VOLUME

2015 National ZIP Code® Directory

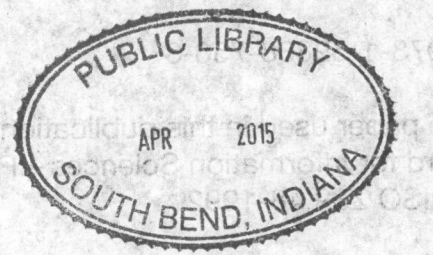

Expires December 31, 2015

Bernan Press is located at 4501 Forbes Blvd., Suite 200, Lanham, MD 20706. Questions concerning this directory can be answered by calling 1-800-462-6420. You may call Monday through Friday, except federal holidays, between the hours of 8:00 a.m. through 5:00 p.m. Eastern Standard Time.

Published by Bernan Press
An imprint of The Rowman & Littlefield Publishing Group, Inc.
4501 Forbes Boulevard, Suite 200, Lanham, Maryland 20706
www.rowman.com
800-462-6420; customercare@bernan.com

ISBN: 978-1-59888-756-3

The paper used in this publication meets the minimum requirements of American National Standard for Information Sciences—Permanence of Paper for Printed Library Materials, ANSI/NISO Z39.48-1992.

Printed in the United States of America

TABLE OF CONTENTS

NATIONAL ZIP CODE DIRECTORY STATE INDEX

U.S. POSSESSION INDEX

INTRODUCTION

Bernan Press publishes the National ZIP Code Directory annually to provide mail users 5-digit ZIP Code and mailing information.

The 5-digit ZIP (Zone Improvement Plan) Code was introduced to the public on July 1, 1963, and was viewed as a positive step for improving the productivity of mail distribution during a period of escalating mail volume and expanding delivery locations. Additionally, 5-digit ZIP Code areas lend themselves to a broad variety of other applications, including geographic and demographic utilization.

Currently, 98 percent of all first-class mail bears a ZIP Code. ZIP Codes support the distribution of letters and other types of mail to 37,000 Post Offices, stations, and branches serving approximately 141 million homes, farms, and businesses across the nation.

How to Use This Directory to Find 5-Digit ZIP Codes

I. Post Offices by State

Each state section begins with a listing of post offices, counties and ZIP Codes. The five-digit ZIP Code for most Post Offices can be found in this section. To find the correct Zip Code:

1. Find the state in alphabetical order.
2. Find the Post Office within the state. The Post Offices are listed in alphabetical order. The name of the county where the Post Office is located follows to the right of the Post Office.
3. To the right of the Post Office and county you will find the corresponding 5-digit ZIP Code.

II. Street Listings by Post Office

Post Offices with more than one delivery area ZIP Code (i.e. large cities)

These pages immediately follow the Post Offices by state listings for each state. Post Offices that have two or more 5-digit ZIP Codes requiring the user to refer to the street address to find the correct 5-digit ZIP Code are included. The listings are in the following order:

1. Post Office boxes at main office, stations and branches
2. Rural routes
3. Highway contracts
4. Named streets
5. Numbered streets

How to Use the Street Listings by Post Office Sections

1. Go to the state list of Post Offices.
2. Find the Post Office in alphabetical order.
3. Go to the page number of the street listings by Post Office section as indicated in the "See Page" reference.
4. Find the street name for which you need a 5-digit ZIP Code.
5. The corresponding 5-digit ZIP Code will be to the right of the street name.

HOW TO WRITE A GOOD RESIDENTIAL ADDRESS

Basic Residential Address Format Table (Important elements are in bold, note differences. Element descriptions are in brackets.)

CORRECT FORMAT	INCORRECT FORMAT
Ms. Mary Jones One Central Plaza 11300 Rockville Pike Ste 1100 Rockville MD 20852	One Central Plaza **Attn: Ms. Mary Jones** 11300 Rockville Pike Ste 1100 Rockville MD 20852
Ms. Mary Jones, RN One Central Plaza 11300 Rockville Pike Ste 1100 Rockville MD 20852	One Central Plaza. 11300 Rockville Pike Ste 1100 Rockville MD 20852 **Attn: Ms. Mary Jones, RN**
Ms. Mary Jones, RN One Central Plaza **Ste 1100** 11300 Rockville Pike Rockville MD 20852	Ms. Mary Jones, RN One Central Plaza 11300 Rockville Pike **Ste 1100** Rockville MD 20852
Ms. Mary Jones, RN One Central Plaza 11300 Rockville Pike Ste 1100 **PO BOX 3005** Rockville MD **20847** [PO Box ZIP Code]	Ms. Mary Jones, RN One Central Plaza **11300 Rockville Pike Ste 1100** PO Box 3005 Rockville MD **20852** [Street ZIP Code]
Ms. Mary Jones, RN 4 Hansen Rd S Brampton Ontario L6W 3H6 **CANADA**	Ms. Mary Jones, RN 4 Hansen Rd S Brampton Ontario L6W 3H6
Marie Jones 13 Rue Duzes **75002** Paris **FRANCE**	Marie Jones 13 Rue Duzes Paris, **France 75002**

Notes: USPS reads an address from bottom to top. The address directly above the city-state-ZIP line is the delivery address. This is the correct format for fastest, most accurate delivery and highest discounts through a presort bureau. Use a 10 pt-12 pt sans serif font without kerning or variable (justified) spacing – Helvetica 10 pt is used in the table. Bold is used in the table for emphasis only. Do not use bold, expanded, condensed, script, stylized or italic fonts in the address itself.

Basic rules: The recipient's name should always be at the top, never in the body of the address and never below. If you can't fit the Ste, Apt or Unit # on the end of the street address line, place the unit information above, not below the street line. It is better not to use a dual address (street and PO Box), but if you must, make sure the ZIP Code you use matches the PO Box or street line directly above the city-state-ZIP – in some larger cities with multiple ZIP Codes there are special ZIP Codes for PO Box sections only. If you are unsure if a special ZIP Code applies, check the address with the recipient or go to the PO Box ZIP Code references – at the beginning of each city listing in this directory. For international addresses put the destination country name at the bottom in all caps. Do not write the address in a U.S. city-state-ZIP format which could cause the piece to be misdirected – the destination code in the incorrectly formatted French address above could cause the piece to be misrouted to Allen, TX. When mailing to Puerto Rico or the U.S. Virgin Islands special formatting may be recommended. See the USPS web site - www.usps.com - and search on "addressing standards for Puerto Rico and the Virgin Islands."

HOW TO WRITE A GOOD BUSINESS ADDRESS

Basic Business Address Format Table (Important elements are in bold, note differences. Element descriptions are in brackets.)

CORRECT FORMAT	INCORRECT FORMAT
John Jones, President Acme Accounting Services, Inc. 11300 Rockville Pike Ste 1100 Rockville MD 20852	Acme Accounting Services, Inc. **Attn: John Jones, President** 11300 Rockville Pike Ste 1100 Rockville MD 20852
John Jones **President** Acme Accounting Services, Inc. 11300 Rockville Pike Ste 1100 Rockville MD 20852	Acme Accounting Services, Inc. 11300 Rockville Pike Ste 1100 Rockville MD 20852 **Attn: John Jones, President**
John Jones, President Acme Accounting Services, Inc. **Ste 1100** 11300 Rockville Pike Rockville MD 20852	John Jones, President Acme Accounting Services, Inc. 11300 Rockville Pike **Ste 1100** Rockville MD 20852
John Jones, President **P&L Division, MC 212** [Dept/Mail Code] Acme Accounting Services, Inc. 11300 Rockville Pike Ste 1100 Rockville MD 20852	John Jones, President Acme Accounting Services, Inc. **P&L Division, MC 212** [Dept/Mail Code] 11300 Rockville Pike Ste 1100 Rockville MD 20852
John Jones, President Acme Accounting Services, Inc. 11300 Rockville Pike Ste 1100 **PO BOX 3005** Rockville MD **20847** [PO Box ZIP Code]	John Jones, President Acme Accounting Services, Inc. **11300 Rockville Pike Ste 1100** PO Box 3005 Rockville MD **20852** [Street ZIP Code]
Charles Smith, GM Canadian Industries 4 Hansen Rd S Brampton Ontario L6W 3H6 **CANADA**	Charles Smith, GM Canadian Industries 4 Hansen Rd S Brampton Ontario L6W 3H6
Henry LaFleur French Impressions 13 Rue Duzes **75002** Paris **FRANCE**	Henry LaFleur French Impressions 13 Rue Duzes Paris **France 75002**

Notes: USPS reads an address from bottom to top. The address directly above the city-state-ZIP line is the delivery address. This is the correct format for fastest, most accurate delivery and highest discounts through a presort bureau. Use a 10 pt-12 pt sans serif font without kerning or variable (justified) spacing – Helvetica 10 pt is used in the table. Bold is used in the table for emphasis only. Do not use bold, expanded, condensed, script, stylized or italic fonts in the address itself.

Basic rules: The recipient's name should always be at the top, never in the body of the address and never below. If you can't fit the Ste, Apt or Unit # on the end of the street address line, place the unit information above, not below the street line. Put department names or internal recipient mail codes above the company name. It is better not to use a dual address (street and PO Box), but if you must, make sure the ZIP Code you use matches the PO Box or street line directly above the city-state-ZIP – in some larger cities with multiple ZIP Codes there are special ZIP Codes for PO Box sections only. If you are unsure if a special ZIP Code applies, check the address with the recipient or go to the PO Box ZIP Code references – at the beginning of each city listing in this directory. For international addresses put the destination country name at the bottom in all caps. Do not write the address in a U.S. city-state-ZIP format which could cause the piece to be misdirected – the destination code in the incorrectly formatted French address above could cause the piece to be misrouted to Allen, TX. When mailing to Puerto Rico or the US Virgin Islands special formatting may be recommended. See the USPS web site - www.usps.com - and search on "addressing standards for Puerto Rico and the Virgin Islands."

TWO-LETTER STATE ABBREVIATIONS

Alabama	AL	Kentucky	KY	North Dakota	ND
Alaska	AK	Louisiana	LA	Ohio	OH
Arizona	AZ	Maine	ME	Oklahoma	OK
Arkansas	AR	Maryland	MD	Oregon	OR
California	CA	Massachusetts	MA	Pennsylvania	PA
Colorado	CO	Michigan	MI	Rhode Island	RI
Connecticut	CT	Minnesota	MN	South Carolina	SC
Delaware	DE	Mississippi	MS	South Dakota	SD
Dist. of Columbia	DC	Missouri	MO	Tennessee	TN
Florida	FL	Montana	MT	Texas	TX
Georgia	GA	Nebraska	NE	Utah	UT
Hawaii	HI	Nevada	NV	Vermont	VT
Idaho	ID	New Hampshire	NH	Virginia	VA
Illinois	IL	New Jersey	NJ	Washington	WA
Indiana	IN	New Mexico	NM	West Virginia	WV
Iowa	IA	New York	NY	Wisconsin	WI
Kansas	KS	North Carolina	NC	Wyoming	WY

U.S. POSSESSION INDEX

American Samoa	AS
Guam	GU
Puerto Rico	PR
Virgin Islands	VI

Nebraska

People QuickFacts	Nebraska	USA
Population, 2013 estimate	1,868,516	316,128,839
Population, 2010 (April 1) estimates base	1,826,341	308,747,716
Population, percent change, April 1, 2010 to July 1, 2013	2.3%	2.4%
Population, 2010	1,826,341	308,745,538
Persons under 5 years, percent, 2013	7.0%	6.3%
Persons under 18 years, percent, 2013	24.9%	23.3%
Persons 65 years and over, percent, 2013	14.1%	14.1%
Female persons, percent, 2013	50.2%	50.8%
White alone, percent, 2013 (a)	89.7%	77.7%
Black or African American alone, percent, 2013 (a)	4.8%	13.2%
American Indian and Alaska Native alone, percent, 2013 (a)	1.3%	1.2%
Asian alone, percent, 2013 (a)	2.1%	5.3%
Native Hawaiian and Other Pacific Islander alone, percent, 2013 (a)	0.1%	0.2%
Two or More Races, percent, 2013	2.0%	2.4%
Hispanic or Latino, percent, 2013 (b)	9.9%	17.1%
White alone, not Hispanic or Latino, percent, 2013	81.0%	62.6%
Living in same house 1 year & over, percent, 2008-2012	83.2%	84.8%
Foreign born persons, percent, 2008-2012	6.2%	12.9%
Language other than English spoken at home, pct age 5+, 2008-2012	10.4%	20.5%
High school graduate or higher, percent of persons age 25+, 2008-2012	90.4%	85.7%
Bachelor's degree or higher, percent of persons age 25+, 2008-2012	28.1%	28.5%
Veterans, 2008-2012	146,852	21,853,912
Mean travel time to work (minutes), workers age 16+, 2008-2012	18.1	25.4
Housing units, 2013	807,034	132,802,859
Homeownership rate, 2008-2012	67.6%	65.5%
Housing units in multi-unit structures, percent, 2008-2012	19.7%	25.9%
Median value of owner-occupied housing units, 2008-2012	$126,700	$181,400
Households, 2008-2012	721,026	115,226,802
Persons per household, 2008-2012	2.46	2.61
Per capita money income in past 12 months (2012 dollars), 2008-2012	$26,523	$28,051
Median household income, 2008-2012	$51,381	$53,046
Persons below poverty level, percent, 2008-2012	12.4%	14.9%

Business QuickFacts	Nebraska	USA
Private nonfarm establishments, 2012	52,294	7,431,808
Private nonfarm employment, 2012	818,289	115,938,468
Private nonfarm employment, percent change, 2011-2012	2.6%	2.2%
Nonemployer establishments, 2012	127,097	22,735,915
Total number of firms, 2007	159,665	27,092,908
Black-owned firms, percent, 2007	1.8%	7.1%
American Indian- and Alaska Native-owned firms, percent, 2007	0.4%	0.9%
Asian-owned firms, percent, 2007	1.4%	5.7%
Native Hawaiian and Other Pacific Islander-owned firms, percent, 2007	0.0%	0.1%
Hispanic-owned firms, percent, 2007	1.9%	8.3%
Women-owned firms, percent, 2007	25.7%	28.8%
Manufacturers shipments, 2007 ($1000)	40,157,999	5,319,456,312
Merchant wholesaler sales, 2007 ($1000)	24,019,868	4,174,286,516
Retail sales, 2007 ($1000)	26,486,612	3,917,663,456
Retail sales per capita, 2007	$14,965	$12,990
Accommodation and food services sales, 2007 ($1000)	2,685,580	613,795,732
Building permits, 2012	6,116	829,658

Geography QuickFacts	Nebraska	USA
Land area in square miles, 2010	76,824.17	3,531,905.43
Persons per square mile, 2010	23.8	87.4
FIPS Code	31	

(a) Includes persons reporting only one race.
(b) Hispanics may be of any race, so also are included in applicable race categories.
FN: Footnote on this item for this area in place of data
NA: Not available
D: Suppressed to avoid disclosure of confidential information
X: Not applicable
S: Suppressed; does not meet publication standards
Z: Value greater than zero but less than half unit of measure shown
F: Fewer than 100 firms
Source: US Census Bureau State & County QuickFacts

Nebraska

3 DIGIT ZIP CODE MAP

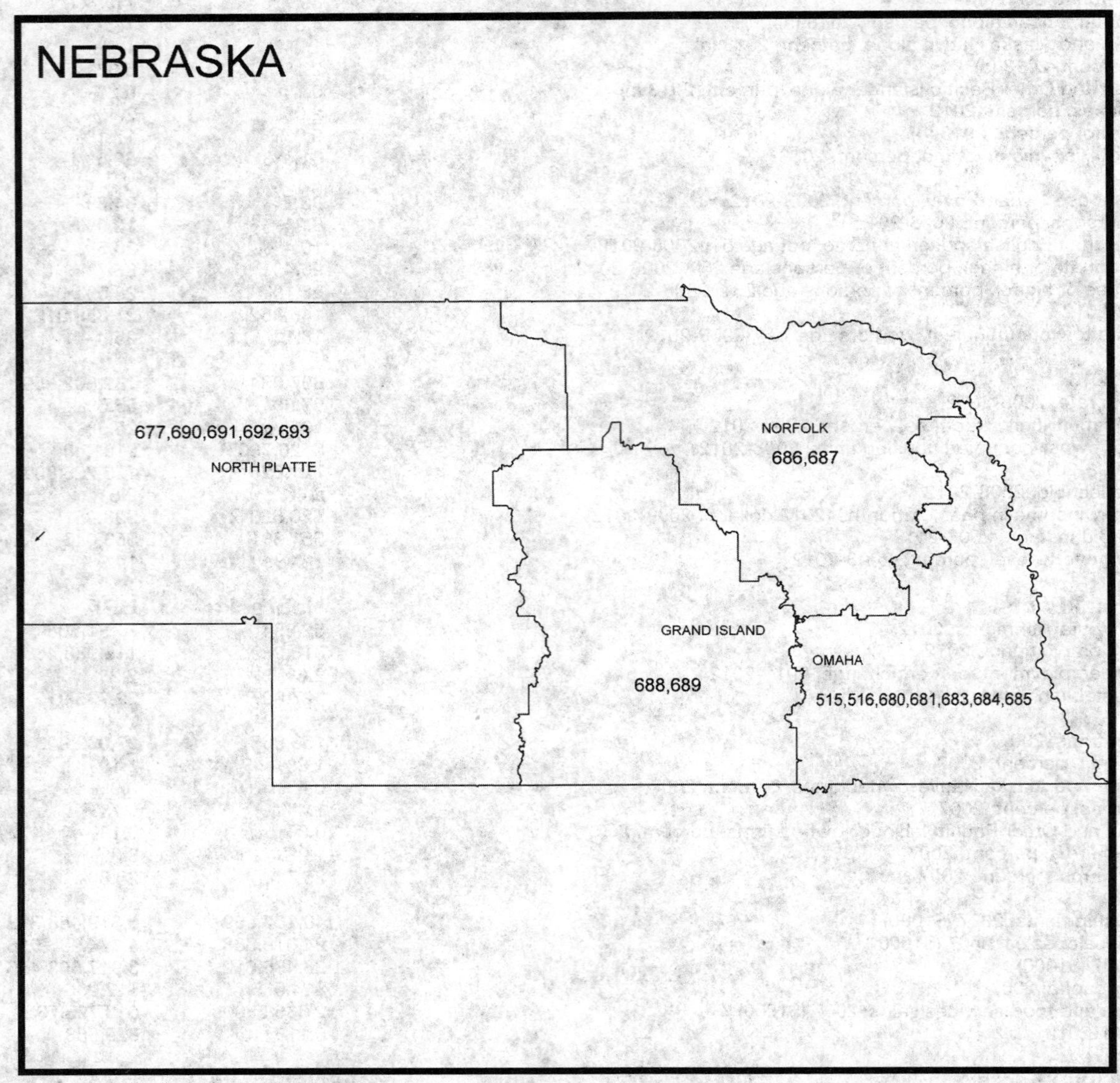

Nebraska

(Abbreviation: NE)

Post Office, County — ZIP Code

Places with more than one ZIP code are listed in capital letters, See pages indicated.

Abie, Butler 68001
Adams, Gage 68301
Agnew, Lancaster 68428
Ainsworth, Brown 69210
Albion, Boone 68620
Alda, Hall 68810
Alexandria, Thayer 68303
Allen, Dixon 68710
Alliance, Box Butte 69301
Alma, Harlan 68920
Almeria, Loup 68879
Alvo, Cass 68304
Amelia, Holt 68711
Ames, Dodge 68621
Amherst, Buffalo 68812
Angora, Morrill 69331
Anoka, Boyd 68722
Anselmo, Custer 68813
Ansley, Custer 68814
Arapahoe, Furnas 68922
Arcadia, Valley 68815
Archer, Merrick 68816
Arlington, Washington 68002
Arnold, Custer 69120
Arthur, Arthur 69121
Ashby, Grant 69333
Ashland, Saunders 68003
Ashton, Sherman 68817
Atkinson, Holt 68713
Atlanta, Phelps 68923
Auburn, Nemaha 68305
Aurora, Hamilton 68818
Avoca, Cass 68307
Axtell, Kearney 68924
Ayr, Adams 68925
Bancroft, Cuming 68004
Barneston, Gage 68309
Bartlett, Wheeler 68622
Bartley, Red Willow 69020
Bassett, Rock 68714
Battle Creek, Madison 68715
Bayard, Morrill 69334
Bazile Mills, Knox 68729
Beatrice, Gage 68310
Beaver City, Furnas 68926
Beaver Crossing, Seward 68313
Bee, Seward 68314
Beemer, Cuming 68716
Belden, Cedar 68717
Belgrade, Boone 68623
BELLEVUE, Sarpy
(See Page 2431)
Bellwood, Butler 68624
Belvidere, Thayer 68315
Benedict, York 68316
Benkelman, Dundy 69021
Bennet, Lancaster 68317
Bennington, Douglas 68007
Bertrand, Phelps 68927
Berwyn, Custer 68814
Big Springs, Deuel 69122
Bingham, Sheridan 69335
Bladen, Webster 68928
BLAIR, Washington
(See Page 2432)
Bloomfield, Knox 68718
Bloomington, Franklin 68929
Blue Hill, Webster 68930
Blue Springs, Gage 68318
Boelus, Howard 68820
Boone, Boone 68620
Boys Town, Douglas 68010
Boystown, Douglas 68010
Bradshaw, York 68319
Brady, Lincoln 69123
Brainard, Butler 68626
Brewster, Blaine 68821
Bridgeport, Morrill 69336
Bristow, Boyd 68719
Broadwater, Morrill 69125
Brock, Nemaha 68320
Broken Bow, Custer 68822
Brownlee, Thomas 69166
Brownville, Nemaha 68321
Brule, Keith 69127
Bruning, Thayer 68322
Bruno, Butler 68014
Brunswick, Antelope 68720
Burchard, Pawnee 68323
Burr, Otoe 68324
Burwell, Garfield 68823
Bushnell, Kimball 69128
Butte, Boyd 68722
Byron, Thayer 68325
Cairo, Hall 68824
Callaway, Custer 68825
Cambridge, Furnas 69022
Campbell, Franklin 68932
Carleton, Thayer 68326
Carroll, Wayne 68723
Cedar Bluffs, Saunders 68015
Cedar Creek, Cass 68016
Cedar Rapids, Boone 68627
Center, Knox 68724
Central City, Merrick 68826
Ceresco, Saunders 68017
Chadron, Dawes 69337
Chambers, Holt 68725
Champion, Chase 69023
Chapman, Merrick 68827
Chappell, Deuel 69129
Chester, Thayer 68327
Clarks, Merrick 68628
Clarkson, Colfax 68629
Clatonia, Gage 68328
Clay Center, Clay 68933
Clearwater, Antelope 68726
Cody, Cherry 69211
Coleridge, Cedar 68727
Colon, Saunders 68018
COLUMBUS, Platte
(See Page 2432)
Comstock, Custer 68828
Concord, Dixon 68728
Cook, Johnson 68329
Cordova, Seward 68330
Cornlea, Platte 68642
Cortland, Gage 68331
Cotesfield, Howard 68835
Cowles, Webster 68930
Cozad, Dawson 69130
Crab Orchard, Johnson 68332
Craig, Burt 68019
Crawford, Dawes 69339
Creighton, Knox 68729
Creston, Platte 68631
Crete, Saline 68333
Crofton, Knox 68730
Crookston, Cherry 69212
Culbertson, Hitchcock 69024
Curtis, Frontier 69025
Dakota City, Dakota 68731
Dalton, Cheyenne 69131
Danbury, Red Willow 69026
Dannebrog, Howard 68831
Davenport, Thayer 68335
Davey, Lancaster 68336
David City, Butler 68632
Dawson, Richardson 68337
Daykin, Jefferson 68338
De Witt, Saline 68341
Decatur, Burt 68020
Denton, Lancaster 68339
Deshler, Thayer 68340
Deweese, Clay 68934
Dickens, Lincoln 69132
Diller, Jefferson 68342
Dix, Kimball 69133
Dixon, Dixon 68732
Dodge, Dodge 68633
Doniphan, Hall 68832
Dorchester, Saline 68343
Douglas, Otoe 68344
Du Bois, Pawnee 68345
Dunbar, Otoe 68346
Dunbar, Otoe 68382
Duncan, Platte 68634
Dunning, Blaine 68833
Dwight, Butler 68635
Eagle, Cass 68347
Eddyville, Dawson 68834
Edgar, Clay 68935
Edison, Furnas 68936
Elba, Howard 68835
Elgin, Antelope 68636
Elk Creek, Johnson 68348
Elkhorn, Douglas 68022
Ellsworth, Sheridan 69340
Elm Creek, Buffalo 68836
Elmwood, Cass 68349
Elsie, Perkins 69134
Elsmere, Cherry 69135
Elwood, Gosper 68937
Elyria, Valley 68837
Emerson, Dakota 68733
Emmet, Holt 68734
Enders, Chase 69027
Endicott, Jefferson 68350
Ericson, Wheeler 68637
Eustis, Frontier 69028
Ewing, Holt 68735
Exeter, Fillmore 68351
Fairbury, Jefferson 68352
Fairfield, Clay 68938
Fairmont, Fillmore 68354
Falls City, Richardson 68355
Farnam, Dawson 69029
Farwell, Howard 68838
Filley, Gage 68357
Firth, Lancaster 68358
Fontanelle, Dodge 68044
Fordyce, Cedar 68736
Fort Calhoun, Washington 68023
Foster, Pierce 68765
Franklin, Franklin 68939
FREMONT, Dodge
(See Page 2432)
Friend, Saline 68359
Fullerton, Nance 68638
Funk, Phelps 68940
Garland, Seward 68360
Garrison, Butler 68632
Geneva, Fillmore 68361
Genoa, Nance 68640
Gering, Scotts Bluff 69341
Gibbon, Buffalo 68840
Gilead, Thayer 68362
Giltner, Hamilton 68841
Gladstone, Jefferson 68352
Glenvil, Clay 68941
Goehner, Seward 68364
Gordon, Sheridan 69343
Gothenburg, Dawson 69138
Grafton, Fillmore 68365
GRAND ISLAND, Hall
(See Page 2433)
Grant, Perkins 69140
Greeley, Greeley 68842
Greenwood, Cass 68366
Gresham, York 68367
Gretna, Sarpy 68028
Guide Rock, Webster 68942
Gurley, Cheyenne 69141
Hadar, Madison 68701
Hadar, Pierce 68738
Haigler, Dundy 69030
Hallam, Lancaster 68368
Halsey, Thomas 69142
Hamlet, Hitchcock 69040
Hampton, Hamilton 68843
Hardy, Nuckolls 68943
Harrisburg, Banner 69345
Harrison, Sioux 69346
Hartington, Cedar 68739
Harvard, Clay 68944
HASTINGS, Adams
(See Page 2434)
Hay Springs, Sheridan 69347
Hayes Center, Hayes 69032
Hazard, Sherman 68844
Heartwell, Kearney 68945
Hebron, Thayer 68370
Hemingford, Box Butte 69348
Henderson, York 68371
Hendley, Furnas 68946
Henry, Scotts Bluff 69358
Herman, Washington 68029
Hershey, Lincoln 69143
Hickman, Lancaster 68372
Hildreth, Franklin 68947
Holbrook, Furnas 68948
Holdrege, Phelps 68949
Holdrege, Harlan 68969
Holland, Lancaster 68372
Holmesville, Gage 68310
Holstein, Adams 68950
Homer, Dakota 68030
Hooper, Dodge 68031
Hordville, Hamilton 68846
Hoskins, Wayne 68740
Howells, Colfax 68641
Hubbard, Dakota 68741
Hubbell, Thayer 68375
Humboldt, Richardson 68376
Humphrey, Platte 68642
Huntley, Harlan 68971
Hyannis, Grant 69350
Imperial, Chase 69033
Inavale, Webster 68952
Indianola, Red Willow 69034
Inglewood, Dodge 68025
Inland, Clay 68954
Inman, Holt 68742
Ithaca, Saunders 68033
Jackson, Dakota 68743
Jansen, Jefferson 68377
Johnson, Nemaha 68378
Johnson, Nemaha 68379
Johnson Lake, Gosper 68937
Johnstown, Brown 69214
Julian, Nemaha 68379
Juniata, Adams 68955
KEARNEY, Buffalo
(See Page 2434)
Kenesaw, Adams 68956
Kennard, Washington 68034
Keystone, Keith 69144
Kilgore, Cherry 69216
Kimball, Kimball 69145
La Vista, Sarpy 68128
La Vista, Sarpy 68138
Lakeside, Sheridan 69351
Lamar, Chase 69023
Laurel, Cedar 68745
Lavista, Sarpy 68128
Lawrence, Nuckolls 68957
Lebanon, Red Willow 69036
Leigh, Colfax 68643
Lemoyne, Keith 69146
Leshara, Douglas 68064
Lewellen, Garden 69147
Lewiston, Pawnee 68380
Lexington, Dawson 68850
Liberty, Gage 68381
LINCOLN, Lancaster
(See Page 2435)
Lindsay, Platte 68644
Linwood, Butler 68036
Lisco, Garden 69148
Litchfield, Sherman 68852
Lodgepole, Cheyenne 69149
Long Pine, Brown 69217
Loomis, Phelps 68958
Lorton, Otoe 68346
Lorton, Otoe 68382
Louisville, Cass 68037
Loup City, Sherman 68853
Lyman, Scotts Bluff 69352
Lynch, Boyd 68746
Lyons, Burt 68038
Macy, Thurston 68039
Madison, Madison 68748
Madrid, Perkins 69150
Magnet, Cedar 68749
Malcolm, Lancaster 68402
Malmo, Saunders 68040
Manley, Cass 68403
Marquette, Hamilton 68854
Marsland, Dawes 69354
Martell, Lancaster 68404
Maskell, Dixon 68751
Mason City, Custer 68855
Max, Dundy 69037
Maxwell, Lincoln 69151
Maywood, Frontier 69038
Mc Cook, Red Willow 69001
Mc Cool Junction, York 68401
Mccook, Red Willow 69001
Mcgrew, Scotts Bluff 69353
Mclean, Pierce 68747
Mead, Saunders 68041
Meadow Grove, Madison 68752
Melbeta, Scotts Bluff 69355
Memphis, Saunders 68042
Merna, Custer 68856
Merriman, Cherry 69218
Milburn, Custer 68813
Milford, Seward 68405
Millard
(See Omaha)
Miller, Buffalo 68858
Milligan, Fillmore 68406
Mills, Keya Paha 68753
Minatare, Scotts Bluff 69356
Minden, Kearney 68959
Mitchell, Scotts Bluff 69357
Monowi, Boyd 68746
Monroe, Platte 68647
Moorefield, Frontier 69039
Morrill, Scotts Bluff 69358
Morse Bluff, Saunders 68648
Mullen, Hooker 69152
Murdock, Cass 68407
Murray, Cass 68409
Naper, Boyd 68755
Naponee, Franklin 68960
Nebraska City, Otoe 68410
Nehawka, Cass 68413
Neligh, Antelope 68756
Nelson, Nuckolls 68961
Nemaha, Nemaha 68414
Nenzel, Cherry 69219
Newcastle, Dixon 68757
Newman Grove, Madison 68758
Newport, Keya Paha 68759
Nickerson, Dodge 68044
Niobrara, Knox 68760
Nora, Nuckolls 68961
NORFOLK, Madison
(See Page 2441)
Norman, Kearney 68959
North Bend, Dodge 68649
North Loup, Valley 68859
NORTH PLATTE, Lincoln
(See Page 2442)
O' Neill, Holt 68763
Oak, Nuckolls 68964
Oakdale, Antelope 68761
Oakland, Burt 68045
Obert, Dixon 68757
Oconto, Custer 68860
Octavia, Butler 68632
Odell, Gage 68415
Odessa, Buffalo 68861
Offutt Afb, Sarpy 68113
Ogallala, Keith 69153
Ohiowa, Fillmore 68416
OMAHA, Douglas
(See Page 2442)
Oneill, Holt 68763
Ong, Clay 68452
Orchard, Antelope 68764
Ord, Valley 68862
Orleans, Harlan 68966
Osceola, Polk 68651
Oshkosh, Garden 69154
Osmond, Pierce 68765
Otoe, Otoe 68417
Overton, Dawson 68863
Oxford, Furnas 68967
Page, Holt 68766
Palisade, Hitchcock 69040
Palmer, Merrick 68864
Palmyra, Otoe 68418
Panama, Lancaster 68419
PAPILLION, Sarpy
(See Page 2454)
Parks, Dundy 69041
Pawnee City, Pawnee 68420
Paxton, Keith 69155
Pender, Thurston 68047
Peru, Nemaha 68421
Petersburg, Boone 68652
Phillips, Hamilton 68865
Pickrell, Gage 68422
Pierce, Pierce 68767
Pilger, Stanton 68768
Plainview, Pierce 68769
Platte Center, Platte 68653
Plattsmouth, Cass 68048
Pleasant Dale, Seward 68423
Pleasanton, Buffalo 68866
Plymouth, Jefferson 68424
Polk, Polk 68654
Ponca, Dixon 68770
Potter, Cheyenne 69156
Prague, Saunders 68050
Primrose, Boone 68655
Prosser, Hall 68883
Purdum, Blaine 69157
Ragan, Harlan 68969
Ralston, Douglas 68127
Randolph, Cedar 68771
Ravenna, Buffalo 68869
Raymond, Lancaster 68428
Red Cloud, Webster 68970
Republican City, Harlan 68971
Reynolds, Thayer 68429
Richfield, Sarpy 68059
Richland, Platte 68601
Rising City, Butler 68658
Riverdale, Buffalo 68870
Riverton, Franklin 68972
Roca, Lancaster 68430
Rockville, Sherman 68871
Rogers, Colfax 68659
Rosalie, Thurston 68055
Rose, Rock 68714
Roseland, Adams 68973
Rosemont, Webster 68930
Royal, Antelope 68773
Rulo, Richardson 68431
Rushville, Sheridan 69360
Ruskin, Nuckolls 68974
Saint Edward, Boone 68660
Saint Helena, Cedar 68774
Saint Libory, Howard 68872
Saint Mary, Johnson 68443
Saint Paul, Howard 68873
Salem, Richardson 68433
Sargent, Custer 68874
Saronville, Clay 68975
Schuyler, Colfax 68661
Scotia, Greeley 68875
SCOTTSBLUFF, Scotts Bluff
(See Page 2455)
Scribner, Dodge 68057
Seneca, Thomas 69161
Seward, Seward 68434
Shelby, Polk 68662
Shelton, Buffalo 68876
Shickley, Fillmore 68436
Sholes, Cedar 68771
Shubert, Richardson 68437
Sidney, Cheyenne 69160
Silver Creek, Merrick 68663
Smithfield, Gosper 68976
Snyder, Dodge 68664
South Bend, Cass 68058
South Sioux City, Dakota 68776
Spalding, Greeley 68665
Sparks, Cherry 69220
Spencer, Boyd 68777
Sprague, Lancaster 68438
Springfield, Sarpy 68059

Springview, Keya Paha 68778
St Columbans, Sarpy 68056
Stamford, Harlan 68977
Stanton, Stanton 68779
Staplehurst, Seward 68439
Stapleton, Logan 69163
Steele City, Jefferson 68440
Steinauer, Pawnee 68441
Stella, Richardson 68442
Sterling, Johnson 68443
Stockville, Frontier 69042
Strang, Fillmore 68444
Stratton, Hitchcock 69043
Stromsburg, Polk 68666
Stuart, Holt 68780
Sumner, Dawson 68878
Superior, Nuckolls 68978
Surprise, Butler 68667
Sutherland, Lincoln 69165
Sutton, Clay 68979
Swanton, Saline 68445
Syracuse, Otoe 68446
Table Rock, Pawnee 68447
Talmage, Otoe 68448
Tarnov, Platte 68642
Taylor, Loup 68879
Tecumseh, Johnson 68450
Tekamah, Burt 68061
Thedford, Thomas 69166
Thurston, Thurston 68062
Tilden, Madison 68781
Tobias, Saline 68453
Trenton, Hitchcock 69044
Trumbull, Clay 68980
Tryon, Mcpherson 69167
Uehling, Dodge 68063
Ulysses, Butler 68667
Ulysses, Butler 68669
Unadilla, Otoe 68454
Union, Cass 68455
Upland, Franklin 68981
Utica, Seward 68456
Valentine, Cherry 69201
Valley, Douglas 68064
Valparaiso, Saunders 68065
Venango, Perkins 69168
Verdel, Knox 68760
Verdigre, Knox 68783
Verdon, Richardson 68457
Virginia, Gage 68458
Waco, York 68460
Wahoo, Saunders 68066
Wakefield, Dixon 68784
Wallace, Lincoln 69169
Walthill, Thurston 68067
Walton, Lancaster 68461
Washington, Washington 68068
Waterbury, Dixon 68785
Waterloo, Douglas 68069
Wauneta, Chase 69045
Wausa, Knox 68786
Waverly, Lancaster 68462
Wayne, Wayne 68787
Weeping Water, Cass 68463
Weissert, Custer 68814
Wellfleet, Lincoln 69170
West Point, Cuming 68788
Western, Saline 68464
Westerville, Custer 68881
Weston, Saunders 68070
Whiteclay, Sheridan 69365
Whitman, Grant 69366
Whitney, Dawes 69367
Wilber, Saline 68465
Wilcox, Kearney 68982
Willow Island, Dawson 69171
Wilsonville, Furnas 69046
Winnebago, Thurston 68071
Winnetoon, Knox 68789
Winside, Wayne 68790
Winslow, Dodge 68072
Wisner, Cuming 68791
Wolbach, Greeley 68882
Wood Lake, Cherry 69221
Wood River, Hall 68883
Wymore, Gage 68466
Wynot, Cedar 68792
York, York 68467
Yutan, Saunders 68073

BELLEVUE NE

General Delivery 68005

POST OFFICE BOXES MAIN OFFICE STATIONS AND BRANCHES

Box No.s
All PO Boxes 68005

NAMED STREETS

Albert St 68147
Albert Raines Ave 68123
Alberta Ave
 800-898 68005
 900-1000 68005
 1002-2198 68005
 1507-1699 68147
 2101-2199 68005
 2500-2799 68147
Alberta Cir 68147
Allied Dr & Rd 68123
Alpine Cir 68123
Altus Pl 68123
Amerado Blvd 68123
N Ameritrade Pl 68005
Amos Gates Dr 68123
Anchor Mill Dr & Rd 68123
Anderson Grv 68123
Angie Dr 68005
Anna Ave & St 68005
Annabelle Dr 68123
Arboretum Dr 68005
Arends Cir 68147
Arenz Dr 68005
Arlington Cir, Pl & St 68123
Armstrong Cir 68147
Arrowhead Ln 68123
Augusta Ave 68005
Avery Rd
 800-998 68123
 801-899 68147
 901-999 68123
 1700-2299 68123
Avian Cir N & S 68005
Baldwin Cir 68147
Bandlytown Pl 68123
Banyan Ct 68005
Bar Harbor Dr 68123
Barbara Ave 68147
Barksdale Ct & Dr 68123
Barretts Dr 68147
Bartmann Dr 68147
Basswood Ct 68005
Bayberry Dr 68005
Bea Cir 68005
Beach Cir 68123
Beale Cir 68123
Beaman Dr 68005
Bellaire Blvd 68005
Bellevue Blvd N & S 68005
Bellevue Medical Center Dr 68123
Bellewood Ct 68005
Bernadette Ave 68147
Bert Murphy Blvd 68005
Betty St 68147
Betz Rd 68005
Biggs Ln & Plz 68123
Birchcrest Rd 68005
Birchwood Dr 68123
Blackhawk Cir & Dr 68123
Bline Ave 68123
Blue Ridge Dr 68147
Bluff St 68005
Bob White Cir 68123
Bogey Ln 68123
Bojanski Dr 68123
Bonnie St 68147
Bordeaux Ave 68123
Breakwater Blvd 68123
Brenda Dr 68005
Brenton Ave 68005
Briar Oak St 68123
Briarwood Ln
 9400-9699 68147
 9700-9899 68123
Brighton Dr 68123
Brook St 68123
Brooks Pl 68005
Brookside Dr 68123
Bruce Cir 68005
Bryan Ave 68005
Buck Dr 68005
Burr Oak Dr 68123
Buttons Dr 68123
Calais St 68123
Caldor Dr 68005
Calhoun St 68005
Calmar Cir 68005
Calvin Dr & St 68123
Camp Brewster Rd 68005
Camp Gifford Rd 68005
Campbell Ct 68123
Canyon Cir 68123
Canyon Dr 68123
Canyon Rd 68005
Cape Cod Lndg 68123
Capehart Rd 68123
Carswell Dr 68123
Cary Cir & St 68147
Cascio Dr 68005
Casey Cir 68123
Castile Dr 68123
Castle Dr 68123
Cedar Cir & St 68005
Cedar Island Rd
 7700-8699 68147
 8701-9199 68147
 9500-10098 68123
 10100-10699 68123
Cedar View Cir, Dr & Ln 68123
Cemetery Rd 68123
Century Rd 68123
Chad Ave & St 68123
Chalet Dr 68123
Chandler Rd E 68005
Chandler Rd W 68147
Chandler Acres Dr 68147
Chandler Hills Dr 68147
Chaput Dr 68005
Charles Cir 68123
Chateau Dr 68005
Chateau St 68123
Chennault Cir & St 68123
Cherry Ln 68147
Cherry Ln E 68005
Chevro Ln 68005
Childs Rd E 68005
Childs Rd W 68147
Circletown Pl 68123
Citta Cir & Dr 68147
Claudene Ct 68005
Clay St
 2200-2298 68005
 2300-2899 68005
 16400-16799 68123
Cobblestone Lane Cir 68005
Coffey Ave 68123
Collins Dr 68005
Colorado St 68005
Columbus Ave 68005
Combs Rd 68005
Comstock Ave & Plz 68123
Constitution Cir 68123
Cornelia St
 1800-1998 68147
 2000-2699 68147
 3100-3199 68005
Cornhusker Rd
 501-997 68005
 999-1099 68005
 1201-1997 68123
 1999-3099 68123
 3101-3899 68123
Cottage Cir 68123
Cottage Rd 68005
Country Club Ct 68005
Courtney Cir & Dr 68123
Coventry Dr 68123
Crappie Cv 68123
Crawford St 68005
Crestridge Dr 68005
Crystal Dr 68123
Culpepper Ave 68005
Cunningham Rd 68005
Dacey Pl 68123
Dagmar Ave 68005
Daisy Cir 68123
Daniell Cir, Rd & St 68123
Day Dr 68005
Denise Cir 68005
Dennis Dr 68005
Denver St 68005
Derby Dr 68123
Dianne Ave 68005
Dogwood Cir 68123
Douglas Dr 68005
Dover Ct 68005
Dow Dr 68123
Dowding Ct 68005
Duane Ave & Plz 68123
Duffer Ct 68123
Dundee Ct 68005
Durand Dr 68005
E & W Dutchman Cir 68123
Dyess Pl 68123
Dyson Hollow Rd 68123
Edgerton Dr 68123
Edgewood Ct 68005
Edna St 68147
Edwards St 68005
Elbow Bend Rd 68005
Ellsworth Ave 68123
Elm Cir & St 68005
Emiline St 68147
Englewood Dr 68005
Esplanada Ct 68123
Eureux Cir & St 68123
Evelyn St 68147
Evergreen Ave 68005
Fairfax Rd 68005
Fairlane Dr 68005
Fairview Rd 68123
Fairview St
 900-999 68147
 2000-2199 68147
 2500-2799 68147
Falcon Dr 68123
Farrell Dr 68005
Faulk Ave 68147
Fawn Ct 68005
Faye Dr 68005
Fisher House Rd 68123
Fleetwood Ln 68005
Florence Dr 68147
Forbes Dr 68123
Forest Dr 68005
Forestdale Dr 68123
Forestview Cir 68005
Fornoff Ave 68123
Fort Crook Rd N 68005
Fort Crook Rd S
 100-1599 68005
 3400-12498 68123
Foster Dr 68005
Fox Meadow Ct 68005
Fox Ridge Cir & Dr 68123
Franklin St 68005
Fraser Ct 68005
Freeman Dr 68005
Front St 68005
Galvin Rd N & S 68005
Garden Ave 68005
Gaslight Ln 68005
Gate Dr 68123
Gates Cir 68123
Gayle Ave 68123
George Cir 68147
Georgetown Pl 68123
Georgia Ave
 1300-1700 68147
 1702-1798 68147
 1901-1997 68005
 1999-2299 68005
 2500-2799 68147
Geri Cir & Dr 68147
Gertrude St & Ter 68147
Giles Rd 68147
Gindy Dr 68147
Ginny Ave 68005
Glendale Cir 68123
Glengarry Cir 68005
Glory Cir 68123
Golden Blvd 68123
Gow Ln 68123
Granada Pkwy 68123
Grandview Ave & St 68005
Greenbriar Ct 68005
Greene Ave & Cir 68147
Greenfield St 68147
Greensboro Ave 68005
Greenwald St 68123
Gregg Cir 68005
Gregg Pl 68005
Gregg Rd
 1001-1497 68005
 1499-1510 68005
 1511-1599 68123
 1512-1908 68005
 1601-1899 68005
 1920-2198 68123
 2200-2299 68123
Grenoble Dr 68123
Griffis Pl 68123
Grove Rd 68005
Groves Cir & Rd 68147
Hackberry Ct 68005
Halifax Dr & St 68123
Hancock St 68005
Hansen Ave & Cir 68005
Hanson Dr 68123
Harlan Dr 68005
Harlan Lewis Rd
 2901-3003 68005
 3005-3500 68005
 3502-14698 68005
 15701-15799 68123
Harmon Cir 68123
Harrington Ave 68005
Harrison Plz & St 68147
Harvell Cir & Dr 68005
Harvell Plaza Dr 68005
Hawk Ridge Cir 68147
Heartland Dr 68123
Helene Dr & Pl 68005
Helwig Ave 68123
Henery Cir & Rd 68123
Herman Dr 68005
Hickory Cir 68005
Hidden Hills Dr 68005
High Meadow Ln 68147
High School Dr 68005
Highway 370
 1600-1698 68005
Highway 370
 1800-1898 68123
Highway 75 S 68123
Hike Cir 68123
Hillcrest Ave & Dr 68005
Hillside Dr 68005
Hogantown Dr 68123
Holloway Ave 68123
Holly St 68147
Hopkins Dr 68005
Hruska Blvd 68123
Hummingbird Cir & Dr 68123
Hunter Dr 68123
Hunters Cv 68123
Imperial Dr 68005
Independence Ln 68123
Independence Ln 68123
Industrial Dr 68005
Innis Cir 68123
Inverness Ct 68005
Ira Cir 68147
Irene St 68147
Iris Cir 68123
Ironwood Ct 68005
Iske Dr & Pl 68123
Ivy Cir 68123
Ivy Ct 68005
Ivy Dr 68123
J F Kennedy Dr 68005
Jack Pine Cir & St 68123
Jackson St 68005
Jamestown Dr 68123
Jan Cir 68123
Janan Dr 68005
Jason Cir, Dr & St 68123
Jeanette Cir 68123
Jefferson Cir & St 68005
Jerry Gilbert Cir 68123
Jessie Marie Dr 68123
Jewell Cir & Rd 68005
Jinings Dr 68005
Joann Ave 68123
Josephine St 68147
Joyce Cir 68005
Julie Cir 68005
Julius Pl 68005
Kansas Dr 68005
Kasper St 68147
Kauii Dr 68005
Kay Lynn Dr 68005
Kayleen Dr 68005
Kelly Dr 68123
Kennedy Blvd 68123
Kensington Cir 68123
Kevin Cir 68005
Kibbon Dr 68005
Kimberly St 68005
Kings Cir & Dr 68005
Kingston Ave 68005
Kirby Ave 68005
Kohl Cir & Rd 68005
Kouba Dr 68005
Kountze Memorial Dr 68005
Kraft Dr 68123
Lafayette Ln 68005
Lakewood Dr 68123
E Laplatte Rd 68123
Larson Cir & Dr 68123
Lasalle Cir 68005
Laura Ave 68123
Laurel Cir & Dr 68005
Lawnwood Dr 68123
Lawre Cir 68005
Lawrence Ln 68005
Layne St 68005
Leawood Cir & Dr 68123
Lee Cir 68147
Lee Dr
 1400-1598 68005
 8900-8999 68147
Leisure Ln 68005
Lemay Dr 68005
Leona Cir & Ln 68123
Lewis And Clark Rd 68123
Lexington Ave 68123
Liam Cir 68123
Lila Ave 68005
Lilley Ln 68123
Lillian St 68147
Lincoln Rd 68005
Linda St 68147
Linden Ave
 9400-9614 68147
 9616-9698 68147
 9700-9899 68123
Linden Plz 68123
Lindy Ln 68005
Lindyview Ln & Rd 68005
Little John Rd 68005
Lloyd Cir & St 68005
Lochmoor Cir 68123
Lockbourne Dr 68123
Logan Ave 68005
Lois Ln 68005
Lola Ave & Cir 68147
Lone Tree Rd 68123
Longo Dr 68005
Longview St 68123
Looking Glass Dr 68123
Lord Blvd 68005
Loring St 68123
Lorraine Ave & Dr 68005
Louisiane Cir 68123
Lucille Dr 68147
Lynnwood Dr 68123
Lynx Cir 68123
Maass Rd 68123
Madison St 68005
Main St
 901-1197 68005
 1199-2599 68005
 16400-16799 68123
March Cir 68123
Margo St 68147
Marian Ave 68005
Marie Dr 68005
Marie St 68147
Mark St 68123
Marlee Dr 68147
Marlene Ln 68123
Mars Cir 68005
Marseille Ave 68123
Martin Dr 68005
Martinview Rd 68005
Mayflower Rd 68123
Mccarty Cir & Dr 68123
Mccarty Loup 68123
Mcconnell Dr 68123
Mccorkindale Ave 68147
Mccoy Dr 68123
Mclaughlin Cir 68005
Mcmahon Ave 68147
Meadowlark Ln 68123
Meghan Dr 68123
Meisinger Rd 68123
Merwood St 68005
Mesa St 68123
Michael St 68005
Michaela St 68123
Micky Dr 68005
Middletown Pl 68123
Mildred Ave & Ct 68005
Miller Rd 68123
Minot Dr 68123
Mirror Cir & Ln 68123
E & W Mission Ave 68005
Missouri River Rd 68005
Mitchell Rd 68123
Modification Rd 68005
Mohanna Pl 68005
Montreal Cir & Dr 68123
Montrovia Blvd 68123
Moore Dr 68005
Morrie Cir & Dr 68123
Mose Ave 68147
Myrtle St 68147
Nantucket Way 68123
Nebraska Cir, Dr & Rd 68005
Nob Hill Ter 68005
Normandy Blvd 68123
Normandy Dr 68005
Nottingham Dr 68123
Nugget Cir 68123
Oak Ave & Cir 68005
Oak Ridge Dr
 9501-9597 68147
 9599-9699 68147
 9701-9797 68123
 9799-9899 68123
Oakridge Ct 68005
Offutt Blvd 68005
Old 36th St 68123
Old Gaelic Cir & St 68123
Olde Hickory Rd 68005
Olive St 68147
Omalley Cir 68005
Orchard Dr 68005
Oriole Dr 68123
Overlook Cir 68147
Paradise Rd 68123
Park Cir 68123
Parkside Dr 68123
Parkway Dr 68005
Patricia Ln 68147
Payne Ave & Dr 68005
Pease Dr 68123
Pelton Ave 68005
Peoples Rd 68005
Perch Dr 68123
Phyllis Cir 68005
Pilgrim Dr 68123
Pinecrest Rd 68123
Pinehill Rd 68123
Platte River Dr 68123
Platteview Rd 68123
Pleasant Dr 68147
Pleasantview Ln 68005
Pluma Dr 68005
Plymouth Pt 68123
Plymouth Rock Rd 68123
Pointer Cir 68123
Ponderosa Cir & Dr 68123
Potter Rd 68005
Power Dr
 2100-2350 68005
 2352-2398 68005
 2900-2999 68123
Prairie Ave 68005
Pratt Ave 68123
Quail Cir & Dr 68123
Rahn Blvd 68123
Railroad Ave 68147
Rainbow Rd 68123
Ramey Ln 68123
Ramsgate Ct 68005
Randall Dr 68005
Rapcon Hill Rd 68005
Raven Ridge Dr 68123
Raynor Pkwy 68123
Rebecca Ct 68123
Redbud Ln 68005
Redwing Cir & Dr 68123
Reed Dr 68005
Reedmont Dr 68005
Rexroad Pl 68005
Ridge Rd 68005
Ridgeview Cir 68123
Ridgewood Ct & Dr 68005
Robbie Ave 68005
Robert St 68147
Robin Dr
 1200-1299 68005
 2300-2499 68147
 2501-3899 68147
Robinson Ave 68005
Robinwood Dr 68005
Rose Lane Rd 68147
Rosewood Cir 68005
Rushton Dr 68005
Rustic Rd 68005
Ryan Ave 68123
Saint Andrews Rd 68005
Saint Joachin Ct 68005
Saint Raphael St 68005
Samson Way 68123
Sandi Ct 68005
Sandra St 68147
Sandy Ln 68123
Sarazen Plz 68123
Sarpy Ave 68147
E Sarpy Ave 68005
W Sarpy Ave 68005
Scarborough Dr 68123
Schilling Dr & Plz 68123
Schneekloth Rd 68123
Schuemann Dr 68123
Scott Dr 68123
Shadow Rd 68005
Shagbark Ct 68005
Shallcross Ln 68005
Sheridan Cir & Rd 68123
Sherman Dr 68005
Sherry Dr 68005
Sherwood Cir & Dr 68147
Sidney St
 1800-1898 68147
 2400-2700 68005
 2702-2798 68005
Sierra Ln & St 68123
Sigmund Dr 68005
Skyview Dr 68005
Smith Rd 68005

Somerset Dr … 68005
Southern Hills Dr … 68147
Spencer Cir & St … 68123
Spring Blvd … 68123
Spring Creek Cir & Dr … 68147
Spruce St … 68147
Stephanie Ln … 68147
Suburban Dr … 68147
Sullivan Cir … 68005
Summit Plaza Dr … 68123
Sunbury Dr … 68005
Sunny Ln … 68005
Sunset Dr … 68005
Sunshine Blvd … 68123
Susie Cir … 68123
Sycamore Ct … 68123
Sycamore St
901-999 … 68123
1500-1699 … 68005
Tamarac Dr … 68147
Tammy St … 68123
Tanglewood Ct … 68005
Tasha Cir … 68123
Terrace Ave … 68005
Terry Ave … 68005
Terry Dr … 68123
Thomas Dr … 68005
Thurston Ave
801-897 … 68123
899-1199 … 68123
1201-1599 … 68123
1700-1999 … 68005
2001-2099 … 68005
Thurston Cir … 68005
Timber Ln … 68005
Tinker Pl … 68123
Towne Center Dr … 68123
Tracon Hill Rd … 68005
Traders Trl … 68005
Tregaron Cir & Dr … 68123
Tregaron Ridge Ave, Ct & Rd … 68123
Trumble Loup E & W … 68123
Tulip Ln
2000-2200 … 68005
2202-2298 … 68005
2500-2800 … 68147
2802-2898 … 68147
Turner Cir … 68123
Turtle Dove Dr … 68123
Twin Creek Dr … 68123
Twinridge Dr … 68005
Valley View Ave … 68147
Valley View Dr … 68005
Van Buren St … 68005
Vandenberg Ave … 68123
Vannornan Dr & Pl … 68005
Ventura Dr … 68005
S Verleade St … 68123
Vernon Ave … 68005
Versaille St … 68123
Vicki Cir … 68005
Victoria Ave
2000-2899 … 68005
4200-4300 … 68123
4302-4498 … 68123
Virginia Ave … 68005
Virginia St … 68147
Vista Cir … 68147
Volt St … 68147
Waldo Cir … 68005
Waldruh Dr … 68005
Walker Dr … 68123
Wall St … 68005
Wallace Ave … 68005
Warren St … 68005
Washington St … 68005
Waterford Ave … 68123
Wayne St … 68005
Westcott Dr … 68005
Westport Cir … 68123
Westridge Ave … 68005
White Cap Ln … 68123
Whiteman Dr … 68123
Whitted Dr … 68123
Wilhelminia Dr … 68123
Williamsburg Ct & Dr … 68123
Willis Ave … 68005
Willow Ave … 68005
Willow Cir
700-799 … 68005
2300-2399 … 68123
Willow St … 68147
Wilroy Rd … 68005
Wilshire Dr … 68005
Wilson Dr … 68005
Winding River Dr … 68123
S Winerney St … 68147
Winnie Dr … 68005
Wolf Ln … 68005
Woodbine Ave & Ct … 68005
Woodland Dr … 68123
Woodlawn Cir … 68005
Woodridge Cir … 68123
Yorktown Pl & St … 68123
Yucca Cir … 68123
Zinsmaster Ct … 68005

NUMBERED STREETS

N 3rd St … 68005
N 4th St … 68005
N 5th St … 68005
S 5th St … 68123
N 6th St … 68005
S 9th Ave … 68147
9700-9999 … 68123
S 9th Cir … 68123
S 9th Ct … 68123
N 9th St … 68005
S 9th St
8300-9099 … 68147
9101-9611 … 68147
9700-9800 … 68123
9802-12898 … 68123
N 10th St … 68005
9500-9699 … 68147
9700-10099 … 68123
N 11th St … 68005
S 11th St
8300-8398 … 68147
8400-8699 … 68147
8701-8799 … 68147
10000-10199 … 68123
E & N 12th … 68005
E 13th Ave … 68005
S 13th St
6900-8298 … 68147
8300-9300 … 68147
9302-9698 … 68147
10000-10198 … 68123
13001-13199 … 68123
E 14th Ave … 68005
W 14th Ave … 68005
S 14th Cir … 68123
S 14th St … 68123
S 15th Ave … 68147
W 15th Ave … 68005
S 15th Cir … 68147
S 15th St
8500-8598 … 68147
10000-10398 … 68123
10400-10700 … 68123
10702-10998 … 68123
E 16th Ave … 68005
W 16th Ave … 68005
S 16th St … 68147
E 17th Ave … 68005
S 17th St
7300-8298 … 68147
8300-9211 … 68147
9213-9311 … 68147
10600-15199 … 68123
W 18th Ave … 68005
S 18th Cir … 68123
S 18th St
6900-7198 … 68147
7200-7599 … 68147
10700-15199 … 68123
E 19th Ave … 68005
W 19th Ave … 68005
S 19th Cir … 68147
S 19th St
7100-7512 … 68147
7514-8498 … 68147
10700-10899 … 68123
E 20th Ave … 68005
S 20th Ave … 68123
W 20th Ave … 68005
S 20th Cir … 68123
S 20th St
6900-7398 … 68147
7400-9599 … 68147
9601-9699 … 68147
9700-15099 … 68123
15101-15105 … 68123
E 21st Ave … 68005
S 21st Ave
6900-7300 … 68147
9700-9800 … 68123
W 21st Ave … 68005
S 21st Cir … 68123
S 21st St
6901-8197 … 68147
10201-13197 … 68123
E 22nd Ave … 68005
S 22nd Ave
7907-9597 … 68147
9701-9797 … 68123
W 22nd Ave … 68005
S 22nd Cir … 68123
S 22nd St
7100-7999 … 68147
13400-15099 … 68123
E 23rd Ave … 68005
W 23rd Ave … 68005
S 23rd St
6900-8500 … 68147
8502-9698 … 68147
9700-14699 … 68123
14701-14899 … 68123
E 24th Ave … 68005
S 24th Ave
7200-7399 … 68147
14600-14698 … 68123
14701-15099 … 68123
W 24th Ave … 68005
S 24th Cir … 68123
S 24th St
7800-9699 … 68147
9700-14700 … 68123
14702-14998 … 68123
S 24th Street Cir … 68123
E 25th Ave … 68005
S 25th Ave
7100-8398 … 68147
9700-14500 … 68123
W 25th Ave … 68005
S 25th St
6900-7398 … 68147
10000-10098 … 68123
S 25th Avenue Cir … 68123
S 26th Ave … 68147
S 26th Ave … 68147
9700-13499 … 68123
S 26th Cir … 68123
S 26th St
7300-9699 … 68147
9700-13607 … 68123
13609-13699 … 68123
S 26th Avenue Cir … 68123
E 27th Ave … 68005
S 27th Ave
9300-9398 … 68147
9700-12499 … 68123
W 27th Ave … 68005
S 27th Cir … 68123
S 27th St
6901-6997 … 68147
9700-14599 … 68123
E 28th Ave … 68005
S 28th Ave
9300-9699 … 68147
9700-13000 … 68123
W 28th Ave … 68005
S 28th Cir … 68123
S 28th Ct … 68123
S 28th St
6900-9699 … 68147
9700-14599 … 68123
S 28th Ter … 68123
S 28th Avenue Cir … 68123
E 29th Ave … 68005
S 29th Ave … 68123
W 29th Ave … 68005
S 29th Cir … 68123
S 29th Pl … 68123
S 29th St … 68123
S 30th Ave … 68123
W 30th Ave … 68005
S 30th St
6900-7098 … 68147
7100-8299 … 68147
11900-12498 … 68123
12500-13499 … 68123
13501-13599 … 68123
W 31st Ave … 68005
S 31st Cir … 68123
S 31st St
7700-7799 … 68147
11500-11598 … 68123
11600-14319 … 68123
14321-14599 … 68123
S 32nd Ave
6900-7099 … 68147
14000-14099 … 68123
W 32nd Ave … 68005
S 32nd Cir … 68123
S 32nd Ct … 68123
S 32nd St
7700-8399 … 68147
11800-13600 … 68123
13602-13698 … 68123
S 32nd Avenue Cir … 68123
S 33rd Ave … 68123
W 33rd Ave … 68005
S 33rd Cir … 68123
S 33rd St
6900-7499 … 68147
11800-13599 … 68123
13601-13699 … 68123
E 34th Ave … 68005
S 34th Ave … 68123
W 34th Ave … 68005
S 34th Cir … 68123
S 34th St
8801-8899 … 68147
11800-14599 … 68123
E 35th Ave … 68005
S 35th Ave … 68123
E 35th St … 68005
S 35th St
7400-7600 … 68147
7602-8898 … 68147
11500-14499 … 68123
S 35th Avenue Cir … 68123
S 36th St … 68147
9809-9911 … 68123
9913-15400 … 68123
15402-16498 … 68123
S 37th Cir … 68123
S 37th St
7701-7997 … 68147
7999-8099 … 68147
11501-11597 … 68123
11599-11899 … 68123
S 38th Ave … 68147
S 38th Cir … 68123
S 38th St
6900-6998 … 68147
7000-8499 … 68147
12700-13800 … 68123
13802-13898 … 68123
S 39th Ave … 68147
S 39th Cir … 68123
S 39th St
6900-7198 … 68147
7200-8699 … 68147
11500-11799 … 68123
S 40th Cir … 68123
S 40th St
7000-8299 … 68147
12500-12599 … 68123
S 41st Ave … 68147
S 41st Cir … 68123
S 41st St
7000-8199 … 68147
13500-13999 … 68123
S 41st Ter … 68147
S 42nd Ave … 68123
S 42nd Cir … 68123
S 42nd St
6900-8700 … 68147
8702-8798 … 68147
11501-11599 … 68123
14500-14598 … 68123
S 43rd Ave … 68123
S 43rd St
6900-7600 … 68147
11400-13799 … 68123
S 44th Ave … 68123
S 44th St
7300-8798 … 68147
11300-13999 … 68123
S 44th Avenue Cir … 68123
370 Plz … 68123

BLAIR NE

General Delivery … 68008

POST OFFICE BOXES MAIN OFFICE STATIONS AND BRANCHES

Box No.s
1 - 800 … 68008
5591 - 5799 … 68009

NAMED STREETS

All Street Addresses … 68008

NUMBERED STREETS

All Street Addresses … 68008

COLUMBUS NE

General Delivery … 68601

POST OFFICE BOXES MAIN OFFICE STATIONS AND BRANCHES

Box No.s
All PO Boxes … 68602

NAMED STREETS

All Street Addresses … 68601

NUMBERED STREETS

1st Ave & St … 68601
S & SE 2nd Ave & St … 68601
E & S 3rd Ave & St … 68601
S & SE 4th Ave & St … 68601
E, S & SE 5th Ave & St … 68601
S & E 6th Ave & St … 68601
E, S & SE 7th Ave & St … 68601
E 8th Ave & St … 68601
E, S & SE 9th Ave & St … 68601
E 10th Ave & St … 68601
E 11th Ave & St … 68601
E 12th Ave & St … 68601
E 13th Ave & St … 68601
E, S & SE 14th Ave & St … 68601
E 15th Ave & St … 68601
E, S & SE 16th Ave & St … 68601
E 17th Ave & St … 68601
E 18th Ave & St … 68601
E 19th Ave & St … 68601
E 20th Ave & St … 68601
E 21st Ave & St … 68601
E 22nd Ave & St … 68601
E 23rd Ave & St … 68601
24th Ave
201-297 … 68601
299-1600 … 68601
1555-1555 … 68602
1602-3598 … 68601
1801-3599 … 68601
E 24th Ave … 68601
24th St … 68601
E 24th St … 68601
S 24th St … 68601
E 25th Ave & St … 68601
E 26th Ave & St … 68601
E 27th Ave & St … 68601
E 28th Ave & St … 68601
E 29th Ave & St … 68601
E 30th Ave & St … 68601
31st Ave & St … 68601
E & S 32nd Ave & St … 68601
S 33rd Ave & St … 68601
S 34th Ave & St … 68601
34th Street Pl … 68601
35th Ave & St … 68601
E & SE 36th Ave & St … 68601
E 37th Ave & St … 68601
E 38th Ave & St … 68601
SE 39th Ave & St … 68601
E 40th Ave & St … 68601
E 41st Ave, Rd & St … 68601
E 42nd Ave & Rd … 68601
43rd Ave & Rd … 68601
E & SE 44th Ave & Rd … 68601
45th Ave … 68601
46th Ave & St … 68601
47th Ave & St … 68601
48th Ave & St … 68601
49th Ave … 68601
50th Ave & St … 68601
51st Ave & St … 68601
E 53rd Ave & St … 68601
54th Ave & St … 68601
55th Ave & St … 68601
56th St … 68601
56th Avenue Pl … 68601
E & SE 59th … 68601
60th Ave & St … 68601
61st Ave … 68601
63rd Ave & St … 68601
65th St … 68601
66th St … 68601
67th Ave … 68601
E 68th … 68601
69th Ave … 68601
S 70th … 68601
78th Ave … 68601
E 83rd … 68601
87th St … 68601
88th St … 68601
94th St … 68601
95th St … 68601
96th St … 68601
97th St … 68601
98th St … 68601
100th Ave … 68601
115th Ave & St … 68601
122nd Ave … 68601
126th Ave … 68601
130th Ave … 68601
140 Rd … 68601
141 Rd … 68601
142 Rd … 68601
144 Rd … 68601
145th Ave & St … 68601
160th Ave & St … 68601
175th Ave & St … 68601
190th Ave & St … 68601
197th St … 68601
205th Ave & St … 68601
220th Ave & St … 68601
223rd St … 68601
227th St … 68601
235th Ave & St … 68601
236th St … 68601
239th Ave … 68601
242nd Ave & St … 68601
246th Ave … 68601
247th Ave … 68601
249th St … 68601
250th Ave … 68601
265th Ave & St … 68601
280th Ave & St … 68601
287th Ave & St … 68601
291st St … 68601
295th Ave & St … 68601
298th St … 68601
308th Ave … 68601
310th Ave & St … 68601
313th St … 68601
317th Ave … 68601
319th St … 68601
325th St … 68601
340th Ave & St … 68601
355th Ave & St … 68601
370th Ave & St … 68601
385th St … 68601
400th St … 68601
44 Ab Rd … 68601

FREMONT NE

General Delivery … 68025

POST OFFICE BOXES MAIN OFFICE STATIONS AND BRANCHES

Box No.s
1 - 816 … 68026
26 - 815 … 68025
901 - 1076 … 68026
922 - 1024 … 68025
1201 - 2448 … 68026
1252 - 10000 … 68025

NAMED STREETS

All Street Addresses … 68025

NUMBERED STREETS

E & W 1st … 68025
E & W 2nd … 68025
2nd Avenue Ct … 68025
E & W 3rd … 68025
E & W 4th … 68025
4th Avenue Ct … 68025
E & W 5th … 68025
E 6th St
100-349 … 68025
348-348 … 68026
351-1599 … 68025
400-1598 … 68025
W 6th St … 68025
E 7th St … 68025
E & W 8th … 68025
E & W 9th … 68025
E & W 10th … 68025
E & W 11th … 68025
E & W 12th … 68025
E & W 14th … 68025
E & W 15th … 68025
E & W 16th … 68025
E & W 17th … 68025
E 18th St … 68025
E & W 19th … 68025
E & W 20th Ave & St … 68025
W & E 21st Ave & St … 68025
E & W 22nd … 68025

E & W 23rd Ave, Dr &
St S 68025
E 24th St 68025
E 25th St 68025
E 27th St 68025
E 28th Cir & St 68025
E 29th Cir & St 68025
E 30th St 68025
E 32nd St 68025
46th St 68025
W 52nd St 68025

GRAND ISLAND NE

General Delivery 68802

POST OFFICE BOXES MAIN OFFICE STATIONS AND BRANCHES

Box No.s
All PO Boxes 68802

RURAL ROUTES

06 68801
01 68803

NAMED STREETS

A Rd 68801
E Abbott Rd
1-299 68803
1400-3598 68801
W Abbott Rd 68803
N Academy Rd 68801
Ada St 68803
N & S Adams St 68801
E Airport Rd
100-299 68803
1000-3999 68801
W Airport Rd 68803
Allegheny Cir 68801
Allen Ave, Ct & Dr 68803
N Alpha St 68803
W Anderson Ave 68801
Ando St 68803
Andrews Ave 68801
W Anna St
600-698 68801
700-1699 68801
1700-2999 68803
Anne Marie Ave 68803
S Antelope Dr 68803
Apache Rd 68801
Arabian Cir 68801
Arapahoe Ave 68803
Arch Ave 68803
Arizona Ave 68803
Arrowhead Rd 68801
Arthur Rd 68801
N Arthur St 68803
S Arthur St 68803
E & W Ashton Ave 68801
Aspen Cir 68803
Aster Dr 68803
Atlanta St 68803
S August St 68801
Augusta Pkwy 68803
Austin Ave 68801
Avon Ave 68803
B Rd 68801
W Bachman St 68803
Baker Ave 68801
Baldwin Ct 68803
Bantam St 68801
Barbara Ave 68803
Bass Rd 68801
Baumann Dr 68803
Beachwood Dr 68803
Beal St 68801
Bearing Pointe Dr 68803
Beck Rd 68801
Bell Blvd 68801
Bellwood Dr 68801
Bighorn Pl 68803
Bischeld St 68801
E & W Bismark Rd 68801
Bison Ct 68803
N Blaine St 68803
S Blaine St
201-597 68803
599-1999 68803
2000-2298 68801
2300-5700 68801
5702-5798 68801
Blake St 68803
Blauvelt Rd 68803
Blender Rd 68803
Bock Ave 68803
N Boggs Ave 68803
Bosselman Rd 68803
Boston Cir 68803
Brahma St 68801
Branding Iron Ct & Ln 68803
Brennen Ln 68803
Brentwood Blvd, Cir,
Ct, Dr, Pl, Sq & Way 68801
Briarwood Blvd 68801
Bridle Ln 68803
N & S Broadwell Ave 68803
Bronco Rd 68801
Brookline Dr 68801
Buckingham Dr 68803
Buffalo Ct 68803
Buffalo Grass St 68803
C Rd 68801
Calvin Dr 68801
Cambridge Rd 68803
Cannon Rd 68803
E Capital Ave 68801
W Capital Ave 68803
Cardinal Dr 68803
Carey St 68803
Carleton Ave 68803
Carol St 68803
Catfish Ave 68801
N & S Cedar St 68801
Cedar Ridge Ct 68803
Centennial Dr 68801
Center Ln 68803
Centre St 68803
Chanticleer St 68801
Chantilly St 68803
E Chapman Rd 68801
W Chapman Rd 68803
E Charles St 68801
W Charles St
100-1699 68801
1700-2700 68803
2702-2798 68803
Chelsea Pl 68803
Cherokee Ave S 68803
N & S Cherry St 68801
Chesapeake Cir 68801
Chisholm Trail Cir 68801
Church Rd 68803
Circle Dr 68801
E Citation Way 68801
N & S Clark St 68801
Claude Rd 68803
Claussen Ave 68801
Claussen Rd 68803
S Clay St 68803
N & S Cleburn St 68801
N & S Cleveland St 68801
Cochin St 68801
College St 68803
Colonial Ln 68803
Colorado Ave 68803
Columbia Cir 68801
Commanche Ave 68803
Commerce Ave 68801
Concord Ave 68801
Conestoga Dr 68803
Congdon Ave 68801
Congressional Pl 68803
Conrad Dr 68801
Cottage St 68803
Cottonwood Rd 68801
W Cougar Dr 68803
E Court St 68801
Coventry Ln & Pl 68803
Craig Dr 68803
Cross Point Dr 68803
Curran Ave 68803
Curtis St 68803
N Custer Ave 68803
D Rd 68801
Dack Ave 68803
Daisy Cir 68803
Dakota Dr 68803
Dallas Ave 68803
N Darr Ave 68803
David Ave 68803
Dean St 68801
Deann Rd 68801
Deerwood Ave 68803
Del Mar Ave 68803
Del Monte Ave 68803
E & W Delaware Ave 68801
Deva Dr 68801
N Diers Ave 68803
E Division St 68801
W Division St
301-397 68801
399-1600 68801
1602-1698 68801
1700-2799 68803
Dixie Sq 68803
Dodge St 68801
Doreen St 68803
Dover Ct 68803
Drake Ln 68801
Driftwood Ct & Dr 68803
E Rd 68801
East Ln 68803
Ebony Ln 68803
N & S Eddy St 68801
Edna Dr 68803
E Eilenstine Rd 68801
Eisenhower Dr 68803
Eldorado St 68801
S Elk Dr 68803
N & S Elm St 68801
Elmwood Dr 68803
N & S Engleman Rd 68803
S Eugene St 68801
Evans St 68803
Evergreen Ln 68801
F Rd 68801
Faidley Ave, Ct & Pl 68803
Fairacres Ln 68801
Fairchild Ln 68801
Farmstead Rd 68801
Firestone St 68803
Fleetwood Cir & Rd 68803
E & W Fonner Park
Rd 68801
Forrest St 68803
Fort Kearney Rd 68801
Fort Worth Ave 68803
Freedom Dr 68803
Frontage Rd 68803
Frostfire Ave 68803
N & S Garfield Ave 68803
Garland St
600-1899 68803
3100-3199 68803
3201-3299 68801
Gateway Ave 68803
Geddes St 68801
George St 68803
Gladstone Cir 68803
Gold Rd 68803
Gold Core Rd 68801
Goldenrod Dr 68801
Good Samaritan Pl 68803
N Grace Ave 68803
Graham Ave 68803
Grand Ave 68801
N Grand Island Ave 68803
N & S Grant St 68803
Grassridge Dr 68803
N & S Greenwich St 68801
Greenwood Dr 68803
E Gregory St 68801
Gretchen Ave 68803
Groff St 68801
W Guenther Rd 68803
E Gulf Stream Dr 68801
N & S Gunbarrel Pl &
Rd 68801
H Rd 68801
Hagge Ave 68801
Hall Ct & St 68801
Hampton Rd 68803
Hancock Ave & Pl 68803
Hanover Ln 68803
N & S Harrison St 68803
Hartford St 68803
Heavenly Dr 68803
W Hedde St 68801
Henry St 68803
Hermitage Ct & Pl 68801
Hiawatha Pl 68803
Hidden Pointe Dr 68803
Hillside Dr 68803
Holcomb St 68801
Holland Dr 68803
N Homestead Dr 68803
Hope St 68803
Horseshoe Pl 68803
Howard Ave, Ct & Pl 68803
Hudson Cir 68803
E Husker Hwy 68801
W Husker Hwy 68803
N Huston Ave 68803
Idaho Ave 68803
Idlewood Ln 68801
Illinois Ave 68801
Imperial Pl 68803
Independence Ave 68803
Indiangrass Rd 68803
Indianhead Dr & Rd 68803
Industrial Ln 68803
Ingalls St 68803
Iowa Ave 68803
Ironwood Ave 68803
Island Cir 68803
Isle Rd 68803
Ivy Hall Ct & Pl 68803
J Rd 68801
Jackson Dr 68803
Jan St 68803
Jay St 68803
N & S Jefferson St 68801
Jerry Dr 68803
Joehnck Rd 68801
Joey Cir 68803
W John St
500-1699 68801
1700-2999 68803
Johnson Dr & Pl 68803
Johnstown Rd 68803
Juergen Rd 68801
Kaufman Ave 68803
Kay Ave 68803
Kelly St 68803
Kennedy Cir, Ct, Dr, Pl &
Way 68803
Kent Ave 68803
N & S Kimball St 68801
Kingston Cir 68803
Kingswood St 68801
Knights Rd 68803
Knott Ave 68801
E Koenig St 68801
W Koenig St
100-1599 68801
1601-1699 68801
1700-2999 68803
N Kruse Ave 68803
Kuester Lk 68801
N Lafayette Ave 68803
Lake St 68801
Lakeside Dr 68801
Lakeview Cir 68803
Lakewood Cir & Dr 68801
Lamar Ave 68803
Lambchop Ln 68803
Lambert St 68801
Langenheder St 68803
S Langenheder St 68801
Laramie Dr 68803
Lariat Ct, Ln & Pl 68803
Laura Ave 68803
Lawrence Ln 68803
Lee St 68803
Legacy Dr 68803
Lexington Cir 68803
Liberty Ln 68803
Lillie Dr 68803
N Lincoln Ave 68801
S Lincoln Ave 68801
W Lincoln Hwy 68803
Linden Ave 68801
Lockwood Rd 68801
N & S Locust St 68801
N & S Logan St 68801
W Louise St
400-1699 68801
1700-2799 68803
2801-2999 68803
Loup River Rd 68801
E Loup River Rd 68801
W Loup River Rd 68803
Lovegrass Dr 68803
Lynn Ln 68801
Macarthur Ave 68803
Macron St 68803
N & S Madison St 68801
Magnolia Ct 68803
S Main St 68801
Mallard Ln 68801
Manchester Rd 68803
Mansfield Rd 68803
Maple St 68801
Maplewood Pl 68801
Marian Rd 68803
Market St 68801
Martin Ave 68801
Mary Ln 68803
Mason Ave 68801
Maywood Dr 68803
Mc Bismark Rd 68801
Mc Capital Ave 68801
Mc Chapman Rd 68801
Mc Highway 30 68801
Mc Martin Ave 68801
Mc Stolley Park Rd 68801
Meadow Rd 68803
Meadow Way Cir &
Trl 68803
Meadowlark Cir 68803
Melody Ln 68803
Memorial Dr 68801
S Memorial Park Rd 68801
Memphis Pl 68803
Merrick Ave & Rd 68801
E Metro St 68801
Meves Ave 68801
Michigan Ave 68803
Midaro Rd 68801
Midway Rd 68801
Mill River Rd 68801
N & S Monitor Rd 68801
N & S Monroe St 68801
Montana Ave 68803
Morrison Dr 68803
Nashville St 68803
Navajo Dr 68803
Nebraska Ave 68801
Nevada Ave 68803
New Mexico Ave 68803
New York Ave 68803
S & W Newcastle Rd 68801
Nordic Rd 68803
Norseman Ave 68803
N & S North Ln & Rd 68801
W North Front St
600-1699 68801
1800-3299 68803
Northview Dr 68803
Northwest Ave 68803
Norwood Dr 68803
O Flannagan St 68803
O Grady St 68803
O Neill Cir 68801
N & S Oak St 68801
E Oklahoma Ave 68801
W Oklahoma Ave
100-1199 68801
1201-1299 68801
1700-2599 68803
Old Fair Rd 68803
W Old Highway 30 68803
W Old Lincoln Hwy 68803
W Old Potash Hwy 68803
E One-R Rd
200-299 68803
1000-2198 68801
2200-3099 68801
3101-3199 68801
W One-R Rd 68803
Orange Rd 68801
Orchardgrass Cir 68803
Orleans Dr 68803
Overland Trail Cir 68801
Oxnard Ave 68801
Palace Dr 68803
Palomino Pl 68801
Park Ave 68803
Park Dr 68801
Parkview Dr 68801
Partridge Cir 68803
Patchwork Pl 68803
Pennsylvania Ave 68803
Pheasant Dr & Pl 68801
E Phoenix Ave 68801
W Phoenix Ave
100-1000 68801
1002-1098 68801
2200-2599 68803
Phoenix Cir 68801
Phoenix Ct 68801
W Pierreda St 68803
N & S Pine St 68801
Pinhurst Pl 68803
Pinnacle Pointe Dr 68803
Pintail Ln 68801
Pioneer Blvd 68801
Piper St 68803
Plantation Pl 68803
Platte Rd 68803
Pleasant View Dr 68801
Pletcher Ter 68803
N & S Plum Rd & St 68801
Ponca Cir 68803
Ponderosa Ct & Dr 68803
Poplar St 68801
Post Pl & Rd 68801
E Prairie Rd
100-598 68803
1200-3798 68801
3800-3999 68801
W Prairie Rd 68803
Prairie Ridge Ln 68803
Primrose Dr 68801
Prospect St 68803
Public Safety Dr 68801
Quail Ln 68801
N Quandt Rd 68801
Raborn St 68801
Rainbow Rd 68801
Ramada Rd 68801
Ravenwood Ct & Dr 68801
Raymond Dr 68803
Redwood Ct & Rd 68803
Reed Rd 68803
Regal Dr 68803
Reuting Rd 68803
Richmond Cir 68803
W Ridge Ln 68803
Ridge Rd 68801
Ridge Point Dr 68803
Ridgewood Ave 68803
Rio Grande Cir 68801
Riverside Dr 68801
Riverview Dr 68801
Roberta Ave 68803
E & W Roberts Ct &
St 68803
Rochdale Cir 68803
Rolling Green Dr 68803
Roselawn Dr 68801
Rosemont Ave 68801
Rosewood Cir 68803
Roth Rd 68803
Roush Ln 68801
Royal Troon Cir 68803
Ruby Ave 68803
Rue De College 68803
Russell Rd 68801
Sacramento Cir 68803
Saddle Horse Ct 68803
Sagewood Ave 68803
Saint James Pl 68803
Saint Patrick Ave 68803
Saint Paul Rd 68801
Sandalwood Dr 68803
Sandra Rd 68801
Santa Anita Dr 68801
Santa Fe Cir 68801
Saratoga Cir 68801
Scheel Dr 68801
E Schimmer Dr 68801
W Schimmer Dr
1000-3299 68801
3401-3697 68803
3699-5999 68803
Schoolhouse Rd 68801
Schroeder Ave 68803
Schuff St 68801
E Seedling Mile Ct &
Rd 68801
N & S Shady Bend Cir,
Rd & Way 68801
Shanna St 68803
Shawnee Ct 68803
Sheridan Ave & Pl 68803
N Sherman Ave, Blvd, Ct
& Pl 68803
Sherwood Rd 68803
Sky Park Rd 68801
Sothman Dr 68803
South Ln 68803
E South St 68801
W South St 68801
E South Front St 68801
W South Front St
200-298 68801
204-204 68802
901-1699 68801
Sparrow Cir 68803
Spring Rd 68801
Springview Dr 68803
Spruce Rd 68801
Spur Ln 68803
St Andrews Cir & St 68803
Stagecoach Cir, Pl &
Rd 68801
Stardust Ln 68803
Starwood Ave 68803
State St
400-698 68801
700-799 68801
1800-3600 68803
3602-3798 68803
Stauss Rd 68803
Stewart Dr 68801
Stockyards Ln 68801
Stoeger Dr 68803
Stolley Park Cir 68803
E Stolley Park Rd 68801
W Stolley Park Rd
200-3199 68801
3300-3900 68803
3902-4148 68803
Stoneridge Path 68801
Stonewood Ave 68803
Stratford Pl 68803
S Stuhr Rd 68801
Summer Cir & Dr 68803
Summerfield Ave 68803
Sun Ridge Ln 68803
Sun Valley Dr & Pl 68801

Sunflower Dr 68801
Sunny Brooke Rd 68801
E Sunset Ave 68801
Superior St 68801
Sutherland St 68801
Swan Ln 68801
Sweetwood Dr 68803
E Swift Rd 68801
N & S Sycamore St 68801
Sylvan St 68801
Taft Ave 68801
Tara Ct & Pl 68801
N Taylor Ave 68803
Teakwood Cir 68803
Terrace Cir 68803
Texas Ave 68803
W Thorindi St 68801
N & S Tilden St 68803
Timberline St 68803
Topeka Cir 68803
Torrey Pines Pl 68803
Tri St 68801
Turn Berry Cir 68803
Union Rd 68801
W Us Highway 2 68803
N Us Highway 281 68803
S Us Highway 281
3700-7998 68803
S Us Highway 281
5501-8299 68801
E Us Highway 30 68801
W Us Highway 30 68803
E & W Us Highway 34 68801
Utah Ave 68803
Valley View Ave 68803
Vandergrift Ave 68803
Vermont Ave 68803
Via Como 68803
Via Milano 68803
Via Trivoli 68803
Vieregg Rd 68801
Viking Ct, Pl & Rd 68803
Villa Mar Dee Ave 68801
N & S Vine St 68801
Virginia Dr 68803
Voss Rd 68801
Wagon Rd 68801
Wainwright St 68801
Waldo Ave 68803
N & S Walnut St 68801
Warbler Cir & Rd 68803
Warren Ln 68801
N & S Washington St 68801
W Waugh St 68803
N Webb Rd
101-397 68803
399-2499 68803
2418-2418 68802
2500-8598 68803
2501-8599 68803
S Webb Rd 68803
Wedgewood Dr 68801
West Ave & Ln 68803
Westgate Rd 68803
Westside St 68803
N Wetzel St 68801
N & S Wheeler Ave 68801
White Ave 68803
E White Cloud Rd
400-499 68803
1001-1497 68801
1499-3399 68801
3401-3699 68801
W White Cloud Rd 68803
Wicklow Dr 68801
E Wildwood Dr 68801
W Wildwood Dr
100-998 68801
1000-3299 68801
3300-3398 68803
3400-4400 68803
4402-5498 68803
William St 68801
Willow St 68801
Wilmar Ave 68803
Windolph Ave 68801
Windridge Ave 68803
Windsor Pl & Rd 68801
W Wood River Rd 68803
S Woodland Dr 68801
Woodridge Blvd, Ct, Ln &
Pl 68801
Worms Rd 68801
Wortman Ave 68801
Wyandotte St 68801
Yund St 68801
Zola Ct & Ln 68803

NUMBERED STREETS

E 1st St 68801
W 1st St
111-197 68801
199-1699 68801
1701-1897 68803
1899-2799 68803
2nd Rd 68801
E 2nd St 68801
W 2nd St
100-1600 68801
1602-1698 68801
1700-3600 68803
3602-3798 68803
3rd Rd 68801
E 3rd St 68801
W 3rd St
100-1500 68801
1502-1620 68801
1622-1798 68803
1800-2699 68803
4th Rd 68801
E 4th St 68801
W 4th St
100-1599 68801
1601-1699 68801
1900-2298 68803
2300-2599 68803
2601-2999 68803
5th Rd 68801
E 5th St 68801
W 5th St
100-1599 68801
1800-1898 68803
1900-2999 68803
6th Rd 68801
E 6th St 68801
W 6th St
100-1599 68801
1801-1897 68803
1899-2450 68803
2452-2598 68803
E 7th St 68801
W 7th St
100-1399 68801
1401-1499 68801
1800-1900 68803
1902-2098 68803
E 8th St 68801
W 8th St
100-1300 68801
1800-2599 68803
E 9th St 68801
W 9th St
100-1399 68801
1800-1900 68803
E 10th St 68801
100-1299 68801
1800-3099 68803
W 11th Ave 68803
E 11th St 68801
W 11th St
100-1199 68801
1201-1299 68801
1800-2499 68803
E 12th St 68801
100-1199 68801
1800-2099 68803
E 13th St 68801
100-1099 68801
1800-5599 68803
E 14th St 68801
W 14th St
100-1099 68801
1800-3200 68803
E 15th St 68801
W 15th St
100-999 68801
1800-1998 68803
2000-3200 68803
3202-3298 68803
E 16th St 68801
100-999 68801
1800-3299 68803
E 17th St 68801
W 17th St
100-899 68801
1800-3299 68803
E 18th St 68801
W 18th St
100-399 68801
401-719 68801
1800-2098 68803
2100-3299 68803
E & W 19th 68801
E & W 20th 68801
E & W 21st 68801
E & W 22nd 68801
E & W 23rd 68801
N & S 60th 68803
N 70th Rd 68803

HASTINGS NE

General Delivery 68901

POST OFFICE BOXES MAIN OFFICE STATIONS AND BRANCHES

Box No.s
All PO Boxes 68902

RURAL ROUTES

01, 02, 03 68901

NAMED STREETS

E & W A St 68901
E Academic Dr 68901
Academy Ave 68901
N & S Adams Central
Ave 68901
Alpha Dr 68901
Apache Ave 68901
N Apple Ave 68901
Arapahoe Ave 68901
N & S Ash Ave 68901
N Aspen Ave 68901
E & W Assumption Rd 68901
Avalon Ln 68901
E & W B St 68901
N & S Baltimore Ave 68901
N Barnes Ave 68901
W Barrows Rd 68901
Bateman St 68901
E Battleship Dr 68901
N & S Bellevue Ave 68901
Bentwood Ln 68901
N Birch Ave 68901
N Blaine Ave 68901
S Boston Ave 68901
Boyce St 68901
E Bravo Dr 68901
Brentwood Ave 68901
Briarwood Ave 68901
N Briggs Ave 68901
E Buffalo Cir 68901
N & S Burlington Ave 68901
Butterfoot Ln 68901
E & W C St 68901
N & S California Ave 68901
N & S Cedar Ave 68901
Centennial Ave 68901
E Charlie Dr 68901
Chestnut Ave 68901
S Chicago Ave 68901
Cimarron Ave & Plz 68901
Circle N 68901
Circle A 68901
Circle B 68901
Circle C 68901
Circle D 68901
Circle F 68901
Circle L 68901
Circle M 68901
Circle O 68901
Circle P 68901
Circle Q 68901
Circle R 68901
E Clark St 68901
Colonial Pl 68901
N & S Colorado Ave 68901
N Columbine Ave 68901
E Community Dr 68901
Cooper Cir 68901
S Cornhusker Ave 68901
W Cottonwood Cv 68901
Country Club Dr 68901
Cranbrook Ln 68901
Crane Ave 68901
Crane Circle Dr 68901
Creighton Ave 68901
Crestmoor Dr 68901
E & W D St 68901
S Deer Trl 68901
N & S Delaware Ave 68901
E Delta Dr 68901
N & S Denver Ave 68901
Dld Rd 68901
Dockside Cv 68901
Durwood Ln 68901
E & W E St 68901
Eastside Blvd 68901
Edgewood Ln 68901
S Elkhorn Rd 68901
N & S Elm Ave 68901
S Emerson Ave 68901
E & W F St 68901
Fantasy Forest Rd 68901
Fisherman Ln 68901
Forest Blvd 68901
W Fork Ave 68901
S Franklin Ave 68901
E & W G St 68901
S Garfield Ave 68901
Glenwood Ave 68901
E Grand St 68901
Greenhouse Ct 68901
N & S Gunpowder Cir 68901
E & W H St 68901
E Hadco Rd 68901
N Hansen Ave 68901
N & S Hastings Ave 68901
Hastings Regional Ctr 68902
Hawthorne Cir 68901
Hay Meadow Rdg 68901
S Heartland Ave 68901
Heritage Dr & Pl 68901
N Hewett Ave 68901
Hickory Ave 68901
N Highland Dr & Rd 68901
E & W Highway 6 68901
Hill St 68901
W Hillangt St 68901
Hillside Dr 68901
S Hilltop Rd 68901
Holly Dr 68901
Home St 68901
Hornet Dr 68901
W I St 68901
W & E Idlewilde Dr &
Rd 68901
Imperial Dr 68901
Indian Acres Dr 68901
E Industry Cir S 68901
E & W J St 68901
Jefferson Ave 68901
Jeffery Ln 68901
W K St 68901
N & S Kansas Ave 68901
E & W Kent St 68901
N Kerr Ave 68901
S Keystone Ave 68901
Kingsdale Rd 68901
Kingston Dr 68901
N Laird Ave 68901
Lake Park Ln 68901
Lakeridge Dr 68901
Lakeside Dr 68901
S Lakeview Ave, Cv, Dr
& Ter 68901
Lane E 68901
Lane A 68901
Lane B 68901
Lane C 68901
Lane D 68901
Lane F 68901
Lane G 68901
Lane H 68901
Lane I 68901
Lane J 68901
Laredo Ln 68901
Laurie St 68901
Lawrence 68901
Leisure Ln 68901
N & S Lexington Ave 68901
S Lifesong Cir 68901
N & S Lincoln Ave 68901
Linden Ave 68901
Loch Loyal Ct 68901
E & W Lochland Rd 68901
Lochview Dr 68901
W M St 68901
Macarthur Rd 68901
Madden Ct & Rd 68901
Magnolia Ln 68901
Mallard Cir & Way 68901
N & S Maple Ave 68901
Maplewood Ave 68901
N & S Marian Rd 68901
Martin Ave 68901
N & S Maxon Ave 68901
Maywood Dr 68901
Mcdonald Ave 68901
S Meadow Ln 68901
E Meadowlark Cir &
Ln 68901
Miller St 68901
N & S Minnesota Ave 68901
Morningside Dr 68901
Nathan Way 68901
S Nebraska Ave 68901
S New York Ave 68901
E & W Oak Ridge Rd 68901
Oakmont Ave 68901
W Olive Knls 68901
E Oliver St 68901
E & W Oregon Trail
Rd 68901
N & S Osage Ave 68901
Osborne Dr E & W 68901
Oswego Ave 68901
Outrigger Dr 68901
Pacific St 68901
Paradise Dr 68901
E Park Ln & St 68901
Park Lane Dr 68901
Park West Dr 68901
E & W Paul St 68901
N & S Pawnee Ave 68901
Pepperridge Dr 68901
Pershing Rd 68901
S Persimmon Ave 68901
Pheasant Cir 68901
Pheasant Run Ave 68901
N & S Pine Ave 68901
Pine Knoll Rd 68901
Pintail Cir 68901
Pleasant St 68901
E & W Prairie Lake
Rd 68901
Quail Cir & Cor 68901
Quail Ridge Ave 68901
S Queen City Ave 68901
Randolph Cir 68901
Regency Dr 68901
Renae Ln 68901
N & S Rhode Island
Ave 68901
Richmond Ave 68901
S Ridge Rd 68901
Ringland Rd 68901
Road 192b 68901
Road 316 68901
Road 3165 68901
Road 3167 68901
Road 3168 68901
Road 318 68901
Road 319 68901
Road A 68901
Road B 68901
Ronan Dr 68901
S Ross Ave 68901
E & W Saddlehorn Rd 68901
N & S Saint Joseph
Ave 68901
Sara Dr 68901
N Saunders Ave 68901
S Sewell Ave 68901
Sheridan Dr & Pl 68901
N & S Shore Dr 68901
Shoreside Cv 68901
N & S Showboat Blvd 68901
Skyeloch 68901
S Smokey Hill Rd 68901
E & W South St 68901
Southern Hills Dr &
Rd 68901
Spanish Trl 68901
N Spruce Ave 68901
Summit Ave 68901
Sumner Ave 68901
Sunset Cir & Dr 68901
Sycamore Ave 68901
S Technical Blvd 68901
Thomas Dr 68901
Tilden Ave 68901
N Turner Ave 68901
University St 68901
S Us Highway 281 68901
Valley Rd 68901
Valley Chase Ave 68901
Valley Road Idlewilde 68901
Village Dr 68901
S Wabash Ave 68901
Walden Cir 68901
N Washington Ave 68901
Wayfair Dr 68901
Waynoka St 68901
N Webster Ave 68901
Wendell Dr 68901
Westchester Dr 68901
Westlawn Ave 68901
Westridge Dr 68901
Westwood Ter 68901
N & S Wildflower Ave 68901
N Williams Ave 68901
Windsor Dr 68901
N & S Woodland Ave 68901
N Yorktown Dr 68901
Yost Ave 68901

NUMBERED STREETS

All Street Addresses 68901

KEARNEY NE

General Delivery 68847

POST OFFICE BOXES MAIN OFFICE STATIONS AND BRANCHES

Box No.s
All PO Boxes 68848

RURAL ROUTES

02 68845
01 68847

NAMED STREETS

A Ave 68847
Airport Rd 68847
Al St 68845
Amherst Rd 68845
Antelope Ave
200-298 68845
401-699 68845
1601-1697 68847
1699-10300 68847
10302-10798 68847
Antelope Rd 68847
Apache Ln 68847
Arapahoe Ln 68847
E & W Arbor Ln 68845
Archway Pkwy 68847
Ash Pl & St 68845
S, E & N Avenue Pl 68847
B Ave 68847
B Avenue Pl 68847
Beall Dr 68845
Bel Air Dr 68845
Bennett Trl 68845
Biehl Rd 68847
Birch St 68845
Birchwood Dr & Pl 68845
Bison Run & St 68845
Blue Mill Rd 68847
Boa Dr 68847
Bonnie Rd 68845
Brandts Lakewood 68845
Buffalo Ave 68845
C Ave 68847
C Avenue Pl 68847
Camelot Way 68845
Canal Heights Dr 68845
Carlton Dr 68847
Catalpa Pl 68845
Cedar Ln, Pl & St 68845
E & W Cedar Hills Dr &
Pl 68845
Centennial Ln 68845
Center Place Rd 68847
S Central Ave 68847
Cherry Ave & Rd 68847
Clearview Dr 68847
Clydesdale Cir 68845
Coal Chute Rd 68847
Cottonmill Ave 68845
E & W Cottonwood Ln,
Pl & Rd 68845
Couniang 68847
Country Club Ln 68845
Crestview Dr 68845
Crestview Pl 68847
Crown Rd 68845
D Ave 68847
Date St 68845
Deerview Dr 68847
Doug St 68845
Dove Hill Ave 68845
E Ave
1003-1003 68847
1005-2300 68847
2302-5498 68847
2401-5499 68847
2401-2401 68848
Eagle Rd 68845
Eastbrooke Dr 68847
Elm Dr, Rd & St 68845
Elmwood Ln 68845
Evergreen Rd 68845
F Ave 68847
F Avenue Pl 68847
Fairacres Rd 68845
Fairway Ave 68845
Farcer Rd 68845
Fawn Woods Trl 68847
Forineri Ave 68845
Front St 68845
Front View Dr 68847
G Ave 68847
G Avenue Pl 68847

Glenwood Rd 68845
Grand Ave 68847
Grandview Hts 68845
Green Hill Rd 68845
Grove Rd 68845
H Ave 68847
H Avenue Pl 68847
Hackamore Dr 68845
Hawk Rd 68847
Heather Ln 68845
Hemlock Dr 68845
Hickory Dr 68845
Hidden Hills Rd 68845
Highland Dr 68845
Highway 10 68847
Highway 30 68845
Highway 30 E 68845
Highway 30 W 68845
W Highway 40 68845
Hillcrest Dr 68845
Homestead Rd 68847
Huron Dr 68847
I Ave 68847
Imperial Ave 68847
Indian Rd 68847
Indian Hills Dr 68847
Iron Horse Rd 68845
K Ave 68847
Kea West Ave S 68845
Keystone Rd 68847
Kimler Ave 68845
Kings Ct 68845
L Ave 68847
L Avenue Pl 68847
La Crosse Dr 68845
W La Platte Rd 68845
La Vista Rd 68845
N Lake Dr 68845
Lakeside Dr 68845
Lakeview Dr 68845
Lakewood Dr 68847
Landon St 68847
Larson Ln 68845
E Lawn Ct 68847
Linden Dr 68847
Linden Drive Pl 68847
Lindsay Rd 68845
Long Island Rd 68845
Loveland Dr 68845
M Ave S 68847
M Avenue Pl 68847
Madison Pl 68847
Magpie Rd 68845
Main Ave 68845
Maple Dr 68845
Maplewood Pl 68847
Meadow Ln 68845
Meadowlark Ln 68845
Mesa Ln 68845
Mustang Trl 68845
N Ave 68847
N-M Ln 68845
Newark St 68847
Northview Dr 68847
O Ave 68847
O Avenue Pl 68847
Oak Ln & Pl 68845
Oakmont Pl 68847
Odessa Rd 68845
Oxen Ave 68845
P Ave 68847
P Avenue Pl 68847
Palamino Rd 68845
Parklane Dr & Pl 68847
Parkwood Ln 68845
Pine Dr 68845
Platte Rd 68847
Plaza Blvd & Dr 68845
Pleasant Valley Dr 68845
Pony Express Dr & Rd 68847
Pony Lake Rd 68847
Poole Ave & Rd 68847
Prairie Hills Rd 68845
Prairie View Pl 68845
Puddle Blvd 68845
Q Ave 68847
Q Avenue Pl 68847
R Ave 68847
E Railroad St 68847
S Railroad St 68847
W Railroad St
9-97 68847
99-111 68847
113-199 68847
301-999 68845
Red Fox Ln 68845
Redwood Dr & Ln 68845
N Regency Pl 68847
Ridgeline Rd 68845
Rio Madera Rd 68845
Rochford St 68845
Rolling Hills Rd 68845
S Ave 68847
E & W Saddlehorse Dr 68847
Sandy Ln 68845
Sartoria Rd 68845
Seminole Ln 68847
Sherwood Cir 68845
Sioux Ln 68847
Skyline Dr 68845
Sleepy Hollow Ln 68847
Stagecoach Ln 68845
Standage Pl 68845
Summerhaven Lk 68847
Summitt Rd 68845
Sunset Trl 68845
Sweetwater Ave & Rd 68847
Sycamore Pl 68847
T Ave & Rd 68847
Tabor Pl 68847
Tahoe Dr 68847
W Talmadge Rd
100-199 68847
201-397 68845
399-599 68845
601-1099 68845
Turkey Ridge Rd 68845
U Ave 68847
U Rd
546-552 68845
700-1099 68847
1101-1199 68847
74600-74699 68845
University Dr 68845
University Drive Cir 68845
V Rd
148-446 68847
448-599 68845
650-746 68847
748-1299 68847
Valleyview Hts 68845
W Villa Dr 68845
Vista View Ln 68845
W Rd 68845
Wedge Way 68845
Wilderness Way 68847
Willow Ln 68845
Windmill Rd 68845
Windy Meadows Rd 68847
Winnipeg Rd 68845
Wood River Rd 68847
Ydc Rd 68845
Yellow Rose Ln 68845

NUMBERED STREETS

1st Ave 68847
1st St 68845
E 1st St 68847
E 1st St S 68847
W 1st St 68845
1st Avenue N 68847
2nd Ave 68847
2nd Ave E 68847
2nd Ave S 68847
2nd Ave W 68847
W 2nd St 68845
W 3rd Ave & St 68845
4th Ave 68845
W 4th St
100-199 68847
320-398 68847
400-501 68845
503-617 68845
W 4th Street Pl 68845
5th Ave 68845
5th Avenue Pl 68845
6th Ave 68845
E 6th St 68847
6th Avenue Pl 68845
7th Ave 68845
8th Ave 68845
E 8th St 68847
W 8th St
1-99 68847
315-397 68845
399-1110 68845
1112-1298 68845
W 9th Ave & St 68845
9th Avenue Pl 68845
W 9th St Pl 68845
10th Ave 68845
W 10th Dr 68845
E 10th St 68847
W 10th St
2-16 68847
600-604 68847
606-704 68845
706-798 68847
10th Avenue Pl 68845
11th Ave 68845
E 11th St 68847
W 11th St
2-98 68847
101-199 68845
301-513 68845
515-4100 68845
4102-4498 68845
11th Avenue Pl 68845
12th Ave 68845
W 12th St
2-98 68847
200-815 68845
12th Avenue Pl 68845
W 12th Street Pl 68845
13th Ave 68845
E 13th St 68847
W 13th St
100-112 68847
201-697 68845
699-1305 68845
1307-1403 68845
W 13th Street Pl 68845
14th Ave 68845
E 14th St 68847
W 14th St
1-99 68847
201-497 68845
499-899 68845
901-999 68845
W 14th Street Pl 68845
15th Ave 68845
E 15th St 68847
W 15th St 68845
W 15th Street Pl 68845
16th Ave 68845
E 16th St 68847
W 16th St
2-198 68847
201-207 68845
209-1721 68845
1723-2915 68845
17th Ave 68845
17th Rd 68845
E 17th St 68847
W 17th St
1-99 68847
101-199 68845
201-211 68845
213-921 68845
923-999 68845
17th Avenue Pl 68845
E 18th St 68847
W 18th St
2-12 68847
14-100 68847
102-198 68847
200-700 68845
702-7098 68845
19th Ave 68845
E 19th St 68847
W 19th St
1-199 68847
200-208 68845
210-1200 68845
1202-1298 68845
20th Ave 68845
E 20th St 68847
W 20th St 68845
E 21st St 68847
W 21st St
9-13 68847
15-99 68847
101-199 68845
200-1400 68845
1402-1498 68845
21st Avenue Pl 68845
22nd Ave 68845
E 22nd St 68847
W 22nd St
2-6 68847
15-99 68847
201-205 68845
207-1499 68845
1501-3199 68845
E 23rd St 68847
W 23rd St
1-99 68847
401-497 68845
24th Rd 68845
E 24th St 68847
W 24th St
17-97 68847
99-106 68847
108-198 68847
201-297 68845
299-2999 68845
E 25th St 68847
W 25th St
1-15 68847
17-199 68847
218-298 68845
300-821 68845
823-6899 68845
25th Avenue Pl 68845
E 26th St 68847
W 26th St
9-105 68847
107-112 68847
114-116 68847
215-219 68845
221-905 68845
907-1299 68845
27th Ave 68845
E 27th St 68847
W 27th St
1-199 68847
200-900 68845
902-998 68845
28th Ave 68845
E 28th St 68847
W 28th St
1-199 68847
200-799 68845
801-899 68845
29th Ave 68845
E 29th St 68847
W 29th St
1-9 68847
11-112 68847
114-198 68847
200-7499 68845
29th Avenue Pl 68845
30th Ave 68845
E 30th Dr 68847
E 30th St 68847
W 30th St
13-13 68847
15-100 68847
102-114 68847
200-6199 68845
E 31st St 68847
W 31st St
5-123 68847
200-298 68845
E 32nd St 68847
115-199 68847
200-499 68845
E 32nd Street Pl 68847
33rd Ave 68845
E 33rd Dr 68847
E 33rd St 68847
W 33rd St
100-198 68847
200-999 68845
1001-1099 68845
E 34th St 68847
W 34th St 68845
W 34th Street Pl 68845
W 35th Rd 68845
E 35th St 68847
W 35th St 68845
35th Avenue Pl 68845
W 36th Dr 68845
E 36th St 68847
W 36th St
1-5 68847
200-2199 68845
W 36th Street Pl 68845
E 37th St 68847
2-4 68847
300-7499 68845
38th Dr & St 68845
39th Rd 68845
E 39th St 68847
W 39th St
9-99 68847
200-2800 68845
2802-5630 68845
W 40th St 68845
E 41st St 68847
W 41st St 68845
E 41st Street Pl 68847
42nd Ave 68845
E 42nd St 68847
W 42nd St 68845
E 42nd Street Pl 68847
E 43rd St 68847
W 43rd St 68845
E 43rd Street Pl 68847
W 43rd Street Pl 68845
44th Ave 68845
E 44th St 68847
W 44th St
1-99 68847
200-2899 68845
E 44th Street Pl 68847
W 44th Street Pl 68845
E 45th St 68847
1-99 68847
1000-1199 68845
46th Ave 68845
E 46th St 68847
W 46th St
2-98 68847
100-199 68847
600-899 68845
901-1005 68845
E 46th Street Pl 68847
W 46th Street Pl 68845
47th Ave 68845
47th St 68845
E 47th St 68847
W 47th St 68845
E 47th Street Pl 68847
W 47th Street Pl 68845
E 48th St 68847
W 48th St
2-98 68847
412-498 68845
W 48th Street Pl 68845
W 49th St 68845
E 49th Street Pl 68847
W 49th Street Pl 68845
W 50th St 68845
E 51st St 68847
E 52nd St 68847
W 52nd St 68845
E 52nd Street Pl 68847
53rd Ave 68845
E 53rd St 68847
E 53rd Street Pl 68847
E 54th St 68847
E 54th Street Pl 68847
55th Ave 68845
56th Ave 68845
56th Rd 68845
E 56th St 68847
W 56th St
2-198 68847
301-1437 68845
1439-6900 68845
6902-7642 68845
E 57th St 68847
E 57th Street Pl 68847
58th Ave 68845
E 58th St 68847
E 59th St 68847
W 60th Ave & St 68845
62nd Ave 68845
E 62nd St 68847
W 62nd St 68845
62nd Avenue Pl 68845
W 62nd Street Pl 68845
E 63rd St 68847
E 63rd Street Pl 68847
64th Avenue Pl 68845
65th Avenue Pl 68845
E 65th Street Pl 68847
W 66th St 68845
66th Avenue Pl 68845
E 66th Street Pl 68847
E 67th St 68847
W 67th St 68845
67th Avenue Pl 68845
68th Ave 68845
68th Avenue Pl 68845
69th Ave 68845
E 69th St 68847
E 69th Street Pl 68847
W 70th St 68845
70th Avenue Pl 68845
71st Ave 68845
72nd Ave 68845
72nd Avenue Pl 68845
W 73rd St 68845
76th Ave 68845
78th Rd 68845
E 78th St 68847
W 78th St 68845
W 81st St 68845
W 82nd St 68845
W 85th St 68845
90th Pl 68845
90th Street Pl 68845
E 92nd St 68847
W 92nd St 68845
E 95th St 68847
W 98th St 68845
E 99th St 68847
99th Street Pl 68845
100th Rd
11600-18499 68845
39900-39998 68847
E 100th St 68847
W 100th St 68845
E 101st St 68847
W 102 Street Pl 68845
E 102nd St 68847
E & W 103rd 68847
W 105th Street Pl 68845
E 106th Street Cir 68847
E 106th St 68847
E 108th St 68847
W 111th Street Pl 68845
W 112th St 68845
115th Rd
23800-24298 68845
24300-26799 68845
26801-28799 68845
29200-36199 68847
128th Rd 68845
130th Rd
26900-28298 68845
32100-37399 68847
145th Rd
24400-28968 68845
29000-34099 68847
160th Rd
25800-25898 68845
25900-25999 68845
29701-32697 68847
32699-35400 68847
35402-36098 68847
167th Rd 68847
170th Rd 68847
175th Rd
28900-28998 68845
29600-29798 68847
29800-31299 68847
31301-32799 68847
190th Rd 68847
20 W 68845
21 Rd 68845
22 Rd 68845
23 Rd 68845
24 Rd 68845
25 Rd 68847
27 Rd 68847
28 Rd 68847
29 Rd 68847
30 Rd 68847
31 Rd 68847
63 Rd 68845
747 Rd 68845
W 96 St 68845

LINCOLN NE

General Delivery 68501

POST OFFICE BOXES MAIN OFFICE STATIONS AND BRANCHES

Box No.s
2200 - 2800 68542
4000 - 4788 68504
5001 - 5994 68505
6001 - 6991 68506
9998 - 9998 68504
9998 - 9998 68509
9998 - 9998 68529
21641 - 23216 68542
29101 - 29816 68529
30004 - 30950 68503
57001 - 57597 68505
67001 - 67296 68506
80001 - 87865 68501
94600 - 98968 68509
830700 - 839809 68583
880100 - 884100 68588

RURAL ROUTES

32 68504
03 68507
11, 15, 25 68521
13 68527

NAMED STREETS

A St
100-400 68502
402-2799 68502
2801-2899 68502
2901-3197 68510
3199-8299 68510
8301-8399 68510
8400-8498 68520
8500-11000 68520
11002-15398 68520
W A St
102-398 68522
400-5405 68522
5407-5599 68522

6005-6697 68532
6699-13399 68532
13401-13999 68532
Aaron Cir 68516
Abbey Ct 68505
Abbott Rd 68516
Aberdeen Ave 68512
Abigail Cir & Dr 68516
Adams St
201-297 68521
299-1500 68521
1502-1898 68521
3400-5599 68504
5600-9799 68507
10500-19399 68527
W Adams St 68524
Addison Ct 68516
W Adriene St 68524
Agate Ct 68516
Agatha Dr 68516
Air Park Rd 68524
Alamosa Dr 68516
Alana Ln 68512
Alden Ave 68502
Aldrich Rd 68510
Alexander Rd 68521
Algonquin St 68524
Ali Dr 68507
Alicia Ln 68506
Alimark Ln 68516
Allen Rd 68516
Allendale Ct & Dr 68516
Alles Cir 68510
W Allison Ct 68521
Almira Ln 68516
Alpha St 68510
Alvo Rd
1200-1298 68531
5001-5299 68514
5301-5400 68514
5402-5498 68514
15200-16099 68527
W Alvo Rd
1400-1999 68531
2000-2699 68524
Amanda Rd 68507
Amber Hill Ct 68526
Amber Hill Rd
7800-8199 68516
8201-8399 68516
8400-8448 68526
8450-8499 68526
Amelia Dr 68516
Amhurst Dr 68510
Ammon Ave
1900-2299 68505
2300-2799 68507
Anaheim Dr 68506
Andermatt Dr 68526
Anderson Dr 68506
Andre Cir 68526
Andrea Pl 68512
Andrew Ct 68512
Andy Dr 68516
Angeline Ct 68526
Anna Pl 68507
Annette Ln 68512
Anns Ct 68516
Antelope Cir 68506
Antelope Creek Rd 68506
Antelope Valley Pkwy 68508
N Antelope Valley Pkwy 68503
S Antelope Valley Pkwy 68510
Anthony Ln 68520
Antler Ct & Dr 68516
Apache Trl 68505
Apple St 68503
Apple Way 68516
Applewood Dr 68516
W Apricot Ln 68522
W Arabian Rd 68523
Arapahoe St 68502
Arbor Rd
1400-2599 68531
4000-5599 68514
5700-7800 68517
7802-7898 68517
Arctic Cir & Dr 68521
Argyll Pl 68512
Aries Dr 68512
Arlene Ave 68502
Arlington Ave 68502
W Arlington Ave 68522
W Arlington Cir 68522
W Arlington St 68522
Arrow Head Cir 68520
Arrow Ridge Pl & Rd 68506
Arrow Wood Rd 68526
Artisan Ct & Way 68516
Ascot Cir 68516
NW Ash Ct 68521
Ash Hollow Ct & Ln 68516
Ashbrook Dr 68516
Ashlee Ln 68516
Ashley Ave & Cir 68524
Aspen Ln 68510
Aspen Canyon Rd 68526
Aster Rd 68521
Atlas Ave & Cir 68521
Atwood Cir & Ln 68521
Aubree Ave 68516
Augusta Cir & Dr 68526
W Aurora St 68524
Austin Dr 68506
Avalon Ct 68526
N Aventint St 68527
Aviation Rd 68524
E & W Avon Ln 68505
Aylesworth Ave
4801-4897 68504
4899-5399 68504
5601-5697 68505
5699-7700 68505
7702-7798 68505
Azalea Pl 68516
Aztec Ct 68516
W B Ct 68522
B St
101-107 68502
109-2699 68502
3300-4499 68510
W B St 68522
Badger Dr 68516
Bair Ave 68504
Baldwin Ave
3500-4899 68504
4901-4999 68504
5600-7799 68507
Ballard Ave 68507
Ballard Cir 68504
Ballard Ct 68504
Bancroft Ave
1800-1898 68502
4500-4598 68506
4600-8299 68506
Barbara Ln 68512
Barjona Pl 68516
Barkley Dr
8300-8399 68516
8500-8599 68526
Barkwood Ln 68516
Barrington Pl & Rd 68516
Barrington Park Dr 68516
Barrow Ct 68521
Bartholomew Cir 68512
Basswood Ct 68506
Baxter Pl 68516
Bayberry Pl 68516
Beacon Hill Cir 68521
Beadle 68588
Beal Cir & St 68521
Bear Creek Rd 68516
Beatrice St 68506
Beaver Creek Ct & Ln 68516
Beaver Hollow Cir 68516
Beckman Cir 68502
Beckys Way Rd 68514
W Bedford St 68521
Bedloe Ct 68505
Beechcraft Rd 68527
Beechwood Dr 68510
Belford St 68521
N Bell St 68528
Bellagio Dr 68516
Bellhaven Dr 68516
Bellville Cir & Dr 68521
W Belmont Ave 68521
Belridge Dr 68521
W Benelli Ln 68532
Benjamin Pl 68516
S Bennington Pl 68516
Bentley Dr 68516
Benton Ct 68521
Benton St
701-797 68521
799-2199 68521
4800-4898 68504
4900-5499 68504
5501-5599 68504
5900-5998 68507
6000-6999 68507
10000-10099 68527
W Benton St
130-498 68521
2500-4798 68524
4800-5499 68524
Benziger Dr 68526
Berg Dr 68505
Berkeley Dr 68512
Berkshire Ct 68505
Berlene Ave 68506
E & S Bermuda Dr 68506
Bernese Blvd 68516
Berrywood Ct & Ln 68516
Bethany Park Dr 68505
Betty Lou Blvd 68516
NW Bewley Ct 68528
Big Horn Dr 68516
Big Tree Cir 68522
Billings Ct & Dr 68516
W Billy Ct 68524
Bilmar Cir 68521
Bingham Cir, Ct & Ln 68516
Birch Creek Cir, Dr & Pl 68516
Birch Hollow Dr 68516
Birchwood Dr 68510
Birmingham Ct 68516
Bison Ct & Dr 68516
Black Forest Ct & Dr 68516
Blackberry Cir 68516
Blackbird Ln 68516
Blackhawk Cir & Dr 68521
Blackpool Rd 68516
Blacksmith Ct & Rd 68507
Blackstone Rd 68526
Blackwater Bay 68505
Blackwood Ave 68526
Blaine Dr 68521
Blanca Dr 68521
Blanchard Blvd 68516
W Blue Bird Ln 68532
Blue Flame Rd 68521
Blue Heron Ct & Dr 68522
Blue Ridge Ln 68516
Blue Sage Blvd 68521
Blue Sky Dr 68505
Blue Spruce Dr 68505
Blue Water Cir 68527
Blue Water Bay Rd 68527
Blueberry Ct 68516
Bluff Rd
500-799 68531
5000-5299 68514
5700-5998 68517
6000-8399 68517
W Bluff Rd
200-999 68531
2700-2799 68524
Bo Creek Ct 68516
Bo Creek Bay 68516
Boat House Rd 68527
Bobcat Cir 68523
Boboli Ln 68516
Bodie Cir 68516
Boeckner Ave 68516
Bolton Rd 68516
Bonacum Dr 68502
Bond Cir & St 68521
Boone Trl 68516
Booth Cir 68521
Bordeaux Cir & Rd 68522
Boston Cir & Dr 68521
Boulder Dr 68516
Boulder Ridge Ct 68526
W Bow Bridge Rd 68523
Bowman Dr 68526
Box Canyon Cir 68516
Boxelder Cir & Dr 68506
NW Boxwood Ct 68521
Bradfield Dr 68502
Bradley Ave 68507
Bradock Ct & Dr 68516
Braemer Rd 68516
Branched Oak Rd
5500-5598 68514
6600-9099 68517
Brandt Cir & St 68506
Brandywine Cir 68516
Branford Pl 68512
Braumfield Cir 68516
Breagan Rd 68526
Breckenridge Dr 68521
Brennen View Ct 68512
Brent Blvd 68506
Brentwood Cir 68506
Bretigne Cir & Dr 68512
Briar Rosa Dr 68516
Briarhurst Cir & Dr 68506
Briarpark Dr 68516
Briarpatch Cir 68516
Briarwood Ave 68516
Bridger Rd 68521
Bridle Ln 68516
Brighton Ave 68506
Bristol Ct 68512
Bristolwood Ln & Pl 68516
W Britt Dr 68521
Brittany Pl 68516
W Brixton Dr 68521
Broadmoore Dr 68506
W Broadview Dr 68505
Broken Spoke Dr 68507
Brome Ln 68512
Brookfield Dr 68506
Brookhaven Dr 68506
Brookside Dr 68528
Brookview Dr 68506
Brower Rd 68502
Browning Ct, Pl & St 68516
Bruce Dr 68510
Brummond Dr 68516
Brushwood Ln 68516
Bryan Cir 68506
Bryson St 68510
Buckboard Dr & Ln 68532
Buckingham Dr 68506
W Bucks Cir & Dr 68523
W Buckthorn Rd 68523
Buffalo Cir 68516
Buffalo Creek Rd 68516
Bunker Hill Rd 68521
W Burgess Ln 68523
Burlington Ave 68507
Burnham St 68502
W Burnham St 68522
Burr St 68502
W Burr Oaks Rd 68523
W Burt Dr 68521
Burton St 68526
Bushclover Rd 68521
Butler Ave 68521
W Butler Ave
300-699 68521
2400-5298 68524
5300-5499 68524
W C Ct 68522
C St
100-2699 68502
3001-3197 68510
3199-4399 68510
4401-4899 68510
W C St 68522
Cable Ave
2700-3099 68502
3400-3499 68506
Cactus Ct 68516
Cademon Cir & Ct 68523
California Ct 68510
Calumet Ct 68502
Calvert Pl 68506
Calvert St
600-700 68502
702-3298 68502
1201-3199 68502
1201-1201 68542
3300-5699 68506
5701-5799 68506
9400-9698 68520
W Calvert St 68522
Cambrian Ct & Dr 68510
Cambridge Ct 68505
Camden Pl 68506
Camellia Ct 68516
Camelot Ct 68512
Cameron Ct 68512
Campbell Dr 68510
Campers Cir 68521
Campfire Cir 68512
Candletree Ln 68506
Candlewood Ln 68521
Cannondale Ct 68516
Canopy St 68508
S Canterbury Ln 68512
Canyon Ct & Rd 68516
Cape Charles Ct, Dr & Rd E & W 68516
Capitol Ave 68510
Capitol Beach Blvd 68528
Capitola Dr 68512
Cardinal Cir 68506
W Cardwell Cir & Rd 68523
Carger Ln 68516
Carlisle Ct 68516
Carlos Dr 68505
Carlsbad Dr 68510
Carlton Cir & Dr 68512
Carmen Dr 68516
Carnelian St 68516
W Carnoustie Ct 68521
Carol Cir 68505
Carolyn Ct 68510
Carriage Way 68510
Carriage Hill Ct 68510
W Carrine Dr 68521
Carson Rd 68516
NW Carver Cir 68521
Casa Grande Ln 68516
Cascade Cir & Dr 68504
Casey Ln 68516
Castle Cir 68524
Cattail Rd 68521
Cavalry Ct 68528
Cavvy Rd 68516
Caymus Ct 68526
Cedar Ave 68502
Cedar Cove Rd 68507
Cedar Creek Cir 68516
Cedar Crest St 68521
Cedarwood Dr 68506
Centennial Mall N & S 68508
Center St 68503
Center Park Rd 68512
Central Park Dr 68504
Cessna Cir & Ln 68527
Chadd Ct 68521
Chadderton Cir & Dr 68521
Chalk Hill Ct & Dr 68526
NW Chambers Dr 68524
W Champion Ct 68524
Champlain Dr 68521
Chanceler Ct & Dr 68521
Chancery Ct, Ln & Rd 68521
Chandon Dr 68526
Channel Dr 68516
Chanticleer Cir 68521
Chaparral Cir 68520
Chapel Hills Ln 68507
Chapin Cir 68506
W Charles Hall Ave 68522
Charleston St 68508
W Charleston St 68528
Chartwell Ln 68516
Chateau Cir 68526
Chatsworth Ln 68516
Chaucer St 68516
Chautauqua Ave 68510
Chelsea Ct 68516
Cheney Ridge Cir & Rd 68516
Cherry Hill Blvd 68510
Cherrycreek Rd 68528
Cherrywood Dr 68510
W Chesapeake Cir 68524
Cheshire Ct N & S 68512
Chester St 68526
N Chester St 68521
Chesterfield Ct 68510
Chestnut Ln 68510
Cheyenne St 68502
Chicago Ave 68527
Chileno Dr 68516
Chisholm Pl & Rd 68516
Chiswick Ct & Dr 68516
W Chitwood Ln 68528
Chloe Ln 68512
Christensen Ct 68510
Christina Ct 68521
Christopher Ct 68516
Cindy Dr 68512
Circle Dr 68506
City View Ct 68521
Claire Ave 68516
W Claire Ave 68523
Claremont St 68508
Clark Ave 68510
Clayton Ct 68507
Clear Creek Dr 68516
Clear Sky Rd 68505
Clearview Blvd 68512
Clearwater Bay 68505
Cleveland Ave
2501-2599 68521
3300-5499 68504
5600-6999 68507
7001-7599 68507
W Cleveland Ave 68524
Clifford Dr 68506
Clinton St 68503
Cloudburst Ln 68521
Clover Cir 68516
Coachmans Ct & Dr 68510
Cobblestone Cir & Dr 68510
N Coddington Ave 68528
S Coddington Ave
101-197 68522
199-3799 68522
3801-4099 68522
4200-4598 68523
4600-6099 68523
6101-6659 68523
Cody Dr 68512
Colby St
5001-5097 68504
5099-5599 68504
5600-9300 68505
9302-9440 68505
Cold Spring Rd 68512
Coldwater Bay 68505
Cole Ct 68506
Colfax Ave
4000-5399 68504
5800-5898 68507
5900-7325 68507
Colfax Cir 68504
E Colfax Cir 68507
College Park Cir & Rd 68505
Collister Rd 68516
Colonial Dr 68502
Colony Ln 68505
Colorado Dr 68521
Colt Ave 68507
NW Columbine Dr 68524
W Commerce Way 68521
W Commodore Blvd 68522
Comoy Cir 68505
Concord Cir & Rd 68516
W Condor Ln 68528
Coneflower Ct 68521
NW Conifer Ct 68521
Connie Rd 68502
Connor Pl & St 68505
Consentino Ct 68526
Constable Ave 68506
Constitution Ave 68521
Cooper Ave, Ct & Pl 68506
Copper Ridge Dr 68516
Coral Dr 68516
Cornell Rd 68516
Cornflower Dr 68504
Cornhusker Hwy
1100-2600 68521
2602-2698 68521
2700-5599 68504
5600-5898 68507
5900-8899 68507
9800-10499 68517
10401-10403 68507
W Cornhusker Hwy 68521
Coronado Dr 68516
N Cotner Blvd
101-387 68505
389-2299 68505
2300-5200 68507
5202-5598 68507
S Cotner Blvd
200-1300 68510
1302-1398 68510
1500-2299 68506
Cotswold Ln 68526
Cottontail Cir 68516
Cottonwood Dr 68510
Country Ln 68517
Country Club Blvd 68502
Country Hill Cir & Rd 68516
Countryside Ln 68521
Countryview Ct, Ln & Rd 68516
County Down Ct 68512
Court St 68508
Courtney Cir 68516
Cove Ct & Dr 68522
Coventry Ct 68512
W Covered Bridge Dr 68523
Covey Ct 68516
Coyote Cir 68516
W & SW Craig Dodge Cir & Rd 68522
W Craw St 68524
Creek View Ct & Dr 68516
Creekside Trl 68512
Crestdale Rd 68510
Cresthaven Dr 68516
Crestline Dr 68506
Crestridge Rd 68506
Crestview Dr 68506
Cripple Creek Rd 68516
Cromwell Dr 68516
Crooked Creek Ct & Dr 68516
Cross Creek Cir, Ct & Rd 68516
Crossbridge Pl 68504
Crosslake Ln 68516
Crown Pointe Cir & Rd 68506
Crystal Ct 68506
Crystal Water Cir 68527
Crystal Water Bay 68527
Culbera St 68521
Cullen Dr 68506
Culpepper Ct 68516
Culwells Ct, Pl & Rd 68516
Cumberland Dr 68516
Cuming St 68507
NW Cuming St 68521
W Cuming St
200-899 68521
3701-3799 68524
Curtis Dr 68506

Cushman Dr ... 68512
Custer Cir ... 68507
Custer St ... 68507
W Custer St ... 68521
Cuthills Cir, Ct & Dr ... 68526
Cypress Pt ... 68520
D St
100-2600 ... 68502
2602-2698 ... 68502
2700-2998 ... 68510
3000-4399 ... 68510
W D St ... 68522
NW Dahlia Dr ... 68524
Dakota Cir & St ... 68502
Dale Dr ... 68510
Dan Ave ... 68504
Danbury Ct & Rd ... 68512
Daniel Rd ... 68506
Danville Cir & Dr ... 68510
Daphne Pl ... 68516
Dargent Ct ... 68526
NW Darkwood Ct ... 68521
Darlington Ct ... 68510
Darren Ave ... 68522
Davenport Cir & Dr ... 68512
Davey Rd ... 68517
David Dr ... 68504
Davies Dr ... 68506
W Dawes Ave & Cir ... 68521
Dawn Ave ... 68516
Dawson Creek Dr ... 68505
Dawson Creek Bay ... 68505
Daybreak Cir & Dr ... 68505
Deer Creek Cir ... 68516
Deer Creek Dr ... 68516
Deer Creek Rd ... 68526
Deer Valley Ln ... 68526
Deerhaven Dr ... 68516
Deerwood Cir & Dr ... 68516
Del Rio Dr ... 68516
Delhay Dr ... 68507
Delphinium Ln ... 68505
Dempster ... 68516
Denby Pl ... 68505
Dennis Dr ... 68506
Densmore Rd ... 68512
W Denton Rd ... 68523
Denver Ct ... 68516
Derby Dr ... 68516
SW Derek Ave ... 68522
Desert Ct ... 68516
Devoe Ct & Dr ... 68506
Devonshire Dr ... 68506
Deweese Dr ... 68504
Dewitt Rd ... 68526
Diablo Cir & Dr ... 68516
Diadem Dr ... 68516
Diamond Ct ... 68506
Diana Dr ... 68506
Dickens St ... 68516
Dilin Cir & St ... 68521
Disbrow Ct ... 68516
Discovery Dr ... 68521
Dixie Trl ... 68527
Doane St ... 68503
Dobbins Dr ... 68505
Dobsons Ct & Rd ... 68516
Docs Dr ... 68507
Dodge Cir & St ... 68521
Doe Cir & Dr ... 68516
Doe Creek Cir ... 68516
Dogwood Cir, Ct & Dr ... 68516
W Dolores Ct ... 68523
Donald Cir & St ... 68505
Donnie Ct & Ln ... 68522
Doonbeg Rd ... 68520
Doral Ln ... 68507
Dorchester Ct ... 68521
Doris Bair Cir ... 68504
Dorothy Dr
2200-2299 ... 68505
2300-2999 ... 68507
Dorset Dr ... 68510
Dotson Rd ... 68505
Dougan Cir & Dr ... 68516
Douglas Cir ... 68504
Douglas Ct ... 68504
Douglas Dr ... 68504
Douglas St ... 68507
S Dove Cir, Ln & Pl ... 68516
Dover Ct ... 68506
Drake Cir & St ... 68516
Drawbridge Ct ... 68516
Drew Pl ... 68516
Driftwood Dr ... 68510
Dryden Pl ... 68516
Duane Ln ... 68505
Dublin Rd ... 68521
Dudley St
1900-4700 ... 68503
4702-4798 ... 68503
4801-4897 ... 68504
4899-5100 ... 68504
5102-5198 ... 68504
6300-7299 ... 68505
Dundee Dr ... 68510
Dunes Ct ... 68507
Dunn Ave ... 68502
Dunraven Ct & Ln ... 68523
Dunrovin Rd
8100-8399 ... 68516
8501-8699 ... 68526
Durado Ct ... 68520
Durango Ct ... 68516
Durham Ct ... 68516
Duxhall Ct & Dr ... 68516
E St
100-1899 ... 68508
1900-4399 ... 68510
W E St
108-136 ... 68508
138-243 ... 68508
245-299 ... 68508
600-732 ... 68522
734-748 ... 68522
Eagle Dr ... 68507
Eagle Crest Rd ... 68505
Eagle Ridge Cir & Rd ... 68516
Eagleton Ln ... 68505
Earl Dr ... 68505
Eastborough Ln ... 68505
Eastgate St ... 68502
Easton Cir ... 68520
Eastridge Dr ... 68510
Eastview Rd ... 68505
Eastwood Ct & Dr ... 68506
NW Ebony Ct ... 68521
Echo Cir & Ct ... 68520
E & N Eden Cir & Dr ... 68506
Edenton Rd ... 68516
Edge Water Ln ... 68527
Edison Cir ... 68504
Edward Ct ... 68502
Edwin Ln ... 68517
Eiger Dr ... 68516
El Avado Ave ... 68504
El Paso Dr ... 68516
Elba Ave ... 68521
Elba Cir ... 68521
Elba Ct ... 68521
W Elba St ... 68524
Elbert Dr ... 68521
Eldon Dr ... 68510
Eldora Ln ... 68505
Eldorado Dr ... 68516
W Elgin Ave ... 68522
Elizabeth Dr ... 68505
Elk Cir ... 68516
Elk Creek Dr ... 68516
Elk Ridge Cir & Rd ... 68516
Elkcrest Cir & Dr ... 68516
Ellendale Rd ... 68510
Ellenridge Rd ... 68526
Ellie Ln ... 68526
Elmwood Ave ... 68510
Emerald Dr ... 68516
Emery Ln ... 68516
Emily Ln ... 68512
Emmawalter Rd ... 68517
Englewood Dr ... 68510
English Dr ... 68516
English Park Ct ... 68516
Enterprise Dr ... 68521
Equestrian Dr ... 68523
Eric Dr ... 68507
Erica Ct ... 68522
Erin Ct ... 68507
Ervin St ... 68504
Essex Rd ... 68512
Euclid Ave ... 68502
Eureka Dr ... 68516
Evans Ave ... 68521
Everett St
2600-2999 ... 68502
3400-6799 ... 68506
Evergreen Dr ... 68510
Exbury Ct & Rd ... 68516
Executive Woods Dr ... 68512
Ezekiel Pl ... 68516
F St
131-1899 ... 68508
1900-4600 ... 68510
4602-4798 ... 68510
W F St
100-227 ... 68508
229-239 ... 68508
4000-4198 ... 68522
4200-4640 ... 68522
4642-4704 ... 68522
S Face Cir ... 68512
Faesy Ln & Pl ... 68528
Fair St ... 68503
Fairacre Ct ... 68506
Fairbanks Ct & Dr ... 68516
Fairbury Ln ... 68516
Fairdale Rd ... 68510
Fairfax Ave ... 68505
W Fairfield St ... 68521
NW Fairway Dr ... 68521
NW Fairwood Ct ... 68521
Falcon Cir ... 68516
Fall Creek Rd ... 68510
Fallbrook Blvd ... 68521
Farmstead Rd ... 68521
Faulkner Ct & Dr ... 68516
Fawn Ct ... 68516
Ferndale Rd ... 68510
Fernhill Pl ... 68516
Fieldcrest Way ... 68512
Fiene Blvd ... 68502
Fiene Cir ... 68506
Finigan Rd ... 68517
Fir Hollow Ct & Ln ... 68516
Firebush Ln ... 68516
Fireplace Cir ... 68523
Firethorn Ct, Ln & Ter ... 68520
NW Flader Ct ... 68528
Flagstone Rd ... 68521
Flat Iron Cir ... 68521
Flat Water Cir ... 68527
Fleetwood Cir & Dr ... 68516
Fletcher Ave
300-1400 ... 68521
1402-2298 ... 68521
2701-2797 ... 68504
2799-2999 ... 68504
3001-3299 ... 68504
5600-9499 ... 68507
9800-19299 ... 68527
19301-19699 ... 68527
W Fletcher Ave
100-198 ... 68521
5100-13199 ... 68524
Flint Ridge Pl & Rd ... 68506
Flintlock Cir ... 68526
Folkways Blvd
1600-1798 ... 68521
1800-2428 ... 68521
2430-2498 ... 68521
2700-3299 ... 68504
Folkways Cir ... 68504
Folkways Pl ... 68504
S Folsom Ct ... 68522
Folsom Ln ... 68522
S Folsom St
1001-1397 ... 68522
1399-4000 ... 68522
4002-4298 ... 68522
4500-6799 ... 68523
Fontaine Dr ... 68526
Fontenelle St ... 68503
W Foothills Rd ... 68523
Forbes Ct & Dr ... 68516
Fords Forest Ct ... 68506
W Foreman Dr ... 68523
Forest Ave ... 68516
Forest Glen Dr ... 68526
Forest Lake Blvd & Pl ... 68516
Forestview Cir ... 68522
Fossil Creek Cir ... 68516
Fox St ... 68527
Fox Hollow Cir & Rd ... 68506
Foxcroft Ct ... 68510
Foxen Cir ... 68526
Foxglove Cir ... 68521
Foxglove Ln ... 68504
Foxtail Dr ... 68526
Framton Cir, Ct & Rd ... 68516
Fran Ave ... 68516
Francis St
4900-5499 ... 68504
5600-7299 ... 68505
Franciscan Dr ... 68526
Franklin St
2200-2698 ... 68502
2700-3099 ... 68502
3300-6699 ... 68506
Frederick Cir ... 68504
Fremont St
4700-4798 ... 68504
4800-5599 ... 68504
5600-6999 ... 68507
Frisco Dr ... 68521
Frontier Rd ... 68516
Frost Ct & Dr ... 68510
Fulton Ave ... 68507
W Furnas Ave ... 68521
G St
100-1899 ... 68508
1900-4399 ... 68510
W G St ... 68508
Gabrielle Dr ... 68526
Gailyn Cir ... 68523
Gallinas Dr ... 68516
Galloway Ave & Cir ... 68512
W Garber Ave ... 68521
Garden Rd ... 68502
Garden Valley Rd ... 68521
W Garfield Cir ... 68522
Garfield St
101-497 ... 68502
499-2999 ... 68502
3400-3498 ... 68506
3500-5999 ... 68506
W Garfield St ... 68522
Garland Ave ... 68527
Garland St
4800-4998 ... 68504
5000-5499 ... 68504
6301-6397 ... 68505
6399-9420 ... 68505
Garret Ln ... 68512
Gary Ct ... 68527
NW Gary St ... 68521
Gaslight Cir & Ln ... 68521
N Gate Cir ... 68521
S Gate Cir ... 68502
N Gate Rd ... 68521
Gateway Mall ... 68505
W Gazebo Rd ... 68523
Georgian Ct ... 68502
Geranium Rd ... 68521
Gertie Ave ... 68516
Gettysburg Ct & Dr ... 68516
Giebenrath Rd ... 68517
Gillan Rd ... 68505
Ginny Ave ... 68516
Glacier Trl ... 68521
Glade Cir & St ... 68506
Gladstone St
3400-4398 ... 68504
4400-5500 ... 68504
5502-5598 ... 68504
5600-7199 ... 68507
Glass Ridge Cir, Ct, Dr &
Pl ... 68526
Glenarbor Cir & Dr ... 68512
Glenbrook Ln ... 68512
Glendale Rd ... 68505
Gleneagle Ct ... 68526
Glenhaven Dr ... 68505
Glenhaven Pl ... 68506
Glenridge Rd ... 68512
Glenview Dr ... 68505
Glenwood Cir ... 68510
Glynn Cir ... 68522
Glynoaks Ct & Dr ... 68516
Godfrey Cir & Dr ... 68521
Goldenrod Cir & Ln ... 68512
Goodhue Blvd
800-1099 ... 68508
1100-1299 ... 68502
1301-1399 ... 68502
W Goodwin Cir ... 68524
Gordon Dr ... 68522
Gott Cir ... 68524
W Gourley St ... 68521
Grace Ave ... 68503
Grace Ln ... 68527
Grainger Pkwy
2200-2499 ... 68512
2501-2509 ... 68512
3200-3298 ... 68516
3300-3499 ... 68516
3501-3699 ... 68516
Granada Ln ... 68528
W Grand Dr ... 68521
N Grand Lake Dr ... 68521
Grand Oaks Cir & Dr ... 68516
Grandview Blvd & Ln ... 68521
Granite Ridge Ct ... 68526
Grassland Ln & Pl ... 68522
Grassridge Rd ... 68512
Grays Peak Ct & Dr ... 68521
Great Falls Rd ... 68516
Green Acres Blvd ... 68522
Greenbriar Ln ... 68506
W Greenfield St ... 68521
Greenlief St ... 68524
Greenspire Cir & Dr ... 68521
Greenwood Ct ... 68507
Greenwood St
4100-5599 ... 68504
5600-5899 ... 68507
Gregory Ave ... 68507
Gregory St ... 68521
Greycliff Dr ... 68516
Griffith St ... 68503
Grimsby Ln ... 68502
Gronerso Rd ... 68526
Grouse Pl ... 68516
Groveland Cir & St ... 68521
Guenevere Ln ... 68512
NW Gum Ct ... 68521
Gunners Ct ... 68522
Gunnison Ct & Dr ... 68521
Gunsmoke Dr ... 68507
H St
101-797 ... 68508
799-1899 ... 68508
2500-3999 ... 68510
Half Moon Bay ... 68527
Hallcliffe Ct & Rd ... 68516
Hallmark Ct & Rd ... 68507
Hallshire Ct & Rd ... 68516
Halsey Ct ... 68516
Hamann Meadows Pl ... 68506
N & S Hampton Rd ... 68506
Hanna Pointe Pl ... 68516
Hanneman Dr ... 68522
Hanover Ct ... 68512
Hanson Ct & Dr ... 68502
Happy Hollow Ct & Ln ... 68516
W Harbour Blvd ... 68522
Harding Ct & Dr ... 68521
Harmony Ct ... 68516
Harold Ct ... 68514
Harrison Ave ... 68502
Hartland Rd ... 68521
Hartley Cir ... 68521
Hartley St
200-1999 ... 68521
4601-4627 ... 68504
4629-5599 ... 68504
5600-6599 ... 68507
Hartman Rd ... 68522
Harvest Cir & Dr ... 68521
Harwood Ct & St ... 68502
Haswell Pl ... 68521
Havelock Ave
5500-5598 ... 68504
5801-5897 ... 68507
5899-9799 ... 68507
10000-17599 ... 68527
W Haven Rd ... 68528
Haverford Cir & Dr ... 68510
Hawkfly Rd ... 68521
Hawkins Bnd ... 68516
Hawthorne Dr ... 68516
Hays Dr ... 68505
Hazel Scott Dr ... 68512
Hazelwood Dr ... 68510
Heather Ln ... 68512
Hedge Apple Ct ... 68521
Heide Ln ... 68512
W Helen Cir ... 68521
Helen Witt Dr ... 68512
Henry St ... 68506
Herel St ... 68512
Heritage Lakes Dr ... 68526
Heritage Pines Ct ... 68506
Heumann Dr ... 68504
Hickory Ln ... 68510
Hickory Crest Cir &
Rd ... 68516
Hidcote Dr ... 68516
Hidden Pines Dr ... 68512
Hidden Valley Dr ... 68526
High St
730-1098 ... 68502
1100-2000 ... 68502
2002-2698 ... 68502
3300-3898 ... 68506
3900-7700 ... 68506
7702-7898 ... 68506
W High St ... 68522
High Plains Cir & Rd ... 68512
High Ridge Cir, Pl &
Rd ... 68522
Highland Blvd ... 68521
Highway 2
1400-1698 ... 68502
Highway 2
2001-2399 ... 68502
6400-6498 ... 68516
6701-6799 ... 68516
W Highway 34 ... 68524
Highway 6 ... 68507
Hill Dr ... 68510
N Hill Rd ... 68504
Hill St ... 68502
W Hill St ... 68522
E Hillcrest Dr ... 68520
Hillsdale Dr ... 68504
Hillside Cir & St ... 68506
Hilltop Rd ... 68521
Hitchcock St ... 68503
Hitching Post Cir & Ln ... 68523
Holdrege St
1600-1698 ... 68508
1800-1898 ... 68503
1900-4399 ... 68503
4401-4799 ... 68503
4800-4898 ... 68504
4900-5599 ... 68504
5600-9500 ... 68505
9502-9598 ... 68505
9800-18699 ... 68527
W Holdrege St ... 68528
Hollow Tree Ct, Dr &
Pl ... 68512
Holltorf St ... 68521
Holly Rd ... 68502
Hollyhock Cir ... 68521
Hollynn Ln ... 68512
Hollywood Ave ... 68504
Holmes Ct ... 68506
Holmes Park Rd ... 68506
Homeland Pl ... 68521
Homestead Ct ... 68521
Hook Dr ... 68507
S Hope Ct ... 68502
Horizon Dr ... 68505
Horseshoe Dr ... 68516
Hoy St ... 68516
W Hub Hall Dr ... 68528
Huddersfield Ct ... 68516
Hudson St ... 68502
Huff St ... 68503
W Hughes St ... 68524
Humann Ct ... 68516
Humphrey Ave & St ... 68521
Hunters Ridge Rd ... 68516
Huntington Ave
3201-3247 ... 68504
3249-4999 ... 68504
5001-5499 ... 68504
5600-7799 ... 68507
W Huntington Ave ... 68524
Hunts Dr ... 68512
Husker Cir ... 68504
Hwy 6 ... 68517
Hyde Park Ct ... 68516
W Ickes Ct ... 68522
Idylwild Dr ... 68503
Imperial Cir & Dr ... 68506
Independence Cir, Ct &
Dr ... 68521
Indian Rd ... 68505
Indian Hills Dr ... 68520
Indigo Ct & Rd ... 68521
Industrial Ave ... 68504
W Industrial Lake Dr ... 68528
Infinity Ct & Rd ... 68512
Innovation Dr ... 68521
Inverness Rd ... 68512
Irish Pointe Pl ... 68521
Iron Gate Ct ... 68526
Irving Cir & St ... 68521
Isaac Dr ... 68521
Ivy Ln ... 68507
J St
100-298 ... 68508
300-1899 ... 68508
1900-5899 ... 68510
W J St ... 68508
W Jacaranda Ct ... 68521
Jack Pine Ct ... 68516
Jackson Dr ... 68502
Jacobs Ct ... 68516
Jacobs Creek Dr ... 68512
Jacquelyn Cir ... 68516
Jacquelyn Dr
2500-2699 ... 68512
4100-4300 ... 68516
4302-5198 ... 68516
Jade Ct ... 68516
Jameson N
2300-2398 ... 68512
Jameson N
2400-2600 ... 68512
2602-2698 ... 68512
2700-2798 ... 68516
2800-2899 ... 68516
2901-2999 ... 68516
Jameson S ... 68512
Jameson Ct ... 68512
Jamestown Ln & Rd ... 68516
Jamie Ln
2201-2219 ... 68512
2221-2511 ... 68512
2513-2699 ... 68512
2700-2849 ... 68516
2851-2899 ... 68516
Jane Ln
2500-2699 ... 68512
2700-2999 ... 68516
Janice Ct ... 68506
Janssen Dr ... 68506
Jasmine Pl ... 68516
Jason Dr ... 68516
Jasper Ct ... 68516
Jean Ave & Cir ... 68522
Jefferson Ave ... 68502
Jeffery Dr ... 68505

Jenna Ln 68512
W Jennifer Ct & Dr 68521
Jersey Cir 68504
Joehank Rd 68521
W Joel St 68521
Johanna Rd 68507
John Ave 68502
Johnson Rd 68516
Jonna Ct 68522
SW Jordan St 68522
Joshua Dr 68507
Joy Ct 68502
Joyce Ave 68505
Judith Dr 68517
Judson St
200-2300 68521
2302-2398 68521
4300-5499 68504
5501-5599 68504
5600-6599 68507
Julesburg Dr 68521
K St
100-1799 68508
1801-1899 68508
1900-2699 68510
Kajan Dr 68506
Kara Ln 68522
Karen Dr 68522
Karl Dr 68516
Karl Ridge Rd 68506
Karlee Dr 68527
W Karwat Ln 68522
Katelyn Cir & Ln 68516
Kathy Ln 68526
W Katleman Dr 68521
Katrina Ln 68512
Katy Cir 68506
Kearney Ave 68507
W Kearney Ave 68524
W Kearney St 68524
Keating Cir & Dr 68521
Keith Cir 68521
Kendall St 68526
Kendra Ln 68512
Kennedy Ct & Dr 68521
Kennelley Ct & Dr 68516
Kensington Dr 68521
Kent St 68521
W Kent St 68524
Kentwell Ln 68516
Kenwood Cir & Rd 68516
Kess Dr 68516
Kessler Blvd & Cir 68502
Keystone Dr 68516
Kimarra Pl 68521
Kimberly Cir 68506
Kimco Ct & Dr 68521
King Ln 68521
King Arthur Ct 68512
King Bird Rd 68521
King Ridge Blvd 68504
Kings Ct 68516
Kings Hwy 68502
W Kingsley St 68524
Kingston Rd 68506
Kingswood Cir 68521
Kipling Cir, Ct, Pl & St 68516
Kirkwood Dr 68516
Kleckner Ct 68503
W Knight Dr 68524
Knights Ln & Pl 68506
Knoll View Ct 68506
Knotting Hill Dr 68527
Knox Ct 68507
Knox St
300-1900 68521
1902-1998 68521
4200-5599 68504
5600-6699 68507
Koi Rock Dr 68526
Kucera Dr 68502
W Kyle Ln 68522
L St
101-497 68508
499-1638 68508
1640-1898 68508
1900-6800 68510
6802-6998 68510
W L St 68522
La Brea Ave 68504
La Salle St 68516
SW Lacey Ln 68522
Lacroix Dr 68526
Lafayette Ave 68502
W Laguna Rd 68522
W Lake Ct 68522
Lake St
1000-2500 68502
2502-2698 68502
3300-3398 68506
3400-8199 68506
W Lake St 68522
Lakeshore Dr 68528
Lakeside Dr 68528
Lakewood Dr 68510
Lambert Pl 68516
Lammle Cir 68526
Lamont Cir & Dr 68528
Lamplighter Cir & Ln 68510
Lancashire Ct & Dr 68510
Lancaster Ln 68505
Lancelot Ln 68512
W Lander Dr 68521
Landmark Cir 68504
Landsberry Ln 68516
Laplata Ct 68521
Laramie Cir & Trl 68521
Larchdale Dr 68506
Laredo Dr 68516
Larges Ct 68512
Larkspur Ln 68521
Larkwood Rd 68516
Laroche Rd 68526
Larry Ln 68506
Larson Blvd 68505
Last Rd 68522
Latham St 68521
Laura Ave 68510
Laura Lynn Ct 68516
Laurel St 68502
Lauren Marie Cir 68512
Laurent Cir 68526
Lavender Cir 68505
Lawnsdale Dr 68506
Lawson Dr 68516
Laytonjohn Ln 68516
Le Gros Ave 68502
Lea Rae Pl 68516
Leavitt Ln 68510
Lee Cir 68506
Leesburg Ct & St 68516
Leichester Ct 68516
Leighton Ave
2800-2998 68504
3000-5499 68504
5600-9799 68507
W Leighton Ave 68524
Lenox Ave 68510
Leo Ln 68505
W Leon Dr 68521
Leonard St 68507
Lester Dr 68521
Lewis Ave 68521
Lexington Ave
5200-5499 68504
6000-8699 68505
Lexington Cir 68505
Liana Ln 68517
Liberty Ln 68516
Liberty Bell Ln 68521
Libra Dr 68512
Lidco Ct 68507
Lilac Dr 68521
Lillibridge St 68506
NW Lime Ct 68521
Limestone Rd N 68512
Lincoln Mall 68508
Lincoln St 68526
Lincolnshire Rd 68506
Linden St 68516
Lindsey Cir 68524
Line Drive Cir 68508
Links Dr 68526
Linwood Ln 68505
Livingston Pl 68510
Lizzie Ln 68527
Lockwood Ct 68528
Locust St 68516
Logan Ave 68507
Loma Cir 68516
Lombard Ct & Dr 68521
London Rd 68516
Londonshire Ct 68516
Lone Tree Cir & Dr 68512
Lonewood Cir & Dr 68516
Longhorn Cir 68516
Longview Ct 68506
Lori Ln 68506
W Loring St 68524
Loveland Dr
2800-3299 68502
3300-4199 68506
Lowell Ave 68506
Lowell Cir 68502
Lowell Ct 68506
Luann Ln 68516
Lucile Cir 68516
Lucile Dr
4200-4298 68506
4400-4698 68516
4700-4799 68516
Lucys Ct 68516
W Ludwig Dr 68528
W Luke St 68524
Lynchburg Ct 68516
Lyncrest Dr 68510
Lynn Cir 68506
Lynn St
2300-2499 68503
6900-6999 68505
Lynnridge Cir & Pl 68521
W M Ct 68522
M St
101-797 68508
799-1800 68508
1802-1898 68508
1900-5899 68510
Mackenzie Rd 68505
Madalyn Rd 68516
Maddie St 68527
Madison Ave
3300-3498 68504
3500-5000 68504
5002-5498 68504
5600-6599 68507
W Madison Ave 68524
W Madison Ct 68524
NW Magnolia Ct 68521
Magnum Cir 68522
Mahoney Dr 68504
N Main St 68521
Malcolm Ct 68521
Manassas Pl 68516
Manatt Ct & St 68521
Manchester Cir & Dr 68528
Mandalay Dr 68516
Mandarin Cir 68516
Manes Ct 68505
Manitou Dr 68521
E & W Manor Ct & Dr 68506
Manse Ave 68502
Maple Village Dr 68510
Mapleview Dr 68512
Maplewood Ct & Dr 68510
Marcel Cir 68526
Marcia Ln 68505
Marcus Rd 68516
Margo Dr 68510
Marie Ln 68516
Marigold Cir & Ct 68521
Marilynn Ave 68502
Marina Bay Pl 68528
Marion St 68502
Mark Ave 68502
Markhorn Ct 68526
Marlborough Rd 68516
Marlene Dr 68512
Marshall Ave 68510
Martin St 68504
Marvs St 68516
Mary Cir 68502
Mary Ct 68522
W Mary Louise Ln 68528
Mason Cir & Dr 68521
Mathew Pl 68516
W Mathis St 68524
Mayflower Ave 68502
Maze Ct 68521
Mcbride Ave 68516
Mccormick Dr 68507
Mcgee St 68516
W Mcguire Rd 68524
Mckelvie Rd 68531
W Mckelvie Rd
100-1899 68531
2000-3298 68524
3300-3500 68524
3502-5498 68524
Mckinty Ln 68516
Mclaughlin Dr 68516
Meadow Ln 68506
Meadow Dale Dr 68505
Meadowbrook Ln 68510
Meadowlark Cir, Ct & Rd 68521
Medicine Hat Rd 68505
Medinah Dr 68526
Meeker Cir 68506
Melrose Ave 68506
Memorial Dr 68502
Merchant Dr 68521
Meredeth Ct, Pl & St 68506
Meridian Dr 68504
Merion Cir 68526
Merrill St 68503
Merritt Dr 68506
Merryvale Dr 68526
Mesa Rd 68505
Mesaverde Dr 68510
Mescal Cir 68516
Mesquite Cir 68516
W Metzger St 68524
Meursault Dr 68526
NW Michael Cir & St 68524
Michelle Ct 68522
Mickaela Ln 68521
Middle Fork Rd 68526
Middleton Ave 68521
Mike Scholl St 68524
Milan Dr 68526
Military Rd 68508
Milkweed Cir 68516
Mill Rd
4000-5599 68514
6600-9799 68517
N Miller Rd 68521
W Millstone Rd 68522
W Milton Rd 68528
Mimosa 68521
Mindoro Dr 68506
Minter Ln 68516
Minuteman Dr 68521
Miranda Ct 68512
Mirwyn Ct 68505
Mission Cir & Ln 68521
Misty Blue Cir 68505
W Mockingbird Ln N & S 68512
Mohave Dr 68516
Mohawk Cir & St 68510
Monarch Cir 68516
Montclair Dr 68521
Montello Rd 68520
Monterey Dr 68506
Monticello Dr 68510
Montini Dr 68521
Moonlight Dr 68527
Moor Dr 68516
Moraine Dr 68510
Moreland Ct 68521
Morgan St 68521
S Moriantr St 68516
Mormon Trl 68521
Morning Glory Ln 68505
Morningside Dr 68506
Morrill Ave 68507
Mortensen Ct & Dr 68526
Morton Ct 68521
Morton St
800-1198 68521
1200-1799 68521
7001-7097 68507
7099-7399 68507
W Mulberry Cir 68522
W Mulberry Ct 68522
Mulberry St 68502
W Mulberry St 68522
Mulder Dr 68510
Music Ln 68516
Mustang Dr 68507
Myrtle St 68506
N St
100-498 68508
500-1899 68508
2000-5499 68510
W Nance Ave 68521
Nancy Dr 68507
Napa Ridge Dr 68526
Naples Ct & Dr 68526
Nashway Rd 68516
Navajo Trl 68520
Neerpark Dr 68506
Nelson St 68521
Nemaha Cir 68506
Nemaha St
1400-1699 68502
7500-7599 68506
Neumann Ln 68516
Neville Ave 68506
New Castle Rd 68516
New Hampshire St 68508
Newport Blvd 68521
Newton Cir & St 68506
Nick Rd 68512
Nighthawk Rd 68521
Nob Hill Rd 68516
Nogalas Cir 68516
Nolan Rd 68512
Norfolk Dr 68505
Normal Blvd 68506
Norman Cir & Rd 68512
Normandy Cir, Ct & Ln 68512
Norris Ln 68516
Northborough Ln 68505
Northern Lights Dr 68505
Northern Sky Rd 68505
Northfork Cir & Dr 68516
Northline Ct 68521
Northlund Dr 68504
Northridge Rd 68516
Northview Rd 68521
Northville Cir 68521
Northwoods Dr 68505
Norval Rd 68520
Norwood Dr 68512
Nottingham Ct 68512
NW Nutwood Ct 68521
O St
103-109 68508
111-1801 68508
1803-1833 68508
1903-1903 68510
1905-5999 68510
6001-8399 68510
6140-6140 68505
6150-8398 68510
8501-8797 68520
8799-17299 68520
17301-18199 68520
W O St 68528
O Reilly Dr 68502
O Street Rd 68528
Oak St 68521
Oakcreek Dr 68528
Oakdale Ave 68506
Oakley St 68512
Oakmont Dr 68526
Oakridge Cir & Dr 68516
Oaks Holw 68516
Oakville Rd 68526
Oakwood Rd 68516
Odessa Ct 68516
Ogden Rd 68521
Ohanlon Dr 68516
Old Cheney Rd
601-697 68512
699-1599 68512
1601-2299 68512
3800-3898 68516
3900-7000 68516
7002-8398 68516
8400-9998 68526
10000-11099 68526
W Old Cheney Rd 68523
Old Creek Rd 68516
Old Dominion Ct & Rd 68516
Old Farm Cir, Ct & Rd 68512
Old Glory Rd 68521
Old Lodge Ct 68516
Old Post Pl & Rd 68506
Old Woodlawn Rd 68524
Oldham St 68506
Oliver Cir 68521
Olivia Dr 68512
W Olympic Cir 68524
Omalley Cir & Dr 68516
Oneil Dr & Pl 68516
Onyx Ct 68516
NW Orange Ct 68521
Orchard St
2200-4600 68503
4602-4698 68503
4800-5599 68504
6300-7299 68505
Orcutt Ave E 68504
Oregon Trl 68521
W Orleans Ct 68524
Orourke Dr 68516
Orwell Cir & St 68516
Osage Ct 68506
Oshea Dr 68516
Oshel Ave 68505
Osullivan Rd 68516
Otoe Cir 68506
Otoe Ct 68506
Otoe Pl 68506
Otoe St
1200-1999 68502
3400-7399 68506
Overland Trl 68503
Oxford Rd 68506
P St
100-298 68508
300-1800 68508
1802-1898 68508
1900-3499 68503
5600-6898 68505
W P St 68528
Pablo Ln 68516
Pace Blvd 68502
Pacific Dr 68506
W Paddock Rd 68523
Pagoda Ct & Ln 68516
Palace Ct 68516
NW Palm Ct 68521
Palmetto Ct & Ln 68521
Palmilla Ln 68516
Palomino Ln 68523
Parducci Dr 68526
Park Ave 68502
W Park Ave 68522
Park Blvd 68502
N Park Blvd 68521
W Park Cir 68522
N Park Rd 68524
Park Crest Ct & Dr 68506
Park Place Ct & Dr 68506
Park Vale St 68510
Park Vista St 68510
Parkridge Cir 68516
Parkside Ln 68521
Parkview Ln 68512
Partridge Ln 68528
Patmore Rd 68516
Patterson Ct & Dr 68522
SW Paul Whitehead Ln 68522
Pawnee St
1200-1999 68502
3300-5800 68506
5802-5898 68506
W Pawnee Park Dr 68524
Paxton Cir & Dr 68521
W Peach Cir 68522
W Peach Ct 68522
Peach St 68502
W Peach St 68522
Pear St 68503
Pearle Rd 68517
Pebble Bch 68520
Pebblebrook Ct 68516
Pecos Rd 68516
Peggy Cir 68507
Pela Verde Cir 68516
Pelican Bay Pl 68528
NW Pemberly Ln 68521
Pennsylvania Ave 68521
Penrose Dr 68521
Pepper Ave 68502
Peregrine Ct 68505
Perkins Blvd 68502
Perry Cir 68516
E Pershing Rd 68502
Pester Ridge Rd 68523
Petersburg Ct 68516
Petunia Rd 68521
Phares Dr 68516
Pheasant Ridge Rd 68532
Pheasant Run Ct, Ln & Pl 68516
Philadelphia Dr 68521
Phillips Dr 68521
Phoenix Dr 68516
Piazza Ter 68510
Piccadilly Ct 68512
Piedmont Rd 68510
Pier 1 68528
Pier 2 68528
Pier 3 68528
Pierce Dr 68504
Pike Pl 68516
Pine Lake Ct 68516
Pine Lake Rd
1401-2197 68512
2199-2600 68512
2602-2640 68512
2700-8299 68516
8301-8399 68516
8700-10799 68526
10801-11199 68526
Pine Ridge Rd 68505
Pine Tree Ln 68521
Pinecrest Dr 68516
Pinedale Ave
1700-2099 68506
8400-8419 68520
Pinedale Ct 68520
Pinehill Ln 68526
Pinewood Ln 68516
Pinnacle Arena Dr 68508
Pinwheel Ct 68516
Pioneer Ct 68520
Pioneer Greens Ct & Dr 68526
Pioneer Woods Dr 68506
Pioneers Blvd
401-697 68502
699-3199 68502
3201-3249 68502
3301-3397 68506
3399-8399 68506
8500-11199 68520
W Pioneers Blvd 68522
Piper Way 68527
Plantation Dr 68516
Platte Ave
5900-6241 68507
6240-6240 68529
6243-7399 68507
6300-7398 68507
W Pleasant Hill Rd 68523

Pleasantview Cir 68504
Plum St 68502
W Plum St 68522
Plum Creek Cir & Dr 68516
Plumridge Rd 68527
Plumwood Ln 68516
Plymouth Ave 68502
E Pointe Cir & Rd 68506
Pomodoro Ct 68516
Ponca St 68506
Pond Cir 68512
Ponderosa Cir & Dr 68510
Pony Hill Ct 68516
Poplar Pl & Rd 68506
Porter Cir 68516
Porter Ridge Rd 68516
Portia St 68521
Portsche Ln 68516
Possum Cir 68506
Postage Due St
2-2 68508
3-3 68510
4-4 68512
5-5 68517
6-6 68514
7-7 68520
8-8 68521
9-9 68522
10-10 68523
11-11 68524
12-12 68526
13-13 68527
14-14 68528
15-15 68531
16-16 68532
Potomac Dr, Ln & Pl 68516
Potter St 68503
Pow Wow Cir 68520
Prairie Ln 68521
Prairie Rd 68506
Prairie Hill Cir 68506
Prairie Rim Rd 68526
Prairie Village Cir, Ct & Dr 68507
Prairieview Dr 68504
Preamble Ct & Ln 68521
Prescott Ave
3000-3299 68502
3300-8399 68506
Prescott Cir 68506
Prescott Pl 68506
Preserve Ct & Ln 68516
Preston Ave 68516
Prestwick Rd 68505
Prince Rd 68516
Princess Margaret Dr 68516
Progressive Ave 68504
Prospect St 68502
Prospector Ct & Pl 68522
Pub Ct 68516
Pueblo Ct 68516
Puritan Ave 68502
Q St
108-726 68508
728-1643 68508
1645-1899 68508
1927-1997 68503
1999-3444 68503
3446-3598 68503
6400-6403 68505
6405-6499 68505
W Q St 68528
Quail Ridge Cir, Ct, Dr & Pl 68516
Quarter Horse Ln 68516
Queens Dr 68516
NW Quincy Ct 68521
R St
600-699 68508
700-708 68501
701-1809 68508
800-828 68508
1400-1498 68588
1500-1788 68508
1800-1898 68588
1900-4600 68503
4602-4798 68503
5000-5198 68504
5200-5599 68504
5700-5898 68505
5900-5999 68505
5945-5945 68503
W R St 68528
W R Street Cir 68528
Rachel Rd 68516
Radcliff St 68512
Rainbow Cir 68516
Rainier Ct & Dr 68510
Rainy River Rd 68505
Rainy River Bay 68505
Raleigh St 68516
Ramona Cir 68516
W Ramsey Rd 68524
Rancho Rd 68502
Ranchview Ct 68516
Randolph St 68510
Ranger Cir 68521
W Ranger Ridge Rd 68532
Raspberry Cir 68516
Rathbone Rd 68502
Raven Cir 68506
Raven Oaks Cir & Dr 68521
Ravenwood Ln 68526
Rawhide Dr 68507
Raymond Rd
5601-5699 68514
5700-11799 68517
11801-14899 68517
Rebel Dr 68516
Red Bird Ln 68532
Red Deer Dr 68516
Red Oak Ct & Rd 68516
Red Rock Ln 68516
Red Tail Cir 68516
W Redberry Ln 68528
Redstone Rd 68521
Redwood Dr & Ln 68510
Regency Dr 68506
Regent Dr 68507
Regina Ct 68522
Remi Ct & Dr 68526
W Remington 68522
W Remington Dr 68532
Renatta Dr 68516
Renewable Dr 68508
Reno Rd 68505
Rent Worth Ct & Dr 68516
Rentfro Dr 68526
Research Dr 68521
Revere Ln 68516
Rexford Dr 68506
Richard Ct 68521
Richard Leyden Cir 68522
S Richland Cir 68516
Richmond Rd 68504
Ricky Rd 68516
Ridge Dr & Rd 68512
Ridge Hollow Dr 68526
Ridge Line Rd 68516
Ridge Park Dr 68504
Ridge Point Cir & Rd 68512
Ridgegate 68516
Ridgehaven Ct 68505
Ridgeline Ct & Dr 68512
Ridgeview Dr
4100-4299 68506
4301-4499 68516
Ridgeway Rd 68506
W Ridgewood Blvd 68523
Rifle Dr 68507
Rim Rock Rd 68526
Ringneck Dr 68506
W Rio Rd 68505
River Cir & Dr 68504
Riviera Dr 68506
Roanoke Ct 68510
Robert Rd 68510
Robin Ct & Rd 68516
Rock Port Dr 68516
Rockcliff Dr 68512
Rockford Dr 68521
Rockhurst Dr 68510
Rockland Cir 68526
Rockledge Rd 68506
Rockwood Ct & Ln 68516
Rocky Ridge Ct & Rd 68526
W Rodeo Cir & Rd 68523
Rogers Cir 68506
Rokeby Rd
800-1198 68512
1200-2699 68512
5601-5697 68516
5699-8199 68516
9300-11000 68526
11002-11398 68526
W Rokeby Rd 68523
Rolf St 68506
Rolling Hills Blvd & Ct 68512
Roose St 68506
Rose St 68502
W Rose St 68522
Rose Hill Ct 68516
Rosebriar Ct 68516
Rosebud Cir & Dr 68516
Roselyn Ter 68502
Rosewood Dr 68510
Round Hill Dr 68526
W Roxbury Ln 68523
Royal Ct 68502
W Royal Dornoch Ct 68521
Ruby Rd 68512
Russell Cir & Dr 68507
Russwood Blvd, Cir, Ct & Pkwy 68505
Rusty Ln 68506
Rutha Ln 68516
Rutherford Dr 68526
Rutland Dr 68512
Rutledge Ave 68507
Ryley Ln 68512
Ryons St 68502
W Ryons St 68522
S St
835-1599 68508
1971-2239 68503
2241-3544 68503
3546-3598 68503
5401-5407 68504
5409-5541 68504
5543-5549 68504
W S St 68528
Saddle Creek Trl 68523
W Saddlehorn Rd 68523
Sage Cir 68520
Sailside Dr 68528
Saint Andrews Pl 68512
Saint Clement Cir 68526
Saint Gregory Cir 68526
Saint James Rd 68506
Saint Marys Ave 68502
Saint Matthew Dr 68526
Saint Michaels Rd 68512
Saint Paul Ave
3300-4900 68504
4902-5098 68504
5600-6099 68507
W Saint Paul Ave 68524
Saint Thomas Dr 68502
Salida Dr 68521
Saline Cir & Dr 68504
Salisbury Ct 68505
W Sally St 68521
Salt Creek Cir 68504
Salt Valley View St 68512
Saltgrass Rd 68521
Saltillo Rd
5600-8399 68516
8600-9599 68526
San Agustin Dr 68516
San Juan Cir 68516
San Mateo Ln 68516
E Sanborn Dr 68505
Sandalwood Dr
7700-8399 68510
8400-8498 68520
8500-8699 68520
Sandhills Ct 68526
W Sandpiper Ln 68528
Sandstone Rd 68512
Santa Monica Ave 68504
Santa Rosa Ln 68516
Sante Fe Trl 68521
Saratoga St 68502
Sardius Ct 68516
NW Satinwood Ct 68521
W Saunders Ave 68521
Savannah Cir 68516
Sawgrass Dr 68526
Sawyer Ct, Pl & St 68505
Saybrook Ln 68512
Saylor Cir & St 68506
Scarborough Dr 68506
Scenic Ln 68505
Schmieding Cir 68521
School House Ln 68512
Schooner Cir 68532
Schweitzer Rd 68507
Schworer Dr 68504
Scotch Pine Trl 68512
Scott Ave 68506
Scottsdale Ln 68516
Sea Mountain Rd 68521
Sedalia Cir & Dr 68516
Sequoia Dr 68516
Serenity Cir 68516
Serra Pl 68516
Set Aside Cir & Ct 68523
Seth Ct 68507
Seward Ave 68507
Sewell St
1700-3100 68502
3102-3198 68502
3300-3899 68506
3901-3999 68506
W Sewell St 68522
Shadow Ln 68516
Shadow Pines Ct, Dr & Pl 68516
Shadow Ridge Rd 68512
Shadowbrook Dr 68516
Shady Creek Ct 68516
Shady Hollow Rd 68516
Shamrock Ct & Rd 68506
W Shane Dr 68522
Shaunte Ct 68507
Sheffield Pl 68512
Sheldon St 68503
Shelley Cir & St 68516
Shenandoah Ct & Dr 68510
Sheridan Blvd
2100-3299 68502
3301-3397 68506
3399-4200 68506
4202-4398 68506
Sheridan Ct 68506
Sherman Pl 68506
Sherman St
2800-2999 68502
4400-7599 68506
Sherwood Dr 68504
Shirl Ct & Dr 68516
Shirley Ct 68507
Shooting Star Dr 68521
E Shore Dr 68516
Shore Front Dr 68527
Short St 68503
Showers St 68526
Sicily Ln 68526
Sierra Dr 68505
W Silver Bell Ct 68523
Silver Brook Pl 68521
Silver Fox Ln 68520
Silver Oak Rd 68526
Silver Ridge Rd 68510
Silverado Ct & Dr 68521
Silverthorn Dr 68512
Simi Ct 68526
Sinclair Ct 68516
Sioux St 68502
Sissel Rd 68516
Sky Bright Rd 68517
Skyhawk Cir 68506
Skylark Cir & Ln 68516
Skyline Dr 68506
Skyway Rd 68505
Smith St
1400-2399 68502
3300-3999 68506
8600-8699 68526
Smoke Tree Holw 68516
Smoky Hill Rd 68520
Snowberry Rd 68521
Somerset Ave 68504
Sonatta Ct & Dr 68516
W Songbird Cir 68528
Sonora Ct 68516
Soukup Cir & Dr 68522
South St
300-498 68502
500-3199 68502
3201-3207 68502
3300-3300 68506
3302-8399 68506
W South St 68522
Southdale Rd 68516
Southern Light Dr 68512
Southern Sky Cir & Rd 68505
Southfork Cir 68516
Southgate Blvd 68506
Southhaven Cir & Dr 68516
Southpass Dr 68512
Southview Cir 68512
Southwood Cir, Dr & Pl 68512
W Sparrow Ln 68528
Speedway Cir 68502
Speidel Ln 68516
Splitrail Ln 68506
Spring Meadow Cir, Ct & Dr 68521
W Springer St 68522
W Springview Rd 68522
Spruce St 68516
Spyglass Ln 68507
Stable Ln 68523
Stacy Ln 68516
W Stallion Cir & Rd 68523
Stanton St 68507
W Stanton St 68524
Starling Cir, Ct & Dr 68516
Starr St
2700-4600 68503
4602-4698 68503
4900-5199 68504
6300-7899 68505
Starview Ln 68512
State Fair Park Dr 68504
N Steamboat Dr 68521
Steele Ave 68510
Steinway Rd 68505
Stephanie Ct & Ln 68516
Stephanos Dr 68516
Stetson Dr 68507
Stevens Ridge Rd 68516
Stewart St 68503
Stillwater Ave 68502
W Stirrup Dr 68523
Stockwell Cir 68506
Stockwell Ct 68506
Stockwell St
1300-2699 68502
3300-8299 68506
W Stockwell St 68522
Stone Creek Loop N & S 68512
Stone Gate Ct 68516
Stonebrook Pkwy 68521
Stonecliffe Ct & Dr 68516
Stonewall Ct 68506
Stony Rapids Bay 68505
Stony Ridge Rd 68507
Stonyhill Rd 68520
Straffan Pl 68516
Stratford Ave 68502
Strauss Ct 68507
Sugar Creek Cir, Ct, Pl & Rd 68516
Sugarberry Ct 68516
Sumac Dr 68516
Summerset Cir & Ct 68516
E, S & W Summit Blvd 68502
W Sumner Cir 68522
Sumner St
100-498 68502
500-3100 68502
3102-3298 68502
3600-6999 68506
W Sumner St
100-198 68502
800-4999 68522
Sun Down Xing 68512
Sun Valley Blvd
200-400 68528
402-598 68528
1000-1098 68508
Sunbeam Ln 68505
Sunburst Ln 68506
Sundance Ct & Dr 68512
Sunlight Ct 68516
Sunny Hill Rd 68502
Sunny Slope Rd 68505
Sunridge Cir & Rd 68505
Sunrise Rd 68510
Sunset Rd 68506
Superior St
200-998 68521
1000-2699 68521
3200-4398 68504
4400-5599 68504
W Superior St 68524
Surfside Cir, Ct & Dr 68528
Surrey Ct 68512
Susan Cir 68506
Sussex Pl 68506
W Swale Rd 68523
Sweetbriar Ln 68516
Swing Cir 68516
Switchback Rd 68512
W Switchgrass Rd 68521
Sycamore Dr
100-1399 68510
7800-7999 68506
T St
2300-3599 68503
5500-5599 68504
Talbot Trl 68506
Talent Plus Way 68506
Taliesin Dr 68520
Talon Ct & Rd 68505
Tamarin Ridge Rd 68512
Tamarisk Ct 68516
Tangeman Ter 68505
Tanglewood Cir, Ct, Ln & Pl 68516
Taylor Park Dr 68510
Teakwood Dr 68510
Teal Cir 68506
Telluride Cir & Dr 68521
NW Tempest Dr 68521
Tennyson Cir & St 68516
Teri Ln 68502
Terrace Rd 68505
Teton Ct & Dr 68510
Thatcher Cir & Ln 68528
Thayer Ave 68527
Thayer St 68507
The Knls 68512
Theresa St 68521
Thies Cove Dr 68516
Thistle Cir 68516
Thomasbrook Cir, Ct & Ln 68516
Thomasville Ave 68521
Thompson Creek Blvd 68516
Thorn Ct 68520
Thornton Dr 68512
Thornview Rd 68506
Thornwood Cir, Ct & Dr 68512
Three Pines Ct 68510
Thunder Bay 68505
Thunderbird Blvd & Cir 68512
Thurston St 68507
Ticonderoga Dr 68521
Tierra Dr 68516
Tiffany Rd 68506
Tihen Cir 68502
Timber Ridge Cir & Rd 68522
W Timberlake Dr 68522
Timberline Ct 68506
Timberview Ct 68506
Tipperary Trl 68512
Tobie Ln 68516
Todd Cir & Ln 68528
Tony Cir 68522
Topaz Ct 68516
Torchlight Ln 68521
Torreys Dr 68521
Touzalin Ave 68507
Tower Rd 68522
Trail Ridge Cir, Ct & Rd 68505
Trails End 68524
Tralee Rd 68520
Tranquility Dr 68504
Transformation Dr 68508
Travis Dr 68516
W Treehaven Dr 68521
Trelawney Dr 68512
Trendwood Dr 68506
Trenridge Rd & Way 68505
Trevor Ct 68512
Trimble St 68522
Troon Dr 68526
Trophy Rd 68516
Tropp Ridge Dr 68512
Trotter Cir & Rd 68516
Truchard Rd 68526
NW Tudor Ln 68521
Tularosa Ct & Ln 68516
Turnberry Cir 68526
Turner St 68504
Turtle Creek Rd 68521
Tuscan Ct 68520
Twin Oaks Rd 68516
Twin Ridge Rd
400-898 68510
900-1399 68510
1400-2099 68506
U St 68503
Union Dr 68516
Union Hill Cir, Ct & Rd 68516
University Ter 68508
W Upland Ave 68521
Upton Grey Cir & Ln 68516
Urbana Ln 68505
Vale Cir 68521
Vale St 68521
W Vale St 68524
Valley Rd 68510
Valley Forge Rd 68521
Valley Stream Dr 68516
Valley View Dr 68505
Van Dorn St
601-697 68502
699-3200 68502
3202-3298 68502
3301-7299 68506
7301-7339 68506
9300-9798 68520
9800-10499 68520
10501-10799 68520
W Van Dorn St
1116-2098 68522
2100-5399 68522
5401-5655 68522
5901-7427 68532
7429-9100 68532
9102-9398 68532
W Vance Rd 68524
Vanderslice Cir & Ln 68516
Vandervoort Dr 68516
Vavak Pl 68516
Vavrina Ln 68512
Vegas Rd 68505
Venice Ln 68526
Venture Dr 68521
Vermaas Pl 68502

Viburnum Dr 68516
Victoria Ave 68510
Victory Ln 68528
Village Ave 68503
Village Blvd 68516
Village Ct 68516
Village Dr 68516
Vine St
1500-1798 68508
1901-2197 68503
2199-4700 68503
4702-4798 68503
4900-4998 68504
5000-5599 68504
5600-8200 68505
8202-8398 68505
W Vine St 68528
Virginia St 68508
W Vista Cir 68522
W Vosler St 68524
W St
800-899 68508
2201-2247 68503
2249-4400 68503
4402-4698 68503
6900-6999 68505
Wagon Ln 68516
Walin Ln & Rd 68532
Walker Ave
4301-4797 68504
4799-5499 68504
5600-7499 68507
W Walker Ave 68524
Walnut Ct 68503
Waltz Pl 68516
Warwick Ct 68516
W Washington Ln 68522
W Washington Pl 68522
Washington St
502-508 68502
510-2899 68502
3300-5199 68506
W Washington St 68522
E Washley Ave 68524
Water Tower Ct 68516
Waterbury Ln 68516
Watercress Ln 68504
Waterford Cir 68506
Waterford Estates Dr 68527
Waterfront Pl 68528
Waters Edge Dr 68526
Waterview Dr 68527
Waverly Rd
4200-5599 68514
5700-10899 68517
W Waverly Rd 68524
Way St 68504
Weaver Ln 68506
Webster St 68507
W Webster St 68524
S Wedgewood Dr 68510
Weeks Dr 68516
Weeping Willow Ln 68506
Wells Ct 68505
W Welter Dr 68522
Wemsha Ct & St 68507
Wendell Way 68516
Wendover Ave 68502
W Wendy Ln 68528
Wenzel Dr 68527
Wesley Dr 68512
Westbrook Cir 68522
Westgate Blvd 68528
Westland Cir 68522
Westminster Ct, Dr & Pl 68510
Westmont Cir 68522
Westridge Rd 68523
Westward Rd 68521
Whispering Creek Rd 68526
Whispering Wind Blvd 68516
Whispering Wind Rd 68512
W Whisperwood St 68528
White Cap Bay 68527
White Dove Cir 68512
White Fish Dr 68516
White Hall Ln 68526
White Pine Rd 68505
Whitehead Dr 68521
Whitestone Cir & Dr 68506
Whitetail Cir 68523
Whitewater Ln 68521
Whitlock Pl & Rd 68516
Whitney Ct 68507
Whittier St 68503
Wildbriar Ln 68516
Wildcat Dr
2500-2598 68521
6700-6798 68504
6800-6899 68504
Wilderness Hill Blvd 68516
Wilderness Ridge Cir & Dr 68512
Wilderness View St 68512
Wilderness Woods Pl 68512
Wildfire Cir & Rd 68512
Wildflower Ct 68516
Wildrye Rd 68521
Wildwood Pl 68512
W Wilkins Cir & St 68524
Willard Ave 68507
William St 68502
Williamsburg Blvd & Dr 68516
Williamson Dr 68516
Willow Ave 68507
Willow Wood Cir & Ln 68506
Willowbrook Ln 68516
Wilshire Blvd
4800-5138 68504
5140-5499 68504
5600-5899 68505
Wimbledon Ct 68506
Winchester N & S 68512
Wind River Trl 68526
Windflower Cir & Rd 68521
Windhaven Dr 68512
Windhoek Dr 68512
Winding Way 68506
Winding Ridge Cir, Ct & Rd 68512
S Windlesham Ct 68516
Windmill Dr 68507
W Windridge Ln 68528
Windsor Dr 68528
W Winfield Ct 68523
W Winfield Rd 68512
W Winners Cir 68524
Winthrop Rd 68502
Wishing Well Dr 68516
Wisteria Pl 68516
Witherbee Blvd 68510
Wolff Ln 68521
SW Woodberry Dr 68523
Woodbine Ave 68506
Woodhaven Dr 68516
Woodland Ave 68516
Woodleigh Ln 68502
Woodridge Ct 68506
Woods Ave 68510
Woods Blvd 68502
Woodscrest Ave 68502
Woodsdale Blvd 68502
Woodshire Pkwy 68502
Woodstock Ave & Cir 68512
Woodsview St
1600-1699 68502
5300-5599 68506
Woodthrush Ln 68516
Woody Creek Cir & Ln 68516
Worthington Ave 68502
Wren Cir & Ct 68506
Wyman Ave 68512
Wyndam Dr 68527
X St
3201-3297 68503
3299-4399 68503
5201-5297 68504
5299-5599 68504
6300-6398 68505
6400-7000 68505
7002-7198 68505
Xavier Cir 68522
Y St
700-1899 68508
1901-2097 68503
2099-4599 68503
4601-4799 68503
5101-5199 68504
6300-7099 68505
Yancy Dr 68507
Yankee Hill Rd
1800-2099 68512
2700-3198 68516
3200-8499 68516
9400-11899 68526
Yankee Woods Dr 68516
Yellow Knife Dr 68505
Yellow Pine Rd 68505
Yellowstone Cir 68510
Yolande Ave 68521
York Ln 68505
Yorkshire Ct 68506
Yorktown Ct 68516
Yosemite Dr 68507
Yukon Ct 68521
Yuma Ln 68516
Zachary Cir 68507
W Zeamer St 68524

NUMBERED STREETS

1st St 68526
N 1st St
100-198 68508
2300-2398 68521
7500-9799 68531
NW 1st St 68521
S 1st St
201-297 68508
1101-1197 68502
4700-4998 68512
SW 1st St 68508
NW 2nd Cir 68521
2nd St 68526
N 2nd St
300-399 68508
2400-2498 68521
NW 2nd St 68521
S 2nd St
101-197 68508
1200-1599 68502
SW 2nd St
901-997 68508
4000-4299 68522
3rd St 68526
N 3rd St
201-299 68508
2300-2598 68521
2600-3699 68521
NW 3rd St 68521
S 3rd St 68502
NW 4th Cir 68521
4th St 68526
N 4th St 68521
NW 4th St 68521
S 4th St 68508
N 4th Street Ct 68521
N 5th St 68521
NW 5th St 68521
S 5th St
1000-1098 68508
1101-1199 68502
SW 5th St 68522
N 6th St
901-919 68508
2601-3099 68521
NW 6th St
500-599 68528
2301-2397 68521
2399-6899 68521
S 6th St
601-1099 68508
1100-1198 68502
1200-3999 68502
SW 6th St 68522
N 7th St
200-1099 68508
3801-3897 68521
8101-8597 68531
NW 7th St
500-599 68528
2301-2309 68521
S 7th St
203-297 68508
1100-1198 68502
5824-5899 68512
S 7th Street Ct 68512
N 8th Cir 68521
N 8th St
100-1099 68508
3600-3898 68521
NW 8th St
500-599 68528
2300-6800 68521
S 8th St
400-698 68508
1100-3999 68502
5400-5599 68512
SW 8th St 68522
N 9th Cir 68521
N 9th St
121-997 68508
2400-6809 68521
NW 9th St
500-599 68528
2300-2398 68521
S 9th St
101-109 68508
1100-3100 68502
SW 9th St
1400-2199 68522
6800-6900 68523
SW 10th Cir 68522
N 10th Ct 68521
N 10th St
100-1700 68508
3201-3297 68521
NW 10th St 68521
S 10th St
201-297 68508
1100-3400 68502
SW 10th St 68522
NW 11th Cir 68521
SW 11th Pl 68522
N 11th St
100-200 68508
2401-2497 68521
NW 11th St 68521
S 11th St
300-1099 68508
1100-3199 68502
SW 11th St 68522
N 12th St
100-198 68508
2400-6699 68521
NW 12th St
2301-2397 68521
7900-10399 68531
S 12th St
301-597 68508
1100-3299 68502
SW 12th St
1800-4299 68522
4400-9299 68523
N 13th St
100-198 68508
3000-6699 68521
NW 13th St 68528
S 13th St
101-127 68508
1100-3499 68502
7300-8199 68512
SW 13th St
1500-2399 68522
7700-7868 68523
SW 13th Street Cir 68522
NW 14th Ct 68521
N 14th St
100-299 68508
312-312 68588
314-314 68508
402-402 68588
501-501 68583
600-1298 68508
2400-6399 68521
7700-11399 68531
NW 14th St
200-499 68528
5600-5799 68521
S 14th St
100-1099 68508
1100-4299 68502
4801-6197 68512
SW 14th St 68522
N 15th St
600-1398 68508
3900-7499 68521
NW 15th St
100-198 68528
3501-3699 68521
S 15th St
1400-3999 68502
7301-7797 68512
SW 15th St 68522
N 16th St
100-398 68508
4900-7499 68521
NW 16th St 68528
S 16th St
100-598 68508
1100-3999 68502
4800-8299 68512
SW 16th St
1400-3899 68522
6700-6999 68523
NW 17th Cir 68528
N 17th Ct 68521
N 17th St
200-298 68508
300-300 68588
301-327 68508
3800-5599 68521
NW 17th St 68528
S 17th St
100-198 68508
1101-1113 68502
7300-8299 68512
SW 17th St
1200-2699 68522
7600-7710 68523
N 17th Street Ct 68521
N 18th Ct 68521
N 18th St
200-320 68508
3900-7399 68521
NW 18th St 68528
S 18th St
101-197 68508
1200-3999 68502
7300-8099 68512
SW 18th St
2001-2097 68522
7801-7897 68523
N 19th St 68508
1201-1297 68503
2701-3197 68521
NW 19th St 68528
S 19th St
300-598 68510
1101-1197 68502
4700-4998 68512
SW 19th St 68522
N 20th Cir 68503
N 20th St
100-198 68503
2700-2798 68521
NW 20th St 68528
S 20th St
200-999 68510
1100-1398 68502
5500-8299 68512
SW 20th St 68522
S 20th Street Cir 68512
N 21st St
200-1699 68503
3900-5900 68521
S 21st St
200-398 68510
1101-1197 68502
6500-7999 68512
SW 21st St 68522
SW 21st Street Ct 68522
N 22nd Ct 68503
N 22nd St
200-698 68503
3400-3498 68521
NW 22nd St 68528
S 22nd St
900-1099 68510
1100-2599 68502
7000-7154 68512
SW 22nd St
1400-1999 68522
7701-7799 68523
S 23rd Ct 68512
N 23rd St
100-198 68503
3900-5999 68521
NW 23rd St 68528
S 23rd St
201-897 68510
1100-2499 68502
7700-7899 68512
SW 23rd St 68522
S 24th Ct 68512
N 24th St
200-1899 68503
4400-4498 68521
NW 24th St 68524
S 24th St
300-898 68510
1100-3000 68502
SW 24th St
901-997 68522
8100-8299 68523
N 25th St
101-197 68503
4100-4198 68521
NW 25th St 68524
S 25th St
101-197 68510
1100-3199 68502
5700-7899 68512
SW 25th St
201-297 68522
6400-8499 68523
N 26th Pl 68521
N 26th St
101-197 68503
2901-3897 68521
S 26th St
200-1099 68510
1101-1197 68502
5400-7698 68512
SW 26th St 68522
N 27th St
100-1899 68503
2500-2598 68521
NW 27th St
201-497 68528
5500-11599 68524
S 27th St
100-999 68510
1200-4299 68502
4300-4398 68512
SW 27th St
201-297 68522
7200-8098 68523
S 28th Cir 68516
S 28th Ct 68516
N 28th St
100-2199 68503
5901-6599 68504
S 28th St
100-1000 68510
1400-3599 68502
6000-9626 68516
SW 28th St 68522
S 29th Cir 68516
N 29th St 68503
S 29th St
100-1099 68510
1500-3599 68502
7100-9499 68516
S 30th Pl 68516
N 30th St 68503
S 30th St
100-1100 68510
1102-1298 68510
1900-3098 68502
3100-4299 68502
4800-9399 68516
SW 30th St 68522
S 31st Pl 68516
N 31st St 68503
S 31st St
100-598 68510
2801-2897 68502
5500-6599 68516
SW 31st St
200-1498 68522
7000-7098 68523
S 31st Street Cir 68502
S 31st Street Ct 68516
S 32nd Cir 68516
S 32nd Ct 68516
S 32nd Pl 68502
N 32nd St
100-2299 68503
4901-4997 68504
S 32nd St
600-1300 68510
4200-4299 68502
5100-7599 68516
SW 32nd St 68522
S 33rd Ct 68516
N 33rd St
101-197 68503
2301-2997 68504
NW 33rd St 68524
S 33rd St
300-398 68510
1400-4299 68506
4300-8399 68516
SW 33rd St
1700-2099 68522
7300-7308 68523
SW 34th Cir 68523
S 34th Ct 68516
SW 34th Ct 68523
N 34th St
100-198 68503
6200-6300 68504
NW 34th St 68524
S 34th St
601-797 68510
1900-3799 68506
5701-6097 68516
SW 34th St
1900-1999 68522
6100-6799 68523
34th Street Cir & Ct 68516
N 35th Cir 68504
SW 35th Cir 68522
S 35th Ct 68516
SW 35th Ct 68522
N 35th St
100-198 68503
2600-2698 68504
NW 35th St 68524
S 35th St
126-132 68510
1501-1997 68506
7200-8099 68516
SW 35th St 68523
SW 36th Ct 68523
N 36th St
301-797 68503
2600-2999 68504
NW 36th St 68524
S 36th St
600-1099 68510
2100-4252 68506
4300-8099 68516
SW 36th St
1400-1999 68522
6100-6199 68523
N 37th St
900-1499 68503
2600-2699 68504
NW 37th St 68524
S 37th St
101-197 68510
1400-1544 68506
4300-8099 68516

SW 37th St
1800-1900 68522
6300-6898 68523
N 38th St
800-1499 68503
2701-2897 68504
NW 38th St 68524
S 38th St
100-999 68510
1600-1698 68506
4300-7699 68516
SW 38th St
1800-1999 68522
6700-6799 68523
S 38th Street Ct 68510
SW 39th Ct 68523
N 39th St
800-898 68503
2601-2697 68504
NW 39th St 68524
S 39th St
400-1000 68510
2101-2297 68506
4501-5197 68516
N 39th Street Cir 68504
SW 39th Street Ct 68523
N 40th St
800-1499 68503
2601-2697 68504
NW 40th St
100-198 68528
5101-7597 68524
S 40th St
100-1399 68510
1501-1597 68506
4300-9399 68516
SW 40th St
200-2599 68522
5701-5797 68523
N 41st St
1000-1499 68503
2600-2698 68504
2700-3300 68504
3302-3398 68504
NW 41st St 68524
S 41st St
400-999 68510
1700-3199 68506
5700-7799 68516
SW 41st St 68523
S 41st Street Ct 68516
N 42nd St
800-1399 68503
2500-4099 68504
NW 42nd St 68524
S 42nd St
100-198 68510
200-831 68510
833-1099 68510
1700-3999 68506
6000-7299 68516
N 42nd Street Cir 68504
S 42nd Street Ct 68516
N 43rd St
1100-1198 68503
2300-2498 68504
NW 43rd St 68524
S 43rd St
400-852 68510
4200-4299 68506
4400-6999 68516
S 43rd Street Ct 68516
N 44th St
100-198 68503
2300-2398 68504
NW 44th St
1800-2099 68528
2300-4200 68524
S 44th St
100-198 68510
1500-4299 68506
4300-6999 68516
SW 44th St
200-1899 68522
6800-6999 68523
N 45th St
801-897 68503
2501-2597 68504
NW 45th St
1600-1714 68528
2300-2499 68524
S 45th St
100-899 68510
1700-2099 68506
4300-7299 68516
SW 45th St 68523
N 45th Street Ct 68504
N 46th St
101-497 68503
2500-3499 68504
NW 46th St
1700-2099 68528
2200-2500 68524
S 46th St
100-900 68510
2200-4199 68506
4300-6199 68516
NW 47th Ct 68528
N 47th St
1000-1098 68503
2501-2797 68504
NW 47th St
1800-1899 68528
2100-2499 68524
S 47th St
300-1299 68510
1700-4000 68506
4300-5099 68516
SW 47th St 68522
N 48th St 68504
NW 48th St
1200-1298 68528
2801-6697 68524
S 48th St
101-297 68510
1401-1497 68506
4300-7499 68516
SW 48th St 68522
N 49th St 68504
NW 49th St
1800-1898 68528
1900-2199 68528
2200-4599 68524
S 49th St
600-1399 68510
1700-4299 68506
4300-6499 68516
6501-6599 68516
N 50th St
201-1297 68504
7310-7422 68514
NW 50th St
1900-2199 68528
2221-2221 68524
S 50th St
200-1399 68510
1400-1698 68506
4300-7499 68516
SW 50th St 68522
S 51st Pl 68506
N 51st St
1000-3499 68504
7400-7440 68514
NW 51st St 68524
S 51st St
600-999 68510
1700-4299 68506
5200-6999 68516
N 52nd St 68504
NW 52nd St
1801-2197 68528
2500-2998 68524
S 52nd St
100-799 68510
1400-1498 68506
4301-4441 68516
S 52nd Street Ct 68516
S 53rd Ct 68516
N 53rd St 68504
NW 53rd St
1901-2097 68528
2099-2199 68528
2400-3899 68524
S 53rd St
101-197 68510
199-799 68510
1700-4099 68506
5100-9699 68516
S 53rd Street Ct 68516
N 54th St 68504
NW 54th St
1900-2199 68528
3601-3697 68524
3699-4599 68524
S 54th St
300-599 68510
2400-4099 68506
4300-5199 68516
S 55th Ct 68516
N 55th St 68504
NW 55th St
1900-2199 68528
2200-2899 68524
S 55th St
300-799 68510
1801-2397 68506
2399-2699 68506
8800-9099 68516
N 56th St
100-5000 68504
7500-16899 68514
NW 56th St 68528
S 56th St
101-397 68510
1501-1797 68506
4400-11400 68516
SW 56th St
1500-1598 68522
5001-5099 68523
NW 57th Ct 68524
N 57th St
401-597 68505
2300-2398 68507
NW 57th St
1800-2299 68528
3600-4100 68524
S 57th St
1901-1997 68506
4400-8399 68516
N 58th Ct 68507
N 58th St
400-498 68505
500-2299 68505
2400-2598 68507
2600-5999 68507
NW 58th St 68528
S 58th St
1400-4299 68506
4301-4397 68516
4399-8399 68516
N 58th Street Cir 68517
N 59th St
800-2299 68505
2500-2899 68507
2901-2999 68507
S 59th St
2100-2400 68506
2402-2998 68506
5500-5598 68516
5600-8099 68516
8101-8199 68516
S 59th Street Cir 68516
S 59th Street Ct 68506
N 60th St
700-2299 68505
2300-6499 68507
S 60th St
2001-2097 68506
2099-2600 68506
2602-2698 68506
4300-11499 68516
N 61st St
1300-1398 68505
1400-2299 68505
2601-2997 68507
2999-4399 68507
4401-4599 68507
S 61st St
2100-2399 68506
4300-8999 68516
S 61st Street Ct 68516
N 62nd St
1500-2299 68505
2300-4599 68507
S 62nd St
2100-2399 68506
5100-8399 68516
N 63rd St
900-998 68505
1000-2299 68505
2300-6200 68507
6202-6298 68507
S 63rd St 68516
SW 63rd St 68532
S 64th Cir 68516
N 64th St
1200-2299 68505
2300-3899 68507
3901-4399 68507
S 64th St 68516
N 65th St
900-2299 68505
2300-4599 68507
S 65th St 68516
S 65th Street Cir 68516
S 66th Pl 68506
N 66th St
100-198 68505
3001-3097 68507
S 66th St
100-199 68510
2100-2299 68506
4800-9999 68516
S 66th Street Cir 68516
N 67th St
600-2299 68505
2300-4199 68507
S 67th St 68516
N 68th St
600-2299 68505
2300-4099 68507
S 68th St 68516
S 68th Street Ct 68516
S 68th Street Pl 68510
N 69th Cir 68507
SW 69th Pl 68532
N 69th St
1000-2199 68505
3200-4500 68507
4502-4598 68507
S 69th St 68516
N 69th Street Ct 68507
N 70th St
200-2299 68505
2300-6600 68507
7500-17799 68517
NW 70th St 68524
S 70th St
201-497 68510
1400-1498 68506
4301-4397 68516
SW 70th St 68532
N 71st St
1500-1999 68505
3101-3197 68507
3199-4999 68507
5001-5099 68507
S 71st St 68516
N 72nd St 68507
S 72nd St
2300-2400 68506
2402-3198 68506
4700-9099 68516
SW 72nd St 68532
N 73rd St
400-2099 68505
2800-5200 68507
5202-5298 68507
S 73rd St 68516
SW 73rd St 68532
N 74th St 68507
S 74th St
2300-3199 68506
5100-6100 68516
6102-9098 68516
SW 74th St 68532
N 75th Ct 68505
N 75th St
400-599 68505
601-699 68505
2601-2697 68507
2699-3599 68507
S 75th St
2300-3699 68506
4800-7699 68516
N 75th Street Ct 68507
S 76th Ct 68516
N 76th St
1500-2299 68505
2301-2397 68507
2399-2599 68507
S 76th St
2400-3700 68506
3702-4098 68506
4700-5099 68516
5101-5499 68516
S 77th Ct 68510
S 77th Pl
200-230 68510
2400-2699 68506
N 77th St 68505
S 77th St
240-298 68510
1400-3800 68506
4800-7741 68516
SW 77th St 68532
N 78th St
1000-2299 68505
2400-2899 68507
S 78th St
2400-4299 68506
4900-6099 68516
6101-9199 68516
SW 78th St 68532
N 79th St
1000-2199 68505
2400-2899 68507
11600-11999 68517
S 79th St
2301-2397 68506
2399-3929 68506
3931-3999 68506
5301-6197 68516
6199-6299 68516
SW 80th Cir 68532
S 80th Pl 68516
N 80th St
1000-1200 68505
2300-2399 68507
S 80th St
1900-4199 68506
4301-4397 68516
SW 80th St 68532
N 81st St
500-2299 68505
2400-2899 68507
S 81st St
3200-4099 68506
5900-8499 68516
S 81st Street Ct 68506
N 82nd Ct 68507
N 82nd Pl 68507
N 82nd St 68505
S 82nd St
2701-4097 68506
4099-4199 68506
5400-7199 68516
S 82nd Street Cir 68506
N 83rd St
1000-1199 68505
2300-2800 68507
2802-2898 68507
S 83rd St
3200-4099 68506
6300-6500 68516
6502-9018 68516
83rd Street Cir & Pl 68506
N 84th St
100-198 68505
2301-4097 68507
7600-17899 68517
NW 84th St
210-2199 68528
2401-2697 68524
S 84th St
101-197 68510
1555-1597 68506
4301-4697 68516
SW 84th St 68532
S 85th Cir 68526
S 85th Ct 68526
S 85th Pl 68526
N 85th St 68507
S 85th St 68526
S 86th Ct 68526
N 86th St 68505
S 86th St 68526
N 86th Street Ct 68505
N 87th St
1500-2299 68505
2300-2699 68507
S 87th St 68526
N 88th St
900-998 68505
1000-1999 68505
2001-2099 68505
2300-2699 68507
S 88th St
4000-4199 68520
5400-6999 68526
N 89th St
2200-2298 68505
2700-2799 68507
S 89th St 68526
SW 89th St 68532
N 90th St 68507
S 90th St 68526
N 91st Ct 68507
N 91st St
1900-1998 68505
2000-2299 68505
2300-2699 68507
NW 91st St 68528
S 91st St
2900-3698 68520
5701-5797 68526
5799-8599 68526
N 92nd St 68505
SW 92nd St 68532
S 93rd Cir 68520
S 93rd Pl 68526
N 93rd St 68505
S 93rd St 68526
S 94th Ct 68526
S 94th St
1100-1399 68520
6100-6199 68526
S 94th Bay 68526
S 95th Ct 68526
N 95th St 68505
S 95th St 68526
S 96th Ct 68526
S 96th Pl 68526
N 96th St 68505
S 96th St 68526
S 96th Bay 68526
S 97th Ct 68526
N 97th St 68505
S 97th St 68526
N 98th St
1501-1697 68505
2301-4597 68507
8400-15499 68517
NW 98th St
100-1899 68528
2400-3199 68524
S 98th St
1500-4099 68520
4300-11499 68526
SW 98th St 68532
N 99th St 68527
100th Cir & St 68527
N 102nd St 68527
NW 105th St 68524
S 105th St 68520
S 107th St 68526
N 112th St
301-497 68527
12200-14999 68517
NW 112th St
200-498 68528
500-1099 68528
5300-7399 68524
S 112th St
200-1399 68520
5700-6799 68526
SW 112th St 68532
S 114th St 68526
S 115th St 68526
NW 118th St 68524
S 120th St
200-1399 68520
8800-9299 68526
NW 122nd Ct 68524
NW 123rd St 68528
5500-5999 68524
NW 126th St
200-898 68528
900-1700 68528
1702-2498 68528
2401-2597 68524
2599-5999 68524
SW 126th St 68532
N 129th Ct 68527
N 131st St 68527
N 134th St 68527
S 134th St 68520
NW 140th St 68528
SW 140th St 68532
N 148th St 68527
S 148th St 68520
N 149th St 68527
N 155th St 68527
N 162nd St 68527
S 162nd St 68520
170th Cir & St 68527
N 176th St 68527
S 176th St 68520
N 179th St 68527
N 181st St 68527
N 182nd Ct 68527
N 190th St 68527

NORFOLK NE

General Delivery 68701

POST OFFICE BOXES MAIN OFFICE STATIONS AND BRANCHES

Box No.s
All PO Boxes 68702

NAMED STREETS

Adams Ave 68701
Adare Rd 68701
Agnes Ave 68701
N & S Airport Rd 68701
Alaska Ave & Cir 68701
Alstadt Dr 68701
Amberwood Dr 68701
Andersen St 68701
Andrews Dr 68701
Andys Lake Cir & Rd 68701
Andys North Shore Dr 68701
Angus Cir & Dr 68701
Ann Ave 68701
Applewood Dr 68701
Aspen Dr 68701
Battle Creek Rd 68701
Bel Air Rd 68701
Bel Ridge Rd 68701
Belmont Dr 68701
E & W Benjamin Ave 68701
E & W Berry Hill Dr 68701
Beverly Rd 68701
N & S Birch St 68701
Blackberry Dr 68701
Blaine St 68701
Blue Stem Cir 68701
E & W Bluff Ave 68701

Bonita Rd 68701
N & S Boxelder Cir & St 68701
E & W Braasch Ave 68701
Brentwood Dr 68701
Bridge Rd 68701
Broadmoor Dr 68701
Buckskin Rd 68701
Campbell Dr 68701
Campus Dr 68701
Carmel Dr 68701
E & W Cedar Ave 68701
Cedar Ridge Rd 68701
Center Dr 68701
S Channel Rd 68701
Charles St 68701
Charolais Dr 68701
S Chestnut St 68701
Clark St 68701
Clearfield Dr 68701
College View Dr 68701
Columbia St 68701
Colwell St 68701
Condenew Ave 68701
E Coolidge Ave 68701
Corto St 68701
Cottage Dr 68701
N Cottonwood St 68701
Country Club Rd 68701
Crestview Rd 68701
Crestwood 68701
Crown Rd 68701
Custer Ave 68701
Darrus Dr 68701
N & S Deer Run Dr 68701
Domar Dr 68701
Dover Dr 68701
Driftwood 68701
Dun Rd 68701
Durland Ave 68701
Eagle Ridge Rd 68701
Eastridge St 68701
N & S Eastwood St 68701
E & W Eisenhower Ave 68701
El Camino Dr 68701
Eldorado Rd 68701
Eleanor Ln 68701
S Elkhorn St 68701
E Elm Ave & St 68701
Elmers Ln 68701
Emerald Dr 68701
Englewood 68701
Fairview Dr 68701
Fieldcrest Dr 68701
Forest Dr 68701
Fox Ridge Ave 68701
N & S Front St 68701
Galeta Ave 68701
Georgia Ave 68701
Gerecke St 68701
Gingerberry Dr 68701
Glenmore Dr 68701
Glenn St 68701
Glenwood Blvd 68701
Gold Strike Dr 68701
Goldenberry Dr 68701
Golf View Dr 68701
S Grandview Dr & Rd 68701
Grant Ave 68701
Greenlawn Dr 68701
Grove Ave 68701
Hackberry Dr 68701
Hadar Rd 68701
Half Mile Rd 68701
Hardison Dr 68701
Harold Cir 68701
Harris Dr 68701
Harrison Ave 68701
Hastings Ave 68701
Hayes Ave 68701
Heather Ln 68701
Hendricks St 68701
Hespe Dr 68701
N & S Hickory St 68701
Highland Dr 68701
E Highway 24 68701
S Highway 81 68701
Hillcrest Cir & Dr 68701
Hillside Dr 68701
Hilltop Dr 68701
Hillview Dr 68701
Homewood Dr 68701
Husker Rd 68701
Impala Dr 68701
Imperial Rd 68701
E & W Indiana Ave 68701
Iron Horse Dr 68701
Isabelle Ave & Cir 68701
J Paul Dr 68701
Jackson Ave 68701
Janet Ln 68701
Jefferson Ave 68701
Jerry Dr 68701
Jo Deb Dr 68701
Joann Dr 68701
Jolean Dr 68701
Jonathan Cir 68701
E & W Kaneb Rd 68701
Kansas St 68701
Kapalar Cir 68701
Kelland Dr 68701
Kimberly Way 68701
Kings Way 68701
E Klug Ave 68701
E Knolls St 68701
Koenigstein Ave 68701
Krenzien Dr 68701
Lake Canyon Rd 68701
Lakeridge Dr 68701
Lakeview Dr 68701
Lakewalk Dr 68701
Lakewood Dr 68701
Larayne Ln 68701
Laurel Ln 68701
Lenton Ln 68701
Lincoln Ave 68701
Linden Ln 68701
Linwood Ln 68701
Lodgeview Dr 68701
Logan St 68701
Longhorn Dr 68701
Lovely Ln 68701
Mach 1 Dr 68701
E & W Madison Ave 68701
Magnet Dr & St 68701
E Main St
100-499 68701
200-299 68738
W Main St 68701
Main Street Enola 68701
E & W Maple Ave & St 68701
Market Ln & Pl 68701
Matrau Ave 68701
Maurer Dr 68701
Mcdonald Dr 68701
Mcintosh Rd 68701
Mckinley Ave 68701
Meadow Dr & Ln 68701
W Meadow Ridge Rd 68701
Meadowlark Ln 68701
E & W Michigan Ave 68701
Milan Dr 68701
Miles Dr 68701
Miller Ave 68701
Mimick Dr 68701
Minnelusa Ave 68701
E & W Monroe Ave 68701
Morningside Dr 68701
Mulberry Dr 68701
E & W Nebraska Ave 68701
Nord St 68701
E & W Norfolk Ave 68701
Northdale Dr 68701
E & W Northwestern Ave 68701
E & W Nucor Rd 68701
Oak St 68701
Oakbrook Dr 68701
Oestreich Rd 68701
Old Hadar Rd 68701
Old Highway 8 68701
E & W Omaha Ave 68701
Opal Ln 68701
E & W Park Ave, Ln & Way 68701
Parker Cir 68701
Parkhill Dr 68701
Parkview Dr 68701
E & W Pasewalk Ave & Cir 68701
Pennsylvania Ave 68701
E & W Phillip Ave 68701
Piedmont Ave 68701
Pierce Dr & St 68701
E Pine St 68701
S Pine Industrial Rd 68701
Pinnacle Dr 68701
Ponca Hills Dr 68701
Portia Dr & Pl 68701
E & W Prairie Ave 68701
E & W Prospect Ave & Cir 68701
Queen City Blvd 68701
Raasch Dr 68701
Random Rd 68701
Regal Way 68701
Regency Cir S 68701
Ridgeway Dr 68701
Riverfront Rd 68701
Riverside Blvd 68701
Rodeo Rd 68701
Roland St 68701
Rolling Hills Dr 68701
Roosevelt Ave 68701
Rose Ln 68701
Ruth Ann Cir 68701
Saddle Rd 68701
Shannon Dr 68701
Sheridan Dr 68701
E & W Sherwood Ln & Rd 68701
Shetland Path 68701
Shorthorn Dr 68701
Silver Fox Ave 68701
Skyline Dr 68701
Skyview Cir 68701
E & W South Airport Rd 68701
Southern Dr 68701
E & W Spruce Ave 68701
Square Turn Blvd 68701
State Highway 13 68701
State Highway 24 68701
N State Highway 35 68701
Suburban Dr 68701
Summit St 68701
Sunnydell Ln 68701
Sunrise Cir & Dr 68701
Sunset Ave 68701
E & W Sycamore Ave & St 68701
Syracuse Ave 68701
Tahazouka Rd 68701
Tara Heights Dr 68701
W Taylor Ave 68701
Tennis Court Dr 68701
Terrace Rd 68701
Timber Meadows Ln 68701
Tomlo Ave 68701
Trailridge Rd 68701
Troon St 68701
Ursula Cir 68701
Us Highway 275 68701
Us Highway 81 68701
Valley Rd 68701
Valley View Dr 68701
Valli Hi Rd 68701
Verges Ave 68701
Vernon Ave 68701
Vicki Ln 68701
N & S Victory Rd 68701
Village Green Dr 68701
Vista Rd 68701
Volkman Dr 68701
E & W Walnut Ave & Cir 68701
Warnerville Dr 68701
Washington Ave 68701
Werner Dr 68701
Westbrook Dr 68701
Western Cir 68701
Westridge Dr 68701
Westside Ave 68701
Westside Plaza Dr 68701
Westview Dr 68701
Westwick Dr 68701
Westwood Dr 68701
E & W Whitney Ave 68701
Wildwood St 68701
Williams St 68701
N & S Willow St & Way 68701
E Wilson Ave 68701
Windsor Dr 68701
Winter Ave 68701
Wood St 68701
Woodcrest Dr 68701
Woodhurst Dr 68701
Woodland Dr 68701
Wyndham Rd 68701

NUMBERED STREETS

N & S 1st Ave & St 68701
N & S 2nd Ave & St 68701
N & S 3rd Ave & St 68701
N 4th Ave 68701
S 4th Ave 68701
N 4th St
100-199 68701
201-399 68701
401-699 68701
401-401 68702
S 4th St 68701
N & S 5th 68701
N & S 6th 68701
N & S 7th 68701
N & S 8th 68701
N & S 9th 68701
N & S 10th 68701
N & S 11th 68701
N & S 12th 68701
N & S 13th Pl & St 68701
S 13th Place Cir 68701
N & S 14th Pl & St 68701
N & S 15th 68701
N & S 16th 68701
N & S 17th Cir & St 68701
N & S 18th 68701
S 18th Street Cir 68701
N 19th Dr & St 68701
S 20th Dr & St 68701
21st Dr 68701
22nd Dr 68701
S 24th St 68701
N & S 25th 68701
N 26th St 68701
N 27th St 68701
N 28th St 68701
N 29th St 68701
N 30th St 68701
N 31st St 68701
N 32nd St 68701
N 33rd St 68701
N 34th St 68701
N 36th St 68701
N & S 37th 68701
N 43rd St 68701
S 45th St 68701
N & S 49th 68701
N & S 61st 68701
546th Ave 68701
547th Ave 68701
548th Ave 68701
549th Ave 68701
550th Ave 68701
551st Ave 68701
552nd Ave 68701
553rd Ave 68701
554th Ave 68701
555th Ave 68701
556th Ave 68701
557th Ave 68701
558th Ave 68701
559th 1/2 Ave 68701
559th Ave 68701
560th Ave 68701
561st Ave 68701
562nd Ave 68701
833rd Rd 68701
834th Rd 68701
835th Rd 68701
836th Rd 68701
837th Rd 68701
838th Rd 68701
839th Rd 68701
840th Rd 68701
842nd Rd 68701
843rd Rd 68701
844th Rd 68701
845th Rd 68701
846th Rd 68701
847 1/2 Rd 68701
847th Rd 68701
848th Rd 68701
849th Rd 68701

NORTH PLATTE NE

General Delivery 69101

POST OFFICE BOXES MAIN OFFICE STATIONS AND BRANCHES

Box No.s
All PO Boxes 69103

RURAL ROUTES

05 69101

HIGHWAY CONTRACTS

35 69101

NAMED STREETS

All Street Addresses 69101

NUMBERED STREETS

W 1st St 69101
E & W 2nd 69101
E 3rd St
100-300 69101
300-300 69103
301-401 69101
403-2021 69101
W 3rd St 69101
E & W 4th 69101
E & W 5th 69101
E & W 6th 69101
E & W 7th 69101
E & W 8th 69101
E & W 9th 69101
E & W 10th 69101
E & W 11th 69101
E & W 12th 69101
E & W 13th 69101
E & W 14th 69101
E & W 15th 69101
E & W 16th 69101
W 17th St 69101
18th Ave & St 69101
W 19th St 69101
W 20th St 69101
W 21st St 69101
W 22nd St 69101

OMAHA NE

General Delivery 68108

POST OFFICE BOXES MAIN OFFICE STATIONS AND BRANCHES

Box No.s
XXXBRM - XXXBRM 68164
XXXXBRM - XXXXBRM 68164
1 - 1629 68101
2000 - 3959 68103
3366 - 3366 68108
3985 - 3995 68103
4001 - 4990 68104
6001 - 6790 68106
7001 - 7910 68107
8001 - 8840 68108
9002 - 9094 68109
9998 - 9998 68101
9998 - 9998 68109
9998 - 9998 68139
11001 - 11999 68111
12001 - 12999 68112
14335 - 14335 68114
19007 - 19473 68119
21000 - 21012 68108
24001 - 24995 68124
27001 - 27999 68127
30000 - 30300 68103
31001 - 32007 68131
34001 - 34999 68134
44000 - 44214 68144
45001 - 45996 68145
68117 - 68117 68117
69001 - 69006 68106
90000 - 90500 68103
111000 - 111636 68111
199500 - 199998 68119
241001 - 249550 68124
271000 - 271059 68127
390001 - 391416 68139
451001 - 459998 68145
540001 - 543099 68154
641001 - 642376 68164

RURAL ROUTES

45, 46 68152

NAMED STREETS

A Cir 68144
A Plz
6701-6899 68106
13100-13198 68144
13901-13999 68144
A St
1801-2025 68108
3100-3198 68105
3200-4499 68105
4500-6699 68106
8500-8799 68124
12301-12397 68144
12399-13799 68144
2025 1/2-2029 1/2 68108
Abbott Dr & Plz 68110
Acorn Ln 68112
Adams Cir
13700-14799 68137
16500-18399 68135
Adams Dr 68127
Adams Plz
9701-9799 68127
11800-11899 68137
Adams St
2500-2599 68107
9100-10299 68127
10301-10399 68127
13300-15599 68137
15601-15797 68135
15799-19899 68135
Adel Cir 68124
Aksarben Dr 68106
Alice Dr 68142
Allan Dr 68137
Allan St 68135
Amelia Earhart Plz 68110
Ames Ave
1300-2100 68110
2102-2298 68110
2400-4200 68111
4202-4498 68111
4501-4597 68104
4599-6599 68104
6601-7199 68104
8500-8502 68134
8504-9699 68134
9701-9999 68134
12900-14200 68164
14202-14398 68164
14400-14698 68116
14700-16699 68116
16701-17599 68116
Ames Cir
7201-7797 68134
7799-7999 68134
17600-17699 68116
Ames Ct 68116
Ames Plz
12600-12700 68164
12702-12798 68164
14401-14649 68116
14651-14699 68116
Amy Cir
5000-5099 68137
17700-17799 68135
Amy Plz 68137
Andresen Plz 68137
Andresen St
13500-13699 68137
19600-19799 68135
Anne St
12000-12098 68137
12100-14300 68137
14302-14398 68137
18600-18999 68135
Arbor Cir
5000-5099 68106
5101-6299 68106
13930-13999 68144
15900-15999 68130
Arbor Ct
100-299 68108
16000-16199 68130
Arbor Plz
6200-6298 68106
17606-17698 68130
Arbor St
1000-2199 68108
2201-2399 68108
2400-4299 68105
4600-6150 68106
6152-6398 68106
8000-9200 68124
9202-9398 68124
11300-15599 68144
16000-16198 68130
16200-17601 68130
17603-17999 68130
Arcadia Ave
3000-3199 68111
4900-4998 68104
5000-5099 68104
9201-9299 68134
Arcadia Plz
10000-10099 68134
16700-16798 68116
Archer Ave
1301-1397 68107
1399-1499 68107
1501-1599 68107
19700-19799 68135
Archer Cir 68135
Arlington Dr 68134
Arlington Plz 68164
Arlington St 68164
Armbrust Dr 68124
Armstrong Plz 68134

Armstrong St 68116
Arrow Rock Dr 68157
Arthur St 68107
Ascot Dr 68114
Ash St 68137
Aspen Cir & Dr 68157
Atlas Cir 68130
Atlas Ct 68137
Atlas Plz 68137
Atlas St
900-1300 68107
1302-1398 68107
18100-19400 68130
19402-20224 68130
S Atlerani St 68136
S Atlernew St 68108
Atwood Ave
2000-2099 68108
12601-12697 68144
12699-13699 68144
Audrey Cir 68136
Audrey St
7000-7299 68138
15700-17000 68136
17002-17298 68136
Augusta Ave 68144
Augusta Cir 68136
Augusta Plz 68144
Aurora Dr 68134
Aurora Plz 68164
Aurora St 68136
N Avenue Plz 68127
Avenue H E 68110
Avenue J E 68110
B Cir 68144
B Plz
6801-6899 68106
13100-13198 68144
B St
1300-2399 68108
2401-2497 68105
2499-2500 68105
2502-4448 68105
4500-6999 68106
8500-8799 68124
12300-13799 68144
18900-20299 68130
Baker St 68122
Bancroft Cir
5000-5099 68106
16200-16299 68130
Bancroft Ct 68130
Bancroft Plz 68108
Bancroft St
100-298 68108
300-2399 68108
2400-2498 68105
2500-4299 68105
4301-4499 68105
4501-4647 68106
4649-6300 68106
6302-6398 68106
16300-16699 68130
Banner St 68136
Barbara Cir 68130
Barbara St
7800-8199 68124
18601-18899 68130
Barker Ave 68105
Barnes St 68118
Barnett St 68116
Barretts Cir & Dr 68138
Bartels Dr 68137
Bartlett St 68122
Battlefield Dr 68152
Bauman Ave
2400-4199 68112
4600-5098 68152
5100-5399 68152
7500-8099 68122
10800-11999 68164
14900-16100 68116
16102-16498 68116
Bauman Cir
11000-11599 68164
16500-16599 68116
Bay Meadows Rd 68127
Baywood Cir & Dr 68130
Bedford Ave
3000-3598 68111
3600-4400 68111
4402-4498 68111
4500-7099 68104
7101-7199 68104
7200-10099 68134
10101-10699 68134
12100-13499 68164
15000-17399 68116
Bedford Cir 68134
Bedford Plz
8000-10598 68134
12001-12099 68164
14701-16197 68116
16199-16299 68116
Bel Ct & Dr 68144
Bel Air Cir 68136
Bel Air Dr 68144
Belmont Dr 68127
Belvedere Blvd 68111
Bemis Cir 68154
Bemis Plz 68114
Bemis St 68154
Bennie Day Rd 68152
Bennington Rd
6200-6398 68152
6400-7199 68152
8601-8697 68122
8699-10600 68122
10602-10698 68122
11200-11298 68142
11300-13600 68142
13602-14198 68142
Benson Gardens Blvd 68134
Bernadette Ave 68157
Berry Ave 68107
Berry Cir 68137
Berry Plz
9600-10799 68127
14101-14199 68137
Berry St
9000-10299 68127
15601-15697 68135
15699-16000 68135
16002-18798 68135
Bert Murphy Ave 68107
Beverly Dr 68114
Binney St
1500-2299 68110
2400-4399 68111
4800-7099 68104
9300-9699 68134
12000-13499 68164
14900-15599 68116
Birch Ave
15400-15499 68138
15900-15998 68136
16000-16599 68136
Birch Dr 68164
Birch Plz 68164
Birch St
6000-6099 68104
10600-10699 68134
10701-10799 68134
15000-15199 68116
Birchwood Ave
13500-13598 68137
13600-14099 68137
18700-18899 68135
Birchwood Cir 68137
Birelia St 68107
Black St 68142
Black Walnut St 68136
Blackwell Dr 68137
Blaine Cir 68135
Blaine St
1101-1197 68107
1199-1299 68107
19300-20099 68135
Blair High Rd 68142
Blake St 68108
Blondo Dr 68134
Blondo St
2401-2497 68111
2499-3999 68111
4500-7000 68104
7002-7198 68104
7200-9599 68134
9601-10799 68134
10800-13499 68164
13501-14149 68164
14401-14997 68116
14999-17799 68116
17801-17999 68116
Bloomfield Dr 68114
Blue Sage Pkwy 68130
Bluebird Ln 68112
Bob Boozer Dr 68130
Bob Gibson Blvd 68108
Boeing Ct 68110
Bohling Dr 68136
Bondesson Cir 68122
Bondesson St
2801-2897 68112
2899-3199 68112
7500-8299 68122
8301-8399 68122
Borman Ave 68137
Borman Cir
10700-10799 68127
14100-14199 68138
16000-16099 68135
Borman St
4500-4899 68157
14500-15599 68138
18600-18799 68135
Bowie Dr 68114
Boyd Cir
9600-9699 68134
13000-13199 68164
16000-16099 68116
Boyd Ct 68116
Boyd Plz
12801-12899 68164
14400-14663 68116
14665-14699 68116
Boyd St
3400-3499 68111
3501-4399 68111
4800-6599 68104
8000-10699 68134
10701-10799 68134
13050-13398 68164
13400-13599 68164
13601-13799 68164
14700-17699 68116
N Branch Dr 68116
Brentwood Rd 68114
Briar St
15400-15499 68138
15600-15798 68136
15800-17099 68136
17101-17199 68136
Bridgeford Rd 68124
Bridle Path 68152
Briggs Cir
13700-14299 68144
19500-19599 68130
Briggs St
1100-1199 68108
5600-5899 68106
7600-7699 68124
19200-19800 68130
19802-19898 68130
Bristol Cir 68164
Bristol Plz 68116
Bristol St 68111
Broadmoor Ct, Dr &
Rd 68114
Brookridge Dr 68137
Brookside Ave 68124
Brookside Cir 68144
Brookside Ln 68124
Browne Cir
11100-14299 68164
16825-17699 68116
Browne St
200-1398 68110
1400-2199 68110
2400-2498 68111
2500-4499 68111
4500-5600 68104
5602-5998 68104
7801-7897 68134
7899-10799 68134
12900-13499 68164
14400-17599 68116
E Browne St 68110
Brownley Cir 68164
Brownley Dr 68134
Buckingham Ave
4400-4498 68107
6000-6299 68117
Burdette Cir
9500-9599 68134
11300-13199 68164
16200-17499 68116
Burdette St
1500-2200 68110
2202-2298 68110
2401-2497 68111
2499-4399 68111
4401-4499 68111
4500-5899 68104
8100-8199 68134
8201-9649 68134
11000-13398 68164
13400-13899 68164
13901-14099 68164
14401-14447 68116
14449-17799 68116
17801-17899 68116
Burke Blvd 68154
Burke St
11500-11899 68154
11901-12699 68154
16700-17407 68118
17409-17999 68118
Burlington Ave 68107
Burlington St 68127
Burr Oak Ln 68122
Burt Cir
10500-10699 68114
14700-14749 68154
Burt Ct 68154
Burt Dr 68154
Burt Plz
8201-8299 68114
12400-12498 68154
Burt St
1500-2199 68102
2201-2399 68102
3001-3197 68131
3199-4399 68131
4800-7099 68132
7101-7199 68132
7200-7598 68114
7600-9499 68114
9501-10799 68114
11500-11598 68154
11600-15599 68154
15600-17999 68118
Butler Ave
4500-4599 68104
14900-16599 68116
C Cir 68144
C Plz 68144
C St
1400-2700 68107
2702-2998 68107
4700-4798 68106
4800-4999 68106
5001-6999 68106
8500-8799 68124
12200-13799 68144
16300-20299 68130
Cady Ave
1400-1500 68110
1502-1598 68110
9200-9999 68134
12900-13099 68164
Cady Cir
11200-11299 68164
16800-17499 68116
Cady Ct 68134
Caldwell St
2400-2899 68131
4901-4949 68132
Caley Ave 68152
Calhoun Rd
9500-9698 68112
9700-10700 68112
10702-10798 68112
10800-14299 68152
14301-14899 68152
California Cir 68154
California Plz 68114
California St
1400-1498 68102
1500-1599 68102
1601-1899 68102
3000-4499 68131
4600-6299 68132
8300-8600 68114
8602-10198 68114
13200-13318 68154
13320-15399 68154
15600-16299 68118
Camden Ave
1800-1899 68110
1901-1999 68110
2400-4399 68111
4500-6399 68104
8000-10399 68134
11300-14199 68164
15000-16942 68116
16944-16998 68116
E Camden Ave 68110
Camden Cir 68116
Camden Ct
1801-1821 68110
14700-14798 68116
14800-14899 68116
Camelback Ave 68136
Camp St 68136
Campbell Ave 68107
Canadian Ln 68112
Canary Ln 68152
Caniglia Plz 68108
Canyon Rd 68112
Canyon Trl 68136
Capitol Ave
1001-1097 68102
1099-1899 68102
4300-4498 68131
4600-5199 68132
8701-9197 68114
9199-9599 68114
11600-11699 68154
15700-16199 68118
16201-16299 68118
Capitol Cir 68118
Capitol Ct 68132
Capitol Plz
6400-6599 68132
12700-12799 68154
16600-16699 68118
Cardinal Ct 68112
Carpenter St 68138
Carroll Dr 68142
Carter Blvd 68110
Carter Lakeshore Dr 68110
Cary Cir
13200-13299 68138
15800-15812 68136
Cary St 68136
Cass Cir 68154
Cass Plz 68154
Cass St
1001-1299 68102
1506-1698 68102
3000-4499 68131
4600-7099 68132
7101-7199 68132
7400-7498 68114
7500-8334 68114
8336-8698 68114
16001-16099 68118
Castelar Cir
11300-15299 68144
17700-17799 68130
Castelar Plz 68144
Castelar St
700-2199 68108
2201-2399 68108
2400-4299 68105
5000-5099 68106
5101-6499 68106
8000-10699 68124
12400-12499 68144
16500-16699 68130
Cedar Cir
13200-15299 68144
15900-19599 68130
Cedar Plz
6300-6346 68106
6348-6352 68106
6354-6498 68106
17000-17199 68130
Cedar St
100-599 68108
601-699 68108
5400-5598 68106
5600-5899 68106
7200-10799 68124
10800-13700 68144
13702-13798 68144
16500-16549 68130
Cedar Valley Ln 68122
N Cedgers St 68134
Centech Rd 68138
Centennial Rd 68138
W Center Rd
7000-7198 68106
7201-7697 68124
7699-10750 68124
10752-10798 68124
10808-11998 68144
12000-15100 68144
15102-15498 68144
15600-17899 68130
17901-19799 68130
Center St
201-397 68108
399-1799 68108
1801-1899 68108
2400-4499 68105
4500-6499 68106
Chalco Pointe Cir &
Dr 68138
Chalco Valley Pkwy 68138
Champion Way 68136
Chandler Cir
12700-12799 68138
17600-17699 68136
Chandler Ct 68138
Chandler Rd 68138
Chandler St
12800-13730 68138
13732-13798 68138
16800-19099 68136
19101-19199 68136
Charles Cir
13500-14999 68154
16300-16399 68118
Charles Plz
10601-10699 68114
12200-14798 68154
14800-14989 68154
Charles St
1901-1999 68102
2801-2897 68131
2899-4356 68131
4358-4358 68131
4500-7099 68132
7500-10700 68114
10702-10750 68114
12200-15599 68154
15600-16099 68118
16101-16199 68118
Cherry Ln 68152
Cherrywood St 68136
Cheshire Ave 68142
Cheyenne Rd 68136
Chicago Cir
3000-3002 68131
3004-3099 68131
11200-15099 68154
16300-16399 68118
16401-17415 68118
Chicago Ct 68114
Chicago Plz
7800-7899 68114
11701-11797 68154
11799-11800 68154
11802-11898 68154
16600-16698 68118
Chicago St
1425-1425 68102
3001-3097 68131
3099-4499 68131
4600-6499 68132
8000-9520 68114
9522-9530 68114
16000-16199 68118
16201-17899 68118
Christensen Ln 68122
Chutney Dr 68136
Cindy Cir 68137
Cinnamon Cir 68135
Cinnamon Dr 68136
Cinnamon St 68135
Circle Dr 68144
Clairmont Ave 68127
Clark St
1001-1597 68110
1599-1699 68110
1701-2199 68110
17001-17097 68118
17099-17199 68118
Clarkson Ave
2900-2999 68105
12400-12498 68144
Clay Cir 68152
Clay St
2800-2848 68112
2850-3199 68112
4601-5247 68152
5249-5499 68152
8101-8197 68122
8199-8299 68122
Clifton Ct & Dr 68134
Cole Creek Cir & Dr 68114
Colonial Ave 68136
Colony Cir & Dr 68136
Commercial Ave 68110
Conagra Dr 68102
Connell Ct 68108
Constitution Blvd 68138
Cook Plz & St 68112
Cooper Cir & St 68138
Copper Creek Rd 68157
Copper Hill Dr 68157
Copper Hollow Rd 68112
Corby Cir
7500-7598 68134
7600-7649 68134
10700-13499 68164
17600-17699 68116
Corby Plz 68164
Corby St
1501-1597 68110
1599-1900 68110
1902-1948 68110
2500-4299 68111
4301-4399 68111
4900-7199 68104
7300-10251 68134
10253-10299 68134
11200-14300 68164
14302-14398 68164
14555-17800 68116
17802-17898 68116
Cornelia Cir 68138
Cornhusker Dr 68124
Cornhusker Rd
12801-14799 68138
16100-18498 68136
18500-18600 68136
18602-18698 68136
Cottage Grove Ave 68131
Cottner St 68137
Cottonwood Ave 68136
Cottonwood Cir 68136
Cottonwood Ln
3000-3499 68134
3501-3599 68134
10800-10899 68164
10901-10999 68164
Cottonwood Plz 68164

Cottonwood St
15400-15499 68138
15603-19099 68136
19101-19199 68136
Country Club Ave 68104
Country Club Cir 68127
Country Club Rd
1-99 68127
6000-6999 68152
7001-7199 68152
Country Club Oaks Pl 68152
Country Squire Ln & Plz 68152
Countryside Plz 68114
County Road 35 68142
County Road 37 68142
County Road 38 68122
County Road 39 68142
County Road 40
7101-7399 68122
County Road 40
10850-10899 68142
County Road 41 68122
County Road 45 68122
County Road 49 68152
County Road 51 68112
County Road P38
3000-3099 68112
3101-3399 68112
3601-3697 68152
3699-3999 68152
4001-4599 68152
7601-7699 68122
9301-9697 68142
9699-9799 68142
9801-10899 68142
County Road P38a 68142
County Road P40
2000-2198 68112
2200-2999 68112
4100-4198 68152
4200-4500 68152
4502-4698 68152
County Road P41 68122
County Road P43 68122
County Road P47 68152
County Road P49 68112
County Road P51 68112
Craig Ave
2400-2698 68112
2700-3500 68112
3502-3798 68112
5801-5999 68152
8000-8599 68122
Craig Cir 68122
Craig St
10600-10699 68122
10701-10799 68122
12700-13199 68142
Crawford Cir & Rd 68144
S Creek Cir 68136
N Crest Dr 68112
Crestfield Dr 68136
Crestline Dr 68134
Crestridge Rd 68154
Crippen Cir 68138
Crown Point Ave
500-899 68110
2400-4499 68111
4500-6799 68104
6801-7099 68104
7400-7498 68134
7500-10518 68134
10520-10598 68134
10801-10897 68164
10899-12899 68164
12901-13099 68164
14700-14800 68116
14802-15498 68116
Crown Point Plz
10000-10099 68134
16700-16798 68116
Cryer Ave 68144
Crystal Fountain Ln 68122
Cuming Cir
7700-7799 68114
14400-15499 68154
Cuming Plz 68114
Cuming St
1200-1298 68102
1300-2300 68102
2302-2398 68102
2400-2898 68131
2900-4217 68131
4219-4499 68131
4500-6999 68132
8300-10699 68114
12200-15399 68154
15900-15998 68118
Curlew Ln
2000-2099 68108
4900-4999 68106
Curtis Ave
3000-4499 68111
4501-4797 68104
4799-6799 68104
7700-7999 68134
8001-10699 68134
10900-13099 68164
14600-16099 68116
Curtis Cir
8900-8999 68134
16200-16299 68116
Curtis Avenue Cir 68164
Custer Rd 68138
Cypress Dr
6200-6699 68137
17100-17119 68136
17121-17199 68136
Cypress St 68136
D Ct 68144
D Plz 68144
D St
900-4223 68107
4225-4251 68107
7501-7799 68124
18300-19600 68130
19602-20198 68130
Dahlman Ave 68107
Daley Dr & Ln 68122
Daly Cir 68127
Davenport Cir 68154
Davenport Plz
6500-6599 68132
11500-11598 68154
11600-12799 68154
16600-16698 68118
Davenport St
1001-1699 68102
2100-2224 68102
2400-3098 68131
3100-4499 68131
4600-6799 68132
7800-9599 68114
11200-13199 68154
16000-17399 68118
David Cir 68138
Davis Cir 68134
Davis Mountain Ln 68112
Dayton Cir
14216-14229 68137
17300-17499 68135
Dayton St
4207-4207 68107
4209-4499 68107
5200-5599 68117
14800-15299 68137
17400-17599 68135
Dean Cir 68105
Deauville Dr 68137
Deborah Cir 68138
Decatur Cir
9100-10399 68114
13500-13899 68154
15600-16399 68118
Decatur Plz
9350-9398 68114
11100-14930 68154
14932-14934 68154
Decatur St
2400-4499 68111
4500-7099 68104
7300-10750 68114
10752-10798 68114
11000-15599 68154
15700-17399 68118
Decatur Plaza Cir 68114
Deer Creek Dr 68142
Deer Hollow Dr 68154
Deer Park Blvd
1300-2399 68108
2400-2599 68105
2601-2699 68105
Deerfield Ln 68152
N Dendince St 68112
Devonshire Dr 68114
Dewey Ave
2300-2399 68102
2600-2698 68105
2700-4351 68105
4353-4401 68105
7800-9399 68114
12800-15299 68154
15700-16098 68118
16100-16199 68118
Dewey Cir
9400-9499 68114
15400-15599 68154
15900-15999 68118
Dick Collins Rd 68112
Dillon Dr 68132
Discovery Dr 68137
W Dodge Rd
7900-9530 68114
9532-9798 68114
10800-15599 68154
15601-15697 68118
15699-16000 68118
16002-16198 68118
Dodge St
900-998 68102
1000-2224 68102
2226-2298 68102
2401-2497 68131
2499-4499 68131
4500-7199 68132
7200-8309 68114
8311-8399 68114
Dodson Cir & Plz 68127
Doolittle Plz 68110
Dora Hamann Pkwy 68116
Dorcas Cir
14900-15299 68144
15900-17799 68130
Dorcas Plz
6200-6299 68106
14000-14099 68144
Dorcas St
500-1999 68108
5600-5700 68106
5702-5998 68106
8000-9299 68124
11800-11899 68144
16000-16599 68130
Douglas Cir
11100-15499 68154
15800-17699 68118
Douglas Ct 68114
Douglas St
1000-1698 68102
1700-2099 68102
2101-2399 68102
2425-2697 68131
2699-4440 68131
4442-4498 68131
4600-4899 68132
7301-8497 68114
8499-9599 68114
11600-11699 68154
16100-17599 68118
17601-17699 68118
Drake Court Walk 68102
Drexel Cir
8700-9199 68127
13800-15399 68137
15600-19199 68135
Drexel Plz 68137
Drexel St
1200-4499 68107
4500-5299 68117
7201-7247 68127
7249-9499 68127
11600-15199 68137
15201-15299 68137
16400-18800 68135
18802-19148 68135
Dumfries Cir & Dr 68157
Dundee Ridge Ct 68132
Dupont Cir 68130
Dupont Ct 68144
Dupont Plz 68144
Dupont St
2001-2099 68108
2700-2999 68105
3001-3099 68105
8000-8799 68124
Durham Research Plz 68105
Dutch Hall Rd
6501-6597 68152
6599-7099 68152
7101-7199 68152
7200-7598 68122
7600-10599 68122
11200-11398 68142
11400-12500 68142
12502-13898 68142
E Cir 68137
E Plz 68137
E St 68107
S Eagerlea St 68137
Eagle Run Dr
12400-12498 68164
12500-14399 68164
14400-14598 68116
Eastridge Dr 68134
Echo Hills Dr 68138
Echo Valley Ln 68142
Ed Creighton Ave 68105
Edgevale Pl 68114
Edinburgh St 68157
Edith Marie Ave 68112
Edna Cir
14100-14199 68138
15600-17499 68136
Edna St
12800-15599 68138
16100-19099 68136
19101-19199 68136
Edward Babe Gomez Ave 68107
Edward R Danner Plz 68110
Ehlers St 68135
Eldorado Dr 68154
S Ellarlet St 68144
Ellison Ave
1001-1097 68110
1099-2399 68110
2400-4499 68111
4600-5398 68104
5400-6499 68104
9101-9297 68134
9299-9899 68134
10801-10897 68164
10899-14300 68164
14302-14398 68164
14400-14898 68116
14900-15000 68116
15002-16698 68116
Ellison Cir
10300-10326 68134
10328-10372 68134
10374-10398 68134
12604-13499 68164
14800-14900 68116
14902-15498 68116
Ellison Plz 68134
Elm Cir
13400-13499 68144
16700-16799 68130
Elm Plz
7900-7999 68124
12501-12597 68144
12599-12699 68144
Elm St
1400-1598 68108
1600-2399 68108
2400-2999 68105
3001-3099 68105
5800-6299 68106
10200-10399 68124
10800-14799 68144
15600-15998 68130
16000-16699 68130
16701-17099 68130
Elmhurst Dr 68157
N Elmwood Rd 68132
Emile Cir 68154
Emile St 68106
Emiline Cir
13600-13699 68138
18706-18798 68136
Emiline St
4600-5399 68157
12600-12698 68138
12700-14799 68138
15700-18700 68136
18702-18704 68136
Emmet Cir 68116
Emmet Plz 68116
Emmet St
1400-2199 68110
2400-4499 68111
4900-6799 68104
8101-8297 68134
8299-10706 68134
10708-10798 68134
10800-10898 68164
10900-12326 68164
12328-12398 68164
15000-17399 68116
17401-17599 68116
Englewood Ave 68137
Englewood Cir 68135
Englewood St 68135
Ernst Cir 68122
Ernst St
2900-2998 68112
3000-3799 68112
5000-5099 68152
7400-7599 68122
Erskine Cir
12100-12399 68164
16200-17499 68116
Erskine Plz 68134
Erskine St
2500-2598 68111
2600-4399 68111
4700-5899 68104
7500-9799 68134
11200-13999 68164
14451-17799 68116
Essex Ct & Dr 68114
Evans Plz
10500-10599 68134
10601-10699 68134
16221-16797 68116
16799-17200 68116
17202-17398 68116
Evans St
1400-2299 68110
2400-4499 68111
4900-6799 68104
6801-6999 68104
7600-7698 68134
7700-10099 68134
11201-11297 68164
11299-12499 68164
15000-15098 68116
15100-17399 68116
F Plz
10404-10404 68127
12100-12298 68137
12300-13000 68137
13002-13098 68137
F St
1901-2097 68107
2099-4499 68107
4500-6000 68117
6002-7198 68117
7200-7398 68127
7400-9800 68127
9802-10398 68127
13200-14511 68137
14513-14799 68137
17200-17398 68135
17400-18299 68135
18301-20299 68135
Fairacres Rd 68132
Fairchild Ct 68110
Fairway Cir 68136
Fairway Dr
7500-7899 68152
10701-10797 68136
10799-17299 68136
Fairwood Ln 68132
Far Hills Ln 68152
S Faralea St 68124
Farnam Cir
11400-15499 68154
15600-17499 68118
Farnam Ct 68114
Farnam Dr
7801-8399 68114
10800-10822 68154
10824-10826 68154
10828-10842 68154
Farnam St
900-998 68102
1000-2299 68102
2400-4499 68131
4500-4598 68132
4600-7099 68132
7101-7199 68132
7201-7297 68114
7299-9200 68114
9202-9298 68114
10901-11097 68154
11099-12649 68154
12651-12699 68154
15670-15698 68118
15700-16699 68118
16701-17599 68118
Fawn Pkwy 68154
Fawn Parkway Plz 68144
Fay Blvd 68117
Ferry St 68112
Ferthenw St 68135
Fieldcrest Cir 68154
Fieldcrest Ct 68114
Fieldcrest Dr
9700-10100 68114
10102-10298 68114
15000-15200 68154
15202-15398 68154
Fillmore Cir 68112
Fillmore St
2900-3098 68112
3100-3199 68112
5600-5699 68152
7600-8099 68122
Florence Blvd
1101-1199 68102
1501-1797 68110
1799-6399 68110
6401-6499 68110
6500-7000 68112
7002-7230 68112
Florence Heights Blvd 68112
Florence Mills Plz 68110
Fnb Pkwy 68154
Foleshill Ln 68122
Fontenelle Blvd
2300-2398 68104
2400-4499 68104
4500-4598 68111
4600-6299 68111
Forest Ave 68108
Forest Lawn Ave
3100-3999 68112
4001-4099 68112
6300-6499 68104
Forrest Dr
10500-10699 68124
10800-10998 68144
Fort Ct 68110
Fort Plz 68134
Fort St
100-398 68110
400-1900 68110
1902-2398 68110
2400-4399 68111
4500-6399 68104
7700-7798 68134
7800-10799 68134
10800-11798 68164
11800-14299 68164
14301-14399 68164
14701-15597 68116
15599-16299 68116
16301-16599 68116
E Fort St 68110
Fountain Hills Dr 68118
Fowler Ave
1451-1697 68110
1699-2399 68110
2400-2498 68111
2500-4399 68111
4500-6500 68104
6502-6548 68104
8500-10699 68134
10800-13999 68164
14400-14498 68116
14500-16899 68116
Fowler Cir
3400-3499 68111
9200-9255 68134
12700-13099 68164
17200-17299 68116
Fowler Plz 68116
Fowler St 68116
Fox Farm Rd 68152
Frances Cir
12400-14799 68144
15900-19599 68130
Frances Plz 68130
Frances St
800-900 68108
902-998 68108
3200-3298 68105
3300-4400 68105
4402-4498 68105
4600-6799 68106
8000-10799 68124
10800-14230 68144
16600-17999 68130
18001-19899 68130
Franklin Cir
10300-10399 68114
12100-12116 68154
12118-12299 68154
15600-15699 68118
Franklin Dr 68118
Franklin Plz
11100-14924 68154
17501-17599 68118
Franklin St
2100-2198 68110
2400-2798 68111
2800-4499 68111
4500-7099 68104
7700-9500 68114
9502-10198 68114
10801-10997 68154
10999-14599 68154
15700-17099 68118
Frederick Ave 68138
Frederick Cir
5000-5099 68106
9500-9799 68124
13300-14199 68138
16500-16799 68130
Frederick Plz 68130
Frederick St
1001-1097 68108
1099-1699 68108
2900-2998 68105
3000-4499 68105
4500-6149 68106
7200-10099 68124
11400-13699 68144
16050-16099 68130
Freedom Park Rd
101-199 68102
1901-1997 68110
1999-2499 68110
2501-2899 68110
Fremont St 68122
Frontier Rd 68138
G Cir
15000-15099 68137

19600-19699 68135
G Ct 68127
G St
1801-1897 68107
1899-4499 68107
4650-6099 68117
8400-8699 68127
14900-14999 68137
19300-20299 68135
Gail Ave
12200-12499 68137
19400-19699 68135
Gail Plz 68137
Galloway St 68157
Gallup Dr 68102
Garden Rd 68124
Garfield St
1300-1499 68107
15200-15499 68144
Garryowen Ln 68112
Garvin Rd 68122
Garvin St 68152
Gary Cir 68138
Geiler Ave 68127
George B Lake Pkwy ... 68130
George Miller Pkwy 68116
Gertrude Cir
13900-14199 68138
17500-17999 68136
Gertrude St
5000-5299 68157
12901-12997 68138
12999-15599 68138
15601-15603 68136
15605-18699 68136
Gibson Rd 68107
Giles Rd
4700-4999 68157
13200-13398 68138
13400-13700 68138
13702-15098 68138
15600-17498 68136
18801-19199 68136
Gilmore Ave 68107
Girard Cir 68122
Girard Plz 68122
Girard St
5800-7199 68152
7300-7398 68122
7400-8499 68122
8501-10799 68122
10801-10847 68142
10849-11299 68142
Glasgow Ave 68157
Glendale Ave 68152
Glenmorrie Cir & Dr 68157
Glenn St 68138
Glenvale Dr 68134
Glenvale Plz 68164
Glenwood Ave 68131
Glenwood Rd 68132
N Gleradw St 68104
Gold Cir
13906-13990 68144
15900-18699 68130
Gold Plz
10500-10699 68124
16000-16099 68130
16101-17699 68130
Gold St
2900-3999 68105
5800-5999 68106
8000-8399 68124
11300-13699 68144
16500-16799 68130
16801-19399 68130
Golfing Green Dr 68137
Gollorth St 68118
Gordon St 68105
Grace St 68110
Graceland Dr 68134
Grain Ave 68107
Grand Ave
1451-1997 68110
1999-2299 68110
2301-2399 68110
3101-3297 68111
3299-4399 68111
4500-6099 68104
6101-6599 68104
8000-8048 68134
8050-10799 68134
11600-13199 68164
14400-17599 68116
17601-17899 68116
Grand Cir
11400-14099 68164
16800-16899 68116
Grand Plz
10000-10198 68134
15701-15797 68116
15799-15899 68116
Grande Ave 68164
Grant Cir
11300-12899 68164
15100-17499 68116
Grant St
1500-2300 68110
2302-2398 68110
2400-4399 68111
4500-7199 68104
7201-7297 68134
7299-9799 68134
11800-11898 68164
11900-14350 68164
14401-14453 68116
14455-17199 68116
Grebe St
2700-2798 68112
2800-3999 68112
4001-4099 68112
4600-4699 68152
12300-12499 68142
12501-12699 68142
Greene Ave
4500-4999 68157
15100-15399 68138
Greenfield Rd 68138
Greenfield St 68136
Greenleaf St
15400-15499 68138
16000-19113 68136
19115-19199 68136
Grenelefe Ave 68136
Gretchen Ave 68104
Grey Fawn Dr 68154
Grissom St 68138
Grover Cir 68144
Grover Plz 68144
Grover St
201-299 68108
400-498 68108
3600-3798 68105
3800-4499 68105
4500-6899 68106
6901-7199 68106
7200-7248 68124
7250-10200 68124
10202-10798 68124
12100-15300 68144
15302-15498 68144
16100-19699 68130
H Cir 68135
H Ct 68127
H St
1600-4499 68107
6000-6299 68117
8000-8999 68127
14800-14999 68137
17650-19899 68135
Hackberry Rd 68132
Hadan St 68142
Hamilton Cir
12200-13099 68154
16300-17099 68118
Hamilton Plz 68114
Hamilton St
2501-2597 68131
2599-4499 68131
4500-7099 68132
7600-8800 68114
8802-8998 68114
12700-15599 68154
15600-15799 68118
Hanover Cir
3500-3599 68112
5300-5398 68152
Hanover Plz 68152
Hanover St
2800-2848 68112
2850-2900 68112
2902-4098 68112
7400-8499 68122
10800-11299 68142
Hanscom Blvd 68105
Hansen Ave
10100-10199 68124
10201-10799 68124
19700-20100 68130
20102-20198 68130
Hansen Plz 68106
Hansen St 68130
N Happy Hollow Blvd
101-397 68132
399-1100 68132
1102-1498 68132
1500-1800 68104
1802-5098 68104
S Happy Hollow Blvd
103-499 68132
501-599 68106
Harender St 68105
Harney Cir 68154
Harney Pkwy N 68114
Harney Pkwy S 68114
Harney St
1100-2099 68102
2101-2399 68102
2400-4000 68131
4002-4098 68131
4800-4848 68132
4850-5799 68132
7401-7797 68114
7799-9099 68114
9101-9599 68114
10800-15500 68154
15502-15598 68154
15900-17999 68118
Harney Plaza Cir 68154
Harris St 68105
Harrison Plz 68137
Harrison St
1300-4398 68147
4500-5199 68157
5201-6499 68157
7800-7898 68128
14300-15300 68138
15302-15598 68138
15601-16697 68136
16699-17900 68136
17902-19198 68136
Harry Andersen Ave 68137
Hartline Ln 68112
Hartman Ave
401-599 68110
2400-3999 68111
4912-4948 68104
4950-6500 68104
6502-6998 68104
7500-10699 68134
10701-10799 68134
11400-11598 68164
11600-14199 68164
14600-16499 68116
16501-16799 68116
E Hartman Ave 68110
Hartman Cir
4000-4099 68111
11300-11399 68164
15100-15199 68116
E Hartman Ct 68110
Hartman Plz 68116
Harvey Oaks Ave 68144
Hascall Cir
12600-14448 68144
15700-15799 68130
Hascall St
100-499 68108
3000-3098 68105
3100-3899 68105
4500-6000 68106
6002-7098 68106
7200-10000 68124
10002-10498 68124
10900-14799 68144
16300-16599 68130
Hawk Woods Cir 68112
Hawthorne Ave
3400-3600 68131
3602-3798 68131
14600-14798 68154
14800-14999 68154
Hawthorne Cir 68154
Hawthorne Ct
13000-13099 68154
17001-17099 68118
Hawthorne Plz 68118
Hayden Ave 68152
Hayes Cir
7500-7599 68127
18700-18999 68135
Hayes Ct 68135
Hayes Plz 68135
Hayes St
7300-7399 68127
15901-15997 68135
15999-16199 68135
Hazel St 68105
Hazeltine Ave 68136
Heather St 68136
Heavenly Dr 68154
Henninger Dr 68104
Heritage Cir & Plz 68127
Hickory Cir
7800-7899 68124
13400-13999 68144
17000-17899 68130
Hickory Plz
6300-6399 68106
17151-17399 68130
Hickory Rd 68144
Hickory St
100-1499 68108
1501-2399 68108
2400-4499 68105
4500-6299 68106
7301-7597 68124
7599-9299 68124
12708-13898 68144
13900-15599 68144
15600-19799 68130
High Point Cir 68112
Highland Blvd 68138
Highland St 68127
Highway 36 68142
Highway 370
12600-12898 68138
Highway 370
15901-15999 68136
18300-18498 68136
Highway 75 68152
Hillcrest Dr 68132
Hillsborough Dr 68164
Hillsdale Ave
3950-3998 68107
4000-4499 68107
6000-6199 68117
14300-15400 68137
15402-15498 68137
Hillsdale Cir 68137
Hillside Cir 68154
Hillside Ct 68154
Hillside Dr
1600-8399 68114
14909-15205 68154
Hillside Plz
9301-9399 68114
14800-14899 68154
Hilltop Ave 68164
Hilltop Rd 68134
Himebaugh Ave
2300-2399 68110
2400-4299 68111
5000-6799 68104
7800-7848 68134
7850-10699 68134
12900-13099 68164
13101-13199 68164
14900-15100 68116
15102-15198 68116
Himebaugh Cir
9400-9499 68134
11700-11799 68164
14800-16399 68116
Himebaugh Plz
10000-10099 68134
14700-14799 68116
Hoctor Blvd
3300-3499 68108
3501-3699 68108
4000-4098 68107
Hoich Dr 68136
Holling Dr 68144
Holly St 68157
Holmes Cir
12400-14499 68137
15600-18699 68135
Holmes Plz
9400-9599 68127
15300-15599 68137
Holmes St
1700-1799 68107
4801-5297 68117
5299-6199 68117
8800-8899 68127
12600-15099 68137
16250-19699 68135
Homer St 68107
N Horaint St 68122
Howard Cir
15500-15599 68154
16600-16699 68118
Howard Plz 68118
Howard Rd 68154
Howard St
1000-2300 68102
2302-2398 68102
2700-3570 68105
3572-3598 68105
5301-5497 68106
5499-5800 68106
5802-6798 68106
7500-8399 68114
15600-17599 68118
Howe Cir 68130
Howe Ct 68144
Howe Plz 68144
Howe St
15200-15499 68144
18600-18999 68130
Howell St
3101-3299 68112
7500-7598 68122
7600-8299 68122
Hugo St 68107
Hummel Rd 68112
Hunt Cir 68152
Huntington Ave
3000-3100 68112
3102-3698 68112
4500-4799 68152
10200-10399 68122
14200-14299 68164
N Hws Cleveland Blvd .. 68116
S Hws Cleveland Blvd
1200-1798 68130
1800-3899 68130
5801-5899 68135
18715-18717 68130
I Cir
13401-13497 68137
13499-15099 68137
16700-16816 68135
I Plz 68127
I St
1200-1212 68107
1214-4399 68107
4401-4499 68107
4600-5000 68117
5002-6298 68117
7850-8498 68127
8500-10700 68127
10702-10798 68127
10801-11097 68137
11099-13399 68137
16851-16879 68135
16881-19899 68135
19901-20299 68135
Ida Plz
1100-1298 68112
12200-12299 68142
Ida St
100-199 68110
1600-4400 68112
4402-4498 68112
5000-5499 68152
9200-9699 68122
14001-14097 68142
14099-14300 68142
14302-14398 68142
Idledale Ln 68112
Indian Hills Dr 68114
Industrial Rd
13300-13598 68137
13600-13999 68137
14000-14335 68144
14337-15599 68144
Iowa Cir 68142
Iowa Ct 68122
Iowa Plz
10600-10798 68122
10800-11399 68142
Iowa St
2200-2498 68112
2500-3999 68112
7001-7047 68152
7049-7199 68152
8250-8499 68122
14200-14299 68142
Irene St 68138
Iron Wood Cir 68152
Irving Ct 68131
Irving Plz 68154
Irvington Rd
6001-6097 68134
6099-6199 68134
6201-6499 68134
6500-7999 68122
8001-8999 68122
Izard Cir 68114
Izard Ct 68131
Izard Plz 68114
Izard St
1200-1598 68102
1600-1800 68102
1802-1898 68102
2800-3998 68131
4000-4400 68131
4402-4498 68131
4500-7099 68132
7300-10699 68114
10701-10799 68114
12200-14999 68154
J Cir
14500-14599 68137
16700-16799 68135
J St
1101-1197 68107
1199-4499 68107
4500-4798 68117
4800-6300 68117
6302-7198 68117
7901-7997 68127
7999-10599 68127
10601-10799 68127
10800-10999 68137
17100-19799 68135
J E George Blvd 68132
Jackson Cir
9450-9499 68114
15500-15599 68154
Jackson Dr 68118
Jackson Plz 68118
Jackson Rd 68154
Jackson St
1000-1098 68102
1100-1799 68102
1801-1999 68102
2900-3799 68105
5000-5699 68106
7800-8399 68114
10900-15399 68154
16600-16799 68118
Jacobs Cir & St 68135
Jaynes Cir
6001-6099 68104
9722-9732 68134
12900-13099 68164
15400-16799 68116
Jaynes Plz 68164
Jaynes St
600-1298 68110
1300-1499 68110
1501-1699 68110
2500-3498 68111
3500-4499 68111
4500-6499 68104
7500-9721 68134
9723-9799 68134
11300-14199 68164
14800-16499 68116
Jefferson Cir
5119-5199 68117
10400-10499 68127
10900-14999 68137
16500-17424 68135
Jefferson Plz
9700-9799 68127
11800-12099 68137
Jefferson St
1300-3499 68107
3501-3599 68107
4501-4599 68117
5000-5118 68117
7200-9299 68127
9301-9399 68127
11000-15299 68137
16200-19700 68135
19702-19798 68135
Jennifer Rd 68138
Jessie Ave 68164
Jessie Cir 68116
Joanne Dr 68136
John A Creighton Blvd . 68111
John D Wear Ave 68154
John Galt Blvd 68137
John J Pershing Dr
6300-6399 68110
6400-11099 68112
Jones Cir
7110-7122 68106
7300-9448 68114
9450-9499 68114
12700-15599 68154
15900-16799 68118
Jones Plz 68105
Jones St
800-898 68102
900-2299 68102
2400-3820 68105
3822-3828 68105
5150-5799 68106
5801-5999 68106
7200-7298 68114
7300-9399 68114
10900-12900 68154
12902-12998 68154
16600-17799 68118
Joseph St 68124
Josephine St
4501-4599 68157
12800-15599 68138
15601-15797 68136
15799-19100 68136
19102-19198 68136
Joshua Rd 68112
Joyce St 68138
K Cir
7700-7800 68127
7802-7898 68127
15000-15099 68137
16700-19399 68135
K Plz 68137
K St
2100-4199 68107
4800-5000 68117
5002-5198 68117
8400-8498 68127
8500-8530 68127

8532-8698 68127
14900-14999 68137
16200-19799 68135
Kameo Dr 68122
Kansas Ave
2300-2399 68110
2401-2697 68111
2699-4471 68111
4473-4499 68111
4601-4649 68104
4651-6999 68104
7800-7832 68134
7834-7999 68134
12601-12899 68164
14600-14799 68116
14801-15399 68116
Kansas Cir 68164
Kansas Plz 68134
Karen Cir
14800-15099 68137
17900-17999 68135
Karen St
6100-6299 68117
14500-14999 68137
16800-16848 68135
16850-17899 68135
Karl St 68137
Karloff Cir 68138
Kathy Dr 68134
Kavan St 68107
Kearney Ave 68138
Kelby Rd 68152
Kent Cir
2300-2399 68144
19100-19199 68130
Kent Plz 68144
Kent St 68105
Keystone Dr 68134
Kimball St 68122
Kimberly Cir 68116
Kimberly Dr 68134
Kimberly Ln 68152
Kincedge St 68127
King St
2800-4000 68112
4002-4198 68112
5400-5500 68152
5502-5998 68152
7800-8600 68122
8602-10798 68122
12200-12299 68142
Kings Dr 68142
Kings Plz 68122
Kingswood Dr 68144
Kristy Plz 68112
Krug Ave
3800-3899 68105
4500-4899 68106
9300-10499 68124
12401-12599 68144
Krug Cir 68144
Kuehl Cir 68137
L Cir 68135
L Plz 68137
L St
2100-2298 68107
2300-4200 68107
4202-4498 68107
4500-7099 68117
7200-10150 68127
10152-10728 68127
11800-12798 68137
12800-14999 68137
15600-19799 68135
Laci Cir 68137
Laci St
10700-10799 68127
19300-19799 68135
Lafayette Ave
3000-4399 68131
4500-7099 68132
7600-10000 68114
10002-10098 68114
12300-15399 68154
15600-16300 68118
16302-16398 68118
Lafayette Cir
12600-14099 68154
17100-17199 68118
Lafayette Ct
6001-6023 68132
11300-11399 68154
Lafayette Plz
9700-9800 68114
9802-10698 68114
11000-14999 68154
Laird St 68110
Lake Cir 68116
Lake St
1600-1698 68110
1700-2299 68110
2400-4399 68111
5000-7050 68104
7052-7198 68104
7200-7298 68134
7300-8999 68134
13251-13297 68164
13299-13699 68164
13701-13949 68164
14600-15999 68116
Lake Cunningham Rd 68122
Lake Forest Dr 68164
Lake Ridge Dr 68136
Lakeshore Dr 68135
Lakeside Cir 68135
Lakeside Dr 68135
Lakeside Plz 68137
Lakeside Hills Ct &
Plz 68130
Lakeview Ct, Dr & St 68127
Lamont Cir 68130
Lamont St
9000-9199 68124
12100-12599 68144
18500-19699 68130
19701-19799 68130
Lamp Cir 68118
Lamp St
11000-11199 68154
16001-16097 68118
16099-16299 68118
16301-16699 68118
Lamplighter Dr 68152
Landon Ct 68102
Laquinta Cir 68136
Larimore Ave
2000-2299 68110
2400-4399 68111
4500-5899 68104
8500-10299 68134
10800-10898 68164
10900-13799 68164
13801-14199 68164
14400-17300 68116
17302-17398 68116
Larimore Cir
10500-10599 68134
12950-13199 68164
16200-16399 68116
Larimore Plz 68116
Lark St 68164
Lathrop Ave 68138
Laurel Ave
2400-4499 68111
4500-6899 68104
6901-6999 68104
9300-10699 68134
12600-12798 68164
12800-13099 68164
14600-15999 68116
Laurel Cir
9400-9499 68134
11000-11199 68164
15400-16599 68116
Laurel Plz
9100-9299 68134
14700-16799 68116
Laurie Cir 68124
Lawndale Dr & Plz 68134
Leavenworth Cir
11300-15399 68154
15900-16799 68118
Leavenworth Ct 68105
Leavenworth Plz 68108
Leavenworth Rd 68154
Leavenworth St
601-997 68102
999-2299 68102
2400-4499 68105
4500-5999 68106
6001-6899 68106
7800-9399 68114
10900-15599 68154
15600-17799 68118
Leawood Dr 68154
Lee Terrace Rd 68112
Legacy Commons Plz 68130
Lilac St 68116
Lillian Cir 68138
Lillian St
4800-4999 68157
12600-13799 68138
17700-19099 68136
Lincoln Blvd 68131
Lincoln Cir 68154
Lindbergh Dr 68110
Lindenwood Ln 68112
Link St 68137
Lisa Cir
12100-12199 68137
13900-13999 68138
Lisa Plz 68137
Lisa St 68138
Lizzie Robinson Ave 68111
Lloyd Cir & St 68144
Lockheed Ct 68110
Lockwood Cir & Ln 68152
Lockwood Plaza Cir 68142
Locust St
1300-2199 68110
2201-2299 68110
12000-12099 68164
14401-14497 68116
14499-15499 68116
15501-17399 68116
E Locust St 68110
Logan Cir 68130
Logan Ln 68157
Logan St 68130
Long St 68152
Longbow Cir & Loop 68136
Longhorn Cir 68136
Loop Cir & St 68136
Lothrop Cir 68116
Lothrop St
1400-2199 68110
2201-2299 68110
2850-3000 68111
3002-3698 68111
Louis Dr
9400-9598 68114
9600-9999 68114
15700-15899 68118
Loveland Dr
500-899 68114
1100-8499 68124
Lucht Ln 68152
Lucia Plz 68108
Lynam Dr 68138
Lynnwood Ln 68152
M Cir
11600-11719 68137
16200-19699 68135
M St
1201-1397 68107
1399-4199 68107
4600-6199 68117
8700-10768 68127
10770-10798 68127
10801-11897 68137
11899-14999 68137
15600-19799 68135
Macc Ln 68142
Mad Hatter Ln 68142
Madison Cir
5100-5122 68117
5124-5199 68117
13700-14799 68137
15700-18599 68135
Madison Plz 68127
Madison St
1300-4499 68107
4500-4599 68117
4601-5121 68117
7301-7347 68127
7349-10499 68127
10501-10699 68127
10800-10998 68137
11000-15299 68137
15900-17599 68135
Maenner Dr 68114
Magnolia St 68137
Main St 68127
Maindinc St 68106
Manchester Dr
4400-4499 68112
4500-5100 68152
5102-5198 68152
Manderson Cir
7700-9399 68134
13800-13899 68164
Manderson Plz
10400-10499 68134
10801-10897 68164
10899-14199 68164
14701-14797 68116
14799-14999 68116
15001-15499 68116
Manderson St
1600-2399 68110
2400-3499 68111
4800-6799 68104
7300-10099 68134
11300-11450 68164
11452-11498 68164
15800-17299 68116
17301-17499 68116
Maple Dr 68134
W Maple Rd
10200-10298 68134
10901-12397 68164
12399-12500 68164
12502-14398 68164
14400-16400 68116
16402-16998 68116
Maple St
1601-1997 68110
1999-2299 68110
2400-4300 68111
4302-4398 68111
4752-4848 68104
4850-7099 68104
7101-7199 68104
7200-10199 68134
Maplewood Blvd 68134
Marbee Dr 68124
March Hare Ln 68142
Marcy Cir
13100-15599 68154
16700-16799 68118
Marcy Plz
1000-1299 68108
10900-11799 68154
Marcy St
400-1298 68108
1300-1599 68108
2500-4499 68105
4500-6899 68106
12700-12999 68154
15600-17800 68118
17802-17898 68118
Margo Cir 68138
Margo Ct 68138
Margo St
4501-4699 68157
12900-15599 68138
17700-19099 68136
Marinda Cir
13200-13899 68144
15900-19199 68130
Marinda Plz 68144
Marinda St
4000-4299 68105
4301-4399 68105
5000-5058 68106
5060-5098 68106
12601-12697 68144
12699-13699 68144
19201-19497 68130
19499-19899 68130
19901-19999 68130
Marshall Dr 68137
Martha Cir
11200-15099 68144
15900-16799 68130
Martha St
500-2099 68108
2101-2199 68108
2401-2597 68105
2599-3999 68105
4601-4997 68106
4999-5099 68106
8000-10700 68124
10702-10798 68124
11000-12799 68144
16500-17799 68130
Martin Ave
2700-3699 68112
10800-11349 68164
15100-15200 68116
15202-15298 68116
Mary Cir
10400-10499 68122
11600-11649 68164
Mary Plz
9000-9099 68122
12200-12299 68142
Mary St
2400-4099 68112
5200-5699 68152
7500-10599 68122
10800-11949 68164
11951-11999 68164
14800-15999 68116
Mason Cir
15500-15599 68154
16700-16799 68118
Mason Plz 68154
Mason St
1001-1697 68108
1699-2299 68108
2301-2399 68108
2500-4399 68105
4500-6899 68106
11300-15099 68154
15101-15199 68154
16400-16699 68118
16701-17799 68118
Mayberry Plz
1000-1299 68108
10900-11799 68154
11801-11999 68154
Mayberry St
4200-4499 68105
4500-6899 68106
9400-9499 68114
11700-11738 68154
Mayfair Dr 68144
Mayfield Ave
800-998 68132
1000-1199 68132
1701-1797 68104
1799-1899 68104
Maywood St 68127
Mckinley St
3400-3598 68112
3600-3800 68112
3802-4498 68112
5200-6398 68152
6400-6500 68152
6502-6898 68152
Meadow Dr 68114
Meadow Rd 68154
Meadow Ridge Rd 68138
Meadows Blvd &
Pkwy 68138
Melissa Ln 68152
Menke Cir 68134
Mercer Blvd 68131
Mercer Park Rd 68131
Mercury St 68138
Mercy Rd
6801-6897 68106
6899-7199 68106
7200-7400 68124
7402-7798 68124
Meredith Ave
2500-4399 68111
4500-4799 68104
7600-9899 68134
11600-13999 68164
14400-17399 68116
Meredith Cir
3500-3599 68111
9100-9121 68134
11500-14099 68164
Meridian St 68136
Merion Dr 68136
Meyer St 68152
Miami Cir
10000-10099 68134
11200-12999 68164
15000-17699 68116
Miami Plz 68134
Miami St
1800-2299 68110
2501-2797 68111
2799-4399 68111
4900-6549 68104
6551-6599 68104
7300-10299 68134
11800-13700 68164
13702-13950 68164
14600-16500 68116
16502-16798 68116
Michael Dr 68157
Mid City Ave 68107
Mike Fahey St 68102
Military Ave
1400-1498 68131
1500-2299 68111
4501-6097 68104
6099-7199 68104
7201-7397 68134
7399-7826 68134
7828-7998 68134
Military Plz 68134
Military Rd
8200-8622 68134
8624-9899 68134
9901-10699 68134
13300-13798 68142
13901-14399 68142
N Mill Ct 68154
Mill Valley Rd 68154
Millard Ave 68137
Millard Airport Plz 68137
Miller Ave 68127
Miller St 68107
Millwood Ln 68142
Minne Lusa Blvd 68112
Miracle Hills Dr 68154
Missouri Ave 68107
Mock Turtle Ln 68142
Mockingbird Dr
9001-9297 68127
9299-10799 68127
10800-11098 68137
11100-11199 68137
11201-11299 68137
Mohr Ln 68142
Monroe Cir
7200-7399 68127
13700-14300 68137
14302-15330 68137
15600-17399 68135
Monroe Plz 68127
Monroe St
1200-4499 68107
4500-4699 68117
8400-10699 68127
11000-15399 68137
15700-17899 68135
Montclair Dr 68144
Morgan Cir 68152
Mormon Cir
3600-3699 68112
4700-4799 68152
Mormon St
2800-3999 68112
12300-12599 68142
Mormon Bridge Rd 68152
Morning View Dr 68137
Morningside Dr 68134
Morris St 68122
Morrison Dr 68154
Morton St 68127
Mullen Cir 68144
Mullen Rd 68124
Musket St 68136
Myrtle Ave 68131
N Ave 68107
N Cir
14900-14999 68137
15600-18699 68135
N Plz
7300-7398 68127
15400-15499 68137
N St
1500-1598 68107
1600-4199 68107
4500-6199 68117
9201-9297 68127
9299-10699 68127
12100-14899 68137
18750-19799 68135
Nancy Cir
10700-10799 68127
11400-11499 68137
Nebraska Ave
3300-4499 68111
4500-6799 68104
7600-10699 68134
12700-13099 68164
14800-15148 68116
15150-15199 68116
15201-16499 68116
Nebraska Cir
11400-11499 68164
14600-14699 68116
Nelsons Creek Dr 68116
Newell St 68138
Newport Ave
2400-4199 68112
4800-5198 68152
5200-6599 68152
6601-7199 68152
7500-10499 68122
10800-14299 68164
14900-15999 68116
Nicholas Cir
7000-7099 68132
7700-7799 68114
13200-13299 68154
Nicholas Ct 68131
Nicholas St
1100-2099 68102
2900-4399 68131
4500-5899 68132
8300-10700 68114
10702-10798 68114
11500-12198 68154
12200-15399 68154
Nina Cir 68130
Nina St
7400-9999 68124
10001-10099 68124
15200-15299 68144
15301-15499 68144
17500-20299 68130
Normandy Cir 68137
Northampton Blvd 68104
Northern Hills Dr 68152
Northland Dr
6800-7199 68152
7200-7208 68122
7210-7399 68122
Northridge Cir 68122
Northridge Dr 68112
Northridge Dr E 68112
Northwest Dr 68104
Northwoods Dr 68152
Norwick Dr
5000-5048 68104
15200-15299 68116
Norwick Plz 68164
Nottingham Dr
9700-9899 68114

15600-16099 68118
O Cir
8700-9930 68127
14706-14739 68137
15700-19799 68135
O Plz 68137
O St
1300-2500 68107
2502-3898 68107
4500-6199 68117
9005-9019 68127
9021-10750 68127
10752-10760 68127
11023-11027 68137
11029-14159 68137
14161-14165 68137
17150-17198 68135
17200-18899 68135
Oak Cir
9500-9699 68124
11500-14599 68144
16200-16399 68130
Oak Dr 68130
Oak Pl 68127
Oak Plz
6900-6999 68106
8401-8499 68124
12500-12598 68144
12601-12699 68144
16000-17999 68130
18001-18799 68130
Oak St
500-1598 68108
1600-2200 68108
2202-2398 68108
2400-2598 68105
2600-4499 68105
4500-7100 68106
7102-7198 68106
7200-10499 68124
10501-10749 68124
10900-10998 68144
11000-14500 68144
14502-14528 68144
16050-16699 68130
16701-18099 68130
Oak Hills Cir, Dr & Plz 68137
Oak View Dr 68144
Oakair Cir, Dr & Plz 68137
Oakbrook Cir
10800-10829 68154
10831-10899 68154
17300-17399 68118
Oakbrook Dr 68154
Oakcrest Plz 68137
Oakmont Dr & St 68136
Oakridge Rd 68112
N Oaks Blvd 68134
Oaks Ln 68137
Oakwood Cir 68107
Oakwood St
7500-8399 68127
19400-19498 68135
Ogden Ave 68104
Ogden Cir
9700-9799 68134
13000-13099 68164
15400-16799 68116
Ogden Plz
4300-4398 68111
10000-10099 68134
11700-11798 68164
Ogden St
1300-2399 68110
4501-5397 68104
5399-6999 68104
9100-9400 68134
9402-9498 68134
12601-12797 68164
12799-14199 68164
14800-14998 68116
16601-16699 68116
Ogden Plaza Cir 68164
Ohern Cir 68135
Ohern Plz
9600-9799 68127
14900-14999 68137
Ohern St
4600-6199 68117
8400-10299 68127
12000-12098 68137
12100-14149 68137
14151-14199 68137
15800-18899 68135
Ohio Cir
12000-12999 68164
15308-16899 68116
Ohio Plz 68134
Ohio St
1200-1398 68110
1400-2200 68110
2202-2298 68110
2400-4399 68111
4900-7099 68104
9000-10299 68134
10301-10317 68134
11200-11300 68164
11302-13698 68164
14500-16399 68116
16401-16499 68116
Old Cherry Cir & Rd 68137
Old Maple Rd
3301-10497 68134
10499-10799 68134
10800-11198 68164
11200-11399 68164
11401-11899 68164
Old Mill Rd 68154
Old Post Ln 68142
Old Smokey Ln 68152
Olin Ave
1500-1599 68108
3600-3699 68105
10900-11099 68144
Olive Cir
13950-14199 68138
16300-16399 68136
Olive St
12800-14999 68138
16400-19099 68136
Olney St 68138
Omaha Trace St 68122
Ontario Cir
9000-9099 68124
16100-19299 68130
Ontario Plz 68130
Ontario St
1700-1999 68108
7200-9999 68124
15200-15299 68144
16801-18097 68130
18099-19699 68130
Orchard Ave
3600-4098 68107
4100-4150 68107
4152-4198 68107
4650-6099 68117
8400-8799 68127
8801-8999 68127
12100-15499 68137
15600-15698 68135
15700-19799 68135
Orchard Cir
9900-9999 68127
12700-14899 68137
16000-16299 68135
Orchard Ln 68131
Orchard Plz 68137
Oregon Trl 68131
Orville Plz 68110
Outback Ln 68152
P Cir 68127
P St
1700-2499 68107
2501-4199 68107
4500-6099 68117
10000-10399 68127
11300-13999 68137
16901-16997 68135
16999-18899 68135
Pacific St
501-797 68108
799-1099 68108
1101-2299 68108
1124-1124 68103
1124-1126 68108
1124-1124 68109
2401-2697 68105
2699-4499 68105
4500-6900 68106
6902-7198 68106
7200-7298 68114
7300-10751 68114
10753-10799 68114
10800-13199 68154
13201-15399 68154
15601-16397 68118
16399-16499 68118
16501-16999 68118
Paddock Plz & Rd 68124
Page St
4000-4050 68131
4052-4198 68131
7400-7499 68114
15300-15399 68154
16300-16399 68118
Palamino Rd 68154
Paleadon St 68131
Palisades Dr 68136
Papillion Pkwy
1101-1919 68154
2100-2198 68164
Papio Cir & St 68138
Park Ave
100-499 68131
500-1399 68105
1401-1999 68105
Park Dr 68127
Park Ln 68127
Park Drive Plz 68127
Park Lane Cir 68164
Park Lane Dr 68104
Park Meadow Plz 68122
Park Meadows Plz 68142
Park View Ln 68104
Park Wild Ave 68108
Parker Cir
2000-2148 68110
2150-2299 68110
12100-15399 68154
15600-15699 68118
Parker Ct 68114
Parker Plz
12001-14797 68154
14799-15399 68154
16800-17498 68118
17500-17699 68118
Parker St
2400-2498 68111
2500-4499 68111
4500-6599 68104
7301-7497 68114
7499-10699 68114
13500-15599 68154
15700-17199 68118
17201-17399 68118
Parkview Dr 68134
Parkwood Ln 68132
Parsonage Dr 68152
Pasadena Ave
1400-1599 68107
7500-9999 68124
15200-15299 68144
18200-18499 68130
Pasadena Cir
7400-7449 68124
16400-19299 68130
Pasadena Ct 68130
Pasadena Plz 68130
Pasadena St 68130
Patrick Ave
2400-2498 68111
2500-4399 68111
11200-14399 68164
14400-17899 68116
Patrick Cir
12500-13199 68164
14600-14699 68116
Patterson Cir 68137
Patterson Dr
15050-15200 68137
15202-15398 68137
16800-17399 68135
Patterson St
3800-4399 68107
6000-6050 68117
6052-6198 68117
19300-19399 68135
Paul Cir 68154
Paul Plz 68154
Paul St
1800-2098 68102
2100-2200 68102
2202-2398 68102
13301-13397 68154
13399-13499 68154
Pauline St 68124
Pawnee Rd
8000-9498 68122
9500-10499 68122
10501-10799 68122
10900-10998 68142
11000-13699 68142
13701-13799 68142
Paxton Blvd 68111
Paxton Ct 68131
Pebble Cir 68136
Pedersen Dr 68144
Pepperwood Dr 68154
Peterson Dr 68130
Phelps Plz 68106
Phelps St 68107
Piedmont Dr 68154
Pierce Cir
7800-7825 68124
15500-15599 68144
16700-18499 68130
Pierce Ct 68144
Pierce Plz
7501-7599 68124
11100-14220 68144
14222-14238 68144
17801-17897 68130
17899-19099 68130
Pierce St
300-2299 68108
2400-4499 68105
4500-6499 68106
7600-7698 68124
7700-9899 68124
11400-14049 68144
16400-20099 68130
Pine Cir
7700-9299 68124
12800-12857 68144
17300-17399 68130
Pine Plz
6351-6399 68106
11100-11300 68144
11302-11330 68144
Pine Rd 68144
Pine St
300-900 68108
902-1598 68108
3300-4499 68105
4500-6826 68106
6828-6902 68106
9100-9899 68124
11332-13398 68144
13400-15300 68144
15302-15598 68144
15600-16298 68130
16300-19799 68130
Pinehurst Ave
10300-10499 68124
17700-17898 68136
19100-19199 68130
Pinehurst Cir
9700-9999 68124
17600-17699 68136
Pinewood Dr 68144
Pinewood Circle Dr 68144
Pinkney St
1400-2200 68110
2202-2398 68110
2400-4499 68111
4700-4898 68104
4900-6999 68104
7200-10099 68134
16101-17599 68116
Plerelan St 68102
N Plersidg St 68116
Polk Cir
11701-15399 68137
15600-18549 68135
Polk Ct 68135
Polk Plz
13601-13799 68137
16801-18097 68135
18099-18195 68135
Polk St
1200-4499 68107
4500-4899 68117
7500-10699 68127
10800-14999 68137
15900-19199 68135
Ponca Rd 68112
Ponderosa Cir & Dr 68137
Pony Ridge Ln 68112
Pooh Bear Ln 68112
Poppleton Ave
400-2299 68108
2400-4499 68105
4500-6500 68106
6502-6598 68106
7800-10799 68124
10800-12599 68144
16300-19799 68130
Poppleton Cir
13700-15599 68144
18400-19599 68130
Poppleton Plz
7500-7698 68124
7700-7799 68124
11900-12298 68144
18000-18099 68130
Portal Dr 68138
Portal St 68136
Post Dr 68114
N Post Rd 68112
Potter Cir 68142
Potter Pkwy 68142
Potter Plz
5400-5499 68152
7800-7999 68122
Potter St
2850-2900 68112
2902-2998 68112
5700-5900 68152
5902-5998 68152
7300-7398 68122
7400-8700 68122
8702-10766 68122
10772-10798 68142
10800-13199 68142
Potwin St 68137
Prairie Ave 68132
Prairie Rd 68134
Prairie Brook Rd 68144
Prairie Corners Rd 68138
Prairie Hills Dr 68144
Prairie Lane Dr 68144
Prairie View Dr 68144
Prairie Village Dr 68144
Pratt Cir 68134
Pratt Ct 68116
Pratt Plz
10501-10599 68134
10800-12898 68164
15300-15398 68116
Pratt St
1600-2299 68110
2400-4449 68111
4451-4499 68111
4800-7000 68104
7002-7098 68104
7200-10099 68134
11300-11399 68164
Prestwick Ave 68136
Primrose Ln 68157
Q Plz
8627-9911 68127
9913-9927 68127
9929-9999 68127
15701-15799 68135
Q St
1801-1997 68107
1999-4149 68107
4151-4499 68107
4501-7199 68117
7300-10799 68127
10800-14899 68137
14901-15599 68137
15600-16398 68135
16400-19199 68135
19201-19799 68135
Queens Dr
11301-11397 68164
11399-11699 68164
14800-14999 68116
Queens Ter 68142
Quest Cir 68112
Quest St 68122
R Ave 68107
R Cir
1700-1799 68107
10700-10799 68127
15900-17199 68135
R Plz
8600-8698 68127
9501-9599 68127
11000-13999 68137
15701-17997 68135
17999-18199 68135
R St
2700-2798 68107
2800-4499 68107
4500-5823 68117
5825-5999 68117
9100-10600 68127
10602-10698 68127
11301-11327 68137
11329-15499 68137
15951-16097 68135
16099-19499 68135
NW Radial Hwy
1000-1199 68132
1201-1399 68132
1500-1598 68104
1600-6199 68104
Railroad Ave 68107
Rainwood Rd
2900-3099 68112
6000-6198 68152
6200-7199 68152
7201-7397 68122
7399-10500 68122
10502-10698 68122
10800-13799 68142
Raleigh Dr 68164
Ralston Ave 68127
Rambleridge Rd 68164
Rampart St 68136
Raven Oaks Cir & Dr 68152
Ray Sapp Dr 68138
Raymond Ave 68104
Read Cir 68142
Read Ct 68142
Read Plz
7800-10599 68122
11300-11325 68142
11327-11399 68142
Read St
1400-1598 68112
1600-3999 68112
4001-4199 68112
5000-6599 68152
8001-8247 68122
8249-8999 68122
12300-12799 68142
Red Rock Ave & Cir 68157
Redick Ave
1601-2297 68112
2299-4499 68112
4500-4999 68152
7500-10399 68122
14200-14299 68164
Redick Cir 68122
Redman Ave
3300-4098 68111
4100-4499 68111
4600-4798 68104
4800-4899 68104
9200-9899 68134
14800-17599 68116
Redman Cir
4000-4099 68111
4101-4399 68111
9300-9399 68134
12955-12999 68164
17300-17399 68116
Redman Plz 68134
Redwood Cir 68138
Redwood St
13400-15399 68138
15600-16600 68136
16602-16698 68136
Rees St
2500-2699 68105
5100-5899 68106
Regency Cir & Pkwy 68114
Regency Parkway Dr 68114
Renfro Cir 68137
Renfro St 68135
Reynolds Cir 68142
Reynolds St
2850-3321 68112
3323-3399 68112
5400-5499 68152
7200-8498 68122
8500-8599 68122
11401-11511 68142
12700-12798 68142
Richland Dr & Plz 68138
Richmond Dr 68134
Ridge Ave 68124
Ridgemont Cir & St 68136
Ridgeway Rd 68134
Ridgewood Ave
500-899 68114
901-1099 68114
1100-2599 68124
Riggs St
13300-13498 68137
13500-13599 68137
16200-17699 68135
River Dr & Ln 68112
Riverfront Dr & Plz 68102
Riverview Blvd 68108
Riviera Dr 68136
Roanoke Blvd 68164
Robertson Dr 68114
Robin Cir 68138
Robin Dr
4800-5000 68157
5002-5098 68157
15100-15198 68138
15200-15499 68138
16000-16200 68136
16202-19098 68136
Robin Hill Ave 68127
Robin Hill Dr 68106
Rock Creek Cir & Dr 68138
Rockbrook Rd 68124
Rogers Rd 68124
Rolling Ridge Rd 68135
Rose Ln 68154
Rose Blumkin Dr 68114
Rose Lane Plz 68154
Rose Lane Rd 68138
Rosewood St
15400-15499 68138
15600-16599 68136
Roxbury Dr & Plz 68137
Royal Wood Dr 68144
Ruggles Cir
8800-8899 68134
11500-11799 68164
Ruggles Plz
10400-10499 68134
10801-12597 68164
12599-12899 68164
Ruggles St
2800-4499 68111
4800-6399 68104
8100-9899 68134
11600-11699 68164
14700-17300 68116
17302-17398 68116

- Rustande St 68117
- Rustrida St 68154
- Ruth St 68157
- S Cir
  - 9000-10799 68127
  - 11300-14599 68137
  - 19000-19099 68135
- S Plz
  - 8636-8648 68127
  - 8650-10099 68127
  - 13900-13999 68137
  - 14001-14099 68137
- S St
  - 1500-1798 68107
  - 1800-4499 68107
  - 4500-5999 68117
  - 9334-9498 68127
  - 14100-15199 68137
  - 15600-19699 68135
- N Saddle Creek Rd
  - 201-297 68131
  - 299-599 68131
  - 600-699 68132
  - 608-608 68131
  - 701-1499 68132
  - 800-1498 68132
  - 1500-1599 68104
- S Saddle Creek Rd
  - 400-499 68131
  - 500-598 68106
  - 600-1599 68106
- Sadler Cir 68127
- Saffron Cir 68136
- Sagarmatha Plz 68152
- Sage St 68136
- Sahler Cir
  - 8200-8299 68134
  - 16000-16049 68116
- Sahler Ct 68116
- Sahler Plz
  - 10400-10599 68134
  - 12700-12798 68164
  - 12800-12899 68164
  - 14401-14597 68116
  - 14599-14666 68116
  - 14668-14670 68116
- Sahler St
  - 1700-1898 68110
  - 1900-2000 68110
  - 2002-2198 68110
  - 2401-2497 68111
  - 2499-3499 68111
  - 4800-6599 68104
  - 8701-9097 68134
  - 9099-9700 68134
  - 9702-9798 68134
  - 10800-14199 68164
  - 14700-17099 68116
  - 17101-17699 68116
- Saint Marys Ave
  - 1700-2299 68102
  - 2400-3100 68105
  - 3102-3198 68105
- Sandra Cir & Ln 68137
- Sapp Brothers Dr 68138
- Saratoga Cir
  - 11700-14099 68164
  - 16800-16899 68116
- Saratoga Plz
  - 10900-11199 68164
  - 14400-14449 68116
- Saratoga St
  - 2200-2298 68110
  - 2401-2597 68111
  - 2599-4399 68111
  - 4500-4999 68104
  - 9600-10299 68134
  - 11300-11499 68164
  - 14450-16499 68116
- Sargent St
  - 3000-3198 68112
  - 5000-5298 68152
  - 5300-5799 68152
  - 5801-5999 68152
- Sarpy Cir
  - 8700-8799 68127
  - 15300-15399 68137
- Sawgrass Cir 68136
- Sawtooth Cir 68157
- Schirra St 68138
- Schooner Rd 68138
- Schram Rd 68138
- Schroeder Cir 68137
- Schroeder Dr 68157
- Schuyler Dr
  - 7400-7499 68114
  - 15300-15499 68154
- Scott Cir
  - 3100-3110 68112
  - 3112-3298 68112
  - 10000-10099 68122
  - 12300-12399 68142
- Scott St
  - 2900-3999 68112
  - 9100-9199 68122
  - 11401-11497 68142
  - 11499-13099 68142
  - 13101-13199 68142
- N Seadis St 68110
- Sedona Cir & St 68136
- Seldin Dr 68144
- Serum Ave 68127
- Seward Cir
  - 10200-10299 68114
  - 12000-13699 68154
  - 15600-16399 68118
- Seward Plz
  - 11100-15399 68154
  - 17500-17599 68118
- Seward St
  - 700-798 68110
  - 800-900 68110
  - 902-998 68110
  - 2800-4399 68111
  - 4500-7099 68104
  - 7300-10099 68114
  - 10800-11098 68154
  - 11100-15599 68154
  - 15700-17299 68118
- Seymour St 68127
- Shadow Ridge Dr 68130
- Shady Lane Cir 68105
- Shamrock Cir 68118
- Shamrock Plz 68154
- Shamrock Rd
  - 8701-9297 68114
  - 9299-9499 68114
  - 12200-12599 68154
  - 15700-15724 68118
  - 15726-15798 68118
- Sharon Dr 68112
- Sharp St
  - 15000-15299 68137
  - 17300-17399 68135
- Sheffield St
  - 3000-3599 68112
  - 5200-5298 68152
  - 5401-5499 68152
  - 8300-8599 68122
  - 8601-10699 68122
- Shepard St 68138
- Sherman Dr 68134
- Sherwood Ave
  - 1400-1499 68110
  - 1501-1599 68110
  - 13400-13499 68164
  - 14450-17199 68116
- Sherwood Cir
  - 13300-13399 68164
  - 15300-16499 68116
- Shirley Cir
  - 7900-7999 68124
  - 13708-14398 68144
  - 14400-15599 68144
  - 17900-17999 68130
- Shirley St
  - 2700-4399 68105
  - 4500-4800 68106
  - 4802-6598 68106
  - 7301-7497 68124
  - 7499-9199 68124
  - 9201-10799 68124
  - 10801-10997 68144
  - 10999-15499 68144
  - 16000-19299 68130
- S Sholisti St 68130
- Shongaska Rd 68112
- Signal Dr 68137
- Sigwart St 68104
- Silver Creek Cir 68152
- Silver Valley Rd 68152
- Sky Park Cir & Dr 68137
- Skylark Dr 68144
- Slayton St 68138
- Sleepy Hollow Ln
  - 2901-2999 68112
  - 10900-10998 68152
  - 11000-11099 68152
- Smokey Cir 68157
- Snowdrift Ln
  - 4200-4499 68112
  - 4500-4598 68152
- Soldier St 68136
- Sorensen Ln 68122
- Sorensen Pkwy
  - 5600-5698 68152
  - 5700-6682 68152
  - 6684-7120 68152
  - 8900-8998 68122
- Southby Plz 68124
- Southdale Cir 68137
- Southdale Dr 68137
- Southdale Plz 68135
- Southern Manor Dr 68117
- Spaulding Cir
  - 8000-10699 68134
  - 16000-16099 68116
- Spaulding Plz
  - 10300-10399 68134
  - 10800-10898 68164
  - 10900-12849 68164
  - 15400-15599 68116
- Spaulding St
  - 2400-4450 68111
  - 4452-4498 68111
  - 4800-6899 68104
  - 8400-10499 68134
  - 11300-11699 68164
  - 14700-17300 68116
  - 17302-17698 68116
- Spencer St
  - 1400-2299 68110
  - 2400-4199 68111
  - 4500-7099 68104
  - 7501-9397 68134
  - 9399-9699 68134
  - 12100-12400 68164
  - 12402-12598 68164
  - 14701-15097 68116
  - 15099-17399 68116
- Spracklin Ln 68152
- Sprague Cir
  - 8800-8899 68134
  - 11700-14299 68164
- Sprague Ct 68116
- Sprague Plz
  - 5101-5113 68104
  - 5188-5190 68104
  - 10500-10599 68134
  - 12500-12598 68164
  - 12600-12899 68164
  - 14651-14699 68116
- Sprague St
  - 1600-1800 68110
  - 1802-2298 68110
  - 2400-4399 68111
  - 4401-4499 68111
  - 4800-6599 68104
  - 6601-7049 68104
  - 8101-8197 68134
  - 8199-10499 68134
  - 13801-13897 68164
  - 13899-14199 68164
  - 14600-14648 68116
  - 14650-17299 68116
- Spring Cir
  - 4000-4099 68105
  - 7900-7999 68124
  - 14400-14499 68144
  - 16300-16800 68130
  - 16802-16820 68130
- Spring Plz
  - 8300-8399 68124
  - 16800-16808 68130
  - 16810-16814 68130
  - 16816-16898 68130
- Spring St
  - 301-1497 68108
  - 1499-2399 68108
  - 3000-4499 68105
  - 4500-7199 68106
  - 7400-10799 68124
  - 10900-13699 68144
  - 13701-13899 68144
  - 15600-15898 68130
  - 15900-16199 68130
- Springfield Dr 68114
- Spruce St 68122
- Spyglass Dr 68136
- St Richards Plz 68111
- Stanford Cir 68108
- Stanford St 68144
- Stargrass Rd 68152
- Starlite Dr 68152
- State Cir 68152
- State St
  - 2800-4499 68112
  - 6000-6598 68152
  - 6601-7199 68152
  - 7500-7724 68127
  - 7725-7727 68122
  - 7726-7938 68127
  - 7731-8399 68127
  - 7940-7998 68122
  - 8000-8398 68127
  - 9400-9898 68122
  - 9900-10499 68122
  - 11100-13398 68142
- State Highway 133 68142
- Sterling Ridge Dr 68144
- Stevens Plz & St 68137
- Stone Ave
  - 3000-3199 68111
  - 14500-14698 68116
  - 14700-14799 68116
- Stone Plz
  - 6000-6099 68104
  - 16600-16698 68116
- Stonegate Cir & Dr 68164
- Stones Throw Dr 68152
- Stoney Brook Blvd 68137
- Stony Cir 68136
- Storage Rd 68136
- Stratford Cir 68137
- Suburban Dr 68157
- Suffolk Cir & Plz 68127
- Summerwood Dr 68137
- Summit Dr 68136
- Summit St 68112
- Summitt St 68122
- Sun Valley Dr 68157
- Sunburst Cir 68134
- Sunburst St 68164
- Sunny Slope Ave 68134
- Sunridge St 68136
- Sunset Dr 68127
- Sunset Ln 68135
- Sunset Trl 68132
- Sunshine Dr 68107
- Surrey Hills Dr 68122
- Susan Cir 68124
- T Ave 68107
- T Cir
  - 9000-10299 68127
  - 10800-15149 68137
  - 16100-18999 68135
- T Plz
  - 8601-9897 68127
  - 9899-10099 68127
  - 11015-13797 68137
  - 13799-13899 68137
- T St
  - 2801-2997 68107
  - 2999-4199 68107
  - 4500-5999 68117
  - 6001-6899 68117
  - 12200-15499 68137
  - 15700-19699 68135
- Tamarisk Ln 68122
- Tammy Trl 68135
- Tangier Way 68124
- Tarragon Cir 68136
- Taylor Cir
  - 6300-6399 68104
  - 8000-8099 68134
  - 12900-14099 68164
- Taylor Ct 68116
- Taylor Plz 68116
- Taylor St
  - 2500-2850 68111
  - 2852-3298 68111
  - 4800-5899 68104
  - 7600-9999 68134
  - 10800-13599 68164
  - 15000-17699 68116
- Tea Party Ln 68142
- Templeton Dr 68134
- Templeton St 68111
- Terrace Dr 68134
- Teton Ave 68157
- Thomas Ln 68152
- Tibbles St 68116
- Tilford Cir 68127
- Timberlane Dr
  - 15400-15498 68138
  - 15500-15599 68138
  - 15600-16599 68136
  - 16601-16699 68136
- Timberline Dr 68152
- Titus Ave 68112
- Tomahawk Blvd 68134
- Trail Creek Ave 68157
- Trail Ridge Cir & Rd 68135
- Tralince St 68111
- N Trelanto St 68152
- Trencenw Rd 68142
- Trendwood Dr 68144
- Troon Cir 68136
- Trumble Ave 68138
- Tucker Cir 68152
- Tucker St
  - 2800-2848 68112
  - 2850-3399 68112
  - 4500-5198 68152
  - 5200-5599 68152
  - 5601-5699 68152
  - 8150-8235 68122
  - 8237-8299 68122
- Turner Blvd
  - 301-399 68131
  - 500-1399 68105
  - 1401-3399 68105
- Twin Ridge Blvd 68105
- Two Knight Ln 68142
- Tyler Cir 68135
- Tyler St
  - 11600-11699 68137
  - 18300-18399 68135
- U Ave 68107
- U Cir 68135
- U Ct 68127
- U Plz
  - 9400-9499 68127
  - 9501-9599 68127
  - 14700-14850 68137
  - 14852-14898 68137
- U St
  - 1300-4199 68107
  - 4501-4597 68117
  - 4599-5399 68117
  - 9900-10198 68127
  - 10200-10599 68127
  - 11000-15499 68137
  - 15700-19699 68135
- Underwood Ave
  - 4801-6899 68132
  - 8300-8600 68114
  - 8602-9498 68114
  - 14801-14899 68154
  - 16300-16399 68118
- Underwood Cir 68118
- Upland Pkwy 68107
- N Us Highway 75 68152
- V Cir
  - 13500-13799 68137
  - 16100-17299 68135
- V Plz
  - 9200-9398 68127
  - 9400-9700 68127
  - 9702-9898 68127
  - 14100-14799 68137
- V St
  - 3000-4100 68107
  - 4102-4198 68107
  - 5600-5900 68117
  - 5902-5998 68117
  - 10200-10799 68127
  - 10800-10898 68137
  - 10900-15499 68137
  - 16600-16998 68135
  - 17000-19699 68135
- Valley Cir
  - 4050-4068 68105
  - 4070-4072 68105
  - 5300-5899 68106
  - 10100-10199 68124
  - 16200-16599 68130
- Valley Dr 68130
- Valley St
  - 300-499 68108
  - 2400-4299 68105
  - 4500-4999 68106
  - 5001-6799 68106
  - 7200-9599 68124
  - 9601-10799 68124
  - 10800-15299 68144
  - 15601-15697 68130
  - 15699-16399 68130
- Valley Ridge Dr 68138
- Valmont Plz 68154
- Van Buren Dr 68135
- Van Camp Ave 68108
- Van Camp Dr 68130
- Vane Cir
  - 5000-5099 68152
  - 12000-12099 68142
- Vane Ct 68122
- Vane Plz 68142
- Vane St
  - 2400-3099 68112
  - 3101-3199 68112
  - 6200-6499 68152
  - 7400-7899 68122
  - 7901-7999 68122
  - 13800-14299 68142
- Ventana Cir 68136
- Verineri St 68138
- Vernon Ave
  - 3900-4499 68111
  - 4800-6799 68104
  - 7700-10399 68134
  - 12900-13099 68164
  - 14900-15098 68116
  - 15100-16099 68116
- Vernon Cir 68104
- Victor Ave 68110
- N View Dr 68134
- Village Ct 68144
- Ville De Sante Dr 68104
- N Vincolle St 68164
- Vinton Cir 68130
- Vinton St
  - 1400-2299 68108
  - 2301-2399 68108
  - 2800-2998 68105
  - 3000-4499 68105
  - 4500-4999 68106
  - 7400-7498 68124
  - 7500-7599 68124
  - 18400-18498 68130
  - 18500-18600 68130
  - 18602-18898 68130
- Virginia Cir 68136
- Virginia St
  - 4500-4899 68157
  - 4901-5099 68157
  - 13800-14399 68138
  - 15900-16499 68136
- S Virginia St 68157
- W Cir 68137
- W Plz 68137
- W St
  - 1501-1897 68107
  - 1899-4099 68107
  - 4101-4199 68107
  - 4850-4898 68117
  - 5051-5099 68117
  - 10201-10203 68127
  - 10205-10500 68127
  - 10502-10598 68127
  - 11000-15499 68137
  - 16000-16098 68135
  - 16100-19699 68135
- Wakeley Cir 68118
- Wakeley Plz
  - 7800-7899 68114
  - 7901-7999 68114
  - 11501-11697 68154
  - 11699-11999 68154
- Wakeley St
  - 4100-4499 68131
  - 4600-4799 68132
  - 16000-16200 68118
  - 16202-16298 68118
- Walling Cir 68144
- Walnut Cir
  - 8101-8101 68124
  - 8103-8421 68124
  - 13300-15599 68144
  - 17000-19499 68130
- Walnut Ln 68127
- Walnut Plz
  - 6300-6398 68106
  - 17100-17298 68130
- Walnut St
  - 201-297 68108
  - 299-499 68108
  - 3300-4400 68105
  - 4402-4498 68105
  - 4500-6299 68106
  - 7500-9899 68124
  - 13557-13849 68144
  - 13851-13899 68144
  - 17301-17397 68130
  - 17399-19449 68130
- Walnut Grove Cir & Dr 68137
- Warwick Cir 68136
- Washington Ave 68152
- Washington Cir
  - 8700-8898 68127
  - 8900-8999 68127
  - 11800-14199 68137
  - 14201-14599 68137
  - 16100-19499 68135
- Washington Dr 68127
- Washington Plz 68137
- Washington St
  - 1300-4499 68107
  - 4500-4599 68117
  - 4601-4999 68117
  - 7200-9199 68127
  - 10900-15299 68137
  - 16400-16552 68135
  - 16554-18899 68135
- Weber Cir 68112
- Weber Plz 68122
- Weber St
  - 2600-3999 68112
  - 7301-7397 68122
  - 7399-9199 68122
  - 10800-14299 68142
- Webster Cir 68154
- Webster Plz
  - 8200-8798 68114
  - 8800-8899 68114
  - 12900-12998 68154
- Webster St
  - 3000-3198 68131
  - 3200-3999 68131
  - 4800-5300 68132
  - 5302-5898 68132
  - 7200-7250 68114
  - 7252-8599 68114
  - 12700-12798 68154
  - 15600-16899 68118
- Wedge Ct 68152
- Weir Cir
  - 12800-14699 68137

18600-18699 68135
Weir Ct 68127
Weir Plz
9800-9898 68127
9900-9999 68127
14900-14999 68137
Weir St
4500-6099 68117
6101-6129 68117
8700-10499 68127
10501-10699 68127
12101-12197 68137
12199-15499 68137
16201-16497 68135
16499-19799 68135
Welch Cir, Plz & St 68135
Wenninghoff Rd
5800-6098 68134
6701-6799 68122
Westbrook Ave 68106
Westchester Cir
15000-15499 68154
15600-15799 68118
Westchester Dr
9700-9999 68114
15200-15399 68154
Westchester Ln 68114
Westchester Plz 68154
Western Ave
5000-7099 68132
7101-7199 68132
7301-7397 68114
7399-9399 68114
15400-15599 68154
15600-17099 68118
Western Cir
9500-9599 68114
12600-14999 68154
17100-17199 68118
Western Plz
9400-9500 68114
9502-9898 68114
10801-10999 68154
Westfield Cir
11800-11899 68144
16300-16699 68130
Westfield Plz 68130
Westgate Cir & Rd 68124
Westmont Dr 68138
Westover Rd
8800-8898 68114
8900-8999 68114
10900-12399 68154
Westport Pkwy 68138
Westridge Dr 68124
Westwood Ln 68144
White Cloud Dr 68157
White Deer Ln 68112
Whitmore Cir
8601-8699 68122
14050-14060 68142
14062-14086 68142
14088-14110 68142
Whitmore Ct
10500-10599 68122
10900-11357 68142
11359-11367 68142
Whitmore Plz
7800-7900 68122
7902-10798 68122
11354-11362 68142
11364-11370 68142
11372-11398 68142
Whitmore St
1600-3399 68112
5000-6499 68152
11700-11999 68142
Wiesman Dr 68134
Wilbur Plz 68110
Wild Rose Ln 68112
Wildewood Dr 68127
William Cir
12200-14299 68144
17200-18499 68130
William Ct 68130
William Plz
7401-7499 68124
11100-12099 68144
12101-12199 68144
15600-15699 68130
William St
301-397 68108
399-1799 68108
4200-4499 68105
4500-6599 68106
8701-8999 68124
11800-15599 68144
16700-16898 68130
16900-19799 68130
Williams St 68130
Willis Ave
1301-1497 68110
1499-2299 68110
13300-13499 68164
Willis Cir 68164
Willit St
2850-3300 68112
3302-4298 68112
4600-5799 68152
8150-8240 68122
8242-8298 68122
Willow Cir & St 68136
Willow Creek Dr 68138
Willow Wood Cir 68152
Wilson Cir 68107
Wilson Dr 68127
Windridge Ln 68152
Windsor Dr
7500-7699 68114
15400-15599 68154
17200-17399 68118
Winslow Pl 68137
Winthrop Cir 68137
Wirt Cir
7200-7298 68134
7300-8099 68134
12500-12599 68164
15000-15499 68116
Wirt Plz 68134
Wirt St
1400-2222 68110
2224-2298 68110
2400-4299 68111
4500-7099 68104
7500-7598 68134
7600-9699 68134
12100-12499 68164
14400-14498 68116
14500-17599 68116
Wood Dr 68130
Wood River Dr 68157
Wood Valley Dr 68142
Woodbine Cir 68127
Woodcrest Cir
12400-12448 68137
16100-16199 68135
Woodcrest Dr 68137
Woodcrest Plz
12701-12799 68137
15701-15799 68135
Woodland Dr
200-299 68108
16200-16599 68136
16601-16799 68136
Woodlawn Ave 68127
Woodney Cir 68122
Woodridge Ln
9700-10399 68124
10801-10899 68144
Woodsdale Cir 68137
Woolworth Ave
300-599 68108
601-2199 68108
2400-4499 68105
4500-6300 68106
6302-6598 68106
7500-10699 68124
10701-10799 68124
11800-13400 68144
13402-15598 68144
15600-19799 68130
Woolworth Cir
13900-14299 68144
16950-19599 68130
Woolworth Plz
7400-7498 68124
11101-11299 68144
World Communications Dr 68122
Worthington Ave 68108
Wright Cir
11200-11399 68144
16200-16699 68130
Wright Plz
6901-6999 68106
15900-17014 68130
17016-17698 68130
Wright St
3201-3297 68105
3299-4099 68105
7400-10499 68124
13400-13899 68144
13901-14799 68144
17200-18499 68130
18501-18599 68130
Wycliffe Dr 68154
Wyoming St
2500-2799 68112
7300-8999 68122
14200-14299 68142
X Cir 68137
X St
2601-2997 68107
2999-4199 68107
10800-11599 68137
16600-19899 68135
Y Cir 68137
Y Plz
9901-9999 68127
12100-12199 68137
Y St
1300-4199 68107
4801-4897 68117
4899-5599 68117
5601-5699 68117
9300-10599 68127
10801-10897 68137
10899-15499 68137
15501-15599 68137
16301-16397 68135
16399-19000 68135
19002-19498 68135
Yates St
1500-1599 68110
1601-2199 68110
9700-9799 68134
12301-12497 68164
12499-12899 68164
15901-15903 68116
15905-16599 68116
Yew Ln 68152
Yort Ave 68116
Yort Cir 68134
Young Cir 68138
Young Plz 68152
Young St
2800-2848 68112
2850-4000 68112
4002-4498 68112
4500-5198 68152
Z Cir
9100-9149 68127
13700-14999 68137
17501-17899 68135
Z Plz 68127
Z St
1300-2699 68107
9150-9198 68127
9200-10399 68127
11000-15300 68137
15302-15398 68137
16100-19599 68135
19601-19699 68135

NUMBERED STREETS

S 1st St 68108
N 2nd St 68110
S 2nd St 68108
E 3rd St 68103
N 3rd St 68110
S 3rd St 68108
S 3rd Street Plz 68108
N 4th Ave 68110
N 4th St 68110
S 4th St 68108
N 5th St 68110
S 5th St 68108
N 6th Ave 68110
N 6th St
301-399 68102
5100-5599 68110
S 6th St 68108
S 7th Ave 68108
S 7th Ct 68108
N 7th St 68110
S 7th St 68108
N 8th St 68110
N 8th St E 68110
S 8th St
1100-2599 68108
4300-4398 68107
N 9th St
100-106 68102
5401-5897 68110
6501-6597 68112
N 9th St E 68110
S 9th St
101-107 68102
1001-1097 68108
3900-4098 68107
S 10th Ct 68108
N 10th St
100-298 68102
1801-1899 68110
N 10th St E 68110
S 10th St
101-411 68102
801-1003 68108
3701-4097 68107
N 11th St
1100-1299 68102
1301-1499 68102
1500-2899 68110
N 11th St E 68110
S 11th St
100-398 68102
400-600 68102
602-698 68102
1100-2799 68108
3901-3999 68107
S 12th Ct 68108
N 12th St 68102
N 12th St E 68110
S 12th St
301-397 68102
399-799 68102
1200-2799 68108
4100-4699 68107
S 13th Ct 68108
N 13th St
501-597 68102
1800-2198 68110
N 13th St E 68110
S 13th St
401-497 68102
800-1098 68108
3700-3898 68107
N 14th Ave
2201-3297 68110
7001-7099 68112
N 14th St
601-1099 68102
2501-4497 68110
N 14th St E 68110
S 14th St
300-614 68102
800-998 68108
3701-3797 68107
N 15th Ave 68110
S 15th Cir 68108
N 15th St
100-104 68102
2600-5299 68110
N 15th St E 68110
S 15th St
106-198 68102
801-897 68108
3901-4297 68107
N 16th St
201-497 68102
1500-6499 68110
6500-6798 68112
S 16th St
200-720 68102
801-1197 68108
3700-5499 68107
N 17th St
321-997 68102
1500-5199 68110
S 17th St
200-298 68102
800-1198 68108
3700-6399 68107
S 18th Plz 68102
N 18th St
100-1199 68102
1501-1797 68110
S 18th St
201-397 68102
801-1397 68108
4200-6199 68107
N 19th Ave 68110
S 19th Ave 68102
N 19th St
101-197 68102
1500-4199 68110
S 19th St
100-632 68102
800-898 68108
4100-4198 68107
S 20th Ave 68108
6000-6098 68107
N 20th Ct 68110
N 20th St
124-598 68102
1500-2699 68110
N 20th St E 68110
S 20th St
100-498 68102
800-3699 68108
4100-6199 68107
N 21st Ave 68110
S 21st Ave 68102
N 21st St
801-1499 68102
1501-2297 68110
N 21st St E 68110
S 21st St
800-3599 68108
4000-4098 68107
N 22nd St
304-898 68102
2300-5100 68110
N 22nd St E 68110
S 22nd St
600-699 68102
800-3200 68108
3700-3998 68107
N 23rd Plz 68110
N 23rd St
301-399 68102
1801-3697 68110
3699-5100 68110
5102-5198 68110
N 23rd St E 68110
S 23rd St
800-3699 68108
3700-6899 68107
S 24th Ave
405-411 68131
500-599 68105
N 24th St
301-897 68102
1500-1598 68110
6500-7199 68112
S 24th St
100-198 68102
800-998 68108
3700-5599 68107
N 24th Avenue Cir 68111
N 25th Ave 68131
3200-6099 68111
S 25th Ave
206-208 68131
601-817 68105
N 25th St
951-999 68131
1501-1697 68111
7151-7199 68112
S 25th St
101-197 68131
700-798 68105
3701-3897 68107
N 26th Ave 68111
S 26th Ave
101-299 68131
514-516 68105
N 26th Cir 68131
N 26th Pl 68111
N 26th St
1300-1399 68131
1800-1898 68111
S 26th St
500-2999 68105
3700-3898 68107
N 27th Ave 68111
S 27th Ave
300-399 68131
2301-2347 68105
S 27th Cir 68107
N 27th St
1101-1299 68131
1901-4897 68111
7601-7699 68112
S 27th St
500-510 68105
3801-3897 68107
N 28th Ave
501-897 68131
2101-2197 68111
2199-5900 68111
5902-5998 68111
6850-7148 68112
7150-8700 68112
8702-8798 68112
2901-3099 68105
5400-5499 68107
5501-5599 68107
N 28th Cir 68111
N 28th St
1500-3198 68111
3200-3300 68111
3302-4198 68111
7403-7403 68112
7405-7800 68112
7802-8398 68112
503-2299 68105
3700-4098 68107
4100-6699 68107
6701-6899 68107
N 29th Ave
2000-2098 68111
10000-10099 68112
S 29th Ave 68107
N 29th Cir 68111
S 29th Cir 68105
N 29th Ct 68112
S 29th Plz 68107
N 29th St
1000-1399 68131
1500-2298 68111
7300-9699 68112
S 29th St
200-298 68131
500-2498 68105
3900-5198 68107
N 30th Ave 68112
S 30th Ave 68105
N 30th Cir 68112
N 30th St
100-1499 68131
1500-6399 68111
6500-6598 68112
S 30th St
500-698 68105
4302-4744 68107
N 31st Ave
101-113 68131
4200-6399 68111
6500-6598 68112
S 31st Ave
120-198 68131
500-699 68105
N 31st St
118-298 68131
1500-1800 68111
7600-10099 68112
S 31st St
500-3600 68105
4600-5198 68107
N 32nd Ave
100-299 68131
2600-2699 68111
13900-13998 68112
S 32nd Ave 68105
N 32nd St
500-516 68131
1500-1598 68111
6500-6799 68112
S 32nd St
1000-3099 68105
3900-4398 68107
N 33rd Ave
2000-6399 68111
7200-7298 68112
S 33rd Ave 68107
N 33rd St
100-1499 68131
1500-6399 68111
6500-7899 68112
S 33rd St
225-499 68131
500-598 68105
3800-6899 68107
N 34th Ave
2200-3698 68111
11401-11597 68112
S 34th Ave 68107
N 34th Cir 68112
N 34th St
100-1499 68131
1600-6399 68111
6500-9927 68112
S 34th St
100-298 68131
500-3099 68105
3800-6199 68107
N 35th Ave 68131
S 35th Ave 68105
N 35th Cir 68112
N 35th St
108-108 68131
1500-6000 68111
6500-6800 68112
S 35th St
400-406 68131
500-3099 68105
3800-6599 68107
N 36th Ave
301-301 68131
3300-6399 68111
7251-7299 68112
S 36th Ave 68107
S 36th Ct 68105
N 36th St
100-1400 68131
1600-6399 68111
6500-12600 68112
S 36th St
100-302 68131
500-3499 68105
3801-3897 68107
N 36th Avenue Cir 68112
N 37th Ave 68111
S 37th Ave 68105
N 37th St
113-113 68131
2000-6399 68111
6500-8399 68112
S 37th St
102-112 68131
500-2699 68105
3900-6499 68107
N 38th Ave
101-441 68131
2200-2249 68111

S 38th Ave
503A-505A 68105
101-117 68131
502-510 68105
N 38th St
105-1499 68131
1501-1597 68111
7700-8199 68112
S 38th St
101-109 68131
500-3199 68105
3900-6899 68107
N 39th Ave 68112
S 39th Ave 68107
N 39th Cir 68111
N 39th St
101-127 68131
2200-6499 68111
6900-7148 68112
S 39th St
100-401 68131
500-1898 68105
3900-6799 68107
N 39th Ter 68112
N 40th Ave 68111
S 40th Ave 68107
N 40th St
100-1499 68131
1500-6317 68111
6500-12599 68112
S 40th St
100-200 68131
600-898 68105
4400-6499 68107
N 41st Ave
307-311 68131
1500-1598 68111
S 41st Ave 68107
N 41st Cir 68112
N 41st St
111-113 68131
115-1022 68131
1024-1398 68131
2600-2698 68111
2700-5199 68111
5201-5299 68111
6601-6697 68112
6699-7400 68112
7402-7498 68112
104-108 68131
110-121 68131
123-415 68131
668-898 68105
900-3599 68105
4400-6800 68107
6802-6898 68107
S 42nd Ave 68107
N 42nd St
100-106 68131
1601-2411 68111
6601-7197 68112
S 42nd St
101-297 68131
708-816 68105
3801-3899 68107
N 43rd Ave
109-907 68131
5700-5798 68111
N 43rd St
100-112 68131
1701-3297 68111
S 43rd St
1100-3499 68105
5401-6197 68107
N 44th Ave 68111
S 44th Ave
3100-3699 68105
4104-4104 68107
N 44th St
201-597 68131
3700-6499 68111
6500-6998 68112
S 44th St
100-498 68131
712-1198 68105
5201-6197 68107
N 45th Ave 68104
S 45th Ave 68157
N 45th Ct 68104
N 45th St
601-997 68132
1500-5400 68104
6800-6898 68152
S 45th St
801-815 68106
4300-4402 68117
6901-6997 68157
S 45th Avenue Cir 68157
N 46th Ave
1801-6097 68104
6500-8599 68152
S 46th Ave
700-798 68106
4400-6899 68117
7400-8699 68157
N 46th St
101-297 68132
4500-5098 68104
6600-8699 68152
S 46th St
101-299 68132
1000-2250 68106
4400-6600 68117
7900-8799 68157
N 47th Ave
901-901 68132
2400-5400 68104
10301-10699 68152
S 47th Ave 68157
N 47th St
300-348 68132
4600-6399 68104
8100-14999 68152
S 47th St
1900-2699 68106
4400-5700 68117
7400-8699 68157
N 48th Ave
800-1326 68132
1800-5500 68104
S 48th Ave
400-499 68132
1900-3799 68106
4401-4497 68117
7200-8499 68157
N 48th Cir 68152
N 48th St
100-116 68132
1501-1697 68104
8800-13599 68152
S 48th St
100-198 68132
601-897 68106
4400-6700 68117
6901-6997 68157
S 48th Ter 68157
S 48th Avenue Cir
3300-3499 68106
7100-7199 68157
N 49th Ave
800-1399 68132
1800-6499 68104
S 49th Ave
100-499 68132
800-3799 68106
4700-6899 68117
7200-8499 68157
S 49th Cir 68157
N 49th St
100-1399 68132
1500-1598 68104
6500-6700 68152
S 49th St
100-499 68132
800-3799 68106
4700-4798 68117
6900-7098 68157
S 49th Ter
6701-6703 68117
8300-8499 68157
S 49th Avenue Cir 68157
N 50th Ave
800-1399 68132
2000-5699 68104
6901-6997 68152
S 50th Ave
100-399 68132
500-2299 68106
4800-5899 68117
8000-8199 68157
S 50th Cir 68157
N 50th Ct 68104
N 50th St
100-799 68132
1500-5800 68104
6601-6997 68152
S 50th St
100-399 68132
500-798 68106
4126-4298 68117
6900-8499 68157
S 50th Ter 68117
S 50th Avenue Cir 68117
N 51st Ave 68104
S 51st Ave
100-499 68132
500-3699 68106
5200-5899 68117
S 51st Cir 68117
N 51st Ct 68152
N 51st Plz 68104
N 51st St
100-1499 68132
1500-5699 68104
6600-6698 68152
S 51st St
100-499 68132
500-3699 68106
4400-4698 68117
N 51st Avenue Cir 68104
S 51st Avenue Cir 68117
N 52nd Ave 68152
S 52nd Ave
1300-1399 68106
6700-6799 68117
N 52nd St
100-1399 68132
1500-6216 68104
6601-6797 68152
S 52nd St
100-499 68132
500-3799 68106
4100-4498 68117
6900-7699 68157
N 53rd St
100-1399 68132
1500-1598 68104
6900-10600 68152
S 53rd St
100-399 68132
500-599 68106
4700-6899 68117
6901-6997 68157
N 54th Ave 68152
N 54th Cir 68104
N 54th Plz 68152
N 54th St
100-1399 68132
1500-5099 68104
6900-7100 68152
S 54th St
100-399 68132
800-3399 68106
4700-5099 68117
N 54th Avenue Cir 68152
N 55th Ave 68104
S 55th Ave 68106
N 55th Cir 68152
N 55th Plz 68152
N 55th St
100-200 68132
1700-5099 68104
6800-6899 68152
S 55th St
100-300 68132
500-3699 68106
5000-5099 68117
S 56th Plz 68106
N 56th St
600-1200 68132
1500-1698 68104
6501-6697 68152
S 56th St
300-400 68132
500-3499 68106
4850-5999 68117
56th Avenue W 68152
N 57th Ave 68132
1701-4897 68104
S 57th Cir 68106
S 57th Plz 68106
N 57th St
600-1399 68132
2900-3198 68104
6900-8899 68152
S 57th St
100-399 68132
500-2299 68106
4101-4197 68117
N 58th Cir 68152
N 58th Plz 68152
N 58th St
600-1499 68132
1500-5100 68104
7000-7699 68152
S 58th St
500-3499 68106
4801-4847 68117
N 58th Plaza Cir 68104
N 59th Cir 68104
N 59th St
600-699 68132
1500-5099 68104
7300-11899 68152
S 59th St
800-3299 68106
4500-4998 68117
5000-5099 68117
N 60th Ave 68104
S 60th Ave 68117
N 60th St
1100-1499 68132
1500-6300 68104
6302-6398 68104
6500-12699 68152
S 60th St
800-3499 68106
4000-6099 68117
6101-6499 68117
N 61st Ave 68104
S 61st Ave
1500-3199 68106
4155-4699 68117
N 61st Cir 68152
N 61st St
101-397 68132
1500-5599 68104
10900-11199 68152
S 61st St
1100-2699 68106
4158-4158 68117
S 61st Avenue Cir 68106
N 62nd Ave 68104
S 62nd Ave
1501-1599 68106
4400-4599 68117
N 62nd St
100-499 68132
2000-5399 68104
10800-11199 68152
S 62nd St
1100-1198 68106
4100-4700 68117
S 63rd Ct 68106
S 63rd Plz 68106
N 63rd St
650-1399 68132
1500-1898 68104
6701-6797 68152
S 63rd St
1101-1197 68106
4400-4699 68117
N 64th Ave 68104
S 64th Ave
1101-1197 68106
8400-8499 68157
S 64th Ct 68106
N 64th Plz 68152
S 64th Plz 68106
N 64th St
1000-1199 68132
2000-5399 68104
6800-6999 68152
S 64th St
1600-1700 68106
8385-8397 68157
N 65th Ave
603-605 68132
2000-4599 68104
6700-6798 68152
N 65th St
500-1499 68132
1501-1597 68104
6501-6697 68152
S 65th St 68157
N 66th Ave 68104
S 66th Cir 68117
S 66th Plz 68117
N 66th St
100-598 68132
1501-1697 68104
8400-13600 68152
S 66th St 68106
S 66th Avenue Cir 68106
N 67th Ave 68132
N 67th Ave 68132
2000-3899 68104
S 67th Ave
100-198 68132
501-501 68106
N 67th Cir 68132
S 67th Ct 68106
N 67th Plz 68152
N 67th St
100-298 68132
2000-3999 68104
S 67th St
300-398 68132
500-3800 68106
4101-4197 68117
S 68th Ave
100-399 68132
500-799 68106
S 68th Ct 68106
N 68th Plz 68152
S 68th Plz 68106
N 68th St
301-303 68132
2000-6434 68104
S 68th St
100-399 68132
500-917 68106
4500-4599 68117
N 69th Ave 68104
S 69th Ave 68106
N 69th Cir 68152
S 69th Ct 68106
S 69th Plz 68106
N 69th St
101-799 68132
1600-1798 68104
10900-12799 68152
S 69th St
100-104 68132
510-1100 68106
5301-5499 68117
N 70th Ave 68132
1500-3799 68104
7205-7211 68152
S 70th Ave 68132
N 70th Cir 68104
S 70th Cir 68117
N 70th Plz 68104
S 70th Plz 68106
N 70th St
2000-2899 68104
7200-7213 68152
S 70th St
100-499 68132
500-3800 68106
5301-5699 68117
N 71st Ave 68152
N 71st Cir 68152
N 71st St 68104
S 71st St
300-499 68132
1100-3298 68106
N 72nd Ave 68114
S 72nd Ave
3000-3499 68124
6200-6400 68127
S 72nd Ct 68124
N 72nd St
101-497 68114
2000-6200 68134
6500-6598 68122
S 72nd St
200-999 68114
1300-1698 68124
4101-4197 68127
N 73rd Ave 68122
S 73rd Ave 68127
N 73rd Cir 68122
N 73rd Plz
6200-6498 68134
6500-13098 68122
N 73rd St
500-1999 68114
2301-2497 68134
7301-7399 68122
S 73rd St
200-298 68114
2101-2397 68124
5300-6198 68127
N 73rd Plaza Cir 68122
S 73rd Street Cir 68127
S 73rd Terrace Cir 68127
N 74th Ave 68114
N 74th Cir
750-799 68114
7000-7099 68122
N 74th Plz 68122
S 74th Plz
800-1098 68114
1400-1498 68124
N 74th St
500-1900 68114
7200-13249 68122
S 74th St
200-298 68114
1700-1798 68124
6200-6399 68127
N 74th Ter 68122
N 75th Ave
1500-1899 68114
2900-3099 68134
8800-8999 68122
S 75th Ave 68127
S 75th Cir 68127
S 75th Plz
1401-1499 68124
5000-5099 68127
N 75th St
500-1699 68114
2000-2098 68134
6500-6800 68122
S 75th St
600-999 68114
1201-1297 68124
5100-6698 68127
S 75th Avenue Cir 68127
N 76th Ave 68122
S 76th Ave
1100-1364 68124
6100-6199 68127
N 76th Cir
5500-6199 68134
7000-7099 68122
S 76th Cir 68127
N 76th Plz 68122
S 76th Plz 68127
N 76th St
101-297 68114
2901-2997 68134
7100-7399 68122
6426 1/2-6448 1/2 68134
S 76th St
600-898 68114
1300-1599 68124
5200-5398 68127
N 77th Ave
500-1032 68114
7350-8899 68122
S 77th Ave
3201-3247 68124
4700-5199 68127
N 77th Cir
501-527 68114
3100-3199 68134
S 77th Cir 68127
N 77th St
805-1099 68114
3600-6499 68134
6500-7399 68122
S 77th St
100-298 68114
3201-3247 68124
5200-6799 68127
N 77th Ter 68122
S 77th Avenue Ct 68127
N 78th Ave 68134
N 78th Ave 68134
6501-6799 68122
1300-1399 68124
4700-4999 68127
N 78th Ct 68122
N 78th St
101-197 68114
199-1899 68114
2510-2518 68134
2520-6101 68134
6103-6435 68134
6501-7397 68122
7399-14799 68122
301-397 68114
399-1099 68114
1300-1598 68124
1600-3799 68124
4720-4726 68127
4728-6100 68127
6102-6898 68127
N 78th Ter
6104-6134 68134
6600-6799 68122
N 78th Avenue Cir 68122
N 79th Ave 68134
8901-8951 68122
S 79th Ave
1600-1699 68124
4700-5199 68127
N 79th Cir 68134
S 79th Cir 68127
N 79th Ct 68122
N 79th Plz 68122
N 79th St
2300-6499 68134
6601-8797 68122
S 79th St
1100-3499 68124
4500-5600 68127
N 80th Ave
4600-4899 68134
7700-7799 68122
S 80th Ave 68124
N 80th Cir 68134
N 80th St
200-299 68114
2900-6300 68134
7100-7799 68122
S 80th St
600-900 68114
1100-3299 68124
4100-5599 68127
N 80th Avenue Cir 68134
N 81st Ave 68134
N 81st Ave 68134
8501-8597 68122
S 81st Ave 68124
N 81st Ct 68134
N 81st Plz 68122
N 81st St
1800-1906 68114
2021-2297 68134
6500-6598 68122
S 81st St 68127
N 81st Avenue Cir 68134
N 82nd Ave 68122

S 82nd Ave ... 68124
N 82nd Cir
4100-4199 ... 68134
7500-7599 ... 68122
N 82nd Plz
701-797 ... 68114
7100-7199 ... 68122
S 82nd Plz ... 68124
N 82nd St
3400-5800 ... 68134
8629-8797 ... 68122
S 82nd St
400-499 ... 68114
3300-3700 ... 68124
4700-4998 ... 68127
N 83rd Ave ... 68122
S 83rd Ave ... 68127
S 83rd Plz ... 68124
N 83rd St
600-650 ... 68114
2000-5599 ... 68134
7700-8999 ... 68122
S 83rd St
401-499 ... 68114
1300-1599 ... 68124
4700-5299 ... 68127
S 83rd Ter ... 68127
N 83rd Avenue Cir ... 68134
N 84th Ave
1600-1799 ... 68114
5200-5299 ... 68134
S 84th Ave ... 68127
N 84th Cir ... 68134
S 84th Ct ... 68127
N 84th St
101-1497 ... 68114
2001-2197 ... 68134
7800-10098 ... 68122
S 84th St
100-398 ... 68114
1100-3699 ... 68124
4000-6599 ... 68127
N 84th Ter ... 68114
N 85th Ave
501-599 ... 68114
3700-3900 ... 68134
S 85th Ave
301-399 ... 68114
1400-2299 ... 68124
6600-6699 ... 68127
N 85th Cir ... 68134
S 85th Cir ... 68127
N 85th St
400-498 ... 68114
2500-5299 ... 68134
7100-7298 ... 68122
S 85th St
100-198 ... 68114
4600-6699 ... 68127
N 86th Ave ... 68122
S 86th Ave ... 68124
N 86th Cir ... 68134
S 86th Cir
1700-1800 ... 68124
5600-5899 ... 68127
S 86th Ct ... 68127
S 86th Pkwy ... 68127
S 86th Plz ... 68127
N 86th St
500-799 ... 68114
3701-4497 ... 68134
S 86th St
200-999 ... 68114
2200-2299 ... 68124
4900-6602 ... 68127
S 86th Avenue Cir ... 68127
N 87th Ave ... 68134
N 87th Ave ... 68134
6900-7099 ... 68122
S 87th Ave
900-999 ... 68114
2000-3799 ... 68124
N 87th Cir ... 68134
S 87th Cir ... 68114
S 87th Plz ... 68127
N 87th St
100-1900 ... 68114
3900-4206 ... 68134
7001-7297 ... 68122
S 87th St
100-199 ... 68114
1101-1697 ... 68124
4100-6799 ... 68127
N 87th Ter ... 68134
N 88th Ave
800-899 ... 68114
3801-3899 ... 68134
6900-7099 ... 68122
N 88th Cir ... 68134
N 88th Plz
500-799 ... 68114
3200-4399 ... 68134
S 88th Plz ... 68127
N 88th St
1101-1197 ... 68114
2000-2899 ... 68134
6900-7499 ... 68122
S 88th St
100-999 ... 68114
1400-1698 ... 68124
4500-6799 ... 68127
N 89th Ave ... 68122
N 89th Cir
800-911 ... 68114
6000-6199 ... 68134
S 89th Cir ... 68127
N 89th Ct ... 68122
S 89th Ct
300-399 ... 68114
2200-2399 ... 68124
N 89th Plz ... 68114
N 89th St
200-1198 ... 68114
6900-7599 ... 68122
S 89th St
100-999 ... 68114
3300-3699 ... 68124
4100-5100 ... 68127
N 90th Ave ... 68114
S 90th Ave ... 68124
N 90th Plz
2200-2298 ... 68134
6600-6699 ... 68122
N 90th St
200-1999 ... 68114
2001-2217 ... 68134
6900-7399 ... 68122
S 90th St
100-1099 ... 68114
1100-3599 ... 68124
4100-4999 ... 68127
N 91st Ave
1400-1499 ... 68114
5200-5300 ... 68134
S 91st Ave
500-798 ... 68114
1100-1799 ... 68124
5600-6799 ... 68127
N 91st Cir
1700-1799 ... 68114
6401-6403 ... 68134
S 91st Cir
400-1099 ... 68114
6505-6512 ... 68127
N 91st Ct ... 68134
N 91st Plz
701-709 ... 68114
2200-2300 ... 68134
6500-6898 ... 68122
N 91st St
307-321 ... 68114
3700-3898 ... 68134
7300-7399 ... 68122
S 91st St
1800-3799 ... 68124
4900-6799 ... 68127
S 91st Avenue Cir ... 68127
N 92nd Ave ... 68134
N 92nd Ave ... 68134
N 92nd Ave ... 68134
6800-7598 ... 68122
S 92nd Ave
800-898 ... 68114
4701-4797 ... 68127
N 92nd Cir ... 68134
S 92nd Cir
1100-1199 ... 68124
5800-6699 ... 68127
N 92nd Ct
701-799 ... 68114
2301-5813 ... 68134
N 92nd Plz ... 68114
S 92nd Plz
2500-2598 ... 68124
5604-5699 ... 68127
N 92nd St
101-107 ... 68114
5600-5999 ... 68134
6700-6799 ... 68122
S 92nd St
100-1099 ... 68114
1300-3799 ... 68124
5000-6599 ... 68127
S 92nd Avenue Cir ... 68127
N 93rd Ave ... 68134
S 93rd Ave
100-699 ... 68114
1100-3199 ... 68124
4800-4999 ... 68127
S 93rd Cir ... 68127
N 93rd Ct
1700-1899 ... 68114
2400-2598 ... 68134
S 93rd Ct ... 68114
S 93rd Plz ... 68124
N 93rd St
100-1826 ... 68114
2600-5899 ... 68134
S 93rd St
100-899 ... 68114
1100-1850 ... 68124
5005-6799 ... 68127
N 94th Ave ... 68134
S 94th Ave
501-597 ... 68114
3400-3699 ... 68124
5000-5199 ... 68127
S 94th Cir
3700-3799 ... 68124
6100-6799 ... 68127
N 94th Ct ... 68114
S 94th Ct ... 68127
N 94th Plz
800-1899 ... 68114
2401-2599 ... 68134
6900-6999 ... 68122
S 94th Plz ... 68127
N 94th St
319-1699 ... 68114
2000-4699 ... 68134
15200-15298 ... 68122
S 94th St
200-999 ... 68114
1100-3699 ... 68124
4100-6399 ... 68127
N 95th Ave ... 68114
S 95th Ave ... 68127
N 95th Cir ... 68134
S 95th Cir
2500-3399 ... 68124
4900-5099 ... 68127
S 95th Ct ... 68127
N 95th Plz ... 68114
S 95th Plz ... 68127
N 95th St
1200-1399 ... 68114
3000-4899 ... 68134
S 95th St
200-999 ... 68114
1100-3799 ... 68124
6000-6499 ... 68127
S 95th Ter ... 68127
N 96th Ave
1400-1499 ... 68114
2000-2099 ... 68134
S 96th Cir ... 68124
S 96th Ct ... 68127
N 96th Dr ... 68134
S 96th Plz ... 68127
N 96th St
200-298 ... 68114
2600-5699 ... 68134
7400-8098 ... 68122
S 96th St
100-198 ... 68114
1100-3799 ... 68124
4000-5700 ... 68127
S 96th Avenue Cir ... 68124
N 97th Ave ... 68134
S 97th Ave ... 68124
N 97th Cir
1300-1313 ... 68114
6900-7099 ... 68122
S 97th Cir ... 68124
N 97th Ct
200-500 ... 68114
7400-7424 ... 68122
S 97th Ct ... 68127
N 97th Plz
1200-1399 ... 68114
7426-7598 ... 68122
S 97th Plz ... 68127
N 97th St
2001-2497 ... 68134
6701-6899 ... 68122
S 97th St
1100-3799 ... 68124
4800-4899 ... 68127
N 98th Ave ... 68134
S 98th Ave ... 68124
N 98th Ct ... 68114
S 98th Ct ... 68127
S 98th Plz ... 68127
N 98th St
515-597 ... 68114
2600-2799 ... 68134
7601-7699 ... 68122
S 98th St
1100-3399 ... 68124
4900-5124 ... 68127
S 98th Avenue Cir ... 68127
S 99th Ave ... 68124
N 99th Cir
1100-1199 ... 68114
3800-3899 ... 68134
S 99th Cir
1106-1131 ... 68124
4700-4742 ... 68127
S 99th Ct ... 68127
N 99th Plz ... 68134
S 99th Plz ... 68127
N 99th St
2000-6100 ... 68134
6600-6698 ... 68122
S 99th St
1204-1598 ... 68124
4901-4997 ... 68127
N 100th Ave ... 68134
S 100th Ave ... 68124
N 100th Cir ... 68114
S 100th Cir ... 68124
N 100th Ct ... 68134
N 100th Plz ... 68134
S 100th Plz ... 68127
N 100th St
1800-1999 ... 68114
2000-4499 ... 68134
S 100th St
2401-2497 ... 68124
6200-6599 ... 68127
S 101st Ave ... 68124
N 101st Cir
1200-1299 ... 68114
2000-2199 ... 68134
S 101st Cir ... 68127
N 101st Plz
6101-6199 ... 68134
7600-7999 ... 68122
S 101st Plz ... 68127
N 101st St
1800-1999 ... 68114
3000-3298 ... 68134
7401-7499 ... 68122
S 101st St ... 68124
N 102nd Ave
1400-1799 ... 68114
2600-6499 ... 68134
6500-6799 ... 68122
S 102nd Ave ... 68127
N 102nd Avenue Cir ... 68122
6900-7000 ... 68122
S 102nd Cir ... 68127
N 102nd Ct ... 68114
N 102nd Plz ... 68134
N 102nd St
700-1999 ... 68114
2000-2298 ... 68134
6012-6012 ... 68164
6015-6099 ... 68134
9100-9598 ... 68122
S 102nd St
2300-3699 ... 68124
4200-6599 ... 68127
S 102nd Ter ... 68127
N 103rd Ave
1701-1797 ... 68114
4900-6399 ... 68134
6501-6599 ... 68122
N 103rd Cir ... 68134
S 103rd Cir ... 68127
N 103rd Ct ... 68134
N 103rd Plz
1120-1122 ... 68114
3301-3997 ... 68134
N 103rd St ... 68134
S 103rd St
1101-1197 ... 68124
6200-6399 ... 68127
N 104th Ave ... 68134
S 104th Ave
3000-3399 ... 68124
5300-5398 ... 68127
N 104th Cir ... 68134
S 104th Avenue Cir ... 68127
5505-5518 ... 68127
N 104th Ct ... 68134
N 104th Plz
1400-1599 ... 68114
3930-3998 ... 68134
N 104th St
4900-6499 ... 68134
6500-6798 ... 68122
S 104th St
2901-2997 ... 68124
5000-5098 ... 68127
N 105th Ave ... 68134
6500-6799 ... 68122
S 105th Ave ... 68124
S 105th Cir ... 68127
N 105th Plz ... 68134
N 105th St
900-1725 ... 68114
3701-3927 ... 68134
6500-6698 ... 68122
S 105th St
1100-1698 ... 68124
5000-5899 ... 68127
N 106th Ave ... 68122
1500-1598 ... 68124
5001-5053 ... 68127
5055-5084 ... 68127
5086-5098 ... 68127
N 106th Cir
6000-6099 ... 68134
6800-6899 ... 68122
S 106th Cir ... 68127
N 106th Ct
1300-1398 ... 68114
7100-7199 ... 68122
N 106th Plz
3301-3697 ... 68134
3699-5699 ... 68134
7000-7100 ... 68122
7102-7198 ... 68122
S 106th Plz ... 68114
N 106th St
1511-1515 ... 68114
1517-1730 ... 68114
4900-6499 ... 68134
6500-7799 ... 68122
1500-3699 ... 68124
5001-5053 ... 68127
5055-6299 ... 68127
N 107th Ave
800-1724 ... 68114
7300-7899 ... 68122
S 107th Ave
900-999 ... 68114
2701-2797 ... 68124
4809-4817 ... 68127
N 107th Plaza Cir ... 68122
S 107th Avenue Cir ... 68124
6625-6699 ... 68127
N 107th Ct
6300-6499 ... 68134
6900-7199 ... 68122
N 107th Plz
3500-5499 ... 68134
6501-7299 ... 68122
N 107th St
1500-1502 ... 68114
3301-4697 ... 68134
7300-7530 ... 68122
S 107th St
1200-3699 ... 68124
4800-6625 ... 68127
N 108th Ave ... 68164
N 108th Ave ... 68154
N 108th Ave ... 68154
N 108th Ave ... 68154
7301-7599 ... 68142
S 108th Ave
101-197 ... 68154
199-200 ... 68154
202-498 ... 68154
6300-6700 ... 68137
6702-6898 ... 68137
N 108th Avenue Cir ... 68164
601-709 ... 68154
4700-4799 ... 68164
N 108th Ct
600-698 ... 68154
711-799 ... 68154
6900-6902 ... 68142
6904-7299 ... 68142
S 108th Ct
6600-6899 ... 68137
N 108th Plz
1100-1198 ... 68154
3700-3998 ... 68164
7000-7299 ... 68142
N 108th St
800-1324 ... 68154
1326-1798 ... 68154
2201-2725 ... 68164
2727-5299 ... 68164
5301-5499 ... 68164
7300-14499 ... 68142
14501-14699 ... 68142
S 108th St
1200-3800 ... 68144
3802-3898 ... 68144
4000-5799 ... 68137
S 108th Ter
6505-6799 ... 68137
N 109th Ave ... 68142
N 109th Cir
4700-6399 ... 68164
N 109th Avenue Cir
5200-5299 ... 68164
S 109th Cir
3400-3499 ... 68144
5900-5999 ... 68137
S 109th Avenue Cir
6014-6220 ... 68137
N 109th Ct
600-748 ... 68154
2515-2597 ... 68164
7100-7198 ... 68142
S 109th Ct
900-999 ... 68154
5400-5499 ... 68137
N 109th Plz
601-617 ... 68154
2501-2507 ... 68164
6900-6999 ... 68142
N 109th St ... 68164
S 109th St
1200-3349 ... 68144
6000-6899 ... 68137
N 109th Ter ... 68164
N 110th Ave
1700-1899 ... 68154
6500-6799 ... 68164
7400-7598 ... 68142
N 110th Avenue Cir ... 68164
5000-6099 ... 68164
S 110th Cir ... 68137
N 110th Ct
2500-2899 ... 68164
7100-7299 ... 68142
S 110th Ct ... 68144
N 110th Plz
1200-1399 ... 68154
3900-3999 ... 68164
7000-7099 ... 68142
S 110th Plz
900-1000 ... 68154
5400-5499 ... 68137
N 110th St
1700-1899 ... 68154
6500-6698 ... 68164
S 110th St
100-299 ... 68154
1200-2300 ... 68144
4400-6699 ... 68137
N 111th Ave ... 68142
N 111th Cir ... 68164
S 111th Cir ... 68144
N 111th Plz
1201-1399 ... 68154
3100-3698 ... 68164
7100-7299 ... 68142
S 111th Plz
900-1098 ... 68154
5301-5325 ... 68137
N 111th St
1600-1842 ... 68154
2200-5498 ... 68164
7400-7599 ... 68142
S 111th St
100-499 ... 68154
1901-3199 ... 68144
5055-5057 ... 68137
N 112th Ave
2600-6699 ... 68164
7300-7399 ... 68142
N 112th Cir ... 68164
N 112th Ct
1300-1313 ... 68154
7100-7299 ... 68142
N 112th Plz
1304-1498 ... 68154
3101-3199 ... 68164
7000-7299 ... 68142
S 112th Plz
800-1099 ... 68154
1100-1299 ... 68144
5300-5498 ... 68137
N 112th St ... 68164
S 112th St
1900-2898 ... 68144
5600-5899 ... 68137
S 113th Ave
600-699 ... 68154
1901-1905 ... 68144
N 113th Cir ... 68164
S 113th Avenue Cir ... 68154
N 113th Ct
1200-1314 ... 68154
3601-3699 ... 68164
7000-7048 ... 68142
S 113th Ct ... 68144
N 113th Plz
1201-1397 ... 68154
3500-3799 ... 68164
7000-7199 ... 68142
S 113th Plz
1108-1647 ... 68144
5201-5299 ... 68137
N 113th St ... 68164
S 113th St
700-1099 ... 68154
1701-1797 ... 68144
5600-5899 ... 68137
N 114th Ave ... 68164
S 114th Ave ... 68144

N 114th Avenue Cir 68164
3700-3799 68164
N 114th St
101-197 68154
4800-6299 68164
7000-7198 68142
S 114th St
101-497 68154
1100-1498 68144
4800-5899 68137
S 115th Ave 68144
N 115th Avenue Cir 68164
5700-6399 68164
S 115th Cir 68137
N 115th Ct 68164
N 115th Plz
1800-1899 68154
2700-2798 68164
N 115th St
200-1100 68154
4800-4998 68164
7000-7098 68142
S 115th St
2100-3599 68144
4801-6097 68137
N 116th Ave 68164
S 116th Ave 68144
N 116th Cir
4000-6830 68164
5600-5699 68164
7400-7499 68142
S 116th Avenue Cir 68144
N 116th Ct
200-298 68154
5200-5299 68164
N 116th St
600-799 68154
4800-5199 68164
7500-7599 68142
S 116th St
400-599 68154
1700-3799 68144
5301-5997 68137
N 117th Ave
200-299 68154
2000-2098 68164
7100-7499 68142
S 117th Ave 68154
N 117th Avenue Cir 68164
4900-6699 68164
7500-7599 68142
S 117th Cir
1000-1099 68154
2200-2299 68144
N 117th Ct
350-452 68154
5300-5499 68164
S 117th Ct 68154
S 117th Plz 68154
N 117th St
100-349 68154
3901-3997 68164
8901-9099 68142
S 117th St
100-200 68154
1200-3799 68144
6500-6799 68137
N 118th Ave 68164
N 118th Cir
2717-2717 68164
6900-7499 68142
S 118th Cir 68137
S 118th Ct 68144
N 118th Plz 68154
S 118th Plz
800-949 68154
2400-2498 68144
5600-6499 68137
N 118th St
200-299 68154
2701-2709 68164
S 118th St
200-599 68154
1100-3799 68144
4800-6899 68137
N 119th Ave
6600-6700 68164
6900-6998 68142
S 119th Cir
200-299 68154
4400-4599 68137
S 119th Ct
900-999 68154
1216-2329 68144
N 119th Plz 68154
S 119th Plz
900-948 68154
2300-2328 68144
5700-5999 68137
N 119th St 68154
S 119th St
400-599 68154
1101-1197 68144
N 120th Ave 68164
S 120th Ave 68154
N 120th Avenue Cir 68164
N 120th Ct 68164
N 120th Plz 68154
S 120th Plz
1200-1224 68144
6200-6499 68137
N 120th St
500-704 68154
2001-3301 68164
7501-7597 68142
S 120th St
1000-1098 68154
1101-1223 68144
4001-4399 68137
N 121st Ave 68164
S 121st Ave 68144
N 121st Cir 68164
S 121st Ct 68137
N 121st Plz 68164
S 121st Plz
1201-1297 68144
4101-4197 68137
N 121st St
800-1799 68154
2100-2599 68164
7000-7200 68142
S 121st St
100-899 68154
1500-3699 68144
4850-5199 68137
N 122nd Ave 68142
S 122nd Ave
1850-3199 68144
5300-5308 68137
N 122nd Avenue Cir 68142
2100-3399 68164
N 122nd Ct
800-899 68154
6801-6897 68142
S 122nd Ct 68137
N 122nd Plz 68154
S 122nd Plz 68144
N 122nd St 68154
S 122nd St
100-899 68154
1500-3599 68144
5100-5699 68137
S 123rd Ave 68144
N 123rd Cir
1200-1299 68154
2600-2799 68164
8300-8399 68142
S 123rd Avenue Cir 68144
1000-1099 68154
N 123rd Ct 68154
S 123rd Ct 68144
N 123rd Plz 68154
N 123rd St
1400-1599 68154
7901-8197 68142
S 123rd St
100-899 68154
1430-3699 68144
5400-5799 68137
N 124th Ave 68164
S 124th Ave
600-699 68154
5100-5199 68137

N 124th Avenue Cir 68164
2000-2799 68164
7200-7216 68142
S 124th Cir 68154
N 124th Ct 68154
N 124th Plz 68154
N 124th St
801-899 68154
3100-3400 68164
7300-8199 68142
S 124th St
600-899 68154
1101-1197 68144
4900-5699 68137
N 125th Ave 68164
S 125th Ave 68144
N 125th Avenue Cir 68164
2100-2799 68164
S 125th Cir 68137
S 125th Ct 68137
N 125th St
3000-3098 68164
3100-3399 68164
7200-7399 68142
S 125th St 68144
N 126th Ave 68164
7101-7499 68142
S 126th Ave
100-199 68154
3200-3799 68144
N 126th Avenue Cir 68164
2700-2799 68164
S 126th Cir
100-199 68154
5600-5699 68137
N 126th Ct 68164
S 126th Ct 68137
N 126th Plz 68164
S 126th Plz
2801-2997 68144
5100-5120 68137
N 126th St
1200-1899 68154
2100-3098 68164
10901-11097 68142
S 126th St
400-699 68154
1101-1197 68144
4800-4899 68137
8901-8999 68138
N 127th Ave 68154
7700-8299 68142
S 127th Ave 68144
N 127th Avenue Cir 68164
1000-1699 68154
2200-2299 68164
S 127th Cir 68144
N 127th Ct 68164
S 127th Ct 68144
N 127th Plz
111-117 68154
4000-4200 68164
S 127th Plz 68154
N 127th St
510-1698 68154
2600-2698 68164
S 127th St
300-799 68154
1400-1498 68144
S 128th Ave 68144
N 128th Avenue Cir 68154
1200-1699 68154
2200-3499 68164
S 128th Cir 68144
N 128th Ct 68164
N 128th Plz
101-299 68154
4101-4297 68164
S 128th Plz 68154
N 128th St
1000-1099 68154
3100-6399 68164
S 128th St
4900-5099 68137
7000-7298 68138
N 129th Ave 68164

N 129th Ave 68164
8050-8052 68142
S 129th Ave
700-835 68154
2700-2798 68144
N 129th Cir
1000-1899 68154
N 129th Avenue Cir
1300-1799 68154
2501-2597 68164
N 129th Avenue Cir
4200-5299 68164
S 129th Avenue Cir 68154
N 129th Ct 68154
N 129th Plz 68154
N 129th St
100-198 68154
2100-6299 68164
S 129th St
101-1499 68154
1400-3298 68144
4700-6799 68137
7000-7099 68138
N 130th Ave 68164
S 130th Ave 68144
N 130th Avenue Cir
1700-1799 68154
1800-1899 68154
3300-5299 68164
N 130th Avenue Cir
4600-4699 68164
S 130th Cir
2400-3299 68144
S 130th Avenue Cir
3200-3399 68144
5050-5099 68137
N 130th Plz 68154
S 130th Plz 68137
N 130th St
100-108 68154
2500-5799 68164
7500-7599 68142
S 130th St
100-999 68154
1800-3599 68144
4700-5049 68137
7000-7300 68138
N 131st Ave
1200-1699 68154
6200-6299 68164
S 131st Ave
800-1099 68154
1800-1999 68144
7000-7099 68138
N 131st Avenue Cir 68154
1300-1799 68154
2500-3399 68164
S 131st Cir
3200-3280 68144
6300-6399 68137
7000-7099 68138
N 131st Ct 68154
N 131st Plz 68154
S 131st Plz 68138
N 131st St
1200-1299 68154
2100-6499 68164
S 131st St
800-1099 68154
4700-5099 68137
N 132nd Ave
800-1521 68154
2500-2699 68164
S 132nd Ave
4850-4856 68137
7000-7299 68138
N 132nd Avenue Cir 68154
S 132nd Ct 68144
N 132nd St
101-799 68154
3401-3897 68164
9200-10398 68142
S 132nd St
107-335 68154
2201-2397 68144
4001-4497 68137
7900-11699 68138

S 133rd Ave 68144
N 133rd Cir 68164
S 133rd Avenue Cir 68144
7000-7099 68138
S 133rd Ct 68137
N 133rd Plz 68164
S 133rd Plz 68144
N 133rd St
800-1599 68154
2400-2599 68164
S 133rd St
1300-3399 68144
4101-4197 68137
4433-4433 68145
4501-5099 68137
7700-7999 68138
N 134th Ave 68164
S 134th Ave 68144
N 134th Cir
1400-1499 68154
3300-3399 68164
S 134th Cir 68138
N 134th St 68164
S 134th St
1300-3499 68144
4400-4899 68137
7300-7498 68138
N 135th Ave 68164
S 135th Ave
1800-2499 68144
5800-5808 68137
7500-7506 68138
S 135th Cir
2270-3599 68144
5811-5899 68137
S 135th Ct 68138
N 135th St
1401-1899 68154
2100-3198 68164
S 135th St
2800-2999 68144
4700-6699 68137
7503-7505 68138
S 135th Ter 68137
N 136th Ave
1200-1399 68154
4800-4999 68164
S 136th Ave 68137
S 136th Cir 68137
N 136th St
1215-1699 68154
2000-4198 68164
S 136th St
1300-3499 68144
4601-4697 68137
5346-5346 68139
5501-6699 68137
7000-7398 68138
N 137th Ave 68164
S 137th Ave
1200-1399 68144
7100-7699 68138
S 137th Cir
5936-6498 68137
8300-8598 68138
S 137th Ct 68137
S 137th Plz 68137
N 137th St
1600-1699 68154
2001-2497 68164
S 137th St
2800-3399 68144
4800-6500 68137
N 138th Ave 68142
S 138th Ave
5600-5699 68137
8700-8799 68138
N 138th Cir
800-1231 68154
4100-4199 68164
7100-7199 68142
2000-2099 68144
7100-7199 68138
N 138th St
1233-1297 68154
2200-2498 68164
8901-10097 68142

S 138th St
1200-3799 68144
4100-5198 68137
7500-8799 68138
N 139th Ave 68164
S 139th Ave 68138
S 139th Avenue Cir 68137
2000-2499 68144
5605-6539 68137
7000-8699 68138
S 139th Ct 68144
S 139th Plz 68137
N 139th St
800-1399 68154
2301-4097 68164
S 139th St
1100-1298 68144
4300-5700 68137
7400-8799 68138
N 140th Ave 68164
S 140th Ave
2519-2599 68144
5600-6899 68137
7000-7499 68138
N 140th Cir 68164
S 140th Avenue Cir 68144
2400-2498 68144
6355-6371 68137
S 140th Plz 68144
N 140th St
1701-1899 68154
2200-2398 68164
S 140th St
2500-2508 68144
4100-4398 68137
7000-9899 68138
N 141st Ave
1200-1599 68154
2001-2097 68164
N 141st Cir
4400-5699 68164
6900-6998 68142
S 141st Avenue Cir 68144
1505-2100 68144
S 141st Ct 68144
S 141st Plz
2200-2298 68144
5700-5798 68137
N 141st St 68164
S 141st St
6200-6299 68137
7100-7299 68138
N 142nd Ave 68164
7000-7398 68142
S 142nd Ave 68138
N 142nd Cir
1400-1499 68154
2200-6599 68164
S 142nd Avenue Cir 68138
1500-1599 68144
S 142nd Ct 68144
S 142nd Plz 68144
N 142nd St
900-998 68154
2301-2397 68164
7001-7599 68142
S 142nd St
4900-6899 68137
7000-9899 68138
N 143rd Ave
1400-1420 68154
2100-2799 68164
S 143rd Ave 68138
N 143rd Cir
904-1599 68154
910-1499 68154
2200-4249 68164
N 143rd Avenue Cir
7500-7599 68142
S 143rd Cir
4100-4199 68137
8900-8999 68138
N 143rd Ct 68154
S 143rd Ct 68144
N 143rd Plz 68154
S 143rd Plz
2200-2400 68144

6800-6898 68137
N 143rd St
1200-1315 68154
2300-2398 68164
7201-7297 68142
S 143rd St
1308-2099 68144
4201-4497 68137
8400-8899 68138
N 144th Ave
601-1699 68154
2100-5167 68116
S 144th Ave 68144
N 144th Avenue Cir 68154
N 144th Ct 68116
N 144th Plz 68116
N 144th St
902-1998 68154
2907-3797 68116
S 144th St
101-199 68154
2323-2597 68144
4026-4098 68137
7021-9897 68138
N 144th Ter 68116
N 145th Ave 68116
S 145th Ave 68144
N 145th Avenue Cir 68154
900-1099 68154
4600-4699 68116
S 145th Cir
2100-2199 68144
4900-4999 68137
N 145th Plz
1200-1499 68154
4101-4197 68116
S 145th Plz 68137
N 145th St
1500-1899 68154
2300-2398 68116
S 145th St
3000-3199 68144
4351-4497 68137
7000-9599 68138
N 146th Ave 68116
N 146th Cir 68154
S 146th Cir
2000-2299 68144
4900-4999 68137
N 146th Ct 68116
N 146th Plz
1200-1499 68154
4162-4298 68116
N 146th St
1500-1899 68154
2900-6199 68116
S 146th St
2800-3099 68144
4350-4350 68137
7000-11499 68138
N 147th Ave
600-699 68154
6000-6004 68116
N 147th Avenue Cir
700-799 68154
3100-3199 68116
N 147th Avenue Cir
4300-4314 68116
S 147th Cir
1849-3049 68144
5100-5199 68137
N 147th Ct 68116
S 147th Ct 68137
N 147th Plz
1200-1499 68154
4150-4598 68116
S 147th Plz 68137
N 147th St
600-699 68154
2301-2397 68116
S 147th St
2200-3999 68144
4000-4348 68137
7301-7497 68138
N 148th Ave 68154
S 148th Ave 68144
N 148th Cir 68116

S 148th Avenue Cir 68144
5100-6799 68137
N 148th Ct 68116
S 148th Ct 68137
N 148th Plz
1300-1799 68154
5701-5899 68116
S 148th Plz 68137
N 148th St
600-999 68154
2400-6799 68116
S 148th St
2500-2999 68144
4000-4699 68137
6901-7197 68138
N 149th Ave 68154
N 149th Ave 68154
5400-6398 68116
S 149th Ave 68137
N 149th Cir
4700-4799 68116
N 149th Avenue Cir
4700-5599 68116
S 149th Cir
1900-2099 68144
4000-4098 68137
S 149th Avenue Cir
4300-4399 68137
7200-7299 68138
N 149th Ct 68154
S 149th Ct 68137
N 149th St
801-999 68154
2300-6699 68116
S 149th St
3600-3700 68144
4200-6500 68137
10700-10799 68138
S 149th Ter 68137
N 150th Ave 68116
S 150th Ave
4251-4267 68137
11201-11399 68138
S 150th Cir 68154
N 150th Ct 68154
N 150th Plz 68154
S 150th Plz
3800-3999 68144
4000-4000 68137
N 150th St
533-847 68154
2400-6799 68116
S 150th St
600-974 68154
4200-4298 68137
7200-11300 68138
N 151st Ave 68116
S 151st Ave
6100-6102 68137
7900-8299 68138
N 151st Cir
600-699 68154
2100-2211 68116
3500-5400 68116
S 151st Cir
300-999 68154
4200-4299 68137
5900-5924 68137
7800-7899 68138
7900-7917 68138
N 151st Plz 68154
S 151st Plz
3900-3999 68144
4000-4099 68137
N 151st St 68116
S 151st St
1800-2499 68144
4300-6699 68137
6901-7097 68138
N 152nd Ave
700-723 68154
2900-5199 68116
S 152nd Ave
5800-5924 68137
8100-8299 68138
N 152nd Avenue Cir
501-557 68154
600-699 68154
2100-4099 68116
S 152nd Cir
400-999 68154
1500-3313 68144
1505-3399 68144
4300-4699 68137
5705-5731 68137
N 152nd Plz 68154
S 152nd Plz
3900-3999 68144
4004-4010 68137
N 152nd St
300-322 68154
2200-6299 68116
S 152nd St
101-297 68154
1600-3800 68144
5500-6200 68137
6901-7997 68138
N 153rd Ave
700-1899 68154
2001-2197 68116
N 153rd Cir
200-1499 68154
N 153rd Avenue Cir
300-1819 68154
2900-4599 68116
S 153rd Cir
400-799 68154
S 153rd Avenue Cir
1700-1799 68144
2500-3999 68144
4350-6799 68137
6900-6999 68138
N 153rd Ct 68116
S 153rd Terrace Ct 68154
900-998 68154
4600-4712 68137
N 153rd Plz 68154
N 153rd St
500-1299 68154
3701-3997 68116
S 153rd St
900-1000 68154
1501-1597 68144
4200-4298 68137
8000-11499 68138
N 154th Ave 68154
2300-4399 68116
S 154th Ave 68138
N 154th Avenue Cir
1100-1199 68154
2900-4321 68116
S 154th Cir
1700-2599 68144
4400-4638 68137
S 154th Avenue Cir
4604-4698 68137
N 154th Ct 68116
S 154th Plz 68137
N 154th St
101-297 68154
2300-6299 68116
S 154th St
300-900 68154
1600-3799 68144
4300-6700 68137
6900-8899 68138
N 155th Ave
600-1899 68154
2900-6299 68116
S 155th Ave
200-399 68154
1715-1717 68144
7100-7306 68138
N 155th Avenue Cir 68116
300-399 68154
2314-2898 68116
S 155th Cir
1700-2599 68144
4600-4699 68137
7000-7099 68138
S 155th Ct 68137
N 155th Plz 68154
S 155th Plz 68137
N 155th St
650-799 68154
2200-6299 68116
S 155th St
400-599 68154
1100-3900 68144
4951-4997 68137
7109-7297 68138
N 156th Ave 68118
N 156th Ave 68118
3900-4099 68116
4101-4399 68116
800-999 68118
6100-6399 68135
7701-7897 68136
7899-7999 68136
N 156th Avenue Cir 68116
S 156th Avenue Cir
600-799 68118
S 156th Cir
2000-2098 68130
4950-6499 68135
7000-7019 68136
S 156th Ct
1300-1399 68130
5200-5298 68135
5300-5399 68135
N 156th St
1301-1399 68118
2001-2497 68116
2499-6099 68116
6101-6599 68116
2701-3599 68130
3700-3898 68130
5100-5198 68135
6601-6699 68135
6900-7000 68136
7002-10898 68136
N 157th Ave 68116
S 157th Ave 68136
N 157th Cir
608-799 68118
3700-6598 68116
N 157th Avenue Cir
6200-6299 68116
S 157th Cir
500-614 68118
S 157th Avenue Cir
550-699 68118
2900-2999 68130
4700-6099 68135
N 157th Ct 68116
S 157th Ct
1200-1322 68130
5255-5299 68135
S 157th Plz
1300-1330 68130
5201-5263 68135
N 157th St
100-1599 68118
2500-6599 68116
S 157th St
300-398 68118
1201-1247 68130
4800-6599 68135
6901-6901 68136
N 158th Ave
1200-1498 68118
1500-1599 68118
4100-5299 68116
S 158th Ave 68118
N 158th Plaza Cir 68116
2500-2599 68116
N 158th Avenue Cir
6200-6299 68116
S 158th Cir
303-423 68118
S 158th Avenue Cir
505-519 68118
1400-2999 68130
4800-5399 68135
S 158th Avenue Cir
7200-7299 68136
N 158th Ct 68116
N 158th Plz 68116
S 158th Plz 68130
N 158th St
600-799 68118
3800-6699 68116
S 158th St
506-699 68118
1500-3098 68130
5600-6399 68135
7100-8199 68136
N 159th Ave 68116
S 159th Ave
400-819 68118
5200-6699 68135
8101-8299 68136
N 159th Cir
200-819 68118
5100-6299 68116
N 159th Avenue Cir
6500-6599 68116
S 159th Cir
505-516 68118
2901-2941 68130
S 159th Avenue Cir
2905-3099 68130
5060-6099 68135
6901-6922 68136
N 159th Plz 68116
S 159th Plz 68130
N 159th St
600-1899 68118
2500-6800 68116
S 159th St
400-499 68118
3100-3399 68130
5600-6599 68135
6922-8599 68136
N 160th Ave
1300-1499 68118
2500-6599 68116
S 160th Ave
3000-3048 68130
8400-8599 68136
N 160th Avenue Cir
1200-1299 68118
5100-5199 68116
N 160th Avenue Cir
5400-5498 68116
S 160th Cir
2900-2999 68130
5050-5099 68135
S 160th Ct 68130
S 160th Plz 68130
N 160th St
201-297 68118
2000-2498 68116
S 160th St
300-398 68118
1800-2399 68130
4800-6299 68135
7100-8599 68136
N 161st Ave
200-299 68118
2600-2698 68116
S 161st Ave
200-299 68118
5401-5497 68135
8109-8299 68136
N 161st Cir
200-1299 68118
400-499 68118
3201-3299 68116
N 161st Avenue Cir
4200-5199 68116
S 161st Cir
509-599 68118
2100-3699 68130
4800-5099 68135
7000-7099 68136
S 161st Plz 68130
N 161st St
700-1499 68118
2200-5000 68116
S 161st St
400-499 68118
1500-3599 68130
5400-6399 68135
7101-7597 68136
N 161st Ter 68116
S 161st Ter 68136
N 162nd Ave
500-599 68118
2100-4899 68116
S 162nd Ave
1300-1499 68130
4400-6749 68135
6900-6998 68136
N 162nd Avenue Cir 68116
400-499 68118
S 162nd Terrace Cir 68135
1600-3499 68130
N 162nd Ct 68116
S 162nd Plz 68130
N 162nd St
200-298 68118
3300-4598 68116
S 162nd St
400-499 68118
1300-1500 68130
4800-5200 68135
7100-7598 68136
N 163rd Ave 68118
4200-4299 68116
1200-1499 68130
5000-6799 68135
8600-9800 68136
9802-9998 68136
N 163rd Cir
1200-1399 68118
4000-4999 68116
1800-3899 68130
6000-6099 68135
6900-6930 68136
N 163rd Plz 68116
S 163rd Plz 68130
N 163rd St
100-198 68118
200-699 68118
701-799 68118
2200-6599 68116
200-299 68118
1300-3599 68130
4400-6749 68135
6931-10199 68136
10201-10299 68136
S 164th Ave
1200-2499 68130
6200-6398 68135
6900-7014 68136
N 164th Cir
601-647 68118
2600-4099 68116
S 164th Cir
2200-2299 68130
6400-6818 68135
7600-7699 68136
N 164th St
600-646 68118
2100-5699 68116
S 164th St
901-999 68118
1250-1299 68130
5000-5799 68135
6900-10299 68136
N 165th Ave 68116
S 165th Ave
1200-3799 68130
6201-6397 68135
N 165th Cir 68116
S 165th Cir
1700-1799 68130
6704-6719 68135
N 165th St 68116
S 165th St
1200-2199 68130
4700-5999 68135
8000-8398 68136
N 166th Ave 68116
S 166th Ave 68135
S 166th Avenue Cir 68135
1700-2699 68130
4600-6499 68135
N 166th Ct 68116
N 166th Terrace Plz 68116
N 166th St 68116
S 166th St
100-600 68118
1101-1197 68130
4800-5999 68135
7301-7697 68136
N 167th Ave 68116
1400-1499 68130
4200-6599 68135
6900-6998 68136
7000-7099 68136
7101-8399 68136
N 167th Cir
2100-5748 68116
N 167th Avenue Cir
5700-5743 68116
S 167th Cir
100-149 68118
1700-2699 68130
S 167th Avenue Cir
1700-2699 68130
4850-4899 68135
S 167th Cir
5700-6199 68135
7100-7135 68136
N 167th Ct 68116
N 167th Terrace Plz 68116
N 167th Plz
301-399 68118
5900-6099 68116
S 167th Plz 68135
N 167th St 68116
150-299 68118
1200-3199 68130
4700-4712 68135
4714-6799 68135
6801-6899 68135
7000-10899 68136
N 168th Ave 68118
2201-2897 68116
2899-5099 68116
1200-1699 68130
4400-4499 68135
4501-4699 68135
7200-10899 68136
N 168th Cir
200-498 68118
N 168th Avenue Cir
4500-4599 68116
S 168th Avenue Cir 68136
N 168th Ct 68116
N 168th St
401-997 68118
999-1300 68118
1302-1998 68118
3001-5997 68116
5999-6099 68116
6101-6699 68116
2301-3497 68130
3499-3699 68130
4501-5397 68135
5399-6200 68135
6202-6798 68135
7700-10310 68136
10501-10799 68136
N 169th Ave 68116
S 169th Ave
1201-1497 68130
6700-6799 68135
S 169th Avenue Cir 68135
200-399 68118
1800-1899 68130
4300-5099 68135
N 169th Plz 68116
S 169th Plz 68130
N 169th St
800-898 68118
2100-5199 68116
S 169th St
1200-1220 68130
5400-5598 68135
7200-9299 68136
N 170th Ave
1201-1297 68118
2500-2699 68116
S 170th Ave 68135
N 170th Cir
1515-1599 68118
2800-2899 68116
S 170th Cir
1500-1599 68130
9901-10099 68136
S 170th Ct 68130
N 170th St
201-1797 68118
2101-2397 68116
S 170th St
1600-1699 68130
4850-4998 68135
7200-9399 68136
N 171st Ave
1600-1699 68118
2900-4299 68116
S 171st Ave
5000-5099 68135
9500-9699 68136
S 171st Cir
1600-1699 68130
5000-6699 68135
S 171st Ct 68130
N 171st St
1101-1597 68118
2400-4399 68116
S 171st St
2301-3399 68130
5500-6399 68135
7200-10099 68136
N 172nd Ave 68116
S 172nd Ave 68135
N 172nd Cir
1900-1999 68118
4300-4399 68116
S 172nd Cir
3200-3299 68130
9900-10200 68136
S 172nd Plz 68130
N 172nd St 68116
S 172nd St
1300-1499 68130
5000-6399 68135
7700-11100 68136
N 173rd Ave 68116
100-199 68118
5400-6599 68135
9500-9899 68136
N 173rd Avenue Cir 68116
N 173rd Cir
1900-1999 68118
4700-4799 68116
4000-4099 68130
5000-6699 68135
9900-10299 68136
S 173rd Ct
805-807 68118
809-903 68118
1700-1799 68130
S 173rd Plz
801-897 68118
899-999 68118
1001-1099 68118
1700-1799 68130
N 173rd St
1600-1899 68118
2401-2497 68116
2499-4399 68116
1400-3399 68130
4100-5999 68135
7000-11199 68136
N 174th Ave 68116
S 174th Ave 68135
N 174th Avenue Cir 68116
S 174th Cir 68130
S 174th Plz
501-599 68118
2501-2599 68130
N 174th St
300-1598 68118
2000-2098 68116
S 174th St
801-899 68118
1300-1499 68130
4100-6499 68135
7000-7400 68136
N 175th Ave 68116

S 175th Ave
1300-4099 68130
4200-4699 68135
N 175th Cir 68116
S 175th Avenue Cir 68135
551-599 68118
5085-5999 68135
9400-10299 68136
N 175th Ct
1700-1899 68118
3500-3530 68116
N 175th Plz
1600-1898 68118
3503-3545 68116
N 175th St
100-199 68118
2200-3098 68116
S 175th St
301-497 68118
1500-1799 68130
4200-6599 68135
S 175th Ter 68135
N 176th Ave 68116
S 176th Ave
3850-3899 68130
4401-4497 68135
6900-9899 68136
N 176th Avenue Cir 68116
1200-1299 68130
3800-4099 68130
4954-5099 68135
7403-10501 68136
N 176th Ct 68118
N 176th Plz
1700-1899 68118
3500-3598 68116
N 176th St 68116
S 176th St
1300-1899 68130
4200-6599 68135
6900-7008 68136
S 177th Ave
1400-1598 68130
7500-7599 68136
N 177th Cir 68118
S 177th Avenue Cir 68136
900-999 68118
1700-1799 68130
4900-4999 68135
N 177th Plz 68118
S 177th Plz 68130
N 177th St
1800-1898 68118
2300-5199 68116
S 177th St
1300-4099 68130
4600-4698 68135
6900-10399 68136
S 178th Ave
300-399 68118
7105-7117 68136
S 178th Avenue Cir 68136
7500-7599 68136
N 178th St 68116
S 178th St
500-1099 68118
1301-1499 68130
4200-6800 68135
7100-10099 68136
S 179th Ave
1500-1799 68130
10301-10497 68136
N 179th Plaza Cir 68118
S 179th Cir
400-499 68118
4110-4122 68135
10300-10313 68136
S 179th Ct
1020-1028 68118
2903-2919 68130
S 179th Plz 68130
N 179th St 68116
S 179th St
1600-2499 68130
4200-6599 68135
7200-7398 68136
S 179th Ter 68130
S 180th Ave 68136
S 180th Avenue Cir 68135
S 180th Plz 68130
S 180th St
1101-1309 68130
4100-5898 68135
8501-9797 68136
S 181st Cir 68130
S 181st Ct 68135
S 181st Plz
1100-1298 68130
1300-1499 68130
5000-5199 68135
S 181st St
1500-3999 68130
5800-6098 68135
6100-6249 68135
7001-7099 68136
S 182nd Ave 68135
S 182nd Avenue Cir 68130
1500-3699 68130
S 182nd Ct 68135
S 182nd St
3700-3900 68130
3902-3998 68130
6150-6199 68135
7300-7399 68136
S 183rd Ave
3801-3897 68130
3899-3999 68130
7000-7199 68136
7201-7299 68136
S 183rd Cir 68130
S 183rd St 68136
S 183rd Ter 68136
S 184th Ave
3200-3999 68130
6400-6599 68135
S 184th Cir 68130
S 184th Plz 68135
S 184th St
3900-3915 68130
3917-3999 68130
4100-6799 68135
S 184th Ter 68130
S 185th Ave
3200-3699 68130
6100-6799 68135
6801-6899 68135
S 185th Cir 68130
S 185th St
2000-3399 68130
3401-3499 68130
5200-5398 68135
5400-5899 68135
S 186th Ave
3700-3899 68130
4700-4798 68135
S 186th Cir 68130
S 186th Plz 68130
S 186th St
1800-3399 68130
6000-6199 68135
7400-7599 68136
S 187th Ave 68135
S 187th Avenue Cir 68135
1500-1699 68130
S 187th Plz 68130
S 187th St
3200-3999 68130
4200-4298 68135
4300-6099 68135
6101-6399 68135
S 188th Ave
3200-3499 68130
4900-6698 68135
6700-6799 68135
S 188th Plz 68130
S 188th St
3200-3399 68130
3401-3999 68130
5300-6799 68135
S 189th Ave
3800-3899 68130
6100-6198 68135
S 189th Avenue Cir 68130
2000-2224 68130
4850-4899 68135
S 189th Ct 68135
S 189th St
1533-1997 68130
4500-6200 68135
7201-7397 68136
S 190th Ave
4901-5099 68135
7800-8299 68136
S 190th Cir
2000-2298 68130
4800-4899 68135
S 190th Plz 68130
S 190th St
3800-3900 68130
4501-4697 68135
S 190th Ter 68135
S 191st Ave
3500-3598 68130
4500-5298 68135
S 191st Cir 68130
S 191st St
2000-3999 68130
5800-6799 68135
7300-7798 68136
S 191st Ter 68135
S 192nd Ave
1300-1498 68130
1500-3999 68130
4801-4999 68135
S 192nd Avenue Cir 68130
S 192nd St
1701-3399 68130
4201-4797 68135
4799-5299 68135
5301-5699 68135
8701-8799 68136
S 193rd Ave 68135
S 193rd Cir 68130
S 193rd St
1200-1498 68130
1500-2200 68130
2202-3798 68130
4101-4497 68135
4499-6299 68135
S 194th Ave
1800-1899 68130
4700-6299 68135
S 194th St
1200-3999 68130
4501-4597 68135
4599-5500 68135
5502-7198 68135
S 195th Cir
1500-1599 68130
5100-5199 68135
S 195th St
1200-1499 68130
1501-2199 68130
5300-6300 68135
6302-6398 68135
S 196th Ave 68130
S 196th Cir 68135
S 196th St
1201-1297 68130
1299-1399 68130
4800-6299 68135
6301-6399 68135
S 197th Ave 68135
S 197th Avenue Cir 68135
3400-3499 68130
6300-6399 68135
S 197th St
1900-3799 68130
4901-4999 68135
S 198th Ave
1404-1504 68130
4201-4297 68135
S 198th Cir 68135
S 198th St
1900-2099 68130
4100-4198 68135
S 199th Ave 68135
S 199th Cir 68135
S 199th St 68135
S 200th Ave 68130
S 200th Cir 68130
S 200th St
1200-1299 68130
4100-4199 68135
201st Ave & Cir 68130
S 201st Avenue Cir 68130
S 202nd Ave
3700-3999 68130
4200-4399 68135
S 202nd Avenue Cir 68135
S 202nd St
3700-3714 68130
3716-3899 68130
4101-4197 68135
4199-4399 68135
4401-4499 68135
203rd Cir & St 68130
N 70 St 68152

PAPILLION NE

POST OFFICE BOXES MAIN OFFICE STATIONS AND BRANCHES

Box No.s
All PO Boxes 68046

NAMED STREETS

Aberdeen Cir 68133
Aberdeen Dr 68133
E Aberdeen Dr 68046
N Aberdeen Dr 68046
Aberdeen Plz 68133
N & S Adams St 68046
Alamoana Cir 68046
Alexandra Rd 68133
Allison Ave 68133
American Pkwy 68046
Anchor Mill Dr & Rd 68133
Anderson Cir 68133
Ann Marie Ct 68046
Antelope Cir 68046
Apache Cir 68046
Apollo Ln 68133
Applewood Dr
1100-1299 68046
1401-1497 68133
1499-1599 68133
Arlene Ave 68046
Ashley Dr 68046
Ashwood Ave 68133
Atlas Dr 68133
Auburn Ln 68046
Azule Cir 68046
Bailey Cir & Dr 68046
Ballpark Way 68046
Barrington Cir & Pkwy 68046
Bay Cir 68133
Bayview Dr 68133
N & S Beadle St 68046
Beaman St 68046
Bear Creek Rd 68133
Bearcreek Cir & Dr 68046
Beaufort Dr 68133
Beechwood Ave & Cir 68133
Berkley Ave & Cir 68046
Beth Ave 68133
Betsy Ave 68133
Big Sky Dr 68046
Bison Cir 68046
Black Forest Dr 68133
Blue Sage Dr 68133
Bluestem St 68046
Bluff Point Cir 68133
Bonnie Ave 68046
Bontath Dr 68133
Bristol St 68046
Broadwater Dr 68046
Brook St 68133
Bryn Mawr Dr 68046
Buckboard Blvd 68046
Capehart Rd
4800-6700 68133
6702-7198 68133
7701-7797 68046
7799-9899 68046
Caribou Cir 68046
Carolina Dr 68133
Carriage Rd 68046
E Cary St 68046
Castana Cir 68046
Castle St 68046
Castle Pine Cir & Dr 68133
Cedardale Rd
100-999 68046
6000-6200 68133
6202-6598 68133
Cedarwoods Dr 68046
E & W Centennial Rd 68046
Charleston Dr 68133
Chennault St 68133
Cherry Tree Ln 68133
Cheyenne Dr 68046
Chisholm Trl 68046
Choke Cherry Ln 68046
Christine St 68133
Cimarron St 68046
Circle St 68046
Citadel Dr 68133
Claudine Ave 68046
Clear Creek Cir & St 68133
Clearwater Cir 68046
Clearwater Dr
700-1199 68046
4500-13899 68133
Coach Rd 68046
Cobblestone Rd 68133
Cody Cir 68046
Coffey St 68133
Colonial Cir 68046
Colt Cir 68046
Concord Cir 68046
Conestoga Rd 68046
Cordes Dr 68046
Cork Dr 68046
Corn Dr 68046
Cornhusker Rd
4500-5398 68133
6801-7199 68133
11000-11098 68046
11100-11200 68046
11202-12298 68046
Corral Cir & St 68046
Cottonwood Cir 68133
Country View Ln 68133
Coyote Cir 68046
Crawford St 68046
Creek Side Dr 68046
Creighton Rd 68046
Crest Cir, Dr & Rd 68046
Crest Ridge Dr 68133
Crestview Dr 68133
Crystal Dr 68046
Crystal Creek Dr 68046
Cumberland Ct 68046
Dana Ln 68133
Dearborn Cir 68046
Deer Run Ln 68046
Deerfield Way 68133
Delmar St 68046
Devon Cir & Dr 68046
Diamond Ln 68133
Diane Dr & St 68046
Donegal Cir & Dr 68046
Driftwood Dr 68046
Dublin Dr 68046
Durham Dr 68133
Eagle Crest Cir, Dr & Plz 68133
Eagle Hills Cir & Dr 68133
Eagle Ridge Dr 68133
Eagle View Dr 68133
Eastlake Cir 68133
Eastview Dr 68046
Edgerton Dr 68133
Edgewater Cir & Dr 68046
Edgewood Blvd 68046
Edward St 68046
Elaine St 68046
Elk Ridge Dr 68046
Elmhurst Dr 68046
Engberg Rd 68046
Erin Cir 68046
Evergreen Dr 68046
Fairview Rd
6401-6509 68133
7201-7797 68046
7799-10199 68046
10201-10399 68046
S Fall Creek Rd 68133
Fenwick Cir, Dr & St 68046
N & S Fillmore Cir & St 68046
Fleetwood Dr 68133
Flint Cir & Dr 68046
Fort Cir & St 68046
Fortune Dr 68046
Fountain Cir & Dr 68133
Fowler Dr 68046
Fox Creek Ln 68046
Fox Run Dr 68046
Franklin Cir & Dr 68133
N Frontier Dr & Rd 68046
Fulkerson Rd 68046
Galway Cir 68046
Garden St 68046
Gayle St 68046
Giles Rd
6601-6899 68133
8501-8599 68046
Glacier Dr 68046
Glenwood Ave 68046
E & W Gold Coast Cir & Rd 68046
Golden Gate Cir & Dr 68046
Gow Cir 68133
Graham Dr 68046
Grand Lodge Ave 68133
N & S Grandview Ave & Plz 68046
E & W Grant Cir & St 68046
Greenwood Ave 68133
Greyson Cir & Dr 68133
Gruenther St 68046
Hackney Dr 68046
E & W Halleck St 68046
Hansen Ave 68133
Harbor Cir 68133
Hardwood Dr 68046
N & S Harrison Cir & St 68046
Harvest Dr 68133
Haverford Dr 68046
Helen Cir 68133
Helwig Ave 68133
Hickory Cir 68133
Hickory Hill Cir & Rd 68046
Hidden Valley Dr 68046
Highland Dr
101-199 68046
5600-5698 68133
5700-11399 68133
Highway 370
5400-5500 68133
Highway 370
5502-5998 68133
10700-11899 68046
11901-12599 68046
Hilltop St 68133
Hilo Cir 68046
Hilton Head Dr 68133
Hogan Dr 68046
Holloway Ave 68133
Horseshoe Cir 68046
Inglewood Cir & Dr 68133
Iron Rd 68046
N & S Jackson St 68046
Jacqueline Cir & Dr 68046
Jake Cir 68133
Jana Cir 68133
Janesview St 68046
N & S Jefferson St 68046
Jersey St 68046
John St 68133
John Schram Dr 68046
Joseph Cir, Dr & Plz 68046
Joy Cir & St 68046
Juniper Cir & Dr 68046
Kara Cir & Dr 68133
Kauai Dr 68046
Kelsey St 68046
Kendel Dr 68046
Kent Cir & Dr 68046
Kentucky Rd 68133
Kilkinny Cir 68046
Killarney Dr 68046
King Dr 68046
Kingston Cir 68046
Knapp Dr 68046
Kona Cir 68046
La Port Dr 68046
Lafayette Dr 68046
Lake Forest Cir & Dr 68133
Lake Tahoe Dr 68046
Lake Vista Cir & Dr 68046
Lakecrest Cir & Dr 68133
Lakeside Cir & Dr 68133
Lakeview Dr 68133
Lakewood Dr 68046
Lambert Cir & Dr 68046
Laplatte Rd 68133
Laramie Cir & St 68046
Laredo Cir & Rd 68046
Lariat Cir 68046
Laura Cir 68046
Le Baron Dr 68133
Leawood St 68046
Legacy St 68046
Leigh Cir, Ln & St 68133
Leprechaun Ln 68046
Lexington Ln 68046
Liberty Ln 68133
Limerick Rd 68046
W & E Lincoln Rd & St 68046
Lockbourne Ave 68133
Locust Ave & Dr 68046
Longview St 68133
Longwood Dr 68133
Lydia Cir 68133
Maass Rd 68133
Macarthur Dr 68046
Mackensey Dr 68046
N & S Madison Cir & St 68046
Magnolia Ave, Cir, Ct & Dr 68046
Makaha Cir 68046
Mallard View Cir 68046
Manor Plz 68046
Margaret Cir 68046
Marilyn Dr 68046
Mark St 68133
Marshall Cir 68046
Matthies Dr 68046
Maui Cir 68046
Merrill Mission Rd 68133
Mesa Cir 68133
Mesquite Cir 68046
Michael Dr 68046
Michelle Pkwy 68046
Mikelluke Cir 68046
S Mineral Dr 68046
Mitchell Rd 68046
Molokai Dr 68046
Monarch Cir 68046
N & S Monroe St 68046
Moore Dr 68046
Normandy Cir 68046
Northwood Cir 68133
Norton Dr 68046
Oahu Cir 68046
Oak Ridge Rd 68046
Oakland Dr 68133
Oakland Ln 68046
Oakmont Cir, Dr & Plz 68133
Oakwood Dr 68133
Oke St 68046
Olson Dr 68046

N & S Osage Dr & St .. 68046
Overland Trl 68046
Overview St 68046
Oxford Cir 68046
Palomino Cir 68046
Papillion Dr
1201-1499 68046
1500-1599 68133
Parc Dr 68046
Park Crest Dr 68133
Patricia Dr 68046
E & W Patton St 68046
W Perry St 68046
Petersen Dr 68046
Pheasant Run Ln 68046
Phoenix Cir 68046
Pierce St 68046
Pine St 68133
Pinehurst Cir & Plz 68133
Pineview Dr 68046
Pinnacle Dr 68046
Pinto Cir 68046
Pioneer Rd 68046
Placid Lake Cir & Dr ... 68046
Platteview Rd
4500-6899 68133
7300-10799 68046
N & S Polk Cir & St 68046
Ponderosa Dr
4701-4999 68133
7501-7597 68046
7599-7999 68046
8001-8199 68046
Port Royal Cir & Dr 68046
Portage Dr 68046
Portal Rd 68046
Prospect Cir, Dr & St ... 68046
Quail Ridge Cir & Rd ... 68046
Quartz Dr 68046
Queen Cir & Dr 68046
Raleigh Cir 68133
Ranch Cir & Dr 68046
Rawhide Cir & Rd 68046
Red Fern Cir 68133
Redwood Ln 68046
Reed Cir & St 68046
Reeve Dr 68046
Reeves Cir 68046
Remington Rd 68046
Renee Ave 68046
Richelieu Ct 68046
Ridgeview Cir 68133
Ridgeview Dr 68046
Ridgeview St 68046
Ridgewood Dr 68133
S River Rock Dr 68046
Rogers Dr 68046
Roland Dr 68046
Rosewood Ave 68133
Rousseau Ct 68046
Royal Dr 68046
Ruby Rd 68133
Russell Emmett Ct 68133
Saddle Dr 68046
Sally St 68046
Sand Hills Dr 68046
Sante Fe Cir 68046
Savannah Dr 68133
Schmid Dr 68046
Schram Rd 68046
Scott Rd 68046
Sea Pines Dr 68133
Shadow Lake Dr &
Plz 68046
Shady Tree Ln 68046
Shamrock Rd 68046
Shannon Dr 68133
Shannon Rd 68046
Shawnee Rd 68046
Shenandoah Dr 68046
Sheridan Rd 68133
E Sheridan St 68046
W Sheridan St 68046
Sheriff Cir 68046
W Sherman Cir & St ... 68046
Sherwood Ln 68046
Shillaelagh Blvd 68046
Shoreline Cir 68133
Sierra St 68133
Sky Hawk Ave 68133
Smith Cir 68046
Socrates Ln 68133
South Dr 68046
Southshore St 68046
Southview Dr 68046
Springview Dr 68133
Spruce Dr 68046
Sterling Dr 68046
Stillwater Dr 68046
Stony Point Dr 68046
Summerset Cir & Dr 68133
Summit Ridge Dr 68046
Sumter Cir 68133
Sunburst Dr 68046
Surrey Rd 68046
Sutley Cir 68133
Suzanne Ave 68046
Swallowtail St 68046
Tara Plz & Rd 68046
N & S Taylor Cir & St .. 68046
Tekamah Ln 68046
Terlerie Dr 68046
Timber Dr 68046
Timberline Dr 68046
Timberridge Dr 68133
Tipperary Dr 68046
Titan Springs Dr 68133
Towne Center Pkwy 68046
Troy St 68133
Tupelo Ln 68133
Turkey Rd 68046
Valentine Ln 68046
Valley Rd 68046
Valleyview Dr 68046
Victoria Ave 68133
Victoria Cir 68046
Victory Cir 68046
Villa Plz 68046
Vivian Cir 68046
Walnut Creek Dr & St .. 68046
N & S Washington St .. 68046
Waterford Ave 68133
Waterford Cir 68046
Western Hills Dr 68046
Westlake Cir 68133
Westshore Cir 68046
Wexford Cir 68046
White Pine Cir & Dr 68046
Whitewater Dr 68046
Whitney Rd 68133
Wicklow Cir & Rd 68046
Wilma Rd 68133
Wilshire Ln 68046
Winchester Cir 68046
Windcrest Ave & Dr 68133
Windsor Cir & Dr 68046
Wood Bridge Cir 68046
Woodbine Cir & Dr 68046
Woodland Ave 68046
Woodlane Dr 68133
Woodview Cir & Dr 68046
Wynnwood Ln 68046

NUMBERED STREETS

E & W 1st 68046
E & W 2nd 68046
E 3rd St 68046
E & W 4th 68046
E & W 5th 68046
E & W 6th 68046
E 7th St 68046
S 45th St 68133
46th Ave & St 68133
S 47th St 68133
S 48th St 68133
49th Ave & St 68133
S 51st St 68133
S 52nd St 68133
53rd Ave & St 68133
S 54th St 68133
S 56th St 68133
57th Ave & St 68133
S 58th St 68133
60th Ct & St 68133
S 61st St 68133
S 63rd St 68133
S 65th St 68133
66th Ave & St 68133
S 67th St 68133
68th Ave & St 68133
S 68th Avenue Cir 68133
69th Cir & St 68133
70th Ave, Cir & St 68133
71st Ave, Plz & St 68133
S 71st Avenue Cir 68133
S 72nd St 68046
73rd Ave, Ct, Plz & St . 68046
S 74th St 68046
75th Cir & St 68046
S 77th St 68046
78th Cir & St 68046
79th Ave, Cir, St &
Ter 68046
S 80th St 68046
81st Ave & St 68046
S 82nd St 68046
S 83rd St 68046
S 84th St 68046
S 87th St 68046
S 90th St 68046
S 96th St 68046
S 99th St 68046
S 105th St 68046
S 108th St 68046
S 109th St 68046
110th Ave & St 68046
111th Ave & St 68046
S 112th St 68046
113th Ave & St 68046
S 114th St 68046
S 120th St 68046
S 124th Ave 68046

SCOTTSBLUFF NE

General Delivery 69361

POST OFFICE BOXES
MAIN OFFICE STATIONS
AND BRANCHES

Box No.s
All PO Boxes 69363

NAMED STREETS

All Street Addresses 69361

NUMBERED STREETS

All Street Addresses 69361

Nevada

People QuickFacts	Nevada	USA
Population, 2013 estimate	2,790,136	316,128,839
Population, 2010 (April 1) estimates base	2,700,552	308,747,716
Population, percent change, April 1, 2010 to July 1, 2013	3.3%	2.4%
Population, 2010	2,700,551	308,745,538
Persons under 5 years, percent, 2013	6.4%	6.3%
Persons under 18 years, percent, 2013	23.7%	23.3%
Persons 65 years and over, percent, 2013	13.7%	14.1%
Female persons, percent, 2013	49.6%	50.8%
White alone, percent, 2013 (a)	76.7%	77.7%
Black or African American alone, percent, 2013 (a)	9.0%	13.2%
American Indian and Alaska Native alone, percent, 2013 (a)	1.6%	1.2%
Asian alone, percent, 2013 (a)	8.1%	5.3%
Native Hawaiian and Other Pacific Islander alone, percent, 2013 (a)	0.7%	0.2%
Two or More Races, percent, 2013	3.9%	2.4%
Hispanic or Latino, percent, 2013 (b)	27.5%	17.1%
White alone, not Hispanic or Latino, percent, 2013	52.2%	62.6%
Living in same house 1 year & over, percent, 2008-2012	77.7%	84.8%
Foreign born persons, percent, 2008-2012	19.2%	12.9%
Language other than English spoken at home, pct age 5+, 2008-2012	29.0%	20.5%
High school graduate or higher, percent of persons age 25+, 2008-2012	84.4%	85.7%
Bachelor's degree or higher, percent of persons age 25+, 2008-2012	22.2%	28.5%
Veterans, 2008-2012	229,570	21,853,912
Mean travel time to work (minutes), workers age 16+, 2008-2012	23.8	25.4
Housing units, 2013	1,186,879	132,802,859
Homeownership rate, 2008-2012	57.8%	65.5%
Housing units in multi-unit structures, percent, 2008-2012	29.9%	25.9%
Median value of owner-occupied housing units, 2008-2012	$190,900	$181,400
Households, 2008-2012	992,896	115,226,802
Persons per household, 2008-2012	2.69	2.61
Per capita money income in past 12 months (2012 dollars), 2008-2012	$27,003	$28,051
Median household income, 2008-2012	$54,083	$53,046
Persons below poverty level, percent, 2008-2012	14.2%	14.9%

Business QuickFacts	Nevada	USA
Private nonfarm establishments, 2012	59,417	7,431,808
Private nonfarm employment, 2012	1,014,570	115,938,468
Private nonfarm employment, percent change, 2011-2012	1.4%	2.2%
Nonemployer establishments, 2012	184,246	22,735,915
Total number of firms, 2007	221,260	27,092,908
Black-owned firms, percent, 2007	3.9%	7.1%
American Indian- and Alaska Native-owned firms, percent, 2007	0.8%	0.9%
Asian-owned firms, percent, 2007	7.9%	5.7%
Native Hawaiian and Other Pacific Islander-owned firms, percent, 2007	0.3%	0.1%
Hispanic-owned firms, percent, 2007	8.1%	8.3%
Women-owned firms, percent, 2007	28.6%	28.8%
Manufacturers shipments, 2007 ($1000)	15,735,787	5,319,456,312
Merchant wholesaler sales, 2007 ($1000)	19,255,893	4,174,286,516
Retail sales, 2007 ($1000)	37,433,983	3,917,663,456
Retail sales per capita, 2007	$14,579	$12,990
Accommodation and food services sales, 2007 ($1000)	28,815,533	613,795,732
Building permits, 2012	9,071	829,658

Geography QuickFacts	Nevada	USA
Land area in square miles, 2010	109,781.18	3,531,905.43
Persons per square mile, 2010	24.6	87.4
FIPS Code	32	

(a) Includes persons reporting only one race.
(b) Hispanics may be of any race, so also are included in applicable race categories.
FN: Footnote on this item for this area in place of data
NA: Not available
D: Suppressed to avoid disclosure of confidential information
X: Not applicable
S: Suppressed; does not meet publication standards
Z: Value greater than zero but less than half unit of measure shown
F: Fewer than 100 firms
Source: US Census Bureau State & County QuickFacts

Nevada

3 DIGIT ZIP CODE MAP

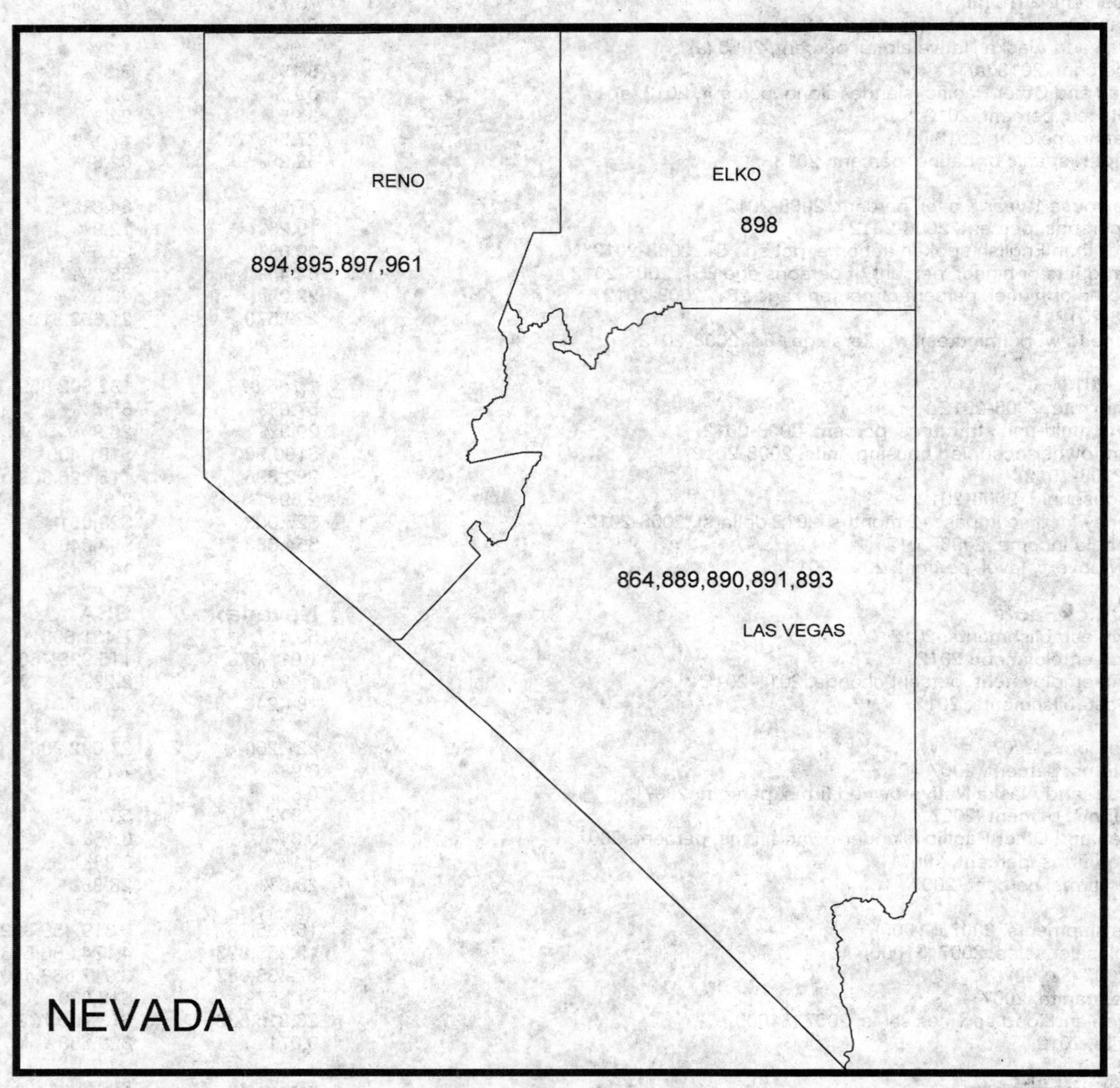

Nevada

(Abbreviation: NV)

Post Office, County — ZIP Code

Places with more than one ZIP code are listed in capital letters, See pages indicated.

Alamo, Lincoln 89001
Amargosa Valley, Nye 89020
Austin, Lander 89310
Baker, White Pine 89311
Battle Mountain, Lander 89820
Beatty, Nye 89003
Beowawe, Eureka 89821
Blue Diamond, Clark 89004
BOULDER CITY, Clark
(See Page 2460)
Bunkerville, Clark 89007
Cal Nev Ari, Clark 89039
Calico Basin, Clark 89124
Caliente, Lincoln 89008
Callville Bay, Clark 89124
Carlin, Elko 89822
CARSON CITY, Carson City
(See Page 2460)
City Center, Clark 89158
Cold Creek, Clark 89124
Corn Creek, Clark 89124
Cottonwood Cv, Clark 89046
Coyote Springs
(See Coyote Springs)
Crescent Valley, Eureka 89821
Crystal Bay, Washoe 89402
Dayton, Lyon 89403
Deeth, Elko 89823
Denio, Humboldt 89404
Duckwater, White Pine 89314
Dyer, Esmeralda 89010
ELKO, Elko
(See Page 2462)
ELY, White Pine
(See Page 2462)
Emigrant Pass, Eureka 89821
Empire, Washoe 89405
Enterprise, Clark 89124
Eureka, Eureka 89316
FALLON, Churchill
(See Page 2462)
Fernley, Lyon 89408
Gabbs, Nye 89409
GARDNERVILLE, Douglas
(See Page 2463)
Genoa, Douglas 89411
Gerlach, Washoe 89412
Glenbrook, Douglas 89413
Golconda, Humboldt 89414
Goldfield, Esmeralda 89013
Goodsprings, Clark 89019
Halleck, Elko 89801
Hawthorne, Mineral 89415
HENDERSON, Clark
(See Page 2464)
Hiko, Lincoln 89017
Imlay, Pershing 89418
INCLINE VILLAGE, Washoe
(See Page 2472)
Indian Springs, Clark 89018
Indian Springs Air Force Aux,
Clark 89191
Jackpot, Elko 89825
Jackpot, Elko 89826
Jarbidge, Elko 89826
Jean, Clark 89019
Jiggs, Elko 89815
Lamoille, Elko 89828
LAS VEGAS, Clark
(See Page 2473)
LAUGHLIN, Clark
(See Page 2510)
Lee, Elko 89801
Lockwood, Washoe 89434
Logandale, Clark 89021
Lovelock, Pershing 89419
Lund, White Pine 89317
Luning, Mineral 89420
Manhattan, Nye 89022
Mc Dermitt, Humboldt 89421
Mc Gill, White Pine 89318
Mccarran, Washoe 89434
Mercury, Nye 89023
MESQUITE, Clark
(See Page 2510)
Midas, Humboldt 89414
Mill City, Pershing 89418
Mina, Mineral 89422
Minden, Douglas 89423
Moapa, Clark 89025
Moapa, Clark 89037
Moapa Valley, Clark 89021
Montello, Elko 89830
Mound House, Carson City 89706
Mount Charleston, Clark 89124
Mountain City, Elko 89831
Mountain Springs
(See Las Vegas)
Nellis Afb, Clark 89191
Nixon, Washoe 89424
NORTH LAS VEGAS, Clark
(See Page 2511)
Oasis, Elko 89835
Orovada, Humboldt 89425
Overton, Clark 89040
Owyhee, Elko 89832
PAHRUMP, Nye
(See Page 2517)
Palm Gardens, Clark 89039
Panaca, Lincoln 89042
Paradise Valley, Humboldt 89426
Pioche, Lincoln 89043
Primm, Clark 89019
RENO, Washoe
(See Page 2519)
Round Mountain, Nye 89045
Ruby Valley, Elko 89833
Ruth, White Pine 89319
Sandy Valley, Clark 89019
Schurz, Mineral 89427
Searchlight, Clark 89039
Searchlight, Clark 89046
Silver City, Lyon 89428
Silver Springs, Lyon 89429
Silverpeak, Esmeralda 89047
Sloan, Clark 89054
Sloan, Clark 89124
Smith, Lyon 89430
Spanish Springs
(See Sparks)
SPARKS, Washoe
(See Page 2526)
Spring Creek, Elko 89815
Stagecoach, Lyon 89429
Stateline, Douglas 89449
Sun Valley, Washoe 89433
The Lakes, Clark 88901
Tonopah, Nye 89049
Tuscarora, Elko 89834
Unionville, Pershing 89418
Valmy, Humboldt 89438
Vc Highlands, Washoe 89521
Verdi, Washoe 89439
Virginia City, Storey 89440
W Wendover, Elko 89883
Wadsworth, Washoe 89442
Walker Lake, Mineral 89415
Washoe Valley, Washoe 89704
Wellington, Lyon 89444
Wells, Elko 89835
Wendover, Elko 89883
West Wendover, Elko 89883
WINNEMUCCA, Humboldt
(See Page 2529)
Yerington, Lyon 89447
Zephyr Cove, Douglas 89448

BOULDER CITY NV

General Delivery 89005

POST OFFICE BOXES MAIN OFFICE STATIONS AND BRANCHES

Box No.s
All PO Boxes 89006

NAMED STREETS

Aaron Way 89005
Adams Blvd 89005
Adobe Cir 89005
Airport Rd 89005
Alpine Dr 89005
America Ct 89005
Amy Ct 89005
Ann Way 89005
Antigua Way 89005
Appaloosa Rd 89005
Arabian Ln 89005
Arapaho Way 89005
Arizona St 89005
Armada Pl 89005
Arrayo Way 89005
Ash St 89005
Aspen Ct & Dr 89005
Avenue A 89005
Avenue B 89005
Avenue C 89005
Avenue D 89005
Avenue F 89005
Avenue G 89005
Avenue H 89005
Avenue I 89005
Avenue K 89005
Avenue L 89005
Avenue M 89005
Aztec Pl 89005
Azul Way 89005
Barcelona Ct & Way 89005
Bay View Dr 89005
Becky Ln 89005
Bender Ct 89005
Benita Pl 89005
Bermuda Dunes Dr 89005
Big Horn Dr 89005
Birch St 89005
Black Canyon Cv 89005
Black Mountain Ct 89005
Blue Lake Ct & Dr 89005
Blue Water Dr 89005
Bonni Pl 89005
Brentwood Dr 89005
Briarstone Dr 89005
Broadmoor Cir & Ct 89005
Bronco Rd 89005
Bryant Ct 89005
Buchanan Blvd 89005
California Ave 89005
Calumet Ln 89005
Canary Way 89005
Canyon Rd 89005
Caperna Ct 89005
Capri Dr 89005
Caria Ct 89005
Carnoustie Ct 89005
Carroll Ln 89005
Carse Dr 89005
Casa Montana Ct & Way 89005
Cats Eye Dr 89005
Cayuga Ct 89005
Cedar Dr 89005
Cherokee Ct 89005
Cherry St 89005
Cheryl Ln 89005
Chestnut Ln 89005
Cheyenne Ct 89005
Christina Dr 89005
Christy Ln 89005
Cindertree Ln 89005
Cindy Ln 89005
Claremont St 89005
Clarice Ln 89005
Clubhouse Dr 89005
Colorado St
1100-1498 89005
1101-1399 89005
1101-1101 89006
Columbia Ct 89005
Comanche Way 89005
Copper Ridge Ct 89005
Coronado Dr 89005
Corral Rd 89005
Cottonwood St 89005
Cottonwood Cove St 89005
Crystal Ct 89005
Cummings Dr 89005
Da Vinci Cv 89005
Darlene Way 89005
Date St 89005
Dee Cir 89005
Del Monte Ln 89005
Del Prado Dr 89005
Del Rey Dr 89005
Del Sol Dr 89005
Della Ct 89005
Denver St 89005
Desert Rose Ct 89005
Desert Valley Dr 89005
Dianne Dr 89005
Don Vincente Ct & Dr 89005
Donner Way 89005
Dorothy Dr 89005
Dreamcatcher Dr 89005
Edie Pl 89005
El Camino Cir & Way 89005
Elm St 89005
Elsa Way 89005
Endora Way 89005
Enterprise Ct 89005
Esther Dr 89005
Fairway Dr 89005
Fir St 89005
Fire Agate Dr 89005
Fleetwood St 89005
Florence Dr 89005
Foothill Ct & Dr 89005
Forest Ln 89005
Freedom Ln 89005
Fuente Way 89005
Garnet Pl 89005
Garrett Ln 89005
Genni Pl 89005
Georgia Ave 89005
Gingerwood St 89005
Gleneagles Ct 89005
Gloria Ln 89005
Golden Ct 89005
Graham Ct 89005
Granada Dr 89005
Granite Ct 89005
Greenbriar Pl 89005
Grillo Way 89005
Gypsum Ct 89005
Hallett Cove Ct 89005
Harbor View Dr 89005
Hazelwood St 89005
Hemenway Cv 89005
Heritage Way 89005
Hermosa Ln 89005
Hidden Cv 89005
Highland Ct & Dr 89005
Highway 93 89005
Hillcrest Ln 89005
Hillside Dr 89005
Hilton Head Dr 89005
Hopi Pl 89005
Hotel Plz 89005
Independence Way 89005
Indian Wells Dr 89005
Industrial Rd 89005
Intrepid Ct 89005
Inverness Ct 89005
Irene Dr 89005
Ironwood St 89005
Isabel Dr 89005
Island Cv 89005
Jani Pl 89005
Jasmine Way 89005
Jasper Way 89005
Jeri Ln 89005
Joy Ln 89005
Judi Pl 89005
Juniper Way 89005
Kaelyn St 89005
Kati Pl 89005
Kay Ct 89005
Kelpwood St 89005
Kendall Ln 89005
Kendrick Pl 89005
Key Biscayne Ct 89005
Key West Ct 89005
Keys Dr 89005
Kingman Cv 89005
Kings Pl 89005
La Mesa Way 89005
La Plata Pl 89005
Laguna Ln 89005
Lake Erie Ln 89005
Lake Havasu Ln 89005
Lake Hill Dr 89005
Lake Huron Ln 89005
Lake Merritt Ln 89005
Lake Michigan Ln 89005
Lake Mountain Dr 89005
Lake Ontario Ln 89005
Lake Shore Rd 89005
Lake Superior Ln 89005
Lake Tahoe Ln 89005
Lake Terrace Dr 89005
Lake Winnebago Ln 89005
Lakes Dr 89005
Laketree Ct 89005
Lakeview Dr 89005
Lantern Bay Dr 89005
Laurel Dr 89005
Lava Ct 89005
Legacy Dr 89005
Lido Dr 89005
Lighthouse Dr 89005
Lillo Ct 89005
Lime Rock Rd 89005
Linda Ln 89005
Lorryn Ln 89005
Los Tavis Way 89005
Lynn Dr 89005
Lynwood St 89005
Magic Cove Ct 89005
Malaga Ct & Dr 89005
Mancha Dr 89005
Marathon Ct 89005
Marina Cv & Dr 89005
Mariposa Way 89005
Marita Ct & Dr 89005
Marjay Ct 89005
Marti Pl 89005
Marwood St 89005
Matecumbe Way 89005
Mead Way 89005
Medical Park Dr 89005
Mendota Dr 89005
Milton Ct 89005
Montego Ln 89005
Montera Ln 89005
Monterey Dr 89005
Moonstone Dr 89005
Morgyn Ln 89005
Mount Antero Way 89005
Mount Bear Way 89005
Mount Blackburn Ln 89005
Mount Bona Way 89005
Mount Elbert Way 89005
Mount Hunter Way 89005
Mount Tamalpais Way 89005
Mount Williamson Way 89005
Mountain View Pl 89005
Mustang Rd 89005
Nadine Way 89005
Nassau Way 89005
Navajo Ct & Dr 89005
Nelson Ct 89005
Nevada Hwy 89005
New Mexico St 89005
Nob Hill St 89005
Northridge Dr 89005
Ocean Mist Ln 89005
Olmo Way 89005
Opal Ct 89005
Otono Dr 89005
Pacifica Way 89005
Paiute Dr 89005
Palmero Way 89005
Palmwood St 89005
Paloma Dr 89005
Park Pl & St 89005
Patti Pl 89005
Pebble Beach Dr 89005
Pinto Rd 89005
Potosi St 89005
Preswick Ct 89005
Providence Ln 89005
Pueblo Dr 89005
Pyramid Ln 89005
Radig Ct 89005
Railroad Ave 89005
Rainbow Dr 89005
Raini Pl 89005
Rainier Ct 89005
Ramona Ln 89005
Ranger Ct 89005
Rawhide Rd 89005
Red Baron Ln 89005
Red Mountain Ct & Dr 89005
Red Rock Rd 89005
Redwood St 89005
Reese Pl 89005
Renaissance St 89005
Ridge Rd 89005
River Mountain Dr 89005
Riviera Ct 89005
Robinson Ln & Way 89005
Roma Ln 89005
Royal Birkdale Dr 89005
Royal Troon Ct 89005
Saddle Ln 89005
Saint Andrews Ct 89005
Saint Judes St 89005
San Felipe Ct & Dr 89005
San Remo Way 89005
Sanchez Cir 89005
Sandra Dr 89005
Sandstone Ct 89005
Sandy Beach Way 89005
Sea Breeze Ln 89005
Seneca Ln 89005
Seno Ct 89005
Shenandoah St 89005
Sherri Ln 89005
Shirley Ln 89005
Shoshone Way 89005
Sierra Vista Pl 89005
Sioux Ct 89005
Sorrel Rd 89005
Stacey Ln 89005
Stone Canyon Rd 89005
Sunrise Cir 89005
Sunset Pt 89005
Swallow Cv 89005
Tamarack Dr 89005
Tamarisk Ln 89005
Tara Ct 89005
Tavernier St 89005
Teakwood St 89005
Temple Rock Ct & Rd 89005
Topsail Dr 89005
Torrey Pines Dr 89005
Tumbleweed Dr 89005
Turnberry Ct 89005
Turquoise Ct 89005
Tuscany Ct & Cv 89005
Utah St 89005
Valencia Dr 89005
Valley View Ln 89005
Vaquero Dr 89005
Venice Ln 89005
Veterans Memorial Dr 89005
Villa Grande Way 89005
Ville Dr 89005
Vista Lago Ct & Way 89005
Walker Way 89005
Walnut Dr 89005
Webster Way 89005
Wells Rd 89005
Wilson Cir 89005
Woodacre Dr 89005
Woodcrest Ct & Dr 89005
Wyoming St 89005
Yates Ln 89005
Yucca St 89005
Yuma Ct 89005

NUMBERED STREETS

All Street Addresses 89005

CARSON CITY NV

General Delivery 89701

POST OFFICE BOXES MAIN OFFICE STATIONS AND BRANCHES

Box No.s
1 - 9050 89702
19981 - 22800 89721

NAMED STREETS

A St 89706
Able Ln 89706
Adair Dr 89706
Adaline St 89703
E Adams St 89706
W Adams St 89703
Adobe Dr 89705
Affonso Dr 89706
Agate Ct 89705
Agate Dr 89706
Airport Rd
801-1597 89701
1599-1600 89701
1602-1698 89701
1700-2048 89706
2050-3399 89706
3401-3499 89706
Akron Way 89701
Albany Ave 89703
Alberta Ct 89703
Alder St 89701
Alexa Way 89706
Alfie Ave 89701
Alfred Way 89703
Allouette Way 89701
Alpine St 89703
Alpine View Ct 89705
Alyce Ct 89701
Amador Cir & Ct 89705
Amberwood Dr 89703
Anderson St 89701
Andorra Dr 89703
Angelo Ct 89706
Angels Camp Dr 89703
Angus St 89703
E Ann St 89701
W Ann St 89703
Annapolis Ave 89703
Antler Dr 89701
Anzac Cir 89701
Apache Dr 89701
Apollo Dr 89706
Appaloosa Ct 89701
E Appion Way 89701
W Appion Way 89703
E & W Applegate Way 89706
Aquifer Way 89701
Arcadia Dr 89705
Arizona Cir 89701
Armagnea St 89701
Armory Ln 89701
Armstrong Ln 89701
Arrowhead Dr 89706
Arroyo Vista Ln 89701
Artemesia Rd 89701
Arthur St 89701
Ash Canyon Rd 89703
Ashby Ct 89701
Ashford Dr 89701
Ashwood Ct 89703
Auburn Ct 89705
Audrey Dr 89706
August Dr 89706
Austin Ln 89701
Avery Rd 89706
Azurite Ln 89705
B St 89706
Baily Ct 89703
Baker Dr 89701
Baldwin Ln 89706
Ballarat Dr 89706
Bandtail Dr 89701
Banjo Cir 89706
Barossa Way 89701
Barrington Cir 89701
Basalt Dr 89705
Basque Way 89706
Bath St 89703
Bavarian Dr 89705
Beaver Ln 89701
Beckworth Ct 89706
Bedford Way 89703
Bel Aire Cir & Way 89706
Belmont Ave 89706
Bennett Ave 89701
Berkenfield Dr 89701
Bernese Ct 89705
Betts St 89703
Beverly Dr 89706
Bigelow Dr 89701
Bighorn Dr 89701
Biltmore St 89706
Birch St 89701
Black Rock Cir & Rd 89706
Blackrock Ct 89706
Bliss Ct 89701
Blossom View Ln 89701
Blue Haven Ln 89701
Blue Ridge Ct & Dr 89705
Bluebell Cir 89706
Bobarly Ct 89706
Bobcat Cir 89703
Bodie Dr 89706
Boeing Way 89706
Bohr Rd 89706
Bolero Dr 89703
E & W Bonanza Dr 89706
Bonnyview Dr 89701
Bordeaux St 89701
Boulder Dr 89706
Bourgogne St 89701
Bowers Ln 89706
Boyle St 89703
Brentwood Dr 89701
Briar Crest Ct 89703
Briarwood Dr 89701
Brick Rd 89701
Bristol Pl 89703
Brittiany Ct 89701
Broadleaf Ln 89706
Brookside Way 89701
Brown Dr 89706
Brown St 89701
Bruce Way 89706
Brunswick Canyon Rd 89701
Brush Dr 89703
Bryan Cir 89706
Bryce Dr 89706
Bucks Way 89705
Bulette Dr 89703
Bullion Dr 89706
Bunch Way 89706
Bunker Hill Dr 89703
Burton St 89706
Butti Way 89701
Buzzys Ranch Rd 89701
C St 89706
Caboose Dr 89701
Cabrolet Dr 89703
Cachet Ct 89706
Calash Dr 89703
Calaveras Dr 89703
Calcite Cir 89705
Calcite Dr 89706
Calico St 89701
California St 89701
Camballeria Dr 89701
Cambridge Ct 89701
Cameron Ct 89706
Camille Dr 89706
Camus Rd 89701
Canter Way 89706
Canvasback Dr 89701
Canyon Dr 89703
Canyon Park Ct 89703
Capitol View Dr 89701
Cardinal Way 89701
Carefree Ct 89705
Carlisle Ct 89703
Carmine St 89706
Carnelian Way 89705
E Caroline St 89701
W Caroline St 89703
Carriage Crest Dr 89706
Carrie Dr 89701
Carroll Dr 89703
Carry Way 89706
N Carson St
100-1999 89701
2000-4300 89706
4302-4698 89706
5400-5498 89706
S Carson St 89701
N & S Carson Meadow Dr 89701
Carson River Rd 89701
Carter Ave 89701
Carville Cir 89703
Cascade Dr 89701
Cash Dr 89706
Cassidy Ct 89701
Castle Way 89706
Catalpa Way 89701
Catherine Cir 89706
Cedar St 89701
Centennial Park Dr 89706
Center Dr 89701
Century Cir & Dr 89706
Chaise Ct & Dr 89703
Challenger Way 89706
Champagne Cir 89701
Champion St 89706
Chanel Ln 89706
Chaparral Dr 89703
Chardonnay Dr 89703
Chari Dr 89706
Charleston Ct 89701
Chateau Dr 89701
Chelsea Pl 89703
Chemus Dr 89703
Cherokee Dr 89705
Chimney Dr 89701
Chinook Cir 89701
Chollar Pl 89706
Christina Cir 89701
Christmas Tree Dr 89703
Christy Ct 89701
Chubasco Way 89701
Cindys Trl 89705
Cinnabar Ave 89706
Circle Dr 89703
Citadel Cir 89703
Classic Ct 89701
Claudia Cir 89701
Clear Creek Ave 89701
Clearview Dr 89701
W Clearview Dr 89703
Clemens Dr 89703
Clordi Ln 89706
Clover Ct 89703
Clubhouse Way 89701
Clydesdale Dr 89703

Cochise St 89703
Coffey Dr 89701
Cognac Ct 89701
Cogorno Way 89703
Cold Spring Way 89701
Colleen Cir 89703
College Dr 89703
College Pkwy 89706
W College Pkwy 89703
Collier Ct 89703
Coloma Dr 89705
Colorado St 89701
Colt Cir 89701
Columbia Way 89706
Columbine Ct 89703
Combs Cir 89703
Combs Canyon Rd 89703
Como St 89701
Comstock Cir 89703
Concord Dr 89706
Condor Cir 89701
Conestoga Dr 89706
Conte Dr 89701
Continental Dr 89701
Convair Dr 89706
Coral Way 89703
Corbett St 89706
Cordero Dr 89703
Coronet Way 89701
Corrinne Ct 89706
Cortez St 89701
Cottonwood Dr 89701
Country Club Dr 89703
Country Village Dr 89701
County Line Rd 89703
Court Side Cir 89703
Coventry Dr 89703
Cowee Dr 89706
Crain Cir & St 89703
Crescent Dr 89701
Crest Dr 89703
Crossett Ln 89706
Crossridge Dr 89706
Crown Point Dr 89706
Crystal Water Way 89701
Cumberland Ct 89703
N & S Curry St 89703
Custer Cir 89703
Cygnet Dr 89706
Dagget Dr 89703
Dale Dr 89706
Damon Rd 89701
Dan St 89706
Dana St 89706
Danielle Dr 89706
Darin Ct 89701
Darla Way 89701
Dartmouth Ct & Dr 89703
Dat So La Lee Way 89701
David St 89706
Dawn Cir 89701
De Ann Dr 89701
De Lah E Deh 89701
Dean Ct 89706
Debbie Way 89706
N & S Deer Run Rd 89701
Delta Cir 89706
Denio Ct 89706
Denise Cir 89701
Denmar Cir 89703
Derby Ct 89703
Desatoya Dr 89701
Desert Ct & Dr 89705
Desert Peach Dr 89703
Diamond Ave 89706
Diamond Back Way 89706
Diane Dr 89701
Dilday Dr 89701
N & S Division St 89703
Divot Rd 89701
Dogleg Rd 89701
Dominic Ct 89703
Donna St 89701
Dori Way 89706
Doubletree Ln 89701
Douglas Dr 89701

Drake Way 89701
Drew Way 89701
Duke Rd 89701
Dyer Ct 89706
Eagle Ct 89701
Eagle Station Ln 89701
Eagle Valley Ranch Rd 89703
Eastgate Siding Rd 89701
Eastridge Ln 89706
Eastwood Dr 89701
Ediza Cir 89706
N & S Edmonds Dr 89701
E Eighth St 89701
W Eighth St 89703
El Rancho Dr 89703
Elaine St 89701
Elizabeth St 89703
Elm St 89703
Elymus Rd 89701
Emerson Dr 89706
Emily Ct 89703
Empire Ln 89706
Empire Ranch Rd
1401-1497 89701
1499-2400 89701
2402-2598 89701
2601-2699 89706
2613-2613 89721
Enterprize Way 89703
Esser Ct 89703
Esther Cir 89706
Ethel Way 89701
Etta Pl 89701
Eureka Dr 89706
Evalyn Dr 89701
Evan St 89701
Evergreen Dr 89703
Executive Pointe Way 89706
F St 89706
Fair Way 89701
Fairmont Way 89706
Fairview Dr 89701
N Fall St 89706
S Fall St 89701
Farady Cir 89706
Feldspar Cir 89706
Fermi Rd 89706
Fern Meadow Cir 89703
Fieldcrest Dr 89703
E Fifth St 89701
W Fifth St 89703
Figuero Way 89701
Firebox Rd 89701
Fleetwood Ave 89701
Fleischmann Way 89703
Flint Dr 89701
Flintwood Dr 89703
Florentine Dr 89701
Folsom Ct 89705
Fonterra Way 89701
Forrest Way 89706
W Fourth St 89703
Fox Creek Rd 89703
Foxhill Dr 89706
Frank Cir 89706
Franklin Rd 89706
Freedom Ct 89703
Fremont St 89701
Fulton Ct 89706
Furgerson Ranch Rd 89701
Furnace Creek Dr 89706
G St 89706
Gabrielle Ct 89706
Galena Pl & Way 89706
Gambrel Dr 89701
E & W Gardengate Way 89706
Gardner Ln 89706
Garnet Cir 89706
Garnet Ct 89705
Garnet Way 89706
Garson Ct 89706
Garys Way 89701
Gay Cir 89703
Genoa Ln 89706

Gentile Ct 89703
Gentry Ln 89701
Gibson Ave 89701
Gillis Way 89701
Ginger Ln 89701
Glacier Dr 89701
Glenbrook Cir 89703
Glenn Dr 89703
Gold Hill Dr 89706
Gold Leaf Ln 89706
Gold Meadow Ct 89703
Golden Eagle Ln 89701
Goldfield Ave 89701
Goni Rd 89706
Gordon St 89701
Gordonia Dr 89701
Goshute Way 89701
Grand View Ct 89705
Grandville Dr 89701
Granite Ct 89705
Granite Way 89706
Grant St 89701
N & S Green Ct & Dr 89701
Green Acres Dr 89705
Greenbriar Dr 89701
Gregg St 89701
Gregory Ct 89705
Grumman Dr 89706
Gs Richards Blvd 89703
Gypsum Dr 89706
H St 89706
Hackamore Way 89701
Halleck Dr 89701
Hamilton Ave & Cir 89706
E & W Hampton Ct & Dr 89706
Hansen Dr 89701
N & S Harbin Ave 89701
Harper Dr 89701
Harriett Dr 89703
Harrison Ln 89706
Harvard Dr 89703
Harvest Dr 89701
Hauser Ct 89701
Havenwood Ct 89706
Hawaii Cir 89701
Hawthorne Ct 89703
Haystack Ct & Dr 89705
Hazelwood Ct 89703
Heather Cir & Way 89701
Heaton Way 89701
Heaven Hill Way 89706
Heidi Cir 89701
Hells Bells Rd 89701
Hematite Dr 89706
Heppner Dr 89706
Heron Rd 89701
Hickory Dr 89701
Hidden Hill Ln 89706
Hidden Meadow Dr 89701
Highland St 89703
Highlands Dr 89706
Hiko Ct 89706
Hillcrest Rd 89703
Hillside Dr
1-99 89706
970-999 89705
1001-1099 89705
Hillside Way 89703
Hilltop Ct 89705
Hilltop Dr
1-99 89706
970-999 89705
Hillview Dr 89701
Hobart Rd 89703
Hobbyhorse Ln 89701
Holly Way 89706
Homann Way 89703
Horizon Dr 89701
Hospitality Way 89706
Hot Springs Rd 89706
Hudson Dr 89701
Humboldt Ln 89706
Hunt Cir 89701
Hunter Ct 89701
Hunterwood Ct 89706

Hytech Dr 89706
I St 89706
Idaho St 89701
Imperial Way 89706
Imus Rd 89706
Indian Dr 89705
Industrial Pkwy 89706
Industrial Park Dr 89701
N & S Iris St 89703
Ivy St 89703
Jacks Valley Rd & Rnch 89705
Jackson Way 89701
Jacobs Way 89701
Jacobson Way 89701
Jacques Way 89701
James Ct & Dr 89706
James Lee Park Rd 89705
Jamie Way 89701
Janas Way 89701
Jarbidge Ct 89706
Jarrard Ct 89701
Jeanell Dr 89703
Jeanette Cir & Dr 89706
Jefferson Dr 89706
Jeffrey Pine Ln 89705
Jenna Ct 89701
Jenni Ln 89706
Jerry Ln 89701
Jewell Ave 89701
Jodi Ln 89701
E John St 89706
W John St 89703
Jones Rd 89706
Joshua Dr 89701
N Julius Ln 89706
Jumbo Ct 89706
June Cir 89706
Juniper Rd 89701
Kansas St 89701
Karin Dr 89706
Kathleen Dr 89706
Kay Ct 89701
Kelly Dr 89706
Kelvin Rd 89706
Kennedy Dr 89706
Kenny Way 89701
Kensington Ct & Pl 89703
Kentuck Ln 89706
Kerinne Cir 89701
Killdeer Rd 89701
Kimberly Cir 89701
E King St 89701
W King St 89703
Kings Canyon Rd 89703
Kingsley Ln 89701
Kingsview Way 89703
Kit Kat Dr 89706
Kit Sierra Loop & Way 89706
Kitchen Dr 89701
Klatt Dr 89701
Knoblock Rd 89706
Knoll Dr 89703
Koontz Ln 89701
La Loma Dr 89701
La Mirada St 89703
Ladera Dr 89701
Lake Glen Dr 89703
Lakeview Ct & Rd 89703
Lander Dr 89701
Lane Cir 89703
Lango Dr 89706
Larry Cir 89706
Latigo Dr 89701
Laurel Rd 89701
Lavender Cir 89703
Laxalt Dr 89706
Laynya Ln 89706
Lee St 89706
Lehigh Cir 89705
Lemon Rd 89706
Lennox St 89706
Leota Cir 89706
Lepire Dr 89701
Levi Gulch 89703
Lewis Dr 89701

Lexington Ave 89703
Liberty Ct 89703
Lida Cir 89706
Lilly Dr 89701
Lincoln Ct 89706
Linda Kay Ct 89701
Lindsay Ln 89706
Line Dr 89701
Linehan Rd 89706
Lisa Way 89706
List Country Rd 89703
Little Ln 89701
Livermore Ln 89701
Loam Ln 89705
Lockheed Way 89706
Loire St 89701
N Lompa Ln
1301-1599 89701
1801-2997 89706
2999-3099 89706
3101-3499 89706
S Lompa Ln 89701
Lone Mountain Dr 89706
Long Dr 89705
E Long St 89706
W Long St 89703
Longridge Dr 89706
Longview Way 89703
Lorraine St 89706
Lotus Cir 89703
Louise Dr 89706
Lovelace Way 89706
Loyola St 89705
Lucas Dr 89701
Lukens Ln 89706
Lyla Ln 89705
Lynne Ave 89703
Lynnett Ln 89701
Mackinly Ct 89701
Macy Ct 89706
Madison Dr 89706
Maison Way 89703
Malaga Dr 89703
Mallard Dr 89701
Mallory Way 89701
Mallow Rd 89701
Manhattan Dr 89703
Manzanita Ter 89706
Maple Creek Ln 89701
Maple Shade Pl 89703
Margarets Ct 89701
Marian Ave 89706
Marie Dr 89706
Marilyns Way 89701
Mark Way 89706
Market St 89706
Marlette Dr 89703
Marsh Rd 89701
Martha Cir 89706
Martin Dr 89706
Martin St
1-15 89706
600-699 89703
Marvin Dr 89703
Mary St 89703
Mathe Dr 89701
Maxwell Rd 89706
Mayflower Way 89706
Mcclellan Peak Dr 89706
Mcdowell Rd 89706
Meadow Ln 89701
Meadow Vista Dr 89705
Meadow Wood Rd 89703
Meadowbrook Ln 89701
Medical Pkwy 89703
Melanie Ln 89706
Menlo Ct & Dr 89701
Mercury Way 89706
Meridian Ct 89701
Meritage Ct 89703
Merrill Rd 89706
Merrimac Way 89706
Merrit Dr 89701
Metric Way 89706
Mexican Dam Rd 89701
Meyer St 89703

Mica Cir 89706
Mica Dr 89705
Michael Ct 89706
Michael Dr 89703
Midas Way 89706
Miles Rd 89706
Millennium Ter 89706
Miller Way 89703
Milliman Way 89706
Mills Park Ln 89701
Mina Way 89706
N & S Minnesota St 89703
Minonee Ln 89701
Miriam Way 89706
E & W Modoc Ct 89701
Molly Dr 89706
Mono Ln 89703
Mont Blanc Ct 89705
Monte Rosa Dr 89701
Montelena Ct 89703
Montez Dr 89706
Moody St 89706
Moonlight Rd 89706
Morgan Mill Rd 89701
Morris Cir 89706
Moses St 89703
Mountain St 89703
Mountain Park Dr 89706
Mouton Dr 89706
Muldoon St 89701
Mulligan Dr 89701
Murphy Dr 89703
E Musser St 89701
W Musser St 89703
Mustang Dr 89701
Myles Way 89701
Nelson Way 89706
Neptune Ct 89706
N & S Nevada St 89703
New Ridge Dr 89706
Newman Ln 89706
Newman Pl 89703
Newton Rd 89706
Nichols Ln 89706
E Ninth St 89701
W Ninth St 89703
Nona Dr 89701
Norfolk Dr 89703
Norrie Dr 89703
Northcreek Ln 89706
Northfield Dr 89706
Northgate Ln 89706
Northill Dr 89706
Northridge Dr 89706
Northview Dr 89701
Norway St 89706
Norwood Pl 89703
Nugget Ct 89706
Numaga Pass 89703
E Nye Ln 89706
W Nye Ln
101-297 89706
299-499 89706
600-899 89703
901-999 89703
Oak St 89701
Oak Ridge Dr 89703
Old Clear Creek Rd 89705
Old Hot Springs Rd 89706
Oneida St 89703
Onyx Ct 89705
Opalite Ct & Dr 89705
Ophir Cir 89703
Ore Ct 89705
Oreana Dr 89701
N & S Ormsby Blvd 89703
Orovada Dr 89701
Osman Cir 89701
Otha St 89706
E Overland St 89701
Overlook Ct 89705
Overview Ct 89705
Oxbow Dr 89706
Oxford Ct 89703
Paiute St 89703
Palo Verde Dr 89701

Panaca Dr 89701
Panamint Rd 89706
Paradise Vw 89703
Park Dr 89706
S Park Dr 89703
E Park St 89706
W Park St 89703
Parker Dr 89701
Parkhill Dr 89701
Parkland Ave 89701
Parkview Ct 89705
Parkview Dr
971-999 89705
3100-3198 89701
Partridge Dr 89701
Pasture Dr 89701
Pat Ln 89701
W Patrick St 89703
Patton St 89703
Paul Way 89706
Pavilion Ct 89701
Pawnee Ave 89701
Pawnee St 89705
Peakwood Ct 89706
Pebbleridge Dr 89706
Penn Cir 89706
Penny Ln 89703
Peridot Ct 89705
Peters St 89706
Pheasant Dr 89701
Philippi St 89701
N Phillips St 89703
Pine Ln 89706
Pine Cone Cir 89703
Pine View Way 89703
Pinebrook Dr 89701
Pinewood Pl 89703
Pinion Hills Dr 89701
Pinion Pine Dr 89706
Pinoak Ln 89703
Pintail Dr 89701
Pinto Ct 89701
Pioche St 89701
Piper Dr 89703
Pittman Pl 89703
Placer Ct 89705
Plantation Dr 89703
N & S Plaza St 89701
Plymouth Dr 89705
Ponderosa Dr 89701
Pontius Pl 89706
Pony Express Cir 89706
Poole Way 89706
Poplar St 89703
Potomac Pl 89703
Ppf Way 89706
N & S Pratt Ave 89701
Princeton Ave 89705
E Proctor St 89701
W Proctor St 89703
Prospect Dr 89703
Pullman Dr 89701
Purple Sage Ct 89706
Pursia Rd 89701
Pyrenees St 89703
Pyrite Dr 89706
Quail Ln 89701
Quail Run Dr 89701
Quartz Cir & Dr 89706
Quinn Dr 89701
Rabe Way 89701
Race Track Rd 89701
Radcliff Dr 89703
Raglan Cir 89701
Railroad Cir & Dr 89701
Ramsey Cir 89706
Ramuda Cir 89701
Ranchview Cir 89705
Rand Ave & Ct 89706
Randell Dr 89701
Rankin Dr 89701
Rapids Ct 89703
Rasner Ct 89701
Rattler Way 89706
Raven Cir 89701
Ravenshorn Dr 89706

Rawhide Way 89701
Read Ct 89706
Reavis Ln 89701
Red Rock Rd 89706
Reds Grade 89703
Reeves St 89701
Regent Ct 89701
Research Way 89706
Retail Dr 89706
Rex Cir 89706
Rhodes St 89703
Rhone St 89701
Rice St 89706
Richard Dr 89703
N & S Richmond Ave 89703
Ridge St 89703
Ridge Point Dr 89706
Ridgecrest Dr
800-899 89705
2400-2599 89706
2601-2999 89706
Ridgefield Dr 89706
Ridgeview Ct & Dr 89705
Ridgeway Ct 89706
Riley Cir 89706
Rio Vista Ln 89701
Riparian Way 89701
Robb Dr 89703
Roberta Way 89706
E Robinson St 89701
W Robinson St 89703
Rock Ct 89701
Rockbridge Dr 89706
E Roland St 89701
W Roland St 89703
Rolando Way 89701
Rolling Hills Dr 89706
Rolling Ridge Ct 89705
Romans Rd 89705
N Roop St
201-397 89701
399-900 89701
902-998 89701
1200-1800 89706
1802-3498 89706
S Roop St
201-1200 89701
1111-1111 89702
1201-2399 89701
1202-2298 89701
Rose Cir 89706
Round House Ln 89701
Roundup Rd 89701
E Roventini Way 89701
W Roventini Way 89703
Roxbury Way 89703
Royal Dr 89706
Ruby Ct 89705
Ruby Ln 89706
Russell Way 89706
Russett Way 89703
Ruth St 89701
Ryan Way 89706
Saddlehorn Rd 89701
Sage St 89706
N Saliman Rd
401-597 89701
599-1099 89701
1101-1299 89701
1401-1499 89706
S Saliman Rd 89701
Salk Rd 89706
Salmon Dr 89701
San Marcus Dr 89703
Sandalwood Dr 89701
Sandstone Dr 89706
Sandy Cir 89703
Sandy Ln 89706
Sarah Dr 89706
Saratoga Way 89703
Savage Cir 89703
Scarlet Cir 89706
Schell Ave 89701
Schneider Ranch Rd 89705
Schulz Dr 89701
Scotch Pine Dr 89706

Sean Dr 89701
E Second St 89701
W Second St 89703
Sedge Rd 89701
Selby St 89701
Sentinel Cir 89701
E Seventh St 89701
W Seventh St 89703
Shadow Ln 89705
Shadow Brook Ct 89703
Shadowridge Dr 89706
Shady Oak Dr 89701
Shady Tree Ln 89706
Sharon Dr 89701
Sharrow Way 89703
Shawnee Dr 89705
Sheep Dr 89701
Sheffield Mnr E & W 89701
Shelbyville Dr 89701
Shenandoah Dr 89706
Sherman Ln 89706
Short Putt Rd 89701
Shoshone St 89703
Shriver Dr 89701
Sierra Ave 89701
Sierra Cir 89703
Sierra Highland Dr 89705
Sierra Nevada Ln 89706
Sierra Vista Ln 89701
Sigstrom Dr 89706
Silver Ln 89706
Silver Oak Dr
600-698 89706
700-799 89706
1400-1699 89703
Silver Sage Dr 89701
Silver Stream Dr 89703
Silverado Dr 89705
Simone Ave 89701
Simons Ct 89703
Singletree Ct 89701
Siskiyou Dr 89701
E Sixth St 89701
W Sixth St 89703
Slide Mountain Dr 89706
Smoketree Ave 89705
Sneddon Way 89706
Snowflake Dr 89703
Snyder Ave 89701
Somerset Dr 89701
Somerset Way 89705
Sonoma St 89701
W Sophia St 89703
Southcrest Rd 89706
Southpointe Dr 89701
Southridge Ct & Rd 89706
Southwest Ct 89701
Spade Bit Ct 89701
Spartan Ave 89701
E Spear St 89701
W Spear St 89703
Spencer St 89703
Spooner Dr 89706
Spring Dr 89701
Spring Meadow Dr 89703
Springview Dr 89701
Spruce Way 89706
St Albans Pl 89703
St George Way 89703
Stafford Way 89701
Stagecoach Ln 89703
Stampede Dr 89701
Stanford Dr 89701
Stanton Dr 89701
Star Way 89706
Starleaf Ct 89705
Starshine Ct 89705
State Route 341 89706
Steamboat Dr 89701
Stephen Ct 89703
N Stewart St
100-198 89701
200-399 89701
401-1099 89701
1201-1497 89706
1499-1900 89706

1902-1998 89706
S Stewart St 89701
Stokes Dr 89706
Stonegate Way 89706
Stonewall St 89701
Sue Cir 89706
Summerfield Dr 89701
Summerhill Rd 89705
Sunburst Dr 89705
Sunchase Ct 89701
Sundance Ct 89701
Sunland Cir & Dr 89706
Sunnycrest Dr 89705
N Sunridge Ct & Dr 89705
Sunrise Dr 89706
E & W Sunset Way 89703
Sunup Ct 89705
Sunview Ct & Dr 89705
Sunwood Dr 89701
Surrey Ln 89706
Sussex Pl 89703
E, N, S & W Sutro
Ter 89706
Sweetland Dr 89701
Sweetwater Dr 89701
Sycamore Glen Dr 89701
Table Rock Dr 89706
Tacoma Ave 89703
Tahoe Dr 89703
Tamarisk St 89701
Tanager Ct 89706
Tangerine Dr 89701
Tara St 89706
Taylor Way 89703
Teague Rd 89701
Teal Dr 89701
Technology Way 89706
E Telegraph St 89701
W Telegraph St 89703
Tenaya Dr 89706
W Tenth St 89703
Terrace St 89703
Tesla Cir 89706
E Third St 89701
W Third St 89703
Thompson St 89703
Thurman Cir 89706
Tiger Dr 89706
Timberline Dr 89706
Tioga Cir 89706
Tissiac Cir 89706
Tonka Ln 89701
Tonni St 89706
Topaz Dr 89703
Topsy Ln 89705
Toscana Way 89701
Tourmaline Dr & Way 89705
Traci Ln 89706
Travis Dr 89701
Trojan Dr 89706
Trolley Way 89701
Truckee Dr 89701
Tucker Ct 89701
Tulip Ct 89703
Tuolumne Way 89706
Turner Ct 89703
Tuscarora Way 89701
Tybo Cir 89706
Upland Ct 89703
Us Highway 395 S 89705
Us Highway 50 E
2600-7799 89701
Us Highway 50 E
7801-8099 89701
9000-9898 89706
9900-12099 89706
Utah St 89701
Valencia Ct 89703
N Valley St 89701
Valley Crest Dr 89705
Valley View Dr 89701
Valley Vista Dr 89705
Van Epps Dr 89701
Vanpatten Ave 89703
Vassar St 89705
Victoria Ln 89703

Viking Way 89706
Village Dr 89701
Vintage Cir 89701
Vista Ln 89703
Vista Ariana Dr 89703
Vista Grande Blvd 89705
Vista Hill Ct 89705
Vista Park Dr 89705
Vista Ridge Ct 89705
Voltaire St 89703
Voltaire Canyon Rd 89703
Wa Pai Shone Ave 89701
Wagner Dr 89703
Wagon Wheel Rd 89703
Walker Dr 89701
Walnut Ct 89703
N Walsh St 89701
Warm Springs Ct 89701
E Washington St 89701
W Washington St 89703
Washoe St 89703
Watercrest Ct & Dr 89703
Waterford Pl 89703
Watt Rd 89706
Wedco Way 89706
Wegotta Way 89706
Weise Rd 89703
Well Way 89701
Wellington E 89703
Wendy Ln 89706
Weninger Dr 89703
Westcreek Ln 89706
Westview Ave 89703
Westwood Dr 89703
Wialaki St 89703
Wild Sage Cir 89703
Willard Ln 89701
E William St 89701
W William St 89703
E Willow St 89701
W Willow St 89703
Wilma Way 89706
Wilson Ct 89701
Windridge Dr 89706
Windtree Cir 89701
Wingate Way 89706
E Winnie Ln 89706
N Winnie Ln 89703
W Winnie Ln 89703
Winters Dr 89703
Woodbend Ct 89701
Woodcrest Ln 89701
Woodridge Cir 89703
Woodside Dr 89701
Woodstock Cir 89703
Wright Way 89701
Yale Dr 89703
Yellow Jacket Ln 89706
Yhvona Dr 89706
Yorktown Dr 89703
Yukon Ct 89706
Zephyr Cir 89706
Zurich Ct 89705

ELKO NV

General Delivery 89801

POST OFFICE BOXES MAIN OFFICE STATIONS AND BRANCHES

Box No.s
All PO Boxes 89803

HIGHWAY CONTRACTS

31 89801

NAMED STREETS

All Street Addresses 89801

NUMBERED STREETS

S 1st 89801
S 2nd 89801
3rd St
100-242 89801
244-300 89801
275-275 89803
301-1399 89801
302-1298 89801
S 3rd St 89801
4 Mile Trl 89801
S 4th 89801
5th St 89801
S 6th 89801
S 7th 89801
S 8th 89801
S 9th 89801
S 10th 89801
S 11th 89801
S 12th 89801
13th St 89801
14th St 89801
30th St 89801

ELY NV

General Delivery 89301

POST OFFICE BOXES MAIN OFFICE STATIONS AND BRANCHES

Box No.s
1989 - 1989 89301
150001 - 159998 89315

HIGHWAY CONTRACTS

10, 31, 32, 33, 34, 64 89301

NAMED STREETS

All Street Addresses 89301

NUMBERED STREETS

All Street Addresses 89301

FALLON NV

General Delivery 89406

POST OFFICE BOXES MAIN OFFICE STATIONS AND BRANCHES

Box No.s
All PO Boxes 89407

NAMED STREETS

E & W A St 89406
N & S Ada St 89406
Adobe Rd 89406
Agate Ln 89406
Agency Rd 89406
Aimee Ln 89406
Airport Rd 89406
Albert St 89406
Alcorn Rd 89406
Alix Cir 89406
Allegre Ln 89406
Allen Rd 89406
N Allen Rd 89406
S Allen Rd
118-120 89406
120-120 89407
N Allen St 89406
S Allen St 89406
Allyn Pl 89406
Amanda Ln 89406
Amber Way 89406
Andrew Ln 89406
Angela Ct 89406
Annette Dr 89406
Anthony Ln 89406
Applewood Cir 89406
Ara Ln 89406
Arizona Ct 89406
Arnold Way 89406
Arrowhead Ln 89406
Arundell Ln 89406
Arvilla Ln 89406
Aspen Cir & Way 89406
Auction Rd 89406
Augusta Ln 89406
Austin Hwy & Rd 89406
W B St 89406
Babb Pl 89406
Bafford Ln 89406
N & S Bailey St 89406
Bango Rd 89406
Bass Rd 89406
Beach Rd 89406
Beacon Way 89406
Bear Paw Ct 89406
Beasley Dr 89406
Beeghly Dr 89406
Bell Aire Ln 89406
Bench Rd 89406
Benson Ln 89406
Berney Rd 89406
Beth Way 89406
Beverly Dr 89406
Bianchi Ln 89406
Bighorn St 89406
Birch Ln 89406
Black Eagle Ct 89406
Blackbird Pkwy 89406
Blue Sage Dr 89406
Blues Ct 89406
Bobby Way 89406
Bobcat Bnd 89406
Bon Accord Ln 89406
Bonanza Ln 89406
Bonnie Ln 89406
Bottom Rd 89406
Boundary Rd 89406
Bourbon St 89406
Bowie Rd 89406
Boyer Rd 89406
Bradley St 89406
Breckenridge Dr 89406
Brent St 89406
Briggs Ln 89406
N & S Broadway St 89406
Brookside Cir 89406
Browns Ln 89406
Brush Garden Dr 89406
Burntwood St 89406
Butte Vw 89406
C J Dr 89406
Caballo Way 89406
Cadet Rd 89406
Calaway Ct 89406
Caleb Dr 89406
California Ct 89406
Calkin Rd 89406
Campus Way 89406
Candee Ln 89406
Cardinal Dr 89406
Carol Dr 89406
Carr Ln 89406
N & S Carson Hwy &
St 89406
Carson River Dr 89406
Casey Rd 89406
Catfish Ct 89406
Cedar Dr 89406
E & W Center St 89406
Chama Cir 89406
Charlys Way 89406

Chavez Dr & Ln 89406
Chelcie St 89406
Cherry Ln 89406
Christie Cir 89406
Christine Way 89406
Chukar St 89406
Chumley Dr 89406
Churchill St 89406
Cicada St 89406
Cimarron Rd 89406
Cin Ber Ln 89406
Cindy Ln 89406
Clark Ln 89406
Classic Way 89406
Claudias Way 89406
Clearview Ct 89406
Cleveland St 89406
Clover Dr 89406
Cloverdale Way 89406
Clyde Ct 89406
Clyde Jr Rd 89406
Cody Rd 89406
Coleman Rd 89406
Colorado Ln 89406
Commercial Way 89406
Concord Ave 89406
Conifer Dr 89406
Conrad Pl 89406
Copperwood Dr 89406
Cora Way 89406
Coral Dr 89406
E & W Corkill Ln 89406
Cornerstone Ct 89406
Cottonwood Dr 89406
Country Club Dr 89406
Country River Dr 89406
Court St 89406
Courtney Marie Ln 89406
Cow Canyon Dr 89406
Cox Rd 89406
Coyote Cir 89406
Cress Pl 89406
N & S Crook Rd 89406
Crystal Ct 89406
Curry Rd 89406
Cushman Rd 89406
W D St 89406
Dalila St 89406
Dallas Dr 89406
Dalton St 89406
Dani St 89406
Davis Ln 89406
Dean Ln 89406
Deena Way 89406
Deer Trl 89406
Deer Creek Cir 89406
Deerfield Dr 89406
Del Rio Dr 89406
Della Cir 89406
Depp Rd 89406
Desatoya Ln 89406
Desert Hills Loop 89406
Desert Springs Ct 89406
Desert View Dr 89406
Dianna Way 89406
Dillon Rd 89406
Discovery Dr 89406
Ditch House Ln 89406
Dixie Dr 89406
Dodge Ln 89406
Dodgion Ln 89406
Doi Dicutta St 89406
Dolores Ln 89406
Dorral Way 89406
Douglas St 89406
N & S Downs Ln 89406
Draper Way 89406
Driftwood Ln 89406
Drumm Ln 89406
Duane Dr 89406
Dundee Ln 89406
Dunmoven 89406
Eagle Feather Ct 89406
Eagle Rock Rd 89406
N & S East St 89406
Edgewater Ln 89406

Edwards Ln 89406
Eider Cir 89406
Elizabeth Pkwy 89406
Elk Horn Way 89406
Ellison St 89406
Elm Dr 89406
Equestrian Dr 89406
Equinox Ln 89406
Erins Way 89406
Ernst Dr 89406
Esmeralda St 89406
Eugene Way 89406
E & W Fairview St 89406
Falcon Dr 89406
Ferguson St 89406
Fischer Pl 89406
Fisherman Rd 89406
Fitz Ln 89406
Flying K Ranch Ln 89406
Franklin St 89406
Freeman Ln 89406
Freeport Cir 89406
E & W Front St 89406
Fruth Way 89406
Fulkerson Rd 89406
Gallo Way 89406
Gary Ln 89406
Getto Cir 89406
Glacier Dr 89406
Gladys Dr 89406
Gloria Way 89406
Golden Cir 89406
Golden Eagle Ct 89406
Golden Park Way 89406
Goldeneye Dr 89406
Graeagle Dr 89406
Graham Ln 89406
Grand Ave 89406
Graystoke Cir 89406
Great Basin Ln 89406
Green Valley Dr 89406
Greenleaf Ln 89406
Grimes St 89406
Gummow Dr 89406
Gwinn Marie Ct 89406
Hammond Dr 89406
N & S Harmon Rd 89406
Harold Ct 89406
Harrigan Rd 89406
Harvey Dr 89406
Hawk Dr 89406
Hayden Ln 89406
Heidi Rd 89406
Helens Way 89406
Henley Ct 89406
Heraind Rd 89406
Heron Ln 89406
Hettinger Pl 89406
Hiatt Loop 89406
Hicks Rd 89406
Highland Dr 89406
Highway 722 89406
Hillsboro Blvd 89406
Hiskett Ln 89406
Hollyhock Cir 89406
Honker Ln 89406
Hooper Pl 89406
Hoover Dr & Rd 89406
Hornby Rd 89406
Horseshoe Dr 89406
Howard Pl 89406
Humboldt St 89406
Hunter Park Way 89406
Idaho Ct 89406
Indian Lakes Rd 89406
Industrial Way 89406
Jacobs Rd 89406
James Ln 89406
Jane Ct 89406
Jarbidge Ct 89406
Jasper Rd 89406
Jensen Ct 89406
Jewell Dr 89406
Joel Way 89406
Jonathan Cir 89406
Jonathon Cir 89406
Jordans Way 89406
Joyce Ct 89406
Julie Ln 89406
June Dr 89406
Kadee Ct 89406
Kaiser St 89406
Kamibo Dr 89406
Karry Way 89406
Kathy St 89406
Keddie St 89406
Ken Ln 89406
Kennedy Ln 89406
Keppel St 89406
Keyes Way 89406
King Dr 89406
Kinsli St 89406
Kirn Rd 89406
La Belle St 89406
Lahontan Dr 89406
Lahontan Dam Rd 89406
Laiolo St 89406
Lakeview Dr 89406
Lammel Pl 89406
Lariat Way 89406
Lattin Rd 89406
N & S Laverne St 89406
Lawrence Ln 89406
Lazy Heart Ln 89406
Lee Ave 89406
Lenore Dr 89406
Leslie Ct 89406
Leter Rd 89406
Lewis Ln 89406
Liberty Ave 89406
Lima Ln 89406
Lincoln St 89406
Linda St 89406
Lizard Ct 89406
London Cir 89406
Lone Tree Rd 89406
Longhorn Dr 89406
Lovelock Hwy 89406
Lucas Rd 89406
Lynnie Ln 89406
Lyons Ln 89406
Macari Ln 89406
Macpherson Ln 89406
Magnolia Rd 89406
N Maine St
67-73 89406
75-97 89406
99-753 89406
120-798 89406
120-120 89407
S Maine St 89406
Mallard Way 89406
Manchester Cir 89406
Manzanita Dr 89406
Maple Way 89406
Margoree Ln 89406
Mark Ave 89406
Marshall Dr 89406
Martin Ln 89406
Mary St 89406
May Ranch Rd 89406
Mckay Ct 89406
S Mclean Rd & St 89406
Meadow Glen Dr 89406
Meadow View Ln 89406
Meadowlark Dr 89406
Medallion Ln 89406
Megan Way 89406
Melanie Dr 89406
Merton Dr 89406
Mesquite Ln 89406
Michael Dr 89406
Michelle Dr 89406
Milburn Ln 89406
Milky Way 89406
Miners Rd 89406
Mission Rd 89406
Moody Ln 89406
Morina Dr 89406
Mount View Dr 89406
Mountain Lion Ct 89406
Nadine Dr 89406
Naval Air Sta 89406
N & S Nevada St 89406
Nevada City Rd 89406
New Pass Rd 89406
New River Pkwy 89406
Nicole Cir 89406
Noel Ln 89406
Nola St 89406
Norcutt Ln 89406
Northview Dr 89406
Nubian Way 89406
Oakwood Cir 89406
Old River Rd 89406
Olive Way 89406
Oran Rd 89406
Orchard Dr 89406
Oregon Dr 89406
Paiute Dr 89406
Pams Pl 89406
E & W Park St 89406
Pasture Rd 89406
Pattie Dr 89406
Paul Pl 89406
Peaceful Way 89406
Peach Tree Rd 89406
Pelican Dr 89406
Penelope Dr 89406
Peraldo Ln 89406
Perazzo Ln 89406
Pflum Ln 89406
Pg Ranch Rd 89406
Pheasant Dr 89406
Phelps Ln 89406
Phritzie Ln 89406
Pine Rd 89406
Pinenut St 89406
Pinion Ln 89406
Pintail Dr 89406
Pioneer Way 89406
Ponderosa Pl 89406
Poplar Trl 89406
Portuguese Ln 89406
Potpourri Dr 89406
Pow Wow Ct 89406
Power Line Rd 89406
Primrose Ln 89406
Purple Sage Ln 89406
Quail Way 89406
Quintin Way 89406
Rachel Ct 89406
Rambling Wind Dr 89406
Rancheria Rd 89406
Ranchland Dr 89406
Rancho Dr 89406
Raven Dr 89406
Red Rd 89406
Red Mountain Ct & Pl 89406
Redwing Dr 89406
Reese Way 89406
Regan Pl 89406
Reno Hwy 89406
Reservation Rd 89406
Reservoir Rd 89406
Rice Rd 89406
E & W Richards St 89406
Rio Vista Dr 89406
River View Dr 89406
River Village Dr 89406
Rivers Edge Dr 89406
Roberson Ln 89406
Roberta Ct 89406
Robin Dr 89406
Rockwood Pl 89406
Rogers Rd 89406
Ronald Way 89406
Rose Cir 89406
Roseman Dr 89406
Rosewood Dr 89406
N & S Russell St 89406
Ryan Way 89406
Sabrina Way 89406
Sage Ln 89406
Saint Clair Rd 89406
Saint Patrick Ct 89406
Saltgrass Trl 89406
Samantha Cir 89406
Sandalwood Dr 89406
Sandhill Rd 89406
Santa Fe Dr 89406
Sapphire Way 89406
Sarah Rd 89406
Sarah Belle Ln 89406
Schaffer Ln 89406
Scheelite Mine Rd 89406
Schindler Rd 89406
Schurz Hwy 89406
Scott St 89406
Serpa Pl 89406
Settlement Rd 89406
Settler Dr 89406
Shady Ct 89406
Sheckler Rd 89406
Sheckler Cut Off 89406
N Sherman St 89406
Sherwood Ct 89406
Shoffner Ln 89406
Shoshone Dr 89406
Sierra Way 89406
Silas 89406
Silver Cir 89406
Silver Sage Ln 89406
Silver Spur Dr 89406
Silver State Ave 89406
Silverado Rd 89406
Sky Ridge Dr 89406
Smart Ln 89406
Smokin Bull Dr 89406
Soda Lake Rd 89406
Solias Rd 89406
Sorensen Ct & Rd 89406
Sprig Ln 89406
Spring Flower Ln 89406
Spruce Trl 89406
Stains Rd 89406
Stark Ln 89406
State St 89406
Steven Dr 89406
E & W Stillwater Ave &
Rd 89406
Stoneberger Pl 89406
Strasdin Ln 89406
Stuart Rd 89406
Sunrise Ter 89406
Sunset Dr 89406
Sunshine Loop 89406
Swope Ln 89406
Tamara Ln 89406
Tamarack Ct 89406
Taos Ct 89406
Tarzyn Rd 89406
N & S Taylor Pl & St 89406
Teal Dr 89406
Tedford Ln 89406
Terry Ln 89406
Testolin Rd 89406
Thomas Ct 89406
Thompson Ln 89406
Thornbird Dr 89406
Thurman Ln 89406
Tiffany Dr 89406
Timber Way 89406
Timothy Way 89406
Toiyabe Ln 89406
W Tolas Pl 89406
Tommy Trl 89406
Topaz Ln 89406
Torrey Pines Ct & Dr 89406
Toyon Dr 89406
Trails End 89406
Tree Line Rd 89406
Trento Ln 89406
Triple E Ln 89406
Tule St 89406
Tumbleweed Rd 89406
Union Ln 89406
Utah Ct 89406
Valley Dr 89406
Van Fleet Rd 89406
Vanessa Dr 89406
Vaughn Rd 89406
Venturacci Ln 89406
Verona Dr 89406
Victor Dr 89406
Vinewood 89406
Violets Rd 89406
E & W Virginia St 89406
Wade Ln 89406
Warwick Ave 89406
Weaver Rd 89406
Western Ave 89406
Westwind Way 89406
Wetland Vw 89406
Whitaker Ln 89406
Whitehawk Dr 89406
Wildes Rd & St 89406
Willdate Dr 89406
E & W Williams Ave 89406
Willow Way 89406
Willow Creek Dr 89406
Winchester Rd 89406
Windmill Dr 89406
Wood Dr 89406
Woodhaven Dr 89406
Woodlands Pl 89406
Woolery Way 89406
Workman Rd 89406
Yeoman Ln 89406
York Ln 89406
Yucca Ln 89406
Zephyr Ln 89406

NUMBERED STREETS

All Street Addresses 89406

GARDNERVILLE NV

General Delivery 89410

POST OFFICE BOXES MAIN OFFICE STATIONS AND BRANCHES

Box No.s
1 - 3196 89410
6001 - 9534 89460

HIGHWAY CONTRACTS

02 89410

NAMED STREETS

Adaline Way 89460
Addler Rd 89460
Alba Vis 89410
Aldersgate Ct 89410
Alex Ct 89460
Alicia Cir 89460
Allerman Ln 89460
Allyn Ct 89460
Amanda Ct 89460
Amarillo Dr 89460
Amber Way 89410
Anderson Ranch Rd 89460
Angora Dr 89460
Ann Way 89460
Annkim Cir 89460
Antares Ave 89410
Anthony Ct 89410
Apaloosa Ln 89410
Apollo Ave 89410
Apple Creek Ln 89460
Arabian Ln 89410
Arlen Ln 89410
Arlene Marie Ln 89460
Arrowhead Dr 89460
Arroyo Dr 89410
Ashley Ct 89460
Aspen Brook Ln 89460
Aspen Hill Ct 89460
Aurora Dr 89410
Austin St 89410
Autumn Hills Rd 89460
E & W Aylesbury Ct 89410
Azul Way 89460
Baltic Ave 89410
Banner Dr 89460
Bar J Rd 89410
Barber Way 89460
Barker Ct 89410
Beatty St 89410
Bell St 89410
Belmont Ct 89460
Bennett Cir 89410
Berning Way 89460
Berry Ln 89460
Beverly Way 89460
Big Jake Ct 89460
Big Valley Rd 89410
Birdie Ct 89460
Bishops Cir 89410
Bitterbrush Ct 89410
Black Bear Trl 89460
Black Sage Cir 89410
Blue Sage 89410
Bluebird Way 89410
Bluerock Rd 89460
Bobwhite Ln 89410
Bobwire Ln 89460
Boddu H Way 89460
Bodie Ct 89460
Bodie Rd 89410
Bolivia Way 89460
Bollen Cir 89460
Bolton Way 89410
Borda Way 89410
Bowers Rd 89410
Bowles Ln 89460
Branden Ln 89410
Bray Way 89410
Brentwood Ct 89410
Broken Arrow Rd 89410
Brooke Way 89410
Bryan Ln 89410
Buckingham Ct 89410
Buckskin Ct & Ln 89410
Buckwheat Ct 89410
Buena Vista Ct 89460
Bumblebee Ln 89410
Burro Ct 89410
Butler Ct 89410
Butterfly Ln 89410
Cabernet Ct 89460
Cahi Cir 89460
Cal Ct & Ln 89410
Calle Del Sol 89410
Calle Hermosa 89410
Calle Ladera 89410
Calle Pequeno 89410
Camas Ct 89410
Camino Vista Montave
Rd 89410
Campbell Ct 89410
Canal Dr 89410
Candy Ln 89410
Canyon Ct 89460
Canyon Creek Ct &
Ln 89460
Cardiff Ct & Dr 89410
Cardinal Ct 89460
Carlson Ct & Dr 89410
Carmel Way 89460
Carrousel Ct 89410
Cary Creek Ct 89460
Casey St 89460
Castle Ln 89410
Catherine Ct 89410
Cavelti Rd 89410
Cayuse Dr 89410
Cedar Brook Ct 89460
Cedar Creek Cir 89460
Centerville Ln
400-1256 89460
1258-1282 89460
1281-1283 89410
1285-1287 89410
1289-1289 89410
1290-1291 89460
1293-1299 89460
1296-1298 89410
1300-1399 89410
Chance Rd 89410
Chardonnay Dr 89460
Charlotte Way 89410
Cheddington Cir 89410
Chestnut Ct 89410
Chichester Dr 89410
Chiltern Ct 89410
China Spring Rd 89410
Chisholm Trl 89460
Choke Cherry Ct 89410
Chukar Ln 89410
Church St 89410
Churchill St 89410
Circle Dr 89410
Claire Ct 89460
Clark Ln 89460
Clydesdale Ct 89410
Cobblestone Dr 89460
Colorado Ct 89460
Colt Ln 89410
Columbia Ct 89460
Como Ct 89460
Comstock Dr 89410
Conejo Ln 89410
Conner Way 89410
Cora Ct 89410
Corie Ct 89460
Cortez Ln 89410
W Cottage Loop 89460
Cottonwood St 89410
Country Ln 89460
Courthouse St 89410
N Courtland Ln 89410
Coyote Rd 89410
Creek Dr 89410
Crestmore Dr 89410
Crockett Ln 89410
Cunningham Ln 89410
Currant Ct 89410
Cutter Ln 89410
Cuttin Loose Ln 89460
Dala Ak Way 89460
Dark Horse Ct 89410
Dayton St 89410
Dean Dr 89460
Deer Path Ln 89460
Delores Way 89460
Derby Ct 89410
Desert Gold Ct 89410
Devenpeck Dr 89410
Dina Ct 89460
Dino Ct 89460
Diorite Rd 89460
Donna Ct 89460
Dora Dr 89460
Douglas Ave 89410
Dove Ct 89410
Drake Ln 89410
Dressler Ln 89460
Dresslerville Rd 89460
Dump Rd 89410
Eagle Ct 89460
Eagle Meadows Ln 89460
Easton Way 89410
Eastside Ln 89410
Eddy St 89410
Edlesborough Cir 89410
Edna Dr 89460
El Dorado Dr 89410
Elges Ave 89410
Ellies Way 89460
Ellis Ln 89460
Ely Way 89460
Eureka St 89410
Eva Ct 89460
Evan Ln 89460
Evening Star Ln 89460
Ezell St 89410
Fahim Dr 89410
Fairchild Ct 89410
Fairs 89410
Fairview Ln 89460
Fairway Dr 89460

Falstaff Ln 89410
Farrier Ct 89410
Fay Ct 89460
Fernley St 89410
Fieldgate Ct & Way 89410
Fifth Green Ct 89460
Finch Dr 89410
Fish Springs Rd 89410
Five Creek Rd 89460
Flying Eagle Ranch Ln 89460
Foothill Rd 89460
Forest Hill Way 89460
Forest View Ln 89460
W Fork Vista Ln 89460
N Forty Rd 89460
Four Place Ln 89410
Franklin Ln 89460
Fred St 89410
Fredricksburg Rd 89460
Fricke Ct 89460
Frontage Rd 89410
Galena Ct 89460
Gansberg Ct 89460
Garden Glen Ct 89410
Gardner Dr 89410
Gemm Ln 89410
Genoa Ln 89410
Georgia Ln 89460
Gilman Ave 89410
Glenwood Dr 89460
Goa Way 89460
Godecke Ln 89410
Goldbug Ct 89460
Golden Eagle Ct 89410
Goldfield Dr 89410
Granborough Dr 89410
Grant Ave 89410
Gray Ct 89410
Green Acres Dr 89460
Grendon Way 89460
Guiness Way 89410
Hackamore Ln 89410
Hansen Ln 89460
Hanslope Way 89410
Harley Ct 89460
Harvest Ave 89410
Hastings Ln 89410
Hawkins Peak Ct 89410
Heavenly View Ct 89460
Helen Ln 89410
Helman Dr 89410
Heriver Dr 89460
Heron Cove Ct 89410
Heybourne Rd 89410
High School St 89410
Highland Way 89410
Hiko Ct 89410
Holly Ct 89460
Home Ln 89410
Homestead Rd 89410
Honey Locust Ave 89410
Honeybee Ln 89460
Hornet Dr 89460
Horsebush Ct 89410
Horseman Ct 89410
Horseshoe Bend Rd 89410
Horsethief Cir 89460
Hussman Ave 89410
Indian Creek Rd 89460
Indian Trail Rd 89460
Industrial Ct & Way 89410
Irene Ct 89460
Irma Ln 89460
Itmahowah Cir 89460
Jackrabbit Rd 89410
Jackson Ranch Rd 89460
Jacobsen Ln 89410
James Rd 89460
Jan Ct 89410
Jane Way 89460
Janelle Ct 89410
Jason Ln 89410
Jeannie Ln 89460
Jessica Ln 89410
Jewel Cir 89410
Jill Dr 89460

Jo Ln 89410
Jobe Ct 89460
Jobes Canyon Ct 89460
Jobs Canyon Ct 89460
Jobs Peak Dr 89460
Jodi Ct 89460
Joette Ct & Dr 89460
Jones Ln 89460
Jones Ranch Rd 89460
Julian Way 89410
Jungo Ct 89410
Juniper Rd 89410
Karnes Dr 89410
Kathy Ct & Way 89460
Keepsake Cir 89460
Kelly Ct 89460
Kerry Ct & Ln 89460
Keystone Ct 89460
Kim Ct 89460
Kimbles Way 89410
Kimmerling Rd 89410
Kingsbury Grade 89460
Kingsland Ct 89460
Kingslane Ct 89410
Kingston Ln & Way 89460
Kittyhawk Ave 89410
Knights Ln 89410
N Knoreda Ln 89410
Kyndal Ct & Way 89460
Lacey Ct & St 89410
Ladera Ln 89460
Lakeside Dr 89460
Lampe Ln 89410
Langley Dr 89460
Larkspur Ln 89460
Lassen Way 89460
Lasso Ln 89410
Laura Springs Cir 89460
Lawrence Ln 89460
Leealan Dr 89460
Lena Ln 89410
Leonard Ct & Rd 89460
Leviathan Mine Rd 89410
Lewallen Ln 89460
Lillian Ct 89460
Linda Dr 89460
Linda Anne Ct 89410
Lisa Ln 89460
Log Cabin Rd 89410
Lois Ct 89460
Lombardy Rd 89410
Lone Eagle Ln 89410
Long Ct 89410
Long Bow Ct 89410
Long Valley Rd 89410
Longfellow Ln 89410
Lorraine Ln 89410
Lost River Ln 89460
Lou Ct 89410
Lupo Ln 89410
Lyell Way 89460
Macenna Ln 89410
Mad Cap Ln 89410
Magpie Ln 89410
Mammoth Way 89460
Manhattan Way 89460
Margo St 89410
Marianne Way 89460
Marion Way 89460
S, E & N Marion Russell
Ct & Dr 89410
Marj Ln 89410
Mark Cir & St 89410
Mark Twain Ave 89410
Marlette Cir 89460
Marron Way 89460
Marsha Ln 89460
Mary Jo Dr 89460
Masonic Dr 89410
Mathew Ct 89460
Mathias Pkwy 89410
Maverick Ct 89460
Me Hu St 89460
Meadow Ct & Ln 89410
Meadow View Dr 89460
Meadowlark Cir 89460

Megan Ct 89410
Meggel Ln 89460
Mel Dr 89410
Memdawee Run 89460
Memory Cir 89410
Merino Cir 89410
Milkweed Ct 89410
Mill St 89410
Mill Creek Cir & Way 89410
Mission St 89410
Mitch Dr 89460
Monarch Ln 89460
Monument Peak Dr 89460
Morgan Ct 89410
Mormon Way 89410
Morning Star Ct 89410
Morning Sun Ct 89460
Morningstar Ct 89460
Moss Cir 89410
Mott Ct 89460
Mottsville Ln 89460
Mottsville Meadows
Way 89460
Mountain Ct 89410
Mountain Ash Ct &
Way 89410
Mountain Clover Rd 89410
Mountain Reach Ct 89460
Mt Como Rd 89410
Mt Siegel 89410
Muir Dr 89460
Mule Ln 89410
Muller Pkwy 89410
Mustang Ln 89410
Myers Dr 89410
Natures Edge Rd 89460
New Hope Dr 89410
Niblick Dr 89460
Nichole Way 89460
Nord Cir & Ct 89460
North Ct 89410
Northampton Cir 89410
Northstar Ct 89410
Old Foothill Rd S 89460
Old Nevada Way 89460
Old Ranch Rd 89410
Old Us Highway 395
S 89410
Olympus Dr 89410
S Orchard Rd 89410
Oreana Peak Ct 89410
Oro Way 89460
Ortega Way 89410
Out R Way 89410
Ox Yoke Ct 89410
Palisade Cir 89460
Palomino Ln 89410
Paradise Mountain Rd
N 89410
Parman Ct 89460
Patdul Negeeh 89460
Patricia Ct & Dr 89460
Patrick Ct 89410
Paula Pl 89410
Pawns Ct 89410
Pbaul St 89460
Peach Ct 89410
E Peak Dr 89460
Peleu Way 89460
Penn Ln 89460
Penrod Ct & Ln 89460
Peoria Trl 89410
Pep Cir 89410
Pepis Dr 89460
Petar Dr 89410
Phillips Way 89460
Pin Oak Dr 89410
Pine Valley Rd 89410
Pinenut Crk & Rd 89410
Pinto Cir 89410
Pioche Ln 89460
Pit Rd 89460
Pleasantview Ct & Dr 89460
Plum Ct 89460
Pollen Ct 89460
Pony Ct 89460

Purple Sage Dr 89460
Purshia Hill Rd 89460
Putter Ln 89460
Qadosh 89410
Quail Ct 89410
Quail Ridge Rd 89460
Quarter Cir 89410
Queens Ct 89410
Raab Ct 89460
Rabbitbrush Dr 89410
Rainshadow Way 89460
Ranch Dr 89460
Rancho Rd 89460
Rawhide Ct 89460
Ray May Way 89460
Red Cedar Ave 89410
Redwood Cir 89460
Reese Ln 89410
Reflection Ct 89460
Regalia Ct 89460
Renee Ct 89410
Richards Ct 89410
Risue Rd 89410
Ritter Dr 89460
S Riverview Dr 89460
Roan Cir 89410
Robin Dr 89460
Rockbottom Rd 89410
Rocking Horse Rd 89410
Rocky Ter 89460
Rojo Way 89460
Ron Ln 89410
Roos Rd 89460
Rose Way 89460
Rubicon Ct 89460
Rubio Way 89460
Rue Ranch Rd 89410
Russell Way 89460
Saddle Ct 89410
Sage Ocean Ct 89460
Sagebrush Ct 89460
Sally Ln 89460
Saltbush Ct 89460
Sanchez Rd 89410
Sandoval Rd 89410
Sandy Bowers Ave 89410
Sawmill Rd 89410
Scarlet Oak Dr 89410
Scotch Pine Way 89460
Scoti Ln 89410
Scott St 89410
Scout Cir 89410
Sego Cir 89410
Selkirk Cir 89460
Service Dr 89410
Shadow Mountain Rd 89460
Shasta Dr 89460
Sheep Camp Rd 89460
Shena Ter 89410
Sheridan Ln 89460
Sheridan Creek Ct 89460
Shetland Cir 89410
Short Ct 89460
W Side Ln 89460
Sierra Country Cir &
Ct 89460
Sierra Shadows Ln 89460
Sierra Vista Ct & Dr 89460
Silver Linden Way 89410
Silver Spur Ct 89410
Silveranch Dr 89460
Skyhawk Ranch Rd 89460
Solitude Ln 89410
Sorensen Ct & Ln 89460
Sorrel Ln 89410
Sotheby Ct 89410
South Ct 89410
Southgate Dr 89410
Spring Valley Dr 89410
Springfield Dr 89460
Springtime Dr 89460
Spruce St 89410
Stagecoach Rd 89410
Stallion Ct 89410
Starlight Ct 89460
State Route 88 89460

Stephen Ct 89410
Sterling Ln 89410
Sterling Ranch Dr 89410
Stodick Ln & Pkwy 89410
Stoen Ct 89410
Stonegate Ct 89410
Stones Throw Rd 89410
Stoney Creek Ct 89460
Stutler Creek Ct 89460
Sugar Maple Ave 89410
Sullivan Dr 89410
Summer Hills Rd 89460
Summit Ridge Way 89460
Sunburst Ct 89460
Sundown Ct 89460
Sunnyside Ct 89460
Sunset Ct & Rdg 89410
Sweetwater Ct & Dr 89460
Taildragger Rd 89410
Tambourine Ranch Rd 89460
Tamzy Ct 89410
Taylor Creek Rd 89460
Tedsen Ln 89410
Tenabo Ln 89410
Thorobred Ave 89410
Tigerwood Ct 89460
Tillman Ln 89460
Timber Ct 89410
Tognetti Aly 89410
Toiyabe Ave 89410
Toler Ave 89410
Topaz Ln
1200-1499 89460
3400-3599 89410
Topaz Park Rd 89410
Townhouse Cir 89410
Trance Acres Ln 89460
Tsam Du Way 89460
Tucke Ct 89460
Tumbleweed Ct 89460
Tybo Ct 89410
Tycoon Ct 89460
Tyndall Way 89460
Uphill Rd 89410
Us Highway 395 N &
S 89410
E Valley Rd 89410
Venture Dr 89410
Vera Way 89410
Verde Way 89460
Victoria Ct, Dr & Way 89460
Victory Cir 89410
View Pointe 89410
Viewmont Ct 89410
Village Way 89410
Violetta Cir 89460
Virginia Ranch Rd 89410
Vista Vallata 89410
Wa She Shu 89460
Wagner Ct 89410
Wagon Dr 89460
Wagon Wheel Ct 89460
E & W Wales Ct 89410
Walker St 89410
Wasp Ct 89460
Watasheamu Rd 89460
Waterloo Ln
900-1208 89460
1232-1234 89410
1236-1244 89460
1245-1249 89410
1250-1298 89460
1251-1399 89410
1300-1382 89410
Watson Ct 89410
Wendover Ct 89410
Westminster Pl 89410
Wheeler Way 89460
Whispering Pine Ct 89460
White Ash Dr 89410
Whitney Way 89460
Wild Iris Ct 89410
Wild Onion Ct 89410
Wildflower Ct 89410
Wildrose Dr 89410
Wilhelm Pl 89460

Willow St 89410
Willow Creek Ln 89410
Wilson Cir 89410
Windmill Rd 89410
Windsor Ct & Dr 89410
Winners Cir 89410
Winter Green Ct & Dr 89460
Winwood Way 89410
Wiseman Ln 89410
Wonder Ct 89460
Woodford Ln 89460
Woodside Ln 89460
Woodys Pl 89460
Yellowjacket Ln 89460
Zinfandel Dr 89460

HENDERSON NV

General Delivery 89015

POST OFFICE BOXES MAIN OFFICE STATIONS AND BRANCHES

Box No.s
55 - 2700 89009
50001 - 50880 89016
90001 - 95075 89009
530001 - 539526 89053
777001 - 778436 89077

NAMED STREETS

Abbeyfield Rose Dr 89052
Abbeystone Cir 89052
Abbington St 89074
Abby Ave 89014
Aberdeen Ln 89014
Abilene St 89002
Ability Point Ct 89012
Abracadabra Ave 89002
Abundance Ridge St 89012
Ackerman Ln 89014
Ackers Dr 89052
Acoustic St 89015
Adagietto Dr 89052
Adagio St 89052
Adams Run Ct 89002
Adcox Ct 89015
Addlyn Ct 89002
Admiralty Ct 89074
Adobe Flat Dr 89011
Adomeit Dr 89074
Adonis Ave 89074
Adorno Dr 89074
Adriana Bend Ct 89052
Adriatic Dr 89074
African Eagle Ave 89015
African Sunset St 89052
African Violet Ave 89074
Afternoon Rain Ave 89002
Ailsa Craig St 89044
Aimless St 89011
Ainslie Lake Ave 89044
Airglow Ct 89014
Airy Hill St 89015
Airy Petals Walk 89044
Al Castello Ct 89011
Alachua St 89011
Aladdin Lamp St 89002
Alanhurst Dr 89052
Alaska Jade St 89074
Albacate St 89015
Albany Way 89015
Albemarle Way 89014
Alberon Gardens Way 89002
Albino Dr 89002
Aldbury Dr 89014
Alder Green Ave 89002
Alder Lake Ct 89052
Aldo Rae Ct 89052
Aldonza Dr 89014

Aldrin Cir 89015
Alfonso Ave 89015
Alias Smith Dr 89002
Alicant Way 89014
Alisal Ct 89074
Aliso Dr 89074
Alla Prima Ave 89044
Allegheny Moon Ter 89002
Allegretto Ave 89052
Allen Ave 89011
Allen Grove Ct 89074
Allendale Cir 89052
Allred Pl 89011
Almart Cir 89014
Almendio Ln 89074
Almond Dr 89074
Almond Ridge Pl 89015
Alnwick Ct 89044
Aloe Yucca Ave 89011
Aloha Dr 89015
Alper Center Dr 89052
Alpine Ct 89074
Alpine Hills Ave 89014
Alpine Meadows Ave 89074
Alta Oaks Dr 89014
Alta Vista Pl 89015
Alterra Dr 89074
Altivo Dr 89074
Alyson Pond Cir 89012
Alyssa Jade Dr 89052
Amador Ln 89012
Amalfi St 89074
Amana Dr 89044
Amarillo Sky Pl 89002
Amarillo Springs Ave 89014
Amarone Way 89012
Amaryllis Ct 89074
Ambassador Dr 89002
Amber Bluff St 89012
Amber Gate St 89002
Amber Horizon St 89015
Amber Light Ct 89074
Amber Moon St 89015
Amber Rock St 89012
Amber Sunset St 89015
Ambermill Ct 89052
Ambling Gait Ave 89015
Ambusher St 89014
American Pacific Dr
800-846 89014
848-999 89014
1000-1299 89074
1301-1699 89074
American Run Ave 89002
Amethyst Ave 89015
Amoretti St 89052
Anaheim Ave 89074
Anamarie Ln 89002
Anani Rd 89044
Anchor Ct & Dr 89015
Anchorgate Dr 89052
Ancient Hills Ln 89074
Ancient Mayan Dr 89015
Ancient Timber Ave 89052
Andada Dr 89012
Anderson Park Dr 89044
Andover Ridge Ct 89012
Andretti Ln 89052
Andromeda Ave 89044
Anelli Ct 89012
Angel Falls Dr 89074
Angelus Oaks Dr 89011
Angus 89012
Animated Ct 89052
Annabelle Ln 89014
Annadale Ct 89052
Annapolis Cir 89015
Anne Ln 89015
Annet St 89052
Annie Oakley Dr 89014
Anserville Ave 89044
Antelope Hill Ct 89012
Antelope Valley Ave 89012
Antelope Village Cir 89012
Antero Dr 89074
Anthem Club Dr 89052

Anthem Creek Cir 89052
Anthem Pointe Ct 89052
Anthem Village Dr 89052
Antienne Dr 89052
Antique Blossom Ave 89052
Antler Point Dr 89074
Antrim Irish Dr 89044
Apache Pl 89015
Apogee Ln 89074
Apollo Ave 89002
Apollo Gardens St 89052
Apostle Dr 89002
Appaloosa Rd 89002
Apparition St 89044
Appian Way 89002
Apple Seed Cir & Ct 89014
Apple Tree Ct 89014
Applecross Ave 89012
Applejack Ct 89002
Apricot Ct 89014
April Breeze Ln 89002
April Mist St 89002
Aqua Ln 89012
Aqua Vista Ave 89014
Arabian Ct & Dr 89002
Arawana Pl 89074
Arbor Way 89074
Arbor Lake Ct 89044
Arborfield Ct 89012
Arcadia Sunrise Dr 89052
Arch Hill St 89074
Archer Glen Ave 89002
Arches Ct 89012
Arcola Ct 89015
Ardchonnel St 89044
Arden Valley Ave 89011
Ardia St 89012
Ardoch Ave 89044
Argenta Ct 89011
Aria Dr 89052
Arimo Dr 89052
Aripeka St 89011
Arizona Way 89015
Arkansas Ave 89015
Arkansas Valley Ave 89044
Armacost Dr 89074
Armadillo Ct 89002
Armenian Pl 89052
Armillaria St 89011
Armstrong Cir 89015
E & W Army St 89015
Arpeggio Ave 89052
Arrow Point Ln 89011
Arrowhead Trl
500-599 89015
700-1299 89002
Arrowhead Canyon Dr 89002
N Arroyo Grande Blvd
101-199 89074
200-398 89014
400-799 89014
S Arroyo Grande Blvd 89012
Arroyo Verde Dr 89012
Arroyo Vista Ter 89052
Artemus Ct 89074
Artesia Wells St 89052
Arthon Ave 89044
Arthur Ave 89015
Arthur Hills Ct 89074
Artistic Flair Walk 89044
Aruba Isle Dr 89002
Asbury Park St 89052
Ascaya Blvd 89012
Ash St 89015
Ashby Hills Ct 89012
Ashdale Way 89074
Ashen Light Dr 89044
Ashford Way 89015
Ashford Hollow Ave 89012
Ashley Rose Ter 89052
Ashmoore Dr 89074
Ashurst Ct 89011
Ashville Ct 89012
Ashwood Ranch Ct 89052
Aspen Bay Ln 89012
Aspen Brook Dr 89074

Aspen Cliff Dr 89011
Aspen Daisy Ave 89074
Aspen Knoll Dr 89074
Aspen Meadows Dr 89014
Aspen Peak Loop 89011
Aspen Wood Ave 89074
Astaire St 89014
Aster Ct 89074
Astounding Hills Dr 89052
Atchley Dr 89052
Athena Hill Ct 89052
E Athens Ave 89015
Athens Ridge Dr 89052
Athol Ave 89011
Atlanta St 89052
E & W Atlantic Ave 89015
Attebury Ct 89074
Atticus Ave 89015
Attingham Park Ave 89002
Aubrey Springs Ave 89014
Auchmull St 89044
Audra Faye Ave 89052
Augusta Pl & St 89074
Augusta Blossom Ct 89074
Augusta Wood Ct 89052
Aura De Blanco St 89074
Austin Rose Ave 89002
Authentic Ct 89012
Auto Mall Dr 89014
Auto Show Dr 89014
Autumn Ct 89002
Autumn Bay Ct 89052
Autumn Blaze Ave 89074
Autumn Blossom St 89052
Autumn Canyon Way 89002
Autumn Chase Ln 89052
Autumn Day St 89012
Autumn Dove Ct 89052
Autumn Eve St 89074
Autumn Grass St 89052
Autumn Hill St 89052
Autumn King Ave 89052
Autumn Oak Ct 89052
Autumn Wind Way 89052
Avacado Ct 89014
Avanti Ln 89074
Avenida Arenas 89074
Avenida Casatino 89011
Avenida Cataluna 89074
Avenida Cortes 89074
Avenida Familia 89074
Avenida Fiori 89011
Avenida Flores 89074
Avenida Gracia 89074
Avenida Picasso 89074
Avenida Sol 89074
Avenida Sorrento 89011
Avenza Dr 89011
Aviance Ct 89074
Aviator Ct 89002
Avon Ave 89014
Award Ct 89014
Awbrey Ct 89052
Ayden Dr 89052
Ayesha Ln 89074
Azalea Ct 89002
Azalea Springs Ave 89002
Aztec Ln 89015
Aztec Lily Ln 89052
Aztec Ruin Way 89044
Azuelo Ct 89015
Azure Springs Ave 89014
Baby Eagle St 89012
Babylon Mill St 89002
Backbone Mountain Dr 89012
Bad Rock Cir 89052
Badlands Ave 89012
Baffetto Ct 89052
Baffin Island Rd 89011
Bailey Island Dr 89074
Baja Ln 89012
Baja Grande Ave 89012
Baked Pottery Ct 89074
Bakersfield Ct 89052
Baldridge Dr 89014
Baldwinville Ct 89044

Balgavies Ct 89044
Balinese Ave 89015
Balintore Ct 89014
Ballerina Dr 89015
Balsa St 89002
Balsam Pear Ct 89074
Bamboo Ct 89074
Bamboo Bay Dr 89012
Banbrook Ct 89014
Banbury Ct 89074
Bannerwood St 89044
Banuelo Dr 89014
Banyon Wood St 89015
Baranek Ave 89044
Barbary Coast Ave 89015
Barberry Ct 89002
Barboursville Ct 89052
Barby Springs Ave 89014
Barclay St 89044
Bareback Ct 89014
Baring Cross St 89074
Barneby Ave 89074
Barnegat Bay St 89052
Barranca Dr 89074
Barrel Cactus Dr 89074
E Barrett St 89011
Barrie Ct 89002
Barron Ct 89002
Barton Manor St 89011
Barton Spring Cir 89074
Basalt Mesa Ave 89012
E & W Basic Rd 89015
Basil Leaf Dr 89074
Bass Dr 89014
Bass Lake St 89052
Bassano Ct 89052
Basswood Ranch St 89052
Bastanchury Ave 89011
Bastrop St 89074
Baton Rouge St 89052
Baychester Dr 89002
Bayleaf Terrace Ave 89014
Baymist Ave 89052
Bayo Canyon Ct 89015
Bayridge Rd 89074
Beach Burr Ct 89002
Beach Oak Ave 89002
Beach Park St 89015
Beaconwood St 89052
Beagle Point Ave 89015
Bear Coat Ct 89002
Bear Cove Ter 89011
Bear Cub Ct 89052
Bear Head St 89011
Bearclaw Ter 89014
Bearden Ave 89011
Beardsley Cir 89052
Bearpaw Catch Ct 89052
Beartooth Falls Ct 89052
Beasley St 89052
Beaver Crest Ter 89015
Bechamel Pl 89044
Beckley Ct 89014
Bedford Park Dr 89052
Beech St 89015
Beechnut Ave 89074
Beechwheat Way 89015
Beechwood Village Ct 89052
Begonia Ct 89074
Begonia Valley Ave 89074
Bekasina Dr 89014
Bel Giorno Ct 89011
Belair View Ct 89074
Belclaire Dr 89052
Belconte Ln 89074
Belfair Ct 89052
Belfast St 89015
Bell Ave 89015
Belle Isle Ct 89012
Belle River Ct 89052
Belleza Ln 89074
Bellini Dr 89052
Belmont Dr 89074
Belmont Canyon Pl 89015
Belt Buckley Dr 89002
Belvedere Dr 89014

Benares Dr 89074
Bench Reef Pl 89052
Benchley Ct 89052
Beneficial Pl 89012
Benevolo Dr 89011
Bensley St 89044
Bensonhurst Ln 89052
Bergamont Dr 89002
Bergholt Crest Ave 89002
Berlin Ave 89015
Bermuda Rd
1400-1599 89052
12101-12199 89044
S Bermuda Rd 89052
Berwick Ct 89014
Beryl Ct 89015
Bet Twice St 89015
Bethany St 89074
Beverly Way 89015
Bicentennial Pkwy 89044
Biddeford Pl 89074
Big Bar Dr 89052
Big Bend Way 89074
Big Bird Ct 89011
Big Delta Ct 89014
Big Horn St 89002
Big Lake St 89002
Big Laurel St 89074
Bighorn Creek St 89002
Bighorn Ridge Ave 89012
Bighorn Station St 89012
Bildad Dr 89044
Billings St 89002
Biloxi Pass 89052
Binary Stars St 89044
Binbrook Dr 89052
Bird Cove Ave 89011
Birdie Ln 89074
Birdseye St 89012
Birkdale Dr 89074
Birmingham St 89074
Bishopsgate Ter 89074
Bismark Way 89015
Bisque Dr 89074
Bitterroot St 89002
Black Eagle Ave 89002
Black Fox Canyon Rd 89052
Black Lava Ct 89011
Black Olive St 89002
Black River Falls Dr 89044
Black Rock Hills Dr 89014
Black Sand Ct 89011
Black Wash Way 89074
Blackberry Ln 89074
Blackburn Hills Ave 89044
Blackcraig St 89044
Blackmore Dr 89015
Blackridge Rd
400-598 89015
600-699 89002
Blaine Ranch St 89012
Blair Castle St 89044
Blairgowrie Dr 89044
Blairlogie Ct 89044
Blakes Field Pl 89011
Blanca Springs Dr 89014
Blanchard Dr 89074
Blanche Ct 89052
Blanco Caballo Way 89015
Blaven Dr 89002
Blazing Creek Way 89052
Bliss Corner St 89044
Blitzen Dr 89012
Bloomfield Hills Dr 89052
Blooming Sage Ct 89015
Blooming Valley Ct 89052
Blossom Glen Dr 89014
Blossom Meadows Pl 89052
Blue Arroyo Dr 89015
Blue Barrel St 89011
Blue Beak Way 89012
Blue Bench Ln 89012
Blue Canyon Ct 89012
Blue Cavern St 89012
Blue Cliffs Ave 89014
Blue Cloud St 89002

Blue Creek Way 89002
Blue Crystal Creek Rd 89002
Blue Fountain Ct 89012
Blue Juniper Ln 89015
Blue Lantern Dr 89015
Blue Palette Ave 89044
Blue Rosalie Pl 89052
Blue Sands Ct 89011
Blue Sierra Ct 89074
Blue Snow River Ct 89002
Blue Springs Dr 89002
Blue Trout Ave 89011
Blue Valley Dr 89002
Bluebell Point Ct 89012
Blueberry Ln 89074
Bluebonnet Dr 89074
Bluefield Ln 89074
Bluegill Way 89014
Bluegrass Ln 89074
Bluff Ridge Ave 89012
Bluffs Dr 89014
Blushing Maple St 89015
Blushing Rose Pl 89052
Blythswood Sq 89044
Bobby Basin Ave 89014
Boboli Ct 89052
Bobtail Cir 89012
Bogey Way 89074
Bogey Crossing St 89074
Boletus Dr 89011
Bolle Way 89012
Bon Papa Ct 89044
Bonanza Plain Ave 89011
Bonaparte Ln 89044
Bonita Ln 89014
Bonita Bluffs Ave 89015
Bonner Springs Dr 89052
Bonnie Brook Pl 89012
Bonnie Claire Ct 89074
Bonniewood Ct 89074
Bonny Lake Ct 89015
Bonsai Tree Ln 89015
Bontemps Ct 89052
Boojum Ct 89011
Book Wagon St 89012
Booted Eagle St 89015
Boothbay St 89074
Bootspur Dr 89012
Boquita Ave 89014
Boris Ave 89015
Borrego Dr 89074
Borthwick Ave 89044
Bosworth Ct & Dr 89015
Bothwell Pl 89044
Botticelli Dr 89052
Bottle Brush Way 89015
N Boulder Hwy
102-398 89015
400-497 89015
499-499 89015
912-998 89011
1000-2199 89011
S Boulder Hwy
100-402 89015
404-404 89009
404-498 89015
500-1424 89015
1426-1618 89015
1700-2899 89002
Boulder Falls St 89011
Boulder Ranch Ave 89011
Boulder Summit Dr 89012
Boulder Summitt Dr 89012
Boundary Line St 89002
Bounty Hunter Ct 89002
Bouret Pl 89012
Boutique Ave 89044
Bowie Cir 89014
Box Elder Way 89015
Box Step Dr 89014
Boysenberry Ln 89074
Bozeman Dr 89012
Brackendale Ave 89052
Brad St 89015
Bradenton Ct 89052
Bradford Dr 89074

Bradley Bay Ave 89014
Braehead Ln 89044
Braelinn Dr 89052
Brahma Ln 89002
Braided Mane Cir 89014
Brandermill Dr 89052
Brands Hatch Ct 89052
Brandy Hill Pl 89052
Brandywine Shoals Pl 89052
Bravado Dr 89002
Braverwood Dr 89015
Brays Island Dr 89052
Breckenham Ct 89002
Breckenridge South Cir 89074
Breeze Way 89015
Breezy Cove Ave 89052
Breezy Orchard St 89015
Breezy Ridge Dr 89002
Breezy Sage Ct 89015
Brenalee Ave 89002
Brent Ct 89074
Brent Park Ct 89002
Brentwood Dr 89074
Brian Dr 89074
Briar Knoll Dr 89074
Briarcliff Ave 89074
Brick Dr 89002
Bridgeford Ct 89011
Bridle Dr 89002
Bridlegate Ave 89012
Brigadier St 89002
Bright Sumac Ct 89015
Bright Valley Pl 89011
Brightmoor Ct 89074
Brighton Point Ave 89044
Brightwater St 89014
Brilliant Summit Cir 89052
Bristlecone Ct 89014
Bristol Wells Ct 89074
Britannia Ave 89014
British Ct 89014
Brittany Mesa Dr 89074
Brockley Cross St 89002
Brockton Way 89074
Brodie Silver St 89044
Broken Arrow Ct 89074
Broken Bell Ln 89002
Broken Hills Dr 89011
Broken Reed Ct 89015
Broken Rock Dr 89074
Broken Shale Cir 89052
Broken Tee Dr 89074
Bronze Patina St 89044
Bronzino Ct 89052
Brook Hollow Ct 89074
Brook Trout Ct 89052
Brookhouse Ct 89011
Brookridge Dr 89052
Brookshire St 89015
Brookside Ct 89015
Broomfield Dr 89074
Broomspun St 89015
Brown St 89015
Brown Hill Ct 89011
Brown Swallow Way 89012
Brownbirds Nest Dr 89052
Brownlee Dr 89015
Bruce Way 89015
E Bruner Ave 89044
Brush Stroke St 89044
Brushback Ave 89074
Bryce Ct 89002
Bubbling Well Ave 89014
Buchanan Ave 89015
Buchanan Rock St 89074
Buckeye Hill Ct 89012
Buckeye Reef St 89002
Buckhorn Cove St 89011
Bucking Horse Ln 89011
Buckingham Ct 89074
Buckskin St 89074
Buena Ct 89074
Buena Adventura Ln 89012
Buffalo Brubaker Ln 89002
Buffalo River Ave 89002

Buffalo Trail Dr 89014
Bugle Bluff Dr 89015
Bugle Boy Dr 89014
Bull Lake Dr 89052
Bullwhip Ct 89011
Bunchberry Ct 89002
Bundy St 89074
Bungalow Ln 89074
Bunker Hollow Ct 89002
Burgundy Dr 89002
Burkholder Blvd 89015
Burns Ave 89011
Burris Hill Dr 89052
Burton St 89015
Burtonsville Dr 89044
Business Center St 89014
Busk St 89011
Bussora Rose Dr 89015
Butch Cassidy Ln 89002
Butterfly Ridge Ave 89014
Buttermilk Dr 89074
Butternut Ct 89014
Butternut Ranch Ct 89052
Butterworth Ct 89052
Caballo Blvd 89014
Cabana Blanca St 89012
Cable View Ave 89011
Cabochon St 89002
Cabrillo Cir & Dr 89015
Cacto Ct 89074
Cactus Garden Dr 89014
Cactus River Ct 89074
Cactus Rock St 89011
Caddy Cir 89074
Cadence St 89052
Cadiz Ave 89015
Cahoon Ct 89014
Calabria Peak Ct 89012
Calamint Hills Ct 89052
Calamity Jane Ln 89002
Calamus Palm Pl 89011
Calanques Ter 89044
Calcione Dr 89011
Calcutta Ln 89015
Calendula Ct 89052
Cali Way 89014
Calico Brook Dr 89002
Calico Ridge Dr 89011
California Way 89015
Calistoga Ct 89052
Callahan Ave 89014
Callaway Cir 89074
Calle Calma 89012
Calle Cantar 89012
Calle De Luz 89012
Calle Palacio St 89012
Calliope Dr 89074
Calm Morning Ave 89002
Calmada Ave 89074
Caltana Ct 89052
Calvert St 89002
Calvert City Dr 89052
Calverton Ct 89052
Calville Estates Ct 89015
Calypso Dr 89002
Camargue Ln 89044
Cambray St 89074
Cambretto Dr 89074
Cambridge Springs Dr 89052
Camelback Ln 89074
Camelback Ridge Ave 89012
Camelia Dr 89011
Cameo Cir 89002
Cameron Hill Ct 89074
Caminito Amore 89011
Camino Barcelona Pl 89011
Camino Capri 89012
Camino Del Ray 89012
Camino Francisco 89012
Camino La Paz 89012
Camino La Venta Ct 89011
Camino Largo Ave 89044
Camino Rico Ave 89044
Camino Sereno Ave 89044
Camino Summit Ave 89012
Camino Viejo St 89012

Street	ZIP
Camino Vista St	89012
Camp Hill Rd	89015
Campassole Ct	89052
Campside Manor Ln	89012
Camrose St	89074
Canadian Goose Cir	89052
Canal Walk Rd	89052
Canarsy Ct	89052
Canberra Ave	89052
Candelaria Dr	89074
Candide St	89002
Candido Garcia Ave	89015
Candle Bright Dr	89074
Candlestick Ave	89052
Candlewyck Dr	89052
Candy Tuft Dr	89011
Canlite St	89015
Cannes St	89015
Canoa Hills Dr	89052
Cantamar St	89074
Canton Hills St	89052
Cantura Mills Rd	89052
Canvas Edge Dr	89044
Canyon Rd	
500-599	89015
600-699	89002
Canyon Blue Ave	89011
Canyon Country Cir	89002
Canyon Retreat Dr	89044
Canyon River Ct	89012
Canyon Spirit Dr	89012
Canyonville Dr	89044
Cape Alan Dr	89052
Cape Horn Dr	89011
Capella Star St	89044
Capital Gains Dr	89074
Capriccio Ave	89052
Caprington Rd	89052
Capstone Ct	89011
Caption Way	89011
Carambala Ln	89044
Caraway Bluffs Pl	89015
Cardamom Ct	89015
Cardelina Ln	89052
Cardinal Point St	89012
Cardino Ct	89052
Carina Way	89052
Carinth Way	89074
Carita Ave	89014
Carleton Dr	89014
Carlisle Corner Ct	89052
Carlsbad Caverns St	89012
Carmel Mesa Dr	89012
Carmel Valley St	89012
Carmelo Dr	89052
Carmona Cir	89074
Carnation Ln	89074
Carnegie St	89052
Carneros Ave	89002
Carnforth Dr	89014
Carole Little Ct	89014
Carolina Blue Ave	89052
Carolina Laurel St	89074
Carolwood Dr	89074
Carousel Pkwy	89014
Carracci Ct	89052
W Carriage Way	89074
Carrington St	89074
Carrizo Way	89052
Carson Way	89015
Carson Run St	89002
Carthage St	89074
Casa Del Fuego St	89012
Casa Palermo Cir	89011
Casa Robles St	89012
Casa Rosa St	89052
Casady Hollow Ave	89012
Cascade Dr	89074
Cascade Meadow Ct	89011
Cascading St	89074
Caserta Ct	89074
Casetto Ct	89052
Cashmere Way	89074
Cassatt Dr	89074
Cassia Way	89014
Castiron Ridge Ct	89052
Castle Canyon Ave	89052
Castle Kennedy St	89011
Castle Point Ave	89074
Castro Hill Ave	89012
Caswell Ct	89074
Cat Creek Ct	89002
Catalan Ct	89002
Catalina Marie Ave	89074
Cathedral Ridge St	89052
Cathy Ln	89015
Cattail Cir	89015
Cattle Ranch Pl	89002
Cattlebaron Ter	89012
Cavalla St	89074
Cave Spring Dr	89014
Cavendish Way	89012
Caves Valley Ct	89052
Cavoli Ct	89012
Cavos Way	89014
Cedar St	89015
Cedar Berry Ct	89012
Cedar Chase Dr	89052
Cedar Hill Ct	89012
Cedar Meadows St	89052
Cedar Pines St	89011
Cedar River Ct	89044
Cedar Tree Dr	89002
Cedar Valley Ct	89052
Celebrate Ct	89074
Celestial Light Dr	89044
Celestial Moon St	89044
Centaurus St	89044
Center St	89015
Center Point Dr	89074
Centerville Ct	89052
Central Falls Ct	89052
Cerchio Alto	89011
Cerchio Basso	89011
Cerchio Centrale	89011
Cervantes Dr	89014
Cervino Cir	89052
Cezanne Dr	89074
Chaco Canyon Dr	89074
Chadwell Ct	89074
Chadwick Cir	89014
Chalet Hills Ter	89052
Chameleon Star Ave	89015
Chamomile Dr	89015
Champlin Ave	89015
Chance Cove Dr	89052
Chandler St	89014
Channel Dr	89002
Chanterelle Dr	89011
E & W Chaparral Dr	89015
Chaplet Ct	89074
Chapman Ranch Dr	89012
Chaps Cir	89002
Character Point Ave	89012
Charlene Ct	89011
Charmartin St	89074
Charming Ct	89052
Charter Oak St	89074
Chartiers Ct	89052
Charwood Cir	89014
Chasma Dr	89044
Chaste Ct	89015
Chateau Dr	89002
Chateau Clermont St	89044
Chateau Napoleon Dr	89044
Chateau Petit Ct	89044
Chatmoss Rd	89052
Chatsworth Ct	89074
Chelsea Dr	89014
Chenal Pass	89052
Chenault Cir	89074
Cherry Dr	89002
Cherry Knolls St	89052
Cherrydale Falls Dr	89052
S & W Chesapeake Way	89015
Cheshire Village Ct	89052
Chesney Dr	89074
Chester Heights Ct	89052
Chesterfield Ave	89014
Chesters Hill Ct	89002
Chestnut St	89011
Chestnut Bluffs Ave	89052
Chestnut Ranch Ave	89052
Chestnut Ridge Cir & Ct	89012
Chestnut View Pl	89052
Chettro Ct	89074
Chevrus Ct	89012
Chickasaw Dr	89002
Childrens Way	89052
Chimney Rock Dr	89002
China Doll Pl	89012
Chinook Breeze Ct	89052
Chiquis Ct	89074
Chislehurst Ct	89002
Choice Hills Dr	89012
Chokecherry Ave	89074
N & S Cholla St	89015
Chorus St	89052
Chris Ave	89074
Christian Rd	89002
Church St	89015
Churchill Cir	89074
Cielito Lindo St	89012
Cilento Ct	89052
Cimarron Ct	89002
Cimarron Hill Dr	89074
Cimarron Village Way	89012
Cimini Ct	89052
Cindy Pl	89015
Cinnamon Ridge Way	89015
Circa St	89015
Circa De Montanas	89011
Citrus Cir	89015
Citrus Garden Cir	89052
Claridge Ave	89074
Clarity Ct	89074
Clark Dr	89074
Clarksville Ct	89052
Claro Ct	89014
Claude Ct	89044
Clayton St	89074
Clear Crossing Trl	89052
Clear Look Ct	89014
Clear Rapid Ct	89012
Clear River Falls Ln	89012
Cleargirl Ct	89052
Clearwater Canyon Dr	89012
Clearwater Lake Dr	89044
Clearwater River Ave	89002
Clemson St	89074
Cliff Branch Dr	89014
Cliffwood Dr	89074
Clint Canyon Dr	89002
Clipper Dr	89015
Clipper Ship St	89074
Clipperton Ave	89074
Cloister Ave	89014
Close Ave	89011
Cloud Cover Ave	89002
Cloudcrest Dr	89015
Cloudy Day Dr	89074
Clove Ct	89012
Clover Glen Ct	89015
Clovercrest Ct	89012
Clown Creek St	89014
Club Crest Way	89014
Club Meadows Dr	89074
Club Point Ct	89052
Club Side Dr	89052
Club Vista Dr	89052
Clubview Dr	89015
Coach House Rd	89002
Coal Valley Dr	89014
Coast Laguna Ct	89002
Coastal Way	89002
Coastal Beach Rd	89002
Coastal Pier Ct	89002
Cobalt Sky Ave	89002
Cocoplum Ct	89015
Codyerin Dr	89074
Coffee Bean Pl	89052
Coffee Cherries Ct	89052
Colfax Creek St	89012
College Dr	
400-599	89015
600-898	89002
Colleton River Dr	89052
Collindale St	89074
Collins Dr	89015
Collinsville Dr	89052
Colloquium Dr	89014
Cologne Ct & Dr	89074
Colonial Cup St	89015
Color Blending Walk	89044
Color Collage Walk	89044
Color Palette Ave	89044
Colorado Way	89015
Colorado Creek Ct	89002
Colour Magic St	89052
Colt Dr	89002
Colt Arms St	89011
Columbia Cir	89014
Colvin Run Dr	89052
Comanche Ct & Pl	89074
Comet Cloud Ct	89044
Comfort Dr	89074
Comfort Hills St	89014
Commerce Center Dr	89014
Commercial Way	89011
Como Ct	89015
Companion Way	89011
Comstock Dr	89014
Concho Dr	89015
Concord Way	89015
Conestoga Way	89002
Confident Crest Ct	89052
Constitution Ave	89015
Continental Ave	89015
Contra Costa Pl	89052
Contrada Fiore Dr	89011
E Coogan Dr	89011
Cook Out Ct	89002
Cool Days Ave	89002
Cool Lilac Ave	89052
Cool Water Dr	89074
Coolidge Ave	89015
Cooper Creek Dr	89074
Coopergrove Dr	89074
Copilico Ter	89052
Coppelia Ct	89052
Copper St	89015
Copper Cove Dr	89074
Copper Flat Ct	89011
Copper Glow Ct	89074
Copper Grass St	89011
Copper Palm Ct	89002
Copper Rock Ct	89012
Copper View St	89052
Coral Cay Ct	89002
Coral Cottage Dr	89002
Coral Dunes St	89014
Coral Fountain St	89014
Coral Ridge Ave	89052
Coral Sea St	89074
Coralino Dr	89052
Cordaville Dr	89044
Cordelia St	89044
Cordero Dr	89074
Cordillera Dr	89074
Corista Dr	89052
E Corn St	89011
Corner Stone Cir	89052
Cornerbrook Cir	89052
Cornet St	89052
Cornsilk Ct	89002
Corolla Ct	89012
Coronado Dr	89015
Coronado Center Dr	89052
Coroneos Dr	89011
Corporate Cir	89074
Corporate Park Dr	89074
Corral De Tierra Pl	89052
Corte Belleza	89011
Corte Madera Ave	89015
Corte Pescado St	89044
Corte Vita	89011
Cortina Ave	89074
Corvallis Ct	89074
Corvus St	89044
Cosmic Dust St	89044
Cosmic Ray Pl	89044
Cosmic Sky St	89015
Cosmic Star Pl	89052
Costa Del Sol Ct	89011
Costa Di Lago	89011
Cottage Lake Ct	89052
Cotton Valley St	89052
Cotton Wind St	89011
Cottonwood Ranch Ct	89052
Coulisse St	89052
Country Club Dr	89015
Country Coach Dr	89002
Country Maple Ave	89074
Country Meadows Dr	89012
Country River Ave	89011
Couperin Dr	89052
Courgette Way	89044
Courier St	89011
Courtland Ave	89074
Courtney Ann Dr	89074
Courtney Valley St	89052
Cove Ct	89002
Coventry Cir & Dr	89074
Coventry Green Ave	89074
Covina Dr	89002
Cow Cove Ave	89011
Cowboy Chaps Pl	89002
Coyote Hills St	89012
Coyote Pass Way	89012
Coyote Pointe Ct	89074
Coyote Run Dr	89014
Cozy Canyon Dr	89002
Cozy Glen Cir	89074
Cozy Hill Cir	89052
Cozy Valley St	89015
Crabapple Dr	89002
Crafty Clint Ln	89002
Craigie Castle St	89044
Craigmark Ct	89002
Craigmillar St	89044
Craigton Dr	89044
Cramond St	89044
Crater Ct	89014
Crater Rock St	89044
Credence Ave	89002
Creekside Rd	89074
Creeping Bend Ct	89052
Crepes Pl	89052
Crescent Bay St	89012
Crescent Falls St	89011
Crescent Heights Ave	89044
Crescent Meadows Ct	89052
Crescent Palm Ct	89002
Crest Valley Pl	89011
Crested Butte St	89052
Crested Creek Ave	89011
Crestway Rd	89015
Cricket Hollow Ct	89074
Cricklewood Ave	89002
Crimson Peak Pl	89011
Crimson Sage Ave	89012
Cripple Creek Ct	89014
Crocodile Ave	89052
Crony Ave	89011
Cross St	89015
Cross Haven Dr	89074
Crossbill Ct	89074
Crossfoot Terrace Ct	89002
Crossview St	89074
Crowfoot Cir	89014
Crown Imperial St	89074
Crown Royale Ct	89002
Crown Valley Dr	89074
Crown View St	89052
Crumbling Ridge St	89011
Crumpler Pl	89052
Crusades Ave	89002
Cryer Ct	89002
Crystal Hill Ln	89012
Crystal Lantern Dr	89074
Crystal Moon Rd	89052
Crystal Ship Ct	89052
Crystal Springs Pl	89074
Crystal Stream Ave	89012
Crystal Tree Pass	89052
Crystalline Ct	89074
Cullen St	89002
Culloden Ave	89044
Culzean Pl	89044
Cumberland Way	89015
Cumberland Hill Dr	89052
Cumulus Ct	89014
Curio Ter	89074
Curly Top Pl	89052
Currant Ln	89074
Cut Bank Trl	89052
Cutlass Dr	89014
Cutter St	89011
Cuzco Ct	89014
E & W Cypress Dr	89015
Cypress Bay Ave	89012
Cypress Gardens Pl	89012
Cypress Greens Ave	89012
Cypress Lake Ct	89012
Cypress Links Ave	89012
Cypress Manor Dr	89012
Cypress Mesa Dr	89012
Cypress Pines Way	89002
Cyrano St	89044
Daffodil Dr	89015
Dagger Dr	89014
Dahlia St	89015
Daisy Ct	89074
Daisy Gold Ct	89074
Daisy Meadow Ter	89074
Dakar St	89015
Dakota Sky Ct	89052
Daks Loden Ct	89044
Dalcross Pl	89044
W Dale Ave	89044
Dalehurst Dr	89074
Dalene Ave	89002
Dalgreen Pl	89012
Dallas Ter	89014
Dalsetter Dr	89044
Dalton Dr	89014
Dan St	89015
Dan Blocker Ave	89011
Danalda Ct	89014
Danbury Crossing Dr	89052
Dancing Cloud Ave	89011
Dancing Hills Ave	89052
Dancing Sage Ct	89015
Dancing Star Ct	89052
Danville Ct	89074
Danzinger Pl	89044
Darcy Ct	89052
Darda St	89044
Darien Ct	89014
Dark Star Ave	89074
Darla St	89002
Dart Brook Pl	89012
Dartington Hall St	89011
Darwin Cir	89014
Datura St	89074
Davina St	89074
Davis Hill Ct	89074
Davis Wright Ct	89044
Dawn Cove Dr	89052
Dawn Crossing Dr	89074
Dawn Ridge Ave	89074
Day St	89074
Day Canyon Ct	89052
Day Marks Ln	89052
Day Trade St	89074
Daylight Blaze Way	89052
Daylin Ct	89015
Dazzling Ter	89012
De Marco Dr	89011
De Narvik Dr	89044
De Rouge Ave	89044
Dean Ct	89002
Deangelis Dr	89015
Deanna Way	89074
Dearport Ct	89052
Decareo Ct	89014
Decidedly St	89015
Deeneric	89011
Deep Well Ct	89011
Deer Crossing Way	89012
Deer Meadow Dr	89012
Deer Season St	89052
Deer Springs Dr	89074
Deerleap Cir	89052
Deerwood Ct	89074
Degas Tapestry Ave	89044
Del Terra Ave	89044
E & W Delamar Dr	89015
Delano Dr	89074
Delfino Way	89074
Dell Way	89015
Delmar Gardens Dr	89074
Delores Ave	89074
Delta Waters St	89074
Denair Way	89074
Denholme St	89044
Denman Valley St	89002
Denmark Ct	89074
Denver Way	89015
Deora Way	89052
Derby Dr	89002
Derringer Ln	89014
Descartes Ave	89002
Desert Arroyo Ct	89012
Desert Castle Ct	89012
Desert Cove Rd	89012
Desert Coyote St	89012
Desert Dawn Ln	89074
Desert Forest Way	89012
Desert Fox Dr	89052
Desert Gallery St	89012
Desert Highlands Dr	89052
Desert Knolls St	89014
Desert Mountain Dr	89002
Desert Olive Ct	89002
Desert Passage St	89002
Desert Pond Ave	89002
Desert Rain Ln	89074
Desert Retreat Ct	89002
E & W Desert Rose Dr	89015
Desert Shadow Trl	89012
Desert Summit Ct	89052
Desert Sunflower Cir	89002
Desert Twilight Ct	89011
Desert Woods Dr	89012
Design Cast Walk	89044
Destino Ln	89074
Destiny Ridge Ct	89074
Devon Way	89074
Devon Downs Ave	89015
Devotion Ct	89052
Devotion Ridge Dr	89052
Diamond Dr	89015
Diamond Crest Ln	89052
Diamond Valley St	89052
Diamondville St	89052
Dibasio Ct	89012
Dilevante Dr	89052
Dipinto Ave	89052
Diplomacy Pointe Ct	89052
Diplomat Ct	89074
Dirleton Pl	89044
Discovery Ct	89014
Discovery Lake Ct	89044
Distinguished Way	89002
Divine Sky Dr	89044
Dixie Down Ct	89002
Dixie Peak Ct	89014
Dockery Pl	89052
Dodee Ct	89015
Dodge St	89002
Doe Run Cir	89012
Dogwood St	89015
Dogwood Ranch Ave	89052
Doherty Way	89014
Dolce Luna Ct	89011
Dolphin Ct	89074
Domani Dr	89074
Domini Veneti Ct	89052
Dominican Ave	89002
Don Tomas Ct	89015
Donavista Ct	89052
Donegal St	89044
Donlon Ct	89012
Donner Pass Dr	89014
Dooley Dr	89015
Doral Ct & Pl	89074
Dornoch Ln	89044
Dorset Ave	89074

Double Tree Ave 89052
Doubleshot Ln 89052
Douglas Cir 89074
Douglas Grove Rd 89052
Dove Forest Ct 89074
Dove Tree Ct 89014
Dover Ridge Ct 89074
Dovetail Cir 89014
Dow Jones St 89074
Downeyville Ave 89052
Dragon Canyon Dr 89012
Dragon Gate Ct 89012
Dragon Glen Dr 89012
Dragon Mountain Ct 89012
Dragon Peak Ct 89012
Dragon Ridge Dr 89012
Dragon Rock Dr 89052
Dragon Stone Pl 89012
Drake St 89015
Drawback St 89012
Dream Valley St 89052
Dresden Ct 89014
Drifting Sand Ct 89074
Driftwood Ct 89015
Driftwood Tide Ave 89052
Drowsy Water Ct 89052
Drumlanrig St 89044
Drummossie Dr 89044
Dry Bed St 89011
Dry Brook Trl 89052
Drysdale Cir 89074
Du Fort Ave 89002
Duarte Dr 89014
Dublin Ave 89015
Duck Pond Ct 89074
Duggan Way 89012
Duke Of Wales Ct 89015
Dulce Fountain Way 89015
Dulcinea Dr 89014
Dunbar Dr 89014
Dunblane St 89012
Dundonald Ct 89044
Dune Drift Rd 89002
Dunford Ct 89012
Dunnam St 89011
Dunnottar Ave 89044
Dunrobin Ct 89014
Dunrobin Garden St 89002
Duppel Ct 89015
Duran St 89015
Durango Station Dr 89012
Durgos Dr 89012
Durini Ct 89011
Durness Ct 89014
Dusan Way 89011
Dusty Canyon St 89052
Dusty Daylight Ct 89052
Dusty Moon Ave 89052
Dusty Palms Ln 89052
Dusty Pines Pl 89052
Dusty Sage Ct 89014
Dutchman Ave 89011
Duxbury Dr 89052
Eagle Chase Ct 89052
Eagle Egg St 89012
Eagle Flight Ln 89012
Eagle Harbor Dr 89052
Eagle Mesa Ave 89012
Eagle Owl Ave 89015
Eagle Perch Pl 89012
Eagle Scout Way 89012
Eagle Sticks Dr 89012
Eagle Village Ave 89012
Eagle Vista Dr 89012
Eagle Watch Dr 89012
Eaglecloud Dr 89074
Eaglehelm Pl 89074
Eaglepath Cir 89074
Eagleridge Dr 89074
Eagleview Ct 89074
Early Frost Ave 89052
Earthen Mesa Ter 89052
Easter Lily Pl 89011
S Eastern Ave 89052
Eastgate Rd
400-7799 89011
8300-8399 89015
Eastminister Ct 89015
Echo Creek St 89052
Echo Dell Ct 89052
Echo Park Pl 89044
Echo Wind Ave 89052
Ecking Ave 89044
Eclipsing Stars Dr 89044
Ecliptic St 89044
Edge Ridge Ct 89052
Edgefield Ridge Pl 89012
Edgemont Dr 89074
Edward Pl 89014
Eiger Way 89014
Ekalaka Rd 89052
El Brio Ct 89014
El Camino Verde St 89074
El Castillo Ct 89074
El Cid Ct 89014
El Cielo Cir 89074
El Corazon Ct 89074
El Fuego Trl 89074
El Lobo Ct 89074
El Macero Ct 89052
El Nido Ct 89012
El Niguel Ct 89052
El Paso Grande Ave 89074
El Pico Dr 89014
El Rio Ct 89012
El Tesoro Ct 89014
El Viento Ct 89074
Elam St 89015
Elation Ln 89002
Elegant Coral Ave 89015
Elegante Way 89074
Elise Ct 89074
Elite St 89002
Elk Cove Ct 89011
Elkhurst Pl 89012
Elkins Cir 89074
Elko Cir 89074
Ellen Tracy Way 89014
Ellensburg St 89052
Elliott Rd 89011
Ellisworth Pl 89074
Elm St 89015
Elm Crest Pl 89012
Elm Hollow Ct 89012
Elsinore Ave 89074
Emanuel St 89002
Embassy Cir 89002
Ember Rock Ave 89015
Emden Dr & St 89015
Emerald Cir 89002
Emerald Crest St 89052
Emerald Dunes Cir 89052
Emerald Idol Pl 89011
Emerald Mountain Ave 89002
Emerald Peak Ave 89012
Emerald Wind St 89052
Emerson Hill St 89012
Empire Mesa Way 89011
Empire Mine Dr 89014
Enadia St 89074
Enchanted Ct 89015
Enchanted Isle St 89052
Enchanted Lakes Dr 89052
Enchanted River Dr 89012
Enchantment Cir 89074
Encima Ct 89014
Encouraging Ct 89052
Energized Ct 89052
Engel Ave & Way 89011
Enloe St 89074
Entrada Ridge Ave 89012
Envoy Cir 89002
Enzo Ave 89052
Epte Poplars St 89044
Equestrian Dr 89002
Equinox Ridge Way 89014
Erastus Dr 89044
Eresma St 89015
Errogie St 89012
Escalante Dr 89015
Escondido Ter 89074
Escoto Pl 89052
Espalda Ct 89014
Esquina Dr 89014
Essex Ave 89015
Estancia Ct 89015
Esteem Ridge Dr 89052
Estherville Ave 89052
Eugene Way 89015
Eureka Dunes Ave 89012
Eureka Falls Ct 89052
European Dr 89052
Evan Picone Dr 89014
Evansdale St 89052
Evansville Ave 89052
Evanwood Ct 89002
Evelyn Ave 89011
Evening Canyon Ave 89014
Evening Lights St 89052
Evening Mist Ave 89052
Evening Ridge St 89052
Evening Sky Dr 89052
Evening Song Ave 89012
Evening Sunset Ct 89044
Evening Twilight Ave 89044
Evening Wind St 89052
Eveningside Ave 89012
Everest Peak Ave 89012
Everett Vista Ct 89012
Evergold Dr 89074
Evergreen St 89002
Evergreen Cove St 89011
Evergreen Oaks Dr 89052
Evvie Ct 89012
Executive Airport Dr 89052
Executive Terminal Dr 89052
Expectation Ct 89002
Extreme Shear Ave 89011
Ezzat St 89052
Fair Play St 89052
Fairbourne Way 89074
Fairbrook Dr 89074
Fairbury St 89052
Fairfield Ave 89044
Fairfield Ter 89074
Fairmeadow St 89012
Fairview Dr 89015
E & W Fairway Rd 89015
Fairweather St 89052
Faith Filled Ct 89052
Falcon Feather Way 89012
Falcon Pointe Ln 89074
Falcons Lair Ln 89012
Fallen Tree Ct 89074
Falling Stones Ct 89012
Fallon Ct & Dr 89074
Fallow Fields Ter 89052
Fallows Fire Ct 89052
Falls City Ct 89044
Fallsburg Way 89002
Falsetto Ave 89052
Fan Palm Ct 89074
Fancrest St 89052
Fantasia Ln 89074
Far Away St 89074
Farlin Cir 89074
Farmington Bay Ct 89044
Faulkner Ct 89014
Faultless St 89015
Favorable Pointe Ct 89052
Fawn Cir 89014
Fayetteville Ave 89052
Feather Bush St 89074
Feather Haven Ct 89011
Feather Point Ct 89011
Feather Ridge Dr 89052
Feather Sound Dr 89052
Feathertree Ave 89052
Featherwood Ave 89015
Federal St 89015
Feliz Contado Ct 89015
Fenwick Ln 89052
Feriverl Dr 89015
Fern Hill Ct 89052
Fernbrook Dr 89002
Ferrand Ct 89044
Fetter Ct 89052
Fiddler Ridge Trl 89011
Fieldbrook St 89052
Fiery Hill Ave 89011
Fiesta Henderson Blvd 89015
Fife St 89015
Finch Island Ave 89015
Findlater St 89044
Finestra Dr 89074
Finlarig St 89044
Fir St 89015
Fircrest Ct 89052
Firebrand Ct 89074
Firedrake Ter 89074
Fireweed Dr 89002
First Light St 89052
Firth Ave 89015
Fish Pond Ave 89014
Fishing St 89011
Flagstone Ranch Ln 89012
Flaming Cliffs Ct 89014
Flapjack Dr 89014
Flare Star Dr 89044
Flat Plains Ave 89012
Flat Ridge Dr 89014
Flat Slate Ave 89011
Flatfoot Ave 89012
Flintrock Rd 89014
Flip Flop Ct 89052
Flirtation Ct 89074
Flodden St 89044
Floral Peak Dr 89074
Floral Vista Ave 89014
Flores Ln 89012
Florindo Walk 89044
Flowering Cactus Ave 89052
Flowing Meadow Dr 89014
Flute Ave 89052
Flutell Ct 89074
Flying M Ct 89002
Foothills Dr 89002
Foothills Mills St 89012
Foothills Village Dr 89012
Forest St 89015
Forest City Dr 89052
Forest Grove Dr 89052
Forest Haven Way 89011
Forest Peak St 89011
Forest Ridge St 89014
Fork Mesa Ct 89015
Forlana Dr 89052
Formia Dr 89052
Foro Romano St 89044
Fort Halifax St 89052
Fort Matanzas Ter 89052
Fort Myer Ave 89052
Fort Sanders St 89052
Fort Stanwix Rd 89052
Fortacre St 89002
Fortifying Crest Ct 89052
Fortuna Ct 89074
Forum Veneto Dr 89052
Fossil Canyon Dr 89052
E & W Foster Ave 89011
Founders Ct 89074
Fountain City St 89052
Fountain Crossing Ln 89074
Fountain Grove St 89012
Fountain Hills Ave 89002
Fountain Ridge Ln 89074
Fountain Springs Dr 89074
Fountain Vista Ln 89074
Fountainhead Cir 89052
Fourth St 89015
Fox Butte Ct 89014
Fox Chapel Ter 89052
Fox Chase St 89015
Fox Coat St 89002
Fox Haven St 89015
Fox Hills Dr 89052
Fox Horn Rd 89052
Fox Links St 89012
Fox Ridge Dr 89014
Fox Trace Ct 89074
Foxfire Ct 89012
Foxhall Rd 89002
Foxmoore Ct 89052
Foxtail Creek Ave 89052
Fragrant Orchard St 89015
Fragrant Sage Ct 89015
Francisco St 89014
Franello Ct 89052
Franklin Chase Ter 89012
Frecco Cavern Ct 89052
Freedom Ct 89014
Freedom Hills Dr 89052
Freeman Ct 89014
French Alps Ave 89044
French Roast Pl 89052
Fresh Pond Ct 89052
Freshly Brewed Ct 89052
Friendly Ct 89052
Friendship Hill Cir 89052
Frisco Peak Dr 89014
Frontera Rd 89074
Frost Ct 89052
Fuente Dr 89014
Fuerte Ct 89015
Fulford Ct 89052
Full Wine St 89074
Fullerton Ave 89015
Furnace Creek Ave 89074
Gabriel St 89044
Gainesborough Ct 89015
Gainsway West Dr 89074
Galactic Halo Ave 89044
Galangate Ave 89015
Galaxy Cluster St 89044
Galena Dr 89074
Galilean Moon St 89044
Galimard Ter 89044
Galindo Ct 89052
Galingale Ct 89015
Gallagher Crest Rd 89074
Gallant Fox Ave 89015
Galleria Dr 89014
E Galleria Dr 89011
W Galleria Dr 89011
Galleria Spada St 89044
Gamboge St 89012
Gamma Ray Pl 89044
Gana Ct 89014
Gannett Peak St 89012
Garberville Pl 89044
Garden Ct 89002
Garden City Ave 89052
Garden Gate Pl 89002
Garden Ridge Ct 89012
Gardenia Blossom St 89015
Garfield Dr 89074
Garmisch Ct 89074
Garnet Garden St 89015
Garnet Star St 89044
Garrett Ct 89012
Garretts Bluff Way 89002
Garwood Ct 89074
Gascony Pl 89011
Gate Dancer Ave 89015
Gatlinburg Ct 89012
Gatsby St 89052
Gayle Ave 89015
Gecko Rd 89002
Genesee Point St 89074
Geneva Ave 89015
Genova Ct 89052
Gentilly Lace Ave 89002
Gentle Bay Ave 89074
Gentle Glow St 89052
Gentle Springs Dr 89012
Gentleslope St 89011
Geranium Dr 89011
Geronimo Ct 89074
Gettysburg Ave 89052
Geyser Peak St 89052
Giant Redwood Ave 89074
N Gibson Rd
2-106 89014
108-399 89014
400-799 89011
S Gibson Rd 89012
Gibson Heights Ave 89074
Gilbertville Ave 89052
Gilespie St 89044
Ginger Lily Ter 89074
Gingerbread St 89012
Ginori Ct 89014
Ginseng Ct 89052
Giverny Bridge Ave 89044
Glacier Dr 89074
Glacier Park Ct 89052
Glacier Rapids Ct 89052
Glade Water Dr 89052
Gladiola Way 89011
Glaring Ct 89002
Glasgow St 89015
Glass Pool Ave 89002
Glen Eden Ct 89074
Glen Falls Ave 89002
Glen Green Ave 89074
Glendevon Cir 89014
Glendive St 89012
Glendon St 89074
Glendora Ct 89052
Gleneagles Ct 89074
Glenoak Dr 89002
Glenwood Ct & Ln 89002
Glistening Cloud Dr 89012
Glistening Grove Ave 89052
Glistening Point Ave 89015
Glocker Ct 89012
Gloria Mountain Rd 89002
Gold St 89015
Gold Bear Dr 89052
Gold Camp St 89002
Golda Way 89011
Goldcreek St 89052
Golden Bay Ct 89052
Golden Corral Trl 89011
Golden Crown Ave 89002
Golden Gardens Ct 89044
Golden Plata Ct 89015
Golden Ridge Ct 89052
Golden Sedum Dr 89011
Golden Shadow Ct &
Dr 89002
Golden Spear Pl 89002
Golden Spike Ct 89014
Golden Splendor Ct 89002
Golden State St 89012
Golden Valley Dr 89002
Golden View St 89012
Goldenrod Ct 89002
Goldfinch Ave 89014
Goldfire Cir 89052
Goldhill Rd 89074
Goldstar St 89012
Golf Crest Ct 89052
Golf View Dr 89074
Gonderville Ct 89044
Gondi Castle Ave 89044
Gondola Way 89074
Gooseberry Ln 89074
Goshawk St 89015
Goshen Ave 89074
Graceful Ln 89052
Graceful Cloud Ave 89011
Graceful Moon Ave 89015
Grafton Ave 89074
Gran Vista Ave 89012
Granados Ave 89014
Grand Anacapri Dr 89011
Grand Corniche Dr 89011
Grand Forks Rd 89052
Grand Helios Way 89052
Grand Hills Dr 89052
Grand Mediterra Blvd 89011
Grand Miramar Dr 89011
Grand Olympia Dr 89012
Grand Teton Dr 89074
Grand Traverse St 89052
Grande Arch St 89044
Grande Sombrero
Way 89015
Grandview Ct & Dr 89002
Grandville Ave 89052
Grange Ave 89074
Granite Bar St 89002
Grantsville Ct 89002
Grantwood Dr 89074
Grape Dr 89015
Grape Vine Ave 89002
Grass Creek Ave 89012
Grass Pond Pl 89002
Grassrange Ln 89052
Gray Fox Rd 89074
Grayson Cir 89014
Graythorn Mountain Ct 89012
Great Dane Ct 89052
Great Elk Dr 89052
Greely Ct 89014
Greely Club Trl 89052
Green Falls Ave 89052
Green Hills Ct 89012
Green Isle Cir 89074
Green Macaw Way 89012
Green Peace Ct 89052
N Green Valley Pkwy
100-598 89074
600-1899 89074
1901-2199 89074
2201-2297 89014
2299-2735 89014
2722-2722 89016
2736-2998 89014
2737-2999 89014
S Green Valley Pkwy
100-399 89012
401-599 89012
600-699 89052
701-799 89052
Greenleaf Glen St 89014
Greens Ave 89014
Greenville St 89015
Greenway Rd
400-599 89015
600-1100 89002
1102-1398 89002
Grenada Lake Ln 89044
Grey Eagle St 89074
Grey Stone Rd 89074
Greycliff Ter 89002
Greyhawk Ct 89074
Grimsby Ave 89014
Grizzly Park Ct 89052
Groft Way 89015
Grosse Pointe Pl 89052
Grossinger Ct 89074
Grove St 89015
Grove Park St 89002
Grub Stake Cir 89014
Guardi Ct 89052
Guidance Ridge Ct 89012
Guided Dancer Ave 89015
Guilford Dr 89014
Guinn Dr 89074
Gumdrop Ave 89074
Gunman Way 89002
Gunnison Pl 89044
Gurneys Eagle Ave 89015
Gusty Sands St 89015
Hacienda Horse Ct 89002
Hacker Dr 89074
Haig Point Ct 89052
Hamlet St 89002
Hammock Dunes Ct 89052
Hamonah Dr 89044
Hampton Rd 89052
Hampton Ridge Ct 89002
Handel Ave 89052
Hanley Way 89074
Hanover Dr 89074
Hansen St 89015
Hanston Ct 89044
Happy Sparrow Ave 89052
Harbor Beach Ct 89002
Harbor Mist Ave 89015
Hardin Dr 89074
Hardin Ridge Dr 89052
Haren Dr 89011
Harlequin Cir 89074
Harmony Hill Dr 89014
Harmony Ridge Way 89052
Harpsichord Way 89012
Harpy Eagle Ave 89015
Harris St 89015
Harrisburg Ave 89052

Hartley Ave 89052
Harts Bluff Pl 89002
Hartsville Rd 89052
Hartwick Pines Dr 89052
Harvard Ct 89074
Harvest Season Ct 89074
Harwood Ave 89012
Hassayampa Trl 89052
Hatten Bay St 89012
Havasu Ct 89014
Haven Green Ct 89012
Havre Ave 89015
Hawk Canyon St 89074
Hawkwood Rd 89014
Hayden Creek Ter 89052
Hayesville Ave 89052
Hazel St 89015
Hazel Valley Ct 89044
Hazelhurst Pass 89052
Hazeltine Ct 89074
Heartland Ave 89074
Hearts Club Dr 89074
Heartstring Ct 89002
Heath Ct 89074
Heather Dr 89002
Heatherstone St
200-299 89052
8600-8799 89074
Heaton Ave 89052
Heaven Sent Ct 89074
Heavenly Ct 89002
Heavenly Harvest Pl 89002
Heavenly View Dr 89014
Heavy Gorge Ave 89011
Heiple Ct 89052
Helmer Ct 89002
Helmsdale Dr 89014
Hennepin Dr 89014
Hera Heights Ct 89052
Herbie Ln 89015
Heritage Cove Dr 89011
Heritage Point Dr 89002
Heritage Springs Dr 89052
Heritage Vista Ave 89015
Heswall Ct 89014
Hexham Ct & Dr 89015
Heydon Ct 89014
Hibiscus Ct 89011
Hickory St 89015
Hickory Valley Rd 89052
Hidden Brook Ct 89015
Hidden Falls Way 89074
Hidden Forest Cir 89074
Hidden Garden Pl 89012
Hidden Hollow Ln 89012
Hidden Meadow Ave 89015
Hidden Mesa Ct 89012
Hidden Mist St 89052
Hidden Ranch Ter 89052
Hidden Sands Ct 89074
Hidden Valley Dr 89002
Hideaway Ter 89002
Hideout Way 89052
High Grass Ct 89011
High Mesa Dr 89012
High Mountain St 89015
High Plains Dr 89002
High Sierra Dr 89074
High Steed St 89011
High Tec Cir 89002
High View Dr 89014
High Vista Cir & Dr 89014
Highbury Grove St 89002
Highgate St 89074
E & W Highland Dr 89015
Highland Cliff Dr 89052
Highland Creek Dr 89052
Highland Trails Ave 89015
Highmore Ave 89052
Hightop Ln 89002
Highwood Ave 89002
Hillcrest Dr 89015
Hillpointe Rd 89074
Hills Of Gold Ct 89052
Hillsboro Dr 89074
Hillside Valley St 89044
Hillstone Ave 89052
Hilltop Rd 89015
Himara Ct 89014
Hitchcock St 89052
Hitchen Post Dr 89011
Hobbyhorse Ave 89012
Hobson Dr 89074
Hocus Pocus Pl 89002
Holdenville St 89052
Holick Ave 89011
Hollow Reed Ct 89011
Hollowvale Ln 89052
Holly Bush Ct 89015
Holly Hunt St 89052
Holly Lake Way 89002
Holly Tree Ct 89052
Hollybrook Ct 89074
Hollyfern St 89074
Hollyhock Dr 89011
Holman Cir 89074
Holmes Sabatini Way 89014
Holmfault St 89044
Holmfield St 89052
Holston Hills Rd 89052
Home Ct 89014
Homestead Ct 89014
Homesteader Ct 89052
Hometown Ave 89074
Honeybee Ct 89002
Honeywood St 89074
Hookcross Cir 89074
Hoopes Ave 89052
Hopeful Ridge Ct 89052
Hopewell Ave 89012
Hopi Ln 89015
E Horizon Dr 89015
Horizon Crest Ct 89012
Horizon Light Ct 89052
Horizon Peak Dr 89012
Horizon Pointe Cir 89012
Horizon Range Ave 89012
E Horizon Ridge Pkwy 89002
W Horizon Ridge Pkwy
2-1574 89012
1575-2099 89012
1575-1575 89053
1576-2098 89012
2200-2999 89052
3001-3099 89052
Horizon View Dr 89015
Horse Creek Cir 89014
Horse Prairie Dr 89052
Horseshoe Bar Ln 89011
Horseshoe Bay Ct 89074
Horseweed Cir 89002
Hoskins Ct 89012
Hotel De Ville Ter 89044
Houdini St 89002
Hourglass Dr 89052
House Blend Ln 89052
Hovenweep St 89052
Huckleberry Ln 89074
Hudson Canyon St 89012
Hudson Falls Ct 89044
Hull St 89015
N & S Humboldt Dr 89074
Hummingbird Cir, Ln &
Way 89014
Hummingbird Hill Ave 89074
Humphreys Peak Ct 89012
Hunt Valley Trl 89052
Hunter Dr 89011
Hunters Peak Ct 89052
Hunters Run Dr 89002
Hunters Valley Way 89015
Huntfield Dr 89074
Huron Ln 89015
Hutch Ct 89015
Hutchings Ln 89074
Hydrus Ave 89044
Hyperion Dr 89011
Hyssop Ct 89015
Ibis Ct 89052
Icarus Dr 89074
Icy Moon St 89044
Idaho Way 89015
Idaho Falls Dr 89044
Ilmenite Way 89015
Impassioned Ct 89052
Imperia Dr 89052
Imposing Knoll Ave 89002
Inca Ln 89015
Incline Village Ct 89074
Indian Bend Dr 89074
Indian Corn Ave 89015
Indian Pony Ct 89052
Indian Row Ct 89011
Indian Trail Ct 89074
Indiana Ct 89015
Indigo Creek Ave 89012
Indigo Island St 89044
Indigo Springs St 89014
Indistre Dr 89014
Industrial Park Rd 89015
Inness Ave 89011
Innsdale Ct 89074
Inropah Dr 89014
Inspired Ct 89052
Integrity Point Ave 89012
Integrity Ridge Dr 89052
Intellectual Ct 89052
Inveraray Ct 89074
Invermark St 89044
Inverness Dr 89074
Investment Way 89074
Iolite Ct 89011
Ione Rd 89074
Iridescent St 89012
Iris Ct 89074
Iris Fields Ave 89044
Iris Point Way 89074
Irish Mittens Ct 89011
Ironbark Dr 89014
Island City Dr 89044
Island Falls Ave 89015
Island Reef Ave 89012
Isleworth Dr 89052
Italian Roast Ct 89052
Ithaca Ave 89015
Ivanpah Dr 89074
Ivy St 89015
Ivy Glen Cir 89074
Jackson Dr 89014
Jada Dr 89044
Jade Cir 89002
Jade Sky St 89044
Jagged Cut St 89011
Jameson Cir 89074
Jamie Ct 89074
Janabi Ct 89002
Jane Ln 89015
Jane Eyre Pl 89002
Janesville Ln 89044
Janice Dr 89015
Jann Dr 89002
Jaramillo Ct 89052
Jasmine Ct 89002
Jasmine Point St 89074
Jasmine Tea Ct 89052
Jasper Wood St 89074
Jay Porter Ave 89002
Jefferson Blvd 89011
Jeffreys St 89052
Jena St 89015
Jenkins Springs St 89014
Jenny Linn Dr 89014
Jensen Dr 89074
Jerez Ct 89052
Jeri Dr 89074
Jesse Harbor Ave 89014
Jessica Grove St 89015
Jessie Rd 89002
Jessup Rd 89074
Jet Stream Dr 89052
Jevonda Ave 89044
Jewelstone Cir 89012
Jib Ct 89074
Jimijo Ct 89052
Joan Of Arc St 89044
Joey Ln 89011
John Henry Dr 89014
John Stuart Mill St 89002
Jonquil Cir 89074
Jordan Valley Ct 89044
Jorge Way 89014
Josephine Dr 89044
Joshua St 89015
Jovita Ct 89074
Joy Creek Ln 89012
Joy Grove Ave 89012
Joy View Ln 89012
Joyce St 89015
Jubilee Rd 89074
Judy Ct & Ln 89015
Jules Ln 89014
Julia St 89014
Julie Rd 89002
Jumbled Sage Ct 89015
Jumping Hills Ave 89052
Jumping Moon Ct 89052
Jumping Springs Pl 89012
June Lake Dr 89052
Junebug Pl 89015
Juniper St 89015
Juniper Ridge Ave 89015
Juniper Springs St 89052
Jupiter Hills Ln 89012
Justin Cir, Ct & Pl 89011
Kabuki Ave 89074
Kachina Dr 89074
Kachina Mountain Dr 89012
Kalkaska Dr 89044
Kanani Ct 89052
Kanarra Ct 89014
Kanel Cir 89074
Kansas Ave 89015
Kantele Cir 89052
Kapelle St 89052
Karen Way 89015
Karsten Creek Ct 89052
Kava Kava St 89015
Kaymin Ridge Rd 89052
Keating St 89074
Keego Harbor St 89052
Keena Dr 89011
Keepsake Ave 89014
Kelsey Creek Ct 89044
Kelso Dunes Ave 89014
Kenerly St 89015
Kennebunk Cir 89015
Kennesaw Rd 89052
Kenneth Ave 89052
Kensingpark Ct 89052
Kentons Run Ave 89052
Kern River Ave 89002
Kernwood St 89002
Kershner Ct 89074
N Kiel St 89015
Kildrummie St 89044
Kilmaron Cir 89014
Kilwinning Dr 89044
E & W Kimberly Dr 89015
Kind Ave 89002
Kindeace Ave 89044
Kindness Crest Ct 89012
Kindred Point Ct 89052
E King St 89011
King Arthur Ct 89002
King Louis St 89044
King Mesa Dr 89012
Kingclaven Dr 89044
Kinghorn Pl 89044
Kings Canyon Ct 89012
Kings Dominion Ct 89052
Kings Links St 89012
Kings Peak Ct 89012
Kings View Ct 89002
Kingston Rd 89074
Kingston Hills Ct 89002
Kinknockie Way 89044
Kinnard Ave 89074
Kiowa Ct 89074
Kirk Ave 89015
Kirkmichael Ln 89014
Kirkton St 89012
Kirkwall St 89002
Kittansett Loop 89052
Klamath River Ave 89002
Klondike Ct 89011
Knightsboro Rd 89074
Knightsbridge Rd 89074
Knob Oak Dr 89052
Knollwood Ct 89074
Knoxville Ct 89052
Knudson Ct 89002
Kokopelli Ct 89074
Kola St 89015
Kona Ct 89074
Kona Crest Ave 89052
Korea Ct 89052
Kory Dunes Ct 89014
Kover Ct 89002
Kransten Dr 89074
Kratzer Cir 89002
Kristin Ln 89011
Kukui Ct 89074
La Alba St 89074
La Amatista St 89014
La Ballena Trl 89074
La Bella Ct 89052
La Boutique St 89044
La Brea Rd 89014
La Casa Dr 89014
La Cienega St 89044
La Colina Cir 89012
La Crosse Ct 89052
La Cruz Dr 89014
La Cuenta Cir 89074
La Entrada St 89014
La Estrella St 89014
La Fiesta St 89012
La Jolla Dr 89015
La Laguna St 89012
La Luna Cir & Dr 89014
La Mancha Way 89014
La Mesa Dr 89014
La Mirada Dr 89015
La Paz Ave 89015
La Pluma St 89014
La Porte Ct 89052
La Ramada Ct 89002
La Serna St 89074
La Suena Ct 89012
Lace Haven Ct 89012
Ladasa Ct 89074
Ladywood Ln 89002
Lago Turchino Ct 89011
Laguna Bay Ct 89052
Laguna Glen Dr 89014
Laguna Hills Ct 89002
Laguna Landing Dr 89002
Laguna Seca Ave 89052
Lairmont Pl 89012
Lake Barkley Rd 89052
Lake Berryessa St 89002
Lake Candlewood Ave 89044
Lake Las Vegas Pkwy 89011
E Lake Mead Pkwy 89015
W Lake Mead Pkwy
63-97 89015
99-699 89015
701-797 89015
841-899 89014
Lake Placid Ter 89014
Lake Wales St 89052
Lakewood Dr 89012
Lambeth Ct 89014
Lamppost St 89074
Land Breeze Ct 89014
Land Rush Dr 89002
Landau Ct 89074
Lander Dr, Pl & Ter 89074
Landfair Ct 89074
Landing Bay Ave 89074
Landmark Ln 89002
Landra Ln 89015
Langford Ave 89052
Langlade Ave 89052
Langston Hughes St 89052
Lanni Ct 89012
Lantern Glow Cir 89074
Laramie Springs Ln 89052
Laramine River Dr 89052
Large Cap Dr 89074
Largo Azul Ave 89015
Lariat Ln 89014
Laricola Ct 89011
Larkside Ct 89014
Larkspur Ranch Ct 89012
Larrimer Ct 89011
Larson Ln 89044
Las Brisas Ct 89074
Las Palmas Entrada
Ave 89012
Las Pasadas Ct 89002
Las Vegas Blvd S 89044
Lasso Ct 89014
Laswell St 89015
Latigo Dr 89002
Latina Ct 89012
Laurel Ave 89014
Laurel Heights Ln 89052
Laurel Wreath Ct 89012
Lauren Patt Ct 89014
E & W Laval Dr 89015
Lawrence Dr 89015
Lawrencekirk Ct 89044
Layla Bay St 89014
Lazy Saddle Dr 89002
Le Arta Dr 89074
Le Conte Ave 89074
Le Pontet Ter 89044
Lead St 89015
Leadville Meadows Dr 89052
Leaf Bud Ct 89074
Leaf Tree Ave 89011
Lefty Garcia Way 89002
Legacy Dr 89014
Legacy Island Cir 89074
Legend Hollow Ct 89074
Lehman Cave Ct 89052
Leicester St 89002
Leighann Rd 89015
Leighton Ave 89052
Leisure Cir 89074
Lembo Di Lago Ct 89011
Lemon Grove St 89052
Lemon Heights Rd 89052
Lemongold St 89012
Lemongrass Ct 89002
Leon Say Ln 89044
Levan Hills Trl 89052
Lewis Ct 89015
Lewisham Ct 89002
Lewiston Pl 89044
Leys Burnett Ave 89044
Libberton St 89044
Liberation Dr 89044
Liberty Heights Ave 89052
Liberty Point Ct 89052
Libretto Ave 89052
Lido Cir & Dr 89015
Lido Nord 89011
Liege Dr 89012
Light Sky Ave 89074
Lilac Ct 89074
Lilac Bud St 89074
Lilium St 89015
Lily Pond Cir 89012
Lily Valley Ct 89074
Lime Cir 89015
Limoges Ter 89014
Lindbrook St 89074
Linden St 89015
Lingering Ln 89012
N & S Lisbon St 89015
Listo Ct 89014
Little Bear Ct 89052
Little Bighorn Dr 89052
Little Bird Ct 89011
Little Dove Ct 89014
Little Falls Cir 89052
Little House Ct 89011
Little Minah Ct 89052
Little Raven St 89002
Lively Fiesta Way 89015
Liverpool Ave 89011
Livery Ct 89011
Living Springs Pl 89012
Livingston Dr 89012
Lloyd George Dr 89052
Lobelias Ct 89002
Lochbroom Way 89044
Lochleven Way 89044
Lochmaben St 89044
Lockerbie St 89044
Lockhaven Ct 89074
Lodgepole Dr 89014
Logan Patrick Dr 89052
Logansport St 89052
Loma Linda Cir 89015
Lombardy Cir 89015
Lomprey Ave & Ct 89002
London Ave 89015
Lone Cliff Dr 89074
Lone Cove Ct 89012
Lone Palm Ct 89002
Lone Pine Ln & St 89014
Lone Pine River Ave 89002
E & W Long Acres Dr 89015
Long Branch Dr 89014
Long Creek Ct 89044
Long Horizon Ln 89074
Long Shadow Ter 89015
Longevity Dr 89014
Longford Ave 89074
Longmeadow St 89002
Longshanks Way 89015
Longtree Ave 89011
Lookout Ave 89002
Lookout Valley Ave 89052
Loring Ave 89074
Lorna Dr 89011
Lorne Green Ave 89011
Los Coches Cir 89074
Losserand Ave 89044
Lost Ball Ct 89074
Lost Eagle Way 89012
Lost Mountain Ct 89074
Lost Pines Cir 89074
Lost Trail Dr 89014
Lothian St 89044
Lotus Garden Ct 89074
Louniang Dr 89012
Lovage St 89002
Lovelady Ct 89074
Lovely Rita Ct 89074
Lovett Rd 89015
Lovington Dr 89074
Lower Meadows Ave 89052
Lowery St 89015
Luau Ct 89074
Lubec Valley Ln 89074
Luberon Dr 89044
Luce Del Sole 89011
Lucerne Cir, Ct & Dr 89014
Lucky Bamboo Dr 89052
Lucky Pine St 89002
Lucy St 89015
Luminous Stars St 89044
Luna Eclipse Ln 89002
Lundgren Ct 89002
Luninborg St 89074
Lupine Ct 89002
Lush Hillside Ct 89002
Lynbrook St 89012
Lynmar Ct 89052
Lynn Ln 89015
Lynnhaven St 89015
Lyon Dr 89074
Lyrical Rd 89052
Mabee Ct 89074
Macdonald Ranch Dr 89012
Machado Dr 89074
Mackay St 89015
Mackenzie Creek Ave 89002
Mackenzie River Ave 89002
Macrory Dr 89044
Madison Heights St 89052
Madrid Ave 89015
Maffie St 89052
Magenta Crest Ct 89052
N Magic Way 89015
S Magic Way
200-299 89015
1800-2099 89002

Magic Canyon Dr 89002
Magic Meadow St 89052
Magical Mystery Ln 89074
Magnesium St 89015
Magnolia Dr 89014
Magnolia Pond Ct 89052
Magnum Ct 89052
Mahaila Cir 89074
Mahalko Ct 89012
Mahogany Grove Ave 89074
Mainsail Ct 89002
Majestic Canyon St 89052
Majestic Park Dr 89052
Majestic Peak Dr 89074
Majestic Ridge Ct 89052
Majestic Shadows Ave 89052
Majestic Sunset Ct 89052
Majesty Ct 89011
N & S Major Ave & Way 89015
Mako Dr 89002
Malachite Ct 89011
Malcolm St 89074
Maleena Mesa St 89074
Mali Heights Ct 89074
Mall Ring Cir 89014
Mallard Creek Trl 89052
Mallard Landing Ave 89074
Mallory St 89015
Mammoth Pools Ct 89012
Mancini Ct 89014
Mandalay Ct 89012
Manganese St 89015
Mango Ct 89015
Mango Rose Ct 89074
Manhattan Rd 89074
Manor Shores Rd 89002
Manosque Ln 89044
Manteno Ct 89052
Manti Pl 89014
Mantua Village Ave 89044
Manzanita St 89014
Manzanita Ranch Ln 89012
Maple St 89015
Maple Heights Ct 89052
Maple Ridge Ct 89052
Maple Shade St 89002
Maple Springs St 89002
Maranello St 89052
Marathon Dr 89074
Marble Cliff Ct 89052
Mardela Springs Ct 89052
Marengo Caves Ave 89044
Margarita Ave 89011
Marie Antoinette St 89044
Marigold Ct 89011
Marina Estates Cir 89015
Marion Center Ct 89052
Mariposa Way 89015
Maritime St 89074
Mark Leany Dr 89011
Market St 89015
Marks St
200-299 89074
400-799 89014
Marlberry Pl 89015
Marlboro Dr 89014
Marlene Ct & Way 89014
Marlin Cove Rd 89012
Marnay Ln 89044
Marsh Creek Ct 89002
Marsh Landing Ct 89052
Marshall Dr 89014
Marsolan Ct 89014
Marston Way 89015
Marstons Mills Ct 89044
Martini Dr 89052
Martinique Ave 89044
Mary Crest Rd
900-998 89014
1000-1199 89074
S Maryland Pkwy 89052
Maryland Hills Dr 89052
Marysville Ave 89052
Marywood Park Ct 89044
Matese Dr 89052
Matrino Ct 89052
Mattie Brook Ave 89015
Mattino Way 89074
Mauna Kea Pl 89011
Mauve St 89012
Maverick Ct 89014
Max Ct 89011
May Valley Way 89052
Mayan Ct & Dr 89014
Mayberry St 89052
Mayfair Ave 89074
Mazatlan St 89074
Mazzanti Way 89014
Mcbride Way 89015
Mccartney Ct 89074
Mckenzie Dr 89015
Mckinley View Ave 89012
Mclaren St 89074
Mcleod Dr 89074
Mcneil Dr 89015
Mcnerney Dr 89012
Meadbury Dr 89014
Meadow Bluffs Ave 89014
Meadow Breeze Ln 89002
Meadow Park Ave 89052
Meadowlark Dr 89014
Meandering Hills Dr 89052
Medina De Leon Ave 89015
Medio Ct 89014
Medway Valley Ln 89074
Megan Dr 89074
Melfi Ct 89012
Melody Vista Ln 89015
Melrose Heights St 89052
Memphis Ave 89052
Menaggio Ct 89011
Menta Ct 89074
Mercury Ave 89002
Meridian Marks Dr 89052
Meridian Mills Rd 89052
Merit Ct 89014
Merivale Ave 89012
E & W Merlayne Dr 89011
Merlin Ct 89002
Merrick Way 89014
Merrimack Valley Ave 89044
Merze Ave 89011
Mesa Pine Ct 89015
Mesa Rivera St 89012
Mesa Verde Ter 89014
Mescalero Trl 89074
Mesquite Ct 89014
Mesquite Canyon Dr 89012
Mesquite Ridge Ln 89012
Mesquite Village Cir 89012
Mesquite Wood Ct 89012
Meteor Shower St 89044
Meteor Stream Ter 89044
Metropolitan Dr 89015
Meyers Ave & Ct 89015
Mezza Ct 89012
Mezza Luna Ct 89011
Mia Isabella Ct 89052
Micah Ave 89074
Michael Ct 89014
Middle Valley St 89052
Middleburgh Ct 89052
Middlegate Rd 89011
E & W Middleton Dr 89015
Midori St 89002
Midvale Ter 89074
Miki Ct 89052
N & S Milan St 89015
Milano Villa Ave 89052
Milicity Rd 89012
Military Tribute Pl 89074
Mill Point Dr 89074
Mill Run Creek Ave 89002
Millbrae Dr 89074
Millcroft Dr 89074
Milldale Ct 89002
Millinocket Ct 89052
Millstream Way 89074
Mimosa Ct 89014
Mineral Hill Ln 89002
Mingary Ave 89044
Minolta Ct 89044
Minor Ave 89015
Mint Orchard Dr 89002
Mintlaw Ave 89044
Minuet St 89052
Mira Montana St 89014
Mirabella St 89052
Mirador St 89074
Mirage Rd 89074
Mirage Lake St 89052
Mirror Ct 89011
Misano Monte St 89044
Mission Dr 89002
Mission Springs St 89052
Mission Verde Ave 89002
Mist Effect Ave 89044
Misty Ct 89074
Misty Garden St 89012
Misty Grove Dr 89074
Misty Moon Ave 89052
Misty Moonlight St 89015
Misty Olive Ave 89052
Misty Rain St 89012
Misty Rose Ave 89074
Misty Sky Dr 89052
Misty Winds Ct 89052
Mizzoni Cir 89052
Moapa Ct 89074
Moccasin Ct 89014
Mocha Mattari St 89052
Modesto St 89014
Mohansic Rd 89052
Mohawk Dr 89015
Mojave Ln 89015
Moliere Ct 89044
Molinard Ct 89044
Moltrasio Ln 89011
Mona Ln 89015
Mona Lisa St 89044
Monachi St 89014
Monarch Pass Dr 89014
Monet Sunrise Ave 89044
Monmouth Ct 89015
Monroe Park Rd 89052
Montagna Mirage St 89012
Montalban Ct 89012
Montana Way 89015
Montana Pine Dr 89052
Montavo Ave 89074
Montclair Ct & Dr 89074
Montcliff Ave 89074
Monte De Luz Way 89012
Monte Etna Ave 89012
Monte Nerone Ave 89012
Monteen Dr 89074
Montefiore Walk 89044
Montelago Blvd 89011
Monteloma Way 89074
Montesol Dr 89012
Montferrat Ln 89044
Montmorency St 89044
Monument Point St 89002
Moon Beam Ave 89052
Moon Vision St 89052
Moondance Ct 89011
Moonlight Mesa Dr 89011
Moonlight Stroll St 89002
Moonlight Valley Ave 89044
Moonlight Village Ln 89012
Moonlit Cliffs Ct 89014
Moonlit Oasis Ln 89002
Moonrise Way 89074
Moonshot St 89074
Moonstar Ln 89052
Moontide Ct 89011
Moore Oaks Ct 89011
Mooreview St 89012
Moorland Bluffs Ave 89014
Moorpark Way 89014
Mora Ct 89074
Moraine Dr 89052
Moreno Ct 89014
Moresca Ave 89052
Morgan City Ave 89052
Morganton Dr 89052
Morning Dr 89012
Morning Crescent St 89052
Morning Melody Ct 89011
Morning Mesa Ave 89052
Morning Mimosa Ct 89012
Morning Skyline Ct 89052
Morning Springs Dr 89074
Morning View Dr 89015
Morning Whisper Dr 89052
Morninglow Pass 89052
Morro Rock Ct 89012
Morrocco Dr 89002
Moser Dr 89011
Moses Lake Ct 89002
Moss Canyon Ave 89014
Moss Springs Ct 89052
Moss View Ct 89074
Mosswood Dr 89002
Motherwell Ave 89012
Motif Ct 89052
Motu Ct 89074
Moulton Ct 89074
Mount Dana Ct 89014
Mount Earl Ave 89012
Mount Hope St 89014
Mount Noble Ct 89074
Mount Saint Helens Dr 89012
Mount Sunflower Ct 89052
Mountain City St 89052
Mountain Cove Ct 89052
Mountain Dell Ave 89012
Mountain Echo Ave 89074
Mountain Heights Ct 89052
Mountain Links Dr 89012
Mountain Ranch Ave 89012
Mountain Song Ct 89074
Mountain Top Ct 89002
Mountain View Rd 89015
Mountain Vista St 89014
Mountainside Dr 89012
Mowbray Ct 89074
Moyer Dr 89074
Muchacha Dr 89014
Muir Ct 89052
Muirfield Ave 89074
E & W Mulberry Dr 89015
Mullen Ave 89044
Mura Del Prato Ave 89044
Mustang Dr 89002
Mustang Breeze Trl 89011
Myrtle Beach Dr 89074
Myrtle Point Way 89052
Mystic River St 89015
Mystic Star St 89044
Mystical St 89052
Nakoa Ct 89002
Nancy Dr 89015
Nantucket Ave 89074
N & S Naples St 89015
Nashira St 89044
Nashville Ave 89052
Natalee Dr 89011
Natchez Ct 89074
National St 89015
Nautical St 89012
Navajo Dr 89015
Navajo Point Pl 89074
Navarre Ln 89014
Navy St 89015
Nebraska Ave 89015
Nectarine Ct 89014
Neidpath Ct 89044
Nellywood Ct 89012
Neon Moon Ct 89052
Nestled Foot St 89011
Neutron Star St 89044
Nevada Way 89015
Nevada State Dr 89002
Nevelson Walk 89044
New Beginnings Dr 89011
New Blossom St 89074
New Creek Ave 89015
New Hope Dr 89014
New Mexico Way 89015
New Morning Ave 89052
New River Cir 89052
New Salem Ave 89052
Newark Valley Ln 89044
Newbury Ct 89015
Newelton Ct 89074
Newmiller St 89002
Neyland Dr 89012
Nickel St 89015
Niddrie Ave 89044
Night Fall Ter 89015
Nightshade Ct 89074
Nikki Pl & Ter 89074
Nimitz Ct 89002
Noah Tyler Ct 89052
Noah Valley St 89052
Noble St 89002
Noble Fir Ave 89074
Noble Isle St 89002
Noblesville Ct 89052
Noche De Paz Ave 89015
Nogales Dr 89014
Noonday Ct 89052
Nora Springs Ct 89052
Nordyke Ave 89015
Norellat Rd 89011
Norfolk Ave 89074
Noritake Ct 89014
Norlina Ct 89014
Normandy Way 89014
Norridgewock St 89074
Norwegian Wood Ln 89074
November Sky St 89074
Nuevo Ct & Rd 89014
Nye St 89074
Oak Canyon Dr 89015
Oak Field Ln 89011
Oak Hollow Ct 89074
Oak Shade Ln 89015
Oak Spring Ct 89002
Oakbrook Ridge Ave 89002
Oakmarsh Dr 89074
Oakwood Ct 89002
Oakwood Station Ct 89012
Oasis Cir 89074
Obscured Light Walk 89044
E Ocean Ave 89015
Ocean Shell St 89052
Ocotillo St 89015
Ocotillo Pointe Ter 89074
Octet Ct 89052
Odyssey St 89074
Oella Ridge Ct 89012
Office Park Dr 89074
Oil Painting Walk 89044
Oklahoma Dr 89015
Old Corral Rd 89052
Old Highlands St 89015
Old Lake Cir 89074
Old Marsh Ct 89052
Old Mill Ln 89014
Oldham Ave 89014
Oleander Pl 89015
Oleta Ave 89074
Olive Tree Ct 89074
Oliveiro Ct 89014
Oliver Springs St 89052
Olivia Pkwy 89011
Olivia Heights Ave 89052
Olsen St 89011
Olympic Ave 89014
Onyx Point Ct 89074
Opal Dr 89015
Opal Valley St 89052
Open Plains Way 89002
Opera House St 89012
Opera Season Ct 89074
Opportunity St 89074
Optimistic Ct 89052
Oracle St 89002
Orange Daisy Pl 89012
Orange Jubilee Rd 89014
Orangeburg Pl 89044
Orangeglory Dr 89052
Orchard Ct 89014
Orchard Meadows Ave 89074
Orchard Mesa Dr 89052
Orchid Tree Ln 89011
Ordaz Ave 89011
Oregon Way 89015
Oribia Ave 89014
N & S Orleans St 89015
Oro Canyon St 89074
Oro Valley Dr 89052
Orphington Ct 89002
Osage Winter St 89052
Osborne Ln 89014
Oslo Ave 89015
Osterville St 89052
Otero Valley Ct 89074
Otsego Ct 89012
Otter Rock Ave 89044
Otto Ridge Ct 89052
Outlook Ct 89002
Outrigger St 89015
Overhang Ave 89011
Overland Dr 89002
Overlook Ct 89074
Oxbow Ct 89014
Oxford Cloth Ct 89074
Ozark Plateau Dr 89044
Ozzie Smith Ave 89074
Pabco Rd 89011
Pacer Ter 89002
E Pacific Ave 89015
W Pacific Ave
1-499 89015
501-599 89015
600-699 89002
Pacific Cascades Dr 89012
Pacific Center Dr 89074
Pacini Ct 89052
Pack Saddle Ct 89014
Pagan St 89011
Paganini Ave 89052
Painted Daisy Ave 89074
Painted Glass Walk 89044
Painted Pony Dr 89014
Painted Rose Ln 89074
Painted Sage Ct 89015
Painted Valley St 89074
Painted View St 89012
Pala Dura Dr 89074
Pala Vista Cir 89074
Paladi Ave 89044
Paladin Ct 89074
Palatine Terrace Dr 89052
Palazzo Ter 89074
Palazzo Reale Ave 89044
Pale Morning St 89052
Pale Vista Ct 89012
Palegold St 89012
Palentina St 89044
Palisade Steep Ln 89015
Palisades Dr 89014
Palleta Dr 89074
Palm St 89011
Palm Wash Ln 89011
Palmar Sur Ct 89074
Palmarosa St 89015
Palmbrook Ln 89052
Palmer Park Ct 89052
Palmetto St 89015
Palmetto Bay Dr 89012
Palmetto Pointe Dr 89012
Palo Verde Dr 89015
Paloma Vista St 89012
Palomino Dr 89002
Palta Ct 89074
Panama St 89015
Pancho Via Dr 89012
Pancole Ct 89052
Pandora Canyon St 89052
Pangloss St 89002
Panhandle Dr 89014
Panini Dr 89052
Panisse Ave 89044
Panorama Ridge Dr 89052
Pansy Pl 89052
Panther Creek Ct 89052
Papaya Pl 89015
Paprika Way 89014
Par Excellence Dr 89074
Paradise Pkwy 89074
Paradise Rd
10800-10999 89052
12800-12898 89044
Paradise Bird St 89074
Paradise Coach Dr 89002
Paradise Desert Ave 89002
Paradise Garden Dr 89002
E Paradise Hills Dr 89002
Paradise Home Rd 89002
Paradise Mountain Trl 89002
Paradise Resort Dr 89002
Paradise River Rd 89002
Paradise Safari Dr 89002
Paradise Valley Ct 89052
Paradise View St 89052
Paradise Vista Dr 89002
N & S Parawan St 89015
Paris Amour St 89044
Parisians Ct 89044
Park Ave & Ln 89015
Park Creek Ln 89052
Park Ridge Ln 89002
Parker James Ave 89074
Parker Ranch Dr 89012
Parkson Rd 89011
Parrot Beak St 89012
Parsons Run Ct 89074
Partlow Ct 89015
Parvin St 89044
Paseo Del Lago Cir 89074
Paseo Hills Way 89052
Paseo Mountain Ave 89052
Paseo Verde Pkwy
1200-1298 89012
1300-1999 89012
2200-2399 89052
2400-2598 89074
2600-2699 89074
Passiflora Dr 89002
Pastel Ave 89074
Pastel Cloud St 89015
Pastel Dusk Ct 89012
Pastis Ct 89044
Patagonia St 89012
Pathfinder Rd 89014
Patrick Ln 89014
Patriot Park Pl 89052
Patti Ann Woods Dr 89002
Paveene Ave 89052
Pawnee Ln 89015
Peaceful Creek St 89011
Peaceful Desert Ct 89052
Peaceful Moon St 89044
Peaceful Pine St 89052
Peaceful Shadows Ct 89052
Peaceful Sky Dr 89044
Peach Bluff Ct 89002
Peach Tree Dr 89014
Pear Meadow St 89012
Pear Tree Cir 89014
Pearl City Ct 89052
Pearl Island Dr 89015
Peat Moss Ave 89074
Pebble Pl 89015
Pebble Rd 89074
Pebble Lake St 89011
Pebble Ridge Rd 89012
Pebble Springs Ct 89074
Pebble View Ct 89074
Pebblegold Ave 89074
N & S Pecos Rd 89074
Pecos Ridge Pkwy 89052
Pecos River Ave 89002
Peekskill Ave 89052
Pelican Bay Ct 89012
Pella Dr 89014
Pendle Priory Ave 89011
Penerly St 89002
Penhill Ct 89002
Penn Cross Ct 89052
Pennsbury Village Ct 89052
Pennyfeather Rd 89015
Pennyrile Forest Ct 89052
Penumbra Dr 89044
Peoria Ave 89052
Pepper Tree Cir 89014

Street	ZIP
Peppercorn Ave	89012
Pepperell Ave	89044
Peregrine Ave	89002
Peregrine Falcon St	89015
Perfect Berm Ln	89002
Peridot Pl	89015
Perlite Way	89015
Perry Ellis Dr	89014
Perry Park Ct	89052
Perrysburg Dr	89044
Pershing Cir	89074
Persian Ave	89015
Petit Tranon St	89044
Pettswood Dr	89002
Petunia Ct	89074
Peyten Park St	89052
Pheasant Ridge Cir, Dr & Pl	89014
Phillip Island St	89052
Piazza Navona	89052
Piazza Telle	89052
Picante Pepper Dr	89015
Picked Petal Ct	89074
Pickwick Dr	89014
Picture Rock Ave	89012
Piedmont Alps St	89012
Pigeon Forge Ave	89015
Pimlico Dr	89015
Pimlico Hills St	89014
Pin High Cir	89074
Pincay Dr	89015
Pine Cove Ct	89011
Pine Field Ln	89011
Pine Flat Ct	89052
Pine Flower Ct	89002
Pine Hollow Dr	89052
Pine Isle Ct	89074
Pine Nut Way	89074
Pine Prairie Ave	89052
Pine Trace Ct	89012
Pinery Ct	89074
Pinetop Lake St	89002
Pinewood Ave	89074
Pinewood Ranch Way	89052
Ping Dr	89074
Pinion Springs Dr	89074
Pinion Woods Ct	89052
Pink Dawn Dr	89014
Pinnacle Ct	89014
Pintale Cir	89074
Pinto Rd	89002
Pinto Horse Ave	89052
Pinyon Tree Cir	89074
Pioneer St	89015
Pioneers Peak Ave	89002
Piping Rock Ln	89052
Pissarro Pl	89074
Pitgaveny Ave	89044
Piute Ln	89015
Piute Valley Ct	89012
Placa De Rei Ct	89011
Placa Santa Maria Ct	89011
Placer Creek Ln	89014
Plain Sight Ave	89014
Plains St	89002
Plantation Acres St	89014
Plantation Rose Ct	89002
Platinum St	89015
Playa Blanca St	89074
Playa Del Coco Ct	89074
Playa Del Sol Way	89015
Playful Glow St	89052
Plaza Capri Ct	89074
Plaza Carmelina Ct	89015
Plaza Marquessa Ct	89074
Plaza Marsala Ct	89074
Plaza Napoli Ct	89074
Pleasant Dale Dr	89074
Pleasant Pebble St	89074
Pleasant Prairie Dr	89052
Pleasant Ridge Ave	89012
Pleasant Run Ct	89011
Pleasant Summit Dr	89012
Pleasing Plateau St	89002
Pleasure Ln	89002
Plentywood Pl	89002
Plockton Ave	89012
Plum Ct	89014
Plum Hollow Dr	89052
Plumpjack Ave	89002
Plumstead St	89002
Pocahontas Ct	89074
Poco Valle Ct	89015
Poetic Valley Cir	89012
Poetry Ave	89052
Point Bluff St	89002
Point Mallard Dr	89012
Point Pleasant Dr	89052
Point Purdue Ct	89074
Point Success Ave	89014
S Pointe Way	89074
Pointe Ranier Ave	89012
Polar Morn Pl	89074
Polynesia Cir	89074
Pomegranate Ct	89014
Pomelo Ct	89074
Ponderosa Dr	89015
Ponderosa Pine Ave	89074
Pont Alma Ct	89044
Pont Marie Dr	89044
Pont National Dr	89044
Ponte Vecchio Ter	89052
Pontiac Pl	89015
Ponticello Dr	89052
Pontine Ct	89052
Pony Ranch Cir	89014
Poppy Ct	89074
Poppywood Ave	89012
Port Lewis Ave	89052
Port Sunlight Ct	89014
Portada Ave	89074
Portezza Dr	89011
Portovenere Pl	89052
Portree Ave	89012
Portsmouth Creek Ave	89052
Portulaca Ct	89011
Poseidon Shore Ave	89052
Positive Point St	89012
Possum Hill St	89014
Potomac St	89015
Potosi Way	89074
Potter Lake Ave	89052
Potters Ct	89074
Pounds Way	89015
Powder Brook Dr	89002
Powder Horn Dr	89014
Powder Springs St	89052
Prairie Creek St	89012
Prairie Dog Dr	89074
Prairie Rose St	89015
Prairie Sky Ct	89074
Prairie Wheat Ct	89052
Preakness Stakes St	89015
Precipice Ct	89002
Preciso Ln	89074
Predera Ave	89052
Prego Ct	89052
Presque Isle St	89074
Prestige Meadows Pl	89052
Preston Dr	89015
Preston Park Dr	89052
Pretty Sunset Ter	89015
Prevost Pass	89002
Price St	89011
Prichard Ave	89052
Prickley Pear Dr	89074
Primero Way	89074
Primrose Ct & Ln	89011
Prince Edward Dr	89052
Princess Ann Ct	89015
Principle Point Ave	89012
Priority Point St	89012
Prism Cavern Ct	89052
Privilege Ct	89052
Professional Ave	89015
Prometheus Ct	89074
Prominent Bluff Ct	89002
Promontory Dr	89014
Prospect Ave	89002
Prosser Creek Pl	89002
Proust Ct	89044
Prudence Ct	89074
Pueblo Blvd & Pl	89015
Puerto Way	89012
Puerto Azul Trl	89074
Puerto Viejo Trl	89074
Pullman Pointe Ct	89012
Pumpkin Way	89015
Punto Vallata Dr	89011
Purple Heather Pl	89052
Purple Lilly Ct	89002
Purple Sage Ter	89015
Putter Pl	89074
Putting Green Dr	89074
Pyramid St	89014
Pyramid Pines Dr	89052
Pyrenees Ct	89011
Pyrite Ave	89011
Qatar Ave	89015
Quail Beak Way	89014
Quail Bird Pl	89052
Quail Canyon Ave	89074
Quail Covey Rd	89002
Quail Crest Ave	89052
Quail Hollow Dr	89014
Quail Ranch Dr	89015
Quail Run Rd	89014
Quail Wood Ct	89074
Quarley Pl	89014
Quarter Horse Dr	89002
Quartz Canyon Dr	89052
Queen Creek Cir	89052
Queen Lake Ct	89052
Queen Marie Ct	89015
Queens Ct	89052
Queensbridge Way	89074
Quest Park St	89074
Quiet Desert Ln	89074
Quiet Fox Way	89012
Quiet Harbor Dr	89052
Quiet River Ave	89012
Quiet Stream Ct	89052
Quiet Summit Pl	89052
Quilt Pl	89052
Quimper Ct	89014
Quince Ct	89002
Quinson Ln	89044
Quintet Ave	89052
Quito Ct	89014
Quiver Point Ave	89012
N & S Racetrack Rd	89015
Radiance Ct	89074
Radiant Flame Ave	89052
Rafkin Pl	89052
Ragusa Ct	89052
Rainbolt Ln	89052
Rainbow Ln	89015
Rainbow View St	89012
Raindance Dr & Pl	89014
Raining Hills St	89052
Rainswept Ave	89052
Rainy Season Ct	89074
Ram Crossing Way	89074
Rampart Ct	89074
Ramrod Ave	89014
Ramsbrook Ave	89052
Ramsgate Dr	89074
E & W Rancho Dr	89015
Rancho Coast Way	89002
Rancho Destino Rd	89044
Rancho Maderas Way	89002
Rancho Navarro St	89012
Rancho Ridge Dr	89012
Random Cloud Ct	89052
Randy Way	89015
Rangely Ave	89052
Ranger Ct	89074
Rapid Falls St	89052
Rapier Dr	89014
Rat Pack Ave	89002
Raton Dr	89074
Rattlesnake Grass Ct	89002
Ravanusa Dr	89052
Ravenglass St	89052
Ravinia Ct	89052
Rawhide Dr	89002
Rawhide Village Ct	89012
Razella Ct	89074
Reading Hills Ave	89052
Rearfield Ct	89052
Reassuring Ct	89052
Reatini Ct	89052
Rebano St	89052
Recognition Pl	89052
Red Alder St	89002
Red Arches Ct	89012
Red Bark Ln	89011
Red Canal Ct	89074
Red Cloud Ter	89015
Red Coral Dr	89002
Red Eucalyptus Dr	89015
Red Fawn Ct	89074
Red Horizon Ter	89015
Red Jade Ct	89014
Red Oak Canyon St	89012
Red Planet St	89044
Red Sand Ct	89002
Red Sea St	89002
Red Shale Ct	89052
Red Snap Dragon Ln	89012
Red Sunset Ave	89074
Red Valley Ave	89044
Red Vista Ct	89074
Red Willow Ln	89014
Redhawk Ct	89074
Redondo St	89014
Redtail Ct	89074
Redwing Village Ct	89012
Redwood Pond Dr	89002
Redwood Valley St	89052
Reebok Ter	89014
Reed Ln	89074
Reed Point Ct	89002
Reflection Ridge Ct	89052
Reflections Rd	89074
Regal Oak Dr	89014
Regal Sunset Ave	89002
Regalia Cir	89074
Regency Hl	89014
Regent Park Ct	89052
Regents Gate Dr	89012
Regina Way	89015
Reims Dr	89012
Reliance Ave	89002
Rene Ln	89015
Renegade Ct	89074
Renoir Way	89074
Renville Ct	89074
Republic St	89015
Respectful Ridge Ct	89012
Rettig Ave	89044
Rettigdale Way	89044
Reunion Ave	89052
Reveille Ct	89011
Revere Ct	89014
Rexford Dr	89011
Reyburn Dr	89074
Rezzonico Dr	89011
Rhonda Ter	89074
Rhyolite Ter	89011
Rhythm St	89074
Ricavoli Ct	89052
Riceville Dr	89052
Rich Flavor Pl	89052
Richard Ct & Dr	89014
Richard Bunker Ave	89015
Richardson Dr	89015
Richgold St	89012
Richland Acres Ct	89074
Richland Hills Ave	89012
Richmar Ave	89074
Rico Guitar Dr	89015
Ricota Ct	89012
Riddle Glen St	89012
Ridge Crossing Ave	89002
Ridge Path Ave	89015
Ridge River St	89011
Ridgegate St	89002
Ridgepointe Way	89074
Ridgewater Cir	89012
Ridgeway Rd	89015
Rifle Dr	89002
Rift Valley St	89044
Riggins St	89011
Rim Fire Cir	89014
Rimbaud St	89044
Ringlore Dr	89015
Rio Poco Ct	89015
Rio Sonora Ct	89074
Ripresa Pl	89052
Rise Canyon Dr	89052
Rising Brook Dr	89011
Rising Cloud Cir	89052
Rising Mesa Ct	89012
Rising Star Dr	89014
Rising Sun Ct	89074
Ritchie Ct	89012
River Dee Pl	89012
River Grove Dr	89044
River Mountain Dr	89015
River Spey Ave	89012
River Walk Ct	89015
Riverband Pl	89052
Riverton Rd	89015
Rivulet Ln	89074
Roan Rd	89002
Roanhorse Ln	89052
Roaring Falls Ave	89052
Roaring River Ave	89002
W Roban Ave	89044
Robbers Roost Ave	89012
Roberts Rd	89002
Robin Ln	89015
Robindale Rd	89074
Robust Ct	89052
E & W Rochell Dr	89015
Rochester Run Ave	89052
Rock Arbor St	89074
Rock Ledge Ct	89012
Rockburne St	89044
Rockcrest Hills Ave	89052
Rockfalls Ln	89074
Rocking Horse Dr	89002
Rockrose Cir	89074
Rockwell Springs Ct	89012
Rocky Rd	89015
Rocky Basin St	89012
Rocky Coast Ct	89002
Rocky Ridge Dr	89052
Rocky Star St	89012
Rocky Trail Rd	89014
Rodarte St	89014
Rolling Cove Ave	89011
Rolling Desert St	89012
Rolling Fields Ct	89012
Rolling Sunset St	89052
Rolling Valley Way	89015
E & W Rolly St	89011
Roma Hills Dr	89012
Romanesca Dr	89052
Romanesque Art Ave	89044
Romano Ln	89012
Romanza Rd	89052
Romarin Ter	89044
Roping Reed Ct	89002
Rosado Springs St	89014
Rose St	89015
Rose Cottage Way	89052
Rose Petal Ct	89012
Rose Pine Ct	89052
Rose Quartz Rd	89002
Rose River Ct	89002
Rosegate Ave	89052
Roseholm Way	89002
Rosemary Ct	89074
Rosendale Village Ave	89052
Rosenhearty Dr	89044
Rosewind Dr	89074
Rossetti Ct	89052
Rossini St	89052
Rothesay Ave	89044
Roughrider Cir	89014
Roxborough St	89074
Roxbury St	89014
Royal Greens Dr	89002
Royal Skyline St	89002
Royal Troon Ct	89074
Royal Valley St	89002
Rubellite St	89011
Ruby Ln	89014
Ruby Ridge Ave	89002
Ruby Sky Ct	89052
Rue Allard Way	89011
Rue Bienville Way	89044
Rue Colette Way	89011
Rue Colmar Dr	89044
Rue De Bourdeaux	89074
Rue De Chateau Pl	89011
Rue De Degas	89074
Rue De Jour St	89044
Rue De Louvre	89074
Rue De Parc	89074
Rue De Versailles	89074
Rue Des Champs	89074
Rue Du Palais Ct	89011
Rue Du Rivoli Pl	89011
Rue Du Ville Way	89011
Rue Grand Paradis Ln	89011
Rue Grimaldi Way	89011
Rue Marquette Ave	89044
Rue Mediterra Dr	89011
Rue Montpellier Ave	89044
Rue Promenade Way	89011
Rue Royale St	89044
Rue Toulouse Ave	89044
Ruffled Feather Way	89012
Ruidoso Ln	89074
Rumford Pl	89074
Running River Rd	89074
Rushing Creek Ct	89014
Rushing Raft Ln	89012
Rustic Desert Pl	89011
Rusticated Stone Ave	89011
Rusty Anchor Way	89002
Rusty Ridge Ln	89002
Rusty Spur Dr	89014
Rutile Way	89015
Ruxton Ave	89074
Ryan Peak Ln	89011
Rye Beach Ln	89052
Rye Creek Ct	89002
Sabatini Dr	89052
Sabine Hill Ave	89052
Sable Chase Pl	89011
Sacred Ct	89052
Saddle Horn Dr	89002
Saddle Rider Ct	89011
Saddle Ridge Ave	89012
Saddle Run St	89012
Saddle Up Ave	89011
Saddleback Ct	89014
Sadie Ln	89074
Sadlers Wells St	89052
Safari Creek Dr	89002
Saffex Rose Ave	89052
Safflower Ct	89015
Safford Pl	89074
Sage Cir	89015
Sage Green Ct	89012
Sagecrest Way	89015
Sagrada Ct	89074
Saigon Dr	89052
Saint Albans Ct & Dr	89015
Saint Andrews Rd	89015
Saint Augustine Ln	89014
Saint Avertine Ln	89044
Saint Croix St	89012
Saint Dizier Dr	89044
Saint Johns Wood Ave	89002
Saint Malo Way	89014
Saint Moritz Dr	89012
Saint Roman St	89044
Saint Rose Pkwy	
2400-2699	89074
2801-2897	89052
2899-3056	89052
3055-3055	89077
3057-3399	89052
3058-3398	89052
3800-3898	89044
4101-4199	89044
Saint Thomas Dr	89074
Saleralt Dr	89052
Salinas Dr	89014
Saloon Ct	89011
Salt Flats Cir	89011
Samantha Rose St	89012
San Andreas St	89002
San Bruno Ave	89002
San Carlos Creek Ln	89002
San Donato Walk	89044
San Eduardo Ave	89002
San Gabriel Ave	89002
San Giorgio Cir	89052
San Jacinto St	89002
San Leandro St	89002
San Lorenzo Ct	89052
San Ramos Ct	89002
Sanctuary Ct	89014
Sand Dune Ct	89074
Sand Lily St	89052
Sand Storm Ct & Dr	89074
Sandalwood Ave	89074
Sandbar Ct	89002
Sandhill Crane Ave	89002
Sandhill Sage St	89052
Sandpiper Village Way	89012
Sandpoint Pond Ln	89002
Sandrock Pointe Ln	89012
Sandsprings St	89011
Sandstone Canyon St	89012
Sandstone Cliffs Dr	89044
Sandwedge Dr	89074
Sandy Dr	89002
Sandy Hook Ter	89052
Sandy Ridge Ave	89052
Sanita Ct	89014
Sankaty Cir	89052
Santa Anna Cir	89015
Santa Helena Ave	89002
Santa Monica Dr	89014
Santa Paula Way	89015
Santa Susana St	89002
Santa Ynez Ave	89002
Santali Ct	89014
Santana Ct	89012
Santeria Star Dr	89044
Santiago Dr	89014
Sapphire Desert Dr	89052
Sapphire Hills Ct	89074
Sapphire Sky Ct	89002
Sapphire Valley Ave	89074
Saragossa Ct	89015
Saratoga Ct	89015
Saratoga Springs St	89015
Sardana Ct	89011
Sardis Ter	89074
Sargon St	89044
Sarina Ave	89074
Sassafras Ct	89074
Satin Saddle Pl	89052
Savannah River St	89044
Savannah Springs Ave	89052
Sawtelle St	89074
Sawtooth Mountain Dr	89044
Sax Fifth Ave	89052
Saxtons River Rd	89044
Scarlet Ave	89002
Scena Ct	89052
Scenic Dr	89002
Scenic Crest Dr	89052
Scenic Lookout Ave	89002
Scenic Terra Dr	89015
Scenic Tierra Ln	89002
Scenic Valley Way	89052
Schaeffer Hills Dr	89052
Schillings Ct	89074
Scholar St	89002
School House Ct	89011
Schooner Dr	89015
Scimitar Dr	89014
Scooter St	89002
Scorpion Ct	89074
Scorpios Island St	89012
Scotch Rose St	89052
Scotgrove St	89074
Scottish St	89014
Scotts Valley Dr	89052
Scottsdale St	89002
Scouts Pine Ln	89011
Sea Bluff Dr	89002

Sea Holly Way 89074
Sea Lavender Ct 89074
Sea Sunset Ct 89074
Sea Wharf St 89012
Seaford Peak Dr 89052
Seagate Ct 89052
Seal Ct 89074
Seaside Daisy Ct 89074
Seasons Ave 89074
Sebastian Ave 89002
Sebring Hills Dr 89052
Secluded Acres Ct 89002
Seclusion Cir 89014
Seco Verde Ave 89015
Secret Canyon Rd 89074
Sedona Rd 89014
Sedona Cedar Ave 89052
Sedona Cliffs Ave 89014
Seine Way 89014
Self Portrait St 89044
Sellers Pl 89011
Seminole Ln 89015
Senator Ct 89015
Sentito Cir 89052
Sentry Ave 89002
September Ave 89002
Sequoia Dr 89014
Sequoia Ruby Ct 89052
Serenade Ct 89074
E Serene Ave 89074
Serene Moon Dr 89044
Serenity Ct 89074
Serenity Crest St 89012
Serenity Hollow Dr 89052
Serenity Ridge Ct 89052
Serpent Rose Ct 89052
Serra Bellisima Ct 89011
Serramonte Ct 89074
Sertata Ct 89074
Seurat Ter 89044
Seven Hills Dr 89052
Severn Ct & St 89002
Sevilla Heights Dr 89074
Sgt Peppers Ct 89074
Shade Valley Ln 89052
Shaded Peak St 89012
Shadow Brook Way 89074
Shadow Canyon Dr 89044
Shadow Dusk Ave 89052
Shadow Pointe St 89074
Shadowfax Rd 89015
Shadows Edge Ct 89052
Shady Charmer Ave 89052
Shady Rest Dr 89014
Shady Run Ter 89011
Shady Side Ct 89052
Shallow Water Ct 89052
Shamrock Dr 89002
Shannon Cove Dr 89074
Shanon Springs St 89014
Sharon Hills St 89052
Sharp Spur Dr 89002
Shasta Glow Ct 89052
Shawna Pl 89015
Shayna Ave 89044
Sheer Paradise Ln 89002
Sheerwater Ave 89052
Sheffield Dr 89014
Shelbyville St 89052
Shelhorn St 89052
Shell Flower Rd 89074
Shellsburg Ave 89052
Shelterbelt Ct 89052
Sheltered Meadows Ln 89052
Shenandoah Ave 89074
Shepherd Mesa Ct 89074
Sheridan Dr 89074
Sheridan Dawn Ct 89052
E & W Sherwood Dr 89015
Shimmering Ave 89011
Shimmering Glen Ave 89014
Shimmering Moon St 89015
Shining Arrows St 89002
Shining Rose Pl 89052
Shining Sun Way 89052
Shoemaker Ave 89015

Shonto Pl 89015
Shootout Pl 89002
Shoreview Dr 89002
Shorewood Hills Ave 89052
Short Crest Ct 89052
Shortstop St 89074
Shoshone Ln 89015
Shoshone Falls Ct 89044
Shotgun Ln 89014
Shubert Ave 89052
Shyley St 89011
Siberia St 89052
Sicily Hills Ct 89012
Sidewinder Ct 89014
Siena Way 89074
Siena Heights Dr 89052
Sierra Ln 89002
Sierra Laurel Ct 89014
Sierra Mesa Cir 89074
Sierra Palms Way 89074
Sierra Peak Ct 89052
Sierra View Ct 89002
Signal Butte Way 89012
Silado Ct 89074
Silent Desert Ct 89012
Silent Echoes Dr 89044
Silent Siesta Dr 89015
Silent Wind Way 89052
Silica Sand St 89012
Silver St 89015
Silver Beach Dr 89052
Silver Blossom Ln 89052
Silver Bullet Ct 89011
Silver Crew Pass 89052
Silver Reef Ct 89002
Silver Retreat Ct 89002
Silver Slipper Ave 89002
Silver Springs Pkwy 89074
Silver Star St 89002
Silver Stirrup Ct 89002
Silver Sunrise Ln 89052
Silver Sunset Dr 89052
Silver Swan Ct 89052
Silver Trace Ct 89011
Silver Wind Ave 89052
Silver Wolf Dr 89011
Silverton Dr 89074
Silvery Shadows Ave 89015
Simms Ave 89074
Simon Bolivar Dr 89014
Sinfonia Ave 89052
Singing Dove Ave 89002
Singing Drum Dr 89002
Singing Sands Ave 89014
Single Petal St 89074
Sioux City Ct 89052
Sir Barton St 89015
Sir Raleigh Ct 89052
Sir Winston St 89052
Sirius Star St 89044
Sisley Pl 89074
Sisley Garden Ave 89044
Sisteron Ct 89044
Sitka Spruce St 89015
Sitting Bull Dr 89014
Skipjack Dr 89015
Skippers Cove Ave 89052
Skowhegan Dr 89074
Sky Mountain Way 89014
Sky Rock Ct 89011
Sky Valley St 89052
Sky Watcher St 89044
Skyforest Dr 89011
Skyline Rd
500-599 89015
600-799 89002
Skysail Dr 89011
Skytop Dr 89015
Slate Crossing Ln 89002
Sleeping Dragon Dr 89012
Sleepy Moon Ave 89012
Slow Bob St 89011
Smiling Cloud Ave 89011
Smoke Canyon Ave 89074
Smoketree Village Cir 89012
Smokey Mountain Ave 89012

Smokey Quartz Ct 89011
Smokey Sky Dr 89052
Smooth Blend Pl 89052
Snapdragon Ct 89074
Snow Bunting Ct 89002
Snow Goose Ave 89002
Snow Roof Ave 89052
Snowy Dove Ct 89052
Snowy Moon Ct 89052
Snowy River Cir 89074
Soaring Peak Ave 89052
Soaring Sky Ave 89011
Socorro Song Ln 89052
Soda Creek Ln 89074
Sodorno Ln 89074
Sojourn Ct 89074
Sol De Sandia St 89015
Solana Crest St 89052
Solar Corona Ln 89044
Solar Flare Ln 89044
Solar Wind St 89014
Solaris Glow St 89052
Solera Moon Dr 89044
Solera Sky Dr 89044
Solitude Point Ave 89012
Solitude Ridge Dr 89012
Somersby Way 89014
Somerset Springs Dr 89052
Somersworth Dr 89044
Sonatina Dr 89052
Songbird Ct 89012
Sonoma Dr 89015
Sonoran Bluff Ave 89014
Sonoran Hope Ct 89052
Sorrelwood St 89014
Spago Ln 89052
Spague St 89011
Spanish Needle St 89002
Sparkling Crystal Ave 89015
Sparkling Light St 89052
Sparkling Point Ave 89015
Sparrow Ct 89014
Sparta Crest St 89052
Spectacular St 89052
Speedy Streak Ave 89015
Spice Ridge Ct 89012
Spiced Wine Ave 89074
Spikenard Dr 89002
Spinnaker Dr 89015
Spirito Ave 89052
Spirits Trail Ct 89002
Split Hoove Ct 89012
Split Rail St 89011
Spode Ave 89014
Spooner Ct 89014
Sport Of Kings Ave 89015
Spotted Bull Ct 89011
Spotted Eagle St 89015
Spottswoode St 89002
Spreading Oak Dr 89014
Spring Hills Ln 89074
Spring Lake Dr 89002
Spring Palms St 89012
Spring Pond Ct 89002
Spring Sage St 89011
Spring Valley Dr 89011
Springfield St 89074
Springtime St 89012
Springville Way 89052
Spruce Brook Dr 89074
Spruce Tree Cir 89014
Spur Cross Cir 89012
Spyglass Dr 89074
Squaw Peak Dr 89014
Stablegate Ave 89012
Staccato St 89052
Stage Stop Dr 89052
Stagecoach Dr 89014
Staghorn St 89012
Stags Leap Ct 89052
Stansbury Ct 89052
Stanwood Ave 89074
Staplehurst Ave 89002
Star Chase Pl 89052
Star Dunes St 89012
Starbrook Dr 89052

Stardust Valley Dr 89044
Stark Springs St 89014
Starlight Valley St 89044
Starstone Ct 89014
Startop St 89052
Steamboat Dr 89014
Stefano Cir 89052
Stella Cilento Ave 89044
Stephanie Pl
1000-1009 89014
1011-1099 89014
1054-1098 89011
N Stephanie St
2-98 89074
100-221 89074
223-299 89074
300-900 89014
902-1048 89014
S Stephanie St 89012
Steppe Eagle Ave 89015
Steprock Ct 89014
Sterling Ct & Dr 89015
Sterling Meadow St 89012
Sterling Point Ct 89012
Stetson Dr 89002
Still Creek Ave 89074
Stillwater Ln 89014
Stippled Clay St 89044
Stirrup Dr 89002
Stock Option St 89074
Stocking St 89052
Stone Arches Dr 89052
Stone Cress Dr 89074
Stone Dry Ave 89011
Stone Lair Ct 89012
Stonemark Dr 89052
Stonequist Ave 89052
Stony Prairie Ct 89052
Storey Cir 89074
Stovall Cress Ct 89012
Strada Cristallo 89011
Strada Di Circolo 89011
Strada Di Villaggio 89011
Strada Nathan 89011
Strada Pecei 89011
Strada Principale 89011
Strasbourg Way 89014
Strathallan Ave 89044
Strathblane Ave 89044
Strathmoor Dr 89074
Strathspey Ct 89044
Stratmoor Hills Ave 89052
Strawberry Pl 89002
Strichen Ave 89044
Strider Dr 89015
Strolling Plains Ln 89011
Strone St 89012
Struan Ave 89044
Stufflebeam Ave 89011
Stunning Summit Ave 89002
Sturm St 89015
Sturrock Dr 89044
Subtle Color Ave 89044
Sudbury Ct 89074
Suffron Hills Ct 89044
Sugar Hill St 89052
Sugarcane Ct 89002
Suguaro Bluffs St 89014
Sumatra Pl 89011
Summer Creek Ct 89002
Summer Dawn Ave 89014
Summer Glow Ave 89012
Summer Meadow St 89074
Summerchase Ln 89052
Summerland Dr 89002
Summerside Ct 89052
Summerview Pl 89074
Summerwind Cir 89052
Summerwood Cir 89012
Summit Dr 89002
Summit Grove Dr 89052
Summit Shadow St 89015
Summit Valley Ln 89011
Summit Vista St 89052
Summit Walk Trl 89052
Sumner Ranch Rd 89012

Sumter St 89052
Sumter Valley Cir 89052
Sun Bridge Ln 89002
Sun Grazer St 89044
Sun Pillars Ave 89014
Sun Rose Cir 89074
Sun Shower Ct 89074
Sun Swept Way 89074
Sunburst Dr 89002
Sunburst View St 89052
Sunday Grace Dr 89052
Sundew Ave 89052
Sundial St 89074
Sundown Dr 89002
Sundown Canyon Dr 89014
Sunfire St 89014
Sunfish Dr 89014
Sunflower Ct 89074
Sunlight Creek St 89052
Sunlight Dunes Ct 89014
Sunlight Peak St 89012
Sunlit Glade Ave 89074
Sunmist Dr 89074
Sunny Slope Cir 89002
Sunny Summit St 89052
Sunnyfield Way 89015
Sunnys Halo Ct 89015
Sunpac Ave & Ct 89011
Sunridge Heights
Pkwy 89052
Sunrise Dr 89014
Sunrise Cliffs St 89014
Sunrise Crossing St 89014
Sunrise Heights Dr 89052
Sunrise Lake Pl 89002
Sunrise Ridge Ct 89052
Sunset Cir 89011
E Sunset Rd
101-297 89011
299-573 89011
575-599 89011
4000-4699 89014
W Sunset Rd
200-799 89011
801-999 89011
1000-2099 89014
Sunset Way 89014
Sunset Bend Dr 89014
Sunset Ridge Ter 89012
Sunset Shower Dr 89012
Sunset Village Cir 89014
Sunset Vista Ave 89052
Sunshine Springs Ct 89014
Sunstar Ct 89012
Sunward Dr 89014
Surrey St 89074
Surrey Meadows Ave 89052
Susanna Way 89011
Sutters Mill Ct & Rd 89014
Sutton Way 89074
Suzanne Peak Ct 89012
Suzette Ct 89044
Swallow Hill Ave 89012
Swan Cir 89074
Swan Ridge Ave 89074
Swans Chance Ave 89052
Sweet Jewel St 89074
Sweet Spot St 89074
Sweet Springs St 89015
Sweet Sugar Pine Dr 89015
Sweet View Ct 89014
Sweetgrass Ct 89002
Sweetspice St 89014
Swift Bear St 89002
Swinford Ct 89002
Swingline St 89002
Sydney Leigh Ln 89074
Tabasco Cat Ct 89015
Table Rock Rd 89074
Tabony Ave 89011
Tabor Hill Ave 89074
Tadpole Ln 89012
Tahiti Dr 89074
Taliput Palm Pl 89011
Talisman Ct 89074
Tall Oak Ave 89074

Tallulah Pl 89052
Talon Ave 89074
Tamarack Dr 89002
Tami Cir 89015
Tangerine Ct 89015
Tangiers Dr 89012
Tanglewood Dr 89012
Tanner Cir 89012
Tapatio St 89074
Tara Murphy Dr 89044
Taragato Ave 89052
Taraway Dr 89012
Tarbert St 89044
Tarbet Ave 89012
Tarrant City St 89052
Tarryall Ter 89074
Tatum Ridge St 89012
Tawney Eagle Ave 89015
Taylor St 89015
Teak Ct 89014
Teakwood Ranch St 89052
Teal Point Dr 89074
Teal Ridge Hills Dr 89014
Teal Wing Way 89002
Tedesca Dr 89052
Tee Box Way 89074
Telegraph Hill Ave 89015
Telfer Ln 89002
Teller St 89074
Temple Canyon Pl 89074
Templeton Dr 89074
Templi Scotia St 89044
Tempo St 89052
Temporale Dr 89052
Tenabo Ct 89011
Tenderfoot Cir 89014
Tentsmuir Pl 89014
Teramo St 89052
Terrabianca Cir 89012
Terranova Ln 89074
Terrytown Ave 89052
Teton Pines Dr 89074
Teton Ranch Ave 89052
Teton Village Ct 89052
E & S Texas Ave 89015
Texas Brand Ct 89002
Texas Moon Ct 89052
Thames View St 89044
Thatcher Ave 89052
Thayer Ave 89074
Thielson Summit Ln 89011
Thomasville Ave 89052
Thoreau Ct 89052
Thornhill Cir 89014
Thoroughbred Rd 89002
Thorton Beach St 89015
Thrill Ct 89002
Thunder Bay Ave 89052
Thunder Canyon Ave 89012
Thunder Mountain Dr 89012
Thunder Plains Way 89012
Thunder Ridge Cir 89012
Thurston St 89074
Tidal Foam Ct 89074
Tidewater Range Ct 89012
Tidwell Ln 89074
Tierra St 89014
Tierra Bonita Ct 89074
Tiger Creek Ave 89012
Tiger Lake Ave 89012
Tiger Lily Way 89015
Tiger Links Dr 89012
Tiger Willow Dr 89012
Tilden Way 89074
Timber Crossing Ct 89074
Timber Hollow St 89012
Timber Walk Dr 89052
Timberline Ct 89015
Timberline Desert Ct 89012
Timeless View Ct 89012
Tin St 89015
Tinted Canvas St 89044
Tionesta Ridge Ln 89012
Tisbury Dr 89052
Tobble Creek Ct 89011
Tofino Ct 89052

Toggle St 89012
Toledo St 89015
Tollbrook Way 89011
Toltec Cir & Ct 89014
Tomahawk Dr 89074
Tomasian Ct 89002
Tomscott Ave 89052
Tonalea Ave 89015
Topaz Ave 89015
Tori Way 89074
Torngate Ave 89002
Toro Hills Ct 89074
Torrey Morgan Way 89074
Tortoise Ct 89074
Toscanella Ave 89052
Toshach Ave 89044
Tossa De Mar Ave 89002
Tottingham Rd 89074
Toucan Ridge Ct 89012
Tour Edition Dr 89074
Tower Mustard Ct 89002
Towering Mesa Ave 89012
Towering Vista Pl 89012
Toyabe St 89015
Tozzetti Ln 89012
Tracey St 89015
Trackers Glen Ave 89015
Trafalgar Ct 89074
Trailside Ct 89012
Trailside Village Ave 89012
Tranquil Moon St 89044
Tranquil Rain Ave 89012
Tranquil Skies Ave 89012
Treasure Lake Ct 89052
Tree Top Ct 89014
Treehouse Ct 89012
Trellis Ave 89074
Tremolo Dr 89052
Trenier Dr 89002
Trentino Alto St 89012
Tressler Ct 89015
Trevin Ct 89074
Trevor Dr 89074
Triana Cir 89074
Triberg Ct 89074
Trickling Descent St 89011
Trimley Ct 89014
Trinity Pond Cir 89002
Triple Bar Ct 89002
Triple Crown St 89015
Triumphant St 89052
Trocadero St 89015
Trojan Way 89074
Trombone Ln 89074
Troon Dr 89074
Tropic Tan Ct 89074
Tropical Dream Ct 89002
Tropical Star Ln 89002
Trossachs St 89044
Trout Stream Ct 89052
Trueno Rd 89014
Truffles St 89015
Truk Lagoon Dr 89002
Trumpet Ct 89074
Tuber Rose Ct 89002
Tuckaway Ct 89074
Tug Boat Ct 89012
Tulip Ct 89074
Tulip Falls Dr 89011
Tulip Grove Ct 89052
Tullio Way 89052
Tumbleweed Dr 89002
Tumbleweed Ridge Ln 89011
Tumbling Falls Pl 89012
Tumbling River Ave 89052
Tungsten St 89015
Turf Dr 89002
Turkey Creek Way 89074
Turner Falls St 89044
Turning Spoke Trl 89011
Turquoise Sky Ct 89011
Turtlebay Ave 89074
Turtlewood Pl 89052
Tuscan Shadow St 89012
Tuscan Sky Ln 89002
Tuscano Ct 89052

Tuscany Ct 89074
Tuscarora Dr 89011
Tuxford Ct 89074
Tv 5 Dr 89014
Twilight Ln 89015
Twilight Crest Ave 89052
Twilight Hills Ave 89052
Twilight Peak Ave 89012
Twin Berry Ct 89002
Twin Creek St 89074
Twin Falls Dr 89044
Twin Pines Ave 89074
Twin Springs Ct 89014
Twinkling Meadows Dr 89012
Twinkling Sky Ave 89015
Twinspur Ct 89002
Tyler Ct & Dr 89074
Tyler Ridge Ave 89012
Tyndrum Ave 89044
Tyneside St 89044
Ullapool Ct 89012
Ultra Dr 89074
Umbria Way 89014
Uplander Steep Ln 89015
Upper Meadows Pl 89052
Upton Ct 89052
Urbana Dr 89074
Urrard St 89044
Utah Way 89015
Vaccaro Pl 89074
Valadon Ave 89044
Valare St 89012
Valarie Way 89074
Valbonne Ter 89044
Valencia Cir & Pl 89074
Valenzano Way 89012
Valerian St 89015
Vallarte Dr 89014
Valle Verde Ct 89014
N Valle Verde Dr
2-4 89074
6-100 89074
102-298 89074
600-799 89014
S Valle Verde Dr 89012
Vallejo Verde St 89012
Valley Basin Ave 89052
Valley Brook Ct 89074
Valley Brush St 89052
Valley Center Dr 89052
Valley Cottage Ave 89052
Valley Falls Way 89052
Valley Forge Ave 89015
Valley Heights Ave 89052
Valley Light Ave 89011
Valley Moon Ct 89052
Valley Rise Dr 89052
Valley View Cir & Dr 89002
Valleywood Rd & St 89014
Value Ridge Ave 89012
Valvent Ct 89044
Van Dornum Ave 89011
Van Gogh Dr 89074
E & W Van Wagenen
St 89015
Vance Ct 89074
Vanier Ct 89052
Vanlier Ln 89015
Vantage Ave 89002
Vegas Vic St 89002
Vegas View Dr 89052
Velez Valley Way 89002
Velodrome Ct 89044
Vendange Pl 89044
Ventana Heights St 89074
Ventana Village Ln 89074
Venus Star St 89044
Vera Cruz Cir 89074
Veramar Ct 89052
Verbena Ave 89015
Verde Canyon Dr 89015
Verde Cape Ave 89052
Verde Domenica Ln 89012
Verde Fields Ln 89015
Verde Ridge Ct 89012
Verde Triandos Dr 89012
Verdite Ave 89011
Verle Ct 89014
Vermillion Dr 89002
Verruca Ct 89011
Versailles Ct 89074
Via Alicante 89044
Via Alloro 89011
Via Alta Ct 89014
Via Angelica 89052
Via Antincendio 89011
Via Appianna 89052
Via Arenula St 89052
Via Avanti St 89074
Via Baglioni 89011
Via Barcelona 89052
Via Barranca St 89044
Via Bel Canto 89011
Via Bel Mondo St 89074
Via Bella Dova St 89052
Via Branchini 89011
Via Breve 89011
Via Brianza 89011
Via Cadoma 89052
Via Calderia Pl 89011
Via Camelia St 89011
Via Canale Dr 89011
Via Capannoli Ter 89052
Via Capassi Way 89011
Via Casa Palermo 89011
Via Casentino 89052
Via Cassia 89052
Via Castelli 89052
Via Cattiva 89052
Via Cellina 89052
Via Cenami Ct 89011
Via Centrale 89011
Via Certaldo Ave 89052
Via Cividino 89011
Via Colmo Ave 89011
Via Columbo St 89011
Via Como 89044
Via Contata St 89074
Via Corso Ave 89052
Via Corto St 89011
Via Dandino Pl 89011
Via De Cortona 89074
Via De Leoni Ave 89052
Via De Luccia 89074
Via De Milano 89074
Via De Pallon Cir 89074
Via De Pellegrini 89011
Via De Pescara 89074
Via Degli 89052
Via Del Campo 89011
Via Del Capitano Ct 89011
Via Del Corallo Way 89011
Via Del Corso 89052
Via Del Duomo 89011
Via Del Foro Dr 89011
Via Del Garda 89011
Via Del Gradi Walk 89044
Via Del Tramonto St 89011
Via Dell Bacio Dr 89052
Via Della Amore 89052
Via Della Costrella 89011
Via Della Curia 89011
Via Della Fortuna 89011
Via Della Scala 89052
Via Delle Arti 89044
Via Di Autostrada 89074
Via Di Citta Dr 89011
Via Di Girolamo Ave 89052
Via Di Lugano 89011
Via Di Mello 89011
Via Di Olivia St 89011
Via Di Parione Ct 89011
Via Di Rienzo St 89052
Via Di Vita 89011
Via Diacceto Ave 89011
Via Dimartini 89052
Via Doccia Ct 89011
Via Dolce 89052
Via Dupre St 89011
Via Empoli 89052
Via Ernesto 89052
Via Fatina Ave 89052
Via Fellini 89052
Via Festiva 89044
Via Firenze 89044
Via Flaminia Ct 89052
Via Florentine St 89074
Via Franciosa Dr 89011
Via Fratelli 89052
Via Fulvia 89011
Via Gaetano 89052
Via Gallia St 89011
Via Gandalfi 89011
Via Garda Dr 89012
Via Garofano Ave 89011
Via Geneva 89052
Via Gregorio 89052
Via Laterna 89052
Via Latina St 89011
Via Lido 89011
Via Lombardi Ave 89011
Via Luminaria St 89074
Via Luna Rosa Ct 89011
Via Malloconni 89011
Via Malorca St 89074
Via Mancinni 89052
Via Mantova 89011
Via Marliana 89052
Via Marradi St 89052
Via Medici 89011
Via Merano St 89052
Via Meridiana 89052
Via Messina 89052
Via Mezza Luna Ct 89011
Via Milan 89052
Via Mira Monte 89011
Via Modena Ct 89011
Via Montale 89052
Via Monticano 89052
Via Morelli 89011
Via Nandina Pl 89011
Via Navona 89052
Via Nomi 89052
Via Pacifico 89012
Via Paladini 89011
Via Palermo Dr 89011
Via Panfilo Ave 89011
Via Paradiso St 89011
Via Pareda Pl 89011
Via Partito 89052
Via Passito Ct 89052
Via Pastini 89052
Via Petrin 89052
Via Piave Ct 89011
Via Piazza 89052
Via Ponte 89052
Via Positano St 89011
Via Potenza Ct 89011
Via Prato Ln 89011
Via Ravello 89011
Via Ravenna Ct 89011
Via Ripagrande Ave 89011
Via Rocca 89052
Via Romantico St 89074
Via Ruscello Way 89011
Via Sacra St 89011
Via Saint Andrea Pl 89011
Via Saint Lucia Pl 89011
Via Salaria Ct 89052
Via Salerno 89011
Via San Gabriella 89011
Via San Gallo Ct 89011
Via San Matteo 89011
Via San Pietro 89011
Via Sanguinella St 89011
Via Santa Croce Ave 89011
Via Santa Maria 89052
Via Sarafina Dr 89052
Via Savona Dr 89052
Via Scula 89052
Via Seranova 89044
Via Siena Pl 89011
Via Sonador 89012
Via Stella St 89074
Via Stellato St 89011
Via Stretto Ave 89011
Via Suzan 89052
Via Tazzoli Ct 89052
Via Tempesto St 89074
Via Terra St 89074
Via Terracina 89052
Via Tiberius Way 89011
Via Tivoli 89052
Via Toscana 89052
Via Trevi 89052
Via Vallisneri 89011
Via Vannucci Way 89011
Via Vasari 89011
Via Venezia 89052
Via Vernio 89052
Via Verona Ct 89011
Via Verso Lago 89011
Via Vicchio 89052
Via Vin Santo 89011
Via Vinci 89052
Via Visione 89011
Via Vita Bella 89011
Via Vittorio Pl 89011
Via Volterra 89052
Viale Aventino 89011
Viale Machiavelli Ln 89011
Viale Marco Polo 89052
Viale Placenza Pl 89011
Victoria Ter 89074
Victorian Hill Ave 89015
E & W Victory Rd 89015
Vienna Bronze Walk 89044
Viento Del Montagna
Ave 89012
Vietti St 89012
View Field Ct 89012
Viewcrest Ave & Rd 89014
Viewmont Dr 89015
Viewpoint Dr 89014
Villa Barolo Ave 89052
Villa Ferrari Ct 89011
Villa Liguria Ct 89011
Villa Marsala Ct 89011
Villa Rica Dr 89052
Villafranca Cir 89052
Village Ct 89015
Village View Dr 89074
Village Walk Dr 89052
Villaggio St 89074
Villandry Ct 89074
Vincents Hollow Cir 89052
Vinci Ct 89052
Vine Cliff Ave 89002
Vineland Ave 89052
Vinewood Ct 89012
Vino Biano Ave 89052
Vino Rosso Ave 89052
Vintage Rose Ave 89052
Viola Cir 89002
Viola Carino Ct 89011
Violet Ln 89074
Violet Note St 89074
Virgin Island Ave 89074
Virginia Lake Ave 89015
Vista Colina St 89014
Vista Del Lago St 89015
Vista Del Mar St 89012
Vista Heights Ln 89074
Vista Pointe Ave 89012
Vista Sereno Ct 89002
Vistoso Cir 89014
Vita Fresco Ct 89011
Vitale Ave 89002
Viva Serenade Way 89015
Vivid Sky Pl 89044
Volante Cir 89052
Voltaire Ave 89002
Volturno Way 89052
Vortex Ave 89002
Voyager St 89002
Wade Hampton Trl 89052
Wagner Valley St 89052
Wagon Box Rd 89012
Wagon Train Dr 89002
Wagon Wheel Dr 89002
Wahine Ct 89074
Walden Ct 89074
Walden Ridge Ct 89014
Walker Ln 89014
Walkerville Ct 89052
Walking Path Ave 89012
Wallingford St 89052
Walnut Park Ct 89052
Walnut Port Pl 89052
Walnut Village Ln 89012
Walsh Glen Ct 89052
Waltham Hills St 89052
Waltrip Ct 89012
Wanda Rd 89002
Wanderer Pl 89052
Wannamaker Way 89015
War Paint Dr 89014
Ward Dr 89011
Ward Frontier Ln 89002
Warm Front St 89014
Warm Rays Ave 89052
E Warm Springs Rd
100-199 89011
700-1199 89015
W Warm Springs Rd
200-798 89011
800-999 89011
1000-1198 89014
1200-2101 89014
2103-3199 89014
Warrington Dr 89052
Warsaw Ave 89015
Washington Way 89015
Washland Dr 89011
Washoe Way 89074
Washtenaw St 89012
N & S Water St 89015
Water Bridge Ct 89012
Water Cove St 89011
Water Irises Walk 89044
Water Mill Ct 89002
Waterbrook Dr 89015
Waterbury Peak Ct 89052
Watercut Ct 89002
Waterlily View St 89044
Waterloo Dr 89002
Watermark Pkwy 89074
Waterton Rivers Dr 89044
Watertown Ct 89052
Waterwheel Falls Dr 89015
Watkins Glen Ave 89052
Wave Ct 89002
Waverly Cir 89014
Wayfarer Ct 89014
Waynesboro Ct 89044
Weatherboard St 89011
Weatherstone Dr 89074
Weatherwood Ct 89074
Weaverville Dr 89044
Webster Way 89074
Wedgewood Dr 89014
Weisbrook Ct 89011
Welkin St 89052
Wellington Ct 89014
Wellington Springs
Ave 89052
Wells St 89011
Wells River Ave 89044
Wellworth Ave 89074
Welpman Way 89044
Wembly Hills Pl 89011
Wentworth Dr 89074
Westheimer Rd 89074
Westin Ln 89002
Westminster Way 89015
Weston Hills Rd 89052
Westwind Rd 89074
Weyburn Ct 89074
Weymouth Ln 89002
Whalers Way 89002
Wharf Landing St 89074
Wheaton Ct 89002
Whirlwind Ter 89012
Whisper Ln 89074
Whispering Cir 89012
Whispering Canyon Ct 89052
Whispering Crest Dr 89052
Whistle Ct 89011
Whistler St 89012
White Butte St 89012
N & S White Cloud
Cir 89074
White Glacier Ave 89002
White Hill Cir 89011
White Knoll Ct 89074
White Mesa Ct 89074
White Mesquite Pl 89012
White Pine Cir & Dr 89074
White Rose Way 89014
White Sage Dr 89052
White Sands Bluff St 89014
White Sparrow St 89052
White Tail Ct 89074
White Thunder St 89002
White Willow Ct 89002
Whitefish Ct 89012
Whiteout Pass 89052
Whites Ferry Ct 89044
Whitewater Falls Ct 89012
Whitewater Village Ct 89012
Whitewood Dr 89052
Whitfeild Ave 89044
Whitney Mesa Dr 89014
Whitney Ranch Dr 89014
Wholesome Ter 89052
Wickenburg St 89015
Wicklow Way 89014
Wide Brim Ct 89011
Wiesner Way 89011
Wigan Pier Dr 89002
Wigwam Pkwy
800-999 89014
1000-2599 89074
2601-2999 89074
Wilbanks Cir 89012
Wild Ambrosia Ave 89074
Wild Grass Ct 89052
Wild Swan St 89052
Wild West Dr 89002
Wild Willey Way 89002
Wildhorn Ct 89074
Wildwood Beach Ave 89052
Wildwood Lake St 89052
William Ave 89074
Williamsburg St 89052
Williamsport St 89052
Willow Ave 89002
Willow Glen Ct 89074
Willow Grove Cir 89014
Willow Wisp Ter 89074
Wiltshire Ave 89052
Winchester Dr 89002
Wind Cave Ct 89012
Wind River Dr 89014
Wind View Ct 89014
Windfall Ave 89012
Winding Rd 89052
Winding Hill St 89002
Winding Oak Ct 89012
Windjammer Ct 89074
Windmere St 89074
Windmill Ln & Pkwy 89074
Window Rock Dr 89074
Windship Ct 89014
Windsong Dr 89074
Windsong Echo Dr 89012
Windsor Dr 89014
Windward Ct 89012
Wingham Ct 89052
Winnipeg Ct 89002
Winnsboro St 89074
Winona Cir, Ct, Dr &
Ter 89015
Winslow Springs Dr 89052
Winter Cliffs St 89052
Winter Creek Ct 89074
Winter Park St 89052
Winter Solstice Ave 89014
Winter Storm Dr 89052
Wintera Ct 89015
Wintercress Dr 89002
Winterport St 89074
Wintersweet Rd 89015
Winthrop Pl 89074
Wisconsin Dells Dr 89044
Wolf Fur St 89002
Wolf Point St 89002
Wolverine Ct 89052
Wolverton Ave 89074
Wood River St 89052
Wood Rose Ct 89015
Wood Village Dr 89044
Woodbine Ave 89074
Woodcarver St 89012
Woodcastle St 89052
Wooded Ave 89011
Wooded Bluff Ct 89014
Woodflower Ave 89052
Woodhaven Dr 89074
Woodridge Dr 89015
Woodshole Ct 89052
Woodside Ct 89015
Woodson Ave 89052
Woodspring Ter 89012
Woodtack Cove Way 89002
Worchester Rd 89074
Workman Ct 89002
Worth Ct 89052
Wrangler Ct 89014
Wrangler Walsh Ln 89002
Wreath Ct 89074
Wright Way 89015
Wynntry Cir & Dr 89074
Wyoming Ave 89015
Xanadu Dr 89014
Yacht Ave 89012
Yellow Marigold Ct 89002
Yellow Orchid St 89002
Yellow Springs Ct 89052
Yellow Tulip Pl 89012
Yellowtail Way 89002
Yerba Santa St 89015
Yesterday Dr 89074
Yew Barrow Ct 89011
Yorkridge Ct 89052
Yorkshire Ave 89074
Yosemite Ct 89074
Youngtown Ave 89052
Yucatan Ct 89012
Yucca St 89015
Yukon Trail Dr 89074
Yuma Ln 89015
Zardini Ct 89052
Zimmerman St 89002
Zinc St 89015
Zinnia Cir 89015
Zirconium Way 89015
Zuber Ave 89011
Zuma Ct 89074
Zurich Ave 89015

NUMBERED STREETS

All Street Addresses 89015

INCLINE VILLAGE NV

General Delivery 89450

POST OFFICE BOXES MAIN OFFICE STATIONS AND BRANCHES

Box No.s
All PO Boxes 89450

NAMED STREETS

Abbey Peak Ln 89451
Ace Ct 89451
Agate Ct 89451
Alden 89451
Alder Ave & Ct 89451
Allen Way 89451
Allison Dr 89451
Alpine View Dr 89451
Altdorf Ter 89451
Anderson Dr 89451

Antler Ct 89451
Apollo Ct & Way 89451
Arosa Ct 89451
Aspen Leaf Ln 89451
Barbara St 89451
Berne Ct 89451
Betty Ln 89451
Bidwell Ct 89451
Birdie Way 89451
Boothill Ct 89451
Bridger Ct 89451
Bronco Ct 89451
Bunker Ct 89451
Burgundy Rd 89451
Caddie Ct 89451
Calcite Ct 89451
Carano Ct 89451
Carinthia Ct 89451
Carson Ct 89451
Cart Ct 89451
Catherine Dr 89451
Champagne Rd 89451
Charles Ct 89451
Chico Ct 89451
Chip Ct 89451
Chipmunk Dr 89451
Chiquita Ct 89451
Cinnabar Ct 89451
Cole Cir 89451
Colleen Ct 89451
College Dr 89451
Cottonwood Ct 89451
Country Club Dr 89451
Crest Ln 89451
Cristina Dr 89451
Crosby Ct 89451
Cross Bow 89451
Crystal Peak Rd 89451
Cynthia Ct 89451
Dale Dr 89451
Dana Ct & Dr 89451
David Way 89451
Debra Ln 89451
Deer Ct 89451
Divot Ct 89451
Doeskin Ct 89451
Donna Dr 89451
Dorcey Dr 89451
Dorothy Ct 89451
Douglas Ct 89451
Driver Way 89451
N & S Dyer Cir 89451
Eagle Ct & Dr 89451
Ellen Ct 89451
E & N Enterprise St 89451
Fairview Blvd 89451
Fairway Blvd 89451
Fairway Park Dr 89451
Fairway View Ct 89451
Fallen Leaf Ct & Way 89451
Farreste Dr 89451
Fifth Green Ct 89451
First Green Dr 89451
Flume Rd 89451
Fourteenth Grn 89451
Fourth Green Dr 89451
Freels Peak Dr 89451
Galaxy Way 89451
Gale St 89451
Garen St 89451
Gary Ct 89451
Geraldine Dr 89451
Glarus Ct 89451
Glen Way 89451
Glenrock Dr 89451
Golfers Pass Rd 89451
Granite Ct 89451
Harold Dr 89451
Harper Ct 89451
Hazel Ct 89451
Hogan Ct 89451
Hook Ct 89451
Ida Ct 89451
Incline Ct & Way 89451
Jackpine Ln 89451
James Ln 89451

Jeffrey Ct & St 89451
Jennifer St 89451
Jensen Cir 89451
Jill Ct 89451
Joyce Ln 89451
Juanita Dr 89451
Judith Ct 89451
Jupiter Dr 89451
Kelly Dr 89451
Knotty Pine Dr 89451
Lake Country Dr 89451
Lakeshore Blvd 89451
Lakeshore View Ct 89451
Lantern Ct 89451
Lariat Cir 89451
Lark Ct 89451
Laura Ct 89451
Len Way 89451
Lichen Ct 89451
Little Burro Ct 89451
Lodgepole Dr 89451
Loma Ct 89451
Lucerne Way 89451
Lucille Dr 89451
Lunar Ct 89451
Lynda Ct 89451
Marlene St 89451
Marlette Way 89451
Martis Peak Rd 89451
Matchless Ct 89451
Mayhew Cir 89451
Mays Blvd
700-761 89451
763-799 89451
770-770 89450
770-774 89451
Mccourry Blvd 89451
Mcdonald Dr 89451
Mercury Ct 89451
Mica Ct 89451
Michael Ct 89451
Mildes Dr 89451
Mill Creek Rd 89451
Miners Ridge Ct 89451
Moritz Ct 89451
Mount Rose Hwy 89451
Mountain Lake Ct 89451
Nadine Ct 89451
Northwood Blvd 89451
Nue Ct 89451
Oneil Way 89451
Ophir Ct 89451
Ophir Peak Rd 89451
Oriole Way 89451
Oxen Rd 89451
Palmer Ct 89451
Pat Ct 89451
Peace Pipe Ln 89451
Peepsight Cir 89451
Pelton Ln 89451
Pinecone Cir & Rd 89451
Pinion Dr 89451
Pinion Pine Way 89451
Pinto Ct 89451
Poco Ct 89451
Ponderosa Ave 89451
Ponderosa Ranch Rd 89451
Puma Ct 89451
Putter Ct 89451
Pyrite Ct 89451
Ralston Ct 89451
Randall Ave 89451
Red Cedar Dr 89451
Redfeather Ct 89451
Rifle Peak Ct 89451
Robin Dr 89451
Rockrose Ct 89451
Rosewood Cir 89451
Rubicon Peak Ln 89451
Saddlehorn Dr 89451
Saint Gallen Ct 89451
Sand Iron Dr 89451
Saturn Ct 89451
Sawmill Rd 89451
Second Creek Dr 89451
Second Tee Dr 89451

Selby Dr 89451
Shoreline Cir 89451
Silvertip Dr 89451
Ski Way 89451
Skylake Ct 89451
Slott Peak 89451
Snead Ct 89451
Southwood Blvd 89451
Spencer Way 89451
Steam Cir 89451
Styria Way 89451
Sugarpine Dr 89451
Susan Ct 89451
Sutro Ct 89451
Sweetwater Rd 89451
Tahoe Blvd 89451
Tanager St 89451
Tee Ct 89451
Third Green Ct 89451
Thurgau Ct 89451
Tiller Dr 89451
Tirol Dr 89451
Titlest Dr 89451
Titlist Dr 89451
Tomahawk Trl 89451
Toni Ct 89451
Tracy Ct 89451
Tramway Rd 89451
Trap Ct 89451
Trent Ct 89451
Tumbleweed Cir 89451
Tunnel Creek Rd 89451
Tyner Way 89451
Uri Ct 89451
Valais Way 89451
Valerie Ct 89451
Valley Dr 89451
Village Blvd 89451
Vivian Ln 89451
Vue Ct 89451
Wander Way 89451
War Bonnet Way 89451
Wedge Ct 89451
Wendy Ln 89451
Wheel Rd 89451
Wilderness Ct 89451
Willow Ct 89451
Wilson Way 89451
Winding Way 89451
Woodridge Cir & Way 89451
Zurich Ln 89451

LAS VEGAS NV

General Delivery 89165

POST OFFICE BOXES MAIN OFFICE STATIONS AND BRANCHES

Box No.s
1 - 2578 89125
3900 - 3980 89127
7301 - 7625 89125
8000 - 8148 89119
9998 - 9998 89160
11001 - 11998 89111
12000 - 13996 89112
14050 - 18450 89114
19001 - 19895 89132
20001 - 20940 89112
24001 - 24449 89101
26001 - 29510 89126
30001 - 32246 89173
33001 - 36920 89133
42001 - 44400 89116
46001 - 46998 89114
60001 - 61740 89160
70001 - 73300 89170
80001 - 82556 89180
93001 - 99995 89193
230001 - 239850 89105
270001 - 271798 89127
370001 - 379909 89137
400001 - 401825 89140
450001 - 459166 89154
570001 - 579006 89157
620001 - 629500 89162
750001 - 759005 89136

HIGHWAY CONTRACTS

30, 38 89124
33 89161
08 89166
03 89178

NAMED STREETS

A St 89106
Aardvark Walks St 89113
Aarondavid Dr 89121
Abaca Ct 89117
Abacus Farms Ct 89131
Abadan St 89142
Abalone Way 89117
Abalone Bay St 89139
Abalone Cove Dr 89128
Abalone Moon Ct 89183
Abalone Shell Ct 89139
Abanico Ct 89117
Abano Ct 89134
Abarth St 89142
Abbeville Meadows Ave 89131
Abbeville River Ct 89122
Abbey Dell Ave 89178
Abbey Door Ct 89122
Abbey Pond Ave 89148
Abbey Ridge Ave 89149
Abbey Rose Ct 89139
Abbeyville Dr
7000-7299 89119
7300-7499 89123
Abbeywood Dr 89110
Abbigal Ct 89131
Abbington St 89120
Abbotsbury Dr 89135
Abbotsford Cir 89156
Abbotsford House Ct 89130
Abbott St 89106
Abdo Ct 89139
Abels Ln 89115
Abercorn Dr 89134
Abercrombe Way 89145
Aberdeen Ln 89107
Aberdeen Ridge Ct 89148
Abernathy Ln 89145
Abernethy Forest Pl 89141
Abilene Gold Ct 89129
Abilene Hills Ave 89178
Abington Valley Ave 89123
Abisso Dr 89135
Abita Cir 89147
Ablette Ave 89122
Abrahams St 89101
Abrams Ave 89110
Abundant Harvest Ave 89131
Acacia Park Pl 89135
Acacia View Ave 89131
Acacia Woods Ct 89113
Academy Dr 89145
Acadia Ct 89142
Acadia Hill Dr 89147
Acapulco Ave 89121
Accademia Ct 89141
Accent Ct 89108
Accentare Ct 89141
Acclamation Ct 89149
Acclamato Ave 89135
Accolade St 89139
Accomplishment Ct 89149
Accurate Dr 89156
Achilpa St 89178
Ackaburg Ct 89130
Ackerman Ave
6100-7399 89131
8800-9099 89143

Aclare Ave 89118
Acme St 89115
Acoma Ct 89145
Acopa Ave 89178
Acorn Ct 89147
Acorn Hill Ave 89115
Acorn Leaf Ct 89115
Acorn Oaks St 89148
Ada Dr 89122
Adabella Ave 89115
W Adams Ave 89106
Adams Bay Ave 89139
Adams Chase St 89183
Adams Grove St 89139
Adams Valley St 89123
Adamshurst Ave 89148
Adamsong Ave 89135
Adavan Ct 89149
Addamo Peak Ct 89141
Addely Dr 89108
Addison Ave 89156
Addison Walk Ct 89149
Adelaide Ave 89156
Adelante Ave 89106
Adeline Ct 89110
Adelman Dr 89123
Adelphi Ave 89120
Ademar St 89148
Adenmoor Ct 89156
Adirondack Ave 89115
Adler Cir 89149
Adobe Ct 89146
Adobe Arch Ct 89148
Adobe Cliffs Cir 89129
Adobe Falls Ct 89113
Adobe Frost Ct 89183
Adobe Grande St 89131
Adobe Hills Ave 89113
Adobe Mountain St 89178
Adobe Summit Ave 89110
Adobe Villa Ave 89142
Adorable Ave 89149
Adornment Ct 89131
Adra Ct 89102
Adrian Cir 89122
Adrian Fog Ave 89141
Adrianna Ave 89129
Adrock Ct 89110
Aduana Ct 89103
Advantage Ct 89129
Adventure Ct 89129
Adventure Bay Ave 89142
Aegean Way 89149
Aesop Ave 89139
Aether St 89148
Affermato St 89131
Affirmed Ct 89113
African Lilly Ct 89130
Afternoon St 89131
Afton Dr 89117
Agapanthus Ct 89113
Agate Ave 89148
E Agate Ave 89123
W Agate Ave
2200-2698 89123
2700-2899 89123
3301-3397 89139
3399-5999 89139
7301-7597 89113
7599-7799 89113
Agate Knoll Ln 89135
Agatha Ln 89121
Agatha Christie Ave 89131
Agave Azul Ct 89120
Aggie Ct 89148
Agnes St 89121
Agnew Valley Ct 89178
Agon Ct 89148
Agonis St 89113
Agora Ct & Way 89110
Agosta Luna Pl 89135
Agreeable Ct 89149
Agua Dr 89103
Agustine Cir 89117
Ahey Rd 89129
Airdale Cir 89103

Airdrie Pl 89122
Aire Dr 89144
Airlands St 89134
Airmont Ct 89128
Airola Peak St 89166
Airshire Ct 89110
Airview Ct 89113
Akron Ct 89142
Al Carrison St
4100-4400 89129
4402-4798 89129
8000-8099 89131
8101-8199 89131
Al De La St 89146
Ala Dr 89103
Alabaster Ct 89149
Aladdin Ln 89102
Alameda Ave 89110
Alameda Creek St 89113
Alameda Falls Ave 89131
Alameda Harbor Ave 89117
Alameda Padre Ave 89139
Alamitos Cir 89120
Alamo Cir 89107
Alamo Ranch Ave 89179
Alamo Summit Dr 89129
Alamosa Way 89128
Alan Shepard St 89145
Alava Ave 89138
Alavesa Ct 89178
Albano Villa Ct 89121
Albatross Cir 89108
Albergotta Ct 89141
Albert Ave
100-158 89109
160-199 89109
400-598 89119
Alberti Ct 89117
Albina Creek St 89149
Albright Pl 89134
Albright Peak Dr 89166
Albrook Cir 89117
Alby Ct 89121
Alcazar Ct 89108
Alcoa Ave 89102
Alcott Ave 89142
Alcova Ridge Dr 89135
Alcove Ave 89118
Alcove Glen Ct 89129
Alcudia Bay Ave 89141
Aldama Rd 89122
Aldarra Canyon Ave 89183
Aldea Cir 89120
Aldea Grande Ave 89147
Aldebaran Ave
3301-3397 89102
3399-3499 89102
3501-3599 89102
4300-4499 89103
Alden Bend Dr 89135
Alden Glen Dr 89135
Alden Pines Ct 89131
Aldenham Dr 89141
Aldenwood Ave 89123
Alder Beech St 89166
Alder Meadows Ave 89131
Alder Springs Ct 89148
Alderbrook Ct 89103
Aldergate Ln 89110
Alderlyn Ave 89122
Aldershot Ct 89147
Alderton Ln 89144
Aldon Ave 89121
Aldrovandi Dr 89141
Alegria Dr 89144
Aleman Dr 89113
Aleppo Pine St 89129
Alerion St 89138
Alessandro Ave 89134
Aleutian St 89178
Alex Creek Ave 89149
Alexa Breanne Ct 89117
Alexander Ave 89106
Alexander Cir 89115
E Alexander Rd 89115

W Alexander Rd
5400-5699 89130
5701-5799 89130
6100-6198 89108
6201-6799 89108
7100-7798 89129
7800-7900 89129
7902-10698 89129
Alexander Darius Ct 89106
Alexander Great Ct 89139
Alexander Hills St 89139
Alexis Dr 89103
Alexito St 89166
Alfa Cir 89142
Alfalfa St 89120
Alfalfa Ridge Ave 89141
Alfano Ct 89117
Alfingo St 89135
Alford Hill Ct 89139
Alfred Dr 89108
Alga Ct 89141
Algerine Ct 89131
Algiers Dr 89115
Algona Cir 89121
Algonquin Cir 89169
Algonquin Dr
3500-3699 89169
3800-3898 89119
3900-3999 89119
Alhambra Cir & Dr 89104
Alhambra Crest Ct 89183
Alhambra Valley St 89178
W Ali Baba Ln
3000-3098 89118
3100-4099 89118
4101-4199 89118
9400-9498 89148
Alia Ct 89102
Alice Ln 89103
Alice Springs Cir 89129
Alicialynn Way 89121
Alido Dr 89147
Alimar Dr 89130
Alina Ave 89145
Alington Bend Dr 89139
Alisa Maria Way 89104
Alishia Cir 89130
Alkaid Ave 89122
All Seasons St 89131
Allanche Ave 89141
Allano Way 89128
Allante Ave 89120
Allegheny Dr 89122
Allegrini Dr 89141
Allegro Ave 89110
Allen Ln 89106
Allen Ranch Ct 89148
Allenford Dr 89147
Allensford Ave 89178
Aller Dr 89119
Allerton Ave 89128
Allerton Park Dr 89135
Alliance St 89129
Allison Ct 89122
Allison Ranch Ave 89148
Alliston Ct 89144
Allon Abraham St 89139
Allspice Ct 89142
Allston Valley Ave 89123
Allthorn Ave 89144
Allure Dr 89128
Alluring Ave 89149
Alluvial Fan Ct 89139
Alma Ridge Ave 89178
Alma White St 89110
Almaden Cir 89120
Almador Vista Ct 89135
Almagordo St 89120
Almansor St 89139
Almenia St 89178
Almeria Ave 89128
Almerta Ave 89178
Almocita Ct 89141
Almond Blossom Ct 89113
Almond Joy Ct 89115
Almond Tree Ln 89104

Almondale Ave 89123
Almondview St 89147
Almondwood Dr 89120
Almost Heaven St 89131
Alness Ln 89141
Alocasia Ct 89149
Aloe Cactus St 89141
Aloe Springs St 89179
Aloha Ave 89121
Alomar Ave 89118
Alondra Dr 89118
Alondra Peak St 89183
Alonzo Ct 89123
Alora St 89141
Alou Dr 89110
Alp St 89120
Alpaca Cir 89142
Alphonse Dr 89122
Alpine Pl 89107
Alpine Way 89124
Alpine Autumn Ct 89149
Alpine Bay Ave 89148
Alpine Bliss St 89123
Alpine Brooks Ave 89130
Alpine Crest Ct 89124
Alpine Edge Ave 89129
Alpine Estates Cir 89149
Alpine Falls Ct 89134
Alpine Fir Ave 89117
Alpine Forest Ct 89149
Alpine Frost Ct 89129
Alpine Grove Ave 89149
Alpine Lily Dr 89141
Alpine Mist St 89148
Alpine Mountain Ct 89148
Alpine Peaks Ave 89147
Alpine Pointe Ln 89134
Alpine Ridge St 89131
Alpine Ridge Way 89149
Alpine Tree Ave 89139
Alpine Winter Ct 89149
Alsop Ct 89156
Alta Dr
1600-1799 89106
1801-2199 89106
2300-6699 89107
6800-10099 89145
10600-10698 89144
Alta Lima Valley Ct 89178
Alta Mesa Way 89122
Alta Monte Ct 89178
Altacrest Dr 89123
Altadena St 89183
Altadonna Ave 89141
Altair St 89117
Altamar Ln 89117
Altamira Rd 89145
Altamont Ridge St 89113
Altaville Ct 89138
Altimeter Ln 89144
Altina St 89147
Alto Ave
3501-4497 89115
4499-4900 89115
4902-4998 89115
5200-5399 89156
Alto Ct 89115
Alto Verde Dr 89119
Alton Downs Dr 89134
Altoona St 89122
Altura Vista Dr 89138
Alvo Ct 89104
Alwill St 89106
Alwoodley Cir 89142
Alydar Cir 89110
Alyse Way 89110
Alysheba Ct 89142
Alyssa Ciara Ct 89123
Alzina Ct 89138
Amadeus Ct 89119
Amador Ranch Ave 89149
Amador Valley Ct 89178
Amagansett St 89166
Amalfi Ct 89117
Amana Oaks Ave 89166
Amanda Ln 89120
Amanda Creek Ct 89149
Amapa Rd 89178
Amapola Dr 89142
Amargosa Way 89115
Amari Ave 89141
Amarillo St 89102
Amarinta Ave 89108
Amaryllis Hills Ave 89149
Amasa Rd 89122
Amato Ave 89128
Amazing Grace Ct 89148
Amazon Ave 89110
Ambassador Ave 89122
Amber Cir 89106
Amber Autumn St 89131
Amber Canyon Ln 89129
Amber Cascade Ct 89149
Amber Crest St 89142
Amber Field St 89178
Amber Flower Ct 89147
Amber Glen Ct 89147
Amber Hills Dr 89123
Amber Hue Ln 89144
Amber Lantern Cir 89147
Amber Mist St 89131
Amber Night St 89183
Amber Peak Ct 89144
Amber Pine St 89144
Amber Ridge Dr 89144
Amber Sky Ave 89156
Amber Star St 89139
Amber Station Ave 89131
Amber Stone Ct 89134
Amber Valley Ln 89134
Amber Vista Dr 89117
Amber Waves St 89123
Ambergate Ct 89147
Amberleigh Ln 89121
Ambershade Ct 89110
Ambersnail St 89139
Amberwood Ln 89147
Amberwood Peak Ct 89166
Ambleshire Ave 89139
Ambleside Ct 89156
Amblewood Way 89144
Amboy Dr 89108
Ambrose Dr 89123
Ambrosia Dr 89138
Ambrosia Stream Ave 89131
Amelia Earhart Ct 89119
American Beauty Ave 89142
American Chestnut Way 89115
American Eagle Ave 89131
American Falls Ln 89144
American Flower St 89148
American Fork Pl 89156
American Mustang Ct 89122
American Pie Ct 89129
American Pride St 89148
American Ranch Ct 89131
American River Ln 89135
Americanwood St 89130
Americas Cup Cir 89117
Amersham Ave 89129
Amesbury Canyon St 89113
Amethyst Ave 89108
Amethyst Creek Ct 89131
Amethyst Glen Ct 89106
Amethyst Park Ct 89139
Ametrine Ct 89139
Amherst Ln 89107
Amherst Ranch St 89131
Amherst Valley St 89123
Amigo Ct 89119
Amigo St
7100-7299 89119
7300-7499 89123
7501-7699 89123
Amirville Ct 89129
Amistad Ct 89115
Amistoso Ln 89138
Amitola Ave 89123
Amour Ln 89121
Ampere Ln 89145
Amphora St 89139
Ampucia Ct 89138
Ampus Pl 89141
Amsterdam Ct 89156
Amtrak Express Ave 89131
Amulet St 89131
Amy Marie Ct 89103
Amy Olivia Ave 89149
Amy Springs St 89113
Anacapa Way 89146
Anacapri St 89138
Anaconda St 89108
Anacostia St 89183
Anaheim Mountain Ave 89178
Analisa Ln 89145
Anasazi Dr 89144
Anasazi Ranch Ave 89131
Anastasia St 89110
Anatolia Ln 89145
Anatolian St 89166
Anatone Dr 89147
Ancala Hollow Ct 89148
Ancestral Hills Ln 89110
Anchor St 89110
Anchor Chain Dr 89128
Anchor Cove Ct 89117
Anchor Point Ave & Cir 89117
Anchorage St 89147
Ancient Creek Ave 89178
Ancient Title Ct 89113
Ancient Valley Ave 89149
Ancona Dr 89141
Andalusia Pl 89146
Andante Ct 89135
Andender Way 89124
Anderson Ln 89106
Anderson Dale Ave 89178
Andes Mountain Ave 89139
Andesite Hollow Ct 89178
Andorra St 89183
Andover Cir & Dr 89122
Andre Dr 89148
Andrea St 89102
Andreas Canyon Ct 89139
Andreola Ct 89141
Andriano Ct 89141
Anembo Ave 89178
Angel Alcove Ave 89144
Angel Crest Cir 89117
Angel Dreams Ave 89144
Angel Falls St 89142
Angel Flight Dr 89115
Angel Forest Ave 89178
Angel Mountain Ave 89130
Angel Peak Ct 89134
Angel Peak Pl 89124
Angel River St 89123
Angel Star Ln 89145
Angel Tree Ct 89147
Angela Robin St 89129
Angelberry St 89117
Angelfire St 89128
Angelfish Dr 89117
Angelica Ct 89134
Angelina St 89120
Angelita View Ave 89142
Angelo Rosa St 89135
Angelo Tenero Ave 89135
Angels Alcove Ct 89131
Angels Camp Ct 89138
Angels Landing Ave 89131
Angels Loft St 89131
Angels Meadow St 89131
Angels Rest Ave 89166
Angels Trace Ct 89148
Angler Cir 89122
Anglia St 89142
Anime Dr 89144
Anise Ct 89142
Ann Dr 89107
Ann Rd 89115
E Ann Rd 89115
W Ann Rd
4800-6899 89130
6901-7199 89130
7700-8498 89149
8500-9500 89149
9502-12098 89149
Ann Arbor Ln 89134
Ann Greta Dr 89108
Anna Bay Dr 89134
Annabeth Ct 89149
Annalee Ave 89110
Annie Oakley Dr
3701-3797 89121
3799-4499 89121
5100-5298 89120
5300-6400 89120
6402-6498 89120
Anniston Ln 89144
Annmillie Ave 89122
Annotto Bay St 89138
Annual Ridge St 89139
Ano Dr 89131
Anoka Ave 89144
Ansley Ct 89148
Ansonia Ct 89118
Ante Up Ct 89122
Antell Cir 89119
Antelope Way 89145
Antelope Bend Ct 89148
Antelope Canyon Ave 89147
Antelope Wells Dr 89129
Anten Gulley Ct 89148
Anteres St 89117
Antero Cir 89128
Anteus Ct 89131
Anthem County St 89178
Anthony Cir 89115
Anthony Dr 89121
Anticipation Ct 89139
Anticline Ave 89139
Antietam St 89122
Antigua Ave 89121
Antigua St 89145
Antilles Ct 89117
Antioch Way 89117
Antique Bay St 89145
Antique Cameo Ave 89147
Antique Garden St 89138
Antique Oak Ct 89139
Antique Olive St 89149
Antique Rose Dr 89135
Antique Sterling Ct 89129
Antler Ct 89149
Antler Peak Ct 89110
Antler Pines Ct 89149
Antler Ridge Ave 89149
Antoinette St 89123
Antonello Way 89123
Antonine Wall Ct 89141
Antonio Dr 89107
Anvils Ring Rd 89161
Anza Ln 89108
Anzio St 89108
Apache Ln
800-999 89110
3600-3899 89107
Apache Cliff St 89113
Apache Mission Ct 89179
Apache Plume Ct 89130
Apache Springs Dr 89117
Apache Tear Ct 89123
Apache Valley Ave 89131
Apache Wells Way 89130
Apache Wing St 89129
Apawana Ln 89108
Apennine Pl 89138
Apenzell Ct 89129
Apex Dr 89147
Apiary Wind St 89131
Aplin Ave 89145
Apollo Heights Ave 89149
Apollos Gate Ct 89142
Apollostar Ct 89115
Aponte St 89121
Appealing Ct 89130
Appellation Ave 89148
Apperson Cir 89123
Applause Way 89147
Apple Barn Ave 89178
Apple Cart Cir 89142
Apple Cider St 89131
Apple Dew Ave 89131
Apple Glaze Ave 89145
Apple Hill Ct 89128
Apple Oak Ct 89115
Apple Orchard Dr 89142
Apple River Ct 89148
Apple Spice St 89143
Apple Springs Ave 89131
Apple Valley Ln 89108
Appleblossom Cir 89117
Applecrest St 89108
Applegate Ln 89110
Applegrove Way 89110
Apples Eye St 89131
Appleton Dr 89156
Appletree Cir 89103
Applevale Ct 89138
Applewood Ave 89121
Appomattox Ave 89166
Apricot Ln 89108
Apricot Ridge Ave 89183
Apricot Rose Pl 89138
Apricot Tree Cir 89142
April Ln 89130
April Blossom St 89113
April Rose Ct 89135
April Shower Pl 89144
April Springs St 89147
April Wind Ave 89131
Apron Ct 89122
Aptos Ct 89113
Aqua Cove Ave 89142
Aqua Ocean Ave 89130
Aqua Spray Ave 89128
Aqua Springs Rd 89148
Aqualine Ct 89117
Aquamarine Way 89103
Aquarena Way 89120
Aquarius Dr 89102
Aqueduct St 89123
Aquifer St 89139
Aquitaine Ct 89145
Arabella St 89169
Arabian Rd 89107
Arabian Filly Ave 89143
Arabian Sand Ct 89144
Aracatuba Ave 89121
Aragon St 89145
Aragon Canyon St 89135
Aragon Crown Rd 89135
Aragon Mist Ct 89135
Aragon Springs Ave 89138
Aram Ct 89120
Arandas Ct 89103
Arapaho Cir 89169
Arapaho Basin St 89179
Arapaho Ranch Ct 89148
Arbol Verde Way 89119
Arbolado Dr 89121
Arbor Way 89107
Arbor Ashbury Ave 89149
Arbor Creek Ct 89123
Arbor Downs Ave 89139
Arbor Forest St 89134
Arbor Glen St 89123
Arbor Oak Cir 89142
Arbor Pine Ave 89144
Arbor Stone Ave 89166
Arbor Valley Ave 89139
Arborcrest Ave 89131
Arborwood Way 89142
Arbour Garden Ave 89148
Arbuckle Dr 89134
Arbury Hall Ct 89130
E Arby Ave 89119
W Arby Ave
2600-2699 89119
3200-3298 89118
3300-6300 89118
6302-6698 89118
7001-8299 89113
8801-8899 89148
Arcade Cir 89110
Arcade Hills Ave 89178
Arcadia Ave & Ct 89118
Arcadia Bluff Ct 89113
Arcadia Heights St 89113
Arcadia Woods Ct 89149
Arcadian Ln 89147
Arcadian Shores St 89148
Arcangelo Ct 89141
Arcata Coast Ave 89178
Arcata Point Ave 89141
Arch Bay Ln 89128
Arch Bluff St 89178
Archcrest Ave & Cir 89147
Archdale St 89135
Arched Rock Ct 89141
Archer St 89108
Archwood Way 89134
Arco Iris Ln 89128
Arcola Ave 89110
Arctic Spring Ave 89115
Arden St 89104
Arden Grove St 89113
Arden Ladder Pl 89117
Arden Landing Pl 89117
Arden Point St 89149
Ardilea St 89135
Ardmore St 89104
Ardsley Ln 89135
Arenas St 89102
Arenoso Dr 89138
Argent Bay Ave 89138
Argent Star Ct 89147
Argenta Habitat Ave 89139
Argents Hill Dr 89134
Arginis St 89108
Argus Reed Ave 89148
Argyle St 89122
Arial Ridge St 89147
Ariba St 89129
Arid Ave 89115
Ariel Pl 89147
Ariel Vista Ct 89178
Aries Cir 89115
Ario Rd 89122
Arivada Ferry Ct 89156
Arizona Ave 89104
Arizona Poppy Ave 89117
Arkansas Diamond Ct 89139
Arkell Ct 89183
Arkose Ct 89123
Arlberg Way 89124
Arlee Ct 89104
Arlene Way 89108
Arletha St 89108
Arlington Ave 89107
N Arlington St 89110
S Arlington St 89104
Arlington Abby St 89183
Arlington Ash St 89148
Arlington Garden St 89166
Arlington Heights St 89110
Arlington Park Ct 89110
Armada Ridge Ct 89129
Armand Ave 89129
Armandito Dr 89138
Armel Ct 89115
Armin Ave 89101
Armistead St 89149
Armitage Ave 89144
Arnica Way 89135
Arno Ct 89121
Arnold Loop 89115
Arnold St 89106
Arnold Palmer Way 89149
Aromatico Ct 89141
Arpa Way 89108
Arrow Pl 89108
Arrow Cottage Ct 89130
Arrow Creek Ct 89156
Arrow Glen St 89113
Arrow Ranch Ct 89131
Arrow Tree St 89130
Arrowcrest Ave 89147
Arrowhead Ave 89106
Arrowhead Bluff Ave 89149
Arrowhead Falls Ct 89148
Arrowhead Lake Ct 89149
Arrowood Dr 89147
Arrowrock Ave 89179
Arrowroot Ave 89110
Arroyo Ave 89103
Arroyo Azul St 89131
Arroyo Crossing Pkwy 89113
Arroyo Dunes Ave 89130
Arroyo Glen Ct 89113
Arroyo Justin Ave 89128
Arroyo Seco Dr 89115
Arroyo Springs St 89113
Artemis St 89117
Artesia Way 89108
Artesia Lake Ct 89118
Artesian Oak Ct 89149
Artful Stone Ave 89149
Arthur Ave 89101
Artic St 89121
Articwood Ct 89183
Artie St 89107
Artist Ct 89115
Artistic Heights Ct 89143
Artistic Walk Ave 89149
Artistry Ct 89117
Artola St 89144
Artrea Pl 89123
Arturo Ct 89120
Aruba Ct 89121
Aruba Beach Ave 89138
Arundel Ave 89135
Arusha Ave 89166
Arvada Way 89122
Arville St
1201-1597 89102
1599-3400 89102
3402-3498 89102
3500-4500 89103
4502-4798 89103
4900-5064 89118
5066-7000 89118
7002-7298 89118
7401-7597 89139
7599-8699 89139
8701-9599 89139
10200-10300 89141
10302-10498 89141
Arwells Corner Ct 89130
Arwen St 89178
Asana St 89178
Asante Cove St 89115
Asbury Ct 89130
Asbury Hill Ave 89110
Ascending Sun Ln 89142
Ascona Ct 89129
Ascona Tide Ct 89141
Ascot Dr 89119
Asgard Ave 89121
Ash Ave
2100-2299 89101
4400-4599 89110
Ash Mountain St 89179
Ash Springs Way 89129
Ashboro Ave 89135
Ashbrook Pl 89147
Ashby Ave 89102
Ashby Gate St 89166
Ashdown Ct 89110
Ashfield Valley Ave 89123
Ashford Grove St 89122
Ashiem St 89183
Ashington St 89147
Ashiwi Ave 89178
Ashkum St 89149
Ashland Ave 89145
Ashland Oaks Ct 89148
Ashlar Point Way 89135
Ashley Creek St 89135
Ashley House Ct 89139
Ashley Park Ave 89148
Ashley Vale St 89131
Ashling St 89129
Ashton Peak Ct 89117
Ashton Pines Ct 89147
Ashwood Ct & Dr 89120
Ashwood Bay Ave 89183
Ashworth Cir 89107

Street	ZIP
Asilo Bianco Ave	89138
Asimov Pl	89115
Askew Pl	89166
Asoleado Cir	89121
Aspect Way	89149
Aspen Ave	89124
Aspen Cir	89101
Aspen St	89147
Aspen Breeze Ave	89123
Aspen Canyon Ct	89148
Aspen Color St	89139
Aspen Cove St	89129
Aspen Dancer Ct	89108
Aspen Falls Cir	89149
Aspen Glow Dr	89134
Aspen Grove Pl	89134
Aspen Hill Cir	89108
Aspen Knoll Ct	89117
Aspen Leaf St	89144
Aspen Marshall St	89178
Aspen Mountain Ave	89141
Aspen Oak St	89134
Aspen Range Ct	89123
Aspen Rose St	89183
Aspen Shade Ct	89123
Aspen Shadow St	89178
Aspen Springs Ave	89115
Aspen Valley Ave	89123
Aspen Village St	89113
Aspenbrook Ave	89145
Aspencrest Dr	89108
Aspendale Dr	89123
Aspiration Ct	89147
Aspire Ct	89113
Assembly Dr	89108
Aster Ln	89101
Aster Crest Ct	89120
Aster Pointe Ct	89123
Asti Pl	89134
Aston Ave	89142
Aston Martin Dr	89117
Astoria Dr	89121
Astoria Pines Cir	89107
Astorville Ct	89110
Astral Ave	89149
Astrology Ct	89128
Astronaut Ave	89145
Astronomy Cir	89128
Atacama Ave	89179
Atessa St	89129
Athena Dr	89156
Athenaville Ct	89129
Athens St	89169
Athens Point Ave	89123
Atherton St	89120
Atlantic St	
1200-1598	89104
1600-2000	89104
2002-2498	89104
2500-2598	89121
2600-2699	89121
Atlantico St	89135
Atlantis St	89121
Atlantis Dream Ave	89139
Atlas Peak Ave	89183
Atmore Ct	89110
Atrium Ave	89108
Atrium Woods Ln	89135
Attavilla Dr	89141
Atterberry Ln	89117
Attic Grace Ave	89149
Attleboro Park Ave	89129
Attraction Ct	89128
Attractive Ct	89149
Atwater Canyon Ave	89123
Atwood Ave	
6100-6398	89108
6400-6899	89108
7300-7398	89129
7400-9699	89129
Aubergine Ct	89115
Aubergine Cove Ct	89149
Auborn Ave	89108
Auburn Dawn Ct	89142
Auburn Fern Cir	89115
Auburn Leaf St	89123
Auburn Shadow St	89129
Auburn Skyline Ave	89139
Auburn Springs Ave	89166
Auburn Valley Ave	89123
Aubusson Ct	89149
Auckland Dr	89110
Auckland Castle St	89135
Auction Ln	89165
Audlington Ave	89148
Audobon St	89147
Audobon Peak Ave	89166
Audrey Hepburn St	89142
Audria Falls Ave	89131
Audrie St	89109
Audubon Canyon St	89131
August Rain Ave	89149
Augusta Dr	89109
Augusta Canyon Way	89141
Augusta Course Ave	89148
Augusta Glen Ave	89123
Aultman Ct	89110
Aurora Ct	89122
Aurora Bay Ct	89149
Aurora Beam Ave	89122
Aurora Cove Ct	89179
Aurora Crest Ave	89139
Aurora Dawn Dr	89142
Aurora Glow St	89139
Aurora Light Way	89123
Aurora Mist St	89113
Aurora Peak Ave	89131
Aussie Ct	89130
Austell St	89129
Auster Park Ave	89148
Austin Ave	89107
Austin Bluffs Ave	89144
Austin John Ct	89122
Austin Peak Ct	89110
Austin Ridge Ave	89178
Australian Ave	89142
Australian Cloud Dr	89135
Austrian Dr	89130
Autumn St	89120
Autumn Creek Dr	89130
Autumn Fire Ct	89117
Autumn Gate Ave	89131
Autumn Glen Cir	89110
Autumn Gold Ave	89123
Autumn Grove Ct	89135
Autumn Harvest Ave	89142
Autumn Haze Ln	89117
Autumn Heights Way	89117
Autumn Hue Ave	89123
Autumn Leaf Ct	89108
Autumn Lull Dr	89146
Autumn Meadow Ave	89130
Autumn Mist Ct	89148
Autumn Moon Dr	89123
Autumn Morning St	89148
Autumn Palace Ct	89144
Autumn Pine Ave	89144
Autumn Rain Ct	89147
Autumn Rose Way	89142
Autumn Royal Ln	89144
Autumn Rust Dr	89119
Autumn Sky Rd	89118
Autumn Star Ave	89145
Autumn Teal Ave	89178
Autumn Valley Ave	89129
Autumn Veil St	89129
Autumn View Ave	89178
Autumn Wreath Ave	89129
Autunno St	89183
Autzen Stadium Way	89115
Avalanche Trl	89124
Avalon Ave & Cir	89107
Avalon Bay St	89139
Avalon Canyon Ct	89138
Avalon Island St	89139
Avalon Mist St	89139
Avalon Valley Ct	89178
Avant Garde Ct	89146
Avebury Pl	89121
Avebury Manor Ln	89135
Avellino Ln	89144
Aveneda Grande	89121
Aveneda Sandia	89121
Avenida Caballo	89108
Avenida Del Diablo	89121
Avenida Del Luna	89119
Avenida Del Sol	89119
Avenida Silla	89108
Avenida Tampico	89108
Avenida Vaquero	89108
Avens Pl	89117
Avent Ferry St	89148
Aventura St	89144
Aventura Canyon Ct	89139
Aventurine Ct	89148
Avenzano St	89141
Avery Dr	89108
Avery St	89161
Avery Meadows Ave	89138
Avery Park Ave	89110
Avery Rock St	89147
Aviano Pines Ave	89129
Aviation St	89115
Avila Cir & St	89103
Avila Beach Ave	89113
Aviston St	89148
Aviv Ct	89121
Avocado Dr	89103
Avon Ct	89108
Avon Park Ave	89149
Avondale Ave & Ct	89121
Avonmore St	89129
Avonwood Ave	89121
Awbury Ave	89110
Awesome Ct	89117
Axis Mountain Ct	89166
Ayita Cir	89169
Aylesbury Ave	89129
Azalea Cir	89107
Azara Rd	89113
Azorella Ct	89149
Aztec Ave	89101
Aztec Way	89169
Aztec Basin Ave	89131
Aztec Cliffs Ct	89128
Aztec Crossing Ct	89142
Aztec Rose Way	89142
Azui Pl	89121
Azul Celeste Pl	89138
E Azure Ave	89115
Azure Dr	89149
W Azure Dr	89130
Azure Bay St	89117
Azure Beach St	89148
Azure Clouds Way	89142
Azure Falls Ct	89117
Azure Heights Pl	89110
Azure Ocean Ave	89166
Azure Ridge Dr	89130
Azure Shores Ct	89117
Azure Sky Dr	89129
Azurelyn Ave	89122
Azurite Dr	89130
Azuza Ave	89122
Azzura Palms Ave	89139
B St	89106
Babbit Dr	89110
Babbs Ct	89123
Babcock Dr	89134
Babson Ave	89110
Baby Bird Ln	89115
Baby Bud St	89183
Baby Jade Ct	89148
Baby Yovani Ave	89129
Babys Breath Ct	89183
Babys Tear Pl	89148
Bacara Ridge Ave	89115
Baccarat Ave	89122
Bacchus Ct	89183
Bachelor Ct	89128
Bachelor Button St	89138
Bachelors Button Dr	89131
Bachelors Fortune St	89128
Bachman Ct	89123
Bacio Bello Ln	89135
Back St	89130
Back Bay Cir	89123
Back Packer Ct	89131
Back Plains Dr	89134
Back Spin Ct	89148
Back Woods Rd	89142
Backstage Blvd	89121
Backstretch Ave	89130
Backwoodsman Ave	89130
Bacolod Ct	89147
Badby Ave	89148
Baden Dr	89142
Badger Ravine St	89178
Badgerbrook St	89129
Badillo St	89104
Badura Ave	
3201-3497	89118
3499-6699	89118
7901-7997	89113
7999-8000	89113
8002-8098	89113
Baer Dr	89115
Baffin Ct	89130
Baffy Cir	89142
Bagdad Ct	89145
Bagnoli Ct	89141
Bagua Ct	89129
Bahama Rd	89145
Bahama Bay Ct	89147
Baile Rd	89146
Bailey Cir	89117
Bailey Dr	89106
Bainberry Ridge Ln	89144
Baja Ct	89122
Baker Ave	89108
Baker Bowl Ct	89148
Baker Hill St	89129
Bakewell Ave	89179
Balanced Rock St	89129
Balaton Lake Ave	89138
Balatta Canyon Ct	89144
Balboa Ave	
1800-2099	89169
4000-4199	89121
Balcony Trellis Ave	89149
Bald Eagle Dr	89134
Bald Hill Ct	89110
Baldosa Ct	89117
Baldoyle Ln	89129
Baldur Run St	89148
Baldurn Ave	89183
Baldwin St	89122
Baldwin Canyon Ln	89131
Baldy Ln	89110
Baldy Mountain Ave	89131
Baleek Point Ct	89123
Balfour Dr	89121
Ballad Ave	89129
Ballantine Dr	89110
Ballarat St	89115
Ballard Dr	89104
Ballet Dr	89107
Ballindarry Ave	89129
Ballineen Ct	89148
Ballinger Dr	89142
Ballroom Ct	89130
Balmoral St	89141
Balmoral Castle Ct	89141
Balmoral Mills Ct	89113
Balsam St	
4501-4597	89108
4599-4700	89108
4702-4798	89108
5600-5699	89130
6600-6800	89131
6802-7698	89131
Balsam Creek Ave	89144
Balsam Mist Ave	89183
Balsam Mountain St	89129
Balsam Pine Dr	89142
Baltic Cir	89121
E Baltimore Ave	89104
W Baltimore Ave	89102
Baltimore Ohio Ct	89131
Baltinglass St	89123
Baluster Ct	89149
Balzac Dr	89156
Balzar Ave	
800-1899	89106
5500-5999	89108
Bamber Dr	89117
Bambola Pl	89135
Bamboo Ct & Pl	89108
Bamboo Forest Pl	89138
Bamboo Rain Ave	89183
Banaba Ln	89156
Banbridge Dr	89103
Banburry Cross Dr	89144
Banbury Heights Way	89139
Bancroft Cir	89121
Bandera Dr	89110
Bandera Creek Ave	89148
Bandera Mountain Ln	89166
Bandinella Ave	89148
Bandit Ct	89119
Bandits Bluff Ave	89143
Bandol Pl	89141
Bandoleer Ct	89131
Bandon Dunes Ct	89141
Banff Ct	89148
Bangor Ct	89134
Banjo St	89107
Bankside Dr	89129
Banneker Park St	89166
Banner Cir	89102
Banner Cloud Ct	89139
Bannie Ave	89102
Banning Creek Dr	89118
Bannister Ln	89130
Bannock Way	89107
Bannockburn St	89145
Banora Point Dr	89134
Bantam St	89131
Banyan Reef St	89141
Banyon St	89101
Barbados St	89110
Barbara Way	
500-599	89104
5200-5299	89119
Barbaradale Cir	89146
Barbary Cir	89103
Barbers Point Pl	89134
Barberton Ct	89138
Barbican Ct	89147
Barbie Ave	89131
Barbuda Rd	89117
Barcelona St	89121
Barcelona Ridge Ct	89129
Barchetta Dr	89134
Barcinas Ln	89138
Bardilino St	89141
Bardmoor Dr	89113
Bardstown Dr	89130
Bare Branch Ave	89123
Bare Rabbit Ct	89178
Bare Rock Ct	89113
Barela Way	89147
Barengo Ave	89129
Bargetto Ct	89141
Bargull Bay Ave	89131
Barham Ln	89128
Barium Rock Ave	89143
Barkentine St	89145
Barkeria Ct	89149
Barkis Ct	89130
Barkstone Ave	89108
Barkwood Ave	89144
Barlett Meadows St	89149
Barletta Ave	89123
Barlow Ln	89110
Barnacle Bay Ave	89178
Barnard Dr	89102
Barnard Bee Ct	89183
Barndance Ct	89149
Barnes Ct	89147
Barney St	89131
Barnsdale Ct	89156
Barnstable Valley Ct	89123
Barnstaple Ct	89129
Barntucket Ave	89147
Barnwell Ave	89149
Barocci St	89131
Barodo Way	89147
Baron Coast St	89178
Baronet Dr	89138
Baronsgate Dr	89110
Baroque Ave	89139
Baroque Gold Ct	89139
Barossa Ct	89117
Barr Ave	89166
Barranca Peak Ct	89139
Barrel Cactus Ct	89108
Barrel Ridge St	89183
Barrel Spring Way	89146
Barrelwood Dr	89147
Barren Vista Ct	89178
Barrier Reef Dr	89117
Barrington Cir	89117
Barrington Bridge Ave	89122
Barrington Hills St	89149
Barrow Downs St	89135
Barry Way	89106
Barrymore Ct	89129
Barstow Ct	89122
Bart St	89131
Bartholomew Park Ct	89139
Bartizan Dr	89138
E Bartlett Ave	89115
W Bartlett Ave	
800-1499	89106
5500-5999	89108
Bartlett Peak St	89166
Bartley Cir	89115
Bartoli Dr	89115
Barton Creek Ct	89113
Barton Green Dr	89128
Barton Rock Ct	89113
Bartona St	89107
Basalt Hollow Ave	89148
Base Camp Ave	89178
Basilone Ave	89122
Basin View Cir	89123
Basketflower Ct	89183
Basque St	89146
Basset Hound Ave	89131
Bassio Ave	89141
Bastille Ave	89130
Basuto St	89122
Bat Masterson Cir	89130
Bataan St	89145
Batavia Dr	89102
Batelli Ct	89121
Bath Dr	
7100-7300	89131
7302-7398	89131
10200-10298	89149
Bathurst Ln	89128
Batik Harbor Ct	89148
Battery St	89129
Battery Park St	89110
Battista Ln	89123
Battle Born Dr	89128
Battle Creek Cir	89108
Battle Mountain Dr	89110
Battlement Ave	89134
Bauble Ave	89128
Baughman Cir	89124
Bavaria St	89128
Bavington Dr	89108
Baxter Pl	89107
Baxter Peak St	89129
Bay Cir	
4100-4299	89122
5700-5799	89108
Bay Colony St	89131
Bay Course Ct	89148
Bay Crest Dr	89128
Bay Dunes St	89131
Bay Ginger Ln	89135
Bay Harbor Dr	89128
Bay Hill Dr	89117
Bay Laurel Ct	89110
Bay Meadows Cir	89108
Bay Pines Ave	89128
Bay Point Dr	89128
Bay Shore Cir	89130
Bay Springs Dr	89128
Bay Tree Dr	89134
Bayakoa Rd	89142
Bayamon St	89129
Bayard St	89148
Bayberry Dr	89110
Bayberry Bend St	89178
Bayberry Creek Ct	89130
Baycliff Ct	89117
Bayfield St	89149
Bayham Abbey Ct	89130
Bayhaven Ct	89131
Bayhead Ct	89138
Bayhead Beach Ave	89135
Bayland Dr	89134
Baylark Ave	89134
Baylor Ranch Ct	89131
Bayo Ct	89102
Bayonne Dr	89134
Bayou Ct	89130
Bays Mountain Ave	89166
Bayside Cir	89117
Baysinger Dr	89129
Baystone St	89141
Baysville Ct	89144
Bayswater Ct	89145
Bayview Cir	89156
Bayview House Ave	89166
Baywood Ave	89103
Bazmorda Ct	89130
Beach Crystal St	89149
Beach Falls Ct	89149
Beach Front Dr	89117
Beach Haven Ave	89183
Beach House Ave	89166
Beach Mill Way	89130
Beach Nest Ave	89130
Beach Pine St	89130
Beach Plum Way	89156
Beach Port Dr	89117
Beach Rose Ct	89148
Beach Shell Ct	89121
Beach Shore Ct	89121
Beach Stone Ct	89147
Beach View Ct	89117
Beach Water Cir	89117
Beachside Ct	89117
Beachwalk Pl	89144
Beachwood Crest St	89166
Beacon Rd	89108
Beacon Cove Ct	89117
Beacon Harbor Ave	89147
Beacon Hill St	89120
Beacon Point St	89129
Beacon Ridge Dr	89134
Beacon Shores Cir	89117
Beacon View St	89178
Beaconfalls Way	89142
Beaconsfield St	89147
Bead Vine Ave	89106
Beadle St	89122
Beallsville St	89141
Beam Dr	89139
Beaming Ct	89149
Bear Basin Ct	89178
Bear Cave Ct	89178
Bear Clan Ct	89131
Bear Cloud St	89143
Bear Creek Dr	89115
Bear Grass St	89144
Bear Island Ct	89147
Bear Lodge Ct	89129
Bear Paw Creek St	89149
Bear Ridge St	89113
Bear River Ct	89139
Bear Tooth Cave Ct	89131
Bear Trap Ct	89178
Bear Valley St	89128
Bearded Iris Ave	89148
Bearden Dr	89106
Bearpaw Ave	89117
Bearpin Gap Ln	89129
Beatrice Ave	89110
Beauchamp Ave	89148
Beaumont St	89106
Beautiful Flower Ct	89149
Beautiful Fruit St	89183
Beaver Bay Ct	89156
Beaver Creek Ct	89117
Beaver Falls Ave	89123
Beaver Mountain Ave	89131

Street	ZIP
Beaver Spring St	89128
Beaverbrook Way	89123
Beaverhead Dr	89120
Beavertail Pond Ave	89122
Beaverton Ct	89129
Becerro Dr	89121
Beckaville Ave	89129
Becke Cir	89104
Becket Ct	89129
Beckett Hill Ct	89135
Beckett Ridge Ave	89149
Beckman Glen Ct	89141
Becks Hill Dr	89134
Beckton Park Ave	89178
Becky Pl	89120
Becoming Ct	89149
Bedding Plane Ct	89139
Bedec Ave	89183
Bedford Rd	89107
Bedford Commons Dr	89135
Bedford Falls Cir	89149
Bedford Hills Ave	89138
Bedford Pine Ct	89113
Bedford Ridge Ct	89166
Bedford Valley Ct	89123
Bedfordshire Pl	89129
Bedrock Cove Ct	89131
Bedrock River Ct	89178
Bedrock Springs Ave	89131
Bedstraw St	89178
Beech Creek St	89141
Beech Family St	89115
Beech Grove Dr	89119
Beech Knoll Ct	89108
Beechcrest Rd	89108
Beecher Park Ave	89166
Beechgate Ave	89110
Beechwood Pl	89108
Beekman St	89147
Beesley Dr	
1-799	89110
1601-1749	89156
1751-1867	89156
1869-1999	89156
5200-5299	89115
5301-5399	89115
Beeson Ct	89130
Beethoven St	89145
Begonia Ct	89108
Begonia Bay Ave	89142
Begonia Blush Dr	89166
Beguiling Ct	89149
Beisner St	89122
Bel Air Cir & Dr	89109
Bel Air Greens Cir	89141
Bel Canto Ct	89139
Bel Etage Ct	89141
Bel Port Dr	89110
Bel Sole Ct	89178
Belcamp Cir	89108
Belcastro St	
1301-1397	89117
1399-3199	89117
3201-3299	89117
5900-8800	89113
8802-9198	89113
9400-9498	89178
Belcher Ln	89110
Belcolla Ln	89122
Belden Ave	89183
Belgate Ct	89129
Belgian Lion St	89139
Belgium Dr	89122
Belgrave Hall Ln	89122
Belgreen St	89135
Belhaven St	89147
Belhurst Ave	89113
Believe Ct	89139
Belinda Ct	89148
Bell Dr	89101
E Bell Dr	89119
W Bell Dr	89118
Bell Loop	89115
Bell Mountain Ct	89129
Bella Calabria Ave	89183
Bella Calera Dr	89148
Bella Camrosa Dr	89141
Bella Cascada St	89135
Bella Citta St	89178
Bella Contada Ln	89141
Bella Di Mora St	89178
Bella Famiglia Ave	89178
Bella Jewel Ave	89178
Bella Kathryn Cir	89117
Bella Lante Ave	89141
Bella Levante St	89183
Bella Loma Ct	89149
Bella Luna St	89183
Bella Matese Ave	89183
Bella Milano Ave	89183
Bella Ordaz Way	89141
Bella Palermo Way	89141
Bella Sovana Ct	89141
Bella Sparkle Ave	89178
Bella Strada Ct	89141
Bella Vacio Ct	89149
Bella Valencia Ct	89141
Bella Veduta Ave	89178
Bella Ventana Ave	89139
Bella Verona Ave	89141
Bella Viera Ct	89141
Belladonna Cir	89142
Bellaria Pl	89156
Bellaterra Ct	89145
Bellatrix Ct	89135
Bellavista Ln	89122
Bellbluff St	89122
Belle Amour Ln	89123
Belle Crest Ct	89123
Belle Esprit St	89123
Belle Essence Ave	89123
Belle Fountain Ave	89123
Belle Glade St	89129
Belle La Blanc Ave	89123
Belle Maison Ave	89123
Belle Marie Ct	89141
Belle Point Ave	89123
Belle Regal St	89123
Belle Reserve St	89123
Belle Rich St	89123
Belle Ridge Ave	89123
Belle Soleil Ave	89123
Belle Springs Ave	89123
Belle Star Ct	89145
Bellefonte Pl	89183
Bellerive St	89113
Bellery Ave	89143
Belleville Ave	89121
Bellglen Dr	89128
Bellingrath Ct	89149
Bellisima St	89118
Bellmead Ct	89135
Bello Circonda Ave	89178
Bellota Dr	89108
Belltower St	89145
Belluno Ct	89117
Bellview St	89134
Bellwood Ct	89118
Belmondo Ln	89128
Belmont Hills Ave	89131
Belmont Lake Dr	89135
Belmont Shores St	89115
Belmont Valley St	89123
Belrose St	89107
Belsay Castle Ct	89178
Belshire Dr	89147
Beluga Way	89117
Belvedere Canyon Ave	89139
Belvedere Park Ln	89141
Ben Hogan Dr	89149
Ben Johnson Ct	89183
Ben Or St	89110
Benbrook Springs Dr	89131
N Bend Dr	89115
Bend St	89122
Bender Ct	89128
Bending River Ave	89129
Bending Wolf Ave	89178
Benecia Way	89122
Benedict Dr	
401-799	89110
410-410	89161
412-798	89110
8800-9699	89161
Benelli Ferry Ct	89156
Benevento Ct	89141
Benezette Ct	89141
Bengal Pl	89145
Benicasim Ct	89178
Benicia Hills St	89144
Benidorm Ave	89178
Benjamin Nicholas Pl	89144
Benlomond Ave	89179
Benmore St	89108
Bennett Dr	89121
Bennett Mountain St	89129
Bennett Spring Ln	89122
Bennington Ct	89134
Benson Ferry St	89149
Bent Branch Ln	89142
Bent Brook Pl	89134
Bent Creek Dr	89107
Bent Oak Ct	89123
Bent Rock St	89108
Bent Sunflower Ct	89106
Bent Tree Ct	89134
Bent Willow Ave	89129
Bent Wood Ct	89108
Bentley Ave	89142
Bentley Oaks Ave	89135
Bentley Wood Ct	89130
Bentonite Dr	89128
Bentonville Ct	89149
Benview Dr	89147
Benvolio Ct	89141
Berchmans Ave	89122
Berendo Dr	89123
Beresford Ave	89123
Beresik Cir	89115
Beretta Ct	89117
Bergamo Ct	89183
Bergin Dr	89110
Bering Sea Cir	89113
Bering Strait Ave	89179
Beringer Dr	89144
Berino Dr	89147
Berkley Ave	
2100-2499	89101
4400-4599	89110
Berkley Hall St	89131
Berkshire Pl	89147
Berkshire Woods Ave	89166
Berman St	89169
Bermuda Rd	
6500-6598	89119
6600-7299	89119
7500-9499	89123
9701-9797	89183
9799-10300	89183
10302-10498	89183
Bermuda Bay St	89117
Bermuda Beach Dr	89128
Bermuda Creek Rd	89123
Bermuda Dunes Ave	89113
Bermuda Island St	89123
Bermuda Nights St	89183
Bernadette St	89122
Bernadine Ct	89117
Bernardo Ln	89102
Berner Ln	89123
Bernice Ct	89149
Bernini Dr	89141
Bernini St	89144
Berrera Ct	89110
Berry Cir	89107
Berry Crest Dr	89108
Berry Fern Cir	89115
Berry Patch Way	89142
Berry Ridge Cir	89110
Berryman Way	89148
Bersaglio St	89135
Berstler Ave	89148
Bertelli Ct	89144
Berthelot Ln	89122
Bertram Ln	89147
Bertsos Dr	89103
Berwick Falls Ln	89149
Berwyck St	89121
Berwyn Cir	89122
Bescano Dr	89122
Bessemer Ct	89129
Best Ct	89178
Beth Ave	89108
Bethalto St	89148
Bethany Dr	89156
Bethany Bend Dr	89135
Bethel Ln	89119
Bethel Cove Ct	89166
Bethel Mill St	89183
Bethel Park Ct	89141
Bethesda Cir	89101
Bethwick Cir	89183
Betsy Ross Dr	89108
Better Way	89110
Bettors Luck Ct	89122
Betty Ln	
101-597	89110
599-1599	89110
1600-3199	89156
Betty Davis St	89142
Beverly Way	89104
Beverly Anne St	89149
Beverly Arbor Ave	89183
Beverly Elms St	89129
Beverly Glen Ave	89110
Beverly Hills Dr	89147
Bevvie Dr	89108
Bewitched Ct	89115
Bewitching Ct	89149
Bianca Ct	89117
Bianca Bay St	89144
Bianco Ridge Ave	89183
Biaritz Ave	89123
Bidens Ct	89149
Bidwell Ct	89183
Biela Ave	89120
Bienville St	89131
Big Bear Pines Ave	89143
Big Bend Ave	89156
Big Bluff Ave	89148
Big Bow Springs Ct	89148
Big Cottonwood Ct	89123
Big Creek Ct	89148
Big Dipper Ct	89115
Big Fawn Ct	89130
Big Green Ln	89134
Big Man St	89123
Big Meadow St	89138
Big Mill Ct	89135
Big Oak Cir	89129
Big Oak Flat Ct	89138
Big Pine Way	89108
Big Plantation Ave	89143
Big Red Ct	89122
Big River Ave	89130
Big Rock Cir	89129
Big Sagebrush Ave	89117
Big Sandy Cir	89129
Big Sea St	89110
Big Sky Ln	89149
Big Springs Ct	89113
Big Stomp Ct	89129
Big Stone Way	89110
Big Sur Dr	89122
Big Sur Mountain St	89178
Big Timber Dr	89134
Big Timber Ridge Rd	89178
Big Top Dr	89123
Big White St	89122
Big Window St	89178
Bigford St	89122
Bighorn Island Ave	89148
Bighorn Narrows Ct	89149
Bighorn Point Ct	89178
Bighorn Ranch Ave	89148
Bighorn River St	89131
Bijah Spring Ave	89122
Biljac St	89145
Billfish Ave	89147
Billman Ave	
3400-3698	89121
3700-4999	89121
5000-5199	89122
Bills Way	89107
Billy Casper Dr	89134
Bilpar Rd	89131
Biltmore Dr	89101
Biltmore Bay St	89147
Biltmore Garden St	89149
Binaggio Ct	89141
Binasco St	89141
Binda Ct	89178
Bindweed Rd	89113
Bing Cherry Dr	89142
Bingham Ave	89110
Birch St	89102
Birch Basin Ct	89148
Birch Bay Ln	89130
Birch Bluff Ln	89145
Birch Creek Cir	89119
Birch Gray Dr	89134
Birch Grove Ct	89134
Birch Hill Ct	89134
Birch Leaf Cir	89156
Birch Ridge Ave	89183
Birch Spring Rd	89124
Birch Tree Ln	89117
Birchbrook Ct	89120
Birchcrest Ct	89108
Birchmont St	89130
Birchview Ct	89147
Birchwood Cir	89120
Birchwood Park Cir	89141
Bird Cherry St	89148
Bird Of Paradise Ct	89123
Bird Springs Dr	89128
Bird View Ct	89129
Birdnest Ct	89123
Birds Nest Ct	89131
Birds Nest Cactus Ct	89106
Birdsong Way	89147
Birdstone Ct	89156
Birdwood Dr	89134
Biriba Pl	89144
Birkland Ct	89117
Biroth Ct	89149
Birtcher Dr	89118
Birthstone Ave	89147
Biscaya Cir	89121
Biscayne Ln	89117
Biscayne Bay Dr	89117
Biscayne Springs Ln	89117
Bishop Dr	89107
Bishop Flowers St	89130
Bishop Pine St	89129
Bishops Lodge St	89117
Bismark Sapphire St	89139
Bison Cir	89145
Bison Creek St	89148
Bisoni St	89149
Bisonwood Ave	89131
Bisset Ave	89118
Bitterroot Crest Ct	89178
Bittersweet Cir	89128
Bitterwood Ln	89118
Bixbee Ct	89129
Black Bart Ct	89143
Black Bear Rd	89149
Black Beard Ave	89147
Black Beauty St	89113
Black Brothers Ct	89117
Black Bush Ln	89156
Black Cherry St	89142
Black Coral Ave	89131
Black Coyote Ct	89139
Black Crow Ave	89123
Black Duck Ct	89117
Black Eagle Ct	89147
Black Elk Ave	89143
Black Forest Dr	89102
Black Friar Ct	89166
Black Island St	89128
Black Knight Cir	89119
Black Lake Pl	89178
Black Ledge Ave	89134
Black Maple Ave	89148
Black Mesa Ct	89142
Black Mulberry St	89178
Black Oil Dr	89122
Black Onyx Ct	89139
Black Opal St	89139
Black Orchid Ave	89131
Black Peak Ct	89129
Black Pine Dr	89134
Black Port Ct	89130
Black River St	89139
Black Rock Way	89110
Black Shadow Ave	89123
Black Slate St	89123
Black Swan Ln	89118
Black Velvet Ave	89122
Black Walnut Ave	89115
Black Water Ct	89117
Black Wolf Ave	89178
Blackberry Field Ave	89142
Blackberry Valley Way	89142
Blackbirch St	89148
Blackbird Ave	89145
Blackburn Ct	89134
Blackcombe St	89128
Blackford Ct & Pl	89102
Blackhawk Rd	89108
Blackhawk Ranch St	89123
Blackheart St	89129
Blacklion Ct	89130
Blackmon Cir	89130
Blackpool Cir	89128
Blacksmith Ct	89145
Blackstone St	89121
Blackstone Ridge Ct	89139
Blackstone River Ave	89148
Blacktail Fork St	89178
Blackthorn Dr	89142
Blacktip Ave	89117
Blackwater Draw St	89179
Bladensburg St	89110
Blair Way	89107
Blair Rock St	89178
Blairsden St	89134
Blairwood Ct	89178
Blake Alan Ave	89147
Blakely Ct	89148
Blanc Vineyard Ct	89138
Blanca Peak Ave	89129
Blanche Ct	89149
Blanco Peak St	89139
Blanda Cir	89124
Blaney Ct	89121
Blank Cir	89115
Blankenship Ave	89106
Blanton Dr	
4701-4797	89121
4799-4999	89121
5000-5200	89122
5202-5298	89122
Blarney Ln	89110
Blatimac Ave	89129
Blazing Fire Ct	89117
Blazing Saddle Ave	89129
Blazing Sand St	89110
Blazing Sky Ct	89131
Blazing Star Ct	89117
Blazing Sun Ave	89129
Bledsoe Ln	
1200-1599	89110
2000-2700	89156
2702-2798	89156
Blended Stitch Ct	89149
Blenheim Ave	89135
Blesbok Ct	89149
Blessed Thistle Ave	89141
Bliss Canyon Ct	89129
Bliss Hill Ct	89149
Blissful Valley Cir	89149
Blissville Ave	89145
Blisworth Ct	89102
Blizzard Ct & Ln	89145
Bloomfield Ct	89134
Blooming Desert Ct	89115
Blooming Grove Ave	89149
Blooming Jasmine Ave	89117
Blooming Rose St	89144
Blooming Sand Ave	89129
Blooming Sun Ct	89142
Bloomingdale Ct	89144
Bloomingfield Ln	89145
Bloomington Dr	89134
Bloomsbury Ave	89123
Blossom Ave	89142
Blossom Knoll Ave	89108
Blossom View Ave	89142
Blossomwood Ave	89108
Blowing Bellows St	89130
Blowing Breeze Ave	89179
Blowing Pines Dr	89143
Blowing Sand Cir	89117
Blue Aloe Ct	89106
Blue Ash Ln	89122
Blue Bay Ct	89141
Blue Bell Dr	89134
Blue Blossom Ave	89108
Blue Breeze Dr	89128
Blue Brook Dr	89147
Blue Calico Dr	89123
Blue Cascade Ave	89128
Blue Charm Ave	89149
Blue Claws Ln	89135
Blue Copper Ct	89113
Blue Cove Ct	89131
Blue Dane Ct	89130
Blue Diamond Rd	
3301-3497	89139
3499-4800	89139
4802-6598	89139
6901-7997	89178
7999-8599	89178
10900-12899	89161
Blue Eagle Way	89128
Blue Evergreen Ave	89131
Blue Fin Cir	89128
Blue Fish Ct	89115
Blue Flax Pl	89148
Blue Ginger Dr	89135
Blue Grouse Trl	89142
Blue Gum Ct	89148
Blue Harbor Ct	89128
Blue Hawaii Ave	89110
Blue Heather Dr	89129
Blue Heron Ct	89121
Blue Hope Diamond Ln	89139
Blue Horizon Ct	89130
Blue Iris Ct	89141
Blue Island Ave	89129
Blue Ivy Ave	89135
Blue Jay Ave	89121
Blue Lagoon Dr	89110
Blue Lake Ave	89115
Blue Lake Peak St	89166
Blue Larkspur Ct	89141
Blue Luster Dr	89119
Blue Magenta Ave	89183
Blue Marlin Ave	89115
Blue Meadow Ave	89178
Blue Mesa Way	89129
Blue Mist Ct	89139
Blue Monaco St	89117
Blue Moon Ln	89147
Blue Mountain Dr	89108
Blue Nile Ct	89144
Blue Oat Ave	89141
Blue Ox Ave	89178
Blue Peak Ave	89131
Blue Rapids Ct	89139
Blue Raven Ave	89143
Blue Ribbon Dr	89142
Blue Ribbon Downs St	89122
Blue Ridge Pkwy	89122
Blue River Dr	89107
Blue Royal Dr	89130
Blue Sage Ct	89129
Blue Sapphire Ave	89110
Blue Sea St	89110
Blue Shadow St	89131
Blue Spruce Cir	89104
Blue Tee Ct	89148
Blue Tropic Ave	89130
Blue Twilight Ct	89108
Blue Venice Ct	89117
Blue Villa Ct	89178
Blue Water Peak Ave	89166
Blue Wave Dr	89115

Street	ZIP
Blue Whirlpool St	89131
Blue Wildrye St	89122
Blue Wolf St	89123
Blue Yucca St	89144
Blue Zenith Cir	89119
Bluebell Garden St	89149
Bluebird St	89121
Bluebird Canyon Pl	89138
Bluecrest Rd	89121
Bluegrass Ln	89123
Bluehill Ave	89156
Bluehurst Ave	89156
Bluejay Cir & Way	89146
Bluemist Mountain Ct	89113
Bluestone Dr	89108
Bluewater Dr	89128
Bluff Cove Cir	89117
Bluff Creek Ave	89131
Bluff Dwellers Ave	89131
Bluff Ledge Ave	89149
Bluff Point Dr	89134
Bluff Valley Ct	89178
Bluffton Ct	89134
Bluffwood Pl	89138
Blume Cir	89108
Blush Ave	89130
Blush Creek Pl	89144
Blushing Bride St	89110
Blushing Den St	89131
Blushing Hearts Rd	89115
Blushing Heights Ave	89131
Bluthe Bridge Ave	89141
Blyth Rock Ave	89147
Boardwalk Way	89123
Bob Fisk Ave	89178
Bobbie Jo Ln	89110
Bobbye Ave	89120
Bobcat Ct	89113
Bobcat Bend Ct	89139
Bobcat Bluffs St	89178
Bobcat Ridge Ave	89122
Bobrich Cir	89110
Boca Dr	89134
Boca Chica Ave	89120
Boca Del Rio St	89131
Boca Grande Ave	89120
Boca Lago Cir	89147
Boca Raton Dr	89113
Boca River Dr	89106
Bocaire Dr	89131
Bocale Ct	89123
Boccelli Ct	89139
Bock St	89119
Bodega Dr	89103
Bodega Bay St	89117
Bodega Point Ct	89113
Bodie Island Ct	89147
Bogart Ct	89117
Bogside Way	89129
Bohemian Forest Ave	89138
Boise St	89121
Bokhara St	89149
Bold Regatta Ct	89139
Bold Venture Ct	89148
Bolero Ave	89121
Bolin Ct	89123
Bolingbrook Ave	89149
Bollentino Ct	89122
Bolles Harbor St	89104
Bollinger Ln	89141
Bologna Dr	89117
Bolsa Dr	89110
Bolting Cloud Dr	89178
Bolton Ct	89148
Bolton Bay Way	89149
Bolton Landing Ct	89178
Bolton Valley Dr	89122
Boltonia Ct	89149
Bolzano Ct	89117
Bombastic Ct	89147
Bombax Ct	89141
Bombay Ct	89110
Bombay Reef Ct	89149
Bomberos Ct	89113
Bon Rea Cir	89110
Bonanza Cir	89107
E Bonanza Rd	
2-200	89101
202-3199	89101
3201-3499	89101
3500-6899	89110
6901-7049	89110
W Bonanza Rd	
300-398	89106
400-2347	89106
2349-2499	89106
2501-3597	89107
3599-4599	89107
4601-4699	89107
Bonanza Way	89101
Bonanza Creek Ave	89148
Bonaventure Dr	89147
Bonchester Hill St	89141
Bond St	89118
Bondeno St	89123
Bonds Flat St	89148
Bonham Ct	89148
Bonillo Dr	89103
Bonita Ave	89104
Bonita Canyon Ave	89142
Bonita Springs Ct	89130
Bonita Una St	89129
N Bonita Vista St	
4201-4399	89129
4800-5800	89149
5802-5998	89149
9301-9599	89143
9800-9898	89143
S Bonita Vista St	
4501-4599	89147
8301-8399	89148
Bonitos Suenos St	89138
Bonk Blvd	89139
Bonn Ct	89130
E Bonneville Ave	89101
W Bonneville Ave	89106
Bonneville Peak Ct	89148
Bonnie Ln	
2-198	89110
2000-2199	89156
Bonnie Blue St	89143
Bonnie Brae Ave	89102
Bonnie Castle Way	89108
Bonnie Doon Ln	89141
Bonnie Rock Dr	89134
Bonnie Springs Rd	89161
Bonnyhill St	89141
Bonta Ct	89134
Bonterra Ave	89129
Bookbinder Dr	89108
Booker Ct	89128
Boom Town Dr	89122
Boomer Beach St	89166
Boomerang Ridge St	89113
Boone Hills Ct	89129
Boothill Ave	89118
Bootlegger Ave	89141
Bootstrap Cir	89117
Borah Park Cir	89178
Borah Peak Ave	89166
Boratko St	89115
Borden Cir	89107
Borealis St	89123
Borgata Bay Blvd	89147
Borla Dr	89117
Borland Ct	89148
Borough Park St	89178
Borrego Springs Way	89129
Boseck Dr	89145
Bosky Springs St	89131
Bossa Nova Dr	89129
Bossart Ct	89102
E Boston Ave	89104
W Boston Ave	89102
Boston Ivy Ct	89130
Boston Springs Ave	89149
Boston Tea St	89149
Boswell Ct	89139
Botanic Gardens Dr	89148
Botanical Ave	89110
Botany Bay Dr	89128
Bottiglia Ave	89141
Bottle Creek Ln	89117
Bottle Palm Ct	89106
Bottle Sage Ave	89130
Bottleneck Ct	89178
Boulder Hwy	
3400-5000	89121
5040-5098	89122
5100-6700	89122
6702-6798	89122
Boulder Brook Ct	89149
Boulder Creek St	89123
Boulder Crossing Cir	89135
Boulder Mesa Dr	89128
Boulder Opal Ave	89148
Boulder Point Ct	89115
Boulder Rise St	89115
Boulder Rock Cir	89135
Boulder Springs Dr	89128
Bouncing Ball St	89178
Boundary Oak Dr	89134
Boundary Peak Way	89135
Bountiful Way	89121
Bounty Ave	89121
Bouquet Canyon St	89139
Bourbon Way	89107
Bourbon Run Ave	89134
Bourne Valley Ct	89123
Bova Matrina Ct	89123
Bow Bridge Dr	89134
Bow Canyon Ct	89147
Bow Creek Ct	89128
Bow Creek Ln	89134
Bow Island Ave	89122
Bow Ridge Ct	89145
Bowen Ct	89135
Bower Basin St	89144
Bowerman Way	89130
Bowler Springs St	89148
Bowles Dr	89130
Bowling Green Cir	89130
Bowman Ave	89106
Bowman Woods Cir	89129
Bowsprit Ct	89183
Bowstring Dr	89142
Box Canyon Dr	89128
Box Cars Ct	89122
Boxberry Ave	89131
Boxer St	89156
Boxerwood Dr	89110
Boxwood Ln	89103
Boyd Ave	
6900-6998	89178
7600-7799	89179
8001-8099	89178
Boyd Ln	89131
Boylagh Ave	89129
Boysen Ct	89156
Bozzolo St	89141
Brabant Ave	89183
Bracana Ct	89141
Bracken Ave	89104
Bracken Cliff Ct	89129
Brackenfield Ave	89178
Bracknell St	89129
Brad Oaks Cir	89123
Bradbury Cir	89128
Braddock Ave	89110
Bradford Ln	89108
Bradford Commons Dr	89135
Bradford Island Ct	89130
Bradford Pear Dr	89122
Bradford Summit St	89183
Bradhurst Ct	89142
Bradley Rd	
3601-4399	89130
6500-6598	89131
6600-8298	89131
8300-8398	89131
Bradley Springs Cir	89108
Bradpoint Dr	89130
Bradshaw Way	89145
Brady Ave	89101
Brady Cir	89120
Brady Ln	89120
Braeburn Dr	89130
Braemar Dr	89130
Braeside Ct	89130
N Braewood Ave	89120
W Braewood Ave	89120
Braewood Cir	89120
Braewood Dr	89121
Brahms Dr	89146
Braided Romel Ct	89131
Braided Yarn Ave	89149
Brair Knoll Ct	89108
Bramante Dr	89141
Bramble Ct	89145
Bramble Ln	89120
Brambleberry Ct	89113
Bramblewood St	89147
Brambly Creek Ct	89129
Bramfield Ct	89102
Branch Ct	89110
Branch Creek Ct	89135
Branch Field Ave	89183
Branded Brook Ave	89156
Branded Bull Ct	89131
Branding Iron Ln	89123
Brandon Ct	89156
Brandonkane Ln	89121
Brandywine Way	89107
Branford Hills St	89123
Brantley Cir	89115
Brasada St	89178
Brass Hills Ct	89122
Brass Ring Rd	89123
Brassica Ct	89148
Brasswood St	89110
Brassy Dr	89142
Brassy Boots Ct	89129
Braswell Dr	89128
Bratcher Point Ct	89166
Brave Voyager Ct	89139
Brave Warrior Ave	89131
Bravo St	89108
Bravura Ct	89139
Brawley Dr	89134
Brazilnut Ct	89145
Brazos St	89169
Brazos Bend St	89178
Brea Blvd	89118
Brea Crest Cir	89123
Break Point Ave	89130
Breakers Ln	89113
Breakers Creek Dr	89134
Breakfast Hill St	89166
Breakthrough Way	89135
Breanna St	89107
Breathtaking Ct	89149
Breazy Meadow Ct	89131
Breckenwood Ct	89115
Breckford Ct	89110
Brecon Mountain Ct	89139
Breechcloth Way	89117
Breecher Ave	89131
Breed Hill St	89149
Breeders Cup St	89130
Breeze Ct & St	89145
Breeze Canyon Dr	89117
Breezewood Dr	89108
Breezy Brown Ave	89143
Breezy Leaf St	89139
Breezy Night Ct	89129
Breezy Point Ln	89115
Breezy Tree Ct	89145
Breman St	89129
Bremerton Cir	89107
Brenda Ln	89156
Brenner Way	89110
Brent Ln	
5000-6198	89131
6200-7700	89131
7702-7798	89131
8400-8800	89143
8802-9398	89143
13300-13399	89166
Brent Leaf Ave	89131
Brent Thurman Way	89148
Brently Pl	89122
Brentmead Dr	89120
Brentwood St	89121
Brentwood Grove Ct	89149
Brescia Dr	89117
Breton Dr	89108
Bretton Oaks St	89166
Brewing Cloud Ave	89148
Brewster St	89135
Brewster Bay St	89179
Brewster Valley St	89123
Brezza Marina Ct	89131
Brian Buscombe Ln	89130
Brian Christopher Ave	89149
Brian Grayson Way	89145
Brian Head St	89122
Briana Renee Way	89123
Brianhurst Ave	89144
Brianna Cheerful Ave	89178
Brianna Peak Ct	89142
Brianwood Ct	89134
Briar Ct	89115
Briar Bay Dr	89131
Briar Meadow Way	89118
Briar Patch Way	89118
Briar Rose Ln	89130
Briarcliff Rd	89115
Briarcreek Cir	89110
Briarcrest Ct	89120
Briarglen Ln	89108
Briarthorne St	89123
Briarwood Ave	89121
Briarwood Bend Ave	89130
Briaton Ct	89118
Brick House Ave	89122
Bridal Cave Ave	89131
Bridal Creek Ave	89178
Bridal Falls Ct	89148
Bridge Creek St	89117
Bridge Gate Dr	89128
Bridge Glen Dr	89108
Bridgefield Ln	89147
Bridgehampton Ave	89130
Bridgepointe Dr	89121
Bridgeport Dr	89121
Bridgeport Bay Ave	89147
Bridgeport Hills Ave	89139
E Bridger Ave	89101
Bridgeton Cross Ct	89148
Bridgetown Ln	89123
Bridgette Way	89122
Bridgeview Ave & Cir	89147
Bridgewater St	89110
Bridgewood Way	89110
Bridle Ct	89121
Bridle Path Way	89145
Bridle Wreath Ln	89156
Bridlehorne Ave	89131
Bridlewood Ct & Dr	89119
Brienholt Ave	89122
Brienza Way	89117
Brier Creek Ln	89131
Brigadoon Dr	89141
Brigantine Way	89128
Briggs Ct	89110
Briggs Hill Ct	89139
Brigham Ave	89178
Bright Dr	89117
Bright Angel Way	89149
Bright Blue Sky Ave	89166
Bright Bush St	89131
Bright Charisma Ct	89178
Bright Eyed Ct	89149
Bright Harbor Ave	89135
Bright Heights St	89131
Bright Hollow Ct	89135
Bright Mountain St	89178
Bright Nimbus Ave	89139
Bright Rose Dr	89122
Bright Sapphire Ct	89148
Bright Sky Ct	89130
Bright Springs Ct	89113
Bright Star Ct	89115
Bright Sun Ct	89130
Bright View Dr	89119
Brighthill Ave	89121
Brighton Dr	89121
Brighton Rd	89145
Brighton Beach Ave	89166
Brighton Creek Ct	89135
Brighton Hill Ave	89129
Brighton Shore St	89128
Brighton Springs St	89128
Brighton Summit Ave	89131
Brighton Village St	89166
Brightridge Dr	89134
Brightwater Dr	89123
Brightwood Dr	89123
Brill St	89108
Brillancy Ave	89147
Brillare Ave	89135
Brilliant Forest St	89131
Brilliant Ore Dr	89143
Brilliant Pompon Pl	89166
Brilliant Prairie Ct	89149
Brilliant Ruby Ct	89139
Brilliant Sky Dr	89178
Brilliant Star Dr	89178
Brilliant View Ct	89129
Brim Canyon Ave	89178
Brindisi Park Ave	89148
Brindle Ct	89117
Briney Deep Ave	89139
Brinkburn Point Ave	89178
Brinkman St	89138
Brinkwood Ave	89134
Brisa Del Mar Ave	89179
Brisbane Pl	89110
Brisbane Hills St	89166
Brisk Ocean Ave	89178
Bristle Canyon Ave	89110
Bristlecone Cir & St	89146
Bristol Way	89107
Bristol Bay Ct	89108
Bristol Bend Ct	89135
Bristol Brush Way	89108
Bristol Crest Ln	89139
Bristol Grove Ln	89135
Bristol Manor Dr	89108
Bristol Peak Ave	89166
Bristol View Ct	89108
Bristow Falls Ct	89148
British Cup Dr	89117
British Isles Ave	89146
Brittany Way	89107
Brittany Harbor Dr	89128
Brittany Nicole Ct	89139
Brittany Shores Dr	89123
Brittany Village Ct	89130
Brittlebush Way	89130
Brittlethorne Ave	89131
Brittlewood Ave	89120
Britton Hill Ave	89129
Britton Rose Dr	89178
Broad Meadow Ct	89129
Broad Oaks Ct	89148
Broad Peak Dr	89131
Broadacres Ranch St	89148
Broadbent Blvd	89122
Broadcast Ave	89183
Broadhead Ct	89135
Broadlake Ln	89122
Broadlands Ct	89147
Broadloom Ct	89149
Broadmead St	89147
Broadmere St	89117
Broadmoor Ave	89109
Broadriver Dr	89108
Broadwater Ln	89130
Brocade Ct	89149
Brocado Ln	89117
Brock Ct	89117
Brock Canyon Ct	89130
Brockington Dr	89120
Brockton Green Ct	89110
Brockwood Dr	89102
Broderick Ave	89130
Brodie Castle Ct	89166
Brody Ct	89147
Brody Marsh Ave	89143
Broken Par Dr	89148
Broken Putter Way	89148
Broken Slate Way	89139
Broken Sound Dr	89110
Broken Spur Ln	89131
Broken Top Ave	89141
Broken Willow Cir	89117
Broken Wood Ave	89148
Bromelia Ct	89149
Bromley Ave	89107
Brompton St	89178
Bronco Rd	89103
N Bronco St	
2601-2797	89108
2799-3699	89108
3701-3799	89108
4900-4998	89130
5901-5999	89130
S Bronco St	
2501-2597	89146
2599-3199	89146
5800-6100	89118
6102-7198	89118
8801-8999	89139
10200-10300	89141
10302-10698	89141
Bronco Billy Ct	89129
Bronco Loco Ct	89108
Bronze Cir	89128
Bronze Hills Ct	89178
Bronze Leaf St	89135
Bronze Meadow Ave	89122
Bronze River Ave	89149
Bronze Treasure Ct	89143
Bronzewood Ave	89149
Broodmare Ave	89143
Brook Bay Ct	89134
Brook Canyon Dr	89147
Brook Cottage Ln	89122
Brook Crest Ave	89131
Brook Valley Dr	89123
Brookdale Ave	89110
Brookfield Dr	89120
Brookfield Cove Ave	89131
Brookhaven Dr	89103
Brookings Ct	89110
Brookline Ct	89123
Brooklyn Bridge St	89135
Brooklyn Heights St	89166
Brookmere Dr	89130
Brookriver Ct	89149
W Brooks Ave	89108
Brooks Lake Ave	89148
Brooks Range St	89129
Brookside Ln	89107
Brookside Way	89121
Brookstone Ct	89117
Brookview Way	89121
Brookway Ln	89169
Brookwood Ave	89131
Broom Hill Dr	89134
Brothers Bay Ct	89145
Broward Ln	89147
Brown Cir	89107
Brown Ln	89115
Brown Bear Falls Ct	89123
Brown Derby Cir	89128
Brown Eagle St	89131
Brown Wolf St	89178
Browndeer Cir	89129
Brownfield St	89148
Browning Way	89130
Browns Mountain Ct	89131
Brownstone Ct	89139
Brownstone Ledge Ave	89149
Brownsville Ave	89129
Brownwood Ave	89122
Broxburn St	89108
Broxden Junction Ave	89166
Broxton Ln	89107
N Bruce St	89101
S Bruce St	
100-218	89101
220-316	89101
318-348	89101
1300-1398	89104
2500-2699	89169
4201-4297	89119
4299-4399	89119
4401-6599	89119
7300-8999	89123

Bruce Dern Ave 89183
Bruin Way 89145
Bruma Ave 89122
Brumana Ct 89141
Brunellos Ave 89123
E Bruner Ave 89183
Brunswick Cir 89107
Brunswick Bay St 89135
Brush St 89107
Brushton Ct 89138
Brushwood Ln 89107
Brushwood Peak Ave 89113
Brushy Creek Ave 89148
Brussels St
3300-3399 89169
4701-4799 89119
Bryandouglas Dr 89121
Bryant Ave 89102
Bryce Canyon Ave 89156
Bryce Rose Ave 89148
Bryce Woodlands St 89148
Bryn Haven Ave 89135
Bryn Mawr Ave 89102
Brynhurst Dr 89156
Bryson Ct 89135
Bubbling Brook Dr 89107
Bubbling Springs Ave 89156
Buccaneer Ln 89145
Buck Island St 89156
Buck Jones Ave 89122
Buckaroo Ave 89108
Buckboard Ln 89123
Buckeye Ave 89102
Buckeye Lake St 89122
Buckhaven Dr 89117
Buckhorn Dr 89134
Buckhorn Butte Ct 89149
Buckingham Dr 89108
Buckland Ct 89129
Buckmaster Ln 89117
Bucknell Dr 89134
Buckpasser Ave 89113
Bucks Lake St 89123
Buckskin Ave
6000-6098 89108
6100-6799 89108
7400-7799 89129
Buckskin Mare Ave 89131
Bucksprings Dr 89129
Buckthorn Cir 89108
Buckthorn Ridge Ct 89183
Buckwood Ct 89149
Bucova Ct 89148
Budding Blossom Ct 89108
Budenny Dr 89122
Budlong Ave 89110
Budnick Cir 89130
Buehler Dr 89102
Buelton Ct 89135
Buena Martina Way 89141
Buena Sera St 89141
Buena Vida St 89166
Buena Vista Dr
3501-3599 89121
4400-4599 89102
Buena Vista Way 89122
Buff Bay St 89148
N Buffalo Dr
201-413 89145
900-3199 89128
3200-3999 89129
4001-4699 89129
4900-5198 89149
6500-7000 89131
7002-8198 89131
S Buffalo Dr
300-598 89145
1001-1099 89145
1100-2900 89117
2902-3298 89117
3700-3798 89147
3901-4599 89147
5500-6298 89113
6300-9099 89113
9101-9199 89113
9201-9299 89178
10700-10798 89179
Buffalo Bill Ave 89110
Buffalo Clan Ct 89131
Buffalo Cloud Ave 89143
Buffalo Hide St 89118
Buffalo Horn Ct 89179
Buffalo Narrows Cir 89129
Buffalo Park Ave 89178
Buffalo Ranch Ave 89147
Buffalo Run Ave 89123
Buffalo Spring Ct 89122
Bufflehead St 89122
Buffwood Ave 89123
Bugbee Ave 89103
Bugle Way 89108
Buglehorn St 89131
Bugsy Siegal Cir 89149
Buhl Ct 89103
Builders Ave 89101
Bull Run Grove Ave 89166
Bull Valley Ct 89139
Bullion Blvd & Ct 89103
Bullring Ln 89130
Bumblebee Cir 89122
Bunch St 89122
Bundella Dr 89134
Bungalow Bay St 89130
Bunker Cir 89121
Bunker Commons Ct 89108
Bunny Run Dr 89128
Buoy St 89110
Burbage Ave 89139
Burcot Ave 89156
Burdel St 89149
Burdette St 89110
Burdock Ct 89129
Burensburg Ave 89135
Burgess Park Ct 89130
Burgesshill Ave 89129
Burgoa Ct 89141
Burgundy Way 89107
Buried Treasure Ct 89139
Burke Ct 89134
Burkehaven Ave 89166
Burkshire Dr 89142
Burleson Ranch Rd 89131
Burlington Ct 89107
Burlwood Way 89108
Burnett Ave 89178
Burnham Ave
1200-1298 89104
1300-2199 89104
2201-2399 89104
2700-3299 89169
4200-5299 89119
7400-7699 89123
Burning Bridge Ct 89131
Burning Bush St 89141
Burning Falls Dr 89131
Burning Hide Ave 89143
Burning Sun Ave 89178
Burning Tree Ct 89113
Burningwood Ln 89108
Burns Allen Ave 89122
Burnt Hills Dr 89130
Burnt Oak Ave 89113
Burnt Sienna St 89123
Burnt Sky Ave 89183
Burnt Umber St 89139
Burntwood Way 89108
Burow Pine St 89131
Burr Oak Dr 89130
Burrell Ct 89148
Burrowing Owl St 89131
Bursera Ct 89141
Burson St 89138
Bursting Nova Ct 89156
Burt Lancaster Ct 89183
Burton Ave 89102
Burton Lake Ct 89148
Burwood St 89178
Bush Clover Ln 89156
Bush Garden Ave 89129
Bush Mountain Ave 89166
Bush Poppy Ave 89147
Bushkill Creek Ct 89142
Bushnell Dr 89103
Bushra Ct 89110
Bushy Tail Ave 89149
Business Ln 89103
Business Center Way 89118
Business Park Ct 89128
Bussero Ct 89138
Buster Brown Ave 89122
Butch Moor Ct 89147
N & S Buteo Woods Ln 89144
N Butler St
4100-4199 89129
4201-4399 89129
5800-5899 89149
5901-5999 89149
Butler Mesa St 89166
Butte Cir 89110
Butterchurn Ave 89143
Buttercreek Way 89117
Buttercup Ct 89149
Butterfield Way 89103
Butterfly Cir 89122
Butterfly Bush St 89117
Butterick Ct 89118
Buttermilk Falls St 89178
Butternut Ln 89115
Butterscotch Cir 89131
Butterton Ct 89139
Butterum Ct 89110
Button Creek Ct 89122
Button Willow Dr 89134
Buttonbrush Ct 89139
Buttons Ridge Dr 89131
Buttonwood Ln 89107
Buzz Aldrin Dr 89149
Byorick Way 89128
Byrne Ave 89122
Byrnes Ave 89106
Byron Dr 89134
Byron Nelson Ln 89149
Byzantine Ct 89149
C St 89106
Cabachon Ave 89121
Caballero Way 89169
Caballo St 89119
Caballo Lake Ct 89148
Caballo Range Ave 89179
Cabana Dr 89122
Cabarita Ave 89178
Cabbage Cove St 89143
Cabeza Dr 89103
Cabin Cove Ave 89148
Cabin Fever St 89149
Cabin Peak St 89123
Cabin Springs Ave 89131
Cabis Bay St 89178
Cabita Beach Ct 89115
Cabo Ln 89121
Cabo Del Mesa Ave 89138
Cabo Del Sol Ct 89138
Cabo Del Verde Ave 89138
Cabo San Lucas Ave 89131
Cabot St 89102
Cabot Falls Ave 89149
Cabot Valley Ct 89123
Cabra Cir & St 89107
Cabrera Ct 89138
Cabrera Cove St 89178
Cabrillo Cir 89108
Cabrito Dr 89103
E Cactus Ave 89183
W Cactus Ave
3201-3397 89141
3399-4899 89141
4901-6399 89141
7300-7398 89178
9301-9399 89178
Cactus Ln 89107
Cactus Bloom Ln 89107
Cactus Brook Ct 89139
Cactus Brush Ct 89141
Cactus Canyon Ct 89128
Cactus Club Dr 89123
Cactus Creek Dr 89129
Cactus Dahlia St 89141
Cactus Flower Ct 89145
Cactus Hill Dr 89156
Cactus Mountain St 89129
Cactus Peak Ct 89113
Cactus Pine Ct 89135
Cactus Point Ct 89115
Cactus Root Ct 89129
Cactus Shadow St 89129
Cactus Springs Dr 89115
Cactus Thorn Ave 89118
Cactus View Ave 89117
Cactus Village Ave 89183
Cactus Wheel Ct 89129
Cactus Wood Dr 89134
Cactus Wren Ln 89129
Cadbury Dr 89121
Caddington Ave 89110
Caddo Creek St 89148
Caddy Cir 89108
Caddy Bag Ct 89148
Caddy Corner St 89139
Cadence Crossing Way 89178
Cadenza Ln 89123
Cadillac Ln 89106
Cadman St 89120
Cadrow Castle Ct 89148
Cadwell Park St 89149
Caesars Cir 89120
Caesars Palace Dr 89109
Cafe Pl 89121
Caffarelli Dr 89115
Cagney Ct 89103
Cahill Ave 89128
Cahlan Dr 89102
Cain Ave 89166
Cainito St 89131
Cairo Cir 89107
Cala Morlanda St 89138
Calabasas Ave 89117
Calabash Tree Ct 89148
Calabria Dr 89104
Calabro Ct 89178
Caladium Ct 89149
Caladonia Ave 89110
Calahonda Ct 89138
Calais Ct 89118
Calanas Ave 89141
Calanda Ct 89102
Calandria Ave 89123
Calaveras Ct 89110
Calavo St 89122
Calcaterra Cir 89119
Calcedonian St 89141
Calcite Cliff Ave 89123
Caldbeck Pl 89183
Calder Ave 89144
Caldera Canyon Ct 89129
Calderwood St 89103
Caldicot Dr 89138
Caldwell Cir 89115
Caledon Ridge Ct 89149
Calella Dr 89103
Caley Canyon St 89166
Calf Creek Ct 89129
Calgary Ct 89118
Caliche Way 89128
Calico Dr 89161
Calico St 89108
Calico Basin Rd 89161
Calico Brook Ct 89147
Calico Canyon Ct 89147
Calico Cove Ct 89147
Calico Creek Ct 89135
Calico Fields St 89149
Calico Flower Ave 89128
Calico Garden Ave 89134
Calico Hearts Ct 89106
Calico Hills Ct 89128
Calico Mountain Ave 89129
Calico Pines Ave 89135
Calico Vista Blvd 89128
Calico Wind St 89131
Caliente Ct & St 89119
Califa Dr 89122
E California Ave 89104
E California St 89104
W California St 89102
Calimesa St 89115
Caliper Dr 89110
Calista Way 89131
Calistoga Springs Ct 89144
Callahan Ave 89120
Callahan Point Dr 89145
Calle De Benito 89121
Calle De Corrida 89102
Calle De El Cortez 89102
Calle De Espana 89102
Calle De Este 89121
Calle De Honra 89120
Calle De Laredo 89102
Calle De Nuevo 89102
Calle De Reynaldo 89119
Calle De Rio Ave 89115
Calle De Sol Dr 89138
Calle De Vega 89102
Calle Del Cajon 89120
Calle Del Mar 89122
Calle Del Oro 89120
Calle Del Oya 89120
Calle Del Sol 89103
Calle Del Torre 89102
Calle Del Valle 89120
Calle Esquina 89103
Calle Fermo 89103
Calle Grande 89120
Calle Mirador 89103
Calle Montery St 89117
Calle Paula 89103
Calle Sedillo 89103
Calle Tereon 89103
Callington Way 89183
Calliope Creek Ct 89148
Callita Ct 89102
Calm Breeze Ave 89108
Calm Brook Ct 89149
Calm Creek Ave 89183
Calm Lagoon Ave 89130
Calm Passage Ct 89139
Calm Sea Ave 89106
Calm Waters St 89131
Calming Waters Ct 89149
Calmosa St 89103
Calmview Pl 89110
Calobar Ln 89110
Calomeria Ct 89149
Calstock Ct 89178
Calvado St 89128
Calvary Ct 89141
Calvert Ct 89121
Calverts St 89130
Calvia St 89138
Calville St 89128
Calvin Cove Dr 89145
Calvin Crest Ave 89129
Calvino Ave 89183
Calypso Ct 89121
Calypso Beach Ct 89115
Calypso Cave St 89141
Calzado Dr 89178
Camara Dr 89123
Camas Ct 89103
Camas Canyon Ave 89130
Cambiata Ct 89139
Cambium Pine Ave 89130
Camborne Ave 89144
Cambria Ave 89108
Cambria Cellars Ct 89139
Cambria Pine Ct 89156
Cambrian Dream Ct 89135
Cambrian Ridge Ct 89144
Cambridge St
3300-3699 89169
3800-3999 89119
Cambridge Blue Ave 89147
Cambridge Crest Ct 89123
Cambridge Cross Pl 89144
Cambridge Glen Ct 89149
Cambridge Grove St 89139
Cambridge Hollows Ct 89135
Cambridge Oaks Ct 89129
Cambridgeshire St 89146
Cambrils Ave 89178
Camden Ave 89122
Camden Bay St 89179
Camden Bridge St 89147
Camden Brook St 89183
Camden Heights Ct 89123
Camden Hills Ave 89145
Camden Pine Ave 89129
Camden Rose Ct 89134
Camel St 89115
Camel Back Dr 89169
Camel Rock Ct 89129
Camelback Peak Ct 89148
Camelia Cir 89108
Camellia Ridge Ct 89129
Camelot Cove St 89147
Cameo Ave 89138
Cameo Cir 89107
Cameo Cove Ave 89139
Cameo Rose Ln 89134
E Camero Ave 89123
W Camero Ave
4000-6699 89139
7100-8499 89113
Cameron St
1700-2200 89102
2202-3298 89102
4100-4399 89103
4401-4799 89103
5000-7299 89118
7300-8699 89139
8701-9099 89139
Cameron Park St 89166
Cameron Paul Ct 89139
Cameron Peak Ct 89156
Camille Flora Ct 89130
Camillo Ct 89146
Caminita Pl 89138
Camino Capistrano Ln 89147
Camino De Rosa Dr 89108
Camino Del Rancho 89130
Camino Gardens Way 89146
Camino Heights Ct 89139
Camino Loma Verde Ave 89117
Camino Ramon Ave 89156
Camino Verde Ln 89119
Camp Bonanza Rd 89124
Camp Fire Rd 89145
Camp Light Ave 89149
Camp Rock Ct 89178
Campana Dr 89147
Campanella St 89123
Campanile St 89141
Campbell Cir 89107
Campbell Dr
200-900 89107
902-998 89107
1100-1300 89102
1302-1698 89102
N Campbell Rd
3200-4399 89129
4401-4599 89129
4801-4897 89149
4899-7199 89149
7201-7399 89149
Campbell Ranch Ave 89179
Campbell Springs Ave 89178
Campers Village Ave 89178
Camphor Tree St 89108
Campo Cir 89130
Campo Seco Ct 89138
Campo Tizzoro Ave 89147
Campo Verde Dr 89121
Campolina Ct 89113
Campsie Fells Ct 89141
Campus Cir 89121
Campus Oaks Ct 89183
Camrose Ridge Pl 89149
Camryn Holly St 89129
Camsore Point Ln 89129
Canaberry Park Ct 89131
Canada Goose St 89115
Canadian Dr 89130
Canadian Lynx Ct 89139
Canal Cir & St 89122
Canalino Dr 89134
Canary Way 89106
Canary Date Ave 89149
Canary Diamond Ave 89139
Canary Ivy Way 89156
Canary Palm Ct 89121
Canary Wharf Dr 89178
Canasta Ct 89117
Cancun Ave 89131
Candia Ct 89141
Candia Rose Ln 89122
Candice St 89156
Candice Creek Ct 89149
Candice Lee Ct 89149
Candilela Ct 89149
Candle Canyon Ct 89147
Candle Maker St 89183
Candle Pine Way 89135
Candleberry Ct & Rd 89103
Candlebrush Ln 89107
Candlefish Ct 89113
Candleglow Ct 89147
Candlelight St 89145
Candlenut Ave 89131
Candlespice Way 89135
Candlewood Ct 89108
Candy St 89166
Candy Apple Cir 89142
Candy Bouquet St 89178
Candy Mint Ave 89183
Candyland Ave 89178
Cane Creek Mill Ct 89131
Cane Hill Dr 89142
Canebrake Ct 89141
Canelo Ct 89118
Canfield Dr 89108
Canfield Canyon Ave 89178
Canfield Point Ave 89183
Canisteo St 89141
Canley Ave 89149
Canna Dr 89122
Cannock St 89131
Cannoli Cir 89103
Cannon Ave 89121
Cannon Blvd 89108
Cannon Cir
3600-3706 89121
3708-3766 89121
4800-4899 89108
Cannon Beach St 89122
Cannon Falls Ave 89138
Cannon Hill Ct 89130
Canoe Ln 89145
Canoe Camp Ct 89129
Canoe Cove Ct 89117
Canoga Canyon Ct 89149
Canoga Peak Ave 89183
Canon Perdido St 89141
Canonero St 89142
Canons Brook Dr 89141
Canopy Ct 89149
Canopy Oak Dr 89135
Canosa Ave 89104
Canova Dossi Ave 89131
Cantabria Ct 89141
Cantabria Heights Ave 89183
Cantada Cir 89130
Cantana St 89123
Cantata Crest Ct 89178
Cantebury Rose Ln 89134
Cantelope Ct 89142
Canter Glen Ave 89122
Canterbury Ct & Dr 89119
Canterbury Bell Ct 89138
Canterbury Creek St 89183
Canterbury Cross Pl 89144
Canterra St 89138
Cantiamo Ct 89135
Cantina Creek Ct 89178
Cantina Terlano Pl 89141
Canto Ave 89147
Cantoria Ct 89141
Cantura Peak St 89143
Canvas Ct 89113
Canvas Canyon Ct 89178
Canvas Vest Ct 89113

Canvasback Ave 89122
Canyon Cir
200-299 89124
309-399 89107
3900-3999 89124
Canyon Dr 89107
Canyon Breeze Dr 89134
Canyon Brook Pl 89145
Canyon Classic Dr 89144
Canyon Cliff Ct 89129
Canyon Cove Way 89108
Canyon Creek Rd 89110
Canyon Crest Dr 89123
Canyon Dawn Ave 89108
Canyon Diablo Rd 89179
Canyon Dunes Ave 89147
Canyon Gate Dr 89117
Canyon Glen Ct 89156
Canyon Greens Dr 89144
Canyon Grove Ct 89131
Canyon Hills Ave 89148
Canyon Hollow Ave 89149
Canyon Lake Dr 89117
Canyon Ledge Ct 89117
Canyon Magic Ave 89129
Canyon Maple St 89148
Canyon Meadows Ct 89129
Canyon Mesa Dr 89144
Canyon Mine Ave 89129
Canyon Oak Cir 89142
Canyon Peak Dr 89147
Canyon Rain St 89139
Canyon Ranch St 89131
Canyon Ridge Dr 89108
Canyon Rim Way 89117
Canyon Rock Pl 89134
Canyon Rose Way 89108
Canyon Run Dr 89144
Canyon Saddle St 89148
Canyon Shadows Ln 89117
Canyon Springs Dr 89117
Canyon Valley Ave 89145
Canyon View Dr 89117
Canyon Vista Ct 89156
Canyon Walk Ave 89147
Canyon Wren Ave 89149
Canyonland Ct 89147
Canyons Eye Cir 89124
Canyons Park Ave 89131
Capaldi Dr 89110
Capanna Rosso Pl 89141
Cape Brett St 89131
Cape Canaveral Ct 89149
Cape Canyon Ct 89141
Cape Cod Dr 89122
Cape Cod Bay Ct 89179
Cape Cod Landing Dr 89135
Cape Coral Cir 89130
Cape Cortez Ct 89138
Cape Elizabeth St 89147
Cape Flattery Ave 89147
Cape Hatteras Ct 89139
Cape Hope Way 89121
Cape Ito Ct 89113
Cape May St 89141
Cape Royal St 89147
Cape Sable Ln 89117
Cape Sand Dr 89108
Cape Shore Ave 89166
Cape Solitude St 89147
Cape Verde Ln 89128
Cape Vista Ln 89128
Cape Wood Ct 89117
Capella Ave
2500-2699 89109
3700-3799 89102
Capella Rico Ave 89117
Caper Tree Ct 89123
Capertino St 89145
Capesthorne Way 89135
Capestone St 89134
Capetown Way 89128
Capeview Ct 89148
Capilla Real Ave 89138
Capistrano Ave
1500-2399 89169
2400-2700 89121
2702-2998 89121
Capistrano Cir 89169
Capistrano Ct 89121
Capistrano Valley Ave 89178
Capistrello Ave 89147
Capitol Hill Ct 89183
Capitol Peak Ave 89166
Capitola Ave 89108
Capo Gallo St 89130
Capo San Vito Ave 89123
E Capovilla Ave 89119
W Capovilla Ave
3201-3897 89118
3899-4499 89118
4501-5299 89118
8300-8398 89113
Cappas St 89115
Cappellini Ct 89141
Capriati Ave 89183
Caprice Ct 89118
Capricorn Dr 89108
Caprino Ave 89108
Caprock Cir 89129
Caprock Canyon Ave 89139
Capsicum Ct 89118
Capstick Ave 89129
Capsule Dr 89115
Captain Jon Ave 89104
Captain Lord Ct 89166
Captain Palmer Ct 89166
Captains Pl 89117
Captains Harbor Dr 89117
Captains Hill Rd 89145
Captivating Ave 89149
Captivation Ct 89128
Cara Mia Ct 89135
Caracas Dr 89145
Caramel Almond Cir 89110
Caramel Crest Ct 89135
Caramel Gorge Ct 89143
Caravelle St 89142
Caraway Ln 89144
Carberry Hill St 89141
Carbine Chapel St 89130
Carbon Heights Ct 89178
Carbondale St 89135
Carbonia Ct 89144
Carbury Ct 89129
Cardiff Ln 89108
Cardigan Bay St 89131
Cardillo Ct 89138
Cardinal Dr & Ln 89121
Cardinal Bluff Dr 89128
Cardinal Climber Ct 89138
Cardinal Crest Ln 89144
Cardinal Peak Ln 89144
Cardinal Ridge Ct 89149
Cardinal Rose Ln 89122
Cardinal View Pl 89134
Cardoness Ct 89139
Carefree Dr 89122
Carefree Peak Ct 89110
Careful Canvas Ave 89149
Caressa Ct 89117
E Carey Ave
3700-4899 89115
4901-5099 89115
5100-7300 89156
7302-7698 89156
Carey Hall St 89110
Cargill Ave 89110
Caribbean Ct 89117
Caribbean Palm Dr 89138
Caribou Way 89108
Caribou Narrows Way 89178
Caribou Ridge St 89149
Carillo St 89104
Carl Ave 89108
Carlin Ave 89110
Carlin Farms St 89179
Carlina Canyon Ct 89149
Carlisle Crest Ln 89139
Carlisle Crossing St 89138
Carlisle Grove Ave 89139
Carlitas Joy Ct 89117
Carlos Dr 89123
Carlotta Cir 89121
Carlsbad Ave & Cir 89156
Carlsbad Beach Ct 89113
Carlton Gate St 89178
Carlton Kay Pl 89144
Carlton Oaks Ct 89113
Carlyle Dr 89115
Carmar Dr 89122
Carmel Ave 89122
Carmel Way 89108
Carmel Heights Ave 89178
Carmel Mountain Ave 89144
Carmel Peak Ln 89145
Carmel Ridge Ct 89113
Carmel Ridge Dr 89134
Carmel River Ave 89141
Carmel Shores Dr 89128
Carmelita Cir 89121
Carmen Blvd
4800-4898 89108
4900-6399 89108
7000-8399 89128
Carmichael Ave 89110
Carmine St 89122
Carnation Ln 89108
Carnation Meadow St 89130
Carnegie Hall St 89135
Carnelian Ct & St 89121
Carnival Ave 89123
Carol Cir
4500-4599 89120
5200-5299 89119
Carol Lark Ct 89129
Carol Steam St 89149
Carolina Cherry Dr 89141
Carolina Dew Ct 89122
Carolina Hills Ave 89144
Caroline Rose St 89183
Carolyn Dr 89103
Carolyn Lee St 89131
Carpenter Dr 89107
Carpenteria Way 89108
Carr Valley St 89131
Carradori Ave 89148
Carrera Cir & Dr 89103
Carriage Ln 89119
Carriage Park Dr 89121
Carriagedale Ct 89110
Carriellen Ln 89110
Carrizo Springs Ave 89148
Carrondale Way 89128
Carrot Ridge St 89139
Carruth Ct 89121
Carruth St
2900-3100 89121
3102-3198 89121
5400-5599 89120
Carsoli Ct 89147
E Carson Ave 89101
Carson Brook St 89183
Carson Creek St 89113
Carson Hills Ave 89139
Cart Crossing Way 89148
Carta Luna St 89135
Cartaro Dr 89103
Cartegena Way 89121
Carter Cir 89106
Carter Ct 89122
Carter St 89106
Carter Creek St 89178
Carter Montgomery Ave 89149
Cartgate Ct 89110
Carthay Cir 89110
E Cartier Ave 89115
W Cartier Ave 89108
Cartwheel St 89178
Cartwright Ave 89110
Cary Grant Ct 89142
Carysford Ave 89178
Casa Bella Ct 89117
Casa Bianca St 89141
Casa Blanca St 89121
Casa Blanco Pl 89121
Casa Christina Ln 89147
Casa Colina Ct 89131
Casa Colorado Ave 89121
Casa Coronado Ave 89131
Casa De Elegante Ct 89117
Casa Del Mar Ct 89138
Casa Del Rey Ct 89117
Casa Encantada St 89118
Casa Grande Ave 89102
Casa Grande Dr 89108
Casa Ladera St 89156
Casa Linda Dr 89103
Casa Loma Ave 89156
Casa Madera Ct 89131
Casa Maria Ave 89141
Casa Mia Cir & Ln 89121
Casa Monica Ct 89141
Casa Palazzo Ct 89141
Casa Real Way 89147
Casa Rustica Ct 89147
Casa Sencia St 89121
Casa Solar Ct 89128
Casa Vegas St 89169
Casa Vista Dr 89146
Casada Way 89107
Casala Ct 89141
Casalvieri St 89113
Casanova Cir 89120
Cascada Piazza Ln 89135
Cascade St 89142
Cascade Bluffs Ct 89123
Cascade Cliffs Ct 89139
Cascade Creek Ln 89113
Cascade Falls Ave 89117
Cascade Hills Dr 89134
Cascade Lake St 89148
Cascade Mist Ave 89123
Cascade Oak Ave 89113
Cascade Pools Ave 89131
Cascade Ridge Ct 89113
Cascade Run Ave 89142
Cascade Valley Ct 89128
Cascadia Ct 89122
Casco Way 89107
Casco Bay St 89179
Casellina Ct 89141
Casey Ct 89119
Casey Dr
1800-2198 89119
2200-2399 89119
2400-3799 89120
Cash Ct 89156
Cashew Ct 89115
Cashman Dr
900-999 89107
1100-1499 89102
Cashmere Mist Ave 89138
Casino Center Blvd 89101
N Casino Center Blvd 89101
S Casino Center Blvd
300-310 89101
312-999 89101
1100-1600 89104
1602-1698 89104
Casitas Way 89122
Casoria Ave 89123
Casper Peak Ct 89117
Caspian Dr 89118
Caspian Moon Dr 89166
Caspian Springs Dr 89120
E & W Cassady Ct 89115
Cassaluce Ave 89141
Cassedy Ln 89122
Casselman Ct 89183
Cassian Ct 89129
Cassis Ct 89117
Cast Pebble Dr 89135
Castano Vista Ct 89179
Castel Martini Ct 89147
Castellane Dr 89141
Castellon Ct 89128
Castillana Ct 89147
Castille St 89121
Castillo Peak St 89139
Castle Bar Dr 89134
Castle Bay Dr 89108
Castle Bid Ct 89129
Castle Brook Ave 89113
Castle Cave Ct 89138
Castle Course Ave 89148
Castle Cove Dr 89108
Castle Creek Ct 89148
Castle Crest Dr 89117
Castle Dome St 89113
Castle Field Ct 89139
Castle Fountain St 89141
Castle Harbor Ave 89130
Castle Hill Ave 89129
Castle Lake Ct 89139
Castle Mountain Ave 89179
Castle Oaks Ct 89141
Castle Pines Ave 89113
Castle Ridge Ave 89129
Castle Rock Ct 89147
Castle Rock Peak St 89166
Castle Springs St 89178
Castle Stone Ct 89123
Castle Valley Ave 89178
Castle View Ave 89129
Castle Vista Ct 89118
Castle Wall St 89117
Castleberry Ln 89156
Castleberry Peak Ave 89131
Castlebridge Ave 89123
Castledowns St 89148
Castleford Pl 89102
Castlemont Ave 89156
Castlesands Way 89121
Castlewood Dr 89102
Castor Tree Way 89108
Castrato Ct 89178
Catalina Aisle St 89138
Catalina Canyon Ave 89147
Catalina Cove Cir 89147
Catalina Harbor St 89131
Catalini St 89107
Catalonia Dr 89117
Catalpa Trl 89108
Cataluna Ct 89143
Catamaran Cir 89121
Catamount Creek Ave 89141
Cataya Ct 89141
Catching Ct 89149
Catclaw Ct 89135
Catfish Stream Ave 89178
Cathedral Ln 89108
Cathedral Way 89109
Cathedral Blue Ave 89118
Cathedral Canyon Ct 89129
Cathedral Peak Ct 89134
Cathedral Pines Ave 89149
Cathedral Range Ct 89139
Cathedral Rock Dr 89128
Cathedral Stairs Ct 89148
Cather Ave 89166
Catherine Ln 89121
Catinga Ct 89178
Catlyn Woods Ave 89141
Catmint St 89113
Catoctin Ave 89139
Catseye Cove Ct 89183
Caumsett Ct 89117
Cavaison Ave 89123
Cavalcade St 89134
Cavalier Cir 89130
Cavalry St 89121
Cavaretta Ct 89103
Cavaricci Ave 89129
Cavatina Ave 89139
Cave Junction Ct 89131
Cave Primrose St 89117
Cave Ridge St 89179
Cave Rock Ave 89110
Cavern Cove Way 89156
Cavern Creek St 89115
Cavern Hills Dr 89178
Cavern Peak Dr 89178
Caverns Mouth Dr 89178
Caviar Dr 89108
Cayley Ct 89110
Cayuga Pkwy 89169
Cazaba Ct 89144
Cazador St 89123
Cecile Ave 89115
Cedar Ave
1700-2999 89101
5300-5398 89110
5400-5874 89110
5876-5898 89110
Cedar Rd 89124
Cedar St 89104
Cedar Basin Ave 89142
Cedar Bluffs Way 89128
Cedar Breaks Ave 89156
Cedar Canyon Ln 89113
Cedar Creek Ave 89134
Cedar Door Ave 89148
Cedar Flat Ln 89134
Cedar Forest Ave 89144
Cedar Fort Ct 89113
Cedar Grove Cir 89130
Cedar Heights Ave 89134
Cedar Hills St 89128
Cedar Island Ct 89147
Cedar Key Ave 89129
Cedar Knolls Dr 89147
Cedar Lake Ct 89110
Cedar Lawn Way 89130
Cedar Leaf Dr 89147
Cedar Log Ct 89135
Cedar Mesa Ave 89149
Cedar Mill Falls Ct 89143
Cedar Mountain St 89117
Cedar Park Ave 89148
Cedar Rae Ave 89131
Cedar Ridge St 89147
Cedar Rock Ln 89128
Cedar Rose St 89183
Cedar Run Ct 89135
Cedarbrook Dr 89146
Cedarcliff Ave 89123
Cedarcrest Ct 89134
Cedardale Pl 89134
Cedaredge Ct 89120
Cedarglen Ct 89103
Cedargulf Ave 89131
Cedarspring Dr 89103
Cedartown St 89129
Cedarview Cir 89146
Cedarwood Ave 89103
Cedeno St 89123
Celadine St 89131
Celcius Pl 89129
Celebration Dr 89123
Celebreeze Ct 89145
Celebrity Cir 89119
Celera Dr 89123
Celeste Ave 89107
Celestial Ave 89128
Celestial Glow St 89123
Celia Pl 89145
Celina Hills St 89131
Celosia St 89113
Celso Ct 89144
Celtic Moon St 89129
Centaur Ave 89123
Centavo Dr 89117
Centennial Cir 89121
Centennial Pkwy 89149
E Centennial Pkwy 89115
W Centennial Pkwy
5700-5798 89131
10600-10699 89166
Centennial St 89121
Centennial Center Blvd 89149
Center Dr 89104
Center St 89106
Center Crossing Rd 89144
Center Green Dr 89148
Center Stage Ave 89129
Centerville Bay Ct 89179
Centocelle Ave 89183
Central Butte Ave 89129
Central Railroad Ct 89131
Central Valley Ave 89149
Centralia St 89149
Centura Ave 89110
Centurion Ct 89122
Century Dr 89110
Century Garden Dr 89119
Century Plant St 89117
Cerbat Ct 89183
Ceremony Dr 89117
Cereus Ave & Ct 89146
Cerise Rose Ave 89144
Cerniglia St 89143
Cerone Ct 89141
Cerotto Ln 89135
Cerrito St 89120
Cerritos Ct 89178
Certitude Ave 89131
Cervantes St 89101
Cessna Ave 89115
Cestrum Rd 89113
Cetus Cir 89128
Ceuta St 89143
Chablis Bay St 89131
Chabot Dr 89107
Chad Cir 89110
Chadford Pl 89102
Chadwick Falls St 89179
Chafer Dr 89121
Chalet Rd 89124
Chalfont Ct 89121
Chalgrove Village Ave 89145
Chalk Hill Ct 89141
Challas St 89110
Challenge Ln 89110
Chalon Pl 89144
Chama Ave, Ct & Pl 89121
Chambersberg St 89147
Chambery Cove Ct 89123
Chambliss Dr 89130
Chambolle Ct 89144
Chambord St 89117
Chamero Mesa St 89110
Champagne Cir 89119
Champagne Bliss Ave 89149
Champagne Isle St 89135
Champion Hills Ln 89134
Champion Run St 89113
Champions Ave & Cir 89142
Championship Ct 89134
Champney Ave 89148
Chandelier Ct 89149
Chandler Ave 89120
Chandler Mews Dr 89108
Chandon Ct 89130
Chandra Ave 89129
Changing Seasons St 89144
Changing Tides Ct 89149
Channel 10 Dr 89119
Channel 8 Dr 89109
Channel Bay Dr 89128
Channel Rock Dr 89117
Channelwood Dr 89110
Chanted Heart Ave 89115
Chantemar St 89135
Chanticleer Ct 89129
Chantilly Ave 89110
Chantilly Island Ct 89123
Chapala Dr 89120
Chaparral Cove Ln 89131
Chaparral Summit Dr 89117
Chapel Bells Ct 89156
Chapel Cove Ct 89106
Chapel Heights Ct 89156
Chapel Hill Ln 89110
Chapel Pines Ln 89117
Chapelle Ct 89131
Chapin Mesa Ave 89139
Chapleton Ct 89178
Chaplin Cove Ave 89183
Chapman Dr 89104
Chapman Pt 89129
Chapman Heights St 89138
Chapman Hill Dr 89128
Chapman Ravine St 89131
Charbonne Pl 89145
Chardonay Way 89108
Chariot Ln 89110
Chariots Path Ct 89142
Charismatic Ct 89141
Charity St 89148

Charlemagne Ave 89130
Charlemont Dr 89134
Charles Ct 89145
Charles Bent Ct 89179
Charles Conrad Cir 89145
Charles Holden Ct 89103
Charles Lam Ct 89117
Charles Ronald Ave 89121
Charles Thomas Ct 89149
Charles Turk Dr 89145
E Charleston Blvd
  1-4899 89104
  4901-5099 89104
  5101-5127 89142
  5129-7099 89142
W Charleston Blvd
  2-6 89102
  8-4720 89102
  4722-4798 89102
  4800-6799 89146
  6800-8999 89117
  9001-9999 89117
  10000-10124 89135
  10126-12299 89135
Charleville Ave 89106
Charlie Ct 89122
Charlie Chaplin Ave 89122
Charlo Dr 89131
Charlottsville Ct 89149
Charlton Valley Ct 89123
Charm Ct 89129
Charm Canyon Ave 89178
Charmaine St 89104
Charmast Ln 89102
Charming Dale Way 89117
Charneta Ct 89130
Charnut Ln 89115
Charreado Ct 89179
Charring Cross Way 89117
Charro Ct 89179
Chartan Ave
  1-399 89183
  4901-4999 89141
  7600-7750 89179
Chartered Cir 89101
Charterhouse Way 89113
Charteroak St 89108
Chartreuse Ct 89122
Chartwell Ct 89135
Chase Canyon Ct 89147
Chase Glen Cir 89121
Chase Hallow St 89149
Chase Tree St 89144
Chasewood Ave 89148
Chasing Heart Way 89115
Chasing Star Ave 89123
Chason St 89107
Chastain Ln 89115
Chastine St 89145
Chatara Way 89148
Chateau Meadow St 89129
Chateau St Jean Dr 89123
Chateau Whistler Ct 89148
Chatfield Dr 89128
Chatham Cir 89119
Chatsworth Ct 89142
Chattanooga Ave 89122
Chaucer St 89135
Chaumont St 89123
Checkerboard Ct 89149
Cheddar St 89117
Cheerful Cir 89147
Cheerful Brook Ave 89143
Cheerful Valley Ave 89178
Chehalis Cir 89107
Chela Cir, Ct & Dr 89120
Chelsea Cir 89107
Chelsea Gardens Dr 89135
Chelsea Grove St 89122
Chelseann St 89110
Cheltenham St 89129
Chenille Ct 89149
Chenin Ave 89129
Chepstow Ave 89178
Cherbourg Ave 89141
Cherico St 89129

Cherish Ave 89128
Cherish River St 89178
Cherokee Ave E 89121
W Cherokee Ave
  5800-5999 89103
  8900-10099 89147
Cherokee Ln
  1200-1399 89106
  1500-1599 89169
  1601-1799 89169
Cherokee Corner Ave 89129
Cherokee Landing St 89179
Cherokee Run Ct 89131
Cherokee Silver Ave 89129
Cherry Ln 89104
Cherry Blossom Ct 89130
Cherry Brook St 89183
Cherry Canyon Ave 89129
Cherry Creek Cir 89135
Cherry Falls Ct 89130
Cherry Glaze Ave 89145
Cherry Glen Pl 89138
Cherry Grove Ave 89156
Cherry Hills Ct 89148
Cherry Meadows Ct 89145
Cherry Melee Ave 89148
Cherry Orchard St 89123
Cherry Ridge Ct 89129
Cherry River Dr 89145
Cherry Springs Ct 89117
Cherry Tree Ln 89108
Cherry Valley Cir 89145
Cherrydale Ct 89147
Cherrystone Ct 89121
Cherrywood St 89108
Cherrywood Forest Ln 89156
Chert Ave 89139
Chertsey Dr 89108
Cherum St 89135
Chervil Valley Dr 89138
Cherwell Ct 89144
Cheryl Lynne Ct 89139
Chesapeake Cir 89108
Chesapeake Cove St 89166
Cheshire Ct 89108
Chessie Ct 89147
Chessington Ave 89131
Chessman Way 89147
Chest Park Ave 89131
Chester Creek Ct 89141
Chesterbrook Ct 89135
Chestermere Ct 89135
Chesterton Dr 89128
Chestnut Ln 89123
Chestnut St 89119
Chestnut Chase St 89138
Chestnut Glen Ave 89131
Chestnut Hill St 89134
Chestnut Hollow Ave 89131
Chestnut Sweet St 89131
Chestnut Timber Ct 89129
Chestnut Valley St 89166
Chestnut Wood Ave 89148
Chestwood Ave 89123
Chettle House Ln 89122
Cheval Lake Way 89148
Chevoit Ct 89129
Chevy Chase Ave 89110
E Cheyenne Ave
  3600-3898 89115
  3900-4699 89115
  4701-4899 89115
  5100-5499 89156
W Cheyenne Ave
  4900-5098 89130
  5201-5397 89108
  5399-6700 89108
  6702-6898 89108
  7300-10100 89129
  10102-10498 89129
Cheyenne Dawn St 89183
Chianti Ln 89117
Chic Ave 89129
Chica Way 89120
E Chicago Ave 89104
W Chicago Ave 89102

Chickasaw Bend Ct 89129
Chickasaw Cedar Ct 89129
Chicopee St 89147
Chicory Falls Ct 89148
Chief Sky St 89178
N Chieftain St
  4001-4297 89129
  4299-4699 89129
  4800-4898 89149
  4900-6899 89149
S Chieftain St 89117
Chigoza Pine Ave 89135
Chikasaw Way 89169
Child Ct 89103
Childers Ave 89178
Childress Dr 89134
Chili Pepper St 89118
Chillingham Dr 89183
Chilly Pond Ave 89129
Chiltern Ave 89129
Chilton Ct 89108
Chimayo Ln 89122
Chimes Tower Ave 89139
Chimney Flat Ct 89129
Chimney Point Ct 89166
Chimney Wood Ave 89130
Chin Cactus Ct 89106
China Dr 89121
China Bend Rd 89118
China Creek Ct 89131
China Rain St 89178
China Ridge Ct 89149
Chinatown St 89166
Chinchilla Ave 89121
Chinese Fir Dr 89141
Chino Peak Ct 89139
Chinook Way 89108
Chinook Candy Ct 89113
Chinook Gale Ct 89183
Chippewa Cir & Dr 89169
Chippindale Ln 89108
Chiquita Dr 89128
Chirr Ln 89121
Chisolm Trl 89118
Chisos Dr 89103
Chloride Ct 89110
Chocolate St 89122
Chocolate Hills Ct 89113
Choctaw Valley Dr 89179
Chokeberry Ct 89108
Cholla Way 89101
Cholla Cactus Ave 89141
Chorleywood Way 89131
Chrisman Ave 89129
Christchurch Ave 89110
Christian Cir 89131
Christinas Cove Ave 89131
Christine Falls Ave 89130
Christine View Ct 89129
Christopher Lee Cir 89129
Christpher Ct 89110
N Christy Ln
  1-197 89110
  199-1599 89110
  1600-2399 89156
S Christy Ln 89142
Chrome Hill St 89139
Chrysalis Dr 89121
Chuparosa Ct 89141
Church Bonnet St 89178
Church Steeple St 89131
Churchfield Blvd, Cir &
Ct 89103
Churchill Ave & St 89107
Churchill Downs Dr 89117
Churnet Valley Ave 89139
Chutney St 89121
Cicada Way 89121
Cicero Pl 89110
Cider Ct 89144
Cider Mill Rd 89135
Cider Springs Ct 89148
Cielo Ln 89130
Cielo Amber Ln 89138
Cielo Oro St 89113
Cielo Vista Ave 89128

N Cimarron Rd
  101-259 89145
  1100-1199 89128
  3200-3998 89129
  4000-4799 89129
  4800-5199 89149
  5201-5699 89149
  7501-7599 89131
S Cimarron Rd
  100-999 89145
  1001-1099 89145
  1101-1997 89117
  1999-2600 89117
  2602-2898 89117
  6601-6897 89113
  6899-8499 89113
  8501-8799 89113
  9201-9297 89178
  9299-9399 89178
Cimarron Cove St 89156
Cimarron Crest St 89144
Cimarron Meadows
Way 89147
Cimarron Ridge Dr 89128
Cimarron River Ct 89149
Cina Ave 89147
E Cincinnati Ave 89104
W Cincinnati Ave 89102
Cinder Ln 89103
Cinder Rock Dr 89128
Cinderella Ln 89102
Cindy Way 89146
Cindysue St 89106
Cinnabar Ave 89110
Cinnabar Ridge Ave 89130
Cinnamon Ave 89122
Cinnamon Bear Ave 89131
Cinnamon Cactus Ct 89106
Cinnamon Crest Pl 89135
Cinnamon Hill Ave 89129
Cinnamonwood Way 89115
Circle Dr 89101
Circus Circus Dr 89109
Cirrus Ave 89121
Cisco Ln 89123
Cita Vista Cir 89149
Citadel Cir 89118
Citation Cir 89123
Citrine Ave 89130
Citroen St 89142
Citrus Hills Ave 89106
Citrus Meadow Ct 89131
Citrus Vine Ct 89129
Cituswood Ct 89106
N City Pkwy 89106
City Clouds Ct 89134
City Hill Ct 89134
City View Ct 89117
Civiletti St 89141
Civita St 89141
Clackamas Ct 89122
Clagett Ln 89110
Claim Jumper Dr 89108
Claire D Ln 89120
Claire Rose Ave 89183
Clairemont St 89110
Clairton Ct 89117
Clairville St 89110
Clamdigger Ln 89117
Clancy St 89156
Clandara Ave 89121
Clapton Way 89148
Clara Bow Ave 89122
Clare Ave 89147
Claremore Ct 89110
Claret Cir 89130
Claretta Dr 89129
Clarges Ln 89110
Clarice Ave 89107
Clarion Ln 89134
Clarion River Dr 89135
Clarita Cavern St 89139
E Clark Ave 89101
Clark St 89122
Clark Petersen Blvd 89165
Clark Point Ct 89134

Clark Towers Ct 89102
Clark Wooldridge Ct 89129
Clarkdale Dr 89128
Clarks Creek St 89131
Clarkson St 89108
Clarkway Dr 89106
Classic Bay Ln 89117
Classic Villa Ct 89128
Classique Ave 89178
Classy Cashmere Ct 89149
Clatsop St 89122
Claudine Dr 89156
Claverton Ct 89148
Clay St 89115
Clay Bluff Ave 89178
Clay Peak Dr 89129
Clay Tablet St 89149
Claybourne Ct 89148
Claybrooke Way 89121
Claymont St 89119
Claystone Ct 89129
Claythorn Rd 89148
Clayton St 89110
Clear Ave 89147
Clear Blue Dr 89117
Clear Brook Pl 89103
Clear Creek Rd 89110
Clear Crest Cir 89123
Clear Crystal St 89183
Clear Day Ln 89178
Clear Diamond Ave 89123
Clear Lake Ct 89115
Clear Meadows Dr 89134
Clear Peak Ct 89156
Clear Range Ave 89178
Clear Sail Ct 89139
Clear Sky Ave 89178
Clear Valley Ave 89142
Clear View Dr 89121
Clearbreeze Ct 89129
Clearview Ave 89124
Clearwater Ave & Cir 89147
Clearweed Ct 89149
Clearwood Ave 89123
Cleary Ct 89108
Cleek St 89142
Cleghorn Canyon Way 89113
Clement Ct 89123
Clementine St 89110
Clemmons Ct 89135
Cleopatra Ave 89115
E Cleveland Ave 89104
W Cleveland Ave 89102
Clewiston Ave 89131
Cliff Crest St 89147
Cliff Edge Ct 89129
Cliff Harbor Dr 89129
Cliff Lake St 89179
Cliff Mountain Ave 89129
Cliff Park St 89178
Cliff Peaks St 89149
Cliff Point Ct 89149
Cliff Ridge Ave 89129
Cliff Shadows Pkwy 89129
Cliff Sieler Ct 89117
Cliff Swallow Ave 89144
Cliff Valley Dr 89148
Cliff View Way 89117
Clifford Ave 89104
Clifford St 89115
Clifford Walk Ave 89148
Cliffords Tower Ct 89135
Cliffrose Dr 89130
Cliffs Edge Cir 89123
Cliffside Ct 89145
Clifftop Dr 89134
Clifton Cir 89108
Clifton Forge Ave 89148
Clifton Gardens St 89166
Clifton Heights Dr 89145
Clifton Hollow St 89113
Clifton Park Ct 89110
Climbing Fern Way 89115
Climbing Lily St 89183
Climbing Rose St 89147
Climbing Vine Ave 89141

Cline St 89145
Cline Cellars Ave 89123
Cline Mountain St 89131
Clinton Ln 89156
Clock Tower Ct 89117
Clonshire Ct 89129
Cloud Cir 89145
Cloud Break St 89178
Cloud Nine Ln 89115
Cloud View Cir 89119
Cloudberry Ct 89147
Cloudburst Ave 89128
Cloudcroft Ave 89134
Cloudland Canyon St 89129
Clouds Rest Ave 89108
Cloudsdale Cir 89117
Cloudy Bay Ct 89141
Cloudy Mountain Pl 89178
Cloudy Ridge Ct 89130
Cloudy Sky Ln 89115
Clove Bud Dr 89142
Clover Canyon Ln 89142
Clover Creek Ct 89130
Clover Field Ct 89183
Clover Path St 89128
Clover Ridge St 89147
Clover Tip Ct 89123
Clover Valley Ct 89149
Clover Wood Ln 89156
Cloverbrook St 89117
Cloverdale Ave 89121
Cloverdale Ct 89117
Cloverhill Ct 89147
Cloverleaf Cir 89142
Cloverstone Ct 89139
Clovery Ct 89183
Clovis Cir 89108
Club Ct 89144
Club House Dr 89142
Club Pacific Way 89128
Clusterberry Cir 89110
Clybourn Ct 89144
Clydene Dr 89156
Clydesdale St 89119
Coach Ln 89101
Coachlight Cir 89117
Coachman Cir 89119
Coal Canyon Ave 89129
Coal Creek Pl 89134
Coaldale Pl 89110
Coast Line Ct 89117
Coast Valley St 89149
Coast Walk Cir 89117
Coastal Breeze Ct 89108
Coatbridge St 89145
Cobal Canyon Ln 89129
Cobalt Ln 89146
Cobb Ln 89101
Cobbhan Dr 89179
Cobble Cove Way 89156
Cobble Creek Ct 89108
Cobble Village Ct 89117
Cobblefield St 89123
Cobblestone Ave 89145
Cobblestone Hill Ct 89166
Cobbs Creek Way 89148
Cobbs Hill St 89139
Cobden Ct 89147
Cobra Ct 89142
Cobre Azul Ave 89108
Cochise Ln 89169
Cochise Bend Ave 89113
Cochran St 89104
Cocktail Dr 89130
Coco Ln 89141
Coco Palms Ave 89123
Cocoa Beach Cir 89128
Coconino Ln 89129
Coconut Ct 89108
Coconut Grove Ct 89145
Codazzi Way 89139
Coder Ct 89118
Cody Pass 89128
Cody Creek St 89149
Coe Estates Ct 89149
Coffee Ave 89147

Coffee Grinder Ct 89129
Coffee Pot Ct 89106
Coffee Tree Ct 89123
Coffeeberry Ct 89183
Coffeeville Creek Dr 89122
Coffeyville Ave 89147
Cog Hill Ln 89134
Cogburn St 89131
Cogswell Ave 89134
Cohasset St 89110
Coke St 89131
Colanthe Ave 89102
Colbath St 89110
Colburn Ln 89123
Colchester St 89117
Cold Brook Ave 89148
Cold Lake St 89148
Cold Mountain Ave 89129
Cold River Ave 89130
Cold Springs Ct 89113
Cold Springs Rd 89124
Cold Stream Dr 89110
Coldwater Dr 89110
Coldwater Bay Dr 89122
Coldwater Canyon Ct 89123
Coldwater Falls Way 89123
Cole Younger Ct 89129
Colebrook St 89115
Coleridge Way 89142
Coleshill St 89135
Coley Ave
  5501-5797 89146
  5799-6799 89146
  6801-6899 89146
  6900-7699 89117
  7701-7799 89117
Colfax Cir 89108
Colfax Crest St 89131
Colgate Ln 89110
Colina Alta Pl 89138
Colina Bella Ct 89142
Colinward Ave 89135
Coliseum Ln 89144
Collanade Ct 89128
Colleen Dr 89107
College Cir & Pl 89156
College Green St 89148
College Park Ln 89110
Collete Cir 89123
Collier Falls Ave 89139
Collier Hills St 89149
Colliers Ct 89131
Collin Crossing St 89130
Collingsworth St 89131
Collingtree St 89145
Collingwood St 89147
Collins Ave 89106
Collinsleap Ct 89123
Collinson Cir 89115
Colonial Cir & Dr 89121
Colonial Springs Ct 89148
Colony Creek Ln 89135
Colony Grant Way 89108
Colony Hills Dr 89134
Colony Pine St 89144
Color Canyon Way 89156
Color Rock Ct 89178
Color Up Ct 89122
E Colorado Ave 89104
W Colorado Ave 89102
Colorado Blue St 89123
Colorado Spruce St 89149
Colored Wind Ave 89148
Colorful Pines Ave 89143
Colorful Rainbow Ave 89166
Colors Ct 89131
Colossal Cave Ave 89131
Colt Pl 89119
Colt Ravine Ct 89178
Colter Bay Ct 89129
Coltman Loop 89115
E Colton Ave 89115
Columbia Crest Ct 89117
Columbia Falls Ct 89149
Columbia Pike Ave 89183
Columbine Way 89108

Street	ZIP
Columbus St	89121
Column Ct	89149
Column Cactus St	89139
Colusa Cir	89110
Coluter Pine Ave	89129
Colwood Ln	89130
Comanche Canyon Ave	89113
Comb Cir & Ct	89104
Comchec Way	89108
Cominskey St	89123
Comiskey Ct	89148
Comiskey Park St	89166
Comitan Ln	89122
Commanche Ave	89121
Commanche Cir	89169
Commanche Dr	89169
Commanche Agate Ct	89179
Commanche Creek Ave	89179
Commanche Moon Ave	89129
Commendation Dr	89117
S Commerce St	
800-1098	89106
1100-1699	89102
1701-1899	89102
Commodore Cove Dr	89142
Common Wealth Dr	89110
Community Ln	89121
Community College Dr	89146
Comnor Hill Ln	89121
Compass Bow Ln	89130
Compass Cove Ave	89142
Compass Point Cir	89117
Compass Rose Way	89108
Compo Ave	89123
Composer Way	89145
Compton Dr	89108
Comstock Dr	89106
Comstock Lode Ln	89118
Comstock Stake Ct	89183
Conan St	89129
Concert Dr	89107
Concertino Ave	89123
Concetta Ave	89129
Conchita St	89108
Concho Ln	89146
Concho River Ave	89148
Concord St	89106
Concord Downs Ave	89117
Concord Heights St	89149
Concord Village Dr	89108
Concordia Pl	89104
Concrete Ct	89110
Condor Ave	89108
Condotti Ct	89117
Conerwood St	89141
Conestoga Trl	89108
Coney Island Ave	89123
Confetti Cir	89145
Congaree St	89141
Conglobate St	89122
Congress Ave	89121
Congressional Ct	89113
Conifer Ln	89145
E Conn Ave	89183
W Conn Ave	89141
Connell St	89129
Connemara Ave	89128
Conners Dr	89107
Connex Ct	89178
Connie Ave	89115
Connie Ct	89107
Connie Dr	89107
Conough Ln	
3400-4400	89129
4402-4598	89129
4800-5199	89149
Conquest Ct	89149
Conquista Ct	89121
N Conquistador St	
4500-4598	89129
4601-4699	89129
4901-5997	89149
5999-6300	89149
6302-7098	89149
S Conquistador St	
5100-5298	89148
5300-5399	89148
5401-5499	89148
9400-9499	89161
Conrad Cir & St	89121
Conroe Ct	89118
Constable St	89135
Constanso Ave	89128
Constantine Ave	89101
Constantinople Ave	89129
Constellation St	89123
Construction Ave	89122
Consul Ave	89142
Contadero Pl	89138
Contera Ct	89120
Contesa Cir	89101
Contessing Way	89108
Continental Ave	89156
Contorno Vista Ct	89138
Contract Ave	89101
Contrada Ct	89148
Contralto St	89139
Convaire Ave	89115
Convention Center Dr	89109
Conville Pl	89120
Convinto St	89131
Cook Bluff Ave	89129
Cook Inlet Ave	89179
Cook Islands Ct	89139
Cookman Ln	89135
Cooks Creek Ct	89148
Cookshack Ln	89118
Cookson Ct	89156
Cool Creek Ave	89147
Cool Dawn Ct	89130
Cool Forest St	89117
Cool Meadows Dr	89129
Cool Melon Ct	89139
Cool Mist St	89178
Cool Springs St	89143
Cool Valley Dr	89110
Coolaire Dr	89117
Coolcrest Ct	89103
Coolidge Ave	89101
Cooper Cir	89101
Cooper Ranch Ct	89123
Cooperville Ct	89123
Copalito Dr	89178
Copano Bay Ave	89148
Copenhagen Way	89147
Copious Cactus Ct	89149
Copley Cir	89120
Copparo Pl	89134
Copper Rd	89110
Copper Basin Dr	89129
Copper Bay Ave	89129
Copper Beach Ct	89117
Copper Bracelet Ave	89122
Copper Cactus Dr	89129
Copper Canyon Rd	89128
Copper Crest Dr	89130
Copper Crown Ct	89129
Copper Falls Ave	89129
Copper Fountain St	89138
Copper Glen St	89129
Copper Harbor Ct	89130
Copper Hill Ct	89110
Copper Island St	89131
Copper Keg Ct	89129
Copper Kettle Ave	89130
Copper Knoll Ave	89129
Copper Mesa Dr	89134
Copper Mine Ave	89129
Copper Mountain Ave	89129
Copper Ridge Ave	89129
Copper River Ave	89130
Copper Sage St	89115
Copper Valley Ct	89144
Copper Villa Ct	89129
Copperfield Ave	89108
Copperhead Creek St	89143
Copperhead Hills St	89129
Copperleaf Dr	89128
Copperlyn St	89122
Coppertip Ave	89179
Coppola St	89141
Copthorn Pl	89178
Cora Hills Ct	89148
Coral Way	89117
Coral Aloe St	89106
Coral Bell Ct	89123
Coral Berry St	89123
Coral Bisque St	89123
Coral Blaze Ct	89143
Coral Cameo Ct	89183
Coral Desert Dr	89123
Coral Falls Cir	89108
Coral Flower Ct	89141
Coral Gables Dr	89130
Coral Gate St	89148
Coral Glow Ct	89149
Coral Harbor Dr	89117
Coral Isle Way	89108
Coral Point Ave	89128
Coral Rainbow Ave	89123
Coral Reef Way	89110
Coral Ribbon Ave	89139
Coral River Dr	89131
Coral Rock Dr	89108
Coral Rose Ct	89134
Coral Sands Dr	89117
Coral Shale St	89123
Coral Shine Ct	89123
Coral Silk Ct	89110
Coral Sky Ct	89142
Coral Springs Cir	89108
Coral View St	89110
Coral Vine Way	89142
Coral Vine Arbor Ave	89144
Coralite Dr	89128
Coralwood Dr	89135
Coran Ln	
2701-3097	89106
3099-3400	89106
3402-3698	89106
3901-4097	89108
4099-4599	89108
4601-4699	89108
Corato St	89123
Corazon Dr	89103
Corbel Ct	89131
Corbett St	
5300-6299	89130
8201-8397	89149
8399-9900	89149
9902-10298	89149
Corbin Ave	89122
Corbridge St	89178
Corby Crossing St	89131
Corcoran St	89148
Cordelle Dr	89156
Cordero Bay Ave	89123
Cordial Cloth Ct	89149
Cordite Rd	89178
Cordoba Ln	89108
Cordoba Bluff Ct	89135
Cordoba Canyon St	89117
Cordonbleu Ct	89122
Cordova St	89104
Cordova Vista Ct	89183
Corey Creek Ct	89148
Cori Rosso Ln	89141
Coriander Ln	89129
Coriander Canyon Ct	89138
Corinne Ct	89103
Corium Ct	89122
Corkfish St	89178
Corkseed Ct	89130
Cormorant Ave	89115
Cormorant Lake Way	89178
Corn Lily Ct	89149
Corncob Cactus Ct	89106
Cornell Ct	89104
Cornellia St	89146
Cornflower Dr	89128
Cornhusk Rd	89142
Corning Dr	89117
Cornish Ct	89123
Cornstalk Cir	89142
Cornwall Ave	89129
Cornwall Crossing Ln	89147
Cornwall Glen Ave	89129
Corona Ave	89169
Corona Del Mar Dr	89108
Corona Hill Ct	89123
Corona Run Ave	89123
Corona Valley St	89144
Corona Vista St	89135
Coronado Ave	89169
Coronado Canyon Ave	89142
Coronado Coast St	89139
Coronado Crest Ave	89139
Coronado Hills Way	89115
Coronado Island St	89139
Coronado Palms Ave	89139
Coronado Peak Ave	89183
Coronation Ave	89123
Corpolo Ave	89141
Corpus Christi Ct	89156
Corral Cir, Ct & Pl	89119
Correen Hills Ct	89139
Corrigan Pl	89138
Corrines Point St	89148
Corsage Ct	89142
Corsaire Ave	89115
Corset Creek St	89131
Corsica Ln	89144
Corsica Crest Ct	89123
Corsica Mist Ave	89135
Corsicana St	89138
Corta Bella Dr	89134
Corte Castillo St	89123
Corte De Casa Cir	89149
Corte Sierra St	89183
Cortez Ct	89145
Cortez Bank Way	89183
Cortile Dr	89134
Cortina Ave	89142
Cortina Rancho St	89147
Cortney Ridge Ct	89149
Cortu Ave	89141
Corvette St	89142
Corvina Ave	89113
Cory Pl	89107
Cosenza Ln	89141
Cosley Dr	89147
Cosmic Dr	89115
Cosmo Ln	89130
Cosmos Ct	89183
Costa Pl	89146
Costa Blanca Ave	89138
Costa Brava Rd	89146
Costa De Oro Ct	89131
Costa Linda Ave	89138
Costa Mesa Ave	89110
Costa Miole Dr	89141
Costa Smeralda Cir	89117
Costa Verde St	89146
Costabella Ln	89130
Costanoa St	89123
Costello Cir	89108
Cote Rd	89161
Cotillion Ct	89147
Cotsfield Ave	89139
Cotswold St	89129
Cottage Cir	89119
Cottage Grove Ave	89119
Cotton St	89110
Cotton Bloom Ct	89149
Cotton Cloud Rd	89117
Cotton Rose Way	89134
Cottoneaster St	89135
Cottonsparrow St	89131
Cottontail Ln	89121
Cottontail Cove St	89130
Cottonwillow St	89135
Cottonwood Pl	89104
Cottonwood Canyon Ct	89141
E Cougar Ave	89123
W Cougar Ave	
3301-3397	89139
3399-6349	89139
6351-6699	89139
7100-8298	89113
8300-8400	89113
8402-8598	89113
8601-8699	89148
11500-12999	89161
Cougar Creek Cir	89123
Cougar Crossing St	89178
Cougar Estates Ln	89123
Cougar Ridge Trl	89124
Coulter Canyon St	89141
Coulthard Dr	89107
Council Ave	89128
Council Crest Ct	89142
Council Heights Way	89142
Count Carlson Cir	89119
Count Fleet St	89113
Count Wutzke Ave	89119
Counterpoint Ln	89123
Country Ct	89145
Country Air Ln	89117
Country Apple Ave	89183
Country Back Rd	89123
Country Cottage Ct	89117
Country Cove Ct	89135
Country Crossings St	89123
Country Day Ln	89119
Country Flats Ln	89135
Country Garden Ave	89110
Country Greens Ave	89148
Country Highlands Ct	89178
Country Hollow Dr	89117
Country Home Cir	89149
Country Knoll Way	89135
Country Lights St	89129
Country Manor Ln	89115
Country Mile Dr	89135
Country Pines Ave	89129
Country Retreat Ct	89131
Country Ridge Ct	89123
Country Scene Way	89117
Country Shadows Way	89123
Country Skies Ave	89123
Country View Ave	89129
Country Village Pl	89113
Country Vista Way	89117
Country Wind Way	89123
Country Wine Ct	89129
Countrywood Cir	89107
Couples St	89128
Courage Ct	89115
Court St	89121
Courtfield Cir	89130
Courtney Cir & Ln	89107
Courtney Cove Ave	89144
Courtside Ln	89108
Cove Rd	89128
Cove Cahill Ct	89130
Cove Haven Ct	89178
Cove Landing Ave	89145
Cove Links Ave	89131
Cove Point Dr	89130
Covek Crossing Ave	89156
Covelo Ct	89146
Covenant Crest Ct	89131
Covent Garden Ct	89145
Coventry Cir	89121
Coventry Gardens Dr	89135
Coventry Glenn Rd	89148
Covered Wagon Ave	89117
Covered Wells Ave	89123
Covey Ln	89115
Covington Ln	89106
Covington Cross Dr	89144
Covington Gardens St	89131
Cow Pony Dr	89123
Cow Town Ln	89118
Cowan Cir	89107
Cowboy Trl	89131
Cowboy Fiddle Ct	89131
Cowboy Inn Ave	89178
Cowboy Rain Dr	89178
Cowboys Dream St	89131
Coyado St	89123
Coyote Brush Ct	89129
Coyote Cave Ave	89113
Coyote Crest Ct	89147
Coyote Crossing St	89129
Coyote Cub Ave	89129
Coyote Falls Ct	89131
Coyote Lakes Ct	89122
Coyote Meadow Ave	89131
Coyote Peak Cir	89147
Coyote Ridge Ct	89129
Coyote Rock Ct	89138
Cozette Ct	89144
Cozumel Pl	89131
Cozy Corner St	89156
Cozy Glen Cir	89117
Cozyloft Dr	89123
Cracker Barrel St	89143
Cradle Mountain Dr	89134
Craftsbury Ct	89130
Cragin Park Dr	89107
E Craig Rd	89115
W Craig Rd	
4800-5900	89130
5902-6098	89130
6400-6998	89108
7001-7097	89129
7099-9699	89129
Craighead Ln	89117
Craigmont Ave	89103
Crakow Ct	89147
Cram Dr	89110
Cranberry Ln	89156
Cranberry Cove Ct	89135
Cranberry Lake Ave	89178
Cranbrook Cir & Way	89103
Cranbrook Cross St	89179
Cranbrook Falls Ct	89148
Cranbrook Hill St	89129
Crandon Park Ave	89131
Cranesbill Ct	89149
Cranston Ct	89135
Cranstonhill Dr	89148
Cranwood Ct	89130
Crassula Pagoda Ave	89139
Crater Cir & St	89122
Craven Ave	89149
Crawfish Bay St	89179
Crazy Train Ct	89131
Crazyhorse Way	89110
Creative Ct	89149
Cree Ave	89123
Creed Mountain Pl	89178
Creedmoor Ct	89148
Creek Bed Ct	89129
Creek Canyon Ave	89113
Creek Forest Ct	89148
Creek River Dr	89129
Creek Village Ave	89183
Creek Water Ln	89123
Creekside Ln	89145
Creekstone Ct	89113
Creekview Ct	89117
Creeping Fig Ct	89129
Creeping Thyme St	89148
Creeping Zinnia Ct	89138
Crellin Cir	89120
Crema Ct	89129
Cremona Dr	89117
Crenshaw Way	89129
Crepe Myrtle Ct	89183
Crescendo St	89129
Crescent Dr	89102
Crescent Canyon St	89129
Crescent Landing St	89113
Crescent Lodge Ct	89178
Crescent Ridge Ln	89134
Crescent Run Ct	89117
Crescentville Ave	89131
Cresco Ct	89141
Cresent Creek Dr	89134
Cresent Mesa Ln	89145
Cresent Valley St	89148
Creslow Ct	89102
Crespo Ct	89122
Cressida Ct	89113
Crest Ave	89119
Crest Basin Ct	89123
Crest Brook Pl	89134
Crest Estates St	89131
Crest Haven Ave	89108
Crest Hill Ave	89145
Crest Horn Dr	89147
Crest Peak Ave	89130
Crest Village Ct	89129
Crestdale Ln	89144
Crestfield Ln	89108
N & S Crestline Dr	89107
Crestline Falls Pl	89134
Crestline Heights Ct	89178
Crestlock Dr	89113
Creston Ave	89103
Crestpoint Way	89134
Crestview Dr	
1-1699	89124
3600-3799	89120
Crestwood Ave	89104
Creswell Ct	89148
Cretan Blue Ln	89128
Crete Ln	89103
Crib Point Dr	89134
Cricket Flat Ct	89131
Crimson Ave	89129
Crimson Canyon Dr	89128
Crimson Clover Way	89134
Crimson Creek Ct	89139
Crimson Crest Pl	89149
Crimson Dusk Ct	89135
Crimson Glory Ln	89130
Crimson Hills Dr	89128
Crimson Leaf Dr	89130
Crimson Mare Rd	89139
Crimson Palisades Pl	89144
Crimson Point St	89149
Crimson Ridge Dr	89130
Crimson Rose Ave	89138
Crimson Sky St	89178
Crimson View Pl	89144
Crinoline Ave	89122
Criollo Dr	89122
Cripple Gulch Ct	89178
Crisp Clover St	89183
Crispinio St	89141
Cristobal Way	89117
Crockery St	89130
Crockett Cir	89108
Crockston Ct	89183
Crocus Hill St	89138
Croft Way	89110
Crofton Cir	89123
Cromberg Ave	89145
Cromwell Ave & Cir	89107
Crooked Ct	89123
Crooked Bow Cir	89149
Crooked Branch St	89143
Crooked Corner St	89134
Crooked Creek Ave	89123
Crooked Mountain Ct	89149
Crooked Path Ct	89129
Crooked Pine Dr	89134
Crooked Putter Dr	89148
Crooked River Cir	89149
Crooked Shell Ave	89143
Crooked Sky Cir	89149
Crooked Stick Way	89113
Crooked Tree Dr	89148
Crooked Valley Dr	89149
Crooked Wood Ave	89148
Crosley Field Ave	89166
Cross Ln	89149
Cross Country St	89144
Cross Creek Way	89117
Cross Meadows Ln	89122
Cross Plains St	89113
Cross Ridge St	89135
Cross Stitch Ct	89149
Crossdale Ave	89142
Crosseto Dr	89141
Crossfield Ave	89122
Crosspointe Ave	89117
Crosstimber Ct	89108
Crossway Dr	89108
Crosswind Way	89145
Crosswood Ave	89108
Crow Butte Ct	89139
Crow Canyon Ave	89179
Crow Creek Ave	89123
Crow Valley Ln	89113

Crowbush Cove Pl 89122
Crowder St 89139
Crowley Way 89142
Crown Ct 89141
Crown Bluffs Ct 89117
Crown Cove Ct 89117
Crown Crest Ln 89135
Crown Cypress St 89149
Crown Jewel St 89130
Crown Palms Ave 89139
Crown Peak Ave 89117
Crown Pines Ct 89123
Crown Point Ave 89110
Crown Ridge Dr 89134
Crown Rock Ct 89139
Crown Vista Ln 89117
Crownbeard St 89149
Crownhaven Ct 89108
Crowntop Cir 89118
Crows Nest Ln 89128
Croyden St 89131
Cruiser Ct 89156
Crusader Ct 89115
Crushed Velvet Pl 89166
Crusoe Creek Ct 89141
Crusted Dome Ct 89139
Cruz Bay Ct 89128
Crying Bird Ave 89178
Crystal Ann Ave 89106
Crystal Arch Ave 89129
Crystal Bay Dr 89117
Crystal Beach Dr 89128
Crystal Brook Ct 89149
Crystal Cascade St 89130
Crystal Cave Dr 89117
Crystal Chimes Dr 89106
Crystal Clear Ave 89113
Crystal Cloud Ave 89129
Crystal Coral Way 89123
Crystal Cove Dr 89117
Crystal Creek Cir 89128
Crystal Crest Ct 89135
Crystal Cup Cir 89117
Crystal Dew Dr 89118
Crystal Downs Ave 89123
Crystal Forrest Dr 89117
Crystal Gem St 89106
Crystal Glass Dr 89117
Crystal Glen Ct 89117
Crystal Haven Ln 89123
Crystal Isle Way 89128
Crystal Lagoon Ct 89147
Crystal Lake Ct 89134
Crystal Lilly Ct 89130
Crystal Mesa Dr 89134
Crystal Mountain Dr 89117
Crystal Ocean St 89130
Crystal Palm Ct 89117
Crystal Peak Dr 89115
Crystal Pool Dr 89117
Crystal Port Ave 89147
Crystal Rapids St 89148
Crystal Ridge Rd 89123
Crystal River Ct 89128
Crystal Rock Cir 89123
Crystal Rose Ct 89106
Crystal Run Ln 89122
Crystal Shadows Cir 89119
Crystal Shore Ave 89138
Crystal Star Ct 89145
Crystal Talon St 89130
Crystal Tower St 89129
Crystal Trip Ct 89129
Crystal Valley Dr 89117
Crystal Village Ln 89113
Crystal Water Way 89117
Crystalaire Ct 89123
Cublington Ct 89102
Culberson Ranch Ct 89131
Culbertson St 89122
Culgoa St 89179
Cull Canyon Dr 89110
Culley St 89110
Cullinan Ln 89139
Culmination Ln 89119
Cultural Ct 89149
Cultured Pearl Ct 89139
Culver Ct 89117
Cumberland Creek Ave 89166
Cumberland Gap Ave 89122
Cunning Fellow Ct 89129
Cunningham Dr
  1000-1299 89106
  4800-4899 89115
Cuno Ct 89117
Cupecoy Point Ave 89141
Cupertino Heights Way 89178
Cupids Dart St 89183
Cupp Dr 89131
Curacao Dr 89156
Curbelo Way 89120
Curdsen Way 89110
Cureton Cir 89145
Curiosity Ave 89131
Curlands Cove Dr 89117
Curlew Dr 89122
Curran Way 89106
Currant Lake Way 89148
Currie Dr 89110
Curtin Ct 89123
Curtis Dr 89104
Curtsy Ave 89148
Cusak Close St 89179
Custer Ct 89117
Custom Weave Ct 89149
Cusumano Ct 89141
Cutlass Bay St 89129
Cutler Dr 89117
Cutting Edge Ct 89149
Cutty Way 89130
Cutty Sark St 89117
Cuva Ct 89110
Cy Cliffview Cir 89121
Cy Young Dr 89110
Cycad Tree St 89108
Cyclone Ave 89110
Cygnus St 89117
Cynthia Joy Dr 89134
Cypress Trl 89108
Cypress Gardens Ln 89119
Cypress Glen Ave 89134
Cypress Grove Ct 89129
Cypress Meadows Ln 89144
Cypress Park Ct 89131
Cypress Point Way 89117
Cypress Pond St 89156
Cypress Ridge Ln 89144
Cypress Run Dr 89131
Cypress Tree St 89123
Cypresswood Ave 89134
D St 89106
Daffodil Sun Ave 89166
Dahlia Ln 89107
Dahlia Grove St 89141
Daily Double Ave 89129
Daily Hope Ave 89129
Daines Dr 89124
Daintree Ct 89113
Dairy Creek Ave 89183
Daisetta St 89110
Daisy St 89119
Daisy Dawn Ct 89129
Daisy Hill Ave 89106
Daisy Lee Ave 89108
Daisy Patch St 89183
Daisy Petal St 89130
Daisy Run Ct 89120
Daisy Springs Ct 89148
Dakota Way 89169
Dakota Hills Ave 89123
Dakota Lodge Ave 89123
Dakota Trace Ct 89131
Dalbergia Ave 89122
Dale Evans Dr 89108
Dale Scotty Ln 89130
Dalecrest Dr 89129
Dalegrove Dr 89129
Dalhart St 89121
Dallas Ct 89139
Dallas Ridge Ave 89178
Dallaswood Ln 89156
Dalmahoy Pl 89145
Dalmatian Ln 89107
Dalton Dr 89119
Dalzell Ct 89120
Damascus Ave 89113
Dames Rocket Pl 89148
Damico Dr 89120
Damon Dr 89110
Dana Way 89103
Dana Hills Ct 89134
Dana Maple Ct
  1100-1199 89123
  7900-7999 89131
Dana Point Ct 89117
Dana Rogers Dr 89110
Dana Springs Way 89130
Danaides Ct 89131
Danborough Ct 89106
Danbrook Ct 89110
Dancer Way 89107
Dancing Ave 89131
Dancing Bear Dr 89113
Dancing Breeze Ct 89178
Dancing Bull Ct 89139
Dancing Daffodil Ave 89129
Dancing Dolphin St 89139
Dancing Lasso Ct 89178
Dancing Leaf St 89131
Dancing Lights Ave 89130
Dancing Orchid Ct 89130
Dancing Pond Way 89178
Dancing Rain Ct 89183
Dancing Snow Ct 89149
Dancing Springs St 89143
Dancing Sunset Ct 89143
Dancing Vines Ave 89183
Dancing Winds Pl 89141
Dandy View Ave 89183
Danehurst Ct 89108
Daneri Pl 89147
Danesbury Ct 89123
Danford Pl 89102
Danforth Ave 89141
Danica Way 89122
Daniel Dr 89117
Daniel Boone Ct 89166
Danielson Ave 89129
Danish Garden St 89148
Danmuir Drop Ct 89148
Dannon Ct 89128
Danny Melamed Ave 89110
Dans Glen Pl 89145
Danskin Dr 89166
Danube Ave 89141
Danville Ln 89119
Danyelle Ct 89117
Danza Del Sol Dr 89128
N Dapple Gray Rd
  4400-4498 89129
  4801-5097 89149
  5099-6599 89149
S Dapple Gray Rd
  3500-3599 89147
  6600-6699 89148
  10200-10398 89178
  10400-10799 89178
Dappled Light Ave 89131
Darby Ave
  5600-5698 89146
  5700-6699 89146
  6900-7999 89117
Darby Falls Dr 89134
Darby Gardens Ct 89146
Dardanelle Ct 89117
Dardanelle Valley St 89139
Dark Bird St 89178
Dark Creek Ave 89183
Dark Forest Ave 89123
Dark Hollow Pl 89117
Dark Peak Dr 89134
Dark Sands Ave 89129
Dark Wolf Ave 89123
Darkfeather Way 89139
Darling Ct 89104
Darling Rd 89131
Darlington Ct 89149
Darmak Dr 89102
Darren Thornton Way 89120
Darrow Ct 89166
Darryl Ave 89123
Dart Dr 89144
Dartle St 89130
Dartmoor Ave 89129
Dartmouth Ct 89104
Dartmouth Hills St 89138
Darwell Dr 89117
Dashing Ct 89149
Date St 89108
Date Creek Ave 89134
Date Palm Cir 89108
Davenport Ln 89107
Daventry St 89123
David Ave 89101
David Allen Ct 89149
Davidson Ct 89110
Davies Dr 89118
Davilla St 89146
Davos Way 89124
Dawes Ct 89110
Dawley Ct & St 89104
Dawn Dr 89110
Dawn Breeze Ave 89131
Dawn Falls St 89148
Dawn Garden Ave 89147
Dawn Heights Ct 89178
Dawn Isle Dr 89145
Dawn Peak St 89129
Dawn Ridge Dr 89123
Dawnbreak Dr 89149
Dawnflower St 89121
Dawning Flower Ave 89131
Dawning Heat St 89178
Dawnlight Ave 89123
Dawns Mist Ave 89129
Day Dawn St 89147
Day Hunt Trl 89113
Day Star Ave 89147
Daybreak Dr 89108
Daybreak Dew Ct 89183
Dayflower St 89121
Daylight Moss St 89135
Daylight Peak Ct 89123
Days Creek Ave 89141
Dayspring St 89128
Dayton Ave & Cir 89107
Daytona Ln 89117
Dazzle Accent Ct 89149
Dazzler Ct 89147
Dazzling Gold St 89138
Dazzling Heights Ln 89110
De Forest St 89103
De Met Dr 89119
De Osma St 89102
De Paz Way 89113
De Silva Dr & Pl 89121
De Soto St 89108
Deacon Ave 89101
Deadwood Rd 89108
Deadwood Bend Ct 89178
Deal Dr 89108
Dealers Choice Way 89122
Dean Martin Dr
  3901-3997 89103
  3999-4800 89103
  4802-4898 89103
  4901-5997 89118
  5999-7299 89118
  7300-7398 89139
  7400-9199 89139
  11300-11399 89141
  11401-12099 89141
Dearborn Ct 89108
Death Valley Dr 89122
Deauville St 89106
Debbie Reynolds Dr 89109
Debellis Creek Ct 89131
Debonair Ct 89147
Debra St 89106
Debrilla Dr 89123
Debutante Ct 89130
Decade St 89121
Decatur Blvd 89141
N Decatur Blvd
  101-497 89107
  499-899 89107
  1101-1597 89108
  1599-2676 89108
  2675-2675 89157
  2678-2798 89108
  2701-2799 89108
  3200-6399 89130
  6400-11399 89131
S Decatur Blvd
  100-298 89107
  300-999 89107
  1001-1099 89107
  1100-1800 89102
  1801-3499 89102
  1801-1801 89114
  1801-1801 89126
  1802-3498 89102
  3500-4899 89103
  4901-4997 89118
  4999-7199 89118
  7300-7398 89139
  7400-9399 89139
  9401-9599 89139
Decibel Ct 89139
Decker Canyon Dr 89128
Deckow Ln 89169
Declaration Dr 89110
Decorative Ct 89149
Decoro St 89139
Decosta Cir 89108
Dedham Ct 89129
Deep Autumn Ave 89131
Deep Creek Ln 89156
Deep Forest Dr 89130
Deep Glen St 89178
Deep Ridge Ct 89178
Deep Sea Ct 89110
Deep Shadow Ct 89148
Deep Spring Ave 89123
Deep Stone Ave 89149
Deep Water Cir 89117
Deepriver Cir 89129
Deepwood Ct 89135
Deer Ct 89134
Deer Clan Ct 89131
Deer Creek Rd 89124
Deer Creek Way 89115
Deer Creek Falls Ct 89118
Deer Flats St 89129
Deer Forest Ave 89139
Deer Haven Ct 89120
Deer Heights St 89178
Deer Hollow St 89149
Deer Isle St 89149
Deer Lake St 89134
Deer Lodge Ln 89129
Deer Park Ave 89148
Deer Point Ct 89131
Deer Springs Way
  5100-5898 89131
  5900-7499 89131
  7501-7999 89131
  8200-9699 89149
  9701-10299 89149
Deer Valley Dr 89156
Deer View Ct 89113
Deerbrook Ln 89107
Deerfield Ave & Cir 89147
Deerfield Beach Ave 89129
Deerfield Ranch Ct 89139
Deerfly Way 89145
Deerford Cir 89110
Deering Bay Dr 89131
Defiance Ave 89129
Dehesa Ct 89122
Deichelmann Loop 89115
Del Almo Dr 89104
Del Amo Dr 89110
Del Cira Ave 89183
Del Font Ct 89117
Del Gado Dr 89103
Del Giorno St 89138
Del Lago Dr 89130
Del Lilly Ln 89123
Del Mar Ave 89169
Del Mar Ct 89169
Del Mar Pl 89169
Del Mar St 89119
Del Mar Heights St 89183
Del Marino Dr & St 89121
Del Mira Dr 89128
Del Monte Ave
  4000-4699 89102
  5100-5499 89146
Del Nido Ln 89110
Del Norte Cir 89110
Del Oro Dr 89102
Del Pappa Ct 89130
Del Pueblo Ave 89141
Del Rey Ave
  4101-4197 89102
  4199-4299 89102
  4301-4399 89102
  5100-6799 89146
  6900-6998 89117
  7000-8599 89117
Del Rosa Ct 89121
Del Rudini St 89141
Del Santos Dr 89121
Del Sueno Dr 89120
Del Sur Ave 89138
Del Vista Ct 89113
Del Webb Blvd 89134
Delabarre Pl 89108
Delamar St 89107
Delamere Way 89123
Delancey Dr 89103
Delaney Creek Ln 89134
Delaware Ln 89169
Delaware Bay Dr 89128
Delbonita Ave 89147
Delderfield Ave 89121
Delectable Ct 89149
Delfern Ln 89169
Delft Blue St 89139
W Delhi Ave 89129
Delicate Dew St 89183
Delicate Petal Ct 89149
Delicious Ct 89149
Delightful Ave 89128
Delina Dr 89134
Delivery Ave 89148
Delker Ct 89179
Dell Cliffs Ct 89144
Dell Ridge Ave 89179
Delling Cir & Ct 89104
Delmue Cir 89101
Delonee Skies Ave 89131
Delorean Cir 89108
Delos Dr 89103
Delphi Ct 89117
Delphinium Ave 89108
Delray Beach Ave 89129
Delta St 89101
Delta Falls St 89166
Delta Lake Ct 89148
Delta Oak Ct 89147
Delta Point Way 89117
Delta Rio St 89138
Delta View Ct 89129
Deluca Ct 89141
Deluge Dr 89129
Deluna St 89141
Delwood St 89147
Demars St 89110
Demetrius Ave 89101
Demoline Cir 89141
Demona Dr 89123
Denali Preserve St 89122
Denali Ridge Ct 89129
Denarius Cir 89101
Denaro Dr 89135
Denberry Way 89123
Denby Ave 89106
Dendrite St 89145
Denevin St 89131
Denham Dr 89134
Denia Cir 89108
Denman St 89178
Denning St 89122
Dennis Way 89121
Dentaria Ct 89149
Denton Ranch Rd 89131
Denton Springs Ct 89138
Denver Cir 89107
Denver Sky Ave 89149
Denwood Dr 89147
Deodar Dr 89108
Depaul Ct 89144
Depew Cir 89129
Deputy Way 89119
Derby Creek Way 89148
Derby Peak Ln 89166
Derby Wharf Ct 89166
Derbyhill Cir 89117
Derbyshire Dr 89117
Derek Dr 89103
Derringer Dr 89119
Derwent Pl 89144
Descano Garden Dr 89148
Descanso Ln 89123
Descanso St 89121
Descending Creek St 89123
Desert Ln
  501-597 89106
  599-1099 89106
  1101-1299 89102
Desert Alcove Rd 89178
Desert Bay Dr 89117
Desert Beach Dr 89128
Desert Bell Ave 89128
Desert Bird Dr 89145
Desert Bloom Ct 89129
Desert Blossom Rd 89107
Desert Breeze Ave 89149
Desert Brook Cir 89149
Desert Butte Dr 89134
Desert Cactus Cir 89149
Desert Candle Way 89128
Desert Canyon Ct 89128
Desert Cliff St 89129
Desert Cloud Ave 89131
Desert Clover Ct 89129
Desert Creek Way 89149
Desert Crest Ct 89129
Desert Crossing Ct 89144
Desert Crystal Dr 89134
Desert Daisy Ct 89178
Desert Dancer Way 89147
Desert Dandelion Ct 89139
Desert Delta Dr 89128
Desert Dove Ave 89144
Desert Eagle Ct 89131
Desert Edge St 89115
Desert Falls Ct 89128
Desert Fir Dr 89130
Desert Flame Ct 89149
Desert Flower Dr 89156
Desert Fort St 89128
Desert Glen Dr 89134
Desert Glow Ct 89115
Desert Green Ct 89149
Desert Haven Rd 89130
Desert Heart Ct 89147
Desert Heat Ave 89178
Desert Hills Dr 89117
Desert Holly Dr 89134
E Desert Inn Rd
  300-798 89109
  800-1199 89109
  1200-2399 89169
  2400-2499 89121
  2478-2478 89160
  2500-4998 89121
  2501-4999 89121
  5100-5200 89122
  5202-5398 89122
W Desert Inn Rd
  2400-2500 89109
  2502-2548 89109
  3200-4899 89102
  4901-5097 89146
  5099-5932 89146
  5934-6598 89146
  6900-8998 89117
  9000-9199 89117

9201-9899 89117
10801-11199 89135
Desert Island St 89149
Desert Jewel Cir 89128
Desert Largo Ave 89128
Desert Lavender Ave ... 89141
Desert Lily Ln 89130
Desert Lime Ct 89148
Desert Lupine St 89139
Desert Marigold Ln 89135
Desert Meadows Way .. 89142
Desert Mission Dr 89134
Desert Mound Dr 89134
Desert Night St 89143
Desert Oak Ct 89145
Desert Oasis Cir 89146
Desert Paintbrush
Way 89129
Desert Palm Dr 89183
Desert Paradise Dr 89130
Desert Peak Rd 89134
Desert Pines St 89134
Desert Plains Rd 89147
Desert Point Dr 89118
Desert Poppy Dr 89130
Desert Porch Rd 89178
Desert Prairie St 89135
Desert Quail Dr 89128
Desert Ranch Ave 89113
Desert Rim Ct 89144
Desert Rock Dr 89123
Desert Sands Dr 89134
Desert Shale Ave 89123
Desert Sky Way 89149
Desert Solitude St 89110
Desert Song Dr 89106
Desert Spring Rd 89149
Desert Star Dr 89130
Desert Storm St 89110
Desert Stream Ct 89156
Desert Sun Dr 89110
Desert Trees St 89141
Desert Troon St 89135
Desert Valley Dr 89149
Desert View St 89107
Desert Village Ave 89147
Desert Vista Rd 89121
Desert Willow Dr 89149
Desert Wind Dr 89144
Desert Zinnia Ln 89135
Desertaire Way 89110
Desertbuck Ct 89149
Desertdeer Ct 89149
Desertscape Ave 89178
Deshields Ave 89123
Designata Ave 89135
Designer Way 89129
Desirable Ct 89149
Desire Ave 89128
Desmond Ave 89121
Desperado St 89131
Destination Ln 89144
Destiny Ave 89129
Development Ct 89115
Devenish Ave 89129
Devers Ct 89118
Devita Cir 89117
Devlin Green Ct 89110
Devon Lake St 89110
Devonhall St 89145
Devonshire Ct 89139
Devonwood Ct 89141
Devry Ln 89156
Dew Mist Ln 89110
Dewberry Ct 89110
W Dewey Dr
3500-3598 89118
3600-6100 89118
6102-6398 89118
6901-6999 89113
7100-7598 89113
Dewhurst Ct 89123
Dewy Falls Ave 89179
Dexter Way 89115
Dexter Cabin Rd 89128
Dexter Falls St 89149

Di Blasi Dr 89119
Di Salvo Dr 89103
Dia Del Sol Way 89128
W Diablo Dr
3501-3857 89118
3859-6599 89118
7300-7699 89113
9001-9397 89148
9399-9799 89148
9801-10199 89148
Diamante Cir & Ct 89121
Diamond Cir 89106
Diamond Bar Dr 89117
Diamond Belle Ct 89129
Diamond Bend Ave 89123
Diamond Bridge Ave 89166
Diamond Brook Ct 89117
Diamond Canyon Ln 89149
Diamond Care Dr 89122
Diamond Creek Ct 89134
Diamond Dust Dr 89147
Diamond Estates Ct 89139
Diamond Falls Dr 89117
Diamond Gem Ct 89129
Diamond Gorge Rd 89178
Diamond Head Cir &
Dr 89110
Diamond Heights St 89143
Diamond Hitch Ct 89129
Diamond Hope Ct 89129
Diamond Lake Ave 89129
Diamond Oaks Ct 89117
Diamond Palm Ct 89122
Diamond Peak Ct 89117
Diamond Pointe St 89156
Diamond Ranch Ave 89131
Diamond Reef Way 89117
Diamond Ridge St 89129
Diamond Rock Way 89128
Diamond Run St 89148
Diamond Sand Ave 89178
Diamond Star Ct 89145
Diamond Summit Ct 89183
Diamond Willow Ct 89178
Diamond Wood Ct 89139
Diamondback Dr 89117
Diamondhead Creek
Ct 89122
Dicentra Rd 89113
Dickens Dr 89119
Diego Dr 89156
Diego Bay Cir 89117
Dieterich Ave 89148
Digger St 89107
Digger Pine Dr 89135
Digne Ct 89141
Dijon Ct 89141
Dike Ln 89106
Dilenium St 89147
Dillingham Dr 89122
Dillseed Dr 89131
Dimick Ave 89130
Dimpled Ct 89149
Dingo Ct 89119
Dinning Ave 89107
Dinsmore Dr 89117
Dio Guardi Dr 89117
Discover Point St 89139
Discovery Dr 89135
Discovery Bay Ct 89117
Discovery Reef Ave 89149
Discus Dr 89108
Distant Mirage Ct 89139
Distant Rain Ct 89183
Distant Star Ct 89145
Distinction Ct 89129
Ditmars St 89166
Diveley Ave 89138
Divernon Ave 89149
Divers Cove Way 89108
Divine Dr 89128
Divine Ridge St 89139
Diving Duck Ave 89117
Divinity St 89142
Divot Pl 89130
Dixie Springs Ct 89148

Dixieland Ct 89129
Diza Ct 89122
Dizzy Petunia Ct 89106
Doane Ave 89143
Dobbs Ave 89166
Dobosh Ave 89123
Dobroyd Dr 89179
Dobson Dr 89115
Doby Peak Dr 89108
Doc Holiday Ave 89130
Docile Ct 89135
Docile Daybreak Ct 89156
Dockside Ct 89145
Dodd St 89122
Dodds Canyon St 89131
Dodge Ridge Ave 89139
Dodger Blue Ave 89123
Doe Ave
5100-5198 89146
5200-5799 89146
5801-5899 89146
7000-7098 89117
7100-7499 89117
Dog Leg Dr 89148
Dogan Ridge St 89131
Doggett Ave 89123
Dogwood Hills St 89148
Doig Ln 89110
Dolan Martin Rd 89166
Dolce Dr 89134
Dolce Flore Ave 89178
Dolce Volpe Ave 89178
Dolcetto Dr 89141
Dolente Ave 89129
Doletto St 89138
Dollar Ct 89148
Dollar Bill Ct 89141
Dollar Pointe Ave 89148
Dollhouse Dr 89145
Dolly Ln 89115
Dolly Varden Ct 89179
Dolomite Ct 89123
Dolomiti Dr 89117
Dolores Dr 89107
Dolorosa St 89110
Dolphin Bay Ct 89128
Dolphin Cove Ct 89117
Dolphin Landing Dr 89128
Dolphine Crest Ave 89129
Doman Ave 89166
Dome Peak Ct 89156
Domina Royal St 89148
Domingo St 89121
Dominic Ln 89117
Dominion Ct 89103
Domino Way 89117
Domnus Ln 89144
Don Bonito St 89121
Don Carlos Dr 89121
Don Gaspar Ave 89108
Don Horton Ave 89178
Don Jose Dr 89123
Don Miguel Dr 89121
Don Quixote St 89121
Don Zarembo Ave 89108
Donald Rd 89131
Donald Nelson Ave 89131
Donald Weese Ct 89129
Donaldson Ct 89118
Donatello Ct 89129
Donde Ave 89135
Donelle Ave 89123
Dongola Ct 89110
Donna Celina St 89110
Donnegal Bay Dr 89117
Donner St 89107
Donner Peak St 89166
Donner Springs Ave 89148
Donnie Ave 89130
Donnington Ct 89123
Donora Ave 89141
Donside Ct 89139
Doobie Ave 89183
Doolittle Ave 89106
Dopo Ct 89135
Dorado Bay Ct 89128

Dorado Vista St 89108
Doral Park Ct 89131
Doran Dr 89123
Doraville Ave 89149
Dorchester Cir 89130
Dorenne St 89166
Dori Ave 89101
Dorian Black Ave 89139
Dorinda Ave 89147
Doris Pl 89120
Doris Joan St 89143
Dorita Ave 89108
Dornoch Castle St 89141
Doroca St 89148
Dorothy Ave 89119
Dorrell Ln
4800-4998 89131
5000-6200 89131
6202-6498 89131
8900-9400 89149
9402-9898 89149
10101-10199 89166
Dorrington Dr 89129
Dorshester Heights Ct .. 89108
Dottie Jewel Ave 89147
Double Arch Ct 89128
Double Arrow Pl 89128
Double Down Dr 89122
Double Eagle Dr 89117
Double Rock Dr 89134
Double Spring Ct 89129
Doubleday St 89118
Doubleday Park St 89166
Doucette Dr 89142
Doug Deaner Ave 89129
Douglas Dr 89102
Douglas Everett St 89120
Douglas Flat Pl 89138
Dougram Ave 89101
Dove Canyon St 89123
Dove Cove Dr 89129
Dove Eagle Ct 89183
Dove Ridge Dr 89117
Dove River Rd 89134
Dove Row Ave 89166
Dove Run Creek Dr 89135
Dove Valley Ct 89134
Dovehill Rd 89148
Dover Pl 89107
Dover Bay St 89129
Dover Canyon Ct 89139
Dover Creek Ave 89134
Dover Landing Ct 89123
Dover Shores Ave 89128
Dover Straight St 89115
Doverwood Ave 89149
Dovewood Ave 89183
Down Way 89106
Down Quilt Ct 89115
Downing Pl 89121
Downpour Ct 89110
Draco Cir 89128
Dracopus Ave 89113
Draga Pl 89115
Dragon Claw Ln 89156
Dragonfly Rock St 89148
Dragonfly Wing St 89183
Dragons Meadow Ct 89148
Dragonslayer Ave 89183
Dragoon Springs St 89135
Drake Cir 89102
Drake Ridge Ave 89166
Dramatic Way 89130
Dramatic Gold Ave 89178
Drappo Ave 89138
Dravite Ct 89148
Drawbridge Ln 89128
Drayton Ave 89148
Drazel Way 89128
Dream St 89108
Dream Bridge Dr 89144
Dream Brook Ct 89149
Dream Catcher Ave 89129
Dream Chaser Ct 89117
Dream Day St 89129
Dream Star Ct 89145

Dream Weaver Ct 89131
Dreaming Shores Ct 89110
Dreamland Cir 89108
Dreiser Park Ave 89166
Dresden Doll St 89110
Dressen Ave 89123
Drew Ct 89117
Drexel Rd 89130
Drift Boat St 89149
Drift Stone Ave 89123
Drifters Peak St 89144
Drifting Bay St 89123
Drifting Cloud Cir 89134
Drifting Creek Ave 89130
Drifting Dunes Dr 89149
Drifting River Ct 89149
Drifting Sands Ct 89149
Drifting Shadow Way 89135
Driftwood Dr 89107
Driftwood Cove Ct 89117
Driftwood Island Ct 89148
Dripping Rock Ct 89131
Driscoll Dr 89128
Driscoll Mountain St 89129
Driving Range St 89122
Dromedary Way 89115
Dronberger Way 89110
Drop Camp St 89123
Droplet St 89110
Droubay Dr 89122
Drover Ave 89101
Druid Hills St 89149
Drumcannon Ave 89129
Drumlin St 89139
Drummond Rd 89130
Drummond Castle Ct 89130
Drury St 89108
Dry Breeze Ct 89108
Dry Cliff Cir 89128
Dry Corral Ln 89113
Dry Creek Ave 89128
Dry Dock Dr 89117
Dry Falls St 89142
Dry Hollow Dr 89122
Dry Lake Ct 89129
Dry Pines Cir 89129
Dry Plains Dr 89134
Dry Point Ct 89144
Dry Ridge Ct 89134
Dry Well St 89113
Dryden Park Ave 89148
Drydust Ct 89149
Dryfork Ave 89129
Dryland Ct 89148
Du Barry Manor Ln 89108
Dublin Valley St 89178
Dubris Dr 89115
Ducale Ct 89141
Ducharme Ave 89145
Duchess Ave 89121
Duchess Of York Ave .. 89166
Duck Arrow Cir 89106
Duck Hill Springs Dr 89122
Duck Hollow Ave 89148
Duck Springs Ct 89147
Duckbill Ave 89123
Duckhorn Ct 89144
Duckwater Ave 89130
Dude Ranch Ln 89156
Dudley Ave 89120
Duece St 89121
Dueces Wild Ct 89122
Duero Way 89103
Duet Ct 89119
Duet Springs St 89149
Dugatz St 89124
Duke Cir 89107
Duke Ellington Way 89119
Dukelley Ct 89131
Dulce Ave 89108
Dulcimer Ln 89123
Duluth Dr 89117
Dumbarton St 89110
Dumbarton Oaks St 89166
Dumont Blvd 89169
Dun Stable Ave 89183

Dunbeck Ct 89156
Duncan Dr
5400-5598 89130
5600-5699 89130
5900-6199 89108
Duncan Barrel Ave 89178
Duncan Peak Ct 89139
Dundee Port Ave 89110
Dundock Ave 89122
Dune Dr 89106
Dune Cove Rd 89117
Dune Grass St 89147
Dune Point Ct 89142
Dune Sunflower Ct 89139
Dunedin Ct 89110
Duneville Ct 89103
Duneville St
1201-1297 89146
1299-3299 89146
3301-3399 89146
3500-3698 89103
3700-3999 89103
4900-4972 89118
4974-6299 89118
7700-8099 89139
Dungaree St 89118
Dunham Ct 89121
Dunham Hills Way 89113
Dunhill Ct 89117
Dunkee Way 89106
Dunkirk Ave, Cir & Ct ... 89121
Dunlap Crossing St 89129
Dunning Cir 89115
Dunoon St 89179
Dunphy Ct 89145
Dunraven Ave 89139
Dunsbach Way 89156
Dunshee Vista Ave 89131
Dunsmuir Cir 89108
Dunstan Way 89123
Dunster Castle Dr 89135
Dupage Ave 89135
Duralite St 89122
Durand Park St 89166
N Durango Dr
100-199 89145
3200-4199 89129
4201-4799 89129
4800-4898 89149
4900-7199 89149
7701-8099 89131
8900-8998 89143
9000-9100 89143
9102-9298 89143
S Durango Dr
300-999 89145
2501-2597 89117
2599-3299 89117
3301-3499 89117
3501-4097 89147
4099-4599 89147
4601-4899 89147
4901-5297 89113
5299-8599 89113
8601-9199 89113
Durango St 89120
Durango Ranch Ct 89113
Durant River Dr 89122
Durante St 89119
Duration Ave 89148
Durell Ln 89146
Durham Ave 89101
Durham Hall Ave 89130
Dusa Dr 89121
Dusk Dr 89110
Dusky Flycatcher St 89122
Dusky Shadows St 89113
Duskyseed Ct 89122
Dusseldorf Way 89147
Dustin Ave 89120
Dustin Lee St 89129
Dusty Cloud St 89149
Dusty Coral St 89147
Dusty Creek St 89128
Dusty Hollow St 89143
Dusty Lake St 89131
Dusty Lynx Ct 89139

Dusty Rose Ln 89130
Dusty Valley Ct 89131
Dusty Wagon Ave 89129
Dusty Winds Ave 89117
Dutch Canyon Ct 89131
Dutch Colony Ave 89183
Dutch Elm Dr 89115
Dutch Flat St 89110
Dutch Fork St 89148
Dutch Gold Ave 89110
Dutch Harbor Cir 89113
Dutch Hill Ct 89128
Dutch Oven Ct 89178
Dutch Valley Dr 89147
Dutch Villas St 89139
Dutch Windmill Ave 89139
Dutchmans Pipe Ct 89106
Duval Dr 89156
Duxbury Valley Ave 89123
Duxford Ave 89123
Dwarf Star Dr 89115
Dwayne Stedman Ave .. 89106
Dwight Ave 89120
Dyker Heights Ave 89178
Dynacraft St 89148
Dynasty Dr 89119
E St 89106
Eagle St 89142
Eagle Bend St 89122
Eagle Bluff Ln 89128
Eagle Cap Ct 89122
Eagle Clan Ct 89131
Eagle Claw Ave 89130
Eagle Cove Ave 89130
Eagle Creek Ln 89156
Eagle Crest St 89131
Eagle Crossing St 89130
Eagle Estates Ct 89131
Eagle Eye Ave 89128
Eagle Feather St 89128
Eagle Glen Rd 89148
Eagle Hills Dr 89134
Eagle Lake Ave 89147
Eagle Meadow Ct 89123
Eagle Mountain Dr 89123
Eagle Nest Cir 89124
Eagle Nest St 89141
Eagle Peak Way 89134
Eagle Point Rd 89108
Eagle Port St 89139
Eagle Ridge Dr 89134
Eagle River Ct 89166
Eagle Rock Ct 89117
Eagle Rock Peak Ct 89166
Eagle Springs Ct 89117
Eagle Trace Way 89117
Eagle Vale Ave 89134
Eagle Valley Dr 89134
Eagledancer Ave 89129
Eaglegate St 89131
Eaglehelm Ct 89123
Eagles Landing Ln 89141
Eagles Pride St 89148
Eaglestone Cir 89128
Eaglewood Dr 89144
Earl St 89101
Earl Grey Ct 89117
Earlsboro St 89139
Early Cir 89101
Early Dawn Ct 89129
Early Grace St 89148
Early Heights Ct 89129
Early Horizon Dr 89178
Early Light Dr 89142
Early Mist Ct 89156
Early Morning Ave 89135
Early Pioneer Ave 89129
Early Sky Ct 89142
Early Sun Ct 89135
Early View St 89129
Early Vista St 89142
Earnshaw Ave 89179
Easement Ln 89156
Easingwold Dr 89113
East Ln 89108
Eastbend Ave 89115

Eastbrook Dr 89142
N Eastern Ave 89101
S Eastern Ave
1142-1198 89104
1200-2299 89104
2301-2499 89104
2500-3899 89169
3900-3998 89119
4000-6499 89119
6501-7299 89119
7300-9600 89123
9602-9698 89123
9701-9999 89183
Eastham Bay Ave 89179
Easton Hills Ct 89123
Eastridge Way 89110
Eastview Dr 89107
Eastwick Cir 89142
Eastwood Dr 89104
Easy Cir, Pl & St 89107
Eaton Dr 89102
Eaton Creek Ct 89123
Ebb Tide Cir 89123
Ebbets Field St 89166
Ebbetts Pass 89110
Eblick Wash Dr 89115
Ebony Hills Way 89123
Ebony Legends Ave 89131
Ebony Peak St 89143
Ebony Rock Ave 89149
Ebony Threads Ct 89149
Ebro Way 89103
Echelon Point Dr 89149
Echelon Resort Dr 89109
Echo Rd 89124
Echo Basin St 89131
Echo Bay St 89128
Echo Canyon Cir 89130
Echo Cave Ave 89131
Echo Cliff Ln 89129
Echo Crest Ave 89130
Echo Falls Ave 89183
Echo Glen Dr 89117
Echo Grande Dr 89131
Echo Hills Dr 89134
Echo Mesa Dr 89134
Echo Peak Ln 89135
Echo Ridge Dr 89117
Echo Shire Ave 89141
Echo Springs St 89156
Echo Valley Way 89123
Echo View Ave 89129
Eclair Cir 89142
Eclat Ct 89131
Eclipse St 89110
Eddingham Ct 89156
Eddington Ave 89129
Eddy Stone Ave 89117
Edelweiss Pl 89124
Edelweiss St 89110
Eden Cir 89107
Eden Falls Ln 89183
Eden Ridge Ave 89135
Edenbridge Ct 89123
Edenville Dr 89117
Edgartown Harbor St 89166
Edge Rock Cir 89117
Edgebrook Dr 89145
Edgecliff Ln 89145
Edgecove Ct 89139
Edgefield Ave 89139
Edgeford Pl 89102
Edgemere Way 89156
Edgemoor Way 89121
Edgerton Dr 89113
Edgeview Pl 89134
Edgewater Ln 89123
Edgewood Ave 89102
Edgewood Cir 89107
Edgeworth Pl 89123
Edifice Ave 89117
Edina Ct 89144
Edinburgh Dr 89103
Edison Ave 89121
Edisto Cir 89130
Edith St 89120
Edmond St
1800-1998 89146
2000-3099 89146
3500-3598 89103
3600-3899 89103
3901-4299 89103
5201-5897 89118
5899-6799 89118
8100-9199 89139
9201-9499 89139
Edmonton Ct 89149
Edna Ave
4900-6800 89146
6802-6898 89146
6900-7799 89117
7801-8599 89117
Ednor St 89183
Edrene Ave 89108
Edward Ave 89108
Edward Baher Ave 89149
Edwardian St 89183
Edwin Pl 89115
Edwin Aldrin Cir 89145
Eel Point St 89147
Effinger St 89101
Effort Dr 89145
Egan Crest Dr
5501-6097 89149
6099-6100 89149
6102-6198 89149
7400-7499 89166
Eginton Ave 89145
Egremont Dr 89115
Egret Cir 89121
Egypt Meadows Ave 89178
Egyptian Ave 89143
Eiffel Ct 89141
Eileen St 89115
Eisner Dr 89131
Ekanger Cir 89106
El Antonio Pl 89121
El Cajon St 89169
El Camino Ave 89102
El Camino Rd
2600-3299 89146
3301-3423 89146
3500-3999 89103
4001-4099 89103
5300-5498 89118
5500-6699 89118
7401-8797 89139
8799-9000 89139
9002-9298 89139
10600-10699 89141
El Camino Cabos Dr 89147
El Camino Real 89121
El Campana Way 89121
E El Campo Grande Ave 89115
W El Campo Grande Ave
4801-4997 89130
4999-6599 89130
6601-6799 89130
8400-10299 89149
El Canasta Way 89121
El Canela Way 89121
N El Capitan Way
4801-4897 89149
4899-6099 89149
6101-6399 89149
7700-7800 89143
7802-9998 89143
S El Capitan Way
4000-4100 89147
4102-4698 89147
7200-7298 89148
El Capote Dr 89147
El Carnal Way 89121
El Caro Ct 89122
El Cartero Way 89121
El Castano Ave 89108
El Cebra Way 89121
El Cederal Ave 89102
El Cedro Cir 89121
El Centro Pl 89104
El Cerrito Cir 89108
El Cerrito Chico St 89179
El Chico Ct 89120
El Cholo Way 89121
El Cid Cir & Way 89121
El Como Way 89121
El Conlon Ave 89102
El Cordobes Ave 89110
El Corriente St 89178
El Cortez Ave 89102
El Diablo St 89131
El Dorado Way 89142
El Escorial Ct & Dr 89121
El Esteban Way 89121
El Greco St 89102
El Jardin Ave 89102
El Loro St 89138
El Malpais St 89118
El Milagro St 89108
El Mirador St 89102
El Molino Cir 89108
El Moor Way 89121
El Morro Ave 89101
El Nuevo Dr 89120
El Oro St 89121
El Parque Ave
3700-4599 89102
5000-5999 89146
6001-6099 89146
6901-6997 89117
6999-7499 89117
7501-7799 89117
El Pasada Ave 89102
El Pasada Ln 89121
El Paseo Cir 89121
El Paso Dr 89121
El Pastor Ln 89121
El Pescador Ave 89108
El Pito Ln 89121
El Playa Dr 89121
El Portal Ave 89102
El Portico Ct 89138
El Prado Dr 89121
El Presidente Dr 89129
El Presidio Dr 89141
El Quinta Ct 89121
El Rito Ct 89122
El Robel Cir 89121
El Roble Ct 89120
El Salto Ln 89122
El Segundo Ave
1500-1699 89169
3900-4199 89121
El Sol Dr 89142
El Tesoro Ave 89121
El Toreador St 89169
El Toro St 89121
El Tovar Ave & Rd 89115
El Valle St 89142
Elaina Ave & Cir 89120
Elaine Dr 89142
Eland Ct 89149
Elated Ct 89149
Elberton Ave 89129
Elbridge Way 89113
Elcadore St 89183
Elche Ct 89178
Elder St 89166
Elderberry Pl 89156
Elderberry Wine Ave 89142
Elderly Ave 89131
Eldon St 89102
Eldora Ave
5001-5397 89146
5399-6899 89146
6900-8498 89117
Eldora Cir 89146
Eldora Estates Ct 89117
E Eldorado Ln
100-2099 89123
2600-2700 89120
2702-3198 89120
W Eldorado Ln
4001-4397 89139
4399-6499 89139
6967-7097 89113
7099-7300 89113
7302-7698 89113
Eldorado Canyon St 89107
Eldorado Hills Ct 89110
Eldorado Pines Ave 89139
Eleanor Ave 89106
Eleanor Cir 89121
Elegant Rose St 89117
Elegant Saint Ct 89115
Elendil St 89178
Elephant Tree St 89117
Elessar Ave 89178
Elfstrom Ave 89166
Elgin Cir 89122
Eliana Ct 89147
Elianto St 89183
Elias Child Ct 89166
Eliminator Dr 89146
Elite Ct 89129
Elizabeth Ave 89119
Elizabeth Ann Ln 89183
Elizabethtown Ave 89110
Elk Cir 89124
Elk Canyon Ct 89117
Elk Clover St 89135
Elk Creek Ln 89156
Elk Falls Ct 89130
Elk Grove Way 89117
Elk Grove Valley St 89178
Elk Lake Dr 89144
Elk Meadows Ct 89131
Elk Mountain St 89113
Elk Point Cir 89147
Elk River Cir 89134
Elk Sands Rd 89179
Elk Springs Ave 89103
Elk Stone Ave 89131
Elk Valley St 89178
Elkhart Ave 89183
Elkhead Creek Way 89148
Elkhorn Rd
4900-5998 89131
6000-7399 89131
7401-7799 89131
9100-9899 89149
Elkin Creek Ave 89131
Elkington Ave 89128
Elko Way 89108
Elkridge Dr 89129
Elkwood Dr 89147
Ella Way 89128
Ellen Way 89104
Ellen Marie Dr 89110
Ellenbrook St 89148
Ellendale Ct 89149
Ellerhurst Dr 89103
Ellingson Dr 89106
Elliot Key Dr 89128
Elliot Peak Ave 89183
Elliott Ave 89106
Ellis Ave 89102
Ellis Island Ct 89130
Ellison Park St 89166
Elliston Rd 89135
Elm Ave
1701-2999 89101
4401-4497 89110
4499-4899 89110
Elm Dr 89169
Elm Creek Dr 89108
Elm Grove Dr 89130
Elm Hill Ct 89131
Elm Ridge Ave 89144
Elm Spring Ct 89148
Elmbrook Ct 89134
Elmdale Pl 89103
Elmhurst Ln 89108
Elmira Dr 89118
Elmrock Pl 89121
Elmstone Pl 89138
Elmwood Pl 89108
Elmwood Glen Ave 89166
Elton Ave 89107
Elvido Ave 89122
Elvis Alive Dr 89166
Elvis Presley Ct 89131
Elwood Ct 89149
Elwood Mead Ave 89156
Elysian Dr 89123
Elysian Plains Ct 89145
Embarcadero Ave 89129
Embassy Ct 89117
Ember Glow Cir 89119
Ember Mist Ct 89135
Embrey Ave 89106
Embroidery Ave 89149
Embry Hills St 89113
Emelita St 89122
Emerald Ave
2400-4599 89120
5801-5897 89122
5899-5999 89122
6001-6099 89122
Emerald Bay Cir 89147
Emerald Beach Ct 89147
Emerald Breeze Dr 89117
Emerald Brook St 89131
Emerald Canyon Dr 89142
Emerald City Ave 89183
Emerald Cove Ct 89117
Emerald Creek Dr 89156
Emerald Edgewater Ct 89178
Emerald Falls Ave 89183
Emerald Forest St 89145
Emerald Gardens Cir 89123
Emerald Glen Way 89117
Emerald Glow St 89123
Emerald Green Ave 89106
Emerald Grove Way 89123
Emerald Harbor Ct 89128
Emerald Heights St 89144
Emerald Hill Way 89117
Emerald Isle Ave 89128
Emerald Path Ave 89166
Emerald Pine Ln 89138
Emerald Pools St 89178
Emerald Ridge Ct 89129
Emerald Springs Ln 89113
Emerald Tint Ct 89144
Emerald Tree Ct 89130
Emerald Twilight St 89178
Emerald View St 89130
Emerald Vista Way 89144
Emerald Waters Ct 89147
Emerald Wood St 89115
Emeraude Ave 89147
Emerson Ave & Ct 89121
Emerson Gardens St 89166
Emery St 89134
Emery Lake St 89123
Emerywheel Cir 89110
Emerywood Ct 89117
Emilia Ave 89108
Eminence Ct 89131
Emma Clare Ct 89149
Emperor Way 89130
Empire Cir 89107
Empire Rock St 89143
Empoli Ct 89134
Empress Dr 89147
Empress Charm Ct 89129
Empress Garden Ct 89148
Emsdale Ct 89147
Encanto Dr 89101
Encanto Cavern Ct 89148
Encarta St 89117
Enchanted Cove Ct 89139
Enchanted Creek Pl 89122
Enchanted Grove Ave 89149
Enchanted Hills Ct 89129
Enchanted Mesa Ct 89129
Enchanted Palms Ave 89139
Enchanted Peak Ave 89110
Enchanted Pool St 89139
Enchanted Rock Ave 89113
Enchanted Valley Ct 89117
Enchanting Ct 89156
Enchantress Ct 89139
Encina Dr 89121
Encino Springs Ave 89139
Encita Ct 89131
Enclave Ct 89134
Encore Way 89119
Encore Paradise Ave 89131
Encorvado St 89138
Endeavor Ct 89134
Enderly Ln 89144
Endicott Ct 89123
Endless Peace Ct 89148
Endora Dr 89103
Enfield Cir 89156
Engleberg Ave 89178
Englewood Ave 89139
Englewood Cliffs Ave 89144
English Daisy Way 89142
English Falls Way 89178
English Heather Dr 89123
English Ivy Ct 89130
English Mist Cir 89128
English Oak St 89117
English Pine Dr 89135
English Rose Dr 89142
English Saddle Cir 89117
English Walnut Ct 89115
Ennis Ct 89121
Enniskeen Ave 89129
Ensworth St
6301-6499 89119
9500-9598 89123
9600-9699 89123
Enterprise Dr 89147
Enticing Ct 89149
Entrada Dr 89121
Entrance Arch St 89179
Entrancing Ave 89149
Enviable Ct 89149
Environment Ct 89149
Epico Way 89179
Epson St 89129
Epworth Ave 89148
Equine Ave 89122
Equinox Ct 89147
Erato Falls St 89148
Ericas Eden St 89131
Erickson Ct 89131
Erie Ave 89183
W Erie Ave 89141
Erie Stream Way 89123
Erin Cir
5200-5299 89122
6900-6999 89145
Erin Glen St 89147
Erins Grove Ct 89147
Ermine Ct 89147
Errol Flynn St 89122
Erskine Ave 89123
Erva St
3301-3397 89117
3399-3499 89117
3501-3797 89147
3799-3999 89147
E & W Erwin Ct 89115
Escada Ln 89145
Escallonia St 89149
Escalon Dr 89108
Escamilla Rd 89135
Escapa Ct 89130
Escarpment St 89139
Escatawpa Bay Ct 89122
Escondido St
4200-4398 89119
4400-6799 89119
6801-6899 89119
8801-9197 89123
9199-9299 89123
Escondido Canyon St 89138
Escuela St 89121
Esk Dr 89144
Eskam St 89156
Esmeralda Ave 89102
Esmont Ln 89117
Espadrille Ct 89138
Espana Ct 89138
Espanita Ave 89121
Espanol Dr 89121
Esparon Ave 89141
Esperanto St 89108
Espinosa Ave 89108
Esplanade Way 89121
Esposito Ave 89141
Essen Ct 89147
Essex Cir 89107
Essex East Dr 89107
Essex Green Ct 89110
Essex West Dr 89107
Esta Ponia Ct 89144
Estaban Ct 89110
Estasi St 89135
Estate View St 89129
Esteem St 89131
Estella Ave 89107
Esterbrook Way 89128
Estero Dr 89147
Estes Park Dr 89122
Estonian Pl 89113
Estornino Ave 89108
Estrada Ave 89129
Estrelita Dr 89128
Estrella St 89117
Estrella Bonita Ct 89147
Estrella De Mar Ave 89131
Estrella Mountain Ct 89122
Estrella Vista St 89138
Eternity St 89138
Ethan Brook St 89183
Ethan Patrick Ct 89149
Ethel May St 89108
Ettenmoor Ave 89135
Eucalyptus Ave 89121
Euclid Ave 89104
Euclid St
3800-3898 89121
3900-4599 89121
5800-6098 89120
Eugene Ave 89108
Eugene Cernan St 89145
Eugene Grayson Ct 89145
N Eula St 89149
Euphorbia Way 89113
Euphoria Rose Ave 89166
Eureka Cir & St 89103
Eureka Coast Way 89141
Eureka Diamond Ct 89139
Eureka Heights Ct 89178
Eureka Pass Ct 89135
Europa Way 89145
Eurorail St 89131
Eurostar St 89131
Evaline St 89120
Evan Lilas St 89148
Evan Ridge Ct 89129
Evangeline Ct 89120
Evanston Ave 89108
Eve Ct 89145
Eve Springs St 89178
Evelyn Lake Ct 89108
Even Money Ct 89122
Evening Breeze Ct, Dr & Pl 89107
Evening Dew Dr 89110
Evening Falls Dr 89131
Evening Fog St 89129
Evening Glow Dr 89134
Evening Hills Ave 89113
Evening Melody Ct 89178
Evening Primrose Ave 89135
Evening Rain Ave 89156
Evening Rock St 89135
Evening Shade Cir 89119
Evening Shadows Ave 89131
Evening Spirit Ave 89183
Evening Star Dr 89134
Evening Sun Dr 89117
Evensail Dr 89156
Evensham Ct 89129
Eventide Way 89107
Ever Clear Ct 89131
Ever View Ct 89148
Everdon Ct 89148
Everest St 89129
Everett St 89101
Everett Basin Ct 89113
Everglade St 89142
Evergreen Ave, Cir & Pl 89107
Evergreen Canyon Dr 89134

Evergreen Creek Ln 89135
Evergreen Glen Dr 89130
Evergreen Meadow
Ave 89130
Evergreen Summit
Ave 89123
Everhart Bay Dr 89135
Everly Ct 89131
Everman Dr 89122
Everston Cir 89123
Evesham Ct 89121
Evident Ct 89131
Evvie Ln 89135
Ewa Beach Dr 89122
Excel Ln 89117
Excelsior Springs Ln 89130
Exeter Dr 89156
Exley Ave 89104
Exodus Ct 89106
Exotic Bloom Dr 89130
Exotic Plum Ave 89147
Exotic Rosette Ave 89139
Expedition St 89131
Exploration Ave 89131
Explorer Dr 89103
Exposition Ave 89102
Exquisite Ave 89110
Exquisite Plains St 89178
Extreme Ct 89129
Exuberance Way 89115
Exultation Ct 89149
Eyebright St 89131
F St 89106
Faberge Ave 89115
Fabiano St 89183
Fable St 89141
Fabled Filigree St 89149
Fabor Way 89147
Fabrica St 89141
Facinas Ave 89141
Factor Ave 89107
Fading Night Ct 89142
Fading Sun St 89135
Fahrenheit Ct 89129
Fair Ave 89106
Fair Bluff St 89135
Fair Falls Ln 89131
Fair Valley St 89148
Fairbanks Cir & Rd 89103
Fairbranch Ln 89135
Faircenter Pkwy 89102
Fairchild St 89110
Faircrest Dr 89134
Fairfax Ave 89120
Fairfax Cir
4200-4299 89119
5200-5299 89120
Fairfax Ridge St 89183
Fairfield Ave
1500-1698 89102
1700-2299 89102
7500-8699 89123
9700-11199 89183
Fairgate Ct 89117
Fairhaven Cir & St 89108
Fairland Ct 89113
Fairlawn Ave 89121
Fairlight Dr 89142
Fairmeade Way 89135
Fairmont Cir 89147
Fairview Ln 89121
Fairway Cir 89108
Fairway Dr 89107
Fairway Woods Dr 89148
Fairwind Acres Pl 89131
Fairwood Ave & Cir 89107
Faiss Dr 89134
Faith Ct 89131
Faith Peak Dr 89108
Falcon Ln 89107
Falcon Ridge St 89142
Falcon Rock Dr 89123
Falcon Springs Dr 89147
Falcon View Ct 89135
Falconer Ave 89122
Falconhead Ln 89128

Falcons Fire Ave 89148
Falconwing Ave 89131
Faldo St 89128
Falesco Ave 89138
Falk Cir & Dr 89115
Falkenberg St 89129
Fall Breeze Dr 89142
Fall Cliff Rd 89149
Fall Creek St 89123
Fall Green Ave 89129
Fall Harvest Dr 89147
Fall Meadows Ave 89130
Fall River Cir 89129
Falla St 89146
Falling Acorn Ct 89123
Falling Heart Ct 89115
Falling Leaf Ln 89142
Falling Needle Ave 89135
Falling Pines Pl 89143
Falling Rain Dr 89142
Falling Snow Ave 89183
Falling Springs Cir 89135
Falling Star Ave 89117
Falling Stream Ave 89131
Falling Timber Ct 89113
Falling Waters Ct 89149
Fallona Ave 89156
Fallowdeer Ct 89149
Falls Church Ave 89144
Falls Peak Ave 89178
Fallwood Ln 89107
Falstaff Way 89142
Falvo Ave 89131
Fam Camp Dr 89115
Fame Ave 89147
Famiglia Dr 89141
Familian Dr 89102
Family Ct 89117
Famous Alcove Ct 89149
Fan Coral Ave 89123
Fanciful Ave 89145
Fancy Ct 89149
Fancy Fern St 89183
Fancy Flight St 89178
Fandango Ct 89123
Fandanso Pl 89146
Fandwood Ln 89107
Fannine Way 89130
Fanwood Ln 89138
Far Hills Ave 89138
Farfalla Ct 89141
Fargo Ave 89107
Fargo Fair Ct 89149
Farkas Ln 89145
Farlington Dr 89147
Farm Rd 89131
Farm Pond St 89131
Farmcrest Dr 89121
Farmhouse Ct 89141
Farmington Ave 89120
Farmington Hall Ct 89129
Farnam Pl 89102
Farndale Ave 89122
Farnsworth Pond Ave ... 89130
Faro St 89146
Farralon Ridge Ct 89149
Farrington Ct 89123
Farris Ave 89183
Farthings Hill Dr 89166
Fascinating St 89149
Fascination St 89128
N Fashion Show Dr 89109
Fassbinder Ct 89129
Fast Ln 89120
Fast Elk St 89143
Fast Green Way 89148
Fast Payout Ct 89122
Fathers Pride Ave 89178
Faucet Ave 89147
Faulkner Run Ave 89166
Faustine Ave 89129
Faversham Ct 89123
Fawn Ave & Cir 89107
Fawn Brook Ct 89149
Fawn Chase Way 89135
Fawn Creek Dr 89115

Fawn Grove Dr 89147
Fawn Heather Ct 89149
Fawn Meadow Ave 89149
Fawn Ridge St 89134
Fawndale Ave 89156
Fay Blvd 89108
Fayette Dr 89123
Faywood St 89134
Feather Way 89108
Feather Cactus Ct 89106
Feather Crest Ct 89117
Feather Duster Ct 89113
Feather Falls Cir 89110
Feather Glen Ct 89117
Feather Pine St 89131
Feather River Ct 89117
Feather Stream Ct 89123
Featherbed Ct 89115
Featherstone Ln 89129
February Falls St 89183
Federman Dr 89123
Feinberg Pl 89138
Feldman St 89118
Feldspar Ave 89120
Felice Ave 89135
Felice Cohn Ct 89179
Felicitas Ave 89122
Feliz Camino Ave 89129
Fellowship Ave 89102
Fence Jumper Ave 89131
Fence Post St 89148
Fencerow St 89131
Fender Ct 89149
Fenmarch St 89135
Fennel Flower Ct 89138
Fenway Ave 89147
Fenway Park Ave 89166
Ferdinand Ct 89129
Ferguson Springs St 89179
Fermata Ct 89178
Fern Canyon Ave 89117
Fern Creek Ln 89183
Fern Hollow Ct 89108
Fern Meadow St 89149
Fern Prairie St 89183
Fern Tree Ct 89183
Fernbrook Rd 89103
Ferndale St 89121
Ferndale Cove Dr 89129
Ferne Dr 89104
Ferngrove Way 89115
Fernleaf Dr 89115
Fernley Way 89110
Fernwood Ln 89169
Ferragamo Ct 89141
Ferrari Ave 89142
Ferrell St 89106
Ferrin Rd 89117
Festival Dr 89134
Festival Plaza Dr 89135
Festivity Cir 89145
Festuca Way 89113
Fewkes Canyon Ct 89139
Fico Ave 89141
Ficus Dr 89113
Fiddlehead Ave 89183
Fidenza Ave 89141
Fidus Dr 89103
Field Breeze St 89148
Field Thistle Ave 89149
Fieldcreek Ct 89113
Fieldcrest Rd 89121
Fieldmouse Ave 89142
Fields St 89142
Fieldstone Rd 89107
Fiero Dr 89134
Fiesole St 89141
Fiesta Way 89121
Fiesta Lakes St 89130
Fiesta Rose Ave 89148
Fife Lake Ct 89148
Fig Ct 89145
Fig Palm Ct 89128
Figaro St 89128
Fighting Fish Way 89118
Figtree Rd 89108

Figueroa Dr 89123
Filmore Ave 89130
Filmore Heights Ct 89135
Finale Ln 89119
Finch Feather St 89143
Finchwood Ln 89110
Findlay Ave 89134
Fine Fern St 89183
Fine Lace St 89148
Finishing Touch Ct 89149
Fintry Hills St 89141
Fionna Ln 89129
Fiore Bella Blvd 89135
Fiorello Ct 89183
Fiorinda Cir 89130
Fire Fly Cir 89122
Fire Island Dr 89120
Fire Lion Ct 89139
Fire Mesa St 89128
Fire Mountain Ct 89129
Fire Night Ave 89122
Fire Opal Dr 89131
Fire Ridge Ct 89148
Fire Rock Ct 89141
Fire Water Ct 89117
Firebird Dr 89134
Firebush Dr 89135
Firecracker Ct 89148
Firecreek Cir 89107
Firefalls Dr 89147
Firenze Ct 89128
Fireside Ln 89110
Fireside Ranch Ave 89131
Firesteed Pl 89141
Firestone Dr 89145
Firethorn Ln 89123
Firewood Dr 89148
First Lady Ave 89148
First On Dr 89148
First View Ave 89142
Firwood Ct 89110
Fish Tail Ave 89149
Fisher Ave 89130
W Fisher Ave 89149
Fisher Creek Ct 89139
Fisherking Dr 89129
Fishers Island St 89141
Fishook Cactus Ct 89106
Fitzpatrick Dr 89115
Fitzroy Dr 89134
Fitzwilliam Ave 89178
Five Pennies Cir & Ln 89120
Flag Cir 89102
Flagler St 89139
Flagship Ct 89121
Flagstaff Ct 89117
Flagstaff Butte Ave 89148
Flagstaff Ranch St 89166
Flagstone Way 89110
Flagwood St 89141
Flambeau St 89131
Flame Cir 89108
Flame Vine Ct 89135
Flamenco Ct 89139
Flametree Ct 89123
Flaming Coral Ln 89130
Flaming Gorge St 89156
Flaming Peak Ct 89129
Flaming Ridge Trl 89147
E Flamingo Rd
120-198 89109
200-378 89169
380-498 89169
500-2399 89119
2400-4899 89121
4901-4999 89121
5300-5798 89122
5800-5899 89122
W Flamingo Rd
3601-3697 89103
3699-6899 89103
7300-7698 89147
7700-9900 89147
9902-10198 89147
11111-11199 89135
Flamingo Arroyo Ct 89121

Flamingo Crest Dr 89121
Flanagan Dr 89131
Flanders Terrace Dr 89123
Flandes St 89121
Flanigan Ct 89142
Flannery St 89166
Flat Creek St 89131
Flat Rock St 89131
Flathead Ave 89122
Flathead Falls St 89156
Flathead River Ave 89179
Flatrock Crossing Way .. 89178
Flatwoods Bay Ct 89122
Flaxen Cir 89107
Fleet Dancer St 89129
Fleeting Twilight Pl 89166
Flickering Star Dr 89103
Flight Wing St 89113
Flint Ridge Ave 89123
Flintstone St 89123
Flippin St 89115
Floating Flower Ave 89139
Floating Lily Ct 89106
Flockenn St 89123
Flokton Ave 89148
Flora Dr 89103
Flora Cove Ct 89123
Flora Plum Ct 89123
Flora Spray St 89130
Flora Springs Ln 89141
Floragold Ct 89147
Floral Fabric Ct 89149
Floralita St 89122
Flore Del Sol St 89120
Florence Ave
2200-2399 89119
2600-2999 89120
Florence Hills St 89141
Florentine Ct 89130
Flores Cir 89123
Florida Keys Dr 89156
Florido Rd 89178
Florine Ave 89129
Florine St 89130
Florio Ct 89138
Florissant Dr 89128
Florisse Ct 89148
Florrie Ave & Cir 89121
Flossmoor St 89115
Flounder Bay Ave 89179
Flourish Springs St 89131
Flower Ave 89101
Flower Cir 89107
Flower St 89101
Flower Dance Ct 89131
Flower Festival St 89139
Flower Hill St 89106
Flower Patch St 89115
Flower Seeds St 89139
Flower Spring St 89134
Flowerdale Ct 89103
Floweret Ave 89117
Flowering Bush Ct 89130
Flowering Meadows
Ave 89131
Flowering Peach Ct 89147
Flowering Plum Ave 89142
Flowering Quince Dr 89179
Flowering Rose Ave 89117
Flowering Tulip Ave 89166
Flowering Willow St 89148
Flowerridge Ln 89129
Flowing Rapids Ct 89131
Flowing Spring St 89122
Flowing Stream Dr 89131
Floyd Ct 89134
Fluffy Fox Ct 89178
Fly Fisher St 89113
Flying Birdie Ave 89122
Flying Cloud Ln 89135
Flying Eagle Ln 89123
Flying Frog Ave 89148
Flying Hills Ave 89148
Flying Pegasus Ct 89131
Fodor Ln 89107
Fog Hollow Ct 89135

Fogg St 89142
N Fogg St 89110
Foggia Ave 89130
Foggy Bay Ln 89117
Foggy Glen Ave 89135
Foggy Mist Ave 89179
Folage Dr 89110
Foley Ln 89138
Folksong Ct 89148
Folkstone Ave 89108
Folsom Dr 89134
Fonchester Ct 89110
Fonseca Dr 89141
Fontainbleu Dr 89145
Fontana Ave 89106
Fontayne Ave 89123
Fontenelle St 89102
Fontera Ct 89139
Fonville Ave 89123
Foolish Pleasure Dr 89113
Fools Gold St 89149
Foothill Blvd 89118
Foothill Ash Ave 89117
Foothill Lodge Ct 89131
Footstep Ave 89149
Forbes Field Ct 89148
E Ford Ave 89123
W Ford Ave
2800-2899 89123
3000-6399 89139
6401-6499 89139
7300-7798 89113
7800-8399 89113
8600-8698 89148
8701-8799 89148
Fords Way 89161
Foredawn Dr 89123
Forefather St 89148
Foremaster 89161
Foremaster Ln
200-1798 89101
8601-8699 89178
Forest Brook Ct 89134
Forest Crossing Ct 89148
Forest Edge Ave 89149
Forest Falls Ct 89156
Forest Frost St 89149
Forest Glen Pl 89134
Forest Heights Ct 89166
Forest Hollow Ct 89149
Forest Ivy St 89131
Forest Knoll Ln 89129
Forest Lake St 89117
Forest Lily Ct 89129
Forest Manor Ct 89134
Forest Meadows Ave 89149
Forest Oaks Dr 89149
Forest Park Dr 89156
Forest Pony Ave 89122
Forest Shadow Ave 89139
Forest Valley Ct 89124
Forest Village Ave 89113
Forest Vista St 89147
Forest Walk Dr 89119
Forest Willow Ave 89149
Forestcrest Dr 89121
Forestdale Ct 89120
S Forester St 89161
Forestina Ct 89122
Foreston Ct 89123
Forever Dawn St 89148
Forever Sunset Ct 89135
Forget Me Not Ln 89142
Formation Ct 89139
Formula Way 89146
Forrest Duke Ct 89108
Forrest Hills Ln 89108
Forsythe Dr 89142
N Fort Apache Rd
3265-4297 89129
4299-4599 89129
4601-4699 89129
5000-6399 89149
S Fort Apache Rd
1100-3399 89117
3501-3621 89147

3623-4899 89147
4900-7100 89148
7102-7298 89148
Fort Bayard Ave 89178
Fort Benton Rd 89122
Fort Bowie St 89179
Fort Concho St 89178
Fort Connah Ct 89178
Fort Crestwood Dr 89129
Fort Defiance Ave 89178
Fort Grey Ct 89139
Fort Hallock Ave 89131
Fort Laramie Ln 89123
Fort Lauderdale Dr 89156
Fort Lincoln Ave 89178
Fort Macarthur St 89178
Fort Mcdermitt Ave 89179
Fort Mchenry Dr 89122
Fort Pike St 89178
Fort Reading St 89179
Fort Ruby Pl 89128
Fort Sedgwick Ave 89131
Fort Slocum Ave 89183
Fort Smith Dr 89122
Fort Tule Ave 89179
Fort Union Ct 89179
Fort Valley Ave 89134
Fort Vasquez St 89179
Fort Verde St 89179
Fort West Rd 89108
Fort Wilkins Dr 89129
Fortney Rd 89161
Fortress Course Ct 89148
Fortress Peak Ct 89166
Fortune Ave 89107
Forum Hills Pl 89144
Forum Peak Ln 89166
Forza Ct 89131
Fosco Ct 89131
Fossil Creek Ln 89145
Fossil Springs St 89135
Foster Springs Rd 89148
Fountain Crest Ave 89113
Fountain Island Dr 89147
Fountain Palm St 89130
Fountain View Dr 89134
Fountain Village Ave 89113
Fountain Walk Ave 89149
Four Leaf Clover Dr 89122
Four Seasons Dr 89129
Four Views St 89143
Fox Cir 89107
Fox Acres Dr 89134
Fox Brook St 89139
Fox Canyon Cir 89117
Fox Creek Ave 89122
Fox Den Ct 89122
Fox Estate St 89141
Fox Forest Ave 89129
Fox Glen Pkwy 89108
Fox Heather Dr 89129
Fox Hollow Ct 89117
Fox Lake Ave 89148
Fox Point Dr 89108
Fox Run Ct 89120
Fox Season Ave 89178
Fox Springs Dr 89117
Fox Tail Way 89123
Foxboro Cir 89121
Foxcroft Ave 89108
Foxdale Way 89107
Foxen Ct 89141
Foxglove Dr 89142
Foxglove Field St 89130
Foxgrove Dr 89147
Foxhunt St 89130
Foxland St 89131
Foxlyn Ave 89122
Foxtail Pine Ave 89129
Foxtrap Ave 89145
Foxwalk Ave 89149
Foxwarren Ct 89130
Foxwood Pl 89145
Foxworth Ct 89183
Fragile Fields St 89183
Fragrant Spruce Ave 89123

Frambrook Ct 89178
Framingham Ct 89123
France Park Falls St 89131
Frances Celia Ave 89122
Francine Ct 89156
Francis Ave 89104
Franciscan Ct & Ln 89121
Francisco Peak Pl 89128
Franco Ct 89123
Frandosa Ln 89117
Franford Ct 89183
Frank St 89104
Frank Aved St 89110
Frank Borman Ave 89145
Frank Derek Ave 89139
Frank Fenlon Ave 89107
Frank Sinatra Dr 89158
Frankfurt Ct 89147
Franklin Ave 89104
Franklin Hills Ave 89135
Frasure Falls Ave 89178
Fratelli Ave 89183
Fraya Dr 89119
Frazier Park Ct 89143
Fred Brown Dr 89106
Frederick Ave 89106
Fredonia Dr 89108
Free Spirit St 89183
Freeburg Pl 89123
Freedom Ave 89121
Freedom Flag Ave 89141
Freedom Heights Ave 89149
Freedom Ring St 89148
Freel Peak Ct 89129
Freeman Ave 89106
Freeport Ln 89117
Fremont St
1-2399 89101
2400-2498 89104
2500-3399 89104
French Cir 89101
French Creek Ct 89156
French Daisy St 89135
French Hill Ct 89139
French Merlot Ct 89144
French Pine Ave 89129
French Springs St 89139
Fresco Ct 89117
Fresh Crown Ct 89148
Fresh Harvest Ave 89131
Fresh Meadows Ln 89108
Fresh Spring Dr 89134
Freshet Ct 89139
Freshwater Dr 89103
Freshwater Pearl St 89139
Fresnal Canyon Ave 89123
Fresno Dr 89120
Friant St 89123
Friar Ln 89130
Friar Tuck Ave 89130
E Frias Ave 89183
W Frias Ave 89141
Frias Point Ct 89122
Friendly Breeze Ct 89123
Friesian St 89143
Fringe Ruff Dr 89148
Fringetree Ct 89123
Frisco Bay Cir 89117
Frittata Ave 89113
Fritzen Ave 89131
Fro Ave 89110
Frogs Leap Ct 89139
Frontier Ave 89106
Frontier St 89102
Frontier Hills Ave 89113
Frontier Ranch Ln 89113
Frostburg Ln 89134
Frosted Dawn Ct 89141
Frostproof St 89128
Frosty Canyon Ct 89183
Frosty Morning Ave 89129
Frozen Springs Ct 89130
Fruit Flower Ave 89130
Fruitful Harvest Ave 89131
Fuchia Cir 89107
Fuchlow Dr 89115

Fuchsia Vine Ct 89131
Fuentes Cir & Way 89121
Fuji Ct 89129
Fujita Way 89115
Fulano Way 89102
Fulbright Ave 89166
Full Moon Dr 89115
Full Sail Dr 89115
Fuller Rd 89108
Fullmoon Maple Ave 89117
Fulstone Way 89115
Fulton Pl 89107
Fulton Meadows Ave 89141
Fulton Ranch St 89131
Fundy Ave 89183
Funny Cide St 89131
Funston Way 89129
Furnace Gulch Ave 89178
Fury Ln 89128
Fusion Dr 89129
Future Dr 89130
Fynn Valley Dr 89148
G St 89106
Gabaldon St 89141
Gabardine Ave 89149
Gabilan Ct 89123
Gable Ln 89145
Gable Crest Ct 89141
Gables Vale Ct 89121
Gaborone Ave 89108
Gabriel Dr
1501-1597 89119
1599-2300 89119
2302-2398 89119
4600-4799 89121
Gabriel St 89183
Gabro Ln 89123
Gadwall St 89108
Gaelic Hills Dr 89141
Gaeta Pl 89134
Gagliano St 89141
Gagnier Blvd 89113
Gainey Ranch Ave 89147
Gains Mill St 89122
Gainsville St 89129
Gaisford St 89149
Gala St 89169
Galahad Point Ct 89147
Galanthus St 89113
Galatea St 89108
Galaxy Ave 89102
Galbraith St 89141
Gale Wind Ct 89129
Galen Glen Ct 89139
Galena Crossing St 89123
Galena Peak Ln 89156
Galena Point St 89130
Galeria Posada Ave 89179
Galeton Ct 89103
Galiceno Dr 89122
Galicia Ave 89143
Galician Pony St 89131
Galileo Dr 89149
Galit Ave 89121
Gallagher Ct 89117
Gallagher Island St 89143
Gallant Cir 89147
Gallant Hills Dr 89135
Gallantry Ct 89145
Galleon Peak Ln 89166
Gallery Course Dr 89148
Gallery Echo St 89141
Gallery Oaks Dr 89123
Gallery Shores Dr 89128
Galley Dr 89147
Galliano Ave 89117
Gallo Dr 89147
Galloping Hills St 89113
Galloping Scout Ct 89131
Gallup Ct 89121
Galore Ave 89115
Galva Ct 89110
Galvani St 89183
Galveston St 89110
Galveston Harbor Ct 89131
Galway Ct 89121

Gambassi Ct 89141
Gambel Oak Ct 89149
Gammila Dr 89141
Ganado Dr 89103
Gannet Cir 89103
Ganzo St 89108
Garamound Ave 89117
Garbo Ct 89142
Garces Ave 89101
Garcia Ct 89130
Garden Cir 89119
Garden Ln 89119
Garden Pl 89107
Garden Arbor Ct 89148
Garden Breeze Way 89123
Garden Cress Ct 89138
Garden East Dr 89121
Garden Flower Pl 89135
Garden Fountain Ave 89149
Garden Fox Ct 89149
Garden Galley St 89139
Garden Glen Ln 89135
Garden Grove Ave 89103
Garden Light Dr 89135
Garden Mist Dr 89135
Garden North Dr 89121
Garden Park Dr 89135
Garden Path Ct 89119
Garden Pond St 89148
Garden Prince Cir 89110
Garden Rain Dr 89135
Garden Rock St 89149
Garden Rose Dr 89135
Garden Sage Ct 89118
Garden Shadow Ln 89135
Garden Shower Pl 89135
Garden South Dr 89121
Garden Springs Ave 89149
Garden State Dr 89135
Garden Stone Ct 89149
Garden Stream Ct 89131
Garden Trellis Ct 89148
Garden Valley Ct 89178
Garden View Dr 89134
Garden Village Ln 89113
Garden Vista St 89113
Gardena Hills Ave 89178
Gardendale St 89121
Gardenia Ln 89107
Gardenside St 89131
Garehime St
3000-3399 89108
7501-7797 89131
7799-8299 89131
Garita Ct & St 89121
Garland Ct 89121
Garland Grove Ln 89183
Garland Grove Way 89135
Garnet Ct 89121
Garnet Canyon Ln 89129
Garnet Creek Ct 89139
Garnet Crown Ave 89145
Garnet Gable Ave 89106
Garnet Haze Dr 89122
Garnet Lake Ave 89113
Garnet Peak Ct 89117
Garnet Point Ct 89123
Garnet Ridge Ct 89123
Garono Way 89104
Garrafon Bay St 89138
Garrett Ranch St 89131
Garrettstone Ct 89149
Garrison St 89107
Garrycastle Ct 89129
Garthmore Ave 89141
Garwood Ave 89107
Gary Ave 89178
E Gary Ave 89123
W Gary Ave
2600-2699 89123
3200-6398 89139
6400-6899 89139
Gary Cooper St 89122
Gary Stewart Ln 89120
Garzota Ave 89108
Gaslight Cir 89119

Gasparville St 89129
Gass Ave 89101
Gate Fall Ct 89149
Gatehouse Ln 89108
Gates Mill Rd 89128
Gatesville Ave 89148
Gateview Ln 89144
Gateway Ave 89104
N Gateway Rd
1301-1599 89110
1601-1697 89115
1699-2799 89115
2801-2999 89115
S Gateway Rd 89120
Gateway Glen Dr 89178
Gatewood Dr 89108
Gatewood Terrace Ln 89129
Gatos Ct 89120
Gatsby House St 89166
Gaucho Dr 89169
Gavilan Ln 89122
Gavin Stone Ave 89145
Gaviota Ave 89110
Gaye Ln 89108
Gaylord Dr 89103
Gazania St 89131
Gaze Ln 89115
Gazebo Way 89142
Gazelle Dr 89108
Geary Pl 89109
Geiger Peak Ct 89148
Geist Ave, Cir & Ct 89115
Gelber Ave 89124
Gem Lake Ct 89130
Gemini Cir 89115
Gemini Bridges St 89130
Gemstar Ln 89135
Gemstone Dr 89134
Gemwood St 89123
Geneive Ln 89108
General Miles Way 89122
General Whipple Ct 89166
Generation Ct 89129
Genesis Ct 89128
Genevieve Ct 89108
Genoa Dr 89141
Genovese Ave 89141
Gentilly Ln 89108
Gentle Breeze St 89108
Gentle Cascade Ave 89178
Gentle Grazer St 89139
Gentle Pines Ct 89130
Gentle Rain Way 89117
Gentle River Ave 89130
Gentle Sky Ct 89113
Gentle Spirit Dr 89148
Gentle Valley St 89149
Gentle Waters Ct 89110
Gentle Winds Ct 89108
Gentlewood Ave 89130
Gentry Ln 89123
Genzer Dr 89145
George Pl 89106
George Crockett Rd 89119
George Hart Ct 89129
Georgeina Dr 89130
Georgeson Ct 89110
Georgetown Pl 89134
Georgetown Cove Ct 89131
Georgia Peach Ct 89130
Georgia Pine Ct 89134
Gerald Ct 89134
Gering Ln 89117
Gerlach Dr 89106
Geronimo Way 89169
Geronimo Springs Ave 89179
Gerri Bay Ln 89147
Gershon Ct 89121
Gerson Ave 89106
Gertrude Ct 89141
Gessler Ct 89118
Geyser Hill Ln 89147
Ghost Dance Cir 89149
Ghost Flower Ct 89128
Ghost Gum St 89183
Ghost Mountain Ave 89129

Ghost Plant Ct 89106
Ghost Ranch Ave 89179
Ghost Rider Ct 89131
Ghost Town Trl 89118
Ghost Trace Ave 89183
Gi Orno Ct 89135
Giant Steps Ct 89141
Giardino Villa St 89148
Gibbon Ave 89149
Gibbous Moon Dr 89129
Gibbs Hill Ave 89138
Gibraltar St & Way 89121
Gibson Falls Ct 89141
Gibson Isle Dr 89166
Giddings Ave 89148
Gifthouse St 89178
Gila Bend Way 89123
Gilanore Ave 89166
Gilbert Ln 89130
Gilbert Ridge St 89143
Gilcrease Ave 89149
Gilded Crown Ct 89117
Gilded Lantern Ave 89139
Gildor Ct 89178
Giles St
3901-3999 89119
7700-8899 89123
9701-9797 89183
9799-12099 89183
Gilespie St
6601-6997 89119
6999-7200 89119
7202-7298 89119
7400-8999 89123
9700-9998 89183
10000-10799 89183
10801-11399 89183
Giliam Ct 89129
Gilleran Ave 89139
Gillette St 89117
Gilliflower Ave 89183
Gilman St 89166
Gilmary Ave 89102
W Gilmore Ave
4801-4997 89130
4999-5099 89130
5101-5299 89130
6100-6199 89108
7400-10699 89129
Gilmore Canyon Ct 89129
Gilmorehill Ct 89148
Gin Hill Ct 89134
Gina Pl 89103
Ginger Way 89123
Ginger Creek St 89108
Ginger Lily Ln 89134
Ginger Root Ct 89110
Ginger Tree Ln 89104
Gingerbread Man Ave 89183
Gingerlyn St 89122
Gingerman Ave 89148
Gipsy Ave 89107
Girard Dr 89147
Gisborn Dr 89147
Glacial Lake St 89122
Glacier Ave 89156
Glacier Basin Ct 89113
Glacier Meadow Rd 89148
Glacier Mist Ave 89149
Glacier Peak Ln 89144
Glacier Point St 89131
Glacier Ridge Ave 89131
Glacier River Ave 89113
Glacier View Ave 89134
Glade Hollow Dr 89135
Glade Minnow Ave 89113
Gladiolus Ct 89108
Gladstone Ct 89134
Gladstone Peak St 89166
Glasbury Ct 89123
Glasgow Green Dr 89141
Glass Gallon Ct 89149
Glass Slipper Ct 89130
Glass Vine Ct 89117
Glassboro Ct 89183
Glassford Ct 89148

Glassy Pond Ave 89183
Gleamstar Ave 89123
Glen Ave 89121
Glen Abbey Cir 89107
Glen Aire Ave 89148
Glen Aspen Dr 89123
Glen Aulin St 89108
Glen Canyon Ct 89110
Glen Eagles Ln 89108
Glen Ellyn Ct 89144
Glen Garden Ct 89135
Glen Heather Way 89102
Glen Iris St 89123
Glen Landing Ave 89130
Glen Malone Ct 89148
Glen Martin Ct 89107
Glen Ora Ave 89134
Glen Park Ave 89183
Glen Port St 89135
Glen Ridge Way 89108
Glen River Cir 89131
Glen Roy Dr 89134
Glen Shire Ct 89149
Glenarden Dr 89130
Glenborough St 89115
Glenbrook Way 89117
Glenbrook Estates Dr 89183
Glenburnie St 89122
Glenchester Dr 89110
Glencliff Dr 89134
Glencoe Harbor Ave 89179
Glendale Ave 89156
Glendale Cir 89107
Glendora Valley St 89178
Glenfield Cir 89129
Glengarry Dr 89129
Glenhaven Pl 89138
Glenhurst Dr 89121
Glenistar Gate Ave 89143
Glenmere Ave 89131
Glenmore Dr 89134
Glenmorgan Ct 89141
Glenmount Dr 89134
Glenna Ln 89107
Glenna Lodge St 89141
Glennaire Way 89123
Glenndavis Dr 89121
Glennon Ave 89148
Glenridding St 89183
Glenrock Dr 89134
Glenview Dr 89134
Glenwillow Dr 89117
Glenwood Ln 89156
Gliding Hawk St 89113
Glimmerglass Ave 89178
Glimmering Light Ave 89139
Glimmering Star Dr 89178
Glimmering Sun Ave 89178
Glisan Ct 89129
Glissando Ct 89139
Glistening Brook Ct 89149
Glistening Dew Ct 89131
Glistening Glen Ave 89131
Glistening Pond St 89131
Glistening Rush St 89131
Glistening Sands Dr 89119
Glitter Glen Ct 89123
Glitter Rock St 89122
Glittering Star Ave 89147
Glittering Star Ct 89130
Globe Ridge Ln 89131
Glorieta Ln 89134
Glorietta Bay Ct 89139
Glorious Linda Ct 89129
Glorious Moon Ct 89178
Glorious Sun Dr 89113
Glory Ct 89103
Glory Canyon Way 89142
Glory Creek Dr 89128
Glory Lily Ct 89123
Glory Rise Ct 89142
Gloucester Cir 89122
Gloucester Gate St 89122
Glow Dr 89115
Glowing Cottage Ct 89139
Glowing Cove Ave 89129

Glowing Ember Ct 89130
Glowing Forge Ct 89183
Glowing Moon Ct 89178
Glowing Peak St 89131
Glowing Sky Ave 89113
Glowing Sunset Ln 89135
Glowing Water St 89143
Gobbler Grove Ct 89143
Gobelin Tapestry Ct 89149
Goddess Ct 89117
Goen Way 89121
Gogo Way 89103
Gold Ave 89106
Gold Bank Dr 89134
Gold Bar Ct 89110
Gold Canyon Dr 89156
Gold Chip St 89129
Gold Coast Dr 89121
Gold Country St 89122
Gold Cup Cir 89117
Gold Dove Ct 89178
Gold Dust Ave 89120
Gold Find Ct 89130
Gold Flash Ave 89129
Gold Glimmer St 89129
Gold Hitt Ct 89179
Gold Inlet Dr 89130
Gold Lake Ave 89149
Gold Mint Ln 89122
Gold Mist Ave 89115
Gold Mountain Dr 89134
Gold Nugget Dr 89122
Gold One Ln 89122
Gold Pan Ct 89183
Gold Point St 89129
Gold Rush Ct 89113
Gold Rush Hill Ct 89183
Gold Shadow Ave 89129
Gold Sunrise Ln 89110
Gold Thorn St 89183
Gold Yarrow St 89148
Goldbrush St 89130
Goldbutte Dr 89115
Golden Ln 89119
Golden Age Ct 89144
Golden Amber St 89139
Golden Antelope Way 89139
Golden Apple St 89142
Golden Arowana Way 89149
Golden Arrow Dr
1500-2399 89169
2400-2452 89121
2454-2599 89121
Golden Aspen Ct 89129
Golden Aster Ave 89135
Golden Barrel Ave 89141
Golden Bell Dr 89139
Golden Birch Pl 89135
Golden Bit Ave 89131
Golden Blossom Ct 89134
Golden Bluff Ave 89148
Golden Cactus Ct 89138
Golden Canyon Rd 89129
Golden Chain Ave 89147
Golden Chestnut Pl 89135
Golden Cliff St 89130
Golden Cypress Ave 89117
Golden Desert Ave 89129
Golden Eagle Dr 89134
Golden Elm St 89147
Golden Falcon St 89131
Golden Feather Ct 89147
Golden Fern Ave 89178
Golden Filly St 89131
Golden Flowers St 89139
Golden Glaze St 89129
Golden Goose Ln 89118
Golden Gossamer St 89149
Golden Grape Ct 89148
Golden Haven Ave 89130
Golden Hawk Way 89108
Golden Hill Ct 89106
Golden Horizon Dr 89123
Golden Idol Ct 89131
Golden Lad Ave 89166
Golden Lantern Ct 89139

Golden Leaf Ave 89122
Golden Lily St 89117
Golden Lotus Dr 89134
Golden Moments Ave 89138
Golden Nectar Way 89142
Golden Oak Dr 89117
Golden Palms Ct 89148
Golden Peak Ct 89113
Golden Pedal St 89129
Golden Pine St 89113
Golden Pond Cir 89108
Golden Poppy St 89110
Golden Prairie Ct 89129
Golden Reflection Ct 89129
Golden Ring Ln 89147
Golden Rod Cir 89146
Golden Saddle St 89130
Golden Sands Dr 89128
Golden Scots Ct 89123
Golden Shimmer Ave 89139
Golden Shore Dr 89123
Golden Sky Dr 89106
Golden Spring Ave 89146
Golden Star Ave 89130
Golden Sunray Ln 89135
Golden Sunset Ct 89115
Golden Talon Ave 89131
Golden Timber Ln 89117
Golden Torch Ct 89147
Golden Trumpet Ave 89123
Golden View St 89129
Golden Villa Ct 89178
Golden Vista Dr 89123
Golden Willow Ln 89135
Golden Wing St 89113
Golden Yucca Dr 89147
Goldenbush Ct 89148
Goldencreek Way 89108
Goldenglow Rd 89108
Goldenmoon St 89108
Goldenspur Ln 89117
Goldensun Ct 89108
Goldhill Ave & Way 89106
Goldmine Dr 89156
Goldmount Ave 89107
Goldridge St 89149
Goldring Ave 89106
Goldsboro Ct 89134
Goldspur St 89129
Goldstone Ave 89143
Goldy Ln 89107
Goldyke St 89115
Goleta Dr 89108
Golf Ln 89108
Golf Club Ave 89145
Golf Course St 89145
Golf Estates Dr 89141
Golf Links Dr 89134
Golf Player Ave 89145
Golf Range St 89145
Golfers St 89142
Golfers Oasis Dr 89149
Golfridge Dr 89130
Golfside Dr 89134
Gomer Rd
6600-6698 89139
7100-7298 89178
7401-7499 89178
Gondolier St 89178
Gonzales Dr 89130
Good Fellows St 89135
Good Fortune Ct 89139
Good Humored Ct 89149
Goodhaven Dr 89134
Goodhope Ct 89134
Goodman Ln 89115
Goodnews Ct 89134
Goodrich Cir 89108
Goodsprings Ct 89110
Goodwill St 89106
Goody Ct 89118
Goose Creek Pl 89108
Goose Lake Way 89149
Goose River Ave 89131
Gordo Way 89117
Gordon Ave 89108

Gordon Creek Ave 89139
Gorgas Ct 89129
Gorham Ave 89110
Gorky St 89121
Gorsky Ave 89131
Gosling St 89117
Gosport Ave 89131
Goss Ranch Ct 89131
Gossamer Fog Ave 89139
Gossamer Wind St 89139
Gothic Ave 89117
Gothic Marigold St 89149
Gourley Ave 89178
Government Point Way 89183
Governors Hill St 89129
Govett Crescent Ct 89130
E Gowan Rd 89115
W Gowan Rd
4800-5099 89130
5101-5399 89130
5700-5798 89108
5800-6399 89108
7000-10599 89129
Goya St 89121
Grace St 89121
Grace Mountain St 89115
Graceda St 89148
Graceful Gold St 89123
Graceful Orchid St 89117
Gracemont Ave 89139
Gracemoor Ct 89149
Graceville Ave 89128
Gracious Lady St 89178
Gracious Pine Ave 89143
Grade Vista St 89135
W Graderle Ave 89113
Grafton Ct 89117
Gragson Ave 89101
Graham Ave 89122
Grammy Dr 89145
Gran Paradiso Dr 89131
Granada Ave & Cir 89107
Granada Bluff Ct 89135
Granada Willows St 89139
Granberg Ct 89131
Granby Ct 89156
Grand Cir 89101
Grand Dr 89169
Grand Augusta Ln 89144
Grand Basin Dr 89156
Grand Canal Dr 89117
N Grand Canyon Dr
4400-4698 89129
4700-4799 89129
4900-6700 89149
6702-6898 89149
8200-8299 89166
S Grand Canyon Dr
2601-2699 89117
4100-4500 89147
4502-4598 89147
5400-5498 89148
5601-5699 89148
8601-8699 89178
8800-8998 89178
Grand Castle Way 89130
S Grand Central Pkwy 89106
Grand Cerritos Ave 89183
Grand Clover Ln 89156
Grand Concourse St 89166
Grand Cru Ave 89123
Grand Cypress Ave 89134
Grand Emerald Ct 89149
Grand Entries Dr 89130
Grand Falls Ct 89113
Grand Fir Ct 89123
Grand Gate St 89143
Grand Grove Ct 89149
Grand Guiness Ct 89130
Grand Gulch Ct 89110
Grand Haven Ave 89134
Grand Height Ave 89149
Grand Heritage St 89130
Grand Island Ct 89117
Grand Isle Ln 89144

Grand Junction Ave 89179
Grand Masters Dr 89141
Grand Mayne Ct 89139
Grand Meadow St 89129
Grand Mesa Dr 89134
Grand Montecito Pkwy 89149
Grand Mountain Cir 89147
Grand Oaks Dr 89156
Grand Pacific Dr 89128
Grand Palace Ave 89130
Grand Palms Cir 89131
Grand Pine Ave 89143
Grand Ridge Ct 89147
Grand Rodeo St 89117
Grand Sequoia St 89139
Grand Sky Ave 89178
Grand Stand Ave 89131
Grand Sunburst Ct 89149
Grand Teton Dr
5100-6098 89131
6100-7700 89131
7702-8398 89131
9700-14799 89166
Grand Viewpoint Ct 89147
Grand Vista Ave 89149
Grand Wash Ct 89129
Grandbank Dr 89145
Grande Ronde Ct 89110
Grande Valley Dr 89135
Grandiose Ct 89130
Grandola Dr 89103
Grandover Ct 89148
Grandross Ct 89130
Grandspur St 89147
Grandview Dr & Pl 89120
Grandview Ridge Ave 89139
Grandview Spring Ave 89166
Granemore St 89135
Granger Farm Way 89145
Grangeville Dr 89108
Granite Ave 89106
Granite City Ct 89166
Granite Creek Ct 89131
Granite Gorge Ct 89148
Granite Lake Dr 89128
Granite Mountain Ln 89129
Granite Peak Ct 89145
Granite Rapids St 89138
Granite Reef Ave 89147
Granite Ridge Dr 89135
Granite River Ln 89122
Granite Springs Ct 89139
Granite Walk Ave 89178
Grannis Ln 89104
Grant St 89106
Grants Arbor Rd 89183
Grants Landing Ct 89141
Grape Arbor Way 89142
Grape Blossom Ave 89142
Grape Ivy Ct 89183
Grape Leaf Ave 89141
Grapefruit Cir 89103
Grapeland Ave 89148
Graphic Center Dr 89118
Grasmere Ave 89121
Grass Ct 89107
Grass Meadows Dr 89142
Grass Valley Pl 89107
Grasshopper Dr 89122
Grassland Cir 89129
Grasswood Dr 89147
Grassy Bank St 89139
Grassy Butte Ct 89149
Grassy Canyon St 89129
Grassy Field Ct 89131
Grassy Knoll St 89147
Grassy Point Cir 89145
Grassy Spring Pl 89135
Grassy Weep Ct 89178
Grassyrock Ct 89129
Gravel Hill St 89117
Gray Ln 89119
Gray St 89145
Gray Aster Dr 89122
Gray Bluff Dr 89129
Gray Duck Ct 89147

Gray Eagle Way 89117
Gray Granite Ave 89123
Gray Horse St 89149
Gray Juniper Ave 89130
Gray Quail Ct 89149
Gray Sea Eagle Ave 89117
Gray Wolf River Way 89149
Grayling Dr 89134
Grays Peak Ct 89156
Grays River Ct 89148
Graystone Canyon Ave 89183
Grazia Ave 89135
Graziano Ave 89141
Grazing Hill Ct 89143
Grazing Meadow Dr 89142
Greasewood Dr 89110
Great Bear St 89147
Great Bend Dr 89117
Great Dover St 89166
Great Duke Ave 89183
Great Eagle Ct 89122
Great Falls Ave 89110
Great Gable Dr 89183
Great Glen Ct 89129
Great Gorge Ct 89149
Great Horizon Dr 89149
Great Oak Ave 89147
Great Pine Dr 89118
Great Plains Way 89121
Great Sioux Rd 89179
Great Smoky Ave 89156
Great Victoria Ave 89179
Greatwood Ave 89113
Grechetto Ct 89141
Grecian Laurel Ct 89183
Greeber Ct 89131
Greek Palace Ave 89178
Green Acres Ave 89156
Green Apple Way 89142
Green Bay Dr 89128
Green Beryl Ct 89131
Green Canyon Dr 89103
Green Cedar Dr 89123
Green Clover Ave 89149
Green Diamond Cir 89118
Green Ferry Ave 89131
Green Finch St 89117
Green Forest Way 89118
Green Frost Dr 89129
Green Gables Ave 89183
Green Heron St 89115
Green Horn St 89118
Green Hunter St 89123
Green Island Ave 89149
Green Jade Dr 89129
Green Leaf Dr 89120
Green Meadow Dr 89129
Green Mesa Ct 89147
Green Mountain Ct 89135
Green Orchard Ct 89183
Green Palms St 89130
Green Pasture Ave 89149
Green Pine St 89143
Green Ridge Ave 89178
Green Ripple Ln 89156
Green River St 89142
Green Sage Way 89138
Green Spruce St 89123
Green Thicket Ct 89123
Green Tree Ave 89142
Green Turtle Ct 89131
Green Vineyard Ave 89148
Green Vista Ct 89156
Green Wave Ct 89134
Green Willow St 89130
Greenbank St 89110
Greenbare Dr 89110
Greenbriar Dr 89121
Greenbriar Townhouse Way 89121
Greenbrook St 89110
Greenbush Dr 89117
Greencombe Ct 89130
Greencreek Dr 89110
Greencrest Dr 89121

Greendale Ct & St 89121
Greene Ln 89119
Greenery Ct 89130
Greenery View Ln 89118
Greenfield Ln 89107
Greenfield Lakes St 89122
Greengrove Dr 89103
Greenham Cir 89117
Greenhedge St 89110
Greenhill Dr 89121
Greenhouse Ct 89134
Greenhurst Rd 89145
Greenlake Way 89149
Greenoak Cir 89145
Greenpoint St 89147
Greensboro Ln 89134
Greensburg Ave 89178
Greenside Dr 89141
Greenslopes Ct 89110
Greenspun Dr 89130
Greenview Ct 89134
Greenway Dr 89108
Greenwich Ct 89129
Greenwich Village Ave 89123
Greenwood Dr 89103
Greenwood Springs Dr 89122
Gregg Pl 89122
Gregory St 89106
Grenache St 89148
Grenfell Dr 89129
Grennock Ct 89115
Grenoble Dr 89142
Grenville Ave 89134
Gresham Dr 89123
Gretel Cir 89102
Gretna Green Ct 89110
Grey Bull Way 89128
Grey Cloud St 89145
Grey Dolphin Dr 89117
Grey Dove Cir 89118
Grey Feather Dr 89135
Grey Havens Ct 89135
Grey Mesa St 89149
Grey Neck Cove Ct 89178
Grey Pebble Ct 89123
Grey Seal Bay St 89179
Grey Spencer Dr 89141
Grey Wolf Ln 89149
Greycrest Ct 89145
Greydawn Dr 89108
Greyhawk Ave 89108
Greyhound Ln 89122
Greymouth St 89110
Greystoke Acres St 89145
Greystone Dr 89108
Gridley Ct 89134
Grier Dr 89119
Grier Woods Ct 89134
Griffin Ave 89129
Griffith Ave 89104
Griffith Peak Dr 89135
Grinding Rock Way 89122
Grindle Point St 89147
Griscom Ct 89145
Grist Mill Ct 89113
Gritty Garnet Ave 89183
Grizzly St 89131
Grizzly Bear Way 89123
Grizzly Creek St 89178
Grizzly Forest Dr 89178
Grizzly Giant St 89139
Grizzly Gorge St 89130
Grobanite St 89131
Groningen Ct 89131
Grossman Ct 89122
Grossmont Ave 89110
Groton Ave 89129
Grotta Azzurra Ave 89138
Grotto Mountain Ave 89166
Grounsel St 89131
Grouse St 89134
Grouse Grove Ave 89148
Grove Cir 89119
Grove Acre Ct 89131
Grove Crest Ln 89134
Grove Hill Ln 89108

Grove Leaf St 89156
Grove Ridge Ave 89148
Groveland Ave 89139
Grovespring St 89135
Groveton Ct 89131
Groveview Ln 89103
Growing Vine Ct 89141
Grumio Ct 89141
Grundy Cir 89110
Gryffin Ave 89123
Guadalimar Way 89122
Guadalupe Ave 89108
Guardian Peak St 89148
Guava Nectar Ave 89131
Guggenheim Ct 89123
Guild Ct 89131
Guinevere Ave 89110
Gulf Breeze Dr 89128
Gulf Island Ave 89156
Gulf Pines Ave 89148
Gulf Shores Dr 89122
Gulf Springs Ct 89130
Gulf Stream Ct 89113
Gulfport Ct 89145
Gulfstar Ln 89147
Gull Dr 89134
Gull Point Ave 89123
Gullane St 89142
Gulliver St 89115
Gulls Perch Dr 89128
Gum Tree Ct 89144
Gumwood Rd 89108
Gunbelt Dr 89123
Gunderson Blvd 89103
Gundy Ct 89134
Gunfighter Ln 89161
Gunn Ct 89156
Gunpowder Falls St 89183
Gunslinger St 89119
Gunsmith Dr 89123
Gunter Hill Ct 89183
Gunther Cir 89145
Gushing Spring Ave 89131
Gusto St 89135
Gusty Ct 89129
Guthrie Dr 89117
Guy Ave
6301-6399 89131
8600-8698 89143
Gwen Pl 89108
Gwynns Falls St 89183
Gym Dr 89119
Gypsum Quarry St 89178
Gypsy Bell Ave 89123
H St 89106
Habanero St 89118
Haberfield Ct 89178
Habersham Ct 89183
Hache St 89103
E Hacienda Ave
200-798 89119
800-2399 89119
2401-2497 89120
2499-4399 89120
5000-5799 89122
W Hacienda Ave
3200-3398 89118
3400-5100 89118
5102-5298 89118
7301-7399 89113
Hacienda Cir 89120
Hacienda Grande Ave 89141
Hackamore Dr 89103
Hackberry Dr 89123
Hackberry Hill Ave 89131
Hackensack Ct 89128
Hackney Ct 89183
Hackney Horse Ct 89122
Haddington Ln 89145
Haddock Ave 89115
Haddon Dr 89134
Hadley Meadow Ct 89131
Hadwen Ln 89135
Haflinger Ct 89122
Hagemann Ln 89110
Haile Sky St 89148

Haileville Dr 89129
Hailey Lynne Rd 89183
Hainsworth Ave 89148
Halbert Ave 89110
Halco Ct 89108
Haldir Ave 89178
Haleakala Dr 89122
W Haleh Ave 89141
Halehaven Dr 89110
Haley Ave
5700-5898 89108
7101-7299 89131
9601-9699 89149
Haley St 89124
Half Dome Cir 89145
Half Moon Point Dr 89113
Half Shell Way 89128
Halfmoon Way 89108
Halfmoon Bay Dr 89115
Halfway Rock St 89147
Halifax Ave & Cir 89107
Halite Ct 89128
Hall Of Fame Dr 89110
Halleck Ct 89110
Hallendale Dr 89147
Hallet Dr 89122
Halleys Comet St 89143
Halloran Springs Rd 89148
Hallston St 89134
Hallwood Dr 89119
Halsey Ct 89129
Halter Dr 89122
Haltwhistle Ct 89178
Halvern Ave 89110
Hamburg St 89147
Hamdem Ave 89129
Hamilton Ave 89122
Hamilton Ln 89106
Hamilton Beach Ln 89128
Hamilton Grove Ave 89122
E Hammer Ln 89115
W Hammer Ln
6400-6699 89130
8000-8198 89149
8200-9199 89149
9201-9899 89149
Hammerschmidt Ct 89135
Hammerwood Dr 89135
Hammett Park Ave 89166
Hammock St 89147
Hammond Ct 89110
Hampshire Cir 89121
Hampshire Bay St 89139
Hampshire Green Ct 89110
Hampstead Ave 89145
Hampstead Heath Ct 89130
Hampstead Hills Ave 89149
S Hampton Ln 89110
Hampton Bluff St 89117
Hampton Cove Ln 89113
Hampton Green Ave 89129
Hampton Grove Ct 89129
Hampton Hills Ln 89144
Hampton Park Ln 89113
Hampton Willows Ln 89113
Hanbury Manor Ln 89145
Hancock St 89110
Hand Pl 89106
Hand Painted Ct 89149
Hand Woven Ct 89149
Handle Bar Ln 89123
Hanford Ave 89107
Hanging Rock Dr 89134
Hanging Tapestry Ct 89149
Hanging Tree Ln 89118
Hanky Panky St 89131
Hannah Clapp St 89179
Hannapah Ct 89110
Hannibal Way 89130
Hanover Grove Ave 89148
Hansel Cir 89102
Hansford Ranch Ave 89131
Hanta Ave 89117
Happy Cir & Ln 89120
Happy Isles Dr 89156
Happy Jack Dr 89115

Happy Pines Ave 89143
Happy Stream Ave 89143
Happy Valley Ave 89121
Hapsburg Ct 89115
Harbison Canyon Ct 89130
Harbor Cliff Dr 89128
Harbor Coast St 89148
Harbor Cove Dr 89128
Harbor Grey Ct 89143
Harbor Heights Dr 89117
Harbor Hills Ln 89117
Harbor Island Dr 89128
Harbor Lights Dr 89130
Harbor Oaks Cir 89128
Harbor Pines Ct 89183
Harbor Pond Dr 89131
Harbor Rain Ave 89117
Harbor Stream Ave 89149
Harbor Tides St 89147
Harbor View Dr 89119
Harbor Vista St 89117
Harbor Wind Ave 89178
Harborside Dr 89117
Harbour Pointe Ave 89122
Harbour Shores Ct 89128
Harbour Towne Ave 89113
Harbow Ridge Pl 89131
Hardesty Ct 89139
Hardrock St 89156
Hardtack Cir 89119
Hardwick Ct 89129
Hardwick Hall Way 89135
Hardy Falls St 89141
Harem Ln 89115
Hargrove Ave 89107
Harley Way 89101
Harlow St 89131
E Harmon Ave
1-199 89109
200-371 89169
373-499 89169
701-897 89119
899-2199 89119
2201-2399 89119
2400-4999 89121
5100-5112 89122
5114-5199 89122
5201-5599 89122
W Harmon Ave
2500-2600 89158
3250-3482 89103
3484-6099 89103
6101-6199 89103
Harmon Cir 89122
Harmonize Ct 89131
Harmony Ave 89107
Harmony Ct 89121
Harmony Green Dr 89149
Harmony Grove Ave 89148
Harmony Hall Ave 89178
Harmony Peak St 89166
Harney Ct 89110
Harney Peak St 89166
Harp Tree St 89139
Harper Cir 89107
Harpers Ferry Ave 89148
Harpoon Cir 89117
Harrahs Ct 89119
Harriet St 89101
Harrington Ave 89110
Harris Ave
1200-1798 89101
1800-2999 89101
3500-3898 89110
3900-5499 89110
5501-5599 89110
Harris Spring Ln 89122
Harris Springs Rd 89124
Harrison Ave 89106
Harrison Dr
4700-4899 89121
4900-6299 89120
6301-6399 89120
Harrison Schmitt Ave 89145
Harrogate Ave 89129
Harrow Rock St 89143
Hart Ave 89106
Hartford Ct & Pl 89102
Hartford Fern Ln 89115
Hartford Hills Ave 89166
Hartford Peak Ct 89166
Hartke Pl 89104
Hartman St 89108
Hartwell Dr 89123
Hartwick Ln 89134
Hartwood Rd 89108
Harvard St 89107
Harvest Dr 89108
Harvest Breeze Rd 89118
Harvest Green Way 89135
Harvest Hill Ln 89135
Harvest Homes St 89123
Harvest Moon Ln 89107
Harvest Night St 89129
Harvest Run Dr 89145
Harvest Spring Pl 89143
Harvest Time St 89130
Harvest Valley Ave 89129
Harvest Wind Dr 89135
Harvester Course Dr 89148
Harwich Ave 89129
Harwich Bay Ave 89179
Harwick Ranch Ct 89131
Hasib Ct 89156
Haskell Flats Dr 89128
Hasley Canyon Ave 89139
Hassell Ave 89106
Hassett Ave 89104
Hast Ct 89156
Hastings Ave
1500-1598 89106
3101-3197 89107
3199-3399 89107
Hat Rock Ct 89129
Hathaway Dr 89156
Hathaway Pines Ln 89138
Hathersage Ave 89139
Hatteras Ct 89145
Hattiesburg Ave 89148
Hauck Cir 89115
Hauck St
2801-3297 89146
3299-3399 89146
3600-3699 89103
6001-6099 89118
7501-7597 89139
7599-9200 89139
9202-9698 89139
Haulover Beach Ct 89131
Haunts Walk Ave 89178
Havana Brown Ct 89166
Havasu Canyon Ave 89166
Havasupai Ave 89148
Havelina St 89108
Havelock Ct 89148
Haven St
5200-7199 89119
7700-8899 89123
9901-10097 89183
10099-11999 89183
Haven Beach Way 89117
Haven Brook Ct 89128
Haven Cove Ave 89113
Haven Hill Ave 89106
Haven Hollow Ave 89130
Haven Hurst Ct 89129
Haven Oaks Pl 89138
Haven Ridge Ct 89117
Havencrest Dr 89110
Havenmist Ct 89113
Havenwood Ln 89135
Havenworth Ave 89123
Havercamp St 89117
Haverford Ave 89121
Haverhill St 89121
Haviland Rd 89123
Havkin Ct 89149
Hawaii Ave 89104
Hawaiian Hills Ave 89183
Hawaiian Sky Ct 89131
Hawaiian Summer St 89123
Hawes End Ct 89183
Hawk Bay Pl 89144
Hawk Clan Ct 89131
Hawk Cliff Ave 89148
Hawk Crest St 89141
Hawk Feather St 89183
Hawk Haven St 89131
Hawk Ravine St 89178
Hawk Ridge Dr 89135
Hawk Shadow Ave 89113
Hawk Valley Ave 89134
Hawks Wing St 89178
Hawksbeard Ct 89135
Hawksbill Ct 89117
Hawksdale Dr 89134
Hawksmore Ct 89142
Hawkstone Ave 89147
Hawley Ct 89118
Hawthorn Woods Ave 89130
Hawthorne Way 89147
Hawthorne Berry St 89141
Hawthorne Creek Ct 89131
Hawthorne Grove St 89183
Hayborn Meadows St 89138
Hayden Ct 89134
Hayden Peak Ln 89156
Hayes Ave 89108
Hayes Pl 89107
Hayloft St 89143
Haymarket St 89166
Haymarket Peak Ave 89166
Haypenny Ct 89123
Haypress Ct 89141
Hayride St 89149
Haystack Dr 89122
Hayward Ave 89122
Hayward Field Rd 89115
Haywood Dr 89135
Hazard Ave 89108
Hazel Beach Ct 89135
Hazel Brooks St 89129
Hazel Dell St 89129
Hazel Plain Ave 89131
Hazel Rock St 89179
Hazel Tree Ct 89142
Hazelcrest Cir & Dr 89121
Hazelmere Ln 89148
Hazelnut Garden St 89131
Hazelridge Dr 89129
Hazeltine Ln 89113
Hazelwood St 89119
Hazelyn Ct 89122
Hazen Ct 89110
Hazy Haven Ct 89149
Hazy Meadow Ln 89108
Headrick Dr 89166
Headwater Ave 89178
Headwind Ave 89129
Heale Garden Ct 89135
Health Aster Ct 89183
Hearst Ct 89117
Hearthfire St 89178
Heartline Dr 89145
Hearts Desire Ave 89115
Heartstone Cir 89129
Heather Breeze Ct 89141
Heather Creek Pl 89122
Heather Downs Dr 89113
Heather Falls Dr 89129
Heather Glen Ct 89123
Heather Knoll Cir 89129
Heather Lilly Ct 89129
Heather Lynnette Ct 89123
Heather Marie Dr 89110
Heather Meadows Ct 89108
Heather Mist Ln 89108
Heather Rock Ct 89117
Heather Valley Dr 89134
Heatherbrook Cir 89120
Heatherdale Ct 89108
Heatherton Ave 89110
Heatherwood St 89149
Heathrow St 89135
Heatwave St 89123
Heaven Delight Ct 89130
Heavenly Hills Ct 89145
Heavenly Joy Way 89147
Heavenly Lights Ave 89123
Heavenly Love Way 89147
Heavenly Peak St 89166
Heavenly Star Cir 89128
Heavenly Valley Ave 89147
Heavenly View Ct 89117
Hebard Dr 89121
Heber Ct 89156
Hebert Cir 89115
Hebron Dr 89147
Heddell Ct 89118
Hedge Way 89110
Hedge Creek Ave 89123
Hedge Rock St 89123
Hedge Top Ave 89110
Hedge View Ave 89129
Hedgeford Ct 89120
Hedgehaven Ct 89120
Hedgehope Dr 89183
Hedgemaple Ct 89148
Hedgemont Ave 89138
Hedingham Ct 89135
Heffner Hills Cir 89117
Heggie Ave 89131
Heidelberg St 89135
Heidi Cir 89102
Heidi St 89119
Heinrick Ct 89118
Heirloom Ct 89134
Heisman Dr 89110
Helaman Ave 89120
Held Rd 89101
Heldron St 89121
Helen Ave
2100-2199 89108
3800-3898 89130
3900-4299 89130
6500-6599 89131
Helen Belle Dr 89110
Helena Ave 89129
Helena Bay Pl 89129
Helena Cove Ct 89129
Helena Hideaway Ct 89129
Heller Dr 89115
Hellman Park St 89166
Helm Dr 89119
Helmhill Ave 89123
Helyne St 89107
Hemet Dr 89134
Hemingway Ct 89149
Hemlock Cir 89145
Hendiso Dr 89122
Hennessy Ct 89123
Henniker Way 89134
Henry Dr 89110
Henshaw Ave 89118
Henson Ln 89156
Hera St 89117
Hercules Dr 89128
Herford Ln 89110
N & S Heritage Ave, Cir, Ct, Dr, Ln, Pl & Way 89121
Heritage Desert St 89178
Heritage Harbor Dr 89131
Heritage Hills Dr 89134
Heritage Oaks St 89119
Heritage Park Ave 89135
Hermes Stables Ct 89131
Hermit Rapids Ave 89148
Hermitage Dr 89108
Hermosa St 89169
Hermosa Canyon Dr 89145
Hermosa Palms Ave 89123
Hermosa Valley St 89178
Hermosillo St 89115
Hernandez Ave 89123
Hernando Dr 89147
Heron Ave 89107
Heron Island Ave 89148
Herons Creek Dr 89134
Herrera Ave 89129
Herring Ave 89147
Herring Cove Ave 89178
Herring Run Ave 89183
Herron Hills St 89156
Hershey Ln 89134
Hesperides Ave 89131
Hetherbrae Ln 89156
Hewitt St 89106
Hexham Abbey Pl 89178
Heyer Way 89161
Heyfield Dr 89134
Hialeah Dr 89119
Hiawatha Rd 89108
Hibbetts Ct & Dr 89103
Hibiscus Dr 89107
Hickam Ave
5100-5799 89130
5801-5999 89130
7500-9300 89129
9302-9398 89129
Hickman Ct 89129
Hickock St 89110
Hickory St 89110
Hickory Bark Rd 89135
Hickory Crest Ct 89147
Hickory Glen St 89179
Hickory Heights Ave 89148
Hickory Hills Dr 89130
Hickory Hollow Ave 89123
Hickory Nut Ave 89142
Hickory Park St 89138
Hickory Post Ave 89179
Hickory Ridge Ct 89147
Hickory Run Ct 89178
Hidden Ct 89145
Hidden Beach Ct 89115
Hidden Bull St 89178
Hidden Cave Ct 89149
Hidden Cellar Ct 89183
Hidden Crossing Ln 89129
Hidden Desert Way 89110
Hidden Gazebo St 89131
Hidden Glen Ct 89134
Hidden Harbor Ave 89148
Hidden Heritage Ct 89110
Hidden Highlands Dr 89110
Hidden Hills Dr 89123
Hidden Hole Dr 89148
Hidden Knoll Ct 89117
Hidden Lake Ave 89124
Hidden Oak Ct 89103
Hidden Oasis Ct 89110
Hidden Palms Pkwy 89123
Hidden Pines Ave 89143
Hidden Plateau St 89130
Hidden Quail Ave 89131
Hidden Ridge St 89129
Hidden Spring Dr 89117
Hidden Treasure Dr 89134
Hidden View St 89156
Hidden Village Ave 89131
Hidden Well Rd 89119
Higger Tor Ave 89139
Higgins Ct 89117
High St 89113
High Alpine St 89178
High Bluff Way 89108
High Breeze Ct 89106
High Cascade Ave 89129
High Chaparral St 89113
High Country Ln 89138
High Desert Dr 89149
High Dormer Ct 89179
High Falls Ct 89178
High Forest Ave 89123
High Grove St 89156
High Horizon Ave 89149
High Meadow Ave 89131
High Noon Ln 89118
High Range Dr 89134
High Sail Ct 89117
High Sierra Ave 89156
High Stream Ave 89131
High Tide Ct 89117
High Valley Ct 89128
High Wager Way 89122
Highacre Dr 89145
Highbridge Ct 89166
Highgate Park Ct 89123
Highland Ave 89102
Highland Dr 89102
S Highland Dr
2500-3365 89109
3367-3499 89109
3501-3597 89103
3599-3699 89103
Highland Bluff Way 89138
Highland Castle Ct 89129
Highland Falls Dr 89134
Highland Hills Ct 89148
Highland Mesa Ct 89144
Highland Park Ct 89144
Highland Pony St 89149
Highland Ranch St 89131
Highland Springs Cir 89147
Highland View Ave 89145
Highland Vista Way 89138
Highlands Point St 89123
Highlands River St 89141
Highline Ln 89134
Highridge Dr 89134
Highside Ct 89110
Highvale Dr 89134
Highview Rock Ct 89149
Higley St 89103
Hilary St 89147
Hildago Way 89121
Hildebrand Ln 89121
Hilgard Ave 89178
Hill Alto Ct 89131
Hill Canyon Ln 89144
Hill Country Ave 89134
Hill Haven Ave 89130
Hill Prince Ct 89142
Hill Valley St 89129
Hill View Ave 89107
Hillary Elan Ct 89139
Hillcrest Ave 89102
Hillcroft Way 89147
Hilldale Ave 89121
Hillgrass Rd 89123
Hillgrove Ct 89145
Hillhead Ct 89148
Hilliard Ave 89128
Hillingdon Ct 89129
Hillman Ave 89142
Hillock Ct 89144
Hillpath Trl 89108
Hillpointe Rd 89134
Hills Dr 89134
Hills Of Red Dr 89128
Hillsboro Ln 89120
Hillsboro Creek Ct 89129
Hillsboro Pines Ct 89131
Hillsdale Ct 89108
Hillsgate St 89134
Hillshire Dr 89134
Hillside Pl 89104
Hillside Bloom Ct 89130
Hillside Brook Ave 89130
Hillside Garden Dr 89135
Hillside Pine St 89148
Hillside View Ct 89149
Hillstop Crest Ct 89131
Hillsway Dr 89110
Hilltop St 89120
Hilltop View Ln 89138
Hilltop Windmill St 89139
Hillwood Dr 89134
Hilo Ave 89104
Hilton St 89121
Hilton Head Ct 89128
Hilverson Ave 89148
Himalayan St 89166
Himalayas Ave 89128
Hines Ave 89143
Hinesville Ct 89129
Hinkle Dr 89101
Hinkle St 89107
Hinsdale St 89115
Hinson St
900-1098 89107
1101-1197 89102
1199-1649 89102
1651-1699 89102
6000-7200 89118
7202-7298 89118
7401-8599 89139
8900-8998 89139
9700-9799 89141
9801-10499 89141
Hipwader Ct 89113
Hirsch Mountain Dr 89131
Historic Legacy Ct 89110
Hitching Rail Dr 89117
Hite Ln 89166
Hobart Ave 89107
Hobbiton Ave 89135
Hobble Creek Dr 89120
Hobbs Dr 89120
Hobiecat Cir 89121
Hoboken Flats Ave 89178
Hodgenville St 89106
Hodges Ave 89123
Hodgson Mill Ct 89131
Hoeker Way 89147
Hogan Dr 89107
Hogan Falls Cir 89123
Hogenmiller Cir 89115
Holbert Ct 89110
Holbrook Dr 89103
Holcomb Cir 89107
Holcomb Bridge Ct 89149
Holden St 89115
Holiday Hills St 89139
Holiday Park Ave 89135
Holland Ave 89106
Holland Heights Ave 89123
Hollander Ave 89148
Hollandsworth Ave 89123
Hollenbeck St 89178
Holleys Hill St 89129
Hollingworth Ct 89117
Hollins Hall St 89145
Hollis Mountain Ave 89148
Hollister Ave 89131
Holliston Cir 89108
Holloran Ct 89128
Hollow Brook Ave 89142
Hollow Creek Ln 89144
Hollow Green Dr 89129
Hollow Pine St 89143
Hollow Rock Ct 89135
Hollow Wharf Dr 89128
Holloway Heights Ave 89129
Holly Ave 89106
Holly Bluff Ct 89122
Holly Grove Dr 89130
Holly Hill Ave 89104
Holly Knoll Ave 89129
Holly River St 89148
Hollyberry Ct 89142
Hollycrest Dr 89117
Hollyhock Ln 89107
Hollyleaf Ct 89115
Hollymead Dr 89135
Hollywell St 89135
N Hollywood Blvd
2-198 89110
200-1500 89110
1502-1598 89110
1800-2599 89156
5801-5997 89115
5999-6599 89115
S Hollywood Blvd
1500-2199 89142
2900-5699 89122
Hollywood Hills Ave 89178
Hollywood Park Ave 89129
Holmby Ave
5100-5499 89146
5501-6799 89146
7401-7499 89117
Holmes St 89106
Holt Ave 89115
Holy Cross Dr 89156
Holyrod Park Ct 89122
Holyrood Ct 89141
Homage Way 89117
Hombard Ave 89148
Home St 89122
Home Light St 89139

Home Run Dr 89130
Homecrest Dr 89121
Homedale Way 89107
Homeland St 89128
Homemade Ct 89149
Homer Ct 89139
Homeria St 89113
Homerun Champ Dr 89113
Homestake Mine Ct 89156
Homestead Rd 89143
Hometown Hero Dr 89113
Homeview Ct 89117
Homeward Cloud Ave 89183
Homewillow Ave 89123
Homewood Dr 89147
Hondo Ct 89121
Honey Crest Dr 89135
Honey Flower Ct 89147
Honey Ginger Ave 89131
Honey Lake St 89110
Honey Maple Ave 89148
Honey Mesquite Ln 89130
Honey Ridge Ct 89135
Honey Tree Dr 89144
Honey Vine Ave 89143
Honeybee Meadow Way 89134
Honeybrook Ct 89147
Honeycomb Dr 89147
Honeydew Cir 89147
Honeygrove Ave 89110
Honeysuckle Ct 89119
Honeysuckle Ridge St 89148
Honeywood Cir 89128
N Honolulu St 89110
S Honolulu St 89104
Honors Ct 89129
Honors Course Dr 89148
Hood River Ave 89179
Hook Creek Ct 89130
Hoop Land Valley Ct 89131
Hoopa Ln 89169
Hooper Bay St 89179
Hoover Ave 89101
Hopcroft Ave 89178
Hope Forest Dr 89134
Hope Island Dr 89134
Hope Mills Dr 89135
Hope Ranch Ln 89134
Hope Valley St 89139
Hopeful Light Ave 89139
Hopi Ln 89110
Hopkins Dr 89156
Hopkinsville Ct 89148
Hopland Cir 89129
Hopscotch St 89131
Horatio Ct 89141
Horizon Cir & St 89121
Horizon Hills Dr 89117
Horizon Homes St 89129
Horizon Hyatt Ave 89178
Horizon Lake Dr 89128
Horizon Mist Ave 89178
Horizon Ridge Ct 89156
Horizon Rock Ave 89179
Horizon Sunset Dr 89123
Horizon Village Ave 89183
Horizon Vista Ln 89117
Horizon Wind Ave 89178
Horn St 89107
Horn Beam Ct 89131
Horn Tail Ct 89131
Hornbeak Ct 89123
Hornblower Ave 89131
Hornbrook Ct 89130
Horned Lark Ct 89117
Hornstone Ct 89149
Horse Dr
5301-5497 89131
5499-6600 89131
6602-7798 89131
8600-8698 89143
13000-13099 89166
Horse Back Cir 89117
Horse Bridle St 89131
Horse Canyon Dr 89178
Horseback Ridge Ave 89144
Horsenettle St 89149
Horseshoe Dr 89120
Horseshoe Basin Ave 89149
Horseshoe Bend Ln 89113
Horseshoe Cliff Ave 89113
Horseshoe Falls Ct 89144
Horseshoe Hills Ave 89131
Horseshoe Mesa St 89147
Horsethief Ranch Ave 89123
Hosner St 89178
Hospitality Pl 89131
Hoss Pl 89131
Hosta Ct 89135
Hostetler Ave 89131
Hot Breeze St 89178
Hot Brook Point St 89134
Hot Creek Dr 89128
Hot Oak Ct 89134
Hot Oak Ridge St 89134
Hot Oak Springs Ave 89134
Hot River St 89134
Hot Springs Ave 89110
Hotchkiss Ct 89110
Houssels Ave 89104
Houston Dr 89104
Houston Peak St 89166
Houston Ridge Ave 89178
Howard Ave & Dr 89104
Howard Dade Ave 89129
Howard Hughes Pkwy 89169
Howdy Wells Ave 89115
Howell Mill Ct 89113
Howestin 89199
Howling Coyote Ave 89135
Hoyt Ave 89104
N Hualapai Way
3400-3898 89129
3900-3999 89129
6200-6298 89149
7001-7199 89166
S Hualapai Way
700-799 89145
1101-3297 89117
3299-3400 89117
3402-3498 89117
3700-4598 89147
5600-5698 89148
5957-5963 89148
Hubbard St 89110
Hubbell St 89156
Huber St 89120
Huber Heights Dr 89128
Huckaby Ave 89179
Hudson Ln 89128
Hudson Bay Ave 89110
Hudson Brook St 89183
Hudson Woods Ct 89156
Huerta Dr 89121
Huff Creek Ct 89178
Huff Mountain Ave 89131
Hugana Pl 89141
Hughes Center Dr 89169
Hughes Springs Dr 89131
Hulme End Ave 89139
Humboldt Ct 89142
Humming Ln 89143
Hummingbird Ln 89103
Humus Ave 89139
Hunnicut St 89110
Hunt St 89146
Hunt Club St 89128
Huntdale Ln 89128
Hunter Brook St 89139
Hunter Flat St 89138
Hunter Hill Ct 89139
Hunter Mountain Ave 89129
Hunter Springs Dr 89134
Hunters Creek Ln 89145
Hunters Green Ave 89166
Hunters Lodge Ct 89113
Hunters Meadow Ave 89144
Hunters Woods Pl 89134
Hunting Arrow St 89123
Hunting Hawk Rd 89179
Hunting Horn Dr 89135
Hunting Lodge Ave 89113
Huntington St 89107
Huntington Cove Pkwy 89178
Huntington Crest Ct 89117
Huntington Hills Dr 89144
Huntington Ridge Ave 89139
Huntly Rd 89145
Hunts Corner St 89166
Huntsville Dr 89134
Hurkling Stone Ave 89139
Hurricane Way 89145
Hurricane Cove Ct 89129
Hurricane River St 89131
Hurtado St 89166
Hussium Hills St 89108
Husson Ct 89142
Hutchinson Dr 89147
Hutton Ln 89145
Huxley St 89123
Huxley Cross Ln 89144
Hyacinth Ln 89107
Hyannis Cir 89129
Hyattsville St 89110
Hyde Ave 89107
Hydra Ln 89128
Hyla Roman Ave 89131
Hyman Pl 89145
I St 89106
Ian Thomas St 89129
Ibanez Ave 89103
Iberia St 89146
Ibizo St 89117
Ice Box Canyon Ct 89117
Ice Fall Ave 89183
Ice Storm Ct 89129
Ice Train Ave 89131
Iceland Spar Ct 89148
Ickworth Ct 89135
Icon St 89129
Icy Mistral Ct 89131
Idaho Ave 89104
Idle Ave 89107
Idle Spring Ct 89131
Idle Spurs Dr 89123
Idledale Ct 89145
Idlewood Ave 89115
Idols Eye Ct 89139
Idylwild Cir 89147
Iginlas Goal Ave 89131
Igou Ln 89156
Iguassu Falls Rd 89149
Ilanos Ln 89108
Illipah Creek St 89178
Illumination St 89113
Illusion Ct 89145
Illusionary Magic Cir 89131
Illustrious St 89147
Images Ct 89107
Imola Ct 89123
Impatients Ave 89131
E Imperial Ave 89104
W Imperial Ave 89102
Imperial Castle Ct 89147
Imperial Cup Dr 89117
Imperial Forest St 89139
Imperial Lakes St 89131
Imperial Orchard St 89130
Imperial Pointe Ave 89134
Imperial Purple Ct 89117
Imperial Treasure St 89139
Impressario Ct 89149
In Vogue Ct 89149
Incline Ave 89103
India Hawthorn Ave 89144
Indian Ln 89108
Indian Blanket St 89143
Indian Bluff St 89145
Indian Breeze Dr 89129
Indian Cane Ave 89178
Indian Cedar Dr 89135
Indian Chief Dr 89130
Indian Cloud Ave 89129
Indian Corn Ct 89178
Indian Cove Ln 89128
Indian Creek Ln 89149
Indian Eagle Dr 89129
Indian Gap Ave 89179
Indian Garden St 89138
Indian Gold St 89129
Indian Head Ave 89179
Indian Hills Ave 89130
Indian Hollow Ct 89134
Indian Meadow Ct 89130
Indian Moon Dr 89129
Indian Path Cir 89128
Indian Princess Dr 89145
Indian Rain Ct 89131
Indian River Dr 89103
Indian Run Way 89148
Indian Run Falls Ln 89123
Indian Sage Way 89108
Indian Shadow St 89129
Indian Summer Dr 89123
Indian Sunset St 89148
Indian Valley Dr 89129
Indian Village Ct 89131
Indian Wells Rd 89110
Indigo Dr 89145
Indigo Bay Way 89131
Indigo Bush Ave 89144
Indigo Cloud Ct 89142
Indigo Gorge Ave 89131
Indigo Gully Ct 89143
Indigo Harbor Ave 89117
Indigo Haven Ct 89117
Indigo Sky Ave 89129
Indigo Valley St 89134
Indios Ave 89121
Indrio Cir 89108
Industrial Rd
1400-2499 89102
2500-3799 89109
Industry Center Dr 89115
Industry Park Ct 89115
Inez Dr 89130
Ingelow Ct 89166
Inglenook Dr 89123
Ingleton Cir 89115
Inglewood Cir 89123
Ingraham St 89101
Inland Ct 89147
Inlet Cove Ct 89117
Inner Cir 89134
Innisbrook Ave 89113
Innsdale Ct 89123
Insignia Ave 89178
Inspiration Dr 89139
Interbay St 89128
Intercoastal Dr 89117
Interlace St 89149
Interlude Dr 89108
Intertwine Ave 89149
Intervale Rd 89135
Intrepid Dr 89130
Intrigue Way 89128
Intriguing Ave 89149
Intro Ave 89135
Invergordon Ct 89110
Inverlochy Ct 89141
Inverness Ave 89102
Invierno Cir 89128
Invitational Dr 89134
Inwood Dr 89145
Inwood Park Ct 89130
Iona Island Ave 89166
Iowa Ave 89107
Ipe Wood Rd 89148
Ipswich Way 89147
Ira St 89130
Ireland St 89149
Irene Ave 89110
Iris Ave & Cir 89107
Iris Canyon Ln 89135
Iris Flat Ct 89178
Iris Garden Cir 89142
Iris Hill Ct 89118
Iris Valley St 89178
Irish Eyes Ct 89149
Irish Moss Ct 89142
Irish Sea Ave 89146
Irish Spring St 89149
Iron Anvil Ct 89129
Iron Bridge St 89178
Iron Cactus Ave 89148
Iron Crossing Ave 89131
Iron Crow Ave 89147
Iron Duke Ave 89183
Iron Hills Ln 89134
Iron Hitch Ave 89143
Iron Horse Ct 89106
Iron Kettle St 89130
Iron Mine St 89183
Iron Mountain Rd
6200-6298 89131
6301-6399 89131
7700-7799 89143
7801-9399 89143
Iron Oak Ave 89113
Iron Ore St 89183
Iron Ridge Dr 89117
Iron Rings Ct 89135
Iron Springs Dr 89144
Iron Wood Peak Ave 89166
Ironbark Ln 89107
Ironbound Bay Ave 89139
Irongate Ct 89120
Ironhorse Lodge Ave 89131
Ironhorse Ranch Ave 89131
Ironsend St 89143
Ironside Dr 89108
Ironstone Ave 89143
Ironton Way 89147
Ironwood Dr 89108
Ironwood Knoll Ave 89113
Ironwood Pass Ave 89166
Irv Marcus Dr 89108
Irvin Ave
201-399 89183
3400-3798 89141
3800-4099 89141
W Irvin Ave 89141
Irvine Bay Ct 89147
Irving Park Ave 89166
Irving Peak Ave 89166
Irwin Ave 89115
Irwin Cir 89119
Irwindale Ave 89123
Isaac Newton Ln 89129
Isaac River Dr 89134
Isabel Cove Ave 89139
Isabella Ave & Cir 89110
Isabelle Ave 89101
Isadora Ct 89108
Isla Vista Valley Ct 89178
Island Breeze Ct 89130
Island Brook Dr 89108
Island Chain Rd 89118
Island Course Ave 89148
Island Dawn St 89123
Island Green Dr 89134
Island Magic Ln 89147
Island Mist St 89130
Island Palm Ave 89118
Island Pond St 89156
Island View Ct 89117
Isle Pointe Ct 89147
Isle Royale Dr 89122
Isleta Ct 89117
Isley Ave 89147
Isola Dr 89117
Isola Bella St 89141
Isola Peak Ave 89122
Isolated Ave 89110
Issac Ave 89156
Istas Ave 89131
Isthmus Cir 89110
Italia Ave 89130
Itasca Ln 89122
Ithaca Ave 89122
Ithaca Falls St 89149
Ivanhoe Way 89102
Ives Ave 89108
Ivory Cir 89130
Ivory Beach Dr 89147
Ivory Cliff Ave 89129
Ivory Coast Dr 89117
Ivory Nut St 89147
Ivory Point Ct 89134
Ivory Reef Ct 89117
Ivoryhill St 89135
Ivy Ln 89106
Ivy Creek Ct 89141
Ivy Garden Ct 89134
Ivy Hollow Ct 89143
Ivy Leaf St 89139
Ivy Patch St 89183
Ivy Point Ln 89134
Ivy Run St 89149
Ivy Russell Way 89115
Ivy Side Ave 89131
Ivy Spring St 89138
Ivy Trellis St 89130
Ivy Vine Ct 89141
Ivybridge Ave 89138
Ivybridge St 89123
Ivycrest St 89108
Ivygate Ave 89183
Ivyhill Ave 89121
Ivylyn Ct 89122
Ivywood Ct 89183
Izabella Ave 89169
J St 89106
Jaboneria Dr 89104
Jacala St 89122
Jacaranda Dr 89117
Jacaranda Arbor St 89144
Jacaranda Bay St 89139
Jacaranda Hill Ct 89139
Jacaranda Leaf St 89139
Jacinta Ct 89108
Jack Frost Rd 89124
Jack Pine Way 89108
Jack Rabbit Way 89128
Jack Russell St 89131
Jackie Dr 89156
Jackpot Cir 89110
Jackpot Winner Ln 89122
Jackrabbit Run Ave 89122
Jackson Ave 89106
Jackson Junction St 89149
Jackson Valley Ct 89131
Jacmar Ct 89120
Jacob Pl 89144
Jacob Lake Cir 89118
Jacobs Field St 89148
Jacobs Ladder Pl 89138
Jacobville Ct 89122
Jacqueline Way 89115
Jacyra Ave 89121
Jade Cir 89106
Jade Canyon Cir 89142
Jade Cliffs Ln 89144
Jade Creek St 89117
Jade Harbor Ct 89143
Jade Hills Ct 89106
Jade Mountain Ct 89139
Jade Plant St 89106
Jadecrest Dr 89134
Jaded Emerald Ct 89183
Jaded Iris Ct 89106
Jadeleaf Ct 89134
Jadelyn Ct 89122
Jadero Dr 89147
Jadestone Ave 89108
Jadewood St 89129
Jagged Peak Ct 89129
Jagged Rock Rd 89123
Jakes Pl 89143
Jalisco Ave 89131
Jalyn Rae Ct 89183
Jamaica Ct 89117
Jamapa Dr 89178
Jamberry Mountain Ct 89138
James St 89101
James Bilbray Dr 89108
James Brandom Way 89128
James Carl Ct 89149
James Grayson Dr 89145
James Harbin Ave 89129
James Lovell St 89145
James Paul Ave 89104
James Raul Ave 89143
James Slagle St 89129
Jamesbury Rd 89135
Jamestown Way 89102
Jamestown Square Ave 89166
Jamie Lee Ave 89149
Jamie Rose St 89135
Jamielinn Ln 89110
Jamies Jewel Way 89149
Jana Ct 89119
Jane Way 89119
Janefield St 89148
Janell Dr 89149
Janfred Ct 89103
Janice Estelle Dr 89107
Jansen Ave 89101
January Dr 89134
Japan Way 89115
Japan Rose Ave 89178
Japonica Ave 89183
Jaquita Ave 89149
Jarbridge Rd 89110
Jarom St 89120
Jarrett Ave 89131
Jarvis Ln 89130
Jasmine Cir 89123
Jasmine Creek Way 89119
Jasmine Falls Dr 89179
Jasmine Garden Dr 89134
Jasmine Hollow Ct 89143
Jasmine Joy Ct 89117
Jasmine Vine Ct 89135
Jason Way 89120
Jasper Ave 89108
Jasper Bluff St 89117
Jasper Butte St 89130
Jasper Creek Pl 89123
Jasper Grove Ave 89138
Jasper Point Ct 89123
Jasper Ridge St 89130
Jasper Rock Ct 89147
Javana Ct 89129
Javelina Ct 89113
Jay Ave 89130
Jaylar Cir 89102
Jaymie Way 89106
Jazzy Ginger Ct 89129
Jazzy June St 89183
Jean Ave 89108
Jean Lee Dr 89108
Jeanette Cir & St 89131
Jeanne Dr 89108
Jeannie Marie Ct 89113
Jebel Ave 89183
Jeeves Cir 89149
Jeff Dr 89110
Jeffcott St 89178
Jefferson Ave 89106
Jeffery Pines St 89108
Jeffreys St
3900-5099 89119
8800-8899 89123
10100-10115 89183
Jelsma Ave 89141
Jelson Falls St 89131
Jemez Pueblo Ave 89118
Jenkins Ave 89124
Jennie Pl 89147
Jennifer Ct 89108
Jennifer Anne Ave 89149
Jennis Silver St 89145
Jenny Lake Ave 89110
Jennydiane Dr 89121
N Jensen St
3600-4198 89129
4200-4799 89129
4901-6097 89149
6099-7299 89149
7301-7399 89149
S Jensen St 89147
Jeran Miles Ct 89147
Jerdon Ct 89129
Jeremiah Grove St 89123
Jeremiahs Lodge Ave 89131
Jeremy Dr 89113
Jeremy Blaine Ct 89139
Jeremy Pointe Ave 89144
Jeremy Ridge Ave 89144

Jericho St 89102
Jerlyn St
  8501-9099 89113
  9700-9798 89178
Jernae Ct 89108
Jerry Dr 89108
Jersey Cir 89108
Jersey Lilly St 89183
Jersey Shore Ave 89135
Jesse Scott St 89106
Jessica Ave 89104
Jessica Joy St 89149
Jett St 89145
Jetty Rock Dr 89128
Jewel Ave 89121
Jewel Canyon Dr 89122
Jewel Cave Dr 89122
Jewel Crystal Ct 89129
Jewel Desert Ct 89179
Jewel Lake Ave 89166
Jewel Mine Ave 89183
Jewel Night St 89129
Jewel Ridge Ave 89148
Jewel Tower St 89178
Jewel Weed Ct 89123
Jewett Lake St 89148
Jicama St 89103
Jim Beckwourth Ct 89179
Jim Dent Way 89149
Jim Hampton Ct 89117
Jimmy Ave 89106
Jimmy Cir 89123
Jimmy Durante Blvd 89122
Jingle Ct 89156
Jo Anne Ln 89156
Jo Marcy Dr 89131
E Jo Rae Ave 89183
W Jo Rae Ave
  2100-2198 89183
  3201-3297 89141
  3299-3999 89141
Joanie Pl 89147
Joann Way 89108
Joaquin Gully Ct 89139
Joaquin Hills Ct 89130
Jobe Cir 89115
Jobear Ave 89118
Jocelyn Dr 89122
Jockey Ave 89130
Jodi Ave & Ct 89120
Jodilyn Ct 89103
Jody Brook Ct 89145
Joe Doumit Way 89110
Joe Michael Way 89108
Joe Robby Ct 89148
Joe W Brown Dr 89109
Joe Willis St 89144
Joella St 89108
Jogging High Ct 89113
Johannson Ln 89115
John Bailey St 89129
John Chapman Pkwy 89115
John Charles Ct 89149
John Glenn Cir 89145
John Wayne St 89183
Johnny Holiday St 89113
Johnny Loftus Ct 89110
Johnson Ave 89110
Jojoba Ct 89144
Jokers Wild Ct 89122
Jolene Pl 89147
Joliet Cir 89108
Jolly Hill Ave 89166
Jolly January Ave 89183
Jon Belger Dr 89145
Jonah Way 89147
Jonathan Dr 89183
Jonathan Glen Way 89145
N Jones Blvd
  240-848 89107
  900-3784 89108
  3786-3898 89108
  4000-4998 89130
  5000-5098 89130
  5100-6210 89130
  6210-6210 89136
  6220-6298 89130
  6701-7497 89131
  7499-7799 89131
  7801-8199 89131
  2-1098 89107
  1200-3499 89146
  3500-4031 89103
  4030-4030 89173
  4032-4898 89103
  4033-4899 89103
  5000-5298 89118
  5300-7299 89118
  7300-8799 89139
  8801-9399 89139
Jones Cir 89107
Jontue St 89115
Joplin Cir 89121
Jordan Bryce Dr 89183
Jordan Frey St 89130
Jordan River Dr 89156
Jordanville St 89129
Jory Trl 89108
Joseph St 89122
Joseph Canyon Dr 89142
Joseph Cary Ct 89145
Joseph Kerwin Dr 89145
Joshua Way 89101
Joshua Star Ct 89138
Joshua Tree Ct 89108
Joshuapoint Ct 89120
Joshuaville Dr 89122
Journal Ct 89117
Journeys End St 89148
Joy Glen Rd 89129
Joy Ridge Ave 89183
Joyce Way 89107
Joyful St 89115
Joylin St 89161
Juana Vista St 89102
Juanita Dr 89102
Jubilation Dr 89145
Jubilee Diamond Ct 89139
Jubilee Gardens Ave 89131
Jubilee Mountain Ave 89129
Judah Way 89147
Judith Ann Ct 89110
Judith Resnik Ct 89103
Judkins Dr 89122
Judson Ave
  3600-5099 89115
  5500-6899 89156
Judson Cir 89156
Judy Ct 89130
Julene Ct 89110
Julesburg Dr 89139
Julia Waldene Ct 89129
Julian St 89101
N Juliano Rd
  4000-4299 89129
  4800-5999 89149
  6001-6399 89149
S Juliano Rd
  3800-3900 89147
  3902-4498 89147
  8601-8699 89148
Juliard Ln 89156
Julie Cir 89107
Julius Ct 89129
July Jewel Ave 89183
Jumpers Bridge St 89143
Jumpin Juniper Ave 89129
Jumping Jacks Ave 89178
Junction Hill Dr 89134
Junction Village Ave 89129
June Ave 89104
June Flower Dr 89141
Junewood St 89129
Jungle Dr 89110
Junior Ct 89120
Juniper Berry Dr 89134
Juniper Brush Ave 89166
Juniper Canyon Ct 89134
Juniper Creek Ln 89145
Juniper Forest St 89139
Juniper Haven Ave 89148
Juniper Hills Blvd 89142
Juniper Myrtle Ct 89183
Juniper Twig Ave 89183
Juniperwood Ct 89135
Juno Ct 89118
Juno Beach St 89129
Juno Hills St 89178
Jupiter Ct 89119
Jupiter Creek St 89156
Jurani St 89131
Justice Ln 89107
Justice Creek Ave 89131
Justin Springs Cir 89108
Justine Ct 89128
Jutland Ave 89122
K St 89106
Kabito Creek Ct 89139
Kachina Cir 89123
Kadena Cir 89110
Kadumba St 89178
Kahala Bay Ln 89147
Kaibab Ave 89101
Kaibab Forest Ave 89141
Kaiser Way 89102
Kalahari Ct 89149
Kalamazoo St 89147
Kalang St 89178
Kalmalii Ave 89147
Kalmia Dr 89103
Kals Way 89103
Kamber Ct 89119
Kamden Way 89119
Kampsville Ave 89148
Kanaka Peak Ct 89156
Kane Ave 89110
Kane Holly St 89130
Kaniksu Ct 89122
Kansas Ave 89107
Kapalua Ln 89113
Kapalua Bay Dr 89129
Kaplan Way 89106
Kapok Tree Ln 89142
Karaoke Ct 89129
Karen Ave
  200-298 89109
  300-999 89109
  1300-2099 89169
  2500-4599 89121
Karen Ct 89109
Kari Lee Ct 89146
Karissa Heights Pl 89115
Karli Dr 89102
Karlsen Ct 89122
Karms Park Ct 89118
Karnes Ranch Ave 89131
Karvel St 89122
Kasmere Falls Dr 89149
Kasper Ave 89106
Kasper Glen Ct 89178
Kassabian Ave 89104
Katella Ave 89118
Kathleen Ct 89110
Kathy Ct 89145
Kathyjo Way 89110
E Katie Ave
  1455-1497 89119
  1499-1599 89119
  1601-1799 89119
  3101-3199 89121
  3800-3998 89121
W Katie Ave
  5500-6600 89103
  6602-6698 89103
  8201-8797 89147
  8799-9599 89147
  9601-9999 89147
Katie Marie Ct 89110
Katmai Dr 89122
Katrina Way 89147
Kaufman Rd 89148
Kavanagh Pl 89123
Kawala Dr 89128
Kay Pl 89107
Kay Lynn Ct 89117
Kayenta Ct 89118
Kayla Ct 89134
Kayla Christine Ct 89123
Kayvani Ct 89117
Kearney St 89147
Kearney Hill Pl 89144
Kearney Mountain Ave 89166
Keating Cir 89147
Keaton Ave 89148
Kedleston St 89135
Keelmans Point Ave 89178
Keenan Ave 89122
Keephills St 89183
Keewatin Ct 89147
Keifer Ln 89128
Keifer Valley St 89178
Keiser Ct 89134
Keith St 89120
Keithann Cir 89110
Kelburn Hill St 89131
Kelitabb Ct 89130
Kell Ln
  3601-3699 89156
  4600-4798 89115
  4800-5099 89115
  5100-6599 89156
Kelley Ln 89119
Kellman Ave 89143
Kellogg Ave 89115
Kelly Barry Way 89121
Kelly Creek Ave 89129
Kelly Johnson Dr 89119
Kellyville Dr 89122
Kelp Ledge Ct 89131
Kelsford Dr 89123
Kelso Way 89107
Keltie Brook Dr 89141
Kemano Ct 89147
Kemble Ct 89115
Kemblefield Ave 89178
Kemper Lakes St 89122
Kempston Ct 89129
Ken St 89106
Kendall Brook Cir 89149
Kendall Hill Ave 89106
Kendall Ridge Ct 89141
Kenicott Pl 89110
Kenilworth Ct 89147
Kenmare Way 89121
Kennedy Dr 89110
Kennedy Heights Ct 89131
Kennedy Peak Ln 89166
Kennet Ct 89144
Kenneth Clyde St 89143
Kennewick Dr 89121
Kennington Cir 89117
Kenny Way 89107
Kenny Heights Ct 89142
Kens Ct 89139
Kensbrook St 89121
Kensett St 89166
Kensington St 89156
Kensington Way 89108
Kent Pl 89110
Kentlands St 89130
Kenton Pl 89144
Kentshire Dr 89117
Kentucky Derby Dr 89110
Kentucky Oaks Dr 89117
Kentwell Ave 89149
Kenwood St 89147
Kenwood Hills Ct 89131
Kenya Rd 89123
Kenyan Sunshine Ct 89138
Kepler Dr 89156
Kepler Cascades St 89141
Keppel Sands Dr 89134
Keren Marie Ave 89110
Kermode Ct 89178
Kern Ridge St 89178
Kernville Dr 89134
Kerr Lake Ct 89128
Ketchikan St 89179
Kettering Pl 89107
Kettle Creek Dr 89117
Kettledrum St 89139
Kevil Cir 89115
Kevin St 89147
Kevin Way
  4200-4399 89129
  4401-4599 89129
  5301-5697 89149
  5699-5999 89149
Kevin Winters St 89120
Kew Gardens Dr 89178
Key Colony Dr 89156
Key Largo Dr 89120
Key Lime St 89142
Key Royale Ct 89131
Key Vista Cir 89130
Keyesport Ct 89148
Keymar Dr 89135
Keynote Dr 89118
Keyport Ln 89138
Keysborough Dr 89134
Keystone Ct 89103
Keystone Pastures St 89183
Keywood St 89123
Khalua Ave 89166
Kiana Crystal Ct 89106
Kickapoo Ave 89149
Kiel Ridge Cir 89117
Kilamanjaro Ln 89128
Kilbarry Ct 89129
Kilda Cir 89122
Kildare Ct 89118
Kilflyn St 89129
Kilgore Dr 89156
Kilkenny Ave 89147
Kilkerran Ct 89141
Killala Ct 89110
Killarney St 89122
Killians Greens Dr 89131
Killington St 89129
Killymoon Ave 89129
Kilmartin Valley Ct 89148
Kilrenny Ave 89122
Kiltie Way 89102
Kim Ave 89145
Kimberly Ave 89122
Kimberly Cir 89107
Kimberly Diamond St 89139
Kimo St 89123
Kimwood Ave 89149
Kincheloe Cir 89115
Kind Sky Ct 89147
Kindle Ct 89131
Kindsland St 89183
King Bird Ct 89147
King Elder St 89117
King Henry Ave 89144
King Hill St 89106
King James St 89144
King John Ct 89149
King Midas Way 89102
King Palm Ave 89115
King Richard Ave 89119
King Solomons Ct 89117
Kingdom St 89117
Kingfisher Way 89103
Kingfisher Daisy Ct 89138
Kings Way 89102
Kings Arms Ln 89138
Kings Beach Ave 89123
Kings Brook Ct 89149
Kings Cove Ct 89145
Kings Gate Ct 89145
Kings Meadow Ct 89138
Kings Ransom St 89139
Kings Row Ct 89148
Kings Town Ave 89145
Kings Wharf Ln 89123
Kingsbarns Ct 89141
Kingsbridge Dr 89130
Kingsclear Ct 89145
Kingsdale Ct 89147
Kingship Ct 89129
Kingsland Ave 89138
Kingsley Ct 89149
Kingsmill Dr 89134
Kingspoint Ave 89120
Kingston Cove St 89166
Kingston Heath Ct 89131
Kingston Springs Way 89123
Kingswood Dr 89147
Kinkenon Dr 89145
Kinley Dr 89115
Kinlock Ct 89117
Kinmount Ct 89118
Kinobe Ave 89120
Kinross Ave 89145
Kinsale Ct 89121
Kinsella Way 89147
Kinsmen St 89101
Kintori Junction St 89139
Kiowa Cir 89149
Kiowa Peak Ave 89179
Kiowa Pointe St 89131
Kip Ct 89115
Kipling St 89107
Kirby Dr 89117
Kirk Ave 89101
Kirkland Ave 89102
Kirkland Ranch Ct 89139
Kirkliston Ct 89110
Kirkstone Way 89123
Kirkwood Dr 89108
Kirwan Heights Way 89108
Kisha Ct 89130
Kishner Dr 89109
Kiska Ave 89123
Kismet Cir 89108
Kisses Ave 89131
Kit Carson Ave 89179
Kit Cove Ct 89131
Kit Fox St 89122
Kite Hill Ln 89138
Kitrin Ct 89147
Kittery Dr 89107
Kitty Hawk Way 89119
Kitty Joyce Ave 89129
Kivas Ct 89129
Kiwi Ln 89123
Kiwi Grove Ct 89142
Klamath Falls Way 89128
Klavans Ct 89183
Kline Cir 89121
Klinger Cir 89121
Klondike Ct 89117
Klosterman Cir 89115
Knickerbocker Ave 89166
Knickknack Ct 89149
Knight Ave 89107
Knob Creek St 89149
Knoll Point St 89156
Knoll View Dr 89119
Knollmist Dr 89147
Knollwood Ct 89121
Knollwood Dr 89147
Knopfler Ln 89148
Knotting Pass 89131
Knotty Pine Ln 89123
Knotty Pine Way 89124
Knotweed Ave 89148
Koa Ave 89122
Koala Forest St 89178
Kobie Creek Ct 89130
Koho Dr 89183
Kokoma Dr 89128
Kolanut Ln 89115
Kolendo Ct 89103
Kolmar Ct 89110
Kolob Ct 89142
Kolson Cir 89119
Kona Coast Way 89121
Kona Peaks Ct 89149
Konami Cir 89119
Konga Dr 89123
Konica Ct 89129
Korbel Blanc St 89178
Kostner St 89149
Koval Ln
  3900-4298 89109
  4500-4599 89169
  4600-4698 89109
  4700-4714 89109
  4716-4898 89109
  5000-5099 89119
Kozak Cir 89115
Kraemer Dr 89107
Kraft Ave
  6200-6299 89130
  6301-6399 89130
  9200-9299 89129
  9301-9899 89129
Kreb Lake Ct 89148
Kressler Ave 89156
Kris Kringle Rd 89124
Krissylouise Way 89121
Kristen Ln 89121
Kristen Lee Ct 89110
Krypton Cir 89108
Kudo Ct 89149
Kuilima Rd 89110
Kulka Rd 89161
Kyland Cove Ave 89123
Kyle Canyon Rd
  1-5399 89124
  10800-14498 89166
  14500-14799 89166
Kyle Springs Cir 89108
Kylemore St 89129
Kylie St 89130
Kyoko Ct 89118
L St 89106
La Barca Ln 89122
La Brea Ct 89110
La Brisa Ave 89169
La Cadena Ave 89179
La Campana St 89179
La Canada St 89169
La Cantera Ct 89144
La Cara Ave 89121
La Carta Ct 89138
La Casita Ave 89120
La Cienega St
  6900-7298 89119
  7700-8799 89123
  9700-11300 89183
  11302-11398 89183
La Coma Way 89130
La Costa Canyon Ct 89139
La Crescenta Ct 89141
La Cruz Ct 89110
La Cumbre Dr 89147
La Flor Ct 89115
La Florentina Ave 89166
La Fonda Dr 89121
La Fortuna Ave 89121
La Harve Dr 89106
La Jara Dr 89120
La Jolla Ave 89169
La Jolla Way 89108
La Junta Dr 89120
La Lima Ct 89130
W La Madre Way
  5800-5900 89130
  5902-6398 89130
  7200-9699 89149
La Madre Ridge Dr 89135
E La Mancha Ave 89115
W La Mancha Ave 89149
La Manga Ave 89147
La Mark Ave 89106
La Mata St 89108
La Menta Dr 89147
La Mirada Ave & Cir 89120
La Mirago Pl 89138
La Mona Ct 89128
La Montana St 89108
La Paca Ave 89117
La Padania Ave 89183
La Palma Pkwy 89118
La Palmera Ave 89138
La Paloma Ave 89121
La Palomas Ct 89120
La Pasada Ave 89102
La Patera Ln 89149
La Perla Ct 89122
La Perm St 89166
La Placita Ave 89142
La Prada Pl 89138
La Puebla St 89120
La Puente St 89115
La Reina Cir 89130
La Roca Cir 89121

La Rue Ct 89145
La Salle St 89106
La Sconsa Dr 89138
La Sendas Ct 89122
La Seyne Ct 89128
La Sierra St 89134
La Solana Way 89102
La Sombra St 89108
La Spezia Way 89141
La Strada Ave 89129
La Sundora Cir 89129
La Tosca St 89138
La Tourette Ct 89148
La Vante Ave 89169
La Venus Ave 89144
La Vid Ct 89117
Labine St 89123
Labrador Dr 89142
Laburnum St 89113
Lacabana Beach Dr 89138
Lace Vine Arbor Ave 89144
Lacebark Ct 89123
Lacebark Pine St 89129
Lacey Landing Ct 89149
Lacey Tree St 89145
Laconia Ave 89121
Lacy Ln 89107
Ladera Ave & Cir 89120
Ladies Tee Ct 89148
Ladue Dr 89128
Lady Angela St 89183
Lady Apple Dr 89148
Lady Barron Ct 89115
Lady Bryan Ln 89110
Lady Bug Cir 89122
Lady Burton St 89129
Lady Finger Ct 89149
Lady Frances Ln 89156
Lady Lake St 89128
Lady Lucille Ct 89115
Lady Marlene Ave 89119
Lady Palm Ct 89147
Ladybank Ct 89110
Ladybug Bend St 89183
Ladyburn Ct 89141
Ladyhawk Way 89118
Lafaette St 89110
Lafite Ct 89117
Lago Ct 89118
Lago Augustine Way 89141
Lago Cantini St 89141
Lago De Coco Ave 89148
Lago Sandia St 89141
Lago Vista Ln 89145
Lagoon Blue St 89139
Lagoon Landing Dr 89129
Laguna Ave 89169
Laguna Del Sol Dr 89121
Laguna Dulce Way 89121
Laguna Garden Ave 89115
Laguna Niguel Dr 89134
Laguna Park Ct 89110
Laguna Shores Ln 89121
Laguna Veneta Ave 89141
Laguna Verde Way 89121
Laguna Vista St 89147
Lahotan Way 89110
Lailani St 89110
Lake Pl 89147
Lake Austin Ct 89148
Lake Chippewa St 89113
Lake Como Ave 89141
Lake Creek St 89123
Lake East Dr 89117
Lake Farm Ave 89131
Lake Fork Peak St 89166
Lake Forrest Ln 89115
Lake Geneva Ct 89113
Lake Hills Dr 89128
Lake Isle Ct 89145
Lake Louise Ave 89131
E Lake Mead Blvd
3500-4900 89115
4902-5098 89115
5100-8099 89156
W Lake Mead Blvd
800-1499 89106
1501-1799 89106
4300-6599 89108
7100-8599 89128
9300-9498 89134
Lake Sahara Dr 89117
Lake Scene St 89148
Lake Shore Ct 89115
Lake Tahoe St 89130
Lake Tahoe View Ct 89143
Lake Windemere St 89138
Lakecrest Dr 89128
Lakefront Color St 89178
Lakehurst Ct & Rd 89145
Lakeland Ct & Rd 89145
Lakeland Bay Dr 89122
Lakepoint Cir 89128
Lakeridge Cir 89117
Lakeshore Ln 89115
Lakeside Dr 89108
Lakestream Ave 89110
N & S Lakewood Ct 89120
Lakewood Garden Dr 89148
Lakota St 89123
Lamarjon Ct 89108
N Lamb Blvd
1-1598 89110
1600-4700 89115
4702-5198 89115
S Lamb Blvd
1200-1500 89104
1502-2398 89104
2601-2797 89121
2799-2899 89121
2901-3299 89121
5700-6099 89120
Lamb Silk Ct 89149
Lambert Dr 89147
Lambert Bridge Ave 89139
Lambourne Ct 89123
Lambrook Dr 89130
Lambtin Quay Ave 89131
Lame Horse Dr 89123
Lames Dr 89122
Lamoille Cir 89120
N Lamont St 89115
S Lamont St 89104
Lamotte Ave 89141
Lampeter Ct 89138
Lampione St 89141
Lamplight Village Ln 89183
Lamplighter Ln 89104
Lamville Canyon Ct 89139
Lana Dr 89121
Lanai Ave 89104
Lancaster Dr 89120
Lanceleaf Ave 89131
Lancer Way 89121
Lancewood Ave 89110
Lancia Ave 89117
Lancome St 89115
E Landberg Ave 89183
W Landberg Ave
3201-3399 89141
3900-3998 89141
7100-7399 89178
Landing Ridge Pl 89135
Landing Strip Ave 89119
Landis Dr N & S 89115
Landons Point Ct 89148
Lands End Ave 89117
Landsdown Pl 89121
Landview Ct 89123
Landy St 89124
Langara Ave 89178
Langhorne Creek St 89139
Langley Estates Dr 89117
Langston Cir 89130
Langtry Dr 89107
Lani Dawn St 89149
Lanning Ln 89108
Lansberry Ct 89147
Lansbrook Ave 89131
Lansdale Rd 89123
Lansing St 89120
Lanta Island Ave 89148
Lantana Breeze Dr 89183
Lantana Falls Ct 89131
Lantern Ln 89107
Lantham Pl 89110
Lanzarote Ct 89178
Lapeer St 89178
Lapford St 89178
Lapilli Ave 89139
Lapis Beach Dr 89117
Lapis Harbor Ave 89117
Laramie Ave 89113
Laramore Dr 89119
Larch Ct 89145
Larchwood Ln 89103
Laredo St
5877-5997 89146
5999-6599 89146
6601-6899 89146
7000-7399 89117
7401-8299 89117
Largo Way 89121
Largo Cantata St 89135
Largo Mar Ave 89131
Largo Sassetta Ct 89135
Largo Verde Way 89121
Lariat Ct & Dr 89121
Larix Rd 89113
Lark Cir 89121
Lark Bunting St 89117
Lark Meadow Ave 89131
Lark Mist St 89131
Larkcrest St 89129
Larkdale St 89120
Larkmead Ave 89149
Larkspur St 89120
Larkspur Point Ct 89138
Larkvale Way 89129
Larkwood Ave 89103
Laronda Ln 89156
Las Alturas Ave 89123
Las Casitas Way 89121
Las Colinas Ave 89179
Las Cruces Dr 89130
Las Flores St 89102
Las Hurdes Ave 89138
Las Lagunas Ln 89129
Las Lanzas St 89138
Las Lomas Ave 89102
Las Lunas Way 89129
Las Manaitas Ave 89144
Las Montanas Ave 89147
Las Nubes Dr 89142
Las Ocas Ct 89138
Las Olivas Ave 89147
Las Palmaritas Dr 89110
Las Palomas Dr 89138
Las Posas Ave 89147
Las Vegas Blvd N
120-200 89101
202-1598 89101
3100-4600 89115
4602-7098 89115
12101-12199 89165
Las Vegas Blvd S
111-125 89101
200-998 89101
201-929 89101
201-201 89125
1100-2461 89104
2463-2499 89104
2500-3713 89109
3715-3899 89109
3716-3752 89158
3756-3778 89109
3780-3788 89158
3790-3850 89109
3900-3934 89119
3936-7299 89119
7300-8252 89123
8254-9656 89123
9658-9698 89123
9777-9797 89183
9799-9999 89183
10001-11999 89183
Las Vegas Studio Ct 89103
Las Verdes St 89102
Las Vista St 89113
Lassen Ct 89142
Lassen Peak Cir 89149
Lasso Cir 89121
Last Hope Ave 89178
Last Point Ave 89129
Latigo Cir & St 89119
Latitudes Ct 89108
Laton Ct 89134
Latour Ct 89117
Latrice Ct 89148
Lattimore Dr 89128
Lauderdale Ct 89128
Lauderhill St 89131
Laughing Brook Ct 89131
Laughing Creek St 89148
Laughlin Way 89110
Laura Kay St 89110
Laurel Ave 89104
Laurel Brook Dr 89147
Laurel Canyon St 89129
Laurel Falls Ct 89149
Laurel Flat Ct 89129
Laurel Grove Ct 89148
Laurel Mountain Ln 89166
Laurel Oak Dr 89123
Laurel Park Ave 89103
Laurel Ridge Way 89142
Laurel Springs Ave 89134
Laureldale Ct 89141
Laurelton Pl 89147
Laurelwood Ave 89122
Laurelwood Lake Ave 89166
Lauren Dr 89134
Lauren Ashton Ave 89131
Laurena Ave 89147
Laurentia Ave 89141
Laurie Dr 89102
Lauter Dr 89145
Lava Ave & Cir 89101
Lava Bluff Ct 89123
Lava Falls Dr 89110
Lava Point St 89131
Lavalette Ct 89113
Lavaliere Ave 89139
Lavandou Dr 89141
Lavarun Ct 89123
Lavender Cloud Pl 89122
Lavender Field Ln 89142
Lavender Heights Ct 89143
Lavender Hills Dr 89135
Lavender Jade Ct 89139
Lavender Mist Ct 89183
Lavender Ridge St 89131
Lavender Rose Ave 89117
Laverne Cir 89108
Laverton Dr 89134
Laveta Ln 89156
Lavina Ct 89123
Lawhon Canyon Ct 89131
Lawman Ct 89119
Lawndale St 89121
Lawnwood Ct 89130
Lawrence Powers Ct 89129
Lawry Ave 89106
Lawsonia Ct 89149
Lawton Ave 89107
Lawton Pine Dr 89129
Laying Up Ct 89148
Lazarro Ct 89139
Lazia St 89131
Lazy Bear St 89131
Lazy Brook Dr 89156
Lazy Creek Ave 89139
Lazy Day Ct 89131
Lazy Days Ct 89141
Lazy Hill Cir 89117
Lazy Pine St 89108
Lazy Posey Ct 89106
Lazy Rabbit Ave 89130
Lazy River Dr 89117
Lazy Sun Ln 89147
Lazy Sunset Ct 89156
Le Agavi Ct 89148
W Le Baron Ave
3200-3898 89141
7101-7397 89178
7399-7400 89178
7402-7498 89178
Le Luberon Ct 89123
Le Mann Cir 89146
Leadbrick St 89143
Leading Ct 89149
Leadville Ave 89130
Leadville Peak Ave 89179
Leafgold Dr 89134
Leafhopper Ct 89178
Leafwood St 89108
Leafy St 89130
Leandro Cir 89120
Leaning Cloud Ct 89113
Leaning Oak Ave 89118
Leaning Pine Way 89128
Leap Frog Ave 89183
Leaping Deer Pl 89178
Leaping Lilly Ave 89129
Leaping Lizard St 89178
Leaping Pad Ct 89148
Leather Harness St 89131
Leatherleaf Dr 89123
Leatherstocking Ave 89166
Leatherwood Cir 89115
Leavorite Dr 89128
Leberger Ave 89129
Ledge View Ct 89145
Ledgecliff Ct 89129
Ledgewood Dr 89103
Ledgewood Creek Ave 89141
Lee St 89156
Lee Canyon Rd 89124
Lee Fairy Ct 89139
Leeann Ln 89121
Leesburg St 89110
Leeward Dr 89117
Leffetto St 89135
Leg Horn Ct 89147
Legacy Arbor St 89139
Legacy Valley Ave 89129
Legalla Ln 89156
Legato Dr 89123
Legato Falls St 89115
Legend Dr 89134
Legend Hills St 89129
Legendary Dr 89121
Leger Dr 89145
Leggett Rd 89149
Lehigh Way 89115
Lehman St 89110
Leia St 89120
Leigh Ave 89120
Leigon Way 89110
Leisel Ave 89148
Leisure Ln 89103
Leisure Springs Dr 89129
Leland Ranch Ave 89178
Lelant Ct 89178
Lemitar Dr 89108
Lemon St 89146
Lemon Balm St 89183
Lemon Gems Ct 89130
Lemon Glaze St 89145
Lemon Mint Ct 89148
Lemon Orchard Dr 89135
Lemon Thyme St 89183
Lemon Valley Ave 89147
Lemonwood Cir 89103
Len Pl 89106
Lena St 89101
Lenaking Ave 89122
Lenamarie Ct 89103
Lenape Heights Ave 89148
Lenapee Ct 89113
Lenna St 89102
Lennox Dr 89123
Lenoir St 89135
Lenora Dr 89122
Lenore Park Ct 89166
Lenox Crater Ct 89148
Lenox Crest Pl 89134
Lenox Hill Ct 89135
Lentil Ct 89129
Leo Dr 89130
Leon Ave
3800-4399 89130
6501-6999 89131
7600-7798 89131
Leon De Oro Dr 89129
Leona St 89106
Leonard Ave 89106
Leonard Ln 89108
Leonetti Ct 89141
Leor Ct 89121
Leota Ct 89103
Leroy Dr 89110
Leslie Ave 89101
Lessona St 89141
Lethbridge Ave 89131
Lettuce Leaf St 89183
Levens Ct 89141
E Levi Ave 89183
W Levi Ave
6100-6499 89141
9200-9299 89178
Levy Ln 89106
Lewis Ave 89101
Lewis Falls Ave 89139
Lewiston St 89183
Lexford St 89123
Lexington St 89106
Lexington Cross Dr 89144
Lexington Pines Ave 89129
Leybourne Ct 89131
Liahona Way 89121
Libbiano Ct 89141
Libby Dr 89103
Liberty Ave & Cir 89121
Liberty Park Ave 89135
Liberty Pride St 89148
Liberty View Rd 89148
Libertyvale Dr 89123
License St 89131
Lida Way 89106
Lido Isle Ct 89117
Liethen Cir 89115
Lift Ct 89117
Light Beam St 89107
Light Bloom St 89131
Light Breeze Dr 89108
Light Springs Ave 89130
Light Tower St 89139
Light Wind Ct 89108
Light Year Dr 89115
Lightgleam Ct 89123
Lightheart Ave 89148
Lighthouse Ave 89110
Lightning Ln & St 89145
Lightning Bay Ct 89123
Lightning Sky St 89179
Lilac Ln 89107
Lilac Arbor St 89144
Lilac Breeze Cir 89108
Lilac Charm Ave 89183
Lilac Cove St 89135
Lilac Creek Ct 89122
Lilac Glen Dr 89129
Lilac Harbor Ct 89143
Lilac Haze St 89147
Lilac Meadow St 89178
Lilac Shadow Ct 89148
Lilac Sky Ave 89142
Lilac Square Ave 89166
Lilac Tree Ave 89135
Lilliput Ln 89102
Lillo St 89103
Lilly Ln 89101
Lillyhammer Ct 89147
Lillywood Ave 89129
Lily Grove Rd 89148
Lily Haven Ave 89120
Lily Pad Cir 89142
Lily Rubin Ave 89138
Lily Touchstone Ct 89148
Limbwood Ct 89131
Lime Grass Ave 89183
Lime Kiln Ave 89139
Lime Point St 89110
Lime Straight Dr 89115
Lime Tree St 89178
Limekin Cir 89115
Limerick Ln 89121
Limestone Rd 89147
Limestone Arch Ave 89178
Limestone Bend Ct 89123
Limewood Cir 89103
Linaria Rd 89113
Lincoln Rd
600-698 89110
700-799 89110
1701-1997 89115
1999-3999 89115
Lincoln Valley St 89123
Lincoln Wood St 89149
Lincourt Ct 89141
Linda Ave 89121
Linda Ln 89103
Linda Vista St 89102
Lindale Ave 89121
Lindell Rd
1201-1597 89146
1599-3499 89146
3601-3697 89103
3699-3700 89103
3702-4098 89103
4901-5197 89118
5199-7099 89118
7101-7199 89118
8200-8999 89139
9001-9599 89139
9800-9899 89141
Linden Ave
1001-1497 89101
1499-2099 89101
6001-6797 89110
6799-7299 89110
Linden Leaf Ave 89144
Linden Tree St 89156
Linden Wood Ct 89134
Lindenhurst Ln 89120
Linderhof Ave 89135
Lindero Pl 89119
Linderwood Dr 89134
Lindo Ct 89121
Lindores Loch St 89166
Lindsay Heights St 89148
Lindsey Cir 89130
Lindy Dr 89107
Lineshack Ln 89110
Linfield Pl 89134
Lingering Breeze St 89148
Lingo St 89129
Linkside Dr 89130
Linkview Dr 89134
Linkwood Dr 89110
Linley Ct 89115
Linn Ln
2-198 89110
200-1599 89110
1600-2249 89156
2251-2399 89156
5600-5699 89115
Linnbaker Ln 89110
Linnington Ct 89135
Linosa Ct 89141
Linq Ln 89109
Linseed Knoll Ct 89178
Linton Hill Ln 89134
Lion Head Way 89118
Lionesse Ct 89130
Lionheart St 89123
Lions Mane Ct 89123
Lions Peak Ct 89139
Lions Rock Way 89128
Lipan Point St 89147
Lipari Ct 89123
Lippizan Cir 89121
Lipton Ct 89121
Liquid Loco St 89178
Lirio Way 89108
N Lisa Ln 89149
S Lisa Ln
1900-2098 89117
2101-2199 89117
8401-8499 89113
8700-8798 89113
Lisa Dawn Ave 89147

Lisa Marie Ct 89113
Lisagayle Ct 89103
Lisandro St 89108
Lisbon Ave 89169
Lisco Ct 89183
Lismore Ct 89135
Litchfield Ave 89134
Little Arrow Ct 89143
Little Aston Cir 89142
Little Blue Heron Ave 89115
Little Boy Blue Ave 89183
Little Brook St 89131
Little Cove Ct 89120
Little Crow Ave 89123
Little Dipper St 89128
Little Doe Cir 89130
Little Fawn Ct 89130
Little Finch Ln 89115
Little Fox St 89123
Little Harbor Ct 89141
Little Horse Ave 89143
Little Horse Creek Ave 89129
Little Lake Ave 89122
Little Laramie St 89131
Little Mac Ct 89118
Little Mesa Way 89120
Little Moon Ave 89178
Little Pine Way 89108
Little River Ct 89156
Little Rock Way 89123
Little Sidnee Dr 89123
Little Spring Ct 89128
Little Springs Rd 89161
Little Star Dr 89156
Little Stream St 89135
Little Valley Ave 89147
Little Wren Ln 89115
Littleton Ave 89128
Littlewater Ln 89108
Littondale St 89139
Live Canyon Ct 89178
Live Oak Dr 89121
Lively Ct 89149
Lively Loom Ct 89149
Livengood Dr 89123
Livermore Ave 89120
Livermore Valley Ave 89178
Liverpool Rd 89107
Living Desert Dr 89119
Living Edens Ct 89148
Living Rock St 89106
Living Rose St 89123
Livorno Ave 89141
Llewellyn Dr 89102
Lloyd Ct 89145
Lo Vista Pl 89110
Lob Wedge Ct 89144
Lobella St 89123
Lobero Ave 89141
Loch Lomond Way 89102
Lochmor Ave 89130
Locke Haven Dr 89123
Lockheed Ave 89183
Lockport St 89129
Loco Weed Ct 89118
Locust Valley Ave 89148
Locustwood St 89110
Lodestone Dr 89117
Lodewyck Dr 89121
Lodge Cir 89129
Lodge Haven St 89123
Lodina Ct 89141
Lofty Hill Ct 89123
Lofty Vista Ave 89148
Log Cabin Way
8401-8497 89143
8499-8599 89143
11800-11899 89166
Log Creek Pl 89139
Log Jam St 89178
Logan Ct & St 89110
Logan Heights Ct 89135
Logan Ridge Ct 89139
Logan Rock St 89129
Loganrun Ln 89110
Logansberry Ln 89145
Loggerhead Rd 89117
Loggers Mill Ave 89143
Loggia Ct 89117
Logging Ct 89110
Logrondo St 89178
Logville St 89113
Lokai Ave 89130
Loma Ct 89130
Loma Alta Cir 89120
Loma Bonita Pl 89138
Loma Del Ray St 89131
Loma Linda Ln 89121
Loma Portal Ave 89166
Loma Verde Ave 89108
Loma Vista Ave 89120
Lomack Ct 89145
Lomaland Ave 89166
Lomas Santa Fe St 89147
Lombard Dr 89108
Lomita St 89121
Lompoc Ct 89135
London Bridge Ave 89130
London Eye Ct 89178
London Porter Ct 89119
Londonderry St 89119
Lone Boulder St 89113
Lone Butte Dr 89156
Lone Creek Cir 89103
Lone Cypress Ct 89141
Lone Desert St 89135
Lone Feather Ln 89123
Lone Grove Dr 89139
Lone Hill St 89106
Lone Jogger Dr 89113
Lone Marble Dr 89139
Lone Mesa Dr 89147
E Lone Mountain Rd 89115
W Lone Mountain Rd
4800-6198 89130
6200-6399 89130
6401-6599 89130
6702-6798 89108
6801-6999 89108
7200-10599 89129
Lone Oak St 89115
Lone Peak Way 89156
Lone Point Ct 89138
Lone Ranch Ave 89131
Lone Ranger St 89178
Lone Shepherd Dr 89166
Lone Tree St 89145
Lone Tree Peak St 89166
Lone Wolf Ave 89131
Lonele Ln 89147
Lonely Heart Ct 89115
Lonely Mountain Ct 89110
Lonesome Cir 89128
Lonesome Biker Ln 89113
Lonesome Cactus St 89130
Lonesome Elk Rd 89124
Lonesome Harbor Ave 89131
Lonesome Lake St 89148
Lonesome Spur Ave 89131
Lonette Ave 89147
Long Ct 89121
Long Barrow Ct 89148
Long Bay St 89148
Long Beach St 89139
Long Buffalo Ave 89131
Long Cattle Ave 89117
Long Grove Ave 89149
Long Horse Ct 89147
Long Island St 89123
Long Lake Ave 89149
Long Leaf Pl 89134
Long Valley Dr 89108
Long View Dr 89120
Long Winter Ct 89131
Longboat Cir 89113
Longbow Dr 89142
Longfellow St 89115
Longford Way 89121
Longhirst Hall Ln 89138
Longhorn Falls Ct 89149
Longhorn Lodge Ave 89113
Longiano Pl 89156
Longley St 89131
Longmont Dr 89123
Longnook Ct 89147
Longoria St 89178
Longoria Garden St 89141
Longridge Ave 89146
Longs Peak Ct 89103
Longshot Dr 89122
Longstock Ct 89130
Longwood Dr 89134
Longworth Rd 89135
Lonigan St 89131
Looking Bear Ct 89178
Looking Glass Ln 89110
Lookout St 89120
Lookout Bridge St 89183
Lookout Canyon Ct 89183
Lookout Hill St 89149
Lookout Mountain Dr 89110
Lookout Peak Way 89108
Lookout Point Cir 89117
Lookout Ridge Dr 89135
Lookout Rock Cir 89129
Lopseed Ct 89149
Lord Crewe St 89138
Lord Latimer Ct 89115
Lordsburg Ln 89134
Lorelei Rock St 89138
Lorenzi St 89107
Loretta Ln 89183
Loretta Jean Ct 89149
Loretto Cove St 89141
Lori Ct 89103
Lori Marie Cir 89149
Lorian St 89183
Lorille Ln 89108
Lorilou Ln 89121
Lorilyn Ave 89119
Lorinda Ave 89128
Lorna Pl 89107
Loro Ct 89117
Lorraine Ln 89120
Los Altos Pl & St 89102
Los Arroyos Ct 89138
Los Banderos Ave 89179
Los Cabos Dr 89144
Los Cotos Ct 89147
Los Dolces St 89138
Los Feliz St
1-397 89110
399-799 89110
1801-1997 89156
1999-2599 89156
S Los Feliz St 89142
Los Hermanos St 89144
Los Lagos Rd 89178
Los Mares Ln 89138
Los Meadows Dr 89110
Los Monteros St 89129
Los Padres Pl 89134
Los Palos St 89108
Los Pinos St 89122
Los Prados Cir 89130
Los Rancheros Ave 89129
Los Reyes Ct 89121
Los Santos Ln 89130
Los Serranos Cir 89130
Lost Ln 89118
Lost Colt Cir 89117
Lost Dutchman Dr 89108
Lost Forest St 89139
Lost Gold Ave 89129
Lost Hills Dr 89122
Lost Lake Ct 89147
Lost Maple St 89115
Lost Miner Ct 89129
Lost Pines Ct 89128
Lost Prospect Ct 89178
Lost Ranger Peak St 89166
Lost River Ct 89108
Lost Shadow Ct 89131
Lost Shanty Ct 89178
Lost Spur St 89131
Lost Treasure Ave 89138
Lost Tree Cir 89130
Lost Valley St 89113
Lots Hills Dr 89179
Lottie Ave 89149
Lotus Blossom Ct 89145
Lotus Elan Dr 89117
Lotus Hill Dr 89134
Lotus Vale Ave 89123
Loud Colors St 89148
Loud Water Way 89148
Loughton St 89178
Louisiana Lakes Ave 89183
Lourdes Ave 89102
Love St 89121
Love Orchid Ln 89138
Lovebird Ln 89115
Loveland Dr 89109
Lovell Ct 89121
Lovely Pine Pl 89143
Lovely Squaw Ct 89179
Lovers Knot Ct 89131
Lovett Canyon St 89148
Low Creek Ct 89123
Low Stakes Ct 89122
Low Tide Ct 89117
Lowden Ln 89107
Lowe Ave 89131
Lowell Ave 89110
Lower Falls Ct 89141
Lower Trailhead Ave 89113
Lowery Point Ct 89147
Lowry Cir 89115
Loxton Cellars St 89139
Loyal Royal Ct 89131
Luanda Ave 89120
Lubbock Ave 89119
Lucaccini Ln 89117
Lucano Ln 89117
Lucas Ave 89120
Lucca Bluff St 89178
Lucerne St 89104
Lucero Ave 89149
Lucia Dr 89128
Lucido Dr 89103
Lucilee St 89101
Lucite Ln 89115
Lucky St 89104
Lucky Boy Dr 89110
Lucky Charm Ct 89149
Lucky Clover St 89149
Lucky Draw Ct 89122
Lucky Gold Ct 89108
Lucky Horseshoe Ct 89129
Lucky Star St 89145
Lucky Strike Way 89108
Lucy Grey Ct 89179
Lucy Thompson St 89107
Ludington Ave 89156
Ludlow Ave 89121
Ludwig Dr 89106
Lufberry Cir 89115
Lufield Ridge Ct 89149
Lufkin Ave 89130
Lugo St 89123
Luke Dr 89115
Lullaby Pine Ct 89130
Lullingstone St 89135
Lulu Ave 89119
Lumberjack Ave 89129
Lumina Ct 89117
Luminal Ln 89147
Luminary Dr 89119
Luminoso St 89138
Luna Way 89145
Luna Alegre St 89115
Luna Bay Ln 89128
Luna Bella Ave 89179
Luna Bonita St 89113
Luna Del Mar Ln 89138
Luna Del Rey St 89123
Luna Magico Ave 89135
Luna Nuevo Ct 89147
Luna Ridge Ct 89129
Luna Sera Ave 89178
Lunar Crest Ave 89129
Lunarlight Dr 89128
Lund Dr 89108
Lunetto Ave 89141
Luning Dr & Way 89106
Lupin Ct 89110
Lupine Bush Ct 89135
Lupine Meadow Dr 89178
Lusitano St 89130
Lusso Ct 89134
Lusterview Ct 89123
Lustrous Ct 89148
Lutts St 89131
Luxaire Ct 89144
Luxembourg Ave 89145
Luxor Way 89115
Luzon Way 89103
Lydia Dr 89107
Lydian Ct 89139
Lyell Canyon Ln 89134
Lyell Mountain Ct 89139
Lyla Rae Cir 89117
Lyle Ln 89120
Lyndhurst St 89178
Lynhurst Dr 89134
Lynnann Dr 89110
Lynnwood St 89109
Lyon Estates Ave 89131
Lyra Ln 89110
Lyric Ln 89119
Lyric Arbor Dr 89135
Lytton Ave 89146
M St 89106
Mabel Rd 89110
Mac Duff Ct 89141
Macadamia Dr 89115
Macarthur Way 89107
Macaw Ln 89145
Macbrey Dr 89123
Maccabe Ave 89123
Maccan St 89113
Macdoogle St 89166
Macedonia Ave 89141
Maceta Ave 89103
Macey Leeann St 89139
Macfarlane St 89101
Macher Way 89121
Mackanos Ave 89148
Mackenzie Ct 89129
Mackenzie Bay Ave 89179
Macklin St 89129
Mackovski Ct 89148
Maclyon Way 89121
Macoby Run St 89148
Macon St 89104
Macsnap Ave 89183
Mad Dog St 89178
Madagascar Ln 89117
Madagascar Palm St 89141
Madama St 89110
Madarang Ave 89178
Maddelena Ave 89183
Maddies Way 89118
Maddingley Ave 89117
Maddington Dr 89134
Maddox Ave 89107
Madeline Dr 89108
Madera Way 89121
Madera Canyon Pl 89128
Madge Ln 89110
Madica Ave 89123
Madigan Ct 89118
Madison Ave 89106
Madison Falls Ave 89130
Madison Grove Ave 89166
Madison Taylor Pl 89144
Madison Walk Ave 89149
Madonna Dr 89156
Madras Cir 89110
Madre Ave 89135
Madre Grande St 89142
Madre Mesa Dr 89108
Madreperla St 89121
Madrid St 89121
Madrid Ridge Ct 89129
Madrigal Way 89122
Madsen Glen Ct 89166
Maenpah Cir, St &
Way 89106
Magazzini Ct 89141
Magdalena Ct 89121
Magellan Way 89103
Magenta Ct 89108
Maggie Ave
6201-6297 89131
6299-6399 89131
6401-7799 89131
8400-8498 89143
8500-8600 89143
8602-8798 89143
Maggie Belle Ct 89123
Maggie Mei Rd 89183
Maggira Pl 89135
Magi Ranch Ct 89131
Magic Cove Ct 89139
Magic Dunes Ave 89149
Magic Flower Ave 89134
Magic Lamp St 89139
Magic Moment Ln 89119
Magic Moon Ln 89146
Magic Peak Ct 89129
Magic Stone Ln 89135
Magic Window Ave 89130
Magical View St 89178
Magini Ave 89141
Magliana St 89183
Magnetic Ct 89149
Magnificent Ave 89148
Magnificent Sky St 89178
Magnifico Cir 89149
Magnolia Ave 89108
Magnolia Arbor St 89144
Magnolia Blossom Ave 89131
Magnolia Crossing St 89148
Magnolia Glen Ave 89128
Magnolia Park Ct 89141
Magnolia Point Ct 89131
Magnolia Ridge Ave 89134
Magnolia Tree Ave 89135
Magnum Bark Ct 89183
Magrath St 89178
Mahogany Dr 89110
Mahogany Forest Ct 89142
Mahogany Grove Ln 89117
Mahogany Meadows
Ave 89122
Mahogany Mountain
Dr 89142
Mahogany Peak Ave 89110
Mahogany Run Pl 89122
Maiden Ct 89130
Maiden Run Ave 89130
Maidenfair Ct 89148
Maidenhair Ct 89139
Maidenhair Fern Ct 89141
Maidenhead Dr 89139
Maidens Wreath Ct 89183
Maidstone Cir 89142
N Main St 89101
S Main St
1-197 89101
199-1099 89101
1100-1799 89104
Mainland Dr 89123
Maitai Ave 89147
Majella Ave 89141
Majestic Dr 89147
Majestic Bay St 89131
Majestic Beauty Ave 89135
Majestic Bluff Pl 89113
Majestic Falls Ln 89110
Majestic Grove Dr 89115
Majestic Heights Ct 89117
Majestic Hills Ave 89141
Majestic Oak St 89145
Majestic Palm Dr 89122
Majestic Pine Ave 89143
Majestic Prince Ct 89178
Majestic Rock Cir 89128
Majestic Springs Dr 89131
Majestic Tide Ave 89131
Majestic View Ave 89129
Majestic Vision Way 89178
Majestic Wind Ave 89122
Majesty Palm Dr 89115
Majorca St 89121
Makenna Ct 89113
Making Memories Pl 89131
Mal Cir 89120
Malabar Ave 89121
Malachite Bay Ave 89130
Malafia Cir 89103
Malaga Dr 89121
Malaga Peak St 89135
Malarga St 89123
Malasana Ct 89147
Malaya Garnet Ct 89148
Maldive Isle Ct 89129
Maldonado Dr 89123
Malerlea Ave 89107
Maleta Ct 89117
Malibu St 89169
Malibu Breeze Pl 89134
Malibu Creek Ct 89183
Malibu Lagoon Ct 89141
Malibu Vista St 89117
N Mallard St 89108
S Mallard St 89107
Mallard Bay Ave 89179
Mallard Nest St 89117
Mallard Ridge Ave 89115
Mallardwood Dr 89129
Mallee Point St 89178
Mallorca St 89144
Malmo Ave 89129
Malner Ln 89130
Malone Ct 89118
Malta Pl 89101
Maltese Way 89117
Maltese Crest Cir 89129
Maltese Cross Ct 89183
Malva Pl 89138
Malvasia Ct 89123
Mambo Vista Ave 89108
Mammoth Ct 89142
Mammoth Cave Ln 89156
Mammoth Creek Dr 89147
Man O War St 89131
Managua Dr 89123
Manalang Rd 89123
Manassas Ave 89122
Manatee Ct 89147
Manchester Cir 89122
Manchester Park Dr 89141
Mancilla St 89130
Mancos Ct 89119
Mandala Peak Ave 89183
Mandalay Springs Dr 89120
Mandarin Dr 89108
Mandarin Zest Ct 89118
Mandarino Ave 89135
Manderley Ct 89123
Manderston Ct 89130
Mandevilla Cir 89117
Mandeville Bay Ave 89148
Mandolina Hills St 89141
Mandrake Ln 89130
Mandrake Falls St 89178
Mandy Scarlet Ct 89148
Maneilly Dr 89110
Manford Cir & Dr 89104
Manfre St 89148
Mango Tree Ct 89115
Mangostone Ln 89147
Mangrove Bay St 89147
Mangrum Cir 89103
Manhattan Dr 89106
Manheim Ln 89117
Manistee Ct 89108
Manito Cir 89130
Manitoba Ave 89123
Mann St
2601-2697 89146
2699-3199 89146
5700-5998 89118
6000-6100 89118
6102-6198 89118
8700-8799 89139
8801-9299 89139
10401-10699 89141
Manning Mountain St 89129
Mannix Ct 89143

Street	ZIP
Manny St	89131
Manor St	89145
Manor Green Ln	89110
Manor Hill Ave	89183
Manor House Ave	89123
Manorwood St	89135
Manse Ranch Ave	89179
Mansfield Ave	89121
Mansfield Park St	89113
Mansion St	89130
Mansion Hall Ct	89129
Mansion Hills Ave	89144
Mansion Oaks St	89149
Manteca Cir	89118
Mantilla Ct	89120
Mantis Way	89110
Mantua Ct	89130
Manuel Dr	89149
Manzanilla Way	89128
Manzanita Way	89101
Manzanita Glen Ave	89130
Manzano Cir	89121
Maple Ave	89104
Maple Bend Ct	89138
Maple Bridge Ave	89131
Maple Hill Rd	89115
Maple Meadow St	89131
Maple Oak Ave	89139
Maple Park St	89131
Maple Red Ct	89139
Maple Rose Dr	89134
Maple Sugar St	89149
Maple Sugar Leaf Pl	89148
Maple Tree Ave	89122
Maple Valley St	89117
Maple Vine Ct	89110
Maple Wood Way	89128
Mapleberry Ct	89135
Maplebrook Ct	89108
Maplegrove Cir	89108
Mapleleaf St	89142
Maplestar Rd	89128
Mapleton Ln	89119
Mapleview Ct	89147
Mar Jay Ct	89107
Mar Vista Way	89121
Maranatha Cir	89103
Marandola St	89141
Marasco Ct	89149
Maratea Ave	89130
Marathon Dr	89108
Marauder Ct	89115
Marbella Cir	89128
Marbella Ridge Ct	89117
Marbelwood Ave	89123
Marble Dr	89134
Marble Bay Cir	89147
Marble City Ct	89139
Marble Falls St	89138
Marble Gorge Dr	89117
Marble Hills Ave	89183
Marble Lake St	89149
Marble Light Ave	89178
Marble Mesa Ct	89149
Marble Mountain St	89129
Marble Peak Ct	89129
Marble Ridge Dr	89135
Marblecrest Ct	89130
Marbledoe St	89149
Marblehead Way	89128
Marbrisas Ln	89130
Marbury St	89166
Marbury Peak Ave	89166
Marc Kahre Ave	89129
Marcasel Dr	89123
Marcasite Pl	89123
Marcelline Ave	89148
March Brown Ave	89149
March Mist Ct	89183
Marcia Ave	89101
Marco St	
700-798	89110
2400-3199	89115
Marco Island St	89148
Marco Rossi Ct	89113
Marco Vista Ave	89142
Marcon Dr	89149
Marcus Dr	89102
Mardagen St	89183
Mardean Ct	89131
E Mardon Ave	89123
W Mardon Ave	89139
Mare Way	89108
Marengo Pl	89147
Margaret Ave	89101
Margarete Ave	89121
Margarita Way	89103
Margo Dr	89122
Margollini St	89148
Maria St	89121
Maria Del Mar St	89130
Maria Elena Dr	89104
Maricopa Way	89169
Maricopa Point Ave	89147
Marida Ct	89120
Marie Fenlon Dr	89107
Marietta Ave	89108
Marigny Ct	89129
Marigold Ln	89107
Marigold Point Ct	89120
Marilyn Monroe Ave	89142
Marin Cir & St	89122
Marin Pointe Ave	89131
Marina Bay Ct	89117
Marina Del Rey Ct	89117
Marina Grande Ct	89138
Marina Port Cir	89117
Marina Valley Ave	89147
Marine Current St	89139
Mariner Dr	89128
Mariner Bay St	89117
Mariner Beach Dr	89129
Mariner Cove Dr	89117
Mariner Village Ct	89147
Marino Hills Dr	89144
Mariola St	89144
Marion Dr	
1-1500	89110
1502-1598	89110
1700-2198	89115
2200-3199	89115
3201-3599	89115
Marion St	89104
Marion Bennet Dr	89106
Marion Morrison Ct	89183
Marionette Ave	89101
Mariposa Ave	89104
Mariposa Grove St	89139
Marissa Dr	89122
Maritime Dr	89117
Marius Cove Ct	89139
Mark Ave	
700-798	89119
4300-4699	89108
Mark Twain Ct	89115
Marka Dr	89108
Markam St	89121
Marker Head Dr	89178
Market Crest Dr	89110
Marketwalk Pl	89135
Markhorn Ct	89149
Markleham Ave	89130
Markley Ave	89141
Marksville St	89149
Markwood Cir	89128
Marla St	89161
Marlboro Ct	89147
Marlborough Ave	89110
Marlena Cir	89108
Marlia St	89123
Marlin Ave	89101
Marlowe Ave	89131
Marluna Ct	89128
Marmalade Ln	89108
Marmo Ave	89148
Marmot Ave	89147
Marmot Ridge Ct	89149
Marnell Dr	89121
Maroney Ave	89104
Maroon Dr	89130
Marquette Dr	89115
Marrow Rd	89108
Mars Black Ct	89131
Marseilles Cir	89145
Marsford Pl	89102
Marsh Ct	89128
Marsh Butte St	89148
Marsh Harbor Ct	89148
Marsh Marigold Ave	89108
Marshall Cir	89108
Marshall Canyon Dr	89166
Marshall Creek St	89178
Marshfield Rd	89135
Martha St	89110
W Martin Ave	
3100-3198	89118
3301-3999	89118
9300-9598	89148
Martin Downs Pl	89131
Martin Hall Dr	89129
N Martin L King Blvd	
612-798	89106
800-1800	89106
1801-2399	89106
1801-1801	89127
1802-2398	89106
S Martin L King Blvd	
1-600	89106
602-998	89106
1100-1298	89102
1501-1599	89102
Martinborough Ave	89131
Martinelli Ct	89130
Martinez Bay Ave	89131
Martingale Ave	89119
Martingale Ct	89119
Martingale Ln	89123
Martinique Bay Ln	89147
Martinsburg Ct	89183
Martinsville Pl	89110
Martita Ave	89108
Marwood Villa Ct	89130
Mary Way	89108
Mary Ann Ave	89101
Mary Jane Dr	89115
Maryland Ave	89121
Maryland Cir	89119
N Maryland Pkwy	89101
S Maryland Pkwy	
100-198	89101
200-554	89101
556-698	89101
1100-2441	89104
2443-2499	89104
2500-3199	89109
3201-3299	89109
3300-3699	89169
3700-4300	89119
4302-4626	89119
4505-4505	89154
4632-4632	89170
4632-4698	89119
4700-5400	89119
5402-5484	89119
8000-9699	89123
9701-9747	89183
9749-10199	89183
10201-10299	89183
Maryland Heights Ave	89183
Marymont Pl	89134
Maryvale Dr	89130
Maryville Ave	89144
Mascaro Dr	89122
Maserati Dr	89117
Masked Duck Ave	89117
Mason Ave	89102
Mason Hill Ave	89166
Masons Creek St	89141
Masotta Ave	89141
Maspalomas St	89178
Massachusetts Ln	89141
Masserta Ct	89183
Mast Dr	89117
Masterful Dr	89148
Masterpiece Dr	89148
Masters Ave & Cir	89142
Matador Way	89128
Matagorda Ln	89128
Matanzas Creek Ct	89139
Mataro Dr	89103
Mater Mea Pl	89161
Matfen Ct	89178
Matfen Hall Ct	89138
Matilda St	89113
Matina Bella St	89135
Matisse Ave	89131
Matogroso Ln	89121
Matterhorn Way	
1-199	89124
2900-3099	89102
4100-4299	89124
Matthew Ave	89123
Matvay St	89121
Maui St	89104
E Maulding Ave	89123
W Maulding Ave	89139
E Maule Ave	
1800-2100	89119
2102-2298	89119
3100-3198	89120
3200-3399	89120
3401-3599	89120
W Maule Ave	
3401-3497	89118
3499-6299	89118
8701-9297	89148
9299-9600	89148
9602-9798	89148
Maurice Ct	89108
Maurice River Ct	89183
Maverick St	
2300-3799	89108
3801-3899	89108
4801-5197	89130
5199-6199	89130
6631-7597	89131
7599-8000	89131
8002-8898	89131
Maverick Valley Pl	89131
Maxley Ct	89145
Maxmar Ct	89108
Maxwell Peak Ct	89139
Maxwood Ct	89122
May Ave	89104
May Basket Ave	89131
May Weed Ct	89138
Maya St	89110
Maybrook Dr	89129
Maycott Ave	89148
Maycrest Cir	89128
Maydelle Pl	89101
Mayfair Pl	89101
Mayfair Park St	89166
Mayfair Walk Ave	89178
Mayfield St	89107
Mayflower Ln	89107
Mayflower Bay Ave	89166
Mayhill Ave	89121
Maymont St	89183
Maynard Ave	89108
Mayport Dr	89131
Mays Cir	89115
Maystar Ln	89135
Maywood Ct	89129
Mcafee Ct	89110
Mcallister Ave	89107
Mcbride Dr	89108
Mccarran Blvd	89115
Mccauley Ranch Ave	89148
Mcclintoc Dr	89147
Mcclure St	89101
Mccoig Ave	
2100-2399	89119
2700-2998	89120
Mccombs St	89123
Mccoy Dr	89134
Mcdermit St	89107
Mcdowell Dr	89129
Mcfall Ct	89121
Mcgill Ave	89122
Mcgill Cir	89121
Mcginnis Ave	89148
Mcgrail St	89110
Mchenry St	89144
Mckellar Cir	89119
Mckendrec Ct	89134
Mckinley Ave & Cir	89121
Mckinley Summit Ct	89110
Mckinney Falls St	89141
Mcknight St	89101
Mclaurine Ave	89121
Mclennan Ranch Ave	89131
Mcleod Dr	
2501-2797	89121
2799-4299	89121
4301-4899	89121
4901-5297	89120
5299-6400	89120
6402-7498	89120
Mcleod St	89104
Mcmillan Rd	89121
Mcmurty Ct	89129
Mcneese Ct	89134
Mcrae Ave	89108
E Mcwilliams Ave	89101
W Mcwilliams Ave	89106
Meadbrook St	89110
Meade Ave	89102
Meadow Bridge Ave	89123
Meadow Brook Ln	89103
Meadow Cove St	89179
Meadow Creek St	89123
Meadow Foxtail Dr	89122
Meadow Garden Ct	89135
Meadow Grove Ave & Ct	89120
Meadow Lark Ln	89103
Meadow Leaf Ave	89144
Meadow Mist Ave	89135
Meadow Ridge Ln	89134
Meadow Rock Ave	89130
Meadow Spring Ct	89156
Meadow Valley Ct, Dr & Ln	89107
Meadow View Ln	89103
Meadow Village St	89183
Meadow Vista Ln	89103
Meadowcrest Dr	89121
Meadowglen Ave, Cir, Dr & Way	89121
Meadowgrass Ln	89103
Meadowhaven Ln	89103
Meadowhawk Ln	89135
Meadowlands St	89129
Meadowleah St	89145
Meadowoak Ln	89147
Meadowood Dr	89134
Meadowpointe Ln	89110
Meadowrobin Ave	89131
Meadows Ave	89101
Meadows Ln	89107
Meadows Encore Ave	89131
Meadows Lilly Ave	89108
Meadowsweet Way	89108
Meadowville Ave	89129
Meander Cir	89117
Meandering Creek Ct	89117
Meandering Light Ave	89131
Meandering Path Ave	89131
Meantmore Ave	89117
Mecham Ave	89107
Medallion Dr	89122
Medford Falls Ave	89149
Medford Hills Ct	89139
Medford Oaks Ct	89129
Medical Center St	89148
Medicine Bow St	89183
Medicine Man Way	89169
Medicine Wheel Ave	89143
Medina Ct	89121
Mediterranean Dr	89117
Medley Ln	89123
Meeks Bay Ave	89148
Megan Ave	89108
Meikle Ln	89156
Meisenheimer Ave	
6101-6497	89131
6499-6500	89131
6502-6598	89131
8800-9099	89143
Meissner St	89115
Melancon Loop	89115
Melbourne Cir & Way	89115
Melbourne Ridge Ct	89141
Melinda Ave	89101
Melissa St	89101
Melissa Meadows St	89131
Mell Cave Ct	89131
Mello Ave	89131
Mellow Breeze St	89117
Mellow Motifs Ct	89149
Melocactus Ct	89149
Melodia Magico Ave	89135
Melodia Songo Ct	89135
Melodic Ct	89139
Melody Ln	89108
Melody Rose Ave	89108
Melon Cactus St	89141
Melonies Dr	89103
Melridge Rd	89148
Melrose Dr	89101
Melrose Abbey Pl	89141
Melrose Park St	89139
Melva Blue Ct	89166
Melville Dr	89102
Melville Grove Ct	89122
Melvin St	89115
Memory Ln	89110
Memory Lake Ave	89178
Menands Ave	89123
Menchaca Ln	89138
Mendacino St	89115
Mendocino Forest St	89122
Mendocino Hill Ave	89139
Mendon Ln	89156
Mendoza Ct	89108
Menelaus Ave	89131
Menifee Ct	89134
Menlo Square Dr	89101
Meno Peak St	89115
Mentesana Ave	89166
Merado Peak Dr	89135
Merano Ct	89123
E Meranto Ave	89123
W Meranto Ave	
3100-3198	89139
3200-5699	89139
5701-5799	89139
7000-7198	89178
7200-7600	89178
7602-9298	89178
Mercado Ct	89128
Mercantile St	89118
Merced St	89148
Merced Grove Ct	89139
Merced Lake Dr	89156
Mercedes Cir	89102
Mercer St	89148
Mercurio Ave	89131
Mercury Springs Dr	89122
Mercutio Ct	89141
Mercy Dr	89156
Meredith Ave	89121
Mereworth Ct	89130
Merialdo Ln	
700-999	89145
1500-1599	89117
Meridale Dr	
3300-3499	89117
3500-3599	89147
Meridian Dr	89147
Meridian Bay Dr	89128
Meridian Park Ave	89147
Meridian Point Ct	89147
Merimack Oaks St	89166
Merimar Dr	89134
Merincha Dr	89108
Meriweather Grove Ave	89166
Merkle Bluff St	89147
Merle St	89119
Merlewood Ave	89117
Mermaid Cir	89103
Mermaid Song Ct	89139
Merope St	89179
Merrill Ave	89120
Merrill Cir	
4800-4899	89121
5100-5299	89120
Merrimack Ave	89166
Merritt Ave	89102
Merriweather Dr	89113
Merry Mullion Ct	89149
Mersault Ct	89144
Merseyside Dr	89178
Meryton St	89178
Mesa Dr	89110
Mesa Canogo Dr	89148
Mesa Capella Dr	89148
Mesa Grove Ct	89120
Mesa Hill Dr	89147
Mesa Linda Dr	89120
Mesa Madera Dr	89148
Mesa Mountain Dr	89135
Mesa Peak Ct	89129
Mesa Ridge Ct	89129
Mesa Rim Ct	89144
Mesa Verde Ct	89142
E Mesa Verde Ln	89123
W Mesa Verde Ln	
3400-4398	89139
4400-4500	89139
4502-5098	89139
7500-7799	89113
Mesa View Dr	89120
E Mesa Vista Ave	89120
W Mesa Vista Ave	
3900-6599	89118
7100-8000	89113
8002-8098	89113
9400-9700	89148
9702-9999	89148
10001-10199	89148
Mescal Way	89110
Mesita Ave	89122
Mesosphere Ct	89110
E Mesquite Ave	
700-2699	89101
6801-6897	89110
6899-7099	89110
W Mesquite Ave	89106
Mesquite Fork Ct	89183
Mesquite Hills St	89139
Mesquite Meadow Ct	89131
Mesquite Ranch St	89113
Mesquite Tree St	89131
Messenger Ct	89108
Messina Ct	89117
Metallic Ct	89183
Metalwood Ct	89142
Meteorite Cir	89128
Meteoro St	89169
Metpark Dr	89110
Metronome Ct	89139
Metropolitan St	89102
Metter St	89129
Mews Ln	89101
Mexican Poppy St	89128
Mexican Rose Ct	89120
Meyer St	89101
Mezlan Ln	89141
Mezpah Dr & St	89106
Mezzana St	89141
Mezzanine View Ave	89178
Mezzanino Ct	89135
Mia Moore Ave	89147
Micahs Canyon Ct	89129
N Michael Way	89108
Michael Collins Pl	89145
Michael Jay Way	89149
Michael Ryan Ct	89149
Michelangelo Ct	89129
Michelena Ave	89147
Michelin Cir	89103
Michelle Ave	89131
Michelle Falls Ave	89149
Michelleanne Rd	89107
Michelli Crest Way	89149
Michigan Ave	89104
Michillinda Ln	89121
Mick Pl	89103
Mickey Mantle Ct	89108

Midas St 89110
Midas Touch Way 89156
Middle Beach St 89138
Middle Creek St 89138
Middle Earth St 89135
Middle Ridge Dr 89134
Middle View Dr 89129
Middlebury Ave 89121
Middleriver Ct 89123
Middlesex Ave 89110
Midfield Ct 89120
Midnight Ave 89143
Midnight Cellars St 89139
Midnight Cowboy Ct 89110
Midnight Gleam Ave 89129
Midnight Glow Ct 89178
Midnight Iris St 89183
Midnight Moon St 89135
Midnight Oil Dr 89122
Midnight Rambler St 89149
Midnight Ride St 89131
Midnight Ridge Dr 89135
Midnight Star Ct 89145
Midnight Sun Ave 89147
Midpark Cir 89145
Midpride St 89144
Midseason Mist St 89183
Midsummer Ave 89183
Midway Ln 89108
Mighty Flotilla Ave 89139
Miguel Way 89124
Miguels Ln 89120
Mihela Ave 89129
Mikasa Point Ct 89123
Mike Cir 89106
Milagro Manor Ct 89135
Milazzo St 89141
Milbank Ave 89135
Mild Weather Ct 89148
Mild Wind St 89148
Milenko Dr 89121
Miles Ct 89129
Milford Pl 89102
Milford Haven St 89122
Milford Pond Pl 89147
Milgate St 89117
Milinane Dr 89107
Milkweed Ct 89149
Milkweed Canyon Ave 89166
Milkwood Ln 89149
Mill Canyon Dr 89128
Mill Cove Ave 89134
Mill Creek Way 89149
Mill Hollow Rd 89107
Mill Pond Ln 89119
Mill Valley Dr 89120
Millbrook Ct 89147
Millbrookshire Way 89139
Millcroft Dr 89120
Miller Ave 89106
N Miller Ln 89149
S Miller Ln
1800-2598 89117
2600-2899 89117
4300-4399 89147
8401-8597 89113
8599-8699 89113
8701-9299 89113
Miller Point Ct 89149
Millers Chase Rd 89183
Millett Dr 89142
Millhopper Ave 89128
Millhouse Way 89117
Millie Ave 89101
Millikan Ave 89148
Mills Cir 89106
Mills Reef Ct 89141
Millsboro Dr 89134
Millsfield St 89166
Millwood Ave 89121
Milo Way 89102
Milonga St 89138
Milorie Ct 89130
Milowski Cir 89115
Milpas Ln 89134
Milstead Ct 89110
Milvio Ave 89141
Mimosa Cir 89123
Mimosa Bloom Ct 89183
Mimosa Leaf Ct 89144
Mimosa Valley St 89131
Minas Ridge Dr 89178
Minden Way 89142
Mindy St 89115
Mine Hill Ct 89147
Mine Shaft St 89131
Mineola Palms St 89139
Miner Way 89104
Mineral Ave 89106
Mineral City Ct 89110
Mineral Lake Dr 89122
Mineral Mine Dr 89129
Mineral Park Ave 89179
Mineral Peak St 89166
Mineral Rock Ave 89131
Mineral Springs Ct 89128
Miners Gulch Ave 89135
Miners Hope Dr 89108
Miners Ridge Dr 89122
Minerva Dr 89130
Miniature St 89143
Mink Creek Dr 89117
N & S Minnesota St 89107
Minots Ledge Ave 89147
Minsk Ct 89147
Minstrel Dr 89123
Mint Frost Way 89108
Mint Julep Way 89142
Mint Leaves St 89183
Minto Ct 89145
Minton Ct 89103
Minturn Ave 89130
Minuteman Ave 89110
Mira Ln 89108
Mira Monte Cir 89120
Mira Vista St 89120
Miracosta Ave 89108
Mirada Dr 89144
Mirada Del Sol Dr 89128
Miradero Ln 89134
Mirado Ct 89121
Miraflores Ave 89102
Mirage Garden St 89130
Miragrande Dr 89108
Miraloma St 89108
Miramar Dr 89108
Miramia Dr 89108
Miratan St 89110
Mirkwood Ave 89178
Mirror Lake Dr 89110
Mirror Pond Dr 89115
Mis Sent 89123
Mis Sequence 89123
Mis Sort 89123
Miss Peach Ave 89145
Mission Bay Dr 89113
Mission Carmel Ln 89107
Mission Catalina Ln 89107
Mission Control Ave 89149
Mission Creek Ct 89135
Mission Creek Inn St 89178
Mission Crest Ave 89131
Mission Del Mar Way 89123
Mission Gorge Ct 89130
Mission Hills Dr 89113
Mission Laguna Ln 89107
Mission Lakes Ave 89134
Mission Meadow Cir 89139
Mission Monterey Ln 89107
Mission Newport Ln 89107
Mission Palm St 89139
Mission Park Ave 89135
Mission Peak Cir 89146
Mission Point Ln 89149
Mississippi Ave 89103
Missoula Ct 89178
Missouri Ave 89122
Missouri Meadows St 89183
Missy Marie Ln 89130
Mist Ct 89135
Mist Flower Cir 89134
Mistfull Ct 89156
Mistral Ave
200-299 89123
8601-8699 89148
W Mistral Ave 89113
Misty Ct 89120
Misty Acres Ct 89148
Misty Bend Ct 89148
Misty Brook Ct 89149
Misty Cloud Ct 89129
Misty Cove Ct 89117
Misty Creek Ave 89129
Misty Evening St 89129
Misty Falls St 89129
Misty Glade Dr 89119
Misty Glow Ct 89131
Misty Harbour Dr 89117
Misty Horizon Ct 89113
Misty Island Cir 89145
Misty Isle Ln 89107
Misty Lake St 89123
Misty Lilac Ct 89122
Misty Meadow Dr 89134
Misty Mill Ct 89149
Misty Moat St 89117
Misty Morning Dr 89118
Misty Peaks Ct 89135
Misty Sage St 89139
Misty Shadows Ave 89128
Misty Springs Ct 89148
Mita Way 89141
Mithril Ave 89178
Mitra Ct 89103
Mitzi Ave 89101
Mizzen Ct 89147
Moaning Cavern St 89131
Moapa Ct 89110
Moapa Water St 89131
E Moberly Ave 89123
W Moberly Ave 89139
Moccasin Point St 89148
Mocha Dr 89128
Mocha Brown Ct 89118
Mock Heather St 89178
Mockingbird Ln 89103
Mocorito Ave 89113
Modena Cir & Dr 89120
Modern Ct 89149
Moenkopi Rd 89161
Mohave Ave 89104
Mohave Trace Ave 89131
Mohawk St
800-1099 89107
1901-1997 89146
1999-2899 89146
5800-5898 89118
6201-6299 89118
8501-8597 89139
8599-9499 89139
Mohawk Cliff Ave 89113
Mohican Canyon St 89113
Mohigan Way
2000-2399 89169
3900-3999 89119
Mojado Ct 89121
N Mojave Rd 89101
S Mojave Rd
100-1098 89104
1100-1899 89104
2601-2797 89121
2799-4799 89121
4801-4899 89121
5300-5699 89120
5701-6299 89120
Mojave Blush Dr 89122
Mojave Canyon St 89139
Mojave Heights Ct 89113
Mojave Ridge Ct 89183
Mokena Ave 89178
Molfetta St 89149
Molino St 89108
Molise Ct 89141
Moller Cir 89107
Mollison Mesa Ct 89131
Molly Ct 89183
Molly Knoll Cir 89123
Molly Malone Ct 89130
Molly Meadows St 89115
Molveno Ct 89130
Momenti St 89135
Momentos St 89149
Momentum Ct 89129
Monaco Rd 89121
Monaco Bay Ct 89117
Monaco Beach Ave 89166
Monaco Shores Dr 89117
Monarcas St 89108
Monarch Bay Dr 89128
Monarch Birch Ave 89117
Monarch Creek St 89130
Monarchy Ct 89129
Moncada Way 89149
Moncinna St 89118
Mondavi Ct 89117
Mondavi Hill Ct 89139
Mondell Rd 89130
Mondell Pines Cir 89146
Mondo Ct 89123
Monessen Ct 89141
Monico Valley Ct 89128
Monika Way 89119
Monja Cir & Ct 89104
Monks Hood Ct 89183
Monkside Ct 89110
Monogram Way 89123
E Monroe Ave 89110
W Monroe Ave 89106
Monrovia Dr 89117
Mont Blanc Way 89124
Montagna Dr 89134
Montagne Marron Blvd 89141
Montago Valley Ave 89117
Montalvo Ct 89128
Montana Ave 89110
Montana Mountain St 89183
Montana Peak Ave 89139
Montana Stream Ave 89113
E & W Montara Cir 89121
Montasola St 89141
Montblanc Ct 89129
Montclair St 89146
Montclair Heights Ct 89178
Montclair Park Ct 89183
Montcliff Ave 89147
Montdale Ave 89121
Monte Carlo Dr
2401-2599 89108
3400-3499 89121
N Monte Cristo Way
4800-5199 89149
6000-6198 89130
7200-7400 89131
7402-8198 89131
S Monte Cristo Way
1200-1298 89117
1300-3199 89117
8200-8298 89113
8300-9099 89113
9101-9199 89113
9301-9727 89178
9729-9799 89178
9801-11199 89178
Monte De Oro Ave 89183
Monte Grande Cir 89108
Monte Mia Cir 89108
Monte Oro Dr 89131
Monte Rio Ct 89128
Monte Rosa Ave 89120
Monte San Savino Ln 89135
Monte Verde St 89121
Montebello Ave 89110
Montecito Cir 89120
Montecito Dr 89120
Montecito Way 89108
Montefino Ct 89117
Montefrio Ave 89113
Montego Cir, Ct & Dr 89121
Montego Bay Dr 89117
Monteleone Ave 89141
Montello Ave 89110
Montemesa Cir 89108
Monterey Ave 89104
Monterey Cir 89169
Monterey Cliffs Ave 89148
Monterey Cypress St 89144
Monterey Loma Ct 89156
Monterey Mesa Ct 89156
Monterey Oaks Ct 89129
Monterey Park Cir 89146
Monterey Pine Dr 89156
Monterey Sunrise Dr 89156
Monterey Vista Ct 89156
Monterra Greens Ave 89123
Monterrey Ave 89121
Montes Vascos Dr 89178
Montessouri St
1455-1497 89117
1499-3200 89117
3202-3398 89117
6000-7299 89113
7301-7399 89113
9201-9299 89178
Montezuma Ct 89119
Montgomery St 89123
Monthaven Ct 89178
Monthill Ave 89121
Monticello Dr 89107
Monticello Mist St 89166
Montour Falls St 89149
Montoya Ave 89120
Montpeliar St 89110
Montsouris Park Ct 89130
Montura Rosa Pl 89138
Montvale Ct 89134
Montvilla Dr 89123
Monument St 89121
Monument Hill Ave 89138
Monument Lake Ct 89113
Monument Valley Rd 89129
Monza Ave 89129
Moody Rd 89123
Moon Cir 89120
Moon Ct 89145
Moon Cactus Ave 89123
Moon Chase St 89110
Moon Crater Ave 89178
Moon Flower Arbor Pl 89144
Moon Garden St 89148
Moon River St 89129
Moon Roses Ct 89108
Moon Shore Dr 89128
Moon Shower Cir 89128
Moon Splash Ct 89129
Moon Tango St 89129
Moon Valley Pl 89134
Moon Vista Ave 89148
Moonbeam Glow Ln 89135
Mooncrest Cir 89129
Moondance Cellars Ct 89139
Moonfire Dr 89135
Moonflower Ct & Dr 89146
Moongate Cir 89103
Moonglow Dr 89156
Moongold Ct 89134
Moonlight Dr
1-4399 89110
6000-6100 89130
6102-6198 89130
Moonlight Bay Ln 89128
Moonlight Beach St 89113
Moonlight Fire Ct 89135
Moonlight Garden St 89130
Moonlight Meadows St 89113
Moonlight Nest Ln 89178
Moonlight Sonata Ave 89122
Moonlight View Ct 89129
Moonlit Beach Ave 89115
Moonlit Rain Dr 89135
Moonlit Sky Ave 89147
Moonlite Dr 89115
Moonmist Ave 89108
Moonraker Ave 89178
Moonridge Ct 89134
Moonscape Ave 89178
Moonshadow Cir 89108
Moonstone Cir 89128
Moonstruck Ave 89107
Moonwood Ct 89123
Moorcroft St 89147
Moore St 89104
Moores Mill Ct 89113
Mooring Ave 89129
Moortown St 89142
Moose Ln 89145
Moose Country Pl 89178
Moose Creek St 89156
Moose Falls Dr 89141
Moose Lake Ave 89124
Moose River Ct 89166
Mooses Ct 89131
Mopan Rd 89178
Mora Ln 89102
Moradi Ave 89131
Morado Hills Ln 89128
Moraga Dr 89103
Morales Cir 89119
Morant Bay Ave 89148
Moratella Ct 89141
Morava St 89138
Morehouse Pl 89123
Morendo Dr 89107
Moreno Ct 89129
Moreno Rd 89161
Moreno Mountain Ave 89122
Moreno Valley St 89149
Morewell St 89117
Morgan Ave 89106
Morgan Cir 89115
Morgan Cashmans
Way 89103
Morisset Ave 89179
Moritz Way 89124
Morlang Ct 89108
Morley Ave 89108
Morning Break Ct 89142
Morning Brook Dr 89131
Morning Canyon St 89147
Morning Cloud Ln 89142
Morning Cove Ct 89131
Morning Creek Ct 89130
Morning Crest Ave 89183
Morning Dew St 89117
Morning Drop Ave 89129
Morning Falls Ave 89131
Morning Flower Ln 89129
Morning Frost St 89179
Morning Gallop Ct 89131
Morning Glen Cir 89108
Morning Glory Ln 89115
Morning Glow Ln 89135
Morning Grove Dr 89135
Morning Harbor Ave 89129
Morning Jewel Ave 89110
Morning Lake Dr 89131
Morning Mauve Ave 89183
Morning Meadow Ct 89156
Morning Mist Ave 89115
Morning Peace St 89115
Morning Port St 89129
Morning Queen Dr 89178
Morning Quiet St 89156
Morning Rain St 89156
Morning Ridge Dr 89134
Morning Sky Ln 89135
Morning Snow Ct 89141
Morning Sorrow St 89183
Morning Splash Ave 89131
Morning Splendor Way 89110
Morning Sun Ct &
Way 89110
Morning Swim Ln 89113
Morning Vista Dr 89110
Morning Water St 89149
Morning Wind Ln 89129
Morningcross St 89130
Mornings Dawn St 89129
Morningside Ave 89106
Morningside Ranch Ct 89113
Moroccan Ct 89141
Morpeth St 89178
Morris St 89122
Morris Bay St 89179
Morrison St 89148
Morrissey Dr 89115
Morro Bay Ave 89108
Morro Creek St 89128
Morro Vista Dr 89135
Morse Arberry Ave 89106
Morton Manor Ct 89130
Mosaic Harbor Ave 89117
Mosaic Sunrise Ln 89166
Mosaic Terrace St 89118
Moselle Ct 89144
Moshi St 89166
Mosport St 89123
Moss Agate Dr 89131
Moss Bluff Ct 89141
Moss Creek Cir 89117
Moss Lake St 89179
Moss Ridge Ct 89147
Moss Rose Ave 89106
Mossback St 89123
Mossman Ave 89108
Mossy Bark Ct 89183
Mossy Hollow Ave 89149
Mossy Oaks Ln 89142
Mossy Rock Ct 89108
Moth Orchid Ct 89183
Mother Of Pearl St 89106
Mothers Joy St 89178
Motley Rd 89178
Mott Cir 89102
Moultrie Ave 89129
Mound House St 89110
Mount Angel Dr 89123
Mount Auburn St 89130
Mount Augusta Ct 89117
Mount Baker Ct 89149
Mount Blackburn Ave 89166
Mount Bret Ave 89129
Mount Brodie Cir 89145
Mount Carmel Ave 89123
Mount Cash Ave 89129
Mount Cherie Ave 89129
Mount Cupertino St 89178
Mount Del Mar St 89178
Mount Diablo Dr 89118
Mount Douglas St 89179
Mount Dutton Dr 89156
Mount Eden Ave 89139
Mount Everest Ct 89110
Mount Flora Ct 89156
Mount Geneva Ct 89131
Mount George St 89179
Mount Gravatt Ct 89110
Mount Hamilton Ct 89117
Mount Harris Ct 89145
Mount Holly Ct 89128
Mount Hood Ct 89129
Mount Hood St
1200-1599 89110
1600-2099 89156
Mount Hope Dr 89156
Mount Hunter St 89179
Mount Jefferson Ave 89166
Mount Julian St 89110
Mount Kearsarge St 89131
Mount Kenyon St 89178
Mount Logan Ct 89131
Mount Lompoc Ct 89178
Mount Madera St 89178
Mount Mariah Dr 89106
Mount Mckinley Ave 89156
Mount Mira Loma Ave 89178
Mount Nido Dr 89147
Mount Olympias Ct 89110
Mount Oroville Ct 89178
Mount Oxford Ave 89166
Mount Palmer Ct 89156
Mount Palomar Ave 89139
Mount Pendleton St 89179
Mount Pleasant Ln 89113
Mount Potosi Canyon
Rd 89161
Mount Princeton St 89166
Mount Rainier Ave 89156
Mount Roy Ln 89156
Mount Royal Ave 89144
Mount Royal Ct 89145
Mount Shasta Cir 89145
Mount Stellar St 89179

Mount Tremblant Ave ... 89123
Mount Vernon Ave ... 89121
Mount Vernon Cir ... 89101
Mount Washington Ave ... 89166
Mount Whitney Cir ... 89145
Mount Wilson St ... 89113
Mountain Trl ... 89108
Mountain Ash Dr ... 89147
Mountain Birch St ... 89147
Mountain Bluebird St ... 89117
Mountain Breeze Ct ... 89128
Mountain Cliffs Ave ... 89129
Mountain Creek Dr ... 89148
Mountain Crest St ... 89129
Mountain Den Ave ... 89179
Mountain Destiny Ave ... 89131
Mountain Elk Ct ... 89148
Mountain Estates Dr ... 89110
Mountain Foliage Dr ... 89148
Mountain Forest Ct ... 89129
Mountain Gap Ct ... 89117
Mountain Gate Dr ... 89134
Mountain Grove Ct ... 89134
Mountain Heather Ct ... 89149
Mountain Hemlock Ave ... 89139
Mountain Hills Ct ... 89128
Mountain Lakes Ave ... 89147
Mountain Lodge Pl ... 89144
Mountain Majesty St ... 89131
Mountain Man Way ... 89113
Mountain Maple Ct ... 89148
Mountain Meadow Ln ... 89147
Mountain Mesa Ave ... 89156
Mountain Mist Ct ... 89117
Mountain Moss Dr ... 89147
Mountain Paradise Way ... 89120
Mountain Park St ... 89129
Mountain Peak Cir ... 89147
Mountain Pepper Dr ... 89148
Mountain Pine Dr ... 89156
Mountain Point Ave ... 89131
Mountain Quail Ave ... 89131
Mountain Range Ave ... 89129
Mountain Rise Ave ... 89129
Mountain River St ... 89129
Mountain Spring Rd ... 89146
Mountain Stream Ct ... 89129
Mountain Thicket St ... 89131
Mountain Top Cir ... 89148
Mountain Trek St ... 89129
Mountain Valley Dr ... 89129
Mountain Valley Rd ... 89121
Mountain View Blvd ... 89102
Mountain View Dr ... 89146
Mountain Villa Dr ... 89110
Mountain Village St ... 89113
Mountain Violet Ct ... 89108
Mountain Vista St
2701-2897 ... 89121
2899-4499 ... 89121
4501-4899 ... 89121
4901-5899 ... 89120
4948-4948 ... 89112
4948-4948 ... 89121
5000-5998 ... 89120
Mountain Waters St ... 89129
Mountain Willow St ... 89179
Mountainair Ave ... 89134
Mountainboro Ln ... 89123
Mountains Edge Pkwy ... 89178
Mountainwood Ln ... 89103
Mountcrest Dr ... 89121
Mountridge Ct & Dr ... 89110
Mozart Dr ... 89146
Mozley Park St ... 89113
Muddy Creek Ave ... 89123
Muddy Waters Ave ... 89178
Muinos St ... 89117
Muir Woods Pkwy ... 89122
Muirfield Dr ... 89147
Muirfield Village Ct ... 89131
Muirlands Ct ... 89130
Mulberry Forest St ... 89166
Mulcahy Ave ... 89145
Muldoon Ct ... 89122
Muldowney Ln ... 89138
Muldrow St ... 89139
Mule Creek St ... 89134
Mule Deer Dr ... 89161
Mule Train Ct ... 89129
Mulgrave Ct ... 89113
Mullinix Ave ... 89166
Mulroona Ct ... 89129
Mulvaney Cir ... 89141
Munich Ct ... 89147
Munstead Woods Ct ... 89130
Murillo St ... 89121
Murmuring Tide Ave ... 89148
Murphys Windmill Ave ... 89139
Murray Ct ... 89134
Murray Canyon Ct ... 89139
Murray Hill Ln ... 89142
Murtiga Ct ... 89141
Muscari Way ... 89141
Muscato Ct ... 89144
Musette Ave ... 89139
Music Ave ... 89144
Musical Ln ... 89145
Musketeer Ln ... 89130
Mustang St
2800-3198 ... 89108
3200-3599 ... 89108
5200-5398 ... 89130
5400-5999 ... 89130
6600-8699 ... 89131
8701-8799 ... 89131
Mustang Canyon St ... 89113
Mustang Creek Way ... 89148
Mustang Hill Ct ... 89131
Mustang Spring Ave ... 89139
My Way ... 89103
My Dream Ct ... 89103
My Gage Ct ... 89123
Mycroft Ct ... 89147
Myerlee Ct ... 89131
Myron Cir ... 89142
Myrsine Ct ... 89149
Myrtle Ave ... 89102
Myrtle Flag Ave ... 89178
Myrtle Grove Ave ... 89166
Myrtle Island Dr ... 89117
Myrtle Springs Ct ... 89148
Myrtlewood Ave ... 89122
Mystere Ct ... 89117
Mystic Arbor St ... 89183
Mystic Cliffs Ave ... 89183
Mystic Dance St ... 89183
Mystic Desert Ave ... 89131
Mystic Lake Ave ... 89148
Mystic Moss St ... 89183
Mystic Night Ave ... 89143
Mystic Pine Rd ... 89135
Mystic Plain Ct ... 89149
Mystic Ridge Ct ... 89129
Mystic Rose Ct ... 89138
Mystic Seaport Ave ... 89129
Mystic Shore Ave ... 89166
Mystic Stream St ... 89131
Mystic Voyage St ... 89139
Mythic Atlantis Ave ... 89139
N St ... 89106
Naco Ct ... 89102
Nadia Ct ... 89108
Naff Ridge Dr ... 89131
Naggio Shores Ave ... 89141
Naha Port Ave ... 89110
Nahatan Way ... 89169
Nakona Ln ... 89169
Nambe Ct & Dr ... 89121
Nancy Ave ... 89120
Nancy Margarite Ln ... 89130
Nantova Ct ... 89141
Nantucket Ridge Ave ... 89166
Naomi Dr ... 89122
Napa Dr ... 89156
Napa Grape Ct ... 89135
Napa Hills Dr ... 89144
Napa Ridge Dr ... 89144
Napatree St ... 89144
Naperville St ... 89130
Napier St ... 89131
E Naples Dr
400-599 ... 89169
600-799 ... 89119
W Naples Dr
3500-3900 ... 89103
3902-3998 ... 89103
9100-9298 ... 89147
Napoleon Dr ... 89156
Napoli Dr ... 89117
Nara Vista Way ... 89103
Narcissus Ln ... 89107
Nardini Ave ... 89141
Nardo Ct ... 89183
Narit Dr ... 89108
Narnia Ave ... 89113
Narod St ... 89121
Narra Pl ... 89144
Narrow Canyon St ... 89129
Narrow Isthmus Ave ... 89139
Narrow Leaf Way ... 89147
Narrow Peak St ... 89149
Nash Ave ... 89110
Nash Peak Ave ... 89166
Nashua Cir ... 89123
Nassau Dr ... 89108
Natalia Ct ... 89130
Natalie Ave
2100-2399 ... 89169
2400-2999 ... 89121
Natchez Trace St ... 89178
National Ave ... 89146
National Park Dr ... 89178
Native Dancer Way ... 89113
Native Winds Ct ... 89149
Natoma Station Pl ... 89123
Natural Bridge St ... 89179
Natural Glass Dr ... 89131
Natural Slope St ... 89148
Natural Springs Ave ... 89129
Natural View St ... 89129
Nature Quest Ct ... 89149
Nature Scene Dr ... 89139
Nature Valley St ... 89149
Natures Dr ... 89122
Natures Song St ... 89131
Natures Touch Ave ... 89131
Naugatuck Cir ... 89129
Naumkeg Ct ... 89115
Nautical Bay Ln ... 89117
Nautical Stone Ct ... 89149
Nautilus Shell St ... 89139
Nautilus Vista Ct ... 89149
Navajo Ln ... 89110
Navajo Way ... 89108
Navajo Gorge Ct ... 89142
Navajo Lake Way ... 89128
Navio Dr ... 89103
Navy Blue Ct ... 89117
Nay Ct ... 89104
Naylor Ct ... 89110
E & W Neal Ave ... 89183
Neath Ave ... 89178
Nebraska Ave ... 89107
Nebula Dr ... 89115
Neches Ave ... 89179
Nectar Cir ... 89147
Nectarine Grove Ct ... 89142
Nedla Ct ... 89104
Needlepoint Ct ... 89149
Needles Ct ... 89130
Neepawa Cir ... 89108
Neets Bay St ... 89179
Negril Ave ... 89130
Neil Armstrong Cir & St ... 89145
Nellie Bell St ... 89118
Nellie Jo Dr ... 89123
Nellie Springs Ct ... 89110
N Nellis Blvd
2-8 ... 89110
10-1599 ... 89110
1600-5899 ... 89115
S Nellis Blvd
1100-1398 ... 89104
1400-2399 ... 89104
2401-2499 ... 89104
2501-2797 ... 89121
2799-4899 ... 89121
Nellis Cir ... 89120
Nellis Oasis Ln ... 89115
Nelson Ridge Ln ... 89178
Nene Ct ... 89144
Neon Ridge Ave ... 89139
Neopolitan Pl ... 89144
Neosho St ... 89120
Nepal Ct ... 89148
Neptune Dr ... 89108
Neptune Beach Ave ... 89128
Neptunian Sky Ct ... 89139
Nerone Ave ... 89148
Nertera Ct ... 89149
Ness Ave ... 89118
Ness Gardens Ct ... 89122
Ness Wood Ln ... 89135
Nesting Way ... 89115
Nesting Pine Pl ... 89143
Nestled Ct ... 89143
Nestled Meadows Ln ... 89128
Nestled Moon Ct ... 89131
Nestled Vista Ave ... 89128
Netherfield Ave ... 89178
Netherseal Ave ... 89139
Netherton Dr ... 89134
Nettie Ave ... 89110
Nettle Way ... 89135
Nettleton Cir ... 89123
Network Cir ... 89156
Nevada Ave
4601-4797 ... 89104
4799-4999 ... 89104
5100-5398 ... 89122
Nevada Classic Cir ... 89108
Nevada Falls Ave ... 89129
Nevada Falls Ct ... 89134
Nevada Sky St ... 89128
Neville Ct ... 89183
W Nevso Dr
4001-4397 ... 89103
4399-4799 ... 89103
4801-4899 ... 89103
7900-8998 ... 89147
New Bedford Cir & Dr ... 89122
New Boro Ave ... 89144
New Boston Ave ... 89166
New Brunswick Ave ... 89110
New Dawn Ct ... 89130
New Dupell Way ... 89147
New Era Ct ... 89103
New Forest Dr ... 89147
New Frontier Ln ... 89144
New Hampton St ... 89166
New Harbor Ave ... 89149
New Hope Way ... 89110
New Horizon Dr ... 89115
New Leaf Ave ... 89131
New London Ct ... 89129
New Moon Way ... 89110
New Mountain Way ... 89123
New Rock Ct ... 89113
New Seabury Ct ... 89122
New Season Ct ... 89123
New Sky Ct ... 89148
New Utrecht St ... 89178
New Wood Ln ... 89108
E New York Ave ... 89104
W New York Ave ... 89102
Newberry Ct ... 89110
Newberry Springs Dr ... 89148
Newbold St ... 89138
Newbury Hills Ave ... 89138
Newby Hall Ct ... 89130
Newcastle Rd ... 89103
Newcastle Bridge Ct ... 89138
Newcastle Hills St ... 89141
Newcombe St ... 89123
Newcomer Cir & St ... 89107
Newcrest Cir ... 89147
Newell Dr ... 89121
Newfane Ct ... 89183
Newhaven Dr ... 89147
Newington Ct ... 89122
Newkirk Ct ... 89130
Newland Ave ... 89121
Newport St ... 89110
Newport Bay Dr ... 89117
Newport Coast Cir ... 89147
Newport Cove Dr ... 89119
Newport Isle Ct ... 89117
Newport Ridge Ct ... 89135
Newport View St ... 89183
Newquay Ct ... 89178
Newridge Ct ... 89103
Newsom Cir ... 89119
Newton Dr
4400-4999 ... 89121
5000-5199 ... 89122
Newton Commons Dr ... 89135
Newton Grove Ct ... 89148
Newview Cir ... 89103
Newville Ave ... 89103
Niagara Falls Ln ... 89144
Nial Cir ... 89115
Niblick Cir ... 89142
Niblick Dr ... 89108
Niccolette Ct ... 89123
Nice Ct ... 89129
Niche Ave ... 89149
Nicholas Dr ... 89115
Nickel Creek Trl ... 89122
Nickel Mine Ave ... 89122
Nickel Ridge Way ... 89122
Nickleby Ave ... 89123
Nicklewood Ave ... 89143
Nicklin St ... 89143
Nicole Ct & St ... 89120
Nicova Ave ... 89148
Nieman Way ... 89146
Night Bloom Ct ... 89148
Night Breeze Dr ... 89128
Night Dance Ct ... 89130
Night Glare St ... 89122
Night Magic Ct ... 89129
Night Mesa St ... 89178
Night Owl Ct ... 89134
Night Rain Ct ... 89130
Night Song Way ... 89135
Night Star St ... 89147
Night Swim Ln ... 89113
Night Wind Dr ... 89117
Nightflower Ln ... 89121
Nightglow Ct ... 89123
Nighthawk Dr ... 89108
Nightingale Ct, Pl & St ... 89107
Nightmoss Ave ... 89183
Nightowl Creek Pl ... 89144
Nightrider Dr ... 89134
Nightwood Ct ... 89149
Nigul Way ... 89117
Nike Way ... 89148
Nikita Ave ... 89123
Nimes Ave ... 89141
Nirvana Dr ... 89110
Nixson Dr ... 89110
No Point Bay St ... 89147
Noahs Star St ... 89145
Noble Mesa Ave ... 89166
Noble Range St ... 89149
Noble Stand St ... 89148
Nocera St ... 89147
Noche Oscura Cir ... 89139
Nocturne Ct ... 89128
Nolan Ln ... 89107
Nolene Stream St ... 89131
Nolinas St ... 89141
Nomo St ... 89123
Nook Way ... 89103
Nook Crest Ct ... 89129
Nookfield Dr ... 89147
Noontide Ave ... 89135
Noorozian Ct ... 89107
Noors Ave ... 89138
Norbeck St ... 89117
Norburn Dr ... 89122
Norco Dr ... 89129
Norcross Ave ... 89129
Nordalpino Ave ... 89178
Nordic Cliff Ave ... 89129
Nordic Lights Dr ... 89119
Nordic Valley Ct ... 89131
Nordic Woods Ln ... 89134
Nordica Ct ... 89117
Nordoff Cir ... 89121
Norfolk Ct ... 89147
Norlen St ... 89107
Norma Joyce Ln ... 89128
Norman Ave ... 89104
Norman Rockwell Ln ... 89143
Normandy Shores St ... 89131
Normanton St ... 89120
Norsemen Ct ... 89134
Norte Cir ... 89130
North Cir ... 89119
North St ... 89124
Northam St ... 89102
Northbridge St ... 89102
Northern Dancer Dr ... 89117
Northern Hills Ave ... 89166
Northern Light Dr ... 89115
Northfield Park Ct ... 89148
Northridge Cir & Ln ... 89122
Northrop Ave ... 89119
Northstar St ... 89107
Northwind Ct ... 89110
Norton Dr ... 89129
Norton Peak Ave ... 89148
Norwalk Ct ... 89110
Norway Ln ... 89130
Norway Maple St ... 89117
Norway Pine Ct ... 89134
Norwegian St ... 89147
Norwich Cir ... 89103
Norwood Ln ... 89107
Norwood Creek Rd ... 89139
Nostalgia Cir ... 89135
Notre Dame Ave ... 89110
Notte Ave ... 89135
Notte Calma St ... 89141
Notte Pacifica Way ... 89141
Nottingham Dr ... 89121
Nottinghill Gate Ct ... 89145
Nottingshire Way ... 89139
Nova Ln ... 89115
Nova Ridge Ct ... 89129
Novak St ... 89115
Novara Ln ... 89144
Novat St ... 89129
Novato Cir & Way ... 89120
Novatoga Dr ... 89120
Novel Ct ... 89149
Novella Ct ... 89135
Novelty St ... 89148
November Breeze St ... 89123
November Rain St ... 89178
Novena St ... 89138
Nu Wav Kaiv Blvd ... 89124
Nugget Creek Dr ... 89108
Null Ln ... 89145
Numaga Rd ... 89178
Numidia Ave ... 89141
Nunca St ... 89107
Nutcracker Ct ... 89115
Nutmeg Ln ... 89115
Nutt Creek Ave ... 89129
Nutwood St ... 89108
Nye St ... 89106
Nyton Dr ... 89108
Oahu St ... 89104
Oak St ... 89120
Oak Apple Ave ... 89144
Oak Bend Dr ... 89135
Oak Country Ln ... 89144
Oak Creek Canyon Ave ... 89147
Oak Crest Ave ... 89144
Oak Fair St ... 89138
Oak Glen Way ... 89115
Oak Grove Ave ... 89117
Oak Hills Course Dr ... 89148
Oak Mist St ... 89139
Oak Moss Pl ... 89144
Oak Park Ave ... 89118
Oak Ridge Ave ... 89142
Oak River St ... 89134
Oak Rock Dr ... 89128
Oak Savanna Ct ... 89141
Oak Shadow Ave ... 89144
Oak Spring Rd ... 89124
Oak Terrace Ave ... 89149
Oak Trail Cir ... 89124
Oak Tree Ln ... 89108
Oak Valley Dr ... 89103
Oak Village Ave ... 89183
Oakbank Ct ... 89130
Oakbrook Ln ... 89169
Oakbury Ct ... 89130
Oakcreek St ... 89110
Oakdale Ave ... 89121
E Oakey Blvd ... 89104
W Oakey Blvd
2-1498 ... 89102
1500-4400 ... 89102
4402-4798 ... 89102
4901-4997 ... 89146
4999-6799 ... 89146
6801-6899 ... 89146
7001-7197 ... 89117
7199-7299 ... 89117
7301-8199 ... 89117
Oakford St ... 89110
Oakglen Ct ... 89108
Oakhaven Ln ... 89108
Oakhill Ave & Cir ... 89121
Oakhurst Ave ... 89145
Oakland Cir ... 89145
Oakland Hills Dr ... 89141
Oakleaf Ln ... 89146
Oakleigh Dr ... 89110
Oakleigh Willow Way ... 89120
Oakmont Ave ... 89109
Oakmont Hills Ln ... 89141
Oakmoor Pl ... 89144
Oakpoint Ln ... 89145
Oakshire St ... 89131
Oakstone Ct ... 89145
Oakton St ... 89130
Oakview St ... 89147
Oakview Falls Ct ... 89148
Oakville Ranch Ct ... 89118
Oakwood Pines Ct ... 89166
Oakwood Ridge St ... 89130
Oasis Ave & Cir ... 89108
Oasis Island St ... 89131
Oasis Palm Ct ... 89117
Oatman Ln ... 89120
Obannon Dr
4700-4998 ... 89102
5001-5097 ... 89146
5099-6899 ... 89146
6900-8199 ... 89117
8201-8599 ... 89117
Oberlin Ct ... 89135
Oberling Bay Ave ... 89113
Obispo Cir ... 89108
Observation Dr ... 89128
Observation Peak St ... 89166
Observer St ... 89123
Obsidian St ... 89145
Obtainable Ct ... 89149
Ocala Ln ... 89122
Ocaso St ... 89138
Ocate Rd ... 89122
Occlusion Ct ... 89129
Ocean Beach Dr ... 89149
Ocean Cliff Ave ... 89147
Ocean Edge Ct ... 89134
Ocean Front Dr ... 89128
Ocean Gate Way ... 89128
Ocean Harbour Ln ... 89148
Ocean Mist Ct ... 89128
Ocean Pines Cir ... 89130
Ocean Port Dr ... 89117
Ocean Sea Dr ... 89131
Ocean Shores Way ... 89130
Ocean Springs Ave ... 89130
Ocean Terrace Way ... 89128
Ocean View Dr ... 89117
Ocean Waters St ... 89129
Oceanside Way ... 89108

Oceanside Slopes Ave 89178
Oceantide Ct 89117
Oceanus Ln 89115
Ocho Rios St 89130
Ochoa St 89143
Ocicat Ave 89166
Ocotillo Ct 89121
Ocotillo Falls Ave 89148
Ocotillo Springs Cir 89147
Octave Ave 89139
Octavia Way 89147
October Oak Ave 89123
Odda Way 89117
Odense Way 89147
Oderzo Ln 89117
Odessa Dr 89142
Odette Ln 89117
Odin Cir 89103
Odoul Ave 89110
Odysseus Ave 89131
Oeste Vista St 89129
Offerman Ave 89123
E Ogden Ave
2-698 89101
700-2499 89101
4000-4599 89110
Ogden Mills Dr 89135
Ogee Dr 89145
Ohana Ct 89129
Ohare Rd
8400-8599 89143
12200-12299 89166
Ohio Ct 89128
Ohrid Lake Ct 89141
Oil Lantern Ln 89145
Ojai Ct 89135
Ojibwa Ave 89149
Okaloosa Dr 89120
Okeefe Ct 89144
Okehampton Ct 89178
Okra Plains St 89149
Olay St 89142
Old Bear Canyon St 89156
Old Cabin Ln 89115
Old Castle Dr 89108
Old Cistern Ct 89131
Old Colonial Way 89108
Old Colony Dr 89139
Old Course St 89122
Old Creek Ranch St 89139
Old English Ct 89139
Old Forge Ln 89121
Old Glory St 89148
Old Harbor Pl 89131
Old Ironsides Ave 89166
Old Lace Ct 89110
Old Majestic St 89108
Old Mine Creek Ln 89134
Old Mission Dr 89128
Old Newbury Ave 89108
Old Orchard Ct 89108
Old Oxford Ave 89108
Old Palms Dr 89123
Old Park Rd 89124
Old Point Ave 89142
Old River Ave 89149
Old Rose Dr 89148
Old Salt Cir 89117
Old Sea Ave 89148
Old Spanish Way 89113
Old Stable Ave 89131
Old Sterling St 89108
Old Storm Ct 89178
Old Time Cir 89128
Old Tradition St 89130
Old Trail Rd 89108
Old Valley St 89149
Old Village Ave 89129
Old West Ct 89110
Old Westbury Ct 89149
Old Woostra Ct 89145
Oldenburg St 89131
Oleg Ct 89141
Oleno Ct 89110
Oleta Ave 89148
W Oleta Ave
4900-4998 89139
5000-5799 89139
5801-6099 89139
7500-7598 89113
Olguin Ln 89110
Olimar Ave 89148
Olive St
2300-2798 89104
2800-3116 89104
3115-3115 89116
3117-4199 89104
3118-4198 89104
Olive Canyon Dr 89128
Olive Mill Ln 89134
Olive Palm Cir 89128
Olive Ridge Dr 89135
Olive Tree Cir 89129
Olivebranch Ave 89144
Olivebrook Ct 89120
Olivegrove St 89108
Oliver Ct 89145
Oliver Sagebrush Dr 89122
Oliver Twist Ln 89113
Olivewood St 89108
Olivine Ct 89130
Olmstead St 89166
Olsen Farm St 89131
Olvera Way 89128
Olympia Dr 89123
Olympia Canyon Way 89141
Olympia Falls Ave 89149
Olympia Fields Ct 89141
Olympia Hills Cir 89141
Olympia Summit Dr 89141
Olympic Mountain Ave 89131
Olympic Pine Dr 89135
Olympic Point Dr 89129
Olympic Spirit Ln 89113
Olympus Ave 89131
Omaha Cir 89169
Omak Cir 89107
Omar Ct 89117
Omega Cir 89130
Omni Ct 89149
Ondoro Ave 89141
One Nation Ave 89121
Oneida Way 89169
Onesto Ave 89148
Onion Creek Ln 89113
Onslow Ct 89135
Ontario Dr 89128
Onyx Way 89106
Onyx Crest St 89145
Opal Bay Ct 89139
Opal Bridge Ct 89178
Opal Cove Dr 89128
Opal Creek Way 89122
Opal Crest Ave 89131
Opal Hills Ln 89178
Opal Splendor Ave 89147
Opalmae Cir 89107
Open Ct 89118
Open Range Ct 89179
Opera Dr 89146
Operetta Way 89119
Ophelia Ct 89113
Ophir Dr 89106
Oppenheimer St 89139
Opulent Ave 89147
Opuntia St 89146
Opus Dr 89117
E Oquendo Rd 89120
W Oquendo Rd
3301-3397 89118
3399-6800 89118
6802-6898 89118
7001-7797 89113
7799-8000 89113
8002-8098 89113
8601-9199 89148
9700-9798 89148
Orange Ave & Cir 89108
Orange Cliff Ct 89123
Orange Dawn St 89122
Orange Grove Ln 89119
Orange Haze Way 89149
Orange Heights St 89129
Orange Hill Dr 89142
Orange Meadow St 89142
Orange Mist Way 89122
Orange Poppy Ct 89120
Orange Port Ct 89129
Orange Sun St 89135
Orange Tree Ave 89142
Orange Vale Ave 89131
Orangeblossom Ct & St 89108
Orangeroot Ct 89130
Orazio Dr 89138
Orbit Ave 89115
Orbiter Ln 89148
Orca St 89123
Orchard Ln 89110
Orchard Course Dr 89148
Orchard Glen Ave 89131
Orchard Harvest Ave 89131
Orchard Hills Ave 89130
Orchard Lodge St 89141
Orchard Mist St 89135
Orchard Oasis Ct 89147
Orchard Pine St 89139
Orchard Port Ave 89131
Orchard Ridge Ave 89129
Orchard Sky Ave 89131
Orchard Spring Ct 89118
Orchard Valley Dr 89142
Orchard View St 89142
Orchard Wood Ct 89131
Orchestra Ave 89123
Orchid Dr 89107
Orchid Bay Dr 89123
Orchid Blossom Dr 89134
Orchid Gardens Rd 89179
Orchid Hill Cir 89108
Orchid Pansy Ave 89148
Orchid Springs St 89148
Orchid Valley Dr 89134
Orchid Vine Ct 89183
Ordrich Pl 89145
Orduno St 89161
Ordway Dr 89139
Ore Cart St 89178
Oread Ave 89139
Oreana Ave 89120
Orense Dr 89138
Organ Pipe Ct 89135
Orient Express Ct 89145
Orinda Ave, Cir & Ct 89120
Oriole Way 89103
Oriole Crest Ct 89117
Orion Ave 89110
Orkiney Dr 89144
Orland St 89107
Orlov Trotter Ave 89122
Orly Ave 89143
Ormond Beach St 89129
Ormsby St 89102
Ornamento Way 89179
Ornate Ct 89129
Ornate Glade Ave 89148
Ornella St 89141
Oro Bullion St 89178
Oro Silver Ct 89178
Orourke Ave 89129
Orovada Pl 89110
Oroville Cir 89108
Ortega Hill Ln 89134
Ortega Spring Ave 89128
Ortiz Ct 89110
Ortiz St 89102
Orto Botanico Ct 89131
Orto Vaso Ave 89131
Orvieto Dr 89117
Orville Wright Ct 89119
Osage Ave 89101
Osage Cir 89169
Osage Canyon St 89113
Osaka Ct 89110
Osaka Bay Ct 89115
Osbiston Way 89110
Osborn Ct 89110
Oscar Ct 89146
Osceola Mills St 89141
Osman Ct 89103
Osmerea Ct 89149
Oso Blanca Rd
7500-7599 89149
8500-8599 89166
Osprey Cir 89107
Osprey Point Ave 89156
Osprey Ridge Ct 89122
Ostend Ave 89166
Ostrander St 89141
Ostrich Fern Ct 89183
Otero Rd 89122
Othello Dr 89121
Otis Ct 89129
Ottawa Cir & Dr 89169
Otter Corner Ct 89122
Otter Creek Ct 89117
Otterburn St 89178
Ottimo Way 89179
Otto Merida Ave 89106
Ouida Way 89108
Outer Banks Ave 89149
Outlaw Ln 89118
Outline Ave 89142
Outpost Dr 89123
Outrigger Ct 89123
Oval Cir 89117
Oval Park Dr 89135
Ovando Way 89122
Ovation Way 89119
Oveja Cir & St 89107
Over Par Ct 89148
Overbrook Dr 89108
Overhill Ave 89129
Overland Ave 89107
Overland Express St 89118
Overlook Ridge Ave 89148
Overton St 89166
Overton Beach St 89156
Overture Dr 89123
Overview Dr 89145
Ovieto Ave 89131
E Owens Ave 89110
W Owens Ave 89106
Owl Pl 89145
Owl Butte Ct 89149
Owl Clan Ct 89131
Owl Ridge Ct 89135
Owls Eyes Ct 89106
Owls Nest St 89178
Owls Peak Ct 89144
Owlshead Mountain St 89129
Owyhee Ct 89110
Oxbow St 89119
Oxbow Lake Ave 89149
Oxendale Ave 89139
Oxford Ln 89121
Oxford Wine Ct 89129
Oxnard Cir 89121
Oxwood St 89141
Oyster Dr 89128
Oyster Bay St 89117
Oyster Cove Dr 89128
Oyster Pearl St 89183
Oyster Shell Dr 89108
Ozuna Ct 89183
Ozzie Harriet Ave 89122
Pacemont Ct 89147
Paces Mill Ct 89113
Pachico Way 89120
Pacific Ave 89121
Pacific St
1300-1999 89104
3701-3797 89121
3799-3899 89121
Pacific Bay Ln 89117
Pacific Breeze Dr 89144
Pacific Brook St 89117
Pacific Castle Pl 89144
Pacific Coast St 89148
Pacific Cove Dr 89128
Pacific Craft Ln 89122
Pacific Creek St 89117
Pacific Crest Ave 89115
Pacific Cruise Ave 89138
Pacific Dogwood Ave 89139
Pacific Echo Ct 89139
Pacific Fountain Ave 89117
Pacific Grove Dr 89130
Pacific Harbors Dr 89121
Pacific Heights Ave 89128
Pacific Hills Ave 89128
Pacific Loon Ct 89122
Pacific Opal Ave 89131
Pacific Palisades Ave 89144
Pacific Panorama Pl 89144
Pacific Peak St 89178
Pacific Ridge Ave 89128
Pacific Rim Ct 89139
Pacific Sageview Ln 89144
Pacific Sandstone Pl 89144
Pacific Shores Dr 89142
Pacific Spring Ave 89117
Pacific Star Ct 89183
Pacific Summerset Ln 89144
Pacific Summit St 89142
Pacific Sun Ave 89139
Pacific Terrace Dr 89128
Pacific Tide Pl 89144
Pacific View Dr 89117
Pacifico Ln 89135
Pack Trl 89118
Pacyna St 89122
Padbury Ct 89102
Paddington Way 89147
Paddle Wheel Way 89117
Paddock Ln 89156
Padleymor St 89139
Padona Hill Ct 89178
Padova Dr 89117
Padre Bay Dr 89108
Padre Island St 89128
Padre Peak Ct 89178
Padre Serra Ln 89134
Padua Way 89107
Page St 89110
Page Mill Ct 89139
Page Ranch Ct 89131
Pagedale St 89118
Pageland Ct 89135
Pago Ct 89117
Pagoda Tree Ct 89183
Pagosa Way 89128
Pagosa Springs Dr 89139
Pahor Dr 89102
Paige Rene Ct 89117
Paine Ct 89134
Painswick Ave 89145
Paint Ct 89122
Paint Water Pl 89129
Painted Bridge St 89179
Painted Butte Ave 89178
Painted Canyon Ct 89130
Painted Clay Ave 89128
Painted Cliffs Dr 89108
Painted Cloud Pl 89144
Painted Dawn Dr 89149
Painted Desert Dr 89108
Painted Dunes Dr 89149
Painted Feather Way 89135
Painted Gorge Dr 89149
Painted Horseshoe St 89131
Painted Lakes Way 89149
Painted Lilly Dr 89135
Painted Mirage Rd 89149
Painted Moon St 89129
Painted Morning Ave 89142
N & S Painted Mountain Dr 89148
Painted Mural Ave 89179
Painted Paradise St 89131
Painted Peak Way 89108
Painted Ridge St 89131
Painted River Ln 89129
Painted Rock Ln 89149
Painted Sands Cir 89149
Painted Shadows Way 89149
Painted Sunrise Dr 89149
Painted Sunset Dr 89149
Painted Vista Ave 89123
Paintedhills Ave 89120
Paisley St 89145
Paiute Cir & Dr 89106
Paiute Meadows Dr 89134
Paiute Pine Ct 89139
Pala Mesa Ct 89123
Palace Ct 89145
Palace Estate Ave 89117
Palace Gate Ct 89117
Palace Heights Ave 89117
Palace Monaco Ave 89117
Palace View Dr 89121
Palacio Ct 89122
Palantine Hill Dr 89117
Palatial Ave 89130
Palatial Palette Ct 89149
Palatine Ct 89144
Palazzi St 89113
Palazzo Marcelli Ct 89147
Pale Buffalo Rd 89139
Pale Moon Ct 89134
Pale Pavilion Ave 89139
Pale Pueblo Ct 89183
Pale Rider St 89131
Pale Sunset Ct 89110
Pale Topaz Ln 89131
Palencia Ave 89121
Palermo Ave 89147
Palini Ct 89123
Palio Ave 89141
Palisade Ave 89110
Palisade Grove Ct 89113
Palisades Canyon Cir 89129
Palisades Quad Ave 89122
Paljay Ct 89103
Palliser Bay Dr 89141
Pallon Ave 89113
Palloni Ct 89135
Palm Ln 89101
Palm Pkwy 89104
Palm St
1000-2299 89104
4900-5098 89120
5100-5599 89120
5601-5899 89120
Palm Ter 89106
Palm Beach St 89129
Palm Canyon Ct 89117
Palm Center Dr 89103
Palm Cove Ct 89129
Palm Creek Ct 89139
Palm Greens Ct 89134
Palm Grove Dr 89120
Palm Island Ct 89147
Palm Leaf Ct 89131
Palm Lilly Way 89147
Palm Mesa Dr 89120
Palm Pinnacle Ave 89139
Palm Shore Ct 89128
Palm Springs Way 89102
Palm Trace Ave 89148
Palm Tree Ct 89131
Palm Valley Ct 89134
Palm View Dr 89130
Palm Village St 89183
Palma Del Rio 89110
Palma Del Sol Way 89130
Palma Vista Ave
1500-2399 89169
2400-2999 89121
Palma Vista Cir 89169
Palmada Dr 89123
Palmadora St 89178
Palmae Way 89128
Palmales Ct 89128
Palmares Ct 89134
Palmas Altas St 89178
Palmdale Ct & St 89121
Palmdesert Way 89120
Palmer St 89101
Palmer House Ave 89149
Palmera Cir & Dr 89121
Palmerston St 89110
Palmetto Park Ct 89123
Palmetto Pines Ct 89131
Palmhurst Dr 89145
Palmridge Dr 89134
Palms Airport Dr 89119
Palmwood Ln 89123
Palmyra Ave
4900-4998 89146
5000-6800 89146
6802-6898 89146
6900-7700 89117
7702-7798 89117
Palmyra Cir 89146
Palo Alto Cir 89108
Palo Duro Canyon St 89179
Palo Real Ct 89179
Palo Verde Cir & Rd 89119
Palomar Ave 89110
Palomino Ln
2000-2098 89106
2300-3100 89107
3102-3398 89107
Palomino Park Ct 89178
Palomino Ranch St 89131
Palora Ave
1500-2399 89169
2400-3199 89121
Palos Verdes St 89119
Pama Ln
1301-1397 89119
1399-2099 89119
2101-2299 89119
3400-3799 89120
E Pamalyn Ave 89119
W Pamalyn Ave 89118
Pamela Way 89115
Pampas Pl 89146
Pamplona Cir & St 89103
Pan Falls St 89178
Pan Pacific Rd 89123
Panaca Spring St 89122
Panache St 89135
Panama Beach Dr 89128
Pancho Villa Dr 89121
Pancho Villa Ln 89110
Panda Bear St 89131
Pandora Dr 89123
Pandur St 89131
Pangea Ave 89139
Panguitch Dr 89122
Panguitch Lake Ct 89178
Panocha St 89121
Panorama Dr 89107
Panorama Cliff Dr 89134
Panorama Crest Ave 89135
Panorama Heights St 89110
Panoramic Ct 89129
Panpipe Ct 89131
Pantara Pl 89138
Pantheon Pl 89144
Panther Hollow St 89141
Panuco Way 89147
Paola Ct 89130
Papago Ln 89169
Papaya Ct 89119
Paper Flower Ct 89128
Papilio St 89108
Pappas Ln 89144
Papyrus Cir 89107
Par St 89119
Par Four Ln 89142
Parade St 89102
Parading Pokey St 89131
Paradise Rd
1901-1997 89104
1999-2299 89104
2600-3199 89109
3201-3299 89109
3300-3898 89169
3900-4799 89169
4900-7298 89119
8000-9498 89123
9500-9699 89123
Paradise Bay Dr 89119
Paradise Peak Dr 89134
Paradise Point Dr 89134
Paradise Ridge Ct 89139
Paradise Skies Ave 89156
Paradise Valley Ave 89156

Paradise Village Way ... 89120
Paradiso Ct 89149
Paragon Dr 89117
Paragon Pointe St 89129
Paraiso St 89117
Parakeet Ave 89145
Paramount St 89115
Parapet Ave 89149
Parasol Ln 89147
Parchment Ct 89117
Pardee Pl 89104
Parete Ct 89141
Paria Canyon St 89147
Parisian Springs Ct 89148
Pariva St 89115
Park Cir 89102
Park Ct 89110
Park St
3600-3698 89121
4100-4199 89110
9000-9086 89178
N Park St
4400-4798 89129
5001-5597 89149
5599-5999 89149
6001-6399 89149
S Park St
3301-3399 89117
3601-3699 89147
Park Way E 89106
Park Way N 89106
Park Way W 89106
Park Bench Ct 89143
Park Bridge Ave 89123
Park Brook Ave 89134
Park Centre Dr 89135
Park City Ave 89122
Park Forest Ct 89134
Park Grove Ct 89120
Park Meadow Ct 89141
Park Mesa Ln 89128
Park Oliver Dr 89110
Park Paseo 89104
Park Plaza Ct 89123
Park Point Ct 89110
Park Run Dr
10000-10199 89145
10500-10699 89144
Park Shadows Ln 89134
Park Sheridan Ln 89134
Park View Dr 89104
Park Villa St 89123
Park Village Pl 89113
Park Vista Dr 89138
Park Walk Ave 89123
Parkchester Cir & Dr ... 89108
Parkdale Ave & Cir 89121
Parker Ln 89115
Parker Cloud Dr 89123
Parker Springs Ct 89166
Parkersburg Ave 89138
Parkhaven Dr 89120
Parkhurst St 89110
Parkmoor Ave 89149
Parkside Village Pl 89134
Parkstone Ave 89178
Parkview Mountain
Ave 89166
Parkwood Cir 89121
Parlay Way 89122
Parleys Cone Ct 89135
Parliament Pl 89110
Parma Ave 89123
Parma Galleria Ave 89141
Parma Ridge Ct 89118
Parnassia Ct 89178
Parnell Ave 89147
Parodia Ct 89149
Parrish Ln 89110
Parrot Cove Ct 89139
Parrot Pointe Ct 89130
Parrot Ridge Ct 89139
Parsifal Pl 89107
Parslow St 89179
Parsons Ridge Ave 89148
Partenio Ct 89183

Parting Clouds Ct 89117
Partridge Ave 89145
Partridge Bluff St 89130
Partridge Hill St 89148
Parvin St
9500-9599 89123
10101-10199 89183
11800-11898 89183
Pasadena Blvd 89156
Pasadera St 89131
Pascal Dr 89156
Paseo Ct 89117
Paseo Cerro Pl 89138
Paseo Del Mar 89108
Paseo Del Prado 89102
Paseo Del Pueblo St 89130
Paseo Del Ray Dr 89121
Paseo Del Vista Ave 89130
Paseo El Rio Dr 89121
Paseo Granada St 89117
Paseo Montana 89108
Paseo Overlook Ct 89128
Paseo Ranchero Ct 89147
Paseo Recallo Ct 89108
Paseo Rocoso Pl 89138
Paseo Vista Dr 89128
Pasilla Ave 89118
Paso Andres St 89146
Paso De Oro Ave 89102
Paso Fino St 89143
Paso Robles Ave 89113
Passing Breeze Ct 89118
Passion Flower Cir 89108
Passion Vine Ct 89135
Passive Elm St 89131
Pastel Pl 89101
Pastel Camellia St 89148
Pastel Colors St 89148
Pastel Sky Ave 89129
Pastel Wing Ct 89148
Pasternak Dr 89115
Pastoral Pl 89145
Pasture Ln 89110
Pat Pl 89118
Patagonia Ridge Ave 89183
Patayan Rd 89146
Patchwood Ct 89130
Paterno Ave 89123
Patina St 89129
Patina Threads Ct 89149
Patinagem Ave 89143
Patmore Ash Ct 89148
Patores St 89141
Patricia Ave 89130
Patricia Gail Ave 89166
E Patrick Ln 89120
W Patrick Ln
3201-4097 89118
4099-6800 89118
6802-6898 89118
6900-7898 89113
7900-7999 89113
Patrick Henry Ave 89149
Patrington Ct 89183
Patriot St 89110
Patriots Point Ct 89108
Patrolina Ave 89141
Pattee Cir 89119
Patterson Ave 89104
Paul Ave 89106
Paul De Weert Ct 89129
Paul Kurtz Way 89108
Paul Robarts Ct 89102
Paul Weitz St 89145
Paula Jean Ave 89149
Pauline Way 89104
Paulson Dr 89123
Pavarotti Ave 89178
Pavero Way 89142
Pavestone Ln 89142
Pavia Dr 89117
N Pavilion Center Dr ... 89144
S Pavilion Center Dr
300-999 89144
1501-2699 89135
Pavilion Lakes Ave 89122

Pavlo St 89121
Pavot Ct 89142
Pawlow Ave 89118
Pawnee Cir & Dr 89169
Pawtucket Ln 89141
Paxon Hollow Ct 89148
Paxton Way 89122
Pay Less Ct 89115
Paya Ct 89120
Payson Ave & Ct 89115
Peace Way 89147
Peace Pipe Ct 89117
Peace River Ct 89148
Peace Rose St 89131
Peace Treaty Ave 89148
Peaceful St 89110
Peaceful Brook St 89131
Peaceful Canyon Dr 89128
Peaceful Dreams St 89139
Peaceful Grove St 89135
Peaceful Harbor St 89129
Peaceful Heights Ln 89129
Peaceful Morning Ln 89129
Peaceful Mountain
Ave 89178
Peaceful Pond Ave 89131
Peaceful Prairie Ct 89135
Peaceful Trellis Dr 89179
Peaceful Village Pl 89143
Peaceful Woods St 89143
Peacemaker Rd 89183
Peach Blossom Ln 89142
Peach Coral St 89183
Peach Creek St 89179
Peach Flare St 89143
Peach Flower Ct 89147
Peach Hill Ave 89106
Peach Nectar Ave 89142
Peach Orchard Rd 89142
Peach Ridge Ct 89129
Peachblossom Ln 89108
Peachgate Ave 89120
Peachtree Ln 89103
Peachtree Creek Ct 89131
Peachtree Hill Ave 89183
Peachwood Rd 89108
Peachy Ct 89183
Peachy Canyon Cir 89144
Peacock Ave & Ct 89145
Peacock Hill Cir 89117
Peak Dr
6300-6398 89108
7200-7299 89128
7301-7499 89128
Peak Lookout St 89178
Peanut Ct 89115
Pear Ct 89110
Pearberry Ave 89183
Pearblossom Ln 89108
Pearblossom Sky Ave 89166
Pearcrest Rd 89108
Peardale Dr 89147
Pearl Ave 89104
N Pearl St 89110
S Pearl St
3900-4899 89121
4900-5198 89120
5200-6199 89120
6201-6299 89120
Pearl Bay Ct 89139
Pearl Beach Ct 89139
Pearl Cotton Ave 89149
Pearl Creek Ct 89131
Pearl Crescent Dr 89113
Pearl Crest St 89134
Pearl Diver Ct 89139
Pearl Harbor Dr 89117
Pearl Hatpin Ct 89106
Pearl Isle Ct 89123
Pearl Oasis Ct 89139
Pearl Peak St 89110
Pearl River Ave 89166
Pearlbush Ct 89123
Pearldrop Ave 89107
Pearlite Ave & Cir 89120
Pearlman Ln 89147

Pearson Ct 89106
Peartree Rd 89108
Pearwood Ct 89123
Peastriv Dr 89145
Peavine Ridge St 89139
E Pebble Rd
1-500 89123
455-455 89105
502-2198 89123
1201-2199 89123
W Pebble Rd
2500-2899 89123
3001-3197 89139
3199-4499 89139
4501-6699 89139
7000-7299 89113
7301-8199 89113
9800-9864 89178
9866-9899 89178
9901-9925 89178
Pebble Beach Blvd 89108
Pebble Brook St 89110
Pebble Canyon Dr 89123
Pebble Creek Ave 89147
Pebble Dunes Ct 89141
Pebble Grey Ln 89130
Pebble Hills Ct 89141
Pebble Path Ct 89148
Pebble River Ct 89123
Pebble Rock Dr 89149
Pebble Shore Ct 89117
Pebble Springs Ave 89117
Pebblecreek Lodge
Way 89148
Pebbleshire Ave 89117
Pebblestone Cir 89117
Pecan Ln 89115
Pecan Grove Ct 89142
Pecan Orchard Ln 89123
Pecan Pie Ct 89115
Pecan Tree Ct 89142
Pecan Valley Ave 89131
Pechavez St 89131
N Pecos Rd
1-1100 89101
1102-1298 89101
1600-4399 89115
S Pecos Rd
3000-3198 89121
3200-4799 89121
4801-4899 89121
5001-5097 89120
5099-7099 89120
7101-7399 89120
Pecos St 89101
Pecos Way 89121
Pecos Mcleod 89121
Pedal Point Pl 89144
Pedro Pl 89108
Pegasus Dr 89135
Peggotty Ave 89130
Peggy Dr 89145
Pelham Ct 89110
Pelham Park Ave 89148
Pelican Cir 89107
Pelican Beach Dr 89117
Pelican Lake Ln 89123
Pemba Ave 89131
Pember St 89143
Pemberry Cir 89123
Pembridge Ct 89121
Pembroke Bay St 89179
Pembrook Falls Ave 89148
Pena Blanca Ct 89183
Pencarrow Ct 89130
Pencester St 89115
Pencil Cedar Ave 89149
Pendini Point Ct 89141
Pendleton Cir 89142
Pendragon Cir 89145
Penedos Dr 89147
Peneplain Ave 89139
Penera Dr 89123
Penfolds St 89183
Pengilly Ct 89147
Penhurst Way 89135

Peninsula Point Ave 89123
Penmar Cir 89115
Penn Station St 89123
Pennant Ave 89166
Penns Creek Ct 89135
Pennsburg Ct 89122
Pennwood Ave 89102
Penny Ln 89178
Pennybrook Ct 89131
Pennypack Ct 89183
Pennyroyal St 89183
Pennystone Ave 89134
Penrith Ave 89144
Penrose Ln 89107
Penrose Falls St 89179
Penryn Ct 89139
Pensacola Ln 89106
Penshaw Bridge Ave 89178
Pensier St 89135
Pensive Ponder St 89178
Pentagon Ave 89115
Pentland Downs St 89141
Penzance Ct 89178
Peony Bush Dr 89156
Pepe Cir 89121
Pepper Ln 89120
Pepperbox Ave 89179
Pepperbrook Ct 89120
Pepperdine Way 89115
Pepperidge Way 89108
Peppermill Dr 89146
Pepperpike Ave 89130
Pepperwood Ln 89107
Pepperwood Grove Ct 89183
Pequeno Ave 89120
Pera Cir 89121
Perceval St 89183
Percheron St 89119
Percussion Ct 89139
Percy Arms St 89138
Perdido Ave 89121
Perennial Ave 89148
Perennial Border Ct 89148
Perennial View Ave 89148
Perez Pl 89123
Perfect Day Ave 89129
Perfect Diamond Ct 89129
Perfect Drift St 89129
Perfect Lure St 89129
Perfect Parsley St 89183
Perfect Peace Ln 89135
Perfect Sunset Ct 89148
Perfect View St 89130
Pergola Peak Ave 89144
Pergola Point Ct 89144
Pericos St 89115
Peridot St 89121
Peridot Point St 89106
Periscope Ct 89117
Periwinkle Dr 89128
Perkins Cir 89106
Perkins Hill St 89166
Perla Bello Ct 89135
Perla Del Mar Ave 89179
Perrone Ave 89141
Perry St 89122
Perryville Ave 89106
Pershing Dr 89107
Persian Violet Ave 89183
Persico Cir 89121
Persimmon Ct 89145
Perthold Ave 89102
Perugia Ct 89141
Perugino Dr 89138
Pesaro Dr 89117
Pescados Dr 89123
Pescara Ct 89123
Peseo Cresta Ave 89117
Peshtigo St 89178
Peso St 89121
Petaca Rd 89122
Petal Ave 89122
Petal Dew Ave 89183
Petaluma Cir 89120
Peter Buol Dr 89106
Petersham Ct 89108

Peterson Dr 89103
Peterson Ln 89115
Petit Chalet Ct 89145
Petite Pillar Ct 89149
Petra Ave 89103
Petricola St 89183
Petron Ct 89139
Petticoat St 89129
Petunia Flower Way 89147
Petya St 89115
Peyton Dr 89104
Phantom Jet Ave 89110
Phantom Rock St 89135
Pheasant Ln 89145
Pheasant Brook St 89183
Pheasant Moon St 89148
Pheasant Trace Ct 89130
Pheasant Valley Way 89123
E Philadelphia Ave 89104
W Philadelphia Ave 89102
Philharmonic Ave 89139
Philippe Allen Ave 89110
Phillip Great Ct 89139
Phillips Ave 89104
Philmar Ave 89120
Philmont Ct 89183
Philomena St 89129
Phlox Rd 89113
Phoenician Ave 89147
Phoenix St 89121
Phoenix Peak St 89166
N Phyllis St 89110
S Phyllis St 89142
Pia Rosetta St 89129
Piazza Cavour Dr 89156
Piazza Del Verano St ... 89138
Piazzale St 89141
Picardie Ln 89123
Picaro Ct 89128
Picaroon Ln 89145
Picasso Cir 89121
Piccadily Dr 89156
Piccata St 89141
Piccolo Way 89146
Picket Fence Ave 89143
Picket Ridge Ct 89143
Pickford Ln 89107
Picnic St 89131
Picnic Hill St 89166
Pico Way 89101
Pico Grande Ct 89147
Pico Rio Ct 89156
Pico Rivera Ave 89178
Picotte St 89144
Picton Ave 89178
Picturesque Ave 89149
Pied Piper St 89113
Piedmont Ave 89102
Piedmont Valley Ave 89144
Pier Harbor Dr 89117
Pier Pointe Ct 89123
Pierce Way 89110
Pierida St 89108
Pierre Milano St 89141
Pieta Ct 89135
Pigeon Point Ct 89147
Pike Ct 89110
Pikedale Dr 89134
Pikes Peak Ct 89110
Pilgrim St 89121
Pillar Pointe St 89115
Pillar Rock Ave 89139
Pillow Talk Ct 89110
Pilot Rd 89119
Pilot Mountain Ct 89129
Pima Ln 89169
Pima Canyon Ct 89144
Pima Crossing Ave 89166
Pima Point Ave 89147
Pimera Alta St 89178
Pin Oak Ave 89101
Pinarello St 89178
Pinchot St 89156
Pindarri Way 89145
Pine Rd 89124

Pine St
1500-1598 89102
1600-1699 89102
6301-6397 89120
6399-7200 89120
7202-7298 89120
Pine Banks Ct 89141
Pine Barrens St 89148
Pine Bay Ct 89148
Pine Bluff Ct 89134
Pine Breeze Ln 89119
Pine Creek Rd 89115
Pine Desert Ave 89108
Pine Falls Dr 89149
Pine Forest Ct 89134
Pine Gardens Ct 89144
Pine Glen Ave 89144
Pine Greens Ct 89144
Pine Harbor St 89166
Pine Haven St 89144
Pine Hill Ave 89156
Pine Island Ct 89134
Pine Knolls Ct 89144
Pine Leaf Dr 89144
Pine Meadows Ct 89134
Pine Mission Ave 89143
Pine Mountain Ave 89139
Pine Needle Ct 89108
Pine Pitch Dr 89143
Pine Pointe Ave 89144
Pine Ranch St 89113
Pine Ridge Dr 89110
Pine Ridge Peak Ave 89166
Pine River Ln 89123
Pine Run Rd 89135
Pine Shadows St 89183
Pine Thickett Ave 89147
Pine Valley Dr 89103
Pine Villa Ave 89108
Pineaire St 89147
Pineapple Tree Ct 89142
Pinebrook Cir & Ct 89147
Pinecliff Dr 89145
Pinecone Pl 89108
E & W Pinecrest Cir &
St 89121
Pinecroft Dr 89135
Pinedale Ave 89145
Pinegrove St 89147
Pineham Ct 89115
Pinehurst Dr 89109
Pinelake Rd 89145
Pinellia Ct 89149
Pineneedle Ridge St 89178
Pinerock St 89156
Pines Glory Dr 89115
Pinetop Ln 89119
Pinetree St 89122
Pineview Pl 89142
Pinewood Ave 89103
Pinewood Hills Dr 89134
Pinewood Ridge St 89178
Piney Summit Ave 89141
Pinion Dr 89161
Pinion Hills Ct 89144
Pinion Jay St 89147
Pinion Juniper Ct 89149
Pinion Mesa Ct 89128
Pinion Valley Dr 89134
Pink Cliff Ct 89128
Pink Cloud Ct 89129
Pink Dogwood Dr 89141
Pink Ginger St 89123
Pink Ice Ct 89106
Pink Panther Ave 89110
Pink Pear Ct 89149
Pink Stargazer Ave 89166
Pinkerton Dr 89134
Pinks Pl 89102
Pinnacle Cove St 89123
Pinnacle Heights Ln 89144
Pinnacle Pass Dr 89117
Pinnacle Peak Ave 89113
Pinnacle View Pl 89134
Pinnate Dr 89147
Pinner Ct 89102

Pinnochio Ave 89131
Pino Cir 89121
Pino Basin Ct 89129
Pinon Dr 89130
Pinon Rd 89124
Pinon Crest Ct 89131
Pinon Peak Dr 89115
Pinon Pine Way 89108
Pinon Pointe Rd 89115
Pinosa Ct 89141
Pinsonso Dr 89120
Pintadas St 89108
Pintail Point St 89144
Pinto Ln
1500-2200 89106
2202-2298 89106
2300-3099 89107
Pinto Bluff St 89131
Pinto Creek Ln 89144
Pinto Mountain Ct 89129
Pinto Rock Ln 89128
Pioche St 89101
Piombino St 89141
Pioneer Ave
3300-4812 89102
4814-4898 89102
5001-5697 89146
5699-5899 89146
9401-9697 89117
9699-9999 89117
Pioneer Cir 89107
Pioneer St 89107
N Pioneer Way
3300-3400 89129
3402-4598 89129
4801-4897 89149
4899-5199 89149
6600-8199 89131
S Pioneer Way
2101-2197 89117
2199-3199 89117
5700-8500 89113
8502-9198 89113
Pioneer Hills St 89113
Pioneer Park Ave 89135
Pioneer Peak Pl 89138
Pioneer Ranch Ave 89113
Pipe Spring Dr 89156
Piper Down Ave 89148
Piper Glen Pl 89134
Piper Peak Ln 89138
Pipers Cove Ln 89135
Pipers Ridge Ave 89113
Pipestone St 89141
Pipestone Pass St 89148
Pipil St 89166
Pirates Cove Rd 89145
Pirates Delight Ave 89139
Pirates Island St 89147
Pisa Ave 89130
Pisan Ln 89148
Pisces Ct 89115
Pismo Beach Dr 89128
Pismo Dunes Ct 89135
Pista Way 89179
Pistachio Nut Ave 89115
Pistolera Cir 89120
Pitch Fork Ave 89143
Pitching Wedge Dr 89134
Pitkin Cir 89108
Pitney Ave 89143
Pittsfield St 89115
Pittston Ave 89123
Placentia Pkwy 89118
Placer Dr 89103
Placer Bullion Ave 89178
Placer Creek Ct 89156
Placerville St 89119
Placid St
6700-6798 89119
6800-7299 89119
7500-8899 89123
9800-11499 89183
Placid Lake Ave 89179
Placid Ravine St 89117
Placita Ave & Ct 89121
Placita Del Lazo 89120
Placita Del Rico 89120
Plaid Cactus Ct 89106
Plain View St 89107
Plainfield Dr 89142
Plainview Ave 89122
Plama Ct 89131
Plane Tree Ct 89178
Planet Ct 89130
Planetary Ln 89115
Plano Dr 89130
Plantain Lily Ave 89183
Plantanus Rd 89113
Plantation Ct 89117
Plantea Ct 89117
Planting Fields Pl 89117
Plata Del Sol Dr 89121
Plata Pico Dr 89128
Plateau Creek Ct 89149
Plateau Heights Pl 89144
Platinum Band St 89156
Platinum Creek St 89131
Platinum Peak Ave 89129
Platis Cir 89103
Platt Dr 89129
Platville St 89139
Playa Bonita Ave 89138
Playa Caribe Ave 89138
Playa Del Rey St 89169
Playa Linda Pl 89138
Player Ct 89130
Players Canyon Ct 89144
Players Club Dr 89134
Plaza St 89121
Plaza Centre Dr 89135
Plaza De Cielo 89102
Plaza De Cordero 89102
Plaza De Ernesto 89102
Plaza De La Candela 89102
Plaza De La Cruz 89102
Plaza De Monte 89102
Plaza De Rafael 89102
Plaza De Rosa 89102
Plaza De Sante Fe 89102
Plaza De Vista St 89120
Plaza Del Cerro 89102
Plaza Del Dios 89102
Plaza Del Fuentes 89102
Plaza Del Grande 89102
Plaza Del Maya 89120
Plaza Del Padre 89102
Plaza Del Paz 89102
Plaza Del Prado 89102
Plaza Del Puerto 89102
Plaza Del Robles 89102
Plaza Pecos Dr 89121
Plaza Verde Pl 89108
Pleasant Rd 89108
Pleasant Brook St 89142
Pleasant Colony Ct 89131
Pleasant Grove Ct 89108
Pleasant Hill Ave 89103
Pleasant Lake Dr 89117
Pleasant Plains Way 89108
Pleasant Slopes Ct 89131
Pleasant Valley Pl 89149
Pleasant View Ave 89147
Pleasant Village Pl 89183
Pleasanton Cir 89120
Pleasantville Ct 89149
Pleasing Ct 89149
Plomosa Pl 89134
Plover Falls Ave 89149
Plum Blossom Ct 89129
Plum Canyon St 89142
Plum Creek Ct 89113
Plum Island Ct 89147
Plum Orchard Cir 89142
Plumas Ct 89108
Plumcrest Rd 89108
Plumflower Ln 89108
Plummer Ct 89129
Plumtree St 89115
Plunging Falls Dr 89131
Plushstone St 89148
Pluto Dr 89108
Plymouth Bay Ct 89141
Pocatello Peak Way 89156
Poco Way 89102
Pocono Way 89108
Pocono Manor Ct 89148
Pocono Palace St 89178
Poe Dr 89115
Poetic Justice Ct 89148
Pohickery Ct 89115
Poinsettia Way 89147
Point Cabrillo Ct 89113
Point Desire Ave 89115
Point Given St 89131
Point Hope Ave 89179
Point Isabel Way 89122
Point Kathy Cir 89147
Point Kirby Ave 89123
Point Kristi Cir 89147
Point Lace Ct 89149
Point Lobos Dr 89108
Point Loma Ct 89122
Point Oaks Ct 89149
Point Powell Ct 89166
Point Ridge Pl 89145
Point Rock Ln 89134
Point Royal Ct 89141
Point Sal Cir 89128
Point Sublime St 89147
Point View Ct 89128
Pointe Vedra Ct 89122
Pointe Willow Ln 89120
Poker Alice Ct 89129
Poker Face Ct 89118
Poker Flat Ln 89118
Poker Hand Ct 89129
Pokeweed Ct 89149
Polar Ct 89121
Polar Express Ct 89131
Polar Lights Ct 89130
Polar Shrimp Ct 89113
Polaris Ave
3100-3499 89102
3500-4700 89103
4702-4798 89103
5200-7299 89118
8600-8898 89139
8900-9300 89139
9302-9498 89139
10401-10499 89141
Polished Jade Ct 89131
Polita Ct 89156
Polizze Ave 89141
Polk Ct 89115
Pollock Dr
7000-7098 89119
7100-7200 89119
7202-7298 89119
7400-7499 89123
9800-9898 89183
Pollux Ave 89102
Polly Cir 89121
Polo Cir 89117
Polo Bay Cir 89117
Polo Grounds St 89148
Polonaise Ave 89123
Polonius Ct 89141
Pomegranate Cir 89107
Pomelo Pl 89156
Pomerado Dr 89128
Pomerol Ave 89123
Pomeroy Cir 89142
Pommel Ave 89119
Pommerelle St 89122
Pomona Ct 89147
Pomona Dr 89156
Pomona Valley Ct 89178
Pompano Cir 89130
Pompano Beach Ln 89128
Pompei Pl 89144
Ponce De Leon Ave 89123
Poncho Cir 89119
Pond Creek St 89139
Pond Run Cir 89117
Ponderosa Ave 89115
Ponderosa Way
3100-6899 89118
7100-7299 89113
Ponderosa Ranch St 89113
Ponderosa Verde Pl 89131
Pont Chartrain Dr 89145
Pontius Cir 89107
Pony Cir 89145
Ponza Ct 89141
Pooh Corner St 89110
Popcorn Flower St 89117
Poplar Ave 89101
Poplar Leaf St 89144
Poplar Park Ave 89166
Poplar Tree St 89148
Popolo Dr 89138
Poppy Ln 89101
Poppy Fields Dr 89129
Poppy Hill St 89106
Poppy Hills Ct 89113
Poppy Meadow St 89123
Poppy Plant St 89141
Poppy Springs Ave 89113
Poppyseed Way 89142
Poppywood Dr 89147
Porch Rocker St 89143
Porch Swings Way 89129
Porchtown Ave 89183
Porcupine Flat St 89108
Porcupine Rim St 89130
Port Ave 89106
Port Astoria Ct 89122
Port Barrington Way 89130
Port Charles Ct 89149
Port Charlotte Ave 89131
Port Douglas Ct 89113
Port Hope Pl 89144
Port Huron Ln 89134
Port Labelle Dr 89141
Port Of Call Dr 89128
Port Of Dreams Dr 89130
Port Orange Ln 89134
Port Orchard Ave 89113
Port Reggio St 89138
Port Ritchey St 89147
Port Side Dr 89117
Port Tack Dr 89110
Port Talbot Ave 89178
Porta Romana Ct 89141
Portabello Rd 89119
Portadown Ln 89121
Portage Ave 89120
Portage Lake Ct 89130
Portavilla Ct 89122
Portchester Ct 89135
Porter Mountain Ct 89129
Porterfield Ln 89183
Portia Ct 89113
Portina Dr 89138
Portland Point Ave 89148
Portland Treaty Ave 89122
Porto Foxi St 89141
Porto Mio Way 89138
Portofino Ct 89117
Portola Rd 89108
Portola Vista Ave 89139
Portraits Pl 89149
Portsmouth Way 89107
Portula Valley St 89178
Poseidon St 89131
Poseidon Quest Ct 89139
Poseidon Valley Ave 89178
Positano St 89141
Positano Hill Ave 89178
Positano Peak Ct 89148
Posse Ave 89110
E Post Rd 89120
W Post Rd
2501-2599 89119
2900-2998 89119
3000-3098 89118
3100-6699 89118
7000-7098 89113
7100-7699 89113
7701-7799 89113
8901-8997 89148
8999-9672 89148
9674-9698 89148
Poston Ln 89144
Pot Of Gold Ave 89149
Potenza Ln 89117
Potosi St 89146
Potters Clay St 89143
Pottery Creek Dr 89128
Pounding Surf Ave 89131
Powder River Ct 89131
Powderham Ave 89117
Powderhorn Cir 89128
Powdermill St 89148
Powell Ave 89121
Powell Plateau Ct 89148
Powell Ridge Ct 89139
Powerbilt Ave 89148
Powers St 89148
Prada Pl 89141
Prada Verde Dr 89138
Pradera Cir 89121
Prado Del Rey Ln 89141
Prague Ct 89147
Prairie Way 89145
Prairie Aster Pl 89148
Prairie Bluff St 89113
Prairie Brush Ct 89141
Prairie Clover St 89148
Prairie Corners Dr 89128
Prairie Dove Ave 89117
Prairie Dunes Dr 89142
Prairie Dusk Dr 89122
Prairie Falcon Rd 89128
Prairie Flower St 89131
Prairie Gold Ct 89129
Prairie Grass Dr 89123
Prairie Grove Rd 89179
Prairie Hill Dr 89134
Prairie Knoll Ct 89113
Prairie Meadow St 89129
Prairie Mountain Ave 89166
Prairie River St 89113
Prairie Run Ave 89149
Prairie Schooner Ave 89129
Prairie Springs Ct 89130
Prairie View Dr 89110
Praline Cir 89142
Prancing Pony Ct 89131
Pratt Way 89147
Prattville Ave 89148
Preakness Pass 89117
Precliffs Ct 89129
Prefontaine Rd 89115
Premia Pl 89135
Premier Ct 89117
Preppy Fox Ave 89131
Prescott St 89110
Prescott Creek Ct 89117
Prescott Downs St 89148
Prescott Pines St 89108
President Cir 89121
Prespa Lake Ct 89141
Prestancia Ave 89144
Presto Ct 89139
Preston Cir 89107
Prestonwood St 89156
Prestwick St 89145
Pretty Fire St 89178
Price Point Ave 89147
Price Ridge Ct 89147
Pride Ln 89103
Pride Dance Ct 89178
Pride Hill St 89183
Prikapa Ct 89118
Primavera St 89122
Prime Ct 89130
Prime View Ct 89144
Primo St 89183
Primrose Path 89108
Primrose Arbor Ave 89144
Primrose Flower Ave 89131
Primrose Hill Ave 89178
Primrose Peak Ct 89130
Primrose Pointe Ct 89135
Primula Ct 89149
Prince Ln 89110
Prince Alan Ct 89110
Prince Cary Ct 89110
Prince Charming Ct 89145
Prince George Rd 89123
Prince Of Tides Ct 89113
Prince Scotty St 89119
Princess Cut St 89183
Princess Jean St 89119
Princess Katy Ave 89119
Princeton St 89107
Princeville Ln 89113
Principi Ct 89183
Priory Gardens St 89130
Priscilla St 89156
Prism Pl 89118
Pristine Falls Ave 89131
Pristine Glen St 89135
Pristine Meadow Ct 89131
Prize Dr 89117
Pro Players Dr 89134
Probst 89110
Processor Ct 89129
Proclamation Pl 89110
Procyon St
3100-3298 89102
3300-3499 89102
3500-4800 89103
4802-4898 89103
5101-5197 89118
5199-7000 89118
7002-7298 89118
7800-9067 89139
9069-9099 89139
10700-10798 89141
Production Ct 89115
Professional Ct 89128
Profeta Ct 89135
Profondo Ct 89135
Progress Cir 89108
Progressive Ct 89149
Progresso St 89135
Promenade Blvd 89107
Promenade Pl 89106
Promenade Park Ct 89135
Prominence Ln 89117
Promised Land Ave 89148
Promising Ct 89149
Promontory Pointe Ln 89135
Promontory Ridge Dr 89135
Promontory Vista Pl 89142
Pronghorn Ct 89149
Pronghorn Ridge Ave 89122
Prospect St 89108
Prospect Claim Ct 89108
Prospect Hill Ct 89129
Prospector Trl 89118
Prospectors Cove Dr 89117
Prospectors Creek Way 89122
Prosperity Ln 89147
Prosperity Point St 89147
Prosperity River Ave 89129
Proud Ct 89149
Proud Clarion St 89178
Proud Eagle Ln 89144
Proud Meadows St 89131
Proud Patriot St 89148
Proud Statue Ave 89148
Proud Waters Ct 89178
Pround Clarion St 89139
Provence Garden Ln 89145
Providence Ln 89107
Provo St 89121
Prudhoe Bay St 89179
Prussian Green St 89139
Puckershire St 89166
Puddle Duck St 89166
Puebla St 89115
Pueblo Cir & Way 89169
Pueblo Amigo Ct 89115
Pueblo Canyon Ave 89131
Pueblo Springs St 89183
Pueblo Vista Dr 89128
Puenta St 89121
Puenta Del Rey St 89138
Puerta Del Sol Dr 89138
Puerto Banus Ave 89138
Puerto Real Ct 89138
Pugatz St 89124
Pulaski Pl 89110
Pulliam Dr 89115
Pulpit Rock Ct 89166
Pulsar Ct 89130
Pumpkin Creek St 89122
Pumpkin Patch Ave 89142
Pumpkin Ridge Ave 89135
Pumpkin Seed Ct 89123
Punch Bowl Falls Ct 89131
Purcell Dr 89107
Purdue Way 89115
Purdy Lodge St 89138
Pure April Ave 89183
Pure Rain Ct 89148
Pure Sapphire Ct 89149
Pureza Ave 89115
Puritan Ave 89123
Purple Ct 89123
Purple Bloom Ct 89122
Purple Finch Dr 89107
Purple Flower Ln 89117
Purple Haze St 89148
Purple Iris Ave 89117
Purple Leaf St 89123
Purple Majesty Ct 89117
Purple Mountain Ave 89131
Purple Orchid Ct 89131
Purple Plum Ct 89147
Purple Primrose Dr 89141
Purple Ridge Ct 89129
Purple Root Dr 89156
Purple Sage Ave 89108
Purple Shadow Ave 89113
Purple Sky Dr 89149
Purple Wisteria St 89131
Pursuit Ct 89131
Purtell Cir 89117
Putnam Ct N & S 89115
E Pyle Ave 89183
W Pyle Ave
2400-2498 89183
3001-3097 89141
3099-5899 89141
Pyracantha Glen Ct 89131
Pyramid Cir 89108
Pyramid Dr
700-798 89107
800-899 89107
900-1499 89108
3600-3799 89107
Pyramid Peak St 89166
Pyrenees Ln 89161
Pyrite Ln 89128
Pyrite Nugget Ave 89122
Pyrope Ct 89148
Quadrel St 89129
Quadro Ct 89134
E Quail Ave 89120
W Quail Ave
3500-6500 89118
6502-6798 89118
7900-7998 89113
10101-10199 89148
Quail Arroyo Ave 89131
Quail Breast Ln 89131
Quail Brook Ave 89117
Quail Cap St 89131
Quail Country Way 89117
Quail Gorge Ave 89131
Quail Harbor St 89131
Quail Head Ave 89131
Quail Heaven St 89131
Quail Heights Ave 89131
Quail Hill St 89106
Quail Hollow Dr 89108
Quail Lakes Ct 89117
Quail Meadow Ct 89131
Quail Mountain Ln 89131
Quail Nest Ave 89131
Quail Point Ct 89117
Quail Prairie St 89131
Quail Ridge Dr 89134
Quail Rise St 89130
Quail Roost Way 89117
Quail Springs Ct 89117

Quail Summit Ln 89131
Quail Turn St 89131
Quail Valley St 89148
Quaint Acres Ave 89183
Quaint Tree St 89183
Quaker Ridge Rd 89142
Quality Ct 89103
Qualla Crest Ct 89129
Quantana Ct 89102
Quantum Ln 89130
Quapaw St 89149
Quarentina Ave 89149
Quarry Dr 89147
Quarry Ridge St 89117
Quarrystone Way 89123
Quarterhorse Ln
6701-7097 89148
7099-7299 89148
7301-8899 89148
9600-10200 89178
10202-10298 89178
Quartz Cliff St 89117
Quartz Landing Ave 89183
Quartz Peak St 89134
Quasar Ct 89130
Quay Ct 89120
Quayside Ct 89178
Quebec Ct 89142
Queen St 89115
Queen Angel Ct 89110
Queen Bee Ct 89134
Queen Charlotte Dr 89145
Queen Irene Ct 89149
Queen Isabel Ct 89115
Queen Palm Dr 89128
Queen Valley Ct 89148
Queen Victoria St 89144
Queens Brook Ct 89129
Queens Canyon Dr 89117
Queens Church Ave 89135
Queens Courtyard Dr 89109
Queens Crescent St 89166
Queens Gate Ct 89145
Queens Walk Cir 89117
Queensborough Ave 89178
Queensbury Ave 89135
Queensland Ave 89110
Queensridge Ct 89145
Queenstown Way 89110
Quencia Ct 89149
Questa Ct 89120
Questa Sera Ct 89135
Quetonia St 89108
Quick Draw Dr 89123
Quick Pine St 89143
Quicksilver Cir 89110
Quiet Breeze Ct 89108
Quiet Canyon St 89113
Quiet Cloud Ct 89141
Quiet Cove Way 89117
Quiet Falls Ct 89141
Quiet Glow Ave 89139
Quiet Mist Ct 89178
Quiet Moon Ln 89135
Quiet Pine St 89108
Quiet Sky St 89123
Quiet Valley Ave 89149
Quill Gordon Ave 89149
Quilt Tree St 89183
Quilted Bear St 89143
Quilting Bear St 89147
Quindio St 89166
Quinella Dr 89103
Quinlan Ave 89130
Quinn Way 89156
Quintana Valley Ct 89131
Quintane Ln 89123
Quintearo St 89115
Quintessa Cir 89141
Quintessa Cove St 89148
Quintillion Ave 89122
Quitman Ave 89149
Rabbit Brush Ct 89135
Rabbit Creek Dr 89120
Rabbit Ridge Ct 89183
Rabbit Springs Rd 89110
Rabbit Track St 89130
Rabitto Ct 89141
Rabnor Cir 89115
Raboso Dr 89141
Raccoon Creek Ln 89143
Raccoon Mountain St 89131
Raccoon Valley Ln 89122
Racel St
6100-7999 89131
8001-8299 89131
13400-13980 89166
Racine Dr 89156
Rackhurst Ave 89134
Racquet St 89121
Radbourne Ave 89121
Radcliff St 89123
Radcliffe Peak Ave 89166
Radiant Beam Ave 89123
Radiant Rapture Ave 89131
Radiant Ruby Ave 89143
Radiant Star St 89145
Radigan Ave 89131
Radio City St 89135
Radkovich Ave 89119
Radley Creek Ct 89148
Radville Dr 89129
Radwick Dr 89110
Rae Dr 89108
Rafael Ridge Way 89119
Rafferty Creek Ln 89156
Rafter Ct 89139
Ragdoll Ave 89166
Raggedy Ann Ave 89183
Raggio Ave 89135
Raging Bull St 89129
Ragland St 89108
Railroad Flat Ct 89138
Railroad River Ave 89139
Railroad Spikes St 89118
Rain Forest Dr 89108
Rain Lily Ct 89117
Rain Shadow Ct 89123
Rain Squall St 89117
Rain Water Dr 89129
N Rainbow Blvd
500-598 89107
600-800 89107
802-882 89107
1101-1897 89108
1899-4699 89108
4701-4799 89108
5000-5800 89130
5802-6198 89130
6600-7599 89131
7601-7899 89131
S Rainbow Blvd
100-1099 89145
1100-3376 89146
3375-3375 89180
3378-3498 89146
3401-3499 89146
3500-4299 89103
4301-4899 89103
4900-5298 89118
5300-7299 89118
7300-7534 89139
7536-8399 89139
8401-9199 89139
10501-11799 89179
Rainbow Bridge Dr 89142
Rainbow Cactus Ct 89106
Rainbow Canyon Blvd 89124
Rainbow Cliff Ct 89123
Rainbow Cove Dr 89131
Rainbow Creek Ct 89122
Rainbow Dream Ave 89183
Rainbow Falls Dr 89134
Rainbow Meadows Dr 89128
Rainbow Ridge Dr 89117
Rainbow River Dr 89142
Rainbow Rock St 89123
Rainbow Sky St 89131
Rainbow Spray Dr 89131
Rainbow Springs Ct 89149
Rainbow Trout Ct 89113
Rainbow Tudor Way 89178
Rainbows End Dr 89149
Rainburst Ct 89115
Raincloud Dr 89145
Raincreek Ave 89130
Raindance Way 89169
Raindrop Canyon Ave 89129
Rainer Ct 89142
Rainfall Ave 89147
Rainford St 89148
Raining Sky St 89178
Rainmaker St 89129
Rainrock Ct 89123
Rainsbrook St 89123
Rainshower Dr 89147
Rainstorm Ridge Ave 89131
Raintree Ln 89107
Rainy Breeze St 89178
Rainy River Rd 89108
Raisin Tree Dr 89148
Raleigh Ave 89108
Ralph Cir 89101
Ralph Mosa St 89138
Ralston Dr 89106
Ram Cliffs Pl 89178
Ram Creek Ln 89178
Rambla Ct 89102
Ramblewood Ave 89128
Rambling Rd 89120
Rambling Rock Ct 89148
Ramhorn Canyon St 89183
Ramillete Rd 89120
Ramon Valley Ave 89149
Ramona Cir 89106
N Rampart Blvd
201-239 89145
1400-2299 89128
S Rampart Blvd 89145
Rampolla Dr 89141
Ramrod St 89108
Ramsey St 89107
Ranch Boss Ct 89113
Ranch Estates Ct 89139
Ranch Hand Ave 89117
Ranch Pines Ave 89178
Ranch Valley St 89179
Ranch View St 89108
Rancher Ave 89108
Ranchito Cir 89120
Rancho Cir 89107
N Rancho Dr
300-1799 89106
1801-2199 89106
2219-2397 89130
2399-4899 89130
4901-4999 89130
7200-7298 89131
S Rancho Dr
101-199 89106
201-909 89106
911-1099 89106
1101-1125 89102
1127-1400 89102
1402-3298 89102
Rancho Ln 89106
Rancho Bel Air Dr 89107
Rancho Bernardo Way 89130
Rancho Camino Ct 89129
Rancho De Taos Ct 89130
Rancho Destino Rd
7400-8899 89123
9900-11100 89183
11102-11498 89183
Rancho Durango Ct 89148
Rancho Hills Dr 89119
Rancho La Costa St 89138
Rancho Lake Dr 89108
Rancho Maria St 89148
Rancho Mirage Dr 89113
Rancho Montanas Ln 89117
Rancho Niguel Pkwy 89147
Rancho Palmas Dr 89117
Rancho Portena Ave 89138
Rancho Rialto Ct 89123
Rancho Rosario Ct 89138
Rancho Santa Fe Dr 89130
Rancho Villa Verde Pl 89138
Rancho Vista Dr 89106
Ranchovilla Ct 89146
Randa Ct & Ln 89104
Randall Dr 89122
Randel Jean Way 89113
Randle Heights Ave 89110
Range Rd
4701-5697 89115
5699-5799 89115
5801-6299 89115
6400-6698 89165
Range Crest Ave 89149
Rani Rd 89139
Ransof Evans Ct 89106
Rapace Ln 89141
Rapallo Ct 89130
Raphael Ct 89129
Rapid Bay Ct 89142
Rapid River Ct 89131
Rappahanock St 89122
Rappeling Ct 89144
Rapunzel Ct 89113
Rarity Ave 89135
Rashelda Ct 89130
Raspberry Hill Rd 89142
Raspberry Ridge Ave 89108
Rassler Ave 89107
Rathburn Ave 89147
Raul Ct 89101
Ravana Ave 89130
Ravel Ct 89145
Raven Ave
3001-3197 89139
3199-6699 89139
6701-6799 89139
7001-7197 89113
7199-8000 89113
8002-8298 89113
9501-9699 89178
Raven Creek Ave 89130
Raven Hills Dr 89149
Raven Horse Dr 89131
Raven Oaks Dr 89124
Raven Springs St 89148
Raven Wing Canyon
Ct 89183
Ravencrest St 89139
Ravendale Cir 89120
Ravenglen Dr 89123
Ravenhollow Ln 89145
Ravenhurst St 89123
Raveno Bianco Pl 89141
Ravens Cry St 89183
Ravenshoe Dr 89134
Ravensmere Ave 89123
Ravenswood Ave 89141
Ravenwood Dr 89147
Ravine Ave 89117
Ravines Ave 89131
Raw Umber Ct 89131
Rawhide Ct 89120
Rawhide St
1200-2299 89119
2301-2399 89119
3301-3397 89120
3399-3679 89120
3681-4499 89120
5100-5153 89122
Rawlins Ct 89128
Ray Charles Ln 89119
Ray Kanel Dr 89156
Raymert Dr 89121
Raymond Ln 89156
Raynham St 89115
Raywood St 89142
Reagan Cir 89115
Reagan Dr 89110
Real Long Way 89148
Real Quiet Dr 89131
Reale Cir 89145
Realeza Ct 89102
Realm Way 89135
Rebecca Rd
5201-5297 89130
5299-5399 89130
5401-5999 89130
6401-6597 89131
6599-6699 89131
6701-7199 89131
Rebecca Raiter Ave 89110
Recital Way 89119
Reckless Wind Ln 89183
Red Ct 89123
Red Apple Ct 89142
Red Arrow Dr 89135
Red Badge Ave 89166
Red Bandana St 89110
Red Barn Dr 89123
Red Bay Way 89128
Red Bear Ct 89117
Red Bluff Dr 89130
Red Boulder Dr 89128
Red Bridge Ave 89134
Red Brook Dr 89128
Red Bud St 89135
Red Camellia Ave 89138
Red Canvas Pl 89144
Red Cider Ln 89130
Red Cinder St 89131
W Red Coach Ave
6901-6999 89108
7600-9800 89129
9802-9898 89129
Red Comet Ct 89156
Red Crest Ln 89144
Red Crossbill Ln 89142
Red Currant Ave 89148
Red Dawn Sky St 89134
Red Deer St 89143
Red Diamond St 89123
Red Eagle St 89131
Red Fern Way 89115
Red Fir St 89135
Red Flower Pl 89134
Red Fox Dr 89123
Red Gable Ln 89144
Red Garnet Ct 89131
Red Glory Dr 89130
Red Gull St 89149
Red Hills Rd 89117
Red Horse St 89143
Red Iron Way 89110
Red Island Ct 89141
Red Jamboree Ct 89130
Red Kansas Ct 89148
Red Knoll St 89113
Red Lake Way 89110
Red Lake Peak St 89166
Red Lava Ct 89123
Red Leaf Dr 89131
Red Lodge Dr 89129
Red Maple Ct 89142
Red Margin Ct 89183
Red Oak Ave 89109
Red Pine Ct 89130
Red Pony Ct 89110
Red Pueblo Pl 89144
Red Raspberry Ct 89142
Red Raven Ct 89123
Red Rio Dr 89128
Red River Dr 89107
Red Robin Ct 89134
Red Rock Cir 89103
Red Rock St
1485-1497 89146
1499-3499 89146
3501-3573 89103
3575-3600 89103
3602-3998 89103
5000-6198 89118
Red Rock Ridge Ave 89179
Red Rooster Ct 89123
Red Rose Ave 89129
Red Rose Ln 89130
Red Ruby Ct 89129
Red Saturn Dr 89130
Red Scott Cir 89117
Red Shores Way 89147
Red Springs Dr 89135
Red Sun Dr 89149
Red Swallow St 89131
Red Tapestry Ct 89149
Red Tee Ln 89148
Red Tide Dr 89131
Red Turtle St 89131
Red Twig Dr 89134
Red Umber Ave 89130
Red Water Ct 89183
Redberry St 89108
Redbird Dr 89134
Redbird Crest Ln 89134
Redbutte Ave 89145
Redcloud Peak St 89166
Reddon Cir 89128
Redeye Ln 89110
Redington Dr 89134
Redlands Cir 89128
Redruth Dr 89178
Redskin Cir 89145
Redstar St 89123
Redstone St 89145
Redwood Cir 89103
Redwood St
1110-1198 89146
1200-3299 89146
3500-3598 89103
3600-3999 89103
5100-5900 89118
5902-6798 89118
8350-9499 89139
9501-9699 89139
Redwood Ash Ave 89144
Redwood Grove Ave 89144
Redwood Point St 89139
Reed Pl 89106
Reed Peak St 89166
Reeder Cir 89119
Reef Dr 89110
Reef Bay Ln 89128
Reef Island Ct 89147
Reef Ridge Ct 89128
Reef View St 89117
Reese St 89107
Reeves Springs Ave 89131
Refectory Ave 89135
Reference St 89122
Refined Ct 89149
Reflecting Waters Ct 89131
Reflection Way 89147
Reflection Brook Ave 89148
Reflection Point Ct 89110
Reflex Dr 89156
Refuge Ct 89135
Refugio St 89141
Regal Ave 89146
Regal Cove St 89117
Regal Hills Ct 89117
Regal Lily Way 89123
Regal Morning Ct 89148
Regal Peak Dr 89118
Regal Plateau Ct 89115
Regal Ridge St 89129
Regal Rock Pl 89138
Regal Springs Ct 89138
Regal Spruce Ln 89130
Regal Stallion Ave 89135
Regal Valley St 89149
Regal Willow Ct 89131
Regalo Bello St 89135
Regatta Dr 89128
Regatta Bay Pl 89131
W Regena Ave
7101-7199 89130
8500-9298 89149
9300-9599 89149
9601-10399 89149
Regency Cove Ct 89121
Regency Park St 89149
Regent Diamond Ave 89106
Regent Pond St 89166
Regents Cir & Ct 89121
Regents Cross Pl 89144
Reggie Cir 89107
Rego Park Ct 89166
Regulus Ave 89102
Rehoboth Bay St 89129
Reiger Ct 89117
Reindeer Ct 89147
Reindeer Lake St 89143
Reining Spur Ave 89143
Reisling Ct 89144
Reiter Ave 89108
Rejoicing Ct 89149
Reka St 89121
Relate Ct 89117
Relente Ct 89117
Relic St 89149
Rema Ct 89131
Rembrandt Dr 89128
Remembrance Hill St 89144
Remington Dr 89110
Remini Ct 89130
Remount Dr 89121
Remsen Ct 89117
Remuda Trl 89146
Renae Nicole Ct 89183
Renaissance Dr 89119
Renate Dr 89103
Renault Ave 89142
Rendon St 89143
Renfrew Dr 89145
Rennes Ct 89131
E Reno Ave
1-1297 89119
1299-2299 89119
2301-2399 89119
2501-2697 89120
2699-4199 89120
4201-4299 89120
W Reno Ave
3401-3497 89118
3499-5446 89118
5448-6698 89118
9500-9598 89148
Reno Ct 89119
Renovah St 89129
Renwick Cir 89117
Renzo St 89183
Requa Ave 89110
Research Ln 89101
Resort Ridge St 89130
Respect Ave 89131
Resplendent Ct 89130
Restful Springs Ct 89128
Resting Pines Ct 89147
Restless Pines St 89131
Retablo Ave 89103
Retriever Ave 89147
Retro Ct 89149
Reuben St 89110
Reveal Ct 89149
Revelry Ln 89138
Revere Dr 89107
Revere St 89106
Revere Crossing Ave 89139
Revital Ct 89131
Revolution Dr 89110
Revolver Ave 89131
Rexburg Cir 89107
Rexford Dr & Pl 89104
Reymore St 89166
Reynard Fox Pl 89113
Rhamus Ct 89149
Rhapsody Ln 89119
Rhea St 89131
Rhett St 89130
Rhine Way 89108
Rhinegold Way 89110
Rhinehart Way 89149
Rhinelander Dr 89108
Rhoda St 89110
Rhodes Ranch Pkwy 89148
Rhodora Peak St 89166
Rhonda Dr 89108
Rhonda Blake Ave 89143
Rialto Rd 89108
Riano Cir 89103
Riata Way 89110
Ribbon Edge St 89139
Ribbon Falls St 89139
Ribbon Garland Ct 89139
Ribbon Grass Ave 89183
Ribbon Ridge Ave 89129
Ribbon Rock Ct 89139

Ribbonwood Ct 89130
Ricardo Ln 89117
Rice Flower Cir 89134
Rice Paper St 89183
Rich Dr 89102
Rich Amethyst Ct 89149
Rich Tapestry Ct 89149
Richard Ct 89102
Richard Allen Ct 89147
Richard Kisling Dr 89115
Richfield Blvd 89102
Richford Pl 89102
Richins Ln 89122
Richland Dr 89134
E Richmar Ave 89123
W Richmar Ave
2400-2799 89123
3000-3098 89139
3100-6500 89139
6502-6598 89139
6900-7398 89178
7400-9198 89178
Richmond Cir 89120
Richmond Heights Dr 89128
Richter Cir 89115
Richtown St 89115
Rick Stratton Dr 89120
Rickenbacker Rd 89115
Ricklebeck Ave 89130
Rickshaw St 89123
Ricky Rd 89130
Rico Peak Ct 89128
Ricochet Ave 89110
Ridge Ave, Ct & Dr 89103
Ridge Blossom Rd 89135
N & S Ridge Club Dr 89103
Ridge Creek Pl 89134
Ridge Heights St 89148
Ridge Hill Ave 89147
Ridge Manor Ave 89148
Ridge Meadow St 89135
Ridge Pine St 89138
Ridge Rim St 89117
Ridge Rock Ct 89134
Ridge Runner St 89131
Ridge Star Ct 89131
Ridge Wolves Ct 89178
Ridgebluff Ave 89148
Ridgecarn Ave 89130
Ridgecliff St 89129
Ridgecrest Dr 89121
Ridgedale Ave 89121
Ridgefield Dr 89108
Ridgeford St 89147
Ridgegrove Ave 89107
Ridgehaven Ave 89148
Ridgeline Ave 89107
Ridgemill St 89178
Ridgemount Dr 89107
Ridgetree Ave 89107
Ridgeview Dr
4200-4299 89103
4900-5099 89120
Ridgeville St 89103
Ridgewood Ave 89120
Riding Heights Ave 89147
Riding Ridge Rd 89123
Rietz Canyon St 89131
Riff Ln 89106
Riflecrest Ave 89156
Rigaletto St 89128
Rigby Ct 89148
Rigel Ave 89102
Riggs Cir 89115
Rigney Ln 89156
Riker Ave 89115
N Riley St 89149
S Riley St
3301-3499 89117
3600-3699 89147
3701-4199 89147
5501-6297 89148
6299-6399 89148
10000-10099 89178
Riley Ann Ave 89139
Riley Cove Ln 89135

Riley Oaks Ct 89108
Rim Rte 89124
Rim Rock Way 89128
Rim View Ln 89130
Rimbey St 89115
Rimcrest Rd 89121
Rimfire Rock Ct 89130
Rimgate Dr 89129
Rimpacific Cir 89146
Rimwood Ct 89147
N & S Ring Dove Dr 89144
Ringe Ln
1001-1197 89110
1199-1599 89110
1600-3199 89156
Ringquist St 89148
Ringtail Ct 89113
Ringwood Ln 89110
Rinker Ln 89147
Rio St 89121
Rio Arriba Dr 89122
Rio Blanco Pl 89121
Rio Camuy Ave 89131
Rio Canyon Ct 89128
Rio De Janeiro Dr 89128
Rio De Thule Ln 89135
Rio Del Mar Dr 89128
Rio Grande St 89115
Rio Grande Falls Ave 89178
Rio Grande Gorge Ct 89130
Rio Mariel Dr 89156
Rio Mayo Dr 89121
Rio Nevada Way 89113
Rio Poco Dr 89156
Rio Rancho Way 89122
Rio Rico Dr 89113
Rio Ridge Ct 89129
Rio Sands Ct 89130
Rio Seco Dr 89156
Rio Tinto Way 89110
Rio Verde Ave 89147
Rio Vista St
5400-5998 89130
6000-6200 89130
6202-6298 89130
6500-7699 89131
7701-7799 89131
Rip Van Winkle Ln 89102
Ripon Dr 89134
Ripple Way 89110
Ripple Ridge Ave 89149
Ripple River Ave 89115
Riscos Hill Rd 89161
Risepine Ct 89110
Rising Cove St 89129
Rising Creek Ct 89148
Rising Harbor Ave 89129
Rising Heights St 89131
Rising Legend Way 89106
Rising Mist St 89134
Rising Moon Ct 89117
Rising Port Ave 89113
Rising Ridge Ave 89135
Rising Rock Cir 89129
Rising Smoke Ct 89183
Rising Sun Dr 89117
Rising Tide Dr 89117
Rising Tree St 89183
Risto Ct 89148
Ristoro St 89148
Rita Cir 89115
Rita Dr 89121
Ritacuba Way 89139
Ritornia Ave 89135
Ritter Ln 89118
Riva De Angelo Ave 89135
Riva De Destino Ave 89135
Riva De Fiore Ave 89135
Riva De Romanza St 89135
Riva De Tierra Ln 89135
Riva Del Garda Pl 89134
Riva Grande Ct 89135
Riva Largo Ave 89135
Riva Ridge St 89149
Rive Gauche St 89115
Rivedro St 89135

Rivenbark Ct 89145
Rivendell Ave 89135
River Beach Ave 89178
River Bed St 89110
River Birch St 89117
River Canyon Rd 89129
River Crest Ct 89106
River Dove Ct 89139
River Glen Dr 89103
River Glorious Ln 89135
River Highlands Pl 89122
River Hills Ln 89135
River Legend St 89122
River Meadows Ave 89131
River Mist Ct 89113
River Oaks Dr 89156
River Pines Ct 89117
River Point Dr 89110
River Ridge Dr 89131
River Rim Ct 89113
River Splash Ave 89131
River Trader St 89178
River Valley St 89107
Riverbank Ln 89110
Riverboat Ct 89130
Riverdale Way 89108
Riverlawn Pl 89138
Rivermeade St 89166
Rivers Edge Dr 89117
Riverside Dr
1200-1399 89106
3000-3398 89108
Riverside Park Ave 89135
Riverstone Ave 89115
Riverwood Ct 89149
Riviera Ave 89107
Riviera Beach Dr 89128
Riviera Ridge Ave 89115
Rizari Ct 89130
Roadrunner Dr 89120
Roamer Pl 89131
Roan Ave 89119
Roanoke Ct 89148
Roanridge Ave 89120
Roaring Springs Cir 89113
Robar St 89121
Robard St 89135
Robbia Dr 89138
Robel Ave 89178
Robert Ct 89120
Robert Dula Ave 89129
Robert Hampton Rd 89120
Robert Mcguire Ct 89129
Robert Randolf Way 89147
Robert Trent Jones St 89141
Roberta Ln 89108
Roberta St 89119
Robin Cir 89121
Robin Ln 89108
Robin St 89106
Robin Hill Ave 89129
Robin Hood Cir 89108
Robin Leaf Ct 89138
Robin Nest Ct 89117
Robin Oaks Dr 89117
Robin Park Ave 89138
Robindale Cir 89123
E Robindale Rd 89123
W Robindale Rd
3401-3597 89139
3599-4900 89139
4902-5398 89139
6900-7698 89113
7700-7900 89113
7902-8198 89113
Robinglen Ave 89131
Robins Creek Pl 89135
Robins Hollow Rd 89183
Robins Ridge Dr 89129
Robins Roost St 89131
Robinson Ridge Dr 89117
Robison Cir 89145
Robusta Ct 89141
Roca Ln 89130
E Rochelle Ave
1401-1597 89119

1599-2200 89119
2202-2398 89119
2501-2897 89121
2899-4799 89121
6000-6098 89122
W Rochelle Ave
4201-4697 89103
4699-5900 89103
5902-6098 89103
7801-7897 89147
7899-9400 89147
9402-10130 89147
Rochelle Ct 89121
Rochelle Ln 89121
Rochester Ave 89115
Rock Castle Ave 89130
Rock Cove Way 89141
Rock Creek Ln 89130
Rock Dove Ave 89122
Rock Face Ct 89129
Rock Garden Ct 89178
Rock Island Ln 89110
Rock Light Ave 89110
Rock Meadows Dr 89178
Rock Port Cir 89128
Rock Run St 89148
Rock Slide Cir 89115
Rock Springs Dr 89128
Rockaway St 89145
Rockaway Beach St 89129
Rockbridge Cir 89128
Rockcrest Dr 89108
Rockefeller St 89123
Rocket St 89131
Rocketman Cir 89149
Rockfield Dr 89128
Rockford St 89134
Rockhampton Ave 89113
Rocking Horse Ave 89108
Rockland Dr 89129
Rockland Break Ct 89147
Rockledge Dr & Way 89119
Rockmine Ct 89118
Rockmoss St 89145
Rockridge Peak Ave 89166
Rockside Ave 89148
Rockvale Dr 89103
Rockview Dr 89128
Rockville Ave 89143
Rockwell Ln 89156
Rockwind Ct 89117
Rockwood Ct 89129
Rocky Ave 89143
Rocky Beach Dr 89115
Rocky Bluff Way 89129
Rocky Cliff Pl 89144
Rocky Gorge Ct 89113
Rocky Hillside Ct 89123
Rocky Mesa Ct 89144
Rocky Mountain Ave 89156
Rocky Park Ct 89123
Rocky Plains Dr 89134
Rocky Point Dr 89145
Rocky Ravine Ave 89131
Rocky River St 89130
Rocky Shore Dr 89117
Rocky Top Ave 89110
Rocky Tree St 89183
Rocky Waters Ave 89129
Rococo Ct 89141
Rod Ct 89122
Roddenberry Ave 89123
Rodeo Dr 89123
Rodman Dr 89130
Rodman Ridge Ct 89130
Roe Ct 89145
Roger Cir 89107
Rogers St
4900-7299 89118
7300-7398 89139
7400-7700 89139
7702-9098 89139
Rolan Ct 89121
Roland Falls Ln 89183
Roland Wiley Rd 89145
Rolling Acres Cir 89117

Rolling Boulder St 89149
Rolling Cloud Dr 89115
Rolling Dunes Ct 89117
Rolling Glen Ct 89117
Rolling Green Dr 89169
Rolling Hills Dr 89156
Rolling Knoll Ct 89134
Rolling Meadow St 89130
Rolling Oaks Ct 89131
Rolling Pasture Ave 89131
Rolling Ridge Ln 89134
Rolling River Dr 89131
Rolling Rock Dr 89123
Rolling Shore Ct 89149
Rolling Springs Dr 89148
Rolling Thunder Ave 89148
Rolling Tree St 89183
Rolling View Dr 89149
Rolling Winds Way 89123
Rollingstone Dr 89103
Rollingwood Cir 89121
Rollingwood Dr 89120
Rollins St 89118
Roma Madre Ave 89135
Roman Tree Ct 89183
Romance Cir 89108
Romantic Sunset St 89131
Romantico Dr 89135
W Rome Blvd
5300-7599 89131
8600-8699 89149
Rome St 89169
Romero Dr 89110
Rometta Ave 89141
Romette Ct 89141
Romine Ct 89149
Romoco Ct 89178
Romola St 89141
Romona Falls Ave 89141
Ron Ct 89115
Ron Evans St 89145
Ronald Ln 89110
Ronan Dr 89110
Roncat Ct 89141
Rondonia Cir 89120
Ronemus Dr 89128
Roohani Ct 89103
Roop St 89131
Ropers Rock Ct 89131
Roping Cowboy Ave 89178
Roping Rodeo Ave 89178
Rory Ct 89129
Rosabella St 89141
W Rosada Way
5700-5999 89130
7200-9599 89149
Rosalba St 89141
Rosalita Ave 89108
Rosamond Dr 89134
Rosanna St
1200-1298 89117
1300-3199 89117
3201-3399 89117
5901-9099 89113
9301-9499 89178
Rosario Cir 89121
Rosarito St 89108
Rosary Rd 89161
Roscoe Ave 89129
Roscommon St 89147
Rose St 89106
Rose Charmont St 89183
Rose Coral Ave 89106
Rose Garden Ln 89142
Rose Hill River Dr 89122
Rose Hills St 89149
Rose Lake St 89148
Rose Mallow St 89148
Rose Park Ave 89135
Rose Petal Ave 89130
Rose Quartz Ct 89139
Rose Reflet Pl 89144
Rose River Falls St 89131
Rose Thicket St 89130
Rose Tiara Dr 89139
Rose Tree Ln 89156

Rose Window Ct 89131
Rosebank Cir 89108
Roseberry Dr 89138
Rosebriar Ct 89131
Rosebud Cir 89108
Rosecrans St 89166
N & S Rosecrest Cir 89121
Rosedale Ave 89121
Roseglen Ct 89108
Rosegrass Way 89129
Roseland Ave 89130
Roselle Ct 89129
Rosellen Ave 89147
Rosemary Ln 89107
Rosemary Park Dr 89135
Rosemeade St 89106
Rosemere Ct 89117
Rosemount Ave 89156
Rosencrantz Ave 89124
Roseridge Ave 89107
Roseville Way 89102
Rosewood Dr 89121
Rosewood St 89103
Rosewood Meadows
Ct 89149
Roseworthy Dr 89134
Rosey Ct 89149
Rosinwood St 89131
Rosita Dr 89123
Roskott Cir 89130
Ross Ave 89110
Rossi Ave 89144
Rossmore Dr 89110
Rossovino St 89183
Roswell St 89120
Rosy Sunrise St 89142
Rotella Dr 89147
Rothbury Ave 89141
Rothmannia Ct 89149
Rothorn St 89178
Rothwell Ct 89102
Rottweiler Ct 89131
Rotunda Ct 89130
Rou Cir 89122
Rouge Rd 89130
Rough Green St 89117
Rough Slate Ct 89178
Round Ct 89123
Round Castle St 89130
Round Hills Cir 89113
Round Lake Dr 89115
Round Stone Ct 89145
Round Table Dr 89110
Round Tree Dr 89128
Round Valley Way 89129
Round Wood St 89147
Roundabout Cir 89161
Roundrock Dr 89142
Roundstone Bog Ave 89139
Roundup Ave 89119
Roundup Ridge St 89131
Rousso Rd 89118
Rowan Tree Dr 89123
Rowdy St 89131
Rowena Cir 89131
Rowland Ave 89130
Rowland St 89108
Rowland Bluff Ave 89178
Rowland Heights Ct 89178
Roxanne Dr 89108
Roxburgh Castle Ave 89117
Roxbury Ln 89119
Roxella Ln 89110
Roxford Dr 89119
Roy Horn Way 89118
Roy Rogers Dr 89108
Royal Ave & Dr 89103
Royal Aberdeen Way 89144
Royal Arches St 89139
N & S Royal Ascot Dr 89144
Royal Bay Dr 89117
Royal Birch Ln 89144
Royal Bridge Dr 89178
Royal Brook Ct 89149
Royal Canyon Dr 89128
Royal Castle Ln 89130

E & W Royal Club
Way 89103
Royal Coach Ct 89134
Royal County Down
Ct 89131
Royal Course Ct 89148
Royal Crest Cir 89169
N Royal Crest Cir 89169
S Royal Crest Cir 89169
Royal Crest St 89119
Royal Crown Ct 89139
Royal Crystal St 89149
Royal Derwent Ave 89138
Royal Desert St 89123
Royal Dolnoch Ct 89141
Royal Elm Ln 89144
Royal Estates Dr 89115
Royal Fern Cir 89115
Royal Glen Ct 89117
Royal Guard Ave 89130
Royal Heritage Ct 89110
Royal Highlands St 89141
Royal Jasmine Ln 89135
Royal Lake Ave 89131
Royal Lamb Dr 89145
Royal Legacy Ln 89110
Royal Lilly Ct 89139
Royal Meadow Pl 89147
Royal Melbourne Dr 89131
Royal Mint Ave 89166
Royal Monarch Ct 89147
Royal Moon Ave 89123
Royal Oaks Rd 89123
Royal Palm Dr 89128
Royal Pine Ave 89144
Royal Plum Ln 89144
Royal Poinciana Ct 89131
Royal Ridge Ave, Blvd,
Ln & Way 89103
Royal Scots Ave 89141
Royal Springs Ave 89131
Royal Stallion Ct 89131
Royal Sunset Ct 89130
Royal View Ave 89144
Royal Viking Way 89121
Royal Vista Ln 89149
Royal Willow Pl 89144
Royal Windsor Ave 89149
Royal Wood Ct 89148
Royalhill Ave 89121
Royalston Falls Ct 89143
Royalton Dr 89144
Royce Ct 89121
Roydale Ave 89183
Royer Ranch Rd 89149
Rozetta Ct 89134
Rubicon Ct 89128
Rubicon Peak Ct 89129
Rubidoux Dr 89108
Rubino St 89183
Ruby Arrow Ct 89178
Ruby Bay Ct 89141
Ruby Cliffs Ln 89144
Ruby Creek Dr 89142
Ruby Finito Ct 89129
Ruby Heights Ave 89117
Ruby Hills Dr 89134
Ruby Kinglet St 89148
Ruby Mountain Way 89128
Ruby Red Cir 89108
Ruby Summit Ave 89110
Ruby Treasure St 89147
Ruby Vista Ct 89144
Rubylyn Ave 89122
Ruckman Ave 89129
Rudica Creek Ave 89149
Rudin Ave & Dr 89124
Rudolf St 89104
Rudy Ln 89120
Rue 13 89101
Ruenda Ct 89147
Ruffian Rd & St 89149
Ruffled Grouse Ct 89130
Rufina St 89148
Rugby Cir 89110
Rugen Ave 89120

Rugged Ave 89131
Rugged Mountain Ave 89166
Rugged Ravine Ct 89183
Ruggles Mansion Ave 89166
Rum Runner Dr 89130
Rumba Ct 89139
Rumrill St
6100-6198 89113
10001-10099 89178
Rumriver St 89134
Rumsfield Ct 89131
Runaway Ct 89117
Runbridge St 89144
Rungsted St 89142
Running Colors Ave 89131
Running Deer Ave 89145
Running Doe Ct 89149
Running Falls St 89178
Running Putt Way 89148
Running Rabbit St 89143
Running Rapids Ave 89130
Running Trout Ave 89131
Running Waters Ct 89123
Running Wind Ct 89131
Runningbear Dr 89108
Runningbrook Rd 89120
Ruperts Ct 89123
E Rush Ave 89183
W Rush Ave 89141
Rush Springs Dr 89139
Rushfield Ave 89178
Rushford St 89103
Rushing Current St 89131
Rushing Waters Pl 89135
Rushing Wind Ave 89148
Rushmore Ave 89131
Rushworth Ave 89178
Ruskin St 89147
Russell Ave 89104
E Russell Rd
1600-1900 89119
1902-2398 89119
2400-2598 89120
2600-4899 89120
4901-4979 89120
5026-7000 89122
7002-7098 89122
W Russell Rd
3400-6799 89118
6801-6899 89118
6900-7398 89113
7400-8000 89113
7925-7925 89140
8001-8599 89113
8002-8098 89113
8800-8898 89148
8900-9699 89148
9701-9999 89148
Russell Peterson Ct 89129
Russell Ranch Ave 89113
Russet Falls St 89129
Russet Hills Ct 89147
Russet Peak Ct 89129
Russet Plains St 89129
Russet Ridge Ct 89183
Russett Wood Cir 89117
Russian Blue Ct 89166
Russian Rider Dr 89122
Russling Leaf Dr 89131
Rustic Canyon Ct 89131
Rustic Charm Ct 89131
Rustic Club Way 89148
Rustic Crest St 89149
Rustic Galleon St 89139
Rustic Haven Ct 89156
Rustic Meadow St 89131
Rustic Raven Ct 89139
Rustic Ridge Dr 89148
Rustic View Ct 89131
Rustler Ct 89119
Rustling Leaves Ln 89143
Rustling Winds Ave 89113
Ruston Rd 89143
Rusty Anchor Ct 89130
Rusty Branch Ave 89123
Rusty Creek St 89123
Rusty Nail Way 89119
Rusty Plank Ave 89148
Rusty Railroad Ave 89135
Rusty Ray Dr 89135
Rusty Rifle Ave 89143
Rusty Sandstone Ct 89131
Rusty Springs Ct 89148
Rustyville Ct 89129
Rutgers Dr 89156
Ruth Dr
2001-2099 89108
3300-3699 89121
Ruthe Duarte Ave 89121
Rutherford Cir 89123
Rutherford Grove St 89148
Rutledge Dr 89120
Rutte Cir 89115
Ryan Ave 89101
Ryan Creek Ave 89149
Ryan Ranch Ave 89130
Ryandale Cir 89145
Ryans Reef Ln 89128
Rye St 89102
Rye Canyon Dr 89123
Rygate Ave 89178
Rymer Ct 89130
Saba Rock Ct 89139
Sabadell St 89121
Sabado St 89121
Sabbotia Ct 89178
Sabine Ranch Rd 89131
Sabino Cir 89110
Sabino Canyon St 89129
Sable Beauty St 89131
Sable Mist Ct 89144
Sable Oaks Ct 89134
Sable Point St 89178
Sable Ridge Ct 89135
Sabora Ave 89122
Sabra Ct 89107
Sabrina Ct 89117
Sabroso St 89156
Sacha Way 89118
Sackett St 89106
Sacks Dr 89122
Sacramento Dr 89110
Sacre Ct 89135
Sacred Bark Ct 89141
Sacred Datura Ave 89139
Sacred Falls Ave 89148
E Saddle Ave 89121
W Saddle Ave
5800-5898 89103
5900-6000 89103
6002-6098 89103
9601-9699 89147
Saddle Pl 89119
Saddle Back Peak St 89166
Saddle Creek Ct 89147
Saddle Horse Ave 89122
Saddle Iron St 89179
Saddle Mountain St 89178
Saddle Peak Trl 89118
Saddle Red Ave 89143
Saddle Rock Cir 89117
Saddle Soap Ct 89135
Saddle Tree Dr 89118
Saddle Valley St 89131
Saddleback Ct 89121
Saddleback Ledge
Ave 89147
Saddlebrook St 89141
Saddlewood Ct 89121
Sadler Dr 89130
Safari Ln 89129
Safeport Cove Ct 89117
Saffredi Ln 89141
Saffron Dr 89142
Sag Harbor Dr 89104
Sagamore Dr 89156
Sagamore Bay Ct 89179
Sage Brush St
4400-4498 89121
5900-6199 89120
Sage Grove Ct 89148
Sage Park Dr 89135
Sage Pines Dr 89118
Sage Pointe Cir 89128
Sage River St 89129
Sage Sparrow Ave 89148
Sage Springs St 89118
Sage Thicket Ave 89178
Sage Tree Ct 89101
Sage Valley Ct 89110
Sageberry Dr 89144
Sagebrook Ln 89121
Sagebrush Bend St 89113
Sagelyn St 89122
Sagewood St 89147
Saginaw Dr 89108
Sagittarius Dr 89135
Sagman St 89101
Sago Palm Ct 89122
Sagtikos St 89122
Saguaro Ln 89110
Saguaro Way 89121
Saguaro Point Ct & St 89115
Sahalee Dr 89148
E Sahara Ave
208-398 89104
400-4999 89104
5000-6599 89142
W Sahara Ave
200-1498 89102
1500-4799 89102
4801-4899 89102
4901-4997 89146
4999-6800 89146
6802-6898 89146
6900-10000 89117
10002-10098 89117
10800-10898 89135
Sahara Way 89108
Sail Bay Dr 89117
Sail Landing Ct 89117
Sail Point St 89147
Sail Port Ct 89129
Sailboat Ln 89145
Sailfish Cir 89117
Sailing Water Ave 89147
Sailor Point Ave 89147
Sailors Delight Ct 89139
Sailplane Ave 89129
Saint Aidans St 89178
Saint Aiden St 89129
Saint Andrews Cir 89107
Saint Andrews Ct 89144
Saint Annes Dr 89149
Saint Augustine St 89183
Saint Bar Ct 89115
Saint Bernard Ct 89131
Saint Clair Dr 89128
Saint Claude Ave 89148
Saint Cloud Ct 89143
Saint Cronan Ct 89129
Saint Elmo Cir 89123
Saint Gregory Dr 89117
Saint Helena St 89121
Saint James Cir 89117
Saint Joseph Cir 89104
Saint Jude Cir 89104
Saint Katherine Cir 89117
Saint Keyne St 89178
Saint Kitts Ct 89128
Saint Lawrence Dr 89108
Saint Lazare St 89130
E Saint Louis Ave 89104
W Saint Louis Ave 89102
Saint Lucia St 89131
Saint Luke Ct 89104
Saint Mark Ct 89104
Saint Nazaire Ave 89141
Saint Paul Way 89104
Saint Petersburg Dr 89142
Saint Pierre Dr 89134
Saint Rafael St 89141
Saint Season St 89178
Saint Tropez St 89128
Saint Whittier Ct 89123
Saintsbury Dr 89144
Sakhalin Ave 89139
Salamanca Cir 89121
Salcio Ave 89183
Salem Dr 89107
Salem Cross Ct 89166
Salem Hills Ct 89134
Salem Mountain Ct 89178
Salem Rose Ct 89144
Salentino Ave 89138
Salernes St 89141
Salerno Ct 89128
Salford Dr 89144
Salida Del Sol Ct 89142
Salimson Way 89110
Salinas Canyon Ave 89139
Salinas Pueblo St 89179
Salinaz Cir 89118
Salinger Ct 89147
Salisbury Pl 89121
Salishan Dr 89147
Sally St 89166
Sally Irene Ct 89113
Sally Rose Ave 89149
Salmon Dr 89115
Salmon Creek Dr 89129
Salmon Falls St 89113
Salmon Leap St 89183
Salmon Mountain Ave 89122
Salmon Rose Pl 89178
Salt Cedar Ln 89121
Salt Marsh Ct 89148
Salt River Ave 89139
Salt Spray Ct 89139
Salt Water Ct 89117
Saltaire St 89120
Saltbush Dr 89134
Saluda Cir 89118
Salvadora Pl 89113
Salvation St 89115
Salvatore St 89148
Salvestrin Point Ave 89148
Salzburg Ave 89183
Sam Jonas Dr 89145
Sam Leone Ct 89138
Samantha St 89110
Samba Ave 89139
Sambar Ct 89149
Samia Ct 89110
Sammis Ave 89110
Sammymel Dr 89115
Samoset Ct 89148
Samoy St 89110
Sampson Dr 89121
San Cir 89120
San Alivia Ct 89141
San Andreas Ave 89121
San Angelo Ave 89102
San Anselmo St 89120
San Antonio Ave 89115
San Ardo Pl 89130
San Arezzo Pl 89141
San Bellacova Ct 89141
San Bellasera Ct 89141
San Benito St 89121
San Bernardino Ave 89102
San Blas Dr 89120
San Capri Way 89141
San Carlos Ave 89115
San Cascina St 89135
San Deluna St 89108
San Dimas Ct 89147
San Domingo Ln 89115
San Felipe St 89115
San Fernando Dr 89108
San Florentine Ave 89141
San Franchesca Ct 89141
San Francisco Ave 89115
San Gabriel Hill Ave 89115
San Gagano Ave 89131
San Gervasio Ave 89147
San Giano Pl 89144
San Gorgonio St 89115
San Grail Ct 89145
San Jacoma Pl 89138
San Joaquin Ave 89102
San Jose Ave 89104
San Juan Dr 89108
San Juan Hills Dr 89134
San Kristia Ave 89141
San Lago Ct 89121
San Laguna Ct 89134
San Leandro Ave 89120
San Lucas Cir 89121
San Luis Cir & St 89115
San Mamete Ave 89141
San Marcello St 89147
San Marcos Ct & St 89115
San Marin St 89123
San Martin Ct 89121
W San Miguel Ave 89130
San Milano Ave 89141
San Onofre Ct 89113
San Pablin St 89139
San Pablo Dr 89104
San Palatina St 89141
San Palazzo Ct 89141
San Palo Way 89147
San Papino Ct 89123
San Pascual Ave 89115
San Pedro Ave, Dr &
St 89104
San Rafael Ave
4400-4899 89120
4901-4999 89120
5000-5099 89122
5101-5199 89122
San Rafael Cir 89122
San Ramon Dr 89147
San Ricardo Ave 89146
San Rosarita Ct 89138
San Rossore Ct 89183
San Sebastian Ave 89121
San Severo St 89147
San Sicily St 89141
San Simeon St 89108
San Terrazo Pl 89141
San Vercelli Ct 89141
San Vincente Ct & St 89115
San Vito St 89147
Sanbury Brook St 89183
Sanction Ave 89131
Sand Bench Ave 89130
Sand Canyon Dr 89128
Sand Castle Ave 89183
Sand Coral Dr 89123
Sand Creek Ave 89103
Sand Dollar Ave 89141
Sand Harbor Ct 89128
Sand Hawk Ct 89129
Sand Key St 89178
Sand Mountain Ave 89166
Sand Pebble Ln 89129
Sand Pier St 89147
Sand Pines Ct 89144
Sand Primrose St 89138
Sand Shark Ct 89147
Sand Tiger Ave 89148
Sand Villa Ct 89147
Sandalwood Ln 89119
Sandana Cir 89123
Sandbar Ct 89117
Sandcastle Dr 89147
Sandcliff Ln 89121
Sandecker Ct 89146
Sanderling Cir 89103
N Sandhill Rd 89110
S Sandhill Rd
1201-1597 89104
1599-1699 89104
1701-1999 89104
2800-2852 89121
2854-4699 89121
4701-4899 89121
5217-5497 89120
5499-6300 89120
6302-6698 89120
Sandhorse Ct 89130
Sandia Ave 89147
Sandilands Dr 89134
Sandinista Dr 89123
Sandirose Way 89122
Sandmark Dr 89145
Sandmist Ave 89134
Sandpiper Ln 89146
Sandpiper Way 89103
Sandra Rd 89110
Sandra Field Ct 89110
Sandridge Ct 89149
Sandringham Ave 89129
Sandrock Ranch St 89113
Sandrone Ave 89138
Sands Ave 89169
Sands Point Cir 89121
Sandspring Dr 89134
Sandstone Dr
1400-1499 89161
5100-5399 89142
Sandstone Mesa Dr 89130
Sandstone Ravine St 89131
Sandstone Ridge Dr 89135
Sandstone Walk St 89178
Sandtrap Ct 89142
Sandy Ln 89115
Sandy Bluff Ct 89134
Sandy Breeze Ln 89115
Sandy Bunker Ln 89148
Sandy Cactus Ln 89149
Sandy Copper Ct 89131
Sandy Cove St 89110
Sandy Creek Dr 89123
Sandy Eagle Ct 89129
Sandy Grove Ave 89144
Sandy Isle Ct 89131
Sandy Peak Ave 89138
Sandy Plains Ave 89131
Sandy Reef Ave 89147
Sandy River Dr 89103
Sandy Rock Cir 89123
Sandy Shale St 89123
Sandy Shores Dr 89117
Sandy Slate Way 89123
Sandy Slope Ct 89113
Sandy Turtle Ave 89149
Sandy Vista Ct 89131
Sandybuck Ct 89149
Sandyfalls Way 89142
Sanford Ct 89107
Sangallo St 89106
Sangay Way 89147
Sangre De Cristo Ave 89118
Sangria Ln 89147
Sanibel Shore Ave 89147
Santa Anita Dr 89119
Santa Barbara St 89121
Santa Candida St 89138
Santa Catalina Ave 89108
Santa Clara Dr 89104
Santa Clarita Ave 89115
Santa Cresta Ave 89129
Santa Cruz Ave 89108
Santa Fe St 89145
Santa Fe Rose St 89123
Santa Isabel Ave 89146
Santa Lorena Ct 89147
Santa Margarita St
1400-3099 89146
5500-6398 89118
6400-6499 89118
Santa Maria Ave 89108
Santa Paula Dr 89104
Santa Ponsa Ct 89178
Santa Rita Dr 89104
Santa Rosa Dr 89104
Santa Terrasa Pl 89121
Santa Ynez Dr 89104
Santana Siesta Ave 89166
Santander Ave 89103
Santerno St 89141
Santiago St 89104
Santina Ave 89123
Santo Ave 89108
Santo Domingo Ave 89178
Santo Marco Ct 89135
Santo Nina Ct 89135
Santo Romeo St 89135
Santo Willow Ave 89141
Santoli Ave 89123
W Santoli Ave
5800-6099 89139
6900-7099 89113
Santolina Dr 89135
Santorini Dr 89141
Santree Cir 89110
Sanucci Ct 89141
Sanwood St 89147
Saphire Stone Ave 89106
Sapodilla Ln 89144
Sapphire St 89108
Sapphire Bay Cir 89128
Sapphire Blue Ct 89108
Sapphire Cove Ave 89117
Sapphire Creek Ct 89131
Sapphire Point Ave 89147
Sapphire Ridge Ave 89129
Sapphire Shores St 89117
Sapphire Springs Cir 89108
Sapphire Valley St 89128
Sapphire Vista Ave 89144
Sapporo Cir 89110
Saputo Ave 89141
Sara Lee Cir 89119
Sarab Ln 89119
Sarajane Ln 89107
Saranac Rd 89130
Saratoga Cir 89120
Saratoga Dr 89120
Saratoga St 89146
Sarazen Cir 89103
Sardinia Sands Dr 89141
Sari Cir & Dr 89110
Sashaying Spirit Ct 89131
Sassa St 89130
Sassy Rose Dr 89122
Satellite Beach Dr 89134
Satin Carnation Ln 89166
Satin Mist Ct 89144
Satin Pond St 89123
Satinwood Dr 89147
Sattes St 89101
Sattley Cir 89117
Sauceda Ln 89103
Sauer Dr 89128
Saugus Dr 89134
Savalli St 89102
Savannah St 89122
Savannah Falls St 89131
Savannah Sky Ave 89131
Savant Ct 89149
Savers Ct 89115
Saville Garden Ct 89130
Savin Cir 89130
Savitar Ave 89117
Savona Cir 89128
Savory St 89131
Savoy Ct 89115
Savvy Seam Ct 89149
Saw Horse St 89143
Sawgrass Ct 89113
Sawhill Pond St 89131
Sawleaf Rd 89135
Sawmill Ave 89134
Sawtooth Dr 89119
Sawyer Ave 89108
Saxondale Ave 89123
Saxony Dr 89119
Saxton Green Ave 89141
Saxton Hill Ave 89106
Sayan Cir 89149
Saybrook Point Dr 89128
Saylor Way
400-898 89107
900-1600 89108
1602-1998 89108
Scalise Ct 89141
Scallop Reef Ave 89147
Scamadella St 89141
Scammons Bay Ct 89129
Scanlon Ferry Ct 89156
Scarborough Ave 89107
Scarlet Flax St 89148
Scarlet Haze Ave 89183
Scarlet Oak Ave 89104
Scarlet Peak Ct 89110
Scarlet Ridge Dr 89128
Scarlet Rose Dr 89134
Scarlet Star Ave 89130

Scarlet Tapestry Ct ... 89149
Scarpa St ... 89178
Scarsdale Dr ... 89117
Scenery Cir ... 89128
Scenic Way ... 89108
Scenic Bay Dr ... 89117
Scenic Desert Ct ... 89131
Scenic Harbor Dr ... 89117
Scenic Hills Dr ... 89128
Scenic Loop Dr ... 89161
Scenic Mountain Ln ... 89117
Scenic Peak St ... 89144
Scenic Pointe Ave ... 89130
Scenic Ridge Dr ... 89148
Scenic Sunrise Dr ... 89117
Scenic Sunset Dr ... 89117
Scenic Walk Ave ... 89149
Schaffer Cir ... 89121
Scherer St ... 89145
Schiff Dr ... 89103
Schilling Ct ... 89117
Schirlls St
  5101-6397 ... 89118
  6399-7100 ... 89118
  7102-7298 ... 89118
  7400-7700 ... 89139
  7702-8598 ... 89139
  10201-10499 ... 89141
Scholar Ln ... 89128
Scholl Dr ... 89107
Scholl Canyon Ave ... 89131
Schooner Cove Ct ... 89117
Schuders Ave ... 89178
Schumann Dr ... 89146
Schuster St
  5000-7199 ... 89118
  7201-7299 ... 89118
  7300-7398 ... 89139
  7400-8700 ... 89139
  8702-8898 ... 89139
  9700-10098 ... 89141
  10100-10299 ... 89141
  10301-10599 ... 89141
Scoby Ct ... 89147
Sconce Ct ... 89149
Sconset Cove Ct ... 89178
Scopes Ave ... 89166
Scoreboard St ... 89130
Scorpion Track Ct ... 89178
Scotch Elm Ave ... 89166
Scotch Heather St ... 89142
Scotch Lake St ... 89134
Scotch Pine Cir ... 89146
Scotland Ln ... 89102
Scotmist Ct ... 89129
Scotscraig Ct ... 89141
Scott Ave ... 89102
Scott Peak Ct ... 89129
Scottie St ... 89166
Scottish Castle Ave ... 89113
Scottish Glen Ct ... 89178
Scotts Crossing St ... 89166
Scottsbluff St ... 89129
Scottsmoor Ct ... 89156
Scottville Ct ... 89148
Scottyboy Dr ... 89113
Scotwood St ... 89121
Scouts Landing Ct ... 89139
Scramble Dr ... 89148
Screaming Eagle Ave ... 89139
Scree Ct ... 89139
Scripps Dr ... 89103
Scroggs St ... 89148
Scrolling Crest Ct ... 89149
Scrub Jay Ct ... 89148
Scuba Cir ... 89108
Sea Anchor Ct ... 89131
Sea Boot Ct ... 89131
Sea Breeze Ave ... 89110
Sea Captain St ... 89178
Sea Cliff Way ... 89128
Sea Cove St ... 89123
Sea Dancer Ct ... 89108
Sea Fog Ct ... 89147
Sea France Ct ... 89130
Sea Glen Dr ... 89128
Sea Hero St ... 89129
Sea Horn Ct ... 89147
Sea Mist Ln ... 89147
Sea Orchard St ... 89131
Sea Palms Ave ... 89134
Sea Pines Ln ... 89107
Sea Rim Ave ... 89148
Sea Rock Rd ... 89128
Sea Shell Ln ... 89110
Sea Spray Ave ... 89128
Sea Venture Dr ... 89128
Sea View Ct ... 89117
Sea Voyage Ave ... 89138
Sea Wind Dr ... 89128
Seabaugh Ave ... 89107
Seabiscuit St ... 89108
Seabourn Ct ... 89129
Seabridge Dr ... 89121
Seabrook Ln ... 89130
Seabury Bay St ... 89179
Seabury Hill Ct ... 89128
Seacraft Way ... 89123
Seaforth St ... 89129
Seagirt Cir ... 89110
Seagull Ave ... 89145
Seahawk St ... 89145
Seahorse Ct ... 89128
Seahurst Dr ... 89142
Seal Beach Dr ... 89108
Seal Rock Ct ... 89147
Sealion Dr ... 89128
Sean St ... 89156
Sean Creek St ... 89149
Sean Darin Cir ... 89146
Searching Bear Ct ... 89149
Searchlight Dr ... 89110
Searles Ave ... 89101
Seascape Dr ... 89128
Seashore Dr ... 89128
Seashore Palm Ct ... 89121
Seaside Park Ave ... 89110
Seaside Treasures Ct ... 89122
Seasmoke Ct ... 89139
Seasonable Dr ... 89129
Seat Wall Rd ... 89148
Seaton Pl ... 89121
Seattle Ave ... 89121
Seattle Shore St ... 89115
Seattle Slew Dr ... 89108
Sebasco Dr ... 89147
Sebastiani Ct ... 89123
Sebring St ... 89103
Secluded Ave ... 89110
Secluded Brook Ct ... 89149
Seclusion Glen Ave ... 89123
Secret Ave ... 89131
Secret Garden St ... 89145
Secret Harbor Ct ... 89128
Secret Island Dr ... 89139
Secret London Ave ... 89178
Secret Rock St ... 89122
Secret Shore Dr ... 89128
Secret Valley St ... 89139
Secretariat Ln ... 89123
Seda Ct ... 89149
Sedalia St ... 89139
Sedgewick Ct ... 89122
Sedimentary St ... 89122
Sedona Creek Cir ... 89128
Sedona Flats St ... 89131
Sedona Hills Ct ... 89147
Sedona Morning Dr ... 89128
Sedona Paseo Ln ... 89128
Sedona Path Way ... 89128
Sedona Shrine Ave ... 89148
Sedona Sunrise Dr ... 89128
Sedona Sunset Dr ... 89128
Sedora Way ... 89156
Sedran Pl ... 89145
Sedro St ... 89144
Sedwick Dr ... 89129
Seedling Way ... 89115
Sego Dr ... 89121
Sego Glen Cir ... 89121
Segolilly Cir ... 89130
Segovia Ter ... 89121
Segura Dr ... 89103
Selby Ct ... 89147
Seldom Scene Ct ... 89148
Selfridge St ... 89145
Selkirk Cir ... 89108
Selleck Ln ... 89120
Semillon St ... 89148
Seminole Cir ... 89169
Sendero Ave ... 89178
Seneca Cir, Dr & Ln ... 89169
Seneca Falls Ct ... 89129
Seneca Shale Ct ... 89139
Seneca Springs St ... 89130
Sentinel Bridge St ... 89130
Sentinel Point Ct ... 89135
Senton Ave ... 89108
Sentry Palm Ct ... 89122
September Flower St ... 89183
September Star Ave ... 89123
Sepulveda Blvd ... 89118
Sequin Dr ... 89130
Sequoia Ave
  3000-3098 ... 89101
  3100-3199 ... 89101
  3600-3999 ... 89110
Sequoia Canyon Pl ... 89148
Sequoia Grove Ave ... 89149
Sequoia Park Ave ... 89139
Sequoia Springs Dr ... 89147
Sequoia Tree Ave ... 89139
Serafina St ... 89102
Serape Cir ... 89169
Serena Veneda Ln ... 89138
Serenada Ave ... 89169
Serenade Pointe Ave ... 89144
Serendipity Ct ... 89183
E Serene Ave ... 89123
W Serene Ave
  2401-2697 ... 89123
  2699-2799 ... 89123
  3100-5500 ... 89139
  5502-6798 ... 89139
  7000-9998 ... 89178
  10300-10399 ... 89161
Serene Dr
  3200-3300 ... 89108
  3302-3398 ... 89108
  4800-4898 ... 89130
  6001-6199 ... 89130
Serene Isle Ct ... 89113
Serene Ranch Ct ... 89139
Serene Star Way ... 89149
Serenidad Dr ... 89123
Serenity Brook Dr ... 89149
Serona Heights Ct ... 89178
Serpentina Ave ... 89123
Serrano Ct ... 89128
Service Ct ... 89122
Sesame Dr ... 89142
Sespe St ... 89108
Sesto Ct ... 89141
Sethfield Pl ... 89145
Seton Hall Ct ... 89110
Setting Sun St ... 89117
Settler St ... 89103
Settlers Bay Ln ... 89134
Settlers Inn Ct ... 89178
Settlers Pointe Ct ... 89148
Settlers Ridge Ln ... 89145
Settlers Run Ave ... 89166
Seven Dwarfs Rd ... 89124
Seventh Heaven Ln ... 89115
Severance Ln ... 89131
Severence Ln
  6400-7198 ... 89131
  7200-7399 ... 89131
  9701-9799 ... 89149
Severiano Way ... 89129
Severn Valley St ... 89139
Seville St ... 89121
Seward St ... 89128
Sewards Bluff Ave ... 89129
Seychelles Ct ... 89129
Shackleton Dr ... 89134
Shad Bush Ave ... 89149
Shaded Arbors St ... 89139
Shadow Ln
  1-1099 ... 89106
  1100-1299 ... 89102
Shadow Bend Dr ... 89135
Shadow Bluff Ave ... 89120
Shadow Boxer Ct ... 89142
Shadow Canyon Ct ... 89141
Shadow Cove Ave ... 89139
Shadow Creek Cir ... 89117
Shadow Crest Dr ... 89119
Shadow Dancer St ... 89128
Shadow Dreams St ... 89130
Shadow Estates Way ... 89113
Shadow Fern Ave ... 89131
Shadow Glen Ln ... 89108
Shadow Grove Ave ... 89148
Shadow Haven Ln ... 89183
Shadow Hill Dr ... 89120
Shadow Hills Dr ... 89141
Shadow Mist Ct ... 89148
Shadow Mountain Pl ... 89108
Shadow Nook Ct ... 89144
Shadow Palm Ct ... 89148
Shadow Peak St ... 89129
Shadow Pines St ... 89123
Shadow Pool Ct ... 89123
Shadow River St ... 89148
Shadow Rock Dr ... 89117
Shadow Run Ln ... 89117
Shadow Valley St ... 89148
Shadow View St ... 89148
Shadow Wood Ave ... 89121
Shadowgate Ct ... 89148
Shadowland Ave ... 89144
Shadowleaf Ct ... 89117
Shadowridge Ave ... 89120
Shadowvale Dr ... 89147
Shadwell St ... 89178
Shady Cir ... 89124
Shady Ct ... 89145
Shady Acre St ... 89148
Shady Bay St ... 89130
Shady Breeze Ct ... 89113
Shady Creek Dr ... 89108
Shady Elm St ... 89135
Shady Glade Ct ... 89148
Shady Glen Ave ... 89131
Shady Grove Ln ... 89130
Shady Hill Ave ... 89106
Shady Lady Ct ... 89131
Shady Oak Dr ... 89115
Shady Peak Way ... 89123
Shady Pines Dr
  8400-8499 ... 89131
  8500-8899 ... 89143
Shady Pond Way ... 89117
Shady Rim Ct ... 89131
Shady Rock St ... 89131
Shady Shores Cir ... 89128
Shady Springs St ... 89131
Shady Timber St ... 89129
Shady Valley Ct ... 89130
Shady Vista Dr ... 89134
Shadybrook Ln ... 89107
Shadycrest Ct ... 89148
Shadymill Ave ... 89148
Shadywood Dr ... 89146
Shagbark Ln ... 89156
Shake Ct ... 89122
Shakespeare Rd ... 89108
Shale St ... 89123
Shale Valley St ... 89123
Shalimar Ave ... 89115
Shalimar Pointe Ct ... 89131
Shallot Ct ... 89183
Shallow Brook Cir ... 89117
Shallow Brush Ave ... 89141
Shallow Creek Ct ... 89108
Shallow Glen Ct ... 89129
Shallow Point Cir ... 89117
Shallow Pond Dr ... 89117
Shallow River Ct ... 89117
Shallow Springs St ... 89130
Shallowford Ave ... 89131
Shamrock Ave ... 89120
Shamrock Lake Ave ... 89141
Shamu Ct ... 89147
Shanad Rd ... 89146
Shanagolden St ... 89129
Shander Ct ... 89123
Shandin Hills Way ... 89149
Shaner Ln ... 89156
Shangri La Ave ... 89147
Shanna Trellis Ave ... 89144
Shannon Christine Dr ... 89104
Shannon River Dr ... 89117
Shark Tank Ct ... 89128
Sharon Rd ... 89106
Sharon Lan Cir ... 89129
Sharon Marie Ct ... 89118
Sharp Horn Ct ... 89149
Sharp Ridge Ave ... 89149
Sharp Rock Ct ... 89139
Sharpei Ct ... 89131
Sharpsburg Ave ... 89141
Shasta Cir ... 89103
Shasta Lake Way ... 89118
Shasta Ridge Ct ... 89135
Shatz St
  1601-2197 ... 89156
  2199-2300 ... 89156
  2302-2598 ... 89156
  6300-6399 ... 89115
S Shaumber Rd ... 89161
Shaver Loop ... 89115
Shaw Cir ... 89117
Shawn Reynolds Ct ... 89129
Shawnee Ave, Ln & Pl ... 89107
Shawnee Mission Ave ... 89178
Shawnee Ridge St ... 89129
Shawnee Springs Ct ... 89139
Shay Mountain Pl ... 89149
Shea Stadium Ave ... 89139
Shear Cliffs Ct ... 89123
Sheared Cliff Ln ... 89149
Sheep Canyon St ... 89122
Sheep Gulch Way ... 89178
Sheep Ranch Ct ... 89143
Sheepshead Bay Ave ... 89166
Sheffield Dr ... 89108
Sheffield Abbot Ct ... 89138
Sheffield Garden Ave ... 89148
Sheila Ave ... 89108
E Shelbourne Ave ... 89123
W Shelbourne Ave
  4500-4698 ... 89139
  4700-5899 ... 89139
  7000-7098 ... 89113
  7100-7500 ... 89113
  7502-8098 ... 89113
Shelby Gene Ct ... 89139
Shell Beach Ct ... 89117
Shellfish Ct ... 89117
Shellmont Ct ... 89148
Shellstone Ave ... 89117
Shelly Rd ... 89123
Shelome Ct ... 89121
Shelter Ln ... 89103
Shelter Cove Ct ... 89117
Shelter Creek Ave ... 89110
Shelter Hill Ct ... 89129
Shelter Island Way ... 89145
Sheltered Valley Dr ... 89128
Sheltering Pines St ... 89115
Shelton Dr ... 89108
Shemtove Ct ... 89121
Shenandoah Ave ... 89156
Shenandoah Springs
Ave ... 89131
Shenley Ct ... 89117
Sheppard Cir ... 89122
Sheppard Dr
  4100-4299 ... 89121
  4500-4899 ... 89122
Sheri Cir ... 89101
Sheri Lyn Ct ... 89121
Sheridan St ... 89102
Sherman Pl ... 89102
Sherman Oaks Ave ... 89129
Sherman Peak Ln ... 89110
Shermer Ct ... 89120
Sherrill Ave & Cir ... 89110
Sherwin Ln ... 89156
Sherwood St ... 89109
Sherwood Park Dr ... 89131
Shetland Rd ... 89107
Shetland Pony St ... 89122
Shewsbury Ave ... 89178
Shifting Breeze Ave ... 89129
Shifting Sands Dr ... 89108
Shifting Winds St ... 89117
Shiloah Dr ... 89110
Shiloh Heights St ... 89178
Shiloh School Ln ... 89129
Shimmering Falls Ct ... 89149
Shimmering Plains St ... 89129
Shingle Beach St ... 89166
Shining Feather Ln ... 89134
Shining Light Ave ... 89139
Shining Moon Ct ... 89131
Shining Sand Ave ... 89142
Shining Star Ln ... 89115
Shiny Bangle Ct ... 89139
Shiny Skies Dr ... 89129
Shinyleaf Cir ... 89142
Shipboard Ct ... 89117
Shipmate Dr ... 89117
Shire Ct ... 89131
Shire Hall St ... 89178
Shirebrook Dr ... 89115
Shirehampton Dr ... 89178
Shirewick Dr ... 89117
Shirley St ... 89119
Shirleyann Ln ... 89128
Shoal Creek Cir ... 89113
Shoalhaven Dr ... 89134
Shockley Cir ... 89115
Shodall Cir ... 89120
Shoen Ave ... 89110
Shogun Ct ... 89128
Shoko Bay Ct ... 89130
Shooting Star St ... 89107
Shore Ln ... 89145
Shore Breeze Dr ... 89128
Shore Haven Dr ... 89128
Shore Pine Ave ... 89129
Shorecliff Dr ... 89134
Shorecrest Dr ... 89128
Shoreham St ... 89117
Shoreheight St ... 89117
Shoreline Dr ... 89117
Shoreline Ridge Ct ... 89166
Short Horse Ct ... 89147
Short Pine Dr ... 89108
Short Putt Dr ... 89134
Short Ruff Way ... 89148
Shortleaf St ... 89119
Showcase Dr ... 89134
Showell Ave ... 89117
Showy Ct ... 89149
Shreve Ave ... 89156
Shropshire St ... 89178
Shrubbery Ln ... 89110
Shumard Oak Ct ... 89149
Shuttle Ct ... 89103
Shy Dandelion St ... 89106
Siamese Ct ... 89166
Sibley Ave ... 89131
Siboney Dr ... 89123
Siboney Villa Cir ... 89121
Siciliano St ... 89138
Sicily Heights Ct ... 89141
Sickle Ln ... 89128
Siddall Ave ... 89183
Sidebrook Ct ... 89129
Sidehill Way ... 89110
Sidewinder Ln ... 89121
Sidewinder Ridge Ave ... 89139
Sidlaw Hills Ct ... 89141
Sidonia Ave ... 89102
Siegfried St ... 89147
Siena Cir ... 89128
Siena Ancora Ln ... 89141
Siena Hills Ln ... 89144
Siena Mist Ave ... 89138
Siena Monte Ave ... 89135
Sienna Canyon St ... 89123
Sienna Hollow Ct ... 89143
Sienna Mesa Dr ... 89117
Sienna Peak Ct ... 89144
Sienna Ridge Dr ... 89117
Sienna Skies Ct ... 89131
Sienna Valley Ave ... 89149
Sienna Vista Dr ... 89117
Sierra Trl ... 89146
Sierra Bello Ave ... 89106
Sierra Blue Ct ... 89141
Sierra Bonita Ct ... 89149
Sierra Brook Ct ... 89149
Sierra Canyon Way ... 89147
Sierra Cascade Ct ... 89117
Sierra Cima Ln ... 89128
Sierra Creek Ln ... 89156
Sierra Diablo Ave ... 89130
Sierra Heights Dr ... 89134
Sierra Hills Way ... 89128
Sierra Kantor St ... 89131
Sierra Knolls Ct ... 89139
Sierra Largo Dr ... 89128
Sierra Linda Dr ... 89147
Sierra Luna Ave ... 89106
Sierra Madre Dr ... 89102
Sierra Medina Ave ... 89139
Sierra Mesa Ave ... 89117
Sierra Mist Ave ... 89139
Sierra Morena St ... 89144
Sierra Oaks Ln ... 89134
Sierra Paseo Ln ... 89128
Sierra Patricia Ave ... 89121
Sierra Pines Ct ... 89130
Sierra Ridge Dr ... 89156
Sierra Rim Dr ... 89131
Sierra Sage St ... 89134
Sierra Seco Ave ... 89106
Sierra Stone Ln ... 89119
Sierra Summit Ave ... 89134
Sierra Sunrise St ... 89156
Sierra Valley Way ... 89128
Sierra Vista Dr ... 89169
Siesta Ave
  2100-2299 ... 89169
  2400-2699 ... 89121
Siesta Grande Ave ... 89129
Siesta Key St ... 89141
Signal Dr ... 89130
Signal Peak St ... 89138
Signal Terrace Dr ... 89134
Signet Ct ... 89142
Sigri St ... 89166
Siki Ct ... 89101
Silandro Dr ... 89117
Silbert Ln ... 89104
Silbury Hill Ct ... 89148
Silent Brook Ct ... 89149
Silent Falls St ... 89123
Silent Hawk Ln ... 89138
Silent Hill Dr ... 89147
Silent Hope Ave ... 89131
Silent Oak Ct ... 89149
Silent Pine Ave ... 89156
Silent Sage Dr ... 89149
Silent Sky Ave ... 89141
Silent Sun Ave ... 89142
Silent Valley Ave ... 89139
Silent Vista Way ... 89122
Silent Water Way ... 89149
Silent Willow Ave ... 89131
Silenzio St ... 89135
Silhouette Ave ... 89142
Silica Chalk Ave ... 89115
Silk Bargain St ... 89131
Silk Bonnet Ct ... 89143
Silk Fire St ... 89131
Silk Oak Ct ... 89148
Silk Tassel Dr ... 89117
Silk Threads Ave ... 89149
Silken Crests Ct ... 89149
Silkwood Ct ... 89134
Silurian St ... 89139
Silvagni Dr ... 89117
Silvaner Ct ... 89123
Silver Ave ... 89102
Silver Arrow Ct ... 89117
Silver Bangle Dr ... 89122

Silver Baron Rd 89179
Silver Bay St 89147
Silver Bear Way 89118
Silver Belle St 89149
Silver Bend Ave 89120
Silver Birch Ln 89104
Silver Bluff Ct 89134
Silver Bough Ct 89183
Silver Bow Dr 89115
Silver Breeze Ave 89183
Silver Brook St 89129
Silver Buckle Ct 89183
Silver Cactus Ct 89183
Silver Castle St 89144
Silver Catfish St 89131
Silver Chaps Ct 89183
Silver Charm Ct 89131
Silver Chimes Ct 89183
Silver Chisel Ave 89130
Silver Cholla Ct 89183
Silver City Dr 89123
Silver Cliff St 89178
Silver Coast St 89139
Silver Creek Ave 89183
Silver Dawn Ln 89118
Silver Desert Ave 89148
Silver Dew St 89183
Silver Dollar Ave 89102
Silver Dusk Ct 89183
Silver Eagle Ave 89122
Silver Falls Ave 89123
Silver Frost St 89123
Silver Glen Ave 89123
Silver Grove St 89144
Silver Harvest Ct 89183
Silver Hawk Ave 89123
Silver Heights St 89130
Silver Hills Way 89123
Silver King Dr 89129
Silver Knoll Ave 89123
Silver Lace Ln 89135
Silver Lake Dr 89108
Silver Lasso St 89183
Silver Leaf Way 89147
Silver Legacy Dr 89122
Silver Magic Ct 89129
Silver Mallard Ave 89131
Silver Meadow Ct 89117
Silver Mesa Cir & Way 89169
Silver Mine St 89123
Silver Mountain Ct 89134
Silver Oaks St 89117
Silver Palm Ave 89117
Silver Peak St 89103
Silver Pebble St 89183
Silver Penny Ave 89108
Silver Perch Ave 89123
Silver Pine Dr 89108
Silver Plateau Ave 89128
Silver Plume Ct 89123
Silver Point Ave 89123
Silver Prairie Ct 89144
Silver Prospect Dr 89108
Silver Pyramid Ct 89144
Silver Rain Ave 89123
Silver Ribbon Ct 89139
Silver Ridge Dr 89128
Silver Ridge Peak St 89166
Silver River St 89130
Silver Rock Ave 89115
Silver Rose Ln 89134
Silver Saber Ct 89129
Silver Saddle St 89169
Silver Sage Cir 89131
Silver Shadow Dr 89108
Silver Sierra St 89128
Silver Sky Dr 89145
Silver Spirit St 89131
Silver Spoon Dr 89108
Silver Spruce Dr 89156
Silver Spur Cir 89119
Silver State Ave 89122
Silver Stone Way 89123
Silver Streak St 89131
Silver Strike Ct 89129
Silver Tip Way 89124
Silver Trout St 89178
Silver Valley St 89149
Silver Wells Rd 89149
Silver Whisper Ave 89183
Silverado Dr 89120
Silverado Pines Ave 89123
E Silverado Ranch Blvd 89183
W Silverado Ranch Blvd 89139
Silverado Sage Ave 89115
Silverdale Ave 89113
Silvered Bark Dr 89135
Silverfield Dr 89103
Silverheart Ave 89142
Silverhorn Ct 89115
Silverman Way 89106
Silvermist Ct 89122
Silverstone Ranch Dr 89131
Silverstream Ave 89107
Silverthorne Ct 89123
Silverton Dr 89134
Silvery Ave 89108
Silvestri Ln 89120
Simmons St 89106
Simone Ave 89147
Simple Life Ave 89148
Simple Promise Ct 89130
Simpson Dr 89122
Simsbury Cir 89129
Sinaloa Ct 89103
Sinatra Sands Ct 89130
Sincerity Ct 89129
Sinclair St 89121
Sindelar Ct 89128
Sinew Ct 89129
Sinfold Park St 89148
Sing Song Way 89106
Singapore Ct 89110
Singing Dunes Ln 89145
Singing Hills Dr 89130
Singing Tree St 89123
Singing View Ct 89129
Singing Wind Pl 89134
Singingwood Ln 89107
Single Leaf Cir 89146
Single Pine Dr 89128
Single Tree Dr 89123
Sioux Way 89169
Sipple St 89141
Sir Arthur Dr 89110
Sir Bret Ct 89104
Sir David Way 89110
Sir Edward Dr 89110
Sir George Dr 89110
Sir James Way 89110
Sir James Bridge Way 89145
Sir Jeffery Cir & St 89110
Sir Lancelot Cir 89108
Sir Monahan St 89119
Sir Payne Ct 89104
Sir Phillip Ct & St 89110
N & S Sir Richard Cir, Ct & Dr 89110
Sir Richard East Dr 89110
Sir Thomas Dr 89110
Sir Turner Dr 89124
Sir William Way 89110
Sirens Song Ct 89139
Sirius Ave 89102
Sirnoble St 89110
Sirocco Ct 89117
Sisk Rd 89131
Sisk St 89108
Sistine St 89144
Sitka Ln 89122
Sitka Trl 89103
Sixshooter Dr 89119
Sixto St 89115
Ski Chalet Pl 89124
Ski Incline Way 89147
Ski Slope Cir 89117
Ski Trail Cir & Rd 89124
Skiers Chalet Ct 89178
Skiff Ln 89128
Skipper Ct 89117
Skipping Stone Ln 89123
Skipton Dr 89134
Skipworth Dr 89107
Skoglund Cir 89108
Skokie Ct 89130
Sky Birch Ct 89147
Sky Canyon Ct 89128
Sky Country Ln 89117
Sky Flower Ct 89123
Sky Gate St 89178
Sky Hollow Dr 89123
Sky Meadows Ave 89134
Sky Of Red Dr 89128
Sky Parlor Rd 89178
Sky Pointe Dr
  5700-5800 89130
  5802-6098 89130
  6400-7099 89131
Sky Ridge Rd 89128
Sky River Ct 89118
Sky Sands St 89147
Skybird Ct 89135
Skybolt St 89115
Skycrest Dr 89123
Skyhawk Canyon St 89147
Skyland Dr 89121
Skylark Pl 89145
Skylight Ln 89123
Skyline Dr 89117
Skyline Peak Ct 89148
Skyline View Ct 89113
Skytop Ledge Ave 89178
Skytrail Ave 89145
Skyview Dr 89104
Skywalker Ave 89120
Skywall Ct 89123
Skyward Ct 89145
Skywood Way 89142
Slate Dr 89134
Slate Harbor Cir 89128
Slate Run Ave 89139
Slate Springs Ct 89122
Slayton Dr 89107
Sleek Ave 89129
Sleeping Cat St 89122
Sleeping Lily Dr 89178
Sleeping Pine St 89143
Sleeping Sun Ct 89129
Sleeping Tree St 89123
Sleepy Ct 89106
Sleepy Canyon Ave 89178
Sleepy Creek Ct 89144
Sleepy Fawn Dr 89142
Sleepy Heaven Pl 89138
Sleepy Hollow Way 89102
Sleepy Meadow Ct 89148
Sleepy Mist Ct 89141
Sleepy Pine St 89130
Sleepy River Ave 89144
Sleepy Spruce St 89113
Sleetridge Dr 89123
Slendermint Ct 89149
Slice Dr 89142
Slide Rock Ave 89113
Sliding Rock St 89149
Sligo St 89130
Slip Point Ave 89147
Slippery Rock Way 89123
Slipstream St 89139
N Sloan Ln
  400-1399 89110
  2201-2399 89156
  4801-4897 89115
  4899-5599 89115
S Sloan Ln 89142
Sloop Dr 89128
Slope Ridge St 89131
Sloping Green Dr 89148
Sloping Hill Ave 89129
Slow Wind St 89134
Sluman Ct 89128
Slumpstone Way 89110
Sly Fox Ct 89130
Small Point Dr 89108
Smart Ct 89149
Smarty Jones Ave 89131
Smiley Rd 89115
Smith Cir 89121
Smith St 89108
Smithsonian Way 89130
Smoke Ranch Rd
  4801-4897 89108
  4899-6499 89108
  6501-6699 89108
  6900-7599 89128
Smoke Signal Ave 89118
Smoke Tree Ave 89108
Smoke Tree Ln 89120
Smokemont Ct 89129
Smokerise Ct 89131
Smokestone Ct 89110
Smokewood Rd 89135
Smokey Dr 89134
Smokey Glen Cir 89110
Smokey Pine Way 89108
Smokey Ridge Ct 89131
Smoking Gun Ct 89129
Smoking Jacket Pl 89166
Smooth Plain Ave 89139
Smugglers Beach Ct 89178
Snake Ln 89118
Snake Eyes St 89122
Snake River Ave 89130
Snead Dr 89107
Snoring Ct 89110
Snorkel Cir 89108
Snow Trl 89134
Snow Angel St 89139
Snow Bank St 89183
Snow Cap Cir 89117
Snow Cloud Ct 89135
Snow Creek Ave 89135
Snow Crest Pl 89134
Snow Drop St 89113
Snow Flat Ct 89134
Snow Flower Ave 89147
Snow Lake St 89179
Snow Mountain St 89144
Snow Petal Ct 89129
Snow Pond Ave 89183
Snow Shoe Way 89128
Snow Spring Ln 89134
Snow White St 89124
Snowberry Ct 89123
Snowbird Ct 89128
Snowden Ln 89128
Snowdon Flat Ct 89129
Snowflake Ln 89115
Snowmass Dr 89128
Snowpoint Ct 89130
Snowtrack Ave 89149
Snowy Canyon Ct 89183
Snowy Pines St 89147
Snug Harbor St 89110
Snugglers Ct 89110
Snughaven Ct 89108
Snyder Ave 89134
Soaring Ct 89134
Soaring Bird Ct 89135
Soaring Brook St 89131
Soaring Gulls Dr
  3101-3199 89128
  3200-3298 89129
Soaring Hawk Ct 89113
Soaring High St 89131
Soaring Hills Ct 89110
Soaring Light St 89131
Soaring Owl Ave 89129
Soaring Palm St 89179
Soaring Springs Ave 89131
Sobb Ave 89118
Socorro Dr 89108
Soda Ash Ave 89110
Soda Canyon St 89139
Soda Springs Dr 89115
Sofferto Ave 89135
Soft Breezes Dr 89128
Soft Horizon Way 89135
Soft Mist Ct 89131
Soft Sand Dr 89117
Soft Springs Ave 89130
Soft Sun Cir 89128
Soggy Ruff Way 89148
Sol Duc St 89139
Sol Vista Ave 89122
Solandra St 89147
Solar Ave
  5300-7399 89131
  9600-9700 89149
  9702-9898 89149
Solar Eclipse Dr 89115
Solar Hawk Ave 89129
Solaris St 89141
Solaron Ave 89156
Soldela Dr 89156
Soldier Creek Ct 89106
Sole Addiction Ave 89183
Soledad Canyon St 89131
Soledad Summit Ave 89139
Solicito St 89110
Solid Horn Ct 89149
Solid Lime St 89183
Solidago Ave 89183
Solimar Ln 89130
Solitary Ave 89110
Solitude Rd 89108
Solitude Canyon Ave 89149
Solitude Summit St 89143
Solomon Spring Way 89122
Soloshine St 89123
Solstice Ave 89123
Solteros St 89103
Solvang Dr 89103
Solvang Mill Dr 89135
Sombra Way 89113
Sombrero Cir & Dr 89169
Sombria Ridge Ave 89139
Somera Way 89113
Somerdale Ct 89148
Somerhill Point Way 89139
Somerset Dr 89120
Somervell Ranch St 89131
Sonador St 89108
Sonata Dr 89121
Sondrio Dr 89134
Soneto Ln 89117
Soneto Creek Ct 89129
Songlight Ct 89117
Songsparrow Ct 89135
Songwood Ct 89129
Sonia Dr 89107
Sonia Rose Ln 89122
Sonnet Ct 89147
Sonoma Cir 89107
Sonoma Creek Ct 89144
Sonoma Station Ave 89139
Sonoma Sunset Ct 89130
Sonoma Valley St 89144
Sonoma View Ct 89139
Sonora St 89102
Sonora Bend Ave 89148
Sonora Canyon Ct 89142
Sonora Hill Ct 89138
Sonora View St 89149
Sonterra Cir 89117
Soothing Surf Dr 89147
Sopra Ct 89135
Soprano Ln 89107
Sorenson Ln 89156
Soria Way 89121
Sorrel St
  2500-2598 89146
  2600-3100 89146
  3102-3198 89146
  5300-6199 89118
  8100-8299 89139
Sorrento St & Way 89121
Sosa Creek Ave 89149
Soso St 89145
Sospel Pl 89141
Sound Barrier St 89110
Sound View Ave 89147
Sour Gum Ct 89131
Sourwood Ave 89135
Southern Comfort Ave 89131
Southern Highlands Pkwy 89141
Southern Hills Ln 89113
Southern Light Dr 89115
Southern Manor Dr 89130
Southern Pine Way 89146
Southern Roundup Ct 89113
Southern Trails Ct 89113
Southerton St 89178
Southpark Ct 89147
Southridge Ave 89121
Souvenir Ln 89118
Souza Dr 89146
Sovereign Way 89130
Spaatz Loop 89115
Spalding Dr 89134
Spangle Dr 89108
Spanish Ct 89108
Spanish Dr 89110
Spanish Armada Rd 89123
Spanish Barb St 89122
Spanish Bay Dr 89113
Spanish Butterfly St 89108
Spanish Garden Ct 89110
Spanish Gate Dr 89113
Spanish Heights Dr 89148
Spanish Hills Dr 89148
Spanish Lake Dr 89113
Spanish Meadows Ave 89131
Spanish Moss Ave 89108
Spanish Mountain Dr 89148
Spanish Mustang Ct 89122
Spanish Oaks Dr 89102
Spanish Peak Ave 89128
Spanish Ridge Ave 89148
Spanish Sky Ave 89183
Spanish Star Ct 89110
Spanish Steps Ln 89117
Spanish Sun Ln 89128
Spanish Trail Ln 89113
Spanish Valor Rd 89135
Spanish View Ln 89110
Spanish Vista Ln 89148
Spanish Winds Ct 89141
Sparkle Ave 89145
Sparkle Ray Ave 89123
Sparklewood Ct 89129
Sparkling Dr 89130
Sparkling Amber Ct 89144
Sparkling Creek Ave 89143
Sparkling Sea St 89117
Sparkling Sky Ave 89130
Sparkling Star St 89123
Sparkling Vine Ave 89131
Sparkling Waters Ave 89129
Sparkling Wing Ct 89148
Sparks Ave 89142
Sparks Summit Ln 89166
Sparky Dr 89102
Sparrow Ln 89103
Sparrow Hawk Ct 89134
Sparrow Ridge Ave 89117
Sparrow Rock St 89129
Sparrow Springs Ct 89129
Sparrowgate Ave 89131
Spartan View Ct 89123
Spartanburg St 89149
Sparwood Dr 89147
Speaking Rock Ave 89131
Spearfish Ave 89145
Spearfish Lake Ct 89148
Spearmint Way 89142
Special Ct 89130
Spectacle Ln 89128
Spectacle Reef Ave 89147
Spectacular Bid St 89113
Spectrum Blvd 89101
Speedway Blvd 89115
Speedwell Cavern St 89139
Spellman Ct 89123
Spencer St
  200-499 89101
  2000-2198 89104
  3400-3600 89169
  3602-3698 89169
  3700-6899 89119
  7300-8900 89123
  8902-8998 89123
  9900-10098 89183
  10100-10200 89183
  10202-10298 89183
Spencer Butte Ct 89113
Spencer Canyon St 89166
Spessard Holland Ct 89131
Sphere Dr 89115
Sphinx Way 89115
Spice Island Ct 89143
Spice Sky Dr 89128
Spice Tree St 89183
Spiceberry Dr 89135
Spiced Strawberry St 89131
Spicenut Dr 89135
Spicewood Cir 89130
Spider Ct 89108
Spider Cactus Ct 89106
Spider Creek Ct 89149
Spider Rock Ave 89135
Spiderlily Ct 89149
Spielburg St 89118
Spiers Ave 89183
Spindle Berry St 89131
Spindleridge Cir 89147
Spindrift Ct 89156
Spindrift Cove St 89139
Spindrift Foam Ave 89139
Spindrift Tide Ct 89139
Spinnaker Cove Dr 89128
Spinnaker Creek Ave 89148
Spinnaker Point Ave 89110
Spinnaker Reach Ave 89130
Spinning Wheel Ave 89143
Spiny Leaf Way 89148
Spire Canyon Rd 89128
Spirit Canyon Ave 89149
Spirit Vale Ave 89117
Spiritual Way 89115
Spitfire St 89115
Spitze Dr 89103
Splashing Falls Dr 89131
Splashing River Ct 89131
Splashing Rock Dr 89131
Splendid Leaf Ct 89178
Splendido Dr 89117
Splendor Ridge Ave 89135
Splendor Sky Ave 89148
Splendor View Dr 89183
Spokane Dr 89121
Spoleto Ave 89141
Sponseller St 89110
Spoon Cir 89142
Spoon River Ct 89139
Spoonbill Ridge Pl 89143
Spooner Lake Cir 89147
Sportsman Dr 89107
Spotless Ct 89149
Spotted Fawn Ct 89131
Spotted Sandpiper St 89122
Spotted Tail Ave 89149
Spotted Wolf Ave 89123
E Spring Ct 89115
W Spring Ct 89115
Spring Rd 89108
Spring Arts Ave 89129
Spring Beauty Ave 89131
Spring Blossom Ct 89118
Spring Blush Ave 89148
Spring Creek Ave 89110
Spring Crest Ln 89129
Spring Day Ct 89147
Spring Flower Ave 89117
Spring Garden Ct 89134
Spring Gate Ln
  1600-1614 89134
  1611-1611 89137
  1616-2098 89134
  1901-2099 89134
Spring Grove Dr 89108
Spring Harvest Dr 89142
Spring Hollow Dr 89148
Spring Leaf Dr 89147
Spring Meadow Dr 89103
Spring Mountain Rd
  3101-3197 89102
  3199-4899 89102

4900-6200 89146
6202-6898 89146
6901-6997 89117
6999-9099 89117
9101-10199 89117
Spring Oak St 89120
Spring Peeper Ave 89148
Spring Rain Rd 89142
Spring Ranch Pkwy 89118
Spring River Ave 89123
Spring Rose St 89134
Spring Shadow Rd 89129
Spring Shower Dr 89147
Spring Star Ct 89148
Spring Summit Ln 89134
Spring Sunset Ct 89149
Spring Vistas Dr 89147
Spring Water Dr 89134
Spring Willow Ct 89147
Springacre Dr 89135
Springbrook Dr 89134
Springbuck Ct 89129
Springbud Dr 89147
Springdale Ave & Ct 89121
Springer Spaniel Ave 89131
Springhill Ave 89121
Springland St 89146
Springridge Dr 89134
Springside St 89178
Springstead St 89134
Springstone St 89142
Springview Dr 89146
Springwood St 89121
Sproul Ct 89145
Spruce Ave 89106
Spruce Cir 89106
Spruce Rd 89124
Spruce Bay Ave 89178
Spruce Bough St 89183
Spruce Canyon St 89144
Spruce Creek Dr 89135
Spruce Fern Ln 89115
Spruce Grove St 89147
Spruce Harbor Ct 89122
Spruce Hill Ct 89148
Spruce Lake Cir 89117
Spruce Meadows Ave 89131
Spruce Mountain Way 89134
Spruce Pine Ct 89123
Spruce Ridge Ln 89156
Spruce Run Ct 89128
Sprucedale Ave 89144
Spruceview Ct 89147
Sprucewood St 89147
Spry Ave 89183
Spumante Ave 89148
Spunsilk Cir 89108
Spur Ct 89145
Spur Creek Ave 89178
Spur Heel Ct 89148
Spurge Laurel St 89183
Spurs Ct 89135
Spyglass Ln 89107
Spyglass Hill Dr 89142
Spyrun Dr 89134
Squall Ct 89129
Square Dance Pl 89178
Square Knot Ave 89143
Squaw Creek Ct 89120
Squaw Mountain Dr 89130
Squaw Springs Ln 89131
Squaw Valley Ave 89128
Squilchuck Ct 89139
Squire St 89135
Squire Boone Ave 89131
Squires St 89146
Squirrel St 89122
Squirrels Nest St 89131
Stable Run Ave 89113
Stacey Ave 89108
Stacey Lyn Dr 89117
Stacked Chips Rd 89122
Stadium Ave 89120
Stadler Ct 89134
Staff Ln 89178
Stafford Dr 89115
Stafford Springs Dr 89134
Staffordshire Cir 89110
Stag Hollow Ct 89139
Staghorn Pass Ave 89183
Stainglass Ln 89110
Stallings St 89148
Stallion Ave 89108
Stampa Ave 89146
Stampede Canyon Ct 89147
Stan Crest Dr 89134
Stanberry Ave 89135
Standard Ave 89129
Standing Bluff Way 89130
Standing Rock Pl 89130
Standing Stone St 89148
Standing Timber Way 89113
Stanford St 89107
Stange Ave 89129
Stanley Ave
4701-4849 89115
4851-5099 89115
5200-5298 89156
Stanley Cup Dr 89110
Stanley Frederick St 89166
Stanley Park Ave 89110
Stanton Heights Ct 89178
Stanwick Ave 89138
Stapleton Ave 89145
Star Cactus Ave 89131
Star Canyon Way 89123
Star Cluster Cir 89145
Star Creek Bay Ln 89115
Star Glow Ct 89118
Star Jasmine Ct 89108
Star Lake Ave 89148
Star Lamb St 89145
Star Lily St 89141
Star Mesa Ct 89144
Star Pine Dr 89144
Star Quest Ave 89144
Star Sapphire Ct 89106
Star Valley Ct 89123
Star View Ct 89118
Star Wind St 89122
Starboard Dr 89117
Starbright Ln 89147
Starbuck Dr 89108
Starburst Dr 89156
Starcrest Dr 89108
Starcross Ln 89147
Stardance Ave 89143
Starfield Ln 89147
Starfinder Ave 89108
Starfire Ct, Ln & Pl 89107
Starfish Ct 89128
Starflower Ct 89107
Stargate St 89108
Stargaze Night Ct 89148
Stargazer Dr 89156
Starks Dr 89107
Starlight Dr 89130
Starlight Canyon Ave 89183
Starlight Evening St 89129
Starlight Express Ave 89131
Starline Meadow Pl 89134
Starling Ct 89147
Starling View Ct 89166
Starling Wing Pl 89143
Starlite Dr 89107
Starmount Dr 89134
E Starr Ave 89183
W Starr Ave 89141
Starridge Way 89142
Starry Beach Ave 89115
Starry Nights Ct 89113
Stars End St 89108
Starshell Bay Ave 89139
Starshell Point Ct 89139
Starship Ln 89147
Starside Dr 89117
Starstruck Ave 89143
Startac Ct 89141
Starter Ave 89156
Starthistle Ln 89135
Starwood Dr 89147
Stassen St 89123
State St 89109
State Hwy 147 89156
State Hwy 160 89161
Stateline Way 89110
Staten Island Ave 89123
Station Creek Cir 89178
Stature Ct 89129
Statz Ct 89101
Stavanger Ln 89147
Steady Breeze Ave 89131
Steamboat Rock Ct 89129
Steamboat Springs Ct 89139
Steamers Ave 89183
Steaming Thunder Ct 89148
Steamship Ct 89130
Steele St 89156
Steeler Dr 89145
Steelhead Ln 89110
Steeltree St 89143
Steep Cliffs Ave 89115
Steeple Ct 89131
Steeple Ridge Dr 89147
Steeplehill Dr 89117
Steinbeck Dr 89115
Steinbrenner Ln 89118
Steinke Ln 89108
Stella Cir 89124
Stella Cadente St 89141
Stella Lake St 89106
Stellar St 89143
Stellar View Ave 89117
Stemrose Way 89122
Step Beach St 89138
Step House Ct 89139
Stephanie St 89122
Stephanie Jean Ct 89149
W Stephen Ave 89149
Stephen Burnet Ct 89102
Steponia Bay St 89141
Steprock Ct 89103
Steptoe St 89122
Sterling Cir 89120
Sterling Cove Dr 89128
Sterling Crest Pl 89135
Sterling Forest Ave 89135
Sterling Harbor Ct 89117
Sterling Heights Dr 89134
Sterling Hill Ave 89148
Sterling Moon Ave 89131
Sterling Peak St 89110
Sterling Ridge Ave 89129
Sterling Rock Ave 89178
Sterling Silver St 89108
Sterling Springs Pkwy 89108
Sterling Thorn Ct 89183
Sterling Valley Ct 89148
Sterlingshire Dr 89146
Stern Dr 89117
Stetson Bluff Ave 89113
Steven Chase Ct 89149
Stevens St
1100-1500 89110
1502-1598 89110
1600-1999 89115
Stevenson Way 89120
Stewart Ave
300-498 89101
500-3000 89101
3002-3398 89101
3700-3798 89110
3800-5100 89110
5102-7098 89110
Stickney Ct 89141
Stiges St 89178
Still Breeze Ave 89130
Still Light St 89142
Stillhouse Ct 89113
Stills Way 89148
Stillwater Ave 89110
Stillwater Bend Ln 89178
Stillwater Bridge St 89142
Stingaree Cir 89110
Stinger Ct 89178
Stingray Ct 89147
Stirrup St 89119
Stivali Ave 89183
Stober Blvd 89103
Stober Ct 89147
Stock St 89178
Stockbridge St 89115
Stockholm Ave 89147
Stockton Ave 89104
Stoddard Ave 89110
Stokes St 89110
Stomping Boots Ave 89118
Stone Dr 89110
Stone Bay Ave 89131
Stone Briar Ct 89144
Stone Cabin Ct 89149
Stone Castle Way 89123
Stone Croft St 89134
Stone Glen Ln 89134
Stone Harbor Ave 89145
Stone Hollow Ave 89156
Stone Lake St 89131
Stone Meadows Ave 89142
Stone Mill Way 89123
Stone Oak Ct 89148
Stone Pine Ct 89134
Stone Tower Ct 89149
Stone Valley Ave 89183
Stone Wall Dr 89123
Stoneborough St 89113
Stonebridge Ln 89108
Stonecliff Way 89123
Stonecott St 89123
Stonefield St 89144
Stonegate Way 89146
Stonehaven Cir & Dr 89108
Stoneheath Ave 89139
Stoneheather Ct 89117
Stonehenge St 89110
Stonehenge Walk Ave 89178
Stonehill Rd 89156
Stonehouse St 89110
Stonestep St 89149
Stonewall Springs Ave 89138
Stonewolf Ct 89148
Stonewood Ct 89107
Stoney Beach Cir & St 89110
Stoney Bluff Ave 89129
Stoney Creek Dr 89117
Stoney Point Dr 89134
Stoney Shore Dr 89128
Stoneybrook Dr 89108
Stonily Ln 89178
Stonington Pl 89108
Stony Ridge Dr 89144
Stonyford Ct 89139
Storici St 89141
Storke Ln 89134
Storkspur Way 89117
Storm Cloud Ave 89129
Storm Mountain St 89130
Storm Peak St 89166
Stormcrest Dr & Ln 89107
Stormson Ct & Dr 89145
Stormy Cir 89119
Stormy Creek Rd 89108
Stormy Falls St 89149
Stormy Hills Dr 89130
Stormy Sky Ave 89110
Stormy Valley Rd 89123
Stormy Weather Ln 89122
Storrie Ct 89103
Story Rock St 89115
Storybook Glen Ct 89139
Storyland St 89139
Stour Ln 89144
Stout Way 89101
Strada Laterina Ct 89135
Strada Mia Ct 89117
Strada Olivero 89117
Straight St 89110
Straight Arrow Dr 89117
Straight Flush Dr 89122
Strait Field Pl 89148
Strand City Ave 89166
Strankman Ave 89131
Strata Ave 89148
Stratford Ave 89121
Stratford Hall Ct 89135
Strathmore Silk Ct 89130
Stratton Ln 89110
Strauss Dr 89146
Straw Hays St 89178
Strawberry Cream Ct 89142
Strawberry Park Dr 89120
Strawberry Spring St 89143
Strawberry Valley Ct 89147
Strawflower Rd 89107
Stray Horse Ave 89113
Strayhorn Ct 89156
Stream Dr 89124
Streamer Cir 89145
Streamside Ave 89129
Stretch Dr 89156
Strike Jumper Ct 89108
Striking Point Ct 89130
Stroh Ln 89178
Strong Dr 89102
Strong Water Ct 89131
Strongbow Dr 89156
Stronghold Ct 89179
Strunk Ln 89115
Strutting Silver Ct 89131
Strutz Ave 89110
Struzzo Ave 89183
Stuckey Ave 89143
Studio St 89115
Stumbling Colt Ct 89131
Sturbridge Cir 89129
Sturgeon Ln 89110
Sturgeon Cape Ave 89179
Stuttgart St 89147
Sublight Ave 89108
Sublime Ave 89130
Sublimity Ave 89131
Suburban Rd 89135
Success Ct 89145
Successful Ct 89149
Sudan Ct 89149
Sudley Ct 89131
Sue Ct 89108
Sueno Ct 89145
Suffolk Ave 89110
Suffolk Hills Ave 89129
Sugar Dr 89147
Sugar Bowl Ct 89128
Sugar City St 89178
Sugar Knoll Ct 89110
Sugar Loaf Ct 89121
Sugar Springs Dr 89110
Sugarberry Ln 89135
Sugarfoot Ave 89107
Sugarhouse Park Ave 89135
Sugarloaf Peak St 89166
Sugarpine Ln 89107
Sugartree Ave 89141
Sugita Ln 89115
Sully Creek Ct 89148
Sulphur Springs Ln 89128
Sultana St 89102
Sumac Ln 89121
Sumac Ridge Ct 89149
Sumatra St 89166
Summa Dr 89135
Summer Air Ave 89179
Summer Ash Ct 89134
Summer Blossom Ct 89134
Summer Blush Ave 89183
Summer Breeze Cir 89108
Summer Cove Ct 89134
Summer Crest Ln 89129
Summer Cypress St 89123
Summer Furnace St 89178
Summer Grove Ave 89117
Summer Harvest Ave 89129
Summer Heights Ln 89110
Summer Holly Way 89156
Summer Home St 89135
Summer Joy St 89113
Summer Lake Dr 89128
Summer Leaf St 89147
Summer Lilac Ct 89123
Summer Mesa Dr 89144
Summer Moon Pl 89129
Summer Oak Ln 89134
Summer Palace Way 89144
Summer Palm Pl 89134
Summer Picnic Ct 89147
Summer Pine Ct 89134
Summer Point St 89134
Summer Quail Ave 89144
Summer Rain Dr 89134
Summer Ridge Dr 89134
Summer River Ave 89144
Summer Solstice St 89131
Summer Splash Ct 89131
Summer Spruce Pl 89134
Summer Squash Ln 89144
Summer Stone Pl 89144
Summer Storm Ct 89144
Summer Sun Dr 89128
Summer Vista Ave 89145
Summer Walk Ave 89183
Summerbell St 89179
Summerdale St 89123
Summerday Ct 89147
Summerfest St 89123
Summerfield Ln 89117
Summerglade Dr 89107
Summerhill Rd 89121
Summerlin Centre Dr 89135
Summers End Ave 89134
Summers Eve Ln 89117
Summers Ranch Ct 89139
Summers Shade St 89147
Summersprings Dr 89129
Summersweet Ct 89123
Summertime Dr 89142
Summerville St 89106
Summit Canyon Dr 89144
Summit Chase St 89156
Summit Cliff St 89129
Summit Gate Ln 89134
Summit Pointe Dr 89117
Summit View Cir 89124
Summitpeak Way 89120
Sun Appello Ave 89122
Sun Briar Ct 89141
Sun Cactus Ct 89106
Sun Canyon Ct 89128
Sun City Blvd 89134
Sun Cliffs St 89134
Sun Cloud Pl 89134
Sun Copper Dr 89117
Sun Cove Cir 89128
Sun Drop Ct 89147
Sun Dusk Ln 89144
Sun Gem Ct 89130
Sun Glory Ct 89130
Sun Glow Ln 89135
Sun Lake Dr 89128
Sun Lemon Ct 89123
Sun Palace Ct 89129
Sun Point Dr 89108
Sun Poppy Ave 89123
Sun Reef Rd 89128
Sun Rhythm St 89129
Sun Ridge Dr 89117
Sun River Cir 89142
Sun Rose Ave 89134
Sun Shimmer Pl 89110
Sun Shores Dr 89128
Sun Stream Ct 89103
Sun Summit Ct 89178
Sun Temple Ave 89139
Sun Terrace Ct 89117
Sun Tree Cir 89110
Sun Valley Cir 89122
Sun Valley Dr
4400-4999 89121
5000-5260 89122
5262-5298 89122
Sun Village Ave 89183
Sun Vista Dr 89104
Sun Wood Dr 89145
Sunair Cir 89110
Sunbeam Dr 89107
Sunbelt Ct 89130
Sunbird Dr 89156
Sunblossom St 89128
Sunblower Ave 89135
Sunblush Ln 89117
Sunbrite Ave 89130
Sunburst Dr 89110
Sunburst Creek Ave 89123
Sunbury Ave 89122
Suncrest Ave 89156
Sundad St 89179
Sundale St 89102
Sundance Ave 89110
Sundance Valley Dr 89178
Sunday River St 89122
Sunderland Ct 89178
Sundial Dr 89134
Sundial Crest Ct 89120
Sundial Peak St 89166
Sundoro Dr 89110
Sundown Dr 89169
Sundown Crest St 89113
Sundown Glen Ave 89113
Sundown Heights Ave 89130
Sundown Hill Ave 89134
Sundown Ridge St 89113
Sundown Vista Ave 89147
Sunflower Ave 89120
Sunflower Hill St 89178
Sungold Dr 89134
Sungrove Ct 89131
Sunhampton Ave 89129
Sunken Meadow Ave 89178
Sunken Reef Cir 89117
Sunken River Trl 89118
Sunking St 89130
Sunkiss Dr 89110
Sunland Ave 89106
Sunlight Canyon Ct 89183
Sunlight Garden Way 89118
Sunnie Dee Ct 89120
Sunningdale Ct 89122
Sunny Pl 89106
Sunny Beach Ln 89118
Sunny Brook Ave 89110
Sunny Countryside Ave 89179
Sunny Days Ln 89113
Sunny Dunes Ct & Dr 89121
Sunny Heights Dr 89134
Sunny Hills Ct 89147
Sunny Mead Ct 89134
Sunny Orchard Ln 89110
Sunny Oven Ct 89178
Sunny Ranch Ave 89129
Sunnyfield Dr 89134
Sunnyside Cir 89123
Sunnyslope Ave 89119
Sunnyvale St 89145
Sunnyview Ct 89147
Sunnywood Dr 89120
Sunpine Ct 89129
Sunporch St 89131
Sunray Ln 89130
Sunrise Ave
1800-3399 89101
3500-3598 89110
3600-6699 89110
Sunrise St 89101
Sunrise Bluff Dr 89142
Sunrise Day Ct 89142
Sunrise Hills Dr 89142
Sunrise Knoll St 89113
Sunrise Meadows Dr 89134
Sunrise Mesa Ct 89149
Sunrise Peak Ln 89144
Sunrise Ranch St 89156
Sunrise Shadow Cir 89118
Sunrise View Dr
1401-1497 89110
1499-1599 89110
1600-1799 89156
Sunrise Villa Dr 89110
Sunrise Vista St 89148
Sunset Dr 89108
E Sunset Rd
101-297 89119
299-399 89119
1001-1003 89199
1001-1001 89193

1301-2399 89119
2400-3999 89120
W Sunset Rd
2500-2598 89119
3100-6599 89118
6601-6699 89118
7000-7198 89113
7200-8500 89113
8502-8598 89113
8800-9799 89148
Sunset Bay St 89148
Sunset Beach Ln 89128
Sunset Blaze Ct 89178
Sunset Cliff Cir 89123
Sunset Corporate Dr 89120
Sunset Cove Dr 89128
Sunset Creek St 89113
Sunset Gardens Dr 89135
Sunset Horizon St 89131
Sunset Mesa Ct 89142
Sunset Mill Dr 89128
Sunset Palisades Way 89183
Sunset Palm St 89121
Sunset Peak St 89142
Sunset Pines St 89148
Sunset Plateau Ct 89142
Sunset Sky Pl 89110
Sunset Spring Ave 89122
Sunset Summit Ave 89141
Sunset Villa Dr 89110
Sunshade Ct 89147
Sunshine St 89118
Sunshine Coast Ln 89148
Sunshine Village Pl 89183
Sunspot Dr 89128
Sunstone St 89128
Suntan Cir 89110
Sunup Dr 89134
Sunvue Cir 89110
Sunwind Ave 89135
Supai Dr 89103
Super Bowl Dr 89110
Super Sonic Ave 89110
Supernova Ct 89123
Supreme Ct 89110
Sur Este Ave 89123
Surf Ln 89110
Surf Breaker St 89147
Surf Spray St 89117
Surf View Dr 89117
Surfboard Ct 89147
Surfcrest Ct 89128
Surfline Dr 89117
Surfrider Ln 89110
Surfs Up Dr 89128
Surfside Ct 89110
Surfwood Dr 89128
Surrey Ct
6800-6899 89119
6900-6999 89145
Surrey Ln 89119
Surrey St 89119
Surrey Downs Ln 89135
Surtees Point St 89144
Surtidor Dr 89117
Surveyor St 89103
Susan St 89106
Susana St 89121
Sussex St 89144
Sutcliffe Cir 89110
Sutro Ln & Way 89106
Sutter Ave 89109
Sutter Crossing Ct 89135
Sutter Hills Ave 89144
Suttle Surf Dr 89147
Sutton Falls St 89135
Suzanne Elaine Ct 89131
Suzy Ct 89110
Suzy Nagle Ave 89106
Suzy Saly Pl 89122
Swaab St 89115
Swale Ln 89144
Swallow Ln 89121
Swallow Point Cir 89117
Swallowtail Ct 89107
Swamp Rose Ave 89149

Swan Ln 89121
Swan Bay Dr 89117
Swan Cove Ct 89166
Swan Hill Dr 89134
Swan Lake Ave 89128
Swan Point Pl 89122
Swan Song Rd 89142
Swanbrooke Dr 89144
Swandale Ave & Ct 89121
Swaps Ln 89108
Swarthmore Ct 89110
Swaying Ct 89147
Swaying Elms Ct 89147
Swaying Ferns Dr 89147
Swaying Palms Dr 89147
Swaying Trees Dr 89147
Sweden St 89129
Sweeney Ave 89104
Sweeping Glen St 89129
Sweeping Ivy Ct 89183
Sweeping Valley St 89129
Sweeping Vine Ave 89183
Sweet Basil Dr 89142
Sweet Cedar Ave 89143
Sweet Cicely Ave 89138
Sweet Clover Ct 89131
Sweet Dreams Ct 89131
Sweet Elderberry Ct 89138
Sweet Fennel Dr 89135
Sweet Gale Ct 89178
Sweet Jasmine Dr 89148
Sweet Juliet St 89183
Sweet Laurel St 89178
Sweet Lily Ct 89141
Sweet Marisa Ct 89139
Sweet Mist Ave 89178
Sweet Nokia St 89183
Sweet Orange St 89142
Sweet Palm Ct 89178
Sweet Pea Ave 89183
Sweet Pea Arbor St 89144
Sweet Pecan St 89149
Sweet Perennial Ct 89149
Sweet Pine St 89108
Sweet Rose Ct 89134
Sweet Sage Ave 89129
Sweet Shade St 89130
Sweet Stone Pl 89147
Sweet Tree Ct 89178
Sweet Willow Ln 89135
Sweet Woodruff Dr 89141
Sweetbriar Ct 89146
Sweetgum St 89108
Sweetheart Cir 89118
Sweetie Ct 89149
Sweetstem Ct 89138
Sweetwater Pl 89145
Sweetwood Ave 89149
Sweetzer Way 89108
Swenson St
3378-3498 89169
3500-3600 89169
3602-3698 89169
3770-3798 89119
3800-4974 89119
4975-4975 89132
4975-5199 89119
4976-5298 89119
Swept Plains St 89129
Swift Fox Ct 89122
Swifton Ct 89104
Swiftwater Ct 89178
Swimmer Dr 89110
Swimming Hole St 89183
Swiss St 89110
Swiss Cottage Ave 89178
Swiss Stone Ct 89123
Swordfish Ct 89115
Sycamore Ln 89101
Sycamore Trl 89108
Sycamore Grove Ct 89139
Sycamore Spring Ct 89128
Sycamore View St 89131
Sylvan Oak Dr 89147
Sylvia St 89121
Sylvia Beach Ct 89148

Symmetry Ct 89149
Symphony Dr 89146
Symphony Park Ave 89106
Syracuse Dr 89121
Syvella Ct 89117
Tabernas Ct 89141
Tabic Dr 89108
Tabitha Ave 89156
Tabitha Lila St 89106
Table Lands Ct 89129
Table Top Ln 89135
Tack St 89122
Tackett St 89148
Tackle Dr 89128
Tackle Box Ct 89113
Tacoma Ave 89121
Tad Moore Ave 89148
Tafalla Ct 89138
Taft Ct 89110
Taggart St 89104
Tahnee Dr 89122
Tahoe Ct & Dr 89142
Tahoe Basin Dr 89129
Tahoe Canyon St 89129
Tahoe Meadows Ct 89120
Tahoe Ridge Ct 89139
Tailor Made Ave 89149
Tailwind Ave 89131
Tait St 89178
Taj Mahal Dr 89130
Tala St 89131
Talavera Ct 89110
Talbot Cir & St 89169
Talking Tree Ave 89129
Tall Arrow Ave 89178
Tall Pine Dr 89108
Tall Ruff Dr 89148
Tall Timber St 89183
Tall Tree St 89147
Tall Wood Ln 89129
Tallard Ct 89141
Talmage Cir & St 89107
Tam Dr 89102
Tam O Shanter 89109
Tamal Ct 89103
Tamalpias Ave 89120
Tamanar Dr 89130
Tamany St 89143
Tamar Ct 89130
Tamar Sage Ct 89149
Tamara Costa Ct 89110
Tamarack Landing Way 89117
Tamareno Cir 89119
Tamarind Ave 89147
Tamarron Cliffs St 89148
Tamaruga Ct 89179
Tamarus St
4100-4198 89119
4200-5799 89119
5801-6899 89119
7600-9399 89123
Tamborine Ct 89128
Tame Pl 89131
Tamerack Ave 89106
Tami Pl 89120
Tampa Ct 89108
Tamworth Ct 89131
Tanager Way 89103
Tanbark Ct 89108
Tandoori Ln 89138
Tangerine Ct 89103
Tangerine Rose Dr 89142
Tangerine Sky Ave 89178
Tangled Spur Ct 89143
Tanglewood Park St 89166
Tango St 89123
Tango Moon Ct 89149
Tanita Ct 89123
Tannenbaum Cir & St 89124
Tanner Rapids Ct 89148
Tanner Valley Cir 89123
Tanning St 89122
Tansy Ct 89183
Tantalizing Ave 89149
Tantalum Ln 89122

Tantalus Ct 89183
Tantilla Ct 89113
Tanto Cir 89121
Tanya Ave 89107
Tanzanite Ave 89130
Taos Ln 89121
Taos Estates St 89128
Taos Paseo Ave 89128
Tapadero Ln 89135
Tapani St 89123
Tapestry Ct 89142
Tapestry Pine St 89178
Tapestry Rose Ct 89148
Tapestry Winds St 89141
Tappaan Lodge Ave 89143
Tappi St 89108
Taps Ct 89148
Tara Ave
3801-4197 89102
4199-4399 89102
5000-5098 89146
5100-6899 89146
6900-8199 89117
Tarata Ct 89144
Taravilla Cir 89146
Tarbell Grove Ave 89166
Tarberts Cottage St 89166
Targhee Ct 89156
Tarkin Ave 89120
Tarpon Dr 89120
Tarpon Glade Ct 89113
Tarpon Springs Ct 89131
Tarrant Ranch Rd 89131
Tarraso Way 89102
Tartan Hill Ave 89141
Tartarus St 89131
Tarzana Ln 89117
Tashmont St 89121
Tassara Way 89108
Tassel Fern Ave 89183
Tasty Ct 89149
Tatiana St 89115
Tatinger Ct 89122
Tattersall Pl 89115
Tattersall Flag St 89139
Taunton St 89178
Taurus Ct 89115
Tavistock Ct 89134
Tavolo Ct 89135
Tawny Buck Ct 89183
Tawny Griffin Ave 89139
Tay River Ct 89166
Tayler Joy Ct 89113
Taylor Ave 89115
Taylor Creek Ave 89130
Taylor Hill St 89106
Taylor Valley Ave 89131
Taylor Woodrow Dr 89117
Taylorville St 89135
Tayman Park Ave 89148
Tazeer St 89131
Tea Garden Dr 89129
Tea Light Ct 89113
Tea Olive Dr 89141
Teaberry Ct 89129
Teahouse St 89138
Teak Crest Dr 89147
Teak Hollow Ct 89147
Teakwood Ave 89110
Teal Ave 89123
Teal Beach St 89117
Teal Harbor Ave 89117
Teal Lake Ct 89129
Teal Sunset St 89129
Tealbrook St 89179
Tealwood St 89131
Teardrop St 89142
Tecate Valley St 89138
Tech Center Ct 89128
Technology Ct 89101
W Teco Ave
3400-5600 89118
5602-5798 89118
7600-7698 89113
Teddington Ct 89102
Teddy Dr 89102

Tee St 89142
N Tee Pee Ln
4000-4699 89129
4701-4799 89129
4900-6599 89149
S Tee Pee Ln
4300-4399 89147
5201-5299 89148
Teedale Ct 89178
Teetering Rock Ave 89143
Tehama Ct 89117
Telegraph Rd 89108
Telescope Peak Ct 89145
Tellima Ct 89149
Temecula Valley Ave 89179
Tempe St 89103
Tempest Ct & Pl 89145
Tempest Point Ct 89147
Temple Dr 89107
Temple Bells Ct 89183
Temple View Dr 89110
Temple Wood Ct 89148
Templemore Ave 89129
Temptation Ln 89128
Tempting Choice Ave 89131
Ten Gallon Ct 89129
Ten Oaks Ave 89145
Ten Palms Ct 89117
N Tenaya Way
100-148 89145
701-897 89128
899-2498 89128
2449-2449 89133
2500-3198 89128
2501-3199 89128
3200-4000 89129
4002-4598 89129
4801-5199 89149
5601-6299 89130
6500-6598 89131
6600-7899 89131
7901-8199 89131
1200-3300 89117
3302-3398 89117
4001-4099 89147
6300-6398 89113
6400-8899 89113
8901-9099 89113
9301-9497 89178
9499-9599 89178
9601-9799 89178
Tender Ct 89149
Tender Tassels St 89149
Tender Tulip Ave 89139
Tenerife St 89178
Tenille Dr 89107
Tennis Court St E 89120
Tennyson Dr 89103
Tenshaw Ave 89145
Tent Rocks Ct 89118
Tenza Ct 89141
Tequesta Rd & St 89108
Terenzio Ct 89183
Teresita Ave 89147
Termas Dr 89117
Termination Ct 89129
Termini Station Ave 89138
Termoli St 89123
Terra Cir 89120
Terra Bella Dr 89108
Terra Grande Ave 89122
Terra Linda Ave 89120
Terra Rosa Dr 89130
Terra Vista Way 89117
Terrace Ct & Dr 89120
Terrace Green Ave 89117
Terrace Grove St 89129
Terrace Hill Rd 89103
Terrace Ridge Ct 89129
Terrace Rock Way 89128
Terrace Stream Ct 89156
Terrace Verde Ave 89138
Terrace View Ct 89144
Terracotta Gulf Ct 89143
Terrapin Mountain Ave 89129
Terrazzo Ave 89115
Terrestrial Ln 89115

Terrill Ave 89183
Territorial St 89149
Territory St 89121
Terry Ln & St 89108
Tersky Ct 89122
Tesara Vista Pl 89128
Tesoras Dr 89144
Tesoro Dr 89144
Teton St 89101
Teton Crest Pl 89143
Teton Diablo Ave 89117
Teton Hills St 89147
Teton Ridge Ave 89149
Teton View Rd 89148
Teton Vista Ave 89117
Teton Wood Ave 89129
Tetonia St 89142
Tevare Ln 89138
Tevere Valley St 89131
Texas Bronco Ave 89129
Texas Ranger Ave 89129
Thackerville Ave 89139
Thackwood Dr 89129
Thai Coast St 89130
Thalia River St 89148
Thames Way 89110
Thataboy Ct 89130
Thatched Sunlight Ct 89178
Theatre Ct 89110
Thelma Ln 89104
Theme Rd 89122
Theresa Ave 89101
Theresa Way 89130
Theseas Ave 89131
Theus Cir 89107
Thicket Willow St 89135
Thiros Cir 89146
Thistle Dew Ave 89148
Thistle Meadow Ave 89139
Thistle Poppy Ave 89139
Thistle Ridge St 89166
Thistle Wind Dr 89135
Thom Blvd
3300-4399 89130
6800-8399 89131
8401-8599 89131
Thomas W Ryan Blvd 89134
Thomaston Ct 89122
Thompson Cir 89107
Thor Cir & Dr 89103
Thor Mountain Ln 89166
Thornapple Ave 89183
Thornbird Ct 89131
Thornbuck Pl 89131
Thornbury Ln 89134
Thorndale Pl 89103
Thorndike Ct 89130
Thorne Bay Ct 89110
Thorne Pine Ave 89131
Thornewood Pl 89123
Thornfield Ln 89123
Thornford St 89178
Thornless Rose Ct 89183
Thornsby Ct 89120
Thornview St 89135
Thousand Oaks Dr 89123
Thousand Palms Ln 89130
Three Bars Ct 89115
Thrush Dr 89145
Thumbelina Cir 89102
Thunder St 89145
Thunder Basin Ave 89149
Thunder Blitz Ave 89131
Thunder Bluff St 89113
Thunder Echo St 89131
Thunder Falls Ct 89149
Thunder Gulch Ave 89141
Thunder Hawk St 89129
Thunder Peak St 89178
Thunder Rapids Ct 89148
Thunder River Cir 89148
Thunder Sky St 89178
Thunder Spirit St 89148
Thunder Twice St 89129
Thunderbolt Ave 89115
Thundercloud Ct 89110

Thurgood Ave 89122
Thurman Ave 89120
Thurman Cir 89115
Thyme Ave 89110
Tiaquinn Ave 89129
Tiara Cove Cir 89128
Tiara Point Cir 89146
Tibana Way 89147
Tiberio Way 89156
Tibet Ct 89117
Tiburtina Ave 89138
Ticonderoga St 89110
Tidal Bay Dr 89117
Tidal Cove Ct 89147
Tidal Pool Ct 89139
Tide Ct 89156
Tide Pool Dr 89128
Tidelands Park Ct 89166
Tidewater Ct 89117
Tie Breaker Ct 89148
Tier Ave 89139
Tierney Ct 89149
Tierney Creek Dr 89183
Tierra Ln 89108
Tierra Baja Way 89110
Tierra Buena Dr 89110
Tierra Del Sol Dr 89113
Tierra Del Verde St 89156
Tierra Hope Ct 89143
Tierra Mesa Ave 89156
Tierra Montanosa Ave 89179
Tierra Santa Ave 89129
Tierra Verde St 89122
Tierra Vista Dr 89128
Tierras Blancos Ct 89138
Tiffanieville Ct 89129
Tiffany Ln 89101
Tiffany Bend Ct 89123
Tiffany Lamp Ct 89149
Tiffin Ct 89129
Tiffollo Ln 89156
Tiger Paws Pl 89183
Tiger Shale Way 89123
Tiger Woods Ave 89128
Tigers Lair Ct 89130
Tigerseye Dr 89134
Tigertail Ct 89131
Tigh Brachen Ct 89166
Tighe Way 89145
Tigress Cir 89115
Tilbury Ave 89123
Tilkuni Dr 89166
Tillamook Ave 89115
Tillis Pl 89138
Tillman Crest Ave 89139
Tillman Falls Ave 89183
Tilted Cart St 89143
Tim Tam Ave 89178
Timaru Dr 89147
Timber Ln 89108
Timber Canyon Ave 89129
Timber Cove Ct 89144
Timber Crest Ave 89131
Timber Gate St 89113
Timber Horn Ct 89147
Timber Mesa St 89139
Timber Mountain Ave 89135
Timber Peak Ln 89113
Timber Pine Ave 89143
Timber Point St 89148
Timber Ridge Ct 89110
Timber Rose Dr 89134
Timber Run St 89149
Timber Stand St 89183
Timber Star Ln 89135
Timber Willow Ave 89135
Timberlake Dr 89115
Timberland St 89123
Timberleaf Ct 89148
Timberline Dr 89124
Timberline Way 89117
Timberline Peak Ave 89166
Timberlodge Ln 89115
Timberview Ct 89118
Timberwolf Ct 89130
Timberwood St 89122

Time Machine Ave 89113
Timely Treasures Ave .. 89178
Timescape Ct 89123
Timpani Dr 89110
Tin Mine Ave 89179
Tin Mountain Ct 89129
Tina Ln 89130
Tina Marie Ct 89149
Tinazzi Way 89141
Tincup Dr 89130
Tindari St 89130
Tingley Ave 89141
Tinker Toy Ave 89139
Tinsley Ct 89134
Tinta Ln 89144
Tinted Mesa Ct 89149
Tiny Pebble Way 89142
Tiny Tortoise St 89149
Tioga Way 89169
N Tioga Way
3301-4197 89129
4199-4399 89129
4800-5199 89149
6500-8199 89131
S Tioga Way
1700-3199 89117
3201-3299 89117
5500-6598 89113
Tioga Pass Ave 89139
Tioga Pines Cir 89117
Tionesta Ct 89141
Tipper Ave 89122
Tipperary St 89130
Tippin Dr 89130
Tirana Way 89103
Tisha Renee Ave 89147
Titan Ct 89108
Titan Hill Ct 89148
Titan Peak Pl 89144
Titania Ct 89147
Titanium Ave & Ct 89120
Titleist Cir 89117
Tittleton Ave 89148
Tiverton Rd 89123
Tivoli Ct 89117
Tivoli Cove Dr 89128
Toad Hollow St 89141
Toadstool Ln 89110
Toast Ave 89148
Tobago Ln 89123
Tobel Springs Dr 89129
Tobias Ln 89120
Tobler Dr 89145
Tocata Dr 89146
Todd Neil Ct 89117
Tohono Canyon St 89147
Toiyabe St 89156
Toiyabe Camino Ct 89179
Tokara Ave 89122
Token Ave 89149
Tokyo Ct 89115
Tolberts Mill Dr 89131
Tolbooth St 89139
Toledo Ave 89121
Tolentino Dr 89156
Tolford Ave 89148
Tolkien Ave 89115
Toluca Ct 89120
Tom Noon Ave 89178
Tom Sawyer St 89113
Tomahawk Bend Ave 89113
Tomahawk Mill Ct 89139
Tomer Ln 89121
Tomich Ave 89145
Tomiyasu Ln 89120
Tomlinson Ln 89156
Tomnitz Ave 89178
Tomorrow Ct 89147
E Tompkins Ave 89121
W Tompkins Ave
3001-3497 89103
3499-4399 89103
9401-9697 89147
9699-9899 89147
Toms River St 89135

N Tomsik St
3600-4799 89129
5000-5199 89149
S Tomsik St
500-599 89145
1800-2098 89117
8300-8898 89113
8900-8998 89113
Tona Cir 89169
Tonada Way 89117
Tone St 89123
Toni Ave 89119
Tonkawa Ave 89178
E Tonopah Ave 89115
N Tonopah Dr 89106
S Tonopah Dr 89106
Tonto Creek Ct 89139
Tonyram Cir 89146
Tonyville Ave 89149
Toofer Winds Ct 89131
Toothwood Ln 89115
Top Hat Ave 89113
Topanga St 89169
Topanza Canyon St 89123
Topawa Dr & St 89103
Topaz Ct 89121
Topaz Sq 89121
Topaz St
2900-4800 89121
4802-4898 89121
4900-5098 89120
5100-6100 89120
6102-7498 89120
Topaz Cliff Pl 89123
Topaz Ravine St 89131
Topaz Springs Ct 89149
Topaz Valley Ave 89130
Topeka Dr 89147
Topley Pike Ave 89139
Topsail Ct 89156
Topsider St 89129
Topweed Ave 89130
Toquima Cir 89120
Torcello Dr 89117
Torchwood Ln 89144
Tordero St 89129
Torington Dr 89108
E Torino Ave 89123
W Torino Ave
3101-3297 89139
3299-6699 89139
6701-6899 89139
7000-7198 89113
7200-7999 89113
8001-8399 89113
8801-9199 89148
11000-11699 89161
Toro Ct 89117
Toro Canyon Ln 89134
Toronto Cir 89121
Toroweap Ridge St 89147
Torre De Nolte St 89141
Torremolinos Ave 89178
Torrence Dr 89103
Torretta Ct 89138
N Torrey Pines Dr
101-197 89107
199-899 89107
1600-1998 89108
2000-3999 89108
4001-4399 89108
4700-6000 89130
6002-6098 89130
6600-8199 89131
8201-8299 89131
S Torrey Pines Dr
201-297 89107
299-400 89107
402-1098 89107
1101-1197 89146
1199-3299 89146
3700-4199 89103
4201-4899 89103
4901-5097 89118
5099-6899 89118
7301-7797 89139
7799-7899 89139

Torrey Point Ct 89145
Torrey Valley Ct 89135
Torreyana Way 89108
Torreys Peak St 89166
Torsby Pl 89119
Tortoise Cactus Ct 89106
Tortoise Greens St 89149
Tortoise Shell St 89149
Tortola Bay Ln 89128
Tory Ct 89110
Tosca St 89128
Toscana Ln 89117
Toscano Gardens St 89141
Total Eclipse St 89129
Totem Pole Ct 89134
Tottenham Ave 89135
Touchstone Ct 89108
Tough Pine Ct 89131
Tour Players Rd 89148
Tourello Ln 89144
Tourmaline St 89130
Tourmaline Blue St 89106
Tournament St 89142
Tournament Canyon
Dr 89144
Tournament Hills Dr ... 89134
Towango Point St 89147
Tower St 89101
Tower Bridge Ave 89117
Tower Falls Ct 89141
Tower Ridge Ave 89129
Towering Pines St 89135
N Town Center Dr
653-1107 89144
1109-1399 89144
1500-1599 89134
S Town Center Dr
600-698 89144
2600-3298 89135
3300-3700 89135
3702-3898 89135
Town Forest Ave 89179
Townbridge Ave 89149
Towngate Ave 89129
Townhouse Dr 89121
Townsend St 89121
Townsend Hall Ct 89135
Townsville Ave 89113
Townview Dr 89129
Townwall St 89115
Toy Soldier St 89178
Trabuco Dr 89110
Trace Hollow St 89149
Traci St 89110
Tracy St 89161
Tracylynn Ln 89121
Traddles St 89130
Trade Center Dr 89119
Tradewind Ct 89123
Trading Post Ln 89128
Tradition Creek Ave ... 89149
Tradition Springs Ct .. 89113
Traditional Ct 89113
Trafalgar Dr 89117
Trail Boss Ct 89113
Trail Dust Dr 89113
Trail Head Dr 89113
Trail Peak Ln 89134
Trail Rider Dr 89117
Trail Roundup Ln 89113
Trail Spring Ct 89138
Trailhead Mesa St 89129
Trailing Daisy St 89183
Trailing Dalea Ave 89135
Trailing Putt Way 89148
Trailing Vine St 89183
Trails End Ave 89143
Trails Park Pl 89113
Trails Village Pl 89113
Trailside Park Ct 89149
Trailwood Dr 89134
Trammel Ct 89103
Tramore St 89148
Tranquil Breeze St 89183
Tranquil Canyon Ct 89147
Tranquil Garden St 89117

Tranquil Glade Ln 89135
Tranquil Meadows Ln ... 89128
Tranquil Seas Ct 89139
Tranquil Stream Ct 89148
Tranquil Waters Ct 89135
Tranquility Dr 89102
Tranquility Ridge Ct .. 89147
Transom Dr 89128
Transvaal Blue St 89139
Transverse Dr 89146
Trap Creek Ct 89156
Trapani Pl 89141
Trapper Mountain St ... 89178
Trattner St 89135
Trattoria St 89178
Trautman Ct 89149
Travelers Ct 89129
Traveling Breeze Ave .. 89178
Traverse St 89120
Traverse Creek Ln 89135
Travertine Ln 89122
Traviata Ave 89141
Travis Jason Ave 89106
Travis Lake Ct 89148
Travois Cir 89119
Tray Mountain Ave 89166
Trea Ave 89147
Treadway Ln 89103
Treak Cliff Ct 89139
Treasure Ave 89122
Treasure Beach Ct 89117
Treasure Bluff Ct 89129
Treasure Chest St 89139
Treasure Island Rd 89128
Treasure Mountain Ct .. 89129
Treasure Ship Ave 89147
Treasure Trove St 89123
Treasured Note Ct 89129
Trebbiano Way 89156
Treble Clef Ave 89139
Tree Bark St 89183
Tree Bridge St 89129
Tree Creek Ct 89183
Tree Haven Ct 89146
Tree Lane Peak Ct 89166
Tree Line Dr 89142
Tree Sap Ave 89183
Treesdale Dr 89134
Treetrunk Ave 89147
Treldert Ave 89121
Trellis Rose Ct 89148
Trellis View Ave 89115
Tremezzo Bay St 89141
Tremolite Ave 89123
Trends Ct 89149
Trendy Ct 89149
Trengrove Pl 89183
Trent Ave 89107
Trenton Pl 89134
Trenton Manor Ct 89131
Trenton Parade Ave 89130
Trentwood Ct 89148
Tres Piedras Rd 89122
Tresor Ct 89135
Tressider Ave 89179
Treto Ave 89141
Tretter Way 89108
Trevet St 89129
Trevi Fountain Ave 89138
Trevino Ave 89131
Trevins Ave 89103
Treviso Way 89117
Trianon Ln 89145
Tribal Cir 89145
Tribeca St 89135
Tribiani Ave 89138
Tribute Ln 89147
Tribute Peak Way 89148
Trickling Brook Ct 89156
Trickling Springs Ct .. 89149
Trickling Stream Cir .. 89117
Trickling Wash Dr 89131
Trident Cir 89117
Trident Maple St 89117
Triest Ct 89110
Trilling Bird Dr 89135

Trillium Dr 89135
Trilly Ln 89156
Trilogy Dr 89108
Trimming Ct 89149
Trimwater Ct 89130
Trineo Ct 89117
Trinidad Ct 89183
Trinity Ct 89146
Trinity Oaks Ct 89139
Trinity Peak St 89128
Trio Way 89119
Triora St 89129
Tripp Ct 89108
Trish Ln 89156
Tristan Flower Ave 89183
Triumph Ct 89117
Trixis Pl 89144
Trogon Way 89103
Trona St 89102
Tronada Way 89128
Trooper St 89120
Trophy Club Dr 89123
Trophy Hills Dr 89134
Trophy Run Ave 89113
Tropic Isle Cir 89128
Tropic Mist St 89130
Tropicaire St 89149
E Tropical Pkwy 89115
W Tropical Pkwy
5300-6198 89130
6200-6600 89130
6602-7298 89130
7701-7797 89149
7799-10299 89149
Tropical Breeze Dr 89117
Tropical Cliff Ave 89130
Tropical Glen Ct 89130
Tropical Island Cir ... 89129
Tropical Knoll Ct 89130
Tropical Meadow Ct 89130
Tropical Peach Dr 89118
Tropical Ridge Ct 89130
Tropical Springs St ... 89130
Tropical Tide Ct 89149
Tropical Toucan Ave ... 89130
Tropical Vine St 89147
E Tropicana Ave
101-199 89109
200-300 89169
302-398 89169
701-1097 89119
1099-2399 89119
2400-4999 89121
5000-5798 89122
5800-6498 89122
W Tropicana Ave
3101-3297 89103
3299-6399 89103
6401-6899 89103
6900-8198 89147
8200-9900 89147
9902-10198 89147
Trotter Cir 89107
Trotter Peak St 89178
Trotters Ridge Dr 89122
Trotting Trigger Ave .. 89131
Trotwood Ln 89108
Troubador Dr 89119
N Trout Canyon Rd 89124
Trout Creek Ct 89123
Trout Lake Ave 89115
Trout Peak Way 89156
Trout River St 89178
Trowbridge St 89178
Troy Pl & St 89103
Truckee Ct 89122
Trudeau Ave 89143
Trudy Ln 89123
Truett St 89128
Truluck Ln 89106
Truman Ct 89107
Trumbull St 89130
Trumbull Point Ct 89166
Trumphet Lilly Ave 89183
Trumpington Ct 89178
Truscott Ct 89130

Trussell St 89141
Tubana Beach Ln 89141
Tuckaway Cove Ave 89139
Tuckaway Harbor St 89139
Tuckermans Ave 89129
Tucumcari Dr 89108
Tudela Ct 89138
Tudor Park Pl 89145
Tudor Rose Ct 89145
Tudur Ln 89119
Tuffer Ln 89130
Tugaloo Ave 89129
Tularosa Ln 89122
Tule Springs Rd 89131
Tulip Ln 89101
Tulip Field St 89142
Tulip Garden Dr 89142
Tulip Hill Ave 89141
Tulip Tree St 89135
Tulip Trestle Ave 89148
Tulip Valley Rd 89179
Tulipan Way 89120
Tulita Dr 89123
Tullamore St 89129
Tully Ave 89110
Tullyroe Ave 89129
Tulsa Cir 89108
Tulsa Peak St 89129
Tulum Ct 89145
Tumberry St 89117
Tumble Brook Dr 89134
Tumble Creek Ct 89134
Tumble Lake Ct 89147
Tumblegrass Ct 89122
Tumbleweed Ave
1100-1300 89106
1302-1398 89106
3800-3999 89121
Tumblewood Ave 89143
Tumbling St 89131
Tumbling Pebble Way ... 89123
Tumbling Tree St 89183
Tumwater St 89121
Tunbridge Ave 89139
Tundra Swan St 89122
Tuni Pueblo Ct 89183
Tunis Ave & Cir 89122
Tunnel Falls Dr 89141
Tupac Ln 89130
Tupelo Ln 89122
Turpelo Ct 89122
Turbys Treehouse Pl ... 89131
Turf Cir 89108
Turf Center Dr 89141
Turhan Cir 89146
Turia Gardens Rd 89135
Turin Pl 89144
Turina Rd 89146
Turkey Ln 89131
Turlington Ln 89135
Turnberry Ln 89113
Turnbridge St 89166
Turner St 89119
Turning Bridge St 89135
Turning Leaf Ave 89129
Turquoise Rd
3000-3099 89106
3101-3297 89108
3299-3599 89108
Turquoise Canyon Ave .. 89106
Turquoise Glass Ct 89178
Turquoise Hill Ct 89130
Turquoise Ridge St 89117
Turquoise Stone Ct 89113
Turquoise Tide Dr 89166
Turquoise Valley Dr ... 89144
Turret Peak Ave 89135
Tursi Lodge Ct 89131
Turtle Cove Ave 89128
Turtle Creek Cir 89113
Turtle Dove Ct 89129
Turtle Haven Ct 89149
Turtle Head Ct 89117
Turtle Head Peak Dr ... 89135
Turtle Hill Rd 89110
Turtle Island Ct 89129

Turtle Mountain Ave ... 89166
Turtle Peak Ave 89148
Turtle Point Dr 89113
Turtle Ridge Ave 89183
Turtle River Ave 89156
Turtle Run Ave 89130
Turtle Vista Cir 89117
Turtle Walk Ave 89149
Turtlerock St 89142
Tuscadora Ct 89110
Tuscan Ct 89141
Tuscan Hill Ct 89141
Tuscan Sun Dr 89178
Tuscany Rose Ct 89129
Tuscany View St 89145
Tuscany Village Dr 89129
Tuscarora Ct 89142
Tuscola Ct 89148
Tuscolana St 89141
Tuxpan St 89131
E Twain Ave
400-448 89169
450-1200 89169
1202-1798 89169
2401-3097 89121
3099-4811 89121
4813-4999 89121
5001-5399 89122
W Twain Ave
3601-3897 89103
3899-5999 89103
6001-6699 89103
9301-9597 89147
9599-10199 89147
10701-10799 89135
Twain Cir 89121
Twain Harte St 89139
Twelve Pins Dr 89129
Twickenham Pl 89108
Twig Ln 89108
Twilight St 89122
Twilight Canyon Ct 89148
Twilight Chase St 89130
Twilight Cove Cir 89131
Twilight Mist Ct 89148
Twilight Point Ct 89148
Twilight Ridge Ct 89148
Twilight Rose St 89138
Twilight Star Dr 89117
Twilight Times Ct 89135
Twilight Valley Ct 89148
Twilight Vista Ave 89148
Twilight Walk Ave 89149
Twiller St 89148
Twin Bridges Ct 89129
Twin Buttes Ave 89129
Twin Feathers Way 89135
Twin Flower Cir 89134
Twin Forks Peak St 89166
Twin Harbor Ct 89141
Twin Lakes Dr 89107
Twin Leaf St 89149
Twin Maples Ct 89148
Twin Mill St 89178
Twin Oaks Ave 89156
Twin Palms Cir 89117
Twin Plant Ct 89129
Twin Ponds Ct 89178
Twin Rivers Ct 89139
Twin Tails St 89149
Twin Towers Ave 89123
Twin View Cir 89121
Twinbreeze St 89129
Twinkle Star Dr 89115
Twinkling Topaz Ave ... 89143
Twirling Yarn Ct 89149
Twisted Pine Ave 89131
Twisted Wood Dr 89148
Twister Trace St 89178
Twistingbow Ln 89121
Two Knights Dr 89156
Twylah St 89115
Tybalt Ct 89113
Tybo Ave & Cir 89110
Tyler St 89104
Tyler Chanel Ct 89106

Tyler Park Ave 89135
Tyler Rose St 89178
Tyler William Ln 89130
Tyne Pl 89144
Tynedale Ct 89123
Typan St 89130
Typecast Rd 89142
Tyrol Way 89124
Uccello Dr 89138
Udine Ct 89117
Ukiah Cir 89118
Ullom Dr
2000-2099 89108
2101-2199 89108
6600-6699 89118
6701-7299 89118
7300-7599 89139
7601-9599 89139
S Ullom Dr 89139
Ulric Ave 89166
Ultima Ct 89144
Umberland Ave 89149
Umberto St 89148
Umbrella Tree Ct 89144
Umbria Gardens Ave 89141
Unbridled Cir 89117
Underhill Ct 89145
Underpar Cir 89142
Underwood Way 89156
Unicorn St 89131
Unicorn Tapestry Ct 89149
Union St 89121
Union Gap Rd 89123
Union Pacific St 89131
Union Park Ct 89183
Unionville Ln 89110
Unique Way 89129
Universal Ave 89142
E University Ave
1361-1397 89119
1399-1700 89119
1702-2298 89119
3100-3348 89121
3350-3398 89121
W University Ave
4700-6200 89103
6202-6298 89103
8501-8599 89147
University Cir 89119
University Rd 89119
University Ridge Ave 89149
Upland Blvd & Pl 89107
Upland Bluff Dr 89142
Upland Heights Ave 89142
Upper Falls Ct 89141
Upper Laurel St 89179
Uppsalla Ave 89129
Urania Ct 89131
Urban Creek Ct 89148
Uribe St 89129
Ursine St 89101
E Utah Ave 89104
W Utah Ave 89102
Ute Ln 89110
Ute Meadows Cir 89129
Utica Cir 89146
Utopia Way 89130
Uvalde St 89130
Uxbridge Dr 89178
Vacanze Ct 89183
Vacation Valley Ave 89183
Vacaville Ave 89139
Vadella Sound Way 89141
Vader Ave 89120
Vahe Cir 89121
Vail St 89122
Val Dechiana Ave 89141
Val Piora St 89178
Val Verde Ct 89122
Vala Cir 89101
N Valadez St
3600-4599 89129
4900-5199 89149
S Valadez St 89117
Valador Ave 89129
Valaris Ct 89178
Valaspen St 89183
Valcour St 89166
Valderas Dr 89123
Valdosta Ave 89129
Valemont Ct 89123
Valencia St 89121
Valencia Canyon Dr 89117
Valencia Crest Ave 89139
Valencia Hills St 89141
Valencia Valley Ave 89178
Valensole Ave 89141
Valentino Ln 89138
Valerie Elaine St 89139
Valerio Ln 89134
Valetta Flat Ave 89183
Valhalla Ln 89123
Valiente St 89144
Valinda Valley Ct 89178
Valla De Bravo St 89131
Valladolid Ave 89178
Vallarta Cir 89121
Vallejo Ave 89110
Vallerosa St 89141
Valles Caldera Ct 89118
Valley Dr 89108
Valley Ln 89106
Valley St 89101
Valley Canyon St 89148
Valley Chase Ave 89138
Valley Creek Dr 89134
Valley Crest St 89108
Valley Downs Dr 89134
Valley Edge Ct 89141
Valley Forge Ave 89110
Valley Glen Ct & St 89119
Valley Green Dr 89149
Valley Grove Ct 89130
Valley Hills Ave 89134
Valley Meadow Dr 89120
Valley Mill St 89148
Valley Nails Ln 89110
Valley Of Fire Ave 89129
Valley Ranch Ave 89178
Valley Ridge Ct 89148
Valley Sand St 89135
Valley Spring Ct 89147
Valley Stream Ave 89131
N Valley View Blvd 89107
S Valley View Blvd
100-298 89107
300-1099 89107
1101-1197 89102
1199-3499 89102
3500-4899 89103
4900-7099 89118
7101-7199 89118
7301-7597 89139
7599-8200 89139
8202-8898 89139
10101-10199 89141
Valley View Ridge Ct 89110
Valley Vision Ct 89149
Valley Wells Way 89113
Valleybreeze Ave 89129
Valleyside Ave 89115
Valmark Dr 89115
Valmeyer Ave 89148
Valmora St 89102
Valparaiso St 89108
Van St 89122
E Van Buren Ave 89110
W Van Buren Ave 89106
Van Buskirk Cir 89121
Van Carol Dr 89147
Van Dyke Ave 89103
Van Eps Ct 89148
Van Halen Ln 89148
Van Patten Pl 89104
Van Patten St 89109
Vancouver Ave 89121
Vancouver Crest Ct 89149
Vandalia St 89106
Vanderbilt Ct 89104
Vanderhoof Ct 89147
Vanessa Dr 89103
Vanishing Point St 89129
Vanity Ct 89149
Vanity Fair Ln 89113
Vanmulligan Ave 89183
Vansville Way 89130
Vantage Ln 89145
Vantage Point Rd 89128
Vantare Ct 89145
Vaquero Way 89169
Varallo St 89129
Varedo Ct 89141
Varenna Ridge Ave 89141
Varese Dr 89141
Varna Ave 89110
Varsity Ave 89146
Vasari Ct 89144
Vasila Dr 89110
Vassar Ln 89107
Vassar Meadow St 89148
Vast Horizon Ave 89129
Vast Valley Ave 89148
Vaughn St 89101
Vecinos Ln 89110
Vedena Pl 89113
Vedra Ct 89135
Veeder Dr 89145
Vega Ln 89130
Vega Carpio Ave 89178
Vega Del Sol Ave 89122
Vegas Dr
1700-2498 89106
2500-3099 89106
3600-6600 89108
6602-6698 89108
7500-7999 89128
Vegas Plaza Dr 89109
Vegas Valley Dr
700-1199 89109
1200-2399 89169
2401-2519 89121
2521-4899 89121
5000-5098 89142
5070-5070 89162
5901-6297 89142
6299-7999 89142
Velarde Ct 89120
Velazco Ln 89130
Velicata Ct 89138
Velino Ave 89123
Vellozia Ct 89149
Velma Ave 89108
Velure St 89122
Velvet Canyon Ave 89128
Velvet Crest Ln 89139
Velvet Dusk Ln 89144
Velvet Hill Ave 89106
Velvet Mist St 89131
Velvet Moon Ct 89178
Velvet Rose St 89135
Velvet Sky St 89131
Vema Dr 89121
Vemoa Dr 89141
Venado Dr 89130
Venalynne St 89156
Veneer Ln 89108
Veneroso St 89148
Venetia St 89123
Venetian Hills Ln 89144
Venice Dr 89108
Venice Cove Ave 89141
Venita Ct & Dr 89120
Ventana Dr 89130
Ventana Canyon Dr 89113
Ventana Hills Dr 89117
Ventosa Way 89128
Ventura Way 89121
Ventura Grass Ct 89135
Ventura Hills St 89144
Ventura Mountain St 89178
Venture Dr 89101
Venus Cir 89101
Venus Lake Ct 89178
Venus Vale Ct 89156
Vera Dell Ct 89110
Veranda Ct 89149
Veranda Falls Ct 89130
Veranda View Ave 89123
Verano Dr 89130
Verbania Dr 89134
Verbena Creek Ct 89131
Vercelli Ct 89117
W Verde Way
5800-6099 89130
7200-9400 89149
9402-9498 89149
Verde Circado Ave 89146
Verde Jardin Way 89146
Verde Mirada Dr 89115
Verde Park Cir 89129
Verde River Way 89149
Verde Springs Dr 89128
Verde Vista Pl 89145
Verdet St 89147
Verdiccio Ave 89141
Verdinal Dr 89146
Verdugo St 89147
Verdugo Peak St 89166
Verdy Ln 89101
Verismo St 89141
Verlaine Ct 89145
Vermeer St 89110
Vermiel Dr 89117
Vermillion Cliffs Ave 89147
Vermont Ave 89107
Vernal St 89139
Vernal Falls Ct 89139
Vernazza Ct 89138
Verneda Ct 89147
Vernon Ave 89108
Vernon Springs Ave 89183
Vero Dr 89134
Verona Ave 89120
Verona Gardens Ct 89141
Verona Wood St 89141
Verplank Ave 89128
Versante Ave 89183
Vertigo Tulip Ct 89106
Vervain Ct 89149
Vespertina Ct 89128
Vestia Ct 89149
Vestibule Ct 89149
Vestone St 89141
Vesuvio Ct 89183
Veterans Ct 89148
Veterans Memorial Dr 89101
Via Alamo Ave 89115
Via Alhambra Ct 89123
Via Amigos Pl 89115
Via Antonia Ave 89119
Via Aquario Dr 89122
Via Austi Pkwy 89119
Via Balizan Ave 89123
Via Bella Luna Ave 89131
Via Bianca Ave 89141
Via Bonita Cir 89147
Via Campanile Ave 89131
Via Capri 89122
Via Costa Bella Ave 89131
Via Costada St 89123
Via Dana Ave 89141
Via De Bellasidra Ct 89123
Via De Palma Dr 89146
Via Del Cerro Ct 89117
Via Del Mar St 89131
Via Del Prado St 89115
Via Del Rey Ct 89115
Via Del Robles Ave 89115
Via Del Viento Ave 89130
Via Delores Ave 89117
Via Delsur Ln 89130
Via Dulcedo St 89124
Via El Monte Ave 89115
Via Esperanza Ave 89138
Via Fernando Ave 89115
Via Fiorentino St 89131
Via La Contera Dr 89122
Via Linda Ct 89144
Via Locanda Ave 89131
Via Lucia Dr 89115
Via Lupine St 89115
Via Madrigal 89103
Via Manigua 89120
Via Margarita Ave 89115
Via Mariposa Ave 89115
Via Marnell Way 89119
Via Mater Misercordia
St 89124
Via Mazarron St 89123
Via Montagna St 89129
Via Napoleone Cir 89143
Via Olivero Ave
4100-4399 89102
5700-5798 89146
6900-7698 89117
7700-7800 89117
7802-8298 89117
Via Paseo Ave 89128
Via Primero St 89115
Via Princessa Ct 89138
Via Provenza Ave 89131
Via Renaldo 89103
Via Rimini St 89131
Via Roma Pl 89144
Via Rosa Ct 89130
Via San Andros 89103
Via San Marco 89103
Via San Rafael 89103
Via Santiago St 89144
Via Segundo Ave 89115
Via Signorelli St 89131
Via Sistina St 89131
Via Sonja Ave 89115
Via Spes Nostra St 89124
Via Spiga Dr 89138
Via Torino 89103
Via Toro Ave 89117
Via Vaquero Ave 89102
Via Ventura Ct 89123
Via Vera Cruz Ct 89138
Via Vista Cir 89147
Via Vita St 89124
Via Zaracoza Ct 89123
Viansa Loma Ave 89149
Viareggio Ct 89147
Viberti Ct 89118
Vibrant Dr 89117
Vibrant Thread Ct 89149
Vicarage Way 89141
Vicenta Ct 89115
Vicenza Ct 89117
Viceroy Ln 89117
Vickers St 89178
Vickers Canyon St 89131
Vicki Ave 89139
Vicksburg Ave 89122
Vicobello Ave 89141
Victor Creek Ave 89149
Victor Hugo Ln 89115
Victoria St 89121
Victoria Beach Way 89130
Victoria Falls Ct 89113
Victoria Medici St 89141
Victoria Oak Ct 89148
Victoria Regina Ave 89139
Victoria Springs Ct 89148
Victorian Lace St 89183
Victorville Ct 89122
Victory Ave 89121
Victory Gallup St 89131
Victory Garden Ave 89149
Vicuna Dr 89146
Vida Nueva Ct 89131
Vida Pacifica St 89115
Vienna Way 89145
Vieno Canyon St 89123
Viento Cir 89147
View Dr 89107
Viewpoint Dr 89156
Vigo Rd 89146
E Viking Rd
1500-1798 89119
1800-2399 89169
2401-2497 89121
2499-4599 89121
W Viking Rd
4001-5497 89103
5499-6500 89103
6502-6598 89103
8901-9097 89147
9099-9399 89147
Viking Garden Cir 89121
Vikings Cove Ln 89117
Vilberti Ct 89144
Villa Cir 89108
Villa Way 89120
Villa Acapulco Ave 89131
Villa Adastra Ave 89148
Villa Alex Ave 89147
Villa Altamura St 89148
Villa Andrade Ave 89131
Villa Arbol Ct 89131
Villa Arceno Ave 89135
Villa Ariel Ln 89147
Villa Armando St 89131
Villa Avada Ct 89113
Villa Belen St 89131
Villa Bellagio Dr 89141
Villa Bonita Rd 89146
Villa Borghese St 89138
Villa Cache Ct 89148
Villa Calera Ave 89148
Villa Camille Ave 89147
Villa Campania Ct 89141
Villa Cano St 89131
Villa Carlotta Ct 89141
Villa Colonade Dr 89128
Villa Creek Ct 89139
Villa Crest Ct 89110
Villa Dante Ave 89141
Villa De Conde Way 89102
Villa De La Paz Ave 89131
Villa De La Playa St 89131
Villa De Medici St 89131
Villa De Palmero Ave 89139
Villa De Paz Ct 89122
Villa De Picasso Ave 89131
Villa De Sol St 89156
Villa Del Cielo St 89131
Villa Del Fuego Ave 89131
Villa Del Mar Ave 89131
Villa Del Sol Ct 89110
Villa Del Viento Dr 89131
Villa Di Firenze Ct 89118
Villa Duenas Ct 89131
Villa Encanto Ave 89131
Villa Faith Ave 89147
Villa Fiesta St 89131
Villa Finestra Dr 89128
Villa Fiori Ave 89141
Villa Flora St 89130
Villa Gabriela Ave 89131
Villa Giovanni Ct 89141
Villa Hermosa Dr 89121
Villa Inn Ct 89110
Villa Jeremiah Ln 89147
Villa Knolls East Dr 89120
Villa Knolls North Dr 89120
Villa Knolls South Dr 89120
Villa Knolls West Dr 89120
Villa La Mora Ave 89147
Villa La Rae Ave 89147
Villa Lante Ave 89113
Villa Lorena Ave 89147
Villa Lucia Ct 89141
Villa Malaparte Ave 89138
Villa Mesa Dr 89107
Villa Modena St 89141
Villa Monica Ln 89147
Villa Montara St 89123
Villa Monterey Dr 89145
Villa Norfolk St 89139
Villa Pablo Ln 89147
Villa Palms Ct 89128
Villa Paola Ct 89141
Villa Park Ct 89110
Villa Pescara St 89147
Villa Pintura Ave 89131
Villa Pulido St 89131
Villa Rafael Dr 89141
Villa Ridge Dr 89134
Villa Rosal St 89108
Villa Rosarito St 89131
Villa Salsa Ave 89131
Villa San Michele Ct 89138
Villa Sovana Ct 89113
Villa Torre St 89141
Villa Toscano Ct 89141
Villa Trentino Ct 89141
Villa Trieste Ct 89113
Villa Trovas Ct 89113
Villa Tuscany Ave 89129
Villa Vasari Ave 89141
Villa Vecchio Ct 89141
Villa Ventana Ave 89131
Villa Vista Way 89128
Village Dr 89142
Village Sq 89121
Village Arbor St 89183
Village Breeze Pl 89183
Village Center Cir 89134
Village Crest Ln 89135
Village Crossing Ln 89183
Village Edge Pl 89183
Village Green Ct 89110
Village Hills St 89147
Village Mist Ln 89113
Village Ridge Ln 89135
Village Shore Ct 89129
Village Spring St 89147
Village Walk Ave 89149
Ville Franche St 89145
Villefort Ct 89117
Villeroy Ave 89141
Vinator St 89138
Vinca Rd 89113
Vincent St 89146
Vincent Way 89145
Vincente Ln 89130
Vinces Lake St 89178
Vincitor St 89135
Vine Creek Pl 89138
Vinecrest Ave 89108
Vineyard Ln 89110
Vineyard Rd 89166
Vineyard Pass St 89141
Vinson Point Ave 89129
Vintage Ct 89113
Vintage Canyon St 89141
Vintage Garden Ct 89148
Vintage Highlands Ln 89110
Vintage Hills Ct 89110
Vintage Ridge Dr 89141
Vintage Valley Dr 89141
Vintage Wine Ave 89148
Vintners Ln 89138
Violet Bay Ct 89131
Violet Blossom Dr 89108
Violet Bouquet Way 89142
Violet Breeze Way 89142
Violet Dawn St 89149
Violet Hill St 89110
Violet Meadow Ct 89117
Violet Peaks St 89117
Violet Pearl St 89183
Violet Rose Ct 89147
Violet Sky St 89149
Violet Sunset Ave 89148
Violet Vista Ave 89130
Vireo Dr 89147
Virgil St 89110
Virginia City Ave 89106
Virginia Dale St 89131
Virginia Falls Ln 89130
Virginia Pine Ct 89123
Virginia Rail St 89115
Virginia Woods Cir 89117
Virgo Dr 89156
Viridine Ct 89122
Virtue Ct 89113
Virtuoso Ct 89139
Visby Ln 89119
Viscanio Pl 89138
Visconti Way 89141
Viscount Carlson Dr 89119
Visibility Ct 89129
Vision St 89123
Vision Quest Ct 89139
Vista Dr 89102
Vista Bonita Dr 89149
Vista Butte Dr 89134
Vista Cache Ct 89148

Vista Cantera Ct 89147
Vista Colorado St 89123
Vista Crest Ave 89148
Vista Del Monte Dr 89121
Vista Del Sol Ave 89120
Vista Diablo St 89117
Vista Famosa Ct 89123
Vista Flora Way 89121
Vista Glen St 89145
Vista Gold Ct 89129
Vista Grande Dr 89149
Vista Greens Way 89134
Vista Hermosa Ave 89108
Vista Hills Dr 89128
Vista Knoll Rd 89178
Vista Ladera Ct 89147
Vista Largo Dr 89121
Vista Linda Ave 89138
Vista Malaga St 89106
Vista Mar Dr 89128
Vista Marbella Ave 89144
Vista Ridge Ave 89129
Vista Royale Ct 89147
Vista Sandia Way 89115
Vista Sunrise Dr 89149
Vista Twilight Dr 89123
Vista Valley St 89110
Vista Verde 89146
Vista Waters Ln 89178
Vital Ct 89149
Vital Crest St 89123
Vitano St 89138
Viterbo St 89183
Viva Cir 89108
Vivaldi Dr 89146
Vivian Cir 89145
Vivid Ave 89144
Vivid Colors Ave 89148
Vivid Vail St 89149
Vivid Violet Ave 89143
Vizcaya Ct 89178
Vizzi Ct 89131
Vogel Ct 89129
Vogue St 89129
Volcanic Garden Ct 89183
Volcanic Rock Ln 89122
Volgi St 89135
Volk Ave 89178
Volonne Ct 89141
Von Bryan Ct 89102
Von Leidner St 89149
Vornsand Dr 89115
Vosburgh Dr 89117
Voxna St 89119
Voyage Cove Dr 89142
Voyager St 89123
Vulcan St 89122
Vulture Peak Trl 89118
Wabusca Way 89142
Wade Lake Ave 89178
Wadsworth Ct
6100-6199 89130
6400-6499 89156
Wagner Ranch Rd 89166
Wagon Trail Ave 89118
Wagonwheel Ave 89119
Wagonwheel Ranch Way 89113
Waikiki Ave 89104
Wailings Ave 89148
Wainscot Ct 89147
Wainwright Ct 89123
Wakashan Ave 89149
Wake Forest Dr 89129
Waking Cloud Ave 89129
Waking View Ave 89129
Walbrook Ln 89148
Walcott Dr 89118
Walden Lake St 89131
Walden Park St 89166
Walden Pond Ct 89148
Waldman Ave 89102
Waldorf Ct 89103
Wales Green Ln 89110
Walhalla Plateau Ct 89148
Walhaven Ct 89103
Walker St 89106
Walker Gardens Pl 89166
Walker Lake Ct 89149
Walker Valley Ct 89139
Walking Spirit Ct 89129
Walking View Ct 89135
Walkinshaw Ave 89148
Wall St 89102
Wall Violet Ct 89183
Walla Walla Dr 89107
Wallaby Ln 89123
N & S Wallace Dr 89107
Wallach Ave 89123
Wallerbee Cir 89156
Wallflower Ave 89135
Wallington Estate St 89178
Walnut Ave
1700-2500 89101
2502-2898 89101
5200-5300 89110
5302-5398 89110
N Walnut Rd 89115
S Walnut Rd 89104
Walnut Bend Ave 89115
Walnut Canyon Dr 89156
Walnut Creek Dr 89147
Walnut Family Ct 89115
Walnut Glen Dr 89115
Walnut Green Ave 89115
Walnut Grove Ct 89104
Walnut Hill Ave 89106
Walnut Knolls Way 89117
Walnut Ridge Cir 89119
Walnut Roast Way 89131
Walnut Star Ln 89115
Walnut Wood St 89129
Walrus St 89117
Walt Lott Dr 89128
Walter Schirra Cir 89145
Walteta Way 89119
Waltham Ln 89122
Walton Heath Ave 89142
Waltons Mill Ct 89131
Waltz St 89123
Waltzing Waters Ct 89147
Walworth Ave 89166
Wanda Ct 89108
Wandercloud Ln 89145
Wandering St 89131
Wandering Doe Ln 89134
Wandering Ivy St 89130
Wandering River Ct 89135
Wandering Star Ct 89131
Wandering Sun Ave 89129
Wandering Violets Way 89138
Wandering Winds Way 89128
Wandering Woods Ct 89149
Wandesforde Ln 89110
Waning Bay Ct 89142
Wapiti Point Ct 89130
War Admiral Ct 89113
War Eagle Cir 89108
War Emblem Ct 89141
Warbonnet Way
1101-1199 89117
4301-4397 89147
4399-4499 89147
8100-8499 89113
8501-8899 89113
Wardelle St 89101
Wardlaw St 89117
Wards Ferry St 89139
Warhawk Ave 89115
Warians St 89118
Warkworth Castle Ave 89178
Warling St 89122
Warm Canyon Way 89123
Warm Eagle Ave 89178
Warm Glow Way 89178
Warm Meadows St 89129
Warm River Rd 89108
E Warm Springs Rd
2-98 89119
100-2299 89119
2301-2399 89119
2401-3299 89120
W Warm Springs Rd
2202-2798 89119
3300-3798 89118
3800-6600 89118
6602-6698 89118
6900-7298 89113
7300-8599 89113
8600-8698 89148
8700-9000 89148
9002-9098 89148
Warm Sun Ct 89110
Warm Walnut Dr 89134
Warm Waters Ave 89129
Warmbreeze Way 89129
Warminster Ave 89178
Warmside Dr 89145
Warner Pl 89115
Warnock Rd 89102
Warren Dr 89106
Warrendale Ct 89183
Warrenville St 89117
Warrior Ct 89135
Wartbug Ct 89131
Warthen Meadows St 89131
Warwick Ct 89110
Warwick Castle Dr 89178
Warwick Falls Ct 89144
Warwickshire Way 89139
Wasatch Ln 89122
Wasatch Cedars St 89122
Wasatch Maple Ave 89117
Wasatch Ridge Cir 89149
Waseca Ave 89144
W Washburn Rd
5800-6399 89130
7201-7697 89149
7699-9499 89149
Washed Pebble Ave 89147
E Washington Ave
2-98 89101
100-505 89101
507-3199 89101
3503-3797 89110
3799-6599 89110
6601-6899 89110
W Washington Ave
300-698 89106
700-2599 89106
2601-2699 89106
2800-6400 89107
6402-6698 89107
7000-7599 89128
7601-7999 89128
Washington Apple St 89122
Washington Oaks St 89128
Washita Ct 89129
Washoe Ave 89107
Watauga Ave 89147
Watch Tower Ave 89178
Watchtide Ct 89166
Water Bucket Ave 89143
Water Crossing Ave 89131
Water Flow Ct 89134
Water Gap Ave 89178
Water Hazard Ln 89148
Water Lily Way 89142
Water Song Dr 89147
Waterbury Ln 89134
Waterdragon Ave 89110
Waterfall Mist Ct 89123
Waterfall Ranch Ct 89131
Waterfalls Ave 89128
Waterfield Ct 89134
Waterford Ln 89119
Waterford Bend St 89123
Waterford Castle Ct 89141
Waterford Falls Ave 89123
Waterhen Cir 89108
Waterhole St 89130
Waterleaf Ct 89130
Watermelon Seed Ave 89143
Waterside Cir 89117
Waterthrush Way 89103
Waterton Dr 89144
Waterton Lakes Ave 89148
Waterview Dr 89117
Waterville Cir 89107
Watkins Dr 89107
Waukegan Ave 89148
Wave Dancer Ln 89118
Wavecrest Dr 89108
Waveland Dr 89130
Wavering Pine Dr 89143
Waving Palm St 89131
Waving Sage Dr 89149
Waving Tree St 89118
Waxberry Ct 89178
Wayburn Way 89103
Waycross Dr 89134
Wayfarer Dr 89156
Wayfaring Tree Ave 89131
Waylon Ave 89178
Waymire Creek Ct 89147
Wayne Cir & St 89121
Wayne Newton Blvd 89111
Waynesvill St 89122
Wayside Ct 89142
Wayward Ct 89129
Wealdston Ct 89178
Wear Ct 89123
Weather Top Ct 89135
Weather View Dr 89110
Weatherford Way 89156
Weatherstone Dr 89110
Weathervane Ct 89110
Weaver Dr 89106
Weavercrest Ct 89166
Weber Ct 89121
Webfoot Rd 89115
Wedge Ct 89122
Wedgebrook St 89183
Wedgewood Way 89147
Wedlock Ln 89129
Weed Willows Ave 89178
Weenap Dr 89108
Weeping Fig Ct 89130
Weeping Hollow Ave 89178
Weeping Pine St 89149
Weeping Springs Ave 89131
Weeping Water Ave 89178
Weeping Willow Ln 89104
Weitzman Pl 89141
Welch Valley Ave 89131
Welcome Ln 89130
Weldon Pl 89104
Welland Ct 89144
Wellesley Ave & Dr 89122
Wellfleet Bay Ave 89179
Wellington Ct 89156
Wellington Manor Ave 89129
Wells Cathedral Ave 89130
Wellsboro St 89147
Wellside Hill Ave 89145
Wellspring Ave 89183
Welsey Ave 89183
Welsey Manor Dr 89156
Welsh Cir 89108
Welsh Mist Ct 89183
Welsh Pony St 89122
Welter Ave 89104
Wenatchee Dr 89107
Wendell Ave 89101
Wendell Williams Ave 89106
Wendover Ave 89110
Wendover Hills Ave 89123
Wendy Ln 89115
Wengert Ave 89104
Wenmarie Ct 89148
Wentworth Cir 89142
Wentworth Springs Ct 89139
Werdco Ct 89115
Wertz Ave 89148
Wesley St 89104
Wesleyan Ct 89113
Wessex Dr 89178
Westbrook Ave 89147
Westbury Rd 89121
Westchester Hill Ave 89148
Westcliff Dr 89145
Western Ave
1101-1219 89102
1221-2499 89102
2600-3400 89109
3402-3498 89109
Western Lily St 89128
Western Saddle Ave 89129
Western Sunset Ct 89117
Westfalen Ct 89131
Westfield Cir & St 89121
Westleigh Ave
3200-3298 89102
3300-3799 89102
5200-5399 89146
Westlund Dr 89102
Westminster Ave 89119
Westmoreland Dr 89108
Westpark Ave & Ct 89147
Westport Cir 89108
Westridge Dr 89107
Westview Dr 89107
Westwind Rd
1200-1272 89146
1274-3499 89146
3700-3799 89103
5201-5697 89118
5699-6299 89118
6301-6499 89118
7801-8497 89139
8499-8699 89139
8701-9499 89139
Westwood Dr
1100-1699 89102
2600-3199 89109
Wetherly Ct 89156
Wetlands Park Ln 89122
Wexford Ln 89129
Weybridge Dr 89121
Weybrook Park Dr 89141
Whale Rock St 89149
Whale Watch St 89113
Whalers Cove Cir 89117
Whalers Landing Ct 89117
Wharton St 89130
Whatley St 89148
Wheat Grass Ct 89129
Wheat Penny Ave 89122
Wheat Ridge Ln 89145
Wheatfield Dr 89120
Wheaties Way 89110
Wheatland Way 89128
Wheatleigh Ct 89115
Wheatsnow Cir 89117
Wheatstone Ct 89129
Wheelbarrow Peak Dr 89108
Wheeler St 89148
Wheeler Peak Dr 89106
Wheelwright Dr 89121
Whipkey St 89183
Whipple Crest Ave 89166
Whipple Manor St 89166
Whippletree Ave 89119
Whipplewood Way 89148
Whippoorwill Cir 89121
Whippoorwill Ln 89121
Whippoorwill Way 89103
Whiptail St 89178
Whirlaway St 89108
Whiskey Moon St 89139
Whiskey River St 89130
Whispa Ct 89183
Whisper Heights Ct 89131
Whisper Lake Ave 89131
Whisper Mare Ct 89131
Whisper Ridge St 89156
Whispering Birch Ave 89123
Whispering Brook Ct 89149
Whispering Clouds Ct 89141
Whispering Creek St 89148
Whispering Glen Cir 89108
Whispering Grove Ave 89123
Whispering Hills Cir 89117
Whispering Marsh Dr 89131
Whispering Meadow Ct 89130
Whispering Palms Dr 89123
Whispering Pine Ave 89142
Whispering Quail Ct 89122
Whispering River St 89131
Whispering Sands Dr 89131
Whispering Spring Ave 89131
Whispering Tree Ave 89183
Whispering Voice St 89110
Whispering Waters Ave 89131
Whispering Willow Ln 89108
Whispering Wind Dr 89117
Whispring Native Ct 89115
Whispy Breeze Ave 89139
Whispy Willow Way 89135
Whistler Ridge Ave 89110
Whistling Acres Ave 89131
Whistling Duck Ave 89115
Whistling Straits St 89141
Whistling Swan Way 89118
Whistling Tree Ct 89148
Whistling Vines Ave 89106
Whitacre Ct 89123
Whitcraft Ct 89141
White Dr 89119
White Ash Ct 89130
White Aspen Ave 89130
White Bark Pine St 89129
White Bison Ct 89149
White Bloom Ave 89117
White Bluffs St 89148
White Cap St 89110
White Cap Mill St 89147
White Carnation St 89147
White Castle St 89129
White Cedar Dr 89115
White Chalk Ave 89115
White Cliffs Ave 89138
White Cloud Dr 89134
White Coyote Pl 89130
White Crane Ct 89139
White Dawn St 89130
White Deer Ct 89131
White Diamond Dr 89129
White Dog Cir 89141
White Dogwood Ct 89148
White Dove Dr 89149
White Dune St 89113
White Eagle Ave 89145
White Eyes Ave 89143
White Falcon St 89144
White Falls St 89128
White Feather Ln 89138
White Fir Way 89148
White Flower Ct 89131
White Gate Ln 89147
White Ginger Ave 89178
White Grass Ave 89131
White Grotto St 89138
White Hawk Ct 89134
White Head Ct 89147
White Heart Rd 89148
White Heath Ct 89144
White Heron Ct 89139
White Horse St 89115
White Ivory Ct 89147
White Lakes Ave 89130
White Landing Ct 89138
White Lilac St 89178
White Lilly St 89183
White Mill Ct 89131
White Mission Dr 89129
White Mist Dr 89134
White Mountain St
3400-3499 89117
3500-3599 89147
White Mulberry Dr 89148
White Mule Ave 89148
White Orchard Ct 89123
White Peppermint Dr 89147
White Pine Way 89108
White Plains Dr 89129
White Point Ct 89139
White Princess Ave 89166
White Ridge Ave 89149
White River Dr 89147
White Rock Dr 89121
White Rock Peak St 89113
White Sands Ave
4200-4299 89121
6800-6899 89145
White Shadow Ct 89123
White Shell Cir 89108
White Shore Cir 89128
White Skies Ct 89156
White Springs St 89123
White Star Dr 89129
White Swan Cir 89108
White Tail Dr 89134
White Tiger Ct 89130
White Truffles Cir 89141
White Waterfall Ave 89149
White Wicker Dr 89147
White Willow Ave 89123
Whitebirch Ln 89134
Whitebird Way 89103
Whitebrush Ave 89144
Whitecap Rains Ct 89148
Whitehills St 89141
Whitekirk Pl 89145
Whiteleaf Ct 89149
Whitelion Walk St 89148
Whiteridge Ave 89107
Whiteriver Plateau Ln 89178
Whitesboro Ct 89139
Whitewater Autumn Ct 89148
Whitewater Canyon Ct 89183
Whitewater Crest Ct 89178
Whitewind Ln 89110
Whitford St 89166
Whiting Ave 89166
Whitlocks Mill Ave 89147
Whitly Bay Ave 89148
Whitman St 89110
Whitman Colonial St 89166
Whitman Falls Dr 89129
Whitney Ave 89122
Whitney Falls Ct 89148
Whiton St 89156
Whittier Ct 89117
Whittingham Ct 89144
Whooping Crane Ln 89144
Wichita Ct 89119
Wicked Wedge Way 89148
Wickstead St 89178
Wide River St 89130
Wiesner Way 89122
Wiggins Bay St 89129
E Wigwam Ave 89123
W Wigwam Ave
2400-2799 89123
3000-3298 89139
3300-6099 89139
7301-7397 89113
7399-8599 89113
8600-8698 89148
11100-11899 89161
Wilborn St 89101
Wilbur St 89119
Wilbur Mcgee Ct 89129
Wild Berry Dr 89142
Wild Bill Ct 89129
Wild Blossom Dr 89129
Wild Bob Way 89108
Wild Briar Ln 89143
Wild Buffalo Ave 89131
Wild Cactus Ct 89156
Wild Calla St 89178
Wild Candlenut Ct 89183
Wild Canyon St 89147
Wild Carrot Ave 89129
Wild Chamomile St 89183
Wild Cherry Ct 89121
Wild Chive Ave 89122
Wild Creek Ct 89117
Wild Creek Falls Way 89141
Wild Crest St 89149
Wild Diamond Ave 89143
Wild Dunes Ct 89113
Wild Eagle Cir 89129
Wild Fern Ct 89183
Wild Geranium St 89108
Wild Ginger Ln 89134
Wild Honey Ct 89147

Street	ZIP
Wild Horse Rd	89108
Wild Horse Mesa Dr	89131
Wild Indigo Ct	89123
Wild Jan Dr	89106
Wild Lariat Ave	89178
Wild Lilac Ct	89141
Wild Lily Ct	89147
Wild Magic St	89129
Wild Marigold Dr	89130
Wild Olive St	89118
Wild Pansy Ct	89147
Wild Peach Ct	89149
Wild Plum Ln	89107
Wild Ridge Ct	89135
Wild River Dr	89108
Wild Roar Ave	89129
Wild Springs St	89129
Wild Stampede Ave	89178
Wild Strawberry Ln	89142
Wild Thing Ct	89131
Wild Thistle Ct	89149
Wild Thyme Ave	89131
Wild Waters Ave	89139
Wild Wave Dr	89131
Wild Willow St	89129
Wild Wind Dr	89128
Wildcat Canyon Ave	89178
Wildcat Hill Ct	89178
Wildcat Springs Ave	89178
Wilde Way	89148
Wildebeest Ct	89149
Wilder Pl	89121
Wilderness Glen Ave	89178
Wildfire St	89123
Wildflower Gully St	89178
Wildheart Ranch St	89131
Wildherd Ave	89149
Wildhorse Ledge Ave	89131
Wildhurst St	89183
Wildroot Rd	89130
Wildrose St	89107
Wildshire Way	89107
Wildwing Ct	89135
Wildwood Dr	89108
Wildwood Glen Dr	89131
Wilhelmina Cir	89128
Willamette Pl	89134
Willard St	89122
Willeford Ct	89123
Willeta Ave	89145
William Anders Ave	89145
William Fortye Ave	89129
William Hill Ave	89148
William Holden Ct	89142
Williams Island Ct	89131
Williams Ranch Rd	89161
Williamville Ct	89129
Willie Saunders St	89120
Willjay Ln	89123
Willoughby Ave	89101
Willow St	89106
Willow Trl	89108
Willow Basin Ct	89131
Willow Basket Ln	89135
Willow Bend Ct	89121
Willow Breeze Ln	89118
Willow Brush St	89166
Willow Cabin St	89131
Willow Cove Cir	89129
Willow Crest Ave	89147
Willow Dove Ave	89123
Willow Glen Dr	89147
Willow Green Dr	89169
Willow Heights Dr	89135
Willow Lake Ct	89108
Willow Meadow Ct	89129
Willow Mist Dr	89147
Willow Oak Cir	89142
Willow Pines Pl	89143
Willow Point Ct	89128
Willow Pond Ct	89148
Willow River Ct	89108
Willow Run Ln	89117
Willow Springs Dr	89103
Willow Trace Ave	89139
Willow Tree Dr	89128
Willow Valley Ct	89135
Willow Village Ave	89183
Willow Wind Ct	89117
Willow Wood Ct	89108
Willowbark Ct	89117
Willowbrook Dr	89106
Willowbrook Pond Rd	89148
Willowbury Dr	89108
Willowcroft St	89149
Willowhaven Ave	89120
Willowhill Ct	89147
Willowleaf Ct	89128
Willowlyn Ct	89122
Willowrich Dr	89134
Willowridge Ct	89149
Willowstone St	89166
Willowview Ct	89147
Willson Sq	89169
Wilma Ave	89108
Wilmington Way	89102
Wilmot St	89102
Wilshire Blvd	89110
Wilshire St	89146
E Wilson Ave	89101
W Wilson Ave	89106
Wilson Cliffs Rd	89128
Wilted Jasmine Ct	89106
Wiltondale Way	89130
Wimberly St	89148
Wimbledon Dr	89107
Wincanton Dr	89134
Winchester Ct & St	89110
Winchester Bluff St	89131
Winchester Ridge St	89139
Wind Cove St	89110
Wind Dancer Dr	89118
Wind Drift Pl	89124
Wind Drift Rd	89149
Wind Prairie St	89130
Wind Ridge Ct	89129
Wind River Dr	89110
Wind Spinner St	89135
Wind Warrior Ave	89143
Wind Whisper St	89148
Wind Willow Ave	89113
Windansea St	89147
Windblown Ct	89129
Windborne Ave	89147
Windchase Ave	89129
Windchime Dr	89106
Windcrest Falls Dr	89135
Windfair Ct	89145
Windfair Village St	89145
Windfresh Dr	89148
Windham Heights Ct	89139
Windhamridge Dr	89139
Windhaven Cir	89117
Windhook St	89144
Winding Canyon Dr	89120
Winding Creek Dr	89113
Winding Ridge Way	89156
Winding River Ct	89129
Winding Sand Ct	89149
Windingwood St	89148
Windjammer Way	89107
Windledge Ave	89134
E Windmill Ln	89123
W Windmill Ln	
2700-2799	89123
4100-6799	89139
6901-6997	89113
6999-8399	89113
8401-8499	89113
12800-12899	89161
Windmill Croft Dr	89148
Windmill Grove Ct	89156
Windmill Island Ave	89139
Windmill Villa St	89139
Windom Point Ave	89129
Window Rock Ln	89123
Windrose Point Ave	89144
Windrush Ave	89117
Windset Ct	89135
Windsford Cir	89117
Windsong Ct	89145
Windsong St	
100-223	89145
4101-4199	89147
Windsor Castle Ct	89138
Windsor Crest Ct	89123
Windsor Forest Ct	89123
Windsor Hill Way	89123
Windsor Locks Ave	89134
Windsor Oaks St	89139
Windsor Ridge Ave	89183
Windstone Ridge Ct	89135
Windstorm Ave	89106
Windswept St	89131
Windward Rd	89147
Windy Rd & St	89119
Windy Bluff St	89129
Windy Breeze Ct	89142
Windy Creek Ave	89123
Windy Gap St	89106
Windy Gorge St	89149
Windy Hollow St	89130
Windy Leaf Dr	89156
Windy Meadow Ave	89178
Windy Oaks Ct	89139
Windy Par Ct	89148
Windy Peak Ct	89113
Windy Point Trl	89142
Windy Reed St	89178
Windy Sands Ct	89110
Windy Seas Ct	89110
Windy Surf Ct	89128
Windy Waters Ct	89110
Windycliff Ct	89117
Wine Cellar Ave	89148
Wine Creek St	89139
Wine River Dr	89119
Wineberry Dr	89119
Winebrook Ave	89148
Winery Ridge St	89144
Winfield Dr	89147
Winfrey Ave	89148
Wing Canyon Ct	89139
Wingate Ln	89110
Wingate Creek Ct	89148
Wingedfoot Ave	89110
Wingrove Ave	89121
Winken Ct	89139
Winnebago Ln	89122
Winner Dr	89120
Winners Choice Pl	89117
Winners Cup Dr	89117
Winnick Ave	89109
Winning Spirit Ln	89113
Winslet St	89183
Winslow Ave	89129
Winslow St	89117
Winston Dr & St	89103
Winston Falls Ave	89139
Winter Ave	89130
Winter Cherry St	89130
Winter Cloud Ct	89115
Winter Cottage Pl	89135
Winter Garden Ct	89145
Winter Grass Dr	89135
Winter Hill St	89106
Winter Lily Ct	89106
Winter Meadow St	89130
Winter Palace Dr	89145
Winter Place St	89122
Winter Ridge St	89149
Winter Scene Ct	89147
Winter Sky Ave	89148
Winter Star Ct	89141
Winter Teal Ave	89144
Winter Valley Ct	89130
Winter View Ave	89135
Winter Whitetail St	89122
Winter Wind St	89134
Winter Wren St	89122
Winterberry Ct	89123
Winterchase Pl	89143
Winterfell Pl	89166
Wintergreen Dr	89128
Winterhaven St	89108
Winterpine Ave	89147
Winters Run Ave	89183
Winterset Dr	89130
Winterthur Ct	89129
Winterwood Blvd	89142
Winthrop Springs Rd	89139
Wintry Garden Ave	89134
Winwood St	89108
Wireless Ct	89129
Wisconsin Ave	89104
Wisdom Ct	89120
Wisdom Valley Ave	89149
Wiseton Ave	89183
Wishing Creek Ave	89178
Wishing Peak St	89178
Wishing Pond Ave	89178
Wishing Rock Way	89123
Wishing Well Rd	89123
Wishingstar Ct	89123
Wispy Sage Way	89149
Wispy Winds St	89148
Wisteria Ave	89107
Wisteria Hills Ct	89135
Wisteria Shade Ave	89115
Wisteria Tree St	89135
Withering Pine St	89123
Wittig Ave	
6000-7599	89131
9200-9899	89149
9901-9999	89149
Wolf St	89124
Wolf Canyon Ct	89128
Wolf Creek Rd	89128
Wolf Cub Ct	89178
Wolf Dancer Ave	89143
Wolf Pack Ln	89178
Wolf Rivers Ave	89131
Wolf Wood Ct	89179
Wolfeboro Ave	89166
Wolves Den Ln	89178
Wonderberry St	89131
Wonderful St	89147
Wonderful Day Dr	89148
Wonderland St	89113
Wonderstone Dr	89107
Wonderview Dr	89134
Wondra Dr	89115
Wood Bark Dr	89119
Wood Cliff Ave	89183
Wood Creek Ct	89141
Wood Fern St	89123
Wood Owl Ct	89144
Wood Petal St	89130
Wood Plank Ln	89135
Wood Shadow Ct	89131
Wood Sorrel St	89135
Wood Stork Ave	89122
Wood Work Ln	89135
Woodbine Way	89103
Woodbridge Dr	89108
Woodbright Way	89166
Woodbrook Ct	89141
Woodbury Ave	89103
Woodcrest Rd	89121
Wooded Heights Ave	89148
Wooded Hills Dr	89148
Wooden Gate Ave	89123
Wooden Pier Way	89117
Wooden Windmill Ct	89131
Woodfall Glen St	89148
Woodfield Dr	89142
Woodglen Ct	89108
Woodgreen Dr	89108
Woodhill Ave	89121
Woodhouse Dr	89134
Woodhue Ln	89147
Woodlake Ave	89147
Woodland Ave	
3000-3099	89106
4600-4799	89121
Woodland Cove Ct	89123
Woodland Moss Rd	89148
Woodland Prairie Ave	89129
Woodland Vase Ct	89131
Woodland Violet Ave	89138
Woodlawn Ln	89130
Woodley St	89106
Woodlore Pl	89144
Woodmore St	89144
Woodmount Dr	89107
Woodpine Dr	89119
Woodridge Rd	89121
Woodruff Pl	89120
Woods Dr	89108
Woods Crossing St	89148
Woodsen Bend Dr	89141
Woodsey Ct	89156
Woodsfield Ct	89183
Woodside Ln	89115
Woodstock Ct	89118
Woodstone Ct	89129
Woodstream Ct	89135
Woodsworth Ave	89108
Woodwell St	89147
Wooland Pines Rd	89148
Woolcomber St	89115
Woolen Hearth Ct	89149
Woolman Rink Ave	89123
Wooly Rose Ave	89106
Wooster Cir	89108
Wordsworth St	89129
World Cup Dr	89117
World Series Ct	89110
Wormwood Ln	89148
Worrell Ave	89123
Worsley Park Pl	89145
Worthen Cir	89145
Worthington Way	89117
Wotans Throne Ct	89148
Wounded Horse Trl	89161
Wounded Star Ave	89178
Woven Memories St	89149
Woven Sands St	89149
Woven Tapestry Ct	89149
Woven Wonders St	89183
Wrangell Mountain St	89122
Wrangler St	89146
Wright St	89115
Wright Brothers Ln	89119
Wright View Dr	89120
Wrigley Ct	89141
Wrigley Field Ave	89166
Wuthering Heights Ave	89113
Wyandotte St	89102
Wyatt Ave	89106
Wyatt Creek Ave	89130
Wyatt Earp Ct	89129
Wycliff Ln	89156
Wyndham St	89115
Wynn Rd	
3100-3298	89102
3300-3399	89102
3401-3499	89102
3500-3698	89103
3700-4800	89103
4802-4898	89103
5201-5397	89118
5399-5899	89118
Wyoming Ave	89142
E Wyoming Ave	89104
W Wyoming Ave	89102
Xavier St	89107
Yacht Basin Rd	89128
Yacht Harbor Dr	89145
Yacht Landing Dr	89129
Yakima Ave	89121
N Yale St	
1-799	89107
900-1099	89108
S Yale St	89107
Yamamoto St	89131
Yamhill St	89123
Yampa River Way	89148
Yang Ct	89129
Yankee Clipper Dr	89117
Yankee Meadow Cir	89130
Yankee Spring St	89122
Yardarm Way	89145
Yardley St	89102
Yarmoth Sea Ct	89166
Yarmouth Dr	89108
Yarmouth Bay Ct	89179
Yarmouth Key Ct	89129
Yarra Valley Ave	89139
Yarrow Ridge Ct	89183
Yarrow Root Ct	89129
Yaupon Ave	89101
Yeager Ave	89123
Yellow Ash St	89118
Yellow Bells Ct	89131
Yellow Canary Ave	89117
Yellow Cosmos Ave	89130
Yellow Cove Ln	89135
Yellow Daisy Ave	89147
Yellow Dawn Ct	89130
Yellow Hair St	89149
Yellow Harbor St	89129
Yellow Hawk Way	89139
Yellow Jasmine Dr	89147
Yellow Pine Ave	89124
Yellow Pine Ln	89130
Yellow Rose St	89108
Yellow Sage Cir	89149
Yellow Sky St	89145
Yellow Warbler St	89148
Yellowcrest Ct	89113
Yellowshale St	89143
Yellowstone Ave	89156
Yellowstone Creek Dr	89183
Yellowwood Dr	89123
Yeoman Cir	89128
Yerba Ln	89108
Yerington Ave	89110
Yew Ave	89110
Yew Blossom Ave	89166
Yolanda Ln	89121
Yondering Ave	89131
Yonie Ct	89117
Yoralis St	89119
Yorba Ct	89103
Yorba Linda Dr	89122
York Manor Ave	89166
Yorkfield Cir	89147
Yorkminster St	89129
Yorkshire Dr	89156
Yosemite St	89107
Young St	89119
Young Doe Ave	89130
Young Harbor Dr	89166
Young Ridge Ct	89139
Young Sky Ave	89142
Youngdale Dr	89134
Youngmont Ave	89103
Youngson Dr	89121
Younts Peak Ct	89178
Your Ave	89108
Yucca Ave	89104
Yucca Blossom Dr	89134
Yucca Fields Ct	89148
Yucca House Ave	89156
Yucca Point Ct	89115
Yucca Springs Dr	89129
Yucca Valley Ct	89142
Yuha Desert Ct	89183
Yukon Hills Ct	89178
Yuma Ave	89104
Yuma Cir	89169
Yvonne Cir	89122
Za Zu Pitts Ave	89122
Zabriskie St	89139
Zachary St	89118
Zaffina Cir	89120
Zafiro Ct	89115
Zafra Ct	89102
Zagarolo Ln	89141
Zamora Dr	89103
Zampino St	89141
Zane Cir	89121
Zane Grey Ct	89129
Zanzibar Ln	89147
Zapotec Way	89103
Zarod Rd	89135
Zavala St	89103
Zawawi Ct	89110
Zelkova Ct	89149
Zen Ct	89129
Zenia St	89103
Zephyr Ct	89121
Zephyr Wind Ave	89139
Zermatt Ave	89129
Zev Ct	89121
Zia St	89145
Zicker Ave	89123
Ziebart Pl	89103
Ziegler Ave	89148
Zingali Ct	89141
Zinkmist Ct	89143
Zinnia Ct & Ln	89108
Zion Dr	89107
Zion Falls St	89131
Zircon Cir	89106
Zircon Ridge Ct	89106
Zodiac Ct	89121
Zodiacal Light St	89129
Zola Cir	89145
Zone Ave	89122
Zorano Cir	89147
Zoroaster St	89148
Zugspitz Way	89124
Zuma Beach Ct	89113
Zuni Cir	89169
Zurich Ct	89147

NUMBERED STREETS

Street	ZIP
N & S 1st	89101
N 3rd St	89101
S 3rd St	
203-297	89101
299-1015	89101
1100-1300	89104
1302-1498	89104
N 4th St	89101
S 4th St	
110-900	89101
1100-1299	89104
5th Pl	89104
N 6th St	89101
S 6th St	
100-198	89101
200-900	89101
902-998	89101
1000-2300	89104
2302-2398	89104
N 7th St	89101
S 7th St	
100-298	89101
300-899	89101
1200-1204	89104
1206-1812	89104
1814-1814	89104
8th Pl	89104
N 8th St	89101
S 8th St	
200-498	89101
500-800	89101
802-898	89101
1101-1197	89104
1199-1816	89104
1818-1998	89104
N 9th St	89101
S 9th St	
119-211	89101
1200-1899	89104
N 10th St	89101
S 10th St	
200-712	89101
714-716	89101
1100-1110	89104
1112-2099	89104
2101-2199	89104
N 11th St	89101
S 11th St	
101-115	89101
117-614	89101
616-632	89101
1301-1797	89104
1799-2099	89104
N 12th St	89101
N 13th St	89101
S 13th St	
123-207	89101
1300-1698	89104
N 14th St	89101
S 14th St	
100-104	89101

1600-1899 89104
N 15th St 89101
S 15th St
112-114 89101
1100-2499 89104
N 16th St 89101
S 16th St
100-415 89101
1100-1999 89104
N 17th St 89101
S 17th St
101-199 89101
1100-2399 89104
N 18th St 89101
N 19th St 89101
N 20th St 89101
N 21st St 89101
N 22nd St 89101
N 23rd St 89101
N 24th St 89101
N 25th St 89101
N 26th St 89101
N 27th St 89101
N 28th St 89101
28th Street Cir 89101
N 29th St 89101
N 30th St 89101

LAUGHLIN NV

General Delivery 89029

POST OFFICE BOXES MAIN OFFICE STATIONS AND BRANCHES

Box No.s
All PO Boxes 89028

NAMED STREETS

Acacia Ct 89029
Aha Macav Pkwy 89029
Alba Dr 89029
Alki Beach Ave 89029
Antigua Dr 89029
Arie Dr 89029
Arroya Ct 89029
Aspen Mirror Way 89029
Athol Way 89029
Avalon Dr 89029
Bay Club Dr 89029
Bay Sands Dr 89029
Bayview Dr 89029
Bayview Loop Dr 89029
Beacon Rock Dr 89029
Benton Cove St 89029
Biscaya Dr 89029
Brian Ct 89029
Brinkley Manor St 89029
Brookfield Bay Ave 89029
Brookings Harbor Dr 89029
Bruce Woodbury Dr 89029
Cactus Springs Dr 89029
Cactus Valley Ln 89029
Cajon Ct 89029
Cal Edison Dr 89029
Calanda St 89029
Camel Mesa Dr 89029
Canyon Song Ave 89029
Canyon Terrace Dr 89029
Carved Canyon Ln 89029
Cascade Canyon Way 89029
S & W Casino Dr 89029
Catalina Dr 89029
Cattail Cove St 89029
Chandler Ranch Pl 89029
Chapels Royal St 89029
Chetco River St 89029
China Cove St 89029
Chinaberry Hill St 89029
Cholla Way 89029
Civic Way 89029
Colleara Dr 89029
Cookies Crossing Ct 89029
Coronado Cherry Ave 89029
Cottage Canyon St 89029
Cottage Hill St 89029
Cottage Meadow Way 89029
Cottage Ridge St 89029
Cottage Stone Ct 89029
Cottage Stream Ct 89029
Cottage Thistle Dr 89029
Cottage View Ct 89029
Cottage Wood St 89029
Cottonwood Dr 89029
Cougar Dr 89029
Country Club Dr 89029
Crook Lake Ct 89029
Crystal Blue St 89029
Dark Canyon Ct 89029
Del Monte St 89029
Delmar Farms Ct 89029
Desert Marina Dr 89029
Dillons Cove Dr 89029
Dry Gulch Dr 89029
Duke Of Earl Ct 89029
Duke Of York Dr 89029
Dunes Ct 89029
Edison Way 89029
El Mirage Way 89029
Ellis Plantation St 89029
Ensalmo Way 89029
Esquina St 89029
Esteban Ave 89029
Fresa Ln 89029
Golf Club Dr 89029
Granada St 89029
Grant Union Ct 89029
High Dunes Ln 89029
High Terrace Ln 89029
Highpointe Dr 89029
Hopewell Landing St 89029
Hunt Woods Ct 89029
Illumination Bay Pl 89029
James A Bilbray Pkwy 89029
Kevin Cir 89029
Kiva Way 89029
La Palma Dr 89029
Las Palmas Ln 89029
Laughlin Blvd 89029
E Laughlin Civic Dr 89029
Leandro Ct 89029
Limestone Cove Ct 89029
Links Dr 89029
Manzanita Ln 89029
Maricopa Dr 89029
Marina Lagoon Dr 89029
Mesa Canyon Dr 89029
Mesquite Ln 89029
Mimosa Ct 89029
Mirador St 89029
Monroe Manor Pl 89029
Morrow Ridge Pl 89029
Mustang Pass St 89029
Needles Hwy
2401-2697 89029
2699-2899 89029
2850-2850 89028
2900-6198 89029
2901-6199 89029
Novato Ct 89029
Oasis Ct 89029
Ocotillo Dr 89029
Palm Dr 89029
Palmera Ct 89029
Palo Verde Dr 89029
Paloma Ave 89029
Partridge Run St 89029
Paseo Canyon Ln 89029
Pebble Creek Ln 89029
Pheasant Canyon Way 89029
Pheasant Hills Way 89029
S Pointe Cir 89029
Port Royal Dr 89029
Quail Song Dr 89029
Quantana Way 89029
Queen Elizabeth Ct 89029
Radiance River Ct 89029
Rialta Ln 89029
Rio Vista Dr 89029
Rippling Springs St 89029
Rippon Landing Ct 89029
Risco Ln 89029
River City Dr 89029
Rosa Canyon Dr 89029
Royal Princess Rd 89029
Ruffed Grouse Way 89029
Rugged Mesa Dr 89029
Shimmering Bay St 89029
Solano Ln 89029
Soledad Dr 89029
Sundance Shores Dr 89029
Sunken Ship St 89029
Terrace View Dr 89029
Thomas Edison Dr 89029
Thornwood Castle Dr 89029
Tullamore Creek Ln 89029
Westcliff Ave 89029
White Salmon Run Ct 89029
Wide Canyon Ct 89029
Willow Bay Rd 89029

MESQUITE NV

General Delivery 89024

POST OFFICE BOXES MAIN OFFICE STATIONS AND BRANCHES

Box No.s
All PO Boxes 89024

NAMED STREETS

Admiral Benbow Way 89027
Adobe Dr 89027
Amen Ct 89027
Angels Landing Trl 89034
Apogee Crst 89027
Appletree Ln 89027
Arguello Cir 89027
N & S Arrowhead Ln 89027
Aruba Hts 89027
Atkins Ln 89027
Augusta Hills St 89027
Auto Mall Cir 89027
Aztec Cir 89027
Babbling Brook Ct 89034
Back Country Trl 89034
Bannock St 89027
Basin Vw 89034
Bay Hill Cir 89027
Beacon Ridge Way 89027
Beehive Ln 89034
Belt Buckle Xing 89034
Bertha Howe Ave 89027
Billy Bones Blf 89027
Bird Rock Run 89027
Bison Trl 89034
Blackfoot St 89027
Blazing Star Xing 89034
Blind Pew Rdg 89027
Bluff Shadow Ct 89034
Bobcat Run 89034
Branding Iron Trl 89034
Bronco Trl 89034
Buckboard Trl 89034
Buena Vista Cir 89027
Buffalo Run 89034
Bull Whip Pt 89034
Bulldog Dr 89027
Bunkhouse Ct 89034
Burns Ln 89027
Buteo Bnd 89027
Calais Cir & Dr 89027
Calle Del Sol 89027
E, N, S & W Camellia Cir 89027
Campfire Ct & Ln 89034
Canal St 89027
Canyon Dr & Way 89027
Canyon View Way 89027
Carrara Ct 89027
Casa Grande Cir 89027
Casa Palmero Way 89027
Cascade Ave 89027
Cassia Ln 89027
Cathedral Canyon Dr 89027
Cedar Ct 89027
Chalet Dr 89027
Chaparral Cir & Dr 89027
Charles St 89027
Cherokee St 89027
Chianti Way 89027
Cholla Way 89027
Chuck Wagon Run 89034
Cimarron Ct 89027
Cinco Ct 89027
Cincy Way 89027
Cindy Sue Ln 89027
Claremont Ave 89027
Clark St 89027
Clear Brk 89027
Clouds Rest Pt 89034
Clover Ln 89027
Cobblestone Way 89027
Cold Creek Bnd 89027
Colleen Ct 89027
Commerce Cir 89027
Concord Dr 89027
Condor St 89027
Conestoga Pkwy 89034
Conestoga Camp Pt 89034
Cool Springs Ln 89034
Copper Springs Dr 89034
Cora Cir 89027
Corona Way 89027
Cottonwood Dr 89027
Cougar Ct 89034
Country Grove Ln 89034
Coventry Ln 89027
Cracker Barrel Cir 89034
Crest View Dr 89027
Crystal Ct 89027
Crystal Canyon Dr 89027
Dairy Ln 89027
Dancing Sky Trl 89027
Dawn Way 89027
Daybreak Ln 89027
Del Lago Dr 89027
Desert Dr 89027
Desert Rose Way 89027
Desert Tortoise Way 89027
Desert Willow Ln 89027
Desert Winds Way 89027
Diamond Cir 89027
Dozier St 89027
Dry Falls Bnd 89034
Duchess Ln 89027
Eagle St 89027
Echo Cyn 89034
El Dorado Rd 89027
Emily Way 89027
Emmarene St 89027
Emperor Ln 89027
Eucalyptus Ln 89027
Fairways Dr 89027
Falcon St 89027
Falcon Glenn Dr 89027
Falcon Nest Ct 89027
Falcon Ridge Pkwy
1-300 89027
302-398 89027
1400-1499 89034
Falls Cir 89027
Fike Cir 89027
Firefly Run 89034
Flat Top Mesa Dr 89034
N Fork Trl 89034
Fountain View Ln 89027
Fox Hills Way 89027
Foxglove St 89027
Francy Ln 89027
Frontier Cyn 89034
Frontier Pass Trl 89034
Garnet Ln 89027
Gazlay Ct 89027
Gean St 89027
Gemini Ln 89027
Glade Rd 89027
Glendale Rd 89027
Golden St 89027
Golden Needle Trl 89034
Golden Rod St 89027
Goshawk Xing 89027
Grand Cyprus Ct 89027
Grande Vista Cir 89027
N & S Grapevine Rd 89027
Grayce Dr 89027
Great Arch Ave 89034
Great Divide Trl 89027
Greens Way 89027
Grist Mill Ln 89034
Grotto Trl 89034
Gypsy Boy Ln 89027
Hacienda Way 89027
Hafen Ln 89027
Hagens Aly 89027
Haley Way 89027
Hanna Ct 89027
Haps Way 89027
Harbour Dr 89027
Hardy Way 89027
Harrier Ln 89027
Hawk St 89027
Heather Ct 89027
Heritage Hts & Trl 89034
Hermosa Way 89027
Hiawatha Way 89027
High Point Cir 89027
Highland Dr 89027
Highland Hills Dr 89027
Highland View Ct 89027
Hillside Dr 89027
Hilltop Trl 89027
Hitching Post Pt 89034
Honeysuckle St 89027
Hughes Ave 89027
Huntington Hts 89027
Ice Box Cyn 89034
Indian Wells Rd 89027
Ironwood Dr 89027
Ivy Lee Crst 89027
Jacaranda Way 89027
Jackrabbit St 89027
Jade St 89027
Jasmine Ct 89027
Jensen Dr 89027
Jessica Dr 89027
Jim Hawkins Trl 89027
Jody Ct 89027
Joseph St 89027
Joshua Dr 89027
Julian Way 89027
Juniper Way 89027
Kalanchoe Way 89027
Kelkim St 89027
Ken Ct 89027
Kerosene Lamp Ct 89034
Kitty Hawk Dr 89027
Kylee Ave 89027
La Paz Ct 89027
La Scala Dr 89027
Lake View Dr 89027
Lakeridge Ct & Dr 89027
Lamp Post Way 89034
Lantana Ln 89027
Lariat Ln 89027
Larkspur Ln 89027
Las Palmas Cir 89027
Laurel Way 89027
Lavender Ln 89027
Leavitt Ln 89027
Lewis St 89027
Lexington Ln 89027
Lilac Ct 89027
Lilly Ln 89027
Lisa Ln 89027
Lolita Ln 89027
Lonesome Dove Dr 89027
Long Iron Ln 89027
Los Altos Cir 89027
Los Padres Cir 89027
Mackenzies Pl 89027
Madison Ave 89027
Madrigal Dr 89027
Manchester Ln 89027
Mayan Cir 89027
Meadowbrook Ct 89027
Megan Cir 89027
Mendicino Ln 89027
Mesa Blvd & Vw 89027
Mesa Springs Dr 89027
Mesa Verde Run & Trl 89027
E Mesquite Blvd 89027
W Mesquite Blvd
12-499 89027
501-899 89027
510-510 89024
510-998 89027
Mesquite Springs Dr 89027
Milky Way 89027
Mimosa Way 89027
Mohave Dr 89027
Monaco Cir 89027
Montpere Cir 89027
Moonbeam Way 89027
Moonlight Terrace Run 89034
Morning Mist Way 89027
Morning Sun Way 89027
Moss Dr 89027
Mountain Rdg 89027
Mountain View Dr 89027
Mountainside Ct 89027
Muirfield Way 89027
Muscat Dr 89027
Myhaley Bnd 89027
Myrtle Ct 89027
Navajo St 89027
Niguel Ct 89027
Nolina Rdg & Way 89027
Normandy Ln 89027
Oakmont Ct & Rdg 89027
Oasis Blvd 89027
Ocotillo Ln 89027
E Old Mill Rd 89027
Olympic Ct 89027
Opal St 89027
Oregon Trl 89027
Orion Ln 89027
Osprey St 89027
Overland Trl 89034
Overlook Ln 89027
Paintbrush Way 89027
Palm St 89027
Palm Cove Ct 89027
Palmer Ln 89027
Paloma Cir 89027
Palomino Cir 89027
Palos Verdes Cir & Dr 89027
Paradise Pkwy 89027
Parkview Dr 89027
Parliament Cyn & Pt 89027
Partridge Ln 89027
Paseo Verde Ct 89027
Peantri Dr 89027
Peartree Ln 89027
Pebble Beach Dr 89027
Pebble Creek Blf, Hts & Run 89027
Pebble View Ln 89027
Perlearb Ave 89034
Pheasant Dr 89027
Pine Meadow Ct 89027
Pine Nut Way 89034
Pinehurst Dr 89027
Pinnacle Cir & Ct 89027
Pinyon Ln 89027
E & W Pioneer Blvd 89027
Piute St 89027
Plateau Rd 89027
Pomegranate Trl 89027
Poppy Ln 89027
Prairie Schooner Ct 89034
Preston Dr 89027
Prestwick Ct 89027
Primrose Ln 89027
Prominence Ln 89034
Prosperity Ln 89027
Pulsipher Ln 89027
Quail Run 89027
Quicksilver Way 89027
Rancho Cir 89027
Rancho Santa Barbara Dr 89027
Raptor Cir 89027
Raven Way 89027
Ravine Ln 89027
Reber Dr 89027
Red Rock Dr 89027
Redd Hills Pkwy 89027
Ridge Crst 89027
Ridgeview Dr 89027
Rim Rock Rdg & Vw 89034
Rio Vly 89027
River Mesa Dr 89027
Rivers Bend Dr 89027
Riverside Rd 89027
Roadrunner Trl 89034
Rodeo Ln 89027
Rolling Hills Dr 89027
Ronnie Way 89027
Royal Flush Ct 89027
Royal Vista Ln 89027
Ruby Cir & Dr 89027
Saddle Way 89027
Saddle Horn Ct & Rdg 89034
Sage Way 89027
Sagebrush St 89027
Sagedell Rd 89027
Saguaro Way 89027
Salerno Cir & Ct 89027
San Juan Ln 89027
San Lucas Way 89027
San Marcos Way 89027
San Marino Way 89027
San Pablo Ct 89027
San Pedro Way 89027
Sanctuary Rdg 89027
Sand Castle Way 89027
Sandbar St 89027
N Sandhill Blvd 89027
Sandstone Bluffs Vw 89034
Sandtrap Ct 89027
Santa Fe Dr 89027
Santa Maria Way 89027
Santa Theresa Way 89027
Sawgrass Way 89027
Sea Pines St 89027
Sedona Dr 89027
Sentinel Rdg 89034
Seven Palms Cir & Way 89027
Shade Tree Ln 89027
Shadow Rdg 89027
Shadow Hawk Rdg 89027
Shane Cyn 89034
Shangrila Ct 89027
Shoshone Cir 89027
Siena Ln 89027
E & W Sierra Vista Cir 89027
Silver Rd 89027
Sioux Cir 89027
Smoke Signal Ct & Trl 89034
Southridge Dr 89027
Spanish Bay Trl 89027
Split Rail Ave 89034
Springdale Ln 89034
Spyglass Way 89027
Stanley Cv 89027
Starlight Terrace Way 89034
Stone Haven Ln 89027
Sublimity Crst 89027
Summit Ct 89027
Sun Star Ln 89027
Sundance Way 89027
Sundial Ln 89034
Sunflower Way 89027
Sunrise Way 89027
Sunset Dr 89027
Sunvalley Dr 89027
Tack Room Xing 89034

Tamarix Way 89027
Tannery Hts 89034
Terrace Dr 89027
Terrace View Ct 89027
Terraces Ct 89027
Tex St 89027
Thistle St 89027
Thompson Dr 89027
Three Springs Cv 89027
Timber Ln 89034
Tivoli Crescent St 89027
Topaz Ln 89027
Torrey Pines Dr 89027
Tortuga Way 89027
Trailside Way 89027
Tucson St 89027
Turquoise Cir 89027
Turtle Cv 89027
Turtle Back Rd 89027
Turtle Shell Ln 89027
Tuscany Cir 89027
Vale View Dr 89027
Valerie Ln 89027
Valley View Cir & Dr 89027
Ventana Cir 89027
Verllonia St 89027
Via Carlotta Ct 89027
Via De Fortuna Way 89027
Via Ventana Dr 89027
Villa La Paz Dr 89027
Vineyard Ln 89027
Vista Dr 89027
Vista Del Ciudad Dr 89027
Vista Del Monte Dr 89027
Vista Del Sol Ct 89027
Wagon Trl 89034
Wagon Wheel Run 89034
Watchmans Pt 89034
Water Lily Ln 89034
Waterfall Ct, Ln & Vw 89034
Watermark Rdg 89034
Wedge Way 89027
Weeping Rock Trl 89034
Wheelwright Ct 89034
Whispering Wind Way 89027
White Rock Rd 89027
White Water Way 89034
Whitey Lee Ln 89027
Wigwam St 89027
Wild Horse Ln 89027
Wildfang Way 89027
N & S Willow St 89027
Willow Bridge Ln 89027
Winder Stock Trl 89034
Woodbury Ln 89027
Woods Ct 89027
Wranglers Rdg 89034
N Yucca St 89027

NUMBERED STREETS

All Street Addresses 89027

NORTH LAS VEGAS NV

General Delivery 89030

POST OFFICE BOXES MAIN OFFICE STATIONS AND BRANCHES

Box No.s
4086 - 4116 89036
335001 - 338480 89033
360001 - 365515 89036

NAMED STREETS

Aaron Scott St 89032
Abbottwood Ave 89031
Abella Gloss St 89081
Ability Ct 89031
Abruzzi Dr 89084
Abundance St 89031
Abyss Ct 89031
Acacia Grove St 89031
Acropolis Ave 89031
Adanon St 89031
Addy Ln 89081
Admiration Ct 89032
Adobe Creek Ct 89084
Adonis Heights Ave 89086
Adorato Dr 89031
Adriel Dr 89032
Advancement Ave 89031
Aerojet Way 89030
Agate Ridge Dr 89081
Agave Ave 89032
Aiken St 89032
Airborne Ct 89032
Airport Dr 89032
Akamine Ave 89031
Akula Bay St 89081
Alachela 89086
Alamo Heights Ave 89031
Alamosa Ridge Ct 89084
Albata St 89030
Albatross Attic St 89084
Albergo St 89031
Alcantara Ln 89084
Alder Creek Ct 89032
Alder Flower Ct 89084
Alder Grove Ct 89081
Alderley Ct 89081
Alderly Ridge Ave 89081
Alderwood Dr 89032
Alecandro Daniel Ave 89031
Alejandro Way 89031
E Alexander Rd
300-399 89032
1000-3299 89030
W Alexander Rd 89032
Alexander Station Ave 89031
Alfa Romero Ave 89031
Aliante Pkwy 89084
Alisa Roberts St 89081
Alise St 89030
Alissa Kim Ct 89086
Alitak Bay St 89081
Allegiance Dr 89032
Allen Ln
3401-4299 89032
4400-4699 89031
4701-5099 89031
Allyson Rae St 89032
Alma Dr 89030
Alma Lidia Ave 89032
Aloha Sue St 89031
Alpenhof Ct 89081
Alpennwood Ct 89084
Alpine Bypass Ave 89081
Alpine Track Ave 89032
Alta Loma Ct 89031
Altamira Cave Dr 89031
Altar Rock Ln 89032
Altissimo St 89081
Alvarez St 89031
Amanda Bay Ave 89081
Amanda Michelle Ln 89086
Amangani St 89081
Amber Crossing St 89031
Amber Falls Ln 89081
Amberdale Ave 89031
Amethyst Stars Ave 89031
Amick St 89081
Amish Ave 89031
Amory St 89081
Amy Lynn St 89031
Ana Raquel Ave 89031
Anchor Dr 89032
Anchorman Way 89031
Ancient Agora St 89031
Andrew Cir 89032
Andrew David Ave 89086
Andrews St 89081
Angel Face St 89032
Angel Field St 89030
Angelbrook Ct 89032
Angelikis St 89031
Ankara Walk Dr 89032
W Ann Rd 89031
Annbriar Ave 89031
Anneke Way 89031
Annendale Ave 89031
Annville Ct 89081
Antelope Creek Ct 89031
Antique Silver Ave 89032
Antler Creek St 89084
Anya Way 89032
Appaloosa Hills Ave 89081
Apple Vista Ave 89031
Appleblossom Time
Ave 89031
Appleside St 89031
Appreciation Ct 89032
April Bend Ct 89084
Apulia Dr 89084
Aqua Blue Ct 89031
Aqua Verde St 89031
Arazi Ln 89031
Arbor Bluff Ct 89084
Arbor Crest St 89081
Arc Dome Ave 89031
Arcadia Creek St 89084
Arcadia Glen Ct 89084
Arcata Way 89030
Arch Stone Ave 89031
Arctic Breeze St 89084
Arden Glade Ct 89084
Aristos Ave 89030
Aristotle Ave 89031
Arizo Ct 89031
Arizona Rosewood
Ave 89085
Arkwright Falls Ave 89032
Arlington Bridge St 89032
Armadale Dr 89031
Armide St 89081
Armor St 89030
Arrow Hill St 89084
Arrow Stone Ct 89031
Arrowbear Ln 89084
Arrowbird Ave 89031
Arrowbrook Way 89032
Arrowhead St 89030
Arrowleaf St 89031
Arrowridge Cir 89032
Arroyo Largo Ct 89031
Arthur St 89030
Ascension Cir 89031
Ash Meadows Way 89031
Ashburn Dr 89032
Ashby Field Ave 89031
Ashcroft St 89084
Asher Ln 89032
Ashley Lynn Ave 89086
Ashwell Ct 89032
Asia Rd 89032
Asiago Ct 89032
Aspen Club Ave 89081
Aspen Creek Ave 89031
Aspen Park Ln 89081
Asphalt Ct 89032
Aspinwall Ct 89081
Astral Beach St 89032
Astro Ct 89030
Athens Bay Pl 89031
Athinas St 89031
Atlas Dr 89030
Attitude Ct 89032
Attributes Ct 89031
Atwater Dr 89032
Auklet Ln 89084
Austin English St 89081
Austin Moore St 89086
Austin Pale Ave 89081
Autumn America Pl 89032
Autumn Crocus Ct 89031
Autumn Damask St 89081
Autumn Ridge Cir 89031
Autumn Sage Ave 89031
Autumndale Ave 89031
Avawatz Ct 89032
Ave Marina Ave 89031
Avenida Fiesta 89031
Avian Ct 89084
Avondale Breeze Ave 89081
Awakening St 89081
Axbridge Ct 89031
Ayers Cliff St 89081
Aztec Heights St 89081
E Azure Ave 89081
W Azure Ave 89031
Azure Banks Ave 89031
Azure Oak Ave 89084
Azure View Ct 89031
Babbler St 89084
Bach Way 89032
Back Country Dr 89031
Badger Canyon Ave 89031
Badger Lake Ct 89084
Badgerglen Pl 89031
Bagpipe Ct 89032
Bahama Point Ave 89031
Bailey Tess Ct 89086
Balch Springs Ct 89031
Balcones Fault Ave 89081
Baltimore Station St 89031
Balzar Ave 89032
Banana Ct 89032
Bangle St 89030
Barada Heights Ave 89081
Barbosa Dr 89031
Bardwell Ct 89084
Bared Eagle Pl 89084
Barhill Ave 89084
Barite Canyon Dr 89081
Baritone Way 89032
Barker Way 89032
Baroda Bay Ct 89032
Baron St 89030
Baronese St 89031
Baronne Prevost St 89081
Barr Ave 89030
Barred Dove Ln 89084
Barrel Bronco Ct 89032
Barrel Oak Ave 89031
Barrel Race Ct 89032
Barrington Oaks St 89084
Barron Creek Ave 89081
Barrow Glen Ct 89084
E Bartlett Ave 89030
Barton Mill Ct 89084
Basil Leaf Ave 89031
Basilicata Ln 89084
Basilwood Ct 89031
Basin St 89030
Basin Brook Dr 89032
Bassae Temple Ave 89031
Bassler Ct & St 89030
Basswood Ave & Cir 89030
Battle Point Ave 89031
Bay Bridge Dr 89032
Bay Horse Ct 89032
Bay Lake Trl 89030
Bay Thrush Way 89084
Bayberry Crest St 89031
Bayhurst Ave 89031
Bayliner Ave 89031
Baywater Ave 89084
Beach Cliff Ave 89031
Beals Dr 89032
Beamery Ct 89032
Beams Ave 89081
Bear Gulch Ct 89031
Bear Mountain Ave 89031
Bear Springs St 89031
Beaufort Ct 89032
Beauty Secret Dr 89081
Beaver Ridge Ave 89031
Beca Faith Dr 89032
Beckwood Ct 89084
Bed Knoll Ct 89031
Bedrock Ct 89031
Beebe Ct 89032
Beefeater Pl 89032
Beeline Ct 89031
Beige Bluff St 89081
Belkin Ct 89032
Bell Canyon Ct 89031
Bell Cord Ave 89031
Bella Legato Ave 89081
Bellington Rd 89030
Bello Cir & Dr 89030
Bellows Beach St 89081
Belmont St 89030
Beluga Bay St 89081
Benchmark Way 89031
Benevolent Dr 89032
Bengal Bay Ave 89081
Bennett St 89030
Benson Ln 89032
Bent Arrow Dr 89031
Bent Grass Ave 89032
Bent Spur Cir 89031
Berg St
2700-3799 89030
4400-4598 89081
4600-4999 89081
Berrien Springs St 89081
Berry Hill Ln 89031
Beth Cir 89030
Bethel Bay St 89032
Bible Cir 89031
Biddle St & Way 89032
Big Ben Ranch St 89084
Big Boulder Dr 89031
Big Cedar Ct 89031
Big Cliff Ave 89031
Big Draw Dr 89031
Big Horn View St 89031
Big Island Ct 89031
Big Mountain Ave 89081
Big Range St 89031
Big Tree Ave 89032
Big Valley Ln 89081
Bilicki St 89032
Birch River St 89032
Birchdale Ct 89032
Bird Man Ln 89084
Birdcall St 89084
Birdhouse St 89084
Birdwatcher Ave 89084
Bishops Bowl St 89081
Bismark Hills St 89084
Bison Mesa Ave 89030
Bistro Bay Ave 89086
Bitterroot Dr 89032
Bizet Ct 89032
Black Eyed Susan Ct 89031
Black Gold St 89031
Black Hills Way 89031
Black Horse Cir 89031
Black Jade Ave 89081
Black Mane Way 89081
Black Oaks St
6300-6399 89031
6500-6699 89084
Black Sand Beach St 89081
Black Sea St 89031
Black Stallion Ave 89031
Black Star Point Ct 89084
Blackbird Knoll Ct 89084
Blackfoot Ct 89030
Blairmoor St 89032
Blake Ave 89030
Blake Canyon Dr 89032
Blanco Dr 89031
Bliss St 89081
Blissful Bluff St 89032
Blizzard Breeze St 89081
Blooming Mesa Ct 89031
Blooming View Ave 89032
Blossom Berry Ct 89031
Blowing Sky St 89081
Blown Glass Dr 89032
Blue Ave 89081
Blue Autumn St 89031
Blue Coral Dr 89032
Blue Dawn Dr 89032
Blue Gull St 89032
Blue Ice Ct 89032
Blue Label St 89081
Blue Lily Ct 89081
Blue Luna St 89081
Blue Magic Way 89031
Blue Manor Ln 89032
Blue Onion Cir 89031
Blue Pearl St 89031
Blue Pimpernel Ave 89081
Blue Reef Dr 89032
Blue Rose St 89081
Blue Sky Ct 89031
Blue Sunrise Ave 89031
Blue View Ct 89031
Blueberry Climber Ave 89031
Blueberry Peak Ln 89032
Bluebird Wing St 89084
Bluebottle Ct 89031
Blues Ln 89081
Bluestar Dr 89032
Bluff Ave
1100-1399 89030
1700-1999 89032
Bluff Ct 89030
Bluff Hollow Pl 89084
Bluff Knoll Ct 89084
Blush Noisette Ave 89081
Blushed Meadows Rd 89031
Blushing Willow St 89081
Boatbill St 89084
Bob Barney Ave 89086
Bob White Dr 89032
Bobby Pollard Ave 89086
Boca Del Mar St 89031
Boca Glen Rd 89081
Bola Dr 89032
Boland Ct 89032
Bolivar Ave 89032
Bonassola Ave 89031
Bonita Desert Ct 89032
Book Cliffs Ct 89031
Booth St 89032
Borderwood Ln 89031
Bordley Way 89032
Bosal Ct 89032
Boston Bell Ct 89031
Boulder Bay St 89081
Boulder Shore Ave 89081
Bourbon Ln 89030
Bowers Hollow Ave 89085
Bowles Creek St 89084
Box Canyon Falls Ave 89085
Box Springs Ave 89031
Bracebridge Falls Ave 89085
Bradford Hill Ave 89081
Bradfox Ln 89032
Braeburn Glen St 89032
Braided River Ave 89084
Brambling Ave 89084
Branchwood Dr 89032
Brand St 89030
Brandy Creek Ct 89032
Branson Ave 89030
Brautigan Ct 89032
Brave Heart Ave 89031
Bravita Dr 89032
Brayton Mist Dr 89081
Brazelton St 89081
Brazil St 89030
Brazil Palm Ct 89032
Breckenridge St 89081
Breckle Key Ave 89081
Breezy Day Dr 89031
Breezy Shore Ave 89031
Breezy Wind Ct 89081
Brenneman St 89081
Brent Scott St 89086
Brentcove Dr 89032
Brick Oven St 89031
Brickland Ct 89081
Bridal Veil Way 89032
Bride St 89081
Bridesmaid Falls Ave 89085
Bridge House St 89032
Bridleton Ave 89081
Briggs Gully St 89085
Briggsdale Ave 89081
Bright Dawn Ave 89031
Bright Leaf Ct 89031
Bright Lights Ave 89031
Bright Moon Ave 89084
Bright Morning St 89084
Brightwork St 89032
Brimstone Dr 89031
Bristlebird St 89084
Bristol Bridge St 89081
Brittany Ann Ct 89031
Brittany Falls Ct 89031
Britz Cir 89030
Broad Arrow Dr 89032
Broad View Ct 89032
Broadway Ave 89030
Broadwing Dr 89084
Broccoli St 89081
Broken Bow Cir 89032
Broken Feather Dr 89031
Broken Lance Ave 89031
Broken Oak Ln 89032
Broken Twig Ct 89032
Brolio Valley Ct 89032
Bronco Buster Ct 89032
Brook Song Ave 89081
E Brooks Ave 89030
W Brooks Ave
11-99 89030
101-500 89030
502-898 89030
1501-1597 89032
1599-1900 89032
1902-2798 89032
Brooks Park Dr 89030
Brown Breeches Ave 89081
Brown Tree Ln 89081
Bruce Cir 89030
N Bruce St
1600-3600 89030
3602-3998 89030
4800-5698 89081
5700-5799 89081
6440-6599 89086
Bruny Island Ave 89081
Brushfire St 89031
Bryan Keith Ave 89031
Bublin Bay Ave 89081
Buchner Ln 89032
Buck Creek Cir 89032
Buck Ranch Ave 89032
Bucking Bronco Rd 89032
Buckwood Mote St 89081
Bucyrus Erie St 89030
Buddy Holly Ct 89031
Buena Tierra St 89031
Buffalo Gap Ct 89084
Bugler Swan Way 89084
Bull Run Ave 89030
Bullboat Ct 89031
Bullet Rd 89032
Bullfinch 89084
Bullhead St 89031
Bulloch St 89030
Bunch Grass Ct 89031
Bunkerhill Dr 89032
Bunting Ct 89084
Burma Rd 89032
Bursting Sun Ave 89031
Buteo Ln 89084
Butterball Ct 89032
Buttercup Creek St 89084
Butterfly Falls Ct 89031
Butterfly Sky St 89084
Button Quail St 89084
Caballo Hills Ave 89081
Cabinhill Cir 89031
Cabrini Ct 89032
Cackling Goose Dr 89084
Cactus Blossom St 89031
Cactus Desert Ct 89084
Cactus Grove Ct 89084
Cactus Mesa Way 89031
Cactus Sands Ave 89031
Caddo Mills Ave 89031
Caddy Ridge St 89031
Cades Cove Ct 89084
Cafe Racer Ct 89031
Calamus Pointe Ave 89081

Calendula Canyon Ct ... 89081
Calf Roper Ct ... 89032
Calico Cactus Ln ... 89031
Calico Cliff Ct ... 89031
Calico Springs Ct ... 89081
California Condor Ave ... 89084
California Holly St ... 89031
Calm Winds Ct ... 89031
Calmness Ct ... 89031
Calumet Farm Cir ... 89031
Calumet Point St ... 89081
Camarillo Dr ... 89031
Cambridge Elms St ... 89032
Camden Cove St ... 89081
Camden Yard Ct ... 89030
Camino Al Norte
4800-4904 ... 89031
Camino Al Norte
4904-4904 ... 89033
4906-5098 ... 89031
5100-5599 ... 89031
Camino Carlos Rey ... 89031
Camino Del Santo Pkwy ... 89031
Camino Del Sol ... 89032
Camino Hermoso ... 89031
Camino Libre St ... 89031
Camino Mirada ... 89031
Camino Monte Sol ... 89031
Camino Pacifico ... 89031
Camino Rosa St ... 89031
Camino Sombrero ... 89031
Campanario Ave ... 89084
Campobello Ave ... 89081
Canary Cedar St ... 89032
Canary Creek Ave ... 89031
Canary Island Ct ... 89031
Canary Lark St ... 89081
Candlas Way ... 89031
Candlebrook Ave ... 89084
Candlecreek Ln ... 89032
Candleglade Ct ... 89084
Candytuft Ridge Ave ... 89081
Caneflower Ct ... 89031
Caney St ... 89030
Cannondale Ave ... 89031
Canoga Ave ... 89030
Cantabella Ct ... 89032
Canter Dr ... 89032
Cantina Ln ... 89031
Cantina Rey St ... 89081
Cantura Bluff Ave ... 89031
Cantura Crest Ct ... 89031
Canyon Edge Rd ... 89031
Canyon Falls Way ... 89031
Canyon Gap Dr ... 89031
Canyon Point Dr ... 89031
Cape Clairmont Ct ... 89031
Cape Eagle Ave ... 89084
Cape Jasmine Ct ... 89031
Cape Petrel St ... 89084
Capehart Falls St ... 89081
Capilano Ln ... 89031
Capistrano Hills St ... 89081
Capitol Reef Dr ... 89032
Caporetto Ln ... 89084
Capri Canyon Ct ... 89031
Captain Kirk Ct ... 89031
Captain Mccall Ct ... 89031
Captain Mcdonald Ct ... 89031
Captain Morgan Ave ... 89031
Cardigan Ave ... 89032
Cardinal Flower Ct ... 89081
Cardinal Walk Ln ... 89084
Cardona Ct ... 89081
Carefree Beauty Ave ... 89081
E Carey Ave ... 89030
W Carey Ave
100-198 ... 89030
200-1399 ... 89030
1500-4100 ... 89032
4102-4198 ... 89032
Carey Grove Ave ... 89030
Caribbean Blue Ave ... 89031
Caribou Creek Ct ... 89031
Carisbrook Ave ... 89081
Carla Ave ... 89030
Carla Ann Rd ... 89081
Carlitos Ave ... 89031
Carlos Julio Ave ... 89031
Carlsbad Heights St ... 89081
Carlton Sea Ct ... 89031
Carmel Bluff St ... 89031
Carmel Sand St ... 89031
Carol Bailey Ave ... 89081
Carolina Ct ... 89031
Carolina Mist St ... 89081
Carolina Moon Ave ... 89081
Carrie Hills Ave ... 89081
Carrier Dove Ave & Way ... 89084
Carroll St ... 89030
E Cartier Ave ... 89030
W Cartier Ave
911-1099 ... 89030
1501-1697 ... 89032
1699-2399 ... 89032
2401-2599 ... 89032
Cartoon Ct ... 89031
Carver Ave ... 89032
Casa Alto Ave ... 89031
Casa Anita Cir ... 89031
Casa Antiqua St ... 89081
Casa Bonita Dr ... 89032
Casa Corona Ave ... 89031
Casa Del Norte Dr ... 89031
Casa Del Oro St ... 89031
Casa Norte Dr ... 89031
Casa Verde Dr ... 89031
Casamar St ... 89086
Cascade Light Ave ... 89031
Casmailia Ave ... 89031
Casper Sands Ct ... 89031
Caspian Tern St ... 89084
Cassandra Dr ... 89032
Castanada St ... 89030
Castle St ... 89030
Castle Butte Ct ... 89031
Catalan Sails Ave ... 89031
Catfish Bend Rd ... 89031
Cathedral Falls Ave ... 89085
Catherine Mermet Ave ... 89081
Catskill Ct ... 89031
Cattleman Ave ... 89031
Cattrack Ave ... 89081
Cayman Beach St ... 89031
Cayuse St ... 89031
Cedar Bend Dr ... 89031
Cedar Bird Dr ... 89084
Cedar Bridge Ct ... 89031
Cedar Dove Rd ... 89081
Cedar Point Way ... 89031
Cedar Ranch Ct ... 89031
Cedar Waxwing St ... 89084
Celebration Cove St ... 89032
Celsion Rock St ... 89081
Celtic Cir ... 89032
E Centennial Pkwy
1-171 ... 89084
173-299 ... 89084
501-2997 ... 89081
2999-3099 ... 89081
W Centennial Pkwy ... 89084
Centisimo Dr ... 89084
Chaffinch St ... 89084
Chamberlain Ln ... 89032
Chambers St ... 89030
Chambers Lake Ct ... 89084
Champagne Flower St ... 89031
Champagne Wood Dr ... 89031
Chandler Cove Ave ... 89081
Channel View Pl ... 89031
Chapel View Ct ... 89081
Chaps Ranch Ave ... 89031
Character Ct ... 89031
Charger Ave ... 89031
Charitable Ct ... 89032
Charm Crest Ave ... 89032
Charter Crest St ... 89084
Chase Glenn Ct ... 89086
Chastain Park Dr ... 89084
Chateau Bella Ave ... 89081
Chatterer St ... 89084
Chavez Ct ... 89031
Chebec St ... 89084
Checker Way ... 89031
Checkmark Ave ... 89032
Chedworth Rd ... 89031
Cheer Pheasant Ave ... 89084
Cheetah Ct ... 89031
Chelsea Ridge Ct ... 89084
Chelton Oaks St ... 89084
Cherokee Rose Ave ... 89031
Cheryl Clay Way ... 89032
Chester Pl ... 89032
Chestnut Bay Ave ... 89031
Chestnut Blaze Dr ... 89032
E Cheyenne Ave ... 89030
W Cheyenne Ave
201-499 ... 89030
501-1200 ... 89030
1202-1498 ... 89030
1500-1598 ... 89032
1600-4600 ... 89032
4602-4798 ... 89032
Cheyenne Gardens Way ... 89032
Chicory Cir ... 89032
Chiefs Ct ... 89032
Chilie Verde Dr ... 89031
Chilly Nights Ave ... 89031
Chimes Dr ... 89032
Chimney Bluffs St ... 89085
China Cloud Dr ... 89031
China Falls St ... 89085
Chinacandle Ct ... 89032
Chinese Cherry Ct ... 89031
Chino Ave ... 89031
Chino Heights St ... 89081
Chipped Rock Dr ... 89031
Chipping Sparrow St ... 89084
Chipplegate Way ... 89032
Chipwood Ct ... 89032
Choctaw Ave ... 89031
Cholla Blossom Ct ... 89031
Chopin Ct ... 89032
Chris Craft St ... 89031
Christina St ... 89030
Christopher View Ave ... 89032
Chuckar St ... 89084
Chula Vista Hills Dr ... 89081
Cicada Flower Ave ... 89081
Cima Dr ... 89032
Cinderwood Ct ... 89032
Cindy Love Ave ... 89081
Cinema Ave ... 89031
Cinnabar Coast Ln ... 89084
Cinnamon Creek Ave ... 89031
Cinnamon Hazlenut St ... 89084
Cinnamon Spice Ct ... 89031
Circling Hawk Dr ... 89031
Citizen Ave ... 89032
Citrus Grove Ct ... 89032
Citrus Heights Ave ... 89081
Citruscedar Way ... 89032
Civic Center Dr ... 89030
Civic Holiday Ave ... 89031
Clarence House Ave ... 89032
Clarendon Ln ... 89081
Clarington Ave ... 89081
Clarks Cove Dr ... 89081
Claxton Ave ... 89084
Clay Ridge Rd ... 89031
Clayton St ... 89032
Clear Canyon Ln ... 89031
Clear Falls St ... 89085
Clear Haven Ln ... 89081
Clear Summit Ln ... 89031
Cliff Breeze Dr ... 89081
Cliff Dancer St ... 89031
Cliff Lodge Ave ... 89081
Cliff Palace Ct ... 89031
Cliff Shore Ct ... 89084
Cliffbrook Hedge Ave ... 89081
Clinging Vine St ... 89031
Clipper Cove Ct ... 89031
Clotidle Soupert Ct ... 89081
Cloud Dance Ct ... 89031
Cloudy Glen St ... 89031
Cloudy Morning St ... 89031
Clove Hitch St ... 89032
Clove Tree Ct ... 89031
Clovelly St ... 89081
Clover Blossom Ct ... 89031
Coast Jay St ... 89084
Coastal Bluff Ave ... 89031
Coastal Dreams Ave ... 89031
Cobble Lake Ave ... 89081
Cobblehill Way ... 89032
Cobblestone Cove Rd ... 89081
Coburn St ... 89032
Cockatiel Dr ... 89084
Cockatoo Dr ... 89084
Coconut Creek St ... 89031
Coff Ct ... 89081
Cohiba Way ... 89031
Colby Creek Ave ... 89081
Cold Harbor Dr & Pl ... 89030
Cole Ave ... 89032
Coleman St
2801-2897 ... 89032
2899-3999 ... 89032
4001-4099 ... 89032
5200-5999 ... 89031
College View Ct ... 89030
Collingswood Way ... 89032
Colombine Dr ... 89031
Colonial Canyon St ... 89031
Colonial Field Ave ... 89031
Colonial Oak Ct ... 89031
Colonnade Row Dr ... 89032
Colorado Breeze Way ... 89031
Colorful Rain Ave ... 89031
E Colton Ave ... 89030
W Colton Ave ... 89032
Colts Ave ... 89032
Columbia Ave & Ct ... 89030
Comet Ave ... 89030
Comida Ln ... 89031
N Commerce St
2000-2800 ... 89030
2802-2998 ... 89030
3800-3899 ... 89032
3901-4299 ... 89032
5100-5198 ... 89031
5801-6399 ... 89031
Commerce Park Ct ... 89032
Commitment Ct ... 89031
Common Ct ... 89032
Companionship Ct ... 89032
Compatibility Ct ... 89032
Comstock Dr ... 89032
Con Carne Ct ... 89031
Concbos Heights St ... 89081
Concord St ... 89030
Confidant Way ... 89031
Consensus Ct ... 89032
Constance Ave ... 89032
Constitution Way ... 89030
Contento Cir ... 89032
Contento Crest Ct ... 89081
Conterra Park Ave ... 89081
Conway St ... 89031
Cooktown Ct ... 89032
Cool Morning Ct ... 89031
Cool River Ct ... 89032
Cool Vista Ct ... 89032
Cool Water Cir ... 89032
Coolidge St ... 89030
Copeland Ct ... 89032
Copper Lakes St ... 89031
Copper Light St ... 89081
Copper Moon Ln ... 89031
Copper Pine Ave ... 89031
Copper Sand Ct ... 89031
Copper Smith Ct ... 89084
Copper Stone Ct ... 89032
Copper Sun Ct ... 89031
Copper Sunset Ave ... 89081
Copper Tree Ave ... 89081
Coral Beach St ... 89031
Coral Cliffs Ct ... 89031
Coral Cove Ct ... 89031
Coral Crystal Ct ... 89032
Coral Flat St ... 89031
Coral Hills St ... 89081
Coral Mist Pl ... 89084
Corinthian Way ... 89030
Cornerstone Pl ... 89031
Cornish Hen Ave ... 89084
Corporate Center Dr ... 89030
Corrie Canyon St ... 89086
Corsica Island St ... 89031
Corte Bella Hills Ave ... 89081
Costa Palma Ave ... 89031
Cotton Creek Ave ... 89031
Cotton Gum Ct ... 89031
Cotton Seed Ct ... 89031
Cougar Falls Ct ... 89085
Council Bluff Ln ... 89031
Count Ave ... 89030
Counter Way ... 89032
Country Breeze Ct ... 89031
Country Dancer Ave ... 89081
Country Gables Ct ... 89031
Country Glen Cir ... 89032
Country Grove Ave ... 89030
Country Hill Dr ... 89031
Country Lake Ln ... 89081
Country Orchard St ... 89030
Country Valley Ct ... 89030
Courlan Dr ... 89084
Courteous Ct ... 89032
Courtney Michelle St ... 89086
Covatta Ct ... 89086
Cove Palisades Dr ... 89031
Covewick Dr ... 89032
Cowboy Cross Ave ... 89081
Cowboy Ranch Ave ... 89031
Cowboy Springs St ... 89085
Cox St ... 89032
Coyote Valley Ct ... 89084
Cozumel Rey Ave ... 89081
Cozy Ct ... 89032
Cozy Cottage Pl ... 89031
Cozy Creek St ... 89031
Cracked Tree Ave ... 89031
Crackling Leaves Ave ... 89031
Cragged Draw St ... 89031
Craggy Ledge Ave ... 89031
E Craig Rd ... 89030
W Craig Rd ... 89032
Craig Creek Ave ... 89032
Craig Crossing Dr ... 89032
Craigmore Ln ... 89031
Crake Ct ... 89084
Crane Ct ... 89084
Craters Edge St ... 89031
Crawford St ... 89030
Creekside Sands Ln ... 89031
Creeping Ivy Ct ... 89031
Creeping Peonies Ave ... 89081
Creosote Way ... 89032
Crescent Moon Dr ... 89031
Crested Cardinal Dr ... 89084
Crested Ibis Ave ... 89084
Crested Moss Ave ... 89081
Crested Quail St ... 89084
Crested Starling Ct ... 89084
Crestline Loop ... 89030
Crestmont Dr ... 89031
Crestpoint Watch Ct ... 89031
Cricket Ln ... 89032
Crimson Rock Way ... 89081
Crimson Tide Ave ... 89031
Crisp Wind Ct ... 89030
Critic Ct ... 89031
Crooked Oak St ... 89032
Cross Anchor Way ... 89032
Cross Ranch St ... 89081
Crown Lodge Ln ... 89084
Crown Valley Ln ... 89032
Crownline Ct ... 89031
Cruz Crest Ct ... 89081
Crying Heart St ... 89031
Crystal Breeze Ln ... 89031
Crystal Cavern Way ... 89031
Crystal Field St ... 89031
Crystal Flower Way ... 89031
Crystal Island Ave ... 89081
Crystal Pond St ... 89031
Crystal Rainey Ave ... 89086
Crystal Sunset Ct ... 89031
Crystal Sword St ... 89031
Crystal View Dr ... 89032
Cuckoo Clock St ... 89084
Cuckoo Shrike Ave ... 89084
Cuddles Ct ... 89081
Cummings Ct ... 89030
Curio Dr ... 89031
Curlews Ct ... 89084
Custis Cir ... 89030
Cutting Diamond Ct ... 89081
Cutting Horse Ave ... 89032
Cypress Ave ... 89030
Cypress Creek St ... 89031
Cypress Falls Ct ... 89081
Cypress Gold Ct ... 89031
Cypress Island Ct ... 89031
Cyprus Dipper Ave ... 89084
Dabney Dr ... 89032
Dagnar Ct ... 89031
Dainty Bess Ct ... 89032
Daisy Field Dr ... 89032
Daisy Meadow Ln ... 89032
Dakota Bay St ... 89081
Dakotah Pointe Ct ... 89031
Dale Bumpers Ct ... 89081
Daley Cir & St ... 89030
Dalle Valley St ... 89031
Dalton Ridge Ct ... 89031
Dandelion Ct ... 89031
Danielle Rebecca Ave ... 89086
Dante Ct ... 89031
Dapple Dr ... 89032
Dara St ... 89081
Darby Way ... 89030
Darby Creek Ct ... 89081
Darnley St ... 89081
Dauntless Dr ... 89031
Dave Pappas St ... 89086
Davis Pl ... 89030
Dawn Break Canyon St ... 89031
Dawn Lily Ct ... 89081
Dawn Valley Dr ... 89031
Dawn View Ln ... 89031
Dawn Wood Ct ... 89031
Dawson Creek St ... 89031
Daydream Bend St ... 89032
Daywood St ... 89031
Dazzling Sparks St ... 89031
De Vinci Ct ... 89031
Debussy Way ... 89032
Debut Ct ... 89031
N Decatur Blvd ... 89084
Deem Dr ... 89031
Deep Blue St ... 89031
Deep Space St ... 89032
Deer Brush Ct ... 89031
Deer Horn Ln ... 89031
Deer Peak Ct ... 89084
Deer Run Ct ... 89031
E Deer Springs Way ... 89086
W Deer Springs Way ... 89084
Del Laguna Ct ... 89031
Del Monico Way ... 89031
Del Rio Dr ... 89030
Del Shannon St ... 89031
Dela Cruz Ave ... 89031
Delaney Falls St ... 89081
E Delhi Ave
300-499 ... 89032
1001-1097 ... 89030
1099-1199 ... 89030
W Delhi Ave ... 89032
Delicate Arch Ct ... 89031
Delighted Ave ... 89031
Delorean Dr ... 89081
Delta Dawn Ln ... 89032
Demille Ct ... 89081
Denali Ave ... 89032
Denvers Dream Ave ... 89081
Desert Columbine Ct ... 89031
Desert Haven Ave ... 89085
Desert Home Ave ... 89085
Desert Leaf St ... 89081
Desert Park Ave ... 89085
Desert Ridge Ave ... 89031
Desert Sage Ave ... 89031
Desert Silk Ct ... 89084
Desert Sparrow Ave ... 89084
Desert Thrasher Dr ... 89084
Desert Wren Ln ... 89084
Devils Canyon St ... 89085
Dewitt Dr ... 89032
Diamond Beach Ct ... 89031
Diamond Bluff Ave ... 89084
Diamond Glen Way ... 89032
Diamond Mine St ... 89031
Diamond Point Ct ... 89084
Diamond Spur Ave ... 89032
E Diana Ct & Dr ... 89030
Diano Marina Ct ... 89081
Dianthus Ct ... 89031
Diazo St ... 89031
Dignified Ct ... 89032
Dillon Ave ... 89030
Dillon Falls Ct ... 89031
Dillon Ridge Dr ... 89081
Dillweed Ct ... 89031
Dilly Cir ... 89031
Dim Stars Ct ... 89031
Dinard Way ... 89031
Dipper Ave ... 89084
Discovery Creek Ave ... 89031
Discovery Downs Ct ... 89081
Disk Ave ... 89084
Distant Drum St ... 89081
Distribution Cir ... 89030
Diver Ave ... 89084
Divers Loons St ... 89084
Diving Petrels Pl ... 89084
Dixon Springs Ave ... 89031
Doe Springs Pl ... 89031
Dogwood Ave & Ct ... 89030
Dogwood Falls Ct ... 89031
Dolphin Beach Ave ... 89081
Dolphin Peak Ct ... 89084
Dolphin Point Ct ... 89081
Don Alberto Ct ... 89031
Don Fernando Cir ... 89031
Don Juan Ct ... 89030
Don Pedro Cir ... 89031
Donato Cir ... 89032
Donica Rose Ct ... 89031
Donna St
2001-2597 ... 89030
2599-3899 ... 89030
3901-3999 ... 89030
4801-5397 ... 89081
5399-5600 ... 89081
5602-5898 ... 89081
6600-6799 ... 89086
Donovan Way
4100-4378 ... 89030
4380-4399 ... 89030
4400-4798 ... 89081
4800-4900 ... 89081
4902-5398 ... 89081
Dorchester Bend Ave ... 89032
Dornie Ave ... 89084
Dorrell Ln ... 89086
Dotted Wren Ave ... 89084
Double Delight Ave ... 89032
Double Oak St ... 89031
Douglas St ... 89030
Dove Ln ... 89032
Dove Creek Rd ... 89032
Dovecote Ave ... 89084
Dover Dove Ct ... 89081
Dover Glen Dr ... 89031
Dover Ridge Cir ... 89032
Dowitcher Ave ... 89084
Dowither Ct ... 89031
Downs Brook Ct ... 89032
Draft Horse Dr ... 89081
Dragon Fly St ... 89032
Dragon Fly Creek Ave ... 89031
Dragonfly Bush Ct ... 89085
Dragonfly Ranch Ln ... 89081
Drakewood Ave ... 89031

Dreamy Hill Ave 89031
Drescina Way 89031
Drifting Pebble St 89081
Drifting Pelican Ct 89032
Dripping Springs Ave 89031
Drumgooley Ct 89032
Dry Valley Ave 89031
Duchess Ave 89030
Duck Harbor Ave 89031
Duffy Cir 89031
Duhamel Way 89032
Duke Ave 89030
Dulce Norte St 89031
Dulcet Dr 89032
Dune Ridge Ave 89031
Dunvegan Ct 89031
Duquesne Ave 89030
Durban Ct 89032
Dusty Chap Ct 89032
Dusty Cowboy Cir 89032
Dusty Glen Ct 89032
Dusty Mile Ct 89031
Dusty Trail St 89031
Dusty View St 89030
Dutchmans Vine Ct 89081
Eagle Way 89031
Eagle Brook Ct 89031
Eagle Glacier Ave 89081
Eagle Pass Ct 89084
Eagle Rose St 89032
Eagle View Way 89032
Eagles Pass Ave 89084
Eaker St 89081
Earth Ct 89032
Earthsong Ct 89081
Easedale Ct 89031
Easter Island Pl 89081
Echo Beach Ave 89086
Echo Hawk St 89031
Edgehill Way 89032
Edgestone Mark Ave 89081
Edinboro Ridge Ave 89081
Edna Crane Ave 89031
Eel River Ct 89031
Eganridge Ct 89081
Eggshell Dr 89084
Egret Ct 89031
Eiderdown Pl 89084
El Cabo Rey Ave 89081
E El Campo Grande
Ave 89081
W El Campo Grande
Ave 89031
El Cubano Ct 89030
El Este Ln 89031
El Nino Ln 89031
El Prado Heights St 89081
El Sur Ct 89031
Elegant Alley Ct 89032
Eliza Ln 89031
Elizabeth Ave 89030
Elkhorn Rd 89084
Elks Peak Ave 89084
Elliot Park Ave 89032
Ellis St 89030
Elmo Garden Ct 89032
Elphin Ct 89031
Elvington Ave 89081
Emerald Basin St 89031
Emerald Stone Ave 89081
Emeritus Cir 89032
Emily Ann Ct 89032
Emma Bay Ct 89031
Emmons Ave 89030
Empress Diamond Dr 89032
Encino Cir 89030
End Run Ln 89032
Energy Way 89030
Engelstad St 89032
Engineers Way 89081
Englestad St 89030
English Aster Ct 89081
English Colony Ct 89031
English Elm Ct 89031
English Lavender Ave 89031
Equador Ave & Ct 89030

Equator Ave 89032
Eric Stocken Ave 89081
Erica Dr 89032
Erin Lee Ct 89031
Erinbird Ave 89084
Ernest St 89032
Esperanza Way 89031
Estate Ranch St 89031
Estrapade St 89031
European Robin St 89084
E Evans Ave 89030
W Evans Ave 89032
Evans Canyon St 89031
Evening Bluff Pl 89084
Evening Fawn Dr 89031
Evening Grosbeak Pl 89084
Evening Storm Ct 89030
Evening View St 89031
Evita Ct 89032
Evora Cir 89032
Extenso Dr 89032
Extravagant Ave 89031
Exulted Valley Ave 89032
Fabulous Finches Ave 89084
Faded Moon Ct 89081
Fair Oaks Pl 89030
Fairport Dr 89032
Falcon Crest Ave 89031
Falcon Hill St 89032
Falcons Flight Ave 89084
Faleantr Ave 89031
Fall Oaks Ct 89032
Fall Pointe Ct 89032
Falling Petals Dr 89031
Falling Sun Ct 89031
Falling Tree Ave 89031
Famoso Dr 89032
Fan Fare Dr 89032
Fantail Dr 89084
Fantastic Tachi St 89081
Farica St 89081
Farina Dr 89032
Farley Feather Ct 89031
Farm Bridge Ave 89081
Farmdale Ave 89031
Farmouth Cir 89032
Farpoint Rd 89031
Favorable Ct 89032
Fawn Hedge Ave 89081
Fawn Kelton Ct 89031
Faye Talor St 89081
Feather Peak St 89084
Featherbrook Ave 89031
Feathering Ct 89084
Felicia Ct 89081
Felix Palm Ave 89032
Fence Rider Ave 89031
Fenton Ln 89032
Feral Dove St 89084
Feral Garden St 89031
Ferguson Ave & Cir 89030
Fern Crest Ave 89031
Fern Forest Ct 89031
Fern Gully Way 89031
Fernbird Ln 89084
Ferrell St
3400-3799 89032
3801-4099 89032
4400-6099 89031
Ferrell Mountain Ct 89031
Ferret Fall Ave 89030
Festive Ct 89032
Fieldfare Dr 89084
Fields St 89032
Fiesta Del Rey Ave 89081
Fiesta Grande Ct 89031
Fighting Falcon Ln 89031
Figler Ct 89030
Fiji Island Ct 89031
Finch Ridge Ave 89032
Fino Cir 89032
Fire Eye Way 89084
Fire Fox Dr 89032
Firecrest Ct 89032
Firefly Ranch Ln 89081
First Sun St 89081

W Fisher Ave 89031
Fishers Landing Ave 89032
Fishtrap Hollow St 89085
Flaming Arrow Rd 89031
Flaming Thorn Dr 89032
Flaminian Ln 89084
Flats Way 89032
Fledgling Dr 89084
Flemington Ct 89031
Flinthead Dr 89084
Flower Ave & Dr 89030
Flower Garden Ct 89031
Flushing River St 89032
Flying Arrow Pl 89031
Flying Colt Ct 89032
Flyway Ct 89084
Focal Point Ave 89031
Fog Run Ct 89031
Folksinger Ct 89081
Fontana Cliffs Ct 89084
Fontana Colony Ct 89031
Forest Creek Rd 89031
Forest Gate St 89084
Forest Mist Ave 89084
Forestville St 89032
Fornax Ct 89032
Forsythia Ct 89031
Fort Dix Cir 89031
Fort Mandan Ct 89081
Fort Niagara Ave 89032
Fort Sumter Dr 89030
Fort Wayne Ct 89031
Fort William St 89084
Fort Worth St 89081
Fortress Dr 89031
Fossil Butte Way 89032
Fountain Ct 89032
Fountain Falls Way 89032
Fountain Valley Way 89031
Fowler Falls Ct 89085
Fox Blitz Ave 89031
Fox Bluff Dr 89032
Fox Crossing Ave 89084
Fox Hair St 89081
Fox Sparrow Ct 89084
Foxtail Ridge St 89031
Foxvale Ave 89032
Frad Ave 89031
Fragrant Jasmine Ave 89081
Frangipani Ct 89031
Franklin Grove St 89081
Frapuccino Ave 89084
Fredrick St 89030
Free Bird Crest Ave 89081
Freestone Ln 89032
Frehner Rd 89030
Freightliner Dr 89081
French Lace Ct 89081
French Landing Rd 89031
French Lavender St 89031
Fresco Breeze Pl 89031
Friarbird Ct 89084
Friendship Ct 89032
Frigate Way 89084
Frigatebird Ln 89084
Frio Cir 89031
Frost Flower Dr 89032
Frostbrook Cir 89032
Frostwood Ln 89031
Fruit Dove St 89084
Full Moon Peak Ct 89084
Fuselier Dr 89032
Gaber Ct 89032
Galapagos Ave 89084
Galendo Dr 89032
Galisteo Ct 89032
Galivan Vista St 89081
Gallowgate Ct 89084
Gallowtree Ave 89081
Galmia Pl 89032
Galway Bay St 89081
Gamez Way 89031
Gander Ct 89084
Gangplank St 89031
Gannon Ridge Ave 89081
Garden Genoa Ave 89031

Gardenia Flower Ave 89031
Garganey Ave 89084
Garnet Heights Ave 89081
Gary Carmena Ave 89081
Gaster Ave 89081
Gaston Ln 89032
Gatepost Ave 89031
Gault Ct 89032
Gazing Stars St 89030
Geese Ave 89084
Geese Gathering St 89084
Gemstone Hill Ave 89031
Gemstone Peak St 89031
Genella Way 89031
Generous Ct 89032
Genesee Gorge Ave 89032
Gentle Bluff Ct 89084
Gentle Brook St 89084
Gentle Creek Ln 89031
Gentle Dawn Ave 89084
Gentle Falls Ln 89084
Gentle Harbor St 89084
George Ave 89030
Giallo Vista Ct 89031
Giant Forest Ln 89031
Giant Oak St 89084
Giant Pine Ave 89031
Giant Rock Pl 89031
Gifford St 89030
Gilbert Creek Ave 89031
Gilday Ave & Ct 89030
Gilded Flicker St 89084
Gilmore Ave 89030
W Gilmore Ave 89032
Ginger Blossom Ave 89031
Gingersnap Way 89032
Gingham St 89031
Gioeli Pl 89032
Glacier Falls St 89085
Glacier Grove Dr 89032
Gladiator Sword Ct 89031
Glamis Cir 89032
Glamorous Ct 89031
Glass Lantern Dr 89032
Glassport Cir 89032
Glastonbury Thorn St 89032
Gleaming Meadows St 89031
Glen Fiditch St 89032
Glendale Ave & Cir 89030
Glenolden St 89081
Glenora Falls St 89085
Glenrosa Dr 89031
Glenwood Springs Ave 89032
Gleriere Dr 89032
Glider St 89030
Gliding Gulls Ave 89084
Glitter Gold Ct 89031
Globe St 89032
Glorious Iris Pl 89084
Glory Ridge Ave 89031
Glory View Ln 89032
Glowing Garnet St 89081
Gnatcatcher Ave 89084
Goal Ct 89031
Godbey Ct 89032
Gold Bird Ct 89032
Gold Horizon St 89031
Gold Run St 89032
Gold Sluice Ave 89032
Golden Dawn Ct 89032
Golden Fields St 89031
Golden Glen Ct 89031
Golden Harmony St 89031
Golden Melody Ln 89081
Golden Palomino Ln 89032
Golden Rain St 89031
Golden Sage Dr 89032
Golden Sea Ln 89032
Golden Sun Ct 89081
Golden Warbler St 89084
Goldeneye Way 89031
Goldenroot Ct 89031
Goldenseal Ct 89031
Goldfield St
1800-1810 89030
1812-1999 89030
3600-3798 89032
3800-3999 89032
4601-4697 89031
4699-5100 89031
5102-5598 89031
6400-7199 89084
Goldleaf Falls Ave 89031
Goosander St 89084
Gosford St 89031
E Gowan Rd
400-410 89032
412-413 89032
415-423 89032
1000-2398 89030
2400-3299 89030
3301-3499 89030
W Gowan Rd 89032
Graceful Grove Ave 89032
Gracewood St 89032
Gracious Crest Ave 89032
Graham Cracker St 89031
Graldela Ct 89085
Gramercy Ave 89031
Granada Gorge Ln 89084
Grand Lake St 89081
Grand Prairie Ave 89032
Grand Prize Ave 89032
Grand Rapids St 89031
Grand Revere Pl 89032
Grand Rock Dr 89081
Grandfalls Bluff Ave 89031
Grandmother Hat St 89081
Granite Ash Ave 89081
Granite Cove Ct 89081
Granite Stone Ave 89032
Grant Hill Ave 89081
Granville Lake St 89031
Grass Sparrow Dr 89084
Grassquit St 89084
Grasswren Dr 89084
Gratefulness Ct 89032
Gratitude Ct 89032
Gravel Rock St 89081
Gray Robin Ave 89032
Grayback Dr 89084
Great Abaco St 89031
Great Auk Ave 89084
Great Divide St 89031
Great Egret Ln 89084
Great Sandy Ct 89081
Great Spirit Ct 89031
Green Hollow St 89031
Green Ice Ave 89081
Green Sparrow Ln 89084
Green Vine St 89031
Greenbriar Bluff Ave 89081
Greenbridge St 89032
Greenfriar Ave 89084
Greenhaven Ct 89031
Greenlet Ave 89084
Greenley Gardens St 89081
Greenwick Dr 89032
Gregorian Way 89032
Gressorial Ln 89084
Greta Garbo St 89031
Gretchen Ct 89081
Grey Goose St 89081
Grey Heron Dr 89084
Grey Hills Dr 89032
Grey Hollow Ave 89031
Grey Hunter Dr 89031
Grey Knoll Cir 89031
Grey Pointe St 89031
Grey Teal St 89084
Grey Wood Way 89031
Grimespound Ct 89031
Griswold St 89030
Groom Ave 89081
Grotto Ct 89031
Ground Robin Dr 89084
Grouse House Ln 89084
Grovestand Ave 89081
Guardsman Ln 89032
Guidance Ct 89031
Guidestar St 89084
Guiding Star Cir 89031

Guillemot Ave 89084
Gullwing Ln 89081
Gum Springs St 89081
Guma Way 89031
Gun Smoke Cir 89031
Gunlock Cir 89031
Hackle Ct 89084
Haddock Ave 89030
Hadley Ct 89031
Hail Storm Ct 89032
Halstead Ct 89081
Hamilton St 89030
Hamilton Falls St 89085
Hamlin Pl 89032
E Hammer Ln 89081
W Hammer Ln 89031
Hammerkop Dr 89084
Hannah Brook St 89084
Hannah Gordon Ct 89081
Hansa Ave 89081
Happiness Ct 89031
Harbor Gulf Ct 89084
Harbor Master St 89031
Hardgate St 89031
Harding St 89030
Harewood Ave & Cir 89030
Harlin Ave 89030
Harmony Point Dr 89032
Harold St 89081
Harp Way 89032
Harrier Ct 89084
Hart Ave 89032
Hartley Cove Ave 89081
Harvard St 89030
Harvest Creek St 89031
Harvest Dance St 89031
Hassell Ave 89032
Hatch St 89032
Hause Ave 89030
Haven Falls Ct 89085
Haven Heights St 89085
Haven Point Ave 89085
Havoc Way 89031
Hawaiian Breeze Ave 89031
Hawkeye Bell St 89081
Hawkeye Falls Ave 89085
Hawks Glide Ave 89084
Hayworth Ave 89032
Hazel Croft Way 89032
Hazelnut Pine Pl 89084
Healing Waters Ln 89031
Heartland Way 89031
Heartland Point Ave 89032
Heather Ave & Ct 89030
Heather Grove Ave 89081
Heather Oaks Way 89031
Heather Ridge Rd 89031
Heathrow Lake Ave 89084
Heavenly Moon St 89084
Heberdeen Ct 89032
Hedge Grove Dr 89032
Hedgewood Dr 89032
Heineken Dr 89031
Helen Ave
1200-1499 89030
1500-1698 89032
1700-1999 89032
Helens Pouroff Ave 89085
Helmsley Ave 89031
Helmsman Dr 89032
Hemmed Hollow St 89085
Hemphill St 89032
Hempsted Glen Ave 89031
Henderson Cir 89030
Hera Temple Ave 89031
Herblinda Ln 89032
Heritage Cliff Ave 89032
Heritage Ridge Ave 89031
Heroic Hills Ln 89032
Herring Gull Ln 89084
Herrod Dr 89030
Hickey Ave 89030
Hickory Grove Cir 89031
Hickorywood Dr 89031
Hidden Rainbow St 89031
Hidden Rock Dr 89031

Hidden Summit St 89031
Hidletow View Ave 89081
High Altitude Ave 89032
High Creek Dr 89031
High Sage Ct 89031
High Uintas Dr 89031
Highfield Ct 89032
Highland Gardens Dr 89031
Hightree St 89030
Hill Bridge Dr 89032
Hill Shine Ave 89031
Hill Spring Ct 89031
Hills Echo St 89031
Hillscroft Ct 89032
Hilmont St 89031
Hobog Ct 89031
Hoke Edward Ct 89031
Hollingshed Ct 89081
Hollis St 89032
Hollow Oak Ave 89031
Hollow Tree Dr 89032
Hollowbluff Ave 89031
Hollowridge Rd 89031
Holly Sprig Ct 89032
Hollycroft Dr 89081
Hollyridge St 89081
Holmes Cir & St 89030
Holster Ave 89032
Home Haven St 89031
Homing Dove St 89084
Homing Pigeon Pl &
St 89084
Honduras Pl 89030
Honey Burst Ave 89032
Honey Locust Dr 89031
Honey Vista Ln 89032
Honeysuckle Ave 89031
Hoover St 89030
Hope St 89081
Hopedale Ave 89032
Hornbill Ct 89084
Hornbrook St 89031
Horned Owl Way 89084
Horse Pointe Ave 89084
Horse Stable Ave 89081
Horsehair Blanket Dr 89081
Hot Cider Ave 89031
House Sparrow St 89084
Hoyt St 89030
Humble Hollow Pl 89084
Hunkins Dr 89030
Hunter Jumper St 89081
Hunters Bluff Dr 89032
Hunters Paradise Ave 89084
Hunters Ridge Way 89032
Hunters Run Dr 89031
Iberville St 89031
Ice Crystal Ct 89032
Iceland Gull St 89084
Icy River Ave 89031
Idaho Springs St 89032
Imperial Beach Ave 89032
Inca Jay St 89084
Indian Hedge Dr 89032
Indian Hollow Ave 89031
Indian Horse Ct 89032
Indian Peak Ct 89084
Indian Ridge Dr 89031
Indian Rock Rd 89031
Indian Rose St 89031
Indian Springs St 89031
Indigo Flower St 89084
Indigo Hills St 89031
Industrial Center Dr 89030
Influential Ct 89031
Ingenue Rd 89031
Ingleside St 89081
Inglewood Point St 89032
Ingraham St 89030
Inlet Bay Ave 89031
Inlet Beach Ct 89031
Inlet Spring Ave 89031
Innovation Ct 89031
Integrity St 89031
Intermezzo Way 89032
Intermission Ct 89031

Internet Ave 89031
Inverness Grove Ave ... 89081
Irene Porter St 89031
Iris Kelly Ave 89081
Iris Pearl Ave 89031
Irish Sea Ct 89031
Iron Stirrup Ave 89081
Iron Summit Ave 89031
Iroquois Ln 89030
Island Dreams Ave 89031
Island Paradise Ave 89031
Island Rail Dr 89084
Iverson Ln 89032
Ivory Jade Ave 89031
Ivory Tusk Cir 89031
Ivorybill Way 89084
Jacarilla Ln 89031
Jacksboro Ct 89084
Jacob Julio Ave 89031
Jade Jaguar St 89086
Jade Ridge St 89081
Jaffa Dr 89032
Jake Andrew Ave 89086
Jamaica Coast Ct 89031
Jamaica Princess Pl 89084
James St 89030
Jamison Park Ln 89032
Jane Austin Ave 89031
Jardine Ave 89032
Jared Ct 89032
Jasmine Heights Ave 89081
Java Sparrow St 89084
Jaybird Way 89084
Jean Harlow Ct 89031
Jean Paul Ave 89031
Jefferson St 89030
Jeffery Ave 89032
Jeremy David St 89031
Jessica Marie St 89032
Jett Canyon St 89031
Jewel Springs Ln 89081
Jim Steele Falls St 89085
Jimmy Buffet St 89031
Johannan Ln 89032
John Bevy Ct 89086
John Peter Lee Ave 89032
Johnny Love Ln 89086
Jonah Clarke St 89086
Jordan Ln 89032
Jose Ernesto St 89031
Jose Leon St 89031
Joshua Jose St 89031
Journey Way 89031
Journey Hills Ct 89084
Joust St 89030
Joyous St 89032
Juanita Cir 89032
Juanita May Ave 89032
Jubilance Point Ct 89032
Judith Dr 89032
Judson Ave 89030
Juelene Way 89030
July Springs Ave 89085
Junction Peak Ave 89031
June Ave 89031
Jungle Fowl St 89084
Jungle Hawk Ln 89084
Jungle Orchard St 89031
Juperana St 89031
Jurupa Ct 89031
Kadena Garden Ct 89031
Kagan Ct 89081
Kami St 89081
Kandahar Ave 89081
Karma Dr 89032
Keasberry Ave 89081
Keefe Falls Ct 89085
Kelcie Marie Ave 89031
Keller Ct 89032
Kemp St 89032
Ken Smith Falls St 89085
Kendall Point Ave 89081
Kenmore St 89031
Kenner Dr 89032
Kenneth Rd & St 89030
N Kenny Way 89031
Kensington Palace Ave 89032
Kenya Springs St 89086
Keswick Rd 89031
Kettle Falls Ave 89085
Kevin Baker Ave 89086
Keystone Crest St 89081
Kidd St 89032
Kiel Way 89030
Kier Rd 89030
Kildare Cove Ct 89081
Kilgores Rocks Ave 89085
Kim Ln 89030
Kinderhook Ct 89081
Kindhearted Ct 89032
Kindness Ct 89031
King Charles St 89030
King Michael Ave 89086
King Revere St 89032
Kingbird Dr 89084
Kingfishers Catch Ave 89084
Kings Ave 89030
Kings Center Ave 89032
Kings Hill Rd 89032
Kingswinford Dr 89032
Kiskadee St 89084
Kitamaya St 89031
Kite Shield Ct 89031
Kittiwake Rd 89084
Klondike River Pl 89081
Knight Hill Pl 89031
Knoll Crest Ave 89032
Knoll Heights Ct 89032
Knoll Ridge Ave 89032
Kodiak Hill Ln 89031
Kohler Way 89032
Kona Mountain St 89031
Kookaburra Way 89084
W Kraft Ave 89031
Kris Cir 89030
Krista Alethea St 89031
Kristina Lynn Ave 89081
Kronos Pl 89032
Krug St 89081
Kruger Ct 89032
Kulawea St 89081
Kyle Stewart Ct 89086
La Brea Keys Ave 89031
La Calera Ave 89084
La Cascada Ave 89031
E La Madre Way
300-398 89031
501-597 89081
599-900 89081
902-2998 89081
W La Madre Way 89031
La Pelusa St 89031
La Pradera Ct 89086
La Princesa Ct 89031
La Quinta Hills St 89081
La Ronda Cir 89032
La Scala Ct 89032
La Villa Dr 89031
Labrusca Vines Ct 89081
Lady Carolina St 89081
Lady Elizabeth Ct 89031
Lael Ct 89032
Laguna Heights Ave 89081
Laguna Palms Ave 89031
Lahaina Ct 89031
Lake Charles St 89031
Lake Martin Ct 89031
E Lake Mead Blvd
601-1499 89030
1414-1414 89036
1501-3599 89030
1600-3540 89030
E Lake Mead Blvd N 89030
E Lake Mead Blvd S 89030
W Lake Mead Blvd
300-738 89030
2600-3999 89032
Lake Victoria Dr 89032
Lakeland Village Dr 89081
Lakeside Villas Ave 89081
Lamance Ct 89031
Lancaster Falls Ave 89085
Lance Ave & Pl 89030
Landau St 89030
Landing Bird Ct 89032
Langdon Way 89032
Langfield Falls St 89085
Langport Dr 89031
Lapalco Ave 89031
Lapwing Dr 89084
Larey Ave 89032
Lark Canyon Ct 89031
Lark Sparrow St 89084
Las Animas Ct 89081
Las Cruces Heights St 89081
Las Vegas Blvd N 89030
Lasha Ct 89032
Lass Cir 89030
Latrobe Bluff St 89031
Lattice Ct 89031
Laughing Larkspur Ave 89081
Laughing Thrush Ct 89084
Laurel Hill Dr 89032
Lava Beds Way 89084
Lava Creek Ct 89031
Lava Rock Ave 89031
Lavender Ct 89031
Lavender Breeze St 89081
Lavender Grove Ct 89031
Lavender Lilly Ln 89084
Lavender Lion St 89086
Lawrence St 89081
Lawry Ave 89032
Laytonstone Way 89081
Lazy Hill Ranch Way 89081
Lazy Leopard Ct 89086
Lazy Meadow Ct 89031
Leadership Ct 89031
Leaning Rock Ct 89031
Leaping Foal St 89081
Leatherbridge Ct 89081
Legend Falls St 89081
Leisure Falls Ct 89031
Lemhi Ct 89031
Lenwood Ave 89030
Leonidas St 89031
Leonor Ct 89031
Leopard Ct 89031
Leopard Spot Ct 89031
Lexington St 89030
Liberal Ct 89032
Liberator Way 89031
Liberty Meadow Ave 89031
Lidia Dr & St 89032
Light Ridge Ct 89031
Lightfoot Ct 89032
Lilac Field Ct 89031
Lillian Wood Ave 89031
Lillis Ave & Cir 89030
Lilly Ave 89030
Lilly Note Ave 89031
Lilly Rose Ct 89031
Lilly Star Ct 89031
Lily Glen Ct 89032
Lily Trotter St 89084
Limelight Ct 89031
Lincoln Ave 89030
Lincoln Rd 89081
Linniki St 89032
Lintwhite St 89084
Lions Den Ave 89031
Little Bay Ave 89081
Little Bend Ln 89031
Little Bow Ave 89084
Little Canyon St 89084
Little Cape Ct 89081
Little Cayman St 89031
Little Crimson Ave 89081
Little Elm St 89031
Little Gull Ct 89084
Little Italy Ave 89031
Little Mountain St 89031
Little Owl Pl 89084
Livia Ave 89031
Lockwood Ave 89030
Lodge Pole Ct 89030
Logan Ave 89032
Logan Creek Ct 89031
Logan Pond Way 89084
Logan Valley Ln 89081
Logsdon Dr 89032
Loida Ct 89031
Lola Ave 89030
Loma Bella Ln 89031
Loma Marsh Ct 89084
Lone Canyon Ct 89031
E Lone Mountain Rd
2-498 89031
501-1497 89081
1499-4199 89081
4201-4299 89081
W Lone Mountain Rd 89031
Lone Prarie Ct 89031
Lone Ridge Ct 89032
Lone Song Rd 89031
Lone Vista Way 89031
Lonejack Ln 89031
Lonesome Drum St 89032
Lonesome Wolf Ct 89031
Longhorn Cattle St 89084
Lookout Crest St 89031
Lookout Lodge Ln 89084
Lord Orville Ct 89031
Los Alamos Dr 89031
Los Amigos Cir 89031
Los Lobos St 89031
Losee Rd
1800-1898 89030
1900-4200 89030
4202-4398 89030
4401-5097 89081
5099-5999 89081
6001-6399 89081
6400-6599 89086
Lost Canyon Dr 89031
Lost Creek Ct 89031
Lost Mesa Ct 89031
Lost Ridge Ct 89031
Louisville Dr 89031
Lovely Ct 89032
Lower Deck Ct 89031
Lower Saxon Ave 89085
Loyola St 89030
Lumber River Ct 89081
Luminous Ct 89032
Luna Vista Pl 89084
Lunar Sky St 89032
Lupita Ct 89031
Lute St 89032
Lydfort Ct 89031
Lynette Ln 89031
Lyrebird Dr 89084
Mabry Pl & St 89030
Macadamia Nut Ave 89084
Macaroon Way 89031
Madador Dr 89031
Madaline Nicole Ave 89086
Madame Plantier Ave 89081
Madison Stone St 89081
Madre Maria Ct 89031
Madrone Dr 89031
Magdelena Ridge Ave 89081
Magenta Hills Dr 89031
Magic Mango St 89031
Magic Mesa St 89031
Magic Oak St 89031
Magnet St 89030
N Main St 89030
Majestic Pearl Pl 89084
Majestic Sand Ave 89031
Majestic Sky Dr 89031
Makushin Bay Ave 89081
Malambro Ct 89032
Malibu Palm Ct 89032
Malibu Sands Ave 89086
Mammoth Canyon Pl 89084
Mammoth Mountain St 89081
Manchester Bay Ave 89031
Mandible St 89084
Mandolin Way 89032
Mango Bay Ave 89031
Manhattan Bridge Pl 89032
Manor Stone St 89081
Manti Peak Ave 89081
Mantle Ave 89084
Manuel Edwardo Ave 89031
Manzanares Dr 89084
Maple Creek Ave 89031
Maple Falls Ct 89032
Maple Mesa St 89084
Maple Pines Ave 89081
Maple Point St 89032
Marathon Keys Ave 89031
Marble Apex Ave 89031
Marcella Ave 89030
Marco Polo St 89031
Mardi Gras Ln 89030
Marigold Oasis Ct 89084
Maritocca Ave 89031
Market Center Dr 89030
Marlock St 89031
Mars Ave 89030
Marsh Sparrow Ln 89084
Marsh Tern Ct 89084
Marshall Island Ct 89031
N Martin L King Blvd 89032
Marvelous Manor Ave 89032
Marvin St 89031
Mary Dee Ave 89030
Masonville St 89081
Masseria Ct 89031
Mast Glorious Ct 89031
Mastercraft Ave 89031
Masterson Ln 89032
Matheson St 89030
Matinee Ave 89031
Mattray St 89032
Maui Surf Ave 89031
Mauna King St 89032
Mavis Ln 89084
Maxwell St 89030
May Time Ave 89081
E & W Mayflower Ave 89030
Mazeno Peak St 89031
Mazzocco Ct 89032
Mccarran St
1800-1898 89030
1900-2599 89030
6300-6398 89081
6501-6699 89086
Mcdaniel St 89030
E Mcdonald Ave 89030
W Mcdonald Ave 89032
Mcdonald Ct 89032
Mcgovern Ave 89030
Mcgregor Way 89032
Mcguire St 89081
Mclennan Ave 89081
Meadow Dale Dr 89031
Meadow Falls St 89085
Meadow Flower Ave 89031
Meadow Green Ave 89031
Meadow Pasture St 89085
Meadow Saffron Ct 89031
Meadowbloom Ave 89085
Meadowlark Wing Way 89084
Mediterranean Sea Ave 89031
Meedeldale St 89031
Megan Faye St 89031
Melador Falls Ave 89081
Melic Way 89032
Mellon Ct 89032
Melon Aroma Ave 89031
Mendenhall Dr 89081
Mensa Ave 89032
Mercer Valley St 89081
Mercury St 89030
Merganser Ct 89084
Meridian Rain St 89031
Merriam Ave 89030
Mesa Blanca Way 89031
Mesa Bloom St 89085
Mesa Landing Ave 89085
Mesa Plains St 89085
Mesquite Creek St 89031
Mexican Flame Ave 89085
Michael Dean St 89081
Michale Ave 89032
Middle Rock St 89081
Middleham St 89031
Midnight Breeze St 89081
Midnight Mist Ct 89081
Midnight Wind Ave 89081
Midwinter Mist St 89031
Milan Peak St 89081
Milange St 89031
Milano Dr 89081
Milgrove St 89081
Mill Point Cir 89032
Mill Ranch Ct 89081
Miller Ave 89030
Miller Ridge Ave 89031
Millerbird St 89084
Millers Run St 89084
Millrun Ct 89032
Mills Bay Ln 89081
Milton Pl 89032
Minaret Way 89031
Mindoro Ave 89031
Mineola Way 89032
Mirasol Way 89031
Mission Cantina St 89081
Mission Del Oro Ave 89081
Mission Rey St 89081
Mistle Thrush Dr 89084
Misty Breeze Cir 89031
Misty Foxglove Ct 89081
Misty Glenn Ct 89032
Misty Ridge Cir 89032
Misty View Ct 89031
Mitchell St 89081
Mizzenmast Ave 89032
Mocine Elm Ct 89031
Mohawk River Ave 89031
Mojave Bend Ct 89081
Monaco View Dr 89032
Monarch Mystic Ave 89081
Mondial Ct 89081
Monitor Way 89031
Monrovia Heights St 89081
Monte Alban Dr 89031
Monte Del Sol Ln 89031
Montessa Ave 89031
Montezuma Castle Ln 89084
Montezuma Creek St 89031
Montina Vines St 89081
Moody Vista Ct 89031
Moon Eclipse St 89032
Moon Wave Ave 89031
Moonglow Peak Ave 89084
Moonlight Bluff Ave 89084
Moonlight Glow Ave 89032
Moonshine Falls Ave 89085
Moorpoint Dr 89031
Moretta Ct 89086
Morgan Manor St 89032
Morgan Springs Ave 89081
Morning Amber St 89032
Morning Breeze Dr 89031
Morning Roses Dr 89031
Morning Song Cir 89031
Morning Wing Dr 89031
Morocco Ave 89031
Morrestown Ave 89084
Morro Dunes Ave 89031
Morton Ave 89032
Mosaic St 89032
Moss Landing St 89031
Mosskag Ct 89032
Motmot Ct 89084
Mott Smith St 89081
Mount Athos St 89031
Mount Ida St 89031
Mount Penteli Ave 89031
Mountain Garland Ln 89081
Mountain Glow Ave 89031
Mountain Rail Dr 89084
Mountain Rock Ct 89031
Mountain Rose Ave 89031
Mountain Skies Ct 89032
Mountain Snow St 89031
Mountain Sunset Ave 89031
Mountain Tree St 89031
Mournful Call Ct 89031
Mourning Warbler Ave 89084
Mulberry Glen Dr 89031
Mullady Ave 89031
Mum Ct 89031
Muskoka Falls St 89085
Myrtle Creek Ct 89032
Mystery View Way 89031
Mystic Canyon Ct 89032
Nagle Ln 89032
Nairobi Ln 89032
Nantucket Clipper Dr 89031
Narada Falls Ave 89085
Native Sunflower St 89031
Nature Loop Ave 89031
Nature Park Dr 89084
Nature Path Cir 89031
Navasota Ct 89031
Nawkee Dr 89031
Nebaum Ct 89032
Nebulous Cir 89032
Neeham Rd 89030
Neighborly Ct 89032
E Nelson Ave 89030
W Nelson Ave
600-1199 89030
1700-1999 89032
Nerine Pass Way 89032
Nest Ct 89031
Nestled Grove Dr 89031
Nestled Oak Ave 89031
Nestos Valley Ave 89031
Neva Ranch Ave 89081
Nevada Blaze Ave 89081
New Journey Way 89031
New Suffolk St 89032
Newbridge Way 89032
Newburg Ave 89032
Newquay Commons Ave 89031
Newton Falls St 89032
Nicki Cometa St 89032
Night Heron Way 89084
Night Owl Bluff Ave 89084
Night Parrot Ave 89084
Night Shadow Ave 89031
Night Storm Ave 89081
Nino Ct 89031
Nipper St 89030
Nobar Cir 89031
Nobility Ave 89032
Noble St 89030
Nobleton Ct 89081
Norma Jean Ln 89031
Norte Del Sol Ln 89031
North St 89030
Nube St 89031
Nuevo Leon St 89031
Nutleaf Ct 89031
Oak Bay Way 89032
Oak Bluffs Ave 89032
Oak Island Dr 89032
Oak Peak Ct 89032
Oakbridge Ct 89032
Oakville Ct 89032
Oakwood Ave 89030
Oasis Bloom St 89085
Oasis Hill Ave 89085
Oasis Plains Ave 89085
Oasis Ridge St 89031
Oasis Valley Ave 89085
Oatfield St 89081
Oberlander Ave 89031
Oberon Ln 89032
Ocatillo Mesa Way 89031
Ocean Breeze Ave 89031
Ocean City Ct 89031
Ocean Spray Ct 89031
Oceanwood Ave 89086
Ocelot Ct 89084
Ocendene Ln 89084
Oconnell Way 89032
Octagon Rd 89030
Octans St 89032
Odlum Point Ln 89032
Old Bridge Ct 89032

Old Canyon Ct 89081
Old Cobble Dr 89081
Old Dominion Ave 89081
Old Field Ave 89081
Old Moccasin Ave 89032
Old Oak Ct 89031
Old Ridge Rd 89031
Old Sorrel Ct 89032
Old Town Dr 89031
Old Vines St 89081
Old Yankee Ave 89031
Olive Dale Ct 89031
Olympic Gold St 89031
Ona Marie Ave 89032
Opal Falls St 89085
Open Door Dr 89032
Opponents Ridge St 89032
Optima Ave 89031
Orange Hue St 89031
Orange Orchid Pl 89084
Orangewood Ln 89030
Orca Lilly St 89031
Orchard Grove Ct 89032
Orchid Jungle Ln 89031
Orchid Lilly Ct 89031
Orchid Moon Ct 89031
Orchid Oasis Ave 89031
Orions Tool St 89031
Orr Ave & Cir 89030
Orvis St 89030
Osaka Pearl St 89031
Oscar Mariano Ave 89032
Osiana Ave 89031
Otter Bay Ct 89031
Otter Falls Ct 89085
Otway Bay Ct 89031
Ouray St 89081
Outlook Point St 89032
Outraker Ct 89031
Outrider Ct 89031
Overlook Ranch St 89031
Overlook Valley St 89081
Overo Ct 89032
Overthere Ln 89032
E & W Owens Ave 89030
Owlet Ct 89084
Oxford Ave 89030
Ozark Way 89031
Ozark Hike St 89031
Pacer Ave 89031
Pacesetter St 89081
Pachand Ave 89030
Pacific Moon Ave 89084
Pacific Screech Pl 89084
Pacific Time Ct 89084
Pack Creek Ct 89031
Packard Pl 89030
Paddleboat St 89031
Padero Dr 89031
Padre Field Ct 89030
Page St 89030
Pageant St 89031
Pageantry Falls Dr 89031
Pagentry Dr 89031
Pahoehoe Way 89031
Painted Hills St 89031
Painted Opus Pl 89084
Painted Pebble St 89081
Painted Woods Ct 89081
Palamos Dr 89032
Palatial Pines Ave 89031
Palatine Hills Ave 89081
Palladio Ave 89031
Pallid Swift Ct 89084
Palmer St 89030
Palmilla St 89031
Palmona St 89031
Palo Pinto Ln 89031
Palomar St 89030
Palomino Estates St 89031
Palomino Farm Way 89081
Panamint Ct 89032
Pandana Cir 89031
Pansy Desert St 89032
Pantego Ave 89031
Panther Pl 89031

Parada Cir 89032
Paradise Harbor Pl 89031
Paradise Hill Ct 89031
Paradise Isle Ave 89031
Paradise Reef Ave 89031
Parasail Point Ave 89031
Paris Meadows Ct 89032
Paris Pearl Ave 89031
Park Hyatt Ave 89081
Park Landing Ct 89032
Park Royal Dr 89031
Park Town St 89032
Parrot Hill Ave 89032
Partegus St 89031
Pasolini Ct 89032
Passage View Ave 89032
Passing Storm Ln 89031
Passionate Ct 89031
Passionfruit St 89032
Pastel Ridge St 89032
Pastori Valley Ct 89032
Patagonia Hills Ave 89081
Patricia St 89030
Patrick Thomas Ct 89086
Patriot Cannon St 89031
Patriot Sword Ave 89031
Patriot Wave St 89031
Patriotic Ln 89032
Pavilions Ave 89031
Pavo Ct 89032
Peaceful Hills Ave 89032
Peaceful Path Ct 89032
Peach Ave 89032
Peacock Pine St 89031
Peak Villa Ave 89031
Pearl Marble Ave 89081
Pearl Mountain Ct 89031
Pearl Sunset Ct 89031
Pearlie May Ct 89081
Pebble Crest Ct 89081
Pebble Rim St 89081
Pecan Lake St 89031
Pecos Rd 89086
N Pecos Rd 89081
Pecos Park Ave 89081
Pele St 89031
Pelican Breeze Ct 89031
Pelican Brief Ln 89084
Pelican Sky Beach Ave 89081
Pella Pompano St 89031
Pen Hollow Ct 89032
Pendergrass St 89081
Penguin Ave 89084
Penney View Ct 89032
Penny Cross Dr 89032
Penthouse Pl 89031
Peony Ct 89031
Pepper Thorn Ave 89081
Perching Bird Ln 89084
Pergola Ct 89031
Periana Ct 89031
Perimeter Rd 89032
Perliter Ave 89030
Petersburg Ln 89031
Petrel St 89084
Petrified Forest St 89084
Petrified Tree Ln 89081
Petrus Ct 89031
Peyton Stewart Ct 89086
Phillip St 89032
Picasso Picture Ct 89081
Piedra Falls Ct 89085
Piercey Ct 89084
Pilar Ave 89032
Pimento St 89032
Pine Blossom Ave 89031
Pine Bough St 89031
Pine Siskin Pl 89084
Pine Terrace Ct 89031
Pine Warbler Way 89084
Pine Willows Ct 89084
Pinehurst Grove St 89081
Pinfeather Way 89084
Pink Chaff St 89031
Pink Coral Dr 89031

Pink Desert St 89085
Pink Flamingos Pl 89084
Pink Frost Dr 89032
Pink Lily Ave 89081
Pinnacle Falls St 89081
Pinnacle Hill Ct 89032
Pinsky Ln 89032
Pinter Way 89032
Pintura Cir 89031
Pioneer Cabin Ct 89031
Pioneer Scout St 89031
Pipeline St 89032
Pipeline Beach Ct 89081
E & W Piper Ave 89030
Pipers Meadow Ct 89031
Pipers Run Pl 89084
Pipers Stone St 89031
Pirate Ship Dr 89031
Pirates Way 89030
Pirates Cave Ct 89032
Playa De Carmen Way 89086
Pleasant Palms St 89081
Plum Horse Ave 89031
Plumb Ridge Ave 89081
Plumeria Ave 89081
Plumwood Ln 89030
Plymouth Ave 89030
Poana Ave 89032
Pocono Ranch Ave 89031
Poem Ct 89081
Point Break St 89084
Point Breeze Dr 89031
Point Loma Ave 89031
Point Morada Ave 89031
Pointe Decatur St & Way 89032
Ponce Royal Ave 89031
Ponderosa Heights St 89081
Pontiac Ave 89030
Pony Express St 89031
Ponycart Ln 89031
Port Antonio Ct 89031
Port Vincent Ave 89081
Portland Ct 89031
Positive Ct 89031
Possum Berry Ln 89081
Post Mountain St 89031
Powell Point Way 89031
Power Quest Way 89031
Prairie Coach Ave 89085
Prairie Moon Ave 89084
Prairie Orchid Ave 89081
Prairie Princess Ave 89081
Prairie Ridge Cir 89031
Precision Dr 89032
Preen St 89084
President Pride Pl 89084
Pretoria Ct 89031
Prevail Dr 89032
Pride Mountain St 89031
Prime Advantage Ave 89032
Princess Ave 89030
Princeton St 89030
Principle Ct 89031
Priority Ct 89031
Prisma Way 89031
Pristine Ct 89032
Prospect Niche St 89031
Prospector Ct 89031
Prospector Mine Ave 89031
Prosperous Ct 89032
Prow Ct 89031
Pueblo Hills Ave 89032
Puesta Del Sol St 89081
Puetollano Dr 89084
Puffer Beach Ct 89081
Puffin Ct 89031
Puglia Ln 89084
Puka Shell St 89031
Puma Ct 89031
Pumpkin Harvest Ave 89031
Punto Del Castello Ct 89081
Purple Martin Ct 89031
Purple Passion Ave 89032
Purple Vista Ct 89031

Putnam Ave 89030
Quail Creek Dr 89032
Quailbush Dr 89031
Quaker Lake St 89032
Quartet Dr 89032
Quartz Crest St 89081
Quartz Ridge Ct 89081
Queenswreath Dr 89031
Quicksand Ln 89032
Quiet Peeps Pl 89084
Quiet Pueblo St 89032
Quinton Ave 89032
Rachel Ann Ave 89031
Radiance Park St 89081
Ragged Robin Ct 89031
Rain Bird Ct 89031
Rain Flower Ln 89031
Rain Storm Ct 89032
Rainbow Draw Ave 89031
Rainbow Glow St 89030
Rainwood Dr 89031
Rainy Sky Ave 89030
Ramirez St 89031
Rams St 89030
Ranch Foreman Rd 89032
Ranch House Rd 89031
Rancho Del Mar Way 89031
Rancho Del Norte Dr 89031
Rancho Del Sol Way 89031
Rancho Domingo Ct 89031
Rancho Linda Ct 89031
Rancho Verde Ct 89031
Randor Ct 89032
Rangeland Ct 89081
Raptor Ct 89084
Raptors View Ave 89031
Ratite Way 89084
Raul St 89030
Raven Hall St 89084
Raven Peak Ave 89081
Ravens Ct 89032
Raymond Ave 89032
Razorbill Ct 89084
Reardon Ct 89031
Recco Ave 89030
Recktenwall Ave 89081
Recollection Ct 89032
Red Blanket Rd 89032
Red Carrousel Ct 89031
W Red Coach Ave 89031
Red Dawn St 89031
Red Fan Palm Ct 89032
Red Fire Ave 89031
Red Gate Ave 89081
Red Glitter St 89031
Red Hollow Dr 89031
Red Imp Ave 89081
Red Ridge Cir 89031
Red Roof St 89081
Red Sox Ave 89030
Red Torador Cir 89031
Red Trumpet Ct 89081
Red Vine St 89031
Redbreast Ct & Ln 89084
Redbud Vine St 89085
Redbull Slice St 89031
Redfield Ave 89032
Redhead Dr 89084
Redquail Cir 89031
Redshank Ln 89084
Redview Ct 89031
Redwood Ridge Way 89031
Reed Station St 89031
Regal Robin Way 89084
Regal Swan Pl 89084
Regal Vista Ave 89032
Regena Rose St 89081
Rejoice Dr 89032
Reliant St 89031
Remembrance Ct 89032
Remex Way 89084
Remington Grove Ave 89081
Renada Cir 89030
Rendava St 89081
Reno Palm Ct 89032
Reseda Cir 89030

Resonance Ct 89032
Respectful Ct 89031
Restful Crest Ave 89032
Resthaven Cir 89032
Rev Wilson Ave 89030
Revere St
- 2000-2498 89030
- 2601-2799 89030
- 5600-5698 89031

Reynolds Ave 89030
Rialto Hills Ave 89081
Riarosa Ct 89086
Ricebird Way 89084
Richborough Ct 89031
Riderwood Ave 89032
Ridge Back Ct 89031
Ridge Mesa Ct 89031
Ridge Vista Way 89031
Riding Crop Ave 89081
Ridosh Cir 89032
Ringbill Ct 89084
Ringstar Rd 89030
Rio Bravo Dr 89031
Rio Colorado Cir 89031
Rio Del Sol Dr 89031
Rio Eldorado Ct 89031
Rio Largo Way 89031
Rio Linda Cir 89031
Rio Paloma Ct 89031
Rio Robles Dr 89030
Rio Royal Way 89031
Ripple Cloud Ct 89031
Ripple Creek St 89031
Ripplestone Ave 89081
Rippling Brook Dr 89032
Rising Cir 89031
Rising Pebble Ct 89031
Riva Del Lago Ct 89081
River Belle St 89031
River Bird St 89031
River Brenta Ct 89031
River Glider Ave 89084
River Ranch Pl 89081
Riverside Run Ct 89081
Riverwalk Falls St 89031
Riviera Regal Ave 89081
Roaming Breeze Rd 89031
Roans Prairie St 89031
Roaring Lion Ave 89031
Roaring Surf Dr 89031
Roaring Wind Ct 89031
Roberta Alecia Ave 89031
Robin Gale Ave 89032
Robin Knot Ct 89084
Robin Tree Ave 89032
Robincrest Ct 89031
Robust Ave 89081
Robust Robin Pl 89084
Roby Grey Way 89081
Rock Cabin Ct 89031
Rock Dove Way 89084
Rock Glen Ln 89032
Rock Pigeon Ave 89084
Rock Quarry Way 89032
Rock Sparrow St 89084
Rock Wren Ct 89084
Rockbottom St 89030
Rocklin Peak Ave 89081
Rockpebble Ave 89030
Rockpine Dr 89081
Rockrose Purple St 89081
Rocky Bluff St 89031
Rocky Brook St 89030
Rocky Countryside St 89030
Rocky Stone Ave 89081
Rolling Creek St 89031
Rolling Rose St 89081
Rolls Royce Rd 89031
Roman Empire Ave 89031
E Rome Blvd 89086
W Rome Blvd 89084
Ronzard Ave 89032
Roosevelt St 89030
Roper Ct 89081
Ropers Ranch St 89032
Rosa Rosales Ct 89031

W Rosada Way 89031
Rosalie Cir 89031
Rose Cir 89030
Rose St 89032
Rose Canyon Dr 89032
Rose Creek Ct 89031
Rose Moss St 89031
Rose Sage St 89031
Rose Valley St 89032
Roseboro Ct 89081
Rosenberg Way 89032
Rosetti Way 89032
Rossmoyne Ave 89030
Round Reign Ave 89081
Round Robin St 89032
Royal St 89030
Royal Antilles Ct 89031
Royal Caribbean Ave 89031
Royal Creek Ct 89031
Royal Gardens Pl 89084
Royal Sands St 89031
Royal Stone Ct 89032
Royal Yacht Way 89031
Royalmile Way 89032
Rubber Tree Ave 89032
Rubio Sun Ave 89081
Ruby Cedar Ct 89031
Ruby Fountain Ave 89031
Ruby Sunset St 89031
Ruddock Dr 89084
Rugosa Alba Ct 89081
Running Creek Dr 89031
Running Fawn Ct 89031
Running Horse Dr 89081
Rushing River Rd 89031
Russian Olive St 89032
Rustic Ct 89031
Rustic Oak Ct 89032
Rustler Ridge Ave 89031
Rustridge Ave 89081
Ryan Lucey Ave 89086
Ryder Ln 89031
Saber Dr 89032
Sable Ct 89031
Sable Palm St 89032
Sacred Mountain Ct 89032
Saddle Hills Ct 89031
Saddlebill Ct 89084
Sadie Lynn Ct 89031
Sagamore Canyon St 89081
Sage Hills Pl 89031
Sage Hollow Cir 89031
Sagebrush Ranch Way 89081
Sagemore Way 89031
Sageridge Cir 89031
Sagerock Way 89031
Saguaro Valley Ct 89030
Sail Rock Pl 89031
Saint Charles Ct 89031
Saint Elias St 89081
Saint Francis St 89031
Saint George St 89030
Saint Peter Ct 89031
Saint Phillip Ct 89031
Salado Creek Ave 89081
Saleen Ct 89031
Salmon Run Ct 89031
Salsbury Cove Dr 89081
Salt Basin St 89084
Salt Lake St 89030
Salutare Ct 89031
Samantha Ct 89030
Sammarra St 89081
Samsara Cir 89032
San Diego St 89032
San Esteban Ave 89084
San Juan Ave 89032
San Mateo St
- 4000-4399 89032
- 4400-4598 89031
- 6300-6399 89084
- 8000-8300 89085
- 8302-8398 89085

W San Miguel Ave 89032
San Niccolo Ct 89031

San Rocco Ct 89031
Sand Swallow St 89084
Sandalo Ct 89086
Sandglass Ave 89032
Sandstone View Way 89084
Sandstone Vista Ct 89031
Sandy Brown Ave 89031
Sandy Point Ct 89031
Sandy Ridge St 89081
Sangara Dr 89031
Sanibel Bay Ct 89031
Santa Fe Heights St 89081
Santa Lucia Dr 89031
Santa Monica Ave 89032
Santa Rosalia Dr 89031
Sapphire Gold St 89031
Sapphire Light St 89081
Sapphire Sands Ct 89031
Sapphire Sea Ct 89031
Sapphire Sea St 89085
Saratoga Reserve St 89081
Sarita Ave & Cir 89030
Satellite Ave 89032
Satre Ct 89031
Saturn Ave 89030
Sawmill Falls St 89085
Saxophone Ln 89081
Scarlet Iris Ct 89081
Scarlet Sage Ave 89031
Scarlet Sea Ave 89031
Scarlet Vista Ct 89031
Scavenger Hunt St 89084
Scissortail Ct 89084
Scotsman Way 89032
Scott Robinson Blvd
- 3900-3999 89032
- 5200-5299 89031

Scott Russell Ct 89031
Screech Owl Ln 89084
Sea Cliff Cove St 89031
Sea Dream Ave 89031
Sea Grass Dr 89032
Sea Harbor Ct 89084
Sea Hunter St 89031
Sea Side Dr 89031
Sea Swallow St 89084
Sea Water Way 89031
Seabirds Pl 89084
Seagull Dive Ct 89084
Seclusion Bay Ave 89081
Seco Adobe Cir 89030
Seneca Heights Ave 89081
Seneca Highland St 89032
Seneca Hill Dr 89032
Seneca Ridge Ave 89084
Senegal Haven St 89081
Sentimental Ct 89031
Serengeti Ct 89032
Serenity Haven St 89081
Sereno Springs St 89081
Sergeant Ct 89031
Sergeant Jordan Ave 89031
Seth Dr 89032
Setting Moon St 89084
Seven Falls St 89085
Seven Pines Pl 89030
Sevier Desert St 89081
Sexton Ave 89031
Seymour Ct 89031
Shaded Field Ave 89081
Shades End Ave 89081
Shadow Bay Ct 89032
Shadow Creek Dr 89081
Shadow Moon Pl 89031
Shadow Oak Dr 89031
Shadow Tree St 89032
Shady Garden Ct 89031
Shady Hollow Ave 89031
Shady Lair Ct 89031
Shady Morning Ave 89031
Shady River Ave 89031
Shady Shopes St 89031
Shallow Dove Ct 89032
Shallow Mist Ct 89032
Shannon Jean Ct 89081
Shannon Valley Ave 89031

Sharp Cir 89030
Sharp Edge Ave 89031
Sharp Tooth Way 89031
Sharpshooter Ln 89031
Shasta Daisy St 89031
Shayla Bay Ave 89086
Shelduck St 89084
Shield St 89030
Shiloh Cir, Pl & Way 89030
Shimmering Creek Ave 89031
Shimmering Peak Way 89031
Shimmering Sands Ave 89031
Shiner Bock Ct 89081
Shining Elm Ct 89031
Ship Wrecked Way 89031
Shockwave Ct 89081
Shonna Way 89032
Shore Ave 89030
Shore Bird Ave 89084
Showdown Dr 89031
Shower Orchid Ct 89031
Shy Albatross Ave 89084
Side Saddle Ct 89032
Sidney Ct 89032
Sidney Spring St 89030
Siena Rose St 89031
Sierra Blanca Ln 89031
Sierra Breeze Ave 89031
Sierra Cliff St 89031
Sierra Lakes St 89031
Sierra Sands St 89086
Sierra Sun St 89032
Silent Path Way 89031
Silent Sunset Ave 89084
Siler Ave & Pl 89030
Silken Saddle St 89031
Silsbee Ct 89084
Silver Bank St 89031
Silver Bark Ave 89081
Silver Bit Ct 89032
Silver Blaze Ct 89031
Silver Bridle Pl 89032
Silver Canyon Ln 89031
Silver Clouds Dr 89031
Silver Crest Ct 89031
Silver Edge St 89031
Silver Lantern Dr 89032
Silver Pony Ct 89084
Silver Rings Ave 89031
Silver Sand Ct 89032
Silver Shore Ct 89081
Silver Silo Ct 89081
Silver Vein St 89031
Silver Vine St 89085
Silvercrest Ct 89032
Silvereye Dr 89084
Silversword Ave 89032
Silverwind Rd 89031
Simmering Sun Ct 89081
Simmons St
- 2701-2997 89032
- 2999-4399 89032
- 4400-6399 89031
- 7300-7399 89084

Simondale Ct 89081
Singer Ln 89084
Singing Bird Ln 89031
Singing Lark Ct 89032
Six Gun Rd 89032
Skimmers Ct 89084
Skinner Cir 89032
Slapton Ave 89031
Slason St 89081
Slate Falls St 89085
Slate Ridge Ct 89081
Sledgehammer Ct 89081
Slide Canyon Ave 89081
Slow Breeze Ave 89081
Smiley Rd 89081
Smokey Fog Ave 89081
Smoking Loon Ave 89031
Snake Charmer Ave 89031
Snap Ridge St 89081
Snow Cactus St 89031
Snow Dome Ave 89031
Snow Finch St 89084
Snow Peak Dr 89031
Snowfire Ave 89032
Snowy Egret Ct 89084
Soaring Bluff St 89031
Sock Hop Way 89031
Sockeye Ln 89032
Socrates St 89031
Soft Whispers St 89031
Solana Del Norte Way 89031
Solar System St 89032
Soledad Way 89030
Sommer Ct 89032
Song Sparrow Ct 89084
Song Thrush St 89084
Songster St 89084
Sonora Crest Ct 89081
Sonoran Heights Ave 89081
Sophia Way 89032
Sorrowing Sparrow Ct 89032
Sorto Lago St 89081
Soto Ln 89032
Southern Cypress Ct 89031
Spanish Fork Ave 89031
Spanish Town Ave 89031
Spanish Wells Dr 89031
Sparkle Crest Ave 89031
Sparkling Meadows Ct 89031
Sparrow Gull Ct 89032
Sparrow Heights Ave 89032
Sparta Way 89032
Spear St 89030
Speckle Summer Pl 89084
Specula Wing Dr 89084
Speranza Del Sol Ct 89081
Spice Stone Ct 89031
Spicebush St 89081
Spiced Butter Rum St 89084
Spindel Ave 89030
Spindletree Ln 89031
Spinet Dr 89032
Spirit Sun Ct 89032
Splinter Rock Way 89031
Split Rock Dr 89031
Spooners Cove Ave 89031
Spotted Pony Dr 89031
Spottswood Ave 89081
Spring Breeze Cir 89031
Spring Canyon St 89081
Spring City Ave 89081
Spring Falls Way 89031
Spring Line St 89032
Springmist St 89031
Sprints Race Ave 89084
Spritlake Ct 89032
Spruce Oak Dr 89031
Spur Ranch Ave 89032
Stable Way 89032
Stable Glen Dr 89031
Stablewood Ct 89084
Stagecoach Ave 89081
Stagecoach Flats Ave 89031
Stampede Ct 89032
Standing Bear Ct 89031
Standing Elm St 89081
Stanford St 89030
Stanley Ave 89030
Stanton Summit Dr 89081
Star Decker Rd 89031
Star Gazing Ave 89030
Star Manor St 89030
Star Meadow Dr 89030
Star Point Ct 89081
Star Shadow St 89031
Starfish Bay Ln 89031
Starlight Peak Ct 89084
Starlight Ranch Ave 89081
Starling Mesa St 89086
Starpoint Rd 89031
Starthroat Ct 89084
Startrain Dr 89031
Statham Ave 89081
Statue St 89081
Statz St
- 1600-2599 89030
- 4501-4597 89081
- 4599-4700 89081
- 4702-4998 89081

Stearman Dr 89031
Steed Cir 89030
Steeplechase Ave 89031
Stelle Amore St 89081
E Stephen Ave 89081
Steppe St 89032
Steppingstone Ct 89031
Sterling Cap St 89081
Sterling Ranch Way 89081
Sterling Spur Ave 89081
Stern Cove Ct 89031
Steubling Glen St 89084
Stibor St 89081
Stocker St 89030
Stockman St 89032
Stockton Edge Ave 89084
Stone Breeze Ave 89031
Stone Cove St 89081
Stone Lagoon St 89031
Stone River Dr & Pl 89030
Stonehurst Dr 89031
Stonesthrow Cir 89031
Stoneypeak Ave 89081
Storks Bundle Ln 89084
Stormy Day Ave 89030
Stormy Ridge St 89081
Stowe Creek Ave 89081
Stratford Bay St 89031
Strato Jet Way 89031
Strawberry Roan Rd 89032
Strawberry Tree St 89031
Styers St 89031
Sudden Valley Ct 89031
Suede Cir 89031
Sugar Creek Dr 89081
Sugar Maple Ct 89031
Sugarbird Ct 89084
Sugarbush Ln 89031
Sullivan Cir 89032
Summer Bluff Ct 89084
Summer Duck Way 89084
Summer Glen Ln 89031
Summer Lily Ave 89081
Summer Night St 89031
Summer Trout St 89031
Summit Creek Ave 89031
Summit Greens St 89081
Sun Ave 89030
Sun Broom St 89081
Sun Harvest Ave 89081
Sun Meadow Ct 89031
Sun Mountain Ave 89031
Sun Prairie St 89081
Sun Seed Ct 89081
Sundance Canyon Ct 89031
Sunny Acres Ave 89081
Sunny Day Ave 89031
Sunnyville St 89031
Sunrise Bay Ave 89031
Sunrise Cove Ave 89031
Sunrise Creek St 89031
Sunrise Falls Ct 89031
Sunrise Rose Ave 89031
Sunrise Shores Ave 89031
Sunrise Springs Ct 89031
Sunset Crater Ct 89031
Sunset Downs St 89081
Sunset Falls Ave 89085
Sunset Harbor Ct 89031
Sunset Hills Ct 89031
Sunset Meadow St 89031
Superior Position St 89032
Support Ct 89031
Surfbird St 89084
Sutter Ridge Ct 89032
Sutters Fort St 89032
Swallow Falls St 89085
Swan Bridge St 89081
Swanson Ave 89086
Sweet Jenny Ct 89086
Sweet Leilani Ave 89031
Sweet Surrender Ct 89032
Sweet William St 89081
Swift Arrow St 89031
Swift Creek Ave 89031
Swift River Ct 89031
Switchback St 89031
Sword St 89030
Sydney Bay Ct 89081
Synergy St 89030
Tabor Ave 89030
Tahiti Isle Ave 89031
Tainted Berry Ave 89031
Talara Ln 89032
Talaverde Heights St 89081
Talbot Springs Ct 89081
Talley Ct 89081
Tallow Tree Ave 89032
Tallulah Falls St 89081
Talmo St 89081
Tamarack Lodge Ln 89031
Tanagrine Dr 89084
Tanna Dove Ct 89084
Taos Pueblo Ct 89031
Tara Leigh Ave 89031
Taramar St 89031
Tartan Ct 89032
Tattler Dr 89084
Tatum Ct 89032
Taylor Ave 89030
Taylor Rock Ct 89031
Taza Verde Ave 89031
Tazewell Ct 89081
Tea Leaf St 89031
Teal Island Dr 89031
Teal Petals Ave 89032
Teal Petals St 89081
Teal Point Dr 89031
Teasdale Ave 89032
Telstar Ct 89032
Tender Hearted Ct 89032
Tennessee Walker Ave 89031
Tercel Way 89084
Tern Ct 89084
Terneza Ave 89081
Terrace Canyon St 89032
Terrace Point Dr 89032
Terraza Mar Ave 89081
Tertulia Ave 89081
Tesoro Del Valle Ct 89031
Tessa Ct 89032
Testarossa Ln 89081
Texas Crude St 89081
Texas Star Ln 89032
Thankfulness Ct 89032
Theatrical Rd 89031
Thicket Ave 89031
Thomas Ave 89030
Thomas Patrick Ave 89032
Thorn Bush St 89031
Thornton St 89081
Threshold Ct 89032
Throstle Dr 89084
Thunder Bird Field Rd 89032
Thunder Storm Ave 89032
Thunder Struck Ct 89030
Tiara Blanca Ct 89031
Tideview St 89081
Tierra Cove St 89081
Tifton Ct 89031
Tiger Cir 89031
Tiger Cub Ct 89031
Tiger Ridge Ln 89084
Tilten Kilt Ave 89081
Tim English St 89031
Timber Glade Pl 89084
Timid Tiger Ave 89086
Timothy Ct 89032
Toasted Almond Ave 89084
Tokalon Pointe Ct 89081
Tomahawk Cir 89030
Tonga St 89031
Tonin Ave 89031
E & W Tonopah Ave 89030
Topaz Hills Dr 89032
Topaz Image St 89031
Topaz Sand St 89081
Torch Ave 89081
Toro Creek Ct 89031
Toscanini Way 89032
Totano Dr 89032
Toulouse Ct 89031
Towboat St 89031
Trade Dr 89030
Trailblazer Dr 89031
Travis St 89030
Treasure Hills St 89031
Tree Vista Ct 89084
Trelack Blvd 89081
Trelawny Ridge Ct 89081
Trembling Hill Ave 89031
Trestle Bridge St 89032
Trigger Way 89032
Trillium Bay Ln 89032
Trinitero St 89032
Trinity River Ct 89081
Triumph Hills Dr 89032
Tropic Blue St 89031
Tropic Breeze St 89081
Tropic Wind Ave 89081
E Tropical Pkwy 89081
W Tropical Pkwy 89031
Tropical Ter 89030
Tropical Palm Ct 89031
Tropical Rain St 89031
Tropical Sands Ave 89031
Tropicbird Dr 89084
Trotting Horse Rd 89032
True Spring Pl 89032
Trumpeter St 89084
Trustworthy Ave 89031
Tufted Duck Way 89084
Tulane Cir 89030
Tumbler St 89084
Turchas Way 89032
Turkey Ridge Ct 89031
Turkey Shoot Pl 89084
Turnbull Ct 89081
Turnstone Ct 89081
Turquoise Waters Ave 89081
Turtle Beach Ave 89081
Turtle Reef Way 89031
Turtleback Dr 89031
Tuscany Ridge Ct 89032
Tuskegee St 89030
Tustin Hills St 89081
Twilight Blue Ave 89032
Twin Peaks Dr 89032
Twining Ave 89030
Twist Cir 89031
Twisted Oak Ave 89032
Ultimate Prize Way 89032
Union Hill Ct 89032
United Ln 89032
Unity Crest Ave 89032
Upper Mesa Ct 89084
Uranus Dr 89031
Ursulines Ct 89031
Valley Dr
- 3600-3998 89032
- 4500-4598 89031
- 4600-4799 89031
- 4801-5899 89031

Valley Flower St 89081
Valley Oaks Dr 89032
Valley Pine Ct 89032
Valley Quail Way 89084
Valley Regal Way 89032
Valley Regents Dr 89032
Valley Royal Dr 89032
Valley Sage Dr 89032
Valley Spruce Way 89032
Value Ct 89031
Van Der Meer St 89030
Van Ert Ave 89030
Van Ness Ave 89081
Vana Ave 89030
Vandenberg Dr 89081
Vanilla Nut Pl 89084
Variety Ave 89031
Veeder Crest St 89081
Vegas Palm Ave 89032
Velvet Leaf Dr 89032
Velvet Silk St 89084
Venadis St 89030
Ventana Rey St 89081
Ventura Way 89030
Venus St 89030
Veranda Hill Ct 89031
Verbena Rose Ct 89081
E & W Verde Way 89031
Veridia Heights Ct 89081
Veronica Ave 89030
Via De Fortuna Way 89031
Via Luis Ct 89031
Via Maria Ct 89031
Via Victoria St 89031
Victoria Garden Ave 89031
Victoria Terrace Ave 89031
Victory Point St 89081
Vidalia Ave 89031
Vigilante Ct 89081
Villa Carmen Cir 89031
Villa Comaro Ct 89086
Villa Cordoba Ct 89086
Villa Elisa Cir 89031
Villa Emo St 89031
Villa Espana Way 89031
Villa Granada Way 89031
Villa Grove Ave 89030
Villa Pisani Ct 89031
Villa Serena Ln 89081
Villa Tironi Ct 89086
Villada St 89084
Village Loft St 89081
Vina Ct 89032
Vincelli Ave 89031
Vincent Hill Ct 89031
Vincents Dream Ave 89031
Vine Hill Ct 89031
Vineyard Vine Way 89032
Violet Bluff Ct 89084
Violetta Ave 89031
Virginia Carmen Ave 89086
Visionary Bay Ave 89081
Vista Creek St 89031
Vista Del Norte Way 89031
Vista Del Oso Way 89031
Vista Del Rancho Way 89031
Vista Del Rey Ct 89031
Vista Del Rio Way 89031
Vista Loma Way 89031
Vista Luna St 89031
Vista Montana Way 89031
Vista Springs Way 89031
Vita Dr 89030
Wabash Ln 89032
Wading Bird Way 89084
Wagner Ave 89030
Walingwood Dr 89031
Walking Stick Ln 89031
N Walnut Rd 89081
Walrus Islands Ct 89031
Walstone Rd 89031
Ward St 89032
Warm Glen Ave 89031
Warm Hearted Ct 89032
Warren Rock St 89032
E Washburn Rd 89081
W Washburn Rd 89031
Watanabe St 89081
Water Ave 89030
Water Birch St 89032
Water Coconut St 89031
Water Pipit St 89084
Water Rail Ave 89084
Water Sport Ave 89031
Watercolor St 89031
Watercreek Dr 89032
Watermelon St 89081
Waving Flower Dr 89031
Waxwing Ct 89084
Wayne Way 89030
Weavers Pl 89084
E & W Webb Ave 89030
Webster Cir & St 89030
Wedgefield St 89081
Wedmore Ct 89031
Wedo Way 89031
Weeping Rock Ave 89031
Wells Fargo St 89031
Wembley Ct 89032
West St 89032
Westbury Square St 89032
Westminster Hall Ave 89032
Wexford Hill Ct 89031
Whalers Drift St 89031
Wheatberry Ct 89031
Wheatley Ct 89031
Whelk Pl 89031
Whisper Bluff St 89031
White St 89030
White Angel Dr 89032
White Barn Ct 89081
White Blanket Ct 89084
White Coconut Ct 89031
White Daisy Way 89081
White Jade St 89081
White Lion Ln 89084
White Oak Rd 89030
White Peaks Ave 89081
White Quail Ct 89032
White Sails Ct 89031
White Shark Ct 89084
White Stallion Ct 89032
White Stork Dr 89084
Whitebridge St 89031
Whitehollow Ave 89031
Whitetail Archery Ave 89084
Whitner St 89031
Whitney Breeze Ave 89031
Whitney Peak Way 89031
Wichita Falls Ave 89031
Wickford Dr 89032
Widewing Dr 89084
Wild Breeze Ct 89031
Wild Draw Dr 89031
Wild Filly Ln 89032
Wild Oak Way 89031
Wild Orchid St 89031
Wild Pony Ave 89031
Wild Sunflower St 89081
Wildcat Brook Ct 89081
Wilderness Way 89030
Wilderness Pack Ct 89084
Wilkinson Way 89030
Williams Ave 89030
Willis St 89031
Willow Warbler St 89084
Willow Wren Dr 89084
Willowcreek Rd 89031
Willowdale Ct 89031
Willowick Ave 89031
Wind Break Ln 89031
Wind Tower St 89031
Windham Hills Ln 89031
Windhurst St 89032
Windsor Ave 89030
Windstone Ct 89032
Windwalker Ave 89081
Windy Ferrell Ave 89081
Windy Hills Ave 89031
Wing Gull Ct 89032
Wingspread St 89084
Winley Chase Ave 89032
Winlock Ct 89032
Winter Breeze Ave 89032
Winter Moon St 89084
Winter Sunset Ave 89081
Winterdale St 89031
Winterhawk Ct 89031
Wisdom Bluff Ave 89084
Withrow Downs St 89081
Wizard Ave 89030
Wizard Wand St 89031
Wolf Lake Ave 89032
Wood Dale Ct 89031
Wood Drift St 89030
Wood Thrush Pl 89084
Woodard St 89030
Woodchat St 89084
Woodland Hills Ct 89032
Woodland Park Ave 89086
Woodlark Ct 89084
Woodpeckers Ct 89084
Woodview St 89031

Woodward Heights Way 89032
Woody Valley St 89031
Wren Ct 89032
Wright Ave 89030
Xavier Ridge Ave 89086
Yale St 89030
Yankee Ave 89030
Yarnell Dr 89031
Yellow Bird Ct 89084
Yellow Bridge Ct 89031
Yellow Flame Ave 89084
Yellow Mandarin Ave 89081
Yellow Peak Ave 89031
Yellowhammer Pl 89084
Yellowwood Cove St 89084
York Ave 89032
Yorkwood Dr 89032
Yountville Ct 89032
Yucca Ridge Ct 89084
Yukon Flats Ct 89031
Zalataia Way 89031
Zapata Ln 89031
Zebra Ct 89031
Zelma St 89030
Zenith Point Ave 89032
Zia Ridge St 89031
Zoee Ave 89030

NUMBERED STREETS

N 5th St
1900-2198 89030
2200-2399 89030
3401-3421 89032
3423-3800 89032
3802-3960 89032
4500-5899 89031
5901-6299 89031
6600-7099 89084

PAHRUMP NV

General Delivery 89041

POST OFFICE BOXES MAIN OFFICE STATIONS AND BRANCHES

Box No.s
1 - 6784 89041
9001 - 9700 89060
9998 - 9998 89041

HIGHWAY CONTRACTS

66 89060
732 89061

NAMED STREETS

Abbe Ln 89048
Acoma Ave 89048
Acorn Cir 89048
Acqua Ln 89061
Adams Rd 89048
E & W Adkisson St 89060
Adobe Ct 89048
S Adriano Way 89061
Agio Ave 89061
E Ailanto Ave 89061
Akita Way 89060
Al Fresco Ave 89061
Alabama St 89048
Alabaster Ct 89060
Alaska Way 89060
Alderwood Ave 89060
Alexander Ave 89060
Alfalfa St 89048
Alfano Ave 89061
Alicia St 89048
Allison Ct 89048
Alvin St 89060
Amarillo Ave 89048
Ambler Way 89060
E & S Ambush St 89048
Andover Ct 89061
Annie Ave 89060
Anns Rd 89048
Antelope Ave 89060
Antelope St 89048
Appaloosa Ln 89060
Applewood Ct 89061
Arabian Way 89061
Arapahoe St 89048
S Arezzo Ave 89061
Arnold Ct 89060
Arrow Ct 89048
Arrowhead St 89048
Arroyo St 89060
Ashley Ave 89061
Ashley Ct 89060
Assay Ln 89060
Atlanta St 89048
Atoll Dr 89060
Augusta St 89048
Autumnwood Dr 89048
Avalon Ave 89048
Ave Of The Stars 89060
Avellaneda St 89060
E Badlands Ln 89061
Bailey Ct 89048
Bakersmill Ct 89061
Balhurst Ct 89061
Balzar St 89060
Banjo St 89048
Bank Ave 89048
N Bannavitch St 89060
S Bannavitch St 89048
Banyon St 89048
Baradonna Rd 89048
Barbara Ave 89060
Barberry Ct 89061
Barley Ct 89048
N Barney St 89060
S Barney St 89048
Barnwood Ct 89061
Bartlett Ln 89048
E & W Basin Ave 89060
Batdorf Ct 89061
Begonia St 89048
Bel Air Ave 89048
E & W Bell Vista Ave 89060
Bello Ln 89061
Belmont Ave 89060
Belville Rd 89048
Bender St 89060
Beniah St 89048
Bennet St 89048
Benson Cir 89060
E & W Betty Ave 89060
Bevs Way 89060
Bientian Way 89061
Big 5 Rd 89048
Big Horn St 89048
Big Oak Ln 89060
Big Sky Way 89048
Bison St 89060
Black St 89060
Black Rock Ave 89060
Blackhorn St 89048
N Blagg Rd 89060
S Blagg Rd 89048
Blanchard St 89048
E & W Blosser Ranch Rd 89060
Blossom Ave 89048
Blue Ln 89048
E & W Bluebird Ave 89060
Bluegrass St 89060
Blueridge St 89061
Boca 89060
S Bolling Rd 89048
Bond St
1800-2199 89048
2201-2899 89048
3000-3500 89061
3502-3698 89061
E & W Bonita Ave 89060
Bonnie St 89048
Bonnie Clair Ct 89048
E & N Boothill Dr 89060
Boston Ln 89060
Bourbon St 89048
Bowler Dr 89048
Boyd Cir 89060
Brents St 89060
Brentwood Dr 89048
Brian Rd 89048
Bride St 89048
Bridger St
1000-1498 89048
1500-2199 89048
2201-2499 89048
3600-3998 89061
4000-6199 89061
Bristle Cone 89048
E Brolio Ct 89061
Bronco St 89048
Brooksby St 89048
Brown St 89060
Bruce St 89048
Buckboard Ln 89060
E Buckeye Dr 89060
Buena Vista Ct 89048
Buffington Ln 89060
Bullseye Ct 89048
Bunarch Rd 89060
S Bunch St 89048
Buol Rd 89048
E Burgundy Dr 89048
Burke St 89048
Burning Tree Ct 89048
Caas Rd 89061
Cabo St 89060
Cactus St 89048
Cajon Ln 89048
California St 89060
E & W Calvada Blvd 89048
Camellia St 89048
Camelot Cir 89061
Candle Way 89048
Candle Stick Ave 89048
E Cansano St 89061
Canyon St 89048
Capa Ln 89060
Capistrano St 89060
Capital Way 89048
Capricorn St 89061
Carberry Ln 89048
Carnation Way 89048
Carrara Pointe St 89061
Carrizo Ln 89060
W Carrol Cir & St 89060
Carson St 89048
E Carter Ln 89061
Casa Ida Ct 89061
Casey Rd 89048
Cash Ave 89048
Castello Way 89061
Castle St 89061
Castlewood Ct 89061
Cathi Ave 89048
Cavalry St 89048
Cavalry Trl 89060
Cazier Ct 89060
Cedarwood St 89048
Centennial Rd 89048
Center St 89048
Central Ave 89060
E & S Chablis St N & W 89048
E Chaffe Ave 89061
Chanele Cir 89060
Chapparel Ave 89060
E & W Charleston Park Ave 89048
Charleston View Ave 89060
E Chasemoor St 89061
Cherend St 89048
Cheryl St 89060
Chevron St 89048
E Cheyenne Way 89061
Chickadee Ct 89048
Chico Ln 89060
China St 89048
Chipmunk Rd 89048
S Chippewa St 89061
Chiquita Ln 89060
Chowchilla Cir 89060
Christian St 89060
Christie Ct 89060
Christine Way 89060
Christopher Ave 89060
Chromium Blvd 89061
Chukar St 89060
Church St 89048
Chyine Way 89048
Cielo Ct 89061
Cimarosa Way 89061
Cimmarron Pl S 89048
Cindy Dr 89048
Clark St 89048
Clementine St 89048
Cline St 89060
Clint Ave 89060
Close St 89060
Clubhouse Dr 89061
Cobalt St 89060
Cody Rd 89048
Colina Ln 89060
Colorado St 89060
E Comanche Dr 89061
Comaradi St 89060
Cometa Ln 89060
Commerce St 89048
Commercial Dr 89048
Comstock Cir & St E, N, S & W 89048
Conestoga Pkwy 89048
Copper Flats Dr 89048
W Corbin Ct 89060
N Corbin St 89060
S Corbin St 89048
E & W Cordova Pl 89060
Corrine St 89048
Cortez Rd 89060
Cortina St 89048
Cosmic Pl 89060
Cottontail Rd 89061
E & W Country Place Rd 89060
Court St 89048
Courtney Ln 89060
Coyote Dr 89061
Craig Ave 89060
Crawford Way 89048
Creb Ct 89060
Curt Ave 89060
Curtis Ct 89048
Cynthia St 89048
Cypress Point Ct 89048
Da Vinci Way 89061
Daag Cir 89061
Dahlia St 89048
Dale Way 89060
Dan Way 89060
Dana Way 89060
E & S Dandelion St 89048
Danielle Ct 89061
Dapple St 89048
Darcy Ln 89060
Dart Dr 89060
N David St 89060
S David St 89048
David Adam 89048
Daytona St 89048
Deacon Ct & St 89048
Deadwood St 89048
Deanna St 89048
Debbie Ct 89048
Deer St 89048
Deer Creek St 89060
Deerfield Ct 89061
E Deerskin St 89048
E Del Sol St 89060
Deliza Dr 89061
Denise Ct 89048
Dennis St 89060
Derby St 89048
Desert Ln 89048
E, N & S Desert Hills Cir N & S 89048
Desert Rose Dr 89060
E Di Bossi Ave 89061
Diamond Cir 89060
Diamond Bar Rd 89048
Dixieland St 89048
Dodge Cir 89048
Dodie Ln 89060
Dollar St 89048
Domingo St 89048
W Donner St 89048
Doral Ct 89048
Doubletree St 89061
Douglas St 89060
Dove St 89060
Driftwood Dr 89048
Duck St 89060
Duck Creek Rd 89048
S Dunn St 89061
Dupont Dr 89060
Dutch Ford St 89048
W Dyer Ct & Rd 89048
Dylan Pl 89048
East St 89048
Eastwind St 89048
Easy St 89061
Edleen Pl 89060
Effinger Rd 89060
E & W Elderberry St 89048
Eldorado Way 89048
Eleganza Ave 89061
Elgin Ln 89060
Elizabeth St 89048
Elk Dr 89060
Ellendale St 89048
Elsie Ln 89060
Elvira St 89048
W Ember St 89048
Emerson St 89048
Emery St 89048
Emma St 89048
Enchanted Mesa St 89048
Encinita St 89048
England Dr 89048
Equestrian Ct 89048
Equus Ct 89060
Erin St 89048
Escuela Ave 89048
Estiva Ct 89061
W Eton St 89048
Evans Rd 89061
Evelyn St 89048
Explorer Ct 89048
Factory Rd 89048
Fairbanks St 89060
Fairmont St 89061
Fairway St 89048
Fairwood Ct 89061
E Falcon St 89048
Fallwood St 89048
Fangio Ln 89060
Faust Pl 89060
Fawn St 89048
Feather St 89048
Fehrs Way 89060
Fern St 89060
Ferndell St 89048
Fernwood Ct 89061
Fieldstone Dr 89061
Fifth St 89048
Finehill St 89060
Finestra St 89061
E Fiore Dr 89061
E Firebird Cir N 89048
Firestone Cir 89048
First St 89048
Fitzroy Ave 89060
Five Feathers St 89048
Flag St 89048
Flagstone Ct 89048
Flamingo Rd 89048
Fleetwood Pl 89060
Florenza St 89060
Florida St 89048
Floyd Dr 89060
Ford Loop Rd 89048
Forest Rd 89048
Fort Carson Ln 89060
Fort Churchill Rd 89060
Fountain Ave 89048
Fourth St 89048
Fox Ave 89061
Francine St 89060
Franklin St 89048
Fremont St 89048
Fritz Ln 89048
Front Sight Rd 89061
N Frontage Rd 89060
S Frontage Rd 89048
Frontier Way 89060
E Fuchsia St 89048
Gahn Dr 89060
Galaxy St 89048
Gallup Ct 89060
Gally Rd 89060
E & W Gamebird Rd 89048
Garden Ln 89048
Gardenia St 89048
E Garfield Dr 89061
Garnet Rd 89060
Garrison 89060
Gay St 89060
Gee St 89060
Geiger Ln 89061
Gemini Dr 89060
Geneva Ct 89060
Genoa Ave 89060
Geoffrey St 89060
Georgene St 89060
Georgia St 89048
Gerald St 89048
Geronimo St 89048
Gertrude Way 89060
S Gilliam St 89061
Gills Way 89061
Gilmore Rd 89060
Gina St 89048
Ginger Cir 89060
Ginseng Ct 89061
Giordano Ct 89061
Glacier Ln 89060
Glen Valley Ave 89048
Glencove Ave 89060
Glenoaks St 89048
Gold Dust Ln 89048
Gold Point Rd 89060
Golden Way 89060
Golden Star Rd 89060
Golden Valley Ave 89061
Goldrush St 89048
Goodale St 89048
Grain Mill Rd 89061
Grandlodge St 89048
Gray Fox Way 89048
Graystone Dr 89061
Greenbriar Ct 89061
Greenwater St 89048
Greenwood Rd 89060
Gregory St 89048
S Gressa St 89061
Greta Blvd 89060
Greyhound St 89060
Grieco Way 89060
Grouse St 89048
Grubstake Ln 89060
Guinn Ct 89060
E Gunnison Ave 89061
Gypsy Ln 89060
Hacienda St 89048
Hafen Ranch Rd 89061
Haiwee St 89048
Hall Ave 89048
Hallsway St 89048
Hamilton St 89048
Hand Ave 89060
W Happy Ln 89048
Happy Canyon Rd 89048
W Hardy Ln 89048
E & W Harris Farm Rd 89060
Harrison Pl 89060
Harwood Ct 89061
Havasu St 89048
Hawkins Way 89061
Hays St 89060
Heather Way 89060
Helen St 89060
Helicopter Ave 89060
Heritage Dr
1000-2400 89048
2402-2598 89048
3001-3099 89061
4200-4298 89061
Hiawatha St 89048
E & W Hickory St 89048
E & S Highland Ave 89048
N Highway 160 89060
S Highway 160
2-398 89048
S Highway 160
400-3699 89048
4500-5698 89061
5700-5899 89061
E & W Highway 372 89048
Higley Rd 89048
Hilton Head St 89048
Hix Ln 89048
Holly St 89060
Homestead Rd
2300-6899 89048
6901-6999 89048
7000-7298 89061
7300-7399 89061
7401-7999 89061
8500-9098 89048
9100-9199 89048
9300-10599 89061
Honey Way 89048
Honey Locust Dr 89061
Honeysuckle St 89048
Hoptree Dr 89061
W Horn Rd 89048
Hornet St 89048
Huascaran St 89060
Huckleberry St 89048
Humahuaca St 89048
Humbolt Pl 89060
Hunt Pl 89060
Huracan St 89048
Huron Ln 89048
Hyde St 89060
Ida St 89060
Idaho St 89048
Idlewild St 89048
Iguana St 89048
Indian Rd 89048
Indian Wells Ct 89060
Indio Ct 89048
Indole St 89048
Industrial Rd 89048
Ingot Ln 89060
Interceptor Dr 89060
Intrepid St 89048
Inverness Ave 89048
E & W Irene Rd & St 89060
Irons 89048
Ironside St 89048
Ironton St 89048
Ironwood Ave 89048
Iroquois Ave 89048
Isaac St 89060
Ishani Ridge Ct 89048
Ivy Ln 89048
Jaborandi Ave 89061
Jacaranda St 89048
Jack Rabbit St 89048
Jackie St 89048
Jacks Dr 89048
Jacksboro Dr 89061
Jacob St 89048
Jake Ct 89060
Jalapa 89060
Jane Ave 89061
Janet Ln 89060

Janice Ave 89060
Jans Pl 89048
Jarvis Rd 89060
Jasmine St 89048
Jason Ln 89060
Java Ave 89048
E & W Jaybird St 89048
Jayco Rd 89048
Jayme St 89048
Jeane Ave 89048
Jennifer St 89061
Jent Rd 89060
Jeremy Ct 89048
Jerome Ln 89048
Jerry Ave 89060
Jesse St 89048
Jessica St 89048
Jet Pl 89060
Jewell Dr 89048
Jill Ave 89060
Jims Ct 89060
Joanita St 89060
Joann St 89060
Jobella Ln 89048
Jodi St 89060
John D Ct 89048
Johnnie Mine St 89060
Jollie Way 89048
Jonquil Ct 89061
Jorgensen Cir 89048
Jornada St 89048
Joseph Dr 89048
Joshua Rd 89060
Joy Ln 89048
Jubilee Ct 89048
Judy Dr 89048
Jujube St 89061
Julia St 89048
Julie St 89061
June St 89060
S Juneau St 89061
Justin Ln 89048
Justine Ct 89048
Jutland Dr 89060
Kachina Moon Ct 89048
Kaibab St 89048
Kansas St 89048
Karen Ct 89048
Katheryn Ave 89060
Katie Ln 89061
Kearney Ct & St 89048
Keenan Way 89048
Keith St 89048
Kelishan St 89060
Keller St 89060
E Kellogg Rd
1500-2098 89048
2100-2599 89048
3001-3097 89061
3001-3001 89041
3099-6299 89061
Kellshan St 89060
Kelly Way 89060
Kelso Way 89060
Kenny Ave 89060
E Kenosha Way 89061
Kens Pl 89060
Kent St 89061
Keomah St 89061
Kick St 89048
S Kid Ave 89048
Kim Ct 89048
Kimberly Ave 89060
Kings Way 89061
Kingston View St 89060
Kiowa St 89048
Kisha Ave 89061
Kismet St 89060
Kite St 89048
Kittyhawk Dr 89060
Krysta Ln 89060
La Grancia Ct 89061
La Romita Ct & St 89061
La Terra Ave 89061
Labrador St 89048
Lafayette St 89048
Laguna St 89048
Lakoda St 89060
Lampshire Ln 89060
Landmark Ave 89060
Lanette Cir 89060
Larsen Dr 89060
Las Casitas St 89048
Laughlin Rd 89048
Laurence Rd 89048
Laute Dr 89061
Lavender Ln 89061
Lazy Lizard Pl 89048
Lea St 89048
E & W Leffner Dr 89060
Leighton Rd 89060
Lemon St 89060
Leonard St 89060
Leone Ave 89061
N Leslie St 89060
S Leslie St 89048
W Leslie St 89060
Lewis St 89048
Lexis Ln 89048
W Liberty St 89048
Lignum Ave 89061
Lil Bit Way 89060
Lilia Ave 89061
Lincolnwood Ct 89061
N Linda St 89060
S Linda St 89048
Lisa Ln 89048
Lockspur Ave 89060
Lois Ln 89060
Lola Ln 89060
N Lola Ln 89060
S Lola Ln 89048
Londonberry Dr 89061
Lone Dove Ct 89061
Lone Pine Rd 89048
Long St 89048
Longhorn Ln 89061
Longmeadow Dr 89061
Lookout Ave 89048
S Loop Rd 89048
Lorelie St 89048
Lorenzo Way 89061
Lost Creek Dr 89048
Lucas Ln 89060
Lucca Ln 89061
E Lucera Ct 89061
Luciano Ave 89061
Luella Rd 89048
Luke St 89060
Lupin St 89048
Mabes St 89061
Machado St 89048
Mack Ct 89060
Madeline Ct 89048
Mae Rd 89060
Magnet Rd 89048
Magnolia Blvd 89048
Mahalo Dr 89061
Majestic View St 89060
Malibou Ave
2900-3298 89048
3300-3900 89048
3902-3998 89048
5101-5897 89061
5899-5999 89061
Mallard Ave 89048
Mandy Ave 89048
Manitoba St 89048
Mankins St 89048
Manse Rd
700-798 89048
800-2899 89048
3001-3997 89061
3999-5500 89061
5502-5898 89061
S Manzanita Dr 89048
Maple Rd 89048
E Marathon Dr 89061
Margaret St 89048
Margarita Ave 89048
Mariah Ct 89060
Maricopa St 89048
Marie St 89060
Marilyn Ct 89048
W Marine Way 89048
Marion Miller 89048
S Mariposa Ave 89048
Marisa St 89048
Mark Rd 89060
Marne Ct 89048
Mars St 89048
Martin Ave 89061
Mary Lou St 89061
Marywood Ct 89061
Mason Dr 89060
Matthew Ln 89048
N Mayfield Ranch Rd 89060
Mazelle Ln 89060
Mcgraw Rd 89061
Mcknight Ave 89060
Mcmurray Dr 89060
Meadow St 89061
W Medicine Man Rd 89048
Megan Ave 89060
Meier Dr 89048
Melanie Ave & Cir 89060
Melissa Ln 89048
Mesa Dr 89048
Mesa Oeste Ln 89048
Mescalero Ave 89048
E & W Mesquite Ave 89060
Mesquite Ranch Rd 89060
Michael Dr 89048
Michelle Ave 89060
Mickey St
1000-2699 89048
3300-3698 89061
Mielzynski St 89048
Mimosa Ct 89060
Ming Tree Ln 89060
Mira Ln 89048
Mitchell Pl 89060
Moapa St 89048
Mojave St 89061
Mondale Ct 89048
Money St 89048
Monique Ln 89061
Monta Ln 89060
Montclair St 89061
Monte Penne Way 89061
Montecito Dr 89048
Monterey Ct 89048
Moon St 89060
Mooncrest Ave 89060
N Mooney St 89048
Moore Rd 89048
Moose St 89048
Morales Ln 89060
Morgan Ln 89048
Morin Way 89060
E Mount Charleston Dr
N 89048
Mountain Falls Pkwy 89061
N Mountain View St 89060
Mourning Dove Ct 89061
Mule Deer St 89060
Munsell Way 89060
N Murphy St 89060
S Murphy St 89048
Murray Ct 89048
My Drive Way 89060
My Way St 89060
Myrtle Beach St 89048
Nanberry Ln 89060
Natalia Ln 89060
National Ave 89048
Navajo Blvd 89061
Naylor Pl 89060
Nellie St 89060
Neptune St 89048
Ness St 89048
Neutral St 89060
Nevada Ave 89048
Nevada West Blvd 89048
Newberry Ave 89048
Newby Ln 89060
Newcomb Ave 89048
Nicholas Way 89048
Nikki Ln 89060
N & W Nopah Vista
Ave 89060
Norway Dr 89048
Novelli Pl 89061
Nyberg Ct 89048
Nye Rd 89060
Oakleaf Ave 89048
Oakley St 89048
Oakridge Ave & Cir 89048
Oasis St 89048
S Oconnor Way 89048
Ogallala St 89048
Ohio Rd 89060
Old Mine Rd 89048
Old Spanish Trl 89061
Old West Ave 89048
Olive Branch Ln 89048
Olivido St 89048
Omaha St 89048
Ophir Ave 89048
Oregon St 89060
Orenda Ln 89048
Oro Ln 89061
Osage St 89060
Our Rd 89060
Owl Cir 89061
Oxbow Ave 89048
Pablo Ln 89060
Pacini Ct 89061
Paddock Ave 89060
Page St 89048
Pahrump Valley Blvd 89048
W Painted Trails Rd 89060
Paiute Blvd 89061
S Palazzo Pl 89061
Palm Dr 89060
Palomino Ln 89060
Palora St 89060
Pampa Ave 89048
Panorama Rd 89060
Panther Way 89060
Papaya Ave 89048
Papigo Ave 89048
Paradiso Pl 89061
Park Retiro 89060
Park Ridge Ave 89048
Parko Ct 89048
Parkwood Ct & Dr 89061
Parque Ave & Pl 89060
E & W Patricia Cir &
Ln 89060
Paula Dr 89048
Pawnee Pl 89061
Peak Ave 89060
Pearl Ln 89060
Pebble Beach Ave 89048
E & W Pechstein Rd 89060
Peggy Ave 89048
Peppertree St 89061
Percheron Ave 89048
Pershing Ave 89048
Peschutes St 89048
Pheasant St 89060
Pilot Pl 89060
Piltz Rd 89060
Pinehurst Ave 89048
Pinewood St 89048
Pinto Ln 89060
Pioche St 89048
Pioneer Ln 89061
Pittman St 89060
Pizarro Pl 89060
Placer Ln 89060
Plain Ln 89060
Plantation St 89048
Platense Ave 89048
Pluto St 89048
Pocahontas Ave 89048
Point Dr 89060
Ponderosa Ave 89048
Pontiac Cir 89048
Postal Dr
2200-2299 89048
2300-2300 89041
2300-2398 89048
2301-2399 89048
Potro Dr 89048
Potter Pl 89048
Powerline Rd 89060
Prairie Ave 89048
Prato Way 89061
Pratt St 89048
Princeton Cir 89060
Promenade Rd 89060
W Prospector Ln 89048
Providence Ct 89048
Pueblo Rd 89048
Quail Run Rd 89060
Quarter Horse Ave 89061
Quartzite Ave 89048
Quebec St 89048
Queenstar St 89048
Queenswood Ct 89061
Quinta Ave 89048
Rabbit Ct 89060
Rachel Ct 89048
S Rainbow Ave 89048
Raindance Dr 89048
Raintree Ct 89061
Ralph Ct 89061
Ramona Ln 89048
Ranch St 89060
Ranch Acres Rd 89061
Ranch Vista St 89060
Ranchita Way 89048
Rancho Rd 89048
Rancho Paradiso St 89060
Rancho View Dr 89060
Rand Ln 89060
Ranger Way 89048
Ravine Ave 89048
Ray Frank Blvd 89060
Raymond St 89060
Rebel Ave 89048
Red Butte St 89048
Red Hawk Ct 89060
Red Planet Ln 89060
Red Rock Dr 89048
N Redelsperger Rd 89060
Redwood Rd 89048
Reno Ln 89060
W Retread Rd 89048
Rhyolite Ave 89060
Riata Pl 89060
Richmar St 89060
Richmond St 89061
Ricksue St 89060
Ridgewood Ct 89061
Rimrock St 89048
Rio Way 89048
Rio Grande St 89060
Rio Rancho Dr 89048
Rio Rico Dr 89048
Riposo Ct 89061
Rita Dr 89060
River Plate Dr 89048
River Run St 89060
Riviera Dr 89048
Robin St 89060
Rockafeller Dr 89060
Rockaway Ln 89048
Rockin Doc Rd 89048
Rod Ln 89060
Rodeo Ave 89048
Ronnie Rd 89060
Rosa St 89061
Rose Ct, Dr & St 89048
Rosewood St 89048
Rossini St 89061
Roumm Ave 89060
Round Up Ct 89048
E Routt Way 89061
Royal Ave 89060
Rudek St 89061
Rudy Rd 89048
Russell Rd 89048
Ruth Rd 89060
Saddle Ln 89048
Saddle Horn Ln 89060
Saddletree Rd 89061
Sadie Way 89048
Sagebrush Ave 89048
Sagehen St 89060
Saginaw Ave 89048
Saif Ct 89061
Saint Andrews St 89048
Sally Cir 89048
Samuel St 89061
San Blas Ln 89060
San Lorenzo St 89048
San Souci Ln 89048
Sandalwood Dr 89061
Sandpebble St 89061
Sandpiper Ct 89061
Sandstone Ct 89048
Sandy Ln 89061
W Santa Fe St 89060
Santa Fiora St 89061
Santa Luc St 89061
Santovito St
1400-1999 89048
4101-4297 89061
4299-6299 89061
Savanna St 89048
Savoy Blvd 89061
Scales Way 89060
Schifrin St 89048
Scott Ave 89060
Sean St 89060
Second St 89048
E Sedgwick Ave 89061
Semifonte Dr 89061
S Senda Pl 89048
Seneca Ave 89048
Serenity Ct 89060
Seymour Ln 89048
Shadow Mountain St 89060
Shady Ln 89060
Sharon St 89060
Sharpe Rd 89060
Shawnee Ave 89048
Shelly Ln 89048
Shenandoah St 89060
Sherry Ave & Ln 89060
Shirley St 89048
Short St 89048
Siegal Cir 89048
N & W Sierra Vista Cir
& Way W, N & S 89060
Siesta Rd 89048
Silver St 89048
Silver Moon Ave 89048
Silver Peak Ave 89048
Silver Sage Dr 89060
E & W Simkins Rd 89060
Simmons St 89048
E Siri Ln 89060
Sisk 89060
Sixshooter Ave 89048
Sky Pl 89060
Slater Cir 89048
Sloan St 89060
N Smart Way 89060
Snail Way 89060
Sommerset Ct 89061
Soplo Ave 89048
Soren St 89048
Southgate St 89061
Soy St 89060
Sparky St 89060
Sparrow Way 89048
Splendido Ave 89061
Spring Mountain Vista
Ave 89060
Springwood St 89048
Spruce Ln 89048
Spy Glass Ave 89048
Squaw Valley Rd 89061
E & W Stagecoach Rd 89060
Stanley Dr 89048
Star Rd 89048
Stardust 89060
Starlight Dr 89048
E State St 89048
Stella St 89048
Stephanie Rd 89060
Steptoe St 89048
Steven Ave 89060
Stirrup Ave 89048
Stonebridge Ct 89061
Stoneham St 89061
Story Ave 89060
Stubblefield Dr 89061
Summer Way 89060
Summerwood St 89048
E Summit Ave 89061
Sumpter Ct 89061
Sundance St 89061
Sundowner Pl 89048
Sunland Ave 89061
Sunny St 89048
Sunrise View St 89060
Sunset St 89060
Suntree Ct 89061
Superior Ln
6000-6099 89061
6100-6199 89048
Surrey Ln 89048
Susan Ave 89060
Susquehanna St 89061
Sutton Dr 89048
Sycamore Ave 89048
Tahachapi Ave 89048
Tamara Ct 89048
Tecopa St 89060
Tecumseh Ave 89048
Teepee Rd 89048
E Teller Dr 89061
Tenderfoot Trl 89048
Tequilla Way 89048
Terry Dr 89060
Tevis Ct 89060
Third St 89048
Thomas Ln 89060
Thorne Dr
1500-1599 89048
6300-6399 89061
Thousandaire Blvd
700-2700 89048
2702-2798 89048
3100-4400 89061
4402-6198 89061
Thundercloud Way 89060
Tiawah Ave 89048
Tiger Rd 89048
Tillman St 89061
Tim Dr 89060
Timothy Ave 89060
Tioga Cir 89060
Tiptop Trl 89048
Tomahawk Ct 89060
Tonopah Trl 89048
Tonya Dr 89060
S Torrey Pines Ave 89048
Tortoise Hill Ln 89048
Toscana Way 89061
Tough Boy Rd 89060
Tough Girl Rd 89060
Tournament Ave 89048
Traci St 89048
W Trade Wind Way 89048
Train Way 89048
Travois St 89048
Triangle Way 89061
Triple E Way 89061
Trudy Cir & St 89060
Tucuman Ave 89048
Tumbleweed Ave 89048
Turner Blvd 89061
Turtle St 89048
Twilight Ave 89048
Ulrich Ct 89060
Underbrush Ave 89048
Unicorn Ave 89048
Union Pacific St 89060
Upland Ave 89048
Ursula Ave 89048
Utah St 89060
Valdez Ct 89060
Valentine Ave 89048
Valerio St 89048
Valero Ct 89060
Valiant Ave 89060

Van Ln 89048
Vandervoort St 89061
Vanguard Ave 89048
Vassar St 89048
Vegas Valley Dr 89048
Venus St 89048
Venza St 89048
Verbena St 89048
Verde Ave 89048
Via Gallo Ct 89061
Via Vinci Ct 89061
Vicki Ann Rd 89048
Victoria Rd 89048
E Vineyard Dr N 89048
Virginia St 89048
Vista Dr 89048
Viva Pl 89048
E Volterra Dr 89061
Vondell Dr 89048
Wagon Ave 89048
Wagon Wheel Ct 89061
Wahkiakum Ave 89048
Wall St 89061
Walt Williams Dr 89048
Walter Way 89060
Ward Ct 89061
Warehouse Rd 89048
N Warren St 89060
S Warren St 89048
Warriell Rd 89061
Washoe Ave 89048
Water Rock Ln 89060
Waterford St 89061
Waterhole Canyon Ave 89048
Weber Way 89048
Wedgewood St 89060
Weeping Willow Ct 89048
Wells Rd 89060
West St 89048
Westmont Ave 89061
Wheatland Dr 89061
Whirlwind Ave 89048
White St 89060
White Burch Ln 89048
White Eagle Dr 89061
Whitman Ave 89048
Wilber Way 89048
Wilderness Way 89048
Wildflower Ct 89060
Wildhorse Rd 89061
Wiley Ct 89061
Williams Ln 89060
Willis St 89048
Willow Tree Ct 89061
E & W Wilson Rd 89048
Winchester Ave 89048
Windmere Ct 89061
W Windsong Ln 89048
Windy Ln 89048
Winery Rd 89048
Winona Way 89060
E Winterwood Rd 89048
Wisteria Way 89048
N Woodchips Rd 89060
S Woodchips Rd 89048
Xenia Ave 89048
Yakima Ave 89048
Yavapai Ln 89048
Yosemite Ave 89048
Yucca Terrace Ave 89048
Yukon St 89048
Z St 89048
Zapata Dr 89048
Zelzah Ave 89048
Zephyr Ave 89048
Zoe Ct 89060
Zolin Ave 89061
Zula Dr 89060
Zuni Ave 89048

NUMBERED STREETS

All Street Addresses 89060

RENO NV

General Delivery 89501

POST OFFICE BOXES MAIN OFFICE STATIONS AND BRANCHES

Box No.s
1 - 1332 89504
1401 - 4130 89505
5001 - 6978 89513
7000 - 7000 89520
7001 - 7850 89510
8001 - 9999 89507
10000 - 12986 89510
10030 - 12000 89520
13000 - 15140 89507
17001 - 19958 89511
20000 - 20000 89520
20001 - 21556 89515
22000 - 31010 89520
32000 - 34980 89533
35000 - 35010 89511
40001 - 41376 89504
50001 - 50895 89513
60001 - 61918 89506
70002 - 71652 89570

RURAL ROUTES

31 89508

NAMED STREETS

Aberdeen Ct 89521
Aberfeldy Rd 89519
Abies Rd 89511
Abilene Rd 89508
Acadia Way 89502
Accacia Way 89503
Achilles Dr 89512
E & W Acoma Rd 89511
Adalinti Dr 89506
Adas St 89509
Adler Ct 89503
Admiral Ct 89523
Adobe Dr 89508
Adobe Rd 89521
Adobe Spur 89521
Aerie Way 89510
Aesop Ct 89512
Agate Rd 89521
Aidan Way 89521
Air Cargo Way 89502
Aircenter Cir 89502
Airmotive Way 89502
Airway Dr 89511
Aitken St 89502
Akard Cir & Dr 89503
Alameda Dr 89506
Alamo Dr 89503
Alamo Square Way 89509
Alaska Way 89506
Albert Way 89506
Albion Way 89502
Albite Ct & St 89506
Albright Ct 89523
E & W Albuquerque Rd 89511
Aldebaran Dr 89508
Alder Dr 89502
Alder Bridge Ct 89521
Alder Creek Ct 89511
Alderwood Ct 89508
Alexander Hamilton Dr 89509
Alexandria Ct & Dr 89508
Algonquin Dr 89521
Alicante Ct 89523
Alicia Way 89506
Alivia Way 89521
Aljo Ct 89506
Allegheny St 89506
Allen St 89509
Allen Glen Dr 89503
Alley Oop 89509
Allison Dr 89519
Almandine Dr 89523
Almond Dr 89502
Almond Creek Dr 89523
Almondleaf Ct 89508
Alpes Way 89511
Alpha Ave 89506
Alpha Butte Rd 89508
Alphabet Dr 89502
Alpine Cir 89509
Alpine Rd 89521
Alpine Creek Rd 89519
Alpine Frost Ct 89511
Alpine Meadows Loop 89523
Alpinista Cir 89511
Alsandair Ct 89506
Alta St 89503
Alturas Ave 89503
Alum Creek Ct 89509
Alum Rock Ct & Rd 89506
Alvaro St 89503
Alydar Ct 89521
Alysheba Ct 89521
Alyssum Ct 89511
Amado Ct 89511
Amador Way 89502
Amarak Way 89523
Ambassador Dr 89523
Amber Cir 89509
Amber Falls Dr 89521
Amber Hill Ct & Ln 89523
Amber Marie Ln 89503
Amberwood Ave 89509
Ambrose Cir & Dr 89519
American Flat Rd 89508
Ames Ln 89521
Amethyst Dr 89508
Ampere Dr 89502
Amston Rd 89511
Amy Rd 89510
Anaho Rd 89510
Anasazzi Ct 89511
Anchor Point Ct & Dr 89506
Anchorage Ct & Dr 89506
Andes St 89506
Andesite Ave 89512
Andorra Ct 89523
Andover Trl 89523
Andraste Way 89506
Andrea St 89503
Andrew Ln 89521
Andrew Cahill Ln 89503
Andromeda Way 89509
Angel St 89503
Angel Falls Ct & Dr 89506
Angel Ridge Dr 89521
Angela Pl 89509
Aniane St 89521
Anitra Dr 89511
Ann St 89506
Anne Marie Ct 89509
Annie Ln 89521
Anniversary Rd 89510
Ansari Ln 89510
Anselmo Ct & Dr 89523
Anson Dr 89503
Antelope Rd 89506
Antelope Creek Ct & Dr 89506
Antelope Trail Ct 89523
Antelope Valley Ct 89506
Antelope Valley Rd
1200-1299 89508
1300-3800 89506
3802-3898 89506
Antero Dr 89523
Anthony James Ct 89503
Antigua Ct 89511
Antler Pointe Ct 89523
Antonio Ln 89523
Antonon Ct 89506
Anza Way 89502
Apache Rose Ct & Dr 89521
Apollo Way 89503
Appaloosa Cir 89508
Appaloosa Dr 89521
Appenzell St 89506
Apple St 89502
Apple Mill Ct & Dr 89521
Applegate Rd 89521
Applewood Ct 89509
Apulia Ct 89506
Aquamarine Ct & Dr 89508
Aquarius Cir 89521
Aquifer Way 89506
Aquila Ave 89509
Arabian Way 89508
Arboleda Ct & Dr 89521
Arbor Ct & Way 89521
Arbor Oak Ct 89509
Arbor Ridge Dr 89523
Arbutus St 89509
Arcane Ave 89503
Arches Ct 89509
Archimedes Ln 89523
Arctic Willow Ct 89511
Arden Cir 89503
Ardmore Dr 89509
Arentz Ct 89523
Arenzano Dr 89521
Argo Way 89509
Argonaught Ct & Way 89506
Argosy Rd 89508
N Argyle Ct 89511
Arid Plains Ct 89506
Ariel Dr 89523
Aries Cir 89521
Aristicon Dr 89523
Aristocrat Way 89506
Aristotle Dr 89512
Arius Ct 89512
Arivaca Ct 89511
Arizona St 89506
Arkansas Dr 89506
Arletta St 89503
N Arlington Ave
100-154 89501
156-399 89501
400-499 89503
501-699 89503
S Arlington Ave
101-217 89501
219-499 89501
500-2299 89509
2301-2399 89509
Arlington Ct 89509
Armin Cir 89511
Armstrong Ln 89509
Army Aviation Dr 89506
Arnold Dr 89512
Arrow Wood Ct & Dr 89521
Arrowcreek Pkwy 89511
Arrowhead Way 89506
Arrowsprings Dr 89511
E Arroyo St 89502
W Arroyo St 89509
Artemesia Way 89503
Artesian Way 89506
Artisan Means Way 89511
Ascot Ln 89502
Ashbrook Dr 89502
Ashbury Ln 89523
Ashfork Dr 89509
Ashland Bluff Way 89523
Ashley Way 89511
Ashworth Ct 89521
E Aspen Cir 89508
W Aspen Cir 89508
Aspen Holw 89511
Aspen Trl 89519
Aspen Creek Rd 89519
Aspen Glen Rd 89519
Aspen Meadows Ct 89519
Aspen View Dr 89523
Aspendale Ct & Dr 89503
Aspenwood Ct 89519
Aster Dr 89502
Atlas Ct 89512
Attridge Pl 89503
Atwood Ct & St 89506
Auburn Way 89502
Audubon Way 89509
Augusta Ave 89509
Aurora Ave 89506
Aurora Rd 89521
Austin Creek Ct & Dr 89523
Austrian Pine Cir & Rd 89511
Automotive Way 89502
Autumn Ct & Ln 89511
Autumn Hills Dr 89511
Autumn Leaf Way 89506
Autumn Ridge Cir 89523
Autumn Valley Ct & Way 89523
Autumn Walk Ct & Ln 89521
Autunite Cir 89521
Avalon Ct 89506
Avalon Terrace Ct 89523
Avelina Ct 89521
Avenida De Landa 89523
Avery Ct 89523
Aviation Blvd 89502
Avocet Ct 89508
Axe Handle Rd 89510
Ayershire Ct 89509
Azalea Dr 89502
Aztec Ct 89511
Azure Cir 89509
Azurite Dr 89508
Azuza Way 89502
Baby Bear Ct 89508
Back Country Ct & Rd 89521
Back Nine Ct & Trl 89523
Backer Way 89523
Bacon Rind Rd 89510
Badger Cir 89519
Badlands Dr 89521
Bagpipe Cir 89506
Bailey Dr 89506
Bailey Canyon Ct & Dr 89521
Bailey Creek Ct 89521
Baileyville Ct 89508
Bain Spring Rd 89521
Baker Ln 89509
Balboa Dr 89503
Ballentyne Way 89502
Balsam St 89509
Balsawood Dr 89511
Balzar Cir 89502
Banbury Ct 89523
Banchory Ct 89519
Bandana Way 89521
Bandolier Ct 89511
Bankside Way 89523
Barbara Cir 89503
Barberry Way 89512
Bargary Way 89511
Barker Cir 89503
Barnes Blvd & Cir 89509
Barnett Way 89512
Barnsdale Rd 89511
Barnwood Ct 89511
Barong Ct 89523
Barrel Springs Rd 89521
Barron Way 89511
Barrow Ct 89506
Barry M Cir 89503
Barrymore Dr 89512
Barstow St 89512
Bartlett St 89512
Bartley Ranch Rd 89511
Basalt Ct 89506
Basin River Ct 89523
Basin Run Ct 89523
Basque Ln 89519
Basque Oven Rd 89510
Basswood Ct 89509
Bates Ave 89502
Bathgate Ct 89519
Baton Ct & Dr 89521
Bauxite Ct 89506
Baxter Village Dr 89521
Bay Meadows Dr 89523
Baypoint Ct 89523
Bayridge Ln 89502
Beach River Dr 89521
Beacon Dr 89506
Beacon Ridge Trl 89523
Bear Creek Ct 89519
Bear Lake Dr 89508
Bear Mountain Pl 89519
Bear River Ct 89508
Bears Ranch Dr 89521
Beaujolais St 89511
Beaumont Pkwy 89523
Becard Ln 89508
Bechtol Ridge Cir 89523
Beck St 89509
Beckfield Ct 89521
Beckwourth Dr 89506
Becky Ct 89503
Bedell Rd 89508
Bedford Ct 89503
Beech St 89512
Beechcraft Dr 89506
Beechwood Ct 89508
Bejay Pl 89509
Belcrest Cir 89512
Beldon Way 89503
Belford Rd 89509
Belgian Way 89508
Belgrave Ave 89502
Bell St 89503
Bella Ct 89519
Bellazza Ct 89519
Bellhaven Rd 89511
Belli Dr 89502
Bellingham Dr 89511
Belmont Dr 89506
Belmore Way 89503
Belsera Ct 89519
Belvedere Dr 89503
Bend Ct 89511
Benjamin Franklin Dr 89509
Benner Dr 89508
Bennie Ln 89512
Bennington Ct 89511
Bentley Ct & Dr 89523
Beringer Way 89521
Berkeley Dr 89509
Bermuda Cir 89509
Bernard Cir 89521
Bernoulli St 89506
Bernwood Ct 89521
Berrum Ln & Pl 89509
Berryhill Dr 89511
Berthoud Ln 89503
Bethal Ct 89521
Bettie Ave 89512
Beverly St 89512
Bexley Sq 89503
Biarritz Ct 89511
Bible Way 89502
Bichon St 89506
Biegler Cir 89509
Big Bend Ln 89509
Big Boulder Ct & Dr 89521
Big Dog Rd 89510
Big Pine Dr 89511
Big River Dr 89506
N & S Big Sage Ln 89511
Big Sky Ct & Dr 89503
Big Smokey Dr 89521
Big Springs Rd 89523
Big Trail Cir 89521
Big Valley Way 89521
Bighorn Dr 89508
Bihler Rd 89511
Billy Dr 89502
Birch St 89506
Birch Point Cir 89521
Bird Springs Rd 89510
Birkdale Ct 89523
Birmingham Pl 89506
Bisby St 89512
Bishop St 89512
Bishop Manogue Dr 89511
Bismarck Dr 89502
Bisset Ct 89503
Bit Ct 89508
Bitter Creek Ct 89519
Bitterbrush Rd 89523
Bittern Ct 89508
Bitteroot Rd 89519
Black Bear Dr 89506
Black Canyon Dr 89506
Black Eagle Ct 89511
Black Pine Ct & Dr 89511
Black Pool Ct 89511
Black Sand Dr 89521
Black Sterling Dr 89521
Black Wolf Ct 89506
Blackberry Ct 89506
Blackbird Ct & Dr 89508
Blackfoot Way 89506
Blackhawk Dr 89508
Blackstone Ct 89509
Blackthorn Dr 89523
Blackwillow Way 89521
Blair Pl 89509
Blake Ct 89508
Blazing Star Dr 89512
Bliss Ct 89521
Blockade Dr 89521
Blue Canyon Ct & Dr 89523
Blue Creek Ct 89508
Blue Falls Cir & Pl 89511
Blue Grouse Ct & Dr 89509
Blue Heron Cir 89523
Blue Hills Ct & Dr 89502
Blue Horizon Ct & Dr 89523
Blue Lakes Ct & Rd 89523
Blue Meadows Ct 89519
Blue Moon Ct 89521
Blue Pine Way 89523
Blue Sage Ct 89506
Blue Spruce Rd 89511
Bluebird Cir 89509
Bluegrass Ct 89509
Bluejay Ct 89509
Bluestone Dr 89511
Bluewater Ct 89519
Bluewood Dr 89523
Bluff View Way 89506
Bob White Way 89502
Bobby Dr 89502
Bobcat Dr 89523
Bobcat Hill Rd 89508
Bobolink Cir 89508
Boca Way 89502
Bodie Dr 89508
Bold Venture Ct 89502
Bolivar Ct 89502
Bolzano Dr 89521
Bombero Ct 89502
Bon Rea Way 89503
Bonanza Ln & Rd 89521
Bond Creek Ct 89519
Bonde Ln 89511
Bondshire Dr 89511
Bonfire Ln 89521
Bonneville Ave 89503
Bonnie Ln 89511
Bonnie Briar Pl 89509
Bonsar Ln 89509
Booth St 89509
Bootstrap Ln 89510
Bordeaux Ct & Dr 89511
Border Ct 89508
Bordertown Rd 89508
Borite Cir 89512
Bornite Ct 89506
Boron Ln 89508
Borzoi Ct 89506
Bottlebrush Cir 89523
Boulder Ct 89509
Boulder Creek Ln 89521
Boulder Field Way 89511
Boulder Glen Way 89511
Boulder Heights Ct 89511
Boulder Patch 89511
Boulder Ridge Ct & Trl 89523
Boulder Springs Ct 89508
Boundary Peak Ct 89508
Bounder Ln 89508

Bowers Dr 89511
Bowie Rd
3301-3397 89503
3399-3499 89503
21800-21899 89521
Bowman Dr 89503
Bowmar Cir 89506
Box Canyon Dr 89521
Boxelder Ct 89508
Boxer Dr 89512
Boyd Pl 89503
Boyer Ct 89503
Boynton Ln 89502
Bozeman Dr 89511
Braddock Ct 89503
Bradford Ct & Ln 89519
Braemore Dr 89521
Bramble Ct & Dr 89509
Branbury Way 89506
Branch Ln 89509
Brander Ct 89509
Branding Iron Rd 89508
Brannan Way 89511
Brant St 89508
Brave Ln 89506
Bravo Ave 89506
Breckenridge Ct & Way 89523
Breen Dr 89509
Breithorn Cir 89511
Brenham Ave 89509
Brentfield Dr 89511
Brentford Way 89521
Brentina Ct 89521
Brentwood Dr 89502
Brentworth Way 89521
Bresson Ave 89502
Bret Harte Ave 89509
Briargate Ct 89523
Briarhills Cir & Ln 89502
Bridge Creek Ct 89519
Bridgeview Ct & Dr 89521
Bridgewater Ct & Dr 89509
Bridgewood Ln 89503
Bridle Way 89519
Bridlewood Path & Way 89509
Brighton Ct & Way 89509
Brightridge Ct & Dr 89506
Brightstone Ct 89521
Brinkby Ave 89509
Brisbane Ave 89503
Bristle Wood Ct 89523
Bristlecone Ct 89502
Britt Rd 89508
Brittania Ct & Dr 89523
Brittany Ave & Ct 89509
Brittany Meadows Dr 89521
Brittany Park Dr 89521
Broadridge Ct 89523
Broadstone Way 89521
Broadview Ct 89521
Broadway Blvd 89502
Brockton Ct 89519
Brockway Ct 89523
Broili Dr 89511
Broken Arrow Cir 89509
Broken Feather Ct 89511
Broken Hill Rd 89511
Broken Spur Rd 89510
Bronc Ct 89521
Bronze Canyon Dr 89521
Bronze Hill Rd 89506
Bronze Wood Ct 89521
Brook Springs Dr 89509
E & W Brookdale Ct & Dr 89523
Brookfield Dr 89503
Brookhollow Ln 89519
Brookmeadow Ln 89511
Brookridge Ct 89509
Brooksboro Cir 89509
Brooksby Ln 89509
Brookshire Dr 89506
Brookside Ct 89502
Brookstone Ct 89523
Brooktrail Dr 89519
Brookview Cir & Ct 89519
Brown St 89509
Brown Eagle Ct 89506
Browning Dr 89506
Browns Creek Ct 89509
Brownstone Dr 89512
Brunswick Mill Rd 89511
Brush Ln 89511
Brush Creek Ct 89506
Brushland Ct & Dr 89508
Brushwood Way 89511
Bryan St 89503
Bryce Canyon Ln 89509
Buck Mountain Rd 89506
Buck Point Ct 89509
Buckaroo Cir 89519
Buckboard Cir 89508
Buckcreek Ct & Dr 89519
Buckeye Ct & Rd 89521
Buckhaven Ct & Rd 89519
Buckhorn Way 89503
Buckingham Sq 89503
Buckland Dr 89511
Buckshot Ct 89508
Buckthorn Ln 89511
Bud Lake Ln 89506
Budger Way 89506
Budrow Dr 89509
Buena Vista Ave 89503
Buffalo Rd 89508
Bugaboo Ct 89511
Bulette Rd 89521
Bull Rd 89506
Bull Rider Ct & Dr 89521
Bullfrog Rd 89521
Bullion Rd 89521
Bullion Hill Rd 89508
Bulluno Dr 89521
Bullwinkle Dr 89512
Burns Gulch Rd 89511
Bunker Point Ct 89511
Bunting Way 89502
Burge Rd 89506
Burghley Ct & Ln 89521
Burgundy Ct 89506
Burks Blvd 89523
Burns St 89502
Burr Ct 89509
Burwood Cir 89521
Butch Cassidy Dr 89511
Butler St 89512
Butte Ct 89508
Butte Pl 89503
Butterfly Ct & Dr 89523
Byington Dr 89509
Caballero Ct 89511
Caballo Dr 89502
Caballo Alto Ct 89502
Cabernet Pkwy 89512
Cabin Creek Trl 89523
Cabrillo Ln 89510
Cache Peak Dr 89512
Cactus Ct 89512
Cactus Canyon Rd 89510
Cactus Creek Ct 89511
Cactus View Dr 89506
Cadence Ct 89523
Cadillac Pl 89509
Cahal Ct 89523
Calavaras Rd 89521
Calcite Cir 89512
Calgary Ct & Dr 89511
Caliente St 89509
California Ave 89509
Calistoga Ct 89508
Caliterra Way 89521
Calla Lily Ct 89511
Callahan Rd 89511
Callahan Ranch Trl 89511
Callaway Trl 89523
Calle Maria St 89508
Calusa Ct & Ln 89523
Cambrian Ct 89503
Cambridge Way 89511
Cambridge Hills Ct 89523
Camden Aly 89502
Camden Cir 89506
Camel Rock Dr 89506
Camella Park Dr 89521
Camellia Dr 89512
Camelot Way 89509
Cameo Ct 89506
Cameron Ct 89508
Camill Dr 89509
Camino Lindo Way 89502
Campfire Pl 89511
Camraderie Way 89521
Canal St 89503
Candlerock Ct 89523
Candy Ave 89509
Cannan St 89512
Canterbury Cir 89502
N & S Cantlon Ln 89521
Canvasback Ln 89508
Canyon Cir & Dr 89519
Canyon Country Ct & Rd 89521
Canyon Creek Rd 89523
Canyon Meadows Dr 89506
Canyon Mesa Ct 89523
Canyon Park Ln 89523
Canyon Ridge Ln 89523
Canyon Shadow Cir 89521
Canyonlands Ct & Way 89521
Capella Dr 89521
Capital Blvd & Ct 89502
Capitan Cir 89511
Capitol Hill Ave 89502
Capricorn Cir 89521
Cardinal Way 89509
Carey Hills Dr 89511
Caribou Rd 89511
Carisbrook Ln 89502
Carl Dr 89511
Carlentini Ct 89519
Carleton Ct 89511
Carlin St 89503
Carlos Ln 89502
Carlsbad Rd 89508
Carlyle Ct & Dr 89506
Carmel Ln 89511
Carnaby Ct 89523
Carnation Ln 89512
Carnoustie Dr 89502
Carolyn Way 89506
Carousel Ct 89523
Carrera Rd 89510
Carriage Dr 89521
Carriage House Way 89519
Carrington Way 89506
Carson Ln 89506
Carter Dr 89509
Cartier Dr 89511
Cartwheel Dr 89512
Cartwright Rd 89521
Carville Dr 89512
Casa Blanca Rd 89502
Casa Linda Ct 89502
Casa Loma Dr 89503
Casazza Dr 89502
Casazza Ranch Ln 89511
Cascade St 89506
Cascade Falls Dr 89521
Casey Ct 89506
Cashill Blvd 89509
Casita Ct 89508
Caspian Ct 89521
Cassandra Ct & Way 89523
Cassas Ct 89511
Cassilis Dr 89506
Castle Way 89512
Castle Peak Rd 89521
Castle Pine Ct & Dr 89511
Castle Rock Dr 89523
Castle Sage Ct 89503
Castlehawk Ct 89523
Castlewood Ct 89509
Caswell Ln 89511
Catalina Dr 89502
Catalpa Ln 89511
Catamaran Dr 89519
Catherine Way 89523
Cathy Ave 89502
Catron Dr 89512
Cattail Cir 89521
Cattlemen Ct 89521
Caughlin Gln, Pkwy, Sq & Xing 89519
Caughlin Creek Rd 89519
Cavalry Cir 89521
Cavanaugh Dr 89509
Cave Rock Rd 89521
Cavern Dr 89521
Cayuse Way 89521
Cedar Ln 89521
Cedar St 89512
Cedar Bend Ct 89521
Cedar Creek Ct 89519
Cedar Crest Ct 89521
Cedar Mountain Ct & Dr 89508
Cedar Ridge Dr 89523
Cedar River Ct 89506
Cedar Rock Dr 89521
Cedar Springs Way 89511
Cedar Trace Ct 89511
Cedar View Ct & Dr 89508
Cedar Waxwing Ct 89523
Cedarbrook Ct & Dr 89502
Cedarhill Ln 89519
Cedarwood Dr 89511
Cee Jay Ct 89508
Celese Cir & Ln 89511
Celeste Dr 89511
Celestial Ct 89523
Cemetery Rd 89503
Centennial Way 89512
Centennial Mill Way 89523
N & S Center St 89501
Centre Pante Ct 89523
Cervino Ct & Dr 89521
Cevenness Ct 89511
Chablis Dr 89512
Chadwell Dr 89521
Chaise Ct 89519
Chalk Hill Ct 89519
Chalk Ridge Ct 89523
Chalkstone Way 89523
Challis Cir 89523
Chambery Cir 89511
Champetre Ct 89511
Champion Hills Dr 89523
Championship Trl 89523
Chamy Dr 89521
Chance Ln 89521
Channel Way 89506
Chanslor Cir 89509
Chanson Way 89511
Chantilly Way 89521
Chantry Flats Rd 89510
Chaparral Ct & Dr 89509
Chapman Pl 89506
N & S Chardonnay St 89512
Chariot Rd 89508
Charismatic Ct 89521
Charlene Dr 89506
Charles Dr & Pl 89509
Charlotte Way 89502
Chartreuse Ct 89511
Chaska Pl 89502
Chateau Ave & Ct 89511
Chatelaine Cir 89511
Chavez Dr 89502
Cheechako Cir & Dr 89519
Chelsea Sq 89509
Cheltenham Way 89502
Cheney St
1-199 89501
200-699 89502
Cherokee Trl 89521
Cherry Ln 89509
Cherryleaf Ct 89508
Cherrywood Dr 89511
Cheryl Ln 89521
Chesapeake Dr 89506
Cheshire Ct 89523
Chesterfield Ct & Ln 89523
Chestnut St 89506
Chevy Chase St 89509
Cheyenne Dr 89521
Chianti Way 89512
Chickadee Dr 89506
Chicory Way 89509
Chieftan Rd 89510
Chimney Ln 89511
China Rose Cir 89502
Chinchilla Ln 89511
Chinook Creek Rd 89519
Chippewa Ave 89506
Chipping Point Ct 89509
Chipshot Trl 89523
Chisholm Trl 89506
Chism St 89503
Chlorite Ct 89521
Choate Ct 89503
Chokecherry Ln 89508
Chris Ln 89502
Christopher Cir 89503
Christy Ln 89521
Christy Way 89519
Chuckwagon Rd 89508
Church Ln 89503
Ciarra Kennedy Ln 89503
Cicada Ct 89521
Cimarron Dr 89508
Cinch Rd 89508
Cinderella Dr 89503
Cindy Ave 89506
Cinnamon Ridge Ln 89523
Circle Dr 89509
Circle Stone Ct 89523
Cisco Way 89502
Citadel Ct & Way 89503
Citation Ct 89523
Citron St 89512
Cityview Ter 89512
Claim Stake Dr 89506
Claremont Cir & St 89502
Clarence Jasmine Dr 89511
Clarens Ct 89511
Claret Ct 89512
N & S Claridge Pointe Pkwy 89506
Clay St 89501
Claymont Ct 89523
Clean Water Way 89502
Clear Acre Ln 89512
Clear Creek Ct & Dr 89502
Clear Lake Ct 89508
Clear Springs Ct 89508
Clear Vista Dr 89521
Clearwater Dr 89511
Clefa Dr 89509
Clemens Rd 89521
Clement Ct 89506
Clementine Ln 89521
Clemson Rd 89502
Cleveland Ave 89503
Clevite Ln 89521
Cliff Park Ct & Way 89523
Cliff View Ct & Dr 89523
Cliffhanger Dr 89521
Clifford Dr 89506
Cliffrose Cir 89511
Clifton Dr 89509
Clos Du Val Ct 89519
Cloud Chaplin Rd 89510
Cloud View Cir 89512
Clough Rd 89509
Clover Way 89509
Clover Creek Ct 89519
Clover Hill Trl 89523
Clover Meadows Ct 89519
Clovis Ct 89523
Clubhouse Dr 89523
Clyde Ct 89509
Clydesdale Dr 89508
Coastal St 89512
Cobalt Ln 89508
Cobb Cir 89506
Cobble Ridge Ct 89511
Cobblestone Ct 89503
Cochise Dr 89521
Cocoa Ave 89506
Cocopah Ct 89511
Codel Way 89503
Cody Ct 89508
Coggins Rd 89506
Cognac Ct 89511
Coit Dr 89523
Colavita Way 89521
Colbert Dr 89511
Colby Ln 89506
Cold Springs Dr 89508
Colegate Ct 89503
Coleman Dr 89503
Coliseum Way 89502
College Ct & Dr 89503
Collins Cir 89506
Colmar Ct 89521
Colombard Way 89512
Colony Cir & Rd 89502
Colorado River Blvd 89502
Colt Dr
600-899 89506
21501-21599 89521
Colton Dr 89521
Columbia Way 89502
Columbia Hill Ct & Rd 89508
Columbus Way 89503
Colusa Dr 89503
Comanche Moon Ct & Dr 89521
Combination Rd 89521
E Commercial Row 89512
W Commercial Row
200-298 89501
1001-1099 89503
Commonwealth Cir 89503
Companion Ct 89511
Compari Ct 89511
Compton St 89506
Comstock Dr 89512
Comstock Estates Dr 89521
Concho Dr 89521
Conestoga Cir & Rd 89521
Conifer Dr 89509
Connemaras Ct 89521
Conness Way 89523
Connie Way 89521
Constellation Ct 89523
Continental Dr 89509
Convair Way 89506
Conway Ln 89503
Cooke Dr 89521
Cool Springs Dr 89509
Cooper Ct 89503
Copenhagen Way 89521
Copper Ct & Rdg 89519
Copper Canyon Rd 89521
Copper Cloud Dr 89511
Copper Creek Ct N & S 89519
Copper Lake Dr 89521
Copper Leaf Dr 89506
Copper Moon Ct 89521
Copper Mountain Cir 89523
Copper Penny Dr 89519
Copper Point Cir 89519
Copper Springs Dr 89521
Copper Vista Ct 89506
Copper Wood Ct 89521
Copperfield Dr 89506
Coral Reef Dr 89506
Corbett Way 89506
Cordero Dr 89521
Cordilla Ct 89523
Cordone Ave 89502
Coretta Way 89506
Corey Dr 89509
Cornerbrook Ct 89511
Corning Ct 89523
Cornwall Cir 89506
Corona Ct 89523
Coronado Way 89503
Coronet Cir & Dr 89509
Corporate Blvd 89502
Corrigan Way 89506
Corsair St 89502
Corsica Ct 89511
Corso St 89506
Corson Ct 89503
Corthenw Dr 89503
Cortono Dr 89521
Corvallis Ct & Dr 89511
Corvus Ct 89502
Cottage Ct 89503
Cottonwood Rd 89511
Cougarcreek Trl 89519
Council Ln 89511
Count Fleet Ct 89502
Country Club Dr 89509
Country Estates Cir & Ct 89511
Country Falls Ln 89521
Country View Ct 89506
Countryside Ave & Ct 89523
Cour Saint Michelle 89511
Court St 89501
Courtney Ln 89523
Cove Pl 89509
Covent Garden Dr 89509
Coventry Way 89506
Covington Way 89503
Cowan Dr 89509
Cowhide Cir 89508
Coyote Cir 89521
Coyote Creek Ct & Dr 89521
Coyote Point Cir 89511
Coyote Ridge Ct & Rd 89523
Coyote Rose Ln 89511
Coyote Run Ct 89508
Craig Ct 89502
Craigmont Dr 89511
Crampton St 89502
Cranbrook Cir & Way 89519
Cranleigh Dr 89512
Cranwood Ct 89521
Crater Ct 89521
Craviasco Ln 89502
Crazy Horse Rd 89510
Creek Pl 89509
Creek Canyon Dr 89506
Creek Crest Dr 89511
Creek Crossing Rd 89511
Creek Haven Cir 89509
E & W Creek Ridge Trl 89519
Creek View Dr 89511
Creekland Dr 89506
Creekside Cir 89502
Creekwood Dr 89502
Creighton Way 89503
Creosote Ct 89506
Crescent Cir 89509
Crescent Moon Ct 89511
Crescent Pointe Ct & Way 89523
Crest Bluff Ct & Dr 89506
Crest Hill Dr 89506
Crest Valley Dr 89511
Crestone Dr 89523
Crestridge Way 89509
Crestview Pl 89509
Crestview Rd 89521
Crickett Ave 89509
Cricketwood Cir 89523
Crimson Dr 89521
Crimson Sky Ct 89506
Crocker Way 89509
Crockett Dr 89508
Crooked Canyon Ct & Dr 89521
Cross Creek Ln 89511
Crossbow Ct 89511
Crossover Rd 89510
Crosswater Ct & Dr 89523
Crotone Ct & Way 89521
Crown Dr 89503
Crown Canyon Ct 89503
Crown Point Ct 89523
Crown View Dr 89523
Crows Nest Pkwy 89519
Crummer Ln 89502

Crystal Ln 89512
Crystal Bay Dr 89521
E & W Crystal Canyon Blvd & Ct 89508
Crystal Shores Dr 89506
Crystal Springs Ct 89519
Crystal Vista Ln 89523
Crystalline Ct & Dr 89506
Cub Ct 89506
Cullen Ct 89519
Cumberland Cir 89511
Cunningham Way 89506
Cuprite St 89506
Curlew Ct 89508
Curnow Canyon Rd 89510
Current Ct 89509
Currie Hills Rd 89506
Curti Dr 89502
Curtis Ln 89511
Custer Rd 89508
Cutting Horse Cir 89519
Cyma Cir 89503
Cynthia Pl 89509
Cypress Way 89502
Cypress Garden Ct 89521
Cypress Point Dr 89502
D Arques Ct 89521
Daffodil Way 89512
Daggett Dr 89511
Dahlia Way 89512
Dakota Way 89506
Dakota Ridge Ct & Trl 89523
Dales Ln 89511
Dalton Ln 89508
Dalwood Ct 89521
Damonte Ranch Pkwy 89521
Damonte View Ln 89511
Damselfly Dr 89523
Dana Kristine Ln 89503
Danbury Ct 89523
Dancing Aspen Dr 89521
Dancing Cloud Ct 89511
Dandelion St 89506
Dandini Blvd 89512
Danette Cir 89511
Daniel Dr 89509
Daniel Paul Ct 89508
Daniel Webster Dr 89509
Dant Blvd & Ct 89509
Darby Ln 89509
Dark Horse Rd 89521
Darlene Cir 89506
Dartmoor Ct 89521
Dartmouth Dr 89509
Darwin Cir 89506
Datewood Ct 89508
Davenport Ct & Ln 89508
David Dr 89521
Davidson Way 89509
Davis Ln 89511
Dawson Dr 89523
Dawson Jacob Ln 89503
Day Lily Ct 89511
Daybreak Dr 89523
Daylin Ct 89523
Dayton Way 89502
De Anza Dr 89511
De Chardin Ln 89511
De Maitre Ct 89511
De Spain Ln 89511
Deadwood Dr 89508
Decade Cir 89512
Deep Bay Dr 89506
Deer Creek Ln 89506
Deer Foot Ln 89506
N & S Deer Meadows Ct 89519
Deer Mountain Rd 89523
Deer Pass Dr 89509
Deer Ridge Ct 89509
Deer River Ct 89506
Deer Run Dr 89509
Deer Valley Ct & Dr 89511
Deerbrook Ct 89523
Deerfield Ct 89519
Deerlodge Rd 89508
Del Curto Dr 89523
Del Mesa Cir 89521
Del Monte Ln 89511
Del Paso Dr 89502
Del Rio Ln 89509
Del Webb Pkwy W 89523
Delacroix 89511
Deli St 89506
Delmar Way 89509
Delta Dr 89521
Delucchi Ln 89502
Demos Ct 89512
Denali Ct & Way 89506
Dendince Dr 89509
Denio Dr 89509
Dennison Dr 89509
Denslowe Dr 89512
Deodar Way 89506
Depaoli St 89512
Derbish Way 89502
Desatoya Ct & Dr 89511
Desert Way 89521
Desert Bloom Dr 89506
Desert Candle Ct 89523
E & W Desert Canyon Dr 89511
Desert Flower Ln 89510
Desert Grass Ct 89506
Desert Jewel Ct 89511
Desert Lake Ct & Dr 89508
Desert Meadow Ct 89502
Desert Sun Ln 89508
Desert Willow Way 89511
Desna St 89512
Desoto Way 89502
Destiny Ct 89506
Deveron Dr 89506
Devon Dr 89506
Devonshire Ln 89511
Diablo Rd 89521
Diamond Country Dr 89521
Diamond Glen Dr 89523
Diamond J Pl 89511
Diamond O Dr 89506
Diamond Peak Dr 89508
Diamond Pointe Way 89506
Diamond Ridge Dr 89523
Diamond Sky Way 89523
Diamond Vista Ct 89506
Dickerson Rd 89503
Dieringer Ln 89511
Dijon Cir 89511
Dillingham Dr 89521
Dillon Way 89506
Diogenes Dr 89512
Diplomat Dr 89523
Discovery Ct & Ln 89506
Dixie Ln 89508
Dixon Ct & Ln 89511
Dog Hollow Ct 89519
Dojack Way 89506
Dolomite Cir 89512
Domingo Ct 89511
Dominic Dr 89521
Donald St 89502
Donalisha Ln 89511
Donnay Ct & Dr 89521
Donner Dr 89509
Donner Peak Dr 89521
Donnybrook Ct 89511
Doral Cir 89509
Doreen Ct 89512
Doretta Ln 89523
Dori Bell Ln 89523
Doric Dr 89503
Doris Cir 89509
Dorset Cir 89506
Dortort Dr 89521
Dos Rios Ct 89502
Double Creek Ct 89511
Double Diamond Pkwy 89521
Double Eagle Ct 89521
Double R Blvd
8000-8098 89511
8301-8599 89511
9000-9298 89521
9300-9999 89521
10001-10899 89521
Doubleback Rd 89506
Douglas Fir Cir & Dr 89511
Dove Cir 89508
Dove Mountain Ct 89523
Downey Ave 89503
Downing Ct 89523
Drake Wood Ct 89523
Dream Sky Ct 89523
Dressage Ct 89521
Drew Dr 89511
Drift Creek Ct 89508
Driftstone Ave 89523
Driscoll Dr 89509
Drop Tine Ct 89511
Drum Horse Ln 89521
Dry Ct 89502
Dry Creek Rd 89511
Dry Falls Cir 89523
Dry Gulch Rd 89521
Dry Lake Rd 89521
Dry Springs Ct 89506
Dry Valley Rd 89508
Drybrush Ct 89506
Dryden Dr 89511
Dublin Ct 89509
Dubrou Ct 89511
Duffney Ln 89506
Duke Way 89502
Dundee Rd 89519
Dunes Cir 89509
Dunkeld Rd 89519
Durango Ct 89503
Dustin Ct 89508
Dutch Creek Ct 89509
Dutch Hollow Trl 89523
Dutch Ravine Ct 89521
Dyal Ct 89508
Dyer Way 89512
Eagle Pl 89510
Eagle Bend Ct & Trl 89523
Eagle Chase Trl 89523
Eagle Claw Ct 89523
Eagle Creek Ct 89519
Eagle Dancer Ln 89521
Eagle Falls Way 89521
Eagle Greens Ct & Dr 89521
Eagle Meadows Ct 89519
Eagle Ridge Ct 89509
Eagle Rock Ct 89511
Eagle Springs Ct 89511
Eagle Valley Cir 89519
Eagle Vista Ct 89511
Eaglecrest Dr 89523
Eagles Landing Ct 89521
Eaglesham Ct 89519
Eaglewood Ct & Dr 89502
Earl Dr 89503
N & S Earlham Ct 89511
Eastmont Ct & Ln 89521
Eastridge Dr 89523
Eastshore Dr & Pl 89509
Eastwood Dr 89509
Easy St 89521
Easy Jet Rd 89510
Eaton Rd 89521
Ebbetts Dr 89503
Echo Ave & Ct 89506
Echo Creek Ct 89519
Echo Pass Rd 89521
Echo Ridge Ct 89511
Echo Valley Pkwy 89521
Edelweiss St 89502
Eden Ct 89509
Edgecliff Dr 89523
Edgehill Ct 89521
Edgemar Cir 89512
Edgerock Rd 89519
Edgewater Pkwy 89519
Edgewood Dr 89503
N Edison Way 89502
Edmands Ct & Dr 89511
Edmonton Dr 89511
Edrie Dr 89502
Egret Ct & Ln 89508
Eichs Rd 89521
Eisan Ave 89506
El Cajon Ct 89502
El Camino Cir 89509
El Campo Ct 89521
El Cerro View Cir 89509
El Gato Way 89502
El Monte Ct 89521
Eldon Ct 89511
Eldorado Dr 89519
Eleanor Ave 89523
Elementary Dr 89512
Elgin Ave 89503
Eli Dr 89511
Elizabeth Dr 89506
Elizabeth St 89509
Elk Ct 89508
Elk Ivory Dr 89511
N & S Elk River Ct & Rd 89511
Elk Run Trl 89523
Elkcreek Trl 89519
Elkhorn Ln 89506
Elko Ave 89512
Ellendale Ct & Rd 89503
Ellicott Ct & Way 89519
Elliot Dr 89512
Ellis St 89502
Elm Ct 89501
Elm St 89503
Elm Glen Ct 89521
Elmcrest Dr 89503
Elmwood Ln 89509
Embassy Cir & Way 89523
Emerald Pl 89502
Emerald Bay Dr 89521
Emerald View Ct 89523
Emery Dr 89506
Emily St 89503
Empire Ct 89508
Empire Rd 89521
Enargite Cir 89521
Enchanted Valley Dr 89523
Energy Way 89502
Englewood Cir 89511
Enterprise Rd
101-199 89512
2000-2499 89521
2601-2697 89512
2699-2700 89512
2702-2898 89512
Epic Ave 89512
Epidote Ct 89521
Equine Ct 89521
Equity Ave 89502
Erbium Cir 89512
Erminia Rd 89523
Ernie Ln 89510
Escalera Ct & Way 89523
N & S Escondido Ct 89502
Escuela Way 89502
Essex Way 89506
Estates Rd 89506
Etral Cir 89506
Eucalyptus Ct 89523
Eureka Ave 89512
Eva Adams Dr 89509
Evans Ave
200-398 89501
400-499 89501
500-1699 89512
1701-1799 89512
Evans Creek Dr & Ter 89519
Evans Ranch Rd 89508
Evelyn Way 89502
Evening Blue Ct 89523
Evening Rock Ct & Trl 89523
Evening Song Ln 89511
Eventer Ln 89521
Everest Dr 89523
Everett Dr 89503
Evergreen Hills Dr 89511
Evergreen Park Dr 89521
Evergreen Ridge Ct & Way 89523
Exeter Way 89503
Exinite Ct 89506
Fair Cir 89503
Fairbanks Ct 89509
Fairfax Ct 89508
Fairfield Ave 89509
Fairhaven Pl 89523
Fairlands Ct & Dr 89523
Fairview Rd 89511
Fairway Chase Trl 89523
Fairway Hills Trl 89523
Fairway Ridge Ct 89523
Fairwood Dr 89502
Faland Way 89503
Falcon Way 89509
Fall Colors Ct 89519
Fall Creek Ct 89519
Fall River Cir 89523
Fallen Leaf Ct 89509
Falling Star Loop 89523
Falling Water Ct & Dr 89519
Fandango Pass 89521
Fantail Cir & St 89508
Far Niente Ct 89519
Faretto Ln 89511
Farkendi Dr 89512
Fawn Ln 89511
Feather Way 89509
Feather Glen Ct 89523
Feather River Ct 89508
N & S Featherstone Cir 89511
Feldspar Ct 89521
Fellowship Way 89511
Fenno Way 89519
Fern St 89506
Ferol Way 89503
Ferrari Mcleod Blvd 89512
Ferret Cir 89523
Ferris Ln 89509
Fescue Ct 89509
Fetlock Dr 89508
Fey Rd 89521
Fieldbrook Cir 89519
Fieldcreek Ln 89511
Fieldstone Pl 89523
Fiesta Ct 89508
Fife Dr 89512
Filbert Rd 89502
Filer Rd 89506
Fillmore Way 89519
Financial Blvd 89502
Findhorn Dr 89506
Finley Dr 89510
Finnsech Dr 89506
Fir Dr 89506
Fire Opal Ln 89506
Fire Poppy Cir 89521
Firefly Ct 89523
Fireside Cir 89509
Firethorn Cir 89523
Fish Springs Rd 89510
Fish Springs Ranch Rd 89510
E & W Five Mile Rd 89521
Flagg Dr 89502
Flagstone Rd 89510
Flamingo Dr 89508
Flanders Rd 89511
Flanigan Rd 89510
Flanigan Chapel Ranch Rd 89510
Flanigan Star Rte 89510
Flat Iron Rd 89521
Fleetwood Dr 89506
Fleur Ct 89511
Flint Rd 89521
Flint St 89501
Flint Ridge Ct 89511
Flintlock Cir 89519
Floreca Way 89511
Florimont Ct 89511
Flower St 89506
Flowering Sage Ct & Trl 89511
Fluorite Cir 89512
Flying Eagle Dr 89510
Foley Way 89509
N & S Folsom Dr 89509
Fontana Ct 89508
Fonti Ct 89508
Foothill Rd 89511
Ford Rd 89508
Forest St 89509
Forest Knoll Ct 89523
Forest View Ct & Ln 89511
Forest Willow Trl 89523
Foret Cir 89511
Forson Dr 89509
Forsythia Way 89506
Fort Churchill Rd 89508
Fort Collins Dr 89511
Fort Morgan Way 89521
Fort Sage Cir 89506
Fortune Ct 89508
Fossil Ct 89508
Foster Dr 89509
Fowler Ave 89506
Fox Ave 89506
Fox Glen Cir & Ct 89521
Fox Glove Ct 89511
Fox Meadows Ct 89523
Fox Run Rd 89523
Fox Trail Dr 89523
Foxcreek Trl 89519
Foxhunter Ln 89521
Foxtail Ct & Dr 89502
Francovich Ct 89519
Frandsen Cir 89509
Frankwood Dr 89521
Freddie Ct 89503
Frederick Dr 89506
Freds Mountain Rd 89508
Fremont Way 89506
French Meadows Way 89521
Friesian Ct 89521
Frontier Ct 89503
Frontier Rd 89508
Frontier St 89503
Frost Ln 89511
Frost Peak Ct 89508
Fryingpan Rd 89521
Fulmar Ct 89508
Fury Ct 89521
Fyvie Ct 89519
Gabro St 89506
Galen Pl 89503
Galena Dr 89506
Galena Canyon Trl 89511
Galena Meadows Dr 89511
Galena Pines Rd 89521
Galilee Dr 89506
Gallaway Ln 89502
Galletti Way 89512
Gallian Ln 89511
Gallup Rd 89511
Gamay Ln 89512
Games Dr 89509
Gannet Ct 89508
Gannon Dr 89506
Gardella Ave 89512
Gardner St 89503
Garlan Ln 89509
Garnet Dr & Pl 89508
Garnet Ridge Ct 89523
Gascony Ct 89511
Gate St 89506
Gateway Dr
9300-9368 89511
9370-9799 89521
9801-9899 89521
Gatewood Dr 89523
Gaucho Ln 89521
Gauguin Dr 89511
Gazelle Rd 89511
Gazin Ct 89506
Gear St 89503
Geary St 89503
Gebser Ct 89511
Geiger Grade Rd 89521
Gellert Dr 89503
Gemini Cir 89521
Gemstone Dr 89511
Gemtown Ct & Dr 89521
Genesee Dr 89503
Genoa Ave 89503
Genovese Ln 89511
Gentry Way 89502
Geode Ct 89523
Georgetown Ct & Dr 89508
Georgia Pl 89509
Georgian Cir 89511
Geronimo Trl 89521
Geyser Rd 89511
Ghettis Way 89521
Ghost Rider Ct & Dr 89511
Gibraltar Dr 89509
Gila Bend Rd 89511
Gildesgard Ranch Rd 89521
Gilvarry St 89506
Gingko Ct 89508
Gipsy Way 89506
Giroux St 89502
Glacier Ct 89503
Glacier Meadow Dr 89521
Gladstone Dr 89506
Glen St 89502
Glen Cove Ct 89521
Glen Eagles Dr 89523
Glen Echo Ct & Ln 89509
Glen Lakes Ct 89508
Glen Oaks Dr 89523
Glen Ridge Dr 89521
Glenda Way 89509
Gleneyre Ct 89509
Glenmanor Dr 89509
Glenmore Ct 89523
Glenshyre Ct 89519
Glenview Dr & Ter 89503
Glenwood Ct & Dr 89509
Globe Rd 89521
Golconda Dr 89509
Gold Ct & Dr 89506
Gold Arrow Dr 89521
Gold Belt Dr 89521
Gold Cliff Ct 89521
Gold Hill Ave 89506
Gold Mine Ct & Dr 89521
Gold Nugget Ct 89506
Gold Ridge Dr 89509
Gold River Ct 89506
Gold Run Ct & Dr 89521
Gold Rush Ct 89523
Gold Strike Ct 89521
Gold Trail Dr 89521
Golden Ln 89502
Golden Creek Rd 89519
Golden Currant Cir 89511
Golden Eagle Ct & Dr 89523
Golden Gate Dr 89511
Golden Highlands Ct 89506
Golden Meadow Rd 89519
Golden Springs Dr 89509
Golden Spur Ct 89521
E & W Golden Valley Rd 89506
Golden Vista Ave & Ct 89506
Golden West Ct & Rd 89506
Goldenrod Dr 89511
Goldfield Rd 89521
Goldfield St 89512
Goldfinch Dr 89508
Goldpan Dr 89511
Goldstone Rd 89508
Goldwood Rd 89506
Goler Wash Ct & Dr 89521
Golf Canyon Ct 89523
Golf Club Dr 89519
Golfwood Ct 89523
Goodher Rd 89510
Gooding Dr 89508
Goodman Rd 89521
Goodsell Ln 89523
Goose Lake Ct & Dr 89508
Gooseberry Dr 89523
Gorc Way 89502
Gordon Ave 89509
Gorham Ct 89508
Goshawk Ct 89523

Gould St 89502
Gracia Deldios Dr 89502
Graham Ln 89508
Gramercy Ln 89509
Grand Canyon Blvd 89502
Grand Falls Dr 89506
Grand Point Way
1400-1579 89523
1580-1898 89523
1580-1580 89533
1581-1899 89523
Grand Summit Dr 89523
Grand Teton Ct 89509
Grand Valley Ct 89508
Grande Rd 89521
Grandview Ave 89503
Granite Dr 89509
Granite Basin Ct 89523
Granite Chief Dr 89521
Granite Mine Dr 89521
Granite Pointe Ct & Dr 89511
Granite Springs Rd 89519
Grant Dr 89509
Graphite Cir 89512
Grass Valley Rd 89510
Grassland Pl 89502
Gravel Ct 89502
Graves Rd 89521
Gray Fox Ct 89511
Graysburg Dr 89523
Grayslake Dr 89521
Great Basin Rd 89523
Great Falls Loop 89511
Greeley Ct 89511
Green Acres Dr 89511
Green Ash Rd 89511
Green Meadow Ct 89506
Green Mountain St 89506
Green Ranch Cir & Rd 89519
Green River Ct & Dr 89503
Green Springs Ct & Dr 89511
Green Tree Ln 89511
Greenbriar Ct 89509
Greenbrook Dr 89511
Greenfield Dr 89509
Greenhorn Cir 89519
Greenleaf Ct 89506
Greenridge Dr 89509
Greensboro Dr & Pt 89509
Greensburg Cir 89509
Greenstone Cir & Dr 89512
Greenview Ct 89502
Greenwich Way 89519
Greenwood Dr 89511
Greg St 89502
Gremlin Way 89506
Greta Pl 89503
Grey Hawk Trl 89511
Grey Rock Ct 89511
Grey Van Rd 89510
Greybull Ct 89519
Greycrest Way 89521
Greyhawk Ct 89508
Greystone Dr 89523
Gridley Ave 89503
Griffon Ct 89506
Grisom Way 89506
Griswold Way 89503
Grizzley Rd 89521
Grizzly Ct 89506
Grizzly Bear Ct 89508
Grizzly Hill Ct 89521
Grosse Point Ct 89506
Grosvenor Park Pl 89509
Grouse Ct & Way 89508
Grousecreek Ct 89519
E Grove St 89502
W Grove St 89509
Grubstake Cir 89519
Grundy St 89506
Gulch Way 89521
Gulf Stream Ct & Ln 89506
Gull St 89508
Gulling Ct & Rd 89503
Gunnison Ct & Dr 89508
Gymkhana Ln 89508
Gypsum Rd 89503
Gypsy Hill Trl 89523
Hacienda Dr 89503
Hackamore Dr 89519
Hackney Dr 89508
Haddock Dr 89512
Hagar Rd 89506
Hahn Cir & Dr 89506
Haida Ct 89506
Halearel Dr 89521
Haleb Ct 89521
Half Dome Dr 89521
Half Mine Rd 89506
Halifax Dr 89506
Halladale Dr 89506
Hamilton Rd 89521
Hammill Ln 89511
Hampshire Dr 89503
Hampton Ln 89519
Hampton Creek Dr 89521
Hampton Park Ct & Dr 89521
Hanaupah Rd 89521
Hannah Ct 89506
Hanover Dr 89523
Happy Canyon Dr 89521
Happy Valley Ct 89511
Harbin Ln 89509
Harbor Cir 89519
Harbottle Dr 89511
Hardesty Dr 89509
Harding Cir & Way 89503
Hardscrabble Rd 89510
Harold Dr 89503
Harris Rd 89506
Harte Rd 89521
Hartford Ct 89503
Harvard Way 89502
Harvest Hill Ln 89523
Harvest Moon Rd 89523
Harvey Ln 89509
Haskell St 89509
Hastings Dr 89503
Hatch St 89501
Havencrest Dr 89523
Hawk Hill Ct 89511
Hawk Meadow Trl 89523
Hawken Rd 89519
Hawkeye Cir 89523
Hawthorne Rd 89502
Hay Canyon Rd 89510
Hayes Cir 89511
Hazelcrest Dr 89521
Hazelnut Dr 89508
Hazelwood Cir 89511
Headgate Trl 89510
Hearthstone Ct 89521
Heartpine St 89506
Heater Ln 89521
Heath Cir 89509
Heathcliff Dr 89511
Heather Field Ln 89521
Heather Glen Dr 89523
Heatheridge Ln 89509
Heatherwood Ct & Dr 89523
Heavenly Valley Ln 89509
Heavenly View Trl 89523
Hebrides Ct 89506
Hedge Ct 89508
Hedgewood Dr 89509
Heights Dr 89503
Heindel Rd 89506
Heitman Ct 89509
Helena Ave 89512
Hellaby Ln 89502
Helm Cir 89503
Helvetia Ave 89502
Hemlock Ct & Way 89509
Hempstead Ct 89523
Hen Ct 89508
Henry Ct 89509
Hensley St 89503
Hereford Way 89521
Heritage Oaks Dr 89523
Heritage Ridge Ct 89523
Herlong Ln 89510
Hermit Rd 89521
Herons Cir 89502
Herons Landing Dr 89502
Herz Blvd 89511
Hibbet Trl 89511
Hickory Hill Way 89523
Hidden Canyon Rd 89510
Hidden Creek Rd 89510
Hidden Green Pt 89502
Hidden Highlands Dr 89502
Hidden Lake Dr 89521
Hidden Meadows Ct & Dr 89502
Hidden Park Dr 89523
Hidden River Ct & Way 89523
E & W Hidden Valley Ct & Dr 89502
High St 89502
High Chaparral Dr & Way 89521
High Ridge Ct 89511
High Terrace Dr 89509
High Vista Dr 89511
Highcrest Dr 89523
Highland Ave 89512
Highland Rd 89521
Highland Spur 89521
Highland Flume Cir 89523
Highland Pines Ct & Dr 89503
Highplains Dr 89523
Highview Ct 89512
Highwood Ct 89509
Hiko Ave 89512
Hill St 89501
Hillboro Ave 89512
Hillcrest Dr 89509
Hillhouse Ct 89512
N Hills Blvd 89506
S Hills Dr 89511
Hillside Dr 89503
Hillside Rd 89521
Hilltop Rd 89509
Hillview Dr 89506
Hilton Ct 89519
Himalaya St 89506
Hinton Dr 89506
History Dr 89502
Hitch Rd 89506
Hockberry Rd 89510
Hodge Dr 89511
Hogadon Way 89523
Hogan Ct 89523
Hoge Rd 89506
Holcomb Ave 89502
Holcomb Ranch Ln 89511
Holiday Ct 89506
Holiday Ln 89511
Holly Canyon Rd 89506
Hollywood Park Dr 89511
Hombre Way 89502
Home Gardens Dr 89502
Homeland Dr 89511
Homestead Pl 89509
Homewood Dr 89509
Honey Ln 89511
Honey Lake Way 89510
Honey Locust Ct 89508
Honey Ridge Dr 89511
Honeysuckle Ct & Dr 89506
Honeywood Ct 89509
Hood Ave 89512
Hope Valley Dr 89521
Hopi Ct & Ln 89506
Hornblende Ct & St 89506
Horse Creek Ct 89506
Horse Prairie Rd 89521
Horseshoe Cir 89508
Hot Springs Rd 89521
Houston Dr 89502
Hoyt St 89509
Hubbard Way 89502
E & W Huffaker Ln & Pl 89511
Huffaker Estates Cir 89511
Hughes Dr 89506
Humboldt St 89509
Humite Ln 89506
Hummer Ct & Dr 89521
Hummingbird Dr 89508
Hungry Mountain Rd 89506
Hungry Valley Rd 89506
Hunter Pl 89519
Hunter Creek Rd 89519
Hunter Glen Ct & Dr 89523
Hunter Lake Dr 89509
Huntington Cir 89509
Huntsdale Dr 89521
Huron Trl 89521
Hurst Park Rd 89502
Hydepark Ct 89502
Hydraulic St 89506
Ibis Ln 89503
Icarus Ct 89512
Ichabod Ct 89502
Idaho St 89506
Ideal Ct 89506
Idlebury Way 89523
Idlewild Dr
1101-1397 89509
1399-3399 89509
3401-3499 89509
4800-4999 89519
Imall Ct 89506
Imperial Blvd 89503
Indian Ln 89506
Indian Cove Way 89523
Indian Ridge Dr 89511
Indian Summer Ct 89511
Indian Wells Dr 89521
Indigo Cir & Ct 89506
Indigo Run Dr 89511
E Indonti Ct E 89511
Indus Dr 89502
Industry Cir 89506
Innovation Dr 89511
Innsbruck Ct 89519
Interlaken Ct 89509
Inverness Dr 89502
Inwood Ln 89502
Iona Way 89502
Ireland Ct 89510
Iris Ct 89512
Iron Eagle Trl 89511
Iron Horse Ranch Ln 89506
Iron Mountain Dr 89521
Iron Point Cir 89521
Iron Ridge Ct 89521
Ironhorse Dr 89511
Ironwood Rd 89510
Iroquois Cir 89502
Irving Park Cir 89503
Isbell Rd 89509
Ishi Point Ct & Dr 89523
Isis Ct 89512
Island Ave 89501
Itasca Ct 89506
Ives Ave & Ct 89503
Ivy Ct 89511
Ivy Gate Ct 89521
Ivywood Ct 89508
Jacana Ct 89508
Jack Hammer Ct & Dr 89521
Jackalope Trl 89510
Jackrabbit Rd 89510
Jackson Pl 89512
Jackson Springs Dr 89523
Jaeger Ct 89508
Jagged Rock Rd 89502
Jake St 89502
Jakes Hill Ct 89519
Jamaica Ave 89502
Jamboree Dr 89521
James Ct & Ln 89503
James Dean Ct 89508
James Madison Dr 89509
Jamil Ct 89511
Jasmine Ct 89506
Jasper Ln 89509
Javalina Ct 89508
Jaybird Rd 89510
Jays Pl 89506
Jean Way 89506
E & W Jeffrey Pine Rd 89511
Jefte Ct 89511
Jenna Way 89511
Jeppson Ln 89511
Jeremy Way 89506
Jerome Ave 89506
Jessica Ct 89521
Jester Ct 89503
Jewel Ridge Ct 89506
Jewel Star Ct 89506
Jigger Bob Way 89510
Jimson Dr 89511
Joanie Ct 89509
Joaquin Miller Dr 89509
Jodi Dr 89512
Joe Ln 89509
John Eugene Ct 89503
John Fremont Dr 89509
John Thomas Ln 89508
Johnson Ln 89511
Johnson Pl 89509
Jolly Ln 89523
Jonada Pl 89509
Jones St 89503
Jonquil Ct 89506
Joshua Dr 89509
Joshuapark Dr 89502
Joule St 89502
Journey Ct 89508
Joy Ln 89512
Joy Lake Rd 89511
Judith Ln 89503
Judy Way 89506
Juliann Way 89509
Julie Ct 89509
June Ave 89512
June Meadows Rd 89519
Junewood Ct 89509
Jung Ct 89511
Juniper St 89506
Juniper Trl 89519
Juniper Creek Rd 89519
Juniper Hill Rd 89519
Juniper Saddle Ct & Dr 89510
Jutewood Ct 89508
Kachina Ct 89511
Kalispell Ct 89503
Kami Ct 89509
Kane Ct 89512
Karsten Ct 89506
Kate Ln 89506
Katherine Dr 89502
Kathleen Denise Ln 89503
Katie Ct 89523
Kauai Ct 89509
Kay Lee Cir 89508
Kaye Way 89509
Kearney Dr 89506
Keaton Ct 89511
Keats Cir 89506
Keegan Cir 89503
Keele Dr 89509
Keever Ct 89509
Kelly Dr 89503
Kelly Ln 89506
Kelpie Ct 89506
Kemmer St 89506
Kenai Dr 89521
Kennedy Dr 89506
Kentfield Pl 89521
Kentwood Ct 89503
Kernite Ct & St 89506
Kerrydale Ct 89521
Keshmiri Pl 89519
Kess Ct & Way 89506
Kessaris Way 89511
Kestrel Ct 89509
Ketchum Ct 89511
Kettle Rock Ct & Dr 89508
Kevin Cir 89511
Kewanna Trl 89521
E & W Key Largo Ct & Dr 89506
Keyhaven Dr 89502
Keystone Ave & Pl 89503
Kietzke Ln
2-98 89502
100-3500 89502
3502-4898 89502
4801-4947 89509
4949-4999 89509
5000-5599 89511
Kilborne Ave & Ct 89509
Kildeer Ln 89502
Killington Ct & Dr 89511
Kimbal Dr 89503
Kindred Ave 89502
King Ln 89521
King Arthur Ct 89503
King Edward Ct & Dr 89503
King Henry Ct 89503
King James Ct 89503
King Richard Ct 89503
Kingbird Ct 89508
Kingfisher Dr 89509
Kingman Ct 89511
Kings Ct & Row 89503
Kingston Ln 89511
Kingsview Ct 89512
Kingswood Ct 89511
Kinney Ct & Ln 89511
Kiowa Way 89506
Kirkham Way 89503
Kirkland Ct 89511
Kirman Ave 89502
Kirston St 89503
Kit Ct 89506
Kitts Way 89521
Kitty Green Ln 89510
Kivett Ln 89521
Kiwi Ct 89508
Klofta Ct 89510
Knight Rd 89509
Knightsbridge Ct 89511
Knob Hill Dr 89506
Knoll Dr 89509
Knox Ave 89509
Kodiak Cir 89511
Koenig Cir & Rd 89506
Kohlepp Ave 89509
Koldewey Dr 89509
Kona Ct 89509
Kristin Ct & Way 89523
Krupp Cir 89509
Kuenzli St 89502
Kumle Ln 89509
Kunde Dr 89511
Kyle Ct 89511
La Briana Ave & Ct 89511
La Casa Ct 89508
La Fond Dr 89509
La France Ln 89506
La Guardia Ln 89511
La Paz Ct 89511
La Rue Ave 89509
La Tierra Ter 89502
Ladonia Ct 89506
Ladybug Ct 89523
Lafayette Ln 89509
Lago Ct 89508
Lahontan Way 89509
Laiolo Dr 89502
S Lake St 89501
Lake Geneva Ct & Dr 89511
Lake Hills Ct 89508
Lake Placid Dr 89511
Lake Powell Dr 89508
E & W Lake Ridge Shrs 89519
Lake Ridge Shores Cir 89519
Lakeland Hills Ct & Dr 89523
Lakeridge Dr & Ter 89509
Lakeridge Terrace Ln 89509
Lakeside Ct 89509
Lakeside Dr
1501-1597 89509
1599-4800 89509
4802-4998 89509
6101-6897 89511
6899-8799 89511
8801-8899 89511
Lakeview Dr 89510
Lakewood Ct 89509
Lamay Cir & Ln 89511
Lamour Ln 89521
Lampe Rd 89511
Lampshire Dr 89506
Lampson Ln 89509
Lancaster Dr 89506
Lanceleaf Ct 89508
Lancelot Way 89509
Lancer St 89523
Lander St 89509
Landerwood Dr 89511
Landybank Ct 89519
Lapwing Ln 89509
E & W Laramie Dr 89521
Larch Rd 89502
Laredo Ct 89503
Lark Bunting Ct 89523
Larkspur St 89512
Larrea Ln 89511
Larson Ranch Rd 89508
Las Brisas Blvd 89523
Lasalle Hts 89523
Lassen Dr 89503
Lasso Dr 89511
Last Chance Ct 89511
Latigo Ct & Dr 89519
Latour Way 89511
Laurel St 89512
Laurel Park Way 89502
Laurel Ridge Ct & Dr 89523
Laurelwood Dr 89519
Laurent Dr 89508
Lausanne Dr 89511
Lavender Way 89521
Leadfield Ave 89506
Leah Cir 89511
Lear Blvd 89506
Leather Ln 89506
Leche Way 89502
Lee Ave 89501
Leeward Ct & Ln 89502
Left Hand Canyon Rd 89510
N & S Legacy Ct 89521
Legacy Village Rd 89521
Legend Vis 89511
Legend View Ct 89511
Lehigh Dr 89502
Leisure Ln 89502
Lemke Ct 89521
Lemming Dr 89523
Lemmon Dr 89506
Len Cir 89511
Lenco Ave 89506
E Leonesio Dr 89512
Leopard St 89506
Leroy St 89523
Lescon Cir 89509
Lester Ave 89502
Lestra Way 89506
Leventina Canyon Rd 89523
Lewis St 89502
E & W Liberty St 89501
Libra Cir 89521
Lighthouse Ct & Ln 89511
Lilac Ln 89512
Lillian Way 89509
Lily Ct 89512
Limber Pine Dr 89506
Limestone Dr 89511
Limkin St 89508
Limnol St 89506
Limonite Ct 89521
Lincoln Meadows Dr 89521
Linden St 89502
Lindley Way 89509
Lindsay Dr 89523
Lingfield Dr 89502
Linwood Pl 89509
Lipizzan Ln 89508
Lisa Ct 89503

Liston Ave 89502
Litch Ct 89509
Little Creek Rd 89508
Little Peak Ct 89508
Little River Ct 89506
Little Sorrel Ct 89521
Little Valley Ct & Rd 89508
Live Oak Ct 89508
Livermore Dr 89519
Livery Rd 89521
Llama Ct 89511
Lloyd Way 89502
Lobelia Ln 89511
Locksley Way 89503
Lockspur Ct 89508
Locust St 89502
Lodestar Ln 89503
Lodge Ave 89503
Lodgepole Pine Ct 89523
Logan Meadow Ln 89511
Logan Ridge Ct 89523
Loki Ct 89512
Loma Vista Ln 89502
Lombardi Rd 89511
Londonderry Ct 89511
Lone Desert Dr 89506
Lone Eagle Ct 89521
Lone Horse Ct & Dr 89502
Lone Oak Trl 89523
Lone Tree Ln 89511
Lone Wolf Cir 89506
Lonepine Ct 89519
Lonesome Spur Dr 89521
Lonestar Cir 89508
Long Hollow Dr 89521
Long River Dr 89506
Long Valley Rd
1000-1499 89508
1500-1598 89521
Longhorn Dr 89508
Longhorn Ln 89510
Longknife Rd 89519
Longley Ln
2000-4999 89502
5001-5197 89511
5199-7599 89511
Longview Ln 89506
Longwood Dr 89509
Lookout Pl 89503
Loon Ct 89508
Loreto Ln 89502
Lorraine Ct 89509
Lost Spring Rd 89510
Lost Valley Rd 89521
Lott Pl 89502
Lotus St 89506
Louie Ln 89511
Louise St 89502
Lousetown Rd 89521
Lovitt Ln 89506
Lucente Way 89521
Luciana Dr 89521
Lucky Ln 89502
Lucy Ave 89512
Lunsford Ct 89511
Lurie Ln 89511
Luxury Ln 89502
Lyman Ave 89509
Lymbery St 89509
Lynnfield Ct & Way 89519
Lynrock Cir 89523
Lynx St 89506
N Lytton Ct & Rd 89506
Macauley Way 89506
Macaw Ln 89508
Macfarlane Rd 89511
Macgregor Ln 89511
Mackay Ct 89503
Mackey Ct 89512
N & S Maddux Dr 89512
Madeline Jane Ln 89503
Madera Ct 89523
Madison Marie Ln 89503
Mae Anne Ave 89523
Maestro Dr 89511
Magellan Ct 89506
Maggie Cir & Ln 89511
Magistrate Ct 89521
Magnetite Dr 89508
Magnolia Way 89506
Magnum Cir 89512
Mahogany Cir & Dr 89511
Mahogany Ridge Dr 89523
Mahon Dr 89506
Maine St 89502
Majestic Ct & Dr 89503
Majestic View Ct & Dr 89521
Makenna Dr 89521
Malachite Ct 89506
Malcolm Ave 89506
Malibu Dr 89506
Mallard Pl 89503
Mallory Ln 89511
Malone Ln 89502
Mama Bear Ct 89508
Mammoth Dr 89521
Man Of War Dr 89502
Manassas Dr 89508
Manciano Way 89521
Mandan Way 89506
Manhattan St 89512
Mankato Dr 89511
Mannington Ave 89512
Manor Dr 89509
Manzanita Cir & Ln 89509
Maple Creek Ct 89511
Maple Leaf Trl 89523
Maplewood Dr 89509
Mar Mac Way 89506
Marango Rd 89521
Marble Canyon Rd 89511
Marble Creek Ct 89506
Marble Ridge Ct 89511
Marbrook Ct 89519
E & W Marchmont Ct & Ln 89511
Margaret Dr 89506
Margarita Ct 89511
Margaux Pl & Rd 89511
Margot Cir 89509
Margrave Dr 89502
Marigene Ct 89509
Marina Cir 89519
Mariner Cove Ct & Dr 89506
Marinette Ct 89523
Mario Rd 89523
Marjay Ct 89512
Mark Allen Cir 89503
Mark Twain Ave 89509
Market St 89502
Markridge Dr 89509
Marla Dr 89509
Marlette Ave 89503
Marlin Dr 89506
Marmot Dr 89523
Marne Dr 89503
Marsh Ave & Ct 89509
Marshal Rd 89508
Marta Way 89503
Marthiam Ave 89509
Martin St 89509
Martingale Ct 89521
Marvel Way 89502
Marvin Way 89503
Mary St 89509
Maryland St 89506
Mason Rd 89506
Masters Dr 89511
Matich Dr 89502
Matley Ln 89502
Matterhorn Blvd & Ct 89506
Matthews St 89506
Maui Ct 89506
Mauldin Ln 89502
Mauna Cir 89502
Maverick Ln 89511
Maxfli Dr 89523
May Rose Cir 89502
Mayberry Dr
1-3699 89509
3701-3797 89519
3799-5099 89519
5101-5599 89519
Mayfield Ct 89508
Mayflower Dr 89509
Mazzone Ave 89502
Mccabe Dr 89511
N Mccarran Blvd
1000-1198 89512
1200-1299 89512
1301-1399 89512
7701-7799 89503
10100-10998 89503
S Mccarran Blvd
1701-3297 89502
3299-4099 89502
4101-5099 89502
6000-6298 89509
6300-6400 89509
6402-6998 89509
9500-9798 89523
Mccauley Ranch Dr 89521
Mccloud Ave 89512
Mcdaniel St 89506
Mcdonald Dr 89503
Mcgee Dr 89523
Mckinley Dr 89509
Mcnevin Ct 89509
Meadow St 89509
Meadow Brook Dr 89519
Meadow Country Dr 89519
Meadow Creek Dr 89519
Meadow Crest Cir 89519
Meadow Edge Ct & Dr 89502
Meadow Glen Ct 89519
Meadow Grass Dr 89502
Meadow Heights Cir 89519
Meadow Hill Cir & Dr 89519
Meadow Rock Ln 89511
Meadow Springs Dr 89509
Meadow Valley Ln 89519
Meadow Vista Ct & Dr 89511
Meadow Wood Ln 89502
Meadowgate Ct & Trl 89519
Meadowlark Dr 89508
Meadowood Mall Cir 89502
Meadowridge Dr 89519
S Meadows Pkwy 89521
Meadowstar Dr 89506
Meadowview Ln 89509
Medford Dr 89511
Medgar Ave 89506
Meeks Way 89503
Meeks Bay Ct 89521
Melarky Way 89511
Melba Dr 89503
Melbourne Ct 89523
Melody Ln 89512
Melrose Dr 89502
Memory Cir & Ln 89509
Menagerie Ave 89511
Mendocino Ln 89502
Mendota Ct 89509
Menlo Ct 89509
Mercury Dr 89521
Meridian Ct & Ln 89509
Meridian Ranch Dr 89523
Mesa Cir & Rd 89511
Mesa Grande Ct 89502
Mesa Park Rd 89523
Mescalero Ave & Ct 89523
Mesquite Ave 89508
Messina Ct & Way 89521
Mexicali Ct 89502
Meyers Ave 89506
Mia Vista Ct & Dr 89502
Miami Way 89502
Michaela Dr 89511
Mick Cir 89511
Microwave Rd 89510
Middlecoff Cir 89502
Miesque Ct 89521
Mildrae Ln 89511
Mile Circle Dr 89511
Military Rd 89506
Mill St
200-398 89501
400-5400 89502
5402-5598 89502
Millbrook Ln 89509
Millenium Cir 89512
Miller Pl 89506
Millie Ln 89511
Millpond Ct 89523
Milton Cir 89506
E Minaret Cir 89523
Mindi Ln 89512
Miner Ln 89521
Mineral Flat Rd 89506
Minerva Ln 89503
Mini Way 89521
Minnetonka Cir 89521
Mira St 89521
Mira Loma Dr 89502
Mirror Lake Ct & Dr 89511
Mission Cir 89503
Missoula Ct 89511
Mistletoe St 89506
Mistral Ct 89511
Misty Ct 89511
Misty Meadows Dr 89521
Mistyridge Ct & Ln 89523
Mitra Way 89523
Mizpah Cir 89508
Moab Ct 89511
E Moana Ln 89502
W Moana Ln 89509
Mobile Manor Dr 89506
Moccasin Ct 89521
Mockingbird Ct & Dr 89508
Model Way 89502
Modoc St 89509
Mogul Rd 89523
Mogul Mountain Cir & Dr 89523
Mohawk Ln 89506
Monitor Dr 89512
Monroe Ct & St 89509
Mont Blanc Ct 89511
Mont Pelier Ct 89511
Montana Dr 89503
Montano Ranch Ct 89511
Montclair Ave 89509
Monte Rosa Ct 89511
Monte Vista Dr 89511
Montego Ct & Dr 89523
Montelena Ct 89521
Montello St 89512
Monterey Cir & Dr 89509
Monterey Shores Dr 89506
Montgomery Way 89506
Monticello Ct 89519
Montreux Ln 89511
Moon Ln 89521
Moon Ridge Cir & Ter 89523
Moon Shadow Ct & Dr 89523
Moondust Ct 89506
Moonrise Ct 89511
Moonset Ct 89506
Moonshine Cir 89523
Moonstone Ln 89508
Moonwalk Ct 89506
Moore Ln 89509
Moose Ridge Dr 89523
Moose River Ct 89523
Moquith Ct 89521
Moraine Way 89503
Moran St
100-299 89501
300-799 89502
Morgan Rd 89521
Morgan Hill Ct 89523
Morgan Pointe Cir & Ct 89523
Moriah Dr 89508
Mormon Tea Way 89511
Morning Breeze Ct & Dr 89508
Morning Dove Rd 89510
Morning Grove Ct 89523
Morning Song Trl 89511
Morning Star Ct & Dr 89523
Morningside Dr 89509
Morrill Ave 89512
Morrill Hall Ct 89512
Moss Creek Ct & Dr 89506
Moss Rock Ct 89521
Moss Wood Ct 89521
Moth Cir 89506
Moulin Rouge Ct 89511
Mount Anderson St 89506
Mount Babcock St 89506
Mount Baldy St 89506
Mount Bismark St 89506
Mount Charleston St 89506
Mount Dana Dr 89506
Mount Diablo Dr 89506
Mount Evans Ct & Dr 89508
Mount Grant Dr 89523
Mount Hood St 89506
Mount Jefferson Dr 89508
Mount Lassen St 89506
Mount Lewis Ct 89508
Mount Logan St 89506
Mount Lola St 89506
Mount Mahogany Ct 89511
Mount Mcclellan St 89506
Mount Olympus St 89506
Mount Pleasant Dr 89523
Mount Rainier St 89506
Mount Rose Hwy 89511
Mount Rose St 89509
Mount Sage Ct 89506
Mount Shasta St 89506
Mount Snow Ct & Dr 89511
Mount Vida St 89506
Mount Whitney St 89506
Mountain Ln 89521
Mountain Air Ct 89511
Mountain Bluebird Dr 89511
Mountain Dew Cir 89523
Mountain Haven Ln 89511
Mountain Lion Dr 89510
Mountain Meadow Ln 89511
Mountain Quail Ct 89502
Mountain Ranch Rd 89511
Mountain Ridge Rd 89523
Mountain Shadow Ln 89511
Mountain Spirit Trl 89523
Mountain Springs Rd 89519
Mountain Sweep Way 89511
Mountain Top Rd 89521
Mountain View Dr 89509
Mountain Vista Way 89519
Mountaingate Dr 89519
Mountainshyre Rd 89519
Mountcrest Ct & Ln 89523
Moya Blvd 89506
Mud Springs Rd 89508
Mueller Dr 89509
Mugo Pine Cir 89511
Muir Dr 89503
Muirfield Ct 89511
Muirwood Cir & Ct 89509
Mule Cir 89521
Mule Creek Cir 89511
Mule Deer Ct & Dr 89523
Mules Ear Ct 89511
Muletail Cir 89508
Munley Dr 89503
Murphy Pl 89521
Murrieta Ct 89521
Muscat Ct 89512
Musket Rd 89521
Mustang Ct 89502
Mustang Rd 89521
Mustang Trail Ct & Dr 89506
Mustengo Ct & Dr 89506
Myrtlewood Cir 89511
Myrtlewood Parklet 89511
Nadia Ct 89511
Nambe Dr 89511
Nancy Cir 89503
Nannette Cir 89502
Nanook Ct 89506
Napoleon Ct & Dr 89511
Narrowleaf Ct 89508
Natalie St 89509
Natasha Way 89512
Nathan Stephen Ct 89503
National Guard Way 89502
Native Dancer Dr & Pl 89502
Nature Trl 89511
Navajo Crest Dr 89506
Navajo Ridge Dr 89506
Navigator Dr 89521
Nectar St 89506
Needles Ct 89521
Neil Cir 89502
Neil Rd
3100-3198 89502
3200-4920 89502
4922-5278 89502
6100-6199 89511
6201-6299 89511
Neil Way 89502
Neilson Rd 89521
Nemaha Creek Ct 89519
Neptune Ct 89512
Nestle Ct 89511
Nevada St 89503
New Mexico Ct 89511
New Pass Rd 89521
Newburgh Way 89523
Newcastle Way 89512
Newcomer Ln 89506
Newlands Cir & Ln 89509
Newport Ct & Ln 89506
Newton Ln 89509
Niagra Ct 89506
Nicholaus Dr 89502
Nicholette Dr 89503
Nicia St 89506
Nighthawk Cir 89523
Nightowl Dr 89523
Niles Ct & Way 89506
Nina Ave 89512
Nine Mile Ct 89508
Nixon Ave
300-398 89501
500-1599 89509
Noche Ln 89502
Nola Way 89506
Nordend Way 89511
Norman Cir & Dr 89509
North Ave 89508
Northcreek Dr 89506
Northern Lights Dr 89506
Northern Pine Ct 89523
Northmont Ln 89521
Northridge Ave 89508
Northrup Ct & Dr 89521
Northshore Dr 89519
Northstar Dr 89503
Northtowne Ln 89512
Norton Dr 89506
Nottingham Ct 89511
Novato Ct 89502
Novelly Dr 89503
Nugget Rd 89521
Nut Tree Ln 89509
Nutmeg Pl 89502
Nyala St 89512
O Farrell Ct & St 89503
O Hara St 89510
Oak St 89503
Oak Creek Dr 89511
Oak Glen Dr 89511
Oak Grass Ct 89511
Oak Hollow Way 89523
Oakbrook Ct & Ln 89508
Oakhaven Dr 89521
Oakhurst Ave 89509
Oakley Ct & Ln 89521
Oakshire Ct 89509
Oakview Ct 89508
Oberholtzer Ct 89506
Obsidian Ct & Dr 89506
Ocelet Pl & Way 89511
Octate Cir 89511
Octavia Ct 89509
Oddie Blvd 89512
Odile Ct 89511
Odin Way 89512
Offenhauser Dr 89511
Ohio St 89506
Ohm Pl 89502
Oklahoma St 89506
Old Coach Ct & Way 89511
Old Virginia Rd 89521
Oldenburg Ct & Dr 89521
Olive Ln & Pl 89511
Oliver St 89512
Olmsted Ct 89519
Olympic Cir 89509
Omaha St 89506
Onyx Way 89509
E & W Opal Ct 89508
Opal Bluff Dr 89506
Opal Glen Way 89506
Opal Ranch Way 89506
Opal Ridge Dr 89506
Opal Star Dr 89506
Opal Station Dr 89506
Opalite Ct 89521
Orange Ln 89502
Orca Way 89506
Orchard Hill Dr 89511
Orchard Park Trl 89523
Orchid Way 89512
Ordway Ave 89509
Oreana Dr 89509
Oregon Blvd 89506
Ormand Ct 89502
Ornellaia Way 89521
Orovada St 89512
Orrcrest Dr 89506
Osage Ct & Rd 89508
Osceola Ct 89506
Osgood Pl 89509
Otter Way 89521
Outback Ln 89510
Outlaw Ln 89508
Outlook Dr 89509
Ouzel Way 89508
Overbrook Ct & Dr 89511
Overland Rd
1300-4299 89521
11500-12099 89506
12900-13298 89521
Overland Park Dr 89521
Overlook Ct 89509
Owens Rd 89506
Owl Ct 89508
Ox Yoke Ln 89521
Oxbow Ct 89511
Oxcart Ct 89521
Ozark St 89506
Paddington Ct 89511
Paddlewheel Ln 89521
Paddock Ln 89521
Page Meadows Dr 89521
Pagni Ln 89521
Pagoda Way 89506
Pah Rah Springs Rd 89510
Painted Trl 89511
Painted River Trl 89523
Painted Rock Trl 89523
Painted Vista Dr 89511
Paisano Ct 89511
Pajaro Pl 89502
Palace Ct & Dr 89506
Palamino Rd 89521
Palisade Dr 89509
Palisade Rd 89521
Palm Cir 89509
Palmer Ct 89502
Palmer Pointe Ct 89511
Palmetto Ct 89523
Palmira Dr 89511
Paloma Way 89506
Palomino Cir 89519
Palos Verdes Cir 89502
Pamela Ave 89502
Pan American Ct & Dr 89506
Pan Zareta Ct 89521
Panamint Dr 89506
Panamint Rd 89521
Panda Bear Ct 89508
Panhandle Rd
15600-15799 89508
21900-22000 89521

22002-22098 89521
Panorama Dr 89511
Panorama Ridge Ct & Dr 89511
Panther Dr 89506
Panther Valley Dr 89506
Papa Bear Ct 89508
Parade Ct 89521
Paradise Dr 89512
Paragon Pl 89509
Paramount Ct 89506
Paris Ave & Ct 89511
Parisian Ct 89511
Park Pl 89523
N Park St 89512
S Park St 89502
Park Hollow Ct 89523
Park Rose Cir 89502
Park Valley Ct 89523
Parkpoint Ct 89502
Parkridge Cir 89509
Parkview St 89502
Parkvista Ct 89502
Parkway Dr 89502
Parma Ct & Way 89521
Parque Verde Ln 89502
Parr Blvd & Cir 89512
Parrot Dr 89508
Partei Valley Rd 89510
Pasado Ct 89508
Paso Fino Ct 89521
Pass Dr 89509
Passa Tempo Dr 89511
Pastantr Dr 89523
Pasture View Rd 89510
Pathfinder Dr 89508
Patidar Dr 89509
Patricia Ln 89512
E & W Patrician Dr 89506
Patrick Ave 89509
E & W Patriot Blvd 89511
Patti Ln 89511
Patton Dr 89512
Paul St 89506
Pawnee Ct & Way 89506
Paxton Ln 89506
Peace Pipe Ct & Loop 89511
Peaceful Valley Dr 89521
Peacock Pl 89508
Peak Rd 89510
Peavine Ct & Rd 89503
Peavine Creek Ct & Rd 89523
Peavine Hills Ave 89523
Peavine Peak Ct 89523
Peavine Pines Ct 89523
Peavine Shadow Ct 89523
Peavine Trail Ct 89523
Peavine Valley Rd 89523
Peavine View Ct 89523
Pebble Ct 89508
Pebble Beach Dr 89502
Pebble Hill Dr 89521
Pebblestone Way 89523
Pecetti Cir 89511
E Peckham Ln 89502
W Peckham Ln 89509
Pedretti Rd 89502
Pelham Dr 89502
Pembroke Dr 89502
Pendleton Pl 89506
Penfield Cir 89502
Pennswood Way 89509
Pennsylvania Dr 89503
Penrose Dr 89503
Pentwater Dr 89521
Pepper Way 89506
Peppermint Ct & Dr 89506
Pepperwood Ct 89523
Pequop St 89512
Percheron Dr 89508
Peregrine Cir & Ct 89508
Perlite Dr 89521
Perro Ct & Ln 89502
Perryville Dr 89521
Persimmon Rd 89502
Pesaro Way 89521
Pescado Way 89502
Peter Cir 89503
Petrel Ct 89508
Pheasant Ln 89509
Phillips St 89509
Philoree Ln 89511
Piazzo Cir 89502
Piccadilly Ct & Dr 89509
Pickard Pl 89501
Pickens Dr 89511
Pickering Cir 89511
Picket Ct 89521
Piedmont Pl 89502
Pierremont Rd 89503
Pike St 89512
Pimlico St 89512
Pin Oak Ct 89508
Pine St 89501
Pine Grove Dr 89506
Pine Knolls Ln 89521
Pine Tree Ct 89506
Pine Valley Dr 89511
Pine View Ct 89511
Pinebluff Trl 89519
Pinebough Ct 89509
Pinebrook Rd 89509
Pinecrest Ct 89523
Pinehaven Ct & Rd 89519
Pinehurst Cir 89502
E Pinenut Ct 89509
W Pinenut Ct 89509
Pinenut Rd 89521
Pineridge Dr 89509
Pinesprings Dr 89509
W Pinewild Rd 89511
Piney Creek Rd 89511
Piney Woods Ct 89519
Pinion Dr 89521
Pinion Wood Ct & Dr 89506
Pinnacle Ct 89523
Pinon Pine Ave 89508
Pinto Dr & Pl 89519
Pintura Ct 89508
Pioche Rd 89510
Pioneer Dr 89509
Pioneer Ridge Ct 89506
Piper Pl 89506
Piping Rock Cir & Dr 89502
Pisa Dr 89509
Pisces Cir 89521
Piute Creek Rd 89510
Placerville Dr 89508
Placerwood Trl 89523
Plainview Ct 89523
Plata Mesa Dr 89508
Plateau Ct & Rd 89519
Platinum Pointe Way 89506
Platinum Ridge Ct 89523
Platora Way 89512
Platte River Ct & Dr 89503
E Plaza St 89501
Pleasant Hills Ct & Dr 89523
Pleasant Valley Dr 89521
Pleasure Dr 89509
Plott Cir 89511
Plover Pl 89502
Plum Hollow Cir 89502
Plum Tree Ct 89523
Plumas St
500-4600 89509
4602-5098 89509
6000-6199 89519
E Plumb Ln 89502
W Plumb Ln 89509
Poeville Ln 89523
Polaris St 89521
Pole Rd 89506
Poleline Rd 89511
Polk St 89503
Polo Park Dr 89523
Polson St 89503
Pomarius Ct 89512
Pomerol Dr 89511
Pomo Dr 89503
Pompe Way 89506
Ponderosa Pine Ct 89519
Pontiac Dr 89506
Pony Springs Rd 89510
Popinjay Dr 89509
Poplar St 89512
Poppy Ln 89512
Porter Cir 89509
Portland Dr 89511
Postre Ct 89502
Posy Lake Ct 89508
Powder Dr 89503
Powder River Ct & Dr 89511
Powderkeg Cir 89519
Powell Ln 89502
Power Plant Rd 89511
Prairie Rd 89510
Prairie Way 89506
Prairie Dog Ct 89508
Prairie Flower Ct 89511
Prairie Rose Pl 89521
Preakness Ct 89521
Prescott Way 89509
Prestige Ct 89506
Preston Burr Ln 89503
Prestwick Cir 89502
Pries Ct 89523
Primavera Ave 89502
Primrose St 89509
Primula Way 89511
Prince Way 89503
Prince Charles Ct 89503
Princequillo Ct 89521
Princess Ave 89502
Princeton Dr 89502
Pringle Way 89502
Prior Rd 89503
Production Dr 89506
Professional Cir 89521
Promontory Dr 89523
Promontory Pointe 89519
Pronghorn Ct 89519
Prospect Rd 89521
Prospect Hill Rd 89506
Prosperity St 89502
Prototype Ct & Dr 89521
Provence Cir 89523
Provo Ct 89511
E Pueblo St 89502
W Pueblo St 89509
Puffin St 89508
Purdue Dr 89502
Purple Sage Dr 89506
Putnam Ct & Dr 89503
Pyramid Way 89510
Quail Bar Ct 89521
Quail Canyon Ranch Rd 89510
Quail Creek Ct 89519
Quail Hollow Dr 89511
Quail Manor Ct 89511
Quail Meadows Ct 89519
Quail Ravine Ct 89511
Quail Rock Ct & Ln 89511
Quail Run Rd 89523
Quail Springs Ct 89511
Quailwood Dr 89521
Quaking Aspen Rd 89510
Quarry Ct 89508
Quarry Rock Ct 89506
Quarterhorse Cir 89508
Quartz Star Ct 89506
Quartzite Dr 89523
Queen Anne Ct 89509
Questa Ct 89511
Quicksilver Dr 89511
S Quiet Meadow Ct & Dr 89511
Quilberry Way 89523
Quilici Ln 89511
Quincy St 89512
Rabbit Brush Ct 89511
Rabbit Ridge Ct 89511
Raccoon Ct 89523
Radar St 89502
Radcliffe Dr 89502
Radford Dr 89511
Raffetto Dr 89512
Raggio Pkwy 89512
Raider Run Rd 89511
Rain Dance Way 89506
E & W Rainbow Ridge Ct & Rd 89523
Rainbow Trout Ct 89523
Rainier Ct & Dr 89508
Rainmaker Ct 89511
Rainna Ct 89509
Rainshadow Ln 89519
Raintree Ct 89511
Rainwood Ct 89509
Ralston St 89503
Ramcreek Trl 89519
Ramona Rd 89521
Rampart Ter 89519
Ramrod Cir 89519
Ramsey Way 89506
Ranch Crest Dr 89509
Ranch Land Cir 89511
N & S Ranch Vista Ct 89509
Rancheros Dr 89521
Ranchita Way 89502
Rancho Dr 89508
Rancho Manor Dr 89509
Rancho Verde Dr 89521
Ranchview Ct 89509
Randolph Ct & Dr 89502
Range Land Rd 89510
Range View Ct & Ln 89519
W Ranger Rd 89506
Rapid Creek Ct 89506
Raptor St 89508
Rauscher Dr 89503
Ravazza Rd 89521
Raven Way 89509
Ravenswood Way 89521
Ravine Ct 89508
Rawhide Dr 89521
Rayburn Dr 89503
Rayma Ct 89503
Raymond Dr 89503
Raytheon Ct 89506
Reactor Way 89502
Reanon Ct 89509
Rebel Cause Rd 89510
Record St 89512
Red Baron Blvd & Ct 89506
Red Bird Dr 89523
Red Corral Trl 89510
Red Fox Ct 89511
Red Gulch Ct 89521
Red Maple Ct 89523
Red Pine Rd 89506
N Red Rock Rd 89508
Red Willow Dr 89521
Reddawn Dr 89523
Redfield Pkwy 89509
Redmond Dr & Loop 89511
Redstone Dr 89512
Redwood Pl 89502
Reed St 89512
Reese Way 89521
Reeves Ave 89503
Regal Ct & Dr 89503
Regency Way 89509
Regent St 89509
Reggie Rd 89502
Relevant Ct 89521
Remington Rd 89506
Renaissance Ct 89523
Renee Way 89503
Renegade Ct 89511
Reno Ave 89509
Reno Corporate Dr 89511
S Reno Park Blvd 89508
Reno View Ct & Dr 89523
Reno Vista Dr 89512
Renzo Way 89521
Reservation Rd 89502
Reservoir St 89506
Resistol Dr 89521
Resource Dr 89506
Reuben Dr 89502
Rewana Way 89502
Rhinestone Cir & Dr 89511
Rhode Island Dr 89503
Rhodes Rd 89521
Rhyolite Cir & Ct 89521
Riata Cir & Ct 89521
Ribeiro Cir 89503
Richter Dr 89509
Rick Cir 89511
Ridge Ln 89523
Ridge St 89501
Ridge Field Trl 89523
Ridge Star Ct 89521
Ridgebrooke Dr 89521
Ridgecrest Cir, Ct & Dr 89512
Ridgegate Cir 89523
Ridgeview Ct 89519
Ridgeview Dr
900-958 89511
960-999 89511
1001-1397 89519
1399-1499 89519
1501-2299 89519
Ridgeview Ter 89519
Ridgeway Ct 89503
Riesling Loop 89512
Riggins Ct 89502
Right Hand Canyon Rd 89510
Riley Ave 89502
Rillough Rd 89511
Rim Rock Dr 89521
Rimfire Cir 89519
Rio Ct 89508
Rio Bravo Ct & Dr 89521
Rio Encantado Ln 89502
Rio Grande Dr 89521
Rio Lobo Ln 89521
Rio Pinar Dr 89509
Rio Poco Rd 89502
Rio Rico Ct 89523
Rio Wrangler Pkwy 89521
Ripple Way 89521
Rising Moon Dr 89506
Rising Sun Ct & Dr 89506
Rissone Ln 89503
River Ln 89519
River Bend Dr 89523
River Birch Dr 89511
River Flow Ct & Dr 89523
River Front Ct & Dr 89523
River Gorge Ct & Dr 89521
River Hill Way 89523
River Oaks Ct 89511
River Park Ct 89523
River Rock St 89501
River Run Pkwy 89509
Riverberry Dr 89509
Riverbrook Ct 89519
Riverhaven Dr & Pl 89519
Riverside Dr 89503
Riverstone Ct 89506
E Riverview Cir 89509
W Riverview Cir 89509
Riverview Rd 89521
Riviera St 89509
Rivolli Ct & Dr 89521
Road Runner Rd 89510
Roan Trl 89511
Roanoke Trl 89523
Robb Ct & Dr 89523
Roberts St 89502
Robilee Ct & Dr 89521
Robin Pl & St 89509
Robinhood Dr 89509
Robinson Ct 89503
S Rock Blvd 89502
Rock Creek Ct 89511
Rock Crossing Dr 89511
Rock Farm Rd 89511
Rock Haven Dr 89511
Rock Hill Cir 89519
Rock Ridge Ct 89512
Rock River Dr 89506
Rock Springs Ct 89511
Rock Wren Cir 89509
Rockchuck Rd 89506
Rockcrawler Dr 89521
Rockhurst Ct 89523
Rockport Ln 89521
Rockview Dr 89519
Rocky Rd 89521
Rocky Cove Ln 89521
Rocky Flats Ct 89502
Rocky Meadow Cir 89511
Rocky Mountain St 89506
Rocky Point Trl 89506
Rocky Vista Ct & Rd 89521
Rodeo Dr 89508
Rodney Dr 89509
Roff Way 89501
Rogue River Ct 89508
Rolling Brook Ct & Ln 89519
Rolling Clouds Dr 89506
Rolling Ridge Ct & Rd 89506
Rolling Rock Ct & Way 89521
Rolling Sage Pl 89506
Roma Ct 89523
Romagnola Ct 89511
Rombauer Ct 89519
Romero Way 89509
Ron Way 89521
Roper Ct & Ln 89508
Rory Cir 89511
Rosalinda Dr 89503
Rose Cir 89509
Rose Creek Ln 89511
Rose Garden Ct 89509
Rose Knob Dr 89508
Rose Meadow Ct 89511
Rose Mist Ct 89521
Rose Peak Ct 89511
Rose Rock Ln 89511
Rose Vista Dr 89502
Roseben Ct 89521
Rosehill Ct 89502
Rosemount Dr 89521
Roseview Ln 89511
Rosewood Dr 89509
Ross Dr 89519
Rossow Ln 89510
Rouge Ct & Dr 89511
Rough Rock Dr 89502
Round Robin Ln 89502
Roundrock Ct 89511
Roundup Rd 89508
Rowel Cir 89508
Rowland Cir & Rd 89509
Roxbury Ct & Dr 89523
Roy St 89506
Royal Dr 89503
Royal Crown Ct 89503
Royal Sage Ct & Dr 89503
Royal Vista Ct & Way 89523
Royal Windsor Ct 89521
Royer Ct 89509
Ruby Ave 89503
Ruby Creek Ct & Ln 89506
Ruby Hill Rd 89506
Ruby Mountain Rd 89506
Ruby Ridge Ln 89506
Ruby Star Ct 89506
Rue D Azur 89511
Rue D Flore 89511
Rue Du Parc 89511
Rue Saint Michelle 89511
Rue St Raphael 89511
Rue St Tropez 89511
Ruffian Ct 89521
Running Bear Ln 89506
Running Dog Cir 89506
Runway Dr 89506
Rushing Flume Dr 89521
Russell Pointe Ct 89523
Rustic Manor Cir 89509
Rusty Rd 89511
Rusty Nail Ct & Dr 89521
Ruth Ct 89509
Rutherford Dr 89506
Ryan Ln 89503
Ryegate Dr 89508
Ryegrass Ct 89509
Ryland St
100-399 89501
401-497 89502
499-1000 89502
1002-1298 89502
Sacred Garden Ct 89511
Saddle Ln & Rd 89508
Saddle Blanket Trl 89510
Saddle Ridge Ct 89509
Saddleback Rd 89521
W Saddlebow Ct & Dr 89511
S Saddlehorn Dr & Pl 89511
Saddlespur Rd 89511
Saddletree Trl 89523
Sadleir Way 89512
Safari Ct 89510
Safe Harbor Way 89512
Sage St 89512
Sage Bluff Ct 89523
Sage Canyon Rd 89510
Sage Flat Rd 89510
Sage Grouse Ct 89523
Sage Hill Rd 89521
Sage Point Ct 89506
Sage Ridge Dr 89509
Sage Rose Way 89502
Sage Sparrow Cir 89509
Sageberry Ct 89509
Sagehen Ln 89506
Sageland Way 89506
Sagewood Dr 89506
Sagittarius Ct & Dr 89509
Saint Alberts Dr 89503
Saint Andrews Ct & Dr 89502
Saint Arms Cir 89506
Saint Lawrence Ave 89509
Salazar Ln 89509
Salem Pl 89509
Salerno Dr 89509
Sally Pl 89509
Salman Way 89506
Salt Brush Ct 89511
Samuel Way 89509
San Clemente Dr 89511
San Donato Loop 89519
San Fernando Rd 89508
San Gabriel Dr 89502
San Joaquin Dr 89521
San Jose Ct 89521
San Juan Cir & Dr 89509
San Lorenzo Dr 89521
San Marcos Ln 89502
San Mateo Ave & Cir 89509
San Pablo Dr 89521
San Ramon Dr 89521
San Simeon Ct 89509
San Sorrento St 89509
Sand Cherry Ct 89511
Sand Hollow Ct 89521
Sand Pebble Dr 89506
Sand Wedge Ln 89523
Sandestin Dr 89523
Sandhaven Ct 89506
Sandhill Rd 89521
Sandia Ct & Dr 89523
Sandlewood Ct 89523
Sandoval Rd 89511
Sandpiper Dr 89508
Sandpoint Cir 89509
Sandra Dr 89503
Sandstone Dr 89511
Sandyhill Ln 89523
Sangre Cir 89511
Santa Ana Dr 89502
Santa Fe Rd 89508
Santa Maria Dr 89502
Sapphire Cir 89509
Sapphire Canyon Ct 89508
Sapphire Ridge Ct & Way 89523
Sarah Ct 89509
Sarah Beth Ln 89503
Sarava Ct 89512
Sarcinella Ct 89509

Sarment Ct 89506
Saturn Cir 89521
Saturno Heights Dr 89523
Sauer Ln 89521
Sauk Ct 89506
Sauvignon Ct & Dr 89506
Sawbuck Rd 89519
Sawtooth Trl 89523
Sazarac Rd 89521
Scarlet Way 89521
N & S Scarsdale Cir 89502
Scattergun Cir 89519
Scenic Hill Cir 89523
Scenic Park Ter 89521
Scepter Ct 89503
Scharr Cir 89509
Schellbourne St 89511
Scholl Dr 89503
Schooner Cir & Dr 89519
Scorpio Cir 89521
Scorpion Rd 89521
Scotch Pine Cir & Rd 89511
Scott Valley Ct & Rd 89523
Scottsdale Rd 89512
Scowens Rd 89506
Seabiscuit Dr 89521
Seal Beach Dr 89506
Searchlite Ct 89503
Seattle Slew Ct 89521
Sebastian Cir 89503
Secluded Cir 89509
Secret Pass Ct & Rd 89521
Secretariat Ct 89521
Security Cir 89506
Selmi Dr 89512
Semillon Ct 89512
Seminary Ave 89503
Seminole Trl 89521
Seneca Dr 89506
Sentinel Cir 89509
September Cir 89523
Sequoia Ln 89502
Serena Dr 89503
Serenity Pl 89510
Serpentine Rd 89506
Serratina Dr 89521
Seth Ln 89510
Settler Ct & Dr 89502
Seven Pines Ct 89521
Severn Dr 89503
Seville Ct 89523
Sewell Dr 89521
Seymour Ave 89506
Shadelands Ct 89523
Shadow Brook Ct 89509
Shadow Creek Ct 89519
Shadow Dancer Trl 89511
Shadow Hills Dr 89521
Shadow Park Dr 89523
Shadow Wood Ct & Rd 89523
Shadowstone Ct & Way 89521
Shady Creek Ct 89523
Shady Lane Ct 89509
Shair Dr 89509
Shale Ct 89503
Shale Creek Dr 89511
Shalestone Way 89523
Shampine Way 89509
Shamrock Ln 89509
Shane Way 89506
Shangri La Dr 89509
Sharlands Ave 89523
Sharon Way 89509
Sharpe Hill Cir 89523
Sharps Cir & Rd 89519
Sharrock Rd 89510
Shawna Ln 89511
Shawnee Cir 89502
Shay Ln 89511
Shearwater Dr 89508
Shelley Cir 89506
Shelter Ct 89521
Shenandoah Dr 89508
Shepherds Bush Ct 89511
Sheri K Bar Ln 89521
Sheridan Rd 89521
Sherman Way 89506
Sherwood Dr & Pl 89509
Shetland Cir 89508
Shewmaker Ct 89509
Shifting Sands Dr 89506
Shiloh Dr 89508
Shinners Pl 89502
Shire Ct 89521
Shirley Ave 89512
Shirley Lake Ct 89519
Shone St 89512
Shooting Star Ct 89506
Shorieri St 89501
Short Ridge Dr 89521
Shoshone Dr 89512
Shotgun Rd 89508
Show Jumper Ln 89521
Sia Ct 89502
Sienna Park Ct & Dr 89512
Sienna Pointe Ct 89512
Sienna Station Way 89512
Sienna Summit Ct 89512
Sienna Vista Ct 89512
N Sierra St
2-299 89501
401-497 89503
499-1600 89503
1602-1998 89503
S Sierra St 89501
Sierra Center Pkwy 89511
Sierra Country Rd 89511
Sierra Crest Way 89519
Sierra Glen Cir 89523
Sierra Highlands Ct & Dr 89523
Sierra Leaf Cir 89511
Sierra Madre Dr 89502
Sierra Manor Dr 89511
Sierra Meadows Ct 89519
Sierra Mesa St 89511
Sierra Oaks Ct 89521
Sierra Pine Ct & Dr 89519
Sierra Ridge Ct 89523
Sierra Rose Dr 89511
Sierra Sage Ln 89509
Sierra Shadows Ave 89506
Sierra View Rd 89508
Sierra Vista Way 89511
Sigg Dr 89509
Silky Sullivan Ln 89502
Silva Ranch Rd 89523
Silver Arrow Ct 89521
Silver Bridle Ct 89521
Silver Cliff Way 89521
Silver Creek Ct 89519
Silver Crest Cir 89523
Silver Dawn Ct & Dr 89506
Silver Desert Ct & Way 89506
Silver Dollar Ln 89506
Silver Falls Ct 89521
Silver Horse Rd 89510
Silver Knolls Blvd 89508
Silver Lake Rd 89506
Silver Mine Ct 89521
Silver Reef Dr 89506
Silver Ridge Dr 89509
Silver Run Dr 89521
Silver Rush Ct 89521
Silver Sage Pl 89506
Silver Shores Dr 89506
Silver Sky Pkwy 89506
Silver Spur Dr 89508
Silver Spur Rd 89511
Silver Star Dr 89521
Silver State Ct 89523
Silver Strike Ct 89523
Silver Vista Dr 89511
Silver Wolf Rd 89511
Silverada Blvd 89512
Silverado Rd 89521
Silverado Creek Dr 89523
Silverkist Ct & Dr 89506
Silverleaf Ct 89508
Silversmith Pl 89511
Silverstone Pl 89512
Silverthread Dr 89521
Silverwood Rd 89506
Simons Dr 89523
Simpson Ave 89503
Sinagua Ct 89511
Sinclair St 89501
Sinelio Dr 89502
Singingwood Dr 89509
Sioux Trl 89521
Sirius Cir & Ct 89506
Siskin Ln 89508
Sitka St 89506
Sitting Bull Cir 89521
Skidoo Ave 89506
Skokie Way 89502
Sky Canyon Ct & Dr 89510
Sky Country Dr 89503
Sky Crest Ct 89508
Sky Eagle Rd 89510
Sky Horse Trl 89511
Sky Mountain Cir & Dr 89523
Sky Tavern Rd 89511
Sky Terrace Ct 89511
Sky Valley Dr 89523
Sky Vista Pkwy 89506
Skylight Ct 89506
Skyline Blvd & Cir 89509
Skyline View Dr 89509
Skyview Dr 89523
Skywatch Ridge Ln 89511
Skyway Dr 89523
Slate Dr 89523
Slater Ave & Ct 89503
Sleepy Hollow Dr 89502
Slide Mountain Cir & Dr 89511
Smith Dr 89509
Smithridge Dr & Park 89502
Smokeridge Dr 89523
Smoketree Ct 89508
Smokewood Ct 89509
Snake River Dr 89503
Snapdragon Way 89512
Snipe Dr 89508
Snoopy Cir 89506
Snow Ln 89506
Snow Bird Ln 89502
Snow Creek Ct 89511
Snow Flower Dr 89511
Snow Partridge Dr 89523
Snow Summit Dr 89523
Snow Valley Dr 89508
Snowball Ct 89511
Snowberry Dr 89511
Snowmass Ct & Dr 89511
Snowshoe Ln 89502
Snowy Owl Ct 89523
Soaring Eagle Dr 89512
Socorro Ct 89511
Socrates Dr 89512
Sofia Ct 89508
Soft Winds Dr 89506
Softwood Cir 89506
Sol Grande Ct 89502
Solano Ct 89521
Solari Dr 89509
Soldier Pass Ct 89523
Solitude Ct & Dr 89511
Somerset Pl 89509
Somersett Pkwy 89523
Sommerville Way 89519
Sondrio Ct & Way 89521
Sonora Cir & Dr 89509
Sonterra Ct & Ln 89523
Sopwith Blvd 89506
Sorcha St 89506
Sordi Ct 89502
Sorrel Ln 89503
Sourdough Cir 89519
South Ave 89508
Southampton Dr 89509
N & S Southmoor Cir 89502
Southridge Dr 89509
Southworth Dr 89512
Souverain Ln 89506
Space Test Rd 89510
Spalding Ct 89523
Spearhead Way 89506
Spearpoint Dr 89509
Spectrum Blvd 89512
Spelling Ct 89521
Spey Dr 89506
Spezia Rd 89511
Spice Wood Cir 89523
Spicer Lake Ct 89508
Spinnaker Dr 89519
Spinner Ct 89523
Spirit Bluff Ct 89511
Spirit Ridge Ct 89511
Spirit Rock Trl 89511
Split Rock Trl 89523
Spokane St 89512
Spoke Rd 89508
Spotted Eagle Ct 89511
Spotted Horse Rd 89521
Spring Dr 89502
Spring Canyon Ct 89508
Spring Creek Cir 89509
Spring Flower Dr 89521
Spring Leaf Cir 89511
Springdale Ct 89523
Springer Ct 89511
Springfield Park Dr 89523
Springhill Dr 89523
Springwood Dr 89523
Spruce Ln 89511
Spruce Creek Ct 89523
Spruce Lake Ct 89508
Spyglass Cir 89509
Squaw Creek Ct 89506
Squaw Tea Ln 89506
Squaw Valley Cir 89509
Squires Ln 89519
Stacie Nicole Ln 89503
Stadium View Ct 89512
Stagecoach Ct 89511
Stagg Ln 89523
Stallion Rd 89521
Stampede Rd 89508
Standard St 89506
Standing Rock Ct 89521
Standing Stone Cir 89523
Stanhope Ln 89502
Stanton Ln 89502
N Star Rd 89521
Star Way 89511
Star Bright Way 89523
Star Fall Dr 89506
Star Pass Loop 89523
Star Pine Ct 89523
Star Wish Ln 89523
Starcrest Ave 89523
Stardust St
1201-1297 89503
1299-1499 89503
1490-1490 89513
1501-1899 89503
1800-2098 89503
Starfire Ln 89523
Stargaze Way 89523
Starks Way 89512
Starlight Cir 89509
Starr Grove Way 89521
Starr Meadows Loop 89519
Starview Cir 89523
Starwood Ct 89519
State St 89501
State Route 445 89510
Statler Cir 89503
Stead Blvd 89506
Steamboat Ct & Pkwy 89521
Steelhead Ct 89523
Steelwood Ln 89512
Steep Climb Ct 89521
Steeplechase Ct 89521
Stephens Rd 89511
Sterling Way 89512
Sterling Crest Ln 89521
Sterling Hill Ct 89521
Sterling Point Ct & Dr 89523
Sterling Ridge Way 89521
Sterling View Ct 89521
Stetson Dr 89521
Stevenson St 89503
Stewart St
2-198 89501
200-299 89501
300-1799 89502
Stillmeadow Ct & Dr 89502
Stillwater Way 89511
Stillwell Ave 89512
Stoddard Dr 89502
Stoker Ave 89503
Stoltz Rd 89506
Stone Bluff Way 89523
Stone Hill Cir 89519
Stone Hollow Dr 89521
Stone Mountain Cir 89519
Stone Pointe Dr 89523
Stone Valley Dr 89523
Stone Vista Ct 89506
Stonebridge Trl 89511
Stonebury Ct 89523
Stonechase Ct 89521
Stonecreek Dr 89511
Stonefield Dr 89521
Stonefly Ct 89523
Stonegate Ct 89506
Stonegate Ln 89523
Stonehaven Cir 89511
Stonehouse Cir 89511
Stoneland Ct & Dr 89511
Stonewall Ct 89511
Stoney Brook Ct & Dr 89511
Stoney Creek Way 89506
Storey Way 89511
Storyteller Ct 89511
Stovak Ct 89511
Stovepipe Rd 89521
Stowe Ct & Dr 89511
Stradella Ct & Way 89521
Strand Pl 89503
Strasbourg Ct 89511
Stratford Dr 89512
Strathmore Ct 89521
Strawberry Ln 89509
Streagle Way 89506
Streamside Ct 89519
Strutter Way 89506
Suda Way 89509
Suffolk Cir 89506
Sugar Bowl Ct 89511
Sugar Creek Trl 89523
Sugar Pine Ct 89523
Sugar Tree Ct 89511
Sugarbrush Ct 89523
Sugarloaf Dr 89511
Sullivan Rd 89521
Sumac St 89509
Summer Field Rd 89521
Summer Glen Dr 89521
Summer Sage Ct 89511
Summer Star Pl & Rd 89511
Summer View Ct 89523
Summershade Ln 89521
Summertime Ln 89508
Summertree Ct 89523
Summerwind Cir 89523
Summit Ridge Ct & Dr 89523
Sumrall Way 89502
Sun Cir 89519
Sun Chaser Ct 89511
Sun Cloud Cir & Ct 89506
Sun Dial Cir 89511
Sun Shadow Ct 89523
Sunbeam Ct & Ln 89521
Sunbird Ln 89508
Sunburst Way 89509
Suncrest Ct & Dr 89506
Sundance Dr 89511
Sunhaven Ct 89521
Sunline Dr 89523
Sunnycrest Dr 89503
Sunnyside Dr 89503
Sunnyvale Ave 89509
Sunray Dr 89503
Sunridge Ct & Dr 89511
Sunrise Dr 89509
Sunrise Meadows Loop 89519
Sunrise Mist Ct 89506
Sunriver Ct 89523
Sunrock Rd 89521
Sunset Dr 89509
Sunset Breeze Dr 89506
Sunset Mountain Rd 89506
Sunset Peak Ct 89508
Sunset Ridge Ct 89511
Sunshine Ln 89502
Sunstone Ct 89508
Sunvilla Blvd 89512
Surf Way 89503
E & W Surge St 89506
Surprise Valley Rd 89510
Surrey Ct & Dr 89521
Susan Way 89506
Susileen Dr 89509
Sutcliffe Dr 89510
Sutcliffe Star Rte 89510
Sutherland Ln 89521
Sutro Dr 89521
Sutro St 89512
Sutter Cir 89503
Sutter Pl 89521
Sutterbrook Way 89521
Sutters Mill Ln 89508
Sutton Way 89512
Suzi Lake Ct 89519
Swaledale Dr 89511
Swan Cir 89509
Swanson Ln 89509
Sweet Clover St 89509
Sweet Gum Ct & Dr 89508
Sweetgrass Ln 89523
Sweetwater Dr 89509
Swift Ct 89508
Swift Creek Ct 89511
Sycamore Way 89502
Sydney Ct 89523
Syler Ct 89511
Sylvester Ct & Rd 89521
Sysonby Ct 89521
T H Ranch Rd 89510
Table Rock Ct 89511
Tacchino St 89512
Tacoma Way 89509
Tagor Dr 89521
Tahiti Way 89502
Tahoe St 89509
Talbot Ln 89509
Tall Oaks Ct 89523
Tallgrass Dr 89506
Talus Way 89503
Tamarack Dr 89509
Tamarisk Dr 89502
Tampa St 89512
Tamra Dr 89506
Tanea Ct & Dr 89511
Tannenbaum Way 89509
Tannerwood Dr 89511
Taos Ln 89511
Taos Ranch Ct 89511
Tapadero Trl 89521
Tappan Ct & Dr 89523
Tara Ridge Trl 89523
Targhee Ct 89511
Tarleton Way 89523
Tarn Way 89503
Tartan Rd 89510
Tasha Ct 89503
Tate Dr 89523
Taurus Cir 89521
Tawleed Rd 89521
E Taylor St
1-99 89501
200-1499 89502
W Taylor St 89509
Technology Way 89521
Teddy Bear Ct 89508
Tee Pee Ln 89506
Telegraph St 89502
Telluride Ct & Dr 89511
Temelec Way 89521
Tempe Ct 89511
Temple Hill Rd 89521
Tenaya Creek Ln 89506
Terabyte Ct & Dr 89521
Teramo Ct & Dr 89521
Terminal Way 89502
Tern Ct 89508
Terra Ct 89506
Terrace Dr 89503
Terrace Heights Ct & Ln 89523
Terrace Knoll Ct 89512
Terracina Way 89521
Terry Way 89521
Tesoro Ct 89523
Tess Way 89511
N & S Tesuque Ct & Rd 89511
Teton St 89506
Tewa Ct 89511
Texas Ave 89506
The Strand 89503
Thelma Pl 89509
Theobald St 89521
Thistle Ct 89506
Thistle Berry Ct 89521
Thistledown Ct 89512
Tholl Dr 89506
Thoma St
100-199 89501
200-1099 89502
Thomas Ave 89523
Thomas Creek Rd 89511
Thomas Jefferson Dr 89509
Thomasville Ct 89508
Thompson Ct & Ln 89511
Thornbury Ct 89523
Thornhill Ct & Dr 89509
Thornridge Ct 89506
Thornwood Ct 89509
Thoroughbred Cir 89508
Thousand Acres Way 89521
Three Mile Dr 89509
Three Wood Ln 89523
Thrush Ln 89508
Thumbs Up Rd 89510
Thunder Mountain Ct & Way 89521
Thunder Ridge Ct 89508
Thunder River Dr 89508
Thunderbolt Dr 89511
Tiberias Ct 89506
Tierra Verde E & W 89512
Tierrapark Ct 89502
Tillamook Ct 89509
Timaru Ct & Trl 89523
Timber Way 89512
Timber Crest Trl 89511
Timber Grove Ct 89508
Timber Ridge Ct 89523
Timbercreek Ct 89511
Timberlake Ct 89511
N Timberline Ct & Dr 89511
Timberline View Ct 89511
Timberwolf Dr 89523
Timoney Ln 89503
Timothy Ct & Dr 89511
Tincup Way 89521
Tinhorn Rd 89521
Tioga Way 89503
Titleist Ct 89523
Toano St 89512
Tobiano Dr 89521
Toiyabe St 89509
Tolica St 89509
Toll Rd 89521
Tom Kite Trl 89523
Tom Sawyer Dr 89512
Tomahawk Way 89506
Tonopah St 89509
Topaz Dr 89502
Torino Ct & Way 89521
Toro Ct 89502
Torrington Dr 89511
Torvinen Way 89511

Tosco Dr 89509
Toucan Ct 89508
Toulouse Ct 89511
Touraco Ct & St 89508
Tourmaline Dr 89521
Tower Falls Rd 89521
Towhee Way 89508
Town Square Ln 89523
Towne Dr 89521
Townsite Rd 89511
Tracy Ln 89509
Trademark Dr 89521
Trail Dr 89506
Trail Creek Way 89523
Trail Head Dr 89521
Trail Hollow Ct 89523
Trail Rider Dr 89521
Trail Ridge Ct 89523
Trailblazer Ct 89511
Trailmaster Dr 89508
Trails End Ln 89511
Trailside Ct 89511
Trainer Way 89512
Traveler Ct 89521
Travis Way 89502
Treasure Cove Ct 89506
Tree Farm Ct & Rd 89510
Trek Trl 89521
Tremont Ln 89509
Trenterl Dr 89502
Trentham Way 89509
Trentwood Ct 89509
Trident Way 89512
Trinity Ln 89511
Triple Creek Ct 89503
Tripp Dr 89512
Troon Ct 89519
Trout Ct 89508
Troy Ln 89509
Truckee Meadows Pl 89521
W Truckee River Ln 89501
Truckee River Trl 89523
Truckee Vista Dr 89501
Trumpeter Ct 89509
Tuck Cir 89506
Tucker Rd 89521
Tucumcari Cir 89511
Tudor Ct 89503
Tufa Rock Rd 89510
Tularosa Ct 89511
Tule Dr 89521
Tulear St 89506
Tulip Ct 89512
Tumbleweed Ct 89510
Tunika Ct 89523
Tunna Tuhugi Rd 89506
Tuolumne Dr 89523
Tupelo St 89506
Turbine Way 89506
Turbo Cir 89502
Turning Leaf Way 89519
Turtle Creek Ct 89506
Tuscany Cir 89523
Tuttle Cir 89509
Tuxon Way 89521
Twin Bridges Way 89521
Twin Creeks Ct & Dr 89523
Twin Eagles Ct 89523
Twin Falls Ct & Dr 89511
Twin Lakes Dr 89523
Twin Oaks Rd 89511
Twin Pines Ct & Rd 89509
Twin Rock Trl 89523
Twin Springs Rd 89510
Twinberry Cir 89511
Two Forty Rd 89510
Tybo Ave 89512
Tybo Rd 89521
Tyrone Rd 89502
Ubaldo Ct 89521
Umber Sky Ct 89506
Underwood Pl 89509
Union Rd 89521
University Pl 89512
University Ter 89503
University Green Ct & Dr 89512
N & S University Park Ct & Loop 89512
University Ridge Ct & Dr 89512
Uplands Ct 89523
Upson Ln 89509
Ural St 89506
Urban Rd 89509
Us Highway 395 N
7400-7448 89506
Us Highway 395 N
16100-19599 89508
Us Highway 395 S 89521
Utah St 89506
Vagabond Ct 89506
Valdez Way 89502
Vale St 89509
Valecito Ct 89508
Valermap Rd 89510
Vallee Way 89512
Valley Rd 89512
Valley Creek Rd 89523
Valley Springs Rd 89511
Valley View Dr 89506
Valley Wood Dr 89523
Valmar Pl 89503
Van Buren Ct & Dr 89503
Van Ness Ave 89503
Van Petten St 89503
Vancouver Ct & Dr 89511
Vantage Way 89502
Vassar St
100-1999 89502
2000-2098 89510
2001-2899 89502
2300-2998 89502
Vega St 89521
Ventana Pkwy 89511
Venus Ave 89521
Vera Dr 89511
Verazae Dr 89521
Verdin Pl 89502
Verelli Ct 89521
Vermillion Rd 89521
Vernon Dr 89509
Vesta St 89502
Veterans Pkwy 89521
Vfw Historic Ln 89509
Via Bianca 89511
Via Como 89511
Via Contento Ct 89511
Via Fiori 89511
Via Mira Monte 89511
Via Ponte 89511
Via Solano 89511
Via Verona 89511
Vicksburg Rd 89508
Victoria Rd 89521
Viento Way 89502
View Crest Ct & Dr 89511
Vikingholm Rd 89521
Villa Way S 89509
Villa Marbella Cir 89509
Villa Verde Dr 89523
Village Pkwy 89508
Village Center Dr 89508
Village Green Pkwy 89519
Villano Ct 89506
Villanova Dr 89502
Villerid Ln 89508
Vincent Ln 89511
Vine St 89503
Vine Creek Ct 89506
Vineyard Ct 89508
Vintage Dr 89506
Vintners Pl 89519
Violet Ct 89512
Virbel Ln 89502
Vireo Ct 89508
N Virginia St
1-97 89501
99-899 89501
901-1597 89503
1599-1677 89503
1674-1674 89507
1678-1698 89503
1679-2199 89503
2700-4698 89506
4700-15099 89506
S Virginia St
2-14 89501
16-99 89501
50-50 89504
50-50 89505
100-798 89501
101-799 89501
800-6199 89502
6200-6398 89511
6400-10399 89511
10400-10448 89521
10401-13999 89511
10450-12098 89511
16000-21099 89521
21101-22799 89521
Virginia Foothills Dr 89521
Virginia Lake Way 89509
Virginia Vista Dr 89521
Viscaya Ct 89523
Vista Trl 89510
Vista Alta Ct & Dr 89521
Vista Bella Ln 89521
Vista Bonita Ln 89521
Vista Citta 89519
Vista Knoll Pkwy 89506
Vista Larga Cir & Ct 89523
Vista Lucci 89519
Vista Occhio 89519
Vista Rafael Pkwy 89503
Vista Ridge Way 89523
Vista Verde Rd 89521
Vista View Dr 89506
Vistacrest Dr 89509
Vitoria Ct 89521
Vivian Ct 89502
Volcano Ave 89506
Volmer Way 89512
Volunteer Ct 89508
Von Way 89509
Vulgamore Cir & Pl 89509
Wa Pai Shone Cir 89502
Wagon Cir 89521
Wagon Ho Ct & Ln 89508
Wagon Wheel Cir 89503
Wagon Wheel Ct 89511
Wagoneer Ct & Dr 89502
Waldron Ln 89506
Walhalla Ct 89511
Walker Ave 89509
Walking Stick Ct & Way 89523
Wall St 89502
Wallsend Dr 89511
Walner St 89506
Walnut St 89502
Walnut Creek Rd 89523
Walnut Ridge Ct & Dr 89521
Walt St 89506
Waltham Ct 89519
Walts Ln 89509
War Paint Cir 89506
Warbler Way 89502
Ward Pl 89503
Warm River Rd 89523
Warren Ct & Way 89509
Warrior Ln 89523
Washington Ct & St 89503
Washington Park Dr 89521
Wassuk Ridge Rd 89506
Water Hole Cir & Rd 89519
Water Lily Ct & Way 89511
Water View Way 89511
Waterash St 89506
Watercress Cir 89523
Waterford Ct 89511
Waterhouse Rd 89521
Waterloo Dr 89509
Waterman Ct 89511
Watt St 89509
Waverly Ct & Dr 89519
Waxwing Ct & St 89508
Wayside Rd 89510
Weatherby Ct 89523
Weaver Pl 89512
Webb Cir 89506
Webster Way 89509
Wedekind Rd 89512
Wedge Pkwy 89511
Wedgewood Ct 89509
Weedachs Rd 89506
Weeping Willow Ct 89502
Welcome Way 89511
Wellington Way 89506
N Wells Ave 89512
S Wells Ave 89502
Wells Fargo Rd 89508
Welsh Dr 89506
Welsh Mountain Ct 89521
Wendy Way 89509
Werth Cir 89506
Wesley Dr 89503
Wessex Cir 89503
West St
100-399 89501
401-697 89503
699-799 89503
Westbrook Ln 89506
Westchester Ct 89523
Westcliff Ln 89523
Western Rd 89506
Western Skies Dr 89521
Western Springs Ct & Dr 89521
Westfield Ave 89509
Westgate Rd 89519
Westglen Ct 89523
Westlake Rd 89523
Westminster Pkwy 89506
Westmont Ln 89521
Weston Pl 89509
N & S Westpoint Dr 89509
Westridge Dr 89511
Westwind Cir 89521
Westwood Dr 89509
Wetzel Ct 89511
Weymoor Ct 89521
Wheatgrass Ct & Dr 89509
Wheatland Ct & Rd 89511
Wheeldale Cir 89511
Wheeler Ave 89502
Whimbleton Way 89511
Whippoorwill Ln 89508
Whirlaway Pl 89502
Whiskey Flat Rd 89521
Whiskey Springs Rd 89510
Whisper Rock Ct & Way 89523
N & S Whisperwood Dr 89521
Whistler Ct 89506
Whistler Ridge Dr 89511
Whistlewood Ct 89509
Whitaker Dr & Way 89503
White Cedar Ct & Dr 89511
White Falls Ct & Dr 89506
White Fir Ct & St 89523
White Fish Dr 89511
White Lake Pkwy 89508
White Mountain Ct 89511
White Owl Dr 89508
White Quartz Dr 89511
White Ridge Cir 89509
White Rock Ct & Dr 89508
White Sage Dr 89506
N White Sands Rd 89511
White Tail Ct 89508
White Water Way 89523
Whitebark Ct 89508
Whitecliff Dr 89521
Whitehawk Dr 89508
Whites Creek Ln 89511
Whitfield Way 89512
Whitmore Ln 89509
Whitney Oaks Ln 89523
Wide Horizon Dr 89509
Wiggins Ct 89506
Wigwam Way 89506
Wilbur Pl 89509
Wilbur May Pkwy 89521
Wilcox Ranch Rd 89510
Wild Eagle Ter 89511
Wild Horse Rd 89510
Wild Mustang Ln 89521
Wild Quail Ct 89511
Wild Rose Rd 89521
Wild Wolf Way 89521
Wilder St 89512
Wildrose Dr 89509
Wildrose Ln 89502
Wildrye Dr 89509
Wildwood Dr 89511
Wilkinson Ave & Ct 89502
Willbuck Rd 89521
Williams Ave & Cir 89503
E & W Willis Ln 89511
Willomonte Rd 89521
Willow St 89502
Willow Brook Dr 89511
Willow Creek Way 89509
Willow Hills Cir 89512
Willow Ranch Trl 89523
Willow Tree Ln 89509
Willowsprings Ct & Dr 89519
Wilmington Ct 89511
Wilshire Dr 89506
Wilson Ave 89502
Winchester Dr 89506
Wind Feather Trl 89511
Wind Ranch Rd 89521
Windcrest Dr 89523
Winding Creek Dr 89506
Winding Ridge Ct 89511
Windmill Dr 89511
Window Rock Trl 89511
E & W Windriver Ln 89511
Windsor Way 89503
Windstar Dr 89523
Windview Ct 89523
Windwood Ln 89523
Windy Creek Ct 89506
Windy Hill Way 89511
Windy Meadow Dr 89519
Winged Foot Ct 89511
Winnemucca Ranch Rd 89510
Winners Cup Dr 89521
Winston Dr 89512
Winter St 89503
Winter Moon Ct 89523
Winter Park Ct 89511
Winter Rose Cir 89502
Winterberry Ct 89511
Winterchase Way 89523
Wintergreen Ct & Ln 89511
Winterhill Ct 89523
Wise Ave 89506
Wisteria Ct & Dr 89511
Wixom Dr 89503
Wolf Creek Dr 89523
Wolf Ridge Way 89521
Wolf Run Ct & Rd 89511
Wolfen Ct 89510
Wonder St 89502
Wood Leaf Ct 89508
Woodbridge Trl 89523
Woodchuck Cir & Ct 89519
Woodcrest Ct 89523
Woodhollow Dr 89521
Woodland Ave 89523
Woods Creek Ct 89519
Wrangler Rd 89510
Wren St 89509
Wrenwood Ct 89523
Wright St 89509
Wrondel Way 89502
Wyatt Ct 89521
Wycliffe Cir 89519
Wynne St 89506
Wyoming Ave & Ct 89503
Xenon Ct 89506
Yale Way 89502
Yankee Blade Rd 89521
Yates Ln 89509
Yeager St 89506
Yearling Ct 89508
Yellow Bird Dr 89523
Yellow Pine Cir & Rd 89511
Yellow Tail Rd 89510
Yellowjacket Rd 89521
Yellowstone Dr 89512
Yori Ave 89502
Yorkshire Dr 89506
Yosemite Pl 89503
Young Cir 89511
Younghans Ct 89511
Youngs Rd 89510
Yuba Ct 89521
Yuma Ln 89509
Zane Grey Ln 89523
Zeolite Dr 89506
Zephyr Heights Dr 89521
Zeppelin Ct 89523
Zermatt Ct 89511
Zeus Way 89512
Zinc St 89502
Zinfandel Ct & Dr 89506
Zinnia Dr 89512
Zion Ln 89503
Zircon Dr 89521
Zoe Ln 89519
Zoeller Ct 89511
Zolezzi Ln 89511
Zuni Ridge Trl 89511

NUMBERED STREETS

E 1st St 89501
W 1st St
2-299 89501
301-497 89503
E 2nd St
36-44 89501
46-194 89501
196-308 89501
400-2599 89502
W 2nd St
1-269 89501
271-299 89501
300-1399 89503
1401-1499 89503
W 3rd St
101-199 89501
501-699 89503
E 4th St
1-259 89501
300-2799 89512
W 4th St
200-204 89501
401-497 89503
2401-3897 89523
E 5th St
201-297 89501
299-400 89501
402-498 89501
500-2700 89512
2702-2798 89512
W 5th St 89503
E 6th St
100-299 89501
300-1699 89512
W 6th St 89503
E 7th St
101-197 89501
199-299 89501
300-1499 89512
W 7th St
701-897 89503
899-4999 89503
5000-5299 89523
E 8th St
101-199 89501
400-898 89512
W 8th St 89503
E 9th St
2-198 89501
301-997 89512
W 9th St 89503
E 10th St 89512
W 10th St 89503
E 11th St 89512
W 11th St 89503
W 12th St 89503
14th St 89503
15th St 89503
18th Hole Ct & Trl 89523

SPARKS NV

General Delivery 89431

POST OFFICE BOXES MAIN OFFICE STATIONS AND BRANCHES

Box No.s
AA - AJ 89432
E - Y 89432
1 - 8635 89432
50001 - 54858 89435

NAMED STREETS

A St 89431
Abacus Ct 89436
Abbay Way 89431
Abbotswood Dr 89436
Abruzzi Ct 89434
Accolade Ct 89436
Acobat Ct 89436
Adara Ct 89441
Adel Way 89431
Adelaide Ct 89436
Adobe Springs Ct & Dr 89436
Adrian Way 89431
Agua Fria Dr 89441
Aguilar Ct 89441
Ahwanee Dr 89436
Ala Tierra Vista Rd 89441
Alamosa Dr 89441
Albatross Way 89441
Albazano Ct & Dr 89436
Alcandre Ct 89436
Alco Ct 89434
Alena Way 89441
Alessandro Ct & Dr 89434
Alexandria Ct 89434
Alexis Ct 89441
Allariz Ct 89436
Allegrini Ct & Dr 89436
Almazan Ct 89436
Almeria Ct 89436
Almonte Ct 89436
Alpland Ct & Ln 89434
Alta Vista Ct & Dr 89434
Altesino Dr 89436
Alvin Ct 89434
S Amanda Cir 89436
Amber Leaf Ct 89434
Amberley Way 89431
Ambonnay Ln 89436
Ambush Cir & Ct 89436
Ambush Ridge Dr 89436
Amico Dr 89434
Amigo Ct 89441
Amsterdam Ct 89434
Ancestor Cir 89436
Ancient St 89436
Andalucia Ct 89441
Annabelle Dr 89436
Anqua Ct & Dr 89434
Antella Ct 89434
Anthem Dr 89441
Antinori Dr 89436
Antonio Ct 89434
Antreka Ct 89436
Apio Ct 89436
April St 89436
Apus Dr 89436
Aquene Ct & Dr 89436
Archer Ct 89441

Street	ZIP
Arcturas Ct	89436
Arianza Ct	89436
Aristedes Dr	89436
Arleen Way	89431
Arndell Way	89431
Arneson Ln	89431
Arona Dr	89434
Arrow Smith Dr	89436
Arsac Ln	89436
Artadi Dr	89436
Ash Ave	89431
Ash Peak Dr	89436
Ash Rock Dr	89436
Ash Springs Ct & Dr	89436
Ashland Ave	89436
Ashley Park Ct & Dr	89434
Ashwood Cir	89434
Aston Cir	89436
Astral Ct	89436
Astronomer Way	89436
Asturius Ct	89436
Aswan St	89441
Atlantic Way	89434
Atomic Ct	89436
Austrina Dr	89436
Autumnwood Ln	89434
Ave De La Argent	89434
Ave De La Bleu De Clair	89434
Ave De La Couleurs	89434
Ave De La Demerald	89434
W Ave Of The Colors	89434
Avella Dr	89434
Avenida Serena Ct	89441
Avian Dr	89441
Avila Ct & Dr	89436
Axis Dr	89436
Azul Ct	89436
Bach Ct	89431
Badelona Ct	89436
Badger Creek Ct	89436
Baldwin Way	89436
Baleares Ct	89436
Bambey Dr	89436
Bandera Ave	89436
Banestone Ct & Rd	89436
Banfi Ct	89436
Bank St	89431
Bankhurst Ct	89436
Bannister Rd	89436
Banyan Ct	89436
Barbados Dr	89436
Barcelona Ct	89436
Bareback Ct & Dr	89436
Baring Blvd	89434
Barranca Dr	89441
Barrett Ct & Way	89436
Bartmess Blvd & Ct	89436
Baxter Way	89431
Baxter Pass Ct	89436
Bayhill Way	89436
Baysheen Ct	89436
Bayshore Dr	89434
Baywood Dr	89434
Beacon Hill Ct	89431
Beatty Cir	89434
Beau Ct & Dr	89436
Beenestr Dr	89434
Belgium Ct	89434
Bella Oaks Ct & Dr	89441
Bellagio Ct	89434
Bellatrix Way	89441
Benedict Dr	89441
Bentgrass Ct & Dr	89431
Bergin Way	89431
Berkshire Ct & Dr	89434
Bermeso Ct	89436
Bernice Ct	89436
Bertini Ct	89434
Betsy Ct & St	89431
Bettina Pl	89431
Big Bang Ct	89436
Big Dipper Ct	89436
Big Fish Dr	89434
Billie Dove Ct	89436
Billow Dr	89441
Birchwood Cir	89434
Black Cinder Ct	89436
Black Deer Ct	89436
Black Diamond Dr	89436
Black Forest Ln	89434
Black Gypsum Ct	89436
Black Hills Ct & Dr	89436
Black Oak Rd	89436
Blancori	89441
Bloomfield Ln	89436
Blossom View Dr	89434
Blue Mountain Cir	89436
Blue Skies Ct & Dr	89436
Bluehaven Dr	89434
Blushing Ct	89436
Boardwalk Pl	89436
Bodega Ct & Dr	89436
Boise Ct & Dr	89431
Bolo Ct	89441
Bonanza Ranch Rd	89434
Bonita Ct	89436
Bonita Vista Dr	89434
Bootes Ct	89436
Borealis Ct & Dr	89436
Bougainvillea Dr	89436
Boulder Peak Ct	89436
Bounty Ct	89431
Boxcar Ln	89431
Boxington Way	89434
Boyle Ct	89436
Brachetto Loop	89434
Bradley Sq	89434
Braidwood Dr	89436
Bramling Cross Dr	89441
Brass Spur Way	89436
Brassie Dr	89431
Breaker Ct & Way	89431
Bria Cir	89436
Briargreen Ct	89434
Briarwood Dr	89434
Bridger Peak Ct & Dr	89436
Bridgetown Loop	89436
Bridgman Ct	89434
Bridle Path Ct & Ter	89441
Brierley Way	89434
Brisa Ct	89436
Bristle Branch Dr	89434
Britain Dr	89434
Brooks Cir	89431
Brooktree Dr	89434
Brunello Dr	89436
Brunetti Way	89431
Brunke Ct	89436
Buckey Way	89431
Budding Oaks Ct	89436
Buffalo Way	89431
Bufflehead Dr	89441
Bunker Hill Ln	89431
Burlington Dr	89436
Burnside Ct & Dr	89434
Burrows Ct	89431
Burtin Dr	89436
Byars Ln	89431
Byrd Dr	89431
C St	89431
Caboose Ct & Way	89434
Caceres Ct	89436
N & S Cactus Hills Ct & Dr	89436
Cadiz Ct	89436
Cal Ln	89431
Calabaza Ct	89436
Calabria Dr	89434
Calaveras Cir	89431
Caldera Dr	89436
Caledonian Dr	89436
Calle Bonito Ct	89441
Calle De La Plata	89441
Calle De Mariposa Ln	89441
Calle Limpio St	89441
Calle Myriam	89436
Calvados Dr	89434
Camelback Dr	89434
Camino De Grato	89441
Camino Real Dr	89434
Camino Verde Dr	89436
Campello Dr	89436
Campo Rico Ct & Ln	89441
Canal Rd	89434
Canary Ct	89441
Candelaria Dr	89434
Candlewood St	89434
Cangrejo Ct	89436
Cannonball Rd	89431
Canoe Hill Ct & Dr	89436
Canoga Ct	89431
Canopus Ct	89436
Cantabria Ct & Dr	89436
Cantamar Ct	89436
Cantara Cir	89436
Cantinia Ct & Dr	89436
Canyon Pkwy	89436
Canyon Way	89434
Canyon Crest Ct	89436
Canyon Dawn Dr	89441
Canyon Point Ct	89436
Canyon Ridge Dr	89436
Canyon Rim Ct	89436
Canyon River Ct	89434
Canyon Run Dr	89436
Canyon Terrace Dr	89436
Canyon View Ct & Dr	89436
Canyon Vista Ct & Dr	89436
Capistrano Dr	89441
Capri Ln	89434
Capriolate Dr	89436
Capurro Way	89431
Carbon Ct	89436
Carefree Dr & Pl	89441
Carema Ct	89436
Carlene Ct & Dr	89436
Carneros Dr	89441
Carson Ave	89431
Carson Pass Ct	89436
Cartago Ct	89436
Carvin Ct	89434
Casarey Ct	89436
Cassiopeia Ct	89436
Caterpillar Ct	89441
Catham Ct & Ln	89434
Cathedral Peak Dr	89436
Catrina Ct	89441
Caymus Dr	89436
Cecilia Ct	89441
Centaurus Dr	89436
Central Ct	89434
Cercle De La Cerese	89434
Cerritos Cir	89436
Cetus Dr	89436
Chacon Ct	89441
Champion Ct	89436
Chancie Way	89431
Chappelet Dr	89436
Chara Ct & Ln	89441
Charolaise Cir	89431
Chatterly Ln	89434
Chaucer St	89431
Cheatgrass Ln	89436
Cherry Springs Ct	89436
Cherry Tree Dr	89434
Chert Ct	89436
Chesney Ct	89441
Chester Sq	89431
Chevalier Ct & Dr	89436
Chilcoot Dr	89434
Chilhowee Ct	89436
Chipwood Dr	89436
Chloris Cir	89431
Chollar Cir	89436
Christina Cir	89436
Chromium Way	89436
Chula Vista Ct & Dr	89436
Churchill Green Dr	89436
Cibola Ct & Dr	89436
Cielo Cir	89436
Cielo Azul Dr	89431
Cielo Vista Dr	89441
Cinnabar Ct	89436
Cinnamon Dr	89436
Cintoia Dr	89436
Circuit Ct	89441
Citori Dr	89436
Cityview Ter	89431
Clan Alpine Dr	89434
Clark Station Rd	89434
Clearsky Dr	89436
Clearwood Dr	89436
Cloud Peak Dr	89436
Clove Hitch Ct	89441
Clover Leaf Dr	89434
Cloverbrook Dr & Pl	89436
Cloverdale Dr	89434
Coachman Ct & Dr	89434
Coal Ct	89434
Cobra Ct & Dr	89436
Cobrita Ct	89436
Cokenee Ct	89436
Cola Ct	89434
Coldwater St	89436
Colina Ct & Dr	89436
Colorado Ct & Ln	89436
Comet Ct	89436
Comet Linear Ct & Dr	89436
Commerce St	89431
Compase Ct	89436
Conductor Ct	89434
Coney Island Dr	89431
Contrail St	89441
Copernicus Ct	89436
Coppa Way	89431
Copper Ann Dr	89436
Copperhead Ct	89436
Cordoba Blvd & Ct	89441
Corleone Dr	89436
Cormorant Ct	89441
Cometa Ct	89436
Cortez Ct	89441
Cosenza Dr	89434
Cosimo Ct	89436
Costa Azul Dr	89436
S Cottage Ln	89434
Country Cir	89434
Country Ridge Dr	89434
Coupler Ct & Way	89434
Cour De La Argent	89434
Cour De La Carabe	89434
Cour De La Cedrant	89434
Cour De La Celedon	89434
Courtland Way	89431
Covered Wagon Ct	89436
Covina Dr	89431
Coyote Springs Ct	89436
Coyote Valley Way	89434
Crabapple Holw	89431
Crabtree Grove Ct	89436
Crane Way	89431
Creation Ct & St	89436
Creekside Ln	89431
Crescent Ct	89431
Crescent Hill Way	89436
Crestline Ct	89434
Crestside Ct & Dr	89436
Crestwood Dr	89434
Cromwell Pl	89436
Crooked Stick Way	89436
Cross Star Ct	89436
Crossing Ct	89434
Culpepper Dr	89436
Cumulus Ct	89441
Curnow Springs Ct	89436
Cuzco Dr	89436
E & W Cygnet Cir	89431
Cygnus Way	89441
D St	89431
N & S D Andrea Pkwy	89434
Dacite Ct	89436
Damon Pl	89431
Dana Way	89431
Dancing Moon Ct & Way	89436
Dansant Ct	89436
Danville Dr	89434
Darby Rose Ln	89436
Darcy Ct	89436
Date Palm Ct & Dr	89441
David James Blvd	89436
Dawn Cir	89431
De Roca Ct	89434
De Wick Ct	89441
Debbie Way	89431
Decoy Dr	89436
Deedee Way	89436
Deep Creek Ct & Dr	89434
Del Fuego Dr	89436
Del Rosa Way	89434
Del Sol St	89436
Delaware Ct	89431
Delna Dr	89431
Demaris St	89436
Deming Way	89431
Denali Peak Dr	89436
Denevi Dr	89434
Denmark Dr	89434
Dermody Way	89431
Descanso Ln	89441
Descent Ct & Dr	89436
N & S Desert Brush Ct	89436
Desert Cove Ct	89436
Desert Dude Ct	89441
Desert Flower Ct	89434
Desert Fox Dr	89436
Desert Highlands Ct & Dr	89436
Desert Hills Ct & Dr	89436
Desert Mirage Ct & Dr	89436
Desert Mountain Dr	89436
Desert Peach Ct & Dr	89436
Desert Peak Ct	89441
Desert Plains Dr	89436
Desert Rain Ct	89436
Desert Rose Ct & Dr	89441
Desert Song Ct	89436
N Desert Springs Cir	89436
Desert View Ct & Dr	89434
Desert Village Ct	89436
Desert Vista Ct & Dr	89436
Desertscape Ct	89441
Desertstone Ct & Dr	89436
Design Pl	89441
Desperado Ct	89436
Deutz Dr	89436
E Devere Way	89431
Diamond Dust Ct	89436
Diamond Oaks Ct	89436
Diamond Wing Ct	89436
Diamondback Ct	89436
Diana Ct	89436
Diorite Ct	89436
Disc Dr	89436
Distribution Dr	89441
Divot Dr	89431
Dodge Dr	89436
Dodson Way	89431
Dogwood Dr	89431
Dolce Dr	89434
Dolores Dr	89436
Domaine Dr	89436
Dome Ct	89436
Dominus Dr	89436
Dondero Ct	89434
Donegan St	89434
Donner Pass Ct	89436
Dorado Ct	89436
Dorchester Dr	89436
Dortmunder Dr	89441
Dover Ct	89434
Doyle Ct	89431
Draco Ct & Dr	89436
N Drexel Dr	89436
S Drexel Dr	89436
Drexel Way	89434
Driftwood Ct & Dr	89431
Dromedary Rd	89441
Dubonnet Dr	89436
Duggan Ave	89431
Dunbar Ct	89436
Dunn Cir	89431
Dutchman Dr	89434
E St	89431
Eagle Canyon Dr	89441
Eagle Mountain Dr	89436
Eagle Peak Dr	89441
Eagle View Ct	89436
Eagle Wing Dr	89436
Eaglenest Rd	89436
Earlsmoore Dr	89436
Early Dawn Ct & Dr	89436
Earmark Ct	89436
Earthstone Dr	89436
Eastbrook Dr	89434
Ebbetts Pass Dr	89436
Ebling Dr	89436
Echaniz Ct	89441
Eclipse Dr	89441
Edna Ct	89431
Egyptian Dr	89441
El Caballo Trl	89441
El Cap Ct	89436
El Capitan Ct	89434
El Cid	89441
El Cortez Way	89434
El Molino Dr	89441
El Paseo Dr	89436
El Portal Ct	89436
El Rancho Dr	89431
Elaine Way	89431
Eldridge St	89436
Electra Ct	89441
Elges Way	89431
Eliza Ct	89441
Emanuel Ct	89441
Ember Ct & Dr	89436
Emblem St	89436
E Emerson Way	89431
Emu Ct	89441
Encanto Dr	89441
Energystone Dr	89436
Engineer Ct	89434
Ephedra Ln	89436
Equation Ct & Dr	89436
Eric Ave	89431
Erin Ct & Dr	89436
Escalon Ct	89436
Espee Ct	89434
Europa Dr	89436
Eutopian Ct	89436
Evening Star Dr	89436
Exchange St	89431
Experiment Ct	89436
Exposition Ct	89436
Express St	89434
F St	89431
Fabric Ct & Dr	89436
Fairlie Ct	89434
Fairway Ct & Dr	89431
Fairway Vista Ln	89436
Falcon Ridge Ct & Dr	89436
Falcon View Ct	89436
Fancy Dance Dr	89441
Fantasy Ln	89441
Fanto Ct	89431
Fargo Way	89434
Farrel Ross Dr	89431
Fernday Ct	89436
Fernwood Ct	89434
Festa Way	89434
Field St	89431
Fieldcrest Dr	89434
Figoni Ranch Rd	89434
Fire Dance Ct	89436
Firebee Ct	89436
Fireburst Dr	89436
Firenze Ct & Dr	89434
Firestone Ct & Dr	89441
Firman Ct	89434
Firtree Ln	89436
Flatcar Ln	89431
Flecha Ct	89436
Flora Glen Dr	89434
Floral Ridge Way	89436
S Florentine Dr	89436
Flycatcher Ct & Dr	89441
Fodrin Way	89431
Forney Ct	89434
Fortunato Loop	89436
Fountain Ct	89431
Fox Wood Ln	89436
Foxford Way	89436
Francesca Way	89436
Frankie Way	89436
Franklin Way	89431
Fraun Ct	89436
Frazer Ave	89431
Freedom Dr	89436
Freeman Way	89436
E Freeport Blvd	89431
Friar Rock Ct	89436
Friedman Cir	89441
Frisco Ct & Way	89434
Fuggles Dr	89441
G St	89431
Gadwall Ct & Way	89441
N & S Gaja Loop	89436
Gallagher Rd	89436
Galleria Pkwy	89436
Galleron Way	89431
Galletti Way	89431
Gamble Dr	89431
Gandolfo Way	89431
Gannet Peak Cir	89436
Ganymede Ct	89436
Garda Ct	89434
Garfield Ct & Dr	89431
Garnet Star Way	89441
Garratt Cir & Ct	89436
Garth Ct	89441
Garzoni Dr	89434
Gato Ct	89436
Gator Way	89431
E Gault Way	89431
General Thatcher Dr	89436
Geneva Ct	89434
Genil Ct	89436
Geraldine Ct	89441
Geranium Way	89436
Germany Cir	89434
Gerona Ct	89436
Giannotti Dr	89436
Gilly Ln	89434
Ginger Quill Ct N & S	89436
Glacier Peak Cir	89436
Gladiola Ct	89436
Gleeson Ct & Way	89431
Glen Abbey Ct	89436
Glen Carran Cir	89431
Glen Martin Ct & Dr	89434
Glen Meadow Dr	89434
Glen Molly Ct & Dr	89434
Glen Valley Dr	89434
Glen Vista Dr	89434
Glenbrook Ct	89434
E Glendale Ave	89431
Glendora Ct & Ln	89436
Globe Ct & Dr	89436
N & S Gobi Cir	89436
Golddust Dr	89436
Golden Dawn Ct	89436
Golden Plover Ct	89441
Golden Spike Dr	89434
Goldy Way	89434
Gomez Ct	89431
Good Hope Ln	89434
Goodwin Ct & Rd	89436
Gorget Ct	89441
Gosling Ct	89441
Grace Ct	89436
Grady Ln	89436
Granada Dr	89431
Grand Cypress Ct	89436
Grand Island Ct & Dr	89436
Granville Dr	89436
Grasswood Dr	89436
Gravity Ct & St	89436
Graymare Ct	89436
Greek Ct	89441
Green Vista Dr	89431
Greenbrae Dr	89431
E Greenbrae Dr	
1-689	89431
691-699	89431
700-1099	89434
Greenwing Dr	89441
E Greg St	89431
Gregory Way	89431
Greyhaven Ln	89431

Groom Way 89434
Grose Ln 89431
Grosmont Dr 89436
Grove Springs Dr 89436
Guerra Ct 89436
Gurr Ct 89431
Gwen Way 89431
Gwynelle Ct 89431
E H St 89431
Haistar Ct & Trl 89441
Halcyon Ct 89436
Hale Bopp Ct 89436
Halentat Way 89431
Hallertau Dr 89441
Hallgarten Dr 89436
Halo Dr 89436
Hamilton Dr 89434
Hamm Ct 89436
Harbor Town Cir 89436
Harbour Cove Ct & Dr 89434
Hardy Dr 89431
Harrison Pl 89441
Harvest Dr 89434
Hawk Bay Ct 89436
Hawkings Ct 89436
Hawks Nest Ct 89431
Hawks View Ct & Dr 89436
Haybale Ct & Dr 89441
Hayfield Dr 89441
Haywood Dr 89434
Healing Stone Ct 89436
Heather Ct 89434
Heaven Dr 89436
Helga Ct 89431
Henry Orr Pkwy 89436
Hercules Dr 89441
Hermosa Dr 89434
Herring Gull Way 89436
Hibernica Ln 89436
Hibiscus Ct 89436
Hidden Hills Dr 89441
High Back Ct 89436
High Desert Ct & Dr 89436
High Hill St 89436
High Pass Dr 89436
High Rock Way 89431
Highgate Ct 89434
Highland Ranch Pkwy 89436
Hillock Ct 89436
Hillsdale Ct 89434
Hillstone Rd 89436
Hobart Cir 89431
Hollyhock Ct 89434
Holman Cir & Way 89431
Home Run Dr 89436
Horizon Ct 89434
Horizon Ridge Rd 89441
Horse Springs Dr 89436
Howard Ct & Dr 89434
Hubble Dr 89436
Hulda Ct & Way 89431
Hunting Creek Way 89436
Hushfield Ct 89436
Hyacinth St 89441
Hymer Ave 89431
E I St 89431
Ian Ct & St 89434
Icehouse Ave 89431
Imperial Ct 89436
Inca Dove Ct 89441
Independence Ave 89434
Independent Ct 89434
Indian Springs Ct & Dr 89436
Industrial Way 89431
Ineisa Ct 89434
Ingenuity Ave 89441
Ingleston Dr 89436
International Pl 89431
Interstate 80 E 89434
Inventors Pl 89441
Ion Dr 89436
Iratcabal Dr 89436
Ireland Dr 89434
Irene Way 89431
Iridium Ct & Way 89436
Iron Stirrup Ct 89436
Ironstone Cir 89436
Isabella Ct & Dr 89434
Isidor Ct 89441
Island Queen Ct & Dr 89436
Isle Of Skye Dr 89431
Istrice Rd 89436
Italy Dr 89434
Ivory Ann Dr 89436
Ivory Gull Ct 89441
E J St 89431
Jacinto Ave 89436
Jacmel Ct 89436
Jacob Patrick Ct 89436
Jacqueline Ave 89431
Jamestown Ct 89431
Jamon Dr 89436
Jana Ln 89436
Janelle Dr 89431
E Janere Ct 89436
Jaquenetta Dr 89436
Jarbidge Way 89434
Jason Dr 89434
Jedediah Smith Dr 89441
Jennifer Lee Ln 89441
Jermann Ct & Dr 89436
Jessie Ave 89431
Jimmy Ct 89436
Jitney Dr 89434
Jordyn Ct 89436
Josefina Ct 89441
Juarez Ct 89431
Junction Ct & Dr 89434
Junction Peak Ct & Dr 89436
E K St 89431
Karnak Cir 89441
Kathy Ter 89436
Kaweah Ct 89436
Kayenta Ct 89436
Keams Ct 89436
Kelly Ranch Dr 89431
Kelsey Ct 89431
Kendal Ct 89434
Kendra St 89436
Kent Dr 89434
Keogh Dr 89431
Kepler Dr 89436
Key Cir 89431
Kiley Pkwy 89436
Kiley Links Dr 89436
Kim Way 89431
Kimberlite Ct & Rd 89436
Kinglet Dr 89441
Kings Peak Cir 89436
Kirby Ct 89434
Kiskadee Dr 89436
Kitty Hawk Dr 89441
Kiva Ct 89436
Klemola Ct 89436
Kleppe Ln 89431
Knoll View Way 89436
Komatite Ct 89436
Koskela Dr 89431
Kresge Ln 89431
Krug Ct & Dr 89436
Kyle Scott Ct 89436
E L St 89431
La Calma Ct 89441
La Colina Ct 89441
La Costa St 89436
La Cresta Ct 89436
La Grange Ct 89431
La Hacienda Dr 89434
La Honda Ct 89436
La Jolla Ln 89441
La Linda Vista Dr 89434
La Loma Way 89441
La Mancha Dr 89441
La Posada Ct & Dr 89441
La Quinta Ct 89436
La Ramba Dr 89436
La Sierra Ct & Dr 89434
La Veaga Ct 89431
La Via Way 89434
Lacerta Dr 89436
Ladera Ct 89436
Lagomarsino Ct & Dr 89431
Laguna Way 89434
Lambic Dr 89441
Lambrays Ct & Ln 89436
Lambrusca Dr 89436
Landmark Dr 89441
Lanstar Dr 89441
Lapida Ct 89441
Lapilli Ct 89436
S Largo Dr 89436
Larkin Cir 89431
Las Plumas Dr 89436
Laser Ct & Dr 89436
N & S Latour 89436
Laughing Chukar Ct & Ln 89441
Lawry Dr 89436
Lawton Ct 89434
Legends Bay Dr 89434
Leilani Ln 89441
Lennox Ln 89431
Lenticular Dr 89441
E Lenwood Dr 89431
Leo Dr 89441
Lepori Way 89431
Lepus Dr 89436
Lerma Ct 89436
Lessini Ct 89434
Lexington Way 89431
Libero Dr 89436
Liberty Springs Ct 89436
Lida Ln 89434
Lightspeed Ct 89436
Lilac Dawn Dr 89436
Lillard Dr 89434
Lincoln Way 89431
E Lincoln Way
- 5-11 89431
- 13-399 89431
- 401-699 89431
- 700-1198 89434
- 1200-1899 89434

Linda Way 89431
Lindberg Ln 89441
Lindsey Ln 89436
Linterna Ln 89441
Lionel Ct 89434
Lisbon Ct 89436
Little Easy Ct & St 89436
Livi Ct 89436
Lobo Ct 89436
Lockwood Rd 89434
Locomotive Ct & Way 89434
Logan Way 89431
Lois Ct 89434
Loma Verde Ct & Dr 89436
London Cir 89431
London Dr 89434
Longridge Dr 89434
Longspur Ct & Way 89441
Lonnie Ct 89436
Lorena St 89431
Lorenzo Ct & Ln 89436
Lorna Ln 89436
S Los Altos Pkwy 89436
Los Amigos Dr 89434
Los Arboles Ln 89441
Los Gatos Ln 89441
Los Lagos Ave 89436
Los Pinos Dr 89441
Louden Ct 89441
Lublin Dr 89441
Lucca Ln 89441
Lucerne Way 89431
Lucinda Ct 89441
Lullabrooke Ct 89436
Lusitano Way 89436
Luther Pass Ct 89436
Lydia Ct 89436
Lynch Ct 89431
Lyyski St 89431
E M St 89431
Mac Rd 89436
Macarthur St 89431
S Mackenzie Cir 89431
Madrid Ct & Dr 89436
Madrone Cir 89434
Magical Dr 89436
Magna Carta Ln 89431
Malapi Way 89431
Mammatus Dr 89441
Manchester Way 89431
Mandarin Ct 89434
Mangosta Ct 89436
Mania Ct 89434
Many Nations Rd 89441
Manzana Ct 89436
Marble Hills Cir 89436
Marbree Dr 89436
Marian Way 89431
Marie Way 89436
Marietta Way 89431
Marilyn Mae Dr 89441
Marissa Anne Ct 89436
Marracco Dr 89434
Martell Pl 89441
Martini Cir & Rd 89434
Mashie Ct & Dr 89431
Mato Ct 89436
Matteoni Dr 89434
Matter Ct & Dr 89436
Maxine Cir 89431
May Dr 89436
Mayacamas Ct 89441
Mayer Way 89431
Maypen Dr 89436
N & S Mccarran Blvd 89431
Mccarran Ranch Rd 89434
Mcclure Cir 89431
Mcgoldrick Way 89431
E Mclean Way 89431
Mclemore Ct 89441
Mcneil Ct 89434
Meadow Park Dr 89436
Meadowlands Ct & Dr 89431
Meadowvale Way 89431
Meagan Dr 89436
Media Ct 89436
Medolla Dr 89434
Megabyte Dr 89434
Mellen Ave 89431
Mercedes Dr 89441
Merchant St 89431
Mercy Ct 89431
Meredith Way 89431
Merganser Ln 89436
Meritage Ct & Dr 89434
Merito Ct & Dr 89436
Mesa Meadows Ct & Dr 89436
Mesa Ridge Dr 89434
Mesa Verde Ct & Dr 89436
Mesa Vista Dr 89434
Metkovich Cir 89441
Mia Ct & Dr 89436
Michael Pl 89441
Michele Way 89431
Milagro Ct 89436
Milan Dr 89434
Milano Dr 89434
Milke Ct & Way 89436
Miller Springs Ct 89436
Millstone Ct 89436
Milroy Ln 89431
Minino Ct 89436
Minkler Ct 89436
Minnow Ct 89436
Mintangt Dr 89436
Mirador Ct 89436
Mirage Pl 89436
Miramar Ct 89436
Miranda Ct 89441
Miro Ct 89436
Missy Dr 89436
Modena Ct & Dr 89434
Mokelumne Way 89436
Mongolo Dr 89431
Monica Ct 89441
Monson Dr 89434
Montague Ct 89436
Monte Rio Ct 89436
Monte Verde Way 89434
Montecito Dr 89431
Montero Ct & Dr 89436
Montezuma Way 89434
Monumental Cir 89436
Moon Vista Dr 89436
Moonbeam Ct & Dr 89441
Moonlit Ct 89436
Morning Dawn Ln 89441
Morning Mist Ct & Ln 89441
Morninglory Dr 89434
Morro Ave 89436
Mount Bachelor Dr 89436
Mount Mckinley Dr 89436
Muir Pass Ct 89436
E Mustang Rd 89434
Myles Dr 89434
Mystery Ct & Dr 89436
Mystic Mountain Dr 89441
Mythical Ct 89436
Napoli Dr 89434
Nash St 89431
E & W Nashua Pl 89436
Neighborhood Way 89441
Nelson Way 89431
Niblick Dr 89431
Nichols Blvd
- 200-599 89431
- 700-798 89434
- 800-899 89434

Nicole Ct & Dr 89436
Nightingale Way 89441
Nimbus Ct 89441
Nives Ct 89441
Noah Ct 89436
Noble Ct 89436
Noreen Dr 89434
Norris Dr 89434
Northview Ct 89434
Northwind Ct 89436
Northwood Dr 89431
Novara Ct & Dr 89434
Nowlin Ln 89431
E Nugget Ave 89431
Numaga Ln 89441
E O St 89431
N O Brien Way 89431
O Callaghan Ct & Dr 89434
O Malley Dr 89434
Oakdale Ct 89434
Oakridge Dr 89436
Oakwood Dr 89431
Oasis Dr 89441
Oasis Park Dr 89436
Ocasa Ct 89431
Ocean View Dr 89441
Oddie Blvd 89431
Ogden Trail Dr 89441
Olancha Ct 89436
Old Pinto Ct 89436
Old Waverly Ct & Dr 89436
Oleander Way 89431
Olinghouse St 89436
Omar Way 89431
Omni Dr 89441
Onyo Way 89441
Oppio Cir & St 89431
Orange Plains Dr 89436
Orbigo Ct 89436
Orchard Rd 89434
Orinda Ct & Dr 89436
Orion Dr 89436
Orlando Ct 89431
Orovada St 89431
Ouray Dr 89436
Overmyer Rd 89431
Oxford Ave 89431
Oxley Dr 89436
E P St 89431
Pacific Ave 89431
Packer Way 89431
Pah Rah Dr 89436
Painted Desert Ct 89436
Painted Rock Rd 89434
Painted Stone Ct 89434
Paisley Ct 89434
Pala Mesa Dr 89436
Palacio Ct 89436
Palermo Dr 89434
Palm Desert Ct & Dr 89441
Palm Springs Ct & Dr 89441
Palmwood Ct & Dr 89434
Palo Alto Cir & Ct 89436
Pam Ln 89431
Panama Ct & Dr 89436
Panther Creek Dr 89436
Panzano Ct & Dr 89434
Par Three Dr 89436
Paradise Hills Ct 89441
Paradise View Dr 89441
Parkland Dr 89434
Parkside Dr 89434
Parlanti Ln 89434
Particles Ct 89436
Pasa Way 89441
Pascus Pl 89431
Paseo Ct 89436
Paso Robles Ct & St 89436
Pasquel Ln 89441
Passage Dr 89436
Path Dr 89436
Patrice Dr 89431
Patrina Way 89436
N & S Patterson Pl 89436
Pauline Ave 89431
Pavo Real Ave 89436
Peach Blossom Way 89436
Peartree Ln 89434
Pebble Bluff Dr 89441
Pebble Creek Dr 89441
Pelican Ct 89441
Penguin Dr 89441
Pennant Ct 89436
E Penny Way 89431
Peppergrass Dr 89436
Peralta Way 89436
Peri Ranch Rd 89434
Perla Ct 89436
Perseus Dr 89436
Peru Dr 89434
Pescadero Dr 89436
Petes Way 89434
Pharaoh Ct 89441
Phenomenon Ct 89436
Phoenix Dr 89436
Piedras Rd 89441
Pileus Rd 89441
Pillary Ct 89436
Pilot Ct & Dr 89436
Pinchot Pass Ct 89436
Pine Meadows Dr 89431
Pinero Ct 89436
Pinewood Ct & Dr 89434
Pinnacle Vista Ct 89436
Pittman Ave 89431
Pittsburgh Ave 89434
Placer Dr 89436
Pleasant View Dr & Pl 89434
Plymouth Way 89431
Poco Bueno Cir 89436
Poco Dove Ct 89436
Poco Rey Ct 89436
Poco Star Ct 89436
Pocono Ct 89434
Point View Way 89431
Poncho Villa Ct 89441
Ponderosa Dr 89431
Poptart Ct 89436
Porto Ct 89436
Pradera Ct & St 89436
Prado Verde Ln 89431
Prairie Dunes Ct 89436
Prairie Moon Ln 89441
Prater Way 89431
E Prater Way
- 1-699 89431
- 701-923 89431
- 1300-2400 89434
- 2402-6898 89434

Pride Dr 89436
Primio Ct & Way 89434
Probasco Way 89431
Promedio Ct 89436
Prospect Ave 89431
Puccinelli Dr 89431
Pullman Ct & Dr 89434
Pumpkin Ridge Dr 89436
Purina Way 89431
Pyramid Way
- 200-298 89431
- 300-3400 89431
- 3402-3498 89431
- 3500-4998 89436
- 5000-8000 89436
- 8002-8198 89436
- 9600-9698 89441
- 9700-11699 89441

S Pyramid Way 89431
Pyramid Peak Cir 89436
E Quail St 89431
Quail Landing Ct 89434
Quail Path Ln 89441
Quantum Ct & Dr 89436
Que Pasa Ct 89441
E Queen Way 89431
Quintero Ln 89441
Quintessa Ct & Dr 89436
Quivera Ln 89441
Rae Ct 89436
Rahonda Dr 89441
Railborne Dr 89434
Railway Ct 89434
Rain Water Ct 89436
Rainier Peak Dr 89436
Ralph Ct 89434
Rama Ct 89436
Rancho Mirage Dr 89436
Rancho Via Dr 89434
Ravello Dr 89436
Rayo Del Sol Ct 89441
Rebecca Dr 89441
Red Blossom Ct 89434
Red Falcon Ct & Way 89441
Red Leaf Ct 89434
Red Sky Ln 89441
Redhead Dr 89441
Redwood Burl Ln 89436
Regier Springs Dr 89441
Rexford Ct 89431
Rey Del Sierra Ct & Dr 89436
Rheingold Ct 89434
Rhine Wine Dr 89436
Rhythm Cir 89436
Ricco Dr 89434
Rice St 89431
Richard Springs Blvd 89436
E Richards Pl & Way 89431
Ridgeland Dr 89434
Ridgetop Ct 89436
Ridgewood Dr 89434
Rincon Ct & Dr 89436
Ringneck Ct & Way 89441
Rio Alayne Ct 89436
Rio Seco Ln 89441
Rio Tinto Dr 89434
Rio Vista Dr 89434
Rioja Ct 89436
Rizzo Dr 89434
Robbie Way 89434
Robert Banks Blvd 89436
Roberta Ln 89431
S Rock Blvd 89431
N Rockdale Dr 89434
Rockin Robin Dr 89441
Rockwell Blvd 89441
Rockwood Dr 89434
Rocky Ridge Blvd & Ct 89431
Rodger Cir 89431
Rodolfo Ct 89436
Rogers Ranch Rd 89441
Rolling Meadows Dr 89436
Roman Dr 89434
Romanga Ct 89436
Rook Ct & Way 89441
Rosecrest Ct 89434
Rosemary Ct & Dr 89434
Roseto Cir 89434
Rosetta Stone Ct & Dr 89441

Rosy Finch Dr 89441
Rota Ct 89436
Round Mountain Cir & Rd 89434
Roundhouse Rd 89431
Roundstone Ct & Dr 89436
Rowe Pl 89441
Roxy Ct 89436
Ruddy Ct & Way 89441
Rue De La Azure 89434
Rue De La Blanc 89434
Rue De La Chartreuse 89434
Rue De La Divoire 89434
Rue De La Fauve 89434
Rue De La Jaune 89434
Rue De La Lavanda 89434
Rue De La Mauve 89434
Rue De La Noir 89434
Rue De La Or 89434
Rue De La Orange 89434
Rue De La Rouge 89434
Rugby Cir 89431
Running Deer Ln 89441
Runnymede Dr 89436
Rusnak Ct 89436
Russell Way 89431
Russian Thistle Dr 89436
Rustler Ct 89436
Ryverson Ct 89441
Sabatino Dr 89434
Sacred Cir 89436
Saddle Shop Ct 89436
Saddleback Ct 89436
Sage Creek Ct 89436
Sage Mountain Ln 89431
Sage Thrasher Way 89436
Sage View Ct & Dr 89434
Sagerdahl Ct 89441
Sahara Ct 89436
Saint George Ct 89441
Saintsbury Ct 89441
Salo Ct 89431
Salomon Cir 89434
Saltern Way 89431
San Diego Ct 89436
San Miguel Way 89434
San Pedro St 89436
San Remo Ct & Dr 89434
Sanchez Ct 89431
N & S Sand Crane Cir 89436
Sand Dune Dr 89441
Sanderling Ct 89441
Sandwood Dr 89434
Sandy St 89431
Sandy Rock Rd 89436
Sansol Ct & Dr 89436
Santa Anita Dr 89436
Santa Barbara Ave 89436
Santa Cruz St 89436
Santa Lupe Ave 89436
Santa Rosa Ave & Ct 89436
Santenay Ln 89436
Santiago Ct 89441
Saratoga Ct 89431
Sartor Ct 89441
Satellite Ct & Dr 89436
Saunto Ct 89436
Savant Ct 89436
Savona Dr 89434
Sawgrass Ct & Ln 89436
Sawyer Way 89431
Saxon Dr 89441
Sbragia Way 89431
Scarborough St 89434
Scarlet Oaks Ct 89436
Scheels Dr 89434
Schroeder Way 89431
Scorpius Dr 89436
Scott Peak Cir 89436
Segre Ct 89436
Segura Ct 89436
Sells St 89431
Sequoia Pass Ct 89436
Serena Springs Ct & Dr 89436
Serenade Dr 89441
Serendipity Ct 89436
Serenghetti Ct & Dr 89436
Setting Sun Ct & Dr 89436
Shaber Ave 89431
Shadow Ct & Ln 89434
Shadow Cast Ct 89434
Shadow Ranch Dr 89434
Shady Oak Dr 89434
Shady Valley Rd 89441
Shady View Ct 89436
Shannon Way 89431
Shari Way 89431
Sharp Springs Ct 89436
Sheena Ct 89436
Sheffield Ct & Way 89431
Shelby Ct & Dr 89436
Sheridan Way 89431
Shriver Blvd 89431
Sienna Ct 89441
Sierra Dust Ct 89436
Siesta Ln 89434
Signa Ct & Dr 89434
Silian Ct 89436
Silicon Dr 89434
Siltstone Way 89436
Silver Coyote Dr 89436
Silver Hills Cir 89431
Silver King Dr 89436
Silver Oak Ln 89441
Silver River Ln 89431
Silver Springs Ct 89436
Silverhorn Ln 89434
Silverton Way 89436
Simms Cir 89431
Singing Hills Dr 89436
Single Foot Ct 89436
Sirach Ct 89436
Situla Ct 89441
E & W Sky Ranch Blvd & Ct 89441
Sky Rocket Ct 89436
Skye Ter 89431
Skyfire Ct 89441
Skylark St 89434
Skyridge Ln 89431
Skystone Dr 89436
Snider Way 89431
Snow Drift Ct 89436
Soar Dr 89441
Soave St 89436
Solaga Ct 89431
Solstice Dr 89436
Sonic Ct 89436
Sonoita Ct 89436
Sonoma Ct 89436
Sonora Pass Ct & Dr 89436
Sorrento Ct & Ln 89434
Southern Way 89431
Southview Dr 89436
Spade Bit Ct & Dr 89434
Spandrell Cir & Ln 89436
Spanish Bay Ct 89436
Spanish Moss Ct & Dr 89436
Spanish Sand 89441
Spanish Springs Ct 89434
Spanish Springs Rd
701-797 89434
799-1499 89434
1501-1799 89434
1801-1897 89436
1899-2400 89436
2402-6798 89436
8901-8999 89441
11000-11098 89441
Spanish Trail Dr 89441
Sparks Blvd
201-497 89434
499-599 89434
601-2399 89434
4600-5098 89436
5100-5198 89436
5200-7098 89436
Sparrow Hawk Dr 89436
Spartan Ct 89436
Specklestone Ct 89436
Sphinx Ct 89441
Spice Islands Ct & Dr 89431
Splitrail Ct 89441
Spoonbill Ct & Dr 89441
Sportoletti Dr 89436
Spring Blossom Ct & Ln 89434
Spring Meadows Dr 89434
N & S Spring Mountain Cir 89436
Spring Ridge Dr 89436
Spring View Ct 89436
Spring Villas Dr 89431
Spring Vista Ct 89436
Springland Ct & Dr 89434
Sprout Way 89431
Spruce Trail Ln 89436
Sprucemont St 89434
Squirreltail Ct & Dr 89436
Stags Leap Cir 89441
S Stanford Way 89431
Star Vista Dr 89436
Starburst Cir & Ct 89441
Starhill Way 89436
Starling Ct 89441
Station St 89434
Steeple Ct 89436
Steffanie Way 89431
Steneri Way 89431
Sterling Ridge Cir 89431
Steven Ct 89431
Sticklebract Dr 89441
Still Brook Ct 89436
Stine Way 89431
Stone View Dr 89436
Stormy Ct 89436
Strasser Dr 89431
Stratus Ct 89436
Strobel Way 89431
Strozzi Ct 89434
Sue Way 89431
Suez Ct 89441
Suki Cir 89441
Sullivan Ln 89431
Summit View Dr 89436
Sun Flag Ct 89436
Sunfield St 89434
Sunkist Dr 89436
Sunlit Ct & Ter 89441
Sunny Slope Dr 89434
Sunnybrook Ct & Ln 89436
Sunset Springs Ln 89441
Sunset Vista Ct 89441
Supreme Ct 89434
Sutter Butte Ct 89436
Suzanne Way 89431
Sweeping View Ct 89441
Sweet Briar Ln 89436
Sweet Cherry Dr 89436
Switch Ct 89434
Sycamore Glen Ct & Dr 89434
E Sydney Dr 89434
Table Mountain Ct & Way 89436
Taft Cir 89431
Tagus Ct 89436
Talking Sparrow Dr 89441
Talladega Ct & Dr 89436
Tallman Rd 89431
Talmedge Cir 89436
Talon Ct & Dr 89441
Tanager Ct 89441
Tangerine St 89434
Tanglewood Dr 89431
Tankersley Ct & Dr 89436
Taryn Dr 89436
Tasker Way 89431
Tavel Ct 89436
Tavira Ct 89436
Teakwood Dr 89431
Tedesco Ct 89434
Teel St 89431
Teglia St 89431
Telehurst Dr 89436
Tempiute Ct 89436
Ten Mile Ct & Dr 89436
Tenabo Way 89434
Tequilla Ct 89441
Teresa Pl 89436
Terra Linda Way 89441
Terrace View Dr 89436
Teruel Ct 89436
Thistle Belle Ct 89436
Thistlewood Ct 89436
Thornton St 89431
Thorpe Ct 89436
Three Bars Ct 89436
Tiburon Ct 89436
Ticino Ct 89434
Tiempo Ct 89436
Tiffany Cir 89431
Tigre Ct 89436
Tina Cir & Ct 89436
Tioga Pass Ct 89436
Titan Ct 89436
Tivoli Ln 89434
Tobago Ct & Dr 89436
Toledo Ct & Dr 89436
Tolusa Ct 89436
Topeka Cir & Ct 89434
Tormes Ct 89436
Toronto Ct 89436
Tortuga Ct 89436
Trabert Cir & Way 89431
Tranquil Dr 89441
Trebol Ct 89436
Tree Swallow Ln 89436
Treeline Ct 89436
Treetop Rd 89436
Trenton Ct 89436
Tres Ahlemeyer Dr 89441
Tres Arroyos Ct & Dr 89436
Trestle Ct 89434
Trevino Ct 89436
Treviso Ct 89434
N & S Tropicana Cir 89436
Tropico Ct 89436
N Truckee Ln 89434
Truckee Canyon Ct 89434
Trujillo Ct 89431
Truth Dr 89436
Turin Ct 89434
Turnberry Dr 89436
Turtledove Ct & Dr 89441
Tuscan Way 89434
Tyler Way 89431
Tyrall Ct 89436
Ulysses Ct & Dr 89436
Umbria Ct 89434
Union Ct & St 89434
United Cir 89431
Upton Way 89431
Usa Pkwy 89434
Valencia Ct & Way 89434
Valerie Cir 89436
Valle De Sol Blvd & Ct 89441
Valle Verde Dr 89441
Valley Forge Way 89431
Valley Vista Way 89431
Valliant Dr 89436
Valparaiso Ct 89441
Van Meter Dr 89434
Vance Way 89431
Vanguard Dr 89436
Varnum Cir 89431
Velda Rose Ln 89441
Venado Ct 89436
Venetian Ct 89436
Veneto Dr 89434
Venezia Dr 89434
Venice Way 89434
Verano Dr 89431
Verbena Way 89431
Verite Ct & Dr 89436
Veronica Ave & Ct 89436
Vicenza Dr 89434
Vickie Ln 89431
E Victorian Ave 89431
Victorian Plaza Cir 89431
Vidette Meadows Dr 89436
Viejo Ct 89436
View St 89431
View Point Dr 89441
Vigo Ct 89436
Village Knoll Dr 89436
Village Meadows Dr 89436
Vintage Hills Pkwy 89436
Virgil Ct & Dr 89441
Virgo Ct & Dr 89436
Vista Blvd
25-97 89434
99-2899 89434
2901-2929 89434
2929-2929 89435
2951-2999 89434
3000-3098 89436
3100-6300 89436
6302-6498 89436
Vista De Lago Dr 89431
Vista Del Rancho Pkwy 89436
Vista Hacienda Way 89436
Vista Heights Dr 89436
Vista Luna Dr 89436
Vista Mountain Ct & Dr 89436
Vista Palomar Way 89436
Vista Serena Way 89436
Vista Terrace Ln 89436
Vivian Dr 89436
Voltice Ct 89436
Voyage Dr 89436
Wabash Cir & Ct 89434
Wagtail Ct & Dr 89441
Waltham Way 89434
Wanbli Ct 89436
Warwick Ct 89431
Washoe Belle 89436
Waterfall Ct & Dr 89434
Waterfield Dr 89434
Watervale Dr 89436
Watson Way 89431
Wave Ct 89436
Wawona Ct 89436
Wayland Dr 89436
Webfoot Ct 89441
Wedekind Rd 89431
Wedgewood Cir 89436
Weizen Dr 89441
Welling Way 89431
Westfall Rd 89436
Westview Blvd & Cir 89434
Wheeler Peak Cir 89436
Whispering Wind Dr & Pl 89436
Whistle Ct 89434
White Dove Ct 89441
White Oak Ln 89436
White Rose Dr & Pl 89441
Whitemare Ct 89436
Whitewood Dr 89434
Whitney Cir & Ct 89436
Whooping Crane Dr 89441
Wicker Ct 89436
Wild Hawk Ct & Dr 89436
Wild Horse Dr 89434
Wild Iris Ct 89436
Wild Island Ct 89434
Wildcat Springs Ct 89436
Wildcreek Dr 89431
William Morby Dr 89434
Willowdale Dr 89434
Wilma Ct & Dr 89431
Windemere Way 89431
Windswept Loop 89436
Wine Cellar Dr 89436
N Wingfield Pkwy 89436
Wingfield Hills Rd 89436
Wingfield Springs Rd 89436
Winter Storm Ct 89436
Winterwood Ave 89436
Wisdom Dr 89436
Wolverine Way 89431
Wood Thrush Ln 89436
Woodberry Dr 89434
Woodburn Ct 89436
Woodglen Dr 89434
Woodhaven Ln 89434
Woodrose Ct 89436
Woodside Dr 89434
Woodstone Dr 89434
Woodtrail Ct & Dr 89434
Woodward Rd 89436
Wright Way 89431
Wunotoo Rd 89434
Xman Way 89431
Yellow Rose Ct 89436
Yellowhammer Ct & Dr 89441
Yonder Ct 89436
York Way 89431
E York Way
1-209 89431
211-694 89431
696-698 89431
700-1099 89434
Zafiro Ct 89436
Zaragoza Ct & Dr 89436
Zephyr Way 89431
Zoroaster Ct 89436

NUMBERED STREETS

1st St 89431
2nd St 89431
3rd St 89431
4th St
200-751 89431
750-750 89432
753-3799 89431
900-3798 89431
5th St 89431
6th St 89431
7th St 89431
9th St 89431
10th St 89431
11th St 89431
12th St 89431
13th St 89431
14th St 89431
S 15th 89431
S 16th 89431
17th St 89431
S 18th 89431
S 19th 89431
20th St 89431
S 21st 89431
22nd St 89431

WINNEMUCCA NV

General Delivery 89445

POST OFFICE BOXES MAIN OFFICE STATIONS AND BRANCHES

Box No.s
All PO Boxes 89446

NAMED STREETS

All Street Addresses 89445

NUMBERED STREETS

All Street Addresses 89445

New Hampshire

People QuickFacts	New Hampshire	USA
Population, 2013 estimate	1,323,459	316,128,839
Population, 2010 (April 1) estimates base	1,316,469	308,747,716
Population, percent change, April 1, 2010 to July 1, 2013	0.5%	2.4%
Population, 2010	1,316,470	308,745,538
Persons under 5 years, percent, 2013	5.0%	6.3%
Persons under 18 years, percent, 2013	20.5%	23.3%
Persons 65 years and over, percent, 2013	15.4%	14.1%
Female persons, percent, 2013	50.6%	50.8%
White alone, percent, 2013 (a)	94.2%	77.7%
Black or African American alone, percent, 2013 (a)	1.5%	13.2%
American Indian and Alaska Native alone, percent, 2013 (a)	0.3%	1.2%
Asian alone, percent, 2013 (a)	2.4%	5.3%
Native Hawaiian and Other Pacific Islander alone, percent, 2013 (a)	Z	0.2%
Two or More Races, percent, 2013	1.6%	2.4%
Hispanic or Latino, percent, 2013 (b)	3.2%	17.1%
White alone, not Hispanic or Latino, percent, 2013	91.6%	62.6%
Living in same house 1 year & over, percent, 2008-2012	86.7%	84.8%
Foreign born persons, percent, 2008-2012	5.3%	12.9%
Language other than English spoken at home, pct age 5+, 2008-2012	7.9%	20.5%
High school graduate or higher, percent of persons age 25+, 2008-2012	91.4%	85.7%
Bachelor's degree or higher, percent of persons age 25+, 2008-2012	33.4%	28.5%
Veterans, 2008-2012	115,415	21,853,912
Mean travel time to work (minutes), workers age 16+, 2008-2012	26.2	25.4
Housing units, 2013	616,537	132,802,859
Homeownership rate, 2008-2012	72.0%	65.5%
Housing units in multi-unit structures, percent, 2008-2012	25.6%	25.9%
Median value of owner-occupied housing units, 2008-2012	$245,600	$181,400
Households, 2008-2012	516,845	115,226,802
Persons per household, 2008-2012	2.47	2.61
Per capita money income in past 12 months (2012 dollars), 2008-2012	$32,758	$28,051
Median household income, 2008-2012	$64,925	$53,046
Persons below poverty level, percent, 2008-2012	8.4%	14.9%

Business QuickFacts	New Hampshire	USA
Private nonfarm establishments, 2012	37,213	7,431,808
Private nonfarm employment, 2012	548,985	115,938,468
Private nonfarm employment, percent change, 2011-2012	-0.9%	2.2%
Nonemployer establishments, 2012	102,310	22,735,915
Total number of firms, 2007	137,815	27,092,908
Black-owned firms, percent, 2007	0.5%	7.1%
American Indian- and Alaska Native-owned firms, percent, 2007	0.4%	0.9%
Asian-owned firms, percent, 2007	1.6%	5.7%
Native Hawaiian and Other Pacific Islander-owned firms, percent, 2007	0.0%	0.1%
Hispanic-owned firms, percent, 2007	1.0%	8.3%
Women-owned firms, percent, 2007	25.8%	28.8%
Manufacturers shipments, 2007 ($1000)	18,592,406	5,319,456,312
Merchant wholesaler sales, 2007 ($1000)	14,564,458	4,174,286,516
Retail sales, 2007 ($1000)	25,353,874	3,917,663,456
Retail sales per capita, 2007	$19,246	$12,990
Accommodation and food services sales, 2007 ($1000)	2,630,968	613,795,732
Building permits, 2012	2,296	829,658

Geography QuickFacts	New Hampshire	USA
Land area in square miles, 2010	8,952.65	3,531,905.43
Persons per square mile, 2010	147	87.4
FIPS Code	33	

(a) Includes persons reporting only one race.
(b) Hispanics may be of any race, so also are included in applicable race categories.
FN: Footnote on this item for this area in place of data
NA: Not available
D: Suppressed to avoid disclosure of confidential information
X: Not applicable
S: Suppressed; does not meet publication standards
Z: Value greater than zero but less than half unit of measure shown
F: Fewer than 100 firms
Source: US Census Bureau State & County QuickFacts

New Hampshire

3 DIGIT ZIP CODE MAP

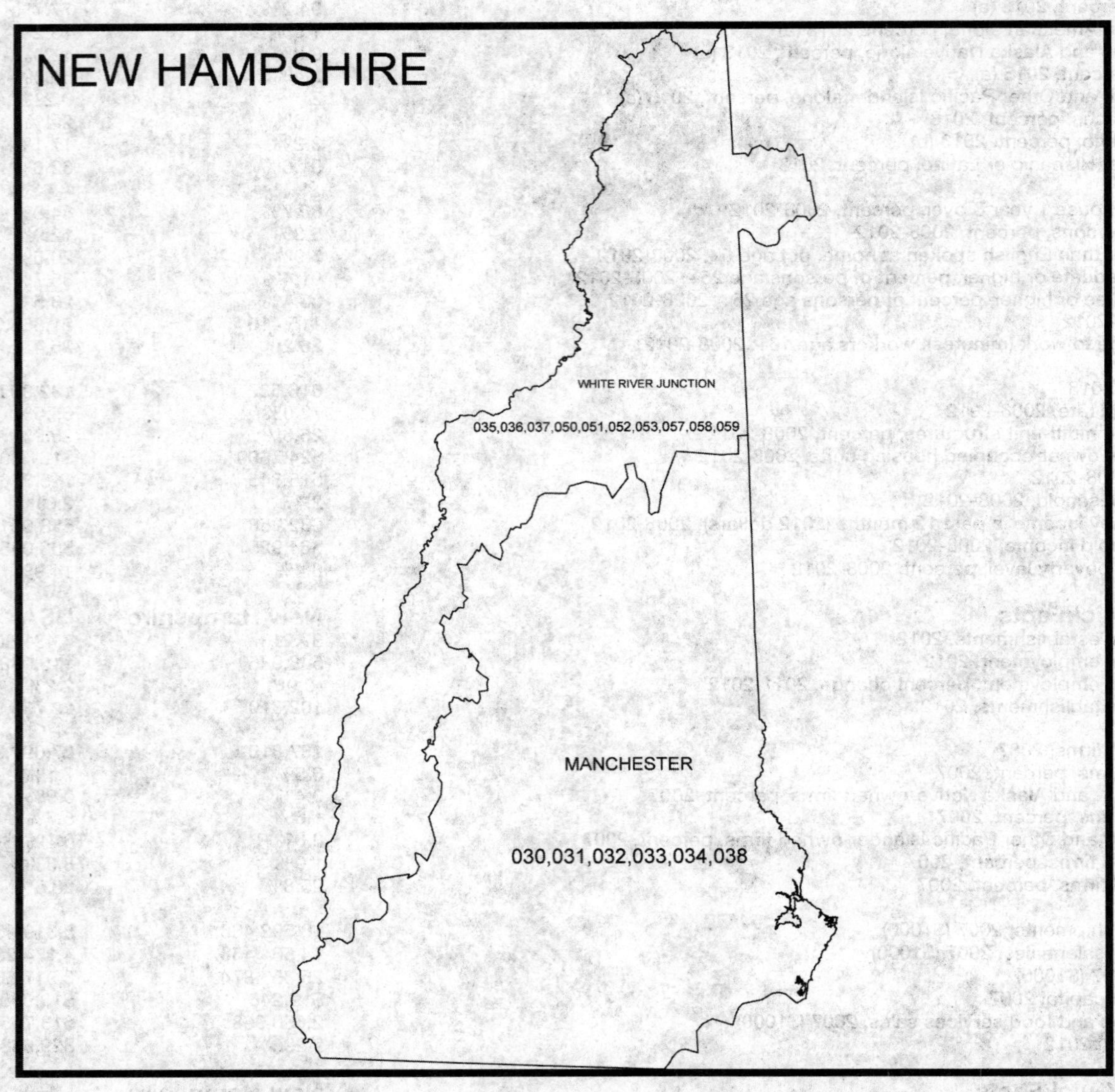

New Hampshire

(Abbreviation: NH)

Post Office, County	ZIP Code

Places with more than one ZIP code are listed in capital letters, See pages indicated.

Acworth, Sullivan ... 03601
Albany, Carroll ... 03818
Alexandria, Grafton ... 03222
Allenstown, Merrimack ... 03275
Alstead, Cheshire ... 03602
Alton, Belknap ... 03809
Alton Bay, Belknap ... 03810
Amherst, Hillsborough ... 03031
Andover, Merrimack ... 03216
Antrim, Hillsborough ... 03440
Ashland, Grafton ... 03217
Ashuelot, Cheshire ... 03441
Atkinson, Rockingham ... 03811
Auburn, Rockingham ... 03032
Barnstead, Belknap ... 03218
Barrington, Strafford ... 03825
Bartlett, Carroll ... 03812
Bath, Grafton ... 03740
Bedford, Hillsborough ... 03110
Belmont, Belknap ... 03220
Bennington, Hillsborough ... 03442
Benton, Grafton ... 03785
Berlin, Coos ... 03570
Bethlehem, Grafton ... 03574
Boscawen, Merrimack ... 03303
Bow, Merrimack ... 03304
Bradford, Merrimack ... 03221
Brentwood, Rockingham ... 03833
Bretton Woods, Coos ... 03575
Bristol, Grafton ... 03222
Brookfield, Carroll ... 03872
Brookline, Hillsborough ... 03033
Campton, Grafton ... 03223
Canaan, Grafton ... 03741
Candia, Rockingham ... 03034
Canterbury, Merrimack ... 03224
Carroll, Coos ... 03598
Center Barnstead, Belknap ... 03225
Center Conway, Carroll ... 03813
Center Harbor, Belknap ... 03226
Center Ossipee, Carroll ... 03814
Center Sandwich, Carroll ... 03227
Center Strafford, Strafford ... 03815
Center Tuftonboro, Carroll ... 03816
Charlestown, Sullivan ... 03603
Chatham, Carroll ... 03813
Chester, Rockingham ... 03036
Chesterfield, Cheshire ... 03443
Chichester, Merrimack ... 03258
Chocorua, Carroll ... 03817
Claremont, Sullivan ... 03743
Clarksville, Coos ... 03592
Colebrook, Coos ... 03576
CONCORD, Merrimack
(See Page 2534)
Contoocook, Merrimack ... 03229
Conway, Carroll ... 03818
Cornish, Sullivan ... 03745
Cornish Flat, Sullivan ... 03746
Croydon, Sullivan ... 03773
Dalton, Coos ... 03598
Danbury, Merrimack ... 03230
Danville, Rockingham ... 03819
Deerfield, Rockingham ... 03037
Deering, Hillsborough ... 03244
Derry, Rockingham ... 03038
Dixville, Coos ... 03576
Dorchester, Grafton ... 03266
DOVER, Strafford
(See Page 2535)
Drewsville, Cheshire ... 03604
Dublin, Cheshire ... 03444
Dummer, Coos ... 03588
Dunbarton, Merrimack ... 03046
Durham, Strafford ... 03824
East Andover, Merrimack ... 03231
East Candia, Rockingham ... 03040
East Derry, Rockingham ... 03041
East Hampstead, Rockingham ... 03826
East Hebron, Grafton ... 03241
East Kingston, Rockingham ... 03827
East Lempster, Sullivan ... 03605
East Wakefield, Carroll ... 03830
Eaton Center, Carroll ... 03832
Effingham, Carroll ... 03882
Elkins, Merrimack ... 03233
Ellsworth, Grafton ... 03223
Enfield, Grafton ... 03748
Enfield Center, Grafton ... 03749
Epping, Rockingham ... 03042
Epsom, Merrimack ... 03234
Errol, Coos ... 03579
Etna, Grafton ... 03750
Exeter, Rockingham ... 03833
Farmington, Strafford ... 03835
Fitzwilliam, Cheshire ... 03447
Francestown, Hillsborough ... 03043
Franconia, Grafton ... 03580
Franklin, Merrimack ... 03235
Freedom, Carroll ... 03836
Fremont, Rockingham ... 03044
Georges Mills, Sullivan ... 03751
Gilford, Belknap ... 03249
Gilmanton, Belknap ... 03237
Gilmanton Iron Works, Belknap ... 03837
Gilsum, Cheshire ... 03448
Glen, Carroll ... 03838
Glencliff, Grafton ... 03238
Goffstown, Hillsborough ... 03045
Gorham, Coos ... 03581
Goshen, Sullivan ... 03752
Grafton, Grafton ... 03240
Grantham, Sullivan ... 03753
Greenfield, Hillsborough ... 03047
Greenland, Rockingham ... 03840
Greenville, Hillsborough ... 03048
Groveton, Coos ... 03582
Guild, Sullivan ... 03754
Hales Location, Carroll ... 03860
Hampstead, Rockingham ... 03841
HAMPTON, Rockingham
(See Page 2536)
Hampton Falls, Rockingham ... 03844
Hancock, Hillsborough ... 03449
Hanover, Grafton ... 03755
Harrisville, Cheshire ... 03450
Harts Location, Carroll ... 03812
Haverhill, Grafton ... 03765
Hebron, Grafton ... 03241
Henniker, Merrimack ... 03242
Hill, Merrimack ... 03243
Hillsboro, Hillsborough ... 03244
Hillsborough, Hillsborough ... 03244
Hinsdale, Cheshire ... 03451
Holderness, Grafton ... 03245
Hollis, Hillsborough ... 03049
Hooksett, Merrimack ... 03106
Hopkinton, Merrimack ... 03229
Hudson, Hillsborough ... 03051
Intervale, Carroll ... 03845
Jackson, Carroll ... 03846
Jaffrey, Cheshire ... 03452
Jefferson, Coos ... 03583
Kearsarge, Carroll ... 03847
Keene, Cheshire ... 03431
Kensington, Rockingham ... 03833
Kingston, Rockingham ... 03848
LACONIA, Belknap
(See Page 2536)
Lancaster, Coos ... 03584
Landaff, Grafton ... 03585
Langdon, Cheshire ... 03602
LEBANON, Grafton
(See Page 2537)
Lee, Strafford ... 03824
Lee, Strafford ... 03861
Lempster, Sullivan ... 03605
Lincoln, Grafton ... 03251
Lisbon, Grafton ... 03585
Litchfield, Hillsborough ... 03052
Littleton, Grafton ... 03561
Lochmere, Belknap ... 03252
Londonderry, Rockingham ... 03038
Londonderry, Rockingham ... 03053
Loudon, Merrimack ... 03307
Lyman, Grafton ... 03585
Lyme, Grafton ... 03768
Lyme Center, Grafton ... 03769
Lyndeborough, Hillsborough ... 03082
Madbury, Strafford ... 03823
Madison, Carroll ... 03849
MANCHESTER, Hillsborough
(See Page 2537)
Marlborough, Cheshire ... 03455
Marlow, Cheshire ... 03456
Mason, Hillsborough ... 03048
Melvin Village, Carroll ... 03850
Meredith, Belknap ... 03253
Meriden, Sullivan ... 03770
Merrimack, Hillsborough ... 03054
Middleton, Carroll ... 03887
Milan, Coos ... 03588
Milford, Hillsborough ... 03055
Milton, Strafford ... 03851
Milton Mills, Strafford ... 03852
Mirror Lake, Carroll ... 03853
Monroe, Grafton ... 03771
Mont Vernon, Hillsborough ... 03057
Moultonborough, Carroll ... 03254
Mount Sunapee, Merrimack ... 03255
Mount Washington, Coos ... 03589
Munsonville, Cheshire ... 03457
NASHUA, Hillsborough
(See Page 2539)
Nelson, Cheshire ... 03457
New Boston, Hillsborough ... 03070
New Castle, Rockingham ... 03854
New Durham, Strafford ... 03855
New Hampton, Belknap ... 03256
New Ipswich, Hillsborough ... 03071
New London, Merrimack ... 03257
Newbury, Merrimack ... 03255
Newfields, Rockingham ... 03856
Newington, Rockingham ... 03801
Newmarket, Rockingham ... 03857
Newport, Sullivan ... 03773
Newton, Rockingham ... 03858
Newton Junction, Rockingham ... 03859
North Conway, Carroll ... 03860
North Hampton, Rockingham ... 03862
North Haverhill, Grafton ... 03774
North Salem, Rockingham ... 03073
North Sandwich, Carroll ... 03259
North Stratford, Coos ... 03590
North Sutton, Merrimack ... 03260
North Swanzey, Cheshire ... 03431
North Walpole, Cheshire ... 03609
North Woodstock, Grafton ... 03262
Northfield, Belknap ... 03276
Northumberland, Coos ... 03582
Northwood, Rockingham ... 03261
Nottingham, Rockingham ... 03290
Orange, Grafton ... 03741
Orford, Grafton ... 03777
Ossipee, Carroll ... 03864
Pelham, Hillsborough ... 03076
Pembroke, Merrimack ... 03275
Penacook, Merrimack ... 03303
Peterborough, Hillsborough ... 03458
Piermont, Grafton ... 03779
Pike, Grafton ... 03780
Pittsburg, Coos ... 03592
Pittsfield, Merrimack ... 03263
Plainfield, Sullivan ... 03781
Plaistow, Rockingham ... 03865
Plymouth, Grafton ... 03264
PORTSMOUTH, Rockingham
(See Page 2542)
Randolph, Coos ... 03593
Raymond, Rockingham ... 03077
Richmond, Cheshire ... 03470
Rindge, Cheshire ... 03461
ROCHESTER, Strafford
(See Page 2543)
Rollinsford, Strafford ... 03869
Roxbury, Cheshire ... 03431
Rumney, Grafton ... 03266
Rye, Rockingham ... 03870
Rye Beach, Rockingham ... 03871
Salem, Rockingham ... 03079
Salisbury, Merrimack ... 03268
Sanbornton, Belknap ... 03269
Sanbornville, Carroll ... 03872
Sandown, Rockingham ... 03873
Sandwich, Carroll ... 03227
Seabrook, Rockingham ... 03874
Sharon, Hillsborough ... 03458
Shelburne, Coos ... 03581
Silver Lake, Carroll ... 03875
Somersworth, Strafford ... 03878
South Acworth, Sullivan ... 03607
South Hampton, Rockingham ... 03827
South Newbury, Merrimack ... 03272
South Sutton, Merrimack ... 03273
South Tamworth, Carroll ... 03883
Spofford, Cheshire ... 03462
Springfield, Sullivan ... 03284
Stark, Coos ... 03582
Stewartstown, Coos ... 03576
Stinson Lake, Grafton ... 03274
Stoddard, Cheshire ... 03464
Strafford, Strafford ... 03884
Stratford, Coos ... 03590
Stratham, Rockingham ... 03885
Sugar Hill, Grafton ... 03586
Sullivan, Cheshire ... 03445
Sunapee, Sullivan ... 03782
Suncook, Merrimack ... 03275
Surry, Cheshire ... 03431
Swanzey, Cheshire ... 03446
Tamworth, Carroll ... 03886
Temple, Hillsborough ... 03084
Thornton, Grafton ... 03223
Thornton, Grafton ... 03285
Tilton, Belknap ... 03276
Troy, Cheshire ... 03465
Twin Mountain, Coos ... 03595
Union, Carroll ... 03887
Walpole, Cheshire ... 03608
Warner, Merrimack ... 03278
Warren, Grafton ... 03279
Washington, Sullivan ... 03280
Waterville Valley, Grafton ... 03215
Weare, Hillsborough ... 03281
Webster, Merrimack ... 03303
Wentworth, Grafton ... 03282
Wentworths Location, Coos ... 03579
West Chesterfield, Cheshire ... 03466
West Lebanon, Grafton ... 03784
West Nottingham, Rockingham ... 03291
West Ossipee, Carroll ... 03890
West Peterborough, Hillsborough ... 03468
West Stewartstown, Coos ... 03597
West Swanzey, Cheshire ... 03469
Westmoreland, Cheshire ... 03467
Whitefield, Coos ... 03598
Wilmot, Merrimack ... 03287
Wilton, Hillsborough ... 03086
Winchester, Cheshire ... 03470
Windham, Rockingham ... 03087
Windsor, Hillsborough ... 03244
Winnisquam, Belknap ... 03289
Wolfeboro, Carroll ... 03894
Wolfeboro Falls, Carroll ... 03896
Wonalancet, Carroll ... 03897
Woodstock, Grafton ... 03293
Woodsville, Grafton ... 03785

CONCORD NH

General Delivery 03302

POST OFFICE BOXES MAIN OFFICE STATIONS AND BRANCHES

Box No.s
1 - 4260 03302
10008 - 10224 03301

NAMED STREETS

A St 03301
Abbott Rd 03303
Abbottville Rd 03301
Academy St
 1-99 03301
 1-99 03303
Acorn Dr 03301
Adonis Ct 03303
Aherns Ct 03301
Airport Rd 03301
Albin St 03301
Alder Creek Dr 03303
Alice Dr 03303
Allard St 03301
Allen Rd & St 03303
Allison St 03301
Alton Woods Dr 03301
Americana Dr 03303
Amoskeag Rd 03301
Amy Way 03303
Angela Way 03301
Antrim Ave 03301
Appaloosa Run 03301
Appleton St 03301
April Ave 03303
Asby Rd 03301
Aster Ct 03303
Auburn St 03301
Autumn Dr 03301
Avon St 03301
B St 03301
Badger St 03301
Bailey Dr 03303
Baileys Lndg 03303
Bainbridge Dr 03301
Baker St 03303
Barberry Ln 03301
Barnett Dr 03303
Barrell Ct 03301
Barrett Ave 03303
Bashan Hollow Rd 03303
Basin St 03301
Batchelder Mill Rd 03301
Battle St 03303
Beacon Ct & St 03301
Bean St 03303
Beaver St 03301
Beaver Dam Dr 03303
Beaver Meadow Dr 03301
Becky Ln 03301
Bela Brook Ln 03301
Bellflower Cir 03303
Benchenw St 03301
Bentwood St 03303
Berle Dr 03303
Best Ave 03303
Beth Dr 03303
Bicentennial Sq 03301
Bill Alice Ln 03303
Birch St 03303
Birchdale Rd 03301
Bishopsgate 03301
Bittersweet Ln 03303
Black Hill Rd 03301
Blackberry Ln 03303
Blackwater Rd 03303
Blake St 03301
Blanchard St 03301
Blevens Dr 03301
Blueberry Ln 03303
Bluebird Ln 03303
Bluffs Dr 03303
Blye Farm Rd 03301
Boanza Dr 03303
Bog Rd 03303
Bonney St 03303
Borough Rd 03303
Bouton St 03301
Bow St 03301
Boyce Ln 03303
Bradley St 03301
Branch Tpke 03301
Brandy Ln 03301
Break O Day Dr 03301
Briar Rd 03301
Bridge St 03301
Bridge House Rd 03303
Bridle Path Trl 03301
Broad Ave 03301
Broad Cove Dr 03303
Broadway 03301
Brodeur St 03303
Broken Bridge Rd 03301
Broken Ground Dr 03301
Brook St 03301
Brookfield Cir 03303
Brookside Dr 03301
Brookwood Dr 03301
Brushwood Dr 03301
Burns Ave 03301
Buxton Pl 03303
Bye St 03303
Cabernet Dr 03303
Call Rd 03303
Call St 03301
Callaway Dr 03301
Cambridge St 03301
Camelia Ave & Dr 03301
Campion Cir 03303
Canal St 03303
Canoe Dr 03303
Canterbury Rd 03301
Canton Cir 03301
Capital Plz 03301
Capitol St 03301
Cardinal Rd 03301
Carpenter St 03301
Carter St 03301
Carter Hill Rd 03303
Cashell Ln 03303
Celtic St 03301
Cemetery St 03301
Centennial Dr 03303
Centerwood Dr 03301
Centre St 03301
Chablis Ter 03303
Chadwick Hill Rd 03303
Chancellor Dr 03303
Chandler St 03303
Chapel St 03301
Chapman St 03303
Charles St
 1-29 03301
 3-7 03303
 9-49 03303
Charles Doe Dr 03301
Chase St 03301
Checkerberry Ln 03301
Chenell Dr 03303
Cherry St 03301
Cheryl Dr 03303
Chesley St 03303
Chesterfield Dr 03301
Chestnut Ct 03303
Chestnut Pasture Rd 03301
Chicory Ct 03303
Christian Ave 03301
Christopher Robert Dr 03303
Church St 03301
Cider Mill Dr 03303
Circle Dr 03303
Clarke St 03301
Clematis Cir 03303
Cleveland Ave 03301
Clinton St 03301
Clothespin Bridge Rd 03303
Clough Sanborn Hill Rd 03303
Clover Ct 03303
College Dr 03301
Columbine Pl 03303
Columbus Ave 03301
Comeared St 03303
Commercial St
 1-1 03301
 1-99 03303
 3-199 03301
S Commercial St 03301
Community Dr 03303
Conant Dr 03301
Concord Dr 03303
Concord Gdns 03301
Concord St 03301
Constitution Ave 03301
Coolidge Ave 03301
Coral St 03303
Corn Hill Rd 03303
Cornell St 03301
Cote St 03301
Cottage Ct 03301
Cottage St 03303
Country Club Ln 03301
Court St 03301
Coventry Rd 03301
Crawford Rd 03303
Cremin St 03303
Crescent St 03301
Crestwood Dr 03301
N Cricket Ln 03301
Crosby St 03301
Cross St 03303
Currier Rd 03301
Curtice Ave 03301
Curtisville Rd 03301
Cypress St 03301
Dakin St 03301
Damante Dr 03301
Daniel Webster Hwy 03303
Daphne Ct 03303
Dartmouth St 03301
Davis St 03301
Dawn Dr 03303
Deer Meadow Rd 03303
Deer Run Rd 03303
Deer Track Ln 03301
Delta Dr 03301
Dempsey Dr 03303
Denis Dr 03301
Depot St 03301
Detour Rd 03303
Devinne Dr 03301
District 5 Rd 03303
Dixon Ave 03301
Dogwood Ter 03303
Dolan St 03301
Dolphin St 03303
Dominique Dr 03303
Donovan St 03301
Douglas Ave 03303
Dove St 03303
Dover St 03301
Downing St 03303
Drew St 03301
Dudley Dr 03301
Duke Ln 03303
Dunbarton Rd 03301
Dunklee St 03301
Dustin Rd 03303
Duston Dr 03301
Dwinell Dr 03301
Eagle Sq 03301
East St 03303
Eastern Ave 03301
Eastman St 03301
Eddy Dr 03303
Edgemont St 03301
Edgewood Dr 03301
Edward Dr 03301
Eel St 03303
Elderberry Pl 03303
Eldridge St 03301
Electric Ave 03303
Elijah St 03303
Elizabeth Dr 03303
Elliot St 03303
Ellsworth St 03301
Elm St 03303
Elmwood Ave 03301
Emerson Rd 03301
Emily Way 03303
N & S Emperor Dr 03303
Engel St 03301
Essex St 03301
Exchange Ave 03301
Fairbanks Dr 03303
Fairbanks St 03301
Fairfield Dr 03301
Fairview Dr 03301
Farmwood Rd 03301
Farnum Ave 03301
Fayette St 03301
Federal St 03301
Fellows St 03301
Fernald St 03301
Fernrock St 03301
Ferrin Rd 03303
Ferry St 03301
Fessenden Dr 03303
Fifield St 03303
Fisher Ave 03303
Fisher St 03301
Fisherville Rd 03303
Fisk Rd 03301
Fiskill Farm 03301
Flaghole Rd 03301
Flamingo Dr 03303
Flume St 03303
Fogg St 03301
Folsom Dr 03303
Forest Ln 03303
Forest St 03301
Fort Eddy Rd 03301
Foster St 03301
Foundry St 03301
Fowler St 03303
Fox Run 03301
Foxcross Cir 03303
Foxglove Ter 03303
Franconia Rd 03303
Franklin St 03301
Franklin Pierce Dr 03303
Freedom Acres Dr 03301
Fremont St 03301
Frost Ln 03303
Frost Rd 03301
N & S Fruit St 03301
Fuller St 03301
Gabby Ln 03301
Gage St 03303
Gale St 03301
Gallen Dr 03303
Garden St 03301
Garrison St 03301
Garvins Falls Rd 03301
Gas St 03301
Gates St 03301
General Stark Dr 03303
Gentian Dr 03303
Gerrish Rd 03303
Gilmore St 03301
Gio Ct 03301
Gladstone St 03301
Glen St 03301
Glendale Rd 03301
Godbout Dr 03301
Goldenrod Ln 03301
Goodhue Rd 03303
Gordon Ct 03301
Governors Way 03303
Graham Rd 03301
Granite Ave 03301
Granite Pl 03301
Granite Way 03303
Grant St 03301
Grappone Dr 03301
Great Falls Dr 03303
Greeley St 03301
Green St 03301
Greenwich St & Trl 03301
Greenwood Ave 03301
Groton Dr 03301
Grove St 03301
Grover St 03301
Guay St 03301
Guide Board Hill Rd 03303
Gulf St 03301
Gully Hill Rd 03301
Haig St 03301
Haines Rd 03301
Hall St 03301
Hammond St 03301
Hampshire Dr 03301
Hampton St 03301
Hannah Dustin Dr 03301
Hanover St 03301
Hardy Ave & Ln 03303
Harrison St 03301
Harrod St 03301
Harvard St 03301
Hayward Brook Dr 03301
Hazel Dr 03301
Hazen Dr 03301
Heartwood Ln 03303
Heather Ln 03301
Hedge Rose Ln 03301
Heights Rd 03301
Henniker St 03301
Herbert St 03301
Higgins Pl 03301
High St 03303
Highland St 03301
Highridge Trl 03301
Hillcrest Ave 03301
Hills Ave 03301
Hillside Rd 03301
Hobart St 03303
Hoit Rd 03301
Hollings Rd 03303
Hollins Ave 03303
Holly St 03301
Holt St 03301
Home Ave 03301
Honey Dr 03303
Hooksett Tpke 03301
Hope Ave 03301
Hopkinton Rd 03301
Horse Hill Rd 03303
Horseshoe Pond Ln 03301
Hot Hole Pond Rd 03301
Hullbakers Pl 03303
Humphrey St 03301
Huntington St 03301
Hutchins St
 1-50 03301
 51-199 03303
 401-499 03301
Hutchinson Ave 03301
Industrial Park Dr 03301
Institute Dr 03301
Integra Dr 03301
Intervale Rd 03301
W Iron Works Rd 03301
Irving Dr 03301
Island Rd 03303
Jackson St
 27A-27B 03301
Jasmine St 03303
Jay Dr 03301
Jefferson St 03301
Jennifer Dr 03301
Jennings Dr 03301
Joffre St 03301
Johnson Ave 03301
Johnson St 03303
Jonathan Dr 03303
Jordan Ave 03301
Josiah Bartlett Rd 03301
Judith Dr 03301
Juniper Ln 03301
Justin Dr 03303
K St 03301
Keanes Ave 03301
Kearsarge St 03301
Ked Dr 03301
Kellom St 03301
Keneval Ave 03303
Kennedy St 03301
Kensington Rd 03301
Kent St 03301
Kesavan Dr 03303
Kimball Ln 03303
Kimball St 03301
King St
 1-99 03301
 100-299 03303
Kipling Cir 03301
Knight St 03301
Knights Meadow Rd 03303
Knoll St 03301
Knowlton Rd 03303
Kozy Trl 03301
Kyle Rd 03303
Ladybug Ln 03301
Lake Rd 03303
Lake St 03301
Lake View Dr 03303
Lamprey Ln 03301
Langdon St 03301
Langley Pkwy 03301
Lantern Ln 03301
Larkspur Pl 03303
Laurel St 03301
Lawrence Ave 03303
Lawrence St 03301
Lawrence Street Ext 03301
Leanne Dr 03303
Ledge Cir 03301
Leighton Ave 03301
Lew Alice Dr 03303
Lewis Ln 03301
Liberty St 03301
Lilac St 03303
Lincoln St
 1-99 03301
 1-99 03303
Linden St 03303
Lisa Ln 03301
Little Hill Rd 03303
Little Pond Rd 03301
Locke Rd 03301
Long St 03303
Long Pond Rd 03301
Longmeadow Dr 03301
Longver Ln 03303
Look Out Cir 03301
Loon Ave 03303
Loop Rd 03301
Lori Ln 03303
Loudon Rd
 1-19 03301
 18-18 03302
 20-498 03301
 21-499 03301
Lovage Pl 03303
Low Ave 03301
Lyndon St 03301
Maccoy St 03303
Madison St 03301
N Main St
 1-299 03301
 12-18 03303
 20-299 03303
S Main St 03301
Maitland St 03301
Manchester Dr 03303
Manchester St 03301
Mandevilla Ln 03301
Manor Rd 03303
Maple Ln & St 03301
Maplewood Ln 03301
Margerie St 03303
Marilyn Dr 03303
Marion St 03301
Market Ln 03301
Marlboro Rd 03303
Marshall St 03301
Martin Ave 03303
Martin St 03301
Mason Ct 03301
Matthew St 03301
Max Ln 03301
Mcguire St 03301
Mckee Dr 03301
Mckinley St 03301
S Meadow St 03301
Merlot Ct 03303
Merrill Corner Rd 03303
Merrimack Cir 03303
Merrimack St
 1-40 03301
 1-199 03303
 42-98 03301
Metalak Dr 03303
Meter St 03303
Middlebury St 03301
S Midland St 03301
Mill St 03301
Millennium Way 03303
Millstone Dr 03301
Millstream Ln 03303
Minot St 03301
Minuteman Way 03301
Misty Oak Dr 03301
Mitchell St 03303
Modena Dr 03303
Monarch Dr 03303
Monitor Dr 03301
Monroe St 03301
Montgomery St 03301
Mooreland Ave 03301
Morrill Ln 03301
Morton St 03301
Mount Vernon Terrace Rd 03303
Mountain Rd 03301
Mulberry St 03301
Mutton Rd 03303
Myrtle St 03301
Nasturtium Ter 03303
New Castle St 03301
New Hampshire Dr 03303
New London Dr 03303
New Meadow Rd 03303
Newbury Rd 03303
Newport Cir 03303
Newton Ave 03301
Nickerson Dr 03303
Nivelle St 03301
Norwich St 03301
Noyes St 03301
Oak St
 1-99 03301
 1-99 03303
Oak Hill Rd 03303
Oakmont Dr 03301
Old Dover Rd 03301
Old Loudon Rd 03301
Old Route 127 03303
Old Suncook Rd 03301
Old Turnpike Rd 03301
Orchard St 03301
Oriole Rd 03301
Orion St 03301
Ormond St 03301
Oscar Blvd 03301
Osgood St 03301
Otter Dr 03301
Overlook Trl 03301
Oxalis Way 03303
Oxbow Dr 03303
Palm St 03303
Palmer Ave 03301
Palomino Ct 03301
W Parish Rd 03303
Park Rdg 03301
Park St
 1-99 03301
 1-99 03303
Parmenter Rd 03303
Partridge Rd 03301
Pavillion Dr 03303
Peabody St 03301
Peaceful Ln 03303
Peach St 03301
Pearl St 03301
Pearson Hill Rd 03303

Pekoe Dr 03301
Pelham Ln 03301
Pembroke Rd 03301
Penacook Cir 03303
Penacook St
1-199 03303
11-11 03301
13-199 03301
Penwood Dr 03303
Perkins Ct & St 03301
Perley St 03301
Perry Ave 03301
Peterson Cir 03303
Phenix Ave 03301
Pierce St 03301
Pillsbury St 03301
Pine St
1-99 03301
1-8 03303
Pine Acres Rd 03301
Pine Crest Cir 03301
Pinehurst St 03303
Pinewood Trl 03301
Piscataqua Rd 03301
Pitman St 03301
Pleasant St
1-399 03301
1001-1097 03303
1099-1599 03303
Pleasant Street Ext 03301
Pleasant View Ave 03301
Plum St 03301
Plymouth Dr 03301
Pond Hill Rd 03303
Pond Place Ln 03301
Poplar Ave 03301
W Portsmouth St 03301
Potash Rd 03303
Prescott St 03301
Primrose Ln 03303
Prince St 03301
Princeton St 03301
Profile Ave 03301
Prospect St
1-99 03301
1-99 03303
Province Rd 03303
Putney Ave 03301
Quail Rdg 03301
Quaker St 03301
Queen St 03303
Quincy St 03301
Railroad St 03301
Randlett St 03303
Randolph Rd 03301
Raymond Rd 03303
Redington Rd 03301
Redwing Rd 03301
Redwood Ave 03301
Regional Dr 03301
Reserve Pl 03301
Rex Dr 03303
Rhodora Ct 03303
Richmond Dr 03303
Ridge Rd 03301
Ridgewood Ln 03301
Ripley St 03301
River Rd 03303
Riverhill Ave 03303
Riverview Ln 03301
Robin Rd 03301
Robin St 03303
Robinson St 03301
Roby Rd 03303
Rochester Ln 03301
Rockingham St 03301
Rockland Rd 03301
Roger Ave 03301
Rolfe Rd & St 03303
Rolinda Ave 03301
Rollins St 03301
Roosevelt Ave 03301
Rosemary Ct 03303
Rosewood Dr 03303
Rosue Dr 03303
Route 103 E 03303
Rowell St 03301
Roy St 03301
Royal Gdns 03301
Rum Hill Rd 03301
Rumford Dr 03303
Rumford St 03301
Rundlett St 03301
Runnells Rd 03303
Russell St 03301
Ryans Way 03301
Saint Catherines St 03303
Saint Johns St 03301
Samuel Dr 03301
Sanborn Rd 03301
Sanders St 03303
Sandquist St 03301
Sawmill Rd 03301
School St
1-199 03301
1-99 03303
Scotts Ave 03301
Sewalls Falls Rd 03301
Sexton Ave 03301
Shaker Rd 03301
Shaw St 03303
Shawmut St 03301
Sheep Davis Rd 03301
Shenandoah Dr 03301
Sherman Dr 03303
Short St 03301
E Side Dr 03301
Silk Farm Rd 03301
Skyline Dr 03303
Snow St 03303
Snow Pond Rd 03301
Songbird Dr 03301
Sorrel Dr 03303
South St 03301
Spaulding St 03301
Spillway Ln 03301
N & S Spring St 03301
Spring Hill Dr 03301
Springfield St 03301
Spruce St 03301
Stark St 03303
N & S State St 03301
Steeple Vw 03303
Stevens Dr 03301
Stickney Ave 03301
Stickney Hill Rd 03301
Stirrup Iron Rd 03303
Stone St 03301
Stone Street Ext 03301
Storrs St 03301
Strawberry Ln 03301
Styles Dr 03301
E & W Sugar Ball Rd 03301
Sulloway St 03301
Summer St 03303
Summit St 03301
Sundance Rd 03301
Sunset Ave 03301
Susan Ln 03301
Swan Cir 03301
Sweatt St 03301
Sylvester St 03303
Tahanto St 03301
Tallant Rd 03301
Tanner St 03303
Tara Dr 03301
Taylor Ln 03303
Temi Rd 03301
Tenney St 03301
Terrace Rd 03301
Terrace Hill Rd 03303
Terrill Park Dr 03301
Thackeray Rd 03301
Thayer Pond Rd 03301
The Acre 03303
Theatre St 03301
Thomas St 03301
Thompson St 03301
Thorndike St 03301
Timberline Dr 03301
Tow Path Ln 03301
Tower Cir 03303
Tremblay Ct 03301
Tremont St
1-99 03301
1-99 03303
Triangle Park Dr 03301
Trinity St 03301
Tuttle St 03301
Ty Ln 03303
Tyler Rd 03303
Union St 03301
Valley St 03301
Valley Of Industry 03303
Venne Cir 03301
Verbena Way 03303
Vernon St 03301
Via Tranquilla St 03301
Victorian Ln 03301
View St 03301
NE Village Rd 03301
Village St 03303
Villanova Dr 03303
Vinton Dr 03303
Walker Ave & St 03301
Walker Pond Rd 03303
Wall St 03301
Walnut St
1-12 03301
13-99 03303
Warner Rd 03303
Warren St 03301
Washington Ct 03301
Washington St
19A-19B 03301
4-199 03303
7-17 03301
19-94 03301
Water St
1-99 03301
1-299 03303
N Water St 03303
Watkins Way 03301
Watson Ct 03301
Waumbec Rd 03301
Waverly St 03301
Webster Ln & Pl 03303
Wedgewood Dr 03301
Weir Rd 03303
Welcome Ave 03303
Welcome Dr 03301
Wentworth St 03301
West St 03301
Westbourne Rd 03301
Westwind Village Rd 03303
Wheaton Ave 03301
White St 03301
White Plains Rd 03303
Whitewater Dr 03303
Whitney Rd 03301
Whittaker Cir 03303
Whittridge Ave 03301
Wiggin St 03301
Wildemere Ter 03301
Wilderness Ln 03303
Wildflower Dr 03303
Wildwind Ter 03303
Wilfred Ave 03301
Willard St 03303
Wilson Ave 03301
Winant St 03301
Windham Dr 03301
Windsor Terrace Rd 03303
Winnepocket Rd 03303
Winsor Ave 03303
Winter St 03303
Winterberry Ln 03303
Winthrop St 03301
Wolf Ln 03303
Wood Ave 03301
Woodbine Ave 03303
Woodbury Ln 03303
Woodcrest Heights Dr 03301
Woodman St 03301
Wyman St 03301
Yale St 03301
Yarrow Way 03303
Yorkshire Ln 03301

NUMBERED STREETS

All Street Addresses 03301

DOVER NH

General Delivery 03821

POST OFFICE BOXES MAIN OFFICE STATIONS AND BRANCHES

Box No.s
All PO Boxes 03821

NAMED STREETS

Abbey Ln 03820
Abbey Sawyer Mem Hwy 03820
Abbott St 03820
Academy St 03820
Addison Pl 03820
Adelle Dr 03820
Alder Ln 03820
Allen St 03820
Alumni Dr 03820
Amy Ln 03820
Angle St 03820
Apache St 03820
Appaloosa Dr 03820
Applevale Dr 03820
Arbor Dr 03820
Arch St 03820
Arcola St 03820
Arlington Dr 03820
Arrowbrook Rd 03820
Ash St 03820
Atina Way 03820
Atkinson St 03820
Atlantic Ave 03820
Auburn St 03820
Augusta Way 03820
Austin Dr 03820
Autumn St 03820
Avon Ave 03820
Ayers Ln 03820
Back Rd 03820
Back River Rd 03820
Baer Rd 03820
Baker St 03820
Baldwin Way 03820
Barry St 03820
Bartlett St 03820
Basils Pl 03820
Bay View Rd 03820
Beacon Cir 03820
Bears Way 03820
Beech Rd 03820
Belanger Dr 03820
Belknap St 03820
Bellamy Rd 03820
Bellamy Woods 03820
Benjamin Way 03820
Berkshire Ln 03820
Berry Brook Ct 03820
Beverly Ln 03820
Birch Dr 03820
Birchwood Pl 03820
Blackwater Rd 03820
Blue Heron Dr 03820
Boston Harbor Rd 03820
Boxwood Ln 03820
Boyle St 03820
Brenda Ave 03820
Briarwood Ln 03820
Brick Rd 03820
Brickyard Dr 03820
Bridle Path 03820
Bristol Ln 03820
Broadway 03820
Brookline Ave 03820
Brookmoor Rd 03820
Browning Dr 03820
Cailey Anna 03820
Canney Ln 03820
Capital Dr 03820
Cardinal Dr 03820
Carriage Hill Ln 03820
Cassily Ln 03820
Cataract Ave 03820
Cedarbrook Dr & Way 03820
Centennial Dr 03820
Center Dr 03820
Central Ave 03820
Central Towers 03820
Chandler Way 03820
Chapel St 03820
Charles St 03820
Chartergrant Rd 03820
Cherokee St 03820
Cherrywood Dr 03820
Chesley St 03820
Chestnut St 03820
Cheyenne St 03820
Childs Dr 03820
Church St 03820
Cielo Dr 03820
Clancy Dr 03820
Clearwater Dr 03820
Clifford St 03820
Cloverdale Cir 03820
Cobble Hill Dr 03820
Cocheco Ct & St 03820
Cold Springs Rd 03820
Columbus Ave 03820
Comanche St 03820
E & W Concord St & Way 03820
Conifer Cmns 03820
Constitution Way 03820
Coolidge Ave 03820
Corbin Dr 03820
Cordeiro Dr 03820
Corner Stone Dr 03820
Cote Dr 03820
Cottonwood Dr 03820
Country Club Est 03820
County Farm Rd 03820
County Farm Cross Rd 03820
Court St 03820
Covered Bridge Ln 03820
Cranbrook Ln 03820
Crane Cv 03820
Crescent Ave 03820
Crestview Dr 03820
Cricketbrook 03820
Crosby Rd 03820
Cross St 03820
Crown Point Dr 03820
Cullen Bay Rd 03820
Cushing St 03820
Daley Dr 03820
Danbury Ln 03820
Danielle Ln 03820
Dean Dr 03820
Deborah Ln 03820
Declan Ln 03820
Deepwood Dr 03820
Deer Creek Run 03820
Deerfield Dr 03820
Digby Ln 03820
Dimon Ln 03820
Dover St 03820
Dover Neck Rd 03820
Dover Point Rd 03820
Dovetail Ln 03820
Dowaliby Ct 03820
Drew Rd 03820
Dudley Ct 03820
Dunns Bridge Ln 03820
Durham Rd 03820
Durrell St 03820
Eagles Bay Dr 03820
Earle St 03820
East St 03820
Edgar Bois Ter 03820
Education Way 03820
Ela St 03820
Elliot Park 03820
Elm St 03820
Elmview Cir 03820
Elmwood Ave 03820
Emerald Ln 03820
Emery Ln 03820
Emmet Rd 03820
Erik Dr 03820
Essex St 03820
Evans Dr 03820
Everett St 03820
Evergreen Vly 03820
Ezras Way 03820
Fairfield Dr 03820
Fairview Ave 03820
Fairway Dr 03820
Falcon Ln 03820
Faraday Dr 03820
Farmington Dr 03820
Federal St 03820
Fern Ct 03820
Fieldstone Dr 03820
Finch Ln 03820
Fisher St 03820
Flanders Ct 03820
Floral Ave 03820
Florence St 03820
Folsom St 03820
Footbridge Ln 03820
Fords Landing Dr 03820
Forest St 03820
Forsythia Dr 03820
Foxtail Rdg 03820
Frances Dr 03820
Franklin Plz 03820
Freedom Dr 03820
Freeman Ct 03820
French Cross Rd 03820
Freshet Rd 03820
Gage St 03820
Garrison Rd 03820
George St 03820
Gerrish Rd 03820
Gerrys Ln 03820
Gilman St 03820
Gina Way 03820
Gladiola Way 03820
Glen Hill Rd 03820
Glencrest Ave 03820
Glenwood Ave 03820
Gold Post Rd 03820
Governor Sawyer Ln 03820
Gradys Ln 03820
Grandview Dr 03820
Granite St 03820
Grapevine Dr 03820
Green St 03820
Greenfield Dr 03820
Grove St 03820
Gulf Rd 03820
Hale St 03820
Hall St 03820
Ham St 03820
Hamilton St 03820
Hampshire Cir 03820
Hancock St 03820
Hanson St 03820
Harlans Way 03820
Harmony Ln 03820
Hartswood Rd 03820
Harvest Dr 03820
Hawthorne Rd 03820
Hayes Ln 03820
Heaphy Ln 03820
Heather Ln 03820
Hemlock Cir & Frst 03820
Henry Law Ave 03820
Hickory Ln 03820
Hidden Valley Dr 03820
High Ridge Dr 03820
Highland St 03820
Hill St 03820
Hillcrest Dr 03820
Hillside Dr 03820
Hilton Rd 03820
Holiday Dr 03820
Homestead Ln 03820
Horne Ct & St 03820
Hotel Dr 03820
Hough St 03820
Hubbard Rd 03820
Hull Ave 03820
Independence Dr 03820
Indian Brook Rd 03820
Industrial Park 03820
Innovation Way 03820
Iona Ave 03820
Ironwood Dr 03820
Isaac Lucas Cir 03820
Ivans Ln 03820
Jack And Jill Trailer Park 03820
Jackson Brook Ter 03820
Jacqueline Dr 03820
James St 03820
Jefferson Dr 03820
Jenness St 03820
Julia Dr 03820
Karens Way 03820
Katie Ln 03820
Katie Lynn Ln 03820
Keating Ave 03820
Kelley Dr 03820
Kelty Dr 03820
Kennedy Cir 03820
Kent Ave 03820
Kings Hwy 03820
Kirkland St 03820
W Knox Marsh Rd 03820
Labrador Ln 03820
Lake St 03820
Lakeview Dr 03820
Lancaster St 03820
Landing Way 03820
Laura Ln 03820
Leathers Ln 03820
Leighton Rd 03820
Lennon Dr 03820
Lexington St 03820
Liberty Way 03820
Lilac Ln 03820
Lillians Ln 03820
Lincoln St 03820
Linda Ave 03820
Lisa Beth Cir & Dr 03820
Littleworth Rd 03820
Locke St 03820
Locust St 03820
Long Hill Rd 03820
Longmeadow Rd 03820
Lowell Ave 03820
Lucy Ct & Ln 03820
Madelyn Dr 03820
Magnolia Dr 03820
Main St 03820
Mallard Ln 03820
Maple St 03820
Maple Street Ext 03820
Maplewood Ave 03820
Marthas Way 03820
Martin Ln 03820
Mast Rd 03820
Mast Road Ext 03820
Mathes Hill Dr 03820
Mccarthy Blvd 03820
Mckenna St 03820
Mckone Ln 03820
Meadow Ln 03820
Mechanic St 03820
Meeting House Way 03820
Melody Ter 03820
Members Way 03820
Meridian Dr 03820
Merry St 03820
Meserve Rd 03820
Middle Rd 03820
Middlebrook Rd 03820
Milk St 03820
Mill St 03820
Mincedg St 03820

- Mineral Park Dr 03820
- Mohawk Dr 03820
- Mones Folly 03820
- Monroe St 03820
- Morgan Way 03820
- Morin St 03820
- Morningside Dr 03820
- Morrison Ln 03820
- Mount Pleasant Rd 03820
- Mount Vernon St 03820
- Mulligan Dr 03820
- Myra Ave 03820
- Nancy Ln 03820
- Nantucket Ct 03820
- Nelson St 03820
- New Bellamy Ln 03820
- New Rochester Rd 03820
- New York St 03820
- Newport Rd 03820
- Newton St 03820
- Nh Route 108 03820
- Nicholas Cir 03820
- Nile Dr 03820
- Niles St 03820
- Northam Dr 03820
- Northway Cir 03820
- Nute Rd 03820
- Nye Ln 03820
- Oak St & Ter 03820
- Oak Hill Dr 03820
- Old Colony Rd 03820
- Old Dover Point Rd 03820
- Old English Vlg 03820
- Old Garrison Rd 03820
- Old Littleworth Rd 03820
- Old Rochester Rd 03820
- Old Rollinsford Rd 03820
- Old Stage Rd 03820
- Olde Madbury Ln 03820
- Olive Meadow Ln 03820
- Orchard St 03820
- Osprey Ln 03820
- Overlook Dr 03820
- Oxbow Ln 03820
- Pacific Dr 03820
- Page Ave 03820
- Palmer Dr 03820
- Park St 03820
- Parker St 03820
- Parsons Ln 03820
- Partridge Ln 03820
- Patriot Dr 03820
- Paul St 03820
- Pearl St 03820
- Pearson Dr 03820
- Pebble Hill Dr 03820
- Penny Ln 03820
- Perimeter Rd 03820
- Phillip St 03820
- Picard Ln 03820
- Pickering Rd 03820
- Picnic Rock Dr 03820
- Pierce St 03820
- S Pine St 03820
- Pinecrest Ln 03820
- Pineview Dr 03820
- Piscataqua Rd 03820
- Plaza Dr 03820
- Pleasant Valley Rd 03820
- Pleasant View Cir 03820
- Polly Ann Park 03820
- Pondview Dr 03820
- Portland Ave 03820
- Preble St 03820
- Production Dr 03820
- Progress Dr 03820
- Prospect Ct & St 03820
- Quail Dr 03820
- Quaker Ln 03820
- Rabbit Rd 03820
- Railroad Ave 03820
- Rainbow Dr 03820
- Redden St 03820
- Redden Street Ext 03820
- Regent Dr 03820
- Renaud Ave 03820
- Reservoir St 03820
- Revolution Dr 03820
- Reyners Brook Dr 03820
- Richardson Dr 03820
- Richmond St 03820
- Ridge St 03820
- Riverdale Ave 03820
- Riverside Dr 03820
- Roberta Dr 03820
- Roberts Rd 03820
- Robinwood Ave 03820
- Rochester Neck Rd 03820
- Rogers St 03820
- Roosevelt Ave 03820
- Rosanna Dr 03820
- Rose St 03820
- Royer Ln 03820
- Ruthies Run 03820
- Rutland St 03820
- Saddle Trail Dr 03820
- Saint Andrews Cir 03820
- Saint John St 03820
- Saint Thomas St 03820
- Salem Ave 03820
- Samuel Hanson Ave 03820
- Sandpiper Dr 03820
- Sandras Run 03820
- Sandy Ln 03820
- Scenic Dr 03820
- School St 03820
- Schooner Dr 03820
- Seaborne Dr 03820
- Shadow Dr 03820
- Shady Ln 03820
- Shamrock Ln 03820
- Shawnee Ln 03820
- Shaws Ln 03820
- Sheffield Dr 03820
- Sherman St 03820
- Shore Ln 03820
- Silver St 03820
- Smith Well Rd 03820
- Snow Ave 03820
- Snows Ct 03820
- Sonia Dr 03820
- Sonnett St 03820
- Southwood Dr 03820
- Spring St 03820
- Spruce Dr & Ln 03820
- Spruce Lane Ext 03820
- Spur Rd 03820
- Spur Road Ext 03820
- Stark Ave 03820
- Station Dr 03820
- Stiles Ln 03820
- Stocklan Cir 03820
- Strafford Rd 03820
- Sullivan Dr 03820
- Summer St 03820
- Sumner Dr 03820
- Sun Hawk Ln 03820
- Sunnybrooke Dr 03820
- Sunset Dr 03820
- Surrey Run 03820
- Susannahs Xing 03820
- Sylvan Dr 03820
- Tamarack Dr 03820
- Tammany Park 03820
- Tanglewood Dr 03820
- Taylor Rd 03820
- Tennyson Ave 03820
- Tetreau Dr 03820
- Thompson Rd 03820
- Three Rivers Farm Rd 03820
- Tideview Dr 03820
- Timrod Rd 03820
- Toftree Ln 03820
- Tolend Rd 03820
- Tolend Road Ext 03820
- Towle Ave 03820
- Townsend Dr 03820
- Trakey St 03820
- Trask Dr 03820
- Trestle Way 03820
- Turnpike Rd 03820
- Tuttle Ln 03820
- Twombly St 03820
- Union Ct, Dr & St 03820
- Upper Factory Rd 03820
- Vallee St 03820
- Varney Rd 03820
- Venture Dr 03820
- Village Dr 03820
- Waldron Ct 03820
- Wallace Dr 03820
- Wallingford St 03820
- Walnut St 03820
- Walt Colby Dr 03820
- Washington St
  - 1-134 03820
  - 133-133 03821
  - 135-499 03820
  - 136-498 03820
- Waterloo Cir 03820
- S & E Watson Ln, Rd & St 03820
- Waverly Dr 03820
- Webb Pl 03820
- Wedgewood Rd 03820
- Weeks Ln 03820
- Wellington Ave & Rd 03820
- Wentworth Ter 03820
- Western Ave 03820
- Westgate Dr 03820
- Westwood Cir 03820
- Whittier St 03820
- Whittier Falls Way 03820
- Wiggin Dr 03820
- Wilbrod Ave 03820
- Wildewood Ln 03820
- Willand Ave 03820
- Willand Pond Rd 03820
- Willard Rd 03820
- Willow St 03820
- Wingate Ln 03820
- Winston Ave 03820
- Winter St 03820
- Winterberry Dr 03820
- Wisteria Dr 03820
- Wolfs Ln 03820
- Woodland Rd 03820
- Woodman Park Dr 03820
- Young St 03820

NUMBERED STREETS

- All Street Addresses 03820

HAMPTON NH

- General Delivery 03843

POST OFFICE BOXES MAIN OFFICE STATIONS AND BRANCHES

Box No.s
- All PO Boxes 03843

NAMED STREETS

- A St 03842
- Academy Ave 03842
- Acadia Ave 03842
- Acorn Rd 03842
- Alakentr Rd 03842
- Alexander Dr 03842
- Alumni Dr 03842
- Anchor Ct & St 03842
- Ancient Hwy 03842
- Anns Ln & Ter 03842
- Ash St 03842
- Ashbrook Dr 03842
- Ashworth Ave 03842
- Atlantic Ave 03842
- Auburn Ave 03842
- Auburn Avenue Ext 03842
- B St 03842
- Bailey Ave 03842
- Ballard St 03842
- Barbour Rd 03842
- Baron Rd 03842
- Bashby Rd 03842
- Battcock Ave 03842
- Bayberry Ln 03842
- Beach Plum Way 03842
- Bear Path 03842
- Beatrice Ln 03842
- Belmont Cir 03842
- Biery St 03842
- Birch Rd 03842
- Bittersweet Ln 03842
- Blake Ln 03842
- Boars Head Ter 03842
- Bock Ln 03842
- Bonair Ave 03842
- Bonnie Ln 03842
- Boston Ave 03842
- Bourn Ave 03842
- Bradford Ave 03842
- Bradstreet Rd 03842
- Bragg Ave 03842
- Briar Rd 03842
- Bride Hill Dr 03842
- Brookes Ln 03842
- Brown Ave 03842
- Bruce St 03842
- Burgundy Dr 03842
- C St 03842
- Campbell Dr 03842
- Carlson Rd 03842
- Carolan Ave 03842
- Cassie Ln 03842
- Cedarview Ln 03842
- Cessna Way 03842
- Charles St 03842
- Chase St 03842
- Church St 03842
- Cliff Ave 03842
- Coffin Dr 03842
- Cogger St 03842
- Colby St 03842
- Cole St 03842
- Colonial Cir 03842
- Concord Ave 03842
- Cora Ave 03842
- Cranberry Ln 03842
- Crest St 03842
- Curtis St 03842
- Cusack Rd 03842
- Cutler Ave 03842
- Dacotah St 03842
- Dalton Rd 03842
- Dearborn Ave 03842
- Depot Sq 03842
- Diane Ln 03842
- Donnas Ln 03842
- Dover Ave 03842
- Dow Ave 03842
- Downer Dr 03842
- Drakes Lndg 03842
- Drakeside Rd 03842
- Driftwood Rd 03842
- Dumas Ave 03842
- Dunvegan Woods 03842
- Dupuis Cir 03842
- Duston Ave 03842
- Eastmor Ln 03842
- Edgewood Dr 03842
- Elaine St 03842
- Elkins St 03842
- Elliott St 03842
- Elm Dr 03842
- Emerald Ave 03842
- Emery Ln 03842
- Epping Ave 03842
- Esker Rd 03842
- Evergreen Rd 03842
- Exeter Rd 03842
- F St 03842
- Fairfield Dr 03842
- Falcone Cir 03842
- Fellows Ave 03842
- Fielding Ln 03842
- Fieldstone Cir 03842
- Fogg Ln 03842
- Forest Dr 03842
- Fox Rd 03842
- Francine St 03842
- Francis St 03842
- Fuller Acres 03842
- G St 03842
- Gale Rd 03842
- Garland St 03842
- Gentian Rd 03842
- George Ave 03842
- Gill St 03842
- Glade Path 03842
- Glen Rd 03842
- Godfrey Ave 03842
- Gookin Ct 03842
- Gray Ave 03842
- Great Boars Head Ave 03842
- Great Gate Dr 03842
- Greene St 03842
- Gulseth Ave & Way 03842
- H St 03842
- Hackett Ln 03842
- Hampton Mdws 03842
- Hampton Towne Est 03842
- Harbor Rd 03842
- Harris Ave 03842
- Haverhill Ave 03842
- Hayden Cir 03842
- Heather Ln 03842
- Hedman Ave 03842
- Hemlock Hvn & St 03842
- Heritage Dr 03842
- Hickory Ln 03842
- Higgins Ln 03842
- High St 03842
- Highland Ave 03842
- Hilda Dr 03842
- Hobbs Rd 03842
- Hobson Ave 03842
- Holly Ln 03842
- Holman Ln 03842
- Homestead Cir 03842
- Huckleberry Ln 03842
- Hunter Dr 03842
- Huntington Pl 03842
- Hurd Ave 03842
- Hutchinson Dr 03842
- I St 03842
- Ice House Ln 03842
- Ina Ave 03842
- Island Path 03842
- J St 03842
- James St 03842
- Jane Appleton Way 03842
- Janet Ln 03842
- Janvrin Rd 03842
- Jeffrey Dr 03842
- Jenness Rd 03842
- Jo Ann Ln 03842
- John Stark Ln 03842
- Johnson Ave 03842
- Jones Ave 03842
- Josephine Dr 03842
- Juniper Ln 03842
- K St 03842
- Katie Ln 03842
- Keefe Ave 03842
- Keene Ln 03842
- Kentville Ter 03842
- Kershaw Ave 03842
- Kings Hwy 03842
- L St 03842
- Lafayette Rd 03842
- Lamprey Ter 03842
- Lamson Ln 03842
- Lancaster St 03842
- Landing Rd 03842
- Langdale Dr 03842
- Laurel Ln 03842
- Lawrence Ct 03842
- Leary Ln 03842
- Leavitt Rd 03842
- Liberty Ln E & W 03842
- Linden Ln 03842
- Little River Rd 03842
- Locke Rd 03842
- Longwood Dr 03842
- Lyons St 03842
- M St 03842
- Mace Rd 03842
- Malek Cir 03842
- Manchester St 03842
- Maple Dr 03842
- Maplewood Dr 03842
- Marston Way 03842
- Mary Ave 03842
- Mary Batchelder Rd 03842
- Mason St 03842
- Mckay Ave 03842
- Meadow Pond Rd 03842
- Merrill Industrial Dr 03842
- Middle Rd 03842
- Milbern Ave 03842
- Mill Rd 03842
- Mill Pond Ln 03842
- Moccasin Ln 03842
- Mohawk St 03842
- Moore Ave 03842
- Mooring Dr 03842
- Morningside Dr 03842
- Morrill St 03842
- Moulton Rd 03842
- Munsey Dr 03842
- N St 03842
- Nathaniel Ct 03842
- Naves Rd 03842
- Nersesian Way 03842
- Newman St 03842
- Noel St 03842
- Noreast Ln 03842
- Norton Rd 03842
- Nudd Ave 03842
- O St 03842
- Oak Rd 03842
- Oakdale Ave 03842
- Ocean Blvd 03842
- Old Stage Rd 03842
- Olde Rd 03842
- Osborne Ter 03842
- Overlook St 03842
- P St 03842
- Page Ln 03842
- Palmer St 03842
- Park Ave 03842
- Parr St 03842
- Patricia St 03842
- Pawnees St 03842
- Pearl St 03842
- Penniman Ln 03842
- Perkins Ave 03842
- Philbrook Ter 03842
- Pine Rd 03842
- Pine Knoll Rd 03842
- Piper Ln 03842
- Playhouse Cir 03842
- Post Rd 03842
- Presidential Cir 03842
- Purington Ln 03842
- Q St 03842
- Quinlan Ln 03842
- Randall St 03842
- Raymond Ln 03842
- Red Coat Ln 03842
- Reddington Lndg 03842
- Redman St 03842
- Reubens Driftway 03842
- Rice Ter 03842
- Richard St 03842
- Ridgeview Ter 03842
- Rings Ter 03842
- River Ave 03842
- Riverview Ter 03842
- Riverwalk 03842
- Roberts Dr 03842
- Robie St 03842
- Robin Ln 03842
- Rosa Rd 03842
- Ross Ave 03842
- Ruth Ln 03842
- Saint Cyr Dr 03842
- Salt Mdws 03842
- Sanborn Rd 03842
- Sapphire Ave 03842
- Schooner Lndg 03842
- Scott Rd 03842
- Seabury 03842
- Seavey St 03842
- Seaview Ave 03842
- Shaw St 03842
- Sherburne Dr 03842
- Shirley Ter 03842
- N Shore Rd 03842
- Sicard St 03842
- Smith Ave 03842
- Springhead Ln 03842
- Spruce St 03842
- State Park Rd 03842
- Stickney Ter
  - 6-26 03842
  - 25-25 03843
  - 27-99 03842
  - 28-98 03842
- Stowecroft Dr 03842
- Summerwood Dr 03842
- Sunsurf Ave 03842
- Susan Ln 03842
- Swain Ct 03842
- Sweetbriar Ln 03842
- Taylor St 03842
- Taylor River Est 03842
- Thayer Rd 03842
- Thomsen Rd 03842
- Thorwald Ave 03842
- Tide Mill Rd 03842
- Tilton St 03842
- Timber Swamp Rd 03842
- Tobey St 03842
- Toppan St 03842
- Tower Dr 03842
- Towle Ave 03842
- Towle Farm Rd 03842
- Trafford Rd 03842
- Tuck Rd 03842
- Tucker Ln 03842
- Tuttle Ave 03842
- Vanderpool Dr 03842
- Verne Rd 03842
- Victor Rd 03842
- Viking St 03842
- Vrylenas Way 03842
- Wall St 03842
- Walnut Ave 03842
- Ward Ln 03842
- Warner Ln 03842
- Watsons Ln 03842
- Wayside Farm Ln 03842
- Wentworth Ave 03842
- Westridge Dr 03842
- Wheaton Lane Ter 03842
- Whitten St 03842
- Wigwam Cir 03842
- Wild Rose Ln 03842
- Williams St 03842
- Willow Ln 03842
- Windmill Ln 03842
- Wingate St 03842
- Winnacunnet Rd 03842
- Witch Island Way 03842
- Woodland Rd 03842
- Yeaton Rd 03842

NUMBERED STREETS

- All Street Addresses 03842

LACONIA NH

- General Delivery 03247

POST OFFICE BOXES MAIN OFFICE STATIONS AND BRANCHES

Box No.s
- All PO Boxes 03247

NAMED STREETS

All Street Addresses 03246

LEBANON NH

General Delivery 03766

POST OFFICE BOXES
MAIN OFFICE STATIONS
AND BRANCHES

Box No.s
All PO Boxes 03766

NAMED STREETS

Abbott St ... 03766
Alden Rd ... 03766
Alice Peck Day Dr ... 03766
Allen St ... 03766
Amsden St ... 03766
Avon Ave ... 03766
Bank St ... 03766
Bank Street Ext ... 03766
Barden Hill Rd ... 03766
Barnes Ave ... 03766
Barrows St ... 03766
Bassy St ... 03766
Baxter Ct ... 03766
Bennett Ct ... 03766
Benton St ... 03766
Bixby St ... 03766
Blacksmith St ... 03766
Bliss St ... 03766
Blueberry Mdws ... 03766
Blueberry Hill Dr ... 03766
Bomhower St ... 03766
Bomhower Street Ext ... 03766
Brook Rd ... 03766
Brookside Dr ... 03766
Buckingham Pl ... 03766
Bush Ave ... 03766
Calvin St ... 03766
Cameron Ave ... 03766
Campbell St ... 03766
Cavendish Ct ... 03766
Cedar St ... 03766
Cedarwood Ln ... 03766
Centerra Pkwy ... 03766
Cherry Cir ... 03766
Chestnut St ... 03766
Child St ... 03766
Church St ... 03766
Churchill Way ... 03766
Clark St ... 03766
Colburn St ... 03766
Colby Ave ... 03766
College Ave ... 03766
Congress St ... 03766
Cooper St ... 03766
Court St ... 03766
Cross Rd ... 03766
Daisy Hill Rd ... 03766
Dartmouth Ave ... 03766
Dartmouth College Anx & Hwy ... 03766
Davis Dr & St ... 03766
Deer Run Ln ... 03766
Dorothy Perley Rd ... 03766
Dorset Ln ... 03766
Downes Ave ... 03766
Dulac St ... 03766
Dulac Street Ext ... 03766
Dunsinane Dr ... 03766
Eagle Rdg ... 03766
Eastman Hill Rd ... 03766
Edwards St ... 03766
Ela St ... 03766
Eldridge St ... 03766
Elm St ... 03766
Etna Rd ... 03766
Evans Dr ... 03766
Excelsior St ... 03766
Fairbanks Ct ... 03766
Fairview Ave ... 03766
Farnum Hill Rd ... 03766
Farr Rd ... 03766
Fellows Hill Rd ... 03766
Flynn St ... 03766
Foch Ave ... 03766
Foliage View Rd ... 03766
Follensbee Ave ... 03766
Forest Ave ... 03766
Fortune St ... 03766
Foundry St ... 03766
Franklin St ... 03766
Freeman Ave ... 03766
Garnet St ... 03766
Gerrish Ct ... 03766
Grandview Ave ... 03766
Granite St ... 03766
Gray St ... 03766
Great Brook Rd ... 03766
Green St ... 03766
Groaderl St ... 03766
Guyer St ... 03766
Hannah St ... 03766
Hanover St ... 03766
Hardy Hill Rd ... 03766
Heater Rd ... 03766
Hetzel Rd ... 03766
High St ... 03766
Hillcrest Dr ... 03766
Hillside Dr ... 03766
Hough St ... 03766
Ice House Rd ... 03766
Jefferson Pl ... 03766
Jenkins Rd ... 03766
Jordan Ct ... 03766
Kendrick St ... 03766
Kimball St ... 03766
Kinne St ... 03766
Labombard Rd N ... 03766
Lafayette St ... 03766
Laplante Rd ... 03766
Lareau Ct ... 03766
Laro St ... 03766
Ledge Ln ... 03766
Lewis Ct ... 03766
Liberty Ln ... 03766
Light St ... 03766
Lilac Ave ... 03766
Little Heater Rd ... 03766
Logan Ln ... 03766
Loomis Rd ... 03766
Lower B St ... 03766
Lower Dorothy Perley Rd ... 03766
Lucent Dr ... 03766
Mahan St ... 03766
Manchester Dr ... 03766
Maple St ... 03766
Maple Hill Rd ... 03766
Mascoma St & Vlg ... 03766
Mason St ... 03766
Mechanic St ... 03766
Medical Center Dr ... 03756
Melrose St ... 03766
Memorial Dr ... 03766
Meriden Rd ... 03766
Merry Ln ... 03766
Messenger St ... 03766
Methodist Hill Rd ... 03766
Michael St ... 03766
Mill Rd ... 03766
Millen Ln ... 03766
Miracle Mile ... 03766
Monica Rd ... 03766
Morgan Dr ... 03766
Morse Rd ... 03766
Moss Rd ... 03766
Moulton Ave ... 03766
Mount Support Rd ... 03766
Mountain View Dr ... 03766
Myra Ave ... 03766
Nottingham Cir ... 03766
Old Etna Rd ... 03766
Old Kings Hwy ... 03766
Ora Ave ... 03766
Orion Dr ... 03766
E, N, S & W Park St ... 03766
Parkhurst St ... 03766
Payne Rd ... 03766
Peabody St ... 03766
Perley Ave ... 03766
Pershing St ... 03766
Pine St ... 03766
Placid Sq ... 03766
Porter Rd ... 03766
Poverty Ln ... 03766
Prospect St ... 03766
Prospect Street Ext ... 03766
Pumping Station Rd ... 03766
Renihan Mdws ... 03766
Reservoir Rd ... 03766
Rita St ... 03766
Riverdale Pkwy ... 03766
Riverside Dr ... 03766
Rolling Ridge Rd ... 03766
Rudsboro Rd ... 03766
School St ... 03766
Shaw St ... 03766
Skylark Rd ... 03766
Slayton Hill Rd ... 03766
South St ... 03766
Spencer St ... 03766
Spring St ... 03766
Stage Coach Rd ... 03766
State Route 120 ... 03766
Stevens Rd ... 03766
Stone Hill Rd ... 03766
Stoney Brook Rd ... 03766
Storrs Hill Rd ... 03766
Summer St ... 03766
Sunset Rock Rd ... 03766
Suzor Ct ... 03766
T Andrew St ... 03766
Tannery Ln ... 03766
Taylor St ... 03766
Thompson St ... 03766
Timber Ln ... 03766
Timberwood Dr ... 03766
Townsend Ter ... 03766
Tuck Rd ... 03766
Union St ... 03766
Us Route 4a ... 03766
Valley St ... 03766
Verona Ave ... 03766
Walhowdon Way ... 03766
Walnut St ... 03766
Water St ... 03766
Wellington Cir ... 03766
West St ... 03766
Westview Ln ... 03766
Wheatley St ... 03766
Whipple Pl & Rd ... 03766
Williams St ... 03766
Winona Cir ... 03766
Winter St ... 03766
Wolf Rd ... 03766
Woodland Rd ... 03766
Woodley Rd ... 03766
Worthen St ... 03766
Young St ... 03766

MANCHESTER NH

General Delivery 03108

POST OFFICE BOXES
MAIN OFFICE STATIONS
AND BRANCHES

Box No.s
1 - 3998 ... 03105
4001 - 9997 ... 03108

NAMED STREETS

A St ... 03102
Aaron Dr ... 03109
Abbott St ... 03102
Abby Rd ... 03103
Acorn Cir ... 03102
N Acres Rd ... 03104
N Adams St ... 03104
Adeline St ... 03102
Agawam St ... 03104
Agnes St ... 03102
Ahern St ... 03103
Ainsworth Ave ... 03103
Airport Rd ... 03103
Aladdin St ... 03104
Albert St ... 03102
Alder Ct ... 03103
Alexander Dr ... 03109
Alfred St ... 03104
Alger St ... 03103
Allamino St ... 03102
Allard Dr ... 03102
Allen St ... 03102
Alliance Way ... 03102
Allied St ... 03109
Almeda St ... 03103
Almond St ... 03102
Alpheus St ... 03103
Alphonse St ... 03103
Alpine St ... 03102
Alsace St ... 03102
Amherst St
1-159 ... 03101
160-899 ... 03104
Ammon Dr ... 03103
Amory St ... 03102
Amoskeag St ... 03102
Andrew St ... 03104
Ann Ave ... 03102
Anthony St ... 03103
Apple Brook Way ... 03109
Apple Hill Ct ... 03104
Applecrest Rd ... 03104
W Appleton St ... 03104
Arah St ... 03104
Arbutus Ln ... 03109
Arch St ... 03103
Arizona St ... 03104
Arline St ... 03102
Arlington St ... 03104
Armand Ave ... 03103
Arms St ... 03101
Arnold St ... 03102
Arrow Head Dr ... 03102
Arthur Ave ... 03104
Ash St ... 03104
Ashland St ... 03104
Ashley Dr ... 03103
Ashmere Dr ... 03109
Aspen Way ... 03104
Auburn St ... 03103
W Auburn St ... 03101
Auclair Ave ... 03102
Aurore Ave ... 03109
Austin St ... 03102
Auto Center Rd ... 03103
Averadw Ave ... 03109
Avon St ... 03102
B St ... 03102
Bailey Ave ... 03104
Baker Ct ... 03101
Baker St ... 03103
W Baker St ... 03103
Balch Ave ... 03102
Balsam Way ... 03102
Bank St ... 03102
Barbara Ln ... 03103
Barnes St ... 03104
Barr St ... 03102
Barrett St ... 03104
Barrette Dr ... 03103
Barry Ave ... 03103
Barstow Way ... 03104
Bartlett St ... 03102
Batchelder Ave ... 03103
Bath St ... 03102
N Bay St ... 03104
Bayberry Ln ... 03104
Beacon St
300-499 ... 03103
500-799 ... 03104
Beaver St ... 03104
Becker St ... 03102
Bedel St ... 03102
S Bedford St ... 03101
Beech St
1-489 ... 03103
490-1499 ... 03104
S Beech St ... 03103
Beech Hill Ave & Dr ... 03103
Beech Plum Dr ... 03109
Belair St ... 03103
Belgrade St ... 03109
Bell St ... 03103
Bellevue St ... 03103
Belmont St
1-539 ... 03103
540-1799 ... 03104
S Belmont St ... 03103
Bemis Savoie Rd ... 03102
N Bend Dr ... 03104
Benjamin St ... 03109
Benton St ... 03103
Bernard St ... 03102
Bernice Ave ... 03109
Bethel Ct ... 03104
Betty Ln ... 03104
Beverly Dr ... 03104
Bicentennial Dr ... 03104
Bildor Dr ... 03103
Billings St ... 03103
Birch View Way ... 03102
Birchwood Rd ... 03104
Biron St ... 03102
Bismark St ... 03102
Bittersweet Dr ... 03109
Blackberry Way ... 03102
Blackstone St ... 03103
Blaine St ... 03102
Blevens Dr ... 03104
Blodget St ... 03104
Blondin Rd ... 03109
Blucher St ... 03102
Blueberry Dr ... 03102
Bodwell Rd ... 03109
Boisvert St ... 03103
Bosse Ave ... 03103
Boston St ... 03104
Bouchard St ... 03103
Bourne St ... 03103
Boutwell St ... 03102
Bow St ... 03103
Bowman St ... 03102
Boynton Ct ... 03103
Boynton St ... 03102
Brad Ct ... 03103
Bradley St ... 03103
Brady Cir ... 03109
Brae Burn Dr ... 03104
Branch St ... 03103
Brandon St ... 03104
Bremer St ... 03102
Brennan St ... 03109
Brent Ct & St ... 03103
Breton Ave ... 03104
Briar Ave ... 03104
Briarcliff Way ... 03109
Brickett Rd ... 03109
Bridge St
1-119 ... 03101
120-1299 ... 03104
Bristol St ... 03104
Broadhead Ave ... 03103
Broadway Ave ... 03104
Brock St ... 03102
Brockton St ... 03102
Brook St ... 03104
W Brook St ... 03101
Brook Hollow Way ... 03103
Brookline St ... 03102
Brooklyn Ave ... 03103
Brown Ave
1-99 ... 03101
100-4799 ... 03103
Bruce Rd ... 03104
Brunelle Ave ... 03103
Bryant Rd ... 03109
Bubier St ... 03104
Buckley Cir ... 03109
Bunker Hill St ... 03102
Burgess St ... 03104
Burnett Ave ... 03103
Burnsen Ave ... 03104
Buzzell St ... 03104
Byledge Rd ... 03104
C St ... 03102
Cahill Ave ... 03103
Calef Rd ... 03103
Callaghan St ... 03109
Calvert Cir ... 03103
Cambridge Ct ... 03103
Camelot Dr & Pl ... 03104
Cameron St ... 03103
Campbell St ... 03104
Canal St ... 03101
Candia Rd ... 03109
Canton St ... 03103
Carl Dr ... 03103
Carnegie St ... 03104
Carolina Way ... 03104
Caroline St ... 03103
Caron St ... 03103
Carpenter St ... 03104
Carriage Way ... 03102
Carroll St ... 03102
Carron Ave ... 03109
Cartier St ... 03102
Carver St ... 03109
Cascade Cir ... 03103
Cass St ... 03103
Castle Dr ... 03104
Catherine St ... 03102
Caye Ln ... 03103
Cedar St
1-139 ... 03101
140-1099 ... 03103
Cedar Hill Dr ... 03109
Celeste St ... 03103
Central St
1-139 ... 03101
140-699 ... 03103
W Central St ... 03101
Chad Rd ... 03104
Chagnon St ... 03102
Chalet Ct ... 03104
Champlain St ... 03102
Chapleau Ave ... 03102
Charles St ... 03101
Charles Chase Way ... 03104
Charleston Ave ... 03102
Charlotte St ... 03103
Chartrand St ... 03103
Chase Ave ... 03103
Chase Way ... 03104
Chauncey Ave ... 03104
Checker Berry Way ... 03102
Chenette Ave ... 03103
Cheney Pl ... 03101
Cherry Ave ... 03103
Chester St ... 03104
Chestnut St
1-549 ... 03101
550-1399 ... 03104
Christy Ln ... 03104
Cilley Rd ... 03103
Circle Rd ... 03103
Circuit St ... 03103
City Hall Plz ... 03101
Claire St ... 03103
Claremont Ave ... 03103
W Clarke St ... 03104
Clay St ... 03103
Clement St ... 03102
Cleveland St ... 03102
Cliff St ... 03103
Clifford Ave ... 03103
Clinton St ... 03102
Clough Ave ... 03103
Cloyde St ... 03104
Cobblestone Ln ... 03109
Coburn St ... 03102
Cody St ... 03109
Cohas Ave ... 03109
Colby St ... 03102
Coldwell St ... 03103
Colin Dr ... 03103
College Ave & Rd ... 03102
Columbia Rd ... 03103
Columbus St ... 03102
Comeau St ... 03102
Commercial St ... 03101
Conant St ... 03102
Concord St
1-139 ... 03101
140-699 ... 03104
Congress St ... 03102
Congressional Ln ... 03104
Constant St ... 03103
Constitution Ln ... 03104
Coolidge Ave ... 03102
Cooper St ... 03102
Coral Ave ... 03104
Corey Pl ... 03104
Corning Rd ... 03109
Cottage Ave & Rd ... 03103
Cotter Ct ... 03103
Country Club Dr ... 03102
Country Walk Dr ... 03109
Countryside Blvd ... 03102
Courtside Way ... 03104
Cranberry Way ... 03109
Cranwell Dr ... 03109
Crawford St ... 03109
Crescent Ln ... 03109
Crescent Rd ... 03103
Crestview Cir & Rd ... 03104
Cricket Ln ... 03104
Crosbie St ... 03104
Cross St
1-5 ... 03102
6-9 ... 03103
10-99 ... 03102
Groteau Ct ... 03104
Crowley St ... 03103
Crusader Way ... 03103
Crystal St ... 03109
Cumberland St ... 03102
Currier Dr ... 03104
Cushing Ave ... 03109
Cutler Ln ... 03104
S Cypress St ... 03103
D St ... 03102
Dale St ... 03103
Dallaire St ... 03104
Danforth Cir ... 03104
Darby Ln ... 03109
Dartmouth St ... 03102
Dave St ... 03104
Davenport Ave ... 03104
Davignon St ... 03102
Davis St ... 03104
Dawson Ave ... 03104
Day St ... 03104
Dean Ave ... 03101
Dearborn St ... 03103
Debbie St ... 03102
Debloice St ... 03102
Delaware Ave ... 03104
Delia Dr ... 03102
Demers St ... 03102
Denis St ... 03102
Depot Rd ... 03103
Depot St ... 03101
Derry St ... 03104
Derryfield Ct ... 03104
Desaulnier St ... 03102
Devco Dr ... 03103
Devon St ... 03103
Devonshire St ... 03103
Dewey St ... 03103
Dexter St ... 03102
Dickey St ... 03102
Dionne Dr ... 03102
Dix St ... 03103
Dixwell St ... 03103
Donahoe St ... 03102

Street	ZIP
Donahue Dr	03103
Donald St	03102
Donna Ave	03103
Dorchester St	03103
Doris St	03103
Douglas St	03102
Dove Ln	03109
Dover St	03102
Dow Ct & St	03101
Drew Ave	03104
Driving Park Rd	03103
Dubisz St	03103
Dubuque St	03102
Duclos St	03102
Dudley St	03103
Dufort St	03104
Dunbar St	03103
Dunbarton Rd	03102
Duncan Farms	03102
Dunham St	03102
Dunlap St	03102
Durette Ct	03102
Dutton St	03104
Dwight St	03104
Dyson St	03102
Eagle Nest Way	03104
Eastern Ave	03104
N Eastgate Way	03109
Eastmeadow Way	03109
Eastwind Dr	03104
Eastwood Way	03109
Eaton St	03109
Eddy Rd	03102
Eden St	03102
Edgar St	03104
Edgemere Ave	03103
Edgewood St	03103
Edmond St	03102
Edna St	03103
Edouard St	03103
Edward J Roy Dr	03104
Effel Ave	03104
Electric St	03102
Elgin Ave	03104
Elizabeth Ave	03103
Ellen Ct	03103
Ellingwood St	03103
Elliot Pl	03104
Elliot Way	03103
Ellis Ave	03109
Elm St	
31B-31C	03101
1-19	03103
20-1089	03101
1000-1000	03105
1090-1698	03101
1091-1699	03101
1700-2999	03104
S Elm St	03103
W Elmhurst Ave	03103
Elmwood Ave	
1-5	03102
2-4	03103
6-8	03102
7-7	03103
7-13	03102
10-14	03102
10-10	03103
15-17	03103
19-299	03103
W Elmwood Ave	03103
Elton Ave	03109
Elwood Ave	03103
Emerald St	03103
Enfield St	03103
English Village Rd	03102
W Erie St	03102
Erskine Ave	03104
Essex St	03102
Estate Dr	03104
Esty Ave	03104
Eugene St	03102
Eve St & Way	03104
Everett St	03104
Exchange Ave	03104
Exeter Ave	03103
Fairbanks St	03102
Fairfield St	03104
Fairmount Ave	03104
Fairview St	03102
Faith Ln	03103
Falcon Crest Way	03104
Falls Ave	03103
Faltin Dr	03103
Farmer Ln	03102
Farmer St	03104
Fenton St	03102
Fern Ln	03109
Fernand St	03103
Ferndale St	03103
Ferry St	03102
Fieldcrest Rd	03102
Filips Glen Dr	03109
Fir St	03101
Fiske St	03104
Flagstone Ter	03109
Flaherty Ln	03102
Fleming St	03104
Flint St	03103
Florence St	03104
Floyd Ave	03103
Foch St	
1-32	03102
33-33	03104
34-48	03102
35-45	03102
47-49	03104
50-55	03102
56-58	03104
57-61	03102
60-62	03104
63-69	03102
64-98	03102
71-99	03104
Fogg Ct	03104
Forest St	03102
Forest Hill Way	03109
Foster Ave	03103
Foundry St	03102
Fowler St	03103
Fox St	03103
Fox Hollow Way	03104
Foxwood Cir	03104
Francis St	03102
Franklin St	03101
Frederick St	03102
S Fremont St	03103
Front St	03102
Frontage Rd	03103
Gabrielle St	03103
Gaines St	03104
Galaxy Way	03103
Gamache St	03102
Gantry St	03103
Garden Dr	03102
Garden St	03103
Garden Walk Dr	03109
Garfield St	03103
Garlact Ave	03109
Garland Ave	03103
Garmon St	03104
Garside Way	03103
Garvin Ave	03109
N Gate Rd	03104
Gates St	03102
Gay St	03103
Gem Dr	03103
Geneva St	03102
George St	03102
Gerard Dr	03104
Gertrude St	03104
Gilford St	03102
Gilhaven Rd	03104
Gingras Ave	03104
Glen Bloom Dr	03109
Glen Forest Dr	03109
Glendale Ave	03103
Glenmore Dr	03109
Glenridge Ave	03102
Glenwood Ave	03102
Goebel St	03103
Goffe St	03102
Goffs Falls Rd	
700-956	03103
955-955	03108
957-2499	03103
958-2498	03103
Goffstown Rd	03102
Gold St	
1-6	03102
7-7	03103
8-8	03102
9-9	03102
10-1199	03103
Golfview Dr	03102
Goodwin St	03104
Gordon St	03109
Gorham St	03102
Gosselin Rd	03103
Gove St	03102
Granby St	03102
Grand Ave	03109
Granite St	
1-199	03101
200-699	03102
Grant St	03104
Gray Ct & St	03103
Greeley St	03102
Green Dr & St	03103
Green Acres Dr	03109
Green Meadow Ln	03109
Greenfield St	03104
Greenleaf St	03103
Greenview Dr	03102
Greenwood Ct	03109
Greer St	03102
Grenier Industrial Park	03103
Greystone Way	03104
Griffin St	03102
Grondin St	03102
Grove Ave	03109
Grove St	03103
Groveland Ave	03104
Gurtner St	03104
Hackett Hill Rd	03102
Haig St	03102
Haines Ct	03104
Hale St	03102
Hall St	
1-549	03103
550-1599	03104
S Hall St	03103
Hamblet St	03103
Hamburg St	03102
Hamel Dr	03104
Hamilton St	03101
N Hampshire Ln	03101
Hampton St	03103
Hancock St	03101
W Hancock St	03102
Hanover St	
1-159	03101
160-1399	03104
Harding St	03109
Harmony Way	03104
Harold St	03104
Harriman St	03102
W Harrington Ave	03103
Harrison St	03104
Hartshorn Way	03109
Hartt Ave	03109
Harvard St	03103
Harvell St	03102
Harvey Rd	03103
W Haven Rd	03104
Hawthorne St	03104
Hayes Ave	03103
Hayward St	03103
Hazel Ln	03109
Hazel St	03104
Hazelton Ave & Ct	03103
Head St	03102
Heald St	03102
Healion St	03109
Heather St	03104
Heathrow Ave	03104
Hecker St	03102
Helen St	03104
Hemlock St	03104
Hemond St	03103
Henriette St	03102
Heritage Way	03104
Hermit Rd	03109
Hester St	03104
Hevey St	03102
Hickory Ct & St	03103
Higgins St	03102
High St	
1-29	03101
30-99	03104
E High St	03104
High Ridge Rd	03104
Highcrest Rd	03104
Highland Ct	03104
Highland Ln	03109
Highland St	03104
Highland Park Ave	03109
Highlander Way	03103
Highview Cir & Ter	03104
Highwood Dr	03104
Hiler St	03109
Hill St	03102
W Hillcrest Ave	03103
Hillcroft Rd	03104
Hillhaven Rd	03104
Hills End Way	03104
Hillsboro St	03104
Hillside Ave	03102
Hilton St	03104
Hitchcock Way	03104
Hobart St	03104
Hollis St	03101
Holly Ave	03103
Holly St	03102
Hollyhock Way	03109
Holmes Dr	03104
Holt Ave	03109
Home Ave	03103
Hooksett Rd	03104
Hosley St	03103
Hospital Ave	03103
Howe St	03103
Hoyt St	03103
Hubbard St	03104
Hudson St	03103
Hulme St	03109
Hunters Village Way	03103
Huntington Ave	03109
Huntress St	03102
Hurd St	03103
Huse Rd	03103
Imelda St	03104
Independence Ln	03104
E Industrial Park Dr	03109
Ingalls St	03102
Iris St	03102
Irwin Dr	03104
Island Pond Rd	03109
Ivy St	03102
Ivywood Ln	03103
Jackson St	03102
James A Pollock Dr	03102
Jane St	03104
Janet Ct	03103
Janet Lee Ct	03102
Jeanine St	03103
Jefferson St	03101
Jenna Way	03104
S Jewett St	03103
Jobin Dr	03103
Joe English Ln	03104
Joffre St	03102
John E Devine Dr	03103
Johnson St	03103
Joliette St	03102
Jonathan Ln	03104
Jones St	03103
Joseph St	03102
Joseph Street Ext	03102
Joshua Dr	03103
Juniper St	03104
Justin Pl	03104
Kalisz Ln	03109
Kara St	03103
Karatzas Ave	03104
Karin St	03103
Karine Ln	03109
Kaunas Cir	03102
Kaye St	03103
Kearney Cir & St	03104
Kearsarge St	03102
Keller St	03103
Kelley St	03102
Kelly Ave	03103
Kenberma St	03103
Kendall Ave	03103
Kennard Rd	03104
Kennedy Ave & St	03103
Kenney St	
1-199	03103
200-299	03104
Kermit St	03102
Kevin St	03103
Keystone Rd	03103
Kidder St	03101
S Kilby St	03103
Killdeer Dr	03104
Kimball St	03102
King St	03102
Kings Ct	03103
Kingston St	03102
Knight St	03104
Knollwood Way	03102
Knowlton St	03103
Koehler St	03102
Kosciuszko St	03101
Krakow Ave	03103
Kristen Ln	03104
Labrecque St	03102
Lacourse St	03104
Lafayette St	03102
Lake Ave	
1-139	03101
140-709	03103
710-799	03109
Lake Shore Rd	03109
Lakeside Dr	03104
Lakeview Ln	03104
Lamonte St	03104
Lamprey St	03102
Lancaster Ave	03103
Lancelot Ave	03104
Langdon St	03101
Lansdowne St	03103
Larch St	
1-24	03102
23-23	03109
26-26	03102
26-26	03109
27-28	03102
29-39	03109
30-98	03102
41-99	03102
Larchmont Rd	03104
Laurel St	
1-52	03102
47-65	03103
54-58	03102
67-69	03103
68-76	03102
70-598	03103
71-599	03103
Lauren Dr	03103
Laurier St	03102
Laurmand Way	03104
Laval St	03102
Lavallee Ln	03104
Lavista St	03103
Lawton St	03103
Laxson Ave	03103
Laydon St	03109
Leandre St	03102
Lebel Ave	03103
Leclerc Cir	03103
Leda Ave	03104
Ledgewood Rd & Way	03104
Lee Ave	03109
Leewood St	03103
Legacy Dr	03102
Leighton St	03102
Lenox Ave	03103
Lenz St	03102
Leo St	03103
Leon Ave	03103
Lewis St	03102
Lexington Ave	03104
Leyte St	03102
Liane St	03102
Libby St	03102
Liberty Ln	03109
Liberty St	03104
Lilac Ct	03103
Lincoln St	
1-539	03103
540-599	03104
S Lincoln St	03103
Linda Ln	03104
Lindahl St	03104
Linden St	03104
Lindstrom Ct & Ln	03104
Line Dr	03101
Lingard St	03103
Lisa Ln	03103
Little Ave	03109
Little Brook Way	03104
Lockwood Ave	03102
Lodge St	03104
Log St	03102
Lois St	03103
Lonchester Way	03103
London St	03104
Londonderry Tpke	03104
Lone Pine Dr	03109
Long Pond Brook Way	03109
Longwood Ave	03109
Loring St	03103
Lorraine St	03102
Louis St	03102
Louise St	03102
Lovering St	03109
Lowell St	
1-109	03101
110-698	03104
Lucas Rd	03109
Lucille St	03103
Lumber Ln	03102
Lupine Way	03109
Lynwood Ln	03109
Lyons St	03103
Mack Ave	03103
Madeline Rd	03104
Madison Way	03109
Magnolia Rd	03104
Maiden Ln	03109
S Main St	03102
Malvern St	03104
Mammoth Rd	
1-449	03109
450-1299	03104
S Mammoth Rd	03109
Manchester St	
1-165	03101
166-599	03103
Manning St	03103
Manor Dr	03103
Maple Ln	03109
Maple St	
1-439	03103
440-899	03104
S Maple St	03103
Maplehurst Ave	03104
Mapleton Rd	03104
Maplewood Ave	03102
Maplewood St	03103
Marathon Way	03109
March Ave	03103
Marguerite St	03103
Market St	03101
Marlborough St	03102
Marston St	03102
Martel Dr	03103
Martin St	03103
Mary Ann Rd	03104
Maryland Ave	03104
Mason St	03102
Massabesic St	03103
Mast Rd	03102
Master St	03102
Maurice St	03103
Maxwell St	03102
Maybrook Ave	03102
Mayflower Dr	03104
Maynard Ave	03103
Mccarthy St	03104
Mccauley St	03104
Mcclintock St	03102
Mcduffie St	03102
Mcgregor St	03102
Mcguigan Ave	03103
Mcilvin St	03103
Mcintyre Ct	03104
Mclane Ln	03104
Mcneil St	03102
Mcphail St	03104
Mcquesten St	03102
Mead St	03104
Meadow Ln	03109
Meadow St	03103
Meadow Glen Dr	03109
Mechanic St	03101
Medford St	03109
Medwick St	03109
Meetinghouse Ln	03109
Megan Dr	03109
Melrose St	03109
Memorial Dr	03103
Mercier Ave	03102
Merrill St	03103
Merrimack St	
1-139	03101
140-699	03103
W Merrimack St	03101
Merritt Nyberg Ln	03104
Merrow St	03104
Miami Ct	03103
Michael St	03104
Michigan Ave	03104
Middle St	03101
Midland St	03103
Milford St	03102
Milky Way	03109
Millstone Ave	03102
Milne Dr	03104
Milton St	
400-499	03103
500-599	03104
Minot St	03109
Mirror St	03104
Missent	03102
Missequenced	03102
Mission Ave	03104
Missort	03102
W Mitchell St	03103
Mollie Dr	03103
Monadnock Ln	03103
Monroe St	03104
Montcalm St	03102
Montgomery St	03102
Moody St	03103
Moore St	03102
Mooresville Rd	03103
Moreau St	03102
Morey St	03103
Morgan St	03102
Morin St	03102
Morning Glory Dr	03109
Morrison St	03104
Morse Rd	03104
Morton St	03104
Moses St	03109
Mountain Laurel Way	03102
Mulsey St	03101
Murphy St	03103
Myrtle St & Way	03104
Mystic St	03103
Mystic Brook Way	03102
Nashua St	03104
Nelson St	03103
New York St	03104
Newbury Rd	03103
Newell St	03101
Newgate Cir	03102

Newstead Way 03104
Norcross St 03109
Norfolk St 03103
Normand St 03109
Norris St 03103
North Ct & St 03104
Northbrook Dr 03102
Norton Ave 03109
Notre Dame Ave 03102
Nourie Park 03102
Oak St 03104
Oak Hill Ave 03104
Oakdale Ave 03103
Oakland Ave 03109
W Oakwood Ave 03103
Ode Way 03103
Ohio Ave 03104
Old Cohas Ave 03109
Old Falls Rd 03103
Old Granite St 03101
Old Hackett Hill Rd 03102
Old Mammoth Rd 03104
Old Orchard Way 03103
Old Wellington Rd 03104
Oliver St 03103
Olmstead Ave 03103
Omalley St 03103
Omega St 03102
Oneida St 03102
Orange St 03104
Orchard Ave 03109
Orchard St 03102
Orms St 03102
Overland St 03103
Overlook Ave 03104
Oxford St 03102
Page St
700-949 03109
950-1399 03104
Pahray Ln 03109
Pamela Cir 03103
Paquette Ave 03104
Parenteau St 03103
Paris Ter 03102
Park Ave 03104
Parker Ave & St 03102
Parkside Ave 03102
Parkview St 03103
Pasture Dr 03102
Patricia Ln 03104
Patterson St 03102
Paule Ave 03104
Payson St 03101
Peabody Ave 03109
Peak St 03104
Pearl St
1-119 03101
120-399 03104
Pelham St 03104
Pennacook St 03104
Pennsylvania Ave 03104
Penny Ln 03104
Pepperidge Dr 03103
Pepsi Rd 03109
Perimeter Rd W 03103
Perkins Ave 03103
Perley St 03104
Pershing St 03102
Petain St 03102
Peterboro St 03103
Pheasant Ln 03109
Phillip St 03102
Phillippe Cote St 03101
Phinney Ave 03109
Picadilly Ct 03104
Pickering St 03104
Pinard St 03102
Pinardville Heights Rd 03102
Pine Ave 03103
Pine Ln 03109
Pine St
1-9 03103
11-369 03103
370-799 03104
Pine Hill Ave 03102
Pine Island Rd 03103

Pine Ridge Ave 03104
Pinebrook Pl 03109
Pinecrest Rd 03104
Pinedale St 03102
Pinehurst St 03103
Plainfield St 03103
Platts Ave 03109
Plaza Dr 03101
Pleasant St 03101
Pleasant Pond Way 03102
Plummer St
1-12 03102
13-23 03103
14-34 03102
23-29 03102
26-28 03103
30-39 03104
40-99 03102
48-56 03103
58-60 03103
Plymouth St 03102
Pond Dr 03103
Pondview Ln 03102
Poor St 03102
Poplar St 03104
S Porter St 03103
S Porter St Ext 03103
Portsmouth Ave 03109
Prairie Ct 03102
Pralinta St 03102
Pratt Ct 03103
Precourt St 03102
Prescott St 03103
President Rd 03103
Primrose Dr 03109
Prince St 03102
Priscilla Cir 03103
Proctor Rd 03109
Prospect St 03104
Prout Ave 03103
Provencher St 03102
Public St 03103
Pullman St 03103
Purchase St 03103
Purdue St 03103
Putnam St 03102
Quail Ct 03109
Quarry Way 03104
Queen City Ave
1-249 03101
2-248 03103
250-399 03102
Quincy St 03102
Quirin St 03102
Radcliffe St 03104
Rambling Rose Dr 03109
Ramsay St 03103
Rand St 03109
Randall St 03103
Ray St 03104
Readey St 03104
N Reading St 03104
Rebel Ln 03104
Red Coat Ln 03104
Reed St 03102
Regent Ave 03104
Renard St 03109
Reservoir Ave 03104
Revere Ave 03109
Reynolds Ave 03103
Rhode Island Ave 03104
Richard St 03103
Riddle Pl & St 03102
S Ridge Dr 03109
Ridge Rd 03104
Ridge St 03102
Ridgewood St 03103
Riley Ave 03103
Rimmon St 03102
W River Dr 03104
River Rd 03104
N River Rd 03106
River Bank Rd 03103
River Bend Way 03103
River Birch Cir 03102
River Front Dr 03102

W Riverbank Rd 03102
Riverdale Ave 03103
Riverview Pl 03104
Riverview Park Rd 03102
Riverwalk Way 03101
Robert Ct 03103
Robert Hall Rd 03103
Robin Hill Rd 03104
Robinson St 03104
Rochambeau St 03102
Rochelle Ave 03102
Rockland Ave 03102
Rockville St 03104
Rockwell St 03103
Rockwood Way 03103
Rogers St 03103
Ronald St 03101
Roosevelt St 03102
Rose Ave 03103
Rose Ter 03102
Roseanne Ln 03103
Rosecliff Ln 03109
W Rosedale Ave 03103
Rosegate Farm Dr 03109
Rosemont Ave 03103
W Rosemont Ave 03103
Rosemont St 03102
Rosewood Ln 03103
Ross Ave 03103
Roundabout Way 03102
Roundstone Dr 03103
Rowell St 03104
Roy Ave 03103
Roy St 03102
Roycraft Rd 03103
Roysan St 03103
Ruggles St 03103
N Russell St 03104
Ruta Cir 03102
Ruth Ave 03109
Sagamore St 03104
Saint Anselm Dr 03102
Saint James Ave 03102
Saint Marie St 03102
Salem St 03103
Salisbury St 03104
Salmon St 03104
Sandy Brook St 03103
Sandys Way 03103
Sargent Rd 03103
Sarto St 03109
Schiller St 03102
School St 03102
Schuyler St 03102
Seadiant St 03103
Seames Dr 03103
Sears Dr 03103
Seminole St 03102
Sentinel Ct 03103
Serenity Way 03104
Settlers Way 03104
Sewall St 03103
Shady Ln 03104
Sharon St 03102
Shasta St 03103
Shaunna Ct 03109
Shaw St 03104
Shawmut St 03102
Sheffield Rd 03103
Shepherd Rd 03104
Sherburne St 03104
Sheridan St 03102
Sherman St 03102
Sherwood Dr 03103
Shirley Hill Rd 03102
W Shore Ave 03109
Sibley Ter 03109
Silver St 03103
Simone St 03103
Sinclair Ave 03104
Sky Meadow Way 03104
Skyline Dr 03109
Skyview Rd 03104
Slade Ave 03103
Smillown St 03104
Smyth Ln & Rd 03104

Smyth Ferry Rd 03103
Somerset Way 03109
Somerville St 03103
South St 03104
Sparks Rd 03103
Sprague St 03103
Spring Garden St 03103
Springdale Rd 03103
Springvalley St 03104
Springview Ave 03103
Springwood Dr 03102
Spruce St 03103
Stagecoach Way 03104
Stanton St 03103
Stark Ln 03102
Stark St 03101
Stark Way 03102
State St 03101
Stearns Cir & St 03102
Steinmetz Dr 03104
Sterling Ave 03103
Stetson St 03104
Stevens St 03103
Stewart St 03102
Stockholm St 03104
Stone Ln 03103
Stoneyview Way 03102
Stonington Dr 03109
Straw Rd 03102
Straw Hill Rd 03104
Streamside Dr 03102
Sugar Hill Ln 03109
Sullivan St 03102
Summer St 03103
Summerside Ave 03102
Sundial Ave 03103
Sunnyside St 03103
Sunset Dr & Way 03104
Sunset Pine Dr 03109
Surrey Ln 03103
Sweeney Ave 03102
Sylvan Ln 03102
Sylvester St 03102
Taggart St 03102
Talbot St 03109
Tamarack Ct 03103
Tanglewood Ct 03102
Tarbell St 03104
Tarrytown Rd 03103
Tavernier Way 03109
S Taylor St 03103
Teaberry Pl 03102
Ted St 03104
Temple Ct 03104
Tennyson Dr 03104
Thayer St 03104
Theodore Rd 03104
Theophile St 03102
Theresa Ct 03103
Thistle Way 03109
Thomas St 03103
Thornton St 03102
Thorp St 03102
Tiffany Ln 03104
Tilden Dr 03103
Tilton St 03102
Titus Ave 03103
Tondreau Ct 03102
Tory Rd 03104
Tougas Ave 03109
Townhouse Rd 03103
Trafford St 03103
Trahan St 03103
Trebor Dr 03104
Treetop Ln 03102
Trenton St 03104
Trestle Ln 03102
Trinity St 03109
Trolley Ct, St & Way 03103
Tufts St 03104
Turner St 03102
Tuttle St 03103
Tyler Ave 03103
Tzinas St 03109
Union St
1-499 03103
500-1699 03104
Upland St 03102
Upton St 03103
Val St 03103
Valentine Dr 03103
Valley St 03103
Valley West Way 03102
Vandora Dr 03103
Varney St 03102
Vassar St 03104
Vernon St 03101
Victoria St 03104
Victorian Way 03104
View St 03103
Villa St 03103
Village Circle Way 03102
Vine St 03101
Vinton St 03103
Violet St 03102
Wagner St 03104
Walden Way 03109
Waldo St 03104
Walker St 03102
Wall St
1-1 03101
1-99 03102
2-2 03101
Walnut St 03104
Walnut Hill Ave 03104
Walsh Ave 03102
Ward St 03104
Warner St 03102
Warren Ave 03102
Warren St 03104
Warsaw Ave 03103
Wason St 03102
Waterford Way 03102
Waterman St 03103
Watson St 03103
Watts St 03104
Waverly St 03109
Wayland Ave 03109
Wayne St 03102
W Webster St 03104
Wedgewood Ln 03109
Welch Ave 03103
Wellesley St 03104
Wellington Ct & Rd 03104
Wellington Hill Rd 03104
Wellington Terrace Dr 03104
Wells St 03104
Wentworth St 03102
West St 03102
Westchester Way 03104
Westland Ave 03103
Westminster St 03103
Weston Rd 03103
Weston St 03104
Westside Ave 03102
Westwind Dr 03104
Westwood Dr 03103
Whalley Rd 03103
Wheelock St 03102
Whig Dr 03104
Whipple St 03102
White Birch Way 03102
White Pine Ln 03102
Whitford St 03104
Whitney Ave 03104
Whittemore Ave 03102
Whittier St 03102
Whittington St 03104
Wild Indigo Ln 03109
Wildwood Ct & St 03103
Wilkins St 03102
Willard St 03109
William St 03102
William Gannon Rd 03104
William Loeb Dr 03109
S Willow St 03103
Wilmot St 03103
S Wilson St 03103
Wind Song Ave 03104
Windflower Dr 03109
Windsor Ave 03104
Windward Ln 03104

Winston St 03103
Winter St 03102
Winthrop St 03103
Witt Ave 03103
Wolcott St 03103
Wolfe St 03109
Woodbine Ave 03109
Woodbury St 03102
Woodcrest Ct 03109
Woodgate Ct 03103
Woodland Ave 03109
Woodlawn Dr 03103
Woodman Ave & St 03103
Woodview Way 03102
Worthen St 03104
Worthley Rd 03102
Wyoming Ave 03103
Young St 03103
Youville St 03102
Yvette St 03102
Zachary Rd 03109

NUMBERED STREETS

1st Ave 03104
2nd St 03102
3rd St 03102
4th St 03102
6th Ave 03104
7th Ave 03104

NASHUA NH

General Delivery 03061

POST OFFICE BOXES MAIN OFFICE STATIONS AND BRANCHES

Box No.s
1 - 4080 03061
7001 - 8260 03060

NAMED STREETS

Abbe Ln 03063
Abbott St 03064
Aberdeen Ln 03062
Abinger Way 03063
Acacia St 03062
Academy Dr 03064
Acton St 03060
Adams St 03064
Addison Dr 03062
W Adelaide Ave 03064
Adella Dr 03063
Aetna Ct 03064
Airport Rd 03063
Alan St 03060
Albury Stone Cir 03063
Alder Dr 03060
Aldgate Dr 03062
Alex Cir 03062
Alford Ln 03062
Algonquin Ln 03063
Alice Dr 03063
W Allds St 03060
Almont St 03060
Alpine St 03060
Alstead Ave 03060
Althea Ln 03062
Amalia Dr 03063
Amble Rd 03062
Amherst St 03064
Amory St 03060
Anders Ln 03060
Andover Down 03063
Annabelle Ct 03062
Anthony Cir 03062
Antrim St 03063
Anvil Dr 03060
Apache Rd 03063

Appaloosa Pl 03062
Appleside Dr 03060
Appletree Grn 03062
April Dr 03060
Archery Ln 03060
Arlington Ave & St 03060
Arrow Ln 03060
Arthurs Ln 03062
Ascot Park 03063
Ash Ct & St 03060
Ashby Cir 03062
Ashland St 03064
Aspen Ct 03062
Aster Ct 03062
Aston St 03063
Atherton Ave 03064
Atwood Ct 03064
Auburn St 03064
Austin Cir 03063
Autumn Glen Cir 03062
Autumn Leaf Dr 03060
Avon Dr 03064
Ayer Rd & St 03064
Azalea Ln 03062
Aztec Rd 03063
Badger St 03060
Bahl St 03063
Bailey St 03063
Baker St 03064
Balcom St 03060
Baldwin St 03064
Ballerina Ct 03062
Baltimore Rd 03062
Bangor St 03063
Barisano Way 03063
Barker Ave 03060
Barnesdale Rd 03062
Barrington Ave 03062
Bartemus Trl 03063
Bartlett Ave 03064
Batchelder St 03060
Bates Dr 03064
Bay Ridge Dr 03062
Bayberry Cir 03062
Baymeadow Dr 03063
Beacon Ct & St 03064
Beard St 03064
Beasom St 03064
Beaujolais Dr 03062
Beausite Dr 03060
Beauview Ave 03064
Beaver St 03063
Beckmann Ln 03062
Bedford St 03063
Beech St 03060
Belfast St 03063
Belgian Pl 03062
Belknap St 03060
Bell St 03064
Bellcrest Rd 03062
Belle Aire Ave 03060
Bellingrath Pl 03063
Belmont St 03060
Bennett St 03064
Bennington Rd 03064
Benrus St 03060
Benson Ave 03060
Benton Dr 03064
Berkeley St 03064
Berkshire Rd & St 03064
Berwick St 03063
Beverlee Dr 03064
Bianchi Ct 03062
Bible Way 03063
Bicentennial Dr 03062
Birch Hill Dr 03063
Birch Ridge Trl 03062
Birchbrow Rd 03060
Birchwood Dr 03064
Biscayne Pkwy 03064
Bishop Ln 03062
Bitirnas St 03064
Bittersweet Rd 03060
Black Oak Dr 03062
Blackfoot Dr 03063
Blacksmith Way 03060

Blackstone Dr 03063
Blaine St 03060
Blanchard St 03060
Bloomingdale Dr 03064
Blossom St 03060
Blue Hill Ave 03064
Blue Jay Hl 03064
Blueberry Ln 03062
Bluestone Dr 03060
Boggs Cir 03060
Bolic St 03062
Bond St 03064
Bonny St 03062
Booth St 03060
Boulder Cir 03062
Bourdeaux St 03060
Bow St 03063
Bowers St 03060
Bowery St 03060
Bowman Ln 03062
Box Mail 03062
Boxwood Ct 03063
Boylston Ave 03064
Brackenwood Dr 03062
Bradford St 03063
Bramble Dr 03062
Brander Ct 03063
Brenda St 03062
Brentwood Ave 03063
Brewster St 03060
Briand Dr 03063
Briarcliff Dr 03062
Briarwood Dr 03063
Brick Manor Dr 03063
Brickyard Ln 03062
Bridge St 03060
Bridle Path 03060
Briggs Ave 03060
Brigham St 03064
Briley Pl 03063
Brinton Dr 03064
Bristol St 03064
Brittany Way 03063
Broad St
6A-6Z 03064
1-149 03064
150-699 03063
Broadcrest Ln 03063
Broadview Ave 03064
Brook St 03060
Brook Village Rd 03062
Brookfield Dr 03063
Brookline St 03064
Brookside Ter 03060
Browning Ave 03062
Bruce St 03064
Brussels Dr 03063
Bryant Rd 03062
Buchanan St 03060
Buck St 03060
Buckmeadow Rd 03062
Bud Way 03063
Buker St 03064
Bulova Dr 03060
Bundled Flats
Endorsed 03062
Burgess St 03064
Burgundy Dr 03062
Burke St 03060
Burley Ave 03062
Burlington Rd 03062
Burnett St 03060
Burnham Ave 03064
Burns St 03064
Burnside St 03064
Burritt St 03060
Burton Dr 03060
Butternut Dr 03063
Byfield Cir 03062
Byron Dr 03062
C St 03060
Cabernet Ct 03062
Cabot Dr 03064
Cadogan Way 03062
Caitlyn Cir 03062
Calais St 03060

Caldwell Rd 03060
Calico Cir 03062
Cambridge Rd 03062
Cameron Dr 03062
Canal St 03064
Candia St 03063
Candlewood Park 03062
Cannon Dr 03062
Cannongate Iii 03063
Canter Ct 03063
Cape Ave 03062
Capitol St 03063
Caraway Ln 03063
Cardiff Rd 03062
Cardinal Cir 03063
Carlene Dr 03062
Carlisle Rd 03062
Carmine Rd 03063
Carnation Cir 03062
Carolina Dr 03060
Caron Ave 03064
Carriage Ln 03063
Carroll St 03063
Carson Cir 03062
Carter Cir 03062
Carver St 03064
Casco Dr 03062
Casey Cir 03063
Cassandra Ln 03064
Castlegate Way 03063
Catalina Ln 03064
Cathedral Cir 03063
Catherine St 03060
Cecile St 03060
Cedar St 03060
Celeste St 03064
Celina Ave 03063
Cellu Dr 03063
Censonta St 03064
Central St 03060
Century Rd 03064
Chablis Ct 03062
Chadwick Cir 03062
Champagne Dr 03062
Chandler St 03064
Chapel Hill Dr 03063
Chapman St 03060
Charles St 03064
Charlotte Ave & St 03064
Charlton Cir 03060
Charron Ave 03063
Chase St 03060
Chatfield Dr 03063
Chatham St 03063
Chaucer Rd 03062
Chautauqua Ave 03064
Chelsea Ct 03062
Cherokee Ave 03062
Cherry St 03060
Cherry Hollow Rd 03062
Cherryfield Dr 03062
Cherrywood Dr 03062
Cheryl St 03062
Chesapeake Rd 03062
Cheshire St 03063
Chester St 03064
Chestnut St 03060
Cheyenne Dr 03063
Chickie St 03062
Chinook Rd 03062
Chokeberry Ln 03062
Christian Dr 03063
Christopher Dr 03060
Chuck Druding Dr 03063
Chung St 03062
Church St 03060
Churchill St 03062
Cider Ln 03063
Cimmarron Dr 03062
Cindy Dr 03062
Circle Ave 03060
Circlefield Dr 03062
Clairmoor Dr 03060
Clark Rd 03062
Clearview Dr 03062
Clement St 03060

Clergy Cir 03063
Cleveland St 03060
Cliff Rd 03062
Clinton St 03064
Clocktower Pl 03060
Clovercrest Dr 03062
Clydesdale Cir 03062
Cobble Hill Rd 03062
Cobbler Ln 03063
Coburn Ave 03063
Coburn Woods 03063
Colby Rd 03064
Coleridge Rd 03062
Colgate Rd 03064
Coliseum Ave 03063
Colleen Rd 03062
Collier Ct 03062
Colonial Ave 03062
Colony Way 03062
Columbia Ave 03064
Columbine Dr 03063
Comanche St 03063
Commercial St 03060
Conant Rd 03062
Concord St 03064
Congress St 03062
Connecticut Ave 03060
Constantine Dr 03062
Copp St 03060
Copperfield Dr 03062
Cornell Rd 03064
Cornwall Ln 03063
Corona Ave 03063
Cortez Dr 03063
Cosworth Cir 03062
Cote Ave 03060
Cotillion Ln 03062
Cottage Ave & St 03060
Cotton Rd 03063
Country Hill Rd 03063
Country Side Dr 03062
Court St 03060
Courtland St 03064
Courtney Ln 03062
Coventry Rd 03062
Covey Rd 03062
Cox St 03064
Cranleigh Mews 03063
Cranwell Ct 03062
Crawford Ln 03063
Creek Pl 03063
Crescent St 03064
Crestview Ter 03060
Crestwood Ln 03062
Crimson Ct 03063
Cross St 03064
Crowley Ave 03060
Crown St 03060
Crystal Dr 03062
Curtis Dr 03062
Cushing Ave 03064
Custer Cir 03062
Custom St 03062
Cutler Way 03063
Cypress Ln 03063
D St 03060
Daffodil Dr 03062
Dale St 03060
Dalton St 03063
Damon Ave 03064
Damper Cir 03063
Danbury Rd 03064
Dane St 03060
Danforth Rd 03060
Daniel Webster Hwy 03060
Daniels St 03060
Darien Cir 03062
Dartmouth St 03064
David Dr 03064
Davis Ct 03064
Dawn St 03064
Daylily Dr 03062
Daytona St 03064
Deacon Dr 03063
Dearborn St 03060
Decatur Dr 03062

Dedham St 03063
Deerhaven Dr 03064
Deerwood Dr 03063
Delaware Rd 03062
Delta Dr 03060
Delude St 03060
Demanche St 03060
Denise St 03063
Denton St 03060
Denver Dr 03063
Depot Rd 03062
Derby Cir 03062
Derry St 03063
E Desilvio Dr 03060
Dexter St 03060
Diamondback Ave 03062
Dianne St 03062
Dickens St 03062
Dickerman St 03060
Diesel Rd 03063
Digital Dr 03062
Dinsmore St 03064
Dion Ln 03062
Divinity Cir 03063
Dixville St 03063
Dobson St 03060
Dodge St 03064
Doggett Ln 03064
Dogwood Dr 03062
Dolan St 03060
Dolphin Cir 03062
Donald Way 03062
Doncaster Dr 03062
Donna St 03060
Donovan Dr 03062
Dora St 03060
Dorchester Way 03064
Douglas St 03064
Dover St 03063
Dow St 03064
Dow Jones Ave 03062
Dray Coach Cir 03062
Drury Ln 03064
Dryden Ave 03062
Dublin Ave 03063
Dubonnet Ln 03062
Ducas Ave 03063
Duchess Rd 03063
Duckford Cir 03063
Dudley St 03060
Dumaine Ave 03063
Dunbarton Dr 03063
Dunlap Dr 03064
Dunloggin Rd 03063
E Dunstable Rd
1A-1B 03060
1-99 03060
100-499 03062
Durham St 03063
Dustin Dr 03062
E St 03060
Earley St 03060
Eastbrook Dr 03060
Eastman St 03060
Eaton St 03060
Echo Ave 03062
Eckler Ave 03060
Edgewood Ave 03064
Edinburgh Dr 03062
Edis Ln 03063
Edith Ave 03064
Edmatteric Dr 03062
Edmond Dr 03063
Edson St 03064
Edwards Ave & St 03060
Edwin St 03060
Egerton Dr 03064
Elaine Dr 03062
Eldorado Cir 03062
Eldridge St 03060
Elgin St 03060
Elliott St 03064
Elm Ct & St 03060
Elmer Dr 03062
Elmhurst Ln 03062
Elystan Cir 03064

Emerald Dr 03062
Emerson Rd 03062
Emmett St 03060
Endorsed Bundled
Letters 03062
Endorsed Individual
Letters 03062
Epping St 03063
Eric Ave 03062
Erie Cir 03062
Erion Dr 03062
Esquire Cir 03062
Essex St 03064
Euclid Ave 03060
Evelyn Cir 03062
Everett St 03060
Evergreen St 03060
Factory St 03060
Fairhaven Rd 03060
Fairlane Ave 03060
Fairmount St 03064
Fairview Ave 03060
Fairway St 03060
Falls Grove Rd 03063
Farley Rd 03063
Farley St 03064
Farmers Trl 03062
Farmington Rd 03060
Farmwood Dr 03062
Fawn Ln 03064
Faxon Ave & St 03060
Federal Hill Rd 03062
Fenwick St 03063
Ferncroft Dr 03063
Fernwood St 03060
Ferry Rd 03064
Ferryalls Ct 03064
Ferson St 03060
Field St 03060
Fifield Ln 03064
Fifield St 03060
Fireside Cir 03063
Fitzpatrick Cir 03063
Flagstone Dr 03063
Fletcher St 03064
Flintlocke Dr 03062
Fordham Dr 03062
Forest St 03064
Forest Hills Dr 03060
Forest Park Dr 03060
Forge Dr 03060
Forsythia Dr 03062
Fossa Ave & Ter 03060
Foster Ct & Sq 03064
Fotene St 03062
Foundry St 03060
Fountain Ln 03062
Fowell Ave 03060
Fox St 03064
Fox Meadow Rd 03060
Foxboro St 03063
Foxglove Ct 03062
Foxmoor Cir 03063
Franconia Dr 03063
Franklin St 03064
Freedom St 03063
Fremont St 03060
French St 03064
Freshwater Ct 03060
Friar Tuck Ln 03062
Front St 03064
Frost Dr 03063
Fulton St 03060
Furnival Rd 03064
Gaffney St 03060
Gagnon Cir 03062
Galway Rd 03062
Garden St 03060
Gary St 03062
Gendron St 03062
George St 03060
Georgetown Dr 03062
Gettysburg Dr 03064
Gilboa Ln 03062
Gillis St 03060
Gilman St 03060

Gilson Rd 03062
Gingras Dr 03060
Girouard Ave 03064
Glacier Dr 03062
Glasgow Rd 03062
Glastonbury Dr 03063
Glen Dr 03062
Glencliff Way 03063
Glendale Dr 03064
Gleneagle Dr 03063
E & W Glenwood St 03060
Gloucester Ln 03063
Goldfinch Ln 03062
Gordon St 03064
Gorman Ave 03060
Gosselin Rd 03062
Governors Ln 03062
Grace Dr 03062
Graham Dr 03060
Grand Ave 03060
Granite St 03064
Grasmere Ln 03063
Gray Ave 03060
Greatstone Dr 03063
Greeley St 03064
Green St 03064
Green Heron Ln 03062
Greenfield Dr 03064
Greenlay St 03063
Greenock Ln 03062
Greenwood Dr 03062
Gregg Rd 03062
Grenada Cir 03062
Grimsby Ln 03063
Groton Rd 03062
N Groton St 03060
S Groton St 03060
Grove St 03064
Gruen Ln 03060
Guilford Ln 03063
Gusabel Ave 03063
Hadley Dr 03062
Haines St 03060
Hall Ave 03064
Hamilton St 03060
Hamlett Dr 03062
Hammar Rd 03062
Hammond Ct 03060
Hampshire Dr 03063
Hampton Dr 03063
Hancock St 03064
Hanover St 03060
Harbor Ave & Ct 03060
Hardy St 03064
Harold Dr 03060
Harris Rd 03062
Harris St 03060
Harrison St 03060
Hartford Ln 03063
Hartwell Brook Dr 03060
Harvard St 03060
Harvest Ln 03063
Hassel Brook Rd 03060
Hastings Ln 03064
Hatch St 03060
Hawkstead Holw 03063
Hawthorne Ln 03063
Hawthorne Village Rd 03062
Hayden St 03060
Hazel Ave 03062
Hearthside Cir 03063
Heathcliff Way 03064
Heather Ct 03062
Heathrow Ct 03063
Heidi Ln 03062
Hemlock Ct 03063
Henry David Dr 03062
Heon Ct 03060
Hereford Dr 03062
Heritage Village Dr 03062
Herrick St 03060
Hibiscus Way 03062
Hidden Trl 03062
Hideaway Rd 03064
High St 03060
High Bridge Hl 03063

High Pine Ave 03063
Highland Pl & St 03064
Hill St 03064
Hillcrest Cir 03064
Hillock Cir & Dr 03062
Hills Ferry Rd 03064
Hillside Dr 03064
Hinsdale Ave 03063
E & W Hobart St 03060
Hobbs Ave 03060
Holbrook Dr 03062
Holden Rd 03063
Holiday Cir 03062
E Hollis St 03060
W Hollis St
1-412 03060
413-1199 03062
Hollow Ridge Dr 03062
Holly Dr 03063
Hollyhock Ave 03062
Holman St 03064
Holmes St 03060
Holt Ave 03060
Honeysuckle Ct 03063
Hooker St 03064
Hopi Dr 03063
Hopkins St 03064
Horizon Cir 03064
Horsepond Ave 03063
Houde St 03060
Houston Dr 03062
Howard Ct 03064
Howard St 03060
Hoyts Ln 03060
Huffey Cir 03062
Hughey St 03064
Hunt St 03060
Hunters Ln 03063
Huntingdon Ln 03062
Huron Dr 03063
Hutchinson St 03064
Hutton St 03060
Hyacinth Dr 03062
Hyannis St 03063
Hydrangea Dr 03062
Inca Dr 03063
Indian Fern Dr 03062
Indian Head Plz 03060
Indian Rock Rd 03063
Indiana Dr 03060
Individual Flats
Endorsed 03062
Industrial Park Dr 03062
Ingalls St 03060
Innovative Way 03062
N Intervale St 03064
Ipswich Cir 03063
Iris Ct 03062
Iroquois Rd 03063
Ivy Ln 03063
Jackson St 03060
Jacoby Cir 03062
Jake Dr 03063
Jalbert Dr 03060
Jamaica Ln 03063
James St 03060
Jared Cir 03063
Jasmine Dr 03063
Jasper Ln 03063
Jayron Dr 03062
Jefferson St 03064
Jennifer Dr 03062
Jenny Hill Ln 03062
Jensen St 03062
Jeremy Pl 03064
Jessica Dr 03060
Jewell Ln 03064
Jill Dr 03062
Joffre St 03060
John St 03060
Jolori Ln 03062
Jones Ct 03064
Jonquil Dr 03062
Judith Dr 03062
June St 03060
Juniper Ln 03063

Street	ZIP
Kanata Dr	03063
Karnoustie Way	03062
Kathy Dr	03062
Katie Ln	03062
Keats St	03062
Kehoe Ave	03060
Keith St	03062
Kelly St	03062
Kendall Way	03062
Kendrick St	03064
Kenmare Rd	03062
Kennedy Dr	03060
Kent Ln	03062
Kern Dr	03060
Kerry Ln	03062
Kessler Farm Dr	03063
Kevin Rd	03062
Killian Dr	03062
Kim Dr	03062
Kincaid Ln	03062
King St	03060
Kingston Dr	03060
Kinsley St	03060
Kipford Way	03063
Kipling St	03062
Kirk St	03064
Kirkwood Dr	03064
Kittery Dr	03062
Klondike St	03060
Knights Bridge Dr	03063
Knollwood Ave	03060
Knowlton Rd	03063
Kona Dr	03062
Kristina Way	03060
Kyle Dr	03062
Labine St	03060
Laconia Ave	03063
Lacy Ln	03062
Lafrance Ave	03064
Lake Ave & St	03060
Lakeside Ave	03060
Lamb Rd	03062
Lamplighter Dr	03064
Lancaster Dr	03062
Landsdown Dr	03062
Langholm Dr	03062
Lansing Dr	03062
Lantern Ln	03062
Laramie Cir	03062
Larchen Ln	03063
Larchmont Dr	03062
Laredo Cir	03062
Larkspur Ct	03062
Laton St	03064
Laurel Ct	03062
Lavoie Ln	03063
Lawndale Ave	03060
Lear Dr	03063
Learned St	03060
Ledge St	03060
Ledgewood Hills Dr	03062
Lee St	03064
Lee Ann St	03062
Leewood Trl	03062
Leith Ct	03063
Lemoine St	03060
Lemon St	03064
Leslie Ln	03062
Lessard St	03064
Lewis St	03060
Liberty St	03060
Lilac Ct	03062
Lille Rd	03062
Lincoln Ave	03060
Linden St	03064
Linjay Cir	03062
Linton St	03060
Linwood St	03060
Lisa Dr	03062
Lisbon Ln	03060
Lochmere Ln	03063
Lock St	03064
Lockness Dr	03062
Locust St	03064
Logan Rd	03063
Lojko Dr	03062
N & S London Dr	03062
Lone Star Dr	03062
Long Ave	03064
Loop Ave	03062
Loop Mail	03062
Loring Dr	03062
Louisburg Sq	03060
Lovell St	03060
Lovewell St	03060
Lowell St	03064
Lowther Pl	03062
Lucier St	03064
Luke St	03063
Lumb Ave	03060
Lunar Ln	03062
Lund Rd & St	03060
Lutheran Dr	03063
Lynde St	03064
Lynn St	03060
Lyons St	03060
Macdonald Dr	03062
Madera Cir	03062
Magnolia Way	03063
Mahogany Dr	03062
Main St	03060
Main Dunstable Rd	
112-199	03060
200-599	03062
Majestic Ave	03063
Major Dr	03060
Manatee Ave	03060
Manchester St	03064
Mandinbarb Cir	03062
Manhattan Ave	03062
Manilla St	03060
Manorcrest Dr	03062
Maple St	03060
Mapleleaf Dr	03062
Mapleshade Dr	03062
Marblehead Dr	03063
March St	03060
Marcia Dr	03062
Margaret Cir	03062
Margate Rd	03062
Marian Ln	03062
Marie Ave	03063
Marina Dr	03062
Mark St	03062
Markar St	03060
Marlowe Rd	03062
Marmon Dr	03060
Marquis Ave	03060
Marshall St	03060
Martha St	03062
Martin St	03064
Masefield Rd	03062
Mason St	03060
Massachusetts Dr	03060
Massasoit Rd	03063
Maurice St	03060
Maxham Ave	03064
May St	03064
Mayfair Ln	03063
Maywood Dr	03064
Mccoy Ave	03064
Mckean St	03060
Mckenna Dr	03062
Mclaren Ave	03060
Mctavish Dr	03063
Meade St	03064
Meadow Ln	03062
Meadowbrook Dr	03062
Meadowview Cir	03062
Medallion Ct	03062
Meghan Dr	03063
Melissa Dr	03062
Mellens Ct	03064
Melrose St	03060
Memory Ave	03062
Mercier Ln	03062
Mercury Ln	03062
Meredith Dr	03063
Merrill St	03060
Merrimack St	03064
Merrit Pkwy	03062
Metropolitan Ave	03064
Miami St	03064
Michael Ave	03062
Michelle Dr	03062
Middle St	03060
Middle Dunstable Rd	03062
Midhurst Rd	03062
Milan St	03063
Milford St	03064
Milk St	03064
Mill St	03060
Mill Pond Dr	03062
Millbrook Dr	03062
Millwright Dr	03063
Milton St	03060
Mindy Pl	03064
Missent	03062
Missequenced	03062
Missort	03062
Missort Flats Non Pref	03062
Missort Flats Pref	03062
Missort Letters	03062
Mitchell St	03064
Mizoras Dr	03062
Moe St	03062
Monadnock St	03064
Monias Dr	03062
Monica Dr	03062
Monroe St	03060
Montclair Dr	03063
Monterey Ave	03064
Montgomery Ave	03060
Monza Rd	03064
Moonstone Ct	03062
Morgan St	03064
Morningside Dr	03060
Morrill St	03064
Morse Ave & St	03060
Morton St	03060
Moselle Ct	03062
Mount Pleasant St	03064
Mount Vernon St	03064
Mountain Laurels Dr	03062
Mountainview St	03060
Mulberry St	03060
Mulvanity St	03060
Murphy Dr	03062
Murray Ct	03060
Musket Dr	03062
Myopia Ln	03063
Myrtle St	03060
Mystic Ct	03062
Nagle St	03060
Nancy Ct	03062
Nashua Dr	03064
Nathan Ct	03064
Natick St	03063
National St	03060
Navaho St	03063
Nelson St	03063
Neptune Ln	03062
Nevada St	03060
New St	03060
New Dunstable Rd	03060
New Hampshire Ave	03063
New Haven Dr	03063
New Searles Rd	03062
Newburgh Rd	03062
Newbury St	03060
Newcastle Dr	03060
Newfield St	03063
Newman Dr	03062
Newton Dr	03063
Nichol Ln	03062
Nigel Ln	03062
Nightingale Rd	03062
Niquette Dr	03062
Norfolk St	03064
Norma Dr	03062
Normandy Way	03063
Northeastern Blvd	03062
Northfield Dr	03063
Northwest Blvd	03063
Northwood Dr	03063
Norton St	03064
Norwich Rd	03062
Norwood St	03063
Notre Dame St	03060
Nottingham Dr	03062
Nova Rd	03064
Nowell St	03060
Nutmeg Dr	03062
Nutt St	03060
Nutting St	03064
Nye Ave	03060
Oak St	03060
Oak Grove Trl	03062
Oak Hill Ln	03062
Oakdale Ave	03062
Oakland Ave	03060
Ohio Ave	03060
Old Balcom Farm Dr	03062
Old Coach Rd	03062
Old House Ln	03062
Old Mill Ln	03064
Oldfield Rd	03060
Oldham Ln	03063
Olympia Cir	03062
Oneida Cir	03060
Oneils Ct	03063
Oracle Dr	03062
Orange St	03064
Orchard Ave	03060
Ordway Ave	03060
Oregon Ave	03060
Oriole Dr	03063
Orlando St	03064
Osgood Rd	03060
E & W Otterson St	03060
Overhill Ave	03064
Overlook Dr	03062
Owls Head Dr	03063
Pacific Blvd	03062
Paige Ave	03064
Palisade Dr	03062
Palm St	03060
Panther Dr	03062
Park Ave	03060
Parker Dr	03062
Parkhurst Dr	03062
Parkinson Ct	03060
Parnell Pl	03060
Parrish Hill Dr	03063
Pasadena Ave	03064
Patten Ct	03060
Paul Ave	03060
Paxton Ter	03064
Peach Dr	03060
E & W Pearl St	03060
Pearson St	03064
Peele Rd	03062
Pelham St	03063
Pell Ave	03060
Pemberton Rd	03063
Pennichuck St	03064
Penny Ln	03062
Penobscot Rd	03062
Pepper Dr	03064
Pepperell Cir	03062
Percheron Cir	03062
Perham St	03064
Perimeter Rd	03063
Perry Ave	03060
Pershing St	03060
Peterborough Pl	03064
Pewter Ct	03063
Pickering Way	03063
Pierce St	03060
Piermont St	03063
Pike St	03060
Pilgrim Cir	03063
Pincongt Dr	03062
Pine St	03060
Pine Grove Ave	03060
Pine Hill Ave	03064
Pine Hill Rd	03063
Pine Street Ext	03060
Pinebrook Rd	03062
Pinehurst Ave	03062
Pioneer Dr	03062
Pitarys Dr	03062
Pitford Way	03063
Pittsburgh Ave & Dr	03062
Plainfield Ln	03062
Pleasant St	03060
Plum Dr	03062
Pluto Ln	03062
Plymouth Ave	03064
Poisson Ave	03060
Poliquin Dr	03062
Pollard Rd	03062
Pond St	03060
Ponderosa Ave	03062
Pondview Cir	03063
Pope Cir	03063
Portchester Dr	03062
Pratt St	03060
W Prescott St	03064
Preserve Dr	03064
Prestonfield Rd	03064
Prestwick Trl	03062
Primrose Dr	03062
Princeton Rd	03064
Proctor St	03060
Profile Cir	03063
Progress Ave	03062
Prospect Ave & St	03060
Pullman Ln	03062
Pulpit Pl	03062
Putnam St	03064
Pyrite Dr	03062
Quaker Rd	03063
Quarry Rd	03062
Queensway Cir	03062
Quincy St	03060
Quinton Dr	03062
Radcliffe Dr	03062
Railroad Sq	03064
Rainbow Dr	03062
Raleigh Dr	03062
Ramsgate Rdg	03063
Rancourt St	03064
Randolph St	03063
Raven St	03060
Raymond St	03064
Reading Rd	03062
Redmond St	03062
Redwood Cir	03062
Reed Ct	03064
Regal Dr	03063
Regent Dr	03063
Rene Dr	03062
Reservoir St	03064
Resurrection Cir	03063
Revere St	03060
Rhode Island Ave	03060
Rice Ave & St	03060
Richmond St	03063
Ridge Rd	03062
Ridge St	03064
Ridgefield Dr	03062
Riesling Pl	03062
Rita St	03060
Ritter St	03060
River Pines Blvd	03062
Riverside Cir & St	03062
Riverview St	03064
Robert Dr	03063
Robin Ln	03064
Robin Hood Rd	03062
Robinson Ct & Rd	03060
Roby Rd	03064
Roby St	03060
Rochette Ave	03060
Rock Island Rd	03062
Rockland St	03064
Rockne Dr	03060
Rocky Hill Dr	03062
Roderick Cir	03062
Rodman St	03064
Roedean Dr	03063
Rogers St	03064
Ronnie Dr	03062
Roseann Cir	03062
Rosecliff Dr	03062
Rosedale Ln	03062
Rosemary Ct	03062
Ross St	03060
Rowley St	03063
Roy St	03060
Royal Crest Dr	03060
Royal Oak Dr	03064
Rugby Rd	03063
Russell Ave & St	03060
Ryan Way	03064
Rye Pl	03063
Sacramento St	03064
Sacred Heart Dr	03060
Sagamore Rd	03062
Saint Andrews Cir	03062
Saint Camille St	03060
Saint James Pl	03062
Saint Josephs Dr	03060
Saint Laurent St	03064
Saint Lazare St	03060
Salem St	03064
Salisbury Rd	03064
Salmon Brook Dr	03062
Salvail Ct	03064
Sanborn Dr	03063
Sanders St	03060
Sands St	03060
Sandstone Dr	03063
Santa Fe Rd	03062
Santerre St	03064
Sapling Cir	03062
Saranac Dr	03062
Sarasota Ave	03060
Sargent Ave	03064
Satin Ave	03062
Saturn Ln	03062
Savoy St	03060
Sawmill Rd	03060
Sawyer St	03060
Saxford Ln	03063
Saxon Ln	03062
Scarborough Dr	03063
School St	03060
Scotia Way	03062
Scott Ave	03062
Scripture St	03060
Searles Rd	03062
Seminole Dr	03063
Seneca Dr	03062
Sequoia Cir	03063
Serotta Ave	03062
Settlement Way	03062
Sexton Ave	03060
Shadowbrook Dr	03062
Shadwell Rd	03062
Shady Ln	03062
Shady Hill Rd	03063
Shadycrest Dr	03062
Shaker Pl	03063
Shakespeare Rd	03062
Shasta Ct	03064
Shattuck St	03064
Shaw Cir	03062
Shawmut Ave	03064
Shawn Ave	03062
Shawnee Dr	03062
Shedds Ave	03060
Sheffield Rd	03062
Shelburne Rd	03063
Shelley Dr	03062
Shelton St	03062
Sheridan St	03064
Sherman St	03064
Sherri Ann Ave	03064
Sherwood Dr	03063
Shetland Rd	03062
Shingle Mill Dr	03062
Shore Dr	03062
Short Ave	03064
Silver Dr	03060
Silverton Dr	03062
Simon St	03060
Sims St	03063
Sioux Ave	03063
Sirelle Ct	03060
Sky Country Dr	03062
Sky Meadow Dr	03062
Skyline Dr	03062
Skyview Dr	03062
Smithfield Ter	03064
Smokey Ln	03062
Snow Cir	03062
Somerset Pkwy	03063
Souhegan Dr	03063
South St	03060
Southfield Dr	03064
Southgate Dr	03062
Southington St	03060
N Southwood Dr	03063
Spalding Ave & St	03060
Spencer Dr	03062
Spindlewick Dr	03062
Spit Brook Rd	
1-89	03060
90-199	03062
E Spit Brook Rd	03060
Spring St	
1-39	03060
38-38	03061
40-98	03060
41-99	03060
Spring Cove Rd	03062
Spruce St	03060
Sprucewood Ave	03062
Squire Dr	03063
Stable Rd	03062
Stadium Dr	03062
Stafford Rd	03062
Stanford Rd	03064
Stanley Ln	03062
Stanstead Pl	03063
Stanwood Dr	03063
E Stark St	03064
State St	03063
Stearns Ct	03064
Stevens Ave & St	03060
Stillwater Dr	03062
Stinson Dr	03063
Stockton Dr	03063
Stonebridge Dr	03063
Stonehaven Rd	03062
Stoneybrook Rd	03063
Stratham Grn	03063
Strawberry Bank Rd	03062
Sudbury Dr	03062
Suffolk Park	03063
Sugar Hill Dr	03063
Sugarberry Dr	03062
Sullivan St	03064
Summer St	03064
Summit St	03060
Sunapee St	03063
Sunblaze Dr	03062
Sunflower Ln	03063
Sunrise Trl	03062
Sunset Ln	03062
Sunshine Ct	03063
Superior Dr	03060
Surrey Ln	03062
Sutherland Dr	03062
Swallow Ln	03063
Swan St	03060
Swart Ter	03064
Sweet Meadow Dr	03063
Sweet William Cir	03062
Sycamore Ln	03063
Syracuse Rd	03064
Tacoma Cir	03062
Taft St	03060
Taggart Dr	03060
Tall Pine Cir	03062
Tammy Cir	03062
Tamora Dr	03062
Tampa St	03064
Tamworth Pl	03063
Tanglewood Dr	03062
Tanguay Ave	03063
Tara Blvd	03062
Taschereau Blvd	03062
Taylor St	03060
Teak Dr	03062
Technology Way	03060
Temple Pl & St	03060
Tempo Dr	03062
Tenby Dr	03062
Tennyson Ave	03062

Ternbury Sq 03060
Terrace St 03064
Terramar Ln 03062
Terry St 03064
Tetreau St 03060
Thayer Ct 03064
Thistle Ct 03063
Tholintr Dr 03063
Thomas St 03060
Thompson Rd 03060
Thoreau Dr 03062
Thorndike St 03060
Thornton Rd 03063
Thresher Rd 03063
Tilton St 03063
Timberline Dr 03062
Timothy Dr 03063
Tinker Rd
2-98 03064
100-299 03063
Titan Way 03063
Todd Rd 03064
Tolles St 03064
Tomolonis Dr 03062
Topaz Dr 03062
Topsfield Dr 03062
Torrey Rd 03063
Townsend W 03063
Tracey Ave 03063
Traders Way 03063
Trafalgar Sq 03063
Travis Rd 03063
Trek St 03062
Trestle Brook Dr 03062
Trinity Dr 03063
Trocha St 03063
Trombly Ter 03062
Troon Cir 03062
Trout Brook Dr 03062
Troy St 03064
Tuckerwood Ct 03064
Tufts Dr 03064
Tumblebrook Ln 03062
Turnbridge Dr 03062
Twilight Dr 03062
Tyler St 03060
Underhill St 03060
Unicorn Way 03063
Union St 03060
Union Way 03063
University Dr 03063
Upstone Dr 03063
Vagge Dr 03060
Valencia Dr 03062
Valhalla Dr 03062
Valiant Ln 03064
Valley Crest Trl 03062
Van Buren St 03060
Vandoner St 03060
Ventura Cir 03062
Venus Ln 03062
Verdun Ave 03060
Vermont Ave 03060
Vernon St 03064
Verona St 03060
Vespa Ln 03064
Victor Ave 03060
Victoria Dr 03063
Vieckis Dr 03062
Vilna Ave 03064
Vine St 03060
Vineyard Pl 03062
Virginia Dr 03060
Wadleigh St 03060
Wagon Trl 03062
Wakefield Dr 03062
Walden Pond Dr 03064
Walkeridge Dr 03062
Walnut St 03060
Waltham Dr 03060
Wanda Ln 03062
Warner St 03063
Warren St 03060
Warton Rd 03062
Wason Ave 03060
Water St 03060
Watersedge Dr 03063
Waterview Trl 03062
Watson St 03064
Waverly St 03060
Wayne Dr 03062
Webster St 03064
Weld St 03060
Wellesley Rd 03062
Wellington St 03064
Wellman Ave 03064
Wentworth St 03060
Westborn Dr 03062
Westbrook Dr 03060
Westchester Dr 03063
Westerdale Dr 03063
Westfield St 03064
Westgate Xing 03062
Westhill Dr 03062
Westminster Dr 03064
Westpoint Ter 03062
Westray Dr 03062
Westwood Dr 03062
Wethersfield Rd 03062
Weymouth Dr 03062
Wheaton Dr 03063
Whipple St 03060
White Ave 03060
White Oak Dr 03063
White Plains Dr 03062
Whites Ct 03064
Whitford Rd 03062
Whitman Rd 03062
Whitney St 03064
Whittemore Pl 03064
Wild Rose Dr 03063
Wilder St 03060
Wildwood Ln 03060
Will St 03060
Williams Ct & St 03060
Willow St 03060
Wilmington St 03062
Wilson St 03060
Wilton St 03063
Winchester St 03063
Windemere Way 03063
Winding Ln 03062
Windsor St 03063
Winn Rd 03062
Winter St 03064
Winwood Ave 03060
Wood St 03064
Woodbury Dr 03062
Woodcrest Dr 03062
Woodfield St 03062
Woodgate St 03063
Woodland Dr 03063
Woodville St 03062
Woodward Ave 03060
Worcester St 03060
Wright Rd 03064
Xenia St 03062
Yale Rd 03064
Yarmouth Dr 03062
York St 03063
Yorkshire Ln 03063
Yorkway Dr 03062
Yvonne St 03060
Zellwood St 03060

NUMBERED STREETS

All Street Addresses 03060

PORTSMOUTH NH

General Delivery 03802

POST OFFICE BOXES MAIN OFFICE STATIONS AND BRANCHES

Box No.s
1 - 1660 03802
2001 - 2511 03804
3003 - 22460 03802

NAMED STREETS

Adams Ave 03801
Airline Ave 03801
Airport Rd 03801
Albacore Way 03801
Albany St 03801
Alder Way 03801
Aldrich Ct & Rd 03801
Alumni Cir 03801
Andrew Jarvis Dr 03801
Anne Ave 03801
Arboretum Dr 03801
Arthur Rd 03801
Arthur F Brady Dr 03801
Artwill Ave 03801
Ash St 03801
Ashland St 03801
Atkinson St 03801
Austin St 03801
Autumn St 03801
Aviation Ave 03801
Ball St 03801
Banfield Rd 03801
Barberry Ln 03801
Bartlett St 03801
Baycliff Rd 03801
Beane Ln 03801
Beaumont St 03804
Bedford Way 03801
Beechstone 03801
Beechwood St 03801
Benson St 03801
Birch St 03801
Bloody Point Rd 03801
Blossom St 03801
Blue Heron Dr 03801
Bluefish Blvd 03801
Borthwick Ave 03801
Boss Ave 03801
Bow St 03801
Boyan Pl 03801
Boyd Rd 03801
Brackett Ln & Rd 03801
Brewery Ln 03801
Brewster St 03801
Brickyard Cir 03801
Bridge St 03801
Brigham Ln 03801
Broad St 03801
Buckminster Way 03801
Burkitt St 03801
Cabot St 03801
Calvin Ct 03801
Campus Dr 03801
Captains Lndg 03801
Carters Ln 03801
Cass St 03801
Cate St 03801
Central Ave 03801
Ceres St 03801
Chapel St 03801
Chase Dr 03801
Chatham St 03801
Chauncey St 03801
Chestnut St 03801
Chevrolet Ave 03801
Church St 03801
Circuit St 03801
Clark Dr 03801
Cleveland Dr 03801
Cliff Rd 03801
Clinton St 03801
Clough Dr 03801
Clover Ln 03801
Coakley Rd 03801
Codfish Corner Rd 03801
Coffins Ct 03801
Coleman Dr 03801
Colonial Dr 03801
Columbia Ct & St 03801
Commerce Way 03801
Commercial Aly 03801
Concord Way 03801
Congress St 03801
Constitution Ave 03801
Coolidge Dr 03801
Cornwall St 03801
Corporate Dr 03801
Cottage St 03801
Country Club Rd 03801
Court St 03801
Crescent Way 03801
Curriers Cv 03801
Custom House Ct 03801
Cutts Ave & St 03801
Daniel St
1-81 03801
80-80 03802
82-198 03801
83-199 03801
Davis Rd 03801
Dearborn St 03801
Decatur Rd 03801
Deer St 03801
Denise St 03801
Dennett St 03801
Desfosses Ave 03801
Diamond Dr 03801
Dodge Ave 03801
Dolphin Dr 03801
Doris Ave 03801
Dover St 03801
Driftwood Ln 03801
Dumpling Cv 03801
Dunlin Way 03801
Durgin Ln 03801
Durham St 03801
Dwight Ave 03801
Eastwood Dr 03801
Echo Ave 03801
Edgewood Rd 03801
Edmond Ave 03801
Edward St 03801
Elm Ct 03801
Elwyn Ave & Rd 03801
Elwyn Road Ext 03801
Essex Ave 03801
Exeter St 03801
F W Hartford Dr 03801
Fabyan Pt 03801
Fairview Ave & Dr 03801
Falkland Pl & Way 03801
Farm Ln 03801
Fells Rd 03801
Fernald Ct 03801
Fields Rd 03801
Fillmore Rd 03801
Fleet St 03801
Fletcher St 03801
Flight Line Ave 03801
Foch Ave 03801
Forrest St 03801
Fox Point Rd 03801
Fox Run Rd 03801
Franklin Dr & St 03801
Freedom Cir 03801
Frenchmans Ln 03801
Friend St 03801
Garden St 03801
Gardner St 03801
Garfield Rd 03801
Gates St 03801
Georges Ter 03801
Gosling Rd 03801
Gosport Rd 03801
Grafton Dr 03801
Granite St 03801
Grant Ave 03801
Green St 03801
Greenland Rd 03801
Greenleaf Ave 03801
Greenleaf Woods Dr 03801
Greenside Ave 03801
Griffin Rd 03801
Gundalow Lndg 03801
Hall Ct 03801
Hampshire Rd 03801
Hampton St 03801
Hancock St 03801
Hannah Ln 03801
Hanover St 03801
Harbour Pl 03801
Harding Rd 03801
Harrison Ave 03801
Harvard St 03801
Haven Ct & Rd 03801
Hawthorne St 03801
Hayes Pl 03801
Heather Ln 03801
Heritage Ave 03801
High St 03801
Highland St 03801
Highliner Ave 03801
Hill St 03801
Hillcrest Dr 03801
Hillside Dr 03801
Hodgdon Ln 03801
Hodgdon Farm Ln 03801
Holiday Dr 03801
Holly Ln 03801
Holmes Ct 03801
Hoover Dr 03801
Howard St 03801
Humphreys Ct 03801
Hunking St 03801
Hunters Hill Ave 03801
International Dr 03801
Islington St 03801
Jackson Hill St 03801
Jenkins Ave 03801
Jewell Ct 03801
Joan Ave 03801
Joffre Ter 03801
Johnson Ct 03801
Jones Ave 03801
Junkins Ave 03801
Kane St 03801
Kearsarge Way 03801
Kensington Rd 03801
Kent St 03801
Ladd St 03801
Lafayette Rd 03801
Lang Rd 03801
Langdon St 03801
Larry Ln 03801
Laurel Ct 03801
Lawrence St 03801
Leavitt Ave 03801
Ledgewood Dr 03801
Lee St 03801
Lens Ave 03801
Leslie Dr 03801
Lincoln Ave 03801
Little Bay Rd 03801
Little Bay Road Ext 03801
Little Harbor Rd 03801
Livermore St 03801
Lois St 03801
Longmeadow Ln & Rd 03801
Lookout Ln 03801
Lovell St 03801
Mackerel Ave 03801
Madison St 03801
Manchester Sq 03801
Mangrove St 03801
Manning St 03801
Manor Dr 03801
Maple St 03801
Maplewood Ave 03801
Marcy St 03801
Mariette Dr 03801
Marjorie St 03801
Mark St 03801
Market Sq & St 03801
Marne Ave 03801
Marsh Ln 03801
Marston Ave 03801
Martha Ter 03801
Martine Cottage Rd 03801
Mashench St 03801
Mason Ave 03801
Mcclintock St 03801
Mcdonough St 03801
Mcgee Dr 03801
Mcintyre Rd 03801
Mckinley Rd 03801
Mcnabb Ct 03801
Meadow Rd 03801
Mechanic St 03801
Meeting House Hl 03801
Melbourne St 03801
Melcher St 03801
Mendum Ave 03801
Meredith Way 03801
Merrimac Dr & St 03801
Michael J Succi Dr 03801
Middle Rd & St 03801
S Mill St 03801
Mill Pond Way 03801
Miller Ave 03801
Mirona Rd 03801
Mirona Road Ext 03801
Moebus Ter 03801
Moffat St 03801
Monroe St 03801
Monroe Street Ext 03801
Monteith St 03801
Morning St 03801
Mott Cove Rd 03801
Mount Vernon St 03801
Myrtle Ave 03801
Nathaniel Dr 03801
Navy Shipyard Rd 03801
New Castle Ave 03801
Newington Park & Rd 03801
Newmarket St 03801
Nh Ave 03801
Nimble Hill Rd 03801
Nixon Park 03801
Northwest St 03801
Northwood Rd 03801
Oak St 03801
Oakwood Dr 03801
Ocean Rd 03801
Octopus Ave 03801
Odiorne Point Rd 03801
Old Dover Rd 03801
Old Parish Way 03801
Old Post Rd 03801
Oleary Pl 03801
Onyx Ln 03801
Opal Ave 03801
Orange St 03801
Orchard Ct & St 03801
Oriental Gdns 03801
Osprey Dr 03801
Oxford Ave 03801
Pamela Dr 03801
Park St 03801
Parker St 03801
Parrott Ave 03801
Partridge St 03801
Patricia Dr 03801
Patterson Ln 03801
Pearl St 03801
Pearson St 03801
Pease Blvd 03801
Penhallow St 03801
Peverly Hill Rd 03801
Pheasant Ln 03801
Pickering Ave & St 03801
Pierce Island Rd 03801
Pine St 03801
Pinecrest Ter 03801
Pinehurst Rd 03801
Piscataqua Dr 03801
Plains Ave 03801
Pleasant St 03801
Pleasant Point Dr 03801
Polk Ave 03801
Porpoise Ln & Way 03801
Porter St 03801
Portsmouth Blvd 03801
Portsmouth Naval Shipyard 03804
Portwalk Pl 03801
Post Rd 03801
Pray St 03801
Preble Way 03801
Princeton St 03801
Prospect St 03801
Raleigh Way 03801
Rands Ct 03801
Ranger Way 03801
Raynes Ave 03801
Redhook Way 03801
Regina Rd 03801
Ricci Ave 03801
Richards Ave 03801
Richmond St 03801
Ridges Ct 03801
River Rd 03801
Robert Ave 03801
Robin Ln 03801
Rochester Ave 03801
Rock St 03801
Rock Street Ext 03801
Rockaway St 03801
Rockingham Ave & St 03801
Rockland St 03801
Rogers St 03801
Round Is 03801
Ruby Rd 03801
Russell St 03801
Ruth St 03801
Rutland St 03801
Rye St 03801
Sagamore Ave, Grv & Rd 03801
Salem St 03801
Salmon Ave 03801
Salter St 03801
Salter Point Cv 03801
Sanderling Way 03801
Sapphire St 03801
Saratoga Way 03801
N & S School St 03801
Schurman Ave 03801
Sewall Rd 03801
Shattuck Way 03801
Shaw Rd 03801
Sheafe St 03801
Shearwater Dr 03801
Sheffield Rd 03801
Sherburne Ave & Rd 03801
Sheridan Ave 03801
Short St 03801
Simonds Rd 03801
Sims Ave 03801
Snug Harbor Ave 03801
South St 03801
Sparhawk St 03801
Spaulding Tpke 03801
Spinnaker Way 03801
Spinney Rd 03801
Spring St 03801
Springbrook Cir 03801
Squid St 03801
Stark St 03801
State St 03801
Staysail Way 03801
Stonecroft 03801
Striped Bass Ave 03801
Sudbury St 03801
Summer St 03801
Summit Ave 03801
Sunset Rd 03801
Sutton Ave 03801
Suzanne Dr 03801
Swan Island Ln 03801
Swett Ave 03801
Sylvester St 03801
T J Gamester Ave 03801
Taft Rd 03801
Tanner Ct & St 03801
Taylor Ln 03801
Thaxter Rd 03801
The Hl 03801
Thornton St 03801
Topaz Pl 03801
Truman Pl 03801
Tuna Ter 03801
Tyler Pl 03801
Union St 03801
Us Highway 1 Byp 03801
Van Buren Ave 03801

Vaughan Mall & St 03801
Verdun Ave 03801
Versailles Ave 03801
Vianiank 03804
Victory Rd 03801
Vine St 03801
Walden St 03801
Walker St 03801
Walker Bungalow Rd 03801
Wallis Rd 03801
Walton Aly 03801
Ward Pl 03801
Washington St 03801
Weald Rd 03801
Webster Way 03801
Wedgewood Rd 03801
Welsh Cove Dr 03801
Wentworth Rd & St 03801
West Rd 03801
Whidden St 03801
Whipple Ct & St 03801
White Cedar Blvd 03801
Wholey Way 03801
Wibird St 03801
Willard Ave 03801
Willow Ln 03801
Wilson Rd 03801
Winchester St 03801
Winsor Rd 03801
Winter St 03801
Witmer Ave 03801
Woodbury Ave 03801
Woodlawn Cir 03801
Woodworth Ave 03801
Worthen Rd 03801
Wright Ave 03801

ROCHESTER NH

General Delivery 03866

POST OFFICE BOXES MAIN OFFICE STATIONS AND BRANCHES

Box No.s
1 - 2080 03866
6001 - 6599 03868
7001 - 7418 03839

NAMED STREETS

Abbott St 03868
Academy St 03867
Adams Ave 03867
Adelia St 03867
Adrien Cir 03867
Airport Dr 03867
Alder Creek Ln 03867
Alexandra Ln 03867
Alice Ln 03867
Allen St 03867
Amanda St 03867
Amarosa Dr 03868
Anctil Ct 03839
Anderson Ln 03867
Angela Ln 03867
Anita St 03867
Antrim Ln 03868
Apple Orchard Rd 03867
Arbor Way 03867
Arrow St 03867
Aruba Dr 03867
Ashencon St 03839
Ashwood Dr 03867
Aspen Ln 03839
Atwood St 03867
Autumn St 03868
Balsam Ln 03867
Barbaro Dr 03867
Barker Ct 03867
Barrington Ln 03839
Beach Ln 03868
Beaudoin Ct 03867
Beauview St 03867
Bermuda Ln 03867
Bernard Rd 03868
Berry St 03867
Betts Rd 03867
Bickford Rd 03867
Bicycle Ave 03867
Big Bear Rd 03868
Bigos Ct 03867
Birch Dr 03867
Birch Hollow Ln 03867
Birchwood Ave 03867
Blackwater Rd 03867
Blair Dr 03868
Blake St 03867
Blossom Ln 03868
Blue Hills Dr 03839
N & S Blueberry Ln 03867
Boulder Ave 03867
Bow Ct 03868
Boysenberry Ln 03867
Bradley Ct 03867
Bramber Ii 03867
Brattle St 03867
Brenda Ln 03867
Briar Dr 03867
Brickyard Dr 03839
Bridge St 03867
Broad St 03867
Broadway St 03868
Brochu Ct 03867
Brock St 03867
Bronze Ct 03868
Brook St 03867
Brook Farm Vlg 03839
Brookfield Dr 03867
Browning Dr 03839
Brownstone Ln 03867
Bryant St 03867
Buffy St 03867
Bunker Dr 03839
Burr Ct 03868
Butterfly Ln 03868
Calef Hwy 03839
Cape Coral Way 03867
Capitol Cir 03867
Cardinal Dr 03867
Caribbean Ln 03867
Carpenter Ln 03867
Catherine St 03867
Cattail Pl 03868
Cecile Ct 03839
Cedarbrook Vlg 03867
Cemetery Rd 03839
Central Ave 03867
Chamberlain St 03867
Champlin Ridge Rd 03867
Channings Ln 03867
Chapman Dr 03839
Charles St 03867
Chasse St 03867
Checkerberry Ct 03867
Cherokee Way 03867
Chesley Hill Rd 03839
Chestnut St 03867
Chestnut Hill Rd 03867
Church St
  1-6 03839
  7-7 03867
  8-198 03839
  9-11 03839
  15-19 03867
  21-199 03839
Cider Hill Rd 03867
Cinder Ct 03868
Claire St 03867
Clamshell Dr 03868
Clayton Ave 03867
Clearview Dr 03867
Cleo Cir 03868
Cleveland St 03867
Clow Ct 03867
Club House Ln 03867
N Coast Rd 03868
Cocheco Ave 03868
Colby St 03839
Cold Spring Cir & Mnr 03867
Coleman St 03867
Collins Cir 03867
Colonial Dr 03839
Columbus Ave 03867
Common St 03867
Concord Way 03867
Congress St 03867
Conifer Cir 03867
Constitution Way 03867
Continental Blvd 03867
Copeland Dr 03867
Copper Ln 03868
Cormier Dr 03867
Cormiers Mobile Home Park 03867
Cornerstone Ct 03867
Corson St 03867
Country Ln 03867
Country Brook Est 03839
Country Ridge Mhp 03867
Court St 03867
Cove Ct 03867
Coxeter Sq 03867
N & S Cranberry Ln 03867
Crane Dr 03867
Crestview Ln 03839
Creteau St 03867
Crimson Ln 03868
Crocker Ct 03867
Crockett St 03867
Cross Rd
  1-31 03868
  32-399 03867
Cross Wind Ln 03867
Crowhill Rd 03868
Crown Point Rd 03867
Cushing Blvd 03867
Daffodil Hill Ln 03868
Daigles Way 03868
Daisy Ln 03868
Damours Ave 03839
Daniel Ct 03867
Darby Ln 03839
Darrell St 03867
Dartmouth Ln 03868
Davis Blvd 03867
Day Lilly Ln 03868
Deerfield Ct 03868
Demeritt St 03839
Denali Dr 03868
Desert Wind Ln 03867
N & S Dewberry Ln 03867
Dewey St 03867
Diamondback Dr 03868
Dockside Ln 03867
Dodge St 03867
Dolphin Dr 03868
Dominicus Ct 03867
Donald St 03839
Dora Dr 03867
Dow Ct 03867
Downfield Ln 03867
Dreyer Way 03867
Drury Dr 03867
Dry Hill Rd
  1-53 03839
  54-199 03867
Dublin Way 03867
Duquette St 03867
Durgin Dr 03868
Durham Ln 03839
Dustin Ter 03867
Dustin Homestead 03867
Eagle Dr 03868
Easter Ln 03867
Eastern Ave
  14A-14B 03867
  1-159 03867
  160-199 03868
Ebony Dr 03867
Echo Brook Rd 03839
Edgerly Way 03867
Edgewood Ln 03867
Efab Ln 03839
Eisenhower Dr 03867
Ela Ct 03867
N & S Elderberry Ln 03867
Elizabeth St 03867
Elmo Ln 03867
Elsie Ln 03867
Emerson Ave 03867
England Rd 03867
Erin Ln 03868
Estes Rd
  1-63 03839
  64-64 03867
  65-65 03839
  66-299 03867
Evans Rd 03867
Evergreen Ln 03867
Factory Ct 03867
Fairway Ave 03867
Falkland Ln 03867
Farmington Rd 03867
Farrington St 03867
Felker St 03839
Fernald Ln 03867
Fiddlehead Ln 03867
Fieldstone Ln & Vlg 03867
Fillmore Blvd 03867
Flagg Rd 03839
Flat Rock Bridge Rd 03868
Florence Dr 03867
Flower Dr 03867
Foch St 03867
Ford Ln 03867
Forest Ave 03868
Forest Mdws 03839
Forest Park Dr 03868
Fortier Dr 03867
Four Rod Rd 03867
Fox Ln 03867
Franklin Hts & St 03867
French Hussey Rd 03867
Fresian Ln 03867
Friendship St 03867
Front St 03868
N & S Fuchsia Dr 03867
Furbush St 03867
Gagne St 03867
Gary Dr 03867
Gear Rd 03839
George Cir 03867
Gerard St 03867
Germaine St 03867
Gerrish Ct 03867
Gina Dr 03867
Given Cir 03867
Glen St 03867
Glenwood Ave 03867
Gloria St 03867
Goldrush Ln 03868
Gonic Rd
  1-26 03867
  28-34 03867
  35-599 03839
Goodwins Way 03867
Gooseberry Cir 03867
Gordon Ln 03867
Governors Rd 03867
Granite St 03867
Granite State Pkwy 03867
Grant St 03867
Great Falls Ave 03867
Green St 03868
Grenada Ln 03867
Grey Ledge Dr 03839
Grondin Ave 03867
Grove St 03868
Haig St 03867
Hale St 03867
Hampshire Ave 03867
Hancock St 03867
Hanson St 03867
Hansonville Rd 03839
Harding St 03867
Harmony Way 03868
Harrison Ave 03867
Harry St 03839
Harvard St 03867
Haskell Ave 03867
Haven Hill Rd 03867
Hawaii Ln 03867
Hawk Ln 03868
Healthcare Dr 03867
Heaton St 03867
Hemingway Dr 03839
Hemlock St 03867
Henrietta St 03867
Henry Dr 03839
Heritage Ave 03867
Hickey St 03868
Hickory Ln 03867
Hidden Path Ln 03839
High St 03867
Highland St 03868
Hillcrest Dr 03867
Hillsdale Rd 03867
Hillside Dr 03867
Hiltons Ln 03868
Hobart St 03867
Hodgkins Way 03868
Hollis Ln 03867
Holly Park Ln 03867
Hoover St 03867
Hope Dr 03868
Horton Way 03867
Howard Brook Dr 03867
Howe St 03867
Hoyt Ct 03867
Huckins Ln 03839
Hunter Ct 03867
Hussey St 03867
Hussey Hill Rd 03867
Hynes Ct 03839
Ians Way 03867
Indian Brook Cir 03839
Industrial Way 03867
Innovation Dr 03867
Ipswich Ln 03868
Ireland Ct 03868
Irish St 03867
Isabelle Ln 03867
Jackson St 03867
Jacobs Dr 03867
Jamaica Ln 03867
Jamey Dr 03868
Jan Ct 03868
Janet St 03867
Jarvis Ave 03868
Jay Way 03868
Jefferson Ave 03867
Jenness St 03867
Jeremiah Ln 03867
Jessica Dr 03839
Jonathan Ave 03839
Joseph Dr 03839
Joshua St 03867
Julia Ave 03867
Juniper St 03867
Justin Ln 03839
Katie Ln 03868
Kelmar Dr 03867
Kendall St 03867
Kennedy Ave 03839
Kenwater Ave 03867
Kim Ln 03867
Kimball St 03867
King St 03867
Kinsale Dr 03868
Kipling Rock Rd 03867
Kirsten Ave 03867
Knight St 03867
Knobby Way 03867
Kodiak Ct 03868
Labrador Dr 03867
Lady Slipper Ct 03867
Lafayette St 03867
Lagasse St 03867
Lambert Ct 03867
Lamy Rd 03839
Lanai Dr 03867
Landry Ln 03839
Lantern Ln 03868
Laredo Ln 03868
Lark Ln 03868
Laura Dr 03867
Lawn Ave 03867
Ledgeview Dr 03839
Leonard St 03867
Letourneau St 03867
Levi St 03839
Liberty St 03867
Lighthouse Ln 03868
Lilac Dr & Mall 03867
Lilac City E 03867
Limestone Ln 03867
Linchalt St 03867
Lincoln St 03867
Linden St 03867
Link St 03867
Lisa Ln 03868
Little Bear Rd 03868
Little Falls Bridge Rd 03867
Lobster Way 03839
Logan St 03867
Lois St 03867
Loon Ln 03867
Loring Dr 03839
Louise St 03867
Lowell St 03867
Lupine Ln 03868
Lynn Ln 03867
Lyons St 03867
Madison Ave 03867
Magic Ave 03868
Main St
  1-9 03868
  10-11 03839
  12-14 03868
  13-15 03839
  16-33 03868
  19-35 03839
  35-35 03868
  37-43 03839
  42-42 03868
  45-51 03839
  46-48 03839
  48-50 03868
  52-53 03868
  55-56 03839
  55-55 03868
  57-57 03868
  58-62 03839
  59-59 03839
  59-59 03868
  61-62 03868
  64-90 03868
  67-72 03839
  71-71 03868
  73-73 03868
  73-73 03839
  74-74 03839
  75-75 03839
  75-77 03868
  83-93 03839
  198A-198Z 03867
  1-299 03867
Manatee Dr 03868
Manchester Ct 03868
Mandela Dr 03868
Maple St 03867
Maplewood Ave 03867
Marcy Dr 03868
Margaret St 03867
Martinique Dr 03867
Mavis Ave 03839
May St 03867
Mayor Roland Roberge Mnr 03867
Mcduffee St 03867
Mcduffee Brook Pl 03839
Mcintire Ct 03867
Mckinley St 03867
Mcneil Dr 03867
Meaderboro Rd 03867
Meadow Ln 03867
Meadowbrook Vlg 03867
Melanie St 03867
Melrose Dr 03868
Michael St 03839
Mill St 03868
Millers Farm Dr 03868
Milton Rd
  1-13 03867
  2-12 03868
  14-267 03868
  269-291 03868
Misty Ln 03839
Moffet Ct 03839
Monadnock Dr 03867
Monogram Pl 03867
Moores Ct 03867
Moose Ln 03867
Morgan Rd 03868
Morning Glory Ln 03868
Morrill Ct 03867
Morton Ave 03867
Mountain View Ln 03867
Murray Dr 03868
Museum Way 03867
Myrtle St 03867
Nadeau Dr 03867
Nashoba Dr 03867
Nature Ln 03867
Nicole St 03867
Nola Ave 03867
Norman St 03839
North St 03867
Norway Plains Rd 03868
Nottingham Ln 03868
Nutter St 03867
Oak St 03839
Ocean Way 03868
Old Dover Rd 03867
Old Gonic Rd 03867
Old Milton Rd 03868
Old Ox Rd 03868
Old Tebbetts Rd 03867
Old Wakefield Rd 03868
Olde Farm Ln 03867
Olianton St 03868
Olsen Way 03867
Orange St 03839
Orchard St 03867
Osborne St 03867
Otter Brook Cir 03839
Outlook Ln 03867
Page St 03867
Paradis Dr 03867
Park St 03867
Partridge Green Way 03867
Patriots Way 03839
Patton St 03867
Pauls Way 03868
Pawtucketts Way 03867
Pearl St
  1-5 03868
  2-2 03867
  4-4 03868
  6-10 03867
  12-15 03867
  16-16 03868
  18-21 03868
  23-23 03868
Peaslee Rd 03867
Pebblestone Ln 03867
Penny Ln 03868
Perimeter Dr 03867
Periwinkle Dr 03868
Phillips Way 03868
Pickering Rd
  1-56 03839
  58-74 03839
  100-600 03867
  602-698 03867
Pierce Dr 03867
Pine Ln & St 03867
Pinecrest Ave 03867
Pineknoll Dr 03867
Pink St 03867
Piper Ln 03839
Plante St 03867
Pleasant St 03867
Politic Dr 03839
Pondview Ln 03867
Portland St
  1-689 03867

690-696 03868
698-858 03868
Post Rd 03867
Pray St 03868
Preston St 03867
Prospect St 03867
Punch Brook Way 03839
Quail Dr 03867
Quaker Ln 03839
Quarry Dr 03867
Raab Ln 03868
Railroad Ave 03839
Ramsey Dr 03839
Rangeway Dr 03868
Ray Dr 03867
Reagan Dr 03839
Rebekah Ln 03839
Regency Ct 03867
Richardson St 03867
Ricker Ct 03867
Ridgewood Dr 03839
Riley Ave 03867
River St 03867
Riverlawn Ave 03868
Riverside Dr 03867
Riverview Dr 03867
Roberts Rd 03867
Rochester Ave & Ter ... 03867
Rochester Hill Rd 03867
Rochester Neck Rd 03839
Rock Ln 03867
Rockledge Rd 03867
Rondas Way 03867
Roseberry Ln 03867
Rouleau Dr 03867
Roulx Dr 03867
Roy St 03867
Royalcrest 03867
Rudman Dr 03839
Russell St 03867
Ryan Cir 03867
Sabrina Ln 03867
Sagamore Ln 03867
Sagebrush Dr 03867
Saint James Ter 03867
Saks Mobile Home Park 03868
Salmon Falls Est & Rd 03868
Sampson Rd 03867
Sandina Dr 03868
Sandstone Ln 03867
Sarah Ct 03867
Sawyer Ave 03867
Schley St 03867
School St 03867
Schultz St 03867
Scott St 03867
Seasons Ln 03867
Seavey Brook Ln 03867
Secretariat Way 03867
Secretariet Way 03839
Seneca St 03867
Sewell Rd 03868
Shady Hill Dr 03867
Shakespeare Rd 03839
Shaw Dr 03868
Sheepboro Rd 03867
Shelby Ln 03839
Sheridan Ave 03867
Sherman St 03839
Shiloh Dr 03867
Sidney St 03867
Signal St 03867
Silver St 03867
Silver Bell Mobile Home Park 03868
Skyline Dr 03867
Sleeper St 03867
Small Ave 03867
Smoke St 03868
Snow St 03867
Soapstone Ln 03867
Sonata Ct 03867
Spaulding Ave 03868
Spencer Ave 03867
Spirit Creek Rd 03839
Split Rock Dr 03839
Spring St 03868
Springfield Ct & Est 03867
Spruce St 03867
Sprucewood Dr 03867
Stacy Dr 03867
Stagecoach Ln 03867
Stair Fls 03868
Stanley Pond Dr 03839
State St 03867
Stephens Dr 03867
Sterling Dr 03867
Stewart Ct 03867
Stillings Ct 03867
Stillwater Cir 03839
Stokes Way 03867
Stone Ridge Dr 03867
Stonewall Dr 03868
Strafford Rd 03867
Strawberry Hill Dr 03867
Sugar Brook Rd 03839
Sullivan Farm Dr 03868
Summer St 03867
Sunrise Dr 03867
Sunset Dr 03867
Sunview Ln 03868
Susan Ln 03867
Sweetbriar Ln 03867
Sylvain St 03867
Tall Pine Ln 03867
Tamarack Ln 03867
Tampa Dr 03867
Tebbetts Rd 03867
Temple Dr 03868
Ten Rod Rd 03867
Tessier Dr 03839
Thomas St 03867
Thorn Dr 03867
Tingley St 03867
Tonka St 03867
Torr Ave 03867
Towle Ln 03867
Towle Street Ext 03867
Townsend Ln 03867
Trade Wind Ln 03867
Trestle Rd 03868
Trinity Cir 03839
Truman Cir 03867
Tumbleweed Dr 03867
Turbo St 03868
Tuttle Ct 03839
Two Rod Rd 03867
Twombly St 03867
Tyler Ln 03867
Union St 03867
Unity St 03868
Upham St 03867
Vernon Ave 03867
Vetter Ln 03867
Victoria Cir 03867
Village Ln 03867
Villanova Ln 03867
Vinewood Ln 03867
Violet Ct 03867
Wadleigh Rd 03867
Wakefield St 03867
Walbridge Ct 03868
Waldron Ave 03867
Wallace St 03867
Walnut St 03867
Walnut Grove Rd 03868
Warren St 03868
Washington St
1-117 03867
118-499 03839
Watercress Dr 03868
Watson Dr 03867
Waverly St 03867
Weare St 03868
Weeping Willow Dr 03867
Wellsweep Cir 03867
Wellsweep Acres 03867
Wentworth Ave 03867
West Ln 03867
Western Ave 03867
Westview Dr 03867
Westwind Est 03867
Whispering Wind Ln 03867
White Birch Ln 03839
Whitehall Rd
2-4 03867
6-79 03867
80-199 03868
Whitehouse Rd 03867
Whitman Dr 03839
Wildflower Way 03868
Wildwood Ln 03867
Willey St 03867
Willowbrook Dr 03867
Wilson St 03867
Winch Way 03868
Windhaven Rd 03867
Winding Path Ln 03839
Winkley Farm Ln 03867
Winter St 03867
Woodland Grn 03868
Woodlawn Rd 03867
Woodman St 03867
Woodside Ln 03867
Wyandotte Fls 03867
Wyvern Ln 03867
Yale St 03867
Yellowstone Ln 03867
York Ct 03868
Young St 03867
Yvonne St 03867

NUMBERED STREETS

All Street Addresses 03867

New Jersey

People QuickFacts	New Jersey	USA
Population, 2013 estimate	8,899,339	316,128,839
Population, 2010 (April 1) estimates base	8,791,909	308,747,716
Population, percent change, April 1, 2010 to July 1, 2013	1.2%	2.4%
Population, 2010	8,791,894	308,745,538
Persons under 5 years, percent, 2013	6.0%	6.3%
Persons under 18 years, percent, 2013	22.7%	23.3%
Persons 65 years and over, percent, 2013	14.4%	14.1%
Female persons, percent, 2013	51.2%	50.8%
White alone, percent, 2013 (a)	73.4%	77.7%
Black or African American alone, percent, 2013 (a)	14.7%	13.2%
American Indian and Alaska Native alone, percent, 2013 (a)	0.6%	1.2%
Asian alone, percent, 2013 (a)	9.2%	5.3%
Native Hawaiian and Other Pacific Islander alone, percent, 2013 (a)	0.1%	0.2%
Two or More Races, percent, 2013	2.0%	2.4%
Hispanic or Latino, percent, 2013 (b)	18.9%	17.1%
White alone, not Hispanic or Latino, percent, 2013	57.6%	62.6%
Living in same house 1 year & over, percent, 2008-2012	90.0%	84.8%
Foreign born persons, percent, 2008-2012	20.8%	12.9%
Language other than English spoken at home, pct age 5+, 2008-2012	29.6%	20.5%
High school graduate or higher, percent of persons age 25+, 2008-2012	87.9%	85.7%
Bachelor's degree or higher, percent of persons age 25+, 2008-2012	35.4%	28.5%
Veterans, 2008-2012	457,724	21,853,912
Mean travel time to work (minutes), workers age 16+, 2008-2012	30.3	25.4
Housing units, 2013	3,578,141	132,802,859
Homeownership rate, 2008-2012	66.2%	65.5%
Housing units in multi-unit structures, percent, 2008-2012	35.9%	25.9%
Median value of owner-occupied housing units, 2008-2012	$337,900	$181,400
Households, 2008-2012	3,186,878	115,226,802
Persons per household, 2008-2012	2.7	2.61
Per capita money income in past 12 months (2012 dollars), 2008-2012	$35,928	$28,051
Median household income, 2008-2012	$71,637	$53,046
Persons below poverty level, percent, 2008-2012	9.9%	14.9%

Business QuickFacts	New Jersey	USA
Private nonfarm establishments, 2012	228,289	7,431,808
Private nonfarm employment, 2012	3,440,470	115,938,468
Private nonfarm employment, percent change, 2011-2012	1.9%	2.2%
Nonemployer establishments, 2012	620,282	22,735,915
Total number of firms, 2007	781,622	27,092,908
Black-owned firms, percent, 2007	7.7%	7.1%
American Indian- and Alaska Native-owned firms, percent, 2007	0.4%	0.9%
Asian-owned firms, percent, 2007	8.7%	5.7%
Native Hawaiian and Other Pacific Islander-owned firms, percent, 2007	0.1%	0.1%
Hispanic-owned firms, percent, 2007	8.7%	8.3%
Women-owned firms, percent, 2007	27.3%	28.8%
Manufacturers shipments, 2007 ($1000)	116,608,094	5,319,456,312
Merchant wholesaler sales, 2007 ($1000)	233,413,004	4,174,286,516
Retail sales, 2007 ($1000)	124,813,580	3,917,663,456
Retail sales per capita, 2007	$14,453	$12,990
Accommodation and food services sales, 2007 ($1000)	19,993,613	613,795,732
Building permits, 2012	17,939	829,658

Geography QuickFacts	New Jersey	USA
Land area in square miles, 2010	7,354.22	3,531,905.43
Persons per square mile, 2010	1,195.5	87.4
FIPS Code	34	

(a) Includes persons reporting only one race.
(b) Hispanics may be of any race, so also are included in applicable race categories.
FN: Footnote on this item for this area in place of data
NA: Not available
D: Suppressed to avoid disclosure of confidential information
X: Not applicable
S: Suppressed; does not meet publication standards
Z: Value greater than zero but less than half unit of measure shown
F: Fewer than 100 firms
Source: US Census Bureau State & County QuickFacts

New Jersey

3 DIGIT ZIP CODE MAP

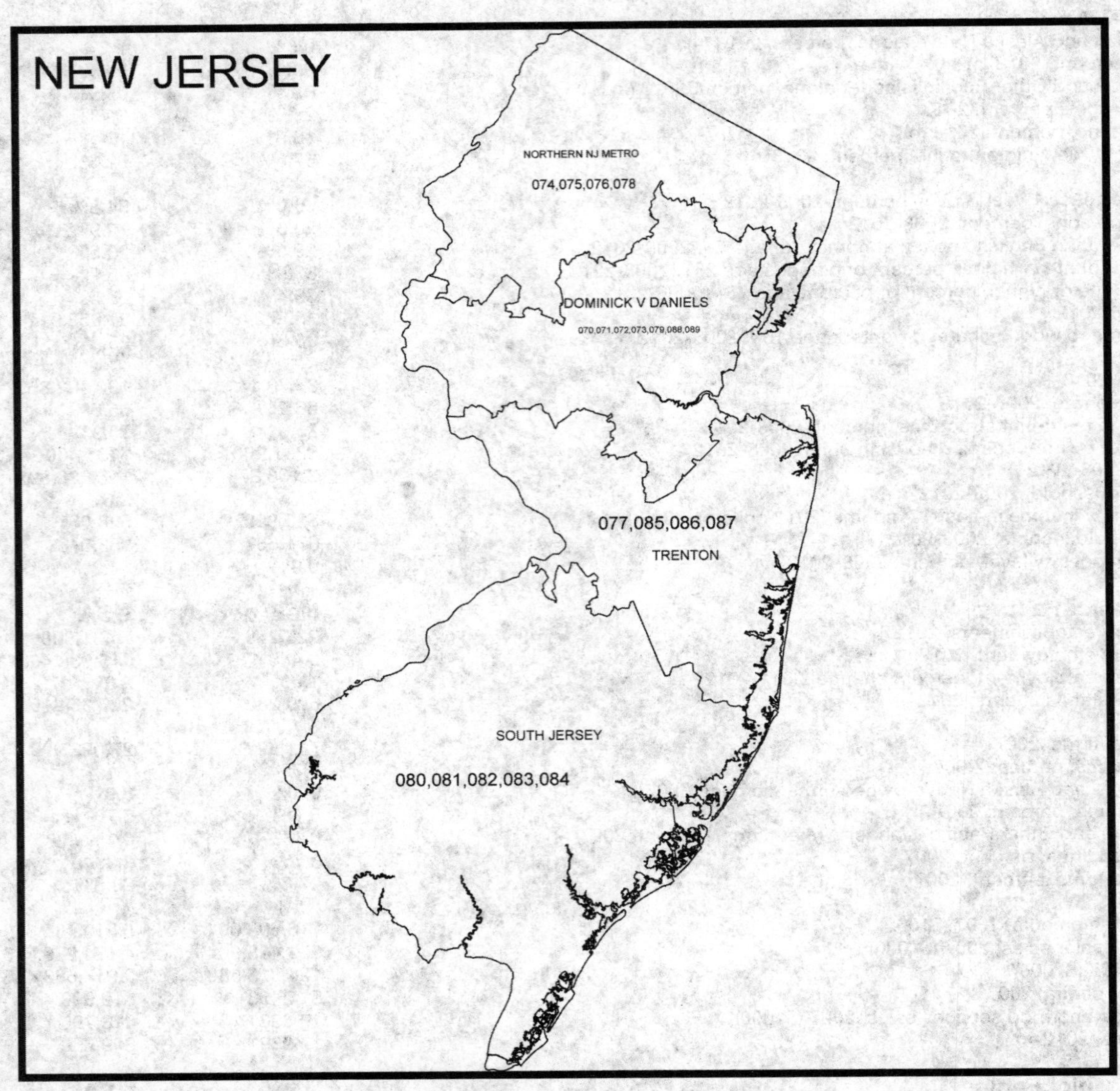

New Jersey

(Abbreviation: NJ)

Post Office, County — ZIP Code

Places with more than one ZIP code are listed in capital letters, See pages indicated.

Aberdeen, Monmouth ... 07747
ABSECON, Atlantic
(See Page 2549)
Adelphia, Monmouth ... 07710
Allamuchy, Warren ... 07820
Allendale, Bergen ... 07401
Allenhurst, Monmouth ... 07711
Allentown, Monmouth ... 08501
Allenwood, Monmouth ... 08720
Alloway, Salem ... 08001
Alpha, Warren ... 08865
Alpine, Bergen ... 07620
Andover, Sussex ... 07821
Annandale, Hunterdon ... 08801
Asbury, Hunterdon ... 08802
Asbury Park, Monmouth ... 07712
Atco, Camden ... 08004
ATLANTIC CITY, Atlantic
(See Page 2549)
Atlantic Highlands, Monmouth ... 07716
Audubon, Camden ... 08106
Augusta, Sussex ... 07822
Avalon, Cape May ... 08202
Avenel, Middlesex ... 07001
Avon By The Sea, Monmouth ... 07717
Baptistown, Hunterdon ... 08803
Barnegat, Ocean ... 08005
Barnegat Light, Ocean ... 08006
Barrington, Camden ... 08007
Basking Ridge, Somerset ... 07920
Basking Ridge, Somerset ... 07939
Batsto, Atlantic ... 08037
Bay Head, Ocean ... 08742
Bayonne, Hudson ... 07002
Bayville, Ocean ... 08721
Beach Haven, Ocean ... 08008
Beachwood, Ocean ... 08722
Bedminster, Somerset ... 07921
Belford, Monmouth ... 07718
Belle Mead, Somerset ... 08502
Belleville, Essex ... 07109
BELLMAWR, Camden
(See Page 2550)
Belmar, Monmouth ... 07715
Belvidere, Warren ... 07823
Bergenfield, Bergen ... 07621
Berkeley Heights, Union ... 07922
Berlin, Camden ... 08009
Berlin Township, Camden ... 08091
Bernardsville, Somerset ... 07924
Beverly, Burlington ... 08010
Birmingham, Burlington ... 08011
Blackwood, Camden ... 08012
Blackwood Terrace, Gloucester ... 08096
Blairstown, Warren ... 07825
Blawenburg, Somerset ... 08504
Bloomfield, Essex ... 07003
Bloomingdale, Passaic ... 07403
Bloomsbury, Hunterdon ... 08804
Bogota, Bergen ... 07603
Boonton, Morris ... 07005
Boonton Township, Morris ... 07005
Bordentown, Burlington ... 08505
Bound Brook, Somerset ... 08805
Bradley Beach, Monmouth ... 07720
Branchburg, Somerset ... 08853
Branchville, Sussex ... 07826
BRICK, Ocean
(See Page 2550)
Bridgeport, Gloucester ... 08014
Bridgeton, Cumberland ... 08302
Bridgewater, Somerset ... 08807

Brielle, Monmouth ... 08730
Brigantine, Atlantic ... 08203
Broadway, Warren ... 08808
Brooklawn, Camden ... 08030
Brookside, Morris ... 07926
Browns Mills, Burlington ... 08015
Budd Lake, Morris ... 07828
Buena, Atlantic ... 08310
Burlington, Burlington ... 08016
Burlington City, Burlington ... 08016
Burlington Township, Burlington ... 08016
Butler, Morris ... 07405
Buttzville, Warren ... 07829
Byram Township, Sussex ... 07821
CALDWELL, Essex
(See Page 2552)
Califon, Hunterdon ... 07830
CAMDEN, Camden
(See Page 2553)
Cape May, Cape May ... 08204
Cape May Court House, Cape May ... 08210
Cape May Point, Cape May ... 08212
Carlstadt, Bergen ... 07072
Carneys Point, Salem ... 08069
Carteret, Middlesex ... 07008
Cedar Brook, Camden ... 08018
Cedar Grove, Essex ... 07009
Cedar Knolls, Morris ... 07927
Cedarville, Cumberland ... 08311
Changewater, Warren ... 07831
Chatham, Morris ... 07928
Chatham Twp, Morris ... 07928
Chatsworth, Burlington ... 08019
CHERRY HILL, Camden
(See Page 2554)
Chesilhurst, Camden ... 08089
Chester, Morris ... 07930
Chesterfield, Burlington ... 08515
Cinnaminson, Burlington ... 08077
Clark, Union ... 07066
Clarksboro, Gloucester ... 08020
Clarksburg, Monmouth ... 08510
Clayton, Gloucester ... 08312
Clementon, Camden ... 08021
Cliffside Park, Bergen ... 07010
Cliffwood, Monmouth ... 07721
CLIFTON, Passaic
(See Page 2556)
Clinton, Hunterdon ... 08809
Closter, Bergen ... 07624
Collingswood, Camden ... 08107
Collingswood, Camden ... 08108
Cologne, Atlantic ... 08213
Colonia, Middlesex ... 07067
Colts Neck, Monmouth ... 07722
Columbia, Warren ... 07832
Columbus, Burlington ... 08022
Convent Station, Morris ... 07961
Cookstown, Burlington ... 08511
Corbin City, Cape May ... 08270
Cranbury, Middlesex ... 08512
Cranford, Union ... 07016
Cream Ridge, Monmouth ... 08514
Cresskill, Bergen ... 07626
Crosswicks, Burlington ... 08515
Dayton, Middlesex ... 08810
Deal, Monmouth ... 07723
Deepwater, Salem ... 08023
Deerfield Street, Cumberland ... 08313
Del Haven, Cape May ... 08251
Delair, Camden ... 08110
Delanco, Burlington ... 08075
Delaware, Warren ... 07833
Delmont, Cumberland ... 08314
Delran, Burlington ... 08075
Demarest, Bergen ... 07627
Dennisville, Cape May ... 08214
Denville, Morris ... 07834
Deptford, Gloucester ... 08096
Dividing Creek, Cumberland ... 08315
Dorchester, Cumberland ... 08316
Dorothy, Atlantic ... 08317

DOVER, Morris
(See Page 2557)
Dumont, Bergen ... 07628
Dunellen, Middlesex ... 08812
East Brunswick, Middlesex ... 08816
East Hanover, Morris ... 07936
East Millstone, Somerset ... 08875
East Newark, Hudson ... 07029
EAST ORANGE, Essex
(See Page 2557)
East Rutherford, Bergen ... 07073
East Windsor, Middlesex ... 08512
Eastampton, Burlington ... 08060
Eastampton Township, Burlington ... 08060
EATONTOWN, Monmouth
(See Page 2558)
Edgewater, Bergen ... 07020
Edgewater Park, Burlington ... 08010
EDISON, Middlesex
(See Page 2558)
Egg Harbor City, Atlantic ... 08215
Egg Harbor Township, Atlantic ... 08234
Egg Harbor Twp, Atlantic ... 08234
Egg Hbr City, Atlantic ... 08215
ELIZABETH, Union
(See Page 2560)
Elizabethport, Union ... 07206
Elmer, Salem ... 08318
Elmwood Park, Bergen ... 07407
Elwood, Atlantic ... 08217
Emerson, Bergen ... 07630
Englewood, Bergen ... 07631
Englewood, Bergen ... 07632
Englewood Cliffs, Bergen ... 07632
Englishtown, Monmouth ... 07726
Erial, Camden ... 08081
Essex Fells, Essex ... 07021
Estell Manor, Atlantic ... 08319
Evesham, Burlington ... 08053
Ewan, Gloucester ... 08025
Ewing, Mercer ... 08560
Fair Haven, Monmouth ... 07704
Fair Lawn, Bergen ... 07410
Fairfield, Essex ... 07004
Fairton, Cumberland ... 08320
Fairview, Bergen ... 07022
Fanwood, Union ... 07023
Far Hills, Somerset ... 07931
Farmingdale, Monmouth ... 07727
Fieldsboro, Burlington ... 08505
Flagtown, Somerset ... 08821
Flanders, Morris ... 07836
Flemington, Hunterdon ... 08822
Florence, Burlington ... 08518
Florham Park, Morris ... 07932
Fords, Middlesex ... 08863
Forked River, Ocean ... 08731
Fort Dix, Burlington ... 08640
Fort Lee, Bergen ... 07024
Fort Monmouth, Monmouth ... 07703
Fortescue, Cumberland ... 08321
Franklin, Sussex ... 07416
Franklin Lakes, Bergen ... 07417
Franklin Park, Somerset ... 08823
Franklinville, Gloucester ... 08322
Fredon, Sussex ... 07860
Fredon Township, Sussex ... 07860
Freehold, Monmouth ... 07728
Frenchtown, Hunterdon ... 08825
Galloway, Atlantic ... 08205
Garfield, Bergen ... 07026
Garwood, Union ... 07027
Gibbsboro, Camden ... 08026
Gibbstown, Gloucester ... 08027
Gillette, Morris ... 07933
Gladstone, Somerset ... 07934
Glassboro, Gloucester ... 08028
Glasser, Sussex ... 07837
Glen Gardner, Hunterdon ... 08826
Glen Ridge, Essex ... 07028
Glen Rock, Bergen ... 07452
Glendora, Camden ... 08029
Glenwood, Sussex ... 07418
Gloucester City, Camden ... 08030

Gloucstr City, Camden ... 08030
Goshen, Cape May ... 08218
Great Meadows, Warren ... 07838
Green Brook, Middlesex ... 08812
Green Creek, Cape May ... 08219
Green Township, Sussex ... 07821
Green Village, Morris ... 07935
Greendell, Sussex ... 07839
Greenwich, Cumberland ... 08323
Grenloch, Gloucester ... 08032
Greystone Park, Morris ... 07950
Guttenberg, Hudson ... 07093
HACKENSACK, Bergen
(See Page 2561)
Hackettstown, Warren ... 07840
Haddon Heights, Camden ... 08035
Haddon Hts, Camden ... 08035
Haddon Township, Camden ... 08104
Haddon Township, Camden ... 08104
Haddonfield, Camden ... 08033
Hainesport, Burlington ... 08036
Hainesport Township, Burlington ... 08036
HALEDON, Passaic
(See Page 2561)
Hamburg, Sussex ... 07419
Hamilton
(See Trenton)
Hamilton Square, Mercer ... 08690
Hammonton, Atlantic ... 08037
Hampton, Hunterdon ... 08827
Hancocks Bridge, Salem ... 08038
Hardwick, Warren ... 07825
Hardyston, Sussex ... 07460
Harrington Park, Bergen ... 07640
Harrison, Hudson ... 07029
Harrisonville, Gloucester ... 08039
Harvey Cedars, Ocean ... 08008
Hasbrouck Heights, Bergen ... 07604
Haskell, Passaic ... 07420
Haworth, Bergen ... 07641
HAWTHORNE, Passaic
(See Page 2562)
Hazlet, Monmouth ... 07730
Hazlet Township, Monmouth ... 07734
Heislerville, Cumberland ... 08324
Helmetta, Middlesex ... 08828
Hewitt, Passaic ... 07421
Hi Nella, Camden ... 08083
Hibernia, Morris ... 07842
High Bridge, Hunterdon ... 08829
Highland Lakes, Sussex ... 07422
Highland Park, Middlesex ... 08904
Highlands, Monmouth ... 07732
Hightstown, Mercer ... 08520
Hillsborough, Somerset ... 08844
Hillsdale, Bergen ... 07642
Hillside, Union ... 07205
Ho Ho Kus, Bergen ... 07423
Hoboken, Hudson ... 07030
Holmdel, Monmouth ... 07733
Hopatcong, Sussex ... 07843
Hope, Warren ... 07844
Hopelawn, Middlesex ... 08861
Hopewell, Mercer ... 08525
Howell, Monmouth ... 07731
Imlaystown, Monmouth ... 08526
Industrial Hillside, Union ... 07205
Interlaken, Monmouth ... 07712
Ironia, Morris ... 07845
Irvington, Essex ... 07111
Iselin, Middlesex ... 08830
Island Heights, Ocean ... 08732
Jackson, Ocean ... 08527
Jamesburg, Middlesex ... 08831
JERSEY CITY, Hudson
(See Page 2562)
Jobstown, Burlington ... 08041
Johnsonburg, Warren ... 07825
Johnsonburg, Warren ... 07846
Juliustown, Burlington ... 08042
Keansburg, Monmouth ... 07734
Kearny, Hudson ... 07032
Keasbey, Middlesex ... 08832
Kendall Park, Middlesex ... 08824
Kenilworth, Union ... 07033

Kenvil, Morris ... 07847
Keyport, Monmouth ... 07735
Kingston, Somerset ... 08528
Kinnelon, Morris ... 07405
Kirkwd Vrhes, Camden ... 08043
Kirkwood, Camden ... 08043
Lafayette, Sussex ... 07848
Lake Como, Monmouth ... 07719
Lake Hiawatha, Morris ... 07034
Lake Hopatcong, Morris ... 07849
Lakehurst, Ocean ... 08733
Lakehurst, Ocean ... 08759
Lakehurst Naec, Ocean ... 08733
Lakewood, Ocean ... 08701
Lambertville, Hunterdon ... 08530
Landing, Morris ... 07850
Landisville, Atlantic ... 08326
Lanoka Harbor, Ocean ... 08734
Laurel Springs, Camden ... 08021
Laurence Harbor, Middlesex ... 08879
Lavallette, Ocean ... 08735
Lawnside, Camden ... 08045
Lawrence, Mercer ... 08648
Lawrence Township, Mercer ... 08648
Lawrenceville, Mercer ... 08648
Layton, Sussex ... 07851
Lebanon, Hunterdon ... 08833
Ledgewood, Morris ... 07852
Leeds Point, Atlantic ... 08220
Leesburg, Cumberland ... 08327
Leonardo, Monmouth ... 07737
Leonia, Bergen ... 07605
Liberty Corner, Somerset ... 07938
Lincoln Park, Morris ... 07035
Lincroft, Monmouth ... 07738
Linden, Union ... 07036
Lindenwold, Camden ... 08021
Linwood, Atlantic ... 08221
Little Egg Harbor, Ocean ... 08087
Little Egg Harbor Twp, Ocean ... 08087
Little Falls, Passaic ... 07424
Little Ferry, Bergen ... 07643
Little Silver, Monmouth ... 07739
Little York, Hunterdon ... 08834
Livingston, Essex ... 07039
Loch Arbour, Monmouth ... 07711
Locust, Monmouth ... 07760
Lodi, Bergen ... 07644
Logan Township, Gloucester ... 08085
Long Beach, Ocean ... 08008
Long Beach Township, Ocean ... 08008
Long Branch, Monmouth ... 07740
Long Valley, Morris ... 07853
Longport, Atlantic ... 08403
Lumberton, Burlington ... 08048
Lumberton Township, Burlington ... 08048
Lyndhurst, Bergen ... 07071
Lyons, Somerset ... 07939
Madison, Morris ... 07940
Magnolia, Camden ... 08049
MAHWAH, Bergen
(See Page 2563)
Malaga, Gloucester ... 08328
Manahawkin, Ocean ... 08050
Manalapan, Monmouth ... 07726
Manasquan, Monmouth ... 08736
Manchester, Ocean ... 08759
Manchester Township, Ocean ... 08759
Mannington, Salem ... 08079
Mantoloking, Ocean ... 08738
Mantua, Gloucester ... 08051
Manville, Somerset ... 08835
Maple Shade, Burlington ... 08052
Maplewood, Essex ... 07040
Margate City, Atlantic ... 08402
Marlboro, Monmouth ... 07746
Marlton, Burlington ... 08053
Marmora, Cape May ... 08223
Martinsville, Somerset ... 08836
Matawan, Monmouth ... 07747
Mauricetown, Cumberland ... 08329
Mays Landing, Atlantic ... 08330

Maywood, Bergen ... 07607
Mc Afee, Sussex ... 07428
Mc Guire Afb, Burlington ... 08641
Mckee City, Atlantic ... 08232
Medford, Burlington ... 08055
Medford Lakes, Burlington ... 08055
Mendham, Morris ... 07945
Mendham Twsp, Morris ... 07945
Mercerville, Mercer ... 08619
Merchantville, Camden ... 08109
Metuchen, Middlesex ... 08840
Mickleton, Gloucester ... 08056
Middlesex, Middlesex ... 08846
Middletown, Monmouth ... 07748
Middleville, Sussex ... 07855
Midland Park, Bergen ... 07432
Milford, Hunterdon ... 08848
Millburn, Essex ... 07041
Millington, Morris ... 07946
MILLSTONE TOWNSHIP, Monmouth
(See Page 2564)
Milltown, Middlesex ... 08850
Millville, Cumberland ... 08332
Milmay, Atlantic ... 08340
Mine Hill, Morris ... 07803
Minotola, Atlantic ... 08341
Mizpah, Atlantic ... 08342
Monmouth Beach, Monmouth ... 07750
Monmouth Junction, Middlesex ... 08852
Monroe, Middlesex ... 08831
Monroe Township, Middlesex ... 08831
Monroeville, Salem ... 08343
Montague, Sussex ... 07827
MONTCLAIR, Essex
(See Page 2565)
Montvale, Bergen ... 07645
Montville, Morris ... 07045
Moonachie, Bergen ... 07074
Moorestown, Burlington ... 08057
Morganville, Monmouth ... 07751
Morris Plains, Morris ... 07950
MORRISTOWN, Morris
(See Page 2565)
Mount Arlington, Morris ... 07856
Mount Ephraim, Camden ... 08059
Mount Freedom, Morris ... 07970
Mount Holly, Burlington ... 08060
Mount Laurel, Burlington ... 08054
Mount Royal, Gloucester ... 08061
Mount Tabor, Morris ... 07878
Mountain Lakes, Morris ... 07046
Mountainside, Union ... 07092
Mullica Hill, Gloucester ... 08062
Mystic Islands, Ocean ... 08087
National Park, Gloucester ... 08063
Navesink, Monmouth ... 07752
NEPTUNE, Monmouth
(See Page 2566)
Neptune City, Monmouth ... 07753
Neshanic Station, Somerset ... 08853
Netcong, Morris ... 07857
NEW BRUNSWICK, Middlesex
(See Page 2567)
New Egypt, Ocean ... 08533
New Gretna, Burlington ... 08224
New Lisbon, Burlington ... 08064
New Milford, Bergen ... 07646
New Monmouth, Monmouth ... 07748
New Providence, Union ... 07974
New Vernon, Morris ... 07976
NEWARK, Essex
(See Page 2567)
Newfield, Gloucester ... 08344
Newfoundland, Passaic ... 07435
Newport, Cumberland ... 08345
Newton, Sussex ... 07860
Newtonville, Atlantic ... 08346
Norma, Salem ... 08347
Normandy Beach, Ocean ... 08739
North Arlington, Bergen ... 07031
North Bergen, Hudson ... 07047
North Branch, Somerset ... 08876

North Brunswick, Middlesex .. 08902
North Caldwell, Essex 07006
North Cape May, Cape May .. 08204
North Haledon, Passaic 07508
North Middletown, Monmouth 07748
North Plainfield
(See Plainfield)
North Wildwood, Cape May .. 08260
Northfield, Atlantic 08225
Northvale, Bergen 07647
Norwood, Bergen 07648
Nutley, Essex 07110
Oak Ridge, Passaic 07438
Oakhurst, Monmouth 07755
Oakland, Bergen 07436
Oaklyn, Camden 08107
Ocean, Monmouth 07712
Ocean City, Cape May 08226
Ocean Gate, Ocean 08740
Ocean Grove, Monmouth 07756
Ocean View, Cape May 08230
Oceanport, Monmouth 07757
Oceanville, Atlantic 08231
Ogdensburg, Sussex 07439
Old Bridge, Middlesex 08857
Old Tappan, Bergen 07675
Oldwick, Hunterdon 08858
Oradell, Bergen 07649
ORANGE, Essex
(See Page 2570)
Osbornville, Ocean 08723
Oxford, Warren 07863
Palisades Park, Bergen 07650
Palmyra, Burlington 08065
PARAMUS, Bergen
(See Page 2571)
Park Ridge, Bergen 07656
Parlin, Middlesex 08859
Parsippany, Morris 07054
Passaic, Passaic 07055
PATERSON, Passaic
(See Page 2571)
Paulsboro, Gloucester 08066
Peapack, Somerset 07977
Pedricktown, Salem 08067
Pemberton, Burlington 08068
Pennington, Mercer 08534
Penns Grove, Salem 08069
Pennsauken, Camden 08109
Pennsauken, Camden 08110
Pennsville, Salem 08070
Pequannock, Morris 07440
Perrineville, Monmouth 08535
PERTH AMBOY, Middlesex
(See Page 2573)
Phillipsburg, Warren 08865
Picatinny Arsenal, Morris 07806
Pilesgrove, Salem 08098
Pilesgrove Township, Salem 08098
Pine Beach, Ocean 08741
Pine Brook, Morris 07058
Pine Hill, Camden 08021
Pine Valley, Camden 08021
PISCATAWAY, Middlesex
(See Page 2574)
Pitman, Gloucester 08071
Pittsgrove, Salem 08318
Pittstown, Hunterdon 08867
PLAINFIELD, Union
(See Page 2575)
Plainsboro, Middlesex 08536
Pleasantville, Atlantic 08232
Pluckemin, Somerset 07978
Point Pleasant Beach, Ocean 08742
Point Pleasant Boro, Ocean .. 08742
Pomona, Atlantic 08240
Pompton Lakes, Passaic 07442
Pompton Plains, Morris 07444
Port Elizabeth, Cumberland ... 08348
Port Monmouth, Monmouth ... 07758
Port Murray, Warren 07865
Port Norris, Cumberland 08349
Port Reading, Middlesex 07064
Port Republic, Atlantic 08241
Pottersville, Hunterdon 07979
PRINCETON, Mercer
(See Page 2576)
Princeton Junction, Mercer .. 08550
Prospect Park, Passaic 07508
Pt Pleasant Beach, Ocean ... 08742
Quakertown, Hunterdon 08868
Quinton, Salem 08072
Rahway, Union 07065
Ramsey, Bergen 07446
Rancocas, Burlington 08073
Randolph, Morris 07869
Raritan, Somerset 08869
Readington, Hunterdon 08870
Red Bank, Monmouth 07701
Richland, Atlantic 08350
Richwood, Gloucester 08074
Ridgefield, Bergen 07657
Ridgefield Park, Bergen 07660
RIDGEWOOD, Bergen
(See Page 2577)
Ringoes, Hunterdon 08551
Ringwood, Passaic 07456
Rio Grande, Cape May 08242
River Edge, Bergen 07661
River Vale, Bergen 07675
Riverdale, Morris 07457
Riverside, Burlington 08075
RIVERTON, Burlington
(See Page 2577)
Rivervale, Bergen 07675
Robbinsville, Mercer 08691
Rochelle Park, Bergen 07662
Rockaway, Morris 07866
Rockleigh, Bergen 07647
Rocky Hill, Somerset 08553
Roebling, Burlington 08554
Roosevelt, Monmouth 08555
Roseland, Essex 07068
Roselle, Union 07203
Roselle Park, Union 07204
Rosemont, Hunterdon 08556
Rosenhayn, Cumberland 08352
Roxbury Township, Morris ... 07836
Rumson, Monmouth 07760
Runnemede, Camden 08078
Rutherford, Bergen 07070
Saddle Brook, Bergen 07663
Saddle River, Bergen 07458
Salem, Salem 08079
Sandy Hook, Monmouth 07732
Sandyston, Sussex 07826
SAYREVILLE, Middlesex
(See Page 2577)
Schooleys Mountain, Morris .. 07870
Scotch Plains, Union 07076
Sea Bright, Monmouth 07760
Sea Girt, Monmouth 08750
Sea Isle City, Cape May 08243
Seaside Heights, Ocean 08751
Seaside Park, Ocean 08752
SECAUCUS, Hudson
(See Page 2578)
Sergeantsville, Hunterdon 08557
Sewaren, Middlesex 07077
Sewell, Gloucester 08080
Shamong, Burlington 08088
Shiloh, Cumberland 08353
Ship Bottom, Ocean 08008
Short Hills, Essex 07078
Shrewsbury, Monmouth 07702
Sicklerville, Camden 08081
Skillman, Somerset 08558
Smithville, Atlantic 08205
Somerdale, Camden 08083
Somers Point, Atlantic 08244
SOMERSET, Somerset
(See Page 2578)
Somerville, Somerset 08876
South Amboy, Middlesex 08879
South Bound Brook, Somerset 08880
South Dennis, Cape May 08245
South Hackensack, Bergen ... 07606
South Harrison Township, Gloucester 08062
South Orange, Essex 07079
South Plainfield, Middlesex ... 07080
South River, Middlesex 08882
South Seaville, Cape May 08246
Southampton, Burlington 08088
Sparta, Sussex 07871
Spotswood, Middlesex 08884
Spring Lake, Monmouth 07762
Springfield, Union 07081
Stafford Township, Ocean 08050
Stanhope, Sussex 07874
Stanton, Hunterdon 08885
Stewartsville, Warren 08886
Stillwater, Sussex 07875
Stirling, Morris 07980
Stockholm, Sussex 07460
Stockton, Hunterdon 08559
Stone Harbor, Cape May 08247
Stratford, Camden 08084
Strathmere, Cape May 08248
Succasunna, Morris 07876
SUMMIT, Union
(See Page 2579)
Surf City, Ocean 08008
Sussex, Sussex 07461
Swartswood, Sussex 07877
Swedesboro, Gloucester 08085
Tabernacle, Burlington 08088
Teaneck, Bergen 07666
Tenafly, Bergen 07670
Tennent, Monmouth 07763
Teterboro, Bergen 07608
Tewksbury Township, Hunterdon 07830
Thorofare, Gloucester 08086
Three Bridges, Hunterdon 08887
Tinton Falls, Monmouth 07701
Titusville, Mercer 08560
TOMS RIVER, Ocean
(See Page 2580)
TOTOWA, Passaic
(See Page 2583)
Towaco, Morris 07082
Townsends Inlet, Cape May .. 08243
Township Of Washington, Bergen 07676
Tranquility, Sussex 07879
TRENTON, Mercer
(See Page 2583)
Tuckahoe, Cape May 08250
Tuckerton, Ocean 08087
Turnersville, Camden 08012
Union, Union 07083
Union Beach, Monmouth 07735
Union City, Hudson 07087
Upper Montclair, Essex 07043
Upper Saddle River, Bergen .. 07458
Vauxhall, Union 07088
Ventnor City, Atlantic 08406
Vernon, Sussex 07462
Verona, Essex 07044
Vienna, Warren 07880
Villas, Cape May 08251
Vincentown, Burlington 08088
VINELAND, Cumberland
(See Page 2587)
Voorhees, Camden 08043
W Caldwell, Essex 07006
Waldwick, Bergen 07463
Wall, Monmouth 07719
Wall Township, Monmouth ... 07719
Wall Township, Monmouth ... 07727
Wallington, Bergen 07057
Wallpack Center, Sussex 07881
Wanaque, Passaic 07465
Wantage, Sussex 07461
Waretown, Ocean 08758
Warren, Somerset 07059
Washington, Warren 07882
Washington Twps, Bergen ... 07676
Watchung, Somerset 07069
Waterford Works, Camden ... 08089
WAYNE, Passaic
(See Page 2589)
Weehawken, Hudson 07086
Wenonah, Gloucester 08090
West Allenhurst, Monmouth .. 07711
West Berlin, Camden 08091
West Caldwell
(See Caldwell)
West Cape May, Cape May .. 08204
West Collingswood, Camden 08107
West Collingswood Heights, Camden 08059
West Creek, Ocean 08092
West Deptford, Gloucester 08051
West Deptford, Gloucester 08063
West Long Branch, Monmouth 07764
West Milford, Passaic 07480
West New York, Hudson 07093
West Orange, Essex 07052
West Paterson, Passaic 07424
West Trenton, Mercer 08628
West Wildwood, Cape May ... 08260
West Windsor, Mercer 08550
Westampton, Burlington 08060
WESTFIELD, Union
(See Page 2590)
Westmont, Camden 08108
Westville, Gloucester 08093
Westwood, Bergen 07675
Westwood, Bergen 07677
Wharton, Morris 07885
WHIPPANY, Morris
(See Page 2591)
Whitehouse, Hunterdon 08888
Whitehouse Station, Hunterdon 08889
Whitesboro, Cape May 08252
Whiting, Ocean 08759
Wickatunk, Monmouth 07765
Wildwood, Cape May 08260
Wildwood Crest, Cape May .. 08260
Williamstown, Gloucester 08094
Willingboro, Burlington 08046
Windsor, Mercer 08561
Winfield Park, Union 07036
Winslow, Camden 08095
Wood Ridge, Bergen 07075
Woodbine, Cape May 08270
Woodbridge, Middlesex 07095
Woodbury, Gloucester 08096
Woodbury, Gloucester 08097
Woodbury Heights, Gloucester 08097
Woodcliff Lake, Bergen 07677
Woodland Park, Passaic 07424
Woodlynne, Camden 08107
Woodstown, Salem 08098
Woolwich Township, Gloucester 08085
Wrightstown, Burlington 08562
Wyckoff, Bergen 07481
Zarephath, Somerset 08890

ABSECON NJ

General Delivery 08201

POST OFFICE BOXES MAIN OFFICE STATIONS AND BRANCHES

Box No.s
All PO Boxes 08201

NAMED STREETS

Ables Run Dr 08201
Abraham Ave 08205
E & W Absecon Blvd ... 08201
Adams Ave 08205
Alameda Ave 08201
S Allen Ln 08205
Ambassador Dr 08201
Amy Ln 08201
S Anderson Ln 08205
Andrea Ln 08201
Angela Ct 08205
Anthony Ln 08205
Apache Ct 08205
Arapaho Pl 08205
Arbor Ct 08205
E Arbutus Ave 08205
Arc Ct 08201
Arlington Ln 08205
Aschwind Ct 08205
S Ash Ave 08205
Aspen Ct 08205
Audubon Ct 08205
Austin Ave 08201
S Avenue A 08205
S Avenue B 08205
S Balboa Ave 08205
E Bartlett Ave 08205
Bayberry Ln 08201
Bayview Dr 08201
E Beanfield Pl 08205
Beech Ave 08205
Beechwood Ave 08205
S Bella Ct 08205
E & W Belmar Ave 08205
Benjamin Ct 08201
E Bergen Ct 08205
Berkley Ave 08201
Berrywood Ln 08205
Birch Cir 08201
E Biscayne Ave 08205
Blackburn St 08205
S Blackman Rd 08205
Blenheim Ave
301-399 08205
700-1199 08201
Blue Rose Ct 08205
Blue Teal Dr 08205
E & W Bolton Ave 08201
Boston Ct 08205
Boulder Ct 08201
E Bradford Ave 08205
Brads Ct 08205
Brampton St 08205
Brandywine Dr 08205
Breaker Dr 08205
Breakers Ave 08201
Brewster Dr 08205
Briarcliff Pl 08201
S Briarwood Ln 08205
E Brook Ln 08205
E Brown Ave 08205
Buchanan Ave 08205
Buck Dr 08205
Burning Tree Blvd 08201
W California Ave 08201
S Cambridge Ct 08205
S Camelback Dr 08205
S Canary Way 08205
Cannon Ave 08201
Cara Mia Ln 08205
Caralena Ct 08201
Cardinal Way 08205
Carlisle Ln 08205
Carvel Ave 08205
N Cavesson Dr 08205
Cedar Hill Dr 08201
Cessna Ln 08201
E Chancery Ln 08205
E Chanese Ln 08205
Charles Dr 08205
Chatham Way 08205
Chelsea Rd 08201
Cheltenham Ave 08205
Cherokee Dr 08205
Cherokee Ln 08201
Cherry Ct 08201
Chesapeake Dr 08205
Cheshire Dr 08205
E Chip Shot Ln 08205
Chris Gaupp Dr 08205
N Chukker Ct 08205
E & W Church St 08201
Claridge Ct 08201
Clearwater Way 08205
Clipper Ct 08205
Club Pl 08205
E Collins Rd 08205
E Colman Pl 08205
Colonial Ct 08205
E & W Colorado Ave ... 08201
Columbus Ave 08205
S Concord Ter 08205
Connecticut Ave 08201
Constitution Ct & Dr 08205
Coolidge Ave
1-99 08205
100-399 08201
E Cooper Ferry Ct 08205
Cordelia Ln 08201
E Cordery Ave 08205
Cordova Dr 08201
E Cornell Ave 08205
Cornwall Dr 08205
Cortez Ave 08201
E Cos Cob Dr 08205
Cotuit Ct 08205
Country Ln 08205
Coventry Way 08205
Creek Ct & Rd 08201
Cresson Ave 08205
Crestview Ave
100-112 08205
100-126 08201
114-399 08205
128-199 08201
Crowndale Pl 08205
Curran Ct 08205
E Curran Dr 08201
N Curran Dr 08201
W Curran Dr 08201
Cynwyd Dr 08201
Damson Ave 08205
Daphne Dr 08205
Davis Ave 08201
S Davis Ave 08205
Deer Run Ct 08205
Delaware Ave 08201
Delmar Ct 08201
Delray Ln 08201
Dennis Dr 08205
Derby Dr 08205
Devon Ct 08205
E Dickinson Ave 08205
Donegal Ln 08205
Doughty Rd 08205
Douglas Ave 08201
Dover Ct 08205
Driftwood Ct 08205
W Duerer St 08205
Eagle Point Ct & Pl 08205
Eaglewood Dr 08205
Earlview Ter 08201
Ebony Tree Ave 08205
S Edgewater Dr 08205
E Egnor Dr 08205
Elaine Dr 08205
Elberon Ave 08201
Elm Ave 08201
E Elm Ave 08205
Elm St 08201
Elton Ln 08205
Emerson Ct 08205
Equestrian Dr 08205
Ethan Ln 08205
Euclid Dr 08201
Everton Pl 08205
Exeter Ct 08205
Ezra Boyce Rd 08205
Fair Haven Hill Ct 08205
Fairway Ln 08205
Falcon Dr 08201
Falcon Crest Ct & Pl ... 08205
Falling Leaf Ct 08205
Falmouth Ct 08205
E & W Faunce Landing Rd 08201
S Fawn Ln 08205
Fays Ct 08205
Federal Ct 08205
W Filmore Ave 08205
S Fir Ave 08205
E Fisher Creek Rd 08205
Flint Pond Pl 08205
Flora Ct 08205
Forest Hill Dr 08201
Forest Park Dr 08205
Forrest Brook Dr 08205
Franklin Blvd 08201
Fulham St 08205
S Gail Ln 08205
Galloway Rd 08205
Garfield Ave 08205
Gatehouse Dr 08205
Genista Ave 08205
Giulia Ln 08205
E Glory Rd 08205
Great Bay Dr 08205
E Great Creek Rd 08205
Greenwich Dr 08205
Griffin Rd 08205
E & N Grist Mill Pl & Way 08205
Gull Wing Ct & Pl 08205
Haddon Ave 08201
Hammel Ln 08201
Hammell Ln 08205
E Harlequin Dr 08205
E Harrison Ave 08205
Harwich Way 08205
Hastings Dr 08205
Haverhill Ct 08205
Havermill Rd 08205
E Haws Ct 08205
Hay Rd 08201
Hayes Ave 08205
Heavenly Valley Ct 08205
Heritage Ct 08205
Hermit Pl 08205
Hickory St 08201
Highbury Ct 08205
Highland Ave 08205
Highland Blvd 08201
Hillside Ave & Cir 08201
Hilltop Dr 08205
Hobart Ave 08201
S Holly Ave 08205
Holly Rd 08201
Holly Brook Dr 08205
Howlett Ln 08201
Huntington Ct 08205
Huron Ave 08201
Hyannis Ct 08205
E & W Illinois Ave 08201
S Independence Pl 08205
Iowa Ave 08201
Ireland Ave 08201
Irish Ln 08205
Iroquois Ave 08201
Iroquois Dr 08205
Ivystone Ct 08205
James Pl 08205
Jersey Woods Rd 08205
E & W Jimmie Leeds Rd 08205
Johnson Ave 08205
Juliana Dr 08201
Juniper Ave 08205
Justine Ln 08205
Katie Ct 08201
Keefer Ave 08201
E Kelly Dr 08205
Kendall Ct 08205
Kensington Dr 08205
Kesler Ave & Ln 08201
Keswick St 08205
E & S Key Dr 08205
Killarney Ln 08205
Kingston Ct 08205
E Lake Front Cir 08205
Lakefront Cir 08205
Lantern Ln 08201
Laurel Ave 08205
Laurel Cir 08201
Lavender Ln 08201
Lazy Ln 08201
E & W Lee Ave 08201
W Leeds Ave 08201
Leeds Point Rd 08205
Lenape Ln 08201
E Lexington Ct 08205
Liberty Ct 08205
Lillian St 08201
E Lilly Lake Rd 08205
Limerick St 08205
Linda Ln 08205
Lindbergh Ave 08205
Linden Pl 08201
Lisbon Ave 08201
Londonderry St 08205
Longfellow Ct 08205
E Lost Pine Way Rd ... 08205
Lostock Ct 08205
S Macarthur Ave 08205
E Magnolia Ave 08205
Mahogany Ct 08205
Malaga Cv 08201
Malibu Way 08205
Manchester St 08205
Manning Ct 08205
Manor Dr 08201
Maria Loretta Ln 08205
Marin Dr 08201
Marlborough Ave 08201
Marlin Rd 08201
Marlowe Ct 08205
S Marshall Ave 08205
Mattix Run 08205
E Mcdevitt Dr 08205
W Mckinley Ave 08205
Meadow Ridge Rd 08205
Meadows Dr 08205
Meadowview Ave 08201
Mechanic St 08201
Miami Ave 08201
Michigan Ave 08201
S Mill Rd 08201
E Millbridge Ct 08205
Minnetonka Ave 08201
Misty Ln 08205
E Mockingbird Way 08205
Mohave Dr 08201
Mohawk Ln 08201
Mohican Ct & Dr 08205
Montrose Ln 08205
Moonraker Ct 08205
Moores Ln 08201
Morton Ave
100-198 08205
101-397 08201
399-1011 08205
1013-1013 08201
W Morton Ave 08205
E Moss Mill Rd 08205
E & N Motts Creek Rd .. 08205
E Mourning Dove Way .. 08205
Nacote Creek Ct & Pl .. 08205
Natalie Ter 08201
Navajo Ave 08201
Navajo Ct 08205
Navasink Ct 08205
Nectar Ave 08205
E & W Nevada Ave 08201
N & S New Rd 08201
New Jersey Ave 08201
New Leaf Ct 08205
New York Ave 08201
N New York Rd 08205
S New York Rd 08205
Newbury Ct 08205
Newcastle Ct 08205
Newport Ct 08205
E Nightingale Way 08205
Northampton Rd 08205
Oak Cir & Ln 08201
E Oakbourne Ave 08205
Oakhurst Ave 08201
E Ocean Ave 08205
Ohio Ave 08201
Old New York Rd 08205
Old Port Republic Rd ... 08205
Old Shore Rd 08205
Orange Tree Ave 08205
W Oregon Ave 08201
Osage Ln 08201
E Oslo Ct 08205
Osprey Ct 08205
Oxford Ct 08205
Oyster Bay Rd 08201
Paget Way 08205
Park Ave 08201
Park Cir 08201
Park Pl 08205
Park St 08205
Patriots Ct 08205
Pelham Dr 08205
Pembrooke Way 08205
Pennsylvania Ave 08201
E Pennsylvania Ave 08205
Peterson Way 08201
Pheasant Meadow Dr .. 08205
Pine Ave 08205
Pine St 08201
Pineview Dr 08205
Pitney Rd 08201
N Pitney Rd 08205
S Pitney Rd 08205
Plaza Pl 08201
Pleasant Ave 08201
Plymouth Landing Rd ... 08201
W Polk Ave 08205
Pomona Rd 08205
Poplar Ave 08205
Price Ln 08205
Prield Ave 08201
E Providence Ct 08205
N & S Quail Hill Blvd ... 08205
Quince Ave 08205
Raleigh St 08205
Ravenwood Dr 08205
Redwood Ave 08205
Reed Rd 08201
Reeds Ct & Rd 08205
E Regency Dr 08205
Revere Ct & Way 08205
Richard Ln 08205
Richmond Cir 08201
E Ridgewood Ave 08205
Ritz Dr 08201
Rolling Stone Dr 08201
Rumson Dr 08205
Ruth Ct 08201
Saint Charles St 08201
Saint Georges Dr 08201
Saint Ives Ct 08205
S Saired Ave 08205
Salem Way 08205
Salisbury Ct 08205
Sander Pl 08205
Sandy Ln 08205
Sara Ann Ct 08205
Saratoga Pl 08205
Scarborough Ct 08205
School St 08201
Schoolview Dr 08201
Schooner Landing Rd .. 08205
Seaside Ave 08201
S Seaview Ave 08205
E Seaview Ridge Dr 08205
Seminole Ave 08201
Seminole Ct 08205
Seminole Dr 08205
Seneca Dr 08205
S Serenity Ln 08205
Shady Ln 08201
Shady Knoll Ln 08205
Sharswood Ave 08205
Shawnee Pl 08205
Sheffield Ct 08205
Shelburne Ave 08201
Shepherd Way 08205
N & S Shore Rd 08201
Short St 08201
Showellton Ave 08201
E Simsbury Ct 08205
N Smith Bowen Rd 08205
Smithville Blvd 08205
S Snake Rd 08205
Snow Mass Ct 08205
Society Hill Dr 08205
E Solitude Pl 08205
E Somers Landing Rd .. 08205
Somerstown Ln 08205
Sooy Ln 08201
Southampton Dr 08205
Southmoor Dr 08205
Southport Ct 08205
E Spencer Ln 08205
Spring Ln 08201
Spring Mill Dr 08205
Spruce Ave 08205
Spruce St 08201
Squaw Valley Ct 08205
S Station Ave 08201
Steamboat Ct 08205
Steeds St 08205
Stepping Stone Ln 08205
Sterling Dr 08205
Stewart Ln 08201
S Stockbridge Ct 08205
Stone Cir 08201
Stonewall Dr 08205
Stoney Hill Rd 08205
Stoneybrook Dr 08201
Strand Ct 08201
Stratton Ct 08205
E Sturbridge Ct 08205
E Summerwood Pl 08205
Summit Ave 08201
Sussex Pl 08205
Sycamore Ave 08201
Sylvan Ave 08205
Tamara Dr 08205
Theresa Ct 08205
S Thoreau Ter 08205
E Timberlane Rd 08205
Tipperary Pl 08205
Traymore Pkwy 08201
Tremont Ave 08201
Trotters Ln 08205
Tulip Ave 08205
Turnbridge Dr 08205
University Ave 08205
Upas Ave 08205
Upland Ave
1-369 08205
200-298 08201
371-399 08205
Vail Ct 08205
Vassar Sq 08201
Vera King Farris Dr 08205
E Victoria Dr 08205
E Village Dr 08205
Vine Ave 08205
Walden Way 08205
Warwick Rd 08205
Washington Ave 08205
Waterview Dr 08205
E Waveland Ave 08205
Webb Rd 08201
Wedgewood Ct 08205
E Weilers Ln 08201
Weston Dr 08205
Whalers Dr 08201
Whalers Cove Ct & Pl .. 08205
E Whispering Ln 08205
White Horse Pike 08201
E White Horse Pike 08205
W White Horse Pike 08205
White Pond Ct 08205
Wicklow Ter 08205
S Willow Ave 08205
Winding Way 08205
Wintergreen Ct 08205
Wochner Ct 08205
S Wood Ln 08205
Woodcrest Ave & Ct 08201
E Woodland Ave 08201
Woods Rd 08201
Wordsworth St 08205
S Wrangleboro Rd 08205
Wynnewood Dr 08201
E & W Wyoming Ave ... 08201
S Xanthus Ave 08205
Yale Ave 08205
S Yam Ave 08205
Yarmouth Ave 08201
Yarmouth Ct 08205
S Zenia Ave 08205

NUMBERED STREETS

1st Ave 08205
S 2nd Ave 08205
3rd Ave 08205
S 4th Ave 08205
4th St 08201
S 5th Ave 08205
S 6th Ave 08205
S 7th Ave 08205
8th Ave 08205
8th St 08201
S 10th Ave 08201
S 10th Ave 08205
12th St 08201
15th St 08201

ATLANTIC CITY NJ

General Delivery 08401

POST OFFICE BOXES MAIN OFFICE STATIONS AND BRANCHES

Box No.s
All PO Boxes 08404

NAMED STREETS

N & S Aberdeen Pl 08401
Absecon Blvd 08401
Adams Ct 08401
Adriatic Ave 08401
N Albany Ave 08401
S Albion Pl 08401
Aliantro Pl 08401
Anchorage Ct 08401
Andowell Ave 08401
N & S Annapolis Ave ... 08401
Anndover Gdns 08401
Arctic Ave 08401
Ariff Ave 08401
Arizona Ave 08401
N Arkansas Ave 08401
Atlantic Ave
114-198 08401
200-1800 08401
1801-4799 08401
1801-1801 08404
1802-4798 08401
N Atlantic Ave 08401
Atlantic City Expy 08401

Atlantic Ocean 08401
Auburn Ter 08401
Augustine Rd 08401
Bacharach Blvd 08401
Bader Ave 08401
Baltic Ave 08401
Baratta Ter 08401
Barkentine Ct 08401
Barrett Ave 08401
N & S Bartram Ave 08401
Bay St 08401
Beach Ave 08401
Beach Thorofare 08401
Belfield Ave 08401
Bella Ter 08401
Belle Haven Ct 08401
N & S Bellevue Ave 08401
S Belmont Ave 08401
S Berkley Sq 08401
Bishop Richard Allen Ave 08401
Blaine Ave 08401
Blake St 08401
Boardwalk 08401
Boardwalk Tower 1 08401
Boardwalk Tower 2 08401
Borgata Way 08401
Born Ter 08401
Boston Ave & Ct 08401
Bowler Ter 08401
Brigantine Blvd 08401
N & S Brighton Ave & Pl 08401
Brights Ct 08401
Brooklyn Ave 08401
Brooks Ct 08401
C Morris Cain Pl 08401
N & S California Ave 08401
Camarotta Pl 08401
Caravel Ct 08401
Carlton Ave 08401
Carolyn Ter 08401
Carson Ave 08401
Caspian Ave & Pl 08401
Castle Blvd 08401
Cedar Ct 08401
Centennial Ave 08401
Center St 08401
S Chalfonte Ave 08401
Charles Ct 08401
N & S Chelsea Ave, Ct & Ter 08401
Chesapeake Bay Ct 08401
N Christopher Columbus Blvd 08401
Church St 08401
City Ave & Pl 08401
Clipper Ct 08401
N Columbia Ave & Pl 08401
Commodore Ave 08401
N & S Congress Ave 08401
N & S Connecticut Ave 08401
Convention Blvd 08401
Crossan Ave 08401
N & S Delancy Pl 08401
N Delaware Ave 08401
Delta Ave 08401
Denny St 08401
Dewey Pl 08401
N & S Dover Ave 08401
N & S Dr Martin Luther King Blvd 08401
Drexel Ave & Pl 08401
Dylan Dr 08401
N & S Elberon Ave 08401
Emerson Ave & Pl 08401
W End Ave 08401
Erie Ave 08401
Evelyn Ct 08401
Fairmount Ave & Ter 08401
Fenton Pl 08401
Filbert Ave 08401
Fisher Ave 08401
N Fleming Ave 08401
N & S Florida Ave 08401
Folsom Ave 08401
Formicas Way 08401
Galleon Ct 08401
Garfield Ave 08401
N & S Georgia Ave & Ter 08401
Graff Ln 08401
Grafton Ave 08401
Grammercy Ave & Pl 08401
Grant Ave 08401
Green St 08401
Halyard Dr 08401
Hamilton Ave 08401
Harbor Rd 08401
Harlem Ter 08401
Harrahs Blvd 08401
Harris Pl 08401
N & S Harrisburg Ave 08401
N & S Hartford Ave & Ct 08401
Hobart Ave 08401
Horace J Bryant Jr Dr 08401
Houston Ave 08401
Howard Ave 08401
Hummock Ave 08401
Huron Ave 08401
Hygeia Ave 08401
N & S Indiana Ave 08401
N & S Iowa Ave 08401
Irving Ave 08401
Island Ave 08401
Italy Ter 08401
N & S Jackson Ave & Ter 08401
Jefferson Pl 08401
Keener Ave 08401
Kennedy Plz 08401
N & S Kentucky Ave 08401
N & S Kingston Ave 08401
Kuehnle Ave 08401
N & S Laclede Pl 08401
Landmark Ct 08401
Lawn Pl 08401
Leopold Ter 08401
Lexington Ave 08401
Liberty Ave & Ter 08401
Lighthouse Ct & Ln 08401
S Lincoln Ave, Pl & Ter 08401
Logan Ave 08401
Longs Ter 08401
Madison Ave 08401
Magellan Ave 08401
N & S Maine Ave 08401
Mainsail Way 08401
N & S Mansion Ave 08401
Marina Way 08401
Marmora Ave 08401
Marshall Ave 08401
Maryland Ave & Ter 08401
N & S Massachusetts Ave 08401
Maxwell Ave 08401
Mckinley Ave 08401
Mediterranean Ave 08401
Melrose Ave 08401
Memorial Ave 08401
S Metropolitan Ave 08401
Mgm Mirage Blvd 08401
N Michigan Ave 08401
Miss America Way 08401
N & S Mississippi Ave 08401
N & S Missouri Ave 08401
Monroe Ave 08401
Monterey Ave 08401
N & S Montgomery Ave 08401
N & S Montpelier Ave 08401
Morningside Ave 08401
N & S Morris Ave 08401
S Mount Vernon Ave 08401
Murray Ave 08401
Nevada Ave 08401
New Gretna Ave 08401
N & S New Hampshire Ave 08401
N New Jersey Ave 08401
N & S New York Ave 08401
N & S Newton Pl 08401
North Dr 08401
N & S North Carolina Ave 08401
N & S Ocean Ave & Ter 08401
Oceanic Ter 08401
N & S Ohio Ave 08401
Ontario Ave 08401
Oriental Ave 08401
Pacific Ave 08401
Park Pl 08401
N & S Parker Ave 08401
Pearl Pl 08401
N & S Pennsylvania Ave 08401
Penrose Ave 08401
Phyllis Ave 08401
N & S Plaza Pl 08401
Pocono Ter 08401
Porter Ave 08401
N & S Presbyterian Ave 08401
N & S Providence Ave & Ct 08401
N & S Raleigh Ave 08401
Reading Ave 08401
Renaissance Plz & Way 08401
Rev Dr Isaac S Coles Plz 08401
Reverend J J Walters Ave 08401
N & S Rhode Island Ave 08401
N & S Richmond Ave 08401
Rider Ave 08401
Ridgeway Ave & Rd 08401
E Riverside Dr 08401
Robinson Ave 08401
Rosemont Pl 08401
Ruffu Ter 08401
Saint Davids Pl 08401
Saint James Pl 08401
N Saint Katherine Pl 08401
Schooner Ct 08401
Seaside Ave 08401
Senate Ave 08401
Sewell Ave 08401
Sextant Dr 08401
Sheldon Ave 08401
Sheridan Ave 08401
Silverman Ave 08401
Siracusa Ter 08401
Sloop Ct 08401
South Blvd & Dr 08401
N & S South Carolina Ave 08401
N & S Sovereign Ave & Ct 08401
Spinnaker Way 08401
S Spray Ave 08401
Stanley Ct 08401
Starboard Ct 08401
N Stenton Pl 08401
Stewart Ave 08401
Sunrise Ave 08401
Sunset Ave 08401
Sussex Ave 08401
N & S Tallahassee Ave 08401
Taylor Ave 08401
N & S Tennessee Ave 08401
N & S Texas Ave & Ct 08401
Theresa Pl 08401
Thompson St 08401
Tindaro Ter 08401
N & S Trenton Ave & Ter 08401
Trenwith Ter 08401
Trinity Ave 08401
Turner Pl 08401
Van Rennslear Ave 08401
Ventnor Ave & Ter 08401
N & S Vermont Ave & Ter 08401
Victoria Ave & Pl 08401
N & S Virginia Ave & Ct 08401
Wabash Ave & Pl 08401
Warrena Rd 08401
Washington Sq 08401
Westcoat Pl 08401
N Westminister Pl 08401
S Westminster Ave 08401
Willow Ave 08401
S Wilson Ave 08401
Winchester Ave 08401
Windjammer Ct 08401
N & S Windsor Ave & Rd 08401
Wine St 08401
Wistar Pl 08401
Wisteria Rd 08401

BELLMAWR NJ

General Delivery 08031

POST OFFICE BOXES MAIN OFFICE STATIONS AND BRANCHES

Box No.s
All PO Boxes 08099

NAMED STREETS

Adams Ave 08031
Alcyon Dr 08031
Anderson Ave 08031
Anthony Dr 08031
Apple Ave 08031
Ash Ter 08031
Aspen Pl 08031
Barielak Ave 08031
Barr Ave 08031
Beaver Dr 08031
Beechwood Pl 08031
S Bell Rd 08031
N & S Bellmawr Ave 08031
Belmont Rd 08031
Benigno Blvd
100-422 08031
421-421 08099
424-598 08031
501-599 08031
Bergen Ave 08031
N & S Black Horse Pike 08031
Booth Dr 08031
Bradley Ave 08031
Braisington Ave 08031
Brooks Ct 08031
Brown Ave 08031
E & W Browning Rd 08031
Buchanan Ave 08031
Campanell Ave 08031
Cardinal Dr 08031
Carter Ave 08031
Catherine Ave 08031
N & S Cedar Ave 08031
Center Ave 08031
Chadwick Ave 08031
Chalmers Ave 08031
Charles Ave 08031
Cherry Pl 08031
Chester Ave 08031
E & W Chestnut Ave 08031
Clover Rd 08031
Collett Ct 08031
Colonial Rd 08031
Coolidge Ave 08031
Cornelia Dr 08031
Creek Rd 08031
Curtis Ave 08031
Cypress Ave 08031
Devenney Dr 08031
Devon Ave 08031
Dewey Rd 08031
Dobbs Ave 08031
Edgewood Ave 08031
Ellen Dr 08031
Elm Pl 08031
Essex Ave 08031
Evergreen Ave 08031
Farragut Rd 08031
Fir Pl 08031
Flanders Rd 08031
Forrest Dr 08031
Garfield Ave 08031
Glenview Ave 08031
Grafton Ave 08031
Grant Ave 08031
Haag Ave 08031
Hall Ave 08031
Hampton Pl 08031
Harbor Rd 08031
Harding Ave 08031
Hart Ave 08031
Heller Pl & Rd 08031
Hendrickson Ave 08031
Hickory Pl 08031
Holly Pl 08031
Howard Ave 08031
Ivy Ridge Rd 08031
Jefferson Ave 08031
Junior Ave 08031
Karr Dr 08031
Kennedy Blvd 08031
W Kings Hwy 08031
Kingston Ave 08031
Lake Dr 08031
Laurel Pl 08031
Leaf Ave 08031
Leed Ave 08031
Lewis Ave 08031
Lincoln Ave 08031
Linden Ave 08031
Logan Ave 08031
N & S Lowell Ave 08031
Lucille Ave 08031
Madison Ave 08031
Majestic Ave 08031
Maloney Ct 08031
E & W Maple Ave 08031
Market St 08031
Mcclelland Ave 08031
Mercer Ave 08031
Meyner Dr 08031
Midway Ln 08031
Monroe Ave 08031
Morris Ave 08031
Murray Ave 08031
Oak Ave 08031
Oakland Ave 08031
Old Kings Hwy 08031
Park Dr 08031
Patterson Ave 08031
Peach Rd 08031
Pine Ter 08031
Poplar Pl 08031
Princeton Ave 08031
Railroad Ave & Ln 08031
Roberts Ave 08031
Rockville Dr 08031
Romano Ave 08031
Rose Ave 08031
Saint Francis Ct 08031
Salem Ave 08031
Saunders Ave 08031
Schaffer Ave 08031
Sheridan Ave 08031
Sherman Ave 08031
Snyder Ave 08031
Spruce Ave 08031
Stanley Ave 08031
Sullivan Ave 08031
Summit Ave 08031
Sunnyside Ln 08031
Thomas Ave 08031
Thompson Ave 08031
Todd Ave 08031
Trinity Pl 08031
Troy Ave 08031
Union Ave 08031
Valley Rd 08031
Vaughn Ave 08031
Victory Dr 08031
Walnut Ave 08031
Warren Ave 08031
Wayne Rd 08031
Wellwood Ave 08031
Welsh Ave 08031
Willow Pl 08031
Wilson Ave 08031
Windsor Dr 08031
Worthington Ave 08031
Worthman Ave 08031

NUMBERED STREETS

All Street Addresses 08031

BRICK NJ

General Delivery 08723

POST OFFICE BOXES MAIN OFFICE STATIONS AND BRANCHES

Box No.s
All PO Boxes 08723

RURAL ROUTES

01, 02 08724

NAMED STREETS

A St 08723
Aarons Way 08723
Abbey Rd 08723
Acapulco Dr 08723
Acorn Dr 08723
Adair Dr 08723
Adams Dr 08724
Adamston Dr & Rd 08723
Addison Ct 08724
Adriana Ct 08724
Aida Way 08723
Alabama Ave 08724
Alameda Dr 08723
Alaska Ave 08724
Albermarle Rd 08724
Albert St 08724
Albert Cucci Dr 08724
Alcala Dr 08723
Alden St 08723
Aldgate Ct & Dr 08724
Alexander Rd 08724
Algonquin Trl 08724
Alhama Dr 08723
Allen Rd 08723
Allison Pl 08723
Allwood Rd 08724
Altier Ave 08723
Amherst Dr 08723
Amy Ct 08724
Andes Ct 08724
Andover Rd 08724
Andrew Ln 08724
Ann Ave 08724
Antoinette Ct 08723
Apache Ln 08724
Applegate Ave 08723
Appleton Dr 08723
Arbor Dr 08724
Arbutus Ave 08723
Arc Ln 08723
Arch Pl 08724
Arctic Ocean Dr 08723
Ardmore Dr 08723
Ariel Pl 08724
Arizona Dr 08723
Arlene Ct 08724
Arms Ct 08723
Arnies Pointe 08724
Arnold St 08724
Arrowhead Dr 08724
Arrowhead Park Dr 08724
Arthur Ct 08724
Aschby Dr 08723
Ashford Dr 08723
Ashland St 08724
Ashwood Dr 08723
Askin Ln 08724
Aspen St 08724
Atlantic Dr 08723
Atrium Dr 08723
Augustus Rd 08723
Aurora Dr & Pl 08723
Austin Ave 08724
Avenue A 08724
Avenue B 08724
Avenue C 08724
Avis Dr 08723
Avon Way 08724
Azalea Dr 08724
B St 08723
B Trl 08724
Bahia Ct 08723
Baker Dr 08724
Balsam St 08724
Baltic Dr 08723
Bancroft Rd 08724
Bara St 08723
Barb Ln 08724
Barbara Ln 08724
Barber Ave 08723
Barberry Dr 08723
Bark Rd 08723
Barker St 08724
Barnegat Ln 08723
Barnes Dr 08723
Barrett Walk 08724
Baser Ln 08724
Basin Ave 08723
Bass Rd 08723
Bates Way 08723
Baxter St 08723
Bay Ave 08724
Bay Way 08723
Bay Bridge Dr 08724
Bay Harbor Blvd 08723
Bay Laurel Dr 08723
Bay Oak Dr 08723
Bay Shore Dr 08723
Bayberry Ave 08723
Baylis Ct 08724
Bayview Ct 08724
Bayview Dr 08723
Baywood Blvd 08723
Beach Ct 08723
Beach Plum Rd 08723
Beacon Ave 08723
Beaton Rd 08723
Beaumont Dr 08723
Beaver Hollow Dr 08724
Beaverson Blvd 08723
Beckert Dr 08723
Bedford Ave 08724
Beechwood Dr 08723
Belinda Ct 08724
Bella Vista Rd E 08724
Bellanca Rd 08723
Berkeley Dr 08724
Berkshire Ct 08724
Bernard Ct 08724
Besante Blvd 08724
Beth Ave 08724
Bethany Ln 08723
Bettys Ln 08723
S Beverly Blvd & Dr 08724
Beverly Beach Rd 08724
Bimini Rd 08723
Binnacle Rd 08723

Birch Ct & Dr 08723
Birch Bark Dr 08723
Birchwood Dr 08723
Black Fox Trl 08723
Blake Cir 08724
Blasius Ave 08724
Blenheim Dr 08724
Blue Cedar Dr 08723
Blue Jay Ln 08723
Blue Ridge Dr 08724
Blue Spruce Pl 08724
Bluefin Dr 08723
Bluff View Dr 08723
Boeing Dr 08723
Boland Ave 08724
Bonair Dr 08723
Bonnie Ln 08723
Boom Ln 08723
Bow Dr 08723
Boxwood Dr 08723
Bradley Ave 08724
Branch Blvd 08724
Brandywine Ct 08724
Brant Dr 08724
Breeze Ct 08724
Brenner Ct 08724
Brentwood Ave 08724
Breton Ct & Rd 08723
Bretonian Dr 08723
Brian Ave 08724
Briar Mills Dr 08724
W Briarcliff Dr 08723
Brick Blvd, Mall & Plz 08723
Bristol Ln 08724
Brompton Ct 08724
Brooke Rd 08724
Brookfield Dr 08723
Brower Dr & Ln 08723
Brown Pl 08724
Browning Ct 08724
Bruce St 08724
Brushy Neck Dr 08724
Bryant Rd 08724
Bryn Mawr Dr 08723
Buckingham Rd 08723
Buena Vista Dr 08723
Burbank Ave 08723
Burdge Ave 08724
Burke Ln 08724
Burlington Dr 08723
Burns Ct 08724
Burnt Bark Rd 08723
Burnt Bridge Ave 08724
Burnt Tavern Rd 08724
Burnt Tavern Road Ext 08724
Burrsville Rd 08724
Burtis St 08723
Burton Pkwy 08723
Bush Ave 08724
Buxton Ct 08724
Byron Rd 08724
C St 08723
C Trl 08724
Cabana Dr 08723
Cadiz Dr 08723
Cajun Ln 08724
California Ave 08724
Callaghan Rd 08724
Calvin Ct 08724
Cambridge Way 08724
Camden Dr 08723
Camille Ct 08724
Campbell Pl 08724
Campion Ct 08724
Canis Dr 08724
Cape Breton Ct 08723
Capri Dr 08723
Captains Ct & Dr 08723
Cardinal Ave 08723
Carey Ct 08724
Carlisa Dr 08723
Carnation Dr 08724
Carole Ave 08724
Carolina Ave 08724
Carroll Fox Rd 08724

Cartagena Dr 08723
Carter Way 08723
Cascade Ct 08724
Catalina Dr 08723
Cayuga Ln 08724
Cedar Ave 08724
Cedar Dr 08724
Cedar Rd 08723
Cedar Bridge Ave 08723
Cedar Island Ct & Dr 08723
Cedar Knoll Dr 08723
Cedar Point Ave 08723
Cedar Village Blvd 08724
Cedarcroft Dr 08723
Cedarhurst Rd 08723
Cedarstream Pl 08724
Cedarwood Dr 08723
Center Dr 08723
Central Ave 08723
Central Blvd 08724
Central Blvd E 08724
Chambersbridge Rd 08723
Channel Dr 08723
Chard Pl 08724
Charles Dr 08723
Charleson Rd 08724
Chatham Ct 08724
Chelsea Dr 08723
Cherie Ct & Dr 08724
N Cherokee Ln 08724
Cherry Ln 08723
Cherry Quay Rd 08723
Cherrywood Cir 08724
Cheryl Ct 08724
Cheryl Ln 08723
Chestnut Ave 08724
Chestnut Ct 08723
Chipmunk Dr 08724
Choctaw Ln 08723
Christopher Ct 08724
Chucks Ct 08724
Church Rd 08723
Cindy Ct 08724
Circle Ct 08723
Circle Dr
1-99 08724
200-299 08723
Clair Ave 08724
Claremont Dr 08723
Clark Dr 08724
Claude Pepper Ct 08723
Claudia Rd 08723
Clay Ave & Cir 08724
Clearwater Dr 08723
Clematis Pl 08724
Cleveland Ave & Ct 08724
Cliff Rd 08724
Clover Rd 08724
Club House Rd 08724
Clubhouse Plz 08723
Coast Dr 08723
Collins Ct 08724
Colonial Dr 08724
Colorado Ave W 08724
Columbus Dr 08724
Commodore Dr 08723
S Community Dr 08724
Compass Ave 08723
Concord Dr 08724
Constable St 08724
Constitution Dr 08723
Conte Ave 08724
Coolidge Dr 08724
Coral Dr 08724
E Coral Dr 08724
W Coral Dr 08723
Cornell Dr 08723
Cottage Pl 08724
Cottontail Dr 08724
Cottonwood Dr 08723
Country Club Ct & Dr 08724
Court E 08724
Court Pl 08723
Court A 08724
Court B 08724
Court C 08724

Court D 08724
Court F 08724
Court M 08724
Courtshire Dr 08723
Coventry Ct 08724
Crabapple Ct 08724
Cranberry Cove Rd 08723
Cranbury Rd 08723
Crane Rd 08723
Cranmore Dr 08723
Crate Pl 08724
Crawford Ave 08724
Creek Rd 08724
Crescent Dr 08724
Crest Dr 08724
Crestview Ter 08723
Cross Trees Rd 08723
Croy Rd 08724
Crystal Dr 08723
Cumberland Dr 08723
Cypress Ave 08723
D St 08723
D Trl 08724
Dahncke Ln 08723
Dakota Ave 08723
Daniel Ct 08724
Darley Cir 08724
Dartmoor Rd 08724
Dartmouth Ct 08723
David Pl 08724
Davids Rd 08724
Davidson Ave 08724
Davos Rd 08724
Daybreak Ct 08723
Debbie Dr 08724
Deer Path 08724
Deer Run Ln 08723
Deerfoot Ln 08723
Dehnz Ln 08723
Dekker Ct 08724
Delaware Dr 08723
Delmar Dr 08723
Delta Pl 08723
Denby Ct 08723
Denise Ct 08724
Dennis Dr 08724
Devin Ln 08723
Diane Dr 08724
Dickinson Rd 08724
Division St 08723
S Dock Rd 08724
Doe Ct 08723
Dogwood Dr 08723
Donald St 08723
Doris Dr 08723
Dorothy Pl 08723
Douglas Rd 08723
Downey Ave 08723
Doyle Ter 08723
Drake Rd 08723
Drew Ave 08724
Driftwood Dr 08723
Driscol Dr 08723
Driver Ave 08723
Drum Point Rd 08723
Drury Ct 08723
Dryden Rd 08724
Duchess Ln 08724
Duck Pond Ln 08723
Duke Ct 08723
Dunbeck Rd 08723
Duquesne Blvd 08723
Durham Ter 08724
Dwight Pl 08723
E St 08723
E Trl 08723
Eagle Ct & Pass 08723
Eagle View Rdg 08724
Earl Dr 08724
East Dr 08723
Eastern Ln 08723
Eastland Rd 08723
Eaton Pl 08723
Ebb Tide Dr 08723
Edge St 08724
Edgewood Dr 08724

Edwards Rd 08723
W Eel St 08724
Elena Ct 08724
Eli Pl 08723
Elizabeth Ave 08724
Ellen Dr 08724
Elliott Ln 08723
Elm Ct 08723
Elm Ln 08723
Elm St 08724
Elmwood Ct, Dr & Pl 08723
Emberly Rd 08723
Emerald Dr 08723
E End Ave 08723
Endora Ct 08724
English Ln 08724
Eric Ct 08723
Ernestine Pl 08723
Esmeralda Ct 08724
E & W Esplanade 08723
Essex Ct, Dr & Pl 08723
Evelyn Ct 08723
Everest Dr N & S 08724
Evergreen Dr 08723
Ezara Ct 08724
F St 08723
Fairfield Ave 08723
Fairmont Ave 08723
Fairview Ave & Ct 08724
Fairway Dr 08724
Fairwood Ln 08724
Falkenberg Rd 08724
Farragut Dr 08724
Fern Ln 08723
Field Pl 08724
Fieldcrest Ln 08724
Finchley Dr 08724
Firehouse Rd 08723
Firwood Dr 08723
Fisher Ave 08723
Fisherman Pl 08723
Flagge Rd 08724
Fletcher St 08724
Flintoft Ave 08724
Flora Ct 08724
Floral Dr 08723
Florida Ct 08724
Folsom Dr 08724
Fontainebleau Dr 08723
Forest Ave & Rd 08724
Forge Pond Rd 08724
Fort St 08724
Fortune Ave 08724
Foxcroft St 08724
Foxwood Ct 08724
France Ave 08723
Francis Rd 08723
Frank Neri Dr 08724
Frede Dr 08724
Freedom Rd 08724
Freeport Rd 08724
Fuller Ln 08724
Fullerton Dr 08724
G St 08723
Gale Rd 08723
Garden Ave 08724
Gardenia Dr 08724
Garland Dr 08723
Georges Rd 08724
Georgia Dr 08723
Gladiola Dr 08723
Glen Rd 08723
Glen Ridge Ct 08724
Glenmere Dr 08724
Glenmore St 08723
Glenn Dr 08723
Glenwood Ave & Pl 08723
Gloria Pl 08724
Gloria Ann Smith Dr 08723
Gloucester Ave 08724
Godfrey Lake Dr 08724
Golden Rod Ct 08724
Graham Ct 08724
E & W Granada Dr 08723
Granite Ct 08723
Grant Ct 08724

Gray Ln 08724
Green Ave 08724
Green Grove Rd 08724
Green Tree Rd 08724
Greenbriar Blvd 08724
Greenhill Dr 08724
Greenville Dr 08723
Greenwood Ln 08723
Greenwood Loop Rd 08724
Gregory Dr 08723
Griggs St 08724
Grove Ave 08723
Halifax Ln 08724
Halsey Dr 08723
Hamilton Dr 08723
S Hampton Pl 08724
Hampton Rd 08723
Hanley Ct 08724
Harbor Pl & Rd 08724
Hardean Rd 08724
Harding Dr 08724
Hardy Ct 08724
Harmony Ln 08724
Harper Ave 08723
Harriot Dr 08724
Harris Ave 08724
Harrison Ave 08724
Hartford Pl 08724
Harvard Ave 08723
Harvey Ave 08723
Havens Dr 08723
Havens Cove Rd 08723
Hawaii Dr 08723
Hawks Nest Rd 08724
Hayes Ave 08723
Hazel Ave 08723
Heather Ln 08723
Helen Dr 08724
Hemlock Dr 08723
Hendrickson Ave 08724
Hendry Ln 08723
Henry Ct 08724
Herbert Ln 08724
Herbertsville Rd 08724
Herborn Ave 08724
Heritage Dr 08723
Herkimer Rd 08724
Heron Rd 08723
Hessler Way 08723
Heywood Ct 08724
Hickory Rd 08723
Higgins Ct 08723
Highland Ct & Ter 08723
Hill Dr 08723
Hillside Ave 08724
Hilltop Dr 08724
Hoffman St 08724
Holly Ct & Rd E 08723
Holly Acres Dr 08723
Holly Berry Ln 08723
Hollycrest Dr 08723
Hollywood Ct & Dr 08723
Holmes Ct 08724
Homestead Dr 08723
Homewood Dr 08723
Honeysuckle Ct 08724
Hooper Ave 08723
Hoover Dr 08723
Horace Ct 08724
Huckleberry Ct 08724
Hudson Dr 08723
Hulse Ave 08724
Hulse Landing Rd 08723
Hunters Rd 08724
Huppert Dr 08723
Huxley Dr 08723
Ida Ln 08724
Illinois Ave 08724
Ilona Ct 08724
Impatiens Ct 08724
Industrial Pkwy 08724
Iowa Ave 08724
Iris Way 08724
Irisado Dr 08723
Iron Ct 08724
Iroquois Dr 08724

Isabella Ct 08724
Isadora Ct 08724
Island Ct & Dr 08724
Ivanhoe Rd 08723
Ivy Pl 08724
Jack Martin Blvd 08724
Jackson Ave 08723
Jacqueline Ave 08724
James Rd 08723
Jane St 08724
Jarome St 08724
Jason Pl 08724
Jay Ave 08724
Jaywood Manor Dr 08724
Jeffers Ct 08724
Jefferson Ct & Dr 08724
Jeffery Ln 08724
Jenny Ct 08724
Jessica Ln 08724
Jetty Ct 08723
Jewel Ave 08724
Jib Cir & Ln 08723
Joanne Ct 08723
John St 08724
John Mcguckin Dr 08724
Johnson Rd 08723
Johnson St 08724
Johnston Ave 08724
Joie Pl 08724
Jordan Rd 08724
Joseph Way 08723
Joseph Byrne Dr 08724
Joyce Ct 08723
Judy Ct 08724
Karen Ln 08724
Kathy Ct 08724
Katie Lynn Ct 08723
Keats Rd 08724
Kelly Ave 08724
Kelly Lynn Ln 08724
Kenmore Rd 08723
Kennedy Mall 08723
Kenneth Pl 08724
Kent Dr 08723
Kentwood Blvd 08724
Kettle Creek Dr 08723
Kevin Ct 08724
Kieser Blvd 08724
Kims Ct 08724
King Ln 08724
Kingfisher Cir 08723
Kingsley Ct 08724
Kirk Ln 08724
Kitty Ct 08724
Knoll Crest Ave 08723
Knollwood Pl & Ter 08724
Koches Ave 08724
Kristi Shay Ln 08723
Kuster Ln 08724
Labanna Ct 08724
Lafayette Dr 08723
Lagoon Dr E & W 08723
E Lagoona Dr 08723
S, E, N & W Lake Ct, Dr & Rd 08724
Lake Oak Pl 08723
Lake Point Dr 08723
N Lake Shore Dr & Way 08723
Lakeland Dr 08723
Lakeside Ter 08723
Lakewood Ave 08724
Lamb Rd 08724
Lamiss Ct 08723
Lancaster Rd 08723
Lance Dr 08723
Lanes Mill Plz & Rd 08724
Larchmont Ave 08724
Larchwood Dr 08724
Lark Ln 08724
Larsen St 08724
Las Olas Dr 08723
Laura Ct 08724
Laurel Ave 08724
Laurel Brook Dr 08724
Laurelhurst Dr 08724

Laurelton St 08724
Laurelwood Rd 08724
Lauren Ln 08723
Laurman Ave 08724
Lawndale Dr 08723
Lawrence Dr 08724
Leah Ct 08724
Leanora St 08723
Lee Dr 08724
Leeds Ct 08724
Lehigh Dr 08723
Lehigh St 08724
Lenape Trl 08724
Lenox St 08724
Leone Dr 08724
Leswing Dr 08723
Lewis Ln 08724
Lexington Dr 08724
Liberty Ln 08723
Lido Ct 08724
Lighthouse Ct 08723
Lilac Dr 08724
Lillian St 08724
Lime Rd 08723
Lincoln Ct 08724
Linda Ct 08724
Lindbergh Dr 08724
Linden Ave & Pl 08723
Linnea Ln 08723
Lions Ln 08723
Lions Head Blvd S 08723
Lisa Dr 08724
Liverpool Rd 08723
Lizzies Ct 08724
Lockheed Rd 08723
Locust Ct 08723
Lodge Ct 08724
Logan Ct 08724
London Rd 08723
Longfellow Ct 08724
Longpoint Dr 08723
Lonna Ct 08724
Lorraine Pl 08724
Lowell Ct 08724
Lynnwood Ave 08723
Macarthur Dr 08724
Madison Ct 08724
Magnolia Ave 08724
Maidenstone Dr 08724
Main Ave 08724
Mako Ct 08724
Malibu Ct & Way 08723
Mallard Dr 08724
Malmy Dr 08724
Mamie Ct & Dr 08723
Manasquan Ct 08724
Manchester Ave 08723
Mandalay Rd 08723
Mandarin Rd 08723
Manhattan Dr 08723
Manor Dr 08723
Manorside Dr 08724
Mansfield Dr 08724
Mantoloking Dr & Rd 08723
Maple Ave 08724
Maple Ct 08723
N Maplewood Cir & Dr 08723
Marbro Ave 08724
Marcy Pl 08724
Margherita Pl 08724
Maria Ct 08724
Marigold Ln 08724
Marilyn Dr 08723
Marina Ln 08724
Mariner Pl 08723
Mark Dr 08723
Mark Manor Dr 08723
Markham Rd 08724
Marlin Ct 08724
Marlow Ave 08724
Marta Ct 08724
Martin Pl 08724
Mary Ann Dr 08723
Marys Dr 08723
Mast Rd 08723
Masters Rd 08724

Mathis Dr 08723
Matterhorn Way 08724
Maxwell Ct 08724
Mayapple Dr 08724
Mayfair Ct 08723
Mcclellan Ave 08724
Mcguire Blvd 08724
Mckay Dr 08723
Mckinley Ct 08724
Mclagan Ave 08724
Meadow Blvd 08723
Meadow Run 08724
Meadow Point Dr 08723
Meadowbrook Rd 08723
Melody Ave 08724
Melrose St 08724
Melville Ln 08724
Mercer Ave 08723
Meredith Ln 08723
Meridian Dr 08724
Merrimac Way 08724
Metedeconk Ave 08724
Metedeconk Rd 08723
Michael Ave 08724
Michelle Pl 08723
Michigan Ave 08724
Midpark Dr 08723
Midstreams Pl & Rd 08724
Midvale Ave 08723
Midway Pl 08724
Midwood Dr 08724
Mill Pond Rd 08724
Millbrook Rd 08724
Miller Ave 08724
Miranda Ct 08724
Mizzen Rd 08723
Moes Ct 08724
Mohawk Dr 08723
Moholo Ct 08723
Molly Ln 08723
Monmouth Ave 08723
Montana Dr 08723
Montclair Dr 08724
Monterey Dr 08723
Monticello Dr 08723
Morey Ln 08723
Morning Glory Ct 08724
Morris Ave 08724
Morsell Dr 08724
Mulberry Pl 08723
Myrtle Ave 08723
Nancy Dr 08723
Nash Ave 08724
Nassau St 08723
Nasto Ter 08724
Natick Trl 08724
National Ave 08724
Nautilus Dr 08723
Navajo Trl 08724
Navarra Dr 08723
Nebraska Ave 08724
Needle St 08724
Neil Ave 08724
Nejecho Dr 08723
Nelson Dr 08723
Neptune Cir 08723
New Brunswick Ave 08724
New Jersey Ave 08724
New York Ave 08724
Newark Dr 08724
Newport Ct 08724
Nicholas Rd 08724
Nicole Dr 08724
Nina Ct 08723
North Dr 08724
Northeast Dr 08724
Northrop Rd 08723
Northrup Dr 08724
Nottingham Dr 08724
Novello Dr 08724
Oak Ave 08724
Oak Ct 08723
Oak St 08724
Oak Forest Ct & Dr 08724
Oak Hollow Rd 08724
Oak Knoll Dr 08724
Oakland Dr 08724
Oakwood Dr 08723
Obispo Dr 08723
Ohio Ave 08724
Oklahoma Dr 08723
Old Adamston Rd 08723
Old Burnt Tavern Rd ... 08724
Old Farm Rd 08723
Old Lanes Mill Rd 08724
Old Silverton Rd 08723
Old Squan Rd 08724
Old Toms River Rd 08723
Olden St 08724
Olive Ct 08723
Olivia Ct 08724
Olympic St 08724
Olympus Way 08724
Orange Rd 08723
Orangewood Ct & Dr ... 08723
Orchard Ct 08724
Orchid Ln 08724
Oregon Ave 08724
Oriole Trl 08724
Orion Dr 08724
Osage Dr 08724
Osborn Ave 08723
Overlook Ct 08724
Owen Ln 08724
Oxford Rd 08724
Pacific Ocean Dr 08723
Page Dr 08724
Palm Ave 08723
E & W Pampano Dr 08723
Paramount Way 08724
Paris Dr 08723
Park Ave & Pl 08724
Parker Ave 08724
Parkway Dr 08723
Patmore Rd 08724
Patriot Ave 08723
Paul Jones Dr 08723
Paula Ct 08724
Pelham Pl 08724
Pello Rd 08724
Penguin Rd 08723
Pennsylvania Ave 08724
Perry Dr 08723
Pershing Ave 08723
Peter Pl 08723
Pheasant Dr 08724
Phillips Rd 08724
Piedmont Ct 08724
Piel Ave 08723
N, S & W Pier Ave 08723
Pilot Dr 08723
Pine Ave 08724
Pine Dr 08723
Pine Dr S 08723
Pine Hammock Rd 08723
Pine Meadow Rd 08724
Pine Tree Dr 08723
Pinecroft Dr 08723
Pinehurst Ct & Rd 08723
Pineland Rd 08724
Pinewood Dr & Trl 08724
Pinta Ct 08724
Pioneer Dr 08724
Pitcairn Rd 08723
Plaza Ter 08723
Pleasant Ave 08724
Pleasant Dr 08723
Plestree Dr 08723
Plymouth Dr 08724
Poe Rd 08724
Point Ave 08724
Point View Rd 08724
Polk Dr 08724
Pompton Plains Dr 08724
Pontiac Ave 08724
Poplar Way 08724
Poppy Ct 08723
Port Rd 08723
Post Rd 08724
Preston St 08723
Primrose Ln 08724
Prince Ln 08724
Princess Ave 08724
W Princeton Ave 08724
Princeton Pines Pl 08724
Prospect Dr 08724
Quadara Blvd 08724
Quail Run 08723
Queen Ann Rd 08723
Quincy Dr 08723
Rabbit Run 08724
Raccoon Ct 08724
Rachel Ct & Rd 08724
Rahway Dr 08724
Rainbow Dr 08724
Rainier Dr 08724
N Raleigh Rd 08723
Ramapo Dr 08724
Rancocas Dr 08724
Ravenswood Pl 08724
Red Cedar Dr 08723
Red Maple Dr 08724
Red Wing Ave 08723
Redwood Dr 08723
Redwood Pl E 08724
Reed Ln 08723
Reedy Dr 08723
Reef Pl 08723
Regent Cir & Ct 08723
Regina Dr 08724
Rena Ct 08724
Reservation Row 08723
Revere Dr 08724
Revolutionary Rd 08724
Reynolds Pl 08723
Rhode Island Ave 08724
Rialto Dr 08723
Rice Ct 08723
Richard St 08724
Ridge Rd 08724
Ripley Ct 08723
Rita Ct 08723
Ritchie Ct 08723
Riva Blvd 08723
River Ave & Ln 08723
River Edge Dr 08724
River Park Dr 08724
Riverside Dr E 08723
Riverside Dr N 08723
Riverside Dr S 08723
Riverside Dr W 08723
Riverview Dr 08723
Riviera Dr 08724
Robbins Ct & St 08724
Robertson Ct 08724
Robinhood Rd 08724
Robinson Rd 08724
Rochester Dr 08723
Rocky Mountain Blvd & Ct 08724
Rodger Rd 08724
Roe Ct 08724
Rolling Hills Ct & Dr 08724
Ronald Ave 08724
Roosevelt Dr 08724
Rosalind Rd 08724
Rose Ave 08724
Rose Manor Ct 08723
Roselle Ave 08724
Rosewood Ave 08724
Rossetti Ct 08724
Round Ave 08723
Route 70
401-497 08723
Route 70
499-799 08723
800-1400 08724
1402-1698 08724
Route 88 08724
Royal Dr 08723
Rozbern Ct 08724
Rushmore Dr 08724
Rutgers Ct 08723
Ryjac Dr 08724
Sabrina Ct 08724
Sager Rd 08723
N & S Sailors Quay Dr 08723
Saint Lawrence Blvd 08723
Salem Rd 08724
Sally Ike Rd 08724
Salmon St 08723
Samantha Ct 08724
Sanctuary Ct 08724
Sandpiper Ct 08723
Sandra Pl 08724
Sandy Trl 08723
Sandy Island Dr 08724
Sandy Point Dr & Rd 08723
Sanford Rd 08724
Santiago Dr 08723
Santrice Ct 08723
Sateroja Rd 08724
Sauers Dr 08723
Sawmill Rd 08724
Scheiber Dr 08723
Schindler Dr 08723
Schoener Dr 08723
Schoolhouse Rd 08724
Scoop Rd 08723
Scott Ave 08724
Seagoin Rd 08723
Seattle Ave 08724
Seaview Ave 08723
Sedge Pl 08723
Seminole Ln 08724
Seneca Ct 08724
Serpentine Rd 08724
Seville Dr 08723
Shadow Way 08724
Shady Ln 08723
Shannon Ct 08724
Shawnee Dr 08723
Shay Ln 08723
Sheldon Ave 08723
Shelley Rd 08724
Sherwood Ln 08724
Shirley Ln 08723
Shore Dr 08723
Shore Line Pl 08723
Shore Pine Dr 08723
Sidney Ct 08724
Sids Ct 08724
Silver Dr 08724
Silver Trl 08723
Silver Sands Way 08724
Silverton Rd 08723
Simon Pl 08723
Skipper Ln 08724
Skoog Ct 08724
Sky Manor Blvd 08723
Skyline Dr 08724
Sleepy Hollow Dr 08724
Sloping Hill Ct & Ter 08723
Smith Rd 08723
Solar Dr 08723
Somerset Dr 08723
South Dr 08723
Southview Ct & Dr 08723
Spark Dr E & W 08723
Spenser Ct 08724
Spiral Dr 08724
Spring Ave 08723
Springhill Dr 08724
Spruce Ct & Dr 08723
Sprucewood Dr 08723
Stapleton Ave 08723
Starboard Ct & Rd 08723
Stearman Rd 08723
Stengel Ave 08724
Stephan Rd 08723
Sterling Ave 08723
Stewart Ave 08723
Stinson Rd 08723
Stoneham Ct & Dr 08724
Stoney Point Rd 08723
Stratford Dr 08723
Sturdy St 08723
Stuyvesant Rd 08723
Suburban Rd 08723
Sullivan Rd 08724
Summit Ave 08724
Sunflower Ln 08724
Sunny Ln 08723
Sunnycrest Dr 08724
Sunnydale Dr 08723
Sunrise St 08723
E Sunset Ct & Rd 08723
Sunshine Ct 08724
Susan Dr 08723
Sussex Dr 08723
Sutton Dr 08724
Swan Rd 08723
Sweeney Ave 08724
Sweetbriar Ln 08724
Sycamore Dr 08723
Sylvan Dr 08723
Sylvia Ct 08724
Tabetha Ct 08724
Tackle Ave 08723
Taft Ave, Ct & Dr 08724
Tall Oaks Dr 08724
Tall Timber Dr 08723
Tamany Ct 08723
Tammy Ct 08724
Tanager Way 08724
Tanglewood Rd 08724
Tanner Ct 08723
Tate Ct 08724
Taylor Blvd 08724
Taylor Dr 08723
Teakwood Dr 08723
Teal Rd 08723
Tennessee Dr 08723
Tennis Ct 08723
Tennyson Rd 08724
Tern Dr 08723
Texas Dr 08723
Thames Pl 08723
The Blvd 08724
The Esplanade 08724
Theodore Ct 08724
Thiele Rd 08724
Thomas Ct 08724
Thoreau Ct 08724
Thoroughfare Rd 08724
Tilford Blvd 08724
Tiller Ln 08723
Tilton Rd 08723
Timberline Pl 08723
Timothy St 08724
Tina Lee Ct 08724
Toledo Dr 08723
Tony Ct 08724
Topsail Rd 08723
Toronto Dr 08723
Towhee Trl 08724
Trangerl Ave 08724
Tremont Pl 08724
Trinity Pl 08724
Trout St 08723
Troy Ct 08724
Truman Dr 08724
Tudor Ct 08723
Tulip Pl 08724
Tunes Brook Dr 08723
Turkey Point Rd 08723
Tuscaloosa Ln 08724
Twilight Dr 08723
Twin Oaks Dr 08724
Unity Dr 08723
University Ct 08723
Utah Trl 08723
Valencia Dr 08723
Valerie Ct 08724
Valley Ct & Way 08723
Van Ave 08724
Van Buren Ave 08724
Van Cortlandt Dr 08723
Van Ness Dr 08723
Van Zile Rd 08723
Vanada Dr 08723
Vanard Dr 08723
Vannote Dr & Pl 08723
Vassar Pl 08723
Vaughn Ct 08724
Venice Dr 08723
Vermont Dr 08723
Vernon Ct 08724
Veronica Dr 08724
Victoria Ct 08724
Victory Ave & Ln 08723
View Dr 08723
Village Way 08724
Vincent Dr 08723
Vine St 08723
Viola Ct 08724
Virginia Dr 08723
Vista Ct 08724
Wabash Ave 08723
Wake Pl 08723
Walden Rd 08724
Wallis Ct 08724
Walnut Ave & Dr 08724
Walsh Pl 08724
Walter Rd 08724
Ward Ave 08724
Ward Dr 08723
Wardell Ave 08724
Warren St 08724
Warwick Rd 08724
Washington Dr 08724
Waterfront Dr 08724
Waters Edge Ct 08724
Waterway Ct 08723
Watkins Rd 08724
Wayne Ln 08723
Wayside Dr 08724
Wedgewood Dr 08723
Wellington Dr 08724
West Dr 08724
Western Ln 08723
Westminster Ave 08724
Westwood Pl 08724
White Oak Ct 08724
White Pine Ct 08724
White Swan Way 08723
Whitecap Way 08723
Whitehorn Ct 08723
Whitman St 08724
Whitney Ct 08724
Whittier Rd 08724
Wilbur Ct 08724
Wildwood Rd 08724
Willetta Dr 08723
Williamsburg Dr 08724
Willow Ave 08724
Wilson Ct 08724
Winchester Dr 08724
Windcrest Ct 08724
Winding Ct & Way 08723
Winding River Ct, Ln & Rd 08724
Windsor Rd 08723
Wintergreen Ave 08723
Wiscasset Trl 08724
Wisteria Dr 08723
Wood Ave 08724
Woodchuck Ln 08724
Woodland Dr 08723
Woodpark Dr 08723
Wordsworth Rd 08724
Worth Rd 08723
Worth St 08724
Wraight Ave 08724
Wren Ave 08724
Yale Pl 08724
Yellowbrick Rd 08724
Yew Dr 08724
York Rd 08724
Yorktowne Blvd 08723
Yorkwood Dr 08723
Younger St 08724
Zachary Ct 08724
Zinnia Ct 08724

NUMBERED STREETS

All Street Addresses 08724

CALDWELL NJ

General Delivery 07006

POST OFFICE BOXES MAIN OFFICE STATIONS AND BRANCHES

Box No.s
1 - 471 07006
501 - 3240 07007
5001 - 5060 07006
6001 - 6879 07007

NAMED STREETS

Academy Rd 07006
Acorn Pl 07006
Aldom Cir 07006
Aldrin Dr 07006
Allen Rd 07006
Amelia St 07006
Andover Dr 07006
Andrea Dr 07006
Angela Ct 07006
Annin Rd 07006
Arbor Rd 07006
Arlington Ave & Ct 07006
Armitage Ln 07006
Ashland St 07006
Aspen Dr 07006
Balsam Pl 07006
Barnsdale Rd 07006
Beachmont Ter 07006
Beechtree Rd 07006
Beechwood Rd 07006
Beekman Hill Rd 07006
Beverly Rd 07006
Birch Ave 07006
Birchwood Rd 07006
Birkendene Rd 07006
Blackberry Ln 07006
Bloomfield Ave 07006
Bond Pl 07006
Borrello Blvd 07006
Bowers Rd 07006
Boxwood Dr 07006
Brentwood Dr 07006
Brian Pl & Rd 07006
Brookside Ave & Ter ... 07006
Brookwood Dr 07006
Byron Rd 07006
Cambridge Dr 07006
Campolattaro Ct 07006
Canterbury Dr 07006
Cascade Pl & Rd 07006
Caton Ter 07006
Cavell Pl 07006
Cedar St 07006
Cedarcrest Dr 07006
Cedars Rd 07006
Central Ave & Pl 07006
Cherry Ln 07006
Chestnut St 07006
Chestnut Hill Rd 07006
Cleveland Rd & St 07006
Clinton Rd
1-299 07006
99-195 07006
155-155 07007
Colony Dr 07006
Coney Rd 07006
Cooks Ln 07006
Coolidge Ave 07006
Coventry Ln 07006
Crane Ave & St 07006
Crossbrook Ln 07006
Crossing Rd 07006
Cypress Ave 07006
Dalewood Rd 07006
Dana Pl & Rd 07006
Dawson Dr 07006
Debaun Ave 07006
Decamp Ct 07006

Dedrick Pl 07006
Deer Trail Rd 07006
Deerfield Rd 07006
Dillon Rd 07006
Distler Ave 07006
Dodd Rd 07006
Dodge Dr 07006
Dogwood Pl 07006
Domessina Ln 07006
Dorset Cir 07006
Drew Ct 07006
Dupont Dr 07006
Eastern Pkwy 07006
Edgewood Ct 07006
Elizabeth St 07006
Ella Rd 07006
Ellis Pl & Rd 07006
Elm Pl & Rd 07006
Elmwood Ter 07006
Erwin Pl 07006
Espy Rd 07006
Essex Pl & Rd 07006
Estella Ave 07006
Eton Dr 07006
Everett Ct 07006
Evergreen Dr & Rd 07006
Fairfield Ave, Cres, Pl & Rd 07006
Fairmount Rd 07006
Fairview Dr 07006
Farmstead Rd 07006
Farrington St 07006
Feldstone Pl 07006
Fells Manor Rd 07006
Fern Ave 07006
Ferndale Rd 07006
Florence Pl 07006
Forest Ave 07006
Four Seasons Dr 07006
Fox Run 07006
Francine Ave 07006
Francis Pl 07006
Francisco Ave 07006
Franklin Ave 07006
Gates Ave 07006
Gladding Rd 07006
Glen Dr 07006
Glenview Rd 07006
Glenwood Way 07006
Gould Ave & Pl 07006
Grandview Ave & Pl 07006
Gray St 07006
Green Pl 07006
E & W Greenbrook Rd 07006
Grove St 07006
Grover Ln W 07006
Gymoty Rd 07006
Hamilton Dr E 07006
Hampton Ct 07006
Hanford Pl 07006
Hanlon Rd 07006
Harding Ave & Rd 07006
Harrison Ave 07006
Hasemann Ct 07006
Hatfield St 07006
Hawthorne Rd 07006
Hemlock Dr 07006
Henderson Dr 07006
Henry Ave 07006
Herbert Pl 07006
Hickory Dr 07006
High Point Pl 07006
Highfield Ter 07006
Highland Dr 07006
Highview Rd 07006
Hill St 07006
Hillcrest Pl & Rd 07006
Hillside Ave 07006
Holderith Rd 07006
Holiday Dr 07006
Howland Cir 07006
Jackson Pl 07006
Jameson Pl 07006
Jasmine Pl 07006
Jennifer Ct 07006
Johnson Ave 07006

Kanouse Pl 07006
Kenwood Ct 07006
Kirkpatrick Ln 07006
Kirkwood Pl 07006
Klimback Ct 07006
Knoll Pl & Ter 07006
Knollwood Dr & Ter 07006
Kramer Ave 07006
Lakeside Ave 07006
Lane Ave 07006
Laurel Ct & Pl 07006
Leaycraft Ln 07006
Lee Dr 07006
Liddy Pl 07006
Lilac Ct 07006
Lincoln Pl & Ter 07006
Lindsley Rd 07006
Linwood Ter 07006
Lockward Rd 07006
Lombard Dr 07006
Long Meadow Ln 07006
Longview Ave 07006
Lougheed Ave 07006
Magnolia Ln 07006
Main Blvd & St 07006
Maple Dr 07006
Marshall St 07006
Martin Rd 07006
Maywood Ct 07006
Mc Nish Way 07006
Mcdonough Pl 07006
Mckinley Ave 07006
Mcrae Ct 07006
Meadow Ln 07006
Melrose Pl 07006
Memorial Rd 07006
Midvale Ave 07006
Mill St 07006
Miller St 07006
Mitchell Ave 07006
Morris Pl 07006
Mount Herman Way 07006
Mountain Ave & Pl 07006
Myrtle Ave 07006
Natalie Dr 07006
North Ter 07006
Norwood Ter 07006
Nutting Pl 07006
Oak Pl & Rdg 07006
Oak Grove Rd 07006
Oak Ridge Rd 07006
Oakland Ave 07006
Oates Ter 07006
Old Carriage Rd 07006
Old Chester Rd 07006
Old Farm Rd 07006
Old Mill Rd 07006
Orchard Sq 07006
Orient Way 07006
Orton Rd 07006
Overlook Ct & Rd 07006
Oxford Rd 07006
Park Ave, Ln, Pl, St & Ter 07006
Parkview Ave 07006
Parkway E & W 07006
Passaic Ave 07006
Patton Dr 07006
Personette St 07006
Piermont Pl 07006
Pin Oak Rd 07006
Pine Pl 07006
Pine Tree Pl 07006
Pleasant Ave 07006
Prospect St 07006
Provost Sq 07006
Ravine Ave 07006
Redman Ter 07006
Reiher Ct 07006
Richard Ave 07006
Rickland Dr 07006
Ridge Ter 07006
Robin Hill Rd 07006
Roosevelt Ave & Blvd 07006
Rose Ave 07006
Roseland Ave 07006

Rosemere Ave 07006
Rosemont Ct 07006
Rubino Rd 07006
Runnymede Rd 07006
Ryerson Ave 07006
Saint Charles Ave 07006
Sanderson Ave 07006
Sanford Ave 07006
Season Dr 07006
Seymour St 07006
Sheffield Rd 07006
Shenandoah Dr 07006
Skyline Dr 07006
Sleepy Hollow Ct 07006
Smull Ave 07006
Soder Rd 07006
Sparrow Dr 07006
Spring Ln 07006
Springdale Rd 07006
Spruce Rd 07006
Squire Hill Rd 07006
Stanley Rd 07006
Stephanie Dr 07006
Stepping Rdg 07006
Stonybrook Dr & Rd 07006
Summit Dr 07006
Sunnie Ter 07006
Sunset Dr & Rd 07006
Sweetwood Ct 07006
Sylvan Way 07006
Tanglewood Rd 07006
Taylor Dr 07006
Tempesta Ter 07006
Terrace Pl 07006
The Xing 07006
Theresa St 07006
Thomas St 07006
Thrumont Rd 07006
Timber Dr 07006
Tobin Ave 07006
Twin Brook Rd 07006
Vale Pl 07006
Valley View Pl 07006
Van Ness Pl 07006
Veazy St 07006
Veranda Ave 07006
Wakefield Pl 07006
Walden Pl 07006
Ward Pl 07006
Washburn Pl 07006
Washington Ave 07006
Welshman Ct 07006
Westbrook Dr 07006
Westover Ave & Ter 07006
Westview Rd 07006
Westville Ave 07006
Whitaker Pl 07006
White Birch Ter 07006
White Oak Dr 07006
Whitfield St 07006
Wildwood Dr 07006
Willow Ln 07006
Willowbrook Dr 07006
Wilson Ter 07006
Winding Way 07006
Windridge Dr 07006
Woodland Ave & Rd 07006
Woodmere Ct & Rd 07006
Woodrow Pl 07006
Woodside Ave 07006
Yoradona Ave 07006
York Ave & Pl 07006

CAMDEN NJ

General Delivery 08101

POST OFFICE BOXES MAIN OFFICE STATIONS AND BRANCHES

Box No.s
1 - 1104 08101
1171 - 1590 08105
1401 - 93990 08101
95001 - 95002 08105
95008 - 99106 08101

NAMED STREETS

A Walk 08104
Abblett Vlg 08105
Adams Ave 08105
Addison Ave 08108
Akron Ave 08108
Alabama Rd 08104
Albany Ave 08108
E & W Albertson Ave 08108
Alton Ave 08108
W America Rd 08104
Aquarium Dr 08103
Arch St 08102
Ardmore Ave 08108
Argus Rd 08104
Arlington St 08104
Arnold St 08104
Arthur Ave 08105
N & S Atlanta Rd 08104
Atlantic Ave 08104
S Atlantic Ave 08108
Auburn St 08103
B Walk 08104
Bailey St 08102
Baird Blvd
1301-1397 08103
1399-1599 08103
2200-2699 08105
Baldwins Ln 08105
Bank St 08105
Baring St 08103
Barivenw Ave 08105
Bartlett Walk 08104
Battleship Pl 08103
Beach St 08102
Beacon St 08105
Beckett St 08103
Beideman Ave 08105
Bella Pl 08103
Belleview Ave 08103
Belmont Ave 08108
Benson Ct 08103
Benson St
301-600 08103
602-698 08103
2700-3099 08105
Bergen Ave 08105
Berkley Ct 08103
Berkley St
300-799 08103
2600-3299 08105
Berwick St 08105
Birch St 08102
Black Horse Pike 08107
Blaine St 08103
Borton St 08102
Boyd St 08105
Bradford Ave 08108
Bradley Ave 08103
Branch Vlg 08104
Braxton Walk 08104
N Broadway 08102
S Broadway
1-1199 08103
S Broadway
1200-2600 08104
2602-2710 08104
Browning St 08104
Budd St 08104
Bulson St 08104
Buren Ave 08105
Burrwood Ave 08108
Burwood Ave 08105
Byron St 08102
C Walk 08104
Calvert Ave 08107
Cambridge Ave
1-42 08108
44-198 08108
1000-1299 08105

Campbell Pl 08103
Canterbury Cir 08104
Carl Miller Blvd & St 08104
Carlton Ave 08108
Carman St 08105
Carpenter St 08102
Carrol Ct 08104
E Cedar Ave 08107
Cedar St 08102
Centennial Vlg 08105
Center St 08108
Central Ave 08104
Chambers Ave 08103
Charles St 08104
Chase St 08104
Chelton Ave 08104
Cherier Pl 08103
Cherry St 08103
N & S Chesapeake Rd 08104
Chester St 08102
Chestnut Ave 08108
Chestnut Ct 08103
Chestnut St 08103
Church St 08105
Claire St 08103
Clark Walk 08104
Cleveland Ave 08105
E Clinton Ave 08107
Clinton St
100-799 08103
2800-3099 08105
Clover St 08103
Clymer Walk 08104
Coates St 08103
Coldsprings Ave 08107
Collings Ave 08107
Collings Rd 08104
E Collingswood Ave 08107
Colorado Rd 08104
Colt St 08103
N & S Common Rd 08104
Concord Ave 08105
Congress Rd 08104
N & S Constitution Rd 08104
Cooper Plz 08103
Cooper St
1-197 08102
1-3 08108
5-710 08108
199-1199 08102
712-810 08108
1900-2099 08105
Cope St 08104
Copewood St 08103
Cornwall Dr 08107
Cramer St 08105
Crescent Blvd 08107
E Crescent Blvd 08103
Crescent Dr 08104
Crestfair Dr 08104
Crestmont Ave 08103
E & W Crystal Lake Ave 08108
Cushing Rd 08104
Cuthbert Blvd 08107
E Cuthbert Blvd 08108
W Cuthbert Blvd 08108
Cuthbert Cir 08108
D Walk 08104
Dallas Rd 08104
Danahower St 08102
Dauphin St 08103
Davis St 08103
E Davis St 08104
Dayton St 08104
Decatur St 08104
Delaware Ave 08102
S Delaware Ave 08103
Denfield St 08104
Denver Ave 08108
Diamond St 08103
Douglass St 08103
N & S Dudley St 08105
Dupont St 08105
E Walk 08104

Eldridge Ave 08107
Elgin Ave & Cir 08108
Ellery Walk 08104
Elm Ave
1-99 08108
1100-1380 08107
Elm St 08102
Emerald Ave 08108
Emerald St 08104
Emma St 08103
Empire Ave 08103
Erie St 08102
Essex Rd 08104
Estaugh Ave 08108
Euclid Ave 08103
Eutaw Ave 08105
Evans St 08103
Everett St 08104
Evergreen Ave 08108
F Walk 08104
Fairfax Dr 08105
Fairmount St 08104
Fairview Ct & St 08104
Farragut Ave 08105
Federal St
1-97 08103
99-1299 08103
1300-1398 08105
1400-4169 08105
4171-4199 08105
Felton St 08103
Fenwick Rd 08104
Fern Ave 08108
Fern St 08102
Ferry Ave
1-99 08103
100-498 08104
500-1799 08104
1801-2199 08104
Filmore St 08104
Florence St 08104
Floyd Walk 08104
Fountain Ave 08105
Fremont Ave 08105
French Ave 08108
Friends St 08102
N Front St 08102
S Front St
1100-1199 08103
1200-1299 08104
G Walk 08104
Galindez Ct 08102
Garden Ave 08105
Garfield Ave 08105
Geneva Ave 08108
Gerry Walk 08104
Girard Pl 08103
Glendale Ave 08108
Glenwood Ave 08108
Gordon Ter 08104
Grand Ave 08105
Grant Ave 08107
Grant St 08102
Green St 08104
Greenwood Ave 08103
E Greenwood Ave 08107
Guilford Ave 08108
Gwinett Walk 08104
H Walk 08104
Haddon Ave
1-344 08108
101-697 08103
346-360 08108
699-1999 08103
Haines St 08103
Hampton Rd 08108
Hancock Walk 08104
Harbor Blvd 08103
Harding Ave 08108
Harrison Ave 08105
Hart Walk 08104
Hartford Rd 08104
Hayes Ave 08105
Hazel Ave & Ter 08108
Hazelton Ct 08104
Heather Rd 08107

Hedgerow Ct 08107
Hemlock Walk 08104
Henry St 08103
High St 08105
Highland Ave
200-300 08108
302-304 08108
3001-3799 08105
Hillside Ave 08105
Holcaine St 08104
E Holly Ave 08107
Hope St 08105
Howard St 08102
Howe St 08104
Howell St 08105
Hudson St 08103
Hull Rd 08104
Hunter Dr & St 08104
I Walk 08104
Idaho Rd 08104
Independence Rd 08104
Ironside Rd 08104
J Walk 08104
Jackson St 08104
Jasper St 08104
Jefferson St 08104
John F Gerry Plz 08102
Johnson Ave 08107
Joint Aly 08103
K Walk 08104
Kaighns Ave 08103
Kansas Rd 08104
Kearsarge Rd 08104
Kenwood Ave 08103
Kimber St 08102
King Ave 08108
Kolo St 08104
Kossuth St 08104
Kraft Ave & Ct 08107
L Walk 08104
Lakeshore Dr
901-1197 08108
1000-1052 08104
1054-1399 08104
Langham Ave 08103
Lansdowne Ave 08104
Larch St 08102
Laurel Ave 08107
Lawnside Ave 08108
Lawrence St 08102
Lee Walk 08104
Lees Ln
1-299 08107
500-798 08108
Lemuel Ave 08105
Leonard Ave 08105
Lester Ter 08104
Liberty St 08104
Lincoln Ave 08105
E Linden Ave 08108
Linden St 08102
Lindis Farne Ave 08108
Line St
200-1100 08103
1102-1198 08103
2900-2999 08105
Linwood Ave 08108
Linwood St 08102
Livingston Walk 08104
Lockland Ave 08108
Locust Ave 08108
Locust St 08103
Lois Ave 08105
Louis St
1000-1199 08103
1200-1699 08104
Lovells Ln 08108
Lowell St 08104
M Walk 08104
Macarthur Blvd 08108
Macarthur Dr 08104
Magnolia Ave 08103
Main St 08102
Mansion Ave 08108
Maple Ave 08108
Maple Walk 08104

Marion St 08103
Market St
1-5 08102
7-400 08102
401-401 08101
401-899 08102
402-898 08102
Marlton Ave 08105
Maryland St 08104
Master St 08104
Maurice St 08103
Mechanic St 08104
Melrose Ave 08108
Memorial Ave 08103
Merivens St 08104
Merrick Ave 08108
Merriel Ave 08105
N & S Merrimac Rd 08104
Mickle Blvd 08103
Mickle St 08105
Middleton Walk 08104
Miller St 08104
Minnesota Rd 08104
Mitchell St 08105
Monitor Rd 08104
Morgan Blvd & St 08104
Morrison St 08105
Morse St 08105
Morton St 08104
Mount Ephraim Ave
101-597 08103
599-1199 08103
1200-2799 08104
2800-3298 08104
2801-3299 08104
Mount Vernon St 08103
Mulford St 08104
Myrtle Ave 08105
N Walk 08104
New St 08103
New Hampshire Ave 08104
New Jersey Ave 08108
New South St 08105
New West St 08105
Newport St 08104
Newton Ave
60-76 08103
78-1099 08103
1100-1399 08107
1101-1199 08103
Newton Ct 08107
Niagara Rd 08104
Norris St 08104
North St 08102
Norwood Ave & Ter 08108
Oak Walk 08104
E Oakland Ave 08107
E, N, S & W Octagon Rd 08104
Old White Horse Pike 08103
Olive St 08104
Olympia Rd 08104
Oneida Ave 08108
Orchard St 08103
Oriental Ave 08108
Ormond Ave 08103
E Ormond Ave 08107
E Park Ave 08107
Park Blvd 08103
Park Ct 08108
Park Dr 08104
S Park Dr 08108
Park Ter 08108
Patton St 08104
Pavonia St 08104
Pearl St 08102
Pelham Pl 08105
Penn Ave 08108
Penn St 08102
Pershing St 08104
Pfeiffer St 08105
Phillips St 08104
Pierce Ave 08105
Pine St 08103
Pleasant St 08105
Point St 08102
Polk Ave 08105
Pontanch St 08102
Porter Rd 08104
Powell Ct 08104
Primas Ct 08104
Princess Ave 08103
Princeton Ave 08103
Pulaski St 08104
Rand St 08105
E Randolph St 08105
Raritan St 08105
Ray St 08102
Raymond St 08102
Reeve Ave 08108
Reeves Ave 08105
Remington Ave 08105
Republic Rd 08104
River Ave & Rd 08105
Riverside Dr 08103
Roanoke Rd 08104
Roberts St 08103
Rodney Walk 08104
Romana Gonzalez St 08103
Roosevelt Plz 08102
Roosevelt Way 08104
Rose St
1100-1199 08103
1300-1499 08104
Rosedale Ave 08105
Ross St 08103
Rowe St 08105
Royal Ave 08105
Royal Court Ln 08103
Royden St
300-799 08103
2900-3099 08105
Rutledge Walk 08104
Saginaw Ave 08108
Saint John St 08103
Salem St 08104
Saunders St 08105
Sayres Ave 08104
Segal St 08102
Senate Ct 08103
Sewell St 08105
Shady Ln 08108
Sheridan St 08104
Sherman Ave 08105
Silver St 08103
Spruce St 08103
State St 08102
E State St 08105
Station Dr 08104
Stevens Ct 08103
Stevens St
300-599 08103
2700-3099 08105
Stewart St 08105
Stokes Ave 08108
Stoy Ave 08108
Stratford Ave 08108
Strawbridge Ave 08108
Summit St 08102
Sumter Rd 08104
Sunset Ln 08108
Sycamore Ct & St 08103
Sylvan St 08104
Teal Ct 08104
Tenford Ct 08104
Terrace Ave 08105
Thompson St 08105
Thorn St 08104
Thorne St 08103
Thurman St 08104
Tilghman Dr 08104
Tioga St 08104
Toledo Ave 08108
Trent Rd 08104
Trenton Ave 08103
Tuckahoe Rd 08104
Tulip St 08104
Tyler St 08105
Utica Ave 08108
Van Buren St 08104
Vesper Ave 08108
Vesper Blvd 08103
Vickerth St 08103
Vine St 08102
Viola St 08104
Virginia Ave 08108
Wainwright St 08104
Waldorf Ave 08105
Walnut Ave 08107
E Walnut Ave 08108
W Walnut Ave 08108
Walnut St 08103
Walton Ave 08108
Ware St 08104
Warsaw St 08104
Washington Ct 08103
Washington St
300-799 08103
2701-2797 08105
2799-2999 08105
3001-3099 08105
Wasp Rd 08104
Watson St 08105
Wayne Ave 08105
Webster St 08104
West Dr 08108
West St 08103
Westfield Ave & Gdns 08105
Westminster Ave 08105
Westmont Ave 08108
Wheatland Ct 08104
Whipple Walk 08104
White St 08103
White Horse Pike
601-1199 08107
1846-1848 08103
Whitman Ave 08104
Wildwood Ave 08103
Willard St 08102
Williams St 08103
Willow Walk 08104
Wilmont Ave 08105
Windsor Ave 08108
Winslow St 08104
Winthrop Walk 08104
Woodland Ave
500-999 08104
6201-6299 08105
Wright Ave 08103
York St 08102
Yorkship Rd & Sq 08104

NUMBERED STREETS

N 2nd St 08102
500-1199 08103
1200-1299 08104
2nd Street Walk 08103
N 3rd St 08102
S 3rd St
300-698 08103
1200-1999 08104
N 4th St 08102
300-1199 08103
1200-2099 08104
N 5th St 08102
S 5th St 08103
N 6th St 08102
S 6th St
201-397 08103
399-1199 08103
1200-1999 08104
2001-2499 08104
N 7th St 08102
400-1199 08103
1500-2499 08104
N 8th St 08102
500-1199 08103
1400-2699 08104
N 9th St 08102
S 9th St
801-1097 08103
1200-2449 08104
N 10th St 08102
S 10th St
201-297 08103
1200-2399 08104
N 11th St 08102
S 11th St 08103
S 12th St 08104
N & S 17th 08105
N 18th St 08105
N 19th St 08105
N & S 20th 08105
N 21st St 08105
N 22nd St 08105
N 23rd St 08105
N & S 24th 08105
N 25th St 08105
N & S 26th 08105
N & S 27th 08105
N & S 28th 08105
N & S 29th 08105
N & S 30th 08105
N 31st St 08105
N & S 32nd 08105
N & S 33rd 08105
N & S 34th 08105
N & S 35th 08105
N & S 36th 08105
S 38th St 08105
S 41st St 08105

CHERRY HILL NJ

General Delivery 08034

POST OFFICE BOXES MAIN OFFICE STATIONS AND BRANCHES

Box No.s
161 - 994 08003
1001 - 6000 08034
8001 - 8632 08002
9004 - 9004 08003

NAMED STREETS

Aaron Ct 08002
Abbey Rd 08003
Abinger Ln 08003
Abington Rd & Ter 08034
Allison Dr 08003
Ambler Rd 08002
Amherst Ct 08003
Anders Dr 08003
Andrew Ln 08003
Ann Dr 08003
Annapolis Ln 08003
Antietam Rd 08034
Anvil Ct 08003
Apley Dr 08003
Appley Ct 08002
Aqua Ln 08034
Aqueduct Ln 08002
Arbor Ave 08034
Arthur Dr 08003
Artisan Way 08003
Ashbrook Rd 08034
Ashford Rd 08003
Ashland Ave 08003
Ashley Ct 08003
Astor Dr 08003
Astoria Blvd 08003
Atlantic Ave 08003
Autumn Ct & Ln 08003
Avon Rd 08034
Badger Ln 08003
Bala Rd 08002
Baldwin Rd 08003
Balfield Ter 08003
Balsam Rd 08003
Bamford Ct & Rd 08003
Bancroft Rd 08034
Banner Rd 08003
Barbara Dr 08003
Barby Ln 08003
Barclay Ct, Ln & Walk 08034
Barclay Pavilion E & W 08034
Barclay Shopping Ctr 08034
Barcroft Dr 08034
Barlow Ave 08002
Bayberry Ct 08003
Beaverbrook Dr 08034
Bedford Ave 08002
Beechwood Ave 08002
Beekman Pl 08002
Beideman Ave 08002
Bel Aire Ave 08034
Belle Arbor Dr 08034
Bellows Ln 08002
Belmont Dr 08002
Bentwood Dr 08034
Berkshire Ave & Ct 08002
Berlin Rd
1-39 08034
41-1299 08034
1301-1401 08034
1400-1498 08003
1500-1999 08003
2001-2999 08003
Beverly Ter 08003
Birch Dr 08003
Birch St 08002
Birchwood Ct 08003
Birchwood Park Dr N & S 08003
Bishops View Cir 08002
Black Baron Dr 08034
Black Latch Ln 08003
Blossom Ct 08003
Blue Bell Dr 08002
Blue Jay Ln 08003
Bobwhite Dr 08003
Bortons Mill Ct & Rd 08034
N & S Bowling Green Dr 08003
Bowood Dr 08034
Box Hill Dr 08003
Brace Rd 08034
Brade Ln 08034
Bradford Rd 08034
Brae Ln 08003
Branch Ct & Dr 08003
Breeders Cup Dr 08002
Brentwood Ave 08002
Brian Dr 08003
Briar Ln 08002
Briar Rd 08034
Brick Rd 08003
Bridle Ct 08003
Brighton Rd 08034
Brittany Ln 08003
Brompton Ct, Dr & Pl 08003
Brondesbury Dr & Pl 08003
W Brook Dr 08003
Brookdale Ct & Dr 08034
N & S Brookfield Ct & Rd 08034
Brookline Ave 08002
Brookmead Dr 08034
Brookville Dr 08003
Browning Ln 08003
Bruce Rd & Ter 08034
Bryant Rd 08003
Bryn Mawr Ave 08002
Buckingham Pl 08003
Bucknell Dr 08034
Bunker Hill Dr 08003
Burning Tree Rd 08034
Burnt Mill Rd 08003
Burroughs Mill Cir & Ct 08002
Buttonwood Dr 08003
Buxton Rd 08003
Byron Ter 08003
Caldwell Rd 08034
Cambridge Rd 08034
Cameo Ct & Dr 08003
Candlewyck Way 08003
Cantor Trl 08002
Capshire Dr 08003
Cardinal Ln 08003
Cardinal Lake Dr 08003
Cardone Ave 08003
Carlisle Ave 08002
Carlton Rd 08034
Carnegie Plz 08003
Carol Ct 08002
Carolina Ave 08003
Carriage House Ct 08003
Castle Dr 08003
Cedarbrook Rd 08034
Center Ave 08003
Chalet Dr 08003
Chambers Ave 08002
Champions 08002
Chandler Ter 08034
Chanticleer 08003
Chapel Ave E 08034
Chapel Ave W 08002
Charlann Cir 08003
Charles Ln 08003
Charleston Rd 08034
Chateau Dr 08003
Chaucer Pl 08003
Chelsea Ct 08003
Chelten Pkwy 08034
Cherry Hill Blvd 08002
Cherry Parke 08002
Cherry Tree Ct & Ln 08002
Cherrywood Ct 08003
Chestnut St & Ter 08002
Chimney Ln 08003
Christian Ln 08002
Church Rd
200-3599 08002
4001-4099 08034
Churchill Rd 08034
Churchill Downs Way 08002
Circle Ln 08003
Citation Rd 08002
Clark Dr 08034
Clemson Rd 08034
S Cleveland Ave 08002
W Cliff Dr 08003
Clover Ave 08034
Coach Ln 08002
Cobble Creek Cir 08003
Cobblestone Ln & Rd 08003
Cohasset Ln 08003
Coleman Ave 08034
Coles Ave 08002
Colgate Dr 08034
Collage Ct & Ln 08003
Collins Dr 08003
Colmar Rd 08002
Colonial Ln 08003
Columbia Blvd 08002
Colwick Rd 08002
Computer Dr 08003
Concord Ln 08003
Connecticut Ave 08002
Conwell Ave 08002
Coolidge Rd 08002
Cooper Ave 08002
Cooper Landing Rd 08002
Cooper Run Dr 08003
Cooperskill Rd 08034
S Cornell Ave 08002
Cornwall Rd 08034
Cotswold Ln 08034
Country Walk 08003
Country Club Ct, Dr & Pl 08003
Courtland Rd 08034
Coventry Ct 08002
Covered Bridge Ct & Rd 08034
Cranberry Ct 08002
Crane Dr 08003
S Cranford Rd 08003
Crescent Way 08002
Crestbrook Ave 08003
Crestview Dr 08003
Cricket Ln 08003
Crofton Commons 08034
Crooked Ln 08034
Cropwell Ct & Rd 08003
Crown Point Ln 08003
Croyden Dr 08003
Cuffys Ln 08003
Cunningham Ln 08003
Curtis Ave 08002
Cuthbert Blvd 08002
Cypress Ln 08003
Dale Ave 08002
Dale Ct 08003
Dalton Ter 08003
Darby Ln 08002
Darien Dr 08003
Dartmouth Rd 08034
Daytona Ave 08034
Dean Ln 08034
Deer Rd 08034
Deerfield Dr 08034
Deland Ave 08034
Delaware Ave 08002
Delicious Way 08003
Dell Dr 08003
Delwood Rd 08002
Derby Ct
245-299 08003
4601-4699 08002
Dewberry Ln 08003
Diamond Spring Ave 08003
Dickens Ct 08034
Dickinson Ave 08002
Dobbs Ln 08034
Dobson Ln 08003
Doe Ln 08034
Dogwood Dr 08003
Donahue Ave 08002
Doncaster Ct & Rd 08003
Dorado Dr 08034
Doral Dr 08003
Doris Dr 08003
Dorset Rd 08003
Douglas Dr 08034
Dove Ln 08003
Dover St 08002
Downing St 08003
Downs Dr 08003
Drake Rd & Ter 08034
Dressage Ct 08003
Drew Ct 08034
Dublin Ln 08003
Dudley Ave 08002
Dumas Rd 08003
Dunbarton Rd 08003
Eagle Ln 08003
Eaton Way 08003
Echo Ct & Pl 08003
Eddy Ln 08002
Edgemoor Rd & Ter 08034
Edgewood Dr 08003
Edison Ave 08002
Edison Rd 08034
Edward Ave 08002
Elbow Ln 08003
Eleanor Ter 08003
Elkins Rd & Ter 08034
Ellis Ave 08003
Elma Ave 08002
Elmhurst Ave 08034
Embassy Ct & Dr 08002
En Provence Ct 08003
Equestrian Ln 08003
Essex Ave 08002
Esterbrook Ln 08003
Europa Blvd & Ct 08003
Evans Ln 08003
Everett Ave 08003
Evergreen Ave 08002
E & W Evesham Rd 08003
Executive Campus 08002
Exton Cir 08003
Fairfax Ave 08003
Fairhaven Ct & Dr 08003
Farmhouse Ct & Ln 08002
Farmington Rd 08034
Farrell Ave 08002
Fatima Ct 08003
Fawn Dr 08034
Fenwick Ct & Rd 08034

Street	ZIP
Fern Ave	08034
Fieldstone Rd	08034
E & W Fireside Cir, Ct & Ln	08003
Firethorne Rd	08003
Folkestone Way	08034
Forage Ln	08003
Forest Rd	08034
Forest Hill Dr	08003
Forge Ln	08002
S Forge Ln	08002
Forge Rd	08034
Fort Duquesne Dr	08003
Fountain Ct	08034
Fox Chase Ln	08034
Fox Hollow Dr	08003
Francine Dr	08003
Franklin Ave	08002
Friendship Ln	08002
Fries Ln	08003
Frontage Rd	08034
Fullwood Rd	08034
Fulton St	08002
Furlong Dr	08003
Gainsboro Rd	08003
Gallery Ln	08003
Galloping Hill Rd	08003
Galway Ln	08003
Garden Ave	08003
Garden Park Blvd	08002
Garden State Dr	08002
Gardner Rd	08034
Garfield Ave	08002
Garwood Dr & Pl	08003
E Gate Dr	08034
SE Gate Dr	08003
W Gate Dr	08034
Gatehouse Ln	08003
Gately Ct	08002
Gatewood Rd	08003
Georgia Ave	08002
Gere Ter	08002
Glen Ln	08002
Glenperth Ln	08003
Glenview Pl	08034
Glenwood Ave	08002
Graham Ave	08002
Grandstand Way	08002
W Grant Ave	08002
Granville Dr	08034
Grass Rd	08034
Gravel Bend Rd	08034
Graydon Ave	08003
N Green Acre Dr	08003
Greenbriar Rd	08034
Greene Ln	08003
Greenleigh Ct	08002
Greensward Ln	08002
Greentree Rd & Way	08003
Greenvale Ct & Rd	08034
Greenwood Rd	08034
Gregory Ct	08034
Grove St	08002
Guilford Rd	08003
Gwen Ct	08003
Haddonfield Rd	08002
Haddontowne Ct	08034
Hadleigh Ct, Dr & Ter	08003
Hampton Rd	08002
Hanover Ave	08002
Hapenny Dr	08034
Haral Pl	08034
Harding Ave	08002
Harrison Ave	08002
Harrowgate Dr	08003
Hart Rd	08034
Harvard Ave	08002
Harvest Rd	08002
Hassemer Ave & Rd	08002
Hastings Rd	08034
Haverford Rd	08002
Haverhill Ave	08002
Hawthorne Ct & Dr	08003
Heartwood Dr & Rd	08003
Heather Ln	08003
Hedgerow Dr	08002
Hedy Ave	08002
Helena Ave	08002
Henfield Ave & Ter	08003
Henszey Ln	08003
Heritage Ct & Rd	08034
Heron Rd	08003
Hessian Way	08003
Hialeah Dr	08002
Hickory Ln	08003
Hidden Ln	08003
W High Ridge Rd	08003
Highgate Ct & Ln	08003
Highland Ave	08002
Hillcroft Ln	08034
Hille Dr	08003
Hillside Dr	08003
Hilltop Ct & Dr	08003
Hinchman Ave	08002
Hoffman Ave	08003
W Hoffman Ave	08002
Holden Rd	08034
Hollis Ave	08002
Holly St	08002
Holly Glen Dr	08034
Hollywood Ave & Pl	08002
Horse Shoe Ct	08034
Howard Rd	08034
Howard Johnson Rd	08034
Hunters Dr	08003
Huntington Dr	08003
Ice House Ln	08034
Imperial Dr	08003
Independence Ln	08003
Indian King Dr	08003
Inskeep Ct	08003
Iris Rd	08003
Iron Master Rd	08034
Isaac Ln	08002
Ivins Ave	08002
Ivy Ln	08002
Jackson Rd	08002
Jade Ln	08002
Jamaica Dr	08002
James Run	08002
Jefferson Ave	08002
Jerome Ave	08002
Jodi Ct	08003
Johns Rd	08034
Jonathan Ct	08003
Jordan Ct	08003
Junewood Dr	08003
Juniper Dr	08003
Justa Ln	08003
Karen Dr	08003
Kassner Ave	08003
Kate Ct	08003
Katherine Ave	08002
Kay Ave & Dr E, S & W	08034
Kaywood Ln	08034
Keats Pl	08003
Kenilworth Ave	08002
Kennebec Rd	08002
Kent Rd	08002
Kenwood Dr	08034
Kevin Ct	08034
Keystone Ave	08003
Kilburn Ct & Dr	08003
King Ave	08002
King George Rd	08034
Kings Dr	08003
Kings Hwy N	08034
Kings Hwy S	08034
Kings Croft	08034
Kings Point Rd	08003
Kingsdale Ave	08003
Kingsley Rd	08034
Kingsport Rd	08034
Kingston Dr & Rd	08034
Kingswood Ct	08034
Kipling Rd	08003
Kitty Hawk Rd	08034
Knight Rd	08034
Knights Pl	08003
Knoll Ln	08002
Knollwood Dr	08002
Kresson Rd	
1-699	08034
700-1926	08003
1928-1998	08003
Lafayette Ln	08003
Lafferty Dr	08002
Lake Dr E & W	08002
Lakeside Ave	08003
Lakeview Ct, Dr, Holw & Pl	08003
Lamp Post Ln	08003
Landover Ln	08002
Lane Of Trees	08003
Lantern Ln	08002
S Lantern Ln	08034
Lark Ln	08003
Larkspur Rd	08003
Larwin Rd	08034
Latches Ln	08003
Laurel Pl & Ter	08002
Laurel Hill Dr	08003
Laurelbrook Rd	08034
Lavender Hill Dr	08003
Lavenham Ct & Rd	08003
Lawrence Ave	08002
Lee Ann Rd	08034
Leith Hill Dr	08003
Lenape Rd	08002
Lewis Ave	08003
Lexington Ct	08002
Liberty Ln	08002
Liberty Bell Dr	08003
Lilac Ln	08003
Lily Ln	08003
Lincoln Ave N & S	08002
Linden Ave	08002
Linden St	08002
Linderman Ave	08002
Lisa Ln	08003
Lloyd Ave	08002
Locust Grove Rd	08003
Logan Dr	08034
Longfellow Dr	08003
Longstone Dr	08003
Longwood Ave	08002
Lourdes Ct	08003
Lowber Dr	08034
Lucerne Blvd & Ct	08003
Lucille Ln	08003
Lynford Ct & Dr	08003
Mackin Dr	08002
N Madison Ave	08002
Main St	08002
Maine Ave	08002
Mall Dr	08002
Manning Ln	08003
Manor House Ct & Dr	08003
Mansfield Blvd N & S	08034
Maple Ave & Ter	08002
Maplebrook Ct	08034
Mara Ct	08002
Market St	08003
Marlboro Ave	08002
Marlkress Rd	08003
Marlowe Rd	08003
Marlton Pike E	
1-3	08034
5-1499	08034
1501-1699	08034
1701-1717	08003
1719-2106	08003
2108-2116	08003
Marlton Pike W	08002
Marshall Ave	08002
Martin Ave	08002
Massachusetts Ave	08002
Mayflower Ln	08003
Mcgill Ave	08002
Mcintosh Rd	08003
Mckinley Rd	08002
Mcphelin Ave	08034
Meadow Ln	08003
Media Rd	08002
Meeting House Ln	08002
Melody Ln	08002
Melrose Ave	08003
Mercer St	08002
Merchant St	08002
Merion Ave	08003
Merion Rd	08002
Meryl Ln	08002
Mews Ct & Ln	08003
E Miami Ave	08034
W Miami Ave	08002
Middle Acre Ln	08003
Midway Dr	08034
Miller Ave	08002
Millhouse Ln	08003
Millstream Dr	08002
Mimosa Dr & Pl	08003
Missouri Ave	08002
Mona Ct	08003
Monmouth Dr	08002
N Monroe Ave	08002
Montana Ave	08002
Monterey Ave	08003
Moore Ave	08034
Morningside Dr	08003
Morrill Ter	08003
Morris Dr & Pl	08003
Mount Carmel Ct	08003
Mount Pleasant Way	08034
Munn Ave & Ln	08034
Murray Ave	08002
Nantucket Dr	08034
Narduc Ave	08002
Narragansett Dr	08002
Nathaniel Ave	08003
Nature Dr	08003
Nevada Ave	08002
New Hampshire Ave	08002
New York Ave	08002
Newell Ave	08034
Niamoa Dr	08003
Northwood Ave	08002
Oak Ave	08002
Oakdale Rd	08034
Oakley Ct & Dr	08003
Oakview Ave	08002
Ocean Ave	08003
Ogden Ave	08002
Old Carriage Rd	08034
Old Cuthbert Rd	08034
Old Marlton Pike	08003
Old Orchard Rd	08003
Old Salem Ct & Rd	08034
Old Town Cir & Rd	08034
Olde Springs Ln	08034
Olive St	08002
N Olney Ave	08003
Orchard Ave	08002
Orchard Ln	
114-114	08003
157-201	08003
1400-1499	08002
Orchid Ln	08002
Oregon Ave	08002
Orlando Rd & Ter	08034
E Ormond Ave	08034
W Ormond Ave	08002
Overbrook Dr	08002
Owl Ct, Ln & Pl	08003
Oxford St	08002
Pacer Ct	08002
Paddock Way	08034
Paige Ct	08002
Palmwood Ave	08003
Pams Path	08034
Papermill Rd	08003
Park Blvd	
2-6	08002
100-100	08034
200-598	08002
600-1799	08002
1801-2099	08002
Park Cir	08034
Park Dr	08002
Park Rd	08034
Park Lane Blvd	08002
Park Place Dr	08002
Parkwood Rd	08034
Parnell Dr	08003
Partree Rd	08003
E Partridge Ct & Ln	08003
Pawtucket Dr	08003
Peacock Dr	08003
Pearlcroft Rd	08034
Pebble Ln	08002
Pelham Ct & Rd	08034
Pembroke Ct	08003
Penchind Rd	08034
Pendleton Dr	08003
Penn Ave	08002
Pennsylvania Ave	08002
Peppermill Dr	08002
Perina Blvd	08003
Perot Ave	08003
Petitt Ave	08002
Philellena Rd	08034
Philmar Ave	08003
Pimlico Pl	08002
Pin Oak Ln	08003
Pine Valley Rd	08034
Pinebrook Rd	08034
Pippin Cir	08003
Pleasant Dr	08003
Plumm Ct	08002
Plymouth Dr	08034
Plymouth Pl	08002
Plymouth Rd	08034
Plymouth Rock Dr	08003
Point Ct & Dr	08003
Pointview Ave	08003
Polo Ct	08003
Poplar Ct & Ter	08002
Portsmouth Rd	08034
Pratt Rd	08002
Preakness Ct	08002
Preston Rd	08034
Prince Dr	08003
Princess Rd	08034
N Princeton Ave	08002
Promenade Ct	08003
Provence Dr	08003
Provincetown Cir & Rd	08034
Purdue Pl	08034
Queen Ann Rd	08003
Queens Ave	08034
Queens Pl	08002
Rabbit Run Rd	08003
Railroad Blvd	08003
Ramble Rd	08034
Ramsgate Rd	08003
Randle Ct & Dr	08034
Randy Ln	08003
Ranoldo Ter	08034
Ravenswood Way	08003
Red Oak Dr	08003
Redstone Rdg	08034
Redwood Ave	08002
Regency Ct	08002
Regent Rd	08003
Renaissance Dr	08003
Rhode Island Ave	08002
Richard Rd	08034
Ridge Cir & Rd	08002
E, N & W Riding Dr & Rd	08003
Roanoke Rd	08003
Roberts Dr	08003
Robin Lake Dr	08003
Robwill Pass	08034
Rockhill Rd	08003
Rockingham Rd	08034
Roland Ct	08003
Rolling Ln	08003
Rooftree Rd	08003
Roosevelt Dr	08002
Rose Ln	08002
Roumfort Ave	08034
Route 38	08002
Royal Oak Ave	08002
Royce Ct	08003
Rue Du Boise	08003
Russell Ter	08034
Russet Dr	08003
Rutgers Rd	08034
Rydal Rd	08034
Rye Rd	08003
Rymill Pl, Run & Ter	08003
Saddle Ln	08002
Saddlebrook Ct	08003
Saddlehorn Dr	08003
Saint Anthony Ct	08003
Saint Davids Rd	08002
Saint James Ave	08002
Saint Johns Dr	08034
Saint Martins Rd	08002
Saint Marys Dr	08003
Saint Michael Ct	08003
Saint Moritz Ct & Ln	08003
Saint Vincent Ct	08003
Salem Rd	08034
Salsbury Rd	08034
Sandringham Pl, Rd & Ter	08003
Santa Anita Pl	08002
Saratoga Dr	08002
Sawmill Ct & Rd	08034
Saxby Ter	08003
Sayer Ave	08002
Scattergood Rd	08003
School Ln	08002
Sea Gull Ln	08003
Secretariat Ln	08002
Sequoia Rd	08003
Severn Ave	08002
Sharrowvale Rd	08034
Sheffield Rd	08034
Shelly Ln	08034
Shepherd Rd	08034
Sherbrooke Ct	08003
Sheridan Ave	08002
Sherry Way	08034
Sherwood Ave	08002
Signal Hill Rd	08003
Silver Hill Rd	08002
Silvertop Ln	08002
Simi Ct	08003
Skylark Ln	08003
Sleepy Hollow Pl	08003
Snowden Pl	08003
Snyder Ave & Ct	08002
Society Hill Blvd	08003
Southview Dr	08034
Southwood Dr	08003
Split Rail Ct & Dr	08034
Split Rock Dr	08003
Spring Ct & Rd	08003
Spring House Ct & Rd	08002
Spring Mill Ln	08003
Springdale Rd	08003
Spruce St	08002
Squire Ln	08003
Staffordshire Rd	08003
Stagecoach Rd	08034
Stanford Rd	08034
Starling Ln	08003
State St	08002
Steeplechase Ct	08003
Stonebridge Rd	08003
Stonehenge Rd	08003
Stratford Ct	08002
Strathmore Dr	08003
Sudely Green Ct	08003
Suffolk Ct	08034
Suffolk Dr	08002
Summer Pl	08003
Sunnybrook Rd	08034
Surrey Ct	08034
Surrey Rd	08002
Sussex Ave	08003
Swallow Dr	08003
N & S Syracuse Dr	08034
Tamara Ct	08002
E Tampa Ave	08034
W Tampa Ave	08002
Tanforan Dr	08002
Tarlton Ct	08034
Tarrington Ct & Rd	08034
Tavistock	08034
Teaberry Dr	08034
Teak Ct	08003
Tearose Ln	08003
Tendring Rd	08003
Thackery Ln	08003
The Woods	08003
The Woods Ii	08003
Thomas St	08002
Thoreau Ct	08003
Thornhill Rd	08003
Ticonderoga Ln	08003
Timothy Ct	08034
Todd Ct	08003
Township Ln	08002
Tracey Ter	08003
Tunbridge Rd	08003
Tuvira Ln	08003
Tyler Ave	08002
Unincou Dr	08003
S Union Ave	08002
Utah Ave	08002
Uxbridge	08034
Valley Pl	08002
Valley Run Dr	08002
E, N & W Valleybrook Ct & Rd	08034
Vanessa Ct	08003
Vassar Ave	08002
Vermont Ave	08002
Versailles Blvd	08003
Victor Ave	08002
Viking Ln	08003
Villagio Ct	08003
Virginia Ave	08002
Wade Dr	08034
Wagon Ln	08002
Walden Ct & Way	08003
Walkaway Ln	08003
Walt Whitman Blvd	08003
Ward Ter	08003
Warfield Rd	08034
Warren Ave	08002
S Washington Ave	08002
Waverly Rd	08003
Wayland Rd	08034
Wayne Ave & Rd	08002
Wayside Ct & Dr	08034
Weather Vane Dr	08002
Webster Ave	08002
Wedgewood Cir	08003
Weld Ave	08002
Wellesley Ct	08003
Wesley Ave	08002
Westbury Dr	08003
Westminster Ave	08002
Weston Ct & Dr	08003
Westover Dr	08034
Westwood Ave	08002
Wexford Ct & Dr	08003
Wheelwright Ln	08003
Whirlaway Ln	08002
Whitby Ct & Rd	08003
White Birch Ct	08003
White Oak Ct & Rd	08034
White Pond Ct	08003
Whitemarsh Way	08034
Whitman Ave	08002
Wicklow Ct	08003
Wilbur Ave	08002
Wilderness Dr & Way	08003
Willard Ave	08034
Williams St	08002
Willis Ave	08002
Willow Ct	08003
Willow Way	08034
Willow Way Ct & Pl	08034
Willowbrook Rd	08034
Willowdale Dr	08003
Wilson Rd	08002
Windgate Rd	08003
Winding Dr	08003
Winding Way	08002
Windsor Cir, Ct, Dr & Mews	08002
Winesap Rd	08003
Winston Way	08034
Winter Pl	08003
Wisteria Ave	08002
Woodbury Dr	08003

Woodcrest Rd 08003
Woodfield Ct 08003
Woodland Ave 08002
N & S Woodleigh Dr 08003
N & S Woodstock Dr 08034
Wyndmoor Rd 08034
Wynnwood Ave 08002
Yale Ave 08002
Yardley Rd 08034
Yearling Ct 08002
York Rd 08034
Yorkshire Rd 08034

NUMBERED STREETS

1st Ave 08003
2nd Ave 08003
3rd Ave 08002
E 3rd Ave 08003
4th Ave 08003
5th Ave 08003
200-299 08002
E 6th Ave 08003
W 6th Ave
2-4 08003
200-299 08002
7th Ave 08003
9 Acre Ct 08003

CLIFTON NJ

General Delivery 07015

POST OFFICE BOXES MAIN OFFICE STATIONS AND BRANCHES

Box No.s
1 - 499 07015
501 - 700 07012
701 - 899 07015
901 - 1137 07014
1201 - 1299 07012
1301 - 2999 07015
3001 - 4437 07012
4700 - 6476 07015

NAMED STREETS

Abbe Ln 07013
Ackerman Ave 07011
Adams St 07011
Adams Ter 07013
Addison Pl 07012
Albury Rd 07013
Alfred St 07013
Allwood Pl 07012
Allwood Rd
1-171 07014
172-1099 07012
Althea St 07013
Alvin Ct 07012
Alyea Ter 07011
Amato Ln 07013
Anderson Dr 07013
Ann St 07013
Annabelle Ave 07012
Anton St 07014
Arcadia Ln 07013
Ardmore Ave
1-30 07012
31-99 07014
Arlington Ave & Pl 07011
Arthur St 07011
Ash St 07011
Athenia Ave 07013
Atkins Ct 07013
Atlantic Way 07012
Austin Pl 07014
Autumn St 07013
Avondale Ave 07013
Bakers Ct 07011
Balsam Ct 07014
Barbara Dr 07013
Barberry Ln 07013
Barkley Ave 07011
Barnsdale Rd 07013
Barrington Ave 07011
Barrister St 07013
Bart Pl 07013
Beech St 07014
Belgrade Ave 07013
Belmont Ave 07012
Belrose Ct 07013
Bender Dr 07013
Bennington Ct 07013
Bergen Ave 07011
Beverly Hill Rd 07012
Birchwood Ter 07012
Bird Ave 07011
Blanjen Ter 07014
Bloomfield Ave 07012
Blue Hill Rd 07013
Bobbink Ct 07013
Bogert Pl 07013
Boll St 07014
Botany Pl 07011
Botany Village Sq W 07011
Bowdoin St 07013
Brannon Ct 07013
Brantwood Pl 07013
Breen Ct 07013
Breezy Hill Ct 07013
Bridewell Pl 07014
Brighton Ave 07013
Brighton Rd 07012
Brittany Ct 07013
Broad St 07013
Broadale Ave 07013
Brookhill Ter 07013
Brookside Dr 07012
Brookwood Rd 07012
Brower Ave 07013
Brownstone Rd 07013
Bruan Pl 07012
Burgess Pl 07011
Burgh Ave 07011
Burlington Rd 07012
Burwood Rd 07013
Butler St 07011
Buttel Dr 07013
Byron Pl 07011
Calstan Pl 07013
Cambridge Blvd 07013
Cambridge Ct 07014
Campbell Ave 07013
Canterbury Ct 07013
Carline Dr 07013
Carol Ln 07012
Carol St 07014
Caroline Ave 07011
Carrington Pl 07013
Catania Dr 07013
Cathay Rd 07013
Center St 07011
Central Ave 07011
Century Dr 07014
Chambers Ct 07013
Chanda Ct 07012
Chaplin Ct 07012
Charlene Dr 07013
Charles Ct & St 07013
Chatham Ter 07013
Chaytor St 07013
Cheever Ave 07011
Chelsea Rd 07012
Cherry St 07014
Chester St 07011
Chestnut St 07011
Chittenden Rd 07013
Chrisibar Dr 07013
Christie Ave 07011
Churchill Dr 07013
Circle Ave 07011
Clair St 07013
Clairmont Rd 07012
Claverack Rd 07013
Clay St 07014
Cliff Hill Rd 07013
Clifton Ave 07012
Clinton Ave 07011
Cloverdale Rd 07013
Cobble St 07013
Colfax Ave 07013
Colin Ave 07014
Collura Ln 07012
Columbia St 07011
Combee Ln 07012
Comfort Pl 07011
Concord St 07013
Conklin Dr 07013
Conover Ct 07012
Coppola Ct 07013
Costello Pl 07011
Cottage Ct & Ln 07012
Country Ln 07013
Coyles Ct 07013
Craig Pl 07013
Cresthill Ave 07012
Crooks Ave 07011
Curie Ave 07011
Cutler St 07011
Dalewood Rd 07013
Dan St 07013
Dando Ct 07013
Daniels Dr 07013
Davidson St 07011
Dawson Ave 07012
Day St 07011
Dayton Ave 07011
Degraw Ave 07013
Delawanna Ave 07014
Delaware St 07011
Demott Ave 07011
Devonshire Dr 07013
Dewey St 07013
Di Donna Ct 07013
Dianne Ct 07012
Dick St 07013
Doherty Dr 07013
Donald St 07011
Donna Dr 07013
Donnalin Pl 07013
Doremus Pl 07013
Duane Rd 07013
Dumont Ave 07013
Durant Ave 07011
Dwasline Rd 07012
Dwight Ter 07013
Dyer Ave 07014
Earnshaw Pl 07013
East Pkwy 07014
Edgewood Ave 07012
Edison St 07013
Edward Ct 07011
Edwards Rd 07013
Ehrle Pl 07013
Eldridge St 07013
Elema Pl 07013
Ellsworth St 07012
Elm St 07013
Elm Hill Rd 07013
Elmwood Dr 07013
E Emerson St 07013
Emma Pl 07013
Englewood Rd 07012
Entin Rd 07014
Essex St 07014
Evergreen Dr 07014
Everson Pl 07013
Exchange Pl 07013
Fair Hill Rd 07013
Fairfield Rd 07013
Fairmount Ave 07011
Federal St 07011
Fenlon Blvd 07014
Fenner Ave 07013
Fern Hill Rd 07013
Ferncliff Ave 07013
Fernwood Ct 07011
Ferris Dr 07013
Field Rd 07013
Fitzgerald Ave 07011
Fleischer Pl 07011
Florence Dr 07011
Fordham Rd 07013
Forest Way 07013
Fornelius Ave 07013
Forstmann Ct 07011
Foster St 07011
Fountain St 07011
Frances St 07014
Franklin Ave 07011
Frederick Ave 07013
Freneran Rd 07012
Friar Ln 07013
Frost Ct 07012
Gail Ct 07013
Galerali Ave 07013
Garden Ct 07012
Garfield Ave 07012
Garrabrant Rd 07013
Garret Ct 07013
Garretsee Pl 07011
E Gate 07013
George St 07011
George Russell Way 07013
Gerald Ave 07012
Getty Ave 07011
Gilbert Pl 07011
Gillies St 07013
Gleeson Dr 07013
Glen Oaks Ct 07012
Glenwood St 07013
Godwin Pl 07013
Gordon St 07011
Goss Pl 07013
Gould St & Ter 07013
Gourley Ave 07013
Grace Ave 07011
Graham Pl 07013
Grant Ave 07011
Graydon Ter 07013
Greenbrier Ct 07012
Greendale Rd 07013
Greenlawn Ave 07013
Greenmeadow Ln 07013
Greentree Rd 07013
Greglawn Dr 07013
Gregory Ave 07011
Grove St 07013
Grunwald St 07013
Hackberry Pl 07013
Haddenfield Rd 07013
Hadley Ave 07011
Hadrys Ct 07013
Haines Ave 07011
Hall St 07014
Hamas St 07013
Hamil Ct 07013
Hamilton Ave 07011
Hammond Ave 07011
Hampton Rd 07012
Harcourt Rd 07013
Harding Ave 07011
Harold Pl 07013
Harrington Rd 07012
Harrison Pl 07011
Harvey Rd 07012
Haussler Ter 07013
Hawthorne Ave 07011
Hazel St 07011
Hazelview Ave 07011
Heights Rd 07012
Helen Pl 07011
Helen St 07013
Hemlock St
1-49 07013
50-199 07012
Henoch Ave 07013
Hepburn Rd 07012
Hemerli Ave 07014
Hickory St 07013
High St 07014
High Park Pl 07011
Highland Ave 07011
Highview Dr 07013
Hillcrest Ave 07013
Hillman St 07011
Hilltop Ct 07012
Hilton St 07011
Hobart Pl 07011
Holden St 07011
Holly St 07013
Hollywood Ave 07014
Holster Rd 07013
Homcy Pl 07011
Home Pl 07011
Homer St 07014
Homestead St 07013
Hooyman Dr 07013
Hope Ave 07011
Howard Ave 07013
Howd Ave 07011
Hudson St 07011
Huemmer Ter 07013
Hugo St 07012
Huron Ave 07013
Hutton Rd 07013
Independence Ct 07013
Industrial St E 07012
Inwood St 07011
Irvington Pl 07013
Isabella St 07012
Ivanhoe Ln 07013
Ivy Ct 07013
Jacklin Ct 07012
James St 07011
Jani Ct 07013
Janice Ter 07013
Jaskot Ln 07012
Jay St 07013
Jefferson St 07014
Jennifer Ct 07013
Jerome Dr 07011
Jewett Ave 07011
Joan Pl 07012
John St 07013
John Alden St 07013
Johnson St 07014
Jones Ct 07013
Josh Ct 07011
Joyce Ln 07012
Juniper Ct 07014
Karen Dr 07013
Kashey St 07013
Katherine Ave 07012
Kathryn St 07013
Kehoe St 07011
Kennebec St 07013
Kennedy Ct 07013
Kensington Ave 07014
Kenter Pl 07012
Kenyon St 07013
Kingsland Ave & Rd 07014
Kipp St 07013
Knapp Ave 07011
Knoll Pl 07012
Knollwood Ter 07012
Knox Pl 07013
Kozy Ln 07013
Kruger Ct 07013
Kulick St 07011
Kuller Rd 07011
La Salle Ave 07013
Ladwik Ln 07013
Lake Ave 07011
Lakeview Ave 07011
Lambert Ave 07013
Landis Pl 07013
Larkspur Ln 07013
Larson Ct 07011
Laurel Ave 07012
Lawrence Ct 07013
Layton Dr 07013
Lee Pl 07011
Leenchal Ave 07011
Lehigh Ave 07012
Lennon Pl 07013
Lenox Ave 07012
Leopold Ter 07011
Lester Pl 07013
Lewis Pl 07013
Lexington Ave 07011
Liberty St 07013
Lincoln Ave & Pl 07011
Lindale Ct 07013
Linden Ave 07014
Linwood Ter 07012
Lio Dr 07013
Lisbon St 07013
Livingston St 07013
Lockwood Dr 07013
Lockwood Pl 07012
Lois Ave 07014
Long Hill Dr 07013
Loretta St 07011
Lorraine Dr 07012
Lorrie Ln 07012
Lotz Hill Rd 07013
Louis Dr 07011
Louise St 07011
Loumar Pl 07012
Lowry Ct 07012
Luddington Ave 07011
Luisser St 07012
Lyall Rd 07012
Lydia Pl 07012
Lynn Dr 07013
Macarthur Dr 07013
Macdonald St 07013
Machias St 07013
Maclean Rd 07013
Madeline Ave 07011
E Madison Ave 07011
Mahar Ave 07011
Main Ave
1-499 07014
900-1143 07011
1114-1114 07015
1144-1698 07011
1145-1699 07011
139-141-139-141 07014
Major St
11-121 07013
123-129 07013
130-136 07012
138-198 07012
Malcolm Ct 07013
Mandeville Ave 07013
Manila St 07011
Manor Dr 07013
Maple Pl 07011
Maple Hill Rd 07013
Maplewood Ave 07013
Marble Ct 07013
Marconi St 07013
Margery Ct 07013
Marie Pl 07013
Marilyn Pl 07011
Market St 07012
Marlboro Rd 07012
Marrion St 07013
Martha Ave 07011
Martin Ave 07012
Martindale Rd 07013
May St 07011
Mayer Dr 07012
Mayfair Pl 07013
Mayflower St 07013
Mcclelland Way 07012
Meadow Ln 07012
Melody Hill Rd 07013
Merrill Rd 07012
Merselis Ave 07011
Miller Ct & Plz 07012
Milosh St 07011
Milton Ave 07013
Mina Ave 07011
Monhegan St 07013
Montclair Ave 07011
Montgomery St 07011
Morris Rd 07012
Mount Prospect Ave
1-211 07013
212-699 07012
Mount Washington Dr 07013
Mountain Park Rd 07013
Mountainside Ter 07013
Mountainview Dr 07013
Myron St 07014
Myrtle Ave 07014
Nash Ave 07011
Nelson St 07013
Nettie Pl 07014
New Brier Ln 07012
Niader Ct 07012
Nino Ct 07013
Noll Ter 07013
Norman Ave 07013
Normandy Rd 07013
North Ct 07013
Northfield Ter 07013
Norwood Ave 07011
Notch Rd 07013
Nottingham Ter 07013
Nugent Dr 07012
Oak St 07014
Oak Hill Rd 07013
Oak Ridge Rd 07013
Oakwood Ct 07012
Olga B Ter 07013
Olympia St 07011
Orange Ave 07013
Orchard Ct 07012
Oregon St 07011
Orono St 07013
Page Rd 07012
Paranya Ct 07013
Park Ave & St 07014
Park Hill Ter 07013
Park Slope 07011
Parker Ave 07011
Parkview Ter 07011
Parkway Ave 07011
Parson Rd 07012
Passaic Ave
500-599 07014
600-839 07012
840-899 07014
Paterson Ave 07014
Patricia Pl 07012
Paulison Ave 07011
Pavan Rd 07014
Paxton St 07013
Pearl Brook Dr 07013
Pebble Brook Dr 07014
Peekay Dr 07014
Pennington Ave 07014
Penobscot St 07013
Pershing Rd
291B-399B 07012
Peru Rd 07012
Peterson Ct 07013
Phyllis Pl 07012
Piaget Ave 07011
Pilgrim Dr 07013
Pine Brae Ln 07012
Pine Hill Rd 07013
Pino Ct 07013
Pleasant Ave 07013
Ploch Rd 07013
Plymouth Rd 07013
Pond St 07013
Portland Ave 07011
Potter Rd 07013
Prescott Ave 07011
Princeton Pl & St 07014
Priscilla St 07013
Prospect Pl & St 07011
Prospect Village Plz 07013
Putnam Pl 07011
Quarry Dr 07013
Rabkin Dr 07013
Randolph Ave 07011
Ravenscroft Rd 07013
Ravine Ct 07013
Ravona St 07012
Raymond Pl 07014
Renaissance Dr 07013
Richfield Ct & Ter 07012
Richland Ct 07012
Richmond St 07011
Ridgewood Rd 07012
River Rd 07014
Riverwalk Way 07014
Robert St 07014
Robin Hood Rd 07013

Robinson Ter 07013
Rock Creek Dr 07014
Rock Hill Rd 07013
Rodgers Pl 07013
Rolling Hills Rd 07013
Rollins Ave 07011
Ronald Dr 07013
Rooney St 07011
Roosevelt Ave 07011
Rosalie Ave 07011
Rose St 07013
Rosedale Ave 07013
Rosemawr Pl 07012
Rowland Ave 07012
Roy Ct 07012
Royal Silk Plz 07011
Runyon Rd 07013
E Russell St 07011
Rutgers Pl 07013
Ruth Ave 07014
Rutherford Blvd 07014
Saco St 07013
Sade St 07013
Sago St 07013
Saint Andrews Blvd 07012
Saint James Pl 07013
Saint Michaels Pl 07013
Saint Philips Dr 07013
Samuel Ave 07013
Samworth Rd 07012
Sanford St 07011
Sargeant Ave 07013
Scales Plz 07013
Scharg Ct 07013
Scoles Ave 07012
Scott Ter 07013
Sears Pl 07011
Sebago St 07013
Sedeyen Ct 07013
Seger Ave 07011
Seidel Ave 07014
Serven Pl 07011
Seton Ln 07013
Sewall Ave 07011
Shafto St 07012
Shale Ln 07013
Sheridan Ave 07011
Sherman Pl 07011
Sherwood St 07013
Short St 07011
Short Hill Rd 07012
Silleck St 07013
Sipp Ave 07013
Sisco Pl 07011
Skyview Ter 07013
Somerset Pl 07012
South Ct 07013
South Pkwy 07014
Speer Ave 07013
Spencer Ave 07013
Sperling Rd 07013
Spring St 07011
Spring Hill Rd 07013
Springdale Ave & Ct 07013
Spruce Ct 07014
Stadtmauer Dr 07013
Stanchak Ct 07014
Standish Dr 07013
Stanley St 07013
Starmond Ave 07013
State Rt 20 07011
State Rt 3
1-621 07014
State Rt 3
622-710 07012
623-711 07014
712-1346 07012
1348-1398 07012
1400-1799 07013
Stefaniak Way 07011
Stevens Rd 07013
Stony Hill Rd 07013
Strangeway Ter 07011
Stuyvesant Ct 07013
Styertowne Plz & Rd 07012
Summer St 07011
Summit Ave 07013
Summit Rd 07012
Sundown Ln 07013
Sunnycrest Ave 07013
Surrey Ln 07012
Susan Ct 07012
Sussex Rd 07012
Sussex St 07011
Svea Ave 07013
Swift Ct 07014
Sycamore Rd 07012
Sylvan Ave 07011
Sylvan Rd 07012
Talus Rd 07013
Tamboer Ave 07013
Tancin Ln 07013
Taylor St 07013
Thanksgiving Ln 07013
The Mdws 07012
Thomas St 07013
Thompson St 07011
Thornton Pl 07012
Timber Dr 07014
Toth Ct 07014
Trella Ter 07013
Tremont Pl 07013
Trenton Ave 07011
Trimble Ave 07011
Tristan Rd 07013
Troast Ct 07011
Tromp St 07011
Tufts Rd 07013
Tulp Ct 07013
Twain Pl 07013
Tyler Ct 07012
Underwood Pl 07013
Unicorn Way 07011
Union Ave 07011
Urma Ave 07013
Us Highway 46
1-474 07011
476-500 07011
573-1299 07013
Vale Ave 07013
Valley Rd 07013
Van Breeman Dr 07013
Van Cleve Ave 07011
Van Houten Ave 07013
Van Ness Ct 07013
Van Orden Pl 07011
Van Riper Ave 07011
Van Vliet Ct 07013
Van Wagoner Ave 07013
Van Winkle Ave 07011
Varettoni Pl 07011
Vernon Ave 07011
View Pl 07013
Village Rd 07013
Village Sq E 07011
Village Sq W 07011
Vincent Dr 07013
Viola Ave 07011
Virginia Ave 07012
Vreeland Ave 07011
Wabash Ave 07011
Waldo St 07013
Walman Ave 07011
Walnut St 07013
Walsh Ct 07013
Wanda Ct 07014
Ward Ave 07014
Ward St 07011
Warren St 07013
Washington Ave 07011
Wayne Pl 07013
Webro Rd 07012
Weeks Ct 07013
Wellington St 07011
Wells Ct 07013
Wesley St 07013
West Pkwy 07014
Wester Pl 07013
Westervelt Pl 07011
Wheeler St 07014
Whiteweld Ter 07013
Whitmore Pl 07011
Wickers St 07014
Wickham Ter 07013
Wiedeman Ave 07011
Willet St 07013
William St 07014
Wilson St 07011
Winchester Ct 07013
Winding Way 07012
Windsor Rd 07012
Wisnev St 07011
Witherspoon Rd 07013
Wonham St 07013
Woodlawn Ave 07013
Woodridge Rd 07012
Woodsend Rd 07012
Woodward Ave 07012
Yereance Ave 07011
Yorkshire Rd 07013
Zeim Dr 07012

NUMBERED STREETS

All Street Addresses 07011

DOVER NJ

General Delivery 07801

POST OFFICE BOXES MAIN OFFICE STATIONS AND BRANCHES

Box No.s
All PO Boxes 07802

NAMED STREETS

Academy St 07801
Adams Ave 07801
Alachelm St 07801
Ann St 07801
Arlene Ln 07801
Art St 07801
Audrey Pl 07801
Baker Ave & St 07801
Bart Pl 07801
Bassett Hwy 07801
Basswood Ave 07801
Beatty St 07801
Beaufort Ave 07801
Beech St 07801
Belmont Ave 07801
Belt Rd 07801
N & S Bergen St 07801
Berkshire Ave 07801
Berry St 07801
Birch St 07801
Blacksmith Rd 07801
E & W Blackwell St 07801
Blakely Ave 07801
Bonnie View Dr 07801
Boonton St 07801
Bowlby St 07801
Brook Dr, Ln & Run 07801
Brown Rd 07801
Buffington Rd 07801
Byram Ave 07801
Caisson St & Way 07801
Carolyn Pl 07801
Carro Ct 07801
Carrol St 07801
Center St 07801
Central Ave 07801
Chestnut St 07801
Christopher St 07801
E & W Chrystal St 07801
Claredon Ter 07801
Clark St 07801
Cleveland Ave 07801
E & W Clinton St 07801
Coghlan Rd 07801
Columbia St 07801
Commerce Center Dr 07801
Conger St 07801
Conrad Pl 07801
Coolidge Ave 07801
E & W Cooper St 07801
Cottage St 07801
Court Dr 07801
Crestmont Dr 07801
Cross St 07801
Curtis St 07801
Daniel St 07801
David St 07801
Davis Ave 07801
Debbie Pl 07801
E Dehart Ave 07801
Depew Ave 07801
Dewey St 07801
E & W Dickerson St 07801
Drake Ave 07801
Edgewood Ter 07801
Edison St 07801
Edwin St 07801
Ekstrom St 07801
Elena Pl 07801
Elizabeth St 07801
N & S Elk Ave 07801
W Elliott St 07801
Elm St 07801
N & S Essex St 07801
Ev Ken Ter 07801
Everett Dr 07801
E & W Fairview Ave 07801
Farley Ave & Ln 07801
Fox Hill Dr 07801
Franklin Rd 07801
Fred Ter 07801
Front St 07801
Garfield Ave 07801
Garrison Ave 07801
Gately Rd 07801
Gaydos St 07801
George St 07801
Glenview Ct 07801
Glenwood Ave 07801
Goodale Ave 07801
Grace St 07801
Grant St 07801
Green Tree Ln 07801
Greenwood Ave 07801
Grover Rd 07801
Guy St 07801
Harding Ave 07801
Harris Ct 07801
Harrison St 07801
Harvard St 07801
Heather Ct 07801
Herrick Dr 07801
High St 07801
S Highland Ave &
Way 07801
Highview Ter 07801
Hillcrest Ave 07801
Hillsdale Dr 07801
Hillside Ave 07801
Hinchman Ave 07801
Hoagland Ave 07801
Hudson St 07801
Irishtown Rd 07801
Ivan St 07801
Jackson Ave 07801
James St 07801
Jardine St 07801
Jefferson Ave 07801
Jessica Ln 07801
John St 07801
Jordan Ter 07801
Joyes Ln 07801
Julia Ter 07801
Kearney St 07801
Kendall Ct 07801
Kensington Ave 07801
King St 07801
Knickerbocker Ave 07801
Kyle Dr 07801
Lake Denmark Rd 07801
Larned Ter 07801
Lawrence St 07801
Lee Ave 07801
Legion Pl 07801
Lehigh St 07801
Lemar St 07801
Leonard Pl & St 07801
Liberty St 07801
Lincoln Ave 07801
N Linden Pl 07801
Linwood Ave 07801
Livingston Ave 07801
Locust Ave 07801
Losey St 07801
Madison St 07801
Main Rd 07801
Maple Ave 07801
Marjorie Ln 07801
Marvin St 07801
Mary St 07801
Mase Ave 07801
Mcdavitt Pl 07801
E & W Mcfarlan St 07801
Meadow Dr 07801
Mechanic St 07801
Mekeel Dr 07801
Mercer St 07801
Michael Ct 07801
Millbrook Ave 07801
Mineral Springs Rd 07801
Moller Pl 07801
Monmouth Ave 07801
Monroe Ave 07801
N & S Morris St 07801
Mount Hope Ave 07801
Mount Pleasant Ave 07801
Mount Prospect Ave 07801
Mountain Ave 07801
E & W Munson Ave 07801
Myrtle Ave 07801
Nelson St 07801
New St 07801
North St 07801
Oak St 07801
Oram Dr 07801
Orchard St 07801
Overlook Ave 07801
Palm St 07801
Park Ave & Pl 07801
Park Heights Ave 07801
Parker Rd & St 07801
Passaic St 07801
Penn Ave 07801
Pequannock St 07801
Perry St 07801
Phipps Rd 07801
Pierson St 07801
Pine St 07801
Pine Hill Ct 07801
Polk Ave 07801
Princeton Ave 07801
Prospect St 07801
Randolph Ave 07801
Reeves St 07801
Replogle Ave 07801
Reservoir Ave 07801
Richard Ave & St 07801
Richard Mine Rd 07801
Richards Ave 07801
Richboynton Rd 07801
River St 07801
Rock Hollow Rd 07801
Rockaway Rd 07801
Rockridge Ter 07801
Roosevelt Ave 07801
Rose Ct 07801
Roswell St 07801
Roy St 07801
Rutan Dr 07801
Rutgers St 07801
Saint Judes Pl 07801
Saint Marys St 07801
N & S Salem St 07801
Sammis Ave 07801
Sampson Ave 07801
Sanford St 07801
Schley St 07801
Schrader Rd 07801
Schwartz Ln 07801
Searing St 07801
Segur St 07801
Sickle St 07801
Simms St 07801
Slope Dr 07801
Snake Hill Rd 07801
South St 07801
Spicer Ave 07801
Spring St 07801
Spruce St 07801
Stanley Ter 07801
Stephen St 07801
Struble Ln 07801
Summer Ave 07801
Sunnyhill Rd 07801
N Sussex St
1-61 07801
22-22 07802
62-298 07801
63-205 07801
S Sussex St 07801
Swede Mine Rd 07801
Sylvan Way 07801
Taft Ave & St 07801
Taylor St 07801
Thompson Ave 07801
Titus St 07801
Towpath Sq 07801
Trenton St 07801
Turner St 07801
Union St 07801
Us Highway 46 07801
Vail St 07801
Van Nostrand Ave 07801
Victory Ct & Hls E 07801
Victory Highlands Way 07801
Walnut St 07801
N & S Warren St 07801
Washington Ave 07801
Watson Dr 07801
Wayne St 07801
Wayside Ave 07801
Welch Ln 07801
White St 07801
William St 07801
Wilson St 07801
Windsor Ave 07801
Winthrop Pl 07801
Yale St 07801

NUMBERED STREETS

All Street Addresses 07801

EAST ORANGE NJ

General Delivery 07019

POST OFFICE BOXES MAIN OFFICE STATIONS AND BRANCHES

Box No.s
All PO Boxes 07019

NAMED STREETS

Abington Ave 07017
Amherst St 07018
Ampere Pkwy & Plz 07017
N Arlington Ave 07017
S Arlington Ave 07018
Arsdale Ter 07018
Ashland Ave 07017
Ashland Pl 07018
Ayr St 07018
Baldwin St 07017
Bedford St 07018
Beech St 07018
Berwyn St 07018
Birchwood Ave 07018
Boyden St 07017
Brick Church Plz 07018
Brighton Ave 07017
Brookwood St 07018
Burchard Ave 07017
N Burnett St 07017
S Burnett St 07018
Cambridge St 07018
Carlton St 07017
Carnegie Ave 07018
Centerway 07017
Central Ave 07018
Charles St 07017
Chauncey Ave 07017
Chelsea Ave 07018
Chelsea Pl 07017
Chestnut St 07018
Church Pl 07017
City Hall Plz
2-24 07017
26-58 07017
26-26 07019
60-99 07017
Clay St 07018
Cleveland Ter 07017
Clifford St 07018
N Clinton St 07017
S Clinton St 07018
College Dr 07017
Colonial Ter 07017
Cottage Pl 07017
Crawford St 07018
Crescent Rd 07017
Davis Ave & Pl 07017
Deldelde Ave 07017
Derby St 07018
Division Pl & St 07017
Dodd St & Ter 07017
Eastwood St 07017
Eaton Pl 07017
Edgar St 07018
Edgerton Ter 07017
Edgewood Rd 07017
Ellington St 07017
Elliot Pl 07018
Elmwood Ave 07018
Ely Pl 07017
Emerson St 07018
Eppirt St 07018
Essex St 07017
Everett St 07017
Evergreen Pl
1-17 07018
19-59 07018
60-198 07018
60-60 07019
61-199 07018
Fair St 07017
Fairmount Ter 07018
Fellowship Cir 07017
Fernwood Rd 07017
Franklin St 07017
Freeman Ave 07018
Freeway Dr E 07018
Fulton St 07017
Garfield Pl 07018
Girard Ave 07017
Glen Park Rd 07017
Glenwood Ave & Pl 07017
Grand Ave 07018
Grant Ave 07017
Greenwood Ave 07017
Grove Pl 07017
N Grove St 07017
S Grove St 07018
Halsted Pl & St 07018
Hamilton St 07017
Hampton Ter 07018
N Harrison St 07017
S Harrison St 07017
Harvard St 07018
Hawthorne Ave & Pl 07018
Hayward St 07017
Hedden Pl 07017
E Highland Ave 07018

Hillcrest Ter 07018
Hillyer St 07017
Hilton St 07017
Hoffman Blvd 07017
Hollywood Ave 07018
Hudson Ave 07018
Irving St 07018
Kearney St 07017
Kenmore Ter 07017
Kensington Pl 07017
Kenwood Pl 07018
La France Ave 07017
Lafayette Ave 07017
Lake St 07017
Laurel Ave 07018
Lawrence St 07017
Lawton St 07017
Lenox Ave 07018
Leslie St 07017
Lincoln St 07017
Linden Ave 07018
Lindsley Pl 07018
Linwood Pl 07017
Little St 07017
Long St 07017
Madison Ave 07017
Madonna Pl 07018
Main St 07018
N Maple Ave 07017
S Maple Ave 07018
Maple Ter 07018
Marcy Ave 07017
Mckay Ave 07018
Meadow St 07017
Melmore Gdns 07017
Melrose Ave 07018
Midland Ave 07017
Monroe Ave 07017
Morris St 07017
Morse Ave 07017
Morton Pl 07017
Mountainview Ave 07018
N Munn Ave 07017
S Munn Ave 07018
Nassau Pl 07018
Netherwood Ter 07017
New St 07017
Newfield St 07017
Norman St 07017
Norwood Pl & St 07018
Oak St 07018
Olive St 07017
S Orange Ave 07018
N Oraton Pkwy 07017
S Oraton Pkwy 07018
E & N Park Ave, Ct, Pl & St 07017
Park End Pl 07018
Parkway Dr E & W 07017
Princeton St 07018
Prospect St & Ter 07017
Renshaw Ave 07017
Rhode Island Ave 07018
Ridgewood Ave 07017
Roosevelt Ave 07017
Ross St 07018
Rowe St 07017
Rutledge Ave 07017
Saint Agnes Ln 07018
Sanford St 07018
Sawyer Ave 07017
Schuyler Ter 07017
Shendong Ave 07018
Shepard Ave 07018
Sherman Ave 07017
Sommer Ave 07017
Springdale Ave 07017
State St 07017
Steuben St 07018
Stockton Pl 07017
Summit St 07017
Sunnyside Ter 07018
Sussex Ave 07018
Telford St 07018
Thomas Blvd 07017
Thornton Pl 07017
Tremont Ave 07018
University Pl 07018
Upsala Ct 07017
Vernon Pl & Ter 07017
N Walnut St 07017
S Walnut St 07018
Warrington Pl 07017
Warwick St 07017
Washington St & Ter 07017
Watson Ave 07018
Wayne Ave 07018
Webster Pl 07018
Westcott St 07017
Whitman Ave 07017
Whitney Pl 07017
Whittier St 07018
Whittlesey Ave 07018
Wilcox Ave 07018
William St 07017
Winans St 07017
Winthrop Ter 07018
Woodland Ave 07017

NUMBERED STREETS

1st Ave 07017
4th Ave 07017
9th Ave 07018
11th Ave 07018
N 14th St 07017
N 15th St 07017
S 15th St 07018
N 16th St 07017
S 16th St 07018
N 17th St 07017
S 17th St 07018
N 18th St 07017
S 18th St 07018
N 19th St 07017
N 20th St 07017
S 20th St 07018
N 21st St 07017
N 22nd St 07017
N 23rd St 07017

EATONTOWN NJ

General Delivery 07724

POST OFFICE BOXES MAIN OFFICE STATIONS AND BRANCHES

Box No.s
All PO Boxes 07724

NAMED STREETS

Academy Ave 07724
Adams St 07724
Admiral Ln 07724
Alameda Ct 07724
Alexandria Ct 07724
Applebey St 07724
Ash St 07724
Azalea Ct 07724
Barker Ave 07724
Barnsdale Way 07724
Bataan Ave 07724
Bayberry Ct 07724
Beacon Ln 07724
Belshaw Ave 07724
Benson Pl & St E 07724
Berkeley Pl 07724
Bernard St 07724
Birch Ln 07724
Brentwood Rd 07724
Broad St 07724
Brook St 07724
Brookwood Dr 07724
Burns Pl 07724
Buttonwood Ave 07724
Byrnes Ln 07724
Cambridge Ct 07724
Campbell Dr 07724
Carmel Way 07724
Carolyn Ct 07724
Carrington Dr 07724
Cedar St 07724
Center St 07724
Chelsea Ct 07724
Christopher Way 07724
Church St 07724
Cliffwood Ave 07724
Clinton Ave 07724
Cloverdale Ave 07724
College Ave 07724
Columbia Dr 07724
Conifer Crest Way 07724
Copperfield Ct 07724
Corbett Way 07724
Corlies Ave 07724
Corrigador Rd 07724
Cortland Rd 07724
Country Club Rd 07724
Crawford St 07724
Crown Ct 07724
Cypress Dr 07724
Daniel Ct 07724
Deannas Way 07724
Dogwood Dr 07724
Eaton Rd 07724
Eatoncrest Dr 07724
Elizabeth Pkwy 07724
Elm Dr & Pl 07724
Emma Pl 07724
Emory Ct 07724
Eton Pl 07724
Evergreen Dr 07724
Fairway Ave 07724
Farm Ln 07724
Ferncliff Dr 07724
Fieldstone Ct 07724
Franklin Ave 07724
Georgetown Rd 07724
Ginger Ct 07724
W Grant Ave & Ct 07724
Guam Ln 07724
Halliard Dr 07724
Hampton Rd 07724
Harvest Ln 07724
Heath St 07724
Helms Dr 07724
Hemphill Rd 07724
Heritage Rd 07724
High St 07724
Hilbert Pkwy 07724
Holly Dr 07724
Holly Glen Way 07724
Hope Rd 07724
Howard Ave 07724
Imperial Ct 07724
Industrial Way E 07724
Industrial Way W
1-306 07724
307-307 07799
308-698 07724
309-623 07724
Iris St 07724
Irving Pl 07724
Jackson St 07724
James Way 07724
Jamestown Rd 07724
Jefferson St 07724
Jeryl St 07724
Judy Rd 07724
Juniper Ln 07724
Kellys Ln 07724
Kent Pl 07724
Kingsley Ct 07724
Knox Ave 07724
Kremer Ave 07724
Lafetra Ave 07724
Laird Rd 07724
Lake Ave & Dr 07724
Lakeview Ter 07724
Lark Spur Dr 07724
Laurel Pl 07724
Lennox Dr 07724
Leonard Pl 07724
Lewis St 07724
Livingston Ct 07724
Locust Ave 07724
Lone Oak Way 07724
Lowther Dr 07724
Mackenzie Rd 07724
Madison St 07724
Magnolia Ln 07724
Main St 07724
Malibu Dr 07724
Maple Ave 07724
Marilyn Ct 07724
Marin Way 07724
Mariveles Rd 07724
Marshall Ct 07724
Maxwell Rd 07724
Mcmenamy Pl 07724
Meadowbrook Ave 07724
Megill Cir & Dr 07724
Meridian Rd 07724
Midway Ln 07724
Mill St 07724
Mill Pond Way 07724
Mindy Ln 07724
Mitchell Dr 07724
Monmouth Rd 07724
Monroe St 07724
Musket Ln 07724
Myrtle Ave 07724
Nelson Dr 07724
Norman J Field Way 07724
Nottingham Dr 07724
Nudd Dr 07724
Oak Ln 07724
Oak View Ter 07724
Old Deal Rd 07724
Old Queens Ct 07724
Old Shark River Rd 07724
Olongapo Ln 07724
Oxford Ln 07724
Palermo Dr 07724
Park Ave 07724
Parker Rd 07724
Paul Ave 07724
Pearce Ave 07724
Phipps Pl 07724
Pine St 07724
Pinebrook Rd 07724
Porter Ave 07724
Princess Ln 07724
Raleigh Ct 07724
Redfern Rd 07724
Redwood Dr 07724
Restantr Dr 07724
Reynolds Dr 07724
Richardson Ave 07724
Rodman Ct 07724
Rose Ct 07724
Rozbern Dr 07724
Rozlyn Ct 07724
Russell Ter 07724
Ruth Pl 07724
Rutland Pl 07724
Ryers Pl 07724
Sam Dr 07724
Sandspring Dr 07724
Sandy Ln 07724
Scheri Ln 07724
Schuber Pl 07724
Shark River Rd 07724
Sheila Dr 07724
Sherwood Dr 07724
South St & Ter 07724
Southbrook Dr 07724
Southern Dr 07724
Squankum Rd 07724
State Route 35 07724
State Route 36 07724
Stirrup Ln 07724
Stonyhill Rd 07724
Subic Ln 07724
Sullivan Ave 07724
Surrey Ln 07724
Taylor Pl 07724
Tess Ct 07724
Thornley Rd 07724
Thors Rd 07724
Throckmorton Ave 07724
Tinton Ave 07724
Todd Dr 07724
Turner St 07724
Valley Forge Rd 07724
Vaughn Ct 07724
Victor Ave 07724
Victoria Dr 07724
Villa Pl 07724
Village Dr 07724
Violante Ct 07724
Wall St 07724
Walter Ave 07724
Washington St 07724
Water St 07724
Watson Pl 07724
Waverly Ct 07724
Waypoint Dr 07724
Wayside Rd 07724
Wedgewood Cir 07724
Wesley Ct 07724
West St 07724
Weston Pl 07724
Whalepond Rd 07724
White St 07724
Willow Ave 07724
Winding Brk 07724
Windsor Dr 07724
Winthrop Ln 07724
Woodmere Dr 07724
Wyckoff Rd 07724
Youmans Ave 07724

NUMBERED STREETS

All Street Addresses 07724

EDISON NJ

General Delivery 08818

POST OFFICE BOXES MAIN OFFICE STATIONS AND BRANCHES

Box No.s
All PO Boxes 08818

NAMED STREETS

Abbott Ct 08820
Acorn Dr 08820
Adams St 08820
Addalia Ln 08820
Adele Ct 08817
Adelphi Ct 08837
Adrian Way 08820
Agatha Dr 08817
Albany St 08837
Albert Ave 08837
Albourne St 08837
Alcoa Ave 08837
Alden Ave 08820
Alderberry Ct 08820
Aldrich Ave 08820
Aldrich Dr 08837
Alexander St 08820
Alexis Ln 08820
Alfred St 08820
Alice Ave 08817
Allison Ct 08820
Almond Ln 08820
Alpine St 08820
Altamont Rd 08817
Alva Ct 08817
Amari Dr 08820
Amboy Ave 08837
Amherst St 08820
Amman Rd 08817
Amy Ave 08817
Andre Ave 08817
Anita Ave 08820
Anna Ln 08820
Annette Dr 08820
Anthony Ave 08820
Apple St 08817
Applewood Dr 08820
Arbor Cir 08837
Ash Rd 08817
Ashbrook Dr 08820
Ashley Rd 08817
Aspen Cir 08820
Audubon Ave 08817
Augusta Ave & Ct 08820
Auld Way 08817
Avennew Ave 08837
Avenue C 08837
Avery St 08817
Avon Rd 08817
Azalea Dr 08820
Aztec Ct 08820
B Ct S 08817
Back Dr 08817
Baldwin Rd 08817
Ballo Pl 08820
Balmoral Ct 08817
Baltic St 08820
Balzano Ct 08817
Bank Pl 08820
Banyan Ct 08820
Barbara Pl 08817
Barlow Rd W 08817
Bartha Ave 08817
Barton St 08837
Bass Ct 08817
Baxter Rd 08817
Bayberry Ct 08820
Beatrice Pkwy 08820
Beaver Ave 08820
Bedford St 08817
Beech Ln 08820
Beech St 08817
Beechwood Ave 08837
Bellavista Ct 08820
Belmont Ave 08817
Belvidere Ave 08820
Bennington Dr 08820
Bergen Pl 08817
Bernard Ave 08837
Bernice St 08820
Berrue Ct 08817
Betty Ann Dr 08820
Beverly St 08820
Birch Rd 08817
Bloomfield Ave 08837
Blossom St 08817
Blue Heron Way 08837
Blueberry Ct 08817
Bluebird Ct 08820
Bobbi Jean Ave 08820
Bodnarik Rd 08837
Boltin St 08817
Bonham Dr 08837
Bonn Ct 08817
Bonnie Brook Ave 08817
Booth Ct 08820
Boulder Dr 08817
Boulevard Of Eagles 08817
Boxwood Cir & Ct 08820
Bradford Rd 08820
Bradley Dr 08817
Brandywine Ct 08820
Brian Rd 08817
Briar Ave 08817
Brida Ct 08817
Broad Ave 08820
Brook Ave 08820
Brookfall Rd 08817
Brookhill Ave 08817
Brookside Rd 08817
Brookville Rd 08817
Brotherhood St 08817
Brower Ave 08837
Brox Rd 08817
Bruce Ct 08820
Brunswick Ave 08817
Bryant Ave 08820
Buchanan Rd 08820
Burchard St N & S 08837
Burlington Ct 08820
Burnett St 08817
Butler Rd 08820
Cabot Ave 08837
Cactus Ct 08820
Caldwell Rd 08817
Calvert Ave E & W 08820
Cambridge Rd 08817
Campbell Ave 08817
Campus Dr 08837
Canary Dr 08820
Candy Ct 08817
Canterbury Ln 08820
Cardinal Ave 08820
Cardownie St 08817
Carlisle Ct 08817
Carlton St S 08837
Carmello Dr 08817
Carnwath Ct 08817
Carol Pl 08817
Carr Ct 08837
Carriage Pl 08820
Carter Dr 08817
Casey Ave 08817
Cedar St 08820
Cedarwood Dr 08820
Celler Rd 08817
Center St 08817
Central Ave 08817
Chandler Rd 08820
Chapel St 08817
Char St 08820
Charles Ct & St 08820
Chatsworth Ct 08820
Chelsea Ct 08820
Cherry St 08817
Chester Ct 08817
Chestnut St 08817
Chokeberry Dr 08837
Christie St 08820
Christopher Ct 08820
Church St 08817
Churchill Rd 08820
Cinder Rd 08820
Clark Ave 08817
Clausen Rd 08817
Clearview Rd 08837
Clemmens Ct 08820
Cleremont Ave 08817
Cleveland Pl 08820
Clif Prescod Ln 08817
Cliff St 08817
Clifford St 08817
Clifton St 08817
Clinton Ave 08820
Clipper Ave 08817
Clive Ct & St 08820
Clive Hills Rd 08820
Clover Pl 08837
Cobblestone Ln 08820
Cody Ave 08820
Colasurdo Ct 08820
Coleman St 08817
Colfax Rd 08817
College Dr 08817
Colletto Ct 08817
Colonial Ct 08820
Colton Rd 08817
Columbus Ave 08817
Columbus Cir 08837
Compton Ave 08820
Comstock Rd 08817
Concord St 08820
Conen St 08820
Conner Ave 08817
Conover Ct 08817
Conway St 08820
Coolidge Ave 08837
Coppertree Ct 08820
Coral St 08837
Cornell St 08817
Cornwall Dr 08820

Corporation Row 08817
Corrine St 08820
Cortlandt St 08837
Cottonwood Ct 08820
Council Pl 08837
Country Ln 08820
Craig St 08817
Cranbury Ct 08820
Crescent Rd 08817
Crestmont Ave 08820
Crestwood Ave 08817
Cricket Cir 08820
Crosby Ave 08817
Crowells Rd 08817
Curtis Ave 08820
Cutter Ave 08820
Cypress Ct 08820
Daffodil Dr 08837
Daisy Ct 08820
Dale Dr 08820
Dalton Pl 08817
Dana Cir 08820
Daniel Rd 08820
Daphne Ct 08820
Darrell Ct 08817
Dartmouth St 08837
Darwin Blvd 08820
David Ct & Dr 08820
Dayton Dr 08820
Dayton Rd 08817
Deborah Dr 08820
Deerfield Dr 08820
Deerwood Ave 08817
Delancey St 08820
Dellview Dr 08820
Dellwood Rd 08820
Delmar Pl 08837
Denise Dr 08820
Denver Blvd 08820
Deri Ct 08820
Desser Pl 08817
Deutsch Ln 08820
Devon Rd 08820
Dewolfe St 08817
Dey Pl 08817
Diamond Dr 08820
Dianne Ct 08817
Dill Ct 08817
Distribution Blvd 08817
Division St 08817
Dix Ave 08817
Dobson Rd 08817
Dock Rd 08837
Dogwood Cir 08817
Dogwood Dr 08820
Dolores Dr 08817
Donna Dr 08820
Doreen Ct 08820
Doris Ct 08820
Dorothy Ave 08837
Dorset Way 08820
Douglas Dr 08817
Duclos Ln 08817
Duley Ave 08817
Dundar Rd 08817
Dunham Ave 08817
Durham Ave & Rd 08817
Eagle Rd 08820
Eardley Rd 08817
East Dr 08820
Eastlick Rd 08817
Easy St 08817
Echo Ave 08837
Eden Ave 08817
Edgegrove St 08837
Edgemount Rd 08817
Edgerald Ave 08817
Edgewood Rd 08820
Edinburgh Ct 08820
Edison Ave 08820
Edison Crossing Dr 08837
Edison Glen Ter 08837
Edith Ave 08817
Edmund St 08817
Edward Ave 08820
Edward Stec Blvd 08837
Egan St 08820
N Eighth Ave 08817
Eileen Way 08837
Elder Dr 08837
Elegante Dr 08820
Elf St 08820
Elizabeth Ave 08820
Elizabeth Ct 08817
Ellen St 08817
Elliot Pl 08817
Ellis Pkwy 08820
Ellison Ave 08820
Ellmyer Rd 08820
Elm St 08817
Elmwood Ave 08837
Elmwood Ter 08817
Elsie St 08820
Ely Pl 08817
Emerson St 08820
Emil Ct 08820
Erie St 08817
Erin Ct 08817
Essex Ct 08817
Estok Rd 08817
Ethel Rd 08817
N Evergreen Ave &
Rd 08837
Executive Ave 08817
Exeter Ave 08817
Fairfax Rd 08817
Fairhill Rd 08817
Fairmount Ave 08820
Fairview Ave 08817
Fairway Ct 08820
Faith Ave 08820
Falcon Dr 08820
Falkirk Ct 08817
Fargo Ct 08820
Farmhaven Ave 08820
Farrington St 08820
Fay St 08837
Fayette St 08817
Feather Bed Ln 08820
Fenakel St 08817
Fern St 08817
Fernwood Ave 08837
Ferris Rd 08817
Fieldcrest Ave 08837
Fielding Pl 08820
N Fifth Ave 08817
Fifth St 08837
Finch Ct 08820
Finley Rd 08817
Firethorn Ct & Dr 08820
First St 08837
First St N 08837
W First St 08820
Fishel Rd 08820
Fitch Rd 08817
Five Acre Dr 08820
Flarlenn Ave 08820
Flatiron Ct 08820
Fleet Ave 08820
Fletcher St 08820
Florence St 08817
Flower Ct 08820
Floyd St 08820
Foley Ave 08820
Forest Dr 08817
Forest Haven Blvd 08817
Forman Ct 08817
Forsythia Dr 08837
Fourth St 08837
Fowler St 08837
Fox Rd 08817
Fox Hill Rd 08820
Foyer St 08817
Frances Rd 08820
Frank St 08820
Franklin Ave 08837
Fred Pl 08817
Frederic St 08820
Freeman St 08820
French St 08817
Frost Ave E & W 08820
Fulton St 08817
Gales Rd 08837
Gallo Way 08820
Garden Pl, St & Ter S 08817
Garfield Park 08837
Garfield St 08820
Gaskill Ave 08817
Gate House Ln 08820
Gates Pl 08817
Genova Ct 08817
Gentore Ct 08820
George Ave E 08820
Georgean Ct 08820
Germantown Ave 08817
Gibian St 08837
Giggleswick Way 08820
Ginesi Ct 08817
Ginger Dr 08837
Gladys Ct 08817
Glencourt Ave 08837
Glendale Ave 08817
Glenville Rd 08817
Gloria Ave 08820
Gogel St 08820
Gold St 08837
Goldpost Rd 08817
Golf Rd 08820
Gooding Ct 08820
Goodluck St 08820
Goodwill Pl 08837
Gourmet Ln 08837
Gracey St 08817
Graham Ave 08820
Grandview Ave W 08837
W Grant Ave 08820
Greek Ln 08817
Green St 08817
Greenwich Rd 08820
Greenwood Ave 08817
Gregory Ct 08820
Gross Ave 08837
Grove Ave 08820
Growney St 08817
Guisborough Way 08820
Gurley Rd 08820
Hackett Dr 08820
Hadfield Rd 08820
Hallo St 08837
Hamilton Ave 08820
Hamlin Rd 08817
Hana Rd 08817
Hansen Dr 08820
Harding Ave 08820
Harley Rd 08837
Harmon Rd 08837
Harold Ave 08820
Harrigan St 08817
Harris Rd 08837
Harrison Ave 08837
Harrison St 08817
Harvey Ave 08820
Hawthorn Dr 08820
Hayduk Dr 08820
Hayes St 08820
Hazel Ave 08820
Hazelwood Ave 08837
Hearthstone Dr 08820
S Heathcote Ave 08817
Heather Ct & Dr 08820
Hector Ave 08817
Hedges Rd 08817
E & W Hegel Ave 08820
Helene Ave 08820
Heller Ct 08817
Heman St 08837
Hemlock Dr 08820
Henry St 08820
Heritage Dr 08820
Herron Rd 08820
Hickory St 08817
Hickory Hollow Ct 08820
Hidden Hollow Ct 08820
Hidden Valley Dr 08820
Highland Ave 08817
Highpoint Dr 08820
Highway Ter 08817
Hill Rd 08817
Hillcrest Ave 08817
Hillsdale Rd 08820
Hillside Ave 08817
Hilltop Rd 08820
Hillwood Ave 08820
Hof Rd 08837
Holly Ct 08820
Holly Pl 08817
Hollywood St 08820
Holmes St 08817
Homestead Rd 08820
Honeysuckle Ln 08820
Hoover Ave 08837
Horizon Dr 08817
Howard Ave 08837
Hull Dr 08817
Hummingbird Ln 08820
Huntington Rd 08820
Idlewild Rd 08817
Independence Dr 08820
Indiana Rd 08820
Industrial Hwy 08837
Inman Ave 08820
Inverness Dr 08820
Ireland Ave 08837
Irene Ct 08820
Iris Ct 08820
Irving St 08817
Jackson Ave 08837
Jacqueline Ct 08820
Jamaica St 08820
James St 08820
Jane Pl 08820
Janina Ave 08820
Jason St 08820
Jay St 08837
Jean Pl 08820
Jeff St 08837
Jefferson Ave 08837
Jefferson Blvd 08817
Jego Ct 08820
Jenna Ln 08820
Jennifer Ct 08820
Jeremy Ct 08817
Jersey Ave 08820
Jill Ct 08817
Joel Ave 08837
John St 08837
Johnstone St 08817
Jonathan Dr 08820
Jones Pl 08817
Joseph Pl 08820
Joshua Ct 08820
Judith Pl 08837
Judson St 08837
Julie Dr 08820
Juniper Ct 08820
Kalmia Ln 08820
Karen Pl 08817
Karnell Ct 08820
Kathleen Pl 08817
Kazcmar Ct 08820
Kean Ct 08837
Kearny Ave 08817
Keen Ln 08820
Kellogg Ct 08817
Kelly Dr 08820
Kenlen Dr 08817
Kenmore Rd 08817
Kester Dr 08817
Keystone Ct 08817
Kilmer Ct 08817
Kilmer Rd
1-20 08817
21-21 08899
21-21 08906
22-98 08817
23-99 08817
Kimble St 08817
King St 08820
King Arthurs Ct 08820
King Georges Post Rd 08837
Kingsbridge Dr 08820
Kingswood Ct 08820
Kinross Ct 08817
Kish Ct 08837
Kitchen Ct 08820
Knapp Ave 08817
Knollwood Rd E & W 08817
Korleen Ct 08817
Koster Blvd 08837
Lafayette Ave & Rd 08837
Lahiere Ave 08817
Lake Pl 08817
Lake View Blvd 08817
Lamar Ave 08820
Lambert Ave 08817
Langholm Ct 08817
Langstaff Ave 08817
Larchmont Rd 08837
Larson Ave 08817
Latonia St 08817
Laura Ave 08820
Laurel Hollow Ct 08820
Laurie Ln 08817
Lavender Dr 08820
Lawlor Ct 08820
Laythan Rd 08817
Lee St 08817
Lehigh Ave 08837
Leiane Ct 08817
Leland Rd 08817
Lench Ave 08820
Lenox St 08817
Leo St 08817
Leslie St 08817
Letson Pl 08817
Lexington Ave 08817
Libby Ct 08820
Liberty St 08837
Library Pl 08820
Liddle Ave 08837
Lilac St 08817
Lillian St 08817
Lily Ct & Rd 08820
Limelight Ct 08820
Limoli Ct 08820
Lincoln Ave 08837
Linda Ln 08820
Linden Ave 08817
Link Pl 08820
Lipnick Ln 08820
Livingston Ave 08820
Lloyd St 08817
Locust Ave 08817
S Locust Ave 08817
W Locust Ave 08820
Lodi Ave 08837
Loeb Ct 08817
Lombardi St 08820
Longview Rd 08820
Lordina Dr 08817
Loring Ave 08817
Louis Ct 08820
Louise Rd 08817
Lucille Ct 08820
Lucinda Ct 08820
Lund Ave 08820
Lydia Ln 08817
Lyle Pl 08820
Lynn Ct 08817
Lynnwood Rd 08820
Lyons Ln 08820
M Ln 08817
Macarthur Dr 08837
Mack Dr 08817
Madaline Dr 08820
Madden Ct 08820
Madison Ave 08837
Magee Rd 08817
Magnolia St 08817
Maida Rd 08820
Main St 08837
Malibu Dr 08820
Malone Ave 08820
Malvern Way 08817
Manning St 08817
Manor Blvd 08820
Manor Ct 08817
Maple Ave & Dr 08837
Maplecrest Rd 08820
Maplewood Ave 08837
Maplewood Ct 08820
Marc Ct 08820
March Pl 08837
Marcols Ct 08820
Marie Ln 08817
Marigold Ct 08820
Marina Dr 08817
Marion St 08820
Market St 08817
Markham Rd 08817
Marlin Ave E & W 08820
Marshall Dr 08817
Martha St 08820
Martin Ave 08837
Mary Ellen Dr 08820
Maryland Ave 08820
Mason Dr 08820
Matson Rd 08817
Matthew Ct 08820
Maureen Ct 08820
May St 08837
Mayercik Ct 08820
Mayfield Ave 08837
Mayling Ct 08837
Mcbratney Ct 08820
Mcevoy Rd 08837
Mcgaw Dr 08837
Mcginnis Rd 08817
Mckinley Ave & St 08820
Meadow Rd
1-320 08817
322-324 08817
326-399 08837
Meadow Brook Rd 08837
Meeker Ave 08817
Megan Ct 08820
Melbourn Ln 08837
Melbourne St 08817
Melissa Ct 08820
Melville Rd 08817
Menlo Park
100-100 08837
100-100 08818
Menlo Ter 08820
Mercer St 08820
Mercury Rd 08817
Meredith Rd 08817
Meridian Rd 08820
Merker Dr 08837
Merriman Pl 08817
Merrywood Dr 08817
Metroplex Dr 08817
Meyer Rd 08817
Michael St 08820
Michelle Cir 08820
Middlesex Ave 08820
Midland Rd 08820
Midvale Rd 08817
Midwood Ave 08820
Miko Rd 08817
Milford Ct 08820
Mill Rd
399A-399B 08837
1-100 08817
101-499 08837
102-598 08817
Miller Ave 08820
Million St 08820
Millpond Way 08820
Milton Ave 08820
Mindy Rd 08820
Minebrook Rd 08820
Mineola Pl 08817
Mitch Snyder Dr 08837
Mockingbird Rd 08820
Monaghan Rd 08817
Monica Dr 08820
Monmouth Ave 08820
Monroe Ave 08820
Montclair Ave 08820
Montview Rd 08837
Moraine Rd 08820
Moretti Ln 08817
Morgan Dr 08817
Morning Glory Ln 08820
Morris Ave 08837
Morse Ave 08817
Moryan Rd 08817
Mount Pleasant Ave 08820
Moyse Pl 08820
Mulberry Ln 08820
Mundy Ave 08820
Municipal Blvd 08817
Murray St 08817
Myra Pl 08817
Myrtle St 08817
Nancy Cir 08817
Nassau Ct 08820
National Rd 08817
Nelson Ave 08817
Netherwood Cir 08820
Nevsky St 08820
New St 08837
New Brooklyn Rd 08817
New Dover Rd 08820
New Durham Rd 08817
New York Blvd 08820
Newburgh Dr 08820
Newfield Ave 08837
Nicholas Ct 08820
Nicholson Ave 08820
Nicole Ter 08820
Nightingale St 08820
Nixon Ln 08837
Noel Ave 08817
Nora Rd 08837
Norman St 08837
Normandy Rd 08820
Northfield Ave 08837
Norton St 08820
Norwood Pl 08817
Nottingham Rd 08820
Now St 08817
Nutmeg Ct 08820
Oak Dr 08837
Oak Ln 08817
Oak Grove Ln 08820
Oak Hills Rd 08820
Oak Tree Rd 08820
Oakland Ave 08817
Oakmont Ct 08820
Oakwood Ave 08837
Oberlin Ct 08820
Ohara St 08837
Old Hickory Ln 08820
Old Post Rd 08817
Old Raritan Rd 08820
Olden Rd 08817
Oliver Ave 08820
Olsen Ave 08820
Olympic Dr 08837
Opatut Ct 08817
Orange St 08817
Orchard St 08837
Orchid Ct 08820
Oriole St 08820
Orlando St 08817
Othen St 08817
Outcalt Rd 08817
Overbrook Ave 08817
Overview Ct 08817
Ovington Ave 08817
Oxford Rd 08820
Pace Dr 08820
Pacific St 08817
Paddock Ct 08820
Paley Pl 08817
Palm Ct 08820
Pannonia Ave 08817
Paris Ave 08820
Park Ave 08820
Park Way 08817
Park Gate Dr 08820
Parker Rd 08820
Parkerson Rd 08817
Parkway Pl 08837
Parkwood Ct 08837
Parsonage Rd 08837
Partch Pl 08817
Patricia Ave 08837
Patrick Ave 08837
Patriot Ct 08820

Patrol Rd 08837
Paul St 08817
Paula St 08820
Pavlocak Ct 08820
Payne Ct 08820
Peace St 08820
Peach Ct 08817
Peake Rd 08837
Ped Pl 08837
Pelham Ave 08817
Pendleton Pl 08820
Penn Ave 08817
Penrose Ct 08820
Periwinkle Ln 08820
Perry Rd 08817
Pershing Ave 08837
Peru St 08820
Peterson Ave 08817
Petti Ln 08820
Pheasant Run 08820
Philip St 08820
Phillip Dr 08820
Phillips Rd 08817
Philo Blvd 08837
Phoenix Ave 08837
Piedmont Rd 08817
Pierson Ave 08837
Pilegis Ct 08817
Pine Dr 08837
Pine St 08817
Pine Ridge Dr 08820
Plafsky Dr 08817
Plainfield Ave 08817
Plainfield Rd 08820
Player Ave 08817
Plaza Pl 08817
Pleasant Ave 08837
Plymouth Pl 08837
Poe Pl 08817
Poll Pl 08817
Poplar St 08817
Porter St 08817
Portland St 08820
W Prescott Ave 08820
Prescott St 08817
Presden St 08820
Preston St 08817
Prestwick Way 08820
Price Dr 08817
Prince St 08837
Private Rd 08817
Proctor St 08817
Progress St 08820
Prospect Ave 08817
Purdue Rd 08820
Putnam Ave 08817
Quaker Ct & St 08820
Quality Pl 08820
Queens Ct 08817
Quincy Rd 08820
Rahway Rd 08820
Rainbow Ct 08820
Rainford Rd 08820
Raleigh Rd 08817
Ramsey Rd 08820
Ranchwood Ct 08817
Raritan Center Pkwy 08837
Raspberry Ct 08817
Ravenswood Ct 08820
Raymond St 08817
Reading Rd 08817
Redfield Vlg 08837
Redwood Ave 08817
Reed St 08817
Regal Rd 08820
Regent Ct 08817
Remington Dr 08820
Renee Ct 08820
Rev Samuel Carpenter Blvd 08820
Revere Blvd 08820
Reynold Ct 08820
Richard Rd 08820
Richmond Rd 08817
Ridge Rd 08817
Rieder Rd 08817
Rinear Dr 08817
Rio Vista Dr 08820
Rivendell Way 08817
Riverview Ave 08817
Roberta Ct 08820
Robin Rd 08820
Rockoff Ct 08837
Rodak Cir 08817
Roger Rd 08817
Rolling Brook Dr 08820
Roney Rd 08820
Roosevelt Blvd, Dr & Ter 08837
Rory Ct 08820
Rose St 08817
Rosewood Rd 08817
Ross Ave 08820
Rosta Rd 08817
Rowan Ct 08837
Roxy Ave 08820
Royale Dr 08820
Runyon Ave 08817
Runyons Ln 08817
Russell Ave 08817
Rutgers St 08817
Rutland St 08817
Ryan Rd 08817
Safran Ave 08837
Sagamore Ave S 08820
Saint Matthews Dr 08817
Salem St 08820
Salka Ct 08817
Sandalwood Dr 08820
Sanders Rd 08817
Sandia Ct 08820
Sandra Dr 08820
Sarah Ct 08817
Savoy Ave 08820
Saw Mill Pond Rd 08817
Schanck Dr 08820
Scheer Ct 08820
Schoolhouse Ln 08817
Schubert Ave 08820
Schuyler Dr 08817
Scotland Ave 08820
Scott Ave 08837
Second St 08837
Seneca St 08837
Seventh St 08837
Seymour Ave 08817
Shady Ln 08820
Shamrock Way 08820
Sharon Ave 08817
Sharp Rd 08837
Sheffield Pl 08837
Sheppard Pl 08817
Sherman Ave & Blvd 08820
Sherry Ct 08820
Sherwood Rd 08820
Sheryl Dr 08820
Shetland Ct 08817
Shifra Ct 08820
W Shirley Ave 08820
Short St 08817
E Side Ave 08817
Silver Lake Ave 08817
Simpson Ave 08817
Sims Rd 08817
Sinclair Rd 08820
Sine Rd 08817
Sixth St 08837
Skytop Rd 08820
Sleepy Hollow Rd 08820
Smalley Rd 08817
Snowflake Ln 08820
Sonia Ct 08820
Southfield Rd 08820
Sovar Ct 08820
Spectrum Dr 08817
Spencer St 08817
Spring St 08820
Spring Brook Dr 08820
Spruce St 08837
Stacey St 08820
Stanley Pl 08817
Stark Pl 08820
Starkin Rd 08837
State Route 27
  1-299 08820
State Route 27
  1500-2100 08817
  2101-2299 08817
  2101-2101 08818
  2102-2298 08817
Stephenville Pkwy 08820
Sterling Ct 08817
Stevens Rd 08817
Stewart Ave 08820
Stiles Rd 08817
Stone St 08817
Stonehedge Rd 08820
Stonewall Dr 08820
Stony Rd W 08817
Stratford Cir 08820
Strawberry Ct 08817
Sturgis Rd 08817
Sulliman Rd 08817
Summer St 08820
Summit Ave 08820
Sunfield Ave 08837
Sunflower Ct 08820
Sunrise Dr 08817
Sunset Ave 08820
Sunshine Ln 08820
Susan Pl 08817
Sussex Ct 08820
Sutton Pl 08817
Suttons Ln 08817
Suydam Ave 08817
Sweetwater Ln 08837
Swiderski Ave 08837
Sycamore Ave 08817
Sylvan Dell Ave 08817
Taft Ave 08817
Tall Oak Rd 08837
Talmadge Rd 08817
Tamagnini Ct 08820
Tamarack Rd 08820
Tarbert Ct 08817
Taurus Ct 08820
Taylor Rd 08817
Teaberry Dr 08820
Technology Dr 08837
Tell Pl 08817
Temple St 08820
Ten Eyck Pl 08820
Tennyson St 08820
Terrill Rd 08817
Terry Ave 08820
Thatcher Ct 08820
Theresa Ct 08837
Third St 08837
Thomas Pl 08837
Thomasine St 08817
Thornall St 08837
Tiffany Dr 08820
Timber Rd 08820
Timber Oaks Rd 08820
Timothy Ct 08837
Tingley Ln 08820
Tived Ln E 08837
Todd St 08817
Toth Ct 08817
Tower Rd 08820
Townsley Ct & St 08837
Traci Ln 08817
Travers Ave 08817
Trenton Ave 08817
Troy St 08820
Truman Dr S 08817
Tulip Ct 08820
Turner Ave 08820
Tuscan Rd 08820
Twin Oaks Dr 08820
Tyler Rd 08820
Tyroler Ave & Ct 08820
Union Ave 08820
Universal Ave 08820
Us Highway 1
  1-1024 08817
  1025-1197 08837
  1026-1198 08817
  1199-1499 08837
  1501-1599 08837
Utica Rd 08820
Valarie Rd 08820
Vale St 08817
Vallata Pl 08820
Valmere Ct 08817
Van Buren Dr 08817
Vassallo Ct 08820
Vauxhall Ct 08820
Velikan Pl 08817
Ventnor Dr 08820
Vernon Rd 08817
Victoria Ct 08817
Victory Pl 08837
Villa Dr 08820
Village Dr 08817
Vinal Ave 08817
Vincent Ct 08820
Vincent Behan Blvd 08837
Vineyard Rd 08817
Vinne Ct 08820
Violet Pl 08817
Visco Dr 08820
Vista Dr 08817
Wagner St 08837
Wainwright St 08837
Wakefield Dr 08820
Waldman Ave 08820
Walker Ave 08820
Wallace St 08817
Walnut St 08817
Walsh Ave 08837
Walton St 08817
Waltuma Ave 08837
Warwick Rd 08820
Washington Ave 08817
Waterford Dr 08817
Watson Ct 08820
Waverly Dr E & W 08817
Wayne Ct 08820
Wayne St 08817
Webb St 08820
Webster Pl 08817
Weldon Rd 08817
Wellington Pl 08817
Wendover Rd 08820
Wendy Ct 08820
West Dr & St 08820
Western Ave 08817
Westervelt Ave 08817
Westgate Dr 08820
Westminster Pl 08817
Weston Forbes Ct 08820
Westover Way 08820
Westwood Cir 08820
Whelan St 08837
White Birch Rd 08837
Whitehall Ave 08820
Whitewood Rd 08820
Whitman Ave & Pl 08817
Whittier St 08820
Wildberry Ct 08817
Wildwood Ave 08837
Wiley Ave 08837
Wilk Rd 08837
Willard Dunham Dr 08837
William Blow Ct 08837
Williams Rd 08820
Willow Ave 08817
Willow Dr 08820
Wilmbelton Ct 08820
Wilshire Rd 08817
Wilson Ave 08817
Winding Brook Way 08820
Windsor Rd 08817
Winnie Ct 08820
Winslow Rd 08837
Winter St 08820
Wintergreen Ave E & W 08820
Winthrop Rd 08817
Wisteria St 08817
Woerner Ct 08817
Wolff Ave 08837
Wood Ave 08820
Wood Acres Dr 08820
Woodbridge Ave
  1600-1798 08817
  1800-2100 08817
  2079-2079 08818
  2101-2825 08817
  2102-2598 08817
  2600-2824 08837
  2826-5099 08837
Woodbrooke Dr 08820
Woodbury Ct & Rd 08820
Woodedge Ave 08817
Woodfern St 08820
Woodhaven Dr 08817
Wooding Ave 08817
Woodland Ave 08820
Woodrow Wilson Dr 08820
Woodruff Rd 08820
Wren Ct 08820
Wright St 08820
Wyndmoor Way 08820
Wynn Rd 08817
Yardley St 08820
Yelencsics Ct 08817
Yolanda Dr 08817
York Dr 08817
Yosko Dr 08817
Yuro Dr 08837
Zaydee Dr 08837

ELIZABETH NJ

General Delivery 07207

POST OFFICE BOXES MAIN OFFICE STATIONS AND BRANCHES

Box No.s
1 - 1399 07207
901 - 978 07208
1425 - 7000 07207
8428 - 8696 07208
8901 - 9060 07201
9141 - 9765 07202
10000 - 10000 07207

NAMED STREETS

Aberdeen Rd 07208
Acme St 07202
Adams Ave 07201
Algonquin Pl 07208
Alina St
  1000-1199 07201
  1200-1399 07208
Allen St 07202
Alton St 07202
Amboy Ave 07202
Amity St 07202
Anna St 07201
Applegate Ave 07202
Arnett St 07202
Aruba St 07201
Augusta St 07201
Bailey Ave 07208
Baker Pl 07208
Baldwin Pl 07208
Bank St 07201
Barnard Pl 07208
Bay Ave 07201
Bayway Ave
  1-97 07202
  99-599 07202
  544-544 07206
  600-898 07202
  601-899 07202
  723-725-723-725 07202
Bayway Cir 07202
S Bayway Terminal 07202
Bellevue St 07202
Bellewood Pl 07208
Bercik St 07201
Berkeley Pl 07208
Berwick St 07202
Bombay St 07201
Bond St 07201
Bonnett St 07202
Boudinot Pl 07201
Boxwood Ct 07202
Boyle Pl 07202
Bridge St 07201
Britton St 07202
Broad St 07201
E Broad St 07201
N Broad St
  200-309 07208
  310-310 07207
  310-920 07208
  311-1099 07208
  813-819-813-819 07208
  919-941-919-941 07208
S Broad St 07202
Broadway 07201
Browning Ave 07208
Brunswick Ave 07202
Burnett St 07202
Burnham Rd 07202
Byron Ave 07208
Cadiz St 07201
Caldwell Pl 07201
Canton St 07202
Carlton St 07202
Carolynn Rd 07201
Carrington St 07208
Carteret St 07202
Catherine St 07201
Cedar Ave 07202
Center Dr 07201
Center St 07202
Chancellor St 07202
Cherry St
  1-199 07202
  201-579 07208
  581-599 07208
Chestnut St 07201
Chetwood St 07202
Chilton St
  1-199 07202
  200-599 07208
Chilton Hall 07202
Christine St 07202
Claremont Ter 07202
Clarkson Ave 07202
Cleveland Ave 07208
Clifton St 07202
Clinton Pl 07208
Clover St 07202
Coakley Cir 07201
Colonia Rd 07208
Commerce Pl 07201
Concord Pl 07208
Coolidge Rd 07208
Corbin St 07201
Country Club Ln 07208
Court St 07201
Crawford Pl 07208
Cross Ave 07208
Cross St 07201
Dakar St 07201
Dayton St 07202
Decker Ave 07208
Dehart Pl 07202
Denman Pl 07208
Devine Ave 07202
Dewey Pl 07202
Dewitt Rd 07208
Dickinson St 07201
Division St 07201
Donald Pl 07208
Dowd Ave 07201
Durant St 07208
Eaton St 07202
Edgar Pl & Rd 07202
Edgewood Rd 07208
Egypt St 07201
Elizabeth Ave 07201
Elizabethtown Plz 07202
Elm Ct & St 07208
Elmora Ave
  1-299 07202
  301-307 07208
  309-499 07208
  59-61-59-61 07202
  61-63-61-63 07202
S Elmora Ave 07202
Elmwood Pl 07208
Ely St 07202
Emerson Ave 07208
Emma St 07201
End Ave & Pl 07202
Erico Ave 07202
Eugenia Pl 07202
Evans St 07201
Fairbanks St 07202
Fairmount Ave
  800-1199 07201
  1200-1299 07208
  851-861-851-861 07201
Fanny St 07201
Fay Ave 07202
Fern Pl 07202
Fernwood Ter 07208
E & N Fleet St 07201
Flora St 07201
Floral Ave 07208
Formosa St 07201
Fralersi St 07202
Franklin St 07201
Fremont Pl 07208
S Front St 07202
Galloping Hill Rd 07208
Garden St 07202
Garfield Pl 07208
Gebhardt Ave 07208
General Karge Ct 07202
Georgian Ct 07208
Gibbons Ct 07202
Gibson Pl 07208
Glenwood Rd 07208
Glimcher Realty Way 07201
E Grand St 07201
W Grand St
  9A-9B 07201
  1-10 07201
  11-17 07202
  12-18 07201
  19-999 07202
  256-258-256-258 07202
Green St 07202
Grier Ave 07202
Grove St
  1-200 07202
  201-299 07208
  202-1098 07202
  601-1099 07202
  645-647-645-647 07202
Halsted Rd 07208
Hamilton St 07208
Hampton Pl 07201
Hand Pl 07201
Harding Rd 07208
Harrison St 07208
Hayes Ave 07202
Hazard Pl 07208
Henry St 07201
Hetfield Ave 07202
High St 07202
Highland Ave 07208
Hillside Rd 07208
Ikea Dr 07201
Irvington Ave 07208
Izmir St 07201
Jackson Ave 07201
Jacques St 07201
Jefferson Ave 07201
Jersey Ave 07202
E Jersey St 07201
W Jersey St
  1-29 07201
  30-56 07202
  58-399 07202
  12-24-12-24 07201
  201-211-201-211 07202

240-242-240-242 07202
40-48-40-48 07202
John St 07202
Johnson Ave 07202
Julia St 07201
Julian Pl 07208
Kapkowski Rd 07201
Keats Ave 07208
Kempshall Pl 07208
Kenneth Ave 07202
Kerlyn Ct 07202
Kilsyth Rd 07208
Kipling Rd 07208
Krakow St 07202
Lafayette St 07201
Laura St 07201
Leenchen Ave 07208
Lexington Pl 07208
Liberty St 07202
Lidgerwood Ave 07202
Lincoln Ave 07208
Linden Ave 07202
Linden St 07201
Livingston Rd 07208
Livingston St 07201
Louisa St 07201
Lowden St 07208
Lower Rd 07208
Lyons Pl 07202
Madison Ave 07201
Magie Ave 07208
Magnolia Ave 07201
Malden Ter 07208
Maple Ave 07202
Marshall St 07201
Martin St 07201
Martin Luther King Plz .. 07201
Mary St 07201
Mckinley St 07202
Mclain St 07202
Mclester St 07201
Meadow St 07201
Mellon Pl 07208
Melrose Ter 07208
Meredith Ave 07202
Meridian St 07201
Miller St 07201
Monmouth Rd 07208
Monroe Ave 07201
Montgomery Pl & St ... 07202
Morrell St 07201
Morris Ave 07208
Morristown Rd 07208
Morses Mill Rd 07202
Mravlag Mnr 07202
Muriel Pkwy 07208
Murray St 07202
Myrtle St 07202
Neck Ln 07201
Nelson Ave 07202
New Point Rd 07201
New York Ave 07202
Newark Ave 07208
Newcomb Pl 07202
Niles St 07202
Norivere St 07201
North Ave
1-539 07208
541-599 07208
1000-1100 07201
1102-1198 07201
1200-1399 07208
1-999 07201
Norwood Ter 07202
Oak St 07201
Oakwood Pl 07208
Ogden St 07202
Okinawa St 07201
Old Rd 07202
Olive St 07201
Orchard St 07208
Palisade Rd 07208
Palmer St 07202
Park Ave 07208
S Park St 07201
Parker Rd 07208
Parkview Ter 07202
Parmalee Pl 07208
Pearl St 07202
Pennington St 07202
Pennsylvania Ave 07201
Pershing Ave 07202
Pingry Pl 07208
Polaris St 07201
Police Plz 07201
Polonia Ave 07202
Prince St 07208
Princeton Rd 07208
Progress St 07201
Prospect St 07201
Pulaski St 07202
Race St 07202
Rahway Ave 07202
Raymond Ter 07208
Rebecca Pl 07201
S Reid St 07201
Relocated Bayway 07202
Reuter Ave 07202
Richford Ter 07202
Richmond St 07202
Riverside Dr 07208
Roanoke Ave 07208
Rockefeller St 07202
Roosevelt St 07202
Rosehill Pl 07202
Rosewood Pl 07208
Russell Pl 07202
Sailer Ct 07201
Salem Ave & Park 07208
Sayre St 07208
Scotland Rd 07208
Seib Ave 07202
Shelley Ave 07208
Sheridan Ave 07208
Sherman Ave 07208
Smith St 07201
South St 07202
Spencer St 07202
Spofford Ave 07202
Spring St 07201
Springfield Rd 07208
Standish St 07202
Stanley Ter 07208
Stanton Ave 07208
Stewart Pl 07202
Stiles St 07208
Summer St 07202
Summit Rd 07208
Thomas St 07202
Thompson Ln 07201
Trenton Ave 07202
Trinity Pl 07201
Tripoli St 07201
Trotters Ln 07208
Trumbull St 07201
Tudor Ct 07208
Union Ave 07208
Union Sq 07201
Union St
100-224 07202
225-299 07208
Ursino Pl 07208
Us Highway 1 07202
Van Buren Ave 07201
Verona Ave 07208
Vine St 07202
Virginia St
1000-1199 07201
1200-1242 07208
1244-1299 07208
1301-1399 07208
Vista Ave 07208
Walnut St 07201
Washington Ave 07202
Watson Ave 07202
Waverly Pl 07208
Westfield Ave 07208
Westminster Ave 07208
Wilder St 07208
Wiley Post Rd 07201
William St 07201
Williams Dr 07202
Williamson St 07202
Wilson Ter 07208
Winfield Scott Plz 07201
Winthrop Pl 07208
Wolski Dr 07202
Woodruff Ln 07201
Wyoming Ave 07208
York St 07201

NUMBERED STREETS

1st Ave 07201
S 1st St 07202
2nd Ave
500-899 07202
900-999 07201
3rd Ave
500-899 07202
900-999 07201
4th Ave 07202
5th Ave 07202
7th St 07201
S 7th St 07202

HACKENSACK NJ

General Delivery 07602

POST OFFICE BOXES MAIN OFFICE STATIONS AND BRANCHES

Box No.s
1 - 1280 07602
1910 - 1910 07601
9998 - 9998 07602

NAMED STREETS

Ackerson St 07601
Allen St 07601
American Legion Dr 07601
Ames St 07601
Anderson St 07601
Arcadia Rd 07601
E Atlantic St 07601
Banta Pl 07601
Beech St 07601
Berdan Pl 07601
Bergen St 07601
Bergen County Plz 07601
Berkshire Pl 07601
E Berry St 07601
Blanchard Ter 07601
Blauvelt Pl 07601
Bloom St 07601
Bonhomme St 07601
Bridge St 07601
Briscolina St 07601
E Broadway 07601
Brook St 07601
Buckingham Dr 07601
Burlews Ct 07601
Byrne St 07601
Cambridge Ter 07601
E & W Camden St 07601
Campbell Ave 07601
Carol Ct 07601
Catalpa Ave 07601
Cedar Ave 07601
Central Ave 07601
Charles St 07601
Chestnut Ave 07601
Church St 07601
Clarendon Pl 07601
Clark St 07601
Clay St 07601
Cleveland St 07601
Clinton Pl 07601
Clubway 07601
Coles Ave 07601
Colonial Ter 07601
Comet Way 07601
Commerce Way 07601
Conklin Pl 07601
Coolidge Pl 07601
County Pl 07601
Court St 07601
Crestwood Ave 07601
Daniel St 07601
Davis Ave 07601
Dean St 07601
Devoe Pl 07601
Dewitt Pl 07601
Dewolf Pl 07601
Dicarolis Ct 07601
Division Pl 07601
Dorchester Rd 07601
Dyatt Pl 07601
Elizabeth St 07601
Elleen Ter 07601
Elm Ave 07601
Emerald St 07601
English St 07601
Esplanade 07601
Essex St 07601
Euclid Ave S 07601
Fair St 07601
Fairmount Ave 07601
W Franklin Pl & St 07601
Frederick St 07601
Gamewell St 07601
Gardner Pl 07601
George St 07601
Golf Pl 07601
Gracie Pl 07601
Grand Ave 07601
Green St 07601
Grove St 07601
Hackensack Ave 07601
Halley Dr 07601
Hamilton Pl 07601
Haynes St 07601
Heath Pl 07601
Henry Pl 07601
Herman St 07601
High St 07601
Hobart St 07601
Holt St 07601
Hopper St 07601
Hospital Pl 07601
Hudson St 07601
Huyler St 07601
Ise St 07601
Jackson Ave 07601
James St 07601
Jay St 07601
Jefferson St 07601
Jersey Pl 07601
John St 07601
Johnson Ave 07601
E Kansas St 07601
Kaplan Ave 07601
E Kennedy St 07601
Kenneth St 07601
Kent St 07601
Kinderkamack Rd 07601
King St 07601
Kipp St 07601
Kotte Pl 07601
Krone Pl 07601
E Lafayette St 07601
S Lake Dr 07601
Lawrence St 07601
Lawton St 07601
Lee Pl 07601
Lehigh St 07601
Lexington Ave 07601
Liberty St 07601
Lincoln St 07601
Linden St 07601
Lodi St 07601
Longview Ave 07601
W Lookout Ave 07601
Louis St 07601
Madison St 07601
Maiden Ln 07601
S Main St 07601
Maple Ave 07601
Maple Hill Dr 07601
Marginal Rd 07601
Marion St 07601
Martin Ter 07601
Marvin Ave 07601
Mary St 07601
Mckinley St 07601
Meadow St 07601
E Mercer St 07601
Michael St 07601
Midtown Pl 07601
Midtown Bridge
Approac 07601
E Moonachie Rd 07601
Moore St 07601
Myer St 07601
New St 07601
S Newman St 07601
Oak St 07601
Old Hoboken Rd 07601
Old River St 07601
Orchard St 07601
Overlook Ave 07601
Owens Rd 07601
Pangborn Pl 07601
S Park St 07601
Parker Ave 07601
Parkway 07601
E Passaic St 07601
Peters Rd 07601
Pine St 07601
Pink St 07601
E & W Pleasantview
Ave 07601
Polifly Rd 07601
Poor St 07601
Poplar Ave 07601
Porter St 07601
Prospect Ave 07601
Pulaski Pl 07601
Railroad Ave & Pl 07601
Reilly Ct 07601
Ricardo Pl 07601
S River St 07601
Riverside Sq Mall 07601
Romaine Ct 07601
Ross Ave 07601
Rowland Ave 07601
Russell Pl 07601
E Salem St 07601
E Salem St Ext 07601
Shafer Pl 07601
Simons Ave 07601
South St 07601
Spring Valley Ave 07601
Standish Ave 07601
Stanley Pl 07601
State St
1-245 07601
226-226 07602
246-498 07601
247-499 07601
252-254-252-254 07601
294-298-294-298 07601
S State St 07601
N & S State Rt 17 07601
State Rt 4 07601
S Summit Ave & Ct 07601
Sussex St 07601
Sutton Ave 07601
Taylor Ave 07601
Temple Ave 07601
Terhune Pl 07601
Terrace Pl 07601
Thompson St 07601
Tracy Pl 07601
Trinity Pl 07601
Troast St 07601
Union St 07601
University Plz 07601
University Plaza Dr 07601
Van Olst St 07601
Van Orden Pl 07601
Van Wettering Pl 07601
Vanderbeck Pl 07601
Vincent Ave 07601
Voorhis Ln & Pl 07601
Vreeland Ave 07601
E Ward St 07601
Warren St 07601
Washington Ave & Pl 07601
Water St 07601
West St 07601
Williams Ave 07601
Willow Ave 07601
Wilson St 07601
Winchester Pl 07601
Woodridge Ave 07601
Worth St 07601
Wysocki Pl 07601
Zabriskie St 07601

NUMBERED STREETS

All Street Addresses 07601

HALEDON NJ

POST OFFICE BOXES MAIN OFFICE STATIONS AND BRANCHES

Box No.s
All PO Boxes 07538

NAMED STREETS

Aberdeen Ct 07508
Ada Ct 07508
Ahnert Ave 07508
Ailsa Ave 07508
Al Lyn Ct 07508
Albanese Rd 07508
Albion Ave 07508
Alpine Dr 07508
Arrow Ter 07508
Arthur St 07508
Aspen Ter 07508
Avenue B 07508
Avenue C 07508
Avenue D 07508
Avenue F 07508
Ballentine Dr 07508
E Barbour St 07508
Bayberry Ln 07508
Beam Pl 07508
Belmont Ave 07508
Bensam Pl 07508
Bernard Ave 07508
Birchwood Ln 07508
Boat St 07508
Bogert Dr 07508
Brian Ct 07508
Briarwood Way 07508
W Broadway 07508
Brookside Ter 07508
Brookview Dr 07508
Brown Ave 07508
Burhans Ave 07508
Buschmann Ave 07508
Carla Ct 07508
Casson Ln 07508
Cedar Ct 07508
Cedar Cliff Ave 07508
Central Ave 07508
Chalmers Ave 07508
Chestnut Ave 07508
Chestnut Hill Rd 07508
Church St 07508
Circle Ave 07508
Clara St 07508
Cliff Ct & St 07508
W Clinton St 07508
Clowes St 07508
Coles Hill Rd 07508
Columbia Ct 07508
Cona Ct 07508
Cook St 07508
Coolidge Pl 07508
Copley Ct 07508
Cranberry Ct 07508
Crest Ct 07508
Crestview Ter 07508
Cypress Ave 07508
Cyril Ave 07508
Darrow Dr 07508
Dater St 07508
Dawn Ave 07508
Degray St 07508
Deroon Ave 07508
Dietrich Ln 07508
Dorothy Dr 07508
Dunkerly Ln 07508
Dykers Farm Rd 07508
Edson Pl 07508
Elizabeth Ct 07508
Ellis Dr 07508
Evergreen Ave 07508
Fairview Ave 07508
Feldman Ter 07508
Florence Pl 07508
Ford Rd 07508
Forest Dr 07508
Frankfort St 07508
Gamba Ct 07508
Gatherings Dr 07508
Gemeinhardt Pl 07508
Geyer St 07508
Gionti Pl 07508
Glen Pl 07508
Glenwood Dr 07508
Graham Ave 07508
Grand Summit Ave 07508
Grandview Dr 07508
Granite Ave 07508
Grant Dr 07508
Greenwood Ave 07508
Grove St 07508
Haledon Ave
104-234 07508
236-258 07508
259-351 07508
260-352 07508
353-439 07508
400-400 07538
440-498 07508
441-499 07508
N Haledon Ave 07508
W Haledon Ave 07508
Haledon Ct 07508
Halsey Ave 07508
Harmon Pl 07508
Harring Ct 07508
Harris St 07508
Harrison Ave 07508
Hartwig Pl 07508
Hearthstone Dr 07508
Heights Dr 07508
Henry St 07508
High Mountain Rd 07508
Highcrest Dr 07508
Highland Rd 07508
Hillcrest Dr 07508
Hillside Dr 07508
Hobart Ave 07508
Hodges Pl 07508
Hopper St 07508
Hoxsey Pl 07508
Hubert Ct 07508
Hunter Rd N & S 07508
Ida St 07508
Indian Trl 07508
Ivy Ct 07508
James Ct & Pl 07508
Jasper St 07508
Joan Pl 07508
John St 07508
John Ryle Ave 07508
Keiller Ct 07508
Kenneth Ave 07508
King St 07508
Kossuth St 07508
Koster Pl 07508

Kuiken Ct 07508
Lake St 07508
Lakeshore Dr 07508
Lakeview Ave 07508
Laurie Dr 07508
Lee Ave & Dr 07508
Legion Pl 07508
Lenox Ave 07508
Leonard St 07508
Leonhard Dr 07508
Lewis St 07508
Linda Vista Ave 07508
Lisa Ct 07508
Lotz Ave 07508
Louise Pl 07508
Lupton Ln 07508
Magnolia Way 07508
E Main Ave & St 07508
Manchester Ave 07508
Mangold St 07508
Manor Rd 07508
Maple Ct 07508
Marilyn St 07508
Marlerle Ave 07508
Mary St 07508
Mason Ave 07508
Meade Ave 07508
Meadow Pl 07508
Melissa Dr 07508
Messerve Pl 07508
Michelle Ct 07508
Moccasin Rd 07508
Morley Pl 07508
Morningside Ave 07508
Morrissee Ave 07508
Morrissee Avenue Ext 07508
Motta Ave 07508
Mountain Ave 07508
Mountainview Dr 07508
Moyer Ct 07508
Myrtle Ave 07508
Nassau St 07508
Norwood St 07508
Oakdale Ct 07508
Oakwood Ave 07508
Onyx Ter 07508
W Overlook Ave 07508
Oxford Ct & St 07508
Park Ave & St 07508
Passaic Ave 07508
Paterson Ave 07508
Peach Tree Ln 07508
Peters Ln 07508
Pettee Ave 07508
Pinecliff Ct 07508
Planten Ave 07508
Pleasantview Dr 07508
Pompton Rd 07508
Post St 07508
Preakness Ave 07508
Prescott Ave, Pl & Ter 07508
Pyramid Way 07508
Reinhardt Ave 07508
Reservoir Dr 07508
Richard St 07508
Richard Scott Ct 07508
Richardson Ave 07508
Ridge Rd 07508
Robert St 07508
Robinson Ct 07508
Rock Ledge Ter 07508
Roe St 07508
Romaine Rd 07508
Roosevelt Ave 07508
Rosewood Ct 07508
Ross Ln 07508
Rosslee Ave 07508
Rothesay Ave 07508
Ruff Ct 07508
Ruth Pl 07508
Ryerson Ave 07508
Sackerman Ave 07508
Savoy Pl 07508
Saw Mill Rd 07508
Schnell Ct 07508
School St 07508
Sherwood Ave 07508
Short St 07508
Sicomac Rd 07508
Skyline Dr 07508
Skyview Dr 07508
Southside Ave 07508
Split Rock Rd 07508
Springbrook Ave 07508
Spruce Ln 07508
Squaw Brook Rd 07508
Stanley Ct 07508
Stansfield Ave & Pl 07508
Stockton Rd 07508
Struyk Ave 07508
Sturr St 07508
Summit Ave 07508
Suncrest Ave 07508
Surrey Pl 07508
Suter Ln 07508
Tamboer Dr 07508
Terrace Ave 07508
Thornton Dr 07508
Tilt St 07508
Tuxedo Ct 07508
Valley View Dr & Rd 07508
Van Dyke Ave 07508
Venna Ave 07508
Verein St 07508
Vine St 07508
Wagaraw Blvd 07508
Walnut Ct 07508
Walray Ave 07508
Wayne Ave & Ct 07508
Weber Ct 07508
Werner Ave 07508
Westervelt Ave 07508
Westside Ave 07508
Wigwam Rd 07508
Willie St 07508
Willow Brook Ct 07508
Woodland Ave 07508
Woodside Ave 07508
Zabriskie St 07508

NUMBERED STREETS

All Street Addresses 07508

HAWTHORNE NJ

POST OFFICE BOXES MAIN OFFICE STATIONS AND BRANCHES

Box No.s
All PO Boxes 07507

NAMED STREETS

Agnes Ter 07506
Alana Dr 07506
Alexandria Ave 07506
Allen St 07506
Annette Ave 07506
Apple Hill Ct 07506
Arlington Ave 07506
Ashley Ct & St 07506
Bamford Ave 07506
Barker Ave 07506
Beverly Ln & Rd 07506
Birchwood Dr 07506
Braen Ave 07506
Brockhuizen Ln 07506
Brook Hollow Ct 07506
Brookside Ave 07506
Browelde Ave 07506
Brownstone Ter 07506
Buena Vista Ave 07506
Calvo Pl 07506
Cathy Ave 07506
Cedar Ave & Pl 07506
Central Ave 07506
Charwalt Dr 07506
Cheryl Hills Dr 07506
Chopin Dr 07506
Cider Mill Rd 07506
Clara Ave 07506
Cobblers Ln 07506
Columbus Ave 07506
Coolidge Pl 07506
Cornell Ave 07506
Coulter St 07506
Crist Ave 07506
Cynthia Ct 07506
De Bruyle Ct 07506
Debra Ct 07506
Devoe Pl 07506
Diamond Bridge Ave
1-81 07506
83-227 07506
226-226 07507
229-399 07506
246-398 07506
Disepo Ave 07506
Division St 07506
Dixie Ave 07506
Dogwood Dr 07506
Douglas Ave 07506
Ekings Ave 07506
Elberon Ave 07506
Emeline Dr 07506
N Ethel Ave 07506
Faber Dr 07506
Fairview Ave 07506
Florence Ave 07506
Forest Ave 07506
Franklin Ave 07506
Frederick Ave 07506
Garden Ave 07506
Garfield Ave 07506
Genevieve Ave 07506
Gibraltar Ter 07506
Glen Ct 07506
Goffle Rd 07506
Goffle Brook Ct 07506
Goffle Hill Rd 07506
Grand Ave 07506
Grandview Ave 07506
Greenwood Ave 07506
Harrison Pl 07506
Hawthorne Ave 07506
Henry Ave 07506
N Highcrest Dr 07506
Highview Ave 07506
Hillcrest Ave 07506
Hillock Ave 07506
Hopper Ave 07506
Horizon Ter 07506
Horton Ave 07506
Hutchinson Ave 07506
Irvington Pl 07506
Ivan Pl 07506
Jefferson Pl 07506
Karl Ave 07506
Kaywin Ave 07506
Keith Ct 07506
Kenwood Rd 07506
Kingston Ave 07506
Knoble Pl 07506
Lafayette Ave 07506
Lafayette Ave Ext 07506
Laggner Ct 07506
Laurel St 07506
Lee Ave 07506
Legion Pl 07506
Lincoln Ave & St 07506
Little St 07506
Llewellyn Ave 07506
Longview Ct 07506
Loretto Ave 07506
Lucille Dr 07506
Lynack Rd 07506
Lynne Ave 07506
Macfarlan Ave 07506
Maitland Ave 07506
Mandon Ter 07506
Mary St 07506
Mawhinney Ave 07506
May St 07506
Mazur Pl 07506
Mckinley Ave 07506
Metro Vista Dr 07506
Midland Ave 07506
Minerva Ave 07506
Missonellie Ct 07506
Mohawk Ave 07506
Mountain Ave & Ln 07506
Nelke Ct 07506
Nelson Ave 07506
New York Ave 07506
Nixon Ct 07506
Norma Ter 07506
Oak Pl 07506
Old Orchard Dr 07506
Orchard Pl 07506
Outlook Ave 07506
Park Ave 07506
Park Slope Ter 07506
Parker Ave 07506
Parmelee Ave 07506
Pasadena Pl 07506
Passaic Ave 07506
Peach Tree Ct 07506
Penney Ct 07506
Pokomoke Pl 07506
Post Ave 07506
Prescott Ave & Pl 07506
Prospect St 07506
Ravine Dr W 07506
Raymond Pl 07506
Rea Ave 07506
Rea Avenue Ext 07506
Regal Ct 07506
Reid Pl 07506
Rhodes Ct 07506
Ridge Rd 07506
Ridgewood Ave 07506
Robertson Ave 07506
Rock Rd 07506
Rockledge Rd 07506
Roosevelt Ave 07506
Royal Ave 07506
Ruth Ave 07506
Schoon Ave 07506
Sherman Ave 07506
Short St 07506
Sicomac Rd 07506
Slotnick Ave 07506
South Ave 07506
Stams Aly 07506
State Rt 208 07506
Summer St 07506
Summit Ave 07506
Sunrise Dr 07506
Surrey Pl 07506
Sylvester Ave 07506
Taylor Ave 07506
Thomas Rd 07506
Todd Ct 07506
Tonia Ter 07506
Tudor Ct 07506
Tuxedo Ave 07506
Union St 07506
Utter Ave 07506
Valley St 07506
Van Winkle Ave 07506
Victor Pl 07506
Vincent Pl 07506
Vreeland Ave 07506
Wagaraw Rd 07506
Wagner Pl 07506
Warburton Ave 07506
Warren Ave 07506
Washington Ave, Pl & St 07506
N Watchung Dr 07506
Westervelt Ave 07506
Woodland Ave 07506
Woodside Ave 07506

NUMBERED STREETS

All Street Addresses 07506

JERSEY CITY NJ

General Delivery 07303

POST OFFICE BOXES MAIN OFFICE STATIONS AND BRANCHES

Box No.s
413A - 413A 07303
470A - 470A 07303
4073A - 4073A 07304
J50 - J55 07306
A25 - A25 07304
J2 - J16 07306
1 - 3960 07303
4000 - 4759 07304
5001 - 5295 07305
6291 - 6942 07306
7001 - 7930 07307
8000 - 8888 07308
9200 - 13240 07303
15001 - 15999 07305
16001 - 16720 07306
17001 - 17400 07307
24001 - 24300 07304
25000 - 25080 07305

NAMED STREETS

Abbett St 07307
Academy St
2-102 07302
104-157 07302
158-399 07306
Aetna St 07302
Alan Ter 07306
Albert Pl 07305
Alder St 07305
Alexander Ct 07305
Allen St 07306
Amity St 07304
Ann St 07307
Apollo St 07306
Arlington Ave
209A-271A 07305
1-272 07305
274-274 07305
275-499 07304
Armstrong Ave 07305
Ash St 07304
Astor Pl 07304
Atlantic St 07304
Atlas Ct 07305
Audrey Zapp Dr 07305
Audubon Ave 07305
Aurora Pl 07305
Baldwin Ave
2-6 07304
8-55 07304
56-599 07306
Barbara Pl 07304
Barrow St 07302
Bartholdi Ave 07305
Bates St 07302
Bay St 07302
Bayside Pl & Ter 07305
Bayside Park Dr & Ter 07305
Bayview Ave 07305
Beach St 07307
Beacon Ave 07306
Beacon Way 07304
Belmont Ave 07304
Belvidere Ave
1-99 07304
100-299 07306
Bennett St 07304
Bentley Ave 07304
Bergen Ave
1-319 07305
320-696 07304
697-999 07306
673-675-673-675 07304
675-673-675-673 07304
Berkeley Pl 07306
Bernius Ct 07304
Bevan St 07306
E Bidwell Ave 07305
Bill Mcewen Dr 07306
Birch St 07305
Bishop St 07304
Bleecker St 07307
Boland St 07306
Boltwood St 07304
Bond St 07306
Booraem Ave 07307
Bostwick Ave 07305
Bowers St 07307
Boyd Ave & Ct 07304
Bramhall Ave 07304
Briarwood Rd 07305
Bright St 07302
Brinkerhoff St 07304
Britton St 07306
Broadman Pkwy 07305
Broadway 07306
Brooks St 07302
Brown Pl 07305
Brunswick St 07302
Bryan Pl 07306
Bryant Ave 07306
Burma Rd 07305
Butternut St 07305
Buttonwood St 07305
Cambridge Ave 07307
Canal Cir 07304
Canal St 07302
Carbon Pl 07305
Carbon St 07304
Carlton Ave
1-48 07307
49-299 07306
Carpenter Ct 07305
Carteret Ave 07305
Cashenso 07311
Casper Ct 07305
Catherine Ct 07305
Cator Ave 07305
Caven Point Ave & Rd 07305
Cedar St 07305
Center St 07302
Central Ave
20-110 07306
112-152 07306
153-523 07307
525-599 07307
325-327-325-327 07307
430-428-430-428 07307
Chapel Ave 07305
Charles St 07307
Charlotte Ave & Cir 07306
Cherry St 07305
Chestnut Ave 07306
Chopin Ct 07302
Christopher Columbus Dr 07302
City Hall 07302
Claremont Ave
1-347 07305
349-371 07305
372-449 07304
450-599 07305
Clarke Ave 07304
Clendenny Ave 07304
Clerk St
1-231 07305
232-399 07304
Cliff St 07306
Clifton Pl 07304
Clinton Ave 07304
Colden St 07302
Coles St
1-179 07302
181-187 07302
189-399 07310
5-11-5-11 07302
Colgate St 07302
Collard St 07306
College Dr & St 07305
Colony Rd 07305
Columbia Ave 07307
Communipaw Ave 07304
Concord St 07306
Concourse St E 07306
Condict St 07306
Congress St 07307
Constellation Pl 07305
Constitution Way 07305
Cook St 07306
Corbin Ave 07306
Corcoran St 07305
Cornelison Ave
1-220 07304
221-299 07302
Cottage St 07306
Cottonwood St 07305
Country Village Rd 07305
County Rd 07307
Court House Pl 07306
Covert St 07306
Crabapple Ct 07305
Crawford St 07306
Crescent Ave 07304
Crossgate Rd 07305
Cubberly Pl 07306
Culver Ave 07305
Cuneo Pl 07307
Custer Ave 07305
Cypress St 07305
Dakota Ave 07305
Dales Ave 07306
Daliangt St 07310
Danforth Ave 07305
Dekalb Ave 07306
Delaware Ave
1-99 07304
100-299 07306
Delmar Rd 07305
Dempsey Ct 07305
Dey St 07306
Division St 07302
Dogwood St 07305
Droyer St 07305
Droyers Pointe Blvd 07305
Dudley St 07302
Duffield Ave 07306
Duncan Ave
1-75 07304
76-599 07306
180-182-180-182 07306
Duncan Ct 07306
Dwight St 07305
East St 07306
Eastern Pkwy 07305
Edward Hart Dr 07305
Ege Ave
1-122 07305
123-499 07304
Elizabeth St 07306
Ellis Is 07305
Elm St 07306
Emerson Ave 07306
Emory St 07304
Ems Plz 07302
Enos Pl 07306
Enterprise Ct 07305
Erie St
1-183 07302
184-184 07310
185-185 07302
186-299 07310
Essex St 07302
Everett St 07304
Evertrust Plz 07302
Exchange Pl 07302
Exeter Rd 07305
Fairmount Ave
1-154 07304
155-499 07306
Fairmount Ter 07306
Fairview Ave 07304
Fayette Ave 07306
Ferncliff Rd 07305
Ferry St 07307
Field Ave 07306
Fir St 07305

Fisk St 07305
Fleet St 07306
Floyd St 07306
Foot Of Colony Rd 07305
Forrest St 07304
Fowler Ave 07305
Fox Pl 07306
Foxhound Ct 07305
Foye Pl 07306
Frances Ct 07305
Franklin St 07307
Freedom Pl 07305
Freedomway 07305
Freeman Ave 07306
Fremont St 07302
Front St 07302
Fulton Ave 07305
G Cannon Dr 07304
Garden Ter 07305
Gardner Ave 07304
Garfield Ave
1-931 07305
932-1199 07304
Garrabrandt St 07304
Garrison Ave 07306
Gates Ave 07305
Gautier Ave 07306
Gifford Ave 07304
Giles Ave 07306
Glenn Ln 07305
Glenwood Ave 07306
Gloria Robinson Ct 07306
Grace St 07307
Graham St 07307
Grand St
1-506 07302
507-507 07304
508-586 07302
509-535 07302
551-585 07304
587-899 07304
81-83-81-83 07302
Grant Ave 07305
Gray St 07302
Gredarai Rd 07311
Greene St 07302
Greenville Ave 07305
Greenwich Dr 07305
Grieco Dr 07305
Griffith St 07307
Grove St
200-368 07302
561-700 07310
Hague St 07307
Half Moon Isle 07305
Halladay St 07304
Halleck Ave 07306
Halstead St 07305
W Hamilton Pl 07302
Hampton Ct 07302
Hancock Ave 07307
Harbor Dr 07305
Harborside Pl 07311
Harmon St 07304
Harrison Ave 07304
Harvey Ave 07306
Hawthorne Ave 07306
Heckman Dr 07305
Hemlock St 07305
Henerth Ave 07304
Henry St 07306
Herbert Pl 07306
High St 07306
Highland Ave 07306
Highview Rd 07305
Highway 440 07305
Hoboken Ave
1-140 07310
276-380 07306
382-499 07306
Hobson St 07307
Holly St 07305
Holmes Ave 07306
Hope St 07307
Hopkins Ave 07306
Howard Pl 07306

Howell St 07306
Hudson Ct 07305
Hudson St 07302
Huron Ave 07306
Hutton St 07307
Independence Way 07305
Industrial Dr 07305
Intrepid Ct & Pl 07305
Iorio Ct 07305
Irene Carson Ct 07304
Irving St 07307
Ivy Pl 07304
James Ave 07306
James Pop Curry Dr 07304
Jefferson Ave 07306
Jersey Ave
1-706 07302
708-716 07302
715-715 07310
717-899 07310
492-498-492-498 07302
705 1/2-705 1/2 07302
Jersey City Blvd 07305
Jewett Ave 07304
John F Kennedy Blvd
1500-2189 07305
2190-2582 07304
2583-3284 07306
3285-3720 07307
3722-3798 07307
2533-2521-2533-2521 07304
3296-94-3296-94 07307
Johnston Ave 07304
Jones Pl & St 07306
Jordan Ave 07306
Journal Sq 07306
Journal Square Plz 07306
Juniper St 07305
Kearney Ave 07305
Kellogg St 07305
Kensington Ave
1-159 07304
160-198 07306
138-140-138-140 07304
Kissam Ct 07305
Lafayette Ln & St 07304
Laidlaw Ave 07306
Lake St 07306
Larch Ave 07306
Laurel Ct 07302
Lee Ct 07305
Lembeck Ave 07305
Leonard St 07307
Lewis Ave 07306
Lexington Ave 07304
Liberty Ave
1-244 07306
245-699 07307
Liberty View Dr 07302
Liggons Ln 07305
Lincoln Park 07304
Lincoln St 07307
Linden Ave & Ct 07305
Lineau Pl
1-15 07306
16-99 07307
Locust St 07305
Logan Ave 07306
Long St 07305
Lott St 07306
Ludlow St 07305
Luis Munoz Marin Blvd 07310
Lyon Ct 07305
Madison Ave 07304
Magnolia Ave 07306
Mall Dr E & W 07310
Mallory Ave
1-55 07305
56-237 07304
421-499 07306
Manhattan Ave 07307
Manila Ave
369-528 07302
529-560 07310
Manischewitz Plz 07302

Manning Ave 07304
Maple St 07304
Marcy Ave 07304
Marcy Pl 07306
Marin Blvd 07302
Marion Pl 07306
Martin Luther King Jr Dr
1-400 07305
401-599 07304
Maxwell St 07302
Mcadoo Ave 07305
Mcdougall St 07304
Mcmartin Ct 07305
Mcpherson Pl 07306
Mcwilliams Pl 07302
Mercer Loop 07302
Mercer St
2-28 07302
30-470 07302
471-599 07306
Merritt St 07305
Merseles Ct & St 07302
Mill Rd 07302
Miller St 07304
Milton Ave 07307
Mina Dr 07305
Minerva St 07304
Monitor St 07304
Monmouth St
100-511 07302
513-535 07302
536-565 07310
570-572 07302
510 1/2-510 1/2 07302
Montgomery Ct 07302
Montgomery St
1A-1A 07302
2-70 07302
69-69 07303
71-601 07302
72-638 07302
639-922 07306
924-998 07306
Monticello Ave
1-243 07304
244-299 07306
115-113-115-113 07304
167-169-167-169 07304
Montrose Ave 07307
Morgan St 07302
Morris Blvd & St 07302
Morris Pesin Dr 07305
Morton Pl 07305
Morton St 07304
Mountain Rd 07307
Msgr Wojtycha Dr 07305
Mulberry St 07305
Murylu Dr 07305
Myrtle Ave 07305
Nardone Pl 07306
Nelson Ave 07307
Neptune Ave 07305
Nesbitt St 07307
Nevins St 07306
New Loop 07302
New St 07305
New Heckman Dr 07305
New Hope Ln 07305
New York Ave 07307
Newark Ave
98-116 07302
118-435 07302
469-509 07306
511-1001 07306
1003-1199 07306
121-125-121-125 07302
Newkirk St 07306
Newport Pkwy 07310
Nj State Hwy 07306
Norcroft Rd 07305
North St 07307
Nunda Ave
1-99 07304
100-299 07306
Oak St 07304
Oakdale Rd 07305
Oakland Ave 07306

Ocean Ave
1-754 07305
755-755 07304
757-899 07304
Ogden Ave 07307
Old Bergen Rd 07305
Olean Ave
1-99 07304
100-299 07306
13-15-13-15 07304
Orchard St 07306
Orient Ave 07305
Oxford Ave 07304
Pacific Ave 07304
Palisade Ave
1-247 07306
248-699 07307
368-370-368-370 07307
76-78-76-78 07306
Pamrapo Ave 07305
Park Ave 07302
Park Ln S 07310
Park St 07304
Parnell Pl 07305
Passaic Ave 07307
Paterson St 07307
Paterson Plank Rd 07307
Path Plz 07306
Paulmier Pl 07302
Paulusen Ct 07305
Pavonia Ave
149-444 07302
445-999 07306
Peace Dr 07305
Peadoner St 07302
Pearsall Ave 07305
Perrine Ave 07306
Perry St 07306
Pershing Plz 07302
Persimmon Ct 07305
Phillip St 07305
Pierce Ave 07307
Pine St 07304
Pinecrest Rd 07305
Plainfield Ave 07306
Plaza Five 07311
Plaza Four A 07311
Plaza One 07311
Plaza Ten 07311
Plaza Three 07311
Plaza Two 07311
Polar St 07305
Pollock Ave 07305
Poplar St 07307
Port Jersey Blvd 07305
Prelaral Ave 07306
Prescott St 07304
Princeton Ave 07305
Prospect St 07307
Provost St
2-30 07302
200-299 07310
Rademan Pl 07310
Randolph Ave
1-203 07305
204-399 07304
Ravine Ave 07307
Redwood St 07305
Reed St 07304
Regent St 07302
Reserve Ave 07307
Reservoir Ave 07307
Richard St 07305
River Ct 07310
River Dr 07310
River Dr S 07310
River St 07302
Riverview Rd 07305
Robinson Dr 07305
Rock St 07306
Romaine Ave 07306
Romar Ave 07305
Roosevelt Ave 07304
Roosevelt Stadium Ct 07305
Rose Ave 07305
Ruby Ct 07305

Ruby Brown Ter 07305
Rutgers Ave 07305
Sackett St 07304
Saddlewood Ct 07302
Saint Pauls Ave 07306
Sal Laf Ct 07304
Sanford Pl 07307
Sayles St 07305
Scott St 07305
Seaman Ave 07306
Searrenc Ave 07305
Seaview Ave 07305
Secaucus Rd 07307
Seidler St 07304
Senate Pl 07306
Shearwater Ct E & W 07305
Sheffield St 07305
Sherman Ave & Pl 07307
Shindara Ave 07307
Shore Ln 07310
W Side Ave
1-424 07305
425-715 07304
716-1282 07306
1284-1298 07306
208-210-208-210 07305
Sip Ave 07306
Skillman Ave 07306
Skyline Dr 07305
Smit Ct 07305
Smith St 07306
Society Hill Dr N 07305
Soho Dr N 07305
South St 07307
Spring St 07305
Spruce St 07306
Stadium Plz 07305
Stagg St 07306
State Hwy 07306
State St 07304
State Rt 169 07305
State Rt 440
201-297 07305
State Rt 440
299-599 07305
600-799 07304
801-899 07304
725-775-725-775 07304
Stegman Ct, Pkwy, Pl, St & Ter 07305
Sterling Ave 07305
Steuben St 07302
Stevens Ave 07305
Storms Ave 07306
Stuyvesant Ave 07306
Suburbia Ct, Dr & Ter 07305
Sullivan Dr 07305
Summit Ave
231A-253A 07304
1-254 07304
255-727 07306
729-873 07307
875-1299 07307
53-55-53-55 07304
Summit Pl 07305
Surry Ct 07305
Sussex St 07302
Suydam Ave 07304
Swan Ct 07305
Sycamore Rd 07305
Tellicherry Ct 07305
Terhune Ave 07305
Terrace Ave 07307
Theodore Conrad Dr 07305
Thomas Gangemi Dr 07302
Thomas Mcgovern Dr 07305
Thorne St 07307
Tidewater St 07302
Tonnele Ave
1-449 07306
450-710 07307
711-711 07306
712-898 07307
713-899 07307
7-11-7-11 07306
Tottenham Ct 07305

Towers St 07305
Town Square Pl 07310
Trenton St 07306
Tribeca Ave 07305
Troy St 07307
Tuers Ave 07306
Tyson Ln 07304
Union St 07304
Us Highway 1 And 9 07306
Utica Ave 07306
Van Cleef St 07305
Van Horne St 07304
Van Houten Ave 07305
Van Keuren Ave 07306
Van Nostrand Ave 07305
Van Reipen Ave 07306
Van Reypen St 07306
Van Vorst St 07302
Van Wagenen Ave 07306
Van Winkle Ave 07306
Varick St 07302
E View Ct 07305
Vine St 07306
Virginia Ave & Ter 07304
Vreeland Pl & Ter 07305
Vroom St 07306
Wade St 07305
Waldo Ave 07306
Wales Ave 07306
Waller St 07307
Wallis Ave 07306
Walnut St 07305
Walter Mays Dr 07304
Warner Ave 07305
Warren St 07302
Washburn St 07306
Washington Blvd 07310
Washington St 07302
Water St
2-48 07305
100-100 07304
Waverly St 07306
Wayne St
1-442 07302
443-499 07306
Webster Ave 07307
Wegman Ct & Pkwy 07305
Weldon St 07306
West St 07306
Western Ave 07307
Westervelt Pl 07304
Westminster Ln 07305
Whitman Ave 07306
Whiton St 07304
Wilkinson Ave 07305
Williams Ave 07304
Willow St 07305
Wilmont Ave 07306
Wilson Ave 07304
Winfield Ave 07305
Woodland Ave 07305
Woodlawn Ave 07305
Woodward St 07304
Wright Ave 07306
Xavier Ct 07305
Yale Ave 07304
York St 07302
Zabriskie St 07307

NUMBERED STREETS

1st St 07302
2nd St 07302
3rd St 07302
4th St 07302
5th St 07302
6th St 07310
160-399 07302
7th St 07302
8th St 07302
9th St 07302
10th St 07302
12th St 07310
13th St 07310
14th St 07310
15th St 07310
16th St 07310
17th St 07310
18th St 07310

MAHWAH NJ

General Delivery 07430

POST OFFICE BOXES MAIN OFFICE STATIONS AND BRANCHES

Box No.s
All PO Boxes 07430

NAMED STREETS

Ackerman Dr 07430
Adirondack Ct 07430
Airmont Ave 07430
W Airmount Rd 07430
Alcott Rd 07430
Alexandra Ct 07430
Anderson Dr 07430
Apache Ct 07430
Appert Ter 07430
Apple Ridge Blvd 07430
Armour Rd 07430
Aronow Pl 07430
Arrowhead Rd 07430
Arthur Ct 07430
Ash Dr 07430
Aspen Ct 07430
Avenue A 07430
Avenue B 07430
Babbit Bridge Rd 07430
Babcock Rd 07430
Banta Ct 07430
Bartholf Ln 07430
N & S Bayard Ln 07430
Bayberry Dr 07430
Bear Swamp 07430
Beatrice Ct 07430
Bedford Rd 07430
Beech Dr 07430
Beehive Ct 07430
Bellgrove Dr 07430
Belmont Pl 07430
Bergen Pl 07430
Beveridge Rd 07430
Beverly Pl 07430
Birch Rd 07430
Black Oak Ln 07430
Blossom Ln 07430
Blue Ridge Ln 07430
Blueberry Ct 07430
Bogert Ct 07430
Boland Ct 07430
Boulder Trl 07430
Boxwood Ct 07430
Brakeshoe Pl 07430
Brams Hill Dr 07430
Breen Pl 07430
Bridle Path Ln 07430
Brook Ct & St 07430
Brookwood Dr 07430
Bush Ln 07430
Byrne Dr 07430
Cambridge Ct 07430
Campgaw Rd 07430
Carlough Pl 07430
Carol St 07430
Cascade Ct 07430
Castle Rd 07430
Catherine Ave 07430
Catskill Ct 07430
Cedar Hill Ave 07430
Chads Barn 07430
Chapel Rd 07430
Charles Ct 07430
Chedworth Cir 07430
Cherokee Ln 07430

Street	ZIP
Chestnut St	07430
Christie Ave	07430
Church St	07430
Cider Ct	07430
Clark St	07430
Clearwater Ct	07430
Clovebrook Rd	07430
Cobbler Ln	07430
Commerce Ct	07430
Concord Ct	07430
Constantine Dr	07430
Continental Blvd	07495
Copperfield Way	07430
Cornwall Rd	07430
Corporate Dr	07430
Cortland Trl	07430
Cottonwood Way	07430
Country Ln	07430
Coventry Way	07430
Cranberry Ct	07430
E & W Crescent Ave	07430
Crescent Ridge Rd	07430
Crocker Mansion Dr	07430
Crown Ct	07430
Cumberland Ct	07430
Cummings Ct	07430
Darlington Ave	07430
Davidson Ct	07430
Day Ct	07430
Decker Ct	07430
Deerfield Ter	07430
W Deerhaven Rd	07430
Degraaf Ct	07430
Degray Ter	07430
Delhagen Ct	07430
Demeduk Ct	07430
Devine Dr	07430
Devon Ct	07430
Diablo Ct	07430
Dickinson Ln	07430
Dodge Ct	07430
Dogwood Ct & Ln	07430
Donner Ct	07430
Doremus Rd	07430
Drake Ct	07430
Duncan Ct	07430
Dundee Ct	07430
Eakens Ct	07430
Eastview Ave & Dr	07430
Edison Rd	07430
Edward Ct	07430
Eileen Dr	07430
Elizabeth Ln	07430
Emerson Ct	07430
Emma Ct	07430
Erskine Ct	07430
Fairmount Ave	07430
Falcon Ct	07430
Fardale Ave	07430
Farmstead Rd	07430
Faulkner Ct	07430
Fawn Hill Dr	07430
Feldman Ct	07430
Fieldstone Ct	07430
Finn Ct	07430
First St	07430
Fisher Rd	07430
Flaming Arrow Rd	07430
Forest Rd	07430
Forest Hill Rd	07430
Fox River Xing	07430
Francis Ct	07430
Frank Ct	07430
Franklin St & Tpke	07430
Frederick Ave	07430
Fromm Ct	07430
Frost Ln	07430
Furman Ct	07430
Fyke Rd	07430
Fyke Hollow Dr	07430
Garden Ct	07430
Gardiner St	07430
Garrison Ct	07430
Geiger Rd	07430
Georgian Ct	07430
N Glasgow Ter	07430
Glasmere Rd	07430
Glen Gray Rd	07430
Glengorra Ct	07430
Glenmere Ter	07430
Grandview Ln	07430
Great Hall Rd	07430
Great Smokey Ln	07430
Green Way	07430
Green Mountain Rd	07430
Greene St	07430
Grenadier Dr	07430
Grist Mill Run	07430
Grove St	07430
Gunston Ct	07430
Halifax Rd	07430
Halstead Way	07430
Hamerind	07495
Hampshire Rd	07430
Haring Ln	07430
Harvin Pl	07430
Hawthorne Ln	07430
Heath Ct	07430
Heather Ln	07430
Heller Ct	07430
Hemingway Ln	07430
Henion Gdn	07430
Henry Ct	07430
Heritage Ln	07430
Herlihy Dr	07430
Hetzel Dr	07430
Hibuscus Ct	07430
High St	07430
Highland Rd	07430
Highwood Rd	07430
N Hillside Ave	07430
Hilltop Rd	07430
Hines Ave	07430
Holly Ct	07430
Homespun Ct	07430
Hopkins Ct	07430
Hopper Ct	07430
Hutton Dr	07430
Hyde Park Ct	07430
Indian Field Ct	07430
Indian Hollow Ct	07430
Industrial Ave	07430
International Blvd	07495
Isabelle Ct	07430
Island Rd	07430
Ivy Ln	07430
Jackson Ln	07430
Jacobean Way	07430
Jahn Ct	07430
James Brite Cir	07430
Janice Ct	07430
Jefferson St	07430
Jersey Ave	07430
Johnson Ave	07430
Jordan Ct	07430
Judith Ann Ct	07430
Juniper Way	07430
Karen Dr	07430
Kent Ct	07430
Kiersted Pl	07430
Kilmer Rd	07430
King St	07430
Knichel Rd	07430
Kohout Dr	07430
Konight Ct	07430
Krinsky Ct	07430
Lakeview Dr	07430
Lambert Trl	07430
Lancaster Ct	07430
Laramie Ln	07430
Larch Ln	07430
Laurel Ct	07430
Lavender Ct	07430
Lawrence Rd	07430
Lehman St	07430
Leighton Pl	07430
Leisure Ln	07430
Leona Ter	07430
Lethbridge Plz	07430
Lilac Ln	07430
Linden St	07430
Litchult Ln	07430
Locust Ln	07430
Long Ave	07430
Longfellow Ln	07430
Lost River Ct	07430
Lottie Ln	07430
Lowell Ct	07430
Lydia Ln	07430
Lynn Ter	07430
Mabie Ct	07430
Macarthur Blvd	07430
Macleish Ct	07430
Macmillan Ct	07430
Macoun Dr	07430
Madison Ave	07430
Mahogany Ct	07430
Mahwah Rd	07430
Malcolm Pl & Rd	07430
Maleszewski Ct	07430
Mallard Rd	07430
Manor Rd	07430
Maple Ave & Rd	07430
Margaret Ct	07430
Marion Dr	07430
Mark Twain Way	07430
Martis Pl	07430
Mary Ct	07430
Masonicus Rd	07430
Matthew Pl	07430
May Ct	07430
Maysenger Rd	07430
Mcintosh Dr	07430
Mckee Dr	07430
Meadow Ave	07430
Meadowlake Dr	07430
Meester St	07430
Melville Ct	07430
Merrill Dr	07430
Micik Ln	07430
Midvale Mountain Rd	07430
Miller Rd	07430
Moccasin Ct	07430
Moffatt Rd	07430
Mohawk Trl	07430
Mohigan Way	07430
Mollie Ct	07430
Monroe Dr	07430
Moramarco Ct	07430
Morris Ave	07430
Mountain Ave & Rd	07430
Mountainside Ave	07430
Mountainview Dr	07430
Mowerson Pl	07430
Mulberry Dr	07430
Murray Ave	07430
Myrtle Ave	07430
Nash Ct	07430
Niagara Dr	07430
Nilsen Ave	07430
Norfolk Rd	07430
Oak Rd & Ter	07430
Oakham Ct	07430
Old Oak Dr	07430
Old Station Ln	07430
Oldwoods Ct	07430
Oliver Ct	07430
Olney Rd	07430
Orchard Dr	07430
Osborne Ct	07430
Overlook Pl	07430
Oweno Pl & Rd	07430
Oxford St	07430
Paddington Rd	07430
Parsloe Ct	07430
Parsons Ct	07430
Patrick Brem	07430
Pelz Farm Ct	07430
Pembroke Ct	07430
Pendleton Rd	07430
Penereda Rd	07430
Penna Ct	07430
Pepperidge Rd	07430
Persimmon Ct	07430
Petersen Pl	07430
Phillip Ct	07430
Pierson Ct	07430
Pine Hill Rd	07430
Plum Ter	07430
Pocono Ct	07430
Poets Way	07430
Polo Ln	07430
Pond Ln	07430
Pulis Ave	07430
Quill Ct	07430
Quince Ct	07430
Rae Ave	07430
N & S Railroad Ave	07430
Raintree Ln	07430
E, N & W Ramapo Ave & Ln	07430
Ramapo Brae Ln	07430
Ramapo Valley Rd	07430
Reich Ave	07430
Reid Ct	07430
Richard Ct	07430
Richmond Rd	07430
Ridge Rd	07430
Rio Vista Dr	07430
Riverview Ter	07430
Robin Rd	07430
Rock Ridge Rd	07430
Romopock Ct	07430
Rozanski Ln	07430
Rutherford Rd	07430
Sage Ct	07430
Sandburg Ct	07430
Santiago Ct	07430
Sargent Ct	07430
Sassafras Ct	07430
Scherer Pl	07430
Second St	07430
Seminary Dr & Rd	07430
Seton Ln	07430
Shadow Mountain Rd	07430
Sharp Plz	07495
Sherwood Ave	07430
Shrewsbury Ct	07430
Shuart Rd	07430
Siding Pl	07430
Sierra Ct	07430
Skytop Dr	07430
E Slope Rd	07430
Smokehouse	07430
Snow Dr	07430
Snow Mountain Ave	07430
South St	07430
Southerland Dr	07430
Sparrowbush Rd	07430
Split Rock Rd	07430
Spruce Rd	07430
Squire Ct	07430
Stabled Way	07430
Stafford St	07430
Stag Hill Rd	07430
Stanhope Ct	07430
State St	07430
State Rt 17	07430
Stephens Ln	07430
Stone Fence Rd	07430
Stone Meadows Ln	07430
Stonewall Ct	07430
Storms Dr	07430
Storrs Ct	07430
Stowe Ln	07430
Strong St	07430
Strysko Ave	07430
Suleski Ct	07430
Summit Rd	07430
Sunnyside Rd	07430
Sunset Ct	07430
Surrey Ln	07430
Swan Rd	07430
Swiatek Ct	07430
Switzer Rd	07430
Sycamore Ln	07430
Sylvan Ct	07430
Tam O Shanter Dr	07430
Tartan Rd	07430
Third St	07430
Thistle Ln	07430
Thoreau Ct	07430
Thunderhead Pl	07430
Trellis Ct	07430
Trommel Dr	07430
Trotters Ln	07430
Tudor Rose Ter	07430
Tuliptree Ct	07430
Turners Lake Dr	07430
Vail Pl	07430
Valentine Ct	07430
Van Bolen Way	07430
Van Brookhaven Ct	07430
Van Mulen St	07430
Van Winkle Ln	07430
Vanderbeck Ln	07430
Victoria Ln	07430
Village Dr	07430
Vista View Dr	07430
Vreeland Ct	07430
Wagon Trl	07430
Walnut St W	07430
Walsh Dr	07430
Wanamaker Ave	07430
Ward Ln	07430
Warhol Ave	07430
Washington Ln	07430
Watch Hill Rd	07430
Weathervane Ct	07430
West Rd	07430
Westervelt Ln	07430
Weyerhauser Rd	07430
Whispering Pines Dr	07430
Whitman Ln	07430
Whitney Rd	07430
Whittier Ct	07430
Willow Bank Ct	07430
Wilmuth St	07430
Wind Hollow Ct	07430
Winding Trl	07430
Windsor Ter	07430
Winter Pl, St & Ter	07430
Witte Pl	07430
Woodbury Ln	07430
Woodcrest Ct	07430
Wyckoff Ave	07430
York St	07430
Youngs Rd	07430

MILLSTONE TOWNSHIP NJ

NAMED STREETS

Street	ZIP
Abate Dr	08510
Agress Rd	
1-96	08535
97-97	08510
99-199	08510
Algonquin Ter	08535
Allen Way	08510
Alpine Dr	08535
Anderson Ct	08510
Applegate Rd	08510
Arrowhead Way	08535
Autumn Ct	08535
Back Bone Hill Rd	08510
Baird Rd	08535
Baldwin Dr	08510
Barc Ln	08535
Battleground Rd	08535
Beechwood Ln	08535
Bergen Mills Rd	08535
Bessie Ct	08535
Birchwood Dr	08535
Bittner Rd	08535
Blacksmith Ln	08510
Blue Spruce Ct	08535
Blueberry Hl	08535
Bowman Ct	08510
Brookside Rd	08535
Bruere Dr	08510
Burns Ct	08535
Burnt Tavern Rd	08510
Candlewood Ct	08535
Carousel Ct	08510
Carriage Way	08510
Carrs Tavern Rd	08510
Cedar Ct	08535
Center Hill Dr	08510
Chadwick Rd	08535
Chamberlain Ct	08535
Chambers Rd	08510
Charleston Springs Rd	08510
Chase Ct	08510
Cheryl Ln	08510
Cindy Ct	08510
Clark Ct	08510
Clarksburg Rd	08510
Clayton Dr	08510
Clearview Ct	08535
Clover Ln	08535
Cole Ct	08510
Compton Ct	08535
Conover Rd	08535
Cottrell Dr	08510
Craig Ct	08535
Cranbury Brook Dr	08535
Crest Circle Dr	08510
Croaderm Rd	08510
Cuomo Ct	08535
Curtins Cor	08510
Danser Dr	08535
David Ct	08535
Dawson Ct	08535
Debow Dr	08535
Deer Run Dr	08510
Deer Trail Dr	08510
Disbrow Hill Rd	08535
Doctors Crk	08510
Doe Ct	08510
Dressage Ct	08535
Dugans Grv	08535
Ella Dr	08510
Elm Ct	08535
Ely Harmony Rd	08510
Emmons Dr	08510
Emory Ct	08535
Ephraim Rd	08510
Equine Run	08510
Evergreen Ct	08535
Fairplay Rd	08535
Fawn Way	08510
Feldsher Rd	08535
Fern Dr	08510
Filmore Ln	08510
Fitzpatrick Run	08535
Forman Rd	08535
Fountain Ln	08510
Fox Hill Dr	08535
Fox Hollow Pl	08510
Francis Ct	08510
Furlong Dr	08535
Gaston Mill Ct	08535
Georgiann Ln	08510
Giant Maple Ct	08535
Gordon Rd	08535
Graham Pl	08535
Gravatt Cir	08510
Greenbriar Ln	08535
Groendyke Cir	08535
Grove School Rd	08510
Halka Way	08510
Hampton Hollow Dr	08535
Hannah Mount Dr	08510
Hartnett Way	08510
Hartshorne Dr	08510
Harvest Ct	08510
Havens Hollow Rd	08510
Haviland Dr	08535
Henry Ct	08535
Hickory Dr	08535
Hidden Pines Dr	08510
Hillside Rd	08535
Hogrefe Way	08510
Holdman Pl	08535
Hooper Ct	08510
Hope Dr	08510
Horseshoe Dr	08535
Huneke Way	08535
Hunt Ln	08510
Imlaystown Rd	08535
Indian Path	08535
Iron Ore Rd	08535
Ivins Ln	08510
Ivy Ct	08535
Jacob Dr	08535
Joan Dr	08510
Kimberly Cir	08510
Koury Ln	08510
Lahaway Creek Ct	08510
Lakeview Dr	08535
Laurel Ct	08510
Laurel Hill Ln	08510
Lawrence Spring Rd	08510
Lebers Ln	08510
Leonard Ln	08535
Lewis Ct	08510
Liberty Ln	08535
Lightfoot Ct	08535
Lisa Ct	08510
Lucas Ln	08510
Lyle Farm Ln	08535
Meadow Ct	08535
Meco Dr	08535
Mercy Mount Way	08510
Merkin Dr	08535
Michael Ct	08510
Millpond Rd	08535
Millstone Rd	
1-299	08535
300-499	08510
Mineral Spring Rd	08510
Mink Hollow Ln	08510
Moccasin Ln	08535
Molsbury Ln	08510
Monmouth Rd	08510
Montgomery Dr	08510
Moonlight Ct	08510
Morse Dr	08535
Mount Dr	08535
Mountain View Ct	08510
Nathaniel Dr	08535
Nolan Dr	08510
Novad Ct	08510
Nurko Rd	08535
Oak Hill Dr	08510
Old Mill Rd	08535
Old Oak Ct	08535
Olde Noah Hunt Rd	08510
Ossener Dr	08535
Paint Island Spring Rd	08510
Palmer Cir	08535
Paradise Pl	08510
Parkside Way	08535
Patterson Ln	08510
Penn Elmer Dr	08510
Perrine Cir	08535
Perrineville Rd	08535
Peters Ct	08535
Pharo Ln	08510
Pheasant Run	08510
Pine Dr	08510
E & W Pine Branch Dr	08510
Pine Hill Rd	08535
Pittenger Ct	08535
Prenered Rd	08535
Preston Dr	08535
Princess Ct	08535
Prodelin Way	08535
Pullen Dr	08535
Quail Hill Rd	08510
Red Mill Ln	08510
Red Owl Ct	08535
Red Valley Rd	08510
Reid Ln	08535
Rike Dr	08535
Rising Sun Tavern Rd	08510
River Dr	08510
Robbins Rd	
8-20	08535
22-22	08535
26-32	08510
34-99	08510
Robbins Nest Dr	08535
Roberts Rd	08535
Rochdale Ave	08535
Rocky Brook Rd	08535

Rooney Ct 08510
Roosevelt Rd 08510
Rue Ct 08535
Running Brook Dr 08535
Saddlebrook Rd 08535
Sawmill Pond Rd 08510
Schoolhouse Rd 08510
Scotto Dr 08510
Scotto Farm Ln 08535
Sedona Ct 08535
Shady Oak Ct 08535
Shield Rd 08535
Soden Farm Ln 08535
Somers Ct 08535
Spring Rd 08510
Squan Rd E & W 08510
Stagecoach Rd 08510
State Route 33 08535
Steeple Chase Rd 08535
Stevenson Ave 08535
Steward Ct 08510
Stillhouse Rd
1-80 08535
81-299 08510
Stone Tavern Dr 08510
Stoney Brook Dr 08510
Strahan Ct 08535
Sugar Loaf Hl 08510
Sweetmans Ln 08535
Timberline Ct 08535
Timmons Hill Dr 08535
Tin Peddler Ln 08510
Trenton Lakewood Rd 08510
Turtle Clan Ct 08510
Valley Dr 08535
Van Arsdale Cir 08535
Van Hise Dr 08535
Vanderveer Ln 08535
Vaughn Ct 08535
Vista Ct 08510
Wagner Farm Ln 08535
Waters Ln 08535
Wetherill Dr 08510
Whispering Spring Dr 08510
White Birch Dr 08510
Willow Tree Dr 08535
Windcrest Ct 08535
Winding Creek Dr 08535
Windsor Rd 08535
Wintergreen Ct 08510
Witches Hollow Rd 08535
Wolcott Ct 08510
Woodville Rd
1-99 08510
113-399 08535
Wright Ct 08510
Yeger Ct 08535
Yellow Meetinghouse Rd 08510
Young Ter 08510

MONTCLAIR NJ

General Delivery 07042

POST OFFICE BOXES MAIN OFFICE STATIONS AND BRANCHES

Box No.s
91 - 1920 07042
3001 - 3520 07043
4203 - 4203 07042
43001 - 43802 07043

NAMED STREETS

Afterglow Way 07042
Alden Rd 07042
Alexander Ave & Ct 07043
Alpine St 07042
Alvin Pl 07043
Amelia St 07042
Amherst Pl 07043
Appleton Pl 07043
Ardsley Rd 07042
Argyle Rd 07043
Aubrey Rd 07043
Baldwin St 07042
Bay Ave & St 07042
Bell St 07042
Bellaire Dr 07042
Bellegrove Dr 07043
Bellevue Ave & Plz 07043
Belvidere Pl 07042
Bentley Pl 07043
Berkeley Pl 07042
Beverly Rd 07043
Bireldel Ave 07043
Bloomfield Ave 07042
Bradford Ave 07043
Braemore Rd 07043
Brainard St 07043
Briar Hill Rd 07042
Brookfield Rd 07043
Brooklawn Rd 07042
N Brookwood Dr 07042
Bruce Rd 07043
Brunswick Rd 07042
Buckingham Rd 07043
Burnside St 07043
Cambridge Rd 07042
Canterbury Dr 07042
Capron Ln 07043
Carey Ct 07042
Carlisle Rd 07043
Carlton Dr 07042
Carolin Rd 07043
Carriage Way 07042
Carteret St 07043
Cedar Ave 07042
Central Ave 07042
Champlain Ter 07042
Charles St 07042
Chester Rd 07043
Chestnut St 07042
Christopher Ct 07042
Christopher St
12-40 07042
42-224 07042
225-299 07043
Church St 07042
Clairidge Ct 07042
Claremont Ave & Pl 07042
Clarewill Ave 07043
Cleveland Rd 07042
Clinton Ave 07042
Cloverhill Pl 07042
Club Rd 07043
Club St 07042
College Ave 07043
Columbus Ave 07042
Cooper Ave 07043
Cornell Way 07043
Cottage Pl 07042
Crestmont Rd 07042
Crestview Ct 07042
Cross St 07042
Curtis Ter 07042
Dantrind Ave 07042
Depot Sq 07042
Dey St 07042
Division St 07043
Dodd St 07042
Draper Ter 07042
Dryden Rd 07043
Duryea Rd 07043
Eagle Rock Way 07042
Edgecliff Rd 07043
Edgemont Rd
1-70 07042
71-73 07043
72-74 07042
75-199 07043
Edgewood Rd & Ter 07042
Elizabeth Rd 07043
Elm St 07042
Elmwood Ave 07042
Elston Rd 07043
Emerson Pl 07042
Enfield Ave 07042
Erie St 07042
Erwin Park 07042
Erwin Park Rd 07042
Essex Ave & Way 07042
Euclid Pl 07042
Fairfield St 07042
Fairmount Ave 07043
Fairview Pl 07043
Ferncliff Ter 07042
Fernwood Ave & Pl 07042
Fessler Pl 07042
Fidelity Pl 07042
Forest St 07042
Francis Pl 07042
Franklin Ave & Pl 07042
Frederick St 07042
Fremont St 07042
Friendship Pl 07042
Frink St 07042
N Fullerton Ave
1-324 07042
326-326 07042
327-499 07043
S Fullerton Ave 07042
Fulton St 07042
Garden St 07042
Gardiner Pl 07042
Garfield Pl 07043
Gates Ave 07042
George St 07042
Glenridge Ave & Pkwy 07042
Glenside Ter 07043
Glenwood Rd 07043
Godfrey Rd 07043
Gordonhurst Ave 07043
Graham Ter 07042
Grandview Pl 07043
Grant St 07042
Gray St 07042
Greenview Way 07043
Greenwood Ave 07042
Grenada Pl 07042
Grove St
1-340 07042
341-799 07043
Grove Ter 07042
Haddon Pl 07043
Hamilton Ter 07043
Harrison Ave 07043
Hartley St 07042
Harvard St 07042
Hawthorne Pl 07042
Heller Dr & Way 07043
Hibben Pl 07043
High St & Ter 07042
Highland Ave
1-198 07042
199-699 07043
Highland Ter 07043
Highmont Ter 07043
Hillside Ave 07042
Hilltop Pl 07043
Hitchcock Pl 07042
Hoburg Pl 07042
Holland Ter 07043
Hollywood Ave 07042
Homewood Way 07042
Howe Ave 07042
Ingleside Rd 07043
Inness Pl 07042
Inwood Ave & Ter 07043
Irving St 07042
James St 07042
Jefferson Pl 07042
Jerome Pl 07043
Kenneth Rd 07043
Label St 07042
Lackawanna Plz 07042
Lane Ct 07043
Lansing Pl 07043
Lasalle Rd 07043
Laurel Pl & Plz 07043
Lee Pl 07043
Lenapee Trl 07043
Lexington Ave 07042
Lincoln St 07042
Linden Ave 07042
Llewellyn Rd 07042
Lloyd Rd 07042
Locust Dr 07042
Lorraine Ave 07043
Macopin Ave 07043
Madison Ave 07042
Manor Ct 07042
Maple Ave 07042
Marion Rd 07043
Marquette Rd 07043
Mccosh Rd 07043
Mcdonough St 07042
Melrose Pl 07042
Mendl Ter 07042
Midland Ave 07042
Miller St 07042
Mission St 07042
Monroe Pl 07042
Montague Pl 07042
Montclair Ave
1-199 07042
200-299 07043
Montclair State University 07043
Morningside Ave 07043
Mount Hebron Rd 07043
Mount Vernon Rd 07043
N Mountain Ave
55A-55C 07042
1-238 07042
239-399 07043
S Mountain Ave 07042
Mountain Pl 07043
Mountain Ter 07043
S Mountain Ter 07042
Mountainside Park Ter 07043
Mountainview Pl 07042
Mulford Ln 07042
Munn St 07042
Myrtle Ave 07042
Nassau Rd 07043
New St 07042
Nishuane Rd 07042
E Normal Ave 07043
Norman Rd 07043
Northview Ave 07043
Norwood Ave 07043
Notting Hill Way 07042
Oak Pl & St 07042
Oakcroft Ave 07043
Oakwood Ave 07043
Orange Rd 07042
Orchard Ct & St 07042
Overlook Rd 07043
Oxford St 07042
Park St
1-249 07042
250-599 07043
S Park St 07042
Park Ter 07043
Parkhurst Pl 07042
Parkside Pl & St 07043
Parkway 07042
Patton Pl 07043
Pierpont Dr 07043
Pine St 07042
Planchet Dr 07042
Pleasant Ave & Way 07042
Plymouth St 07042
Porter Pl 07042
Portland Pl 07042
Potter Ct 07043
Prescott Ave 07042
Preston Pl 07043
Princeton Pl 07043
Prospect Ave & Ter 07042
Ramsey Rd 07042
Ridgewood Ave 07043
Riverview Dr W 07043
Rockledge Rd 07042
Roosevelt Pl 07042
Rosedale Ave 07042
Roswell Ter 07042
Russell Ter 07042
Rutgers Pl 07043
Rydal Pl 07042
Saint Lukes Pl 07042
Sears Pl 07042
Seneca Pl 07043
Seymour St 07042
Sherman St 07042
Sherwood St 07042
Skytop Ter 07043
Southern Ter 07042
Squire Hill Rd 07043
Stanford Pl 07042
Stephen Ct 07043
Stephen St 07042
Stonebridge Ct & Rd 07042
Stonehenge Rd 07043
Summit Ave 07043
Sunset Park 07043
Sutherland Rd 07042
Sylvan Pl 07042
Talbot St 07042
The Cres 07042
The Fairway 07043
Tichenor Pl 07042
Tremont Pl 07042
Trinity Pl 07042
Tuers Pl 07043
Tuxedo Rd 07042
Undercliff Dr & Rd 07042
Union St 07042
University Ave 07043
Upper Montclair Plz 07043
Upper Mountain Ave
1-221 07042
222-699 07043
Valley Pl 07043
Valley Rd
1-317 07042
400-1299 07043
1301-1399 07043
134-136-134-136 07042
622-624-622-624 07043
Valley Way 07042
Van Breeman Ct 07043
Van Vleck St 07042
Vera Pl 07042
Victoria Ter 07043
Vincent Pl 07042
Virginia Ave 07042
Walden Pl 07042
Walnut Cres, Pkwy, Pl & St 07042
Ward Pl 07042
Warfield St 07043
Warman St 07042
Warren Pl 07042
Washington Ave & St 07042
Watchung Ave 07043
Watchung Plz 07042
Waterbury Rd 07043
Wayside Pl 07042
Wellesley Rd 07043
Wendover Rd 07042
Westview Rd 07043
Wheeler St 07042
Wilde Pl 07042
Wildwood Ave 07043
Wilfred St 07042
Willard Pl 07042
William St 07042
N & S Willow St 07042
Willowdale Ave & Ct 07042
Willowmere Ave 07042
Windermere Rd 07043
Windsor Pl 07043
Woodland Ave 07042
Woodlawn Ave 07043
Woodmont Rd 07043
Yale Ter 07042
Yantacaw Brook Rd 07043

MORRISTOWN NJ

General Delivery 07960

POST OFFICE BOXES MAIN OFFICE STATIONS AND BRANCHES

Box No.s
1 - 929 07963
1001 - 5000 07962
9001 - 9998 07963
50000 - 50000 07962

NAMED STREETS

Abbett Ave 07960
Abbington Way 07960
Abby Rd 07960
Airport Rd 07960
Albert Ave 07960
Alexandria Rd 07960
Allen Dr 07960
Alpine Dr & Trl 07960
Altamont Ct 07960
Alvord Rd 07960
Ames Pl & Rd 07960
Amy Dr 07960
Anderson St 07960
Andrew Ln 07960
Ann St 07960
Anthony Wayne Rd 07960
Applewood Ln 07960
Arbor Way 07960
Arborview Way 07960
Armstrong Rd 07960
Arrowhead Rd 07960
Ascot Ln 07960
Ash Ln 07960
Ashley Ct 07960
Aspen Way 07960
Atno Ave 07960
Baer Ct 07960
Bailey Hollow Rd 07960
Baileys Mill Rd 07960
Baker St 07960
Bank St 07960
Barberry Rd 07960
Barnstable Ct 07960
Battlefield Dr 07960
Baxter Farm Rd 07960
Beach Trl 07960
Bedford Pl 07960
Beech Ln 07960
Beechwood Dr 07960
Beekman Pl 07960
Bell Dr 07960
Bellevue Ter 07960
Bennington Rd 07960
Bettin Dr 07960
Bickford Dr 07960
Birch Ln 07960
Bishop Ct 07960
Black Watch Trl 07960
Blackberry Ln 07960
Blackwell Ave & Pl 07960
Blue Mill Rd 07960
Blue Stone Ter 07960
Bockoven Ln 07960
Boxwood Dr 07960
Bradford Ct 07960
Bradley Rd 07960
Bradwahl Dr 07960
Braidburn Way 07960
Brandywine Ter 07960
Briarwood Ln 07960
Brigade Hill Rd 07960
Brook Dr N & S 07960
Brookfield Way 07960
Brothers Pl 07960
Buckingham Ct 07960
Buckley Hill Rd 07960
Budd St 07960
Buddy Ln 07960
Burnett Rd 07960
Burnham Pkwy & Rd 07960
Butterworth Dr 07960
Byron Ave 07960
Cabell Ct 07960
Cadence Ct 07960
Cambridge Rd 07960
Canfield Rd, Ter & Way 07960
Canterbury Way 07960
Carla Ct 07960
Carlton St 07960
Caroline Foster Ct 07960
Carolyn Ct 07960
Carriage Hill Dr 07960
Carrington Way 07960
Carton Rd 07960
Catalpa Rd 07960
Catherine Ln 07960
Cattano Ave 07960
Cedar Ln & St 07960
Cedar Hill Dr 07960
Center Ave 07960
Chadwell Pl 07960
Chatham Walk 07960
Cherry Ln & St 07960
Chestnut St 07960
Chimney Ridge Dr 07960
Cleveland Ave & St 07960
Clinton Pl & St 07960
Clyde Potts Ct & Dr 07960
Coal Ave 07960
Cobb Pl 07960
Cobblestone Ln 07960
Cold Hill Rd 07960
Colles Ave 07960
Collins Dr 07960
Colonel Evans Dr 07960
Colonial Dr & Rd 07960
Colonial Drive At Harding 07960
Columba St 07960
Columbia Rd 07960
Community Pl 07960
Concord Ln 07960
Condict Pl 07960
Conklin Ave 07960
Connie Pl 07960
Constitution Way 07960
Continental Ave 07960
Convent Rd 07960
Copperfield Way 07960
Corn Hill Dr 07960
Cory Rd 07960
Cottage Pl 07960
Cottonwood Rd 07960
Country Dr 07960
Court St 07960
E Cove Ln 07960
Craig Ct & Rd 07960
Crescent Dr 07960
Crestview Ter 07960
Crestwood Rd 07960
Cromwell Dr W 07960
Croydon Rd 07960
Cutler St 07960
Cypress Cir 07960
Dale Dr 07960
Darnay Rd 07960
Davenport Pl 07960
Deborah Dr 07960
Deer Chase Rd 07960
Deer Ridge Dr 07960
Defarge Way 07960
Degan Ln 07960
Dehart St 07960
Dekalb Pl 07960
Delaware Rd 07960
Dellwood Ave 07960
Devonshire Ct 07960
Dickens Ct 07960
Doehill Rd 07960
Dogwood Dr & Rd 07960
Dorado Dr 07960
Dorothy Dr 07960
Doughty St 07960

Douglas Rd 07960
Duke Ct 07960
Dumont Pl 07960
Dwyer Ln 07960
Eagle Nest Rd 07960
Early St 07960
Easley Ter 07960
East Dr 07960
Edgar Pl 07960
Edgehill Ave 07960
Edgewood Rd 07960
Edward Shippen Ln 07960
Egbert Ave 07960
Egbert Hill Rd 07960
Elder Dr 07960
Elliott St 07960
Ellsworth Ave 07960
Ellyn Ct 07960
Elm Pl, St & Trl 07960
Emerson Ct 07960
Emmet Ave 07960
Entrance Ave 07960
Erin Ave 07960
Erskine Dr 07960
Evans Farm Rd 07960
Evergreen Pl 07960
Exeter Ln 07960
Fairchild Ln 07960
Fairfield Dr 07960
Fairmount Ave 07960
Fairview Pl 07960
Fanok Rd 07960
Farmhouse Ln 07960
Farragut Pl 07960
Farrelly Pl 07960
Fawn Hill Dr 07960
Featherleigh Rd 07960
Ferndale Ave 07960
Fieldstone Dr 07960
Flagler St 07960
Flintlock Run 07960
Florence Ave 07960
Footes Ln 07960
Ford Ave 07960
Forest Dr 07960
Forest Dale Dr 07960
Fox Chase Ln 07960
Fox Hollow Rd 07960
Franklin Pl & St 07960
Fraser Ln 07960
Frederick Pl & St 07960
Gallagher Rd 07960
Garden St 07960
Garfield St 07960
Gaston Rd 07960
Gate House Ct 07960
George St 07960
Georgian Ct & Rd 07960
Gillespie Ln 07960
Glen Airlee Ct 07960
Glen Alpin Rd 07960
Glenwood Rd 07960
Glimpsewood Ln 07960
Gloucester Pl 07960
Godet Pl 07960
Goose Down Dr 07960
Grace Way 07960
Grant St 07960
Great Oaks Rd 07960
Green St 07960
Green Hill Rd 07960
Green Knolls Rd 07960
Gregory Ter 07960
Griffin Ln 07960
Gulick Rd 07960
Guy Ct 07960
Hadley Way 07960
Hamilton Ave, Dr & Rd 07960
Hancock Dr 07960
E & W Hanover Ave 07960
Harding Rd & Ter 07960
Harding Green Dr 07960
Harding Terrace At Fen 07960
Harrison St 07960
Harter Rd 07960
Hartley Farms Rd 07960
Harvey Ct 07960
Harwich Rd 07960
Hawthorne Ct 07960
Hays Dr 07960
Hazel St 07960
Hazlett St 07960
Headley Rd 07960
Headquarters Plz 07960
Hearthstone Way 07960
Heather Ln 07960
Hemlock Ln 07960
Henry St 07960
Heritage Ln 07960
Herms Pl 07960
Hervey St 07960
Hickory Ln 07960
High Street Ct 07960
Highland Ave 07960
Hill Ct & St 07960
Hillairy Ave & Ct 07960
Hillcrest Ave 07960
Hillside Ter 07960
Hilltop Cir 07960
Hillview Ter 07960
Hingham Ct 07960
Hoffman Ct 07960
Holly Hills Ln 07960
Holmes Ct 07960
Homestead Rd 07960
Homewood Dr 07960
Honeymoon Ln 07960
House Rd 07960
Howland Ter 07960
Humphrey Rd 07960
Hunter Dr 07960
Inamere Rd 07960
Independence Ct & Way 07960
Indianhead Rd 07960
Ironwood Rd 07960
Jacob Arnold Rd 07960
James St 07960
Jardine Rd 07960
Jason Ln 07960
Jean St 07960
Jefferson Ave 07960
Jenks Ct & Rd 07960
Jenks Hill Rd 07960
Jenni Ln 07960
Jerome Ave 07960
Jersey Ave 07960
Jockey Hollow Rd 07960
John St 07960
John Glenn Rd 07960
Johnston Dr 07960
Jonathan Smith Rd 07960
Jones Dr 07960
Junard Dr 07960
Kahdena Rd 07960
Kahn Rd 07960
Kary Way 07960
Keats Way 07960
Kenilworth Rd 07960
Kenmuir Ave 07960
Kennedy Ln 07960
Kensington Ct 07960
Ketch Rd 07960
Kimberwick Ct 07960
King Pl & St 07960
King Hill Ct 07960
Kings Ct 07960
Kinney St 07960
Kissel Ln 07960
Kitchell Pl & Rd 07960
Knollwood Dr & Rd 07960
Knox Rd 07960
Knox Hill Rd 07960
Koch Rd 07960
Lackawanna Pl 07960
Lafayette Ave 07960
E & W Lake Blvd, Rd & Trl E & W 07960
Lake Valley Rd 07960
Lakeside Pl 07960
Langdon Ln 07960
Laura Ln 07960
Lawndale Ave 07960
Legion Pl 07960
Leslie Ct 07960
Leva Dr 07960
Liberty St 07960
Lidgerwood Pkwy & Pl 07960
Lincoln St 07960
Linden St 07960
Lindsley Dr 07960
Livingston Rd 07960
Loantaka Ln N & S 07960
Locust St 07960
Log Rd 07960
Logan Ln & Pl 07960
Lohman Rd 07960
Longview Pl & Ter 07960
Longwood Rd 07960
Lord Stirling Dr 07960
Lord William Penn Dr 07960
Loree Brook Ln 07960
Lovell Ave 07960
Lumber St 07960
Lynn Ct 07960
Lynnfield Dr 07960
Lyons Pl 07960
Macculloch Ave 07960
Macdougall Ln 07960
Mackenzie Rd 07960
Madison Ave, Ct & St 07960
Magnolia Ct 07960
E & W Main St 07960
Malcolm St 07960
Manchester Ct 07960
Manette Rd 07960
Manor Dr 07960
Maple Ave 07960
Marian Pl 07960
Marianna Pl 07960
Mark Twain Dr 07960
Market St 07960
Martha Dr 07960
Martin Luther King Ave S 07960
Martins Ln 07960
Max Dr 07960
Maxine Dr 07960
Maxwell Ct 07960
Mayfield Rd 07960
Meadow Ln 07960
Mendham Ave & Rd 07960
Merrywood Ct 07960
Midland Dr 07960
Military Hill Dr 07960
Miller Rd & St 07960
Millers Farm Rd 07960
Mills St 07960
Millstone Ct 07960
Milton Pl 07960
Minnisink Rd 07960
Molly Stark Dr 07960
Monroe St 07960
Morgan Ct 07960
Morris Ave 07960
Morris St
1-299 07960
1-1 07963
Morton St 07960
Mount Airy Pl 07960
Mount Kemble Ave 07960
Mount Pleasant Rd 07960
Mountainside Dr 07960
Netherton Ter 07960
New St 07960
Nichols Rd 07960
Normandy Blvd & Pkwy E & W 07960
Normandy Heights Rd 07960
Northbridge Pl 07960
Norwood Ct 07960
Nottingham Ct 07960
Oak Ln & St 07960
Oak Park Dr 07960
Ogden Pl 07960
Old Army Post Rd 07960
Old Glen Rd 07960
Old Harter Rd 07960
Old Mendham Rd 07960
Old Orchard Rd & Ter 07960
Old Turnpike Rd 07960
Olmstead Rd 07960
Olyphant Dr, Pkwy & Pl 07960
One Bridge Ct 07960
Orchard St 07960
Overlook Rd 07960
Oxford Ln 07960
Parindel Rd 07960
E, N, S & W Park Ave & Pl 07960
Parker Rd 07960
Parkview Plz 07960
Paula Ct 07960
Peachcroft Rd 07960
Peachtree Ln 07960
Pear St 07960
Pembrooke Pl 07960
Pepperidge Rd 07960
Perry St 07960
Persian Ct 07960
Philip Pl 07960
Phoenix Ave 07960
Picatinny Rd 07960
Piedmont Ct 07960
Pilgrim Ct 07960
Pine St 07960
Pioneers Ln 07960
Pippins Way 07960
Pitney Pl 07960
Pletcher Pl 07960
Plum St 07960
Plymouth Rd 07960
Pocahontas St 07960
Pond Hill Rd 07960
Poplar Ln 07960
Post House Rd 07960
Powder Horn Dr 07960
Primrose Trl 07960
Prospect Pl & St 07960
Prudence Ln 07960
Pudding Stone Ct 07960
Punch Bowl Rd 07960
Quaker Ridge Rd 07960
Queens Ct 07960
Raleigh Ct 07960
Ralph Pl 07960
Rambling Woods Dr 07960
Randolph Dr 07960
Ranney Hill Rd 07960
Raskin Rd 07960
Raven Dr 07960
Ravenswood Dr 07960
Raynor Rd 07960
Red Gate Rd 07960
Redner Rd 07960
Redwood Rd 07960
Reed Rd 07960
Reservoir Ridge Rd 07960
Revere Rd 07960
Richlyn Ct 07960
E Ridge Rd 07960
Ridgedale Ave
1-1 07960
3-169 07960
150-150 07962
170-206 07960
171-299 07960
Roberts St 07960
Robertson Ct 07960
Robin Ct 07960
Rolling Hill Dr 07960
Rona Rd 07960
Rosemilt Pl 07960
Rowe St 07960
Saint Clair Rd 07960
Sand Hill Rd 07960
Sand Spring Ln & Rd 07960
Schoolhouse Ln 07960
Schuyler Pl 07960
Searing Ave 07960
Shadowbrook Ln 07960
Shady Ln 07960
Shadyside St 07960
Shalebrook Dr 07960
Shelley Pl 07960
Shenandoah Pl 07960
Shephard Pl 07960
Sherman Pl 07960
Sherwood Dr 07960
Silverbrook Rd 07960
Skyline Dr 07960
South St 07960
Southern Slope Ter 07960
Southgate Pkwy 07960
Sparrow Ct 07960
Speedwell Ave & Pl 07960
Spencer Dr & Pl 07960
Spring Pl & St 07960
Spring Brook Rd 07960
Spring Hill Ln 07960
Spring House Ln 07960
Spring Valley Rd 07960
Spring View Dr 07960
Spruce Ln 07960
Squirrel Run 07960
Standish Dr 07960
N Star Dr 07960
Stark Dr 07960
Starlight Dr 07960
Steeplechase Way 07960
Stephen Crane Way 07960
Stonehenge Rd 07960
Stoney Brook Way 07960
Stratford Ct 07960
Strawberry Ln 07960
Sudberry Dr 07960
Summit Rd 07960
Sunderland Dr 07960
Sunset Pl 07960
Sussex Ave & Pl 07960
Sycamore Ln 07960
Sylvan Way 07960
Symor Dr 07960
Taft Ln 07960
Tall Pines Rd 07960
Tall Timber Dr 07960
Tanager Ln 07960
Tempe Wick Rd 07960
Tennyson Ct 07960
Terry Dr 07960
Thanksgiving Rd 07960
Thomas Trl 07960
Thomas Paine Rd 07960
Thompson Ct & St 07960
Three Gables Rd 07960
Tiffany Rd 07960
Tiger Lily Ln 07960
Tikvah Way 07960
Timothy Ct 07960
Tingley Rd 07960
Todd Pl 07960
Tower Ln 07960
Tracy Ct 07960
Trails End 07960
Tree Top Ter 07960
Trent Ct 07960
Tulip Ln 07960
Turnbull Ln 07960
Turtle Rd 07960
Tuxedo Pl 07960
Twombly Ct 07960
Upperfield Rd 07960
Vail Pl 07960
W Valley View Dr & Rd 07960
Valleyview St W 07960
Van Beuren Rd 07960
Vanderpool Dr 07960
Ventosa Dr 07960
Victoria Ln 07960
Village Dr 07960
Vom Eigen Dr 07960
Walker Ave 07960
Wallace Ave 07960
Walnut Ln & St 07960
Walt Whitman Trl 07960
Warwick Rd 07960
Washington Ave, Pl & St 07960
Washington Valley Rd 07960
Water St 07960
Waters Edge Rd 07960
Weathervane Dr 07960
Wedgewood Ln 07960
West Dr 07960
Western Ave 07960
Westminster Pl 07960
Wetmore Ave 07960
Wexford Ln 07960
Wheatsheaf Farm Rd 07960
Whippany Rd 07960
Whispering Meadows Dr 07960
White Birch Rd 07960
White Deer Ln 07960
Whitehead Rd 07960
Whitney Ave 07960
Whitney Farm Pl 07960
Wildflower Ln 07960
Willard Pl 07960
Willison Park Rd 07960
Willow St 07960
Willow Acres Ln 07960
Willow Spring Dr 07960
Wilmot St 07960
Wilrich Glenn Rd 07960
Winding Way 07960
Windmill Dr 07960
Windsor Way 07960
Windward Dr 07960
Wisteria Ter 07960
Witherspoon Ct 07960
Wood Rd 07960
Woodcrest Dr 07960
Wooded Acres Ln 07960
Woodland Ave & Rd 07960
Woodlawn Dr & Ter 07960
Woodley Rd 07960
Woodruff Rd 07960
Woodside Rd 07960
Wren Ct 07960
Wychwood Rd 07960
Wyndmoor Dr 07960
Yorke Rd 07960
Zamrok Way 07960

NUMBERED STREETS

All Street Addresses 07960

NEPTUNE NJ

General Delivery 07753

POST OFFICE BOXES MAIN OFFICE STATIONS AND BRANCHES

Box No.s
All PO Boxes 07754

NAMED STREETS

Adams Way 07753
Albany Rd 07753
Alberta Ave 07753
Alfred Ct 07753
Allenhurst Ave 07753
Alpine Trl 07753
Ambassador Ct 07753
Amparo Way 07753
Anelve Ave 07753
Anthony Dr 07753
Arnold Ave & Pl 07753
Asbury Ave 07753
Ash Dr 07753
Atkins Ave 07753
Audrey Pl 07753
Augusta Ct 07753
Avondale Ave 07753
W Bangs Ave 07753
Bay Breeze Way 07753
Bayard Pl 07753
Beach Rd 07753
Belle Pl 07753
Belmar Ave & Blvd 07753
Bennett Ave & Rd 07753
N Benton Pl 07753
Berkeley Ln 07753
Bernard Dr 07753
Beverly Way 07753
Bingham St 07753
Birch Dr 07753
Blackwell Way 07753
Bloomfield Ave 07753
Bob Ter 07753
Borden Ave 07753
Boston Rd 07753
Bradfiske Ave 07753
Bradford Ave 07753
Bradley Ave & St 07753
Brighton Ave 07753
Brixton Pl 07753
Brockton Ave 07753
Brook Dr 07753
Brooklawn Dr 07753
Brookside Dr & Rd 07753
Buford Ct 07753
Campbell Ave 07753
Candice Ct 07753
Captains Way 07753
Cardinal Rd 07753
Carol Ave 07753
Carton Ave 07753
Cedar Pl & Ter 07753
Cedarbrook Dr 07753
Cedarcrest Dr 07753
Center St 07753
Chadwell Ct 07753
Champions Dr 07753
N Chaphagen Dr 07753
Chapman Ave 07753
Chelsea Ct 07753
Cherry Ln 07753
Cindy Ln 07753
Clayton Ave 07753
Cliffwood Dr 07753
Clinton Pl 07753
Coastal Dr 07753
Colgate Ave 07753
Colleen Way 07753
Columbia Rd 07753
Columbus Ave 07753
Commerce Dr 07753
Commons Dr & Way 07753
Compass Ct 07753
S & W Concourse 07753
Cora St 07753
Coral Way 07753
Cornell Ave 07753
Cottage Pl 07753
Cotter Ave 07753
Country Club Dr 07753
Courtland St 07753
Couse Rd 07753
Crescent Dr 07753
Crest Dr 07753
Cypress St 07753
Cypress Point Dr 07753
Dale Pl 07753
Daly Pl 07753
Dartmouth Rd 07753
Davis Ave 07753
Deal Ave 07753
Denbo Dr 07753
W Dianne Dr 07753
Division St 07753
Donald Pl 07753
Doral Way 07753
Doris Ter 07753
Douglas Dr 07753
Drummond Ave 07753
Durand Rd 07753
Dykeman Pl 07753
Edgemere Rd 07753

Edgeware Ln 07753
El Dorado Way 07753
Elizabeth Ter 07753
Elm Dr 07753
Elmwood Dr 07753
Ely Rd 07753
Embury Ave 07753
Emerson Pl 07753
E & W End Ave 07753
Essex Rd 07753
Eton Way 07753
Evergreen Ave 07753
Fabio Ct 07753
Fairfield Way 07753
Fairview Ave & Pl 07753
Fairway Ln 07753
Fenchurch Way 07753
Fern Pl 07753
Filly Way 07753
Filmore Ave 07753
Fisher Ave & Pl 07753
Fletcher Dr 07753
Fordham Rd 07753
Forest Dr 07753
Fortunato Pl 07753
Fountain Pl 07753
Foxchase Dr 07753
Frankfort Ave 07753
Frederick Ave 07753
Fulham Pl 07753
Fulton Pl 07753
Gables Ct 07753
Gail Dr & Pl 07753
Gary Dr 07753
George St 07753
Glenmere Ave 07753
Glestri Ave 07753
Golf Ct 07753
Golfview Dr 07753
Graham Ave 07753
Gray Pl 07753
Green Ave 07753
Green Grove Pl & Rd 07753
Greenlawn Pl 07753
Greenwood Ave & Pl 07753
Grove Pl 07753
Gully Rd 07753
Halton Ct 07753
Hamilton Ave 07753
Hampshire Ct 07753
Hampton Ct 07753
Harding Ave 07753
Harrow Ct 07753
Hart Ter 07753
Harvard Ave 07753
Harvey Ave 07753
Hawthorne Ave & St 07753
Hazel St 07753
Heath Dr 07753
Heck Ave 07753
Helen Ter 07753
Hemlock Dr 07753
Heritage Ct 07753
Highland Ave 07753
Hill Dr 07753
Hillcrest Ave 07753
Hillside Ave, Dr & Rd 07753
Hillview Dr 07753
Hobart Pl 07753
Holborn Ln 07753
Holly St 07753
Hollywood Ave 07753
Holmes Ct 07753
Home St 07753
Hoover Rd 07753
Huntington Ave 07753
Irene Pl 07753
Iris Dr 07753
Ivins Rd 07753
Ivy Pl 07753
Jackson Pl 07753
Jagger Ave 07753
Jamie Ct 07753
Janet Rd 07753
Jeanne Dr 07753
Jeanne Nicole Ct 07753
John Ter 07753
Jonathan Pl 07753
W Jumping Brook Dr & Rd 07753
Karen Ave 07753
Kenneth Ter 07753
Knox Blvd 07753
Lafeyette Ave 07753
Laird Ave 07753
W Lake Ave 07753
Lakeview Ave 07753
Lakewood Rd 07753
Larsen Dr 07753
Laurel Ave & Pl 07753
E & W Lawn Dr 07753
Lawrence Dr 07753
Leonard Ave 07753
Lexington Ave 07753
Lincoln Ave 07753
Lipman Pl 07753
Lloyd Ter 07753
Locust Ave & St 07753
Lorraine Dr 07753
Louisville Ave 07753
Lynn Dr 07753
S Main St 07753
Manor Dr & Pl 07753
Mansfield Ct 07753
Maple Ave 07753
Maplecrest Dr 07753
Marcy Dr 07753
Margert Ave 07753
Marie Pl 07753
Marion Rd & St 07753
Marlow Pl 07753
Marsha Dr 07753
Marvin Ct 07753
May Pl 07753
Mayfair Ln 07753
Mcaneny St 07753
Mcbride Ave 07753
Mcclelland Pl 07753
Mcdermott Rd 07753
Melrose Ave 07753
Memorial Dr 07753
Merritt Ave 07753
Michelle Ct 07753
Midwood St 07753
Milford Rd 07753
Millbrook Ave 07753
Milton Ave & Ln 07753
Monmouth Ave 07753
Monroe Ave 07753
Montclair Ave 07753
Moore Rd 07753
Morris Ave 07753
Morrisey Rd 07753
Moss Pl 07753
Murray Ln 07753
Myron Ave 07753
Myrtle Ave 07753
Nathan Pl 07753
Neptune Ave 07753
Neptune Blvd
2-49 07753
50-50 07754
51-1099 07753
52-898 07753
Neptune Blvd S 07753
New York Rd 07753
Newgate Ln 07753
Nicholas Dr 07753
Norman Dr 07753
Oak St & Ter 07753
Oakcrest Dr 07753
Oakdale Dr 07753
Ohagen Ter 07753
Old Corlies Ave 07753
Olden Ave 07753
Olive St 07753
Oliver Dr 07753
Oriole Rd 07753
Overbrook Dr & Pl 07753
Overlook Dr 07753
Oxford Way 07753
Oxonia Ave 07753
Palmer Ave 07753
Park Ave & Pl 07753
Patricia Dr 07753
Pharo St 07753
Phoebe Dr 07753
Pine Dr & Ter 07753
Pinebrook Dr 07753
Pinewood Dr 07753
Pittenger Pl 07753
Pond Rd 07753
Poplar Pl 07753
Poppy Ave 07753
Princeton Ave 07753
Prospect Ave, Pl & St 07753
Provincial Pl 07753
Rachel Ct 07753
Randi Way 07753
Reef Dr 07753
Remsen Mill Rd 07753
Rhodes Ter 07753
Richardson Pl 07753
Rider Ln 07753
Ridge Ave, Pl & Ter 07753
Ridgeway Ter 07753
Riley Rd 07753
Riverdale Ave 07753
N & S Riverside Dr 07753
Riverview Ave & Ct 07753
Robbins Rd 07753
Roberta Dr & Rd 07753
Roberts Dr 07753
Robin Rd 07753
Rosewood Pl 07753
Rowland Pl 07753
Russex Rd 07753
Rutgers Ter 07753
Ruth Dr 07753
Rutherford Ave 07753
Salem Ct 07753
Sand Pl 07753
Sandra Ln 07753
Saratoga Ct 07753
Sarian Dr 07753
Sayre St 07753
Schindler Ct 07753
Schock Ave 07753
Schoolhouse Rd 07753
Schooner Cir 07753
Sea Spray Ct & Ln 07753
Seaboard Way 07753
Sean Dr 07753
Seaview Ave, Cir & Ct N 07753
Sewall Ave 07753
E Shadowlawn Dr 07753
Shafto Rd 07753
Shark Pl 07753
Shark River Rd 07753
Sheldon Ave 07753
Shell Rd 07753
Sherry Ln 07753
Sherwood Dr 07753
Shorebrook Cir 07753
Slocum Ave 07753
Smith Ln 07753
Smock Ave & St 07753
Spinnaker Way 07753
Spray Blvd 07753
Springdale Ave 07753
W Squirrel Rd 07753
Stamford Dr 07753
State Route 33 07753
State Route 35 N & S 07753
State Route 66 07753
Steiner Ave 07753
Stephen Ter 07753
Stockwell Ln 07753
Stratford Ave 07753
Summerfield Ave, Ln & Pl 07753
Summerlan Pl 07753
Summit Ave & Rd 07753
Sunnyfield Ter 07753
Sunset Dr 07753
Sunshine Pkwy 07753
Surrey Ln 07753
Sycamore St 07753
Sylvan Dr 07753
W Sylvania Ave 07753
T F H Plz 07753
Tall Pines Dr 07753
Taylor Ave N & S 07753
Terrier Ct 07753
The Plz 07753
Tide Pl 07753
Tilton Pl 07753
Timber Ridge Ct 07753
Toomin Dr 07753
Tremont Dr 07753
Trent Rd 07753
W Trident Blvd 07753
Tucker Dr 07753
Union Ave 07753
Valley Dr & Rd 07753
Vanada Ct & Dr 07753
Vanderbilt Pl 07753
Vernon Ave 07753
Victor Pl 07753
Victoria Ln 07753
Village Pl 07753
Volunteer Way 07753
Wakefield Rd 07753
Walker Rd 07753
S & W Wall St 07753
Walnut St 07753
Wardell Rd 07753
Washington Ave & St 07753
Waterview Ct 07753
Wayside Rd 07753
Wells Ave 07753
Westwood Pl 07753
White Dr & Ln 07753
Whitesville Rd 07753
Williams Rd 07753
Willow Dr 07753
Wilson Ave & Rd 07753
Winding Ridge Cir, Ct & Dr 07753
Windsor Ct & Ter 07753
Woodfield Rd 07753
Woodland Ave 07753
Woodmere Ave 07753
Woodward Ct 07753
Woolley Dr 07753
Worth Rd 07753

NUMBERED STREETS

All Street Addresses 07753

NEW BRUNSWICK NJ

General Delivery 08901

POST OFFICE BOXES MAIN OFFICE STATIONS AND BRANCHES

Box No.s
1 - 5965 08903
10001 - 18001 08906

NAMED STREETS

Abeel St 08901
Adams Pl 08901
Ag Extension Way 08901
Albany St 08901
Alder Ct 08901
Alexander St 08901
Antile Rd 08901
Baldwin St 08901
Ball St 08901
Bartlett St 08901
Bayard St
1-43 08901
45-87 08901
86-86 08903
88-198 08901
89-199 08901
Bergen Ct 08901
Bethany St 08901
Biel Rd W 08901
Birch Ct 08901
Bishop Pl & St 08901
Bowser Rd 08901
Brookside Ave 08901
Buccleuch Pl 08901
Burnet St 08901
Camner Ave 08901
Carman St 08901
Carpender Rd 08901
Carter Rd 08901
Cedar Ct 08901
Central Ave 08901
Chapel Dr 08901
Charles St 08901
Chester Cir 08901
Church St 08901
Class Pl 08901
Clifton Ave 08901
Cobb Rd 08901
Cogswell Pl 08901
College Ave 08901
College Farm Rd 08901
Columbus Pl 08901
Commercial Ave 08901
Comstock St 08901
Condict St 08901
Conger Ave 08901
Constitution Sq 08901
Cook Rd 08901
Cotter Dr 08901
Courtland St 08901
Cpo Way 08901
Crescent Ct 08901
Crest Rd 08901
Curtis Pl 08901
Delafield St 08901
Delavan Ct & St 08901
Dennis St 08901
Dewey Dr 08901
Division St 08901
Dix St 08901
Dogwood Ct 08901
Dpo Way 08901
Drift St 08901
Dudley Rd 08901
Duke St 08901
Easton Ave 08901
Edgebrook Rd 08901
Edgeworth Pl 08901
Edpas Rd 08901
Elizabeth St 08901
Ellen St 08901
Elm Row 08901
Evergreen Ct 08901
Fernwood Ct 08901
Florence St 08901
Freeman St 08901
French St 08901
Fulton Ct & St 08901
Gatling Ct 08901
George St 08901
Georges Rd 08901
Gibbons Cir 08901
Golden Triangle Plz 08901
Goodale Cir 08901
Guilden St 08901
Hale St 08901
Halstead Rd 08901
Hamilton St 08901
Hampton Rd 08901
Handy St
1-332 08901
333-399 08901
333-333 08903
334-398 08901
Hardenberg St 08901
Hartwell St 08901
Harvey St 08901
Hassart St 08901
Hay St 08901
Hazelhurst St 08901
Henry St 08901
High St 08901
Hildebrand Way 08901
Hiram Sq 08901
Hoffman Blvd 08901
Home News Row 08901
Hope Manor Dr 08901
How Ln 08901
Howard St 08901
Huntington St 08901
Industrial Dr 08901
Indyk Engel Pl 08901
James St 08901
Janine Pl 08901
Jefferson Ave 08901
Jelin St 08901
Jennings Ct 08901
Jersey Ave 08901
John St 08901
John F Kennedy Sq 08901
Johnson And Johnson Plz 08901
Jones Ave 08901
Joyce Kilmer Ave N 08901
Jules Ln 08901
Juliet St 08901
Kempton St 08901
Kirkpatrick St 08901
Labor Center Way 08901
Lafayette St 08901
Lake St 08901
Landing Ln 08901
Langley Pl 08901
Lansing Pl 08901
Larch Ave 08901
Laurel Pl 08901
Lawrence Ln & St 08901
Lee Ave 08901
Liberty St 08901
Lincoln Pl 08901
Linsout St 08901
Lipman Dr 08901
Little Albany St 08901
Livingston Ave 08901
Llewellyn Pl 08901
Log Cabin Rd 08901
Longfield Rd 08901
Lorain St 08901
Loretto St 08901
Louis St 08901
Lufberry Ave 08901
Manor Cres & Ct 08901
Maple St 08901
Mason Ave 08901
May St 08901
Memorial Pkwy 08901
Mine St 08901
Mitchell Ave 08901
Monument Sq 08901
Morrell St 08901
Morris St 08901
Neilson St 08901
New St 08901
New York Ave 08901
Newell Ave 08901
Nichol Ave 08901
Oak St 08901
Oliver Ave 08901
Oxford St 08901
Palmetto Ct 08901
Park Blvd 08901
Parkview Dr 08901
Paterson St 08901
Paulus Blvd 08901
Penn Plz 08901
Pennington Rd 08901
Phelps Ave 08901
Pine St 08901
Plum St 08901
Poultry Ln 08901
Powers St 08901
Prentiss Rd 08901
Prospect St 08901
Prosper St 08901
Quentin Ave 08901
Railroad Ave & Plz 08901
Ray St 08901
Redmond St 08901
Reed St 08901
Regency Manor Dr 08901
Remsen Ave 08901
Renaissance Ln 08901
Reservoir Ave 08901
Richardson St 08901
Richmond St 08901
Riverside Dr 08901
Robert Wood Johnson Pl 08901
Roberts Rd 08901
Robinson St 08901
Roosevelt St 08901
Rpo Way 08901
Rutgers Plz & St 08901
Ryders Ln 08901
Sandford St 08901
Scott St 08901
Seaman St 08901
Seminary Pl 08901
Senior St 08901
Sheepfold Ln 08901
Sicard St 08901
Simplex Ave 08901
Somerset St 08901
Spring St 08901
Squibb Dr 08901
Starlight Ct 08901
State Route 18 08901
Stockton Rd 08901
Stone St 08901
Stratford Pl 08901
Suydam St 08901
Tabernacle Way 08901
Talmadge St 08901
Taylor Dr 08901
Terminal Rd 08901
Throop Ave 08901
Townsend St 08901
Triangle Rd 08901
Tunison Rd 08901
Tuthill Rd 08901
Union St 08901
Us Highway 1 08901
Van Dyke Ave 08901
Voorhees Rd 08901
Wall St 08901
Ward St 08901
Wellington Pl 08901
Welton St 08901
Wilcox Rd 08901
Wirt St 08901
Woodbridge St 08901
Woodnor Ct 08901
Wright Pl 08901
Wyckoff St 08901

NUMBERED STREETS

All Street Addresses 08901

NEWARK NJ

General Delivery 07102

POST OFFICE BOXES MAIN OFFICE STATIONS AND BRANCHES

Box No.s
420A - 420A 07101
1362A - 1362A 07101
20260A - 20260A 07101
20290A - 20290A 07101
22410A - 22410A 07101
20410A - 20410A 07101
1171A - 1171A 07101
1 - 1995 07101
1 - 23 07105
2001 - 2700 07114

3000 - 3974 07103
4001 - 4318 07112
5001 - 5999 07105
6001 - 6480 07106
7001 - 7905 07107
8001 - 8809 07108
9001 - 9960 07104
10001 - 31099 07101
32001 - 32719 07102
33001 - 48399 07101
50000 - 50138 07105
50000 - 57049 07101
200001 - 200599 07102
400001 - 400360 07104

NAMED STREETS

Abbotsford Ave 07106
Abinger Pl 07106
Abington Ave
1-99 07104
100-399 07107
193-195-193-195 07107
Academy St
1-199 07102
200-399 07103
Adams St
1-364 07105
365-499 07114
133-135-133-135 07105
193-195-193-195 07105
225-231-225-231 07105
233-235-233-235 07105
267-269-267-269 07105
310-312-310-312 07105
33-35-33-35 07105
358-364-358-364 07105
41-39-41-39 07105
419-425-419-425 07114
45-43-45-43 07105
Agate Pl 07104
Airis Dr 07114
Albert Ave 07105
Aldine St 07112
Alexander St 07106
Algiers St 07114
Alling St 07102
E Alpine St 07114
W Alpine St 07108
Alyea St 07105
Amity Pl 07104
Amsterdam St 07105
Ann St 07105
Anthony St 07107
Arlington Ave 07104
Arlington St 07102
Arsdale Pl 07106
Ashby Ln 07103
Ashland St 07103
Astor St 07114
Atlantic St 07102
Austin St 07114
Avenue A 07114
Avenue B 07114
Avenue C 07114
Avenue I 07105
Avenue K 07105
Avenue L 07105
Avenue P 07105
Avon Ave 07108
Ayr St 07106
Backus St 07105
Badger Ave
1-341 07108
342-499 07112
106-108-106-108 07108
114-116-114-116 07108
152-158-152-158 07108
159-161-159-161 07108
163-165-163-165 07108
167-169-167-169 07108
209-207-209-207 07108
225-223-225-223 07108
233-231-233-231 07108
237-239-237-239 07108
286-288-286-288 07108
370-372-370-372 07112
428-430-428-430 07112
Baldwin Ave 07108
Baldwin St 07102
Ball St 07105
Ballantine Pkwy 07104
Bank St 07102
Barbara St 07105
Barclay St
1-74 07103
76-82 07103
83-141 07108
143-199 07108
Bathgate Pl 07107
Bay Ave 07105
Bayard Pl 07106
Bayview Ave 07112
Beacon St 07103
Beardsley Ave 07107
Beaumont Pl 07104
Beaver St 07102
Bedford St 07103
Beecher St 07102
Belgium St 07103
Bellair Pl 07104
Belmont Ter 07112
Belmont Ruyon Way 07108
Bergen St
1-81 07107
83-87 07103
89-418 07103
419-814 07108
815-1180 07112
1033-1047-1033-
1047 07112
1061-1065-1061-
1065 07112
204-206-204-206 07103
399-411-399-411 07103
409-411-409-411 07103
421-429-421-429 07108
516-518-516-518 07108
569-571-569-571 07108
773-775-773-775 07108
798-800-798-800 07108
801-805-801-805 07108
893-895-893-895 07112
921-923-921-923 07112
968-970-968-970 07112
Berkeley Ave
1-100 07104
101-299 07107
156-158-156-158 07107
171-173-171-173 07107
207-209-207-209 07107
215-217-215-217 07107
238-240-238-240 07107
Bertha Ct 07103
Bessemer St 07114
Beverly St 07108
E Bigelow St 07114
W Bigelow St 07108
Birks Pl 07112
Blanchard St 07105
Bleeker St
1-119 07102
121-147 07103
149-187 07103
189-199 07103
Bloomfield Ave
1-249 07104
300-599 07107
125-127-125-127 07104
129-131-129-131 07104
132-134-132-134 07104
136-138-136-138 07104
216-218-216-218 07104
37-39-37-39 07104
399-403-399-403 07107
40-48-40-48 07104
527-529-527-529 07107
Blum St 07103
Bock Ave 07112
Bond St 07103
Boston Ct & St 07103
Boyd St
1-134 07103
135-199 07108
Boyden St 07103
Boylan St 07106
Bragaw Ave 07112
Branch Brook Pl & Plz 07104
Branford Pl 07102
Branford St 07114
Brenner St 07108
Brewster Rd 07114
Bridge St 07102
Bright Ct 07104
Brill St 07105
Brinsmaid Pl 07105
Broad St
1-415 07104
416-1090 07102
1091-1091 07114
1092-1092 07102
1093-1299 07114
105-107-105-107 07104
1093-1091-1093-
1091 07114
1101-1107-1101-
1107 07114
1118-1124-1118-
1124 07114
1199-1201-1199-
1201 07114
1215-1221-1215-
1221 07114
193-195-193-195 07104
201-217-201-217 07104
221-223-221-223 07104
271-275-271-275 07104
272-274-272-274 07104
295-293-295-293 07104
301-317-301-317 07104
372-374-372-374 07104
401-417-401-417 07104
441-443-441-443 07102
501-517-501-517 07104
608-610-608-610 07102
78-80-78-80 07104
863-865-863-865 07102
881-887-881-887 07102
Broadway 07104
Brookdale Ave 07106
Broome St
1-222 07103
239-299 07108
Brown St 07105
Bruce St 07103
Bruen St 07105
Brunswick St 07114
Bryant St 07104
Buffington St 07112
Burnet St 07102
Cabinet St
1-110 07103
111-147 07107
149-199 07107
Calcutta St 07114
Callahan Ct 07103
Calumet St 07105
Camden St 07103
Cameron Rd 07106
Camp Pl & St 07102
Carmella Ct 07104
Carmen Ct 07105
Carolina Ave 07106
Carrington St 07114
Carson Rd 07114
Carteret St 07104
Cathedral Ct 07104
Catherine St 07105
Cedar Ave 07106
Cedar Ln 07107
Cedar St 07102
Center St 07102
Center Ter 07114
Central Ave
1-142 07102
143-399 07103
400-699 07107
14-20-14-20 07102
252-224-252-224 07103
256-262-256-262 07103
294-296-294-296 07103
40-42-40-42 07102
418-426-418-426 07107
439-443-439-443 07107
461-463-461-463 07107
513-515-513-515 07107
526-528-526-528 07107
Centre Pl 07102
Chadwick Ave
1-282 07108
283-499 07112
153-155-153-155 07108
304-306-304-306 07112
60-62-60-62 07108
91-93-91-93 07108
Chambers St 07105
Chancellor Ave 07112
Chapel Ct 07102
Chapel St 07105
Chapman St 07106
Charlton St
1-169 07103
190-224 07108
Chelsea Ave 07106
Chester Ave 07104
Chestnut St
1-78 07102
79-499 07105
103-105-103-105 07105
111-113-111-113 07105
13-15-13-15 07102
17-19-17-19 07102
21-23-21-23 07102
266-272-266-272 07105
274-278-274-278 07105
294-296-294-296 07105
383-385-383-385 07105
China St 07114
Christie St 07105
Church Ter 07114
City Dock St 07102
Clarion Ln 07103
Clark St 07104
Clay St 07104
Cleveland Ave 07106
Cliff St 07106
Cliff Hill Pl 07106
Clifford St 07105
Clifton Ave
1-10 07103
12-14 07103
23-187 07104
189-999 07104
383-389-383-389 07104
484-486-484-486 07104
655-657-655-657 07104
897-899-897-899 07104
9-13-9-13 07103
Clifton St 07114
Clinton Ave
23-61 07114
63-144 07114
146-148 07114
158-166 07108
168-856 07108
858-868 07108
117-119-117-129 07114
146-148-146-148 07114
202-204-202-204 07108
265-267-265-267 07108
324-326-324-326 07108
360-370-360-370 07108
380-384-380-384 07108
600-610-600-610 07108
634-640-634-640 07108
677-681-677-681 07108
691-693-691-693 07108
695-697-695-697 07108
699-701-699-701 07108
75-95-75-95 07114
821-823-821-823 07108
825-827-825-827 07108
845-847-845-847 07108
849-851-849-851 07108
862-864-862-864 07108
Clinton Pl
2-10 07108
12-125 07108
139-529 07112
531-537 07112
210-216-210-216 07112
234-236-234-236 07112
242-244-242-244 07112
246-248-246-248 07112
389-391-389-391 07112
446-448-446-448 07112
459-461-459-461 07112
46-48-46-48 07108
58-60-58-60 07108
Clinton St 07102
Clipper St 07114
Clover St 07105
Coastal St 07114
Coastwise St 07114
Coeyman St 07104
Colden St 07103
Colgate Dr 07103
Colleen St 07106
College Pl 07103
Colonnade Pl 07104
Columbia Ave 07106
Columbia St 07102
Commerce Ct 07102
Commerce St
1-172 07102
173-299 07105
Commercial St 07105
Commonwealth Ave 07106
Concord St 07114
Congress St 07105
Conrad Rd 07114
Corbin St 07114
Cornelia St 07105
Cornerstone Ln 07103
Cortland Pl & St 07105
Cossio Dr 07103
Cottage St 07102
Court St
1-119 07102
120-299 07103
130-128-130-128 07103
Crane St 07104
Craneway St 07114
Crawford St 07102
Crescent Ave 07112
Crescent Ct 07106
Crittenden St 07104
Crown St 07106
Custer Ave & Pl 07112
Cutler St 07104
Cypress St 07108
Dandridge Dr 07108
Darcy St 07105
Dassing Ave 07106
Davenport Ave 07107
Dawson St
1-43 07105
44-99 07114
Dayton Pl, St & Ter 07114
De Rosa Ct 07105
Degraw Ave 07104
Delancey St 07105
Delavan Ave
1-45 07104
47-282 07104
284-398 07104
401-599 07107
132-136-132-136 07104
158-160-158-160 07104
164-166-164-166 07104
33-35-33-35 07104
77-79-77-79 07104
Delavan Pl 07104
Demarest St 07112
Denbigh St 07105
S Devine St 07106
Dewey St 07112
Dey St 07103
Dickerson St
1-104 07103
105-299 07107
163-165-163-165 07107
167-169-167-169 07107
40-42-40-42 07103
43-63-43-63 07103
50-60-50-60 07103
Dillard Ct 07104
Distribution St 07114
Doby Pl 07103
Dodd Aly 07105
Dolphin St 07114
Doremus Ave
8-38 07105
40-304 07105
306-704 07105
325-325 07114
329-703 07105
705-1099 07114
41-85-41-85 07105
Dover St 07106
Downing St 07105
Duryea St 07103
Eagle St 07102
Eagles Pkwy 07103
Earhart Dr 07114
Earl St 07114
Eastern Pkwy 07106
Eaton Pl 07107
Eckert Ave 07112
Edison Pl
1-142 07102
143-199 07105
Edmonds Pl 07112
Education Way 07108
Edwin Pl 07112
Elizabeth Ave
1-287 07108
288-899 07112
43-45-43-45 07108
663-665-663-665 07112
Ellery Ave 07106
Elliott St 07104
Elm Rd 07105
Elm St
1-18 07102
20-42 07102
52-62 07105
64-399 07105
166-168-166-168 07105
Elwood Ave & Pl 07104
Emerson Pl 07114
Emmet St 07114
Empire St 07114
W End Ave 07106
N End Ter 07104
Erie Pl 07104
Essex St 07102
Esther St 07105
Euclid Ave 07105
Evencori Ave 07106
Evergreen Ave 07114
Evergreen Ln 07107
Export St 07114
Fabyan Pl
1-78 07108
79-290 07112
292-498 07112
111-113-111-113 07112
117-119-117-119 07112
12-14-12-14 07108
129-131-129-131 07112
134-136-134-136 07112
19-21-19-21 07108
204-206-204-206 07112
33-35-33-35 07108
34-36-34-36 07108
39-41-39-41 07108
8-10-8-10 07108
9-15-9-15 07108
Fairlawn Walk 07104
Fairmount Ave
1-99 07107
123-499 07103
12-14-12-14 07107
175-177-175-177 07103
202-206-202-206 07103
445-447-445-447 07103
Fairview Ave 07103
Faith Ct 07103
Farley Ave 07108
Federal Sq
1-99 07102
2-10 07101
2-98 07102
Fenwick St 07114
Ferdinand St 07103
Ferdon St 07105
Ferguson St 07105
Ferliani St 07105
Ferry St 07105
Fessenden Pl 07112
Field Pl 07112
Fillmore St 07105
Finlay Pl 07106
Firmench Way 07114
Flagpole Rd 07114
Fleetwood Pl 07106
Fleming Ave 07105
Flexon Plz 07114
Floral Ave 07114
Florence Pl 07106
Forest Pl 07112
Forest Hill Pkwy 07104
Fortuna St 07106
Foster St 07114
Foundry St 07105
Franklin Ave 07107
Franklin St 07102
Freeman St 07105
Frelindi Ave 07107
Frelinghuysen Ave
1-513 07114
514-514 07112
514-998 07114
515-999 07114
126-140-126-140 07114
189-195-189-195 07114
217-219-217-219 07114
283-299-283-299 07114
30-36-30-36 07114
307-327-307-327 07114
315-317-315-317 07114
41-43-41-43 07114
439-451-439-451 07114
699-701-699-701 07114
717-719-717-719 07114
85-87-85-87 07114
90-92-90-92 07114
Frontage Rd 07114
Fuel Farm Rd 07114
Fulton St 07102
Garden St 07105
Gareis St 07103
Garibaldi Ave 07114
Garrison St 07105
Garside St 07104
Gateway Ctr 07102
George St 07105
Georgia King Vlg 07107
Gillette Pl 07114
Gilligan St 07114
Girard Pl 07108
Gladstone Ave 07106
Goble St 07114
Gold St 07103
Goldsmith Ave 07112
Goodwin Ave 07112
Gotthardt St 07105
Gould Ave 07107
Gouverneur St 07104
Governor St 07102
Grafton Ave 07104
Grain St 07103
Grand Ave 07106
Grant Ave 07112
Grant St 07104
Gray St 07107
Greek Way 07103
Green St
1-117 07102
118-199 07105
Greenwood Lake St 07104
Grove St 07103
Grove Ter 07106
Grumman Ave 07112
Hackett St 07102

Halleck St 07104
Halsey St 07102
Halstead St 07106
Hamilton St
1-77 07102
79-110 07105
112-198 07105
Hanford St 07114
Hanover St 07105
Hansbury Ave 07112
Harding Ter 07112
Harper St 07114
Hartford St 07103
Hawkins Ct & St 07105
Hawthorne Ave
28-74 07112
76-599 07112
225-227-225-227 07112
245-247-245-247 07112
305-309-305-309 07112
314-316-314-316 07112
315-317-315-317 07112
342-344-342-344 07112
349-351-349-351 07112
360-364-360-364 07112
363-365-363-365 07112
367-369-367-369 07112
376-378-376-378 07112
457-459-457-459 07112
70-72-70-72 07112
76-78-76-78 07112
77-79-77-79 07112
81-83-81-83 07112
82-84-82-84 07112
85-87-85-87 07112
88-90-88-90 07112
89-91-89-91 07112
93-95-93-97 07112
N Hawthorne Ln 07107
S Hawthorne Ln 07107
Hayes St 07103
Haynes Ave 07114
Hazel Pl 07108
Hazelwood Ave 07106
Hearrind Ave 07108
Hecker St 07103
Hedden Ter 07108
Helen Pl 07106
Heller Pkwy
1-199 07104
2-2 07107
4-198 07104
201-299 07107
3-5-3-5 07104
55-57-55-57 07104
60-62-60-62 07104
70-78-70-78 07104
89-91-89-91 07104
Hemlock Pl 07104
Hennessey St 07105
Hensler St 07105
Herbert Pl 07104
Herbert St 07105
Hermon St
1-77 07105
78-99 07114
37-39-37-39 07105
45-47-45-47 07105
Highland Ave 07104
Hill St 07102
Hillside Ave
2-30 07108
32-218 07108
272-298 07112
300-399 07112
163-165-163-165 07108
165-163-165-163 07108
175-177-175-177 07108
198-200-198-200 07108
2-12-2-12 07108
203-205-203-205 07108
207-211-207-211 07108
35-37-35-37 07108
Hillside Ter 07106
Hinsdale Pl 07104
Hobson St 07112
Holiday Ct 07104
Holiday Plz 07114
Holland St 07103
Homestead Park 07108
Honiss Pl 07104
Horatio Ct & St 07105
Hotel Rd 07114
Houston St 07105
Howard Ct & St 07103
Howell Pl 07106
Hoyt St 07103
Hudson St 07103
Humboldt St 07107
Hunter St 07114
Hunterdon St
100-409 07103
410-806 07108
807-1099 07112
192-194-192-194 07103
592-596-592-596 07108
820-822-820-822 07112
913-915-913-915 07112
Huntington Ter 07112
Hyatt Ave 07105
Ingraham Pl 07108
Intercoastal St 07114
International Way 07114
Irvine Turner Blvd
1-164 07103
165-569 07108
570-699 07112
470-472-470-472 07108
476-478-476-478 07108
493-495-493-495 07108
497-499-497-499 07108
506-508-506-508 07108
550-552-550-552 07108
586-588-586-588 07112
590-592-590-592 07112
Irving Ave 07112
Irving St 07104
Irvington Ave 07106
Isabella Ave 07106
Ivy St 07106
Jabez St 07105
Jackson St 07105
Jacob St 07103
James St
1-97 07102
98-199 07103
Jay St 07103
Jefferson St
1-341 07105
342-399 07114
401-401 07114
335-337-335-337 07105
367-369-367-369 07114
387-393-387-393 07114
Jelliff Ave
1-400 07108
401-499 07112
200-202-200-202 07108
204-206-204-206 07108
208-210-208-210 07108
366-370-366-370 07108
381-383-381-383 07108
413-415-413-415 07112
Jennie Ct 07103
Jersey St 07105
Johnson Ave
1-3 07108
5-247 07108
249-263 07112
265-399 07112
206-208-206-208 07108
212-214-212-214 07108
34-36-34-36 07108
38-40-38-40 07108
Johnson St
18-22 07105
24-140 07105
142-194 07105
100-102-100-102 07105
20-22-20-22 07105
25-27-25-27 07105
26-28-26-28 07105
32-32-32-34 07105
33-31-33-31 07105
37-39-37-39 07105
50-52-50-52 07105
54-56-54-56 07105
90-92-90-92 07105
96-98-96-98 07105
Jones St 07103
Joseph St 07105
Kearny St 07104
Keer Ave 07112
Kellogg St 07114
Kenmore Ave 07106
Kent St 07108
Kerrigan Blvd 07106
E Kinney St
1-1 07102
3-79 07102
109-123 07105
125-499 07105
130-132-130-132 07105
136-138-136-138 07105
142-144-142-144 07105
17-21-17-21 07102
190-194-190-194 07105
190-196-190-196 07105
401-403-401-403 07105
45-47-45-47 07102
53-55-53-55 07102
W Kinney St
2-20 07102
22-99 07102
101-113 07102
122-299 07103
301-303 07103
177-195-177-195 07103
72-74-72-74 07102
Kipp St 07108
Kitchell Pl 07102
Knoldeld St 07114
Komorn St 07105
Kossuth St 07105
Krueger Ct 07103
Labella Ct 07105
Lackawanna Ave
1-127 07102
128-299 07103
236-240-236-240 07103
Lafayette St
1-133 07102
134-499 07105
101-103-101-103 07102
Lake St 07104
Lanark Ave 07106
Lang St 07105
Laurel Pl 07106
Lawton 07112
Learning Ct 07108
Legal St 07114
Lehigh Ave 07112
Lenox St 07106
Lentz Ave 07105
Leo Pl 07108
Leslie St
1-100 07108
101-499 07112
111-113-111-113 07112
123-125-123-125 07112
140-142-140-142 07112
153-155-153-155 07112
164-166-164-166 07112
236-238-236-238 07112
413-415-413-415 07112
416-418-416-418 07112
417-419-417-419 07112
420-422-420-422 07112
424-426-424-426 07112
425-427-425-427 07112
428-430-428-430 07112
429-431-429-431 07112
432-434-432-434 07112
433-435-433-435 07112
455-453-455-453 07112
457-459-457-459 07112
471-473-471-473 07112
480-482-480-482 07112
Lexington St 07105
Libella Ct 07105
Liberty St 07102
Lillie St 07103
Lincoln Ave 07104
Lincoln Park 07102
Lincoln St 07103
Linden St 07102
Lindenberg Rd 07114
Lindsley Ave 07106
Lisa Ct 07112
Lister Ave 07105
Little St 07107
Littleton Ave
1-106 07107
107-397 07103
399-499 07103
183-185-183-185 07103
220-222-220-222 07103
Livingston St
1-148 07103
149-299 07108
Lock St 07103
Lockwood St 07105
Lombardy St 07102
Longfellow Ave 07106
Longworth St 07102
Loretto St 07112
Lowell Pl 07114
Ludlow Pl & St 07114
Lum Ln 07105
Lyons Ave 07112
Madison Ave 07108
Madison St 07105
Magazine St 07105
N Magnolia Ln 07107
S Magnolia Ln 07107
Magnolia St
1-64 07103
65-99 07108
Mahogany Ct 07104
Maiden Ln 07102
Main St 07105
Malvern St 07105
Manchester Pl 07104
Manor Dr 07106
Manufacturers Pl 07105
Mapes Ave, Pl & Ter 07112
Maple Ave & Pl 07112
Maracaibo St 07114
Margaretta St 07105
Marion Ave 07106
Marion Pl 07102
Maritime St 07114
Market St
1-312 07102
314-330 07102
372-394 07105
396-700 07105
702-798 07105
224-226-224-226 07102
234-236-234-236 07102
283-299-283-299 07102
418-428-418-428 07105
548-550-548-550 07105
551-553-551-553 07105
584-586-584-586 07105
W Market St
1-47 07102
49-58 07102
91-229 07103
231-331 07103
333-620 07107
622-642 07107
Marlin St 07114
Marne St 07105
Marrow St 07103
Marsac Pl 07106
Marsh St 07114
Martens Ave 07106
Martha Ct 07103
Martin Luther King Jr Blvd
1-180 07104
182-184 07104
185-799 07102
1-7-1-7 07104
108-136-108-136 07104
138-162-138-162 07104
36-38-36-38 07104
52-54-52-54 07104
54-56-54-56 07104
56-58-56-58 07104
667-669-667-669 07102
78-80-78-80 07104
Mary St 07105
Matthews Dr 07103
May St 07104
Maybaum Ave 07106
Mccarter Hwy
201-461 07114
463-735 07102
737-1146 07102
1147-2199 07104
1173-1225-1173-1225 07104
1256-1262-1256-1262 07104
1279-1283-1279-1283 07104
1369-1373-1369-1373 07104
1400-1422-1400-1422 07104
1425-1437-1425-1437 07104
1475-1489-1475-1489 07104
1487-1495-1487-1495 07104
1489-1495-1489-1495 07104
435-439-435-439 07114
701-703-701-703 07102
752-766-752-766 07102
Mcclellan St 07114
Mcwhorter St 07105
Mead St 07106
Meeker Ave
1-47 07114
49-219 07114
221-399 07112
179-181-179-181 07114
255-257-255-257 07112
259-261-259-261 07112
Melrose Ave 07106
Mercer St 07103
Merchant Pl & St 07105
Metroplex Rd 07114
Midland Pl 07106
Mildred Helms Pl 07108
Milford Ave 07108
Miller St 07114
Millington Ave 07108
Mitchell Pl 07114
Mohawk St 07114
Monmouth St 07108
Monroe St 07105
Montclair Ave 07104
Monte Irvine Way 07103
Monteith Ave 07107
Montgomery Ave 07108
Montgomery St 07103
Monticello Ave 07106
Montrose St 07106
Morris Ave 07103
Morton St 07103
Mott St 07105
Mount Olivet Ave 07114
Mount Pleasant Ave 07104
Mount Prospect Ave & Pl 07104
Mount Vernon Pl 07106
Mountain View Ave & Pl 07106
Muhammad Ali Ave
1-300 07108
301-399 07103
Mulberry St
1-423 07102
424-533 07114
535-599 07114
128-144-128-144 07102
Mulford Pl 07112
N & S Munn Ave 07106
Murray St 07114
Myrtle Ave 07107
Nairn Pl 07108
Napoleon St 07105
Navy St 07114
Nelson Pl 07102
Neptune St 07114
Nesbitt St 07103
Netherwood Pl 07106
Nevada St 07102
New St
2-34 07102
36-93 07102
95-161 07102
162-413 07103
414-499 07107
New Fairview Ave 07108
New Jersey Railroad Ave
27-285 07105
325-599 07114
149-151-149-151 07105
251-253-251-253 07105
261-263-261-263 07105
New York Ave 07105
Newark Ctr 07102
Newark St 07103
Newark Airport 07114
Newton St 07103
Niagara St 07105
Nichols St 07105
Noble St 07114
Noll Pl 07106
Norfolk St 07103
Norman Rd 07106
Norwood Pl & St 07106
Nursery St 07104
Nuttman St 07103
Nye Ave 07112
Oak St 07106
Oakland Ter 07106
Oceania St 07114
Ogden St 07104
Old Road To Bloomfield 07104
Oliver St
1-24 07102
25-364 07105
366-398 07105
182-184-182-184 07105
55-57-55-57 07105
67-69-67-69 07105
Olympia Dr 07114
S Orange Ave
22-46 07103
48-509 07103
511-571 07103
573-587 07106
589-1199 07106
285-289-285-289 07103
396-398-396-398 07103
448-450-448-450 07103
527-531-527-531 07103
543-545-543-545 07103
826-828-826-828 07106
830-832-830-832 07106
904-906-904-906 07106
916-924-916-924 07106
Orange St
1-15 07102
17-126 07102
128-138 07102
139-344 07103
370-420 07107
422-678 07107
680-698 07107
174-176-174-176 07103
272-274-272-274 07103
300-302-300-302 07103
302-300-302-300 07103
505-507-505-507 07107
607-609-607-609 07107
Oraton St 07104
Orchard St
1-168 07102
169-199 07114
13-15-13-15 07102
132-134-132-134 07102
23-25-23-25 07102
27-29-27-29 07102
58-68-58-68 07102
Oriental Pl & St 07104
Osborne Ter
1-149 07108
150-499 07112
17-19-17-19 07108
181-183-181-183 07112
259-257-259-257 07112
311-315-311-315 07112
324-326-324-326 07112
54-56-54-56 07108
Oxford St 07105
Pacific St
2-14 07105
16-158 07105
160-188 07105
189-299 07114
129-133-129-133 07105
92-94-92-94 07105
97-99-97-99 07105
Palm St 07106
Panama St 07114
Paris St 07105
Park Ave
2-14 07104
16-199 07104
201-390 07107
Park Pl 07102
Park Plz 07102
E Park St 07102
W Park St 07102
Parker St 07104
Parkhurst St 07114
Parkside Pl 07114
Parkview Ter 07112
Passaic St 07104
Paterson St 07105
Patten Pl 07112
Peabody Pl 07104
Pearl St 07102
Peat St 07103
Peck Ave 07107
E Peddie St 07114
W Peddie St 07112
Peerless Pl 07114
Penn Plz E 07105
Pennington Ct 07105
Pennington St
1-63 07102
64-199 07105
201-299 07105
145-147-145-147 07105
15-31-15-31 07102
23-25-23-25 07102
27-29-27-29 07102
38-40-38-40 07102
43-45-43-45 07102
51-53-51-53 07102
88-90-88-90 07105
Pennsylvania Ave
1-19 07102
20-199 07114
78-88-78-88 07114
97-99-97-99 07114
Pensey Pl 07114
Perez Dr 07103
Permapl St 07102
Pershing Ave 07114
Peshine Ave
187A-187B 07108
1-345 07108
346-499 07112
134-136-134-136 07108
Pierce St 07103
N & S Pine Ln 07107
Pine Grove Ter 07106
Plymouth St 07106
Poe Ave 07106
Poinier St 07114
Polk St 07105
Pomona Ave 07112
E Port St 07114
Porter Ave & Pl 07112
Prince St
2-82 07103
84-223 07103
225-233 07103

234-299 07108
30-40-30-40 07108
Prondar Ave 07104
Prospect Row & St 07105
Providence St 07105
Pulaski St 07105
Putnam St 07106
Queen St 07114
Quitman St
2-18 07103
20-83 07103
84-167 07108
169-177 07108
98-100-98-100 07108
Radar St 07114
Randolph Pl 07108
Rankin St 07103
Ray Dandridge Way 07103
Raymond Blvd
1-1 07105
3-544 07105
546-998 07105
1037-1083 07102
1085-1245 07102
1247-1299 07102
1338-1499 07103
11-43-11-43 07102
223-245-223-245 07105
820-822-820-822 07105
Raymond Plz W 07102
Read St 07105
Rector St 07102
Reeves Pl 07108
Renner Ave 07112
Reynolds Pl 07106
Richards St 07105
Richelieu Pl & Ter 07106
Richmond St 07103
Ricord St 07106
Rider Ct 07103
Ridge St 07104
Ridgewood Ave
1-212 07108
214-260 07108
261-399 07112
176-178-176-178 07108
198-200-198-200 07108
208-210-208-210 07108
56-58-56-58 07108
61-63-61-63 07108
90-92-90-92 07108
93-95-93-95 07108
River St 07102
Riverfront Plz 07102
Riverside Ave, Ct & Mews 07104
Riverview Ct, Pl & Ter 07105
Roanoke Ave & Ct 07105
Rockland Ter 07106
Romaine Pl 07104
Rome St 07105
Ropes Pl 07107
Rose Ave 07107
Rose St 07108
Rose Ter 07108
Roseville Ave 07107
Ross St 07114
Route 21 Plz 07104
Rowland St 07104
Rowley St 07103
Ruby Pl 07104
Ruggerio Plz 07104
Runiak St 07114
E Runyon St 07114
W Runyon St
2-10 07108
12-399 07108
215-217-215-217 07108
219-221-219-221 07108
222-224-222-224 07108
223-225-223-225 07108
243-245-243-245 07108
249-251-249-251 07108
252-254-252-254 07108
303-305-303-305 07108
324-326-324-326 07108
73-75-73-75 07108
Rutgers Dr 07103
Rutherford St 07105
Saint Charles St 07105
Saint Francis St 07105
Saint James Pl 07112
Saint Paul Ave 07106
Salem St 07106
Sanford Ave & Pl 07106
Sarah Vaughan Pl 07112
Sayre St 07103
Schalk St 07105
Scheared Ave 07112
Scheerer Ave 07112
Schley St 07112
School St 07103
Schuyler Ave 07112
Scofield St 07106
Scontond St 07103
Scott St 07102
Seabury Ct & St 07104
Selvage St 07112
Seth Boyden Ter 07114
Seton Hall Dr 07103
Seymour Ave
1-237 07108
239-251 07108
253-499 07112
129-131-129-131 07108
162-160-162-160 07108
280-282-280-282 07112
282-280-282-280 07112
Shanley Ave 07108
Sharah Voaghan Pl 07112
Shaw Ave 07112
Sheffield Dr 07104
Sheffield St 07103
Sheldon Ter 07106
Shephard Ave 07112
Sherman Ave 07114
Shipman St 07102
Silver St 07106
Smith St 07106
Somerset St
1-56 07103
57-199 07108
Somme St 07105
South St
1-85 07102
86-337 07114
338-368 07105
369-369 07114
370-598 07105
371-599 07105
105-109-105-109 07114
111-113-111-113 07114
126-128-126-128 07114
175-181-175-181 07114
18-20-18-20 07102
259-261-259-261 07114
358-360-358-360 07105
392-394-392-394 07105
47-49-47-49 07102
51-53-51-53 07102
55-57-55-57 07102
58-60-58-60 07102
59-61-59-61 07102
Speedway Ave 07106
Spencer St 07106
Spring St
1-68 07104
69-100 07102
Springdale Ave 07107
Springfield Ave
1-57 07102
58-291 07103
290-290 07108
292-718 07103
293-725 07103
168-176-168-176 07103
302-324-302-324 07103
343-359-343-359 07103
399-443-399-443 07103
474-476-474-476 07103
668-670-668-670 07103
685-687-685-687 07103
Springline St 07114
Spruce St
1-76 07102
77-147 07108
149-299 07108
150-178 07103
180-298 07108
87-89-87-89 07108
Stanton St 07114
Star Ledger Plz 07102
Starboard St 07114
Starboard Export 07114
State St 07104
Stecher St 07112
Stengel Ave 07112
Stirling St 07103
Stockton St 07105
Stone St 07104
Stratford Pl 07108
Stuyvesant Ave 07106
Suez St 07114
Summer Ave & Pl 07104
Summit Ave 07112
Summit St 07103
Sumo Village Ct 07114
Sunset Ave 07106
Sussex Ave
1-226 07103
228-242 07103
243-399 07107
116-132-116-132 07103
119-111-119-111 07103
140-142-140-142 07103
163-161-163-161 07103
168-170-168-170 07103
289-291-289-291 07107
391-397-391-397 07107
64-68-64-68 07103
E Sylvan Ave 07104
Synott Pl 07106
Taylor St 07104
Telford St 07106
Terminal A 07114
Terminal B 07114
Terminal C 07114
Thomas St 07114
Thomas Carmichael Dr 07112
Thorne St 07114
Thornton St 07105
Tichenor Ln 07114
Tichenor St
13-29 07102
31-63 07102
64-199 07105
155-157-155-157 07105
23-25-23-25 07102
25-23-25-23 07102
27-29-27-29 07102
41-43-41-43 07102
45-55-45-55 07102
55-57-55-57 07102
89-87-89-87 07105
Tiffany Blvd 07104
Tillinghast St 07108
Toler Pl 07114
Tompkins Point Rd 07114
Treacy Ave 07108
Treadwell St 07104
Treat Pl 07102
Tremont Ave 07106
Triton Pl & Ter 07104
Tuxedo Pkwy 07106
Tyler St 07114
Underwood St 07106
Union St 07105
Unity Ave 07106
University Ave 07102
Us Highway 1 And 9 07114
Us Highway 21 And 22 07114
Us Highway 22 07114
Us Highway 9 And Intl Way 07114
Vail St 07106
Vailsburg Ter 07106
Val Sumo Ln 07105
Valley St 07106
Van Buren St 07105
Van Duyne St 07114
Van Ness Pl 07108
Van Vechten St 07114
Van Velsor Pl 07112
Van Wagenen St 07104
Vanderpool St 07114
Varsity Ct & Rd 07106
Vassar Ave 07112
Vaughan Dr 07103
Vermont Ave 07106
Vernon Ave 07108
Verona Ave 07104
Vesey St 07105
Victoria Ave 07104
Victoria St 07114
Victory Plz 07102
Viking St 07114
Village Pl 07103
Vincent Ct & St 07105
Vine St 07102
Virginia St 07114
Voorhees St 07108
Wainwright Pl & St 07112
Wakeman Ave 07104
Wall St 07105
Walnut St
2-58 07102
60-107 07102
108-499 07105
10 1/2-10 1/2 07105
121-123-121-123 07105
323-325-323-325 07105
438-436-438-436 07105
67-69-67-69 07102
71-73-71-73 07102
Warren Pl 07102
Warren St
1-31 07102
33-112 07102
114-138 07103
140-399 07103
156-182-156-182 07103
19-21-19-21 07102
226-230-226-230 07103
Warwick St 07105
Washington Park, Pl & St 07102
Watchung Ave 07107
Watson Ave 07112
Waydell St 07105
Webster St 07104
Weequahic Ave 07112
Wellington Way 07103
West St 07103
Westbrooks Ave 07103
Wharton St 07114
Wheeler Point Rd 07105
White Ter 07108
Whitney St 07106
Whittier Pl 07114
Wicker Ct 07104
Wickliffe St 07103
Wilbur Ave 07112
Wilburton Pl 07104
Wiley Post Rd 07114
William St
1-136 07102
178-182 07103
168-190-168-190 07103
Willoughby St 07112
Wilnora Holman Way 07108
Wilsey St 07103
Wilson Ave 07105
Winans Ave 07108
Winthrop St 07104
Wolcott Ter 07112
Wood St 07104
Woodbine Ave 07106
Woodland Ave 07103
Woodside Ave & Pl 07104
Wright St 07114
Wyndmoor Ave 07112
Yancy Dr 07103
Yates Ave 07112

NUMBERED STREETS

1st Ave & St W 07107
2nd Ave 07104
2nd Ave W 07107
2nd St 07107
3rd Ave 07104
3rd Ave W 07107
3rd St 07107
4th Ave 07104
4th Ave W 07107
4th St 07107
5th 07107
6th Ave W 07107
N 6th St 07107
S 6th St
119A-119A 07107
121-430 07103
7th Ave 07104
7th Ave W 07107
N 7th St 07107
S 7th St
3-5 07107
152-461 07103
133-135-133-135 07107
181-183-181-183 07103
8th Ave 07104
N 8th St 07107
S 8th St
1-174 07107
176-232 07103
234-499 07103
202-204-202-206 07103
9th Ave W 07107
N 9th St 07107
S 9th St
3-65 07107
215-265 07103
115-117-115-117 07107
N 10th St 07107
S 10th St
62-236 07107
237-596 07103
598-622 07108
108-110-108-110 07107
256-258-256-258 07103
610-614-610-614 07108
96-98-96-98 07107
11th Ave 07103
11th Ave W 07107
N 11th St 07107
S 11th St
16A-16A 07107
269-766 07103
767-899 07108
226-228-226-228 07107
381-383-381-383 07103
849-853-849-853 07108
12th Ave
30-41 07103
103-241 07107
379-387 07103
136-138-136-138 07107
379-381-379-381 07103
N 12th St 07107
S 12th St
5-7 07107
262-314 07103
759-899 07108
10-12-10-12 07107
747-749-747-749 07103
826-828-826-828 07108
13th Ave
1-7 07102
80-98 07103
100-579 07103
581-599 07103
N 13th St
2-522 07107
524-572 07107
100-102-100-102 07107
124-126-124-126 07107
128-130-128-130 07107
136-138-136-138 07107
140-140-140-144 07107
144-146-144-146 07107
328-330-328-330 07107
66-70-66-70 07107
81-83-81-83 07107
S 13th St
46-52 07107
54-140 07107
142-192 07107
419-423 07103
425-767 07103
768-899 07108
107-109-107-109 07107
111-113-111-113 07107
722-724-722-724 07103
728-730-728-730 07103
731-733-731-733 07103
734-736-734-736 07103
824-826-824-826 07108
828-830-828-830 07108
840-842-840-842 07108
857-859-857-859 07108
14th Ave
1-9 07103
456-466 07106
241-243-241-243 07103
N 14th St 07107
S 14th St
6-144 07107
400-776 07103
777-899 07108
109-111-109-111 07107
670-672-670-672 07103
790-792-790-792 07108
15th Ave 07103
S 15th St
1-101 07107
103-199 07107
363-397 07103
399-768 07103
769-899 07108
831-835-831-835 07108
876-878-876-878 07108
16th Ave 07103
S 16th St
400-794 07103
795-999 07108
418-420-418-420 07103
815-817-815-817 07108
17th Ave 07103
S 17th St
400-790 07103
800-999 07108
430-432-430-432 07103
829-827-829-827 07108
18th Ave
899A-899B 07106
200-433 07108
466-634 07103
893-1099 07106
343-345-343-345 07108
466-468-466-468 07103
921-925-921-925 07106
S 18th St
231-391 07103
802-939 07108
331-333-331-333 07103
838-840-838-840 07108
19th Ave 07103
S 19th St
200-800 07103
801-999 07108
280-282-280-282 07103
839-841-839-841 07108
S 20th St
200-328 07103
330-803 07103
804-999 07108
238-240-238-240 07103
250-260-250-260 07103
286-288-286-288 07103
364-366-364-366 07103
632-630-632-630 07103
680-682-680-682 07103
686-690-688-690 07103
695-697-695-697 07103
791-795-791-795 07103

ORANGE NJ

General Delivery 07051

POST OFFICE BOXES MAIN OFFICE STATIONS AND BRANCHES

Box No.s
All PO Boxes 07051

NAMED STREETS

Adrianne Ct 07050
Alden Pl & St 07050
Argyle Ave 07050
Austin Pl & Rd 07050
Baldwin Ter 07050
Beach St 07050
Beechwood Ter 07050
Bell St 07050
Berg Pl 07050
Berkeley Ave & Rd 07050
Berryman Pl 07050
Berwick St 07050
Berwyn St 07050
Bradford St 07050
Brook Aly 07050
Burnside Pl & St 07050
Canfield St 07050
Capuchin Way 07050
Carroll St 07050
Carteret Pl & Ter 07050
Cary St 07050
N & S Center St 07050
Central Ave & Pl 07050
Chapel St 07050
Chapman St 07050
Chestnut St 07050
W Christopher St 07050
Clairmont Ter 07050
Claredon Pl 07050
E Clark Cir 07050
Cleveland St 07050
Codner St 07050
Columbia St 07050
Conover Ter 07050
Crane St 07050
N & S Day St 07050
Dodd St 07050
E Duane St 07050
Elizabeth St 07050
Elliot Pl 07050
Elm St 07050
Elmwynd Dr 07050
N & S Essex Ave 07050
Fairview Ave 07050
Flagg St 07050
Forest St 07050
Frankfort St 07050
Freeman St 07050
Freeway Dr W 07050
Fuller Ter 07050
Generli St 07050
Gist Pl 07050
Glebe St 07050
Glenwood Ave 07050
Gray St 07050
Hampton Ter 07050
S Harrison St 07050
Hawthorne St 07050
Haxton Ave 07050
Hayward St 07050
Henry St 07050
Heywood Ave 07050
Hickory St 07050
High St 07050
E Highland Ave & Ter 07050
Hill St 07050
Hillside Ave 07050
Hillyer St 07050
Irving Ter 07050
Ivy Ct 07050
Jackson St 07050

N & S Jefferson St 07050
Joyce St 07050
Keasby Rd 07050
Lafayette St 07050
Lakeside Ave 07050
Langdon St 07050
Laurel St 07050
Lawnridge Rd 07050
Liberty St 07050
Lincoln Ave & Pl 07050
Linden Pl 07050
Lindsley Pl 07050
Madison St 07050
Main St
1-385 07050
384-384 07051
386-598 07050
387-599 07050
150-160-150-160 07050
187-189-187-189 07050
70-80-70-80 07050
Manor Ter 07050
Maryland Pl & St 07050
Matthew St 07050
Mcchesney St 07050
Mclaughlin Pl 07050
Meade St 07050
Mechanic St 07050
Merrill Ct 07050
Minton Pl 07050
Mitchell St 07050
Monroe St 07050
Morris St 07050
Morrow St 07050
Mosswood Ave & Ct 07050
Mount Vernon Ave 07050
Mountainview Ave 07050
Nassau St 07050
New St 07050
New England Ter 07050
Oakwood Ave & Pl 07050
Ogden St 07050
Olcott St 07050
Orange Rd 07050
Oxford St 07050
Park Ave, Pl & St 07050
Parkinson Ter 07050
Parkview Ter 07050
Parrow St 07050
Pierson St 07050
Prince St 07050
Reock St 07050
Reynolds St & Ter 07050
Ridge Ct & St 07050
Roberts Rd 07050
Russ Monica Ct 07050
Scotland Rd 07050
Seven Oaks Ct, Rd & Way 07050
Snyder St 07050
South St 07050
Spring St 07050
Stetson St 07050
Stirling Ave & Dr E, N & W 07050
Summer St 07050
Sylvan Way 07050
Taylor St 07050
Thomas Blvd & St 07050
Tompkins Pl & St 07050
Tony Galento Plz 07050
Tremont Ave, Ct & Pl 07050
Union St 07050
Valley Rd & St 07050
Vernon Pl 07050
Vose Ave 07050
Wallace St 07050
Walsh Ave 07050
Ward St 07050
Washington St 07050
Watchung Ave 07050
Waverly Pl 07050
Webster Pl 07050
White St 07050
William St 07050
Willow St 07050
Wilson Pl 07050
Windsor Pl 07050

PARAMUS NJ

General Delivery 07652

POST OFFICE BOXES MAIN OFFICE STATIONS AND BRANCHES

Box No.s
All PO Boxes 07653

NAMED STREETS

A And S Dr 07652
Abbott Rd 07652
Acorn Dr 07652
Adams Ln 07652
Addison Pl 07652
Adler Way 07652
Alan Dr 07652
Alberta Dr 07652
Albradt St 07652
Albright Ln 07652
Alden Rd 07652
Alpine Dr 07652
Amherst Ct 07652
Andrea Ct 07652
Ann Ct 07652
Arbor Rd & Way 07652
Arcadian Way 07652
Arcola Ave 07652
Ardale Rd 07652
Arnot Pl 07652
Arthur Ter 07652
Arundel Rd 07652
Ashley Pl 07652
Aspen Ct 07652
Aster Ct 07652
Azalea St 07652
Bailey Rd 07652
Balsam Ct 07652
Bancroft Pl 07652
Barnard Rd 07652
Barry Way 07652
Bay Ct 07652
Beasley Ter 07652
Bedford Rd 07652
Beech Ave & Ln 07652
Beechwood Dr 07652
Behnke Ave 07652
Bennington Ter 07652
Benton Rd 07652
Bergen Town Ctr 07652
Berkley Pl 07652
Berry Ln 07652
Bertha Ct 07652
Beverwyck Pl 07652
Birch Ln 07652
Birchwood Rd 07652
Blauvelt Ct 07652
Bluebell Ct 07652
Bogert Pl 07652
Bona Ln 07652
Boyd Rd 07652
Briarcliff Ln 07652
Bridle Way 07652
Broad Ave 07652
Broadview Ter 07652
Broadway Blvd 07652
Brock Ct 07652
Brook Dr & St 07652
Brookfield Ave 07652
Brown Cir 07652
Bruce Dr 07652
Bryant St 07652
Bryn Mawr Ct 07652
Buchanan Ct 07652
Buckthorn Ct 07652
Budd Rd 07652
Buehler Pl 07652
Bullard Ave 07652
Burke Pl 07652
Burlington Rd & St 07652
Burnet Pl 07652
Bush Pl 07652
Buttonwood Dr 07652
Cadmus Ave 07652
Cambridge Rd 07652
Cardinal Pl 07652
Carl Pl 07652
Carletta Ct 07652
Carlough Dr 07652
Caroline Rd 07652
Carter Ln 07652
Cathy Ann Ct 07652
Cedar Ave & Ln 07652
Central Ave 07652
E Century Rd 07652
Chadwick Dr 07652
Chelsea St 07652
Chestnut St 07652
Chimes Rd 07652
Circle Dr 07652
Clark Rd 07652
Clarkson Ct 07652
Clauss Ave 07652
Clayton Ter 07652
Cleenput Ter 07652
Cleveland Ave 07652
Clinton Rd 07652
Clover Rd 07652
Cloverdale Ave 07652
Coe Rd 07652
Colby Pl 07652
Colgate Ave 07652
College Rd 07652
Colorado Rd 07652
Columbia Ter 07652
Columbine Rd 07652
Columbus Way 07652
Concord Dr 07652
Continental Ave 07652
Coolidge Pl 07652
Coombs Dr 07652
Cooper Pl 07652
Cornell Rd 07652
Cottonwood Ct 07652
Crabtree Ln 07652
Craig Ave 07652
Crain Rd 07652
Crest Dr 07652
Croton Pl 07652
Cumberland Ct 07652
Curley Ct 07652
Curry Ln 07652
Cypress Ln 07652
Daisy Way 07652
Dansen Ave 07652
Dartmouth Ct 07652
Decker Pl 07652
Demarest Rd 07652
Denver Rd 07652
Diane Pl 07652
Diaz Pl 07652
Dogwood Ct 07652
Douglas Dr 07652
Dover St 07652
Drew Ave 07652
Drexel Rd 07652
Duke Dr 07652
Dunkerhook Rd 07652
East Dr 07652
Edmund Ter 07652
Edstan Way 07652
Ehret St 07652
Eisenhower Dr 07652
Ellen Pl 07652
Elliot Pl 07652
Elmwood Dr 07652
Emerald Ct 07652
Engle Rd 07652
Erie Rd 07652
Essex Rd 07652
Eton Ct 07652
Evans St 07652
Evelyn St 07652
Evergreen Pl 07652
Fairfield Dr 07652
Fairmount Pl 07652
Fairway Ter 07652
Falmouth Ave 07652
Farmington Ln 07652
N & S Farview Ave & Ter 07652
Fashion Ctr 07652
Ferandia Rd 07652
Fern Pl 07652
Ferndale Rd 07652
Fielding Ter 07652
Filippe Ct 07652
Fillmore Ct 07652
E Firehouse Ln 07652
Flint Pl 07652
Fordham Pl 07652
Forest Ave 07652
Forsythia Ln 07652
Frank Ln 07652
Franklin Pl 07652
Fredrick St 07652
Freeland Ave 07652
Frisch Ct 07652
From Rd 07652
Galda Rd 07652
Garden Ave 07652
Garden State Plz 07652
Garden State Plaza Blvd 07652
Gary St 07652
Geering Ter 07652
Georgian Dr 07652
Gerald St 07652
Geranium Ct 07652
Gertrude Ave 07652
Gettysburg Pl 07652
Gilbert Ave 07652
Glen Ave 07652
Godwin Rd 07652
Golf Rd 07652
Gorden Dr 07652
Grant Pl 07652
Green Valley Rd 07652
Greenbriar Rd 07652
Greglawn Dr 07652
Gregory Rd 07652
Grist Trl 07652
W Grove St 07652
Haase Ave 07652
Halco Dr 07652
Hall Rd 07652
Halsey St 07652
Hamilton Ct 07652
Hampshire Rd 07652
Harmon Dr 07652
Harold St 07652
Harrison St 07652
Harvey Ave 07652
Harwood Pl 07652
Haywood Dr 07652
Heather Ln 07652
Hebberd Ave 07652
Heights Rd 07652
Helen Ave 07652
Hemlock Dr 07652
Henry St 07652
Herbert Pl 07652
Hickory Ave 07652
Highland Ave & Ct 07652
Highview Ter 07652
Hillcrest Dr 07652
Hillside Ave 07652
Hilton Pl 07652
Hobart Rd 07652
Holly Ave 07652
Hollybrook Rd 07652
Homestead Rd 07652
Hoover Ct 07652
Hoppers Ln 07652
Howland Ave 07652
Idaho St 07652
Ikea Dr 07652
Iona Pl 07652
Iris Ct 07652
Island Rd 07652
Ivanhoe Dr 07652
Iverson Ct 07652
Ivy Pl 07652
Jackson Pl 07652
Janet Ave 07652
Jasper Rd 07652
Jay Dr 07652
Jefferson Ave 07652
Jerome Ave 07652
Jersey Pl 07652
Jockish Sq 07652
Johnson Ct 07652
Jolene Ct 07652
Jonquil Ct 07652
Josephine Ave 07652
June Dr 07652
Juniper Ln 07652
Justin Ct 07652
Kalisa Way 07652
Kaywin Rd 07652
Kearney Pl 07652
Kendrick St 07652
Kennedy Ct 07652
Kenwood Rd 07652
King Rd 07652
Knollwood Dr 07652
Knox Pl 07652
Koman Dr 07652
Kossuth St 07652
Kramer Dr 07652
Lafayette St 07652
Lambert Pl 07652
Laurel Ct 07652
Lawrence Dr 07652
Lawson Pl 07652
Lee Pl 07652
Legion Pl 07652
Lentz Ave 07652
Leonard Pl 07652
Lilac Ln 07652
Lincoln Dr 07652
Linden St 07652
Linwood Ave E & W 07652
Livingston Ct 07652
Lockwood Dr 07652
Locust Ave 07652
Longview Ct 07652
Lotus Ln 07652
Lozier Ct 07652
Lucky Hollow Dr 07652
Lyncrest Dr 07652
Lynn Dr 07652
Mack Centre Dr 07652
Mackay Ave 07652
Madison Ave 07652
Maitland Ave 07652
Mall At Iv 07652
Manchester Way 07652
Manning Rd 07652
Maple St 07652
Maplewood Dr 07652
Maril Ct 07652
Marion Ln 07652
Marquette Ct 07652
Maryann Ct 07652
Maryland Rd 07652
Mason Pl 07652
Mayfair Rd 07652
Mazur Ave 07652
Mchenry Dr 07652
Mckinley Blvd 07652
Meadow Ln 07652
Melton Pl 07652
Merrimack Ct 07652
Middlesex Ave 07652
E Midland Ave
1-66 07652
33-33 07653
67-399 07652
68-398 07652
W Midland Ave 07652
Midwood Rd 07652
Mill Run 07652
Millar Ct 07652
Minogue Ter 07652
Monroe Ave 07652
Montana St 07652
Morningside Rd 07652
Morristown Pl 07652
Mulberry Ct 07652
Myrna Rd 07652
Nevada St 07652
Nichols Dr 07652
Nimitz Rd 07652
Norman Way 07652
Nugent St 07652
Oakwood Dr 07652
Oliver Rd 07652
Olympia Blvd 07652
Oradell Ave 07652
Oregon St 07652
Otto Pl 07652
Owen Pl 07652
Oxford Ct 07652
Palm Ct 07652
S Paramus Park & Rd 07652
Paramus Park Mall 07652
Park Pl 07652
Parkside Dr 07652
Pascack Rd 07652
Paul Ct 07652
Pelican Ct 07652
Pepperidge Rd 07652
Pierce Dr 07652
Plaza Way 07652
Pleasant Ave E 07652
Polly Ann Ter 07652
Pond Pl 07652
Poplar Dr 07652
Powers Dr 07652
Prescott Pl 07652
Primrose Ln 07652
Princeton Ter 07652
Prospect St 07652
Purdue Ct 07652
Ramille Ct 07652
Redwood Rd 07652
Reeder Rd 07652
Regis Ct 07652
Reid Way 07652
Ridgeland Rd 07652
E & W Ridgewood Ave 07652
Robert St 07652
Robin Rd 07652
Roedel Pl 07652
Roosevelt Blvd 07652
Rose Dr 07652
Rosemont Ct 07652
Ross Rd 07652
Rutgers Pl 07652
Salem St 07652
Sandor Ct 07652
Sayre Ln 07652
Scarlet Oak Ln 07652
Schimmel St 07652
Schubert Ln 07652
Seagull Dr 07652
Sears Dr 07652
Seneca Ct 07652
Seton Hall Dr 07652
Sette Dr 07652
Sharp Plz 07652
Shelby Ave & Ct 07652
Sherwood Dr 07652
Short Way 07652
Silver Rod Ct 07652
Skie Dr 07652
Skylark Ct 07652
Soldier Hill Rd 07652
Sorbello Rd 07652
South Dr 07652
Southcrest Ave 07652
Spencer Pl 07652
Split Rock Rd 07652
Spring Ln 07652
S Spring Valley Ave & Rd 07652
Springfield Ave 07652
Standish Rd 07652
Starling Ct 07652
N & S State Rt 17 07652
E & W State Rt 4 07652
Stella Ct 07652
Stevens Ct 07652
Stony Ln 07652
Stuart St 07652
Summer Ln 07652
Summit Dr 07652
Sunflower Ave 07652
Swan Ct 07652
Swarthmore Ln 07652
Sweetbriar Pl 07652
Sycamore St 07652
Taft Ct 07652
Taylor Rd 07652
S Terhune Ave 07652
Terrace Dr 07652
Tether Ln 07652
Thistle Dr 07652
Thomas Dr 07652
Timothy Pl 07652
Trinity Ct 07652
Troast Rd 07652
Truman Ter 07652
Tryon Pl 07652
Tuers Ln 07652
Tufts Ct 07652
Tulane Ct 07652
Tulip Ln 07652
Twinberry Ct 07652
University Way 07652
Utah St 07652
Valley Health Plz 07652
Valley View Ave 07652
Van Binsberger Blvd 07652
Van Buren Dr 07652
Vanderbilt Ct 07652
Vassar Dr 07652
Vera Pl 07652
Vermont Dr 07652
Verona Way 07652
Veronica Ct 07652
Veterans Way 07652
Victoria Ave & Ter 07652
Village Cir E & W 07652
Villanova Dr 07652
Viola Way 07652
Virginia Ct 07652
Vivien Ct 07652
Wagner Ct 07652
Walnut St 07652
Washington Pl 07652
Wedgewood Dr 07652
Wendy Ann Ct 07652
West Dr 07652
Westbrook Ct 07652
Westview Ave 07652
White Pine Ct 07652
Willard Rd 07652
Willowbrook Ct 07652
Wilsey Ct 07652
Wilson Ave 07652
Windsor Rd 07652
Winslow Pl 07652
Winters Ave 07652
Woodcrest Ave 07652
Woodland Ave 07652
Wynetta Pl 07652
Wyoming Rd 07652
Yale Ct 07652
Yorktown Pl 07652
Yuhas Dr 07652

NUMBERED STREETS

All Street Addresses 07652

PATERSON NJ

General Delivery 07510

POST OFFICE BOXES MAIN OFFICE STATIONS AND BRANCHES

Box No.s
C - V 07509

AE - AZ 07509
BB - BE 07509
1 - 860 07543
2 - 447 07544
151 - 237 07533
472 - 679 07544
701 - 1057 07533
701 - 1757 07544
1101 - 28680 07509

NAMED STREETS

Acorn St 07512
Adams Dr 07512
Alabama Ave
2-6 07503
8-199 07503
201-257 07513
259-281 07513
259-271-259-271 07513
80-82-80-82 07503
Albert M Tyler Pl 07501
Albion Ave 07502
Alden Ter 07522
Alois Pl 07514
Amethyst Ln 07501
Amity St 07522
Anderson Ave 07512
Angela Ln & Pl 07502
Ann Pl 07524
Ann St 07501
Arch St 07522
Arlington Ave 07502
Arlington St 07522
Artillery Park Rd 07512
Atlantic St 07503
Auburn St 07501
N Barclay St 07503
Barnert Ave 07512
Barnert Pl 07522
Barnes St 07501
Battle Ridge Trl 07512
Baysteel Cir 07512
Beckwith Ave 07503
Beech St 07501
Belle Ave 07522
Belmont Ave 07522
Bergen St 07522
Berkshire Ave 07502
Bersongs Ave 07512
Birch St 07522
Bleeker St 07524
Bloomfield Ave 07503
Bogert St 07512
Bomont Pl 07512
Boulder Run Rd 07501
Boyle Ave 07512
Branch St 07524
Braun St 07503
Bridge St 07501
N Bridge St 07522
Broadway
1-200 07505
Broadway
201-452 07501
453-857 07514
859-899 07514
280-282-280-282 07501
35-37-35-37 07505
39-41-39-41 07505
40-42-40-42 07505
60-62-60-62 07505
65-67-65-67 07505
730-2-730-2 07514
82-84-82-84 07505
W Broadway
1-95 07505
96-337 07522
339-565 07522
187-189-187-189 07522
2-4-2-4 07505
217-221-217-221 07522
Brookman Ln 07512
Buffalo Ave 07503
Burhans Ave 07522
Burlington Ave 07502

Butler St 07524
Caldwell Ave 07501
California Ave 07503
Cambridge Rd 07512
Camden St 07503
Campus Rd 07512
Canal St 07503
Cannon Hill Rd 07512
Caraderl Ave 07502
Carbon St 07522
Carlisle Ave 07501
Carr Pl 07512
Carrelton Dr 07522
Carroll Pl 07512
Carroll St 07501
Catherine St 07512
Cedar Ct 07512
Cedar St 07501
Centennial Ct 07512
Center Ct 07512
Chadwick St 07503
Chamberlain Ave
1-430 07502
431-499 07522
505-505 07502
Charles St 07512
Chatham Ave 07502
Cherba Pl 07512
Chestnut St 07501
Christina Pl 07502
Church St
1-15 07505
1-199 07512
17-99 07505
19-21-19-21 07505
20-22-20-22 07505
23-25-23-25 07505
Cianci St 07501
Circle Ave 07522
Claremont Ave 07512
Clark St 07505
Cliff St 07522
Clinton St 07522
College Blvd 07505
Colonial Ave 07502
Colonial Ct 07512
Colt St 07505
Columbia Ave 07503
Columbus Ave 07512
Commanders Ct 07512
Commerce Way 07512
Congressional Ln 07512
Constitution Ln 07512
Continental Cir 07512
Coolidge Ave 07512
Coral St 07522
Courtland St 07503
Craig Ct 07512
Crescent Ave 07512
Crestwood Ct 07512
Crews St
1-99 07512
20-20 07511
Crooks Ave 07503
Crosby Ave
1-435 07502
101-299 07512
436-499 07522
190-1-190-5 07502
Crosby Pl 07501
Crystal Ln 07501
Cumberland Ave
1-99 07512
140-398 07502
Dakota St 07503
Dale Ave
1-54 07505
55-199 07501
Danforth Ave 07501
Dayton St 07501
Degrasse St 07505
Delaware Ave 07503
Denora Dr 07512
Derrom Ave 07504
Dewey Ave 07512
Dey St 07503

Dey Hill Trl 07512
Dill Plz 07501
Dixon Ave 07501
Don Bosco Ave 07502
Doremus St 07522
Dover St 07501
Duffus Ave 07512
Dundee Ave 07503
Dunkerly St 07512
Eagle Ave 07503
Edmund Ave 07502
Elberon Ave 07502
Elizabeth Pl 07512
Elizabeth St 07503
Elk St 07503
Ellison Pl 07504
Ellison St
1-43 07501
44-229 07505
230-232 07501
234-518 07501
150-154-150-154 07505
153-155-153-155 07505
295-315-295-315 07501
508-514-508-514 07501
58-60-58-60 07505
Elm St
1-99 07501
10-34 07502
510-534 07512
Emerson Ave 07502
W End Rd 07512
Erie St 07524
Essex St 07501
Fair St 07501
Falls Bridge Dr 07512
Federal Plz 07505
Fellner Pl 07512
Flintlock Ct 07512
Florida Ave 07503
Floyd Dr 07512
Frances St 07512
Franklin Pl 07512
Franklin St 07524
Front St 07522
Fulton Pl 07514
Fulton St 07501
Furler St 07512
Furman St 07505
Furrey Pl 07522
Garfield Ave 07522
Garfield Pl 07512
Garret St 07501
Garretson Ave 07512
Garrison St 07522
Gatherings Dr 07501
Generals Ln 07512
Genessee Ave 07503
George St 07503
Getty Ave 07503
Glen Ter 07512
Glover Ave 07501
Godwin Ave & St 07501
Gordon Ave & Dr 07512
Goshen St 07503
Gould Ave 07503
Governor St
1-309 07501
310-399 07514
195-197-195-197 07501
36-38-36-38 07501
41-43-41-43 07501
Graham Ave 07524
Grand St
1-315 07501
316-451 07505
453-499 07505
183-229-183-229 07501
325-327-325-327 07505
357-359-357-359 07505
96-98-96-98 07501
Granite Ave
1-149 07502
150-210 07522
Grant Ave 07512
Gray St 07501

Green St 07501
Greene Ave 07512
Grimes Pl 07514
E Grockens St 07514
Grove St 07503
Haledon Ave 07522
Halpine St 07522
Hamilton Ave
2-380 07501
77-79 07505
87-381 07501
382-388 07514
390-499 07514
356-358-356-358 07501
Hamilton Plz 07505
Hamilton St 07505
Hamilton Trl 07512
Harding Ave 07512
Harris Pl 07514
Harrison St 07501
Haven Ave 07512
Hazel St 07503
Headenti St
1-99 07503
701-799 07505
Hemlock St 07503
Henderson St 07501
Henry St 07502
Heritage Ct 07512
Heritage Pl 07513
Hickory Hill Blvd 07512
Highland St 07524
Highview Ave 07512
Hill St 07502
Hillman St 07522
Hillside Dr 07512
Hine St 07503
Hobart Pl 07512
E Holsman St 07522
Hopper St 07522
Hospital Plz 07503
Howard St 07501
Hoxey St 07501
Hudson Ave 07512
Hudson St 07522
Huizenga Ln 07512
Huntington Ter 07512
Hydeway Dr E 07512
Illinois Ave 07503
Independence Trl 07512
Industrial Plz 07503
Inglis Pl 07522
Iowa Ave 07503
Jackson Rd 07512
Jackson St
1-157 07501
158-199 07503
James St 07502
Jane St 07522
Jasper St 07522
Jefferson Pl 07512
Jefferson St 07522
Jelsma Pl 07501
Jersey St 07501
John St 07522
Kathys Ct 07501
Katz Ave
1-61 07522
62-199 07502
2-4-2-4 07522
Kearney St 07522
Keen St 07524
Kent Ct & Rd 07502
Kentucky Ave 07503
Killian Pl 07512
Kings Rd 07512
Kipp Pl 07513
Knickerbocker Ave 07503
Knollwood Rd 07512
Knox Ter 07512
Lackawanna Ave 07512
Lafayette Cir 07512
Lafayette St
1-206 07501
207-227 07524
229-299 07524

Lake Ave 07503
Lake St 07501
Lakeview Ave 07503
Laurel St 07522
Lawrence Pl 07514
Lawrence St 07501
Lee Pl 07505
Lehigh Ave 07503
Lenox Ave 07502
Leslie St 07503
Levine St 07503
Lewis Pl 07512
Lewis St 07501
Lexington Ave 07502
Liberty St 07522
Liberty Ridge Trl 07512
Lily St 07522
Lincoln Ave 07512
Lincoln St 07501
Lind Rd 07512
Lindbergh Pl 07503
Linden Rd 07514
Linwood Ave 07502
Look Out Pt 07512
Loretta Pl 07512
Lynden Pl 07512
Lyon St 07524
Madison Ave
1-480 07524
481-655 07514
656-685 07504
686-1064 07501
1065-1299 07503
217-219-217-219 07524
252-254-252-254 07524
464-466-464-466 07514
54-56-54-56 07524
875-3-875-4 07501
Madison Rd 07512
Madison St 07501
Magees Aly 07501
Main St
1-352 07505
354-378 07505
380-509 07501
510-1199 07503
120-122-120-122 07505
123-125-123-125 07505
134-132-134-132 07505
210-212-210-212 07505
213-215-213-215 07505
222-224-222-224 07505
256-258-256-258 07505
319-321-319-321 07505
336-338-336-338 07505
346-344-346-344 07505
349-351-349-351 07505
366-368-366-368 07505
560-566-560-566 07503
607-609-607-609 07503
71-73-71-73 07505
821-825-821-825 07503
956-958-956-958 07503
977-975-977-975 07503
997-999-997-1001 07503
E Main St 07522
N Main St 07522
Mair Ave 07512
Maitland Ave 07502
Malerriv Ave 07503
Maltese Dr 07512
Manchester Ave 07502
Manor Rd 07514
Maple Ln 07512
Maple St 07522
Margaret St 07512
Marion St 07522
Market St
1-25 07501
26-34 07505
27-35 07501
36-262 07505
263-528 07501
529-1099 07513
1013-1019-1013-1019 07513
369-371-369-371 07501

37-35-37-35 07505
447-449-447-449 07501
48-46-48-46 07505
76-78-76-78 07505
850-852-850-852 07513
Marshall St
437A-437B 07503
1-151 07501
152-599 07503
323-325-323-325 07503
49-57-49-57 07501
53-57-53-57 07501
Martin St 07501
Mary St 07503
Maryland Ave 07503
Masklee Ct 07512
Matlock St 07522
May St 07524
Mcbride Ave 07501
Mclean Blvd
1-57 07514
58-58 07513
59-119 07514
60-98 07514
100-100 07513
102-110 07514
120-160 07504
162-319 07504
321-335 07504
337-353 07513
355-357 07513
359-371 07513
364-364 07514
373-457 07514
380-598 07513
243-247-243-247 07504
375-385-375-385 07513
Meadow Dr 07512
Melissa Dr 07512
Memorial Dr 07505
Mercer St 07524
Michigan Ave 07503
Mill St 07501
Millarke Ave 07504
Minnisink Rd 07512
Mitchell Ave 07512
Montclair Ave 07503
Montgomery St 07501
Morris St 07501
Morris Canal Way 07512
Morton St 07501
Mountain Ave 07501
Mountainview Ct 07512
Mountainwood Ct 07512
Murphy Ct 07512
Murray Ave 07501
Nagle St 07501
New St 07501
Newark Ave 07503
News Plz 07501
Norwood Ter 07512
Oak St 07501
Olive St 07501
Oliver St 07501
Otillio Ter 07502
Overlook Ave 07504
Oxford St 07522
Pacific St 07503
Pamela Dr 07512
Park Ave
1-260 07501
261-300 07513
301-700 07504
33-37-33-37 07501
51-57-51-57 07501
E Park Dr 07504
Park Pl 07524
Park Rd 07514
Park St 07503
Passaic St 07501
Paterson Ave
1-91 07522
92-299 07502
301-301 07502
Paterson St 07501
Pathelde St 07501
Patriots Trl 07512

Paxton St 07503
Peach St 07503
Pearl St 07501
Peel St 07524
Pennington St 07501
Pennsylvania Ave 07503
Perendia Ave 07513
Perry St 07501
Peterson Rd 07512
Piercy St 07522
Plesinger Pl 07514
Ploch St 07503
Plum St 07503
Plymouth Rd 07502
Pope Rd 07514
Potomac Ave 07503
Preakness Ave
2-124 07522
126-139 07522
140-799 07502
423-425-423-425 07502
74-76-74-76 07522
Presidential Blvd 07522
Prince St
1-71 07505
72-199 07501
Prospect St 07505
Putnam St 07524
Quartz Ln 07501
Quinn St 07501
Railroad Ave
1-66 07505
67-299 07501
118-130-118-130 07501
74-102-74-102 07501
E & W Railway Ave 07503
Ramsey St 07501
Raphael Rd 07512
Raritan Ave 07503
Redman Pl 07512
Redwood Ave 07522
Reenstra Ct 07522
Reservoir Ave 07501
Richmond Ave 07502
Ridge Ter 07514
River St
1-69 07505
70-80 07501
71-81 07505
82-267 07501
268-899 07524
165-185-165-185 07501
294-302-294-302 07524
429-431-429-431 07524
445-447-445-447 07524
456-458-456-458 07524
478-480-478-480 07524
520-522-520-522 07524
River Ter 07502
Riverview Dr 07512
Robert St 07503
Rockland St 07501
Roosevelt Ave 07512
Rosa Parks Blvd 07501
Rose St 07501
Roseda Dr 07512
Roseland Ave 07512
Rosengren Ave 07512
Rossiter Ave 07502
Rutherford Ct 07512
Ryerson Ave 07502
Ryle Ave & Rd 07522
Saint James Pl 07512
Salem Rd 07502
Sandra Dr 07512
Sandy Ct 07522
Sassafras St 07524
Scrivens St 07512
Seeley St 07501
Sentry Way 07512
Shady Ln 07512
Shady Pl 07512
Shady St 07524
Shepherds Ln 07512
Sheridan Ave 07502
Sherman Ave 07502

Sherwood Ave 07502
Short St 07522
Slater St 07501
Smith St 07505
Southard St 07501
Sparrow St 07524
Spring St
1-153 07501
154-299 07503
193-195-193-195 07503
258-262-258-262 07503
Spruce St 07501
Stanford Ct 07512
State St 07501
Stewart Ter 07512
Stirling Ter 07512
Stout St 07522
Straight St
1-480 07501
481-599 07503
389-391-389-391 07501
421-423-421-423 07501
5-7-5-7 07501
N Straight St 07522
Summer St
1-59 07524
60-599 07501
230-232-230-232 07501
419-421-419-421 07501
Summit St 07501
Suntrens St 07524
Sussex St 07503
Sutton Ave 07512
Swinburne St 07503
Taft Ct & Rd 07512
Temple St 07522
Thistle Ct 07512
Thomas St 07503
Timothy St 07503
Totowa Ave
1-441 07502
442-546 07522
548-598 07522
323-325-323-325 07502
385-391-385-391 07502
541-543-541-543 07522
Totowa Rd 07512
Tow Path Cres 07512
Tracy Ave 07512
Trenton Ave
1-179 07513
180-499 07503
426-430-426-430 07503
Turner St 07501
Tyler St 07501
Union Ave
1-440 07502
441-599 07522
194-196-194-196 07502
Union Blvd 07512
Us Highway 46 07512
Valley Rd 07503
Van Blarcom St 07524
Van Houten St
2-12 07505
14-140 07505
230-499 07501
13 1/2-15 1/2 07505
314-316-314-316 07501
343-359-343-359 07501
Van Winkle Ave 07503
Vangerma St 07522
Vernon Ave 07503
Vesper St 07503
Veterans Pl 07505
Vistas Ter 07522
Vita Rd 07512
Vreeland Ave
1-271 07504
1-99 07512
272-399 07513
308-310-308-310 07513
Wabash Ave 07503
Waite St 07524
Walker St 07501
Wall Ave 07504
Walnut St 07522
Walton St 07501
Ward St
1-44 07501
45-53 07505
55-160 07505
162-180 07505
181-184 07501
194-194 07510
194-194 07509
194-194 07544
Warren St 07524
Washington Ave 07503
Washington Pl 07512
Washington St
1-79 07501
80-80 07505
81-81 07501
82-130 07505
132-198 07505
48-50-48-50 07501
88-86-88-86 07505
Watson St 07522
Wayne Ave
1-99 07522
100-399 07502
1-7-1-7 07522
279-283-279-283 07502
3-1-3-1 07522
7-5-7-5 07522
Webster Ave 07501
Weiss St 07503
Welcome St 07522
Weldon Ct 07512
Wentick St 07512
N West St 07522
E Westside Ave 07501
White St 07522
Willard Ave 07512
William Pl 07512
William St 07514
Willow Ct 07512
Wilson Ave 07512
N & S Winifred Dr N 07512
Wood St 07524
Woodruff Pl 07522
N York St 07524
Yorktown Ln 07512
Young Ave 07512

NUMBERED STREETS

1st Ave
1-24 07524
25-99 07514
7-9-7-9 07524
N 1st St 07522
2nd Ave
1-42 07524
43-199 07514
N 2nd St 07522
3rd Ave
1-75 07524
76-299 07514
N 3rd St 07522
4th Ave
1-156 07524
157-299 07514
171-177-171-177 07514
30-36-30-36 07524
81-83-81-83 07524
N 4th St 07522
5th Ave
2-26 07524
28-305 07524
306-599 07514
245-247-245-247 07524
249-251-249-251 07524
297-299-297-299 07524
E 5th St 07524
N 5th St 07522
6th Ave
1-360 07524
361-499 07514
185-199-185-199 07524
E 6th St 07524
N 6th St 07522
7th Ave
1-135 07524
136-299 07514
79-85-79-85 07524
E 7th St 07524
N 7th St 07522
8th Ave
1-145 07524
146-299 07514
80-82-80-82 07524
N 8th St 07522
9th Ave
1-290 07524
291-499 07514
N 9th St 07522
10th Ave 07524
315-599 07514
N 10th St 07522
11th Ave 07514
E 11th St 07524
N 11th St 07522
12th Ave
1-226 07501
227-599 07514
1001-1005 07501
73-71-73-71 07501
E 12th St 07524
13th Ave 07504
E 13th St 07524
14th Ave 07504
15th Ave 07504
E 15th St 07524
16th Ave 07501
E 16th St
1-370 07524
371-397 07514
399-499 07514
1-3-1-3 07524
17th Ave
1-59 07501
60-148 07513
149-599 07504
86-88-86-88 07513
E 17th St 07524
18th Ave
1-95 07513
96-466 07504
E 18th St
1-450 07524
451-590 07514
591-799 07501
357-359-357-359 07524
359-357-359-357 07524
504-506-504-506 07514
786-790-786-790 07501
19th Ave
1-170 07513
171-499 07504
458-462-458-462 07504
E 19th St
1-479 07524
480-649 07514
651-769 07501
771-1099 07501
446-60-446-60 07524
20th Ave
1-300 07501
301-524 07513
525-799 07504
200-214-200-214 07501
367-369-367-369 07513
E 20th St 07513
21st Ave
1-135 07503
136-375 07501
381-385 07513
497-497 07543
501-899 07513
E 21st St
1-46 07504
47-499 07513
22nd Ave 07513
E 22nd St
1-645 07514
646-753 07504
754-1199 07513
56-58-56-58 07514
60-62-60-62 07514
23rd Ave 07513
E 23rd St
1-645 07514
646-775 07504
776-802 07513
777-783 07504
804-1199 07513
305-307-305-307 07514
816-818-816-818 07513
E 24th St
1-645 07514
646-799 07504
800-1199 07513
670-672-670-672 07504
E 25th St
1-615 07514
616-799 07504
800-1099 07513
138-140-138-140 07514
E 26th St
1-590 07514
591-799 07504
800-1099 07513
E 27th St
100-567 07514
568-799 07504
800-1099 07513
E 28th St
200-540 07514
541-754 07504
800-1099 07513
682-684-682-684 07504
E 29th St
200-515 07514
516-785 07504
786-899 07513
E 30th St
1-240 07514
241-547 07504
549-559 07504
561-799 07513
E 31st St
1-230 07514
231-545 07504
546-799 07513
E 32nd St
1-176 07514
181-540 07504
541-799 07513
509-511-509-511 07504
33rd St 07504
E 33rd St
2-8 07514
10-170 07514
171-540 07504
542-558 07513
560-699 07513
E 34th St
1-130 07514
131-512 07504
650-690 07513
E 35th St
1-130 07514
131-512 07504
E 36th St
1-130 07514
131-474 07504
476-598 07504
600-699 07513
E 37th St
1-130 07514
131-599 07504
E 38th St
1-130 07514
131-530 07504
531-699 07513
E 39th St
1-130 07514
131-530 07504
531-599 07513
26-48-26-48 07514
E 40th St
1-130 07514
131-530 07504
E 41st St 07504
E 42nd St
290-530 07504
531-599 07513
E 43rd St
1-99 07514
201-300 07504

PERTH AMBOY NJ

General Delivery 08861

POST OFFICE BOXES MAIN OFFICE STATIONS AND BRANCHES

Box No.s
All PO Boxes 08862

NAMED STREETS

Adams Ave 08861
Albert St 08861
Alpine St 08861
Alta Vista Pl 08861
Amboy Ave 08861
Amy Way 08861
Andrews Dr 08861
Anton St 08861
Armstrong Ln 08861
Arnold Ave 08861
Ashley St 08861
Atlantic Ave 08861
Augustine Pl 08861
Baker Pl 08861
Barclay St 08861
Barnes Ct 08861
Barracks St 08861
Barry Ave 08861
Bertrand Ave 08861
Bingle St 08861
Birch St 08861
Boggs St 08861
Brace Ave 08861
Brighton Ave 08861
Broad St 08861
Broadhead Pl 08861
Bruck Ave 08861
Buckingham Ave 08861
Bud Ct 08861
Carlock Ave 08861
Carson Ave 08861
Catalpa Ave 08861
Catherine St 08861
Cedar St 08861
Center St 08861
Central Pl 08861
Chamberlain Ave 08861
S Charles St 08861
Chauncey St 08861
Chester St 08861
Christopher Ct 08861
S Church St 08861
Clark Ave 08861
Clembil Ct 08861
Clyde Ave 08861
Coddington Ave 08861
Colfax St 08861
Colgate Ave 08861
Columbus Cir & Dr 08861
Commerce St 08861
Compton Ave 08861
Convery Blvd 08861
Cornell St 08861
Cortlandt St 08861
Court Ave 08861
Crencoun St 08861
Dally Ct 08861
Davidson Ave 08861
Dayna Ct 08861
De Kalb Ave 08861
Dillon Ln 08861
Division St 08861
Dobranski Dr 08861
Donald Ave 08861
Dorsey St 08861
Drahos Ave 08861
Eagle Ave 08861
East Ave 08861
Edward Pl 08861
Elizabeth St 08861
Ellen Ave 08861
Elm St 08861
Emmett Ave 08861
Erin Ave 08861
Fayette St 08861
Federal Ct 08861
Florida Grove Rd 08861
Forbes Ave 08861
Francis St 08861
Franklin Dr 08861
Front St 08861
Gadek Pl 08861
Garretson Ave 08861
Gifford St 08861
Goodwin St 08861
Gordon St 08861
Gornik Dr 08861
Grace St 08861
Grant St 08861
Great Beds Ct 08861
Groom St 08861
Grove Ave & St 08861
Hall Ave 08861
Hamilton Ave 08861
Hanson Ave 08861
Harbor Ter 08861
Harbortown Blvd 08861
Harding Ave 08861
Harned Ave & St 08861
Harrington St 08861
Harrison Pl 08861
Hartford St 08861
Hazel Ave 08861
Herbert St 08861
Hickory St 08861
Hidden Village Dr 08861
High St 08861
Hobart St 08861
Holly Dr 08861
Hommann Ave 08861
Hornsby Ave 08861
Howard St 08861
Hunter Ave 08861
Huntington St 08861
Inslee St 08861
Jacques St 08861
James St 08861
Jefferson St
1-206 08861
205-205 08862
207-299 08861
208-298 08861
Jeffries St 08861
Jennetty Ct 08861
John St 08861
Johnstone St 08861
Juliette St 08861
Kamm St 08861
Kearny Ave 08861
Keene St 08861
Kelly Ave 08861
Kelsey Ave 08861
Kennedy St 08861
King St 08861
Kirkland Pl 08861
Koczusko St 08861
Kosciusko St 08861
Kreil St 08861
Krockmally Ave 08861
Laura Pl 08861
Laurel St 08861
Lawrence St 08861
Lawrie St 08861
Lawton Pl 08861
Lee Ave & St 08861
Lehigh Ave 08861
Leon Ave 08861
Lewis St 08861
Lincoln Dr 08861
Lindberg Ave 08861
Linden St 08861
Long Ferry Rd 08861
Loretta St 08861
Louis St 08861
Luther Ave 08861
Lynd St 08861
Madison Ave 08861
Maple St 08861
Market St 08861
Mary St 08861
Maurer Rd 08861
May Ave & St 08861
Mcclellan St 08861
Mcguire Pl 08861
Mckeon St 08861
Meade St 08861
Mechanic St 08861
Meinzer St 08861
Meredith St 08861
Miller St 08861
Mitchell Pl 08861
Morris St 08861
Myrtle St 08861
Neville St 08861
New St 08861
New Brunswick Ave 08861
Oak St 08861
Ogden Pl 08861
Olive St 08861
Otlowski Ct 08861
Pacific Ave 08861
Packer Pl 08861
Paderewski Ave 08861
N & S Park Ave & Dr 08861
Parker St 08861
Patterson St 08861
Pearl Pl 08861
Penn St 08861
Pennsylvania Ave 08861
Pershing Pl 08861
Peterson Ct 08861
Pfeiffer Blvd 08861
Pine St 08861
W Pond Rd 08861
Prospect St 08861
Pulaski Ave 08861
Quincy Ct 08861
Raritan Ave 08861
Rathburn Pl 08861
Reade St 08861
Rector St 08861
Richard Ave 08861
Ridgeley St 08861
Riverview Dr 08861
Robbins St 08861
Route 440 Connection 08861
Rowson Ave 08861
Rudyard Dr 08861
Sadowsky Pkwy 08861
Sayre Ave 08861
Seaman St 08861
Shannon Ave 08861
Sheridan St 08861
Sherman St 08861
W Side Ave 08861
Silzer St 08861
Smith St 08861
Sofield Ave 08861
Spruce St 08861
Stanford St 08861
State St 08861
Steadman Pl 08861
Stephen Ave 08861
Sterling Ct 08861
Steurwald Pl 08861
Stevenson Pl 08861
Stockton St 08861
Summit Ave 08861
Sutton St 08861
Thomas St 08861
Truxton Dr 08861
Union Ct 08861
Us Highway 9 N 08861
Valley Pl 08861
Vincent Pl 08861
Wagner Ave 08861

Walnut St 08861
Waltrous Ave 08861
Washington St 08861
Water St 08861
Watson Ave 08861
Wayne St 08861
Weirup St 08861
William St 08861
Wilson St 08861
Wisteria St 08861
Wolff St 08861
Woodruff Pl 08861
Worden Ave 08861
Zambory St 08861

NUMBERED STREETS

All Street Addresses 08861

PISCATAWAY NJ

General Delivery 08854

POST OFFICE BOXES MAIN OFFICE STATIONS AND BRANCHES

Box No.s
All PO Boxes 08855

NAMED STREETS

Abbot Ct 08854
Academy St 08854
Adams St 08854
Adrian Ave 08854
Agatha Dr 08854
Albert St 08854
Allen St E & W 08854
Allison Rd 08854
Amanda Ct 08854
Amaryllis Ln 08854
Ambrose Valley Ln 08854
Ames St 08854
Anderson Pl 08854
Andrews Way 08854
Angela Ct 08854
Anita Dr 08854
Ann St 08854
Anthony Ave 08854
Apple Way 08854
Arlington Pl 08854
Art Pl 08854
Aspen Ct 08854
Astor Pl 08854
Atlanta Ave 08854
Autumn Dr 08854
Avenue E 08854
Avon St 08854
Azalea Pl 08854
Baekeland Ave 08854
Balch Ave 08854
Baldwin St 08854
Ballas Ln 08854
Baltimore Ave 08854
Barbour Pl 08854
Barclay Ct 08854
Barnett Pl 08854
Bartholomew Rd 08854
Bay St 08854
Bayberry Close 08854
Beatty St 08854
Beaver Creek Ct 08854
Bedford Ct 08854
Begonia Ct 08854
Behmer Rd 08854
Bell St 08854
Bella Dr 08854
Ben Pl 08854
Benjamin Ter 08854
Bennington Pl 08854
Berkshire Ct 08854
Berrue Cir 08854
Berwick Way 08854
Bev Ave 08854
Beverly Rd 08854
Bevier Rd 08854
Bexley Ln 08854
Birch Run Dr 08854
Birchview Dr 08854
Birchwood Dr 08854
Blackford Ave 08854
Blue Ridge Ave 08854
Blueberry Ct 08854
Bohdan St 08854
Boston Ave 08854
Bound Brook Ave 08854
Bowler Ct 08854
Bowser Rd 08854
Boxwood Rd 08854
Bpo Way 08854
Brandywine Cir 08854
Brearly Pl 08854
Breckenridge Ct 08854
Brentwood Dr 08854
Brett Rd & St 08854
Brewster Ave 08854
Brian Ct 08854
Briarwood Ct 08854
Bristol Rd 08854
Brook Ave 08854
Brook Hollow Rd 08854
Brookside Rd 08854
Brotherhood St 08854
Brunella Ave 08854
Buchman St 08854
Buckingham Dr 08854
Buena Vista Ave 08854
E Burgess Dr 08854
Buttonwood Dr 08854
Caladium Ct 08854
Cambridge St 08854
Camelot Ct 08854
Cameron Rd 08854
Canterbury Ct 08854
Carlton Ave 08854
Carlton Club Dr 08854
Caroll Ave 08854
Carpathia St 08854
Carpenter Rd 08854
Carriage Dr 08854
Castle Pointe Blvd 08854
Cedarwood Dr 08854
Centennial Ave 08854
Center St 08854
Central Ave 08854
Chadovoyne Dr 08854
Chariot Ct 08854
Charles Ter 08854
Charlton Ave 08854
Charter St 08854
Chelsea Dr 08854
Cherrywood Dr 08854
Cheryl Ct 08854
Chester Way 08854
Chesterfield Dr 08854
Chestnut Pl 08854
Chicago Ave 08854
Chippenham Ct 08854
Christina Ct 08854
Christopher Ct 08854
Church St 08854
Circle Dr N 08854
Clara Dr 08854
Clarendon Pl 08854
Clark Pl 08854
Clawson St 08854
Clay Ave 08854
Colonial Dr 08854
Colson Ct 08854
Commonwealth Ave 08854
Concord Ave 08854
Constitution Ave 08854
Cooper St 08854
Corporate Pl S 08854
Coventry Cir 08854
Craig Ave 08854
Crestwood Dr & St 08854
Crocus Ct 08854
Cromwell Ct 08854
Cumberland Rd 08854
Curtis Ave 08854
Custer St 08854
Cypress Ct 08854
Dahlia Ct 08854
Danterli Ave 08854
Darby Ln 08854
Davidson Rd 08854
Davis Ave 08854
Day Ave 08854
Deborah Dr 08854
Deep Brook Ct 08854
Deerfield Ave 08854
Dell Rd 08854
Demarest Pl 08854
Dennis Ct 08854
Desna St 08854
Devon Dr 08854
Dewey Ct 08854
Dey St 08854
Dial Ave 08854
Dickerson Dr 08854
Digian Ct 08854
Diiorio Ct 08854
Division Ave 08854
Dogwood Dr 08854
Donna Ct 08854
Doral Ct 08854
Dorset Ct 08854
Dover St 08854
Doyle Ct & St 08854
Draco Rd 08854
Drake Ln 08854
Dryden St 08854
Duffie Pl 08854
Duke Rd 08854
Dunbar Ave 08854
Dunellen Ave 08854
Dunn Ave 08854
Dupont Ave 08854
Durango Dr 08854
Eastview St 08854
Edgewood St 08854
Edmond Ct 08854
Edna Pl 08854
Edwards Ave 08854
Eiseman Ave 08854
Elizabeth Ave 08854
Elk St 08854
Ellis Pkwy 08854
Elwood St 08854
Emerson St 08854
Emma Pl 08854
Emmet Ct 08854
Ethel Rd W 08854
Eva St 08854
Evans Ave 08854
Evergreen Ct 08854
Evona Ave 08854
Ewing Dr 08854
Exeter Ct 08854
Fairview Ave 08854
Fairways Blvd 08854
Farmland Ct 08854
Farragut Dr 08854
Fawn Ct 08854
Fellowship Ln 08854
Fernwood Dr 08854
Fisher Ave 08854
Fitzrandolph Rd 08854
Fleming St 08854
Florence Ave & Ter 08854
Forest Dr 08854
Foster St 08854
Fountain Ave 08854
Fox Chase Dr 08854
Fox Hollow Dr 08854
Frances St 08854
Franklin St 08854
Franko Ave 08854
Freedom Ave 08854
Frelinghuysen Rd 08854
Fuller Ave 08854
Gail Ct 08854
Gallini Dr 08854
Gates Ave 08854
Gemma Ct 08854
Gibson St 08854
Gilman Dr 08854
Glenwood Dr 08854
Goldfinch Ct 08854
Golf Links Ave 08854
Gordon Rd 08854
Grace Pl 08854
Gramercy Dr 08854
Grandview Ave E 08854
Grant Ave 08854
Greenwood Dr 08854
Grove St 08854
Hadley St 08854
Haight Ave 08854
Haines Ave 08854
Hall St 08854
Halley Ct 08854
Hamilton Blvd 08854
Hampshire Ct 08854
Hancock Rd 08854
Hanover St 08854
Hanson Ave 08854
Harmony St 08854
Harold Pl 08854
Harper St 08854
Harte Pl 08854
Harvard St 08854
Harwick Ct 08854
Hawthorne Rd 08854
Hayford St 08854
Haywood Ave 08854
Hazelwood Pl 08854
Hedgerow St 08854
Heffernan St 08854
Heidy Ct 08854
Helen Ct 08854
Hendrick Pl 08854
Henry Pl 08854
Hicks St 08854
Hidden Hollow Ct 08854
Hidden Woods Ct 08854
High St 08854
High Point Way 08854
Highland Ave 08854
Hillcrest Dr 08854
Hillside Ave 08854
Hoes Ln 08854
Holly Ln 08854
Hopkinson Ave 08854
Hospital Rd 08854
Howard St 08854
Howe Pl 08854
Howell Ave 08854
Hudson St 08854
Hughes Ter 08854
Hunt Dr 08854
Independence Ct 08854
International Ave 08854
Irving Pl 08854
Ivy St 08854
Jackson St 08854
James Ave 08854
Jarrard St 08854
Jasmine Dr 08854
Jay St 08854
Jefferson Dr 08854
Jeffrey Way 08854
Jennie Pl 08854
Jennifer Ct 08854
Jerome St 08854
Jersey Ave 08854
Jesse Way 08854
Johanna Ct 08854
Johnfield Ct 08854
Johnson Ave 08854
Joyce Dr 08854
Joyce Kilmer Ave 08854
Juniper Ln 08854
Justice St 08854
Karen Ct 08854
Karnell Dr 08854
Kate Ter 08854
Keller Ln 08854
Kensington Dr 08854
Kent St 08854
Kerwin St 08854
Keswick Dr 08854
Kilmer Ct 08854
Kim Ct 08854
Kingsbridge Rd 08854
Knightsbridge Rd 08854
Knollwood St 08854
Kossuth St 08854
Kroeger Ln 08854
Lackland Ave 08854
Lafayette St 08854
Lake Ct & Way 08854
Lake Park Dr 08854
Lakeside Dr N & S 08854
Lakeview Ave & Rd 08854
Lancaster Ct 08854
Lavender Dr 08854
Lee Pl 08854
Lehigh Ave 08854
Lenox Ct 08854
Leslie Ave 08854
Lester Pl 08854
Levgar St 08854
Lewis Ct & Pl 08854
Lexington Dr 08854
Liberty Ct 08854
Lilac Way 08854
Lillian Ter 08854
Lily Ln 08854
Lincoln Ave 08854
Linda Ct 08854
Linden St 08854
Lioni Ct 08854
Locust Ave 08854
Lodge St 08854
Logan Ln 08854
Long St 08854
Longfellow Ave 08854
Lpo Way 08854
Luca Dr 08854
Lucille Ct 08854
Ludlow St 08854
Lunar Rd 08854
Lund Ct 08854
Lynnwood St 08854
Mabel St 08854
Madison Ave 08854
Mae Ln 08854
Magnolia Ct 08854
Manchester Ct 08854
Manor Blvd 08854
Mansfield Rd 08854
Maple Ave 08854
Maplehurst Ln 08854
Marcel Ln 08854
Marion Ct 08854
Marisa Ct 08854
Martin Ln 08854
Marvin Ln 08854
Masters Blvd 08854
Matthew Ct 08854
May Ct 08854
Mayfield Ln 08854
Mcclellan Ct 08854
Mckinnon St 08854
Meade Ct 08854
Meadowbrook Ln 08854
Meister St 08854
Melrose Ave 08854
Meredith Pl & Rd 08854
Metlars Ln 08854
Michael St 08854
Michelle Ct 08854
Middlesex Ave 08854
Mill Brook Rd 08854
Miller St 08854
Milton Pl 08854
Mimosa Ln 08854
Mindy Ln 08854
Mitchell Ave 08854
Mohill Pl 08854
Montgomery St 08854
Moonlight Dr 08854
Moore Ave 08854
Morris Ave & Ln 08854
Mountain Ave 08854
Muriel Ave N 08854
Murray Ave 08854
Musket Way 08854
Mynipoti Ct 08854
Myrtle Ave 08854
Nancy Ln 08854
Naomi Way 08854
Nebula Rd 08854
Nelson Ave & Pl 08854
Netherwood Ave 08854
New Brook Ct & Dr 08854
New Brunswick Ave 08854
New Durham Rd 08854
New England Ave 08854
New Market Rd 08854
Newark Ave 08854
Normandy Dr 08854
Norwich Ct 08854
Nova Dr 08854
Nye Ct 08854
Oak Pl 08854
Oakwood Way 08854
Ode Pl 08854
Old New Brunswick Rd 08854
Old Randolphville Rd 08854
Olive St 08854
Orchard Rd & St 08854
Orion Rd 08854
Orris Ave 08854
Overbrook Rd 08854
Owen Pl 08854
Oxford St 08854
Palisade Ave 08854
Park Ave 08854
Parkside Ave 08854
Patron Ct 08854
Patton Ave 08854
Peabody St 08854
Pearl Pl 08854
Pegasus Rd 08854
Pelham Ave 08854
Pelmont Pl 08854
Penrose Ln 08854
Perrine Ave 08854
Pershing Pl 08854
Pickett Pl 08854
Piluso Way 08854
Pine Valley Way 08854
Pinelli Dr 08854
Pinewood Dr 08854
Pittsburgh Ave 08854
Plainfield Ave N 08854
Plane St 08854
Pleasant Ave 08854
Pleasantview Dr 08854
Plum St 08854
Plymouth Ct 08854
Poe Pl 08854
Pond Ln 08854
Poplar Pl & Rd 08854
Possumtown Rd 08854
Postal Plz 08854
Powderhorn Pl 08854
Prescott Pl 08854
Primrose Ln 08854
Princeton Rd 08854
Prospect Ave 08854
Putnam Ave 08854
Quick Way 08854
Quincy St 08854
Rachel Ter 08854
Ralston Ave 08854
N & S Randolphville Rd 08854
Raven Ave 08854
Rea Ct 08854
Rebecca Pl 08854
Redbud Rd 08854
Redwood Dr 08854
Retta Ct 08854
Revere Rd 08854
Richard Ter 08854
Richards Ave 08854
Ripley Ct 08854
River Rd 08854
Rivercrest Dr 08854
Riverview Ave 08854
Road 1 08854
Road 3 08854
Roberts Ave E & W 08854
Robin Ct 08854
Rock Ave 08854
Rockafeller Rd 08854
Roma Blvd 08854
Roosevelt Ave 08854
Rose Pl 08854
Rosewood Dr 08854
Ross Hall Blvd N & S 08854
Royal Dr 08854
Ruby Ct 08854
Runyon Ave 08854
Rushmore Ave 08854
Rutgers Rd 08854
Ruth Pl 08854
Ryan Ln 08854
Rye St 08854
Sabrina Ln 08854
Saint Marks Ave 08854
Saint Michael St 08854
Saint Olga Pl 08854
Salem St 08854
Saratoga Ct 08854
Sawgrass Ct 08854
Scarlet Knight Way 08854
School St 08854
Scott St 08854
Seeley Ave 08854
Sefton Cir 08854
Seward Ave 08854
Sewell Ave 08854
Seymour Ter 08854
Shady Oak Ct 08854
Sheffield Ct 08854
Sheldon Pl 08854
Sherman Ave 08854
Sherwood Dr 08854
Shirley Pkwy 08854
Short St 08854
Sidney Rd 08854
Silas Pl 08854
Silverton Pl 08854
Simon Ct 08854
Skiles Ave
1-99 08854
3-3 08855
Smalley St 08854
Smith St 08854
Smock Pl 08854
Smoke Tree Close 08854
Snowdrift Dr 08854
South Ave 08854
Southview Ct 08854
Spear St 08854
Spencer St 08854
Springfield Ave 08854
Spruce Ln 08854
Stafford Dr 08854
Stanton Ave 08854
Steamboat Way 08854
Stelton Rd 08854
Sterling Dr 08854
Stratton St N & S 08854
Strawberry Ln 08854
Street 1603 08854
Strong Rd 08854
Stuart St 08854
Sturbridge Dr 08854
Summers Ave 08854
Summershade Cir 08854
Sumner Pl 08854
Sunbrite Ln 08854
Sunburst Ln 08854
Sunset Rd 08854
Sunshine Dr 08854
Surrey Ln 08854
Susan Ct 08854
Suskin Pl 08854
Suttie Ave 08854
Sutton Ln 08854

Suttons Ln 08854
Sycamore Ln 08854
Sylvan Ave 08854
Tabb Ave 08854
Tammy Ct 08854
Tanglewood Dr 08854
Taylor Rd 08854
Telcordia Dr 08854
Telluride Dr 08854
Terrace Ct 08854
Thames Ave 08854
Theresa Ct 08854
Thornton Ln 08854
Timan Pl 08854
Tina Ct 08854
Titsworth Pl 08854
Tower Blvd 08854
Townsend Ct 08854
Traci Ln 08854
Truman Ter 08854
Turner Pl 08854
Underwood St 08854
Union St 08854
Upson Ln 08854
Vail Ave 08854
Valmere Ave 08854
Van Winkle Pl 08854
Vasser Dr 08854
Veghte Pl 08854
Ventnor Ct 08854
Vera St 08854
Vernon Ct 08854
Victoria Ave 08854
Vocisano Ct 08854
Vogel Ave 08854
Wade St 08854
Wagner Ave 08854
Wakefield Ln 08854
Waldhaven Ct 08854
Wall St 08854
Walnut St 08854
Ward Pl 08854
Warehouse Rd 08854
S Washington Ave 08854
Washington Plaza Dr 08854
Water St 08854
Wayne Ave & St 08854
Webster Ave 08854
Wedgewood St 08854
Welles Ct 08854
Wembly Pl 08854
Westfield Ave 08854
Whispering Pines Way 08854
Whittier Ave 08854
Wickley Ave 08854
Wildwood Dr 08854
Wilkens Dr 08854
William St 08854
Willow Ave 08854
Wills Way 08854
Winans Ave 08854
Winchester Rd 08854
Winterberry Cir 08854
Wisteria Ct 08854
Witherspoon St 08854
Woodlake Dr 08854
Woodland Rd 08854
Woodrow Ave W 08854
Wyckoff Ave 08854
Wyndham Way 08854
Wyndmere Rd 08854
Wynnwood Ave 08854
Yorktowne Dr 08854
Zirkel Ave 08854

NUMBERED STREETS

All Street Addresses 08854

PLAINFIELD NJ

General Delivery 07061

POST OFFICE BOXES MAIN OFFICE STATIONS AND BRANCHES

Box No.s
1 - 1830 07061

2401 - 2699 07060
2701 - 2999 07062
3001 - 3270 07063
5001 - 5668 07061
6200 - 6320 07062

NAMED STREETS

Abbond Ct 07063
Abbotsford Rd 07062
Academy Ave 07062
Adam Cir 07062
Albert St 07063
Alden Pl 07062
Allen Pl 07060
Allenwood Dr 07060
Alletta St 07060
Almont Pl 07060
Andover Ave 07062
Anna Pl 07063
Answorth Ave 07062
Arlington Ave 07060
Arnold Ave 07063
Astor Pl 07063
Ayres Ave 07063
Azalea Ct 07060
Barbara Dr 07062
Beech Ln 07060
Beechwood Ct 07060
Belleview Ave & Ct 07060
Belmont Ave 07060
Belvidere Ave
  500-799 07062
  800-999 07060
Berckman St 07062
Bergen St 07063
Berkeley Ave & Ter 07062
Berry Hill Ct 07060
Birch Ave 07062
Blue Ridge Cir 07060
Bradford St 07063
Brentwood Ter 07060
Brewster Ct 07060
Brokaw Blvd 07063
Brook Ave
  1-360 07060
  361-499 07062
Brook Ct 07060
Brook Ln 07060
Brookside Pl 07060
Buttfield Dr 07060
Cambridge Ave 07062
Cameron Ave 07060
Carlisle Ter 07062
Carlton Ave 07060
Carnegie Ave 07060
Carol Rd 07062
Catalpa Ave 07063
Cedar Ct & St 07060
Cedarbrook Rd 07060
Central Ave 07060
Central St 07062
Challenger Ct 07060
Charlotte Rd 07060
Chatham Pl & St 07060
Chelsea Blvd 07062
Chestnut Ave 07063
Chestnut St 07060
Chetwynd Ave 07060
Church Pl 07063
Church St 07060
Clawson Ave & Ct 07060
Cleveland Ave 07060
Clinton Ave & Pl 07063
Coddington Ave 07060
Colonial Cir 07060
Colonial Pl 07062
Columbia Ave
  100-299 07060
  1200-1499 07062
Compton Ave 07063
Coolidge Ave 07063
Coolidge St 07062
Corbett Pl 07060
Cottage Pl 07060
Court Pl 07060

Crabapple Ln 07060
Craig Pl 07060
Crescent Ave 07060
Crosson Pl 07063
Crystal Ter 07060
Cushing Pl & Rd 07062
Dahlia Ter 07060
Darrow Ave 07060
Deborah Ct 07062
Deforest Ave 07062
Dekalb Ave 07063
Delacy Ave & Dr 07060
Denmark Rd 07062
Denninger Rd 07063
Depot Park 07060
Division Ave 07063
Dixie Ln 07062
Dorbett Pl 07062
Dorsey Pl 07062
Duer St 07060
Dumas Ave 07063
Dupont St 07060
Earle Pl 07062
Edgerria Ave 07060
Edgewood Ave & Ct 07060
Edward Pl 07060
Edwin Pl 07062
Elaine Ct 07063
Ellsworth Ct 07060
Elmwood Pl 07060
Emerson Ave 07062
Emma St 07063
W End Ave
  1-49 07060
  50-225 07060
  227-297 07063
  299-449 07063
  450-499 07060
S End Pkwy 07060
Essex St 07060
Everett Pl 07063
Evergreen Ave 07060
Evona Ave 07063
Fairview Ave 07060
Farragut Pl & Rd 07062
Fayette Pl 07060
Fernwood Ave 07062
Fernwood Ln 07060
Field Ave 07060
Fillmore Ave 07060
Fisk Pl 07063
Flontanc Ave 07063
Florence Ave 07060
Forest Brook Dr 07060
Forest Hill Rd 07060
Frances Ln 07062
Franklin Pl 07060
Frederick St 07062
Fritz Pl 07060
E Front St
  418A-418E 07060
  100-699 07060
  701-715 07060
  704-714 07062
  716-1499 07062
  135-139-135-139 07060
  149-151-149-151 07060
  155-157-155-157 07060
  185-187-185-187 07060
  190-196-190-196 07060
W Front St
  100-799 07060
  800-1740 07063
  1742-1898 07063
  120-124-120-124 07060
Galbraith Pl 07063
Garden St 07062
Garfield Ave 07062
Gate House Ln 07060
Gavett Pl 07060
Gavin Pl 07060
Geneva Pl 07062
George St 07062
Geraud Ave 07060
Germain St 07060
Glen Ct 07063

Glendale Rd 07063
Glenside Pl 07060
Glenwood Ave 07060
Grace Pl 07063
Grandview Ave 07060
Grant Ave 07060
Graybar Dr 07062
Green Ct 07060
Greenbrook Rd
  1-312 07060
  314-330 07060
  332-398 07063
  400-799 07063
Greenock Ave 07062
Gresham Rd 07062
Grove St 07060
Halsey St 07063
Hamilton Ave 07063
Harding Ave 07063
Harmony St 07060
Harold St 07060
Harrington Ave 07063
Harrison Ave 07060
Hartridge Pl 07060
Harvey Ave 07063
Harvey Pl 07062
Hazel Ave 07060
Hazelwood Ter 07060
Helene Ave 07062
Henry Ct 07060
Hidden Trl 07060
Highland Ave 07060
Hill St 07062
Hillcrest Ave 07062
Hillman Pl 07063
Hillside Ave 07060
Hilltop Rd 07060
Hobert Ave 07063
Hollywood Ave 07060
Howard St 07060
Hudson Ave 07060
Hunter Ave 07063
Huntington Ave
  400-799 07060
  800-899 07063
Hurley Ave 07060
Interhaven Ave 07060
Inwood Pl 07062
Ironbound Ave 07060
Irving Pl 07060
Ivy Pl 07062
N Jackson Ave 07060
Jean Ter 07062
Jefferson Ave 07060
Jeffries Pl 07060
Jennings Ln 07060
Johannis Pl 07063
John St 07060
Johnston Ave 07062
Johnston Dr Ext 07060
Judges Ln 07063
Kennedy Ct 07062
Kensington Ave 07060
Kent Pl 07063
Kenyon Ave 07060
Knollwood Ct 07062
Lafayette Pl 07060
Lake St 07060
Lakeview Ter 07060
Lansdowne Ter 07062
Laramie Rd 07060
Lawrence Ave 07063
Lee Pl 07063
Leland Ave 07062
Lenox Ave 07060
Leonard Pl & St 07060
Lewis Ave 07063
Lewis St 07060
Lexington Pl 07063
Liberty St 07060
Linbarger Ave 07062
Lincoln Pl 07060
Linda Ln 07060
Linden Ave 07060
Little Pl 07060
Locust Ave & Pl 07060

Loraine Ave 07062
Loretta Ter 07062
Louise Ave 07060
Lyman Pl 07063
Mable St 07063
Madison Ave 07060
Magnolia Ave 07060
Malcolm Ave 07063
Mali Dr 07062
Maltby Ave 07063
Manning Ave 07060
Manson Pl 07063
Maple Ave & Ter 07060
Maplewood Ter 07060
Mariners Ct & Pl 07063
Marion Ave 07060
Marlborough Ave 07060
Marsh Pl 07060
Marshall Pl 07062
Martine Ave 07060
Martins Way 07060
Mayfair Way 07060
Mccrea Pl 07062
Mcdowell St 07063
Mckinley Pl 07062
Meadowbrook Dr & Rd 07062
Melrose Ave & Pl 07063
Melvin Pl 07060
Mercer Ave 07060
Milton Pl 07062
Mobus Ave 07060
Moffett Ave 07060
Monroe Ave 07063
Morris St 07063
Mountain Ave
  1-335 07060
  336-587 07062
  588-588 07060
  589-599 07062
Mountainview Dr 07063
Muhlenberg Pl 07060
Muriel Ave & Pl 07060
Murray Ave 07060
Myrtle Ave
  1-199 07060
  900-1899 07063
Netherwood Ave 07062
New St 07060
New Walnut St 07060
Newton St 07060
North Ave
  100-699 07060
  700-1499 07062
North Dr 07060
Norwood Ave 07060
Oak Ln 07060
Oakland Ave 07060
Oakridge Ave 07063
Oakwood Pl 07060
Oneida Ave & Pl 07060
Orange Pl 07060
Orchard Ave & Pl 07060
Osborne Ave 07062
Oxford Ave 07062
Oxford Pl 07060
Pacharad Ave 07062
Pacific St 07062
Park Ave 07060
Park Ln 07062
Park Pl
  18-26 07060
  28-111 07060
  113-113 07060
  1100-1199 07062
Park Ter 07062
Parkside Rd 07060
Parkview Ave 07063
Pearl St 07060
Pemberton Ave 07060
Penn Pl 07063
Pine St 07060
Pineview Ter 07062
Plainfield Ave 07060
Pond Pl 07063
Post Dr 07062

Prescott Pl 07063
Princeton Ln 07063
Prospect Ave & Pl 07060
Putnam Ave 07060
Race St 07060
Radcliffe Pl 07062
Rahway Rd 07060
Randolph Rd 07060
Rangewood Ct 07060
Ransome Pl 07063
Ravine Rd 07062
Raymond Ave 07062
Redfield Rd 07063
Redmont Rd 07063
Reeve Ter 07062
Regent St 07060
Remington Ave 07060
Richard St 07063
Richard Way 07062
Richmond St 07060
Ridge Ave 07060
Rock Ave
  1-209 07063
  160-334 07063
  211-299 07063
  344-1198 07060
  1200-1399 07060
Rockview Ave
  1-182 07060
  183-699 07063
Rockview Ave W 07063
Rockview Ter 07060
Roosevelt Ave 07060
Rose St 07060
Rushmore Ave 07063
Russell Pl 07062
Rutledge Ct 07060
Saint Marks Pl 07062
Saint Marys Ave 07062
Saint Nicholas Blvd 07062
Salem Rd 07060
Sandford Ave 07060
Seneca Pl 07062
Shady Ct 07060
Sheridan Ave 07060
Sherman Ave
  600-698 07060
  700-799 07060
  800-1099 07063
Shiloh Ct 07063
Shirley St 07062
Slavin St 07063
Sleepy Hollow Ln 07060
Sloane Blvd 07060
Somerset Pl & St 07060
South Ave
  500-599 07060
  600-1499 07062
  1428-1432-1428-1432 07062
Spooner Ave 07060
Spring St 07060
Spruce St 07060
Stahls Way 07060
Stebbins Pl 07063
Steiner Pl 07060
Stelle Ave
  101-197 07060
  199-799 07060
  800-999 07063
Sterling St 07062
Stilford Ave 07060
Stillman Ave 07060
Stone St 07060
Stoney Brook Pl 07060
Summer Ave 07062
Summit Ave 07060
Sumner Ave 07062
Sunnyside Pl 07060
Sunset Rd 07063
Susan Ct 07060
Sweetbriar Ln 07060
Sycamore Ave 07060
Taft Ave 07063
Tappan Ave
  100-199 07060

  400-499 07063
Tate Ct 07060
Terrill Rd 07062
Thornton Ave 07060
Townsend Pl 07063
Tremont Ave 07063
Trinity St 07063
Union St 07060
Us Highway 22 07060
Verdon St 07060
Vermeule Pl 07063
Victory Ave 07060
View Ave 07063
Vine St 07060
Vivian St 07060
Wadsworth Ave
  400-798 07060
  800-898 07063
Wald Dr 07062
Wallace Pl 07060
Walnut St 07060
Warfield Rd 07063
Warren St 07060
Washington Ave 07060
Watchung Ave
  46A-46B 07060
  1-202 07060
  50-431 07060
  201-201 07061
  204-1798 07060
  225-1799 07060
  433-443 07060
  1800-1899 07062
  50-54-50-54 07060
  7-9-7-9 07060
Watson Ave 07062
Waynewood Park 07060
Webster Pl 07060
Wells Rd 07062
Westervelt Ave 07060
Whitewood Ave 07060
Whitewood Ct 07062
Whittingham Ter 07060
Wiley Ave 07062
Willard Pl 07060
Willever St 07063
Willow Ave
  1-139 07060
  141-199 07063
Willow Ave Ext 07063
Wilson Ave 07060
Windsor St 07060
Wood Pl 07060
Woodbine Ave 07060
Woodland Ave
  500-799 07062
  800-1400 07060
Woodmere Pl 07062
Worth Dr 07062

NUMBERED STREETS

1st Pl 07060
2nd Pl 07060
E 2nd St
  100-198 07060
  200-699 07060
  700-1499 07062
S 2nd St
  600-799 07060
  800-1699 07063
W 2nd St 07060
3rd Pl 07060
E 3rd St
  200-228 07060
  230-699 07060
  701-797 07062
  799-1200 07062
  1202-1398 07062
W 3rd St
  200-799 07060
  800-1699 07063
E 4th St 07060
  100-799 07060
  800-1499 07063

E 5th St 07060
100-599 07060
800-1399 07063
E 6th St
100-699 07060
700-899 07062
W 6th St
100-599 07060
800-1299 07063
E 7th St
100-699 07060
700-1499 07062
409-411-409-411 07060
517-523-517-523 07060
W 7th St
729A-729B 07060
100-799 07060
800-1299 07063
W 8th St
100-198 07060
800-1199 07063
E & W 9th 07060

PRINCETON NJ

General Delivery 08540

POST OFFICE BOXES MAIN OFFICE STATIONS AND BRANCHES

Box No.s
AB - AQ 08542
1 - 713 08542
1 - 631 08543
821 - 1705 08542
1777 - 9839 08543

NAMED STREETS

Academy St 08540
Acadia Ct 08540
Acken Ln 08540
Acre Ln 08540
Adams Dr 08540
Aiken Ave 08540
Airpark Rd 08540
Airport Pl 08540
Aldgate Ct 08540
Alexander Park, Rd & St 08540
All Saints Rd 08540
Allison Rd & Way 08540
Alta Vista Dr 08540
Anderson Ln 08540
Andover Cir 08540
Andrews Ln 08540
Angelica Ct 08540
Armour Rd 08540
Arreton Rd 08540
Astor Ct 08540
Audubon Ln 08540
Autumn Hill Ln & Rd 08540
Avery Ln 08542
Azalea Ct 08540
Bailey Dr 08540
Bainbridge St 08540
Baker Ct 08540
Balcort Dr 08540
Baldwin Ln 08540
Balsam Ln 08540
Bank St 08542
Bannister Dr 08540
Barbieri Ct 08540
Barclay Blvd 08540
Barkley Dr 08540
N & S Barrow Pl 08540
Barsky Ct 08540
Basin St 08540
Battle Rd 08540
Battle Road Cir 08540
Battlebrook Ln 08540
Bayard Ln 08540
Bayberry Dr & Rd 08540
Bear Brook Rd 08540
Beatty Ct 08540
Beech Hill Cir 08540
Beech Hollow Ln 08540
Beechtree Ln 08540
Belford Dr 08540
Bellaire Dr 08540
Belleview Ter 08540
Bellflower Ct W 08540
Benedek Rd 08540
Benjamin Rush Ln 08540
Bentley Dr 08540
Bergen Ave 08540
Berkshire Dr 08540
Berrien Ct 08542
Bertrand Dr 08540
Billie Ellis Ln 08540
Birch Ave 08542
Birchwood Ct & Dr 08540
Biscayne Ct 08540
Blackstone Dr 08540
Blue Spring Rd 08540
Bogart Ct 08540
Bolton Cir 08540
Bongerne St 08542
Borrowby Cir 08540
Boudinot St 08540
Bouvant Dr 08540
Boxwood Dr 08540
Bradley Ct 08540
Braeburn Dr 08540
Braemer Dr 08540
Brearly Rd 08540
Brentwood Blvd 08540
Brian Ct 08540
Briarwood Ct 08540
Brickhouse Rd 08540
Broadmead St 08540
Broadripple Dr 08540
Brook Dr E & W 08540
Brookline Ct 08540
Brooks Bnd 08540
Brookside Dr 08540
Brookstone Dr 08540
Brookwood Ct 08540
Brown Hall 08540
Buckingham Dr 08540
Bullock Dr 08540
Bunker Hill Rd 08540
Bunn Dr 08540
Burr Dr 08540
Burton Cir 08540
Butler Ave & Rd 08540
Butternut Row 08540
Caitlin Ct 08540
Calder Ct 08540
Caldwell Dr 08540
Caleb Ln 08540
Cambridge Ct 08540
Camelot Ct 08540
Cameron Ct 08540
Campbell Woods Way 08540
Campbelton Cir & Rd 08540
Campus Dr & Rd 08540
Canal Rd 08540
Canal Pointe Blvd 08540
Canterbury Way 08540
Caraway Ct 08540
Carlton Cir 08540
Carlyle Ct 08540
Carnahan Pl 08540
Carnegie Ctr
101-212 08540
213-213 08543
214-902 08540
215-711 08540
Carnegie Dr 08540
Caroline Dr 08540
Carriage Trl & Way 08540
Carson Rd 08540
Carter Rd 08540
Carter Brook Ln 08540
Cascade Ct 08540
Casselberry Way 08540
Castle Howard Ct 08540
Castleton Rd 08540
Catelli Rd 08540
Cedar Ln 08540
Cedar Brook Ter 08540
Chambers St 08542
Charlton St 08540
Chauncey Rd 08540
Chelsea Ct 08540
Cherry Brook Dr 08540
Cherry Hill Rd 08540
Cherry Valley Rd 08540
Chestnut Ct 08540
Chicopee Dr 08540
Christopher Dr 08540
Claridge Ct 08540
Clarke Ct 08540
Clay St 08542
Clearview Ave 08540
Cleveland Ln & Rd 08540
Clover Ln 08540
Clubhouse Dr 08540
Cold Soil Rd 08540
Colebrook Ct 08540
College Rd 08540
Colts Run Rd 08540
Commons Way 08540
Commonwealth Ct 08540
Conifer Ct 08540
Coniston Ct 08540
Constitution Dr & Hl 08540
Coolidge Way 08540
Coppermine Rd 08540
Coppervail Ct 08540
Cordova Rd 08540
Coriander Dr 08540
Cotswold Ln 08540
E & W Countryside Dr 08540
County Road 518 08540
Courtside Ln 08540
Coventry Cir 08540
Coventry Farm Ln 08540
Coverdale Dr 08540
Crabapple Ct 08540
Cradle Rock Rd 08540
Craftwood Dr 08540
Cranberry Ct 08540
Crescent Dr 08540
Creststone Cir 08540
Crestview Dr 08540
Cricket Hill Cir 08540
Cromwell Ct 08540
Crooked Tree Ln 08540
Cuyler Rd 08540
Cynthia Ct 08540
Dana Ct 08540
Danby Ct 08540
David Brearly Ct 08540
Dean Mathey Ln 08540
Deer Path & Run 08540
Delamere Dr 08540
Dempsey Ave 08540
Dennick Ct 08540
Derwent Dr 08540
Devereux Ave 08540
Devonshire Dr 08540
Dickinson St 08540
Division St 08540
Dodds Ln 08540
Dogwood Hl & Ln 08540
Dorann Ave 08540
Dorchester Ct 08540
Dorset Ct 08540
Douglas Fir Ct 08540
Douglass Dr 08540
Drakes Corner Rd 08540
Duffield Pl 08540
Eagles Pass 08540
Earle Ln 08540
Eden Way 08540
Edgehill St 08540
Edgerstoune Rd 08540
Edwards Pl 08540
Einstein Dr 08540
Eisenhower St 08540
Elm Ln & Rd 08540
Elm Ridge Rd 08540
Emmons Dr 08540
Empress Ct 08540
English Ln 08540
Erdman Ave 08540
Essex Ct 08540
Esterbrook Dr 08540
Esther Plz 08542
Ettl Cir 08540
Evelyn Pl 08540
Evergreen Cir 08540
Evert Ct 08540
Ewing St 08540
Executive Dr 08540
Exeter Ct 08540
Fackler Rd 08540
Faculty Rd 08540
Fair Acres Ct 08540
Fairfield Rd 08540
Fairview Ave 08540
Fairway Dr 08540
Farber Rd 08540
Farrand Rd 08540
Federal Ct 08540
Fernwood Dr 08540
Fieldcrest Dr 08540
Fieldston Rd 08540
Fieldwood Ct 08540
Finley Rd 08540
Firestone Ct 08540
Fisher Ave & Pl 08540
Fitch Way 08540
Fitzrandolph Rd 08540
Fleming Way 08540
Flexner Ln 08540
Florence Ln 08540
Forest Ave 08540
Forester Dr 08540
Forrestal Rd S 08540
Foulet Dr 08540
Founders Ln 08540
Fountayne Ct 08540
Fox Hill Rd 08540
Foxboro Ct 08540
Foxcroft Dr 08540
Foxfield Ct 08540
Franklin Ave 08540
Franklin Ter 08542
Fredrick Ct 08540
Fringe Tree Ct 08540
Gabriella Ct 08540
Gallup Rd 08540
Garfield Way 08540
Garrett Ln 08540
George Rd 08540
Ginger Ct 08540
Glen Dr 08540
Glenview Dr 08540
Goldman Ln 08540
Goldstar Dr 08540
Golf View Dr 08540
Goodrow Ct 08540
Gordon Way 08540
Gossamer Ct 08540
Governors Ln 08540
Grant Way 08540
Grasmere Way 08540
Great Rd 08540
Green St 08542
Green Leaf Ct 08540
Greenbriar Row 08540
Greenholm St 08540
Greenhouse Dr 08540
Greenland Ct 08540
Greenshadows Ln 08540
Greenview Ave 08542
Greenway Ter 08540
Greylynne Dr 08540
Griffin Way 08540
Griggs Dr 08540
Griggstown Cswy 08540
Grover Ave 08540
Gulick Rd 08540
Guyot Ave 08540
Hageman Ln 08540
Hale Dr 08540
Halsey Ct & St 08540
Halstead Pl 08540
Hamilton Ave
1-31 08542
33-49 08542
100-399 08540
Hampstead Ct 08540
Hanover Ct 08540
Hanson Ct 08540
Harcross Ct 08540
Hardin Rd 08540
Hardy Dr 08540
Harriet Dr 08540
Harris Rd 08540
N & S Harrison Ln & St 08540
Harrogate Cir 08540
Hartley Ave 08540
Harvard Cir 08540
Haslet Ave 08540
Haverhill Ct 08540
Hawthorne Ave 08540
Heath Ct 08540
Heather Ln 08540
Hedge Row Rd 08540
Hedley Dr 08540
Hemlock Cir & Ct 08540
Henderson Ave 08540
Henry Ave 08540
Heritage Blvd 08540
Herrontown Cir, Ln & Rd 08540
Hibben Rd & Ter 08540
Hibben Apartment 08540
Hickory Ct 08540
Highland Rd & Ter 08540
Hill Top Dr 08540
Hillside Ave & Rd 08540
Hodge Rd 08540
Hodge Hall 08540
Holly House 08540
Honey Lake Dr 08540
Honeybrook Dr 08540
Honeyman St 08540
Hoover Ave 08540
Hornor Ln 08540
Horseshoe Ct 08540
Houghton Rd 08540
Howe Cir 08540
Huckleberry Dr 08540
Hulfish St 08542
Humbert Ln & St 08542
Hun Rd 08540
Hunt Dr 08540
Hunter Rd 08540
Hunters Run 08540
Hutchinson Dr 08540
Independence Dr & Way 08540
Inverness Dr 08540
Ivy Ln 08540
Jackson Ave 08540
James Ct 08540
Jasmine Way 08540
Jefferson Ct, Plz & Rd 08540
Jochris Dr 08540
John St 08542
Jonathan Ct 08540
Jonathon Dayton Ct 08540
Jones Dr 08540
Journeys End Ln 08540
Juliet Ct 08540
Juniper Row 08540
Justice Ct 08540
Karin Ct 08540
Katies Pond Rd 08540
Kean Ct 08540
Kennedy Ct 08540
Kensington Ct 08540
Kent Ct 08540
Ketley Pl 08540
Kimberly Ct 08540
King St 08540
Kingston Ter 08540
Kingsway Cmn 08540
Kirby Cir 08540
Knoll Dr 08540
Lafayette Rd W 08540
Lake Dr & Ln 08540
Lakeview Ave & Ter 08540
Lambert Dr 08540
Landfall Ln 08540
Larch Way 08540
Lassen Ct 08540
Laurel Cir & Rd 08540
Lavender Dr 08540
Lawrence Dr 08540
Lawrenceville Rd 08540
Leabrook Ln 08540
Leavitt Ln 08540
Lehigh Ct 08540
Leicester Ct 08540
Leigh Ave 08542
Leiv Eirikson Ave 08540
Lenmore Ct 08540
Leonard Ct 08540
Leslie Ct 08540
Lexington Ct 08540
Library Pl 08540
Lilac Ln 08540
Lincoln Ave 08540
Lincoln Ct 08542
Linden Ave & Ln 08540
Linwood Cir 08540
Littlebrook Rd N 08540
Lockwood Dr 08540
Locust Ln 08540
Loetscher Pl 08540
Lois Ct 08540
Longview Dr 08540
Loomis Ct 08540
Lovers Ln 08540
Lowell Ct 08540
Lower Harrison St 08540
Lytle St 08542
Maclean Cir 08540
Maclean St 08542
Madison St 08542
Magie Apartment 08540
Magnolia Ln 08540
Maidenhead Rd 08540
Main St 08540
Mandon Ct 08540
Manor Ave & Dr 08540
Mansfield Rd 08540
Mansgrove Rd 08540
Maple St & Ter 08542
Mapleton Rd 08540
Margerum Ct 08542
Marigold Ct 08540
Marion Rd E & W 08540
Market Hall 08540
Markham Rd 08540
Marshall Ave 08540
Marten Rd 08540
Mason Dr 08540
Mather Ave 08540
Maxwell Ln 08540
Maybury Hill Rd 08540
Mccomb Rd 08540
Mccosh Cir 08540
Mckinley Ct 08540
Meadow Rd 08540
Meadowbrook Dr 08540
Meetinghouse Ct 08540
Melrose Ct 08540
Mercer Rd & St 08540
Merit Ln 08540
Mershon Dr 08540
Merwick Rd 08540
Michelle Ct 08540
Michelle Mews 08542
Mimosa Ct 08540
Monroe Ct & Ln 08540
Montadale Cir & Dr 08540
Monument Dr 08540
Moore St
2-36 08542
38-79 08542
81-299 08540
Moran Ave 08542
Morgan Pl 08540
Morning Glory Ct 08540
Morning Sun Ave 08540
Morris Dr 08540
Morrison Rd 08540
Morse Ln 08540
Morven Pl 08540
Mosher Rd 08540
Mount Lucas Rd 08540
Mountain Ave 08540
Mountain View Rd 08540
Mulberry Row 08540
Muriel Ct 08540
Murray Pl 08540
Mya Dr 08540
Nassau St
342A-342B 08540
2-58 08542
60-234 08542
235-267 08540
236-268 08542
269-499 08540
Nassau Park Blvd 08540
Needham Way 08540
Neil Ct 08540
Nelson Ridge Rd 08540
Nestlewood Way 08540
Newlin Rd 08540
Nippert Way 08540
Norbridge Dr 08540
North Rd 08540
Norwood Ct 08540
Nottingham Cir 08540
Oak Pl 08540
Oakland St 08540
Oakridge Ct 08540
Ober Rd 08540
Old Rd 08540
Old Georgetown Rd 08540
Old Nursery Rd 08540
Old Orchard Ln 08540
Old Vliet Rd 08540
S Olden Ln & St 08540
Olympic Ct 08540
Oppenheimer Ln 08540
Orchard Cir 08540
Orchid Ct 08540
Overbrook Dr 08540
Overlook Ctr 08540
Palmer Sq E & W 08542
Panofsky Ln 08540
Pardee Cir 08540
Pardoe Rd 08540
Park Knl 08540
Park Ln 08540
Park Pl 08542
Parkside Dr 08540
Patton Ave 08540
Paul Robeson Pl
1-99 08540
16-36 08542
Peck Pl 08540
Pelham St 08540
Pennyroyal Ct 08540
Pepper Rd 08540
Pettit Pl 08540
Pheasant Hill Rd 08540
Philip Dr 08540
Pickering Cir 08540
Pierson Ave 08540
Pine St 08542
Players Ln 08540
Poe Rd 08540
Poor Farm Rd 08540
Potters Run 08540
Preservation Pl 08540
Pretty Brook Rd 08540
Primrose Cir 08540
Prince William Ct 08540
Princeton Ave & Pike 08540
Princeton Highlands Blvd 08540
Princeton Kingston Rd 08540
Princeton Walk Blvd 08540
Prospect Ave & St 08540
Province Line Rd 08540
Puritan Ct 08540

Quail Crk 08540
Quaker Rd 08540
Quakerbridge Rd 08540
Quarry Ln 08540
Quarry St 08542
Queenston Pl 08540
Quincy Ct 08540
Race St 08542
Ragany Ln 08540
Rainier Ct 08540
Randall Rd 08540
Random Rd 08540
Raymond Rd 08540
Red Hill Rd 08540
Red Oak Row 08540
Redding Cir 08540
Regatta Row 08540
Renfield Dr 08540
Research Way 08540
Richard Ct 08540
Rider Ter 08540
Ridge Blvd & Rd 08540
Ridgeview Cir & Rd 08540
Ridings Pkwy 08540
River Rd 08540
River Birch Cir 08540
Riverside Dr 08540
Robert Rd 08540
Rockingham Row 08540
Rocky Hill Rd 08540
Rodney Ct 08540
Rollingmead St 08540
Roper Rd 08540
Rosedale Ln & Rd 08540
Ross Stevenson Cir 08540
Roszel Rd 08540
Route 27 08540
Roxbury Ct 08540
Running Cedar Rd 08540
Russell Rd 08540
Rutgers Ln 08540
Rydal Rd 08540
Sage Ct 08540
Saint Clair Ct 08540
Salem Ct 08540
Sandor Dr 08540
Sassafras Row 08540
Sayre Dr 08540
Scarlet Oak Dr 08540
School House Ln 08540
Schuh Rd 08540
Scott Ln 08540
Scribner Ct 08540
Seminary Dr 08540
Sequoia Ct 08540
Sergeant St 08540
Shadybrook Ln 08540
Shirley Ct 08542
E Shore Dr 08540
E & W Shrewsbury Pl 08540
Skyfield Dr 08540
Snowden Ln 08540
Somerset Ct 08540
Southern Way 08540
Spring St 08542
Springdale Rd 08540
Springwood Ct 08540
Spruce Cir 08540
Spruce Ln
1-3 08540
2-2 08542
4-6 08540
5-11 08540
6-6 08542
8-16 08540
Spruce St 08542
Stanford Pl 08540
Stanhope St 08540
Stanley Ave 08540
E, N & S Stanworth Dr & Ln 08540
State Rd 08540
Stellarator Rd 08540
Stephen Dr 08540
Sterling Rd 08540
Stetson Way 08540
Stillbrook Ln 08540
Stirrup Way 08540
Stockton Ave & St 08540
Stone Cliff Rd 08540
Stonebridge Ln 08540
Stonehouse Dr 08540
Stonewall Cir 08540
Stoney Brook Ln 08540
Stout Rd 08540
Stuart Rd 08540
Stuart Close 08540
Stump Rd 08540
Sturges Way 08540
Summerfield Dr 08540
Sunset Ave 08540
Supra Ct 08540
Sycamore Pl & Rd 08540
Taft Ct 08540
Talbot Ln 08540
Tall Timbers Dr 08540
Tanner Dr 08540
Tarkington Ct 08540
Taylor Rd 08540
Teak Ln 08540
Tee Ar Pl 08540
Terhune Rd 08540
Thanet Cir & Rd 08540
Thorngate Ct 08540
Three Acre Ln 08540
Toftrees Ct 08540
Tomlyn Dr 08540
Torrey Ln 08542
Towpath Ct 08540
Tree Swallow Dr 08540
Treetops Cir 08540
Trewbridge Ct 08540
Trinity Ct 08540
Truman Ave 08540
Trumbull Ct 08540
N & S Tulane St 08542
Tupelo Row 08540
Turner Ct 08540
Tyson Ln 08540
Union St 08540
University Pl 08540
University Square Dr 08540
Us Highway 1 08540
Valley Rd 08540
Van Dyke Rd 08540
Van Kirk Rd 08540
Van Marter Ct 08540
Vandeventer Ave 08542
Vanteran Rd 08540
Varsity Ave 08540
Vaughn Dr 08540
Veblen Cir 08540
Vernon Cir 08540
Victoria Mews 08542
Village Blvd 08540
Vista Dr 08540
Von Neumann Dr 08540
Vreeland Ct 08540
Waldorf Dr 08540
Walker Dr 08540
Wall St 08540
Wallingford Dr 08540
Walnut Ln 08540
Warren Ct 08540
Washington Ave & Rd 08540
Watertown Ct 08540
Wedgewood Ct 08540
Wellington Park Dr 08540
Wendover Dr 08540
Wenlock Ct 08540
Wessex Dr & Pl 08540
West Dr 08540
Westcott Rd 08540
Westerly Rd 08540
Western Way 08540
Westfield Ct 08540
Weyl Ln 08540
Wheatsheaf Ln 08540
Wheeler Way 08540
White Oak Dr 08540
White Pine Ln 08540
Wiggins St 08540
Wildbriar Ln 08540
Wilder Ave 08540
Wilkinson Way 08540
William St 08540
William Livingston Ct 08540
William Patterson Ct 08540
Willow St 08542
Wilson Rd 08540
Wilton St 08540
Winant Rd 08540
Windermere Way 08540
Windham Ct 08540
Winding Way 08540
Windridge Ct 08540
Windrow Dr 08540
Winfield Rd 08540
Winterberry Way 08540
Winthrop Way 08540
Witherspoon Ln 08542
Witherspoon St
1-222 08542
224-498 08542
237-281 08540
283-399 08542
Wittmer Ct 08540
Woodfield Ct 08540
Woodland Dr 08540
Woods Way 08540
Woodside Ln 08540
Worlidge Ct 08540
Worths Mill Ln 08540
Wrangel Ct 08540
Yale Ter 08540
York Dr 08540

RIDGEWOOD NJ

General Delivery 07451

POST OFFICE BOXES MAIN OFFICE STATIONS AND BRANCHES

Box No.s
All PO Boxes 07451

NAMED STREETS

Abbey Ct 07450
Ackerman Ave 07450
Addison Pl 07450
Alanon Rd 07450
Albert Pl 07450
Albin Ct 07450
Allen Pl 07450
Allison Ct 07450
Alpine Ter 07450
Amsterdam Ave 07450
Andover Ter 07450
Arcadia Rd 07450
Arden Ct 07450
Arrow Ln 07450
Auburn Ave 07450
Avondale Rd 07450
Banta St 07450
Barnes Dr 07450
Barnett Pl 07450
Barrington Rd 07450
Bartell Pl 07450
Bedford Rd 07450
Beechwood Rd 07450
Bellair Rd 07450
Belmont Rd 07450
Bennington Ter 07450
Bergen Ct 07450
Berkshire Rd 07450
Best Ct 07450
Betty Ct 07450
Beveridge Rd 07450
Beverly Rd 07450
Bingham Rd 07450
Bogert Ave 07450
Boyce Pl 07450
Brainard Pl 07450
Briarcliff Rd 07450
N & S Broad St 07450
Brookmere Ct 07450
Brookside Ave 07450
Bryden Pl 07450
Burnside Pl 07450
Busteed Dr 07450
California St 07450
Cambridge Rd 07450
Cameron Ln 07450
Canterbury Pl 07450
Cantrell Rd 07450
Carlisle Ter 07450
Carlton Ter 07450
Carolina Pl 07450
Carriage Ln 07450
Cathleen Ter 07450
Cedar Ave 07450
Cedarcroft Rd 07450
Centrend Rd 07450
Chelsea Pl 07450
Cherry Ln 07450
Chesterfield St 07450
Chestnut St 07450
Christopher Pl 07450
Circle Ave 07450
Claremont Rd 07450
Cliff St 07450
Clinton Ave 07450
Collingwood Pl 07450
Colonial Rd 07450
Colwell Ct 07450
Concord Rd 07450
Corella Ct 07450
Corona Pl 07450
Corsa Ter 07450
Cottage Pl 07450
Coventry Ct 07450
Crest Rd 07450
Daniel Ct 07450
Darby Ct 07450
Dayton St 07450
Deerfield St 07450
Delaware Ave 07450
Demarest St 07450
Devon Ct 07450
Dorchester Rd 07450
Doremus Ave 07450
Doris Pl 07450
Douglas Pl 07450
Downing St 07450
Downs St 07450
Durar Ave 07450
Eastbrook Rd 07450
Eastern Ct 07450
Eastgate Rd 07450
Eastside Ave 07450
Edwards St 07450
Elaine Ter 07450
Eldon Ct 07450
Ellington Rd 07450
Elm Ct 07450
Elmsley Ct 07450
Emker Ter 07450
Emmett Pl 07450
W End Ave 07450
Ethelbert Pl 07450
Eton Ct 07450
Evergreen Pl 07450
Fairfield Ave 07450
Fairmount Rd 07450
Fairway Rd 07450
Farview St 07450
Fernwood Ct 07450
Ferris Pl 07450
Foster Ter 07450
Fox Ct 07450
Franklin Ave & Tpke 07450
Frederick St 07450
Garber Sq 07450
Gardner Rd 07450
Garfield Pl 07450
Gateway Rd 07450
George St 07450
Gilbert St 07450
E & W Glen Ave 07450
Glenview Rd 07450
Glenwood Rd 07450
Godwin Ave 07450
Goffle Rd 07450
Gordon Rd 07450
Grandview Cir 07450
Grant St 07450
Graydon Ter 07450
Greenway Rd 07450
Grove St 07450
Hamilton Rd 07450
Hammond Rd 07450
Hampshire Rd 07450
Hampton Pl 07450
Hanks Ave 07450
Hawthorne Pl 07450
Heermance Pl 07450
Heights Rd 07450
Hempstead Rd 07450
Henrietta Ct 07450
Hickory St 07450
High St 07450
Highland Ave 07450
Highview Ter 07450
Highwood Ave 07450
S Hill Rd 07450
Hillcrest Rd 07450
N & S Hillside Pl 07450
Hope St 07450
Hopper Ave 07450
Howard Rd 07450
Hudson St 07450
Hunter Rd 07450
N & S Irving St 07450
Ivy Pl 07450
Jackson Ter 07450
James St 07450
Jeffer Ct & St 07450
Jefferson St 07450
Jemco Pl 07450
John St 07450
Katherine Rd 07450
Kemah Rd 07450
Kenilworth Rd 07450
Kensington Dr 07450
Kenwood Rd 07450
Kingsbridge Ln 07450
Kira Ln 07450
Knickerbocker Rd 07450
Knollwood Rd 07450
Lake Ave 07450
Lakeview Dr 07450
Laurel Rd 07450
Lawrence Ct 07450
Lenox Ave 07450
Leonard Pl 07450
Leroy Pl 07450
Libby Ave 07450
Liberty St 07450
Lincoln Ave 07450
Linden St 07450
Linwood Ave 07450
Litchfield St 07450
Lockwood Rd 07450
Lotte Rd 07450
Lotus Rd 07450
Lucille Ct 07450
Lynn St 07450
Madison Pl 07450
Maltbie Ave 07450
Manchester Rd 07450
Manor Rd 07450
N & S Maple Ave & Ct 07450
Marshall St 07450
Mary Ann Pl 07450
Mastin Pl 07450
Maxwell Pl 07450
Maynard Ct 07450
Mcguire Ct 07450
Mckinley Pl 07450
Meadowbrook Ave 07450
Melrose Pl 07450
Midvale St 07450
Midwood Rd 07450
N & S Monroe St 07450
Monte Vista Ave 07450
Morningside Rd 07450
Mountain Ave 07450
Mulberry Pl 07450
N & S Murray Ave 07450
Nagle St 07450
Nauset Ln 07450
Newcomb Rd 07450
Norgate Dr 07450
Norman Dr 07450
North Rd 07450
Northern Pkwy 07450
Oak St 07450
Old Stone Rd 07450
Olivia St 07450
Orchard Pl 07450
Orville Pl 07450
Overbrook Rd 07450
Oxford Ct 07450
Palmer Ct 07450
Paramus Rd 07450
Park Slope 07450
Parsons Rd 07450
Passaic St 07450
Patricia Ct 07450
Paul Ct 07450
Pearsall Ave 07450
Pershing Ave 07450
Phelps Rd 07450
Pine St 07450
N & S Pleasant Ave 07450
Pomander Walk 07450
Ponfield Pl 07450
Preston Pl 07450
Prospect St 07450
Quackenbush Pl 07450
Queens Ct 07450
Racetrack Rd 07450
Randolph Pl 07450
Red Birch Ct 07450
Red Rock Ct 07450
Reynen Ct 07450
Richards Rd 07450
Richmond Ave 07450
Ridge Rd 07450
E Ridgewood Ave
1-144 07450
143-143 07451
146-1250 07450
169-1115 07450
65-67-65-67 07450
W Ridgewood Ave 07450
Rivara Ct 07450
Robert St 07450
Robinson Ln 07450
Rock Rd 07450
Rose Ct 07450
Roslyn Rd 07450
Rugby Ct 07450
E & W Saddle River Rd 07450
Salem Ln 07450
Shadowbrook Rd 07450
Sheffield Rd 07450
Shelbourne Ter 07450
Shelton Rd 07450
Sheridan Ter 07450
Sherman Pl 07450
Sherwood Rd 07450
Smith Pl 07450
Sollas Ct 07450
Somerville Rd 07450
Southern Pkwy 07450
Spencer Pl 07450
Spring Ave 07450
Standish Rd 07450
Stanley Pl 07450
State Rt 17 07450
Station Plz 07450
Steilen Ave 07450
Sterling Pl 07450
Stevens Ave 07450
Stillwell Pl 07450
Stonycroft Rd 07450
Stratford Rd 07450
Stuart St 07450
Summit St 07450
Sunset Ave 07450
Taylor Rd 07450
Terhune Rd 07450
The By Way 07450
Theyken Pl 07450
Thompson Pl 07450
Unadilla Rd 07450
Undercliff Ct 07450
Union St 07450
Upper Blvd 07450
Valley View Ave 07450
Van Buren St 07450
N & S Van Dien Ave 07450
Van Dyke St 07450
Van Emburgh Ave 07450
Van Neste Sq 07450
Vesta Ct 07450
Waiku Rd 07450
Wall St 07450
N & S Walnut St 07450
Walthery Ave 07450
Walton St 07450
Warren Pl 07450
Washington Pl 07450
Wastena Ter 07450
Waverly Rd 07450
Wellington Rd 07450
Westbrook Rd 07450
Westfield Ave 07450
Westgate Rd 07450
Wickham Way 07450
Wildwood Rd 07450
William St 07450
Willow Ct 07450
Wilsey Sq 07450
Wilson St 07450
Windsor Ter 07450
Witthill Rd 07450
Wood Hollow Ln 07450
Woodbine Ct 07450
Woodfield Ct 07450
Woodland Ave 07450
Woodside Ave 07450
Wyndemere Ave 07450

NUMBERED STREETS

All Street Addresses 07450

RIVERTON NJ

General Delivery 08077

POST OFFICE BOXES MAIN OFFICE STATIONS AND BRANCHES

Box No.s
All PO Boxes 08077

NAMED STREETS

All Street Addresses 08077

NUMBERED STREETS

All Street Addresses 08077

SAYREVILLE NJ

General Delivery 08872

POST OFFICE BOXES MAIN OFFICE STATIONS AND BRANCHES

Box No.s
All PO Boxes 08871

NAMED STREETS

All Street Addresses 08872

NUMBERED STREETS

All Street Addresses 08872

SECAUCUS NJ

General Delivery 07094

POST OFFICE BOXES MAIN OFFICE STATIONS AND BRANCHES

Box No.s
All PO Boxes 07096

NAMED STREETS

Acorn Rd 07094
Allan Ter 07094
American Way 07094
Aquarium Dr 07094
Arch Ave 07094
Arn Ter 07094
Averrins Ave 07094
Blanche St 07094
Blondel Dr 07094
Blue Heron Dr 07094
Born St 07094
Broadcast Plz 07094
Castle Rd 07094
Cedar Ave & Ln 07094
Central Ln 07094
Centre Ave 07094
Century Way 07094
Charles St 07094
Chestnut Pl & St 07094
Clarendon St 07094
County Ave
1-301 07094
300-300 07096
303-799 07094
330-798 07094
252-254-252-254 07094
County Rd Ext 07094
Cove Ct 07094
Creekside Ct 07094
Daffys Way 07094
Donosaur Way 07094
Dorigo Ln 07094
Dunlin Plz 07094
Edna Pl 07094
Egret Ln 07094
Electric Ave 07094
Elizabeth Ct 07094
Emerson Ln 07094
N End Dr 07094
Enterprise Ave N & S .. 07094
Fairview Ave 07094
Farm Rd 07094
Fisher Ave 07094
Flanagan Way 07094
Floral Ter 07094
Franklin St & Ter 07094
Front St 07094
Gail Pl 07094
Garry Ter 07094
Gillis Pl 07094
Golden Ave 07094
Grace Ave 07094
Green Valley Ct 07094
Hagan Pl 07094
Harbor Ky 07094
Harmon Blvd & Plz 07094
Harmon Cove Tower ... 07094
Harmon Meadow Blvd .. 07094
Hartz Way 07094
Helen St 07094
Henry St 07094
Hops Ln 07094
Hops Commons Ct 07094
Huber St 07094
Hudson Ave 07094
Humboldt St 07094
Irving Pl 07094
James Pl 07094
Jane Ct 07094
Jefferson Ave 07094
John St 07094
Julianne Ter 07094
Kiesewetter Ln 07094
Koch Pl 07094
Koelle Blvd 07094
Kroll Ter 07094
Lanza Ln 07094
Laurel Ct 07094
Laurel Hill Ave 07094
Lausecker Ln 07094
Liberty Ct 07094
Lighting Way 07094
Lincoln Ave 07094
Louis St 07094
Lucht Pl 07094
Luhman Ter 07094
Luhrs Ct 07094
Mainsail Ln 07094
Mallard Pl 07094
Mansfield Ave 07094
Maple St 07094
Marianne Ter 07094
Marina Ky 07094
Meadow Ln 07094
Meadowlands Pkwy 07094
Metro Way 07094
Mill Creek Dr 07094
Millridge Rd 07094
Minnie Pl 07094
Moller St 07094
Msnbc Plz 07094
Mutillod Ln 07094
Myrtle Ave 07094
New County Rd 07094
New County Rd Ext 07094
Oak Ln 07094
Osprey Ct 07094
Panasonic Way 07094
Pandolfi Ave 07094
Park Dr & Pl 07094
Park Plaza Dr 07094
Paterson Plank Rd 07094
Paulanne Ter 07094
Penhorn Ave 07094
Pikeview Ter 07094
Plaza Ctr & Dr 07094
Poplar St 07094
Post Pl 07094
Radio Ave 07094
Raydol Ave 07094
Reidel Ct 07094
River Rd 07094
Riverside Station Blvd .. 07094
Riverview Ct 07094
Roosevelt Ave 07094
Sampson Pl 07094
Sandcastle Ky 07094
Sanderling Ct 07094
Sandpiper Ky 07094
Schmidts Pl 07094
Schopmann Dr 07094
Schultz Pl 07094
Sea Isle Ky 07094
Seaview Dr 07094
Secaucus Rd 07094
Sinvalco Rd 07094
Sparman Pl 07094
Spinnaker Ct 07094
State Rt 3 07094
Statewide Ct 07094
Stonewall Ln 07094
Sunset Ky 07094
Syms Way 07094
Teal Plz 07094
Terminal Rd 07094
Topsail Ln 07094
Ups Dr 07094
Valley Ct 07094
Venture Way 07094
Village Pl 07094
Walter Pl 07094
Washington Ave 07094
Weigands Ln 07094
Whimbrel Ln 07094
Windsor Dr 07094
Wood Ave 07094

NUMBERED STREETS

All Street Addresses 07094

SOMERSET NJ

General Delivery 08873

POST OFFICE BOXES MAIN OFFICE STATIONS AND BRANCHES

Box No.s
All PO Boxes 08875

RURAL ROUTES

02, 03, 05 08873

NAMED STREETS

Abate Ct 08873
Abbey Dr 08873
Abbott Rd 08873
Abrams Ct 08873
Academy Rd 08873
Adams St 08873
Aimwick Ct 08873
Alcorne St 08873
Aldeburgh Ave 08873
Alerica Ln 08873
Alex Pl 08873
Alfred Ave 08873
Alma Ct 08873
Almond Dr 08873
Alton Dr 08873
Ambassador Ct 08873
Ambrose St 08873
Amwell Rd 08873
Angel Pl 08873
Annapolis St 08873
Apgar Dr 08873
Appleman Rd 08873
April Ln 08873
Archer Ave 08873
Arden St 08873
Ari Dr 08873
Arlington Ave 08873
Arrow Head Ln 08873
Arthur Ave 08873
Ashley Ct 08873
Atlantic Rd 08873
Atrium Dr 08873
Austin Ave 08873
Avalon Ct 08873
Avebury Pl 08873
Avery Ct 08873
Azalea Ln 08873
Baier Ave 08873
Baker St 08873
Baldwin Ave 08873
Bamburgh Ct 08873
Barclay Ct 08873
Barge Ln 08873
Barker Rd 08873
Barmouth Ct 08873
Barron Cir 08873
Bartle Rd 08873
Bates Ct 08873
Bathgate Ave 08873
Battle Pl 08873
Bayard Rd 08873
Bayberry Dr 08873
Beaconsfield Pl 08873
Beatrice St 08873
Beck Ave 08873
Beckett Pl 08873
Bedford Rd 08873
Bell St 08873
Belmar St 08873
Belmont Dr 08873
Benjamin St 08873
Bennetts Ln 08873
Berger St 08873
Bering Way 08873
Berkely Pl 08873
Berry St 08873
Bertram Ave 08873
Beverly Ave 08873
Biltmore Ln 08873
Birch Ter 08873
Blackwells Mills Rd 08873
Blair Ave 08873
Blairsden Ct 08873
Blake Ave 08873
Bloomfield Ave 08873
Bloomsbury Ct 08873
Bob Franks Way 08873
Bolton Ct 08873
Booker St 08873
Bort Rd 08873
Boston Way 08873
Boudinot Ln 08873
Boulder Ln 08873
Boxgrove Pl 08873
Boyard Ct 08873
Bray Ct 08873
Breakers Ln 08873
Brenner Ct 08873
Briarwood Dr 08873
Bridington Ln 08873
Bridle Ct 08873
Bristol Blvd 08873
Brook St 08873
Brookline Ave 08873
Brushwood Ct 08873
Buckingham Way 08873
Buell St 08873
Buffa Dr 08873
Burnham St 08873
Burns St 08873
Burr Pl 08873
Buttonwood Dr 08873
Byron Pl 08873
Callaway Ter 08873
Cambridge Ln 08873
Camner Ave 08873
Campus Dr 08873
Canal Rd 08873
Canal Walk Blvd 08873
Canterbury Cir 08873
Canvass Ct 08873
Carlisle Ct 08873
Carmen St 08873
Carol Ct 08873
Carson Ct 08873
Castle Ct 08873
Castleton Ave 08873
Cedar Ave 08873
Cedar Brook Dr 08873
Cedar Grove Ln 08873
Center St 08873
Chandler Rd 08873
Chapel Hill Rd 08873
Charles St 08873
Chatsworth Dr 08873
Cheddar Pl 08873
Cherrywood Dr 08873
Cheshire Ct 08873
Chester Ave 08873
Chesterwood Way 08873
Chestnut Cir 08873
Churchill Ave 08873
Classon Ct 08873
Clifford Cir 08873
Clifton St 08873
Clinton St 08873
Clover Hills Dr 08873
Club House Rd 08873
Clyde Rd 08873
Coburn Ln 08873
Coddington Ave 08873
Coldspring Ct 08873
Colgate Ct 08873
Colony Ct 08873
Commerce Dr 08873
Commons Way 08873
Como Dr 08873
Concord Dr 08873
Conerly Rd 08873
Congress Ct 08873
Conrad Way 08873
Constitution Way 08873
Continental Rd 08873
Cooper Ave 08873
Copley Sq 08873
Cornelius Way 08873
Corporate Park Dr 08873
Cortelyou Ln 08873
Cortland Dr 08873
Corwen Ct 08873
Cotswold Pl 08873
Cottontail Ln 08873
Courtney Ln 08873
Coventry Ln 08873
Crossfields Ln 08873
Crown Rd 08873
Croyden Ct 08873
Culver St 08873
Cumberland Ct 08873
Cypress Rd 08873
Dahlia Rd 08873
Dahmer Rd 08873
Darby Rd 08873
Dartmoor Dr 08873
Darwin Rd 08873
Daulton Dr 08873
Davidson Ave 08873
Davinci Ct 08873
Davis Ave 08873
Dayton Ave 08873
Deborah Dr 08873
Debow St 08873
Deerfield Rd 08873
Dekalb St 08873
Delaware Xing 08873
Dellwood Ln 08873
Delmonico Ave 08873
Demott Ln
1-501 08873
500-500 08875
503-599 08873
Den Herder Dr 08873
Denbigh Dr 08873
Denise Ct 08873
Dennett Rd 08873
Depalma Ct 08873
Derbyshire Ln 08873
Dermer Pl 08873
Devonshire Dr 08873
Dewald Ave 08873
Dickens Ct 08873
Dina Ln 08873
Disbro Ln 08873
Dochery Pl 08873
Domino Rd 08873
Donald Ave 08873
Doria Rd 08873
Dorset Ct 08873
Douglas Ave 08873
N & S Dover Ave 08873
Drake Rd 08873
Driftwood Dr 08873
Driscoll Ct 08873
Dumont St 08873
Dunbar St 08873
Dunham Ave 08873
Dutch Rd 08873
Dutton St 08873
Easton Ave 08873
Edgeware Ct 08873
Edith Pl 08873
Edna Ct 08873
Elizabeth Ave 08873
Ellen St 08873
Ellison Rd 08873
Elm St 08873
Elmwood St 08873
Emerald Pl 08873
Emerson Rd 08873
Enclave Cir 08873
Epping Ct 08873
Equator Ave 08873
Esplanade Dr 08873
Ethel St 08873
Eton Way 08873
Eugene Ave 08873
Evans Ct 08873
Evergreen Rd 08873
Executive Dr 08873
Exeter Ct 08873
Fairfield Rd 08873
Fairmount St 08873
Farrell St 08873
Farrington Plz 08873
Fehervari Ct 08873
Fir Ct 08873
Flower Rd 08873
Ford Ave 08873
Fordham Rd 08873
Fort St 08873
Fountain Dr 08873
Foxwood Dr 08873
Fraley Dr 08873
Francis St 08873
Frank St 08873
Franklin Blvd
1-601 08873
602-798 08873
602-602 08875
603-799 08873
Franklin Ct 08873
Franklin Grns S 08873
Franklin St 08873
Franklin Square Dr 08873
Fredrick St 08873
Freedom Ln 08873
Freeman Rd 08873
Freemont Ct 08873
French St 08873
Fuller St 08873
Fulton Rd 08873
Gallop Ln 08873
Garden Hills Dr 08873
Garfield Ave 08873
Gary Ct 08873
Gates Rd 08873
Gauguin Way 08873
Gifford Rd 08873
Ginkgo Ct 08873
Girard Ave 08873
Glastonbury Ln 08873
Glouchester Dr 08873
Gold St 08873
Grace Rd 08873
Grailli St 08873
Grandview Ave 08873
Grant St 08873
Grantham Dr 08873
Green St 08873
Grier Rd 08873
Griggs St 08873
S Grosser Pl 08873
Grouser Rd 08873
Grove St 08873
Gunther Loop 08873
Gurley St 08873
Hadler Dr 08873
Hageman Rd 08873
Hale Plz 08873
Hall St 08873
Halsey St 08873
Hamilton St 08873
Hamlet Ct 08873
Hampton Ct 08873
Hancock Pl 08873
Hardenbergh St 08873
Harlech Way 08873
Harper St 08873
Harrison St 08873
Harrow Dr 08873
Haven Way 08873
Haverhill Pl 08873
Hawkshead Way 08873
Haworth Pl 08873
Hawthorne Dr 08873
Hazlitt Way 08873
Heather Dr 08873
Heinrich Rd 08873
Heller Park Ln 08873
Hemlock Ln 08873
Hempstead Dr 08873
Henley Dr 08873
Henry St 08873
Hexham Dr 08873
Hickory Rd 08873
High St 08873
Highland Ave 08873
Highwood Rd 08873
Hill Ave 08873
Hillcrest Ave 08873
Hilltop Ln 08873
Holland Dr 08873
Holly St 08873
Hollywood Ave 08873
Home St 08873
Hopkinson Ln 08873
Howard Ave 08873
Hughes Rd 08873
Hunt Rd 08873
Hunters Crossing Rd 08873
Hyde Park Rd 08873
Independence Ct 08873
Indiana Rd 08873
Inwood Ct 08873
Iris Ct 08873
Irving St 08873
Irvington Ave 08873
Jacob Rd 08873
Jacques Ln 08873
Jarvis Pl 08873
Jays Cor 08873
Jean Ct 08873
Jefferson St 08873
Jensen Dr 08873
Jeremy Ct 08873
Jerome Ave 08873
Jiffy Rd 08873
Jill Ct 08873
Jimmy Ct 08873
Joan Rd 08873
John E Busch Ave 08873
John F Kennedy Blvd 08873
Johnson Rd 08873
Jonathan Pl 08873
Jordans Cir 08873
Julie Ct 08873
Juliet Ave 08873
Julip Ct 08873
Juniper Ct 08873
Jurocko Ave 08873
Kasey Ct 08873
Kassul Pl 08873
Kathryn St 08873
Kaufman St 08873
Kee Ave 08873
Keenan St 08873
Kent St 08873
King Rd 08873
Kingsberry Dr 08873
Kingsbridge Rd 08873
Kirkstall Ct 08873
Knollcrest Ct 08873
Knox Ave 08873
Koolidge Ct 08873
Kossuth St 08873
Kristen Ct 08873
Kuhn St 08873
Kyle Rd 08873
Lafayette Ave 08873
Laird Ter 08873
W Lake Ave & Ct 08873
Lakeside Rd 08873
Lander St 08873
Landry Rd 08873

Larsen Rd 08873
N & S Lawrence Ave 08873
Layne Rd 08873
Leahy Ct 08873
Learnington Way 08873
Lebed Dr 08873
Lee Dr 08873
Lenape Dr 08873
Lenox Pl 08873
Leona St 08873
Leupp Ln 08873
Lewis St 08873
Lexington Rd 08873
Liam St 08873
Liberty Ln 08873
Lilac Ln 08873
Lillian St 08873
Link Rd 08873
Lisi Ct 08873
Livingston Ave 08873
London Pl 08873
Longwood Ln 08873
Lori Ct 08873
Louis Ave 08873
Lovers Ln 08873
Lowell Pl 08873
Luton Way 08873
Lynch St 08873
Lyndhurst Dr 08873
Maak Ct 08873
Macafee Rd 08873
Madison Ave 08873
Magnolia Rd 08873
Maher Rd 08873
Main St 08873
Majesty Ln 08873
Manville Cswy 08873
Maple Ave 08873
Marcy St 08873
Margaret Dr 08873
Mariano Ct 08873
Marigold Ln 08873
Mark St 08873
Market St 08873
Markham Rd 08873
Marlowe Ct 08873
Marshall St 08873
Marswillo Way 08873
Martin St 08873
Martine St 08873
Martino Way 08873
Marvin Ave 08873
Masada St 08873
Matilda Ave 08873
Matlook Pl 08873
Mattawang Dr 08873
Maxwell Ln 08873
Mayflower Ct 08873
Maynard Rd 08873
Mcauliffe Ct 08873
Mcguffy Rd 08873
Mckinley Pl 08873
Mcnair Ct 08873
Meade Ct 08873
Meadow Hills Dr 08873
Medici Dr 08873
Meister St 08873
Memorial Dr 08873
Mercury St 08873
Merriewold Ln 08873
Mettlers Rd 08873
Michael J Smith Ct 08873
Michelangelo Ct 08873
S Middlebush Rd 08873
Miller Ave 08873
Miller Farm Rd 08873
Millstone Rd 08873
Mindy Dr 08873
Minetta Rd 08873
Monet Ct 08873
Montrose Rd 08873
Mustang Trl 08873
Myrtle St 08873
Nantwich Ct 08873
Napoleon Ct 08873
Nassau Ave 08873

Nepote Pl 08873
Neptune Ct 08873
Neuville Dr 08873
Neville Ct 08873
Nevius Pl 08873
New Brunswick Rd 08873
Newkirk Rd 08873
Newport Ave 08873
Newton Ct 08873
Nicole Dr 08873
Nina Ct 08873
Norfolk Rd 08873
Norma Ave 08873
Norris Rd 08873
Nortwick Ct 08873
Norwich Pl 08873
Nostrand Way 08873
Nottingham Way 08873
Oak Pl 08873
Oakbrook Pl 08873
Oakcroft Ln 08873
Oakland Ave 08873
Olcott St 08873
Old Amwell Rd 08873
Old Hamilton St 08873
Old Lane Highwood 08873
Oliver St 08873
Onizuka Ct 08873
Orchid Ct 08873
Osborne Ct 08873
Oswestry Way 08873
Overbrook Rd 08873
Oxford Pl 08873
Park St 08873
Parkside St 08873
Pasture Trl 08873
Patriots Way 08873
Patton Dr 08873
Peak Pl 08873
Pearl Pl 08873
Pembrook Ct 08873
Penn Ct 08873
Peoples Line Rd 08873
Pershing Ave 08873
Phillips Ct & Rd 08873
Phythian Ct 08873
Picadilly Pl 08873
Picasso Ct 08873
Pickering Pl 08873
Pierce St 08873
Pin Oak Ln 08873
Pine St 08873
Pine Grove Ave 08873
Pinecrest Rd 08873
Pitcher Pt 08873
Plum Tree Ln 08873
Plymouth Pl 08873
Poe Ave 08873
W Point Ave 08873
Pony Ct 08873
Post Ln 08873
Prescott Ct 08873
Prestbury Ln 08873
Prospect St 08873
Pucillo Ln 08873
Queens Pl 08873
Quick Ct 08873
Radio Ct 08873
Railroad Ave 08873
Ralph St 08873
Randolph Rd 08873
Ray St 08873
Red Oak Ct 08873
Reeve St 08873
Regent St 08873
Regina Pl 08873
Reins Ct 08873
Reler Ln 08873
Renaissance Blvd 08873
Renfro Rd 08873
Renoir Way 08873
Republic Row 08873
Resnik Ct 08873
Revere Ln 08873
Richmond Dr 08873
Rieder Ct 08873

Riverview Dr 08873
Robbins Ave 08873
Robert C Keri Ct 08873
Roberts Rd 08873
Rodney Ave 08873
Rogers Ave 08873
Rolling Rd 08873
Rolling Hills Dr 08873
Ronald Dr 08873
Roosevelt Ave 08873
Rose St 08873
Rosecliff Ct 08873
Rosewood Ct 08873
Royal Ct 08873
Rue Cezanne 08873
Rue Chagall 08873
Rue Matisse 08873
Runyon Ave 08873
Ruppert Dr 08873
Russett Rd 08873
Rutledge Trl 08873
Saddle Ct 08873
Saint Anns Ct 08873
Saint Giles Ct 08873
Samuel Pl 08873
Sanders Ave 08873
Saratoga Ct 08873
Saw Mill Dr 08873
Scaletti Ct 08873
Schenck Ln 08873
Schindler Ct 08873
School Ave 08873
Schoolhouse Rd 08873
Scobee Ln 08873
Scott St 08873
Sebring Rd 08873
Seelys Run 08873
Selby Ct 08873
Shadowlawn Dr 08873
Shannon Ct 08873
Sheffield Ct 08873
Shelly Dr 08873
Shenandoah Pl 08873
Sherborne St 08873
Sherman Cir 08873
Sherwood Ct 08873
Shevenchenko Ave 08873
Shilling Dr 08873
Shirley Ave 08873
Silcox Pl 08873
Simpson Rd 08873
Sinclair Blvd 08873
Skillmans Ln 08873
Skipton Pl 08873
Smith Rd 08873
Smithwold Rd 08873
Somerset St 08873
Spader Way 08873
Spangenberg Ln 08873
Spencer St 08873
Spooky Brook Rd 08873
Spring St 08873
Springfield Ave 08873
Spruce St 08873
Stallion Ct 08873
Stanwick Ct 08873
State Route 27 08873
Staudt Ct 08873
Steeplechase Ct 08873
Stone Pl 08873
Stone Leigh Way 08873
Stone Manor Dr 08873
Stonehedge Ct 08873
Stothoff St 08873
Stratford Dr 08873
Stryker Rd 08873
Stuyvesant Ave 08873
Summerall Rd 08873
Sumner Ave 08873
Sunflower Rd 08873
Sunny Ct 08873
Sunnyvale Ct 08873
Surrey Rd 08873
Susan Dr 08873
Sussex Ct 08873
Suydam Rd 08873

Sweetbriar Rd 08873
Sydney Pl 08873
Talbot St 08873
Tall Oaks Rd 08873
Tallman Ln 08873
Tamarack Rd 08873
Temple St 08873
Terry Ter 08873
Thistle Hill Ln 08873
Thomas Rd 08873
Thompson Pkwy 08873
Tintern Ct 08873
Treptow Rd 08873
Tripplet Rd 08873
Tudor Dr 08873
Tunnell Rd 08873
Ulysses Rd 08873
Unami Ct 08873
Upperpond Rd 08873
Valley Wood Dr 08873
Van Cleef Rd 08873
Van Doren Ave 08873
Vanderbilt Ave 08873
Varga Ln 08873
Vassar St 08873
Vernon Ave 08873
Veronica Ave 08873
Victor St 08873
Victoria Dr 08873
Viking Ave 08873
Village Dr 08873
Vince Rd 08873
Virginia Ct 08873
Viscaya Ct 08873
Voorhees Ave 08873
Wade Ave 08873
Waldorf St 08873
Walnut Ave 08873
Warren St 08873
Waterlou Ct 08873
Webster Rd 08873
Welshs Ln 08873
Wendham Pl 08873
Westminster Ave 08873
Weston Rd 08873
Weston Canal Rd 08873
Westover Way 08873
Wexford Way 08873
Wheeler Pl 08873
Whitby Cir 08873
Whittier Ave 08873
Wiley Dr 08873
William St 08873
Willocks Cir 08873
Willow Ave 08873
Wilson Rd 08873
Winchester Way 08873
Windfall Ln 08873
Windsor Ct 08873
Winslow Ave 08873
Winston Dr 08873
Winthrop Rd 08873
Wisbech Pl 08873
Witherspoon Way 08873
Woodhill St 08873
Woodlawn Rd 08873
Worlds Fair Dr 08873
Wortman St 08873
Wycombe Pl 08873
Yates Ave 08873
Zapf Ct 08873
Zarephath Rd 08873
Zeller Dr 08873

NUMBERED STREETS

All Street Addresses 08873

SUMMIT NJ

General Delivery 07901

POST OFFICE BOXES MAIN OFFICE STATIONS AND BRANCHES

Box No.s
All PO Boxes 07902

NAMED STREETS

Acorn Dr 07901
Arden Pl 07901
Argyle Ct 07901
Ascot Way 07901
Ashland Rd 07901
Ashwood Ave & Ct 07901
Aubrey St 07901
Badeau Ave 07901
Baltusrol Pl & Rd 07901
Bank St 07901
Beacon Rd 07901
Beauvoir Ave & Pl 07901
Bedford Rd 07901
Beech Spring Dr 07901
Beechwood Rd 07901
Beekman Rd & Ter 07901
Bellevue Ave 07901
Beverly Rd 07901
Blackburn Pl & Rd 07901
Blair Pl 07901
Brainerd Rd 07901
Brantwood Dr 07901
Briant Pkwy 07901
Broad St 07901
Brook Ct 07901
Butler Pkwy 07901
Caldwell Ave 07901
Canoe Brook Pkwy & Pl 07901
Canterbury Ln 07901
Carleen Ct 07901
Cedar St 07901
Cedric Rd 07901
Chapel St 07901
Chatham Rd 07901
Chestnut Ave 07901
Clark St 07901
Clearview Dr 07901
Cleveland Rd 07901
Club Dr & Ln 07901
Colonial Rd 07901
Colony Ct & Dr 07901
Colt Rd 07901
Constantine Pl 07901
Cottage Ln 07901
Countryside Dr 07901
Crescent Ave 07901
Crest Dr 07901
Crest Acre Ct 07901
Crestwood Ln 07901
Cromwell Pkwy 07901
Dale Dr 07901
Dayton Rd 07901
De Bary Pl 07901
Deforest Ave 07901
Denman Pl 07901
Dennis Pl 07901
Devon Rd 07901
Division Ave 07901
Dogwood Dr 07901
Dorchester Rd 07901
Doremus St 07901
Dorset Ln 07901
Druid Hill Rd 07901
Drum Hill Dr 07901
Dunnder Dr 07901
Eaton Ct 07901
Edgar St 07901
Edgemont Ave 07901
Edgewood Dr & Rd 07901
Edison Dr 07901
Eggers Ct 07901
Elm Pl & St 07901
W End Ave 07901
Essex Rd 07901
Euclid Ave 07901
Evergreen Rd 07901
Fairview Ave 07901
Faitoute Ct 07901
Fay Pl 07901
Fernwood Rd 07901
Franklin Pl 07901
Fremont Rd 07901
Friar Tuck Cir 07901

Garden Rd 07901
Gary Rd 07901
Gates Ave 07901
George St 07901
Glen Ave 07901
Glen Oaks Ave 07901
Glendale Rd 07901
Glenside Ave 07901
Glenwood Pl 07901
Gloucester Rd 07901
Greenbriar Dr 07901
Greenfield Ave 07901
Grove St & Ter 07901
Harrison Ct 07901
Hartley Rd 07901
Harvard St 07901
Harvey Ct & Dr 07901
Hawthorne Pl 07901
Henry St 07901
Hickory Rd 07901
High St 07901
Highland Dr 07901
Hillcrest Ave 07901
Hillside Ave & Ter 07901
Hillview Ter 07901
Hobart Ave & Rd 07901
Hughes Pl 07901
Huntley Rd 07901
Industrial Pl 07901
Iris Rd 07901
Irving Pl 07901
Joanna Way 07901
John St 07901
Karen Way 07901
Kendrick Rd 07901
Kenneth Ct 07901
Kent Place Blvd 07901
Kings Hill Ct 07901
Knob Hill Dr 07901
Lafayette Ave 07901
Larch Pl 07901
Larned Rd 07901
Laurel Ave 07901
Lavina Ct 07901
Lee Ln 07901
Lenox Rd 07901
Lewis Ave 07901
Lincoln Ave 07901
Linda Ln 07901
Linden Pl 07901
Little Wolf Rd 07901
Llewelyn Rd 07901
Locust Dr 07901
Londonderry Way 07901
Lorraine Pl & Rd 07901
Lowell Ave 07901
Lower Overlook Rd 07901
Madison Ave 07901
Magnolia Pl 07901
Malvern Dr 07901
Manor Hill Rd 07901
Maple St
1-62 07901
61-61 07902
63-199 07901
64-198 07901
Meade Ct 07901
Meadowbrook Ct 07901
Michigan Ave 07901
Middle Ave & Way 07901
Midland Ter 07901
Miele Pl 07901
Milton Ave 07901
Montrose Ave 07901
Montview Rd 07901
Morris Ave, Ct & Tpke 07901
Mount Vernon Ave 07901
Mountain Ave 07901
Myrtle Ave 07901
Nassau Dr 07901
New England Ave 07901
New Providence Ave 07901
North St 07901
Norwood Ave 07901
O Shea Ln 07901
Oak Forest Ln 07901

Oak Knoll Rd 07901
Oak Ridge Ave 07901
Oakland Pl 07901
Oaklawn Rd 07901
Oakley Ave 07901
Old Coach Rd 07901
Old Oak Dr 07901
Old Springfield Ave 07901
Orchard St 07901
Overhill Rd 07901
Overlook Rd 07901
Oxbow Ln 07901
Pacheank Ave 07901
Park Ave & Pl 07901
Parkview Ter 07901
Parmley Pl 07901
Passaic Ave 07901
Pearl St 07901
Pembroke Rd 07901
Pine Grove Ave 07901
Pine Ridge Dr 07901
Plain St 07901
Plymouth Rd 07901
Portland Rd 07901
Primrose Pl 07901
Princeton St 07901
Prospect St 07901
Prospect Hill Ave 07901
Railroad Ave 07901
Ramsey Dr 07901
Ridge Rd 07901
Ridgedale Ave 07901
Risk Ave 07901
River Rd 07901
Robin Hood Rd 07901
Rose Ln 07901
Rotary Dr & Ln 07901
Rowan Rd 07901
Russell Pl 07901
Ruthven Pl 07901
Sayre St 07901
Seven Oaks Dr 07901
Shadyside Ave 07901
Sheffield Rd 07901
Sheridan Rd 07901
Sherman Ave 07901
Shunpike Rd 07901
Silver Lake Dr 07901
South St 07901
Springfield Ave 07901
Stacie Ct 07901
Stanley Ave 07901
Stiles Rd 07901
Stockton Rd 07901
Stone Ridge Rd 07901
Stony Hill Ct 07901
Summit Ave 07901
Sunset Dr 07901
Surrey Rd 07901
Sweetbriar Rd 07901
Sylvan Rd & Ter 07901
Tall Oaks Dr 07901
Tanglewood Dr 07901
Templar Way 07901
Tulip St 07901
Twombly Dr 07901
Union Pl 07901
Upper Dr 07901
Upper Overlook Rd 07901
Valemont Way 07901
Valley View Ave 07901
Van Dyke Pl 07901
Wade Dr 07901
Waldron Ave 07901
Wallace Rd 07901
Walnut St 07901
Warwick Rd 07901
Washington Ave 07901
Watchung Pl 07901
Weaver St 07901
Webster Ave 07901
Wentworth Rd 07901
West Ln 07901
Westminster Rd 07901
Whitesell Ct 07901
Whitewood Dr 07901

Whittredge Rd 07901
Wildwood Ln 07901
William St 07901
Willow Rd 07901
Winchester Rd 07901
Winchip Rd 07901
Windsor Rd 07901
Woodcroft Rd 07901
Woodfern Rd 07901
Woodland Ave 07901
Woodmere Dr 07901
Yale St 07901

TOMS RIVER NJ

General Delivery 08753

POST OFFICE BOXES MAIN OFFICE STATIONS AND BRANCHES

Box No.s
B - H 08754
1 - 2677 08754
3001 - 4174 08756
4501 - 5456 08754

RURAL ROUTES

10 08753
07 08755

NAMED STREETS

Abaco St 08757
Abbott Ave 08753
Aberdeen Ln 08753
Abergele Ct & Dr 08757
Acacia Row 08755
Acapulco Pl 08753
Acorn Dr 08753
Ada Ct 08753
Adafre Ave 08753
Adams Ave 08753
Adamsway Ct 08753
Adelphi Rd 08757
Adirondack Pl 08753
Admiral Ave 08753
Agincourt Rd 08755
Alabama Ave 08753
Albert Ave 08753
Alberta St 08757
Albonito Dr 08757
Albright Ave 08757
Alden Dr 08753
Aldo Ct & Dr 08753
Aldous St 08755
Alexandria Dr 08753
Alfred Dr 08757
Alfred Ln 08753
Alfred Rd 08757
Alissa Dr 08753
Allaire Dr 08753
Allen St 08753
Alligator Dr 08753
Almeda Dr 08753
Almond Dr 08753
Alpen Ln 08755
Alpina Ter 08757
Alton Ct 08757
Amanda Ct 08753
Ambassador Dr 08753
Americana Ct 08753
Amethyst Dr 08753
Amherst Rd 08757
Amsterdam Ave 08757
Amy Ct 08755
Anchor Sq 08753
Anchorage Dr 08753
Andover Ct 08757
Andros St 08757
Anegada Ave 08753
Anguilla Ln 08757
Ann Rd 08755
Annapolis Ct & Rd 08757
Annette Ln 08753
Anthony Ave 08753
Antiqua Ave 08753
Anvil Ct & Way 08755
Apache Dr 08753
Apple Ct 08753
Apple Blossom Ct 08755
Appleby Way 08757
Applegate Ave 08757
Aqueduct Ct 08755
Arapaho Ct 08755
Arbar Ct 08755
Arcadia Dr 08755
Ardmore Ave 08757
Aria Rd 08755
Arima Ct 08757
Arizona Ave 08753
Ark St 08755
Arkansas Ave 08753
Arlene Ct 08755
Arlington Dr 08755
Arrow Dr 08753
Arthur St 08755
Aruba Ct 08757
Arvell St 08755
Ascot Ct 08755
Ashcroft Ln 08757
Ashdown Forest Ln 08755
Asheville St 08753
Ashewood Ct 08755
E & W Ashfield Ct 08755
Ashford Rd 08755
Ashlar Way 08753
Aspen Ct & Dr 08753
Aster Dr 08753
Astoria Dr 08753
Atlantic City Blvd 08757
Atsion Way 08753
Attison Ave 08757
Auburn Rd 08757
Audrey Ave 08755
Audubon Dr 08753
Augusta Ct 08757
Autumn Dr 08753
Ava Rd 08755
Aviary Way 08755
Avon Ct 08753
Avrum Dr 08753
Azalea Ct 08753
Aztec Ct 08757
Badger Dr 08755
Bahama Ave 08753
Bahamia Dr 08757
Bailey Ave 08753
Bakoua Ct 08757
Balfrey Dr 08753
Balmoral Ct 08757
Baltusrol Ct 08753
Bamberry Ln 08755
Bananier Dr
2-4 08757
6-8 08757
10-198 08757
49-55 08755
101-199 08757
Bandon Rd 08753
Banning Ct 08757
Barbados Ave 08753
Barbados Dr N 08757
Barbados Dr S 08757
Barbara Cir & Ln 08753
Barbuda St 08757
Barcelona Dr 08753
Bark St 08753
Barnegat Ave 08753
Barnes Ln 08753
Baron St 08753
Bartine St 08753
Bartlett Cir & Pl 08755
Bash Rd 08753
Basset Ct & Dr 08757
Basseterri St 08753
Basswood Ct 08755
Basswood Hollow Dr 08755
Batchelor St 08753
N Bay Ave & Ter 08753
Bay Breeze Dr W 08753
Bay Creek Ln 08753
Bay Point Dr 08753
Bay Ridge Ave 08753
Bay Shore Dr 08753
Bay Stream Dr 08753
Baylor St 08757
Bayview Dr 08753
Baywood Dr 08753
Beachview Dr 08753
Beachwood Ave 08753
Beacon St 08757
Bear Mountain Ct 08753
Beauchamps Pl 08753
Beaumont Ct 08757
Beaver Hollow Dr 08755
Beaverbrook Dr 08757
Bedford Ct 08757
Bedivere Ct 08757
Beech St 08757
Beechmont St 08757
Beechtree Dr 08753
Begonia Ct 08753
Bel Aire Ct 08753
Bell Ct & St 08753
Bellflower Ct 08755
Bellwood Dr 08753
Belmont Ct 08753
Belmont Dr 08757
Beltane Rd 08755
Benjamin St 08755
Bennington Dr 08757
Bent Trl 08753
Bent Hook Rd 08755
Bequia Ct 08757
Bergen Ave 08753
Berkeley Ave 08753
Berkshire Ct 08753
Bermuda Dr 08753
Bernice Ct 08753
Berry Ave 08753
Bertha Rd 08755
Beverly Ct 08755
Bewick St 08753
Bey Lea Rd 08753
Biabou Dr 08757
Big Enough Way 08755
Bimini Dr 08757
Binnacle Ln 08753
Biondo St 08753
Birch Ln 08753
Birch St
2A-98A 08757
2B-98B 08757
2C-98C 08757
2D-98D 08757
1A-99A 08757
1B-99B 08757
1C-99C 08757
1D-99D 08757
3100-3199 08753
Birchbark Pl 08753
Birmingham Ave 08757
Birr Ct 08753
Biscayne St 08757
Bismarck St 08757
Black Birch Ct 08753
Black Oak Ct 08753
Blackfoot Ct 08753
Blackpool Way 08757
Blissfield Ln 08755
Blossom Dr 08753
Blue Heron Dr S 08753
Blue Jay Dr 08753
Blue Sea Ln 08753
Blue Spruce Ct 08753
Blyth Ct 08757
Boca Raton St 08757
Bolans Ct 08757
Bolingbroke Ct & Dr 08757
Bolton Ct 08757
Bonaire Dr 08757
Bonasse St 08757
Bookbinder Ct 08753
Bordeaux Ct 08757
Bough Ct 08753
Boundary St 08753
Bounty Ct 08753
Bow Rd 08753
Bowling Green Dr 08753
Boxelder Dr 08753
Boxer St 08753
Boxwood Ter 08755
Boyd St 08753
Braddock Rd 08755
Braden Ct 08755
Bradley Blvd 08753
Brakenbury Ct & Dr 08757
Branch Dr 08755
Branch Brook Ct 08755
Brand Rd 08753
Brandies Ct & Rd 08757
Brandywine Dr 08753
Breckenridge Pl 08755
Breezy Oaks Dr 08753
Brenton Ln 08755
Brentwood Ave 08753
Breton Harbor Dr 08753
Brett Pl 08753
Brian Ct 08757
Briar Ave 08753
Briarcliff Dr 08753
Bricksburg Ct 08755
Bridgetown Ct 08757
Bridport Dr 08755
Brightwood Dr 08753
Brisbane Ct 08757
Briscoe Dr 08753
Bristol Ct 08753
Brittany Ln 08755
Broad St 08753
Broadway Blvd 08757
Brook Harbor Ln 08753
Brookdale Ct 08755
Brookewood Dr 08755
Brookfield Ct 08757
Brookforest Dr 08757
Brooks Rd 08753
Brookside Ct & Dr 08753
Brookville Rd 08753
Brower Ave 08755
Brown Ct 08753
Brussels Ct 08757
Bryant Ave 08753
Buchanan St 08753
Buckingham Dr 08753
Bucknell Dr 08757
Bucks Ct 08757
Bud Ct 08753
Buena Visa Ct & Dr 08757
Buenaventura Ct 08753
Buermann Ave 08753
Buffalo Ct 08753
Bugle Ct 08757
Bunker Hill Dr 08755
Buoy Pl 08753
Burgess Ct 08757
Burlington Ct 08757
Burns Ave 08755
Burnside St 08757
Burntwood Trl 08753
Burr Oak Rd 08755
Buttercup Ct 08755
Buttonwood Ave 08755
Buxton Rd 08755
Cabernet Ct 08753
Cable Dr 08755
Cabrillo Blvd 08757
Cadillac Dr 08755
Cahill Rd 08755
Calalou Ct 08757
Caldwell Ct & Dr 08757
Calico Ln 08757
California Ct 08753
Calm Way 08755
Cambourne Dr 08753
Cambridge Ct
1-2 08757
3-5 08753
4-4 08757
6-6 08753
6-8 08757
7-7 08753
10-10 08757
11-11 08753
11-11 08757
12-12 08753
12-14 08757
15-15 08753
15-17 08757
16-16 08753
16-18 08757
19-19 08753
19-21 08757
20-20 08753
20-22 08757
23-24 08753
26-48 08757
Camelot Dr 08755
Camino De Contento 08755
Camino Del Node 08755
Camino Hermosa 08755
Camino Medio 08755
Camino Real 08755
Camino Real Ct 08757
Camino Redondo 08755
Camino Rio 08755
Camino Roble 08755
Camino Verde 08755
Camrose St 08757
Canandaigua Rd 08753
Canaries Ct 08757
Cancun St 08757
Canterbury Ln 08753
Canton Dr 08753
Cape Ct 08753
Capri Ct 08757
Capstan Dr 08753
Captains Dr 08753
Caracas Ct 08757
Carann Dr 08753
Cardiff Ct 08757
Cardigan Dr 08757
Cardinal Dr 08755
Caribbean Ct 08753
Caribbean St 08757
Carlisle Rd 08757
Carlow Dr 08753
Carlsbad Dr 08757
Carmacks Way 08757
Carmen Ct 08755
Carnaby Ln 08753
Carnation Cir 08753
Carnegie St 08757
Carol Dr 08753
N Carolina Ct 08753
Caroline Ln 08755
Carrazal Ct 08757
Carriage Ct 08753
Carter St 08753
Casablanca Ct 08753
Castle Dr 08753
Castle Harbor Dr 08757
Castlebuono Ave 08753
Castleton Dr 08757
Castries St 08757
Castro Grove Dr 08753
Catalina Ct 08753
Cathedral Ct 08755
Catskill Ct 08753
Cattus St 08753
Cattus Island Blvd 08753
Caudina Ave 08753
Cavan Dr 08753
Cayman Ave 08753
Cayuga Ct 08755
Cedar Dr 08753
Cedar Row 08753
Cedar St 08757
Cedar Berry Ln 08753
Cedar Brook Dr 08753
Cedar Creek Ln 08753
Cedar Crest Dr 08753
Cedar Grove Rd 08753
Cedar Hill Ln 08755
Cedar Inn Dr 08755
Cedar Point Ct 08753
Cedar Stream Ct 08755
Cedar Tree Ln 08753
Cedarhurst Dr 08753
Cedarview Dr 08757
Cedarwood Dr 08755
Center Pl 08753
Center St 08757
Central Ave 08753
N Central Ave 08753
Central St 08757
Chadwick Ave 08753
Chamberlain Ct, Dr & St 08757
Champlain St 08757
Chancellor Ct 08757
Channel Rd 08753
N & S Chanticleer Ct 08755
Chapel Ct 08753
Charlen Rd 08755
Charles Ave 08757
Charles Dr 08753
Charlotte St 08753
Charlotteville Dr N & S 08757
Charlton Cir 08755
Chateux Ln 08757
Chatham Ct & Dr 08753
Chaucer Ln 08755
Cheddar Pink Cv 08755
Chelsea Ct 08753
Cherbourg St 08753
Cherokee Ct 08753
Cherry Ct 08753
Cherry St 08757
Cherry Cove Ct 08753
Cherryvale Ct 08755
Cheryl Dr 08753
Chesterfield Ct & Ln 08757
Chestnut St
2A-8A 08757
Chestnut Hill Dr 08755
Cheyenne Ct 08755
Chipmunk Ct & Ln 08755
Chippewa Rd 08753
Chisholm Ct 08753
Chivas Dr 08753
Choir Ct 08755
Chopin Ct 08757
Christian Ct 08753
Christiansted St 08757
Christoffer Ter 08753
Church Rd
1000-1658 08755
1659-2499 08753
Churchill Dr 08753
Chutney St 08757
Circle Dr 08753
Citadel Ave & Ct 08757
Citta Ct 08753
Claremont St 08757
Claridge Ct 08753
Clarkson Dr 08753
Clayton Ave 08755
Clear Lake Blvd 08753
Clearwater Way 08753
Clement Pl 08755
Cleveland St 08755
Cliffside Dr 08755
Clifton Ave 08753
Clinton Ave 08753
Clipper Ct 08753
Clover Hill Ln 08755
Cloverdale Ct 08755
Cobblestone Ct 08755
Cobham Ct 08757
Coborca Way 08757
Cody Rd 08753
Cohansey Dr 08757
Cokes Dr 08753
Colby St 08757
Colfax St 08753
Colgate Dr 08757
Colleen Ct 08755
College Dr 08753
Colonial Dr 08753
Colorado Dr 08753
Columbia Rd 08753
Columbine Cir 08755
Columbus St 08755
Colwyn Way 08757
Commons Way 08755
Commonwealth Blvd 08757
Compass Ct 08753
Concord Ln 08757
Concord Way 08753
Condor St 08753
Congress St 08753
Conifer St 08753
Conroy Ave 08753
Constable Pl 08753
Constitution Ave 08753
Contempo Dr 08753
Continental Ave 08753
Coolidge Ave 08753
Cooper Dr 08753
Copperfield Ln 08755
Coral Bell Holw 08755
Coral Leaf Rd 08755
Cordoba Ct 08757
Corfu Ct 08757
Corinth Pl 08757
Cornell Ave 08753
Cornell Rd 08757
Cornwallis Rd 08755
Corporate Cir 08755
Cortlandt Dr 08757
Corwill Ter 08753
Cory Dr 08755
Costa Mesa Dr 08757
Cotswold Close 08753
Cottonwood Dr 08753
Coulter St 08755
Country Trce 08753
Country Club Ln 08753
Court House Ln 08753
Courtier Dr 08753
Courtney Ct 08753
Cove Rd 08753
Cove Point Rd 08753
Coventry Dr 08753
Coventry Rd 08757
Cox Cro Rd 08755
Cozy Way 08755
Crabbe Rd 08757
Craig Rd 08753
Cranberry Rd 08753
Crane Way 08753
Cranmoor Dr 08753
Craven Rd 08753
Creek Rd 08753
Crescent Ct 08755
Crescent Dr 08757
Crest Rd 08753
Crest Hill Rd 08755
Crest Ridge Dr 08753
Crestview Ln 08755
Crimson Ct & Rd 08755
Crisfield Cir & St 08755
Cromwell Dr 08753
Crowder Dr 08753
Crowell St 08753
Cruiser Ct 08753
Crystal Dr 08753
Crystal Mile Ct 08753
Culebra Ave 08753
Culpepper Dr 08753
Cumana St 08757
Cumberland Blvd 08757
Curacao St 08757
Curaco Ave 08753
N Curtis Pl 08753
Cutty Ct 08753
Cynthia Ln 08755
Cypress Rd 08753
W Cypress Rd 08753
Cypress St 08757
Cypress Point Dr 08753
Daffodil Ct 08753
Dahlia Ln 08753
Daisy Rd 08753

S Dakota Ave 08753
Dale Dr 08753
Dallas Dr 08753
Dalton Ln 08755
Dam Rd 08755
Danbury Ln 08755
Danube Ct 08757
Darren St 08753
Dartmouth Dr 08757
Darye Ct 08755
Dauphin Ct 08753
Dave Marion Rd 08753
Davenport Rd W 08757
Dawn Way 08757
Day Lilly Nook 08755
Dayna Ct 08753
Dayton Ave 08753
Deauville Ave 08757
Debbie Ct 08753
Deep River Ln 08755
Deer Ln 08753
Deer Hollow Dr 08753
Delaware Ave 08753
Dell St 08755
Delos Dr 08753
Demont St 08753
Derby Ln 08757
Derry Dr 08753
Devonshire Rd 08753
Dewey St 08753
Dickinson Ave 08753
Dillon Ct & Ln 08755
Dino Blvd 08755
Disalvo St 08753
Discovery Way 08755
Disney Dr 08755
Dittmar Dr 08757
Division St 08753
Dock St 08753
Dockage Ave 08753
Doe Rd 08753
Dogwood Ln 08753
Dolly Rd 08753
Dominica Dr 08757
Donegal Ct 08753
Donna Dee Ct 08755
Doral Ct & Dr 08757
Dorchester Dr 08753
Dorothy Rd 08753
Dorset Psge 08753
Double Trouble Rd 08757
Dove St 08753
Dover Rd 08757
Dover St 08753
Dover Walk 08753
Dover Chase Blvd 08755
Dover Pines Ave 08755
Down Ct 08757
Down Hill Run 08755
Downing St 08755
Drake Ln 08757
Drake Way 08753
Drew Ln 08757
Drew Pl 08753
Drexel Ct 08753
Drexel Dr 08757
Dreyfus Ct 08757
Driftwood Pl 08753
Driscoll Rd 08753
Dublin Ct 08753
Duchess Ct 08753
Dugan Ln
1-99 08755
100-200 08753
202-1498 08753
Duke Ct 08753
Duke Dr 08757
Dunedin St 08753
Dunham Ave 08753
Dupont Ct 08757
Duxbury Rd 08757
Eagle Ct 08755
Eagle Point Dr 08753
Eaglehurst Ct & Rd 08753
E & W Earl Ct 08753
East Dr 08753
Easton Rd 08757
Eastwind Ave 08753
Easy St 08757
Echo Pl 08755
Edgebrook Dr E 08757
Edgemere Ct & Dr 08755
Edgemont Ter 08757
Edgewater Ct & Dr 08757
Edgewood Ct & Dr 08755
Edinburgh Ct 08757
Edinburgh Dr
1-99 08757
900-999 08753
Edith Ct 08753
Edken Ave 08753
Edna Ct 08755
Edwards Ln 08753
Egret Dr 08753
Eileen Ct 08753
Eisenhower Rd 08753
Elderberry Ln 08753
Eldorado St 08757
Elevthera St 08757
Elizabeth Ave 08753
Elkton Ct 08757
Ellicott Ave 08753
Elm St 08757
Elmhurst Ct 08753
Elmswell Ct 08757
Elmwood Dr 08755
Elsinore St 08757
Ely Ct 08757
Emerald Ct 08753
Emerson Ct 08753
Emma Dr 08755
Encinitas Dr 08757
N End Ave 08753
Englemere Blvd 08757
English Ln 08753
Ensign Ct 08753
Equality Ct 08755
Equestrian Way 08755
Eric Ct 08753
Ernst St 08753
Esher Ct 08757
Essex Ct 08755
Estate Point Rd 08753
Esto Ct 08755
Eton Ct & Rd 08757
Eugene Dr 08753
Eve Pl 08757
Evelyn Dr 08753
Everett St 08753
Evergreen Dr 08753
Evesham Ct 08755
Executive Dr 08755
Exitir St 08757
Fairacres Dr 08753
Fairfield Rd & St 08757
Fairview Dr 08753
Fairway Dr
1-99 08753
100-199 08757
Falcon Ln 08755
Falconcrest Ct 08755
Falling Oaks Rd 08753
Falmouth St 08757
Farragut Ave 08753
Fawn Dr 08753
Feathertree Dr 08753
Federal Way 08753
Fellowship Ct 08755
Fern St 08753
Fernwood Dr 08753
Ferro Ln 08755
Ferry Ln 08753
Fiddlers Run 08755
Field St 08753
Fieldcrest Ln 08755
Fielders Ln 08755
Fireside Blvd & Ct 08755
Firestone Rd 08753
Firethorn Way 08755
Fischer Blvd 08753
Flaam St 08753
Flack St 08753
Flag Point Rd 08753
Flagstone Ct 08755
Flamingo Way 08757
Flint Rd 08757
Flintlock Dr 08753
Flitsch Dr 08753
Floral Way 08755
Florence Ct 08753
Fontana St 08757
Foothill Ct 08753
Forelle Ln 08755
Forest Cir 08755
Forest Glen Ct 08755
Forest Grove Ave 08753
Forest Ridge Ct 08755
Forest Valley Dr 08755
Forge Ln 08753
Formicola St 08753
Forrest Trail Cir 08753
Fort De France Ave 08757
Fortune Ct 08755
Foster Rd 08753
Fountain Dr 08753
Fox Glove Run 08755
Fox Hollow Dr 08755
Foxwood Ter 08755
France Ct & St 08753
Francis Dr 08753
Frankies Ln 08753
Franklin Ave 08753
Frann Rd 08753
Frederiksted St 08757
Freeman Ct 08753
Freeport Blvd & Ct 08757
Friar Ct 08753
Friendship Ln 08753
Fritz Dr 08755
Frontage Rd 08753
Froriep Ln 08755
Galloping Hill Ln 08755
Garden Ave 08753
Garden Ct 08757
Garden St 08753
Gardenia Way 08755
Garfield Ave 08753
Garnet Ct 08753
Garrett Rd 08757
Gary Rd 08753
E, N, S & W Gateway 08753
Gem Ave 08755
Gemstone Ln 08755
Genes Dr 08753
Genoa Ave 08753
George Rd 08753
Georgetown Dr & Rd 08757
Georgia Dr 08753
Gerald Dr 08753
Geranium Ct 08753
Germania Ct 08755
Germania Station Rd 08755
Gilbert Ave 08753
Gilford Ave & Pl 08753
Gillian Ct 08753
Gilmores Island Rd 08753
Girard Rd 08753
Gladney Ave 08753
Gladstone St 08757
Glasgow Ave 08753
Glen Oak Dr 08753
Glendale Dr 08753
Gleniffer Hill Rd 08755
Glenwood Cir & Rd 08753
Gloucester Dr 08753
Gold St 08753
Golden Dr 08753
Golden Glow Circus 08755
Golden Hemlock Way 08753
Goldspire Rd 08755
Golf View Blvd 08753
Goose Pl 08753
Goose Creek Rd 08753
Gorginio Dr 08757
Gouveneur Ave 08753
Gower Ct & Rd 08757
Goyave St 08757
Grace Dr 08753
Gramercy Ct 08757
Grand Ave 08753
Grand View Dr 08753
Grande River Blvd 08755
Grande Woodlands
Way 08755
Grant Ave 08753
Grantwood Dr 08753
Grassy Hollow Dr 08755
Green Dr 08755
Green Hill Blvd & Ct 08753
W Green Island Rd 08753
Green Ridge Dr 08757
Green Twig Dr 08753
Green View Way 08753
Greendale Ct 08755
Greenleaf Ct 08753
Greenspire Ct 08755
Greenville Ct 08757
Greenwich Ct 08753
Greenwood Rd 08753
Gregory Ter 08753
Grenada St 08757
Grinnell Ave 08757
Grover Rd 08753
Guadalajara Dr 08757
Guadeloupe Dr 08757
Gudvangen St 08753
Gulfstream Way 08755
Gwyn Ct 08757
Hadley Ave 08753
Haifa Ct 08753
Haines Rd 08753
Haines Cove Dr 08753
Haiti Ct 08757
Halsey Rd 08753
Hamilton Ct 08757
Hamilton Dr 08753
Hamlet Ct 08753
Hampshire Ct & Rd 08757
Hancock Rd 08753
Hanincot Rd 08755
Hannibal St 08757
Harbor Rd 08753
Harbor View Ln 08753
Hardenbrook Ave 08753
Harding Ave 08753
Hare Bell Holw 08755
Harley Rd 08755
Harmony Rd 08757
Harpers Ferry Rd 08753
Harrington Dr N & S 08757
Harrison Rd 08753
Harrow Ct 08757
Harvey Rd 08753
Hatfield Ct & Rd 08757
Havelock Ter 08757
Haverhill Ct 08755
Hawser Pl 08753
Hawthorne Pl 08753
Hazelwood Rd 08753
Hearth Way 08755
Hearthstone Rd 08753
Heather Rd 08753
Heather Narrows 08755
Heatherleaf Ln 08755
Hecht Dr 08755
Hedge St 08753
Helen St 08753
Hemlock St 08757
Hemlock Hill Dr 08753
Herald Ct 08757
Herbert Rd 08753
Hereford Close 08753
Herflicker Blvd 08753
Heritage Way 08753
Hickory St
1A-99A 08757
Hickory Hill Rd 08753
Hidden Brook Ct 08753
Hidden Pond Ln 08755
Hiering Rd 08753
Highland Pkwy 08753
Highmeadow Dr 08753
Hightstown Ln 08753
Hill Rd 08753
Hillgrass Ct 08753
Hillside Dr 08753
Hilltop Rd 08753
Hinds Rd 08753
Hoffman Dr 08753
Holiday Ct 08753
Holly St
2A-12A 08757
Holly Creek Ln 08753
Holly Hill Dr 08753
Holly Tree Ln 08753
Holly Village Ln 08753
Hollyberry Dr 08753
Hollybrook Dr 08753
Hollycrest Dr 08753
Hollywood Ave 08753
Holmes Ave 08753
Homestead Rd 08753
Honey Locust Dr 08755
Honeysuckle Ct 08753
Honeywell Dr 08753
Hooper Ave 08753
Horizon Dr 08755
Hospital Dr 08755
Hovsons Blvd 08753
Huckleberry Ln 08753
Huddy Dr 08755
Hugo Dr 08753
Hummel Dr 08757
Hummingbird Ln 08755
Hundred Oaks Dr 08755
Hunt Dr 08753
Hunters Ct 08755
Huntington Ct 08753
Hyannis St 08757
Hyers St 08753
Iberis Ln 08753
Ilexberry Ln 08753
Impatiens Ct 08753
Imperato Ct 08753
Indian Head Rd
1-199 08753
1256-1256 08755
Indian Hill Rd 08753
Industrial Way S 08755
Innkeeper Ln 08753
Innsbruck Dr 08757
Intermediate North
Way 08753
Inverell Dr 08757
Inverness Dr 08753
Iovino St 08753
Iris Ct 08753
Iron Kettle Rd 08753
Irons St 08753
Iroquois Ct S 08755
Irving Pl 08755
Isaac Ct 08753
Isabella Ct 08753
Island Rd 08753
Ivan Rd 08753
Jacks Way 08755
Jackson Ave 08753
Jacqueline Ct 08753
Jade Ct 08755
Jamaica Ave 08753
Jamaica Blvd 08757
James St 08753
Jamesport Dr 08753
Jane Ct 08755
Janet Rd 08753
Jasam Ct 08755
Jay St 08753
Jay Bird Ln 08755
Jeff Ct 08753
Jefferson Ave 08753
Jerah Ct 08753
Jericho Rd 08757
Jessica Ct 08753
Jill Ct 08753
Joanna Dr 08753
Jobson Ct 08757
Jockey Hollow Dr 08755
Jonquil Ln 08753
Jordan Dr 08755
Joshua Ct 08755
Jouet Ct 08753
Joyce St 08753
Julia Ct 08755
Jumping Brook Dr 08755
June Ct 08753
Juniper Pl 08753
Justice Ct 08755
Kahala Ter 08757
Kaitlyn Ct 08753
Kalvel Ct 08755
Karen Ct 08755
Kathleen Ct 08755
Katni Ct 08753
Keats Ave 08753
Kells Ct 08753
Kelowna Ct 08757
Kendal Dr 08757
Kenilworth Ct 08753
Kensington Cir 08755
Kenton Dr 08753
Kettle Creek Rd 08753
Key West Ct 08753
Kildare Dr 08753
Kilkormic St 08753
Killarney Dr 08753
Killington Rd 08757
Kilrush Ct 08753
Kim Ct & Ln 08755
King St 08753
King George Ln 08753
Kingfisher Ln 08753
Kingsley Ct 08753
Kingston Ave 08753
Kinkora Ct E & W 08757
Kinsale St 08757
Kira Ct 08755
Kirby Ct 08757
Kirkwood Ct 08757
Knight St 08753
Knightsbridge Close 08753
Knollwood Ct 08753
Kresson Ct 08757
Kris Ct 08755
Kwansan Ct 08755
La Casta Ct 08757
La Combe Ter 08757
La Dunette Dr 08757
La Terraza Dr 08757
La Tourette Ct 08757
Lacebark Ct & Rd 08755
Lafayette Ave 08753
Lafite Ct 08753
Lagoon Dr E & W 08753
Lagos Ct 08757
Lake Dr 08757
W Lake Dr 08753
Lake Placid Dr 08753
Lake Ridge Blvd 08755
Lake Spring Ct 08755
Lakehurst Rd 08755
Lakeview Ct 08753
Lakeview Dr 08757
Lambert Way 08757
Lamdan Ln 08753
Lamplighter Dr 08753
Lancaster Ln 08755
Lancer Ct 08753
Landers St 08753
Lands End Dr 08755
Langley Ct & Rd 08757
Larboard St 08753
Larch Ct & Dr 08753
Larchmont St 08757
Lark Rd 08753
Larkspur Ct 08755
Larue Ln 08753
Las Croabas Ln 08757
Latache Ct 08753
Laurel Ave & Dr 08753
Lauren Ln 08755
Lavenham Ct 08755
Lawn St 08753
Lawrence Ave & Pl 08757
Le Diamant St 08757
Le Lamentin Dr 08757
Leadership Ct 08755
Leaf Ln 08753
League Rd 08753
Leahy St 08753
Leawood Ave 08755
Lee Ter 08753
Leeward St 08757
Legion Ct 08753
Leighton Ct 08757
Lena Ave 08755
Lenape Trl 08753
Lenox St 08755
Leonard Dr 08755
Leone Rd 08755
Lester Rd 08753
Lewis Ave 08753
Lewison Dr 08753
Lexington Ave 08753
Liberta Dr 08757
Liberty Bell Rd 08755
Lien St 08753
Lighthouse Ln 08753
Lilac Dr 08753
Lillian Ln 08755
Lillie Rd 08753
Lincoln Ave 08753
Linda Dr 08753
Linden Rd 08753
Lindsay Ln 08755
Linstead Ct 08757
Lisa Ct 08753
E Lisbon Ave 08753
Lismore Dr 08757
Little Pine Ct 08755
Littleton Rd 08757
Liverpool Ct 08753
Lloyd Rd 08753
Lockhart St 08757
Logan Ct 08755
Loganberry Ln 08753
London Ct 08753
Long Dr 08757
Long Point Dr 08753
Longdenville St 08757
Longest Dr 08755
Longewood Ln 08755
Longfellow Ave 08753
Longman St 08753
Longview Dr 08753
Lonny Ct 08753
Lookout Dr 08753
Louise St 08753
Lowell Ave 08753
Lower Circle Dr 08753
Loxley Dr 08753
Luane Rd W 08755
Lucaya Ct 08753
Lucy Ln 08753
Lumsden Ct & St 08757
Lyford Ct 08757
Lynn Dr 08753
Lynne Ln W 08755
Lynwood Pl 08753
Macarthur Rd 08753
Mackenzie Rd 08755
Madera Ct 08757
Madison Ave
1-599 08753
600-1899 08757
3100-3199 08753
Madras Ct 08757
Magnolia Ave 08757
Magnolia Ln 08753
Magnolia St 08757
Mahlon Ct 08753
Maiden Ln 08753
Maidstone Ct 08757
Maimone St 08753
Main St 08753
S Main St 08757
Main Bayway 08753
Maine St 08753
Maison Way 08757
Majorca Ct 08753
Malcolm St 08753
Malta Ct 08753
Manassas Dr 08757

Manchester Ave	08755
Manchester St	08757
Manitoba Ct	08757
Maniwaki Ct & Dr	08757
Manor Rd	08753
Mantle Way	08755
Maple Ave	08753
N Maple Ave	08755
Maple St	
2A-6A	08757
2B-6B	08757
2C-6C	08757
2D-6D	08757
1-3	08753
5-5	08753
7-7	08757
11-11	08753
13-199	08753
Maple Manor Ct	08755
S Maplecrest Ct & Rd	08753
Mapleton Rd	08757
Mapletree Rd	08753
Maplewood St	08757
Maracaibo Pl	08757
Marathon St	08757
Marbil Ave	08753
Marc Dr	08753
Marco Island Dr	08753
Margaret Ct	08753
Margarita St	08757
Maria Dr	08753
Marian St	08753
Marie St	08753
Marigold Ct	08753
Marigot Ct	08757
Marisa Dr	08755
Maritime Dr	08753
Marjorie Dr	08755
Marlane Rd	08753
Marom Dr	08753
Marquis St	08757
Marshall Rd	08753
Martin Rd	08753
Martinique Dr	08757
Mary Ln	08753
Maryann Pl	08753
Masada Ct	08753
Massachusetts Ave	08755
Matso Dr	08753
Mayaguana St	08757
Mayaquez Ln	08757
Mayo Dr	08753
Maypink Dr	08753
Mccormick Dr	08753
Mcguire Dr	08753
Mckinley Ave	08753
Mclean Ct	08755
Mcpherson St	08755
Meadow St	08753
Meadow Lake Dr	08753
Meadowbrook Ct	08753
Meadowlands Ct	08755
Medallion Ln	08753
Medjay Ln	08755
S Mehar Ct	08753
Mello Ln	08753
Melrose Dr	08753
Menlow Ct	08755
Mercedes Bnd	08755
Mercer Dr	08753
Meredith Dr	08753
Mermaid Rd	08753
Merrilee Ln	08757
Merrimac Dr	08753
Messenger Ct & St	08753
Mica Ct	08753
Michael Dr	08753
Michele Dr	08755
Michigan Ave & Ct	08753
Middle Dr	08753
Middlesex St	08757
Midship Dr	08753
Midway Ave	08757
Midwood Dr	08753
Miles Pond Rd	08757
Mill St	08757
Millbrook Ct & Dr	08757
Millen Dr	08753
Millennium Ct	08753
Millstone Ct	08753
Mimosa Ct	08753
Mink Ct	08755
Minnesota Ave	08753
Minturn Rd	08753
Mirador Ct	08757
Miramar Ct	08757
Mississippi St	08755
Mistletoe Ct	08753
Mitchell Dr	08755
Mizzen Rd	08753
Mobile Ln	08755
Mocorito Way	08757
Mohawk Dr	08753
Molde Ct	08753
Monaco Ct	08757
Monitor Dr	08753
Monmouth Ave & Pl	08757
Monroe Ave	08755
Montana Dr	08753
Monte Carlo Dr	08753
Montego St	08757
Montgomery Ave	08757
Montgomery Rd	08753
Monticello Ct	08755
Montreal Ct	08757
Montserrat St	08757
Monty Rd	08753
Moonlight Ct	08753
Moore Rd	08753
Morgan Rd	08755
Morning Glory Ct	08755
Morningdale Blvd	08755
Morningside Dr	08755
Morningside St	08757
Morongo Ct	08757
Morrell Dr	08753
Morris Blvd	08753
Morristown Dr	08753
Mott Pl	08753
Mount Ln	08753
Mount Ararat Ln	08753
Mount Blanc Ln	08753
Mount Carmel Blvd	08753
Mount Dashan Ln	08753
Mount Everest Ln	08753
Mount Fairweather Ln	08753
Mount Gannet Ln	08753
Mount Hood Ln	08753
Mount Hope Ln	08753
Mount Idenburg Ln	08753
Mount Juliano Ln	08753
Mount Katadin Dr	08753
Mount Kilimanjaro Ln	08753
Mount Kisco Dr	08753
Mount Logan Ln	08753
Mount Matterhorn Ln	08753
Mount Nebo Ln	08753
Mount Rainier Dr	08753
Mount Rushmore Dr	08753
Mount Vernon Dr	08755
Mountainview Dr	08753
Muirhead St	08757
Mulberry Pl	08753
Mule Rd	
1-99	08755
600-630	08757
Musket Pl	08753
Muskflower Ct	08753
Myron Ct	08755
Myrtle Ln	08755
Mystic Port Pl	08753
Nakiska Ct	08755
Nanlyn Ter	08753
Nantucket Ct	08753
Napoli Ct	08757
Narberth Way	08757
Nassau Dr	08753
Nature Way	08755
Nautilus Dr	08753
Navajo Ct	08753
Neal St	08753
Nebraska Ave	08753
Nelson Ct	08757
Neptune Rd	08753
Nevada Dr	08753
Neville St	08753
Nevis Ct	08757
New St	08753
New Castle Ct	08753
New Hampshire Ave	08755
New Jersey Ave	08753
Newbury Ct	08757
Newcastle Ct	08757
Newington Ln	08755
Newman Dr	08753
Newport Pl	08753
Niagara Dr	08753
Niles Ct	08755
Nimitz St	08753
Nobility Ct	08755
Nocturn Ct & Way	08755
Noranda St	08757
Norfolk Ct & Dr	08757
Norma Pl	08755
Normanton Ct & Way	08757
North St	08753
Northampton Blvd	
1-99	08755
100-2299	08757
Northstream Dr	08755
Northumberland Dr	08757
Norway Rd	08757
Norwich Dr	08757
Norwood Dr	08755
Nostrand Dr	08757
Nottaway Ln	08755
Nottingham Ct	08753
Notts Ct	08757
Novins Dr	08753
Oak Ave	08753
Oak Crest Dr	08753
Oak Dale Rd	08753
Oak Dale St	08757
Oak Glen Rd	08753
Oak Hill Dr	08753
Oak Knoll Dr	08757
Oak Leaf Ln	08755
Oak Ridge Pkwy	08755
Oak Tree Ln	08753
Oakengates Dr	08757
Oakfield Rd	08757
Oakham Ct	08757
Oakmont Dr	08753
Oakside Dr	08755
Oakview Dr	08753
Oakwood Ave	08753
Oakwood Hollow Ln	08755
Ocean View Dr	08753
Oceanic Dr	08753
Odyssey Way	08753
Old St	08753
Old Church Rd	08753
Old Freehold Rd	
901-997	08753
999-1499	08753
1500-1899	08755
Old Orchard Rd	08755
Oliver St	08755
Olstins Ct	08757
Olympic St	08757
Onyx Dr	08753
Opal Ter	08753
Opatut Ct	08753
Oranjestad St	08757
Orchard St	08753
Orchid Ct	08753
Orien Rd	08755
Oriole Ct	08755
Orlando Blvd	08757
Osage Ln	08755
Osborne Ter	08753
Oslo Ct	08757
Osprey Dr	08753
Otley Ct	08757
Ottawa Ct	08753
Otter Dr	08755
Overlook Dr	08753
Owen Ct	08755
Oxford Dr	08757
Oxford St	08755
Paavo Ct	08755
Paddock Pl	08755
Page Ct	08753
Pala St	08757
Palermo Ct	08757
Palisades Dr	08753
Palm Springs Ct	08753
Palmer Ave	08755
Palmerson Ct	08753
Palmetto Dr	08753
Palmetto Point St	08757
Pamela Ct	08755
Panama Ct	08757
Paradise Blvd	08757
Parisian Ct	08757
Parisian Dr	08753
Park St	08753
Park Crest Rd	08753
Parkside Ave	08753
Parkview Blvd	08757
Parkview Ln	08753
Parkway Blvd	08757
Parkway Dr	08753
Parkwood Ave	08753
Partridge St	08753
Patmas Dr	08755
Patrician Dr	08753
Patton Rd	08753
Paul Dr	08753
Pavilion St	08757
Peaceful Way	08755
Peacock Pl	08755
Pearl Dr	08753
Pebble Beach Ct	08757
Pechanga St	08757
Peddie St	08753
Pegasus Ct	08755
Pemberton St	08757
Pembroke Ln	08757
Penbrook Ct	08755
Pennington Ct	08753
Pepperbush Ct	08755
Peppertree Dr	08755
Percy Ave	08753
Periwinkle Ln	08753
Peter Ave	08753
Petunia Way S	08755
Pheasant Ln	08753
Pheasant Hollow Ln	08755
Phoebe St	08753
Picasso Ct	08757
Piccadilly Ct	08757
Piermont Rd	08757
Pierson Rd	08753
Pigalle St	08757
Pilot Rd	08753
Pin Oak Ct	08753
Pine St	
1A-1D	08757
Pine Acres Mnr	08757
Pine Bluff Rd	08753
Pine Brook Dr	08753
Pine Crest Dr	08753
Pine Fork Dr	08755
Pine Grove Ave	08753
Pine Hill Rd	08755
Pine Meadow Ave	08753
Pine Needle Dr	08753
Pine Shore Rd	08753
Pine Tree Rd	08753
Pine Valley Dr	08757
Pineview Dr	08755
Pinewood Rd	08753
Pinta Ct	08757
Pioneer Dr	08753
Pirogue St	08757
Plante Ave	08755
Plaza Dr	08757
Pleasant Ct	08753
Plymouth Ct & Dr	08757
Pocono Pl	08753
Poe Ave	08753
S Point Ct	08757
Point Rd	08753
Point Blanche Ct	08757
Point O Woods Dr	08753
Polhemus Rd	08753
Pollys Dr	08753
Pollys Park Dr	08753
Polonaise Dr	08757
Pontiac Ct	08753
Ponybrook Way	08755
Poplar Pl	08753
Porlamar Ct	08757
Porpoise Ct	08753
Port Au Prince St	08753
Port Royal Dr	08757
Portobello Rd	08753
Portsmouth Dr	08757
Powder Horn Rd	08755
Prado Ct	08757
Precious Ct	08755
Presidential Blvd	08753
Preston Ct	08757
Primrose Ct	08755
Prince St	08753
Prince Charles Ct & Dr	08757
Princess Ct	08753
Princeton Ct	08753
Priscilla Ct	08753
Prosperity Ct	08755
Providence Ct	08755
Pueblo Ct	08755
Puerto Vallarta St	08757
Pulaski Blvd	08757
Pumpshire Rd	08753
Purnell St	08757
Quail Rd	08753
Quartz Dr	08753
Queen Anne Ln	08753
Quiet Way	08755
Quimby Ct	08755
Quince Pl	08755
Quiver Ct	08753
Raccoon Dr	08755
Raider Way	08753
Rail Pl	08755
Rainbow Way	08755
Raleigh Dr	08753
Ramona Dr	08757
Ramsey Ct	08753
Ranch Rd	08753
Randalls Dr	08757
Randolph St	08753
Raven Ct	08753
Ravenna Ct	08757
Ravenwood Dr	08757
Ray Dr	08753
Raymond Ave	08755
Red Cedar St	08753
Red Maple Ct	08757
Red Oak Ct	08753
Redhook Bay Dr	08757
Redlands Ct	08757
Redwood Dr	08753
Reed Dr	08753
Reflection Rd	08753
Regal Ct	08753
Regency Ct	08753
Regina Ct	08755
Reney Ct & St	08753
Reno Ct	08753
Revere Ct	08753
Reynolds Ave	08755
Rickard Ct	08753
Rico Ave	08753
Ridge Dr	08753
W Ridge Rd	08755
Ridge Hill Dr	08755
Ridgemont Ct	08755
Ridgeview Ct	08753
Ridgeway Rd	
1500-1599	08755
1600-2399	08757
Ridgewood Dr	08755
Rio Ct	08757
Rio Grande Dr	08755
Riparian Way	08753
Ripley Ct	08757
River Dr	08753
River St	08757
River Ter	08755
River Bend Dr	08753
Riverbrook Ct	08753
Rivercrest Dr	08753
Rivers Edge Ln	08755
Rivers Glen Ter	08755
Riverside Ave	08757
Riverside Dr	08753
Riverton Rd	08757
Riverwood Ct	08757
Riverwood Dr	08755
Riviera Ave & Dr	08753
Roanoke Dr	08753
Robbins Pkwy & St	08753
Roberts Ave	08753
Roberts Rd	08753
Robin Ln	08755
Roca Sola St	08757
Rock Hill Ln	08755
Rockport Ln	08755
Rodhos St	08757
E Rolling Hills Ct	08755
Rolling Ridge Ln	08755
Rolls Ct	08755
Roman St	08757
Romana Ln	08755
Romford Ct	08757
Ronda Rd	08755
Roosevelt Ave	08753
Rose Ct	08753
Roseau Ct	08757
Roseville Ct	08755
Rosewood Dr	08753
Ross St	08753
Roundtree Dr	08753
Route 166	08753
Route 37 E	08753
Route 37 W	
1-9	08753
Route 37 W	
11-33	08753
39-97	08755
99-1601	08755
1603-1699	08755
1700-1999	08757
Route 70	08755
Route 9	08755
Roxbury Ln	08753
Roxton Pl	08757
Royal Ln	08753
Royal Oaks Dr	08753
Royal Sire Ct	08755
Ruby Dr	08753
Rue Ln	08753
Rugby Ct	08757
Runyon Dr	08755
Russell St	08753
Russo Pl	08753
Rutland Dr	08757
Ryan Run	08753
Sabinas St	08757
Sachs Ave	08755
Saddle Back Ln	08755
Sage Rd	08753
Sahara Ct	08753
Saint Andrews Ct	08757
Saint Catherine Blvd	
1-9	08757
100-199	08755
Saint Christopher Ct	08755
Saint Clande Way	08757
Saint Croix St	08757
Saint David Dr	08757
Saint Eustatius St	08757
Saint Francois Ct	08757
Saint George St	08757
Saint John Ave	08753
Saint Kitts Dr	08757
Saint Lucia Ct	08757
Saint Martin Pl	08757
Saint Moritz Pl	08753
Saint Nicholas Ct	08757
Saint Pierri Ct	08757
Saint Thomas Ave	08753
Saint Thomas Dr	08757
Saint Tropez Ct	08757
Saint Vincent Ct	08757
Salem Dr	08753
Salerno Ct	08757
Salisbury Ct	08757
Samantha Way	08753
San Carlos Ct & St	08757
San Jacinto St	08757
San Juan Ct	08757
San Juan Dr	08753
San Salvador St	08757
Sand Creek Ln	08753
Sandhurst Ct	08757
Sands Point Dr	08755
Sandy Ln & Pl	08753
Sanish Ct	08755
Santa Anita Ln	08755
Santa Fe Ct	08757
Santiago Ct & Dr	08757
Santo Domingo Dr	08757
Sapling Ct	08753
Saratoga Pl	08753
Satinwood Ln	08755
Sauvignon Dr	08753
Savannah Cir	08753
Savannah Rd	08757
Savannah St	08753
Sawmill Ct	08755
Scarborough Pl	08757
Scarlet Ct	08753
Scarlet Oak Ave	08755
Schencks Mill Line Rd	08753
Schley Ave	08755
Schoeberlein Ave	08753
Scholar Pl	08755
Schoolhouse Ln	08753
Schooner Dr	08753
Scrimshaw Ct	08753
Sea Breeze Rd	08753
Sea Island Dr	08753
Seabury Ct	08753
Seafoam Ct	08753
Seaman Ct	08753
Seaton Rd	08755
Secretariat Pl	08755
Selena Pl	08753
Selkirk Ave	08757
Seminole St	08757
Senaroth Ct	08757
Sequoia Cir	08753
Serene Way	08755
Serenity Pl	08755
Serrata Way	08755
Seville Pl	08757
Seward Ave	08753
Shadow Brook Dr	08753
Shadow Oaks Dr	08753
Shady Ln	08753
Shady Nook Dr	08755
Shannon Ct	08757
Sharon Dr	08753
Shasta Ln	08753
Shaw Ct	08757
Shawnee Dr	08753
Sheepshead Dr	08757
Sheffield Dr	08757
Sheila Dr	08753
Shelly St	08755
Shelton Ct	08755
Shenandoah Blvd	08753
Shepherd Ct	08755
Sheridan Ave	08753
Sheridan Rd	08757
Sherwood Ct	08757
Sherwood Ln	
1-99	08757
100-199	08753
Sherwood Forest Dr	08755
Shining Way	08753
Ship Ct	08753
S Shore Blvd & Dr	08753
Shoshone Ct	08753
Sica Ln	08753
Sierra Dr	08753
Signal Ln	08755

Silver Bay Rd 08753
Silver Creek Ln 08753
Silver Hill Ln 08755
Silver Lagoon Dr 08753
Silver Ridge Dr 08755
Silverton Rd
1000-1599 08755
1601-1697 08753
1699-1999 08753
Silverwood Ct 08753
Simmons Dr 08753
Simot Ln 08753
Skiff Ct 08753
Sky Harbor Ct 08757
Skylark Dr 08755
Sleepy Hollow Rd 08753
Sloop Ct 08753
Smith Rd 08755
Smokerise Ln 08755
Snowberry Ct 08755
Snowdon Ct 08757
Snug Ct 08753
Snyder St 08753
Somerset Dr 08753
Sonoma Ct 08753
Sophia Ct 08757
Sorrento Ct 08757
South St 08753
Southampton Blvd & Rd 08757
Spanish Wells St 08757
Speighstown Pl 08757
Spinnakers Cv 08753
Spirit Bear Rd 08755
Spring St 08753
Spring Hill Dr 08755
Springer Ln 08755
Springfield Dr 08753
Springwater Ct 08755
Spruce St 08753
Spruce Hill Dr 08753
Sprucewood Dr 08755
Squire Ct 08753
St Joseph Pl 08753
St Maximilian Ln 08757
Stacy Ct 08755
Stafford Dr 08753
Stamler Dr 08753
Standish Rd 08753
Stanford Ct & Dr 08757
Stanley Dr 08753
Stanley Ln 08755
Starboard Ct 08753
Starc Rd 08755
Starling Pl 08755
Steeplechase Ct 08755
Stephan Ave 08753
Stepping Stone Ct 08753
Sterling St 08753
Stevens Rd 08755
Stockport Dr 08757
Stockton Dr 08755
Stonehedge Dr 08753
Stowe St 08753
Stratford Ct 08753
Strawberry Ln 08753
Strichi St 08757
Stroud Ct 08757
Stuart Ave 08755
Suburban Dr 08753
Sudsbury Rd 08757
Sugarbush Ct 08755
Summit Ave & Pl 08753
Sumner Ave 08755
Sun Ray Dr 08753
Sun Valley Rd 08755
Sunflower Ln 08755
Sunrise Blvd, Ct & Way 08753
Sunset Ave 08755
Superior Ct 08755
Surrey Ct 08757
Susan St 08753
Susanna Ct 08753
Susquehanna St 08755
Sussex Ct 08753
Sutherland Ct 08757
Sutter St 08753
Sutton Pl 08755
Swain Ave 08755
Swan Blvd 08753
Sweet Williams Ct 08755
Sweetbay Dr 08755
Swindon Ct 08757
Sycamore Ct & Ln 08753
Sylvan Dr 08753
Sylvia Ct 08755
Tahoe Ct 08757
Taj Mahal Ct 08757
Tall Oak Ln 08755
Tall Ships Ct 08755
Tampa Ln 08757
Tanager Dr 08755
Tanglewood Rd 08753
S Tapestry Ct 08755
Tapola Rd 08757
Tara Ct 08755
Tarworth Ct 08757
Tavernier St 08757
Taylor Rd 08753
Teaberry Ct 08753
Teakwood Rd 08753
Templeton St 08757
Tennyson Ave 08753
Terrace Ave 08753
Terry Ln 08755
Texas Dr 08753
Thames Way 08755
Thatcher Ln 08753
Theresa Ct 08753
Thicket Ct 08755
E Thistle Ave 08753
Thomas St 08753
Thornton Rd 08757
Thronbury Ct 08757
Ticonderoga Dr 08755
Tiffany Walk 08753
S Tiiu Ct 08755
Tijuana Ct 08757
Tilbury Ct 08757
Tiller Dr 08753
Tilton Ave 08757
Tilton St 08753
Timberline Rd 08753
Tina Ct 08753
Tinsmith Ct 08753
Titan Dr 08753
Tivoli St 08757
Tobago Ave 08753
Toby Ct 08755
W Todd Rd 08755
Togo Rd 08757
Tolerance Ct 08755
Tolly Ct 08757
Tomera Pl 08755
Tonbridge Ct 08757
Topaz Dr 08753
Torremolinos Ct 08753
Torrey Pines Dr 08757
Torrington Dr 08755
Tortola St 08757
Toshi Ct 08753
Tova Ct 08753
Tradewinds Ave & Ct 08753
Tralee Dr 08753
Transom Ct 08753
Trent Dr 08757
Trinity Pl 08753
Troja St 08753
Tropicana Ct 08757
Trotters Way 08755
Troumaka St 08757
Tudor Ct & Dr 08753
Tulip Pl 08755
N Tunesbrook Dr 08753
Tunney Point Dr 08753
Turnberry Cir 08753
Tuyahov Blvd 08755
Twilight Ct 08753
Twin Oaks Dr 08753
Twin Rivers Dr 08753
Tyler Dr 08753
Union St 08753
Upton Ct 08757
Utah Dr 08753
Vail St 08757
Valencia St 08757
Valley Ln 08753
Valley Stream Rd 08753
Van Gogh St 08757
Vanada Dr 08753
Vans Way 08755
Vaughn Ave 08753
Vauxhall Rd 08753
Veeder Ave 08753
Venetian Ct 08753
Venezia St 08757
Venus Ln 08753
Vera Cruz Ct 08757
Verdant Rd 08753
Vermont Ave 08755
Vernon St 08755
Vicari Ave 08755
Victor Ave 08753
Victoria Rd 08753
Vienna Dr 08757
Villa Bella Ct 08757
Village Rd 08755
Village Green Ct 08755
Vincent St 08753
Vincenzo Dr 08753
Vine Ave 08753
Violet Ct 08753
Virgin Islands Dr 08757
Viscount Dr 08753
Vision Ave 08753
Vivian Dr 08753
Wainwright Rd 08753
Wakan Ct 08757
Wake Forest Dr 08753
Walchest Dr 08753
Walden Woods Dr 08755
Waldron Rd 08753
Waldwick Ct 08757
Wales Ln 08753
Walesa Ct 08757
Wall Cress Ct 08755
Wallach Dr 08755
Walnut St
2A-16A 08757
Walnut Creek Ln 08753
Walton St 08753
Ward Ave 08755
Warner Ct, St & Way 08755
Warren St 08753
Warren Point Rd 08753
Washington St 08753
E Water St 08753
W Water St
1-99 08753
101-399 08753
130-130 08754
200-598 08753
Waterberry Ct 08755
Waterberry Ct N 08757
Waterberry Ct S 08757
Waterline Rd 08755
Waters Edge Dr 08753
Wave Way 08753
Wave Crest Ct 08753
Webster Rd 08755
Wedgeport Dr 08757
Wedgewood Dr 08753
Weeping Willow Ct 08753
Wellington Ave & Pl 08757
Wendy Ln 08753
West Dr 08753
Westbrook Dr 08757
Westfield Dr 08753
Westgate Ct 08757
Westminster Dr 08753
Weston Dr 08755
Westport Dr 08757
Westwood Dr 08753
Weybridge Ct 08757
Whilshire Ln 08753
Whitaker Dr 08757
White Cedar Dr 08753
White Knoll Dr 08755
White Oak Ct 08753
White Oak Bottom Rd 08755
White Spruce Dr 08753
White Water Ct 08755
Whitesville Rd
2-20 08753
1200-2599 08755
Whitetail Ln 08753
Whitmore Ct & Dr 08757
Whittier Ave 08753
Whitty Rd 08753
W Whitty Rd 08755
Whitty Pine Ct 08753
Wicklow Ct 08755
Wiley Way 08757
Wilkins Rd 08753
Wilkinson Dr 08755
Willemstad St 08757
William Ter 08753
Williamsburg Ct & Dr 08755
Willoughby Ct 08757
Willow Rd 08753
Willow St 08757
Wills Ct 08753
Wilson Ave 08753
Wiltshire Ct 08757
Winchester Dr 08753
Windham Ct 08755
Winding River Dr 08755
Windjammer Ct 08753
Windsor Ave & Ct 08753
Windward Ct 08753
Wingate Ct 08755
Winston Ct 08755
Winterton Dr 08757
Wisteria Ct 08755
Witham Ct 08757
Wojtyla Ct 08757
Wood St 08753
Wood Spring Ln 08755
Woodberry Dr 08753
Woodbine Ln 08755
Woodbury Ct 08757
Woodchuck Ln 08755
Woodcrest Dr 08753
Woodfern Ct 08755
Woodhaven Rd 08753
E & W Woodland Ave & Dr 08753
Woodlark Rd 08755
Woodleigh Pl 08755
Woodridge Ave 08755
Woodside Pl 08753
Woodstock Dr 08757
Woodview Ct & Rd 08755
Worth St 08757
Wrangle Brook Rd 08755
Wren Pl 08755
Wright Ave 08753
Wycombe Ct 08757
Wyeth Way 08755
Wyoming Dr 08753
Yellowbank Rd 08753
Yellowstone Dr 08753
York Ct
1-99 08757
1000-1099 08753
York St 08757
Yorkshire Dr 08753
Yorktowne Blvd 08753
Yucatan Way 08757
Yucca Ct 08755
Yvonne Dr 08753
Zapata Ct 08757
Zeeland Dr 08757
Zilg Dr 08753
Zircon Dr 08753

NUMBERED STREETS

1st Ave 08757
1st Ave
2200-2499 08753
1st St 08757
1st Bayway 08753
2nd Ave 08757
2nd Ave
2200-2899 08753
2nd Bayway 08753
3rd Ave 08757
3rd Ave
2200-2202 08753
2216-2216 08757
2219-2499 08753
2232-2232 08757
2300-2498 08753
3rd St 08757
3rd Bayway 08753
4th Ave 08757
2200-2999 08753
4th St 08757
4th Bayway 08753
5th Ave 08757
5th Ave
2200-2499 08753
5th St 08757
5th Bayway 08753
6th Ave 08757
2200-2999 08753
6th Bayway 08753
7th Ave 08757
2400-2499 08753
7th St 08757
7th Bayway 08753
8th Ave & St 08757
8th Bayway 08753
9th Ave 08757
9th Bayway 08753
10th Ave 08757
10th St
1-99 08753
18-18 08757
50-98 08753
10th Bayway 08753
11th Ave 08757
11th St
2-16 08757
27-27 08757
51-51 08753
53-73 08753
72-72 08757
74-90 08753
75-99 08753
11th Bayway 08753
12th Ave 08757
12th St 08753
13th St 08753
14th St 08753
15th St 08753
16th St 08753
17th St 08753

TOTOWA NJ

POST OFFICE BOXES MAIN OFFICE STATIONS AND BRANCHES

Box No.s
All PO Boxes 07511

NAMED STREETS

TRENTON NJ

General Delivery 08650

POST OFFICE BOXES MAIN OFFICE STATIONS AND BRANCHES

Box No.s
C - C 08690
A - A 08691
1 - 180 08601
1 - 134 08625
34 - 105 08691
128 - 128 08628
143 - 152 08691
150 - 150 08650
157 - 256 08625
191 - 328 08602
228 - 228 08628
247 - 247 08691
290 - 549 08625
317 - 518 08603
328 - 328 08628
360 - 360 08602
428 - 428 08628
485 - 487 08691
516 - 759 08604
528 - 528 08628
600 - 671 08625
628 - 628 08628
650 - 650 08650
700 - 729 08625
728 - 728 08628
750 - 750 08650
750 - 867 08625
752 - 970 08605
828 - 828 08628
905 - 991 08625
928 - 928 08628
971 - 1210 08606
1028 - 1128 08628
1205 - 2494 08607
1228 - 1428 08628
1450 - 1450 08650
1528 - 2228 08628
2501 - 2699 08690
2701 - 2811 08607
2800 - 2999 08690
2851 - 2852 08607
3001 - 3499 08619
3501 - 3999 08629
4001 - 4596 08610
4394 - 4394 08650
4501 - 4575 08611
4614 - 4999 08650
5000 - 5990 08638
5850 - 6650 08650
7001 - 7478 08628
7050 - 7050 08650
7500 - 7992 08628
7950 - 10650 08650
11036 - 11336 08620
11350 - 11350 08650
11362 - 11441 08620
12000 - 12149 08650
16001 - 16176 08641
17201 - 17205 08690
18550 - 18550 08650
22001 - 23903 08607
33000 - 33320 08629
34500 - 34770 08619
50002 - 57001 08638
77001 - 77430 08628
444601 - 444718 08610

RURAL ROUTES

03 08691

NAMED STREETS

Aaa Dr 08691
Abbey Pl 08610
Abbington Ln 08691
Abbott Rd 08690
Abbott Farm Ct 08610
Abby Ct 08691
Aberfeldy Dr 08618
Aberfoyle Dr 08690
Abernethy Dr 08618
Acacia Ave 08691
Academy St
100-199 08608
200-399 08618
Acres Dr 08690
E Acres Dr 08620
Adam Ave 08618
Adams Ct 08690
Adeline St
1-799 08611
800-898 08610
900-1299 08610
Adella Ave 08609
Adirondack Blvd 08619
Afton Ave 08618
Agabiti Ct 08610
Agress Ct 08619
Aidan Ct 08691
Albemarle Rd 08690
Albert E Bonacci Dr 08690
Alberta Ave 08619
Alden Ave 08618
Alessio Ter 08620
Alexander Ave 08619
Alfred Ave 08610
Allen St
1-99 08620
101-105 08620
123-197 08618
199-266 08618
268-298 08618
Allinson Dr 08691
Alpha Rd 08610
Althea Ave 08620
Alton Rd 08619
Amalfi Ct 08691
Amber Dr 08691
Amberfield Rd 08691
American Metro Blvd 08619
Amesbury Ct 08691
Amherst Ave 08619
Ammo Rd 08641
Amsterdam Rd 08620
Amy Ct 08691
Anastasia Ct 08690
Anderson Ln 08691
Anderson St 08611
N Anderson St 08609
Andover Pl 08691
Andover Way 08610
Andrea Ln 08619
Andree Pl 08619
Andrew St 08610
Andrews Ct & Ln 08641
Ang Rd 08641
Angelique Ct 08619
Anita Way 08610
Ann Marie Dr 08610
Annabelle Ave 08610
Annie Ln 08691
Apollo Dr 08620
Apone Ct 08641
Applegate Dr
1-99 08691
100-299 08690
Appleton Dr 08610
Aqua Ter 08620
Arbor Ave 08619
Arbor Ct 08620
Archer Ct 08619
Ardmore Ave 08629
Arena Dr 08610
Argonne Ave 08620
Argyle Dr 08618
Arlington Ave
1-200 08620
2-32 08618
34-42 08618
44-98 08618
202-298 08620
Armour Ave 08619
E Arnold Ave 08641
W Arnold Ave 08641
Arnold Ln 08691
Arrowwood Dr 08690
Artisan St 08618
Asbury Pl & St 08611
Ashelari St 08611
Ashford Ct 08691
Ashford Dr 08610

Ashmore Ave 08611
Ashwood Rd 08610
Aspen Ct 08619
Assunpink Blvd 08619
Aster Rd 08690
Atkins Ave 08610
Atlantic Ave
100-299 08609
300-899 08629
Atrium Dr 08620
Atterbury Ave 08618
Audrey Pl 08619
Austin Ave 08629
Axford Ct & Rd 08610
Azalea Way 08690
Back Creek Rd 08691
Baggaley Rd 08690
Bainbridge Ct 08690
Baltusrol St 08690
Banbury Ct 08691
Banbury Rd 08690
Bank St 08618
Barbados Ct 08691
Barbara Dr 08619
Barbara St 08618
Barbara Lee Dr 08619
Barnes St 08618
Barnt Ave 08611
Barnt Deklyn Rd 08610
Barrack St 08608
Barricklo St 08610
Barry Way 08619
Barto Way 08691
Basin Rd 08619
Bayard St 08611
W Baylor Cir, Ct, Dr & Rd 08610
Beacon Ct & Pl 08691
Beal St 08610
Bear Ct 08620
Bear Branch Rd 08610
Bear Meade Dr 08691
Beatrice Ct 08690
Beatty St 08611
Beaumont Rd 08620
Beech Ave 08610
Beech St 08691
Beechwood Ave 08618
Beechwood Dr 08691
Belfast Ct 08610
Bell Ave 08619
Bellevue Ave 08618
Belmont Cir 08618
Belmont Dr 08691
Belvidere St 08618
Benson Ave & Ln 08610
Bentley Ave 08619
Benton Rd 08610
Benton St 08609
Berg Ave 08610
Bergen St 08610
Berkeley Ave 08618
Berkley St 08619
Bernadine Ave 08610
Bernard St 08618
Bernath Dr W 08690
Berrel Ave 08619
Berrywood Dr 08619
Bert Ave 08629
Bethany Ct 08610
Bethel Ave 08620
Betsy Ct 08620
Beverly Ct 08691
Beverly Pl 08619
Bigelow Rd 08610
Billington Rd 08690
Birch St 08610
Birkshire Rd 08619
Birtin Ave 08619
Bismarck Ave 08629
Bismark Ave 08610
Black Forest Rd 08691
Black Pine Dr 08610
Blackbird Dr 08619
Blairmore Dr 08690
Blarli Ave 08629

Bldg 1801 08641
Bldg 2202 08641
Bldg 2216 08641
Bldg 2424 08641
Bldg 2620 08641
Bldg 2623 08641
Bldg 2841 08641
Bldg 3209 08641
Bldg 3452 08641
Bldg 5353 08641
Bloomfield Ave 08618
Blue Bell Ln 08691
Blue Devil Ln 08619
Blyman Ct 08690
Boatwright Ct 08641
Boeing Ave 08628
N & S Bolling Blvd & Ct 08641
Bolton Rd 08610
Bon Air Pl 08620
Bond St 08618
Bonnie Ave 08629
Bonnie Rae Dr 08620
Borden Ave 08610
Borden Way 08608
Boudinot St 08618
Bow Rd E 08690
Bow Hill Ave 08610
Boxwood Ave 08619
Bozarth Ct 08690
Bradford Ave 08610
Bradley Ct 08620
Brafman Dr 08610
Brampton Way 08690
Brandywine Way 08690
Branford Dr 08691
Braver Dr 08610
Brecht Rd 08690
Bree Dr 08690
Bresnahan Rd 08691
Breunig Ave 08638
Brian Dr 08619
Brianna Ct 08619
Bridge St 08611
Brighten Dr 08619
Briner Ln 08690
Brinton Ave 08618
Britton Ln 08691
N Broad St
1-299 08608
300-398 08618
S Broad St
3347A-3347D 08610
3355A-3355D 08610
3363A-3363D 08610
3371A-3371D 08610
3379A-3379D 08610
3387A-3387D 08610
3391A-3391D 08610
3399A-3399D 08610
3407A-3407D 08610
3415A-3415D 08610
3423A-3423D 08610
3431A-3431D 08610
3439A-3439D 08610
3447A-3447D 08610
3451A-3451D 08610
3459A-3459D 08610
3467A-3467D 08610
1-399 08608
400-1199 08611
1200-3700 08610
3702-3798 08610
3800-5999 08620
Brockton Rd 08619
Broidy Rd 08641
Bromley Ave 08629
Bromley Ct 08691
Bromley Pl 08691
Brook Ln 08619
Brooks St 08618
Brookshire Dr 08691
Brookside Ave 08609
Brookwood Rd 08619
Brown Ave 08619
Brown Ct 08641

Brown Dr 08690
Brown St 08610
E Brown St 08610
Bruce Way 08609
Bruce Park Dr 08618
Bruin Dr 08619
Bruno Cres 08620
Brunswick Ave
100-400 08618
401-403 08638
402-404 08618
405-1000 08638
1002-1498 08638
Bryn Mawr Ave 08618
Buchanan Ave 08610
Buck Rd 08620
Buckalew Ct 08610
Buckeye Dr 08619
Buckingham Ave 08618
Buckley Ln 08691
Bucknell Ave 08619
Buford Rd 08691
Building 2624 08641
Bulldog Ln 08619
Bunting Ave 08611
Burholme Dr 08691
Burke Rd 08691
Burleigh Way 08619
Burleson Ave 08619
Burnet Cres & Walk 08691
Burnside Ave 08620
N & S Burtis Ave 08690
Burton Ave 08618
Burtonwood Ct & Dr 08641
Bushler Aly 08611
Butler St 08611
Buttonwood St 08619
Byron Ave 08610
Bywater Ave 08610
Cabot Dr 08691
Cadillac Ct 08690
Cadwalader Dr & Ter 08618
Cain Ave 08638
Cairn Ct 08619
Cairns Way 08610
Caitlin Ln 08691
California Ave 08619
Cambria Ct 08690
Camden Ave 08610
Camden St 08618
Camp Ave 08610
Can Do Way 08641
E Canal St 08609
W Canal St 08608
Canary Way 08690
Cannon Dr 08690
Canterbury Dr 08691
Capitol St 08618
Capner St 08610
Capri Ln 08690
Captiva Ct 08691
Cardiff Ln 08690
Cardigan Rd 08690
Cardinal Rd 08619
Carl Sandburg Dr 08690
Carlisle Ave
1-73 08620
75-107 08620
108-108 08619
109-299 08620
118-202 08620
230-298 08619
300-399 08619
401-499 08619
Carlyle Ct 08691
Carmen Ave 08610
Carnegie Ave 08619
Carney Way 08620
Caroline Ave 08610
Carriage Way 08691
Carroll St 08609
Carrousel Ln 08619
Carson St 08691
Carteret Ave 08618
Cartlidge Ave 08610
Carver Ln 08618

Cass St 08611
Castle Ct 08620
E Castle Dr
4201A-4201H 08641
4224A-4224H 08641
4228A-4228H 08641
4251A-4251H 08641
4266A-4266D 08641
4270A-4274A 08641
4270B-4274B 08641
4270C-4274C 08641
4270D-4274D 08641
4271A-4273A 08641
4271B-4273B 08641
4271C-4273C 08641
4271D-4273D 08641
4411-4431 08641
4433-4550 08641
4552-4558 08641
W Castle Dr 08641
Catawba Dr 08690
Cathy Dr 08691
Cavalier Dr 08619
Cavell St 08618
Cedar Ln 08610
Centennial Ave 08629
Central Ave 08610
Centre St 08611
Century Way 08690
S Cessna Ave 08628
Chadwick Ct 08691
Chadwick St 08638
Chaffee Ave 08641
Chambers Ct 08691
Chambers St
1-401 08609
403-499 08609
600-1099 08611
1100-1999 08610
Chambers Farm Rd 08691
Chambord Ct 08619
Chancery Ln 08618
Chapel St 08618
Chapman Ave 08610
Charlene Ct 08691
Charles Blvd 08641
Charles St 08611
Charles Way 08609
Charles Ewing Blvd 08628
Charlotte Ave 08629
Chase Ct
2-2 08638
2-2 08691
4-4 08638
4-4 08691
6-6 08638
6-6 08691
8-8 08638
8-10 08691
Chase St 08638
Chatham Ct 08691
Chelten Way 08638
Chennault Ct & Ln 08641
Cherry St 08638
Chester Ave 08619
Chestnut Ave
1-399 08609
400-1999 08611
Chestnut Dr 08691
Cheverny Ct 08619
Chewalla Blvd 08619
Chickadee Way 08690
Chinnick Ave 08619
Chippin Ct 08691
Chris Ct 08619
Christina Ln 08691
Christine Ave 08619
Christoph Ave 08618
Church St
2-2 08620
4-99 08620
200-314 08618
316-342 08618
321-397 08620
340-398 08620
399-499 08620
Churchill Ave 08610

Circle Dr
3700A-3700B 08641
1-99 08691
101-599 08691
Claire Ln 08690
Clarendon Ave 08620
Clarion Ct 08690
Clark St 08611
Clarksburg Robbinsville Rd 08691
Claude Rd 08620
Clay St 08611
Clayton Ave 08619
Clearfield Ave 08618
Clearview Ave 08619
Cleveland Ave
1-199 08609
200-499 08629
Cliff St 08611
Clifford Ave 08619
Clifford E Harbourt Dr 08690
N Clinton Ave
1-254 08609
256-268 08609
300-799 08638
S Clinton Ave
1-499 08609
500-1399 08611
1400-4299 08610
Clocktower Dr 08690
Clover Ave 08610
Coates St 08611
Cold Spring Rd 08619
Coleman Rd 08690
Coleridge Ave 08620
College Ct & St 08611
Collier Ave 08619
Collins Rd 08619
Colonial Ave
1-59 08618
24-32 08610
34-78 08610
61-63 08618
100-499 08610
Colony Ct & Dr 08619
Colson Ave 08610
Colton Ct 08619
Colts Neck Ter 08620
Columbia Ave 08618
Columbus Ave 08629
Combs Rd 08690
N Commerce Sq 08691
Commerce St 08618
Commerce Way 08691
Commonwealth Ave 08629
Comp St 08619
Compton Cir 08691
Compton Way 08690
Concord Ave 08619
Connecticut Ave
200-299 08609
300-499 08629
Connor Ct 08690
Conovers Aly 08611
Conrad St 08611
Constance Dr 08620
Control Tower Dr 08628
N Cook Ave 08609
S Cook Ave
1-199 08609
200-499 08629
Cook Pl 08609
Cook Rd 08690
Coolidge Ave
1-70 08619
72-76 08619
100-299 08618
Cooney Ave 08619
Copperfield Dr 08610
Coral Dr 08619
Cornell Ave 08619
Cornflower Dr 08691
Cornflower Rd 08620
Cornwall Ave 08618
Coronet Ct 08619
Corporate Blvd 08691

Corral Dr 08620
Corson Ave 08619
Cortland St 08638
Cottage Ct 08690
Cottage Pl
1-15 08618
2-6 08691
14-18 08618
Cottage Place Dr 08691
Country Ln 08690
Country Meadow Ct 08691
Court St 08620
Cove St 08611
Cranbrook Rd 08690
Crawford Ct 08690
Creamery Pl 08620
Creekview Ave 08610
Crescent Ave 08619
N Crest Ave 08690
Crestpoint Dr 08690
Crestwood Dr 08690
Cromwell Dr 08691
Crossroads Dr 08691
Crosswicks Ct 08610
Crosswicks Hamilton Sq Rd
3800-4899 08691
4900-5099 08620
Cubberly Ave 08690
Culbertson Ave 08609
Cullen Way 08620
Cumberland Ave 08618
Cumberland Rd 08690
Cummings Ave & Pl 08611
Cunningham Ave 08610
Cuyler Ave
1-199 08609
200-499 08629
Cynthia Ln 08619
Cynthia Way 08620
Cypress Ln 08619
Cypress St 08691
Dailey Dr 08620
Dakota Dr 08619
Dale St 08618
Damon Ave 08610
Dan Rd 08620
Dancer Dr 08610
Daniels Ave
1-699 08619
700-799 08690
Darcy Ave 08629
Darien Ct 08620
Dark Leaf Dr 08610
Davis Ave 08629
Daymond St 08611
Dayton St 08610
Deacon Dr 08619
N & S Dean Ave 08618
Deborah Ct 08691
Deerwood Dr 08619
Deklyn Ave
1-499 08611
500-600 08610
602-698 08610
Delawareview Ave 08618
Delotto Dr 08619
Denise Dr 08690
Desiree Dr 08690
Deutz Ave 08611
Devon Ct 08691
Dewar Dr 08620
Dewberry Dr 08610
Dewey Ave 08610
Dexter St 08638
Diamond Blvd 08691
Diana Ct 08609
Dickinson Ave 08629
Ditmar Aly 08611
Division St 08611
Dixon St 08641
Doanes Aly 08611
Dodge Dr 08610
Doe Dr 08620
Dogwood Ln 08690
Dolphin Ln 08619

Donald Dr 08619
Donald Lilley Ct 08690
Doncaster Ave 08609
Donna St 08691
Doolittle Cir, Ct & Dr 08641
Doreen Rd 08690
Dorm 2612 08641
Dorm 2619 08641
Dorm 2620 08641
Dorm 2623 08641
Dorm 2624 08641
Dorm 2720 08641
Dorothy Dr 08610
Douglas Ave 08619
Douglas Ct 08690
Dove Ct 08690
Dover Rd 08620
Downing Rd 08690
Dresden Ave 08610
Dube Rd 08619
Dukoff Dr 08690
Duncan Dr 08690
Dunham St 08618
Dunmoor Ct N & S 08690
Dunston Ln 08691
Durand Ave 08611
Dye St 08611
Eagleson St 08641
Eastbridge Dr 08691
Eastburn Ave 08638
N & S Eastfield Ave 08618
Eaton Ave 08619
Eddrie Ct 08690
Edgebrook Rd 08691
Edgemere Ave 08618
Edgemont Rd 08620
Edgewood Ave 08618
Edgewood Rd 08691
Edinburg Rd
1-799 08619
810-866 08690
868-929 08690
931-939 08690
Edmund St 08610
Edward Ave 08610
Edward Ct 08609
Edwards Plz 08618
Edwin Ave 08610
Egglington Rd 08691
Eisenhower Ave 08618
Eisenhower Dr 08691
Eldridge Dr & Rd 08691
Eleanor Ave 08629
Electronics Dr 08619
Elizabeth Ave
1-299 08610
1300-1599 08629
Elkshead Ter 08620
Elkton Ave 08619
Elliot Ct 08620
Ellis Ave 08638
Ellsworth Ave 08618
Ellwood St 08610
Elm St 08611
Elmer St 08611
Elmhurst Ave 08618
Elmont Rd 08610
Elmore Ave 08619
Elmwood Ave 08629
Elton Ave 08620
Ely Cres 08691
Ely Ct 08690
Emaline Ave 08610
Emanuel St 08610
Emerald Rd 08691
Emily Ct 08691
Emily Pl 08690
Emmett Ave 08629
Emory Ave 08611
W End Ave 08618
Endicott Rd 08690
Endsleigh Ct & Pl 08691
Engineer Dr N & S 08641
Englewood Blvd 08610
Enterprise Ave 08638
Erica Cir 08691

Erica Lynne Way 08690
Erie Ave 08619
Erin Ct 08691
Erman Ct 08629
Ernies Ct 08690
Ervin Dr 08620
Escher St 08609
Estates Blvd
100-199 08610
700-832 08619
833-835 08690
834-836 08619
837-1153 08690
Euclid Ave 08609
Evans Ave
1-99 08610
1-199 08638
Evelyn Ave 08619
Everett Aly 08611
Everett St 08691
Evergreen Ave 08619
Evergreen Ln 08690
Ewing St 08609
Exeter Dr 08610
Exmoor Ln 08690
Extender Ct 08641
Exton Ave
1-97 08618
99-199 08618
1600-1899 08610
Extonville Rd 08620
Fair Ln 08690
Faircrest Ave 08609
Fairgrounds Rd 08619
Fairlawn Ave 08619
Fairmount Ave
300-399 08610
800-998 08629
1000-1099 08629
Fairview Rd 08691
Fairway Dr 08618
Falcon Ct 08690
Falcon Ln 08641
Fallview Ct 08690
Falmouth Rd 08620
Farm Brook Dr 08690
Farragut Ave 08629
Fawn Ln 08620
Faxon Dr 08691
Federal St 08611
Feeder St 08608
Fell St 08638
Fennimore Rd 08690
Fenway Rd 08620
Fenwood Ave 08619
Fern Ct 08690
Ferndale Ave 08619
Fernwood Ave 08610
Ferry St 08611
Fetter Ave 08610
Fiebelkon Rd 08641
Field Ave 08610
Fillmore St 08638
Finley Ave 08610
Fire Ln 08641
Firth St 08638
Fisher Pl
2-6 08620
8-57 08620
15-17 08618
19-42 08618
59-85 08620
Fitzrandolph Ave 08610
Flagger Ln 08619
Fleetwood Dr 08690
Fletcher Ave 08629
Flock Rd
1-499 08619
500-699 08690
Floral Ave 08619
Florence St 08610
Florister Dr 08690
Fogarty Dr 08619
Ford Dr 08690
Fordham Dr 08690
Forman Ct 08641
Forman Dr 08690
Forman St 08641
Forrest St 08611
Forsyth Ct 08641
Fountain Ave 08618
Fowler St 08618
Fox Ln 08620
Fox Runne 08691
Foy Dr 08690
Francine Dr 08610
Francis Ave 08629
Francis Ct 08691
Franklin St
1-699 08611
700-1199 08610
E Franklin St 08610
Frazier St 08618
Frederick Ave 08620
Freedman Ln 08609
Fritche Ave 08641
E Front St
1-199 08608
200-299 08611
W Front St 08608
Fss 08641
Fuld St 08638
Fulton St 08611
Furman St 08611
Gail Ct 08691
Galaxy Trailer Park 08641
Gallavan Way 08619
Galway Rd 08620
Gander Way Ave 08641
Garden Ave 08610
Garden Pl 08691
Gardner Ave 08618
Garfield Ave
1-199 08609
200-499 08629
Garnet Ln 08691
Garton Ct 08691
Gary Dr 08690
Gaskill Ave 08610
Gates Mill Ct 08690
Gena Ct 08690
General Greene Ave 08618
Genesee St
100-799 08611
800-2299 08610
George St
1-99 08638
100-100 08691
102-121 08691
E George St
4212E-4260E 08641
4212F-4260F 08641
4212G-4260G 08641
4212H-4260H 08641
4213E-4259E 08641
4213F-4259F 08641
4213G-4259G 08641
4213H-4259H 08641
4050A-4260A 08641
4050B-4260B 08641
4050C-4260C 08641
4050D-4260D 08641
4049A-4259A 08641
4049B-4259B 08641
4049C-4259C 08641
4049D-4259D 08641
W George St
4012A-4012H 08641
4013A-4013H 08641
4014A-4060A 08641
4014B-4060B 08641
4014C-4060C 08641
4014D-4060D 08641
4014E-4060E 08641
4014F-4060F 08641
4014G-4060G 08641
4015E-4045E 08641
4015F-4045F 08641
4015G-4045G 08641
4023A-4023D 08641
4045H-4046H 08641
4048H-4060H 08641
4015A-4051A 08641
4015B-4051B 08641
4015C-4051C 08641
4015D-4051D 08641
George Dye Rd
1-299 08690
300-367 08691
369-399 08691
Gerard Rd 08620
Gerson Rd 08691
Getz Ave 08619
Gibbs Ave 08611
Gilbert Aly 08618
Girard Ave 08638
Gla Dean Ct 08610
Gladstone Ave 08629
Glendon Rd 08610
Glenn Rd 08641
Glenn Ridge Rd 08620
Glenwood Ave 08618
Globemaster Ct 08641
Godfrey Dr 08610
Goeke Dr 08610
N & S Gold Dr 08691
Golden Crest Ct 08691
Goldenrod Ct 08690
Goldey Ave 08610
Goldfinch Dr 08690
Gordon Ave 08618
Gordon Rd 08691
N & S Gouverneur Ave 08618
Grace Dr 08610
Grady Ave 08610
Graffam Ave 08610
Grand Ave
1-22 08620
20-40 08610
100-517 08610
519-519 08610
Grand St
1-599 08611
600-999 08610
Grand Central Dr 08619
Grandview Ave 08620
Grant Ct 08619
Grant St 08609
Grapevine Ct 08691
Grayson Ave 08619
Great Oak Rd 08690
Green Ct 08610
Green Pl 08618
Greenbriar Dr 08690
Greening Ct 08641
Greentree Rd 08619
Greenwald Ave 08618
E & W Greenway 08618
Greenwood Ave
1-24 08611
26-98 08611
300-2299 08609
Gregory Dr 08690
Grell Pl 08691
Grenville Ct 08690
Gress Ct 08619
Gridley St 08610
Grissom Rd 08641
Gropp Ave 08610
Grover Ave 08610
Groveville Rd 08620
Groveville Allentown Rd 08620
Grumman Ave 08628
Guilford Ln 08619
Gwenyth Way 08609
Hadley Dr 08691
Haines Dr 08691
Halifax Pl 08619
Halley Dr 08691
Hamid Ct 08619
Hamilton Ave
2-78 08611
80-99 08611
100-136 08609
138-599 08609
601-797 08629
799-1699 08629
1700-2699 08619
N Hamilton Ave 08619
Hamilton Health Pl 08690
Hamilton Lakes Dr 08619
Hampton Ave 08609
Hamton Ct E & W 08691
Hancock St 08611
Handeland Dr 08690
Hanford Pl 08609
Hangar Rd 08641
Hanover Pl 08608
E Hanover St 08608
W Hanover St 08618
Hansen Ave 08610
Harcourt Dr & Pl 08610
Harding St 08611
Harlington Dr 08610
Harmon Rd 08641
Harold Ave 08618
Harold Dr 08610
Harriet Ct 08691
Harris Ave 08618
Harrison Ave 08610
Hart Ave 08638
Hartley Ave 08610
Hartman Dr 08690
Harvest Bend Rd 08691
Harwick Dr 08619
Haslach Ave 08629
Hastings Rd 08620
Hauser Ave 08620
Hawthorne Ct 08690
Hayes Ave 08618
Heatherstone Ln 08620
Heathwood Ln 08620
Heights Ter 08620
Heil Ave 08638
Heiser Ave 08610
Heisler Ave 08619
Helma Way 08609
Hemlock Ct 08619
Hempstead Rd 08610
Henchark Rd 08691
Henry St 08611
Henry Marshall Dr 08620
Herbert Ave 08690
Herbert Rd 08691
Heritage St 08691
Herman Ct 08691
N & S Hermitage Ave 08618
Hess Way 08610
Hewitt Ave & St 08611
Hibiscus Ln 08691
Hickman Dr 08610
Hickory Way 08691
Hidden Hollow Dr 08620
Higgins Ave 08641
High St
1-99 08609
100-199 08611
Highbridge Rd 08620
Highland Ave
1-299 08620
200-299 08618
Highway 33
1-400 08619
Highway 33
339-339 08690
401-899 08619
402-898 08619
900-2223 08690
2225-2299 08690
2300-2379 08691
S Hill Dr 08610
Hillcrest Ave 08618
Hillhurst Ave 08619
Hills Pl 08611
Hillside Ave 08638
Hillside Dr 08691
Hilltop Dr 08620
Hilltop Pl 08691
Hillwood Ave 08620
Hilvista Blvd 08618
Hine Ct 08641
Hirsch Ave 08690
Hirth Dr 08620
Hluchy Rd 08691
Hobart Ave 08629
Hobbs Ct 08691
Hobbs Rd 08619
Hobson Ave 08610
Hoffman Ave 08618
Hoffman Dr 08690
Hogarty Aly 08618
Hogback Rd 08620
Holden Way 08691
Holland Ter 08610
Holly Ct 08619
Hollyhock Way 08619
Hollynoll Ct & Dr 08619
Hollywood Ave & Dr 08609
Holmes Ave 08610
Holt Ave & Cir 08619
Homan Ave 08618
Home Ave 08611
Homer Ct 08641
Homestead Ave
1-21 08620
25-199 08610
Honey Flower Dr 08620
Honeysuckle Dr 08691
Hoover Ave 08619
Horizon Dr 08691
Houghton Ave 08638
Hovey Ave 08610
Howard St 08611
E Howell St 08610
Howland Cir 08690
Hubert Ave 08619
Hudson Ct 08611
Hudson St
2-40 08609
42-70 08609
72-98 08609
100-1099 08611
Huff Ave 08618
Hughes Ave 08619
Hughes Dr 08690
Hulse St 08691
Humboldt St 08618
Hummingbird Dr 08690
Hunt Ave 08610
Hunter Ave 08610
Hurley St 08638
Hustons Aly 08611
Hutchins Ave 08610
Hutchinson Rd 08691
Hutchinson St 08610
Imlaystown Hightstown Rd 08691
Imperial Dr 08690
Indelarn Ave 08618
Independence Ave 08610
Independence Way 08618
Indiana Ave 08638
Industrial Dr 08619
E & W Ingham Ave 08618
Ingleton St 08611
Innocenzi Dr 08690
Intervale Rd 08620
Iorio Dr 08620
Iron Bridge Rd 08620
Iron Works Way 08611
Irving Ct 08610
Irvington Ave 08620
Irvington Pl 08610
Isa Ct 08691
Ithaca Ct 08690
Ivanhoe Dr 08691
Ivy Ct 08618
Jack St 08619
Jackson St 08611
Jacob Ct 08690
Jaffrey Way 08620
Jamaica Way 08610
James Pl 08690
James Cubberly Ct 08610
Japril Dr 08619
Jared Dr 08691
Jarvie Dr 08690
Jarvis Pl 08618
Jean Dr 08690
Jed Ct 08609
Jefferson Ave 08619
Jeffrey Ln 08619
Jencohallo Ave 08619
Jennett St 08638
Jenny Jump Rd 08619
Jeremiah Ave 08610
Jeremy Pl 08620
Jericho Dr 08690
Jersey St 08611
Jesse Dr 08619
Jimarie Ct 08620
Joan Ter
1-99 08609
100-299 08629
Joe Dimaggio Dr 08620
John Ct 08620
John Way 08609
John Fitch Plz & Way 08611
John Henry Dr 08691
John Lenhardt Rd 08690
John Paul Dr 08690
Johnston Ave 08629
N Johnston Ave 08609
S Johnston Ave 08609
Jonathan Dr
1-199 08619
1-99 08691
Joni Ave 08690
Joseph St 08610
Josiah Ln 08691
Julia Ave 08610
June Ave 08619
Junior Ave 08619
Juniper Way
1-99 08619
101-103 08691
105-115 08691
117-199 08691
Justice Samuel Alito Jr Way 08619
Kafer St 08618
Karl Suess Dr 08609
Katie Way 08690
Kay Rd 08620
Kearney Ave 08629
Kelly Ct 08690
Kelsey Ave 08618
Kendall Rd 08690
Kenith Way 08691
Kenneth Ct 08620
Kensington Ave 08618
Kensington Way 08620
Kent St 08611
Kentucky Ave 08619
Kenwood Ter 08610
Kerr Dr 08610
Kettering Ct 08691
Kiernan Way 08690
Kim Valley Rd 08620
Kindley Ct & Pl 08641
Kingsbury Sq 08611
Kingston Blvd 08690
Kino Blvd & Ct 08619
Kinter Ave 08610
Kirby Ave 08610
Klagg Ave 08638
Klein Ave 08629
Klein Dr 08620
Klockner Rd
1-1999 08619
2000-3399 08690
3500-3699 08691
Knapp Ave 08610
Kosco Ct 08610
Kremper Ct 08619
Kristin Way 08690
Kristopher Dr 08620
Krueger Ln 08620
Kulp Ave 08618
Kuser Rd
1-1600 08619
1602-1698 08619
1700-2499 08690
2500-2799 08691
Kyle Ct 08690
Kyle Ln 08691
Labarre Ave 08618
Lacey Ave 08610
Laclede Ave 08618
Lafayette Ave 08610
E Lafayette St 08608
W Lafayette St 08608
Lajes Loop 08641
Lake Ave 08610
Lake Cir 08691
Lake Dr 08691
Lake Dr E 08691
Lake Dr W 08691
Lakeside Ave & Blvd 08610
Lakeview Ct & Dr 08620
Lalor St
1-690 08611
691-697 08610
692-698 08611
699-1099 08610
Lambert Ln 08691
Lamberton Rd & St 08611
Lambo Ct 08620
Lamerenw Ave 08610
Lamont Ave 08619
Lancaster Ave 08641
Lander Dr 08619
Landing St 08611
Landview Ct 08691
Langham Way 08620
Lansing Ave 08619
Lasalle Ave 08618
Laura Ave 08619
Laurel Ave 08618
Laurel Ct 08690
Laurel Dr 08691
Laurel Pl 08618
Lauren Ln 08620
Laurie Ct 08690
Lawrence Industrial P 08638
Lawton Ave 08629
Lea Dr 08690
Lee Ave 08618
N Lee Ave 08618
Lee Ct
1-99 08619
3718-3722 08641
Leese Ave 08609
Lehavre Ct 08619
Lehigh Ave 08619
Lemay Ln 08641
N & S Lenape Ave 08618
Lenhardt Ave 08619
Lenox Ave 08620
Lenox Way 08611
Lenwood Ct 08690
Leonard Ave
1-200 08610
202-298 08610
345-347 08619
349-355 08619
357-365 08619
Leuckel Ave 08619
Levitow Dr 08641
Lewis Ave 08629
Lexington St 08611
Libby Ct 08619
Liberty Ave 08620
Liberty St
1-1100 08611
1102-1198 08611
1300-2699 08629
2701-2799 08629
Lida St 08610
Lilac Ter 08691
Lillian Ave 08610
Lilly Ln 08638
Lily St 08610
Limewood Dr 08690
Lincoln Ave
1-99 08609
100-298 08610
101-199 08609
Lincoln Ct 08629
S Lindbergh St 08641
Linden Ave 08610

Line Rd 08690
Linton Ave 08619
Lionel Ln 08619
Lions Rd 08619
Lipton Ave 08618
Lisa Ct 08690
Livingston Dr 08619
Livingston St 08611
Llewellyn Pl 08620
Locust Ave
1-174 08610
18-38 08620
40-299 08620
176-194 08610
Locust St 08609
Locust Hill Blvd 08691
N Logan Ave 08609
S Logan Ave
1-199 08609
200-599 08629
Lohli Dr 08690
Lola Way 08610
Lone Bugler Way 08620
Longleaf Dr 08690
Longwood Dr 08620
Loomis Ave 08610
Lori Ct 08619
Lorraine Dr 08619
Louise Ln 08618
Lowell Ave 08619
Lucaya Cir 08691
Lyndale Ave 08629
Lynwood Ave
200-299 08609
300-599 08629
Macon Dr 08619
Maddock Ave 08610
Madeline Ct 08619
Madison Ave 08619
Madison St 08611
Mae Dr 08620
Magnolia Ln 08610
Magowan Ave 08619
Maguire Rd 08690
Main St
1-9 08691
11-28 08691
30-40 08691
55-75 08620
77-571 08620
573-573 08620
Maitland Rd 08620
Malencor Ave 08638
Mallory Way 08610
Malone St 08611
Malsbury St 08691
Mandl St 08619
Manor Blvd 08620
Manor Rd
1-99 08690
1810-1810 08641
1812-1899 08641
W Manor Way 08691
Maple Ave 08618
Maple St 08691
Maple Shade Ave
15-19 08690
18-34 08610
21-184 08690
36-148 08610
150-152 08610
186-186 08690
Marbella Ct 08691
Marcia Dr 08610
Margo Pl 08620
Marietta Ln 08619
Mario Dr 08690
Marion St 08618
Marjorie Way 08690
Mark Twain Dr 08690
Market St 08611
Marketplace Blvd 08691
Marksboro Way 08610
Marlen Dr 08691
Marlon Pond Rd 08690
Marlow Ct 08610

Marshall Ave
2-20 08619
16-16 08610
18-178 08610
22-399 08619
Marshall Ct 08611
Martha Dr 08610
Martin Ln 08619
Martin Luther King Jr Blvd
400-799 08618
800-1299 08638
Martins Ln 08620
Marvin Way 08620
Mary St 08610
Mason Ave 08610
Mason Ct 08690
Massachusetts Ave
200-299 08609
300-499 08629
Masterson Ct 08618
Matthew Dr 08690
Maxwell Dr 08610
May Ln 08641
Mayers Ct 08611
Mcadoo Ave 08619
Mccabe St 08691
Mcclellan Ave 08610
Mccoy Ave 08619
E & W Mcgalliard Ave 08610
Mcguire Blvd 08641
Mckinley Ave 08609
Meade Dr 08619
Meade St 08638
Meadowbrook Rd 08691
Meadowlark Dr 08690
N Meanchil Ct 08641
Mechanics Ave 08638
Medford Ave 08619
Medical Group Blvd 08641
Meeting House Rd 08620
Mellon St 08618
Melody Ct 08691
Melrose Ave 08629
Mercer St
1-699 08690
100-262 08611
264-298 08611
Merchant St 08608
Meredith Rd 08610
Merham Ct 08619
Merovan Ave 08619
Merrick Rd 08691
Mervine Pl 08609
Meyer Ct 08691
Miami Ave 08610
Michael Dr 08609
Michael Mccorristin Rd 08690
Michele Ct 08619
Michigan Ave 08638
Middle Rose St 08618
Middleton Dr 08620
Mifflin St
1-199 08611
200-220 08629
Milburne Ln 08691
Mildred Ct 08609
Miles Ave 08610
Mill Rd
1-5 08618
2-8 08620
10-24 08620
Mill Bend Rd 08690
Millenium Ct 08619
Miller Ave
300-599 08610
600-699 08619
Miller St 08638
W Miller St 08638
Millside Dr 08691
Milton Ave 08610
Mint Leaf Dr 08690
Miry Cir 08619
Miry Brook Rd 08690
Mission Rd 08620
Misty Pine Ln 08690

Mitchell Rd 08641
Mockingbird Dr 08690
Model Ave 08609
Moffatt Ave 08629
Mohawk Way 08610
Monaco Dr 08691
Monmouth Pl & St 08609
Monroe Dr 08619
Monroe St 08618
Montana Ave 08619
Monte Carlo Dr 08691
Montgomery Pl 08618
N Montgomery St
1-299 08608
300-499 08618
S Montgomery St
1-99 08608
20-20 08601
20-20 08602
20-20 08603
20-20 08604
20-20 08605
20-20 08606
20-20 08607
20-98 08611
100-199 08611
Montgomery Way 08691
Monument Ave 08619
Monument Pl 08618
Moorsleigh Way 08691
Moose St 08620
Moreland Ave 08618
Morgan Ave 08619
Morningside Dr 08618
Moro Dr 08619
Morris Ave 08611
Morris Cir 08618
Morton Ave 08610
Mott St 08611
Mount Ave 08620
Mount Dr 08619
Mount Vernon Ave 08618
Mowat Cir 08690
Msgr Cardelia Ln 08611
Muirhead Ave 08638
Mulberry Ct 08619
Mulberry St 08638
Murray Ave 08620
Murray St 08618
Nalbone Ct 08620
Nami Ln 08619
Nan Way 08620
Nancy Dr 08619
Nassau St 08638
Natrona Ave 08619
Nebraska Ave 08619
Neely Rd 08641
Negron Rd 08691
Nelson Ave 08619
New St
1-7 08691
9-27 08691
18-38 08619
40-99 08619
New Canton Way 08691
New Cedar Ln 08610
New Colony Dr 08619
New Rose St 08618
New Trent St 08638
New Willow St 08618
New York Ave 08638
Newell Ave 08618
Newkirk Ave
1-99 08629
100-699 08610
Newtown Blvd 08691
Nicklin Aly 08611
Nicole Ct 08620
Nightingale Dr 08690
Noa Ct 08690
Norcross Cir 08619
Nordacs Pl 08618
Norman Ave 08618
Norman Ct 08629
North St 08691
Norton Ave 08610

Norway Ave
1-399 08609
400-1099 08629
Norwood Aly 08611
Nottingham Way
1438A-1438B 08609
Nottinghill Ln 08619
Nurko Rd 08691
Nursery Ln 08620
Oak Ln 08638
Oak St
6-8 08691
10-10 08638
10-10 08691
12-12 08638
12-14 08691
15-15 08638
15-15 08691
16-16 08691
16-16 08638
17-19 08638
18-18 08691
20-22 08638
21-22 08691
21-21 08638
23-23 08638
23-23 08691
24-24 08638
24-24 08691
25-27 08638
26-28 08691
29-29 08638
29-29 08691
30-30 08691
31-31 08638
31-31 08691
32-32 08638
32-32 08691
33-33 08638
33-33 08691
34-34 08638
34-34 08691
35-35 08638
35-35 08691
36-36 08638
36-36 08691
37-37 08638
37-37 08691
38-38 08638
38-38 08691
39-39 08638
39-39 08691
40-40 08638
40-40 08691
41-41 08638
41-41 08691
42-42 08638
42-42 08691
43-43 08638
43-43 08691
44-44 08638
44-44 08691
45-45 08638
45-45 08691
46-46 08638
46-46 08691
47-47 08638
47-47 08691
48-48 08638
48-48 08691
49-51 08638
50-50 08691
53-89 08638
39 1/2-39 1/2 08638
Oaken Ln 08619
Oakland St 08618
Oakton Ct 08691
Oakwood Ct 08620
Ogden St 08609
Old Amboy Rd 08620
Old Olden Ave 08610
Old Post Ln 08620
Old Rose St 08618
Old Stock Ln 08611
Old Trenton Rd 08690
Old York Rd
2-32 08620
34-599 08620
1200-1599 08691
N Olden Ave
1-75 08609
77-99 08609
100-198 08638
200-1399 08638
S Olden Ave
1-199 08609
200-799 08629
800-2299 08610
Olden Ter 08610
Oldfield Ave 08610
Olive St 08618
Oliver Ave 08618
Olszak Ct 08691
Olympia Ave 08610
Omaha Ct 08619
Opal Dr 08691
Orange St 08611
Orchard Ave 08610
Oregon Ave 08610
Orly Ct & Pl 08641
Orourke Dr 08691
Osage Ave 08619
Oscar Way 08620
Ott St 08638
N & S Overbrook Ave 08618
Overlook Ave & Ct 08610
Overton Rd 08690
Ovington Dr 08620
Oxcart Ln 08619
Oxford St 08638
Pacific Ave 08629
Pannick Dr 08610
Papps Dr 08620
Parent Ave 08610
Park Ave
10-12 08638
32-36 08690
38-299 08690
800-1100 08629
1102-1198 08629
E Park Ave 08610
W Park Ave 08610
Park Ln 08609
Park St 08691
Parker Ave & Pl 08609
Parkinson Ave 08610
Parkside Ave 08618
Parkway Ave 08618
Parrotta Dr 08691
Partridge Ave 08610
Pasadena Dr 08619
Pashley Ave 08618
Paso Dr 08619
Passaic St 08618
Patricia Ln
1-99 08610
200-299 08691
Patrick Ct E 08691
Patrick Ct W 08691
Patrick Way 08620
Patriot Dr 08691
Patterson Ave 08610
E & W Paul Ave 08638
Paxson Ave
10-30 08690
32-498 08690
499-699 08619
Paxson Avenue Ext 08690
Payne Dr 08691
Peabody Ln 08619
Peace St 08608
Peacock Ct 08619
Pearl St 08609
Pearson Dr 08610
Pennfield Rd 08691
Pennington Ave 08618
Pennsylvania Ave 08638
Penny Ln 08691
Percy West Dr 08690
Perdicaris Pl 08618
Perilli Dr 08610
Periwinkle Ln 08619
Perrine Ave 08638

Perrineville Rd 08691
Perro Pl 08690
Perry Ave 08629
Perry St 08618
Pescia Ln 08619
Petal Way 08610
Peter Rafferty Dr 08690
Petito Ct 08691
Petticoat Way 08619
Petty Ridge Rd 08620
Phaeton Dr 08690
Pheasant Ln 08690
Phillips Ave
1-199 08610
1-299 08638
Phillips Blvd 08618
Phillips Ct 08618
Philmont Ave 08610
Philrich Dr 08619
Pickering Dr 08691
Pierce Ave 08629
Pilgrim Way 08620
Pine St
100-199 08691
600-899 08638
Pine Brook Ct 08620
Pinedale Ct 08690
Pinehurst Ct 08690
Pinewood Dr 08690
Pintinalli Dr 08619
E & W Piper Ave 08628
Pitcairn Ave 08628
Pitman Ave 08610
Pizzullo Rd 08690
Pleasant Dr 08620
Plum St 08638
Polking Rd 08641
Pollman Ave 08619
Pond Rd 08691
Pope Ave 08619
Poplar St 08638
Portofino Dr 08691
Potter Ave 08619
Potts Rd 08691
Pow Mia Blvd 08641
Powell Pl 08610
Power St 08611
Prestile Pl 08691
Preston Way 08619
N & S Prestwick Rd 08641
Prince St 08638
Princess Diana Dr 08638
Princeton Ave
1-499 08619
1300-1598 08638
Pritchard St 08638
Proctor Ave 08618
Prospect Ave 08620
Prospect St 08618
Prospect Vlg 08618
Psc 08641
Pullen Aly 08611
Quaint Ln 08690
Quakerbridge Plz & Rd 08619
Quay Ct 08620
Quimby Ave 08610
Quincy Ave 08629
Quinton Ave 08629
Race St 08638
Rachel Ln 08691
Radin Rd 08641
Rafting Way 08611
Railroad Ave 08691
Raintree Dr 08690
Ranchwood Dr 08618
Randall Ave
1-299 08611
200-599 08610
Randolph Dr 08691
Ravine Dr 08620
Ray Dwier Dr 08690
Razorback Dr 08619
Reading Ave 08618
Reagan Ln 08691
Red Cedar Dr 08690

Redalloc Dr 08690
Redfern St 08610
Redwood Ave 08610
Reed Ave 08610
Reed Ln 08691
Reeger Ave 08610
Reeves Ave 08610
Regal Ct 08690
Regina Ave 08619
Reichert Ave 08610
Remsen St 08610
Renfrew Ave 08618
Rennie St 08610
Reservoir St 08618
Rev S Howard Woodson Jr Way
1-899 08618
900-1899 08638
1901-2099 08638
Revere Ave 08629
Rex Ct 08609
Ribsam St 08619
Richardson Rd 08691
Richbell Rd 08620
Richey Pl 08618
Richland Ave 08629
Richmond Ave 08619
Ridge Ave 08610
Riley Ave 08610
Ringold St 08618
Ritz Ave 08610
River Dr 08618
River View Plz 08611
Riverside Ave & Dr 08618
Rivulet Way 08619
Robbinsville Allentown Rd 08691
Robbinsville Edinburg Rd 08691
Robert Frost Dr 08690
Robert Pearson Ct 08610
Roberts Ave 08609
Robin Dr 08619
Robin Rd 08691
Rock Royal Rd 08620
Rockhill Ave 08619
Rockleigh Dr 08638
Rockwood Ave 08619
Roebling Ave
1-922 08611
924-998 08611
1001-1005 08629
Rogers Ave 08618
Rogers Cir 08610
Rolf Ave 08610
Rolling Ln 08690
Ronald Way 08609
Roosevelt Ave 08620
Roosevelt St 08618
Roosevelt Way 08691
Rose Ct 08691
Rose Everett Ct 08690
Rosemont Ave 08618
Rosewood Ter 08620
Roslyn Rd 08610
Rossell Ave 08638
Rotunda Dr 08610
Route 156 08620
Rowan Ave 08610
N & S Rudd Ct 08641
Rudner Ave 08619
Rugby Way 08620
Runyon Cir & Dr 08610
Ruskin Ave 08610
Rusling St 08611
Rutgers Ave 08619
Rutgers Pl 08618
Ruth Ave 08610
Rutherford Ave 08618
Ryan Ave 08610
Ryerson Dr 08690
Sadie St 08619
Saint Clair Ave 08619
Saint Francis Ave 08629
Saint Joes Ave 08638
Sairelar Rd 08628

Salem Pl 08619
Sallie St 08610
Salzano Dr 08690
Sam Naples Rd 08619
Samantha Ln 08619
Samdin Blvd 08610
Sams Way 08620
Samuel St 08610
San Fernando Dr 08619
Sanbert Cir 08690
W Sancheld St 08608
Sandalwood Ave 08619
Sandtown Ter 08690
Sandy Ln 08610
Sanford St 08618
Sanhican Dr 08618
Sanibel Ln 08691
Santa Fe Ct 08619
Sapphire Rd 08691
Sara Dr 08691
Saranac Rd 08619
Sawmill Rd 08620
Saxony Ln 08691
Saybrook Ave 08619
Sayen Dr 08690
Scalia Ct 08690
Scammel Ave 08629
Scattergood Ave 08619
Schenck St 08611
Schenk Pl 08691
Schiller Ave 08610
School Ln 08618
School House Rd 08641
Scobey Ct 08690
Scobey Ln 08610
E & W Scott St 08641
Scottie Ct 08619
Scullin Dr 08620
Scully Ave 08610
Sculptors Way 08619
Secretario Way 08690
Sedgwick Rd 08690
Sedona Blvd 08691
Seneca Ln 08690
Senf Dr 08620
Sequoia Rd 08619
Service Rd 08641
Setter Way 08610
Seward Ave 08609
Sewell Ave 08610
Shackamaxon Dr 08690
Shady Ln 08619
Sharon Rd 08691
Sharon Station Rd 08691
Sharps Ln 08610
Shawnee Dr 08690
Sheffield Rd 08619
Shelbourne Ave 08618
Shell Turn 08690
Shellflower Ln 08690
Shelly Ln 08690
Shepards Aly 08618
Sheridan Ave 08609
Sheridan Rd 08619
Sherman Ave 08638
Sherwood Ave 08619
Shibla Ave 08610
Shinceda Ave 08619
Shirley Ln 08610
Short St 08618
Siegel Ave 08638
Sierra Dr 08619
Silver Ct 08690
Silver Spruce Way 08690
Simpson St 08619
Sloan Ave 08619
Smith Ave
1-99 08619
101-199 08619
102-104 08611
104-104 08619
106-112 08611
112-112 08619
114-120 08611
126-134 08619
200-899 08611

Smith St 08610
Smythe Ave 08610
Snowball Ln 08619
Soden Ct & Dr 08620
Soem Dr 08620
Soloff Dr 08610
Sommers Rd 08638
Southard St
1-399 08609
400-1299 08638
Spaatz Dr 08641
Sparrow Dr 08690
Spencer Way 08691
Spicer Ave 08610
Sprague Turn 08610
Spring St 08618
Spring Garden Rd 08691
Spring Valley Ln 08638
Springdale Ave 08620
Springmeadow Dr 08638
Spruce Ct 08610
Spruce St
500-514 08691
501-501 08638
501-525 08691
530-598 08638
600-833 08638
835-1099 08638
1501-1597 08610
1599-1899 08610
1900-2098 08638
2100-2399 08638
Stacey Ave 08618
Stacy Ave 08619
Stafford Ct 08690
Stamford Rd 08619
Stamy Dr 08618
Stanley Ave 08618
Stanley Dr 08691
Stanton St 08610
Stanwyck Ct 08691
Stark Dr 08691
Starlifter Ct 08641
E State St
1-441 08608
443-499 08608
500-1805 08609
W State St
1-1 08608
3-299 08608
300-312 08618
314-1599 08618
1601-1699 08618
E State Street Ext 08619
Steamboat St 08611
Steel St 08611
Steiner Ave 08619
Steinert Ave 08619
Stella Ave 08610
Stenton Ct 08610
Stephanie Ln 08691
Sterling Ave 08619
Steven Ave 08619
Stevens Aly 08609
Stevenson Ave 08619
Steward St 08610
Stillwell Ct 08690
Stockton St 08619
N Stockton St
1-22 08608
24-38 08608
35-41 08618
43-199 08618
S Stockton St
25-99 08608
101-199 08611
Stokely Ave 08611
Stoneridge Dr 08691
Story Pl 08691
Strassberg Ct 08690
Stratton Ct 08691
Stratton Dr 08690
Strawberry St 08638
Stults Ave 08619
Stuyvesant Ave 08618
Summer St 08618

Summer Hill Dr 08620
Sun Valley Rd 08690
Sundance Dr 08619
Sundew Way 08691
Sunflower Ln 08620
Sunnybrae Blvd 08620
Sunset Ave 08610
Sunset Blvd 08690
Sunset Ct 08690
Surrey Dr 08690
Sutton Dr 08690
Sven Dr 08691
Swallow Dr 08690
Swan St 08611
Sweetbriar Ave 08619
Sweets Ave 08618
Switlik Rd 08690
Sycamore Dr 08691
Sycamore Way 08690
Sykes Ave 08629
Sylvan Ave 08610
Sylvester St 08638
Sylvia Way 08691
Tacoma Ln 08619
Taft Ave
1-1 08620
14-22 08610
24-199 08610
Talbot Way 08691
Tally Rd 08619
Tamiterm Ave 08609
Tampa Ave 08610
Tanager Ln 08691
Tanglewood Dr 08619
Tantum Dr 08610
Tappan Ave 08690
Tar Heels Rd E 08619
Tara Ct 08619
Tartear Dr 08610
Tasley Ct 08691
Tattletown Rd 08620
E Taylor Ave 08610
W Taylor Ave 08610
Taylor St 08638
Tea Rose Ln 08620
Tekening Way 08690
Temple St 08611
Tennis Ct 08619
Tennyson Dr 08610
Terrapin Ln 08619
Terrill Ave 08619
Terry Ct 08620
Tettemer Ave 08610
Thistle Pl 08691
Thomas J Rhodes Indust
Dr 08619
Thompson Ave 08619
Thompson St 08609
Thompson Way 08690
Thoreau Rd 08690
Thropp Ave 08619
Thunder Rd
1-99 08611
3300-3399 08641
Tiberi Ct 08690
Tidewater Ct 08610
Tigers Ct 08619
Tilia Ct 08690
Tilton Aly 08611
Timber Wolf Dr 08620
Timberlake Dr 08618
Tindall Ave 08610
Tindall Rd 08691
Tioga St 08609
Tipton St 08629
Titus Ave 08618
Toby Ln 08620
Topaz Ln 08690
Toronita Ave 08610
Towne Ln 08618
Travis Cir 08641
Treelawn Ter 08619
Trellis Way 08691
Tremont St 08611
Trent Ave 08618
Trenton Ave 08619

E Trenton Ave 08638
Trinity Ave 08619
Trotter Ct 08619
Truman Ct 08691
Tucker St 08618
Tudor Dr 08690
Tunner Ct 08641
Turnbull Ave 08610
Turpin St 08611
Tuskegee Airmen Ave 08641
Tuttle Ave 08629
Twig Ln 08620
Tyler St 08609
Tyndale Rd 08690
Tynemouth Ct 08691
Tyrell Ave 08638
Uncle Petes Rd 08691
Union St
351A-371A 08611
University Dr 08619
Unwin Dr 08610
Upper Pond Ct 08690
Upton Way 08610
Us Highway 130
1-399 08620
Us Highway 130
401-499 08620
500-532 08691
534-679 08691
680-680 08620
680-1274 08691
681-1239 08691
Us Highway 206
526A-526B 08610
100-116 08610
118-585 08610
587-699 08610
594-602 08620
604-606 08610
Uxbridge Dr 08691
Vahlsing Way 08691
Valerie Ln 08690
Valley Rd 08690
Valley View Ct & Rd 08620
Valli Ct 08690
Van Kannel Ave 08620
Van Nostrand Ct 08691
Van Sant Dr 08690
Vandenberg Ave 08641
Ventana Ct 08619
Verona Ave 08619
Versailles Ct 08619
Vetterlein Ave 08619
Vicky Ct 08610
Victor Ave 08609
Victoria Ave 08610
Villa Pl 08620
Village Ct 08690
Village Dr E 08620
Village Dr W 08620
Vincent Ave 08619
Vine St 08638
Vintage Ct 08619
Violet Ln 08691
Violet St 08618
Virginia Ave
1-199 08611
200-299 08610
301-399 08610
Vista Rd 08690
Volk St 08618
Volusia Ave 08610
Vroom St 08610
Wagner St 08610
Wainwright Ave 08618
Walden Cir 08691
Walker Ave 08629
Walkletts Aly 08611
Wall St 08609
Waln Ave 08620
Walnut Ave 08609
Walnut St
1-99 08610
400-499 08691
Walt Whitman Way 08690
N Walter Ave 08609

S Walter Ave
1-199 08609
200-299 08629
Walters Rd 08691
Waltham Ct 08690
War Memorial 08608
Ward Ave
1-199 08609
301-397 08619
399-499 08619
Warehouse Rd 08641
Warner Dr 08609
N Warren St
1-199 08608
200-222 08618
224-299 08618
301-399 08618
S Warren St
--- 08611
830A-850A 08611
830B-850B 08611
1-399 08608
800-821 08611
823-899 08611
Warrior Way 08690
Washington Blvd 08691
Washington Ct 08629
Washington St 08611
Water View Dr 08691
Watson Ave 08610
Watson St 08611
Waverly Ct 08691
Waverly Pl 08609
Wayne Ave 08618
Weathersfield Dr 08620
Webster St 08638
Wedge Dr 08610
Wegner Ave 08619
Weinberg Pl 08638
Welland Rd 08690
Weller Ave 08610
Wellington Ct 08620
Wells Dr 08690
Wendover Way 08690
Wert Ave 08610
Wesley Ave 08610
Wesleyan Dr 08690
West St 08611
Westbury Ct 08691
Westcott Ave 08610
N & S Westfield Ave 08618
Westminister Ave 08618
Weston Ave 08619
Weyburne Rd 08690
Weymouth Dr
1-2 08690
3-99 08610
Wharian Ct 08620
Whatley Rd 08690
White St
1-99 08618
2200-2299 08641
White Horse Ave 08610
White Stag Dr 08620
Whitehall Rd 08690
Whitehead Rd 08619
Whitehorse Hamilton
Square Rd
400-1099 08610
1100-1598 08690
1600-2699 08690
Whitehorse Mercerville
Rd 08619
Whitman Rd 08619
Whittaker Ave 08611
Whittier Ave 08618
Whittlesey Rd 08618
Wickom Ave 08690
Wilbert Way 08610
Wilbur Ct 08609
Wildflower Trl 08691
Wiley Ave 08638
Wilfred Ave 08610
Wilkinson Pl 08618
William St
1-5 08611

2-6 08619
8-99 08619
100-199 08611
200-1499 08610
Willow Ct 08619
Willow St 08691
N Willow St
1-99 08608
100-399 08618
401-599 08618
801-897 08638
899-1399 08638
1401-1799 08638
Willow Bend Dr 08690
Wilson Ave
1-23 08620
2-16 08620
16-32 08619
34-399 08619
Wilson Ct 08691
Wilson St 08618
Winder Ave 08609
Windfall Ln 08690
Winding Way 08620
Windmere Ct 08620
Windmere Path 08690
Windsor Ct 08638
Windsor Ln 08620
Windsor Rd 08691
Windswept Dr 08690
Windward Way 08690
Winslow Ave 08619
Winterberry Ter 08690
Winterset Dr 08690
Winthrop Ct 08618
Wisteria Ln 08690
Witmer Way 08691
Wittenborn Ave 08619
Wolf Dr 08610
Wolfpack Ct & Rd 08619
Wolverton St 08611
Wonnacott Ave 08641
Wood St 08618
Woodcliffe Dr 08690
Woodcroft Dr 08690
Woodland Ct 08610
Woodland St
1-299 08611
300-599 08610
601-799 08610
Woodlawn Ave 08609
Woods Edge 08691
Woodside Ave
16-22 08618
22-22 08620
24-220 08618
31-399 08610
222-298 08618
400-699 08620
Woodside Rd 08691
Woodvine Ave 08610
Woolsey St 08610
Wren Ln 08690
Wycklow Ct & Dr 08691
Wyndham Pl 08691
Yankee Peddler Path 08620
Yard Ave 08609
Yard St 08691
Yardville Allentown Rd 08620
Yardville Groveville Rd 08620
Yardville Hamilton Squ
Rd
1-9 08620
11-299 08620
300-398 08691
400-1399 08691
1766-1838 08690
1840-2599 08690
Yellow Jacket Ln 08619
Yorkshire Rd 08610
Youngs Rd 08619
Zachary Ln 08620
Zelley Ave 08620
Zieglers Ln 08690

NUMBERED STREETS

1st Ave 08619
2nd Ave 08619
2nd St 08611
E 2nd St 08641
3rd Ave
1-199 08619
600-699 08691
3rd St 08611
E 3rd St 08641
W 3rd St 08641
4th Ave
1-199 08619
800-899 08691
E 4th St 08641
5th Ave 08619
E 6th 08619
7th Ave 08619

VINELAND NJ

General Delivery 08360

POST OFFICE BOXES MAIN OFFICE STATIONS AND BRANCHES

Box No.s
All PO Boxes 08362

RURAL ROUTES

01, 05, 70 08360
02, 03, 04, 06 08361

NAMED STREETS

Acorn St 08360
Adams Ave 08360
Adler Ln 08361
Aino Ln 08360
Alberic St 08360
Alexander Dr 08361
Allegheny Ave 08360
Allen Ave 08360
W Almond Rd & St 08360
Alpha Pl 08360
Alpine Way 08360
Alps Pl 08361
Amanda Ct 08360
Amber Ln 08360
Amos Ave 08360
Annlo Ln 08361
Anthony Dr 08360
Apache Ct 08361
E & W Arbor Ave & Ct E
& W 08360
Arcadia Pl 08360
Ardsley Ter 08360
Arlene Dr 08360
Arrowhead Trl 08361
Ascher Rd 08361
Ashwood Ct 08360
Athens Way 08361
August Dr 08361
Autumncrest Dr 08361
Avas Ct 08361
Avon Pl 08360
Axtell Ave 08360
Barbara Dr 08361
Barred Owl Ln 08361
Barry Dr 08361
Bartholomew Dr 08361
Bayberry Ln 08361
Baylor Ave 08360
Baywood Dr 08361
Beacon Ave 08360
Bear Branch Ct 08361
Becker Dr 08361
Beechwood Dr 08361
Bella Rosa Ct 08361
Bellair Ave 08360
Belvedere Ave 08360
Berkeley Dr 08361

Street	ZIP
Berkshire Dr	08360
Bethpage Ct	08361
Beverly Dr	08360
Birch St	08360
Bird St	08360
Blackburn Ct	08361
Blackwood Dr	08361
Blue Ct	08361
S Blue Bell Rd	08360
Boody Dr	08360
Bortle Ave	08360
Boxwood Dr	08361
Bracco Dr	08360
Bradford Dr	08360
Brandywine Dr	08361
Brentwood Dr	08361
N Brewster Rd	
1-41	08361
43-99	08361
100-100	08360
101-1605	08361
110-1628	08361
S Brewster Rd	
40-42	08361
63-89	08361
104-104	08360
106-110	08360
111-119	08361
112-122	08360
121-123	08361
124-136	08360
125-137	08361
138-142	08360
144-202	08360
157-205	08361
207-209	08361
210-218	08360
211-227	08361
224-292	08361
231-233	08360
241-295	08361
302-304	08360
306-309	08360
311-311	08360
312-312	08361
314-315	08361
317-351	08361
320-326	08360
334-336	08361
357-359	08360
365-367	08361
378-378	08360
380-381	08360
382-384	08361
383-603	08360
386-406	08360
406-406	08361
412-426	08360
426-426	08361
428-474	08360
484-486	08361
504-604	08360
606-664	08361
666-1099	08361
Briar Trl	08360
Broad Ln	08360
Broadlawn Ter	08360
Broadway	08360
N & S Brookfield Ct & St	08361
Brookhaven Dr	08361
Brunetta Dr	08360
Bruun Ave	08360
Bryant St	08361
Bucks Run	08360
Buckwood Ln	08361
Buena Dr	08360
Burns Ave	08360
Burnt Mill Dr	08360
E Butler Ave	
1-147	08360
149-599	08360
703-711	08361
713-1299	08361
W Butler Ave	08360
Buttonwood Dr	08361
Caitlin Dr	08360
Cambridge St	08360
Canberra Ct	08361
Candlewood Dr	08361
Cannon Range Ave	08360
Canterbury Ln	08361
Carlisle Dr	08360
Carlton Pl	08360
Carmel Ave	08360
Carol Dr	08360
Carpy Ave	08361
Carteret St	08361
Castpa Pl	08360
Catherine St	08360
Cavallo Dr	08361
Cayuga St	08360
Cedar Ave	08360
Cedarbrook Ct	08361
Cedarwood Dr	08360
S Central Ave	08360
Chalet Ln	08360
Chambers Pl	08360
Chammings Ct	08360
Chapel Dr	08361
Charles St	08360
Chelseas Way	08360
Cheltenham Dr	08360
Cherokee Ln	08361
E & W Cherry St	08360
Chestnut Ave	08360
E Chestnut Ave	
500-1145	08360
1147-1181	08360
1301-1397	08361
1399-5199	08361
5201-5299	08361
W Chestnut Ave	08360
Chestnut Ter	08360
Chimes Ter	08360
Chris Ct	08361
Christy Ln	08361
Cimino Blvd	08360
Cindy Dr	08360
City Line Ave	08360
Civil War Rd	08361
Clarendon Ave	08360
Clayville Switch	08360
Cliffside Dr	08361
Clover Ave	08361
Cobblestone Ln	08361
College Dr	08360
Columbia Ave	08360
Comanche Rd	08361
Concetta Ln	08361
Coney Ave	08360
Conley Dr	08361
E & W Cornell St	08360
Cornucopia Ave	08361
Cornwall Dr	08361
Coronado Ave	08360
Cottonwood Dr	08361
Country Ln	08361
Crane St	08361
E & W Crescent Dr	08360
Crystal Ave	08360
Cumberland Rd	08360
Cypress Ct & Dr	08360
Dahliadel Dr	08361
Daldon Ln	08361
Damask Rose Ct	08360
Dante Ave	08361
Dauphin Rd	08361
David St	08360
Deborah Ct	08361
Deerberry Ct	08361
Defalco Ave	08360
Delmar Ave	08360
N & S Delsea Dr	08360
Demarco Dr	08360
Derosa Dr	08360
Deshibe Ter	08360
Diamond Dr	08361
Diane Ct	08360
Dippolito Dr	08360
Dirk Dr	08360
Division St	08360
Dogwood Ln	08360
Dolly Dr	08361
Doral St	08361
Doren Ter	08360
Dorothy St	08360
Douglas Ln	08360
Dove Ct	08361
Downs Dr	08360
Driftwood Ln	08361
Duchess Ct	08361
Dukes Rd	08361
Eagles Ct	08361
E & W Earl Dr	08360
N East Ave	08360
S East Ave	08360
N East Blvd	08360
S East Blvd	
27-515	08360
517-2800	08360
2802-2914	08360
2809-3503	08360
2809-2809	08362
Eastwood Dr	08361
Edgewood Dr	08361
Edna Dr	08361
Edrudo Rd	08360
Edward Ln	08360
Eglantine Dr	08360
Eilene Dr	08360
Elizabeth Dr	08360
Elm Rd	08360
E Elmer Rd	
45-67	08360
69-989	08360
991-999	08360
1100-1134	08361
1136-1999	08361
W Elmer Rd	08360
E Elmer St	08360
W Elmer St	08360
Elmwood Ave	08360
Elty Ave	08360
Embassy Ter	08360
Erin St	08360
Estrose St	08360
Eureka St	08361
Evelyn Ave	08360
Evergreen Ave	08360
Ewan Ter	08360
Fairmount Ave	
1100-1200	08360
1202-1298	08360
1531-1799	08361
Falcon Way	08360
Fava Dr	08360
Fawn Dr	08360
Fela Dr	08361
Fenimore St	08360
Fernwood Dr	08361
Ferrari Dr	08361
Fina Pl	08361
Finch St	08361
Fiocchi Dr	08360
Flora Rd	08360
Florence Ave	08360
Forbes Dr	08360
Forest Grove Rd	08360
Fornataro Ave	08360
Forsythia Dr	08361
Foster Ave	08360
Fowler Ave	08360
Fox Ln	08360
Foxmoor Dr	08361
Francine Dr	08360
Franklin Dr	08361
Freddy Ln	08360
Frederick Ct	08361
Friendship St	08360
Fruit St	08361
Gallagher Dr	08360
Galli Dr	08361
Garden Rd	08360
Gardner St	08361
Garrison Rd	08360
Garry Ave	08360
Garwood Ln	08361
Genoa Ave	08361
George Ln	08360
Gerow Ave	08360
Gettysburg Dr	08361
Gheysens Ave	08360
Gianna Ct	08360
Gilmore St	08360
Glenn Ter	08360
Glenwood Ct & Dr	08361
Golda Ln	08361
Gordons Pl	08360
Grace Ann Dr	08360
Graiffs Way	08361
Grandview Ave	08360
E Grant Ave	
1-63	08360
65-799	08360
801-803	08360
900-928	08361
930-1643	08361
1645-1799	08361
W Grant Ave	08360
E & W Grape St	08360
Green Valley Ct	08361
Greenwillows Dr	08361
Greenwood Ct & Dr	08361
Grove Ln	08360
Hadsell Ave	08360
Halsey Ct	08361
Hamilton Dr	08360
Hance Bridge Rd	08361
Harding Hwy	08360
N Harding Hwy	08360
Harding Rd	08361
Harvard St	08360
Harvest Ct	08361
Hawks Way	08360
Hawthorn Ct	08361
Hazel Ave	08360
Heatherwood Dr	08360
Heights Pl	08360
Helen Ave	08360
Hendee Rd	08360
Hendricks Rd	08360
Heritage Dr	08361
Heron St	08361
Hickory Dr & Pl	08360
Hideaway Ct	08361
Highland Ave	08361
Hillwood Ln	08360
Hoffman Dr	08361
Holly Hill Ter	08360
Holmes Ave	08361
Homecrest Dr	08360
Hope St	08361
Howard St	08360
Hubbard Ln	08360
Humbert St	08360
Ida Ln	08361
Independence Ct & Rd	08361
Indian Dr	08361
Industrial Way	08360
Inverness Rd	08361
Iowa Ave	08360
Iris Ave	08361
Iroquois Ct	08361
Isabel Rd	08361
Italia Ave	08361
Ithaca St	08360
Jackson Dr	08360
James Ct	08361
Jamic Rd	08361
Janet St	08360
Jay Ter	08361
Jefferson Ave	08361
Jennifer Ln	08360
Jeremy Ct	08361
Jesse Rd	08361
Jewel St	08360
Joel St	08361
John St	08360
Josephs Ct	08361
Joshua Dr	08360
Joyce Ln	08361
Juliana Dr	08360
Junior Dr	08361
Juniper St	08361
Justin Ct	08361
Karin St	08360
Karls Rd	08361
Kay Pl	08360
Kay Ter	08361
Kickapoo Trl	08361
Kingman Ave	08360
Kings Rd	08361
Kirkwood Dr	08361
Knoll Dr	08361
N Korff Dr	08360
Kristian Dr	08360
La Valle Ave	08360
Lafrance St	08360
Laielli Ct	08360
Landis Ave	08360
E Landis Ave	
500-721	08360
722-1198	08360
722-722	08362
723-1199	08360
1601-1673	08361
1675-4699	08361
4701-4717	08361
W Landis Ave	08360
Larchwood Ln	08361
Lasalle St	08360
Laurel Ct	08361
Laurel St	08360
Lawrence St	08361
Lee Dr	08360
Lejan Ter	08360
Leroys Pl	08360
Liberty Ave	08360
Lilac Dr	08360
Lincoln Ave	08360
N Lincoln Ave	
1-575	08361
102-198	08360
226-580	08361
S Lincoln Ave	08361
Linda Ln	08360
Linden Blvd & Ct	08361
Lindsey Rd	08361
Linwood Ave	08361
Lisa Ln	08360
Lisbon Ln	08361
Livia Ln	08360
Lois Ln	08360
London Ln	08361
Longwood Dr	08361
Loretta Ln	08361
Louis Dr	08360
Louisa Ln	08360
Luciano Ave	08360
Lynn Ave	08360
Madison Ave	08361
Magnolia Rd	
600-1037	08360
1039-1099	08360
1133-1133	08361
1135-2899	08361
N & S Main Ave & Rd	08360
Mainview Ter	08360
Manaway Ln	08360
Manchester Dr	08360
Maple Ave	
1100-1199	08360
1500-1998	08361
2000-4099	08361
N Maple Dr	08360
S Maple Dr	08360
Margo Dr	08360
Marion St	08361
Marla Pl	08361
Marlyn Ave	08360
Mars Pl	08360
Marshall St	08361
Mart Ave	08361
Mary Lou Ln	08361
Mathew Ln	08361
Maurice River Pkwy	08360
Mayer St	08360
Mayfair Ct & St	08360
Mays Ave	08361
Mays Landing Rd	08361
Mcclain Dr	08361
Mcmahan Dr	08361
Meade Dr	08361
Meadow Dr	08361
Medina St	08361
Megan Ct	08361
Melrose St	08360
Menantico Rd	08361
Mercury Way	08360
Michael Ave	08360
Michelon Ct	08361
Michigan Ave	08360
Mildred Ln	08361
N & S Mill Rd	08360
Mona Dr	08361
Monarch Ln	08361
Monroe Ave	08361
E & W Montrose St	08360
Morning Glory Dr	08361
Mosswood Dr	08360
Mount Vernon St	08360
Moyer St	08360
Mulberry St	08360
Mullen Dr	08361
Musterel Ln	08361
N & S Myrtle St	08360
Nathan Ln	08361
Nelson Ave	08360
Neptune Ter	08360
New Magnolia Rd	08360
New Panther Rd	08361
New Peach St	08360
New Pear St	08360
Nicolette Ct	08360
Nona Dr	08361
Norris Dr	08360
North St	08360
Northwood Dr	08360
Nottingham Dr	08360
Nylund Dr	08361
Oak Ln	08360
Oak Rd	08360
E Oak Rd	
67-111	08360
113-1520	08360
1522-1564	08360
1600-3435	08361
W Oak Rd	08360
Oaklawn Ter	08361
Ok Ln	08361
Old Farm Dr	08361
Old Forest Rd	08360
Old Union Rd	08361
N & S Orchard Rd	08360
Osborne Ave	08360
Oslo Ct	08361
Overbrook Rd	08360
Owle St	08361
Oxford St	08360
Palermo Ave	08361
Panther Rd	08361
Paris Pl	08361
E & W Park Ave, Dr & Ln	08360
Paterson Dr	08361
Pats Ln	08361
Paul St	08360
Peace St	08361
E & W Peach St	08360
E & W Pear St	08360
Pennsylvania Ave	08361
Pentrain Ave	08360
Percy Ln	08361
Perna Ln	08361
Phillip St	08361
Piacenzia Ave	
4400-4498	08361
4500-5599	08361
6000-6098	08360
Pilgrims Way	08361
Pine Ave & St	08360
Pine Grove Ave	08360
Pinehurst Rd	08361
Pixwhey Ct	08361
Pleasant Dr	08360
E & W Plum St	08360
Post Rd	08360
Princess Ln	08361
Prospect Ave	08360
Prospect St	08361
Quail St	08361
Queens Rd	08361
Quigley Ave	08360
E & W Quince St	08360
Rae Dr	08360
Rainbow Ln	08360
Rainforest Dr	08360
Ramblewood Dr	08360
Raven Ct	08360
Ravenna Ln	08361
Rebecca Dr	08360
Redcrest St	08361
Redwood Dr	08361
Regina Elena Ave	08360
Reilly Ct	08360
Renee Dr	08361
Reviam Ct	08360
Ridgewood Dr	08361
Rieck Ter	08361
Rios Ave	08360
Rita Ave	08361
Riverside Dr	08360
Riviera Blvd	08361
Roberts Blvd	08360
Rogers Ave	08361
Rolfhausen Ct	08361
Rome Rd	08361
Roosevelt Ave	08360
Roosevelt Blvd	08361
Rosalie Ln	08360
Rosemary Ave	08361
Rosewood Ave	08360
Rostan Ct	08361
Royal Dr	08360
Rudolph Dr	08361
Russell Ave	08360
Saddlebrook Dr	08361
Sally Dr	08361
Samuel Dr	08360
Sandy Ct	08360
Sanford Dr	08361
Sarah Pl	08360
Sassafras Dr	08360
Sawyer Ave	08360
Scarpa Dr	08361
School Ln	08361
Sequoia Dr	08361
Serene Dr	08360
Seville St	08361
Shadow Ln	08361
Shady Creek Ln	08360
Sharon Ct	08361
Sharp Rd	08360
Sheridan Ave	
101-187	08360
189-466	08360
468-470	08360
500-1532	08361
1534-1684	08361
E Sherman Ave	
49-235	08360
237-698	08360
700-706	08360
789-809	08361
811-2699	08361
W Sherman Ave	08360
Sherwood Dr	08361
Shirley Ct	08360
Siena Way	08361
Silverwood Ln	08361
Simca Ter	08360
Simonelli Dr	08361
Singer Ln	08361
Smith St	08360
Solona Ave	08360
Sonnys Trl	08361
Southwood Dr	08361
N & S Spring Rd	08361
Spruce St	08360
Starlet Dr	08360
N & S State St	08360

Steven Dr 08360
Stewart St 08361
Strathmore Ter 08361
Strawberry Ave 08360
Streamview Ln 08360
Summer Ave 08360
W Summit St 08360
Sunrise Ave 08360
Sunset Ave 08360
Sutliff Ave 08360
Swallow Dr 08361
Swan Dr 08361
Swenlin Dr 08360
Sycamore Ln 08361
Sylvan Lake Rd 08361
Sylvester Dr 08360
Tammie Ter 08360
Tanglewood Ln 08360
Tatanka Ct 08361
Taylor Ave 08360
Temm Ct 08360
Temple Rd 08360
Thornhill Rd 08361
Thorview Ct 08360
Timber Brook Dr 08360
Tomahawk Ct 08361
Tori Ln 08361
Torino Ct 08361
Trento Ave 08361
Tuckahoe Rd 08360
Tulip St 08360
Tuttlegrove Rd 08361
Union Rd 08360
S Union Rd 08361
Utopia Ln 08361
Valentine St 08360
Valhalla Rd 08361
N & S Valley Ave 08360
Vassar Pl 08360
Venetia Ave 08361
Venezia Ave 08361
Venturi Ln 08361
Venus Dr 08360
Victoria Ct 08361
Victory Ave 08360
Villa Ave 08360
Vine Rd
1800-2799 08361
2800-3199 08360
Vineland Ct 08361
Virano Ln 08360
Virginia Ave 08360
Wallace St 08360
E Walnut Rd
2-30 08360
32-1199 08360
1201-1297 08361
1299-1999 08361
W Walnut Rd 08360
Warren Dr 08360
Washington Ave
600-1099 08360
1300-1398 08361
1400-2499 08361
Wayne Ave 08360
Wellington Ct 08360
Wendy Ln 08360
N & S West Ave & Blvd 08360
Westmont Ln 08360
Westwood Dr 08360
Wexley Way 08361
Weymouth Rd 08360
Wheat Rd 08360
E Wheat Rd
1-111 08360
113-1725 08360
1727-1799 08360
1800-2199 08361
2201-2299 08361
W Wheat Rd 08360
Whispering Woods Way 08361
White St 08360
White Deer Ln 08360
White Pine Way 08360
Wilderness Dr 08361
Wills Pl 08361
Wilson Ave 08360
Winchang Ave 08361
Wisteria Ave 08361
E & W Wood St 08360
Woodcrest Dr
1000-1199 08360
1500-1799 08361
Woodlawn Ave 08360
Woodstock Ct 08361
Wren St 08361
Wynnewood Dr 08361
Yale Ter 08360
Yankee Ct 08361
Yelkca Ave 08360

NUMBERED STREETS

All Street Addresses 08360

WAYNE NJ

General Delivery 07470

POST OFFICE BOXES MAIN OFFICE STATIONS AND BRANCHES

Box No.s
All PO Boxes 07474

NAMED STREETS

Abbott Rd 07470
Aberdeen Ave 07470
Adams Rd 07470
Adelphia Rd 07470
Adobe Dr 07470
Agatha Ln 07470
Agawam Dr 07470
Alden Pl 07470
Alder Ave 07470
Ales Pl 07470
Alexandria Ave 07470
Algonquin Trl 07470
Allen Dr 07470
Allison Ct 07470
Allwood Ter 07470
Almadera Dr 07470
Almroth Dr 07470
Alpine Dr 07470
Alps Rd 07470
Ambassador Dr 07470
Amboy Rd 07470
Amherst Ct 07470
Amy Way 07470
Anderson Dr 07470
Andover Dr 07470
Angell St 07470
Ann St 07470
Apache Rd 07470
Apollo Dr 07470
Apple Ln 07470
Arbor Rd 07470
Archung Rd 07470
Armstrong Ave 07470
Arundel Rd 07470
Ashburn Rd 07470
Ashlyn Ct 07470
Ashwood Ln 07470
Aspen Ct 07470
Atherton Ct 07470
Atwood Pl 07470
Audubon Pkwy 07470
Augusta Dr 07470
Azusa Ct 07470
Baker St 07470
Baldwin Ter 07470
Balsam Rd 07470
Barbara Way 07470
Barbour Pond Dr 07470
Barker Pl 07470
Barnsdale Rd 07470
Basswood Ter 07470
Baywood Ave 07470
Beatrice Ln 07470
Beech Ter 07470
Beechwood Dr 07470
Belair Ter 07470
Bella Ct 07470
W Belt Plz 07470
Benson Dr 07470
Benwell Ave 07470
Berdan Ave 07470
Bergen St 07470
Berkley Ct 07470
Berkshire Dr 07470
Berry Dr 07470
Bertrand Dr 07470
Beverly Way 07470
Big Horn Dr 07470
Billrose Ln 07470
Birch Ln 07470
Birchwood Ter 07470
Birdseye Cir 07470
Birkett Ct 07470
Bitola Dr 07470
Black Briar Ln 07470
Black Oak Ridge Rd 07470
Blackfoot Cir 07470
Blandford Rd 07470
Bobolink Ct 07470
Bodie Rd 07470
Bolton Rd 07470
Bonita Ter 07470
Boonstra Dr 07470
Borzotta Blvd 07470
S Boulevard Dr 07470
Bouningt Rd 07470
Bourbon St 07470
Bowfell Ct 07470
Braemar Dr 07470
Brandon Ave 07470
Brandywine Rd 07470
Breckenridge 07470
Breen Ter 07470
Brentwood Ct 07470
Briarwood Rd 07470
Brighton Ter 07470
Bristol Pl 07470
Brittany Dr 07470
Broadway 07470
Brook Ter 07470
Brookdale Rd 07470
Brookside Rd 07470
Brookwood Dr 07470
Bryan Ct 07470
Budd Way 07470
Buen Ln 07470
Bullens Ave 07470
Bunker Hill Rd 07470
Burgess Pl 07470
Burgundy Way 07470
Burke Rd 07470
Burnside Pl 07470
Butternut Dr 07470
Buttonwood Dr 07470
Byrne Ct 07470
Cadmus Pl 07470
Cambridge Pl 07470
Camden St 07470
Camillo Dr 07470
S Canal St 07470
Canterbury Way 07470
Canton Rd 07470
Cardinal Way 07470
Carey Arthur Dr 07470
Caribou Cir 07470
Carlisle Rd 07470
Carlton Ct 07470
Carol Pl 07470
Casey Ln 07470
Castles Dr 07470
Cathyann Ct 07470
Cauley Rd 07470
Cayuga Trl 07470
Cecilia Dr 07470
Cedar Pl 07470
Cedarcliffe Dr 07470
Central Ave 07470
Cezar Ct 07470
Chadwick Rd 07470
Chandler Dr 07470
Chapel Pl 07470
Charlotte Ter 07470
Chatham Ct 07470
Cherry Way 07470
Cherrywood Dr 07470
Chestnut Dr 07470
Cheyenne Way 07470
Chicopee Dr 07470
Chimney Ln 07470
Chopin Dr 07470
Christine Ct 07470
Church Ln 07470
Ciccone Dr 07470
Circle Ave 07470
Claire Ct 07470
Claremont Ter 07470
Clark St 07470
Clearwater Dr 07470
Cliff Rd 07470
Clifford Dr 07470
Clinton Ln 07470
Clove Pl 07470
Cobble Stone Ct 07470
Colburn Ct 07470
Cole St 07470
Colfax Rd 07470
Colombo Ln 07470
Colona Rd 07470
Colonial Rd 07470
Colville Rd 07470
Colyer Ter 07470
Concord Pl 07470
Coniston Ct 07470
Continental Dr 07470
Cook Rd 07470
Copley Ct 07470
Corporate Dr 07470
Corvair Pl 07470
Cosden Ln 07470
Cottonwood Rd 07470
Cougar Cir 07470
Court Ln 07470
Courter Ave 07470
Coventry Rd 07470
Cracco Ln 07470
Craig Ct 07470
Crane Ter 07470
Crescent Rd 07470
Crest Ct 07470
Crossing Way 07470
Crow Trl 07470
Dakota Ave 07470
Dalewood Rd 07470
Daly Ave 07470
Danielle Dr 07470
Darlington Dr 07470
Dartmouth Rd 07470
Dave Espie Way 07470
David Scott Dr 07470
Davies Ct 07470
Dawn Pl 07470
Debbie Ct 07470
Deerfield Rd 07470
Dehart Ct 07470
Delaware Dr 07470
Demarest Dr 07470
Dey Rd 07470
Diane Ct 07470
Diaz Ct 07470
Diorio Ct 07470
Divan Way 07470
Dixon Pl 07470
Dogwood Ter 07470
Doig Rd 07470
Donald Ct 07470
Donna Ln 07470
Doreen Ln 07470
Doremus Ln 07470
Dorsa Ave 07470
Douglas Way 07470
Dowitcher Ct 07470
Drayton Pl 07470
Dubel Rd 07470
Dudley Ct 07470
Duncan Ln 07470
Dupont Ter 07470
Dwight St 07470
Dwyer Rd 07470
Eagle Dr 07470
Easedale Rd 07470
Echo Ct 07470
Eden Pl 07470
Edgemont Cres 07470
Edison Dr 07470
Edith Ct 07470
Eider Ct 07470
Eldorado Dr 07470
Eleron Pl 07470
Ella Ln 07470
Ellen Ln 07470
Ellicott Ln 07470
Elmary Pl 07470
Elmwood Ter 07470
Emanuel Ave 07470
Emerson Pl 07470
Erie Ave 07470
Erli St 07470
Eros Ct 07470
Eton Ct 07470
Evelyn Ter 07470
Everett Pl 07470
Evergreen Pl 07470
Evers Ct 07470
Fair Ridge Ct 07470
Fairfield Rd 07470
Fairmount Rd 07470
Fairpark Pl 07470
Fairview Ter 07470
Falcon Pl 07470
Farm View Ct 07470
Farmingdale Rd 07470
Farmstead Ln 07470
Fay Ct 07470
Fayette Ave 07470
Fenner Pl 07470
Fern Ter 07470
Fern River Rd 07470
Ferndale Rd 07470
Ferrara Ave 07470
Ferri St 07470
Fieldstone Pl 07470
Finley Ln 07470
Finns Dr 07470
Fisk Rd 07470
Flynn Pl 07470
Ford St 07470
Forest Ter 07470
Forest Hill Dr 07470
Four Seasons Dr 07470
Fox Boro Rd 07470
Fox Hill Dr 07470
Fox Hollow Ct 07470
Franklin Ave 07470
Frederick Ct 07470
French Hill Rd 07470
Friar Way 07470
Furman Dr 07470
Furno Pl 07470
Gaede Pl 07470
Galesi Dr 07470
Gannett Ct 07470
Garfield Rd 07470
Garside Ave 07470
Garvey Rd 07470
Gates Pl 07470
Geneva Ct 07470
Geoffrey Way 07470
Georgia Dr 07470
Giannone Rd 07470
Gibbs Dr 07470
Gina Marie Ct 07470
Glen Rd 07470
Gorge Way 07470
Gorham Ct 07470
Gow Rd 07470
Grace Ct 07470
Graham Ave 07470
Grand St 07470
Grandview Dr 07470
Grantwood Rd 07470
Green Knolls Dr 07470
Greenbrier Ct 07470
Greenrale Ave 07470
Greenup Ct 07470
Greenwood Ave 07470
Greg Ct 07470
Gressinger Rd 07470
Grieves Ter 07470
Grove Pl 07470
Grover Dr 07470
Haddon Rd 07470
Hadley Ln 07470
Hall St 07470
Halsey Rd 07470
Hamburg Tpke 07470
Hamilton Ave 07470
Hampton Ter 07470
Hanes Dr 07470
Hanover Pl 07470
Hanson Pl 07470
Hardwick Ln 07470
Harlan Ter 07470
Harmer Ter 07470
Harmony Ln 07470
Harrier Ct 07470
Harrison Rd 07470
Harwood Pl 07470
Haul Rd 07470
Hawthorne Rd 07470
Hazen Ct 07470
Hearthstone Ct 07470
Heights Rd 07470
Helene Ct 07470
Hemlock Ter 07470
Herfort Rd 07470
Heritage Manor Dr 07470
Herrick Rd 07470
Hershey Rd 07470
Hickory Pl 07470
High St 07470
Highfield Ct 07470
Highland Ter 07470
Highpoint Dr 07470
Highview Ct 07470
Hillcrest Dr 07470
Hillside Ter 07470
Hilltop Ter 07470
Hinchman Ave 07470
Hobson Ave 07470
Hollow Brooke Ct 07470
Holmes Ln 07470
Holy Cross Way 07470
Holyoke Rd 07470
Hoover Pl 07470
Hopper Ln 07470
Horizon Dr 07470
Howe Ave 07470
Hubbardton Rd 07470
Huff Rd 07470
Hunter Pl 07470
Huron Ave 07470
Hurst Ter 07470
Independence Ave 07470
Indian Rd 07470
Ingraham Ter 07470
Iowa Rd 07470
Irene Pl 07470
Iroquois Trl 07470
Island St 07470
Ivy Pl 07470
Jackson Ave 07470
Jacobus Ave 07470
James St 07470
Jane Pl 07470
Jansen Ln 07470
Jason Ct 07470
Jean Ter 07470
Jefferson Pl 07470
Jeffrey Rd 07470
Jenny Ln 07470
Jerome Pl 07470
N Jersey Ln 07470
Jessica Way 07470
Joan St 07470
Joseph Pl 07470
Joyce Ln 07470
Judith Pl 07470
Julie Pl 07470
Juniper Rd 07470
Kane Ct 07470
Karen Ct 07470
Kathleen Ct 07470
Katrina Ct 07470
Keilana Dr 07470
Kelly St 07470
Kennedy Ct 07470
Kenneth St 07470
Kent Ave 07470
Kenwood Rd 07470
Kevin Pl 07470
Kievit Rd 07470
Kimberly Pl 07470
Kime Ave 07470
King Ct 07470
Kingston Rd 07470
Kipp Ct 07470
Kirk Ter 07470
Kiwanis Dr 07470
Knight Rd 07470
Knoll Rd 07470
Knox Ter 07470
Kossuth Pl 07470
Kram Ct 07470
Kristen Ct 07470
Kuiken Ct 07470
Kurland St 07470
Laauwe Ave 07470
Lafayette Ct 07470
Laguna Dr 07470
Lake Dr, Rd & Trl E & W 07470
Lakeside Ave 07470
Lamoureux Ln 07470
Lancaster Ct 07470
Langdale Rd 07470
Larkspur Rd 07470
Laurel Dr 07470
Lauren Ct 07470
Lavina Ter 07470
Lawrence Rd 07470
Laytham Dr 07470
Ledge Rd 07470
Legion Pl 07470
Legrande Ter 07470
Leisure Ln 07470
Lenape Trl 07470
Lenox Rd 07470
Leo Pl 07470
Leonard Ter 07470
Leslie Dr 07470
Levinberg Ln 07470
Lewis St 07470
Lexington Ln 07470
Leystra Ln 07470
Lillian Ct 07470
Lilro Ct 07470
Lincoln Pl 07470
Linda Ct 07470
Linden Ln & Rd 07470
Lindy Rd 07470
Linwood Ave 07470
Lions Head Blvd & Dr 07470
Lisa Ln 07470
Little Pl 07470
Little Pond Rd 07470
Littlewood Ct 07470
Lockley Ct 07470
Locust Pl 07470
Lois Ct 07470
Longell Dr 07470
Longport Rd 07470
Longwood Ct 07470
Lorenz Pl 07470
Lorrie Ct 07470
Louisa Ct 07470
Lowell Dr 07470
Lucas Ln 07470
Ludlum Rd 07470

Street	ZIP
Lyle Ave	07470
Lyncrest Ter	07470
Lyons Ave	07470
Macdonald Dr	07470
Mack St	07470
Madero Ln	07470
Madison St	07470
Maghee Rd	07470
Magnolia Pl	07470
Main Ave & Rd	07470
Maljim Ct	07470
Manchester Ct	07470
Mandeville Dr	07470
Mandon Dr	07470
Manhattan Ave	07470
Manor Dr	07470
Mansard Ct	07470
Maple Ave & Ln	07470
Maplewood Ave	07470
Marc Rd	07470
Margaret St	07470
Market St	07470
Marling Dr	07470
Marlo Rd	07470
Marlton Dr	07470
Matthew Rd	07470
Maybrook Ct	07470
Mayfair Dr	07470
Mcclelland Ave	07470
Mcdevitt Dr	07470
Mcgrogan Ct	07470
Mckernan Ct	07470
Mead St	07470
Meadow Rd	07470
Medford Pl	07470
Melanie Ln	07470
Meyer Ln	07470
Michael Dr	07470
Michardy Pl	07470
Michele Ct	07470
Micheline Ct	07470
Midwood Pl	07470
Miller Rd	07470
Milton Dr	07470
Minnisink Rd	07470
Minns Ave	07470
Mohawk Trl	07470
Moiyas Rd	07470
Monhegan Ave	07470
Monmouth Ave	07470
Montauk Trl	07470
Monterey Dr	07470
Morgan Ct	07470
Morning Watch Rd	07470
Moro Ter	07470
Morris Ave	07470
Mountain Rd	07470
Mountain Ridge Dr	07470
Mountainside Dr	07470
Mountainview Blvd	07470
Mulford Dr	07470
Munster Pl	07470
Myrtle Ave	07470
Nancy Ct	07470
Nathan Way	07470
Navajo Ave	07470
Ned Rd	07470
Nellis Dr	07470
Nevins Rd	07470
New St	07470
New York Ave	07470
Newark Ave	07470
Newark Pompton Tpke	07470
Newton Rd	07470
Nimitz Rd	07470
Noreen Ln	07470
Normandy Dr	07470
North Rd	07470
Nostrand Ave	07470
Nottingham Rd	07470
Nuthatcher Ct	07470
Oak Ln & St	07470
Oak Hill Dr	07470
Oak Tree Ln	07470
Oakley Way	07470
Oakwood Dr	07470
Old Homestead Rd	07470
Old Newark Pompton Tpke	07470
Old Turnpike Rd	07470
Oldham Rd	07470
Olga St	07470
Omaha Rd	07470
Oneida Trl	07470
Orange Pl	07470
Orchard Pl	07470
Oriskany Pl	07470
Osage Rd	07470
Osborne Ter	07470
Osceola Rd	07470
Otis Pl	07470
Overhill Rd	07470
Overlook Ave	07470
Owens Dr	07470
Oxbow Pl	07470
Packanack Lake Rd	07470
Pal Dr	07470
Palmer Dr	07470
Pancake Hollow Dr	07470
Parclake Ct	07470
Parish Dr	07470
Park Ln	07470
Parkhurst St	07470
Parkside Ct	07470
Parkview Dr	07470
Parkwood Dr	07470
Patricia Ct	07470
Patton Ct	07470
Paul St	07470
Pauline Ct	07470
Peach Way	07470
Pelham Rd	07470
Penny Ct	07470
Perera Ave	07470
Perrin Dr	07470
Peslin Ct	07470
Peter Pl	07470
Peterson Rd	07470
Petrie Ln	07470
Phyllis Ct	07470
Piermont Ter	07470
Pike Dr	07470
Pilgrim Way	07470
Pine Ter	07470
Pine Tree Dr	07470
Pinecrest Ter	07470
Pines Lake Dr E & W	07470
Pitman Pl	07470
Pleasantview Dr	07470
Pocahontas Trl	07470
Point Rd	07470
Point View Pkwy	07470
Pompton Rd	07470
Pompton Plains Xrd	
1-199	07470
150-150	07474
201-299	07470
Pond Cir	07470
Pontiac Dr	07470
Poplar Rd	07470
Post Ln	07470
Powderhorn Dr	07470
Power Rd	07470
Preakness Ave	07470
Preakness Shopping Ctr	
1-199	07470
42-42	07474
300-300	07470
Prince Ct	07470
Princeton Pl	07470
Prospect Rd	07470
Pueblo Cir	07470
Queens Ln	07470
Quincy Ct	07470
Railroad Ave	07470
Raleigh Ln	07470
Ralph St	07470
Randall Ter	07470
Rande Dr	07470
Ratcliffe Rd	07470
Ratzer Rd	07470
Ravine Ln	07470
Raymar Ln	07470
Rays Ct	07470
Redwood Ave	07470
Reed Ct	07470
Reinhardt Rd	07470
Rene Ct	07470
Reston Rd	07470
Richard Ln	07470
Ridge Pl	07470
Ridgeview Ter	07470
Rigby Ct	07470
Rillo Dr	07470
Rinaldo Ln	07470
River Rd	07470
Riverlawn Dr	07470
Riverside Dr	07470
Riverview Dr	07470
Robin Rd	07470
Robin Hood Way	07470
Rock Rd	07470
Rockledge Ter	07470
Roland Pl	07470
Rolling Hills Dr	07470
Ronnie Rd	07470
Rose Ter	07470
Royal Ct	07470
Rumana Rd	07470
Runnymede Dr	07470
Ruskin Ct	07470
Russell Ter	07470
Rutgers Ct	07470
Ryder Rd	07470
Ryerson Ave	07470
Saint Moritz Pl	07470
Salem Rd	07470
Salisbury Rd	07470
Sandra Ln	07470
Saniewski Ln	07470
Saralyn Ct	07470
Saratoga Sq	07470
Saxon Ave	07470
Schindler Ln	07470
Schuyler Rd	07470
Scribner Pl	07470
Sears Pl	07470
Sell Pl	07470
Seminole Ave	07470
Seneca Trl	07470
Sequoia Pl	07470
Seven Trails Ln	07470
Shadow Ridge Run	07470
Shady Ter	07470
Shasta Rd	07470
Shawn Ct	07470
Shearwater Ln	07470
Sheffield Rd	07470
Shephard Ln	07470
Sherman St	07470
Sherry Ct	07470
Sherwood St	07470
Shore Rd	07470
Shoshone Trl	07470
Siena Vlg	07470
Sierra Ter	07470
Siesta Dr	07470
Sikkema Ave	07470
Simmons Pl	07470
Sinclair Dr	07470
Sisco St	07470
Skyview Rd	07470
Sleepy Hollow Dr	07470
Sloping Hill Ter	07470
Smith Ln	07470
Soldatovic Ct	07470
Somers Pl	07470
South Rd	07470
Southhall Ct	07470
Spring Rd	07470
Spring Hill Cir	07470
Spruce Ter	07470
Squire Ln	07470
Stacy Ct	07470
Stagg Rd	07470
Stalter Dr	07470
Stanford Pl	07470
Starview Ct	07470
State Route 23	07470
Steeple Chase Ct	07470
Stirling Ln	07470
Stone Hill Rd	07470
Stonycroft Rd	07470
Stratton Dr	07470
Stuart Ln	07470
Stuckler Ln	07470
Sturbridge Cir	07470
Styles Ter	07470
Stylon Rd	07470
Summer Hill Rd	07470
Summerhill Rd	07470
Summit Dr	07470
Sunburst Ln	07470
Sundance Dr	07470
Sunny Knolls Ct	07470
Sunnyridge Rd	07470
Sunrise Dr	07470
Sunset Ter	07470
Surrey Dr	07470
Susan Ave	07470
Sussex Rd	07470
Suters Ln	07470
Swan Ter	07470
Swiss Ter	07470
Sycamore Ter	07470
Sylvan Ter	07470
Tall Grass Dr	07470
Tall Oaks Dr	07470
Talsman Ct	07470
Tamarack Rd	07470
Tammy Ter	07470
Tanager Ct	07470
Taylor Dr	
20-32	07470
34-36	07470
35-35	07474
38-50	07470
Teak Rd	07470
Terhune Dr	07470
Terrace Rd	07470
Teton Cir	07470
Thomas Ter	07470
Thorne Hl	07470
Ticonderoga Ter	07470
Tilghman Dr	07470
Timberline Dr	07470
Timothy Rd	07470
Todd Ter	07470
Tomahawk Dr	07470
Toms Lake Rd	07470
Torbet Dr	07470
Tosch Ave	07470
Totowa Rd	07470
Toucan Ct	07470
Tower Rd	07470
Towsen Rd	07470
Traphagen Rd	07470
Travelo Dr	07470
Trenton Ter	07470
Tripoli St	07470
Tulip Ter	07470
Tuxedo Dr	07470
Umberto St	07470
Upton Ct	07470
Urban Club Rd	07470
Us Highway 46	07470
Vale Rd	07470
Valhalla Way	07470
Valley Rd	
1270A-1270B	07470
Valley View Ter	07470
Van Allen Ct	07470
Van Duyne Ave	07470
Van Ness Pl	07470
Van Riper Rd	07470
Vanderelinde Rd	07470
Vans Ln	07470
Varick St	07470
Verkade Dr	07470
Vernon Ct	07470
Veteri Pl	07470
Viewpoint Rd	07470
Village Dr	07470
Vincent St	07470
Viola Ln	07470
Virginia Ct	07470
Vista Trl	07470
Vizcaya Ct	07470
Waling Dr	07470
Walker Ave	07470
Wanda Ave	07470
Warbler Dr	07470
Warner Way	07470
Warren Pl	07470
Water St	07470
Waterford Ct	07470
Waterway Rd	07470
Wayne St	07470
Wayne Hills Mall	07470
Wayne Towne Ctr	07470
Webster Dr	07470
Wedgewood Dr	07470
Weinmanns Blvd	07470
Wellington Dr	07470
Welsh Ct	07470
Wendt Ln	07470
N West Rd	07470
Westbelt	07470
Westervelt St	07470
Weston Ct	07470
Westview Rd	07470
Wheeler Rd	07470
Whimble Ct	07470
Whipple Rd	07470
White Birch Ct	07470
White Oak Ln	07470
Whitmore Ave	07470
Whittaker Ct	07470
Wiessmann Way	07470
William St	07470
Williamsburg Ct	07470
Willowbrook Blvd & Mall	07470
Wills Ave	07470
Wilson Ave	07470
Winding Way	07470
Windsor Pl	07470
Winonah Ave	07470
Winters Dr	07470
Witkowski Way	07470
Wittig Ter	07470
Wood St	07470
Woodhaven Dr	07470
Woodland Ct	07470
Woodlot Rd	07470
Woodridge Ter	07470
Woods End Ct	07470
Woodstock Dr	07470
Worcester Dr	07470
Yellow Brick Rd	07470
Yorktown Rd	07470

NUMBERED STREETS

Street	ZIP
All Street Addresses	07470

WESTFIELD NJ

Street	ZIP
General Delivery	07091

POST OFFICE BOXES MAIN OFFICE STATIONS AND BRANCHES

Box No.s	ZIP
J - P	07091
1 - 897	07091
216 - 416	07090
995 - 3076	07091
2038 - 2038	07090

NAMED STREETS

Street	ZIP
Alden Ave	07090
Amy Dr	07090
Archbold Pl	07090
Ardsleigh Dr	07090
Arlington Ave	07090
Austin St	07090
Avon Rd	07090
Ayliffe Ave	07090
Azalea Trl	07090
Bailey Ct	07090
Baker Ave	07090
Barchester Way	07090
Bates Way	07090
Bayberry Ln	07090
Beechwood Pl	07090
Bell Dr	07090
Belmar Pl & Ter	07090
Belvidere Ave	07090
Bennett Pl	07090
Benson Pl	07090
Beverly Dr	07090
Birch Ave & Pl	07090
Boulevard	07090
Boynton Ave & Ct	07090
Bradford Ave	07090
Bradson Ct	07090
Brandt	07090
Breezeknoll Dr	07090
Brightwood Ave	07090
E & W Broad St	07090
Brown Ave	07090
Bryant Ave	07090
Burgess Ct	07090
Burrington Gorge	07090
Byron Ct	07090
Cacciola Pl	07090
Cambridge Rd	07090
Canterbury Ln & Rd	07090
Cardinal Dr	07090
Carleton Rd	07090
Carol Rd	07090
Castleman Dr	07090
Cayuga Way	07090
Cedar St & Ter	07090
Central Ave	
101-107	07090
109-154	07090
153-153	07091
155-1999	07090
156-2424	07090
Channing Ave	07090
Charles St	07090
Cherokee Ct	07090
Cherry Ln	07090
N & S Chestnut St	07090
Clarence St	07090
Clark St	07090
Cleveland Ave	07090
Clifton St	07090
Clover St	07090
Codding Rd	07090
Coleman Pl	07090
Colonial Ave	07090
Columbus Ave	07090
Connecticut St	07090
Coolidge St	07090
Cornwall Dr	07090
Cory Pl	07090
N Cottage Pl	07090
Cowperthwaite Pl & Sq	07090
Cranford Ave	07090
Crescent Pkwy	07090
Crossway Pl	07090
Cumberland St	07090
Dakota St	07090
Dartmoor	07090
Davis Ct	07090
Delaware St	07090
Dickson Dr	07090
Dorian Ct, Pl & Rd	07090
Doris Pkwy	07090
Dorset Hill Rd	07090
Downer St	07090
Drake Pl	07090
Drummond Rd	07090
E & W Dudley Ave & Ct	07090
Duncan Hl	07090
Dunham Ave	07090
Eaglecroft Rd	07090
Eastgate Sq	07090
Edgar Rd	07090
Edgewood Ave	07090
Effingham Pl	07090
Elizabeth Ave	07090
Elm St	07090
S Elmer St	07090
Embree Cres & Ct	07090
Eton Pl	07090
N & S Euclid Ave	07090
Evergreen Ct	07090
Everson Pl	07090
Everts Ave	07090
Fairacres Ave	07090
Fairfield Cir	07090
Fairhill Dr & Rd	07090
Fairmont Ave	07090
Fanwood Ave	07090
Faulkner Dr	07090
Ferris Pl	07090
Floral Ct	07090
N Florence Ave	07090
Florida St	07090
Folkstone Dr	07090
Forest Ave	07090
Forest Glen Ct	07090
Francis Ter	07090
Franklin Ave	07090
Frazee Ct	07090
Gallowae	07090
Gallows Hill Rd	07090
Garfield Ave	07090
Genesee Trl	07090
Girard Ave	07090
Glen Ave	07090
Golf Edge Dr	07090
Graceland Pl	07090
Grandview Ave	07090
Grant Ave	07090
Green Briar Ct	07090
Greene Pl	07090
E Grove St	07090
Hamilton Ave	07090
Hampton Ct	07090
Hancock St	07090
Hanford Pl	07090
Harding St	07090
Hardwick Ave	07090
Harrison Ave	07090
Harrow Rd	07090
Hawthorn Dr	07090
Hazel Ave	07090
Hiawatha Dr	07090
Highgate Ave	07090
Highland Ave	07090
Hillcrest Ave	07090
Hillside Ave	07090
Hort St	07090
Hyslip Ave	07090
Irving Ave	07090
Jefferson Ave	07090
John St	07090
Karen Ter	07090
Kensington Dr	07090
Kent Pl	07090
Kimball Ave & Cir	07090
Kimball Turn	07090
Kirkstone Cir	07090
Kirkview Cir	07090
Knollwood Ter	07090
Lambert Cir	07090
Lamberts Mill Rd	07090
Landsdowne Ave	07090
Lawnside Pl	07090
Lawrence Ave	07090
Leigh Dr	07090
Lenape Trl	07090
Lenox Ave	07090
Liberty Ave	07090
Lincoln Plz & Rd	07090
Linden Ave	07090
Livingston St	07090
Longfellow Ave	07090
Ludlow Pl	07090

Lynn Ln 07090
Lynwood Pl 07090
Madison Ave 07090
Manchester Dr 07090
Manitou Cir 07090
Maple St 07090
Marcellus Dr 07090
Marion Ave 07090
Marlboro St 07090
Marlin Ct 07090
Maryland St 07090
Massachusetts St 07090
Max Pl 07090
Maye St 07090
Michael Dr 07090
Midvale Ter 07090
Midwood Pl 07090
Minisink Way 07090
Mohawk Trl & Way 07090
Mohican Dr 07090
Montauk Dr 07090
Morris Ave 07090
Moss Ave 07090
Mountain Ave 07090
Mountainview Cir, Dr & Ter 07090
Munsee Way 07090
Myrtle Ave 07090
Nancy Way 07090
Naworth Pass 07090
Nelson Pl 07090
Nevada St 07090
New St 07090
New England Dr 07090
Newark Ave 07090
Nomahegan Dr 07090
Norgate 07090
Norman Pl 07090
Normandy Dr 07090
North Ave E & W 07090
Norwood Dr 07090
Nottingham Pl 07090
Oak Ave 07090
Oak Tree Pass 07090
Oneida Dr 07090
Orchard St 07090
Orenda Cir 07090
Osborne Ave 07090
Otisco Dr 07090
Overhill St 07090
Oxford Ter 07090
Palsted Ave 07090
Park Dr & St 07090
Parkview Ave 07090
Pearl St 07090
Pennsylvania Ave 07090
Pierson St 07090
Pine Ct & St 07090
Pine Grove Ave 07090
Plymouth Rd 07090
Poe Ave 07090
Priscilla Ln 07090
Prospect St 07090
Quantuck Ln 07090
Quimby St 07090
Radley Ct & Rd 07090
Rahway Ave 07090
Ramapo Way 07090
Raymond St 07090
Ripley Ave & Pl 07090
Roanoke Rd 07090
Robin Hood Way 07090
Rodman Ln 07090
Roger Ave 07090
Roosevelt St 07090
Ross Pl 07090
Rutgers Ct 07090
Saint Georges Pl 07090
Saint Johns Pl 07090
Saint Marks Ave 07090
Saint Paul St 07090
Salter Pl 07090
Sandford Ave 07090
Sandra Cir 07090
Sandy Hill Rd 07090
Saunders Ave 07090
Scotch Plains Ave 07090
Scudder Rd 07090
Sedgewick Ave & Ct ... 07090
Seneca Pl 07090
Settlers Ln 07090
Seward Ave 07090
Shackamaxon Dr 07090
Shadowlawn Dr 07090
Shawnee Pass 07090
Sherbrooke Dr 07090
Sherman St 07090
Sherwood Pkwy 07090
Short Hills Ct 07090
Sinclair Pl 07090
South Ave E & W 07090
Springfield Ave 07090
Standish Ave 07090
Stanley Ave & Oval 07090
Stanmore Pl 07090
Starlite Ct 07090
Stevens Ave 07090
Stirling Pl 07090
Stoneleigh Park 07090
Summit Ave & Ct 07090
Sunnywood Dr 07090
Sunset Ave 07090
Surrey Ln 07090
Sussex St 07090
Sycamore St 07090
Sylvania Pl 07090
Talcott Rd 07090
Tamaques Way 07090
Temple Pl 07090
Terrace Pl 07090
Thomas Ct 07090
Tice Pl 07090
Topping Hill Rd 07090
Trails End Ct 07090
Tremont Ave 07090
Trinity Pl 07090
Tudor Oval 07090
Tuttle Pkwy 07090
Tuxford Turn 07090
Twin Oaks Ter 07090
Unami Ter 07090
Union St 07090
Vermont St 07090
Vernon Pl & Ter 07090
Village Cir & Grn 07090
Virginia St 07090
Wallberg Ave 07090
Walnut St 07090
Warren St 07090
Washington St 07090
Watchung Frk 07090
Watterson St 07090
Webster Pl 07090
Welch Way 07090
Wells St 07090
West Ct 07090
Westbrook Rd 07090
Westfield Ave 07090
Whittier Ave 07090
N & S Wickom Dr 07090
Willow Grove Pkwy & Rd 07090
Winchester Way 07090
Windsor Ave 07090
Winyah Ave 07090
Woodbrook Cir 07090
Woodland Ave 07090
Woodmere Dr 07090
Woods End Rd 07090
Wyandotte Trl 07090
Wychview Dr 07090
Wychwood Rd 07090
Wyoming St 07090

NUMBERED STREETS

All Street Addresses 07090

WHIPPANY NJ

General Delivery 07981

POST OFFICE BOXES MAIN OFFICE STATIONS AND BRANCHES

Box No.s
All PO Boxes 07981

NAMED STREETS

Academy Dr E & W 07981
Adams Dr 07981
Addie Ln 07981
Adela Ct 07981
Alanon St 07981
Algonquin Pkwy 07981
Alpine Ln 07981
Altaview Ct 07981
Andrew Rd 07981
Anna Ter 07981
Apollo Dr 07981
Appleton Way 07981
Baird Pl 07981
Baldwin Ct 07981
Bayer Blvd 07981
S Beaumont Pl 07981
Beaverbrook Ter 07981
Bee Meadow Pkwy 07981
Beech Ter 07981
Beekman Pl 07981
Behrens Dr 07981
Berkshire St 07981
Birch Hill Dr 07981
Black Brook Dr 07981
Boxwood Ct 07981
Brandywine Ct 07981
Branford Rd 07981
Briarwood Ct 07981
Brook Hollow Dr 07981
Brookview Ct 07981
Buckingham Rd 07981
Bunker Hill Pl 07981
Cambridge St 07981
Cedar Knolls Rd 07981
Chandler Ln 07981
Clay St 07981
Clemens Ter 07981
Cobblestone Way 07981
Concord Rd 07981
Constitution Pl 07981
Convergence Way 07981
Cortland Ln 07981
Cortright Rd 07981
Cove Lane Rd 07981
Crescent Dr 07981
Crestview Ter 07981
Daniel Ter 07981
David Dr 07981
Dawson Pl 07981
Deerfield Rd 07981
Dellwood Ln 07981
Dogwood Rd 07981
Dorchester St 07981
Druetzler Ct 07981
Eden Ln 07981
Edgehill Ter 07981
Elizabeth St 07981
Emerson Dr 07981
Erna Pl 07981
Ertman Dr 07981
Evergreen Ct 07981
E Fairchild Pl 07981
Fanok Rd 07981
Fawnridge Pl 07981
Fenwick Rd 07981
Fieldstone Dr 07981
Fischer Pl 07981
Ford Hill Rd 07981
Forest Hill Ct 07981
Foxchase Ln 07981
Frank Ter 07981
Glenbrook Ct 07981
Glenn Pl 07981
Gloria Ave 07981
Grandview Ct 07981
Griffith Dr 07981
Grove Pl 07981
Hamilton Ct 07981
Handzel Rd 07981
Hanover Ave 07981
Harriet Dr 07981
Harvest Ct 07981
Heritage Ln 07981
Highland Ave 07981
Hillary Ct 07981
Hillcrest Rd 07981
Hilltop Cir 07981
Howell St 07981
Hubert St 07981
Independence Dr 07981
Jackento Rd 07981
Jacque Ter 07981
Jefferson Park 07981
N Jefferson Rd 07981
S Jefferson Rd
1-53 07981
54-54 07999
54-198 07981
55-199 07981
Jeffrie Trl 07981
John St 07981
Joseph St 07981
Karla Dr 07981
Kathryn Dr 07981
Kearney Ave 07981
Kensington Ct 07981
Kitchell Pl 07981
Knollwood Rd 07981
Lafayette Ct 07981
Leamoor Dr 07981
Lefke Ln 07981
Legion Pl 07981
Leo Pl 07981
Leslie Ct 07981
Lexington Ct 07981
Lionel Pl 07981
Llewelyn Ct 07981
Longview Dr 07981
Louis St 07981
Lynn Ter 07981
Magnolia Dr 07981
Malapardis Rd 07981
Manchester Dr 07981
Mapleshade Dr 07981
Marlin Dr 07981
Martin Rd 07981
Meadow Brook Ct 07981
Melanie Ln 07981
Mount Pleasant Ave 07981
Mount Vernon Way 07981
Nemic Ln 07981
Northcrest Ter 07981
Norwood Way 07981
Nye Ave 07981
Oak Glen Pl 07981
Oakwood Ct 07981
Old Stone Ln 07981
Papermill Dr 07981
Park Ave 07981
Parsippany Rd 07981
Perry St 07981
Pleasant Valley Rd 07981
Polhemus Ter 07981
N Pond Rd 07981
Prince Rd 07981
Railroad Plz 07981
Regina Pl 07981
Reynolds Ave 07981
Ridgedale Ave 07981
River Park Ct 07981
Riveredge Ln 07981
Rosemont Ln 07981
Runnymede Ct 07981
Salem Dr E 07981
Schindler Ct 07981
School St 07981
Seamount Dr 07981
Sharon Dr 07981
Sherry Ln 07981
Skurla Ln 07981
Slattery Ln 07981
Smithfield Rd 07981
Springbrook Ct 07981
State Route 10 07981
Sterling Ct 07981
Stone Creek Ct 07981
Sunrise Dr 07981
Sunset Dr 07981
Tanglewood Pl 07981
Thea Pl 07981
Tompkins Pl 07981
Troy Rd 07981
Troy Hills Rd 07981
Vale Rd 07981
Valley Forge Dr 07981
Vermont Ter 07981
Veterans Pl 07981
Victoria Rd 07981
Vincent Ter 07981
Walnut Rd 07981
Warren St 07981
Washington Ave 07981
Westview Dr 07981
Whippanong Way 07981
Whippany Rd 07981
Wilson Pl 07981
Windemere Ct 07981
Woodcrest Rd 07981
Woodfield Dr 07981
Woodland Ave 07981
Yardley Pl 07981

New Mexico

People QuickFacts	New Mexico	USA
Population, 2013 estimate	2,085,287	316,128,839
Population, 2010 (April 1) estimates base	2,059,183	308,747,716
Population, percent change, April 1, 2010 to July 1, 2013	1.3%	2.4%
Population, 2010	2,059,179	308,745,538
Persons under 5 years, percent, 2013	6.7%	6.3%
Persons under 18 years, percent, 2013	24.3%	23.3%
Persons 65 years and over, percent, 2013	14.7%	14.1%
Female persons, percent, 2013	50.4%	50.8%
White alone, percent, 2013 (a)	82.9%	77.7%
Black or African American alone, percent, 2013 (a)	2.5%	13.2%
American Indian and Alaska Native alone, percent, 2013 (a)	10.4%	1.2%
Asian alone, percent, 2013 (a)	1.6%	5.3%
Native Hawaiian and Other Pacific Islander alone, percent, 2013 (a)	0.2%	0.2%
Two or More Races, percent, 2013	2.4%	2.4%
Hispanic or Latino, percent, 2013 (b)	47.3%	17.1%
White alone, not Hispanic or Latino, percent, 2013	39.4%	62.6%
Living in same house 1 year & over, percent, 2008-2012	84.8%	84.8%
Foreign born persons, percent, 2008-2012	9.8%	12.9%
Language other than English spoken at home, pct age 5+, 2008-2012	36.0%	20.5%
High school graduate or higher, percent of persons age 25+, 2008-2012	83.4%	85.7%
Bachelor's degree or higher, percent of persons age 25+, 2008-2012	25.6%	28.5%
Veterans, 2008-2012	175,832	21,853,912
Mean travel time to work (minutes), workers age 16+, 2008-2012	21.7	25.4
Housing units, 2013	905,135	132,802,859
Homeownership rate, 2008-2012	68.9%	65.5%
Housing units in multi-unit structures, percent, 2008-2012	15.0%	25.9%
Median value of owner-occupied housing units, 2008-2012	$161,500	$181,400
Households, 2008-2012	763,844	115,226,802
Persons per household, 2008-2012	2.63	2.61
Per capita money income in past 12 months (2012 dollars), 2008-2012	$23,749	$28,051
Median household income, 2008-2012	$44,886	$53,046
Persons below poverty level, percent, 2008-2012	19.5%	14.9%

Business QuickFacts	New Mexico	USA
Private nonfarm establishments, 2012	43,883	7,431,808
Private nonfarm employment, 2012	602,715	115,938,468
Private nonfarm employment, percent change, 2011-2012	0.9%	2.2%
Nonemployer establishments, 2012	120,916	22,735,915
Total number of firms, 2007	157,231	27,092,908
Black-owned firms, percent, 2007	1.2%	7.1%
American Indian- and Alaska Native-owned firms, percent, 2007	5.3%	0.9%
Asian-owned firms, percent, 2007	2.1%	5.7%
Native Hawaiian and Other Pacific Islander-owned firms, percent, 2007	0.1%	0.1%
Hispanic-owned firms, percent, 2007	23.6%	8.3%
Women-owned firms, percent, 2007	31.7%	28.8%
Manufacturers shipments, 2007 ($1000)	17,122,725	5,319,456,312
Merchant wholesaler sales, 2007 ($1000)	10,589,286	4,174,286,516
Retail sales, 2007 ($1000)	24,469,997	3,917,663,456
Retail sales per capita, 2007	$12,429	$12,990
Accommodation and food services sales, 2007 ($1000)	3,734,300	613,795,732
Building permits, 2012	4,672	829,658

Geography QuickFacts	New Mexico	USA
Land area in square miles, 2010	121,298.15	3,531,905.43
Persons per square mile, 2010	17	87.4
FIPS Code	35	

(a) Includes persons reporting only one race.
(b) Hispanics may be of any race, so also are included in applicable race categories.
FN: Footnote on this item for this area in place of data
NA: Not available
D: Suppressed to avoid disclosure of confidential information
X: Not applicable
S: Suppressed; does not meet publication standards
Z: Value greater than zero but less than half unit of measure shown
F: Fewer than 100 firms
Source: US Census Bureau State & County QuickFacts

New Mexico

3 DIGIT ZIP CODE MAP

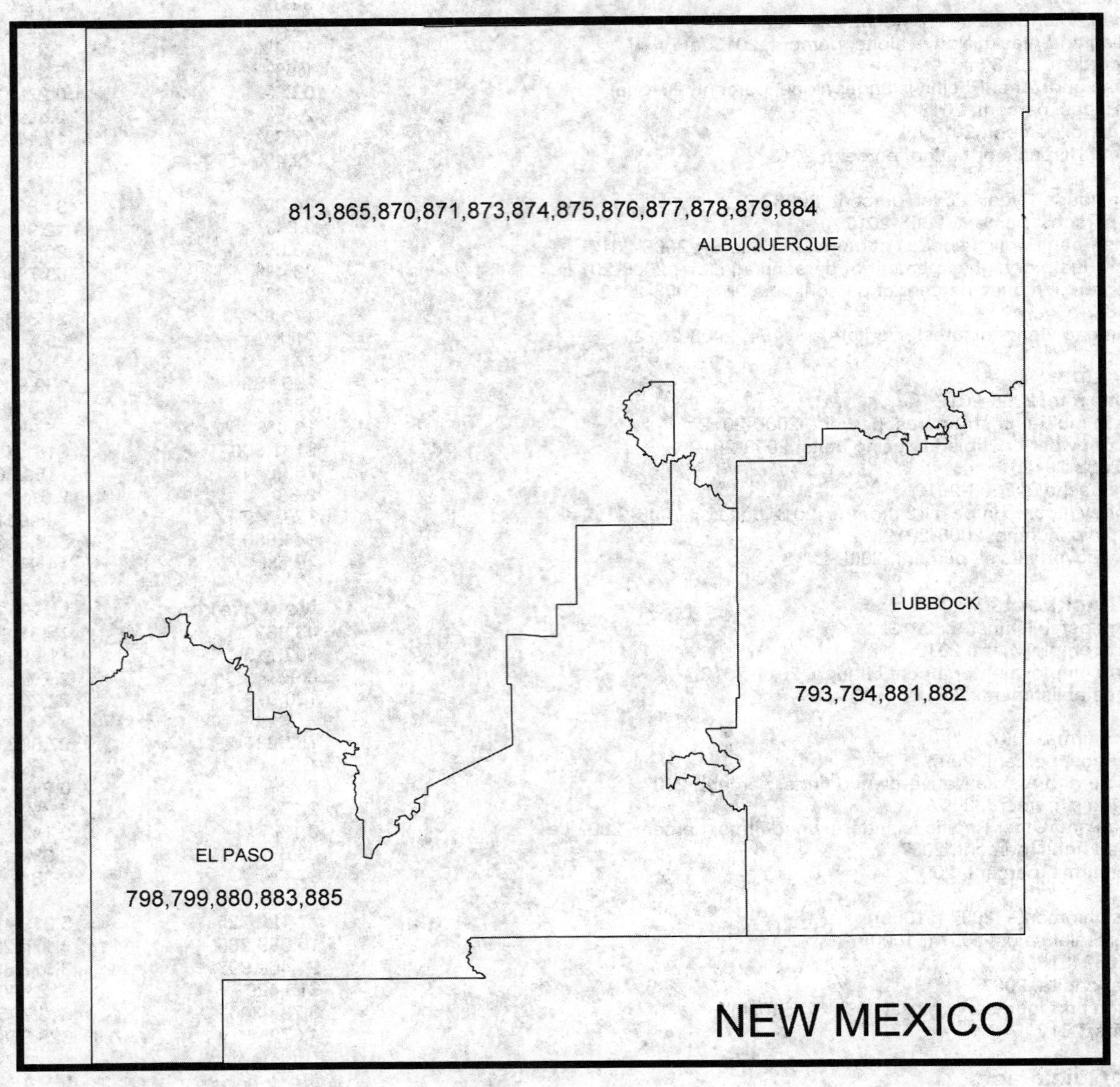

New Mexico

(Abbreviation: NM)

Post Office, County — ZIP Code

Places with more than one ZIP code are listed in capital letters, See pages indicated.

Abiquiu, Rio Arriba 87510
Acoma, Cibola 87034
Alameda
(See Albuquerque)
Alamo, Socorro 87825
ALAMOGORDO, Otero
(See Page 2596)
Albert, Harding 87733
ALBUQUERQUE, Bernalillo
(See Page 2597)
Alcalde, Rio Arriba 87511
Algodones, Sandoval 87001
Alto, Lincoln 88312
Amalia, Taos 87512
Amistad, Union 88410
Ancho, Lincoln 88301
Angel Fire, Colfax 87710
Angus, Lincoln 88316
Animas, Hidalgo 88020
Anthony, Dona Ana 88021
Anthony, Dona Ana 88024
Anton Chico, Guadalupe 87711
Arabela, Lincoln 88351
Aragon, Catron 87820
Arenas Valley, Grant 88022
Arrey, Sierra 87930
Arroyo Hondo, Taos 87513
Arroyo Seco, Taos 87514
ARTESIA, Eddy
(See Page 2612)
Aztec, San Juan 87410
Bard, Quay 88411
Bayard, Grant 88023
Belen, Valencia 87002
Bell Ranch, Guadalupe 88431
Bellview, Curry 88112
Bent, Otero 88314
Berino, Dona Ana 88024
Bernalillo, Sandoval 87004
Bingham, Socorro 87832
Blanco, San Juan 87412
Bloomfield, San Juan 87413
Bluewater, Cibola 87005
Border Hill, Chaves 88201
Bosque, Valencia 87006
Bosque Farms, Valencia 87042
Bosque Farms, Valencia 87068
Brimhall, Mckinley 87310
Broadview, Curry 88112
Buckhorn, Grant 88025
Budaghers, Sandoval 87001
Buena Vista, Mora 87712
Bueyeros, Union 88415
Caballo, Sierra 87931
Canjilon, Rio Arriba 87515
Cannon Afb, Curry 88101
Cannon Afb, Curry 88103
Canoncito, Cibola 87026
Canones, Rio Arriba 87516
Capitan, Lincoln 88316
Caprock, Lea 88213
Capulin, Union 88414
CARLSBAD, Eddy
(See Page 2612)
Carrizozo, Lincoln 88301
Carson, Taos 87517
Casa Blanca, Cibola 87007
Causey, Roosevelt 88113
Cebolla, Rio Arriba 87518
Cedar Crest, Bernalillo 87008
Cedarvale, Torrance 87009
Central, Grant 88026
Cerrillos, Santa Fe 87010
Cerro, Taos 87519
Chacon, Mora 87713
Chama, Rio Arriba 87520
Chamberino, Dona Ana 88027
Chamisal, Taos 87521
Chaparral, Dona Ana 88021
Chaparral, Dona Ana 88081
Chimayo, Rio Arriba 87522
Church Rock, Mckinley 87311
Cimarron, Colfax 87714
Claunch, Socorro 87011
Clayton, Union 88415
Cleveland, Mora 87715
Cliff, Grant 88028
Clines Corners, Torrance 87070
Cloudcroft, Otero 88317
Cloudcroft, Otero 88350
CLOVIS, Curry
(See Page 2612)
Cochiti Lake, Sandoval 87083
Cochiti Pueblo, Sandoval 87072
Columbus, Luna 88029
Conchas Dam, San Miguel 88416
Continental Divide, Mckinley 87312
Cordova, Rio Arriba 87523
Corona, Lincoln 88318
Corrales, Sandoval 87048
Costilla, Taos 87524
Counselor, Sandoval 87018
Coyote, Rio Arriba 87012
Crossroads, Lea 88114
Crownpoint, Mckinley 87313
Cuba, Sandoval 87013
Cubero, Cibola 87014
Cuchillo, Sierra 87901
Cuervo, Guadalupe 88417
Cundiyo, Rio Arriba 87522
Datil, Catron 87821
DEMING, Luna
(See Page 2613)
Derry, Sierra 87933
Des Moines, Union 88418
Dexter, Chaves 88230
Dixon, Rio Arriba 87527
Dona Ana, Dona Ana 88032
Dora, Roosevelt 88115
Dulce, Rio Arriba 87528
Duran, Lincoln 88301
Eagle Nest, Colfax 87710
Eagle Nest, Colfax 87718
Edgewood, Santa Fe 87015
El Prado, Taos 87529
El Rito, Rio Arriba 87530
Elephant Butte, Sierra 87935
Elida, Roosevelt 88116
Embudo, Rio Arriba 87531
Encinal, Cibola 87038
Encino, Torrance 88321
ESPANOLA, Rio Arriba
(See Page 2613)
Estancia, Torrance 87016
Eunice, Lea 88231
Fairacres, Dona Ana 88033
Fairview, Rio Arriba 87533
FARMINGTON, San Juan
(See Page 2613)
Faywood, Grant 88034
Fence Lake, Cibola 87315
Flora Vista, San Juan 87415
Floyd, Roosevelt 88118
Flying H, Otero 88339
Folsom, Union 88419
Fort Bayard, Grant 88036
Fort Stanton, Lincoln 88323
Fort Sumner, De Baca 88119
Fort Wingate, Mckinley 87316
Fruitland, San Juan 87416
Galisteo, Santa Fe 87540
Gallina, Rio Arriba 87017
GALLUP, Mckinley
(See Page 2615)
Gamerco, Mckinley 87317
Garfield, Dona Ana 87936
Garita, San Miguel 88421
Gila, Grant 88038
Gladstone, Union 88422
Glencoe, Lincoln 88324
Glenrio, Quay 88434
Glenwood, Catron 88039
Glorieta, Santa Fe 87535
Golden, Bernalillo 87047
Gonzales Ranch, San Miguel 87560
Grady, Curry 88120
Grants, Cibola 87020
Grenville, Union 88424
Guadalupita, Mora 87722
Hachita, Grant 88040
Hagerman, Chaves 88232
Hanover, Grant 88041
Hatch, Dona Ana 87937
Hernandez, Rio Arriba 87537
High Rolls Mountain Park, Otero 88325
Hillsboro, Sierra 88042
HOBBS, Lea
(See Page 2615)
Holloman Air Force Base, Otero 88330
Holman, Mora 87723
Hondo, Lincoln 88336
Hope, Eddy 88250
House, Quay 88121
Hurley, Grant 88043
Ilfeld, San Miguel 87538
Isleta, Bernalillo 87022
Jaconita, Santa Fe 87506
Jal, Lea 88252
Jamestown, Mckinley 87347
Jarales, Valencia 87023
Jemez Pueblo, Sandoval 87024
Jemez Springs, Sandoval 87025
Kenna, Roosevelt 88122
Kewa, Sandoval 87052
Kirtland, San Juan 87417
Kirtland Afb, Bernalillo 87117
La Jara, Sandoval 87027
La Joya, Socorro 87028
La Loma, Guadalupe 87724
La Luz, Otero 88337
La Madera, Rio Arriba 87539
La Mesa, Dona Ana 88044
La Plata, San Juan 87418
Laguna, Cibola 87026
Lake Arthur, Chaves 88253
Lake Sumner, De Baca 88119
Lakewood, Eddy 88254
Lamy, Santa Fe 87540
LAS CRUCES, Dona Ana
(See Page 2616)
Las Tablas, Rio Arriba 87581
Las Vegas, San Miguel 87701
Las Vegas, San Miguel 87745
Ledoux, Mora 87732
Lemitar, Socorro 87823
Lincoln, Lincoln 88338
Lindrith, Rio Arriba 87029
Lingo, Roosevelt 88123
Llano, Taos 87543
Llaves, Sandoval 87027
Loco Hills, Eddy 88255
Logan, Quay 88426
Lon, De Baca 88136
Lordsburg, Hidalgo 88009
Los Alamos, Los Alamos 87544
Los Lunas, Valencia 87031
Los Ojos, Rio Arriba 87551
Los Ranchos De Abq
(See Albuquerque)
Los Ranchos De Albuquerque
(See Albuquerque)
Los Rnchs Abq
(See Albuquerque)
Loving, Eddy 88256
Lovington, Lea 88260
Lumberton, Rio Arriba 87528
Luna, Catron 87824
Madrid, Santa Fe 87010
Magdalena, Socorro 87825
Malaga, Eddy 88263
Maljamar, Lea 88264
Manuelito, Mckinley 87301
Maxwell, Colfax 87728
Mayhill, Otero 88339
Mcalister, Quay 88427
Mcdonald, Lea 88262
Mcintosh, Torrance 87032
Medanales, Rio Arriba 87548
Melrose, Curry 88124
Mentmore, Mckinley 87319
Mescalero, Otero 88340
Mesilla, Dona Ana 88046
Mesilla Park, Dona Ana 88047
Mesita, Cibola 87026
Mesquite, Dona Ana 88048
Mexican Springs, Mckinley 87320
Miami, Colfax 87729
Milan, Cibola 87021
Mills, Harding 87730
Milnesand, Roosevelt 88125
Mimbres, Grant 88049
Mogollon, Catron 88039
Montezuma, San Miguel 87731
Monticello, Sierra 87939
Monument, Lea 88265
Mora, Mora 87732
Moriarty, Torrance 87035
Mosquero, Harding 87733
Mount Dora, Union 88424
Mountainair, Torrance 87036
Mule Creek, Grant 88051
Nageezi, San Juan 87037
Nambe, Santa Fe 87506
Nara Visa, Quay 88430
Navajo, Mckinley 87328
Navajo Dam, San Juan 87419
New Laguna, Cibola 87038
Newcomb, San Juan 87455
Newkirk, Guadalupe 88431
Nogal, Lincoln 88341
Ocate, Mora 87734
Ohkay Owingeh, Rio Arriba 87566
Oil Center, Lea 88240
Ojo Caliente, Taos 87549
Ojo Encino, Sandoval 87013
Ojo Feliz, Mora 87735
Ojo Sarco, Taos 87521
Old Laguna, Cibola 87026
Organ, Dona Ana 88052
Orogrande, Otero 88342
Oscuro, Lincoln 88301
Paguate, Cibola 87040
Paraje, Cibola 87007
Pastura, Guadalupe 88435
Pecos, San Miguel 87552
Pena Blanca, Sandoval 87041
Penasco, Taos 87553
Pep, Roosevelt 88126
Peralta, Valencia 87042
Peralta, Valencia 87068
Petaca, Rio Arriba 87554
Picacho, Lincoln 88343
Pie Town, Catron 87827
Pine Lodge, Chaves 88201
Pinehill, Cibola 87357
Pinon, Otero 88344
Pinos Altos, Grant 88053
Placitas, Sandoval 87043
Playas, Hidalgo 88009
Pojoaque, Santa Fe 87501
Polvadera, Socorro 87828
Ponderosa, Sandoval 87044
Portales, Roosevelt 88123
Portales, Roosevelt 88130
Prewitt, Mckinley 87045
Pueblo Of Acoma, Cibola 87034
Puerta De Luna, Guadalupe 88435
Quay, Quay 88433
Quemado, Catron 87829
Questa, Taos 87556
Radium Springs, Dona Ana 88054
Rainsville, Mora 87736
Ramah, Mckinley 87321
Ramah, Cibola 87357
Ranchos De Taos, Taos 87557
Raton, Colfax 87740
Red River, Taos 87558
Redrock, Grant 88055
Regina, Sandoval 87046
Rehoboth, Mckinley 87322
Reserve, Catron 87830
Ribera, San Miguel 87560
Rincon, Dona Ana 87940
Rio Communities, Valencia 87002
RIO RANCHO, Sandoval
(See Page 2621)
Road Forks, Hidalgo 88045
Rociada, San Miguel 87742
Rodeo, Hidalgo 88056
Rogers, Roosevelt 88132
ROSWELL, Chaves
(See Page 2624)
Rowe, San Miguel 87562
Roy, Harding 87743
RUIDOSO, Lincoln
(See Page 2625)
Ruidoso Downs, Lincoln 88346
Rutheron, Rio Arriba 87551
Sacramento, Otero 88347
Saint Vrain, Curry 88133
Salem, Dona Ana 87941
San Acacia, Socorro 87831
San Antonio, Socorro 87832
San Antonito, Bernalillo 87047
San Cristobal, Taos 87564
San Felipe Pb, Sandoval 87001
San Fidel, Cibola 87049
San Ildefonso Pueblo, Santa Fe 87506
San Jon, Quay 88411
San Jon, Quay 88434
San Jose, San Miguel 87565
San Juan Pueblo, Rio Arriba 87566
San Lorenzo, Grant 88041
San Mateo, Cibola 87020
San Miguel, Dona Ana 88058
San Patricio, Lincoln 88348
San Rafael, Cibola 87051
San Ysidro, Sandoval 87053
Sandia Park, Bernalillo 87047
Sandia Pueblo, Sandoval 87004
Sanostee, San Juan 87461
Santa Ana Pueblo, Sandoval 87004
Santa Clara, Grant 88026
Santa Cruz, Santa Fe 87567
SANTA FE, Santa Fe
(See Page 2625)
Santa Rosa, Guadalupe 88435
Santa Teresa, Dona Ana 88008
Santo Domingo Pueblo, Sandoval 87052
Sapello, San Miguel 87745
Seama, Cibola 87007
Seboyeta, Cibola 87014
Sedan, Union 88436
Sena, San Miguel 87560
Seneca, Union 88415
Serafina, San Miguel 87569
Sheep Springs, San Juan 87364
Shiprock, San Juan 87420
SILVER CITY, Grant
(See Page 2631)
Smith Lake, Mckinley 87365
Socorro, Socorro 87801
Solano, Harding 87746
Spaceport City, Sierra 87654
Springer, Colfax 87729
Springer, Colfax 87747
Stanley, Santa Fe 87056
Stead, Union 88415
Sunland Park, Dona Ana 88063
Sunspot, Otero 88349
Taiban, De Baca 88134
Tajique, Torrance 87016
Tamaya, Sandoval 87004
Taos, Taos 87571
Taos Ski Valley, Taos 87525
Tatum, Lea 88213
Tatum, Lea 88267
Tererro, San Miguel 87573
Tesuque, Santa Fe 87574
Texico, Curry 88135
Thoreau, Mckinley 87323
Tierra Amarilla, Rio Arriba 87575
Tijeras, Bernalillo 87059
Timberon, Otero 88350
Tinnie, Lincoln 88351
Tohajiilee, Cibola 87026
Tohatchi, Mckinley 87325
Tome, Valencia 87060
Torreon, Torrance 87061
Trampas, Taos 87576
Trementina, San Miguel 88439
Tres Piedras, Taos 87577
Truchas, Rio Arriba 87578
Truth Consq, Sierra 87901
Truth Or Consequences, Sierra 87901
Tucumcari, Quay 88401
Tucumcari, San Miguel 88416
Tularosa, Otero 88352
Tyrone, Grant 88065
Univ Of New Mexico, Bernalillo 87196
Unm
(See Albuquerque)
Ute Park, Colfax 87749
Vadito, Taos 87579
Vado, Dona Ana 88072
Valdez, Taos 87580
Vallecitos, Rio Arriba 87581
Valmora, Mora 87750
Vanadium, Grant 88023
Vanderwagen, Mckinley 87326
Vaughn, Guadalupe 88353
Veguita, Socorro 87062
Velarde, Rio Arriba 87582
Village Of Los Ranchos
(See Albuquerque)
Villanueva, San Miguel 87583
Virden, Hidalgo 88045
Wagon Mound, Mora 87735
Wagon Mound, Mora 87752
Waterflow, San Juan 87421
Watrous, Mora 87750
Watrous, Mora 87753
Weed, Otero 88354
White Oaks, Lincoln 88301
White Rock, Los Alamos 87544
White Sands Missile Range, Dona Ana 88002
Whites City, Eddy 88268
Willard, Torrance 87063
Williamsburg, Sierra 87942
Winston, Sierra 87943
Yatahey, Mckinley 87375
Yeso, De Baca 88136
Youngsville, Rio Arriba 87064
Zia Pueblo, Sandoval 87053
Zuni, Mckinley 87327

ALAMOGORDO NM

General Delivery 88310

POST OFFICE BOXES MAIN OFFICE STATIONS AND BRANCHES

Box No.s
All PO Boxes 88311

NAMED STREETS

Abbott Ave 88310
Abuelito Dr 88310
Acoma Ave 88310
Adams Ave 88310
Adobe Rdg 88310
Adobe Ranch Ct, Dr & Trl 88310
Aero Loop 88310
Airport Ave & Rd 88310
Alamo Ave & St 88310
Alamo Canyon Rd 88310
Alamogordo Dr 88310
Alamotero Ln 88310
Alaska Ave 88310
Alberta Dr 88310
Alta Vista Dr 88310
Amber Skies Ave 88310
American Way 88310
Andergill Ave 88310
Apache Ln 88310
April Lea Ln 88310
Arapaho Trl 88310
Arizona Ave 88310
Arlan Ct 88310
W Arnold Ln 88310
Arroyo Ln 88310
Arroyo Ridge Rd 88310
Arroyo Seco 88310
Arthur Ct 88310
Ascot Parade 88310
Aspen Dr 88310
Avenida Amigos 88310
Avenida Aveta 88310
Azelia St 88310
Bakers Pl 88310
Bandolier 88310
Bassett St 88310
Basswood Dr 88310
Battersby Ave 88310
Baylor Ave 88310
Beecher Rd 88310
Bellamah Dr 88310
Beverly Ln 88310
Bidwell 88310
Birdie Ct & Loop 88310
Black St 88310
Boeing Blvd 88310
Bonnell Ave 88310
Bosque 88310
Boulder Rd 88310
Boyce Ave 88310
Brady Dr 88310
Brentwood Dr 88310
Briarwood Ct 88310
Broken Spoke 88310
Brookdale Dr 88310
Brooks Ave 88310
Brown St 88310
Bucko Rd 88310
Buena Vista Ct 88310
Burnage Ln 88310
Byrd Ave 88310
Cactus Ct 88310
Cactus Wren 88310
Cady Ln 88310
Calle De Gallegos 88310
Calle De Juana 88310
Calle De Oro 88310
Calle De Paz 88310
Calle De Sol 88310
Calle De Suenos 88310
Calle De Vistas 88310
Calle Verde 88310
Cambridge Ave 88310
Cameo Dr 88310
Camino Bonita Vis 88310
Camino De Paz 88310
Camino De Suenos 88310
Camino Del Centro 88310
Camino Del Norte 88310
Camino Del Rey 88310
Camino Del Sol 88310
Camino Del Sur 88310
Camino Ranchitos 88310
Camino Real 88310
Camino Valle Verde 88310
Campbell Pl 88310
W Canal St 88310
Canary Ln 88310
Candlewood Ct 88310
Caneadea Loop 88310
Cano St 88310
N & S Canyon Pl & Rd 88310
Canyon Draw 88310
Caprock Ct 88310
Carmel Dr 88310
Carpenter 88310
Casa Bonita 88310
Casa De Reina 88310
Casa De Suenos 88310
Casady Ct & Dr 88310
Catalina Ln 88310
Cauthen Ln 88310
Cedar Ave 88310
Center St 88310
Cerrillos St 88310
Chaco Dr 88310
Chalk Ln 88310
Challenger Ave 88310
Chamisa Ln 88310
Champion 88310
Chantel Ave 88310
Chapparral Loop & Rd 88310
Charles Ave 88310
Charlotte Ln 88310
Cherokee Trl 88310
Cherry Ln 88310
Cherry Hills Ct, Dr & Loop 88310
Chicory 88310
Choctaw Trl 88310
Cholla Cir & Dr 88310
Christina Pl 88310
Cielo Vis 88310
Cielo Bonito 88310
Cielo Grande Ct 88310
Cielo Montana 88310
Circle Dr 88310
Claraboya Loop 88310
Cloud Mountain Rd 88310
Cobble Stone 88310
College Ave 88310
Collie Ln 88310
Collins Ave 88310
Columbia Ave 88310
Columbus Rd 88310
Comanche Ct & Trl 88310
Constant Dr 88310
Copper Rdg 88310
Cornell Ave 88310
Coronado Dr 88310
Corte Alegre 88310
Corte Del Ranchero 88310
Corte Del Sol 88310
Cotton Ave 88310
Cottontail Run 88310
Cottonwood Dr 88310
Country Ln 88310
Coyote Run 88310
Coyote Flats Rd 88310
Cree Pl 88310
Crescent Dr 88310
Crestwood Ln 88310
Crews Ave 88310
Critter 88310
Cross Bow Trl 88310
Crouch Dr 88310
Cuba Ave 88310
Dale Scott Ave 88310
Danley Ranch Rd 88310
Datura Dr 88310
David Dr 88310
Debbie Ln 88310
Del Cerro 88310
Del Norte Dr 88310
Del Prado Ct 88310
Del Sur 88310
Delaware Ave 88310
Delphia St 88310
Desert Hvn 88310
Desert Air Rd 88310
Desert Bloom Ct 88310
Desert Breeze Ct 88310
Desert Dawn Dr 88310
Desert Dunes Rd 88310
Desert Eve Dr 88310
Desert Hills Dr 88310
Desert Jay 88310
Desert Lakes Rd 88310
Desert Pine Dr 88310
Desert Sands Rd 88310
Desert Sun Ct 88310
Desert View Ct 88310
Desert Vista Dr 88310
Desert Willow Dr 88310
W Dewey Ct & Ln 88310
Dexter Ln 88310
Diablo Dr 88310
Digger Ln 88310
Dingo Rd 88310
Dirt Devil Rd 88310
Discovery Ave 88310
Divers Cv 88310
Dog Canyon Rd 88310
Dog Patch Rd 88310
Dog Ranch Rd 88310
Dooley St 88310
Dora Ave 88310
Douglas Dr 88310
Dr Martin Luther King Jr Blvd 88310
Driftwood Ave 88310
Dublin Ln 88310
Dulce 88310
Dungan Ave 88310
Duran Ave 88310
Eagle Ct, Dr & Loop 88310
Eagle Ranch Rd 88310
Earhart Ave 88310
East Rd 88310
Eastmont Ct 88310
Eastridge Dr 88310
Eddy Dr 88310
Edgington Rd 88310
El Dorado 88310
El Nido Dr 88310
El Paso Dr 88310
Elizabeth Ln 88310
Elkins Pl 88310
Elm St 88310
Encantado Dr 88310
Endeavor Ave 88310
Enterprise Ave 88310
Equus 88310
Era St 88310
Estrella Norte Park 88310
Eudora St 88310
Fairgrounds Rd 88310
Fayne Ln 88310
Fernwood Ave 88310
Filipino Ave 88310
Filmore Ave 88310
Fire Thorn Rdg 88310
Fleetwood Cir 88310
N & S Florida Ave 88310
Foothills Dr 88310
Forsyth Rd 88310
Galway Dr 88310
Garcia Ave 88310
Garden Ave 88310
Garner Ave 88310
George St 88310
Gila Ct 88310
Gill Dr 88310
Glacier Dr 88310
Glenn Ave 88310
Globewillow Rd 88310
Goodyear Dr 88310
Gopher Rd 88310
Grady St 88310
Granada 88310
Grand View Rd 88310
Grant St 88310
Gray St 88310
Greasewood Ave 88310
Green Trl 88310
Greenfield Rd 88310
Greenwood Ln 88310
Griffin Rd 88310
Grosvenor Ct 88310
Guardian Angel Ln 88310
Hamilton Rd 88310
Hamilton Ridge Rd 88310
Harris Ave 88310
Harvard Ave 88310
Hawaii Ave 88310
Heather Ln 88310
Heights Cir 88310
Hendrix Ave 88310
Hermoso El Sol 88310
Hickory Dr 88310
High Mesa Rd 88310
High Sierra Ave & Dr 88310
Highland Dr 88310
Highway 54 S
  1900-3400 88310
  3402-5978 88310
  5980-5980 88311
  5982-6198 88310
Highway 54 70 88310
Highway 70 W 88310
Highway 82 88310
Hitching Post Ln 88310
Hobo Ln 88310
Holloman Ave & Blvd 88310
Homestead Trl 88310
Hondo Rd 88310
Honey Suckle 88310
Hopi Trl 88310
Hubbard Dr 88310
Hughes Dr 88310
Hyde Park Pl 88310
Ida Way 88310
Idaho Dr 88310
Incredible Ct & Dr 88310
Indian Loop 88310
Indian Maid Ln 88310
Indian Wells Rd 88310
Indiana Ave 88310
Indigo Loop 88310
Iowa Ave 88310
Ironwood Ave 88310
Ivy Rd 88310
Jackson Ave 88310
James St & Way 88310
Jeane Ct 88310
Jefferson Ave 88310
Jody Lee Dr 88310
John Dr 88310
Johnese Marie Dr 88310
Joy Dr 88310
Juniper Dr 88310
K C Rd 88310
Kelly Dr 88310
Kennedy St 88310
Kerry Ave 88310
Khj Rd 88310
Kingston Dr 88310
Kiowa Ct 88310
La Bajada Dr 88310
La Codorniz Dr 88310
La Cresta 88310
La Escopita Ct 88310
La Luz Pl 88310
La Luz Gate Rd 88310
La Mesa 88310
La Puerta 88310
La Sala Del Centro 88310
La Sala Grande 88310
La Sala Redondo 88310
Lackland Ave 88310
Lady Of The Mountain Rd 88310
Lamar Cir 88310
Larkspur Ave 88310
Las Alturas Ct 88310
Las Lomas 88310
Las Palomas Rd 88310
Lavelle Rd 88310
Lawndale Ave 88310
Lawrence Blvd 88310
Lemin Ave 88310
Les Ct 88310
Liberty Dr 88310
Lilac Ln 88310
Lincoln Ave 88310
Linda Vista Dr 88310
Lindberg Ave 88310
Lockheed Dr 88310
Loma Verde 88310
Loma Vista Dr 88310
Lonesome Dove Dr 88310
Los Robles 88310
W Lovers Ln 88310
Lucky Dr & St 88310
Lulu Ave 88310
Madera 88310
Madison Ave 88310
Magnolia St 88310
Maple Dr 88310
Marble Canyon Dr 88310
Marble Top Dr 88310
Margarita Loop 88310
Maricopa Trl 88310
Mariposa Dr 88310
Mars Ave 88310
Maryland Ave 88310
Mason Dr 88310
Matthews 88310
Mayflower Rd 88310
Mcdonald Rd 88310
Mcdonnell Dr 88310
Mcgill Ave 88310
Mckinley Ave 88310
Mclean Ave 88310
Mcnutt Ave 88310
Meadow Lark Ln 88310
Meadowland Rd 88310
Medical Dr 88310
Melanie Ln 88310
Melody Ln 88310
Memory Ln 88310
Mercados Dr 88310
Mercury Ave 88310
Mesa Ln & Vlg 88310
Mesa Grande 88310
Mesa Verde Pl 88310
Mesa Verde Ranch Rd 88310
Mescal Loop 88310
Mescalero Ave 88310
Mesquite St 88310
Mi Casa Ln 88310
Miami Ave 88310
Michael Pkwy 88310
Michel St 88310
Michigan Ave 88310
Miguel Pl 88310
Mimosa Ave 88310
Mira Vista Loop & Trl 88310
Miracerros Ln 88310
Mission Cir 88310
Mobile Ct & Ln 88310
Monjeau 88310
Monroe Ave 88310
Montana Vis 88310
Monte Vista Corte 88310
Montlake Ter 88310
Montwood Ct & Dr 88310
Moondale Rd 88310
Moondust 88310
Moonglow Ave 88310
Moonlight Trl 88310
Moonshine Trl 88310
Moonwalk 88310
Moor Pl 88310
Moore Ave 88310
Mosswood Dr 88310
Mountain Meadows Rd 88310
Mountain View Ave & Rd 88310
Municipal Ave 88310
Nevada Dr 88310
S New York Ave 88310
Nogal St 88310
None Rd 88310
Not A Ln 88310
Oak Dr 88310
Oakcreek St 88310
Oakmont Dr & Pl 88310
Oaktree Ct 88310
Ocotillo Dr & Ln 88310
Ohio Ave 88310
Old El Paso Hwy 88310
Old Mill Rd 88310
Old Spanish Trl 88310
Oliver Rd 88310
Oregon Ave 88310
Oro Vista Dr 88310
Osage Ln 88310
Otero Pl 88310
Owens Rd 88310
Paiute Trl 88310
Pajarito Dr 88310
Palm Harbor Dr 88310
Palo Duro 88310
Palo Verde Dr 88310
Panorama Blvd & Cir 88310
Papago Rd 88310
Paradise Ave 88310
Park Ave 88310
Pasa Por Aqui Ln 88310
Patricia Ln 88310
Pecan Dr 88310
Peden Ave 88310
Pena Ct 88310
Pennsylvania Ave 88310
Perry Rd 88310
Pg Ranch Rd 88310
Pheasant Ln 88310
Phillips Ave 88310
Piedra 88310
Pine Dr 88310
Pinehurst Ct 88310
Pinon Dr 88310
Plainview Dr 88310
Playa Azul St 88310
Playa Del Ray Dr 88310
Plaza Del Prado 88310
Poco Grande 88310
Pontiac Dr 88310
Post Ave 88310
Prell Dr 88310
Princeton Ave 88310
Pueblo Trl 88310
Pueblo De Luna 88310
Pueblo Del Sol 88310
Puerto Rico Ave 88310
Puesta Del Sol 88310
Quail Trl 88310
Railroad Ave 88310
Raincloud Dr 88310
Rancho Ln 88310
Rathgeber Dr 88310
Red Arroyo 88310
Redman St 88310
Rena Rd 88310
Riata Rd 88310
Ridge Ct & Ln 88310
Ridgecrest Ct & Dr 88310
Rio Rancho Rd 88310
Roadrunner Ln 88310
Robert H Bradley Dr 88310
Rockwood 88310
Rocky Mountain Rd 88310
Rolland Ave & Ct 88310
Roosevelt Ave 88310
Rosalia Ln 88310
Rose Ave 88310
Rosewood Ave 88310
Ross Rd 88310
Ruby Ln 88310
Running Indian Dr 88310
Russell Ct 88310
Rutz Cir 88310
Ryan Dr 88310
Sacramento St 88310
Saddle Ct 88310
Saguaro Loop 88310
Saint Andrews Ct 88310
San Andres St 88310
San Carlos St 88310
San Cristo St 88310
San Juan Dr 88310
San Miguel 88310
San Pedro Dr 88310
San Simon Dr 88310
San Thomasa 88310
Sandalwood Ct 88310
Santa Anna Rd 88310
Santa Clara Ct 88310
Santa Cruz Dr 88310
Santa Fe Dr 88310
Santa Florence Rd 88310
Santiago St 88310
Saturn Cir 88310
Scenic Dr & Pl 88310
Scorpion Rd 88310
Sedona Rdg 88310
Sendero Dr 88310
Sequoia Ave & Loop 88310
Serrano 88310
Shadow Mountain Dr 88310
Shady Ct 88310
Shawnee Trl 88310
Shenandoah Pl 88310
Sherwood Dr 88310
Shiprock 88310
Sierra Loop 88310
Sierra Blanca Dr 88310
Sierra Verde 88310
Sierra Vista Ct 88310
Siesta Dr 88310
Silverado 88310
Simon Ln 88310
Simpson Ave 88310
Sims Ave 88310
Sioux Trl 88310
Sky Rnch 88310
Sleepy Hollow Ave 88310
Smith Ave 88310
Snow Dr 88310
Sol Del Oriente Rd 88310
Solana Dr 88310
South Rd 88310
Southend Rd 88310
Southgate 88310
Southland Rd 88310
Southwind Dr 88310
Spanish Daggers Dr 88310
Spruce Ave 88310
Stafford Ct 88310
Stanford Ave 88310
Stapp Ave 88310
Star Thistle Ln 88310
Stardust Ct 88310
Starlight Ct 88310
Stonecliff 88310
Stonewood Dr 88310
Summer Ave 88310
Sunbeam Ave 88310
Sundial Ave 88310
Sundown Ave 88310
Sunglow Ave 88310
Sunland Dr 88310
Sunny Cir 88310
Sunnyside Ave 88310
Sunrise Ave 88310
Sunset Ave 88310
Sunshine Ave 88310
Suzy Ana 88310
Swinson Ave 88310
Taft Ave 88310
Taylor Rd 88310
Taylor Ranch Rd 88310
Teakwood Dr 88310

Telles Ave 88310
Terall Trl 88310
Teresa Ln 88310
Texas Ave & Trl 88310
Thomas 88310
Thunder Rd 88310
Tierra Bella Dr 88310
Tierra De Suenos 88310
Tierra Royos 88310
Tobosa Rd 88310
Toots Dr 88310
Tovar Acres Rd 88310
Tractor Rd 88310
Travis Ave & Ct 88310
Trawood Ave 88310
Tres Lagos 88310
Tulane Ave 88310
Tularosa Dr 88310
Tumbleweed Ct 88310
Tumbleweed Draw 88310
Turquoise Ct 88310
Turri Ave 88310
Turtle Trl 88310
Twilight Dr 88310
Unicorn Ln 88310
Union Ave 88310
Uranus Dr & Pl 88310
Utah Ave 88310
Ute Pl 88310
Valle Vis 88310
Valle Verde Ct 88310
Valmont Dr 88310
Van Ct 88310
Venus Ave 88310
Vermont Ave 88310
Via Roches 88310
Vingeran Ave 88310
Virginia Ave 88310
Vista Bonita 88310
Wagner Ave 88310
Wagon Wheel Rd 88310
N & S Walker Ave 88310
Walnut Dr 88310
Washington Ave 88310
Webster Dr 88310
Wedgewood Ct 88310
West Rd 88310
Western St 88310
Westminster Ave 88310
White St 88310
White Oaks Ct & St 88310
N & S White Sands
Blvd 88310
Wicker Ave 88310
Wiest Rd 88310
Wildcat Ln 88310
Wildwood Dr 88310
Willow Dr 88310
Wilson Ave 88310
Winchester Ct 88310
Winterhaven Dr 88310
Wood Loop & Rd 88310
Wright Ave 88310
Wyatt Way 88310
Yale Ave 88310
Yeates St 88310
Yellowstone 88310
Young Ct 88310
Yucca Cir & Ln 88310
Zia Ave 88310
Zuni Dr & Pl 88310

NUMBERED STREETS

All Street Addresses 88310

ALBUQUERQUE NM

General Delivery 87101

POST OFFICE BOXES MAIN OFFICE STATIONS AND BRANCHES

Box No.s
AA - AA 87103
JT - JT 87103
D - Z 87103
1 - 2350 87103
3001 - 3996 87190
3327 - 3327 87110
4001 - 4999 87196
5001 - 5800 87185
6001 - 6998 87197
7001 - 7999 87194
8001 - 8998 87198
9043 - 9998 87119
9997 - 9997 87196
10001 - 10990 87184
11001 - 11999 87192
12001 - 12998 87195
13000 - 13976 87192
14001 - 16858 87191
18001 - 18076 87185
19001 - 19836 87119
20001 - 22118 87154
23001 - 23476 87192
25001 - 27960 87125
30001 - 33900 87190
35001 - 37518 87176
40000 - 40754 87196
50000 - 52576 87181
53001 - 53658 87153
56001 - 57196 87187
65001 - 69140 87193
70001 - 70602 87197
72001 - 73278 87195
80001 - 84936 87198
90001 - 97500 87199

RURAL ROUTES

09 87105

NAMED STREETS

Aaron Ct SW 87105
Abajo Rd SE 87102
Abaskin Farm Ln SW 87105
Abbey Ct NW 87120
Abbie Ln SW 87105
Abbot Pl NW 87120
Abby Jean Pl NW 87104
Abe Sandoval Ln SW 87121
Abees St SW 87121
Abeyta Rd SW 87121
Abilene Ave SE 87102
Abiquiu Pl NE 87111
Abis Ct NE 87113
Abo St SW 87105
Acacia St NW 87120
Academic Pl SE 87106
Academy Ct NE 87109
Academy Pkwy NE 87109
Academy Rd NE
5350-5412 87109
5414-6603 87109
6605-7803 87109
8000-10798 87111
10800-12203 87111
12205-12251 87111
Academy Rd NW 87114
Academy Trl NE 87109
Academy Hills Dr NE 87111
Academy Knolls Dr
NE 87111
Academy Parkway East
NE 87109
Academy Parkway North
NE 87109
Academy Parkway South
NE 87109
Academy Parkway West
NE 87109
Academy Ridge Ct, Dr,
Pl & Rd NE 87111
Acapulco Dr NE 87111
Access Road C SE 87106
Accipitrine Ct SE 87123
Acequia Dr SW 87105
Acequia Trl NW 87107
Acequia Escondida
NW 87104
Acoma Rd SE
5301-6297 87108
6299-7000 87108
7002-7098 87108
9400-10999 87123
11001-11299 87123
Acton Ct NW 87114
Ada Ct & Pl 87106
Adams Pl SE 87108
Adams St NE
101-197 87108
199-599 87108
600-3099 87110
3101-3299 87110
8900-8999 87113
Adams St SE 87108
Addis Ave SE 87106
Adele Pl NE 87109
Adelita Dr NE 87112
Adina Ln NW 87114
Adirondack Pl SE 87123
Admiral Dewey Ave
NE 87111
Admiral Emerson Ave
NE 87111
Admiral Halsey Dr NE 87111
Admiral Lowell Ave &
Pl 87111
Admiral Nimitz Ave
NE 87111
Admiral Rickover Dr
NE 87111
Adobe Rd NW 87107
Adonai Rd NW 87121
Adonis Ct NE 87112
Adrian St SW 87121
Aerospace Pkwy NW 87120
Affirmed St SW 87121
Agate Ave & Ln 87120
Agate Hills Rd NW 87114
Agave Verde Way NE 87113
Agnes Ct NE 87112
Agua Fresca Ave NW 87104
Agua Sarca Ct NE 87111
Aguacate Dr NW 87120
Aida Rd NW 87114
Airbase Way 87115
Aircraft Ave SE 87106
Airpark Rd SE 87106
Airport Dr NW & SW 87121
Airway Rd SW 87105
Akutan Ct NW 87120
Al St NW 87120
Aladdin Ct NW 87120
Alameda Blvd NE
301-4297 87113
4299-6699 87113
6701-7499 87113
8201-8597 87122
8599-8799 87122
8801-10399 87122
Alameda Blvd NW 87114
Alameda Park NE 87113
Alameda Pl NE 87113
Alameda Rd NE 87113
Alameda Rd NW 87114
Alamillo Rd NW 87114
Alamo Ave SE
100-461 87102
463-499 87102
1300-2599 87106
Alamo Rd NW 87120
Alamogordo Dr NW 87120
Alamosa Rd & Way 87107
Alaska Pl NE 87111
Alba Pl NW 87114
Albany Ct NW 87114
Albero Rosso Dr NW 87114
Alberta Ln NW 87120
Alcalde Pl SW 87104
Alcazar St NE
100-499 87108
900-998 87110
1000-3199 87110
3201-3299 87110
4100-4199 87109
Alcazar St SE 87108
Aldea Ave NW 87114
Alder Dr NW 87114
Alderman Dr NW 87120
Alegre Dr NE 87123
Alegria Ct & Rd 87114
Alejandro Ln NW 87104
Alejandro Rd NE 87123
Alejandro St NW 87105
Alene Ct NE 87123
Alexander Blvd & Rd NE
& NW 87107
Alexandra St SW 87121
Alexandria Dr & Rd 87122
Alexis Ave & Ct 87121
Alfredo Garcia Ct NW 87107
Algiers Dr NE 87111
Algodones Ct & St 87112
Alhambra Ave SW 87104
Alicante Ave SW 87121
Alice Ave NE
5400-5599 87110
5601-5999 87110
12700-12898 87112
12900-13200 87112
13202-13298 87112
Alice Ct NE 87112
Aliso Dr NE
100-198 87108
200-599 87108
1400-3199 87110
Aliso Dr SE 87108
Aliyah Ln NW
301-399 87121
500-599 87107
All Saints Rd NW 87120
Allande Rd NE 87109
Allano Ct NW 87114
Allegheny Ct NW 87114
Allegiance St NW 87114
Allegretto Trl NW 87104
Allegro Way NW 87104
Allen Ct NW 87114
Allison Ct NE 87112
Alma Dr SW 87105
Alma Encantada Ct
NW 87114
Almeria Dr NW 87120
Aloe Rd NW 87120
Alondra Ln NW 87114
Aloysia Ln NW 87104
Alpha Ave & Ct 87120
Alpine Ct NE 87111
Alpine Rd SW 87105
Alpine Trail St NE 87111
Alps Way NE 87111
Alta Dr NW 87114
Alta Loma Ln NE 87113
Alta Mesa NW 87114
Alta Monte Ave NE
3200-3299 87107
3301-3499 87107
3600-6399 87110
Alta Monte Ave NW 87107
Alta Monte Ct NE 87107
Alta Monte Pl NW 87107
Alta Vista Ct SW 87105
Altamonte Ave NE 87111
Altez St NE
100-499 87123
1100-1398 87112
1400-2999 87112
3000-3698 87111
3700-3899 87111
Altez St SE 87123
Altima Pl NW 87120
Altos Ct & Way 87121
Altura Ave & Pl 87110
Altura Azul Ln NE 87110
Altura Mesa Ln NE 87110
Altura Verde Ln NE 87110
Altura Vista Ln NE 87110
Alvarado Dr NE
100-918 87108
920-998 87108
1001-1097 87110
1099-3700 87110
3702-3798 87110
Alvarado Dr SE
100-112 87108
111-111 87198
114-1198 87108
301-1099 87108
Alvarado Pl NE 87110
Alvera Ave & Ct 87121
Alvis Cir & Rd 87105
Alwood Dr NW 87120
Alyssa Dr SW 87105
Amado St NW 87104
Amalia Rd SW
2501-2597 87105
2599-2699 87105
2800-2900 87121
2902-2998 87121
3101-3115 87105
3117-3199 87105
3201-3999 87105
Amatista St NW 87114
Ambar Ct NW 87114
Ambassador Rd NE 87112
Amber Dr NW 87107
Amberly Rd SW 87121
Amberside Rd NW 87120
Amberstone Rd SW 87121
American Heritage Dr
NE 87109
Americare Ct NW 87120
Americas Pkwy NE 87110
Amherst Dr NE
101-115 87106
117-1999 87106
3101-4197 87107
4199-4399 87107
Amherst Dr SE 87106
Amherst Pl NE 87107
Amigante Dr NE 87111
Amigo Way NE 87111
Amistad Rd NE 87111
Amman Ave NE 87122
Amole Dr SW 87121
Amole Vista St SW 87121
Amor Dr NW 87120
Amraam Ln NE 87122
Amy Ave NW 87120
Amy Kay Ct NW 87107
Amy Marie Ct NW 87120
Ana Ct NW 87120
Anacapa Ave NW 87121
Anaconda St SW 87121
Anador Ct NW 87114
Anaheim Ave NE
4400-6099 87113
6101-6699 87113
7601-8297 87122
8299-11800 87122
11802-12598 87122
Anasazi Dr NE 87111
Anasazi Ridge Ave
NW 87114
Anaya St SW 87121
Ancala Trl NE 87111
Ancho Ct NW 87105
Ancients Rd NW 87114
Andalucia NE 87111
Andalusian Ave SW 87121
Anderson Ave SE
101-197 87102
199-999 87102
3400-3599 87106
3700-6200 87108
6202-6598 87108
Anderson Pl SE 87108
Andesite Dr NW 87114
Andretti Ave SW 87121
Andrew Dr NE
3700-3998 87110
4300-4599 87109
Andromeda Ave NW 87114
Angel Dr NW 87120
Angel Baby Ct SW 87105
Angel Peak Rd NW 87114
Angelina Pl NE 87123
Angelina Daisy St SW 87121
Aniceto Rd NW 87114
Animas Pl NW 87120
Aniston Ct & St 87111
Anita Ln NE 87123
Ankara Rd NE 87122
Ann Ave SW 87105
Anna Maria Pl SW 87105
Annapolis Ct, Dr & Rd 87111
Antares Rd NE 87111
Antelope Ave NE 87122
E Antelope Cir SE 87123
W Antelope Cir SE 87123
Antelope Dancer Trl
NE 87112
Antequera Rd NW 87120
Anthony Ln & Pl 87105
Antigua St NE 87111
Antique Ln SE 87123
Antler Tool Rd SW 87121
Anton Cir NE 87122
Antone Loop Rd SW 87105
Antonia Ct NW 87120
Antonio Dr NE 87112
Apache Ave NE
7605-7799 87110
7801-8208 87110
8210-8306 87110
9500-12299 87112
Apache Ave NW 87102
Apache Ct NE
1904-1908 87106
1910-1917 87106
1919-1925 87106
12517-12529 87112
Apache Pl NE 87112
Apache Pine Way NE 87122
Apache Plume Pl NE 87111
Apodaca St SW 87121
Apollo Ct & Dr 87120
Appalachian Way NE 87111
Appaloosa Dr NW 87120
Appian Way NE 87111
Apple Ln NW 87104
Apple Valley Ave SW 87105
Appleton Rd SW 87105
Applewood Ln NW
1-99 87107
7701-7899 87120
Appomattox Pl NE 87109
April St SE 87123
April Flower Pl & Rd 87121
Aqua Marine Rd NE 87113
Aquarius Ave NW 87114
Aqueduct Rd SE 87123
Arabella Dr NW 87114
Arabian Dr & Pl 87120
Aragon Rd SW 87105
Aragon St SE 87123
Arapahoe Ave NW 87114
Arboleda Senda NE 87111
Arbor Pl & Rd NE &
NW 87107
Arbordale Ln NW 87107
Arbus Dr SE 87106
Arbustos Ct NE 87111
Arcadia Rd NE 87123
Arcadian Trl NW 87107
Arch Ct NE 87112
Archuleta Dr NE 87112
Arco Ct NW 87120
Arenal Rd SW
700-2805 87105
2807-2809 87105
2825-2899 87121
3001-3077 87105
3079-3200 87105
3202-3298 87105
3900-3998 87121
Arenas Pl SE 87123
Arenoso Pl NW 87120
Arezzo Dr NW 87114
Argon Ave NE 87112
Argonite Dr NW 87114
Arguello Trl NE 87123
Argus Ave NW 87120
Argyle Ave NE 87109
Arias Ave NW 87104
Aritas Rd SW 87105
Arizona Pl NE 87110
Arizona St NE 87110
Arizona St SE 87108
Arizona Rose Dr SW 87121
Arkansas Rd NW 87120
Arlington Ave NW 87114
Arlolane Ave SW 87121
Arlote Ave SE 87108
Armand Ct & Rd 87120
Armijo Ln, Pl & Rd 87105
Armistice Rd NE 87109
Arno St NE
100-198 87102
200-1024 87102
1026-1026 87102
2900-6700 87107
6702-6798 87107
Arno St SE 87102
Arrington Pl & St 87105
Arrow Point Rd NW 87120
Arrowhead Ave NW 87114
Arroyo Bend Dr NW 87114
Arroyo Chamisa Rd
NE 87111
Arroyo Crest Dr NW 87114
Arroyo De Vis NE 87111
Arroyo Del Oso Ave
NE 87109
Arroyo Falls St NW 87120
Arroyo Hondo St SW 87121
Arroyo Lupine Cir SE 87116
Arroyo Seco St NE 87113
Artesanos Ct NW 87107
Arthur Dr SW 87105
Artie Rd NW 87114
Arvada Ave NE
200-368 87102
370-398 87102
6901-7297 87110
7299-7599 87110
9200-11299 87112
Arvada Ave NW 87102
Arvilla Ave NE
5200-5298 87110
5300-6499 87110
9300-10599 87111
Arvilla Ave NW 87107
Arvilla Ct NE 87111
Arvilla Pl NE 87110
Asbury Ct & Ln 87114
Ash Ct & St 87106
Ashfall Pl NW 87120
Ashland St NW 87114
Ashton Loop & Pl 87122
Aspen Ave NE
301-307 87102
309-515 87102
517-599 87102
3401-3497 87106
3499-3599 87106
3700-8199 87110
8500-10599 87112
Aspen Ave NW
200-298 87102
300-899 87102
1200-2699 87104
Aspen Ct NE 87112
Aspen Ct SE 87116
Aspen Glade Dr NW 87114
Aspenwood Ave NW 87120
Asper Ct NE 87111
Astair Ave NW 87120
Aster Ct SE 87116
Aster Rd SW 87121
Atanacio Rd NE 87123
Athens Dr NE 87111
Atherton Way NW 87120
Atkinson Pl NE 87112
Atlantic Ave SW 87102
Atlantic City Ave NE 87111
Atrisco Dr NW
220-408 87105
410-1628 87105
1630-1720 87105

1800-2998 87120
3000-4400 87120
4402-6902 87120
Atrisco Dr SW 87105
Atrisco Pl NW 87105
Atrisco Pl SW 87105
Atrisco Ranch Rd SW 87121
Atrisco Vista Blvd NW 87120
Atrisco Vista Blvd SW 87121
Aubol SW 87105
Aubright Rd NE 87112
Auburn Ave NE 87112
August Dr SW 87105
Augusta Ave NE 87111
Austin Ave NW 87120
Autumn Breeze Rd SW 87121
Autumn Canyon Rd SW 87121
Autumn Rose Dr NE 87113
Autumn Sage Ct SE 87116
Autumn Sage Dr NW 87114
Autumn Sky Rd SW 87121
Autumnwood Pl SE 87123
Avalon Pl NW 87105
Avalon Rd NW
3800-6499 87105
6501-6599 87105
9900-10000 87121
10002-10398 87121
Avanti St SW 87121
Avedon Ave SE 87106
Avenales Ave NE 87111
Avenida Almendro NE 87123
Avenida Alturas NE 87110
Avenida Arturo NW 87120
Avenida Cesar Chavez SE
200-698 87102
Avenida Cesar Chavez SE
700-800 87102
802-1098 87102
1200-1598 87106
1600-2000 87106
2002-2098 87106
Avenida Cesar Chavez SW 87102
Avenida Charada NW 87107
Avenida Chiquita NW 87120
Avenida Cielito NE 87110
Avenida Cristo Rey NW 87107
Avenida Cuesta NE 87111
Avenida Curvatura NW 87107
Avenida De La Luna NE 87111
Avenida Del Oso NE 87111
Avenida Del Sol NE 87110
Avenida Estrellita NE 87110
Avenida La Barranca Ct & Pl 87114
Avenida La Costa NE 87109
Avenida La Cuchilla NW 87107
Avenida La Mirada NW 87114
Avenida La Prestina NE 87109
Avenida La Resolana NE 87110
Avenida Las Campanas NW 87107
Avenida Los Griegos NW 87107
Avenida Madrid NW 87114
Avenida Manana NE 87110
Avenida Nevada NE 87110
Avenida Real NW 87105
Avenida Serena Dr & Pl 87114
Avenida Seville NW 87114
Avenida Vista Cerros NW 87114
Avenida Vista Sol NW 87114
Avenida Vista Ventana NW 87114
Aventura Ct NW 87114
Avestruz St SW 87121
Avignon Ct NW 87114
Avital Dr NE 87123
Avocet Rd NW 87114
Avon St NW 87107
Avondale Pl NW 87120
Axtell St SE 87105
Ayrshire Ct SW 87105
Azaleas Rd NW 87114
Azar Pl NW 87104
Aztec Ct NE 87111
Aztec Rd NE
2100-3499 87107
3600-7399 87110
7401-8399 87110
8400-9999 87111
Aztec Rd NW 87107
Azuelo Ave NW 87120
Azure Ave NE 87109
Baby Deena St NW 87114
Baccarat Ln NE 87111
Baco Noir Dr SW 87121
Badger Ln SE 87123
Baer Pl NW 87120
Bahama St NE 87111
Baja Ct & Dr 87111
Bajada Dr NW 87114
Baker Ave NE 87109
Baker Ct NW 87114
Baker Ln NE 87113
Balcon Ct NW 87120
Bald Eagle Rd NW 87114
Baldwin Ave NE 87112
Balearic Ave SW 87121
Bali Ct NE 87111
Balloon Fiesta Pkwy NE 87113
Balloon Museum Dr NE 87113
Balloon Park Rd NE 87109
Balsa Ct & Pl 87111
Balsam Glade Rd NW 87114
Bancroft Ct NE 87111
Bandelier Dr NW 87114
Baneberry Dr NE 87113
Banff Dr NE 87111
Bangor Ave NW 87120
Banyan Ave NW 87114
Bar Harbor Pl NE 87111
Barbara Ellen Ave NE 87111
Barbara Vista Ave SW 87121
Barbed Wire Dr SW 87121
Barber Pl NE 87109
Barberry St SW 87121
Barboa Ct, Pl & Rd 87105
Barcelona Cir SW 87105
Barcelona Pl SW 87121
Barcelona Rd SW
1400-3699 87105
3701-3705 87105
3800-4200 87121
4202-4298 87121
Bareback Pl SW 87105
Barelas Ct & Rd 87102
Barlane Pl NW 87107
Barnhart Ct & St 87109
Baronet Pl NE 87123
Barr Ave & Rd SE & SW 87105
Barranca Dr SW 87121
Barranca Oso Ct NE 87111
Barranca Vista Ct NE 87111
Barrett Ave NW 87114
Barrett Dr NW 87120
Barrinson NE 87111
Barro Rd SE 87105
Barstow St NE
6901-6997 87111
6999-7000 87111
7002-7098 87111
7500-7598 87109
8100-9298 87122
Bart Ave & Ct 87109
Bartlett St NE 87109
Bartolo Ave, Ct & Pl 87105
Bartonwood Pl NE 87111
Basalt Ave NW 87120
Basalt Peak Dr NW 87114
Basehart Rd SE 87106
Basha St NW 87114
Basin St NE 87111
Basin Creek Ct & Trl 87120
Basket Weaver Ave NW 87114
Basswood Ct & Dr 87120
Bataan Dr SW 87121
Bates Ct NW 87114
Bates Ln SE 87105
Bates Rd SE 87105
Battle Creek Trl NW 87114
Bauer Rd NE 87123
Baxter Ct NW 87114
Bay Ct NE 87111
Bay Mare Ave SW 87121
Baybrook Rd NW 87120
Bayita Ln NW 87107
Baylor Dr SE 87106
Bazan Ct SW 87102
Beach Rd NW 87104
Beacon Knoll Ct NW 87114
Beaker Rd SW 87121
Beall Ct & Rd 87105
Bear Ln SW 87105
Bear Canyon Ln NE 87113
Bear Canyon Rd NE 87109
Bear Claw Rd NW 87120
Bear Dancer Trl NE 87112
Bear Mountain Trl NE 87113
Beargrass Ct NE 87111
Beau Chene NE 87111
Beaver Trl SE 87123
Beaver Wood Ct NW 87120
Beck Dr NE 87109
Beck Rd SW 87105
Bedrock Ct NW 87114
Beebe St NE 87111
Beeson St SE 87123
Bel Air Ct, Dr & Pl 87110
Bel Vedere Ln NE 87102
Belcher Ave & Ct 87109
Bell Ave SE
100-712 87102
714-798 87102
2100-2198 87106
5600-8199 87108
8201-8299 87108
9600-9698 87123
9700-10200 87123
10202-10298 87123
Bell Ave SW 87102
Bell Park Cir SE 87108
Bella Vista Pl NW 87120
Bellamah Ave NE
5700-8047 87110
8049-8099 87110
9600-13299 87112
Bellamah Ave NW
401-497 87102
499-899 87102
900-1198 87104
1200-1899 87104
1901-1999 87104
Bellamah Ct NE 87110
Bellehaven Ave, Ct & Pl 87112
Bellevue Ct & St 87114
Bellflower Ln NE 87113
Bellini Ln NW 87114
Bellrose Ave NE
6501-6897 87110
6899-7200 87110
7202-7598 87110
8501-8599 87111
Bellrose Ct NE 87110
Belmont Rd SW 87105
Belnap Ct & Pl 87114
Belrose Ave NW 87107
Benavides Ave & Rd 87121
Benge Pl NW 87114
Benicia Ln SW 87102
Benito St SW 87121
Benjamin Pl NE 87122
Benny Rd SW 87105
Benson Ct NW 87120
Bent Rd NE 87109
Bent Tree Dr NW 87120
Bentley Ct NW 87114
Benton Ave & St 87114
Bentwood Trl NE 87109
Beresford Ln NW 87120
Beringer Ave NE 87122
Berkeley Pl NE 87106
Berm St NW 87120
Bermuda Dr NE 87111
Bermuda Dunes NE 87111
Bernalillo Ct & Pl 87123
Bernard Thomas Ave SW 87105
Bernardino Rd NW 87104
Bernardo Ct NE 87113
Bernice Ave SW 87105
Berquist Pl NW 87105
Berry Rd NW 87107
Berryessa Rd NE 87122
Beryl Ct NW 87104
Besler Ln SW 87105
Bethel Ave SE 87102
Bette Clair St SE 87123
Betts Ct NE 87112
Betts Dr NE 87111
Betts Pl NE 87112
Betts St NE 87112
Beulah Dr SE 87123
Beverly Rd SW 87105
Beverly Hills Ave NE
5301-7599 87113
7600-7698 87122
7700-8999 87122
9001-9099 87122
Bianca Ct SW 87121
Bice Rd NW 87105
Bien Mur Dr NE 87113
Big Bend Rd NE 87111
Big Cottonwood Ct SE 87105
Big Horn Ridge Cir, Ct, Dr & Pl NE 87122
Big Pine Dr NW 87120
Big Sage Dr NW 87114
Big Sky Dr NE 87111
Big Springs St SW 87121
Biggs Ave SE 87115
Bighorn Rd NE 87111
Bilboa St NW 87114
Bill Cody Dr NW 87120
Billy The Kid Rd SW 87121
Binbrook Rd NW 87114
Bing Pl NE 87111
Birch Ct SE 87116
Bisbee Pl NW 87114
Biscayne Dr NE 87111
Bishop Ct SW 87105
Bison Trl NW 87120
Bison Springs St SW 87121
Bitter Creek Dr NW 87114
Bixby St NW 87120
Black Dr NW 87120
Black Arroyo Blvd NW 87114
Black Bear Loop, Pl & Rd 87122
Black Farm Ln NW 87114
Black Gold St SE 87123
Black Hawk Dr NE 87122
Black Hills Ct & Rd 87111
Black Mesa Loop SW 87105
Black Oak Ct NE 87122
Black Pine Pl NE 87109
Black Ridge Dr NW 87120
Black Rock Rd NW 87120
Black Stallion Rd SW 87121
Black Volcano Rd NW 87120
Black Willow Dr NE 87122
Blackbird Dr SW 87121
Blackstone Rd NE 87111
Blair Ct & Dr 87112
Blake Rd SW
1300-3499 87105
3800-4504 87121
4506-4598 87121
Blanco Dr NW 87114
Blanda Ct NW 87114
Blanford Ave SW 87121
Blanket Flower Pl NE 87111
Blazick St SW 87121
Blazing Star Ct & Rd 87116
Bledsoe Rd NW 87107
Bletcher Rd SW 87105
Blevin Ct NE 87112
Bloodstone Rd NE 87113
Blossom Pl NE 87111
Blossom Wood Pl NW 87120
Blue Avena Ave SW 87121
Blue Cypress Ave NE 87113
Blue Feather Ave NW 87114
Blue Flax Ct NE 87111
Blue Holly Ct NE 87113
Blue Jay Ln NE 87109
Blue Jay Ln NW 87120
Blue Meadow Trl SW 87121
Blue Mesa Dr NE 87113
Blue Moon Ln NE 87113
Blue Pine Ave NW 87120
Blue Quail Rd NE 87112
Blue Ribbon Rd SE 87123
Blue Ridge Pl NE 87111
Blue Sage Pl NE 87113
Blue Sky St SW 87121
Blue Stone Rd NW 87114
Bluebell Dr & Pl 87122
Blueberry Ln NW 87120
Bluebird Ln NE 87122
Bluebonnet Rd SE 87116
Bluecorn Maiden Ct & Trl 87112
Bluegrass Ct NE 87113
Bluemist Ln NE 87111
Bluestem Ct NW 87114
Bluethorn Ct SW 87121
Bluewater Rd NW
3500-5799 87105
5801-6399 87105
6600-8599 87121
8601-8999 87121
Bluewood Ln NE 87122
W Bluff St NW 87121
Bluff Springs Dr NE 87113
Bluffs Edge St NW 87120
Bluffside Dr & Pl 87105
Blume St NE
1601-1697 87112
1699-1899 87112
3100-3399 87111
10000-10299 87112
Blumenshine Cir SW 87105
Blush Rd NW 87120
Boatright Dr NE 87112
Bobby Foster Rd SE 87106
Bobby Foster Rd SW 87105
Bobcat Blvd & Pl 87122
Bobcat Hill Pl NE 87111
Bobwhite Ln NE 87109
Boca Negra Pl NW 87120
Boddy Rd SW 87121
Boe Ln NE 87113
Bogan Ave NE 87109
Bogart Ct & St 87120
Bohemia Ct SW 87105
Bolack Dr NE 87109
Bold Ruler St SE 87123
Boliver Ln SW 87105
Bona Terra Loop & Pl 87114
Bonaguidi Rd SW 87105
Bond Ct NW 87120
Bondings Dr NE 87111
Bonita Plz NE 87110
Bonita Rosas Rd NW 87107
Bonito Cir, Ct, Pl & Rd SW 87105
Bonito Suenos Ct NW 87107
Bonnie Ct NE 87110
Bonnie Ann Ct NE 87111
Boone St NE 87109
Borg Rd NE 87111
Borrego Creek Dr NW 87114
Bosque Cir NW 87114
Bosque Plz NW 87120
Bosque Rd NE 87113
Bosque St NW 87114
Bosque Del Rio Ln NW 87120
Bosque Del Sol Ln NW 87120
Bosque Entrada Trl NW 87120
Bosque Meadows Pl NW 87120
Bosque Pointe Ave SW 87121
Bosque Verde Ln NW 87104
Bosque Vista Dr NE 87111
Boton De Oro Rd NW 87114
Botts St SE 87123
Boulder Ct & St 87114
Bourke-White Dr SE 87106
Bouvardia Ave NW 87120
Bowe Ln SW 87105
Bowers Rd SW 87105
Bowie Rd SW 87121
Box Canyon Pl NW 87114
Boxwood Ave NE 87113
Brackett Dr SW 87121
Brackley Dr NW 87120
Brad Pl NW 87114
Bradbury Dr SE 87106
Bradford Pl NW 87114
Brady Rd NW 87120
Brahma Dr NW 87120
S Branch Dr SW 87121
Brand Ave NE 87109
Branding Iron St SE 87123
Brandon Ct SW 87121
Brandywine Loop & Rd 87111
Braniff Ave NW 87114
Braveheart Dr NW 87120
Bray Ct NW 87120
Brayton Rd NW 87105
Brazos Ct NE 87109
Brazos Ct SE 87123
Brazos Pl SE 87123
Breckenridge Dr & Rd 87114
Breece Rd SW 87105
Breezy Ct NW 87120
Breezy Point Rd NW 87120
Brenda Ave, Ct & St 87109
Brendan Ct NW 87120
Brenton Dr NW 87120
Brentwood Ct NE 87112
Brentwood Ln NE 87109
Brentwood Hills Blvd NE 87112
Brentwood Park Dr NE 87112
Bret Pl NE 87109
Breton Rd SW 87121
Brezza Dolce Ave NW 87114
Brian Ave & Ct 87121
Brian Meadows Pl NW 87120
Brianna Loop NE 87113
Brianne Ave NW 87114
Briar Ridge Ave NW 87114
Briarcliff NE 87111
Briarwood Ter NE 87111
Bridge Blvd SW
501-599 87102
700-2908 87105
2910-2998 87105
3000-7800 87121
7802-8298 87121
Bridgepointe Ct NE 87111
Bridgeport Rd NW 87120
Bridges Ave NW 87120
Bridgewater Pl NW 87120
Bridle St NW 87120
Bridle Falls Ave SW 87121
Bridle Gate Trl SW 87121
Bridle Wood Rd NE 87113
Bright Way NW 87105
Bright Star Dr NW 87120
Brighton Dr NE 87122
Brindisi Pl NW 87114
Briscoe Ranch Trl NW 87114
Bristlebrush St SW 87121
Bristol St NW 87121
Britt Ct NE 87112
Britt St NE
1800-2599 87112
3100-3699 87111
Britt St SE 87123
Brittany Ave NE 87109
Broadbent Pkwy NE 87107
Broadcast Plz SW 87104
Broadmoor Ave NE 87108
Broadview Pl NW 87107
Broadway Blvd NE
100-710 87102
712-2424 87102
1135-1137 87101
1135-1135 87125
1201-2415 87102
2701-2897 87107
2899-6799 87107
Broadway Blvd SE
101-103 87102
105-3099 87102
3200-14051 87105
631 1/2-631 3/4 87102
Broadway Pl NE 87102
Brock Ln NE 87122
Brockmont Ave NE 87108
Brockton Ct NE 87111
Broeas Dr NW 87114
Broken Arrow Ln NW 87120
Bromley Ct NW 87114
Bromo Ln SW 87105
Brook Pl & St 87113
Brookdale Ct NE 87113
Brookhaven Pl NW 87120
Brookline Pl NW 87114
Brookside Ln SW 87121
Brooksmoor Dr SW 87121
Brookstead Dr NW 87120
Brookstone Dr NW 87120
Brookville St NW 87114
Brookwood St NE 87109
Brosman Ave SW 87121
Brother Rd SW 87105
Brother Mathias Pl NW 87102
Brown Dr SW 87121
Brown Rd SW 87105
Browning Rd NE 87109
Brownsville Ln NE 87113
Bruce Ct NW 87114
Brunswick Pl NW 87114
Brush Pl NE 87123
Brushfield Rd NW 87114
Brushwood St NE 87122
Brussels Ave & Ct 87111
Bryan Ave NW 87114
Bryan Ct NW 87114
Bryan Ct SW 87105
Bryce Ave & Ct 87112
Bryce Canyon St SE 87123
Bryn Mawr Dr NE
101-197 87106
199-1940 87106
1942-1998 87106
3400-4399 87107
Bryn Mawr Dr SE 87106
Bryn Mawr Pl NE 87106
Buchanan Ct NW 87120
Buck Ct NW 87105
Buck Trl SE 87123
Buck Island Rd SW 87121
Buckboard Ave NE 87109
Buckboard St NW 87114
Buckeye St NW 87114
Bucking Bronco Trl SE 87123
Buckingham Ct NW 87120
Buckskin Rd NE 87111
Buena Ventura Ct, Pl & Rd 87123
Buena Vista Ave NW 87114
Buena Vista Dr SE 87106
Buenos Aires Pl NW 87120

Buffalo Cir SE 87123
Buffalo Dancer Ct & Trl 87112
Buffalo Grass Ct NE 87111
Buffalo Hills Dr NE 87111
Buffalo River Rd SE 87123
Buford Way SW 87121
Burgan Ave NE 87111
Burgos Ave NW 87114
Burgundy Way NE 87122
Burham Rd NW 87114
Burke St NE 87109
Burkett Ave NW 87120
Burlison Dr NE 87109
Burma Dr NE 87123
Burnhamwood Pl NE 87111
Burniece St SW 87105
Bursera Dr NW 87120
Burton Ave SE
2700-3299 87106
3301-3399 87106
3701-4597 87108
4599-4999 87108
Bush Ct SE 87123
Busher St SE 87123
Butch Cassidy Dr SW 87121
Buteos Dr NW 87120
Butler Ave NW 87114
Butler Ln SW 87121
Butte Pl NW 87120
Butte Volcano Rd NW 87120
Butterfield Trl NW 87120
Butterfly Dr NW 87114
Butterfly Maiden Trl NE 87112
Button Quail Ave NW 87114
Byron St SW 87105
C De Baca Ln NW 87114
C J Ct SW 87121
Caballero Dr SE 87123
Caballero Pkwy NW 87107
Caballo Canyon Dr NE 87112
Caballo De Fuerza Rd SE 87123
Cabernet St SW 87121
Cabin Ct NW 87120
Cabral Trl SW 87121
Cabrillo Cir NW 87120
Cacahuate SW 87105
Cache Creek Dr NW 87114
Cactus Ave NW 87114
Cactus Canyon Trl NE 87111
Cactus Flower Dr NW 87120
Cactus Hills Pl NW 87114
Cactus Point Dr SW 87121
Cactus Pointe Dr NW 87114
Cactus Trail Rd NW 87114
Cacy Ave NW 87107
Caddie St NW 87114
Cadiz St NW 87114
Cagua Dr NE
200-999 87108
1200-3499 87110
Cagua Dr SE 87108
Cagua Pl NE 87110
Cairo Dr NE 87111
Caitlin Ct NW 87120
Calabacillas Ct NW 87114
Calandrias St NW 87114
Caley Ave NW 87120
Calhoun Ave SE 87105
Calhoun Dr NE 87109
Caliber Rd SW 87121
Calico Pl NW 87114
California St NE
101-197 87108
199-299 87108
1008-1010 87110
1012-3619 87110
3621-3625 87110
California St SE 87108
Calistoga Ave NE 87122
Calla Lily Cir NE 87111
Callaway Cir NE 87111
Calle Abajo Way SW 87121
Calle Acanta NW 87114
Calle Adolanto NE 87113
Calle Alameda NE 87113
Calle Alava NW 87114
Calle Alba NW 87114
Calle Alegre NW 87120
Calle Alegria NE 87113
Calle Allegro NW 87114
Calle Alma NW 87114
Calle Almeria NE 87113
Calle Alta NE 87111
Calle Amado NE 87111
Calle Amarillo SW 87121
Calle Amor SE 87123
Calle Amorada Ct NW 87114
Calle Arbol NW 87114
Calle Armonia NE 87113
Calle Arroyo Seco NW 87120
Calle Avila NW 87114
Calle Avion NE 87113
Calle Azul SE 87123
Calle Azulejo NW 87120
Calle Barbarita NW 87107
Calle Bella NW 87114
Calle Bonito NE 87111
Calle Calma NE 87113
Calle Candela NW 87107
Calle Canta NW 87114
Calle Carisma NE 87113
Calle Castano Ct 87111
Calle Cedro NE 87111
Calle Cereza NE 87111
Calle Chamisa NW 87114
Calle Chulita NW 87114
Calle Cielo SW 87121
Calle Comodo NE 87113
Calle Contento NW 87114
Calle Corazon Ct NW 87114
Calle Cordoba NW 87114
Calle Coronado SE 87123
Calle Corta SW 87105
Calle Corvo NE 87113
Calle Cuervo NW 87114
Calle Cumbre NW 87120
Calle De Alamo NW 87104
Calle De Alondra NW 87120
Calle De Amole SW 87121
Calle De Carino NE 87111
Calle De Cobre NE 87109
Calle De Daniel NW 87104
Calle De Deborah NW 87104
Calle De Estella NW 87104
Calle De Gabriel NE 87122
Calle De La Noche NE 87109
Calle De Laura NW 87104
Calle De Los Hijos NW 87114
Calle De Luna NE 87111
Calle De Oro NE 87109
Calle De Paloma NW 87104
Calle De Panza NW 87104
Calle De Plata NE 87109
Calle De Rafael NE 87122
Calle De Real NW 87104
Calle De Sancho NW 87104
Calle De Sandias NE 87111
Calle De Tierra NE 87111
Calle De Vida NW 87114
Calle Del Bosque NW 87104
Calle Del Cielo NE 87111
Calle Del Contento NE 87110
Calle Del Corte NE 87110
Calle Del Dominica SW 87105
Calle Del Estavan NW 87104
Calle Del Fuego NE 87113
Calle Del Monte NE
3400-3499 87106
Calle Del Monte NE
3501-3599 87106
3600-3899 87110
Calle Del Oso Pl NE 87111
Calle Del Pajarito NW 87114
Calle Del Prado SW 87105
Calle Del Ranchero NE
1100-3599 87106
3600-3699 87110
Calle Del Rey NW 87114
Calle Del Rey SW 87121
Calle Del Rio NW 87104
Calle Del Rio SW 87105
Calle Del Sol NE
1100-3599 87106
3600-3699 87110
Calle Del Sueno Way SW 87121
Calle Del Vista Rd NW 87105
Calle Dichoso Ct NW 87114
Calle Diez NW 87107
Calle Divina NE 87113
Calle Dolce NW 87114
Calle Elena NE 87113
Calle Encina NE 87113
Calle Ensueno NW 87120
Calle Facio NW 87104
Calle Feliz NW 87114
Calle Floresta Ct NW 87120
Calle Fuerte NE 87113
Calle Gandia NW 87114
Calle Garza NE 87113
Calle Grande NW 87104
Calle Hermosa Ct & Pl 87114
Calle Hidalgo NW 87114
Calle Laguna NE 87113
Calle Leon NW 87114
Calle Loma Parda NW 87120
Calle Los Vecinos NW 87107
Calle Maravilla Ct NW 87114
Calle Margarita NE 87113
Calle Merida NW 87114
Calle Meseta NE 87113
Calle Mirlo NW 87114
Calle Montana NE 87113
Calle Monte Aplanado NW 87120
Calle Montosa Ct NW 87120
Calle Nuestra NW 87120
Calle Nueve NW 87107
Calle Ocho NW 87107
Calle Olas Altos NE 87109
Calle Olivo NE 87111
Calle Oveja Ct NW 87120
Calle Pajaro Azul NW 87120
Calle Paraiso NE 87113
Calle Pequeno NW 87107
Calle Perdiz NW 87114
Calle Perro NW 87114
Calle Petirrojo NW 87120
Calle Picaflor NW 87120
Calle Pino NE 87111
Calle Pinon NW 87114
Calle Placido NW 87114
Calle Playa Del Sol NE 87109
Calle Primera NW 87120
Calle Pueblo Pinado NW 87120
Calle Quieta NW 87120
Calle Redonda NW 87120
Calle Rosa NW 87114
Calle Salinas SW 87121
Calle San Angel NW 87107
Calle San Blas NE 87109
Calle San Ysidro NW 87107
Calle Santiago NE 87113
Calle Serena NW 87120
Calle Sol Se Mete NW 87120
Calle Sombra NW 87114
Calle Sonrisa NE 87113
Calle Soquelle NE 87113
Calle Tesoro NW 87114
Calle Tranquilo NW 87104
Calle Vadito NW 87120
Calle Verde SE 87123
Calle Vigo NW 87104
Calle Vizcaya NW 87114
Calle Zagal NE 87111
Callejon Dr NE 87112
Callow St NE 87109
Calyx Ct & Dr 87120
Cam Fella St SE 87123
Cambria Rd NW 87120
Cambridge Pl NE 87112
Camden Ct NW 87114
Camelback Rd NW 87114
Camelia Ct SW 87105
Camelot Pl NE 87122
Cameo Dr SE 87105
Camero Ave NE 87111
Cameron St NW 87114
Camille Ave NW 87120
Camilo Ln NW 87104
Caminito Ct & Dr 87111
Caminito Coors NW 87120
Camino Vis NW 87120
Camino Alameda SW 87105
Camino Amparo NW 87107
Camino Aplauso NW 87107
Camino Arbustos NE 87111
Camino Azul NW 87121
Camino Bello SW 87121
Camino Bonito NW 87114
Camino Caballette NW 87107
Camino Canada NW 87114
Camino Capistrano NE 87111
Camino Cepillo NW 87107
Camino Cerrito SE 87123
Camino Cinco SW 87105
Camino Cometa NE 87111
Camino Contento NW 87120
Camino Corto NW 87120
Camino Cuatro SW 87105
Camino De Aguila NW 87120
Camino De Amador NW 87107
Camino De Compania NW 87107
Camino De Esperanza SW 87105
Camino De La Luna NW 87120
Camino De La Sierra NE
100-198 87123
200-599 87123
1600-1799 87112
1801-2599 87112
3000-4114 87111
4116-4198 87111
Camino De Los Artesanos NW 87107
Camino De Luciano NW 87114
Camino De Monte NE 87111
Camino De Pacheco NE 87113
Camino De Paz Rd NW 87120
Camino De Salud 87106
Camino De Salud NE 87102
Camino Del Arrebol NW 87120
Camino Del Bosque NW 87114
Camino Del Cielo NE 87123
Camino Del Norte NE 87123
Camino Del Oeste NE 87123
Camino Del Oso NE 87111
Camino Del Prado NW 87114
Camino Del Rey NE 87123
Camino Del Rio NW 87114
Camino Del Sol NE 87111
Camino Del Valle SW 87105
Camino Del Venado NW 87120
Camino Don Diego NE 87111
Camino Dos SW 87105
Camino Ecuestre NW 87107
Camino El Alto NE 87123
Camino Espanol NW 87107
Camino Etereo NE 87122
Camino Floretta NW 87107
Camino Gallo NW 87107
Camino Gusto NW 87107
Camino La Morada NW 87114
Camino Montano NE 87111
Camino Ocho SW 87105
Camino Osito NE 87111
Camino Paisano NW 87120
Camino Paseo Corto NE 87123
Camino Perfecto NE 87113
Camino Placido NE 87109
Camino Quieto NW 87120
Camino Ranchitos NW 87114
Camino Raso NW 87107
Camino Real Ct NE 87111
Camino Rosario NW 87107
Camino Sacramento NE 87111
Camino San Martin Ct 87121
Camino Sandia NE 87111
Camino Segundo NE 87123
Camino Seis SW 87105
Camino Siete SW 87105
Camino Soledad NW 87120
Camino Tres SW 87105
Camino Uno SW 87105
Camino Valle Trl NW 87120
Camino Viejo NW 87114
Camino Viento NW 87120
Campana Ct SW 87105
Campbell Ct & Rd 87104
Campbell Farm Ln NW 87104
Campfire Ln NW 87120
Campo De Maiz Rd NW 87114
Campo Del Oso Ave NE 87123
Campo Del Sol Ave NE 87123
Campus Blvd NE 87106
Canada Pl NW 87114
Canada De Los Alamos Rd & Trl 87123
Canada Del Oso Pl NE 87111
Canada Vista Pl NW 87120
Canal Rd SW 87105
Canario Ct NW 87120
Canary Ln NE 87109
Cancelar Dr NE 87111
Candelaria Rd NE
101-211 87107
213-3500 87107
3502-3520 87107
3600-3899 87110
3901-7899 87110
8400-8498 87112
8500-9600 87112
9602-13298 87112
9717-9719 87111
9719-9719 87154
9719-9719 87191
9741-13199 87112
Candelaria Rd NW 87107
Candelarias Ln NW 87107
Candelia Ave NW 87114
Candelita Ct NE 87112
Candle Ln NE 87111
Candleglow Dr NE 87111
Candlelight Ct & Dr 87111
Candlestick Dr NE 87109
Candlewood Ct NE 87111
Canelo Ct NW 87114
Canis Ave NW 87114
Cannon Rd SW 87105
Cannonade Ct SE 87123
Canoncito Dr NE 87122
Canoncito Pl NE 87113
Canoncito Pl NW 87120
Cantacielo Dr NW 87114
Cantariello Ct NW 87120
Cantata St NW 87114
Canter St SW 87121
Cantera Dr NW 87120
Canterbury NE 87111
Canyon Ct NE 87111
N Canyon Rd SW 87121
S Canyon Rd SW 87121
Canyon Trl SW 87121
Canyon Bluff Trl NE 87111
Canyon Cliff Rd NW 87114
Canyon Creek Dr NE 87111
Canyon Crest Pl NE 87111
Canyon Edge Trl NE 87111
Canyon Gate Trl SW 87121
Canyon Hills Dr NE 87112
Canyon Pointe Ct NE 87111
Canyon Ridge Pl NE 87111
Canyon Rim Dr NE 87112
Canyon Run Rd NE 87111
Canyon Sage Dr NE 87113
Canyon View Ct NE 87123
Canyon Vista Dr NE 87111
Canyonlands Ct, Pl & Rd 87123
Canyonview Pl NE 87123
Capistrano Ct NE 87111
Capitan Ave NE 87109
Capitol Dr NE 87109
Capri Ct NW 87114
Capriccio Rd NW 87114
Capricorn Pl NW 87114
Caprock Rd NW 87114
Capulin Rd NE 87109
Caramel Dr NE 87113
Carbine Ct NE 87109
Carbondale Ct NW 87114
Cardenas Dr NE
100-921 87108
1021-1197 87110
1199-3499 87110
Cardenas Dr SE 87108
Cardenas Pl NE 87110
Cardiff Ave NE 87109
Cardigan Ct NW 87120
Cardinal St NW 87114
Carefree Ave NW 87120
Carfax Pl SW 87121
Cargo Ave NE 87109
Caribou Ave NE 87111
Carl Ct NE 87112
Carl Hatch Pl NW 87114
Carla Ct & St 87121
Carlisle Blvd NE
101-197 87106
199-917 87106
919-999 87106
1300-3799 87110
3800-4499 87107
4500-4598 87109
4600-4699 87109
Carlisle Blvd SE 87106
Carlisle Pl SE 87108
Carlito Rd NE 87113
Carlito Rd NW 87107
Carlos Ct SW 87121
Carlos Rd NE 87113
Carlos Rd NW 87114
Carlos Rey Cir & Dr 87121
Carlota Rd NW 87104
Carlsbad Ct NW 87120
Carlton St NW 87107
Carmel Ave NE
5600-5698 87113
5700-6100 87113
6102-7520 87113
7600-9698 87122
9700-12500 87122
12502-12598 87122
Carmel Ct NE 87122
Carmelita Dr NE 87111
Carmelito Loop NE 87113
Carmellia Ct SE 87123
Carmen Rd NW 87114
Carmona Rd NW 87114
Carmony Ln NE 87107
Carney Ave NW 87120
Carol Pl & St 87112
Carolina St NE 87110
Carousal Ave NW 87120
Carraro Pl NW 87114
Carreta Dr NW 87114
Carriage Rd NE 87109
Carrick St NW 87120
Carrie Pl SE 87123
Carriveau Ave NE 87110
Carrizo Rd NW 87114
Carruthers St NE 87111
Carson Rd NW 87104
Carson Trl NW 87120
Carson Mesa Dr NW 87114
Cartagena Ave SW 87121
Cartouche Dr SW 87105
Casa Amarilla Rd NW 87120
Casa Azul Ct NW 87120
Casa Blanca NW 87120
Casa Bonita Dr NE 87111
Casa De Luz Ct NW 87120
Casa De Vida NE 87111
Casa Del Norte Ct NE
2600-2799 87112
3100-3199 87111
Casa Del Norte Dr NE
2800-2999 87112
3000-3099 87111
Casa Del Oso NE 87111
Casa Del Rio Trl NW 87120
Casa Elena Dr NE 87113
Casa Feliz NE 87111
Casa Florida Pl NW 87120
Casa Grande Ave, Ct & Pl 87112
Casa Gris Ct NW 87120
Casa Hermosa Dr NE 87112
Casa Linda Ct NW 87120
Casa Loma NE 87109
Casa Maria Rd NE 87113
Casa Morena Ct NW 87120
Casa Negra Ct NW 87120
Casa Roja Pl NW 87120
Casa Tomas Rd NE 87113
Casa Verde Ave NW 87120
Casa Vistosa Ct NW 87120
Casador Del Oso NE 87111
Cascabel Trl SE 87123
Cascada Rd NW 87114
Cascada Azul Pl NW 87114
Cascade Pl NW 87105
Cascade Park Ave NW 87120
Cascajo Dr NE 87111
Casey Jones Pl NE 87113
Casita Vista Ct & Pl 87105
Casitas Ct SW 87121
Cassandra St SW 87121
Cassidy Dr NW 87114
Cassiopeia St NW 87114
Castanada St SW 87105
Castaneda Rd NW 87107
Castellano Ct & Rd 87123
Castellon Ave SW 87121
Castillo St SW 87121
Castle Pl SE 87116
Castle Dome Pl NW 87114
Castlerock Ct NW 87120
Catalina Ct & Pl 87121
Catalonia Ct NW 87114
Catamount Dr NW 87114
Cathy Ave NE 87109
Catron Ave & Ct 87123
Catskill Way NE 87111
Cattail Ct SW 87121
Cattail Willow Ave NE 87122
Cattleya Rd NW 87120
Caughran Pl NE 87123
Cavenaugh Dr NW 87114
Cayenne Dr NW 87120
Cayetana Pl NW 87120
Cayman Ct NW 87120
Cebolleta Ct SW 87105
Cecilia Dr SW 87105
Cedar Ct SE 87116
Cedar Ln NE 87122
Cedar St NE 87106
Cedar St SE 87106
Cedar Canyon Ct, Pl & Rd 87122

Cedar Creek Dr & Pl 87120
Cedar Hill Ct, Ln, Pl & Rd NE 87122
Cedar Ridge Dr NE 87112
Cedar Springs Pl NW 87114
Cedar Waxwing Pl NW 87114
Cedarbrook Ave, Ct & Pl 87111
Cedarcroft Rd NW 87120
Cedarwood Ave NW 87120
Celeste Rd SW 87105
Celestial Ave NW 87114
Cenaroca Ct NE 87123
Cenote Rd SW 87121
Central Ave NE
300-399 87102
401-817 87102
1001-3599 87106
3601-8623 87108
8711-10197 87123
10199-10299 87123
10301-13317 87123
Central Ave NW
123-1215 87102
1401-2603 87104
3901-6411 87105
7017-15225 87121
16001-16003 87120
16701-17599 87121
18000-18998 87121
Central Ave SE
520A-520B 87102
2132A-2132B 87106
202-808 87102
1100-3502 87106
3600-8614 87108
8700-15602 87123
Central Ave SW
100-1304 87102
1404-2060 87104
2016-2016 87194
2100-2702 87104
3900-6432 87105
6600-18998 87121
Central Park Dr NE 87123
Centre Ave SE 87106
Century Ave NE 87107
Cerrillos Rd SW 87121
Cerro Colorado SW 87121
Cerro Crestado Dr NW 87114
Cerro Largo Pl NW 87114
Cerro Vista Rd SW 87105
Cerros Pl NW 87114
Cerros De Morado SE 87123
Cesar Chavez Ct SW 87121
Cesars Palace Dr NW 87121
Chaco Rd NE 87109
Chaco Canyon Ln NE 87111
Chaco Cliff Trl SE 87123
Chaco Mesa Loop NW 87114
Chaco Ridge Pl NE 87111
Chaco Terrace St NW 87114
Chacoma Pl SW 87104
Chacon Pl NW 87104
Chadwick Rd NW 87120
Chalmers Rd SW 87105
Chama St NE
100-532 87108
534-608 87108
900-2999 87110
4101-4199 87109
Chama St SE 87108
Chamaigne Ct SE 87105
Chambers Ct & Pl 87111
Chamblee Ct NE 87111
Chambourcin Rd SW 87121
Chamisa Ct NW 87120
Chamisal Rd NW 87107
Chamiso Ln NW 87107
Chamisoso Ct SE 87116
Chanate Ave SW 87105
Chance Ct NW 87114
Chandelle Ct & Loop 87112
Chandler Dr NW 87114
Chantilly Rd NW 87114

Chanute St SE 87116
Chapala Ct, Dr & Pl 87111
Chaparral Cir & Ct 87114
Chaparro Dr NW 87114
Chapel Ct & Dr 87114
Chaplin St NW 87120
Chapman Ln NW 87104
Chappell Dr NE 87107
Chappell Rd NE 87113
Chaps St SW 87121
Chapulin Rd SW 87105
Charger Trl NE 87109
Charla Ct SE 87123
Charles Pl NW 87107
Charleston St NE
200-799 87108
800-2598 87110
2600-3199 87110
Charleston St SE 87108
Charlevoix St NW 87104
Charlotte Ct NE 87109
Charwood Rd NW 87114
Chase Ranch Pl SW 87121
Chateau Dr NE 87122
Chavez Rd NW 87107
Chelon Pl NW 87114
Chelton Ct NE 87111
Chelwood Ct NE 87112
Chelwood Dr NE 87111
Chelwood Pl NE 87112
Chelwood Rd NE 87111
Chelwood Trl NE 87112
Chelwood Park Blvd NE
301-397 87123
399-600 87123
602-898 87123
900-998 87112
1000-2799 87112
2801-2999 87112
3500-5610 87111
5612-5612 87111
Chenoa Rd NW 87120
Cheraz Rd NE 87111
Cherokee Ct NW 87107
Cherokee Rd NE
3400-3498 87107
3600-5299 87110
9101-9197 87111
9199-9299 87111
Cherokee Rd NW 87107
Cherry Ln NW 87104
Cherry Blossom Ln NE 87111
Cherry Hills Dr, Loop, Pl & Rd NE 87111
Cherry Sage Ct NE 87111
Cherry Tree Ln SW 87105
Cherrydale Ct NW 87107
Chesapeake Rd NW 87120
Chester Ln SW 87105
Chetwood Ln SW 87105
Cheyenne Ct NW 87120
Chia Way NE 87122
Chianti Ave SW 87121
Chickadee Ln NE 87109
Chico Rd NE
7601-7997 87108
7999-8499 87108
9600-11098 87123
11100-13599 87123
Chicobush Dr NW 87114
Chicory Dr NW 87120
Chihuahua Ave NE 87112
Childers Dr NE 87112
Childs Dr & Pl 87105
Chilili Dr NW 87114
Chilte Pine Rd NW 87120
Chimayo Dr NW 87120
Chinlee Ave NE 87110
Chiricahua Ct & St 87123
Chisholm Trl NW 87120
Chitalpa Pl NE 87111
Choctaw Trl NW 87120
Choke Cherry Ct SE 87116
Cholla Pl SE 87123
Chris Ct NW 87120

Christine St NE
1200-2999 87112
3100-3299 87111
Christopher Rd SW 87121
Christy Ave NE 87109
Chuckar Dr SW 87121
Chuckwagon Trl NW 87120
Chula Vista Pl NE 87108
Church St NW 87104
Churchill Ln SW 87121
Churchill Rd SW
5100-5199 87105
5401-5497 87121
5499-6699 87121
6701-6799 87121
Ciani Ct SW 87121
Cibola Loop NW 87114
Cibola Village Dr NE 87111
Cielito Ct NE 87111
Cielito Lindo NE 87111
Cielito Lindo Ct NW 87114
Cielito Lindo Pl NW 87114
Cielito Norte Way NE 87122
Cielito Oeste Way NE 87122
Cielo Ct NE 87111
Cielo Grande NE 87109
Cielo Linda Ct SW 87121
Cielo Oeste Pl NW 87120
Cienega Rd NW 87120
Ciguena St SW 87121
Cilantro Ln NW 87104
Cimarron Rd NW 87120
Cimino Rd NW 87107
Cinder Pl NW 87120
Cinder Cone Dr NW 87120
Cindy Dr NE 87109
Cinnamon Dr NW 87120
Cinnamon Teal Ct NW 87120
Circle Dr NE 87122
Circulo Del Monte NE 87112
Circulo Floretta NW 87107
Circulo Gallegos NW 87107
Circulo Largo Ct 87112
Cirrus Dr NW 87120
Cisco Rd NW 87120
Cita Rd NW 87114
Citation Dr SW 87105
City Lights Dr NE 87111
City View Dr SW 87105
Ciudad Ct NE 87123
Civic Plz NW 87102
Claire Ct NW 87104
Claire Ln SW 87121
Clancy Dr NE 87112
Claremont Ave NE
101-2097 87107
2099-2499 87107
2501-3499 87107
3901-5297 87110
5299-7600 87110
7602-7998 87110
8400-12399 87112
Claremont Ave NW 87107
Claremont Ct NE 87112
Claremont Pl NE 87110
Claridge Pl NW 87114
Clarita Way SW 87121
Clark Cir & Rd 87105
Clark Carr Loop SE 87106
Clarks Fork Rd NW 87120
Classic Ave NE 87109
Claudine St NE
600-899 87123
1000-1099 87112
Claveles St NW 87104
Clay St SE 87105
Clear St SW 87121
Clearwater Ct & St 87114
Cleghorn Ct & Rd 87120
Clemente Ct, Pl & St 87121
Cleo Rd SW 87121
Cleopatra Ct & Pl 87112
Cletsoway Dr SW 87105
Cliff Rd NW 87120
Cliff Base Dr NW 87120
Cliff Dwellers Rd NW 87114

Cliffbrush Ln NE 87111
Clifford Ave NE 87112
Cliffrose Dr NE 87122
Cliffrose Rd NW 87120
Cliffside Ct & Dr 87105
Cliffview Ave NW 87120
Clifton Ave SE 87102
Clinton Blvd SW 87105
Clinton Anderson Dr NW 87114
Cloud Ct NW 87114
Cloud Burst Dr NW 87120
Cloudcroft Rd NW 87105
Cloudveil Pl NW 87114
Cloudview Ave NE 87123
Cloudy Rd NW 87120
Clover Ln SW 87105
Clovis Pl SE 87123
Club Ct NW 87114
Club Cholla Ct NE 87111
Clyburn Park Dr NE 87123
Clyde St NW 87107
Coachman St NE 87109
Coal Ave SE
400-400 87102
402-800 87102
802-820 87102
1000-2699 87106
2701-3299 87106
3901-4209 87108
4211-5599 87108
Coal Ave SW
200-1399 87102
1400-1498 87104
Coal Pl SE 87106
Cobalt Dr NW 87114
Cobblestone Pl NE 87109
Coca Rd NW 87104
Cochiti Ct NW 87120
Cochiti Dr NW 87120
Cochiti Rd SE
6301-6397 87108
6399-7099 87108
9600-12999 87123
Cockatiel Dr SW 87121
Cockatoo Ln NE 87109
Coconino Rd SE 87123
Cocono Cir & Dr 87105
Coda Pl NE 87111
Cody Ct & St 87114
Coe Ct NE 87110
Coe Dr NE 87110
Coe Rd SW 87105
Colby Ct NW 87114
Cold Creek Ave NW 87114
Cole Ln SW 87105
Cole Springs Dr SW 87121
Colfax Ave NE 87109
Colima Ave NW 87120
Colinas Ave NE 87113
Colleen Ave NE 87109
Colleens Way NE 87111
College St NW 87120
College Heights Dr NW 87120
Collier Ct NE 87112
Colonial Cir NE 87111
Colonnade Ct NW 87107
Colony Pl NE 87122
Colorado Ct & St 87110
Colt Ln SE 87123
Colt Rd NE 87113
Columbia Dr NE
1000-1599 87106
3300-3400 87107
3402-3498 87107
Columbia Dr SE 87106
Columbine Ave NE 87113
Columbus Cir NW 87114
Colville Rd SE 87123
Comanche Ct NE 87110
Comanche Rd NE
501-597 87107
599-3500 87107
3502-3598 87107
3600-8336 87110
8338-8338 87110
8400-13300 87111
13302-13398 87111
Cometa Ct & Pl 87111
Comfrey Dr NW 87120
Commerce Dr NE 87107
Commercial St NE
301-1797 87102
1799-2513 87102
2515-2599 87102
2900-3900 87107
3902-6498 87107
Commercial St SE 87102
Commons Ave NE 87109
Commons North Ln NW 87114
Community Ln SW 87105
Como Dr NW 87114
Compa Ct NE 87112
Compadre Ct & Ln 87111
Compound North Ct NW 87107
Conchas Ct NE 87123
Conchas St NE
100-450 87123
452-498 87123
1400-1600 87112
1602-2698 87112
3000-3099 87111
Conchas St SE 87123
Concord Pl SW 87105
Concordia Rd NE 87111
Conder Ln NW 87107
Condershire Dr SW 87121
Condesa Ct & Dr 87114
Condor Dr NW 87114
Coneflower Dr NW 87114
Conejo Rd NE 87123
Conestoga Dr NW 87120
Conestoga Dr SE 87123
Confederate Dr NE 87109
Congress Ave NW 87114
Conita Real Ave SW 87105
Connecticut St NE 87110
Connemara Dr SW 87121
Conner Ct NE 87112
Conrad Ave NW 87120
Conrado Ln NE 87113
Conrado Ln NW 87107
Constance Pl NE 87109
Constitution Ave NE
2900-3599 87106
3701-3997 87110
3999-8303 87110
8305-8499 87110
8500-13104 87112
13106-13198 87112
Constitution Ave NW 87102
Constitution Ct NE 87112
Constitution Pl NE 87110
Consuelo Ln & Pl 87104
Consuelo Point St NE 87111
Contess Rd NW 87114
Contessa Pl SW 87105
Continental Loop SE 87108
Contreras Pl NW 87104
Cook Ave SW 87105
Cook Ct NE 87112
Cook Ranch Pl SW 87121
Cool Springs Dr SW 87121
Coors Blvd NW
100-1600 87121
1602-1698 87121
2500-9182 87120
9184-9198 87120
9201-9297 87114
9299-10199 87114
10201-10799 87114
Coors Blvd SW 87121
Coors Byp NW 87114
Coors Pl SW 87121
Coors Trl NW 87120
Copeland Pl & Rd 87105
Coppell Ct NE 87113
Copper Ave NE
400-402 87102
404-614 87102
616-714 87102
1000-1199 87106
1201-1599 87106
3601-3797 87108
3799-8600 87108
8602-8698 87108
9101-9797 87123
9799-14199 87123
14201-14299 87123
Copper Ave NW 87102
Copper Pl NE 87123
Copper Creek Ct SW 87121
Copper Grass Ct NE 87113
Copper Rose Ct SE 87116
Copper Rose St NE 87111
Copperfield Dr NE 87109
Copperhead Ct NE 87113
Copperleaf Trl NE 87122
Copperwood Dr NE 87123
Coppice Dr NW 87120
Coral Ct NW 87120
Coral Dawn Rd NE 87122
Coral Satin Ct NE 87122
Coralita Ct NE 87122
Cordelia St SW 87105
Corder Ln NW 87107
Cordero Rd NE 87102
Cordero Mesa Dr NW 87120
Cordoniz St NW 87120
Cordova Ave NE 87112
Cordova Ave NW 87107
Cordova Pl NW 87107
Cordova Rd SW 87105
Corel Dr SW 87121
Corfield Ln & Pl 87105
Corianda Ct NW 87104
Corn Mountain Pl NW 87114
Cornelia Ct SW 87121
Cornell Dr NE 87106
Cornell Dr SE
100-116 87106
115-115 87196
118-2198 87106
201-2199 87106
Corona Ave NE
5701-5797 87113
5799-6500 87113
6502-7522 87113
7900-7998 87122
8000-11799 87122
11801-11899 87122
Corona Dr NW 87120
Corona Loop NE 87113
Corona Ranch Rd SW 87121
Coronado Ave NE
5701-6199 87109
9601-9997 87122
9999-12599 87122
Coronado Fwy SW 87121
Corral Gate Ln SW 87121
Corrales Rd NW
10200-10702 87114
10701-10731 87114
10701-10701 87187
Corregidor Rd SW 87105
Corriz Dr SW 87121
Corsica Ave NW 87114
Corsico Pl NW 87114
Cortaderia Pl & St 87111
Corte Adelina St SW 87105
Corte Alzira NW 87114
Corte Bonito NW 87105
Corte De Aguila NW 87120
Corte De Apio NW 87104
Corte De Azucena NW 87104
Corte De Caballo NW 87120
Corte De Calabaza NW 87104
Corte De Chamisa NW 87120
Corte De Loma NW 87120
Corte De Pimienta NW 87104
Corte De Ristra NW 87104
Corte Del Sol NW 87105
Corte Del Viento NW 87120

Corte Dorada NW 87120
Corte Eduardo St SW 87105
Corte Elicia St SW 87105
Corte Florentino St SW 87105
Corte Mirabal Rd NW 87104
Corte Ocaso NE 87113
Corte Plateada NW 87120
Cortez Dr SW 87121
Corto Ct NW 87114
Cortona Ln NE 87122
Corundum Ct NW 87114
Cosmos Dr SW 87121
Coso Ave SE 87105
Costa Blanca Ave NW 87114
Costa Brava Ave NW 87114
Costa Calida Ave NW 87114
Costa Del Sol NE 87111
Costa Garraf Rd NW 87120
Costa Maresme Dr NW 87120
Costa Uasca Dr NW 87120
Costa Uerde Rd NW 87120
Cote Ave NE 87123
Cottontail Pl SW 87105
Cottontail St SW
600-698 87121
1000-1099 87105
Cottonwood Ct NW 87107
Cottonwood Ct SE 87123
Cottonwood Dr NW 87107
Cottonwood Ln SW 87105
Cottonwood Park NW 87114
Cottonwood Pl NW 87107
Cottonwood Rd NE 87111
Cottrell Ln SW 87105
Cougar Ln SE 87123
Cougar Loop NE 87122
Coulson Dr NE 87109
Coulterville St NW 87114
Count Fleet St SE 87123
Country Clb NE 87111
Country Club Ln NW 87114
Country Cove Pl NW 87114
Country Glen Ct NW 87114
Country Hills Ct NW 87114
Country Knoll Ct NW 87114
Country Manor Pl NW 87114
Country Meadows Dr NW 87114
Country Sage Ct & Dr 87114
Country View Rd SW 87105
Countryside Ln NW 87114
Countrywood Ave NW 87120
Countrywood Rd NE 87109
Courtney Ave NE 87108
Courtyard Dr NE 87112
Cove Ct NW 87114
Covered Wagon SE 87123
Covert Ln SW 87121
Covina Pl NW 87104
Coyote Hls, Ln & Trl 87123
Coyote Canyon Dr SE 87123
Coyote Canyon Pl NW 87114
Coyote Hill Way NW 87120
Coyote Run Rd NE 87122
Coyote Springs Rd SE 87123
Coyote Willow Ave NE 87122
Crabtree Ct NW 87120
Cranbrook St NE 87111
Crandall Rd SW 87121
Crane Dr SW 87121
Creek Pl NW 87114
Creek St NE 87113
Creekwood Ave NW 87120
Creggs St NW 87120
Crepe Myrtle Rd SW 87121
Crescent Dr NW 87105
Crespin Ave NE 87102
Cresswell Rd SW 87105
Crest Ave SE
3400-3599 87106
3600-4598 87108
4600-4899 87108
Cresta Del Sur Ct NE 87111
Cresta Luna Ct NE 87111

Cresta Park Ave NW 87114
Crested Butte Dr NE 87112
Crested Moss Rd NE 87122
Crestline Ave NE 87112
Crestridge Ave & Ct 87114
Crestside Ln SW 87121
Crestview Dr SW 87105
Crestview Pl SW 87105
Crestview Trl NE 87122
Crestwood Ave NE 87112
Cricket Pl SW 87121
Cricket Hill Dr NE 87113
Crimson Ave NW 87120
Crimson Glory Rd NE 87122
Crimson Rose Ln SW 87121
Cripple Creek Rd NW 87114
Cripple Creek Rd SE 87123
Criss Rd SW 87105
Crissy Field Way NE 87123
Cristalino Rd SW 87121
Cristo Rey Ct SW 87105
Cristobal Rd SW 87105
Cromwell Ave SE & SW 87102
Crooked Creek Ave NW 87114
Crosscut Dr NW 87114
Crossroads Pl SE 87116
Crosswinds Trl NW 87114
Crown Ridge Rd NW 87114
Crownpoint Ct NW 87120
Croyden Ave NW 87114
Cruz St SW 87121
Crystal Ave NW 87120
Crystal Ridge Rd SW 87121
Crystalaire Ave NW 87120
Cuadro St SE 87123
Cuarzo Ave NW 87114
Cuatro Cerros Trl SE 87123
Cuatro Milpas Rd SW 87105
Cuba Rd NW 87114
Cubero Dr NE 87109
Cuchillo Rd NW 87114
Cuervo Ct NW 87107
Cuervo Dr NE 87110
Cuesta Pl NW 87120
Cuesta Abajo Ct NE 87113
Cuesta Arriba Ct NE 87113
Cueva Del Oso NE 87111
Cueva Escondida NW 87120
Cuevita Ct NE 87113
Cuevita Oeste Dr NE 87122
Cullen Ln NE 87112
Cumberland Pl & Rd 87120
Cumbre Del Sur Ct NE 87111
Cumbres St NE 87112
Cumulus Pl NW 87120
Cunningham Ave SE 87106
Curry Ave NE 87109
Curt Walters Ct NE 87122
Cutler Ave NE
200-407 87102
2200-3099 87106
4100-8300 87110
8302-8398 87110
Cutler Ave NW 87102
Cutler Ct NE 87106
Cutler Pl NE 87110
Cutting Ave NW 87114
Cyan Ct NW 87120
Cydni Ct NE 87112
Cygnus Ave NW 87114
Cynthia Ct & Loop 87114
Cyonus Ave NW 87114
Cypress Cir & Dr 87105
Cypress Point Way NE 87111
D And H Cir NE 87123
D Reed Ct NE 87122
Daisy Summer Ave SW 87121
Dakota St NE 87110
Dakota St SE 87108
Dakota Ridge Rd SW 87121
Dale Ave SE 87105

Dallas St NE
100-799 87108
801-1297 87110
1299-3199 87110
Dallas St SE 87108
Damacio Rd NW 87104
Dan Ave SE 87102
Dan Patch Rd SE 87123
Dana Ct NE 87122
Dancing Eagle Ave & Ct 87113
Dancing River Dr NW 87114
Dancing Star Way NW 87120
Dandas Dr NW 87114
Daniel Cir & Rd 87107
Danielito Ave NW 87120
Dans Rd SE 87123
Dante Ln NW 87114
Danube Ct & Dr 87111
Dark Mesa Ave NW 87120
Darla Ct SW 87121
Darlene Pl SW 87105
Darlington Pl NW 87114
Dartmouth Dr & Pl 87106
Daskalos Dr NE 87123
Datum St SW 87121
Datura Trl NE 87122
Davenport St NW 87114
David Ct NW 87107
David Ct SW 87105
Dawn View Dr NE 87111
Day Dreamer Rd NW 87114
Dayflower Dr NW 87114
Daylily Ct SE 87116
Daytona Pl NW 87121
Daytona Rd NW 87105
De Baca Cir SW 87105
De La Cruz NW 87107
De Leon Ct NE 87109
De Soto St SE 87123
De Trevis St SW 87121
De Vargas Loop NE 87109
De Vargas Rd SW 87121
De Vita Rd SW 87105
Dean Blvd SW 87105
Dean Dr SW 87121
Deanna St NE 87112
Deborah Ave NW 87120
Deborah Ln NE 87111
Decatur Ave SE 87108
Decker Ave NW 87107
Dee Dr NE 87111
Deer Dr NE 87122
Deer Canyon Ave NE 87113
Deer Dancer Trl NE 87112
Deer Lodge Pl & Rd 87123
Deer Meadow Trl NW 87120
Deer Trail Ct & Pl 87111
Deerbourne Rd NW 87114
Deerfield Rd NW 87120
Deergrass Cir NW 87120
Del Agua Ct NE 87111
Del Aker Rd NW 87107
Del Arroyo Ave & Ct 87122
Del Campo Pl NE 87109
Del Carmen St NW 87114
Del Chaparral Ct NE 87111
Del Cielo Dr NW 87105
Del Frate Pl NW 87105
Del Fuego Cir NE 87113
Del Haven St SW 87121
Del Mar St NE 87113
Del Mastro Ct & Dr 87121
Del Monte Ct & Trl 87121
Del Norte Dr SW 87105
Del Oeste Rd NW 87105
Del Oso Ct NE 87109
Del Pasado NW 87120
Del Rey Ave NE 87122
Del Rey Pl SW 87121
Del Rey Rd SW 87121
Del Rio Rd SW 87105
Del Sol Park Dr NW 87114
Del Sur Dr SW 87105
Delamar Ave NE
3300-3599 87107

3800-4799 87110
8700-8999 87111
Delamar Ave NW 87107
Delamar Loop NW 87107
Delamar Pl NW 87107
Delano Ave & Pl 87106
Delaware St NE 87110
Delbert Ave NW 87114
Delforado Dr SW 87121
Delgado Dr SW 87121
Delhi St NE 87111
Delia Ct NW 87104
Delia Rd SW 87121
Delicado Pl NE 87111
Delilah Dr SW 87121
Della Ct SW 87105
Della Dr SW 87105
Della Rd NE 87109
Della Longa Ln NE 87111
Dellwood Ct & Rd 87110
Dellyne Ave & Ct 87120
Delmar Ct & Dr 87111
Delta Ct NW 87114
Deluvina Dr & Pl 87105
Delvitto Ct NE 87111
Demica Pl NE 87109
Deming Ct NE 87109
Democracy Rd NE 87109
Dempsey Dr NE 87109
Denali Rd NE 87111
Denise Ct NE 87111
Dennis Chavez Ave NW 87114
Dennis Chavez Blvd SW 87121
Dennison Rd SW
1300-1599 87105
6000-6499 87121
Denton Rd SW 87121
Deputy Dean Miera Dr SW 87121
Derby Ct NW 87114
Derickson Ave NE 87109
Derramadera Ave NE 87113
Derringer Ct SW 87121
Derry Ct NW 87114
Descanso Rd SE 87102
Deschutes St SE 87123
Descollado Dr NW 87114
Desert Ct NE 87122
Desert Dr SW 87105
Desert Rd SE 87105
Desert Aster Ln NE 87122
Desert Bloom Ave, Ct & St 87120
Desert Bluff Dr SW 87121
Desert Breeze Dr SW 87121
Desert Cactus Dr SW 87121
Desert Canyon Pl SW 87121
Desert Classic Ln NE 87111
Desert Dawn Ct & Dr 87113
Desert Dreamer St NW 87114
Desert Dusk Ct NE 87113
Desert Eagle Rd NE 87113
Desert Finch Ln NE 87122
Desert Flower Pl NE 87111
Desert Fox Way NE 87122
Desert Garden Ln SW 87105
Desert Hills Pl NE 87111
Desert Holly Pl SE 87116
Desert Lily Ln NE 87122
Desert Maize Dr SW 87121
Desert Marigold Ln NE 87111
Desert Mesa Rd SW 87121
Desert Mist Dr SW 87121
Desert Moon Pl NE 87111
Desert Morning Rd SW 87121
Desert Mountain Rd NE 87122
Desert Mountain Rd SE 87123
Desert Orchid Dr SE 87123
Desert Pine Ave SW 87121

Desert Plume Ln NE 87122
Desert Pointe Ave SW 87121
Desert Poppy Ln NE 87122
Desert Rain Rd NW 87120
Desert Ridge Rd SW 87121
Desert Rim Rd SW 87121
Desert Rock Dr SW 87121
Desert Rose Ave NE 87111
Desert Sage Ct NW 87120
Desert Sand Pl NW 87120
Desert Shadow Way NE 87122
Desert Sky Ave NE 87111
Desert Sky Rd SE 87123
Desert Spirits Rd NW 87114
Desert Springs Ct & Dr 87121
Desert Star Rd NE 87111
Desert Sun Rd NE 87113
Desert Sunrise Rd NE 87122
Desert Surf Cir NE 87107
Desert Tree Dr SW 87121
Desert Willow Ct NE 87113
Desert Wood Dr SW 87121
Desert Zinnia Ct NE 87111
Desiderio Rd SW 87105
Desperado Rd SW 87121
Development Rd SE 87123
Devils Tower St SW 87121
Devon Ln NW 87107
Diablo Trail Pl NW 87114
Diamantes NW 87120
Diamond Pl SW 87121
Diamond Mesa Trl SW 87121
Diamondback Dr NE 87113
Diana Pl NE 87123
Dickerson Dr SE 87106
Diego Pl SW 87105
Diers Rd NW 87114
Dietz Ct, Loop & Pl 87107
Dietz Farm Cir & Rd 87107
Diolinda Ln SW 87121
Diomedea Ln NW 87107
Disney Pl NE 87122
Dixon Rd SE 87108
Dobson Ln NE 87112
Docena Pl NW 87114
Dodd Pl NE 87110
Dodge Ave NW 87114
Dodge Trl NW 87120
Doe Ln SE 87123
Dogwood Trl NE 87109
Dolly Ave SW 87105
Dolores Dr NW 87105
Dolores Dr SW 87121
Domingo Rd NE
5500-5598 87108
5600-7500 87108
7502-7898 87108
8901-9297 87123
9299-14299 87123
Don Dr NE 87110
Don Andres Ct, Pl & Rd 87105
Don Cipriano Ct NE 87102
Don Diego St NE 87109
Don Enrico Dr SW 87121
Don Felipe Ct, Pl & Rd 87105
Don Francisco Pl NW 87107
Don Gabal Loop & Pl 87104
Don Gaspar Dr NE 87109
Don Giovanni Pl NW 87114
Don Gregorio Rd SW 87105
Don Isidro Ln NW 87107
Don Juan Ct NW 87107
Don Juan Loop NW 87104
Don Lorenzo Ct & Dr 87121
Don Luciano Ct & Rd 87121
Don Luis Rd SW 87105
Don Mariano Rd SW 87105
Don Miguel Pl SW 87105
Don Onofre Trl NW 87107
Don Pablito Pl SW 87121
Don Pablo Rd NW 87104
Don Pancho Rd NW 87104

Don Pasquale Dr SW 87121
Don Pedro NW 87104
Don Pedro Padilla Rd SW 87121
Don Quixote Ct & Dr 87104
Don Reynaldo St SW 87121
Don Romero Dr SW 87105
Don Santos St SW 87121
Don Tomas Ln NE 87109
Don Xavier Ave SW 87121
Dona Adelina Ave SW 87121
Dona Angelica Ave SW 87121
Dona Arcelia St SW 87121
Dona Carmen St SW 87121
Dona Delia Ave SW 87121
Dona Elena Dr SW 87121
Dona Esmera Ave SW 87121
Dona Juanita Dr SW 87121
Dona Katalina Dr SW 87121
Dona Linda Pl NW 87120
Dona Luisa St SW 87121
Dona Marguerita Ave NE 87111
Dona Rowena Ave NE 87111
Dona Teresa Pl SW 87121
Donahoo Ct NE 87111
Donald Rd SW 87105
Donaven Ln NW 87114
Donette Ct & Pl 87112
Donia Ave NW 87120
Donna Ct NE 87112
Donna Alberta Dr SW 87121
Donna Maria Dr SW 87121
Donna Marlane Ct & Dr 87121
Dora Ave NW 87104
Dorado Bch NE 87111
Dorado Ct SE 87123
Dorado Dr SE 87123
Dorado Pl SE 87123
Doral Ct NE 87111
Doris Ave SW 87105
Doris Steider St NE 87122
Doroteo Pl NE 87111
Dorothy Pl NE 87111
Dorothy St NE
200-298 87123
300-600 87123
602-698 87123
1000-2999 87112
Dorothy Lois Dr NE 87112
Doty St SW 87105
Double Eagle NE 87111
Douglas Ct NW 87114
Douglas Rd SW 87121
Douglas Macarthur Rd NE 87110
Douglas Macarthur Rd NW 87107
Dover Ct NW 87114
Dover Pl NW 87114
Dover Rd SW 87105
Dover St NW 87114
Downey St NE 87109
Dr Martin Luther King Jr Ave NE
301-497 87102
499-800 87102
802-898 87102
1000-1699 87106
Draco Ave SW 87105
Dragonfly Ln SW 87105
Dragoon Rd NW 87114
Drake Ave & Ct 87114
Draxton Ave SW 87105
Drayton St NE 87111
Dream Weaver Dr NW 87114
Dreamy Way Dr NW 87114
Driftwood Ave & Pl 87114
Driscoll Ave NE 87109
Drolet Ave & Dr 87114
Dru Ave SE 87108
Dry Creek Pl NW 87114
Dry Gulch St SW 87121
Duchess Dr NE 87123

Duerksen Rd NW 87120
Duero Pl NW 87114
Duerson Trl SW 87121
Duffer Pl NW 87114
Duke Ave SW 87121
Dumas Dr NE 87109
Dunbar St NW 87114
Dunes Ct, Pl & Rd 87123
Dungan St NE 87109
Dunhill Ave SW 87121
Durand Rd SW 87105
Duranes Rd NW 87104
Durango Ct NE 87109
Durant Ave NE 87112
Durham St NW 87114
Duro Ct NE 87110
Duskfire Dr NW 87120
Dustin Ct NW 87120
Dusty Miller Rd SE 87116
Dusty Rose Rd NE 87122
Dusty Trail Ct NW 87120
Eagle Ave NW 87114
Eagle Canyon Rd NE 87113
Eagle Creek Dr NE 87113
Eagle Crest Ave NE 87113
Eagle Dancer Trl NE 87112
Eagle Eye Dr NW 87120
Eagle Feather Dr NE 87113
Eagle Hills Dr NW 87114
Eagle Mesa Rd NE 87113
Eagle Nest Ct & Dr 87122
Eagle Ranch Rd NW
9109-9121 87120
9200-9699 87114
9701-9799 87114
Eagle Ridge Ct, Dr, Ln, Pl, Rd & Ter NE 87122
Eagle River Rd NW 87120
Eagle Rock Ave NE
5201-5297 87113
5299-5699 87113
5701-6799 87113
7600-7614 87122
7616-12599 87122
Eagle Springs Dr NE 87113
Eagle View Ave NE 87113
Eagle Vista Dr NE 87113
Eakes Ct & Rd 87107
Eames Rd SW 87105
Easterday Dr NE 87112
Eastern Ave SE
3400-3599 87106
4600-5098 87108
5100-6499 87108
6501-6899 87108
Eastford Pl NW 87114
Eastman Ave SE 87106
Easton Pl NW 87114
Eastridge Ct NE 87112
Eastridge Dr NE
800-900 87123
902-998 87123
1500-12999 87112
Eastridge Pl NE 87112
Eastridge Trl NE 87112
Eastview St SW 87105
Easy Ct, Pl & St 87114
Easy Goer Rd SE 87123
Echo Park Dr NE 87123
Eddy Ave NE 87109
Eden Ct & Dr 87112
Edgebrook Pl NW 87120
Edgewood Dr NW 87107
Edie Pl NW 87114
Edison Rd NW 87114
Edith Blvd NE
112-118 87102
120-1903 87102
1905-2403 87102
2801-2997 87107
2999-6499 87107
6501-6599 87107
6600-11099 87113
Edith Blvd SE 87102
Edmon Rd NE 87107
Edmunds St SE 87102

Edna Ave NW 87104
Eduardo Pl & Rd 87121
Education NW 87114
Edward Ln SE 87105
Edwardo Ave NW 87120
Edwardo Y Juanita Ct NW 87107
Edwards Ct NE 87123
Edwards Dr NE 87111
Edwin Mechem Ave NW 87114
Edwina Ave & Ct 87110
Egret Ct SW 87121
Eiffel Ave SW 87121
Ekarma Dr NW 87120
El Aguila Pl NW 87120
El Alhambra Cir NW 87107
El Arco Dr NE 87123
El Bordo Dr SW 87102
El Caballero Dr SW 87121
El Cajon Ct NW 87120
El Caminito De Guadalupe Rd NW 87107
El Camino Real St NE 87111
El Centro Familiar Blvd SW 87105
El Cerquito Ct 87120
El Charro Pl SW 87121
El Conde Ave NE 87110
El Corte Cajon NE 87111
El Corte Miramar NE 87111
El Corto Dr SW 87105
El Dorado Dr NW 87114
El Dorado Pl NE 87111
El Encanto Pl NE 87110
El Ensueno Cir & Rd 87107
El Llano Ln NW 87107
El Malecon Rd NW 87120
El Marta Ct NE 87111
El Modesto Ct NE 87113
El Monte Ln NE 87113
El Morro Rd NE 87109
El Navajo St SW 87105
El Nido Ct NW 87104
El Nido Amado Rd SW 87121
El Ojito Ct NW 87114
El Oriente Rd SW 87105
El Paraiso Rd NE 87113
El Paraiso Rd NW 87107
El Paseo Dr NW 87107
El Patio Pl SW 87105
El Patron Rd SW 87121
El Pinon St SW 87105
El Portal NW 87107
El Porvenir Cir & Ct 87105
El Prado Rd NW 87107
El Pueblo Rd NE 87113
El Pueblo Rd NW 87114
El Rancho Dr SW 87121
El Rito Ave NW 87105
El Segundo Ave NE 87113
El Serrano Ct SW 87105
El Shaddai St NW 87121
El Solindo Ave & Ct 87111
El Tesoro Escondido NW 87120
El Toboso Dr NW 87104
El Toro Pl NW 87120
El Vado Ave NE 87112
Elaine Pl NE 87112
Elata Ct NE 87111
Elder Ct SW 87121
Elderberry Ct NE 87111
Elderwood Dr NW 87120
Eldridge Rd NW 87114
Electric Ave SE 87105
Elena Cir SW 87105
Elena Dr NE
7100-7598 87113
7700-12519 87122
12521-12521 87122
Elena Gallegos Pl NE 87111
Elfego Pl & Rd 87107
Elfego Baca Dr SW 87121
Eliyah Ct NW 87120

Elizabeth St NE
101-199 87123
1100-2499 87112
Elizabeth St SE 87123
Elk Dr SE 87123
Elk Creek Rd NE 87113
Elk Horn Dr NE 87111
Elk Ridge Rd NE 87113
Ellen Ct NE 87112
Ellington Rd SW 87105
Elliott Ct & Rd 87120
Ellis Pl NE 87109
Ellison Dr NW 87114
Ellison Rd NW 87114
Ellison St NE 87109
Elm Ct SE 87116
Elm St NE
100-505 87102
507-507 87102
6200-6399 87113
Elm St SE 87102
Elmhurst Dr NW 87114
Elmwood Dr NE 87109
Elna Ct NE 87110
Elohim Ct NW 87121
Eloise Ct SW 87105
Elona Dr NE 87109
Elvin Ave & Pl 87112
Elwood Dr NW 87107
Elwood Pl NE 87112
Elyse Pl SE 87123
Embarcadera Dr SW 87121
Embudito Dr NE 87111
Embudito View Ct NE 87111
Embudo Ct & Dr 87112
Emerald Dr NW 87120
Emerald Sky Ave SW 87121
Emery Point Ave NE 87111
Emily St NE 87109
Emmason Rd SW 87105
Emory Oak Pl NE 87111
Emperor Dr NE 87123
Encantado Rd NE 87123
Enchanted Sky Ln NE 87113
Enchanted Valley Pl & Rd 87107
Enchantment Ln NE 87111
Encino Pl NE 87102
Enclave Ln NE 87111
Enclave Way NE 87122
Endeavour Rd NW 87114
Endee Rd NW 87120
Enebro St NE 87112
Enfield Ct SW 87121
Engel Dr NE 87107
Englewood Ln SE 87102
Ensenada Pl NW 87107
Entrada Pl NW 87114
Entrada Bonita St SW 87105
Entrada Vista Ave NW 87120
Equestrian Ct & Dr 87120
Erbbe St NE
100-400 87123
402-498 87123
1301-1397 87112
1399-2199 87112
3100-4099 87111
Eric Ct NE 87112
Eric Dr NE 87109
Erin St NE 87109
Erlitz Dr NW 87114
Ermemin Ave NW 87114
Ernesto Ct NE 87112
Eroy Ave SW 87102
Erratic St SW 87121
Ervien Ln SW 87121
Erwin Pl NW 87114
Escalante Ave SW 87104
Escarpa Dr NW 87120
Escarpment Ave NW 87120
Escavada St SW 87105
Escena St SE 87123
Escensia St NW 87114
Escobar Ct SW 87121
Escoviel St NW 87120
Escuela Rd SW 87105

Esequiel Rd SW 87105
Esmail Ct NE 87113
Esmeralda Dr NW 87114
Espalin Ln NE 87113
Espanola St NE
100-799 87108
900-998 87110
1000-3099 87110
Espanola St SE 87108
Espejo St NE
100-499 87123
1000-1599 87112
3400-3899 87111
Esperanza Ct & Dr 87105
Espira Ct & Dr 87114
Esquire Ct NE 87123
Essex Dr NW 87114
Estancia Dr NW
100-600 87105
602-1098 87105
2201-4097 87120
4099-4200 87120
4202-4398 87120
Estates Dr NE 87122
Estes Park Ave NW 87114
Esther Ave NE 87109
Estrada Ct NE 87122
Estrella Brillante St NW 87120
Estrellita Del Norte Rd NE 87111
Estribo St NW 87114
Ethel Ave SW 87105
Ethlyn Ave SE 87102
Eton Ave SE 87106
Eubank Blvd NE
101-297 87123
299-899 87123
900-2999 87112
3000-6300 87111
6302-6398 87111
7101-7199 87122
7500-8100 87122
Eubank Blvd SE 87123
Eucariz Ave SW
1701-1997 87105
1999-2199 87105
5900-6000 87121
6002-9810 87121
Euclid Ave NE
2800-2899 87106
2901-3099 87106
5300-5398 87110
5400-7799 87110
9300-9799 87112
Euclid Ave NW 87102
Euclid Ct NE 87112
Eugene Ct SE 87123
Eulalia Dr SW 87105
Eusebio Ln SW 87105
Evangeline Ave NE 87111
Evangeline Ct NE 87109
Evans Ct & Rd 87105
Evansdale Rd NW 87105
Eve Ct NE 87110
Evelyn Ct NE 87112
Evening Fire St SW 87121
Evening Star Dr NE 87111
Evergreen Hls NE 87122
Evergreen St SW 87105
Everitt Ct & Rd 87120
Everton Ave NE 87111
Evesham Rd NW 87120
Evita Way SW 87121
Executive Dr NE 87109
Executive Hills Ln & Way 87123
Executive Ridge Dr NE 87112
Eyota Dr NW 87120
Facio Ct SW 87121
Faindert Ave SE 87116
Fairbanks Rd NE 87112
Faircroft Rd NW 87120
Fairfax Ct & Dr 87114
Fairfield Greens Ct NE 87111
Fairhaven Ave SW 87105

Fairington Way NE 87111
Fairmont Ct & Dr 87120
Fairmount Park Ave NE 87123
Fairoak Trl NE 87109
Fairway Rd NW 87107
Faith Ct NE 87112
Falcon Pl SE 87116
Fallbrook Pl NW 87120
Family Rd SW 87105
Fantozzi Ct & Rd 87105
Farola Dr NW 87114
Farragut Dr NE 87111
Father Sky Ct & St 87112
Fawn Trl SE 87123
Fay St SW 87105
Faye Ave & Pl 87112
Feather Dalea Ave NW 87114
Feather Edge St SW 87121
Feather Rock Pl NW 87114
Feathertop Rd SW 87121
Felicitas Rd SW 87105
Feliz Ln SW 87105
Fence Post Rd SW 87121
Fence Rail St SW 87121
Fencik Ln SW 87121
Fennel Ct SE 87123
Fentiman Pl SE 87105
Fenwick Pl SW 87121
Ferguson Ave SE 87123
Fermin Rd NE 87123
Fern Spring Dr SW 87121
Ferndale Rd SE 87123
Ferris Ave SW 87105
Ferro Rd SW 87105
Field Dr NE 87112
Field St SW 87121
Field Hawk Trl NW 87114
Fieldstone Ave NW 87120
Fiesta Park NW 87114
Figaro Dr NW 87114
Figueroa Ct NE 87112
Figueroa Dr NE 87112
Figueroa St NE 87123
Fileberto Ln SE 87123
Filvera Rd SW 87105
Finch Dr SW 87121
Firenze Dr NW 87114
Firestone Ln NE 87113
Firewheel Rd NW 87120
Firman Ct SW 87121
First Plaza Ctr NW 87102
Fitzgerald Rd NW 87107
Five Points Pl & Rd 87105
Flagstaff Dr NW 87114
Flagstone Pl NW 87114
Flamingo Ave NW 87120
Flat Rock Ct NW 87114
Flightway Ave SE 87106
Flint Ave SW 87121
Flint Ct NW 87120
Flint Ridge Trl SE 87123
Flintlock Ct SW 87121
Flip Ln SW 87121
Flor De Mayo Pl NW 87120
Flor De Rio Ct 87120
Flor Del Rey NW 87120
Flor Del Sol Pl NW 87120
Flor Silvestre NW 87120
Flora St SW 87121
Flora Vista Ave SW 87121
Flora Vista Dr SW 87105
Floral Pl & Rd 87104
Florence Ave NE
5800-5998 87113
7600-8099 87122
8101-8121 87122
8128-8220 87109
8221-8221 87122
8222-8234 87109
8223-8241 87109
8301-8397 87122
8399-11100 87122
11102-11198 87122
Florence Pl NE 87109

Floretta Dr NW 87107
Florida St NE 87110
Florida St SE 87108
Flower Pl NE 87112
Flowers Rd NE 87113
Floyd Ave SW 87121
Flushing Meadows Dr NE 87111
Flynn Ave NW 87120
Foley Ct SW 87105
Fonner Dr SE 87123
Fontana Pl NE 87108
Foothill Dr SW 87105
Foothills Cyn & Trl 87111
Foradown Rd SW 87121
Foraker Pl NW 87107
Ford St SE 87123
Fordham Dr NW 87114
Forest Rd NW 87114
Forest Hills Ct & Dr 87109
Forest View Dr NE 87122
Forestal Ct NW 87120
Forman Rd SW 87105
Forrester Ave NW
800-1099 87102
1100-1499 87104
Forsythe Rd SW 87121
Fort Point Ln NE 87123
Fort Scott Trl NE 87123
Fortuna Rd NW
5401-5597 87105
5599-6099 87105
6500-6598 87121
6701-7799 87121
Forty Niners NE 87111
Fossil Rd NW 87114
Fossil Ridge Pl NW 87114
Foster Ct SW 87121
Fostoria Rd NE 87111
Fountain Ct NW 87114
Fountain Hill Ln NE 87111
Four Hills Ct & Rd 87123
Four Mile Rd SW 87121
Fox Ln SE 87123
Fox Briar Ct NW 87120
Fox Hill Dr & Pl 87121
Fox Hollow Pl NW 87114
Fox Point Ave NE 87112
Fox Sparrow Trl NW 87120
Foxford Ave & Ct 87120
Foyt Dr SW 87121
Francella Dr NW 87104
Frances St NE 87112
Francisca Rd NW 87107
Franciscan St NE
900-1431 87102
1433-2499 87102
2900-6499 87107
Frank Ave SE 87108
Frank Pl NE 87109
Franklin Ave SE 87102
Franklin Ct SW 87105
Frantz Dr NE 87109
Franz Huning Ave SW 87104
Franzen Rd SW 87105
Fraser Dr SE 87123
Frazier Ln SW 87121
Frederick Ct NW 87104
Frederick Ln SW 87121
Frederick Pl NW 87104
Freedom Ct & Way 87109
Freeman Ave NW 87107
Freeway Pl NE 87123
Fremont Pl NW 87121
Fremont Ellis Ct NE 87122
Fresam St SW 87121
Fresca Ct NW 87120
Fresno Way NE 87122
Fresquez Ln NE 87113
Frieda St NE 87109
Friendly Ct & Pl 87120
Fringe Sage Ct NE 87111
Fritts Xing SE 87106
Fritzie St NW 87120
Front Royal Ct NW 87120

Frontage Rd NW & SW 87121
Frontier Ave NE 87106
Frost Ave SE 87116
Fruit Ave NE
401-497 87102
499-599 87102
8000-8098 87108
8100-8399 87108
13101-13297 87123
13299-13499 87123
Fruit Ave NW
700-1299 87102
1300-1699 87104
Fuentes Rd SW 87105
Fuji Ct NW 87120
Full Moon Ave NW 87114
Fulmer Dr NE 87111
Fulton Ct NE 87111
Furman Ave & Ct 87114
Gabaldon Ct, Dr, Ln & Pl NW 87104
Gabbro Ave NE 87113
Gable Ln NE 87123
Gable St NW 87120
Gabriel Rd SW 87105
Gabrielita Ln NW 87104
Gait St SW 87121
Galacia St SE 87123
Galataneau St NW 87121
Galatin Ct NW 87120
Galaxia Way NE 87111
Galaxia Park Dr NW 87114
Gale Ct NW 87120
Galena St SE 87102
Galeras St NW 87120
Gallant Fox Rd SE 87123
Gallatin Pl NW 87121
Gallegos Rd SW 87105
Galleon Dr NW 87121
Galleta Rd NW 87120
Gallileo St NW 87114
Gallinas Ave NE 87109
Gallup Ave SW 87104
Gambel Oak Ct NE 87111
Ganado Ct SE 87123
Gandert Ave SE 87106
Garcia Rd NE 87113
Garcia Rd NW 87114
Garcia Rd SW 87105
Garcia St NE
100-499 87123
1000-2999 87112
3400-3999 87111
Garden Rd SW 87105
Garden Gate Ln SW 87121
Garden Park Cir NW 87107
Gardenbrook Pl NW 87120
Gardenia Rd SW 87105
Garduno Dr NW 87114
Garfield Ave SE
100-699 87102
701-717 87102
2200-2398 87106
2400-2899 87106
3700-3798 87108
Garland Ct SW 87121
Garner Rd SW 87105
Garnet Ave SW 87121
Gary Ct NE 87110
Gary Ln SW 87121
Gaslight Ln SW 87121
Gatewood Ave SW 87105
Gatling Dr NE 87109
Gault Trl SW 87121
Gavilan Pl NW 87107
Gavin Dr NW 87120
Gaviota NW 87120
Gay Ave SW 87105
Gazelle Pl NE 87111
Geiger Rd SW 87105
Gelfand Pl NW 87114
Gem Ct SW 87121
Gem Pointe Rd SW 87121
Gemini Ave & Ct 87114
Gemstone Rd SW 87121

Gene Ave NE 87109
Gene Ave NW 87107
Gene Ct NW 87107
General Arnold St NE
100-399 87123
2301-2397 87112
2399-2699 87112
3601-3697 87111
3699-3799 87111
General Bradley St NE
100-399 87123
2300-2699 87112
3600-5013 87111
5015-5099 87111
General Chennault St NE
100-198 87123
200-499 87123
2600-2999 87112
3000-3799 87111
3801-3999 87111
General Chennault St SE 87123
General Hodges Dr NE 87111
General Hodges St NE 87123
General Hodges St SE 87123
General Kearny Ct & Dr 87109
General Marshall St NE
100-399 87123
2300-2699 87112
General Patch St NE
100-499 87123
3600-3698 87111
3700-3799 87111
General Patch St SE 87123
General Somervell St NE
100-499 87123
2000-2099 87112
3801-3897 87111
3899-3900 87111
3902-4098 87111
General Somervell St SE 87123
General Stilwell St NE
101-197 87123
199-499 87123
2901-2997 87111
2999-3799 87111
Geneva Dr NW 87114
Genoa St NE 87111
Gentry Ln SW 87121
Geode Rd NW 87114
George Rd SE
2100-2199 87106
2100-2100 87119
Georgene Dr NE
400-899 87123
1100-2799 87112
Georgetown Ave NW 87120
Georgia St NE 87110
Georgia St SE 87108
Gerald Ave SE 87106
Germania Ln NE 87122
Gettysburg Rd NE 87109
Ghiradelli St NE 87106
Ghost Flower Trl NE 87111
Ghost Ranch St SW 87121
Gibbs Rd SW 87105
Gibson Blvd SE
400-899 87102
1300-1498 87106
1500-3499 87106
3500-3598 87116
3501-3599 87106
4601-5397 87108
5399-6499 87108
6501-6599 87108
8100-8198 87116
11100-11198 87123
25000-25098 87116
Gibson Blvd SW 87121
Gibson Rd SE 87123
Giddings Ave NE 87109
Gila Rd NE 87109

Gila Cliff Dr SW 87121
Gila Gulch Rd SW 87121
Gill St NE 87109
Gillingham Dr NW 87120
Gilmer Pl NE 87110
Ginger Ct NW 87120
Giomi Pl NW 87105
Girard Blvd NE
101-127 87106
129-1999 87106
2700-3599 87107
Girard Blvd SE 87106
Giraudo Pl SW 87105
Gisele Dr NE 87109
Glacier Rd NW 87114
Glacier Bay Pl & St 87123
Gladden Ave & Ct 87110
Gladiolas Pl NW 87114
Gladys Ct NE 87109
Gleann Ln SW 87105
Gleason Ave NW 87120
W Glen Dr SW 87105
Glen Canyon Ct & Rd 87111
Glen Oak NE 87111
Glenarbor Ct NW 87107
Glenbrook Pl NW 87120
Glencroft Ave NW 87114
Glenda Ct NW 87107
Glendale Ave NE 87122
Glendale Pl NW 87105
Glendale Rd NW 87105
Glendora Dr NE 87109
Glenlochy Way NE 87113
Glenn Dr SE 87105
Glenridge Pl NW 87114
Glenridge Park Ln NE 87123
Glenrio Rd NW
5401-5497 87105
5499-5799 87105
5801-5899 87105
6100-6110 87121
6801-7399 87121
Glenturret Way NE 87113
Glenwood Ct & Dr 87107
Glenwood Hills Ct & Dr 87111
Glenwood Pointe Ln NE 87111
Globe Willow Ave NE 87122
Globus Ct NW 87114
Gloria Ct & Pl 87112
Glorieta St NE
100-499 87123
1000-2599 87112
3400-3498 87111
3500-3799 87111
Glory Ct SW 87105
Glyndon Trl NW 87114
Glynview Ct NW 87120
Go West Rd NW 87120
Goddard St SE 87106
Goff Blvd SW 87105
Gold Ave SE
100-108 87102
110-799 87102
801-803 87102
1400-2199 87106
Gold Ave SW
100-1399 87102
1400-1499 87104
Gold Rush Dr NW 87120
Golden Ave NW 87120
Golden Barrel Rd NW 87114
Golden Eagle Dr & Pl 87109
Golden Gate Ave & Ct 87111
Golden Glow Ln & Way 87113
Golden Meadow Dr NW 87114
Golden Rod Cir SE 87116
Golden Sky Ave SW 87121
Golden Smoke Dr SE 87116
Golden Spike Dr NW 87120
Golden Thread Dr NE 87113
Golden View Dr SW 87121
Goldenrod Dr NE 87122

Goldfield Pl NE 87111
Goldfinch Ct SW 87121
Golf Course Rd NW
6400-6402 87120
8201-8399 87120
8501-9197 87114
9199-10399 87114
10401-10511 87114
Goliad Ct & St 87107
Golinda Rd SW 87121
Golondrina NW 87120
Golondrina Rd NE 87123
Gomez Ave NE 87102
Gomez Dr NW 87107
Gonzales Ln NE 87123
Gonzales Rd SW
1300-3299 87105
5701-5797 87121
5799-6400 87121
6402-6998 87121
Goodrich Ave NE 87110
Gooseberry Rd NW 87120
Gordon Snidow Ct NE 87122
Gore Ave SE 87105
Gorrion St NW 87120
Gorry Ct NW 87107
Goshawk Ave NW 87114
Grace Ct NE 87123
Grace St NE
600-821 87123
823-899 87123
1000-1199 87112
Grace Vigil Rd SW 87121
Graceland Dr NE
200-299 87108
2500-2502 87110
2504-2506 87110
2505-2505 87176
2505-2505 87190
2508-3198 87110
2601-3199 87110
Graceland Dr SE 87108
Gracia Ct NE 87110
Grady Ct & Pl 87123
Grama Ct NW 87120
Gran Quivira Rd NW 87120
Granada Ct & Rd 87105
Granada Hills Ct & Dr 87123
Granby Ct NW 87114
Grand Ave NE
3400-3498 87106
3500-3599 87106
3600-6000 87108
6002-8698 87108
11600-14399 87123
Grand Ct NE 87123
Grand Mesa Rd SE 87123
Grande Ct & Dr 87107
Grande Vista Ct & Pl 87120
Grandview Dr SE 87108
Grange Ave NW 87120
Granite Ave NE
301-303 87102
305-331 87102
333-609 87102
5300-5599 87110
12700-13000 87112
13002-13098 87112
Granite Ave NW
100-1299 87102
1300-1398 87104
1400-2699 87104
Granite Point Trl SE 87123
Granite Ridge Dr NW 87114
Grant Pl NE 87123
Grant Rd SW 87121
Grape Ave & Cir 87105
Grape Arbor Ct NE 87122
Grape Harvest Ct NE 87122
Grape View Ct NE 87122
Grape Vine Ct NE 87122
Grasshopper Dr SW 87121
Grassland Dr SW 87121
Grassy Ct SW 87121
Gray Hills Rd NE 87111
Gray Rock Pl NE 87112
Grayson Rd NW 87120

Grayware Rd SW 87121
Great Pl NE 87113
Grecian Ave & Ln 87107
Green Acres Pl NW 87104
Green Meadows Dr
NW 87114
Green River Pl NW 87114
Green Valley Ct NW 87107
Green Valley Dr SE 87123
Green Valley Pl NW 87107
Green Valley Rd NW 87107
Greenarbor Rd NE 87122
Greenbrier Rd NE 87111
Greene Ave & St 87114
Greenhouse Pl SE 87116
Greenly Ave NE 87111
Greenmont Ct NE 87109
Greenview NE 87111
Greenwich Rd SW 87105
Greenwood St NE 87109
Greer Loop SW 87105
Gretta Ct NE
700-799 87123
4600-4699 87111
Gretta St NE
600-699 87123
1100-2800 87112
2802-2898 87112
Grey Hawk Ct NW 87120
Greyleaf Trl NE 87111
Greythorn Rd SW 87121
Greywolf Rd SW 87121
Griegos Pl & Rd 87107
Griffin Rd SW 87105
Griffith Park Dr NE 87123
Griffon Dr NW 87114
Griggs Ct NE 87112
Grogan St NW 87120
Groman Ct NE 87110
Gros Ventre Ct NW 87114
Groundsel Rd NW 87120
Groundstone Rd SW 87121
Grove St NE
200-799 87108
900-1299 87110
Grove St SE 87108
Grover Ct SW 87121
Gruber Ave NE 87109
Gschwind Pl SW 87121
Gto Dr SW 87105
Guadalajara Ave NE 87111
Guadalupe Cir NW 87114
Guadalupe Ct NW 87114
Guadalupe Pl NW 87107
Guadalupe Trl NW
4700-4798 87107
4800-6100 87107
6102-6198 87107
6401-6597 87107
6599-7899 87107
7900-8899 87114
8900-10199 87114
Guadalupe Del Prado St
NW 87107
Guadiana Pl SW 87121
Guaymas Pl NE
701-797 87108
799-899 87108
1300-1499 87110
Guernsey Ct SW 87105
Gulton Ct NE 87109
Gun Club Rd SW
1900-2900 87105
2901-2909 87121
2902-2910 87105
2911-3999 87121
4001-7299 87121
Gunn Ave SW 87121
Gunnison Pl NW 87120
Guthrie Ave SW 87121
Gutierrez Rd NE 87111
Guzman Ave SW 87105
Gwin Rd SW 87121
Gypsy Dr NE 87122
H Ave SE 87116
Habanero Way SE 87123

Habershaw Rd NW 87120
Hacienda Dr & Rd 87114
Hackamore Ave & Pl 87121
Hackberry Trl SE 87123
Hackney Rd NE 87109
Hagen Rd NE 87111
Hager Ave SE 87108
Hagerman Ave NE 87109
Hagland Ave & Pl 87112
Hahn Ct NE 87110
Haines Ave NE
2600-3599 87106
4600-8499 87110
8900-11599 87112
11600-13998 87112
11600-11600 87153
11600-11600 87192
11601-13599 87112
Haines Ave NW 87102
Haines Pl NE 87112
Halcon Pl SW 87105
Hale Cir SW 87105
Hall Ct SW 87105
Hallmark Ave & Ct 87109
Hallston Trl NW 87114
Halter Dr SW 87121
Halyard Rd NW 87121
Hamilton St NE 87122
Hamlet Ct NE 87112
Hampton Ave NE 87122
Hanalei Ave NE 87111
Hancock Ct NE 87109
Hannett Ave NE
400-498 87102
2201-2297 87106
2299-3599 87106
3600-8199 87110
8500-11599 87112
Hannett Ave NW 87102
Hannett Pl NE 87112
Hanosh Ct SE 87123
Hanover Rd NW
5200-5799 87105
6101-6497 87121
6499-6599 87121
7300-7398 87120
Harbor Rd NW 87121
Hardin Ct & Dr 87111
Hardware Dr NE 87109
Hardy Ave & Ct 87105
Harmony Ln NW 87107
Harold Pl NE 87106
Harper Ct NE 87109
Harper Dr NE
5700-6899 87109
8001-8199 87111
8800-8898 87111
Harper Pl NE 87109
Harpers Ferry Ct NW 87120
Harrier Ave NW 87114
Harrington Rd SE 87123
Harris Rd SW 87105
Harrisonburg Ct NW 87120
Hartford Pl NW 87114
Hartline Ave SW 87105
Hartman Dr SW 87121
Harvard Ct & Dr 87106
Harvest Ln NW 87104
Harvest Maiden Way
NW 87120
Harwood Ave NE
7101-7597 87110
7599-8300 87110
8302-8398 87110
8500-8999 87111
9001-9199 87111
Harwood Ct NE 87110
Harzman Rd SW 87105
Hastings Dr NE 87106
Hatch Dr NW 87114
Hatteras Pl NW 87121
Hattiesburg Ave NW 87120
Havasu Ave NW 87120
W Haven NW 87114
Havenwood Ct & Rd 87120
Hawk Dr SW 87121

Hawk Eye Rd NW 87120
Hawking Dr SE 87106
Hawkins St NE 87109
Hawkwatch Rd NW 87114
Hawthorn Ave NE 87113
Hawthorne Ct NE 87113
Hayden Pl NW 87120
Hayes Dr NW 87120
Hayley Ct NE 87112
Hazeldine Ave SE
202-218 87102
220-799 87102
900-1299 87106
1301-1899 87106
Hazeldine Ave SW 87102
Headingly Ave NE
3600-5199 87110
9100-9208 87111
Headingly Ave NW 87107
Headingly Ct NE 87111
Hearaill Ave SE 87106
Hearth Dr NW 87120
Hearthstone Rd NW 87114
Heather Ln & Pl 87105
Heights Rd NE 87111
Helen Ct SW 87121
Helen Hardin St NE 87122
Helmick Pl NE 87122
Hemlock Ave NW 87114
Hemlock Ct SE 87116
Hendola Dr NE 87110
Hendren Ln NE 87123
Hendrix Ave NE 87111
Hendrix Ct NE 87111
Hendrix Rd NE
3500-3599 87107
4000-7899 87110
7901-7999 87110
8900-8998 87111
9000-10399 87111
Hendrix Rd NW 87107
Henrie Pl SW 87105
Henriette Wyeth Dr
NE 87122
Henry Cir & Rd 87105
Hensch Ave NE 87109
Heritage Ct, Pl & Way 87109
Herman Roser Ave
SE 87123
Hermanas Ln SW 87105
Hermanson Pl NE 87110
Hermosa Dr NE
200-599 87108
700-4199 87110
Hermosa Dr SE 87108
Hermosa Creek Dr
SW 87121
Hernandez Rd NE 87113
Heron Ct & Rd 87121
Herrera Dr SE 87123
Herrera Ln SE 87123
Herrera Rd NW 87105
Herrera Rd SE 87123
Hertz Dr SE 87108
Hiawatha Ct & Dr 87112
Hickory Ct NE 87111
Hidalgo Cir NW 87105
Hidden Spring Ave
SW 87121
Hidden Valley Ct NE 87111
Hidden Valley Dr SE 87123
Hidden Valley Rd NE 87111
Hidden Valley Rd SE 87123
Hideaway Ln SE 87123
Hideout Ln SW 87121
High St NE
117-199 87102
201-1510 87102
1512-1528 87102
3600-3799 87107
High St SE 87102
High Assets Way NW 87120
High Canyon Trl NE 87111
High Desert Pl NE 87111
High Place Ct NW 87120
High Point Ct NE 87112

High Range Rd SW 87121
High Ridge Pl NE 87111
High Rock Pl NE 87112
Highland Park Cir SE 87102
Highway 66 E 87123
W Highway 66 NW 87121
Highway 85 North NW 87114
Hilda Ct NW 87105
Hildegarde Dr NE 87109
Hilgenberg Ln SW 87121
Hill St SE 87105
Hillcrest Ave NW 87120
Hilldale Rd NE 87123
N Hills Blvd NE 87109
S Hills Dr SW 87121
N Hills Pl NE 87109
Hillsboro Ct NW 87120
Hillshire Pl NW 87114
Hillspire Ave & Ct 87120
Hilltop Pl NE 87111
Hillview Ct NE 87123
Hilton Ave NE
3800-4999 87110
8400-9325 87111
9327-9339 87111
Hilton Ave NW 87107
Hilton Pl NE 87111
Himalayan Way NE 87111
Hines Dr NE 87111
Hinkle St SE 87102
Hodgin Ln NW 87120
Hoffman Dr NE 87110
Hogle Rd NE 87112
Hokona Pl NW 87120
Holbrook St NE 87122
Holiday Ave & Ct 87111
Holiday Breeze Pl NE 87111
Hollis St NE 87109
Holly Ave NE
5501-5597 87113
5599-7599 87113
8800-8998 87122
9000-12599 87122
Hollywood Ave NW 87104
Holm Bursun Dr NW 87114
Holstein Ct SW 87105
Homeland Rd NW 87114
Homesite Ln NW 87114
Homestead Cir NW 87120
Homestead Rd NE 87110
Homestead Trl NW 87120
Hondo Valley Pl SW 87121
Honeck Rd SW 87105
Honeylocust Ave, Ct &
Pl 87121
Honeysuckle Dr NE 87122
Hood Rd NW 87114
Hooper Rd SW 87105
Hope Ct & Pl 87123
Hopi Rd NE 87123
Hops Ct NW 87120
Horacio Ct & Pl 87111
Horizon Blvd NE 87113
Hornbill Ct SW 87121
Horseshoe Trl SE 87123
Horton Ln NW 87114
Hosher Ave SE 87102
Hospital Loop NE 87109
Hotel Ave & Cir 87123
Howe Dr SW 87105
Hoyle Rd NE 87110
Hubbell Cir SW 87105
Hudson Ave & Cir 87107
Huerfano Rd NE 87123
Huerto Ave NW 87120
Hugh Graham Rd NE 87111
Hughes Ave NE 87112
Hughes Rd SW 87105
Humbolt St SE 87123
Hume Ave NE 87112
Hummingbird Ln NW 87120
Hummingbird Ln SW 87105
Hummingbird Pl SW 87105
Hummock Rd NW 87114
Humphries Ln SW 87121
Hunters Ct SW 87105

Huntington Dr NE 87111
Hupmobile Dr NE
1100-1199 87123
1200-1299 87112
Hurley Dr NW 87120
Huron Ct SE 87123
Huseman Pl SW 87121
Huyana Dr NW 87120
Hyder Ave SE 87106
I 40 Frontage Rd E 87123
Ian Ave NW 87120
Ibex Ave NE 87111
Ibis Rd SW 87121
Ida Pl NE 87123
Idlewilde Ln SE 87108
Ignacio Ct NW 87114
Ilfield Rd SW 87105
Iliff Rd NW
5200-5799 87105
6000-6199 87121
6401-6403 87120
Illinois St NE 87110
Imperata St NE 87111
Imperial Ct NE 87111
Ina Dr NE 87109
Inca Ct & St 87111
Independence Dr NW 87120
Indian Pl & Trl 87112
Indian Farm Ln NW 87107
Indian Gold Pl NE 87122
Indian Plaza Dr NE 87106
Indian School Rd NE
10-1098 87102
1100-1504 87102
1506-1698 87102
2701-2797 87106
2799-3400 87106
3402-3598 87106
3901-4697 87110
4699-8400 87110
8402-8498 87110
8500-13999 87112
Indian School Rd NW
500-698 87102
1000-2600 87104
2602-2608 87104
Indian Springs Dr NE 87109
Indian View Pl NE 87112
Indiana St NE 87110
Indiana St SE 87108
Indigo Ct NE 87122
Indigo Dr NW 87120
Indigo Sky Trl SW 87121
Industrial Ave NE 87107
Industry Way SE 87105
Inez Dr NE 87110
Inman Ct NE 87110
Inniskillin Ave SW 87121
Innovation Pkwy SE 87123
Innsbrook Ct NE 87111
Inspiration Dr SE 87108
International Ave SE 87106
Inverness Ct NE 87111
Inwood Ct NW 87120
Iona Rd SW 87105
Irbid Rd NE 87122
Irene Ave NE 87112
Iris Rd NW 87104
Irish Mist Rd NE 87122
Iron Ave SE 87102
Iron Ave SW
111-215 87102
217-1399 87102
1410-1440 87104
Iron Gate Trl SW 87121
Iron Rock Dr NW 87114
Ironshore NE 87111
Ironside Ave NE 87109
Ironwood Ct SE 87116
Ironwood Dr NW 87114
Iroquois Pl NE 87112
Irving Blvd NW 87114
Irwin St NE 87109
Isidro Garcia Rd NE 87123
Isla Pl NE 87111
Isle Royale Ct, Pl &
Rd 87123

Isleta Blvd SW 87105
Ivy Pl SW 87121
Ivy Lawn Ct NW 87107
Izabel Rd SW 87105
Ja Ct NW 87120
Jacal Ct NW 87114
Jackie St NE 87109
Jackrabbit St NE 87113
Jacks Creek Rd NW 87114
Jackson Rd SW 87105
Jackson St NE 87108
Jackson St SE 87108
Jacobo Dr NE 87109
Jacobson Ln NW 87107
Jaconita Pl SW 87121
Jacqueline Dr SW 87121
Jacs Ln NE 87113
Jade Dr NW 87120
Jade Park Ave NE 87109
Jaffa Rd NE 87112
Jaime Rd SW 87105
Jal Pl NW 87120
Jalisco Rd NW 87114
Jamaica Dr NE 87111
Jamers Dr NW 87120
James Ave NE 87111
James Ave NW 87107
James Pl NE 87111
James Allen Pl SE 87105
James Moore St SE 87123
Jameson St NW 87114
Jamestown Rd NW 87114
Jamesway Dr SW 87121
Jane Ct NE 87112
Jane Pl NE 87111
Jane St NE
200-298 87123
300-699 87123
1000-2500 87112
2502-2912 87112
Janis Dr NE 87109
Jarales Ct NW 87114
Jaramillo Rd SW 87105
Jarash Pl NE 87122
Jardin Plz NE 87110
Jardin Rd SW 87105
Jarmel Dr NW 87114
Jarosa Creek Pl NW 87114
Jasmine St NW 87120
Jason Ct & Pl 87123
Jasons Way NE 87111
Jasper Dr NE 87113
Javelina Rd SW 87121
Javier Way SW 87121
Jaynes Ct SW 87105
Jazmin Pl NW 87114
Jean Parrish Ct NE 87122
Jeanette Ave SW 87105
Jeanne Ct NE 87110
Jefferson Ln NE 87109
Jefferson Plz NE 87109
Jefferson St NE
100-599 87108
600-2999 87110
4700-7900 87109
7902-7998 87109
8200-8298 87113
8300-8699 87113
8701-8903 87113
Jefferson St SE 87108
Jeffery Ave NE 87109
Jemez St NE 87109
Jenaro Ct & St 87121
Jennie Rd SW 87121
Jennifer Dr NE 87109
Jenny Ave & Ct 87121
Jensen Ct NE 87112
Jensen Dr NE 87112
Jensen Rd SW 87105
Jerry Cir, Ct, Pl & Rd
SW 87105
Jersey Ct SW 87105
Jesse James Dr SW 87121
Jessica Ct NW 87120
Jessie Dr NE 87111
Jesus St SE 87102

Jet Rd NE 87113
Jetty Ct NW 87121
Jewel Pl NE 87123
Jewel Cave Rd SE 87123
Jewett Dr NE 87112
Jicama Way SE 87123
Jicarilla Pl NE 87110
Jiles Dr NE 87111
Jill Patricia St NW 87114
Jo Ln NE 87111
Jo Ann Pl NE 87109
Joanne Ct SW 87121
Joe Dan Pl NE 87110
Joe Montoya Pl NW 87114
Joe Sanchez Rd SW 87105
Joel Ct, Pl & St 87121
Joelle Rd NE 87112
Joem Ln NW 87107
John St NE & SE 87102
John Henry Ct SE 87123
John Thomas Dr NE 87111
Johncock Ave SW 87121
Johnice Dr SW 87121
Johnville Pl NE 87107
Joli Ct NE 87111
Jones Pl NW 87120
Jordan Ave NE 87122
Jornada St SW 87105
Joseph Sharp St NE 87122
Joshua Tree Pl SE 87123
Journal Center Blvd
NE 87109
Joy Pl NE 87109
Joyce Dr NE 87109
Juan Rd NE 87123
Juan Herrera 87121
Juan Tabo Blvd NE
100-899 87123
900-998 87112
1000-2999 87112
3000-3098 87111
3100-5199 87111
5201-5899 87111
Juan Tabo Blvd SE 87123
Juan Tabo Pl NE 87111
Juan Valdez St SE 87123
Juanita Dr SW 87105
Juanita Ln NW 87107
Judith Ln SW 87121
Judy Pl NE 87111
Judy Rd SW 87105
Julene St NE 87111
Julia Ln SW 87121
Julian Robles St NE 87122
Julie Rd SW 87105
Julie St NE 87110
Julie Romero Rd SW 87121
Juliet Ct NW 87104
Junco Pl NW 87114
June Ct NE 87111
June St NE
1000-2999 87112
3100-3330 87111
3332-3332 87111
Juneberry St NW 87120
Juniper Ct SE 87116
Juniper St NW 87120
Juniper Canyon Trl
NE 87111
Juniper Hill Ct, Loop, Pl
& Rd NE 87122
Jupiter St NW 87107
Justin Dr NW 87114
Justo Rd SW 87105
Kaas Trail Ct NE 87111
Kacey Ln SW 87105
Kachina Pl NE 87112
Kachina St NW 87120
Kafka Pl NW 87120
Kaibab Rd SE 87123
Kally Ct NE 87123
Kanaga Dr NW 87120
Kandace Dr NW 87114
Kane Ct NW 87120
Karak Rd NE 87122
Karen Ave NE 87111
Karlson Dr NE 87113
Karrol SW 87121
Karsten Ct SE 87102
Karthala Ave NW 87120
Kaseman Ct NE 87110
Kashmir St NE 87111
Kathleen Ave NE 87110
Kathryn Ave SE
200-800 87102
802-898 87102
2301-2497 87106
2499-2900 87106
2902-3598 87106
4100-4798 87108
4800-8299 87108
Kathryn Cir SE 87108
Katie St NE 87110
Katrina Dr SW 87121
Katson Ave NE 87109
Kayenta Pl NW
6200-6299 87120
10500-10599 87114
Kaylyn Dr SE 87123
Kayser Mill Rd NW 87114
Kearney Trl NW 87120
Keel Ave NW 87120
Keeling St NW 87120
Keely Rd SE 87123
Keeping Dr NW 87114
Keeran Ln NE 87122
Keesha Jo Ave SE 87123
Keith Cir SW 87105
Kelarth St NW 87102
Keleher Ave NW 87102
Kellia Ln NE 87111
Kelly Ave NE 87109
Kelly Ave SW 87105
Kelly Rd SW
2200-2399 87105
2500-2798 87121
2800-2900 87121
2902-2998 87121
Kelly Ann Rd NE 87109
Kelsey Rd SW 87105
Kelso Ct SE 87123
Kencoriv Ave NE 87110
Kensington Dr NW 87107
Kent Ave NW 87102
Kentucky Ct NE 87110
Kentucky St NE 87110
Kentucky St SE 87108
Kentwood Ave NW 87114
Kenwood Ct NW 87120
Kenyon Pl NW 87107
Kepler St NW 87120
Kestrel Ct NW 87107
Keswick Pl & Rd 87120
Ketch Dr NW 87121
Kettle Rd NW 87120
Kevin Ct NW 87105
Key West Dr NE 87111
Keystone Dr NE 87109
Khamsin Dr NW 87114
Kibo Dr NW 87120
Kielich Ave NE 87111
Kilauea Ave NW 87120
Killington Rd NW 87114
Kilmer Ave NW 87120
Kimberlite Dr NW 87120
Kimberly Ct NW 87120
Kimela Ct & Dr 87121
Kimo Dr NE 87110
King Ct NE 87112
King Rail Rd SW 87121
King Ranch Ln SW 87121
Kingfisher Ct NW 87114
Kings Ct NW 87121
Kings Row NE 87109
Kings Canyon Pl & Rd 87123
Kingsbury Rd SW 87105
Kingston Ave NE 87109
Kingsway Ct NW 87120
Kinley Ave NE
400-722 87102
724-798 87102
12205-12321 87112
12323-12323 87112
Kinley Ave NW
201-297 87102
299-700 87102
702-898 87102
900-918 87104
920-1106 87104
Kinley Ct NE 87112
Kinley Pl NE 87112
Kinney St SE 87105
Kiowa Ave NE 87110
Kipuka Dr NW 87120
Kirby Ct & St 87112
Kirk Ln SW 87121
Kirks Ct NW 87107
Kirkview Dr SW 87121
Kirsten Rd SW 87121
Kirtland Dr SE 87106
Kiska St NW 87120
Kit Carson Ave SW 87104
Kitrin Rd NW 87114
Kiva Dr SE 87123
Kiva St NW 87120
Klondike St NE 87111
Knight Ln SE 87123
Knight Rd NE 87109
Knightsway Ave NW 87120
Knollwood Dr NE 87109
Knox Ct & Pl 87123
Kochis Rd NW 87120
Kokopelli Ct & Dr 87114
Kola Ct NW 87120
Krick Ct NE 87110
Krim Dr NE 87109
Kriss Pl NE 87112
Krista Dr NE 87109
Krogh Ct NW 87104
Kyle Rd NW 87120
La Anita St NW 87105
La Arista Pl NE 87111
La Bajada Ct & Rd 87105
La Barranca Ave NE 87111
La Bienvenida Pl NW 87120
La Brea St NE 87113
La Cabra Ct & Dr 87123
La Camila Rd NE
2900-2999 87111
8300-8399 87110
8400-8499 87111
La Canada Dr NW 87114
La Casa Bonita NE 87110
La Caverna Ave NE 87122
La Chamisal Ln NW 87107
La Charles Ave NE 87111
La Charles Dr NE
400-899 87123
900-2799 87112
3800-3899 87111
La Cienega Ln & St 87107
La Colonia Dr NW 87120
La Comunidad NW 87114
La Condesa Ave NE 87110
La Corrida Rd NE 87110
La Costa Dr NE 87111
La Cueva Ave NE 87123
La Cueva Ln NE 87123
La Cueva Trl NE 87122
La Entrada NE 87113
La Espina Pl NE 87113
La Fiesta Dr NE 87109
La Fonda Ct & Dr 87105
La Font Rd SW 87105
La Habra Ln NE 87113
La Hacienda Dr NE 87110
La Hacienda Pl NE
3500-3599 87106
3600-3721 87110
3723-3737 87110
La Jara Ct NE 87109
La Jolla Pl NE 87123
La Joya Pl NW 87120
La Junta Rd SW 87105
La Loma Rd SW 87105
La Lucena Ave NE 87113
La Luz Dr NW 87107
La Luz Trl NE 87122
La Luz De Cielo NW 87120
La Madera Rd NE 87109
La Mancha Ct, Dr &
Pl 87104
La Mariposa Pl NE 87109
La Media Rd SW 87105
La Merced Ave & Pl 87105
La Merido Ave NE 87113
La Mesa Ct NW 87120
La Mesita Rd NE 87112
La Milpita St NE 87113
La Mirada Pl NE 87109
La Mora Ln SW 87105
La Morada NW 87120
La Orilla Rd NW 87120
La Paloma Ct & Rd 87120
La Palomita Rd NE 87111
La Paz Dr NW 87114
La Perouse St SW 87121
La Plata Rd NW 87107
La Playa St NE 87111
La Plaza Dr NW 87107
La Poblana Rd NW
1-1499 87107
1501-1597 87104
1599-1899 87104
1901-1999 87104
La Posada Dr SW 87105
La Puente St NE 87113
La Rambla St NW 87120
La Rocca Ct & Rd 87114
La Ronda Pl NE 87110
La Rueda Ct NW 87107
La Sala Cuadra NE 87111
La Sala Del Centro
NE 87111
La Sala Del Este NE 87111
La Sala Del Norte NE 87111
La Sala Del Oeste NE 87111
La Sala Del Sur NE 87111
La Sala Grande NE 87111
La Sala Redonda NE 87111
La Salle Pl NW 87114
La Senda Ln NW 87107
La Sombra Rd SW 87105
La Subida St NW 87105
La Terra Bella Rd NW 87114
La Tierra Ct NE 87122
La Traviatta Pl NW 87114
La Tuna Pl SE 87123
La Vega Ct & Dr 87105
La Venita Ave NW 87120
La Ventura Ct NW 87120
La Veta Ct NE 87110
La Veta Dr NE
100-999 87108
1101-1797 87110
1799-3599 87110
La Vida Ln SW 87121
La Vida De Jean SW 87105
La Vida De Ryan SW 87105
La Vida Nueva Del Este
SW 87105
La Vida Nueva Del Norte
SW 87105
La Vida Nueva Del
Oeste
SW 87105
La Vida Nueva Del Sur
SW 87105
La Villita Cir NE 87112
La Villita Ct NE 87112
La Villita Pl NE 87111
La Villita Tres St NE 87112
La Vista Ct NW 87120
La Vista Grande Dr &
Pl 87111
Lace Rd SE 87102
Lacy Spine Rd NW 87114
Ladder Ranch Ln SW 87121
Ladera Ct NE 87111
Ladera Dr NW 87120
Ladrillo Pl NE 87113
Ladron Dr NW 87114
Ladrones Ct & Pl 87121
Lafayette Dr NE
600-1899 87106
3200-3398 87107
3400-4000 87107
4002-4098 87107
Lafayette Pl NE 87106
Lafving St NE 87109
Lagrange Park Dr NE 87123
Lagrima De Oro Rd
NE 87111
Laguayra Dr NE 87108
Laguna Blvd & Pl NW &
SW 87104
Laguna Seca Ln NW 87104
Lagunitas Ln & Rd 87105
Lahar Ave NW 87120
Lake Dr SW 87105
Lake Spur Ct SE 87116
Lake Tahoe Rd NW 87114
Lakeshore Dr NE 87112
Lakeview Rd SW 87105
Lakewood Ave NW 87120
Lamar Ave NW 87120
Lamberton Pl NE 87107
Lamp Post Cir SE 87123
Lamplighter Ln NE 87109
Lamy St NW 87120
Lancaster NE 87111
Lanceleaf Ct NW 87114
Landau St NE 87111
Landman Dr NE
800-899 87123
1100-2599 87112
Landman Pl NE 87123
Landmark St NW 87121
Landon Dr SW 87105
Landry Ave NW 87120
Lane Ct NW 87107
Lanes End NW 87114
Laney Ave SW 87105
Lang Ave NE 87109
Lanier Dr SE 87123
Lansing Dr SW 87105
Lantana Ave NW 87114
Lantern Rd NE 87109
Lara Dr NE 87111
Larailly Rd SW 87105
Laramie Dr NW 87120
Larchmont Dr NE 87111
Lariat Ave NW 87120
Lark Ave SW 87105
Larkin Ln SW 87105
Larkspur Ln NE 87113
Larnaca Rd NE 87122
Larrazolo Rd SW 87105
Las Animas Ave NE 87110
Las Cadenas Rd NW 87120
Las Calabazillas Rd
NE 87111
Las Camas Rd NE 87111
Las Casitas Ct NE 87111
Las Casitas Ct NW 87107
Las Casitas St NE 87111
Las Colinas Ln & Pl 87113
Las Crestas Dr NW 87120
Las Cruces Rd NE 87110
Las Estancia Dr 87121
Las Garzas Rd SW 87105
Las Glorietas SW 87105
Las Golondrinas Ct
NW 87107
Las Hermanas St NW 87107
Las Humanas Rd NW 87120
Las Lomas Rd NE
900-1008 87102
1010-1099 87102
1101-1117 87106
1119-1924 87106
Las Lomitas NE 87113
Las Nutrias NW 87114
Las Palmas St NW 87114
Las Trampas Way NW 87120
Las Vegas Ave NE 87110
Las Vegas Dr SW 87105
Lassen Ct SE 87123
Laster Ave NE 87109
Latigo Ave SW 87121
Latir Mesa Rd NW 87114
Laura Ct SW 87121
Laura Lee Pl NW 87114
Laurel Cir SE 87108
Laurel Ct SE 87116
Laurel Dr SE 87108
Laurel Loop NE 87122
Laurel Pl NE 87122
Lauren Ave SW 87121
Laurene Ct NW 87120
Lava Bluff Dr NW 87120
Lava Reach Ave NW 87120
Lava Rock Dr NW 87120
Lavender Lace Ct NE 87122
Lawrence Ct & Dr 87123
Lawson Ct NE 87112
Lawton St NW 87114
Layton Ave, Ct, Loop &
Pl NE 87111
Lazo St NW 87114
Lazy Brook Ct NE 87113
Lazy Day Dr SW 87121
Le Ave & Rd 87105
W Lea Dr SW 87105
Lead Ave SE
306-312 87102
314-783 87102
785-883 87102
1000-2700 87106
2702-2798 87106
3800-4499 87108
Lead Ave SW 87102
Leah Ct NE 87112
Leah Dr NE 87110
Leander Ave NE 87109
Leanne St NE 87109
Learning Rd NW 87120
Leatherwood Ln NW 87107
Lee Ct NW 87107
Lee Pl NW 87114
Leeward Dr NW 87121
Legends Ave NW 87120
Legion Rd NE 87102
Lehr Pl NW 87114
Lejano Ave NE 87109
Lemitar Pl NE 87113
Lemmons Ln NE 87113
Lena Rd SW 87105
Lento Way NW 87104
Leo Ct NE 87109
Leo Pl NE 87109
Leo Rd SW 87105
Leon Ct NW 87107
Leona St NE 87109
Leonard Euler Ct SW 87121
Leonora Dr NW 87104
Leopoldo Rd NW 87104
Leslie Pl NE 87109
Leslynne Dr NE 87109
Lester Dr NE 87112
Leta Rd NE
5800-5899 87107
6600-6699 87113
Levy Ct NW 87120
Lew Wallace Dr NE 87109
Lewis Ave SE 87102
Lewis Ave SW 87102
Lewis Ct NW 87114
Lewisburg Ct & Dr 87120
Lexie Ln NE 87122
Lexington Ave, Ct &
Pl 87112
Leyendecker Rd NE 87112
Leymon Ct NW 87114
Libby Ave SW 87121
Liberty Dr NE 87109
Libia St NE 87112
Libro Iluminado Ct SW 87121
Lilac Dr NW 87104
Lillian Pl NE 87112
Lily Ave SE 87102
Lima Ct & Pl 87123
Limestone Ave NE 87113
Lincoln Rd NE 87109
Linda Ln & Pl 87105
Linda View Ct & Pl 87123
Linda Vista Ave SE 87106
Linden Ln NE 87111
Lindgren Rd NW 87107
Lindsay Pl SW 87121
Link St NW 87120
Linn Ave NE
6300-6399 87108
6401-6499 87108
11300-11799 87123
11801-12499 87123
Linn Way NE 87123
Lipizzan Ave SW 87121
Lirios St NW 87114
Lisa Ct NE 87110
Lisa Rd SW 87121
Lito Rd NW 87114
Little Joe Pl NW 87120
Little Park St NW 87105
Littleton Ave NW 87120
Live Oak Ct, Ln, Loop,
Pl & Rd NE 87122
Lizard Ln SW 87121
Lizard Flats Rd SW 87105
Llano Ct NW 87107
Llano Del Sur SE 87105
Llano Encantado NW 87120
Llano Vista Ave SW 87121
Llave Ln NE 87122
Lobelia Rd NW 87120
Lobo Ct & Pl 87106
Lobos Creek Way NE 87123
Lochnager Ln NE 87113
Lochside Ln NE 87113
Lockhaven Ln NE 87111
Lockwood Ct NW 87120
Locura Pl & Rd 87121
Locust Pl NE 87102
Locust St NE
201-299 87102
6300-6399 87113
6401-6499 87113
Locust St SE
401-499 87102
801-999 87106
Lodestone Trl SE 87123
Loftus Ave NE 87109
Logan Rd NW 87114
Lola Dr NE 87109
Loma Alta Ct NW 87105
Loma De Caliza NE 87123
Loma Del Norte Rd
NE 87109
Loma Hermosa Ct, Dr &
Pl 87105
Loma Linda Pl SE 87108
Loma Pedregosa NW 87120
Loma Vista Dr & Pl 87106
Lomas Blvd NE
101-1603 87102
1700-3599 87106
4000-4098 87110
4100-8500 87110
8502-8630 87110
8601-8797 87112
8799-13100 87112
13101-13103 87123
13101-13101 87181
13102-13498 87112
13201-13699 87112
Lomas Blvd NW
111-197 87102
199-1204 87102
1206-1218 87102
1300-2000 87104
2002-2098 87104
Lomas Ct NE 87112
Lomas De Atrisco Rd
NW 87105
Lomas Verdes Ave
NE 87123
Lombard Ln NE 87123
Lombardy Rd NW 87105
Lomita Ct & Pl 87105
Lona Ln NE 87111
Londene Ln SW 87105
London Ave SW 87121
Lone Draw St SW 87121

Lone Mountain Ave SW 87121
Lone Pine Dr SW 87121
Lone Prairie Ave SW 87121
Lone River Trl SW 87121
Lone Tree Rd SW 87121
Lonesome Dove Trl SW 87121
Long Ln SW 87105
Long Mesa Pl NW 87114
Longmont Pl NW 87114
Longview Dr NW 87120
Loop One NW 87120
Lopez Rd SW 87105
Lora Ct NW 87107
Lorelei Ln NE 87111
Loren Ave NW 87114
Lorete Rd NW 87114
Loretta Dr NW 87114
Lori Pl NE 87111
Loro Ave NW 87114
Lorraine Ct NE 87113
Los Abuelos Ct SW 87105
Los Alamos Ave SW 87104
Los Alisos Ct NW 87120
Los Altos Pl SW 87105
Los Anayas Rd NW 87104
Los Arboles Ave NE
2800-3098 87107
3100-3299 87107
3301-3399 87107
3801-5197 87110
5199-7200 87110
7202-7598 87110
8400-12499 87112
Los Arboles Ave NW 87107
Los Arboles Ct NE 87112
Los Arboles Pl NE 87112
Los Cansados Rd NW 87114
Los Cantos Ave NW 87114
Los Compadres St NW 87120
Los Faisanes Rd SW 87105
Los Garcias Ln SE 87123
Los Hermanos Ct NE 87111
Los Jardines Pl NW 87104
Los Lagos NE 87111
Los Luceros Rd NW 87104
Los Lunas Dr NE 87109
Los Metates Rd NW 87120
Los Nietos Ct NW 87107
Los Padillas Rd SW
2100-2700 87105
2702-2798 87105
2800-2999 87121
3001-7999 87121
Los Padres Pl & St 87123
Los Picaros Rd SE 87105
Los Pinos Rd SW 87105
Los Poblanos Cir, Ln & Pl 87107
Los Poblanos Ranch Rd NW 87107
Los Prados Rd NW 87114
Los Prados De Guadalupe Dr NW 87107
Los Pueblos Pl NW 87114
Los Puentes Dr SW 87105
Los Ranchos Rd NE 87113
Los Ranchos Rd NW 87107
Los Reyes Ct NW 87120
Los Riscos Rd NW 87120
Los Ritos Ct NW 87120
Los Santos NW 87114
Los Serranos Ct NW 87120
Los Suenos Ct NW 87114
Los Tomases Dr NW
1101-1107 87102
1109-1699 87102
1701-1799 87102
2600-4199 87107
Los Trechos Ct NE 87109
Los Tretos St NW 87120
Los Valles Dr NW 87120
Los Viejitos St NW 87120
Los Viejos Dr SW 87105

Los Volcanes Rd NW 87121
Lost Arrowhead Ave SW 87121
Lost Desert Dr SW 87121
Lost Dutchman Ave & St 87111
Lost Horizon Dr NW 87121
Louanne Ln NW 87114
Louise Pl NE 87109
Louise Rd SW 87105
Louisiana Blvd NE
120-898 87108
900-4004 87110
4006-4098 87110
4100-8003 87109
8005-8005 87109
8100-8198 87113
8200-8300 87113
8302-9798 87113
Louisiana Blvd SE 87108
Lovato Rd SW 87105
Love Ave NE 87112
Love St SW 87121
Lovejoy Rd SW 87105
Lovelace Rd SE
1700-1799 87106
6101-6397 87108
6399-6499 87108
Loveland Dr NW 87114
Lowe St NE 87111
Lowell Dr NE 87122
Lowell St NE 87111
Lower Meadow Ave & Trl 87121
Lower Terrace Cir NE 87111
Loyola Ave & Pl 87112
Luana St NE 87109
Luas Ln NW 87107
Lucca Ave SW 87121
Lucca Ln SW 87121
Lucca Rd SW 87105
Lucerne St NE 87111
Lucero Rd SW 87105
Luchetti Rd SW 87105
Lucia Ave SW 87105
Lucille Dr NE 87111
Lucretia St SW 87121
Lucyle Pl NW 87114
Luecking Park Ave NE 87107
Luella Anne Ct & Dr 87109
Luis Sanchez Pl SW 87105
Luke Cir NW 87107
Lulac Ave NW 87104
Lumber Ave NE 87109
Luminoso Dr NW 87121
Luna Blvd NW 87102
Luna Cir NW 87102
Luna Rd SW 87105
Luna Azul Ave SW 87121
Luna Del Oro Ct & Rd 87111
Luna Ladera Ave SW 87121
Luna Nuestra NW 87120
Lundy Ln SW 87105
Lura Pl SW 87105
Lutes Ct NW 87114
Luthy Cir, Ct, Dr & Pl NE 87112
Luttrell Ct NE 87111
Luz De La Luna Pl NW 87114
Luz Del Dia Dr NW 87114
Luz Del Sol Ct & Pl 87114
Lykes Dr NE 87110
Lyman Rd SW 87121
Lynch Ct & Pl 87104
Lyndale Ln NW 87114
Lyndsi Ave NW 87120
Lynette Ct SW 87121
Lynne Ct NE 87112
Lynnhaven Pl NW 87120
Lynwood Dr NW 87120
Lynx Loop NE 87122
Lyon Blvd NW 87114
Lyria Rd NW 87114
Mabry Ave, Ct & Ln 87109
Macallan Rd NE 87109

Macaw Dr SW 87121
Macbeth Ct NE 87112
Maciel Dr NW 87104
Mackland Ave NE
3000-3599 87106
3600-4299 87110
Macnish Dr NE 87109
Maddux Pl NW 87114
Madeira Dr NE
100-398 87108
400-918 87108
920-920 87108
1101-1797 87110
1799-3999 87110
Madeira Dr SE 87108
Madeira Pl NE 87110
Madeline Dr NW 87114
Madison Ct NE 87110
Madison Pl SE 87108
Madison St NE
101-197 87108
199-599 87108
600-2999 87110
Madison St SE 87108
Madras Dr NE 87122
Madre Ave NE 87111
Madre Ct NE 87111
Madre Dr NE 87112
Madrid Dr NE 87111
Madrina Ct NW 87114
Mae Ave SW 87105
Mafraq Ave NW 87114
Magdalena Ln SW 87121
Magenta Rd NW 87120
Magic Mist Rd NE 87122
Magic Sky Ct NW 87114
Magid St NW 87114
Magin St SE 87123
Magma Pl NW 87120
Magnolia Ct & Dr 87111
Mahlon Ave NE 87112
Mahogany Pl NE 87111
Mahonia Rd NW 87120
Maiden Grass Rd NW 87120
Main St NW 87104
Mainsail Dr NW 87121
Mairend Ave NE 87123
Maisey Ct SW 87121
Major Ave NW 87107
Makian Pl NW 87120
Malachite Dr SW 87121
Malaga Dr NE 87109
Malaguena Ln NE 87111
Mallard Ave NW 87114
Malpais Ct, Ln & Rd 87105
Malpais Park Ave NW 87114
Man O War St SE 87123
Mananitas NW 87104
Manchester Ct, Dr & Pl 87107
Mandarin Pl NW 87120
Mandy Rd SW 87121
Maness Ln SW 87121
Manganite Ct NW 87114
Mangas Trl NE 87111
Manhattan Pl NW 87104
Manistee St SE 87123
Manitoba Ct & Dr 87111
Mankin St NE 87123
Manor Ct NE 87123
Mansfield Pl NW 87114
Mansout Rd NW 87104
Manuel Ave SW 87102
Manuel Cia Ct & Pl 87122
Manuel Sanchez Pl SW 87105
Manuel Torres Ln NW 87107
Manzanillo Ave & Loop 87111
Manzano Ct NW 87102
Manzano St NE
101-197 87108
199-499 87108
600-698 87110
700-3199 87110
Maple Ct SE 87116

Maple St NE 87106
Maple St SE 87106
Maplewood Ct SW 87121
Maplewood Dr NW 87120
Maplewood Dr SW 87121
Maplewood Ln SW 87121
Marapi St NW 87120
Maravillas Dr NW 87114
Marbella Dr NW 87120
Marble Ave NE
301-397 87102
399-621 87102
2600-2998 87106
3000-3099 87106
4100-8200 87110
8202-8598 87110
12900-13199 87112
13201-13299 87112
Marble Ave NW
101-197 87102
199-1299 87102
1300-2699 87104
Marble Pl NE 87112
Marble Stone Dr NW 87114
Marcadas Rd NW 87114
Marcato Ln NW 87104
Marcelino Rd SW 87105
Marcella Pl NE 87123
Marcella St NE
700-899 87123
1000-1499 87112
Marcos Ln NE 87113
Maren Ln SW 87105
Mares Rd SW 87105
Margarita Ct 87121
Margerum Trl SW 87121
Margo Rd SW 87105
Maria Cir NW 87114
Maria Ct SE 87102
Mariah Ct & Rd 87120
Mariano Trl SW 87121
Maricopa Rd SW 87105
Marie Pl NW 87104
Marie Park Dr NE
800-899 87123
2000-2098 87112
2100-2899 87112
Marigold Ct NW 87120
Marigold Dr NE 87122
Marigold Dr NW 87120
Marigot Ct & Rd 87120
Marilyn Ave NE 87109
Marin Dr NW 87114
Marina Gate Trl NE 87123
Mariner Ln NE 87111
Marino Rd SW 87105
Mariola Pl NE 87111
Mariposa Dr & Pl 87120
Maritca Dr NW 87114
Mark Dr NE 87123
Market St NW 87120
Markham Rd SW 87105
Marla Dr NE 87109
Marlborough Ave SW 87121
Marlowe Ct & Ln 87113
Marmac Ave NE 87106
Marna Lynn Ave NW 87114
Maroa St NW 87120
Marquette Ave NE
400-409 87102
411-499 87102
1000-1099 87106
1101-3299 87106
3701-4097 87108
4099-8599 87108
11400-11598 87123
11600-11900 87123
11902-13398 87123
Marquette Ave NW
101-397 87102
399-1200 87102
1202-1298 87102
1300-1399 87104
Marquette Dr NE 87123
Marquette Pl NE 87106
Marquez Ln SW 87102
Marquis Ct & Dr 87123

Marron Cir NE 87112
Mars Rd NE 87107
Marseille Pl NE 87122
Marshall Ct NE 87112
Marston St SW 87105
Marta Rd NW 87114
Marta Way SW 87121
Martha St NE
300-699 87123
1400-2499 87112
Martin Ct NE 87109
Martin Pl NW 87114
Martin Rd NW 87104
Martin Rd SW 87105
Martinez Dr NE 87102
Martinez Ln NE 87107
Martinez Rd SW 87105
Martingale Ln SE 87123
Martinsburg Rd NW 87120
Marva Pl SE 87123
Mary Ave SW 87105
Mary Ellen Ct NE 87111
Mary Ellen Pl NE 87111
Mary Ellen St NE
1000-1098 87112
1100-2899 87112
3401-3497 87111
3499-3799 87111
3801-3999 87111
Maryetta St SW 87105
Marys Way NW 87107
Masini Ln NW 87114
Masters Dr NE 87111
Masthead St NE 87109
Mata Ortiz Dr SW 87121
Matador Dr NE 87111
Matador Dr SE 87123
Matchlock Ct SW 87121
Mateo Prado NW 87107
Mather Ave NE 87112
Matia Ct NE 87123
Matisse Rd NE 87123
Matthew Ave NE
3200-3299 87107
3301-3399 87107
8900-10399 87112
Matthew Ave NW
901-1299 87107
2001-2097 87104
2099-2499 87104
Matthew Pl NW 87104
Mauna Loa Dr NW 87120
Maverick Ct, Ln & Trl 87123
Maxim Ct NW 87120
Maximillian Rd NW 87104
Maxine St NE
200-899 87123
1000-2999 87112
Maya Ct NE 87111
Mayfair Pl SW 87121
Mayflower Rd NE 87109
Mayflower Rd SW 87105
Mayhill Ct NW 87120
Mayo St NW 87120
Maywood Rd SE 87123
Mazatlan Dr NE 87111
Mccall Ct NE 87123
Mccloskey Dr SW 87121
Mccoy Pl NE 87106
Mccracken Rd SW 87105
Mcdonald Rd NW 87107
Mcdonnell St SE 87123
Mcduffie Cir NE 87110
Mcearl Ave SE 87106
Mcewen Ct SW 87105
Mckay Way NE 87111
Mckee Ct & Dr 87112
Mckinney Dr NE 87109
Mckinnon Way SW 87121
Mcknight Ave NE
307-337 87102
4700-4900 87110
4902-7798 87110
9500-11199 87112
Mcknight Ave NW 87102
Mcleod Rd NE 87109

Mcmahon Blvd NW 87114
Mcmichael Ln SW 87121
Mcmullen Dr NW 87107
Mcnary Ct NW 87120
Mcnerney Ave NE 87110
Meade Pl SW 87121
W Meadow Dr SW 87121
Meadow Rd SW 87105
Meadow Gate Trl SW 87121
Meadow Green Ct SE 87123
Meadow Hills St NE 87111
Meadow Lake Dr NW 87120
Meadow View Ct, Dr & Pl 87104
Meadowbrook Ave NW 87120
Mechem St SE 87102
Mechenbier Ln SW 87105
Medford Ct NW 87120
Medical Arts Ave NE 87102
Medicine Bow Pl SE 87123
Medinah Ln NE 87111
Megafauna Rd SW 87121
Mel Smith Ct & Rd 87123
Melinda Ave SW 87121
Menaul Blvd NE
101-197 87107
199-3599 87107
3600-8299 87110
8301-8399 87110
8400-12599 87112
12601-12899 87112
Menaul Blvd NW 87107
Menaul Rd NE 87102
Mendius Ave NE 87109
Mendocino Ct & Dr 87122
Mendoza Ave & Ct 87109
Meoqui Ct NW 87107
Mercantile Ave NE 87107
Mercury Cir SE 87116
Meridian Pl NW 87121
Merion Cir NE 87111
Merissa Ln NE 87122
Meriwether Ave NE 87109
Merle Dr NE 87109
Merlida Ct & St 87121
Merlot Dr SW 87121
Merrimac Ct NE 87109
Merritt Rd SW 87104
Mervosh Ave & Pl 87105
Merz Rd SW 87105
Mesa Pl NW 87114
Mesa St SE 87106
Mesa Alegre Ave NW 87120
Mesa Antigua Pl NW 87120
Mesa Arriba Ave & Ct 87111
Mesa Bonita Ct NW 87120
Mesa Camino Ave SW 87121
Mesa De Arena NW 87120
Mesa De Oro Rd NW 87114
Mesa De Romero SW 87121
Mesa Del Oso Rd NE 87111
Mesa Del Rio St NW 87121
Mesa Dura Dr NW 87120
Mesa Encantada Ct NW 87120
Mesa Entrada Ave SW 87121
Mesa Escondida Ct NW 87120
Mesa Grande Pl SE 87108
Mesa Linda Dr NE 87112
Mesa Marcada Ct NW 87120
Mesa Mariposa Pl NW 87120
Mesa Pointe Rd SW 87121
Mesa Prieta Ct NW 87120
Mesa Rain Rd NW 87120
Mesa Real Ave SW 87121
Mesa Ridge Rd NW 87114
Mesa Rincon Dr NW 87120
Mesa Roja Ave SW 87121
Mesa Solana Pl NW 87120
Mesa Sombra Pl NW 87120
Mesa Springs Ave SW 87121
Mesa Sunset Ave SW 87121
Mesa Terraza Pl NW 87120
Mesa Top Rd NW 87120

Mesa Verde Ave NE 87110
Mesa Viejo St SW 87121
Mesa Viento Rd NW 87120
Mesa View Dr SW 87121
Mesa Vista Rd NE 87106
Mesa Vista Trl NW 87120
Mesa Wood Pl NW 87120
Mescalero Ct NE 87110
Mescalero Rd NE
4000-5399 87110
9100-9299 87111
Mescalero Rd NW 87107
Mesilla St NE
100-616 87108
900-2999 87110
4101-4199 87109
Mesilla St SE 87108
Mesita Cliff Rd NE 87112
Mesquite Dr NE 87109
Mesquite Dr NW 87120
Mesquite Wood Dr NW 87120
Messervy Ave NE 87109
Mete Sol Dr NW 87120
Meteor Ct NW 87120
Metro Ln NE 87123
Metzgar Rd SW 87105
Mezcal Cir NW 87105
Mezzano Ln SW 87105
Mi Cordelia Dr NW 87120
Mia St NE 87109
Miami Rd NW 87120
Michael Hughes Dr NE 87112
Michelangelo Ln NW 87114
Michelle Loop NE 87111
Michelle Pl NW 87107
Michelle Rd SW 87105
Michelle St SW 87121
Mickelsen Ave SE 87123
Microlith Rd SW 87121
Middleberry Way NW 87120
Midge St NE 87109
Midnight Vista Ave NW 87114
Midtown Pl NE 87107
Midway Pl NE 87109
Midway Park Blvd & Pl 87109
Miera Dr NW 87114
Miguel Ct NE 87111
Miguel Chavez Ln SW 87105
Mijas Dr NW 87120
Mikell Ct NW 87114
Milagro SW 87105
Milan Ct 87121
Milano St NW 87114
Mildred Ave NW 87107
Mildred St NE 87123
Miles Rd SE 87106
Milky Way St NW 87114
Mill Rd NW 87120
Miller Cir NW 87107
Millstream Pl NW 87120
Millwood Ct NW 87120
Milne Rd NW 87120
Milton Ct & Rd 87104
Mimbres St SW 87121
Mimbres Canyon Pl NE 87112
Mimi Ct NW 87105
Mimosa Ct & Pl 87111
Minaret Dr SW 87121
Mindy Ln SW 87121
Minehead Ct & St 87120
Miner Rd SW 87121
Minge Rd NW 87120
Minnie St SW 87105
Mint Pl NW 87121
Minuteman Dr NE 87109
Miracerros Pl NE 87106
Mirada Ct & Dr 87120
Mirador Dr NW 87120
Mirage Ct NW 87120
Miramar Dr & Ln 87114
Miramon Ave SW 87105

Mirandy Ct NE 87122
Mirasol Ave NW 87120
Mirasol Ct NW 87120
Mirasol Pl NW 87114
Miravista Pl SE 87123
Mirto St NE 87112
Mis Abuelitos Dr NW 87104
Mission Ave NE 87107
Mission Ridge Dr NW 87114
Mistletoe Ct SE 87123
Mistral Dr NW 87114
Misty Sage Ct NW 87114
Mitchell Ave SE
300-399 87105
6101-6297 87108
6299-6499 87108
Moab Ln NE 87111
Mocho Ave & Pl 87123
Mock Heather Rd NW 87120
Modesto Ave NE
5600-5698 87113
7601-8497 87122
8499-12599 87122
Mogollon Dr NW 87114
Mojave Ct & St 87120
Mojave Aster Way NE 87111
Molinero Ct SW 87105
Molino Ct & Way 87121
Molly Brown Ave NE 87111
Molokai Ave NE 87111
Molten Pl NW 87120
Monaco Dr NE 87111
Monahiti Pl NE 87109
Monarch Dr NE 87123
Moncloa Ct NW 87120
Moneda Dr NW 87120
Monell Dr NE 87123
Mongollow Way NE 87111
Monitor Dr NE 87109
Monk Ct NW 87107
Monolith Dr NW 87114
Monroe Ct NE 87110
Monroe Pl SE 87108
Monroe St NE
100-499 87108
600-600 87110
602-3899 87110
Monroe St SE 87108
Montano Dr NW 87120
Montano Rd NE 87107
Montano Rd NW
100-1733 87107
1735-1899 87107
1776-1798 87107
4200-7399 87120
Montano Plaza Dr NW 87120
Montano Pointe Pl & Rd 87120
Montara Ct NW 87114
Montbel Pl NE 87107
Montclaire Dr NE
200-532 87108
534-598 87108
600-698 87110
700-3599 87110
Montclaire Dr SE 87108
Monte Rd NE 87123
Monte Alto Ct, Dr & Pl 87123
Monte Bello Ct NW 87114
Monte Carlo Dr NW 87120
Monte De Neve Dr NW 87114
Monte Frio Dr NW 87120
Monte Largo Ct NE 87123
Monte Largo Dr NE
100-1199 87123
1300-2099 87112
Monte Rosso Pl NW 87114
Monte Serrano NE 87111
Monte Verde Dr NE 87112
Monte Vista Blvd NE 87106
Montecillo Dr NW 87114
Montecito Ct NW 87114
Montego Pl NE 87111
Montera Pl NW 87114
Monterey Ave SE 87106
Monterey Bay Ct NW 87114
Monterey Cove Ave NW 87114
Monterey East Ave NE 87109
Monterey Pier Dr NW 87114
Monteria Ct NW 87114
Montezuma Ct NW 87114
Montford St NW 87114
Montgomery Blvd NE
3200-3599 87107
3601-3797 87109
3799-8399 87109
8400-13200 87111
13202-13298 87111
Montgomery Pkwy NE 87111
Monticello Dr NE 87123
Montoya St NW 87104
Montreal St NE 87111
Montrose Pl SW 87105
Monument Dr NW 87120
Moon St NE
100-198 87123
200-399 87123
1300-2199 87112
2201-2999 87112
3100-5699 87111
5701-6199 87111
Moon St SE 87123
Moon Dance Pl NE 87111
Moon Eagle Dr NE 87113
Moon Glow Ct NE 87111
Moon Ridge Trl NE 87122
Moon Shadows Dr NW 87120
Moon Valley Ct NE 87111
Moonbeam Ct NE 87111
Moonlight Ct NE 87111
Moonlight Dr SW 87105
Moonrise Ave SW 87121
Moonstone Dr NE 87113
Moontree Ct NE 87111
Moore Dr SW 87121
Mora Rd SW 87105
Moraga Way NE 87123
Morenci Ave NE 87112
Morgan Ln NW 87120
Morina Ct NE 87112
Morning Dew St SW 87121
Morning Glory Rd NE 87122
Morning Mist Ave NE 87111
Morning Star Ct & Dr 87111
Morning Sun Trl SW 87121
Morningrise Pl SE 87108
Morningside Dr NE
100-198 87108
200-599 87108
700-3900 87110
3902-4298 87110
Morningside Dr SE 87108
Morningside Pl SE 87108
Morocco Rd NE 87111
Morris Ct NE 87112
Morris Pl NE 87112
Morris St NE
500-600 87123
602-798 87123
900-2800 87112
2802-2998 87112
3020-3198 87111
3200-4701 87111
Morris Rippel Pl NE 87122
Morrissey St SW 87121
Morrow Ave NE
7400-8399 87110
9301-9597 87112
9599-12699 87112
Morrow Rd NE 87106
Morton Ln SW 87105
Mosca Ct NW 87114
Mosher Ct NW 87120
Mosquero Ave NE 87109
Mosquero Ct NW 87120
Mosquero Pl NW 87120
Mossman Pl NE 87110
Mount Carmel Rd NE 87113
Mount Everest Ave NE 87111
Mount Rainier Dr NE 87111
Mountain Pl NE 87112
Mountain Rd NE
101-297 87102
299-999 87102
1001-1217 87102
2801-3297 87106
3299-3399 87106
4500-4598 87110
4600-7912 87110
7914-8202 87110
8501-10197 87112
10199-13399 87112
Mountain Rd NW
121-497 87102
499-1224 87102
1226-1298 87102
1300-3199 87104
3201-3499 87104
Mountain Gate Ln SW 87121
Mountain Haze Rd NE 87122
Mountain Laurel Cir SE 87116
Mountain Park Pl NW 87114
Mountain Ridge Ct & Pl 87112
Mountain Road Pl NE 87110
Mountain Shadow Rd NE 87111
Mountain Top Dr SW 87121
Mountain View Ave NE 87123
Mountain West Ct SE 87123
Mountaineer Dr SE 87123
Mountainside Pkwy & Way 87111
Mountvale Ave NW 87114
Mourning Dove Pl NW 87120
Moya Rd NW 87104
Muir Dr NW 87120
Mulberry St NE & SE 87106
Mule Farm Pl SW 87105
Muledeer Rd SW 87121
Mullen Rd NE & NW 87107
Mullhacen Pl NW 87114
Mundo Ct NE 87112
Muniz Ln & Rd 87105
Murchison Ave SW 87121
Murcia Ave NW 87114
Muriel St NE
200-899 87123
1000-2799 87112
2801-2999 87112
Murifield Ct NE 87111
Murrelet Dr NE 87113
Murry Rd SE 87105
Muscatel Ave NE 87107
Mustang Ln NW 87120
Mustang Trl SE 87123
Myers Rd NW 87114
Myra Pl NE 87112
Myrtle Dr SW 87105
Na Pali St NE 87111
Nabor Rd NW 87107
Nacimiento St NW 87114
Nacional Rd NW 87114
Nakomis Ct NE 87112
Nakomis Dr NE
700-899 87123
901-997 87112
999-2899 87112
Namaste Rd NW 87120
Namath Ave NW 87120
Nambe Ave & Ct 87123
Nancy St SW 87105
Nandina Ct NW 87120
Nandina Ln SE 87123
Nandina Way SE 87123
Napa Valley Rd NE 87122
Naples St NE 87111
Napoli Pl & St 87114
Nara Visa Ct & Rd 87107
Narcisa Ct NW 87107
Narcisco Ct & St 87112
Narcissus Pl SE 87123
Nardos Rd NW 87114
Nasci Dr NE 87111
Nashua Rd SE 87123
Nashville Ave SW 87105
Nasrullah St SE 87123
Nassau Dr NE 87111
Nassif Ct NW 87120
Natalie Ave NE
5800-7000 87110
7002-7398 87110
8800-9099 87111
Natalie Ave NW 87107
Natalie Ct NE 87111
Natalie Janae Ln NE 87109
Nathan St SE 87123
Nationwide St NW 87114
Native Dancer Rd SE 87123
Native Flower Dr & Pl 87121
Navajo Willow Dr NE 87122
Navarra Way SE 87123
Neal Ave NE 87113
Neal Ln SW 87121
Neat Ln SW 87105
Nebula Ct NW 87114
Ned St NE 87109
Neetsie Dr SW 87105
Nelle Ave NE 87111
Nelson Pl NW 87114
Nemesia Pl NE 87112
Neon Ave NE 87112
Neptune St NW 87114
Nerisa Ct SW 87121
New Cave Rd NW 87114
New Dawn Ct & Rd 87122
New Hampshire St NE 87110
New Hampton Rd NE 87111
New Vistas Ct NW 87114
New York Ave NW & SW 87104
Newberry Way NW 87120
Newcomb Ave NE 87111
Newport Ct SE 87123
Newsome Park Rd NE 87123
Newton Pl NE 87106
Niagara Ct & Rd 87113
Nicklaus Dr SW 87121
Nico Trl NW 87114
Nicodemus Ln SW 87105
Nicolas Rd NW 87104
Nicole Ct SW 87105
Nido Gavilan St NW 87120
Niels Dohr Ct SW 87121
Niese Ct & Dr 87121
Nieves Rd SE 87123
Night Hawk Rd NW 87114
Night Rose Ave NW 87114
Night Shadow Ave NW 87114
Night Sky Ln NE 87122
Night Whisper Rd NW 87114
Nightingale Ct NW 87114
Nikanda Rd NE 87107
Niquel Pl NW 87120
Nita Pl NE 87111
Noah Ave SW 87121
Noble Dr NE
5800-6099 87107
6700-6799 87113
Noble Pl NE 87107
Noche Clara Ave NW 87114
Noche Vista Dr NW 87114
Nogal Pl NW 87114
Noisy Brook Rd NW 87114
Nolina Ct NW 87120
Noor Ave NE 87122
Nordica St NE 87111
Noreen Ct & Dr 87111
Norma Dr NE 87109
Norman Ave NE 87112
Norment Pl & Rd 87105
Norte Vista Rd NW 87114
North St SW 87105
Northeastern Blvd NE 87112
Northern Trl NW 87120
Northern Sky Ave NE 87111
Northfield Ct NW 87107
Northland Ave NE 87109
Northlands Dr SE 87123
Northpointe Dr NW 87114
Northridge Ave NE
7400-8299 87109
8500-9599 87111
Northridge Ct NE 87109
Northridge Pl NE 87111
Northview Ln NW 87120
Northwest Cir NW 87104
Northwood Ct NW 87107
Norwich Ct NW 87114
Notre Dame Dr NE 87106
Nova Ct NW 87120
Novak Ln NW 87114
Noval Pl NW 87114
Nowicki Ln SW 87105
Nuanes Ln SW 87102
Nube Blanca NE 87111
Nueva Espana Ct & Rd 87114
Nueva Sevilla St NW 87114
Nuevo Hacienda Ln NW 87107
Nuez Ct NE 87111
Nugget Ave, Ct & St 87111
Nutrias Pl SW 87105
Nuves Ct NW 87105
Oahu Dr NE 87111
Oak Ct SE 87116
Oak Hl NE 87111
Oak St NE 87106
Oak St SE 87106
Oak Butte Rd NE 87112
Oak Ridge Ct NE 87122
Oakbrook Dr NW 87120
Oakcrest Pl NW 87114
Oakdale Pl NW 87120
Oakham Dr NW 87120
Oakland Ave NE
5200-5298 87113
5300-7599 87113
7600-12199 87122
12201-12599 87122
Oakland Ct NE 87122
N Oakland Ct NE 87122
Oakledge Ct NW 87120
Oakmont Rd NE 87111
Oakwood Pl NE 87123
Oasis Dr SW 87105
Oasis Canyon Rd NW 87114
Obsidian St NE 87113
Ocala St SE 87123
Ocean Breeze Dr NE 87112
Oceola Rd SE 87123
Oconee Ct SE 87123
Ocotillo Ct NE 87111
Ocotillo Rd SW 87105
Odelia Rd NE 87102
Odessa Ct SW 87121
Odin Rd SW 87121
Odlum Dr SE 87108
Office Blvd NE 87109
Ogle St SE 87102
Oja De Arbole Ct SW 87105
Ojo Feliz St SW 87121
Ojo Sarco St SW 87121
Ojos Azul Ct NW 87120
Ojos Negros Dr NW 87120
Ojos Prieto Dr NW 87120
Old Rd SE 87123
Old Adobe Trl NW 87120
Old Airport Rd NW 87114
Old Aspen Rd SW 87121
Old Caballero Ave SW 87121
Old Coors Dr SW 87121
Old Cottonwood Ave SW 87121
Old Glory Ct NE 87109
Old Mesa Dr NW 87120
Old Mill St NW 87114
Old Orchard Ln NE 87111
Old Pecos Trl NE 87113
Old Town Rd NW 87104
Ole Ct NE 87111
Oliver Ross Dr NW 87121
Olivine St NE 87113
Olivo Ct NE 87111
Olsen Pl NW 87114
Olympia Rd NW 87105
Olympic Ct, Pl & St 87114
Omaha St NE
700-899 87123
1000-1099 87112
Onate Ct NE 87109
Onate Pl SW 87105
Onate St NE 87109
Onava Ct NE 87112
One Civic Plz NW 87102
Ongais Ave SW 87121
Onyx Ct NW 87120
Opal Pl NE 87112
Opal Mist Ct SW 87121
Opalo Dr NW 87114
Open Sky Dr NW 87120
Ophelia Ave NW 87120
Opportunity Dr NE 87109
Oralee St NE 87109
Orchard Ct NW 87107
Orchard Pl NW
1000-1299 87102
1300-1399 87104
1401-1599 87104
Orchard Garden Rd SW 87105
Oregon Trl NW 87120
Orfeo Trl NW 87114
Oriente Ave NE 87123
Orilla Rd NW 87120
Oriole Ct SW 87121
Orion Ave NW 87120
Orlando Pl NE 87111
Ornella Ln NW 87104
Oro Real NE 87123
Oro Viejo NW 87120
Oro Vista Rd NW 87107
Orphelia Ave NE 87109
Orr Ave NE 87111
Ortega Ct NW 87114
Ortega Rd NE 87113
Ortega Rd NW 87114
Ortiz Ct NE 87110
Ortiz Dr NE
400-918 87108
920-920 87108
2900-3299 87110
Ortiz Dr SE 87108
Oryx Pl NE 87111
Osage Ave, Pl & Rd 87105
Osage Orange Rd NE 87111
Oscura St NW 87114
Osito Ct NE 87111
Oso Ct NE 87111
Oso Abrazo Dr NE 87122
Oso Corridor Pl NW 87114
Oso Escondido Dr NE 87122
Oso Feliz Dr NE 87122
Oso Grande Ct, Pl & Rd 87111
Oso Loco Dr NE 87122
Oso Redondo NE 87111
Oso Rico Rd NE 87122
Oso Ridge Pl NW 87114
Osullivan Pl SW 87105
Osuna Ct NE 87109
Osuna Pl NE 87111
Osuna Rd NE
201-297 87107
299-399 87107
500-2199 87113
3600-8199 87109
8201-8299 87109
8400-9999 87111
Osuna Rd NW 87107
Otero Ave NE 87109
Otero Mesa Rd SW 87121
Othello Ct NE 87112
Otono Ct NW 87120
Otra Vez Ct NW 87107
Ottawa Rd NE 87110
Ouray Rd NW 87120
Oveja Ct SE 87123
Overland St NE 87109
Overlook Dr NE 87111
Owen Rd SW 87121
Owl Ct SE 87123
Oxbow North Trl NW 87120
Oxbow Village Ln NW 87120
Oxford Ave SE 87106
Ozark St SE 87123
Paakweree Blvd SW 87121
Pablo Ct NE 87112
Pacaya Dr NW 87120
Pace Rd NW 87114
Pacheco Ln NW 87104
Pacific Ave SE & SW 87102
Packaway Rd NW 87114
Paddington NE 87111
Padilla Rd SW 87121
Padre Ct NE 87111
Padre Roberto Rd NW 87107
Paese Pl NW 87114
Paganica Way NE 87111
Page Ave NE 87102
Page Ct SW 87105
Pago Pl NW 87120
Pagosa Dr NW 87114
Paige Pl NE 87112
Paint Brush Dr NE 87122
Painted Pony Ct, Dr & Trl 87120
Painted Rock Dr NW 87120
Painted Sky Pl NW 87120
Paisano Ct NE 87112
Paisano St NE
301-397 87123
399-699 87123
1101-1197 87112
1199-2599 87112
Paja Pl NE 87111
Pajarito Mdws SW 87105
Pajarito Rd SW
2100-2800 87105
2802-2898 87105
3401-8999 87121
9001-9999 87121
Pajarito Meadows Ct SW 87105
Pala Mesa Ct NE 87111
Palacio Dr, Ln & Pl 87105
Palacio Del Rio Grande NW 87107
Palacio Real Ave NW 87120
Palazzo Rd NW 87114
Palermo St NW 87114
Palisades Dr NW 87105
Palm Ave SW 87121
Palm Bch NE 87111
Palm Cir SE 87116
Palm Ln SW 87121
Palm Springs Ave & Ct 87111
Palm Yucca Dr NE 87113
Palma Pl NW 87120
Palmer Ct NW 87114
Palmer Park Dr NE 87123
Palmilla Pl NW 87114
Palmyra Ave NW 87114
Palo Ct NE 87110
Palo Alto Ave SE 87108
Palo Alto Dr NE
2700-2999 87112
3000-3100 87111
3102-3198 87111
Palo Duro Ave NE
3601-3797 87110
3799-8199 87110
8400-8500 87111
8502-9298 87111
Palo Duro Ave NW 87107
Palo Duro Dr NE 87111
Palo Verde Dr NE 87112
Palo Verde Dr NW 87114
Palo Verde Pl NW 87114
Palomar Ave & Ct 87109
Palomas Ave NE
6501-6597 87109
6599-9699 87109

9700-11998 87122
12000-12499 87122
Palomas Ct NE 87110
Palomas Dr NE
100-917 87108
1800-3899 87110
Palomas Dr SE 87108
Palomas Park Ave NE .. 87109
Palomino Dr & Pl 87120
Palomita Ct NW 87114
Pam Dr SW 87121
Pamela Pl NE 87111
Pamela Marie Way NE 87122
Pampas Dr & Pl 87108
Pamplona St NW 87114
Pan American Fwy NE
1901-2697 87107
2699-4400 87107
4402-4498 87107
8200-8398 87113
8400-9300 87113
9302-10098 87113
Pan American Pl NE 87109
Pan American East Fwy NE 87109
Pan American West Fwy NE 87109
Pandora Ln NW 87114
Panicum Rd NW 87120
Panmunjon Rd NW 87104
Panola St SW 87121
Panorama Loop & Pl 87123
Papaya Ct & Pl 87111
Paper Flower Pl NE 87111
Paradise Blvd NW
4500-4600 87114
4600-4600 87193
4601-4697 87114
4699-6568 87114
6570-6598 87114
Paradise Ln SW 87105
Paradise Rd SW 87105
Paragon Ct NW 87107
Paragon Rd SE 87105
Paramount Ct NE 87122
Paris Ave NE 87111
Parisian Way NE 87111
Park Ave SW
800-1098 87102
1100-1399 87102
1401-1497 87104
1499-1800 87104
1802-1898 87104
Park Ct NW 87114
Park Ln NW 87114
Park Sq 87110
Park Heights Rd NW 87120
Park Hill Ave NW 87114
Park North St NW 87114
Park Pointe Pl NW 87120
Park Ridge Rd NW 87120
Park South Pl NW 87114
Parkland Cir & Pl 87108
Parkland View Dr & St . 87120
Parkside Dr & Pl NE & SE 87123
Parktree Pl NE 87111
Parkview Ave NE 87123
Parkway Dr NW 87120
Parkwest Dr NW 87120
Parkwood Dr NW 87120
Parnelli Dr SW 87121
Parrot Run Rd NE 87109
Parsifal Ct NE 87112
Parsifal Pl NE 87111
Parsifal St NE
100-198 87123
200-399 87123
1000-2999 87112
3300-3398 87111
3400-4999 87111
Parsons St NE 87112
Pasadena Ave NE 87113
Pasaje Pl NW 87114
Paseo Vis NE 87123
Paseo Alameda NE 87113
Paseo Alegre Rd SW 87105
Paseo Bueno Ct SW 87105
Paseo Circulo NE 87123
Paseo De Canto Dr SW 87121
Paseo De Ladera NW .. 87120
Paseo Del Banco Ct SW 87105
Paseo Del Bosque NW 87114
Paseo Del Mar NE 87123
Paseo Del Norte NE
300-3498 87113
Paseo Del Norte NE
3500-7599 87113
8000-8398 87122
8400-9600 87122
9602-12498 87122
Paseo Del Norte NW 87114
Paseo Del Oso NE 87111
Paseo Del Prado NW .. 87104
Paseo Del Rey NE 87111
Paseo Del Rey NW 87120
Paseo Del Rio Pl SW .. 87105
Paseo Del Sol NE 87123
Paseo Del Volcan NW .. 87121
Paseo Verde Rd NE 87113
Paso Del Puma NE 87111
Paso Fino Ave & Pl 87121
Pasquale Dr NW 87114
Pastime Ave NW 87114
Pastorcito Dr NW 87120
Pastura Pl NW 87107
Patio Market St NW 87104
Patricia Dr NE 87109
Patrick Pl NW 87107
Pattie Ln SE 87123
Patton Rd SW 87105
Paul Rd SW 87105
Paulette Rd SW 87105
Pauline Ave NW 87107
Pavon Pl NW 87114
Pawnee St NE
800-999 87123
1000-1099 87112
Pawnee Creek Trl NE .. 87123
Payne Rd SW 87121
Payson Ct NW 87120
Payton Trl SW 87121
Paz Rd SE 87123
Peachtree Pl NE 87111
Peacock Dr SW 87121
Pear Dr & Rd 87105
Pearl St SW 87121
Pebble Ct & Rd 87114
Pebble Beach Dr NE 87111
Pebble Stone Pl NE 87113
Pecan Ave SW 87105
Pecos Pl SW 87121
Pecos Trl NW 87120
Pedregoso Ct & Pl 87123
Pedroncelli Ct & Rd 87107
Pegasus Dr & Pl 87120
Pelican Ct SW 87121
Penasco Rd NE 87123
Penelope Pl NE 87109
Penfield Ln NE 87111
Penn Ave SE 87106
Pennsylvania Cir NE 87110
Pennsylvania Ct NE 87109
Pennsylvania Ct SE 87108
Pennsylvania Ln NE 87110
Pennsylvania Pl NE 87110
Pennsylvania St NE
100-110 87108
112-499 87108
501-599 87108
801-1097 87110
1099-3508 87110
3510-3898 87110
4100-4198 87109
Pennsylvania St SE 87108
Pennyback Park Dr NE 87123
Peno Pl NW 87114
Penstemon Ct SE 87116
Pentura Dr NW 87120
Peony Ct NE 87113
Pepperdine St NE 87111
Peppertree Pl NE 87111
Pepperwood Ct NW 87120
Pequeno Rd NW 87107
Pequin Trl SE 87123
Peralta Rd NE 87109
Peregrine Rd NE 87113
Perez Ln SE 87123
Perez Rd S 87123
Perez Rd SW 87105
Peridot Ave SW 87121
Periwinkle Ct NW 87120
Periwinkle Pl SE 87116
Perry Rd SW 87105
Perseus Ave NW 87114
Pershing Ave SE
3101-3297 87106
3299-3400 87106
3402-3498 87106
3700-3998 87108
4000-5099 87108
Persimmon Ave & Ct 87111
Petaluma Dr NE 87122
Petosky NW 87120
Petra Ct NE 87122
Petra Pointe Cir NW 87120
Petroglyph Ave NW 87120
Petronas Ave SW 87121
Petros Ave NW 87120
Pheasant Ave NW 87120
Pheasant Run Dr SW .. 87121
Phillips Dr SW 87121
Phoenix Ave NE
2200-2600 87107
2602-2698 87107
5201-5297 87110
5299-7800 87110
7802-8398 87110
8501-8597 87112
8599-12599 87112
Phoenix Ave NW 87107
Phoenix Pl NW 87107
Photinia Pl NW 87121
Phyllis St NE 87109
Picacho Ln NW 87114
Pickard Ave & Ct 87110
Pico La Cueva Rd NE .. 87122
Pictograph Rd SW 87121
Picture Rock Pl NW 87120
Piedra Ct NW 87114
Piedra Dr NW 87114
Piedra Rd NE 87123
Piedra Blanca St NE 87111
Piedra Colina Ct NW 87114
Piedra Grande Pl NE 87111
Piedra Larga Pl NE 87123
Piedra Lisa St NE 87111
Piedra Negra St NE 87111
Piedra Quemada Rd NW 87114
Piedra Rosa St NE 87111
Piedra Vista Rd NE 87123
Piedras Rd NE 87123
Pierce Arrow Rd NE 87112
Piermont Dr NE 87111
Pierre Dr SW 87105
Pilar Ave SW 87121
Pilares St NW 87114
Pilgrim Ct NE 87109
Pima Dr & Pl 87120
Pimenton Dr & Pl 87113
Pimlico Pl SW 87105
Pinata Pl NE 87109
Pinatubo Pl NW 87120
Pine St NE & SE 87106
Pine Butte Rd NE 87112
Pine Forest Pl NE 87111
Pine Park Pl NE 87109
Pine Springs Ct NE 87113
Pine Top Ln NE 87111
Pinecrest Dr NW 87114
Pinehurst Ave NE 87111
Pineleaf Pl NW 87114
Pineridge Ave NE 87112
Pinewood Dr NW 87120
Pinnacle Ct NE 87112
Pinnacle Peak Ct NW .. 87114
Pinnacle View Dr & Pl .. 87112
Pino Ave NE
5201-5397 87109
5399-6799 87109
6801-6899 87109
10501-10597 87122
10599-12599 87122
Pino Arroyo Ct NE 87111
Pino Canyon Pl NE 87111
Pino Pond Ct NE 87111
Pino Ridge Ct & Pl 87111
Pinon Ct NW 87107
Pinon Pl NE 87122
Pinon Altos Rd NW 87114
Pinon Azul St NW 87114
Pinon Blanco Rd NW 87114
Pinon Creek Ct & Rd 87123
Pinon Dulce Rd NW 87114
Pinon Encantada Trl NW 87104
Pinon Flats Rd NW 87114
Pinon Grande Rd NW 87114
Pinon Hill Pl NE 87122
Pinon Jay Ct NW 87120
Pinon Park Ct NW 87114
Pinon Vista Ct NE 87113
Pinonwood Ave NW 87120
Pinos Altos Ave NE 87111
Pinot Nor Ave SW 87121
Pinsouni Rd NW 87107
Pintado Ct NW 87114
Pinto Ln NE 87113
Pinto Pl SW 87105
Pintura Pl NW 87114
Pinzon Ave NW 87114
Pioneer Pl NW 87120
Pioneer Trl NE 87109
Pipe Spring St SW 87121
Pipestone Rd SW 87121
Piru Blvd SE 87123
Pisa Dr NW 87114
Pisces Ct NW 87114
Pitt Ct NE 87111
Pitt Pl NE 87111
Pitt St NE
1200-1899 87112
3100-4599 87111
4601-4699 87111
10100-10199 87112
Pittard Dr SW 87121
Pizzo Dr NW 87114
Placer Dr NE 87111
Placer Creek Ct NE 87113
Placid Ave NE 87112
Placido Dr NE 87111
Placido Martinez Ct NE 87102
Placitas Rd NE & NW .. 87107
Planeta Ct NE 87111
Plano Ct NW 87105
Plateau Ln & Pl 87120
Platero Pl NW 87120
Platinum St SW 87102
Platt Pl NW 87114
Playa De Tranquilidad NE 87109
N & S Plaza St 87104
Plaza De La Noche NE 87109
Plaza Encantada NW 87107
Plaza Olas Altos NE 87109
Plaza Paseo St NW 87114
Plaza San Blas NE 87109
Plaza Sonada NW 87107
Plaza Vizcaya NW 87104
Pleasant Ave NW 87107
Pleasanton Dr SE 87123
Plerelak Rd NE 87113
Plum St NW 87104
Plume Rd NW 87120
Plunkett Dr NW 87114
Plymouth Rock Rd NE . 87109
Poblanos Ct NW 87107
Poco Cerro Ct SE 87123
Poco Loco Dr SW 87105
Pocono Rd SE 87123
Poinsettia Ct & Pl 87123
Pojoaque Dr NW 87120
Pojoaque Rd NE 87110
Polo Pl NW 87114
Polvadera Pl NE 87113
Polvo De Oro Pl NW 87120
Pomelo Pl NW 87120
Pompano Pl SE 87123
Ponderosa Ave NE 87110
Ponderosa Ave NW 87107
Ponderosa Ct NE 87110
Pontiac Pl SW 87105
Pony Ln SW 87121
Pony Express Trl NE 87109
Pony Hills Pl NW 87114
Pool St NW 87120
Pope St NE 87107
Pope Valley Dr NE 87122
Poplar Ln SW 87105
Popo Dr NW 87120
Poppy Pl NW 87121
Porlamar Ct & Rd 87120
Port Rd NW 87121
Portales St NE 87109
Porto St SW 87121
Porto Fino Ct 87121
Portofino Dr NW 87114
Portulaca Dr NW 87120
Posada Ct SE 87123
Potentilla Ct NW 87120
Potomac Cir SW 87105
Potomac Ct NE 87109
Potomac Dr SW 87105
Powder Ct NW 87120
Powderhorn St SW 87121
Powell Rd SW 87105
Powers Way Rd SW 87121
Poza Rica Ct NW 87107
Prairie Ct & Rd 87109
Prairie Clover Pl SE 87116
Prairie Clover Way NE . 87111
Prairie Dunes St NE 87111
Prairie Falcon Ave NW 87114
Prairie Hill Pl NW 87114
Prairie Loft Way NE 87111
Prairie Night Ln NW 87120
Prairie Sage Dr NW 87120
Prairie View Rd NW 87120
Prairie Vista Dr NE 87113
Prenda De Oro NW 87120
Prenda De Plata NW 87120
Prescott Ct & Dr 87114
Presidential Pl NE 87109
Presidents Pl NE 87113
Presidio Pl SW 87105
Presley Pl NE 87111
Prestige Ct NW 87114
Prestina Pl NE 87111
Presto Way NW 87104
Preston Trl NE 87111
Prestwick NE 87111
Prickly Brush St NW 87114
Prickly Pear St NW 87114
Primrose Ct NE 87122
Primrose Ct SE 87116
Primrose Dr NW 87120
Prince St SE 87105
Princess Jeanne Ave NE
5600-8199 87110
8500-13399 87112
Princeton Ct NE 87106
Princeton Dr NE
1000-1813 87106
1815-1815 87106
2400-3799 87107
Princeton Dr SE 87106
Pristine Ct & Dr 87122
Procopio Pl SW 87105
Pronghorn Rd SW 87121
Propps St NE 87112
Prospect Ave NE
200-405 87102
2600-3498 87107
3501-3599 87107
4100-4108 87110
4110-8199 87110
9500-9598 87112
9600-12599 87112
405 1/2-407 1/2 87102
Prospect Ave NW
101-405 87102
407-899 87102
1600-1900 87104
1902-1998 87104
Prospect Ct NE 87112
Prospect Pl NE 87110
Prospector Way NW 87114
Prosperity Ave SE 87105
Provo Ct & Pl 87123
Pruitt Dr NE 87112
Puccini Trl NW 87114
Pueblo Pl NW 87114
Pueblo Bonito Ct NW 87104
Pueblo Grande Trl NW 87120
Pueblo Luna Dr NW 87107
Pueblo Solano Rd NW . 87107
Pueblo Verde NE 87111
Puerco Ridge Rd NW .. 87114
Puesta Del Sol Trl SW . 87121
Puffin Ct & St 87121
Puma Pl NE 87111
Pumice St NE 87113
Punta Alta Ave NW 87105
Punta De Vista Dr & Pl 87112
Purcell Dr NE 87111
Purdue Pl NE 87106
Puritan Ct NE 87109
Purple Aster Ln NE 87111
Purple Canyon Dr SW .. 87121
Purple Cone Rd SW 87121
Purple Fringe Rd SW 87121
Purple Rock Pl SW 87121
Purple Sage Ave NW 87120
Pyrenees Ct NW 87114
Pyrite Pl NW 87114
Q St NE 87110
Quail Ct NW 87114
Quail Ct SW 87105
Quail Holw NE 87109
Quail Rd NW 87120
Quail Creek Ct NE 87113
Quail Pointe Dr NW 87120
Quail Ridge Dr NW 87114
Quail Run Ct, Dr, Loop & Rd NE 87122
Quail Springs Pl NE 87113
Quailbrush Dr NW 87121
Quailwood Dr NE 87122
Quaker Heights Pl NW . 87120
Quaking Aspen Pl NE .. 87111
Quarai Ave NE 87111
Quarterhorse Ln NW 87120
Quartz Dr SW 87121
Quartzite Ave NW 87114
Quasar St NW 87114
Quebec Dr NE 87111
Quebrada Ln & Pl 87113
Queens Ct & Way 87109
Quemado Ct & Dr 87109
Questa Ct SW 87121
Quetzal Dr SW 87105
Quiet Ln SW 87105
Quiet Desert Dr SW 87121
Quimera Trl SE 87123
Quincy Pl SE 87108
Quincy St NE
100-499 87108
601-697 87110
699-3199 87110
Quincy St SE 87108
Quintana Dr NE 87109
Quintessence Rd NE 87122
R C Gorman Ave NE 87122
Rabadi Castle Ave NW 87114
Rabbit Brush Ave NW .. 87120
Rachel Rd SE 87123
Racheleigh Rd NE 87109
Radcliffe Rd NW 87114
Rael St SW 87121
Rafael Rd SW 87121
Rafelita Ln NW 87114
Raglin Ave & Ct 87121
Rain Pl NW 87120
Rainbow Blvd NW 87114
Rainbow Ct SE 87123
Rainbow Rd NE 87113
Rainbow St NW 87114
Rainier Way NE 87111
Rainmaker Rd SW 87121
Rainridge Ct NE 87111
Raintree Dr NE 87122
Rainwater Rd SW 87121
Ralph Ave & Ct 87112
Ram Trl SE 87123
Ramah Dr NW 87114
Ramirez Ct & Rd 87105
Ramona Ave NW 87114
Ramsey Ln NW 87114
Ranch Ct & Trl 87123
Rancher Rd SW 87121
Ranchitos Loop NE 87113
Ranchitos Rd NE
300A-310A 87113
300B-310B 87113
310J-310J 87113
100-300 87113
302-310 87113
6500-6598 87109
6600-6899 87109
9701-10497 87122
10499-12599 87122
Ranchitos Rd NW 87114
Rancho Rd NW 87107
Rancho Alegre Rd NW 87120
Rancho Bonito Dr NW .. 87120
Rancho Centro Ct 87120
Rancho Cielo NW 87120
Rancho Colina NW 87120
Rancho De Palomas NE 87109
Rancho De Roberto Rd NW 87114
Rancho Del Cerro Dr NE 87113
Rancho Del Oro Pl NE 87113
Rancho Del Rey Rd NE 87113
Rancho Del Rio Dr NE 87113
Rancho Diego Pl NE 87113
Rancho Dorado Ct NW 87120
Rancho Encanto Rd NW 87120
Rancho Felice Ct NW 87120
Rancho Grande Pl NW 87120
Rancho Guadalupe Trl NW 87107
Rancho Gusto NW 87120
Rancho Ladera Rd NE . 87113
Rancho Lago Ct NW 87120
Rancho Largo Rd NW .. 87120
Rancho Lindo Ct NW 87120
Rancho Lucido NW 87120
Rancho Mirage Dr NE .. 87113
Rancho Paraiso NW 87120
Rancho Pleno NW 87120
Rancho Quieto Ct NW .. 87120
Rancho Redondo NW .. 87120
Rancho Santa Fe Pl NE 87113
Rancho Seguro NW 87120
Rancho Solano Ct NW . 87120
Rancho Sueno Ct NW .. 87120
Rancho Vecino Ct NW . 87120
Rancho Ventoso Ct NW 87120
Rancho Verano Ct NW 87120

Rancho Verde Ct NW .. 87120
Rancho Viejo Ct NW .. 87120
Rancho Vista Pl NE 87113
Rancho Vistoso NW 87120
Rancho West Pl SW ... 87121
Ranchwood Dr NW 87120
Randolph Ave SE 87116
Randolph Ct SE 87106
Randolph Dr SW 87105
Randolph Rd SE 87106
Range Rd SW 87121
Rankin Ln & Rd 87107
Rapallo Ct NW 87114
Raton Ave SE 87123
Raven Ln SW 87105
Raven Ridge Dr NE 87113
Ravenwood Ct, Ln &
Pl 87107
Rawhide Ave SW 87121
Rawlings Rd NE 87111
Ray Ct SW 87105
Ray Ln SW 87121
Ray St NE 87109
Ray Barr Rd SW 87105
Rayado Pl NW 87114
Rayito Del Luna Ln
NE 87111
Raymac Ct & Rd 87105
Raymac Dam Ln SW ... 87121
Raymond Dr NE 87109
Rayner Dr NW 87114
Raynolds Ave SW 87104
Rayo Del Sol Dr SW ... 87121
Reading Ave SE 87105
Reba Ave SW 87121
Rebecca Ct SW 87105
Rebonito Ct & Rd 87112
Red Bluff Ave SW 87105
Red Finch Ct NW 87114
Red Hawk Rd NE 87113
Red Mesa Ave SW 87105
Red Mile Rd SE 87123
Red Oaks Loop NE 87122
Red Polard Ct NW 87120
Red River Ct & Rd 87114
Red Robin Rd SW 87121
Red Rock Park NW 87114
Red Rock Rd SW 87121
Red Rum Ct SE 87123
Red Sky Ct, Pl & Rd ... 87111
Red Sun Dr NE 87110
Red Tail Ct NW 87114
Red Thunder Rdg SW .. 87121
Red Yucca Ave NE 87111
Redberry St NW 87120
Redbud Ct SE 87116
Redbud St NW 87114
Redlands Rd NW 87120
Redmont Rd NE 87109
Redondo E 87106
Redondo Ct 87106
Redondo Ct NW 87107
Redondo Dr E 87106
Redpoll Rd NW 87114
Redwing Pl SE 87116
Redwood Dr NW 87120
Reese St NE 87107
Regal Mist Loop SW ... 87121
Regal Ridge Dr NE 87111
Regent Ave NE 87112
Regina Cir, Dr, Pl & Rd
NW 87105
Reilly Ct SW 87121
Reina Ct & Dr 87112
Relampago St NW 87120
Rembert Trl SW 87121
Remington Dr NE 87109
Rempas Ct & Dr 87114
N & S Renaissance
Blvd 87107
Renard Pl SE 87106
Rencher St SE 87105
Renee Ave NE 87109
Reo Rd NE 87112
Republic Dr NE 87109
Research Rd SE 87123

Retama Ct SE 87123
Retanas Pl NW 87114
Revi Don Dr NE 87111
Rex Ct NE 87112
Rhode Island Dr NE 87110
Rhode Island Pl NE 87109
Rhode Island St NE
100-120 87108
122-499 87108
1100-2999 87110
Rhode Island St SE ... 87108
Rhonda Ave & St 87121
Rialto Ave SW 87121
Ribera St 87121
Ricardo Rd NW 87104
Rice Ave NW 87104
Ricegrass Pl NE 87111
Rich Ct NE 87122
Richardson Way SW ... 87121
Richfield Ave NE 87122
Richmond Dr NE
100-1999 87106
2701-2797 87107
2799-3300 87107
3302-3598 87107
Richmond Dr SE 87106
Richmond Pl NE 87106
Richmond Hill Rd NW .. 87120
Richwood Rd NW 87120
Riddle Rd NE 87123
Ridge Pl NE 87106
Ridge Pointe Loop NE .. 87111
Ridge Rock Ave NW ... 87114
Ridge Stone Dr SW 87121
Ridge Top Ct NW 87114
Ridgecircle Dr NW 87114
Ridgecrest Cir, Dr,
Loop & Pl SE 87108
Ridgefield Ave, Ct &
Pl 87109
Ridgeley Ave NE 87108
Ridgeline Ave NE 87111
Ridgemont Ave NW 87114
Ridgerunner Rd NW 87114
Ridgeside Trl SW 87121
Ridgeview Dr NW 87120
Ridingcircle Rd NW 87114
Riesling St SW 87121
Rigel St SW 87105
Rigoletto Dr NW 87114
Riley Rd SW 87121
Rim Ct SW 87105
Rim Dr SW 87105
E Rim Dr NW 87114
W Rim Dr NW 87114
N Rim Rd NE 87112
S Rim Rd NE 87112
Rimera Ave NW 87114
Rimfire Ct SW 87121
Rimrock Cir NW 87120
Rincon Ct, Pl & Rd 87105
Rincon Del Rio Ct NW . 87107
Rinconado Ln SW 87105
Riner Ct SW 87105
Rio Rd SE 87123
Rio Abajo Rd SE 87105
Rio Arriba Ave SE 87123
Rio Azul Ln NW 87104
Rio Bonito Dr SW 87121
Rio Bravo Blvd SE &
SW 87105
Rio Camino Ave SW ... 87121
Rio Canon Ave & Ct ... 87121
Rio Cebolla Ct NW 87114
Rio Chiquito Ct NW 87114
Rio Colorado Ct & Rd .. 87120
Rio Corto Ave SW 87121
Rio Del Norte Ct NW ... 87114
Rio Del Sol Ct NW 87114
Rio Encantado Ct NW .. 87107
Rio Fonda Ave & Ct 87121
Rio Galisteo Pl NW 87114
Rio Grande Blvd NW
9710A-9710B 87114
100-198 87104
200-2799 87104

2800-4299 87107
4300-7899 87107
7900-9099 87114
8903-9197 87114
9199-10111 87114
10113-10133 87114
Rio Grande Blvd SW ... 87104
Rio Grande Ct NW 87107
Rio Grande Ln NW 87107
Rio Grande Pl NW 87107
Rio Grande Del Sol Ct
NW 87107
Rio Guadalupe Pl NE .. 87122
Rio Hondo Dr NE 87109
Rio Largo Dr SW 87121
Rio Las Vacas Pl NW .. 87114
Rio Linda Dr SW 87121
Rio Los Pinos Dr NW .. 87114
Rio Madre Ave & Ct 87121
Rio Maria Dr SW 87121
Rio Orilla Ln NW 87120
Rio Penasco Ct NW 87120
Rio Plata Dr SW 87121
Rio Pueblo Dr NW 87120
Rio Puerco Trl SW 87121
Rio Salado Ct NW 87120
Rio San Diego Pl SW .. 87121
Rio Seco Dr SW 87121
Rio Segura Ave NW 87114
Rio Senda Dr SW 87121
Rio Trumperos Ct NW .. 87120
Rio Valle Ave SW 87121
Rio Verde Pl NW 87120
Rio Vista Cir SW 87105
Rio Vista Ct SW
2800-2899 87105
2901-2999 87105
5900-5999 87121
Rio Vista Pl SW 87105
Risa Springs Dr SW 87121
Rising Star Pl NE 87122
Rita Ct & Dr 87106
Riva Ridge Ct SE 87123
River St NE 87113
River Ridge Ave & Pl ... 87114
River Stone Dr SW 87121
River Willow Trl NW 87120
Rivera Ct SW 87105
Riverbend Ave SW 87121
Riverdale Ln NW 87114
Riverfront Rd NW 87114
Riverhill Dr NW 87120
Riverside Dr SW 87105
Riverside Rd NW 87114
Riverside Plaza Ln
NW 87120
Riverton Dr NW 87120
Riverview Ct, Dr, Pl &
Rd NW 87105
Riverwalk Dr NW 87120
Riviera Pl & Rd 87111
Rivulet Dr SW 87121
Roadrunner Ln NE 87122
Roadrunner Ln NW 87107
Roadrunner Ln SW 87105
Roadrunner Pl SW 87105
Roan Ave SW 87121
Roanoke Ave NW 87120
Roaring Fork Pl NW 87120
Robby Ave SW 87121
Robert Dale Dr NE 87112
Roberta Pl NE 87109
Roberts St NE 87109
Robertson Rd SW 87105
Robin Ave NE
4500-8300 87110
8302-8398 87110
8800-9999 87112
Robin Cir SW 87105
Robin Meadow St NW .. 87114
Roble Blanco Rd SW ... 87105
Robs Pl NE 87122
Roca Fiel St NW 87120
Rocinada Ln SW 87121
Rock Creek Park Ave
NE 87123

Rock Daisy Ct NW 87120
Rock Dove Trl NW 87120
Rock Point Pl NE 87122
Rock Ridge Ct & Dr 87122
Rock Springs Rd SW ... 87121
Rock View Dr NW 87114
Rock Way Ct NW 87114
Rockcliff Ct & Dr 87114
Rockcress Ct & Dr 87120
Rockingham Ct SE 87123
Rockrose Rd NE 87122
Rocksberg Ct & St 87111
Rockwood Rd SW 87121
Rocky Rd SW 87121
Rocky Trl NW 87107
Rocky Crest Dr NW 87114
Rocky Mountain Dr
NW 87114
Rocky Point Ct NE 87123
Rodeo Ave SW 87121
Roehl Ct & Rd 87107
Rogers Ave NE 87110
Rohan Rd NW 87114
Rolling Ridge Dr SW ... 87121
Rolling Rock Pl SW 87121
Roma Ave NE
300-399 87102
401-599 87102
1001-1097 87106
1099-3399 87106
4001-4197 87108
4199-8599 87108
12701-12897 87123
12899-13499 87123
Roma Ave NW
100-300 87102
302-1199 87102
1201-1299 87102
1300-1398 87104
1400-1599 87104
Romadora Ln SW 87121
Romana Ave SE 87102
Romero St NW 87104
Ronald Trl SW 87121
Ronda De Lechusas
NW 87120
Rosalba St NE 87112
Rosalee Rd NW 87107
Rosalind Dr NE 87109
Rosas Ave & Ct 87121
Rose Ave NW 87104
Rose Park Ave NW 87114
Rose Quartz Ave NW .. 87114
Rose Rock Rd NW 87114
Rosebeary Rd SW 87105
Rosebud Dr NW 87121
Rosecliff Ave NW 87114
Rosefinch Dr NW 87114
Rosemary Ct SE 87116
Rosemary Dr NW 87120
Rosemont Ave NE
101-197 87102
199-508 87102
5300-5599 87110
11400-11598 87112
11600-12599 87112
Rosemont Ave NW
500-502 87102
507-699 87102
1200-1498 87104
1500-1599 87104
Rosendo Ct SW 87105
Rosendo Garcia Rd
SW 87105
Rosetree Pl NE 87111
Rosette Dr NW 87120
Rosewood Ave NW 87120
Rosewood Ct NW 87120
Rosewood Rd NE 87111
Rosie Ct SW 87105
Rosita Pl SW 87105
Ross Ave SE
801-897 87102
899-999 87102
2401-2497 87106
2499-3599 87106
5200-5298 87108

5301-6699 87108
Ross Ct SE 87106
Ross Pl SE 87108
Rossmoor Ave SW 87105
Rosson Ct SE 87105
Rough Rider Rd NE 87109
Round Rock Rd SW 87121
Round Up Pl SW 87121
Rover Ave NE 87112
Rowe Ave NW 87114
Rowen Rd SW 87121
Roxbury Ave NE 87111
Roy Ave NE 87113
Royal Crst & Dr 87111
Royal Birkdale NE 87111
Royal Glo Dr NE 87122
Royal Oak Ave, Ct, Dr,
Pl & St NE 87111
Royal Point Ct NE 87111
Royal Ridge Ct NE 87111
Royal Troon NE 87111
Royal Winslow Pl NE ... 87111
Royene Ave & Ct 87110
Rozinante Ct & Dr 87104
Ruby St NE 87109
Rudy Rd SW 87121
Ruffian Ct SE 87123
Ruffin Ave SW 87105
Ruger Rd SW 87121
Ruidoso Ct & Rd 87109
Ruiz Ln NW 87120
Rumaldo Ln SW 87105
Running Bird Pl NW 87120
Running Water Cir SE .. 87123
Rushing Rd SW 87105
Rushing Brook Ave
SW 87121
Russell Dr NW 87114
Russian Sage Ct NE ... 87111
Rustler Ct & Rd 87120
Rusty Rd NW 87114
Ruth Ave NE 87109
Rutledge Rd NE 87109
Ryan Pl NW 87107
Ryan Patrick Dr NW 87114
Ryno Ct SW 87121
Saavedra Rd SW 87105
Sabina St NE 87112
Sabinal Dr NW 87114
Sabre Ct NW 87107
Sabrina Ln SW 87105
Sabrosa Dr NE 87111
Sacate Ave NW 87120
Sacate Alto St NW 87120
Saddle Blanket Trl SW . 87121
Saddleback Rd NW 87114
Saddlebrook Ave NW ... 87120
Sadora Rd SW 87105
Safford Pl NW 87114
Sagan Loop SE 87106
Sage Rd SW 87121
Sage Hill Ct NW 87120
Sage Point Ct NE 87111
Sagebrush Ct SE 87123
Sagebrush St SW 87105
Sagebrush Trl SE 87123
Sagewood Ct SE 87123
Saguaro St NW 87114
Sahar Ct NE 87113
Saint Ct & St 87112
Saint Andrews Ct NE ... 87111
Saint Annes St NE 87111
Saint Clair St NE 87109
Saint Croix Dr NW 87120
Saint Cyr Ave SE 87106
Saint Francis Rd NW ... 87114
Saint James Pl SW 87121
Saint Josephs Ave, Ct,
Dr & Pl NW 87120
Saint Marys Ave & Dr .. 87111
Saiz Rd NW 87104
Sala De Tomas Dr
NW 87120
Salamanca Ct & St 87107
Salazar Ct SE 87102
Salem Rd NE 87112

Salerno St NW 87114
Salida Rd NW 87114
Salida Del Sol SW 87105
Salida Sandia SW 87105
Salinas St SE 87123
Sally Anne Ln NE 87122
Salome Dr NW 87114
Salt Brush Ct SE 87116
Salt Cedar Trl NW 87120
Saltbrush Rd SW 87121
Saltbush Ct NE 87111
Saltillo St NW 87114
Salvador Rd SW 87105
Salvator Dr SE 87123
Sam Bowen Ct SW 87121
Sam Bratton Ave NW .. 87114
Samantha Dr NE 87109
Samar Rd NE 87122
Samara Rd NW 87120
Samia St NW 87114
Sammy Ln SW 87105
San Adan Ave NW 87120
San Andres Ave NE
3500-3599 87107
4000-4699 87110
San Andres Ave NW ... 87107
San Antonio Dr NE
5200-6256 87109
6255-6255 87199
6258-7398 87109
6501-7399 87109
10400-10598 87122
10600-12199 87122
12201-12599 87122
San Antonio Pl NE 87109
San Antonio St NW 87104
San Augustine St NW .. 87120
San Benito St NW 87120
San Bernardino Ave
NE 87109
San Bernardino Dr NE . 87122
San Blas Pl NW 87120
San Carlos Ct & Rd 87104
San Clemente Ave
NW 87107
San Cristobal Rd SW .. 87104
San Diego Ave NE 87122
San Diego Ave SE 87106
San Diego Ct NE 87122
San Diego Rd NE 87113
San Felipe St NW 87104
San Fernando Pl NW .. 87104
San Fidel Rd NW 87107
San Francisco Rd NE
5100-9099 87109
9600-12500 87122
12502-12598 87122
San Francisco Rd NW .. 87104
San Francisquita Ct
NW 87120
San Gabriel Ct & Rd ... 87111
San Gavilon St NE 87113
San Gregorio Dr NW ... 87114
San Ignacio Ct NE 87102
San Ildefonso Dr NW ... 87120
San Isidro Ct NW 87107
San Isidro Dr NW 87104
San Isidro St NW 87107
San Jacinto Ave NE
10301-10397 87112
10399-11599 87112
11701-11899 87123
San Joaquin Ave SE
2700-3199 87106
8000-8599 87108
San Jon Ct SW 87121
San Jorge Ave NW 87120
San Jose Ave SE
100-450 87102
452-612 87102
1300-1499 87106
1501-1599 87106
San Juan Ave NE 87123
San Juan Pl NW 87107
San Juan Rd NE 87108
San Leandro Ln NW ... 87114

San Lorenzo Ave & Pl .. 87107
San Luis Pl NW 87107
San Luis Obispo Ave
NE 87109
San Luis Rey Pl NE 87111
San Marcial St NW 87104
San Marcos Pl NE 87111
San Marino Ct, Pl &
Rd 87111
San Martin Pl NW 87107
San Mateo Blvd NE
201-297 87108
299-999 87108
1100-4399 87110
4401-4697 87109
4699-6899 87109
8600-9600 87113
9602-9698 87113
San Mateo Blvd SE 87108
San Mateo Ln NE 87109
San Mateo Pl NE 87110
San Miguel Ct NE 87109
San Nicholas Ave NW .. 87121
San Pablo St NE
101-197 87108
199-799 87108
900-3099 87110
San Pablo St SE 87108
San Pancho Rd SW 87105
San Pasquale Ave NW &
SW 87104
San Patricia Pl NW 87107
San Patricio Ave SW ... 87104
San Pedro Ct NE 87109
San Pedro Dr NE
100-311 87108
313-925 87108
1000-1198 87110
1200-4003 87110
4100-4198 87109
4200-7999 87109
8100-9399 87113
9401-9699 87113
San Pedro Dr SE 87108
San Rafael Ave NE
1-1427 87122
1429-1499 87122
9300-9699 87109
10500-10598 87122
10600-12600 87122
12602-12798 87122
San Rafael Ave SE 87106
San Rafael Ct NE 87122
San Rafael Pl NE 87122
San Rio Ct & Pl 87107
San Saulo Rd SW 87105
San Tesoro St NE 87113
San Timoteo Ave NW .. 87114
San Tomas Ln SW 87121
San Venito Rd NW 87104
San Victorio Ave NE ... 87111
San Ygnacio Pl SW 87105
San Ygnacio Rd SW
1700-2899 87105
2900-2998 87121
3000-3098 87105
3001-3059 87121
3061-3099 87105
3100-3298 87121
3300-3999 87121
Sanchez Rd NW
101-199 87114
200-558 87107
560-598 87107
Sanchez Rd SW 87105
Sancho Panza Way
SW 87121
Sand Cherry Pl NE 87111
Sand Hill Ave SW 87121
Sand Piper Ct NW 87120
Sand Sage Dr NW 87114
Sand Sage Pl SE 87116
Sand Springs Cir &
Rd 87114
Sand Verbena Trl NE .. 87122
Sandalwood Pl NE 87111
Sandcreek St NW 87114

Sanderling Rd NW 87114
Sandhurst Dr NW 87114
W Sandia Cir SE 87116
Sandia Ct NW 87107
Sandia Dr NE 87122
Sandia Rd NW 87107
Sandia Glow Ct NE 87122
Sandia Heights Dr NE 87122
Sandia Point Rd NE 87111
Sandia Ridge Pl NE 87111
Sandia View Rd NW 87107
Sandler Ct NE 87112
Sandler Dr NE
500-699 87123
1100-1198 87112
1200-2699 87112
Sandlewood Dr NW 87120
Sandman Dr NW 87114
Sandoval Ct & St 87122
Sandpiper Dr SW 87121
Sandpoint Rd NW 87114
Sandra Ave NE 87109
Sandreed St NW 87114
Sandstone Pl NE 87111
Sandstone Pl NW 87114
Sandstone Pl SE 87116
Sandwater Rd NW 87120
Sandy Dr NW 87120
Sandy Creek Rd SW 87121
Sandy Flats Ave SW 87121
Sandy Ridge Rd SW 87121
Sandy Spring Ave SW 87121
Sandy Trail Rd SW 87121
Sanford Ave SW 87105
Sanrod Rd SE 87105
Santa Ana Ave SE 87123
Santa Anita Rd SW 87105
Santa Barbara Rd NE 87109
Santa Catalina Ave
NW 87121
Santa Catarina Ct NW 87120
Santa Clara Ave SE 87106
Santa Clarita St NE 87113
Santa Cruz Ave SE 87106
Santa Elena St NE 87113
Santa Fe Ave SE 87102
Santa Fe Ave SW 87102
Santa Fe Trl NW 87120
Santa Isabel Ct NW 87120
Santa Lucia Ave NE 87122
Santa Lucia St NW 87120
Santa Maria Ave SW 87105
Santa Maria Ct NE 87111
Santa Maria Ct NW 87120
Santa Marisa St NE 87113
Santa Martha Ct NE 87113
Santa Monica Ave NE 87109
Santa Monica Ave SE 87106
Santa Monica Dr NE 87122
Santa Paula Ave NE 87111
Santa Rachel St NE 87113
Santa Rita Pl NE 87113
Santa Rosa Rd SW 87105
Santa Rosalia St NW 87120
Santa Susana Pl & Rd 87111
Santa Teresa St NW 87120
Santala Pl NW 87114
Santander St SW 87121
Santiago Rd SW 87105
Santo Domingo St NW 87120
Santo Lina Trl NW 87120
Santo Tomas Ct NW 87120
Santolina Dr NW 87120
Sapphire St SW 87121
Saragossa St NW 87114
Sarah Ct & Ln 87114
Sarasota St NE 87111
Saratoga Ct, Dr & Pl 87120
Sardinia Dr NE 87122
Sarita Ave NW 87104
Sartan Way NE 87109
Sasebo St NE 87112
Satellite St NW 87114
Saturn Ct & Pl 87112
Saturnia Dr & Rd 87114
Saul Bell Rd NW 87121
Saunders Rd SW 87105
Sausalito Dr SW 87105
Sauza Dr SW 87121
Savage Dr NE 87109
Savoy Dr NW 87114
Sawgrass Pl NW 87121
Sawmill Rd NW 87104
Sawtooth St SE 87123
Saxton Ct NW 87104
Scarlet Pl NW 87120
Scarlet Bloom Dr SW 87121
Scarlet Gem Ct NE 87122
Scarlet Night NE 87122
Schell Ct & Pl 87106
Schenley Park Dr NE 87123
Schist Ave NE 87113
Schooner Rd NW 87121
Schulte Rd NW 87107
Schumacher St NW 87120
Scoresby Dr NE 87109
Scoria Dr NW 87120
Scorpio Ave NW 87114
Scottish Broom Rd
SW 87121
Scotts Pl NE 87109
Scottsdale Ave NW 87114
Scotty Ct SW 87121
Sea Biscuit Dr SE 87123
Sea Breeze St NW 87120
Sea Foam St NW 87120
Seaborn Dr SW 87121
Seabrook Dr NE 87111
Seagull St NE 87109
Seaside Rd NW 87121
Seattle Slew Ave SE 87123
Seco Ct NE 87111
Seco Rd SW 87121
Secret Oasis Ave SW 87121
Secret Valley Ct & Dr 87121
Secretariat Ave SE 87123
Sedan Rd NW 87114
Sedge Ave NW 87120
Sedona Dr NE 87111
Sedrev Rd NE 87123
Sefton Rd SW 87105
Sego Ct NW 87120
Segovia Ave NW 87114
Segunda St NW 87114
Seligman Ave NE 87109
Sellers Dr NE 87112
Selway Pl NW 87120
Seminole Rd NE 87110
Senac Pl NE 87123
Sendero Rd NW 87114
Seneca Dr NW 87114
Senecu Ct NW 87114
Sentinal Ct NE 87111
Sepulveda Ave NE 87113
Sequoia Ct NE 87111
Sequoia Ct NW 87120
Sequoia Pl NW 87120
Sequoia Rd NW 87120
Serena Cir NE 87111
Serenata Pl NW 87114
Serenity Ct SE 87123
Serenity Hills Ct & Pl 87123
Sereno Dr NE 87111
Serna Rd NW 87104
Serpentine Ct NW 87114
Serrano Pointe NW 87120
Sesame St SW 87121
Setaria Rd NW 87120
Setter Dr NE 87112
Settlement Way NW 87120
Seven Bar Loop Rd
NW 87114
Seven Falls Ct & Pl 87121
Seven Springs Rd NW 87114
Severo Rd SW 87105
Sevilla Ave NW 87120
Seville Pl NW 87120
Seward Park Ave NE 87123
Sgt Pepper Ct NW 87114
Shadetree Dr SW 87121
Shadow Ave NW 87114
Shadow Leader Pl SE 87123
Shadow Mountain Rd
NE 87123
Shadow Ridge Dr NW 87120
Shadow Rock Rd NW 87114
Shadowcast Dr SW 87121
Shady Ln SW 87105
Shady Spring Dr SW 87121
Shady Trails Ln 87105
Shadyside Dr SW 87105
Shaffer Ct SE 87123
Shaheen Ct NE 87113
Shale Ave NE 87113
Shamrock Way NW 87120
Shana Ln SW 87121
Shangri La Ct NW 87107
Shannon Pl NW 87107
Shannon St NE 87109
Shari Vista Rd SW 87105
Sharon Dr NE 87123
Sharp Spur St SW 87121
Sharps Rd NE 87109
Shasta Rd SW 87105
Shaw Dr SW 87105
Shawna St NW 87114
Shawndra Dr SW 87121
Shawnee Ct & Pl 87108
Sheffield Pl NW 87120
Shelburn Rd SW 87105
Sheldon St SE 87105
Shelly Rd SW 87121
Shelly Rose Rd NW 87114
Shenandoah Pl NE 87111
Shepard Pl & Rd 87110
Sheridan St NW 87104
Sherre Dr NE 87111
Sherry Ann Rd NW 87114
Sherwood Dr NW 87120
Sherwood St NE 87109
Shetland Pl SW 87121
Shiloh Dr & Pl 87111
Shipman Rd SW 87105
Shiprock Ct NW 87120
Shiraz Rd SW 87121
Shire St SW 87121
Shirk Ln SW 87105
Shirlane Pl NE 87112
Shirley St NE
101-197 87123
199-899 87123
1000-2999 87112
Shone Ave & St 87121
Shooting Star St NW 87114
Shorewood Dr NW 87121
Shoshone Rd NE
6900-7199 87110
8800-9699 87111
Showlow St NW 87114
Shropshire Ave NW 87107
Siboney Loop NE 87111
Sicily Rd NW 87114
Sidewinder Dr NE 87113
Sidney Ave NE 87111
Siempre Verde Dr NE 87123
Sienna St NW 87120
Sierra Ct NE 87123
Sierra Dr NE
100-198 87108
2501-2597 87110
2599-3499 87110
Sierra Dr SE 87108
Sierra Pl NE 87108
Sierra Pl SE 87108
Sierra Altos Pl NW 87114
Sierra Azul Ave NE 87110
Sierra Bonita Ave & Pl 87111
Sierra Grande Ave NE 87112
Sierra Hill Dr NW 87114
Sierra Larga Dr NE 87112
Sierra Linda Ave NW 87120
Sierra Madre Dr NE 87111
Sierra Morena St NW 87114
Sierra Nevada Cir NW 87114
Sierra Oscura Ave NE 87111
Sierra Rica Dr NW 87120
Sierra Vista Ct NE 87111
Sierra Vista St NW 87107
Siesta Pl NE 87113
Sigma Chi Rd NE 87106
Signal Ave NE
5800-7300 87113
7302-7598 87113
8201-8209 87122
8211-12299 87122
Signal Ct NE 87122
Siguard Ct NE 87109
Silas Ct NE 87111
Silent Meadows Pl
SW 87121
Silica Ave NW 87120
Silk Tassel Rd NW 87120
Silkwood Ave NW 87121
Silver Ave SE
100-298 87102
300-718 87102
720-898 87102
1001-1197 87106
1199-3399 87106
3401-3499 87106
3600-5599 87108
Silver Ave SW
100-398 87102
400-1399 87102
1400-1599 87104
Silver Arrow Dr NW 87114
Silver Creek Rd NW 87121
Silver Fox Dr SE 87105
Silver Grade Ct NW 87114
Silver Hair Rd NW 87114
Silver Leaf Trl NE 87111
Silver Peak Pl NE 87111
Silver Saddle Rd NE 87113
Silver Sage Ct SE 87116
Silver Sage Dr NE 87113
Silver Sage Rd SE 87116
Silver Sky Ct & Dr 87121
Silver Star Dr SW 87121
Silverado Ave SW 87121
Silverberry Cir SE 87116
Silverberry Rd SW 87121
Silverberry Way SE 87116
Silvercrest Ct NW 87114
Silverhills Ln SE 87123
Silverlace Trl NE 87111
Silverthorne Rd NW 87114
Silverton Dr NW 87114
Silverton Rd SE 87105
Silverwood Dr NE 87113
Silvery Minnow Pl NW 87120
Simi Ln NE 87113
Simms Ave & Ct 87108
Simon Ct SW 87121
Simon Dr NW 87114
Simon Ln SW 87105
Simpier Ln SW 87102
Sin Nombre Ct NE 87113
Sincho Ave NW 87114
Singapore Cir NE 87111
Singer Blvd NE 87109
Singing Arrow Ave &
Rd 87123
Singletary Dr NE 87112
Sioux St NW 87107
Sipapu Ave NW 87120
Sir Barton Rd SE 87123
Sirius Ave SW 87105
Sirocco Pl NW 87114
W Sky St SW 87121
Sky Court Cir NE 87110
Sky Tower St SW 87121
Sky Trail Ct NW 87114
Sky Valley Way NE 87111
Sky Watcher St NW 87114
Skybrook Dr NW 87120
Skylight Ave SW 87121
Skyline Ct NE 87111
Skyline Rd NE 87123
Skyline Ridge Ct NE 87111
Skyline View Ct NE 87111
Skyview Ave & Pl 87123
Skyview Crest Rd NW 87114
Skyway Ct SW 87105
Slate Ave NE 87102
Slate Ave NW
401-499 87102
501-999 87102
1700-1899 87104
Slateridge Pl NE 87111
Sleeping Bear Dr NW 87120
Sleepy Nights Rd NW 87114
Slickrock Ct NW 87114
Sloan Ct & Pl 87105
Slumber Ct NW 87114
Smarty Jones St SE 87123
Smith Ave SE
200-799 87102
2800-3398 87106
3400-3599 87106
3600-4099 87108
Smokerise Ave NW 87120
Smokey Mountain Way
NE 87111
Snakedance Ct NE 87111
Snapdragon Rd NW 87120
Snaproll NE 87109
Snipes Rd SW 87121
Snow Ave NE 87110
Snow Ct NE 87112
Snow Creek Ct NW 87114
Snow Goose Ct NW 87120
Snowberry St NW 87120
Snowbird Dr NW 87114
Snowdrop Pl NE 87112
Snowflake Ct & Dr 87114
Snowheights Blvd &
Cir 87112
Snowmass Way NE 87111
Snowridge Ct NE 87111
Snowvista Blvd SW 87121
Snowy Egret Ct & Pl 87114
Snyder St SE 87123
Soaring Eagle Dr NE 87113
Sobra Ct SE 87123
Socorro St NW 87104
Sol De Sandia Pl SW 87105
Sol De Vida NW 87120
Sol Poniente Rd NW 87120
Sol Rio Ct NW 87107
Solano Ct NE 87110
Solano Dr NE
200-599 87108
601-697 87110
699-3213 87110
Solano Dr SE 87108
Solano Pl NE 87110
Solar Rd NW 87107
Sole Grande Rd NW 87114
Sole Rosso Ct NW 87114
Soledad Ct SE 87123
Solitude Rd SW 87121
Soltana Ct SW 87105
Solterra Pl NE 87111
Sombra Pl NW 87114
Sombra De Guadalupe
Trl NW 87114
Sombra Del Rio NW 87107
Sombrero Loop NE 87113
Sombrillo Ave SW 87121
Somerset Dr NW 87120
Somervell Ct & St 87112
Sonata Dr NE 87111
Sonoma Ave NW 87121
Sonoma Valley Rd NE 87122
Sonora Ave NW 87120
Sonrisa Pl NE 87113
Sontero Ave NW 87120
Sonya Ave SW 87121
Sooner Trl NW 87120
Sophia Polito Ln SW 87105
Soplo Rd SE 87123
Soria Ave NW 87114
Sorrel Ln SW 87105
Sorrento Dr NW 87114
Soula Dr NE 87123
Southdale Dr SW 87105
Southeast Cir NW 87104
Southern Ave SE
200-700 87102
702-798 87102
2000-2099 87106
4700-8299 87108
9901-10399 87123
Southfield Dr SW 87105
Southfort SW 87105
Southwood Ct NW 87107
Spain Rd NE
7801-8399 87109
8400-11099 87111
Spanish Bit NE 87111
Spanish Broom Ave &
Ct 87120
Spanish Pointe Pl NW 87114
Spanish Sun Ave NE 87110
Sparrow Hawk Ct SE 87123
Speakman Dr SE 87123
Speedway Blvd SW 87121
Spence Ave SE 87106
Spencer Rd NE 87109
Speronelli Rd NW 87107
Spinnaker Dr NW 87121
Spinning Wheel Rd
NW 87120
Spirit Dr SE 87106
Spirit Trail Pl NE 87112
Spotted Pony Ave SW 87121
Sprenger Dr NE 87109
Spring Ave NE 87110
Spring Canyon Dr SW 87121
Spring Creek Ct, Dr, Ln
& Pl NE 87122
Spring Flower Pl & Rd 87121
Spring Sage Ct & Rd 87121
Spring Vale Rd NW 87114
Spring Valley Cir SW 87105
Springcroft Rd NW 87120
Springfield Dr NE 87109
Springhill Dr NW 87114
Springwood Rd NW 87120
Spruce St NE & SE 87106
Sprunk Rd NE 87102
Spur Ct NW 87104
Spyglass Hill Ln NE 87111
Stadler Ave NW 87114
Stafford Pl NW 87120
Stagecoach Ln & Rd 87123
Staghorn Dr NW 87120
Stalgren Ct NE 87123
Stallion Dr NW 87120
Standfier Ct SW 87105
Stanford Dr NE
1000-1002 87106
1004-1899 87106
2801-2897 87107
2899-3499 87107
Stanford Dr SE 87106
Stanley Dr NW 87114
Star Ct NW 87114
Star Pl SW 87105
Star Bright Rd NW 87120
Star Kachina St NW 87120
Star Light St SW 87105
Starboard Rd NW 87121
Stardust Ct & Dr 87110
Starfire Pl NW 87120
Stargazer Ave NW 87114
Starling Rd SW 87121
Starshine St NE 87111
Starwood Dr NW 87120
State Highway 303 SE 87105
State Highway 528
NW 87114
State Road 314 SW 87105
State Road 45 SW 87105
State Road 47 SE 87105
Staubach Ave NW 87120
Staunton Pl NW 87120
Steamboat St SE 87123
Stela St SW 87121
Stella Ln & Rd 87105
Steller Ct NW 87114
Stephan Rd SW 87121
Stephanie Dr NE 87111
Stephen Moody St SE 87123
Sterling Rd SW 87105
Stern Dr NW 87121
Stetson Dr SW 87121
Stevens Dr NE 87112
Steward St NW 87114
Stieglitz Ave SE 87106
Still Brooke Ave NW 87120
Stilwell Dr NE 87112
Stinson St SW 87121
Stipa St NW 87120
Stirrup Ct SW 87121
Stock Dr SE 87105
Stockbridge Ave NW 87120
Stone Ct NW 87114
Stone St NE 87102
Stone St NW 87114
Stone Canyon Rd NE 87113
Stone Creek Ave NW 87120
Stone Hedge Ct NW 87114
Stone Hills Rd NW 87114
Stone Hollow Pl NW 87114
Stone Mountain Pl &
Rd 87114
Stone Peak Rd NW 87114
Stone Ridge Dr NW 87114
Stonebrook Pl NW 87114
Stoneham Pl NW 87120
Stoner St SW 87105
Stoneway Dr NW 87120
Stoney Pl NE 87122
Stoney Bluff Ct NW 87120
Stoneybrook Pl NW 87120
Stony Creek Rd SW 87121
Storm Cloud Ave NW 87120
Storrie Pl NE 87109
Story Rock St NW 87120
Storyteller Rd NW 87120
Stoughton Pl & Rd 87114
Stovall Ct & Pl 87112
Stover Ave SW 87102
Stowe Rd NW 87114
Strada Tuscano NE 87112
Strand Loop SE 87106
Strasburg Ct NW 87120
Stratford Ave NW 87114
Stream Ct & St 87113
Stream Stone Ave NW 87114
Stuart Rd NW 87114
Stutz Dr NE
1100-1199 87123
1200-1300 87112
1302-1498 87112
Suerte Pl NE 87113
Suffolk Ave & Ct 87121
Sugarbear Ct NW 87120
Sulky Dr NE 87109
Sullins Pl SW 87105
Sullivan Ct NW 87114
Sumac Cir SE 87116
Sumac Dr NW 87120
Summer Ave NE
4601-4797 87110
4799-7799 87110
8500-8598 87112
8600-13099 87112
Summer Ave NW
100-799 87102
1200-1599 87104
Summer Pl NE 87112
Summer Breeze Dr
NW 87120
Summer Hill Ln NW 87120
Summer Night Pl NW 87120
Summer Ray Ct, Dr &
Rd 87120
Summer Ridge Rd
NW 87114
Summer Sage Dr SW 87121
Summer Shower Pl
NW 87120
Summercrest Dr NW 87114
Summerfield Ct & Pl 87121
Summerlin Rd NW 87114
Summerside Rd SE 87123
Summersville Dr NW 87120
Summertree Rd NE 87111
Summerwind Pl NE 87122
Summerwood Ct & Rd 87120

Summit Dr & Pl 87106
Summit Hills Dr, Pl & Rd 87112
Summit Park Rd NW 87120
Sun Ave NE 87109
Sun Ave SW 87121
Sun Cir SW 87105
Sun Ct SW 87121
Sun Canyon Ln SW 87121
Sun Chaser Trl SW 87121
Sun Cove Rd NE 87110
Sun Dancer Dr NW 87114
Sun Gate Trl SW 87121
Sun Light St SW 87105
Sun Mountain Trl SW 87121
Sun Valley Dr SW 87105
Sun View Dr NW 87120
Sunbeam Rd SW 87105
Sunbear Dr SW 87121
Sunbird Ct SW 87121
Sunbird Dr NW 87120
Sunbird Rd SW 87121
Sunbow Ave SW 87121
Sunburst Rd SW 87121
Suncrest Ave & Ct 87121
Suncup Ct NW 87120
Sundance Trl NW 87120
Sundance Kid Dr SW 87121
Sundeck Ct SW 87121
Sundew Ct NW 87120
Sundial Pl SW 87121
Sundial St NE 87122
Sundoro Pl NW 87120
Sundown Pl SE 87108
Sundrop Pl NW 87114
Sundrop Pl SE 87116
Suneast Dr SW 87121
Sunfish Ave SW 87121
Sunflower Rd SW 87105
Sunglow Rd NE 87123
Sunland Cir NW 87107
Sunlight Ln SW 87105
Sunningdale Ave, Ct & Pl 87110
Sunny Cir SW 87105
Sunny Brook St NE 87113
Sunny Day Ct & Pl 87120
Sunny Morning Dr NW 87120
Sunny Sky Ln SW 87121
Sunnyslope Rd & St SE & SW 87105
Sunport Blvd & Pl 87106
Sunray Ct & Rd 87120
Sunridge Rd SW 87121
Sunrise Ct SW 87121
Sunrise Dr SW 87121
Sunrise Pl SE 87108
Sunrise Trail Pl NE 87111
Sunrise West Dr SW 87121
Sunrose Dr NW 87120
Sunset Dr SW 87121
Sunset Loop SW 87105
Sunset Pl SW 87105
Sunset Rd SW
177-397 87105
399-1051 87105
1050-1050 87195
1053-1399 87105
1054-1498 87105
Sunset Canyon Dr & Pl 87111
Sunset Farm Pl & Rd 87105
Sunset Gardens Rd SW
1500-4099 87105
4100-4198 87121
4101-5599 87105
5300-5398 87105
5801-6097 87121
6099-11800 87121
11802-11898 87121
Sunset Ridge Pl NE 87111
Sunset Strip St NE 87122
Sunshine Pl SW 87105
Sunshine Rd SW 87105
Sunshine Ter SE 87106
Sunshine Mesa Dr NW 87114

Sunshine West Plaza Dr SW 87121
Sunspot Rd SW 87121
Sunstar Blvd SW 87105
Sunstone Dr NW 87120
Suntrail Rd NW 87114
Sunward Dr SW 87121
Sunwest Dr SW 87121
Sunwise Ave SW 87121
Suny Bay Rd SE 87123
Supernova St NW 87114
Supper Rock Dr NE 87123
Supreme Ct NE 87109
Sur Vista Rd NW 87114
Surrey Rd NE 87109
Susan Ave SE 87123
Susy St SW 87105
Sutton St NW 87114
Suzanne Ln SE 87123
Swallow Dr SW 87121
Sweetbrier Ave NW 87120
Sweetwater Ct & Dr 87120
Swoose Ct SW 87105
Swope Park Ave NE 87123
Sycamore St NE & SE 87106
Sydney Ln NW 87107
Sylvia Rd SW 87105
Taft Ct NW 87114
Tafwood Rd NW 87120
Tahiti Ct NE 87112
Tahiti Pl NE 87111
Tahiti St NE
2800-2925 87112
2927-2999 87112
3000-3199 87111
3201-3399 87111
Tahoe Pl NE 87107
Tahoe St NE 87111
Talang St NW 87120
Talara Pl NW 87114
Talea Ct NE 87122
Tall Rock Ct NW 87114
Talladega St SE 87123
Tallsman Dr NW 87120
Tally Ho Ave NW 87114
Talmadge Ave NW 87114
Tamarac Trl NE 87111
Tamarisk Pl NW 87120
Tamariz Dr NW 87120
Tamarron Pl NE 87109
Tambora St NW 87120
Tanager Dr SW 87121
Tanbark Ct NW 87120
Tangerine Pl NW 87120
Tanglewood Pl NW 87120
Tanoan Dr NE 87111
Tansion Ct NE 87112
Tanzanite Dr NW 87114
Taos Pl SW 87121
Tapatio Dr NW 87114
Tapia Blvd & Pl 87105
Tara Ct & Dr 87111
Target Ln NW 87120
Tarrington Dr NW 87120
Tasco Dr NE 87111
Tascosa Ln NW 87107
Tassy Ct SE 87123
Taurus Ave & Ct 87114
Tauton Pl & Rd 87120
Taylor Ranch Rd NW 87120
Taylor Ridge Rd NW 87120
Tb Catron Ave NW 87114
Teagan Ct NE 87112
Teakwood Dr NW 87120
Teakwood Trl NE 87111
Teal Rd SW 87121
Tecolote NW 87120
Tejana Mesa Pl NE 87112
Telesfor Dr SW 87105
Telesfor Sanchez Rd NW 87107
Telluride Ct NW 87114
Telstar Loop NW 87121
Temile Hill Pl NE 87112
Tempe Ave NW 87114
Tempest Dr NW 87120

Templeton Ave SW 87121
Tempur-Pedic Pkwy NW 87120
Tenabo Rd NW 87120
Tenemaha Ave SW 87121
Tennessee Pl SE 87108
Tennessee St NE
100-700 87108
702-998 87108
2600-3399 87110
4700-4799 87109
Tennessee St SE 87108
Tennis Ct NW 87120
Tennyson St NE
6601-6699 87111
7101-7797 87122
7799-8700 87122
8702-9698 87122
Teodocio St NW 87107
Teodoro Rd NW 87107
Tephra Ave NW 87120
Tepin Trl SE 87123
Teree Ct SW 87121
Teresa Ct NW 87120
Teresina Ct NW 87114
Terra Bella Ln SE 87123
Terra Bonita Way SE 87123
Terra Dolce Ave NW 87114
Terra Forte Rd NW 87114
Terra Vista Trl SE 87123
Terrace St SE 87106
Terracita Ln SE 87123
Terracotta Pl SW 87121
Terragon Dr & Pl 87112
Terraza Dr SE 87123
Terrazas Rd NW 87114
Territorial Rd NW 87120
Terry Ct NE 87110
Terry Rd SW 87105
Tesoro Pl NE 87113
Tessa Dr NW 87120
Tesuque Ct NW 87120
Tesuque Dr NE 87113
Tesuque Dr NW 87120
Teton Pl NW 87114
Tewa Ct & Dr 87111
Texas St NE
100-599 87108
1000-1098 87110
1100-3399 87110
Texas St SE 87108
Teypana Rd NW 87114
Thais St NW 87114
Thaxton Ave SE
101-197 87102
199-899 87102
901-999 87102
3400-3599 87106
3600-3698 87108
3701-4099 87108
Thayer Ln SW 87121
The 25 Way NE 87109
The American Rd NW 87114
The Lane At 25 NE 87109
Theresa Pl NE 87111
Theresa Rd SW 87105
Thicket St NW 87120
Thiel Ct NW 87114
Thistle Ave NW 87120
Thistledown Rd SE 87123
Thomas Ct NE 87111
Thomas Dr NE 87111
Thomas Ln NW 87114
Thomas Pl NE 87111
Thompson Ln SW 87105
Thompson Loop NW 87104
Thompson Rd NW 87104
Thomte Rd NE 87112
Thor Rd SW 87121
Thorn Ct SE 87116
Thornton Ave NE 87109
Thornwood Dr NW 87120
Thoroughbred Dr SW 87121
Thunder Rd NW 87120
Thunder Basin Rd SE 87123
Thunderbird Cir NW 87120

Thunderbird Ct NW 87121
Tia Christina Dr NW 87114
Tiburon St NE 87109
Ticonderoga Rd NE 87109
Tieran Ct NE 87112
Tierra Dr NW 87107
Tierra St NE 87111
Tierra Alegre Dr NE 87122
Tierra Amada St NW 87120
Tierra Antigua St NE 87111
Tierra Bonita Pl NE 87122
Tierra De La Luna Dr SW 87121
Tierra Del Oro SW 87105
Tierra Del Oso Dr & Pl 87120
Tierra Del Rio NW 87107
Tierra Del Sol NW 87114
Tierra Del Sol Ave SW 87121
Tierra Encantada Ct NE 87109
Tierra Linda Pl NE 87122
Tierra Luna Ct NW 87120
Tierra Madre Ct NW 87120
Tierra Montana NE 87122
Tierra Montanosa Ct & Dr 87112
Tierra Monte St NE 87122
Tierra Morena Pl NE 87122
Tierra Prieta Ave NW 87120
Tierra Sandia Ct NW 87120
Tierra Serena Pl NE 87122
Tierra Verde Ct & Pl 87105
Tierra Vida Pl NW 87107
Tierra Vieja St NW 87120
Tierra Vista Ave NW 87120
Tierra Viva Ct & Pl 87107
Tiffany Rd SW 87121
Tiffany Bud Ct NE 87122
Tigers Eye Rd NW 87114
Tigerwood Ct NW 87120
Tijeras Ave NE
101-297 87102
299-411 87102
1000-1599 87106
1601-1699 87106
Tijeras Ave NW 87102
Tijeras Creek Rd NW 87114
Tiley Dr NE 87110
Timan Ave & Pl 87114
Timberfalls Rd NW 87114
Timberidge Pl NW 87114
Timberline Ave NW 87120
Timothy Ct SW 87121
Tina Dr NE 87109
Tingley Dr SW 87104
Tinnin Rd NW 87107
Tintara Ave SW 87121
Tio Carlos St SW 87105
Tioga Rd NW 87120
Tiovivo Cir NW 87107
Tippett St NE 87112
Titleist Dr NE 87112
Tivoli Ave NE 87111
Tobacco Rd SW 87105
Todd St NE 87109
Todos Santos St NW 87120
Tohatchi Trl NW 87104
Tokachi Dr NW 87120
Tokay Ct NE 87113
Tokay Rd NE 87107
Tokay St NE
5800-5898 87107
5900-5999 87107
6301-6697 87113
6699-6824 87113
6826-6898 87113
Toledo St NW 87114
Tolleson Ave NW 87114
Toltec Rd NE 87111
Tomas Ct NW 87107
Tomas Ct SW 87121
Tomas St SW 87121
Tomasita Ct NE 87112

Tomasita St NE
500-698 87123
700-800 87123
802-898 87123
900-1799 87112
Tomatillo Ln SE 87123
Tombstone Rd NW 87114
Tome Ct NW 87114
Tomlinson Dr SE 87123
Tommie Ln SW 87105
Tompiro Dr NW 87120
Tony Barboa Rd SW 87105
Tony Sanchez Dr SE 87123
Topacio St NW 87114
Topanga Ct NE 87122
Topaz Ave NW 87114
Topeka St SE 87102
Topke Ct & Pl 87109
Tor Ln NE 87122
Toratolla Ct NW 87120
Toreador Dr NE 87111
Torin Dr NE 87122
Tornasol Ln NE 87113
Toro St SE 87123
Torpedo Pl NW 87120
Torrance St SE 87108
Torreon Ave SE 87102
Torreon Dr NE 87109
Torres Rd SW 87105
Torretta Dr SW 87121
Torribio Dr NE 87112
Torriso Ct SW 87121
Tortuga Way SW 87121
Tosca Rd NW 87114
Toscali Ct SW 87121
Toscana St NW 87114
Tottle Ave NW 87114
Toucan Pl NW 87114
Toulon Dr NE 87122
Tourmaline Dr NW 87114
Tourmaline Rd NE 87113
Tovar Pl SW 87121
Tower Rd SW 87121
Towne Center Ln NE 87106
Towne Park Dr NE 87123
Towner Ave NE
400-498 87102
4400-4499 87110
9600-12600 87112
12602-12698 87112
Towner Ave NW
400-498 87102
500-899 87102
1600-1800 87104
1802-1898 87104
Townsend Ave & Pl 87121
Trace Way Ave NW 87120
Tracy Ct & St 87111
Tradewind Rd NW 87121
Trading Post Trl SE 87123
Tradition Ln NE 87111
Trail Ct NW 87107
Trail Boss Dr NW 87114
Trail Ridge Rd NE 87109
Trail Vista Ct NE 87111
Trail Wind Rd NE 87113
Trailing Pl NW 87114
Trails End St NW 87120
Tramway Blvd NE
415-901 87123
1001-1497 87112
1499-1502 87112
1504-1550 87112
4700-4799 87111
7100-7838 87122
7840-7900 87122
7902-9698 87122
9601-9603 87113
Tramway Blvd SE 87123
Tramway Cir NE 87122
Tramway Ln NE 87122
Tramway Loop NE 87122
Tramway Pl NE 87122
Tramway Rd NE 87122
Tramway Lane Ct NE 87122
Tramway Ridge Dr NE 87111

Tramway Terrace Ct & Loop 87122
Tramway Vista Ct, Dr, Loop & Pl NE 87122
Tranquilino Ct NE 87102
Tranquilo Rd NE 87111
Transport St SE 87106
Travilla Dr NW 87114
Travina Ct SW 87121
Travis Rd NW 87114
Treasure Ct NW 87114
Treasure Stone Dr SW 87121
Tree Line Ave NW 87114
Trellis Dr NW 87107
Tres Gracias Dr NW 87120
Tres Lagunas Ln NE 87113
Tres Luceros Ct NW 87104
Tres Pinos Ln NW 87107
Tres Pistolas Trl NE 87123
Tres Ritos St SW 87121
Tres Vistas Ct & Rd 87120
Trevi Pl NW 87114
Trevino Loop NW 87114
Treviso Ct NE 87113
Triad Loop NE 87123
Triana Pl NW 87114
Tribal Road 40 SW 87105
Tribal Road 41 SW 87105
Tribal Road 54 SW 87105
Tribal Road 62 SW 87105
Tribal Road 63 SW 87105
Tribal Road 65 SW 87105
Tribal Road 66 SW 87105
Tribal Road 67 SW 87105
Tribal Road 70 SW 87105
Tribal Road 71 SW 87105
Tribal Road 72 SW 87105
Tribal Road 73 SW 87105
Tribal Road 74 SW 87105
Tribal Road 76 SW 87105
Tribal Road 78 SW 87105
Tribal Road 82 SW 87105
Tribal Road 83 SW 87105
Tribal Road 84 SW 87105
Tribal Road 86 SW 87105
Tribal Road 88 SW 87105
Tribal Road 90 SW 87105
Tricia Rd NE 87113
Trieste Ct NW 87114
Trillium Trl NE 87111
Trimble Blvd NE 87123
Trinidad St NE 87111
Trinity Pl NW 87107
Tristani Rd SW 87121
Trocadero Pl SW 87105
Trotter Rd SW 87121
Troy Ct & Pl 87123
Truchas Dr NE 87109
Trujillo Rd SW
1200-1599 87105
6000-6599 87121
Truman St NE
100-499 87108
600-3199 87110
3201-3399 87110
Truman St SE 87108
Trumbull Ave SE
100-198 87102
200-512 87102
514-698 87102
4500-8600 87108
8602-8698 87108
9000-9198 87123
9200-10299 87123
Trumbull Ave SW 87102
Tucker NE 87106
Tucson Rd NW 87120
Tuffs Ct NW 87114
Tulane Dr NE
100-1099 87106
3200-3398 87107
3400-4499 87107
Tulane Dr SE 87106
Tulane Pl NE 87106
Tularosa Trl NE 87111

Tulip St SW 87105
Tulipan Rd NW 87114
Tumbleweed NW 87120
Tumulus Dr NW 87120
Tuna Pl NW 87114
Tundra Swan Ct NW 87120
Tunnabora Ave SW 87121
Tunnell St SW 87105
Turing Dr SE 87106
Turnberry Ln NE 87111
Turner Ct, Dr & Pl 87123
Turquoise Ave & Ct 87123
Turrietta Ln SW 87105
Turtledove Ln NE 87109
Tuscany Ct & Dr 87114
Tuscarora Rd NW 87114
Twilight Ln NE 87122
Twilight Trail Pl NE 87111
Twin Harbor Ave NW 87121
Twin Oaks Dr NW 87120
Twin Peaks Rd SE 87123
Twisted Branch St NE 87113
Tyler Rd NE 87113
Tyler Rd NW 87107
Tyndall Ct SW 87121
Tyrone Ave NW 87107
Tyson Pl NE 87107
Union St NE 87109
Union Way NE 87107
Union Square St SE 87102
Unionville Ct NW 87114
Unitas Ct & Ln 87114
Universe Blvd NW 87114
University Blvd NE
201-397 87106
399-500 87106
502-798 87106
1100-1699 87102
1701-1999 87102
2500-2600 87107
2602-2898 87107
University Blvd SE 87106
University West Blvd SE 87106
Unser Blvd NW
300-399 87121
2200-5998 87120
6000-6004 87120
6006-6498 87120
10660-10798 87114
10800-10803 87114
10805-10805 87114
Unser Blvd SW 87121
Upland Ct & Dr 87112
Upper Canyon Ct NW 87120
Upper Meadow Ave SW 87121
Uptown Blvd & Loop 87110
Ursa Ave NW 87114
Utah Pl SE 87108
Utah St NE
100-900 87108
902-998 87108
1024-1030 87110
1032-3799 87110
Utah St SE 87108
Ute Dr NW 87105
Vail Ave SE
2800-3599 87106
3600-3699 87108
Vail Ct SE 87106
Vail Pl SE 87106
Val Verde Dr NE 87110
Val Verde Pl SW 87105
Val Verde Rd SW 87105
Valdez Ct & Dr 87112
Valdora Rd SW 87105
Valencia Dr NE
100-999 87108
1200-3599 87110
Valencia Dr SE 87108
Valencia Pl NE 87110
Valentino St NW 87120
Valerian Pl NE 87111
Valerie Pl NE 87111
Valle Ln NW 87107

Valle Alegre Rd NW 87120
Valle Alto Ct NW 87107
Valle Bonita Ln NW 87120
Valle Bosque Way NW 87120
Valle Caldera Rd SW 87121
Valle Del Sol Ct, Pl & Rd 87105
Valle Grande Rd SW 87105
Valle Rio Trl NW 87120
Valle Romantico Way NW 87120
Valle Santo Trl NW 87120
Valle Verde Rd NW 87114
Valle Vidal Pl SW 87121
Valle Vista Dr NW 87120
Vallecito Dr NW 87114
Vallejo Pl NE 87122
Valletta St NW 87120
Valley Rd SW 87105
Valley Forge Pl & Rd 87109
Valley Garden Cir & Dr 87105
Valley Haven Ct NW 87107
Valley High Ave & St SE & SW 87105
Valley Park Dr SW 87105
Valley View Dr NW 87114
Valley View Dr SW 87121
Valplano Rd SE 87105
Valtierra Ct & Pl 87121
Valverde Dr SE 87108
Van Ct SW 87105
Van Buren Pl SE 87108
Van Buren St NE 87110
Van Christopher Dr NE 87111
Van Cleave Rd NW 87107
Van Horne Way SW 87121
Vancouver Ave NW 87114
Vanwhy SW 87121
Vasilion Pl NW 87120
Vassar Dr NE
400-1999 87106
2301-2717 87107
2719-3500 87107
3502-4098 87107
Vassar Dr SE 87106
Vassar Pl NE 87107
Vecchio Dr NW 87114
Vega Verde St SW 87105
Vega Vista Dr NW 87114
Velarde Ct & Rd 87107
Velma Ct & Pl 87112
Vendaval Ave NW 87114
Vendaval Hills Rd NW 87114
Venetian Way SW 87105
Venice Ave NE
5201-5597 87113
5599-7599 87113
7600-8399 87122
Ventana Ct SW 87105
Ventana Azul Ave NW 87114
Ventana Cielo Ave NW 87114
Ventana Hills Rd NW 87114
Ventana Oeste Dr NW 87114
Ventana Sol Dr NW 87114
Ventana Village Rd NW 87114
Ventanita Ct NW 87114
Venticello Dr NW 87114
Ventose Pl NW 87114
Ventura Ct NE 87122
Ventura Pl NE 87123
Ventura St NE
8001-8099 87109
8100-8198 87122
9201-9399 87122
Venus Ct NE 87112
Vera Rd SW 87105
Veranda Rd NE
3700-7199 87110
8901-8997 87111
8999-9099 87111
Veranda Rd NW
100-499 87107
424-424 87197
500-2798 87107
501-699 87107
Verano Ct NW 87120
Verbena Ct NE 87113
Verbena Pl NE 87112
Verdad Del Luz Ct SW 87121
Verde Rd SW 87105
Verdi Way NW 87114
Vermejo Dr NW 87107
Vermejo Park Dr SW 87121
Vermilion Ct NW 87120
Vermont St NE
100-599 87108
1000-3799 87110
Vermont St SE 87108
Vernon Ct NW 87114
Vernon Dr SE 87123
Verona St NW 87120
Veronica Dr NE 87111
Versailles Ave NE 87111
Vervain Dr NW 87114
Vesuvius Pl NW 87120
Via Alegre NE 87122
Via Arbolado SW 87121
Via Asombro NE 87122
Via Belleza SW 87121
Via Bueno NE 87113
Via Cadiz Ct NW 87104
Via Canale SW 87121
Via Chamisa NE 87113
Via Cometa SW 87121
Via Conejo NE 87111
Via Contenta NE 87113
Via Corta St SW 87105
Via Corta Del Sur Ct 87120
Via De Calma NE 87113
Via De Luna NE 87110
Via De Paz NE 87113
Via Del Cerro NE 87113
Via Del Oro SW 87121
Via Del Sol NE 87110
Via Del Sueno NE 87113
Via Desierto NE 87113
Via Elegante NE 87113
Via Encantada NE 87122
Via Granada Pl NW 87104
Via Macduffee Rd NE 87111
Via Madrid Ct & Dr 87104
Via Patria SW 87121
Via Paz SW 87121
Via Porto Rd NW 87104
Via Posada SE 87123
Via Serenita SW 87121
Via Sereno SW 87121
Via Seville Ct & Rd 87104
Via Tomas NE 87113
Via Tranquilo SW 87121
Via Vista St SE 87123
Via Vista Mesa NW 87114
Via Vista Norte NW 87114
Via Vista Parque NW 87114
Vic Rd NE 87112
Vicenza Dr NW 87114
Vicic Rd NW 87104
Vickrey Dr NE 87109
Vicksburg Dr NW 87120
Victoria Dr NW 87120
Victoria Falls Dr NE 87111
Vidal Pl NE 87123
Vidal Rd SW 87105
Vienna Dr NE 87111
Vierra Ave SW 87105
View Ct NE 87112
Viewcrest Pl NE 87112
Vigil Pl SW 87105
Vigo Ave SW 87121
Viking Dr SW 87121
Villa Dr NE 87111
Villa Camilla NE 87113
Villa Campo NE 87113
Villa Candela NE 87113
Villa Canela Ct NW 87107
Villa Celaje NE 87113
Villa Chamisa NE 87113
Villa Clavel NE 87113
Villa Corrales NE 87113
Villa Del Rey NE 87111
Villa Del Valle NE 87113
Villa Doro Way NW 87104
Villa Firenze Ln NE 87122
Villa Guadalupe NW 87114
Villa Lila St NE 87113
Villa Loma Ln NE 87111
Villa Los Ranchos NE 87113
Villa Montana NE 87113
Villa Rosado NE 87113
Villa Sandia Pl & Rd 87112
Villa Serena Pl 87121
Villa Sonrisa NE 87113
Villa Tulipan NE 87113
Villa Ventosa NE 87113
Village Ave NE 87122
Village Green Dr NE 87111
Villanueva Dr NE 87109
Villarrica St NW 87120
Ville Ct NE 87113
Vina Del Sol Dr NE 87122
Vinca Trl NE 87112
Vincent Ct NW 87105
Vincente SW 87105
Vinemont Pl NW 87120
Vineyard Rd NE 87113
Vineyard Rd NW 87107
Vineyard Ridge Ct & Rd 87122
Vinnie Rd SW 87105
Vintage Dr NE 87122
Vintner Ct & Dr 87122
Vinton St SW 87121
Viola Dr SW 87105
Violet St SW 87105
Violet Orchid Trl SW 87121
Violetas Rd NW 87104
Viramontes Rd NW 87114
Virginia St NE
100-611 87108
613-999 87108
1000-2999 87110
Virginia St SE 87108
Virgo Ct & St 87114
Visalia Way NE 87122
Vista Ct NE 87123
Vista Pl SE 87105
Vista Abajo Dr NE 87123
Vista Alameda NE 87113
Vista Alegre St NW 87120
Vista Alta Rd NW 87114
Vista Antigua Dr NW 87120
Vista Bella Pl NW 87114
Vista Bonita NE 87111
Vista Campo Rd NE 87109
Vista Cantera Ln NW 87114
Vista Casitas Dr NW 87114
Vista Cedro Ct NE 87109
Vista Chamisa Ln SW 87121
Vista Cielo Ave NW 87120
Vista Clara Ln SW 87121
Vista Clara Loop NW 87114
Vista De Luz Dr NW 87120
Vista De Paseo Rd NW 87120
Vista Del Angel SW 87121
Vista Del Arroyo Ave NE 87109
Vista Del Camino St SW 87105
Vista Del Cerro NE 87111
Vista Del Escuela Pl NE 87113
Vista Del Monte NE 87109
Vista Del Norte Dr & Rd 87113
Vista Del Oso Ct NE 87109
Vista Del Pueblo St SW 87121
Vista Del Rancho Rd NE 87113
Vista Del Rey Ct 87112
Vista Del Rio Rd SW 87105
Vista Del Sol Ct NW 87114
Vista Del Sol Dr NW
6700-6900 87120
6902-7198 87120
10400-10525 87114
10527-10529 87114
Vista Del Sur St NW 87120
Vista Del Valle Ct & St 87121
Vista Estrella Ln SW 87121
Vista Faisan Trl NW 87107
Vista Grande Dr NW
1000-1199 87105
2301-2397 87120
2399-3699 87120
Vista Hermosa Ct SW 87121
Vista Larga Ave & Ct 87106
Vista Lejana NE 87111
Vista Lejos Ln SW 87121
Vista Luna Ln SW 87121
Vista Manzano Ave SW 87121
Vista Maravillosa NW 87120
Vista Montano St NW 87120
Vista Monte Dr NE 87113
Vista Oeste NW 87120
Vista Oriente NW 87120
Vista Penasco Ave SW 87121
Vista Point Ct NE 87123
Vista Sandia NE 87111
Vista Sandia Dr NW 87120
Vista Serena Ln SW 87121
Vista Sierra St NW 87120
Vista Terraza Dr NW 87120
Vista Tijeras Ln SW 87121
Vista Valle Ave NW 87120
Vista Verde Pl NW 87120
Vista Viva Ln SW 87121
Vista Volcan Ln SW 87121
Vistas Dr NE 87113
Vistazo Pl SE 87123
Vito Romero Rd SW 87105
Vivaldi Trl NW 87114
Vivian Dr NE 87109
Volcano Rd NW 87121
Volunteer St NE 87109
Vulcan NW 87120
Vulcan Vista Dr NE 87111
Wade Cir & St 87112
Wadi Musa Dr NE 87122
Wagon Gate Trl SW 87121
Wagon Mound Ct, Dr & Trl 87120
Wagon Train Ct, Dr & Ln 87123
Wagon Wheel St SE 87123
Walden Ln NE 87111
Waldie Rd SW 87105
Wales Ave NE 87111
Walker Dr NE 87112
Walkerway St NE 87111
Wallace Ave NE 87109
Wallace St SE 87105
Walnut Ave SW 87105
Walnut Canyon Rd SW 87121
Walter St NE & SE 87102
Walter Bambrook Pl NE 87122
War Admiral Dr SE 87123
Ward Dr NW 87120
Ward Rd SW 87121
Warm Sands Ct, Dr & Trl 87123
Warm Springs Rd NW 87120
Warm Wind Pl NW 87120
Warren Ln SW 87105
Wasatch Rd SE 87123
Washington Pl NE 87113
Washington St NE
200-599 87108
600-2999 87110
4300-6698 87109
6700-7300 87109
7302-7498 87109
8200-9099 87113
Washington St SE 87108
Water Stone Rd SW 87121
Waterbury Ave & Pl 87120
Watercress Dr NE 87113
Waterfall Dr SE 87123
Waterford Pl NE 87122
Waterlily Ct SE 87123
Waters Dr SW 87121
Watershed Dr NW 87120
Waterwillow Pl NW 87120
Watson Dr SE 87106
Waverly Dr NW 87120
Way Cross Ave NW 87120
Wayne Rd NW
200-303 87114
304-399 87114
5600-6599 87120
Waynesboro Pl & Rd 87120
Wedgewood Ave & Ct 87120
Weems Ave SW 87121
Wellesley Ct NE 87107
Wellesley Dr NE
100-198 87106
200-1599 87106
2400-4399 87107
Wellesley Dr SE 87106
Wellesley Pl NE 87106
Wellington NE 87111
Wells Dr NE
200-300 87123
302-398 87123
1400-1799 87112
Wells Fargo Trl NW 87120
Wellsburg Ave & Ct 87120
Welton Ct & Dr 87109
Wendell Rd SW 87121
Wenk Rd SW 87105
Wenonah Ave SE 87123
Wentworth NE 87111
Wesley Ct SW 87121
Wesmeco Rd SE 87102
Westbound Ave SW 87121
Westbrook Dr NW 87120
Westcourt Pl NW 87105
Westcreek Pl NW 87120
Westdale Way NW 87114
Westerfeld Dr NE
1000-1299 87112
3400-9699 87111
Western Ave SW 87121
Western Trl NW 87120
Western Breeze Ct NW 87120
Western Meadows Ct & Rd 87114
Western Skies Dr SE 87123
Westford Pl NW 87114
Westgate Ln NW 87107
Westlake Dr NE 87112
Weston Pl NW 87114
Westover Pl NW 87120
Westridge Ct NW 87114
Westridge Pl NE 87111
Westridge Pl NW 87114
Westside Dr NW 87114
Westview Ave & Ct 87123
Westward Ln NW 87120
Westwind St NE 87111
Westwood Ave NW 87120
Wexford St NW 87120
Wheeler Ave SE
100-198 87102
200-599 87102
1300-1799 87106
Wheelwright Ave NW 87120
Whimbrel Ct SW 87121
Whinerna St SE 87108
Whippoorwill Ln NE 87109
Whisper Dr SW 87121
Whisper Mesa St SW 87121
Whisper Pointe St SW 87121
Whisper Ridge Dr NW 87120
Whisper Wind St NW 87120
Whispering St SW 87121
Whispering Sands Ct SE 87123
Whisperwood Ct & Pl 87109
Whistler Ave NW 87114
White St NE 87109
White Cloud St NE 87112
White Pine Pl NE 87109
White Reserve Ave SW 87105
White Rim Pl NE 87112
White Rock Pl NE 87112
Whitehorn St SW 87121
Whiteman Dr NW 87120
Whiteoaks Dr NE 87122
Whitetail Dr & Rd 87122
Whitewood Ct NE 87109
Whiting Rd SW 87105
Whittier Pl SE 87123
Wickenburg St NW 87114
Wilbur Ave & Rd 87105
Wild Dunes Rd NW 87120
Wild Horse Trl SE 87123
Wild Olive Ave NE 87113
Wild Onion Ave NW 87114
Wild Plum Way NW 87120
Wild Turkey Dr NW 87114
Wilda Dr & Pl 87114
Wilder Ln NW 87104
Wilderness Pl & Trl 87111
Wildfire Rd NW 87114
Wildflower Trl NE 87111
Wildstream St NW 87120
Wildwood Ct NE 87111
Wildwood Ln NE 87111
Wildwood Ln SW 87105
Wilford Rd SW 87105
Wilkinson Rd SW 87105
Willard Rd NW 87114
William St SE 87102
William Moyers Ave NE 87122
Williams St SE 87105
Williamsburg Rd NW 87114
Willis Pl SW 87104
Willow Cir SE 87116
Willow Ct SE 87123
Willow Rd NE 87113
Willow Rd NW 87107
Willow Creek Pl NW 87114
Willow Run Dr NE 87113
Willow Springs Ct & Rd 87113
Willow View Ln NW 87120
Willow Wood Dr NW 87120
Willowbrook Pl NW 87114
Wills Way SW 87121
Willys Knight Rd NE 87112
Wilma Rd NW 87104
Wilmington NE 87111
Wilmoore Dr SE 87106
Wilshire Ave NE
4900-5098 87113
5100-6101 87113
6103-7199 87113
7801-9299 87122
9301-11899 87122
11901-12599 87122
Wilshire Ct NE 87122
Wilshire Dr SW 87105
Wilson Pl NE 87106
Wilson Hurley Ct & Pl 87122
Wilway Ave NE 87106
Wimbledon Dr NE 87111
Winans Dr NE 87109
Winchester Rd SW 87121
Winchester St NW 87120
N Wind Dr SW 87121
Wind Rd NW 87120
Wind Cave Dr NW 87114
Wind Mountain Rd NE 87112
Wind River St SE 87123
Windmill Ct & Rd 87114
Window Rock Ct NW 87120
Windridge Dr NW 87120
Windsong Pl & Rd 87121
Windsor Pl NE 87123
Windward Dr NW 87120
Winema Ct SE 87123
Wingate Ave NW 87120
Winn Dr SW 87105
Winncrest Trl NW 87114
Winnetka Ct NE 87111
Winona Ct NE 87112
Winslow Pl NW 87114
Winter Ave NE 87110
Winter Haven Dr NW 87120
Winter Sage Rd SW 87121
Winterwood Way SE 87123
Wisconsin St NE
100-599 87108
1600-2999 87110
Wisteria Ct SE 87116
Witcher Ave NE 87112
Witkin St SE 87106
Wolcott Ave NE 87109
Wolf Creek Rd SE 87123
Wolfberry Pl NE 87122
Wolters Pl NE 87106
Wolverine Dr NW 87120
Wood Ct NE 87112
Wood Rd SW 87105
Wood Duck Dr SW 87121
Wood Stork Ct NW 87114
Woodal St NE 87109
Woodburne Rd NW 87114
Woodcroft Dr NW 87114
Woodford Dr & Pl 87110
Woodhaven Dr NE 87109
Woodhill Dr NW 87120
Woodhollow Pl NW 87120
Woodland Ave NE 87112
Woodland Ave NW 87107
Woodleaf Dr NE 87109
Woodmar Ln NE 87111
Woodmount Ave NW 87114
Woodquail Dr NW 87114
Woodridge Dr NE 87109
Woodrose Rd NW 87114
Woodstar Ave NW 87114
Woodward Ave, Ctr & Pl SE, SW & NE 87102
Woodwind Dr NE 87109
Wren Ln NE 87109
Wren Walk Dr NE 87109
Wynview Ct NW 87120
Wyoming Blvd NE
100-703 87123
705-899 87123
1200-2699 87112
2700-4800 87111
4802-5298 87111
5301-5497 87109
5499-7999 87109
8001-8097 87113
8099-8300 87113
8302-8598 87113
Wyoming Blvd SE
110-699 87123
21001-21099 87116
Yakima Rd SW 87105
Yale Blvd NE
1001-1199 87106
4201-4297 87107
4299-4399 87107
4401-4499 87107
Yale Blvd SE 87106
Yankee Dr NE 87109
Yao Dr SW 87121
Yarbrough Pl NW 87120
Yarrow Trl NE 87112
Yarwood St NE 87109
Yeager Dr NE 87109
Yellow Pine Ln SW 87121
Yellowstone Rd NE 87111
Yellowwood Ct SE 87116
Yerba Rd SW 87121
Yipee Calle Ct NW 87120
Yorba Linda Dr SE 87123
Yorktown Ave NE 87109
Yosemite Dr NE 87111
Young Ave SW 87105
Yucatan Dr NE 87111
Yucca Cir NW 87120
Yucca Dr NW
100-499 87105

3600-3699 87120
Yucca Pl NW 87105
Yucca Hills Ct NW 87114
Yuma Ct NW 87120
Yuma Rd SW 87105
Yvonne Marie Dr & Pl 87114
Zafrio St NW 87114
Zaltana Rd NW 87120
Zambra Pl NE 87111
Zapateco St NW 87107
Zaragoza St SW 87121
Zartman Rd SW 87105
Zarzamora Ave NW 87120
Zarzuela Ave NW 87120
Zearing Ave & Pl 87104
Zelkova Cir SE 87116
Zena Lona Ct NE 87112
Zena Lona St NE
200-500 87123
502-598 87123
1100-1198 87112
1200-2599 87112
Zephyr Pl NW 87120
Zia Rd NE
5801-5899 87108
12000-12099 87123
12101-12199 87123
Zickert Pl & Rd 87104
Zimina Dr NW 87120
Zimmerman Ave NE 87110
Zinfandel Ave NE 87122
Zinnia Pl NW 87121
Zion Ct NE 87111
Zircon Pl SW 87121
Zorro Dr SE 87105
Zuni Rd SE
4301-4397 87108
4399-8699 87108
9000-9098 87123
Zurich Pl NE 87111
Zydecko Ave SW 87121

NUMBERED STREETS

1st St NW
2-514 87102
516-2599 87102
2700-3000 87107
3002-8098 87107
1st St SE 87116
1st St SW 87102
2nd St NW
110-122 87102
2601-2697 87107
8100-8298 87114
2nd St SW
106-112 87102
2900-3198 87105
3rd St NW
101-197 87102
199-1525 87102
1527-1899 87102
2700-4699 87107
3rd St SW
100-212 87102
214-1600 87102
1602-1612 87102
4900-5099 87105
4th St NW
100-106 87102
2600-2698 87107
7900-8956 87114
9132-9132 87184
9135-11099 87114
4th St SW
105-341 87102
4900-5199 87105
5th Ct NW 87107
5th St NW
315-603 87102
2601-2697 87107
8900-8999 87114
5th St SW
100-200 87102
201-201 87103
202-906 87102
4900-5107 87105
6th Ct NW 87107
6th St NW
106-110 87102
112-2299 87102
2301-2599 87102
2600-5464 87107
5466-5498 87107
6401-6499 87107
8900-8999 87114
6th St SW 87102
7th Ct NW 87107
7th St NW
111-217 87102
219-2299 87102
3500-4199 87107
8900-8999 87114
7th St SW 87102
8th Ct NW 87107
8th St NW
204-218 87102
220-2000 87102
2002-2098 87102
2600-4699 87107
8900-8999 87114
8th St SW 87102
9th St NW
200-206 87102
208-2400 87102
2402-2598 87102
2900-5499 87107
5501-5599 87107
8900-8999 87114
9th St SW 87102
10th Ct NW 87107
10th St NW
120-312 87102
314-315 87102
317-323 87102
1111-1111 87104
1113-1147 87104
2800-2998 87107
3000-4699 87107
10th St SW 87102
11th St NW
201-311 87102
313-936 87102
938-938 87102
1000-1225 87104
1227-1239 87104
3000-4699 87107
11th St SW 87102
12th Ct NW 87107
12th St NW
110-198 87102
200-914 87102
1003-1007 87104
1009-2309 87104
2311-2499 87104
2601-2797 87107
2799-5199 87107
12th St SW 87102
13th NW & SW 87102
14th Ct NW 87107
14th St NW
200-799 87104
801-999 87104
4800-4999 87107
14th St SW 87102
15th Ct NW 87107
15th St NW
312-1430 87104
1432-1502 87104
3901-3999 87107
15th St SW 87104
16th Ct NW 87107
16th St NW 87104
16th St SW 87104
17th Ct NW 87107
17th St NW 87104
18th St NW 87104
19th St NW 87104
20th St NW 87104
21st St NW 87104
22nd St NW 87104
23rd St NW 87104
40th St NW 87105
45th Ave SE 87116
46th NW & SW 87105
47th NW & SW 87105
48th St SW 87105
49th St NW 87105
50th St NW 87105
51st St NW
300-399 87105
2900-2999 87120
52nd NW & SW 87105
53rd NW & SW 87105
54th St NW 87105
55th St NW 87105
55th St SW 87121
56th St NW 87105
56th St SW 87121
57th Pl NW 87105
57th St NW 87105
57th St SW 87121
58th St NW 87105
59th St NW 87105
59th St SW 87121
60th St NW 87105
60th St SW 87121
61st St NW 87105
61st St SW 87121
62nd St NW 87105
62nd St SW 87121
63rd St NW 87105
63rd St SW 87121
64th St NW
100-399 87105
900-1000 87121
1002-1098 87121
4201-4299 87120
64th St SW 87121
65th St NW
100-299 87105
4100-4299 87120
65th St SW 87121
66th St NW 87120
67th St NW 87120
67th St SW 87121
68th St NW
901-999 87121
2000-3898 87120
68th St SW 87121
69th St NW 87121
70th St NW 87120
71st St NW 87120
72nd St NW 87121
1800-3798 87120
75th St NW 87120
75th St SW 87121
80th St NW 87120
81st St NW 87120
82nd St SW 87121
86th St SW 87121
90th St SW 87121
93rd St SW 87121
94th NW & SW 87121
97th St SW 87121
98th NW & SW 87121
106th St NW 87121
110th St SW 87121

ARTESIA NM

General Delivery 88210

POST OFFICE BOXES MAIN OFFICE STATIONS AND BRANCHES

Box No.s
All PO Boxes 88211

NAMED STREETS

All Street Addresses 88210

NUMBERED STREETS

All Street Addresses 88210

CARLSBAD NM

General Delivery 88220

POST OFFICE BOXES MAIN OFFICE STATIONS AND BRANCHES

Box No.s
All PO Boxes 88221

HIGHWAY CONTRACTS

66 88220

NAMED STREETS

All Street Addresses 88220

NUMBERED STREETS

All Street Addresses 88220

CLOVIS NM

General Delivery 88101

POST OFFICE BOXES MAIN OFFICE STATIONS AND BRANCHES

Box No.s
All PO Boxes 88102

NAMED STREETS

Acoma Dr 88101
Adams St 88101
Adenmor Ct 88101
N & S Aderholt Loop 88103
Adkins Ct 88101
N Air Commando Way 88103
S Air Commando Way 88103
W Air Commando Way 88101
Alabama St 88101
Alaska Ct 88101
W Allison Ave 88101
Alma St 88101
Almond Tree Ln 88101
Alphon St 88101
Altos Dr 88101
Ann Ave 88101
Anthony Dr 88101
Anvil Pl 88101
Anzio Ct 88101
Apache Rd 88101
Apollo Ct 88101
Appaloosa Dr 88101
Arbor Dr 88101
E Arcadia Ave 88103
W Arcadia Ave 88103
Arcadia Ct 88101
Arcineiga Dr 88101
Ardennes St 88101
E Argentia Ave 88103
Arizona St 88101
Arkansas Ct 88101
Armstrong 88101
Arrowhead Rd 88101
Ash St 88101
Asher Dr 88101
Ashford Dr 88101
Ashton St 88101
Aspen St 88101
Autumnwood Ct 88101
Avalanche Loop 88101
Avenue M 88101
Avery St 88101
Avondale Blvd 88101
Axtell St 88101
Baronne Ct 88101
Barton Ct 88101
Bataan Ct 88101
Belair Ave & Rd 88101
Belvoir Cir 88101
Ben Crenshaw Ct 88101
Ben Hogan Dr 88101
Benjamin Davis Dr 88101
N & S Beta St 88101
Billys Cir 88101
Birch St 88101
Bison Rd 88101
Blaine Cir 88101
Bluebird Pl 88101
Bob Jay Dr 88101
Bobwhite Ct 88101
Bolero Loop 88101
Bonney Ln 88101
Borneo Ct 88101
Bosc Ct 88101
E & W Brady Ave 88101
Brentwood Dr 88101
Brians Way 88101
Bridle Pl & Rd 88101
Briggs Ave 88101
Brionne Dr 88101
Brynhurst Ct 88101
Buccaneer Loop 88101
Buffalo Rd 88101
Burch Pl 88101
Burro Trl 88101
Cactus Dr 88101
Cades Ct 88101
Cain Ave 88101
Calan Ct 88101
Calhoun St 88101
California Ct 88101
Calle De Oro 88101
Cameo St 88101
Canton Ct 88101
Carmel Ln 88101
Carolina Ct & Loop 88101
E Casablanca Ave 88103
W Casablanca Ave
101-199 88101
208-298 88103
Cassino Ct 88101
Castle Ct & Rd 88101
Cedar St 88101
Cesar Chavez Dr 88101
Chama St 88101
Chanticleer Pl 88101
Chapman St 88101
Chapparal Ave & Cir 88101
Charles Reese Cir 88101
Charlotte St 88101
Chase Mdws 88101
Cherry Dr 88101
Cheyenne Dr 88101
N & S Chindit Blvd 88103
E & W Christopher Dr 88101
Circle Dr 88101
Circlewood Pl 88101
Claremont Ter 88101
Clarion Loop 88101
Clovis Ct 88101
Cobblestone Cir 88101
E & W Cochran Ave 88101
College Park Dr 88101
Collins Ave 88101
Colonial Est & Pkwy 88101
Columbia Ln 88101
Comer Dr 88101
Commerce Way 88101
Concord Rd 88101
Conestoga Trl 88101
Connecticut Ct 88101
N & S Connelly St 88101
Cooper Ct 88101
Corlington Ln 88101
Corrales Rd 88101
Cottonwood Dr 88101
Country Meadows Dr 88101
Courtland Cir 88101
Cr E 88101
Cr 10 88101
Cr 11 88101
Cr 12 88101
Cr 13 88101
Cr 14 88101
Cr 15 88101
Cr 16 88101
Cr 17 88101
Cr 17 1/2 88101
Cr 18 88101
Cr 19 88101
Cr 20 88101
Cr 21 88101
Cr 22 88101
Cr 23 88101
Cr 27 88101
Cr 29 88101
Cr 3 88101
Cr 4 88101
Cr 5 88101
Cr 6 88101
Cr 7 88101
Cr 8 88101
Cr 9 88101
Cr 9.3 88101
Cr 9.5 88101
Cr D 88101
Cr E 1/2 88101
Cr F 88101
Cr G 88101
Cr H 88101
Cr I 88101
Cr J 88101
Cr J.1 88101
Cr K 88101
Cr L 88101
Cr M 88101
Cr M.1 88101
Cr O 88101
Cr P 88101
Cr Q 88101
Cr R 88101
Cr T 88101
Cr U 88101
Cr V 88101
Cr X 88101
Cr Y 88101
Cravy Dr 88101
Crescent Dr 88101
Crimson Ave 88101
Crm 88101
Crossbow Cir 88101
Crusader Ct 88101
Curlew Pl 88101
Curran Dr 88101
Curry Ave 88101
Cypress St 88101
W D L Ingram Ave 88101
E D L Ingram Blvd 88103
N D L Ingram Blvd 88103
S D L Ingram Blvd 88103
W D L Ingram Blvd 88103
Dakota St 88101
Dale St 88101
Dartmouth St 88101
N & S Davis St 88101
Dawn Loop 88101
Daybreak Trl 88101
Debra St 88101
Delaware Ct 88101
Dellfield Ln 88101
Delores Dr 88101
N & S Delta St 88101
Dennis Pl 88101
Diamondhead Dr 88101
Diane Dr 88101
Dillon Rd 88101
Dixie Dr 88101
Dominion Way 88101
Don January Ave & Ct 88101
Dove Ct 88101
N & S Dr Martin Luther King Jr Blvd 88101
Duckworth Ave 88101
Dusk Ln 88101
Eagle Way 88101
Earlmont Ln 88101
Eastridge Dr 88101
Echols Ave 88101
N & S Edwards St 88101
El Camino St 88101
Elizabeth Ct 88101
Elm St 88101
Engineers Way 88103
Enloe Dr 88101
S Enterprise Dr & Rd 88101
Erinn Pl 88101
Ernst Pl 88101
Ethan Ave 88101
W Eureka Ave 88103
Ewing St 88101
Fairfield Ave 88101
Fairlane Dr 88101
Fairmont Ct 88101
Fairway Ter N 88101
Falcon 88101
Fireball Dr 88101
Fitzhugh Ave 88101
Flagstone Dr 88101
N Flaricks Blvd 88103
Florida Loop 88101
S Fork Dr 88101
Franklin Dr 88101
Fred Daugherty Ave 88101
Frontier Rd 88101
Gail Jackson Ct 88101
Galeadel St 88101
N Gamma St 88101
Garrett Dr 88101
Gary St 88101
Gayland Dr 88101
Gayle St 88101
Gene Littler Ln 88101
Georgia St 88101
Gerry Dr 88101
Gidding St
100-198 88101
200-500 88101
417-417 88102
501-3499 88101
502-3498 88101
Gila St 88101
Gladstone St 88101
Glenarm Dr 88101
Glenfield Dr 88101
Golden St 88101
Golf Dr 88101
E & W Grand Ave 88101
Grayson Ct 88101
Green Acres Rd 88101
Grove Dr 88101
Guadalcanal Pl 88101
Gunstock Rd 88101
Hachita Hills Dr 88101
Hali Ln 88101
Hall St 88101
Hallum St 88101
E Hammett St 88101
Hammond Blvd 88101
Happy Ln 88101
Harrison Ave 88101
Hartley Blvd 88101
Harvard St 88101
Hawaii Ct 88101
Hawken Rd 88101
Heaslet St 88101
Hemlock St 88101
Herb St 88101
Heritage Rd 88101
Hickory St 88101
Hidalgo Cir 88101
Highland Dr 88101
Hillcrest Dr 88101
Hinkle St 88101
Hl Ave 88101
Hockenhull Ave 88101
Holmberg Dr 88101
Homestead St 88101
Hondo St 88101
Horn Ave 88101
Hound Ct 88101

E Howard St ... 88101
Howard Cowper Dr ... 88101
N & S Hull St ... 88101
Hummingbird Pl ... 88101
Humphrey Rd ... 88101
Huntington Way ... 88101
Husky Loop ... 88101
Illinois St ... 88101
Imperial Ct ... 88101
Indiana Ct ... 88101
Industrial Park Rd ... 88101
Innsdale Ter ... 88101
Iris Arbor Dr ... 88101
Jackrabbit Run ... 88101
Jadyn Ln ... 88101
Janeway St ... 88101
Jeanie Dr ... 88101
Jill Rd ... 88101
Joes Ln ... 88101
John Doe St ... 88101
Johnson St ... 88101
Jones St ... 88101
Jonquil Park Dr ... 88101
Juggler Loop ... 88101
June Ave ... 88101
Justin St ... 88101
Kaleigh Cir ... 88101
Kansas St ... 88101
Kasserine Pl ... 88101
Kathie Dr ... 88101
Katy Rd ... 88101
Kearny ... 88101
Kelli Rd ... 88101
Kelso Ave ... 88101
Kent Pl ... 88101
Kentucky Ct ... 88101
Kershner Dr ... 88101
Kimberly Ln ... 88101
Kingston Ave & Pl ... 88101
Kiowa Trl ... 88101
L Casillas Blvd ... 88101
La Fonda Rd ... 88101
La Linda St ... 88101
La Luz Rd ... 88101
La Salle Dr ... 88101
Lakeview Ter ... 88101
Lancaster Dr ... 88101
Las Palomas Rd ... 88101
Lasso Rd ... 88101
Laura Ln ... 88101
Laurelwood Dr ... 88101
Layton Ct ... 88101
Lazy Ln ... 88101
N & S Lea St ... 88101
Lesley St ... 88101
Lew Wallace Dr ... 88101
Lexington Rd ... 88101
Liberator Ave ... 88103
Lilac Dr ... 88101
Limestone ... 88101
Lincoln Ave ... 88101
Linkwood Ln ... 88101
Lisa Ave ... 88101
E & W Llano Estacado Blvd ... 88101
Llano Verde Cir ... 88101
Llano Vista Dr ... 88101
Lockwood Dr ... 88101
Locust St ... 88101
Lomas Pl ... 88101
Long Island St ... 88101
Lore St ... 88101
Lori D James Ct ... 88101
Lost Silver Trl ... 88101
Louisiana St ... 88101
Lowe Ave ... 88101
Lucile Ln ... 88101
Luzon Ct ... 88101
Lydia St ... 88101
Lynn Ave ... 88101
Mable St ... 88101
Mabry Dr ... 88101
Madison Rd ... 88101
N & S Main St ... 88101
E & W Manana Blvd ... 88101
Mandell Cir ... 88101
Manila Ct ... 88101
Manson Dr ... 88101
S Maple St ... 88101
Marco Rd ... 88101
Marcus St
1400-1499 ... 88101
1404-1498 ... 88103
Mareth Pl ... 88101
Mariah Dr ... 88101
Marie Reese Ct ... 88101
Mariposa Dr ... 88101
Market Loop ... 88101
Marlene Blvd ... 88101
Martin Ave ... 88101
Marvin Hass Blvd ... 88101
Mary St ... 88101
Maryland Ct ... 88101
Matador Ct ... 88101
E & W Mcdonald Ave ... 88101
Melrose St ... 88101
Mendenhall Ave ... 88101
Mercury Pl ... 88101
Merrill Dr ... 88101
N Merriwether St ... 88101
Mesa Ave ... 88101
Michigan Ct ... 88101
Midway Cir ... 88101
Miller St ... 88101
Mindoro Ct ... 88101
Mississippi St ... 88101
N Missouri St ... 88101
Mitchell St ... 88101
Moberly Dr ... 88101
Mockingbird Ln ... 88101
Mollie Cir ... 88101
Monterrey Dr ... 88101
Mora St ... 88101
Morse Ave ... 88101
Murray Dr ... 88101
Myrle St ... 88101
Nancy Lopez Dr ... 88101
Navajo Rd ... 88101
Nebraska Ct ... 88101
Neptune Ct ... 88101
New Jersey Ct ... 88101
New York Ct ... 88101
Newman Dr ... 88101
Nicklaus Dr ... 88101
Normandy Loop ... 88101
N & S Norris St ... 88101
North Dr ... 88101
Northglen Dr ... 88101
N & S Oak St ... 88101
Oakhurst Rd ... 88101
E & W Octagon St ... 88103
Olive Dr ... 88101
Ora Dr ... 88101
Oxbow Ln ... 88101
P R Lyons Ave ... 88101
Palmer Ct ... 88101
Pantelleria Pl ... 88101
Park Dr ... 88101
Parkland Dr ... 88101
Paseo Vlg ... 88101
Peacock Pl ... 88101
Pecos St ... 88101
Pennsylvania Ct ... 88101
Pettibone St ... 88101
Piedmont Dr ... 88101
Piersall Ave ... 88101
S Pile St ... 88101
Pine St ... 88101
Pineway Blvd ... 88101
Pinon St ... 88101
N Pioneer St ... 88101
E & W Plains Ave ... 88101
Playa Dr ... 88101
Player Pl ... 88101
E & W Plaza Dr ... 88101
Ploesti Ct ... 88101
Point Blank Loop ... 88101
Portales Ct ... 88101
Prado Rd ... 88101
Prairieview Dr ... 88101
N & S Prince St ... 88101
Providence Cir ... 88101
Pueblo Pt & Rd ... 88101
Purdue Ave ... 88101
Putnam Dr ... 88101
Quail Ct ... 88101
Raintree ... 88101
Ralph Boone ... 88101
Ranchero ... 88101
Raven Dr ... 88101
Ray Hardy Dr ... 88101
Rebaul Ct ... 88101
Redcloud Pl ... 88101
Redwing ... 88101
Redwood St ... 88101
Reese Dr ... 88101
N & S Reid St ... 88101
Remuda Dr ... 88101
Rencher St ... 88101
Rhode Island Ct ... 88101
Rio St ... 88101
Robbles St ... 88101
Robin Ct ... 88101
Rodeo Dr ... 88101
N Roosevelt Road 3 ... 88101
N Roosevelt Road F ... 88101
N Roosevelt Road G ... 88101
N Roosevelt Road H 1/2 ... 88101
Rope Rd ... 88101
Rosa Blvd ... 88101
Rose Dr ... 88101
Rosemont St ... 88101
Rosewood Dr ... 88101
S Ross St ... 88101
Ruth St ... 88101
Ryan Rd ... 88101
Saddle Rd ... 88101
Saint Andrews Dr ... 88101
Sam Snead Pl ... 88101
San Vincente Cir ... 88101
Sandia Dr ... 88101
N & S Sandoval St ... 88101
Sandpiper Ct ... 88101
Sandstone Dr ... 88101
Sandy Ln ... 88101
Sandzen Dr ... 88101
Santa Fe Ave ... 88101
Sara Layne ... 88101
Sasser Dr ... 88101
Saturn Cir ... 88101
Savannah Ct ... 88101
Schepps Blvd ... 88101
Scottsdale Dr ... 88101
Seaton Dr ... 88101
Settler Pl ... 88101
E Sextant Ave ... 88103
Shady Ln ... 88101
Sharondale Dr ... 88101
Sharps Ave ... 88101
Shay Marie Ct ... 88101
Sheffield Dr ... 88101
Sheldon St ... 88101
Sheridan St ... 88101
W Sheriff Ave ... 88101
Shingle Loop ... 88101
Siesta Ln ... 88101
Simmons St ... 88101
Sir Echo Dr ... 88101
Skyline Dr ... 88101
Smith Ave ... 88101
Sombrero ... 88101
Southland Dr ... 88101
Sparrow Ct ... 88101
Springfield Dr ... 88101
Springwood Dr ... 88101
Spur Rd ... 88101
Sr 19 ... 88101
Sr 209 ... 88101
Sr 245 ... 88101
Sr 288 ... 88101
Sr 289 ... 88101
Sr 311 ... 88101
Sr 467 ... 88101
Sr 523 ... 88101
Sr 77 ... 88101
Stagecoach Trl ... 88101
Stanton Pl ... 88101
Starkey Rd ... 88101
Starlite Dr ... 88101
State Ave ... 88101
Sterling Ave ... 88101
Stone Pl ... 88101
Stratford Ln ... 88101
Sugarbeet Rd ... 88101
Sumac Trl ... 88101
Summer Ct ... 88101
Sunland Dr ... 88101
Sunrise Blvd ... 88101
Sunset Dr ... 88101
Sutter Pl ... 88101
S Sycamore St ... 88101
Tallgrass Ln ... 88101
Tanning Way ... 88101
Tatum Ave ... 88101
Taylor Ln ... 88101
N & S Tennessee St ... 88101
W Terminal Ave ... 88103
Texas St ... 88101
Tharp St ... 88101
N Thomas St ... 88101
N & S Thornton St ... 88101
Tidal Wave Loop ... 88101
E & W Tierra Blanca Rd ... 88101
Tiffani Ln ... 88101
Timona St ... 88101
Tom Watson Dr ... 88101
Torreon Dr ... 88101
Townsgate Plz ... 88101
Traver St ... 88101
E & W Trident Ave ... 88103
Tucker Ave & Cir ... 88101
Tulane St ... 88101
N & S Upsilon St ... 88101
Us 60 70 84 ... 88101
Us 60 84 ... 88101
Us 70 ... 88101
Utah St ... 88101
Ute Rd ... 88101
S Valley Dr ... 88101
Varsity Loop ... 88101
Vega ... 88101
Ventura St ... 88101
Venus Ave ... 88101
Vermont Ct ... 88101
Victoria Ave ... 88101
Victory Loop ... 88101
N Village Dr ... 88101
Vinton St ... 88101
Virginia Ave ... 88101
Vivian Ave ... 88101
Vohs Pl ... 88101
W St ... 88103
Wade Blvd ... 88101
Waldell Massey Blvd ... 88101
Waldhauser St ... 88101
Wallace St ... 88101
N & S Walnut St ... 88101
Waneta Cir ... 88101
Washington St ... 88101
Waters Ct ... 88101
Weatherford St ... 88101
Weeden Dr ... 88101
West St ... 88101
Westchester St ... 88101
Westerfield Pl ... 88101
Western Ct ... 88101
Westgate St ... 88101
Weston St ... 88101
N & S Wheaton St ... 88101
Wheatridge Dr ... 88101
N & S Whippoorwill Way ... 88101
Wicks Ave ... 88101
Wilclark Rd ... 88101
W Wilhite Rd ... 88101
Williams Ave ... 88101
Willow St ... 88101
Wilmington Cir ... 88101
Wilshire Blvd ... 88101
Winchester St ... 88101
Windsor Way ... 88101
Wisconsin Ct ... 88101
Woodlark Rd ... 88101
Woods ... 88101
Woodson Way ... 88101
Wrangler Way ... 88101
Wright St ... 88101
Wyoming Ct ... 88101
Yale St ... 88101
York Dr ... 88101
E & W Yucca Ave ... 88101
Zia Pl ... 88101
Zulek St ... 88101

NUMBERED STREETS

E & W 1st ... 88101
E & W 2nd ... 88101
E & W 4th ... 88101
E & W 5th ... 88101
E & W 6th ... 88101
E & W 7th ... 88101
E & W 8th ... 88101
E & W 9th ... 88101
E & W 10th ... 88101
E & W 11th ... 88101
E & W 12th ... 88101
E & W 13th ... 88101
E & W 14th ... 88101
W 15th St ... 88101
E 16th St ... 88101
W 17th St ... 88101
W 18th St ... 88101
E & W 19th ... 88101
W 20th St ... 88101
E 21st St ... 88101
W 21st St
100-498 ... 88101
500-1225 ... 88101
1224-1224 ... 88102
1227-4099 ... 88101
1300-4098 ... 88101
E & W 22nd ... 88101

DEMING NM

General Delivery ... 88030

POST OFFICE BOXES MAIN OFFICE STATIONS AND BRANCHES

Box No.s
All PO Boxes ... 88031

HIGHWAY CONTRACTS

66, 69 ... 88030

NAMED STREETS

All Street Addresses ... 88030

NUMBERED STREETS

All Street Addresses ... 88030

ESPANOLA NM

General Delivery ... 87532

POST OFFICE BOXES MAIN OFFICE STATIONS AND BRANCHES

Box No.s
1 - 2999 ... 87532
3001 - 5240 ... 87533
5800 - 5800 ... 87532

RURAL ROUTES

01, 03, 04, 05 ... 87532

NAMED STREETS

All Street Addresses ... 87532

FARMINGTON NM

General Delivery ... 87401

POST OFFICE BOXES MAIN OFFICE STATIONS AND BRANCHES

Box No.s
1 - 6860 ... 87499
15001 - 15297 ... 87401
45850 - 45850 ... 87499

NAMED STREETS

Abbey Rd ... 87402
Acacia St ... 87401
Acoma Pl ... 87401
Afton Pl ... 87401
Airport Dr ... 87401
Albert Pl ... 87401
Alder St ... 87402
Alise Ave ... 87401
N & S Allen Ave ... 87401
Almon St ... 87401
Alpine Ave & Pl ... 87401
Alta Vista Dr ... 87402
Alyssa Ct ... 87402
Amoco Ct ... 87401
Amsden Dr ... 87401
Anasazi Trl ... 87402
Andrea Dr ... 87401
Angel Pl ... 87402
E & W Animas St ... 87401
Anna Ln ... 87401
Antelope Jct ... 87402
E & W Apache St ... 87401
Apple Ln ... 87402
Applewood Dr ... 87402
Arch Ln ... 87402
Arctic Ct & St ... 87402
Aredo De Carlos ... 87401
E & W Arrington St ... 87401
Arroyo Dr ... 87402
Ashurst Dr ... 87401
N Aspen Dr ... 87401
Atlantic St ... 87402
N & S Auburn Ave ... 87401
Augusta Dr ... 87402
Avery Ln ... 87402
Azalea St ... 87402
Bailey Ave ... 87401
Baltic Ave ... 87402
Barcelona Cir & Ct ... 87401
N Barliant Ave ... 87401
Bartens St ... 87402
Basin Rd ... 87401
Bayhill Dr ... 87402
Beckland Dr ... 87402
Beech St ... 87402
N & S Behrend Ave ... 87401
Bell Rd ... 87401
Bella Donna Ln ... 87401
Bella Vista Cir ... 87401
Bellflower Cir ... 87401
Bent Tree Cir & Ct ... 87402
Bering St ... 87402
Best St ... 87402
Big Cedar Ave ... 87402
Billie St ... 87401
Birmingham St ... 87402
Bishop Ln ... 87401
Blake Rd ... 87401
Bloomfield Blvd & Hwy ... 87401
Bluebell Ct ... 87401
Bluestone Ave ... 87401
S Bluffview Ave ... 87401
Bogie Ave ... 87402
Bonnie Cir ... 87401
S Bowen Ave ... 87401
N Bowman Ave ... 87401
E & W Boyd Dr ... 87401
Boyle St ... 87401
Bramble Ave ... 87401
Brenna Pl ... 87401
E Brentwood Cir ... 87401
Brenwood Dr ... 87401
Brianna Pl ... 87401
Briarwood Cir ... 87402
Brimhall Pl ... 87401
Bristol Ave ... 87402
Brittany Pl ... 87401
Brittlebrush Dr ... 87402
E & W Broadway St ... 87401
Brooke Pl ... 87401
Brookside Ct & Dr ... 87401
Brothers Ave ... 87402
Brown Ave ... 87401
S Browning Pkwy & Rd ... 87401
Brynie St ... 87401
Buckingham St ... 87402
Budding Ln ... 87402
N Buena Vista Ave ... 87401
Bunker Ct ... 87402
Burnham Rd ... 87401
Burson Ln ... 87402
N & S Butler Ave ... 87401
Cactus Trl ... 87402
Calla Lilly ... 87401
Calle De Suenos ... 87402
Calle Mio Ave ... 87401
Calle Norte Trl ... 87402
Camaron Ave ... 87402
Camellia St ... 87402
Camina Contenta ... 87401
Camina Entrada ... 87401
Camina Flora ... 87401
Camina Hermosa ... 87401
Camina Placer ... 87401
Camina Vega ... 87401
Camino Largo ... 87401
Camino Monte ... 87401
Camino Morro ... 87401
Camino Oro ... 87401
Camino Real ... 87401
Camino Rio ... 87401
Camino Sol ... 87401
Campana Way ... 87401
Cannery Ct ... 87401
N Canyon Pl ... 87401
Canyonview Cir & Dr ... 87401
Cardinal St ... 87401
Cardon Dr ... 87401
Caribbean Ave ... 87402
Carl St ... 87402
N & S Carlton Ave ... 87401
Carmel Dr ... 87401
Carolcreste Dr ... 87402
Casa Bonita ... 87401
Casa Linda Ct ... 87401
Caspian Ave ... 87402
Castle Pl ... 87402
Castle Rock Cir & Ct ... 87402
Catalina Ct ... 87401
Cedar Dr ... 87402
E Cedar St ... 87401
W Cedar St ... 87401
Cedarview Dr ... 87402
Cedarwood Dr & St ... 87402
Celtic Ave ... 87402
Centenary Ave ... 87402
Cerrillos Dr ... 87401
N Chaco Ave ... 87401
Chamisa Ln ... 87402
Chantelle St ... 87401
Chaparral Ave & Cir ... 87402
Charloff Pl ... 87401
Cherry Ave & Ln ... 87401
Cherry Hills Dr & Pl ... 87402

Cheva Ct 87402
Chico 87401
Chilton Ct 87401
Chimayo Ct 87402
Choke Cherry Trl 87401
Cillessen Ct 87401
Cimarron Cir 87402
Circle Dr 87401
Clark Ave 87401
N Clayton Ave 87402
Cleone Pl 87402
Cliffside Dr
1600-1698 87401
1700-2699 87401
2701-3497 87402
3499-3699 87402
3701-3999 87402
Club House Dr 87402
N Cochiti Ave 87401
Coggins St 87401
Colgate Ave 87402
Colibri Pl 87402
College Blvd 87402
E & W Comanche St 87401
S Commercial Ave 87401
Concho Dr & Pl 87401
Condor Pl 87401
Cooper St 87401
Copper Ave 87402
E Corcorran Dr 87401
Cordoba Way 87402
N Coronado Ave 87401
Cortez Way 87402
Cortland Dr 87401
Country Club Dr & Rd 87402
N & S Court Ave 87401
Coy Ave 87401
W Coyote Dr 87401
N Crescent Ave 87401
Crestridge Dr 87401
E Crestview Cir & Dr 87401
Crestwood Dr 87402
Cristo Rey St 87401
Criterion St 87402
Cuervo St 87401
Culpepper Ln 87401
Cunningham St 87401
Curtis Pl 87401
Cypress St 87402
Darby Ln 87402
Darlas Ln 87401
Daybreak Dr 87401
Dee St 87402
Deer Trail St 87401
Dekalb Rd 87401
Del Rio Ct 87402
Delhi Ave & Ter 87401
Dellwood Ct 87402
Desert Rose Trl 87401
E Diamond St 87401
W Dodd St 87401
Don Rovin Ln 87401
E Douglas St 87402
W Douglas St 87401
Dowell Rd 87401
S Drake Ave 87401
Driftwood Dr 87402
Drinen Ln 87402
N & S Dustin Ave & Rd 87401
Eastridge Ct 87401
Eastwind Ave 87401
Echo Ln 87401
Edgecliff Cir, Dr & Pl 87402
El Paso Dr 87401
El Redondo Cir 87401
Electric Ave 87401
Elk Ridge Ct 87401
E & W Elm St 87401
Emerald 87401
Emerrain Dr 87402
Enchantment Way 87401
Energy Ct 87401
English Dr, Pl & Rd 87402
Ensenada Way 87402
Escalante Trl 87402
Escondido Trl 87401
Espacio St 87401
Evans St 87402
Evergreen Dr 87402
Fairfax Ave 87402
Fairgrounds Rd 87401
N & S Fairview Ave & Pl 87401
Fairway Dr 87402
Falcon Pl 87401
Farmington Ave 87401
Farmview Ln 87401
Fawcett Ct 87401
Fawn Dr 87402
Fern Dr 87401
Figueroh Ave 87401
Finch Ave 87401
Foothills Dr 87402
Footjoy Rd 87402
Forrest Pl 87401
Fortuna Dr 87402
Four Seasons Pkwy 87401
Foutz Rd 87401
Fox St 87402
Francis Ave 87401
Franks Ln 87402
Game Refuge Rd 87401
Garnet 87401
N Gibson Ave 87401
Gila St 87402
N Giles Ave 87401
E & W Gladden Dr 87401
Glade Ln, Pl & Rd 87401
N Gladeview Dr 87401
Gold Ave 87402
Goldenrod Ave 87401
S Gooding Ln 87401
S Gower Rd 87401
Graham Rd 87401
Greenbriar Ave 87402
Greens Ct 87402
Greenwood Dr 87402
Griffin Ave 87401
Gulledge Rd 87401
Hall Pl 87401
Hallett Ave & Cir 87401
Hallmarc Dr 87402
Halls Way 87402
Hannon Dr 87402
Harbor Ln 87401
Harmony Dr 87402
Harper Hill Rd 87401
Harvard Dr 87402
Hawk Pl 87401
Hawk Eye St 87402
Hawkins Rd 87401
Head St 87401
Heights Dr 87401
Herrera Rd 87402
Hickory Ave 87402
Hicks Ave 87401
Hidden Acres Dr 87401
N & S Hidden Glenn St 87401
High Point Dr 87402
Highland Pl 87401
Highland View Dr 87402
Highway 170 87401
Hill N Dale Dr 87402
Hillcrest Pl 87402
Hillside Dr 87401
Hilltop Ct 87402
Hines Rd 87401
Hogan Ave & Pl 87401
Holiday Dr 87402
Hollyhock Cir 87401
Hollywood St 87401
Holmes Dr 87402
Homestead Rd 87401
Hood Mesa Trl
5301-5397 87401
5399-6300 87401
6302-6398 87401
7800-8298 87402
8300-8500 87402
8502-8698 87402
Hope Ave 87401
E & W Hopi St 87401
Hubbard Rd 87402
Hudson St 87402
N Huntzinger Ave 87401
Hutton Ave 87402
Hutton Rd 87402
S Hutton Rd 87401
Hydro Plant Rd 87401
Iles Ave 87402
Illinois Ave 87401
Indian Wells Ct 87402
Industrial Ave 87401
Inland St 87401
Inverness Dr 87402
Ironwood Ave 87402
E & W Isleta St 87401
Iva Dr 87401
S Ivie Ave 87401
Jack Rabbit Jct 87402
Janice Pl 87402
Jefferson Ave 87401
Jeffrey Dr 87401
Jemez Ave 87402
Johnson Ter 87402
Juneau St 87401
Juniper Pl 87402
Katherine Ave 87401
Kathleen Pl 87401
Katrina St 87402
Kayenta Cir & Dr 87402
Kenwood Cir 87401
Kerney Dr 87401
Kevin Cir 87402
Kingsway Dr 87402
Kira Dr 87402
Knollcrest Dr 87402
Knudsen Ave 87401
Kokopelli Trl 87401
Kristy St 87401
Kylie Pl 87401
La Belle Ave 87401
La Canada Ave 87401
La Colina Ct 87401
La Crosse Ave 87401
La Cuesta Ave 87401
La Grange Ave 87401
La Habra St 87401
La Luz Trl 87402
La Napa St 87401
La Palma Pl 87401
E & W La Plata Dr, Hwy & St 87401
La Puente Pl & St 87401
La Rue Ave 87401
La Salle St 87401
La Sierra Pl 87401
La Veta Dr 87402
Ladera Dr 87401
N & S Laguna Ave 87401
Lajoya Dr 87402
S Lake St 87401
Lakewood Dr 87402
Largo Cir & St 87402
Lark Ave 87401
Las Brisas Trl 87402
Laurel Ct 87402
Lauren St 87401
Laurie St 87401
Lee Ave & Ln 87402
Leighton Ave 87401
Leslie Pl 87402
N Lincoln Ave 87401
Linda Dr & Ln 87402
Linden Dr 87401
Lions Trl
1900-2098 87401
2100-2299 87401
2600-2698 87402
2700-3003 87402
3005-3099 87402
Little Eagle Ct 87401
Little Rabbit Dr 87401
Lobo Ridge Dr 87401
N & S Locke Ave 87401
Logans Cove Pl 87402
Lola Ln 87402
Loma Alto Dr 87402
N Loma Linda Ave 87401
Lomas St 87401
W Lonewolf Dr 87401
N & S Lorena Ave 87401
Los Arcos 87402
Los Ninos Pl 87402
Lupine Ln 87401
Lyle Ave 87402
Lynwood Dr 87401
Mable Dr 87402
Madison Ln 87401
Magnolia Ln 87402
E Main St
100-2699 87401
2700-8199 87402
W Main St 87401
Majesta Pl & St 87402
Malone Pl 87402
Malta Ave 87401
Manana Pl 87401
Manchester St 87402
Mancos Ln 87402
E & W Maple St 87401
Marcy Pl 87402
Maricopa Pl 87401
Marilyn Dr 87402
Marlene Ct 87402
Marlow Cir 87402
Marquette Ave 87402
Marseille Blvd 87402
Martello St 87402
Masonic Dr 87401
Mayfair Dr 87402
Mccarty Ave 87402
Mccolm Dr 87402
Mccormick School Rd 87401
Mcdonald Rd 87401
Mchenry Dr 87401
Mckinsey Ave 87402
Mead Ln 87402
Meadow Lark Ave 87401
Meadowview Dr 87401
Mediterranean Pl 87402
Melba Ln 87401
Melbourne Pl 87402
Melissa Ave 87401
N Melrose Dr 87401
Merino Kraal St 87401
Merlin Pl 87401
N Mesa Dr 87401
Mesa Del Oso 87402
N & S Mesa Verde Ave 87401
Mesa Vista Dr 87401
Meseta St 87401
Messina Dr 87402
Mickey Dr 87402
S Miller Ave 87401
Mirabel St 87401
E & W Mojave St 87401
Monarch St 87401
Monroe Rd 87401
Monteagle Dr 87402
N & S Monterey Ave & Cir 87401
Moonlight Mesa Dr 87401
Morgan Pl 87401
Morning Star Dr 87401
Mortensen Rd 87402
Mossey Cup Dr 87401
N Mossman Dr 87401
N Mountain View Dr 87401
Mountview Ave 87401
Mulligan Rd 87402
Municipal Dr 87401
E & W Murray Dr 87401
E & W Nambe St 87401
Naples Dr 87402
Natane Ave 87401
Nathan Ave 87401
E & W Navajo St 87401
Nelson Ave 87401
Nm 170 87401
Northgate Ln 87401
Northridge Ct & Dr 87401
Northwood Cir & Dr 87401
Oak St 87401
Ocio Pl & St 87401
Old Aztec Hwy 87402
Old Butler Ave 87401
Old Course Dr 87402
Old Mission Rd 87401
N & S Orchard Ave & Dr 87401
E Orchard Homes Dr 87401
Oriole Ave 87401
Oscar Ln 87401
Otono Cir 87401
Ouray Ave 87401
Pacific St 87402
Padilla Dr 87401
Pallas St 87401
Palo Verde St 87401
Palomas Cir 87401
Paralee Dr 87401
N Park Pl 87401
Parkland Cir 87401
Parque De Oeste Dr 87401
Parque Del Norte Dr 87401
Paseo Del Rancho 87402
Peace Valley Rd 87402
Peach St 87401
Peargrove Ln 87401
Pecos St 87402
Pheasant Ct 87401
Phillips Rd 87401
Picuris Ave 87402
Piedra Vista Dr 87402
W Piedras St 87401
Pima Ave 87402
Pine St 87402
Pinecroft 87402
Pinehurst 87402
E & W Pinon St 87401
Pinon Frontage Rd 87402
E Pinon Frontage Rd 87402
Pinon Hills Blvd 87402
Placitas Trl 87401
Plaza Dr 87402
Plum St 87401
N Pontiac Dr 87401
Poplar St 87401
Poquita St 87402
Positive Way 87401
Precept Way 87402
Primavera Dr 87401
Primrose Pl 87401
Princeton Ave 87402
Pryor Ln 87402
Putter Pl 87402
Quail Run 87402
Queens Way Dr 87402
Quince St 87401
Rabbit Run Ct 87401
Rabbitbrush Dr 87402
Rail Rd 87402
Ranch Ct & Dr 87401
Rancho De Animas Ct & Dr 87402
Randolph Ave 87401
Ravella Dr 87402
Rayos Del Sol Dr 87401
Red Rock Ct & Dr 87402
Reilly Ave 87401
Resource Ave 87401
Ridge Lea Ct 87401
Ridgecrest Dr 87401
Ridgeview Dr 87401
Ridgeway Pl 87401
Rimview Pl 87402
Rinconada St 87402
Rio St 87402
Rio Vista Ct & Way 87401
Rita St 87401
River Rd 87401
River Ranch Rd 87401
Riverside Dr 87401
Riverstone Rd 87401
Riverview Ln 87401
Road 1633 87401
Road 1634 87401
Road 1636 87401
Road 1639 87401
Road 1738 87401
Road 1740 87401
Road 1741 87401
Road 1764 87401
Road 1768 87401
Road 1783 87401
Road 1788 87401
Road 1790 87401
Road 1798 87401
Road 1799 87401
Road 1800 87401
Road 1947 87401
Road 1948 87401
Road 1952 87401
Road 1956 87401
Road 1990 87401
Road 3000 87401
Road 3333 87401
Road 350 87401
Road 3720 87401
Road 3721 87401
Road 3773 87401
Road 3775 87401
Road 3776 87401
Road 3777 87401
Road 3778 87401
Road 3779 87401
Road 3780 87401
Road 3781 87401
Road 3782 87401
Road 3783 87401
Road 3785 87401
Road 3786 87401
Road 3787 87401
Road 3788 87401
Road 3791 87401
Road 390 87401
Road 3900 87401
Road 3934 87401
Road 3935 87401
Road 3936 87401
Road 3937 87401
Road 3938 87401
Road 3939 87401
Road 3940 87401
Road 3942 87401
Road 3943 87401
Road 39431 87401
Road 3944 87401
Road 3945 87401
Road 3950 87401
Road 39509 87401
Road 3953 87401
Road 3954 87401
Road 3955 87401
Road 3956 87401
Road 3957 87401
Road 3958 87401
Road 3959 87401
Road 3960 87401
Road 3961 87401
Road 3962 87401
Road 3965 87401
Road 5209 87401
Road 5211 87401
Road 5217 87401
Road 5235 87401
Road 5243 87401
Road 5267 87401
Road 5270 87401
Road 5290 87401
Road 5291 87401
Road 5292 87401
Road 5293 87401
Road 5294 87401
Road 5295 87401
Road 52951 87401
Road 5296 87401
Road 5297 87401
Road 5299 87401
Road 5322 87401
Road 5323 87401
Road 5324 87401
Road 5330 87401
Road 5334 87401
Road 5336 87401
Road 5364 87401
Road 5367 87401
Road 5368 87401
Road 5370 87401
Road 5371 87401
Road 5374 87401
Road 5377 87401
Road 5387 87401
Road 5398 87401
Road 5402 87401
Road 5431 87401
Road 5433 87401
Road 5441 87401
Road 5455 87401
Road 5457 87401
Road 5466 87401
Road 5467 87401
Road 5468 87401
Road 5470 87401
Road 5472 87401
Road 5473 87401
Road 5474 87401
Road 5476 87401
Road 5478 87401
Road 5479 87401
Road 5480 87401
Road 5481 87401
Road 5482 87401
Road 5483 87401
Road 5485 87401
Road 5487 87401
Road 5490 87401
Road 5499 87401
Road 5500 87401
Road 5568 87401
Road 5569 87401
Road 5570 87401
Road 5571 87401
Road 5572 87401
Road 5573 87401
Road 5574 87401
Road 5575 87401
Road 5577 87401
Road 5578 87401
Road 5579 87401
Road 5580 87401
Road 5581 87401
Road 5582 87401
Road 5583 87401
Road 5584 87401
Road 5585 87401
Road 5586 87401
Road 5587 87401
Road 5588 87401
Road 5589 87401
Road 5590 87401
Road 5591 87401
Road 5720 87401
Road 5723 87401
Road 5753 87401
Road 5756 87401
Road 5758 87401
Road 5759 87401
Road 5760 87401
Road 5761 87401
Road 5769 87401
Road 5772 87401
Road 5775 87401
Road 5777 87401
Road 5778 87401
Road 5779 87401
Road 5787 87401
Road 5793 87401
Road 5795 87401
Road 5803 87401
Road 5809 87401
Road 5817 87401
Road 5821 87401
Road 5841 87401
Road 5859 87401
Road 5860 87401
Road 6015 87401
Road 6050 87401

Road 6052 87401
Road 6054 87401
Road 6055 87401
Road 6065 87401
Road 6067 87401
Road 6070 87401
Road 6071 87401
Road 6100 87401
Roberts Rd 87402
Robin Ave 87401
Rochester Ave 87402
Rockcress Pl 87401
Rollo Way 87401
Rosa St 87401
W Ross St 87401
Rowe Ave 87402
Rustic Pl 87401
Sage Ct & Dr 87401
Sagebrush Dr 87402
Saguaro Trl 87401
Saint Andrews Dr 87402
Saint James Pl 87401
Saint Michaels Dr 87401
Salida Del Sol Dr 87401
Samantha Ln 87402
San Juan Blvd & Pl 87401
San Lucas Ct 87402
San Marcos Dr 87402
San Medina Ave 87401
San Miguel St 87401
N San Paula Ave 87401
Sand Ave 87402
Sandalwood Dr 87402
Sandia Ct 87401
Sandra Ln 87402
Sandstone Ave 87401
Santa Ana Dr 87402
Santa Barbara Dr 87401
Santa Clara Dr 87402
Santa Fe Ct 87401
Santa Theresa Ct 87402
N Santiago Ave 87401
Santo Domingo Dr 87402
Sapphire St 87401
Scanlon Dr 87402
Schmitt Rd 87402
Schofield Ln 87401
N & S Schwartz Ave 87401
Scott Ave 87402
Sea Pines Ct 87402
Sedona Ct 87401
Self Ln 87402
Shadow Valley Ln 87401
Shady Ln 87401
Shannon Ln 87401
Sherwood St 87402
Shiprock St 87401
Sierra Vista Dr 87402
Silver Ave 87402
S Silver St 87401
Skyline Ct & Dr 87401
Smith Ln 87401
Snowdrift Ln 87401
Soaring Eagle Dr 87401
Sol Rey Ct 87402
Southside River Rd 87401
Spencer Dr 87401
Spring Ave 87402
Spring Mist Ln 87401
Springfield Way 87401
E Spruce St 87401
Staghorn Pl 87401
Stanford Ave 87402
Star Ln 87402
Sullivan Ave 87401
Summer Solstice 87401
Summer Wind 87401
Summit Dr 87401
Sundance Rd 87401
Sundown Rd 87401
Sunrise Cir, Ct & Pkwy 87401
N & W Sunset Ave & Pl 87401
N Suntuoso Ct 87401
Sycamore St 87401
Tamarack St 87401
Tampico Ct, Pl & Way 87402
Taos Ave 87401
Tarry Terrace Dr 87402
Taylor Dr 87401
Tear Drop Ct 87402
Tee Ct & Dr 87402
Terence Ave 87402
Terrace Dr 87402
Tesoro Pl 87401
Teton Cir & Dr 87401
Thomas Dr 87402
Tierra Ct 87401
Tijeras Ave 87402
Titleist Ct 87402
Tory Ave 87401
Tosha St 87401
Tranquility Ct 87401
Troy King Rd 87401
N & S Tucker Ave 87401
Tulane Ave 87402
Turning Leaf Ln 87401
Tuscany Ct & Way 87402
E & W Twilight Dr 87401
Twin Peaks Blvd 87401
E & W Tycksen Dr 87401
Us 64 87401
E & W Ute St 87401
Utton Ln 87401
Valentine Rd 87401
Valle Bonita Dr 87401
Valle Vista Dr 87401
Valley View Ave 87402
Veda Ln 87402
Venada Cir 87401
Ventana Cir 87401
Via Del Oro Dr 87402
Victoria Way 87402
Villa View Dr 87402
N & S Vine Ave 87401
Virden St 87401
N Vista Cir 87401
Vista Grande Dr 87401
Vista Hermosa Trl 87401
Vista Pinon Dr 87401
N & S Wagner Ave 87401
N Wall Ave 87401
Walnut Dr 87401
Washington Ave 87402
N Watson Ave 87401
Webb Rd 87401
Wellington Pl & St 87402
N Western Ave 87401
Westland Park Dr 87401
Westview Ln 87401
Westwind Ave 87401
Wildflower Dr 87401
Wildflower Mesa Dr 87401
Wildwood St 87402
Williams Dr 87401
Willow St 87401
Wilshire Dr 87402
Windsor Dr 87402
Winnifred Dr 87402
Winter Ct & Park 87401
Winter Solstice 87401
Wolf Ct 87401
Woodland Ct 87402
Yale Dr 87402
Yarrow Trl 87401
York Ave 87401
Yorkshire St 87402
Yucca Ave 87401
Zia Ct 87401
Zuni Dr & Pl 87401

NUMBERED STREETS

1st Ave 87402
E 10th St 87401
E 11th St 87401
E 12th St 87401
E 13th St 87401
E 14th St 87401
E 15th St 87401
E 16th St 87401
E 17th St 87401
E 18th St
- 300-398 87401
- 2700-2999 87402

E 19th St
- 1801-1997 87401
- 1999-2099 87401
- 2700-2798 87402
- 2800-2999 87402

E 20th St
- 300-2699 87401
- 2700-3000 87402

W 20th St 87401
E 21st St 87401
E 22nd St
- 700-2699 87401
- 2700-3099 87402

E 23rd St
- 701-797 87401
- 2900-3099 87402

E 24th St
- 800-2699 87401
- 2900-3099 87402

W 24th St 87401
E & W 25th 87401
E & W 26th 87401
E & W 27th 87401
E 28th St 87401
E 30th Cir 87402
E 30th Pl 87402
E 30th St
- 100-2399 87401
- 2401-2599 87401
- 2600-4099 87402

W 30th St 87401
E & W 31st 87401
E & W 32nd 87401
E & W 33rd 87401
E & W 35th 87401
E 36th St 87401
E 37th St 87401
E & W 38th 87401
39th Pl & St 87401

GALLUP NM

General Delivery 87301

POST OFFICE BOXES MAIN OFFICE STATIONS AND BRANCHES

Box No.s
All PO Boxes 87305

HIGHWAY CONTRACTS

30, 31, 32, 33, 57 87301

NAMED STREETS

Abel Ct 87301
E & W Adams Ave 87301
Adobe Ct 87301
Aida Ct 87301
Alexander Cir 87301
All American Dr 87301
N Alma Dr 87301
Alto St 87301
Anthony Ave 87301
Anton St 87301
Apache Cir & Ct 87301
Arizona St 87301
Arnold Cir, Pl & St 87301
E Aztec Ave 87301
W Aztec Ave
- 100-951 87301
- 950-950 87305
- 953-1803 87301
- 1000-1998 87301

Aztec Ct 87301
Baca Ct 87301
Baja Ct 87301
Baker Ave 87301
Barbara Ave 87301
Basileo Dr 87301
Belle Dr 87301
Bishop Dr 87301
Black Diamond Canyon Dr 87301
Blue Hill Ave & Dr 87301
Boardman Dr 87301
Bobelu Cir 87301
Boggio Dr 87301
Bonito Ct 87301
Bortot Dr 87301
Boulder Cir, Dr & Rd 87301
Box Canyon Ave 87301
Boyd Ave 87301
S Bradley St 87301
W Buena Vista Ave 87301
Burke Dr 87301
Cabezon Ct 87301
Cactus Rd 87301
Caesar Dr 87301
Calle Pinon 87301
Camino De Los Caballos 87301
W Camino Del Monte 87301
Camino Del Sol 87301
Camino La Tierra 87301
Camino Rancheros 87301
Canoncito Ave 87301
Canyon Dechelly St 87301
Canyon View Dr 87301
N Carver St 87301
E Cedar Ave 87301
Cedar Hills Dr 87301
Cerrito Dr 87301
Chaco Dr 87301
Chamisal Ave 87301
Chee Dodge Blvd 87301
Church Rock Pl & St 87301
Cindy Ln 87301
Ciniza Ct & Dr 87301
S Clark St 87301
Clay Ave 87301
N & S Cliff Dr 87301
E & W Coal Ave 87301
Coal Basin Rd 87301
College Dr 87301
Copper Ave 87301
Cora Lee Dr 87301
S Country Club Dr & Pl 87301
County Road 1 87301
Coyote Canyon Dr 87301
Crestwood Ct 87301
Curtis Ave 87301
Dairy Dr 87301
Dakota Ln 87301
Dallago St 87301
Dani Cir & Dr 87301
Day St 87301
S Dean St 87301
Debra Dr 87301
Dee Ann Ave 87301
Defiance Ave 87301
Diamond Cir 87301
Donna Jean St 87301
Dulce Ct 87301
Edith Ave 87301
S Eighth St 87301
N Eleventh St 87301
Elizabeth St 87301
Elm Cir 87301
Elva Dr 87301
Escalante Rd 87301
Fairway Dr 87301
Fairways Cir 87301
N & S Fifth St 87301
N & S First St 87301
S Florence St 87301
Foothills Ave & Pl 87301
S Ford Dr 87301
N & S Fourth St 87301
Frances St 87301
Freedom Dr 87301
Fuhs Ave 87301
Garcia St 87301
George Ln 87301
Georgiana Dr 87301
Giant Crossing Rd 87301
Giovanetti Cir 87301
Gladden Ave 87301
Glenn St 87301
Gold Ave 87301
Gomez Dr 87301
N & S Grandview Dr 87301
E & W Green Ave 87301
Grey Hill Cir 87301
Gurley Ave 87301
Hamilton Rd 87301
Hasler Valley Rd 87301
Hazel Dr 87301
Helena Dr 87301
Hemlock Canyon Trl 87301
Henrietta Dr 87301
Hidden Cv 87301
N High St 87301
Highway 264 87301
E & W Hill Ave 87301
E & W Historic Highway 66 87301
Hopi Ct 87301
Hospital Dr 87301
W I-40 Frontage Rd 87301
Idaho Cir 87301
Ignacio St 87301
Jay St 87301
Jeff King St 87301
E & W Jefferson St 87301
Jm Montoya Blvd 87301
Julie Dr 87301
Kachina 87301
Kestral Rd 87301
Kevin Ct & Dr 87301
Kit Carson Dr 87301
Kiva Dr 87301
Klagetoh Dr 87301
Lacima Cir & Rd 87301
Laguna Cir 87301
Lance St 87301
Lewann Dr 87301
E & W Lincoln Ave 87301
Linda Dr 87301
Linda Vista Rd 87301
E & W Logan Ave 87301
Lookout Ave 87301
Lopez 87301
Low Mountain St 87301
E & W Maloney Ave 87301
Manuelito Dr 87301
Maple Ave 87301
Marcella Cir 87301
Marcy Cir, Ct & Ln 87301
Marguerite St 87301
Mariyana Ave & St 87301
Mark Ave 87301
Martinelli Dr 87301
Maya Dr 87301
Mazon Ave 87301
Mcbride Cir 87301
Mcdevitt Pl 87301
Mckee Dr 87301
N & S Mckinley Dr 87301
Mentmore Rd 87301
Merritt 87301
E & W Mesa Ave 87301
Mesquite Dr 87301
Metro Ave 87301
Middleton Cir 87301
Milda Ave 87301
Mine Run St 87301
N Mission St 87301
Mollica Dr 87301
Monterey Ct & Dr 87301
E Montoya Blvd 87301
E & W Morgan Ave & Cir 87301
Mossman Ave 87301
Mount Carmel Ave 87301
Mountain Loop 87301
Mountain View Cir & Dr 87301
Murray Dr 87301
S Navajo Cir & Dr 87301
Nevada Cir 87301
N & S Ninth St 87301
E & W Nizhoni Blvd 87301
Nm Highway 564 87301
Ortega 87301
Padre Canyon Rd 87301
W Park Ave 87301
Parmelee St 87301
Patton Dr 87301
Pecan Cir 87301
Peggy Ann Dr 87301
Peretti St 87301
Pershing Ave 87301
Philipina Ave 87301
Piano Ave 87301
E Pine Ave 87301
Pinon Ln 87301
Placida Dr 87301
Plateau Cir & Dr 87301
Pony Cir 87301
E & W Princeton Ave 87301
Pueblo Ct 87301
N & S Puerco Dr 87301
Pyramid Trail Rd 87301
Radosevich Dr 87301
Rancho Rd 87301
Red Bluff Ct 87301
Red Hill Dr 87301
Red Rock Dr 87301
Red Rock Park Dr 87301
Rico St 87301
Ridgecrest Ave 87301
Rimrock Dr 87301
Robin Rd 87301
Rocco Cir 87301
Rocky Point Cir 87301
Rocky View Cir 87301
S Romero Cir 87301
Round House Rd 87301
Rudy Dr 87301
Rupe Rd 87301
Ryan Ln 87301
Sage Ave 87301
Sagebrush Ln 87301
Saguaro Dr 87301
Sands Ct 87301
Sandstone Dr & Pl 87301
Sanostee Dr 87301
Sarracino Ct 87301
Schenso Dr 87301
Scott Dr 87301
N & S Second St 87301
N & S Seventh St 87301
Sierra Dr 87301
N & S Sixth St 87301
Sophie Ave 87301
Stagecoach Cir, Ct & Rd 87301
State Highway 602 87301
State Road 602 87301
N & S Strong Dr 87301
Sunde St 87301
Sunset Dr 87301
Susan Ave & Cir 87301
Tafoya Dr 87301
Tanner Ave 87301
N Tenth St 87301
N & S Third St 87301
Tocito Trl 87301
Todd Dr 87301
Toltec Dr 87301
Turquoise Ln 87301
Twin Butte 87301
Us Highway 491 87301
Utah Cir 87301
Ute Cir 87301
Valentina Dr 87301
S Valley View Rd 87301
Vandenbosch Pkwy 87301
Vega Ave 87301
Verdi Dr 87301
W Victoria Ave 87301
Villani Dr 87301
Viro Cir 87301
Vista Ave 87301
Wagon Rd 87301
Walnut Cir 87301
S We St 87301
Western Skies Rd 87301
Williams St 87301
E & W Wilson Ave 87301
S Woodrow Ave 87301
Wrangler 87301
Wyatt St 87301
Yei Ave 87301
Zane Dr 87301
Zecca Dr 87301
Zia Ct & Dr 87301
Zorena Ave 87301
Zuni Rd 87301

HOBBS NM

General Delivery 88240

POST OFFICE BOXES MAIN OFFICE STATIONS AND BRANCHES

Box No.s
All PO Boxes 88241

HIGHWAY CONTRACTS

61, 69, 76 88240
72, 73, 74, 75, 77 88242

NAMED STREETS

W Abby Rd 88242
E Abella Ln 88240
E Abo Dr 88240
Absher Dr 88240
N & W Acoma Ct & Dr 88240
N Adobe Dr 88240
Airport Rd 88240
E Alabama St 88242
W Alabama St
- 100-4899 88242
- 6500-8599 88240

E Alameda St 88240
E, N & W Albertson Cir & Dr 88240
W Alegre St 88242
E & W Alston St 88240
E Alto Dr 88240
Alvardo Ln 88240
W Antelope Ln 88242
E & W Apache Dr 88240
N Apodaca St 88240
E Arbors Ave 88240
E & W Arco Rd 88240
W Arizona St 88242
W Arkansas St 88242
W Armijo Ave 88242
E & W Arriba Dr 88240
E Arrow Ln 88240
E Ash St 88240
N Asher Rd 88242
S Asher Rd 88240
E Aspen St 88240
N & S Avenue A 88240
N & S Avenue B 88240
N & S Avenue C 88240
N Azotea St 88240
N Aztec St 88242
W Azul Dr 88240
N Baggett St 88242
E & W Baja Dr 88240
E Baregrass Ln 88242
N Bataan St 88240
Bay Dr 88240
Beard St 88240

Bel Aire Ct 88240
E Bell Pl 88240
Belmont Pl 88240
E & W Bender Blvd 88240
W Bendisti St 88242
N Bensing Rd
1700-8899 88240
10200-14499 88242
S Bensing Rd 88240
E & W Berry Dr 88240
N Billy St 88242
Billy Walker Rd 88240
N & W Blanco Dr 88240
Blue Quail Dr 88240
E Bond St 88240
N Bond St 88240
W Bond St 88242
Bradley Ct 88240
N Brand Dr 88240
N Braniff St 88242
E & N Brazos Ave & Pl 88240
Breanna St 88242
N Breckon Dr 88240
E Briarwood St 88240
W Brittany Dr 88242
Broadmoor Park 88240
W & E Broadway Pl & St 88240
E Bronc Rd 88240
S Bronco Dr 88240
W Broom Dr 88240
Bucknell Ct 88240
E Buena Suerta Dr 88242
W Burgess St 88242
N & S Burk St 88240
Business Park Blvd 88240
N Butler Dr 88242
E Butte St 88242
E & W Byers St 88240
W & N Cactus Ct & Ln 88242
E & W Cain St 88240
W California St 88242
N Calle Alto St 88242
N Calle Bonita St 88242
N Calle Chiquita Rd 88242
N Calle Grande 88240
W Calle Sur St 88240
N Camelot Dr 88242
W Camino Del Arco 88240
Camino Real 88240
E Campbell St 88240
N Campus St 88240
E Cannedy St 88242
N & W Canterbury Ln & St 88242
W Caprock St 88240
W Carlsbad Hwy 88240
S Carlton St 88240
Carr Ln 88240
N Carriage Rd 88242
E Carter Rd 88240
Casa Bonita 88242
W Casa Verde 88242
E & W Castle Ave 88240
Cat Claw 88242
W Catalpa St 88240
N Catchings 88242
N Catherine Dr 88240
Cattle Call Dr 88240
N & S Cecil St 88240
N Central Dr 88240
N Chama Dr 88240
W Chance Dr 88242
Charlcia Blvd 88240
N Chenault St 88242
E Cherokee Dr 88240
E Chickasaw St 88242
W Chico Dr 88240
E & S Childers Dr 88242
W Christopher Ln 88240
Chuckwagon Dr 88240
E Church Dr 88240
W Church St 88242
E Chuska St 88242
N Cibola Ave 88240
N & W Cielo Dr 88240
W Cielo Bonita 88242
E Cimarron Rd 88240
W & E Clearfork Cir & Dr 88240
E & W Clinton St 88240
Coal Ave & St 88240
N Cobb Dr 88240
W Cochiti Ave 88240
N Cochran St
201-297 88240
299-1299 88240
1301-1599 88240
5000-6099 88242
S Cochran St 88240
E Cody Ln 88240
N & S Coleman St 88240
W College Ln 88242
E College St 88240
E & W Colorado Ave 88242
W Comanche Dr 88240
Commerce Dr 88240
W Connecticut St 88242
N Conner St 88240
E Conquistador Ln 88240
S Continental Dr 88240
N Cook Ln 88242
W Cope Pl 88242
E & W Copper Ave 88240
E Corbett St 88240
Cordoba Ln 88240
N Cortez St 88240
Corto Cir 88240
E Cottonwood Ln 88242
N Cottrell St 88240
N Country Rd 88242
W Country Road 61 88240
NW & SW County Rd 88240
W Coyote Ln 88242
E Crosswhite St 88242
N Dairy St 88240
N Dal Paso St
100-4899 88240
4900-9199 88242
S Dal Paso St 88240
N Dalmont St
101-197 88240
199-1099 88240
7300-7499 88242
S Dalmont St 88240
Dartmouth Ct 88240
N Davis Ln 88242
W Dawson Dr 88240
W De Baca St 88242
W De Vargas St 88242
E Decker Rd 88240
W Delaware Ave 88242
N Delta St 88240
N Denson Dr 88240
N Denver City Hwy 88242
Desert Sage 88242
N Desert Willow Ln 88240
E Desoto St 88240
Donahue Ave 88240
S Douglas Ave 88240
W Drake St 88242
E Dunn St 88240
E & W Dunnam St 88240
E Eagle Dr 88240
N & S Eastern St 88240
S Edwards St 88240
El Caminito Dr 88240
El Centro 88240
El Nido 88240
N Eleanor Cir 88240
N & S Elm Blvd, Pl & St 88240
N Enterprise Dr 88240
N Eugenia Ln 88242
S Eunice Hwy 88240
W Eva St 88242
N Evans St 88240
E Everglade St 88240
Fairmont Ct 88240
S Farquhar St 88240
W Faught St 88242
S Fellowship Ln 88240
N Ferrett St 88242
Fiesta Dr 88240
N Finley Dr 88242
N Flamingo Dr 88240
W Florida St 88242
N Ford Pl 88240
N Fowler St
301-397 88240
399-4199 88240
4201-4299 88240
5000-5299 88242
5700-5799 88240
6000-6299 88242
S Fowler St 88240
N French Dr 88240
W Frey Ave 88242
E Gamblin St 88240
Gantt Ave 88240
Garcia Pl 88242
N Gardner Rd 88242
N Garfield Ln 88240
N Gary Ln 88240
S Gasper St 88240
W Georgia Ave 88242
Gerwick Ln 88240
S Gibbs St 88240
N Gila Dr 88240
N Gilbert Ave 88240
E Glorietta Dr 88240
Goff Pl 88240
Goins Ln 88240
E, W & N Gold Ave & Ct 88240
N Grayson St 88240
E Greebon St 88240
E & N Green Acres Dr 88240
Green Valley Trl 88240
N Greenwood Pl 88242
N Gregory St 88240
N Greyhound Pl 88242
W Grief St 88242
N Grimes St
100-4899 88240
5000-8499 88242
S Grimes St 88240
W Guadalupe St 88242
N Gulf St 88240
E & W Gypsy St 88240
Hallam St 88240
N Hamilton Dr 88242
S Hannah Rd 88240
E & W Harden Blvd 88240
E Hardy St 88240
N Harris St 88240
Harvard Ct 88240
Heizer Pkwy 88240
Heritage Ln 88240
Hermosa St 88240
W Hickman Dr 88240
E Hicks St 88240
E Highland Dr 88240
W Hightower Dr 88242
S Highway 18 88240
N Hillcrest Dr 88242
Hogue Pl 88240
W Hollis Dr 88240
N Hope Rd 88240
S Houston Ct 88240
N Houston St
100-3099 88240
7300-7599 88242
S Houston St 88240
E & W Humble St 88240
W Hunter St 88242
W Idaho Ave 88242
E Illinois St 88242
W Illinois St
500-4699 88242
6000-6999 88240
W Indiana St 88242
Industrial Dr 88240
W Iowa Ave 88242
W Iron Ave 88240
N Isaacs St 88242
E Isabella Ln 88242
N Ja Rob Ln 88242
Jack Gomez Blvd 88240
E Jackson Rd 88240
N Jade Ave 88240
W Jason St 88242
N & S Jefferson Pl & St 88240
Jemez Dr & St 88240
Jennifer Ln
7400-7599 88240
13200-13999 88242
W Jernigan Dr 88242
N & S Jerry Ln 88240
Jicarilla St 88240
W Joe Harvey Blvd 88240
N Johnson Rd 88242
S Johnson Rd 88240
W Jones Ln 88240
W Jones Rd 88242
N Judy Ln 88242
N Juniper Ln 88240
E Kansas St 88242
W Kansas St
400-798 88242
800-4999 88242
6200-6299 88240
W Kara St 88242
E Katy Ln 88242
E Keith Ln 88240
Khleem Rd 88240
N Kingsley Dr 88240
W Kiowa Ave 88240
E Kiva Dr 88240
Kk Ranch Rd 88242
E Knapp 88240
N Knowles Rd 88242
N Kornegay Ln 88242
W Kyleigh 88242
N La Mesa St 88242
Laguna 88240
W Lakeview Dr 88240
S Landfill Rd 88240
W Lanehart Dr 88240
W Laughlin Dr 88240
E & W Lawrence Rd 88242
E & W Lea St 88240
W Lead Ave 88240
Leanne St 88240
N & S Leech St 88240
Lewis Ln 88242
N & S Linam St 88240
E Lincoln Rd 88240
E Linda Ln 88240
E Llano Dr 88240
E & W Llano Grande Dr 88240
N Llewelyn St 88240
N Lobo Ct 88240
N Locust Ln 88240
E Lora Dr 88240
W Lorene Dr 88240
W Lost Horizons St 88240
E & W Lovelady Rd 88242
N Lovington Hwy 88240
W Lucky Cir 88240
E Luna Dr 88240
Lynn St 88240
W Macaw Ln 88242
W Mackenzie Dr 88240
Magdum Dr 88240
Magnolia 88240
W Mahan Dr 88240
E Main St 88240
W Mallard Ln 88242
E Manning St 88242
Maple St 88240
Marathon Rd 88240
N, S, E & W Marland Blvd, Pl & St 88240
Marquis Ln 88240
W Marr St 88242
N Martha St 88240
W Martin St 88242
N Matt Dr
2000-2099 88240
7900-8599 88242
Matthews Ct 88240
N Mauri Ln 88240
N & S Mckinley St 88240
N Meadowbrook St 88240
N Meadowlark St 88242
N Meadows Cir 88242
W Medlin St 88242
E & W Mesa Dr 88240
W Mesa Verde Dr 88240
Mescalero Dr 88240
E & W Mesquite Dr 88240
E Michigan Dr 88240
E & W Midwest St 88240
W Millen Dr
100-800 88242
802-2498 88242
3801-3999 88240
N Mimosa Ln 88240
Mini Ranch Rd 88240
N Mobile St 88240
N Mockingbird Ln 88242
N Mohawk St 88240
N Monarch St 88242
N Monsey St 88240
Montgomery St 88240
Monument Hwy 88240
Moose 88240
N Mora Dr 88240
W Morales St 88242
Morgan Ct 88240
N Morris Dr 88240
N Morris St
200-799 88240
801-899 88240
7300-7599 88242
S Morris St 88240
Mosely Cir 88240
N Mulberry Ln 88240
N Murray St 88240
E Nadine Rd 88240
Nambe St 88240
N National Dr 88242
E & W Navajo Dr & Loop 88240
N Nelson St 88242
E Nicks Ln 88240
N Northacres Dr 88240
N Northeast Dr 88240
N Northwest Dr 88240
N Noyes Dr 88242
E Oak St 88240
Oak Grove Ln 88242
N Oriole Dr 88240
W Oro Dr 88240
N Owens Pl 88240
W Paige Dr 88240
E & W Palace Ave 88240
Palo Verde 88242
N Paradise Ave 88242
W Paradise Ln 88242
E & W Park Pl & St 88240
S Parkway Dr 88240
Pawnee St 88242
N Peaches Ln 88240
Peacock 88240
N Pearl St 88242
N Pearl Valley Rd 88240
N Pecan Dr 88240
E Pecos Dr 88240
E Pedigree Ln 88240
E Penasco Dr 88240
N Pennington Dr 88240
E & W Permian Dr & Pl 88240
S Perrin St 88240
S Perry Dr 88240
Pevey Ln 88240
E Phantom Trce 88240
N Piedras Dr 88242
W & N Pine Dr & St 88240
Pinon Dr 88240
E & W Pinson St 88242
N Plainfield Dr 88242
W Ponderosa Dr 88242
N Pondinta St 88240
N Pool St 88242
Prairie Ln 88240
N & W Prairie Dog Ln 88242
W Princess Jeanne Dr 88240
Propps Dr 88240
W Pueblo Ave 88240
N Quiroz Dr 88240
W Ragsdale St 88240
E Rahe St 88240
W Rainbow Dr 88240
N Ralph Ct 88240
E Rancho Rd 88242
Randy Pl 88240
S Rash St 88240
N Red Oak Dr 88240
Redbud St 88242
Regency Sq 88242
Richards Rd 88240
N Ridge Ln 88242
W Roanway St 88242
N Robert Rd 88240
Roberts Camp Ln 88240
W Rogers Ln 88242
N & W Rojo Dr 88240
N Rolling Meadows St 88242
E Rose Ln 88240
E Rose Rd 88242
N Roth Rd 88240
N Roundup Dr 88242
E & W Roxana St 88240
Running Horse Ln 88240
E Rushin Rd 88242
N Russell Ave 88240
S Ryco Ln 88240
N Sacramento St 88242
Saddle Club Dr 88240
W Sage Dr 88242
Sage Brush St 88242
E Saint Anne Pl 88242
W Sally Ln 88240
N San Andres Dr 88240
San Joaquin 88242
W San Jose St 88242
N San Juan St 88242
N San Martin St 88242
N San Mateo St 88240
W San Miguel Dr 88242
E Sandcrest Dr 88242
Sandia Dr 88240
N Sandridge Dr 88240
S Sandy Ln 88240
E, N & W Sanger Pl & St 88240
E & W Santa Fe St 88242
W Sayers Dr 88240
Scenic Dr 88240
E & W Scharbauer St 88240
W Scott Pl 88242
E Seco Dr 88240
N & S Selman St 88240
E Seminole Hwy 88240
N Shady Ln 88242
N Shannon Rd 88242
W Shed Ln 88240
W Shell Rd 88240
W, N & S Shipp Dr & St 88240
S Short St 88240
E Siler Rd 88242
E & W Silver Cir & Dr 88240
E & W Skelly St 88240
W Smith Ln 88240
Smith Ranch Rd 88240
E & W Snyder St 88240
W Sockwell St 88242
E & W Spears Dr 88240
E & W Stanolind Rd 88240
Starlight Rd 88240
S Starling Dr 88240
Startem Rd 88240
N State Line Rd
7500-11099 88242
N Steven Dr 88240
E & W Stiles Rd 88242
Stonecrest Ct 88240
W Sunrise Cir 88240
Sunset Cir & Dr 88240
Sydney Ln 88242
T Bird Rd 88242
E & W Taos St 88240
N Tasker Dr 88240
N Tatum St 88242
E & W Taylor St 88240
E Teague Dr 88242
S Telephone Pole Rd 88240
E & W Temple Ave 88240
Terry Ct 88240
S Texaco Rd 88242
E Texas St 88240
N Thomas Dr 88240
Thompson Dr 88240
N Thorp St
100-198 88240
200-1299 88240
1301-1499 88240
13800-14499 88242
S Thorp St 88240
Thunderbird Cir 88240
Tipton Dr 88240
Tombly Ln 88240
N Tomlinson St 88242
W Toro 88240
E Townsend Pl 88240
Traditions Dr 88240
N Trail Ride Ln 88240
N Travis Dr 88240
N Tres Amigo Dr 88240
W Trevino Rd 88240
N Truman St 88240
W Tucker St 88242
E Tulsa St 88242
W Tumbleweed Dr 88242
N & S Turner St 88240
W Us Highway 62 180 88240
N & W Ute Pl & St 88240
Valdez Ct & St 88242
E, N & W Vega Ct & Dr 88240
E Vera St 88240
W Victoria Ln 88240
W & N Vista Ct & Dr 88240
N Wagon Wheel Dr 88242
E Walker Dr 88240
S Ward Ln 88240
N Warpath St 88240
N Waylon Rd 88240
E & W White St 88240
N & S Willow St 88240
Winker Rd 88240
E & N Wittman Dr 88242
E & W Wolfcamp Dr 88240
W Woodfin Dr 88242
W Woods Dr 88240
N World Dr 88242
E & W Yeso Cir, Dr & Pl 88240
E & N Yucca Dr 88240
E Yuciapa St 88242
E Zia Dr 88240
Zuni St 88240

NUMBERED STREETS

All Street Addresses 88240

LAS CRUCES NM

General Delivery 88001

POST OFFICE BOXES MAIN OFFICE STATIONS AND BRANCHES

Box No.s
1 - 2876 88004
3000 - 5850 88003
6001 - 8758 88006
9000 - 9000 88004

13001 - 14318 88013
15001 - 20007 88004
30001 - 30006 88003

NAMED STREETS

A J Miller Rd 88011
Aberdeen Angus Way 88012
Abiding Pl 88011
Abilene Ct 88011
Acacia Rd 88011
Academy Ct 88007
Acala St 88005
Achenbach Ct 88011
Achenbach Canyon Rd 88011
Acoma St 88001
Adaro Way 88011
Addington Rd 88005
Adobe Ln 88007
Adriatic Rd 88012
Advancement Ave 88007
Aegean Rd 88012
Aerosmith Ct 88012
Agate St 88012
Agave Dr 88001
Agave Ln 88012
Agave Pl 88001
Aggie Rodeo Dr 88011
Agua Azul Ct 88012
Agua Caliente Dr 88012
Agua Clara 88012
Agua De Vida Dr 88012
Agua Ladoso Ave 88012
Aguilera Ct 88007
Aguirre Ct 88011
Akers St 88005
N Alameda Blvd
101-147 88005
149-2111 88005
2113-2199 88005
2158-2198 88007
2200-2298 88005
S Alameda Blvd 88005
Alamo St 88001
Alamo Mine Trl 88011
Alamosa Ave 88005
Alba Rd 88012
Alberta Way 88011
Aldrich Rd 88011
Alhambra Ct 88007
Aliance Blvd 88007
Aliyah Rd 88007
Allande St 88012
Alma Rd 88011
N & S Almendra St 88001
Aloe Ct 88012
Aloe Vera Ln 88007
Alpine Ct 88011
Alta Mira Ct 88007
Alta Vista Pl 88011
Altura Ave 88001
Alumni Hall 88003
Alvillar Rd 88007
E Amador Ave 88001
W Amador Ave
100-198 88001
200-2899 88005
Amapola St 88007
Amarantha Ct 88007
Amarillo Del Sol 88007
Amber Dr 88012
Amethyst St 88012
Amis Ave 88005
Amistad Dr 88005
Amity Ct 88012
Ampere Rd 88007
Amy Pl 88005
Anasazi Ct 88012
Anasazi Trl 88011
Ancho Ave 88007
Ancona Ct 88007
Anderson Dr 88001
Andrews Dr 88001
Angel Fire Ct & Pl 88011
Anita Ct & Dr 88001
Answer Dr 88012
Antares St 88012
Antelope Trl 88001
Antelope Pass Dr 88012
Antonito Rd 88011
Apache Dr 88007
Apache Trl 88012
Apache Canyon Ct & Dr 88007
Apache Plume Ct 88011
Apex Mine Rd 88011
Apodaca Rd 88005
Apollo Dr 88005
Apple Cross Pl 88005
Apple Orchard Rd 88007
Apple Tree Ln 88007
Apple View Pl 88007
Applejack Ln 88005
April Pl 88007
Aquamarine Pl 88012
Arabela Dr 88012
Archuleta Rd 88005
Arcila Pl 88005
Arco De Goya 88007
Arco Iris St 88012
Ardis Dr 88011
Arena Dr 88012
Argus St 88005
Aries Ave 88005
Arizona Ave 88001
Arlington Ave 88001
Armadillo Ln 88007
N Armijo St 88005
N Armory Rd 88007
Armstrong Rd 88007
Arnold Palmer Ct 88011
Arrowhead Rd
3100-3300 88011
3302-3698 88011
9200-9699 88012
Arroyo Rd 88012
Arroyo Seco 88011
Arroyo Verde Ct & St 88011
Artifact Ln 88007
Artist Rd 88011
Ascencion Cir 88012
Ash Ave 88001
Aspen Ave & Ct 88005
Asteroid Ct 88011
Astor Dr 88001
Aswan Ct 88005
Athenian Way 88011
Atlas St 88012
Augustine Ave 88001
Augustus Rd 88001
Auriga Ct 88011
Aurora Pl 88012
Austin Dr 88001
Australite Ct 88012
Ava Ave 88012
Avalon Dr & Pl 88005
Avenida Blanco 88005
Avenida De Antigua 88005
Avenida De Mercado 88005
Avenida De Mesilla 88005
Avenida De Quintas 88005
Avenida Del Sol 88011
Avenida Encantada 88001
Avenida Sonrisa 88011
Avis Rd 88007
Avondale Dr 88005
Azalea Dr 88005
Aztec Dr 88011
Azteca Rd 88012
Azure Hills Rd 88011
B And J Ln 88007
Baca Rd
100-198 88007
200-299 88007
301-649 88007
690-714 88001
716-799 88001
Bad Archer Ln 88007
Baldwin St 88001
Baldy Peak Way 88011
Bales Rd 88007
Balsam Rd 88011
Bamert Rd 88007
Banegas Rd 88007
Banna Ct 88005
Baraka Ct 88011
Barcelona Ridge Rd 88007
Barclay Ct 88001
Barela Cir & Dr 88007
Barker Rd 88005
Barksdale Loop 88012
Barrel Cactus Ct 88011
Barry St 88005
Bask Ln 88005
Bason Dr 88005
Bataan Memorial E 88011
Bataan Memorial W 88012
Baudin Pl 88007
Bay Leaf Rd 88011
Bayard Ct 88001
Baylor Canyon Rd 88011
Baylor Peak Rd 88011
Bazille Pl 88007
Bear Claw Ln 88007
Bearcat Dr 88001
Beehive Ln 88012
Belen Pl 88005
Bell Ave 88005
Bell Rd 88012
Bella Sierra Ct & Dr 88011
Bellamah Cir & Dr 88001
Beltran Rd 88007
Ben Boldt Pl 88012
Benavidez Rd 88012
Bencomo Ln 88007
Benisa Pl 88011
Benito Juarez 88012
Bentley Dr 88001
Benton Ave 88001
Benz Dr 88001
Berkshire Ct 88005
Berry Patch Ave 88011
Bertals Ln 88012
Beryl St 88012
Betty Cir 88001
Beverly Pl 88001
Bex Ct & St 88005
Beyer Rd 88011
Bienes Pl 88007
Big Jim 88012
Big Sky Dr 88012
Big Spring St 88012
Big Tree Rd 88007
Bilbo Ln 88005
Birch Ct & Dr 88001
Bisbee Ct 88001
Bison Trl 88001
Bitter Creek Ln 88011
Black Hills Rd 88011
Black Quartz Rd 88011
Blackhawk St 88001
Blacktail Deer Ave 88007
Blair Canyon Dr 88011
Blazing Trail Rd 88007
Bleimeyer Rd 88007
Bloomdale Dr 88005
Blue Hawk Rd 88007
Blue Jay Rd 88007
Blue Mountain Dr 88012
Blue Topaz Ave 88012
Blueridge Ln 88005
Bluestone Trl 88011
Bluewater Ct 88012
Bogart Ln 88007
Boggy Ln 88005
Boise Dr 88001
Boldt St 88005
Boling Ln 88007
Bon Burt Ln 88005
Bonita Cir 88005
Borinquen Ct 88012
Borroughs St 88007
Bosque Seco Rd 88005
Boston Dr 88001
Bosworth Rd 88012
Bougainvillea Ct 88011
Boulder Cyn 88011
Boulder Canyon Ln 88011
Boulders Dr 88011
E Boutz Rd
100-132 88005
134-200 88005
202-370 88005
500-1699 88001
W Boutz Rd 88005
E Bowman Ave 88001
W Bowman Ave 88005
Bowman St 88005
Bowra Ln 88007
Boxster Way 88001
Boxwood Ln 88012
Brahman Rd 88012
Branding Iron Cir 88005
Brandy Ln 88007
Branson Ave 88001
Brass Way 88007
Bravia Dove Loop 88001
Bravo Rd 88012
Breeze Ln 88007
Brian Pl 88007
Briareus Dr 88005
Briarwood Ln & Loop 88005
Bridger Ave 88001
Bridle Path 88007
Bright Star Ave & Pl 88011
Bright View Rd 88007
Bristol Ave & Ct 88001
Broadmoor Dr 88001
Broadview Ct, Pl & Rd 88005
Broken Stone Rd 88011
Bromilow St 88001
Bronco Way 88005
Brook Cir 88001
Brook Haven Ct 88005
Brown Rd 88005
Brownlee Ave 88005
Bruins Ln 88007
Bubbling Wells Ct 88011
Buchanan Ave 88001
Buckhorn Dr 88005
Bud Way Ln 88007
Buena Tierra Ct 88005
Buena Vida Cir & Ct 88011
Buffalo Estates Rd 88007
Bugatti Dr 88001
Buildtek Ct 88005
Bumpy Ln 88012
Bunkhouse Rd 88011
Burgers Dr 88007
Burke Rd 88007
Burley Ct 88005
Burmite Ct 88012
Burnut Rd 88012
Bushland Ave 88012
Butler St 88001
Butterfield Blvd 88011
Butterfield Ridge Dr 88007
Butterfly Ln 88011
Buttonwillow Ct 88011
C A Ridge Rd 88007
Caballo Ct 88011
Cabin Creek Ave 88012
Cactus Ave 88001
Cactus Gulch Way 88011
Cactus Patch Way 88007
Cadiz Ct 88011
Calabazilla Dr 88011
Calais Ave 88011
Calcite St 88012
Calico Dr 88012
California Ave 88001
Calle Allegre 88011
Calle Amarilla 88011
Calle Americana 88005
Calle Aplanado 88012
Calle Arcos 88007
Calle Arriba 88012
Calle Bedado 88007
Calle Bella Ave & Ct 88012
Calle Belleza
3600-3698 88012
Calle Belleza
4000-4199 88011
Calle Bellisima Rd 88011
Calle Bonita Ln 88011
Calle Bronce 88012
Calle Calmado 88007
Calle Cazador 88012
Calle Chica 88012
Calle Cobre 88012
Calle Contendo 88011
Calle Contento 88007
Calle Corte 88011
Calle De Vis 88007
Calle De Alegra 88005
Calle De Alvarez 88005
Calle De Cuarzo 88012
Calle De El Paso 88005
Calle De Estrellas 88012
Calle De Fira 88007
Calle De Fuerte 88011
Calle De Guadalupe 88005
Calle De Lano 88012
Calle De Las Margaritas 88005
Calle De Luna 88012
Calle De Mercado 88005
Calle De Ninos 88005
Calle De Nubes 88012
Calle De Oro 88007
Calle De Oso 88005
Calle De Paradise 88011
Calle De Paz 88012
Calle De Plata 88007
Calle De Pompe 88007
Calle De Rosa 88001
Calle De Rosas 88007
Calle De Salud 88011
Calle De Sierra 88012
Calle De Suenos 88001
Calle De Valezquez 88007
Calle Del Centro 88007
Calle Del Encanto 88005
Calle Del Norte 88005
Calle Del Ranchero 88011
Calle Del Sol 88005
Calle Del Valle 88007
Calle Desperta 88012
Calle Escondida 88007
Calle Estados 88005
Calle Estancias 88007
Calle Feliz 88001
Calle Fielder 88001
Calle Florista 88005
Calle Griega 88011
Calle Hierro 88012
Calle Lajas 88007
Calle Lamina 88012
Calle Las Lomas 88012
Calle Libertad 88005
Calle Linda 88012
Calle Nuestra 88005
Calle Paraiso 88012
Calle Pastura 88012
Calle Pico Gemelo 88012
Calle Plomo 88012
Calle Porton 88007
Calle Princesa 88012
Calle Querido 88007
Calle Ranchito 88007
Calle Rancho Caballo 88012
Calle Sereno 88007
Calle Sonesta 88011
Calle Sosa 88001
Calle Tenebroso 88005
Calle Unidos 88005
Calle Ventanas 88007
Calle Verde 88012
Calle Vista Bella 88007
Callejon De Mecho 88007
Calo Ln 88007
Calvary Trl 88007
E Cambridge Dr 88001
W Cambridge Dr 88005
Camelot Dr 88005
Caminito Amigo 88005
Camino Blanco 88007
Camino Bodegas 88005
Camino Bonito 88011
Camino Castillo 88005
Camino Coyote 88011
Camino De Flores 88007
Camino De Nosotros 88007
Camino De Pavos 88005
Camino Del Rex 88001
Camino Del Rey 88005
Camino Dos Vidas 88012
Camino Escondida 88011
Camino Leon Ct 88011
Camino Lindo Ct 88011
Camino Nuevo Mejico 88007
Camino Real 88001
Camino Seco St 88005
Camino Verde 88012
Camp Cody 88007
Campana Ct 88011
Campbell Rd 88007
Campesino Ct 88007
N & S Campo St 88001
N Campus Housing 88003
Canary Ct 88007
Candeleras St 88011
Candlelight Dr 88011
Candlewood Cir 88011
Cantabria Ct 88007
Canterbury Arc 88005
Canterra Arc 88011
Canyon Ct 88011
Canyon Bonito Ct 88011
Canyon De Oro 88011
Canyon Point Rd 88011
Canyon Ridge Arc 88011
Canyon Verde 88011
Canyon Vista Rd 88011
Capistrano Ave & Ct 88011
Capitan Ave 88001
Capri Arc & Rd 88005
Carebear Ln 88012
Carefree Ct 88011
Carjac Rd 88011
Carlen Ct 88001
Carlton Rd 88007
Carlyle Dr & Pl 88005
Carmel Ct 88011
Carol Ann Ct 88007
Carr Ln 88007
Carreon Pl 88005
Carretas Ct 88007
Carrillo Ct & St 88001
Carson Ct 88011
Carter Dr 88011
Carver Rd 88005
Casa Dr 88007
Casa De Pueblo St 88001
Casablanca Ln 88005
Cashmere Ct 88011
Casita Ct 88007
Cassatt Pl 88007
Castile Ct 88007
Catalana 88007
Catalonia Ct 88007
Catalpa Dr 88001
Catamount Dr 88011
Cats Eye Rd 88012
Cattleguard Trl 88012
Cave Creek Mnr 88011
Cave Springs Trl 88011
Cayenne Ct 88012
Cecilia Ct 88012
Cedardale Dr & Loop 88005
Cedarwood Ct 88012
Centennial St 88011
Central Rd 88012
Century Ln 88012
Ceres Ct 88011
Cerro Ln 88007
Certified Pl 88007
Cervantes Vlg 88001
Chacoma Ct 88012
Chagar Ct 88007
Challenger Pl 88012
Chama Dr 88012
Chamisa Ct 88011
Chamisa Vlg 88001
Chamiso Pl 88012
Chamizal Rd 88011
Chante Ct 88011
Chaparral St 88001
Chaparrita Ct 88011
Chaparro St 88001
N Charles St 88005
Charles Russell Rd 88011
Charolais Dr 88012
Charro St 88011
Chase Pl 88011
Chateau Dr 88005
Chato Ct 88012
Chavez Rd 88007
Chelsea Rd 88005
Cherokee Cir 88011
Cherry St 88005
Cherry Cider Ln 88007
Chesney Rd 88012
E Chestnut Ave 88001
W Chestnut Ave 88005
W Chestnut Pl 88005
Cheyenne Ct & Dr 88011
Chickasaw Trl 88012
Chile Ct & Ln 88001
Chilton Dr 88001
Chimayo Dr 88011
Chimney Rock Rd 88011
Chinook 88007
Chinook Pl 88011
Chippewa Trl 88011
Chippewa Summit Dr 88011
E Chiquita St 88001
Chiricahua Trl 88012
Chisholm Trl 88005
Chivalry Ln 88005
Choctaw Trl 88012
Cholla Rd 88011
Christine Ct 88001
Chromite Ct 88012
Chuckwagon Rd 88011
Chukar Ct 88012
Chula Vista Rd 88012
Chuparosa Ct 88011
N & S Church St 88001
Churchill Ave 88011
Cielo Cir 88007
Cielo Bonito Ct 88005
Cielo Grande Ct 88005
Cielo Manso 88011
Cielo Vista Ct 88005
Cimarron Ct & Dr 88011
Cindy Pl 88001
Cinnabar Ln 88001
Circle Dr 88005
Circuit Ln 88011
Cisco Way 88011
Citrine Ave 88012
City Lights Pl 88007
City View Dr 88011
Clark Ln & Rd 88007
Clarke Ln 88007
Claude Dove Dr 88011
Clavel St 88007
Clear Creek Ln 88007
Clearview Dr 88011
Clearwater Ct 88012
Cliff Ln 88007
Cliffhanger Ct 88012
Clifford Ave 88012
Cloister Ct 88005
Cloud Dance Dr 88012
Cloudcroft Cir 88011
Clover Dr 88001
Cobre Ct 88012
Cochise Trl 88012
Cochita Ln 88007
Codorniz St 88007
Cody Cir 88011
Cole Vlg 88001
Coleen Ave & Ct 88001
W College Ave 88005
College Dr 88003
College Pl 88005
College St 88001
Colorado Ave 88001
Colosseo Cir 88012

Street	ZIP
Colt Rd	88011
Columbia Ave	88012
Columbus Dr	88011
Comanche Trl	88012
Comet St	88012
Commerce Dr	88011
Compas Rd	88011
N & S Compress Rd	88005
Comstock Ct	88011
Conchas Ln	88011
Concho Pl	88012
Concord Ave	88001
Condor St	88011
Conejo Way	88012
Conlee Ln	88005
Connie Lou Dr	88001
Conocito Pl	88012
Conroy Trl	88007
Constitution Rd	88007
Contana Ct	88007
Conway Ave	88005
Copa Ln	88007
Copper Loop	88005
Copper Bar Rd	88011
Coral Rd	88007
Corbett Ctr	88003
Corbett Dr	88001
Cordova Cir	88007
Corley Dr	88001
Corn Dr	88001
Corona Rd	88012
Corona Del Campo Loop	88011
Coronado St	88005
Corralones Rd	88007
Cortabella	88005
Corte Dios	88011
Cortez Ave	88012
Cortez Dr	88011
Cortina Mnr	88011
Costales Trl	88012
Cotorro Ct	88005
Cotton Ave	88001
Cotton Bloom Ct	88007
Cottontail Ln	88005
Cottonweed Rd	88007
Cottonwood St	88001
Coues Deer Ave	88007
Cougar Ln	88012
Council Oak Rd	88011
Country Pl	88007
Country Club Cir	88001
Country Pride Rd	88012
County Road D65	88012
County Road D66	88012
County Road D68	88012
E Court Ave	88001
W Court Ave	88005
Coventry Rd	88011
Covina Blvd	88011
Cowboy Ave	88012
Cox Ln	88007
Coyote Rd	88012
Coyote Trl	88001
Coyote Flats St	88012
Coyote Peak Pl	88012
Coyote Ridge Dr	88011
Craig Ave & Ct	88001
Crawford Blvd	88007
Cree Ct	88005
Creed Ave	88005
Creek Trl	88012
Creekstone	88001
Creosote Ct	88012
Creosote Run Rd	88011
Crescent Dr	88005
Crescent Creek Cir	88011
Cresta Ct	88005
Crestview Dr	88011
Crianza Way	88011
Cripple Creek Rd	88011
Critter Ln	88007
E & W Crocus Ct	88007
Crossley Ln	88005
Crow Rd	88007
Crown Point Ct	88011
Cruse Ave	88005
Crystal Ct & Pl	88012
Cuates Canyon Rd	88011
Cuesta Rd	88007
Cumbres Ct	88011
Cummings Ct	88001
Curnutt St	88011
Custer Way	88011
Custus Wren Ct	88007
Cymbeline Ct	88011
Cypress Ct	88012
D Banegas Rd	88007
Daffodil Ln	88007
Dakota Dr	88011
Dale Ln	88001
Dalrymple Rd	88007
Damonite Ct	88012
Daniel Ct	88007
Danny Ln	88007
Darlene Dr	88001
Dartmouth Ave	88005
Datil Ct	88007
Davis Ave	88005
Davis Rd	88011
Dawn Ln	88012
Day Dreamer Dr	88005
De Anza Pl	88007
De Beers	88007
De Vaca Ct	88012
De Vargas Ave	88011
Deadwood Camp Ct	88011
Death Valley Ct	88011
Debby Cir	88005
Debra St	88001
Deer Ridge Ct	88007
Defiance Ave	88001
Degas Dr	88007
Del Mar Ave	88005
Del Monte St	88001
Del Norte Ct	88007
Del Prado Way	88011
Del Rey Blvd	88012
Del Rio Ct & Dr	88007
Del Rose Ct	88007
Delano Dr	88011
Delphi Ln	88007
Delta Dr	88001
Demos Ave	88011
Derby Ave	88007
Derringer Rd	88011
Desert Cir & Dr	88001
Desert Blossom Rd	88007
Desert Broom Ct	88011
Desert Cove Pl	88011
Desert Edge Rd	88007
Desert Fox	88007
Desert Greens Dr	88011
Desert Hills Rd	88012
Desert Mesa Pl	88012
Desert Mirage	88011
Desert Park Ave	88011
Desert Peak Pl	88012
Desert Plum Ln & Rd	88012
Desert Rose Ct	88005
Desert Shadow Pl	88011
Desert Spriggs Rd	88012
Desert Springs Ct	88011
Desert Star Rd	88005
Desert Valley Ct	88007
Desert Walk Ct	88011
Desert Willow Ct	88011
Desert Wind Way	88012
Devendale Ave & Dr	88005
Devils Claw Rd	88012
Dia Y Noche Ave	88012
Diamante Ct	88012
Diamond Cir	88012
Diamond Dr	88001
Diamond Mine Rd	88011
Diamond Springs Dr	88011
Diamondback Dr	88011
Diana Maura Dr	88001
Diane Ln	88012
Diaz Rd	88007
Dies Ave	88005
Divot Ave	88001
Doc Bar Ct	88007
Dodgen Ct	88007
Doe Ln	88001
Dogwood St	88001
Don Miguel Ave	88007
S Don Roser Dr	88011
Dona Ana Rd	88007
N Dona Ana St	88001
S Dona Ana St	88001
Dona Ana School Rd	88007
Dona Elayna Ct	88011
Dona Villa Dr	88007
Doniphan Pl	88007
Doolittle Dr	88007
Dorado Ct & Dr	88011
Doral Ct	88011
Doree Ct	88001
Dormilon Rd	88007
Dorothy Cir	88001
Dos Equis Rd	88012
Dos Lobos Rd	88005
Dos Sapros	88012
Dos Vistas	88012
Doubletree St	88012
Douglas Ave	88011
Douglas Dr	88005
Dove Ln	88001
N & S Downtown Mall	88001
Dr King Way	88001
Dragonfly Ave	88012
Drake Ct	88005
Dressage Ct	88007
Driftwood Cir	88011
Dripping Springs Rd	88011
Dry Canyon Rd	88007
Dry Creek Pl	88011
Dry Harbor Ct	88012
Dulcinea Dr	88005
Dune Dr	88012
Dunlop	88005
Dunn Dr	88011
Durango Ct	88011
Durazno St	88001
Dusty Prints Rd	88007
Dyer St	88011
Dyne Ave	88005
Eagle Rd	88012
Eagle Pass Rd	88011
Eagle Ridge Dr	88012
Eagle Wings Rd	88007
Eagles Nest Rd	88007
Eason Ln	88011
East St	88005
Eastridge Rd	88005
Eastview Ave	88007
Easy Ln	88011
Easy Living Dr	88005
Ebony Ave	88001
Echo Ln	88011
Echo Canyon Rd	88011
Eclipse Rd	88012
Eclipse Ridge Ln	88011
Edgewood Ave	88005
Edison Pl	88007
Efrain Ln	88007
Egyptian St	88005
Eider Ln	88007
El Caminito Ave	88001
El Camino Real	88007
El Centro Blvd	88012
El Dorado Ct	88011
El Faro St	88005
El Llano Rd	88012
El Molino Blvd	88005
El Nido Rd	88007
El Paseo Rd	88001
El Prado Ave	88005
El Presidio	88011
El Segundo Trl	88011
Elder St	88001
Elena Way	88011
Elkridge Ln	88005
Elks Dr	
2700-4099	88005
4201-4397	88007
4399-4599	88007
4601-5599	88007
Ellendale Dr	88005
Elm St	88005
Embarcadero Rd	88007
Embassy Dr	88005
Emerald St	88012
Emilia Ave	88001
Enchanted Dr	88011
Encino Ave	88001
Englehardt Rd	88012
Engler Rd	88007
Enriquez Ln	88007
Enterprise Ave	88012
Entrada Del Sol	88001
Enzie Dr	88001
Erickson Rd	88012
Erminda St	88005
Ermita Rd	88012
Escalante Dr	88012
Escalera Rd	88012
Escenico Ct	88012
Escondido Ln	88005
Escuela Ct	88011
Espalin Ct	88007
Espana Way	88011
S Espanola St	88001
Espejo Ct	88007
N & S Esperanza St	88001
N Espina St	88001
S Espina St	
100-198	88001
200-3111	88001
3113-3499	88001
3140-3498	88003
Estancia Ct	88007
Estancia Pl	88005
Estancia Real Pl	88007
Esterlina Pl	88005
Estrada Rd	88005
W Ethel Ave	88005
Eucalyptus Dr	88001
Eugene Dr	88001
Eugenio St	88001
Evans Dr & Pl	88001
Evelyn St	88001
Evening Star Ave	88011
Eventing Ct	88007
Evon Dr	88012
Evy Ln	88012
Ewe Ln	88001
Executive Pl	88011
Executive Hills Rd	88011
Fair Lady Ln	88005
N & S Fairacres Rd	88005
Fairbanks Dr	88001
Fairfax Ave	88001
Fairpark Rd	88007
Fairway Cir & Dr	88011
Fairway Village Dr	88007
Faith Rd	88012
Falcon Dr	88011
Fallbrook Way	88011
Fallow Deer St	88007
Fandango Ct	88007
Farney Ln	88005
E Farney Ln	88001
Farside St	88007
Faulkner Rd	88007
Fawn Ln	88001
Featherstone Dr	88011
Feliz Real	88011
Ferguson Rd	88007
Ferndale Dr	88005
Fiesta Dr	88005
Fillmore Cir	88001
Fir Ave	88001
Fire Mountain Ct	88011
Firefly Rd	88011
Firethorn Ct	88011
Fireweed Dr	88007
Fischer Rd	88007
Fite Dr	88001
Flatland Rd	88012
E Fleming Ave	88001
W Fleming Ave	88005
Flintstone Loop	88012
Flora Cir	88001
Flora Vista Dr	88007
Florence Dr	88011
Flores Ct	88007
Floret Ln	88011
Florida Dr	88005
Fluorite Rd	88012
Fontana Way	88007
Foothills Rd	88011
Forest Park Dr	88007
N & S Fork Arc & Rd	88012
Fort Bayard Rd	88007
Fort Cummings Rd	88007
Fort Furlong	88007
Fort Marcy Trl	88007
Fort Mclane Rd	88007
Fort Mcrae Rd	88007
Fort Selden Rd	88007
Fort Thorn Rd	88007
Fossil Ct	88012
Fossil View Rd	88007
Foster Ln	88007
Foster Rd	88001
E Foster Rd	88005
Foster Canyon Rd	88007
Found Ave	88011
Fountain Ave & Loop	88007
Four Winds Pl	88011
Fox Rd	88012
Fox Canyon Rd	88011
Fox Den Ct	88007
Fox Tract Ct	88007
Foxboro Ct	88007
Foxtail Pine Dr	88012
Fran Dr	88007
Francine Ct	88007
Francis Way	88007
Frank Maes Ave	88005
Franklin Pl	88007
Franzia Ct & Rd	88011
Frascati Ave	88012
Fred Way	88007
Freedom Dr	88007
Freese Ln	88007
Frenger Mall	88003
Fresno Trl	88012
Frida Dr	88012
Friendship Dr	88007
Frodo Pl	88007
N Frontage Rd	88007
Frontier Dr	88011
Ft Sumner Way	88005
Gadwall Pl	88012
Galaxy Dr	88012
Galaz Rd	88011
Galicia Way	88011
Galina Ct, Dr & Pl	88012
Galisteo Loop	88011
E Gallagher Ave	88001
W Gallagher Ave	88005
Galvan Dr	88005
Gamble Ct	88011
Gandy Ln	88005
Garcia Anx	88003
Garcia Dr	88007
Garcia St	88001
Garcia Hall	88003
Gardenia St	88007
Gardner Ave	88001
Garnet Pl & St	88012
Garrison Rd	88001
Gasline Rd	88012
Gem Ct, Pl & St	88012
Genesis Ln	88012
George Catlin Rd	88011
Georgia Okeeffe Rd	88011
Georgianna Ct	88007
Geothermal Dr	
1001-2099	88011
4001-4099	88003
4501-4599	88011
Gerald Dr	88007
Geronimo Trl	88012
Gila Trl	88005
Gila Bend Loop	88011
Gilmer Way	88005
Girault Ave	88012
Giron Rd	88007
Gladys Dr	88001
Glass Rd	88005
Glendale Dr	88005
Glenn Ln	88007
Glorieta Pl	88011
Gobi Ln	88011
Gold Ct	88007
Golden Dr	88005
Golden Rod Ct	88007
Golden Sage Ct	88011
Goldeneye Ct	88007
Golf Club Rd	88011
Golondrina Ct	88012
N Gonzales St	88001
Gonzalez St	88005
Good News Way	88007
Good Shepherd Rd	88005
Good Times Dr	88005
Gopher Rd	88012
Graham St	88001
Grampas Farm Rd	88005
Granada St	88007
Grand Teton Way	88011
Grandview St	88012
Granite St	88012
Grant Rd	88007
Grape Vineyard Rd	88007
Grapevine Canyon Ct	88011
Gray Fox Ct	88007
Great Basin Ln	88011
Great Sandy Dr	88011
Greek Row	88003
Green Hill Ct	88012
Green Ridge Ct	88005
W Greening Ave	88005
Gregg St	88001
Grenada Pl	88012
Grider Rd	88007
E Griggs Ave	88001
W Griggs Ave	
100-199	88001
200-599	88005
Grindell Rd	88001
Grooms Rd	88011
Grouse Run Dr	88012
Grover Dr	88005
Grover Pl	88012
Guadalupe St	88001
Guamis Rd	88012
Gunsight Peak Dr	88012
Guthrie Pl	88001
Gypsy Rd	88007
Habanero Dr	88012
Hachita Dr	88012
Hacienda Ave	88011
E Hadley Ave	88001
W Hadley Ave	
200-1799	88005
1800-1998	88007
2000-2199	88007
2201-2799	88007
Hagerty Rd	88001
Haines Rd	88007
Halfmoon Dr	88005
Hall Ave	88005
Hamiel Dr	88001
Hammerand Ct	88011
Hanger Lake Rd	88012
Hanks Dr	88005
Hansen Ave	88005
Happy Pl	88007
Happy Trl N	88005
Happy Trl S	88005
Happy Trails Dr	88005
Happy Valley Ln	88005
Hardrock Rd	88011
Hare Rd	88007
Harmony Ct	88012
Harmony Ridge Ln	88011
Harmony Wells Cir	88011
Harp Ct	88011
Harrelson St	88005
Harris Rd	88007
Harrison St	88005
Harvard Dr	88005
Harvey Farm Rd	88007
Hatchet Ct	88012
Hatfield Rd	88007
Hawk Rd	88012
Hawk Eye Pl	88012
Hayner Ave	88005
Hayride Rd	88007
Hazen Ct	88011
Heather Ave & Cir	88005
Helios Farm Ct	88005
Hellenic Dr	88011
Hembrillo Canyon Ct	88011
Heno Mine Rd	88011
Herbrillo Pass Rd	88011
Hereford Blvd	88012
Heritage Ridge Dr	88011
Hermia Ct	88011
N Hermosa St	88001
Hermosillo Ct, Dr & Pl	88005
E Hernandez Rd	88001
Hess Ter	88005
Hickory Dr & Loop	88005
Hidden Ln	88007
Hidden Springs Ct	88011
Higgins Ln	88011
High St	88011
High Desert Dr	88012
High Hopes Rd	88012
Highland Ave	88005
Highridge St	88012
N Highway 28	88005
N Highway 292	88005
Hilda Dr	88007
Hildalgo Ct	88012
Hillcrest Ave	88007
Hillrise Cir, Ct & Dr	88011
Hillsboro Loop	88012
Hillsdale St	88005
Hilltop Ave	88007
Hixon Dr	88005
Hoagland Rd	88005
Hoffmann Dr	88005
Holcomb Rd	88007
Holiday Ave	88005
Holliday Ln & Pl	88007
Hollinger St	88001
Holly Dr	88005
Hollyhock	88005
Holman Rd	88012
Holsome Rd	88011
Holy Cross Rd	88001
Homestead Cir & Ct	88011
Hondo Rd	88012
Hope Rd	88007
Hopi Ct	88011
Horace Ln	88011
Horizon Arc	88007
Horizon View Dr	88011
Horner Rd	88007
Horny Toad Rd	88001
N Horseshoe	88003
S Horseshoe	88003
Horseshoe Cir	88007
Hoskins Ln	88007
Hot Rd	88012
Howard Pl	88011
Howell Ave	88005
Humbert St	88005
Hummingbird Dr	88007
Hunt Rd	88012
Hunters Ct	88011
Hunters Chase Rd	88011
Huntington Dr	88011
Hurt Rd	88007
Hyacinth St	88007
Ice Canyon Ln	88011
E Idaho Ave	
100-300	88005
302-398	88005
500-2499	88001
2501-2597	88011
2599-2899	88011
2901-2999	88011
Idyll Ct	88007
Imperial Dr	88012

Imperial Rdg 88011
Inca Ave 88005
Inca Dove Ave 88012
Independence Loop 88005
Indian Head Rd 88012
Indian Hollow Rd 88011
Inez Ln 88007
Inspiration Ln 88011
International Mall 88003
Ironshoe Rd 88007
Ironwood Ct 88012
Ironwood Dr 88001
Iroquois 88007
Isaacks Ave 88011
Isaacks Ln 88007
Isabella Ct 88012
Island Ct 88007
Isleta Ct 88011
Isolation Point Rd 88012
Ithaca Ct 88011
Ivory Ct 88012
Ivory Wing Ln 88012
Ivydale Dr 88005
J H Sharp Rd 88011
Jack Nicklaus Dr 88011
Jack Rabbit Rd 88012
Jackson Ln 88007
Jacobs Rd 88012
Jade Ave, Ct & Pl 88012
Jaeger Pl 88012
Jalapeno Dr 88012
Jamie Pl 88007
Jamison Dr 88012
Jan Ln 88012
Jana Ct 88005
Janet Ann Ln 88007
Jaradite Dr 88012
Jasmine Dr 88005
Jasper Ct 88012
Jasper Dr 88001
Jayne Ln 88001
Jeanie Ct 88007
Jefferies St 88012
Jefferson Ln 88011
Jemez Way 88012
Jenice Ct 88001
Jennifer St 88005
Jerry St 88005
Jester Pl 88012
Jett Ave 88001
Jewel Ct 88012
Jill Cir 88001
Jimmie St 88012
Jj Ln 88007
Jody Dr 88007
John St 88001
John Muir Rd 88011
Johnson Ln 88011
Johnson St 88005
Jordan Rd 88001
N Jornada Rd 88012
S Jornada Rd 88011
Joseph H Ln 88012
Joshua Ct 88012
Journey Ct 88012
Joy Ln 88001
Joyce Ln 88011
Juan Diego Ave 88001
June Ct 88001
Juniper Ave 88001
Jupiter Rd 88012
Justin Ct & Ln 88007
Kachina Canyon Rd 88011
Kalahari Ln 88011
Kalancho Ct 88011
Kalvin Pl 88007
Kangaroo Ct 88012
Kansas Ave 88001
Karen Ave 88007
Karen Dr 88001
Karen Pl 88001
Karrie Ln 88007
Katrina St 88005
Kay Ln 88005
Kearny Pl 88007
Keathley Dr 88005
Keel Rd 88012
Keelo Rd 88007
Kelli Cir 88007
Kenerral Rd 88012
Kenmore Rd 88012
Kennedy Rd 88007
Kenner Way 88012
Kensington Way 88012
Kent Rd 88001
E Kentintr Row 88003
Kentwood Ct 88011
Kenwood Rd 88012
Kerry Ann Pl 88012
Kevin Dr 88001
Key Deer Ct 88007
Kilbourne Hole Dr 88012
Kilmer St 88001
Kinerend Ave 88001
King Bird Ct 88007
King Edward Ave 88007
King Gregs Ct 88007
King James Ave 88007
Kings Rd 88012
Kingsbury Ct 88005
Kingston Ct & Rd 88012
Kiskadee Pl 88012
Kismet Pl 88005
Kissiah Dr 88012
Klein Ave 88001
Kokopelli Ln 88005
Kristin Dr 88007
Kuhnley Farm Rd 88007
Kyle Ln 88012
Kyler Rd 88012
L B Lindbeck Rd 88007
La Camelia 88011
La Cienaga Pl 88011
La Colonia St 88005
La Cueva Mine Trl 88011
La Fleche Pl 88007
La Fonda Cir, Ct & Dr 88001
La Jolla Ave 88005
La Luz St 88007
La Melodia Dr 88011
La Mirada Ct 88011
La Paloma Ct 88007
La Paloma Dr 88011
La Paloma St 88007
La Plata Dr 88007
La Posada Ln 88005
La Pradera Rd 88005
La Puente Ln 88005
La Purisima Dr 88011
La Quinta St 88007
La Redonda 88011
La Reina Rd 88012
La Senda Dr 88011
La Supita 88007
La Union Ct 88007
La Vida Nueva Ct 88005
Ladder Ct 88012
Ladera Ave 88007
Ladera Canyon Rd 88011
Ladera Seca Ct 88011
Laguna Ct & Dr 88005
Lake City Ave 88012
Lake Lucero 88011
Lake Tahoe St 88007
Lake Valley Ave 88007
Lakeside Dr
2400-2599 88007
2600-2698 88005
Lamanite Ct 88012
Lamar Rd & St 88005
Lamske Ln 88005
Lane St 88005
Lantana Ave 88005
Laramie Dr 88011
Laredo Ave 88011
Lariat Dr 88011
Larimer Ln 88011
Lark Pl 88007
Lark Spur Ct, Dr &
Way 88007
Larry Dr 88001
Las Alturas Dr 88011
Las Casitas 88007
Las Colinas Dr 88012
E Las Cruces Ave
201-297 88001
201-201 88004
201-201 88006
299-1300 88001
1302-1898 88001
W Las Cruces Ave
100-198 88001
200-298 88005
300-799 88005
Las Golondrinas 88007
Las Laureles 88007
Las Lilas Way 88005
Las Palmas St 88007
Las Piedras Rd 88011
Las Placitas Rd 88011
Las Tunas Dr 88011
Las Vegas Ct 88007
Las Vistas Dr 88005
Lassiter Rd 88001
Latigo Ln 88007
Laurel St 88001
Lavender Dr
4100-4194 88005
4201-4209 88007
Lazo Del Norte 88011
Lazo Del Sur 88011
Lea Ranch Dr 88012
Leaping Lizard Loop 88012
Leasburg Dm & Dr 88007
Lebanon Arc 88005
Lee Ave 88011
Leebarry Ln 88012
Lees Dr 88001
Leghorn Loop 88007
Lemo Rd 88012
Lenox Ave 88005
Leonard Bryan Aly 88007
Leroy Ln 88007
Lester Ave & Ct 88001
Lettuce Ln 88001
Levante Dr 88011
Lewis St 88001
Libra Dr 88005
Lilac Dr 88005
Lilla Rd 88011
Lillian Ct 88007
Linda Vista Rd
300-599 88005
6000-6100 88007
6102-6198 88007
Linden Ave 88005
Lion Den Canyon Way 88011
Lisa Ln 88012
Little Creek Ct 88011
S Locust St 88001
E Lohman Ave
100-2399 88001
2500-2513 88011
2515-4499 88011
2532-2598 88001
3000-4498 88011
W Lohman Ave 88005
Loma Bella Dr 88011
Loma Real Rd 88011
Loma Verde Ln 88011
Lomas Del Valle 88012
Lomita Ave 88001
Lone Tree Ln 88011
Lonesome Rd 88007
Lonesome Pine Rd 88007
Lonewolf Ct 88011
Long Bow Dr & Loop 88011
Long Canyon Ct 88011
Long River Ln 88007
Longhorn Dr 88012
Longview Ln 88012
Lookout Ridge Dr 88011
Loomis Rd 88007
Lopez Rd 88007
Lores Gonney Way 88012
Lori Dr 88005
Lorrea Ct 88011
Los Alamos Ct 88011
Los Amigos Ct 88011
Los Arboles Ct & Dr 88011
Los Misioneros 88011
Los Morenos Ct 88007
Los Nogales Dr 88001
Los Vaqueros Dr 88011
Lost Ln 88007
Lost Padre Mine Rd 88011
Lost Wrangler Way 88007
Louise Cir & Ct 88001
Love Ct 88005
Lowell Rd 88001
Loya Ln 88007
Lt Ralph J Silva St 88007
Lucerne Ct & Way 88005
E Lucero Ave 88001
W Lucero Ave 88005
Lucky Lindy Ln 88007
Lucky Oak Ct 88011
Lujan St 88001
Lujan Hill Rd 88007
Luna St 88001
Luna De Oro 88011
Luna Sereno Ct 88011
Luna Vista Rd 88012
Lunarridge St 88012
Lupton Pl 88001
Luz Bonita Ln 88012
Lyles Rd 88007
Lynch Dr 88001
Lynx Trl 88001
Lyon Pl 88001
Lyra Ct 88011
Lytton Cir 88001
Macarthur Rd 88012
Macaw Cir 88001
Macleod Rd 88001
Madera Vieja Ct 88007
Madero Ave 88005
E Madrid Ave 88001
W Madrid Ave 88005
Maese Ln 88007
Mages St 88005
Magnolia Dr 88001
Magoffin Pl 88007
Mahalo Ct 88012
Mahaney Dr 88005
Mahogany Dr 88001
N Main St
101-297 88001
299-3299 88001
3855-8199 88012
2521-1-2521-9 88001
2525-1-2525-9 88001
S Main St
100-751 88001
753-805 88001
800-804 88005
806-2499 88005
2501-3999 88005
Majestic Rdg 88011
Majestic Shadow Loop &
Way 88011
Majestic Terrace Dr 88011
Malachite Ave 88012
Malaga St 88011
Mall Dr 88011
Malleanc Rd 88007
Mangas Trl 88012
Manor Way 88005
Manso Ave 88005
N & S Manzanita St 88001
Maple St 88001
Marble View Dr 88012
Marconi Pl 88007
Marcy St 88001
Margaret St 88001
Maricopa Cir 88011
Marigold St 88007
Marilissa Ln 88005
Marion Ln 88012
Mariposa Dr 88001
Market Pl 88007
Marmara 88012
Marquess St 88005
Marron Ct 88007
Mars Ave 88012
Martha Dr 88001
Martin St 88005
N & S Martinez St 88001
Marwood Ln 88007
Mary Cir 88001
Mateo Pl 88011
Matisse Ct 88007
Mauer Rd 88005
Maura Ln 88012
Maverick Trl 88007
Maxim Ct 88011
E May Ave 88001
W May Ave 88005
Mayfield Ln & Rd 88007
Mayflower Dr 88007
Mayfly Ln 88011
Mcarthur Dr 88001
Mcclane Ct & Rd 88001
Mcclure Rd
300-499 88005
501-599 88005
600-799 88007
801-1299 88007
Mccoy Ave 88007
Mcdowell Pl & Rd 88005
Mcfie Ave 88005
Mcguffey St 88012
Mcrae Ave 88001
Mcswain Dr 88005
Meador Dr 88007
Meadow Cir & Ln 88007
Meadow Park Ct 88007
Mechem Ave 88005
Med Park Dr 88005
Medina Dr 88007
Melanite Ct 88012
N & S Melendres St 88005
Melody Ln 88012
Memorial Ct 88011
Mercury Ln 88012
Meriwether St 88007
Mervs Ln 88007
E Mesa Ave
1100-1499 88001
5700-5799 88012
Mesa Dr 88012
Mesa Central Dr 88011
Mesa De Santa Fe 88012
Mesa Grande Dr
4800-4898 88012
4900-5399 88012
5401-6299 88012
5700-5798 88011
6200-6998 88012
Mesa La Jolla Ave 88012
Mesa Moreno Dr 88011
Mesa Point Rd 88011
Mesa Prieta Dr 88011
Mesa Rico Dr 88011
Mescal Bean Ct 88011
Mescalero Trl 88012
N & S Mesilla St 88005
Mesilla Acres Rd 88005
Mesilla Dam Rd 88005
Mesilla Hills Dr 88005
Mesilla Verde Ter 88005
Mesita St 88012
N & S Mesquite St 88001
Mican Ct 88005
Mickey Ln 88011
Micro Rd 88011
Midnight Ridge Dr 88011
Midway Ave 88012
Milestone Ct 88007
Millard Ave 88012
Millennium St 88011
Miller Rd 88007
Millstone Ct 88012
Milton Ave 88005
Milton Rd 88001
Mimbres Ct & St 88001
Mimosa Ln 88001
Minniec Rd 88011
Minnow Ln 88007
Mira Montes 88007
Mira Valle Ct 88011
Miramar Arc 88011
N & S Miranda St 88005
Mirasol Dr 88007
Missile Ln 88011
Mission Ln 88012
Mission Rd 88011
Mission Bell Ave 88011
Mission Nuevo Dr 88011
Missouri Ave
1301-1397 88001
1399-2499 88001
2500-3299 88011
Misty Way 88007
Mitchell Cir 88012
Mockingbird St 88011
Modoc Trl 88011
Mogollon Rd 88007
Mohawk 88007
Mohegan Trl 88005
Mohican 88007
Mojave 88007
Mojave Dr 88005
Monagle Hall 88003
Mondale Loop 88005
Montana Ave
201-297 88005
299-399 88005
600-2399 88001
Monte Bello Dr 88011
Monte Lindo Ct 88012
Monte Luna Ct 88012
Monte Luz St 88012
Monte Sol St 88012
Monte Sombra Ave 88012
Monte Verde Pl 88012
Monte Vista Ave
400-799 88005
1000-1098 88001
1100-1599 88001
Montecito Ct 88011
Monterey Dr 88005
Montezuma Ave 88011
Monticello Dr 88011
Montoya Rd 88007
Moon River Loop 88007
Moon Shadow Pl 88011
Moon View Dr 88012
Moongate Rd 88012
Moonlight Ridge Arc 88011
Moonrise Arc & Vis 88012
Moonstone St 88012
Moore Cir & Ct 88012
Moose Ct 88007
Moraga Ct 88007
Moreno Rd 88007
Moret 88011
Morgan Pl 88001
Morganite Ct 88012
Morisat Pl 88007
Mormon Dr & Pl 88011
Morning Dove Pl 88001
Morning Glory Ln 88007
Morning Light Pl 88011
Morning Star Dr 88011
Morning Sun Way 88012
Morningside Rd
5001-5197 88011
5199-5232 88011
5234-5298 88011
5285-5315 88012
5347-5357 88011
5365-5385 88012
Morton Ln 88007
N & S Motel Blvd 88007
Mother Lode Trl 88011
Motor Ln 88007
E Mountain Ave 88001
W Mountain Ave 88005
Mountain Shadow St 88001
Mountain View Ave 88001
Mountain Vista Pkwy 88007
E Mulberry Ave 88001
Mule Creek Dr 88007
Mule Deer Dr 88005
Munoz Rd 88011
Murano Ct 88007
Music Ln 88007
Muskrat Ln 88001
Myles Rd 88007
Myrtle Ave 88001
Mystic Ct 88011
Mystic View Ct 88011
Nachas Pl 88007
Nambe Arc & Ct 88011
Nana Trl 88012
Nancy Lopez Ct 88011
Nasa Rd 88012
Navajo Rd 88007
Navajo Trl 88012
Nebula Way 88011
Nehemiah Ct 88001
Neleigh Dr 88007
Nemesh Dr 88005
Nena Ct 88007
Nephite Ct 88012
Neptune Dr 88012
Nevada Ave 88001
Nevarez Ct 88012
N Nevarez St 88001
S Nevarez St 88001
New Mexico Ave 88001
Newberry Ln 88001
Newcomb Ave 88005
Newton St 88001
Nicely Ct 88012
Nieve Ln 88005
Night Shade Ct 88007
Nighthawk Ln 88007
Nike Ave 88011
Nizhoni Trl 88005
Nmsu 88003
No Name Ct 88007
No Problem Dr 88005
Noche Bella Loop 88011
Nogal Canyon Rd 88011
Nopalito Rd 88011
Norte Luz Dr 88012
Norte Vista Dr 88012
Northfield Rd 88007
Northgate Rd 88012
Northpointe Dr 88012
Northridge Dr 88005
Northrise Dr 88011
Northstar Ct 88012
Northview Ave 88007
Northwind Rd 88007
Nosotros Ln 88007
Nunatak Pl 88012
O Joy Pl 88005
Oak St 88005
Oakridge Dr 88005
Oasis Ave 88001
Oban Ct 88001
Ocotillo Rd 88011
Odonnell Dr 88001
Ohair Dr 88001
Ojo Caliente Cir 88011
Old Farm Rd 88005
Old Mill Rd 88007
Old Picacho Rd 88007
Old River Rd 88005
Old West Way 88005
Olde Country Rd 88007
Oleander Dr 88001
Oleta Dr 88001
Olive St 88001
Olla De Oro Ln 88005
Omaha Ct 88005
Omaha Saddle Pl 88011
Onate Rd 88007
Oneida Dr 88005
Onyx Cir & Ct 88012
Orange Ave 88005
Orchard Ave 88005
E Organ Ave 88001
W Organ Ave 88005
Organ Mesa Loop 88011
Organ Mountain Trl 88011
Organ Peak Dr 88012
Organview Ave 88005
Oriole Rd 88011

Street	ZIP
Orion St	88012
Oro Piedras Dr	88011
Oro Viejo Rd	88011
Ortega Rd	88012
Osage Ct	88005
Osos Del Sol Rd	88012
Ottawa Ct	88005
Otter Ln	88001
Outback Dr	88012
Outlaw Rd	88012
Outpost	88007
Overlook Ln	88007
Owls Nest Rd	88012
Ox Cart Ct	88007
Oxbow Ct	88012
Oxford Dr	88005
Pacana Trl	88007
Paetz Ln	88011
Pagosa Hills Ave	88011
Paisano Rd	88005
Pajaro Rd	88005
Palm St	88001
Palm Canyon Ct & Dr	88011
Palmer Rd	88005
W Palms	88007
Palo Verde Ave	88001
Palomas Ave	88001
Pamela Pl	88007
Panlener Ave	88001
Panorama Ct	88007
Panorama Dr	88011
Pantera Cir	88007
Pantera Pond Ln	88007
Panther Peak Dr	88012
Papago Ct	88005
E Papen Memorial Plz	88001
Papillon Ln	88005
Paradise Ln	88007
Parakeet Rd	88007
Park Dr	88005
E Park Dr	88001
N Park Dr	88005
W Park Dr	88001
Park Ridge Pl	88005
Parker Rd	88005
Parkhill Dr	88012
Parkview Dr	88001
Paroquia St	88001
Parrigin Way	88012
Party Time Pl	88005
Paseo Azul	88011
Paseo Del Oro	88007
Patagonia Dr	88011
Patricia Ct	88001
Paula Pl	88001
Pawnee	88007
Paxton St	88001
Payan Rd	88012
Payne Ct & St	88001
Peachtree Hills Rd	88012
Pearl Ct & Pl	88012
Pebble Beach Rd	88011
Pebble Brook Rd	88001
Pecan Dr	88001
Pecan Ln	88011
Pecos St	88001
Pedro Madrid Rd	88007
Pelicano Trl	88012
Pena Blanca Loop	88011
Penasco Pl	88011
Penny Pl	88001
Pepper Rd	88007
Pepper Post Ave	88011
Peralta Pl	88007
Percha Creek Way	88011
Peri Ann Dr	88001
Perkins Dr	88005
Pettes Blvd	88012
Petunia Ln	88007
Phenakite Ct	88012
Phillips Dr	88005
Phoenix St	88012
Phyllis Ln	88001
E Picacho Ave	88001
W Picacho Ave	
3100-C-3100-C	88007
3030-B-3030-D	88007
100-198	88005
200-1999	88005
2000-2098	88007
2100-6599	88007
Picacho Hls	88007
Picacho Peak Vw	88011
Picacho Vistas Ct	88007
Picuris Ct	88011
Piedras Negras Dr	88012
Pigeon Rd	88007
Pine Hollow Ct	88007
Pine Needle Bnd & Way	88012
Pine Valley St	88011
Pinecone Way	88012
Pinedale Ave	88005
Pinehurst St	88011
Pineridge Run	88012
Pines St	88001
Pinetrail St	88012
Pineview Rd	88007
Pinkerton Ct	88007
Pinnacle View Dr	88011
Pinon St	88001
Pinon Jay Ct	88007
Pinta Rd	88012
Pinto Ct	88012
Pioneer Ave	88011
Pioneer Pl	88005
Piqueito Rd	88011
Piro Ave	88001
Pissarro Dr	88007
Pittsburg Ave	88005
Plain St	88001
Playground Ct	88012
Pleasant Hill Ct	88012
Pluto Rd	88012
Plymouth Rock Rd	88007
Pocolomas Ct	88011
Poe Dr	88001
Polaris St	88012
Polder Ln	88007
Pomegranate Ln	88007
Pomona Dr	88011
Ponderosa Pine Pl	88007
S Ponerang Ln N	88005
Pony Express Ct	88007
Poose Creek Rd	88011
Poplar Ave	88001
Porcupine Ct	88007
Porisont Dr	88011
Portales Pl	88007
Porter Dr	
4500-4698	88011
4700-4999	88011
5245-5269	88012
5445-5449	88011
5475-6199	88012
Portico Trl	88011
Portland Dr	88007
Posada Ct	88011
Powder Horn Ct	88012
Powers Dr	88012
Pradera Dorada Arc	88007
Prado Del Sol Ave	88011
Prairie Dog Rd	88012
Prairie Falcon St	88012
Prairie Lilly Dr	88007
Prentice	88011
Primavera St	88007
Princess Jeanne Dr	88001
Princeton Dr	88005
Prophet Cir	88012
Providence Rd	88007
Pueblo St	88005
Pueblo Trl	88012
Pueblo Vis	88007
Pueblo Gardens Ct	88007
Pueblo Mesa Dr	88007
Puerta De Picacho	88007
Puerta Vieja Pl	88007
Puesta De Sol	88005
Puffin St	88012
Puma Trl	88001
Purdue Ct	88005
Purfly Rd	88011
Purple Mtn	88007
Purple Sage Dr	88011
Pyramid Peak Ct	88011
Pyramid Peak Dr	88012
Pyramid Peak Ln	88011
Pyrite Rd	88012
Quail Brush Ct	88011
Quail Run Ave	88011
Quail Valley Pl	88012
Quannah Wild Dr	88011
Quartz Mountain Rd	88012
Quasar Dr	88011
Queen Ann Ct	88012
Queensryche Ct	88012
Quesenberry Ln	88007
Quesenberry St	88005
Raasaf Cir & Dr	88005
Rabbit Run Rd	88012
Radiant Ct	88011
Raevin Ct	88007
Rainbow Dr	88005
Rainbow Ridge St	88007
Raintree Ln	88007
Raleigh Rd	88005
Ralls Rd	88012
Ralph Dr	88001
Ram Trl	88001
Ramrod Frg	88012
Ranchers Rd	88012
Rancho Algodones Rd	88007
Rancho Grande Ave	88012
Raseyn Ct	88005
Rayos De Luna	88007
Rea Blvd	88007
Real Del Norte	88012
Real Del Sur	88011
Real La Luz	88012
Red Bird Ct	88011
Red Canyon Sage Ct	88011
Red Deer Ct	88007
Red Fly Rd	88011
Red Hawk Golf Rd	88012
Red Roof Ct	88012
Red Wing Ave	88012
Red Wolf	88007
Red Yucca Ct	88011
Redfox Rd	88007
Redland Dr	88011
Redman Rd	88011
Redwood St	88001
Reeves Dr	88005
Reflection Plz	88011
Reflections Ln	88011
Regal Rdg	88011
Regal Mist Ct	88011
Regency Ct	88007
Reina Dr	88007
Rel Ln	88007
Remington Rd	88011
Rena Mae Ct	88005
Renoir Ct, Dr & Loop	88007
Renteria St	88001
Rentfrow Ave	88001
Research Dr	88003
Research Park Cir	88001
Rexview Rd	88012
N & S Reymond St	88005
Reyna Ct	88011
Reynolds Dr	88011
Rgh	88003
Rhapsody Ln	88007
Rhea Pl	88012
Rhodes Pl	88007
Rhonda Ln	88012
Rich Pl	88012
Richard Dr	88007
Ricker Ct	88012
Ricochet St	88012
Ridgecrest St	88005
Ridgeline Dr	88005
Ridgemont Dr	88011
Ridgetop Ave	88001
Ridgeway Ct	88011
Rigel St	88012
Rigsby Rd	88005
Rillito Dr	88007
Rimrock Ct & Dr	88012
Rincon De Amigos	88012
Rinconada Blvd	
3331-3331	88011
3502-3514	88012
Ringneck Dr	88001
Rio Arriza Loop	88012
Rio Bravo Ct & Way	88007
Rio Grande St	88001
Rio Vista Dr	88007
Rising Sun Rd	88011
Risner St	88011
Ritter Rd	88005
River Ct	88007
River Heights Dr	88007
Rivers Edge Ln	88007
Riverside Dr	88007
Riverwalk Rd	88007
Riverwood Rd	88007
Roadrunner Cir	88011
Roadrunner Ct	88011
Roadrunner Ln	
535-899	88005
1000-2000	88007
2002-2098	88007
1875-1-1875-2	88007
N Roadrunner Pkwy	88011
S Roadrunner Pkwy	88011
Robert Larson Blvd	88007
Roberts Dr	88005
Robin Rd	88007
Robin Wing Rd	88012
Robledo Rd	88012
Robledo Vista Rd	88007
Rocca Secca Rd	88012
Rociante Dr	88005
Rock Ct	88012
Rock Canyon Loop	88011
Rock House Rd	88011
Rock Springs Rd	88011
Rocky Rd	88001
Rocky Acres Trl	88007
Roe Deer Ct	88007
Rolling Hills Ln	88011
Rolling Stone Ct	88012
Roma Dr	88012
Ronna Dr	88001
Roosevelt St	88001
Rosales Farm Rd	88007
Rosalie Ave	88005
Rose Ln	88005
Rosedale Dr	88005
Rossman Ave	88011
Rouault Ave	88005
Round Up Rd	88011
Roundtable Ct	88012
Roundtree Pl	88005
Royal Dr	88011
Rubina Ct	88007
Ruby Ct	88007
Ruby Dr	88001
Ruby Mine Rd	88011
Run Along Rd	88007
Russian Sage Dr	88011
Rusty Ln	88007
Sable Cir	88001
Sacramento Cir, Ct & St	88001
Saddle Fork Ct	88012
Saddle Mountain Rd	88012
Saddle Ridge Ct	88011
Saddle Rock Rd	88011
Sage Rd	88011
Sagecrest Ave	88011
Saguaro Ct	88011
Saint Anthony Rd	88012
Saint Francis Rd	88012
Saint James	88005
Saint Michaels Rd	88011
Sal Si Puedes Rd	88012
Salado Creek St	88012
Salida Del Sol Ct	88005
Salina Rd	88012
Salinas Dr	88011
Sallee Rd	88011
Salopek Blvd	88001
Salopek Rd	88005
Saltillo Pl	88007
Salvia Loop	88011
Sambrano Ave	88001
Sambrero Ct	88007
San Acacio St	88001
San Andres Dr	88007
San Augustin Dr	88012
San Bonifacio Arc	88005
San Carlos Ct	88011
San Clemente Ave	88012
San Elizario Ct	88007
San Felipe	88011
San Felipe Ave	88001
San Fernando Dr	88011
San Francisco St	88001
San Juan Ave	88001
San Leonardo Ct	88005
San Lorenzo Ct	88007
San Luis Rey Ave	88011
San Marcos Ct	88007
San Miguel Ct	88007
San Pablo Rd	88005
San Patricio Ct & Loop	88011
N & S San Pedro St	88001
San Savino Ct	88007
San Vicente Ct	88005
San Ysidro Rd	88007
Sanban Dr	88005
Sanchez Pl	88005
Sandalwood Dr	88011
Sandcastle Ave	88012
Sanddollar Ct & Way	88007
Sandell Rd	88001
Sandhill Rd	88012
Sandia Ct	88012
Sandigale Dr	88011
Sandstone Ln	88007
Sandy St	88012
Sandy Beach Rd	88005
Sandy Hill Dr	88007
Santa Adriana Ave	88012
Santa Ana	88011
Santa Barbara Ct	88012
Santa Cecilia Ave	88012
Santa Clara Ln	88007
Santa Cruz	88012
Santa Cruz Rd	88005
N & S Santa Fe St	88001
Santa Gertrudis Dr	88012
Santa Ines St	88011
Santa Lucia Arc	88005
Santa Marcella Ave	88012
Santa Minerva Ave	88012
Santa Monica	88007
Santa Sabina Ave	88012
Santanova Arc	88005
Santiago Way	88011
Santo Domingo Ave & Ct	88011
Sapillo Dr	88012
Saragossa Ct	88007
Sarah Lee Wooten Ct	88007
Saromi Ln	88011
Saturn Cir	88012
Sauco Ln	88005
Scale Ct	88011
Scenic Cir	88011
Scenic Crest Loop	88011
Scenic Ridge Loop	88011
Scenic View Dr	88011
Schaffner Rd	88012
Schooner Loop	88012
Scoggins Ave	88005
Scorpio Loop	88005
Scott Ln	88012
Scottland Ct	88005
Scout Ln	88007
Sedona Hills Pkwy	88011
Seldon Ave	88001
Selene Ct	88005
Sells Pl	88007
Seminole Trl	88012
Seneca Dr	88005
Senita Dr	88011
Senna Dr	88011
Sequoia Ave	88005
Serrano Dr	88012
Settlers Bnd N & S	88012
Seville Way	88011
Sexton Ln	88012
Sexton St	88001
Shadow Hills Rd	88012
Shadow Mountain Rd	88011
Shadow Run Ave	88011
Shadow Valley Dr	88007
Shady Pl	88007
Shady Brook Ct	88005
Shady Glen Ave	88005
Shady Grove Ln	88007
Shadywood Ln	88007
Shakespeare Ln	88007
Shalem Colony Trl	88007
Shannon Rd	88011
Shannon St	88001
Sharon Cir	88001
Sharon Q	88007
Shawnee	88007
Sheep Springs Rd	88011
Shenandoah Trl	88007
Sherri Ct	88005
Sherwood Rd	88012
Sheryl Way	88001
Shining Star Ct	88011
Shoestring Ranch Rd	88012
Shorthorn Dr	88012
Shorty Pl	88007
Shoshone	88007
Sierra Alta Pl	88012
Sierra Bella Pl	88012
Sierra Bonita Ave	88012
Sierra De Luna Pl	88012
Sierra De Oro Pl	88012
Sierra Del Sol Ave	88012
Sierra Linda Ct	88012
Sierra Luz Dr	88012
Sierra Prado Ct	88012
Sierra Vista Ave	88012
Silk Oak Ct	88011
Silver Rd	88001
Silver Creek Rd	88007
Silver Hawk Ave	88011
Silver King Rd	88011
Silver Sage Dr	88011
Silvermoon Ct	88012
Silverton Ct	88011
Sim Ave	88005
Singer Rd	88007
Singletree	88012
Sioux Trl	88012
Sirena Ln	88012
Siri Ln	88011
Sirius St	88012
Sisley Pl	88007
Sitka Deer St	88007
Skylark Ln	88012
Skyline Dr	88007
Skyview Ln	88007
Skyway Dr	88001
Slate Ave	88012
Sleepy Hollow Rd	88007
Smith Ave	88001
Smokethorn Dr	88007
Snow Rd	88005
Snowy Egret Ct	88007
Soda Spring Dr	88011
N & S Solano Dr	88001
Solar Way	88001
Solarridge St	88012
Soldier Ct	88007
Soledad Ave	88001
Soledad Canyon Ct & Rd	88011
Solid Comfort Pl	88005
Soloeste Way	88012
Solstice St	88012
Sombra Arbol Ct	88012
Sombra Azul St	88012
Sombra Morada Rd	88012
Sombra Prieta Ct	88012
Sommerset Arc	88011
Sonnet Ct	88007
Sonoma Ranch Blvd	
1884-4598	88011
4600-4699	88011
4801-4899	88012
S Sonoma Ranch Blvd	88011
Sonoma Springs Ave	88011
Sonrisa Loop	88007
Sorrel Dr	88012
Sorrento Pl	88005
Sotol Ct & Dr	88011
Southern Canyon Loop	88011
Southern Star Loop	88011
Southgate Ct	88005
Southridge Dr	88005
Southview Ave	88007
Southwind Rd	88007
Space Murals Ln	88011
Spanish Trl	88001
Spanish Dagger St	88011
Spanish Pointe Rd	88007
Sparrow Rd	88007
Spirit Hunter Ct	88011
Spirit Ridge Rd	88007
Spirit Rock Dr	88011
Spirit Winds	88012
Spitz St	88005
Spotted Dove Dr	88001
Spring Water Way	88011
Springfield Ct	88007
E Springs Rd	88011
Spruce Ave	88001
Spur Ln	88012
Spur Ridge Rd	88011
Squaw Mountain Dr	88011
Squirrel Rd	88007
Stagecoach Dr & Ln	88011
Staghorn Ct	88012
Standley Dr	
700-1599	88001
1600-1698	88003
Stanford St	88005
Stanley Rd	88012
Stanton Ave	88001
Star View Dr	88012
Starburst	88012
Starfly Rd	88011
Starlite Ct	88012
Starview Rd	88012
Steeler Ln	88012
Stefanie Ct	88005
Steins Dr	88012
Stellar Way	88011
Stern Dr	
700-800	88005
802-2398	88005
3800-5398	88001
5400-5500	88001
5502-5898	88001
Stetson Pl	88011
Stewards Dr	88012
Stewart Ln	88005
Stewart St	88003
Stithes Rd	88005
Stone Canyon Dr	88011
Stone Crop Ct	88007
Stone Mountain Ln	88011
Stone Pine Dr	88012
Stoneway Rd	88012
Stoney Brook Cir & Ct	88005
Stout Ln	88007
Strange Rd	88007
Stryker Rd	88005
Stull Dr	88001
Sue Ct	88007
Sugar Loaf Rd	88011
Sugar Pine Way	88012
Sugar Sand Trl	88007
Summit Ct & Ln	88011
Summit Ridge Ct	88011
Sumner Ave, Ct & Pl	88001
Sun Ct	88012
Sun Canyon Ct & Rd	88011
Sun Chaser Pl	88011

Sun Shadow Pl 88011
Sun Stone Way 88011
Sun Valley Ln 88007
Sunbonnet Ln 88007
Suncreek Ct 88012
Suncrest Arc 88011
Sundance Cir 88011
Sundown Ct & Rd 88011
Sunflower Pl 88007
Sunglow Ct 88012
Sunken Train Pl 88007
Sunland Ave 88012
Sunny Ln 88011
Sunny Acres Dr 88012
Sunray St 88012
Sunridge Dr 88012
Sunrise Ave 88001
Sunrise Point Rd 88011
Sunrise Vista Ln 88007
Sunrunner Ave 88012
Sunset Dr 88005
Sunset Pl 88011
Sunshine Valley Ct 88007
Sunspot Ct 88012
Superstition Dr 88011
Supreme Ct 88007
Suzanne Ave 88005
Swartz Rd 88007
Sweet Ave 88001
Sweetwater Ct 88012
Sycamore Dr 88005
Talavera Ave 88011
Tall Tree Ct 88012
Tamarack Dr 88005
Tamarisk Rd 88011
Tamariz Ct 88007
Tammy Ln 88012
Tamony Ln 88007
Tanglewood Pl 88012
Tanzanite Rd 88012
Taos Ln 88005
Tapestry Cir 88005
Tashiro Dr 88007
Tasmania Ave 88012
Taurus Dr 88005
E Taylor Rd 88007
W Taylor Rd 88007
Taylor St 88001
Tayvis Rd 88012
Teal Drake Ct 88012
Techo Alto Ct 88007
Tecolote Trl 88012
Tejean Trl 88007
Tel High Rd 88007
Tellbrook Ct & Rd 88011
N & S Telshor Blvd & Ct 88011
Temple St 88005
Tepeyac St 88001
Teresita St 88005
Terrace Arc, Ct & Dr 88011
Territorial St 88012
Terry Dr 88007
Tesota Dr & Rd 88011
Tesuque Pl 88011
Tetakawi Ct 88007
Tewa Ct 88011
Texas Ave 88001
Thielman Rd 88005
Thomas Dr 88001
Thomas Moran Rd 88011
Thorpe Rd 88012
E Thorpe Rd 88007
W Thorpe Rd 88007
Three Crosses Ave 88005
Threeawn Ct 88012
Thunder Way 88012
Thunderbird St 88011
Thurmond Rd 88012
Thurston Ct 88012
Tierra Rd 88005
Tierra Alta Dr 88011
Tierra Blanca Rd 88011
Tierra De Mesilla 88005
Tierra Del Sol Ct & Dr 88007
Tierra Grande Ct 88011

Tierra Roja Ct 88012
Tierra Sagrada 88011
Tiffany Dr 88011
Tiger Eye Dr 88012
Tiger Woods Dr 88011
Tigua Dr 88001
Tile Ave 88001
Tingley Dr 88007
Tingo Cir 88007
Titania Ct 88007
Tobosa Rd 88011
Tonja Ct 88005
Topaz Pl 88001
Topaz Rd 88012
Topley Ave 88005
Tor Ln 88005
Tornado Ct 88012
N & S Tornillo St 88001
Tortugas Dr 88001
Totonic 88007
Towhee Ave 88012
Townsend Ter 88005
Townview Ln 88007
S Track Trl 88007
Trails End Rd 88007
Tranquilo Ln 88012
Travis Ln 88007
Tres Amigos Rd 88007
Tres Hijos Pl 88007
Tres Hombres 88005
Tres Infantes 88011
Tres Ninos 88011
Tres Piedras Way 88012
Tres Pinos Ln 88005
Tres Sendas Rd 88005
Tres Yuccas Rd 88012
Trillium Dr 88007
Trinity Ln 88012
Triplett Rd 88011
Triumph Ct 88011
N & S Triviz Dr 88001
Trojan Loop 88007
Troybrook Rd 88012
Trucha Dr 88007
Tucson Ave 88012
Tularosa Dr 88007
Tulip Cir 88007
W Tundra Rd 88007
Turkey Knob Dr 88012
Turn Here Rd 88012
Turner Ave 88005
Turquoise Ave & Loop 88001
Turrentine Dr 88005
Turtle Creek Ave 88005
Tuscan Hills Ln 88011
Tuscany Dr 88007
Twighlight Ridge Way 88011
Twin Peaks Rd 88012
Tyre Cir 88001
Unicorn Ln 88012
E Union Ave 88001
W Union Ave 88005
E University Ave
  201-699 88005
  600-698 88001
  700-1499 88001
  1501-1799 88001
  1700-2998 88003
  3000-3099 88011
  3101-3299 88011
W University Ave 88005
Uranus Ave 88012
E Us Highway 70
  8701-9799 88012
E Us Highway 70
  17400-18499 88011
Usana 88012
Utah Ave & Ct 88001
Vajillo Ln 88005
Valdes Rd 88005
Valencia Dr 88001
Valle Vis 88011
Valle Alegre 88007
Valle Bonita Dr 88007
Valle Del Luz 88007
Valle Grande 88005

Valle Hermosa 88005
Valle Sonrisa 88007
N Valley Dr
  340-372 88005
  374-1068 88005
  1070-1250 88005
  1300-1698 88007
  1700-23499 88007
  3940-1-3940-9 88007
S Valley Dr 88005
Valley View Ave 88005
Valverde Loop 88012
Van Ess Ct 88012
Van Patten Ave 88005
Vanegas Ct & Dr 88007
Vaquero Pl 88007
Vassar Ct 88005
Velarde Pl 88011
Venetian Loop 88011
Ventana View Rd 88011
Ventura Cir 88012
Venture Dr 88007
Venus St 88012
Verbinia St 88007
Vereda Granate 88012
Verona Ct 88007
Via Campestre 88007
Via De Vl 88007
Via De Valle 88012
Via Diamante 88007
Via Emma 88007
Via Estrella 88011
Via Norte 88007
Via Rubi 88007
Via Segura 88011
Via Sierra Sagrado 88011
Via Sombra 88005
Via Tesoro 88005
Via Turquesa 88007
Victorio Trl 88012
View Ct & Dr 88011
Villa Chiquita 88007
Villa Mora Ave 88001
Villa Napoli Loop E & W 88011
Village Dr 88012
Villita Loop 88007
Vintage Ct 88007
Violet Way 88001
N & S Virginia St 88001
Virginia Pine Pl 88012
Virgo Dr 88005
Vista Ct 88005
Vista Bella 88011
Vista Belleza Ave 88012
Vista Chico Loop 88012
Vista Cuesta 88001
Vista De Dios 88005
Vista De Luz Ct 88011
Vista De Oeste Pl 88012
Vista De Oro 88007
Vista De Sobre Dr 88012
Vista De Tierra 88012
Vista Del Cerro 88007
Vista Del Monte
  100-199 88001
Vista Del Monte
  1200-1300 88007
  1302-1398 88007
Vista Del Norte St 88012
Vista Del Reino 88007
Vista Del Sol Pl 88007
Vista Del Valle 88007
Vista Estrella Ct 88011
Vista Hermosa 88007
Vista Hills Dr 88011
Vista Lejano 88005
Vista Montana Rd 88005
Vista Primera Rd 88011
Vista Real Dr 88007
Vista Sierra Ct 88005
Vista Sureste 88011
Vista Valley Trl 88007
Vista Verde Rd 88005
Wade St 88001
Wagon Wheel Trl 88005

Wagonmound Trl 88012
Wagons East Trl 88012
Walden Dr 88001
Walker Trl 88007
Wall Ave 88001
S Walnut St 88001
Walter Ln 88007
Walton Blvd 88001
Waltz Ln 88007
Waring Rd 88007
Warm Sands Ct 88011
Warm Springs Ln 88011
Warrior Ln 88007
N & S Water St 88001
Waterfall Cyn 88011
Waterhole Cyn 88011
Watson Ln & Pl 88005
Weaver Trl 88012
Webb Rd 88012
Webster Ave 88001
Weddell St 88003
Weinrich Rd 88007
Weisner Rd 88012
Wells St 88003
Wendale Ave 88001
Wendall Rd 88012
Wendy Ln 88007
Wesley Dr 88012
West St 88005
Westdin 88011
Western Ct 88007
Western View Rd 88007
Westgate Ct & St 88005
Westmoreland Ave 88012
Westridge Dr 88005
Westview Ave 88007
Westway Ave 88005
Westwind Rd 88007
Whispering Pines Ct & Ln 88007
White Fox Rd 88012
White Horse Ct 88007
White Lightning Dr 88007
White Thorn Rd 88012
White Wing Rd 88012
Whitney Pl 88012
Whitstone Dr 88012
Wild Bill Ln 88011
Wild Hollow Ct 88012
Wild Horse Rd 88011
Wildcat Canyon Dr 88011
Wildflower Rd 88011
Wildwind Rd 88007
Wildwood Pl 88011
Wiley Ave 88007
William Bonney Rd 88007
Williams Ln 88005
E Willoughby Ave 88001
W Willoughby Ave 88005
N & S Willow St 88001
Willow Brook Ct 88005
Willow Creek Ln 88007
Willow Glen Dr 88005
Wilson Ave 88005
N Wilt Ave 88012
S Wilt Ave 88011
Wimberly St 88001
E Winchester Rd 88011
Wind Ln 88007
Wind Chime Ln 88007
Wind Dancer Trl 88011
Wind Summit Pl 88011
Windflyer Ln 88007
Windmill Ct 88011
Windmill Dr 88011
Windmill Rd 88012
Windridge Cir 88012
Windrose Ct 88007
Windsong Ln 88005
Windsor Ct & Pl 88005
Wingate Ct & Rd 88001
Wingspan 88007
Winston Ave 88005
Winterhaven Dr 88007
Winters St 88005
Winterset Rd 88005

Winton Cir & Ct 88007
E Wisconsin Ave 88001
Witt St 88005
Wofford Dr 88001
Wolf Crk 88012
Wolf Trl 88001
Wonder Ln 88005
Wooten Dr 88001
Wrangler Pl 88011
Wyatt Dr
  100-199 88005
  300-398 88001
Wyoming Ave 88001
Yale Ct & Dr 88005
Yavapai Ct 88011
Yellowstone Dr 88011
Yeso Ln 88005
Yucca Hts 88012
Yuma St 88012
Zacatecas Ct 88012
Zachary Ln 88012
Zeno Pl 88012
Zertuche Ln 88007
Zeus Ave 88011
Zia Blvd 88007
Zircon Ct 88012
Zorro Trl 88007
Zuni 88007

NUMBERED STREETS

All Street Addresses 88005

RIO RANCHO NM

General Delivery 87124

POST OFFICE BOXES MAIN OFFICE STATIONS AND BRANCHES

Box No.s
All PO Boxes 87174

NAMED STREETS

Abbey Ct SE 87124
Aberdeen Dr SE 87124
Abeto Ln SE 87124
Abra Pl NE 87124
Abrazo Rd NE 87124
Abril Cir NE 87124
Acadia Ct SE 87124
Acapulco Ct & Rd 87144
Ace Way SE 87124
Acebo NE 87124
Acetin Ct NE 87124
Acicate Pl NE 87124
Acorn Loop NE 87144
Adema Rd NE 87124
Afuste Rd NE 87124
Ag Pl SE 87124
Agora Rd NE 87124
Agua Dulce Dr SE 87124
Agua Fria Dr NE 87144
Aguila Rd SE 87124
Akita Ct NE 87144
Alama Dr NE 87124
Alamo Dr SE 87124
Albany Hills Ct & Dr 87144
Alberta Ave NE 87144
Alberti Ct NE 87144
Albor Cir NE 87124
Alcano Cir NE 87124
Alda Rd SE 87124
Aldaba Cir NE 87124
Aldan Dr NE 87144
Alder Dr NE 87144
Alero Cir NE 87124
Alexa Way NE 87144
Algodones Ct SE 87124
Alif Rd NE 87144

Allegheny Dr NE 87144
Aloe Cir NE 87144
Alpha Ct & Rd 87124
Alpine Cir & Ct 87124
Alta Vista Ct SE 87124
Ambrose Alday Loop SE 87124
Amethyst Dr NE 87124
Anchiote Rd NE 87144
Angela Dr NE 87144
Animas Ct NE 87144
Anitori Rd SE 87124
Ann Cir SE 87124
Annette Dr NE 87124
Antigua Rd SE 87124
Apache Ct & Loop 87124
Apache Plume Rd NE 87144
Apex Ct SE 87124
Apple Ct NE 87144
Applewood Park Dr SE 87124
Aqua Marine Dr NE 87124
Aragon Ct NE 87144
Arapahoe Rd NE 87144
Arbolera Loop SE 87124
Arce Ln SE 87124
Archibeque Ave SE 87124
Arcturus Ave SE 87124
Argus Ct SE 87124
Arizona St SE 87124
Arizona Sunset Rd NE 87124
Arkansas Ct & St 87124
Arlene Ct, Pl & Rd 87124
Arlin Ct NE 87124
Arrowhead Ridge Dr SE 87124
Asbury Rd NE 87124
Ashberry Ct SE 87124
Ashkirk Loop & Pl 87124
Aspen Leaf Ct SE 87124
Aspen Meadows Dr NE 87144
Assisi Hills Rd NE 87144
Aster Dr SW 87124
Asturia Ct NE 87144
Athens Ct SE 87124
Atlanta Hills Dr NE 87144
Atlantic Rd SE 87124
Aubry Hills Dr NE 87144
Audh Ct NE 87144
Augusta Dr SE 87124
Augusta Hills Dr NE 87144
Aurora Rd NE 87144
Autumn Meadows Dr NE 87144
Autumn Sage Ave NE 87144
Avenida Castellana SE 87124
Avenida Comunidad SE 87124
Avenida Corazon SE 87124
Aztec Ct NE 87144
Aztec Sun Ct SE 87144
Azure Sky Ave NE 87144
Bachmann Ct NE 87144
Bahama Dr SE 87124
Baldy Loop NE 87144
Bali Rd SE 87144
Balsa Rd NW 87144
Baltic Ave & Way 87124
Baranca Rd NE 87144
Baranca Overlook Ct & Pl 87144
Barbara Loop SE 87124
Barona Ave SE 87124
Basin Ct SE 87124
Bay Ct & Rd 87124
Bay Hill Loop SE 87124
Bayas Rd SE 87124
Bayou Rd NE 87144
Beaver Ct NE 87144
Bellflower Dr NE 87144
Benjamin Ct & Dr 87124
Benson Park Ct SE 87124
Bentgrass Mdws NE 87144
Bermuda Dr SE 87124
Bertha Rd SE 87124

Beth Way NE 87144
Bhutan Dr SE 87124
Big Hawk Rd NE 87144
Birch Ct SE 87124
Birdie Ct SE 87124
Biscayne Way SE 87124
Bismark Hills Way NE 87144
Black Hawk Dr NE 87144
Black Hills Rd NE 87124
Black River Ct & Dr 87144
Blackberry Rd NE 87144
Blackbird Rd NE 87144
Blackhawk River Dr NE 87144
Blanca Peak Trl NE 87144
Bloomfield Meadows Dr NE 87144
Blue Moon Dr NE 87144
Blue Quail Ct & Rd 87144
Blue River Ct NE 87144
Blue Sage Rd NE 87144
Blue Sky Loop NE 87144
Blue Spruce Dr NE 87144
Blueberry Dr NE 87144
Bogie Rd SE 87124
Borealis Ave SE 87124
Boromir NW 87144
Boulder Rd NE 87144
Box Lake Dr NE 87144
Bramble Ct SE 87124
Branco Dr NE 87144
Branding Iron Rd SE 87124
Bravo Ct SE 87124
Brazos Ct NE 87144
Brazos Dr SE 87124
Brenda Rd SE 87124
Bridger Rd NE 87144
Brierwood Ct SE 87124
Brighton Hills Dr & Pl 87144
Broadmoor Blvd NE
  700-704 87124
  706-770 87124
  3001-3005 87144
Broadmoor Blvd SE 87124
Brook Meadows Dr NE 87144
Brown Bear Dr NE 87144
Buckaroo Rd NE 87144
Buckboard Rd SE 87124
Buckeye Ct NE 87144
Buckskin Loop NE 87144
Buena Vista Ct SE 87124
Bulb Ct NE 87124
Bunker Rd SE 87124
Bunker Hill Ct SE 87124
Bursum Ln SE 87124
Burton Meadows Dr NE 87144
Caballo Ct & Pl 87144
Cabeza Negra Ct & Dr 87124
Cabezon Blvd SE 87124
Cabezon Dr NE 87144
Cabo Way NE 87124
Cabot Hills Ct NE 87144
Cactus Dr NE 87144
California Pine Rd NE 87124
Calle De Roja Dr SE 87124
Calle Suenos SE 87124
Calming Meadows Ct NE 87144
Calvillo Ct SE 87124
Camacho Rd SE 87124
Camino Catalonia SE 87124
Camino Cordoba SE 87124
Camino Pyrenees SE 87124
Camino Seville SE 87124
Campeche Rd NE 87124
Campfire Ct & Rd 87124
Campus NE 87144
Cancun Loop NE 87124
Candlelight Dr SE 87124
Canelo Ct SE 87124
Cantera St SE 87124
Canvasback Ct & Rd 87144
Canyon Gate Pl NE 87144

Capri Ct SE ... 87124
Caprock Ct & Dr ... 87144
Caramel Ct SE ... 87124
Caramesa Ct & Dr ... 87124
Carin Ct SE ... 87124
Carina Ct SE ... 87124
Carr Way NE ... 87144
Carrizo Dr NE ... 87144
Carson Rd NE ... 87144
Cascade Ct, Rd & Way ... 87124
Cascades Trl SE ... 87124
Casper Rd SE ... 87124
Castile Ct NE ... 87144
Castle Peak Loop NE ... 87144
Castle Rock Rd SE ... 87124
Cattail Rd NE ... 87144
Cattle Dr NE ... 87144
Cave Primrose Ct SE ... 87124
Cedar Ln SE ... 87124
Cedro Ln SE ... 87124
Celina Ct & Rd ... 87124
Ceniza Ln SE ... 87124
Cereza Dr SE ... 87124
Cerro Chafo Rd SE ... 87124
Cerro De Ortega Dr SE ... 87124
Cerro Parrido Rd SE ... 87124
Chaco Loop NE ... 87144
Chaco Canyon Ct & Dr ... 87144
Chama Meadows Dr NE ... 87144
Chama River Ct NE ... 87144
Chamisa Rd NE ... 87144
Chandra Ln SE ... 87124
Chaparral Loop SE ... 87124
Chapingo Rd NE ... 87144
Chaps Rd SE ... 87124
Chardon Meadows Dr NE ... 87144
Charlene Rd SE ... 87124
Charles Dr NE ... 87144
Chayote Rd NE ... 87144
Cherish Ct SE ... 87124
Cherokee Dr SW ... 87124
Cherry Rd NE ... 87144
Chesapeake Pl NE ... 87144
Chessman Dr NE & SE ... 87124
Chetah Rd NE ... 87124
Chicoma Rd NE ... 87144
Chihuahua Rd NE ... 87144
Chimayo Meadows Dr NE ... 87144
Chino Ct NE ... 87144
Chip Ct SE ... 87124
Chippewa Ct & Dr ... 87124
Chisholm Trl NE ... 87144
Cholla Dr NE ... 87144
Chow Ct NE ... 87144
Christine Dr NE ... 87124
Christopher Ct NE ... 87144
Chromium Dr NE ... 87124
Chuckwagon Rd SE ... 87124
Cibola Dr NE ... 87144
Cielo Azul Dr NE ... 87144
Cielo Grande Dr NE ... 87144
Cimarron Meadows Ct & Dr ... 87144
Cimmarron Ct NE ... 87144
Cipres Ln SE ... 87124
Civic Center Cir NE ... 87144
Clark Hills Dr NE ... 87144
Clayton Meadows Dr NE ... 87144
Clear Creek Ct, Pl & Rd ... 87144
Clearwater Loop NE ... 87144
Cliff Dr NE ... 87144
Clovis Ct NE ... 87144
Coba Rd SE ... 87124
Cochise Cir SE ... 87124
Cochiti St NE ... 87144
Cody Rd NE ... 87144
Colfax Pl NE ... 87144
Colina Roja NE ... 87124
Colina Serena Pl NE ... 87124
College Ave NE ... 87144
Collie Dr NE ... 87144
Colmor Meadows Cir & Dr ... 87144
Colorado Ct NE ... 87144
Colorado Mountain Rd NE ... 87124
Colores Ct SE ... 87124
Columbia Ct NE ... 87144
Comanche Ct & Rd ... 87124
Commercial Dr SE ... 87124
Concord Hills Loop NE ... 87144
Conejos Dr SE ... 87124
Conestoga Rd SE ... 87124
Confection Ct SE ... 87124
Contreras Rd NE ... 87144
Copper Dr NE ... 87124
Copper Creek Rd SE ... 87124
Coral Dr NE ... 87124
Coronado Ct SE ... 87124
Corsica Dr SE ... 87124
Corte Castellana SE ... 87124
Corte Castellon SE ... 87124
Corte Cordillera SE ... 87124
Corte De La Villa SE ... 87124
Corte Marbella SE ... 87124
Corte Palos SE ... 87124
Corte Seville SE ... 87124
Corte Toledo SE ... 87124
Cortina Loop SE ... 87124
Corvara Dr SE ... 87124
Costilla Rd NE ... 87144
Cottontail Rd NE ... 87144
Coulter St NE ... 87144
Count Dr NE ... 87144
Country Club Dr SE ... 87124
Coventry Hills Dr NE ... 87144
Coyote Ct & Way ... 87144
Coyote Bush Rd NE ... 87144
Cozumel Way NE ... 87124
Crane Pl SE ... 87124
Cree Ct NE ... 87144
Crescent Moon Dr NE ... 87144
Crest Pl SE ... 87124
Crestview Dr SE ... 87124
Cripple Creek Dr SE ... 87124
Crook Pl SE ... 87124
Crow Ct & Rd ... 87144
Crown Ct NE ... 87124
Crownpoint Dr NE ... 87144
Daffodil Dr SW ... 87124
Dakota St SW ... 87124
Dakota Morning Rd NE ... 87144
Dal Ct NE ... 87144
Dalmation Pl NE ... 87144
Dalmuir Ct SE ... 87124
Danzante Dr SE ... 87124
Dara Dr NE ... 87144
Darlene Rd SE ... 87124
Dauphine Ct NE ... 87144
David Ct NE ... 87124
Daybreak Rd SE ... 87124
De Baca Ct NE ... 87144
De Vinci Blvd NE ... 87144
Dearborn Hills Dr NE ... 87144
Deborah Rd SE ... 87124
Debra Pl NE ... 87144
Deer Trail Loop NE ... 87144
Del Carmen Dr NE ... 87144
Del Rey Ct SE ... 87124
Delaina Dr NE ... 87144
Deledda Rd NE ... 87144
Delfinio Dr SE ... 87124
Delicias Rd SE ... 87124
Demasiado Rd SE ... 87124
Demavend Rd NE ... 87144
Deming Meadows Dr NE ... 87144
Denchit Dr NE ... 87124
Denise Dr NE ... 87124
Dennison Park Loop SE ... 87124
Desert Ave NE ... 87144
Desert Broom Rd NE ... 87144
Desert Chicory Ct SE ... 87124
Desert Lily Ct SE ... 87124
Desert Lupine Dr NE ... 87144
Desert Marigold Rd NE ... 87144
Desert Paintbrush Loop NE ... 87144
Desert Pinon Dr NE ... 87144
Desert Ridge Dr SE ... 87124
Desert Sky Ct & Pl ... 87144
Desert Sunflower Dr NE ... 87144
Desert View Ct & Rd ... 87144
Desert Willow Ct, Dr & Pl ... 87144
Desert Zinnia Rd NE ... 87144
Devon Ct SE ... 87124
Dexter Ct NE ... 87144
Diamond Peak Dr NE ... 87144
Diez Y Ocho Ct SE ... 87124
Dillon Dr NE ... 87124
Doe Ct NE ... 87124
Dogwood Trl SE ... 87124
Dolores Hidalgo Dr SE ... 87124
Dolphin Rd NW ... 87144
Domain Loop SE ... 87124
Dona Ana Loop NE ... 87144
Donet Ct & Dr ... 87144
Donora Ct NE ... 87144
Doral Park Rd SE ... 87124
Dove Ct NE ... 87144
Dream Dancer Dr NE ... 87144
Dry Creek Ct NE ... 87144
Ducale Dr SE ... 87124
Dulce Dr NE ... 87144
Dundee Way SE ... 87124
Durango Rd SW ... 87124
Dynamite Rd NE ... 87144
Eagle Nest Ct SE ... 87124
Eastlake Ct & Dr ... 87124
Eaton Rd SE ... 87124
Eddy Dr NE ... 87144
El Alamo Ct SE ... 87124
El Alto Ct SE ... 87124
El Bardo Ct SE ... 87124
El Cajon Ct SE ... 87124
El Camino Loop NW ... 87144
El Campo St NW ... 87144
El Dedo Ct SE ... 87124
El Fresno Ct SE ... 87124
El Granado Ct SE ... 87124
El Hachero Ct SE ... 87124
El Higo Ct SE ... 87124
El Morro Dr SE ... 87124
El Olmo Ct SE ... 87124
El Paseo St NW ... 87144
El Picador Ct SE ... 87124
El Prado St NW ... 87144
El Puno Ct SE ... 87124
El Rio Ct SE ... 87124
El Torero Ct SE ... 87124
Elder Meadows Dr NE ... 87144
Elizabeth Ann Rd NE ... 87144
Elkslip Dr NE ... 87144
Elm Ct SE ... 87124
Emerald Dr NE ... 87124
Emperador St NW ... 87144
Encantado Ridge Ct NE ... 87124
Enchanted Hills Blvd NE ... 87144
N & S Ensenada Cir ... 87124
Enterprise Rd NE ... 87124
Epic Ct SE ... 87124
Erie Ct NE ... 87144
Erlinda Rd SE ... 87124
Escudo Rd NE ... 87144
Esplanade Cir & Pl ... 87124
Essex Dr NE ... 87124
Estrellita Rd SE ... 87124
Eucalyptus Rd NE ... 87144
Evelyn Dr NE ... 87144
Eventide Rd SE ... 87124
Everest Rd SE ... 87124
Exeter Ct SE ... 87124
Fairbanks Dr NE ... 87144
Fairway Loop SE ... 87124
Falesco Rd SE ... 87124
Falkirk Ct & Rd ... 87144
Feldspar Dr NE ... 87124
Fence Lake Dr NE ... 87144
Fennel Rd NE ... 87144
Fiat Ct SE ... 87124
Finnigan Ct NE ... 87144
Fireweed Dr NE ... 87144
Flagstone Rd NE ... 87144
Flat Iron Rd NE ... 87144
Fleet Rd NE ... 87124
Foraker Rd SE ... 87124
Forest Trail Rd SE ... 87124
Fornax Rd SE ... 87124
Fountain Ct SE ... 87124
Fowler Meadows Dr NE ... 87144
Foxmoore Ct & Dr ... 87144
Foxwood Trl SE ... 87124
Fran Pl & Rd ... 87124
Franklin NE ... 87144
Franzen Hills Ct NE ... 87144
Fraser Dr SE ... 87124
Freemont Hills Loop NE ... 87144
Fringe Ct SE ... 87124
Fringe Sage Rd NE ... 87144
Frontage Rd NE ... 87124
Frontier Rd NE ... 87144
Fruta Rd NE
500-798 ... 87124
800-899 ... 87124
1600-1648 ... 87144
Fulcrum Way NE ... 87144
Full Moon Ct NE ... 87144
Gadwall Rd NE ... 87144
Galacia Ct NE ... 87144
Gallinas Rd NE ... 87144
Gallup Rd SW ... 87124
Galway Rd NE ... 87144
Gambel Quail Rd NE ... 87144
Gambia Dr NE ... 87144
Garden Rd NE ... 87124
Garnet Dr NE ... 87124
Gay Cir SE ... 87124
Gazelle Rd NE ... 87144
Gemini Rd NE ... 87144
Georgia Pl NE ... 87144
Geraldine Loop, Pl & Rd ... 87124
Gila River Rd NE ... 87144
Girasol Rd SE ... 87124
Gladstone Dr NE ... 87144
Glen Hills Dr NE ... 87144
Glendale Ct SE ... 87124
Globe Ct NE ... 87124
Glorieta Meadows Dr NE ... 87144
Golden Ct SE ... 87124
Golden Eye Loop NE ... 87144
Goldfinch Way NE ... 87144
Golf Course Rd SE ... 87124
Golfers Ln SE ... 87124
Goya Rd SW ... 87124
Gral Trevino Dr SE ... 87124
Granada Rd NE ... 87144
Grand Ridge Ct SE ... 87124
Grande Blvd & Ct ... 87124
Grande Vista Rd NE ... 87144
Granite Ct SE ... 87124
Grants Dr NE ... 87144
Gray Hawk Dr NE ... 87144
Grays Peak Trl NE ... 87144
Grayson Hills Dr NE ... 87144
Green Lake Rd NE ... 87124
Greenock Dr SE ... 87124
Greenview Way NE ... 87144
Gregg Rd NE ... 87144
Gregory Ct NE ... 87144
Greystone Ct SE ... 87124
Greystone Ridge Dr SE ... 87124
Gros Ventre Dr NE ... 87144
Guadalajara Rd NE ... 87144
Guava Ct NE ... 87144
Gunpowder Ct NE ... 87124
Gypsum Ct & Dr ... 87124
Halo Cir SE ... 87124
Hampton Ct SE ... 87124
Hanley Rd NE ... 87144
Hapsburg Rd NE ... 87144
Harding Rd NE ... 87144
Harrison Dr NE ... 87144
Hartford Hills Dr NE ... 87144
Harvard Dr SE ... 87124
Havasu Falls Ct & St ... 87144
Hawk Rd NE ... 87144
Hayworth Hills Dr NE ... 87144
Hermit Falls Dr SE ... 87124
Hewlett Dr NE ... 87124
Hidalgo Rd NW
900-998 ... 87124
1701-1899 ... 87144
High Desert Cir & Ct ... 87144
High Mesa Rd SE ... 87124
High Plains Rd NE ... 87144
High Resort Blvd SE ... 87124
High Ridge Trl SE ... 87124
Highland Meadows Ct, Pl & Rd ... 87144
Hill Rd NE ... 87144
Hillcrest Dr SE ... 87124
Hobbs Ct & Dr ... 87144
Hollow Park Ct SE ... 87124
Holly Ct NE ... 87124
Hollyberry Ct & Dr ... 87144
Holt Ct NE ... 87124
Hondo Rd SW ... 87124
Honduras Rd NE ... 87144
Hood Ct, Pl, Rd & Way SE ... 87124
Hook Ct SE ... 87124
Hope Ct NE ... 87124
Hopi Rd SE ... 87124
Hp Way NE ... 87124
Hudson River Rd NE ... 87144
Hummingbird Rd NE ... 87144
Hunter Ct NE ... 87124
Hunters Meadows Cir NE ... 87144
Hurley Ct NE ... 87144
Huron Dr NE ... 87144
Huron Rd SE ... 87124
Husky Dr NE ... 87144
Hydra Rd SE ... 87124
Icarian Rd NE ... 87144
Idaho Creek Rd NE ... 87124
Idalia Rd NE
1500-1598 ... 87124
1800-2698 ... 87124
3000-7198 ... 87144
Idalia Rd SW ... 87124
Iglesia St SW ... 87124
Ilford Rd NE ... 87144
Inca Rd NE
1001-1999 ... 87124
2400-2699 ... 87144
Inca Rd SW ... 87124
Indio Rd SW ... 87124
Industrial Park Loop & Pl ... 87124
Innovation Way NE ... 87144
Inverness Dr SE ... 87124
Ira Dr NE ... 87144
Iris Rd NE ... 87144
Iroquois Ct SW ... 87124
Island Dr & Loop ... 87124
Isleta Ct NE ... 87144
Istle Rd NE ... 87124
Itasca Rd SE ... 87124
Ivan Ct NE ... 87144
Ivory Ct & Rd ... 87124
Jacinto Rd SW ... 87124
Jack Rabbit Rd NE ... 87144
Jackie Rd SE ... 87124
Jackson Loop NE ... 87144
Jacob Dr NE ... 87144
Jade Ct NE ... 87124
Jager Dr NE ... 87144
Jane Cir SE ... 87124
Jane Pl NE ... 87144
Japura Ct NE ... 87144
Jean Pl SE ... 87124
Jeffrey Rd NE ... 87144
Jemez Loop NE ... 87144
Jessica Dr NE ... 87144
Jewel Ct SE ... 87124
Jinsen Ct NE ... 87144
Jon Ct NE ... 87144
Joshua Dr SE ... 87124
Joshua Tree Dr NE ... 87144
Juan Aldama Ct & Rd ... 87124
Juneau Hills Dr NE ... 87144
Kafka Ct & Rd ... 87144
Kaiser Pl & Rd ... 87144
Kalgan Rd NE ... 87144
Karen Ln SE ... 87124
Kathy Rd SE ... 87124
Kelly Way NE ... 87144
Kenai Dr NE ... 87144
Kennard Rd NE ... 87144
Kent Rd NE ... 87144
Kenya Rd SE ... 87124
Kim Rd NE ... 87144
Kiowa Ct NE ... 87144
Kiva Vw NE ... 87124
Kiwi Ct NE ... 87144
Kokopelli Ct & Dr ... 87144
Kraft Pl SE ... 87124
La Cantora Ct SE ... 87124
La Casa De Prasa Dr SE ... 87124
La Cieba Rd NE ... 87144
La Colorada Ct SE ... 87124
La Encina Ct SE ... 87124
La Frente Ct SE ... 87124
La Luz Cir NE ... 87144
La Merced Ct SE ... 87124
La Mirage Ct SE ... 87124
La Nuez Ct SE ... 87124
La Pacana Ct SE ... 87124
La Paz Rd NE ... 87144
La Pera Ct SE ... 87124
La Pinta Ct SE ... 87124
La Resolana Ave NW ... 87144
La Verja Ct SE ... 87124
Laban Rd NE ... 87144
Labrador Dr NE ... 87144
Laguna Ct NE ... 87144
Laird Ct SE ... 87124
Lakeview Cir & Way ... 87124
Lam Ct NE ... 87144
Landing Ct & Trl ... 87124
Laredo Rd NE ... 87144
Lariat Rd SE ... 87124
Lark Dr NE ... 87144
Lark Spur Dr NE ... 87144
Las Brisas Cir SE ... 87124
Las Casas Ct SE ... 87124
Las Cimbras Ct SE ... 87124
Las Colinas Ave NE ... 87124
Las Marias Dr SE ... 87124
Las Medanales Ct NE ... 87124
Las Ramblas Ave NW ... 87144
Laser Rd NE ... 87144
Latigo Trl SE ... 87124
Laurel Meadows Dr NE ... 87144
Lavender Meadows Dr NE ... 87144
Lawrence Dr NE ... 87144
Lazy River Ct NE ... 87144
Lee Loop NE ... 87144
Lema Rd SE ... 87124
Leo Ct NE ... 87144
Leon Ct NE ... 87144
Leon Grande Ave SE ... 87124
Leonard St SE ... 87124
Lepus Ct SE ... 87124
Lerma Rd NE ... 87144
Lewis Dr NE ... 87144
Libra Rd NE ... 87144
Lil Ave NE ... 87144
Lilac Pl NE ... 87144
Limestone Ct & Dr ... 87124
Lincoln Ave NE ... 87144
Linda Vista Ave & Ct ... 87124
Links Ln SE ... 87124
Lisbon Ave SE ... 87124
Littler Dr & Pl ... 87124
Llano Mesa Rd NE ... 87124
Llano Vista Loop ... 87124
Lockerbie Dr SE ... 87124
Logan Meadows Dr NE ... 87144
Loire Dr NE ... 87144
Loma Alta Rd NE ... 87124
Loma Colorado Blvd NE
300-900 ... 87124
1201-1213 ... 87144
1600-1702 ... 87144
Loma Linda Ct & Loop ... 87124
Loma Pinon Loop NE ... 87144
Lonesome Ridge Ct & St ... 87144
Longhorn Rd SE ... 87124
Longwood Dr & Loop ... 87124
Lorry Ln NE ... 87124
Los Alamos Dr NE ... 87144
Los Altos Ave NE ... 87124
Los Balcones Pl NE ... 87124
Los Miradores Dr & Pl ... 87124
Los Reyes Ct & Rd ... 87124
Lost Tree Rd SE ... 87124
Lucid Meadows Dr NE ... 87144
Luna Dr NE ... 87144
Lupin Rd NE ... 87144
Lupine Dr NE ... 87144
Luz De Sol Dr SE ... 87124
Lyndsey Hills Pl NE ... 87144
Lynwood Dr SE ... 87124
Lyra Ct SE ... 87124
Mackenzie Ct, Dr & Pl ... 87144
Madeira Dr SE ... 87124
Magdalena Rd NE ... 87144
Magnet NE ... 87144
Magpie Way NE ... 87144
Malaga Ct SE ... 87124
Mallard Ct NE ... 87144
Manitoba Rd NE ... 87144
Manitou Springs Dr SE ... 87124
Mansart Ct NE ... 87144
Manzanita Ct SE ... 87124
Manzano Loop NE ... 87144
Maple Ct SE ... 87124
Maple Meadows Dr NE ... 87144
Mara Way NE ... 87144
Marble Sky Ave NE ... 87144
Margarita Dr SE ... 87124
Margie Ct & Rd ... 87124
Maria Ct SE ... 87124
Maricopa Dr SE ... 87124
Marigold Dr SW ... 87124
Marino Dr SE ... 87124
Mariposa Pkwy NE ... 87144
Mark Rd NE ... 87144
Marlow Meadows Dr NE ... 87144
Martin Meadows Dr NE ... 87144
Mason Meadows Dr NE ... 87144
Matamoros Rd NE ... 87144
Mate Ct NE ... 87144
May Cir SE ... 87124
Mayapan Rd SE ... 87124
Mayhill Ct & Pl ... 87144
Meadowlark Ct, Ln & Way ... 87124
Meadows Point Pl NE ... 87144
Medina Meadows Dr NE ... 87144
Merlot Dr NE ... 87144
Mesa Rd SE ... 87124
Mesa Crotalo Rd SE ... 87124
Mesa Grande Loop NE ... 87144
Mesa Verde Dr SE ... 87124
Mesa Vista Ct SE ... 87124

Meseta Ct NE … 87124
Meteor Ave NE … 87144
Mica Dr NE … 87124
Michaelangelo Ct NE … 87144
Michelle Ct NE … 87144
Michigan Ct NE … 87144
Milagro Ridge Ct NE … 87124
Milan Hills Rd NE … 87144
Miller Rd NE … 87144
Milpa Alta Rd NE … 87144
Mim Ct NE … 87144
Mindoro Dr SE … 87124
Minor Ln SE … 87124
Minturn Ct & Loop … 87124
Mira Ct SE … 87124
Mira Vista Dr NE … 87144
Mirador Loop NE … 87144
Mirage Ct SE … 87124
Misty Meadows Dr NE … 87144
Mohawk St SW … 87124
Montana Vista Ct SE … 87124
Montana Wells Rd NE … 87124
Monte Vista Dr NE … 87124
Montego Ct & Dr … 87124
Monterrey Rd NE … 87144
Montevine Ave & Ct … 87124
Montiano Loop SE … 87124
Monticello Park Dr SE … 87124
Montreal Loop & Way … 87144
Moon Glow Dr NE … 87144
Moon Shadow Dr NE … 87144
Moonstone Dr NE … 87124
Morgan Meadows Dr NE … 87144
Morning Meadows Dr NE … 87144
Morning Sky Ave NE … 87144
Mosca Rd NE … 87144
Mountain Hawk Loop & Way … 87144
Mountain Vista Dr SE … 87124
Muskrat Ct NE … 87144
Nacelle Rd NE … 87144
Nagoya Rd NE … 87144
Nambe Rd NE … 87144
Nantucket Ct NE … 87124
Napoleon Rd NE … 87144
Nativitas Rd NE … 87144
Navajo Ln SE … 87124
Newcastle Dr SE … 87124
Nez Perce Loop NE … 87144
Nickel Dr NE … 87124
Nicklaus Dr SE … 87124
Night Hawk Ct & Dr … 87144
Night Sky Ave NE … 87144
Nightglow Ave NE … 87144
Nita Pl NE … 87144
Nogales Rd NE … 87144
Nome Dr NE … 87144
Norfolk Ct SE … 87124
Northern Blvd NE & NW … 87124
Northern Lights Way NE … 87144
Northwest Loop NE … 87144
Nova Ct SE … 87124
Nun Ct NE … 87144
Nyasa Rd SE … 87124
Oak Hills Dr SE … 87124
Oakmount Dr SE … 87124
Oakwood Ct SW … 87124
Oasis Springs Rd NE … 87144
Obeah Ct NE … 87144
Obregon Rd NE … 87144
Obsidian Pl NE … 87124
Ocate Meadows Ct & Dr … 87144
Ochre Rd NE … 87124
Ocotillo Dr NE … 87144
Octavia Ct NE … 87144
Oculus Loop NE … 87144
Odell Ct NE … 87124
Oersted Rd NE … 87144
Ohio Ct NE … 87144
Old Mill Rd NE … 87144
Oldenburg Ct & Rd … 87144
Onies Ct NE … 87144
Ontario Pl NE … 87144
Onyx Ct NE … 87124
Opal Dr NE … 87124
Orange Dr SE … 87124
Orbit Ct SE … 87124
Orchid Dr SW … 87124
Oreja De Oro Dr SE … 87124
Orinoco Dr SE … 87124
Osceola Rd SE … 87124
Osprey Dr NE … 87144
Ottawa Ct & Dr … 87144
Pagosa Meadows Dr NE … 87144
Paiute Rd SE … 87124
Pajarito Rd NE … 87144
Paladin Ct NE … 87144
Palenque Dr SE … 87124
Palermo Ct NE … 87144
Palmas Altas Dr SE … 87124
Palo Alto Dr NE … 87144
Panorama Way SE … 87124
Panorama Heights Dr SE … 87124
Paradise Ct SE … 87124
Parkside Rd SE … 87124
Parkview Way NE … 87144
Parkway Ave NE … 87144
Parr Rd SE … 87124
Paseo De La Villa SE … 87124
Paseo Roja Pl NE … 87144
Paseo Vista Ct, Loop & Pl … 87124
Pasilla Rd NE … 87144
Paso Llano Dr … 87124
Pasterid Ave NE … 87144
Patchogue Rd NE … 87144
Patti Pl NE … 87144
Pawnee Ct NE … 87144
Peaceful Meadows Dr NE … 87144
Peach Rd NE … 87144
Peach Tree Rd SE … 87124
Pearl Ct & Dr … 87144
Pecan Ct NE … 87144
Pechora Ct & Dr … 87144
Pecos Loop SE … 87124
Pecos Trail Dr NE … 87144
Pedragal Ave SE … 87124
Pegasus Ave SE … 87124
Peggy Rd SE … 87124
Pelizzano Dr SE … 87124
Pelona Ct NE … 87144
Penasco Rd NE … 87144
Peony Ct NE … 87144
Pepe Ortiz Rd SE … 87124
Peppoli Loop SE … 87124
Peridot Way NE … 87124
Perma Dr & Way … 87144
Perry Meadows Dr NE … 87144
Petunia Ct SE … 87124
Picabo St NE … 87144
Picea Ln SE … 87124
Piedras Pase Rd NE … 87124
Pikes Peak Loop NE … 87144
Pin Ct SE … 87124
Pine Ct SE … 87124
Pine Rd NE … 87144
Pine Bough Rd NE … 87124
Pine Forest Dr SE … 87124
Pinehurst Rd SE … 87124
Pinetree Rd SE
  700-900 … 87124
  900-900 … 87174
  902-998 … 87124
Pinewood Dr SE … 87124
Pinnacle Dr SE … 87124
Pinon Meadows Dr NE … 87144
Pisa Hills Rd NE … 87144
Placita De La Casas SE … 87124
Placita Del Suenos SE … 87124
Plano Vista Rd NE … 87124
Plata Dr SE … 87124
Platina Ct & Rd … 87124
Platinum Dr & Loop … 87124
Platte River Rd NE … 87144
Player Ct & Loop … 87124
Playful Meadows Cir & Dr … 87144
Plaza Colina NE … 87144
Plum Rd NE … 87144
Pojaque Ct NE … 87144
Polaris Blvd SE … 87124
N Pole Loop NE … 87144
Pomona Hills Ct NE … 87144
Ponderosa Ct SE … 87124
Pontiac Dr SW … 87124
Portafino Ave SE … 87124
Powder River Dr NE … 87144
Prado Alto Ave NE … 87144
Prado Hermosa Ct NE … 87124
Prairie Sage Way SE … 87124
Premier Pkwy SE … 87124
Prestige Way NE … 87144
Prestwick Ct SE … 87124
Procyon Ct SE … 87124
Pubela Ct NE … 87144
Puenta Alto Ave NE … 87144
Pumice Dr & Loop … 87124
Putt Ct SE … 87124
Pyrite Ct & Dr … 87124
Quail Run Rd NE … 87144
Quantum Rd NE … 87124
Quartz Dr NE … 87124
Quay Dr NE … 87144
Questa Rd NE … 87144
Quixote Dr SE … 87124
Rachel Ct & Rd … 87144
Rae Ct NE … 87144
Rainbow Blvd NE
  800-998 … 87124
  1201-1399 … 87144
Rainbow Blvd NW
  801-999 … 87124
  6400-7098 … 87124
Raleigh Hills Dr NE … 87144
Ramadan Ct NE … 87144
Rancher Loop NE … 87144
Rancho Oro Ave SE … 87124
Rancho Plata Ave SE … 87124
Rancho West Ct & Dr … 87124
Range Ct SE … 87124
Raptor Rd NE … 87144
Raspberry Ct & Dr … 87144
Rebecca Ct, Loop & Rd … 87144
Red Canyon Rd NE … 87144
Red River Rd NE … 87144
Red Rock Ct NE … 87144
Redondo Peak Rd NE … 87144
Redondo Santa Fe NE … 87144
Redondo Sierra Vis NE … 87144
Redwood Pl & St … 87124
Regency Park Rd SE … 87124
Renaissance Dr & Loop … 87124
Reserve Ct NE … 87144
Reynosa Loop SE … 87124
Rhein Dr SE … 87124
Riata Trl SE … 87124
Ricasoli Dr SE … 87124
Ridge Ct NE … 87144
Ridge Rock Rd SE … 87124
Ridgecrest Dr SE … 87124
Ridgeline Pl NE … 87144
Ridgeway Ct SE … 87124
Ridgewood Dr NE … 87144
Rincon De Romos Dr SE … 87124
Rio Animas Rd NE … 87144
Rio Arriba Ct & Rd … 87144
Rio Hondo Rd NE … 87144
Rio Lama Rd NE … 87144
Rio Mimbres Rd NE … 87144
Rio Norte Dr NE … 87144
Rio Oso Rd NE … 87144
Rio Pinos Rd NE … 87144
Rio Rancho Dr NE & SE … 87124
Rio Ruidoso Rd NE … 87144
Rio Salado Loop NE … 87144
Rio Vista Dr NE … 87144
Riva Ct NE … 87124
Rivers Edge Dr NE … 87144
Riverview Dr SE … 87124
Roadrunner Loop NE … 87144
Roanoke Dr NE … 87144
Robert Ct NE … 87124
Robin Pl & Rd … 87124
Robles Dr SE … 87124
Rock Rd NE … 87144
Rockaway Blvd NE
  300-398 … 87124
  400-609 … 87124
  611-641 … 87124
  1000-1011 … 87144
  1013-1013 … 87144
  4800-4898 … 87124
  4901-4999 … 87124
Rockaway Loop NE … 87124
Rodeo Loop SE … 87124
Rolling Meadows Dr NE … 87144
Roosevelt Ct & Loop … 87144
Rooster Point Ct, Pl & Rd … 87144
Rosarito Rd SE … 87124
Rose Cir SE … 87124
Rosswood Dr SE … 87124
Rough Ct SE … 87124
Round Up Dr NE … 87144
Russel Ct NE … 87124
Sabana Loop SE … 87124
Sabana Grande Ave SE … 87124
Saddlewood Trl SE … 87124
Saffin Dr SE … 87124
Sage Brush Ct SE … 87124
Sagecrest Loop NE … 87144
Saint Andrews Dr SE … 87124
Salem Ct NE … 87144
Salida Sol Dr SE … 87124
Salinas Ave SE … 87124
Sally Cir SE … 87124
Salt Cedar Rd NE … 87144
Salt River Ct & Loop … 87144
Saltillo Rd NE … 87144
San Ildefonso Loop NE … 87144
San Jose Rd SE … 87124
San Juan Ct NE … 87144
San Juan De Rio Dr SE … 87124
San Miguel Dr NE … 87144
San Pablo Rd NE … 87144
San Pedro Rd NE … 87144
Sanbusco Ct & Dr … 87144
Sand Dune Rd NE … 87144
N Sandia Ct NE … 87144
S Sandia Ct NE … 87144
Sandia Loop NE … 87144
Sandia Rd … 87124
Sandia Vista Ct SE … 87124
Sandia Vista Pl NE … 87144
Sandia Vista Rd NE … 87144
Sandoval Dr NE … 87144
Sandpiper Trl NE … 87144
Sandstone Dr NE … 87124
Sandy Loop NE … 87144
Sandy Lane Ct SE … 87124
Santa Ana Rd NE … 87144
Santa Clara Rd NE … 87144
Santa Elena Rd SE … 87124
Santa Fe Hills Blvd NE … 87144
Santa Fe Meadows Dr NE … 87144
Santa Fe Trail Dr NE … 87144
Santa Fe Vista Rd NE … 87144
Santana Ct SE … 87124
Santolino Dr SE … 87124
Sapphire Dr NE … 87124
Sara Rd & Way … 87124
Sarasota Rd NE … 87144
Saratoga Dr NE
  400-799 … 87124
  800-1800 … 87144
  1802-1998 … 87144
Sava Dr SE … 87124
Savannah Ct & Dr … 87144
Saw Mill Rd NE … 87144
Sea Rd NE … 87144
Sedona Meadows Dr NE … 87144
Serena Dr SE … 87124
Seven Falls Dr SE … 87124
Shadow Meadows Dr NE … 87144
Shane Ct NE … 87144
Shavano Peak Dr NE … 87144
Shelby Meadows Dr NE … 87144
Sheltie Ct NE … 87144
Shenandoah River Ct NE … 87144
Shepherd Ct NE … 87144
Shiloh Rd NE … 87144
Shin Ave NE … 87144
Shiprock Ct & Dr … 87144
Shore Meadows Dr NE … 87144
Shoshone Trl NE … 87144
Sicomoro Ln SE … 87124
Sidewinder Rd NE … 87144
Sienna Ct NE … 87124
Sierra Ln NE … 87144
Sierra Alta Ave NE … 87124
Sierra Norte Ct & Loop … 87144
Sierra Verde Way NE … 87124
Silent Spring Dr NE … 87124
Silver Ct NE … 87124
Silver Creek Dr NE … 87144
Silver Mountain Loop NE … 87144
Silver Saddle Rd SE … 87124
Sioux Dr NE … 87144
Skagway Dr NE … 87144
Skylar Dr NE … 87144
Skyview Cir NE … 87144
Slice Ct SE … 87124
Snead Loop SE … 87124
Snow Ct SE … 87124
Snow Heights Cir & Ct … 87124
Snowberry Dr NE … 87144
Snowden Ct NE … 87124
Snowflake Ct SE … 87124
Snowy Owl Rd NE … 87144
Soave Dr SE … 87124
Solano Del Sol Dr NE … 87144
Solano Meadows Dr NE … 87144
Solar Ct SE … 87124
Soldotna Dr NE … 87124
Sombrerete Rd SE … 87124
Somerset Meadows Dr NE … 87144
Sommerset Dr SE … 87124
Sonora Rd NE … 87144
Soothing Meadows Dr NE … 87144
Sophia Hills Ct NE … 87144
Southern Blvd SE & SW … 87124
Spring Dr & Rd SE & NE … 87124
Spring Valley Rd NE … 87144
Sprint Blvd NE … 87144
Spruce Meadows Dr NE … 87144
Spruce Mountain Loop NE … 87144
Spruce Needle Rd SE … 87124
Spur Ct, Pl, Rd & Way SE … 87124
Spyglass Loop & Pl … 87124
Stagecoach Rd SE … 87124
Stallion Ct, Loop & Rd … 87124
Stanley Dr NE … 87144
Stapleton Ave NE … 87144
Star Villa Cir SE … 87124
Starry Sky Ave NE … 87144
State Highway 528 NE
  101-199 … 87124
State Highway 528 NE
  1000-3498 … 87144
  3500-3700 … 87144
  3702-4298 … 87144
State Highway 528 SE … 87124
State Highway 550 NE … 87144
Stephanie Rd SE … 87124
Stony Meadows Cir NE … 87144
Storm Mountain Rd SE … 87124
Strawberry Ct, Dr & Pl … 87144
Subio Rd SE … 87124
Sue Cir SE … 87124
Sugar Rd SE … 87124
Sugar Ridge Ct & Loop … 87124
Summer Winds Dr NE & SE … 87124
Sun Ct SE … 87124
Sundance Ct & Dr … 87144
Sundt Ct & Rd … 87124
Sunflower Ct & Dr SE & SW … 87124
Sunlight Peak Dr NE … 87144
Sunny Meadows Dr NE … 87144
Sunset Rd SE … 87124
Sunstone Way NE … 87124
Superior Ct NE … 87144
Superstition Dr SE … 87124
Suttle Ct NE … 87124
Syr Ct & Dr … 87144
Tahoe Ct SE … 87124
Tajo Ct SE … 87124
Talon Ct & Dr … 87144
Tampico Rd NE … 87144
Taos Meadows Dr NE … 87144
Tapatio St SE … 87124
Tarpon Ave SE … 87124
Taurus Rd NE … 87144
Teal Pl NE … 87144
Tecamec Rd NE … 87144
Tecolote Way SE … 87124
Teresa Ct SE … 87124
Terra De Sol Dr SE … 87124
Terrace Dr NE … 87144
Tesuque Ct NE … 87144
Teton Ave NE … 87144
The American Rd SE … 87124
Thoreau Meadows Dr NE … 87144
Threadgrass Rd NE … 87144
Thunder Rd SE … 87124
Tierra Abierta Pl NE … 87124
Tierra Roja Pl NE … 87124
Tierra Rosa Pl NE … 87124
Tierra Vista Pl NE … 87124
Tiffany Ln SE … 87124
Tiffin Meadows Dr NE … 87144
Tigris Rd NE … 87124
Timor Rd SE … 87124
Tin Cup Rd NE … 87144
Tiny Sparrow Rd NE … 87144
Tiwa Ln NE … 87124
Toadlena Meadows Dr NE … 87144
Tobol Ct NE … 87144
Topeka Hills Dr NE … 87144
Torino Hills Rd NE … 87144
Torrey Pines Rd SE … 87124
Toscana Rd SE … 87124
Towhee Ct NE … 87144
Tramview Ct & Ln … 87144
Tranquil Meadows Dr NE … 87144
Trapper Creek Rd NE … 87144
Treasure Ct & Dr … 87124
Trenton Hills Dr NE … 87144
Trevino Dr SE … 87124
Treviso Dr SE … 87124
Trinity Dr NE … 87124
Triumph Rd NW … 87144
Troon Dr SE … 87124
Trout Creek Dr NE … 87144
Truchas Meadows Dr NE … 87144
Truchas Peak Trl NE … 87144
Tula Ct & Dr … 87124
Tulip Rd SE … 87124
Tulipan Loop SE … 87124
Turf Ln SE … 87124
Turquoise Dr NE … 87124
Turquoise Trl NE … 87144
Twilight Rd SE … 87124
Twin Buttes Dr NE … 87144
Twinberry Dr NE … 87144
Twisted Juniper Rd SE … 87124
Tyler Loop NE … 87144
Umber Ct NE … 87124
Union Dr NE … 87144
Unser Blvd NE & SE … 87124
Upland Meadows Rd NE … 87144
Uranium Ct & Dr … 87124
Utah Meadow Rd NE … 87124
Valencia Dr NE … 87144
Valle Alto Dr NE … 87124
Valley Meadows Dr NE … 87144
Valley Vista Ct SE … 87124
Valmera Rd NE … 87144
Value Ct SE … 87124
Vancouver Ct, Pl & Rd … 87124
Vargas Rd SE … 87124
Vatapa Rd NE … 87144
Vaughn Dr NE … 87144
Veja Baja Dr SE … 87124
Venada Ct & Rd … 87144
Vera Cruz Rd NE … 87144
Veranda Rd SE … 87124
Verbena Dr NE … 87144
Verde Pl SE … 87124
Veridian Dr SE … 87124
Verona Rd NE … 87144
Via Esterlina Ave SE … 87124
Via Sonata Rd SE … 87124
Via Virane Dr SE … 87124
Victor Ln SE … 87124
Viga Pl & Rd … 87124
Villa Dr, Pl, Rd & Way SE … 87124
Villa Verde Dr SE … 87124
Violeta Cir, Ct & Way … 87124
Virgin Wood Rd SE … 87124
Virginia Ct NE … 87144
Vista Rd NW … 87144
Vista Borde Dr NE … 87124
Vista De Colinas Ct, Dr & Pl … 87124
Vista Este NE … 87124
Vista Hermosa Pl NE … 87124
Vista Larga Pl NE … 87124
Vista Manzano Ct & Loop … 87144
Vista Roja Pl NE … 87124
Vortex Rd NE … 87144
Wagon Train Dr SE … 87124
Walsh Ct, Loop & St … 87124
Wasilla Dr NE … 87144
Waterfall Dr NE … 87144
Wayne Rd NE … 87144
Weeping Willow Ct & Rd … 87144
Wellspring Ave SE … 87124
Western Hills Dr NE & SE … 87124
Westfield Ct & Dr … 87144
Westphalia Loop NE … 87144
Westside Blvd & Dr … 87144
Wheeler Peak Dr NE … 87144
Whippet Ct NE … 87144
Whispering Meadows Dr NE … 87144
White Horse Dr SE … 87124
White Owl Ct & Way … 87124
White Pine Dr NE … 87144
Whitewater Dr NE … 87144

Whitney Rd SE 87124
Wilder Loop NE 87144
Wildflower Pass NE 87144
Wilkes Way SE 87124
Willow Ct SE 87124
Willow Rd NE 87144
Willow Creek Rd NE ... 87144
Willow Trace Ct SE 87124
Windsor Ct SE 87124
Wingate Meadows Dr
NE 87144
Winged Foot Ct SE 87124
Winston Meadows Dr
NE 87144
Withington Peak Dr
NE 87144
Wolf Creek Ct NE 87144
Woodhaven Dr NE 87144
Wrangell Loop NE 87144
Wrangler Ct SE 87124
Wyoming Autumn Rd
NE 87124
Yucatan Dr SE 87124
Yucca St SE 87124
Yukon Rd NE 87144
Zaragoza Rd SE 87124
Zenith Ct NE 87144
Zia Ct & St 87144
Zirconia Ct & Dr 87124
Zuni Ct & Rd 87124

NUMBERED STREETS

1st Ave & St 87124
2nd Ave NW 87124
3rd Ave & St 87124
4th Ave & St NE, NW &
SW 87124
5th Ave SW 87124
5th St NE 87124
5th St NW 87144
5th St SE 87124
5th St SW 87124
6th Ave & St 87124
7th Ave & St 87124
8th St NE 87124
9th Ave NE 87124
9th Ave NW 87124
9th St NE 87124
9th St NW 87144
9th St SW 87124
10th Ave NE 87144
10th Ave NW
500-999 87144
3400-3417 87124
3418-3598 87144
3419-3499 87124
10th Ave SE 87124
10th Ave SW 87124
10th St NE
2-598 87124
901-997 87144
10th St NW 87144
10th St SE 87124
10th St SW 87124
11th Ave NW 87144
11th Ave SE 87124
11th Ave SW 87124
11th St SE 87124
11th St SW 87124
12th Ave NW
1-999 87144
3480-3482 87124
12th Ave SE 87124
12th Ave SW 87124
12th St SE 87124
12th St SW 87124
13th Ave NW 87144
13th Ave SE 87124
13th St NE 87144
13th St SE 87124
13th St SW 87124
14th Ave NW 87144
14th Ave SE 87124
14th St SE 87124
14th St SW 87124
15th Ave NE 87144
15th Ave SE 87124
15th Pl SE 87124
15th St SE 87124
15th St SW 87124
16th Ave NE 87144
16th Ave SE 87124
16th St NW 87144
16th St SW 87124
17th Ave NE 87144
17th Ave SE 87124
17th St NW 87144
17th St SE 87124
17th St SW 87124
18th Ave SE 87124
18th St NE 87144
18th St SE 87124
19th Ave SE 87124
19th St NW
205-913 87124
1000-1006 87144
1008-1013 87144
1015-1513 87144
19th St SE 87124
19th St SW 87124
20th Ave SE 87124
20th St NW
100-798 87124
800-840 87124
842-920 87124
1000-1002 87144
1004-1008 87144
1010-1698 87144
20th St SW 87124
21st Ave SE 87124
21st St NW
830-926 87124
1201-1213 87144
1500-2706 87144
2121-2123 87124
21st St SE 87124
22nd Ave & St 87124
23rd Ave NE 87144
23rd Ave SE 87124
23rd Ave SW 87124
23rd St NW 87144
23rd St SW 87124
24th Ave NW 87144
24th St NW 87144
24th St SE 87124
24th St SW 87124
25th Ave NE 87144
25th Ave NW 87144
25th St NW 87144
25th St SE 87124
25th St SW 87124
26th Ave NE 87144
26th St NW 87144
26th St SE 87124
26th St SW 87124
27th Ave NE 87144
27th St NW 87124
27th St SW 87124
28th Ave NE 87144
28th St NW 87124
28th St SE 87124
28th St SW 87124
29th SE & SW 87124
30th NW & SW 87124
31st SE & SW 87124
32nd Cir & St 87124
33rd Ave NE 87144
33rd Cir SE 87124
33rd St NE 87144
33rd St SE 87124
34th Ave NE 87144
34th Ave NW 87144
34th Cir SE 87124
34th St SE 87124
35th Cir & St SE, NE &
SW 87124
36th Cir, Pl & St 87124
37th St SE 87124
38th St SE 87124
39th Ave NW 87144
39th Pl NE 87144
39th St NE 87144
39th St SE 87124
40th St NW 87124
41st St NW 87124
43rd NE & NW 87144
44th St NE 87144
45th St NE 87144
46th Ave & St 87144
47th St NE 87144
48th St NE 87144
50th St NE 87144
51st St NE 87144
52nd St NE 87144

ROSWELL NM

General Delivery 88201

POST OFFICE BOXES MAIN OFFICE STATIONS AND BRANCHES

Box No.s
All PO Boxes 88202

RURAL ROUTES

01, 03, 04 88201

HIGHWAY CONTRACTS

12, 30, 31 88201
02, 05 88203
30 88203

NAMED STREETS

A St 88203
Abbott Pl 88201
Acacia Rd 88201
Adams Ave & Dr 88203
Adobe Mesa Rd 88201
Agate Rd 88201
E & W Alameda St 88203
E & W Albuquerque
St 88203
Alden Pl 88203
Alhambra Dr 88201
Alicia Ln 88201
Allen Ave 88201
Allison Dr 88201
Alta Vista Ln 88203
Alto Rd 88201
Amherst Dr 88201
Andrews Pl 88203
Angus Rd 88201
Anna J Dr 88201
Antelope Rd & Run 88201
Apache Hills Dr 88201
E Apple Ln & St 88201
Arlene Rd 88201
S Ash Ave 88203
N Aspen Ave 88201
S Aspen Ave 88203
Aspen Pl 88203
N Atkinson Ave
100-199 88203
300-6199 88201
S Atkinson Ave 88203
Atoka Trl 88203
Auburn Dr 88203
Autumn Wind Pl 88201
Avenida De Amigos 88201
Avenida De Vista Rd ... 88201
Avenida Del Sumbre ... 88203
Avenida Manana 88203
Avenue E 88203
Avenue A 88203
Avenue B 88203
Avenue C 88203
Avenue D 88203
Avenue F 88203
Avenue G 88203
Azalea Trl 88203
Aztec Rd 88201
B St 88203
Badger Rd 88201
Bahia St 88201
Bailey Pl 88203
S Baker Rd 88203
E Ballard St 88203
S Balsam Ave 88203
Bandolina Ave 88201
Bar L St 88203
Barberry Rd 88201
Barcelona Dr 88201
Barlow Pl 88203
Barnett Dr 88203
Baton Rouge Ct 88201
Bay Meadows Dr 88201
Baylor Ave 88203
Bayou Ct 88201
Beargrass Rd 88201
Beaver Pl 88201
N Beech Ave 88201
S Beech Ave 88203
E Beech St 88203
Bel Aire Dr 88201
Belmont Dr 88201
Beloit St 88201
Bent Tree Rd 88201
Berkley Dr 88203
E & W Berrendo Rd 88201
Berrendo Meadows Cir . 88201
Beverly Ave 88201
Billy Jack Rd 88201
Billy Mitchell Pl 88203
S Birch Ave 88203
Birdsall Pl 88201
Bitter Lakes Rd 88201
Blanca Rosa Ln 88201
Blanchard St 88203
E & W Bland St 88203
Blue Mountain Rd 88201
Bluebell Rd 88201
Boley Pl 88203
Bonham Ln 88201
S & W Bonita Dr 88203
W & E Bonney Dr &
St 88203
Bosque Rd 88201
Boss Ln 88201
Bottomless Lakes Rd ... 88203
Bradley Dr 88201
Brandon Way 88201
E & W Brasher Rd 88203
Brazos Cir, Ct, Pl & St . 88201
Brenda Rd 88201
Brentwood Rd 88201
Brewer Pl 88203
Briarwood Pl 88201
Briggs Rd 88201
Bright Sky Rd 88201
Broken Arrow Rd 88201
Brown Pl 88203
N Brown Rd 88201
S Brown Rd 88203
E Brown St 88203
Browning Pl 88201
Buchanan Draw Rd 88203
E & W Buena Vista St . 88203
E & W Burkette Rd 88203
E & W Byrne St 88203
Caballo Rd 88201
Cactus Ave 88201
Cactus Ln 88201
S Cahoon Ave 88203
Cajun Ct 88201
Calle Del Sol 88201
Calumet Rd 88201
Camas Rd 88201
N Cambridge Ave 88201
Camilla Dr 88203
Caminisito 88203
Caminito Dr 88201
Camino Real 88203
Camper Trl 88203
Campus Cir 88201
Cane Ln 88203
Cannon Rd 88203
Canoncito Dr 88201
Capitan Ave 88203
Capitan Pl 88203
Capitan Rd 88201
Carol Ann Way 88201
Carolina Way 88201
Carrizozo Rd 88201
Carrol Ave 88203
Carter Dr 88203
Carver Dr 88203
Cass Rd 88203
Cat Rd 88201
Catalina Dr 88201
Catclaw Ave 88201
N Cedar Ave 88201
S Cedar Ave 88203
Cedar Dr 88201
Cedarvale Rd 88203
E & W Challenger St ... 88203
S Chamisal Ave 88203
Chapparal Rd 88201
Charing Cross Ct 88201
E & W Charleston Rd .. 88203
Cherokee Rd 88201
E Cherry St 88201
Chesser Rd 88203
Chickweed Rd 88201
Chico Dr 88201
Chiquita Ln 88201
E & W Chisum Rd &
St 88203
Cholla Dr 88201
Christian Rd 88203
Chrysler Dr & Pl 88201
E & W Church St 88203
Cielito Dr 88201
Cielo Ln 88201
Cimarron Pl 88201
Circle Cross St 88201
N Circle Diamond Dr ... 88201
Circle Diamond St 88203
Clayton Rd 88201
Clearview Rd 88201
S Clorangt Ave 88203
Clover Ln 88203
Clovis Hwy 88201
Cobean Dr 88201
Coddington Rd 88203
N Cole Ave 88201
E & W College Blvd ... 88201
Columbia Rd 88201
Conchas Pl 88201
Concord Rd 88203
Conde Pl 88203
E Conner St 88203
Corn Rd 88203
Cornell Dr 88203
Cornflower Rd 88201
Coronado Cir 88203
Coronado Dr 88201
N Coronado Dr 88201
Corrales Rd 88203
Corralitos Rd 88201
Cortez Ct 88201
Cotton Rd 88201
S Cottonwood Dr 88203
Cottonwood Ln 88203
Cottonwood Rd 88201
E & W Country Club
Rd 88201
Country Hill Pl 88201
Cow Chip Rd 88201
Coy Ln 88201
Crenshaw Dr 88203
Crescent Dr 88201
Crooked Creek Rd 88201
E & W Crossroads 88203
Cumbres Ave 88201
Curry Rd 88201
S Cypress Ave 88203
Daisy Rd 88201
Dandelion Ln 88201
Davidson Dr 88203
N Davis Ave 88201
De Bremond Dr 88201
Deborah Dr 88201
Deer Trail Rd 88201
Del Norte Dr 88201
N Delaware Ave
100-199 88203
500-598 88201
600-1799 88201
S Delaware Ave 88203
Delicado Dr 88201
E & W Deming St 88203
Desert Hill Rd 88203
Desert Rose 88201
Desert Springs Cir 88201
Desosa Ct 88201
Detta Loop 88201
Devonian St 88201
Diamond A Dr 88201
Diamond A St 88203
Diana Dr 88203
Dirt Rd 88201
Dogwood Rd 88201
Dona Ana Rd 88201
Dove Trl 88201
Dow Dr 88201
Drake Trl 88201
Draper Rd 88201
Driftwood Pl 88201
Dunbar Pl 88203
Dunken Rd 88203
Dusty Miller Rd 88201
E St 88203
Eagle Pl 88201
E & W Earl Cummings
Loop 88203
Ec Tucker Ct 88201
Eden Valley Rd 88201
Edgewood Ave & Dr 88201
N Eisenhower Rd 88201
S Eisenhower Rd 88203
El Arco Way 88203
El Arco Iris Dr 88201
El Camino Ave 88203
El Dorado 88203
El Rosal St 88203
Eldora Dr 88201
Elizabeth Dr 88203
E Elm Ave 88203
N Elm Ave 88201
S Elm Ave 88203
Emerald Dr 88203
Encanto Dr 88201
Enterprise St 88203
Escalante Ct & Rd 88201
Estrellita Dr 88201
Everglade Ct 88201
S Evergreen Ave 88203
E & W Eyman St 88203
F St 88203
Fairway Ct & Dr 88201
Farmington Rd 88201
Farris Pl 88203
Fawn Rd 88203
Felts Rd 88201
Fern Dr 88203
Fern Rd 88201
N Fir Ave 88201
S Fir Ave 88203
Fitzgerald Pl 88203
N Flint Ave 88201
Flying H St 88203
Foothill Blvd 88203
E & W Forest Dr, Pl &
St 88203
Fort Sumner Rd 88201
Fowler Rd 88201
Fox Glove Rd 88201
E & W Frazier St 88203
S, E & W Fruitland Dr &
St 88203
Fulkerson Dr 88203
Futura Dr 88203
G St 88203
Gail Harris St 88203
E & W Gallina Rd 88201
N Garden Ave
100-198 88203
201-297 88201
299-3999 88201
S Garden Ave 88203
Garden Pl 88201
Gary Dr 88203
Gaviota Trl 88201
Gaye Dr 88201
E & W Gayle St 88203
Geiger Pl 88203
Georgia Rd 88203
Gillespie Pl 88203
Glen Dr 88203
Glenwood Rd 88201
Golondrina Dr 88201
Gramma Ave 88201
N Grand Ave 88201
S Grand Ave 88203
Grand Avenue Plz 88201
E Grand Plains Rd 88203
Granite Cir & Ct 88201
S Graves Rd 88203
Green St 88203
Greenbriar St 88203
Greenfield Rd 88201
E & N Greenwood Ave &
Dr 88201
Grove St 88201
H St 88203
Hackberry Rd 88201
Hahn St 88203
S Hale Ave 88203
Haley Cir 88201
Hall Dr 88201
Hamilton Dr 88201
E Hammond St 88203
Harding Dr 88203
Harral Rd 88203
Harris Pl & Rd 88203
Harvard Dr 88203
Hawkweed Rd 88201
Hawthorn Rd 88201
Hawthorne Ln 88201
Heather Dr 88203
Heflin Rd 88203
Heights Dr 88203
S Hemlock Ave 88203
E & W Hendricks St 88203
Hermosa Dr 88201
W & E Hervey Dr &
St 88203
Hickory St 88203
Highland Rd 88201
Hillcrest St 88201
Hinkle St 88203
Hoagland St 88203
E & W Hobbs Pl & St .. 88203
E & W Hobson Rd 88203
E & S Holland Dr 88203
Holloman Pl 88203
Holly Loop 88201
Hollyhock Ln 88201
Hondo Dr 88201
Honeysuckle Rd 88201
Horizon Rd 88201
Horse Center Rd 88203
Horton Rd 88203
Howard Dr 88203
Howard Cook Rd 88201
Huerta Ct 88201
S Hummingbird Ln 88203
Hunsicker Pl 88203
Huskey Rd 88201
Hyman Pl 88203
I St 88203
Irene Ave 88203
Ironwood Rd 88201
Isla Ct 88201
Isler Rd 88201
Ivy Dr 88203
Jack Mcclellan Dr 88201
Jackson Dr & Pl 88203
W Jaffa St 88203
Jal Rd 88201
Janus Dr 88203

Jardin Ct 88201
E & W Jefferson St 88203
Jemez Ct 88201
Jennifer Ln 88203
Jenny Ln 88201
Jerry Smith Cir 88203
Jicarilla Rd 88201
Jingle Bob St 88203
S Johnson Rd 88203
Juanito Dr 88203
Judy St 88201
W Juniper St 88203
Juno Dr 88203
Kachina Dr 88201
Kallahin Rd 88203
N Kansas Ave
101-199 88203
200-1899 88201
S Kansas Ave 88203
Karabella Way 88201
Kay Bar St 88203
E Keith St 88203
Kelly Pl 88203
Kenlea Dr 88203
Kensington Ct 88201
N Kentucky Ave
100-199 88203
300-598 88201
600-2999 88201
3001-3299 88201
S Kentucky Ave 88203
Kessler Pl 88201
Kincaid Rd 88203
Kings Dr 88201
Kiva Ln 88201
Knubbin Rd 88201
La Fonda Dr 88201
La Jara Rd 88201
La Jolla Ln 88201
La Joya Rd 88201
La Luz Rd 88201
E & W La Paloma Ln & Pl 88201
La Paz St 88201
La Placita Dr 88201
La Quinta Rd 88203
La Tierra Dr 88201
Ladrones St 88201
Lafayette Loop 88201
Lamay St 88203
Langley Pl 88203
Largo Dr 88203
Larry Ave 88201
Las Flores Dr 88203
Latigo Cir & Ln 88201
Latimer Ln 88203
Lazy O J Rd 88203
Le Ann Dr 88201
N Lea Ave
100-199 88203
200-398 88201
400-2999 88201
S Lea Ave 88203
Leslie Ln 88201
E Lewis Rd & St 88203
E Lfd St 88203
Lighthall Pl 88203
Lily Rd 88201
S Lincoln Ave 88203
Linda Cir 88201
Linda Dr 88203
E & W Linda Vista Blvd 88201
Lipan Rd 88201
Loma Linda Dr 88203
Loma Verde Ln 88203
Loma Vista Rd 88201
London Ct 88201
Lone Cedar Rd 88201
Lopez Morley Ln 88203
Los Alamos Rd 88201
Los Padrinos 88203
Lost Adobe Rd 88201
Lost Trail Rd 88201
N Louisiana Ave 88201
S Louisiana Ave 88203
Lovers Ln 88203
Luebke Pl 88203
Lupita Ln 88201
Lusk St 88203
Lynnwood Ave 88203
Madison Ave 88203
Madrid St 88201
Magdelena Rd 88201
N Main St
5500A-5500C 88201
100-199 88203
200-8799 88201
S Main St 88203
SE Main St 88203
E & W Malamute Rd 88201
Mallard Ave 88201
Mann Ave 88203
N Maple St 88201
Marion Richards Rd 88201
Mark Rd 88201
E Marker Rd 88203
Marley Rd 88201
Marrujo Rd 88201
E & W Martin St 88203
N Maryland Ave 88201
Mason Dr 88201
E & W Mathews St 88203
Maya Rd 88201
Mayapple Rd 88201
Mccall Loop 88203
E & W Mccune St 88203
Mcdonald Pl 88203
Mcfadin Rd 88201
E & W Mcgaffey St 88203
Mckay Pl 88201
Mclean Rd 88201
Mcpherson Rd 88201
Meadow Ln & Pl 88203
Meadow Brook Rd 88203
Meadowlark Dr 88203
Melrose St 88201
Membres Rd 88201
Mercedes Ct & Dr 88201
N Mesa Ave 88201
Mesa Dr 88203
Mesa Verde St 88201
Mescal Rd 88201
E & W Mescalero Rd 88201
Miami Rd 88203
N Michigan Ave
100-199 88203
200-4999 88201
S Michigan Ave 88203
Military Heights Dr 88201
Milky Way Rd 88203
Miller Xing 88201
Mills Dr 88203
Mimosa Dr 88201
Mission Arch Dr 88201
N Mississippi Ave 88201
S Mississippi Ave 88203
N Missouri Ave
100-199 88203
200-1899 88201
S Missouri Ave 88203
Mistico Ln 88203
Mockingbird Rd 88203
Monksdale Rd 88203
S Monroe Ave 88203
N Montana Ave 88201
S Montana Ave 88203
Monterrey Dr 88201
Montgomery Rd 88203
Monument Canyon Rd 88203
Moore Ave & Dr 88201
Moose Rd 88201
Morningside Dr 88201
Mossman Dr 88201
Mossman Rd 88203
E & W Mountain View Rd 88203
N Mulberry Ave 88201
S Mulberry Ave 88203
Mullis St 88201
Murphy Pl 88203
Nanticoke Rd 88203
Navajo Dr 88201
Neiss Pl 88201
Nettle Rd 88201
N Nevada Ave 88201
S Nevada Ave 88203
New Mexico Dr 88203
Newell Dr 88203
Night Sky Ln 88201
Nighthawk Rd 88201
Nogal Rd 88201
Nola Ln 88201
Norris Pl 88201
Northwood Dr 88201
Notting Hill Ave 88201
O Connor Rd 88203
Oak Dr 88203
Oakwood Dr 88201
S Oasis Rd 88203
Ocotillo Ave 88201
Offutt St 88203
N Ohio Ave
100-199 88203
201-597 88201
599-1799 88201
S Ohio Ave 88203
Old Clovis Hwy 88201
Old Dexter Hwy 88203
Old Hondo Channel Rd 88203
Oliver St 88203
Oljato Rd 88203
Omaha Rd 88203
Onate Rd 88201
One Horse Rd 88201
W & E Onyx Dr & St 88203
E Orange St 88201
N Orchard Ave 88201
Oscura Ave 88201
Outlaw Trl 88201
Pack Rd 88203
Palacio St 88203
Palomar Dr & Pl 88203
Pampas Ave 88201
Paradise Ln 88201
Park Dr, Pl & Rd 88201
Parkview Rd 88203
Paul St 88201
S Pawhatan Rd 88203
Pawnee Dr 88203
Peaceful Valley Rd 88201
Peach St 88201
Peachtree Ct 88201
Pear St 88201
Pearson Dr 88201
Pecan Dr & Pl 88201
Pecos Dr 88203
Pecos Diamond Rd 88201
Pecos View Rd 88201
Penasco Rd 88201
N Pennsylvania Ave
803A-803B 88201
100-199 88203
200-298 88201
300-414 88201
415-2725 88201
415-415 88202
416-2798 88201
S Pennsylvania Ave 88203
Penoak Rd 88201
Pequeno Camino 88203
Petro Dr 88201
Pima Dr 88203
Pine Ave & Pl 88203
E & W Pine Lodge Rd 88201
S Pinon Ave 88203
Pioneer St 88201
Plains Park Dr 88203
E Plaza Dr 88201
Plaza Del Sol 88203
E Plum St 88201
E & W Poe St 88203
Pontiac Dr 88201
S Poplar Ave 88203
Poppy Rd 88201
Portales Rd 88201
Positano Loop 88201
Powell Pl 88203
Prager St 88203
N Prairie Ave 88201
Primrose Rd 88201
Princeton Dr 88203
Purdue Dr 88203
Purdy Dr 88203
Quemado Rd 88201
Radcliff Dr 88203
N Railroad Ave 88201
Ranchito Dr 88201
Rancho Rd 88203
Raney Ln 88201
Ransom Rd 88203
Ray Pl 88203
Red Bluff Rd 88203
N Red Bridge Rd 88201
S Red Bridge Rd 88203
Red Sky Ln 88201
Redwood St 88203
E & W Reed St 88203
Regents Ct 88201
Remy Pl 88203
Resolana Dr 88201
Reynolds Pl 88203
N Richardson Ave
100-198 88203
200-298 88201
300-3299 88201
S Richardson Ave 88203
Ridgecrest Dr 88203
Riley Dr 88203
Rincon Rd 88201
Rio Bonito Cir 88201
Ristra Rd 88201
River Rd 88203
Riverside Dr 88201
Riverview Cir 88201
Robins Dr 88203
Robins Nest Pl 88201
Rock House Rd 88201
Rocking Chair Rd 88203
Rocoso Rd 88201
Rosebud Ln 88201
Rosemary Ln 88201
Rowland Dr 88201
Ruohonen Pl 88203
Ruth Rd 88201
Ryan Rd 88203
Sacaton St 88201
Sage Rd 88201
Saint Marys Pl 88203
Sallee Loop 88201
Salt Creek Rd 88201
Salt Lick Trl 88201
Saltillo Dr 88201
San Juan Dr 88201
Sandhill St 88201
Santa Rosa Rd 88201
Saquaro Rd 88201
Sarsaparilla Rd 88201
S Saucedo Ave 88203
Saunders Dr 88201
Schneider Rd 88203
School Rd 88203
Seminole Rd 88203
Sena Rd 88201
N Sequoia Ave 88201
S Sequoia Ave 88203
Serena Dr 88201
Serenata Dr 88201
Seville St 88201
Seward Ave 88201
N Shartell Ave 88201
Shepards Way 88203
Sheperd Rd 88201
N Sherman Ave 88201
S Sherman Ave 88203
Sherrill Ln 88201
Shinkle Dr 88201
Sierra Blanca Cir & Dr 88201
N Sillond Ave 88201
Silverado Rd 88203
Silverweed Rd 88201
Simpson Dr 88201
Sioux Dr 88201
Skidmore Rd 88201
E & N Sky Loop 88201
Smith Ave 88203
Solana Ln 88201
Sorrento Dr 88201
Southridge Rd 88203
Southwest Way 88203
S Spencer Ave 88203
S Spring Loop 88203
E Spring St 88201
Spring Branch Dr 88203
Spring River Rd 88203
Springfield Rd 88201
N Spruce Ave 88201
S Spruce Ave 88203
Stacy Dr 88203
S Stanton Ave 88203
Star Dr 88201
Stargrass Rd 88201
Stephens Cir 88201
Stone St 88201
Studdard Rd 88201
Sumac Rd 88201
Summer Wind Pl 88201
E & W Summit St 88203
S Sundance Loop 88201
Sunflower Rd 88201
Sunrise Rd 88201
Sunset Ave & Pl 88203
Sunset Plaza Ct 88203
Sunshine St 88203
Suzanne Dr 88201
Swinging Spear Rd 88201
N Sycamore Ave
100-199 88203
500-6099 88201
S Sycamore Ave 88203
N Sycamore Ct 88201
Sydney Ave 88201
Tamarack Dr 88201
Tamarish Rd 88201
Taos Ct 88201
Taylor Dr 88203
Tee Pan St 88203
Tesuque 88203
Teton Rd 88201
N Texas Ave 88201
Thiel Pl 88203
Thistle Rd 88201
Thomas Ln 88203
Thompson Rd 88203
Three Cross Dr 88201
Thunder Rd 88201
Thunderbird Ln 88203
Thunderbird Rd 88201
Tierra Berrenda Dr 88201
Tierra Grande Blvd 88203
Tijeras Rd 88201
E & W Tilden St 88203
Tome Rd 88201
Topaz Dr 88203
Tottenham Ct 88201
Townsend Trl 88201
Trail Rd 88201
Trailing Heart Rd 88201
Tulane Dr 88203
Tumbleweed Rd 88203
Turkey Track St 88203
Turquoise Ave 88201
Twin Diamond Rd 88201
N Union Ave
100-198 88203
201-297 88201
299-1900 88201
1902-2098 88201
S Union Ave 88203
University Blvd 88203
Urton Rd 88201
Us Highway 70 88203
S Utah Ave 88203
E & W Van Buren St 88203
Vanderslice Pl 88203
Vassar Dr 88203
Vaughn Pl 88203
Venus Dr 88203
Verbena Rd 88201
Verde Dr 88201
Verle Dr 88203
Via Blanco Dr 88203
Via Del Sol Dr 88203
Via Verde 88203
Viale Bond 88201
Victoria Ct 88201
Violet Rd 88201
N Virginia Ave
100-199 88203
200-1399 88201
S Virginia Ave 88203
E & W Vista Ln & Pkwy 88201
Vista Parkway Cir 88201
Von Leuven Pl 88203
Wagon Trl 88201
Walker Pl 88203
Walker Rd 88201
Walking Cane Ln 88201
E & W Walnut St 88203
N Washington Ave
100-199 88203
200-5499 88201
S Washington Ave 88203
Weiss Pl 88203
Welch Rd 88201
E Wells St 88203
Werkeister Pl 88203
Western Ave 88203
Western Briar Rd 88201
Westminister Ct 88201
Westover Dr 88201
White Dove Dr 88201
White Mill Rd 88203
Whitehead Rd 88203
Whitney Ln 88203
Wiggins Rd 88201
E & W Wildy Dr & St 88203
Will Pl 88203
Will Rogers 88203
Willow Dr 88203
E Wilshire Blvd 88201
N Wind Loop 88201
Wintercres Rd 88201
Wonder Ln 88201
Woodbine Way 88203
S Woody Dr 88203
Wool Bowl Ct 88201
Wooldridge Margaret Rd 88203
Wrangler Rd 88201
N Wyoming Ave 88201
S Wyoming Ave 88203
X Ell St 88203
Xanadu Pl 88201
Y O Rd 88203
Yale Dr & Pl 88203
Yeso Rd 88201
Yorkshire St 88201
Young Pl 88203
Yriart Rd 88201
Yucca Mesa Rd 88201
Zeb Chewning Pl 88203
Zettle Pl 88203
Zia Dr 88201
Zinnia Rd 88201
Zuni Dr 88201

NUMBERED STREETS

E & W 1st 88203
E & W 2nd 88201
E & W 3rd 88201
E & W 4th 88201
E & W 5th 88201
E & W 6th 88201
E & W 7th 88201
E & W 8th 88201
E & W 9th 88201
E & W 10th 88201
W 11th St 88201
E & W 12th 88201
E & W 13th 88201
W 14th St 88201
W 16th St 88201
E & W 17th 88201
E & W 18th 88201
E & W 19th 88201
W 21st St 88201
E 22nd St 88201
E & W 23rd 88201
E 24th St 88201
W 25th St 88201
W 27th St 88201

RUIDOSO NM

General Delivery 88345

POST OFFICE BOXES MAIN OFFICE STATIONS AND BRANCHES

Box No.s
All PO Boxes 88355

HIGHWAY CONTRACTS

66 88345

NAMED STREETS

All Street Addresses 88345

NUMBERED STREETS

All Street Addresses 88345

SANTA FE NM

General Delivery 87501

POST OFFICE BOXES MAIN OFFICE STATIONS AND BRANCHES

Box No.s
A - T 87504
C5160 - C5160 87502
C5439 - C5439 87502
C609 - C609 87504
C728 - C728 87504
C909 - C909 87504
C1028 - C1028 87504
C1148 - C1149 87504
C1269 - C1269 87504
C1840 - C1840 87504
C2048 - C2048 87504
C2228 - C2228 87504
C2267 - C2268 87504
C2408 - C2408 87504
C8390 - C8390 87504
C9054 - C9054 87504
C20009 - C20009 87504
C276 - C276 87504
C630 - C630 87504
C1059 - C1059 87504
C25101 - C25140 87504
C2107 - C2107 87504
C2307 - C2307 87504
C5212 - C5212 87502
C5469 - C5469 87502
1 - 2990 87504
4001 - 6990 87502
8001 - 9955 87504
9998 - 9998 87592
10101 - 12050 87504
15001 - 16776 87592
20002 - 20009 87504
22001 - 24458 87502
25000 - 25150 87504
25110 - 27118 87502
28001 - 30816 87592

31001 - 34174 87594

RURAL ROUTES

39 87505
01, 04, 05, 11, 32, 49 87506
06, 08, 10, 20, 21, 27, 36, 41 87507
02, 34 87508

NAMED STREETS

A N B Ln 87507
A Van Nu Po 87508
Aaron Y Veronica Rd 87506
Abanico Rd 87508
Abeyta St 87505
Abierto Way 87506
Abs Rd 87506
Academy Rd 87507
Acequia Ln 87507
Acequia Borrada W 87507
Acequia De Las Joyas 87505
Acequia Madre 87505
Acote Ct 87508
Adenois Lujan Rd 87506
Adobe Crk 87506
Adobe Loop 87508
Adolfo St 87501
Aggie Rd 87507
Agoyo Po 87506
Agua De Oro 87507
Agua Dulce 87506
Agua Fria St
5360A1-5360A2 87507
Agua Fria Park Rd 87507
Agua Viviendo 87508
Aguila Pl 87508
Airport Rd 87507
E Alameda St 87501
W Alameda St
2214A2-2214H2 87507
2214F1-2214F1 87507
201-497 87501
499-1999 87501
2100-4899 87507
Alamo Dr 87501
Alamo Ln 87507
Alamo Rd 87507
Alamo Creek Dr 87506
Alamosa Dr
2500-2799 87505
2800-2930 87507
2932-2998 87507
Alamosa Pl 87505
Alarid St
500-599 87501
600-899 87505
901-999 87505
Alba Ct 87508
Alcalde Loop & Rd 87508
Alcaldesa St 87501
Alegre Pass 87508
Alegre St 87501
Alejandro St 87501
Alfalfa Fields Ln 87506
E & W Alicante Rd 87505
Alicia St
500-599 87501
600-699 87505
All Trades Rd 87507
Allahna Way 87501
Allendale St 87505
Alley Ranch Trl 87505
Allondra Ln 87508
Alma Ct 87508
Aloe Cir 87506
Alondra Rd 87508
Alta Vista St 87505
Altazano Dr 87505
Alteza 87508
Altezita 87508
Alto Ln & St 87501
Altura Dr 87508
Altura Rd 87508
Altura Vis 87507
Amada Romero Rd 87506
Amadeo Lujan Ct 87506
Amado St 87501
Amado Sueno 87507
Amanda Ln 87507
Amarante Rd 87507
Amber Ln 87507
Amberwood Loop 87506
Ambrosio St 87501
Amigos Ln 87508
Amistad Pl 87508
Anastacio Ln 87506
Angel Peak 87508
Angelitos Rd 87506
Anita Pl 87505
Anna Jean Ct 87505
Anna Maria Ln 87506
Annex 87508
Antelope Hl 87508
Antigua Ct, Pl & Rd 87508
Antonio Ln 87507
Apache Ave 87505
Apache Crk 87505
Apache Knl 87507
Apache Pt 87505
Apache Rd 87508
Apache Trl 87505
Apache Canyon Trl 87505
Apache Creek Rnch 87505
Apache Plume Dr 87508
Apache Ridge Rd 87505
Apodaca Hill St 87501
Arapahoe Rd 87507
Arbol Grande 87506
Ardor St 87505
Arenal Ct 87501
Armenta St 87505
N & S Armijo Ln & St 87501
Arquero Rd 87508
Arriba Cir 87506
Arrow Head Ranch Rd 87507
E Arrowhead Cir 87506
W Arrowhead Cir 87506
Arrowhead Ct 87507
Arroyo Rdg 87508
Arroyo Trl 87508
Arroyo Vis 87505
Arroyo Calabasas Rd 87506
Arroyo Canyon Rd 87508
Arroyo Chamiso 87505
Arroyo Chico 87507
Arroyo Coyote Rd 87508
Arroyo Cuyamungue Rd 87506
Arroyo De Las Cruces Rd 87505
Arroyo De Las Cuevas 87506
Arroyo El Fego Gomez 87506
Arroyo Escondido 87507
Arroyo Griego 87506
Arroyo Hondo Rd & Trl 87508
Arroyo Jaconita 87506
Arroyo Los Lopez 87506
Arroyo Nambe 87506
Arroyo Negra 87506
Arroyo Pacifico 87507
Arroyo Pequeno 87506
Arroyo Piedra 87501
Arroyo Privado 87507
Arroyo Risueno 87507
Arroyo Salado 87508
Arroyo San Antonio 87506
Arroyo Sonrisa 87507
Arroyo Tenorio St 87505
Arroyo Viejo Rd 87508
Artifact Pl 87508
Artisan Ln 87507
Artist Rd 87501
Ash St 87507
Aspen Dr 87505
Aspen Loop 87507
Aspen Vw 87506
Aspen Compound 87501
Asta Ter 87508
Aster Rd & Way 87508
Astor Cir 87506
Atalaya Hill Trl 87505
Aula Ct 87508
Aurora Way 87508
Autumn Leaf Ln 87507
Autumn Light Pl 87508
Avalon Pl & Rd 87508
Avanyu Po 87506
Avelina Ln 87506
Avenger Way 87507
Avenida Alamosa 87507
Avenida Aldea 87507
Avenida Aliso 87501
Avenida Angeles 87507
Avenida Azul 87508
Avenida Buena Ventura 87508
Avenida Campo Verde 87506
Avenida Casa Del Oro 87508
Avenida Casa Del Oso 87508
Avenida Castellano 87501
Avenida Celaya 87506
Avenida Chamisa 87507
Avenida Chaparral 87505
Avenida Christina 87507
Avenida Codorniz 87507
Avenida Colima 87506
Avenida Contenta 87507
Avenida Cristobal Colo 87505
Avenida Cristobal Colon 87501
Avenida De Amistad 87508
Avenida De Clotilde 87506
Avenida De Compadres 87508
Avenida De Garcia 87507
Avenida De Isidro 87505
Avenida De La Scala 87506
Avenida De Las Alturas 87505
Avenida De Las America 87507
Avenida De Las Campanas 87507
Avenida De Las Casas 87506
Avenida De Las Estrellas 87507
Avenida De Luis 87506
Avenida De Luna 87506
Avenida De Melodia 87506
Avenida De Mercedes 87506
Avenida De Montoya 87507
Avenida De Rey 87506
Avenida De Ricardo 87507
Avenida De Sesario 87507
Avenida De Sevilla 87506
Avenida Del Monte Alto 87508
Avenida Del Oro 87507
Avenida Del Sol 87505
Avenida Del Sur 87508
Avenida El Nido 87507
Avenida Eldorado 87508
Avenida Frijoles 87507
Avenida Hermosa 87507
Avenida Herrera 87506
Avenida Juliana 87507
Avenida Las Nubes 87508
Avenida Linda 87507
Avenida Madison 87506
Avenida Malaguena 87506
Avenida Maya 87508
Avenida Morelia 87506
Avenida Oso Ct 87508
Avenida Pita 87505
Avenida Primera S 87501
Avenida Rincon 87506
Avenida San Diego 87507
E & W Avenida Sebastian 87506
Avenida Sonrisa 87507
Avenida Torreon 87508
Avenida Villa Hermosa 87506
Avenida Vista Esquisita 87508
Avenida Vista Grande 87508
Aventura Rd 87508
Aviation Dr 87507
Avila Ct & Rd 87508
Aztec St 87501
Azul Ct, Dr, Loop, Pl & Way 87508
E & W Azulejo Ct 87508
B Leal Rd 87505
Baca Ln 87507
Baca St 87505
Bajada Pl 87508
Balboa Rd 87505
Balde Rd 87508
Balsa Ct, Dr, Pl & Rd 87508
Banana Ln 87506
Banco Ln 87506
Bandilier Ct 87505
Bandolina Rd 87501
Bar D Four Rd 87506
E & W Barcelona Ln & Rd 87505
Barela Ln 87505
Barela St 87501
Barosa Rd 87507
Barra Del Oro 87508
Barranca Dr & Rd 87501
Barranca De Oro 87501
Barranquenos Ct & Rd 87506
Barrone Ln 87506
Bartlet Ct 87501
Barton Rd 87507
Basin View Ct 87506
Basket Maker Ct 87508
Bataan Blvd 87508
Battleship View Rd 87506
Bauer Rd 87506
Baya Ct & Rd 87508
Bear Mtn 87508
Bella Dr 87507
Bella Loma 87506
Bellamah Ct & Dr 87507
Ben Ln 87507
Ben Hur Dr 87501
Bens Ct 87506
Bent Hl 87501
Berardinelli St 87505
E & W Berger St 87505
Berrendo 87508
Berry Ave 87505
Betatakin Cir 87507
Big Bear Pl 87508
Big Bluestem 87508
Big Sky Rd 87507
Big Tesuque Cyn 87506
Birch St 87507
Birdwatch Ridge Ln 87506
Birla Ct 87508
Bisbee Ct & Ln 87508
Bishops Trl 87506
Bishops Dome Rd 87506
Bishops Lodge Rd
301-397 87501
399-1230 87501
1232-1298 87501
1297-1297 87506
1299-1300 87506
1301-1311 87501
1302-1598 87506
1313-1599 87506
Bison Ct & Loop 87506
Black Canyon Rd 87508
Black Mesa Vw 87506
Blanket Flower Cir 87506
Blazing Star Cir 87506
Blue Hl 87508
Blue Bird Ct 87508
Blue Canyon Trl, Vis & Way 87507
Blue Corn Rd 87506
Blue Corn Trce 87506
Blue Feather Rd 87508
Blue Jay Dr 87506
Blue Juniper Loop 87507
Blue Mesa Rd 87508
Blue Raven Rd 87508
Blue Spruce Dr 87507
Blue Tesuque Ln 87506
Blue Wing Pl 87508
Bluebell Ct 87508
Bluebonnet Cir 87506
Bluesky Cir 87506
Bluestem Dr 87506
Bluffs Ln 87506
Bob St 87501
Bob Cat Trl 87505
Bob Cat Xing 87508
Bonanza Trl 87508
Bonanza Creek Ln & Rd 87508
Bonito Cir 87507
Bonito Ct 87508
Bonito Dr 87508
Bonito Rd 87508
E & W Booth St 87505
Borrego Pass 87507
Bosque Loop 87508
Bosque Azul 87507
Bosquecillo 87508
Botulph Ln & Rd 87505
Bouquet Ln 87506
Boylan Cir & Ln 87507
Boylan County Rd 87507
Brae St 87505
Brahma Ln 87506
Brass Horse Ln & Rd 87508
Brazos Ct 87508
Brazos River Rd 87507
Brianna Ln 87506
Brillante Ln & St 87505
Brillantes Arenas St 87501
Brilliant Sky Dr 87508
Brimhall Wash 87508
Brisa Cir 87507
N & S Brisa Fresca Dr 87506
Broken Rock Pl 87508
Broken Sherd Trl 87506
Bronerli 87506
Bronze Trl 87508
Bronze Sky 87506
Brooks Way 87508
Brother Abdon Way 87505
Brother Luke Pl 87505
Brothers Rd 87505
Brown Castle Rnch 87508
Brownell Howland Rd 87501
Brownie Ln 87505
Brunn School Ln & Rd 87505
Bucking Horse Ct 87508
Buckman Rd
703A-703B 87507
701-703 87507
1000-1002 87507
1045-1049 87506
1051-1117 87506
1119-1123 87506
2674-3256 87507
Buckskin Cir 87506
Buen Pastor 87508
Buena Ventura Pl 87508
E & W Buena Vista St 87505
Buffalo Cyn 87505
Buffalo St 87506
Buffalo Trl 87506
Buffalo Draw 87508
Buffalo Grass Rd 87507
Buffalo Thunder Trl 87506
Bundy Rd 87506
Burro Ln 87507
Burro Alley St 87501
Burro Bend Rd 87505
Buster Rdg 87505
Butterfly Bush Ct 87508
Buu Pin Gae Po 87506
C De Baca Ln 87505
Caballito 87508
Caballo Viejo 87508
Caballos Trl 87508
Cabana Ct 87501
Cactus Ln 87505
Cactus Flower Ln 87507
Cadiz Rd 87505
Cagua Ct & Rd 87508
Caja Del Oro Grant Rd 87507
Caja Del Rio 87507
Caja Del Rio Rd 87506
Caliente Pl & Rd 87508
Calientito Loop 87507
Calimo Cir 87505
Calle Vis 87507
Calle Abeja 87506
Calle Adelina 87506
Calle Agar 87505
Calle Agua Clara 87508
Calle Aguila 87508
Calle Alejandra 87508
Calle Alexia 87508
Calle Altamira 87501
Calle Altura 87507
Calle Alvarado 87505
Calle Amanda 87507
Calle Amelia 87505
Calle Amistosa 87507
Calle Anaya N & S 87505
Calle Andreita 87506
Calle Andrew 87507
Calle Angelina 87507
Calle Anna Jean 87505
Calle Arbusto 87506
Calle Arco 87501
Calle Aventura 87507
Calle Azulejo 87505
Calle Bajo 87501
Calle Baronesa 87507
Calle Basilica 87508
Calle Beatrice 87501
Calle Belicia 87508
Calle Bella 87505
Calle Blanca 87507
Calle Bonita 87505
Calle Brocha 87505
Calle Caballero 87507
Calle Cabito 87508
Calle Cacique 87505
Calle Cal 87508
Calle Calmo 87505
Calle Camarico 87505
Calle Campeon 87505
Calle Canoncito 87505
Calle Cantando 87508
Calle Capulin 87507
Calle Carino 87506
Calle Carla 87507
Calle Carmilita 87505
Calle Carolina 87507
Calle Cascabella 87508
Calle Casitas 87506
Calle Catalina 87501
Calle Cazuela 87507
Calle Cedro 87505
Calle Celestial 87506
Calle Cerrada 87505
Calle Chiquita 87501
Calle Chuparosa 87507
Calle Cielo 87506
Calle Cimarron 87506
Calle Cisco 87507
Calle Colibri 87505
Calle Colina 87501
Calle Compa 87507
Calle Conejo 87501
Calle Contento 87505
Calle Contessa 87505
Calle Corazon 87507
Calle Corazzi 87507
Calle Corrado 87508
Calle Corta 87507
Calle Corto 87507
Calle Corvo 87501
Calle Cristiano 87508
Calle Cristo 87507
Calle Cristoval 87507
Calle Cuesta 87505
Calle Culebra 87507
Calle Curioso 87506
Calle Daniel 87507
Calle David 87506
Calle De Agua 87501
Calle De Anza 87501
Calle De Arce 87505
Calle De Bonita 87507
Calle De Carlotta 87507
Calle De Cinco 87506
Calle De Comercio 87507
Calle De Familia 87508
Calle De Francisco 87505
Calle De Gatos 87506
Calle De Juan 87507
Calle De La Vuelta 87505
Calle De Leon 87505
Calle De Los Alamos 87506
Calle De Los Cerros 87508
Calle De Los Ninos 87505
Calle De Los Trujillo 87506
Calle De Luz 87506
Calle De Marcos 87505
Calle De Molina 87507
Calle De Montanas 87507
Calle De Ocho Vacas 87508
Calle De Oriente 87507
Calle De Oriente Norte 87507
Calle De Ovejas 87505
Calle De Pinata 87507
Calle De Pinos Altos 87507
Calle De Quiquido 87507
Calle De Rincon Bonito 87505
Calle De Romero 87506
Calle De Saiz 87507
Calle De Sebastian 87505
Calle De Sonoro 87507
Calle De Suenos 87507
Calle De Valdez 87505
Calle De Valle 87505
Calle De Vecinos 87506
Calle De Vigil 87508
Calle Debra 87507
Calle Del Arroyo 87507
Calle Del Barrio 87505
Calle Del Cielo 87507
N & S Calle Del Oro 87507
Calle Del Pajarito 87507
Calle Del Prado 87508
Calle Del Res 87505
Calle Del Resplandor 87505
Calle Del Rey 87506
Calle Del Sol 87505
Calle Del Sur 87507
Calle Delfino 87505
Calle Derecha 87505
Calle Don Enrique 87506
Calle Don Jose 87501
Calle Don Roberto 87507
Calle Don Tomas 87506
Calle Dorthia 87506
Calle Dulcinea 87505
Calle El Gancho 87507
Calle Electra 87508
Calle Elena 87506
Calle Eloisa 87507
Calle Eloy 87501
Calle Encanto 87506
Calle Enlace 87505
Calle Enrique 87507
Calle Ensenada 87505
Calle Espejo 87505
Calle Estado 87501
Calle Estevan 87507
Calle Estrella 87506
Calle Eugenio 87507
Calle Feliz 87507
Calle Festiva 87507
Calle Florinda 87507
Calle Francisca 87507
Calle Galisteo 87508
Calle Garcia 87506
Calle Gary 87507
Calle Giraso 87501
Calle Golondrina 87505

Calle Grillo 87505
Calle Guillermo 87507
Calle Gurule 87505
Calle Hacienda 87506
Calle Halcon 87505
Calle Hermosa 87508
Calle Hernandez 87507
Calle Inez 87507
Calle Jacinta 87508
Calle Jaime 87507
Calle Jenah 87507
Calle Jessica 87507
Calle Josephina 87506
Calle Joya 87501
Calle Juanita 87501
Calle Katarina 87507
Calle Kokopelli 87501
Calle Kryshanna 87507
Calle La Mirada 87507
Calle La Paz 87505
Calle La Pena 87505
Calle La Resolana 87507
Calle Largo 87501
Calle Larranaga 87507
Calle Las Casas 87507
Calle Lazo Errante 87507
Calle Lejano 87501
Calle Lema 87507
Calle Lemita 87507
Calle Lento 87501
Calle Lila 87506
Calle Linda 87505
Calle Lisa 87507
Calle Loma 87507
Calle Loma Bonita 87507
Calle Loma Norte 87501
Calle Lomita Blanca 87506
Calle Lorca 87505
Calle Lucero 87505
Calle Luminoso 87505
Calle Luna 87501
Calle Maes 87507
Calle Manzano 87508
Calle Margarita 87507
Calle Margosa 87508
Calle Maria N & S 87508
Calle Maria Luisa 87507
Calle Marie 87507
Calle Marisol 87505
Calle Matilde 87506
Calle Medico 87505
Calle Mejia 87501
Calle Melecio 87505
Calle Melita 87505
Calle Mi Gusto 87506
Calle Miquela 87505
Calle Nava 87505
Calle Navidad 87505
Calle Nopal 87507
Calle Nopalitos 87507
Calle Norte 87507
Calle Nueva Vis 87507
Calle Nuves 87507
Calle Ojitos 87506
Calle Ojo Feliz 87505
Calle Orilla 87506
Calle Oso 87501
Calle Otra Banda 87506
Calle Pacifica 87505
Calle Pagosa 87506
Calle Paisano 87505
Calle Palomita 87505
Calle Paula 87505
Calle Pava 87505
Calle Peligroso 87505
Calle Perdiz 87505
Calle Perezoso 87507
Calle Petaca 87505
Calle Pia Tixier 87507
Calle Picacho 87505
Calle Pico 87507
Calle Pinonero 87505
Calle Pintura 87505
Calle Plazuela 87507
Calle Po Ae Pi 87507
Calle Poco 87501
Calle Ponciano 87506
Calle Prado 87507
Calle Preciosa 87505
Calle Primavera 87505
Calle Princesa Juana ... 87507
Calle Privado 87508
Calle Pulido 87505
Calle Quedo 87505
Calle Querido 87506
Calle Quieta 87507
Calle Quintana 87506
Calle Ramon 87501
Calle Raquel 87508
Calle Redondo 87505
Calle Reina 87507
Calle Rivera 87506
Calle Roble 87501
Calle Romolo 87505
Calle Royale 87505
Calle San Acacia 87506
Calle San Martin 87506
Calle San Simon 87505
Calle Santa Maria 87501
Calle Santo Nino 87501
Calle Saragosa 87505
Calle Serena 87505
Calle Sierpe 87501
Calle Siete Casas 87507
Calle Sinsonte 87507
Calle Sombra 87505
Calle Sotero 87507
W Calle Suerte 87507
Calle Suzanna 87507
Calle Tablas 87505
Calle Tangara 87507
Calle Tecolote 87505
Calle Tia Louisa 87506
Calle Torreador 87505
Calle Torreon 87501
Calle Tranquillo 87505
Calle Tres Pinos 87508
Calle Turquesa 87507
Calle Unidad 87507
Calle Vado 87507
Calle Varada 87507
Calle Vecinos 87507
Calle Venado 87506
Calle Vencejo 87507
Calle Ventoso E & W .. 87506
Calle Vera Cruz 87507
Calle Verde 87507
Calle Vianson 87508
Calle Vibora 87501
Calle Viejo 87507
Calle Vistoso 87501
Calle Volver 87505
Calle Zaguan 87505
Calle Zanate 87507
Callecita Pl 87501
Callecita Jicarilla 87505
Callecita Membreno 87505
Callecita Pecos 87505
Calleja Shannon 87507
Callejon Alegre 87506
Callejon Arias 87501
Callejon Colibri 87506
Callejon Cordelia 87501
Callejon De Atanacio ... 87506
Callejon De Rita 87507
Callejon Emilia 87501
Callejon Faisan 87507
Callejon Garza 87507
Callejon Hermosa 87505
Callejon Lechuza 87507
Callejon Lomitas 87507
Callejon Nambe 87506
Callejon Norte 87507
Callejon Picaflor 87507
Callejon Tisnado 87501
Callejon Urraca 87507
Callejon Valdez 87506
Callejon Veronica 87501
Callejon Zenaida 87501
Callejoncito Rd 87506
Calmo Ct 87505
Calvin Rd 87508
Camel Rock Rd 87506
Camerada Loop & Rd .. 87508
Cameron Ln 87505
Caminito Alegre 87501
Caminito Carlitos 87505
Caminito Corto 87506
Caminito De Gracia 87506
Caminito De Norbert 87505
Caminito De Pinon 87505
Caminito Del Donaldo .. 87505
Caminito Del Rincon 87506
Caminito Del Sol 87505
Caminito Monica 87501
Caminito Montano 87501
Caminito Nevado 87501
Caminito Quintana 87507
Caminito Ramon 87507
Caminito Romero 87507
Caminito San Lucas 87507
Caminito Santera 87505
Caminito Sena 87506
Caminito Sonrisa 87507
Caminito Tranquilo 87507
Caminito Valdez 87506
Caminito Vigil 87507
Camino Acoma 87505
Camino Acote 87508
Camino Adela 87505
Camino Agua Azul 87507
Camino Aj 87506
Camino Alfredo 87505
Camino Alhambra 87507
Camino Alire 87501
Camino Alondra 87507
Camino Altito 87501
Camino Alto 87506
Camino Amado 87505
Camino Amansador 87508
Camino Amor 87506
Camino Anasazi 87505
Camino Anastacio 87508
Camino Ancon 87506
Camino Apolonia 87505
Camino Arbustos 87506
Camino Archuletas 87506
Camino Artesano 87505
Camino Artista 87505
Camino Atalaya 87505
Camino Aurelia 87506
Camino Azul
1A-29A 87508
Camino Azulejo 87508
Camino Bajo 87508
Camino Barranca 87507
Camino Benavidez 87507
Camino Bonito 87506
Camino Botanica 87507
Camino Brisa 87508
Camino Cabestro 87505
Camino Cabo 87508
Camino Cabra 87505
Camino Cacto 87505
Camino Calabasas 87506
Camino Campanario 87506
Camino Capilla Vieja ... 87507
Camino Capitan 87505
Camino Carlita 87507
Camino Carlitos 87505
Camino Carlos Rael 87507
Camino Carlos Rey 87507
Camino Caruso 87506
Camino Catalina 87506
E Camino Cerrado 87506
Camino Cerrito 87505
Camino Cerro
Escondido 87508
Camino Cerro Lindo 87507
Camino Chaco 87501
Camino Chamisa 87501
Camino Charro 87507
Camino Chico 87505
Camino Chueco 87505
Camino Chupadero 87506
Camino Cielo 87506
Camino Cielo Vis 87507
Camino Cielo Alto 87505
Camino Cielo Azul 87508
Camino Cieneguilla 87507
Camino Cimarron 87505
Camino Claro 87505
Camino Colores 87507
Camino Consuelo 87507
Camino Corrales 87505
Camino Corto 87501
Camino Costadino 87508
Camino Crosby 87506
Camino Cruz Corta 87507
Camino Cuervo 87507
Camino De Agua 87506
Camino De Baros 87507
Camino De Chelly 87505
Camino De Colores 87506
Camino De Cruz
Blanca 87505
Camino De Elfego 87506
Camino De Fabian 87506
Camino De Griego 87507
Camino De
Guadalupita 87505
Camino De Hermanos .. 87507
Camino De Jacobo 87507
Camino De Jemez 87501
Camino De La Familia .. 87501
Camino De La Luz 87505
Camino De La Sierra ... 87501
Camino De La Vega ... 87506
Camino De La Vuelta .. 87501
Camino De Las
Animas 87505
Camino De Las
Crucitas 87501
Camino De Las Minas .. 87508
Camino De Las
Trampas 87501
Camino De Levante 87501
Camino De Los
Caballos 87507
Camino De Los
Marquez 87505
Camino De Los
Montoyas 87506
Camino De Los
Roybals 87506
Camino De Manuel 87507
Camino De Mi Angel ... 87507
Camino De Milagro 87506
Camino De Monte
Rey 87505
Camino De Pabilo 87505
Camino De Pastores ... 87506
Camino De Rey Cir 87506
Camino De Romeros ... 87506
Camino De Roybal 87506
Camino De Vaca 87507
Camino De Vecinos 87507
Camino De Verdad 87508
Camino De Vida 87505
Camino De Viento 87507
Camino Debra 87507
Camino Del Alba 87506
Camino Del Bosque 87507
Camino Del Campo 87501
Camino Del Centro 87507
Camino Del Cerezo 87506
Camino Del Este 87501
Camino Del Griego 87507
Camino Del Gusto 87507
Camino Del Leo 87508
Camino Del Monte 87508
Camino Del Monte Sol
300-399 87501
Camino Del Monte Sol
400-800 87505
802-898 87505
Camino Del Norte 87501
Camino Del Ojito 87506
Camino Del Olmo 87501
Camino Del Oso 87501
Camino Del Poniente ... 87505
Camino Del Prado 87507
Camino Del Rincon 87506
Camino Del Sol 87508
Camino Del Valle 87506
Camino Delilah 87506
Camino Delora 87505
Camino Dimitrio 87508
N & S Camino Don
Carlos 87506
Camino Don Emilio 87507
Camino Don Fidel 87507
Camino Don Miguel 87505
Camino Don Patron 87506
Camino Dos Antonios .. 87507
Camino Dos Perros 87506
Camino El Toro 87505
Camino Encantado 87501
Camino Entrada 87507
Camino Escondido
16A-16B 87508
1-11 87508
13-99 87508
100-199 87501
Camino Espejo 87507
Camino Esperanza 87507
Camino Espuela 87505
Camino Esquelipa 87505
Camino Esquinas 87507
Camino Estrada 87505
Camino Estrellas 87508
Camino Estribo 87505
Camino Felix 87506
Camino Francisca 87506
Camino Giron 87506
Camino Hasta Manana . 87506
Camino Haulapai 87505
Camino Iglesia 87506
Camino Iris 87505
Camino Jalisco 87507
Camino Juliana 87507
Camino Justicia 87508
Camino La Canada 87501
Camino La Familia 87506
Camino La Llorona 87505
Camino La Tierra 87506
Camino Ladera 87506
Camino Lado 87505
Camino Lagunitas 87507
Camino Largo 87507
Camino Las Cuatas 87506
Camino Las Joyas 87506
Camino Lazo 87505
Camino Lazo Del Sol ... 87507
Camino Lejo 87505
Camino Lila 87507
Camino Lisa 87501
Camino Loma 87507
Camino Los Abuelos ... 87508
Camino Los Altos 87501
Camino Los Arboles ... 87506
Camino Los Gardunos . 87506
Camino Los Suenos ... 87506
Camino Lumbre 87505
Camino Manana 87501
Camino Manzano 87505
Camino Maria Feliz 87507
Camino Mariquita 87508
Camino Matias 87501
Camino Mayancita 87507
Camino Mcmillin 87507
Camino Medianoche 87506
Camino Meliton 87507
Camino Miguel 87506
Camino Militar 87501
Camino Mio 87505
Camino Mirada 87505
Camino Mocho 87507
Camino Monte Vis 87505
Camino Monte Feliz 87505
Camino Monte Y Cielo . 87507
Camino Montebello 87501
Camino Montoso 87508
Camino Montoya 87507
Camino Montuoso 87506
Camino Nevoso 87505
Camino Ocaso Del
Sol 87505
Camino Oraibi 87505
Camino Oriente 87508
Camino Ortiz 87507
Camino Osito 87505
Camino Otilia 87506
Camino Pacifico 87508
Camino Pequeno 87501
Camino Peralta 87507
Camino Piedra
Lumbre 87505
Camino Pinon 87508
Camino Pinones 87505
Camino Pintores 87505
Camino Placitas 87507
Camino Polvoso 87507
Camino Porvenir 87505
Camino Prado Vis 87507
Camino Principe 87507
Camino Quien Sabe ... 87505
Camino Quieto 87508
Camino Rancheros 87505
Camino Ranchitos 87505
Camino Rancho
Siringo 87505
Camino Rancho Verde . 87505
Camino Real 87501
Camino Real Loop 87507
Camino Redondo 87505
Camino Ribera 87505
Camino Rio 87501
Camino Rizo 87505
Camino Rojo 87507
Camino Sabanero 87508
Camino Sabio 87506
Camino Samuel
Montoya 87507
Camino San Acacia 87506
Camino San Acacio 87505
Camino San Andres ... 87505
Camino San Carlos 87507
Camino San Jose 87507
Camino San Juan 87507
Camino San Patricio ... 87505
Camino San Ysidro 87506
Camino Sanador 87505
Camino Santa Ana 87505
Camino Santander 87505
Camino Santiago 87501
Camino Serpiente 87507
Camino Sierra Vis 87505
Camino Sin Ganas 87506
Camino Sin Luz 87506
Camino Sin Nombre 87505
Camino Sin Salida 87501
Camino Solano 87505
Camino Sudeste 87508
Camino Teofanio 87508
Camino Teresa 87505
Camino Tetzcoco 87508
Camino Tierra Alta 87501
Camino Tierra Real 87507
Camino Torado 87507
Camino Torcido Loop ... 87507
Camino Tortuga 87505
Camino Tres Arroyos ... 87507
Camino Tres Cruces ... 87506
Camino Trujillo 87506
Camino Unido 87507
Camino Urban 87507
Camino Vado 87507
Camino Valle 87508
Camino Ventura 87507
Camino Verde 87507
Camino Vista Aurora ... 87507
Camino Vista Grande ... 87508
Camino Vista Verde 87507
Camino Vistas
Encantada 87507
Camino Zozobra 87505
Campana Pl 87501
Campeon Ct 87505
Campo De La Vega 87506
Campo Del Viento 87506
Campo Montoso 87506
Campo Rancheros 87506
Campo Verde 87505
Campo Villenos 87506
Canada Ancha 87501
Canada De Santa Fe ... 87508
Canada Del Humo 87505
Canada Del Rancho 87508
Canada Del Sur 87501
Canada Valley Rd 87505
Canada Village Rd 87505
Candela St 87505
Candelario St 87501
Candelero St 87505
Canjilon Ct 87508
Canon Del Cerro 87506
Cantera Cir 87501
Canto Del Pajaro 87508
Canyon Rd 87501
Canyon Cliff Dr 87508
Canyon Hill Ln 87501
Canyon Vista Ct 87506
Capital Peak 87508
S Capitol Pl 87501
Carissa Rd 87508
Carlito Rd 87508
Carlson Ct & Rd 87508
Carmello Way 87505
Carson Valley Way 87508
Casa De Ortiz 87506
Casa Del Oro Ct, Ln,
Loop, Pl & Way 87508
Casa Rinconada 87507
Casa Rufina Rd 87507
Casados St 87501
Casas De Milagros 87507
Casas De San Juan 87506
Casas Escondidos 87506
Case Rd 87507
Castillo Pl 87501
Cathedral Pl 87501
Catron St 87501
Cayuse Pl 87508
Cedar Rd 87508
Cedar St 87501
Cedarcrest Cir 87507
Cedros Cir 87505
Centaurus Ranch Rd ... 87507
Center Ct, Dr & Pl 87507
Ceramic Ct 87508
Cerrado Ct, Dr, Loop, Pl,
Rd & Way 87508
Cerrillos Rd
400-599 87501
600-2699 87505
2701-4251 87507
4250-4250 87592
4252-8380 87507
4253-7521 87507
Cerrito Lindo 87507
Cerro Contento 87505
Cerro De La Paz 87501
Cerro De Palomas 87506
Cerro Del Alamo 87507
Cerro Escondido 87501
Cerro Gordo Rd 87501
Cerro Gurule 87505
Cerros Altos 87501
Cerros Colorados 87501
Cerros Grande Pl 87507
Cerros Grandes Dr 87507
Chalan Rd 87507
Chama Ave 87505
N Chamisa Dr 87508
S Chamisa Dr 87508
Chamisa St 87505
Chamisa Path Rd 87507
Chamiso Ln 87505
Chamisos Ct 87505
Chapala Rd 87508
Chaparral N 87507
Chaparral S 87507
Chaparral Ct 87508
Chaparral Dr 87508
Chaparron Pl 87507
Chapelle St 87501
Chaquaco 87508
Charlie Bentley Dr 87507
Chavez Pl & Trl 87505
Chelsea Ln 87505
Chestnut Cir 87506

Chestnut St 87507
Chet Smith Ln 87506
Cheyenne Cir 87507
Chicoma Vis 87507
E & W Chili Line Rd 87508
Chippewa Cir 87506
Chisholm Trl 87506
Chocolate Flower Cir 87506
Cholla Cir 87506
Christmas Ln 87506
Christopher Ct 87508
Chula Vista St 87501
Churchill Rd 87508
Chusco Rd 87508
Cibola Cir
1-99 87505
1300-1399 87501
Cibola Dr 87501
Cibolita Peak 87508
Cielo Ct 87507
Cielo Azul St 87501
Cielo Cumbre Rd 87505
Cielo De Oro 87508
Cielo Del Oeste 87507
Cielo Encantado 87506
Cielo Grande 87505
Cielo Lindo 87507
Cielo Rosado 87507
Cielo Tranquilo Ct 87508
Cielo Vista Ct 87507
Cienega St 87501
Cimarron Pass 87508
Cinco Pintores 87506
Circita Del Norte 87507
Circita Del Sur 87507
Circita En Medio 87507
Circle Dr 87501
Circle Drive Rdg 87501
Circle Drive
Compound 87501
Circulo De Morelia 87506
Cities Of Gold Rd 87506
City Lights St 87507
Clark Ct & Rd 87507
Clematis Cir 87506
Cleveland St 87501
Cliff Palace 87507
Closson St 87501
Cloud Loop 87506
Cloud Way 87508
Cloud Dance 87507
Cloud March E & W 87506
Cloudstone Dr 87505
Cloudview Ct 87506
Clove Cir & Ct 87506
Clubhouse Dr 87506
Cochiti E 87508
Cochiti W 87508
Cochiti St 87505
Cole Ct 87507
Cole Ln 87508
Colibri Tierra 87506
Colina Verde 87501
Colinas Rd 87508
College Dr 87508
Colonitas Campestres 87501
Colony Ct & Dr 87507
Colores Del Rey 87507
Colores Del Sol 87507
Colour De Lila 87507
Columbia St 87505
Columbine Ln 87506
Comanche Dr 87508
Conchas Ct, Loop &
Pl 87508
Condesa Ct & Rd 87508
Conejo Dr 87505
Conejo Trl 87506
Conestoga Trl 87508
Constellation Way 87507
Contenta Rdg 87507
Cooks Ln & Rd 87507
Copita Ln 87505
Copper Trl 87508
Coppermallow Rd 87506
Coral St 87506
Coral Bell Ct 87508
E & W Cordova Ln, Pl &
Rd 87505
Coreopsis Ct 87508
Coriander Rd 87507
Corn Maiden 87506
Cornerstone Ln 87506
Corona St 87501
E & W Coronado Ln &
Rd 87505
Corral Blanco Rd 87508
Corrales Trl 87505
Corrida De Agua 87507
Corriente Cir 87507
Corte Ct 87507
Corte Corazon 87506
Corte De Espuelas 87505
Corte De Pinon 87505
Corte De Princessa 87507
Corte Del Becerro 87505
Corte Del Potro 87505
Corte Del Pozo 87505
Corte Gracia 87507
Corte La Canada 87501
Corte Ojo De Agua 87505
Corte Patricia 87508
Cortez Pl 87501
Cortez St
500-599 87501
600-699 87505
701-799 87505
Cosmos Cir 87506
Cosmos Ct 87508
Cottontail Rd 87507
Cougar Rdg 87505
Cougar Canyon Rd 87508
Cougars Walk 87505
Country Club Rd 87507
County Road 101b 87506
County Road 101c 87506
County Road 101e 87506
County Road 104 87507
County Road 106 87506
County Road 113 S 87506
County Road 113b 87506
County Road 117 N 87506
County Road 119 N &
S 87506
County Road 62 87507
County Road 68a 87507
County Road 72h 87506
County Road 74 87506
County Road 84 87506
County Road 84a 87506
County Road 84b 87506
County Road 84c 87506
County Road 84d 87506
County Road 84f 87506
County Road 84g 87506
County Road 89d 87506
Courtney Ln 87507
Coyote Ln 87507
Coyote Pass 87508
Coyote Spgs 87508
Coyote Trl 87508
Coyote Xing 87508
Coyote Hills Ln 87505
Coyote Loco Rd 87508
Coyote Moon Ln 87507
Coyote Mountain Rd 87505
Coyote Ridge Ct, Rd &
Trl 87507
Coyote Wash 87508
Coyotillo Ct 87507
Crabapple Ct 87505
Craftsman Rd 87508
Crazy Horse Rd 87505
Crazy Rabbit Ct, Dr &
Rd 87508
Cree Cir 87507
Cresencio Ln 87506
Cresta Del Angel 87505
Cresta Pequena 87505
Crestview Cir 87506
Crimson Ridge Pl 87508
Cristo Rey St 87505
Cristobal Ln 87505
Cristos Rd 87507
Cross St 87505
Crossroads Ct 87506
Crouch Ct 87507
Crows View Pl 87508
Cruz Blanca Ct 87505
Crystal Mesa Rd 87508
Cuates Y Rabo 87506
Cuatro Vientos Rd 87507
Cuerno De Vaca Dr 87507
Cuesta Ln & Rd 87508
Cuesta Del Norte 87501
Cumbre Vista Dr 87501
Cumbres Pass 87508
Cundiyo Rd 87506
Cypress St 87507
Dail Cir 87507
Daisy Cir & Ct 87506
Dancing Ground Rd 87507
Dandelion Cir 87506
Daniel St 87501
Darlene Ct 87508
Dawn Trl 87508
Daybreak 87507
Dayflower Dr 87506
De Fouri St 87501
E & W De Vargas St 87501
Deans Ct 87508
Declovina St 87505
Deer Cir 87506
Deer Dancer 87506
Deer Tank Rd 87508
Del Monte 87506
Del Norte Ln 87501
Del Rio Dr 87501
Del Ross Ln 87507
Delantera Ct 87506
Delaware Ln 87508
Delgado Ln 87505
Delgado St 87501
Delilah Ln 87506
Delora Estates Rd 87505
Demas Rd 87508
Demora Ct & Rd 87508
Descanso Rd
1-99 87508
700-799 87501
Desert Mtn 87508
Desert Blossom 87508
Desert Plume Trl 87508
Desert Rain 87508
Desert Rose Ct 87506
Desert Sun Cir 87507
Destierro Trl 87506
Devoys Peak 87508
Dinosaur Trl 87508
Diolinda Rd 87505
Dlp Rd 87506
Dogwood Cir 87506
Dolores St 87501
Domingo Ct, Pl & Rd 87508
Dominguez Ln 87507
Dominic Ln 87507
Don Bernardo 87506
Don Canuto St 87505
Don Cubero Aly, Ave &
Pl 87505
Don Diego Ave 87505
Don Felix St 87501
Don Fernando Rd 87505
Don Filomeno Rd 87506
Don Gaspar Ave
100-400 87501
402-498 87501
500-1599 87505
1601-1699 87505
Don Gaspar Ln 87505
Don Jose Loop 87505
Don Juan St 87501
Don Manuel St 87505
Don Miguel Pl 87505
Don Quixote 87505
Dos Hermanos 87507
Dos Lobos Loop 87508
Double Arrow Rd S 87505
Douglas St 87505
Dovela Ct, Pl & Rd 87508
Dream Catcher 87506
Droege Rd 87508
Dry Creek Rd 87506
Dry Dock Pl 87508
Duende Rd 87508
Dulce Rd 87508
Dunlap St 87501
Duran St 87501
Durango Dr 87507
Dutch Rd 87508
Eagle Rdg 87508
Eagle Feather Ct 87506
Eagle Nest Cir 87506
Eagle Peak 87508
Eagle Thorn Pl 87508
Early St 87505
Eastlook 87507
Easy St 87506
Eccola Ln 87506
Eddy Rd 87506
Edwardo Ortiz Dr 87506
El Alamo St 87501
El Alto 87506
El Calle Joncito 87506
El Callejon 87506
El Callejoncito Rd 87506
El Caminito St 87505
El Cerro Trl 87508
El Cuero Way 87508
El Duane Ct 87501
El Nido Ln 87506
El Paseo 87501
El Pueblito Rd 87506
N & S El Rancho Ln &
Rd N 87501
El Sol Ct 87507
El Trebol Ct 87507
Eldorado Cir, Pl &
Way 87508
Elena Ct 87508
Elena St 87501
Eliza Rd 87508
Elk Cir 87506
Elk Horn Rd 87507
Ellis Ranch Loop &
Rd 87505
Elm St 87507
Emblem Rd 87507
Embudo Del Sol 87508
Emilia Ct 87507
Emiliano Pl 87506
Emily Rd 87508
Emory Pass 87508
Encantado Cir 87508
Encantado Ct 87508
Encantado Dr 87501
Encantado Loop 87508
Encantado Pl 87508
Encantado Rd 87508
Encina Rd 87505
End Of The Trail Rd 87508
Enebro Ct, Pl, Rd &
Way 87508
Enmedio Pl 87508
Ensenada Dr 87508
Entrada 87507
Entrada Capulin 87506
Entrada Celedon Y
Nestora 87506
Entrada Corte 87506
Entrada De Colores 87508
Entrada De Duran 87506
Entrada De Gonzales 87506
Entrada De Gutierrez 87507
Entrada De Milagro 87507
Entrada De Montoya 87506
Entrada De Santiago 87508
Entrada Descanso 87506
Entrada Empinada 87506
Entrada Enrique 87506
Entrada Fabian 87507
Entrada Hermosa 87506
Entrada La Cienega 87507
Entrada Sonata 87507
Ephriam St 87501
Erica 87507
Ernesto Rd 87508
Errett St 87501
Escalante St 87505
Escondida Ct 87507
Escondido Mtn 87508
Escopeta Ct & Pl 87506
Escudero St 87505
Escuelita Ln 87506
Espejo Pl 87505
Esperanza Ln 87501
Esperanza Noel 87508
Espinacitas St 87505
Espinoza Ln 87506
Espira Ct & Rd 87508
Esplendor St 87505
Esquila Rd 87508
Esquina Rd 87508
Estacada Ct & Rd 87508
Estambre Ct, Pl & Rd 87508
Estancia Ct 87506
Estates Dr 87506
Este Ln 87501
Este Es El Camino 87508
Estrada Calabasa W 87506
Estrada Maya 87506
Estrada Redonda 87506
Estrella Ct 87501
Estrella Brillante 87507
Estrella De La
Manana 87508
Estrellas Rd N & S 87507
Estrellas De Tano 87506
Evergreen Ln 87506
Fair Way 87507
Fairly Rd 87507
E Faithway St 87501
Fajada Wash 87508
Faldas De La Sierra 87501
Falling Star Cir 87506
Falling Star Ln 87507
Family Ln 87505
Farmers Pond Rd 87507
Faubion Ln 87508
Fayette St 87505
Feather Rd 87506
Feather Bush Ct 87508
E Feather Catcher 87506
S Federal Pl
2-198 87501
120-120 87504
Felipe St 87505
Ferguson Ln 87505
Fermina Dr 87506
Fido Ln 87508
Fields Ln 87507
Fiesta St 87501
Fin Del Sendero 87506
Finch Cir 87506
Fire Pl 87508
Fire Gard 87508
Fire Hearth Pl 87508
Firerock Pl & Rd 87508
Firewheel Ct 87508
First Lgt 87506
Five Jays Ln 87508
Flagman Way 87505
Flora Dr 87505
Floral Dr 87507
Floras Del Sol St 87507
Florence Rd 87507
Florencio Trl 87506
Floresta Dr 87508
Flower Garland Rd 87508
Fonda Ct, Pl, Rd &
Way 87508
Foothills Rd & Trl 87505
Forest Cir 87505
N & S Fork Ext 87508
Forrest Ln 87508
Fort Union Dr 87505
Fortuna Rd 87508
Fox Rd 87507
Foxglove Ct 87508
Foxtail Cir 87506
Frances Ln 87506
Francisco Ln 87506
Franklin Ave
500-599 87501
600-799 87505
Frasco Ct, Pl, Rd, Ter &
Way 87508
E Frontage Rd 87508
W Frontage Rd 87507
Fuego Sagrado 87505
Fulton Ln 87505
Gabaldon Ln 87508
Galisteo Ct 87505
Galisteo Ln 87505
Galisteo Pkwy 87505
Galisteo Rd 87505
Galisteo St
108-114 87501
116-410 87501
412-526 87501
600-2099 87505
Gallegos Dr & Ln 87505
Galleria Grande St 87507
Gallina Rd 87508
Gallina Peak 87508
Gambel Oak 87505
Gan Eden Rd 87508
Garbosa Rd 87508
Garcia St
300-399 87501
500-999 87505
Garfield St 87501
Garkentr 87507
Gavilan Ct, Pl & Rd 87508
Gaviota Rd 87508
General Dempsey St 87501
General Sage Dr 87505
George Hayes Sr Pl 87506
Gildersleeve St 87505
Gilmore St 87505
Gils Way 87507
Glass Ln 87506
Glorieta Rd 87508
Glowing Star Rd 87506
Gold Trl 87508
E & W Gold Canyon
Rd 87508
Golden Eagle Rd 87508
E Golden Eagle Rd 87506
W Golden Eagle Rd 87506
Golden Feather Pl 87508
Golden Mesa 87507
Golden Ray Cir 87507
Golden Ridge Rd 87505
Goldpoppy Cir 87506
W Gomez Rd 87505
Gonzales Ct 87501
Gonzales Ln 87506
Gonzales Rd 87501
Goodnight Trl E & W 87506
Goodrich Rd 87507
Gormeley Ln 87501
Governor Dempsey Dr 87501
Governor Lindsey Rd 87505
Governor Mabry Ct 87505
Governor Mechem Rd 87505
Governor Miles Rd 87507
Grace Vigil Rd 87506
Graham Ave 87501
Gran Quivira 87501
Granada St 87505
Grandpas Ranch Rd 87507
Grant Ave 87501
Grasslands Trl 87508
Gray Fox Ln & Rd 87505
Grayhawk Pl 87508
Graythorn Dr 87506
Grazing Elk Dr 87506
Green Way 87507
Green Gorge 87505
Green Meadow Loop 87506
Gregg Ave 87501
Gregory Ln 87505
Greiser Ln 87506
Grey Wolf 87506
Griego Hl 87506
Griffin St 87501
Grillo Loco 87506
Gringo Aly 87506
N Guadalupe St
100-599 87501
534-534 87594
600-698 87501
S Guadalupe St 87501
Gualdo Rd 87508
Gunnison Rd 87507
Gurule Ln 87505
E & W Gutierrez 87506
Gwendolyn Ct 87506
Hacienda Ct 87506
Hacienda Loop 87508
Hacienda Caballero 87506
Hacienda Del Canon 87506
Hacienda Rincon 87506
Hacienda Vaquero 87506
Hadisway Ave 87501
Halona St 87505
Halpin Ct 87507
Hammond Cir & Rd 87507
Hampton Rd 87505
Hano Rd 87505
Hansen Ln 87507
Haozous Rd 87508
Happy Trl 87505
Harkins Ln 87501
Harkle Rd 87505
Haroldsville 87507
Harriets Rd 87506
Harrison Rd 87507
Hart Rd 87507
Hawthorne Cir 87506
Hay Gan Po 87506
Hazadel Cerrino 87506
Headquarters Trl 87506
Heartstone Dr 87506
Heiwa 87506
Henry Ln 87507
Henry Lynch Rd 87507
Hereford Ln 87506
Herencia De Prada 87505
Hernandez Ln 87507
Herrada Ct, Pl, Rd, Ter
& Way 87508
Herradura Rd 87505
Herrera Dr 87507
Herrera Rd 87506
Hickory St 87507
Hickox St 87505
Hidalgo Ct 87508
Hidden Vis 87506
Hidden Cricket 87507
Hidden Valley Rd 87505
High Country Rd 87508
High Noon Rd 87508
High Ridge Rd 87506
High View Ln 87508
Highland Way 87508
Highlands Ct & Loop 87507
N & S Hijo De Dios 87508
Hillcrest Dr 87501
Hillside Ave 87501
Hollyhock Cir & Ln 87506
E & W Hondo Ln, Trl &
Vis 87508
Hondo Ridge Rd 87508
Honeysuckle Cir 87506
Hopewell St 87505
Hopi Rd 87505
Horcado Ranch Rd 87506
N Horizon Ln 87507
Horse Peak 87508
Horse Thief Cyn 87501
Hospital Dr 87505
E & W Houghton St 87505
Hounds Ln 87507
Housing Dr 87507
Housta Ct 87508
Howling Wolf Ln 87507
Huddleson St 87501
Huerfana Ln 87506
Huey Rd 87507
Hummingbird Ct 87501

Hunters Pass 87508
Hyde Park Rd 87501
I 25 East Frontage Rd 87508
Ilea Way 87507
Immanuel 87508
Indian Cir 87507
Indian Pony 87506
Indian Ridge Rd 87501
Indian Rock Ln 87501
Indian Summer Ln 87507
Indigo Ct 87506
Industrial Rd
1-99 87506
2800-2899 87507
Inez Ct 87508
Irvine St 87501
Isabel St 87505
Isidro Rd 87508
Isleta Ave 87505
Ivjohaje Ranch Rd 87506
J R Dr 87506
Jacinto Ct & Rd 87508
Jack Rabbit Ln 87508
Jacona Cir 87507
Jacona Plz 87506
Jacona Rd 87506
Jaguar Dr & Loop 87507
James Ave 87507
Jaramillo Ln 87507
Jardin Ln 87507
Jay St 87505
Jefferson St 87501
Jemez Rd 87507
Jennifer Way 87508
Jennings Ct 87506
Jericho Ln 87505
Jicarrilla Ridge Rd 87505
Jimenez St 87501
Jimenez Romero Rd 87506
Jimson Weed Ct 87508
Jiron St 87505
Joaquin Ln 87505
Johnson Ln 87505
Johnson St 87501
Johnson Mesa 87508
Johnsons Ranch Rd 87505
Jon Kim Ln 87507
Jordan Logan Rd 87507
Jorgensen Ln 87507
Jornada Ct, Loop, Pl & Way 87508
Jose Ct 87508
Jose St 87501
Jose Alfredo Ln 87506
Josephine Rd 87508
Joshua Ln 87507
Joy Ln 87508
Joya Ct 87508
Juan Climaco Ct 87508
Juan De Dios 87501
Juan De Gabaldon Trl 87506
Juan Lujan Ln 87506
Juanita St 87501
Juego Ct, Pl & Rd 87508
Julia Ct 87508
Julians Ln 87506
Juniper 87508
Juniper Dr 87501
Juniper Ln 87501
Juniper Hill Ln 87507
Kachina Ct 87501
Kachina Loop 87507
Kachina Rd 87508
Kachina Ridge Dr 87507
Katarina Rd 87506
Katassee Way 87508
Kathryn Ave
500-599 87501
600-799 87505
Kathryn Pl 87501
Kearney Ave & Rd 87501
Kelincou Rd 87508
Kellogg Ln 87507
Kenny Ln 87506
Kia Rd 87506
Kimberli Ct 87508

Kiva Ct 87505
Kiva Rd 87505
N Kiva Rd 87506
S Kiva Rd 87506
Klarrisa Ct 87508
Ko Pin Po 87506
Kokopelli Dr 87506
Kokosori Ln 87507
Koshari 87506
Ksk Ln 87507
Kuu Ka Ave Po 87506
Kuu Pin Po 87506
Kwahe Ridge Rd 87506
Kwanpo Poe 87506
L Ln 87507
La Vis 87505
La Avenida De San Marcos 87507
La Bajada 87505
La Barberia Rd & Trl 87505
La Carrera 87507
La Cieneguita 87507
La Cruz Rd 87501
La Cuchara Rd 87506
La Cumbre Ln 87507
La Entrada 87501
La Espia Ct 87508
La Jara Ct 87508
La Jara Rd 87507
La Joya Rd 87501
La Joya St
300-398 87501
400-499 87501
500-599 87505
La Junta St 87507
La Junta Del Alamo 87507
La Loma Vis 87501
La Lomita 87507
La Lumbre Ct 87508
La Luna Rd 87507
La Luz Ln 87505
La Madera St 87501
La Mancha Ct 87501
La Marta Ct & Dr 87501
La Mesita Dr 87506
La Mesita Del Rey 87507
La Mesita Ranch Rd 87506
La Paloma St 87505
La Paz Ln 87507
La Paz Loop 87508
La Piedra Blanca 87508
La Pintera Pl 87508
La Placita Cir 87505
La Placita Dr 87506
La Posta Way 87505
La Pradera 87508
La Rambla 87505
La Salle Cir 87505
La Senda St 87505
La Serena Trl 87506
La Silla Dorada 87505
La Tierra Nueva 87506
La Traviata 87506
La Tusa St 87505
La Vela Rd 87507
La Venida Ln 87506
La Ventana 87508
La Vereda St 87501
La Vereda Este 87501
La Vereda Norte 87501
La Vida Ct 87506
La Vida Trl 87507
La Villa Escondida 87505
La Viveza Ct 87501
Ladera Ln, Pl & Rd 87508
Ladera Del Norte 87508
Laguna Ln 87508
Laguna St 87505
Lalo Ln 87505
Lamy Dr 87506
Larson Loop 87507
Las Caballeros 87508
Las Campanas Dr 87506
Las Casitas 87507
Las Colinas Dr 87501
Las Crucitas St 87501

Las Cuarto Milpas 87507
Las Estrellas 87507
Las Golondrinas Rd 87507
Las Joyas Ln 87506
Las Lomas Dr 87508
Las Mananitas St 87501
Las Nubes 87507
Las Nueves 87507
Las Soleras Dr 87507
Latir Ct 87508
Laughing Crow Ln 87507
Laughing Horse Ln 87508
Laughing Raven Rd 87508
Laughlin St 87505
Laurel Cir 87506
Laurens Ln 87507
Lauro Pl & Rd 87508
Lavadero Rd 87506
Lazo Corte 87505
Leaping Powder Rd 87508
Leaping Rabbit Ln 87507
Ledd Rd 87507
Legacy Ct 87507
Lejano Ct & Ln 87501
Lena St 87505
Letrado St 87505
Lewis Ln 87508
Lightning Loop 87506
Lightning Ridge Rd 87505
Likely Pl & Rd 87508
Lilac Cir 87506
Lincoln Ave 87501
Linda Vista Rd 87505
Lino Ln 87507
Little Arrow Rd 87505
Little Bird Rd 87506
Little Bluestem 87508
Little Island Rd 87505
Little Lous Ave 87506
Little Tesuque Crk 87506
Lizard Ln 87508
Llano St 87505
Llano Largo St 87501
Lluvia De Oro 87506
Lobo Ln 87508
Locust St 87507
Lodge Cir & Trl 87506
Lois Ln 87507
Lolita St 87501
Loma Arisco 87501
Loma Blanca 87506
Loma Boreal St 87501
Loma De La Vida 87506
Loma De Oro 87506
Loma Del Tanque 87507
Loma Encantada 87506
Loma Entrada 87501
Loma Manzanita 87506
Loma Oriente 87508
Loma Serena 87506
Loma Verde 87507
Loma Vieja Ln 87506
Lomas De Tesuque 87506
Lomita St 87505
Lone Butte Dr 87508
Lone Coyote Rdg 87508
Lone Pine Rdg & Spur 87505
Lone Raven Ln 87507
Long Shadow Ln 87507
Longhorn Ln 87506
Lookout Ln 87506
Lookout Mtn 87508
Lopez Ln 87507
Lopez St 87501
Lorca Ct & Dr 87505
Lorenzo Ln, Rd & St 87501
Los Altos Way 87501
Los Altos Norte 87501
Los Arboles Dr & Ln 87501
Los Cielos Ln 87507
Los Coyotes 87506
Los Gatos Ln 87507
Los Georges Rd 87505
Los Huertas 87506
Los Jimenez Rd 87506
Los Katrinas 87506

Los Lovatos Rd 87501
Los Milagros 87507
Los Nidos Dr 87501
Los Ojitos Rd 87506
Los Pinoneros Ct 87508
Los Pinos Ct 87505
Los Pinos Rd 87507
Los Prados 87506
Los Romeros 87507
Los Suenos Ct & Trl 87506
Los Tapias Ln 87508
Los Tres Vecinos 87507
Lost Feather Ln 87507
Louis Rd 87508
Louraine Cir & St 87507
Lovato Ln 87505
Lowlands Ln 87506
Luana St 87505
Lucerito Ct 87507
Lucero Rd 87508
Lucia Ln 87507
Luciander Rd 87507
Lucy Rd 87508
Lugar De Charco 87507
Lugar De Jose 87507
Lugar De Madison 87506
Lugar De Monte Vis 87505
Lugar De Oro 87501
Lugar De Pacifica 87506
Lugar De Padilla 87507
Luisa Ct, Ln, Pl & St 87505
Lujan St 87505
Lujan Country Ln 87506
Lujo Pl 87508
Lumbre Ct 87505
Lumbre Del Sol 87507
N Luna Cir 87501
S Luna Cir 87501
Luna Dr 87508
Luna Vis 87506
Luna De Miel 87507
Luna Grande Ln 87507
Luna Y Sol 87507
Lupine Ct 87506
E & W Lupita Rd 87505
Lustre Ct 87505
Luz De Amado 87506
Luz De Estrella 87507
Luz Del Dia 87506
Luz Del Monte 87506
Luz Del Mundo 87508
Luz Del Sol 87507
M J Tapia Dr 87508
Maclovia Cir, Ln & St 87505
Madison Rd 87507
Madre Mtn 87508
Madre De Dios 87505
Madrid Ln, Pl & Rd 87505
Madrona Cir 87506
Maez Ct & Rd 87505
Magdalena Rd 87501
Magee Ln 87501
Mago Rd 87508
Makena Ln 87506
Malaga Ln & Rd 87505
Mallard Way 87507
Mamies Mile 87506
Mandy Ln 87505
W Manhattan Ave 87501
Mann St 87505
Mansion Dr 87501
Mansion Ridge Rd 87501
Manuel Medrano Rd 87505
Manuelito Ln 87507
Manzana Ct 87507
Manzano Ct & Ln 87508
Maple St 87507
E & W Marcy St 87501
Mariano Rd 87508
Mariposa Rd 87508
Mariquita Ct 87508
Marissa Ln 87508
Market St 87501
Marquez Pl 87505
Marquez Ville Rd 87508
Martin Mora Rd 87507

Martinez Ln 87505
Martinez St 87501
Mateo Cir N 87505
Mayas Rd 87506
Maynard St 87501
Mckenzie St 87501
Meador Ln 87508
Meadow Ct 87505
S Meadows Rd 87507
Media Luna 87508
Medico Ln 87505
Medio St 87501
Medrano Ln 87505
Mejor Lado 87508
Melado Dr 87508
Melody Ln 87506
Menford Ln 87507
Mercantile Ct & Rd 87507
Mercedes Ct 87506
Mercer St 87505
Meredith Dr 87506
Mesa 87508
Mesa Bonito Rd 87507
Mesa Del Oro Ct, Ln & Loop 87507
Mesa Encantado 87506
Mesa Pino 87508
Mesa Top Farm Loop 87508
Mesa Verde St 87501
Mesa Vista St 87501
Mescalero Rdg & Trl 87505
Mesilla Rd 87501
Mesita Huerfana Rd 87506
Metate Way 87505
Metro Blvd & Ct 87508
Mi Ranchito 87506
Michelle Ct & Dr 87501
Middle Ct 87505
Midnight Owl 87507
Miguel Chavez Rd 87505
Milagro Rd 87507
Milagro Estrella 87507
Milagro Luna 87507
Milagro Oro 87507
Miles Ln 87507
Miller St 87505
Millers End 87508
Mimbres Ln 87507
Mimosa Ct & Rd 87508
Mineral Hl 87508
Miners Trl 87508
Mint Cir 87506
Miracerros Ln & Loop N & S 87505
Miramonte St 87501
Mirasol Ct 87507
Mission Bnd 87507
Mission Rd 87501
Mojave Pl 87508
Moki Ln 87507
Molino De Viento 87505
Molino Viejo 87506
Montana Ct 87508
Montana Vis 87507
Montana Verde Rd 87507
Montano St 87505
Monte Alto 87501
Monte Alto Cir 87508
Monte Alto Ct 87508
Monte Alto Ln 87508
Monte Alto Pl 87508
Monte Alto Rd 87508
Monte Alto Way 87508
Monte Azul Loop & Pl 87507
Monte Carlo 87507
Monte Enebro 87506
Monte Luz 87506
Monte Rosa St 87507
Monte Serena 87501
Monte Sereno Dr 87506
Monte Verde 87501
Monte Verde Pl 87507
Monte Vista Pl 87501
Montecito 87506
Monterey Dr 87505
Monterey Pl 87505

Monterey Rd 87508
Montez St 87501
Montezuma Ave 87501
Montoya Cir 87501
Montoya Pl 87505
Montoya St 87501
Moore St 87501
Mora Ln 87507
Morelia St 87505
Morning Dr, Ln & St 87507
Morning Breeze 87506
Morning Glory Cir 87506
Morris Pl 87505
Mosca Peak 87508
Mount Carmel Rd 87505
Mountain Rd 87505
Mountain Top Rd 87505
Moya Ln, Loop, Pl & Rd 87508
Mule Deer Rd 87508
Murales Rd 87501
Muscat Dr 87507
Muscle Car Ln 87507
Mustang Mesa 87506
Mutt Nelson Rd 87507
My Way 87507
Myranda Ct 87508
Mystic Ln 87506
Nacimiento Peak 87508
Nambe E 87508
Nambe W 87508
Nambe St 87505
Nancys Trl 87507
Narbona Pass 87508
Narrows Wash 87508
Navajo Dr 87505
Nazario St 87501
Nelson Loop 87507
Nevado Rdg 87501
New Mexican Plz 87507
New Moon Cir 87507
New Village Ave 87508
New West Ct 87506
Nicholas Pl 87507
Nicole Pl 87505
Nido Ln 87508
Nighthawk Cir 87506
Ninas Dr 87506
Nine Mile Rd 87508
Ninita St 87505
Nix Ln 87507
Nizhoni Dr 87507
No Trespassing Rd 87507
Noble Vis 87506
North Ct 87505
Notorious Way 87507
Nova Rd 87507
Np 100 87506
Np 101 W 87506
Np 102 E & W 87506
Np 117 87506
Np 118 87506
Nublado 87505
Nuestro Callejon 87506
Nueva Ct 87501
Nuevo Milenio 87507
Nursery Rd 87506
Nusbaum St 87501
O Toh Nah Po 87506
Oak 87508
Oak Ave 87501
Oasis St 87508
Ocaso 87508
Ocate Rd 87507
Ocotillo Pl 87508
Odo Po 87506
Office Court Dr 87507
Ogo Wii 87506
Ojo Ct 87505
Ojo Azul 87501
Ojo De La Vaca Rd & Trl 87508
Ojo Verde 87501
Ojos De Jo 87507
Old Agua Fria Rd E & W 87508

Old Airport Rd 87507
Old Arroyo Chamiso 87505
Old Bridge Ct 87505
Old Callejon Rd 87506
Old Canoncito Rd 87508
Old Coach Rd 87506
Old Cochiti Rd 87507
Old Dinosaur Trl 87508
Old Dog Run 87508
Old Forest Trl 87505
Old Galisteo Rd, Trl & Way 87508
Old Las Vegas Hwy 87505
Old Pecos Ct 87508
Old Pecos Ln 87508
Old Pecos Trl
4020A-4020B 87508
902-2003 87505
2005-3199 87505
4000-4021 87508
4023-4025 87508
Old Pueblito Rd 87506
Old San Marcos Trl 87508
Old Santa Fe Trl
53-101 87501
103-119 87501
121-495 87501
140-140 87505
200-492 87501
501-515 87505
517-7923 87505
Old Santa Fe Way 87505
Old Sunset Trl 87501
Old Taos Hwy 87501
Olive Ln 87506
Olive St 87507
Oliver Dr 87507
Onate Pl 87501
Onate St 87505
Opera Dr 87506
Orchard Dr 87501
Oriente Ct 87508
Oro Pl 87508
Ortiz Ln 87508
Ortiz Rd 87505
Ortiz St 87501
Osage Ave, Cir, Dr & Ln 87505
Oshara Blvd 87508
Osito Pl 87505
Oso Ct 87506
Otero St 87501
Otowi Rd 87505
Otto Rd 87508
Overlook Rd 87505
Owl Pl 87506
Owl Creek Rd 87505
Pablina St 87505
Pablo Dr 87508
Pacheco Ct 87505
Pacheco St 87505
S Pacheco St
2000-2006 87505
2008-2056 87505
2058-2198 87505
2071-2071 87502
2071-2099 87505
Pacheco Canyon Rd 87506
Pacheco Meadows Ln 87506
Padre Kino 87501
Paintbrush Cir & Ct 87506
Painted Horse 87506
Painted Pony Cir 87507
Painted Sky 87507
Pajarito Loop 87506
Pajarito De Azul 87506
Pajarito Peak 87508
Pajaro Blanco Rd 87508
E & W Palace Ave 87501
Palacio Ln 87505
Palacio Rd 87508
Palentine Rd 87506
Palo Duro Rd 87506
Palomino Ct & St 87505
Palomita Dr 87506
Pam Y Eutilia 87507

Pan De Vida 87508
Panda Ln 87507
Panorama Ln 87501
Panther Peak 87508
Park Ave 87501
Park Ct 87508
Park Ln 87508
Parkside Dr 87506
Parkway Dr 87507
Parque De Villa 87507
Parsley Cir 87506
Pasada Del Ben 87507
Pasada San Juan 87507
Pasaje Del Herrero 87505
Pasco Las Terraza 87506
Paseo Vis 87508
Paseo Aragon 87506
Paseo Barranca 87501
Paseo C De Baca 87507
Paseo Corto 87501
Paseo Coyote 87506
Paseo Cresta 87501
Paseo De Vis 87501
Paseo De Aguila 87506
Paseo De Andres 87501
Paseo De Angel N & S 87507
Paseo De Antonio 87506
Paseo De Canto 87505
Paseo De Don Carlos 87501
Paseo De Enrique 87505
Paseo De Estrellas 87506
Paseo De Florencio 87501
Paseo De Gallegos 87506
Paseo De La Acequia 87507
Paseo De La Conquistadora 87501
Paseo De La Cuma 87501
Paseo De La Joya 87506
Paseo De La Loma 87501
Paseo De La Luz 87505
Paseo De La Reina 87507
Paseo De La Serna 87505
Paseo De La Tierra 87506
Paseo De Los Chamisos 87505
Paseo De Los Pueblos 87507
Paseo De Martinez 87507
Paseo De Pajarito 87506
Paseo De Peralta 87501
Paseo De Rincon 87508
Paseo De River St 87507
Paseo De San Antonio 87507
Paseo De Tercero 87507
Paseo De Tularosa 87505
Paseo De Ulibarri 87507
Paseo De Valentine 87507
Paseo De Zamora 87508
Paseo Del Antilope 87506
Paseo Del Arroyo 87501
Paseo Del Caballo E & W 87508
Paseo Del Canon 87507
Paseo Del Conejo 87506
Paseo Del Coyote 87506
Paseo Del Fondo 87506
Paseo Del Halcon 87506
Paseo Del Monte 87501
Paseo Del Oso 87506
Paseo Del Paisano 87506
Paseo Del Pajaro 87506
Paseo Del Paloma 87506
Paseo Del Pinon 87508
Paseo Del Rancho 87506
Paseo Del Rey 87507
Paseo Del Sol W 87507
Paseo Del Sur 87501
Paseo Del Valle 87508
Paseo Del Venado 87506
Paseo Dolores 87506
Paseo Encantado NE & SW 87506
Paseo Feliz 87507
Paseo Galisteo 87508
Paseo Iglesia 87501
Paseo La Vida 87506
Paseo Las Terrazas 87506
Paseo Los Pereas 87507
Paseo Luna Blanca 87508
Paseo Margarita 87507
Paseo Mel Senaida 87507
Paseo Nopal 87507
Paseo Norteno 87507
Paseo Patrocino 87506
Paseo Patron 87506
Paseo Ponderosa 87501
Paseo Primero 87501
Paseo Real 87507
N Paseo San Pasqual 87507
Paseo Segunda 87501
Paseo Sol Y Sombra 87506
Pasillo Chico 87508
Patrocino Romero Rd 87506
Paulin St 87505
Pawprint Trl 87506
Paycheck Ln 87508
Payupki Cir 87507
Peacock Aly 87507
Peak Pl 87506
Pedregal Pl 87501
Pelona Ct 87508
Pen Rd 87505
Pena Pl 87501
Penasco Cir 87506
Penitentiary Rd 87508
Penny Ct & Ln 87507
Penstemon Ct 87508
Peregrine 87506
Perez Ln 87506
Perilla Ct 87505
Periwinkle Pl 87508
Petroglyph Cir 87506
Picacho Peak Dr 87506
Picaflor Path 87506
Piedra Alto 87501
Piedra Rondo 87501
Piedras Negras 87505
Piedras Rojas 87501
Pin Cushion Pl 87508
Pine 87508
Pine E 87508
Pine W 87508
E Pine Ext 87508
Pine St 87501
Pine Ridge Pl 87507
Pino Pl 87508
Pino Rd 87505
N Pinon 87508
N Pinon N 87508
S Pinon S 87508
Pinon Dr 87501
Pinon St 87505
Pinon Way 87508
Pinon Bluffs Dr 87506
Pinon Doblado 87508
Pinon Farm 87508
Pinon Jay Trl 87505
Pinon Ridge Ln 87506
Pinon Vista St 87501
Pinos Verdes St 87501
Pintado Cir 87507
Piute Rd 87505
Placita Anita 87506
Placita Chaco 87505
Placita Chueco 87508
Placita Dalinda 87508
Placita De Luna 87506
Placita De Oro 87501
Placita De Quedo 87505
Placita De Vida 87505
Placita Del Este 87501
Placita Don Andres 87501
Placita Halcon 87505
Placita La Condesa 87507
Placita La Marquesina 87507
Placita Loma 87501
Placita Lorenzo 87505
Placita Lucinda 87508
Placita Rafaela 87505
Placita Real Loop 87507
Placita Santa Fe 87505
Placita Verdad 87507
Plano Arbolito 87506
Plant Farm Rd 87506
N & S Plata Cir 87501
Platinum 87508
N Platte Rd 87507
Plaza Amarilla 87507
Plaza Azul 87507
Plaza Balentine 87501
Plaza Blanca 87507
Plaza Bosque 87505
Plaza Canada 87501
Plaza Central 87507
Plaza Chamisal 87505
Plaza Del Centro 87506
Plaza Del Corazon 87506
Plaza Del Sur Dr 87505
Plaza Fatima 87501
Plaza La Prensa 87507
Plaza Lomas 87505
Plaza Lopez 87506
Plaza Molleno 87506
Plaza Montana 87505
Plaza Montoya 87507
Plaza Nueva 87507
Plaza Ortega 87506
Plaza Rojo 87507
Plaza Sonata 87507
Plaza Thomas 87505
Plaza Velasquez 87506
Plaza Verde 87507
Plazuela Vis 87505
Plazuela Intimo 87506
Plazuela Serena 87505
Plestont 87501
Poco Ln 87507
Poe Pin Po 87506
Poh See Buh Rd 87506
Pohuuupoe Rd 87506
N Point Dr 87501
Pojoaque Rd 87506
Pojoaque Po Box 87501
Pojoaque Ridge Rd 87506
Polaco St 87501
Polaris Rd 87506
Pollito Rd 87508
Polmood Farm Rd 87506
S Polo Dr 87507
Ponces Rd 87506
Ponderosa 87508
Ponderosa Ln 87505
Ponderosa Ridge Rd 87505
Poplar St 87507
Poppy Pl 87508
Portavela St 87505
Porvenir Ln 87505
Potencia St 87505
Povi Kaa Dr 87506
Povi Pin Poe 87506
Practilliano Dr 87505
Pradera Ct 87505
Prairie Crest Dr 87508
Prairie Dog Loop 87507
Prairie Vista Pl 87508
Price Ranch Rd 87505
Primavera Ct 87505
Primo Colores 87507
Primrose Cir 87506
Prince Ave 87501
E Prince Rd 87507
W Prince Rd 87507
Principe De Paz 87508
Proctor Ct 87505
Promenade Blvd 87507
Puccini Plz 87506
Pueblo Dr 87505
Pueblo Rd 87508
Pueblo Alto 87507
Pueblo Bonito 87507
Pueblo De Cielo 87506
Pueblo Garcia Rd 87508
Pueblo Grande 87507
Pueblo Halona 87507
Pueblo Hawikuh 87507
Pueblo Jacona 87507
Pueblo Pintado 87507
Pueblo Puye 87507
Pueblo Quemado 87507
Pueblo San Lazaro 87507
Pueblo Sapawe 87507
Pueblo Tsankawi 87507
Puerto Ct, Rd & Way 87508
Puerto Bonito 87505
Puerto De Luna 87507
Puesta Del Sol 87508
Pulitzer Trl 87506
Puma Cir 87506
Punabay Po 87506
Punta De Vis 87507
Punta De Cazador 87506
Punta Sonrisa 87507
Purple Aster 87507
Purple Crow Pl 87508
Puu Poe 87506
Puwanini 87506
Puye Rd 87505
Quail Run Dr 87508
Quail View Ln 87507
Quapaw Pl & St 87505
Quartz Trl 87505
Quedo Rd 87508
Quemado St 87505
Quintana St 87501
Rabbit Mtn, Rd & Run E & W 87508
Rabbitbrush 87506
Rael Ln 87507
Rael Rd 87505
Rafael St 87505
Railfan Way 87505
Rain Dance Ct 87506
Rainbow Cir 87506
Rainbow Ridge Ln 87505
Raindance Ln 87507
Ramada Ct & Way 87508
Ramon Ln 87507
Ramon Gomez Ln 87506
Ramon Rivera Dr 87506
Ranch Estates Rd 87506
Ranch House Rd 87506
Ranchito De Marina 87506
Ranchitos De Baca 87507
Rancho Alegre Rd 87508
Rancho Ancon Ln 87506
Rancho Cholla Ln 87508
Rancho De Chavez 87507
Rancho De Leandro 87506
Rancho De Ortiz 87506
Rancho De Siesta 87508
Rancho Del Alamo 87506
Rancho El Barranco 87506
Rancho Enrique 87506
Rancho Escondido 87506
Rancho Las Acequias 87506
Rancho Las Lagunas 87506
Rancho Los Vigils 87505
Rancho Manana 87506
Rancho Santo Valle 87506
Rancho Siringo Ct, Dr & Rd 87505
Rancho Verano Rd 87508
Rancho Viejo Blvd 87508
Ranchos Canoncito 87508
Ranchos Sin Vacas Rd 87507
Rattlesnake Rd 87508
Raudo Pl & Rd 87508
Raven Ravine 87507
Ravens Ridge Rd & Trl 87505
Ravenswood Ln 87507
Ravine Rd 87507
Rawhide Ct 87506
Rayon Dr 87507
Rays Cor 87507
Read St 87501
Reata Rd 87507
Rebecca Ln 87505
Recado Rd 87508
Red Bluff Draw 87508
Red Hills Ln 87505
Red Raven Rd 87508
Red Sky Trl 87505
Red Thorn Pl 87508
Redondo Ct 87508
Redondo Peak 87508
Redwood St 87507
Reeds Peak 87508
Rees Ct 87507
Relampago 87508
Rendon Rd 87501
Reno Pl & Rd 87508
Rey De Reyes 87508
Ricardo Rd 87501
Ricardos Ct 87506
Richards Ave 87507
S Richards Ave
2001-2897 87507
2899-3224 87507
3226-3370 87507
5400-5498 87508
6401-6599 87508
Richards Ln 87507
Rico Ct 87508
W Ridge Dr & Rd 87505
Ridge Canyon Rd 87506
Ridgecrest Dr 87505
Ridgeline Rd 87507
Ridgepoint Ln & Loop 87506
N & S Ridgetop Cir & Rd 87506
Ridgeview Cir 87505
Rim Rd 87501
Rim Rock 87501
Rincon Ct 87505
Rincon De Aragon 87507
Rincon De Marquez 87508
Rincon De Torreon 87501
Rinconada Cir 87507
Rio Way 87506
Rio Del Luna 87507
Rio Del Sol 87507
Rio En Medio Rd 87506
Rio Grande Ave & Pl 87501
Rio Seco 87501
Rio Vista Pl & St 87501
Rising Moon 87506
Rito Guicu 87507
River Song Ln 87507
River Valley Rd 87506
Rivera Cir & Ln 87507
Rivers Edge Ln 87507
Riverside Dr & Loop 87507
Roadrunner Ct & Ln 87507
Rock Castle Ln 87507
Rock Pile Rd 87508
Rocking Horse Rd 87506
Rocky Slope Dr 87508
Rodeo Ln 87507
Rodeo Rd
281-421 87505
296-298 87507
402-1516 87505
995-997 87507
1851-1853 87505
2801-3509 87507
3511-4204 87507
4206-4470 87507
Rodeo Park Dr E & W 87505
Rodriguez St 87501
Rogelios Ln 87506
Rojo Caliente 87505
Romero St 87501
Romeroville Rd 87506
Rons Rd 87508
Rosa De Castia Ln 87505
Rosalinda 87507
Rosanna 87506
Rosario Blvd & Hl 87501
Rosendo Y Senida Dr 87506
Rosewood St 87507
Rosina St 87505
Rosita St 87505
Roy Crawford Ln 87505
Roybal St 87501
Roys Way 87507
Rudolfo Rd 87507
Rudy Rodriquez Dr 87508
Rufina Cir, Ct, Ln & St 87507
Rumble Rd 87508
Rumbo Al Sur 87507
Running Horse Trl 87508
Russell Rd 87508
Rusty Spur Pl 87508
Ruta Corta St 87507
Ruta Sin Nombre 87507
Saa Paa Po 87506
Sabina Ln 87508
Sabroso Ct, Pl & Rd 87508
Saddle Ct & Rd 87508
Saddle Blanket Rd 87508
Saddle Horn Pl 87508
E & W Saddleback Mesa 87508
Sage Cir 87506
Sagebrush Rd 87507
Saint Francis Dr 87505
N Saint Francis Dr 87501
S Saint Francis Dr
100-599 87501
700-1599 87505
1601-3099 87505
1098 1/4-1098 1/2 87505
Saint James Crst 87507
Saint Michaels Dr 87505
Salako Way 87506
Salas Ln 87505
Salazar Pl 87501
Salazar St
500-599 87501
600-699 87505
Salt Creek Wash 87508
Saltbush Rd 87508
Saltillo Ct 87506
Salva Tierra 87506
Salvador Pl 87501
Sam St 87501
Sambra Dr 87507
San Angelo St 87507
San Antonio St 87505
San Antonio Peak 87508
San Benito St 87507
San Carlos Ln 87505
San Felipe Ave 87505
San Felipe Cir 87505
San Felipe Rd 87505
E & W San Francisco St 87501
San Gabriel St 87507
San I Senior Rd 87506
San Ignacio 87507
San Ildefonso Rd 87505
San Isabel Rd 87505
San Jose Ave 87505
San Juan Dr 87505
San Juan Ranch Rd 87506
San Lorenzo Dr 87505
San Luis St 87507
San Marcos Loop, Rd & Trl E & W 87508
San Mateo Ct 87508
San Mateo Ln 87505
E San Mateo Rd 87505
W San Mateo Rd 87505
San Mateo Way N 87508
San Mateo Way S 87508
San Pasqual St 87505
San Patricio Ct & Plz 87505
San Pedro Way 87508
San Rafael Dr 87506
San Salvador Ln 87501
San Sebastian Rd 87505
San Ysidro Ct, Ln, Pl & Xing 87507
Sanchez St 87505
Sand Dunes 87508
E & W Sand Sage 87506
Sandia 87508
Sandia Cir 87507
Sandia Ln 87508
Sandia St 87501
Sandia Vista Ct & Rd 87507
Sandoval St 87501
Sands Ln 87507
Sandy Ln 87505
Sandy Way 87506
Sandy Creek Rd 87507
Sangre De Cristo Dr 87506
Sangre De Cristo St 87501
Santa Barbara Dr 87505
Santa Clara Dr 87507
Santa Cruz Dr 87505
Santa Elena St 87507
E & W Santa Fe Ave 87505
Santa Fe River Rd 87501
Santa Fe Studios Rd 87508
Santa Lucia 87507
Santa Rosa Dr 87505
Santander Ln 87505
Santeros Rd 87507
Santiago Loop 87507
Santo Domingo Cir 87506
Santo Domingo St 87507
Santo Nino Pl 87501
Santos Ln 87506
Saratoga Ct & Ln 87507
Sarma Ln 87506
Sawmill Rd 87505
Scarlett Ln 87507
Scenic Mesa Rd 87508
Scotts Pl 87507
Sculpture 87508
Sena St 87505
Senda Ln 87507
Senda Corva Ct & Rd 87507
Senda De Andres 87501
Senda De Daniel 87501
Senda De Elueterio 87501
Senda De Fuego 87506
Senda Del Espectro 87506
Senda Del Puerto 87505
Senda Del Valle 87507
Senda Jarosa 87505
Senda Mescal 87508
Senda Sauza 87508
Senda Sonrisa 87506
Senda Torcida 87508
Sendero Alegre 87506
Sendero De Corazon 87505
Sendero De La Vida 87506
Sendero Del Oro 87506
Sendero Del Oso 87506
Sentiero Ceutro 87506
Sentiero Della Villa 87506
E & W Serena Ln & Rd 87508
Serenity Ln 87507
Sereno Dr 87501
Sereno Loop 87507
Serna Ln 87506
Seton Plz 87508
Seton Castle Trl 87508
Seton Village Rd 87508
Seville Rd 87505
Shaggy Peak Trl 87505
Shalako Way 87507
Shalako Xing 87508
Shalom 87506
Shaman 87506
Shannon Ct 87508
Shasta Ln 87506
Shawnodese 87508
Shelby St 87501
Shenandoah Trl 87508
Sheridan Ave 87501
Shilo Rd 87508
N Shining Sun 87506
Shiprock Peak 87508
Shoofly St 87505
Short Rd 87506
Shorthorn Ln 87506
Shrub Rd 87507
Shumaa Po 87506
Sibley Rd 87508
Sicomoro St 87501
Sierra Ct 87506
Sierra Pl N 87508
Sierra Pl S 87508
Sierra Azul 87507

Sierra Blanca ... 87507
Sierra Dawn Rd ... 87508
Sierra Del Este ... 87501
Sierra Del Norte ... 87501
Sierra Del Sol ... 87508
Sierra Grande Rd ... 87508
Sierra Lavanda ... 87507
Sierra Lejana ... 87508
Sierra Nevada ... 87507
Sierra Pinon ... 87501
Sierra Rosa ... 87507
Sierra Rosa Loop ... 87506
Sierra Verde ... 87507
Siesta Ln ... 87507
Silent Rdg ... 87508
Silent Wing ... 87507
Siler Ln & Rd ... 87507
Siler Park Ln ... 87507
Silva St ... 87505
Silver Mdw ... 87506
Silver Trl ... 87508
Silver Buckle Rd ... 87508
Silver Hills Rd ... 87508
Silver Mesa Cir & Ct ... 87506
Silver Rock Rd ... 87508
Silver Water Rd ... 87506
Sin Pena Park ... 87507
Singer Rd ... 87506
Sipapu Ln ... 87507
Siri Dharma Ct ... 87501
Siringo Ct ... 87507
Siringo Ln ... 87505
Siringo Rd
94-98 ... 87505
100-2700 ... 87505
2702-2798 ... 87505
2800-3399 ... 87507
Siringo Rondo E & S ... 87507
Skeeter Ln ... 87507
Sky Island Rd ... 87505
Sky Ridge Dr ... 87508
Sky Show ... 87506
Skytop Rd ... 87508
Sleeping Bear Ln ... 87507
Sleeping Dog Rd ... 87508
Sloman Ct, Ln & Trl ... 87507
Smokey Hill Dr ... 87506
Snow Bird ... 87507
Snow Blossom Rd ... 87507
Soaring Eagle Ct ... 87506
Soaring Eagle Ln ... 87507
Soaring Hawk Trl ... 87508
Sobradora Dr ... 87508
Sobre Los Cerros ... 87506
Socorro Ct ... 87508
Softwynd Dr ... 87508
Sol Y Lomas Dr ... 87505
Sol Y Luz Loop & St ... 87505
Sol Y Nubes ... 87505
Solana Dr ... 87501
Solano Ct ... 87508
Soleado Ln ... 87508
Solecito Cir, Loop & Way ... 87507
Solona St ... 87501
Sombra Ct
1-99 ... 87508
1900-1999 ... 87505
Sombra De Jose ... 87506
Sombrio Dr ... 87501
Sonrisa Ct & Trl ... 87506
Sonrisa Del Cielo ... 87506
Sosaya Ln & St ... 87505
South Ct ... 87505
Southard Rd ... 87508
Southern Exposure ... 87508
Spanish Hl ... 87501
N Sparrow Ln ... 87506
Sparrow Way ... 87508
Spearpoint Knl ... 87506
Spencers Knl ... 87501
Spirit Ct ... 87506
Spirit Mtn ... 87505
Spirit Vly ... 87508
Spirit Run Pl ... 87508
Spruce ... 87508
Spruce St ... 87501
N & S Spur Rd ... 87505
Spur Cross Pl ... 87508
Staab St ... 87501
Stacy Rd ... 87505
Stag Pt ... 87505
Stagecoach Cir, Dr & Rd ... 87501
Star Ct ... 87507
Star Dancer Trl ... 87506
N & S Star Gazer ... 87506
Star Splash ... 87506
Star Vista Rd ... 87505
Starfire Ln ... 87505
Starlight Cir ... 87506
Starview ... 87507
State Highway 14 ... 87508
State Road 502 ... 87506
State Road 503 ... 87506
State Road 592 ... 87506
State Road 599 Frontage Rd ... 87507
State Route 502 ... 87501
Stereophile Way ... 87505
Stone Cabin Rd ... 87505
Stone Ridge Rd ... 87505
Stonegate Cir ... 87506
Storm View Ln ... 87506
Storyteller ... 87506
Strawberry Cir ... 87506
Sudeste Pl ... 87508
Sueno De Santa Fe ... 87505
Suenos De Ts Anaya ... 87507
Summer Rd ... 87506
Summer Night ... 87506
Summer Storm Cir ... 87506
N & S Summit Dr & Rdg ... 87501
Sun Mountain Dr ... 87505
E & W Sunbird Ln ... 87506
Sundance Cir ... 87506
Sundance Ct ... 87506
Sundance Dr ... 87506
Sundance St ... 87507
Sundance Ridge Cir ... 87506
Sundial Way ... 87507
Sundog Dr ... 87508
Sunflower Cir & Dr ... 87506
Sunlight Vw ... 87506
Sunlit Dr E & W ... 87508
Sunnyslope St ... 87501
E Sunrise Dr ... 87506
Sunrise Pl ... 87507
Sunrise Rd ... 87507
Sunrise Vis ... 87506
Sunset Cir ... 87507
Sunset Rd ... 87507
Sunset Rdg ... 87507
Sunset Spgs ... 87507
Sunset St ... 87501
Sunset Trl E ... 87508
Sunset Trl W ... 87508
Sunset Vw ... 87506
Sunset Canyon Ln ... 87508
Sunset Hills Rd ... 87508
Sunshine Way ... 87507
Swartz Ln ... 87508
Sweet Swan Ln ... 87508
Sycamore Loop ... 87507
Synergia Rd ... 87508
T Anna Ln ... 87507
Tamarisk Trl ... 87506
Tango Rd ... 87506
Tano Rd & Trl ... 87506
Tano Alto ... 87506
Tano Compound Dr ... 87506
Tano Del Este ... 87506
Tano Escondido ... 87506
Tano Norte ... 87506
Tano Point Ln ... 87506
Tano Ridge Rd ... 87506
Tano Vida ... 87506
Tanoito ... 87506
Taos St ... 87505
Tapia Est ... 87508
Tapia Entrada ... 87508
Tarro Rd ... 87508
Tasa Pl ... 87508
Taylor Loop, Mtn & Rd ... 87508
Tecolote Cir ... 87506
Teddy Bear Trl ... 87505
Temblon St ... 87501
Tequila Sunset ... 87506
Terary Ct ... 87506
Terelist ... 87505
Terra De Coral St ... 87507
Terrazas Ln ... 87507
Teseque Overlook ... 87506
Tesuque Dr ... 87505
Tesuque Ln ... 87506
Tesuque Rdg ... 87501
Tesuque Vis ... 87506
Tesuque Creek Rd ... 87501
Tesuque Hill Rd ... 87506
Tesuque Village Rd ... 87506
Tetilla Rd ... 87508
Tewa Rd ... 87505
Tewa Butterfly Rd ... 87506
Than Povi Po ... 87506
The High Rd ... 87507
The Red Rd ... 87505
Theresa Ln ... 87507
Thistle Ln ... 87506
Thomas Ave ... 87505
Thomas Rd ... 87507
Thorpe Way ... 87506
Three Rock Rd ... 87506
Thunder Ridge Rd ... 87501
Thunderbird Ct ... 87501
Thundercloud Rd ... 87506
Thunderhead Dr ... 87505
Thyme Ct ... 87506
Tierra Dr ... 87505
Tierra Adentro ... 87508
Tierra De Tano ... 87506
Tierra Grande ... 87506
Tierra Hermosa Ct ... 87507
Tierra Rica Dr ... 87505
Tierra Verde ... 87506
Tijeras Rd ... 87505
Tijeras Creek Ln Dr ... 87508
Timberwick Rd ... 87508
Tobasco Ln ... 87507
Todos Santos St ... 87507
Toltec Rd ... 87505
Tom Romero Ct ... 87506
Tony St ... 87501
Topeka St ... 87505
Torch Flower Ct ... 87508
Torneo Ct & Rd ... 87508
Toro Ln ... 87508
Torreon Ct & Pl ... 87508
Tortola Trl ... 87507
Totavi Loop ... 87506
Towa Golf Rd ... 87506
Towa Golf Course Ln ... 87506
Tp 804 ... 87506
Trades West Rd ... 87507
Trail Cross Ct ... 87505
Trails End Ct ... 87508
Tranquil Trl & Way ... 87508
Traviesa De Camilo E & W ... 87508
Tree House Rd ... 87505
Tren Via ... 87508
Tres Cientos ... 87508
Tres Hermanas Rd ... 87508
Tres Montanas ... 87508
Tribal Works Rd ... 87506
Trinidad Ln ... 87506
Trinity Rd ... 87508
Triple Spur ... 87508
Trujillo Ln & Loop ... 87506
Tse Aa Po ... 87506
Tse Wang Loop ... 87506
Tunyo Loop ... 87506
Tunyo Po ... 87506
Turquoise Ct ... 87508
Turquoise Trail Ct ... 87508
Turtle Cir ... 87506
Tusa Dr ... 87508
Twin Rd ... 87506
Twin Yuccas Ln ... 87507
Two Bears Rd ... 87505
Two Horse Trl ... 87508
Two Trails Rd ... 87505
Unity Way ... 87506
Upper Pond Rd ... 87505
Urioste St ... 87501
Urraca Ln ... 87506
Us 285 ... 87508
Us 84/285 ... 87506
Ute Cir & Ln ... 87505
Vail Rd ... 87508
Val Verde Dr ... 87508
Valencia Ct ... 87508
Valencia Loop ... 87508
Valencia Rd ... 87505
Valentine Loop & Way ... 87507
Valerie Cir ... 87507
Valle Bonita ... 87507
Valle Chamiso Ln ... 87505
Valle De Suerte ... 87506
Valle Del Sol Dr ... 87501
Valle Duran ... 87506
Valle Pinon ... 87506
Valle Rio St ... 87505
Valle Romero ... 87506
Valle Sereno ... 87506
Valle Tapia ... 87506
Valle Vista Blvd ... 87508
Valle Vista Ct ... 87508
Valle Vista St ... 87505
Vallecita Dr ... 87501
Vallecito Rd ... 87506
Valley Dr ... 87501
Valmora Rd ... 87505
Vaquero Rd & Trl ... 87508
Vargas Ct ... 87508
Vegas De Suenos ... 87507
Vegas Verdes ... 87507
Vela St ... 87505
Velarde Rd ... 87507
Velarde St ... 87505
Velocity Way ... 87508
Venado Ln ... 87505
Ventoso ... 87505
Vera Dr ... 87501
Verano Ct, Dr, Ln, Loop, Pl & Way ... 87508
Vereda Alta ... 87507
Vereda Baja ... 87507
Vereda Corta ... 87507
Vereda De Encanto ... 87505
Vereda De Pueblo ... 87507
Vereda De San Antonio ... 87507
Vereda De Valencia ... 87507
Vereda Josefita ... 87507
Vereda Mesita ... 87508
Vereda Oriente ... 87507
Vereda Poniente ... 87507
Vereda Rodiando ... 87505
Vereda Romero ... 87506
Vereda Serena Rd ... 87508
Via Cyn ... 87506
Via Altera ... 87507
Via Antigua ... 87505
Via Arista ... 87506
Via Bella ... 87507
Via Berrenda ... 87505
Via Bosque ... 87506
Via Brisa ... 87507
Via Caballero Del Norte ... 87505
Via Caballero Del Sur ... 87505
Via Chiquita ... 87505
Via Colibri ... 87501
Via De Estrellas ... 87506
Via De Las Yeguas ... 87506
Via De Los Romero ... 87507
Via De Zorritos ... 87506
Via Del Sol ... 87508
Via Del Vaquero ... 87508
Via Diamante ... 87506
Via Don Toribio ... 87507
Via Estancia ... 87506
Via Feliz Loop ... 87506
Via Janna ... 87507
Via Magdalene ... 87507
Via Manzana ... 87507
Via Maria Albina ... 87507
Via Nova ... 87507
Via Optima ... 87507
Via Orilla Dorado ... 87508
Via Pampa ... 87506
E & W Via Plaza Nueva ... 87507
Via Prima ... 87507
Via Punto Nuevo ... 87508
Via Quarta ... 87507
Via Quinta ... 87507
Via Robles ... 87501
Via Sagrada ... 87508
Via Seconda ... 87507
Via Summa ... 87507
Via Tertia ... 87507
Via Tessera ... 87507
Via Vecino ... 87506
Via Venado ... 87505
Via Verde Ct ... 87507
Viaje Pavo Real ... 87505
Viale Ct ... 87505
Viale Cetona ... 87505
Viale Seravezza ... 87505
Viale Tresana Ct ... 87505
Viarrial ... 87506
Victoria St ... 87505
Victorio Peak ... 87508
Viejo Rastro ... 87505
Viento Cir & Dr ... 87501
Viento Segundo Dr ... 87501
View Hvn ... 87508
W View Ter ... 87507
Vigil Ln ... 87505
Villa Alegre St ... 87501
Villa Strada ... 87506
Village Ln ... 87505
Village Loop ... 87507
Village Way ... 87507
Villas Loop ... 87506
Villeros St ... 87501
Violet Cir ... 87506
Violeta Virtuoso St ... 87507
Virginia Ln ... 87508
Vista Alondra ... 87508
Vista Barrancas ... 87506
Vista Bonita ... 87505
Vista Calabasas ... 87506
Vista Canada Ln ... 87501
Vista Catedral ... 87501
Vista Chicoma Rd ... 87506
Vista Chupadero ... 87506
Vista Colorado ... 87506
Vista Coyote ... 87506
Vista De Cristo ... 87507
Vista De Esperanza ... 87506
Vista De Jemez ... 87505
Vista De La Ciudad ... 87501
Vista De La Vida ... 87506
Vista De Luna ... 87508
Vista Del Cerro ... 87508
Vista Del Cielo ... 87506
Vista Del Fuego ... 87506
Vista Del Monte ... 87508
Vista Del Mundo ... 87506
Vista Del Norte ... 87507
Vista Del Prado Ct ... 87507
Vista Del Rey ... 87506
Vista Del Sol ... 87507
Vista Del Sur ... 87505
Vista Grande Cir, Ct & Dr ... 87508
Vista Hermosa ... 87506
Vista Hermosa St ... 87501
Vista Herrera ... 87506
Vista Jemez Ct ... 87505
Vista Joya ... 87505
Vista Lagunitas ... 87507
Vista Linda Grande ... 87506
Vista Morada ... 87506
Vista Point Rd ... 87508
Vista Preciosa ... 87507
Vista Redonda ... 87506
Vista Sandia ... 87506
Vista Serena ... 87506
Vista Tesuque ... 87506
Vista Valle Grande ... 87506
Vista Vallecito ... 87508
Vista Verde Ct ... 87501
Vistoso Pl ... 87501
Vitalia St ... 87505
Vitrina Ct ... 87501
Vivigen Way ... 87505
Vuelta Pl ... 87501
Vuelta Chamisa ... 87506
Vuelta Colorada ... 87507
Vuelta De La Luz ... 87507
Vuelta De La Tusa ... 87506
Vuelta De Las Acequias ... 87507
Vuelta Del Sur ... 87507
Vuelta Dorado ... 87507
N & S Vuelta Herradura ... 87506
Vuelta Horcado ... 87506
Vuelta Linda ... 87506
Vuelta Maria ... 87506
Vuelta Montuoso ... 87506
Vuelta Muerdago ... 87506
Vuelta Otra Banda ... 87506
Vuelta Real ... 87507
Vuelta Roble ... 87501
Vuelta Rosal ... 87506
Vuelta Sabio ... 87506
Vuelta San Marcos ... 87505
Vuelta Susana ... 87506
Vuelta Tomas ... 87506
Vuelta Ventura ... 87507
Vuelta Vistoso ... 87507
Vuelta Yucca ... 87506
Wagon Rd ... 87507
Wagon Meadow Ln ... 87505
Wagon Wheel Ln ... 87508
Waking Sky ... 87507
Waldo St ... 87505
Walking Rain Rd ... 87507
Walnut St ... 87507
Wandering Trail Ln ... 87507
E & W War Chief Ln ... 87506
Warner St ... 87505
Washington Ave ... 87501
Watchpoint ... 87507
E & W Water St ... 87501
Water Garden Way ... 87508
Webber St ... 87505
Well Tank Rd ... 87508
Westwind Rd ... 87508
Whispering Wing Rd ... 87507
Whistling Moon Ln ... 87507
White Bear Ct & Trl ... 87506
White Boulder Ln ... 87506
White Cloud Ct ... 87505
White Feather Rd ... 87508
White Sands Blvd & Ct ... 87506
Whitewater Ct ... 87508
Wide View Ln ... 87508
Wild Turkey Way ... 87505
Wild West Ln ... 87506
Wilder Ln & Pl ... 87508
Wilderness Cv, Rdg, Vw & Way ... 87505
Wilderness Arroyo ... 87505
Wilderness Gate Rd ... 87505
Wilderness Heights Rd ... 87505
Wilderness Meadow Rd ... 87505
E & W Wildflower Dr & Way ... 87506
Wildhorse ... 87506
Wildlife Way
1-3 ... 87507
149-149 ... 87506
Williams St ... 87501
Willow ... 87508
Willow Way
5-7 ... 87508
1000-1199 ... 87507
Willow Back Rd ... 87508
Willow Branch Rd ... 87508
Willy Rd ... 87507
Wilowa Ln ... 87505
Winding Rd ... 87505
Winding Rdg ... 87506
Winding Ridge Loop ... 87507
Windridge Cir ... 87506
Windspirit Rd ... 87505
Windstone Dr ... 87508
Winische Way ... 87505
Withers Peak ... 87508
Wo Peen Rd ... 87506
Wofford Ln ... 87507
Wolf Rd ... 87508
Wolf Creek Rd ... 87507
Wood Flower Pl ... 87508
Woods Loop ... 87505
Woodson Dr ... 87506
Wymas Dr ... 87506
Ya Callete Ln ... 87507
Yan Tsidae Dr ... 87506
Yana Dr ... 87506
Yo Povi Po ... 87506
Young St ... 87505
Yucatan ... 87507
Yucca St ... 87505
Yucca Way ... 87508
Zacate Verde ... 87506
Zafarano Dr ... 87507
Zambra Way ... 87506
Zepol Rd ... 87507
E Zia Rd ... 87505
W Zia Rd
100-2504 ... 87505
2506-2698 ... 87505
2800-2898 ... 87507
Zonie Way ... 87505
Zorrito Ct ... 87508
Zozobra Ln ... 87505
Zuni St ... 87505

NUMBERED STREETS

All Street Addresses ... 87505

SILVER CITY NM

HIGHWAY CONTRACTS

60 ... 88022

NAMED STREETS

N A St ... 88061
Acorn Dr ... 88061
Adams Ln ... 88061
Adobe Ln ... 88061
Agave Ln & St ... 88061
N Alabama St ... 88061
Alamo St ... 88022
Alegre St ... 88022
E & W Alice St ... 88061
Allen Spgs ... 88061
Aloe Vereda ... 88061
Alpine Cir ... 88061
Amber Dr ... 88061
Angus Dr ... 88061
Antelope Run ... 88061
E Apache Cir & St ... 88061
Apache Mound Rd ... 88061
Arenas Valley Rd ... 88022
N & S Arizona St ... 88061
Armijo Rd ... 88061
Armistad ... 88061
N & W Arrowhead Rd ... 88061
Arroyo Ln ... 88061
Arroyo Seco Rd ... 88061
Archer Rd ... 88061
Autumn Ln ... 88061
Avenida De Paso ... 88022
Axle Canyon Rd ... 88061

Street	ZIP
N B St	88061
Babbling Brk	88061
Bandoni Dr	88061
Bar 6 Dr	88061
Bar D Rd	88061
Bar Ranch Rd	88061
S Bard Ave	88061
N Bartlett St	88061
Basalt Dr	88061
N & S Bayard St	88061
Bear Canyon Rd	88061
Bear Grass Ln	88061
Bear Mountain Rd	88061
Beck Rd	88061
Bell St	88061
Bella Vista Rd	88061
Bellwood Cir	88061
N Ben Lilly Dr	88061
N & S Bennett St	88061
Big Bend Rd	88061
Big Joe Rd	88061
Bighorn Trl	88061
E Birch St	88061
N Black St	88061
N Blackhawk Rd	88061
N Bluejay Ln	88061
Bob White Dr	88061
S Bonita Ave	88061
N Bonney Trl	88061
Bosworth Dr	88061
Boulder Trl	88061
Branding Iron Trl	88061
W Bremen St	88061
Brianna Way	88061
Briarwood Ln	88061
E & W Broadway St	88061
Broken Arrow Dr	88061
Broken Bow St	88061
Brookhollow Dr	88061
Brookside Ln	88061
Buckboard Ln	88061
Buffalo Bur Rd	88022
N & S Bullard St	88061
Burke Loop	88061
Burnham St	88022
N Burning Tree Ln	88061
Burnside Rd	88061
Burro Spgs	88061
Busy St	88022
Butterfield Ln	88061
Bypass Rd	88061
N C St	88061
Caballero	88061
N Cactus St	88061
E & W Cain Dr	88061
N California Ave	88061
Camino Amarillo	88022
Camino Azteca	88061
Camino Azul	88022
Camino Blanco	88022
Camino De La Montana	88022
Camino De Suenos	88061
Camino De Viento	88061
Camino Del Bosque	88061
Camino Moreno	88022
Camino Oro	88022
Camino Seco	88061
Camino Serna	88061
Camino Tolteca	88061
Camino Verde	88022
N Canal St	88061
Cantada Creek Rd	88061
N Cardinal Ln	88061
Carl Pl	88061
Carpenter Rd	88061
Casa Loma Rd	88061
Cattlemans Trl	88061
Cecilia St	88061
N Cedar Ave	88061
Chamise Rd	88061
Chaparral Trl	88061
Charolais	88061
Charro Trl	88061
Chavez Ln	88061
Cherokee Trl	88061
Cherry St	88022
N Cherry Hills Pl	88061
N Cheyenne Ave	88061
W Chihuahua St	88061
Chimboraza Pt	88061
Chisholm Trl	88061
Chitalpa Ct	88061
Chloride Flts	88061
Chrisitan Ranch Rd	88061
Christian Flury Dr	88061
Christopher Rd	88061
Chukar Rd	88061
Cielo Azul	88061
Cimarron Trl	88061
Cinc Dr	88061
Circle A	88061
Claw Rd	88061
Cleveland Mine Rd	88061
S Cobre Ct	88061
N Cochise Cir	88061
Coffey Cir	88061
W Cold Springs Ranch Rd	88061
Coleman Dr	88061
E & W College Ave	88061
Coloradas Rd	88061
E Comanche Rd	88061
Combs Cir & St	88061
Cook St	88061
N & S Cooper St	88061
Cooper Vista Rd	88061
Copper Ridge Dr	88061
N & S Corbin St	88061
Corona Ct	88061
Corto Dr	88061
Corua Way	88061
Cottage San Rd	88061
Cotton Tail Dr	88061
Cottontail Trl	88061
Cottonwood Rd	88061
Cougar Way	88061
Country Rd	88061
Country Club Dr	88061
Cove Rd	88061
Cow Trl	88022
Cowan Rd	88061
Coye Ln	88061
E Crescent St	88061
N Crestway Dr	88061
Cripple Creek Rd	88061
Cullum Dr	88061
Cumorah Hls	88061
Cygnet Rd	88061
N D St	88061
E & W Daniel St	88061
N Debby Dr	88061
Deer Trail Rd	88061
Delk Dr	88061
Descanso	88061
Desert Rose Ln	88061
Dewey Rd	88061
Diamond A Rd	88061
Dickson Rd	88061
Dividing Line Rd	88061
Dogwood Cir	88061
E & W Dorothy St	88061
Dream Catcher	88022
N Durango St	88061
N E St	88061
Eagle Nest Dr	88061
Eckles Hall	88061
N Eddie Ward Way	88061
Elder Ln	88061
S Elias Ave	88061
Elias Rd	88022
Ells	88022
Elmer Boyett	88061
Emerald Dr	88061
Enchanted Trl	88061
Encina St	88022
Escobedo Ln	88061
Ethel Ln	88061
Euphoria Rd	88061
Evergreen Dr	88061
F St	88061
Fairway Dr	88061
Faith Rd	88061
Fargo Trl	88061
Farley Rd	88061
Fast Ln	88061
Fawn Ct & Trl	88061
E Filaree Rd	88061
Fir St	88061
Flamingo St	88061
Fleming Tank Rd	88061
W Florence St	88061
N Florida St	88061
Flury Ln	88061
Forest Dr	88061
Forest Rd 172	88061
Forest Ridge Trl	88061
W Fork Rd	88061
N Fork Walnut Creek Rd	88061
Fotis Rd	88061
N Fowler Ave	88061
Fran Dr & Pl	88061
Franics Rd	88022
Franks Rd	88022
Fraser Dr	88061
Freedom Trl	88061
Fuller Dr	88061
E & W Garcia St	88061
Gatlin Rd	88061
N Georgia St	88061
N Gideon Truesdell Ln	88061
W Gila St	88061
Glenda Cir	88061
Goathead Path	88061
N & S Gold St	88061
Golf Course Dr	88061
Goodnight Trl	88061
W Gordon St	88061
Grand Mesa St	88061
N Grandview Rd	88061
N Grant St	88061
Green Valley Dr	88061
Greene Rd	88061
Greenwood Canyon Rd	88061
Grenfell Dr	88061
Gulch Ln	88061
H Bar M	88061
Half Moon Cir	88061
Harris St	88061
Heart Cross Dr	88061
Heavens Gate	88061
Helen Lynch Pl	88061
Hereford Dr	88061
Heritage Ln	88061
Hermana Rd	88022
W Hester St	88061
Hidden Way	88061
Hidden Valley Ln	88061
Hide Away Ln	88061
High Lonesome Rd	88061
Highway 15	88061
Highway 180 E	
900-1098	88061
1100-11650	88061
11652-11698	88061
11675-11697	88022
11699-11999	88022
Highway 180 W	88061
Highway 35 N	88061
Highway 90 S	88061
W Hill St	88061
Hilltop Rd	88061
Hl Watkins Rd	88061
Holly Ln	88061
Hood St	88061
Horseman Trl	88061
Horseway	88022
W Howell St	88061
N Hudson St	
100-198	88061
200-399	88061
401-1505	88061
500-1598	88061
500-500	88062
S Hudson St	88061
N Huff St	88061
Hugh Mckeen Dr	88061
W Idaho St	88061
W Indiana St	88061
Iron Dr	88061
Ironwood Ln	88061
Jack Frost Dr	88061
Jack Rabbit Dr	88061
Jacob Dr	88061
Jade Dr	88061
Jason St	88061
Jasper Dr	88061
Jazmine Rd	88061
Joe Ray Dr	88061
Johnson Rd	88061
Jomar Ranch Rd	88022
Joseph Blane Rd	88061
N Juniper Ave	88061
Kachina Cir	88061
Katheryne Cir	88061
Kathleen Dr	88061
E & W Kelly St	88061
N Kentucky St	88061
Kidder Rd	88061
Kilimanjaro Ct	88061
N Kimberly Dr	88061
Kirkland Rd	88061
N Kiva Pl	88061
Kohdy Ln	88022
N Kokopelli Dr	88061
E Kris Cir	88061
Kristine Ln	88061
La Montana	88061
E Lamb St	88061
S Lamina Loop	88061
E Lance Dr	88061
Lane Rd	88061
W Langstroth Dr	88061
Latigo Trl	88061
N Leslie Rd	88061
Lesson Ln	88061
E Lisa Pl	88061
Little Walnut Rd	88061
Little Wing Rd	88061
Logan St	88061
Loma Linda Dr	88061
Loma Verde Dr	88061
Lomita Dr	88061
E Lori Pl	88061
Los Encinos St	88061
Los Pinos St	88061
N Louisiana St	88061
W Luck St	88061
Lynx Ln	88061
N Lyon St	88061
Madison Rd	88061
Mahogany Dr	88061
N & S Main St	88061
Manganese Dr	88061
Mangus Valley Rd	88061
N Mann Dr	88061
E Maple St	88061
Maplewood Cir	88061
Marchele Dr	88061
Margaret Dr	88061
Marguerite St	88061
E & W Market St	88061
Mathers Rd	88061
Mcginty Pl	88061
Mckinley St	88061
Mckinney St	88061
Mcmillan Rd	88061
Meadow Hawk Ln	88022
Memory Ln	88061
Mesa Rd	88061
Mesa Trl	88022
Mesita Cir	88061
Mesquite Dr	88061
Michelle Ln	88061
W Michigan St	88061
S Mill St	88061
Mineriew	88022
Mira Loma	88022
N Mississippi St	88061
Mitchell	88022
E Mobile Dr	88061
Mogollon Trl	88061
W Montana St	88061
Monte St	88022
Moonshine Ln	88061
Morales Dr	88061
Mount Olympus Rd	88061
Mountain View Dr, Ln & Rd	88061
Muir Hts	88061
Mulberry Dr	88061
N Newsham St	88061
Nichols Dr	88061
Nickle	88061
Niki Rd	88061
Nizhoni Loop	
1-99	88061
100-199	88022
101-199	88061
North Loop	88061
E Oak St	88061
Oakgrove	88061
Oakridge Dr	88061
Oakwood Ave	88061
Offutt Cyn	88061
Ohio St	88061
Old Little Walnut Rd	88061
Olympus St	88061
N Omega Pl	88061
Onyx Dr	88061
Opal Dr	88061
Orchard Dr	88061
W Oro Dr	88061
Otis Ln	88061
Owens Rd	88061
Owl Hoot Trl	88061
Oxbow Dr	88061
W Pacific Rd	88061
Pack Rat	88022
Painted Sky Rd	88061
Paisano Dr	88022
Palo Verde Dr	88061
Paloma St	88022
Panorama Dr	88061
Partridge Ave	88061
E Paul Pl	88061
Pearce Rd	88061
Peeler St	88022
N Pertherr St	88061
Peterson Dr	88061
Petes Pass	88061
Pewter Rd	88061
E & N Pheasant Dr	88061
Piedra Vis	88061
Pike St	88061
E Pine Loop & St	88061
Pine Point Trl	88061
Pinon Dr, Ln & St	88061
N & S Pinos Altos Rd & St	88061
Pioneer Rd	88061
Pitchfork Ranch Rd	88061
Plata Rd	88061
Ponderosa St	88061
Pony Express Rd	88061
N Pope St	88061
Pueblo	88022
Quail Run	88061
Quail Canyon Rd	88061
Quartz Dr	88061
Racetrack Rd	88022
Rachel Rd	88061
Railroad Dr	88061
Rainier St	88061
Rams Horn Rd	88061
Ramuda Way	88061
Ranch Club Rd	88061
Range Fire Rd	88061
Ranzo Way	88061
E Raven Dr	88061
Realta Dr	88061
Red Hill Rd	88061
Red Rock Rd	88061
Redwood Cir	88061
Regents Row	88061
Reynolds Cir & St	88061
W Rhoda Rd	88061
E & W Richard St	88061
S Ridge Rd	88061
Ridge Crest Cir & Dr	88061
N Ridge Loop Dr	88061
Rio De Arenas	88022
S Robert St	88061
Robson St	88061
Rocky Acres	88061
Rocky Creek Rd	88061
Rodeo Rd	88061
Rogers Rd	88061
Rosedale Rd	88061
Rosewood Cir	88061
Round Mountain Rd	88061
N Royal Dr	88061
Running Iron Rdg	88061
Rustlers Trl	88061
Rusty Dime	88022
Saavedra Rd	88061
Saddle Rock Rd	88061
Salars Rd	88061
W San Vicente St	88061
Sanctuary Rd	88061
Sandalwood Ave	88061
N Santa Rita St	88061
Sara Ct	88061
W Sawyer Cir	88061
Schiff Trl	88061
W Scholl Pl	88061
Separ Rd	88061
Serinna Ct	88061
Seven Sons Rd	88022
N Shadow Mountain Rd	88061
Shady Grv	88061
Shale Dr	88061
Shannon Dr	88061
Shasta St	88061
Sheriffs Posse Rd	88061
W Short St	88061
N Silver St	88061
Silver Bell Rd	88061
Silver Heights Blvd	88061
Simmens Ranch Rd	88022
Six Shooter Dr	88061
Skarn Way	88061
E Skyview Dr	88061
Slag Rd	88061
Slash Dr	88061
Smith Ranch Rd	88061
Snow Shoe Cv	88061
W Sonora St	88061
Sotol St	88061
E Spear Dr	88061
E & W Spring St	88061
Spring Creek Rd	88061
Spur Dr	88061
Stag Rd	88061
Starlight Way	88061
W State St	88061
Summit Rd	88061
Sunburst Trl	88061
Sundown Trl	88061
Sunlight Trl	88061
Sunset Ln & Trl	88061
Suntanner Rd	88061
E Superior St	88061
N & S Swan St	88061
N Swarthmore St	88061
Sycamore St	88061
T Bar T Dr	88061
Table Butte Rd	88061
S Tabor Dr	88061
Talissa Dr	88061
Tanglewood Cir	88061
N & S Texas St	88061
S Theodore St	88061
Thomas Rd	88061
Thunder Rd	88061
Tigers Lode	88061
Timber Dr	88061
E Timmer Way	88061
N Todd Cir	88061
W Tom Lyons Dr	88061
Tomahawk Rd	88061
N Tracy Cir & Pl	88061
Trail Ridge Rd	88061
E Trailing Heart Dr	88061
Trapper Rd	88061
Truck By Pass Rd	88061
Trudy Dr	88061
Turner Rd	88061
Twin Sisters Rd	88022
Tyrone Rd	88061
Unit 18	88061
Unit 19	88061
Unit 21	88061
Unit 51	88061
Unit 53	88061
Unit 55	88061
Unit 63	88061
Unit 64	88061
Unit 66	88061
Unit 67	88061
Unit 79	88022
Unit 84	88022
Ursa Major	88061
Ursa Minor	88061
Ut Dr	88061
E Valle Dr	88061
Valley Dr	88061
Valley Vista Dr	88061
Ventana Dr	88061
Ventana De Sierra	88061
Vesuvius Way	88061
Vic Culberson Dr	88061
S Vicente Pl	88061
N Vicki Pl	88061
E & W Victoria St	88061
Village Dr & Rd	88061
N Virginia St	88061
Vista Grande	88061
Wagon Wheel Ln	88061
N Walnut Dr	88061
Watts Ln	88061
Wayne Rd	88061
Welsh St	88022
Wendy Rd	88061
N West St	88061
Western Dr & Hls	88061
Western Heritage	88061
Whiskey Creek Rd	88061
Whispering Hills Rd	88061
White Water Rd	88061
Wide Canyon Trl	88061
Wildwood Cir	88061
Willow Flat Rd	88061
Winchester Rd	88061
Wind Canyon Rd	88061
Woodland	88061
Wrangler Way	88061
X Bar X	88061
Xyz Ranch Rd	88022
E & W Yankie St	88061
Yellow Arrow Ln	88061
N Yucca St	88061
Yucca Pod Ln	88022
Yucca Stalk Ln	88022
Yucca Valley Dr	88022
N Zia Cir	88061

NUMBERED STREETS

Street	ZIP
All Street Addresses	88061

New York

People QuickFacts	New York	USA
Population, 2013 estimate	19,651,127	316,128,839
Population, 2010 (April 1) estimates base	19,378,105	308,747,716
Population, percent change, April 1, 2010 to July 1, 2013	1.4%	2.4%
Population, 2010	19,378,102	308,745,538
Persons under 5 years, percent, 2013	6.0%	6.3%
Persons under 18 years, percent, 2013	21.6%	23.3%
Persons 65 years and over, percent, 2013	14.4%	14.1%
Female persons, percent, 2013	51.5%	50.8%
White alone, percent, 2013 (a)	70.9%	77.7%
Black or African American alone, percent, 2013 (a)	17.5%	13.2%
American Indian and Alaska Native alone, percent, 2013 (a)	1.0%	1.2%
Asian alone, percent, 2013 (a)	8.2%	5.3%
Native Hawaiian and Other Pacific Islander alone, percent, 2013 (a)	0.1%	0.2%
Two or More Races, percent, 2013	2.3%	2.4%
Hispanic or Latino, percent, 2013 (b)	18.4%	17.1%
White alone, not Hispanic or Latino, percent, 2013	57.2%	62.6%
Living in same house 1 year & over, percent, 2008-2012	88.7%	84.8%
Foreign born persons, percent, 2008-2012	22.0%	12.9%
Language other than English spoken at home, pct age 5+, 2008-2012	29.8%	20.5%
High school graduate or higher, percent of persons age 25+, 2008-2012	84.9%	85.7%
Bachelor's degree or higher, percent of persons age 25+, 2008-2012	32.8%	28.5%
Veterans, 2008-2012	957,004	21,853,912
Mean travel time to work (minutes), workers age 16+, 2008-2012	31.5	25.4
Housing units, 2013	8,126,026	132,802,859
Homeownership rate, 2008-2012	54.5%	65.5%
Housing units in multi-unit structures, percent, 2008-2012	50.5%	25.9%
Median value of owner-occupied housing units, 2008-2012	$295,300	$181,400
Households, 2008-2012	7,230,896	115,226,802
Persons per household, 2008-2012	2.6	2.61
Per capita money income in past 12 months (2012 dollars), 2008-2012	$32,104	$28,051
Median household income, 2008-2012	$57,683	$53,046
Persons below poverty level, percent, 2008-2012	14.9%	14.9%

Business QuickFacts	New York	USA
Private nonfarm establishments, 2012	527,001	7,431,808
Private nonfarm employment, 2012	7,556,521	115,938,468
Private nonfarm employment, percent change, 2011-2012	2.5%	2.2%
Nonemployer establishments, 2012	1,612,106	22,735,915
Total number of firms, 2007	1,956,733	27,092,908
Black-owned firms, percent, 2007	10.4%	7.1%
American Indian- and Alaska Native-owned firms, percent, 2007	0.7%	0.9%
Asian-owned firms, percent, 2007	10.1%	5.7%
Native Hawaiian and Other Pacific Islander-owned firms, percent, 2007	0.1%	0.1%
Hispanic-owned firms, percent, 2007	9.9%	8.3%
Women-owned firms, percent, 2007	30.4%	28.8%
Manufacturers shipments, 2007 ($1000)	162,720,173	5,319,456,312
Merchant wholesaler sales, 2007 ($1000)	313,461,904	4,174,286,516
Retail sales, 2007 ($1000)	230,718,065	3,917,663,456
Retail sales per capita, 2007	$11,879	$12,990
Accommodation and food services sales, 2007 ($1000)	39,813,499	613,795,732
Building permits, 2012	24,872	829,658

Geography QuickFacts	New York	USA
Land area in square miles, 2010	47,126.40	3,531,905.43
Persons per square mile, 2010	411.2	87.4
FIPS Code	36	

(a) Includes persons reporting only one race.
(b) Hispanics may be of any race, so also are included in applicable race categories.
FN: Footnote on this item for this area in place of data
NA: Not available
D: Suppressed to avoid disclosure of confidential information
X: Not applicable
S: Suppressed; does not meet publication standards
Z: Value greater than zero but less than half unit of measure shown
F: Fewer than 100 firms
Source: US Census Bureau State & County QuickFacts

New York

3 DIGIT ZIP CODE MAP

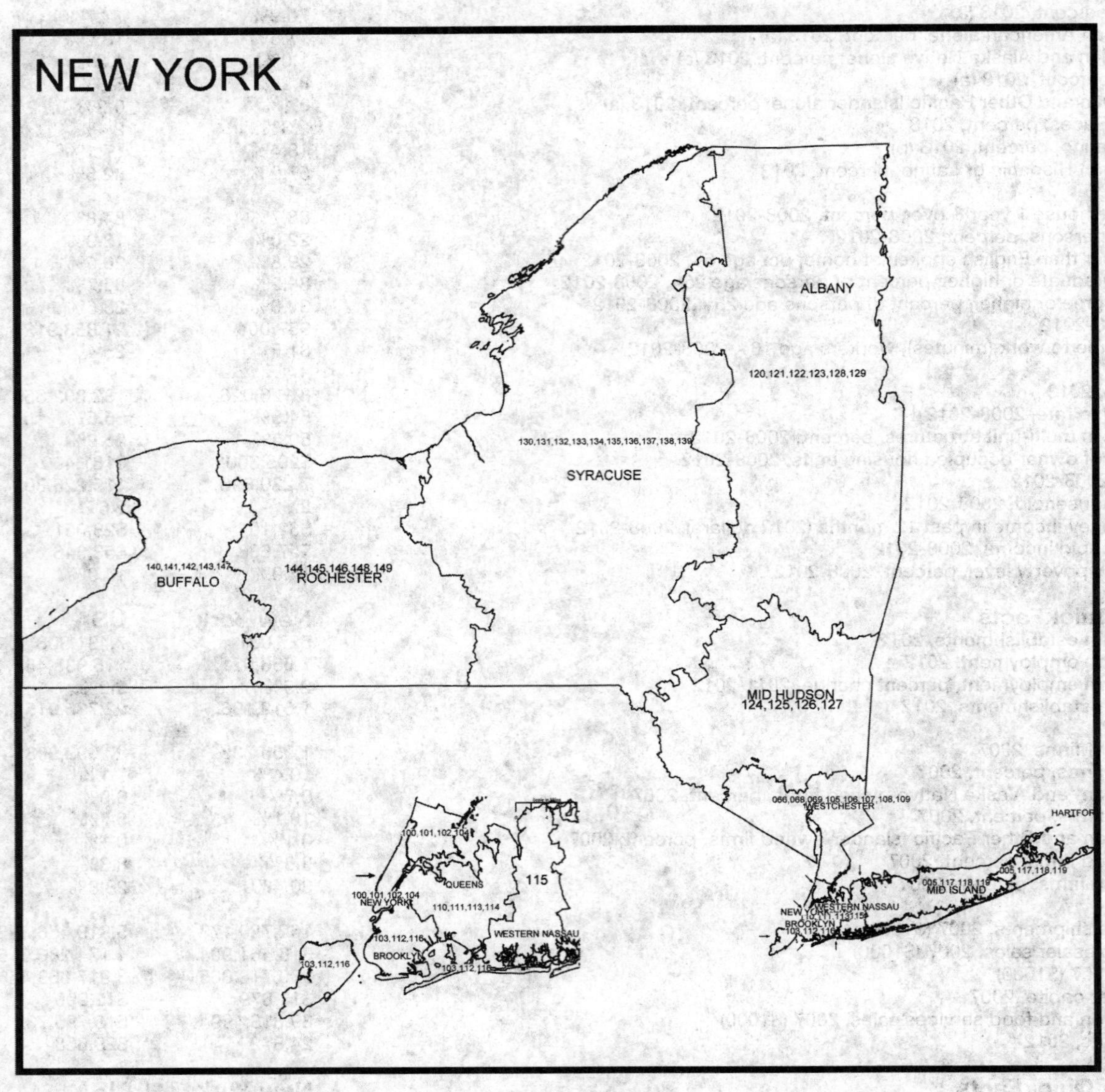

NEW YORK
ALBANY
120,121,122,123,128,129
130,131,132,133,134,135,136,137,138,139
SYRACUSE
140,141,142,143,147
BUFFALO
144,145,146,148,149
ROCHESTER
MID HUDSON
124,125,126,127
066,068,069,105,106,107,108,109
WESTCHESTER
HARTFOR
005,117,118,119
005,117,118,119
MID ISLAND
WESTERN NASSAU
NEW YORK
BROOKLYN
103,112,116
100,101,102,104
QUEENS
115
100,101,102,104
NEW YORK
110,111,113,114
103,112,116
BROOKLYN
WESTERN NASSAU
103,112,116
103,112,116

New York

(Abbreviation: NY)

Post Office, County — ZIP Code

Places with more than one ZIP code are listed in capital letters, See pages indicated.

Accord, Ulster 12404
Acra, Greene 12405
Adams, Jefferson 13605
Adams Basin, Monroe 14410
Adams Center, Jefferson 13606
Addisleigh Park
(See Jamaica)
Addison, Steuben 14801
Adirondack, Warren 12808
Afton, Chenango 13730
Airmont, Rockland 10901
Akron, Erie 14001
Akwesasne, Franklin 13655
Alabama, Genesee 14013
ALBANY, Albany
(See Page 2640)
Albertson, Nassau 11507
Albion, Orleans 14411
Alcove, Albany 12007
Alden, Erie 14004
Alden Manor, Nassau 11003
Alder Creek, Oneida 13301
Alexander, Genesee 14005
Alexandria Bay, Jefferson 13607
Alfred, Allegany 14802
Alfred Station, Allegany 14803
Allegany, Cattaraugus 14706
Allentown, Allegany 14707
Alma, Allegany 14708
Almond, Allegany 14804
Alpine, Schuyler 14805
Alplaus, Schenectady 12008
Altamont, Albany 12009
Altmar, Oswego 13302
Alton, Wayne 14413
Altona, Clinton 12910
Amagansett, Suffolk 11930
Amawalk, Westchester 10501
Amenia, Dutchess 12501
Ames, Montgomery 13317
Amherst
(See Buffalo)
Amity Harbor, Suffolk 11701
Amityville, Suffolk 11701
Amsterdam, Montgomery 12010
Ancram, Columbia 12502
Ancramdale, Columbia 12503
Andes, Delaware 13731
Andover, Allegany 14806
Angelica, Allegany 14709
Angola, Erie 14006
Annandale On Hudson, Dutchess 12504
Antwerp, Jefferson 13608
Apalachin, Tioga 13732
Appleton, Niagara 14008
Apulia Station, Onondaga 13020
Aquebogue, Suffolk 11931
Arcade, Wyoming 14009
Arden, Orange 10910
Ardsley, Westchester 10502
Ardsley On Hudson, Westchester 10503
Argyle, Washington 12809
Arkport, Steuben 14807
Arkville, Delaware 12406
Arlington, Dutchess 12603
Armonk, Westchester 10504
Arverne, Queens 11692
Ashland, Greene 12407
Ashville, Chautauqua 14710
ASTORIA, Queens
(See Page 2643)
Athens, Greene 12015
Athol, Warren 12810
Athol Springs, Erie 14010
Atlanta, Steuben 14808
Atlantic Beach, Nassau 11509
Attica, Wyoming 14011
Au Sable Chasm, Clinton 12911
Au Sable Forks, Clinton 12912
AUBURN, Cayuga
(See Page 2643)
Auburndale, Queens 11358
Auriesville, Montgomery 12016
Aurora, Cayuga 13026
Austerlitz, Columbia 12017
Ava, Oneida 13303
Averill Park, Rensselaer 12018
Avoca, Steuben 14809
Avon, Livingston 14414
Babylon, Suffolk 11702
Bainbridge, Chenango 13733
Baiting Hollow, Suffolk 11933
Bakers Mills, Warren 12811
Baldwin, Nassau 11510
Baldwin Place, Westchester 10505
Baldwinsville, Onondaga 13027
Ballston Lake, Saratoga 12019
Ballston Spa, Saratoga 12020
Balmat, Saint Lawrence 13642
Bangall, Dutchess 12506
Bangor, Franklin 12966
Bardonia, Rockland 10954
Barker, Niagara 14012
Barnes Corners, Lewis 13626
Barneveld, Oneida 13304
Barrytown, Dutchess 12507
Barryville, Sullivan 12719
Barton, Tioga 13734
Basom, Genesee 14013
BATAVIA, Genesee
(See Page 2644)
Bath, Steuben 14810
Bay Shore, Suffolk 11706
Bayberry, Onondaga 13090
Bayport, Suffolk 11705
BAYSIDE, Queens
(See Page 2645)
Bayside Hills, Queens 11364
Bayville, Nassau 11709
Beacon, Dutchess 12508
Bear Mountain, Rockland 10911
Bearsville, Ulster 12409
Beaver Dams, Schuyler 14812
Beaver Falls, Lewis 13305
Beaver Fls, Lewis 13305
Beaver River, Lewis 13367
Bedford, Westchester 10506
Bedford Corners, Westchester 10549
Bedford Hills, Westchester 10507
Beechhurst, Queens 11357
Belfast, Allegany 14711
Belle Harbor, Queens 11694
Bellerose, Queens 11426
Bellerose Manor
(See Queens Village)
Bellerose Village, Nassau 11001
Belleville, Jefferson 13611
Bellmore, Nassau 11710
Bellona, Yates 14415
Bellport, Suffolk 11713
Bellvale, Orange 10912
Belmont, Allegany 14813
Bemus Point, Chautauqua 14712
Bergen, Genesee 14416
Berkshire, Tioga 13736
Berlin, Rensselaer 12022
Berne, Albany 12023
Bernhards Bay, Oswego 13028
Bethel, Sullivan 12720
Bethpage, Nassau 11714
Bible School Park, Broome 13737
Big Flats, Chemung 14814
Big Indian, Ulster 12410
Billings, Dutchess 12510
BINGHAMTON, Broome
(See Page 2645)
Black Creek, Allegany 14714
Black River, Jefferson 13612
Blasdell, Erie 14219
Blauvelt, Rockland 10913
Bliss, Wyoming 14024
Blodgett Mills, Cortland 13738
Bloomfield, Ontario 14469
Blooming Grove, Orange 10914
Bloomingburg, Sullivan 12721
Bloomingdale, Essex 12913
Bloomington, Ulster 12411
Bloomville, Delaware 13739
Blossvale, Oneida 13308
Blue Mountain Lake, Hamilton 12812
Blue Point, Suffolk 11715
Bluff Point, Yates 14478
Bohemia, Suffolk 11716
Boiceville, Ulster 12412
Bolivar, Allegany 14715
Bolton Landing, Warren 12814
Bombay, Franklin 12914
Boonville, Oneida 13309
Boston, Erie 14025
Bouckville, Madison 13310
Bovina Center, Delaware 13740
Bowling Green, New York 10004
Bowmansville, Erie 14026
Bradford, Schuyler 14815
Brainard, Rensselaer 12024
Brainardsville, Franklin 12915
Branchport, Yates 14418
Brant, Erie 14027
Brant Lake, Warren 12815
Brantingham, Lewis 13312
Brasher Falls, Saint Lawrence 13613
Breesport, Chemung 14816
Breezy Point, Queens 11697
Brentwood, Suffolk 11717
Brewerton, Onondaga 13029
Brewster, Putnam 10509
Briarcliff Manor, Westchester 10510
Briarwood, Queens 11435
Bridgehampton, Suffolk 11932
Bridgeport, Onondaga 13030
Bridgewater, Oneida 13313
Brier Hill, Saint Lawrence 13614
Brighton
(See Rochester)
Brightwaters, Suffolk 11718
Brisben, Chenango 13830
Broad Channel, Queens 11693
Broadalbin, Fulton 12025
Brockport, Monroe 14420
Brocton, Chautauqua 14716
BRONX, Bronx
(See Page 2647)
Bronxville, Westchester 10708
Brookfield, Madison 13314
Brookhaven, Suffolk 11719
BROOKLYN, Kings
(See Page 2651)
Brooklyn Heights, Kings 11201
Brooktondale, Tompkins 14817
Brookview, Rensselaer 12033
Brownville, Jefferson 13615
Brushton, Franklin 12916
Buchanan, Westchester 10511
BUFFALO, Erie
(See Page 2658)
Bullville, Orange 10915
Burdett, Schuyler 14818
Burke, Franklin 12917
Burlingham, Sullivan 12722
Burlington Flats, Otsego 13315
Burnt Hills, Saratoga 12019
Burnt Hills, Saratoga 12027
Burt, Niagara 14028
Buskirk, Washington 12028
Byron, Genesee 14422
Cadosia, Delaware 13783
Cadyville, Clinton 12918
Cairo, Greene 12413
Calcium, Jefferson 13616
Caledonia, Livingston 14423
Callicoon, Sullivan 12723
Callicoon Center, Sullivan 12724
Calverton, Suffolk 11933
Cambria Heights, Queens 11411
Cambridge, Washington 12816
Camden, Oneida 13316
Cameron, Steuben 14819
Cameron Mills, Steuben 14820
Camillus, Onondaga 13031
Campbell, Steuben 14821
Campbell Hall, Orange 10916
Canaan, Columbia 12029
Canajoharie, Montgomery 13317
Canal Street, New York 10013
Canandaigua, Ontario 14424
Canandaigua, Ontario 14425
Canaseraga, Allegany 14822
Canastota, Madison 13032
Candor, Tioga 13743
Caneadea, Allegany 14717
Canisteo, Steuben 14823
Canton, Saint Lawrence 13617
Cape Vincent, Jefferson 13618
Captree Island, Suffolk 11702
Carle Place, Nassau 11514
Carlisle, Schoharie 12031
Carmel, Putnam 10512
Caroga Lake, Fulton 12032
Carthage, Jefferson 13619
Cassadaga, Chautauqua 14718
Cassville, Oneida 13318
Castile, Wyoming 14427
Castle Creek, Broome 13744
Castle Point, Dutchess 12511
Castleton On Hudson, Rensselaer 12033
Castorland, Lewis 13620
Cato, Cayuga 13033
Catskill, Greene 12414
Cattaraugus, Cattaraugus 14719
Cayuga, Cayuga 13034
Cayuta, Schuyler 14824
Cazenovia, Madison 13035
Cedarhurst, Nassau 11516
Celoron, Chautauqua 14720
Cementon, Greene 12414
Center Moriches, Suffolk 11934
Centereach, Suffolk 11720
Centerport, Suffolk 11721
Centerville, Allegany 14029
Central Bridge, Schoharie 12035
Central Islip, Suffolk 11722
Central Islip, Suffolk 11749
Central Square, Oswego 13036
Central Valley, Orange 10917
Ceres, Allegany 14721
Chadwicks, Oneida 13319
Chaffee, Erie 14030
Champlain, Clinton 12919
Chappaqua, Westchester 10514
Charlotteville, Schoharie 12036
Charlton, Saratoga 12019
Chase Mills, Saint Lawrence 13621
Chateaugay, Franklin 12920
Chatham, Columbia 12037
Chaumont, Jefferson 13622
Chautauqua, Chautauqua 14722
Chazy, Clinton 12921
Cheektowaga
(See Buffalo)
Chelsea, Dutchess 12512
Chemung, Chemung 14825
Chenango Bridge, Broome 13745
Chenango Forks, Broome 13746
Cherry Creek, Chautauqua 14723
Cherry Grove, Suffolk 11782
Cherry Plain, Rensselaer 12040
Cherry Valley, Otsego 13320
Chester, Orange 10918
Chestertown, Warren 12817
Chestnut Ridge, Rockland 10977
Chichester, Ulster 12416
Childwold, Saint Lawrence 12922
Chinatown, New York 10013
Chippewa Bay, Saint Lawrence 13623
Chittenango, Madison 13037
Churchville, Monroe 14428
Churubusco, Clinton 12923
Cicero, Onondaga 13039
Cincinnatus, Cortland 13040
Circleville, Orange 10919
Clarence, Erie 14031
Clarence Center, Erie 14032
Clarendon, Orleans 14429
Clark Mills, Oneida 13321
Clarkson, Monroe 14430
Clarksville, Albany 12041
Claryville, Sullivan 12725
Claverack, Columbia 12513
Clay, Onondaga 13039
Clay, Onondaga 13041
Clayton, Jefferson 13624
Clayville, Oneida 13322
Clemons, Washington 12819
Cleveland, Oswego 13042
Cleverdale, Warren 12820
Clifton, Monroe 14428
Clifton Park, Saratoga 12065
Clifton Springs, Ontario 14432
Climax, Greene 12042
Clinton, Oneida 13323
Clinton Corners, Dutchess 12514
Clintondale, Ulster 12515
Clintonville, Clinton 12924
Clockville, Madison 13043
Clyde, Wayne 14433
Clymer, Chautauqua 14724
Cobleskill, Schoharie 12043
Cochecton, Sullivan 12726
Cochecton Center, Sullivan 12727
Coeymans, Albany 12045
Coeymans Hollow, Albany 12046
Cohocton, Steuben 14826
Cohoes, Albany 12047
Cold Brook, Herkimer 13324
Cold Spring, Putnam 10516
Cold Spring Harbor, Suffolk 11724
Colden, Erie 14033
College Point, Queens 11356
Colliersville, Otsego 13747
Collins, Erie 14034
Collins Center, Erie 14035
Colonie, Albany 12205
Colton, Saint Lawrence 13625
Columbiaville, Columbia 12050
Commack, Suffolk 11725
Comstock, Washington 12821
Concord, Erie 14055
Conesus, Livingston 14435
Conewango Valley, Cattaraugus 14726
Congers, Rockland 10920
Conklin, Broome 13748
Connelly, Ulster 12417
Constable, Franklin 12926
Constableville, Lewis 13325
Constantia, Oswego 13044
Coopers Plains, Steuben 14827
Cooperstown, Otsego 13326
Copake, Columbia 12516
Copake Falls, Columbia 12517
Copenhagen, Lewis 13626
Copiague, Suffolk 11726
Coram, Suffolk 11727
Corbettsville, Broome 13749
Corfu, Genesee 14036
Corinth, Saratoga 12822
Corning, Steuben 14831
Cornwall, Orange 12518
Cornwall On Hudson, Orange 12520
Cornwallville, Greene 12418
Corona, Queens 11368
Cortland, Cortland 13045
Cortlandt Manor, Westchester 10567
Cossayuna, Washington 12823
Cottekill, Ulster 12419
Cowlesville, Wyoming 14037
Coxsackie, Greene 12051
Cragsmoor, Ulster 12420
Cranberry Lake, Saint Lawrence 12927
Craryville, Columbia 12521
Crittenden, Erie 14038
Croghan, Lewis 13327
Crompond, Westchester 10517
Cropseyville, Rensselaer 12052
Cross River, Westchester 10518
Croton Falls, Westchester 10519
CROTON ON HUDSON, Westchester
(See Page 2667)
Crown Point, Essex 12928
Crugers, Westchester 10521
Cuba, Allegany 14727
Cuddebackville, Orange 12729
Cutchogue, Suffolk 11935
Cuyler, Cortland 13158
Dale, Wyoming 14039
Dalton, Livingston 14836
Dannemora, Clinton 12929
Dansville, Livingston 14437
Darien Center, Genesee 14040
Davenport, Delaware 13750
Davenport Center, Delaware 13751
Davis Park, Suffolk 11772
Dayton, Cattaraugus 14041
De Kalb Junction, Saint Lawrence 13630
De Peyster, Saint Lawrence 13633
De Ruyter, Madison 13052
De Witt, Onondaga 13214
Deansboro, Oneida 13328
Deer Park, Suffolk 11729
Deer River, Lewis 13627
Deerfield, Oneida 13502
Deferiet, Jefferson 13628
Degrasse, Saint Lawrence 13684
Delancey, Delaware 13752
Delanson, Schenectady 12053
Delevan, Cattaraugus 14042
Delhi, Delaware 13753
Delmar, Albany 12054
Delphi Falls, Onondaga 13051
Denmark, Lewis 13631
Denver, Delaware 12421
Depauville, Jefferson 13632
Depew, Erie 14043
Deposit, Broome 13754
Derby, Erie 14047
Dewittville, Chautauqua 14728
Dexter, Jefferson 13634
Diamond Point, Warren 12824
Dickinson Center, Franklin 12930
Dix Hills, Suffolk 11746
Dobbs Ferry, Westchester 10522
Dolgeville, Herkimer 13329
Dormansville, Albany 12055
Douglaston
(See Little Neck)
Dover Plains, Dutchess 12522
Downsville, Delaware 13755
Dresden, Yates 14441
Dryden, Tompkins 13053
Duanesburg, Schenectady 12056
Dundee, Yates 14837
Dunkirk, Chautauqua 14048
Dunkirk, Chautauqua 14166
Durham, Greene 12422
Durhamville, Oneida 13054
E Atlantic Beach, Nassau 11561
E Yaphank, Suffolk 11967
Eagle Bay, Herkimer 13331
Eagle Bridge, Rensselaer 12057
Eagle Harbor, Orleans 14411
Earlton, Greene 12058
Earlville, Chenango 13332
East Amherst, Erie 14051
East Atlantic Beach, Nassau 11561
East Aurora, Erie 14052
East Berne, Albany 12059
East Bethany, Genesee 14054
East Bloomfield, Ontario 14443
East Branch, Delaware 13756
East Chatham, Columbia 12060

East Concord, Erie 14055
East Durham, Greene 12423
EAST ELMHURST, Queens
(See Page 2667)
East Fishkill, Dutchess 12533
East Freetown, Cortland 13040
East Greenbush, Rensselaer 12061
East Greenwich, Washington 12865
East Hampton, Suffolk 11937
East Homer, Cortland 13056
East Homer, Cortland 13158
East Islip, Suffolk 11730
East Jewett, Greene 12424
East Marion, Suffolk 11939
East Meadow, Nassau 11554
East Meredith, Delaware 13757
East Moriches, Suffolk 11940
East Nassau, Rensselaer 12062
East Northport, Suffolk 11731
East Norwich, Nassau 11732
East Otto, Cattaraugus 14729
East Palmyra, Wayne 14513
East Patchogue, Suffolk 11772
East Pembroke, Genesee 14056
East Pharsalia, Chenango 13758
East Quogue, Suffolk 11942
East Randolph, Cattaraugus 14730
East Rochester, Monroe 14445
East Rockaway, Nassau 11518
East Schodack, Rensselaer 12063
East Setauket, Suffolk 11733
East Springfield, Otsego 13333
East Syracuse, Onondaga 13057
East Williamson, Wayne 14449
East Williston, Nassau 11596
East Windham, Greene 12439
East Worcester, Otsego 12064
East Yaphank, Suffolk 11967
Eastchester, Westchester 10707
Eastchester, Westchester 10709
Eastport, Suffolk 11941
Eaton, Madison 13334
Eddyville, Ulster 12401
Eden, Erie 14057
Edgemere, Queens 11690
Edgewood, Suffolk 11717
Edmeston, Otsego 13335
Edwards, Saint Lawrence 13635
Eggertsville, Erie 14226
Elba, Genesee 14058
Elbridge, Onondaga 13060
Eldred, Sullivan 12732
Elizabethtown, Essex 12932
Elizaville, Columbia 12523
Elka Park, Greene 12427
Ellenburg, Clinton 12933
Ellenburg Center, Clinton 12934
Ellenburg Depot, Clinton 12935
Ellenville, Ulster 12428
Ellicottville, Cattaraugus 14731
Ellington, Chautauqua 14732
Ellisburg, Jefferson 13636
Elma, Erie 14059
ELMHURST, Queens
(See Page 2667)
ELMIRA, Chemung
(See Page 2667)
Elmira Heights, Chemung 14903
Elmira Hgts, Chemung 14903
Elmont, Nassau 11003
Elmsford, Westchester 10523
Elwood, Suffolk 11731
ENDICOTT, Broome
(See Page 2668)
Endwell, Broome 13760
Endwell, Broome 13762
Erieville, Madison 13061
Erin, Chemung 14838
Esopus, Ulster 12429
Esperance, Montgomery 12066
Essex, Essex 12936
Etna, Tompkins 13062
Evans Mills, Jefferson 13637
Fabius, Onondaga 13063
Fair Harbor, Suffolk 11706

Fair Haven, Cayuga 13064
Fairport, Monroe 14450
Falconer, Chautauqua 14733
Fallsburg, Sullivan 12733
Fancher, Orleans 14452
FAR ROCKAWAY, Queens
(See Page 2669)
Farmersville Station, Cattaraugus 14060
Farmingdale, Nassau 11735
Farmington, Ontario 14425
Farmingville, Suffolk 11738
Farnham, Erie 14061
Fayette, Seneca 13065
Fayetteville, Onondaga 13066
Felts Mills, Jefferson 13638
Ferndale, Sullivan 12734
Feura Bush, Albany 12067
Fillmore, Allegany 14735
Findley Lake, Chautauqua 14736
Fine, Saint Lawrence 13639
Fineview, Jefferson 13640
Fire Island Pines, Suffolk 11782
Fishers, Ontario 14453
Fishers Island, Suffolk 06390
Fishers Landing, Jefferson 13641
Fishkill, Dutchess 12524
Fishs Eddy, Delaware 13774
Flanders, Suffolk 11901
Fleetwood, Westchester 10552
Fleischmanns, Delaware 12430
FLORAL PARK, Nassau
(See Page 2670)
Florida, Orange 10921
FLUSHING, Queens
(See Page 2670)
Fly Creek, Otsego 13337
Fonda, Montgomery 12068
Forest Hills, Queens 11375
Forestburgh, Sullivan 12777
Forestport, Oneida 13338
Forestville, Chautauqua 14062
Fort Ann, Washington 12827
Fort Covington, Franklin 12937
Fort Drum, Jefferson 13602
Fort Drum, Jefferson 13603
Fort Edward, Washington 12828
Fort Hamilton, Kings 11252
Fort Hunter, Montgomery 12069
Fort Jackson, Saint Lawrence 12965
Fort Johnson, Montgomery 12070
Fort Montgomery, Orange 10922
Fort Plain, Montgomery 13339
Fort Salonga, Suffolk 11768
Fort Tilden, Queens 11695
Fort Totten, Queens 11359
Frankfort, Herkimer 13340
Franklin, Delaware 13775
Franklin, Delaware 13846
Franklin Springs, Oneida 13341
Franklin Square, Nassau 11010
Franklinville, Cattaraugus 14737
Fredonia, Chautauqua 14063
Freedom, Cattaraugus 14065
Freehold, Greene 12431
Freeport, Nassau 11520
Freeville, Tompkins 13068
Fremont Center, Sullivan 12736
FRESH MEADOWS, Queens
(See Page 2671)
Frewsburg, Chautauqua 14738
Friendship, Allegany 14739
Frontenac, Jefferson 13624
Fulton, Oswego 13069
Fultonham, Schoharie 12071
Fultonville, Montgomery 12016
Fultonville, Montgomery 12072
Gabriels, Franklin 12939
Gainesville, Wyoming 14066
Gallupville, Schoharie 12073
Galway, Saratoga 12074
Gansevoort, Saratoga 12831
GARDEN CITY, Nassau
(See Page 2671)
Garden City Park, Nassau 11040

Garden City South, Nassau 11530
Gardiner, Ulster 12525
Garnerville, Rockland 10923
Garrattsville, Otsego 13342
Garrison, Putnam 10524
Gasport, Niagara 14067
Gates
(See Rochester)
Geneseo, Livingston 14454
Geneva, Ontario 14456
Genoa, Cayuga 13071
Georgetown, Madison 13072
Germantown, Columbia 12526
Gerry, Chautauqua 14740
Getzville, Erie 14068
Ghent, Columbia 12075
Gilbertsville, Otsego 13776
Gilboa, Schoharie 12076
Gilgo Beach, Suffolk 11702
Glasco, Ulster 12432
Glen Aubrey, Broome 13777
Glen Cove, Nassau 11542
Glen Head, Nassau 11545
Glen Oaks, Queens 11004
Glen Park, Jefferson 13601
Glen Spey, Sullivan 12737
Glen Wild, Sullivan 12738
Glendale, Queens 11385
Glenfield, Lewis 13312
Glenfield, Lewis 13343
Glenford, Ulster 12433
Glenham, Dutchess 12527
Glenmont, Albany 12077
Glens Falls, Warren 12801
Glens Falls, Saratoga 12803
Glenville
(See Schenectady)
Glenwood, Erie 14069
Glenwood Landing, Nassau 11547
Gloversville, Fulton 12078
Godeffroy, Orange 12729
Goldens Bridge, Westchester 10526
Gorham, Ontario 14461
Goshen, Orange 10924
Gouverneur, Saint Lawrence 13642
Gowanda, Cattaraugus 14070
Grafton, Rensselaer 12082
Grahamsville, Sullivan 12740
Grand Gorge, Delaware 12434
Grand Island, Erie 14072
Grandview On Hudson, Rockland 10960
Granite Springs, Westchester 10527
Granville, Washington 12832
Great Bend, Jefferson 13643
GREAT NECK, Nassau
(See Page 2671)
Great Neck Plaza, Nassau 11021
Great River, Suffolk 11739
Great Valley, Cattaraugus 14741
Greece
(See Rochester)
Green Island, Albany 12183
Greene, Chenango 13778
Greenfield Center, Saratoga 12833
Greenfield Park, Ulster 12435
Greenhurst, Chautauqua 14742
Greenlawn, Suffolk 11740
Greenport, Suffolk 11944
Greenvale, Nassau 11548
Greenville, Greene 12083
Greenwich, Washington 12834
Greenwood, Steuben 14839
Greenwood Lake, Orange 10925
Greig, Lewis 13345
Grenell, Jefferson 13624
Groton, Tompkins 13073
Groveland, Livingston 14462
Groveland, Livingston 14545
Guilderland, Albany 12084
Guilderland Center, Albany 12085
Guilford, Chenango 13780
Hadley, Saratoga 12835
Hagaman, Montgomery 12086

Hague, Warren 12836
Hailesboro, Saint Lawrence 13645
Haines Falls, Greene 12436
Halcott Center, Delaware 12430
Halcottsville, Delaware 12438
Halesite, Suffolk 11743
Hall, Ontario 14463
Hamburg, Erie 14075
Hamden, Delaware 13782
Hamilton, Madison 13346
Hamlin, Monroe 14464
Hammond, Saint Lawrence 13646
Hammondsport, Steuben 14840
Hampton, Washington 12837
Hampton Bays, Suffolk 11946
Hancock, Delaware 13783
Hankins, Sullivan 12741
Hannacroix, Greene 12087
Hannawa Falls, Saint Lawrence 13647
Hannibal, Oswego 13074
Harford, Cortland 13784
Harford Mills, Tioga 13835
Harpersfield, Delaware 13786
Harpursville, Broome 13787
Harpursville, Broome 13826
Harriman, Orange 10926
Harris, Sullivan 12742
Harrison, Westchester 10528
Harrisville, Lewis 13648
Hartford, Washington 12838
Hartsdale, Westchester 10530
Hartwick, Otsego 13348
Hartwick Seminary, Otsego 13326
Hastings, Oswego 13076
Hastings On Hudson, Westchester 10706
Hauppauge, Suffolk 11749
Hauppauge, Suffolk 11788
Haverstraw, Rockland 10927
Hawthorne, Westchester 10532
Hayt Corners, Seneca 14521
Heathcote, Westchester 10583
Hector, Schuyler 14841
Helena, Saint Lawrence 13649
Hemlock, Livingston 14466
HEMPSTEAD, Nassau
(See Page 2672)
Henderson, Jefferson 13650
Henderson Harbor, Jefferson 13651
Henrietta, Monroe 14467
Hensonville, Greene 12439
Herkimer, Herkimer 13350
Hermon, Saint Lawrence 13652
Heuvelton, Saint Lawrence 13654
Hewlett, Nassau 11557
HICKSVILLE, Nassau
(See Page 2673)
High Falls, Ulster 12440
Highland, Ulster 12528
Highland Falls, Orange 10928
Highland Lake, Sullivan 12743
Highland Mills, Orange 10930
Highmount, Ulster 12441
Hillburn, Rockland 10931
Hillsdale, Columbia 12529
Hillside Manor, Nassau 11040
Hilton, Monroe 14468
Himrod, Yates 14842
Hinckley, Oneida 13352
Hinsdale, Cattaraugus 14743
Hobart, Delaware 13788
Hoffmeister, Hamilton 13353
Hogansburg, Franklin 13655
Holbrook, Suffolk 11741
Holland, Erie 14080
Holland Patent, Oneida 13354
Holley, Orleans 14470
Hollis, Queens 11423
Hollis Hills, Queens 11364
Hollowville, Columbia 12530
Holmes, Dutchess 12531
Holtsville, Suffolk 00501
Homer, Cortland 13077
Honeoye, Ontario 14471

Honeoye Falls, Monroe 14472
Hoosick, Rensselaer 12089
Hoosick Falls, Rensselaer 12090
Hopewell, Dutchess 12533
Hopewell Junction, Dutchess 12533
Hopkinton, Saint Lawrence 12965
Hornell, Steuben 14843
Horseheads, Chemung 14845
Hortonville, Sullivan 12745
Houghton, Allegany 14744
Howard Beach, Queens 11414
Howells, Orange 10932
Howes Cave, Schoharie 12092
Hubbardsville, Madison 13355
Hudson, Columbia 12534
Hudson Falls, Washington 12839
Hughsonville, Dutchess 12537
Huguenot, Orange 12746
Hulberton, Orleans 14470
Huletts Landing, Washington 12841
Hume, Allegany 14745
Hunt, Livingston 14846
Hunter, Greene 12442
Huntington, Suffolk 11743
Huntington Station, Suffolk 11746
Hurley, Ulster 12443
Hurleyville, Sullivan 12747
Hyde Park, Dutchess 12538
Ilion, Herkimer 13357
Indian Lake, Hamilton 12842
Industry, Monroe 14543
Inlet, Hamilton 13360
Interlaken, Seneca 14847
Inwood, Nassau 11096
Ionia, Ontario 14475
Irondequoit
(See Rochester)
Irving, Chautauqua 14081
Irvington, Westchester 10533
Ischua, Cattaraugus 14743
Island Park, Nassau 11558
Islandia, Suffolk 11749
Islip, Suffolk 11751
Islip Terrace, Suffolk 11752
ITHACA, Tompkins
(See Page 2674)
Jackson Heights, Queens 11372
Jacksonville, Tompkins 14854
JAMAICA, Queens
(See Page 2675)
Jamesport, Suffolk 11947
JAMESTOWN, Chautauqua
(See Page 2677)
Jamesville, Onondaga 13078
Jasper, Steuben 14855
Java Center, Wyoming 14082
Java Village, Wyoming 14083
Jay, Essex 12941
Jefferson, Schoharie 12093
Jefferson Valley, Westchester 10535
Jeffersonville, Sullivan 12748
Jericho, Nassau 11753
Jewett, Greene 12444
Jf Kennedy Ap, Queens 11430
John F Kennedy Airport, Queens 11430
Johnsburg, Warren 12843
Johnson, Orange 10933
Johnson City, Broome 13790
Johnsonville, Rensselaer 12094
Johnstown, Fulton 12095
Jordan, Onondaga 13080
Jordanville, Herkimer 13361
Kanona, Steuben 14856
Kaser, Rockland 10952
Katonah, Westchester 10536
Kattskill Bay, Warren 12844
Kauneonga Lake, Sullivan 12749
Keene, Essex 12942
Keene Valley, Essex 12943
KEESEVILLE, Clinton
(See Page 2677)
Kendall, Orleans 14476

Kenmore
(See Buffalo)
Kennedy, Chautauqua 14747
Kenoza Lake, Sullivan 12750
Kent, Orleans 14477
Kent Cliffs, Putnam 10512
Kent Lakes, Putnam 10512
Kerhonkson, Ulster 12446
Keuka Park, Yates 14478
Kew Gardens, Queens 11415
Kew Gardens, Queens 11424
Kew Gardens Hills, Queens 11367
Kiamesha Lake, Sullivan 12751
Kill Buck, Cattaraugus 14748
Killawog, Broome 13794
Kinderhook, Columbia 12106
King Ferry, Cayuga 13081
Kings Park, Suffolk 11754
Kings Point, Nassau 11024
KINGSTON, Ulster
(See Page 2677)
Kirkville, Onondaga 13082
Kirkwood, Broome 13795
Kiryas Joel, Orange 10950
Kismet, Suffolk 11706
Knapp Creek, Cattaraugus 14760
Knickerbocker, New York 10002
Knowlesville, Orleans 14479
Knox, Albany 12107
Knoxboro, Oneida 13362
Krumville, Ulster 12461
La Fargeville, Jefferson 13656
La Fayette, Onondaga 13084
La Guardia Airport, Queens 11371
Lackawanna, Erie 14218
Lacona, Oswego 13083
Lagrangeville, Dutchess 12540
Lake Clear, Franklin 12945
Lake George, Warren 12845
Lake Grove, Suffolk 11755
Lake Hill, Ulster 12448
Lake Huntington, Sullivan 12752
Lake Katrine, Ulster 12449
Lake Lincolndale, Putnam 10541
Lake Luzerne, Warren 12846
Lake Peekskill, Putnam 10537
Lake Placid, Essex 12946
Lake Pleasant, Hamilton 12108
Lake Ronkonkoma, Suffolk 11779
Lake Success, Nassau 11020
Lake View, Erie 14085
Lakemont, Yates 14857
Lakeville, Livingston 14480
Lakewood, Chautauqua 14750
Lancaster, Erie 14086
Lanesville, Greene 12450
Lansing, Tompkins 14882
Larchmont, Westchester 10538
Latham, Albany 12110
Latham, Albany 12128
Laurel, Suffolk 11948
Laurelton, Queens 11413
Laurens, Otsego 13796
Lawrence, Nassau 11559
Lawrenceville, Saint Lawrence 12949
Lawtons, Erie 14091
Lawyersville, Schoharie 12043
Le Roy, Genesee 14482
Lebanon, Chenango 13332
Lebanon Springs, Columbia 12125
Lee Center, Oneida 13363
Leeds, Greene 12451
Leicester, Livingston 14481
Leon, Cattaraugus 14751
Leonardsville, Madison 13364
Levittown, Nassau 11756
Lew Beach, Sullivan 12758
Lewis, Essex 12950
Lewiston, Niagara 14092
Lexington, Greene 12452
Liberty, Sullivan 12754
Lido Beach, Nassau 11561
Lily Dale, Chautauqua 14752
Lima, Livingston 14485
Limerick, Jefferson 13657

Limestone, Cattaraugus 14753
Lincolndale, Westchester 10540
Lindenhurst, Suffolk 11757
Lindley, Steuben 14858
Linwood, Genesee 14486
Lisbon, Saint Lawrence 13658
Lisle, Broome 13797
Little Falls, Herkimer 13365
Little Genesee, Allegany 14754
LITTLE NECK, Queens (See Page 2678)
Little Valley, Cattaraugus 14755
Little York, Cortland 13087
LIVERPOOL, Onondaga (See Page 2678)
Livingston, Columbia 12541
Livingston Manor, Sullivan 12758
Livonia, Livingston 14487
Livonia Center, Livingston 14488
Lloyd Harbor, Suffolk 11743
Loch Sheldrake, Sullivan 12759
Locke, Cayuga 13092
LOCKPORT, Niagara (See Page 2680)
Lockwood, Tioga 14859
Locust Valley, Nassau 11560
Lodi, Seneca 14860
Loehmanns Plaza, Monroe 14618
Long Beach, Nassau 11561
Long Eddy, Sullivan 12760
LONG ISLAND CITY, Queens (See Page 2681)
Long Lake, Hamilton 12847
Loon Lake, Franklin 12989
Lorraine, Jefferson 13659
Loudonville, Albany 12211
Lowman, Chemung 14861
Lowville, Lewis 13367
Lycoming, Oswego 13093
Lynbrook, Nassau 11563
Lyndonville, Orleans 14098
LYON MOUNTAIN, Clinton (See Page 2681)
Lyons, Wayne 14489
Lyons Falls, Lewis 13368
Lysander, Onondaga 13027
Mac Dougall, Seneca 14541
Macedon, Wayne 14502
Machias, Cattaraugus 14101
Madison, Madison 13402
Madrid, Saint Lawrence 13660
Mahopac, Putnam 10541
Mahopac Falls, Putnam 10542
Maine, Broome 13802
Malba, Queens 11357
Malden Bridge, Columbia 12115
Malden On Hudson, Ulster 12453
Mallory, Oswego 13103
Malone, Franklin 12953
Malta, Saratoga 12020
Malverne, Nassau 11565
Mamaroneck, Westchester 10543
Manchester, Ontario 14504
Manhasset, Nassau 11030
Manhasset Hills, Nassau 11040
Manlius, Onondaga 13104
Mannsville, Jefferson 13661
Manorville, Suffolk 11949
Maple Springs, Chautauqua 14756
Maple View, Oswego 13107
Maplecrest, Greene 12454
Marathon, Cortland 13803
Marcellus, Onondaga 13108
Marcy, Oneida 13403
Margaretville, Delaware 12455
Marietta, Onondaga 13110
Marilla, Erie 14102
Marion, Wayne 14505
Marlboro, Ulster 12542
Martinsburg, Lewis 13404
Martville, Cayuga 13111
Maryknoll, Westchester 10545
Maryland, Otsego 12116
Masonville, Delaware 13804
Maspeth, Queens 11378
Massapequa, Nassau 11758
Massapequa Park, Nassau 11762
Massawepie, Franklin 12986
Massena, Saint Lawrence 13662
Mastic, Suffolk 11950
Mastic Beach, Suffolk 11951
Mattituck, Suffolk 11952
Mattydale, Onondaga 13211
Maybrook, Orange 12543
Mayfield, Fulton 12117
Mayville, Chautauqua 14757
Mc Connellsville, Oneida 13401
Mc Donough, Chenango 13801
Mc Graw, Cortland 13101
Mc Lean, Tompkins 13102
Meacham, Nassau 11003
Mechanicville, Saratoga 12118
Mecklenburg, Schuyler 14863
Medford, Suffolk 11763
Medina, Orleans 14103
Medusa, Albany 12120
Mellenville, Columbia 12544
Melrose, Rensselaer 12121
Melville, Suffolk 11747
Memphis, Onondaga 13112
Menands, Albany 12204
Mendon, Monroe 14506
Meredith, Delaware 13753
Meridale, Delaware 13806
Meridian, Cayuga 13113
Merrick, Nassau 11566
Merrill, Clinton 12955
Mexico, Oswego 13114
Mid Hudson, Orange 12555
Middle Falls, Washington 12848
Middle Granville, Washington 12849
Middle Grove, Saratoga 12850
Middle Island, Suffolk 11953
Middle Village, Queens 11379
Middleburgh, Schoharie 12122
Middleport, Niagara 14105
Middlesex, Yates 14507
MIDDLETOWN, Orange (See Page 2681)
Middleville, Herkimer 13406
Milan, Dutchess 12571
Milford, Otsego 13807
Mill Neck, Nassau 11765
Millbrook, Dutchess 12545
Miller Place, Suffolk 11764
Millerton, Dutchess 12546
Millport, Chemung 14864
Millwood, Westchester 10546
Milton, Ulster 12547
Mineola, Nassau 11501
Minerva, Essex 12851
Minetto, Oswego 13115
Mineville, Essex 12956
Minoa, Onondaga 13116
Model City, Niagara 14107
Modena, Ulster 12548
Mohawk, Herkimer 13407
Mohegan Lake, Westchester 10547
Moira, Franklin 12957
Mongaup Valley, Sullivan 12762
MONROE, Orange (See Page 2682)
Monsey, Rockland 10952
Montauk, Suffolk 11954
Montebello, Rockland 10901
Montezuma, Cayuga 13117
Montgomery, Orange 12549
Monticello, Sullivan 12701
Monticello, Sullivan 12777
Montour Falls, Schuyler 14865
Montrose, Westchester 10548
Mooers, Clinton 12958
Mooers Forks, Clinton 12959
Moravia, Cayuga 13118
Moriah, Essex 12960
Moriah Center, Essex 12961
Moriches, Suffolk 11955
Morris, Otsego 13808
Morrisonville, Clinton 12962
Morristown, Saint Lawrence 13664
Morrisville, Madison 13408
Morton, Monroe 14508
Mottville, Onondaga 13119
Mount Kisco, Westchester 10549
Mount Marion, Ulster 12456
Mount Morris, Livingston 14510
Mount Sinai, Suffolk 11766
Mount Tremper, Ulster 12457
Mount Upton, Chenango 13809
MOUNT VERNON, Westchester (See Page 2683)
Mount Vision, Otsego 13810
Mountain Dale, Sullivan 12763
Mountainville, Orange 10953
Mumford, Monroe 14511
Munnsville, Madison 13409
Murray Isle, Jefferson 13624
N Baldwin, Nassau 11510
N Merrick, Nassau 11566
N White Plains, Westchester 10603
Nanuet, Rockland 10954
Napanoch, Ulster 12458
Naples, Ontario 14512
Narrowsburg, Sullivan 12764
Nassau, Rensselaer 12123
Natural Bridge, Jefferson 13665
Nedrow, Onondaga 13120
Nelliston, Montgomery 13410
Nelsonville, Putnam 10516
Neponsit, Queens 11694
Nesconset, Suffolk 11767
Neversink, Sullivan 12765
New Baltimore, Greene 12124
New Berlin, Chenango 13411
New City, Rockland 10956
New Hamburg, Dutchess 12590
New Hampton, Orange 10958
New Hartford, Oneida 13413
New Haven, Oswego 13121
NEW HYDE PARK, Nassau (See Page 2684)
New Kingston, Delaware 12459
New Lebanon, Columbia 12125
New Lisbon, Otsego 13415
New Milford, Orange 10959
New Paltz, Ulster 12561
NEW ROCHELLE, Westchester (See Page 2685)
New Russia, Essex 12964
New Square, Rockland 10977
New Suffolk, Suffolk 11956
New Windsor, Orange 12553
New Woodstock, Madison 13122
NEW YORK, New York (See Page 2686)
New York City, New York 10259
New York Mills, Oneida 13417
Newark, Wayne 14513
Newark Valley, Tioga 13811
NEWBURGH, Orange (See Page 2689)
NEWCOMB, Essex (See Page 2691)
Newfane, Niagara 14108
Newfield, Tompkins 14867
Newport, Herkimer 13416
Newton Falls, Saint Lawrence 13666
Newtonville, Albany 12110
Newtonville, Albany 12128
NIAGARA FALLS, Niagara (See Page 2691)
Niagara University, Niagara 14109
Nichols, Tioga 13812
Nicholville, Saint Lawrence 12965
Nineveh, Broome 13813
Niobe, Chautauqua 14758
Niskayuna, Schenectady 12309
Niverville, Columbia 12130
Norfolk, Saint Lawrence 13667
North Babylon, Suffolk 11703
North Baldwin, Nassau 11510
North Bangor, Franklin 12966
North Bay, Oneida 13123
North Bellmore, Nassau 11710
North Blenheim, Schoharie 12131
North Boston, Erie 14110
North Branch, Sullivan 12766
North Brookfield, Madison 13418
North Castle, Westchester 10504
North Chatham, Columbia 12132
North Chili, Monroe 14514
North Cohocton, Steuben 14808
North Collins, Erie 14111
North Creek, Warren 12853
North Evans, Erie 14112
North Granville, Washington 12854
North Greece, Monroe 14515
North Hills, Nassau 11040
North Hoosick, Rensselaer 12133
North Hornell, Steuben 14843
North Hudson, Essex 12855
North Java, Wyoming 14113
North Lawrence, Saint Lawrence 12967
North Massapequa, Nassau 11758
North Merrick, Nassau 11566
North New Hyde Park (See New Hyde Park)
North Norwich, Chenango 13814
North Pitcher, Chenango 13124
North River, Warren 12856
North Rose, Wayne 14516
North Salem, Westchester 10560
North Syracuse, Onondaga 13212
North Tarrytown, Westchester 10591
North Tonawanda, Niagara 14120
Northport, Suffolk 11768
Northville, Fulton 12134
Norton Hill, Greene 12083
Norwich, Chenango 13815
Norwood, Saint Lawrence 13668
Nunda, Livingston 14517
Nyack, Rockland 10960
Oak Beach, Suffolk 11702
Oak Hill, Greene 12460
Oak Island, Suffolk 11702
Oakdale, Suffolk 11769
Oakfield, Genesee 14125
Oakland Gardens, Queens 11364
Oaks Corners, Ontario 14518
Obernburg, Sullivan 12767
Ocean Beach, Suffolk 11770
Oceanside, Nassau 11572
Odessa, Schuyler 14869
Ogdensburg, Saint Lawrence 13669
Ohio, Herkimer 13324
Olcott, Niagara 14126
Old Bethpage, Nassau 11804
Old Chatham, Columbia 12136
Old Forge, Herkimer 13420
Old Westbury, Nassau 11568
Olean, Cattaraugus 14760
Olivebridge, Ulster 12461
Oliverea, Ulster 12410
Olmstedville, Essex 12857
Onchiota, Franklin 12989
Oneida, Madison 13421
Oneonta, Otsego 13820
Ontario, Wayne 14519
Ontario Center, Wayne 14520
Orangeburg, Rockland 10962
Orchard Park, Erie 14127
Orient, Suffolk 11957
Oriskany, Oneida 13424
Oriskany Falls, Oneida 13425
Orwell, Oswego 13426
Ossining, Westchester 10562
Oswegatchie, Saint Lawrence 13670
Oswego, Oswego 13126
Otego, Otsego 13825
Otisville, Orange 10963
Otto, Cattaraugus 14766
Ouaquaga, Broome 13826
Ovid, Seneca 14521
Owasco, Cayuga 13021
Owego, Tioga 13827
Owls Head, Franklin 12969
Oxbow, Jefferson 13608
Oxbow, Jefferson 13671
Oxford, Chenango 13830
Oyster Bay, Nassau 11771
OZONE PARK, Queens (See Page 2692)
Painted Post, Steuben 14870
Palatine Bridge, Montgomery 13428
Palenville, Greene 12463
Palisades, Rockland 10964
Palmyra, Wayne 14522
Panama, Chautauqua 14767
Panorama, Monroe 14625
Paradox, Essex 12858
Paris, Oneida 13456
Parish, Oswego 13131
Parishville, Saint Lawrence 13672
Parksville, Sullivan 12768
Patchogue, Suffolk 11772
Patterson, Putnam 12563
Pattersonville, Schenectady 12137
Paul Smiths, Franklin 12970
Pavilion, Genesee 14525
Pawling, Dutchess 12564
Pearl River, Rockland 10965
Peck Slip, New York 10038
Peconic, Suffolk 11958
Peekskill, Westchester 10566
Pelham, Westchester 10803
Penfield, Monroe 14526
Penn Yan, Yates 14527
Pennellville, Oswego 13132
Perkinsville, Steuben 14529
Perry, Wyoming 14530
Perrysburg, Cattaraugus 14129
Perryville, Madison 13032
Peru, Clinton 12972
Peterboro, Madison 13134
Petersburg, Rensselaer 12138
Petersburgh, Rensselaer 12138
Phelps, Ontario 14532
Philadelphia, Jefferson 13673
Phillipsport, Sullivan 12769
Philmont, Columbia 12565
Phoenicia, Ulster 12464
Phoenix, Oswego 13135
Piercefield, Saint Lawrence 12973
Piermont, Rockland 10968
Pierrepont Manor, Jefferson 13674
Piffard, Livingston 14533
Pike, Wyoming 14130
Pilot Knob, Warren 12844
Pine Bush, Orange 12566
Pine City, Chemung 14871
Pine Hill, Ulster 12465
Pine Island, Orange 10969
Pine Plains, Dutchess 12567
Pine Valley, Chemung 14872
Piseco, Hamilton 12139
Pitcher, Chenango 13136
Pittsford, Monroe 14534
Plainview, Nassau 11803
Plainville, Onondaga 13137
Plandome, Nassau 11030
Plattekill, Ulster 12568
PLATTSBURGH, Clinton (See Page 2692)
Pleasant Valley, Dutchess 12569
Pleasantville, Westchester 10570
Plessis, Jefferson 13675
Plymouth, Chenango 13832
Poestenkill, Rensselaer 12140
Point Lookout, Nassau 11569
Point O Woods, Suffolk 11706
Point Vivian, Jefferson 13607
Poland, Herkimer 13431
Pomona, Rockland 10970
Pompey, Onondaga 13138
Pond Eddy, Sullivan 12770
Poolville, Chenango 13332
Poplar Ridge, Cayuga 13139
Port Byron, Cayuga 13140
Port Chester, Westchester 10573
Port Crane, Broome 13833
Port Ewen, Ulster 12466
Port Gibson, Ontario 14537
Port Henry, Essex 12974
Port Jefferson, Suffolk 11777
Port Jefferson Station, Suffolk 11776
Port Jervis, Orange 12771
Port Jervis, Sullivan 12785
Port Kent, Essex 12975
Port Leyden, Lewis 13433
Port Washington, Nassau 11050
Portageville, Wyoming 14536
Porter Corners, Saratoga 12859
Portland, Chautauqua 14769
Portlandville, Otsego 13834
Portville, Cattaraugus 14770
Potsdam, Saint Lawrence 13676
Pottersville, Warren 12860
POUGHKEEPSIE, Dutchess (See Page 2693)
Poughquag, Dutchess 12570
Pound Ridge, Westchester 10576
Pratts Hollow, Madison 13409
Prattsburgh, Steuben 14873
Prattsville, Greene 12468
Preble, Cortland 13141
Preston Hollow, Albany 12469
Prince, New York 10012
Prospect, Oneida 13435
Pulaski, Oswego 13142
Pulteney, Steuben 14874
Pultneyville, Wayne 14538
Purchase, Westchester 10577
Purdys, Westchester 10578
Purling, Greene 12470
Putnam Station, Washington 12861
Putnam Valley, Putnam 10579
Pyrites, Saint Lawrence 13677
Quaker Street, Schenectady 12141
QUEENS VILLAGE, Queens (See Page 2695)
Queensbury, Warren 12801
Queensbury, Warren 12804
Quogue, Suffolk 11959
Rainbow Lake, Franklin 12976
Randolph, Cattaraugus 14772
Ransomville, Niagara 14131
Raquette Lake, Hamilton 13436
Ravena, Albany 12143
Ray Brook, Essex 12977
Raymondville, Saint Lawrence 13678
Reading Center, Schuyler 14876
Red Creek, Wayne 13143
Red Hook, Dutchess 12504
Red Hook, Dutchess 12507
Redfield, Oswego 13437
Redford, Clinton 12978
Redwood, Jefferson 13679
Rego Park, Queens 11374
Remsen, Oneida 13438
Remsenburg, Suffolk 11960
Rensselaer, Rensselaer 12144
Rensselaer Falls, Saint Lawrence 13680
Rensselaerville, Albany 12147
Retsof, Livingston 14539
Rexford, Saratoga 12148
Rexville, Steuben 14877
Rhinebeck, Dutchess 12572
Rhinecliff, Dutchess 12574
Richburg, Allegany 14774
Richfield Springs, Otsego 13439
Richford, Tioga 13835
Richland, Oswego 13144
Richmond Hill, Queens 11418
Richmondville, Schoharie 12149
Richville, Saint Lawrence 13681
Ridge, Suffolk 11961
Ridgemont, Monroe 14626
RIDGEWOOD, Queens (See Page 2696)
Rifton, Ulster 12471
Riparius, Warren 12862
Ripley, Chautauqua 14775
Riverhead, Suffolk 11901
Rochdale Village, Queens 11434
ROCHESTER, Monroe (See Page 2696)

Rock City Falls, Saratoga 12863
Rock Glen, Wyoming 14550
Rock Hill, Sullivan 12775
Rock Stream, Schuyler 14878
Rock Tavern, Orange 12575
Rockaway Beach, Queens 11693
Rockaway Park, Queens 11694
Rockaway Point, Queens 11697
ROCKVILLE CENTRE, Nassau (See Page 2704)
Rocky Point, Suffolk 11778
Rodman, Jefferson 13682
Roessleville, Albany 12205
ROME, Oneida (See Page 2705)
Romulus, Seneca 14541
Ronkonkoma, Suffolk 11749
Ronkonkoma, Suffolk 11779
Roosevelt, Nassau 11575
Roosevelt Island, New York 10044
Rooseveltown, Saint Lawrence 13683
Roscoe, Sullivan 12776
Rose, Wayne 14542
Roseboom, Otsego 13450
Rosedale, Queens 11413
Rosedale, Queens 11422
Rosendale, Ulster 12472
Roslyn, Nassau 11576
Roslyn Heights, Nassau 11577
Rossburg, Wyoming 14536
Rotterdam, Schenectady 12306
Rotterdam Junction, Schenectady 12150
Round Lake, Saratoga 12151
Round Top, Greene 12473
Rouses Point, Clinton 12979
Roxbury, Delaware 12474
Ruby, Ulster 12475
Rush, Monroe 14543
Rushford, Allegany 14777
Rushville, Yates 14544
Russell, Saint Lawrence 13684
Rye, Westchester 10580
Rye Brook, Westchester 10573
S Bloomng Grv, Orange 10914
Sabael, Hamilton 12864
Sackets Harbor, Jefferson 13685
Sag Harbor, Suffolk 11963
Sagaponack, Suffolk 11962
Saint Albans, Queens 11412
Saint Albans, Queens 11413
Saint Bonaventure, Cattaraugus 14778
Saint Huberts, Essex 12943
Saint James, Suffolk 11780
Saint Johnsville, Montgomery 13452
Saint Regis Falls, Franklin 12980
Saint Remy, Ulster 12401
Salamanca, Cattaraugus 14779
Salem, Washington 12865
Salisbury Center, Herkimer 13454
Salisbury Mills, Orange 12577
Salt Point, Dutchess 12578
Saltaire, Suffolk 11706
Sanborn, Niagara 14132
Sand Lake, Rensselaer 12153
Sands Point, Nassau 11050
Sandusky, Cattaraugus 14065
Sandusky, Cattaraugus 14133
Sandy Creek, Oswego 13145
Sangerfield, Oneida 13455
Sanitaria Springs, Broome 13833
Saranac, Clinton 12981
Saranac Lake, Franklin 12983
Saratoga Springs, Saratoga 12866
Sardinia, Erie 14134
Saugerties, Ulster 12477
Sauquoit, Oneida 13456
Savannah, Wayne 13146
Savona, Steuben 14879
Sayville, Suffolk 11782
Scarborough, Westchester 10510
Scarsdale, Westchester 10530
Scarsdale, Westchester 10583
Schaghticoke, Rensselaer 12154
SCHENECTADY, Schenectady (See Page 2705)
Schenevus, Otsego 12155
Schodack Landing, Rensselaer 12156
Schoharie, Schoharie 12157
Schroon Lake, Essex 12870
Schuyler, Herkimer 13340
Schuyler Falls, Clinton 12985
Schuyler Lake, Otsego 13457
Schuylerville, Saratoga 12871
Scio, Allegany 14880
Scipio Center, Cayuga 13147
Scotchtown (See Middletown)
Scotia, Schenectady 12302
Scottsburg, Livingston 14545
Scottsville, Monroe 14546
Sea Cliff, Nassau 11579
Seaford, Nassau 11783
Selden, Suffolk 11784
Selkirk, Albany 12158
Seneca Castle, Ontario 14547
Seneca Falls, Seneca 13148
Setauket, Suffolk 11733
Severance, Essex 12872
Shady, Ulster 12409
Shandaken, Ulster 12480
Sharon Springs, Schoharie 13459
Shelter Island, Suffolk 11964
Shelter Island Heights, Suffolk 11965
Shenorock, Westchester 10587
Sherburne, Chenango 13460
Sheridan, Chautauqua 14135
Sherman, Chautauqua 14781
Sherrill, Oneida 13461
Shinhopple, Delaware 13755
Shirley, Suffolk 11967
Shokan, Ulster 12481
Shoreham, Suffolk 11786
Shortsville, Ontario 14548
Shrub Oak, Westchester 10588
Shushan, Washington 12873
Sidney, Delaware 13838
Sidney Center, Delaware 13839
Siena, Albany 12211
Silver Bay, Warren 12874
Silver Creek, Chautauqua 14136
Silver Lake, Wyoming 14549
Silver Springs, Wyoming 14550
Sinclairville, Chautauqua 14782
Skaneateles, Onondaga 13152
Skaneateles Falls, Onondaga 13153
Slate Hill, Orange 10973
Slaterville Springs, Tompkins 14881
Sleepy Hollow, Westchester 10591
Slingerlands, Albany 12159
Sloan, Erie 14212
Sloansville, Schoharie 12160
Sloatsburg, Rockland 10974
Smallwood, Sullivan 12778
Smith Point, Suffolk 11967
Smithboro, Tioga 13840
Smithtown, Suffolk 11787
Smithtown, Suffolk 11788
Smithville, Jefferson 13605
Smithville Flats, Chenango 13841
Smyrna, Chenango 13464
Snyder (See Buffalo)
Sodus, Wayne 14551
Sodus Center, Wayne 14551
Sodus Point, Wayne 14555
Solsville, Madison 13465
Solvay, Onondaga 13209
Somers, Westchester 10589
Sonyea, Livingston 14556
Sound Beach, Suffolk 11789
South Bethlehem, Albany 12161
South Butler, Wayne 13154
South Byron, Genesee 14557
South Cairo, Greene 12482
South Cheektowaga, Erie 14227
South Colton, Saint Lawrence 13687
South Corning, Steuben 14830
South Dayton, Cattaraugus 14138
South Edmeston, Chenango 13411
South Fallsburg, Sullivan 12779
South Farmingdale, Nassau 11735
South Floral Park, Nassau 11001
South Glens Falls, Saratoga 12803
South Hempstead, Nassau 11550
South Jamesport, Suffolk 11970
South Kortright, Delaware 13842
South Lima, Livingston 14558
South New Berlin, Chenango 13843
South Otselic, Chenango 13155
South Ozone Park, Queens 11420
South Ozone Park, Queens 11436
South Plymouth, Chenango 13844
South Richmond Hill, Queens 11419
South Rutland, Lewis 13626
South Salem, Westchester 10590
South Schodack, Rensselaer 12033
South Setauket, Suffolk 11720
South Wales, Erie 14139
South Westerlo, Greene 12083
SOUTHAMPTON, Suffolk (See Page 2709)
Southfields, Orange 10975
Southold, Suffolk 11971
Sparkill, Rockland 10976
Sparrow Bush, Orange 12780
Sparrowbush, Orange 12780
Speculator, Hamilton 12164
Spencer, Tioga 14883
Spencerport, Monroe 14559
Spencertown, Columbia 12165
Speonk, Suffolk 11972
Sprakers, Montgomery 12166
Spring Brook, Erie 14140
Spring Glen, Ulster 12483
Spring Valley, Rockland 10977
Springfield Center, Otsego 13468
Springfield Gardens, Queens 11413
Springville, Erie 14141
Springwater, Livingston 14560
Staatsburg, Dutchess 12580
Stafford, Genesee 14143
Stamford, Delaware 12167
Stanfordville, Dutchess 12581
Stanley, Ontario 14561
Star Lake, Saint Lawrence 13690
STATEN ISLAND, Richmond (See Page 2710)
Steamburg, Cattaraugus 14783
Stella Niagara, Niagara 14092
STEPHENTOWN, Rensselaer (See Page 2716)
Sterling, Cayuga 13156
Sterling Forest, Orange 10979
Stewart Manor, Nassau 11530
Stillwater, Saratoga 12170
Stittville, Oneida 13469
Stockton, Chautauqua 14784
Stone Ridge, Ulster 12484
Stony Brook, Suffolk 11790
Stony Creek, Warren 12878
Stony Point, Rockland 10980
Stormville, Dutchess 12582
Stottville, Columbia 12172
Stow, Chautauqua 14785
Stratford, Fulton 13470
Strykersville, Wyoming 14145
Stuyvesant, Columbia 12173
Stuyvesant Falls, Columbia 12174
Stuyvesant Plaza, Albany 12203
Suffern, Rockland 10901
Sugar Loaf, Orange 10981
Summit, Schoharie 12175
Summitville, Sullivan 12781
Sundown, Sullivan 12740
Sunnyside, Queens 11104
Surprise, Greene 12176
Swain, Allegany 14884
Swan Lake, Sullivan 12783
Swormville, Erie 14051
Sylvan Beach, Oneida 13157
Syosset, Nassau 11773
SYRACUSE, Onondaga (See Page 2716)
Taberg, Oneida 13471
Taconic Lake, Rensselaer 12138
Taghkanic, Columbia 12521
Tahawus, Essex 12879
Tallman, Rockland 10982
Tannersville, Greene 12424
Tannersville, Greene 12485
Tappan, Rockland 10983
Tarrytown, Westchester 10591
Thendara, Herkimer 13472
Theresa, Jefferson 13691
Thiells, Rockland 10984
Thompson Ridge, Orange 10985
Thompsonville, Sullivan 12784
Thomson, Washington 12834
Thornwood, Westchester 10594
Thous Is Pk, Jefferson 13692
Thousand Island Park, Jefferson 13692
Three Mile Bay, Jefferson 13693
Thurman, Warren 12885
Ticonderoga, Essex 12858
Ticonderoga, Essex 12883
Tillson, Ulster 12486
Tioga Center, Tioga 13845
Tivoli, Dutchess 12583
Tomkins Cove, Rockland 10986
TONAWANDA, Erie (See Page 2721)
Town Of Tonawanda (See Buffalo)
Treadwell, Delaware 13846
Tribes Hill, Montgomery 12177
Trinity, New York 10006
Troupsburg, Steuben 14885
Trout Creek, Delaware 13847
TROY, Rensselaer (See Page 2721)
Trumansburg, Tompkins 14886
Truxton, Cortland 13158
Tuckahoe, Westchester 10707
Tully, Onondaga 13159
Tunnel, Broome 13848
Tupper Lake, Franklin 12986
Turin, Lewis 13473
Tuscarora, Livingston 14510
Tuxedo Park, Orange 10987
Tyrone, Schuyler 14887
Ulster Park, Ulster 12487
Unadilla, Otsego 13849
Union Hill, Wayne 14563
Union Springs, Cayuga 13160
UNIONDALE, Nassau (See Page 2723)
Unionville, Orange 10988
Upper Jay, Essex 12987
Upper Saint Regis, Franklin 12945
Upton, Suffolk 11973
UTICA, Oneida (See Page 2724)
Vails Gate, Orange 12584
Valatie, Columbia 12184
Valhalla, Westchester 10595
Valley Cottage, Rockland 10989
Valley Falls, Rensselaer 12185
VALLEY STREAM, Nassau (See Page 2725)
Valois, Schuyler 14841
Van Buren Bay, Chautauqua 14048
Van Buren Point, Chautauqua 14166
Van Etten, Chemung 14889
Van Hornesville, Herkimer 13475
Varysburg, Wyoming 14167
Venice Center, Cayuga 13147
Verbank, Dutchess 12585
Vermontville, Franklin 12989
Vernon, Oneida 13476
Vernon Center, Oneida 13477
Verona, Oneida 13478
Verona Beach, Oneida 13162
Verplanck, Westchester 10596
Versailles, Cattaraugus 14168
VESTAL, Broome (See Page 2726)
Veterans Administration, Steuben 14810
Victor, Ontario 14564
Victory Mills, Saratoga 12884
Village Of Garden City, Nassau 11530
Voorheesville, Albany 12186
W Amherst, Erie 14228
W Harrison, Westchester 10604
W Windsor, Broome 13865
Waccabuc, Westchester 10597
Waddington, Saint Lawrence 13694
Wadhams, Essex 12993
Wading River, Suffolk 11792
Wadsworth, Livingston 14533
Wainscott, Suffolk 11975
Walden, Orange 12586
Wales Center, Erie 14169
Walker Valley, Ulster 12588
Wall Street, New York 10005
Wallace, Steuben 14809
Wallkill, Ulster 12589
Walton, Delaware 13856
Walworth, Wayne 14568
Wampsville, Madison 13163
Wanakena, Saint Lawrence 13695
Wantagh, Nassau 11793
Wappingers Falls, Dutchess 12590
Warners, Onondaga 13164
Warnerville, Schoharie 12187
Warrensburg, Warren 12885
Warsaw, Wyoming 14569
Warwick, Orange 10990
Washington Mills, Oneida 13479
Washingtonville, Orange 10992
Wassaic, Dutchess 12592
Water Mill, Suffolk 11976
Waterford, Saratoga 12188
Waterloo, Seneca 13165
Waterport, Orleans 14571
WATERTOWN, Jefferson (See Page 2726)
Waterville, Oneida 13480
Watervliet, Albany 12189
Watkins Glen, Schuyler 14891
Wave Crest, Queens 11690
Waverly, Tioga 14892
Wawarsing, Ulster 12489
Wayland, Steuben 14572
Wayne, Schuyler 14893
Webster, Monroe 14580
Webster Crossing, Livingston 14560
Weedsport, Cayuga 13166
Wellesley Island, Jefferson 13640
Wells, Hamilton 12190
Wells Bridge, Otsego 13859
Wellsburg, Chemung 14894
Wellsville, Allegany 14895
West Amherst, Erie 14228
WEST BABYLON, Suffolk (See Page 2727)
West Bangor, Franklin 12966
West Bloomfield, Ontario 14585
West Brentwood, Suffolk 11717
West Burlington, Otsego 13482
West Camp, Ulster 12490
West Charlton, Montgomery 12010
West Chazy, Clinton 12992
West Clarksville, Allegany 14786
West Coxsackie, Greene 12192
West Danby, Tioga 14883
West Davenport, Delaware 13860
West Eaton, Madison 13484
West Edmeston, Madison 13485
West Ellicott, Chautauqua 14701
West Exeter, Herkimer 13491
West Falls, Erie 14170
West Fishkill, Dutchess 12590
West Fulton, Schoharie 12194
West Gilgo Beach, Suffolk 11702
West Harrison, Westchester 10604
West Haverstraw, Rockland 10993
West Hempstead, Nassau 11552
West Henrietta, Monroe 14586
West Hurley, Ulster 12491
West Islip, Suffolk 11795
West Kill, Greene 12492
West Lebanon, Columbia 12195
West Leyden, Lewis 13489
West Monroe, Oswego 13167
West Nyack, Rockland 10994
West Oneonta, Otsego 13861
West Park, Ulster 12493
WEST POINT, Orange (See Page 2727)
West Rush, Monroe 14543
West Sand Lake, Rensselaer 12196
West Sayville, Suffolk 11796
West Seneca (See Buffalo)
West Shokan, Ulster 12494
West Stockholm, Saint Lawrence 13696
West Valley, Cattaraugus 14171
West Windsor, Broome 13865
West Winfield, Herkimer 13491
Westbrookville, Sullivan 12785
Westbury, Nassau 11568
Westbury, Nassau 11590
Westdale, Oneida 13483
Westerlo, Albany 12193
Westernville, Oneida 13486
Westfield, Chautauqua 14787
Westford, Otsego 13488
Westgate, Monroe 14624
Westhampton, Suffolk 11977
Westhampton Beach, Suffolk 11978
Westmoreland, Oneida 13490
Westons Mills, Cattaraugus 14788
Westport, Essex 12993
Westtown, Orange 10998
Wevertown, Warren 12886
Whallonsburg, Essex 12936
Wheatley Heights, Suffolk 11798
Whippleville, Franklin 12995
White Creek, Rensselaer 12057
White Lake, Sullivan 12786
WHITE PLAINS, Westchester (See Page 2727)
White Sulphur Springs, Sullivan 12787
Whiteface Mountain, Essex 12997
Whitehall, Washington 12887
Whitesboro, Oneida 13492
Whitestone, Queens 11357
Whitesville, Allegany 14897
Whitney Point, Broome 13862
Wiccopee, Dutchess 12533
Willard, Seneca 14588
Willet, Cortland 13863
Williamson, Wayne 14589
Williamstown, Oswego 13493
Williamsville (See Buffalo)
Williston Park, Nassau 11596
Willow, Ulster 12495
Willsboro, Essex 12996
Willseyville, Tioga 13864
Wilmington, Essex 12997
Wilson, Niagara 14172
Wilton, Saratoga 12831
Windham, Greene 12496
Windsor, Broome 13865
Wingdale, Dutchess 12594
Winthrop, Saint Lawrence 13697
Witherbee, Essex 12998
Wolcott, Wayne 14590
Woodbourne, Sullivan 12788
Woodbury, Nassau 11797
Woodgate, Oneida 13494
Woodhaven, Queens 11421
Woodhull, Steuben 14898

Woodmere, Nassau 11598
Woodridge, Sullivan 12789
Woodside, Queens 11377
Woodstock, Ulster 12498
Woodville, Jefferson 13650
Worcester, Otsego 12197
Wurtsboro, Sullivan 12790
Wyandanch, Suffolk 11798
Wykagyl, Westchester 10804
Wynantskill, Rensselaer 12198
Wyoming, Wyoming 14591
Yaphank, Suffolk 11980
YONKERS, Westchester
(See Page 2729)
York, Livingston 14592
Yorkshire, Cattaraugus 14173
Yorktown Heights,
Westchester 10598
Yorkville, Oneida 13495
Youngstown, Niagara 14174
Youngsville, Sullivan 12791
Yulan, Sullivan 12792

ALBANY NY

General Delivery 12201

POST OFFICE BOXES MAIN OFFICE STATIONS AND BRANCHES

Box No.s
1 - 1999 12201
270 - 1979 12212
2000 - 2999 12220
3002 - 3980 12203
4001 - 4480 12204
5001 - 5956 12205
6001 - 6998 12206
7101 - 7353 12224
8211 - 8976 12208
9001 - 9220 12209
10001 - 10896 12201
11001 - 11825 12211
12001 - 16414 12212
22001 - 22222 12201
38001 - 39998 12203
50001 - 50275 12205
61000 - 61000 12212
66001 - 66699 12206
209998 - 209998 12220
249998 - 249998 12224

NAMED STREETS

Ableman Ave 12203
Academy Park 12207
Academy Rd 12208
Access Rd 12205
Acorn Dr 12211
Adams Dr 12205
Adirondack St 12203
Admiral St 12205
Ahl Ave 12205
Airline Dr 12205
W Albany Dr 12205
Albany St
1-99 12204
4100-4316 12205
4318-4398 12205
Albany International Airport 12211
Albany Shaker Rd
298-298 12211
300-490 12211
475-475 12204
492-898 12211
493-737 12211
Albert Dr 12203
Albion Ave 12209
Albright Ave 12203
Alden Ave 12209
Aldershoot Rd 12205
Alexander St 12202
Alfred Dr 12205
Alfred Dr E 12205
Alfred St 12209
N Allen St
1-123 12203
125-127 12203
133-133 12206
135-299 12206
S Allen St 12208
Allyson Ct 12205
Alsen St 12205
Alta Rd 12205
Altamont Ave 12205
Alton Rd 12203
Alvina Blvd 12203
Alyssa Ct 12205
Amboy Dr 12205
Amherst Ave 12208
Amsterdam Ave 12204
Amy Ln 12205
Amy Marie Ct 12205
Anderson Dr 12205
Andover Dr 12211
Andriana Ln 12204
Anthony Ln 12205
Antoinette Ln 12205
Apollo Dr 12205
Apple Blossom Ln 12205
Arbor Ct 12211
Arbor Dr 12207
Arcadia Ave
1-99 12209
100-199 12203
Arcadia Ct 12205
Arch Ave 12203
Arch St 12202
Arden Ct 12205
Arden Craig Dr 12203
Ardsley Rd 12203
Arlene Ave 12203
Arthur Dr 12208
Ash Grove Pl 12202
Ashford Dr 12203
Ashwood Ct 12208
Aspen Cir 12208
Aspen Ct 12203
Aspinwall Rd 12211
Atrium Dr 12205
Ausable Frks 12205
Austain Ave 12205
Automation Ln 12205
Avalon Ct 12211
Avenue A
3-99 12209
Avenue A
100-199 12208
Avenue B
1-9 12209
2-8 12208
10-99 12208
Aviation Rd 12205
Avon Ct 12208
Avon Pl 12203
Avon St 12203
Avondale Ter 12209
Ayre Dr 12203
Azalea Ct 12205
Bacon Ln 12211
Balsam Way 12205
Bancker St 12208
Bancroft St 12208
Barclay St 12209
Barker St 12205
Barnard Ave 12203
Barnet St 12208
Barrows St 12209
Barry Ct 12211
Bartes Ct 12211
Barthol St 12205
Bassett St 12202
Batcher St 12202
Batterman Ln 12203
Bauer Dr 12205
Beach Ave 12203
Beacon Ave 12203
Beatrice Ln 12205
Beaver St 12207
Beaver Pond Rd 12211
Bedford Sq 12203
Beekman Ct 12211
Beekman St 12209
Beltrone Dr 12205
Belvidere Ave 12203
Bender Ave 12208
Benjamin Ln 12205
Benjamin St 12202
Benson St 12206
Benton Ln 12203
W Bentwood Ct 12203
Berkeley House 12203
Berkshire Blvd
27-299 12203
30-34 12208
84-298 12203
Berkshire Dr 12205
Berncliff Ave 12208
Bertha St 12209
S Bertha St 12209
Bertha Ter 12211
Besch Ave 12209
Bethwood Dr 12211
Betwood St 12209
Beverly Ave 12206
Beverly Dr 12203
Bick Ln 12205
Bingham St 12202
Binghampton St 12202
Birch Ave 12205
Birch Dr 12203
Birch Hill Rd 12211
Birch Tree Rd 12205
Birchwood Ct 12211
Bittersweet Ln 12211
Blanchard Ave 12203
Bleecker Pl 12202
Bleecker Ter 12206
Bleeker St 12202
Blockhouse Creek Ct 12203
Bluebell Ln 12211
Blurry Ave 12205
Boat St 12202
Boenau St 12202
Bogardus Rd 12208
Bogart Ter 12202
Bohl Ave 12209
Boice St 12202
Bonheim St 12204
Booth Ln & St 12205
Bosher Dr 12205
Boucci Mctague Dr 12202
Bower St 12208
Bradford St 12206
Bradford House 12203
Braintree St 12205
Brandon Ter 12203
Brayton St 12205
Breeman St 12205
Brenda Ct 12203
Brent St 12205
Brevator St
2-48 12203
50-149 12203
150-199 12206
Briar Ave 12203
Briarwood Rd 12211
Briarwood Ter 12203
Brickley Dr 12205
N Bridge Dr 12203
Bridge Rd 12204
Bridge St 12204
Bridle Path 12205
Bridlepath Ext 12205
Brigadier St 12205
Brighton Ct 12211
Brinker Way 12211
Broad St 12202
Broadway
1-11 12204
Broadway
2-48 12202
13-1400 12204
50-99 12202
101-199 12202
300-342 12207
344-961 12207
963-981 12207
1402-1798 12204
57-85-57-85 12204
N Broadway 12204
Broderick St 12205
Brookland Ave 12203
Brookline Ave 12203
Brooks Rd 12203
Brookside Ave 12204
Brookwood Ave 12203
Brown Rd 12205
Browne St 12202
Bryn Mawr Ct 12211
Buchanan St 12206
Buchman Dr 12211
Buckingham Dr 12208
Buckingham House 12203
Buell St 12206
Burdick Dr 12205
Burlwood Dr 12205
Burton Ln 12211
Buttercup Ln 12211
Cadillac Ave 12205
Caldwell St 12208
California Ave 12205
Callaway Cir 12211
Cambridge Rd 12203
Camp Ter 12203
Campagna Dr 12205
Campbell Dr 12205
Campus View Dr 12211
Canal Rd S 12204
Candlewood Ct 12205
Canterbury Ct 12205
Cardinal Ave
1-91 12208
92-92 12209
93-93 12208
94-199 12209
Carlisle Ct 12209
Carlton Ter 12211
Carnevale Dr 12205
Carol St 12205
Carol Ann Dr 12205
Caroline St 12203
Carpenter St 12209
Carriage House 12203
Carroll Ave 12203
Carroll Ter 12209
Cary Ave 12208
Casey Ct 12205
Castle Ct 12211
Catalpa Dr 12209
Catherine St
1-239 12202
240-246 12209
241-247 12202
248-299 12209
91-93-91-93 12202
Catskill St 12203
Caveson Ln 12205
Cayuga Ct 12208
Cedar Dr 12205
Cemetery Ave 12204
Center St 12204
Central Ave
1095A-1095E 12205
1-38 12210
39-925 12206
926-932 12205
927-933 12206
934-2057 12205
2059-2073 12205
Central Term Warehouse 12207
Centre Dr 12203
Centre St 12207
Cerone Commercial Dr 12205
Chainyk Dr 12203
Champlain St 12204
Chanelle Ct 12211
Chapel Dr 12205
Chapel St
1-33 12210
46-98 12207
Chapman Dr 12203
Charles Ave 12205
Charles Pl 12205
Charles St 12202
Charming Ln 12211
Chateau Ct 12211
Chatham Cir 12211
Chelsea House 12203
Cherry St 12205
Cherry Hill St 12202
Cherry Tree Rd 12211
Cheshire Ct 12209
Cheshire Way 12211
Chestnut St
2-4 12205
6-10 12205
58-64 12210
66-199 12210
700-899 12203
Chestnut Hill Rd N & S 12211
Chris Pl 12205
Christian Ct 12203
Church Rd 12203
Church St 12202
Circle Ln 12203
Clara Barton Dr 12208
Clare Ave 12202
Clare Castle Dr 12205
Clarendon Rd 12203
Clark Pkwy 12203
Clayton Pl 12209
Clermont St 12203
Cleveland St 12206
Cliff St 12208
Cliff Top Dr 12211
Clifford Rd 12204
Clinton Ave
9-31 12207
33-37 12207
36-36 12210
38-321 12210
323-339 12210
326-338 12206
340-799 12206
Clinton Sq 12207
Clinton St 12202
Clit Ct 12205
Clover Ln 12211
Clover Field Dr 12211
Cobble Ct 12211
E & W Cobble Hill Rd 12211
Cobee Ln 12205
Colatosti Pl 12208
Colby St 12206
Cole Ave 12205
Colleen Dr 12211
W Colleen Dr 12205
College View Dr 12211
Collins Pl 12208
Colonial Ave
1-99 12203
101-115 12203
141-141 12208
143-299 12208
Colonial Grn 12211
Colonie Ctr 12205
Colonie St
1-9 12207
100-148 12207
150-182 12210
184-350 12210
351-399 12206
Colt Rd 12205
Columbia Cir 12203
Columbia Pl 12207
Columbia St
1-60 12207
61-95 12210
97-99 12210
101-107 12210
Colvin Ave 12206
Commerce Ave 12206
Commerce Plz 12260
Commercial Ave 12205
Commodore St 12205
Compass Ct 12205
Computer Dr E 12205
Conrad St 12205
Consaul Rd 12205
Conway Cir 12211
Copperfield House 12203
Coral Berry Cir 12203
Coralberry Ct 12203
Corlear St 12209
Cornell Ave 12203
Cornell Dr 12204
Corning Pl 12207
Corning St 12205
Cornwall House 12203
Corporate Cir 12203
Corporate Woods Blvd & Dr 12211
Corthell St 12205
Cortland Dr 12211
Cortland Pl 12203
Cortland St
299-400 12208
402-638 12208
645-697 12203
699-1050 12203
1052-1098 12203
Cottage Ave 12203
Cottonwood Pl S 12205
Country Rd 12203
Court St 12205
Craigie Ave 12205
Crailo Ct 12211
Cramond St 12205
Crescent Dr 12208
Cresthaven Ave 12205
Crestone Rd 12205
Crestwood Ct 12208
Crestwood Ter 12203
Crisafulli Dr 12205
Criswood Dr 12205
Crosby St 12205
Cross St 12203
Croswell St 12206
Crown Ct 12211
Crown Ter 12209
Crumitie Rd 12211
Culver Ave 12205
Cuyler Ave 12209
Cuyler St 12202
Cypress Dr 12211
Cypress St 12205
Daisy Ln 12211
Dale St 12203
Dana Ave 12208
Danbury Ct 12205
Danforth St 12205
Daniel Ln 12205
Danielwood Dr 12211
Danker Ave 12206
Darrens Way 12205
Dartmouth St 12209
Dauphin Dr 12205
David Ct 12205
Davis Ave
1-42 12203
44-148 12203
150-299 12208
Davis Ct 12208
Dawn Dr 12205
Daytona Ave 12203
De Lucia Ter 12211
De Voe Dr 12205
De Witt St 12207
Debbie Ct 12205
Deer Path Dr 12205
Deerwood Ct 12208
Deerwood Dr 12205
Delafield Dr 12205
Delaware Ave
1-40 12210
41-169 12202
170-172 12209
171-173 12202
174-1000 12209
Delaware St 12202
Delaware Ter 12209
Delee Ave 12203
Dennin Dr 12204
Dennis Ave 12211
Derby Ct 12211
Devonshire Dr 12205
Dewberry Ct 12203
Dewey St 12205
Dianna St 12211
E & W Dillenbeck Dr 12203
Dogwood Ln 12211
Dongan Ave 12202
Donna Dr 12205
Dorlyn Rd 12205
Dorwood Dr 12211
Dory Ln 12205
Dott Ave 12205
Douglas Ln 12211
Dove St
116A-116A 12210
5-117 12210
118-199 12202
S Dove St 12202
Dowling Rd 12205
Drake Ct 12205
Drawbridge Dr 12203
Dresden Ct 12203
Driftwood Dr 12205
Dudley Hts 12210
Duffy Ln 12205
Duncliff Ct 12205
Dunham Dr 12202
Dunning Ave 12205
Dutch Vlg 12204
Eagle St
2-22 12207
24-26 12207
28-98 12207
100-299 12202
Eastland Cir 12203
Eastwood Dr 12205
Echo Ln 12203
Ecomm Sq 12207
Eden Ln 12211
Edenburg Ave 12203
Edgecomb St 12209
Edgewood Ave 12203
Edgewood Cir 12204
Edison Ave 12208
Eduardo Ct 12203
Edward Ter 12208
Eileen St 12203
Eisenhower Ct 12205
Elbel Ct 12209
Elberon Pl 12203
Elderberry Ct 12203
Elgin St 12205
Eliot Ave 12203
Elizabeth St 12202
Elk St
1-38 12207
55-185 12210
187-230 12210
231-599 12206
Ellendale Dr 12205
Elm Ct 12205
Elm Pl 12203
Elm St 12202
Elmendorf St 12202
Elmhurst Ave
1-99 12203
1-99 12205
N Elmhurst Ave 12205
Elmo St 12205
Elmwood Rd 12204
E Elmwood Rd 12204
Elmwood St 12203
Emerick Ln 12211
Emery Ave 12205
Emmett St 12204
Empire State Plz 12223
Englewood Pl 12203
Enorom Dr 12211
Ensign Pl 12205
Enterprise Dr 12204
Equality Ct 12205
Erie Blvd
2-4 12204
2-10 12207
6-41 12204
43-99 12204
Erie St 12204
W Erie St 12208
Essex Ave 12205
Essex Cir 12209
Essex St 12206
Essex House 12203
Ethel Dr 12211
Euclid Ave
1-149 12203
150-162 12208
164-299 12208
Eustis Rd 12208
Eva St 12205
Everett Rd 12205
Everett Rd Ext 12205
Evergreen Ct 12211
Evergreen Ln 12203
Exchange St 12205

Street	ZIP
Exchange Street Ext	12205
Executive Park E	12203
Executive Centre Dr	12203
Executive Park Dr	12203
Fairfield Ave	12205
Fairfield House	12203
Fairlawn Ave	12203
Fairmont Dr	12205
Fairview Ave	12208
Fairview Rd	12211
Fairway Ct	12208
S Family Dr	12205
Farnam Pl	12205
Fay St	12203
Federal St	12209
Felicia Ct	12205
Fenway Ct & Dr	12211
Fermac St	12205
Fern Ave	12205
Ferndale St	12208
Fernwood Dr	12211
N Ferry St	12207
S Ferry St	12202
Fielding Way	12203
Fleetwood Ave	
1-64	12208
65-71	12209
66-72	12208
73-199	12209
Fletcher Rd	12203
Fliegel Ave	12203
Folmsbee Dr	12204
Fordham Ct	12209
Forest Ave	12208
Forest Dr	12205
Forsythia Ct	12205
Foss Ave	12203
Fountain Ave	12203
Four Lincoln Sq	12202
Frances Dr	12205
Frances Ln	12203
Francis Ave	12203
Franklin St	12202
Frantone Ln	12211
Frederick Ave	12205
Freeman Rd	12208
Friar Tuck Rd	12203
Friebel Ct & Rd	12208
Frisbee Ave	12209
Fritz Blvd	12205
Front Ave	12203
Frost Pl	12205
Fuller Pl	12205
Fuller Rd	
37A-37B	12205
1-199	12205
201-297	12203
299-332	12203
334-398	12203
Fuller Ter	12205
Fullerton St	12209
Furlong Dr	12205
Gabriel Ter	12203
Gabriel Way	12205
Gadsen Ct	12205
Gage Ave	12203
Gail Ave	12205
Gansevoort St	12202
Garden Aly	12210
Garden Ave	12203
Garden St	12209
Garden Ter	12205
Garden Pathway	12205
Garfield Ave	12205
Garfield Pl	12206
Garland Ct	12202
Gaskill Ave	12203
Gaslight Dr	12205
Gay Lyn Dr	12205
Geisel Ln	12203
Georgetown Ct	12203
Georgian Ter	12211
Gert Ln	12205
Gertrude St	12203
Gibbs Cir	12204
Gingerbread Ln	12208
Gipp Rd	12203
Gladwish Ave	12203
Glendale Ave	12208
Glenwood Rd	12204
Glenwood St	
1-15	12203
2-24	12208
2-38	12203
17-39	12203
17-25	12208
26-99	12208
Glynn St	12203
Golder St	12209
Goodwin Ln	12203
Gorman Rd	12204
Governor Cir	12208
Grace St	12205
Gracemore St	12203
Graffunder Dr	12204
Grain St	12202
Grand St	
49-59	12207
61-63	12207
65-65	12207
66-199	12202
Grandview Ter	12202
Grandy St	12205
Granito Dr	12205
Grant Ave	12206
Gray Fox Ln	12203
Graylon Pl	12203
Graystone Rd	12211
Great Oaks Blvd	12203
Green St	
10-18	12207
100-299	12202
Green Meadows Ln	12211
Greenhill Ct	12203
Greenhouse Rd	12205
Greentree Ln	12208
Greenway	12208
Greenwich Dr	12203
Gregory Ln	12211
Greyledge Dr	12211
Grounds Pl	12205
Grove Ave	12208
Grove St	12203
Guilder Ct	12211
Guildford House	12203
Hackett Ave	12205
Hackett Blvd	
265A-265D	12208
266A-266B	12208
270A-270D	12208
274A-274F	12208
280A-280D	12208
283A-283D	12208
284A-284D	12208
333A-333D	12208
335A-335B	12208
336A-336D	12208
338A-338D	12208
339A-339F	12208
340A-340F	12208
342A-342D	12208
343A-343B	12208
345A-345D	12208
346A-346B	12208
351A-351D	12208
353A-353D	12208
355A-355F	12208
359A-359D	12208
361A-361D	12208
365A-365D	12208
369A-369F	12208
370A-370D	12208
371A-371B	12208
375A-375D	12208
380A-380D	12208
1-499	12208
2-250	12209
252-498	12208
Haley Ct	12205
Hall Pl	12210
Halsdorf St	12208
Hamilton St	
34-148	12207
200-411	12210
413-445	12203
447-599	12203
340-338-340-338	12210
Hampshire House	12203
Hampton St	
1-99	12209
1-49	12204
51-73	12204
Hanes St	12203
Hanifin Ave	12205
Hanley Ln	12203
Hansen Ave	12208
Hardie Ave	12205
Harding St	12208
Harmony Hill Rd	12203
Harriet St	12205
Harriman Campus Rd	12206
Harris Ave	12208
Hartman Rd	12208
Harts Ln	12204
Hartwood St	12205
Harvard Ave	12208
Harvest St	12205
Harvester Ct	12211
Harwich Dr	12205
Hathaway House	12203
Hawk St S	12202
N Hawk St	12210
Hawley Ave	12205
Hawthorn Cir	12203
Hawthorne Ave	12203
Hawthorne Ct	12211
Haydenwood Ct	12211
Hazelhurst Ave	12203
W Hearthstone Dr	12205
Heatherton Ct	12205
Helderberg Ave	12208
Helen Ter	12211
Hemlock Ln	12208
Henderson Ln	12203
Hendrick Ave	12204
Henry Ave & St	12203
Henry Johnson Blvd	12210
Herkimer St	12202
Herman St	12205
Hialeah Dr	12205
Hidden Hollow Rd	12208
High Dune Dr	12203
Highfield Ln	12208
Highland Ave	
1-46	12205
7-41	12203
43-45	12203
47-55	12203
48-64	12205
Highland Ct	12203
E Highland Dr	12203
Highland St	12204
Highwood Cir	12203
Hilander Dr	12211
Hillcrest Ave	12203
Hills Blvd & Rd	12211
Hillside Ave	12205
Hillview Rd	12211
Hilmor Rd	12205
Hilton Ct	12211
Hilton Ln	12203
Hitching Post Rd	12205
Hoffman Ave	12209
Holland Ave	
1-3	12205
2-14	12209
5-30	12205
16-31	12209
32-36	12205
41-41	12208
43-113	12208
115-199	12208
Hollywood Ave	
1-149	12208
150-299	12209
Holmes Ct	12209
Holmes Dl	
1-99	12203
100-299	12208
Home Ave	12208
Homes Ter	12203
Homestead Ave	
1-170	12203
171-179	12206
172-180	12203
181-200	12206
202-298	12206
Homestead St	12203
Honey Ct	12205
Hope Ln	12205
Hopewell St	12208
Hopi St	12208
Howard St	12207
Huckleberry Ln	12205
Hudson Ave	
1-46	12205
28-58	12207
45-45	12201
45-45	12209
45-45	12207
48-48	12205
200-390	12210
391-699	12203
701-799	12203
Hughson Pl	12211
Hummel Ter	12202
Hungerford Rd	12203
Hunter Aly	12210
Hunter Ave	12206
Hunter St	12202
Hunting Rd	12205
Huntington Ct	12203
Huntleigh Dr	12211
Hunts End Ln	12211
Hurlbut St	12209
Huron St	12203
Hurst Ave	12208
Hutton St	12204
Ichabod Ln	12211
Ida Yarbrough Apts	12207
Ildra Ln	12203
Imperial Dr	12211
Industrial Rd	12205
Industrial Park Rd	12206
Inman Ave	12203
Interstate Ave	12205
Iris Ln	12205
Irons Ln	12203
Iroquois Dr	12208
Irving Pl	12204
Irving St	12202
Isbestor St	12205
Ivaloo Ave	12203
James Dr	12211
James St	12207
Jameson Ln	12211
Janet Ln	12203
Jase Ct	12208
Jay St	
100-299	12210
401-499	12203
501-899	12203
Jean Ave	12211
Jean Ln	12203
Jeanette St	12209
Jefferson St	12210
Jeffrey Ln	12211
Jeffrey Ter	12203
Jennings Dr	12204
Jermain St	12206
Jetway Dr	12211
Jo Ann Ct	12205
Joan Ln	12203
Joanne Ct	12209
Jodiro Ln	12205
Joelson Ct	12209
John David Ln	12208
Johnston Rd	12203
Johnston House	12203
Joliun House	12203
Jon Michael Ter	12205
Jones Ct	12204
Joseph Ave	12205
Joseph Ter	12203
Joy Dr	12211
Judson St	12206
Jules Dr	12205
June Dr	12211
Jupiter Ln	12205
Kaine Dr	12203
Kaine Ter	12208
Kairnes St	12205
Kakely St	12208
Karen Ct	12211
Karl Ct	12205
Karner Rd	
121A-121E	12205
30-30	12212
32-40	12205
42-122	12205
Kasper Dr	12211
Kate St	12209
Katherine Rd	12205
Kathy Dr	12205
Keane St	12202
Keeler Dr	12208
Kehoe St	12209
Keller St	12205
Kelly Ave	12203
Kelton Ct	12209
Kenjack Ter	12205
Kenlyn Dr	12205
E & W Kenmar Rd	12204
Kennedy Dr	12205
Kenosha St	12209
Kensington Pl	12209
Kent Pl	12203
Kent St	12206
Kent Ter	12203
Kent House	12203
Kenyon Dr	12205
Kerry Ln	12211
Keystone Ct	12205
Killean Park	12205
Kim Dr	12211
Kimberly St	12205
Kinder Ln	12205
King Ave	12206
King St	12203
Kings Ct	12211
Kings Mill Ct	12205
Kingston St	12204
Klaasen Way	12211
Klink Rd	12203
Knapp Ter	12205
Knauf Ln	12211
Kneeland St	12205
Knights Way	12203
Knob Hill Rd	12211
Knollwood Ter	12203
Knowles Ter	12203
Knox St	12208
Kraft Ave	12205
Krank St	12202
Kraus Rd	12203
Kristole Ct	12205
Kross Keys Dr	12205
Krug Ct	12211
Krumkill Ct E	12208
Krumkill Rd	
1-121	12208
123-199	12208
364-900	12203
902-948	12203
Lacy Ln	12211
Laing St	12205
N Lake Ave	
1-45	12203
46-199	12206
201-205	12206
S Lake Ave	
1-23	12203
25-93	12203
94-125	12208
127-199	12208
Lake Rd	12205
Lancaster St	
100-299	12210
700-899	12203
901-999	12203
Lanci Ln	12205
N Lansing St	12207
Lapham Dr	12205
Lark Dr	12210
Launfal St	12205
Laurel Dr	12211
Laureldale Ter	12211
Laurendale St	12205
Lawn Ave	12204
Lawnridge Ave	12208
N Lawrence St	12207
W Lawrence St	
418A-418B	12208
6-28	12206
117-121	12203
123-199	12203
200-599	12208
Lawton Ter	12203
Leach Ave	12205
Learned St	12207
Ledgewood Dr	12205
Leedale St	12209
Lehner Rd	12203
Leighton St	12209
Lena Dr	12203
Lenox Ave	
1-149	12203
150-299	12208
Leonard Pl & St	12202
Leslie Ct	12211
Lester St	12205
Leto Rd	12203
Lexington Ave	12206
Liberty St	12207
Liberty Way	12211
Liebel St	12202
Lily St	12205
Limerick Dr	12204
Lincoln Ave	12205
Linda Ct	12208
Linda Dr	12205
Lindbergh Ave	12204
Linden Rd	12208
Lindsey House	12203
Link St	12208
Linton Ave	12205
Lisa Ct	12205
Lishakill Rd	12205
Little Ln	
1-22	12202
2-6	12211
8-30	12211
24-24	12202
Little Falls Pl	12203
Little John Rd	12203
Living Resources Ln	12203
Livingston Ave	
65-65	12207
67-101	12207
103-123	12207
125-133	12210
135-282	12210
283-899	12206
Lockrow Blvd	12205
Locksley Ct	12203
Locust Ln	12211
Locust Park	12205
Locust St	12203
Locust Hill Rd	12203
Lodge St	12207
Lois Ct	12205
Lois Ln	12211
Longwood Dr	12211
Loralee Dr	12205
Loren Ave	12203
Lorini Ct	12205
Lorna Ln	12211
N & S Loudon Hts, Ln,	
Pkwy & Rd N & S	12211
Loudonville Rd	12204
Loudonwood E	12211
Loughlin St	12203
Louis Ave	12204
Louis Dr	12205
Lowell St	12205
Lower Sage Hill Ln	12204
Ludlow Aly	12210
Lupine Cir & Ct	12203
Lynn Ct & Dr	12205
Lynnwood Dr	12211
N & S Lyons Ave	12204
Lyric Ave	12205
Macaffer Dr	12204
Mack Dr	12205
Madison Ave	
1-1	12205
3-42	12205
44-44	12205
82-116	12202
118-176	12202
178-180	12202
300-433	12210
434-698	12208
435-499	12210
700-1100	12208
1102-1198	12208
Madison Pl	12202
Madison Avenue Ext	12203
Magazine St	12203
Magnolia Ter	12209
Maid Marion Rd	12203
Maiden Ln	12207
N Main Ave	
35A-35B	12203
1-90	12203
100-108	12206
110-199	12206
S Main Ave	
1-308	12208
310-328	12208
313-327	12209
329-399	12209
Main St	12204
Majestic Ct	12211
Malpass Rd	12203
Manchester House	12203
Manning Blvd	
1-165	12203
166-224	12206
226-499	12206
590-608	12210
610-700	12210
702-798	12210
900-900	12207
N Manning Blvd	
1-99	12206
100-898	12207
101-199	12206
900-1099	12207
S Manning Blvd	
1-152	12203
153-399	12208
Manning Sq	12206
Manor St	12207
Maple Ave	
1-8	12205
2-22	12208
24-40	12208
Maple Dr	12205
N Maple Ln	12211
S Maple Ln	12211
Mapleridge Ave	12209
Maplewood Ave	
1-1	12205
3-27	12205
9-79	12203
29-51	12205
81-89	12203
Maplewood Ct	12205
Maplewood St	12208
Marcus Blvd	12205
Margaret Dr	12211
Maria Dr	12211
Marian Ln	12211
Mariana Ln	12203
Marie Ave	12203
Marie Pkwy	12211
Marietta Dr	12205
Mariette Pl	12209
Marilou St	12205
Marinello Ter	12209
Marini Ct	12205
Marion Ave	
1-100	12203

Street	ZIP
102-104	12203
106-299	12208
Marjorie Dr	12203
Marjorie Rd	12205
Marlborough Ct	12209
Marlene Dr	12205
Marriner Ave	12205
Marsdale St	12208
Marshall Pl	12207
Marshall St	12209
S Marshall St	12209
Martin Pl & Ter	12205
Martingale Dr	12205
Marvill Dr	12211
Marwill St	12209
Marwood St	12209
Maryland Ave	12205
Mason Ct	12211
Massachusetts Ave	12205
Matilda St	12209
Maxwell St	12208
Mayflower Dr	12205
Mayhall St	12205
E Maynes Ave	12203
Maywood Ave	12205
Mcalpin St	12209
Mcardle Ave	12206
Mccartney Dr	12211
Mccarty Ave	
1-116	12202
118-198	12202
200-399	12209
Mccormack Rd	12208
Mccrossin Ave	12206
Mcdonald Cir	12204
Mcdonald Rd	12209
Mckinley St	12206
Mckown Rd	12203
Mckown St	12209
Mcnutt Ave	12205
Mcpherson Ter	12206
Meade Ave	12203
W Meadow Dr	12203
Meadow Ln	12208
Medinah Ct	12205
Meeting House Rd	12211
Melissa Ct	12205
Melrose Ave	12203
Menands Rd	
1-138	12204
139-299	12211
Menger Ln	12203
Mercer St	
1-15	12202
1-99	12203
2-14	12202
2-98	12203
500-899	12208
901-931	12208
Mercy Ct	12205
Mereline Ave	12209
Merrill St	12205
Metro Park Rd	12205
Michael Ter	12203
Michigan Ave	12205
Midland Ave	12203
Midway Dr	12205
Mill St	12204
Miller Ave	12203
Milner Ave	
1-99	12203
100-299	12208
Milo Ln	12211
Milton Ct & St	12205
Miracle Ln	12211
Mohawk St	12204
Mohican Pl	12208
Momrow Ct & Ter	12204
Mona Ter	12209
Monroe Ave	12203
Monroe St	12210
Montgomery St	12207
Moon Dr	12205
Moore St	12202
Mordella Rd	12205
Moreland Ave	12203
Morone Pl	12205
Morris St	12208
Morton Ave	
1-264	12202
266-268	12202
270-300	12209
302-398	12209
Mount Hope Dr	12202
Mountain St	12209
Mountain Vw	12204
Mountain View Ave	12205
Mountainview Ave	12208
Mulberry Dr	12205
Myers Ct	12205
Myrtle Ave	
1-252	12202
253-359	12208
361-949	12208
950-999	12203
Myton Ln	12204
Nancy Theresa Ter	12205
Nash Pl	12205
Natick St	12205
Neal Dr	12205
New Hope Ter	12204
New Karner Rd	
90-98	12203
191-197	12205
199-599	12205
New Scotland Ave & Rd	12208
New Shaker Rd	12205
Newcomb Dr	12211
Newell Ct	12204
Newman Rd	12203
Newton St	12205
Niblock Ct	12206
Nicholas Dr	12205
Nicole Dr	12205
Nicolla Ave	12211
Nina Dr	12205
Noble Path	12205
Nolan Rd	12205
Noonan Ln	12209
Norbrick Dr	12205
Norfolk St	
4-6	12203
8-16	12203
11-15	12209
17-39	12203
18-36	12203
Norman Ave	12203
Norman Dr	12205
Normanside Dr	12208
Normanskill Dr	12209
Normanskill St	12202
North Ct	12205
North Ln	12211
North St	
1-32	12205
20-26	12204
28-45	12204
34-38	12205
Northern Blvd	
225-323	12210
300-322	12204
324-400	12204
402-602	12204
Northgate Dr	12203
Norton St	12205
Norwood Ave	12208
Norwood Dr	12204
Norwood St	12203
Notre Dame Dr	12208
Nottingham Rd	12203
Noxon Ct	12211
Nutgrove Ln	12202
S O Connell St	12209
Oak Cir	12205
Oak Dr	12203
Oak Rdg	12204
Oak St	
1-5	12205
5-9	12206
7-19	12205
Oakland Ave	
1-2	12205
3-3	12204
3-99	12205
4-98	12205
N Oakland Ave	12205
Oakmont Ter	12205
Oaks Ct	12203
Oakwood Dr	12205
Oakwood Dr W	12205
Oakwood St	12208
Odell St	12202
Old Birch Ln	12205
Old Hickory Dr	12204
Old Karner Rd	12205
Old Myers Dr	12205
Old Niskayuna Rd	12211
Old Pine Ave	12205
Oleary Blvd	12203
Olive Tree Ln	12208
Oliver Ave	12203
Oliver St	12205
Olympus Ct	12208
Omah Ter	12205
Onderdonk Ave	12208
One Keycorp Plz	12207
One Lincoln Sq	12202
Oneida Ter	12209
Oneil Rd	12208
Ontario St	
1-181	12206
182-202	12203
204-267	12203
269-295	12203
297-301	12208
303-472	12208
474-476	12208
Orange St	
1-99	12207
81-155	12210
157-335	12210
336-342	12206
337-343	12210
344-499	12206
425-423-425-423	12206
Orchard Ave	12203
Orchard Grv	12211
Orford St	12205
Oriole St	12209
Orlando Ave	12203
Ormond St	
1-99	12203
101-149	12203
150-299	12208
Osborne Rd	
1-251	12205
252-399	12211
Osborne St	
1-190	12202
191-193	12209
192-194	12202
195-202	12209
204-298	12209
Oxford Hts, Pl & Rd	12203
Paddock Ln	12208
Paden Cir	12203
Palisades Dr	12205
Palma Blvd	12203
Palmer Ave	12205
Pansy St	12205
Par Cir & Dr	12208
Park Ave	
3-19	12202
19-39	12203
20-20	12202
22-22	12203
30-36	12202
34-36	12203
38-38	12202
40-40	12203
44-73	12202
75-299	12202
500-999	12208
201-209-201-209	12202
Park Dr	12204
Park Hl	12204
Park Ln E	12204
Park Ln S	12204
Park Ln W	12204
Park Pl	12205
Park St	12207
Parkwood Dr	12205
Parkwood St	
1-25	12203
1-45	12208
4-24	12203
14-54	12208
E Parkwood St	12203
W Parkwood St	12203
Partridge St	
1-99	12206
178-194	12203
196-222	12203
224-228	12208
230-499	12208
Pateman Cir	12204
Patricia Ave	12203
Patricia Dr	12205
Patricia Ln	12203
Patroon Pl	12211
Patroon Creek Blvd	12206
Patten Dr	12211
Paul Holly Dr	12211
Pauline Ave	12203
Pawling St	12204
Peachtree Ln	12205
N Pearl St	
1-414	12207
416-438	12207
435-437	12204
439-800	12204
802-898	12204
403-409-403-409	12207
84-86-84-86	12207
S Pearl St	
1-119	12207
120-132	12202
121-133	12207
134-899	12202
Pembroke House	12203
Pembrooke Ct	12211
Pennsylvania Ave	12206
Pepper Ln	12211
Perkins Ave	12203
Peter Dr	12205
Peter Kiernan Plz	12207
Petra Ln	12205
Pettibone Dr	12205
Peyster St	12208
Pfeil Ave	12205
Pheasant Ln	12204
Pheasant Ridge Dr	12211
Philbrick St	12209
Philip St	
40-54	12207
51-53	12202
55-199	12202
49 1/2-49 1/2	12202
Picotte Dr	12208
Pierce St	12205
Pieter Schuyler Ct E & W	12210
Pilgrim Dr	12211
Pine Ave	12205
N Pine Ave	12203
S Pine Ave	12208
Pine Ln	12203
Pine St	
1-5	12203
4-15	12207
6-6	12203
8-17	12203
16-16	12207
18-22	12203
19-31	12203
99-199	12207
Pine Knob Dr	12203
Pine Stump Rd	12205
Pine Tree Ln	12208
Pine West Plz	12205
Pinehurst Ave	
3A-3B	12203
2-2	12203
3-19	12205
4-119	12203
21-29	12205
121-123	12203
Pinehurst Rd	12205
Pines Ct	12203
Pinewood Ave	
1-95	12208
2-12	12203
14-22	12208
16-26	12203
24-94	12208
Pinewood Pl	12205
Pitch Pine Rd	12203
Plant Pl	12205
Plarani Ave	12205
Pleasant St	12207
Pleasantview Ave	12203
Plum St	12202
Plymouth St	12205
Point Of Woods Dr	12203
Pommel Rd	12205
Poplar St	12205
Port Rd & St	12202
Port Of Albany	12202
Porter Ct	12202
Post Rd	12205
Prescott St	12205
Primrose Ln	12211
Prince Ct	12211
Princess Grn & Ln	12211
Princess Taylor Ln	12203
Proctor Ct	12211
Prospect Ave	
1-45	12206
2-2	12205
4-16	12205
18-18	12205
Prospect Rd	12206
Prospect Ter	12208
Providence Pl	12202
Providence St	
1-99	12203
500-699	12208
701-709	12208
Putnam St	12202
Quackenbush Sq	12207
Quadrini Dr	12208
Quail St	
114A-114E	12206
Quarry Dr	12205
Queens Ct	12211
Quincy St	12205
Rachlin Ln	12211
Raffaele Ct	12205
Raft St	12202
Railroad Ave	
5-5	12205
7-31	12205
32-32	12204
32-158	12205
33-157	12205
Railroad Avenue Ext	12205
Ramsey Pl	
1-107	12208
108-199	12209
Ramundo Dr	12205
Rapp Rd	12203
Rapp Rd N	12205
Rapple Dr	12205
Ravenwood Dr	12205
Rawson St	12206
Raymo St	12209
Reamer St	12205
Reber St	12205
Red Fox Dr	12205
Red Lane Dr	12211
Reddy Ln	12211
Regal Ct	12211
Regent St	12202
N Reineman St	12203
Reinemann Ave	12203
Rene Dr	12205
Rensselaer St	12202
Reynolds St	12205
Richard J Conners Blvd	12204
Richards Dr	12205
Richland Dr	12205
Richmond St	12205
Ricky Blvd	12203
E Ridge Rd	12211
Ridge Ter	12205
Ridgefield St	12208
Ridgewood Cir & Ter	12203
Rielton Ct	12203
Rifle Range Rd	12205
Rita Ln	12211
Rizzo Ln	12203
Robert Dr	12205
Robin St	12206
Robinhood Rd	12203
Robinia Dr	12211
Robinson Ln	12211
Roe Ave	12205
Roland Dr	12208
Roman Ct	12211
Rondack Rd	12205
Rooney Ave	12205
Rooney Rd	12204
Roosevelt St	12206
Rose Ct	12209
Rosebud Ln	12211
Rosemary Cir & Dr	12211
Rosemary Drive Ext	12211
Rosemont St	
139A-139A	12203
1-139	12203
140-199	12206
Ross Ct	12211
S Royal Dr	12205
Ruso Dr	12204
Russell Rd	
3-599	12203
4-18	12205
20-82	12205
84-120	12205
N Russell Rd	12206
Rustyville Rd	12211
Ruth Rd	12205
Ruth Ter	12203
Rutland Ave	12205
Rutland St	12209
Ryckman Ave	12208
Sage Ct & Est	12204
N Sage Hill Ln	12204
Salem Ct	12203
Salem St	12205
Samaritan Rd	12208
Sand St	12209
Sand Creek Rd	12205
Sand Pine Ln	12203
Sandalwood Ct	12208
Sandalwood Dr	12211
Sandra Sue Dr	12211
Saradale Ave	12211
Sarah Ct	12205
Sard Rd	12209
Sawyer Pl	12208
School St	12205
Schoolhouse Rd	12203
Schuyler Rd	
1-9	12203
1-5	12211
7-77	12211
11-11	12203
79-87	12211
Schuyler St	12202
Schuyler Hills Rd	12211
Schuyler Meadow Rd	12211
Scott St	12202
Seabee Ln	12203
Seandari St	12209
Sebring Ave	12205
Seeley Dr	12203
Selina Dr	12205
Seminole Ave	12203
Seneca Pl	12208
Seward St	12203
Shady Ln	12203
Shaker Dr	12211
Shaker Rd	
2-58	12204
60-91	12204
92-114	12211
93-115	12204
116-295	12211
297-299	12211
Shaker Run	12205
Shaker El	12211
Shaker Park Dr	12211
Shalimar Ct	12211
Sharon Dr	12205
Sheffield Cir	12211
Sheffield House	12203
Shelbourne Dr	12211
Shephard Ave	12203
Sherbourne House	12203
Sheridan Ave	
1-13	12207
14-22	12210
24-282	12210
283-299	12206
284-300	12210
301-499	12206
124-126-124-126	12210
Sherman St	
1-49	12210
50-499	12206
Sherwood Forest Rd	12203
Shinnecock Hills Dr	12205
Short St	12203
Silas Ave	12205
Silverberry Pl	12211
Simmons Ln	12204
Sir Charles Way	12203
Sky Hollow Dr	12204
Sligo St	12209
Slingerland St	12202
Sloan St	12202
Smith Ave	12205
Smith Blvd	12202
Snaffle Ring	12205
South Ln	12211
South St	12204
Southern Blvd	12209
Southgate Rd	12211
Southwest Way	12205
Southwoods Blvd	12211
Space Blvd	12205
Sparkill Ave	12209
Sparrowhill	12203
Spencer St	12207
Sprague Pl	12203
Spring Holw	12203
Spring St	
1-99	12210
100-440	12203
442-476	12203
Spring Street Rd	12211
Springsteen Rd	12203
Springwood Manor Dr	12211
Spruce St	
11A-11B	12205
1-99	12205
200-299	12210
Spur Cir	12205
Spy Glass Ct	12203
Spyglass Hl	12204
St Agnes Ln	12211
St George Pl	12202
St James Pl	12209
St Josephs Ter	12210
St Micheals Ter	12205
Stafford St	12211
Stanford Ct	12209
Stanwix St	12209
State St	
1-199	12207
200-241	12210
240-240	12220
242-398	12210
243-399	12210
401-1199	12203
38-40-38-40	12207
Stedman Way	12211
Stella Ter	12205
Stephen St	12202
Steuben Pl & St	12207
Steve Ln	12205
Stewart St	12205

Stirrup Dr 12205
Stonegate Ct 12205
Stonehenge Dr & Ln 12203
Stoneridge Dr 12211
Stover Pl 12205
Strathmore Dr 12211
Summit Ave 12209
Sumpter St 12205
Sumter Ave 12203
Sundance Ln 12211
Sunflower Ln 12205
Sunnyside Ave 12205
Sunset Ave 12203
Sunset Blvd 12205
Surcingle 12205
Surfwood Dr 12205
Susan Ln 12205
Sutton Pl 12203
N Swan St 12210
S Swan St
1-161 12210
162-174 12202
163-175 12210
176-299 12202
122-126-122-126 12210
Swartson Ct 12209
Swinton St 12206
Swiss Ct 12205
Sycamore Dr 12205
Sycamore St
1-166 12208
167-299 12209
Taft Ave 12203
Tallmadge Ave & Pl 12208
Tampa Ave
1-47 12203
49-100 12203
102-148 12203
150-299 12208
Tanglewood Rd 12205
Tanner Hollow Dr 12205
Taprobane Ln 12211
Tattersall Ln 12205
Teacup Cir 12208
Ten Broeck Pl & St 12210
Ten Broeck Manor Lark Dr 12210
Ten Eyck Ave 12209
Tennessee Ave 12205
Terminal St 12206
Terrace Ave 12203
Terry Ct 12205
Teunis Ave 12208
Teunis St 12202
Thatcher St 12207
The Concourse 12203
Theatre Row 12210
Thelma St 12205
Theresa Ann Ct 12205
Thistledown Ct 12211
Thomas St 12204
Thompson St 12205
Thorandi St 12202
Thornton St 12206
Thoroughbred Ln 12205
Three Lincoln Sq 12202
Thunder Rd 12205
Thurlow Ter 12203
Tice Rd 12203
Tiernan Ct 12203
Tillinghast Ave 12204
Timberland Dr 12211
Timberside Ct 12203
Tina Ct 12205
Tioga Ter 12208
Tipton Dr 12211
Tipton House 12203
Tivoli St 12207
Toll Ln 12203
Top Ridge Dr 12203
Torquay Blvd 12203
Tower Hts 12211
Tower Pl 12203
Townwood Dr 12203
Traditional Ln 12211
Traffic Rd 12205
Tremont Dr & St 12205
Trillium Ln 12203
Trinity Pl 12202
Tryon Ct, Pl & St 12203
Tubman Cir 12204
Tudor Rd 12203
Tull Dr 12205
Turf Ln 12211
Turnberry Ln 12211
Turner Ln 12211
Turner Pl 12209
Turnpike Ln 12203
Turnstile Dr 12203
Twilight Ter 12211
Twiller St 12209
Twitchell St 12208
Two Lincoln Sq 12202
Ulenski Dr 12205
Undine St 12205
Union Dr 12208
United Way 12205
University Pl 12203
University St 12205
Upland Rd 12204
Upper Ball Ct 12204
Upper Hillcrest Ave 12203
Upper Loudon Rd 12211
Upton Rd 12208
Valerie Ln 12211
Valley Ln 12203
Valleyview Dr 12208
Van Buren Ave 12205
Van Buren St 12206
Van Dyke Rd 12205
Van Heusen St 12205
Van Orden Ave 12202
Van Patten Ln 12203
Van Rensselaer Blvd 12204
Van Rensselaer Rd 12205
Van Schoick Ave
1-82 12208
83-91 12209
84-92 12208
93-199 12209
Van Tassel Ct 12211
Van Tromp St 12207
W Van Vechten St 12209
Van Wie Ter 12203
Van Zandt St 12207
Vanessa Ct 12205
Vatrano Ln 12211
Vatrano Rd 12205
Vaughn Dr 12203
Veeder Dr 12205
Velina Dr 12203
Venezio Ave 12203
Venus Dr 12211
Ver Planck St 12206
Vfw Dr 12205
Vics Ct 12205
Victor Dr 12203
Victor St 12206
Victoria Way 12209
Victory Dr 12205
View Ave 12209
Vigars Pl 12205
Villa Ave 12203
Villa Rd 12204
Village Park Dr 12205
Vincent Ave 12205
Vincenzo Ct 12203
Vine St
8-20 12203
26-26 12202
Virginia Ave 12205
Vly Rd 12205
Waldens Pond Rd 12203
Walker Way 12205
Wall St 12205
Walnut St 12205
Walter St 12204
Walter Way 12211
Warbler Way 12203
Wards Ln 12204
Warehouse Row 12205
Warmington St 12205
Warren Ave 12203
Warren St
1-14 12203
15-15 12202
15-23 12203
16-24 12203
25-25 12202
25-27 12203
500-899 12208
650-658-650-658 12208
Warwick Ave 12205
Washington Ave
566A-566B 12203
5-9 12205
11-40 12205
42-78 12205
99-107 12210
109-196 12210
198-260 12210
262-1026 12203
265-1017 12206
1019-1021 12206
1023-1499 12206
1028-1082 12203
1200-1398 12226
1400-1498 12206
Washington Sq 12205
Washington Avenue Ext
101-399 12205
120-398 12203
Water St 12207
Waterman Ave 12205
Watervliet Ave 12206
Watervliet Avenue Ext 12206
Watervliet Shaker Rd
800-1198 12205
801-899 12211
901-1199 12205
Waverly Pl 12203
Webster St 12208
Wedgewood Dr 12211
Wedgewood House 12203
Weis Rd 12208
Wellesley Ct 12211
Wellington Ave 12203
Wells Blvd 12205
Wembley Ct 12205
Wendell Dr 12205
Wendfair Ter 12205
Wendom Rd 12203
Wendys Path 12211
Wertman Ln 12211
West St 12206
Westchester Dr 12205
Westerlo St 12202
Western Ave 12203
Westford St 12208
Westlyn Ct & Pl 12203
Westmere Ter 12203
Weymouth St 12205
Whip Cir 12205
White Fir Dr 12211
White Oak Ln 12208
White Pine Dr 12203
White Rock Cir 12205
Whitehall Rd
1-326 12209
327-337 12208
328-338 12209
339-451 12208
453-453 12208
Whitetail Ln 12203
Wicken Sq 12205
Wilan Ln 12203
Wilbur St
1-3 12202
1-20 12205
5-23 12202
22-98 12205
Wildwood Dr 12211
Wildwood Rd 12205
Wilkins Ave
1-35 12206
1-35 12205
2-30 12205
2-30 12206
32-34 12205
36-53 12205
48-52 12206
54-134 12205
55-61 12205
55-61 12206
63-71 12205
73-73 12206
75-131 12205
Willett St 12210
Willey St 12203
Williams Ct 12203
Williams Park Rd 12211
Williamsburg Ct 12203
Willo Ln 12211
Willoughby Dr 12205
Willow Ave 12205
Willow St 12206
Willowdale Ter 12205
Wilshire Dr 12205
Wilson Ave 12205
Wilson Ct 12205
Wilson St 12207
Winchester Pl 12211
Winchester House 12203
Windsor Dr 12205
Windsor Pl 12209
Windsor House 12203
Winifred Dr 12205
Winners Cir 12205
Winnie St 12208
Winston Pl 12205
Winthrop Ave
1-170 12203
171-199 12206
Winthrop St 12205
Witte Rd 12203
Wolf Rd 12205
Wolfert Ave 12204
Wood St 12203
Wood Ter 12208
Wood Plot Rd 12211
Woodlake Rd 12203
Woodlawn Ave 12208
Woodridge Ct 12203
Woodridge Dr 12211
Woodridge St 12203
Woods Ln 12204
Woodscape Dr 12203
Woodside Ave 12205
Woodside Dr 12208
Woolard Ave 12205
Yardboro Ave 12205
Yardley Ct 12211
Yates St 12208
York Rd 12203
Zoar Ave
4-15 12205
5-15 12209
6-6 12203
8-8 12209
10-12 12203
12-14 12209
16-22 12203
17-31 12205
24-31 12203
33-37 12205
Zorn Rd 12203
Zuni St 12208

NUMBERED STREETS

1st Ave 12202
1st St
1-238 12210
239-239 12206
240-240 12210
241-599 12206
N 1st St 12204
2nd Ave
1-220 12202
221-500 12209
502-598 12209
2nd St
216A-216A 12210
1-214 12210
215-215 12206
216-216 12210
217-699 12206
76-82-76-82 12210
3rd Ave 12202
3rd St
1-194 12210
195-205 12206
196-206 12210
207-899 12206
901-999 12206
74-76-74-76 12210
N 3rd St 12204
4th Ave 12202

ASTORIA NY

POST OFFICE BOXES MAIN OFFICE STATIONS AND BRANCHES

Box No.s
2000 - 2685 11102
3000 - 3549 11103
5000 - 5999 11105
6000 - 6655 11106
9001 - 39027 11103
56000 - 59024 11105
69001 - 69005 11106

NAMED STREETS

Astoria Blvd
100-3299 11102
3300-3900 11103
3902-4898 11103
4001-4799 11105
Astoria Park S 11102
Berrian Blvd 11105
Broadway
1100-3699 11106
Broadway
3700-4800 11103
4802-4898 11103
Brooklyn Queens Expy E & W 11103
Crescent St
2000-2399 11105
2400-3099 11102
3100-3600 11106
3602-3698 11106
30100-30102 11102
Ditmars Blvd 11105
Dorothy Pl 11102
Farlett St 11102
Gopost
318-318 11103
Gopost
607-607 11106
Hoyt Ave S 11102
Main Ave 11102
Newtown Ave 11102
Newtown Rd 11103
Pierells St 11106
Shalindo St 11103
Shore Blvd
2001-2199 11105
2540-2598 11102
Sound St 11105
Steinway Pl 11105
Steinway St
1700-1834 11105
1836-2399 11105
2400-3299 11103
Vernon Blvd
3000-3099 11102
3101-3197 11106
3199-3499 11106
3501-3699 11106
Watholle St 11105
Welling Ct 11102

NUMBERED STREETS

1st St 11102
2nd St 11102
3rd St 11102
4th St 11102
8th St 11102
9th St
2500-2598 11102
2600-2699 11102
3300-3600 11106
3602-3698 11106
10th St 11106
11th St 11106
12th St
2500-3099 11102
3100-3699 11106
13th St 11106
14th Pl 11102
14th St
2500-3099 11102
3100-3400 11106
18th St
2000-2099 11105
2500-2700 11102
19th Ave 11105
19th St
2000-2199 11105
2401-2459 11102
20th Ave, Rd & St 11105
21st Ave 11105
21st Dr 11105
21st Rd 11105
21st St
2000-2399 11105
2400-3099 11102
3100-3699 11106
22nd Dr 11105
22nd Rd 11105
22nd St
2500-2599 11102
3601-3699 11106
23rd Ave 11105
23rd Dr 11105
23rd Rd 11105
23rd St
2000-2399 11105
2400-3099 11102
3100-3699 11106
23rd Ter 11105
24th Ave
1900-3200 11102
3202-3298 11102
3300-3699 11103
3701-3799 11103
24th Dr 11102
24th Rd 11102
24th St
2000-2399 11105
2400-2499 11102
3400-3699 11106
25th Ave 11103
25th Rd 11102
26th Ave 11102
26th Rd 11102
26th St
2000-2399 11105
2400-2499 11102
27th Ave 11102
27th Rd 11102
27th St
2000-2399 11105
2400-2799 11102
28th Ave
1400-3200 11102
3202-3298 11102
3300-4899 11103
28th Rd 11102
28th St
2000-2399 11105
2400-2699 11102
3300-3699 11106
29th Ave 11102
29th St
2000-2332 11105
2334-2398 11105
2400-3099 11102
3100-3699 11106
30th Ave
1100-3299 11102
3300-4899 11103
30th Dr 11102
30th Rd
1100-2599 11102
4400-4498 11103
4500-4699 11103
30th St
2600-3099 11102
3100-3699 11106
31st Ave
1100-3640 11106
3642-3698 11106
3700-4849 11103
31st Dr 11106
31st Rd 11106
31st St
2000-2399 11105
2400-3099 11102
3100-3108 11106
32nd St
2000-2399 11105
2400-3099 11102
3100-3108 11106
3110-3699 11106
33rd Ave 11106
33rd Rd 11106
33rd St
2000-2399 11105
2400-3099 11102
3100-3699 11106
34th Ave 11106
34th St
2500-3099 11103
3101-3103 11106
35th Ave 11106
35th St
2000-2399 11105
2400-3099 11103
3100-3699 11106
36th Ave 11106
36th St
2000-2399 11105
2400-3099 11103
3100-3653 11106
3655-3699 11106
37th St
1900-2399 11105
2400-2430 11103
38th St
1900-2399 11105
2400-3299 11103
41st St 11105
41st St 11105
2400-2406 11103
2408-3299 11103
42nd St
1800-2399 11105
2400-3299 11103
43rd St
1800-2299 11105
2301-2399 11105
2400-3299 11103
44th St 11103
45th St 11105
2400-3299 11103
46th St
1901-1999 11105
2001-2299 11105
2400-3299 11103
47th St
2000-2299 11105
2400-3299 11103
48th St
1900-2008 11105
2010-2299 11105
2301-2337 11103
2339-3299 11103
49th St
1900-2299 11105
2400-3250 11103

AUBURN NY

General Delivery 13021

POST OFFICE BOXES MAIN OFFICE STATIONS AND BRANCHES

Box No.s
1 - 6980 13021

7001 - 7480 13022

RURAL ROUTES

06 13021

NAMED STREETS

Acorn Ln 13021
Adams Ave & St 13021
Aiken Dr 13021
N & S Albany St 13021
Alden Ave 13021
Aldrich Ave 13021
Allen St 13021
Almond Dr 13021
Amherst Ave 13021
Amherst Avenue Ext 13021
Anderson Cir 13021
Anna St 13021
Arch St 13021
Archie St 13021
Arlington Ave 13021
Arnold Rd 13021
Arterial E & W 13021
Ashbaugh Ave 13021
Aspen St 13021
Auburn Ave & Hts 13021
Auburn Correctional Facility 13021
Augustus St 13021
Aurelius Ave 13021
Austin Dr 13021
Bailey St 13021
Baker Ave & Rd 13021
Baptist Corner Rd 13021
Barber St 13021
Barrington Way 13021
Barski Rd 13021
Basswood Rd 13021
Beach Ave & Rd 13021
Beardsley St 13021
Beech Rd 13021
Beech Tree Cir & Rd 13021
Belle Ave 13021
Bellevue Pl 13021
Bellnier Ln 13021
Belmont Ave 13021
Benham Ave & Rd 13021
Benson Rd 13021
Benton St 13021
Bevier Rd 13021
Bevior Rd 13021
Birch Dr 13021
Birchwood Ln 13021
Blanchard Rd 13021
Bluefield Mnr & Rd 13021
Bonnie Lynn Ter 13021
Boston Ave 13021
Bostwick Ave 13021
Bowen St 13021
Boyle Ave & Ctr 13021
Bradford St 13021
Bradley St 13021
Brae Ridge Rd 13021
Briggs Dr 13021
Brister Ave 13021
Bristol Ave 13021
Broadway Rd 13021
Brogan Mnr 13021
Brookfield Pl 13021
Brookhollow Dr 13021
Brookshire 13021
Brookside Dr 13021
Buck Point Rd 13021
Bundy Ave 13021
Burgess St 13021
Burkhart Dr 13021
Burt Ave 13021
Burtis Point Rd 13021
Butera Dr 13021
Butler Dr 13021
Button St 13021
Byrne Rd 13021
Cady St 13021
Calemad Dr 13021
Calloway Dr 13021
Cambridge Cir 13021
Cameron St 13021
Camp St 13021
Campbell Pl 13021
Canal St 13021
Canoga Rd & St 13021
Capitol St 13021
Capitol Street Ext 13021
Carpenter St 13021
Carrie Ct 13021
Case Ave 13021
Catlin St 13021
Cayuga St 13021
Cedar Swamp Rd 13021
Center St 13021
Center Street Rd 13021
Centerport Rd 13021
Chamberlain Rd 13021
Chapel St 13021
Chapman Ave 13021
Charles St 13021
Chase St 13021
Chase Street Ext 13021
Chedell Pl 13021
Cherry Street Rd 13021
Chestnut Pl & St 13021
Chestnut Ridge Rd 13021
Church St 13021
Cindy Ln 13021
Clark St 13021
Clark Street Rd 13021
Cliffside Dr 13021
Clymer St 13021
Colburn Ave 13021
Columbus St 13021
Commerce Way 13021
Connors Rd 13021
Conroy Jackson Xing 13021
Copley St 13021
Corcoran Dr 13021
Cork St 13021
Cornwall Ave 13021
Corporate Dr 13021
Cottage St 13021
Cottonwood Ln 13021
Cottrell St 13021
County House Rd 13021
County Line Rd 13021
Court St 13021
Crane Brook Dr 13021
Crescent Ave 13021
Cross St 13021
Curtis Pl 13021
Dawson Ave 13021
Day Rd 13021
Dayton St 13021
Deer Run Rd 13021
Deerview Dr 13021
Delevan St 13021
Denman Cv 13021
Dennis St 13021
Densmore Ave 13021
Depew St 13021
Depot Rd 13021
Derby Ave 13021
Devon Ave 13021
Dewey Ave 13021
Dexter Ave 13021
Dill St 13021
N Division St 13021
N Division Street Rd 13021
Donovan Rd 13021
Dougall Rd 13021
Drummond St 13021
Dublin Rd 13021
Dunning Ave 13021
Eagle Dr 13021
East Dr & Rdg 13021
Easterly Ave & Pl 13021
Eastern Pkwy 13021
Eastwood Ave 13021
Elaine Est 13021
Elizabeth St 13021
Ellis Dr 13021
Elm St 13021
Elmhurst Cir & Dr 13021
Emily Dr 13021
Emma St 13021
Englewood Ave 13021
Eric Ln 13021
Evans St 13021
Exchange St 13021
Experimental Rd 13021
Fairway Dr 13021
Finger Lakes Mall 13022
Fire Lane 12a 13021
Fire Lane 12b 13021
Fire Lane 14 13021
Fire Lane 15 13021
Fire Lane 16a 13021
Fire Lane 17 13021
Fire Lane 1b 13021
Fire Lane 20 13021
Fire Lane 21 13021
Fire Lane 23 13021
Fire Lane 24 13021
Fire Lane 26 13021
Fire Lane 3 13021
Fire Lane 5 13021
First Ave 13021
Fitch Ave 13021
Fitzpatrick Rd 13021
Fleming St 13021
Fleming Scipio Townline Rd 13021
Florence St 13021
Foote St 13021
Forest Hill Dr 13021
Fort St 13021
Fosterville Rd 13021
Fourth Ave 13021
Foxcroft Cir 13021
Frances St 13021
Frank Smith St 13021
Franklin Rd & St 13021
Franklin Street Rd 13021
Frazee St 13021
Frederick St 13021
Freeman Rd 13021
French Ave 13021
N & S Fulton St 13021
Gable Rd 13021
Gahwiler Rd 13021
E & W Garden St 13021
Garfield St 13021
Garrow St 13021
Garrow Street Ext 13021
S Gate Dr 13021
Gates Rd 13021
Gaylord St 13021
E Genesee Gdns, Pl & St 13021
E & W Genesee Street Rd 13021
Gillings Rd 13021
Giza Rd 13021
Glanville Rd 13021
Gleason Dr 13021
Glenbrook Dr 13021
Glenwood Ln 13021
Goulds Dr 13021
Grant Ave & St 13021
Grant Avenue Rd 13021
N Green St 13021
Green Links Turn 13021
Greenview Cir 13021
Griffin Rd 13021
Grove Ave 13021
Grove Ave Ext 13021
Grover St 13021
Guilfoil Ave 13021
Halcomb Dr 13021
Half Acre Rd 13021
Hamilton Ave 13021
Hardenburg Ave 13021
Harnden St 13021
Harter Rd 13021
Harvard Ave 13021
Havens Ave 13021
Hazelhurst Ave 13021
Healy Rd 13021
Henry Dr 13021
N & S Herman Ave 13021
Hickory Ln & St 13021
Hidden Brook Way 13021
Hidden Valley Blvd 13021
Highland Bch & St 13021
Highland St Ext 13021
Hillside Ter 13021
Hobart Ave 13021
Hobson Ave 13021
Hockeborne Ave 13021
Hoffman St 13021
Holland Dr 13021
Holley St 13021
Honeysuckle Rd 13021
N & S Hoopes Ave 13021
Horan Ave 13021
Howard St 13021
Hulbert St 13021
Hume Ln 13021
N & S Hunter Ave 13021
Hurd Cir 13021
Indarria St 13021
Irish Rd 13021
James St 13021
Janet St 13021
Jarvis St 13021
Jefferson St 13021
John St 13021
John Smith Ave 13021
Johnson Dr 13021
Justin Dr 13021
Karlin Mnr 13021
Kearney Ave 13021
Kennedy Ln 13021
Kensington Ave 13021
Kenwood Rd 13021
Ketchell St 13021
Kijowski Rd 13021
Kitty Ln 13021
Koenig Ct 13021
Koenigs Point Rd 13021
Koon Rd 13021
Kristy Ln 13021
Lafayette Pl 13021
E & W Lake Ave & Rd 13021
Lake Avenue Ext 13021
W Lake Mobile Home Park 13021
Lakehurst Dr 13021
Lakeshore Dr 13021
E Lakeview Dr 13021
Lansing St 13021
Large Rd 13021
Lasher Rd 13021
Lawton Ave 13021
Leavenworth Ave 13021
Letchworth St 13021
N & S Lewis Rd & St 13021
Lexington Ave 13021
Liberty St 13021
Lime Kiln Rd 13021
Lincoln St 13021
Linen St 13021
Linn Ave 13021
Lizette St 13021
Lockwood Rd 13021
Locust St 13021
Logan St 13021
Longpoint On Owasco 13021
Loop Rd 13021
Lorraine Ave 13021
Macdougall St 13021
Madison Ave 13021
Mahaney St 13021
Mandy Rue 13021
Mann St 13021
Manor House Dr 13021
Manrow Rd 13021
Maple St 13021
Market St 13021
Martin Rd 13021
N & S Marvine Ave 13021
Mary St 13021
Mattie Pl & St 13021
Mcclelland Dr 13021
Mcconnell Ave & Ter 13021
Mccormick Way 13021
Mcdonald Rd 13021
Mcintosh Dr 13021
Mcmaster Pl & St 13021
Mead St 13021
Meadow Ln 13021
Meadow View Ln 13021
Meadowbrook Dr 13021
Melone Vlg 13021
Melrose Pkwy & Rd 13021
Metcalf Dr 13021
Mill St 13021
Miller Rd & St 13021
Milligan St 13021
Mobbs Rd 13021
Montross Ln 13021
Moraine Mnr 13021
Morningside Dr 13021
Morris St 13021
Mullen Dr 13021
Mundt Ave 13021
Munro Ave 13021
Murphy Dr & Way 13021
Murray Hl & St 13021
Mutton Hill Rd 13021
Myrtle Ave 13021
Near Pl 13021
Nelson Rd & St 13021
Nesbit Ln 13021
Noonan Ln 13021
Norma Dr 13021
Norman Ave 13021
Norris Ave 13021
North Park, Rd & St 13021
Northrup Rd 13021
Nugent Rd 13021
Oak St 13021
Oak Creek Town Houses 13021
Oakridge Rd 13021
Oakwood Ave & Rd 13021
Old State Rd 13021
Olympia Ave & Ter 13021
Oneil Rd 13021
Orchard Ave & St 13021
Osborne St 13021
Overbrook Dr 13021
Owasco Dr, Rd, St & Ter 13021
Paige Rd 13021
Palm Dr 13021
Palmer St 13021
Parcell Rd 13021
W Park Ave & Pl 13021
Parker St 13021
Parkwood Ln 13021
Parsons St 13021
Patriot Way 13021
Paul St 13021
Peach Tree Rd 13021
Peacock St 13021
Pearce Ave 13021
Pennrose Est 13021
Perrine Ave & St 13021
Perry St 13021
Petre Dr 13021
Pimm Ave 13021
Pinckney Rd 13021
Pine St 13021
Pine Ridge Rd 13021
Pinfeather Pl 13021
Plaza Dr 13021
Pleasant St 13021
Poplar Bch & Cv 13021
Potter Rd 13021
Powers Rd 13021
Prospect St 13021
Pulaski St 13021
Pulsifer Dr 13021
Quarry Rd 13021
Quicksilver Dr 13021
Quill Ave 13021
Rathbun Ave 13021
Red Tape Dr 13021
Reyer Rd 13021
Rice Rd 13021
Richardson Ave 13021
Ridge Rd 13021
Riester Rd 13021
Riverside Dr 13021
Roberts Rd 13021
Robinson Rd 13021
Rochester St 13021
Rock Ave 13021
Rockefeller Rd 13021
Rockingham Rd 13021
Roselawn Ln 13021
Rosewood Dr 13021
Ross Pl, St & Way 13021
Ross Street Ext 13021
Saint Anthony St 13021
Sam Adams Ln 13021
Sand Beach Dr & Rd 13021
Scammell Ave 13021
Schell Ln 13021
School St 13021
Schwartz Dr 13021
Schwartz Towers 13021
Second Ave 13021
Seminary Ave & St 13021
Seneca Pkwy 13021
Sevior Rd 13021
N & S Seward Ave 13021
Seymour St 13021
Sharon Dr 13021
Shearin St 13021
Sheldon Ave 13021
Sheridan St 13021
Sherman Rd & St 13021
Sherwood St 13021
Shevchenko Ave 13021
Shine Ln 13021
Silver Ave 13021
Silver Street Rd 13021
Sine Rd 13021
Sittser Rd 13021
Skillett Rd 13021
Sloan Rd 13021
Somerset Ave 13021
South St 13021
Southfield Apt 13021
Spencer Dr 13021
Spring St 13021
Standart Ave 13021
Standart Woods 13021
State St 13021
State Route 326 13021
State Route 34 13021
State Route 34b 13021
State Route 38a 13021
State Street Rd 13021
Steel St 13021
Stillmeadow Ln 13021
Stone School Rd 13021
Strawberry Ln 13021
N & S Street Rd 13021
Stryker Ave 13021
Stryker Homes 13021
Sumner St 13021
Sunrise Trl 13021
Sunset Beach Rd 13021
Swamp Rd 13021
Swartout Rd 13021
Sweetwater Way 13021
Swift St 13021
Swift Street Ext 13021
Taber Dr 13021
Taylor Rd 13021
Technology Park Blvd 13021
Tehan Ave 13021
Teller Ave 13021
Third Ave 13021
Thompson Rd 13021
Thornton Ave 13021
Throop Ave 13021
Town Hall Rd 13021
Town Line Rd 13021
Townsend Ln & Rd 13021
Train Dr 13021
Tubman Ln 13021
Turnpike Rd 13021
Tuxill Sq 13021
Twelve Corners Rd 13021
Tyler Dr 13021
Underwood St 13021
Union St 13021
Upper Dr 13021
Valentine Rd 13021
Van Anden St 13021
Van Duyne Ave 13021
Van Patten St 13021
Vandenbosch Ave 13021
Vanderstow Rd 13021
Vanliew Rd 13021
Venice St 13021
Victory Dr 13021
Vista St 13021
Wadsworth St 13021
Waldron Rd 13021
Walker Rd 13021
Wall St 13021
Wallace Ave 13021
Walnut St 13021
Walnut Street Ext 13021
Ward Ln 13021
Wards Rd 13021
Warren Ave 13021
Washington St 13021
Water St 13021
Waterford Ln 13021
Waters Edge 13021
Webb Rd 13021
Webster Ln & Rd 13021
Weedsport Sennett Rd 13021
Wegman St 13021
Weimans Cv 13021
West Dr & St 13021
Westlake Ave 13021
Westwood Dr 13021
Wheeler St 13021
White Birch Ln 13021
White Bridge Rd 13021
Whitehead Ln 13021
Wide Waters Ln 13021
Wiggins Rd 13021
Wilbur Ave 13021
Willard St 13021
Willey St 13021
William St 13021
Willis Dr 13021
Willow Dr 13021
Willowbrook Dr & Rd 13021
Wilson Ave 13021
Windsong Way 13021
Wisteria Ln 13021
Wood St 13021
Woodhollow Dr 13021
Woodlawn Ave 13021
Woodruff Pl 13021
Worden Ave 13021
Wright Ave & Cir 13021
Wyckoff Rd 13021
Yale Ave 13021
York St 13021
Youngs Rd 13021
Zoar St 13021

BATAVIA NY

General Delivery 14020

POST OFFICE BOXES MAIN OFFICE STATIONS AND BRANCHES

Box No.s
All PO Boxes 14021

NAMED STREETS

Adams St 14020

Agpark Dr N & W 14020
Alexander Rd 14020
Allanview Dr 14020
Allen St 14020
Alva Pl 14020
Apollo Dr 14020
Arena Pkwy 14020
Bank St 14020
Bank Street Rd 14020
Batavia Bethany Townl Rd 14020
Batavia Byron Rd 14020
Batavia City Ctr 14020
Batavia Elba Townline Rd 14020
Batavia Oakfield Town Rd 14020
Batavia Stafford Town Rd 14020
Beckwith Rd 14020
Belvedere Ln 14020
E, N, S & W Bennett Hts 14020
W Bethany Rd 14020
Birchwood Dr 14020
Blakely Pl 14020
Bogue Ave 14020
Briarwood Ter 14020
Broadlawn Ave 14020
Brooklyn Ave 14020
Brown Rd 14020
Bryant St 14020
Buell St 14020
Burke Dr 14020
Buxton Ave 14020
Call Pkwy 14020
Carolwood Dr 14020
Cecere Dr 14020
Cedar St 14020
Center St 14020
Central Ave 14020
Chandler Ave 14020
Charles St 14020
Chase Park 14020
Cherry St 14020
Cheryl Ln 14020
Chestnut St 14020
Clifton Ave 14020
Clinton Park & St 14020
Clinton Street Rd 14020
College Mdws & Rd 14020
Collegeview Dr 14020
Colonial Blvd 14020
Colorado Ave 14020
Columbia Ave 14020
Commerce Dr 14020
Cone St 14020
Cone Dorman Rd 14020
Court St 14020
Court Street Plz 14020
Creek Rd 14020
Crescent Ct 14020
Crystal Ln 14020
Davis Ave 14020
Dawson Pl 14020
Dellinger Ave 14020
Denio St 14020
Dennis Dr 14020
Dewey Ave 14020
Donahue Rd 14020
Douglas St 14020
Downey Rd 14020
East Ave & Rd 14020
Edgewood Dr 14020
Edwards St 14020
Eleanor Pl 14020
Elizabeth St 14020
Ellicott Ave, Pl & St 14020
Ellicott Street Rd 14020
Ellsworth Ave 14020
Elm St 14020
Elmwood Ave 14020
Eugene St 14020
Evans St 14020
Evergreen Dr 14020
Fairmont Ave 14020
Fairway Dr 14020
Farwell Dr 14020
Federal Dr 14020
Fisher Park 14020
Florence Ave 14020
Fordham Dr 14020
Forest Edge Dr 14020
Fotch Rd 14020
Francis Rd 14020
Franklin St 14020
Galloway Rd 14020
Ganson Ave 14020
Garden Dr 14020
Garfield Ave 14020
Gaslite Ln 14020
Gateway Dr 14020
Genesee St 14020
Goade Park 14020
Graham St 14020
Grandview Ter 14020
Hall St 14020
Haller Pl 14020
Halstead Rd 14020
Harrold Sq 14020
Hart St 14020
Harvester Ave 14020
Haven Ln 14020
Hewitt Pl 14020
Highland Park 14020
Hillcrest St 14020
Hillside Dr 14020
Holland Ave 14020
Holmes Ave 14020
Hopkins Rd 14020
Horseshoe Lake Rd 14020
Howard St 14020
Hull Park 14020
Hutchins Pl & St 14020
Hyde Park 14020
Industrial Blvd & Plz 14020
S Jackson Ave & St 14020
James St 14020
Jamitann St 14020
Jefferson Ave 14020
Jerome Pl 14020
Kelsey Rd 14020
Kibbe Ave 14020
Kieffer Rd 14020
Kingsbury Ave 14020
La Crosse Ave 14020
E, NW, S & W Lake Rd 14020
Law St 14020
Lear Rd 14020
Lehigh Ave & Rd 14020
Lewis Ave & Pl 14020
Lewiston Rd 14020
Liberty St 14020
Lincoln Ave 14020
Linwood Ave 14020
Lovers Lane Rd 14020
N & S Lyon St 14020
Macarthur Dr 14020
Macomber Rd 14020
Madison Ave 14020
Main St 14020
E Main St 14020
S Main St 14020
W Main St
1-499 14020
2-2 14021
4-498 14020
244-248-244-248 14020
E Main Street Rd 14020
Manhattan Ave 14020
Maple Rd & St 14020
Margaret Pl 14020
Masse Pl 14020
Mckinley Ave 14020
Meadowcrest Dr 14020
Med Tech Dr 14020
Mill Rd & St 14020
Miller Ave & Rd 14020
Mix Pl 14020
Montclair Ave 14020
Morse Pl 14020
Morton Ave 14020
Naramore Dr 14020
New York Pl 14020
Noonan Dr 14020
Norris Ave 14020
North Park & St 14020
Northern Blvd 14020
Oak St 14020
Oak Orchard Rd 14020
Oakland Ave 14020
Old Creek Rd 14020
Old Meadow Ln 14020
Olyn Ave 14020
Orange Grove Dr 14020
Orleans Ave 14020
Osterhout Ave 14020
Otis St 14020
Overlook Dr 14020
Park Ave & Rd 14020
Pearl St 14020
Pearl Street Rd 14020
N Pembroke Rd 14020
Pickthorn Dr 14020
Pike Rd 14020
Pine Hollow Dr 14020
N Pointe Dr 14020
Porter Ave 14020
Powers Rd 14020
Pratt Rd 14020
Prestige Xing 14020
Pringle Ave 14020
Prole Rd 14020
Prospect Ave 14020
Prune St 14020
Putnam Rd 14020
R Stephen Hawley Dr 14020
Raymond Ave 14020
Redfield Pkwy 14020
Richmond Ave 14020
River St 14020
Rollin Cir E & W 14020
Roosevelt Ave 14020
Rose Rd 14020
Ross St 14020
E & W Saile Dr 14020
School St 14020
Seneca Ave 14020
Seven Springs Rd 14020
Shady Ln 14020
Shepard Rd 14020
Slusser Rd 14020
Soccio St 14020
Spencer Ct 14020
N & S Spruce St 14020
State St 14020
State Street Rd 14020
Stegman Rd 14020
Stringham Dr 14020
Summit St 14020
Sumner St 14020
Sunset Ter 14020
S Swan St 14020
Terry Hills Dr 14020
Thomas Ave 14020
Thorpe St 14020
Tracy Ave 14020
Treadeasy Ave 14020
Trojan Cir 14020
Trumbull Pkwy 14020
Union Sq & St 14020
Upton Rd 14020
Valle Dr 14020
Valley View Dr 14020
Vernon Ave 14020
Verona Ave 14020
Veterans Memorial Dr 14020
Victorian Dr 14020
Vine St 14020
Violet Ln 14020
Wade Ave 14020
Walden Creek Dr 14020
Walker Ave & Pl 14020
Wallace St 14020
Walnut Pl & St 14020
Warren St 14020
Washington Ave 14020
Watson St 14020
Webster Ave 14020
West Ave 14020
Wiard St 14020
Wilkinson Rd 14020
Williams St 14020
Willow St 14020
Wood St 14020
Woodcrest Dr 14020
Woodland Dr 14020
Woodrow Rd 14020
Woodstock Gdns 14020
Wortendyke Rd 14020

BAYSIDE NY

POST OFFICE BOXES MAIN OFFICE STATIONS AND BRANCHES

Box No.s
1 - 704 11361
4001 - 605127 11360
610001 - 610704 11361

NAMED STREETS

Abbott Rd 11359
Bay Club Dr 11360
Bayside St 11359
Bell Blvd
1200-1298 11360
1300-2999 11360
3200-4799 11361
Bonnie Ln 11360
Brian Cres 11360
Chapel Rd 11359
Circle Dr 11359
Clearview Expy
2600-2799 11360
2801-2899 11360
3200-4299 11361
4301-4599 11361
Corbett Rd 11361
Corporal Kennedy St
1800-3099 11360
3200-3298 11361
3300-4399 11361
Corporal Stone St 11361
Cross Island Pkwy 11360
Darren Dr 11360
Diane Pl 11360
Duane Rd 11359
Emily Rd 11360
Estates Dr & Ln 11360
Francis Lewis Blvd 11361
General Rw Berry Dr 11359
Hicha St 11360
Jordan Ct & Dr 11360
Lee Rd 11359
Little Bay Rd 11359
Little Neck Blvd 11360
Lori Dr 11360
Melissa Ct 11360
Michael Ct & Pl 11360
Murray Ave 11359
North Loop 11359
Northern Blvd 11361
Oceania St 11361
Ordinance Rd 11359
Pratt Ave 11359
Robert Rd 11360
Robin Ln 11360
Rocky Hill Rd 11361
Sgt Beers Ave & Ln 11359
Shore Rd 11359
Silleriv St 11361
Springfield Blvd 11361
Story Ave 11359
Totten Ave 11359
Virelins Rd 11359
Walter Reed Rd 11359
Waters Edge Dr 11360
Weaver Ave 11359
Weeks Ln 11361
Westaway Rd 11359
Whistler Ave 11359
Willets St 11359
Willets Point Blvd 11360

NUMBERED STREETS

14th Ave 11360
15th Ave, Dr & Rd 11360
16th Ave 11360
17th Ave 11360
18th Ave 11360
19th Ave 11360
22nd Ave 11360
23rd Ave & Rd 11360
24th Ave & Rd 11360
26th Ave 11360
27th Ave 11360
28th Ave & Rd 11360
29th Ave 11360
30th Ave 11360
31st Rd 11360
32nd Ave & Rd 11361
33rd Ave & Rd 11361
34th Ave & Rd 11361
35th Ave 11361
36th Ave 11361
37th Ave 11361
38th Ave 11361
39th Ave 11361
40th Ave 11361
41st Ave & Rd 11361
42nd Ave 11361
43rd Ave 11361
44th Ave 11361
45th Ave, Dr & Rd 11361
46th Ave & Rd 11361
47th Ave & Rd 11361
200th St
1500-2999 11360
3200-3499 11361
201st St
1500-2999 11360
3200-4799 11361
202nd St
1500-2198 11360
3200-4799 11361
203rd Pl 11360
203rd St
2600-2999 11360
3200-4746 11361
204th St
2300-2400 11360
3200-4799 11361
205th St
2300-2399 11360
3200-4399 11361
206th St
2300-2399 11360
4600-4799 11361
207th St
2300-2399 11360
4301-4697 11361
208th Pl 11360
208th St
1500-3099 11360
3200-3298 11361
209th Pl 11360
209th St
1300-1599 11360
3300-3318 11361
210th Pl 11360
210th St
2600-2900 11360
2902-2998 11360
3201-3297 11361
3299-4799 11361
211th St
1800-2999 11360
3200-4799 11361
212th St
1300-2999 11360
3200-4799 11361
213th St
2600-2999 11360
3200-4799 11361
214th Pl
2800-2999 11360
3200-4399 11361
214th St
2800-2971 11360
2973-3399 11361
215th Pl
2800-2999 11360
3200-3498 11361
3500-4799 11361
215th St
1500-2999 11360
3200-4799 11361
216th St
1500-2999 11360
3500-4799 11361
217th St 11361
218th St
2900-3199 11360
3600-4699 11361
219th St 11361
220th Pl & St 11361
221st St 11361
222nd St 11361
223rd St 11361

BINGHAMTON NY

General Delivery 13902

POST OFFICE BOXES MAIN OFFICE STATIONS AND BRANCHES

Box No.s
F1706 - F1706 13902
D1017 - D1017 13902
1 - 320 13903
1 - 305 13905
2 - 232 13904
301 - 1980 13902
345 - 390 13905
401 - 480 13903
445 - 777 13905
2001 - 90490 13902

RURAL ROUTES

08 13901

HIGHWAY CONTRACTS

61 13903
06, 07 13904
04 13905

NAMED STREETS

A Cline Rd 13903
Abbott St 13904
Aberystwyth Pl 13905
Acre Pl 13904
Adams Dr & St 13905
Addison Ct 13904
Adriance Rd 13903
Afton St 13903
Ahern Rd 13903
Airport Rd
2-30 13901
32-299 13901
1001-1097 13905
1099-2299 13905
1732-1-1732-2 13905
Aitchison Rd 13905
Aldrich Ave 13903
Alfred St 13903
Alice St
1-11 13901
1-25 13904
2-10 13901
10-10 13904
12-14 13901
12-28 13904
7-9-7-9 13904
Alida Ave 13901
Allen St 13901
Allendale Rd 13903
Alpine Rd 13903
Amsbry St 13901
Andrews Ave 13904
Angela Ct 13903
Annette Ave 13905
Anoka Rd 13905
Aquinas St 13905
Arbutus Ln 13901
Ardsley Rd 13904
Arthur St 13905
Asbury Ave 13901
Asbury Ct 13905
Athan St 13903
Atherly Park 13903
Audubon Ave 13903
Avalon Rd 13901
Avenue A 13901
Avenue B 13901
Avon Rd 13905
Ayres St 13905
Badger Dr 13901
Badger Rd 13904
Baird Ave 13901
Baker Rd 13901
Balcom Ave 13905
Baldwin St 13903
Ball Ave 13901
Ballard St 13904
Baltimore Ave 13903
Banford Rd 13901
Barbara Ave 13903
Barlow Rd 13904
Barney Ct 13903
Barrier Rd 13905
Barry Way 13901
Bartell Rd 13905
Baxter Ave & St 13905
Bayless Ave 13903
Beacon St 13901
Beckwith Ave 13901
Bedford St 13903
Beech St 13903
Beechknoll Rd 13903
Beers Rd 13901
Beethoven St 13905
Belair Dr 13901
Belden St 13903
Belknap Ave 13905
Bellaire Ave 13905
Bellevue Ave & Hts 13905
Bellview Rd 13904
Beman St 13901
Bennett Ave 13905
Berlin St 13905
Bernice Blvd 13903
Berwick Ave 13904
Bevier Ct 13901
Bevier St
1-23 13901
25-67 13901
89-577 13904
579-581 13904
Bigelow St 13904
Billata Dr 13901
Bingham St 13904
Birch St 13903
Birchwood Dr 13905
Bishop Rd 13901
Blackstone Ave 13903
Blanchard Ave 13901
Bobs Blvd 13901
Boland Rd 13905
Bond St 13903
Bonita Dr 13904
Booth Rd 13905
Boulevard Ter 13905
Bradley St 13904

Street	ZIP
Brady Hill Rd	13903
Brandywine Ave & St	13901
Brevity Ct	13905
Briar Ct	13905
Briarwood Rd	13904
Brick Ave	13901
Bridge St	13901
Brigham Rd	13905
Brigham St	13903
Brinkman Rd	13903
Brintnall Pl	13905
Broad Ave	13904
Broad St	
2-2	13901
3-3	13904
11-11	13901
13-13	13904
15-30	13904
35-45	13901
N Broad St	13901
Broad Acres Dr	13901
Bromley Ave	13901
Brook Ave	
1-7	13901
1-7	13903
2-20	13901
2-98	13903
9-17	13901
19-99	13903
Brookfield Rd	13903
Brooks Rd	13905
Brookside Rd	13903
Brookview Dr	13901
Broome St	13903
N Broome St	13901
Brotzman Rd	13901
Brown Rd	13903
Brown St	13905
Brownell Ave	13905
Brownson St	13901
Buckley Rd	13901
Burdick Rd	13903
Burlington St	13903
Burr Ave	13903
Burton Ave	13904
Butchs Blvd	13901
Bystrak Dr	13905
Calgary Ln	13901
Campbell Rd	13905
Campbell Rd Ct	13905
Canfield Rd	13904
Capwell Ave	13901
Carhart Ave	13905
Carlton St	13903
Carman Rd	13903
Carmichael Rd	13901
Carol Ct	13903
Carroll St	13901
Cary St	13901
Castle Creek Rd	13901
Catherine St	
1-11	13905
52-52	13904
E Catherine St	13904
Cedar St	13905
Centenary St	13901
Center St	13901
Chadwick Rd	13903
Chamberlain St	13904
Chambers St	13903
Chapel Pl	13905
Chapin St	13905
Charles Pl & St	13905
Charlotte St	13905
Charmel Dr	13901
Chase Ave & Ct	13901
Chelsea Sq	13905
Chenango Ln	13901
Chenango Pl	13901
W Chenango Rd	
5-5	13901
401-439	13905
441-734	13905
736-798	13905
Chenango St	
679A-679B	13901
1-85	13901
87-1303	13901
120-120	13902
212-1398	13901
777-779-777-779	13901
87-89-87-89	13901
Chenango Bridge Rd	13901
Cherese Ln	13905
Cherry Ln	13901
Cheryl Dr	13903
Cheshire Rd	13903
Chester St	13901
Chestnut St	13905
Chitanne Rd	13903
Chris Ct	13901
Christopher St	13903
Church St	13901
Circle Dr	13905
E Clapham St	13904
Clarence St	13903
Clarendon Dr	13901
Clark Ave	13901
Clarke St	13905
Clayton Ave	13904
Clearview Ave	13903
Clearview Pl	13901
Cleveland Ave	13905
Cliff Ave	13905
Clifford St	13901
Clifton Ave	13905
Clifton Blvd	13903
Cline Rd	13903
Clinton St	13905
E Clinton St	13901
Clubhouse Rd	13903
Clyde Gruver Rd	13901
Cobblestone Ct	13903
Cohoes St	13903
Colchester Dr	13903
Coleman Rd	13903
Colesville Rd	13904
Colfax Ave	13905
College St	13905
College View Rd	13905
Collier St	13901
Columbia Ave	13903
Columbine Dr	13901
Columbus Park E	13901
Columbus St	13905
Commercial Aly	13901
Commercial Dr	13905
Congdon Pl	13901
Conklin Ave & Rd	13903
Conklin Forks Rd	13903
Conti Ct	13905
Corbett Ave	13903
Cornell Ave	
1-99	13903
1100-1299	13901
Cornell Ct	13901
Cornish Ave	13901
Corporate Dr	13904
Councilman Rd	13901
Country Trl	13905
Country Knoll Dr	13901
Court St	
2-2	13901
4-227	13901
229-273	13901
293-333	13904
335-500	13904
502-528	13904
111-115-111-115	13901
184-186-184-186	13901
218-222-218-222	13901
7-9-7-9	13901
Coventry Ln	13903
Crandall St	13905
Crary Ave	13905
Crestmont Rd	13905
Crocker Hill Rd	13904
Cross St	13903
Curran Ave	13903
Cushman Blvd	13901
Cutler Pond Rd	13905
Cynthia Dr	13903
Cypress St	13905
Daisy Dr	13905
Dale Ct	13901
Daniel Dr	13901
Dau Ct	13904
David Ave	13901
David Ct	13903
Davis Rd	13901
Davis St	13905
Deborah Dr	13901
Decatur St	13903
Decker Rd	13903
Dedrick Hill Rd	13905
Deer Run Ln	13903
Deforest St	13901
Delavan Ave	13903
Dellwood Pl & Rd	13903
Delmar St	13903
Dennison Ave	13901
Denton Rd	13903
N Depot St	13901
Depot Hill Rd	13904
Devon Blvd	13903
Dewey Ave	13903
Diane Dr	13904
Dickinson Ave	13901
Dickinson St	13905
Dimmock Hill Rd	13905
Division St	13905
Dogwood Dr	13903
Donna Ct	13901
Donna Ln	13903
E Dorman Rd	13901
Dorothy St	13901
Doubleday St	13901
Douglas Dr	13903
Downs Ave	13905
Druid Pl	13905
Duane Ave	13903
Duell Rd	13904
Duffy Ct	13905
Duke Rd & St	13903
Dunham Hill Rd	13905
Duryea Rd	13901
Dutchess Rd	13901
Earle Dr	13903
East Ave	13903
East St	13904
Eaton Pl	13905
Edelweiss Ln	13901
Edgebrook Rd	13903
Edgecomb Rd	13905
Edgewood Rd	13903
Edison Ave	13903
Edna Ave	13903
Edwards Ln	13901
Edwards Rd	13904
Edwards St	
1-15	13901
1-15	13905
2-12	13901
2-98	13905
17-17	13901
17-99	13905
Edwin Ln	13901
Elaine Dr	13905
Eldredge St	13901
Elizabeth Ln	13903
Elizabeth St	13901
Ellen St	13901
Ellis Rd	13904
Ellsworth Rd	13903
Elm St	13905
Elwell Ave	13901
Elwood Ave	13901
Ely St	13904
N Ely St	13901
Ely Park Blvd	13905
Emerson Pkwy	13905
Emma St	13905
Emmett St	13901
W End Ave	13905
English St	13904
Equipment Dr	13904
Erie St	13905
Espial Dr	13903
Esther Ave	13903
Ethel St	13905
Euclid Ave	13903
Evans St	13903
Evelyn Pl	13903
Everett Rd	13901
Everett St	
2-2	13905
4-18	13905
20-20	13905
25-33	13901
35-42	13901
44-98	13901
Everline St	13903
Exchange St	13901
Fairview Ave & Ter	13904
Farrell Dr	13901
Farview Ave	13903
Fayette St	13901
Fazon Ct	13905
Fellows Ave	13904
Felters Rd	13903
Fenton Ave	13901
Ferndale Dr	13905
Fernwood Ln	13901
Field St	13905
Flagg Rd	13904
Flint Rd	13905
N Floral Ave	13905
Florence Ave	13905
Florence St	
1-11	13905
13-99	13905
3400-3498	13903
3500-3599	13903
Flower St	13904
Foland Rd	13903
Forest St	13903
Forest Hill Rd	13903
Forest Hills Blvd	13905
Fowler Pl	13903
Fox Ln	13901
Fox Rd	13905
Fox Hollow Rd	13904
Francis St	13905
Frank St	13905
Franklin Ave	13901
Franklin St	
1-99	13905
1901-1947	13903
1949-2099	13903
Franklin Avenue Ext	13901
Frederick Rd	13901
S Frederick Rd	13901
Frederick St	13901
E Frederick St	13904
French Ct	13904
Front St	13905
Fuller Rd & St	13901
Fuller Hollow Rd	13903
Gage Rd	13905
Gaines St	13905
Gar Glen Dr	13904
Garden Ave	13904
Gardner Rd	13903
Garfield Ave	13905
Gary St	13905
Gates St	13903
Gaylord St	13904
Gee St	13903
Genesee Ave	13903
Geneva St	13903
George St	13904
Gerard Ave	13905
Gilbert St	13903
Giles St	13905
Gillen Dr	13903
Gillespie Rd	13903
Gilmore Ave	13901
Ginny Ln	13901
Glen Ave	13904
Glenwood Ave & Rd	13905
Goethe St	13905
Gold St	13904
Gorden St	13901
Gordon Dr	13901
Gordon Pl	13905
Grace St	13905
Gradinda Pkwy	13902
Grand Ave	13905
Grand Blvd	13905
Grand St	13903
Grandview Ave	13904
Grandview Dr	13905
Grandview St	13903
Grant Ave	13905
Grant Rd	13901
Grant St	
1-11	13901
2-6	13904
8-16	13901
8-12	13904
14-45	13904
47-47	13904
Gratsinger Rd	13903
Gray Ct	13903
Gray St	13904
Green St	13901
Green Meadow Ln	13901
Gregory Ave	13901
Gregory Ln	13905
Gregory Rd	13903
Griffis St	13904
Griswold St	13904
Grummon St	13903
Guilfoyle Ave	13903
Hadsell Ct & Rd	13901
Haendel St	13905
Halford St	13905
Hall St	13903
Hallam St	13903
Hamilton St	13905
E & W Hamton Rd	13903
Hance Rd	13903
Hancock St	13903
Hand Rd	
1-99	13905
101-199	13905
3900-4099	13903
Harding Ave	
1-1	13901
1-19	13903
20-22	13901
21-65	13903
28-98	13903
Harding Ln	13901
Harmony Ln	13901
Harris Rd	13905
Harrison St	13905
Hartley Rd	13901
Haskins Ave	13904
Hastings St	13901
Hawkins Rd	13904
Hawley St	13901
Hawleyton Rd	13903
Hawthorne Rd	13903
Hayden St	13905
Hayes Rd	13905
Hayes St	13903
Hazard Hill Rd	13903
Hazel St	13905
Heath Dr	13901
Heavy Equipment Rd	13904
Heights Ct	13905
Helen St	13905
Hemlock Ln	13901
Henry St	
1-26	13901
28-298	13901
115-115	13905
211-211	13901
Herman Ave	13905
Hiawatha Trl	13901
Hickory Ln	13903
Hickory Rd	13905
Hidden Pine Ct	13903
High St	13903
Highland Ave	13905
Highland Rd	13901
Highover Rd	13901
E Hill Rd	13901
Hill St	
1-3	13901
2-2	13904
4-14	13901
5-15	13901
Hillcrest Ave	13901
Hillside Ave	13903
Hillside Dr	13905
Hinds St	13901
Hiner Rd	13904
Hodge Ave	13901
Hoffman Dr	13901
Hogan Rd	13903
Holland Ave & St	13905
Holmes Pl	13903
Home Ave	13903
Homer St	13903
Horthol St	13901
Hospital Hill Rd	13901
Hotchkiss Ave	13901
Hotchkiss St	13903
Houdlum Hill Rd	13905
Howard Ave	13904
Howard Dr	13901
Howell Rd	13903
Hoyt Ave	13901
Hughes St	13903
Hunters Landing Rd	13903
Indiana St	13903
Industrial Park	13904
Industrial Park Dr	13904
Ingraham Hill Rd	13903
Iris Dr	13905
Irving Ave	13901
Isbell St	13901
Iva Ave & St	13903
Ivan Ln	13901
Ivanhoe Rd	13903
J T Blvd	13905
Jackson Rd & St	13903
Jacobs Hwy	13901
James Ave	13901
James St	13903
Jameson Rd	13905
Janette Ave	13905
Jarvis St	13905
Jason Dr	13901
Jay St	13901
Jean Ct	13901
Jefferson Ave	13905
Jefferson St	13903
Jeffrey Dr	13901
Jerome Ave	13905
Jessie Dr	13901
Jewell Ave	13901
John St	
1-99	13903
200-220	13905
John Smith Rd	13901
Johnson Ave, Rd & St	13905
Jolen Dr	13905
Jones St	13905
Jr Blvd	13903
Judson Ave	13905
Julian St	13905
June St	13903
Jutland Rd	13903
Kabanek Rd	13903
Kane Ave	13903
Karen Ct	13903
Karlada Dr	13905
Kattelville Rd	13901
Keeler Ave	13901
Kendall Ave	13903
Kenilworth Rd	13903
Kennedy Rd	13901
Kennedy St	13903
Kimball St	13903
King Ave	13905
Kings Row	13901
Kinney St	13901
Kirkwood Ave	13901
Knapp Rd	13905
Kneeland Ave	13905
Kolb Rd	13905
Kostyshak Rd	13903
Krager Rd	13904
Kress St	13903
La France Rd	13901
La Grange St	13905
Lake Ave	
1-11	13905
2-8	13901
2-12	13905
13-17	13901
13-71	13905
14-14	13901
14-68	13905
Lakeview Ter	13904
Lamont St	13903
Lanesboro St	13903
Larchmont Rd	13903
Lathrop Ave	13905
Lathrop Rd	13903
Laurel Ave	13905
Laurie Brook Dr	13903
Lawson Ct	13905
Lawton Ave	13905
Leekville Rd	13905
Lennox Dr	13903
Lenox Ln	13901
Leon Ave	13904
Leonard Ln	13901
Leroy St	13905
Lewis Rd	13905
Lewis St	13901
Liberty St	13901
Lillian Dr	13903
Lincoln Ave	13905
Lincoln St	13901
W Lincoln St	13905
Linda Dr	13905
Linden St	13901
Lindows Dr	13905
Link Dr	13904
Lisi Ln	13903
Lisle Ave	13901
Livingston St	13903
Locke Dr	13903
Lockwood St	13901
Lois St	13901
Lolita St	13901
Longview Ave	13905
Lookout St	13903
Loretta Dr	13905
Lori Ln	13903
Lorraine Ave	13905
Lotus Ave	13903
Loughlin Rd	13904
Louisa St	13904
N Louisa St	13901
Lourdes Rd	13905
Lowell Dr	13901
Lower Stella Ireland Rd	13905
Lt Vanwinkle Dr	13905
Lucy St	13903
Lydia St	13905
Lyon St	13901
Mac George Ave	13903
Macomber Ave	13901
Macon St	13903
Maiden Ln	13905
Main St	13905
Manier Ave	13903
Manor Dr	13905
Maple Ave	
1-5	13901
1-7	13903
2-12	13901
2-12	13903
9-9	13901
11-11	13903
13-13	13901
13-13	13903
Maple St	13905
Maplewood Dr	13901
Margaret St	13905
Margery St	13903
Maria Blvd & Mnr	13903
Marian Ter	13901
Marilyn Ave	13903
Marine Midland Plz	13901
Marion Ct	13903

Marion St 13905
Markay Ct 13905
Market St 13905
Martha St 13903
Mary Dr 13901
Mary St 13903
Mason Ave 13904
Mather St 13905
Matias Rd 13903
Matis St 13905
Matthew Ct & Dr 13901
Matthews Rd 13901
Matthews St 13905
Maxian Rd 13903
May St 13905
Maye St 13901
Mcdonald Ave 13905
Mcnamara Ave 13903
Mead Rd 13901
Meadow St 13905
Meadowood Ln 13901
Medford St 13903
Melcher St 13904
Mendelssohn St 13905
Merrick St 13904
Merrill Rd 13901
Merrill St 13905
Merritt St 13904
Michael Rd 13901
W Middle Ave 13905
Middle Stella Ireland Rd 13905
Midway Dr 13903
Midwood Dr 13903
Mildred Ave 13905
Mildred St 13903
Miles St 13905
Milford St 13904
Milks Rd 13903
Mill Rd
2-8 13901
10-99 13901
1400-2299 13903
2301-3809 13903
Mill St
1-1 13903
2-8 13901
2-16 13903
3-11 13901
3-15 13903
17-17 13901
17-3805 13903
18-18 13901
18-3804 13903
1/2-1/2 13901
Millard Ave 13905
Miller St
1-1 13903
2-8 13901
5-7 13903
10-98 13901
11-99 13901
Minden Ave 13905
Minerva Ave 13905
Mitchell Ave 13903
Moeller St 13904
N Moeller St 13901
Moffatt Ave 13901
Mohawk St 13903
Monroe St 13904
Montague St 13901
Montgomery St 13901
Montour St 13903
Montrose Ave 13903
Moody St 13904
Moore Ave & St 13903
Moran Ct 13903
Morgan Rd 13903
Morgan St 13901
N & S Morningside Dr 13905
Morris St 13903
Morrison Ave 13901
Mountain Park, Rd & Ter 13903
Mountainview Dr 13901
Mozart St 13905
Muckey Rd 13903
Mulberry St 13901
Munsell St 13901
Murphy Ave 13905
Murphy Rd 13903
Murray St 13905
Mygatt St 13905
Nash St 13904
New St
1-11 13901
2-12 13903
14-22 13903
24-98 13903
Newman Ave 13901
Newton Ave 13903
Newton St 13901
E Niles Rd 13901
Norfolk Rd 13903
Norman Rd 13901
Normandy Ct 13903
North Ave 13901
North Rd 13904
North St 13905
Norton Dr 13905
Norton Rd 13901
Nowlan Rd
1-121 13901
123-131 13901
151-187 13904
189-663 13904
665-699 13904
Noyes Rd 13903
Oak Dr 13901
Oak St 13905
Oak Hill Rd 13901
Oak Tree Dr 13903
Oakridge Dr 13903
Oconnell Rd 13903
Ogden St 13901
Old Pennsylvania Ave 13903
Old River Rd 13901
Old State Rd
2-140 13901
142-146 13901
200-202 13904
204-1699 13904
1701-1799 13904
Oliver St 13904
Olmstead St 13901
Oneonta St 13903
Orchard Ave 13904
Orchard Rd 13905
Orton Ave 13905
Oswego St 13903
Otseningo St 13903
Ouaquaga Rd 13904
Overbrook Ave 13903
Overbrook Dr 13901
Overland Dr 13903
Packard St 13905
Page Rd 13904
Palmer Rd & St 13901
Pamela Dr 13901
Panorama Dr 13901
Park Ave 13903
Park Rd 13901
Park St 13905
Park Terrace Pl 13903
Parkway Pl 13905
Parkway St 13903
Parkwood Ln 13903
Parsons St 13903
Partridge Ln 13903
Patch Rd 13901
Patricia St 13905
Patrick St 13901
Paul Dr 13901
Paula St 13901
Payne Way 13903
Pearl Ave 13903
Pearne St 13901
Peckham Rd 13903
Peer St 13901
Pembroke Dr 13901
Peninsula Dr 13901
Penn View Dr 13901
Pennsylvania Ave 13903
Penny Ln 13905
Penny St 13901
Penston Rd 13903
Perkins Ave 13901
Perry Rd & St 13905
Peterson Rd 13901
Phelps St
1-1 13901
1-3 13905
4-8 13901
4-14 13905
5-9 13905
11-11 13901
11-11 13905
15-15 13901
17-100 13901
102-110 13901
11 1/2-11 1/2 13905
2 1/2-2 1/2 13905
Phillips Way 13903
Phinn Ave 13903
Pierce St 13903
Pierce Creek Rd 13903
Pine Dr & St 13901
Pine Camp Dr 13904
Pinewood Dr 13901
Pleasant Ave 13901
Pleasant Ct 13905
Pleasant St 13901
Pleraina Rd 13904
Poland Ave 13905
Popes Ravine Rd 13904
Poplar Hill Rd 13901
Port Rd 13901
Porter Ave 13901
Powderhouse Rd 13903
Powers Rd 13903
Prague St 13905
Pratt Ct 13903
Prentice Blvd & Rd 13901
Prentice Hill Rd 13904
Prescott Rd 13905
Proctor St 13903
Progy Rd 13903
Prospect Ave 13901
Prospect St 13905
Pulaski St 13905
Quaker Lake Rd 13903
Queen St 13904
Quinn Rd 13901
Ransom Rd 13901
Renole Dr 13903
Republic St 13905
Reservoir St 13903
Rexford St 13903
Rexleigh St 13903
Reynolds Cir 13903
Rhodes Rd 13905
Richard Ave 13903
Richard Rd 13901
Richmond Ave 13903
Ridge St 13905
Ritchie Rd 13901
River Rd & St 13901
Riverside Dr 13905
Riverside St 13904
Riverview Ave 13904
Riverview Ln 13905
Riverview Rd 13901
Riverview St 13905
Roberts Rd 13903
Roberts St 13901
Robinson St
1-93 13901
94-369 13904
371-425 13904
216-218-216-218 13904
261-265-261-265 13904
276-280-276-280 13904
Rochelle Rd 13901
Rogers Mountain Way 13901
Rollins St 13903
Ronan St
1-3 13905
2-2 13901
4-6 13901
5-12 13905
8-10 13901
9-9 13901
11-36 13901
14-14 13905
38-42 13901
Roosevelt Ave 13901
Rosedale Dr 13905
Ross Hill Rd 13903
Rossmore Pl 13904
Rotary Ave 13905
Rowe Ave 13903
Rubin Ave 13904
Rugby Pl & Rd 13905
Rundall Pl 13905
Rush Ave 13903
Russell Rd 13901
Ruth Ct 13903
Ruth St 13905
Rutherford St 13901
Saddlebrook Dr 13901
Saddlemire Rd 13903
Saint Clair Ave & Rd 13903
Saint Cyril Ave 13905
Saint John Ave 13905
Saluda St 13901
Sandy Ln 13901
Sanitaria Springs Rd 13904
Saratoga Ave & Hts 13903
Savitch Rd 13901
Schiller St 13905
Schubert St 13905
Sears Rd 13905
Seminary Ave 13905
Seneca St 13903
Serrell Ave 13905
E & W Service Hwy 13901
Seymour Ave & St 13905
Shaw Pl 13901
Sheldon St 13903
Sherwood Ave 13903
Shipman Rd 13903
Shore Acres Dr 13901
Silver St 13904
Sky View Ln 13905
Slauson Ave 13905
Smith Ave 13904
Smith Rd 13903
Smith Hill Rd 13905
Snow Ave 13905
South St 13901
Sowden St 13905
Spaulding Rd 13903
Spellicy Blvd 13904
Spring Ln & St 13903
Spring Forest Ave 13905
Springer Rd 13904
Spruce St 13905
Spud Ln 13904
Spurr Ave 13903
Stacy Dr 13905
Standish Ave 13901
Stanford Pl 13905
Stanford Rd 13903
Stanley St 13905
Starr Ave 13905
W State St 13901
State Line Rd 13903
State Route 12 13905
State Route 369 13904
State Route 7b 13904
Stearns Rd 13905
Stephanie Ln 13903
Stephen Dr 13905
Stevens Rd 13903
Stever Dr 13901
Stokes Ave 13905
Stone Rd & St 13903
Stonecrest Ct 13903
Stratford Pl 13905
Stratmill Rd 13904
Stuart St 13901
Sturges St 13901
Stuyvesant St 13901
Summer St 13901
Summit Ave 13904
Sumner Ave 13905
Sundew Way 13901
Sunrise Dr 13905
Sunset Ave 13904
Sunset Dr 13905
Sunset Way 13901
Susan St 13901
Susquehanna St 13901
Swift Rd 13905
Taft Ave 13901
Taylor Pl 13905
Teeburn Blvd 13901
Telegraph St 13903
Terrace Ave 13901
Terrace Dr
1-99 13905
10-10 13903
28-36 13905
42-42 13903
48-54 13905
60-60 13903
64-98 13905
Terry Ave 13901
The Arena St 13903
The Circuit St 13903
Theresa Blvd
2-10 13901
12-134 13901
136-198 13901
2400-2499 13903
Thistle Way 13901
Thistlewood Dr 13903
Thomas Rd 13905
Thomas St 13901
E Thomas St 13901
Thompson St 13903
Thorp St 13905
Timber Bluff Ct 13903
Timberland Dr 13903
Titchener Pl 13905
Tokos Rd 13905
Tompkins St 13903
Tony St 13901
Towpath Rd 13904
Track Dr 13904
Tracy St 13905
Trafford Rd 13901
Travis Ave & Dr 13904
Treadwell Rd 13905
Tremont Ave 13903
True Ave 13905
Truesdell St 13901
Tudor St 13901
Twining St 13905
Unadilla St 13903
Upper Court St 13904
Upper Front St
800-1233 13905
1235-1265 13905
1250-1276 13901
1278-1452 13901
Upper Stella Ireland Rd 13905
Upper Taft Ave 13901
Upper Vine St 13903
Utica Ave 13901
Valley St 13905
Valley View Ct 13904
Valley View Dr 13905
Valleyview Ave 13901
Van Etten Rd 13905
Van Ness Rd 13905
Vankuren Dr 13901
Varick St 13901
Vermont Ave 13905
Verneth Dr 13901
Vestal Ave 13903
Vestal Pkwy
--- 13902
--- 13903
4400-4400 13902
Via Yezzi 13903
Victoria Dr 13904
Victory Ave 13903
Vincent Ct & St 13905
Vine St 13903
Virgil St 13901
Virginia Ave 13905
Wagner St 13904
Waldorf St 13904
Wales Ave 13901
Wall St 13901
Wallace Rd 13905
Walnut St 13905
Walter Ave 13901
Warner Rd 13901
Washington St 13901
S Washington St 13903
Water St 13901
Watson Ave 13901
Way St 13901
Wayman Rd 13901
Wayne Ave 13901
Webb Rd 13903
Webster Ct & St 13903
Weslar Ct 13903
West St 13905
Westerly Way 13903
Westland Ct 13905
Westmoor Pl 13905
Westwood Ct 13905
Whitcomb Dr 13901
White St 13901
Whiting St 13904
Whitney Ave 13901
Wightman Dr 13901
Wilcox Rd 13903
Wilcox St 13904
Willard St 13904
William Rd 13901
William St 13904
Williams Pl 13903
Willis Rd 13905
Willow Ln 13901
Wilson St 13905
Wilson Hill Rd 13905
Winding Way 13905
Windy Hill Rd 13904
Winston Dr 13901
Wisconsin Dr 13901
Wittman Ln 13901
Wolfinger Way 13904
N & S Woodhill Ave & Ct 13904
Woodland Ave 13903
Woodland Dr 13901
Woodland Rd 13901
Woodlawn Dr 13904
Woodruff Ave 13901
Woodside Ave 13903
Woodworth Rd 13903
Wynne Rd 13901
Yager St 13901
Zane Rd 13903

NUMBERED STREETS

All Street Addresses 13903

BRONX NY

General Delivery 10451

POST OFFICE BOXES MAIN OFFICE STATIONS AND BRANCHES

Box No.s
95A - 121A 10451
307A - 307A 10451
414A - 414A 10451
444A - 444A 10451
790A - 800A 10451
871A - 875A 10451
950A - 950A 10451
357A - 357A 10451
597A - 597A 10451
172A - 204A 10451
674A - 674A 10451
1 - 1680 10451
1 - 630 10457
1 - 1020 10458
1 - 750 10461
1 - 1320 10462
1 - 1020 10467
1 - 432 10469
1 - 628 10470
1 - 557 10471
1 - 1380 10472
1 - 1110 10473
1 - 780 10460
1 - 852 10455
1 - 720 10475
1 - 600 10463
1 - 1036 10465
1 - 923 10468
1 - 1580 10453
1 - 1606 10459
1 - 804 10456
1 - 334 10464
500 - 576 10469
600 - 600 10471
600 - 1100 10469
636 - 800 10471
820 - 879 10457
900 - 900 10471
901 - 960 10455
901 - 904 10470
1000 - 1360 10471
1002 - 1008 10455
1005 - 1007 10468
1321 - 1371 10475
1402 - 1414 10471
1405 - 1407 10475
1500 - 1500 10473
1709 - 1794 10451
2000 - 2047 10461
2000 - 2012 10460
2000 - 2000 10451
2000 - 2010 10462
2000 - 2003 10466
2001 - 2009 10467
2001 - 2011 10469
2001 - 2007 10457
2001 - 2010 10463
2002 - 2014 10458
2004 - 2004 10472
2005 - 2005 10465
3000 - 3006 10453
5000 - 5007 10460
5007 - 5086 10451
5011 - 5011 10463
6001 - 6420 10451
6600 - 6605 10459
370001 - 371750 10458
520001 - 524656 10452
540001 - 542026 10454
563000 - 563004 10456
580001 - 580360 10458
610001 - 610360 10461
622301 - 622660 10462
630001 - 630360 10463
660001 - 661620 10466
670001 - 672480 10467
681008 - 681009 10468
690001 - 690480 10469
740001 - 742020 10474
753001 - 753336 10475

NAMED STREETS

Abbot St 10470
Acorn Pl 10465
Adams Pl
2200-2289 10457
2290-2299 10458
Adams St 10460
Adee Ave
600-899 10467
900-1999 10469
Adee Dr 10465
Adler Pl 10475
Admiral Ct & Ln 10473

Adrian Ave 10463
Agar Pl 10465
Alan Pl 10465
Albany Cres 10463
Alcott Pl 10475
Alden Park 10465
Alden Pl 10457
Alderbrook Rd 10471
Aldrich St 10475
Aldus St 10459
Alexander Ave 10454
Allen Pl 10475
Allerton Ave
601-609 10467
611-899 10467
900-1799 10469
Amethyst St 10462
Ampere Ave 10465
Amundson Ave 10466
Anderson Ave 10452
Andrews Ave
1600-2249 10453
2250-2399 10468
Angelas Pl 10465
Anthony Ave 10457
Anthony J Griffin Pl 10451
Antin Pl 10462
Aqueduct Ave 10468
Aqueduct Ave E 10453
Archer Rd 10462
Archer St
1800-1861 10460
1863-1879 10460
1880-1999 10462
Arlington Ave
2600-3299 10463
3900-6099 10471
Armand Pl 10463
Arnow Ave
600-899 10467
900-1999 10469
Arnow Pl 10461
Arthur Ave
1998A-1998B 10457
1700-2299 10457
2301-2303 10458
2305-2599 10458
Arthur Murphy Sq 10457
Asch Loop 10475
Aster Pl 10465
Astor Ave
700-899 10467
900-1899 10469
Austin Pl 10455
Avenue Saint John 10455
B St 10461
Bailey Ave & Pl 10463
Bainbridge Ave
2500-3029 10458
3030-3699 10467
Baisley Ave
2800-3099 10461
3100-3299 10465
Baker Ave 10460
Balcom Ave
100-1202 10465
1204-1298 10465
1300-1499 10461
Baldwin St 10470
Balesto Ave 10452
Balinche Ave 10458
Balsam Pl 10465
Banes Ct 10473
Bantam Pl 10469
Banyer Pl 10473
Barker Ave 10467
Barkley Ave 10465
Barnes Ave
1600-2199 10462
2300-3899 10467
3900-4599 10466
4600-4899 10470
Barnett Pl 10462
Barrett Ave 10473
Barretto St
200-899 10474
900-999 10459

Barry St 10474
Bartholdi St 10467
Bartow Ave
1600-1999 10469
2000-2299 10475
Bassett Ave
1300-1699 10461
2000-2099 10475
Bassford Ave
2200-2289 10457
2290-2399 10458
Bathgate Ave
1500-2289 10457
2290-2599 10458
E Bay Ave 10474
Bay St 10464
E Bay Avenue Ext 10474
Baychester Ave
100-2200 10475
2202-3498 10475
3201-3499 10469
3500-4499 10466
Bayshore Ave 10465
Bayview Ave 10465
Beach Ave
300-799 10473
1000-1399 10472
1400-1599 10460
Beach St 10464
Beacon Ln 10473
Beaumont Ave
2200-2299 10457
2300-2499 10458
Beck St
500-809 10455
810-999 10459
Bedford Park Blvd 10458
Bedford Park Blvd E 10468
Bedford Park Blvd W 10468
Beech Pl 10465
Beech Ter 10454
Beekman Ave 10454
Belden St 10464
Bell Ave 10466
Bellamy Loop 10475
Belmont Ave
1800-2299 10457
2300-2599 10458
Benchley Pl 10475
Benedict Ave 10462
Benson St 10461
Bergen Ave 10455
Betts Ave 10473
Bevy Pl 10465
Billingsley Ter 10453
Birchall Ave 10462
Bivona St 10475
Blackrock Ave
1900-2299 10472
2300-2348 10462
2350-2499 10462
Blackstone Ave
3700-3800 10463
3900-5399 10471
Blackstone Pl 10471
Blair Ave 10465
Blondell Ave 10461
Bogart Ave 10462
Boller Ave
2100-3499 10475
3500-3799 10466
Bolton Ave 10473
Bolton St 10462
Bonner Pl 10456
Bontri Ave 10461
Boone Ave
1300-1459 10459
1460-1899 10460
Boscobel Ave 10452
Boston Rd
2559A-2559B 10467
900-1432 10456
1433-2163 10460
2164-2199 10462
2200-2734 10467
2735-2747 10469
2736-2748 10467

2749-3600 10469
3601-4339 10466
3602-3798 10469
3800-4340 10475
Botanical Sq 10458
Bouck Ave 10469
Bowne St 10464
Boyd Ave 10466
Boynton Ave
800-999 10473
1000-1399 10472
Bradford Ave 10461
Bradley St 10470
Brady Ave 10462
Brandt Pl 10453
Bridge St 10464
Briggs Ave 10458
Brinsmade Ave 10465
Bristow St 10459
Britton St 10467
Broadway
5171-5970 10463
Broadway
5971-6799 10471
Bronx Blvd
3200-3899 10467
3900-4399 10466
4400-4799 10470
Bronx Park E
2000-2199 10462
2200-3099 10467
Bronx Park S 10460
Bronx St 10460
Bronx Park Ave 10460
Bronx Park Zoological 10460
Bronx River Ave
300-999 10473
1000-1499 10472
1500-1699 10460
Bronx River Pkwy 10462
Bronx Science Blvd 10468
Bronx Terminal Market 10451
Bronxdale Ave 10462
Bronxwood Ave
2200-3899 10469
3900-4399 10466
Brook Ave
1-434 10454
436-438 10454
440-738 10455
739-1016 10451
1017-1504 10456
1505-1505 10457
1507-1599 10457
Broun Pl 10475
Brown Pl 10454
Browns Ln 10464
Bruckner Blvd
1-419 10454
420-799 10455
800-1409 10459
1410-2498 10473
1411-2299 10472
2500-2900 10465
2901-3699 10461
2902-3298 10465
Bruner Ave
2300-3499 10469
4000-4499 10466
Brush Ave 10465
Bryant Ave
300-949 10474
950-1453 10459
1454-2199 10460
Buchanan Pl 10453
Buck St 10461
Buckley St 10464
Buhre Ave 10461
Bullard Ave
4300-4399 10466
4400-4799 10470
Burke Ave
600-899 10467
900-1999 10469
Burnett Pl 10474
E Burnside Ave
1-199 10453

200-399 10457
W Burnside Ave 10453
Burr Ave 10461
Bush St
100-199 10453
200-299 10457
Bussing Ave & Pl 10466
Butler Pl
2300-2399 10462
2400-2599 10461
Buttrick Ave 10465
Byron Ave 10466
Caesar Pl 10473
Calhoun Ave 10465
Cambreleng Ave
2200-2289 10457
2290-2599 10458
Cambridge Ave 10463
Cameron Pl 10453
Camp St 10466
Campbell Dr 10465
Canal Pl & St W 10451
Cannon Pl 10463
Capuchin Way 10467
Cardinal Spellman Pl 10466
Carlisle Pl 10467
Carpenter Ave
3800-3899 10467
3900-4399 10466
4400-4899 10470
Carr St 10455
Carroll Pl 10456
Carroll St 10464
Carter Ave 10457
Carver Loop 10475
Casals Pl 10475
Casanova St 10474
Casler Pl 10465
Castle Hill Ave
1-999 10473
1000-1105 10472
1106-1799 10462
Catalpa Pl 10465
Cauldwell Ave
500-736 10455
738-754 10456
756-1099 10456
Cayuga Ave 10471
Cedar Ave
1800-2059 10453
2060-2299 10468
Cedar Ln 10451
Cedar Pl 10465
Cendonde Ave 10468
Centre St 10464
Centre Edgewater Park
Dr 10465
Chaffee Ave 10465
Charlotte St 10460
Chatterton Ave
1900-2338 10472
2339-2499 10462
Chesbrough Ave 10461
Chester St 10469
Chestnut Dr & St 10467
Chisholm St 10459
Choctaw Pl 10461
Cicero Ave 10473
Cincinnatus Ave 10473
City Island Ave & Rd 10464
Claflin Ave 10468
Claremont Pkwy 10457
Clarence Ave 10465
E & W Clarke Pl 10452
Clason Point Ln 10473
Clay Ave
900-1505 10456
1506-1899 10457
Clementine St 10466
Clerrann Ave 10453
E & W Clifford Pl 10453
Clinton Ave
1300-1499 10456
1500-2199 10457
Clinton Pl 10453
Close Ave
900-999 10473

1000-1199 10472
Co Op City Blvd 10475
Coddington Ave 10461
Colden Ave
1500-2199 10462
2300-3499 10469
Coles Ln 10458
Colgate Ave
800-999 10473
1000-1299 10472
College Ave
401-445 10451
447-499 10451
928-1449 10456
1450-1499 10457
College Rd 10471
Collis Pl 10465
Colonial Ave 10461
Commerce Ave
1000-1299 10462
1300-1499 10461
Commonwealth Ave
400-799 10473
1100-1419 10472
1420-1599 10460
Compton Ave 10473
Concord Ave
300-413 10454
414-699 10455
Concourse Vlg E & W 10451
Connell Pl 10465
Conner St
2100-2256 10466
2258-2298 10466
3200-3599 10475
Continental Ave 10461
Cooper Ave 10461
Cooper Pl 10475
Corlear Ave 10463
Cornell Ave 10473
Cornell Pl 10461
Corsa Ave 10469
Coster St 10474
Cottage Pl 10456
Country Club Rd 10465
Courtlandt Ave 10451
Cove Ct 10473
Cranford Ave
700-849 10470
850-999 10466
Crantinc St 10464
Craven St 10474
Crawford Ave 10466
Crescent Ave 10458
Creston Ave
1900-2293 10453
2294-2899 10468
Crimmins Ave 10454
Croes Ave
700-999 10473
1000-1499 10472
Croes Pl 10473
Cromwell Ave
200-699 10451
890-1499 10452
Crosby Ave 10461
Cross St 10464
Cross Bronx Expy
203-269 10457
450-478 10457
760-1199 10460
1201-1899 10460
1600-2298 10472
1901-2499 10462
2500-4499 10465
Crotona Ave
1300-1499 10456
1700-2289 10457
2290-2599 10458
Crotona Park E 10460
Crotona Park N
600-759 10457
760-899 10460
Crotona Park S 10456
Crotona Pkwy 10460
Crotona Pl 10456

Cruger Ave
1900-2199 10462
2215-2219 10467
2221-3399 10467
Cypress Ave 10454
Cyrus Pl 10458
Daisy Pl 10465
Daly Ave 10460
Daniel St 10461
Dare Pl 10465
Dark St 10466
Darrow Pl 10475
Dash Pl 10463
Davidson Ave
2099A-2099B 10453
1600-2270 10453
2271-2699 10468
Davis Ave 10465
Davit Ct 10473
Dawson St
600-809 10455
810-999 10459
De Kruif Pl 10475
De Reimer Ave
2100-3499 10475
3500-4499 10466
Dean Ave 10465
Debs Pl 10475
Decatur Ave
2500-3029 10458
3030-3599 10467
Deepwater Way 10464
Defoe Pl 10475
Dekalb Ave 10467
Delafield Ave, Ln, Pl &
Way 10471
Delancey Pl 10462
Delanoy Ave 10469
Delavall Ave 10475
Demeyer St 10469
Dendinda Ave 10470
Devoe Ave 10460
Devoe Ter 10468
Dewey Ave 10465
Dewitt Pl 10469
Deyo St 10469
Digney Ave 10466
Dill Pl 10465
Ditmars St 10464
Dodge Ln 10471
Dodgewood Rd 10471
Dolen Park 10461
Dolphin Ct 10473
Donizetti Pl 10475
Doris St 10462
Dorothea Pl 10458
Dorsey St 10461
Douglas Ave
3100-3299 10463
4400-4699 10471
Dr Martin L King Jr Blvd
900-1500 10452
1501-1577 10453
1502-1578 10452
1579-2249 10453
Drake St 10474
Dreiser Loop 10475
Dudley Ave 10461
Duncan St 10469
Duncomb Ave 10467
Dune Ct 10473
Dupont St 10474
Duryea Ave 10466
Dwight Pl 10465
Dyre Ave 10466
Eagle Ave
500-739 10455
740-742 10456
744-999 10456
Eames Pl 10468
Earhart Ln 10475
Earley St 10464
East Ave 10462
Eastburn Ave 10457
Eastchester Pl 10475
Eastchester Rd
1600-2199 10461

2200-3649 10469
3650-3799 10466
Eastchester Rd Pelham
Pkwy S 10461
Echo Pl
100-199 10453
200-399 10457
Edenwald Ave 10466
Edgehill Ave 10463
Edgewater Park 10465
Edison Ave
500-1099 10465
1100-1999 10461
Edsall Ave 10463
Edson Ave
2300-3499 10469
3500-4499 10466
Edward L Grant Hwy 10452
Edwards Ave 10461
Effingham Ave 10473
Eger Pl 10465
Einstein Loop 10475
Elder Ave
900-999 10473
1000-1399 10472
Elgar Pl 10475
Elliot Pl 10452
Ellis Ave
1900-2024 10472
2026-2036 10462
2038-2599 10462
Ellis Pl 10465
Ellison Ave 10461
Ellsworth Ave 10465
Elm Pl
1-99 10465
2400-2499 10458
Elsmere Pl 10460
Elton Ave
480-598 10455
600-739 10455
741-743 10455
744-899 10451
901-999 10451
Ely Ave
2300-3499 10469
3500-4499 10466
Emerson Ave 10465
Erdman Pl 10475
Ericson Pl 10461
Erskine Pl 10475
Esplanade Ave
1000-1199 10461
2200-2499 10469
Evelyn Pl 10468
Evergreen Ave
900-999 10473
1001-1001 10473
1002-1299 10472
Exterior St
1-1000 10451
1601-1799 10468
2800-2900 10463
2902-2910 10463
Faile St
200-939 10474
940-1099 10459
Fairfax Ave 10465
Fairfield Ave 10463
Fairmount Ave 10465
Fairmount Pl
700-759 10457
760-899 10460
Faraday Ave 10471
W Farms Rd
1000-1381 10459
1382-1999 10460
W Farms Square Plz 10460
Father Zeiser Pl 10468
Fearn Pl 10465
Featherbed Ln 10452
Fenton Ave 10469
Fern Pl 10465
Ferris Pl 10461
Field Pl
1-199 10468
200-299 10458

Fielding St 10469
Fieldston Rd
3600-3899 10463
3900-6199 10471
Fieldston Ter 10471
Fillmore St 10460
Findlay Ave 10456
Fink Ave 10461
Fish Ave 10469
Fleet Ct 10473
Fletcher Pl 10457
Flint Ave 10475
Folin St 10457
Food Center Dr 10474
Ford St 10457
Fordham Pl 10464
Fordham Plz 10458
E Fordham Rd
1-199 10468
200-799 10458
W Fordham Rd 10468
Fordham St 10464
Fordham Hill Oval 10468
Forest Ave
730-743 10455
745-745 10455
747-775 10456
777-1199 10456
Forichea Ave 10457
Fort Charles Pl 10463
Fort Independence St 10463
Foster Pl 10471
Fowler Ave 10462
Fox St
500-799 10455
800-1199 10459
Fox Ter 10469
Franklin Ave 10456
Freeman St 10459
Frisby Ave 10461
Fteley Ave
900-999 10473
1000-1499 10472
Fuller St 10461
Fulton Ave
1000-1501 10456
1502-1504 10457
1503-1505 10456
1506-1799 10457
Furman Ave
4300-4499 10466
4500-4699 10470
Gabriel Dr 10469
Gale Pl 10463
Garden Pl 10470
Garden St
600-759 10457
760-799 10460
Garfield St 10460
Garrett Pl 10466
Garrison Ave 10474
Gates Pl 10467
George St 10461
Geranium Pl 10465
Gerard Ave
200-871 10451
872-1299 10452
Gerber Pl 10465
Giegerich Pl 10465
Gifford Ave 10465
Gilbert Pl 10474
Gildersleeve Ave 10473
Giles Pl 10463
Gillespie Ave 10461
Givan Ave
1200-1999 10469
2000-2399 10475
Gleadere Ave 10462
Gleason Ave
1600-2038 10472
2039-2049 10462
2040-2050 10472
2051-2499 10462
Glebe Ave
2100-2399 10462
2400-2599 10461
Glennon Pl 10465

Glenz Est 10473
Glover St 10462
Goble Pl 10452
Godwin Ter 10463
Goodridge Ave 10471
Goulden Ave 10468
Gouverneur Ave 10463
Gouverneur Pl 10456
Grace Ave
2400-3499 10469
3500-4499 10466
Gradonew Ave 10466
Graff Ave 10465
Graham Pl 10462
Grand Ave
1600-2270 10453
2271-2699 10468
Grand Concourse
200-900 10451
Grand Concourse
901-1679 10452
902-1036 10451
1038-1448 10456
1450-2298 10457
1681-2299 10453
2300-3298 10458
2301-3399 10468
Grandview Pl 10452
Grant Ave
800-940 10451
941-1284 10456
1286-1294 10456
Green Ave 10461
Greene Pl 10465
E Greliann St 10454
Grenada Pl 10466
Greystone Ave
3400-3900 10463
3901-4599 10471
Grinnell Pl 10474
Griswold Ave 10465
Grosvenor Ave 10471
Grote St
600-759 10457
760-799 10460
Guerlain St
1800-1879 10460
1880-1999 10462
Guion Pl 10460
E Gun Hill Rd
1-899 10467
900-2099 10469
W Gun Hill Rd 10467
Gunther Ave
2200-3499 10469
4000-4399 10466
Hadley Ave 10471
Haight Ave 10461
Hall Pl 10459
Hall Of Fame Ter 10453
Halleck St 10474
Halperin Ave 10461
Halsey St 10461
Hammersley Ave 10469
Hampden Pl 10468
Hancharr Ave 10475
Harding Ave 10465
Harding Park 10473
Harper Ave & Ct 10466
Harrington Ave 10461
Harrison Ave 10453
Harrod Ave 10472
Hart St 10473
Haskin St 10461
Hatting Pl 10465
Havemeyer Ave
500-999 10473
1000-1039 10472
1040-1399 10462
Haviland Ave
1900-2166 10472
2167-2399 10462
Hawkins St 10464
Hawkstone St 10452
Hawthorne St 10469
Hazel Pl 10465
Hearridg Ave 10455

Heath Ave 10463
Heathcote Ave 10475
Hegney Pl
700-739 10455
740-742 10451
741-743 10455
744-799 10451
Hendal Ave 10473
Hennessy Pl 10453
Henry Hudson Pkwy
2600-3756 10463
3758-3798 10463
3900-4599 10471
4600-5398 10471
4601-5399 10471
Henwood Pl 10453
Heraínda Ave 10469
Hering Ave
1500-2099 10461
2200-3299 10469
Herkimer Pl 10470
Hermany Ave 10473
Heron Ln 10473
Herschell St 10461
Hewitt Pl
701-737 10455
739-809 10455
810-899 10459
Hicks St 10469
Hill Ave 10466
Hillman Ave 10463
Hobart Ave 10461
Hoe Ave
900-1459 10459
1460-1799 10460
Hoffman St 10458
Holland Ave
1600-2199 10462
2200-3699 10467
Hollers Ave 10475
Holly Pl 10465
Hollywood Ave
1-1099 10465
1200-1599 10461
Holt Pl 10467
Home St
700-801 10456
802-820 10459
822-1099 10459
Homer Ave 10473
Hone Ave
1500-2199 10461
2500-3399 10469
Honeywell Ave 10460
Hornaday Pl 10460
Horton St 10464
Hosmer Ave 10465
Howe Ave 10473
Hoxie St 10470
Hubbell St 10461
Hudson Manor Ter 10463
Hudson River Rd 10471
Hugh J Grant Cir
1-99 10462
2-198 10472
Hughes Ave
1900-2270 10457
2271-2599 10458
Huguenot Ave 10475
Hull Ave 10467
Hunt Ave 10462
Hunter Ave
400-499 10464
2200-3499 10475
Huntington Ave 10465
Hunts Point Ave
400-918 10474
919-925 10459
920-998 10474
Hunts Point Co Op
Mkt 10474
Hunts Point Term Mkt 10474
Husson Ave 10473
Hutchinson Ave 10475
Hutchinson River Pkwy
1-1099 10465
1300-3099 10461

Hutchinson River Pkwy
E 10475
Huxley Ave 10471
Independence Ave
2500-3999 10463
4500-6099 10471
Indian Rd 10471
Indian Trl 10465
Industrial St 10461
Intervale Ave 10459
Inwood Ave 10452
Irvine St 10474
Irwin Ave 10463
Iselin Ave 10471
Ittner Pl 10457
Ivy Pl 10465
Jackson Ave
809A-809C 10456
Jacobus Pl 10463
Jarret Pl 10461
Jarvis Ave 10461
Jefferson Pl 10456
Jennings St
700-899 10459
900-1099 10460
Jerome Ave
900-1649 10452
1650-2280 10453
2281-3299 10468
3300-3899 10467
Jesup Ave & Pl 10452
John Mcnamara Sq 10465
Johnson Ave 10463
Kappock St 10463
Katonah Ave 10470
Kearney Ave 10465
Kelly St
600-799 10455
800-1199 10459
Kencomar Ave 10474
Kennellworth Pl 10465
Kepler Ave 10470
Kilroe St 10464
Kimberly Pl 10463
King Ave 10464
Kings College Pl 10467
Kingsbridge Ave 10463
E Kingsbridge Rd
1-199 10468
200-399 10458
W Kingsbridge Rd
1-131 10468
133-147 10468
149-399 10463
Kingsbridge Ter 10463
Kingsland Ave 10469
Kingsland Pl 10453
Kinsella St 10462
Kirby St 10464
Knapp St 10469
Knolls Cres 10463
Knox Pl 10467
Kossuth Ave 10467
Lacombe Ave 10473
Laconia Ave
2200-3899 10469
3900-4199 10466
Ladd Rd 10471
Lafayette Ave
1699A-1699B 10473
Lafontaine Ave 10457
Lakeview Pl 10471
Lakewood Pl 10461
Lamport Pl 10465
Landing Rd 10468
Landing Way 10464
Lasalle Ave 10461
Latting St 10461
Laurie Ave 10461
Lawton Ave 10465
Layton Ave 10465
Lebanon St 10460
Leeward Ln 10464
Leggett Ave
900-1079 10455
1080-1199 10474

Leland Ave
842A-842C 10473
Lester St 10467
Libby Pl 10461
Library Ave 10465
Liebig Ave 10471
Light St 10466
Lighting Pl 10474
Lincharl Ave 10471
Lincoln Ave 10454
Linden Ave 10465
Lisbon Pl 10458
Litantat Ave 10465
Little League Pl 10461
Livingston Ave 10471
Locust Ave 10454
Locust Point Dr 10465
Lodovick Ave 10469
Logan Ave 10465
Lohengrin Pl 10465
Longfellow Ave
300-979 10474
980-1454 10459
1455-1999 10460
Longstreet Ave 10465
Longwood Ave
800-1079 10459
1081-1089 10459
1090-1180 10474
1182-1198 10474
Lontrani Ave 10459
Loomis St 10461
Loop Dr 10474
Lorillard Pl 10458
Loring Pl N
2100-2249 10453
2250-2399 10468
Loring Pl S 10453
Louis Nine Blvd 10459
Lowell St 10459
Lowerre Pl 10466
Lucerne St 10465
Lurting Ave
1500-2199 10461
2400-3399 10469
Lustre St 10466
Lydig Ave
600-1023 10462
1024-1299 10461
Lyman Pl 10459
Lyon Ave 10462
Lyvere St 10461
Mabel Wayne Pl 10451
Mac Cracken Ave 10453
Mac Donough Pl 10465
Mace Ave
600-899 10467
900-1899 10469
Maclay Ave
2300-2399 10462
2400-2599 10461
Macombs Rd
1400-1602 10452
1603-1799 10453
Macombs Dam Park 10452
Macy Pl 10455
Magenta St
600-899 10467
900-999 10469
Magnolia Pl 10465
Mahan Ave 10461
Maitland Ave 10461
Major Deegan Expy 10470
Manhattan College
Pkwy 10471
Manida St 10474
Manning St 10462
Manor Ave 10472
Mansion St 10460
Mapes Ave 10460
Maple Ave 10465
Maran Pl 10462
Marble Hill Ave 10463
Marcy Pl
1-199 10452
200-299 10456

Marina Dr 10465
Marine St 10464
Marion Ave 10458
Marisa Ct 10465
Marmion Ave 10460
Marolla Pl 10466
Martha Ave 10470
Marvin Pl 10461
Mathewson Rd 10453
Matilda Ave
4300-4399 10466
4400-4799 10470
Matthews Ave
1600-2199 10462
2300-3099 10467
Mayflower Ave 10461
Mc Owen Ave 10475
Mcclellan St
1-159 10452
160-299 10456
Mcdonald St 10461
Mcgraw Ave
1800-1859 10472
1860-2099 10462
Mead St 10460
Meagher Ave 10465
Melrose Ave
500-742 10455
743-751 10451
753-999 10451
Melville St 10460
Mercy College Pl 10462
Mermaid Ln 10473
Merriam Ave 10452
Merrill St 10460
Merritt Ave
3300-3399 10475
3700-3999 10466
Merry Ave 10461
Metcalf Ave
700-999 10473
1000-1499 10472
Metropolitan Ave &
Oval 10462
Meyers St 10461
Mickle Ave 10469
Middletown Rd
2800-3149 10461
3150-3299 10465
Miles Ave 10465
Milton Pl 10465
Minerva Pl 10468
Minford Pl 10460
Minnieford Ave 10464
Miriam St 10458
Mitchell Pl 10465
Mohegan Ave 10460
Monroe Ave 10457
Monsignor Halpin Pl 10465
Monterey Ave 10457
Montgomery Ave 10453
Montgomery Pl 10461
Monticello Ave 10466
Moore Plz 10466
Morgan Ave 10469
Morris Ave
200-928 10451
929-1449 10456
1450-1799 10457
1800-2293 10453
2294-2899 10468
Morris Park Ave
300-644 10460
646-646 10460
647-1023 10462
1024-1399 10461
Morrison Ave
800-899 10473
1000-1399 10472
Morton Pl 10453
Mosholu Ave 10471
E Mosholu Pkwy N 10467
E Mosholu Pkwy S 10458
W Mosholu Pkwy N 10467
W Mosholu Pkwy S 10468
E Mount Eden Ave 10452
W Mount Eden Ave 10452

Mount Eden Pkwy 10457
Mount Hope Pl
1-199 10453
200-299 10457
Mulford Ave 10461
Muliner Ave 10462
Mullan Pl 10465
Mulvey Ave 10466
Mundy Ln 10466
Munn Ave 10462
Murdock Ave
3900-4799 10466
4800-4899 10470
Murray Ct 10473
Napier Ave 10470
Naples Ter 10463
Narragansett Ave 10461
Needham Ave
1300-1599 10469
1700-2199 10466
Neill Ave
700-1023 10462
1024-1299 10461
Nelson Ave
1000-1599 10452
1600-1799 10453
Neptune Ct & Ln 10473
Nereid Ave
550-699 10470
700-2099 10466
2101-2199 10466
Netherland Ave
2600-3699 10463
3900-6099 10471
New England Thru 10475
New England Thruway 10469
Newbold Ave
1900-1999 10472
2000-2599 10462
Newman Ave 10473
Newport Ave 10461
Noble Ave
700-999 10473
1100-1499 10472
1500-1599 10460
Noell Ave 10475
Noricken Ave 10467
North St 10468
Norton Ave 10473
Nuvern Ave 10466
Oak Ave 10465
N Oak Dr 10467
S Oak Dr 10467
Oak Ter 10454
Oak Tree Pl 10457
Oakland Pl 10457
Oakley St 10469
Oakpoint Ave 10474
Obrien Ave 10473
Ocensont Ave 10460
Odell St 10462
Ogden Ave 10452
Ohm Ave 10465
Old Kingsbridge Rd 10460
Olinville Ave 10467
Oliver Pl 10458
Olmstead Ave
300-398 10473
400-999 10473
1000-1199 10472
1200-1599 10462
Oneida Ave 10470
Oneill Pl 10469
Orchard Beach Rd 10464
Orloff Ave 10463
Osbourne Pl 10453
Osgood St 10470
Osman Pl 10470
Otis Ave 10465
Outlook Ave 10465
Overing St 10461
Oxford Ave 10463
Paine St 10461
Palisade Ave
2300-3899 10463
4500-5999 10471

Street	ZIP
Palisade Pl	10453
Palmer Ave	
2198-2198	10475
2200-3399	10475
3500-3699	10466
Paraingt Ave	10472
Park Ave	
2300-3267	10451
3268-3799	10456
3800-4546	10457
4547-4551	10458
4548-4552	10457
4553-4799	10458
Park Dr	10464
Parkchester Rd	10462
Parker St	10462
Parkside Pl	10467
Parkview Ave	10461
Parkview Ter	10468
Parsifal Pl	10465
Patricia Ln	10465
Patterson Ave	10473
Paul Ave	10468
Paulding Ave	
1500-1549	10461
1550-2199	10462
2300-3899	10469
3900-4199	10466
Paulis Pl	10464
Pawnee Pl	10461
Peace St	10464
Pear Tree Ave	10475
Pearsall Ave	10469
Pelham Pkwy N	
601-899	10467
901-1799	10469
Pelham Pkwy S	
600-948	10462
950-1998	10461
Pelham Bay Park W	10475
Pelham Bay Rd	10464
Pell Pl	10464
Penfield St	10470
Pennyfield Ave & Cp	10465
Perot St	10463
Perry Ave	
2900-3029	10458
3030-3599	10467
Peters Pl	10470
Phelan Pl	10453
Philip Ave	10465
Pierce Ave	
900-1023	10462
1024-1199	10461
Pilgrim Ave	10461
Pilot St	10464
Pinchot Pl	10461
Pinkney Ave	10475
Pitman Ave	10466
Plaza Dr	10452
Plaza Pl	10465
Plimpton Ave	10452
Ploughmans Bush	10471
Plymouth Ave	10461
Poe Pl	10458
Polo Pl	10465
Pond Pl	10458
Pontiac Pl	10455
Ponton Ave	10461
Popham Ave	10453
Poplar Ave	10465
N Poplar Ave	10465
Poplar St	10461
Post Rd	10471
Powell Ave	
1900-2139	10472
2140-2399	10462
Powers Ave	10454
Pratt Ave	10466
Prentiss Ave	10465
Prospect Ave	10459
Provost Ave	
2300-2399	10466
3300-3399	10475
3600-3999	10466
Pugsley Ave	
1-999	10473
1000-1269	10472
1270-1399	10462
Purdy St	10462
Puritan Ave	10461
Putnam Ave W	10463
Putnam Pl	10467
Quarry Rd	10457
Quimby Ave	10473
Quincy Ave	10465
Radcliff Ave	
1500-2199	10462
2500-3399	10469
Radio Dr	10465
Rae St	10455
Randall Ave	
1100-1399	10474
1600-2499	10473
2675-3299	10465
Randolph Pl	10465
Rawlins Ave	10465
Reed Pl	10465
Reeds Mill Ln	10475
Reiss Pl	10467
Research Ave	10465
Reservoir Ave	10468
Reservoir Oval E	10467
Reservoir Oval W	10467
Reservoir Pl	10467
Rev James A Polite Ave	10459
Revere Ave	10465
Review Pl	10463
Reville St	10464
Reynolds Ave	10465
Reynolds St	10464
Rhinelander Ave	
601-637	10462
639-1023	10462
1024-1599	10461
Richardson Ave	
4300-4399	10466
4400-4799	10470
Richman Plz	10453
Rider Ave	10451
Risse St	10468
Ritter Pl	10459
River Ave	
400-870	10451
871-1299	10452
River Rd	10463
Rivercrest Rd	10471
Riverdale Ave	
1-3899	10463
5400-6302	10471
6304-6398	10471
Roberto Clemente State Brg	10453
Roberts Ave	10461
Robertson Pl	10465
Robertson St	10470
Robinson Ave	10465
Rochambeau Ave	10467
Rochelle St	10464
Rockwood St	10452
Rodman Pl	10460
Rodmans Nck	10464
Roebling Ave	10461
Rogers Pl	10459
Rohr Pl	10465
Rombouts Ave	
3201-3301	10475
3303-3599	10475
3600-4099	10466
Roosevelt Ave	10465
Ropes Ave	10475
Rose Feiss Blvd	10454
Rosedale Ave	
400-899	10473
1000-1419	10472
1420-1599	10460
Roselle St	10461
Rosewood St	10467
Rowe St	10461
Rowland St	10461
Rudd Pl	10473
Ruppert Pl	10451
Ryawa Ave	10474
Ryer Ave	
1900-2299	10457
2300-2499	10458
Sackett Ave	
900-1023	10462
1024-1299	10461
Sagamore St	10462
Saint Anns Ave	
1-439	10454
440-740	10455
741-899	10456
Saint Georges Cres	10458
Saint Lawrence Ave	
400-799	10473
1100-1419	10472
1420-1599	10460
Saint Marys St	10454
Saint Ouen St	10470
Saint Paul Ave	10461
Saint Pauls Pl	10456
Saint Peters Ave	10461
Saint Raymonds Ave	
2000-2399	10462
2400-2699	10461
Saint Theresa Ave	10461
Salvatore R Naclerio Plz	10466
Samantha Way	10465
Sampson Ave	10465
Sands Pl	10461
Santo Donato Pl	10461
Saxon Ave	10463
Scenic Pl	10463
Scharansky Sq	10471
Schieffelin Ave & Pl	10466
Schley Ave	10465
Schofield St	10464
Schorr Pl	10469
Schurz Ave	10465
Schuyler Pl	10461
Schuyler Ter	10465
Scott Pl	10465
Screvin Ave	10473
Seabury Ave	
1200-1299	10462
1301-1499	10461
Seabury Pl	10460
Secor Ave	10466
Seddon St	10461
Sedgwick Ave	
900-1499	10452
1500-2199	10453
2200-3099	10468
3100-3999	10463
Selwyn Ave	10457
Seminole Ave & St	10461
Seneca Ave	10474
Senger Pl	10465
Seton Ave	10466
Seward Ave	10473
Sexton Pl	10469
Seymour Ave	10469
Shakespeare Ave	10452
Sheridan Ave	
938B-938B	10451
870-939	10451
940-1449	10456
1450-1599	10457
Sheridan Expy	10459
Sherman Ave	
802-940	10451
941-1299	10456
Shore Dr	10465
Shore Rd	10464
Shrady Pl	10463
Siegfried Pl	10465
Sigma Pl	10471
Silver St	10461
Simpson St	10459
Sommer Pl	10465
Soundview Ave	
1-999	10473
1000-1099	10472
Soundview Ter	10465
Southern Blvd	
300-419	10454
420-799	10455
800-1459	10459
1460-2399	10460
2400-2999	10458
Spaulding Ln	10471
Spencer Ave	10471
Spencer Dr	10465
Spencer Pl	10471
Spencer Ter	10471
Split Rock Rd	10464
Spofford Ave	10474
Stadium Ave	10465
Stanton Ct	10473
Starboard Ct	10473
Starling Ave	10462
Stearns St	10462
Stebbins Ave	10459
Stedman Pl	10469
Steenwick Ave	10475
Stell Pl	10469
Stephens Ave	10473
Steuben Ave	10467
Stevenson Pl	10463
Stickball Blvd	10473
Stickney Pl	10469
Stillwell Ave	
1500-1699	10461
1700-1999	10469
2000-2099	10475
Story Ave	10473
Strang Ave	10466
Stratford Ave	10472
Strong St	10468
Suburban Pl	10460
Sullivan Pl	10465
Summit Ave	10452
Summit Pl	10463
Sunset Blvd	10473
Sunset Trl	10465
Surf Dr	10473
Sutherland St	10464
Swinton Ave	10465
Sycamore Ave	10471
Sylvan Ave	10471
Tameadin Ave	10451
Taylor Ave	
300-999	10473
1100-1359	10472
1360-1799	10460
Teasdale Pl	10456
Teller Ave	
800-933	10451
934-954	10456
935-955	10451
956-1449	10456
1450-1599	10457
Tenbroeck Ave	
1600-2099	10461
2200-3299	10469
Tenny Pl	10453
Terrace St	10464
Terrace View Ave	10463
Teumissin Pl	10463
Thieriot Ave	
1265A-1265B	10472
300-999	10473
1000-1359	10472
1360-1599	10460
Throggmorton Ave	10465
Throggs Neck Blvd & Expy	10465
Throop Ave	10469
Thurman Munson Way	10451
Thwaites Pl	10467
Tibbett Ave	
2975-2997	10463
2999-3899	10463
4400-5099	10471
5101-5199	10471
Tiebout Ave	
2000-2299	10457
2300-2500	10458
Tiemann Ave	10469
Tier St	10464
Tierney Pl	10465
Tiffany St	
300-849	10474
850-1199	10459
Tilden St	
700-899	10467
900-999	10469
Tillotson Ave	
1500-1899	10469
2000-2499	10475
Tim Hendricks Pl	10463
Timpson Pl	10455
Tinton Ave	
852A-852C	10456
446-494	10455
496-743	10455
744-1299	10456
Tomlinson Ave	10461
Topping Ave	10457
Torry Ave	10473
Townsend Ave	
1400-1649	10452
1650-1799	10453
Trafalgar Pl	10460
Tratman Ave	10461
E Tremont Ave	
1-199	10453
200-759	10457
760-1879	10460
1880-2399	10462
2400-3400	10461
3401-4399	10465
W Tremont Ave	10453
Trinity Ave	
810A-810C	10456
Truxton St	10474
Tryon Ave	10467
Tudor Pl	10452
Tulfan Ter	10463
Turnbull Ave	10473
Turneur Ave	10473
Tyndall Ave	10471
Undercliff Ave	
1300-1499	10452
1500-1899	10453
Underhill Ave	
847A-847C	10473
Union Ave	
805A-805C	10459
Unionport Rd	10462
University Ave	10468
Valentine Ave	
1800-2299	10457
2300-3099	10458
Valhalla Dr	10465
Valles Ave	10471
Van Buren St	10460
Van Corlear Pl	10463
Van Cortlandt Ave E	
150-199	10458
200-300	10467
Van Cortlandt Ave W	10463
E Van Cortlandt Ave	
1-149	10468
Van Cortlandt Park	10471
Van Cortlandt Park E	10470
Van Cortlandt Park S	10463
Van Hoesen Ave	10461
Van Nest Ave	
400-646	10460
647-1023	10462
1024-1201	10461
1203-1299	10461
Vance St	10469
Varian Ave	10466
Verveleen Pl	10463
Victor St	10462
Viele Ave	10474
Villa Ave	10468
Vimont Rd	10471
Vincent Ave	10465
Vineyard Pl	10460
Vireo Ave	10470
Virgil Pl	10473
Virginia Ave	
1000-1299	10472
1300-1399	10462
Vreeland Ave	10461
Vyse Ave	
1100-1455	10459
1456-1458	10460
1457-1459	10459
1460-2199	10460
Wade Sq	10457
Waldo Ave	
3500-3899	10463
4401-4407	10471
4409-5099	10471
Wales Ave	
300-415	10454
416-699	10455
Wallace Ave	
1600-2199	10462
2200-3299	10467
3301-3399	10467
Walton Ave	
200-890	10451
891-1649	10452
1650-2293	10453
2294-2499	10468
Ward Ave	10472
Waring Ave	
600-899	10467
900-1899	10469
Washington Ave	
800-929	10451
930-932	10456
934-1506	10456
1507-1509	10457
1508-1510	10456
1511-2289	10457
2290-2599	10458
Waterbury Ave	
2200-2599	10462
2600-3099	10461
3100-3305	10465
3307-3399	10465
Waterloo Pl	10460
Waters Pl	10461
Waterstone Dr	10461
Watson Ave	
1400-2199	10472
2200-2499	10462
Watt Ave	10465
Wayne Ave	10467
Webb Ave	10468
Webster Ave	
1505A-1505A	10456
1000-1505	10456
1506-2285	10457
2286-3011	10458
3013-3025	10458
3016-3024	10467
3026-3600	10467
3900-4399	10470
Weeks Ave	10457
Weiher Ct	10456
Wellman Ave	10461
Wenner Pl	10465
West Ave	10462
Westchester Ave	
959A-959B	10459
798A-798B	10455
400-839	10455
840-1327	10459
1328-1398	10472
1329-1399	10459
1400-1899	10472
1900-2379	10462
2380-3299	10461
Westchester Sq	10461
Westervelt Ave	10469
Whalen St	10471
Wheeler Ave	
800-999	10473
1000-1399	10472
White Plains Rd	
4399A-4399A	10466
2-999	10473
1000-1299	10472
1300-2199	10462
2200-3899	10467
3900-4399	10466
4400-4899	10470
Whitehall Pl	10466
Whitlock Ave	10459
Whittier St	10474
Wickham Ave	
2200-3499	10469
4000-4499	10466
Wilcox Ave	10465
Wilder Ave	
3900-4699	10466
4800-4899	10470
Wilkins Ave	10460
Wilkinson Ave	10461
Willett Ave	10467
William Ave	10464
William Pl	10461
Williamsbridge Rd	
1400-1422	10461
1424-2199	10461
2200-2799	10469
2900-3099	10467
Willis Ave	
1-439	10454
440-599	10455
Willow Ave	10454
Willow Ln	10461
Wilson Ave	
2000-2099	10461
2200-3599	10469
Wincoria Ave	10463
Windward Ln	10464
Winters St	10464
Wissman Ave	10465
Wood Ave	
1800-1879	10460
1880-1999	10462
Wood Rd	10462
Woodhull Ave	10469
Woodmansten Pl	10462
Woodycrest Ave	10452
Worthen St	10474
Wright Ave	10475
Wyatt St	10460
Wythe Pl	10452
Yates Ave	
1500-2099	10461
2300-3299	10469
Yorainso Ave	10456
Young Ave	10469
Yznaga Pl	10465
Zerega Ave	
300-999	10473
1000-1799	10462
Zulette Ave	10461

NUMBERED STREETS

Street	ZIP
3rd Ave	10454
2401-2773	10451
2740-2770	10455
2772-3041	10455
3042-3044	10451
3043-3045	10455
3046-3245	10451
3247-3249	10451
3248-3248	10456
3250-3799	10456
3800-4423	10457
4424-4498	10458
4425-4529	10457
4502-4522	10457
4524-4528	10458
4530-4799	10458
E 132nd St	
200-239	10451
240-999	10454
E 133rd St	
200-239	10451
600-999	10454
E 134th St	
200-239	10451
240-999	10454
E 135th St	
100-249	10451
250-999	10454
E 136th St	
200-269	10451
270-999	10454
E 137th St	
417AF-417AS	10454

419AF-419AS 10454
200-269 10451
270-999 10454
E 138th St
483AF-483AS 10454
485AF-485AS 10454
100-269 10451
270-999 10454
E 139th St
476AF-476AS 10454
478AF-478AS 10454
200-269 10451
270-999 10454
E 140th St
100-289 10451
290-999 10454
E 141st St
200-305 10451
307-309 10451
308-308 10454
310-999 10454
E 142nd St
200-299 10451
300-799 10454
E 143rd St
200-334 10451
335-599 10454
E 144th St
100-339 10451
340-841 10454
E 145th St
300-349 10451
350-599 10454
700-876 10455
878-898 10455
E 146th St
100-359 10451
360-599 10455
E 147th St 10455
E 148th St
200-353 10451
354-599 10455
E 149th St
298A-298B 10451
E 150th St
1-353 10451
354-899 10455
E 151st St
1-353 10451
354-900 10455
E 152nd St
200-353 10451
354-899 10455
E 153rd St
1-353 10451
354-599 10455
E 154th St
200-353 10451
354-499 10455
E 155th St 10455
E 156th St
161-175 10451
177-353 10451
354-1099 10455
1100-1299 10474
E 157th St 10451
E 158th St 10456
1-569 10451
570-799 10456
E 159th St
100-569 10451
570-599 10456
E 160th St
791A-791C 10456
795A-795C 10456
200-569 10451
570-808 10456
809-899 10459
E 161st St
823A-823C 10459
829A-829C 10459
1-569 10451
570-808 10456
809-899 10459
W 161st St 10452
E 162nd St
1-159 10452
160-599 10451
810-899 10459
W 162nd St 10452
E 163rd St
160-569 10451
570-811 10456
812-1099 10459
W 163rd St 10452
E 164th St
1-159 10452
160-649 10456
810-899 10459
W 164th St 10452
E 165th St
1-159 10452
160-809 10456
810-1199 10459
W 165th St 10452
E 166th St
100-159 10452
160-810 10456
811-811 10459
812-812 10456
813-899 10459
W 166th St 10452
E 167th St
1-150 10452
152-178 10452
180-809 10456
810-1099 10459
W 167th St 10452
E 168th St
1-197 10452
198-212 10456
199-199 10452
214-801 10456
802-899 10459
W 168th St 10452
E 169th St
1-199 10452
200-799 10456
800-808 10459
801-809 10456
810-999 10459
W 169th St 10452
E 170th St
1-199 10452
200-208 10456
210-796 10456
797-899 10459
W 170th St 10452
E 171st St
1-199 10452
200-599 10457
W 171st St 10452
E 172nd St
1-199 10452
200-599 10457
800-1099 10460
1400-1799 10472
W 172nd St 10452
E 173rd St
100-599 10457
800-1099 10460
1500-1599 10472
E 174th St
2-100 10452
101-599 10457
900-1099 10460
1500-1802 10472
W 174th St 10453
E 175th St
1-149 10453
150-759 10457
760-999 10460
W 175th St 10453
E 176th St
1-153 10453
154-759 10457
760-887 10460
889-929 10460
W 176th St 10453
E 177th St
1-199 10453
1100-1299 10460
W 177th St 10453
E 178th St
100-199 10453
200-759 10457
760-1299 10460
E 179th St
1-199 10453
200-759 10457
760-1199 10460
W 179th St 10453
E 180th St
100-199 10453
200-759 10457
760-1499 10460
W 180th St 10453
E 181st St
2-4 10453
6-199 10453
200-759 10457
760-999 10460
W 181st St 10453
E 182nd St
1-199 10453
200-759 10457
760-899 10460
W 182nd St 10453
E 183rd St
1-199 10453
200-759 10458
760-799 10460
W 183rd St 10453
E 184th St
1-199 10468
200-549 10458
W 184th St 10468
E 185th St
400-599 10458
760-799 10460
E 186th St 10458
E 187th St 10458
E 188th St 10468
E 188th St 10468
200-799 10458
W 188th St 10468
E 189th St
100-199 10468
400-799 10458
E & W 190th 10468
E 191st St 10468
500-552 10458
W 191st St 10468
E 192nd St
100-199 10468
200-299 10458
W 192nd St 10468
E 193rd St
1-199 10468
300-399 10458
W 193rd St 10463
E 194th St
200-399 10458
2800-2999 10461
E 195th St
300-399 10458
2800-2899 10461
W 195th St 10468
E 196th St
1-199 10468
200-399 10458
2800-2999 10461
E 197th St
100-199 10468
200-400 10458
2800-2899 10461
W 197th St 10468
E 198th St
1-199 10468
200-400 10458
W 198th St 10468
E 199th St
1-99 10468
200-499 10458
E 201st St 10458
E 202nd St
200-399 10458
400-499 10467
E 203rd St
200-399 10458
400-499 10467
223-5-223-5 10458
E 204th St
1-199 10468
200-269 10458
270-499 10467
E 205th St
1-149 10468
150-219 10458
220-399 10467
W 205th St 10468
E 206th St
150-219 10458
220-399 10467
E 207th St 10467
E 208th St 10467
E 209th St 10467
E 210th St 10467
E 211th St
100-899 10467
900-1199 10469
E 212th St
1-799 10467
900-1199 10469
E 213th St
1-899 10467
900-1199 10469
E 214th St
700-899 10467
900-1200 10469
E 215th St
700-899 10467
900-1199 10469
E 216th St
600-899 10467
900-1199 10469
E 217th St
700-899 10467
900-1099 10469
E 218th St
700-899 10467
900-1199 10469
E 219th St
600-899 10467
900-1199 10469
E 220th St
600-899 10467
900-1099 10469
E 221st St
600-899 10467
900-1200 10469
E 222nd St
550-899 10467
900-1599 10469
E 223rd St 10466
E 224th St 10466
E 225th St 10466
W 225th St 10463
E 226th Dr & St S 10466
226th Street Dr 10466
E 227th St 10466
W 227th St 10463
E 228th St 10466
W 228th St 10463
229th Dr S 10466
E 229th St 10466
W 229th St 10463
E 230th St 10466
W 230th St 10463
E 231st St 10466
W 231st St 10463
E 232nd St 10466
W 232nd St 10463
E 233rd St
1-549 10470
600-1799 10466
W 233rd St 10463
E 234th St
200-549 10470
550-899 10466
W 234th St 10463
E 235th St
1-549 10470
600-899 10466
W 235th St 10463
E 236th St
1-549 10470
550-799 10466
W 236th St 10463
E 237th St
1-549 10470
550-799 10466
W 237th St 10463
E 238th St 10470
W 238th St 10463
E 239th St
100-699 10470
700-799 10466
W 239th St 10463
E 240th St 10470
200-499 10463
600-799 10471
E 241st St
200-869 10470
870-1099 10466
242nd St And Van Cortlandt Park E 10470
E 242nd St 10470
W 242nd St 10471
E 243rd St 10470
W 245th St 10471
W 246th St 10471
W 247th St 10471
W 249th St 10471
W 250th St 10471
W 251st St 10471
W 252nd St 10471
W 253rd St 10471
W 254th St 10471
W 255th St 10471
W 256th St 10471
W 258th St 10471
W 259th St 10471
W 260th St 10471
W 261st St 10471
W 262nd St 10471
W 263rd St 10471

BROOKLYN NY

General Delivery 11201

POST OFFICE BOXES MAIN OFFICE STATIONS AND BRANCHES

Box No.s
926A - 926A 11202
1197A - 1197A 11202
1680A - 1680A 11202
29193A - 29193A 11202
2000C - 2000C 11202
70801A - 70801A 11202
M - M 11207
33A - 33A 11202
1 - 256 11204
1 - 459 11205
1 - 719 11206
1 - 388 11208
1 - 670 11209
1 - 624 11212
1 - 360 11213
1 - 372 11214
1 - 819 11215
1 - 636 11216
1 - 360 11217
1 - 264 11218
1 - 352 11220
1 - 600 11221
1 - 446 11222
1 - 572 11225
1 - 306 11228
1 - 860 11230
1 - 840 11231
1 - 270 11232
1 - 959 11233
1 - 464 11235
1 - 416 11236
1 - 900 11238
1 - 1020 11211
1 - 182 11223
1 - 420 11203
1 - 619 11224
1 - 742 11237
1 - 769 11229
1 - 440 11219
1 - 921 11207
1 - 680 11226
1 - 3388 11202
1 - 560 11234
243 - 314 11223
300 - 419 11218
301 - 459 11204
401 - 423 11217
471 - 471 11210
500 - 619 11217
500 - 559 11219
500 - 559 11222
500 - 619 11235
600 - 1219 11219
601 - 660 11234
607 - 640 11225
701 - 760 11234
929 - 929 11210
938 - 938 11235
3501 - 4000 11202
5001 - 5714 11220
5001 - 5700 11224
9099 - 29222 11202
30001 - 39010 11203
40001 - 49026 11204
50001 - 59065 11205
60001 - 60719 11206
70001 - 79412 11207
80001 - 89006 11208
90001 - 99057 11209
100001 - 109016 11210
110001 - 119031 11211
120001 - 129005 11212
130001 - 139016 11213
140001 - 149082 11214
150001 - 159681 11215
160001 - 169013 11216
170001 - 179030 11217
180001 - 189120 11218
190001 - 199045 11219
200001 - 209289 11220
210001 - 219010 11221
220001 - 229061 11222
230001 - 239060 11223
240001 - 249005 11224
250001 - 259008 11225
260001 - 260680 11226
280001 - 289003 11228
290001 - 299033 11229
300001 - 309046 11230
310001 - 319044 11231
320001 - 329087 11232
330001 - 339011 11233
340001 - 349038 11234
350001 - 359630 11235
360001 - 369022 11236
370001 - 379051 11237
380001 - 389007 11238
470001 - 474295 11247
609001 - 609049 11206

NAMED STREETS

Abbey Ct 11229
Aberdeen St 11207
E Adallanc St 11234
Adams St 11201
Adarenew Ave 11237
Adelphi St
1-326 11205
327-483 11238
485-499 11238
Adler Pl 11208
Agate Ct 11213
Ainslie St 11211
Airendis Ave 11215
Aitken Pl 11201
Alabama Ave 11207
Albany Ave
1-33 11216
34-469 11213
470-1387 11203
1389-1449 11203
1501-1999 11210
Albee Sq 11201
Albemarle Rd
1-97 11218
99-1299 11218
1300-2999 11226
Albemarle Ter 11226
Alice Ct 11213
Allen Ave 11229
Alton Pl 11210
Amber St 11208
Amboy St 11212
Amersfort Pl 11210
Amherst St 11235
Amity St 11201
Angela Dr 11223
Anthony St 11222
Apollo St 11222
Applegate Ct 11223
Ardsley Loop 11239
Argyle Rd
1-530 11218
531-799 11230
Arion Pl 11206
Arkansas Dr 11234
Arlington Ave
2-22 11207
24-240 11207
241-399 11208
Arlington Pl 11216
Ash St 11222
Ashford St 11207
Ashland Pl
100-153 11201
155-169 11201
170-299 11217
301-399 11217
Aster Ct 11229
Atkins Ave 11208
Atlantic Ave
1-346 11201
347-644 11217
646-750 11217
785-835 11238
837-1082 11238
1083-1129 11216
1084-1130 11238
1131-1404 11216
1406-1516 11216
1455-1515 11213
1517-1588 11213
1590-1800 11213
1777-1799 11233
1801-2426 11233
2428-2450 11233
2465-2485 11207
2487-2951 11207
2952-2956 11208
2953-2957 11207
2958-3511 11208
3513-3549 11208
3700-4499 11224
Atlantic Commons 11217
Auburn Pl 11205
Aurelia Ct 11210
Autumn Ave 11208
Avenue N
105-105 11230
Avenue N
107-1910 11230
1912-1998 11230
2000-2999 11210
3001-3199 11210
3201-3297 11234
3299-7300 11234
7302-7398 11234
8300-8398 11236
8400-10852 11236
10854-10898 11236
Avenue S
1-1199 11223
1200-3099 11229
3203-3297 11234
3299-5199 11234

5201-5499 11234
Avenue W
15-47 11223
49-1099 11223
1200-3200 11229
3202-3398 11229
6900-7599 11234
Avenue A 11236
Avenue B 11236
Avenue C 11218
Avenue D
2300-3200 11226
3202-3298 11226
3300-5900 11203
5902-5998 11203
8701-8797 11236
8799-10799 11236
10801-10899 11236
Avenue F 11218
Avenue H
600-614 11230
616-1999 11230
2901-3197 11210
3199-4299 11210
4301-4399 11210
4400-5799 11234
Avenue I
2-98 11230
100-1999 11230
2001-2097 11210
2099-4399 11210
4400-5799 11234
Avenue J
1-1999 11230
2000-4399 11210
4400-5699 11234
5701-5899 11234
8000-8298 11236
8300-10799 11236
Avenue K
601-609 11230
611-1999 11230
2000-2098 11210
2100-4299 11210
4301-4399 11210
4400-5499 11234
5501-5599 11234
8001-8097 11236
8099-10599 11236
Avenue L
400-1916 11230
1918-1998 11230
2000-3899 11210
3901-3999 11210
4401-4497 11234
4499-5900 11234
5902-7098 11234
8001-8097 11236
8099-10599 11236
Avenue M
1-115 11230
117-1999 11230
2000-3399 11210
3500-3598 11234
3600-7300 11234
7302-7398 11234
8101-8197 11236
8199-10599 11236
Avenue O
2-30 11204
32-199 11204
200-1999 11230
2000-2499 11210
2501-2699 11210
4700-5999 11234
Avenue P
2-78 11204
80-360 11204
362-390 11204
392-1099 11223
1100-2964 11229
3000-4299 11234
Avenue R
401-497 11223
499-1199 11223
1200-3064 11229
3065-4299 11234
Avenue T
1-1199 11223
1200-1216 11229
1218-3099 11229
3300-7400 11234
7402-7598 11234
Avenue U
25-59 11223
61-1199 11223
1200-3104 11229
3106-3198 11229
3300-3398 11234
3400-7500 11234
7502-7598 11234
Avenue V
18-22 11223
24-1199 11223
1200-3172 11229
3174-3198 11229
3901-6897 11234
6899-7599 11234
Avenue X
1-47 11223
49-499 11223
500-510 11235
512-3062 11235
3064-3092 11235
6901-7097 11234
7099-7599 11234
Avenue Y
2-60 11214
300-550 11223
551-2960 11235
2962-3048 11235
6901-7399 11234
Avenue Z
101-209 11214
211-282 11214
283-753 11223
755-813 11235
815-3099 11235
Aviation Rd 11234
Bainbridge St 11233
Balfour Pl 11225
Baltic St
50-399 11201
400-699 11217
Bancroft Pl 11233
Bank St 11236
Banker St 11222
Banner Ave 11235
Banner 3rd Rd & Ter 11235
Barbey St 11207
Barlow Dr N & S 11234
Bartlett Pl 11229
Bartlett St 11206
Barwell Ter 11209
Bassett Ave 11234
Batchelder St
1002-1898 11229
1900-2399 11229
2400-2498 11235
2500-2899 11235
Bath Ave
1400-1599 11228
1600-2773 11214
2775-2799 11214
Battery Ave
1-83 11228
84-350 11209
Baughman Pl 11234
Bay Ave
1700-1898 11230
1900-1999 11230
2000-2299 11210
Bay Pkwy
4600-5499 11230
5800-5898 11204
5900-7300 11204
7302-7498 11204
7500-7698 11214
7700-9000 11214
9002-9098 11214
Bay St 11231
Bay 10th St 11228
Bay 11th St 11228
Bay 13th St 11214
Bay 14th St 11214
Bay 16th St 11214
Bay 17th St 11214
Bay 19th St 11214
Bay 20th St 11214
Bay 22nd St 11214
Bay 23rd St 11214
Bay 25th St 11214
Bay 26th St 11214
Bay 28th St 11214
Bay 29th St 11214
Bay 31st St 11214
Bay 32nd St 11214
Bay 34th St 11214
Bay 35th St 11214
Bay 37th St 11214
Bay 38th St 11214
Bay 40th St 11214
Bay 41st St 11214
Bay 43rd St 11214
Bay 44th St 11214
Bay 46th St 11214
Bay 47th St 11214
Bay 48th St 11214
Bay 49th St 11214
Bay 50th St 11214
Bay 52nd St 11214
Bay 53rd St 11214
Bay 7th St 11228
Bay 8th St 11228
Bay Cliff Ter 11220
Bay Ridge Ave
1-899 11220
901-917 11219
919-1599 11219
1600-2199 11204
Bay Ridge Pkwy
2-699 11209
900-1599 11228
1600-2199 11204
Bay Ridge Pl 11209
Bayard St
2-50 11211
52-124 11222
126-199 11222
Bayview Ave 11224
Bayview Pl 11236
Beach Pl 11236
Beach 38th St 11224
Beach 40th St 11224
Beach 42nd St 11224
Beach 43rd St 11224
Beach 44th St 11224
Beach 45th St 11224
Beach 46th St 11224
Beach 47th St 11224
Beach 48th St 11224
Beach 49th St 11224
Beach 50th St 11224
Beach 51st St 11224
Beach Reservation 11224
Beacon Ct 11229
Beadel St 11222
Beard St 11231
Beaumont St 11235
Beaver St 11206
Bedell Ln 11236
Bedford Ave
1-2 11222
4-70 11222
72-684 11249
101-679 11211
681-683 11206
685-724 11206
725-729 11205
726-730 11206
731-1030 11205
1031-1057 11216
1032-1058 11205
1059-1536 11216
1538-1546 11216
1548-1576 11225
1578-2005 11225
2006-2609 11226
2611-2639 11226
2640-3663 11210
3664-4444 11229
4445-4529 11235
4446-4446 11229
4531-4899 11235
Bedford Pl 11216
Beekman Pl 11225
Bell Point Dr 11234
Belmont Ave
1-121 11212
123-199 11212
202-398 11207
400-698 11207
700-718 11208
720-1199 11208
1201-1299 11208
Belvidere St 11206
Bennett Ct 11209
Benson Ave
1394-1498 11228
1500-1599 11228
1600-2624 11214
2626-2698 11214
Bergen Ave 11234
Bergen Ct 11234
Bergen Cv 11234
Bergen Pl 11220
Bergen St
1-132 11201
133-135 11217
134-136 11201
137-559 11217
560-945 11238
946-948 11216
947-949 11238
950-1159 11216
1160-1662 11213
1664-1730 11213
1732-1810 11233
1812-2179 11233
2181-2199 11233
Bergen Beach Pl 11234
Berkeley Pl 11217
Berriman St
1-759 11208
761-899 11208
1100-1198 11239
Berry St 11249
Bethel Loop 11239
Beverley Rd
100-1299 11218
1300-1598 11226
1600-3299 11226
3300-5999 11203
Bevy Ct 11229
Bijou Ave 11229
Billings Pl 11223
Bills Pl 11218
Blake Ave
1-39 11212
41-457 11212
459-479 11212
482-502 11207
504-958 11207
959-977 11208
979-1499 11208
Blake Ct 11235
Blanders St 11206
Bleecker St
1-182 11221
184-250 11237
252-449 11237
Bliss Ter 11220
Boardwalk W 11224
Boerum Pl 11201
Boerum St 11206
Bogart St 11206
Bokee Ct 11223
Bond St
1-50 11201
51-273 11217
275-285 11217
287-293 11231
295-426 11231
428-450 11231
Borinquen Pl 11211
Bouck Ct 11223
Bowery St 11224
Bowne St 11231
Box St 11222
Boynton Pl 11223
Bradford St 11207
Bragg St
2000-2399 11229
2400-2900 11235
2902-2966 11235
Branton St 11236
Brevoort Pl 11216
Bridge St 11201
Bridgewater St 11222
Brigham St
2100-2399 11229
2400-2500 11235
2502-2842 11235
W Brighton Ave 11224
Brighton Ct
1-30 11223
62-64 11235
66-81 11235
83-89 11235
Brighton 10th Ct, Ln, Path, St & Ter 11235
Brighton 11th St 11235
Brighton 12th St 11235
Brighton 13th St 11235
Brighton 14th St 11235
Brighton 15th St 11235
Brighton 1st Ct, Ln, Path, Pl, Rd, St, Ter & Walk 11235
Brighton 2nd Ln, Path, Pl, St & Walk 11235
Brighton 3rd Ct, Ln, Pl, Rd, St & Walk 11235
Brighton 4th Ct, Ln, Pl, Rd, St, Ter & Walk 11235
Brighton 5th Ct, Ln, Pl, St & Walk 11235
Brighton 6th Ct & St 11235
Brighton 7th Ct, Ln, St & Walk 11235
Brighton 8th Ct, Pl & St 11235
Brighton Beach Ave 11235
Brightwater Ave & Ct 11235
Bristol St
1-610 11212
655-799 11236
Broadway
16-22 11249
Broadway
24-134 11249
135-506 11211
507-933 11206
934-944 11221
935-945 11206
946-1558 11221
1559-1609 11207
1560-1560 11221
1611-2000 11207
2002-2098 11207
Brookdale Plz 11212
Brooklyn Ave
11-53 11216
55-118 11216
119-119 11213
120-120 11216
121-334 11213
336-374 11213
411-545 11225
547-567 11225
569-1400 11203
1401-1861 11210
1863-1899 11210
Brooklyn Terminal Market 11236
Broome St 11222
Brown St
1800-2399 11229
2401-2597 11235
2599-2899 11235
Buffalo Ave
2-18 11233
20-130 11233
131-299 11213
Bulwer Pl 11207
Burnett St 11229
Bush Plz 11232
Bush St 11231
Bushwick Ave
1-74 11211
76-96 11211
98-168 11206
170-639 11206
640-640 11221
641-641 11206
642-1242 11221
1244-1799 11207
Bushwick Ct 11206
Bushwick Pl 11206
Butler Pl 11238
Butler St
1-132 11231
134-188 11217
190-419 11217
421-431 11217
Cadman Plz E
101-299 11201
271-271 11202
Cadman Plz W 11201
Calder Pl 11215
Calyer St 11222
Cambridge Pl 11238
Cameron Ct 11204
Campus Pl 11208
Campus Rd 11210
Canal Ave 11224
Canarsie Rd 11236
Canda Ave 11235
Canton Ct 11229
Carlton Ave
1-341 11205
342-699 11238
Carroll St
8-410 11231
412-422 11215
424-874 11215
875-897 11225
876-898 11215
899-1226 11225
1227-1251 11213
1228-1252 11225
1253-1799 11213
Cass Pl 11235
Cathedral Pl 11201
Catherine St 11211
Caton Ave
2-298 11218
300-900 11218
902-1198 11218
1300-1698 11226
1700-2199 11226
2201-2299 11226
Caton Pl 11218
Cedar St
1-99 11221
1600-1699 11230
Celeste Ct 11229
Central Ave
1-49 11206
51-106 11206
108-110 11206
111-526 11221
527-549 11207
528-550 11221
551-799 11207
Centre Mall & St 11231
Chapel St 11201
Charles Pl 11221
Chauncey St
1-69 11233
71-576 11233
578-600 11233
601-799 11207
Cheever Pl 11231
Cherry St 11222
Chester Ave 11218
Chester Ct 11225
Chester St
1-89 11212
91-699 11212
700-737 11236
739-799 11236
Chestnut Ct & St 11208
Christopher Ave 11212
Church Ave
1-1299 11218
1300-3299 11226
3300-5999 11203
8900-9098 11236
9100-9200 11236
9202-9298 11236
9300-9799 11212
Church Ln 11236
City Pt 11201
Clara St 11218
Clarendon Rd
2161-2169 11226
2171-3299 11226
3300-5700 11203
5702-5898 11203
Clark St 11201
Clarkson Ave
2-340 11226
342-366 11226
367-397 11203
399-900 11203
902-978 11203
981-1001 11212
1003-1199 11212
Classon Ave
71-343 11205
344-358 11238
345-359 11205
360-846 11238
848-852 11238
877-999 11225
Claver Pl 11238
Clay St 11222
Clear Water Rd 11234
Clermont Ave
1-338 11205
339-549 11238
551-599 11238
Cleveland St 11208
Clifford Pl 11222
Clifton Pl
2-2 11238
4-176 11238
177-399 11216
Clinton Ave
1-326 11205
327-339 11238
328-340 11205
341-599 11238
Clinton St
2-30 11201
32-300 11201
301-313 11231
302-314 11201
315-684 11231
686-750 11231
Clove Rd 11225
Clymer St
2-66 11249
68-141 11249
142-142 11211
143-143 11249
144-199 11211
Cobeck Ct 11223
Coffey St 11231
Colby Ct 11223
Coleman St 11234
Coleridge St 11235
Coles St 11231
Colin Pl 11223
College Pl 11201
Colonial Ct 11209
Colonial Gdns 11209
Colonial Rd
6601-6797 11220
6799-6899 11220
6900-6998 11209
7000-9199 11209
Columbia Ct 11235
Columbia Hts 11201
Columbia Pl 11201
Columbia St
1-115 11201
117-183 11231

185-700 11231
Columbus Pl 11233
Comerenn Ave 11221
Commerce St 11231
Commercial St 11222
Concord St 11201
Conduit Blvd 11208
Coney Island Ave
301-307 11218
309-910 11218
911-911 11230
912-912 11218
913-1940 11230
1941-2668 11223
2669-3206 11235
3208-3398 11235
Congress St 11201
Conklin Ave 11236
Conover St 11231
Conselyea St 11211
Conway St 11207
Cook St 11206
Cooke Ct 11207
Cooper St
1-252 11207
253-399 11237
E Coradens St 11236
Corbin Ct 11230
Corbin Pl 11235
Cornelia St
1-300 11221
301-449 11237
Corso Ct 11223
Cortelyou Rd
1-97 11218
99-1299 11218
1300-3100 11226
3102-3298 11226
3300-4698 11203
Court St
16-16 11241
22-24 11201
26-26 11242
32-42 11201
44-242 11201
244-248 11201
250-260 11231
262-750 11231
752-764 11231
Cove Ln 11234
Coventry Rd 11236
Covert St
1-270 11207
271-349 11237
351-359 11237
Cox Pl 11208
Coyle St
1900-1998 11229
2000-2199 11229
2401-2497 11235
2499-2899 11235
Cozine Ave
2-192 11207
194-401 11207
403-413 11207
416-454 11208
456-716 11208
718-724 11208
Cralench Ave 11205
Cranberry St 11201
Crawford Ave 11223
Creamer St 11231
Crescent St 11208
Crooke Ave 11226
Cropsey Ave
1325-1353 11228
1355-1548 11228
1601-1649 11214
1651-3019 11214
3020-3199 11224
Crosby Ave 11207
Croton Loop 11239
Crown St
1-9 11225
11-492 11225
493-851 11213
853-899 11213
Crystal St 11208
Cumberland St
1-276 11205
277-291 11238
278-292 11205
293-499 11238
Cumberland Walk 11205
Cypress Ave
1-36 11237
38-194 11237
3700-3999 11224
Cypress Ct 11208
Cyrus Ave 11229
Dahill Rd
1-33 11218
35-699 11218
800-898 11204
900-1580 11204
1582-1600 11204
1601-1799 11223
Dahl Ct 11204
Dahlgren Pl 11228
Dakota Pl 11234
Danforth St 11208
Dank Ct 11223
Dare Ct 11229
De Koven Ct 11230
De Sales Pl 11207
Dean St
2-135 11201
136-572 11217
573-1049 11238
1050-1419 11216
1421-1433 11213
1435-1730 11213
1731-2499 11233
Debevoise Ave
1-60 11211
61-117 11222
Debevoise St 11206
Decatur St
1-141 11216
142-146 11233
143-147 11216
148-799 11233
801-901 11233
902-1312 11207
1313-1399 11237
Degraw St
1-59 11231
61-398 11231
399-423 11217
400-424 11231
425-702 11217
704-728 11217
Dekalb Ave
1-117 11201
118-120 11217
119-121 11201
122-166 11217
167-608 11205
609-693 11216
610-616 11205
695-763 11216
764-764 11221
765-765 11216
766-1388 11221
1389-1799 11237
Delevan St 11231
Delmar Loop 11239
Delmonico Pl 11206
Dennett Pl 11231
Denton Pl 11215
Desmond Ct 11235
Devoe St 11211
Dewey Pl 11233
Dewitt Ave
299-301 11236
303-335 11207
337-442 11207
444-498 11207
Diamond St 11222
Dictum Ct 11229
Dikeman St 11231
Ditmars St 11221
Ditmas Ave
1-1299 11218
1300-2227 11226
2229-2299 11226
8301-8397 11236
8399-9899 11236
Division Ave
1-89 11249
90-102 11211
91-103 11249
104-299 11211
301-399 11211
Division Pl 11222
Dobbin St 11222
Dodworth St 11221
Dontreld St 11256
Dooley St 11235
Doone Ct 11235
Dorchester Rd
1000-1199 11218
1201-1299 11218
1301-1497 11226
1499-2100 11226
2102-2198 11226
Dornerli Ave 11226
Dorset St 11236
Doscher St 11208
Doubleday Ln 11209
Doughty St 11201
Douglass St
1-119 11231
120-178 11217
121-121 11231
180-419 11217
Dover St 11235
Downing St 11238
Drew St 11208
Driggs Ave
14-316 11222
318-330 11222
400-999 11211
Duffield St 11201
Dumont Ave
1011A-1011B 11208
1-97 11212
99-480 11212
481-491 11207
482-492 11212
493-967 11207
968-1599 11208
Dunham Pl 11249
Dunne Ct & Pl 11235
Dupont St 11222
Durland Pl 11236
Duryea Ct 11219
Duryea Pl 11226
Dwight St 11231
Eagle St 11222
Eastern Pkwy
5-99 11238
101-201 11238
203-327 11238
212-618 11225
329-617 11216
619-1209 11213
1211-1289 11213
1291-2010 11233
2011-2099 11207
Eaton Ct 11229
Ebony Ct 11229
Eckford St 11222
Egan St 11239
Eldert Ln 11208
Eldert St
1-299 11207
300-349 11237
351-439 11237
Ellery St 11206
N Elliott Pl 11205
S Elliott Pl 11217
N Elliott Walk 11205
Elm Ave 11230
Elm Pl 11201
Elmira Loop 11239
Elmwood Ave 11230
Elton St
1-1053 11208
1055-1097 11239
1099-1180 11239
Emerald St 11208
Emerson Pl 11205
Emmons Ave 11235
Empire Blvd
17-29 11225
31-581 11225
583-587 11225
589-841 11213
843-899 11213
W End Ave 11235
Engert Ave 11222
Erasmus St 11226
Erskine St 11239
Essex St
1-1000 11208
1002-1050 11208
1064-1108 11239
1110-1132 11239
1134-1154 11239
Etna St 11208
Euclid Ave 11208
Evans St 11201
Everanin 11223
Evergreen Ave
2-64 11206
66-142 11206
143-205 11221
144-174 11206
207-586 11221
587-639 11207
588-640 11221
641-800 11207
802-898 11207
Everit St 11201
Exeter St 11235
Fairview Pl 11226
Falmouth St 11235
Fanchon Pl 11207
Fane Ct 11229
Farragut Rd
2600-4199 11210
4200-4899 11203
4901-5299 11203
5600-5712 11234
5714-5898 11234
6000-8598 11236
8600-10799 11236
Fayette St 11206
Fenimore St
2-60 11225
62-452 11225
453-799 11203
Ferris St 11231
Fillmore Ave
2600-2698 11229
2701-2999 11229
3001-3197 11234
3199-5699 11234
5701-5799 11234
Fillmore Pl 11211
Fiske Pl 11215
Flatbush Ave
1-303 11217
304-342 11238
305-343 11217
344-410 11238
432-458 11225
460-714 11225
715-721 11226
716-722 11225
723-1297 11226
1298-1338 11210
1299-1339 11226
1340-1945 11210
1946-1948 11234
1947-1949 11210
1950-3000 11234
3002-3650 11234
Flatbush Avenue Ext 11201
Flatlands Ave
3400-5999 11234
6000-6498 11236
6500-10805 11236
10807-10841 11236
11000-12012 11207
12014-12299 11207
12301-12399 11207
12411-12799 11208
12480-12504 11239
12506-12798 11208
Flatlands 10th St 11236
Flatlands 1st St 11236
Flatlands 2nd St 11236
Flatlands 3rd St 11236
Flatlands 4th St 11236
Flatlands 5th St 11236
Flatlands 6th St 11236
Flatlands 7th St 11236
Flatlands 8th St 11236
Flatlands 9th St 11236
Fleet Pl & Walk 11201
Florence Ave 11229
Floyd Bennett Fld 11234
Flushing Ave
63-67 11205
69-519 11205
520-540 11206
521-535 11205
542-1003 11206
1004-1028 11237
1005-1029 11206
1030-1349 11237
Folsom Pl 11208
Forbell St
1-999 11208
1000-1050 11256
1001-1199 11208
Force Tube Ave 11208
Ford St
1-50 11213
1900-2399 11229
2600-2899 11235
Forest Pl 11209
Forrest St 11206
Fort Greene Pl 11217
Fort Hamilton Pkwy
2800-4000 11218
4002-4098 11218
4100-6899 11219
6900-7299 11228
7301-7799 11228
8200-8398 11209
8400-10099 11209
Fort Hill Pl 11228
Foster Ave
100-102 11230
104-1999 11230
2000-2999 11210
3001-3599 11210
3701-4097 11203
4099-5299 11203
5401-5697 11234
5699-5999 11234
6000-7998 11236
8000-10399 11236
10401-10699 11236
Fountain Ave 11208
Fralewood Ave 11203
Frank Ct 11229
Franklin Ave
1-20 11249
21-297 11205
298-302 11238
299-303 11205
304-803 11238
804-818 11225
805-819 11238
820-922 11225
924-1098 11225
Franklin St 11222
Freeman St 11222
Freeport Loop 11239
Friel Pl 11218
Front St 11201
Frost St
1-256 11211
257-259 11222
258-260 11211
261-352 11222
Fuller Pl 11215
Fulton St
340-406 11201
408-543 11201
544-624 11217
545-625 11201
626-713 11217
714-884 11238
715-781 11217
886-1133 11238
1134-1148 11216
1135-1149 11238
1150-1359 11216
1360-1558 11216
1360-1360 11247
1361-1569 11216
1560-1568 11213
1570-1630 11213
1632-1752 11213
1701-1751 11233
1753-2449 11233
2451-2469 11207
2471-2958 11207
2959-3499 11208
Furman Ave 11207
Furman St 11201
Gain Ct 11229
Gallatin Pl 11201
Garden Pl 11201
Garden St 11206
Gardner Ave
1-33 11237
35-207 11237
208-252 11211
398-508 11222
510-542 11222
544-598 11222
Garfield Pl 11215
Garland Ct 11229
Garnet St 11231
Gates Ave
1-29 11238
31-261 11238
262-272 11216
263-273 11238
274-529 11216
530-550 11221
531-551 11216
552-1423 11221
1424-1545 11237
1547-1603 11237
Gateway Dr 11239
Gatling Pl 11209
Gaylord Dr N & S 11234
Gelston Ave 11209
Gem St 11222
General Lee Ave
1-300 11252
301-399 11209
302-398 11252
400-499 11252
Geneva Loop 11239
George St
2-96 11206
100-157 11237
159-199 11237
Georgetown Ln 11234
Georgia Ave 11207
Gerald Ct 11235
Gerritsen Ave 11229
Gerry St 11206
Gilmore Ct 11235
Girard St 11235
Glen St 11208
Glendale Ct 11234
Glenmore Ave
1-199 11212
201-675 11207
677-695 11207
697-1199 11208
1201-1299 11208
Glenwood Rd
1100-1999 11230
2000-4399 11210
4400-4499 11203
4501-4599 11203
4700-5999 11234
6001-8197 11236
8199-10699 11236
10701-10799 11236
Gold St 11201
Goodwin Pl 11221
Gopost
147-147 11201
Gopost
506-506 11205
610-610 11206
815-815 11208
1109-1109 11211
1412-1412 11214
1953-1953 11219
2413-2413 11224
Gopost St
1808-1808 11218
2913-2913 11229
Gotham Ave 11229
Grace Ct 11201
Grace Court Aly 11201
Grafton St 11212
Graham Ave
1-270 11206
271-450 11211
451-463 11222
452-454 11211
465-599 11222
Graillea Ave 11238
Grand Ave
1-118 11205
120-234 11205
273-647 11238
649-699 11238
Grand St
30-171 11249
172-1399 11211
Grand Army Plz 11238
Granite St 11207
Grant Ave 11208
Grant Sq 11216
Grattan St
1-46 11206
47-199 11237
Gravesend Neck Rd
16-24 11223
26-900 11223
902-1044 11223
1045-1055 11229
1057-2900 11229
2902-2998 11229
Green St 11222
Greene Ave
1-29 11238
31-347 11238
348-352 11216
349-353 11238
354-599 11216
600-1282 11221
1283-1550 11237
1552-1598 11237
Greenpoint Ave 11222
Greenwood Ave 11218
Grimes Rd
1-219 11252
221-223 11209
235-299 11252
Grimes Rd N 11252
Grove St
22-48 11221
50-159 11221
211-449 11237
Guernsey St 11222
Guider Ave 11235
Gunnison Ct 11235
Gunther Pl 11233
Hale Ave 11208
Haleners St 11219
Hall St 11205
Halleck St 11231
Halsey St
1-362 11216
363-399 11233
364-400 11216
401-900 11233
902-970 11233
972-1206 11207
1207-1261 11237
1208-1262 11207
1263-1399 11237
Hamilton Ave
2-58 11231

60-382 11231
384-406 11231
407-500 11232
502-600 11232
Hamilton Walk 11209
Hampton Ave 11235
Hampton Pl 11213
Hancock St
2-52 11216
54-433 11216
434-438 11233
435-439 11216
440-970 11233
971-1298 11221
1299-1459 11237
Hanover Pl 11201
Hanson Pl
1-1 11243
2-99 11217
Harbor Dr 11234
Harbor Ln 11209
Harbor View Ter 11209
Harden St 11234
E Harielli St 11230
Haring St
1700-2399 11229
2400-2899 11235
Harkness Ave 11235
Harman St
2-34 11221
36-190 11221
191-499 11237
Harrison Aly 11201
Harrison Ave
1-67 11211
69-77 11211
79-97 11206
99-151 11206
153-299 11206
Harrison Pl
1-41 11206
42-199 11237
201-299 11237
Hart Pl 11224
Hart St
1-396 11206
397-411 11221
398-412 11206
413-739 11221
740-1099 11237
Harway Ave 11214
Hastings St 11235
Hattie Jones Pl 11213
Hausman St 11222
Havemeyer St 11211
Haven Pl 11233
Hawthorne St
1-400 11225
401-699 11203
Hazel Ct 11229
Hegeman Ave
1-197 11212
199-270 11212
272-330 11212
332-420 11207
422-850 11207
851-1099 11208
Hemlock St 11208
Henderson Walk 11224
Hendrickson St 11234
Hendrix St 11207
Henry St
1-423 11201
424-424 11231
425-425 11201
426-722 11231
724-780 11231
N Henry St 11222
Heralist Ave 11228
Herbert St 11222
Herkimer Ct 11216
Herkimer Pl 11216
Herkimer St
1-313 11216
315-363 11216
365-535 11213
537-609 11213
700-1500 11233
1501-1517 11207
1502-1518 11233
1519-1542 11207
Herzl St 11212
Hewes St
1-49 11249
51-107 11249
108-114 11211
109-115 11249
116-391 11211
393-499 11211
Heyward St
1-61 11249
62-74 11206
63-75 11249
76-399 11206
Hicks St
2-24 11201
26-435 11201
437-449 11201
451-597 11231
599-832 11231
834-860 11231
Highland Ave 11224
Highland Blvd 11207
Highland Pl 11208
Highlawn Ave 11223
Hill St 11208
Hillel Pl 11210
Himrod St
1-27 11221
29-180 11221
181-469 11237
Hinckley Pl 11218
Hinsdale St 11207
Hitchings Ave 11235
Holly St 11208
Holmes Ln 11236
Homecrest Ave
1900-2399 11229
2600-2799 11235
Homecrest Ct 11223
Hooper St
1-51 11249
53-99 11249
100-384 11211
386-498 11211
Hope St 11211
Hopkins St 11206
Horace Ct 11218
Horinera Ave 11214
Hornell Loop 11239
Howard Ave
2-18 11221
20-60 11221
62-76 11221
78-78 11233
80-570 11233
571-890 11212
892-898 11212
Howard Pl 11215
Hoyt St
1-89 11201
90-266 11217
268-286 11217
287-425 11231
427-499 11231
Hubbard Pl 11210
Hubbard St 11235
Hudson Ave & Walk 11201
Hull St 11233
Humboldt St
2-2 11206
4-290 11206
291-478 11211
479-487 11222
480-488 11211
489-899 11222
Hunterfly Pl 11233
Huntington St 11231
Hunts Ln 11201
Huron St 11222
Hutchinson Ct 11223
Hyman Ct 11229
Imlay St 11231
Independence Ave 11228
India St 11222
Indiana Pl 11234
Ingraham St
1-56 11206
58-58 11237
60-299 11237
Ira Ct 11229
Irving Ave 11237
Irving Pl 11238
Irvington Pl 11230
Irwin St 11235
Ivan Ct 11229
Jackie Robinson Pkwy 11207
Jackson Ct 11209
Jackson Pl 11215
Jackson St 11211
Jaffrey St 11235
Jamaica Ave
1-29 11207
31-364 11207
366-442 11207
444-568 11208
570-1000 11208
1002-1004 11208
Jardine Pl 11233
Java St 11222
Jay St 11201
Jefferson Ave
1-35 11238
36-344 11216
345-1366 11221
1367-1599 11237
Jefferson St
1-218 11206
219-388 11237
390-498 11237
Jerome Ave 11235
Jerome St 11207
Jewel St 11222
Jewell Mckoy Ln 11213
Jodie Ct 11203
John St 11201
Johnson Ave
100-405 11206
406-410 11237
407-411 11206
412-604 11237
606-698 11237
Johnson St 11201
Jones Walk 11224
Joralemon St 11201
Joval Ct 11229
Judge St 11211
Juliana Pl 11249
Junius St 11212
Just Ct 11229
Kane Pl 11233
Kane St 11231
Kansas Pl 11234
Karweg Pl 11208
Kathleen Pl 11235
Kaufman Pl 11236
Kay Ct 11229
Keap St
2-14 11249
16-50 11249
52-62 11249
100-499 11211
Keen Ct 11229
Kenilworth Pl 11210
Kenmore Ct 11235
Kenmore Ter 11226
Kensington St 11235
Kent Ave
1-770 11249
771-999 11205
Kent St 11222
Kermit Pl 11218
Kiely Pl 11208
Kimball St 11234
King St 11231
Kings Hwy
74-98 11214
100-108 11214
110-124 11214
125-949 11223
951-999 11223
1100-3099 11229
3100-5301 11234
5302-5899 11203
9000-9799 11212
Kings Pl 11223
Kings Plz 11234
Kingsborough 1st Walk 11233
Kingsborough 2nd Walk 11233
Kingsborough 3rd Walk 11233
Kingsborough 4th Walk 11233
Kingsborough 5th Walk 11233
Kingsborough 6th Walk 11233
Kingsborough 7th Walk 11233
Kingsland Ave
2-12 11211
14-77 11211
78-82 11222
79-83 11211
84-416 11222
418-598 11222
Kingston Ave
1-377 11213
378-382 11225
379-383 11213
384-541 11225
542-699 11203
Kingsway Pl 11234
Knapp St
2100-2399 11229
2400-2899 11235
Knickerbocker Ave
1-495 11237
497-517 11237
519-731 11221
733-751 11221
763-781 11207
783-879 11207
881-999 11207
Knight Ct 11229
Kosciuszko St
1-88 11205
90-90 11205
92-172 11216
174-230 11216
231-618 11221
620-698 11221
Kossuth Pl 11221
Krier Pl 11236
Lacon Ct 11229
Lafayette Ave
446A-446A 11238
1-119 11217
120-128 11238
121-129 11217
130-447 11238
448-574 11205
575-585 11216
576-586 11205
587-696 11216
697-697 11221
698-698 11216
699-1199 11221
Lafayette Walk 11209
Lake Ave 11235
Lake Pl 11223
Lake St 11223
Lama Ct 11223
Lamont Ct 11225
Lancaster Ave 11223
Landis Ct 11229
Langham St 11235
Laurel Ave 11224
Lawn Ct 11235
Lawrence Ave 11230
Lawrence St 11201
Lawton St 11221
Lee Ave
1-197 11211
198-198 11206
199-199 11211
200-299 11206
Lefferts Ave
14-22 11225
24-557 11225
558-770 11203
772-884 11203
Lefferts Pl 11238
Legion St 11212
Lenox Rd
2-12 11226
14-374 11226
400-950 11203
951-1199 11212
Leonard St
5-97 11206
99-210 11206
211-395 11211
397-399 11211
401-409 11222
411-799 11222
Lester Ct 11229
Lewis Ave
1-103 11206
105-115 11206
117-119 11221
121-332 11221
333-333 11233
334-334 11221
335-412 11233
414-498 11233
Lewis Pl 11218
Lexington Ave
2-8 11238
10-121 11238
122-124 11216
123-125 11238
126-411 11216
412-424 11221
413-425 11216
426-899 11221
Liberty Ave
2-60 11212
62-171 11212
173-175 11212
176-675 11207
676-716 11208
718-1299 11208
Liberty Way 11209
Lincoln Ave 11208
Lincoln Pl
1-252 11217
267-561 11238
562-570 11216
563-571 11238
572-872 11216
873-1540 11213
1541-1701 11233
1703-1799 11233
Lincoln Rd 11225
Lincoln Ter 11235
Linden Blvd
5-19 11226
21-323 11226
325-335 11226
336-966 11203
968-1000 11212
1002-1649 11212
1651-1719 11212
1721-2250 11207
2252-2298 11208
2300-2868 11208
2870-2898 11208
Linden St
2-10 11221
12-253 11221
254-449 11237
Linwood St
1-1080 11208
1082-1100 11208
1141-1189 11239
Little St 11201
Livingston St
32-56 11201
58-254 11201
255-269 11217
256-270 11201
271-308 11217
310-398 11217
Livonia Ave
2-70 11212
72-337 11212
339-399 11212
451-799 11207
801-999 11207
Lloyd Ct 11223
Lloyd St 11226
Locust Ave 11230
Locust St 11206
Logan St 11208
Lois Ave 11229
Lombardy St 11222
Lorimer St
1-475 11206
477-479 11206
481-740 11211
832-902 11222
904-1199 11222
Loring Ave 11208
Lorraine St 11231
Losee Ter 11235
Lott Ave 11212
Lott Pl 11234
Lott St 11226
Louis Pl 11233
Louisa St 11218
Louise Ter 11209
Louisiana Ave
1-71 11207
73-127 11207
129-399 11207
400-598 11239
600-699 11239
701-899 11239
Love Ln 11201
Ludlam Pl 11225
Luquer St 11231
Lyme Ave 11224
Lynch St
1-17 11249
2-16 11206
18-246 11206
Macdonough St
1-210 11216
211-219 11233
212-220 11216
221-899 11233
Macdougal St 11233
Mackay Pl 11209
Mackenzie St 11235
Macon St
1-321 11216
322-338 11233
323-339 11216
340-778 11233
780-898 11233
Madeline Ct 11220
Madison Pl 11229
Madison St
1-76 11238
77-350 11216
351-1299 11221
1300-1449 11237
Madoc Ave 11229
Main St 11201
Malbone St 11225
Malcolm X Blvd
2-232 11221
233-237 11233
234-238 11221
239-359 11233
361-399 11233
Malta St 11207
Manhattan Ave
2-18 11206
20-232 11206
233-239 11211
234-240 11206
241-410 11211
411-413 11222
412-414 11211
415-1199 11222
1201-1299 11222
4000-4399 11224
Manhattan Ct
2-2 11223
4-59 11223
60-99 11235
Manor Ct 11235
Maple Ave 11224
Maple St
1-530 11225
532-548 11225
545-547 11203
549-899 11203
Marconi Pl 11233
Marcus Garvey Blvd
383A-383A 11221
1-35 11206
37-165 11206
166-383 11221
385-401 11216
403-499 11216
Marcy Ave
2-118 11211
120-308 11211
310-344 11211
333-343 11206
345-665 11206
667-713 11216
715-999 11216
Margaret Ct 11235
Marginal St E & W 11207
Marine Ave 11209
Marine Pkwy 11234
Marion St 11233
Marlborough Rd
1-638 11226
639-699 11230
Marshall Dr 11252
Marshall Dr N 11209
Marshall Dr S 11209
Martense Ct & St 11226
Martin Luther King Jr Pl 11206
Maspeth Ave 11211
Matthews Ct 11218
Matthews Pl 11236
Maujer St 11206
Mayfair Dr N & S 11234
Mcarthur Rd 11252
Mcclancy Pl 11207
Mcdonald Ave
1-279 11218
281-953 11218
954-968 11230
970-1799 11230
1800-2599 11223
Mcguinness Blvd S 11222
Mckeever Pl 11225
Mckibben Ct & St 11206
Mckinley Ave 11208
Meadow St
1-61 11206
63-85 11206
201-299 11237
Meeker Ave
200-226 11211
228-334 11211
336-370 11211
388-926 11222
928-998 11222
Melba Ct 11229
Melrose St
1-300 11206
301-400 11237
402-498 11237
Menahan St
1-170 11221
171-395 11237
397-499 11237
Meredarb St 11209
Merestan Ave 11224
Merit Ct 11229
Mermaid Ave 11224
Mesereau Ct 11235
Meserole Ave 11222
Meserole St
1-378 11206
380-392 11206
497-599 11237

Metropolitan Ave
51-204 ... 11249
205-1125 ... 11211
1126-1302 ... 11237
1304-1348 ... 11237
Metrotech Ctr N ... 11201
Miami Ct ... 11225
Micieli Pl ... 11218
Middagh St ... 11201
Middleton St ... 11206
Midwood St
5-7 ... 11225
9-545 ... 11225
546-899 ... 11203
Milford St ... 11208
Mill Ave ... 11234
Mill Ln ... 11234
Mill Rd ... 11214
Mill St ... 11231
Miller Ave & Pl ... 11207
Milton St ... 11222
Minna St ... 11218
Moffat St
1-230 ... 11207
232-290 ... 11207
285-289 ... 11237
291-399 ... 11237
Monaco Pl ... 11233
Monitor St ... 11222
Monroe Pl ... 11201
Monroe St
1-64 ... 11238
65-338 ... 11216
339-353 ... 11221
340-354 ... 11216
355-899 ... 11221
Montague St & Ter ... 11201
Montana Pl ... 11234
Montauk Ave ... 11208
Montauk Ct ... 11235
Montgomery Pl ... 11215
Montgomery St
1-668 ... 11225
669-1099 ... 11213
Montrose Ave
1-15 ... 11211
16-399 ... 11206
Monument Walk ... 11205
Moore St ... 11206
Morgan Ave
1-266 ... 11237
268-270 ... 11237
272-272 ... 11211
274-419 ... 11211
420-442 ... 11222
421-423 ... 11211
444-699 ... 11222
Morton St ... 11249
Mother Gaston Blvd
2-12 ... 11233
14-226 ... 11233
231-999 ... 11212
Moultrie St ... 11222
Murdock Ct ... 11223
Myrtle Ave
100-154 ... 11201
156-202 ... 11201
204-278 ... 11201
279-317 ... 11205
319-752 ... 11205
754-754 ... 11205
756-830 ... 11206
832-1133 ... 11206
1134-1170 ... 11221
1135-1171 ... 11206
1172-1351 ... 11221
1352-1372 ... 11237
1353-1373 ... 11221
1374-1599 ... 11237
Narrows Ave
6800-6899 ... 11220
6900-8699 ... 11209
8701-8999 ... 11209
Nassau Ave ... 11222
Nassau St ... 11201
National Dr ... 11234
Nautilus Ave ... 11224
Navy St & Walk ... 11201
Nelson St ... 11231
Neptune Ave
2-10 ... 11235
12-390 ... 11235
391-437 ... 11224
392-396 ... 11235
439-3999 ... 11224
Nevins St
2-24 ... 11217
26-303 ... 11217
304-399 ... 11215
New Dock St ... 11201
New Jersey Ave ... 11207
New Lots Ave
1-66 ... 11212
68-146 ... 11212
195-760 ... 11207
761-783 ... 11208
785-1047 ... 11208
1049-1099 ... 11208
New Utrecht Ave
3000-6899 ... 11219
6900-7299 ... 11228
7300-7499 ... 11204
7500-8499 ... 11214
8501-8599 ... 11214
New York Ave
2-28 ... 11216
30-298 ... 11216
299-317 ... 11213
319-392 ... 11213
394-468 ... 11225
470-584 ... 11225
585-1349 ... 11203
1350-2152 ... 11210
2154-2198 ... 11210
2201-2299 ... 11234
E New York Ave
401-449 ... 11225
451-600 ... 11225
601-945 ... 11203
947-961 ... 11203
963-1001 ... 11212
1003-1757 ... 11212
1758-1760 ... 11207
1759-1761 ... 11212
1762-1900 ... 11207
1902-2598 ... 11207
Newell St ... 11222
Newkirk Ave
200-1399 ... 11230
1400-2999 ... 11226
3001-3299 ... 11226
3100-3198 ... 11210
3301-3397 ... 11203
3399-3599 ... 11203
Newkirk Plz ... 11226
Newport St
1-310 ... 11212
312-398 ... 11212
401-499 ... 11207
Newton St ... 11222
Nichols Ave ... 11208
Nixon Ct ... 11223
Noble St ... 11222
Noel Ave ... 11229
Nolans Ln ... 11236
Noll St
1-158 ... 11206
159-199 ... 11237
Norfolk St ... 11235
Norman Ave ... 11222
Northside Piers ... 11249
Norwood Ave ... 11208
Nostrand Ave
762A-762B ... 11216
1-135 ... 11206
2-166 ... 11205
168-260 ... 11205
261-289 ... 11216
262-290 ... 11205
291-792 ... 11216
794-832 ... 11216
799-831 ... 11225
833-1262 ... 11225
1263-1267 ... 11226
1264-1268 ... 11225
1269-1926 ... 11226
1927-2800 ... 11210
2801-2801 ... 11229
2802-2802 ... 11210
2803-3694 ... 11229
3695-4099 ... 11235
Nova Ct ... 11229
Ny Area Command ... 11252
Oak St ... 11222
Oakland Pl ... 11226
Obrien Pl ... 11208
Ocean Ave
15-145 ... 11225
147-151 ... 11225
153-325 ... 11225
327-329 ... 11226
331-1052 ... 11226
1054-1060 ... 11226
1061-1079 ... 11230
1081-2099 ... 11230
2100-2812 ... 11229
2813-4220 ... 11235
4222-4398 ... 11235
Ocean Ct
11-51 ... 11223
53-59 ... 11235
61-99 ... 11235
Ocean Pkwy
1-7 ... 11218
9-620 ... 11218
621-629 ... 11230
622-630 ... 11218
631-1600 ... 11230
1601-1607 ... 11223
1602-1608 ... 11230
1609-2399 ... 11223
2400-3199 ... 11235
Ocean View Ave
100-1099 ... 11235
1101-1123 ... 11235
3801-4997 ... 11224
4999-5199 ... 11224
Oceana Dr E & W ... 11235
Oceanic Ave ... 11224
Old Fulton St ... 11201
Old Mill Rd ... 11208
Old New Utrecht Rd ... 11204
Olean St ... 11210
Olive St ... 11211
Oliver St ... 11209
Opal Ct ... 11229
Orange St ... 11201
Orient Ave ... 11211
Oriental Blvd ... 11235
Osborn St ... 11212
Otsego St ... 11231
Ovington Ave
200-208 ... 11209
210-699 ... 11209
1000-1599 ... 11219
Ovington Ct ... 11204
Owls Head Ct ... 11220
Oxford St ... 11235
N Oxford St ... 11205
S Oxford St ... 11217
N Oxford Walk ... 11205
Pacific St
100-331 ... 11201
332-562 ... 11217
564-748 ... 11217
750-846 ... 11238
848-1121 ... 11238
1122-1144 ... 11216
1123-1145 ... 11238
1146-1461 ... 11216
1462-1502 ... 11213
1463-1503 ... 11216
1504-1751 ... 11213
1752-1794 ... 11233
1753-1795 ... 11213
1796-2499 ... 11233
Paerdegat Ave N ... 11236
Paerdegat 10th St ... 11236
Paerdegat 11th St ... 11236
Paerdegat 12th St ... 11236
Paerdegat 13th St ... 11236
Paerdegat 14th St ... 11236
Paerdegat 15th St ... 11236
Paerdegat 1st St ... 11236
Paerdegat 2nd St ... 11236
Paerdegat 3rd St ... 11236
Paerdegat 4th St ... 11236
Paerdegat 5th St ... 11236
Paerdegat 6th St ... 11236
Paerdegat 7th St ... 11236
Paerdegat 8th St ... 11236
Paerdegat 9th St ... 11236
Paidge Ave ... 11222
Pallinde St ... 11222
Palm Ct ... 11225
Palmetto St
1-280 ... 11221
281-381 ... 11237
383-399 ... 11237
Parade Pl ... 11226
Park Ave
101-171 ... 11205
173-548 ... 11205
550-560 ... 11205
562-568 ... 11206
570-899 ... 11206
Park Pl
1-160 ... 11217
161-167 ... 11238
162-168 ... 11217
169-638 ... 11238
639-912 ... 11216
913-1570 ... 11213
1571-1863 ... 11233
1865-1999 ... 11233
Park St ... 11206
Parkside Ave & Ct ... 11226
Parkville Ave ... 11230
Parkway Ct
1-9 ... 11223
11-28 ... 11223
30-40 ... 11223
42-99 ... 11235
Parrott Pl ... 11228
Patchen Ave
1-177 ... 11221
178-178 ... 11233
179-179 ... 11221
180-391 ... 11233
393-399 ... 11233
Paterenw Ave ... 11213
Pathoriv Ave ... 11239
Pearl St ... 11201
Pearson St ... 11234
Pembroke St ... 11235
Pence St ... 11209
Penn St
1-96 ... 11249
98-116 ... 11249
101-115 ... 11211
117-300 ... 11211
302-398 ... 11211
Pennsylvania Ave
2-14 ... 11207
16-1140 ... 11207
1141-1600 ... 11239
1602-1798 ... 11239
Pentrang St ... 11233
Perri Ln ... 11234
Perry Ter ... 11209
Pershing Loop N ... 11252
Pier 1 ... 11201
Pier 12 ... 11231
Pier 3 ... 11201
Pier 5 ... 11201
Pierrepont Pl, Plz & St ... 11201
Pilling St ... 11207
Pine St ... 11208
Pineapple St & Walk ... 11201
Pinerlen Ave ... 11208
Pioneer St ... 11231
Pitkin Ave
1401-1403 ... 11233
1405-1454 ... 11233
1455-1813 ... 11212
1815-1899 ... 11212
1933-2385 ... 11207
2386-2790 ... 11208
2792-2998 ... 11208
E Plancoll St ... 11210
Plaza St E ... 11238
Plaza St W ... 11217
Plearlin St ... 11231
Pleasant Pl ... 11233
Pleriche Ave ... 11207
Plumb 1st St ... 11229
Plumb 2nd St ... 11229
Plumb 3rd St ... 11235
Plymouth St ... 11201
Polar St ... 11224
Polhemus Pl ... 11215
Poly Pl ... 11209
Poplar Ave ... 11224
Poplar St ... 11201
Portal St ... 11233
Porter Ave
1-99 ... 11237
501-599 ... 11222
N Portland Ave ... 11205
S Portland Ave ... 11217
Post Ct ... 11229
Powell St ... 11212
Powers St ... 11211
Prallak Ave ... 11235
Prescott Pl ... 11233
President St
30-410 ... 11231
412-436 ... 11231
437-959 ... 11215
960-968 ... 11225
961-969 ... 11215
970-1262 ... 11225
1263-1799 ... 11213
Preston Ct
1-5899 ... 11234
5901-5907 ... 11234
8000-8099 ... 11236
Prince St ... 11201
Prospect Ave
1-303 ... 11215
305-592 ... 11215
594-618 ... 11215
1100-1299 ... 11218
1301-1399 ... 11218
Prospect Park SW
1-78 ... 11215
79-299 ... 11218
Prospect Park W ... 11215
Prospect Pl
2-140 ... 11217
141-149 ... 11238
142-150 ... 11217
151-613 ... 11238
614-878 ... 11216
879-1546 ... 11213
1547-1999 ... 11233
Prospect St ... 11201
Provost St ... 11222
Pulaski St
1-410 ... 11206
411-419 ... 11221
412-420 ... 11206
421-499 ... 11221
Putnam Ave
1-5 ... 11238
7-129 ... 11238
130-150 ... 11216
131-151 ... 11238
152-423 ... 11216
424-1396 ... 11221
1398-1472 ... 11237
1474-1506 ... 11237
1508-1598 ... 11237
Quay St ... 11222
Quentin Rd
1-23 ... 11223
25-1099 ... 11223
1100-3008 ... 11229
3009-4299 ... 11234
Quincy St
1-106 ... 11238
107-396 ... 11216
397-899 ... 11221
Radde Pl ... 11233
Raleigh Pl ... 11226
Ralph Ave
1-127 ... 11221
128-156 ... 11233
158-600 ... 11233
602-620 ... 11233
626-757 ... 11212
758-918 ... 11236
920-1742 ... 11236
1744-1864 ... 11236
1855-1863 ... 11234
1865-2508 ... 11234
2510-2598 ... 11234
Randolph St ... 11237
Rantralt St ... 11211
Rapelye St ... 11231
Red Hook Ln ... 11201
Reed St ... 11231
Reeve Pl ... 11218
Regent Pl ... 11226
Remsen Ave
1-419 ... 11212
421-479 ... 11212
480-1700 ... 11236
1702-1798 ... 11236
Remsen St ... 11201
Renaissance Ct ... 11206
Revere Pl ... 11213
Rewe St ... 11211
Richards St ... 11231
Richardson St
1-154 ... 11211
155-159 ... 11222
156-160 ... 11211
161-344 ... 11222
Richmond St ... 11208
Ridge Blvd
6600-6899 ... 11220
6900-9499 ... 11209
Ridge Ct ... 11209
Ridge Crest Ter ... 11209
Ridgewood Ave
26-26 ... 11207
28-72 ... 11207
73-699 ... 11208
Ridgewood Pl ... 11237
Riverdale Ave
1-300 ... 11212
302-314 ... 11212
426-454 ... 11207
456-699 ... 11207
701-799 ... 11207
Rochester Ave
1-19 ... 11233
21-54 ... 11233
56-126 ... 11233
128-286 ... 11213
288-498 ... 11213
Rock St ... 11206
Rockaway Ave
18-20 ... 11233
22-325 ... 11233
326-955 ... 11212
957-985 ... 11212
1022-1253 ... 11236
1255-1299 ... 11236
Rockaway Pkwy
1-599 ... 11212
602-2299 ... 11236
Rockwell Pl
1-99 ... 11217
32-60 ... 11201
62-98 ... 11217
Roder Ave ... 11230
Rodney St
16-16 ... 11249
18-38 ... 11249
40-44 ... 11249
133-135 ... 11211
137-200 ... 11211
202-498 ... 11211
Roebling St ... 11211
Rogers Ave
22-177 ... 11216
179-199 ... 11216
196-212 ... 11225
214-634 ... 11225
635-1283 ... 11226
1284-1337 ... 11210
1339-1399 ... 11210
Roosevelt Ave ... 11252
Roosevelt Ct ... 11232
Roosevelt Pl ... 11233
Rose St ... 11236
Ross St
1-19 ... 11249
21-131 ... 11249
132-299 ... 11211
Rost Pl ... 11236
Royce Pl & St ... 11234
Ruby St ... 11208
Rugby Rd
24-40 ... 11226
42-530 ... 11226
531-799 ... 11230
Russell St ... 11222
Rutherford Pl ... 11214
Rutland Rd
2-399 ... 11225
401-914 ... 11203
915-937 ... 11212
939-1199 ... 11212
Rutledge St
1-119 ... 11249
120-335 ... 11211
Ryder Ave ... 11230
Ryder St ... 11234
Ryerson St ... 11205
Sackett St
2-60 ... 11231
62-478 ... 11231
480-516 ... 11231
518-528 ... 11217
530-722 ... 11217
724-738 ... 11217
Sackman St
1-160 ... 11233
162-204 ... 11212
206-899 ... 11212
Saint Andrews Pl ... 11216
Saint Charles Pl ... 11216
Saint Edwards St
36-44 ... 11205
46-125 ... 11205
126-198 ... 11201
Saint Felix St ... 11217
Saint Francis Pl ... 11216
Saint James Pl
1-50 ... 11205
51-399 ... 11238
Saint Johns Pl
1-267 ... 11217
268-624 ... 11238
625-925 ... 11216
926-1572 ... 11213
1573-1587 ... 11233
1574-1588 ... 11213
1589-1816 ... 11233
1818-1898 ... 11233
Saint Jude Pl ... 11236
Saint Marks Ave
1-136 ... 11217
137-143 ... 11238
138-144 ... 11217
145-538 ... 11238
539-551 ... 11216
540-552 ... 11238
553-760 ... 11216
761-777 ... 11213
762-778 ... 11216
779-1316 ... 11213
1317-1799 ... 11233
Saint Marks Pl ... 11217
Saint Nicholas Ave ... 11237
Saint Pauls Ct & Pl ... 11226
Sandford St ... 11205
Sands St ... 11201
Sansongs Ave ... 11220
Sapphire St ... 11208
Saratoga Ave
1-475 ... 11233
477-495 ... 11212
497-999 ... 11212
Schaefer St
1-257 ... 11207

258-258 11237
259-259 11207
260-399 11237
Schenck Ave 11207
Schenck Ct 11207
Schenck Pl 11236
Schenck St 11236
Schenectady Ave
2-48 11213
50-430 11213
431-1529 11203
1530-2271 11234
2273-2299 11234
Schermerhorn St
1-251 11201
252-256 11217
253-257 11201
258-360 11217
362-398 11217
Scholes St
1-376 11206
475-475 11237
477-554 11237
556-596 11237
Schroeders Ave 11239
Schum Ave 11252
Scott Ave
1-199 11237
400-599 11222
Sea Breeze Ave 11224
Sea Gate Ave 11224
Sea View Ave 11239
Seabring St 11231
Seacoast Ter 11235
Searieli Ave 11218
Seaview Ave & Ct 11236
Seba Ave 11229
Sedgwick Pl 11220
Seeley St 11218
Seigel Ct & St 11206
Senator St 11220
Seton Pl 11230
Shalesti St 11217
Sharon St 11211
Sheepshead Bay Rd
600-698 11224
1000-1149 11229
1150-1152 11235
1151-1153 11229
1154-1780 11235
1782-1898 11235
Sheffield Ave 11207
Shell Rd
2601-2819 11223
2842-2898 11224
2900-2999 11224
Shepherd Ave 11208
Sheridan Ave 11208
Sheridan Loop 11252
Sherlock Pl 11233
Sherman St
1-70 11215
71-399 11218
Shore Blvd 11235
Shore Ct 11209
Shore Pkwy
923-1117 11228
1119-1597 11214
1599-1951 11214
1953-2199 11214
2343-2799 11223
2800-2898 11235
2900-3999 11235
5901-5999 11236
7000-7020 11234
Shore Rd
6700-6798 11220
6801-6839 11220
6901-7097 11209
7099-9099 11209
9101-9999 11209
Shore Road Ln 11209
Sidney Pl 11201
Sigourney St 11231
Sillonta Ave 11204
Skidmore Ave & Ln 11236
Skillman Ave 11211
Skillman St 11205
Sloan Pl 11223
Slocum Pl 11218
Smith St
1-221 11201
222-222 11231
223-223 11201
224-699 11231
Smiths Ln 11236
Snediker Ave 11207
Snyder Ave
2-4 11226
6-3299 11226
3300-5900 11203
5902-5998 11203
Somers St 11233
Southgate Ct 11223
Spencer Ct 11205
Spencer Pl 11216
Spencer St 11205
Stagg St
1-376 11206
499-599 11237
Stanhope St
1-141 11221
143-155 11221
150-154 11237
156-449 11237
Stanley Ave
200-820 11207
821-827 11208
829-1247 11208
1249-1499 11208
Stanton Rd 11235
Stanwix St 11206
Starr St
1-50 11221
51-399 11237
State St
21-37 11201
39-310 11201
311-333 11217
312-334 11201
335-599 11217
Stephens Ct 11226
Sterling Dr
300-399 11209
400-498 11252
Sterling Pl
1-160 11217
161-183 11238
162-184 11217
185-650 11238
651-940 11216
941-1604 11213
1605-1609 11233
1606-1610 11213
1611-1989 11233
1991-1999 11233
Sterling St 11225
Steuben St 11205
Stewart Ave
1-200 11237
202-298 11237
500-590 11222
592-598 11222
7201-7399 11209
Stewart St 11207
Stillwell Ave
1600-2649 11223
2650-3050 11224
3052-3098 11224
Stillwell Pl 11236
Stockholm St
2-32 11221
34-154 11221
155-499 11237
Stockton St 11206
Stoddard Pl 11225
Stonewall Jackson Dr 11209
Story Ct & St 11218
Stratford Rd 11218
Strauss St 11212
Strickland Ave 11234
Strong Pl 11231
Stryker Ct & St 11223
Stuart St 11229
Stuyvesant Ave
1-288 11221
289-299 11233
290-300 11221
301-421 11233
423-499 11233
Sullivan Pl 11225
Sullivan St 11231
Summit St 11231
Sumner Pl 11206
Sumpter St 11233
Sunintow Ave 11225
Sunnyside Ave & Ct 11207
Suntondi Ave 11216
Surf Ave 11224
Sutter Ave
1-470 11212
471-950 11207
951-973 11208
975-1500 11208
1502-1598 11208
Sutton St 11222
Suydam Pl 11233
Suydam St
1-200 11221
201-499 11237
Taaffe Pl 11205
Tabor Ct 11219
Tampa Ct 11225
Tapscott St 11212
Taylor St
1-125 11249
127-199 11211
Tehama St 11218
Temple Ct 11218
Ten Eyck St 11206
Tennis Ct 11226
Terrace Pl 11218
Thames St
1-41 11206
42-199 11237
Thatford Ave 11212
Thomas St 11222
Thomas S Boyland St
2-22 11233
24-390 11233
392-418 11233
403-417 11212
419-1049 11212
1050-1199 11236
Thornton St 11206
Throop Ave
1-326 11206
327-349 11221
328-350 11206
351-544 11221
545-573 11216
546-574 11221
575-699 11216
Tiffany Pl 11231
Tilden Ave
2100-2198 11226
2200-3200 11226
3202-3298 11226
3300-3398 11203
3400-5999 11203
Tillary St 11201
Tompkins Ave
1-33 11206
35-203 11206
205-207 11206
209-221 11216
223-494 11216
496-498 11216
Tompkins Pl 11231
Troutman St
1-147 11206
149-199 11206
200-499 11237
Troy Ave
1-19 11213
21-430 11213
431-1575 11203
1590-1632 11234
1634-2299 11234
Trucklemans Ln 11236
Truxton St 11233
Tudor Ter 11224
Turner Pl 11218
Twin Pines Dr 11239
Underhill Ave 11238
Union Ave
1-152 11206
170-184 11211
186-607 11211
609-627 11211
Union St
1-51 11231
53-477 11231
479-515 11231
500-514 11215
516-923 11215
924-970 11225
925-971 11215
972-1301 11225
1302-1324 11213
1303-1325 11225
1326-1851 11213
1852-1900 11233
1853-1901 11213
1902-1992 11233
1993-1997 11212
1994-1998 11233
1999-2199 11212
University Plz 11201
Utica Ave
21-49 11233
51-69 11213
71-440 11213
441-1460 11203
1461-1497 11234
1499-2169 11234
2171-2399 11234
Van Brunt St 11231
Van Buren St 11221
Van Dam St 11222
Van Dyke St 11231
Van Sicklen St 11223
Van Siclen Ave
1-5 11207
7-1022 11207
1500-1598 11239
Van Siclen Ct 11207
Van Sinderen Ave 11207
Vandalia Ave 11239
Vanderbilt Ave
103A-103D 11205
1-331 11205
333-371 11238
373-671 11238
673-681 11238
Vanderbilt St 11218
Vanderveer Pl 11226
Vanderveer St 11207
Vandervoort Ave
251-297 11211
299-349 11211
351-385 11211
401-507 11222
Varet St 11206
Varick Ave
1-258 11237
500-599 11222
Varick St 11222
Varkens Hook Rd 11236
Verandah Pl 11201
Vermont Ct & St 11207
Vernon Ave
1-399 11206
400-498 11221
Verona Pl 11216
Verona St 11231
Veronica Pl 11226
Veterans Ave 11234
Vianiank Dr 11252
Village Ct & Rd E, N & S 11223
Virginia Pl 11213
Visitation Pl 11231
Vista Pl 11220
Voorhies Ave 11235
Wainwright Dr 11252
Wakeman Pl 11220
Waldorf Ct 11230
Wallabout St
2-64 11249
66-98 11249
99-147 11206
100-148 11249
149-399 11206
Wallaston Ct 11204
Walsh Ct 11230
Walton St 11206
Walworth St 11205
Warren Pl 11201
Warren St
69-396 11201
397-445 11217
447-699 11217
Warsoff Pl 11205
Warwick St 11207
Washington Ave
16-350 11205
351-812 11238
814-860 11238
880-1001 11225
1003-1199 11225
Washington Park 11205
Washington Rd 11209
Washington St 11201
Washington Walk 11205
Water St 11201
Waterbury St 11206
Wathold St 11232
Watkins St 11212
Waverly Ave
1-335 11205
337-377 11238
379-599 11238
Webers Ct 11235
Webster Ave 11230
Webster Pl 11215
Weirfield St
1-237 11221
239-289 11221
290-451 11237
Weldon St 11208
Wellington Ct 11230
Wells St 11208
West Ave 11224
West St
1-200 11222
202-298 11222
2000-2566 11223
2568-2698 11223
Westbury Ct 11225
Westminster Rd
1-530 11218
531-799 11230
Whale Sq 11232
Wharton Pl 11208
Whincenw Ave 11212
Whipple St 11206
White Ave 11252
White St 11206
Whitman Dr 11234
Whitney Ave 11229
Whitney Pl 11223
Whitty Ln 11203
Whitwell Pl 11215
Will Pl 11207
Williams Ave 11207
Williams Ct 11235
Williams Pl 11207
Williamsburg St E 11211
Williamsburg St W
1-191 11249
192-199 11211
Willmohr St 11212
Willoughby Ave
11-438 11205
439-441 11206
440-442 11205
443-840 11206
841-1098 11221
1099-1099 11237
1100-1100 11221
1101-1499 11237
Willoughby St 11201
Willow Pl & St 11201
Wilson Ave
1-319 11237
320-332 11221
321-333 11237
334-513 11221
514-550 11207
515-527 11221
552-640 11207
642-668 11207
Wilson St
1-95 11249
97-135 11249
137-210 11211
Windsor Pl
1-254 11215
255-399 11218
Winthrop St
8-370 11225
401-439 11203
441-965 11203
966-992 11212
994-1122 11212
Withers St
1-273 11211
275-275 11211
401-499 11222
Wogan Ter 11209
Wolcott St 11231
Wolf Pl 11223
Woodbine St
1-280 11221
281-379 11237
381-424 11237
Woodhull St 11231
Woodpoint Rd 11211
Woodrow Ct 11232
Woodruff Ave 11226
Woods Pl & St 11226
Woodside Ave 11223
Wortman Ave
73-123 11207
125-408 11207
410-432 11207
433-455 11208
457-780 11208
782-798 11208
Wyckoff Ave 11237
Wyckoff St
1-130 11201
131-193 11217
195-299 11217
Wyona St 11207
Wythe Ave & Pl 11249
York St 11201

NUMBERED STREETS

1st Ave
4000-5199 11232
5301-5597 11220
1st Ct 11223
1st Pl 11231
1st St
8-62 11231
107-197 11215
E 1st St 11223
N 1st St
1-150 11249
151-155 11211
152-156 11249
157-199 11211
S 1st St
1-137 11249
138-146 11211
139-147 11249
148-384 11211
W 1st St
1500-1599 11204
1600-2500 11223
3000-3098 11224
2nd Ave
1-196 11215
501-3997 11232
5300-5799 11220
2nd Pl 11231
2nd St
2-142 11231
282-699 11215
E 2nd St
1-792 11218
900-1668 11230
1669-2599 11223
S 2nd St
1-136 11249
137-499 11211
W 2nd St
1500-1599 11204
1600-2699 11223
3rd Ave
25-25 11217
27-230 11217
251-599 11215
621-647 11232
649-1000 11232
1002-4398 11232
4400-5398 11220
5400-6899 11220
6900-9956 11209
3rd Pl 11231
3rd St
2-4 11231
167-699 11215
E 3rd St
1-820 11218
918-1699 11230
1700-2499 11223
N 3rd St
2-42 11249
155-155 11211
156-158 11249
159-199 11211
S 3rd St
2-12 11249
129-129 11211
130-130 11249
131-499 11211
W 3rd St
1400-1498 11204
1600-2600 11223
2949-2999 11224
4th Ave
2-22 11217
215-221 11215
216-220 11217
223-618 11215
619-629 11232
620-630 11215
631-4399 11232
4400-6899 11220
6900-10100 11209
10102-10198 11209
4th Pl
1-199 11231
N 4th Pl
1-99 11249
4th St
2-2 11231
4-106 11231
108-112 11231
308-599 11215
E 4th St
1-805 11218
807-897 11230
899-1699 11230
1700-2499 11223
N 4th St
1-117 11249
119-139 11249
141-149 11211
151-299 11211
S 4th St
1-127 11249
128-128 11211
129-129 11249
130-499 11211
W 4th St
1400-1599 11204
1600-2099 11223
5th Ave
22-26 11217
28-206 11217
207-723 11215
724-4100 11232
4102-4398 11232

4400-6899 ... 11220
6900-9399 ... 11209
5th St
7-75 ... 11231
78-336 ... 11215
E 5th St
2-148 ... 11218
801-897 ... 11230
1700-2399 ... 11223
N 5th St
10-70 ... 11249
140-299 ... 11211
S 5th St
1-139 ... 11249
141-249 ... 11211
W 5th St
1400-1600 ... 11204
1601-2261 ... 11223
2700-2936 ... 11224
6th Ave ... 11215
6th Ave ... 11217
6th Ave ... 11220
6th Ave ... 11215
6th Ave ... 11232
6th Ave ... 11232
6th Ave ... 11217
6th Ave ... 11217
6th Ave ... 11215
6900-8300 ... 11209
6th St ... 11215
E 6th St ... 11235
N 6th St
1-152 ... 11249
153-159 ... 11211
154-160 ... 11249
161-300 ... 11211
S 6th St ... 11249
W 6th St
1300-1599 ... 11204
1600-2299 ... 11223
7th Ave
7-93 ... 11217
95-604 ... 11215
606-630 ... 11215
3900-4099 ... 11232
4101-4399 ... 11232
4400-6599 ... 11220
6601-6899 ... 11220
6901-8599 ... 11228
7000-7898 ... 11209
8100-9298 ... 11209
7th St ... 11215
E 7th St
1-7 ... 11218
736-798 ... 11230
1677-1687 ... 11223
1678-1688 ... 11230
1689-2416 ... 11223
2417-2699 ... 11235
N 7th St
1-158 ... 11249
159-399 ... 11211
W 7th St
1300-1600 ... 11204
1601-2317 ... 11223
8th Ave
1-5 ... 11217
7-72 ... 11217
73-1999 ... 11215
3801-3897 ... 11232
4400-6825 ... 11220
6900-7299 ... 11228
8th St ... 11215
E 8th St
1-649 ... 11218
676-726 ... 11230
1600-2299 ... 11223
N 8th St
47-49 ... 11249
160-399 ... 11211
S 8th St
27-61 ... 11249
123-129 ... 11211
124-130 ... 11249
131-199 ... 11211
W 8th St
1400-1599 ... 11204
1601-1611 ... 11223
2800-2954 ... 11224
9th Ave
3800-3898 ... 11232
3900-4399 ... 11232
4400-6399 ... 11220
9th St
1-16 ... 11231
26-599 ... 11215
E 9th St
200-599 ... 11218
700-1600 ... 11230
1601-2199 ... 11223
N 9th St
1-160 ... 11249
161-299 ... 11211
S 9th St
2-36 ... 11249
118-124 ... 11211
119-125 ... 11249
126-198 ... 11211
W 9th St
1-176 ... 11231
1400-1402 ... 11204
1600-2199 ... 11223
10th Ave
1501-1799 ... 11215
3801-3897 ... 11219
6900-8599 ... 11228
10th St ... 11215
E 10th St
1-100 ... 11218
700-710 ... 11230
1600-1799 ... 11223
N 10th St
1-127 ... 11249
161-299 ... 11211
S 10th St ... 11249
W 10th St
1401-1599 ... 11204
1600-2199 ... 11223
11th Ave
1501-1597 ... 11215
1679-1749 ... 11218
4500-4598 ... 11219
6900-8526 ... 11228
11th St ... 11215
E 11th St ... 11235
N 11th St
1-47 ... 11249
145-299 ... 11211
S 11th St ... 11249
W 11th St
1500-1599 ... 11204
1600-2399 ... 11223
12th Ave
3300-4099 ... 11218
4100-6799 ... 11219
6900-8599 ... 11228
12th St ... 11215
E 12th St
800-1599 ... 11230
1600-2357 ... 11229
2400-2799 ... 11235
N 12th St
1-49 ... 11249
200-298 ... 11211
W 12th St
1501-1599 ... 11204
1600-2399 ... 11223
2701-2837 ... 11224
13th Ave
3601-4099 ... 11218
4100-6899 ... 11219
6900-8599 ... 11228
13th St ... 11215
E 13th St
800-1599 ... 11230
1600-2399 ... 11229
2401-2497 ... 11235
N 13th St ... 11249
W 13th St ... 11223
14th Ave
3401-3497 ... 11218
4100-6899 ... 11219
6900-8850 ... 11228
14th St ... 11215
E 14th St
800-1599 ... 11230
1600-2399 ... 11229
2401-2700 ... 11235
N 14th St ... 11249
15th Ave
3500-3598 ... 11218
4100-6899 ... 11219
6900-8999 ... 11228
W 15th Pl ... 11214
15th St ... 11215
E 15th St
700-1599 ... 11230
1600-2399 ... 11229
2400-2699 ... 11235
N 15th St ... 11222
W 15th St
2500-2659 ... 11214
2661-2697 ... 11224
16th Ave
3800-3898 ... 11218
4100-7299 ... 11204
7500-8919 ... 11214
16th St
1-47 ... 11215
560-586 ... 11218
561-587 ... 11215
588-599 ... 11218
E 16th St
2-8 ... 11226
800-1599 ... 11230
1600-2399 ... 11229
2400-2799 ... 11235
W 16th St
2401-2497 ... 11214
2700-2899 ... 11224
17th Ave
4200-7499 ... 11204
7500-8899 ... 11214
17th St
110-114 ... 11215
561-565 ... 11218
562-566 ... 11215
567-699 ... 11218
E 17th St
7-23 ... 11226
641-1606 ... 11230
1607-2399 ... 11229
2400-2599 ... 11235
W 17th St
2500-2599 ... 11214
2800-2941 ... 11224
18th Ave
3701-4399 ... 11218
4400-7499 ... 11204
7500-8999 ... 11214
18th St
2-108 ... 11232
110-114 ... 11215
569-799 ... 11218
E 18th St
9-17 ... 11226
634-1603 ... 11230
1604-2399 ... 11229
2400-2699 ... 11235
19th Ave
4701-4797 ... 11204
7500-8900 ... 11214
19th Ln ... 11214
19th St
1-236 ... 11232
237-300 ... 11215
542-636 ... 11218
E 19th St
1-7 ... 11226
616-1599 ... 11230
1600-2399 ... 11229
2400-2700 ... 11235
W 19th St ... 11224
20th Ave
4900-4998 ... 11204
7500-8902 ... 11214
20th Dr ... 11214
20th Ln ... 11214
20th St
1-236 ... 11232
237-492 ... 11215
541-699 ... 11218
W 20th St ... 11224
21st Ave
5300-5598 ... 11204
7600-8819 ... 11214
21st Dr ... 11214
21st St
1-236 ... 11232
238-399 ... 11215
E 21st St
5-9 ... 11226
691-1716 ... 11210
1717-2446 ... 11229
2447-2799 ... 11235
W 21st St ... 11224
22nd St
1-236 ... 11232
237-399 ... 11215
E 22nd St
154-324 ... 11226
326-615 ... 11226
616-1652 ... 11210
1653-2399 ... 11229
2400-2799 ... 11235
W 22nd St ... 11224
23rd Ave
5800-5898 ... 11204
7801-7897 ... 11214
23rd St
100-236 ... 11232
237-295 ... 11215
E 23rd St
201-217 ... 11226
501-1599 ... 11210
1600-2399 ... 11229
2400-2770 ... 11235
W 23rd St ... 11224
24th Ave
6000-6499 ... 11204
8100-8899 ... 11214
24th St ... 11232
E 24th St
400-1551 ... 11210
1553-1597 ... 11229
1599-2399 ... 11229
2400-2498 ... 11235
2500-2699 ... 11235
W 24th St ... 11224
25th Ave ... 11214
25th St ... 11232
E 25th St ... 11226
W 25th St ... 11224
26th Ave ... 11214
26th St ... 11232
E 26th St
166-212 ... 11226
214-490 ... 11226
491-529 ... 11210
531-1500 ... 11210
1501-2399 ... 11229
2400-2899 ... 11235
27th Ave ... 11214
27th St ... 11232
E 27th St
700-1500 ... 11210
1501-2399 ... 11229
2400-2899 ... 11235
W 27th St ... 11224
28th Ave ... 11214
28th St ... 11232
E 28th St
1-490 ... 11226
491-1489 ... 11210
1491-1497 ... 11229
1499-2399 ... 11229
2400-2899 ... 11235
W 28th St ... 11224
29th St ... 11232
E 29th St
2-38 ... 11226
40-490 ... 11226
491-1459 ... 11210
1460-2399 ... 11229
2400-2700 ... 11235
2702-2968 ... 11235
W 29th St ... 11224
30th St ... 11232
W 30th St ... 11224
31st St ... 11232
E 31st St
2-400 ... 11226
402-490 ... 11226
491-1400 ... 11210
1402-1412 ... 11210
1413-1899 ... 11234
W 31st St ... 11224
32nd St ... 11232
E 32nd St
1-401 ... 11226
403-489 ... 11226
491-1399 ... 11210
1400-1899 ... 11234
1901-1999 ... 11234
W 32nd St ... 11224
33rd St ... 11232
E 33rd St ... 11234
W 33rd St ... 11224
34th St ... 11232
E 34th St
101-185 ... 11203
187-710 ... 11203
711-1445 ... 11210
1446-2199 ... 11234
35th St
1-199 ... 11232
1400-1499 ... 11218
E 35th St
71-99 ... 11203
101-710 ... 11203
711-1370 ... 11210
1371-2199 ... 11234
W 35th St ... 11224
36th St
200-499 ... 11232
1100-1499 ... 11218
E 36th St
1000-1269 ... 11210
1270-2199 ... 11234
W 36th St ... 11224
37th St
201-297 ... 11232
299-499 ... 11232
1100-1500 ... 11218
1502-1598 ... 11218
E 37th St
1-97 ... 11203
99-718 ... 11203
719-1402 ... 11210
1403-2199 ... 11234
W 37th St ... 11224
38th St
301-499 ... 11232
1000-1099 ... 11219
1100-1500 ... 11218
E 38th St
1-657 ... 11203
658-666 ... 11210
659-667 ... 11203
668-1273 ... 11210
1302-2199 ... 11234
39th St
50-298 ... 11232
900-1099 ... 11219
1100-1599 ... 11218
E 39th St
2-98 ... 11203
100-720 ... 11203
721-1399 ... 11210
40th St
200-899 ... 11232
900-1099 ... 11219
1100-1699 ... 11218
E 40th St
1-47 ... 11203
49-668 ... 11203
670-746 ... 11210
748-1299 ... 11210
1300-1399 ... 11234
41st St
100-899 ... 11232
900-1099 ... 11219
1100-1699 ... 11218
E 41st St ... 11234
42nd St
1-97 ... 11232
900-1599 ... 11219
1600-1700 ... 11204
1702-1798 ... 11204
E 42nd St
1-744 ... 11203
745-1199 ... 11210
43rd St
1-899 ... 11232
900-1599 ... 11219
1600-1799 ... 11204
E 43rd St
1-744 ... 11203
776-798 ... 11210
800-1199 ... 11210
1591-1597 ... 11234
1599-1699 ... 11234
44th St
100-198 ... 11232
200-299 ... 11232
300-899 ... 11220
900-1599 ... 11219
1600-1799 ... 11204
45th St
200-899 ... 11220
900-1599 ... 11219
1600-1799 ... 11204
E 45th St
1-1094 ... 11203
1095-1103 ... 11234
1096-1104 ... 11203
1105-1799 ... 11234
46th St
200-899 ... 11220
900-1599 ... 11219
1600-1799 ... 11204
E 46th St
1-1099 ... 11203
1100-1799 ... 11234
47th St
1-199 ... 11232
200-899 ... 11220
900-1599 ... 11219
1600-1999 ... 11204
48th St
1-199 ... 11232
200-899 ... 11220
900-1599 ... 11219
1600-1899 ... 11204
E 48th St
2-198 ... 11203
200-980 ... 11203
982-1052 ... 11203
1054-1899 ... 11234
49th St
1-97 ... 11232
99-199 ... 11232
200-899 ... 11220
900-1599 ... 11219
1601-1603 ... 11204
E 49th St
2-98 ... 11203
1052-1162 ... 11234
50th St
1-199 ... 11232
200-899 ... 11220
900-1599 ... 11219
1600-1999 ... 11204
51st St
101-199 ... 11232
200-899 ... 11220
900-1599 ... 11219
1600-1999 ... 11204
E 51st St
2-999 ... 11203
1071-1924 ... 11234
52nd St
2-198 ... 11232
200-899 ... 11220
900-1599 ... 11219
1600-2099 ... 11204
E 52nd St
1-949 ... 11203
951-1015 ... 11234
1017-2099 ... 11234
E 53rd Pl ... 11234
53rd St
1-1 ... 11232
3-199 ... 11232
200-899 ... 11220
900-1599 ... 11219
1600-2099 ... 11204
E 53rd St
1-899 ... 11203
900-2099 ... 11234
54th St
100-899 ... 11220
900-998 ... 11219
1000-1599 ... 11219
1600-1999 ... 11204
E 54th St
1-556 ... 11203
558-660 ... 11203
817-2099 ... 11234
55th St
100-198 ... 11220
200-899 ... 11220
900-1599 ... 11219
1600-1899 ... 11204
E 55th St
1-499 ... 11203
501-615 ... 11203
711-2099 ... 11234
56th Dr ... 11234
56th St
100-198 ... 11220
200-899 ... 11220
900-1599 ... 11219
1600-1799 ... 11204
E 56th St
1-599 ... 11203
701-2099 ... 11234
E 57th Pl ... 11234
57th St
100-899 ... 11220
900-1599 ... 11219
1600-2199 ... 11204
E 57th St
2-10 ... 11203
12-441 ... 11203
443-499 ... 11203
580-2099 ... 11234
58th St
100-899 ... 11220
900-1599 ... 11219
1601-1629 ... 11204
1631-2199 ... 11204
E 58th St
1-410 ... 11203
655-2099 ... 11234
E 59th Pl ... 11234
59th St
200-208 ... 11220
210-899 ... 11220
900-1599 ... 11219
1600-2299 ... 11204
E 59th St
1-584 ... 11203
585-2099 ... 11234
E 60th Pl ... 11234
60th St
200-899 ... 11220
900-1599 ... 11219
1600-2999 ... 11204
E 60th St ... 11234
61st St
1-799 ... 11220
801-899 ... 11220
901-1397 ... 11219
1399-1500 ... 11219
1502-1598 ... 11219
1600-2399 ... 11204
E 61st St ... 11234
62nd St
200-700 ... 11220
702-898 ... 11220
900-966 ... 11219
968-1599 ... 11219
1600-2400 ... 11204
2402-2498 ... 11204
63rd St
201-297 ... 11220
299-851 ... 11220

853-899 ... 11220
900-1599 ... 11219
1600-2499 ... 11204
E 63rd St ... 11234
64th St
200-800 ... 11220
802-898 ... 11220
900-1599 ... 11219
1600-2499 ... 11204
E 64th St ... 11234
65th St
200-899 ... 11220
900-1599 ... 11219
1600-2599 ... 11204
E 65th St ... 11234
66th St
501-899 ... 11220
901-941 ... 11219
1600-2199 ... 11204
E 66th St ... 11234
67th St
100-300 ... 11220
302-898 ... 11220
937-1599 ... 11219
1700-2999 ... 11204
E 67th St ... 11234
68th St
66-98 ... 11220
100-899 ... 11220
932-999 ... 11219
1600-2199 ... 11204
E 68th St ... 11234
E 69th St ... 11234
70th St
1-99 ... 11209
701-797 ... 11228
1600-2199 ... 11204
E 70th St ... 11234
71st St
2-44 ... 11209
46-699 ... 11209
800-1570 ... 11228
1600-2199 ... 11204
E 71st St ... 11234
72nd Ct ... 11209
72nd St
11-27 ... 11209
29-699 ... 11209
800-1579 ... 11228
1600-2199 ... 11204
E 72nd St ... 11234
73rd St
1-699 ... 11209
801-897 ... 11228
899-1599 ... 11228
1600-2199 ... 11204
E 73rd St ... 11234
74th St
1-27 ... 11209
29-699 ... 11209
700-1599 ... 11228
1600-1616 ... 11204
1618-2199 ... 11204
E 74th St ... 11234
76th St
2-8 ... 11209
10-699 ... 11209
701-897 ... 11228
899-1599 ... 11228
1600-2199 ... 11214
E 76th St ... 11236
77th St
2-4 ... 11209
6-699 ... 11209
900-1599 ... 11228
1600-2199 ... 11214
E 77th St ... 11236
78th St
1-699 ... 11209
900-1599 ... 11228
1600-2299 ... 11214
E 78th St ... 11236
79th St
2-4 ... 11209
6-699 ... 11209
900-1599 ... 11228
1601-1697 ... 11214
1699-2300 ... 11214
2302-2398 ... 11214
E 79th St ... 11236
80th St
1-7 ... 11209
9-699 ... 11209
900-1599 ... 11228
1600-2371 ... 11214
2373-2399 ... 11214
E 80th St ... 11236
81st St
1-679 ... 11209
680-898 ... 11228
900-1599 ... 11228
1600-2399 ... 11214
E 81st St ... 11236
82nd St
2-28 ... 11209
30-599 ... 11209
601-667 ... 11209
669-1599 ... 11228
1600-2499 ... 11214
E 82nd St ... 11236
83rd St
1-97 ... 11209
99-599 ... 11209
664-1599 ... 11228
1600-2499 ... 11214
E 83rd St ... 11236
84th St
1-599 ... 11209
651-1599 ... 11228
1600-2500 ... 11214
2502-2598 ... 11214
E 84th St ... 11236
85th St
2-98 ... 11209
100-599 ... 11209
601-655 ... 11209
657-1599 ... 11228
1600-2599 ... 11214
E 85th St ... 11236
86th St
1-577 ... 11209
579-673 ... 11209
612-672 ... 11228
674-1599 ... 11228
1600-2599 ... 11214
2600-2999 ... 11223
E 86th St ... 11236
87th St ... 11209
E 87th St ... 11236
88th St
1-599 ... 11209
624-752 ... 11228
E 88th St ... 11236
89th St ... 11209
E 89th St ... 11236
90th St
1-599 ... 11209
621-671 ... 11228
91st St ... 11209
E 91st St
1-431 ... 11212
433-479 ... 11212
480-1801 ... 11236
1803-1807 ... 11236
92nd St
1-599 ... 11209
600-671 ... 11228
673-699 ... 11228
E 92nd St
1-499 ... 11212
500-528 ... 11236
530-1899 ... 11236
93rd St ... 11209
E 93rd St
1-521 ... 11212
522-1800 ... 11236
94th St ... 11209
1-542 ... 11212
543-1699 ... 11236
95th St ... 11209
1-571 ... 11212
572-1660 ... 11236
96th St ... 11209
E 96th St
1-588 ... 11212
589-1649 ... 11236
97th St ... 11209
98th St ... 11209
E 98th St
1-470 ... 11212
472-598 ... 11212
641-1608 ... 11236
1610-1698 ... 11236
99th St ... 11209
E 99th St ... 11236
100th St ... 11209
E 100th St ... 11236
101st Ave ... 11208
101st St ... 11209
E 101st St ... 11236
E 102nd St ... 11236
E 103rd St ... 11236
E 104th St ... 11236
E 105th St ... 11236
E 106th St ... 11236
E 107th St ... 11236
E 108th St ... 11236

BUFFALO NY

General Delivery ... 14240

POST OFFICE BOXES MAIN OFFICE STATIONS AND BRANCHES

Box No.s
A - D ... 14240
172A - 172A ... 14217
A - H ... 14217
A - D ... 14218
9A - 9A ... 14217
H3201 - H3201 ... 14240
H0002 - H0002 ... 14240
O15 - O15 ... 14240
1 - 940 ... 14205
1 - 980 ... 14220
1 - 180 ... 14223
1 - 3490 ... 14240
1 - 247 ... 14217
1 - 117 ... 14218
1 - 1430 ... 14224
1 - 1250 ... 14231
1 - 1094 ... 14207
1 - 120 ... 14226
1 - 926 ... 14213
1 - 700 ... 14212
1 - 1040 ... 14209
1 - 1740 ... 14215
1 - 1300 ... 14201
1 - 1 ... 14219
1 - 2278 ... 14225
141 - 3779 ... 14226
212 - 212 ... 14219
281 - 515 ... 14223
301 - 389 ... 14218
400 - 755 ... 14217
640 - 699 ... 14223
900 - 900 ... 14217
949 - 2754 ... 14213
1001 - 1940 ... 14220
1001 - 1415 ... 14205
1271 - 1430 ... 14231
1451 - 1880 ... 14224
1451 - 1490 ... 14231
1501 - 1676 ... 14205
1511 - 2144 ... 14231
1800 - 1800 ... 14215
1901 - 2554 ... 14219
1990 - 1990 ... 14220
2165 - 2238 ... 14231
2300 - 2300 ... 14201
4001 - 4125 ... 14240
4121 - 4237 ... 14217
4200 - 4730 ... 14240
5000 - 5000 ... 14225
5008 - 5030 ... 14205
5008 - 5019 ... 14240
5100 - 5299 ... 14205
5100 - 5198 ... 14240
5108 - 5207 ... 14213
5356 - 5356 ... 14240
6000 - 6000 ... 14207
6001 - 7263 ... 14240
7955 - 8005 ... 14225
8000 - 8000 ... 14240
8000 - 8000 ... 14207
8000 - 8000 ... 14201
8041 - 8041 ... 14207
8100 - 8900 ... 14201
9001 - 9077 ... 14231
9001 - 9077 ... 14240
9001 - 9009 ... 14224
9003 - 9016 ... 14225
9100 - 9100 ... 14201
9500 - 9530 ... 14226
9998 - 9998 ... 14231
14273 - 704612 ... 14240

NAMED STREETS

A St
1-59 ... 14211
60-99 ... 14218
Abbington Ave ... 14223
Abbott Pkwy ... 14219
Abbott Rd
1-1200 ... 14220
1201-2299 ... 14218
Abbott Hall ... 14214
Abbottsford Pl ... 14213
Abby St ... 14220
Abeles Ave ... 14225
Aberdeen St ... 14225
Abt St ... 14221
Acacia Dr ... 14228
Academy Rd ... 14211
Academy St ... 14221
Ada Pl ... 14208
Adams St
1-50 ... 14210
51-280 ... 14206
281-505 ... 14212
506-699 ... 14211
Addison Ave ... 14226
Adlon Pl ... 14225
Admiral Rd ... 14216
Admirals Walk
1-199 ... 14228
201-1103 ... 14202
Adrian Ave
1-99 ... 14226
1-99 ... 14218
Aegean Ave ... 14228
Aero Dr ... 14225
Affinity Ln ... 14215
Agassiz Cir ... 14214
Ahepa Dr ... 14227
Ainsley Ct ... 14221
Airborne Pkwy ... 14225
N Airport Dr ... 14225
Alabama St ... 14204
Alamo Pl ... 14220
Alaraley St ... 14213
Alaska St ... 14206
Albany St ... 14213
Albemarle St ... 14207
Albert Ave ... 14207
Alberta Dr ... 14226
Albion Ave ... 14226
Albion Pl ... 14220
Alcona Ave ... 14226
Alden Ave ... 14216
Alder Pl ... 14223
Aldrich Pl ... 14220
Alexander Ave ... 14211
Alexander Pl ... 14208
Alexander Rd ... 14224
Alexia Ct ... 14221
S Alfred St ... 14219
Algiers Ln ... 14225
Alice Ave ... 14215
Alice Ct ... 14203
Allegany Ave ... 14217
Allegany St ... 14220
Allen Ave ... 14219
Allen St
1-90 ... 14219
1-99 ... 14202
92-98 ... 14219
100-299 ... 14201
E Allen St ... 14219
Allen Hall ... 14214
Allendale Ct ... 14215
Allendale Pkwy ... 14219
Allendale Rd
1-199 ... 14215
1-399 ... 14224
Allenhurst Rd
435A-435B ... 14226
Alliance Dr ... 14218
Allied Dr ... 14227
Allison Dr ... 14225
Alma Ave ... 14215
Alma Dr ... 14224
Almeda Ave ... 14226
Almont Ave ... 14224
Almont Pl ... 14220
Alpine Pl ... 14225
Alran Dr ... 14221
Alsace Ave ... 14220
Alsace Pl ... 14219
Alsace St ... 14224
Alton Ct ... 14219
Altruria St ... 14220
Alwin Pl ... 14211
Alyssum Ct ... 14221
Amana Pl ... 14224
Amber Ct ... 14219
Amber St ... 14220
Amberwood Dr ... 14228
Ambrose Ct ... 14228
Amelia St ... 14220
N America Dr ... 14224
American Campus Dr ... 14228
Amherst Ct ... 14225
Amherst St
1-700 ... 14207
701-1450 ... 14216
1451-1750 ... 14214
E Amherst St
1-275 ... 14214
276-799 ... 14215
Amherst Manor Dr ... 14221
Amherst Villa Rd ... 14225
Amherstdale Rd ... 14226
Amherston Dr ... 14221
Amistad Ln ... 14201
Amsterdam Ave
1-99 ... 14226
1-99 ... 14215
Amurra Ct ... 14225
Ana Woods ... 14221
E And West Rd ... 14224
Anderson Pl ... 14222
Anderson Rd ... 14225
Andover Ave ... 14215
Andover Ln ... 14221
Andres Pl ... 14225
Andrew Aly ... 14210
Andrews Ave ... 14225
Angela Ln ... 14225
Angelacrest Ln ... 14224
Angle Rd ... 14224
Angle St ... 14214
Anna Ct ... 14225
Annamarie Ter ... 14225
Annette Dr ... 14224
Ansley Ct ... 14224
Ansonia Ct Ct ... 14228
Anthony Ave ... 14225
Anthony Dr ... 14218
Anthony Tauriello Dr ... 14201
Antwerp St ... 14211
Apollo Dr ... 14228
Appenheimer Ave ... 14214
Apple Ave ... 14218
Applefield Dr ... 14221
Appletree Ct ... 14227
Applewood Rd ... 14225
Arbour Ln ... 14220
Arcade Ave ... 14226
Arcade St ... 14224
Arcadian Dr ... 14228
Archer Ave ... 14210
Archie St ... 14204
Arden Ave ... 14215
Ardmore Ct ... 14219
Ardmore Pl ... 14213
Ardsley Ln ... 14221
Arend Ave ... 14221
Argonne Dr ... 14217
Argosy Dr ... 14226
Argus St ... 14207
Argyle Ave ... 14226
Argyle Park ... 14222
Arielle Ct ... 14221
Aris Ave ... 14206
Arkansas St ... 14213
Arlington Pl ... 14201
Arlington Rd ... 14221
Armbruster St ... 14212
Armin Pl ... 14210
Arnold Pl ... 14218
Arnold St ... 14213
Arondale Dr ... 14221
Arrowhead Dr ... 14224
Arsenal Pl ... 14204
Arthur Ave ... 14219
Arthur St
1-199 ... 14207
1-99 ... 14225
Arthur Musarra Pkwy ... 14225
Arty Dr ... 14221
Arundel Rd ... 14216
Ash St ... 14204
Ashby Ct ... 14221
Ashdale Cir ... 14228
Ashland Ave ... 14222
Ashleaf Dr ... 14227
Ashley Dr
S3200-S3399 ... 14219
1-199 ... 14224
3200-3399 ... 14219
Ashley St ... 14212
Ashton Pl ... 14220
Ashworth Ct ... 14228
Aspen Ct ... 14226
Aspinwood Pl ... 14223
Astor Ridge Dr ... 14228
Athens Blvd ... 14223
Athol St ... 14220
Atlantic Ave
1-99 ... 14222
1-50 ... 14206
100-399 ... 14212
Atwood Pl ... 14225
Auburn Ave
1-500 ... 14213
501-899 ... 14222
Auchinvole Ave ... 14213
Auden Ct ... 14221
Audet Dr ... 14227
Audley End ... 14226
Audrey Ln ... 14211
Audubon Dr ... 14226
Augusta Ave ... 14225
Augusta St ... 14220
Aurora Ave ... 14224
Aurora Dr ... 14215
Austin St ... 14207
Autumn Ln ... 14219
N Autumn St ... 14221
S Autumn St ... 14221
Autumnview Rd ... 14221
Autumnwood Dr ... 14227
Auxaire Dr ... 14221
Ava Ln ... 14221
Avalon Dr ... 14226
Avenue B ... 14224
Avery Ave
1-199 ... 14216
1-99 ... 14218
Avery Pl ... 14225
Avignon Ct ... 14224
Avon Dr ... 14224
Avon St ... 14219
Avondale Pl ... 14210
Awood Pl ... 14225
Ayer Rd ... 14221
Ayrault Dr ... 14228
Azalea Dr ... 14224
Azure Pine Ct ... 14228
B St ... 14211
Babcock St
1-365 ... 14210
366-499 ... 14206
501-515 ... 14206
Bahama Ln ... 14225
Bailey Ave
1-165 ... 14220
166-500 ... 14210
501-1499 ... 14206
1500-1720 ... 14212
1721-2350 ... 14211
2351-2359 ... 14215
2352-2360 ... 14211
2361-3496 ... 14215
3498-3500 ... 14215
3800-3868 ... 14226
3870-4599 ... 14226
N Bailey Ave ... 14226
Bain Pkwy ... 14219
Baitz Ave ... 14206
Baker Ct ... 14218
Bakos Blvd ... 14211
Balbach Dr ... 14225
E & W Balcom St ... 14209
Balen Dr ... 14218
Bame Ave ... 14215
Bangel Ave ... 14224
Baraga St ... 14220
Barbados Dr ... 14227
Barbara Pl ... 14225
Barberry Ln ... 14221
Bardol St ... 14211
Barker St ... 14209
Barlow Ave ... 14218
Barnard St ... 14206
Barnett Dr ... 14224
Barnett Pl ... 14215
Barnsdale Ave ... 14224
Barone Cir ... 14225
Barry Pl ... 14213
Barrymore Rd ... 14225
Barthel St ... 14211
Barton Ct ... 14217
Barton St ... 14213
Bassett Rd ... 14221
Basswood Dr ... 14227
Batavia Dr ... 14221
Bauder St ... 14218
Bauman Ct & Rd ... 14221
Baxter St ... 14207
Bay Ln ... 14225
Bayberry Ave ... 14224
Baynes St ... 14213
Bayview Rd ... 14219
Baywood Dr ... 14227
Beach Rd ... 14225
Beacon Park ... 14228
Beacon St ... 14220
Beale Ave ... 14225
Beard Ave ... 14214
Beatrice Ave ... 14207
Beaumaris Pl ... 14207
Beaumont Dr ... 14228
Beck St ... 14212
Beck Hall ... 14214
Beckford Ct ... 14221
Beckwith St ... 14212
Bedford Ave
1-399 ... 14216
1-199 ... 14218
Bedford Ct ... 14204
Beech Rd ... 14226
Beech St
1-99 ... 14204
1-199 ... 14218
Beechwood Dr ... 14224

Beechwood Pl 14225
Beiter Walk 14215
Belcourt St 14226
Belgia Pl 14210
Bell Ave
1-199 14220
1-99 14218
Bell Rd 14225
Bellevue Ave 14227
Bellingham Dr 14221
Bellwood Ave 14224
Belmont Ave 14223
Belmont Dr 14224
Belmont Pl 14221
Belmont St 14207
Belmore Ct 14228
Belvedere Rd 14220
Belvoir Rd 14221
Benbro Dr 14225
Bender Ave 14206
Bennett Ct 14227
Bennett Ln 14203
Bennett Rd 14227
Bennett St 14204
Bennett Village Ter 14214
Bennington Rd 14226
Benson Ave 14224
Bentham Pkwy E 14226
Bentley Ct 14221
Benwood Ave 14214
Benzinger St 14206
Berehaven Dr 14228
Beresford Ct 14221
Berg Rd 14218
Bering Ave 14223
Berkley Pl 14209
Berkley Rd 14221
Berkley St 14223
Berkshire Ave 14215
Bernadette Ter 14224
Bernhardt Dr 14226
Bernice Dr
1-199 14225
1-199 14224
Berry Ave 14218
Berryman Dr 14226
Bert Rd 14225
Bertha Pl 14220
Berwin Dr 14226
Berwyn Ave 14215
Beryl Dr 14225
Best St
1-225 14209
226-390 14204
391-600 14208
601-899 14211
Bethford Dr 14219
Bethlehem St 14218
Betina Ave 14226
Betty Lou Ln 14225
Beverly Rd 14208
Beyer Pl 14210
Bickford Ave 14215
Bidwell Pkwy 14222
Big Tree Rd 14219
Bigelow Rd 14225
E & W Bihrwood Dr 14224
Bink St 14227
Binner Rd 14225
Biomedical Education Bldg 14214
Biomedical Res Bldg 14214
Birch Pl 14215
Birch St 14218
Birchwood Ave 14224
Birchwood Ct 14221
Birchwood Dr
1-99 14227
1-299 14221
Birchwood Sq 14224
Bird Ave
1-470 14213
471-699 14222
700-899 14209
Bird Walk Ln 14221
Birkdale Rd 14225

Biscayne Dr 14225
Bismarck St 14206
Bison Pkwy 14227
Bissell Ave 14211
Bissell Dr 14226
Bixler Ave 14225
Black Friars Yard 14222
Black Rock Hbr 14207
Black Spruce Ct 14228
Blaine Ave 14208
Blair Ct 14219
Blair Ln 14224
Blake St 14211
Blantyre Rd 14216
Blick St 14212
Block St 14211
Bloomfield Ave 14220
Blossom Rd 14224
Blossom St 14203
Blossom Heath Rd 14221
Blossom Wood Ln 14227
Bluebird Ln 14228
Blum Ave 14216
Boardman Rd 14218
Bobbie Ln 14221
Boehm Pl 14211
Bogardus St 14206
Boland Dr 14218
Boll St 14212
Bolton Pl 14210
Boncrest Dr E & W 14221
Boncroft Dr 14224
Bond St
S4000-S4099 14219
1-145 14210
146-299 14206
4000-4099 14219
Bondcroft Dr 14226
Bonview Ter 14221
Boone St 14220
Bordeaux Ct 14224
Borden Rd
1-465 14224
466-900 14227
Bosse Ln 14224
Botsford Pl 14216
Boulevard Mall 14226
Bourbon Ct 14224
Box Ave 14211
Boxelder Ln 14228
Boxwood Ln 14227
Boyd St 14213
Boynton St 14206
Bradenham Pl 14226
Bradford St
1-99 14210
1-99 14224
Bradley St 14213
Bradwood Rd 14224
Bragg Ct 14221
Bramble Ct & Rd 14221
Brambly Ct 14221
Brandon Ct 14228
Brandywine Dr 14221
Brant St 14226
Brantford Pl 14222
Brantwood Dr 14224
Brantwood Rd 14226
Brauncroft Ln 14226
Brayton St 14213
Breckenridge St
1-540 14213
541-699 14222
Bremen St 14213
Brendan Ave 14217
Brenon Rd 14228
Brentwood Dr
1-199 14227
4500-4799 14221
Brewster St 14214
Brian Ave 14221
Brian Ln 14224
Brianwood Dr 14224
Briar Row 14221
Briarcliff Rd 14225
Briarhill Dr 14224

Briarhill Rd 14221
Briarhurst Rd 14221
Briarwood Dr 14224
Bridge St 14207
Bridgehampton Cir 14221
Bridgeman St 14207
Bridle Path 14221
N Brier Rd 14228
Briggs Ave 14207
Bright St 14206
Brighton Ave 14212
Brimfield Ct 14224
Brinker Rd 14218
Brinkman Ave 14211
Brinton St
1-140 14214
141-299 14216
Brisbane Bldg 14203
Briscoe Ave 14211
Bristol Ct 14228
Bristol Dr 14228
Bristol Pkwy 14219
Bristol Rd 14219
Bristol St 14206
Britt Ave 14220
Brittany Ct 14224
Brittany Dr 14228
Brittany Ln 14222
Broad St 14225
Broadcast Plz 14202
Broadway St
1-152 14203
1-199 14224
153-540 14204
541-2313 14212
2315-2449 14212
2451-3297 14227
3299-3943 14227
Brockett Dr 14223
Brockton Rdg 14221
Brompton Cir 14221
Brompton Dr 14219
Brompton Rd 14221
Brompton Woods 14221
Bronx Dr 14227
Brook Ln 14224
Brookdale Dr 14221
Brookedge Ct
1-99 14224
1-99 14221
Brookedge Dr 14221
Brookfield Ln 14227
Brookhaven Dr 14225
Brooklane Dr 14221
Brooklyn St 14208
Brookpark Dr 14228
Brookside Dr
1-399 14220
1-99 14221
Brookwood Dr 14224
Brost Dr 14220
Brown St
1-99 14211
1-99 14227
1-199 14218
Brownell St 14212
Bruce St 14214
Brunswick Blvd 14208
Brush Creek Rd 14221
Bryant St
S4000-S4199 14219
1-100 14209
101-399 14222
4000-4199 14219
Bryant And Stratton Way 14221
Bryant Woods N & S 14228
Brynstone Ct 14228
Bryson St 14212
Buckeye Rd 14226
Bucyrus Dr 14228
Bud Mil Dr 14206
Buell Ave 14225
Buffalo Ave 14219
Buffalo St 14220
Buffalo China Rd 14210

Buffalo River Pl 14210
Buffum St 14210
Bullis Rd 14224
Burbank Dr
1-299 14226
17-21 14214
23-25 14214
N Burbank Dr 14226
Burbank Ter 14214
Burch Ave 14210
Burdette Dr 14225
Burgard Pl 14211
Burgess Blvd 14225
Burgundy Cir 14224
Burgundy Ter 14228
Burke Dr
1-399 14215
1-199 14218
Burke Pkwy 14219
Burlington Ave 14215
Burnie Ln 14203
Burroughs Dr 14226
Burton St 14203
Bush St 14207
Bushnell St 14206
Busti Ave
1-197 14201
199-600 14201
601-859 14213
861-999 14213
Butler Ave 14208
Butler Annex A 14214
Butler Annex B 14214
Butternut Rd 14227
Button Bush Ct 14228
Byrd Way 14204
Byron Ave 14223
Bywater Ct 14221
C St 14211
Cable St
1-99 14206
1-89 14223
2-98 14206
2-88 14223
90-164 14223
100-250 14206
165-199 14223
251-399 14206
Cadman Dr 14221
Caesar Blvd 14221
Caitlin Ter 14219
Caladium Ct 14221
Calais Ct 14224
Calais St 14210
Calderwood Dr 14215
Caldwell Dr 14224
Caldwell Pl 14218
California Dr 14221
California St 14213
Calla Way 14225
Callodine Ave 14226
Calumet Pl 14207
Cam Ct 14224
Cambria St 14206
Cambridge Ave
1-599 14215
1-199 14224
Cambridge Blvd 14226
Cambridge Ct 14204
Cambridge Sq 14221
Cambridge Sq S 14219
Cambridge St 14223
Cambrook Row 14221
Camden Ave 14216
Camel Rd 14225
Camelot Ct 14214
Camelot Dr 14224
Cameron Dr 14221
Camp St 14204
Campbell Ave 14216
Campbell Blvd 14228
Campbell Ln 14224
Campbell Rd 14215
Campus Dr
1-499 14226
1-199 14224

Campus Dr E 14226
Campus Dr N 14226
Campus Dr W 14226
Campus Ln 14226
Campwood Ct 14215
Camwood Dr 14224
Canalview Ter 14228
Candlewood Ln 14221
Cannas Ct 14227
Canterbury Ct
1-99 14226
100-199 14221
Canterbury Ln 14217
Canterbury Trl 14224
Cantwell Dr 14220
Capen Blvd
1-60 14214
61-599 14226
Caprice Dr 14227
Caraway Ct 14228
Cardinal Dr 14221
Cardinal Ln 14224
Cardinal Rd 14227
Carefree Ln 14227
Carl St 14215
Carla Ln 14224
Carleton Ct 14221
Carlton St
1-159 14203
160-400 14204
401-518 14211
520-598 14211
Carlyle Ave 14220
Carmel Rd 14214
Carmen Rd 14226
Carmolite Dr 14224
Carol Ct 14219
Carol Dr
1-199 14215
1-99 14224
Carolina St 14201
Carolyn Ct 14225
Carpenter Ave 14223
Carriage Cir 14221
Carriage Hl E 14221
Carriage Hl W 14221
Carriage Park 14224
Carriage Hill Ct 14221
Carroll St
100-140 14203
141-399 14204
700-899 14210
Carter St 14220
Cary St 14201
Cary Hall 14214
Cascade Dr 14228
Case Way 14225
Casimer St 14206
Casimir St 14206
Caspian Ct 14228
Cass Ave 14206
Castle Ct 14226
Castle Pl 14214
Castle Creek Trl 14221
Castlebrook Ln 14221
Castlewood Dr 14227
Cathedral Ct 14224
Cathedral Dr 14224
Cathedral Ln 14225
Cathedral Park 14202
Catherine St 14221
E & W Cavalier Dr 14227
Cayuga Rd 14225
N Cayuga Rd 14221
S Cayuga Rd 14221
Cayuga St 14211
Cayuga Creek Rd 14227
Cazenovia St
1-60 14220
62-130 14220
131-299 14210
Cecil St 14216
Cedar Ct 14224
Cedar Rd 14215
Cedar St 14204
S Cedar St 14204

Cedar Ridge Dr 14224
Cedargrove Cir 14225
Cedarwood Dr 14221
Ceil Dr 14227
Celina St 14206
Celtic Pl 14208
Centennial Ct 14224
Center Ave
1-199 14227
200-298 14223
Center Ln 14207
Center Rd 14224
E Center Rd 14224
Center St 14218
Center Pine Ln 14221
Centerpoint Cir 14224
Centerview Dr & Ln 14224
Central Ave
1-399 14206
1-99 14218
N Central Ave 14212
Central Blvd 14225
Central Park Plz 14214
Century Dr 14224
Century Rd 14215
S Century Rd 14215
Chadduck Ave 14207
Chadway Ct 14221
Chalmers Ave
2-70 14223
70-78 14214
80-198 14223
Chalmers St 14221
Chamberlin Dr 14210
Chambers Rd 14224
Chancellor Ln 14224
Chandler St 14207
Chapel Ave 14225
Chapel Ln 14224
Chapel Rd 14217
Chapel Woods Ct 14221
Chapin Pkwy 14209
Chaplin Dr 14223
Char Del Way 14221
Chardon Dr 14225
Charles St 14206
Charlescrest Ct 14224
Charleston Ave 14217
Charlestown Rd 14226
Charlotte Rd 14225
Charming Ln 14221
Charnwood Ct & Dr 14215
Charter Oaks Dr 14228
Chassin Ave 14226
Chateau Ter E, N & S 14226
Chatham Ave 14216
Chatsworth Ave 14217
Chaumont Dr 14221
Chauncey St 14206
Cheekwood Dr 14227
Chelsea Pl
100-260 14211
261-399 14215
Chelsea St 14223
Cheltenham Dr 14216
Chemical Bank Bldg 14202
Chenango St 14213
E & W Cherbourg Dr 14227
Cherokee Dr
1-199 14224
200-499 14225
Cherokee Pl 14206
Cherry Ave 14218
Cherry Ln 14225
Cherry St 14204
Cherry Laurel Ln 14228
Cherrywood Ct 14221
Cherrywood Dr
1-199 14227
1-299 14221
Cheryl Dr 14218
Cheryl Rd 14224
Chester St 14208
Chesterfield Dr 14215
Chestnut Ave 14224
Chestnut Hill Ct & Ln 14221

Chestnut Ridge Ln & Rd 14228
Chicago St 14204
Chincome Dr 14227
Chippewa Ct 14224
E Chippewa St 14203
W Chippewa St
1-147 14202
148-198 14201
Choate Ave 14220
Chopin Pl 14211
Christa St 14225
Christian Dr 14225
Christine Dr 14228
Christopher Dr 14224
Church St
1-27 14218
28-98 14202
29-35 14218
100-199 14202
Churchcroft Ln 14221
Churchill St 14207
Cid Del Way 14221
Cimarand Dr 14221
Cindy Dr 14221
Cindy Ln 14224
Circle Ct 14221
Circle Ln 14218
Circle End Dr 14224
City Hall 14202
City View Ave 14219
Clansour Ave 14208
Clardon Dr 14221
Clare St
1-40 14210
41-199 14206
Claremont Ave
1-31 14222
1-73 14223
2-30 14222
2-72 14223
32-139 14222
74-162 14223
140-299 14222
163-599 14223
Clarence Ave 14215
Clarendon Pl 14209
Clarion Ct 14221
Clark St
1-49 14206
1-99 14223
1-99 14218
2-50 14206
2-100 14223
51-105 14212
101-197 14223
106-209 14212
198-299 14223
210-299 14212
300-399 14223
Clark Hall 14214
Claude Dr 14206
Claudette Ct 14225
Clay St
1-13 14218
14-199 14207
Clayton St
1-99 14207
101-165 14207
215-299 14216
Clearfield Dr 14221
Clearvale Dr 14225
Clearview Dr 14221
Clearview Way 14219
Clearwater Dr 14228
Clement Hall 14214
Clemo St 14206
Cleveburn Pl 14222
Cleveland Ave
1-41 14222
1-199 14218
43-299 14222
Cleveland Dr
1-10 14215
2-8 14223
10-111 14223
11-120 14215

112-220 14223
121-225 14215
221-321 14223
226-336 14215
322-425 14223
337-425 14215
426-1599 14225
W Cleveland Dr 14215
Cliff St 14206
Clifford Hts 14226
Clifford St 14210
Clinton St
1-53 14218
54-160 14203
161-550 14204
551-955 14210
956-2275 14206
2276-2412 14227
2413-5099 14224
Clio Ave 14220
Cloister Ct
1-11 14226
2-10 14219
12-99 14219
Clover Pl 14225
Cloverdale Ave 14215
Cloverdale Rd 14225
Cloverleaf Ave 14218
Cloverside Ct & Dr 14224
Clyde Ave 14215
Cobb Aly 14201
Cobb Rd 14218
Cobblestone Ln 14221
Coburg St 14216
Cochrane St 14206
Coe Pl 14209
Coit St
1-165 14206
166-399 14212
S Colby St 14206
Colden Ct 14225
Coleen Ct 14224
Colette Ave 14227
Colfax Ave 14215
Colgate Ave 14220
Collaton St 14207
College Pkwy 14221
College St 14201
Collingwood Ave 14215
Collins Ave 14224
Collins Walk 14215
Colonial Ave 14217
Colonial Cir
1-99 14222
2-98 14213
Colonial Dr 14226
Colonial Manor Ct 14224
Colony Ct 14226
Colorado Ave
1-150 14211
151-299 14215
Colton Ave 14218
Colton Dr 14216
Colton St 14206
Columbia Blvd 14217
Columbia Dr 14221
Columbia Pkwy 14224
Columbia St 14204
Columbine Dr 14221
Columbus Ave 14220
Columbus Park W 14213
Columbus Pkwy 14213
Columbus St 14227
Colvin Ave 14216
Colvin Blvd
651-1000 14217
1001-1800 14223
N Colvin Blvd 14223
Colvinhurst Dr 14223
Comet Ave 14216
Commerce Dr
1-699 14228
1-399 14218
Commercial St 14219
Commodore Ter 14225
Commonwealth Ave 14216
Community Dr
1-99 14218
1-8 14225
Como Ave 14220
Como Park Blvd 14227
Comstock Ave 14215
Conant Dr 14223
Concord Dr 14215
Concord Pl 14226
Concord St 14212
Concourse Center Dr 14225
Condon Ave 14207
Congress St 14213
Congressional Walk 14215
Coniston Rd 14226
Connecticut St 14213
Connection Dr 14221
Connelly Ave 14215
Conner Ct & Dr 14224
Connie Trl 14219
Connors Way 14219
Constance Ln 14227
Constitution Ave 14224
Contessa Ct 14221
Convention Center Plz 14202
Cooke St 14218
Coolidge Dr 14226
Coolidge Rd 14220
Copeland Pl 14207
Copley Sq 14221
Copper Hts 14226
Copsewood Ave 14215
Coralwood Ct 14215
Cordage Aly 14213
Cordova Ave 14214
Corey Ct 14225
Corfu Cir 14228
Cornelia St 14210
Cornell Ave 14226
Cornell St 14214
Cornwall Ave 14215
Coronada St 14220
Coronation Dr 14226
Corporate Pkwy 14226
Corral Row 14221
Cortland Ave 14223
Corwin Dr 14224
Costin Rd 14226
Cottage Pl 14218
Cottage St 14201
Cottonwood Dr 14221
Countess Ave 14211
Country Ln 14224
Country Pkwy 14221
Country Meadows Ln 14221
Countryside Ct & Ln 14221
Courier Blvd 14217
Court St 14202
Courtland Ave 14215
Cove Holw 14224
Cove Creek Run 14224
Covent Garden Ln 14221
Coventry Rd
1-399 14217
1-199 14221
Coventry Green Cir 14221
Covington Dr 14220
N Covington Dr 14220
Covington Rd 14216
Cox Dr 14219
Coyote Ct 14221
Crabapple Ln 14227
Craigmore Dr 14221
Cranburne Ct & Ln 14221
Crandon Blvd 14225
W Cranwood Dr 14224
Crawford Dr 14206
Cree Ton Dr 14228
N Creek Dr 14225
S Creek Dr 14225
Creek Hts 14221
Creek Rd 14221
Creek Walk 14227
Creekside Ave 14218
Creekside Dr
1-599 14228
1-99 14227
Creekview Dr
1-99 14225
1-199 14224
Creekward Dr 14224
Crescent Ave
1-625 14214
626-799 14216
Crescent Ct 14225
Crescent Pl 14218
Cresthaven Dr
1-199 14225
1-199 14224
Crestview Ave 14225
Crestwood Ave 14216
Crestwood Ln 14221
Crestwood Pl 14225
Crisfield Ave
1-50 14227
51-299 14206
Crocker St 14212
Crofton Ct & Dr 14224
Crosby Ave 14217
Crosby Blvd 14226
Crosby Cir 14226
Crosby Hall 14214
S Crossman Ave & St 14211
Crowley Ave 14207
Crown Pl 14223
Crown Point Ln 14221
Crown Royal Dr 14221
Crownland Cir 14224
Croy Ave 14215
Crystal Ave 14220
Crystal Ln 14224
Crystal Tree Ct 14224
Culpepper Rd 14221
Culver Rd 14220
Cumberland Ave 14220
Cunard Ave 14225
Cunard Rd 14216
Currant Ave 14218
Currier Ave 14212
Curry Walk 14204
Curtain Up Aly 14202
Curtis Pkwy 14223
Curtiss St 14212
Curtwright Dr 14221
Cushing Pl 14220
Custer St 14214
Cypress Ct 14221
Cypress Rd 14227
Cypress St 14204
Daisy Ln
1-99 14228
4800-5099 14219
Daisy Pl 14208
Dakota St 14216
Dale Rd 14225
Dalewood Dr 14228
Dallas Rd 14220
Dalton Dr 14223
Dan Troy Dr 14221
Dana Rd 14216
Danbern Ln 14221
Danbury Dr 14225
Danbury Ln 14217
Danebrock Dr 14226
Danforth St
1-99 14213
1-99 14227
Dania Dr 14225
Daniel Ave 14225
Danielle Dr 14227
Dann St 14207
Dante Ct 14221
Darcy Ln 14221
Darien Pl 14216
Darlington Dr 14223
Dart St 14213
Dartmouth Ave 14215
Dartwood Dr 14227
Darwin Dr
1-430 14226
431-599 14225
Das Ct 14221
Dash St 14220
Date Ave 14218
Dauer Dr 14224
Dauphin Dr 14221
Davey St 14206
David Ave 14225
David Ct 14221
David Rd 14221
Davidson Ave 14215
Davinci Ct 14221
Davis Rd 14224
Davis St 14204
Dawnbrook Ln 14221
Days Park 14201
Daytona Pl 14210
Dean St 14219
Dearborn St 14207
Deborah Ln 14225
Debra Ln 14207
Decatur Rd 14223
Decker St 14215
Dee Ter 14227
Deepwood Ct 14228
Deer Path 14224
Deer Run 14221
Deer St 14207
Deer Trl 14227
Deer Lakes Dr 14228
Deer Run Ct 14221
Deerchase Rd 14224
Deerfield Ave 14215
Deerhurst Park Blvd
1-245 14217
246-399 14223
Deerwood Dr 14221
Delamere Rd 14221
Delaney Ave 14216
E Delavan Ave
1-360 14208
361-480 14214
481-630 14211
631-1799 14215
W Delavan Ave
1-500 14213
501-800 14222
801-1199 14209
Delaware Ave
1-7 14202
9-670 14202
671-1700 14209
1900-1938 14216
1940-2735 14216
2736-4000 14217
Delaware Rd
1-440 14217
441-1099 14223
Delaware Park Casino 14222
Delham Ave 14216
Della Dr 14218
Dellwood Pl 14225
Dellwood Rd 14226
Delmar Ave
1-99 14225
3900-3999 14219
Delmar Mitchell Dr 14204
Delphi Dr 14227
Delray Ave 14224
Delray Dr 14225
Delsan Ct 14216
Delta Rd 14226
Delwood Rd 14217
Dempster St 14206
Denerind Ave 14218
Denise Dr 14227
Dennis Ln 14227
Dennybrooke Ln 14224
Denrose Dr 14228
Densmore St 14220
E Depew Ave 14214
Depot St 14206
Derby Rd 14221
Deshler St 14212
Detroit St
1-165 14206
166-399 14212
Deumant Ter 14223
Devereaux Ave 14214
Deville Cir 14221
Devon Grn 14204
Devon Ln 14221
Devonshire Rd 14223
Dewberry Ln 14227
Dewey Ave 14214
Dewitt St 14213
Diane Ct 14224
Diane Dr
1-299 14225
1-99 14224
Dick Rd 14225
Dickens Rd 14219
Diefendorf Anx 14214
Diefendorf Hall 14214
Dignity Cir & Ln 14211
Dingens St 14206
Dirkson Ave 14224
Dismonda St 14210
N Division St
2-26 14203
28-199 14203
400-549 14204
550-665 14210
667-799 14210
S Division St
1-19 14203
21-167 14203
168-570 14204
571-899 14210
Dixon Dr 14223
Doat St 14211
Dodge St
1-210 14209
211-599 14208
Dogwood Dr 14227
Dogwood Rd 14221
Dole St 14210
Dolphin Dr 14219
S Domedion Ave & St 14211
Dona St 14218
Donald Dr
1-199 14225
1-99 14224
Donaldson Rd 14208
Doncaster Rd 14217
Donlen Dr 14225
Donna Pl 14221
Donna Lea Blvd 14221
Donovan Dr 14211
Dorchester Rd
1-99 14226
1-75 14222
76-199 14213
4400-4599 14219
Doris Dr 14224
Dorothy Pl 14219
Dorothy St 14206
Dorr St 14210
Dorrance Ave
1-165 14218
166-200 14220
202-400 14220
401-480 14218
482-698 14218
Dorris Ave 14215
Dorset Dr 14223
Doster Pl 14224
Doucette St 14224
Douglas Dr 14227
Dover Dr 14224
Dover St 14212
Downing Ln 14221
Downing St 14220
Doyle Ave 14207
Doyle Ct 14225
Draden Ln 14228
Drake Dr 14225
Drexel Rd 14214
Driftwood Ct 14221
Drummond Ct 14221
Duane Ct 14219
Duane Ter 14214
Duchess Ct 14225
Duchess Dr 14224
Duerstein St 14210
Duke Rd 14225
Duluth Ave 14216
Dundee St 14220
Dunlop Ave 14215
Dunston Ave 14207
Dupont St 14208
Durant St 14220
Durham Ave 14215
Durham Ct
1-99 14204
12-22 14228
Durham Dr 14228
Dushane Dr 14223
Dutchmill Dr 14221
Dutton Ave 14211
Dwyer St 14224
Dyke Rd 14224
Dyouville Sq 14201
Eagan Dr 14218
Eagle St 14221
E Eagle St
1-164 14203
165-299 14204
500-999 14210
W Eagle St 14202
Eaglebrook Dr 14224
Eagles Trce 14221
Eaglewood Ave 14220
Earhart Dr 14221
Earl Pl 14211
East Ave
1-19 14218
20-299 14224
East St 14207
Eastbrooke Pl 14221
Eastland Pkwy 14225
Easton Ave 14215
Eastvale Ct 14225
Eastwick Dr 14221
Eastwood Dr 14224
Eastwood Pl 14208
Eaton St
1-70 14209
1-99 14218
71-299 14208
Ebenezer Dr 14224
Echols Ln 14204
Eckhert St 14207
Eden Ln 14225
Eden St 14220
Edgar Ave 14207
Edge Park Ave 14216
Edge Park Dr 14225
Edgebrook Est 14227
Edgewater Dr 14228
Edgewood Ave
1-99 14220
1-109 14223
2-98 14220
2-110 14223
100-199 14220
111-399 14223
Edgewood Pl 14218
Edison Ave 14215
Edison St 14218
Edith St 14215
Edmund St 14227
Edna Pl
1-199 14209
1-99 14218
Edson St 14210
Edward Ct 14225
Edward St
1-96 14202
1-99 14221
97-130 14201
132-298 14201
Efner St 14201
Eggert Rd
1-775 14215
776-2170 14226
2171-2299 14223
Ehinger Dr 14224
Eileen Ct 14227
Eiseman Ave 14217
Eiss Pl 14226
Elaine Ct 14225
Elam Pl 14214
Elderwood Ct 14228
Eldon Rd 14215
Eldred Ave 14224
Electric Ave
1-199 14206
1200-1900 14218
1901-2499 14219
Eley Pl 14214
Elgas St 14207
Elk St 14210
Elk Terminal 14204
Elkhart St 14218
Elkhurst Dr 14225
Elkins Dr 14225
Ellen Dr 14225
Eller Ave 14211
Ellicott Rd 14227
Ellicott St
1-885 14203
886-1199 14209
N Ellicott St 14221
S Ellicott St 14221
Ellicott Creek Rd 14225
N Ellicott Creek Rd 14228
S Ellicott Creek Rd 14228
Ellsworth Dr 14225
Ellwood Ave 14223
N Ellwood Ave 14223
Ellwood Pl 14225
Elm Ave 14224
Elm Cir 14226
Elm Ct 14226
Elm Rd 14226
Elm St
1-799 14203
1-199 14218
Elm And Carlton St 14203
Elma Rd 14221
Elmer Ave 14215
Elmhurst Pl 14216
Elmhurst Rd 14226
Elmleaf Dr 14227
Elmsford Ct & Dr 14224
Elmview Ave 14218
W Elmview Ave 14218
Elmview Pl 14207
Elmwood Ave
1-199 14201
200-1301 14222
1303-1375 14222
1376-1400 14216
1401-2150 14207
2151-2255 14216
2256-4099 14217
4200-4399 14219
S Elmwood Ave
2-88 14202
90-130 14202
132-188 14201
190-399 14201
Elsie Pl 14208
Eltham Dr 14226
Elton Pl 14208
Elwood Dr 14224
Emerald Dr 14224
Emerald Ln 14227
Emerald Trl 14221
Emerling Dr 14219
Emerson Dr 14226
Emerson Pl 14209
Empire Dr 14224
Empire St 14212
Emporium Ave 14224
Empress Ave 14226
Emslie St
1-175 14210
176-415 14206
416-599 14212
Emsworth Ave 14223
E End Ave 14225
N End Ave 14217
Endicott Dr 14226
Englewood Ave
1-290 14214

291-1199 14223
Enola Ave 14217
Ensign St 14210
Erb St
1-30 14211
31-199 14215
Eric Trl 14219
Erickson Rd 14217
Ericson Ave 14215
Ericson Dr 14221
Erie St 14202
Ermann Dr 14217
Ernst Ave 14211
Erskine Ave 14215
Erwin Dr 14224
Esperar St 14201
Esser Ave 14207
Essex Ln 14204
Essex St 14213
Essjay Rd 14221
Estelle Dr 14225
Eton Ln 14226
Euclid Ave
1-99 14211
1-399 14217
Euclid Pl 14210
Eugene Ave
1-75 14216
76-399 14217
Eureka Pl 14204
Evadene St 14214
Evans St 14221
Evanshire Ln 14221
Evanston Pl 14220
Evelyn Ave 14224
Evelyn St 14207
Evergreen Pl 14225
Evermay Ln 14221
Exchange St
2-24 14203
26-179 14203
180-565 14204
566-1099 14210
Exeter Ct 14215
Exeter Rd 14221
Fair Woods Dr 14221
Fairbanks Ave 14223
Fairchild Dr 14226
Fairchild Pl 14216
Fairdale Dr 14221
Fairdale Rd 14218
Fairelm Ln 14227
Fairfax Dr 14224
Fairfield Ave
1-24 14223
2-22 14214
24-40 14214
26-28 14223
30-38 14223
40-87 14223
42-48 14214
50-89 14214
88-162 14223
89-89 14223
90-198 14214
91-199 14214
91-161 14223
163-499 14223
Fairfield Dr 14221
Fairgreen Dr 14228
Fairhaven Dr 14225
Fairlawn Dr 14226
Fairmount Ave
1-99 14223
1-199 14218
Fairoaks Ln 14227
Fairvale Dr 14225
Fairview Ave 14218
Fairview Pkwy 14219
Fairview Pl 14210
Fairways Blvd 14221
Falianto Ave 14223
Fallwood Ct 14223
Falmouth Ln 14221
Fancher Ave 14223
Faraday Rd 14223
Farber Ln 14221

Farber Hall 14214
Farber Lakes Dr 14221
Farenti St 14210
Fargo Ave
1-199 14201
200-274 14213
276-699 14213
Farmer St 14207
Farmingdale Rd 14225
Farmington Rd 14221
Fath Dr 14225
Fawn Ct 14227
Fawn Trl 14224
Fawnwood Dr 14221
Fay St 14211
Fayette Ave 14223
Fbi Plz 14202
Federal Ave
1-199 14215
1-199 14225
Fennimore Ave 14215
Fenton St 14206
Fenwick Rd 14221
Ferenti St 14210
Ferguson Ave 14213
Fernald Ave 14218
Ferndale Ave 14217
Ferndale Rd 14221
Fernhill Ave 14215
Fernleaf Ct 14221
Fernleaf Ter 14228
Fernwood Ave 14206
Fernwood Pl 14225
E Ferry St
1-125 14209
126-570 14208
571-1399 14211
W Ferry St
25-500 14213
501-850 14222
851-999 14209
Fieldcrest Ct 14224
Fieldgate Ct 14221
Fields Ave 14210
Fig Ave 14218
Fillmore Ave
1-225 14210
226-535 14206
536-895 14212
896-1770 14211
1771-2399 14214
S Fireside Dr 14221
Firestone St 14218
Fisher Rd
1-203 14218
204-899 14224
S Fisher Rd
1-100 14218
101-199 14224
Fisher St
1-50 14211
51-199 14215
Fisher Pond Ct 14221
Fitzgerald St 14210
Fleetwood Ter 14221
W Fleming St 14206
Flickinger Ct 14228
Flint Rd
1-99 14226
100-199 14221
Flohr Ave 14224
Flora Rd 14225
Floral Pl 14225
Floreis Ct 14225
Florence Ave
1-199 14214
1-99 14224
Florette Dr E & W 14227
Florida St 14208
Floss Ave
1-105 14211
106-299 14215
Flower St 14214
Foisset Ave 14225
Folger St 14220
Fonda Dr 14225
Fontaine Dr 14215

Foot Of W Ferry St 14213
Fordham Dr 14216
Forest Ave
1-500 14213
501-700 14222
701-899 14209
Forest Dr 14224
N Forest Rd 14221
S Forest Rd
1-399 14221
400-410 14225
Forest Hill Dr 14221
Forest Stream Rd 14221
Forestglen Cir & Dr 14221
Forestview Ct & Dr 14221
Forman St 14211
Forrestal Ln 14210
Forrester Ct 14228
Fosdick St 14209
Foster Hall 14214
Fougeron St 14211
Foundry St 14207
Fountain Park 14223
Fountain Plz
1-3 14203
2-50 14202
Fountainview Ct 14228
Four Seasons Cir & Rd 14226
Four Winds Way 14226
Fowler Ave 14217
Fowler St 14218
Fox St
1-140 14212
141-499 14211
Fox Trce 14221
Fox Chapel Ct & Rd 14221
Fox Den 14221
Fox Meadow Dr 14221
Foxcroft Ln 14221
Foxpoint Rd W 14221
Foxwood Ln 14221
Fradine Dr 14227
Fraleana Dr 14221
Francine Ln 14227
Francis Ave 14212
Frank Ave 14210
Frank Ct 14224
Frankfort Ave 14211
Frankhauser Rd 14221
Franklin Ave 14212
Franklin Park N 14202
Franklin St
1-99 14221
1-299 14218
3-35 14202
37-599 14202
Frantzen Ter 14227
Freda Ave 14225
Frederick Dr 14225
Frederick Pl 14211
Frederick St 14227
Fredro St 14206
Freedom Dr 14224
Freeman Rd 14221
Freeman St 14215
Freemont Ave 14226
Frelac Ave 14209
Fremont Ave
1-29 14218
30-299 14224
French Rd
1-1180 14227
1-499 14224
N French Rd 14228
French St 14211
French Lea Rd 14224
Freund St
1-65 14211
66-199 14215
Fronckowiak Ave 14227
Front Park 14213
Front St 14218
Frontenac Ave 14216
Frontera Ct 14224
Frontier Dr 14219

E Frontier Dr 14219
Frontier Rd 14228
Fruehauf Ave 14226
Fruitwood Ter 14221
Fuhrmann Blvd 14203
Fuller Ave 14219
Fuller St 14207
Fulton St
1-350 14204
351-699 14210
Furlong Rd 14215
Gabrielle Dr 14227
Gaby Ln 14227
Gail Ave 14215
Galbraith Rd 14221
Galileo Dr 14221
Gallatin Ave 14207
Galleria Dr 14225
Galloway St 14210
Ganna Ct 14224
Ganson St 14203
Garden Aly 14201
Garden Ave 14224
Garden Ct 14226
Garden Pkwy 14221
Garden Rd 14225
Garden Village Dr 14227
Gardenvale Dr 14225
Gardenville Pkwy W 14224
Gardenville On The Grn 14224
Gardenwood Ln 14223
Garfield Rd 14221
Garfield St 14207
Garland Ave 14206
Garland Dr 14226
Garner Ave 14213
Garnet Dr 14227
Garnet Rd 14226
Garrison Rd 14221
Garrock Rd 14221
Garry Dr 14224
Garvey Ave 14220
Gary Ln 14227
Gaslight Trl 14221
Gaspe Dr 14228
Gatchell St 14212
Gates Ave 14218
N Gates Ave 14218
Gates Cir 14209
Gates St 14212
Gatewood Ln 14221
Geary St 14210
Gelston St 14213
Gemcor Dr 14224
Gencendo St 14212
Genesee St
1-19 14203
21-230 14203
231-600 14204
601-2280 14211
2281-5199 14225
W Genesee St
201-247 14202
225-229 14201
249-299 14202
Geneva St 14212
Genoa Pl 14216
Gentwood Dr 14221
George Dr 14224
George St 14204
George Karl Blvd 14221
George Urban Blvd 14225
Georgetown Ct 14221
Georgia St 14201
Georgian Ln 14221
Gerald Ave 14215
Gerard Dr 14224
Gerhardt St 14208
Germain St 14207
Germania St 14220
Gervan Dr 14224
Gesl St 14214
Gettysburg Ave 14223
Getzville Rd 14226
Gibbons St 14218

Giblin Dr 14224
Gibson St
1-85 14206
86-499 14212
Gierlach St 14212
Gilbert Ave 14219
Gilbert St 14206
Gill Aly 14222
Gillette Ave 14214
Gilmore Dr 14225
Girard Ave
1-99 14218
1-199 14227
E Girard Blvd 14217
W Girard Blvd 14217
Girard Pl 14211
Gittere St 14211
Gladstone St 14207
Gladys Holmes Blvd 14204
Glen Ave 14221
Glen Eagle Ct 14221
Glenbourne Ct 14221
Glencove Rd 14223
Glendale Ln 14225
Glendale Pl 14208
Glendhu Pl 14210
Glendon Pl 14221
Glenfield Dr 14224
Glenhaven Dr 14228
Glenmar Dr 14224
Glenn St 14206
Glenny Dr 14214
Glenside Ave & Ct 14223
Glenwood Ave
1-155 14209
1-99 14218
156-599 14208
700-999 14211
3100-3221 14219
3223-3299 14219
Glenwood Ct 14225
Glenwood Dr 14221
Gleradow Ave 14216
S Glidden St 14206
Glor St 14207
Godfrey St 14215
Goembel Ave 14211
Goering Ave 14225
Goethe St
1-300 14206
301-499 14212
Gold St 14206
Gold Cup Dr 14221
Golden Oak Cir 14221
Goldfinch Ct 14228
Gollorne St 14202
Good Ave 14220
Goodell St
1-175 14203
176-298 14204
Goodrich Rd 14218
Goodrich St 14203
Goodyear Ave
1-140 14212
141-699 14211
Goodyear Hall 14214
Gordon Ave 14224
Gordon St 14221
Gorham St 14210
Gorski St 14206
Gorton St 14207
Gothic Cir 14228
Goulding Ave 14208
Grace Ave 14226
Grace St 14207
Grafton Ave 14219
Grand Blvd 14225
Grand Prix Dr 14227
Grandview Ave 14223
Grandview Dr 14228
Granger Pl 14222
Grant Blvd 14218
Grant Rd 14226
Grant St
1-670 14213
672-844 14213

846-1099 14207
Grape Ave 14218
Grape St 14204
Grasspointe Dr 14228
Grattan St 14206
Gravel Pl 14218
Great Arrow Ave
1-145 14216
146-300 14207
Greeley St 14207
Green St 14218
Greenaway Rd 14226
Greenbranch Rd 14224
Greenbriar Rd 14221
Greenbrier Rd 14226
Greencastle Ln 14221
Greene St
1-87 14206
89-425 14206
426-499 14212
Greenfield Ave 14224
Greenfield Pkwy 14219
Greenfield St 14214
Greenhill Ter 14224
Greenhurst Rd 14221
Greenleaf Ln 14225
Greenmeadow Dr 14224
Greenway Blvd 14225
Greenwich Dr 14228
Greenwood Ave 14218
Greenwood Pl 14213
Gregory Dr 14224
Greiner Rd 14221
Gren Way Aly 14222
Gresham Dr 14226
Grey St
1-120 14212
121-299 14211
Greymont Ave 14224
Grider St 14215
Griffith St 14212
Grimes St 14212
Grimsby Rd W 14223
Griswold St 14206
Groell Ave 14227
Grosvenor Rd 14223
Grosvenor St 14210
Grote St 14207
Groton Dr 14228
Grove St
1-199 14207
1-99 14221
340-399 14216
Groveland St 14214
Grover Cleveland Hwy 14226
Gruner Rd 14227
Gualbert Ave 14211
Guernsey St 14207
Guilford Ln 14221
Guilford St
1-140 14212
141-499 14211
Gull Lndg 14202
Gull St 14213
Gunnell Ave 14216
Hagen St
1-150 14211
151-299 14215
Hager St 14208
Halbert St 14214
Haley Ln 14227
Hallam Rd 14216
Haller Ave 14211
Hallmark Ct 14221
Halstead Ave 14212
Halwill Dr 14226
Hamburg St 14204
Hamburg Tpke 14218
Hameangt St 14201
Hamilton Ave 14218
Hamilton Blvd 14217
Hamilton Dr 14226
Hamilton St 14207
Hamlin Rd 14208
Hamlin Sq 14221
Hammerschmidt Ave 14210

Hampshire St 14213
Hampton Ct 14221
Hampton Pkwy 14217
Hampton Hill Dr 14221
Hancock Ave 14220
Hancock Ter 14226
Hannah St 14206
Hanover St 14202
Hansen Ave 14220
Harbour Ln 14225
Harbour Pointe Cmn 14202
Harbridge Mnr 14221
Harcroft Ct 14226
Harding Ave 14217
Harding Rd
1-299 14220
1-599 14221
Hardt Ln 14226
Hardwood Pl 14210
Hareenes Ave 14217
Haridern St 14207
Harlem Rd
1-1040 14224
1041-1250 14227
1251-1800 14206
1801-1887 14212
1889-2100 14212
2101-3261 14225
3263-3577 14225
3578-3875 14215
3876-5099 14226
Harlow Pl 14208
Harmonia St 14211
Harmony Ln 14225
Harp Pl 14207
Harper Rd 14226
Harriet Ave 14215
Harriman Hall 14214
Harris Ct 14225
Harris Hill Rd 14221
Harrison Ave
S3500-S3799 14219
1-799 14223
3500-3799 14219
Harrison St 14210
Harrogate Sq 14221
Hartford Ave 14223
Hartford Rd 14226
Hartman Pl 14207
Hartwell Rd 14216
Harvard Ct
1-99 14225
1-99 14221
Harvard Pl 14209
Harvest Ave 14216
N Harvest St 14221
S Harvest St 14221
Harvey Pl 14210
Harwood Ave 14219
Harwood Dr 14226
Harwood Pl 14208
Harwood Rd 14224
Hastings Ave 14215
Hatch Ct 14225
Hauf St 14208
Haven St 14211
Haverford Ln 14221
Haverton Ln 14228
Hawley Rd 14219
Hawley St 14213
Hawthorne Ave
1-399 14223
1-99 14227
Hayden St 14210
Hayes Pl 14210
Hayes A 14214
Hayes B 14214
Hayes C 14214
Hayes D 14214
Hayes Hall 14214
Hayward St 14204
Hazel Ct 14224
Hazel Pl 14211
E & W Hazeltine Ave 14217
Hazelwood Ave 14215
Hazelwood Dr 14228

Heath St 14214
Heath Ter 14223
Heather Dr 14221
Heather Rd 14225
Heather Hill Dr 14224
Heathrow Ct 14221
Heathwood Rd 14221
Hecla St 14216
Hedge Ct 14226
Hedgewood Dr 14221
Hedley Pl 14208
Hedley St 14206
S Hedley St 14206
Hedstrom Dr 14226
Hedwig Ave 14211
Heim Rd 14221
Helen Ave 14219
Helen St
1-99 14213
1-25 14227
26-299 14206
Helenwood Dr 14221
Hemdale Dr 14221
Hemenway Rd 14225
Heminway St 14211
Hemlock Dr 14224
Hemlock Ln 14226
Hemlock Rd 14226
Hempstead Ave 14215
Henderson Ave 14217
Hendricks Blvd 14226
Henel Ave 14226
Henley Rd 14216
Hennepin Rd 14228
Hennepin St 14206
Henrietta Ave
1-199 14207
1-99 14224
S Henry St 14227
Herbert Ave
1-99 14215
1-199 14225
Heredam Ave 14214
Heritage Ct 14225
Heritage Rd E 14221
Heritage Rd W 14221
Heritage Farm Rd 14218
Herkimer St 14213
Herman St
1-140 14212
141-499 14211
Hershey Ct 14221
Hertel Ave
1-805 14207
806-1865 14216
1866-2099 14214
Hetzel Rd 14221
Heussy Ave 14220
Heward Ave 14207
Hewitt Ave 14215
Hi View Ter 14224
Hichindi St 14204
Hickory St 14204
Hickory Grove Ln 14227
Hickory Hill Rd 14221
Hidden Creek Ct 14221
Hidden Pines Ct 14221
Hidden Pond Ln 14226
Hidden Ridge Cmn 14221
Hidden View Ct 14221
High Ct 14226
High St
1-101 14203
103-169 14203
170-399 14204
400-616 14211
618-698 14211
High Park Blvd 14226
High View Ter 14220
Highgate Ave
1-165 14214
166-699 14215
Highland Ave
1-99 14224
1-350 14222
1-99 14218

351-357 14223
352-358 14222
359-1050 14223
1052-1198 14223
Highland Dr 14221
Highland Pkwy
1-340 14223
4200-4400 14219
E Highland Pkwy 14219
W Highland Pkwy 14219
Highview Cir 14219
Highview Ct 14215
Highview Rd 14215
Hiler Ave 14217
N Hill Dr 14224
Hill St 14214
Hillcrest Dr
1-299 14226
1-99 14224
Hillcrest Hts 14224
Hilldale Ave 14224
Hillery Ave 14210
Hillpine Rd 14227
Hillsboro Rd 14225
Hillside Ave
1-99 14210
1-99 14225
Hillside Dr 14221
Hilltop Cts 14224
Hillview Ter 14224
Hillwood Dr 14227
Hilton Blvd 14226
Hilton St 14212
Hines St 14220
Hinman Ave 14216
Hirschbeck St 14212
Hirschfield Dr 14221
Hirschwood Dr 14221
Hitching Post Ln 14228
Hobart St 14206
Hobmoor Ave 14216
Hodge Ave 14222
Hoerner Ave 14211
Hoffman Pl 14207
Holbrook St 14218
Holden St 14214
Holland Ave
1-199 14218
1-99 14225
1-99 14224
Holland Pl 14209
Holling Dr 14216
Hollister St 14204
Holloway Blvd 14209
Holloway Creek Ln 14228
Holly Ln 14227
Holly St 14206
Hollybrook Dr 14221
Hollywood Ave 14220
Holmes St 14207
Holt St 14206
Holtz Dr 14225
Home Pl 14218
Homecrest Dr 14226
Homer Ave 14216
Homer Ln 14221
Homesgarth Ave 14225
Homestead St 14218
Homewood Ave
1-199 14227
100-399 14217
Homewood Ct 14221
Homeworth Pkwy 14225
Honduras Ln 14225
Honeybee Ln 14228
Hoover Ave 14217
Hoover Rd 14219
Hope Way 14201
Hopkins Rd
1-1649 14221
2700-3399 14228
Hopkins St 14220
Horizons Plz 14202
Horton Ave 14219
Horton Pl 14209
Houghton Ave 14212

Houston St 14220
Howard Ave 14221
Howard Dr 14221
Howard St 14206
Howe Lab 14214
Howell St 14207
Howlett St 14211
Hoyer Pl 14216
Hoyt St 14213
Hubbard St 14206
Hubbardston Pl 14228
Hubbell Ave 14220
Hudson St
S4000-S4199 14219
1-399 14201
4000-4199 14219
Huetter Ave 14207
Hughes Ave 14208
Hugo Pl 14219
Humason Ave 14211
Humber Ave 14215
Humboldt Pkwy
176-480 14214
177-1099 14208
482-1098 14211
W Humboldt Pkwy 14214
Hummingbird Ln 14228
Humphrey Rd 14207
Hunt Ave 14207
Hunters Cv & Ln 14221
Hunting Rd 14215
Huntington Ave
1-499 14214
1-199 14224
Huntington Ct 14221
Huntleigh Cir 14226
Huntley Rd 14215
Hurd St 14206
Hurlock Ave 14211
E Huron St 14203
W Huron St
25-57 14202
59-101 14202
103-139 14202
141-299 14201
Hutchens Dr 14227
Hutchinson Ave 14215
S Huth Rd 14225
Huxley Dr
1-370 14226
371-599 14225
S Huxley Dr 14225
Hybank Dr 14224
Hydraulic St 14210
Hyland Pl 14224
Hyledge Dr 14226
Ideal St 14206
Idlebrook Dr 14225
Idlewood Dr 14224
Illinois St 14203
Imperial Dr 14226
Imson St 14210
In The Woods Ln 14224
Indian Rd 14227
Indian Church Rd
1-371 14210
372-1399 14224
Indian Orchard Pl 14210
Indian Trail Rd 14221
Industrial Pkwy 14227
Ingham Ave 14218
Inn Keepers Ln 14228
Inner Dr 14218
Innes Rd 14224
Innsbruck Dr 14227
Inter Dr 14224
Inter Park Ave 14211
International Dr 14221
Inwood Pl 14209
Irene St 14207
Iris Ave 14224
Iroquois Aly 14204
Iroquois Ave
1-139 14206
4000-4099 14219
Irving Pl 14201

Irving Ter 14223
S Irving Ter 14223
Irvington Dr 14228
Irwin Rd 14228
Isabelle Rd 14225
Isabelle St 14207
Ivanhoe Rd 14215
Ivy St 14211
Ivy Green Ct 14226
Ivy Lea 14223
Ivyhurst Cir & Rd 14226
Jack Rd 14221
Jacks Ln 14224
Jacks Trl 14219
Jackson Ave
1-199 14212
1-199 14218
Jackson Ter 14209
Jaktram Ct 14209
Jamaica Ln 14225
James Ct 14221
James St
1-299 14210
2-28 14218
30-298 14210
3400-3799 14219
James D Griffin Plz 14203
James E Casey Dr 14206
James P Coppola Sr
Blvd 14210
Jamstead Ct 14221
Jane Dr 14227
Janet St 14215
Janice St 14207
Janine Ct 14227
Jarvis St 14219
Jasmine Ave 14224
Jasper Dr 14226
Jasper Parrish Dr 14207
Jean Ter 14225
Jeanmoor Rd 14228
Jefferson Ave
1-249 14210
2-248 14204
250-1050 14204
1051-1899 14208
Jeffrey Blvd 14219
Jeffrey Dr 14228
Jenawood Ln 14221
Jenny Ct & Ln 14225
Jerome Ct 14227
Jersey St
1-345 14201
347-379 14213
381-499 14213
Jewett Ave & Pkwy 14214
Joanie Ln 14228
Joann Dr 14224
Joanne Ln 14227
Jody Ct 14219
Joe Mccarthy Dr 14228
John Brian Ln 14227
John Glenn Dr 14228
John James Audubon
Pkwy 14228
John Muir Dr 14228
John Paul Ct 14206
Johnson Park 14201
N Johnson Park 14201
S Johnson Park 14201
Johnson St
1-140 14212
1-99 14218
141-391 14211
393-499 14211
4000-4299 14219
Joliet Ln 14226
Jonathan Pl 14228
Jones St 14206
Jordan Rd 14221
Joseph Ct 14218
Joseph St 14225
Josephine St 14211
Josie Pl 14220
Joslyn Pl 14207
Judith Dr 14227

Julian Ave 14218
Julianna Ct 14228
Julius St 14220
June Rd 14217
Juniata Pl 14210
Junior Ave 14210
Juniper Ln 14227
Kail St 14207
Kalayne Ln 14221
Kamper Ave 14210
Kane St
1-99 14204
1-99 14218
Kapoor Hall 14214
Karen Pl 14221
Katherine St 14210
Kathleen Dr 14225
Kathy Ln 14224
Katie Ln 14221
Kauderer Pl 14224
Kaufman Dr 14225
Kay St 14215
Kaymar Dr 14228
Keever Ave 14218
Kehr St 14211
Keitsch Aly 14211
Kelburn St 14206
Keller Ave 14217
Kellogg St 14210
Kelly Dr 14227
Kellybrook Ct 14224
Kelsey Dr 14224
Kelvin Dr 14223
Kemp Ave 14225
Kendale Rd 14215
Kenefick Ave 14220
Kenfield Ct 14215
Kenmore Ave
1-175 14226
176-511 14223
512-1920 14216
513-965 14223
967-1919 14217
1921-1999 14217
2100-2350 14207
Kennedy Dr 14218
Kennedy Rd 14227
Kenova St 14214
Kensington Ave
1-610 14214
611-1975 14215
1976-2599 14226
Kent St
1-99 14219
1-199 14212
Kenton Rd 14217
Kentucky St 14204
Kenview Ave 14217
Kenview Blvd 14215
Kenwood Rd 14217
Keph Dr 14228
Keppel St 14210
Kermit Ave 14215
Kerns Ave 14211
Keswick Rd 14226
Ketchum Pl 14213
Kettering Dr 14223
Kevin St 14218
Keystone St 14211
Kiefer St 14211
Kilbourne Rd 14225
Kilhoffer St 14211
Kim Cir 14221
Kimball Tower 14214
Kimberly Ave 14220
Kimberly Ln 14218
Kimberly Rd 14221
Kimmel Ave 14220
King St 14206
King Peterson Rd 14204
Kings Hwy 14226
Kings Trl 14221
Kingsgate Rd S 14226
Kingsley St 14208
Kingston Ln 14225
Kingston Pl 14210

Kingsview Ct & Rd 14221
Kingswaye Dr 14221
Kingswood Dr 14225
Kinsey Ave 14217
Kirby Ave 14218
Kirkover St 14206
Kirkpatrick St 14215
Kirkwood Dr 14224
Klas Ave 14224
Klauder Rd 14223
Klaus St 14206
W Klein Rd 14221
Klink Pl 14224
Knoerl Ave 14210
Knollwood Dr 14227
Knollwood Ln 14221
Knotty Pine Ct 14221
Knowlton Ave
1-499 14217
1-99 14218
Knox Ave
1-116 14216
1-399 14224
118-198 14216
Koester St 14220
Kofler Ave 14207
Koons Ave
1-140 14212
142-268 14211
270-499 14211
Kopernik St 14206
Kosciuszko St 14212
Kossuth Ave 14218
Koster Row 14226
Krakow St
1-199 14206
1-99 14218
Krehmore Pl 14223
Krettner St
1-165 14206
166-299 14212
Kron Ave 14224
Krupp Ave 14212
Kuhn Rd 14225
La Force Pl 14207
La Riviere Dr 14202
Labelle Ave 14219
Labelle Ter 14228
Lackawanna Ave 14212
Ladner Ave 14220
Lafayette Ave
1-470 14213
471-800 14222
801-1099 14209
Lafayette Blvd 14221
Lafayette Sq 14203
Laird Ave 14207
Lake Ave 14219
Lake Ledge Dr 14221
Lake Shore Rd 14219
Lakefront Blvd 14202
Lakeside Ct 14224
Lakeside Dr
1-199 14224
1-99 14221
Lakeview Ave
1-3799 14219
1-99 14201
Lakewood Ave 14220
Lakewood Pkwy 14226
Lamacha Ln 14228
Lamarck Dr
1-385 14226
386-599 14225
Lamont Dr 14226
Lamont Pl 14207
Lamson Rd 14223
Lancaster Ave 14222
Landers Rd 14217
Landing Creek Ct 14221
Landings Dr 14228
Landon St
1-275 14208
276-399 14211
Lang Ave 14215
Langfield Dr 14215

Langmeyer Ave 14215
Langner Rd 14224
Lanoche Ct 14221
Lansdale Pl 14211
Lansing St 14207
Lantern Ln 14228
Larch Rd 14226
Larchmont Rd 14214
Lark St 14211
Larkin St 14210
Larkspur Ln
2-8 14221
10-199 14228
Larkwood Rd 14224
Larrabee St 14220
Larsen Ln 14224
Lasalle Ave
1-235 14214
1-299 14217
236-799 14215
Lathrop St
1-200 14212
201-399 14211
Latona Ct 14220
Latour St 14211
Laura Ct 14227
Laura Ln 14221
Laurel Ln 14221
Laurel Run 14225
Laurel St
1-140 14209
141-299 14208
Laurelton Dr 14224
Laurentian Dr 14225
Laurie Lea 14221
Laux St 14206
Lavender Ln 14225
Lawn Ave 14207
Lawnwood Dr 14228
Lawrence Ln 14221
Lawrence Pl 14213
Lawrence Bell Dr 14221
Layer Ave 14207
Layton Ave 14226
Le Havre Dr 14227
Leacliff Ln 14224
Leah Ct 14221
Leamington Pl 14210
Leaside Dr 14224
Lebanon St 14218
Lebrun Cir 14226
Lebrun Rd
1-149 14215
150-999 14226
Leddy St 14210
W Ledge Ln 14221
Ledge View Ter 14221
Ledger St 14216
Lee St 14210
Lee Entrance 14228
Leennewo St 14203
Legion Dr 14217
N Legion Dr 14210
S Legion Dr 14220
Legion Pkwy 14224
Lehigh St
1-99 14206
1-299 14218
Lehn Springs Dr 14221
Leicester Rd 14217
Lein Rd 14224
Leland Dr 14220
Lemay Ct 14221
Lemoine Ave 14227
Lemon St
1-299 14204
27-48 14218
Lemon Tree Ct 14228
Lena Ave 14225
Lena Ct 14224
Leni Ln 14225
Lennox Ave 14226
Lenox St 14224
Leo Ct 14224
Leo Pl
1-99 14218

20-40 14225
Leocrest Ct 14224
Leonard St
1-199 14215
1-199 14218
Leonard Post Dr 14211
Leonore Rd 14226
Leroy Ave
1-410 14214
411-500 14215
502-598 14215
Leroy Rd 14215
Leslie St 14211
Lester St 14210
Letchworth St 14213
Lewis St 14206
Lexington Ave 14222
Lexington Grn 14224
Lexington Ter 14226
Leydecker Rd 14224
Liberty Ave 14215
Liberty Ln 14224
Liberty Ter 14215
Liddell St 14212
Lilac St 14220
Lilac Ter 14225
Lille Ln 14227
Lillis Ln 14224
Limestone Dr 14221
Lincoln Ave 14218
Lincoln Blvd 14217
Lincoln Pkwy
1-200 14222
201-499 14216
Lincoln Rd 14226
Lincoln Park Dr 14223
Lincoln Woods Ln 14222
Lincroft Rd 14218
Lind Ave 14224
Linda Dr 14225
Lindbergh Ct 14225
Linden Ave
1-29 14217
2-78 14214
2-98 14217
31-79 14214
35-99 14217
80-106 14214
100-189 14217
108-160 14214
190-699 14216
191-199 14217
Linden Park 14208
Linden St
1-199 14206
1-99 14218
N Linden St 14221
Lindner Dr 14224
Lintredg Dr 14225
Linview Ter 14216
Linwood Ave
1-799 14209
1-199 14221
4100-4399 14219
Linwood Ter 14209
Lisa Ln 14219
Lisa Ann Ln 14224
Lisbon Ave
1-185 14214
186-699 14215
Liston St 14223
Litchfield Ave 14215
Littell Ave 14210
Little Ln 14227
Little Robin Rd 14228
Littlefield Ave 14211
Livingston Pkwy 14226
Livingston St 14213
Lloyd Dr 14225
Lloyd St 14202
Lobue Ln 14225
Loch Lee 14221
Lochland Dr 14225
Lockhart Cir 14228
Lockhart Rd 14224
Lockwood Ave 14220
Locust St 14204
Loepere St
1-175 14212
176-399 14211
Logan Ave 14223
Lois Dr 14227
Lombard St
1-65 14206
66-299 14212
Long Ave 14225
N Long St 14221
S Long St 14221
Longleat Dr 14226
Longmeadow Rd 14226
Longnecker St 14206
Longview Ave 14211
Lonsdale Rd 14208
Lord St
1-145 14210
146-299 14206
Lord Byron Ln 14221
Lordan Dr 14227
Loretta St 14223
Loretto Dr 14225
Lorfield Dr 14226
Loring Ave
S4000-S4199 14219
100-175 14208
176-299 14214
4000-4199 14219
Lorraine Ave 14220
Lorraine Ln 14225
Lorraine Pl 14224
Lorry Dr 14224
Los Robles St 14221
Losson Rd 14227
Losson Garden Dr 14227
Louis Ave 14224
Louis St 14225
Louise Dr
1-10 14224
11-99 14227
Louisen St 14211
Louisiana St 14204
Louvaine Dr 14223
Love Ter 14218
Lovejoy St 14212
E Lovejoy St 14206
Lovering Ave 14216
Lowell Ln 14224
Lowell Pl 14213
Lowell Rd 14217
Lower East Ln 14207
Lower Terrace St 14202
Loxley Ct 14224
Loxley Rd 14225
Lucerne Ct 14227
Lucid Dr 14225
Lucille Dr 14225
Lucy Ln 14225
Ludel Ter 14218
Ludington St 14206
Ludwig Ave
1-599 14227
1-99 14224
Lydia Ln 14225
Lyman Ave 14225
Lyman Rd 14226
Lyman St 14206
Lyndale Ave 14223
Lyndale Ct 14224
Lyndhurst Ave 14216
Lyndhurst Rd 14221
Lynette Ln 14228
Lynn St 14218
Lynn Lea St 14221
Lynncrest Ter 14225
Lynndon Ln 14221
Lynnette Ct 14227
Lynwood Ave 14219
Lyth Ave 14208
Lyth Rd 14218
S Lyth St 14219
M And T Plz 14203
Mable Ct 14203
Macamley St 14220
Macarthur Dr 14221
Mackinaw St
1-253 14204
255-275 14204
276-399 14210
Madison Ave
1-199 14219
1-199 14218
Madison St
1-50 14210
51-280 14206
281-470 14212
471-599 14211
Madonna Ln 14225
Mafalda Dr 14215
Magnolia Ave 14220
Magnolia St 14218
Mahogany Dr 14221
Main St
1-1045 14203
1-999 14224
2-1044 14202
1046-1730 14209
1731-2110 14208
2111-3499 14214
3500-3638 14226
3640-5050 14226
5051-8900 14221
Main Place Mall 14202
Main Place Tower 14202
Maishoss St 14227
Maitland Dr 14221
Majestic Cir 14226
Majestic Ter 14218
Mallard Ct 14228
Mallard Roost 14221
Malsch St 14207
Malta Pl 14201
Manchester Pl 14213
Mandan St 14216
Mang Ave 14217
Manhart St 14215
Manhasset St 14210
Manhattan Ave
1-202 14215
203-399 14214
Manitoba St 14206
Manko Ln 14227
Manlon Ter 14225
Mann St 14206
Manning Rd 14226
Manor Oak Dr 14228
Manser Dr 14226
Mansion Ave 14206
Mansperger Pl 14224
Manton Pl 14207
Maple Ave 14219
Maple Ct 14226
N Maple Dr 14221
Maple Rd
1-2399 14221
3800-4699 14226
Maple St
1-99 14218
59-97 14204
99-399 14204
Maple Grove Ave 14218
Maple Ridge Ave 14215
Mapleleaf Dr 14221
E, N & W Maplemere Rd 14221
Mapleton Dr 14221
Mapleview Dr 14226
Mapleview Rd 14225
Maplewood Ave 14224
Mar Del Way 14221
Marann Ter 14206
Marbeth Ct 14220
Marcia Ln 14221
Margaret Rd 14226
Maria Ln 14227
Maricrest Dr 14228
Marie Ave 14227
Mariemont Ave 14220
Marigold Ave 14215
Marilla St 14220
Marilyn Dr
1-99 14225
1-199 14224
Marina Park S 14202
Marine Dr
1-299 14228
1-299 14202
Mariner St 14201
Marion Rd 14226
Marion St 14207
Marjann Ter 14223
Marjorie Dr 14223
Mark St 14204
E & W Market St 14204
Markham Pl 14216
Markus Dr 14225
Marlene Dr 14225
Marlin Dr 14224
Marlow Rd 14224
Marlowe Ave 14219
Marne Rd 14215
Marquette Ave 14217
Marrano Pkwy 14227
Marsdale Rd 14215
Marseille Ave 14224
Marshall St 14211
Martha Ave 14215
Martha Jackson Pl 14214
Martin Ave 14219
Martin Rd 14218
Martin Luther King Park 14211
Martinique Dr 14227
Martinvale Rd 14225
Marvin St 14204
Mary B Talbert Blvd 14204
Mary Johnson Blvd 14204
Marycrest Ln 14224
Maryknoll Dr 14218
Maryland St 14201
Maryner Homes 14201
Maryner Towers 14201
Maryon Dr 14220
Maryvale Dr 14225
Mason St 14213
Massachusetts Ave 14213
Masten Ave
1-65 14204
66-699 14209
Matejko St 14206
Matthew Ln 14225
Matthews St 14204
Maurice St 14210
May St 14211
Mayberry Dr E & W 14227
Mayer Ave 14207
Mayfair Ct 14225
Mayfair Ln
1-24 14201
2-22 14221
24-199 14221
Mayfield Ct & Dr 14224
Maynard Dr 14226
Mayville Ave 14217
Maywood Pl 14210
Mccarley Walk 14204
Mccarthy Dr 14211
Mcclellan Cir 14220
Mcconkey Dr 14223
Mcdonald Hall 14214
Mcguire St 14218
Mcgurk Ave 14219
Mcintosh Pl 14228
Mckenzie Ct 14227
Mckesson Pkwy 14225
Mckibben St 14211
Mckinley Ave
1-499 14217
1-499 14221
Mckinley Mall 14219
Mckinley Pkwy
S3261-S4225 14219
1-1100 14220
1101-1399 14218
3261-4225 14219
Mckinley Plz 14219
Mckinley Parkway Ext 14218
Mcnair Rd 14221
Mcnaughton Ave 14225
Mcneeley Way 14204
Mcparlin Ave 14225
Meadow Dr 14224
N Meadow Dr 14214
Meadow Ln
1-299 14223
1-99 14218
Meadow Pl 14225
Meadow Rd 14216
Meadow Lea Dr 14226
Meadow Stream Ct & Dr 14226
Meadowbrook Dr 14218
Meadowbrook Pkwy
1-210 14206
4200-4299 14219
N Meadowbrook Pkwy 14206
Meadowbrook Rd 14221
Meadowdale Ln 14224
Meadowlawn Rd 14225
Meadowview Ln 14221
Meadowview Pl 14214
Meaford Rd 14215
Medford Pl 14216
Medina St 14206
Meech Ave 14208
Melbourne Ct & Pl 14222
E & W Melcourt Dr 14225
Melissa Renee Ct 14221
Melody Ln 14225
Melrose Rd 14221
Melrose St
1-130 14220
131-299 14210
Melroy Ave 14218
Melvin Pl 14210
Memorial Dr
1-200 14206
201-499 14212
Mendola Ave 14215
Merallew Ave 14215
Mercer Ave 14214
Mergenhagen St 14210
Meriden St 14220
Merrihurst Dr 14221
Merrimac St 14214
Merrymont Rd 14225
Mesmer Ave 14220
Metcalfe St 14206
Meyer Rd
1-499 14226
101-397 14224
399-499 14224
Miami Pkwy 14225
Miami St 14204
Michael Ave 14212
Michael Pl 14218
Michael Rd 14224
Michael Hall 14214
Michelle Dr 14218
Michigan Ave
1-230 14204
231-1069 14203
1070-1599 14209
S Michigan Ave 14203
Middlebury Ln 14216
Middlesex Rd 14216
Midland Ave 14223
Midland Dr 14225
Midland St 14220
Midshore Dr 14219
Midvale Ave 14215
Midway Ave 14215
Milburn St 14212
Mildred Dr 14225
Mildred St 14214
Milestrip Rd 14219
Milford St 14220
Military Rd
1-695 14207
696-785 14216
786-1999 14217
Mill Rd 14224
Mill St 14221
Millbrook Ct & Dr 14221
Miller Ave
1-199 14219
1-140 14212
100-299 14224
141-299 14211
Millersport Hwy
600-1299 14226
1300-2185 14221
3900-3912 14228
3914-4399 14228
Millhurst Rd 14218
Millicent Ave 14215
Millrace Ct & St N 14221
Mills St
2-175 14212
176-399 14211
Milnor Ave 14218
E Milnor Ave 14218
Milnor St 14204
Milsom Ave 14227
Milton Ave 14224
Milton St
1-199 14210
1-199 14221
Mineral Springs Rd
1-375 14210
376-1399 14224
Ming Ct 14225
Minnesota Ave
1-210 14214
211-699 14215
Minnetonka Rd 14220
Minton St 14210
Miriam Ave 14219
Mississippi St 14203
Mitchell Pl 14218
Mockingbird Ct 14228
Modern Ave 14218
Moeller St 14211
Mohawk St 14224
E Mohawk St 14203
W Mohawk St 14202
Mohican Ave
1-99 14208
100-199 14211
Mohr St 14212
Molnar Ct & Dr 14224
Mona Dr 14226
Monarch Dr 14226
Monroe Ave 14224
Monroe Dr 14221
Monroe St
1-13 14210
2-12 14218
14-31 14218
28-50 14210
33-49 14218
51-280 14206
281-490 14212
491-599 14211
Montana Ave 14211
Montcalm St 14214
Montclair Ave 14215
Monterey Ln 14225
Montfort Dr 14225
Montgomery St
1-50 14210
51-199 14206
Monticello Pl 14214
Montrose Ave
1-175 14214
176-799 14223
Moore Ave 14223
Moore St 14204
Moorman Dr 14225
Moreland St 14206
Morgan Pkwy 14221
Morgan Rd 14220
Morgott Ave 14224
Morley Pl 14209
Morningside Ln 14221
Morningstar Ct 14221
Morris Ave 14214
E Morris Ave 14214
Morris Cres 14224
Mortimer St 14204
Morton Dr 14226
Moselle St
1-395 14211
396-699 14215
Mosey Ln 14219
Mosside Loop 14224
Moulton Ave 14223
Mount Vernon Ave 14210
Mount Vernon Rd
1-550 14226
551-799 14215
Msgr Valente Dr 14206
Muck St 14218
Mulberry St 14204
Mumford St 14220
Mundy Ave 14219
Muriel Dr 14224
Museum Ct 14216
Myers Rd 14218
Myers St 14211
Myron Ave 14217
Myrtle Ave
1-399 14204
1-99 14218
Mystic St 14220
Nadine Dr 14225
Nagel Dr 14225
Nancy Ln 14228
Nancy Pl 14227
Nancycrest Ln 14224
Nandale Dr 14227
Nantucket Dr E & W 14225
Naples Cir 14228
Naples Dr 14224
Naples Ln 14228
Narragansett Rd 14220
Nash Rd 14217
Nash St
1-9 14204
2-8 14206
10-30 14206
31-31 14204
32-32 14206
33-36 14204
37-199 14206
Nason Pkwy 14218
Nassau Ave 14217
Nassau Ct 14225
Nassau Ln 14225
Nature Cove Ct 14221
Navaho Pkwy 14210
Naval Park Cv 14202
Navel Ave 14211
Neibert Pl 14225
Nelson Ave 14219
Nelson Pl 14218
Neubauer Ct 14224
Neumann Pkwy 14223
Nevada Ave 14211
New Rd 14228
New Amsterdam Ave 14216
New Babcock St 14206
New Southgate Rd 14215
Newburgh Ave
1-160 14211
161-499 14215
Newcastle Dr 14221
Newell Pl 14224
Newell St 14206
Newfield St 14207
Newgate Rd 14226
Newman Pl 14210
Newman St 14218
Newport Ave
1-74 14216
75-99 14225
News Plz 14203
Newton St 14212
Niagara Plz 14202
Niagara Sq 14202
Niagara St
50-119 14202
120-650 14201
726-776 14213
778-1620 14213

1621-2959 14207
Niagara Falls Blvd
1-150 14214
151-1409 14226
152-998 14223
1411-2779 14228
2781-3599 14228
Niagara Frontier Food Termin 14206
Nicholson St
1-140 14214
141-199 14216
Nickel Way 14228
Niles Ave 14219
Nina Pl 14215
Nina Ter 14224
Noel Dr 14221
Nokomis Pkwy 14225
Nora Ln 14209
Norfolk Ave 14215
Norfred Dr 14218
Norine Dr 14225
Norma Dr 14218
Norma Pl 14214
Normal Ave
1-65 14201
66-142 14213
144-599 14213
Norman Ave 14210
Norman Pl 14226
Norman Way 14218
Normandy Ave 14225
Normandy Ct 14224
Norris St 14207
North Ave 14224
North Dr
1-199 14226
1-313 14216
1-499 14218
315-399 14216
North Ln 14207
North St
1-99 14202
100-399 14201
4200-4299 14219
E North St
1-174 14203
175-400 14204
401-539 14211
541-699 14211
Northampton St
1-200 14209
201-630 14208
632-674 14211
676-1099 14211
Northcrest Ave 14225
Northern Pkwy 14225
Northfield Pl 14226
Northland Ave
1-440 14208
441-820 14211
821-1299 14215
Northledge Dr 14226
Northpointe Pkwy 14228
Northridge Dr 14224
W Northrup Pl 14214
Northumberland Ave 14215
Northwood Ave 14224
Northwood Dr
1-499 14223
1-2299 14221
Norwalk Ave 14216
Norway Park 14208
Norwood Ave 14222
Norwood Dr
1-299 14224
4500-4699 14221
Nottingham Ct 14216
Nottingham Ter
1-55 14216
57-399 14216
8400-8799 14221
Nugget Dr 14225
Oak Ct 14226
Oak St 14203
N Oak St 14203
Oak Leaf Ln 14221
Oakbrook Dr
1-399 14221
1-399 14224
Oakdale Ln 14221
Oakdale Pl 14210
Oakfield Ln 14221
Oakgrove Ave
1-100 14208
101-199 14214
Oakgrove Dr 14221
Oakhill Dr 14224
Oakhurst Ave 14220
Oakland Pl 14222
Oakland Rd 14221
Oakmont Ave 14215
Oakridge Ave 14217
Oakridge Dr
1-99 14221
1-99 14224
Oakvale Blvd 14223
Oakview Dr 14221
Oakway Ln 14221
Oakwood Ave 14219
Oakwood Dr
1-399 14221
1-99 14227
4100-4299 14221
E Oakwood Pl 14214
W Oakwood Pl 14214
Oberlin Ave 14211
Oconnell Ave
1-170 14204
171-299 14210
Oconnor Ave 14220
October Ln 14228
Odell St 14218
Oehman Blvd 14225
N Ogden St
1-375 14206
376-499 14212
S Ogden St
1-149 14210
150-799 14206
Ohio St
1-200 14203
201-525 14204
526-899 14203
Ojibwa Cir 14202
Okell St 14220
Olcott Ave 14220
Olcott Pl 14225
Olcott St 14218
Old Bailey Ave 14210
Old Broadway 14227
Old Farm Cir
1-99 14218
1-199 14221
Old Hickory Ln 14221
Old Indian Rd 14227
Old Lyme Dr 14221
Old Maryvale Dr 14225
Old Niagara Falls Blvd 14228
Old Orchard St 14221
Old Spring Ln 14221
Old Union Rd 14227
Olde Ivy Dr 14221
Olean Ave 14224
Olga Pl 14206
Olin Ln 14218
Olive Ln 14221
Olney Dr W 14226
Olsen St 14206
Olympic Ave
1-499 14215
4900-5199 14219
Olympic Towers 14202
Oneida St 14206
Onondaga Ave 14220
Ontario Dr 14225
Ontario St
1-700 14207
701-899 14217
Ora Wrighter Dr 14204
Oraderiv Ave 14219
Orange Ave 14218
Orange St 14204
Orbit Dr 14228
Orchard Ave
1-199 14219
1-199 14224
Orchard Dr 14223
Orchard Pl
1-299 14225
1-99 14214
1-399 14218
Orchard St 14221
Orchard Walk 14221
Orchard Park Rd 14224
Oregon Pl 14207
Organ Cres 14224
Oriole Pl 14225
Orlando St 14210
Orleans Ct 14224
Orleans St 14215
Orman Pl 14210
Orson Pl 14216
Orton Pl 14201
Oschawa Ave 14210
Osgood Ave 14224
Otis Pl 14209
Overlook Dr 14221
Owahn Pl 14210
Oxford Ave
1-299 14226
1-299 14209
Oxford Ct 14204
Pacecrest Ct 14224
Pacific Ave 14218
Pacific St 14207
Paderewski Dr 14212
Page St 14207
Paige Ave 14223
Palermo Cir 14228
Palm St 14218
Palmdale Dr 14221
Palmer Ave 14217
Palos Pl 14215
Pamela Ct 14224
Panama Ln 14225
Pannell St 14214
Pansy Pl 14208
E Parade Ave 14211
N Parade Ave 14211
W Parade Ave 14208
E Parade Cir 14211
Paradise Ct 14225
Paramount Pkwy 14223
Parish Rd 14225
Park Ave 14219
N Park Ave
1-399 14216
1-99 14225
S Park Ave
1-202 14203
203-575 14204
576-928 14210
930-1074 14210
1076-2440 14220
2441-3360 14218
3361-4599 14219
Park Cir 14226
Park Dr 14221
Park Ln 14224
Park Pl 14227
Park Rd 14223
Park St
1-199 14201
1-99 14227
Park Club Ln 14221
Park Edge Dr 14225
Park Forest Dr 14221
Park Lane Ct 14221
Park Lane Villas Ct & Dr 14224
Park Meadow Dr 14224
Parkdale Ave 14213
Parker Ave
1-10 14206
11-111 14214
113-147 14214
200-251 14206
228-251 14214
252-284 14206
253-265 14214
267-287 14214
285-285 14206
287-310 14206
289-295 14214
297-395 14216
311-395 14206
312-340 14206
312-388 14216
390-398 14206
397-599 14216
N Parker Ave 14216
Parker Blvd 14223
Parker Hall 14214
Parkhaven Dr 14228
Parkhurst Blvd 14223
Parkledge Dr 14226
Parkridge Ave 14215
Parkside Ave
1-380 14214
381-1060 14216
1062-1088 14214
1090-1199 14214
Parkside Cir 14227
Parkside Ct 14214
Parkside Dr 14224
Parktrail Ln 14227
Parkview Ave
1-199 14210
1-99 14218
Parkview Ter 14225
Parkwood Ave 14217
Parkwood Dr 14226
N & S Parrish Ct & Dr 14228
Partridge Ln 14224
Partridge Run 14228
Parwood Dr 14227
Pasadena Pl 14221
Pasha Ct 14221
Passagrille Dr 14228
Patrice Ter 14221
Patricia Dr 14224
Patricia Ln 14227
Patrick Ln 14225
Patton Ln 14225
Patton Pl 14221
Paul Dr 14228
Paul Pl
1-2 14219
3-99 14210
Paula Dr 14225
Pauline St 14214
Pavonia St 14207
Pawnee Pkwy 14210
Paxford Pl 14224
Payne Ave 14220
Payson Ave 14220
Peabody St 14210
Peace St 14211
Peace Bridge Plz 14213
Peach St
1-27 14218
26-28 14204
29-29 14218
30-399 14204
Peach Tree Rd 14225
Peachrow Ln 14225
Peadeld St 14206
Pearce Dr 14226
Pearl Ave
1-199 14219
5-5 14218
7-69 14218
71-85 14218
91-109 14219
Pearl St
1-299 14224
65-599 14202
N Pearl St 14202
Pebble Creek Dr 14227
Peck St 14212
Peckham St 14206
W Peckham St 14204
Peconic St 14220
Peinkofer Dr 14225
Pelham Dr 14214
Pellman Pl 14218
Pembina St 14220
Pembroke Ave 14215
Pendennis Pl 14225
Pendlewood Dr 14225
Penfield St 14213
Penhurst Park 14222
Pennington Ct 14228
Pennock Pl 14225
Pennsylvania St 14201
Penny Ln 14228
Penwood Dr 14227
Peoria Ave 14206
Peoria St 14207
Peppertree Dr 14228
Peppy Pl 14225
Peremont Pl 14210
Peridot Pl 14227
Perkins Pl 14213
Perry St
1-99 14203
100-525 14204
526-1399 14210
Pershing Ave
1-130 14211
131-299 14208
Persia St 14211
Person St 14212
Peru Pl 14206
Petan Dr 14225
Peter St 14207
Peters Cir 14224
Peterson St 14211
Pfohl Pl 14221
Pfohl Rd 14225
Pfohl Ter 14221
Pharaohs Ct 14221
Pheasant Ln 14227
Pheasant Run Rd 14228
Phelps St 14214
Philadelphia St 14207
Philip Dr
1-20 14227
9-19 14228
21-99 14228
Phillips Pl 14218
Phyllis Ave 14215
Phyllis Dr 14224
Pickford Ave 14223
Pielaren Rd 14226
Piellone Dr 14228
Pierce Ct 14209
Pierce St
1-199 14206
1-99 14218
S Pierce St 14206
Pierpont Ave 14221
Pin Oak Dr 14221
Pinchot Ct 14228
Pinderiv Ave 14222
Pine Cir 14225
Pine Ct 14221
Pine Ct N 14224
Pine Park 14225
Pine St
1-399 14204
1-199 14218
N Pine St 14204
Pine Acres Ct 14221
Pine Cove Dr 14224
Pine Harbor Walk 14201
Pine Loch Ln 14221
Pine Ridge Rd
1-95 14211
97-149 14211
151-415 14225
Pine Ridge Ter 14225
Pine Ridge Heritage Blvd 14225
Pine Tree Ln 14224
Pine Valley Ct 14224
Pinebrook Ave 14221
Pinehurst Ave 14225
E Pinelake Ct & Dr 14221
Pinestone Ct 14221
Pinevale Ct 14225
Pineview Ct 14224
Pineview Dr 14228
Pinewood Dr 14224
Pinewood Ter 14225
Pink St 14206
Pino Alto Ct 14221
Pino Verde Ln 14221
Plarlest St 14211
Playter St 14212
Plaza Dr 14221
Pleasant Pkwy 14206
N Pleasant Pkwy 14206
Pleasant Pl 14208
Pleasant St 14225
Pleasantview Ln 14224
Plymouth Ave
1-140 14201
142-170 14201
171-799 14213
Plymouth Pl 14221
Poinciana Pkwy 14225
Point St 14218
Polish Ct & Pl 14210
Pomeroy St 14210
Pomona Pl 14210
Ponderosa Dr 14221
S Pontiac St 14206
Pontrado Rd 14224
Pool Plz 14223
Pooley Pl 14213
Poplar Ave 14211
Poplar Ct 14226
Portage St 14208
Porter Ave 14201
Portland St 14220
Portside 14202
Post Rd 14221
Potomac Ave
1-500 14213
501-750 14222
751-899 14209
Potters Rd
1-189 14220
191-575 14220
576-799 14224
Poultney Ave 14215
Powers Rd 14219
Prairie Ave 14207
Pratt St 14204
Preble Ct 14224
Prenatt St 14210
Presidents Walk 14221
Presidio Pl 14221
Preston Rd 14215
Pries Ave 14220
Prime St 14202
Primrose Dr 14225
Primrose Ln 14221
Prince Of Wales Ct 14221
Princess Dr 14225
Princess Ln 14224
Princeton Ave 14226
Princeton Blvd 14217
Princeton Ct 14225
Princeton Pl 14210
Pritchard St 14210
Pritchard Hall 14214
Privet Dr 14221
Proctor Ave 14215
Progressive Ave 14207
Promenade Ln 14221
Prospect Ave
55-540 14201
541-671 14213
673-925 14213
927-999 14213
Prospect Pl 14218
Pulaski St
1-199 14206
1-99 14218
Pullman Ave 14217
Pullman Pl 14212
Purdy St 14208
Putnam St 14213
S Putnam St 14213
Putnam Way 14228
Quantico Ct 14221
Queen St 14206
Queen Anns Gate 14222
Queens Dr
1-99 14225
1-99 14224
Quincy St 14212
Rabin Ter 14201
Race St
1-299 14207
1-99 14224
Rachel Ct 14228
Rachel Vincent Way 14216
Rachelle Dr 14227
Radcliffe Rd 14214
Raintree Ct 14221
Ralston Ave 14217
Ramona Ave 14220
Ramsdell Ave 14216
Rana Ct 14221
Ranch Trl W 14221
Rand Ave 14216
Randolph Ave 14211
Randwood Dr 14221
Randwood Dr N 14221
Randwood Ln 14216
Randy Way 14227
Rankin Rd 14226
Rano St 14207
Ransier Dr 14224
Raphael Ct 14221
Rapin Pl 14211
Ravenswood Ter 14225
Rawlins Ave 14211
Raymond Ave 14227
Raymond Dr 14219
Reading St 14220
Rebecca Dr 14221
Rebecca Park 14207
Rebecca Way 14224
Red Clover Ave 14221
Red Jacket Pkwy 14220
Red Jacket St 14210
Red Maple Ct 14228
Red Oak Dr
1-99 14227
1-499 14221
Red Tail Run 14221
Reddon St 14218
Redmond Ave 14216
Redwood Dr 14225
Redwood Ter 14221
Reed Ave 14218
Reed St
1-140 14212
141-399 14211
Rees St 14213
Regency Ct 14226
Regent St 14206
Regina Pl 14208
Reiman St
1-200 14206
201-599 14212
Rein Rd 14225
Reist St 14221
Rejtan St 14206
Relich Ave 14218
Remington Pl 14210
Remoleno St 14220
Renaissance Dr 14221
Rene Dr 14224
Rensch Rd 14228
Renwood Ave 14217
Reo Ave 14211
Republic St 14204
Reservation St 14207
Reserve Rd 14224
Revere Pl 14214
Review Pl 14207
Rex Pl 14211
Rey St 14204
Reynolds Rd 14224
Rhode Island St 14213
Rich Pl 14218
Rich St 14211
Richard Dr 14206

Richfield Ave 14220
Richfield Rd 14221
Richlawn Ave 14215
Richmond Ave
- 1-999 14222
- 4900-5199 14219

Richmond Rd 14226
Rickert Ave 14211
Ridge Ct N 14221
Ridge Rd
- 1-1412 14218
- 1414-1598 14218
- 1700-3099 14224

Ridge Lea Rd
- 3800-4200 14228
- 4201-4399 14226

Ridge Park Ave 14211
Ridgewood Cir 14218
Ridgewood Dr 14226
Ridgewood Rd 14220
Riffel Ter 14227
Riggs St 14219
Riley St
- 1-185 14209
- 186-630 14208
- 631-799 14211

Rinewalt St 14221
Ripley Pl 14213
Ritt Ave 14216
Rittling Blvd 14220
River Rd 14207
River Rock Dr 14207
Riverdale Ave 14207
Rivermist Dr 14202
Riverside Ave & Park 14207
Riverview Pl 14210
Roanoke Pkwy 14210
Robert Ct 14225
Robert Rich Way 14213
Roberts Ave 14206
Robie St 14214
Robin Ct 14224
Robin Ln 14224
Robin Rd
- 501A-501D 14228
- 502E-502L 14228
- 503M-503P 14228
- 504A-504B 14228
- 505C-505F 14228
- 506G-506J 14228
- 507A-507D 14228
- 508E-508H 14228
- 509A-509B 14228
- 510C-510F 14228
- 511G-511J 14228
- 825A-825H 14228
- 826A-826H 14228
- 827A-827H 14228
- 828A-828H 14228
- 847A-847H 14228
- 848A-848H 14228
- 849A-849H 14228
- 860A-860H 14228
- 861A-861H 14228
- 862A-862H 14228
- 910E-910H 14228
- 911A-911D 14228
- 912M-912P 14228
- 913G-913N 14228
- 914C-914F 14228
- 915A-915B 14228
- 916M-916P 14228
- 917E-917L 14228
- 918A-918D 14228
- 919Q-919R 14228
- 920M-920P 14228
- 921E-921L 14228
- 922A-922D 14228
- 923E-923H 14228
- 924A-924D 14228
- 926I-926J 14228
- 927E-927H 14228
- 928A-928D 14228
- 930M-930P 14228
- 931E-931L 14228
- 932A-932D 14228
- 933E-933H 14228
- 934A-934D 14228
- 935I-935J 14228
- 936E-936H 14228
- 937A-937D 14228
- 1-960 14228

Robin Hill Dr 14221
Robins St 14220
E Robinson Rd 14228
Rock St 14221
Rockdale Dr 14228
Rockford Pl 14221
N & S Rockingham Way 14228
Rockleigh Dr 14225
Rockne Rd 14223
Rockwell Rd 14213
Rodman Rd 14218
Rodney Ave 14214
Roebling Ave 14215
Roeder St 14211
Roehrer Ave 14208
Roesch Ave 14207
Roetzer St 14211
Roger Chaffee Dr 14228
Rogers Ave 14211
Rogers Dr 14225
Rohe St 14211
Rohr St 14211
Roland Ave 14218
Roland St 14212
Rolling Hills Dr 14224
Rolling Woods Ln 14224
Rollingwood St 14221
Roma Ave 14215
Roman Ln 14226
Rommel Ave 14212
Rondelay Ct & Dr 14227
Roosevelt Ave
- 1-199 14215
- 1-99 14224

Rosalia St 14216
Rosary Ave 14218
Rosary Blvd 14225
Rose Ave 14224
Rose Ct 14226
Rose St 14204
Rosedale Blvd 14226
Rosedale Dr 14225
Rosedale St 14207
Rosemary Ave 14216
Rosemead Ln 14227
Rosemont Ave 14217
Rosemont Dr 14226
Rosetta Petruzzi Way 14201
Roseview Ave 14219
Roseville St 14210
Rosewood Dr
- 1-99 14221
- 1-299 14224

Rosewood Ter 14225
Rosie Ln 14225
Roslyn St
- 1-160 14211
- 161-399 14215

Ross Ave 14207
S Rossler Ave 14206
Roswell Ave 14207
Roswell Rd 14215
Rotary Row 14201
Rother Ave
- 1-200 14212
- 201-399 14211

E & W Rouen Dr 14227
Round Trail Rd 14218
Rounds Ave 14215
Roundwood Ct 14228
Rowan Rd 14215
Rowland Ave 14225
Rowley Ave 14217
Rowley Holw 14227
Rowley Rd 14227
Roxborough Ave 14225
Roxbury Dr 14221
Royal Ave 14207
Royal Pkwy 14221
Royal Pkwy E 14221
Royal Pkwy W 14221
Royal Coach Rd 14224
Royal Palm Dr 14225
Royal York Cir 14224
Royalwoods Ct 14221
Roycroft Blvd
- 1-450 14226
- 451-699 14225

S Roycroft Blvd 14225
Roycroft Dr 14224
Rubino Ct 14221
Rudolph St 14218
Rue Madeleine 14221
Rugby Rd 14216
Ruhl Ave 14207
Ruhland Ave 14211
Rumsey Ln & Rd 14209
Rumson Rd 14228
N Rushford Ln 14227
Rushford Hollow Dr 14227
Ruskin Rd 14226
Ruspin Ave 14215
Russell St 14214
Rustic Pl 14211
Ruth Ave 14226
Ruth Dr 14225
Rutland Ave 14212
Rutland St 14220
S Ryan St 14210
Saber Ln 14221
Sable Palm Dr 14225
Sagamore Ter 14214
Sage Ave 14210
Sagewood Ter 14221
Saint Andrews Walk 14222
Saint Boniface Rd 14225
Saint Catherines Ct 14222
Saint Charles Ct 14221
Saint Clair St 14204
Saint Davids Dr 14224
Saint Felix Ave 14227
Saint Florian St 14207
Saint Francis Pl 14207
Saint Georges Sq 14222
Saint Gregory Ct 14221
Saint James Pl
- 1-299 14222
- 1-99 14218

Saint James Rd 14225
Saint Joan Ln 14227
Saint Johns Ave 14223
Saint Johns Pl
- 1-99 14201
- 1-99 14218

Saint Johns Parkside St 14210
Saint Joseph Ave 14211
Saint Jude Dr 14218
Saint Jude Ter 14224
Saint Lawrence Ave 14216
Saint Louis Ave 14211
Saint Louis Pl 14202
Saint Lucia Ln 14225
Saint Lucian Ct 14225
Saint Margarets Ct 14216
Saint Martins Pl 14220
Saint Marys Dr 14218
Saint Marys Rd 14211
Saint Marys St 14225
Saint Paul Ct 14225
Saint Paul Mall 14209
Saint Paul St 14218
Saint Ritas Ln 14221
Saint Stephens Pl 14210
Salem Dr 14219
Salem St 14220
Salisbury Ave 14219
Sally Mae Cunningham Dr 14201
Samantha Way 14227
Samuel Dr 14225
Sanctuary Ct 14221
Sand St 14218
Sanders Rd 14216
Sandhurst Ct & Ln 14221
Sandpiper Ct 14228
Sandra Dr
- 1-199 14218
- 1-199 14225

Sandrock Rd 14207
Sandstone Dr 14225
Sandy Ln 14227
Sanford St 14214
Santin Dr 14225
Sarabel Ct 14225
Sarah Pl 14218
Saranac Ave 14216
Saratoga Rd 14226
E Saratoga Rd 14221
Saratoga St 14207
Sargent Dr 14226
Satinwood Dr 14225
Sattler Ave 14211
Savona St 14210
Saxony Pl 14219
Saybrook Pl 14209
Sayre St 14207
Scajaquada St
- 200-250 14215
- 252-498 14211

Scamridge Curv 14221
Scarbora Dr 14221
Schaefer Rd 14218
Schauf Ave 14211
Scheu Park 14211
Schiller St
- 1-300 14206
- 301-499 14212

Schlenker Ave 14225
Schlenker St 14212
Schmarbeck Ave 14212
Schoedel Ave 14225
Schoelles Rd 14228
Schoellkopf Hall 14214
School St
- 1-99 14224
- 1-99 14221
- 1-75 14217
- 2-98 14218
- 17-81 14213
- 77-99 14217
- 80-98 14217
- 83-125 14213
- 100-161 14217
- 100-199 14218
- 102-126 14213
- 128-129 14213
- 131-159 14213
- 162-399 14217

Schreck Ave 14215
Schuele Ave 14215
Schultz Rd 14224
Schuster Ave 14225
Schutrum St 14212
Schuyler St 14210
Scotia Rd 14218
Scott Dr 14221
Scott Pl 14225
Scott St
- 1-96 14203
- 97-399 14204

Scoville Ave 14206
Scrivner Dr 14227
Seabrook Dr 14221
Seabrook St 14207
Seal Pl 14218
Sears St 14212
Seattle St 14216
Sedgemoor Ct 14221
Segsbury Rd 14221
N & S Seine Dr 14227
Selkirk St 14210
Seminole Ln 14225
Seminole Pkwy
- 1-99 14210
- 1-199 14225

Seneca St
- 1-180 14203
- 181-570 14204
- 571-2540 14210
- 2541-5709 14224

N Seneca St 14224
Seneca Creek Rd 14224
Seneca Parkside 14210
Seneca Tower 14203
Service Bldg 14214
Seton Rd 14225
Seward St 14206
Seymour St 14210
Seymour H Knox Iii Plz 14203
Shade Tree Ct 14221
Shadow Rdg 14221
Shamokin Dr 14218
Shamrock Dr 14218
Shanley St 14206
Shannon Dr 14218
Sharon Ct 14225
Sharon Dr 14224
Sharon Pkwy 14218
Shawnee Ave 14215
Shawnee Pl 14224
Sheffield Ave 14220
Shelbourne Ct 14221
Shelby Dr 14225
Shenandoah Rd 14220
Shepard Ave 14217
Shepard St 14212
Sherbrooke Ave 14221
Sheridan Ave 14211
Sheridan Dr
- 1251-1650 14217
- 1651-2299 14223
- 2981-4095 14226
- 4096-8860 14221

Sheridan Hill Dr 14221
Sherman St
- 1-165 14206
- 166-425 14212
- 426-799 14211

Sherman Hall 14214
Sherrelwood Ct 14221
Sherwood Ct 14224
Sherwood Ln 14224
Sherwood St 14213
Shetland Dr 14221
Shevchenko Dr 14228
Shields Ave 14213
Ship Canal Pkwy 14218
Shirley Ave
- 1-599 14215
- 1-99 14225

Shirley Dr 14218
W Shore Ave 14211
S Shore Blvd 14218
N Shore Dr 14219
S Shore Dr 14219
Shoreham Pkwy 14216
Short St 14207
Shoshone St 14214
Shumway St
- 1-165 14206
- 166-299 14212

Siberling Dr 14225
Sibley Dr 14224
Sibley St 14220
Sidney St 14211
Sidway St 14210
Siegfried Dr 14221
Sienkiewicz Pl 14212
Sierra Dr 14225
Silo City Row 14203
Silver Ave 14219
Silver Fox Ct 14221
Silver Thorne Dr 14221
Silverdale Pl 14210
Simon Ave 14218
Simon St 14207
Simpson Dr 14225
Simsbury Dr 14225
Singer Dr 14224
Sirret St 14220
Skillen St 14207
Skinnersville Rd 14228
Sky Hi Dr 14224
Slade Ave 14224
Slate Creek Dr 14227
Smallwood Dr
- 1-399 14226
- 1-99 14224

Smallwood Ter 14225
Smith Dr 14218
Smith Rd 14228
Smith St
- 1-690 14210
- 1-99 14225
- 702-975 14206
- 976-1099 14212

Snyderwoods Ct 14226
W Sobieski Ave 14225
Sobieski St
- 1-192 14212
- 193-399 14211

Soldiers Pl 14222
Somersby Ct 14221
Somerton Ave 14217
Sonwil Dr 14225
South Ave 14224
South Dr
- 1-199 14226
- 1-199 14218

South Ln 14207
South St
- 1-9 14218
- 10-52 14204
- 54-198 14204

Southampton St
- 1-140 14209
- 141-299 14208

Southcrest Ave 14225
Southern Pkwy 14225
Southgate Dr 14224
Southgate Rd 14215
Southridge Dr 14224
Southside Pkwy
- 1-400 14220
- 401-599 14210

Southwestern Blvd 14224
Southwind Trl 14221
Southwood Dr
- 1-499 14223
- 1-199 14224

Spann St 14206
Spaulding St 14220
Spicebush Ln 14221
Spiess St 14211
Spillman Pl 14208
Spindrift Ct & Dr 14221
Sprenger Ave 14211
Spring St
- 1-699 14204
- 1-99 14218

E Spring St 14221
W Spring St 14221
Spring Meadow Dr 14221
Springfield Dr N & S 14225
Springville Ave 14226
Springwood Ct 14223
Spruce Rd 14226
Spruce St
- 1-199 14204
- 1-199 14218

Sprucewood Dr 14227
Sprucewood Ter 14221
Squire Hall 14214
Staats St 14202
Stamford Rd 14221
Standard Pkwy 14227
Standish Rd 14216
Stanislaus Ave 14225
Stanislaus St 14212
Stanley St 14206
Stanton St
- 1-165 14206
- 1-99 14221
- 166-299 14212

Starcrest Dr 14225
Starin Ave
- 1-260 14214
- 261-650 14216
- 651-999 14223

Starlite Ave 14227
Starwood Dr 14227
State St 14219
Stearns Ave 14218
N Steelawanna Ave 14218
Steiner Ave 14224
Steinway Ct 14221
Stephenson Ave 14224
Sterling Ave 14216
Stetson St 14206
Steven Dr 14227
Stevens Ave 14215
Stevenson Blvd 14226
Stevenson St
- 1-130 14220
- 131-299 14210

Stewart Ave 14211
Stewart St 14219
Stillwell Ave 14217
Stockbridge Ave 14215
Stone St 14212
Stoneboro Ave 14214
Stonecroft Ln 14226
Stonegate Ln 14221
Stonehaven Dr 14221
Stoneledge Ct 14221
Stoneleigh Ave 14223
Stoney St 14218
Stonham Way 14221
Stonybrook Ln 14221
Storz Ave 14208
Stradtman St
- 1-189 14206
- 190-299 14227

Straley Ave 14211
Strasbourg Dr 14227
Stratford Pl 14225
Stratford Rd 14216
Strathmore Ave 14220
Strauss St
- 1-160 14212
- 161-399 14211

Strawn Ave 14206
Sturbridge Ln 14221
Suburban Ct 14224
Sudbury Ln 14221
Sudbury Rd 14218
Suffolk St 14215
Sugar Berry Ln 14221
Sugnet Rd 14215
Sultans Ct 14221
Summer St
- 1-100 14209
- 101-350 14222
- 351-499 14213

Summer Hill Ct & Ln 14221
E & W Summerset Ln 14228
Summerview Rd 14221
Summerwood Ct 14223
Summit Ave
- 1-399 14214
- 1-399 14224

Summit Meadow Ave 14224
Sumner Pl 14211
Sun St 14215
Sunbriar Dr 14224
Sunbury Ct 14221
Sundown Trl 14221
Sundridge Dr 14228
Sunmist Sq 14228
Sunnyside Dr 14224
Sunnyside Pl 14207
Sunrise Blvd 14221
Sunrise Dr 14219
Sunrise Ter 14224
Sunset Ct 14228
Sunset Dr 14221
Sunset Rd 14227
Sunset St 14207
Sunset Creek Dr 14224
Sunshine Dr 14228
Surfside Pkwy 14225
Surrey Run 14221
Susan Dr 14221
W Susan Dr 14221
Susan Ln
- 1-99 14220
- 1-199 14225

Susquehanna Dr 14218
Sussex Ct 14204
Sussex St 14215

Sutherland Ct ... 14221
Sutton Ln ... 14214
Suzette Dr ... 14227
Swan Pl ... 14221
Swan St
1-93 ... 14203
94-136 ... 14218
95-167 ... 14203
95-145 ... 14218
138-138 ... 14203
140-146 ... 14218
148-166 ... 14203
168-570 ... 14204
571-799 ... 14210
Swanson Ter ... 14221
Sweeney St ... 14211
Sweet Ave
1-355 ... 14212
356-499 ... 14211
Sweet Bay Ln ... 14221
Sweet Home Rd
400-1199 ... 14226
1200-3599 ... 14228
Sweethaven Ct ... 14228
Sweetwood Dr N ... 14228
Swinburne St ... 14212
Swygert St ... 14218
Sycamore St
1-82 ... 14203
83-455 ... 14204
456-1165 ... 14212
1166-1499 ... 14211
Sydni Ln ... 14204
Sylvan Pkwy ... 14228
Symphony Cir ... 14201
Tacoma Ave
1-852 ... 14216
854-890 ... 14216
922-952 ... 14214
954-999 ... 14214
Tadio Pkwy ... 14225
Taft Pl ... 14214
Tamarack St ... 14220
Tamark Ct ... 14227
Tammy Ln ... 14225
Tampa Dr ... 14220
Tanglewood Dr
1-99 ... 14228
1-99 ... 14224
Tartan Ln ... 14221
Taunton Pl
1-430 ... 14216
432-684 ... 14216
686-714 ... 14214
716-799 ... 14214
Taverly Dr ... 14221
Taylor Ct ... 14224
Taylor Dr ... 14224
Taylor Pl ... 14220
Teakwood Ter ... 14221
Tech Dr ... 14221
Tee Ct ... 14221
Telfair Dr ... 14221
Temple Dr ... 14225
Templeton Ter ... 14202
Tennessee St ... 14204
Tennyson Ave ... 14216
Tennyson Ct ... 14221
Tennyson Rd ... 14221
Tennyson Ter ... 14221
Teresa Dr ... 14218
Teresa Pl ... 14210
Terrace Blvd ... 14224
Terri Trl ... 14219
Terry Ln ... 14225
Texas St
1-75 ... 14211
76-299 ... 14215
Thamesford Ct & Ln ... 14221
Thatcher Ave ... 14215
The Ave ... 14225
The Cmn ... 14221
The Grn ... 14224
The Spur ... 14221
The Courtyards ... 14221
The Paddock ... 14221
The Tradewinds ... 14221
The Village Grn ... 14221
Theatre Pl ... 14202
Theodore St ... 14211
Theresa Ct ... 14224
Theresa Dr ... 14227
Thielman Dr ... 14206
Thistle Ct ... 14224
Thistle Lea ... 14221
Thomas Dr ... 14224
Thomas St ... 14206
Thomas Ter ... 14218
Thomas Jefferson Ln ... 14226
Thompson St ... 14207
Thorncliff Rd ... 14223
Thorndale Ave ... 14224
Thornton Ave ... 14215
Thornwood Dr ... 14227
Thornwood Ln ... 14221
Thruway Ct & Mall ... 14225
Thruway Plaza Dr ... 14225
Thurston Ave
1-199 ... 14217
4900-5299 ... 14219
Tiernon Park ... 14223
Tifft St ... 14220
Tillinghast Pl ... 14216
Tillotson Ave ... 14225
Tillotson Pl ... 14223
Tim Tam Ter ... 14224
Tim Tam Trl ... 14219
Timberlane Ct & Dr ... 14221
Timon St
1-62 ... 14211
64-130 ... 14211
131-299 ... 14208
Timothy Ct ... 14224
Tindle Ave ... 14224
Tioga St ... 14216
Titus Ave
1-140 ... 14212
141-299 ... 14211
Tobey Hill Dr ... 14224
Toelsin Rd ... 14225
Toledo Pl ... 14216
Tolsma Pl ... 14225
Tomcyn Dr ... 14221
Tommie Ct ... 14224
Tonawanda St ... 14207
Tonawanda Creek Rd ... 14228
Topaz Dr ... 14227
Torraine Ct ... 14224
E & W Toulon Dr ... 14227
Tower St ... 14215
Towers Blvd ... 14227
Town Rd ... 14224
Townsend St
1-120 ... 14206
121-299 ... 14212
Townsend Hall ... 14214
Tracy Pkwy ... 14218
Tracy St ... 14201
Tracy Lynn Ln ... 14224
Trailing Dr ... 14221
Trammell Walk ... 14204
Transit Rd
1700-3398 ... 14224
4001-6597 ... 14221
6599-7000 ... 14221
7002-8530 ... 14221
Travers Blvd & Cir ... 14228
Traverse Blvd ... 14223
Traymore St ... 14216
Treebrooke Ct ... 14221
Treehaven Rd
1-299 ... 14215
1-199 ... 14224
E Treehaven Rd ... 14215
Trella Pl ... 14218
Trellis Ln ... 14226
Tremaine Ave ... 14217
Tremont Ave
1-99 ... 14213
1-499 ... 14217
Trent Sq ... 14225
Trenton Ave ... 14201
Trier Pl ... 14224
Trinity Pl ... 14201
Tristan Ln ... 14221
Trooper Paul Kurdys
Way ... 14225
Troupe St ... 14210
Trowbridge St ... 14220
Troy Del Way ... 14221
Troy View Ln ... 14221
Trudy Ln ... 14227
Truesdale Rd ... 14223
Tudor Blvd ... 14220
Tudor Pl ... 14222
Tudor Rd ... 14215
Tulane Rd ... 14217
Tupelo Ln ... 14228
E Tupper St ... 14203
W Tupper St
1-100 ... 14202
117-117 ... 14201
119-399 ... 14201
Turnberry Ct & Dr ... 14221
Turner Ave ... 14220
Tuscarora Rd ... 14220
Tuxedo Pl ... 14207
Twin Bridge Ln ... 14221
Twyla Pl ... 14223
Tyler St ... 14214
Tyrol Dr ... 14227
Uaw Grn Blvd ... 14207
Ullman St ... 14207
Unger Ave ... 14210
Union Cmn ... 14221
Union Pl
1-45 ... 14213
1-99 ... 14221
Union Rd
100-2350 ... 14224
2260-2272 ... 14227
2274-3300 ... 14227
3301-4999 ... 14225
N Union Rd ... 14221
S Union Rd ... 14221
S Union Ter ... 14221
Unionvale Rd ... 14225
University Ave
1-210 ... 14214
211-599 ... 14223
University Ct ... 14226
Upper East Ln ... 14207
Upper Terrace St ... 14202
Urban St ... 14211
E Utica St
1-165 ... 14209
166-590 ... 14208
591-799 ... 14211
W Utica St
1-100 ... 14209
101-425 ... 14222
426-614 ... 14213
616-698 ... 14213
Valerenw St ... 14220
Valley Dr ... 14224
Van Gorder St ... 14214
Van Rensselaer St ... 14210
Van Wyck St ... 14219
Vandalia St ... 14204
Vanderbilt St ... 14206
Vegola Ave ... 14225
Venice Cir ... 14228
Vera Ave ... 14225
Verdun Ave ... 14214
Verdun Pl ... 14225
Verel Ave ... 14218
Vermont Pl ... 14224
Vermont St ... 14213
Vern Ln ... 14227
Vernon Cir ... 14221
Vernon Dr ... 14225
Vernon Pl ... 14214
Verona St ... 14220
Verplanck St ... 14208
Veterans Pl ... 14227
Via Del Sole ... 14221
Via Foresta Ln ... 14221
Via Marina ... 14221
Via Pinto Dr ... 14221
Victor Pl ... 14208
Victoria Ave ... 14214
Victoria Blvd
1-316 ... 14217
1-199 ... 14225
317-499 ... 14217
Victory Ave ... 14218
Villa Ave ... 14216
Villa Park ... 14227
Villa Maria Rd ... 14224
Villa Moraine Dr ... 14225
Village Ln ... 14212
Village Gate Ct ... 14221
Village Park Dr ... 14221
Village Pointe Ln ... 14221
Village Station Cir ... 14221
Villas Dr E & W ... 14228
Vincennes St ... 14204
Vincent Ave
1-99 ... 14218
1-99 ... 14225
Vine Ln ... 14228
Vinewood Dr ... 14221
Viola Dr ... 14227
Viola Park ... 14208
Violet Ave ... 14226
Virgil Ave ... 14216
Virginia Pl ... 14202
Virginia Rd ... 14225
Virginia St
2-162 ... 14201
164-455 ... 14201
457-487 ... 14202
489-550 ... 14202
551-726 ... 14203
727-999 ... 14204
Viscount Dr ... 14221
Vista Ave ... 14221
Vita Ave ... 14227
Voorhees Ave
1-260 ... 14214
261-499 ... 14216
Vulcan St ... 14207
Wabash Ave
S3500-S3799 ... 14219
1-134 ... 14206
1-499 ... 14217
100-3799 ... 14219
Wade Ave ... 14214
Wadsworth St ... 14201
Wagner Ave
1-50 ... 14206
51-399 ... 14212
Wagner St ... 14206
Wainwright Ct ... 14221
Wainwright Rd ... 14215
Wakefield Ave ... 14214
Walden Ave
1-35 ... 14211
37-1359 ... 14211
1361-1399 ... 14211
1401-2899 ... 14225
Walden Ter ... 14211
Walden Galleria ... 14225
Wallace Ave
1-199 ... 14227
2-64 ... 14214
66-160 ... 14214
161-299 ... 14216
Walnut Rd ... 14224
Walnut St
1-129 ... 14218
130-399 ... 14204
Walter St ... 14210
Waltercrest Ter ... 14224
Walton Dr
1-380 ... 14226
381-599 ... 14225
Wanda Ave ... 14211
Wansfell Rd ... 14226
Warburton Pl ... 14223
Ward Ct ... 14220
Wardman Rd ... 14217
Warren Ave
1-299 ... 14224
1-199 ... 14212
1-499 ... 14217
S Warren Ave ... 14224
Warring Ave ... 14211
Warsaw St
1-99 ... 14206
1-299 ... 14218
Warwick Ave ... 14215
Washington Ave ... 14217
Washington Hwy ... 14226
Washington St
1-99 ... 14224
1-10 ... 14203
11-11 ... 14218
12-12 ... 14203
13-94 ... 14218
95-109 ... 14203
96-98 ... 14218
111-704 ... 14203
701-701 ... 14205
705-999 ... 14203
706-998 ... 14203
Wasmuth Ave ... 14211
Wasson Ave ... 14218
Wasson St ... 14210
Waterford Park ... 14221
Waterfront Cir ... 14202
Waterway Ln ... 14228
Watson St
1-50 ... 14210
51-290 ... 14206
291-399 ... 14212
Waverly Ave ... 14217
Waverly St ... 14208
Wayne Ave ... 14228
Wayne St ... 14207
Wayne Ter ... 14225
Wayside Ct ... 14226
Weaver St ... 14206
Weber Ave ... 14215
Weber Rd ... 14218
Wecker St ... 14215
Wedgewood Dr
1-299 ... 14227
1-60 ... 14224
61-256 ... 14221
62-198 ... 14224
Wedgewood Ter ... 14226
Wehrle Dr
1-775 ... 14225
776-8699 ... 14221
Weigand St ... 14224
Weimar St ... 14206
Weiss St
1-399 ... 14206
1-100 ... 14224
102-198 ... 14224
Welker St ... 14208
Wellington Ave ... 14223
Wellington Ct ... 14221
Wellington Rd
1-399 ... 14216
1-99 ... 14225
Wells Ave ... 14227
Wellworth Pl ... 14225
Welwyn Cir ... 14223
Wende St ... 14211
Wende Hall ... 14214
Wendel Ave ... 14223
Wendover Ave ... 14223
Wenner Rd ... 14221
Wenro Pl ... 14210
Wescott St ... 14210
Wesley Ave ... 14214
West Ave
S4100-S4199 ... 14219
1-399 ... 14201
300-499 ... 14224
401-1499 ... 14213
4100-4199 ... 14219
West Ln ... 14207
Westbrook Dr ... 14225
Westchester Blvd ... 14217
Westchester Dr ... 14225
Westchester Rd ... 14221
Westcliff Dr ... 14224
Westcliffe Dr ... 14228
Westfield Rd N ... 14226
Westgate Blvd ... 14224
Westgate Rd ... 14217
Westland Pkwy ... 14225
Westminster Ave ... 14215
Westminster Rd ... 14224
Westmoreland Rd ... 14226
Weston Ave ... 14215
Westport Ct ... 14221
Westvale Ct ... 14225
Westview Dr ... 14224
Westwind Ln ... 14228
Westwood Dr ... 14224
Westwood Rd ... 14221
Wetherstone Dr ... 14224
Wex Ave ... 14211
Weyand Ave ... 14210
Wheaton Dr ... 14225
Wheelock St ... 14206
White Ave ... 14219
White Rd ... 14225
Whitehall Ave ... 14220
Whitfield Ave ... 14220
Whitney Pl
1-299 ... 14201
1-299 ... 14227
Wichita Rd ... 14224
Wick St ... 14212
Wickendon Ct ... 14221
Wickham Dr ... 14221
Wiesner Rd ... 14218
Wik St ... 14221
Wilber Ave ... 14217
Wilbury Pl ... 14216
Wildwood Dr ... 14221
Wildwood Pl ... 14210
Wildy Ave ... 14211
Wiley Pl ... 14207
Wilkes Ave ... 14215
Wilkesbarre St ... 14218
Willert Park Ct ... 14204
Willet Rd
100-400 ... 14219
402-532 ... 14218
534-899 ... 14218
Willett St ... 14206
William St
1-100 ... 14203
101-465 ... 14204
466-1119 ... 14206
1121-2575 ... 14206
1200-1200 ... 14240
1202-2574 ... 14206
2576-3199 ... 14227
William L Gaiter Pkwy ... 14215
William Price Pkwy ... 14214
Williamsburg Sq ... 14221
Williamstowne Ct ... 14227
Willink Ave ... 14210
Willow Ct ... 14225
Willow Dr ... 14224
Willow Ln ... 14228
Willow Pl ... 14208
Willow St ... 14218
Willow Breeze Rd ... 14223
Willow Green Dr ... 14228
Willow Lane Ct ... 14228
Willow Ridge Dr ... 14228
Willow Wood Dr ... 14225
Willow Wood Park N ... 14226
Willow Wood Park S ... 14226
Willowbrook Dr ... 14221
Willowcrest Dr ... 14224
Willowdale Ave ... 14219
Willowdale Dr ... 14224
W Willowdale Dr ... 14224
Willowlawn Pkwy ... 14206
N Willowlawn Pkwy ... 14206
Willowlawn St ... 14214
Wilmuth Ave ... 14218
Wilshire Rd
1-99 ... 14217
1-199 ... 14225
Wilson Rd ... 14221
Wilson St
1-99 ... 14224
1-13 ... 14218
2-8 ... 14206
10-100 ... 14206
15-199 ... 14218
101-445 ... 14212
446-599 ... 14211
Wilton Pkwy ... 14223
Wiltshire Rd ... 14221
Wimbledon Ct & Ln ... 14224
Winchester Ave ... 14211
Winchester Pl ... 14217
Windcrest Dr ... 14225
Windermere Blvd ... 14226
Windham Way ... 14228
N Windmill Rd ... 14218
Windridge Ct ... 14221
Windsor Ave
1-199 ... 14226
1-299 ... 14209
Windsor Ct ... 14228
Windtree Ln ... 14224
Windwood Cts ... 14225
Winegar Pl ... 14210
Winfield Dr ... 14224
Wing Ct ... 14225
Wingate Ave ... 14216
Winkler Rd ... 14225
Winona St ... 14210
Winslow Ave
1-275 ... 14208
276-699 ... 14211
Winspear Ave
1-130 ... 14214
131-699 ... 14215
W Winspear Ave ... 14214
Winspear Rd ... 14224
Winstead Rd ... 14218
Winston Rd ... 14216
Winter St ... 14213
Wintergreen Pl ... 14218
Winterwood Ct ... 14223
Wisconsin Pl ... 14211
Wisteria Ave ... 14226
Woeppel St ... 14211
Wohlers Ave ... 14208
Woltz Ave
1-175 ... 14212
176-399 ... 14211
Wood Ave ... 14211
Wood St ... 14218
Woodbine Ave ... 14224
Woodbine Ct ... 14221
Woodbine Pl ... 14225
Woodbridge Ave ... 14214
Woodbury Dr ... 14226
Woodcliffe Ter ... 14215
Woodcrest Blvd ... 14223
Woodcrest Ct ... 14225
Woodcrest Dr
1-399 ... 14226
1-399 ... 14220
Woodell Ave ... 14211
Woodette Pl ... 14207
Woodgate Dr ... 14227
Woodhaven Rd ... 14226
Woodhurst Rd ... 14221
Woodland Dr ... 14223
Woodland Ter ... 14225
Woodlane Dr ... 14224
Woodlawn Ave
S3200-S4099 ... 14219
1-140 ... 14209
141-570 ... 14208
571-899 ... 14211
3101-3997 ... 14219
3999-4099 ... 14219
E Woodlawn Ave ... 14211
Woodlee Rd ... 14221
Woodley Rd ... 14215
Woodmar Ter ... 14224
Woodpointe Run ... 14221
Woodridge Ave ... 14225
Woodridge Dr ... 14228
Woodrow Pl ... 14225
Woodsedge Ct ... 14221
Woodside Ave ... 14220
W Woodside Ave ... 14220
N Woodside Ln ... 14221

S Woodside Ln ... 14221
Woodview Ct ... 14221
Woodward Ave
1-499 ... 14214
1-599 ... 14217
Woodward Cres ... 14224
Woodward Ct ... 14224
Woodward Dr ... 14224
Woodyard Way ... 14218
Worcester Pl ... 14215
World Ministry Ctr ... 14223
Worth St ... 14223
Wright Ave ... 14215
Wyandotte Ave ... 14207
Wynngate Ln ... 14221
Wyoming Ave ... 14215
Yale Ave ... 14226
Yale Pl ... 14210
Yeager Dr ... 14225
York St ... 14213
Yorktown Rd
1-199 ... 14226
1-99 ... 14225
Young St ... 14212
S Youngs Rd ... 14221
Yvette Dr ... 14227
Yvonne Ave ... 14225
Zeller Ln ... 14227
Zelmer St ... 14211
Zenner St ... 14211
Zent Ct ... 14225
Zimmerman Blvd ... 14223
Zittel St ... 14210
Zoerb Ave ... 14225
Zollars Ave ... 14220

NUMBERED STREETS

1st St ... 14227
3500-3799 ... 14219
2nd St
1-99 ... 14227
3600-3799 ... 14219
3rd Ave ... 14221
3rd St ... 14219
4th St
1-99 ... 14202
400-699 ... 14201
3600-3799 ... 14219
5th Ave ... 14221
5th St ... 14219
6th Ave ... 14221
6th St ... 14219
7th St
1-600 ... 14201
808-875 ... 14213
877-999 ... 14213
3600-3799 ... 14219
10th St ... 14201
14th St ... 14213
15th St ... 14213
16th St ... 14213
17th St ... 14213
18th St ... 14213
19th St ... 14213

CROTON ON HUDSON NY

General Delivery ... 10520

POST OFFICE BOXES MAIN OFFICE STATIONS AND BRANCHES

Box No.s
1 - 394 ... 10520
400 - 580 ... 10521
601 - 696 ... 10520
701 - 759 ... 10521
801 - 1001 ... 10520
8000 - 9998 ... 10521

NAMED STREETS

All Street Addresses ... 10520

EAST ELMHURST NY

POST OFFICE BOXES MAIN OFFICE STATIONS AND BRANCHES

Box No.s
1 - 599 ... 11369
1001 - 1440 ... 11370
690001 - 690800 ... 11369
701001 - 701440 ... 11370

NAMED STREETS

Astoria Blvd
7506-7998 ... 11370
8000-8599 ... 11370
8600-8798 ... 11369
8800-11100 ... 11369
11102-11298 ... 11369
Astoria Blvd N ... 11370
Astoria Blvd S ... 11370
Buell St ... 11369
Butler St ... 11369
Construction Way ... 11370
Couch Pl ... 11369
Curtis St ... 11369
Ditmars Blvd
4900-7799 ... 11370
9000-9998 ... 11369
10000-11000 ... 11369
11002-11098 ... 11369
Duntonso St ... 11369
Ericsson St ... 11369
Executive Cir ... 11370
Gillmore St ... 11369
Grand Central Pkwy
8000-8099 ... 11370
9000-10798 ... 11369
10801-10899 ... 11369
Hazen St ... 11370
Humphrey St ... 11369
Jackson Mill Rd ... 11369
Junction Blvd ... 11369
Kearney St ... 11369
Mandinici Rd ... 11370
Mcintosh St ... 11369
N & W Perimeter Rd ... 11370
Pindinta St ... 11370
White Oak Ct ... 11370

NUMBERED STREETS

E 1st St ... 11370
E 4th St ... 11370
W 5th St ... 11370
W 8th St ... 11370
19th Ave, Dr & Rd ... 11370
20th Ave ... 11370
21st Ave ... 11370
23rd Ave ... 11370
8601-8697 ... 11369
8699-10100 ... 11369
10102-10198 ... 11369
24th Ave
7700-8199 ... 11370
8201-8511 ... 11370
8901-9097 ... 11369
9099-10099 ... 11369
10101-10199 ... 11369
24th Rd ... 11369
25th Ave
7201-7305 ... 11370
7307-8199 ... 11370
8201-8599 ... 11370
8600-9200 ... 11369
9107-9107 ... 11371
9201-9899 ... 11369
9202-9998 ... 11369
27th Ave ... 11369
29th Ave ... 11369
30th Ave ... 11370
30th Ave ... 11370
8601-8697 ... 11369
8699-8900 ... 11369
8902-9498 ... 11369
31st Ave
7000-8399 ... 11370
8500-8798 ... 11369
31st Dr ... 11369
32nd Ave
7000-7298 ... 11370
8601-8697 ... 11369
8699-10799 ... 11369
70th St ... 11370
71st St ... 11370
72nd St ... 11370
73rd St ... 11370
74th St ... 11370
75th St ... 11370
76th St ... 11370
77th St ... 11370
78th St ... 11370
79th St ... 11370
80th St ... 11370
81st St ... 11370
82nd St ... 11370
83rd St ... 11370
84th St ... 11370
85th St ... 11370
86th St ... 11369
87th St ... 11369
88th St ... 11369
89th St ... 11369
90th Pl & St ... 11369
91st St ... 11369
92nd St ... 11369
93rd St ... 11369
94th St ... 11369
95th St ... 11369
96th St ... 11369
97th St ... 11369
98th St ... 11369
99th St ... 11369
100th St ... 11369
101st St ... 11369
102nd St ... 11369
103rd St ... 11369
104th St ... 11369
105th St ... 11369
106th St ... 11369
107th St ... 11369
108th St ... 11369
110th St ... 11369
111th St ... 11369
112th Pl & St ... 11369

ELMHURST NY

POST OFFICE BOXES MAIN OFFICE STATIONS AND BRANCHES

Box No.s
1 - 357 ... 11380
501 - 739055 ... 11373
800001 - 808803 ... 11380

NAMED STREETS

Albion Ave ... 11373
Alstyne Ave ... 11373
Ankener Ave ... 11373
Aske St ... 11373
Barnwell Ave ... 11373
Baxter Ave ... 11373
Benham St ... 11373
Booth St ... 11373
Britton Ave ... 11373
Broadway
7400-7498 ... 11373
7500-8100 ... 11373
8027-8027 ... 11380
8101-8659 ... 11373
8102-8698 ... 11373
Calamus Ave & Cir ... 11373
Case St ... 11373
Claremont Ter ... 11373
Codwise Pl ... 11373
Cornish Ave ... 11373
Corona Ave ... 11373
Denman St ... 11373
Dongan Ave ... 11373
Elbertson St ... 11373
Elks Rd ... 11373
Elmhurst Ave ... 11373
Forley St ... 11373
Gleane St ... 11373
Goldsmith St ... 11373
Gorsline St ... 11373
Grand Ave ... 11373
Hampton St ... 11373
Haspel St ... 11373
Hillyer St ... 11373
Hoffman Dr ... 11373
Ireland St ... 11373
Ithaca St ... 11373
Jacobus St ... 11373
Judge St ... 11373
Junction Blvd ... 11373
Justice Ave ... 11373
Ketcham St ... 11373
Kneeland Ave & St ... 11373
Lamont Ave ... 11373
Layton St ... 11373
Macnish St ... 11373
Manilla St ... 11373
Oconnell Ct ... 11373
Pettit Ave ... 11373
Poyer St ... 11373
Queens Blvd ... 11373
Reeder St ... 11373
Saint James Ave ... 11373
Seabury St ... 11373
Simonson St ... 11373
Van Horn St ... 11373
Van Kleeck St ... 11373
Van Loon St ... 11373
Vietor Ave ... 11373
Vindarel Ave ... 11373
Warren St ... 11373
Wetherole St ... 11373
Whitney Ave ... 11373
Woodhaven Blvd ... 11373
Woodside Ave ... 11373

NUMBERED STREETS

All Street Addresses ... 11373

ELMIRA NY

General Delivery ... 14901

POST OFFICE BOXES MAIN OFFICE STATIONS AND BRANCHES

Box No.s
1 - 1999 ... 14902
2000 - 2343 ... 14903
3001 - 3500 ... 14905
4001 - 5020 ... 14904
9998 - 9998 ... 14902

NAMED STREETS

Abbey Rd ... 14905
Abbott St ... 14901
Academy Pl ... 14901
Acorn Rd ... 14905
W Acres Ln ... 14905
Adams St ... 14904
Admiral Pl ... 14901
Albermarle Ave ... 14905
Albert St ... 14904
Alexander Pl ... 14901
Allen St ... 14904
Alvord Dr ... 14905
Arcadia Ave ... 14905
Arcadia Rd ... 14904
Ashland Ave ... 14903
Aspen Rdg ... 14904
Austin Ln ... 14904
Badger Path ... 14901
Baldwin St ... 14901
Balsam St ... 14904
Bancroft Rd
1-5 ... 14901
7-11 ... 14901
13-19 ... 14901
120-140 ... 14905
Batavia St ... 14904
Baty St ... 14904
Baylor Cir & Rd ... 14904
Beach St ... 14901
Beecher St ... 14904
Benedict Blvd ... 14903
Benita Ave ... 14903
Benjamin St ... 14901
E Bennett Cir ... 14903
W Bennett Cir ... 14903
Bennett St ... 14904
Bennett Circle Ext ... 14903
Benton Pl ... 14901
Billings Dr ... 14905
Birch St ... 14904
Birchwood Ave ... 14903
Bloomer Ave ... 14901
Boardman St ... 14904
Bohemia Ln ... 14903
Bonaview Ave ... 14904
Bond St ... 14903
Bonview St ... 14905
Bower Rd ... 14905
Bowlby Rd ... 14901
Bowman Rd ... 14905
Boyd Dr ... 14901
Braden St ... 14901
Brady St ... 14904
Brand St ... 14904
Brant Rd ... 14901
Breesport N Chemung Rd ... 14901
Briar Ln ... 14903
Bridgeman Rd ... 14901
Bridgman St ... 14901
Brimfield Dr ... 14904
Broadway St ... 14904
Brookline Ave ... 14905
Brookside Cir ... 14903
Budd St ... 14904
Burdick St ... 14904
Buzzard Hill Rd ... 14901
Cadet Ter ... 14904
Caldwell Ave ... 14904
California Ave ... 14903
Canal St ... 14901
Canton St ... 14904
Cardinal Ln ... 14903
Carl St ... 14904
Carpenter Rd ... 14903
Carpenter St ... 14901
Carriage Cir ... 14903
Carroll St ... 14901
Carrollton Ave ... 14905
Carson Dr ... 14903
Carter St ... 14904
Casey St ... 14904
Catherine St ... 14904
Caton Ave ... 14904
Cedar St ... 14904
E & W Center St ... 14901
Chamberlain St ... 14904
Chapman Pl ... 14901
Charles St ... 14904
Charles Storch Rd ... 14903
Charlesmont Rd ... 14904
Chatham Ln ... 14905
E & W Chemung Pl ... 14904
Chemung Canal Plz ... 14901
Cherrywood Manor Dr ... 14904
Cheryl St ... 14903
Chester St ... 14904
Chestnut St ... 14904
E Church St ... 14901
W Church St
1-499 ... 14901
500-1799 ... 14905
Circuit Dr ... 14904
Clairmont Ave ... 14904
Clemens Sq ... 14901
Clemens Center Pkwy ... 14901
Cleveland Ave ... 14905
Cleveland St ... 14903
E Clinton St ... 14901
W Clinton St
100-619 ... 14901
620-1239 ... 14905
1241-1299 ... 14905
Cobbles St E & W ... 14905
Coburn St ... 14904
Coldbrook Dr ... 14904
Coleman Ave
4-12 ... 14905
14-136 ... 14905
138-158 ... 14905
160-399 ... 14903
401-627 ... 14903
College Ave
102-108 ... 14901
110-2010 ... 14901
2012-2028 ... 14901
2030-2206 ... 14903
2208-2208 ... 14903
Collins St ... 14904
Columbia St
100-199 ... 14901
200-299 ... 14905
300-699 ... 14901
701-799 ... 14901
Combs Hill Rd ... 14905
Congdon St ... 14904
Conklin St ... 14905
Connelly Ave ... 14904
Copley St ... 14905
W Corentat St ... 14905
Cornell Rd ... 14905
Corning Rd ... 14903
E Cottage Dr ... 14903
W Cottage Dr ... 14903
Cottage Pl ... 14904
Country Club Dr ... 14905
County Road 64 ... 14903
County Route 60 ... 14901
Cowan Rd ... 14901
Craige St ... 14905
Crane Rd ... 14901
Crescent Ave ... 14901
Crest Dr ... 14903
Crestwood Rd ... 14905
Crete Ave ... 14901
Cross Rd ... 14901
Curren Dr ... 14905
Curren Rd ... 14903
Curtis St ... 14904
Cypress St ... 14904
Davis St
100-199 ... 14905
300-2099 ... 14901
Dawn Dr ... 14904
Days Ln ... 14901
Decker Ave ... 14904
Decker Pkwy E ... 14905
Decker Pkwy W ... 14905
Decker Pl ... 14901
Deerfield Rd ... 14905
Delaware Ave ... 14904
Demarest Pkwy ... 14905
Devonshire Dr ... 14903
Dewitt Ave ... 14901
Dininny Pl ... 14905
Diven Ave ... 14901
Division St ... 14901
Doane St ... 14901
Dogwood Ln ... 14905
Draht Hill Rd ... 14901
Draper Ave ... 14905
Drive A ... 14905
Drive B ... 14905
Drive C ... 14905
Dublin Dr ... 14905
Dubois St ... 14904
Dug Rd ... 14901
Durland Ave ... 14905
Eagle View Dr ... 14903
East Ave ... 14901
Edgewood Dr ... 14905
Eldridge Park Dr ... 14903
Elizabeth St
500-599 ... 14901
650-699 ... 14905
Ellancor St ... 14901
Elm St
100-299 ... 14905
300-499 ... 14901
N Elm St ... 14901
Elmwood Ave ... 14903
Elston Hollow Rd ... 14901
Epworth Cir ... 14901
Erie St ... 14904
Estates Dr ... 14903
Esty St ... 14904
Euclid Ave
304-348 ... 14905
350-599 ... 14905
600-899 ... 14901
Evergreen Ave ... 14905
Fair St ... 14904
Fairfield Ave ... 14904
Fairmont Rd ... 14905
Fairway Ave ... 14904
Falck St ... 14904
Farm Ln ... 14901
Farnham St ... 14901
Farr Ln ... 14903
Fassett Rd
650-699 ... 14901
700-999 ... 14905
Fayette St ... 14901
Federal St ... 14904
Fern Dell Dr ... 14905
Fernwood Ave ... 14905
Ferris St ... 14904
Fisherville Rd ... 14903
Fitch St
300-399 ... 14901
501-597 ... 14905
599-600 ... 14905
602-698 ... 14905
Foothill Rd ... 14903
Forest Hills Dr ... 14905
Foster Ave ... 14905
Fountain Dr ... 14905
Fox St ... 14901
Foxwin Ln ... 14901
Frank St ... 14904
Franklin Pl & St ... 14904
Fred St ... 14904
Friendly Pl ... 14901
Front St ... 14901
Fulton St ... 14904
Gaines St ... 14904
Garden Rd ... 14905
Garfield St ... 14903
Garrison Pl ... 14903
Gates Pl ... 14901
Genesee Rd ... 14905
Geneva St ... 14905
German St ... 14901
Gildea Pl ... 14901
Gleason St ... 14904
Glen Ave ... 14905
Glenwood Ave ... 14905
Glider Ave & Cir ... 14903
Golden Glow Dr ... 14905
Golf Course Rd ... 14903
Gordon Cir ... 14905
Goss Rd ... 14903

Gould St 14905
Grace St 14901
Grand Central Ave
900-1599 14901
1600-1614 14903
1616-1999 14903
Grandview Ave 14905
Grant St 14901
E Gray St 14901
W Gray St
1-97 14901
99-349 14901
350-999 14905
Graycliff Dr 14903
Graylea Cir 14905
Graystone Dr 14903
Greatsinger Rd 14901
Greenaway Rd 14905
Greenlawn Ave 14905
Greenridge Dr E & W 14905
E & W Gridley Ln & Pl
E 14904
Griswold St 14904
Groff Ave 14905
Grove St
1-599 14905
600-999 14901
Guinnip Ave 14905
Gunderman Rd 14901
Haines Ter 14905
Halderman Hollow Rd 14903
Hall St 14901
Halls Ln 14901
Hammond Ter 14904
Hampton Rd 14904
Harcourt Dr 14904
Hardscrabble Rd 14901
Harmon St 14904
Harper St 14901
Harriet Ct & St 14901
Harrington Rd 14901
Harris Hill Rd 14903
Harrison St 14903
Hart St 14905
Harwood Rd 14901
Haskell St 14904
Hatch St 14901
Hathorn Ct & St 14901
Hawley St 14903
Hazel St 14904
Hazelwood Ave 14905
Hendy Ave 14905
Hendy Creek Rd 14905
W Henry St 14904
Herrick St 14904
Hibbard Pl 14901
Hibbard Rd 14903
S Hibbard Rd 14903
Hickory Tree Ter 14905
High St 14901
High Pond Rd 14901
Highland Ave 14905
W Hill Rd 14903
W Hill St 14905
W Hill Road A 14903
Hillbrook Rd 14905
Hillcrest Rd
1-50 14905
57-314 14903
316-352 14903
Hillside Dr 14903
Hillview Dr 14904
N Hoffman Rd
1202-1233 14905
1235-1235 14905
1239-1265 14903
1267-1704 14903
1706-1710 14903
Hoffman St 14905
S Hoffman St 14904
Holdridge St 14904
Holecek Ave 14904
Holley Rd 14905
Home St 14904
Homewood Ave 14904
Honeysuckle Ln 14903
Hope St 14903
Hopkins St 14904
Horner St 14904
Horseheads Blvd 14903
Howard St 14904
E & W Hudson St 14904
Hynes Pl 14903
Industrial Park Blvd 14901
Irvine Pl 14901
Ivy St 14905
Jacob Rhode Dr 14901
James St 14904
Jay St 14901
Jefferson St 14904
Jerusalem Hill Rd 14901
John St 14901
Johnson St 14901
Joyell Dr 14903
Juanita St 14904
Judson St 14901
Junction St 14904
Kahler Rd S 14903
Keefe St 14904
Kendall Pl 14901
Kentucky Ave 14903
Kingsbury Ave 14901
S Kinyon St 14904
Kiwanis Rd 14905
La France St 14904
Lackawanna Ave 14901
Lafayette St 14904
Lake Ave 14904
Lake Rd 14903
Lake St 14901
Lamoreaux Pl 14903
Lancelot Dr 14903
Larchmont Cir & Rd 14905
Lattabrook Rd 14901
Laurel St 14904
Laurentian Pl 14904
Legion Rd 14903
Leland St 14905
Lena Pl 14905
W Lenox Ave 14903
Lew Storch Rd 14903
Lewis St 14904
Lexington Ave 14905
Liberty St 14904
Lincoln St 14901
Linden Pl 14901
Linden Place Ext 14901
Livingston St 14904
Locust St 14904
Log Cabin Rd 14903
Log Haven Acres Dr 14901
Logan St 14901
Lone Pine Ter 14905
Longford Farm Dr 14903
Longmeadow Dr 14905
Lorenzo Pl 14901
Lormore St 14904
Lounsbury Ave 14903
Lovell Ave & Ter 14905
Lowe Rd 14903
Lowecroft Rd 14905
Lower Maple Ave 14901
Luce Pkwy & St 14904
Lynwood Ave 14903
Lyon St 14904
Lyons Rd 14901
Mackey Pl 14904
Madison Ave 14901
S Magee St 14901
Magnolia St 14904
N Main St 14901
S Main St 14904
Manor Cir 14903
Manor Dr
5-8 14903
1100-1198 14904
Maple Ave
1552A-1552B 14904
300-348 14904
350-1550 14904
1551-1551 14901
1552-1552 14904
1553-1604 14901
Maple Dr 14904
Maple Manor Dr 14904
Marciel Ln 14903
Marian Ave 14903
Marion St 14904
E Market St 14901
Mary St 14901
Marywood Dr 14904
Mastrive Ave 14903
Matthew St 14901
Maxwell Pl 14901
May Rd 14901
Mcambley Ave 14903
E & W Mccanns Blvd 14903
Mccauley Ave 14903
Mcconnell Ave 14903
Mcdowell Pl 14904
Mchenry St 14904
Mckinley Pl 14901
Mechanic St 14904
Medina St 14904
Merrill Pl 14904
Michigan Ave
900-999 14901
3500-3599 14903
Mid Ave 14904
Midtown Plz 14901
Mill Rd 14901
Millard St 14901
E & W Miller St 14904
Milton St 14904
Monkey Run Rd 14901
Moore St 14904
Mooreland Pl 14904
Morley Pl 14904
Morningside Cir & Dr 14905
Morrow St 14904
Morrowfield Ave 14904
Mount Zoar St 14904
Mulberry Ave 14903
Nancy St 14903
Neilly Pl 14904
Newhall St 14904
Newtown St 14904
Nice Dr 14903
Noble St 14901
Northcrest Rd 14903
Norton St 14901
Nottingham Way 14903
Oak St 14901
Oak Hill Dr 14905
Oakdale Ave 14904
Oakdale Dr 14905
Oakwood Ave 14903
Ogden Ave 14905
Ogorman St 14904
Ohanlon Ave 14903
Ohio Ave 14905
Old Narrows Rd 14903
Oneida Rd 14901
Orchard St 14901
Orchard Hill Rd 14903
Overland St 14904
Ovid St 14901
Owens Ave 14903
Palisades Blvd 14903
Palomino Mnr 14901
Park Ave 14901
Park Ln 14903
S Park Ln 14903
Park Pl 14901
Parker Cir 14901
Parker Dr 14901
Parker Rd 14905
Parkside Dr 14904
Parkwood Ave 14903
Partridge St 14904
Passmore Rd 14901
Pattinson St 14901
Pear Tree Ln 14901
Pearl Pl 14901
Pennsylvania Ave 14904
Pepin Dr 14901
Perine St 14904
Philo Rd W 14903
Phoenix Ave 14904
Pine St 14904
Pinehurst St 14905
Pineview Dr 14903
Pinewood Cir 14905
Pinnacle Rd 14905
Pleasant St 14904
Plymouth Ave 14904
Pomeroy Pl 14901
Post St 14904
Potter Pl 14901
Powell St 14904
Pratt St 14901
Prescott Ave 14903
Quail Run 14903
Race St 14904
Raecrest Cir 14904
Railroad Ave 14901
Ralph St 14904
Rambler Rd 14905
Ranch Rd 14901
Rathbun St 14904
Redfield Dr 14905
Redwood Dr 14904
Reservoir St 14905
Reynolds St 14904
Richard St 14904
Riderren St 14904
Ridgewood Dr 14905
Rilla St 14903
River Dr 14905
River St 14904
Riverside Ave 14904
Riverview Cir 14904
Robert St 14904
Robinson St 14904
Robinwood Ave 14903
Roe Ave
200-599 14901
600-819 14905
821-899 14905
Roman Rd 14901
Roricks Glen Pkwy 14905
Rowan St 14901
Rudy Ln 14901
Rustic Ave 14905
Saddleridge Dr 14903
Saint Josephs Blvd 14901
Schuyler Ave 14904
Scio St 14901
Scott Ave 14905
Scottwood Ave 14903
Sears Rd 14903
Seneca Pl 14904
Shady Knoll Dr 14905
Shannon Ave 14904
Sharr Ave 14904
Sheely St 14904
Shepler St 14904
Sherman Ave 14904
Sickles Rd 14901
Simkin Rd 14901
Sliter St 14904
Sly St 14904
Smith St 14904
Snell Rd 14901
Soaring Hill Dr 14903
Soaring Ridge Way 14903
Sommerset Dr 14903
Soper St 14904
South Ave 14904
Southport St 14904
Spaulding St 14904
Spruce St 14904
W Squires Rd 14901
Stacia Dr 14904
Standish St 14901
Stanley Roberts Rd 14901
Stannard Rd 14901
State St 14901
State Route 17 14901
State Route 352 14903
Stephens Pl 14901
Stermer Rd 14901
Stiles Rd 14901
Stony Brook Rd 14905
Stowell Pl & St 14901
Suburban Dr 14903
Sullivan St 14901
Sullivan Crest Rd 14901
Summit Dr 14905
Sunnyside Dr 14905
Sunset Cir 14903
Sunset Dr
780-784 14905
786-833 14905
835-841 14905
1900-1999 14903
Sunset Ter 14903
Sutton St 14904
Sycamore Cir & St 14904
Sylvester Pl 14904
Symonds Pl 14901
Taylor St 14901
Thompson St 14904
Thornapple Dr 14903
E & W Thurston St 14901
Timber Ln N & S 14904
Tompkins St 14901
Tory Meadow Dr 14901
Townsend Way 14903
Tracy Pl 14901
Travis Dr 14903
Tremaine Pl 14904
Turner Rd 14905
Tuttle Ave 14901
Underwood Ave 14905
Union Pl 14901
Universal Ave 14904
Upland Dr 14905
Upper Oakwood Ave 14903
Valentine St 14904
Valley View Dr 14903
Vanderhoff Rd 14903
Vermont Ave 14903
Verona St 14903
Virginia Ave 14903
Vixon Cir 14903
Wall St 14905
Wallace Pl 14904
Walnut St
100-299 14905
300-1048 14901
1049-1299 14905
S Walnut St 14904
Warner Ave 14905
Warnick St 14901
E & W Warren St 14901
E & W Washington Ave,
Ct & St 14901
E Water St 14901
W Water St
100-198 14901
200-332 14901
334-348 14901
350-1865 14905
1867-1875 14905
Watercure Hill Rd 14901
Watercure Run Rd 14901
Webber Pl 14901
Welles St 14901
Wells Ln 14903
West Ave 14904
Westfield Rd 14904
Westmont Ave 14905
Westside Ave 14901
Whitetail Dr 14903
Wilawana Rd 14901
Wilcox Dr 14903
Wildwood Rd 14905
William St 14901
S William St 14904
Williams Rd 14901
Willys St 14904
Windswept Rd 14901
Winsor Ave, Cir & Ter 14905
Winter St 14905
Winters Rd 14903
Wisner St 14901
Woodbine Ave 14904
Woodland Est 14903
E Woodlawn Ave 14901
Woods Ln 14905
Woodside Dr 14903
Woodsview Dr 14903
Wuthering Dr 14903
Yale St 14904
York Ave
1-92 14905
94-98 14905
201-299 14903
Zeigler Dr 14901

NUMBERED STREETS

W 1st St
100-499 14901
500-1399 14905
E 2nd St 14901
100-599 14901
600-1299 14905
E 3rd St 14901
W 3rd St
101-147 14901
600-1299 14905
W 4th St 14901
E & W 5th 14901
W 6th St 14901
E & W 7th 14901
E & W 8th 14903
E & W 9th 14903
E & W 10th 14903
E & W 11th 14903
W 12th St 14903
W 13th St 14903
E & W 14th 14903
W 15th St 14903
W 16th St 14903
W 17th St 14903
E & W 18th 14903
W 19th St 14903
22nd St 14903

ENDICOTT NY

General Delivery 13760

POST OFFICE BOXES MAIN OFFICE STATIONS AND BRANCHES

Box No.s
1 - 5000 13761
5541 - 5920 13763
7001 - 9030 13761

NAMED STREETS

N Adams Ave 13760
Airey Ave 13760
Airport Rd 13760
Alameda Ln 13760
Alexander St 13760
Alexandra Pl 13760
Alfred Dr 13760
Alice Ave 13760
Allan Ct 13760
Alma Pl 13760
Alpine Dr 13760
Andover Rd 13760
Andrews Ave 13760
Anna Dr 13760
Annabelle St 13760
Anne Ln 13760
Anson Rd 13760
Antoinette Dr 13760
Antonio Ct 13760
Arbor Dr 13760
Ardmore St 13760
Argonne Ave 13760
Arnold Dr 13760
N Arthur Ave 13760
Ash Ave 13760
Ashton Ct 13760
Auburn St 13760
Audrey Ct 13760
Autumn Dr 13760
N & S Avenue B 13760
Aylesworth Ave 13760
Badger Ave 13760
Barnes Ave 13760
Barteau St 13760
Bassett Ave 13760
Bean Hill Rd 13760
Beatrice Ln 13760
Beckwith Ave 13760
Beechwood Dr 13760
Belknap Rd 13760
Bella Ct 13760
Berkley St 13760
Bermond Ave 13760
Bernard Blvd 13760
Bernetta St 13760
Betty St 13760
Birdsall St 13760
Biscayne Ter 13760
Booth Ave 13760
Bornt Hill Rd 13760
Boswell Hill Rd 13760
Bradley Creek Rd 13760
Brainard St 13760
Briar Ln 13760
Briarwood Dr 13760
Brieves Dr 13760
Brink St 13760
Broad St 13760
Brookcrest Dr 13760
N & S Brookside Ave 13760
Buckingham Rd 13760
Buffalo St 13760
Bundy Ave & Cir 13760
Burt Ave 13760
Byford Blvd 13760
Cafferty Ln 13760
N Cafferty Hill Rd 13760
Calumet St 13760
Camelot Rd 13760
E Campville Rd 13760
Canterbury Dr 13760
Carden St 13760
Carl St 13760
Carol Ct 13760
Carolyn Ct 13760
Carrie Ave 13760
Carrie Ann Dr 13760
Case Rd 13760
Casterline Ave & Rd 13760
Catalina Blvd 13760
Catherine Ave 13760
Cedar Ct 13760
Central St 13760
Chatham Rd 13760
Chaumont Dr 13760
Cherry Dr 13760
Cheryl Dr 13760
Chestnut St 13760
Christina Ct 13760
Christopher St 13760
Chrysler Rd 13760
Church St 13760
Cieri Dr 13760
Circle Dr 13760
Clara St 13760
Clark St 13760
Clearview Dr 13760
Clernerm Rd 13760
N Cleveland Ave & Pl 13760
Club House Rd 13760
Colgate Dr 13760
Colonial Dr 13760
Colorado Ave 13760
Columbia Dr 13760
Columbus Ave 13760
Corey Ave 13760
Cornell Ave 13760
Cornell Hollow Rd 13760
Corsica Ct 13760
Country Club Rd 13760
Country Knoll Dr 13760
Coventry Rd 13760

Crescent Dr & Pl 13760
Crest Ct 13760
Crestview Dr 13760
Crestwood Ct 13760
Cummings Rd 13760
Cyprus Ln 13760
Dallas Ct 13760
Dante Dr 13760
Daren Dr 13760
Darlene Dr 13760
Daugherty Rd 13760
David Ln 13760
Davis Ave 13760
Day Pl & St 13760
Day Hollow Rd 13760
Dean Dr 13760
Debonair Dr 13760
Dehart Ave 13760
Delaware Ave 13760
Deming Dr 13760
Dencary Ln 13760
Denver Ct E & W 13760
Depot St 13760
Destin Dr 13760
Devon Dr 13760
Dickson St 13760
Dittrick St 13760
Dogwood Ct 13760
Domenica Dr 13760
Donna Ave 13760
Dorchester Dr 13760
Dorothy St 13760
Douglas Dr 13760
Dover Dr 13760
Doyleson Ave 13760
N & S Duane Ave 13760
Dudley Ave 13760
Duke St 13760
Dutchtown Rd 13760
Dwight Ave 13760
Eagle Dr 13760
Echo Ln 13760
Edgebrook Dr 13760
Edgewood Rd 13760
Edson Rd 13760
E & W Edwards St 13760
Ellen Dr 13760
Elliott St 13760
Ellis Ave 13760
Elm St 13760
Elmira St 13760
Elmwood Dr 13760
Elsie Dr 13760
Elton Dr 13760
Emerald Ln 13760
Endicott Plz 13760
Endwell Plz 13760
English Rd 13760
Enterprise Cir 13760
Ethel St 13760
Evergreen Ave 13760
Exchange Ave 13760
Executive Cir 13760
Exeter Dr 13760
Fairlane Dr 13760
Fairmont Ave 13760
Farm To Market Rd 13760
Felicia Blvd 13760
Fillmore Ave 13760
Firth St 13760
Flora St 13760
Florence St 13760
Ford Rd 13760
Forest Rd 13760
Foster St 13760
Foster Valley Rd 13760
Foxboro Ln 13760
Francis Ave 13760
E & W Franklin St 13760
Frazier Dr 13760
Fredericks Rd 13760
Frey Ave 13760
Frost Rd 13760
Gabriella Ave 13760
Garfield Ave 13760
George F Hwy 13760
Georgia St 13760
Gladys St 13760
Glenbrook Ct & Dr 13760
Glendale Dr 13760
Governeurs Ln 13760
Grandview Pl 13760
Grant Ave & St 13760
Green Lantern Blvd 13760
Green Meadow Ln 13760
Greenwood Ct, Gln & Rd 13760
N & S Grippen Ave 13760
Groats St 13760
Groveland Ave 13760
Hall St 13760
Hamilton Dr 13760
Hannah St 13760
Harding Ave 13760
Harmony Rdg 13760
Harpur Dr 13760
Harrison Ave 13760
Harvard St 13760
Hastings Ave 13760
Hayes Ave 13760
Hazel Ave & Dr 13760
Hearthstone Dr 13760
Heath St 13760
Helen St 13760
Hickory Ln 13760
High Ave 13760
Highland Ave 13760
Highview Dr 13760
Hill Ave 13760
Hilldale Dr 13760
Hillside Ct & Ter 13760
Hilltop Rd 13760
Holiday Hl 13760
Hollerith Ave 13760
Holly Ln 13760
Hooper Rd 13760
Hoover Ave 13760
Ideal Aly 13760
Industrial Park Blvd 13760
Irma Ave 13760
Ironwood Dr 13760
Irving Ave 13760
Ivon Ave 13760
N Jackson Ave 13760
Jade Dr 13760
Jamaica Blvd 13760
James Dr 13760
Jane Lacey Dr 13760
Janice St 13760
Jayar St 13760
Jeanette Rd 13760
Jefferson Ave 13760
Jenkins St 13760
Jennifer Ln 13760
Jennings St 13760
Jfk Blvd 13760
Jill Ave 13760
Joel Dr 13760
John St 13760
Jon Ln 13760
Jonas Ln 13760
Joyce Ct 13760
June St 13760
N Kathleen Dr 13760
Kay Rd 13760
Keeler St 13760
N & S Kelly Ave 13760
Kemp Dr 13760
Kenneth Dr 13760
Kensington Rd 13760
Kent Ave 13760
Kentucky Ave 13760
Kevin Blvd 13760
Kim Dr 13760
King St 13760
King Hill Rd 13760
Kinney Rd 13760
Kirk Rd 13760
N & S Knight Ave 13760
Knightlee Ave 13760
Knoll Dr 13760
La Rue Ave 13760
La Salle Dr 13760
Lacey Dr 13760
Laguna Dr 13760
Lake Ave 13760
Lakeview Dr 13760
Lancaster Dr 13760
Landmark Dr 13760
Larch Cir 13760
Latourette Ln 13760
Laurelton Dr 13760
Lawndale St 13760
Lee Ave 13760
Leon Dr 13760
Leona Ave 13760
Leonard Dr 13760
Leroy St 13760
Lewis St 13760
N & S Liberty Ave 13760
Lillian Ave 13760
Lincoln Ave 13760
N & S Loder Ave 13760
Lodge Blvd 13760
London Ln 13760
Loomis Rd 13760
Lorne Dr 13760
Lott St 13760
Louisiana Ave 13760
Lowell Dr 13760
Ludington Dr 13760
Luther St 13760
Lyncourt Dr 13760
Lyndale Dr 13760
Madeline Dr 13760
Madison Ave 13760
Magnolia St 13760
E & W Main St 13760
Malverne Rd 13760
Manhattan Dr 13760
Manor Entrance 13760
Mansfield Dr 13760
Maple Ave, Dr, Ln & St 13760
Maplehurst Dr 13760
Marcella St 13760
Marion Ave & St 13760
Marjorie Ln 13760
Marlboro Dr 13760
Marne Ave 13760
Marshall Dr 13760
Martin St 13760
Mary St 13760
Maryland Ave 13760
Massachusetts Ave 13760
Matthews Dr 13760
May St 13760
N Mckinley Ave 13760
Mechanic Ave 13760
Merrit Rd 13760
Mersereau Ave 13760
Metz Ave 13760
Michael Dr 13760
Midway Ct 13760
Milan Ave 13760
Mill Gln 13760
Mills Ave 13760
Miner Cir 13760
Mitchell St 13760
Monforte Dr 13760
Monroe St 13760
Monterey Dr 13760
Moore Ave 13760
Morlando Dr 13760
Moss Ave 13760
Mountain View Dr 13760
Mulberry Cir 13760
Murphy Ave 13760
N & S Nanticoke Ave & Dr 13760
Nantucket Dr 13760
Neal Rd 13760
Nebraska Ave 13760
Newark Valley Rd 13760
Newberry Dr 13760
Newell Rd 13760
North St 13760
Northwood Dr 13760
Norton Ave 13760
Nottingham Dr 13760
Nuel Ct 13760
N & S Oak Ave 13760
Oak Hill Ave 13760
Oday Dr 13760
Odell Ave 13760
Old Newark Valley Rd 13760
Oneida St 13760
Orman St 13760
Oscar Ter 13760
Overlook Ter 13760
Overton St 13760
Oxford Dr & St 13760
Paden St 13760
N & S Page Ave 13760
Park St 13760
Park Hill Dr 13760
Park Manor Blvd 13760
Parkview Ct 13760
Parmerton Dr 13760
Parsons Ave 13760
Partridge Pl 13760
Patio Dr 13760
Patterson Ct 13760
Paul St 13760
Payne Rd 13760
Paynter Ave 13760
Pearl St 13760
Pelican Ln 13760
Pembroke Dr 13760
Perimeter Rd E & W 13760
Pheasant Ln 13760
Phyllis St 13760
Pierce Ave 13760
Pietro Dr 13760
Pine St 13760
Pine Knoll Rd 13760
Pinecrest Rd 13760
Plaza Dr 13760
Pleasant Dr 13760
Pollard Hill Rd 13760
Prescott Ave 13760
Prince Edward Ct 13760
Princeton St 13760
Prospect St 13760
Pruyne St 13760
Quail Ridge Rd 13760
Rath Ave 13760
Redwood Rd 13760
Renee Ct 13760
Rennie Dr 13760
Richmond Rd 13760
Ricky Dr 13760
Ridgefield Rd 13760
River Dr, Rd & Ter 13760
Riverview Dr 13760
Robble Ave 13760
Roberts St 13760
Robins St 13760
Robinson Hill Rd 13760
Rochester St 13760
Rodman Rd 13760
N Rogers Ave 13760
N Roosevelt Ave 13760
Rosendale Dr 13760
Rosewood Ter 13760
Royal Rd 13760
Rustic Ridge Rd 13760
Sally Piper Rd 13760
Sandra Dr 13760
Sapphire Dr 13760
Sarah Ln 13760
Scarborough Dr 13760
Schuyler St 13760
Scribner Dr 13760
S Seward Ave 13760
Shadowbrook Dr 13760
Shady Dr 13760
Shale Dr 13760
Sheffield Dr 13760
Sherder Rd 13760
Sherman Dr 13760
Sherwood Dr 13760
Simon Dr 13760
Skye Island Dr 13760
Skylane Ter 13760
Sliter Pl 13760
Smith Dr 13760
Smithfield Dr 13760
Somerset Dr 13760
South St 13760
Southerland Rd 13760
Southern Pines Dr 13760
Spring St 13760
Springview Dr 13760
Squires Ave 13760
Stack Ave 13760
Stanton Rd 13760
Stark Ave 13760
State Route 17c 13760
State Route 26 13760
State Route 38b 13760
Stein Dr 13760
Stoddard Pl 13760
Stonefield Rd 13760
Stony Hill Dr 13760
Struble Rd 13760
Sugarpine Pl 13760
Summit St 13760
Sunrise Dr 13760
Sunset Dr & Ter 13760
Sutton Rd 13760
Swartwood Ave 13760
Sweetbriar Ct 13760
Sylvia Dr 13760
Syracuse St 13760
Taft Ave 13760
Talan Dr 13760
Taylor Ave 13760
Terra Marr Ct 13760
Terrace Rd 13760
Tilbury Hill Rd 13760
Tracy St 13760
Tudor Dr 13760
Turner Dr 13760
Twilight Dr 13760
Twining Cir 13760
Twist Run Rd 13760
Ulmer St 13760
E & W Union St 13760
Union Center Maine Hwy 13760
University Ave & Cir 13760
Utica St 13760
Valley St 13760
Valley View Dr 13760
Valleyview Dr 13760
Ventura Blvd 13760
Verdun Ave 13760
Verna Dr 13760
Vestal Ave 13760
Vidka Ln 13760
Villa Cir 13760
Village Dr 13760
Virginia Ave 13760
Vistaview Ln 13760
Waldo Ave 13760
Walker Rd 13760
Wallace St 13760
Walnut Ave 13760
Ward Ave 13760
Warrick Rd 13760
Washington Ave
1-199 13760
200-200 13761
201-299 13760
202-298 13760
38-40-38-40 13760
Watson Blvd 13760
Wayne St 13760
Weber Rd 13760
Wellington Ct & Dr 13760
E & W Wendell St 13760
West Ave 13760
Western Heights Blvd 13760
Westminster Rd 13760
Wheeler Pl 13760
White Birch Ln 13760
Whittemore Hill Rd 13760
Wildwood Dr 13760
William Reuben Dr 13760
Williams St 13760
N & S Willis Ave 13760
Wilma St 13760
Wilson Ave 13760
Winchester Dr 13760
Winding Ridge Rd 13760
Windsor Dr 13760
Winston Dr 13760
Witherill St 13760
Woodford Ave 13760
Woodrow Ave 13760
Yale St 13760
Youngs Ave 13760
Zeggert Rd 13760
Zimmer Ave 13760

FAR ROCKAWAY NY

General Delivery 11690

POST OFFICE BOXES MAIN OFFICE STATIONS AND BRANCHES

Box No.s
1 - 298 11693
1 - 268 11695
276 - 1040 11690
291 - 398 11695
1100 - 903005 11690
930001 - 930560 11693
950001 - 950398 11695

NAMED STREETS

Almeda Ave 11691
Almont Rd 11691
Alonzo Rd 11691
Anchor Dr 11691
Annapolis St 11691
Augustina Ave 11691
Aztec Pl 11691
Bailey Ct 11691
Battery Rd 11691
Bay Ct 11691
Bay 24th St 11691
Bay 25th St 11691
Bay 27th St 11691
Bay 28th St 11691
Bay 30th St 11691
Bay 31st St 11691
Bay 32nd Pl & St 11691
Baypark Pl 11691
Bayport Pl 11691
Bayside Dock 11693
Bayswater Ave & Ct 11691
Beach 11th St 11691
Beach 12th St 11691
Beach 13th St 11691
Beach 14th St 11691
Beach 15th St 11691
Beach 16th St 11691
Beach 17th St 11691
Beach 19th St 11691
Beach 20th St 11691
Beach 21st St 11691
Beach 22nd St 11691
Beach 24th St 11691
Beach 25th St 11691
Beach 26th St 11691
Beach 27th St 11691
Beach 28th St 11691
Beach 29th St 11691
Beach 30th St 11691
Beach 31st St 11691
Beach 32nd St 11691
Beach 35th St 11691
Beach 36th St 11691
Beach 37th St 11691
Beach 38th St 11691
Beach 39th St 11691
Beach 3rd St 11691
Beach 40th St 11691
Beach 41st St 11691
Beach 42nd St 11691
Beach 43rd St 11691
Beach 44th St 11691
Beach 45th St 11691
Beach 46th St 11691
Beach 47th St 11691
Beach 48th St 11691
Beach 49th St 11691
Beach 4th St 11691
Beach 51st St 11691
Beach 6th St 11691
Beach 79th St 11693
Beach 7th St 11691
Beach 80th St 11693
Beach 81st St 11693
Beach 84th St 11693
Beach 85th St 11693
Beach 86th St 11693
Beach 87th St 11693
Beach 88th St 11693
Beach 89th St 11693
Beach 8th St 11691
Beach 90th St 11693
Beach 91st St 11693
Beach 92nd St 11693
Beach 93rd St 11693
Beach 94th St 11693
Beach 95th St 11693
Beach 96th St 11693
Beach 97th St 11693
Beach 9th St 11691
Beach Channel Dr
1100-5199 11691
5201-5315 11691
8101-8397 11693
8399-9199 11693
9201-9699 11693
Beacon Pl 11691
Beatrice Ct 11691
Beck Rd 11691
Bert Rd 11693
Bessemund Ave 11691
Birdsall Ave 11691
Bolton Rd 11691
Briar Pl 11691
Brookhaven Ave 11691
Brunswick Ave 11691
Caffrey Ave 11691
Camp Rd 11691
Cedar Hill Rd 11691
Cedar Lawn Ave 11691
Central Ave 11691
Chandler St 11691
Channel Rd 11693
Channing Rd 11691
Church Rd 11693
Coldspring Rd 11691
Collier Ave 11691
Cornaga Ave & Ct 11691
Coronado Ct 11691
Cross Bay Blvd & Pkwy 11693
Davies Rd 11691
De Sota Rd 11693
Deerfield Rd 11691
Delia Ct 11691
Demerest Rd 11693
Dickens St 11691
Dinsmore Ave 11691
Dix Ave 11691
Dorian Ct 11691
Dunbar St 11691
Dune St 11691
Dwight Ave 11691
Edgemere Ave 11691
Eggert Pl 11691
Egmont Pl 11691
Elk Dr 11691
Elvira Ave 11691
Empire Ave 11691
Enright Rd 11691
Everdell Ave 11691
Faber Ter 11691
Falcon Ave 11691

Far Rockaway Blvd 11691
Fernside Pl 11691
Foam Pl 11691
Frisco Ave 11691
Garden Ct 11691
Garianto St 11691
Gateway Blvd 11691
Gerson Ct 11691
Gipson St 11691
Granada Pl 11691
Grandview Ter 11691
Grassmere Ter 11691
Greenwood Ct 11691
Grove Ct 11691
Hanson Ct 11691
Harbour Ct 11691
Harris Ave 11691
Hartman Ln 11691
Hassock St 11691
Healy Ave 11691
Henry Rd 11691
Heyson Rd 11691
Hicksville Rd 11691
Highland Ct 11691
Holland Ave 11693
Hollywood Ct 11691
Hurley Ct 11691
Ives Ct 11691
Jarvis Ave & Ct 11691
Jaydee Ct 11691
Lanark Rd 11693
Lanett Ave 11691
Lewmay Rd 11691
Loretta Rd 11691
Mador Ct 11691
Maradeld St 11693
Martin Ct 11691
Marvin St 11691
Mcbride St 11691
Meehan Ave 11691
Minton St 11691
Mobile Rd 11691
Morse Ct 11691
Moss Pl 11691
Mott Ave 11691
Muhlebach Ct 11691
Nameoke Ave & St 11691
Nasby Pl 11691
Neilson St 11691
New Haven Ave 11691
Noel Rd 11693
Norton Ave & Dr 11691
Oak Dr 11691
Oceancrest Blvd 11691
Old Beach 88th St 11693
Ostend Pl 11691
Pearl St 11691
Pinson St 11691
Plainview Ave 11691
Plunkett Ave 11691
Point Breeze Pl 11691
Power Rd 11693
President St 11691
Reads Ln 11691
Redfern Ave 11691
Regina Ave 11691
Rockaway Fwy 11691
Rockaway Beach Blvd
3701-3797 11691
3799-5399 11691
7900-8498 11693
8500-9700 11693
9702-9798 11693
Roosevelt St 11691
Rose St 11691
Sage St 11691
Samantha Dr 11691
Scott A Gadell Pl 11691
Seagirt Ave & Blvd 11691
Shad Creek Rd 11693
Shore Front Pkwy 11693
Smith Pl 11691
Sunnyside Ave 11691
Tammy Dr 11691
Trist Pl 11691
Van Brunt Rd 11693
Virginia St 11691
Walton Rd 11693
Waterloo Pl 11691
Waterview St 11691
Watjean Ct 11691
West Rd 11693
Westbourne Ave 11691
Wheatley St 11691
Williams Ct 11691
Willow Ct 11691

NUMBERED STREETS

All Street Addresses 11693

FLORAL PARK NY

POST OFFICE BOXES MAIN OFFICE STATIONS AND BRANCHES

Box No.s
All PO Boxes 11002

NAMED STREETS

Adams St 11001
Adelaide St 11001
Argyle Rd 11001
Arthur Ave 11001
Ash St 11001
Aspen St 11001
Atlantic Ave 11001
Barwick St 11001
Beech St 11001
Beechhurst Ave 11001
Bellmore St 11001
Belmont Ave 11001
Bergen St 11001
Bertha St 11001
Beverly Ave 11001
Birch St 11001
Boston Rd 11001
Brokaw Ave 11001
Bryant Ave 11001
Calla Ave 11001
Carnation Ave 11001
Caroline Pl 11001
Cedar Pl & St 11001
Charles St 11001
Chelsea St 11001
E Cherry Ln & St 11001
Chestnut Ave 11001
Childs Ave 11001
Cisney Ave 11001
Clarence St 11001
Clayton Ave 11001
Clover Ave 11001
Colonial Rd 11001
Commonwealth Blvd 11001
Concord St 11001
Covert Ave 11001
Crest Ave 11001
Crocus Ave 11001
Crown Ave 11001
Cunningham Ave 11001
Cypress St 11001
Daisy Ave 11001
Delaware Rd 11001
Depan Ave 11001
Drew Ave 11001
Earl St 11001
E & W Elder Ave & Pl 11001
Elizabeth St 11001
Elm Ave 11001
Emerson Ave 11001
Eweler Ave 11001
Fern St 11001
Floral Blvd & Pkwy 11001
Florence St 11001
Flower Ave 11001
Frederick Ave 11001
Fuller Ave 11001
Geranium Ave 11001
Gilbert Ct 11001
Gilmore Blvd 11001
Gladiolus Ave 11001
Gordon Blvd 11001
Grand Central Pkwy 11005
Granger Ave 11001
Green St 11001
Hanover St 11001
Harvard St 11001
Hawthorne Ave 11001
Hazel Pl 11001
Helen Ct 11001
Hemlock St 11001
Heradong Ave 11001
Hickory St 11001
Hill St 11001
Hillside Ave 11001
Hinsdale Ave 11001
E & W Hitchcock Ave 11001
Holland Ave 11001
Holly Pl 11001
Hudson Rd 11001
Huron Rd 11001
Iris Ave 11001
Irving Ave 11001
Jamaica Ave 11001
Jamerney Pkwy 11005
Jefferson St 11001
Jericho Tpke 11001
Keene Ave 11001
Kenneth Ct 11001
King St 11001
Kingston Ave 11001
Landau Ave 11001
Larch Ave 11001
Laurel St 11001
Lesoir Ave 11001
Lexington St 11001
Lily St 11001
Linden Ave 11001
Little Neck Pkwy 11001
Locust St 11001
Louis Ave 11001
Lowell Ave 11001
Magnolia Ave 11001
Main St 11001
Maple Ave 11001
Marguerite Ave 11001
Marshall Ave 11001
Martha Ter 11001
Massachusetts Blvd 11001
Mayfair Ave 11001
Mayflower Pl 11001
Mckee St 11001
Memphis Ave 11001
Michigan Rd 11001
Mildred Ct 11001
Miller Ave 11001
Monroe St 11001
Nassau St 11001
North St 11001
Oak St 11001
Ontario Rd 11001
Orchid Ct & St 11001
Pansy Ave 11001
Park Pl 11001
Pennsylvania Blvd 11001
Pine Ave 11001
Plainfield Ave 11001
E & W Poplar St 11001
Poppy Pl 11001
Press St 11001
Primrose Ave 11001
Raff Ave 11001
Reed Ave 11001
Remsen Ln 11001
Revere Ct & Dr 11001
Rogers Pl 11001
Roquette Ave 11001
Roscoe Pl 11001
Rose Ave 11001
Schenck Blvd 11001
Spooner St 11001
Spruce Ave 11001
Star St 11001
Stewart St 11001
Superior Rd 11001
Sycamore Ave 11001
Tennessee St 11001
Terrace Ave 11001
Tulip Ave
1-90 11001
35-35 11002
91-567 11001
92-790 11001
Tunnel St 11001
N & S Tyson Ave 11001
Van Buren Ave 11001
Van Siclen Ave 11001
Vanderbilt Ave 11001
Vanderwater Ave 11001
Verbena Ave 11001
Vernon St 11001
Violet Ave 11001
Virginia Rd 11001
Walnut Ave 11001
Ward St 11001
Webster St 11001
Whitney Ave 11001
Whittier Ave 11001
Willis Ave 11001
E Williston Ave 11001
Willow St 11001
Woodbine Ct 11001
Zinnia Ave 11001

NUMBERED STREETS

All Street Addresses 11001

FLUSHING NY

General Delivery 11355

POST OFFICE BOXES MAIN OFFICE STATIONS AND BRANCHES

Box No.s
1 - 825 11352
1 - 476 11367
1 - 356 11358
1 - 258 11371
401 - 460 11358
426 - 488 11371
501 - 554 11367
666 - 666 11371
801 - 994 11354
901 - 1099 11352
1101 - 1198 11354
1200 - 1480 11352
1301 - 1678 11354
1801 - 5250 11352
5401 - 5458 11354
7001 - 528320 11352
540050 - 548012 11354
580001 - 580912 11358
670001 - 679002 11367
710001 - 718104 11371

NAMED STREETS

Aguilar Ave 11367
Ash Ave 11355
Ashby Ave 11358
Auburndale Ln 11358
Avery Ave 11355
Bagley Ave 11358
Banchelm Ave 11355
Barclay Ave 11355
Barton Pl 11354
Bayside Ave 11354
Bayside Ln 11358
Beech Ave 11355
Berallea 11371
Blossom Ave 11355
Booth Memorial Ave 11355
Bowne St
3600-3900 11354
3902-4098 11354
4100-5299 11355
Budd Pl 11354
Building 11371
Burling St 11355
Byrd St 11355
Carlton Pl 11354
Central Terminal 11371
Cherry Ave 11355
Colden St 11355
College Point Blvd
2500-4099 11354
4100-4999 11355
5001-5899 11355
Collins Pl 11354
Courtney Ave 11358
Craleadw Ave 11354
Crocheron Ave 11358
Crommelin Ave 11355
Dahlia Ave 11355
Delaware Ave 11355
Delong St 11355
Delta Terminal 11371
Depot Rd 11358
Downing St 11354
Effington Ave 11358
Elder Ave 11355
Elm Ave 11355
Fairchild Ave 11358
Farrington St 11354
Fowler Ave 11355
Frame Pl 11355
Francis Lewis Blvd 11358
Franklin Ave 11355
Fresh Meadow Ln 11358
Fuller Pl 11355
Georgia Rd 11355
Geranium Ave 11355
Gopost 11355
Graham Ct 11354
Gravett Rd 11367
Gurino Dr 11354
Haight St 11355
Hanger N 11371
Hawthorne Ave 11355
Higgins St 11354
Hollis Court Blvd 11358
Holly Ave 11355
Hollywood Ave 11355
Horace Harding Expy
13000-15498 11367
13801-13899 11355
14201-15799 11367
Janet Pl 11354
Jasmine Ave 11355
Jewel Ave 11367
Jordan St 11358
Juniper Ave 11355
Kalmia Ave 11355
King Rd 11354
Kissena Blvd
4100-6099 11355
6400-7400 11367
7402-7598 11367
Laburnum Ave
13700-15799 11355
15800-16299 11358
Latimer Pl 11354
Lawrence St
5700-6099 11355
6101-6199 11367
Leavitt St 11354
Linden Pl 11354
Linnaeus Pl 11354
Main St
3600-4099 11354
4100-4164 11355
4165-6099 11355
4165-4165 11352
4166-6098 11355
6100-6198 11367
6200-7999 11367
Main Terminal 11371
Maple Ave 11355
Marine Air Terminal 11371
Melbourne Ave 11367
Miller St 11354
Mulberry Ave 11355
Murray Ln 11354
Murray St
2500-4099 11354
4100-4399 11355
Negundo Ave 11355
New York Times Plz 11354
Northern Blvd
13201-13397 11354
13399-15700 11354
15702-15798 11354
15800-19699 11358
Oak Ave
13700-15799 11355
15800-15899 11358
15901-16349 11358
Park Dr E 11367
Parsons Blvd
2500-3900 11354
3902-4098 11354
4100-4108 11355
4110-5199 11355
5201-5299 11355
Peck Ave 11355
Phlox Pl 11355
Pidgeon Meadow Rd 11358
Pleareen St 11367
Poplar Ave 11355
Pople Ave 11355
Prince St 11354
Quince Ave 11355
Reeves Ave 11367
Robinson St 11355
Roosevelt Ave 11354
Rose Ave 11355
Sancondo St 11358
Sanford Ave
13100-15799 11355
15800-16499 11358
16501-16599 11358
Saull St 11355
Smart St 11355
Station Rd
15700-15798 11355
15900-15998 11358
16000-19599 11358
19601-19699 11358
Stratton St 11354
Summit Ct 11355
Syringa Pl 11355
Thompson Pl 11367
Ulmer St 11354
Union St
2500-4000 11354
4002-4098 11354
4100-4799 11355
Union Tpke 11367
Us Air Terminal 11371
Utopia Pkwy 11358
Vleigh Pl 11367
Whitestone Expy 11354

NUMBERED STREETS

20th Ave 11351
25th Dr
14400-15799 11354
16000-16699 11358
25th Rd 11354
26th Ave
11900-15799 11354
16000-19899 11358
27th Ave
11901-11913 11354
16000-19899 11358
28th Ave
11900-15799 11354
15800-19999 11358
28th Rd 11354
29th Ave
11800-15199 11354
15201-15799 11354
15801-15897 11358
15899-19899 11358
29th Rd 11354
30th Ave
12301-12399 11354
19800-19899 11358
31st Ave, Dr & Rd 11354
32nd Ave
13200-13298 11354
13300-15500 11354
15502-15798 11354
15800-15898 11358
15900-19999 11358
32nd Rd 11358
33rd Ave
13200-15699 11354
15800-19999 11358
33rd Rd 11354
34th Ave
13200-15199 11354
19900-19999 11358
34th Rd 11354
35th Ave
13200-15799 11354
15800-19299 11358
36th Rd 11354
37th Ave
13300-14499 11354
18900-19599 11358
38th Ave 11354
39th Ave
13101-13297 11354
13299-13650 11354
13652-13698 11354
17000-17198 11358
17200-19599 11358
40th Rd 11354
41st Ave 11355
15000-15400 11354
41st Rd 11355
42nd Ave & Rd 11358
43rd Ave
15600-15698 11355
15701-15799 11355
15900-16900 11358
16902-17098 11358
43rd Rd 11358
44th Ave 11358
45th Ave
13700-15799 11355
15800-19699 11358
45th Dr 11358
45th Rd 11358
46th Ave
14700-15720 11355
15800-19799 11358
46th Rd 11358
47th Ave 11358
56th Ave & Rd 11355
57th Ave & Rd 11355
58th Ave & Rd 11355
59th Ave 11355
60th Ave 11355
61st Rd 11367
62nd Ave & Rd 11367
63rd Ave & Rd 11367
64th Ave & Rd 11367
65th Ave 11367
68th Ave, Dr & Rd 11367
69th Ave & Rd 11367
70th Ave & Rd 11367
71st Ave & Rd 11367
72nd Ave, Cres, Dr & Rd 11367
73rd Ave & Ter 11367
75th Ave & Rd 11367
76th Ave & Rd 11367
77th Ave & Rd 11367
78th Ave, Dr & Rd 11367
79th Ave 11367
119th St 11354
120th St 11354
121st St 11354
122nd St 11354
123rd St 11354
124th St 11354
125th St 11354

126th St 11354
127th St 11354
133rd St 11355
134th St
5501-5597 11355
6100-6199 11367
135th St 11355
136th St
5600-6000 11355
6122-7399 11367
137th St
2900-3499 11354
5500-5699 11355
6300-7600 11367
7602-7698 11367
138th St
2900-3098 11354
3100-3200 11354
3202-3898 11354
5500-6099 11355
6100-7830 11367
7832-7878 11367
139th St
2900-2998 11354
7200-7299 11367
140th St
3100-3112 11354
3114-3199 11354
6800-6900 11367
6902-6998 11367
141st Pl 11367
141st St
2600-2700 11354
2702-2898 11354
5601-5799 11355
6800-7799 11367
7801-7899 11367
142nd St 11355
143rd St 11354
145th Pl & St 11354
146th Pl 11367
146th St
2500-2558 11354
2560-3599 11354
5700-6099 11355
6100-6199 11367
6201-7999 11367
147th Pl 11354
147th St
2501-2797 11354
2799-4099 11354
4100-4399 11355
6700-7999 11367
148th Pl 11367
148th St
2500-3499 11354
5600-6098 11355
6100-6199 11367
149th Pl
3300-4099 11354
4100-4299 11355
149th St
2500-2898 11354
2900-4099 11354
4100-4599 11355
6100-7999 11367
150th Pl 11354
150th St
2500-4099 11354
4100-5899 11355
5901-6099 11355
6100-7999 11367
151st St 11355
152nd St
3000-3299 11354
5400-5499 11355
6700-7999 11367
153rd St
3000-3599 11354
5400-5500 11355
5502-6098 11355
7000-7999 11367
154th Pl 11355
154th St
2500-2526 11354
7900-7999 11367
155th St
2900-3198 11354
3200-4099 11354
4200-5999 11355
6100-6599 11367
156th St
2800-3599 11354
4100-5999 11355
6100-6199 11367
157th St
2500-4099 11354
4100-5999 11355
6100-6199 11367
158th St 11358
159th St 11358
160th St 11358
161st St 11358
162nd St 11358
163rd Pl & St 11358
164th St 11358
165th St 11358
166th St 11358
167th St 11358
168th St 11358
169th St 11358
170th St 11358
171st Pl & St 11358
172nd St 11358
187th St 11358
188th St 11358
189th St 11358
190th St 11358
191st St 11358
192nd St 11358
193rd St 11358
194th St 11358
195th St 11358
196th Pl & St 11358
197th St 11358
198th St 11358
199th St 11358

FRESH MEADOWS NY

POST OFFICE BOXES MAIN OFFICE STATIONS AND BRANCHES

Box No.s
1 - 658005 11365
660001 - 660176 11366

NAMED STREETS

Booth Memorial Ave 11365
Francis Lewis Blvd 11365
Fresh Meadow Ln 11365
Gladwin Ave 11365
Hollis Court Blvd 11365
Horace Harding Expy 11365
Jewel Ave 11365
Lanchins St 11366
Lithonia Ave 11365
Metcalf Ave 11365
Millonge St 11365
Park Ave 11365
Parsons Blvd
5700-7299 11365
7301-7497 11366
7499-7999 11366
Peck Ave 11365
Pidgeon Meadow Rd 11365
Sutton Pl 11365
Underhill Ave 11365
Union Tpke 11366
Utopia Pkwy
4801-4897 11365
4899-7000 11365
7002-7098 11365
7300-7600 11366
7602-7798 11366
Weeks Ln 11365

NUMBERED STREETS

48th Ave 11365
49th Ave 11365
50th Ave 11365
51st Ave 11365
53rd Ave 11365
56th Ave 11365
58th Ave 11365
59th Ave 11365
64th Ave & Cir 11365
65th Ave & Cres 11365
67th 11365
68th Ave 11365
69th Ave 11365
71st Ave & Cres 11365
72nd Ave 11365
73rd Ave 11366
74th Ave 11366
75th Ave & Rd 11366
76th Ave & Rd 11366
77th Ave & Rd 11366
78th Ave & Rd 11366
79th Ave 11366
159th St 11365
160th St
5700-7299 11365
7300-7899 11366
161st St 11365
162nd St
5700-7200 11365
7300-7899 11366
163rd St 11365
164th St
4801-5697 11365
7300-7899 11366
165th St
6100-7199 11365
7800-7899 11366
166th St
4900-7199 11365
7201-7299 11365
7301-7497 11366
7499-7899 11366
167th St
4900-7199 11365
7300-7498 11366
168th St
4900-7199 11365
7301-7497 11366
169th St
4900-7199 11365
7300-7799 11366
170th Pl 11365
170th St
4900-7199 11365
7300-7799 11366
171st St
4800-7199 11365
7300-7799 11366
172nd St
6000-7199 11365
7300-7699 11366
173rd St
6100-7099 11365
7300-7700 11366
174th St
5600-7099 11365
7300-7699 11366
175th Pl 11365
175th St
5000-7099 11365
7300-7398 11366
176th St 11366
177th St 11366
178th St
6900-6999 11365
7300-7599 11366
179th St
6700-6999 11365
7300-7599 11366
180th St
6500-6999 11365
7300-7599 11366
181st St
6400-6999 11365
7300-7583 11366
182nd St
5801-6097 11365
7300-7599 11366
183rd St
5800-6979 11365
7300-7599 11366
184th St
5000-6999 11365
7300-7599 11366
185th St
5000-6999 11365
7300-7599 11366
186th Ln 11365
187th St
4800-5899 11365
7300-7599 11366
188th St
6911A-6913A 11365
189th St
4800-5899 11365
7300-7599 11366
190th Ln 11365
192nd St
6402B-6752B 11365
193rd Ln 11365
194th Ln 11365
195th Ln 11365
196th Pl
4800-5899 11365
7300-7599 11366
196th St
4800-5899 11365
7300-7599 11366
197th St
5300-6999 11365
7300-7599 11366
198th St
5300-6999 11365
7300-7599 11366
199th St
5000-5700 11365
7300-7598 11366

GARDEN CITY NY

General Delivery 11530

POST OFFICE BOXES MAIN OFFICE STATIONS AND BRANCHES

Box No.s
1 - 1851 11530
2000 - 5019 11531
7121 - 9998 11530
9997 - 9997 11531

NAMED STREETS

Adams St 11530
Amherst St 11530
Andover Ct 11530
Ardsley Blvd 11530
Argyle Rd 11530
Arthur St 11530
Ash St 11530
Atlantic Ave 11530
Avalon Rd 11530
Avenue U 11530
Axinn Ave 11530
Bane Rd 11530
Barnes Ln 11530
Bayberry Ave 11530
Beech St 11530
Birch Ln 11530
Bluebell Ct 11530
Boulevard Pl 11530
Boylston St 11530
Brixton Rd S 11530
Bromleigh Rd N 11530
Brompton Rd S 11530
Brook St 11530
Butler Pl 11530
Cambridge Ave 11530
Camearri Ave 11530
Carlton Ter 11530
Caroline Ave 11530
Carteret Pl 11530
Cathedral Ave 11530
Cedar Pl 11530
Charles Lindbergh Blvd 11530
Chelsea Rd 11530
Cherry Valley Ave 11530
Chester Ave 11530
Chestnut St 11530
Childs Ave 11530
Claydon Rd 11530
Clinch Ave 11530
Clinton Rd 11530
College Pl 11530
Colonial Ave 11530
Colvin Dr 11530
Commander Ave 11530
Commercial Ave 11530
Coventry Pl 11530
Covert Ave & Pl 11530
Croyden Rd 11530
Damson St 11530
Dartmouth St 11530
Davis Ave 11530
Devereaux Pl 11530
Dibblee Dr 11530
Dorchester Rd 11530
Dover Ave & Pkwy 11530
Duncan Ave 11530
East Dr & Rd 11530
Edgemere Rd 11530
Education Dr 11530
Ellington Ave E & W 11530
Elm St 11530
Elton Rd N 11530
Emmet Pl 11530
Endo Blvd 11530
Eton Rd 11530
Euston Rd S 11530
Fair Ct 11530
Fairmount Blvd 11530
Fenimore Ave 11530
Fernwood Ter N 11530
Filbert St 11530
Flower Rd 11530
Franklin Ave & Ct E & W 11530
Garden Blvd & St 11530
Garden City Plz 11530
Garfield St 11530
S & E Gate Blvd 11530
Glen Rd 11530
Godfrey Ave 11530
Golf Club Ln 11530
Greenridge Ave & Park 11530
Grove St 11530
Hamilton Pl 11530
Hampton Rd S 11530
Harmon Ave 11530
Harrison St 11530
Harvard Rd & St S 11530
Harvey Hall 11530
Hathaway Dr 11530
Hawthorne Rd 11530
Hayes St 11530
Hazelhurst Ave 11530
Heath Pl 11530
Hilton Ave 11530
Homestead Ave 11530
Hudson Rd 11530
Huntington Rd 11530
Iris Ln 11530
Ivy Ct 11530
Jackson St 11530
Jefferson St 11530
John St 11530
Keenan Pl 11530
Kellum Pl 11530
Kenmore Rd 11530
Kensington Ct & Rd 11530
Kenwood Rd 11530
Kilburn Rd S 11530
Kildare Rd 11530
Kingsbury Rd 11530
Laurel St 11530
Lee Rd 11530
Lefferts Rd 11530
Levermore Hall 11530
Lincoln St 11530
Lindbergh St 11530
Linden St 11530
Locust St 11530
Lydia Ln 11530
M H Plz 11530
Magnolia Ave 11530
Main Ave & St 11530
Manor Rd 11530
Maple St 11530
Maria Ln 11530
Maxwell Rd 11530
Mayfair Ave 11530
Meadbrook Rd 11530
Meadow St 11530
Merrilon Ave 11530
Middleton Rd 11530
Miller Ave 11530
Mitchel Field Way 11530
Mitchell Fld 11530
Monroe St 11530
Mulberry Ave 11530
Nassau Blvd & Pl 11530
New Hyde Park Rd 11530
Newmarket Rd 11530
North Ave & Rd 11530
Oak St 11530
Old Country Rd
2-630 11530
630-630 11531
640-1098 11530
Osborne Rd 11530
Oxford Blvd S 11530
Pell Ter 11530
Pine St 11530
Plattsdale Rd 11530
Plaza Rd 11530
Poplar St 11530
Prescott St 11530
Primrose Ct 11530
Princeton Ave & St S 11530
Prospect Ave 11530
Quentin Roosevelt Blvd 11530
Raymond Ct 11530
Rice Cir 11530
Ring Rd W 11530
Rockaway Ave 11530
Roderick Ln 11530
Roosevelt St 11530
Roxbury Rd S 11530
Russell Rd 11530
Sackville Rd 11530
Saint James St N & S 11530
Saint Pauls Cres & Pl 11530
Salisbury Ave 11530
Sandy Ct 11530
Seabury Rd 11530
Selfridge Ave 11530
Somerset Ave 11530
South Ave & St 11530
Spruce St 11530
Stewart Ave
830A-830A 11599
3-5 11530
7-791 11530
56-56 11530
793-1299 11530
830-830 11599
900-1298 11530
Stratford Ave 11530
Suffolk Ln 11530
Sunset Ln 11530
Surrey Ln 11530
Tanners Pond Rd 11530
Terrace Ave & Park 11530
Transverse Rd 11530
Tremont St 11530
Tulip Ave 11530
Tullamore Rd 11530
Vanderbilt Ct 11530
Vassar St 11530
Waldo Hall 11530
Warren Blvd 11530
Warton Pl 11530
Washington Ave 11530
Wellington Rd S 11530
Westbury Rd 11530
Westminster Rd 11530
Wetherill Rd 11530
Weyford Ter 11530
Wheeler Ave 11530
Whitehall Blvd & Rd 11530
Wickham Rd 11530
Willow St 11530
Wilmar Pl 11530
Wilson St 11530
Woodoak Pl 11530
Wyatt Rd 11530
Wydler Ct 11530
Yale Rd & St 11530
Zeckendorf Blvd 11530

NUMBERED STREETS

All Street Addresses 11530

GREAT NECK NY

General Delivery 11022

POST OFFICE BOXES MAIN OFFICE STATIONS AND BRANCHES

Box No.s
1 - 497 11022
1001 - 1322 11023
2001 - 2270 11022
4001 - 4912 11023
220001 - 229005 11022
230401 - 235003 11023

NAMED STREETS

Albert Ct 11024
Alger Rd 11023
Allen Dr 11020
Allen Ln 11024
Allenwood Rd 11023
Amherst Rd E 11021
Andover Rd 11023
Appletree Ln 11024
Arbor St 11021
Arcadia Ln 11020
Ardsley Pl 11021
Arleigh Rd 11021
Arrandale Ave 11024
Ascot Ridge Rd 11021
Ash Dr & Pl 11021
Aspen Pl 11021
Aster Ln 11020
Austin Pl 11020
N Avalon Rd 11021
Baker Hill Rd 11023
Ballantine Ln 11024
Bancroft Ln 11024
Barincon Rd 11020
Barstow Rd 11021
Bates Rd 11020
Bayport Ln N 11023
Bayside Dr & Ter 11023
Bayview Ave
1-100 11021
102-136 11023
138-171 11023
173-199 11023
Beach Rd 11023
Beadwate Rd 11023
Bearenti Rd 11021

Beech Dr & Ln 11024
Bell Cv 11024
Bellingham Ln 11023
Belmont Rd 11020
Bentley Rd 11023
Berkshire Rd 11023
Bernard St 11023
Betsy Ct 11021
Beverly Rd 11021
Birch St 11023
Birch Hill Rd 11020
Birchwood Ln 11024
Blossom Rd 11024
Blue Bird Dr 11023
Blue Sea Ln 11024
Bly Ct 11023
Bond St 11021
Bowers Ln 11020
Boxwood Dr 11021
Brampton Ln 11023
Brentwood Ln 11023
Breuer Ave 11023
Briar Ln 11024
Briarfield Dr 11020
Bridle Path 11021
Bridle Path Ln 11020
Broadlawn Ave 11024
Broadway 11021
Brokaw Ln 11023
Bromley Ln 11023
Brompton Rd 11021
Brook Ln 11023
Brookbridge Rd 11021
Brown Ct & Rd 11024
Buckingham Pl 11021
Burbury Ln 11023
Buttonwood Rd 11020
Byron Ln 11023
Cambridge Rd 11023
Candy Ln 11023
Canterbury Rd 11021
Carlin Pl 11023
Carlton Rd 11021
Carriage Rd 11024
Cary Rd 11021
Catalina Dr 11024
Cathy Ln 11024
Cedar Dr 11021
Central Dr 11024
Centre Dr 11024
Chadwick Rd 11023
Channel Dr 11024
Chapel Pl 11021
Chelsea Pl 11021
Cherry Ln 11024
Cherry Brook Pl N & S 11020
Chester Dr 11021
Chestnut Dr 11021
Church St 11023
N & S Circle Dr 11021
Clair St 11021
Clark Dr 11020
Clent Rd 11021
N Clover Dr 11021
Colgate Rd 11023
Colonial Rd 11021
Community Dr 11021
Concord Ave 11020
Cooper Dr 11023
Cornelia Ave 11024
Cornell Dr & Pl 11020
Country Pl 11021
Cove Ln 11024
Cow Ln 11024
Crampton Ave 11023
Creek Rd 11024
Crescent Rd 11021
Crestwood Pl 11024
Crickett Ln 11024
Crosswood Rd 11023
Croyden Ave 11023
Crystal Dr 11021
Cumberland Ave 11020
Cuttermill Rd 11021
Cypress Ave 11024
Dale Carnegie Ct 11020
Darley Rd 11021
Day Ct 11021
Deepdale Dr 11021
Deer Park Rd 11024
Denton Ct & Rd 11024
Devon Rd 11023
Devonshire Ln 11023
Dickenson Pl 11023
Dock Ln 11024
Dodford Rd 11021
Dogwood Rd 11024
Dorset Rd 11020
Drury Ln 11023
Dunster Rd 11021
Duxbury Rd 11023
Dwight Ln 11024
Eagle Point Dr 11024
East Rd 11024
Edgewater Ln 11023
Edgewood Pl 11024
Effron Pl 11020
Ellard Ave 11024
Elliot Rd 11021
Elm Ln 11020
Elm Pl 11024
Elm St 11021
Elmridge Rd 11024
Embassy Ct 11021
Emerson Dr 11023
W End Ave 11023
W End Dr 11020
Essex Rd 11023
Fairfield Rd 11024
Fairview Ave 11023
Fairway Dr 11020
Farm Ln 11020
Farmers Rd 11024
Fayette Pl 11020
Fieldstone Ln 11020
Fir Dr 11024
Fleetwood Ct 11024
Florence Ave 11024
Florence St 11023
Flower Ln 11024
Floyd Pl 11024
Forest Ave 11023
Forest Ln 11024
Forest Row
1-28 11023
29-99 11024
Fox Hunt Ln 11020
Foxwood Rd 11024
Franklin Pl 11023
Franklin Rd 11024
Gallagher Ct 11021
Garden St 11021
N & S Gate Rd 11023
Gateway Dr 11021
Gatsby Ln 11024
Gay Dr 11024
Genevieve Pl 11021
George St 11024
Georgian Ln 11024
Gilbert Rd 11024
Gilchrest Rd 11021
Glamford Rd 11023
Glenwood Dr & St 11021
Gloucester Ct 11021
Gould St 11023
Governors Ct 11023
Grace Ave & Ct 11021
Gracefield Dr 11024
Grady Ct 11023
Grandview Ave 11020
Grassfield Rd 11024
Great Neck Rd 11021
Greenacre Ct 11021
Greenleaf Hl 11023
Grenfell Dr 11020
Grenwolde Dr 11024
Gristmill Ln 11023
Grosvenor Pl 11021
Gussack Plz 11021
Gutheil Ln 11024
Hale Dr 11024
Hall Ct 11024
Hampshire Rd 11023
Hampton Ct & Rd 11020
Hamptworth Ct & Dr 11024
Harbor Way 11024
Harbour Rd 11024
Harris Ct 11021
Hartley Rd 11023
Hawthorne Ln & Ter 11023
Hayden Ave 11024
Helen Ln 11024
Hemlock Dr 11024
Hemsley Ln 11023
Henhawk Rd 11024
Henry St 11023
Hereford Rd 11020
Heritage Ln 11024
Hewlett Ln & Pl 11024
Hickory Dr 11021
Hicks Ln 11024
Highland Ave 11021
Highland Pl 11020
Hill Park Ave 11021
Hillcrest Dr 11021
Hillside Ave 11021
Hilltop Dr 11021
Holleys Ln 11023
Horace Harding Blvd 11020
Horizon Rd 11020
Horizon Way 11024
Horseshoe Ln 11020
Hutchinson Ct 11023
Imperial Ct 11023
Iowa Rd 11020
Ipswich Ave 11021
Iris Ln 11020
Jayson Ave
71A-71B 11021
18-99 11021
4500-4799 11021
Jeffrey Ln 11020
Johnstone Rd 11021
Jordan Dr 11021
Juniper Dr 11021
Keats Ln 11023
Kenneth Ct 11024
Kennilworth Ter 11024
Kensington Ct 11021
Kensington Pl 11020
Kensington Gate 11021
Kent Pl 11020
Kings Ct & Pl 11024
Kings Point Rd 11024
Kings Terrace Rd 11024
Knightsbridge Rd 11021
Lake Rd N, S & W 11020
Lakeview Dr 11020
Lakeville Rd 11020
Larch Dr 11021
Laurel Dr 11021
Lawson Ln 11023
Lee Ave 11021
Lee Ct 11024
Lee Ct W 11024
Lighthouse Rd 11024
Lincoln Rd 11021
Linden Blvd, Pl & St 11021
Linford Rd 11021
Links Dr 11020
Locust Dr 11021
Locust St 11023
Locust Cove Ln 11024
Lodge Rd 11021
Longfellow Rd 11023
Longview Pl 11021
Magnolia Dr 11021
Manor Dr & Pl 11020
Maple Dr 11021
Maple St 11023
Maple Grove St 11023
Margaret Ct 11024
Margot Pl 11023
Market Ln 11020
Marshall Ct 11021
Martin Ct 11024
Masefield Way 11023
Mcknight Dr 11021
Meadow Woods Rd 11020
Melbourne Rd 11021
Melville Ln 11023
Merrivale Rd
1-15 11021
16-16 11020
18-100 11020
Merrivale Ter 11020
Meryl Ln 11024
Middle Neck Rd
2-8 11021
10-226 11021
228-298 11021
261-417 11023
419-701 11023
702-704 11024
703-705 11023
706-999 11024
S Middle Neck Rd 11021
E & W Mill Dr 11021
Millbrook Ct 11021
Mirrielees Cir & Rd 11021
Mitchell Dr 11024
Moline Ct 11024
Moreland Ct 11024
Morris Ln 11024
Myrtle Dr 11021
Nassau Dr & Rd 11021
Nirvana Ave 11023
Norfolk Rd 11020
North Dr 11021
North Rd 11024
Northern Blvd 11021
Nottingham Pl 11023
Oak Dr 11021
Oakland Pl 11021
Oakley Pl 11020
Oaks Hunt Rd 11020
Old Colony Ln 11023
Old Cuttermill Rd 11021
Old Farm Rd 11020
Old Field Ln 11020
Old Lakeville Rd 11020
Old Mill Rd 11023
Old Pond Rd 11023
Old Tree Ln 11024
Olive St 11020
Orchard Ln 11024
Orchard Rd 11021
Orchard St 11023
Overlook Ave 11021
Overlook Rd 11020
Oxford Blvd 11023
Paddock Ln 11020
Pallorin Rd 11024
Park Cir 11024
Park Pl
1-7 11024
2-6 11024
8-99 11024
9-11 11021
13-30 11021
32-34 11021
W Park Pl 11023
Parkside Dr 11021
Parkwood Dr 11023
Patsy Pl 11023
Pearce Pl 11021
Pembroke Ave 11020
Pheasant Run 11024
Piccadilly Rd 11023
Pickwood Ln 11024
Pilvinis Dr 11024
Pine Dr 11021
Pine Hill Rd 11020
Pine Tree Dr 11024
Plymouth Rd 11023
Polo Rd 11023
Polo Field Ln 11020
Pond Rd 11024
Pond Hill Rd 11020
Pond Park Rd 11023
Pond View Rd 11023
Pont St 11021
Poplar Ct 11024
Portico Ct & Pl 11021
Potters Ct & Ln 11024
Preston Rd 11023
Prospect Pl & St 11021
Radcliff Dr 11024
Radnor Rd 11023
Ramsey Rd 11023
N Ravine Rd 11023
Red Brook Rd & Ter 11024
Reed Ct 11024
Remsen Rd 11024
Ridge Dr E & W 11021
Ridgeway Dr 11024
Rivers Dr 11020
Road On The Hl 11023
Robbins Ln 11020
Robin Way 11021
Robin Hill Rd 11024
Rodney Ln 11024
Rogers Rd 11024
Romola Dr 11024
Rose Ave 11021
Rosemont Pl 11023
Roseth Pl 11020
Round Hill Rd 11020
Russell Woods Rd 11021
Ruth Ct 11023
Rutland Rd 11020
Ruxton Rd 11023
Saddle Rock Ter 11023
Saint George Rd 11021
Saint Pauls Pl 11021
Sands Ct 11023
Schenck Ave 11021
School House Ln 11020
N Service Rd 11020
Shadow Ln 11021
Shady Brook Rd 11024
Sheffield Rd 11021
Shelly Ln 11023
Shelter Bay Dr 11024
Shore Dr
1-12 11021
1-32 11024
33-99 11024
34-98 11024
E Shore Rd
90-98 11023
100-397 11023
399-399 11023
400-600 11024
W Shore Rd 11024
Shore Park Rd 11023
Shorecliff Pl 11023
Shoreward Dr 11021
Sinclair Dr 11024
Singley Ct 11021
Somerset Dr N & S 11020
Soundview Dr 11020
Soundview Ln 11024
Soundview Rd 11020
South Dr 11021
South St 11023
Spinney Hill Dr 11020
Split Rock Dr 11024
Spring Ln 11024
Spruce Pl & St 11021
N Station Plz 11021
S Station Plz 11021
Station Rd 11023
Steamboat Rd 11024
Stepping Stone Ln 11024
Sterling Rd 11024
Steven Ln 11024
Stevenson Dr 11023
Stewart Dr 11021
Stonehenge Rd 11023
Stoner Ave 11021
Stony Run Rd 11023
Strathmore Rd 11023
Stream Ct 11023
Stuart St 11023
Summer Ave 11020
Summer St 11021
Summit Rd 11024
Sunset Rd 11024
Surrey Ln 11023
Surrey Rd 11020
Susquehanna Ave 11021
Sussex Rd 11020
Sutton Ct 11021
Sycamore Dr 11021
Tain Dr 11021
Talbot Dr 11020
Tanners Rd 11020
W Terrace Cir, Dr & Rd 11021
The Cir 11020
Tideway St 11024
Tobin Ave 11021
Town House Pl 11021
Tuddington Rd 11023
Tulip Dr 11021
Turtle Cove Ln 11024
Twin Ponds St 11024
Udall Dr 11020
University Pl & Rd 11020
Upland Rd 11020
Valley View Rd 11021
Van Nostrand Ave 11024
Vanderbilt Dr 11020
Vista Dr 11021
Vista Hill Rd 11021
Walden Ave & Pl 11020
Walnut Pl 11021
Walters Pl 11023
Warwick Rd 11023
Watermill Ln 11021
Waterview Rd 11024
Webb Hill Rd 11020
Wedgewood Ct 11023
Weigt Ct 11021
Welwyn Rd
1-9 11021
1-9 11022
2-8 11021
10-99 11021
Wensley Dr
1-50 11021
52-99 11020
Wesey Ct 11024
West Dr 11021
Westbrook Rd 11024
Westcliff Dr 11020
Westminster Rd 11020
Weybridge Rd 11023
White Pine Ln 11023
Whitman Rd 11023
Wilbur Dr 11021
Wildwood Dr & Rd 11024
William St 11023
William Penn Rd 11023
Willow Ln 11023
Willow Pl 11021
Wilshire Dr 11020
Wilwade Rd 11020
Wimbleton Ln 11023
Windsor Rd 11021
Windsor Gate 11020
Winfield Ter 11023
Wood Ct & Rd 11024
Woodbourne Rd 11023
Woodcrest Rd 11024
Woodland Pl 11021
Woodlawn Ave 11023
W Woods Rd 11020
Wooleys Ln 11023
Wooleys Ln E 11021
Wycham Pl 11021
Wyngate Pl 11021
York Dr 11021

NUMBERED STREETS

All Street Addresses 11021

HEMPSTEAD NY

General Delivery 11551

POST OFFICE BOXES MAIN OFFICE STATIONS AND BRANCHES

Box No.s
All PO Boxes 11551

NAMED STREETS

Acacia Ave 11550
Adams Ave 11550
Alabama Ave 11550
Albemarle Ave 11550
Alicia Ct 11550
Allen St 11550
Amherst St 11550
Angevine Ave 11550
Ann St 11550
Ash Ct 11550
Astor Ct 11550
Atlantic Ave 11550
Attorney St 11550
Azalia Ct 11550
Baldwin Rd 11550
Beatrice Ct 11550
Bedell Ave & St 11550
Bedford Rd 11550
Beebe Ave 11550
Beech St 11550
Bell St 11550
Belmont Pkwy 11550
Bennett Ave 11550
Bernhard St 11550
Beverly Rd 11550
Blemton Pl 11550
Booth St 11550
Botsford St 11550
Boylston St 11550
Brickstone Ct 11550
Broadfield Rd 11550
Brooklyn Rd 11550
Brower Ln 11550
Brown Ave 11550
Burnett St 11550
Burr Ave 11550
Burston St 11550
Butler Pl 11550
Byrd St 11550
California Ave 11550
Cameron Ave 11550
Carman St 11550
Carolina Ave 11550
Cathedral Ave & Ct 11550
Catherine St 11550
Cedar St 11550
Central Ave 11550
Centre St 11550
Chamberlain St 11550
Chase St 11550
Chasner St 11550
Chelsea Pl 11550
Cherry Ln 11550
Chester St 11550
Christie St 11550
Church St 11550
Circle Dr 11550
Clarendon Rd 11550
Clark Pl 11550
Cleaves Ave 11550
Clemente Pl 11550
Clermont Ave 11550
Cliff Ave 11550
Clinton St 11550
Clowes Ave 11550
Clyde Ave 11550
E & W Columbia St 11550
Commander Ave 11550
Cooper St W 11550
Cornell St 11550
Cornwall Ln 11550

Cottage Pl 11550
Courtenay Rd 11550
Covert St 11550
Crowell St 11550
Cruikshank Ave 11550
Curtis Ave 11550
Cynthia Ct 11550
Dakota Pl 11550
Dale Ave 11550
Darina Ct 11550
Dartmouth St 11550
Delaware Pl 11550
Denton Grn 11550
Devon Rd 11550
Dicks Ln 11550
Dietz St 11550
Dikeman St 11550
Dorlon St 11550
Dover Pl 11550
Downs Rd 11550
Duncan Rd 11550
Duryea Pl 11550
Edgewood Ct 11550
Eldridge Ave & Pl 11550
Elizabeth Ave & Ct 11550
Elk Ct & St 11550
Elm Ave 11550
Elmwood Ave 11550
Emery St 11550
Evans Ave 11550
Fairview Blvd 11550
Fairway Dr 11550
Fern St 11550
Flint Ave 11550
Florence Ave 11550
Flower St 11550
Fordham Pl 11550
Foster Pl 11550
N & S Franklin St 11550
Frazier St 11550
Front St 11550
Fulton Ave
1-203 11550
182-202 11551
204-1098 11550
205-731 11550
Garden Pl 11550
Garfield Pl 11550
Georgia St 11550
Gertrude St 11550
Gladys Ave 11550
Glenmore Ave 11550
E & W Graham Ave 11550
Grand Ave 11550
Grant St 11550
Green Ave 11550
Greenlawn Ct 11550
Greenwich St 11550
Grove St 11550
Hamilton Pl & Rd 11550
Hapsburg Pl 11550
Harold Ave 11550
Harriet Ave 11550
Harriman Ave 11550
Harrison Ave 11550
Harry Ct 11550
Harvard St 11550
Heath Pl 11550
Hedgeway Ct 11550
Helen Keller Way 11550
Helena Dr 11550
Hempstead Ave 11550
Hendrickson Ave 11550
Henry St 11550
Hewlett St 11550
High St 11550
Highland Ave 11550
Hilbert St 11550
Hilton Ave & Pl 11550
Hoff Ct 11550
Holly Ave 11550
Homan Blvd 11550
Hope St 11550
Hudson Pl 11550
Ingraham Blvd, Ln & St 11550
Intersection St 11550
Irene St 11550
Jackson Ct & St 11550
James L L Burrell Ave 11550
Jane St 11550
Jean Ave 11550
Jefferson Pl 11550
Jerusalem Ave 11550
Johnson Pl 11550
Kane Ave 11550
Kellum Pl 11550
Kendig Pl 11550
Kennedy Ave 11550
Kensington Ct 11550
Kernochan Ave 11550
Koeppel Pl 11550
Lafayette Ave 11550
Lancaster Pl 11550
Laurel Ave 11550
Lawrence Rd 11550
Lawson St 11550
Lent Ave 11550
Leverich St 11550
Lewis Pl 11550
Lexington Cir 11550
Liberty Ct 11550
Lincoln Blvd & Rd 11550
Lindbergh St 11550
Linden Ave & Pl 11550
Locust St 11550
Long Dr 11550
Long Beach Rd 11550
Lucille St 11550
Macdonald St 11550
Madison Ave 11550
Main St 11550
Manor Ave & Ct 11550
Maple Ave 11550
Maplewood Ave 11550
Margaret Ct 11550
E & W Marshall St 11550
Martin Ave 11550
Martin Luther King Dr 11550
Marvin Ave 11550
Maryland Ave 11550
Mason St 11550
Maude St 11550
May St 11550
Mead Ter 11550
Meade St 11550
Meadowbrook Rd 11550
Meriam St 11550
Midwood St 11550
Milburn Ave 11550
Milford St 11550
Miller Pl 11550
Mirschel St 11550
Mitchell Ct 11550
Monroe Pl 11550
Moore Ave 11550
Morrell St 11550
Morton Ave 11550
Mulford Pl 11550
Myrtle Ave 11550
Nassau Pkwy & Pl 11550
New Ct 11550
Newmans Ct 11550
Nichols Ct 11550
Nostrand Pl 11550
Oak Ave & St 11550
Oakland St 11550
Oakmont Ave 11550
Old Franklin St 11550
Olive Blvd 11550
Olsen Pl 11550
W Orchard St 11550
Ormond St 11550
Page Ave 11550
Park Pl 11550
Parsons Dr 11550
Patterson Ave 11550
Peninsula Blvd 11550
Pennsylvania Ave 11550
Perry St 11550
Peters Ave 11550
Phoenix St 11550
Pierson Ave 11550
Pilot St 11550
Pine St 11550
Polk Ave 11550
Powell Pl 11550
President St 11550
Primrose Ln 11550
Princeton St 11550
Prospect Pl 11550
Remsen Ave 11550
Rev Clinton C Boone Pl 11550
Revere Ct 11550
Rhodes Ave 11550
Richardson Pl 11550
Robinwood Ave 11550
Robson Pl 11550
Roger St 11550
Roosevelt St 11550
Rose Ave 11550
Rundle Ct 11550
Rutland Rd 11550
Ryan Ct 11550
Saint James Pl 11550
Saint Pauls Pl & Rd 11550
Saint Regis Pl 11550
Sammis Pl 11550
Saratoga Cir 11550
Seabury St 11550
Sealey Ave 11550
Seaman Ave 11550
Searing St 11550
Seitz Ave 11550
Sewell St 11550
Shady St 11550
Short Pl 11550
Smith St 11550
Spencer Pl 11550
Stanley Pl 11550
Station Plz 11550
Sterling Pl 11550
Stevens Ave 11550
Stewart Ave 11550
Stowe Pl 11550
Stratford Rd 11550
Sunnyside Ave 11550
Sunset Dr 11550
Surrey Ln 11550
Sutton St 11550
Sycamore Ave 11550
Taft Ave 11550
Taylor Pl 11550
Tennessee Ave 11550
Teresa Pl 11550
Terrace Ave 11550
Thomas St 11550
Thorne Ave 11550
Tompkins Pl 11550
Totten St 11550
Tower Ct 11550
Truro Ln 11550
Turnwood Ct 11550
Tyler Ave 11550
Union Pl 11550
Valentine Pl 11550
Valtond Ave 11550
Van Cott Ave 11550
Vanata Ct 11550
Vermont Ave 11550
Villa Ct 11550
Virginia Ave 11550
Warner Ave 11550
Washington Ct & St 11550
Webb Ave 11550
Webber Ave 11550
Weekes Ave 11550
Weil Pl 11550
Weir St 11550
Wellesley St 11550
Wellington Pl & St 11550
Wendell St 11550
Westbury Blvd 11550
Whitson St 11550
William St 11550
Willis St 11550
Willow Ave & St 11550
Windsor Pkwy 11550
Winthrop St 11550
Witley Ct 11550
Woodland Dr 11550
Yale St 11550

HICKSVILLE NY

General Delivery 11802

POST OFFICE BOXES MAIN OFFICE STATIONS AND BRANCHES

Box No.s
All PO Boxes 11802

NAMED STREETS

Abbot Ln 11801
Abode Ln 11801
Access Ln 11801
Acre Ln 11801
Adams St 11801
Adelphi Rd 11801
Admiral Ln 11801
Alan Crest Dr 11801
Albany St 11801
Albert Rd & St 11801
Alexander Ave 11801
Allen St 11801
Alling St 11801
Alpha Plz 11801
Alpine Ln 11801
Amherst Ln & Rd 11801
Andover Ln 11801
Andrews Rd 11801
Angle Ln 11801
Anne Dr 11801
Apex Ln 11801
Apollo Ln 11801
April Ln 11801
Arbor Ln 11801
Arcadia Ln 11801
Arch Ln 11801
Ardsley Gate 11801
Arnold St 11801
Arpad St 11801
Arrow Ln 11801
Ash Ln 11801
Aster Dr 11801
Atlas Ln 11801
Auburn Ln 11801
August Ln 11801
Autumn Ln 11801
Ball Park Ln 11801
Ballad Ln 11801
Balsam Dr & Ln 11801
Bamboo Ln 11801
Bank Ln 11801
E & W Barclay St 11801
Barrel Ln 11801
Barrister Rd 11801
Barry Ct 11801
Barter Ln 11801
Basket Ln 11801
Bay Ave 11801
Beacon Ln 11801
Beech Ln & St 11801
Belfry Ln 11801
Belle Ct 11801
Belmart Ct & Rd 11801
Belmont Pl 11801
Benjamin Ave 11801
Berkshire Rd 11801
Bernadette Ct 11801
Berry Ln 11801
Bethpage Ct, Dr & Rd 11801
Birchwood Ln 11801
Bird Ln 11801
Bishop Ln 11801
Bloomingdale Rd 11801
Blueberry Ln 11801
Boblee Ln 11801
Bobwhite Ln 11801
Boehme St 11801
Bond Ln 11801
Bonnie Ct 11801
Border St 11801
Boulder Ln 11801
Boulevard Dr 11801
Boxwood Ln 11801
Brewster Pl 11801
Bridge Ln 11801
Bridle Ln 11801
Briggs St 11801
Brighton Pl 11801
Brittle Ln 11801
N & S Broadway Mall & Pl 11801
Brooks St 11801
Bruce Ave 11801
Buckner Ave 11801
Buffalo St 11801
Bunker Ln 11801
Burkland Ln 11801
Burns Ave 11801
Byron Pl 11801
Cable Ln 11801
California St 11801
Cambridge Dr 11801
Campus Pl 11801
Cantiague Rock Rd 11801
Carino Dr 11801
E & W Carl St 11801
Carlton Pl 11801
Carol Ct 11801
Carroll St 11801
Cecil Pl 11801
Cedar St 11801
Center St 11801
Chain Ln 11801
Chance St 11801
Charles St 11801
Charlotte Ave 11801
Chatham Ct 11801
E & W Cherry Ln & St 11801
Chestnut St 11801
Cinder Ln 11801
Clarissa Dr 11801
Cliff Dr 11801
Clinton Ln & St 11801
Cloister Ln 11801
Clotilde Ct 11801
Clove Ln 11801
Coe Pl 11801
Colony St 11801
Columbia Rd 11801
Combes Ave 11801
Commerce Pl 11801
Commercial St 11801
Cornell Ave & Ln 11801
Cornwall Ln 11801
Cortland Ave 11801
Cottage Blvd 11801
Country Ct 11801
Crescent St 11801
Crown St 11801
Croyden Ln 11801
Cumberland Rd 11801
Dairy Ln 11801
Dakota St 11801
Dale Ct 11801
Dante Ave 11801
Dartmouth Dr 11801
David Ave 11801
Dawn Ln 11801
S Dean St 11801
Deer Ln 11801
Derby Rd 11801
Desmond Pl 11801
Dikeman Ct 11801
Division Ave 11801
Doris Rd 11801
Dorothy St 11801
Dove St 11801
Duffy Ave 11801
East Ave & St 11801
Edgewood Dr 11801
Edward Ave 11801
Eli Rd 11801
Elliot Dr 11801
S Elm St 11801
Elmira St 11801
Elwood Ave 11801
Emmet Pl 11801
E End Ave 11801
Engel St 11801
Engineers Dr 11801
Enterprise Pl 11801
Ernst Ave 11801
Essex Ln 11801
Eton Ln 11801
Evers St 11801
Fairview Ct 11801
Farm Ln 11801
Farrell Way 11801
Felice Cres 11801
Fern Ct 11801
Ferndale Dr 11801
Ferney St 11801
Field Ave & Ct 11801
Fireplace Ln 11801
Flamingo Rd 11801
Flower St 11801
Foran Pl 11801
N & S Fordham Ave & Rd 11801
Fork Ln 11801
Fountain St 11801
Fox Ct & Pl 11801
Frances Ln 11801
Frank Ave & Rd 11801
Franklin Ct & St 11801
Frederick Pl 11801
Frevert Pl 11801
Friendly Rd 11801
Froehlich Farm Rd 11801
Fuchia Ln 11801
Fulton Ave 11801
Gables Dr & Rd 11801
Garden Blvd & St 11801
Gardenia Ln 11801
Gardner Ave 11801
Gate Ct 11801
Gem Ct 11801
Genesee St 11801
George Ave 11801
Georgia St 11801
Gerald Ave 11801
Ginamarie Ct 11801
Gladys Pl 11801
Glenbrook Rd 11801
Glow Ln 11801
Grand Ave 11801
Grant Ct 11801
Grape Ln 11801
Greenbriar Ln 11801
Grondela Ave 11801
Grove St 11801
Gull Rd 11801
Halsey Ave 11801
Hanover Pl 11801
Harding Ave 11801
Harkin Ln 11801
Harnat Ct 11801
Harrison Ave 11801
Hastings Ln 11801
Hattie Ct 11801
Haverford Rd 11801
Hawks Ct 11801
Hawthorne St 11801
Hazel St 11801
Heitz Pl 11801
Hemp Ln 11801
Henrietta St 11801
Henry Ave & Pl 11801
Herald Ln 11801
Herman Ave 11801
Herzog Pl 11801
Hewitt St 11801
Hicks Cir 11801
High St 11801
Hilton Ct 11801
Hollins Rd 11801
Holly St 11801
Holman Blvd 11801
Holyoke Rd 11801
Home Ln 11801
Honved St 11801
Hope Ln 11801
Horn Ln 11801
Howard St 11801
Hudson Pl & St 11801
Hunter Ln, Pl & St 11801
Hus Pl 11801
Ida Ave 11801
Indiana St 11801
Ingram Dr 11801
Iris Ct 11801
Irving Ct & St 11801
Jackson Pl 11801
James St 11801
Jay St 11801
Jefferson Ave 11801
Jefry Ln 11801
Jerome Ave 11801
Jersey St 11801
N Jerusalem Ave 11801
E John St 11801
W John St
1-222 11801
147-221 11802
223-599 11801
224-600 11801
Jolan Ave 11801
Jonathan Ave 11801
Jordan Ln 11801
Joseph Ln 11801
Julian St 11801
Juniper St 11801
Kansas St 11801
Karin Ln 11801
Keats Pl 11801
Kenneth Ct 11801
Ketcham Ave & Rd 11801
Key Ln 11801
King Ct & St 11801
Kingston Ave 11801
Kolmer Ave 11801
Kraemer St 11801
Kuhl Ave 11801
Lantern Rd 11801
Larch St 11801
Lauman Ln 11801
Laurel St 11801
Lawn Pl 11801
S Lawnside Ave & Dr 11801
Lawnview Ave 11801
Lawrence Ct & St 11801
Layton Ave 11801
Lee Ave & Pl 11801
Lehigh Ln 11801
Lenore Ave 11801
Lenox Ave 11801
Lesley Ct 11801
Levittown Pkwy 11801
Lewis St 11801
Libby Ave 11801
Liberty Ave 11801
Lilac Ln 11801
Linden Blvd & Ct 11801
Link Ln 11801
Liszt St 11801
Locust St 11801
Loretta Ln 11801
Lottie Ave 11801
Louis St 11801
Lowell Pl & St 11801
Ludy St 11801
Lyon Ct 11801
Mabel St 11801
Mack Ave 11801
Madison Ave 11801
Magenta St 11801
Maglie Dr 11801
Malone St 11801
Mangan Pl 11801
Maple Pl 11801
E & W Marie Ct & St 11801

Marion Pl & St 11801
Marvin Ave 11801
Max Ave 11801
Mayfair Ln 11801
Mayflower Dr 11801
Mcalester Ave 11801
Mckinley Ave 11801
Mead Ave 11801
Meadow Ln 11801
Meeting Ln 11801
Memory Ln 11801
Mercury Pl 11801
Michigan Dr 11801
Midland Ave 11801
Milano St 11801
Milburn St 11801
Mill Rd 11801
Miller Cir, Pl & Rd 11801
Millwood Gate 11801
Milton St 11801
Mineola Ave 11801
Mitchell Ct 11801
Moeller St 11801
Monroe Ave 11801
Montana St 11801
Morgan St 11801
Mulberry St 11801
Murray Rd 11801
Myers Ave 11801
Nancy Ln 11801
Narcissus Ave 11801
Narkin Ct 11801
Nelson Ave 11801
Nevada St 11801
New South Rd 11801
Newbridge Rd 11801
E & W Nicholai St 11801
North Dr 11801
Notre Dame Ave 11801
Oak St 11801
Ohio St 11801
E & W Old Country Rd 11801
Ormond Pl 11801
Oxford Pl & St 11801
S Oyster Bay Rd 11801
Page Dr 11801
Palermo St 11801
Parc Ln 11801
Park Ave 11801
Paula St 11801
Peachtree Ln 11801
Peg Ct 11801
Pen Ln 11801
Petal Ln 11801
Peter Rd 11801
Pewter Ln 11801
Pickwick Ct & Dr N & S 11801
Picture Ln 11801
Pierce St 11801
Pine St 11801
Pinetree Ave 11801
Pintle Ct 11801
Plainview Rd 11801
Plover Ln 11801
Po Ln 11801
Poet Ln 11801
Police Plz 11801
Pollok Pl 11801
Potter Ln 11801
Power St 11801
Preston Ln 11801
Primrose Ave 11801
Prince St 11801
Princess St 11801
Prose St 11801
Prospect St 11801
Quality Plz 11801
Queen St 11801
Radnor Ct 11801
Railroad Ln 11801
Railroad Station Plz 11801
Rave St 11801
Ray St 11801
Raymond St 11801
Regent St 11801
Regina St 11801
Reiter Ave 11801
Rhodes Ln 11801
Richard Ave & St 11801
Richfield Ave 11801
Ridge Ct 11801
Rim Ln 11801
Rising Ln 11801
Robert St 11801
Robin Ct 11801
Rockcrest 11801
Roma St 11801
Ronald Ave 11801
Roosevelt Ave 11801
Root Ln 11801
Rover Ln 11801
Roy Ave 11801
Ruth Dr 11801
Sackett St 11801
Saint Johns Ave 11801
Salem Rd 11801
Salem Gate 11801
Sara Pl 11801
Saurer Ct 11801
Savoy Pl 11801
Schiller St 11801
Schrimpe Ct 11801
Scooter Ln 11801
Seth Ln 11801
Seymour Ln 11801
Shady Ln 11801
Shari Ct 11801
Sleepy Ln 11801
Smith St 11801
Somerset Ave 11801
South Ct 11801
Spencer St 11801
Spindle Rd 11801
Spray Ln 11801
Spruce St 11801
Stanford Ln 11801
Stanley St 11801
Stephen Ln 11801
Sterling Pl 11801
Stewart Ave 11801
Story Ln 11801
Straw Ln 11801
Strong St 11801
Suggs Ln 11801
Summer Ln 11801
Summit St 11801
Sunnyfield Rd 11801
Sunset Ave 11801
Susan St 11801
Sussex St 11801
Sutherland Rd 11801
Switzerland Rd 11801
Table Ln 11801
Tanager Ln 11801
Tec St 11801
Terrace Pl 11801
Terrell Ln 11801
Terry St 11801
Texas St 11801
Thimble Ln 11801
Thorman Ave 11801
Tile Ln 11801
Tinker St 11801
Tiptop Ln 11801
Tobias St 11801
Townsend Ln 11801
Trezza Ct 11801
Tudor Rd 11801
Turnbull Ln 11801
Twig Ln 11801
Twinlawns Ave 11801
Underhill Ave 11801
University Pl 11801
Utica Ave 11801
Valerie Ave 11801
Valley Ct & Ln 11801
Vassar Ln 11801
Verbena Ct 11801
Victor Ct 11801
W Village Grn 11801
Vincent Rd 11801
Violet Ave 11801
Walnut Ln 11801
Walter Ave 11801
Ward St 11801
Washington Ave, Pkwy & St 11801
Waters Ave 11801
Wellesley Ln 11801
West Ave & St 11801
Westmoreland Rd 11801
Wicks Ct 11801
Wildwood Rd 11801
Wilfred Blvd 11801
Willet Ave 11801
William St 11801
Willis Ct 11801
Willoughby Ave 11801
Willow Ave & Pl 11801
Willy Ln 11801
Winding Rd 11801
Windsor St 11801
Winter Ln 11801
Wishing Ln 11801
Woodbine Dr E 11801
Woodbury Ct & Rd 11801
Woodcrest Rd 11801
Wyckoff St 11801
York St 11801

NUMBERED STREETS

All Street Addresses 11801

ITHACA NY

General Delivery 14850

POST OFFICE BOXES MAIN OFFICE STATIONS AND BRANCHES

Box No.s
DH - DH 14852
1 - 960 14851
1 - 960 14852
2300 - 2300 14851
3241 - 5998 14852
6401 - 9998 14851

NAMED STREETS

Abbott Ln & Rd 14850
Ad White House 14853
Adam Ave 14850
Adams St 14850
Administrative Anx 14850
Aidans Ln 14850
Akwe Kon 14853
N & S Albany St 14850
Albrectsen Rd 14850
Alessandro Dr 14850
Alex Way 14850
Alice Cook House 14853
Alice Miller Way 14850
Alison St 14850
Alumni Hall 14850
Amber Ln 14850
Amy Ln 14850
Anabel Taylor Hall 14853
Anchor Dr 14850
Anna Comstock Hall 14853
Appel Commons 14853
Apple Blossom Dr 14850
N & S Applegate Rd 14850
Arrowood Dr & Ln 14850
Asbury Dr 14850
Ascot Pl 14850
Ashley Pl 14850
Aspen Way 14850
Auburn St 14850
N & S Aurora St 14850
Autumn Ridge Cir, Dr & Ln 14850
Ayla Way 14850
Babcock Hall 14853
Bailey Hall 14853
N & S Baker 14853
Baker Lab 14853
Baker Tower 14853
Balch Hall 14853
Bald Hill Rd 14850
Bard Hall 14853
Barnes Hall 14853
Barr Rd 14850
Barton Pl 14850
Barton Hall 14853
Bauer Hall 14853
Bean Hill Ln 14850
Beardsley Ln 14850
Beckett Way 14850
Beebe Hall 14853
Beechnut Ter 14850
Bella Vista Cir & Dr 14850
Bellwood Ln 14850
Belvedere Dr 14850
Benny Ln 14850
Berkshire Rd 14850
Besemer Ln & Rd 14850
Besemer Hill Rd 14850
Bio Tech Building 14853
Birchwood Dr N 14850
Black Oak Rd 14850
Blackchin Blvd 14850
Blackstone Ave 14850
Blair St 14850
Bluegrass Ln 14850
Boardman Pl 14850
Bogart Hall 14850
Boldt Hall 14853
Boldt Tower 14853
Bolton Point Rd 14850
Bomax Cir & Dr 14850
Bool St 14850
Boothroyd Hall 14850
Bostwick Rd 14850
Boyce Thompson Inst 14853
Bradfield Hall 14853
Brandon Pl 14850
Brandywine Dr 14850
Brentwood Dr 14850
Brewery Ln 14850
Brianna Dr 14850
Briarwood Dr 14850
Bridge St 14850
Brindley St 14850
Brook Dr, Ln & Way 14850
Brook Tree Ln 14850
Brookfield Rd 14850
Brookhaven Dr 14850
Brooktondale Rd 14850
Brown Rd 14850
Bryant Ave 14850
E & W Buffalo St 14850
Bundy Rd 14850
Burdick Hill Rd 14850
Burleigh Dr 14850
Burns Rd 14850
Bush Ln 14850
Buttermilk Ln 14850
Buttermilk Falls Rd E & W 14850
Caldwell Rd 14850
Caldwell Hall 14853
Calkins Rd 14850
Cambridge Pl 14850
Campbell Ave 14850
N Campus 14853
Campus Rd
1-99 14850
200-299 14853
Candlewyck Park 14850
Captains Walk 14850
Cardinal Dr 14850
Carl Becker House 14853
Carls Way 14850
Carpenter Hall 14853
Cascadilla Ave & St 14850
Cascadilla Hall 14853
Cascadilla Park Rd 14850
Catherine St 14850
Catherwood Rd 14850
N & S Cayuga Ave & St 14850
Cayuga Heights Rd 14850
Cayuga Hills Rd 14850
Cayuga Park Cir & Rd 14850
Cecil Malone Dr 14850
Cedar Ln 14850
Center St 14850
Center For Health Sciences 14850
Center For Natural Sciences 14850
Center For Public Safety 14850
Central Ave 14853
Ceracche Ctr 14850
Charles St 14850
Chase Ln 14850
Chelseas Walk 14850
Cherry Rd & St 14850
Chestnut St 14850
Christopher Cir & Ln 14850
Churchill Dr 14850
Cinema Dr 14850
Clara Dickson Hall 14853
Clark Hall 14853
Clarke Hall 14850
Class Of 17 Hall 14853
Class Of 18 Hall 14853
Class Of 22 Hall 14853
Class Of 26 Hall 14853
Class Of 28 Hall 14853
Cleveland Ave 14850
Cliff St 14850
Cliff Park Cir & Rd 14850
E & W Clinton St 14850
Clover Ln 14850
Cobb St 14850
Coddington Rd 14850
Colegrove Rd 14850
College Ave
100-499 14850
500-599 14853
College Cir
1A-1D 14850
2A-2D 14850
3A-3D 14850
4A-4D 14850
5A-5B 14850
6A-6B 14850
7A-7B 14850
8A-8B 14850
9A-9B 14850
10A-10B 14850
11A-11B 14850
12A-12B 14850
13A-13B 14850
14A-14B 14850
15A-15B 14850
16A-16B 14850
17A-17B 14850
18A-18B 14850
19A-19B 14850
20A-20B 14850
21A-21B 14850
22A-22B 14850
28A-28B 14850
29A-29B 14850
30A-30B 14850
31A-31B 14850
34A-34B 14850
35A-35B 14850
36A-36B 14850
37A-37B 14850
38A-38B 14850
39A-39B 14850
40A-40B 14850
41A-41B 14850
23-34 14850
Columbia St 14850
Comfort Rd 14850
Commercial Ave 14850
Compton Rd 14850
Comstock Rd 14850
Comstock Hall 14853
Concord Pl 14850
Conifer Cir & Dr 14850
Cook St 14850
N & S Corn St 14850
Cornelius Rd 14850
Cornell Ave, St & Walk 14850
Cornell Campus Store 14853
Cornell Communications 14853
Cornell Library 14853
Cornell University 14853
Corson Pl 14850
Corson Hall 14853
Cottage Pl 14850
Country Club Rd 14850
E & W Court St 14850
Court Hall 14853
Coventry Walk 14850
Coy Glen Rd 14850
Craft Rd 14850
Crescent Pl 14850
Crest Ln 14850
Culligan Dr 14850
Culver Rd 14850
Curtis Rd 14850
Cutters Path 14850
Cypress Ct 14850
Danby Rd 14850
Dart Dr 14850
Dates Dr 14850
Day Hall 14853
Dearborn Pl 14850
Decann Dr 14850
Deer Run Rd 14850
Deerfield Ln & Pl 14850
Deerhaven Dr 14850
Delaware Ave 14850
Della St 14850
Delong Ave 14850
Department Comm Arts 14853
Devon Rd 14850
Dewitt Pl 14850
Dey St 14850
Dillingham Ctr 14850
Dobson Rd 14850
Dodge Rd 14850
Dolgen Hall 14853
Donalds Dr 14850
Donlon Hall 14853
Dove Dr 14850
Drew Rd 14850
Dryden Ct & Rd 14850
Duboise Rd 14850
Duffield Hall 14853
Dunmore Pl 14850
Durfee Hill Rd 14850
Dutch Mill Rd 14850
Eagleshead Rd 14850
East Ave 14853
Eastern Heights Dr 14850
Eastlake Rd 14850
Eastman Hall 14850
Eastwood Ave & Ter 14850
Eddy St 14850
Edgecliff Pl 14850
Edgemoor Ln 14850
Edgewood Pl 14850
Egbert Hall 14850
Eldridge Cir 14850
Ellis Hollow Rd 14850
Ellis Hollow Creek Rd 14850
Elm St 14850
Elm Street Ext 14850
Elmcrest Cir 14850
Elmira Rd 14850
Elmwood Ave 14850
Elston Pl 14850
Emerson Hall 14850
Enfield Center Rd E & W 14850
Enfield Falls Rd 14850
Enfield Main Rd 14850
Essex Ct 14850
Estates Dr 14850
Esty Dr & St 14850
Etna Rd 14850
Evergreen Ln 14850
Fair St 14850
Fairgrounds Memorial Pkwy 14850
Fairmount Ave 14850
Fairview Sq 14850
Fairway Dr 14850
Fairwinds Way 14850
Fall Creek Dr 14850
E & W Falls St 14850
Fallview Ter 14850
Farm St 14850
Farrell Rd 14850
Farrier Rd 14853
Fayette St 14850
Fernow Hall 14853
Ferris Pl 14850
Fidler Rd 14850
Fieldstone Cir & Ln 14850
Fish Rd 14850
Fitness Ctr 14850
Five Mile Dr 14850
Flora Rose House 14853
Floral Ave 14850
Forest Dr & Ln 14850
Forest Acres Dr 14850
Forest Home Cir 14850
Forest Home Dr
1-99 14853
100-404 14850
406-498 14850
Forest Park Ln 14850
Founders Hall 14853
Fountain Pl 14850
Fox Hollow Rd 14850
Franklin St 14850
Freese Rd 14850
N & S Fulton St 14850
Game Farm Rd 14850
Gannett Ctr
--- 14853
1-640 14853
1000-1299 14850
Garden Apartment 25 14850
Garden Apartment 26 14850
Garden Apartment 27 14850
Garden Apartment 28 14850
Garden Apartment 29 14850
Garrett Rd 14850
Gaslight Vlg 14850
Gates Hall 14853
N & S Geneva St 14850
Genung Cir & Rd 14850
German Cross Rd 14850
Gilbert Rd 14850
Giles St 14850
Glen Pl 14850
Glenside Rd 14850
Glenwood Rd 14850
Glenwood Heights Rd 14850
Goldwin Smith Hall 14853
Goodwin Dr 14850
Goss St 14850
Graduate Dr 14850
Graham Rd W 14850
Grandview Ave, Ct, Dr & Pl 14850
Gray Rd 14850
E & W Green St 14850
Grove Pl & Rd 14850
Gunderman Rd 14850
Gussie St 14850
Gussie Street Ext 14850
Guterman Lab 14853
Hackberry Ln 14850
Halcyon Hill Rd 14850
Hall Rd 14850
Haller Blvd 14850
Hallwoods Rd 14850
Halseyville Rd 14850
Hammond Health Ctr 14850
Hampton Rd 14850

Hampton Hill Ln 14850
Hancock St 14850
Hans Bethe House 14853
Hanshaw Rd 14850
Happy Ln 14850
Harbor Cir 14850
Hartwood Rd 14850
Harvard Pl 14850
Harvey Hill Rd 14850
Harwick Rd 14850
Hasbrouck Apartments 14850
Hawthorne Cir & Pl 14850
Hayts Rd 14850
Hector St 14850
Heights Ct 14850
Helen Newman Hall 14853
Helens Way 14850
Hemlock Ln 14850
Heron Dr 14850
Hickory Cir, Pl, Rd & Trl 14850
Hickory Hollow Ln 14850
High Rise 5 14853
Highgate Cir, Pl & Rd NE 14850
Highland Ave, Pl & Rd 14850
Highland Park Ln 14850
S & W Hill Cir, Ctr, Rd & Ter 14850
Hillard Hall 14850
Hillcrest Dr & Rd 14850
Hillside Dr 14850
Hilltop Rd 14850
Hillview Pl 14850
Hinging Post Rd 14850
Ho Plz 14850
Hollister Hall 14853
Holly Creek Ln 14850
Holmes Hall 14850
Homestead Cir, Rd & Ter 14850
Honness Ln 14850
Hood Hall 14850
Hook Pl 14850
Hopkins Pl & Rd 14850
Hopper Pl 14850
Horizon Dr 14850
Hornbrook Rd 14850
Horvath Dr 14850
Houghton Rd 14850
Howard Rd 14850
Hubbell Dr 14850
Hudson Hts, Pl & St 14850
Hudson Street Ext 14850
Hughes Hall 14853
Humphreys Service Bldg 14853
Hungerford Rd 14850
Hunt Grove Rd 14850
Hunt Hill Rd 14850
Hunter Ln 14850
Hurd Rd 14850
Hyers St 14850
Ilr Bldg 14853
Indian Creek Rd 14850
Iradell Rd W 14850
Iroquois Pl & Rd 14850
Irving Pl 14850
Ithaca Rd 14850
Ithaca Beer Dr 14850
Ives Hall 14853
Jacobs Dr 14850
Jacobs Drive Ext 14850
Jake St 14850
James St 14850
James L Gibbs Dr 14850
Jameson Hall 14853
Janivar Dr 14850
E & W Jay St 14850
Jennings Pond Rd 14850
W Jersey Hill Rd 14850
Joanne Dr 14850
Job Hall 14850
John St 14850
Johnson Museum 14853
Jon Stone Cir 14850
Jordan Ave 14850
Judd Falls Rd
--- 14853
1-101 14853
103-105 14850
107-199 14850
Juniper Dr 14850
Kay St 14850
Kay Hall 14853
Keith St 14850
Kelaridg Rd 14850
Kelvin Pl 14850
Ken Post Lab 14853
Kendall Ave 14850
Kennedy Hall 14853
Kimball Hall 14853
E & W King Rd & St 14850
Kings Way 14850
Kinzelberg Hall 14853
Kline Rd 14850
Klinewoods Rd 14850
Knight Lab 14853
Knoll Tree Rd 14850
Kraft Rd 14850
Krums Corners Rd 14850
Lagrand Ct 14850
Lake Ave & St 14850
Lake Country Ave 14850
Lancashire Dr 14850
Landmark Dr 14850
N Landon Rd 14850
Landon Hall 14853
Landsman Way 14850
Larisa Ln 14850
Laura Ln 14850
Layen Rd 14850
Leeland Lab 14853
Leifs Way 14850
Lenox Rd 14850
Leslie Ln 14850
E & W Lewis St 14850
Lexington Dr 14850
Lieb Rd 14850
Lilly Dr 14850
E & W Lincoln St 14850
Lincoln Hall 14853
Linden Ave 14850
Lindsay Ln 14850
Linn St 14850
Lisa Ln & Pl 14850
Llenroc Ct 14850
Lodge Way 14850
Lois Ln 14850
Lone Oak Rd 14850
Longview Dr 14850
Loomis Ct 14850
Love Lab 14853
Low Rise 10 14853
Low Rise 6 14853
Low Rise 7 14853
Low Rise 8 14853
Low Rise 9 14853
Lowell Pl 14850
Lower Creek Rd 14850
Lyon Hall 14853
Lyons Hall 14850
Madison St 14850
Makarainen Rd 14850
Mallard Dr 14850
Malott Hall 14853
Mann Library 14853
Maple Ave 14850
Maple Grove Pl 14850
Maplewood Dr, Pt & Rd 14850
Marcy Ct 14850
Markerid 14853
Marsh Rd 14850
Marshal Rd 14850
E & W Marshall St 14850
Mary Ln & St 14850
Mary Ann Wood Dr 14853
Mary Anne Wood Dr 14850
Maxs Dr 14850
Mcfaddin Hall 14853
Mcgraw Pl 14850
Mcgraw Hall 14853
Mcgraw House 14853
Mcintyre Pl 14850
E, W, N & S Meadow Dr & St 14850
Meadow Wood Ter 14850
Meadowlark Dr 14850
Mecklenburg Rd 14850
Mennen Hall 14853
Mews Hall 14853
Midway Rd 14850
Millcroft Way 14850
E & W Miller Rd & St 14850
Mitchell St 14850
Monkey Run Rd 14850
Monroe St 14850
Morrill Hall 14853
Morris Ave & Hts 14850
Morrison Hall 14853
Mount Pleasant Rd 14850
Mudd Hall 14853
Muller Chapel 14850
Muller Faculty Ctr 14850
Murfield Dr 14850
Muriel St 14850
Mussell St 14850
Muzzy Rd 14850
Mvr Hall 14853
Myron Taylor Hall 14853
Needham Pl 14850
Neimi Rd 14850
Nelson Rd 14850
New Buisness School 14850
Newman Lab 14853
Nor Way 14850
W Northview Rd 14850
Northway Rd 14850
Nottingham Dr 14850
Noyes Ldg 14853
Noyes Community Recreation Ctr 14853
Oak Ave 14850
Oak Brook Dr 14850
Oak Hill Pl & Rd 14850
Oakcrest Rd 14850
Oakwood Ln 14850
Observatory Cir 14850
Ogden Rd 14850
Old Gorge Rd 14850
Olde Towne Rd 14850
Olin Hall 14853
Orchard Pl & St 14850
Orchard Hill Rd 14850
Osmun Pl 14850
Overlook Rd 14850
Oxford Pl 14850
E Palm Rd 14850
Park Ctr, Ln, Pl & St 14850
Park Hall 14850
Parker St 14850
Parkside Gdns 14850
Parkway Pl 14850
Pats Pl 14850
Pauls Way 14850
Peaceful Dr 14850
Peach Tree Ln 14850
Pearl St 14850
Pearsall Pl 14850
Pembroke Ln 14850
Pennsylvania Ave 14850
Penny Ln 14850
Peregrine Way 14850
Peridot Cir 14850
Perry Ln 14850
Perry City Rd 14850
Pheasant Ln, Walk & Way 14850
Phillips Hall
--- 14853
Phillips Hall
1-99 14853
100-199 14850
200-428 14853
Physical Plant Admin 14850
Pier Rd 14850
Pinckney Rd 14850
Pine Tree Rd 14850
Pineview Ter 14850
Pinewood Pl 14850
Placid Ter 14850
N & S Plain St 14850
Plant Science Building 14853
Plantations Rd 14850
Pleasant St 14850
Pleasant Grove Ln & Rd 14850
Poole Rd 14850
Porter Hill Rd 14850
Prospect St 14850
N & S Quarry Rd & St 14850
Queen St 14850
Rachel Carson Trl & Way 14850
Rainbow Dr 14850
Rand Hall 14853
Randolph Rd 14850
Reach Run 14850
Redwood Ln 14850
Regency Ln 14850
E & W Remington Rd 14850
Renwick Dr & Pl 14850
Renwick Heights Rd 14850
Renzetti Pl 14850
Research Park 14850
Reuben St 14850
Rhodes Hall 14853
Rice Hall 14853
Rich Rd 14850
Richard Pl 14850
Ridgecrest Rd 14850
Ridgedale Rd 14850
Ridgewood Rd 14850
Riley Robb Hall 14853
Ringwood Ct, Knl & Rd S & W 14850
Risley Hall 14853
Roat St 14850
Robert Purcell 14853
Roberts Pl 14850
Roberts Hall 14853
Rockcress Ln 14850
Rockefeller Hall 14853
Rocky Ln 14850
Rosehill Rd 14850
Rosina Dr 14850
Rothermich Rd 14850
Rowland Hall 14853
Royal Rd 14850
Rumsey Hill Rd 14850
Ryans Way 14850
Sage Pl & Rd 14850
Sage Chapel 14853
Sage Hall 14853
Saint Catherines Cir 14850
Saint Joseph Ln 14850
Salem Dr 14850
Sanctuary Dr 14850
Sandbank Rd 14850
Sandpiper Dr 14850
Sandra Pl 14850
Sapsucker Woods Rd 14850
Saranac Way 14850
Saunders Rd 14850
Savage Farm Dr 14850
Savage Hall 14853
Schaber Dr 14850
Schickle Rd 14850
Schuyler Pl 14850
Schwan Dr 14850
Sears St 14850
E & W Seneca St & Way 14850
Sesame St 14850
Settlement Rd & Way 14850
Seven Mile Dr 14850
Sharlene Rd 14850
Sheffield Rd 14850
Sheldon Ct 14853
Sheldon Rd 14850
Sheraton Dr 14850
Sherwood Dr 14850
Shore Cir & Dr 14850
Short St 14850
Shudaben Rd 14850
Sibley Hall 14853
Siena Dr 14850
Simsbury Dr 14850
Sisson Pl 14850
Sky Acres Dr 14850
Skyvue Rd 14850
Slaterville Rd 14850
Slim St 14850
Smiddy Hall 14850
Smugglers Path 14850
Snee Hall 14853
Snyder Hts 14850
Snyder Hill Ct & Rd 14850
Sodom Rd 14850
South Ave & St 14850
Southwoods Dr 14850
Space Science Bldg 14853
Sparrow Crest Dr 14850
E & W Spencer Rd & St 14850
Sperry Hall 14853
Spring Ln 14850
Springbrook Cir 14850
Spruce Ln & Way 14850
Spyglass Rdg 14850
E & W State St 14850
Statler Hall 14853
Statler Hotel 14853
Steam Mill Rd 14850
Stevenson Rd 14850
Stewart Ave
--- 14853
100-600 14850
601-699 14853
602-1098 14850
701-1099 14850
Stewart Park 14850
Stimson Hall 14853
Stocking Hall 14853
Stone Creek Dr 14850
Stone Quarry Rd 14850
Stonehaven Dr 14850
Stormy View Rd 14850
Strawberry Ln 14850
Strawberry Hill Cir & Rd 14850
Sugarbush Ln 14850
Summerhill Dr & Ln 14850
Summit Ave 14850
Sun Downs Rd 14850
Sun Path Rd 14850
Sunny Knoll Rd 14850
Sunnyhill Ln 14850
Sunnyslope Rd & Ter 14850
Sunnyview Ln 14850
Sunrise Rd 14850
N Sunset Dr & Park W 14850
Sunset West Cir 14850
Surge I 14853
Surge Iii 14853
Sycamore Dr 14850
Taber St 14850
Tallcott Hall 14850
Tareyton Dr 14850
Taughannock Blvd 14850
N Taylor Pl 14850
Teagle Hall 14853
Teeter Rd 14850
Terrace Pl 14850
Terrace 1 14850
Terrace 10 14850
Terrace 11 14850
Terrace 12 14850
Terrace 2 14850
Terrace 3 14850
Terrace 4 14850
Terrace 5 14850
Terrace 6 14850
Terrace 7 14850
Terrace 8 14850
Terrace 9 14850
Terrace Dining Hall 14850
Terrace View Dr 14850
Teton Ct 14850
Texas Ln 14850
The Knls, Pkwy & Trl 14850
The Byway 14850
The Insectory 14853
The Strand 14850
Thomas Rd 14850
Thornwood Dr 14850
Thurston Ave 14850
Thurston Hall 14853
Tibet Dr 14850
Tigerlily Ln 14850
Tioga St 14851
N Tioga St 14850
S Tioga St 14850
N & S Titus Ave 14850
Tjaden Hall 14853
Toboggan Ldg 14853
E & W Tompkins St 14850
E Tower 14850
W Tower 14850
Tower Rd 14853
Towers Concourse 14850
Townhouse Apartments 14853
Townline Rd 14850
Toxic Chemical Lab 14853
Treva Ave 14850
N Triphammer Ln, Rd & Ter 14850
Troy Rd 14850
Trumansburg Rd 14850
Trumbulls Corners Rd 14850
Tudor Rd 14850
Turkey Hill Rd 14850
Turner Pl 14850
Twin Glens Rd 14850
Tyler Rd 14850
University Ave & Park 14850
Updike Rd 14850
E & W Upland Rd 14850
Upson Hall 14853
Uptown Rd & Vlg 14850
Uris Hall 14853
Uris Library 14853
Us Nutrition Lab 14853
Utica St 14850
Valentine Pl 14850
Valley Rd 14850
Valleyview Rd 14850
Van Dorn Rd N & S 14850
Van Dorn Corners Rd 14850
Vera Cir 14850
Veterinary College 14853
W Village Cir & Pl 14850
Vine St 14850
Vinegar Hl 14850
Vista Ln 14850
Votapka Rd 14850
Wait Ave 14850
Wakefield Dr 14850
Walnut St 14850
Ward Lab 14853
Warren Dr 14850
Warren Pl 14850
Warren Rd
100-756 14850
757-757 14852
758-1298 14850
759-1299 14850
Warren Hall 14853
Warwick Pl 14850
Washington St 14850
Water St 14850
Waterview Cir & Hts 14850
Waterwagon Rd 14850
Wedgewood Dr 14850
West Ave
100-299 14850
300-399 14853
Westbourne Ln 14850
Westfield Dr 14850
Westhaven Dr & Rd 14850
Westmount Dr 14850
Westview Ln 14850
Westwood Knls 14850
Whalen Center For Music 14850
Whispering Pines Dr 14850
White Hall 14853
White Hawk Ln 14850
White Park Pl & Rd 14850
Whitetail Dr 14850
Whitted Rd 14850
Wiedmaier Ct 14850
Wildflower Dr 14850
Wilkins Rd 14850
Willard Way 14850
Willard Straight Hall 14853
Willets Pl 14850
William Keeton House 14853
Williams St 14850
Williams Glen Rd 14850
Williams Hall 14850
Willow Ave 14850
Willow Creek Rd 14850
Willow Creek Point Rd 14850
Willow Hill Dr 14850
Willow Point Rd 14850
Wilson Lab 14853
Windjammers Way 14850
Wing Hall 14853
Winners Cir 14850
Winston Ct & Dr 14850
Winthrop Dr & Pl 14850
Wood St 14850
Woodcrest Ave & Ter 14850
Woodgate Ln 14850
Woodland Pl, Rd & Way 14850
Woodlane Rd 14850
Woolf Ln 14850
Worth St 14850
Wyckoff Ave & Rd 14850
Yaple Rd 14850
Yardley Grn 14850
E & W Yates St 14850
E & W York St 14850

NUMBERED STREETS

1st St 14850
2nd St 14850
3rd St 14850
4th St 14850
5th St 14850
410 Thurston 14853

JAMAICA NY

General Delivery 11431

POST OFFICE BOXES MAIN OFFICE STATIONS AND BRANCHES

Box No.s
1 - 1320 11431
1 - 671 11434
1 - 412 11435
1 - 960 11430
501 - 580 11435
501 - 587 11424
601 - 900 11435
701 - 968 11434
2001 - 32560 11431
240501 - 249001 11424
300001 - 307051 11430
310001 - 319500 11431
340001 - 345010 11434
350001 - 359008 11435

NAMED STREETS

Aberdeen Rd 11432
Adelaide Rd 11433
Allendale St 11435
Amelia Rd 11434

Anderson Rd 11434
Archer Ave
13901-14697 11435
14699-14999 11435
15801-16497 11433
16499-16600 11433
16602-16698 11433
Arlington Ter
14500-14799 11435
15001-15399 11433
Aspen Pl 11432
Atari Ln 11433
Augusta Ct 11434
Ava Pl 11432
Aviation Plz 11434
Avon Rd & St 11432
Baisley Blvd 11434
Barrington St 11432
Bascom Ave 11436
Beaver Rd 11433
Bedell St
11200-11299 11433
11400-13499 11434
Bennett Ct & St 11434
Beraindi St 11436
Bergen Rd 11430
Bergen Basin Area 11430
N Boundary Rd 11430
N Brafinso Rd 11430
Brisbin St 11435
Broadway 11434
Brocher Rd 11434
Burden Cres 11435
Burdette Pl 11432
Cambridge Rd 11432
S Cargo Plz & Rd 11430
Cargo Service Rd 11430
Cedarcroft Rd 11432
Central Terminal Area 11430
Chapin Ct & Pkwy 11432
Charlecote Rdg 11432
Charter Rd 11435
Chelsea St 11432
Cheney St 11434
Chevy Chase St 11432
Claude Ave 11433
Clinton Ter 11432
Commissary Rd 11430
Compass Rd 11430
N Conduit Ave
14501-14899 11436
15101-18099 11434
S Conduit Ave
13000-13298 11430
15300-17898 11434
Coolidge Ave
13500-14799 11435
15000-15099 11432
Crandell Ave 11434
Cranston St 11434
Cresskill Pl 11435
Croydon Rd 11432
Dalny Rd 11432
Daniels St 11435
Deencoma Ave 11433
Dennis St 11434
Devonshire Rd 11432
Dillon St 11433
Doncaster Pl 11432
Douglas Ave 11433
Dumphries Pl 11432
Edgerton Blvd & Rd 11432
Eton St 11432
Eveleth Rd 11434
Farmers Blvd 11434
Federal Cir 11430
Fern Pl 11433
Ferndale Ave 11435
Foch Blvd
13801-13997 11436
13999-14799 11436
15000-17099 11434
17101-17199 11434
Garrett St 11434
Glassboro Ave 11435
Goethals Ave 11432
Gopost 11430
Gothic Dr 11432
Grand Central Pkwy
13500-13898 11435
13900-14799 11435
15000-18700 11432
18702-18798 11432
Guinzberg Rd 11433
Guy R Brewer Blvd
9200-11300 11433
11302-11398 11433
11400-15099 11434
15101-145199 11434
Haddon St 11432
E Hangar Rd 11430
Harry Douglass Way 11434
Hendrickson Pl 11434
Henley Rd 11432
Herianto St 11434
Highland Ave 11432
Hillside Ave
13800-14856 11435
14858-14898 11435
15000-18799 11432
Homelawn St 11432
Hoover Ave
13500-14799 11435
15000-15099 11432
Hovendon Rd 11432
Inwood St
10400-11199 11435
11400-13399 11436
Irwin Pl 11434
Jamaica Ave
13701-13725 11435
13727-14999 11435
15000-18099 11432
Jamaica Center Plz 11432
James Ct 11434
Kendrick Pl 11432
Kent St 11432
Kildare Rd 11432
Kingston Pl 11432
Kruger Rd 11432
Lakeview Blvd & Ln 11434
Lakewood Ave 11435
Lander St 11435
Latham Ln 11434
Lefferts Blvd 11430
Leslie Rd 11434
Liberty Ave
13701-14197 11435
14199-14899 11435
15000-18099 11433
Linden Blvd
13800-14999 11436
15001-15029 11434
15031-17999 11434
18001-18099 11434
Liverpool St 11435
Lloyd Rd 11435
Long St 11434
Lowe Ct 11435
Lux Rd 11435
Main St 11435
Manton St 11435
Marne Pl 11433
Mars Pl 11434
Marsden St 11434
Mathewson Ct 11434
Mathias Ave 11433
Mayfield Rd 11432
Meadow Dr & Rd 11434
Merrick Blvd
8750-8798 11432
8800-9199 11432
9200-9398 11433
9400-11399 11433
11400-11420 11434
11422-13299 11434
13301-13499 11434
Merrill St 11434
Meyer Ave
15700-15798 11434
15900-15999 11433
Midland Pkwy 11432
Murdock Ave 11434
Nadal Pl 11433
Nat Ct 11433
Normal Rd 11432
Odonnell Rd 11433
Old Rockaway Blvd 11430
Oradenda St 11435
Paige Ct 11433
Pan Am Rd 11430
Park Cres 11432
Parsons Blvd
8000-9099 11432
9201-9299 11433
Pershing Cres 11435
Perth Rd 11432
Phroane Ave 11433
Pilot Rd 11430
Pinegrove St 11435
Polhemus Ave 11433
Porter Rd 11434
Princeton St 11435
Queens Blvd
12001-12099 11424
13700-14055 11435
14057-14099 11435
Radar Rd 11430
Radnor Rd & St 11432
Remington St 11435
Rex Rd 11433
Ring Pl 11434
Rockaway Blvd
13700-13998 11436
14000-14700 11436
14702-14998 11436
15200-15999 11434
16001-17799 11434
Roe Rd 11434
Ruscoe St 11433
Sanders Pl 11435
Sayres Ave 11433
Selover Rd 11434
N & S Service Ct & Rd 11430
Shore Ave
14300-14699 11435
15000-15099 11433
Sidway Pl 11434
Smedley St 11435
Smith St 11434
Somerset St 11432
South Rd
14400-14799 11435
15000-15498 11433
15500-15600 11433
15602-16598 11433
Spa Pl 11435
Styler Rd 11433
Sunbury Rd 11434
Surrey Pl 11432
Sutphin Blvd
8700-8766 11435
8768-11399 11435
11400-12400 11434
12402-12598 11434
Sutter Ave 11436
Thurston St 11434
Tiff Ct 11433
Troon Rd 11432
Troutville Rd 11434
Tryon Pl 11432
Tuckerton St 11433
Tudor Rd 11432
Union Hall St 11433
Ursina Rd 11434
Utopia Pkwy 11432
Van Wyck Expy
111-120 11430
122-146 11430
8401-11199 11435
11401-13499 11436
Vaswani Ave 11434
Victoria Dr & Rd 11434
Village Rd
14400-14799 11435
15000-15099 11432
Vintrair St 11432
Waltham St 11435
Wareham Pl 11432
Warwick Cres 11432
Watson Pl 11433
Wexford Ter 11432
Wicklow Pl 11432
Wren Pl 11433
Yates Rd 11433
Zoller Rd 11434

NUMBERED STREETS

80th Dr & Rd 11432
81st Ave 11435
16400-16999 11432
82nd Ave
13500-13899 11435
17000-17398 11432
82nd Dr
13500-13798 11435
13800-14199 11435
15800-15898 11432
16001-16099 11432
82nd Rd 11432
83rd Ave
13501-13915 11435
17001-17197 11432
84th Ave
14300-14899 11435
15000-17299 11432
84th Dr
13800-14899 11435
15000-17099 11432
84th Rd
14100-14298 11435
14300-14799 11435
15000-17199 11432
17201-17299 11432
85th Ave
14401-14797 11435
14799-14899 11435
15000-16499 11432
16501-16599 11432
85th Dr
13900-14999 11435
15000-15299 11432
85th Rd 11435
86th Ave
13800-13898 11435
13900-14899 11435
15000-16299 11432
86th Cres 11432
86th Rd
13900-13999 11435
16201-16397 11432
16399-16499 11432
87th Ave
13800-14899 11435
15000-15099 11432
87th Dr 11432
87th Rd
13900-14899 11435
15000-18799 11432
88th Ave
13900-14849 11435
14851-14899 11435
15000-17599 11432
88th Rd 11435
89th Ave
13900-14899 11435
15201-15297 11432
90th Ave
13700-14899 11435
15300-15498 11432
15500-17999 11432
18001-18099 11432
90th Rd 11432
91st Ave
13701-13797 11435
13799-14699 11435
16600-17299 11432
17301-17399 11432
92nd Rd 11433
93rd Ave 11433
94th Ave 11435
94th Ave 11435
15001-15199 11433
95th Ave 11435
97th Ave 11435
101st Ave 11435
102nd Ave 11435
103rd Rd 11433
104th Ave 11435
16800-17400 11433
104th Rd 11433
105th Ave
14300-14899 11435
16800-17799 11433
106th Ave
13800-14398 11435
14400-14799 11435
16800-17799 11433
106th Rd 11433
107th Ave
13800-14699 11435
15000-17899 11433
107th Rd 11435
108th Ave
14700-14799 11435
15000-17499 11433
108th Dr 11433
109th Ave
13800-14799 11435
15000-17599 11433
17601-17699 11433
109th Dr 11433
109th Rd
13900-13999 11435
15000-16999 11433
110th Ave
14201-14297 11435
14299-14799 11435
15300-17799 11433
17801-17999 11433
110th Rd
14700-14799 11435
15300-16999 11433
111th Ave
13800-14899 11435
15300-17599 11433
111th Rd 11433
112th Ave
14800-14899 11435
15000-17800 11433
112th Rd 11433
113th Ave 11433
114th Rd 11434
115th Ave 11436
115th Ave 11436
15000-17750 11434
17752-17798 11434
115th Dr 11434
115th Rd 11434
116th Ave
13800-13998 11436
14000-14899 11436
15000-17399 11434
116th Dr 11434
116th Rd
14200-14299 11436
15000-15599 11434
118th Ave & Rd 11434
119th Ave 11436
15000-17299 11434
119th Dr 11434
119th Rd
14200-14299 11436
15000-17999 11434
120th Ave
14200-14799 11436
15000-17851 11434
121st Ave 11436
122nd Ave 11436
15000-16399 11434
123rd Ave
14000-14799 11436
15000-15399 11434
124th Ave 11434
125th Ave 11434
126th Ave 11434
127th Ave 11434
128th Ave 11434
129th Ave 11436
129th Ave 11436
15400-17700 11434
17702-17798 11434
130th Ave
13700-14999 11436
15800-15998 11434
16000-17900 11434
17902-17998 11434
130th Pl 11430
130th Rd 11434
131st Ave
13700-14299 11436
15900-17850 11434
131st St 11430
132nd Ave
13700-13799 11436
15000-15098 11434
132nd St 11430
133rd Ave
13700-14999 11436
15100-17598 11434
17600-17699 11434
17701-17899 11434
133rd Rd 11434
134th Ave
13700-13799 11436
15100-17999 11434
134th St
143-143 11430
180-402 11430
8000-8098 11435
8201-8299 11435
14800-14998 11430
15000-15099 11430
135th Ave
13701-13797 11436
13799-14499 11436
14501-14599 11436
15100-17999 11434
135th St 11435
136th Ave 11434
137th Ave 11434
138th Ave 11434
138th Pl 11435
138th St 11435
139th Rd 11434
139th St
8101-8497 11435
8499-11199 11435
11400-11699 11436
11701-11799 11436
140th Ave 11434
140th St
11100-11199 11435
11400-13599 11436
141st Ave 11434
141st St
8200-11199 11435
11400-12099 11436
142nd Ave 11434
142nd Pl 11436
142nd St
10401-10597 11435
10599-11199 11435
11400-13339 11436
13341-13399 11436
143rd Ave 11434
143rd Rd 11434
143rd St
8400-8498 11435
8500-11199 11435
11401-11497 11436
11499-13399 11436
144th Ave 11434
144th Dr 11434
144th Pl 11435
144th Rd 11434
144th St
8500-11199 11435
11400-13099 11436
144th Ter 11434
145th Ave 11434
145th Dr 11434
145th Rd 11434
145th St
8800-11199 11435
11400-13399 11436
146th Ave 11434
146th Dr 11434
146th Rd 11434
146th St
8700-11199 11435
11400-13399 11436
146th Ter 11434
147th Ave 11434
147th Pl 11435
147th St
124-128 11430
11100-11199 11435
11400-13399 11436
148th Ave 11434
148th Rd 11434
148th St
125-127 11430
204-206 11430
8400-11299 11435
11400-13399 11436
149th Ave 11434
149th Rd 11434
149th St
108-110 11430
8500-9599 11435
11400-13399 11436
150th Ave
13000-13099 11430
17701-17799 11434
17900-17998 11434
150th Rd 11434
150th St
8000-8398 11435
8400-10799 11435
12600-13398 11436
151st St 11432
152nd St
8431-8439 11432
11800-12399 11434
153rd Ct 11434
153rd Ln 11434
153rd St
8700-8799 11432
8801-9041 11432
10600-11127 11433
11129-11199 11433
11800-12499 11434
12501-12999 11434
154th St
10600-10899 11433
11800-13499 11434
155th St
9000-9098 11432
10600-11199 11433
11201-11399 11433
11400-14565 11434
14567-14599 11434
156th St
10600-11199 11433
13200-14599 11434
157th St
9500-10598 11433
10600-11200 11433
11202-11398 11433
11400-14599 11434
158th St
9400-10998 11433
11400-14599 11434
159th St
8000-8599 11432
9400-10598 11433
10600-11299 11433
11400-14100 11434
14102-14598 11434
160th St
8000-9099 11432
9200-11199 11433
12700-14099 11434
161st Pl 11434
161st St
8000-9099 11432
12700-14099 11434
162nd St 11432
163rd St 11432
164th Pl
8000-8300 11432
10400-11099 11433
164th St
7900-7998 11432

8840-8840 11431
8900-8998 11432
10400-11099 11433
11700-12099 11434
165th St
8000-8999 11432
9200-10799 11433
11400-12099 11434
166th Pl 11434
166th St
8000-8749 11432
10700-11199 11433
11400-14499 11434
167th St
8000-8799 11432
10800-10826 11433
10828-11299 11433
11400-14599 11434
14601-14649 11434
168th Pl
8300-8999 11432
9200-10399 11433
168th St
8000-9199 11432
9200-9298 11433
9300-11299 11433
11400-14450 11434
169th Pl 11433
169th St
8000-9099 11432
9101-9199 11432
10300-11299 11433
11301-11399 11433
11400-14099 11434
170th St
8000-8198 11432
8200-9099 11432
9200-10800 11433
10802-11198 11433
11400-14399 11434
171st Pl 11433
171st St
8400-9099 11432
10300-10899 11433
11600-14099 11434
172nd St
8200-9199 11432
9200-11121 11433
11123-11199 11433
11400-14099 11434
173rd St
8700-8798 11432
8800-9199 11432
9200-11199 11433
11400-14099 11434
174th Pl 11434
174th St
10800-11199 11433
11400-14299 11434
175th Pl
11200-11299 11433
11400-11499 11434
175th St
8700-8898 11432
8900-9199 11432
9200-9204 11433
9206-11399 11433
11400-14799 11434
14801-14899 11434
176th Pl 11434
176th St
9000-9099 11432
9200-11299 11433
11400-14799 11434
177th Pl 11434
177th St
9200-10298 11433
10300-11299 11433
11400-14799 11434
14801-14999 11434
178th Pl
9201-11097 11433
11099-11299 11433
11400-145199 11434
178th St
8701-8797 11432
8799-9099 11432
9201-10297 11433
10299-11299 11433
11400-13199 11434
13201-13299 11434
179th Pl
8800-9099 11432
9200-11149 11433
11151-11199 11433
179th St
8800-9099 11432
11000-11299 11433
11400-14599 11434
14601-14699 11434
180th St
8800-9099 11432
9200-11299 11433
11400-14564 11434
14566-14698 11434

JAMESTOWN NY

General Delivery 14702

POST OFFICE BOXES MAIN OFFICE STATIONS AND BRANCHES

Box No.s
All PO Boxes 14702

RURAL ROUTES

01, 02, 03, 04, 05, 06 .. 14701

NAMED STREETS

All Street Addresses 14701

NUMBERED STREETS

E & W 1st 14701
E & W 2nd 14701
E 3rd St
1-301 14701
300-300 14702
303-399 14701
W 3rd St 14701
E & W 4th 14701
E & W 5th 14701
E & W 6th 14701
E & W 7th 14701
E & W 8th 14701
E & W 9th 14701
E & W 10th 14701
11th St 14701
12th St 14701
13th St 14701
14th St 14701
E 15th 14701
16th St 14701
17th St 14701
18th St 14701
21st St 14701
22nd St 14701
23rd St 14701

KEESEVILLE NY

General Delivery 12944

POST OFFICE BOXES MAIN OFFICE STATIONS AND BRANCHES

Box No.s
All PO Boxes 12944

NAMED STREETS

Acorn Ln 12944
Augur Lake Rd 12944
N Ausable St 12944
Ausable Hotel Rd 12911
Balsam Dr 12944
Basket Ave 12944
Beach St 12944
Bens Ln 12944
Blaise Ln 12944
Boathouse Rd 12944
Bond Rd 12944
Boulder Ledge Way 12944
Brinton Rd 12944
Burke Rd 12944
Bushey Rd 12944
N Camp Rd 12944
Caridenc Rd 12944
Carver Ln 12944
Cassidy Rd 12944
Cedar Ct 12944
Cemetary Rd 12944
Chasm Rd
1-99 12911
100-499 12944
Chesterfield St 12944
Church St 12944
Cinnamon Rdg 12944
Clark Rd 12944
Clinton St 12944
Clintonville Rd 12924
Cold Spring Rd 12944
Connell Rd 12944
Corlear Bay Rd 12944
Dellwood Ln 12944
Derek Dr 12944
Dicks Pl 12944
Dion Dr 12944
Division St 12944
Dog Hill Rd 12944
Doty Ln 12944
Dugway Rd 12944
Dusty Rd 12944
Easton Rd 12944
Elks Ln 12944
Evans Rd 12944
Finney Rd 12944
Friendly Park 12944
Front St 12944
Frontage Rd 12944
Gilbert Cameron Ln 12944
Glomann Rd 12944
Green St 12944
Grove St 12944
Hallock Hill Rd 12944
Hamilton Ter 12944
Harms Way 12944
Heather Ln 12944
Heron Pt 12944
Herron Point Ln 12944
Highland Rd 12944
Hill St 12944
Hollywood Ave 12944
Industrial Park Rd 12944
Jackson St 12944
Jewel Rock Rd 12944
June Dr 12944
Kencomai Rd 12924
Kent St 12944
Kessel Park 12944
La Mountain Rd 12944
Laflure Ln 12944
Lakeview Meadows Rd ... 12944
Lamplighter Mobile Home Park ... 12944
Latourelle Ln 12944
Less Traveled Rd 12944
Lewis Rd 12944
Liberty St 12944
Lindsay Dr 12944
Little Sandy Rd 12944
Locust Ln 12944
Lorraine Way 12944
Lower Rd 12924
Mace Chasm Rd
1-1000 12944
1001-1021 12911
1002-1022 12944
1023-1199 12911
Main St 12944
Margaret St 12944
Mays Ln 12944
Meeker Dr 12944
Merrilee Ln 12944
Mill St 12944
Moore Ln 12944
Morrow Ln 12944
Nicolis Rd 12944
Niesen Rd 12944
Nixie Bay Rd 12944
Nys Route 22 12944
Old Ice House Rd 12944
Old State Rd 12911
Ouelette Cir 12944
Ovencene Rd 12911
Parrish Rd 12924
Patnode Ln 12944
Pill Row 12944
Pine St 12944
Pine Estate Cir 12944
Pine Grove Trailer Ct ... 12944
Pine Tree Dr 12944
Pleasant St 12944
Pond St 12944
Port Douglas Rd 12944
Pray Rd 12944
Prescott Rd 12944
Prospect Rd 12944
Randolph Rd 12944
Rectory St 12924
Renas Ln 12944
Ritas Way 12944
River St 12944
Robare Rd 12944
Rocky Cove Way 12944
Rogers Ln 12944
Route 22 12944
Route 373 12944
Route 9
100-1615 12944
Route 9
2000-2084 12911
Route 9n
100-1199 12944
1200-1699 12924
Sand Hill Rd 12924
Sandy Pine Trailer Park ... 12944
Santor Ln 12944
School St 12944
Schuyler Rd 12944
Scott Ln 12944
Shady Ln 12944
Shunpike Rd 12944
Smart St 12944
Smith St 12924
Smyth Dr 12944
Soper Rd 12944
Spring St 12944
Taylor Hill Rd 12944
Thompson Rd 12944
Tierney Rd 12944
Tony Ln 12944
Trembleau Rd 12944
Trout Pond Rd 12944
Twa Ln 12944
Valleyview Dr 12944
Vine St 12944
Virgina Dr 12944
Water Edge Rd 12944
Whip Linc Ln 12944
White St 12944
Whitney Ln 12944
Woodlawn Dr 12944

KINGSTON NY

General Delivery 12401

POST OFFICE BOXES MAIN OFFICE STATIONS AND BRANCHES

Box No.s
All PO Boxes 12402

NAMED STREETS

Aaron Ct 12401
Abbey St 12401
Abeel St 12401
Abruyn St 12401
Adams St 12401
Adas Way 12401
Addis St 12401
Albany Ave 12401
Albert St 12401
Alberts Ave 12401
Alcazar Ave 12401
Alda Dr 12401
Alder Ct 12401
Aleo Post Rd 12401
Alison Ct 12401
Ameribag Dr 12401
Amherst St 12401
Amsterdam Ave 12401
Amy Ct 12401
Amy Kay Pkwy 12401
Anand Pl 12401
Andrew St 12401
Anita Ct 12401
Apple St 12401
Ardsley St 12401
Arlington Pl 12401
Arlmont St 12401
Armory Dr 12401
Arnold Dr 12401
Arts Cir 12401
Ash Ct 12401
Ashokan Rd 12401
August Hill Ln 12401
Augusta St 12401
Avalon Hl 12401
Barbara Ter 12401
Barbarossa Ln 12401
Barberry Rd 12401
Barmann Ave 12401
Basten Ln 12401
Beaverkill Rd 12401
Becket St 12401
Beech Ct 12401
Beesmer Rd 12401
Belmont St 12401
Belvedere St 12401
W Bend Dr 12401
Beth Dr 12401
Beyersdorfer St 12401
Binnewater Ln & Rd 12401
Birch St 12401
Birmingham Ln 12401
Blacks Rd 12401
Blue Heron Dr 12401
Bluestone Ct 12401
Bogart St 12401
Boices Ln 12401
Boices Lane Ext 12401
Bond St 12401
Boulder Ave 12401
Boulevard 12401
Brabrant Rd 12401
Breezy Hill Rd 12401
Brewster St 12401
Brian A Steeves Cir ... 12401
Bridge Rd 12401
Brigham St 12401
N Broadway 12401
Brook St 12401
Brown Ave 12401
Browning Ter 12401
Bruyn Ave 12401
Buckley St 12401
Burgevin St 12401
Burhans Blvd 12401
Burnett St 12401
Burns Pl 12401
Calumet Rd 12401
Camini Way 12401
Canal St 12401
Canary Hill Rd 12401
Canfield St 12401
Cantine Rd 12401
Carle Ter 12401
Cascade Dr 12401
Cassidy St 12401
Catherine St 12401
Catskill Ave 12401
Cedar St 12401
Cemetary Rd 12401
Center St 12401
Chambers Dr 12401
Chapel St 12401
Charles Rider Park Rd . 12401
Charlotte St 12401
Charming Barn Rd 12401
Cheryl Ct 12401
E & W Chester St 12401
E Chester Street Ext ... 12401
E & W Chestnut St 12401
W Chestnut Street Ext .. 12401
Church Hill Rd 12401
Circle Ave 12401
City View Ter 12401
Clarendon Ave 12401
Clearhorn Rd 12401
Clifton Ave & Ter 12401
S Clinton Ave 12401
Codwise St 12401
Coffey Pl 12401
Colfax Pl 12401
Colonial Dr 12401
Columbia St 12401
Condie St 12401
Conifer Ln 12401
Conners Rd 12401
Conway Pl 12401
Cook Ave 12401
Cora Ter 12401
Coral Ln 12401
Cordts St 12401
Cornell St
1-91 12401
90-90 12402
92-998 12401
93-999 12401
Corporate Dr 12401
Costello Ln 12401
Country Club Ln 12401
Court Ave 12401
Coyote Ct 12401
Crane St 12401
Creek Locks Rd 12401
Creekside Rd 12401
Cross St 12401
Crown St 12401
Cummings Ave 12401
Cutler Hill Rd 12401
Dalewood St 12401
Danny Cir 12401
Davis St 12401
Decker Ave & St 12401
Dederick St 12401
Deer Run Rd 12401
Delaware Ave 12401
Dellay Ave 12401
Delta Pl 12401
Denver Rd 12401
Depew Ln 12401
Derrenbacher St 12401
Development Ct 12401
Dewitt St 12401
Dewitt Lake Rd 12401
Dewitt Mills Rd 12401
Deyo St 12401
Dietz Ct 12401
Dirk Ln 12401
Division St 12401
Dock St 12401
Dogwood Ln, Pl & St ... 12401
Downs St 12401
Dubois St 12401
Duflon St 12401
Dunn St 12401
Dunneman Ave 12401
Dunwoodie Dr 12401
Eastwoods Dr 12401
Edlin Dr 12401
Edwards Ln 12401
Elaine Dr 12401
Elisa Landi Dr 12401
Elissa Landi Dr 12401
Elizabeth St 12401
Elm St 12401
Elmendorf St 12401
Elmwood St 12401
Emerick St 12401
Emerson St 12401
Enterprise Dr 12401
Erin Ln 12401
Esopus Ave 12401
Evergreen Ln & St 12401
Everson Ln 12401
Fair St 12401
Fairmont Ave 12401
Fairview Ave 12401
Fairview Avenue Ext 12401
Family Practice Dr 12401
Farm To Market Rd 12401
S Farrelly St 12401
Fawn Hill Ct 12401
Field Ct 12401
Fischer Ave 12401
Fitch St 12401
Flatbush Ave & Rd 12401
Florence St 12401
Flowerhill 12401
Fording Place Rd 12401
Forest Hill Dr 12401
Fort St 12401
Fortuna St 12401
Foxhall Ave 12401
Frank Sottile Blvd 12401
Franklin St 12401
Frog Aly 12401
N Front St 12401
Furnace St 12401
Gage St 12401
Gallis Hill Rd 12401
Garden St 12401
Garraghan Dr 12401
Garrison St 12401
German St 12401
Gilead St 12401
Gill St 12401
Glen St 12401
Golden Hill Dr & Ln 12401
Goldrick Landing Ct & Rd ... 12401
Golf Ter 12401
Grand St 12401
Grandview Ave 12401
Granite Ct 12401
Grant St 12401
Green St 12401
Greenbrook Ln 12401
Greenkill Ave & Rd 12401
Greywood Ct 12401
Groff St 12401
Gross St 12401
Grove St 12401
Guyton St 12401
Hallihans Hill Rd 12401
Hamilton St 12401
Hanratty St 12401
Harding Ave 12401
Harrison St 12401
Harwich St 12401
Hasbrouck Ave & Pl 12401
Hayes St 12401
Hazel St 12401
Heath Rd 12401
Heather Ln 12401

Hemlock Ave 12401
Hemlock Avenue Ext 12401
Henry St 12401
Heritage Ct 12401
Hewitt Pl 12401
Hickory Bush Rd 12401
Hidden Valley Rd 12401
High St 12401
Highland Ave 12401
Hill Rd 12401
Hillcrest Ave 12401
Hillside Ct & Ter 12401
Hillsworth Ave 12401
Hilton Pl 12401
Hinel Rd 12401
Hinsdale St 12401
Hoffman St 12401
Holiday Ln 12401
Hone St 12401
Hooker St 12401
Hovi Ln 12401
Howland Ave 12401
Hudson St 12401
Hudson Valley Lndg 12401
Hudson View Ct 12401
Hunter St 12401
Hurley Ave 12401
Hurley Mountain Rd 12401
Hutton St 12401
Indian Springs Ln 12401
Irving Pl 12401
Janet St 12401
Jansen Ave 12401
Jarrold St 12401
Jean Pl 12401
Jefferson Ave 12401
Jervis Ave 12401
Jockey Hill Rd 12401
John St 12401
Johnson Hill Rd 12401
Johnston Ave 12401
Josephine Ave 12401
Joys Ln 12401
Jumping Brook Ln 12401
Kachigan St 12401
Kallop Rd 12401
Kemble Ter 12401
Kerry Ln 12401
Kieffer Ln 12401
Kiersted Ave & Ln 12401
Kiln Ln 12401
Kings Mall Ct 12401
Kingston Plz, St & Ter 12401
Kingswood Knls 12401
Klingberg Ave 12401
Koskie Ln 12401
Krastin Dr 12401
Kukuk Ln 12401
Lafayette Ave 12401
Lainey Ln 12401
Lake Hill Rd 12401
Lakeside Garden Dr 12401
Lakeview Ave & Ter 12401
Lansing Ln 12401
Lantreli St 12401
Lapla Rd 12401
Larch St 12401
Lauren Ct 12401
Lawrenceville St 12401
Lay St 12401
Lazzaro Rd 12401
Lebert St 12401
Ledge Rd 12401
Lee Woods Dr 12401
Lefever Falls Rd 12401
Lem Boice Ln 12401
Len Ct 12401
Lenox Pl 12401
Levan St 12401
Liberty St 12401
Lily Ln 12401
Lincoln St 12401
Lincoln Park Pl 12401
Linden Ln 12401
Linderman Ave 12401
Linderman Avenue Ext 12401
Lindsley Ave 12401
Links Ln 12401
Linwood Pl 12401
Lipton St 12401
Lisa Ln 12401
Livingston St 12401
Locust St 12401
Lohmaier Ln 12401
Loughran Ct 12401
Lounsbury Ct & Pl 12401
Lucas Ave 12401
Lucas Avenue Ext 12401
Lynette Blvd 12401
Madden St 12401
Maddy Ln 12401
Madison Ave 12401
Magic Dr 12401
Maiden Ln 12401
Main St
1-61 12401
50-50 12402
62-1198 12401
63-1199 12401
N & S Manor Ave, Lk & Pl 12401
Maple Ln & St 12401
Maple Hill Rd 12401
N Marbletown Rd 12401
Marcotte Rd 12401
Marius St 12401
Marshall Pl 12401
Marys Ave & Ln 12401
Massa Dr 12401
Maxs Pl 12401
Maxwell Ln 12401
Mcentee St 12401
Meade St 12401
Meadowbrook Dr 12401
Melissa Rd 12401
Melvin Dr 12401
Memorial Dr 12401
Mentnech Ct 12401
Merilina Ave 12401
Merilina Avenue Ext 12401
Merritt Ave 12401
Meyers Rd 12401
Miggins Rd 12401
Millers Ln 12401
Minuet Ln 12401
Miron Ln 12401
Montrepose Ave 12401
Moore St 12401
Morey Hill Rd 12401
Morton Blvd 12401
Mountain Rd 12401
Mountain View Ave & Ct 12401
Munchkin Ln 12401
Murray Rd & St 12401
Nancy Ct 12401
Navara St 12401
New St 12401
New Salem Rd 12401
Newkirk Ave & St 12401
Nicholas Ave 12401
Night Owl Rd 12401
Noone Ln 12401
Norma Ct 12401
North Ct & St 12401
Northfield St 12401
Oak St 12401
Oak Ridge Ter 12401
Oakwood Dr 12401
Ohio St 12401
Old Ballpark Rd 12401
Old Country Ln 12401
Old County Rd 1 12401
Old Flatbush Rd 12401
Old Lucas Tpke 12401
Old Neighborhood Rd 12401
Old North Broadway 12401
Old Sawkill Rd 12401
Old State Route 32 12401
Old Whiteport Rd 12401
Olde Zena Ln 12401
Oneil St 12401
Ora Pl 12401
Orchard Ave & St 12401
E & W Oreilly St 12401
Orlando St 12401
Otis St 12401
Overlook Dr 12401
Park Rd & St 12401
Parsell St 12401
Patriots Pl 12401
Pearl St 12401
Penn Ct 12401
Perry Hl 12401
Peter St 12401
Petit Ave 12401
Petronella Rd 12401
W Pierpont St 12401
S Pine Pl & St 12401
Pine Grove Ave 12401
Pine Tree Dr & Ln 12401
Plainfield St 12401
Platt Ln 12401
Plaza Rd 12401
Plymouth Ave 12401
Ponckhockie St 12401
Poplar Ct 12401
Post St 12401
Powder Mill Bridge Rd 12401
Powells Ln 12401
Presidents Pl 12401
Prince Ct, Ln & St 12401
Princeton St 12401
Privatewood Ct & Rd 12401
Progress St 12401
S Prospect St 12401
Pulaski St 12401
Pupwood Ln 12401
Purvis St 12401
Putt Ln 12401
Quail Dr 12401
Quarry Rd & St 12401
Railroad Ave 12401
Ravine St 12401
Reynolds St 12401
Richmond Pkwy 12401
Ridge Dr & St 12401
Ringtop Rd 12401
Riseley St 12401
Riverview Ter 12401
Robert St 12401
Robin Ln 12401
Rock St 12401
Rock Ledge Ln 12401
Rockwell Ln & Ter 12401
Rodney St 12401
Rogers St 12401
Romanus St 12401
Rondout Dr, Lndg & St 12401
Roosevelt Ave 12401
Rose St 12401
Rosendale Ave 12401
Rowe Ct & Rd 12401
Ruby Rd 12401
Russell St 12401
Rymrock Rd 12401
Saccoman Ave 12401
E Saint James Ct & St 12401
Sandy Rd 12401
Sari Ct 12401
Savoy St 12401
Sawdust Ave 12401
Sawkill Rd 12401
Sawkill Park Rd 12401
Sawkill Ruby Rd 12401
Schryver Ct 12401
Schultz Ln 12401
Schwenk Dr 12401
Scudder Ave 12401
Shady Ln 12401
Shamrock Ln 12401
Sharon Ln 12401
Sheehan Ct 12401
Sherman Rd & St 12401
Sherry Ln 12401
Sherwood Dr 12401
Shining Path 12401
Shufeldt St 12401
Silvertone Ln 12401
Skytop Dr 12401
Smith Ave 12401
Snyder Ave 12401
South Rd 12401
Southfield St 12401
Spencer Ln 12401
Spring St 12401
Spring Lake Dr 12401
Spruce St 12401
Stahlman Pl 12401
Stanley St 12401
Staples St 12401
State Route 209 12401
State Route 213 12401
State Route 28 12401
State Route 32 12401
Station Rd 12401
Stephan Rd & St 12401
S Sterling St 12401
Steward Ln 12401
Stewart Ln 12401
Stickles Ave & Ter 12401
Stockade Dr 12401
Stoll Ct 12401
Stone Church Rd 12401
E & W Strand St 12401
Stuyvesant St 12401
Summer St 12401
Sunrise Ave 12401
Susan St 12401
Sweet Mdws 12401
Sycamore St 12401
Sylvester St 12401
Szymanski St 12401
Tall Oaks Ct & Dr 12401
Tammany St 12401
Taylor St 12401
Teller St 12401
Ten Broeck Ave 12401
Terrace Ave 12401
Terrance St 12401
Terry Ln 12401
Thomas St 12401
Tietjen Ave 12401
Tompkins St 12401
Tongore Rd & Way 12401
Tooley Dr 12401
Tremper Ave 12401
Trenton St 12401
Trinity Way 12401
Tubby St 12401
Twin Ponds Dr 12401
Ulster Ave & St 12401
Ulster Landing Rd 12401
E & W Union St 12401
Union Center Rd 12401
Upland Rd 12401
Urbana St 12401
Valentine Ave & Ct 12401
Valley St 12401
Valley View Rd 12401
Van Buren St 12401
Van Deusen St 12401
Van Gaasbeck St 12401
Van Keuran Hwy 12401
Van Kleeck Ln 12401
Van Steenburg Ln 12401
Van Voorhis Ln 12401
Van Wagenen Ln 12401
Vestal Hills Dr 12401
Victory Ln 12401
Village Ct 12401
Vincent St 12401
Virginia Dr 12401
Vista Dr 12401
Voorhees Ave 12401
S Wall St 12401
Walnut St 12401
Warren St 12401
S Washington Ave 12401
Washington Avenue Ext 12401
Watson Ln 12401
Waughkonk Rd 12401
Wayside Dr 12401
Webster St 12401
Welles Ln 12401
Westbrook Ln & Pl 12401
Westrum St 12401
Whiteport Rd 12401
Wiedy Rd 12401
Wilbur Ave 12401
Wilkie Ave 12401
Williams Ln 12401
Williams Lake Rd 12401
Willow St 12401
Wilson Ave 12401
Wiltwyck Ave 12401
Winchell Ave 12401
Wintergreen Hill Rd 12401
Wood St 12401
Woodland Ave & Dr 12401
Woods Rd 12401
Wrentham St 12401
Wuchte Ln 12401
Wurts St 12401
Wynkoop Pl 12401
Yale Ct 12401
Yarmouth St 12401
Yeoman St 12401
York Pl 12401
Zena Rd 12401
Zena Highwoods Rd 12401

NUMBERED STREETS

All Street Addresses 12401

LITTLE NECK NY

POST OFFICE BOXES MAIN OFFICE STATIONS AND BRANCHES

Box No.s
1 - 447 11363
701 - 620820 11362
630001 - 639008 11363

NAMED STREETS

Alameda Ave 11362
Alston Pl 11363
Annandale Ln 11362
Ardsley Rd 11363
Arleigh Rd 11363
Barrows Ct 11362
Bates Rd 11362
Bay Ave 11363
Bayview Ave 11363
Beechknoll Ave 11362
Berenced Ave 11363
Beverly Rd 11363
Brancona Ave 11362
Brattle Ave 11362
Brookside St 11363
Browvale Ln 11362
Cambria Ave 11362
Carolina Rd 11362
Cedar Ln 11363
Center Dr 11363
Cherry St 11363
Church St 11363
Circle Rd 11363
Commonwealth Blvd 11362
Concord St 11362
Cornell Ln 11363
Cullman Ave 11362
Deepdale Ave & Pl 11362
Depew Ave 11363
Douglas Rd 11363
Douglaston Pkwy
3800-4499 11363
4500-7299 11362
7301-7599 11362
East Dr 11363
W End Dr 11362
Forest Rd 11363
Gaskell Rd 11362
Glenwood St
3900-4200 11363
4202-4398 11363
4500-4899 11362
Grand Central Pkwy 11362
Grosvenor St 11363
Hamilton Pl 11363
Hand Rd 11362
Hanford St 11362
Hewlett St 11362
Hillcrest Ave 11363
Hollywood Ave 11363
Horace Harding Expy 11362
Iowa Rd 11362
Jessie Ct 11363
Kenmore Rd 11363
Knollwood Ave 11363
Leeds Rd 11362
Leith Pl & Rd 11362
Little Neck Pkwy
3401-3697 11363
3699-4499 11363
4500-6200 11362
6202-6398 11362
Little Neck Rd 11363
Manor Rd 11363
Marathon Pkwy
4200-4399 11363
4501-4597 11362
4599-6699 11362
Marinette St 11363
Maryland Rd 11362
Melrose Ln 11363
Morenci Ln 11362
Morgan St 11363
Nassau Blvd 11362
Northern Blvd
22500-23198 11362
23200-25099 11362
25010-25010 11363
25100-25598 11362
25101-25599 11362
Oak Ln 11363
Oak Park Dr 11362
Orient Ave 11363
Overbrook St 11362
Overlook Rd 11362
Park Ln 11363
Pembroke Ave 11362
Pine St 11363
Poplar St 11363
Prospect Ave 11363
Redfield St 11362
Regatta Pl 11363
Richmond Rd 11363
Ridge Rd 11363
Rushmore Ave & Ter 11362
Sandhill Rd 11363
Shore Rd 11363
Stuart Ln 11363
Thebes Ave 11362
Thornhill Ave 11362
Upland Rd 11362
Van Nostrand Ct 11362
Van Zandt Ave 11362
Walden Ave 11362
Warwick Ave 11363
West Dr 11363
Westmoreland Pl & St 11363
Willow Pl & St 11363
Zion St 11362

NUMBERED STREETS

34th Ave 11363
37th Ave 11363
38th Ave, Dr & Rd 11363
39th Ave & Rd 11363
40th Ave 11363
41st Ave, Dr & Rd 11363
42nd Ave 11363
43rd Ave 11363
44th Ave 11363
51st Ave 11362
52nd Ave & Rd 11362
53rd Ave 11362
54th Ave 11362
57th Ave & Dr 11362
58th Ave 11362
59th Ave 11362
60th Ave & Rd 11362
61st Ave 11362
62nd Ave 11362
63rd Ave 11362
64th Ave 11362
65th Ave 11362
66th Ave 11362
67th Ave 11362
68th Ave 11362
69th Ave 11362
70th Ave 11362
72nd Ave 11362
73rd Ave 11362
233rd Pl & St 11363
234th St 11363
235th St 11363
240th Pl 11362
240th St
3801-3897 11363
5201-5399 11362
241st St 11362
242nd St 11362
243rd St 11362
244th St 11363
4500-7399 11362
245th Pl & St 11362
246th Cres, Pl & St 11362
247th St 11363
4600-6699 11362
248th St
4000-4399 11363
4500-5399 11362
249th St 11363
250th St 11362
251st Pl & St 11362
252nd St 11362
253rd St 11362
254th St 11363
4500-5298 11362
5300-6400 11362
6402-6698 11362
255th St
3300-3899 11363
5700-6399 11362
256th St 11362
260th St 11362
262nd St 11362
263rd St 11362
264th St 11362

LIVERPOOL NY

General Delivery 13088

POST OFFICE BOXES MAIN OFFICE STATIONS AND BRANCHES

Box No.s
1 - 820 13088
2001 - 3180 13089
7001 - 7020 13088
8089 - 8089 13090

NAMED STREETS

Acton Ln 13090
Admiral Dr 13090
Alban Ct 13090
Albernathy St 13088
Albion Ave 13088
Albury Ct 13090
Aldenwood Dr 13088
Alder Ln 13090

Alder St 13088
Aldgate Ct 13090
Aldwych Ct 13090
Alexis Dr 13090
Alfred Dr 13090
Alperton Ct 13090
Altair Crse 13090
Amersham Ct 13090
Anadale Ln 13090
Anchor Dr 13090
Anguilla Dr 13090
Anita Ave 13088
Anlane Cir 13090
Antler Ln 13090
Apache Ln 13090
Apple Tree Ln 13090
Apricot Ln 13090
Ardencrest Rd 13090
Arlington Cir 13090
Arrowhead Ln 13090
Aspen St 13088
Aster Dr 13088
Astilbe Path 13088
Aurora Path 13090
Ausable Run 13088
Autumnal Ln 13088
Avon Ave 13088
Avon Pkwy 13090
Bainbridge Dr 13090
Balboa Dr 13090
Baldpate Ln 13090
Balsam St 13088
Balsamwood Ln 13090
Baltic Dr 13090
Banbury Ct 13090
Barclay Rd 13090
Barnyard Cir 13088
Bartlett Ave 13088
Bass St 13088
Bay Cir 13090
Bay Chapel Cir 13088
Bay Park Dr 13090
Bayberry Cir 13090
Beacon Hill Cir 13090
Bear Rd 13088
Beechwood Ave 13088
Beehive Cir 13090
Bel Harbor Dr 13090
Beling Ct 13090
Belmont Dr 13090
Berkley Ct 13090
Bermond Ct 13090
Berners Ct 13090
Berrywood Rd 13090
Bethnal Ct 13090
Betsy Ross Way 13088
Big Cone Path 13090
Birch St 13088
Birchwood Dr N & S 13090
Bitternut Ln 13090
Black Brant Dr 13090
Black Hawk Cir 13088
Black Oak Cir & Dr 13088
Black Willow 13090
Blackberry Rd 13090
Blacksmith Path 13088
Blackwood Dr 13090
Blue Beech Ln 13090
Blueberry Rd 13090
Blumer Rd 13088
Bordeaux Ave 13090
Bowdoin Ln 13090
Bradley St 13088
Braemar Dr 13090
Braintree Dr 13088
Bramblebush Cir 13090
Branchwood Dr 13090
Brompton Ln 13090
Brookview Ln 13088
Brookville Cir 13090
Brow St 13088
Buckeye Rd 13088
Buckley Rd
99-1300 13088
1302-7228 13088
4401-4425 13090
4451-7227 13088
Bufflehead Ln 13090
Bunny Ln 13090
Burdett Ct 13090
Burnham Ct 13090
Burningtree Rd 13090
Burr Dr 13088
Buttonwood Trl 13090
Cactus Cir 13090
Cadenza Ln 13088
Calypso Cir 13088
Cambridge Ct 13090
Cameco Cir 13090
Candlelight Cir & Ln 13090
Canoe Creek Ln 13090
Canvasback Dr 13090
Capricorn Dr 13090
Caraway Dr 13090
Cardinal Path 13090
Carling Rd 13090
Carmel Dr 13090
Carolyn Ave 13090
Carriage Pkwy 13088
Casimir Cir 13088
Cassidy Ln 13090
Casual Est 13090
Cedar Cir 13090
Cedar Post Rd 13088
Cedarcrest Cir 13090
Cepheus Crse 13090
Chancery Ln 13090
Chariot Ln 13090
Chelsea Ct 13090
Cherry Tree Cir 13090
Cheshire Ct 13090
Chestnut Heights Dr 13088
Chestnut Hill Dr 13088
Chiffon Path 13090
Choke Cherry Way 13090
Cinnamon Path 13090
Clacton Ct 13090
Clayton Manor Dr S 13088
Cleveland Ave & St 13088
Cloister Ct 13090
Cloverfield Cir 13090
Coachlight Ln 13088
Coconut Tree Dr 13090
Coffeemill Cir 13088
Cold Springs Rd
1000-1223 13088
1225-1299 13088
1300-2099 13090
2101-2199 13090
Colony Park Dr 13088
Commander Cir 13090
Commerce Blvd 13088
Commodore Cir 13090
Condor Cir 13090
Constable Dr 13090
Constitution Ln 13088
Continuum Dr 13088
Coppel Cir 13090
Corkins Ln 13088
Corsair Path 13090
Coton Ct 13090
Cotswold Ct 13090
Cottington Dr 13088
Cottonwood Ct 13090
Council Pl 13088
Cranberry Dr 13088
Cromwell Ct 13090
Cross Creek Dr 13090
Crossroads Park Dr 13088
Crown Rd 13090
Crystalwood Dr 13088
Cullen St 13088
Curlew Path 13090
Cypress St 13088
Dahlia Cir 13088
Dampier Cir 13090
Damson Ln 13090
Daniel Dr 13088
Darien Dr 13088
Dayton Dr 13090
Deborah Dr 13088
Deerfield Rd 13090
Delconte Cir 13088
Dell Center Dr 13090
Deptford Ct 13090
Devon Ct 13090
Dewline Rd 13090
Dexter Ave 13088
Dey Rd 13088
Diamond Rd 13088
Dollin St 13088
Dominion Pkwy 13090
Donald Pl 13090
Doncaster Ct 13090
Donegal Way 13088
Donlin Dr 13088
Dorando Way 13090
Douglas Ave 13088
Dove Path 13090
Drexler Ave & St S 13088
Driftwood Dr 13088
Duerr Rd 13090
Eagles Point Cir 13090
Ealing Ct 13090
Eastgate Cir 13090
Easton Rd 13090
Ebury Ct 13090
Echo Park Rd 13088
Edgecomb Dr 13088
Eider Down Path 13090
Elaine Cir 13090
Elderberry Ln 13090
Electronics Pkwy 13088
Elmcrest Cir & Rd 13090
Elwood Davis Rd 13088
Emerald Dr 13088
Ensign Cir & Dr 13090
Erica Ln 13090
Esperance Trl 13090
Ethel Ct 13090
Evergreen Cir 13090
Executive Dr 13088
Exeter Ave 13088
Eynsford Rd 13088
Fairmount Ave 13088
Fairway Dr E 13088
Falcon Ct & Dr 13090
Farmstead Rd 13088
Fenimore Ct 13090
Fern Hollow Dr 13088
Ferncliff Ave 13088
Finch Path 13090
Fireside Cir & Dr 13090
Fitzpatrick Dr 13088
Floradale Rd 13088
Florian Way 13088
Footprint Cir 13088
Forestbrook Dr 13090
Forester Rd 13088
Forestway Ct 13090
Forichit Rd 13090
Foster Rd 13090
Four Seasons Dr 13088
Fox Run Cir 13090
Foxberry Ln 13090
Foxmeadow Dr 13088
Foxtail Pnes 13090
Frandin Path 13090
Frayer Ln 13090
Frederick Dr 13088
Freestone Rd 13090
Fruitwood Dr 13088
Gabion Way 13090
Galbraith Ct 13090
Gale Ave 13088
Galloway Dr 13090
Gallowgate Ct 13090
Gallowhill Ct 13090
Galt Ct 13090
Gardner Ct 13090
Garfield Ave 13088
Garloch Ct 13090
Garnoch Ct 13088
Gembrook Ln 13088
Gemini Path 13090
Georgian Ct 13090
Gerviston Ct 13090
Gillis Ave 13088
Ginger Rd 13090
Girvan Ct 13090
Glenburn Rd 13090
Glencairn Ct 13090
Glencove Ct 13090
Glencrest Ave 13088
Glendale Ave 13088
Glenlynn Ct 13090
Glenwood Dr N & S 13090
Goguen Dr 13090
Golden Larch Ln 13090
Gooseberry Ln 13090
Gopher Cir 13090
Graham Ct 13090
Grampian Rd 13090
Grampton Ct 13090
Grandy Dr 13088
Grant Ct 13090
Grapewood Ln 13088
Gray Ave 13088
Gray Fox Run 13088
Grayhill Ct 13090
Great Muskrat 13090
Greeley Cir 13090
Green Acres Dr 13090
Green River Way 13090
Greenfield Pkwy 13088
Greenpoint Ave 13088
Gregor Ct 13090
Grenadier Dr 13090
Greystone Dr 13088
Gristmill Cir 13090
Grosvenor Rd 13090
Gulfline Rd 13090
Gull Path 13090
Halfmoon Cir 13090
Hanley Rd 13090
Hanover Ave 13088
Harbor Cir 13090
Harding Ave S 13088
Harvest Ln 13088
Harvest Home Pl 13088
Haverton Ln 13090
Hawthorne Dr 13090
Hazel St 13088
Hearthstone Ln 13088
Hemlock Cir 13090
Henry Clay Blvd
7000-7098 13088
7100-7527 13088
7529-7699 13088
7701-7797 13090
7799-8099 13090
Heritage Dr 13090
Hiawatha Trl 13088
Hickory St 13088
Hiram Ave 13088
Hollow Brook Dr 13090
Holly Ln 13090
Hollywood Cir 13088
Homeview Dr 13088
Honeysuckle Dr 13090
Hopkins Rd 13088
Huckleberry Ln 13090
Hummingbird Path 13090
Hunter Ave 13088
Ibis Path 13090
Ilex Ln 13090
Indian Orchard Ln 13090
Indigo Path 13090
Inglesid Ln 13090
Innovation Ln 13090
Inverrary Dr 13090
Iris Ln 13088
Iron Oak Cir 13090
Ironwood Cir 13090
Iroquois Ln 13090
Irving Ave 13088
Jackson Dr 13088
Jaguar Path 13090
Janus Park Dr 13088
Japine Dr 13090
Javelin Trl 13090
Jay Path 13090
Jennings Rd 13090
Jewell Dr 13088
Joel Ave 13088
Joewood Dr 13090
Jonquil Ln 13090
Joyce Pl 13090
Juanita Dr 13090
Junco Trl 13090
Juneberry Ln 13090
Juneway Dr N & S 13088
Juniper Ln 13090
Kearney Ave 13088
Kellars Ln 13088
Kettle Rd 13088
Kidron Ln 13090
Kies Dr 13090
Kingman Rd 13090
Kings Park Dr 13090
Kings Park Drive Ext 13090
Kingsdown Dr 13088
Kiwi Path 13090
Knowland Dr 13090
Kumquat Ln 13090
Labatts Way 13090
Lace Bark Ln 13090
Lake Dr 13088
Lakeview Ter 13088
Lancewood Dr 13090
Landsend Ln 13090
Lantern Cir 13088
Lark Path 13090
Larkin St 13088
Laurel Ave 13088
Laurie Ln 13090
Lazybrook Cir 13088
Lee St 13088
Lemontree Ln 13090
Ley Creek Dr 13088
Libby St 13088
Libra Ln 13090
Liffey Ln 13088
Lighthouse Village Cir 13088
Limestone Dr 13088
Limetree Ln 13090
N & S Lincoln Ave 13088
Lobelia Ln 13088
Lobos Ln 13090
Lockheed Martin Dr 13088
Long Branch Cir & Rd 13090
Long Leaf Trl 13090
Longdale Dr 13090
Longwood Dr 13088
Look Kinney Cir 13088
Lorraine Cres 13090
Loveland Dr 13090
Lowell Rd 13090
Lucan Rd 13090
Lueck Ln 13088
Lumber Way 13090
Luna Crse 13090
Luther Ave 13088
Lyra Crse 13090
Majestic Dr 13090
Mallard Path 13090
Maltlage Dr 13090
Mango Ln 13090
Mann Dr 13088
Manor Ln 13088
Marble Dr 13088
Marietta Pl 13090
Marlton Cir 13090
Marsh Pointe 13090
Marshfield Ct 13090
Maryland Ln 13090
Matchwood Ln 13090
Mayers St 13088
Mayfair Cir 13090
Mcardell Rd 13088
Mcintosh St 13090
Mcmahon Pl 13090
Meadow River Dr 13090
Melvin Ave 13088
Memphis St 13088
Mercury Cir 13088
Merganser Dr 13090
Merrill Dr 13090
Mesa Ln 13090
Metauro Dr 13090
Metropolitan Park Dr 13088
Meyers Rd 13088
Midwood Dr 13088
Mill Run Rd 13090
Millwood Cir 13090
Minuteman Ln 13088
Mistral Cir 13090
Moccasin Path 13090
Molson Way 13090
Monarch Dr 13088
Montezuma Crse 13090
Moonvalley Dr 13088
Morgan Pl & Rd 13090
Moses Dr 13090
Moss Creek Cir 13090
Moss Oak Trl 13090
Mountain Ash 13090
Moyer Heights Dr 13088
Muench Rd 13088
Nectarine Ln 13090
Needle Pine Path 13090
Nelson Rd 13090
Nestling Duck 13090
New Hope E 13090
Nightingale Path 13090
Norstar Blvd 13088
Norwood Ave E 13088
Nutcracker Trl 13090
Nutmeg Ln 13090
Oakledge Dr 13090
Oakpost Rd 13088
Oakridge Ter 13088
Odonnell St 13088
Office Park Dr 13088
Okeefe Ln 13090
Old 7th North St 13088
Old Cove Rd 13090
Old Liverpool Rd 13088
Old Wetzel Rd 13090
Oldbury Rd 13090
Onondaga Lake Pkwy 13088
Ontario Pl 13088
Opal Dr 13088
Orange Tree Ln 13090
Orangewood Dr 13090
Oriole Path 13090
Orion Path 13090
Oswego Rd
7100-7647 13090
7608-7608 13089
7648-8450 13090
7649-8399 13090
Oswego St 13088
Otis St 13088
Ourteds Cir 13090
Palomino Path 13088
Park Ridge Path 13090
Parker Ave 13088
Patrick Pl 13090
Patriot Ln 13088
Pawnee Dr 13090
Pearl St 13088
Pebblestone Ln 13088
Pedham Pl 13088
Penelope Ln 13090
Peppermill Ln 13088
Perch Dr 13090
Persimmon Path 13090
Pine Hollow Dr 13090
Pinewood Dr 13090
Pinkerton St 13088
Pintail Path 13090
Pinyon Pine Path 13090
Pisces Cir 13090
Plantation Blvd 13090
Platinum Dr 13088
Plaxdale Rd 13090
Plaza Rd 13090
Pleasantview Dr 13088
Plinius Way 13088
Plum Hollow Cir 13090
Plum Yew Cir 13090
Polaris Crse 13090
Poplar Dr 13090
Portobello Way 13090
Poseidon Cir 13090
Pranchin St 13088
Princess Path 13090
Provo Dr 13090
Quail Path 13090
Queenmar Cir 13090
Quincy Pl 13088
Rabbit Run 13090
Radar Dr 13088
Railroad St 13088
Rancho Park Dr 13090
Ravenswood Dr 13090
Ray St 13088
Red Barn Cir 13088
Reddeer Rd 13090
Redhead Ter 13090
Redwing Dr 13090
Regulus Crse 13090
Renfrew Dr 13090
Retford Dr 13088
Reval Ct 13088
Revolutionary Path 13088
Ridge Ave 13088
Rigel Crse 13090
Ritman Dr 13090
River Park Dr 13090
River Ridge Rd 13090
Rivercrest Rd 13090
Riverdale Rd 13090
Riverglen Rd 13090
Riverine Rd 13090
Rivers Pointe Way 13090
Roberta Dr 13090
Rocky Rd 13090
N & S Roosevelt Ave 13088
Roseanne Dr 13088
Rosemary Ln 13088
Rosewood Dr & Pl 13090
Royal Rd 13088
Royal Meadow Dr 13090
Ruby Rd 13088
Russell Ave 13088
Rusty Pine Ln 13090
Sagamore Dr N & S 13090
Salina St 13088
Saltmakers Rd 13088
Saltwell Rd 13090
Sampan Way 13090
Sandalwood Ln 13088
Sandbar Ln 13090
Sandpiper Ln 13090
Sargent Ln 13090
Saslon Park Dr 13088
School Rd 13088
Scotia Ln 13090
Scott Ln 13088
Scottsdale Cir 13088
Seabreeze Dr 13090
Sesame Path 13090
Shallowcreek Rd 13090
Shannon Way 13088
Shawnee Cir 13090
Sheridan Rd 13090
Shoreview Dr 13090
Shoveler Ln 13090
Silver Spruce Cir 13090
Silverado Dr 13090
Skyview Dr 13088
Snappy Ln 13090
Songbird Ln 13090
Sotherden Dr 13090
Soule Rd 13090
Spicebush Trl 13090
Springmoor Dr 13088
Spruce Tree Cir 13088
State Route 31 13090
Steelhead Dr 13090
Steelway Blvd N & S 13090
Stepping Stone Ln 13090
Stillwood Ln 13088
Stonedale Dr 13090
Stonehurst Rd 13090
Stormy Ln 13088
Streamwood Dr 13090
Sudbury Dr 13088
Sugar Pine Cir 13090
Summerhurst Dr 13088

Summerwood Pl 13090
Summit Cedar Ln 13090
Sun Harbor Dr 13088
Sunflower Dr 13088
Sunrise Ter 13088
Sunset Ct 13090
Surrey Ln 13088
Sutcliffe Dr 13090
Swallow Path 13090
Sweet Gum Ln 13090
Sycamore St 13088
W Taft Rd 13088
Tamarack St 13088
Tannis Ter 13090
Tempo Cir 13088
E & W Terminal Rd 13088
Thomas Dr 13088
Thornwood Dr 13088
Thrush Ln 13090
Thunderbird Rd 13088
Thyme Cir 13090
Tigerwood Dr 13090
Tirrell Hill Cir 13090
Todd Way 13088
Tommys Trl 13090
Tomwood Dr 13090
Torrey Ln 13090
Town Garden Dr 13088
Traister Dr 13088
Transistor Pkwy 13088
Trawler Crse 13090
Treadmill Cir 13090
Tree Line Dr 13090
Trellis Brook Ln 13090
Trivet Dr N & S 13088
Troyon St 13088
Tulip St
100-1199 13088
1200-1299 13090
Tuna Path 13090
Turnpike St 13088
Turtle Cove Rd 13090
Tyler Ter 13088
Underbrush Trl 13090
Ursa Crse 13090
Valley Rd 13088
Vardon St 13088
Vega Crse 13090
Ventura Cir 13088
Victoria Park Dr 13088
Viking Pl 13088
Vincent Ave 13088
Vine St 13088
Vine Meadow Rd 13090
Virgo Crse 13090
Voorhies Ln 13088
Wafer Ash Way 13090
Walking Stick Way 13090
Walnut Pl 13090
Walters Dr 13088
Warbler Way 13090
Westgate Ln 13090
Wetzel Rd 13090
Whiffletree Ln 13090
White Birch Cir 13090
White Cedar Cir 13090
Whitman Way 13090
Wild Turkey 13090
N & S Willow St 13088
Willowbrook Ct, Dr & Ln 13090
Wilson Ave 13088
Winchester Dr 13088
Windgate Rd 13088
Winterberry Way 13090
Winterhaven Dr 13088
Winterpark Dr 13090
Wintersweet Dr 13088
Woerner Ave 13088
Woodard Way 13088
N & S Woodland Dr & Ter 13088
Woodmark Dr 13088
Woodside Ln 13090
Woodspath Rd 13090
Wrentham Dr 13088
Wyant Way 13088
Wyker Cir 13088
Yager Dr 13088
Zodiac Cir 13090

NUMBERED STREETS

All Street Addresses 13088

LOCKPORT NY

General Delivery 14094

POST OFFICE BOXES MAIN OFFICE STATIONS AND BRANCHES

Box No.s
All PO Boxes 14095

NAMED STREETS

Aaron Dr 14094
Academy Ln 14094
N Adam St 14094
Aiken Rd 14094
Akron Rd & St 14094
Alabama Pl 14094
Alanview Dr 14094
Alexander St 14094
Allen St 14094
Amanda Ln 14094
Ambleside Dr 14094
Amelia St 14094
Amy Ln 14094
Angela Dr 14094
Ann St 14094
Applewood Dr & Ln 14094
Arbor Dr 14094
Arrowhead Dr 14094
Ash Ct & St 14094
Ashley Pl 14094
Autumnvale Dr 14094
Bacon St 14094
Badger Dr 14094
Bartz Rd 14094
Beach Dr 14094
Beach Ridge Rd 14094
Bear Ridge Rd 14094
Beattie Ave 14094
Ben Way 14094
Berkley Dr 14094
Beverly Ave 14094
Bewley Pkwy 14094
Bewley Building 14094
Bickert Pl 14094
Birch Holw 14094
Birchwood Dr 14094
Blackley Ct 14094
Blackman Rd 14094
Block Church Rd 14094
Bob O Link Ln 14094
Bonner Dr 14094
Bordino Dr 14094
Bowen Rd 14094
Bowmiller Rd 14094
Boyer Rd 14094
Branch St 14094
Brian Walk 14094
Briarwood Dr 14094
Bridlewood Dr 14094
Bright St 14094
S Bristol Ave 14094
Brockton Dr 14094
Brookside Dr 14094
Budd Rd 14094
Buell Dr 14094
Bulmore Rd 14094
Bunker Hill Rd 14094
Butler St 14094
W Caledonia St 14094
Cambria Rd 14094
Cambria Wilson Rd 14094
Cambridge Dr 14094
Cameron Dr 14094
Campbell Blvd 14094
E, N & W Canal Rd & St 14094
Candlewood Dr 14094
Carleton Lake Dr 14094
Carlton Pl 14094
Carolina Ave 14094
Carriage Ln 14094
Carter Dr 14094
Case Ct 14094
Cave St 14094
Cedar St 14094
Center St 14094
Central Ave 14094
Chapel St 14094
Charles St 14094
Charlotte St 14094
Checkered Tavern Rd 14094
Cherry St 14094
Cherrywood Ln 14094
Chestnut Dr & St 14094
Chestnut Ridge Rd 14094
Christiana Ct 14094
Church Rd & St 14094
N Circle Dr 14094
Cleveland Pl 14094
Clinton St 14094
Cloverleaf Dr & Ln 14094
Club House Dr 14094
Cold Springs Rd 14094
Collins Dr 14094
Colonial Dr 14094
Colony Ct 14094
Columbia St 14094
Commerce Dr 14094
Comstock Rd 14094
Congressional Dr 14094
Continental Dr 14094
Coolidge Ave 14094
Corinthia St 14094
Corwin Rd 14094
Cottage Ct, Ln, Rd & St 14094
Creek Holw 14094
Creekview Dr 14094
Crescent Dr 14094
Crestfield Ln 14094
Crestwood Ct & Dr 14094
Crosby Ave & Rd 14094
Crown Dr 14094
Dale Rd 14094
Davies Ln 14094
Davison Ct & Rd 14094
Day Rd 14094
Dayton St 14094
Dedi Dr 14094
Del Ct E & W 14094
Desales Cir 14094
Devereaux Ct 14094
Devonshire Ln 14094
Dewhirst Rd 14094
Dogwood Dr 14094
Donner Rd 14094
Dorchester Rd 14094
Dunnigan Rd 14094
Dysinger Rd 14094
East Ave
1-137 14094
138-138 14095
139-799 14094
140-798 14094
Eastview Dr 14094
Eastwood Dr 14094
Edgewood Dr 14094
Eisenhower Dr 14094
Elizabeth Dr 14094
Ellicott Rd 14094
Elm Ct & St 14094
Elmhurst Dr 14094
Elmira St 14094
Elmwood Ave 14094
Emily Ln 14094
Enterprise Dr 14094
Erica Ln 14094
Erie St 14094
Erna Dr 14094
Ernest Rd 14094
Ertman Rd 14094
Escarpment Dr 14094
Euclid Ave 14094
Evans St 14094
Evergreen Dr 14094
Ewings Rd 14094
Exchange St 14094
Fairfax St 14094
Fairview Dr 14094
Fairway Dr 14094
Fayette St 14094
Feigle Rd 14094
Fernwood Dr 14094
Fieldcrest Dr 14094
Fisk Rd 14094
Forest Hill Rd 14094
Forestview Dr 14094
Fox Cir 14094
Franklin Ave 14094
Frontier Pl 14094
Frost St 14094
Gabriel Dr 14094
Gaffney Rd 14094
Garden St 14094
Gardenwood Dr 14094
W Genesee St 14094
Georgetown Ct 14094
Georgia Ave 14094
Glendale Dr 14094
Glenwood Ave 14094
Gooding St 14094
Gothic Ln 14094
Gothic Hill Rd 14094
Gothic Ledge 14094
Grand St 14094
Grant St 14094
Grasmere Rd 14094
Green Rd & St 14094
Green Valley Ln 14094
Greenview Dr 14094
Groff Rd 14094
Grosvenor St 14094
Grove Ave & Rd 14094
Haines St 14094
Hallmark Ln 14094
Hamilton Dr 14094
Hamm Rd 14094
Harding Ave 14094
Harding Avenue Ext 14094
Harrington Rd 14094
Harrison Ave 14094
Hartford Dr 14094
Harvest Ridge Way 14094
Harvey Ave 14094
Harwood St 14094
Hawley Ct & St 14094
Heath St 14094
Heather Dr 14094
Heritage Ct & Pt 14094
Hess Rd 14094
Hi Point Dr 14094
Hidden Lake Dr 14094
Hidden Lane Dr 14094
Hidden Oak Dr 14094
Hidden Pond Ln 14094
High St 14094
Highland Dr 14094
Hildreth St 14094
Hill St 14094
Hillcrest Dr 14094
Hinman Rd 14094
Hollenbeck Rd 14094
Hollywood Dr 14094
Homewood Dr 14094
Hoover Pkwy 14094
Hope Ln 14094
Hopi Ct 14094
Howard Ave 14094
Hyde Park 14094
I D A Park Dr 14094
Independence Dr 14094
Irish Rd 14094
Iroquois Dr 14094
Irving St 14094
W Jackson St 14094
Jacques Rd 14094
Jefferson Dr 14094
Jeffrey Dr 14094
Jennifer Dr 14094
Jesson Pkwy 14094
John St 14094
Johnson Rd 14094
Juniper St 14094
Keck Rd 14094
Keswick Rd 14094
Kimberly Dr 14094
King St 14094
Kingston Cir 14094
Kinne Rd 14094
Knotty Pine Dr 14094
Lagrange St 14094
Lake Ave 14094
Lakeview Pkwy 14094
Lea Ln 14094
Leete Rd 14094
Levan Ave 14094
Lewis St 14094
Lexington Ct 14094
Lilac Dr 14094
Lincoln Ave, Dr & Pl 14094
Lincoln Avenue Ext 14094
Lincolnshire Dr 14094
Lindhurst Dr 14094
Livingston Pl 14094
Lock St 14094
Lock Haven Dr 14094
Lockport Rd 14094
Lockport Junction Rd 14094
Lockport Olcott Rd 14094
Locks Plz 14094
Lockwood Ct, Dr & Ln 14094
Locust St 14094
Locust Street Ext 14094
Longcroft Dr 14094
Longview Dr 14094
Lower Mountain Rd 14094
Magnolia Dr 14094
W Main Rd & St 14094
Maple St 14094
Mapleton Rd 14094
Maplewood Ct & Dr 14094
Marion Dr 14094
Marjorie Dr 14094
Market St 14094
Marnerth St 14094
Marshall Pl 14094
Massachusetts Ave 14094
Matthew Dr 14094
Mccollum St 14094
Mccue Ave 14094
Mcintosh Dr 14094
Meadow Ln 14094
Meadowview Dr 14094
Meahl Rd 14094
Michelle Dr 14094
Michigan St 14094
Middleton Dr 14094
Mill St 14094
Millar Pl 14094
Miller Rd 14094
Minard St 14094
Minnick Rd 14094
Monroe St 14094
Morrow Ave 14094
Morton Ave 14094
Mount View Dr 14094
Moyer Rd 14094
Mulberry Ln 14094
Mulligan Dr 14094
Murphy Rd 14094
Neil Dr 14094
S New York St 14094
Newcastle Dr 14094
S Niagara Ct & St 14094
Niagara Street Ext 14094
Nichols St 14094
Nixon Pl 14094
North St 14094
Northledge Dr 14094
Northview Dr 14094
Norwood Dr 14094
Oak Ln & St 14094
Oakhurst St 14094
Obrien Dr 14094
Oconnor Dr 14094
Ohio St 14094
Olcott St 14094
Old Beattie Rd 14094
Old Beebe Rd 14094
Old Dysinger Rd 14094
Old English Rd 14094
Old Niagara Rd 14094
Old Saunders Settlemen Rd 14094
Oliver St 14094
Ontario St 14094
Orchard St 14094
Otto Park Pl 14094
Outwater Dr 14094
Oxford Ln 14094
E Park Ave, Dr & Pl 14094
Park Lane Cir 14094
Parkwood Dr 14094
Passaic Ave 14094
Pennsylvania Ave 14094
Penrith Rd 14094
Pepper Tree Ct 14094
Pheasant Holw 14094
Phelps St 14094
Pine St 14094
Pinecrest Dr 14094
Pinegrove Ter 14094
Piper Ln 14094
Plank Rd 14094
Porter St 14094
Pound St 14094
Prentice St 14094
Presidential Way 14094
Price St 14094
Priscilla Ln 14094
Professional Pkwy 14094
Prospect St 14094
Purdy Rd 14094
Ransom Ct & St 14094
Rapids Rd 14094
Rathke Hts 14094
Raymond Rd 14094
Rebecca Rd 14094
Reed St 14094
Regent St 14094
Reger Dr 14094
Remick Pkwy 14094
Renassance Dr 14094
Rene Pl 14094
Richfield St 14094
Riddle Rd 14094
N Ridge Rd 14094
Ridgelea Dr 14094
Ridgewood Dr 14094
Robert Breen Pkwy 14094
Robinson Pl & Rd 14094
Roby St 14094
Rochester Rd & St 14094
Rogers Ave 14094
Roosevelt Dr 14094
Royal Ct, Ln & Pkwy N & S 14094
Ruhlmann Rd 14094
Russell St 14094
Rydalmount Rd 14094
Saint Joseph Dr 14094
Sanders Rd 14094
Sandy Ln 14094
Sargent Dr 14094
Saunders Settlement Rd 14094
Saxton St 14094
Scovell St 14094
Sebastian Dr 14094
Seneca Ct 14094
Shaeffer St 14094
Shaffer Rd 14094
Sharon Dr 14094
Sheetram Rd 14094
Sherman Dr 14094
Sherwood Dr 14094
Shimer Dr 14094
Short St 14094
Shunpike Rd 14094
Simms Rd 14094
Simonds St 14094
Singer Rd 14094
Slayton Settlement Rd 14094
Snyder Dr 14094
South St 14094
Southview Dr 14094
Southwood Dr 14094
Spalding St 14094
Spring St 14094
Spruce Ct & St 14094
Standish Rd 14094
State Rd 14094
Stevens St 14094
Stone Rd 14094
Strauss Rd 14094
Sturbridge Ln 14094
Subbera Rd 14094
Summer St 14094
Summit St 14094
Sunnyside St 14094
Sunset Ct & Dr 14094
Susanne Dr 14094
Sweetwood Dr 14094
Sycamore St 14094
The Cmn 14094
Thrall Rd 14094
Timberwood Ct 14094
Tonawanda Creek Rd 14094
Townline Rd 14094
Tracy Ct 14094
N & S Transit Rd & St 14094
Treehaven Dr 14094
Trowbridge St 14094
Tudor Ln 14094
Twilight Ln 14094
Underwood Ct 14094
E Union St 14094
Upper Mountain Rd 14094
Utica St 14094
Valley Way 14094
Van Buren St 14094
Van Dusen Rd 14094
Vermont Ave 14094
Victoria Ln 14094
Vine St 14094
Vinewood Dr 14094
Vintage Ct 14094
Virginia Ct 14094
Wakeman Pl 14094
Walnut Ln & St 14094
Washburn St 14094
Washington St 14094
Water St 14094
Waterford Pl 14094
Waterman St 14094
Webb St 14094
Weld St 14094
Wendy Cir 14094
West Ave 14094
Westwood Dr 14094
Wheeler Rd 14094
Wick Rd 14094
William St 14094
Willow St 14094
Willow Wood Dr 14094
Willowbrook Dr 14094
Wills Holw 14094
Wilson Pkwy & Rd 14094
Windermere Rd 14094
Windsor St 14094
Wisterman Rd 14094
Woodbury Dr 14094
Woodhaven Dr 14094
Woodlawn Ave 14094
Woodmore Ct 14094
Works Pl 14094
Wynkoop Rd 14094
Young Rd 14094

LONG ISLAND CITY NY

General Delivery ... 11101

POST OFFICE BOXES MAIN OFFICE STATIONS AND BRANCHES

Box No.s
All PO Boxes ... 11101

NAMED STREETS

Austel Pl ... 11101
Borden Ave ... 11101
Bradley Ave ... 11101
Center Blvd ... 11109
Court Sq ... 11101
Crane St ... 11101
Crescent St ... 11101
Davis Ct & St ... 11101
Dutchkills St ... 11101
Flachenn Ave ... 11101
Gale Ave ... 11101
Gopost ... 11101
Greenpoint Ave ... 11101
Honeywell St ... 11101
Hunter St ... 11101
Hunters Point Ave ... 11101
Jackson Ave ... 11101
Met Life Plz ... 11101
Northern Blvd ... 11101
Orchard St ... 11101
Pearson Pl & St ... 11101
Purves St ... 11101
Queens Blvd, Plz & St N & S ... 11101
Railroad Ave ... 11101
Review Ave ... 11101
Skillman Ave ... 11101
Starr Ave ... 11101
Steinway St ... 11101
Thomson Ave ... 11101
Van Dam St ... 11101
Vernon Blvd ... 11101
West St ... 11101
Woodside Ave ... 11101

NUMBERED STREETS

2nd St ... 11101
5th St ... 11101
9th St ... 11101
10th St ... 11101
11th St ... 11101
12th St ... 11101
13th St ... 11101
21st St ... 11101
22nd St ... 11101
23rd St ... 11101
24th St ... 11101
25th St ... 11101
27th St ... 11101
28th St ... 11101
29th St ... 11101
30th Pl & St ... 11101
31st Pl & St ... 11101
32nd Pl & St ... 11101
33rd St ... 11101
34th Ave & St ... 11101
35th Ave & St ... 11101
36th Ave & St ... 11101
37th Ave & St ... 11101
38th Ave & St ... 11101
39th Ave ... 11101
40th Ave & Rd ... 11101
41st Ave & St ... 11101
42nd Rd & St ... 11101
43rd Ave, Rd & St ... 11101
44th Ave, Dr, Rd & St ... 11101
45th Ave, Rd & St ... 11101
46th Ave, Rd & St ... 11101
47th Ave & Rd ... 11101
48th Ave ... 11109
  501-997 ... 11101
48th St ... 11101
49th Ave ... 11101
50th Ave ... 11101
51st Ave ... 11101
53rd Ave ... 11101
54th Ave ... 11101

LYON MOUNTAIN NY

General Delivery ... 12952

POST OFFICE BOXES MAIN OFFICE STATIONS AND BRANCHES

Box No.s
All PO Boxes ... 12952

NAMED STREETS

Archie Way ... 12955
Bella Vista Way ... 12952
Bigelow Rd ... 12955
Birch Way ... 12955
Blanche Rd ... 12955
Boomhower Rd ... 12952
Brooks Way ... 12955
Buckhorn Way ... 12955
Catalan Forge Rd ... 12952
County Route 54 Rd ... 12955
Cross St ... 12952
Depot St ... 12952
Donterth Rd ... 12955
Gadway Rd ... 12955
Harris Rd ... 12955
Hemlock Ln ... 12952
W Hill Rd ... 12955
Holtzman Way ... 12955
Keysor St ... 12952
Larrindo Rd ... 12952
Light Post Way ... 12955
Loon Point Way ... 12952
Mcpherson Way ... 12955
Middle St ... 12952
Narrows Rd ... 12955
Norcross Way ... 12955
Peets Rd ... 12955
Saxe Way ... 12955
Shutts Rd ... 12955
Spear Hill Rd ... 12955
Split Rock Point Way ... 12955
Standish Rd ... 12952
State Route 374
  3800-3999 ... 12952
  4000-6099 ... 12955
Sunset Rd ... 12952
Tacy Rd ... 12955
Tallman Way ... 12955
Tamarack Ln ... 12952
Trillium Way ... 12952
Trillum Way ... 12952
Wolf Pond Rd ... 12952
Youngs Rd ... 12955

MIDDLETOWN NY

General Delivery ... 10940

POST OFFICE BOXES MAIN OFFICE STATIONS AND BRANCHES

Box No.s
1 - 3135 ... 10940
4001 - 4840 ... 10941
5000 - 7088 ... 10940

NAMED STREETS

Abingdon Mews ... 10940
Abraham Joseph Cir ... 10940
Abrahamson Rd ... 10940
Academy Ave ... 10940
Acorn Ave ... 10941
Adams Ave ... 10940
Agin Court Sq ... 10940
Airport Rd ... 10940
Alabama Pl ... 10940
Alaska Ave ... 10940
Albert St ... 10940
Alberta Dr ... 10941
Alex Ct ... 10940
Allan Park Mews ... 10940
Allen Dr & St ... 10940
Allerton Ave ... 10940
Alvaran Ln ... 10941
Amchir Ave ... 10940
Amster Rd ... 10940
Amy Ln ... 10941
Anna Ct ... 10941
Annis Ct ... 10940
Anthony St ... 10940
Apache Trl ... 10940
Apple Ln ... 10940
Apple Lane Dr ... 10940
Arbor Way ... 10940
Arden Ct ... 10940
Arlington Pl ... 10940
Arnott Ln ... 10941
Ash Ln ... 10940
Ashland Ave ... 10940
Ashley Ave ... 10940
N & S Aspen Rd ... 10940
Aster Way ... 10940
Avenue E ... 10940
Avenue A ... 10940
Avenue B ... 10940
Avenue C ... 10940
Avenue D ... 10940
Avenue F ... 10940
Avian Acres Ln ... 10940
Avoncroft Ln ... 10940
Badami Dr ... 10941
Baker Rd ... 10941
Baldwin Hill Rd ... 10941
Ballard Rd ... 10941
Barra Rd ... 10940
Bart Bull Rd ... 10941
Bartlett Dr ... 10941
Bayea Ln ... 10940
Beacon Rd ... 10941
Beacon St ... 10940
N Beacon St ... 10940
Beakes Ave & St ... 10940
Bear Cave Ln ... 10940
Beattie Ave ... 10940
Bedford Ave ... 10940
Beers Dr ... 10940
Belgrave Mews ... 10940
Bellevernon Ave ... 10940
Belmont Ave ... 10940
Ben Lomond Dr ... 10941
Benedict St ... 10940
Benjamin Ave ... 10940
Bennett St ... 10940
Benny Ln ... 10940
Benton Ave ... 10940
Berkman Dr ... 10941
Bert Crawford Rd ... 10940
Beth Dr ... 10941
Beth Pl ... 10940
Beverly Dr ... 10941
Beyers Rd ... 10941
Birch Ct ... 10940
Birch Dr ... 10940
Birch Pl ... 10941
Birch St ... 10940
Birchwood Ln ... 10940
Bisch Rd ... 10940
Black Stallion Ct ... 10940
Blake Ln ... 10940
Blanchard St ... 10940
Bloomingburg Rd ... 10940
Blumel Rd ... 10941
Boak Ave ... 10940
Bonnell Pl & St ... 10940
Bonnie Brae Dr ... 10941
Boorman Rd ... 10940
Bowery Ln ... 10940
Bowser Rd ... 10940
Bradner Ave ... 10940
Brae Mar Rd ... 10941
Breslin Pl ... 10940
Brewster Dr ... 10940
Briarwood Dr ... 10940
Brick Pond Rd ... 10940
Brimstone Hill Rd ... 10941
Brink Ave ... 10940
Bristol Dr ... 10941
Brittany Dr ... 10940
Broad St ... 10940
Brola Rd ... 10940
Brook Rd ... 10941
Brookline Ave ... 10940
Brown Ave ... 10940
Brown Rd ... 10941
Buckingham Mews ... 10940
Buckley Ln ... 10940
Budd Ave ... 10940
Bull Rd ... 10941
Burnt Corners Rd ... 10940
California Ave & Dr ... 10940
Camellia Ln ... 10940
Camp Orange Rd ... 10941
Camp Stadie Rd ... 10940
Canal St ... 10940
Canterbury Dr ... 10940
Cantrell Ave ... 10940
Carboy Rd ... 10940
Cardinal Ln ... 10940
Carl Pl ... 10940
Carmelite Dr ... 10940
Carole Ct ... 10940
Carpenter Ave ... 10940
Carrie Ln ... 10940
Casey Ln ... 10940
Casimer Rd ... 10941
Caskey Ln ... 10940
Castle High Rd ... 10940
Cedar Ct & Ln ... 10940
Cedarcrest Dr ... 10940
Cemetery Rd ... 10940
Center St ... 10940
S Centerville Rd ... 10940
Certified Dr ... 10940
Chancery Mews ... 10940
Chappell Pkwy ... 10940
Charles Ct ... 10941
Charles St ... 10940
Charlotte Ln & Mews ... 10940
Chattel St ... 10940
Chaucer Ct ... 10941
Cherry Ave ... 10941
Cherry St ... 10940
Chestnut Ave & St ... 10940
Christopher Ct ... 10941
Church St ... 10940
Cindy Ln ... 10941
Circle Dr ... 10941
Claremont Ct ... 10940
Clarence Mews ... 10940
Clark St ... 10940
Clemson Park ... 10940
Clinton St ... 10940
Clover Pl ... 10940
Club Way ... 10940
Cobb Ln ... 10940
Cobblestone Ln ... 10940
Columbia Ave ... 10940
Columbine Ct ... 10940
Comfort Rd ... 10941
Commercial Ave ... 10941
Commonwealth Ave ... 10940
Concord Ln ... 10940
E & W Conkling Ave ... 10940
Conning Ave ... 10941
Connors Rd ... 10941
Coolidge Ct ... 10940
Cornelia St ... 10940
Cornfield Rd ... 10940
Cornwall Ln ... 10940
Cortright Rd ... 10940
Corwin Ave ... 10940
Cottage St ... 10940
Cottage St Ext ... 10940
Country Club Dr ... 10940
Country Side Ct ... 10941
County Highway 78 ... 10940
County Route 22 ... 10940
County Route 49 ... 10940
County Route 50 ... 10940
County Route 56 ... 10940
County Route 65 ... 10940
County Route 70 ... 10940
Courtland Pl & St ... 10940
Crabapple Ln ... 10941
Crane Rd ... 10941
Crans Rd ... 10941
Crawford Pl ... 10940
Creeden Dr ... 10940
Creeden Hill Rd ... 10940
Crescent Pl ... 10940
Cross Rd ... 10941
Crotty Rd ... 10941
Crystal Run Rd & Xing ... 10941
Dakota Dr ... 10940
Daly Rd ... 10940
Danielle Ct ... 10940
David St ... 10940
Davidge Rd ... 10940
De Block Rd ... 10940
Decker Dr & Rd ... 10940
Deer Ct Dr ... 10940
Denman Rd ... 10940
Denton Ave ... 10941
Depot St ... 10940
Derby Rd ... 10940
Dewitt St ... 10940
Disco Dr ... 10941
Dodge Dr ... 10940
Dogwood Dr
  1-47 ... 10940
  2-54 ... 10940
  2-2 ... 10941
  3-17 ... 10941
  19-99 ... 10941
Dogwood Ln ... 10940
Dolaway Ln ... 10940
Dolson Ave ... 10940
Dolsontown Rd ... 10941
Dominick St ... 10941
Dorothea Dix Dr ... 10940
Dosen Rd ... 10940
Drago Ln ... 10940
Drake Rd ... 10940
Dubois St ... 10940
Dulcie Ct ... 10940
Dun Donald Cir ... 10941
Dundee Cir ... 10941
Dunning Rd ... 10940
Durham Ct ... 10940
Eagles Way ... 10940
Earle St ... 10940
East Ave ... 10940
Eaton Ct ... 10940
Eatontown Rd ... 10940
Ebert Rd ... 10941
Ebury Mews ... 10940
Edgewater Dr ... 10940
Edinburgh Rd ... 10941
Edward Ct ... 10940
Eisenhower Dr ... 10940
Eldred St ... 10940
Electric Ave ... 10940
Elise Dr ... 10941
Elizabeth Ave ... 10941
Elm Rd & St ... 10940
Elman Pl ... 10940
Emma Ave ... 10940
Enterprise Pl ... 10941
Eric Dr ... 10940
Erie Ave ... 10940
Erin Ct ... 10941
Estate Dr ... 10940
Euclid Ave ... 10940
Evan Ct ... 10940
Evergreen Dr ... 10940
Excelsior Ave ... 10940
Fair Ave ... 10940
Fair Oaks Rd ... 10940
Fairfax Ave ... 10940
Fairgrounds Ave ... 10940
Fairlawn Ave ... 10940
Fairview Ave ... 10940
Fairways Dr ... 10940
Fanchers Trailer Park ... 10941
Faulkner St ... 10940
Fawn Ct ... 10940
Fay Ln ... 10940
Feiertag Rd ... 10941
Fern St ... 10940
Ferrara Dr ... 10941
Fifth Ave ... 10941
Finch Rd ... 10940
Finchville Tpke ... 10940
Fini Dr ... 10941
First Ave ... 10941
Fitzgerald Dr ... 10940
Fitzherbert Mews ... 10940
Forest Ave & Dr ... 10940
Fortune Rd E & W ... 10941
Foster Rd ... 10941
Fourth Ave ... 10941
Fox Hill Dr ... 10940
Foxfire Estates Rd ... 10940
Francis Dr ... 10940
Franklin Ln & St ... 10940
Frederick St ... 10941
Freendon Rd ... 10941
Freezer Rd ... 10941
Fulton St ... 10940
Gabby Ln ... 10940
Gail Myra Ln ... 10940
N Galleria Dr ... 10941
Gardner Ave ... 10940
Gardner Ave Ext ... 10940
Gavin Ave ... 10940
Gaybar Cir ... 10940
Gene Rd ... 10941
Genung St ... 10940
Georges Rd ... 10941
Gertrude Dr ... 10940
Gibbs Ct ... 10940
Gillen Rd ... 10940
Glazer Dr ... 10940
Glen Ave ... 10940
Glen Cove Ct ... 10940
Godwin Rd ... 10941
Goffredo Ct ... 10940
Golf Links Rd ... 10940
Gordon Rd ... 10941
Goshen Tpke ... 10941
Gould St ... 10940
Grahamtown Rd ... 10940
Grand Ave ... 10940
Grandview Ave ... 10940
Granite Ct ... 10940
Grant St ... 10940
Green Ct ... 10940
Greencrest Dr ... 10941
Greenville Tpke ... 10940
Greenway Ter ... 10941
Greenwood Ct ... 10940
Groo St ... 10940
Grosvenor Mews ... 10940
Grove St ... 10940
Guymard Tpke ... 10940
Haelen Ter ... 10940
Hampton Ct ... 10941
Hanford St ... 10940
Hanover Mews ... 10940
Harcourt Mews ... 10940
Harding St ... 10940
Harriet Tubman Dr ... 10940
Harrison St ... 10940
Harry Ln ... 10940
Harvest Hill Ln ... 10940
Hasbrouck St ... 10940
Haven Ln ... 10940
Hawthorne Dr ... 10940
Heather Ct ... 10941
Heather Ln ... 10940
Heidt Ave ... 10940
Helen Dr ... 10940
Henry St ... 10940
Herallea Ave ... 10940
Hermanette Ave ... 10940
Hickory Pl ... 10941
Hickory Ter ... 10940
Hidden Dr ... 10941
High Barney Ln & Rd ... 10940
High Ridge Ln ... 10940
Highland Ave & Pl ... 10940
Highland Ave Ext ... 10940
Highland Lake Rd ... 10940
Highland View Pl ... 10940
Highrose Ridge Way ... 10940
Highview Ave ... 10940
Highview Dr ... 10941
Hill Rd
  1-6 ... 10941
  4-5 ... 10940
  8-24 ... 10941
  9-25 ... 10941
  27-31 ... 10941
  30-32 ... 10940
  33-71 ... 10941
  34-38 ... 10941
  38-50 ... 10940
  42-52 ... 10941
  54-58 ... 10940
  56-70 ... 10941
  57-59 ... 10940
  61-199 ... 10940
  201-299 ... 10940
  300-399 ... 10941
  400-499 ... 10940
Hill St ... 10940
Hillcrest Dr & Rd ... 10940
Hillside Ave ... 10940
Hillside Dr ... 10941
Hilltop Ave ... 10940
Hoffman St ... 10940
Holly Hill Ln ... 10941
Hollywood Rd ... 10941
Homestead Ave ... 10941
Homestead Ln ... 10940
Hoover Dr ... 10940
Horseshoe Way ... 10940
Horton Ave ... 10940
Houston Ave ... 10940
Houston Avenue Ext ... 10940
Howard Dr ... 10941
Howells Rd & Tpke ... 10940
Hufcut Rd ... 10941
Hulle Rd ... 10941
Hulse Ave & St ... 10940
Imperial Pk Dr ... 10941
Independence Ave ... 10940
Indian Trail Rd ... 10941
Industrial Dr ... 10941
Industrial Pl ... 10941
Ingalls St ... 10940
Ingrassia Rd ... 10940
Inwood Rd ... 10941
Iris Ln ... 10940
Irwin Ave ... 10940
Ivory Ln ... 10940
W Jackson Ave & St ... 10940
James Ct ... 10941
James St ... 10940
James Clark Dr ... 10940
James P Kelly Way ... 10940
Janice Dr ... 10941
Jasmine Dr ... 10940
Jason Pl ... 10940
Jay St ... 10940
Jean Ridge Rd ... 10940
Jimal Dr ... 10940
Jogee Rd ... 10940
John St ... 10940
Johns Rd ... 10941
Jonathan Ct ... 10941
Jordan Ln ... 10940
Jorie Ct ... 10941
Juniper Cir ... 10940

Karen Dr 10940
Karen Joy Dr 10940
Karmin Dr 10940
Keasel Rd 10940
Keats Rd 10941
Kelly St 10941
Kendal Ln 10940
Kennedy Ter 10940
Kenny Dr 10941
Kensington Mnr 10941
Kensington Way 10940
Kent Ct 10940
Keystone Park 10940
King Rd 10941
King St 10940
Kings Dr 10941
Kinne Ln 10940
Kirby Pl 10940
Kirbytown Rd 10940
Kirchner Ln 10940
Knapp Ave 10940
Knox Ave 10940
Kohler Rd 10940
Kyleigh Way 10940
La Grange St 10940
Laddie Rd 10941
Lafayette Ave 10940
Lake Ave 10940
Lake Claire Dr 10940
Lake Ridge Dr 10940
Lake View Dr 10940
Lakeview Ave 10941
Langton Mews 10940
Last Rd 10941
Laurel Pl 10940
Laurie Ann Dr 10941
Lawrence Ave 10940
Leaf Haven Ct 10941
Ledge Rd 10940
Leewood Dr 10941
Leighton Ct 10940
Lenox Pl 10940
Leonard St 10940
Lewis Ln & Rd 10940
Lewis Landing Rd 10940
Lexington Way 10940
Liberty St 10940
Lilac St 10940
Lincoln St & Ter 10940
Linden Ave & Pl 10940
Little Ave 10940
Little Monhagen Ave 10940
Livingston St 10940
Lloyds Ln 10940
Loch Invar Ln 10941
Loch Lomond Ln 10941
Lodi St 10941
Lone Indian Trl 10940
Longview Ln 10941
Lopresti Rd 10940
Lorelei Dr 10940
Low Ave 10940
Lybolt Rd 10941
M And M Rd 10940
Mabel Rd 10941
Macintosh Dr 10941
Madelaine Ter 10940
Madison Ave 10940
Magar St 10940
Magdalene Close 10940
Main Dr 10941
E Main St 10940
W Main St 10940
Maltese Dr 10940
Manhattan Ave 10940
Manning Rd 10940
Manor Mews 10940
Mapes Rd 10940
Maple Ave 10940
Maple Dr
2-20 10941
9-47 10940
15-199 10941
22-32 10940
26-98 10941
34-42 10940
100-198 10941
Maples Ln & Rd 10940
Maplewood Dr 10940
Marc Craig Blvd 10940
Marcy Ln 10941
Margaret Ter 10940
Marie Ln 10941
Marion Ct 10941
Mark Dr 10940
Marsham Ct 10940
Martin St 10940
Maryland Ave 10940
Matthews Ct 10940
Maureen Dr & Ln 10940
Mayer Dr 10940
Mccombs Dr 10940
Mckenzie Ct 10940
Meadow Lake Dr 10941
Meadows Ln 10941
Melissa Ter 10941
Mercer St 10940
Mermaid Rd 10940
Meyer Rd 10940
Michele Ct 10941
Midland Ave 10940
Midland Ave Ext 10940
Midland Lake Rd 10941
Midland Lake Rd S 10940
Midway Rd 10940
Midway Park Dr 10940
Mila Dr 10940
Mill St 10940
Miller Heights Rd 10940
Mills Ave
1-99 10940
101-113 10940
Mills Ave N 10941
Mills Rd 10941
Millsburg Rd 10940
Milo Dr 10941
Monhagen Ave 10940
Monica Ct 10941
Montgomery St 10940
Moriah Ln 10940
Morningside Dr 10941
Motel Rd 10941
Mountain Ave & Rd 10940
Mt Hope Rd 10940
Mt Joy Rd 10941
Mt Joy Hill Rd 10941
Mt Orange Rd 10940
Mud Mills Rd 10940
Mulberry St 10940
Mulford Rd 10940
Mullock Rd 10940
Murray Rd 10940
My Valley Dr 10940
Myrtle Ave 10940
Neeley St 10940
Neptune Ln 10940
New St 10940
New Vernon Rd 10940
New York Ave 10940
Newton Dr 10940
Nicaj Ct 10941
Nicole Pl 10940
North St 10940
Northwoods Rd 10940
Norwich Ct 10940
O Brian Rd 10940
Oak Cir 10940
Oak Ct 10940
Oak Dr 10940
Oak Ln 10940
Oak Rd 10941
Oak St 10940
Oak Ter 10940
Oak Hill Rd 10941
Oak Ridge Rd 10940
Ogden St 10940
Ohaire Rd 10941
Ohio Ave 10940
Old Anvil Ln 10940
Old Stage Rd 10940
Old Timers Rd 10940
Oliver Ave 10940
Ontario Ave 10940
Orange Ter 10940
Orange Plaza Ln 10940
Orchard Hl 10941
Orchard St 10940
Otis Rd 10940
Overhill Rd 10940
Overlook Dr 10940
Palmer Ave & Dr 10940
Par Ct 10940
Park Ave 10940
Park Ct 10940
Park Pl 10940
Park Row 10941
Park Circle Dr 10940
Parkview Dr 10940
Parsons Ln 10940
Patio Rd 10941
Patricia Rd 10941
Paula Ln 10940
Peace Dr 10941
Peach Pl 10940
Pennsylvania Ave 10940
Perrins Mews 10940
Peterson Ct 10941
Philcox Rd 10940
Phillips St 10940
Phillipsburg Rd 10940
Pierson Hill Rd 10940
Pilgrim Pl 10940
Pilgrim Corners Rd 10940
Pine Ct 10941
Pine St 10940
E Pine St 10940
Pine Grove Rd 10940
Pinto Rd 10941
Placid Ave 10941
S Plank Rd 10940
Pleasant Ave 10940
Pocatello Rd 10940
Polly Kay Dr 10940
Pondview Dr 10941
Poplar Ln 10941
Preston St 10940
Prince Ln 10941
Prince St 10940
Private Ln 10940
Prospect Ave 10940
W Prospect Ave 10940
Prospect Rd 10941
Prospect St 10940
Prosperous Valley Rd 10940
Pufftown Rd 10941
Putters Way 10940
Queen Anna Ln 10940
Quigley Rd 10940
R Hunter Pl 10940
S Railroad Ave 10940
Raleigh Close 10940
Randall Hts & Ter 10940
Rdean Pl 10940
Rebecca Dr 10940
Red Barn Ln 10940
Red Maple Ln 10940
Red Oak Ct 10941
Red Oak Rd 10940
Regency Ct 10940
Reinhardt Rd 10940
Reiss Rd 10940
Remey Rd 10940
Renfrewshire Dr 10941
Republic Plz 10940
Reservoir Rd 10940
Restorative Ln 10940
Revere Dr 10940
Rhode Island Ave 10940
Richmond Pl 10940
Ridge Ave, Dr, Rd &
St 10940
Ridgewood Ave 10940
Riverside Dr 10941
Rivervale Rd 10940
Robbins Rd 10940
Robert Bruce Pl 10941
Robert Burns Ct 10941
Roberts St 10940
Robertson Dr 10940
Robinn Dr 10940
Robins Dr 10941
Rock Hill Rd 10941
Rockwell Ave 10940
Rockwood Cir, Dr & Pl 10941
Rodman St 10940
Roger Ave 10940
Rolling Meadows Rd 10940
Rome School Rd 10940
Rondack Rd 10941
Roosevelt Ave 10940
Rose Ln
1-9 10940
1-24 10941
12-14 10940
16-99 10940
26-38 10941
Ross Ln 10941
Route 17m 10940
Route 211 E
229-239 10940
Route 211 E
241-499 10940
500-889 10941
890-890 10940
891-1999 10941
892-1998 10941
Route 211 W 10940
Route 302 10941
Route 6 10940
Rowan St 10940
Royal Acres Dr 10940
Royal Oak Ave 10940
Royce Ave 10940
Russell Mews 10940
Rutan Ln 10940
Ruth Ct 10940
Rykowski Ln 10941
Saint Eve Ct 10940
Saint James Dr 10940
Saint Louis Ave 10940
Saint Stephens Close 10940
Salisbury Rd 10940
Sandburg Ct 10941
Sands Rd 10941
Sands Rd W 10940
Sands Station Rd 10940
Santee St 10940
Sarah Ln 10941
Sayer Ln 10940
School St 10940
School House Rd 10940
Schutt Rd 10940
Schutt Road Ext 10940
Scotchtown Ave, Dr, Ln
& Pl 10941
Scotchtown Collabar
Rd 10941
Scott Dr 10941
Seaman Rd 10941
Second Ave 10941
Seniors Way 10940
Seward Ave 10940
Shagbark St 10941
Shale Dr 10940
Sharon Dr 10941
Shaw Rd 10941
Shawangunk Rd
1-88 10941
83-93 10940
90-122 10941
91-95 10941
97-113 10940
115-132 10940
133-145 10941
134-398 10940
135-399 10941
Sheffield Dr 10940
Shelley Ct 10941
Sherwood Dr N & S 10941
Shirley Ln 10940
Shoddy Hollow Rd 10940
S Shore Dr 10940
Silo Ln 10940
Silo Farm Pl 10941
Silver Lake Scotchtown
Rd
1-299 10940
300-999 10941
Silver Mine Estate Rd 10940
Slaughter Rd 10941
Smith Rd 10941
Smith St 10940
South St 10940
Sprague Ave 10940
Spring St 10940
Sproat St 10940
Spruce Rd 10940
Spruce Peak Rd 10940
St Andrews Ct 10941
Stage Rd 10941
Stagecoach Dr & Trl 10940
Standish Ave 10940
Stanton St 10940
Stapleton Ct 10940
Starhaven Ave 10940
State St 10940
State Route 17k 10941
State Route 302 10941
Stephens Ave 10941
Sterling St 10940
Stern Scenic Dr 10940
Stivers Pl & Rd 10940
Stoneridge Rd 10941
Stony Ford Rd 10941
Stratford Ln 10940
Stratton Ave 10940
Stub St 10940
Sullivan Ln 10941
Sun Glow Ter 10941
Sunflower St 10940
Sunnyside Ave 10940
Sunrise Ct & Dr 10940
Sunset Ave & St 10940
Susan Dr 10940
Sutton Hill Dr 10940
Sweezy Ave 10940
Sycamore Dr 10940
Talcott Pl 10940
Tall Oaks Dr 10940
Tally Ho Rd 10940
Tamms Rd 10941
Tammy Dr 10941
Tarbell Rd 10940
Tetz Ln 10941
The Ln 10940
Third Ave 10941
Thistle Ln 10940
Thomas Jefferson Pl 10940
Tice Ln 10941
Timothy Collard Rd 10940
Toad Pasture Rd 10940
Todd Dr 10941
Top Notch Rd 10940
Tower Dr 10941
Tower Ridge Cir 10941
Truman Ct 10940
Tucci Rd 10941
Tudor Rd 10940
Turfler Ter 10941
Turner Dr 10941
Twin Wells Ct 10940
Uhlig Rd 10940
Underhill Rd 10940
Union St 10940
Union School Rd 10941
Upper Rd 10940
Vail Ave 10940
Valley View Dr 10940
Valley View Trailer
Park 10941
Van Burenville Rd 10940
Van Dewark Rd 10941
Van Duzer Rd 10940
Vermont Ln 10940
Vetosky Rd 10940
Victory St 10940
Vincent Dr 10940
Vincenzo Ct 10940
Virginia St 10941
Vista View Ter 10941
Vogt Ln 10940
Wades Ln 10940
Wallington Ct 10940
Wallkill Ave 10940
Walnut Ln 10940
Walter Scott Cir 10941
Warren St 10940
Washington St 10940
Watkins Ave 10940
Waverly Pl 10940
Wawayanda Ave & Pl 10940
Wayne Ct 10941
Wayne Dr 10940
Wayne Pl 10940
Weather Vane Way 10940
Webb Rd 10940
Weber Rd 10940
Wedgewood Ln 10940
Weld Rd 10941
Wells Ave 10940
Wes Warren Dr 10941
Wesley Ct 10941
Western Ave 10940
Westminster Dr 10940
Whipple Rd 10940
White Bridge Rd 10940
White Horse Rd 10940
White Oak Ct 10941
Whitlock Rd 10940
Whitman Ct 10941
Wickham Ave 10940
Wilbur Ave 10940
Wilcox Ave 10940
Wilkes Ave 10940
Wilkin Ave 10940
William St 10940
William Kirby Dr 10940
Willow Pl & St 10940
Wilson Dr 10941
Wilson Rd 10941
Wilson St 10940
Winchester Ave & Pl 10940
Winding Ridge Ln 10940
Windsor Mews 10940
Winner Ave 10940
Winters Ln 10940
Winterton Rd 10940
Winthrop Ave 10940
Wishe Cir 10940
Wisner Ave & Pl 10940
Wisner Avenue Ext 10940
Witte Dr 10940
Woodcrest Dr 10940
Woodlake Dr 10940
Woodland Ave & Rd 10940
Woodlawn Ave 10940
Woods Pl 10940
Woodside Knolls Dr 10940
Woodstock Ln 10941
Wyoming Ln 10940
Yereance Ln 10941
York Rd S 10940
Young Ln 10941

NUMBERED STREETS

1st St 10940
2nd St 10940
3rd St 10940
4th St 10940
5th St 10940
6th St 10940
7th St 10940
84 Ln 10941

MONROE NY

General Delivery 10950

POST OFFICE BOXES MAIN OFFICE STATIONS AND BRANCHES

Box No.s
All PO Boxes 10949

NAMED STREETS

Acres Rd 10950
Adams Ct 10950
Akita Rd 10950
Alamo Ct 10950
Albert Ct 10950
Alden Rd 10950
Aldo Ct 10950
Alex Smith Ave 10950
Alexander Rd 10950
Alley Rd 10950
Allison Dr 10950
Amy Todt Dr 10950
Anderson Pl 10950
Angel Rd 10950
Anipoli Dr 10950
Ann Pl 10950
Apta Way 10950
Aquarius St 10950
Arbor Trl 10950
Arcadian Trl 10950
Archer Dr 10950
Arden Trl 10950
Arlin Rd 10950
Arlington Dr 10950
Ascension Trl 10950
Ash St 10950
Ashmore Pl 10950
Augusta Ct 10950
Austin Ct 10950
Autumn Ln 10950
Bailey Farm Rd 10950
Bailie Ln 10950
Bakertown Rd 10950
Balder Ct 10950
Barnett Dr & Rd 10950
Barr Ln 10950
Bayberry Dr 10950
Bear Ct 10950
Beech Tree Round 10950
Bell Rd 10950
Belmont Rd 10950
Berdans Rd 10950
Berkley Ter 10950
Berry Rd 10950
Beverly Rd & Trl 10950
Billwood Dr 10950
Birch Dr 10950
Bliss Ter 10950
Block Aly 10950
Blythelea Rd 10950
Bnai Yoel Dr 10950
Bollenbach Dr 10950
Bonney Ct 10950
Bonnie Brook Rd 10950
Boyd Rd 10950
Boyles Ct 10950
Bramley Ct 10950
Branch St 10950
Brennan Rd 10950
Brentwood Pl 10950
Brewster Rd 10950
Briarway St 10950
Briarwood Ave 10950
Bridge St 10950
Brook Dr & Trl 10950
Brooks Ave 10950
Brookside Rd & Trl 10950
Brookview Dr 10950
Brower Rd 10950
Buchanan Ct 10950
Buffi Ln 10950
Burgess Dr 10950
Burr Dr 10950
Byrnes Rd 10950
Callaway Dr 10950
Cambridge Cir 10950
Camp Monroe Rd 10950
Candle Rd 10950
Capt Carpenter Dr 10950
Cardinal Dr 10950
Carol Dr 10950
Carpenter Pl 10950
Carriage Hill Ct 10950
Carter Ln 10950

Carvel Rd 10950
Cascade Trl 10950
Case Ct 10950
Catskill Ave 10950
Cedar Rd & Trl 10950
Cedar Cliff Rd 10950
Celtic Pl 10950
Center Hill Rd 10950
Charlotte Pl 10950
Charlton Pl 10950
Chatham Rd 10950
Cheesecock Dr 10950
Chernobyl Ct 10950
Chester St 10950
Chestnut Cir & Dr 10950
Chevron Rd 10950
Circle Dr 10950
Circle Drive Ext 10950
Claire Dr 10950
Clancy Rd 10950
Claremont Trl 10950
Clark St 10950
Cliff Ct 10950
Clinton Aly & Ct 10950
Clove Rd 10950
Coffey Rd 10950
Colony Dr 10950
Concetta Ct 10950
Conklin Ct & Rd 10950
Continental Dr 10950
Cooper Dr, Rd & St 10950
Corinne Ct 10950
Corlear Ct 10950
Country Ct 10950
County Route 105 10950
County Route 5 10950
Cox Dr 10950
Cregan Pl 10950
Crescent Pl 10950
Crestwood Trl 10950
Cromwell Rd 10950
Cromwell Hill Rd 10950
E Crossman Ave 10950
Crotty Ct 10950
Cunningham Dr 10950
D A Weider Blvd 10950
Daley Ln 10950
Dallas Dr 10950
Dana Dr 10950
Dara Ct 10950
Davenport Ct 10950
David Ln 10950
David Lester Dr 10950
Deangelis Dr 10950
Deer Path Way 10950
Deerfield Rd 10950
Delano Grv 10950
Devan Dr 10950
Dinev Ct & Rd 10950
Dogwood Ln 10950
Donna Jean Dr 10950
Dorn Dr 10950
Dorothy Dr 10950
Dry Hill Lake Rd 10950
Duelk Ave 10950
Dunderberg Rd 10950
Durant Dr 10950
Eagle St 10950
Eagleton Dr 10950
Eahal Ct 10950
Ebby Way 10950
Echo Trl 10950
Edgewood Trl 10950
Edward Pl 10950
Elm Rd & St 10950
Elmwood Dr 10950
Emerald Ln & Trl 10950
Emily Ln 10950
Estybrook Trl 10950
Ethan Cir 10950
Evergreen Dr & Ln 10950
Fairway Dr 10950
Felter Hill Rd 10950
S Field Fls 10950
Fillmore Ct 10950
Fini Rd 10950

First Ave & St 10950
Fischer Dr 10950
Fitzgerald Ct 10950
Flag Dr 10950
Ford Ct 10950
Forest Ave, Rd & St 10950
Forest Glen Rd 10950
Forestdale Ave 10950
Forge Rd 10950
Forshee St 10950
Fort Worth Pl 10950
Fountain Rd 10950
Fourth St 10950
Frances Ln 10950
Frank Ct 10950
Frankfurt Rd 10950
Franklin Ave 10950
Fredrick Dr 10950
Freeland St 10950
Front St 10950
Galveston Dr 10950
Garfield Rd 10950
Garland Trl 10950
Gatehouse Rd 10950
Georges Ln 10950
Getzil Berger Blvd 10950
Gilbert St 10950
Gilbert St Ext 10950
Giles Pl 10950
Gillian Ct 10950
Giovanni Ct 10950
Glen Ave 10950
Gleneagles Ct 10950
Glenwood Rd & Trl 10950
Gloria Trl 10950
Goldman Rd 10950
Gorlitz Ct 10950
Graham Pl 10950
Grandview Trl 10950
Grant Dr 10950
Greene Rd 10950
Greenwood Ave 10950
Haight Rd 10950
Hain Dr 10950
Hala Dr 10950
Half Hollow Turn 10950
Hall Ct 10950
Hamaspik Way 10950
Hamburg Way 10950
Hanison Pl 10950
Harding Way 10950
Harriman Heights Rd 10950
Harrison Pl 10950
Hawks Nest Rd 10950
Hawthorne Dr 10950
Hawxhurst Rd 10950
Hayes Ct 10950
Heaton Rd 10950
Heights Rd & Trl 10950
Herbst Dr 10950
Heritage Ln 10950
Hewson Rd 10950
Hickory Ln 10950
Hickory Hollow Rd 10950
Hidden Dr 10950
Hidden Creek Blvd 10950
Higgins Trl 10950
High St 10950
High Ridge Rd 10950
Highland Ave, Rd & Trl 10950
Highview Rd 10950
Hill Ln 10950
Hillcrest Ave & Trl 10950
Hillside Ave, Dr, Rd, Ter & Trl 10950
Hilltop Dr, Pl, Rd & Trl 10950
Hobard Ward Dr 10950
Hoffman Dr 10950
Holland Ct & Rd 10950
Hoover Ct 10950
Houston Ave 10950
Hudson Pl 10950
Hudson Pointe 10950
Hyland Rd 10950
Hyler Dr 10950

Industrial Park Rd 10950
Interlochen Pkwy 10950
Irene Dr 10950
Iron Hill Plz 10950
Ironworks Rd 10950
Island View Ave 10950
Israel Zupnick Dr 10950
Ivy Ln 10950
Jacobs Ldg 10950
James Rd 10950
Jamps Rd 10950
Jane Ct 10950
Jarmain Rd 10950
Jay Mar Ct 10950
Jean Dr 10950
E & W Jeanibo Rd 10950
Jefferson Dr 10950
Jenna Dr 10950
Jmd Dr 10950
Joseph Ct 10950
Julien Ct 10950
Juniper Ln 10950
Jupiter Dr 10950
Kahan Dr 10950
Kalev Way 10950
Kalvin Ter 10950
Karen Dr 10950
Karlin Blvd 10950
Kasch Ct 10950
Kates Ln 10950
Keith Ln 10950
Kenna Dr 10950
Kennedy Dr & Ln 10950
Kenny Dr 10950
Kiefer Dr 10950
Kimberly Ter 10950
King St 10950
Kingsville Dr 10950
Kintrend Rd 10950
Kit Ct 10950
Knight St 10950
Knoll Ct 10950
Koritz Ct 10950
Kosnitz Dr 10950
Krakow Blvd 10950
Krolla Dr 10950
Lake Ave & St 10950
Lake Region Blvd 10950
Lake Shore Dr 10950
Lakes Rd 10950
Lakeview Dr 10950
Lambros Dr 10950
Lamplight Village Rd 10950
Lanzut Ct 10950
Laredo Ct 10950
Lark Dr & Rd 10950
Larkin Dr 10950
Laroe Rd 10950
Laura Rd 10950
Laurel Trl 10950
Lawrence Rd 10950
Leah Ln 10950
Lee Ave 10950
Leipnik Way 10950
Lemberg Ct 10950
Lemko Ln 10950
Lenox Rd 10950
Letts Cir 10950
Lily Pond Ln 10950
Lincoln Rd 10950
Linden Ln & Trl 10950
Links Ct 10950
Lionel Psge 10950
Lipa Friedman Ln 10950
Lisa Ln & Way 10950
Liska Way 10950
Lizensk Blvd 10950
Loch Lomond Ct 10950
Lois Ln 10950
Lone Oak Cir 10950
Lookout Trl 10950
Lotus Ln 10950
Lublin Way 10950
Lucy Ln 10950
Ludlam Rd 10950
Ludwig Dr 10950

Lues Ct 10950
Mack Pl 10950
Madison Cir 10950
Maidstone Ln 10950
N Main St 10950
Mainey Dr 10950
Makan Rd 10950
Mangin Rd 10950
Mansion Rd 10950
Mansion Ridge Blvd 10950
Mapes Ln 10950
Maple Ave & Ln 10950
Marc Ter 10950
Margaret Rd 10950
Marie Ct 10950
Mcbee Ct 10950
Mcelroy Pl 10950
Mcgarrah Rd 10950
Mcgarrah Road Ext 10950
Mcgill Rd 10950
Memory Ln 10950
Menendian Ln 10950
Mercury Ave & Ct 10950
Meri Ln 10950
Meron Dr 10950
Merriewold Ln N & S 10950
Mezabish Pl 10950
Michael Ct & Ln 10950
Mid Oaks Dr, Rd & St 10950
Midland Ct 10950
Midway Dr 10950
Midwood Ter 10950
Mill St 10950
Millard Cir 10950
Miller Ln 10950
Millpond Pkwy 10950
Mine Rd 10950
Minnow Ln 10950
E & W Mombasha Rd 10950
Monroe Ave & St 10950
Montauk Rd 10950
Moran Trl 10950
Mordche Sher Blvd 10950
Moulton Cir 10950
Mount Ridge Ct 10950
Mountain Ave & Rd 10950
Mountain Laurel Dr 10950
Mountain Lodge Rd 10950
Mountain Park Rd 10950
Mountainview Dr 10950
Museum Village Rd 10950
Nancy Ct 10950
Natalie Ct 10950
Nelson Dr & Rd 10950
Neptune Ct & Dr 10950
Newbury St 10950
Nicklesburg Rd 10950
Nininger Rd 10950
Norwich Ln 10950
O Sullivan Ln 10950
Oak Dr, Rd & St 10950
Oak Hill Rd 10950
Oakland Ave 10950
Oakwood Trl N & S 10950
Old Country Rd 10950
Old Dutch Hollow Rd 10950
Old Quaker Hill Rd 10950
Old Town Rd 10950
Old Tuxedo Rd 10950
Oneil Cir 10950
Orange Tpke 10950
Orchard Cir, Dr, St, Ter & Trl 10950
Orchard Hill Rd 10950
Orchard Lake Dr 10950
Oreco Ter 10950
Orion Ave 10950
Orshava Ct 10950
Osseo Park Rd 10950
Overlook Rd 10950
Owen Dr 10950
Paddock Ln 10950
Paksh Pl 10950
Palamar Dr 10950
Palmer Ave 10950
Paradise Trl 10950

Park Ave, Pl & Ter 10950
Patterson Pass 10950
Pavek Cir 10950
Pawtuxet Ave 10950
Pearsall Dr 10950
Pebble Ln 10950
Pecos Ct 10950
Peddler Hill Rd 10950
Penaluna Rd 10950
Pennsylvania Ave 10950
Penny Ct 10950
Perl Plz 10950
Peter Bush Dr 10950
Peter Turner Rd 10950
Peters Ter 10950
Peterson Rd 10950
Phelps Dr 10950
Pickerel Rd 10950
Pike Ct 10950
Pine Hill Rd 10950
Pine Tree Rd 10950
Pinecrest Ln 10950
Pinehurst Cir 10950
Pioneer Trl 10950
Placid Ln 10950
Pleasant View Rd 10950
Ponderosa Ln 10950
Pondside Ln 10950
Pope Ln 10950
Poplar Dr & Trl 10950
Post Rd 10950
Posten Hill Rd 10950
Prag Blvd 10950
Premishlan Way 10950
Premium Point Rd 10950
Preshburg Blvd 10950
Prestwick Dr 10950
Prospect Rd & St 10950
Pt O Pne 10950
Quaker Hill Rd 10950
Quickway Rd 10950
Rabbit Hill Rd 10950
Radomsk Way 10950
Rainbow Ln 10950
Ralphie Ln 10950
Ramapo Ave & St 10950
Rande Rd 10950
Raywood Dr 10950
Rea Ct 10950
Red Bird Dr 10950
Reed Rd 10950
Reiher Rd 10950
Reilly Rd 10950
Reinheimer Rd 10950
Revere Rd 10950
Reynolds Rd 10950
Ridge Rd 10950
Rieger Dr 10950
Riley Ct 10950
Rimenev Ct 10950
Roanoke Dr 10950
Roberts Dr 10950
Robyn Dr & Rd 10950
Rocky Rd 10950
Roe Cir 10950
Romeo Dr 10950
Rosa Ct 10950
Rose Hill Rd 10950
Rosemarie Ln 10950
Rosemont Rd 10950
Rosmini Ln 10950
Round Hill Rd 10950
Round Lake Ave & Ter 10950
Round Lake Park Dr & Rd 10950
Rovna Ct 10950
Ruby Rd 10950
Rumsey Ln 10950
Runco Crst 10950
Rupshitz Rd 10950
Ruzhin Rd 10950
Ryan Ct 10950
Rye Hill Rd 10950
Salvatore Ct 10950
San Antonio Cir 10950

San Marcos Dr 10950
Sandra Ln 10950
Sanz Ct 10950
Sapphire Rd 10950
Sasev Ct 10950
Satmar Dr 10950
Scenic View Rd 10950
School Rd 10950
Schunnemunk Rd & St 10950
Scott St 10950
Seals Dr 10950
Seamanville Plz 10950
Sears Rd 10950
Second Ave 10950
Seeley Bull St 10950
Sergio Rd 10950
Seven Springs Rd 10950
Seven Springs Mountain Rd 10950
Shadowmere Rd 10950
Shannon Ln 10950
Shinev Ct 10950
W Shore Dr 10950
Siget Ct 10950
Silas Seaman St 10950
Silver Trl 10950
Singh Rd 10950
Sleepy Hollow Rd 10950
Smithfield Ct & Spur 10950
Snoop St 10950
Southside Dr 10950
Sparrow St 10950
Spinnaker Ct 10950
Spring St 10950
Spruce Ct 10950
St Georges Ave 10950
Stage Rd 10950
Stahl Way 10950
Stainton Fareway 10950
Stair Way 10950
Standish Rd 10950
Stanton Trl 10950
Starr Ln 10950
State Route 17m
1-786 10950
787-787 10949
788-1298 10950
789-1299 10950
State Route 208 10950
Station Rd 10950
Stephen Ln 10950
Steven Ct 10950
Still Rd 10950
Stillman Wye 10950
Stone Crest Dr 10950
Stonegate Dr 10950
Stonewall Rd 10950
Stralisk Ct 10950
Strawberry Dr & Ln 10950
Stropkov Ct 10950
Summit Pl, St & Trl 10950
Sunfish Ln 10950
Sunny Ln 10950
Sunrise Trl 10950
Sunset Hts, Ter & Trl 10950
Sunset Ridge Rd 10950
Sutherland Dr 10950
Suttie Ave 10950
Swan Hollow Rd 10950
Swezey Pl 10950
Sylvan Trl 10950
Sylvia Ln 10950
Taitch Ct 10950
Talmadge Ct 10950
Tanager Rd 10950
Tanyas Ct 10950
Tappan Dr 10950
Taurus Ave 10950
Taylor Ct 10950
Tephanic Ave 10950
Terry Rd 10950
Teverya Way 10950
Tiedemann Ct 10950
Toby Pl 10950
Toltchav Way 10950

Trazino Dr 10950
Treza Ln 10950
Triangle Trl 10950
Trout Brook Rd 10950
Tulip Ln 10950
Turnberry Ct 10950
Turner Rd 10950
Turtle Knls 10950
Twin Lakes Rd 10950
Tyler Pl 10950
Tzfas Rd 10950
Underhill Trl 10950
Utopia Trl 10950
Utopian Trl 10950
Valley Trl 10950
Valley View Ave 10950
Van Buren Dr 10950
Van Keuren Ct 10950
Vayoel Moshe Ct 10950
Velove Ct 10950
Veteran Cir 10950
Via Lipari 10950
Village Gate Way 10950
Vincenzo Ct 10950
Virginia Ave 10950
Vista Ln 10950
Walton Ter 10950
Walton Lake Park Rd 10950
Washington Rd 10950
Water Plant Rd 10950
Way Cross Trl 10950
Webb Ct 10950
Webb Farm Rd 10950
Webster Ct 10950
Wenzel Dr 10950
Westwind Dr 10950
Whippoorwill Trl 10950
Whitman Pl 10950
Wildwood Trl 10950
Willard Pl 10950
William Cory Rd 10950
Williams Ct & Dr 10950
Wilson Rd 10950
Winchester Dr 10950
Windgate Ct 10950
Windmill Ct 10950
Windridge Mws 10950
Windsor Rd 10950
Woodard Rd 10950
Woodcock Rd 10950
Woodland Cir, Rd & Trl N & S 10950
Woodycrest Trl 10950
Yankee Ct 10950
Yoel Klein Blvd 10950
Zenta Rd 10950
Ziggy Ct 10950
Zlotchev Way 10950

MOUNT VERNON NY

General Delivery 10551

POST OFFICE BOXES MAIN OFFICE STATIONS AND BRANCHES

Box No.s
1 - 749 10551
1 - 660 10552
1001 - 3000 10551
3001 - 3903 10553
4445 - 6050 10551
8000 - 8000 10553
9001 - 9038 10552
9998 - 9998 10551
10001 - 10002 10552

NAMED STREETS

Adams St 10550
Aetna Pl 10552

Alameda Pl 10552
Alta Dr & Pkwy 10552
Amsterdam Pl 10553
Amundson Ave 10550
Anderson Ave 10550
Archer Ave 10550
Arden Ter 10552
Atlas Pl 10552
Audrey Ave 10553
Audubon Ave 10552
Bateman Pl 10552
Beach St 10550
Bedford Ave 10553
Beechwood Ave 10553
Beekman Ave 10553
Bell Ave 10550
Berg St 10552
Bertel Ave 10550
E Birch St 10552
N & S Bleeker St 10550
N & S Bond St 10550
Bonita Vista Rd 10552
Bradford Rd 10553
Bradley Ave 10552
Broad St E & W 10552
Bronx St 10552
Brookdale Pl 10550
Brookfield Rd 10552
Brookside Ave 10553
Bruce Ave 10552
Burkewood Rd 10552
Bushnell Pl 10550
California Rd 10552
Canal St 10550
Carleton Ave 10550
Carpenter Pl 10553
Carwall Ave 10552
Cedar Ave 10553
E Cedar St 10552
Central Pkwy 10552
Centre St 10552
Charles Pl 10550
Chester St 10552
Chesterwood Ave 10552
Chestnut Pl 10553
S Claralli Ave 10550
Claremont Ave
  1-199 10550
  200-399 10552
Claremont Pl
  1-19 10550
  20-99 10553
Clinton Pl 10550
Clinton St 10552
Collins Ave 10552
Colonial Pl 10550
Columbia Pl 10552
N Columbus Ave
  1-98 10553
  99-99 10552
  100-200 10553
  101-199 10553
  201-699 10552
S Columbus Ave
  1-499 10553
  500-999 10550
Commonwealth Ave 10552
Cooley Pl 10550
Cortlandt St 10550
Cottage Ave 10550
Crary Ave 10550
Crest Ave 10550
Darling Ave 10553
Darwood Pl 10553
Del Rey Dr 10552
Dell Ave
  1-99 10553
  100-199 10550
Denman Pl 10552
E & W Devonia Ave 10552
Dock St 10550
Douglas Pl 10552
Drake St 10550
Dunham Ave 10553
Duryea Ave 10550
Eastchester Ln 10550

Eastfield Rd 10552
Edenwald Ave 10550
Edgewood Ave 10552
Edison Ave 10550
Egmont Ave 10553
Ehrbar Ave 10552
Elliot St 10553
Ellwood Ave 10552
Elm Ave & St 10550
Elmsmere Rd 10552
Esplanade 10553
Euclid Ave 10552
Fairway St 10552
Faralew Ave 10552
Farrell Ave 10553
Fisher Dr 10552
Fiske Pl 10550
Fleetwood Ave 10552
Fletcher Ave 10552
Forster Ave & Pkwy 10552
Franklin Ave
  1-230 10550
  231-499 10553
  500-699 10550
Frederick Pl 10552
N Fulton Ave
  1-199 10550
  200-599 10552
S Fulton Ave
  1-234 10550
  235-499 10553
  500-899 10550
Fulton Ln 10550
Garden Ave
  200-499 10553
  500-699 10550
  424-422-424-422 10553
George Pl 10550
Glen Ave 10550
Gramatan Ave
  1-299 10550
  300-899 10552
E & W Grand St 10552
Grandview Ave 10553
Greendale Ave 10553
Grove St 10550
Hamilton Ave 10552
Hancock Ave 10553
Hanover Pl 10552
Harding Pkwy 10552
Harrison St 10550
Hartford Ave 10553
Hartley Ave 10550
Haven Ave 10553
Hawthorne Ter 10552
Hayward Ave 10552
Hesper Pl 10550
N High St
  1-399 10550
  400-599 10552
S High St 10550
Highland Ave 10553
Hill St 10552
Hillcrest Rd 10552
Hillside Ave 10553
Homestead Ave
  400-499 10553
  500-599 10550
Homewood Rd 10553
Howard St 10550
Hudson Ave 10553
Huntwood Pl 10552
Hussey Rd 10552
Hutchinson Ave 10553
Hutchinson Blvd 10552
Irving Pl 10550
Jackson St 10553
Jefferson Pl 10550
Johnson St 10550
Kenyon Pl 10552
Kimball Pl 10550
E & W Kingsbridge Plz & Rd 10550
Knollwood Ave 10550
Labelle Rd 10552
Lafayette Ave 10552

Lane St 10550
Langdon Ave 10553
Laporte Ave 10552
Laurel Ave 10552
Lawrence St 10552
Lenox Ave 10552
Lexington Ave 10552
E Lincoln Ave 10552
W Lincoln Ave 10550
Linden Ave 10552
Livingston St 10552
Locust Ln 10552
Locust St
  300-399 10550
  400-799 10552
Lorraine Ave
  1-199 10553
  200-299 10552
Lorraine Ter 10553
Lyons Pl 10553
N Macquesten Pkwy
  1-399 10550
  400-899 10552
S Macquesten Pkwy 10550
Madison St 10550
Magnolia Ave
  1-199 10553
  200-299 10552
Maple Pl 10552
Marion Ave & Pl 10552
Martens Pl 10550
Mcclellan Ave 10553
Melrose Ave 10552
Mersereau Ave 10553
Miller Pl 10550
Millington St 10553
Monroe St
  1-99 10550
  100-199 10553
Monterey Dr 10552
Morrison Pl 10550
Mount Vernon Ave 10550
Mundy Ln 10550
New Haven Rr St 10550
New Rochelle Rd 10552
Newton Pl 10550
North St 10550
Nuber Ave
  1-499 10553
  500-599 10550
Nuvern Ave 10550
Oak Dr 10552
Oak St 10550
Oakland Ave 10552
Oakley Ave & Pl 10550
Oakwood Ave 10553
Oneida Ave 10553
Orchard St 10552
Overhill Rd 10552
Overlook St 10552
Packman Ave 10552
Palmer Ave 10552
Palo Alto Pl 10552
Park Ave 10550
Park Ln 10552
Park Pl 10552
Parkway Cir E, S & W 10552
Pasadena Pl 10552
Pathmark Plz 10550
Pearl St 10550
Pearsall Dr 10552
Pease St 10553
Pelhamdale Ave 10553
Pennsylvania Ave 10552
Pondfield Pkwy 10552
Portugal Pl 10550
Pratt St 10550
Primrose Ave 10552
E Prospect Ave
  1-279 10550
  280-599 10553
W Prospect Ave 10550
Putnam St 10550
Raynor Ave 10552
Rhynas Dr 10552

Rich Ave
  1-199 10550
  200-499 10552
Ridgeway St 10552
Rochelle Ter 10550
Rockledge Ave 10550
Rockridge Rd 10552
Roosevelt Sq 10550
Roslyn Pl 10550
Sageman St 10550
Saint Pauls Pl 10550
E Sandford Blvd
  1-439 10550
  440-598 10550
  440-440 10553
  441-599 10550
W Sandford Blvd 10550
Sargent Pl 10550
Seneca Ave 10553
Seton Ave 10550
Sheridan Ave 10552
Sherman Ave 10552
Short St 10550
E Sidney Ave
  1-275 10550
  276-499 10553
W Sidney Ave 10550
South St 10550
Southfield Rd 10552
Station Pl 10552
Stevens Ave 10550
Stuyvesant Plz 10552
Summit Ave
  1-98 10550
  99-99 10552
  100-198 10550
  101-199 10550
  200-499 10552
Sycamore Ave 10553
Tamerton St 10552
Tecumseh Ave 10553
N Terrace Ave
  1-399 10550
  400-698 10552
S Terrace Ave 10550
Tower Pl 10552
Union Ave 10550
Union Ln 10553
Urban St 10552
Valentine St 10550
Valerali Ave 10553
Valois Pl 10552
Vernon Ave 10553
Vernon Pkwy 10552
Vernon Pl 10552
Villa St 10552
Vista Pl 10550
Wales Pl 10552
Wallace Ave 10552
Walton Pl 10550
Warren Pl 10550
Wartburg Pl 10552
Warwick Ave 10553
Washington Blvd 10550
Washington Pl 10550
Washington St
  100-199 10550
  200-399 10553
N & S West St 10550
Westchester Ave 10552
Westchester Towers 10550
Wildwood Ave 10550
Willard Ave 10553
William St 10552
Willow Pl 10550
Wilson Pl 10550
Wilson Block 10552
Winfield Ave 10552
Wyndmere Rd 10552

NUMBERED STREETS

S 1st Ave
  1-14 10550
  15-599 10550
  15-15 10551
  16-598 10550
E 1st St 10550
W 1st St 10550
S, E & W 2nd Ave & St 10550
N 3rd Ave 10550
S 3rd Ave 10550
E 3rd St
  1-199 10550
  200-599 10553
  474-484-474-484 10553
W 3rd St 10550
S 4th Ave 10550
E 4th St
  1-199 10550
  200-499 10553
W 4th St 10550
N 5th Ave 10550
S 5th Ave 10550
E 5th St
  1-99 10550
  100-599 10553
W 5th St 10550
N & S 6th 10550
N, S, E & W 7th Ave & St 10550
N, S, E & W 8th Ave & St 10550
N & S 9th 10550
N & S 10th 10550
S 11th Ave 10550
S 12th Ave 10550
S 13th Ave 10550
N & S 14th 10550
S 15th Ave 10550
S 16th Ave 10550

NEW HYDE PARK NY

General Delivery 11040

POST OFFICE BOXES MAIN OFFICE STATIONS AND BRANCHES

Box No.s
1 - 494 11040
148 - 148 11042
700 - 3999 11040
5001 - 5605 11042
7000 - 403606 11040

NAMED STREETS

Aberdeen Rd 11040
Aladdin Ave 11040
Albert St 11040
Allen St 11040
Argon Pl 11040
Armstrong Rd 11040
Ash Pl 11040
Ashland Ave 11040
Aspen Ln 11040
Aster Dr 11040
Astoria Bank Plz 11042
Atlantic Ave 11040
Atlas Ct 11040
Avon Rd 11040
Baer Pl 11040
Baxter Ave 11040
Beaumont Ct 11040
Bedford Ave 11040
Beech St 11040
Beechwood Ln 11040
Bellwood Dr 11040
Belmont Ave 11040
Betty Rd 11040
Birch Dr & Ln 11040
Birchwood Dr 11040
Bixley Dr 11040
Blossom Ln 11040
Bly Ct 11040

Bolton Rd 11040
Bregman Ave 11040
Bretton Rd 11040
Brian St 11040
Brill Pl 11040
Brisbane St 11040
Broadway 11040
Brook Ct N & S 11040
Brookfield Rd 11040
Brooklyn Ave 11040
Brown Pl 11040
Brussel Dr 11040
Bryant Ave 11040
Bryn Mawr Rd 11040
Camden Pl 11040
Campbell St 11040
Carling Dr 11040
Carole Ave 11040
Cary Rd 11040
Cedar Dr & Ln E, N, S & W 11040
Celler Ave 11040
Center Dr 11040
Central Ave & Blvd 11040
Charles Rd & St 11040
Cherrywood Dr 11040
Churchill Dr 11040
Claudy Ln 11040
Clausen Pl 11040
Clyde St 11040
Continental Dr 11040
Conway Rd 11040
Corbin Ave 11040
Cornelia Ave 11040
Corwin Ave 11040
Country Village Ct & Ln 11040
County Courthouse Rd 11040
Covert Ave 11040
Crest Rd 11040
Croyden St 11040
Dail St 11040
Dakota Dr 11042
Daley St 11040
Dallas Ave 11040
Delano Ct 11040
Delaware Dr 11042
Dennis St 11040
Denton Ave S 11040
Devonshire Dr 11040
Dogwood Ln 11040
Duke Dr 11040
Dunhill Rd 11040
Durham Rd 11040
Dyckman Ave 11040
East Ln & St 11040
Eastern Dr 11040
Edgewood Dr 11040
Elm Ct, Dr & Ln 11040
Emmett St 11040
W End Ave 11040
Eric Ln 11040
Eton Rd 11040
Evans St 11040
Evergreen Ave & Ln 11040
Executive Dr 11040
Fairfield Ln 11040
Falmouth Ave 11040
Farrel St 11040
Fir Dr 11040
Flag Ln 11040
Flower Ln 11040
Foxhurst Ct 11040
Franklin Ave 11040
Fulton Ave 11040
Garden Ct 11040
Gerard Ave 11040
Gilford Ave 11040
Gould St 11040
Grattan St 11040
Greenway 11040
Haddon Rd 11040
Hancori Ave 11040
Heather Ln 11040
Herbert Dr 11040
Herkomer St 11040

Herrick Ct 11040
Herricks Rd 11040
Hewlett St 11040
Heywood St 11040
Hickory Rd 11040
Highland Ave 11040
Hillside Ave, Blvd, Ct, Dr & Ln S 11040
Hillside Park Dr 11040
Hilton Ave 11040
Hoffman Rd 11040
Holiday Gate 11040
Hollow Ln 11042
Howard Ave 11040
Hull Ave 11040
Hunting Hill Rd 11040
Imperial Ave 11040
Independence Dr 11040
Ingraham Ln 11040
Iris Ln 11040
Irons Pl 11040
Irving Ln 11040
Irwin St 11040
Ivy Pl 11040
Jackson Ave 11040
James St 11040
Jara Ct 11040
Jasmine Ave 11040
Jefferson St 11040
Jeffrey Pl 11040
Jericho Tpke 11040
Jones St 11040
Joseph Rd & St 11040
Joy Dr 11040
Kalda Ave 11040
Kamda Blvd 11040
Kate Dr 11040
Kemp Ln 11040
Kenneth Pl 11040
Kent Rd & St 11040
Kings Ln 11040
Kingston St 11040
Knolls Dr N 11040
Lahey St 11040
Lake Dr 11040
Lakeville Dr 11040
Lakeville Rd
  36-96 11040
  98-141 11040
  143-2099 11040
  400-460 11042
  470-2098 11040
  2200-2298 11042
Langdale St 11040
Larch Dr 11040
Laurel Dr 11040
Lawrence St 11040
Leamar Dr 11040
Leonard Blvd & Cir 11040
Leslie Ln 11040
Lewis Ave 11040
Lincoln Ave 11040
Linden St 11040
Lloyd St 11040
Locust Ln 11040
Long Island Expy 11040
Lords Way 11040
Lowell Ave 11040
Madison Ave 11040
Magnolia Dr 11040
Majestic Ct 11040
Major Ln 11040
Manly Pl 11040
Manor Ct S 11040
Maple Cir, Ct, Dr & Ln W 11040
Mapleleaf Ln 11040
Maraintr Ave 11042
Marcus Ave
  45-45 11040
  47-1001 11040
  1003-1077 11040
  1020-1022 11042
  1030-1698 11040
  1101-2009 11042
  2200-3098 11042

Mason St 11040
Mayfair Rd 11040
Mcnulty Pl 11040
Meadowfarm Rd 11040
Michael Ln 11040
Midland Dr 11040
Millers Ln 11040
Monterey Dr 11040
Moore St 11040
Morris Dr 11040
Nassau Blvd & Dr 11040
Nassau Terminal Rd 11040
Nevada Dr 11042
New Hyde Park Dr 11040
New Hyde Park Rd
2-2099 11040
2101-2199 11040
2201-3399 11042
Norman St 11040
Nortema Ct 11040
North Dr & St 11040
Norton Ave 11040
Nottingham Ct & Rd 11040
Nugent St 11040
Oak Dr & Ln 11040
Ohio Dr 11042
Old Broadway 11040
Old Courthouse Rd 11040
Old Farm Rd N & S 11040
Old Stewart Ave 11040
Olive Ln 11040
Orchid Ln 11040
Oxford St 11040
S Park Ave, Cir & Pl E & W 11040
Patton Blvd 11040
Paul Ave 11040
Pearl St 11040
Peter Ln 11040
Pilgrim St 11040
Pine St 11040
Pinewood Ln 11040
Plaza Ave 11040
Plymouth St 11040
Pond Ln 11040
Powell Pl 11040
Premier Blvd 11040
Primrose Dr 11040
Prince St 11040
Pubins Ln 11040
Quaker St 11040
Queens Ln 11040
Railroad Ave 11040
Redwood Rd 11040
Regent Ln 11040
Rhodes Dr & St 11040
Robby Ln 11040
Rose Ln & Pl 11040
Rowe Pl 11040
Royal Way 11040
Ruxton St 11040
Schumacher Dr 11040
Scott St 11040
S Service Rd 11040
Shelbourne Ln 11040
Shelter Rock Rd 11040
Soma St 11040
South Dr & St 11040
Sperry Blvd & Ct 11040
Spruce Ln 11040
Stanley Ln 11040
Stanwood Rd 11040
Stephan Marc Ln 11040
Stephen Ave 11040
Stewart Ave 11040
Stoothoff Dr 11040
Strattford Rd 11040
Suburban Gate 11040
Summit Ln 11040
Surrey Ln & Rd 11040
Sutton Hill Ln 11040
Sycamore Dr 11040
Sylvia Ln 11040
Talbot St 11040
Tenafly Dr 11040
Terrace Blvd 11040
Thorens Ave 11040
Tottenham Pl 11040
Tryon Ct 11040
Tudor Dr 11040
Tulip Ln & Pl 11040
Tuxedo Ave 11040
Union St & Tpke 11040
Vale Ct 11040
Valentine Dr 11040
Vermont Dr 11042
Villa Pl 11040
Washington Ave 11040
Wayne Ave 11040
West St 11040
White Ave 11040
Whitehall Ln 11040
Whittier Ave 11040
Wicks Rd 11040
Wilben Ct 11040
William St 11040
Willow Rd 11040
Wilson Blvd 11040
Wilton St 11040
Windsor Gate Dr 11040
Winthrop St 11040
Woodland Dr 11040
Yale Blvd 11040
Yorkshire Rd 11040

NUMBERED STREETS

All Street Addresses 11040

NEW ROCHELLE NY

General Delivery 10802

POST OFFICE BOXES MAIN OFFICE STATIONS AND BRANCHES

Box No.s
A - E 10802
A - D 10804
1 - 845 10802
1 - 500 10804
991 - 9998 10802

NAMED STREETS

Aberfoyle Rd 10804
Acacia Ter 10805
Acorn Ter 10801
Adams St 10801
Agar Ave 10801
Albermarle Ave 10801
Albert Pl 10801
Albert Leonard Rd 10804
Alfred Ln 10804
Allard Ave 10805
Alpha Pl 10805
Alpine Rd 10804
Amanda Ln 10804
Amherst Dr 10804
Anderson St 10801
Andrea Ct 10804
Andrew Ln 10804
Antler Pl 10804
Arbor Dr 10804
Arbor Gln 10801
Argyll Ave 10804
Ashland St 10801
Askins Pl 10801
Aspen Rd 10804
Aurora Ln 10804
Aviemore Dr 10804
Avis Dr 10804
Avon Rd 10804
Badeau Pl 10801
Bailey Pl 10801
Bally Pl 10801
Bancker Pl 10805
Barbara Hall Ct 10801
Barberry Ln 10804
Barnard Rd 10801
Bartels Pl 10801
Bayard St 10805
Bayberry Ln 10804
Bayeau Rd 10804
Bayview Ave
1-1 10801
2-99 10805
Beachfront Ln 10805
Beattie Ln 10805
Beaufort Pl 10801
Beech Rd 10804
Beechmont Dr & Pl 10804
Beechwood Ave 10801
Belleau Ave 10804
Belleview Pl 10801
Belmont Ave 10801
Belvidere Pl 10805
Bergholz Dr 10801
Berrian Rd 10804
Beverly Rd 10804
Biehn St 10801
Birch St 10801
Bon Air Ave 10804
Bonnefoy Pl 10805
Brady Ave 10805
Braemar Ave 10804
Brewster Ter 10804
Briar Cir 10804
Bridge St 10801
Brittany Ln 10805
Broadcast Plz 10801
Broadfield Rd 10804
Broadview Ave 10804
Brook Ln & St 10801
Brookdale Ave & Cir 10801
Brookridge Rd 10804
Brookside Pl 10801
Brookwood Rd 10804
Burling Ln 10801
Byworth Rd 10804
Cadillac Dr 10804
Calhoun Ave 10801
Calton Ln & Rd 10804
Cambridge Ct 10804
Cameron Pl 10804
Carlisle Rd 10804
Carol Ln 10804
W Castle Pl 10805
Cedar St 10801
Centre Ave
1-114 10801
115-399 10805
Charles St 10801
Chatham Rd 10804
Chatsworth Pl 10801
Chauncey Ave 10801
Chelsea Rd 10805
Cherry Ave 10801
Cherry Lawn Blvd 10804
Chester Pl 10801
Chestnut Ln 10805
Church St
1-44 10801
45-399 10805
Circuit Rd 10805
Claire Ave 10804
Cleveland Ave & Ct 10801
Cliff St 10801
Clinton Ave & Pl 10801
Clove Rd
1-202 10801
203-264 10804
265-265 10801
266-398 10804
267-399 10804
Clover Pl 10805
Club Way 10805
Colangelo Pl 10801
Cole Ter 10801
Coligni Ave 10801
Colonel Lee Archer Blvd 10801
Colonial Pl 10801
Colonial Lee Archer Ave 10801
Columbus Ave 10801
Commerce Dr 10801
Congress St 10801
Cooper Dr 10801
Copper Beech Cir 10804
Cornell Pl 10804
Cortlandt Ave 10801
Cottage Pl 10801
Coutant Dr 10804
Coventry Ln 10805
Crawford Ter 10804
Crescent Ave 10801
Crestview St 10801
Crestwood Ln 10801
Croft Ter 10804
Crosby Pl 10801
Daisy Farms Dr 10804
Darling Ave 10804
Davenport Ave 10805
David Dr 10804
Davis Ave 10805
De Veau Ln 10805
Dearborn St 10801
Decatur Rd 10801
Dennis Dr 10804
Devonshire Rd 10804
Dewey Ave 10801
Dewitt Pl 10801
Disbrow Cir & Ln 10804
Division St 10801
Division St S 10805
Dock Pathway 10801
Donald Dr 10804
Dora Ln 10804
Drake Ave 10805
Driftwood Ln 10805
Durand St 10801
Dusk Dr 10804
Earle Pl 10801
East Pl 10801
Eastchester Rd 10801
Echo Ave 10801
Echo Bay Dr & Pl 10805
Eck Pl 10804
Edgewood Park 10801
Edna Pl 10804
Eighth St 10801
Elizabeth Rd 10804
Elk Ave 10804
Ellenton Ave
1-58 10801
59-99 10804
Elm St 10805
Emerson Ave & Pt 10801
Emmett Ter 10805
Erroll Pl 10804
Euclid Pl 10805
Evans St 10801
Everett St 10801
Evergreen Ave 10801
Fairview Pl 10805
Faneuil Pl 10801
Farlisti Rd 10804
Fenimore Rd 10804
Ferdinand Pl 10801
Fern St 10801
Field Ave 10805
Fieldmere St 10804
Fir Pl 10801
Flandreau Ave 10804
Flower St 10801
Forest Ave, Cir & Pl 10804
Fort Slocum Rd 10805
Fountain Pl 10801
Frank Davis Ct 10801
Franklin Ave 10805
Frederic B Powers Sq 10801
French Rdg 10801
Gaby Ln 10804
Gail Dr 10805
Gaillard Pl 10801
Garden St 10801
Gerada Ln 10804
Gladstone Rd 10804
Glen Pl 10801
Glen Island Park 10805
Glenbrook Rd 10804
Glencar Ave 10801
Glenfruin Ave 10804
Glenmore Dr 10801
Glenorchy Pl 10804
Glenwood Ave & Pl 10801
Gloucester Pl 10801
Glover Johnson Pl 10801
Gramercy Pl 10801
Grand St 10801
Grant St 10801
Green Pl 10801
Greens Way 10805
Griffon St 10801
Grove Ave 10801
Guion Pl 10801
Halcyon Ter 10801
Halligan Pl 10801
Hamilton Ave 10801
Hampton Oval 10805
Hanford Ave 10805
Hanson Ln 10804
Harbor Ln W 10805
Harding Dr 10801
Harlan Dr 10804
Harmon Ave 10801
Harold Ct 10801
Harrison St 10801
Hawthorne Dr 10801
Hayhurst Rd 10804
Hemingway Ave 10801
Hemlock Pl 10805
Heritage Ln 10801
Hertford St 10801
Hickory St 10805
High St 10801
Highland Ave 10801
Highpoint Rd 10804
Highridge Rd 10804
Highview Ave 10801
Hilary Cir 10804
Hill St 10801
Hillandale Dr 10804
Hillcrest Ave 10801
Hillside Ave 10801
Hillside Cres 10804
Hillside Ln 10804
Hilltop Ave 10801
Holly Dr 10801
Homestead Pl 10801
Hon Rhoda Quash Ln 10801
Horton Ave 10801
Howard Pkwy 10801
Hubert Pl 10801
Hudson Pk Rd 10805
Huguenot St 10801
Humane Pl 10805
Hunt Path 10804
Hunter Ave 10801
Huntington Pl 10801
Icard Ln 10805
Indian Trl 10804
Indian Hill Rd 10804
Industrial Ln 10805
Interlaken Ave 10801
Inverness Rd 10804
Inwood Pl 10801
Irving Pl 10801
Iselin Dr 10804
Island View Pl 10801
Jackson St 10801
James Dr 10804
Jefferson St 10801
Jerome Ave 10804
John St 10805
John Alden Rd 10801
Jones St 10801
Joyce Rd 10801
Karen Ln 10805
Kensington Oval 10805
Kenwood Dr 10804
Keogh Ln 10805
Kewanee Rd 10804
Kings Hwy 10801
Kingsbury Rd 10804
Knoll Pl 10801
Koch St 10801
Kress Ave 10801
Lafayette Ave 10801
Lafayette St 10805
Lake Ave 10801
Laken Ter 10801
Lakeshore Dr 10804
Lakeside Dr 10801
Lakeview Rd 10804
Lambert Ln 10804
Lane Crest Ave 10805
Laron Dr 10804
Lasalle Dr 10801
Lathers Park 10801
Laurel Pl 10801
Lawn Ave 10801
Lawrence Pl 10801
Lawton St 10801
Le Fevres Ln 10801
Lecount Pl 10801
Lee Ct 10805
Leffingwell Pl 10801
Leland Ave 10805
Lemke Pl 10801
Leroy Pl 10805
Leslie Pl 10804
Lester Pl 10804
Leviness Pl 10801
Lewis Pl 10804
Liberty Ave
1-70 10801
71-299 10805
Library Plz 10801
Lincoln Ave & St 10801
Linden Pl 10801
Linwood Rd 10804
Lispenard Ave 10801
Lockwood Ave 10801
Locust Ave
59A-59B 10801
1-107 10801
108-199 10805
Lomond Pl 10804
London Ter 10804
Longvue Ave 10804
Lord Kitchener Rd 10804
Lorenz Ave 10801
Lotus Rd 10804
Lovell Ln & Rd 10804
Lyncroft Rd 10804
Lynette St 10801
Lynns Way 10805
Lyons Pl 10801
Madeleine Ave 10801
Madison St 10801
Maid Stone Ct 10804
Main St
209-209 10801
211-744 10801
746-748 10801
747-747 10805
749-798 10805
799-1099 10801
E Main St 10801
Malysana Ln 10805
Manhattan Ave 10801
Manor Pl 10801
Maple Ave 10801
Marion Dr 10804
Marvin Pl 10801
Maul Pl & St 10801
May St 10801
Mayflower Ave 10801
Maywood Rd 10804
Meadow Ln 10805
Meadowood Path 10804
Melrose Dr 10804
Memorial Hwy 10801
Mereland Rd 10804
Merton St 10801
Mildred Pkwy 10804
Mill Rd 10804
Mill Pond Ln 10805
Mohegan Pl 10804
Monroe St 10801
Montgomery Cir & Pl 10804
Moran Pl 10801
Morgan St 10805
Morris St 10801
Morrison Dr 10804
Mount Etna Pl 10805
Mount Joy Pl 10801
Mount Tom Rd 10805
Mountain Ave 10804
Muir Pl 10801
Mulberry Ln 10804
Nardozzi Pl 10805
Nautilus Pl 10805
Neptune Ave 10805
New Roc City Plz 10801
Nob Ct 10804
Norman Rd 10804
Normandy Ln 10804
North Ave
1-69 10805
70-254 10801
255-255 10802
256-798 10801
257-799 10801
800-1600 10804
1602-1698 10804
Northfield Rd 10804
Northwood Cir & Ct 10804
Oak St 10801
Oakdale Ave 10801
Odell Pl 10801
Old Boston Post Rd 10801
Old Country Rd 10804
Old Orchard Rd 10804
Orchard Pl 10801
Ormonde Pl 10801
Otsego Ave 10804
Overhill Rd 10804
Overlook Cir & Rd 10804
Overman Pl 10801
Owen Rd 10804
Oxford Rd 10804
Paine Ave 10804
Palmer Ave 10801
Pamela Ln 10804
Parcot Ave 10801
Park Ave 10805
Park Pl 10801
Park Ridge Ave 10805
Parkview Ave 10805
Pebbleway Rd 10804
Pelham Rd
1-26 10801
27-799 10805
Pelhamdale Ave 10801
Pelhamside Dr 10801
Pell Pl 10804
Pembroke St 10801
Pengilly Dr 10804
Pershing Ave 10801
Perth Ave 10804
Petersville Rd 10801
Pierce St 10801
Pine Ct & St 10801
Pine Pk Dr 10804
Pinebrook Blvd 10804
Pinebrook Rd 10801
Pinebrook Hollow Dr 10804
Pintard Ave 10801
Piping Rock Way 10804
Plain Ave 10801
Pleasant St 10801
Pondview Ln 10804
Poplar Pl 10805
Portman Rd 10801
Portnellan Ave 10804
Potter Ave 10801
Potters Ln 10805
Pratt St 10801
Premium Pt 10801
President St 10801
Prince St 10801
Prospect St 10805
Pryer Pl & Ter 10804
Putnum Rd 10801

Quaker Ridge Rd 10804
Radisson Plz 10801
Railroad Ave & Pl 10801
Ralph Rd 10804
Ramona Ct 10804
Randistr Ave 10801
Ranger Pl 10804
Regal Dr 10804
Relyea Pl 10801
Remington Pl & Ter 10801
Renewal Pl 10801
Retiro Ln 10804
Reyna Ln 10804
Rhodes St 10801
Richmond Ln 10804
Ridge Rd 10804
Risley Pl 10801
River St 10801
Robert Dr 10804
Robins Cres & Rd 10801
Rochelle Pl 10801
Rock Ridge Cir 10804
Rockdale Ave 10801
Rockland Pl 10801
Rockledge Pl 10801
Rockwood Pl 10804
Rodman Oval 10805
Rogers Dr 10804
Rolling Way 10804
Ronalds Ave & Ln 10801
Ronbru Dr 10804
Rosedale Ave & St 10801
Rosehill Ave 10804
Rotunno Pl 10801
Rugby Rd 10804
Russell Ave 10801
Saint Johns Pl 10801
Saint Joseph St 10805
Saint Pauls Pl 10801
Saldo Cir 10804
Sara Ln 10804
Saxon Way 10804
Schley Ave 10801
Schoen Ln 10804
Schudy Pl 10801
Schuyler St 10801
Seacord Rd 10804
Seaview Ave 10801
Seton Dr 10804
Shadow Ln 10801
Shady Glen Ct 10805
Sharot St 10801
Shea Pl 10801
Sheldon Ave & Pl 10801
Sheldrake Ln & Pl 10804
Sherman St 10801
Shinnecock Way 10804
Shore Ave 10801
Shore Club Dr 10805
Short Ln 10804
Sicard Ave 10804
Sickles Ave & Pl 10801
Sidney St 10801
Siebrecht Pl 10804
Silver Birch Dr 10804
Skyview Ln 10804
Slocum St 10801
Somerset Rd 10804
Soulice Pl 10804
Soundview St 10805
Spencer Dr 10801
Split Rock Ln 10804
Springdale Rd 10804
Spruce St 10805
Stanton Cir 10804
Starr Ter 10804
State St 10801
Station Plz 10801
Stephenson Blvd 10801
Stone Cabin Rd 10801
Stonelea Pl 10801
Stony Run 10804
Stony Gate Oval 10804
Storer Ave 10801
Stratford Rd 10804
Stratton Rd 10804
Stuart Dr 10804
Summit Ave 10801
Sun Haven Dr 10801
Sunnyridge Rd 10804
Sunnyside Way 10804
Surrey Dr 10804
Sussex Rd 10804
Sutton Manor Rd 10801
Sycamore Ave 10801
Sylvan Pl 10801
Tall Spruce Loop 10804
Tall Trees Rd 10804
Tamindo Ave 10805
Taymil Rd 10804
Terrace Park Ln 10805
The Blvd, Cir & Ct E .. 10801
The Esplanade 10804
The Serpentine 10801
Thomas Pl 10801
Town Dock Rd 10805
Treno St 10801
Trenor Dr 10804
Trevon Pl 10804
Trinity Pl 10805
Troy Ln 10801
Tulip Ln 10804
Turner Dr 10804
Union Ave 10801
Union St
1-50 10805
51-51 10801
52-98 10805
53-99 10805
Upland Rd 10804
Valley Pl 10801
Valley Rd 10804
Van Etten Blvd 10804
Van Guilder Ave 10801
Van Meter Fens 10804
Van Meter Fenway 10804
Vaneck Dr 10804
Vaughn Ave 10801
Verdun Ave 10804
Victory Blvd 10804
Villus Ave 10801
Walnut St 10801
Ward Dr 10804
Warren St 10801
Washington Ave 10801
Water St 10805
Watkins Pl 10801
Weaver St 10804
Webster Ave
1-752 10801
753-1199 10804
Weeks Pl 10801
Wellington Ave 10804
West Way 10801
Westchester Pl 10801
Westminster Ct 10801
Westwood Ave 10801
Weyman Ave 10805
White Oak St 10801
White Stone Pl 10801
Whitewood Ave 10805
Whitfield Ter 10801
Wickford Rd 10801
Wildcliff Rd 10805
Wildwood Rd 10804
Willow Dr 10805
Wilmot Rd 10804
Wilputte Pl 10804
Wilson Dr 10801
Winchester Oval 10805
Winding Brook Rd 10804
Windsor Oval 10805
Winfield Pl 10801
Winthrop Ave 10801
Winyah Ter 10801
Wood Ln 10804
Wood Pl 10801
Wood Hollow Ln 10804
Woodbine Ave 10801
Woodbury St 10805
Woodcut Ln 10804
Woodland Ave 10805
Woodlawn Ave 10804
Wykagyl Ter 10804

NUMBERED STREETS

All Street Addresses 10801

NEW YORK NY

General Delivery 10001

POST OFFICE BOXES MAIN OFFICE STATIONS AND BRANCHES

Box No.s
A - X 10028
A - H 10159
A - S 10034
401A - 401A 10024
1 - 1260 10002
1 - 2652 10009
1 - 1070 10014
1 - 538 10024
1 - 1440 10025
1 - 720 10028
1 - 1120 10030
1 - 1840 10035
1 - 1178 10040
1 - 460 10044
1 - 1852 10150
1 - 1066 10272
1 - 644 10034
1 - 1260 10037
1 - 680 10031
1 - 696 10012
1 - 1230 10029
1 - 3660 10027
1 - 1200 10039
1 - 1970 10156
1 - 4020 10185
1 - 1740 10274
1 - 613 10013
1 - 743 10276
1 - 1408 10008
1 - 822 10018
1 - 749 10032
1 - 457 10033
1 - 5063 10163
1 - 1127 10268
1 - 960 10101
1 - 776 10113
1 - 835 10159
1 - 1088 10021
1 - 1149 10108
1 - 1198 10116
1 - 1859 10026
50 - 200 10023
501 - 780 10033
603 - 630 10024
637 - 740 10013
701 - 1060 10024
766 - 820 10276
770 - 2100 10013
800 - 822 10028
807 - 824 10113
844 - 864 10018
845 - 870 10276
856 - 864 10113
857 - 971 10159
879 - 879 10017
889 - 915 10018
898 - 925 10276
901 - 2038 10113
961 - 1439 10018
971 - 1660 10276
981 - 1021 10101
1001 - 1660 10028
1007 - 1009 10034
1079 - 1099 10101
1101 - 2060 10159
1119 - 2538 10021
1131 - 1154 10101
1156 - 1168 10268
1182 - 1268 10101
1190 - 1380 10268
1253 - 1287 10116
1296 - 1325 10101
1313 - 1377 10116
1368 - 1368 10101
1400 - 1405 10116
1401 - 1470 10268
1411 - 1416 10101
1430 - 3998 10008
1438 - 1466 10116
1442 - 2324 10101
1501 - 1624 10268
1502 - 1550 10116
1561 - 2140 10025
1575 - 1608 10116
1604 - 1604 10023
1614 - 1871 10019
1651 - 1754 10268
1668 - 1668 10116
1681 - 1760 10037
1695 - 1703 10116
1700 - 1712 10023
1748 - 1780 10116
1805 - 1805 10023
1816 - 1942 10116
1944 - 1944 10023
1966 - 2050 10116
1999 - 2099 10156
2001 - 2700 10108
2001 - 2016 10002
2001 - 2127 10272
2002 - 2015 10035
2080 - 2192 10116
2152 - 2175 10272
2215 - 2225 10116
2233 - 2250 10272
2251 - 2323 10116
2301 - 2362 10272
2366 - 2550 10116
2515 - 2515 10272
2622 - 2973 10116
3000 - 3067 10108
3000 - 3032 10116
3001 - 3005 10012
3001 - 3005 10009
3002 - 3004 10040
3002 - 3014 10025
3080 - 3515 10116
3729 - 3729 10017
4002 - 4120 10023
4621 - 5597 10185
5002 - 5212 10274
5011 - 5090 10150
5093 - 5177 10163
5112 - 5176 10150
5200 - 5213 10163
5200 - 5217 10150
5200 - 5251 10008
5238 - 5354 10150
5243 - 5300 10163
5375 - 5375 10150
5462 - 5496 10163
5521 - 5582 10027
5548 - 5959 10163
6000 - 6461 10249
6001 - 8559 10150
6491 - 6874 10249
7001 - 8720 10116
7001 - 7200 10008
7401 - 7401 10101
7777 - 7777 10108
7900 - 7912 10242
8000 - 8020 10008
8001 - 8090 10027
9595 - 14616 10101
19000 - 19018 10249
20001 - 20720 10011
20001 - 21080 10023
20001 - 20776 10021
20001 - 20216 10014
20001 - 20478 10001
20001 - 21192 10025
20001 - 20240 10017
20181 - 20960 10009
20481 - 20514 10017
24231 - 24943 10242
28823 - 28833 10028
30001 - 30974 10011
37021 - 37021 10037
130001 - 130426 10013
182004 - 182008 10018
225003 - 225396 10150
230001 - 237210 10023
250001 - 250900 10025
286001 - 287560 10128
293000 - 293010 10029
302001 - 302010 10030
321701 - 322097 10032
373000 - 373020 10037
3620001 - 3621016 10129

NAMED STREETS

Abingdon Sq 10014
Abp Fulton J Sheen Pl . 10017
Academy St 10034
Adam Clayton Powell Jr Blvd
1800-2000 10026
2001-2259 10027
2260-2499 10030
2500-2699 10039
Albany St
1-13 10006
15-99 10006
200-399 10280
Alex Rose Pl 10033
Allen St 10002
Altschul 10027
American Express Plz .. 10004
Amsterdam Ave
1-339 10023
340-639 10024
640-1099 10025
1100-1138 10027
1101-1139 10025
1140-1479 10027
1480-1880 10031
1881-2268 10032
2269-2565 10033
2566-2699 10040
Ann St 10038
Arden St 10040
W Ashanins St 10031
E Asharai St 10022
Asser Levy Pl 10010
Astor Pl 10003
Attorney St 10002
Audubon Ave
1-160 10032
161-439 10033
440-599 10040
Avenue A 10009
Avenue B 10009
Avenue C 10009
Avenue D 10009
Avenue Of The Americas
2-8 10013
Avenue Of The Americas
10-204 10013
206-210 10014
212-335 10014
336-414 10011
337-415 10014
416-650 10011
653-653 10010
655-773 10010
774-960 10001
961-1080 10018
1081-1219 10036
1220-1279 10020
1280-1289 10019
1290-1298 10104
1291-1339 10019
1300-1440 10019
1341-1359 10105
1361-1499 10019
Bank St 10014
Barclay 10279
Barclay St 10007
Barrow St 10014
Baruch Dr & Pl 10002
Battery Park 10004
Battery Pl
2-6 10004
8-24 10004
25-99 10280
101-101 10280
Battery Park Plz 10004
Baxter St 10013
Bayard St
1-38 10002
39-191 10013
193-199 10013
Beach St 10013
Beak St 10034
Beaver St
11A-11C 10004
1-54 10004
55-75 10005
56-74 10004
77-99 10005
Bedford St 10014
Beekman Pl 10022
Beekman St 10038
Beliste St 10128
Bennett Ave
1-131 10033
132-299 10040
301-399 10040
Benson St 10013
Beradia 10279
Bernard Baruch Way 10010
Bethune St 10014
Bleecker St
1-226 10012
227-499 10014
Bloomfield St 10014
Boat Basin 10024
Bogardus Pl 10040
Bond St 10012
Bowery
1-279 10002
Bowery
2-148 10013
150-364 10012
281-363 10003
365-399 10003
Bowling Grn 10004
Bradhurst Ave
1-59 10030
61-61 10030
64-299 10039
W Brallarl St 10011
Bridge St 10004
Brinerle Plz 10112
Broad St
12-12 10005
14-23 10005
25-25 10004
27-109 10004
111-241 10004
Broadway
3778A-3778B 10032
Broadway
1-28 10004
29-115 10006
30-56 10004
72-108 10005
120-120 10271
122-148 10005
150-222 10038
173-225 10007
233-238 10279
239-332 10007
334-334 10007
335-487 10013
488-695 10012
696-696 10003
697-697 10012
698-901 10003
902-1139 10010
1140-1314 10001
1316-1328 10001
1331-1450 10018
1451-1590 10036
1591-1591 10019
1592-1592 10036
1593-1810 10019
1811-2159 10023
2160-2459 10024
2460-2919 10025
2920-2958 10027
2921-2959 10025
2960-3299 10027
3300-3699 10031
3700-4100 10032
4101-4113 10033
4115-4379 10033
4380-4759 10040
4760-5170 10034
E Broadway
1-11 10038
12-14 10002
16-399 10002
W Broadway
2-2 10007
4-94 10007
96-98 10007
100-369 10013
370-372 10012
371-373 10013
374-484 10012
486-488 10012
Broadway Aly 10016
Broadway Ter 10040
Broome St
354A-354B 10013
109-113 10002
115-338 10002
339-599 10013
Bryant Park 10036
Cabrini Blvd
1-250 10033
251-399 10040
Canal St
1-143 10002
144-150 10013
145-151 10002
152-349 10013
350-350 10012
350-598 10013
351-599 10013
Cannon St 10002
Cardinal Hayes Pl 10007
Carlisle St 10006
Carmine St 10014
Catherine Ln 10013
Catherine St 10038
Catherine Slip 10038
Cedar St
2-14 10005
16-88 10005
89-199 10006
Central Park S 10019
Central Park W
1-160 10023
161-296 10024
298-310 10024
311-499 10025
Centre St
153C-153D 10013
1-57 10007
59-69 10007
70-72 10013
71-73 10007
74-299 10013
Centre Market Pl 10013
Chambers St
2-200 10007
202-250 10007
301-343 10281
345-400 10282
Charles Ln & St 10014
Charlton St 10014
Chase Manhattan Plz ... 10005
Chatham Sq 10038
Chelsea Piers 10011
Cherokee Pl 10075
Cherry St 10002
Chisum Pl 10037
Chittenden Ave 10033
Christopher St 10014

Chrystie St 10002
Church St
185A-185E 10007
City Hall 10007
E Clantang St 10016
Claremont Ave 10027
Clarkson St 10014
Cleveland Pl 10012
Cliff St 10038
Clinton St 10002
Clontr 10167
Coenties Slip 10004
Collister St 10013
Colonel Robert Magaw Pl 10033
Columbia St 10002
Columbus Ave
2-18 10023
20-339 10023
340-639 10024
640-1099 10025
Columbus Cir
2-25 10019
36-99 10023
Columbus Pl 10019
Comeari St 10014
Commerce St 10014
W Coneriso St 10036
Confucius Plz 10002
Convent Ave
1-116 10027
117-480 10031
482-498 10031
Cooper Sq 10003
Cooper St 10034
Cornelia St 10014
Cortlandt Aly 10013
Cortlandt St 10007
W Cournern St 10032
Cradowe Ave 10168
Crennew Ave 10035
Crosby St
2-2 10013
4-40 10013
41-199 10012
Cumming St 10034
Dag Hammarskjold Plz 10017
E Dandenti St 10017
W Dantranc St 10023
Davered Ave 10199
Delancey St 10002
W Dendongs St 10039
Desbrosses St 10013
Dey St 10007
Division St 10002
Dodge Hall 10027
Dominick St 10013
Dongan Pl 10040
W Dorideld St 10119
E Dorielis St 10010
Dover St 10038
Downing St 10014
Doyers St 10013
Duane St
1-40 10007
41-89 10278
42-124 10007
91-125 10007
126-199 10013
Dutch St 10038
Dyckman St
1-99 10034
100-217 10040
218-399 10034
Earl Hall 10027
Edgar St 10006
Edgecombe Ave
1-231 10030
232-394 10031
395-699 10032
Edward M Morgan Pl 10032
Eldridge St 10002
Elizabeth St
1-136 10013
137-399 10012
Elk St 10007
Ellis Is 10004
Ellwood St 10040
Emerrall 10045
E End Ave
1-19 10075
21-23 10075
25-156 10028
157-159 10128
158-160 10028
161-182 10128
184-200 10128
N End Ave 10282
S End Ave 10280
W End Ave
1-7 10023
9-341 10023
342-638 10024
639-639 10025
640-640 10024
641-999 10025
Ericsson Pl 10013
Essex St 10002
Exchange Pl
20-28 10005
30-43 10005
45-67 10005
62-66 10004
68-99 10004
Exchange Plz 10006
Extra Pl 10003
Fairchild Ctr 10027
Fairview Ave 10040
Fashion Ave
450-460 10123
462-576 10018
Fdr Dr
2-611 10002
612-1225 10009
2100-2600 10010
2602-25100 10010
Federal Plz 10278
W Fermaill St 10025
S Ferry 10004
Financial Sq 10005
Fletcher St 10038
Foley Sq 10007
Forsyth St 10002
Fort George Ave & Hl 10040
Fort Washington Ave
2-6 10032
8-300 10032
301-599 10033
600-799 10040
Frankfort St 10038
Franklin Pl & St 10013
Frederick Douglass Blvd
2031-2037 10026
2039-2224 10026
2225-2225 10027
2226-2226 10026
2227-2482 10027
2483-2487 10030
2484-2488 10027
2489-2728 10030
2729-2999 10039
Freedom Pl 10069
Freeman Aly 10002
E Freendo St 10009
Front St
1-74 10004
75-75 10005
76-76 10004
77-152 10005
153-153 10038
154-154 10005
155-299 10038
Fulton St
1-159 10038
160-166 10007
161-167 10038
168-199 10007
Fulton Fish Market 10038
Galeandi St 10007
Gallondi Ave 10029
Gansevoort St 10014
Gansevoort Market 10014
E Garaliso St 10003
Gay St 10014
Gendark Ave 10170
Gold St 10038
Golleass St 10006
Gopost
211-211 10002
Gopost
1302-1302 10013
1333-1333 10013
1712-1712 10017
2704-2704 10027
3701-3701 10037
Gopost St 10007
Gouverneur St 10002
Gouverneur Slip 10002
Gracie Sq & Ter 10028
Gramercy Park E 10003
Gramercy Park N 10010
Gramercy Park S 10003
Gramercy Park W 10003
Grand St
2-20 10013
22-235 10013
236-599 10002
Grand Central Terminal 10017
Great Jones St 10012
Greene St
2-12 10013
14-55 10013
56-199 10012
229-299 10003
Greenwich Ave
1-127 10014
2-198 10011
Greenwich St
348A-348B 10013
11-39 10004
41-165 10006
167-169 10006
224-228 10007
230-293 10007
294-300 10013
295-301 10007
302-550 10013
551-617 10014
552-552 10013
619-899 10014
Grelarry St 10005
Grove Ct & St 10014
Gustave L Levy Pl 10029
Hamill Pl 10007
Hamilton Pl & Ter 10031
W Hancharr St 10019
Hancock Pl 10027
Hanover Sq
1-3 10004
4-6 10005
5-7 10004
8-99 10005
Hanover St 10005
Harkness Plz 10023
Harlem River Dr 10039
Harrison St 10013
Haven Ave
40-50 10032
52-162 10032
163-324 10033
326-340 10033
Haven Plz 10009
Henderson Pl 10028
Henry St
2-11 10038
12-399 10002
Henry Hudson Pkwy 10034
Henshaw St 10034
Herald Sq 10001
Hester St
42-42 10002
44-135 10002
136-148 10013
137-149 10002
150-299 10013
149 1/2-149 1/2 10002
Hillside Ave 10040
Hogan Pl 10013
E Holinern St 10021
Horantr Ctr 10281
Horatio St 10014
Horthold 10155
E Houston St
1-71 10012
73-81 10012
83-91 10012
90-90 10002
92-599 10002
W Houston St
2-16 10012
18-86 10012
88-148 10012
172-176 10014
178-399 10014
Howard St 10013
Hubert St 10013
Hudson St
1-340 10013
341-343 10014
342-344 10013
345-699 10014
Indian Rd 10034
Irving Pl 10003
Isham St 10034
W Jacheadw St 10033
Jackson St 10002
James St 10038
Jane St 10014
Jay St 10013
Jefferson St 10002
Jersey St 10012
Joe Louis Plz 10001
John St
1-115 10038
114-114 10272
116-198 10038
117-199 10038
Jones St 10014
Journalism Building 10027
Jumel Pl & Ter 10032
Kenmare St 10012
King St
1-5 10012
6-199 10014
La Salle St 10027
Lafayette St
2-34 10007
36-38 10013
40-193 10013
194-372 10012
373-499 10003
Laguardia Pl 10012
Laight St 10013
Laraderm Ave 10034
Laurel Hill Ter
1-120 10033
121-199 10040
Leenchig Ave 10165
Lenox Ave 10039
Leonard St 10013
Lerner Hall 10027
Leroy St 10014
Lewis St 10002
Lexington Ave
1-79 10010
80-353 10016
354-373 10017
374-390 10168
375-403 10017
392-418 10017
405-405 10174
407-537 10017
420-420 10170
422-458 10017
450-450 10163
460-538 10017
539-589 10022
590-590 10154
591-765 10022
592-762 10022
764-764 10065
766-942 10065
943-1078 10021
1079-1163 10075
1164-1170 10028
1165-1171 10075
1172-1289 10028
1290-1290 10128
1291-1291 10028
1292-1487 10128
1488-1488 10029
1489-1489 10128
1490-1870 10029
1871-2169 10035
2170-2198 10037
Liberty Is 10004
Liberty Pl 10038
Liberty Plz 10006
Liberty St
2-76 10005
19-51 10045
53-75 10005
77-199 10006
201-201 10281
203-299 10281
Lincoln Ctr, Plz & Sq 10023
Lincoln Center Plz 10023
Lispenard St 10013
Litatte Plz 10278
Little West St 10004
Little West 12th St 10014
Low Libr 10027
Ludlow St 10002
Macdougal Aly 10011
Macdougal St
2-6 10012
8-142 10012
143-153 10011
144-154 10012
155-180 10011
Macombs Pl 10039
Madison Ave
1-39 10010
41-61 10010
62-278 10016
279-279 10017
280-280 10016
281-339 10017
340-340 10173
341-429 10017
344-430 10017
432-434 10022
436-651 10022
652-825 10065
827-827 10065
828-971 10021
972-972 10075
973-973 10021
974-1048 10075
1049-1055 10028
1050-1056 10075
1057-1189 10028
1190-1208 10128
1191-1209 10028
1210-1379 10128
1380-1767 10029
1768-2056 10035
2057-2200 10037
2202-2298 10037
Madison St
1-17 10038
19-68 10038
69-71 10002
70-72 10038
73-399 10002
Maiden Ln 10038
Main St 10044
Malcolm X Blvd
663A-663B 10037
1-199 10026
200-399 10027
401-401 10037
403-699 10037
Mancend 10175
Mangin St 10002
Manhattan Ave
2-48 10025
50-239 10025
240-480 10026
481-487 10027
482-488 10026
489-599 10027
Manhattan Pl 10007
Mansonso Ave 10065
Maradenc Ave 10040
Maraintr St 10038
Margaret Corbin Dr 10040
Market St 10002
Market Slip 10002
Marketfield St 10004
W Mellenda St 10018
Mercer St
1-63 10013
64-260 10012
261-399 10003
Midarriv 10169
Mill Ln 10004
Milligan Pl 10011
Mincenne Ave 10037
W Mindenco St 10001
Minetta Ln & St 10012
Mitchell Pl 10017
Monroe St 10002
Montgomery St 10002
N Moore St 10013
Morningside Ave
1-52 10026
59-199 10027
Morningside Dr
2-59 10025
60-200 10027
Morris St
1-9 10004
2-8 10006
10-99 10006
Morton Sq & St 10014
Mosco St 10013
Mott St
1-171 10013
172-172 10012
173-173 10013
174-399 10012
Mount Carmel Pl 10016
Mount Morris Park W 10027
Mulberry St
177A-177C 10013
10-10 10013
12-177 10013
178-399 10012
176 1/2-176 1/2 10013
Murray St
1-199 10007
200-299 10282
Nagle Ave
1-169 10040
170-299 10034
Nassau St
1-41 10005
42-54 10045
43-47 10005
49-53 10038
55-199 10038
Nathan D Perlman Pl 10003
Nevada Plz 10023
New St 10004
New York Plz 10004
Norfolk St 10002
Odell Clark Pl 10030
Old Broadway 10027
Old Slip 10005
Oliver St 10038
Orchard St 10002
Overlook Ter
1-65 10033
66-199 10040
Pace Plz 10038
Paladino Ave 10035
W Palerall St 10027
Pareende Blvd 10069
Park Ave
1-99 10016
100-198 10017
101-101 10178
117-199 10017
200-200 10166
230-230 10169
241-245 10167
242-248 10017
250-250 10177
259-259 10017
261-272 10017
274-282 10017
277-277 10172
299-299 10171
300-338 10022
340-518 10022
341-373 10154
375-375 10152
389-519 10022
520-699 10065
700-837 10021
839-839 10021
840-915 10075
916-922 10028
917-923 10075
924-1059 10028
1060-1241 10128
1242-1244 10029
1243-1245 10128
1246-1637 10029
1638-1906 10035
1908-1914 10035
1916-1918 10037
1920-2299 10037
Park Ave S
200-250 10003
251-362 10010
364-384 10010
365-383 10016
385-471 10016
473-499 10016
Park Pl 10007
Park Row
3-43 10038
44-166 10007
45-299 10038
168-198 10038
Park Ter E 10034
Park Ter W 10034
Patchin Pl 10011
Payson Ave 10034
Pearl St
1-101 10004
102-116 10005
103-117 10004
118-195 10005
196-196 10038
197-197 10005
198-463 10038
464-599 10007
Peck Slip 10038
Pell St 10013
Penn Plz
1-1 10119
2-2 10121
5-7 10001
8-10 10121
9-15 10001
12-12 10001
Perrelar Ave 10020
Perry St 10014
Pershing Sq 10017
Peter Cooper Rd 10010
Philosopy Hall 10027
Pier 59 10011
Pier 60 10011
Pier 61 10011
Pier 62 10011
Pike St 10002
Pike Slip 10002
Pine St
1-13 10005
15-65 10005
67-79 10005
70-70 10270
72-88 10005
S Pinehurst Ave 10033
Pitt St 10002
Plarree 10177
Platt St 10038
Pleasant Ave
263-299 10029
300-399 10035
Police Plz 10038
Pomander Walk 10025
Post Ave 10034
W Pralearn St 10030
W Pranchal St 10024

Street	ZIP
Prenwo Ave	10028
Prince St	10012
Ranchine St	10002
Randalls Is	10035
Reade St	
1-83	10007
84-199	10013
Rector Pl	10280
Rector St	10006
Renwick St	10013
Ridge St	10002
River Pl	10036
River Rd	10044
River Ter	10282
E River Piers	
2-8	10004
E River Piers	
10-14	10005
15-26	10038
36-36	10002
55-68	10009
N River Piers	
3-11	10006
21-36	10013
37-54	10014
56-56	10014
65-75	10001
76-80	10018
81-86	10036
88-99	10019
Riverside Blvd	10069
Riverside Dr	
1-40	10023
41-182	10024
184-190	10024
191-439	10025
440-442	10027
444-474	10027
475-475	10115
476-568	10027
477-569	10027
570-762	10031
763-1150	10032
1151-1499	10033
1600-1700	10040
1702-1780	10040
1781-1899	10034
Riverside Dr W	10032
Riverview Ter	10022
Rivington St	10002
Robert F Wagner Sr Pl	10038
Rockefeller Plz	
1-7	10020
9-19	10020
21-43	10020
24-38	10112
40-52	10020
45-47	10111
51-73	10020
75-75	10019
Rutgers St	10002
Rutgers Slip	10002
Rutherford Pl	10003
Ryders Aly	10038
Saint Andrews Plz	10007
Saint Clair Pl	10027
Saint James Pl	10038
Saint Johns Ln	10013
Saint Lukes Pl	10014
Saint Marks Pl	
1-83	10003
84-84	10009
85-85	10003
86-199	10009
Saint Nicholas Ave	
1-37	10026
39-199	10026
200-200	10027
202-456	10027
457-691	10030
692-698	10031
693-699	10030
700-861	10031
862-1259	10032
1260-1539	10033
1540-1699	10040
Saint Nicholas Pl	
2-20	10031
22-60	10031
61-99	10032
Saint Nicholas Ter	
1-55	10027
57-99	10031
Schangto	10044
Seaman Ave	10034
Seanche	10107
Searieli Ave	10075
Seminary Row	10027
Sheridan Sq	10014
Sheriff St	10002
Sherman Ave	
1-84	10040
86-98	10034
100-299	10034
Sherman Sq	10023
Shindern	10111
Sickles St	10040
Sniffen Ct	10016
South St	
1-39	10004
40-75	10005
76-199	10038
203-399	10002
39 1/2-39 1/2	10004
Spriande Ave	10176
Spring St	
1-220	10012
221-399	10013
Spruce St	10038
Staff St	10034
Stanton St	10002
Staple St	10013
State St	10004
Stone St	10004
Stuyvesant Oval	10009
Stuyvesant St	10003
Suffolk St	10002
Sullivan St	10012
Sutton Pl & Sq	10022
Sylvan Ct	10035
Sylvan Pl	10035
Sylvan Ter	10032
Taras Shevchenko Pl	10003
Temerth St	10013
Thames St	10006
W Thames St	10280
Thayer St	10040
Thomas St	
1-42	10007
43-49	10013
44-50	10007
51-99	10013
Thompson St	
1-49	10013
50-299	10012
Tiemann Pl	10027
Time Warner Ctr	10019
Times Sq	10036
Trallank	10173
Trelacha St	10282
Trimble Pl	10007
Trinity Pl	10006
Tudor City Pl	10017
Union Sq E	10003
United Nations Plz	10017
University Pl	10003
Uris Hall	10027
Valintr	10270
Vandam St	10013
Vanderbilt Ave	
1-62	10017
63-79	10169
64-98	10017
81-99	10017
Varick St	
2-8	10013
10-170	10013
171-171	10014
172-172	10013
173-299	10014
Vermilyea Ave	10034
Vesey St	
1-30	10007
32-198	10007
201-299	10282
202-298	10281
Vestry St	10013
W Viangt St	10026
Vichendi	10118
Wadsworth Ave	
1-279	10033
280-380	10040
382-398	10040
Wadsworth Ter	10040
Walker St	10013
Wall St	10005
Wall Street Ct	10005
Wallontr	10174
Wards Is	10035
Warkenso St	10004
Warren St	
1-108	10007
110-120	10007
201-201	10282
Washington Mews	10003
Washington Pl	
1-60	10003
61-90	10011
91-199	10014
Washington Sq E	10003
Washington Sq N	
1-13	10003
14-27	10011
Washington Sq S	10012
Washington Sq W	10011
Washington St	
2-32	10004
34-38	10006
40-170	10006
200-218	10007
220-225	10007
287-531	10013
532-899	10014
Washington Ter	10033
Washington Square Vlg	10012
Water St	
2-48	10004
55-55	10041
58-74	10005
76-153	10005
154-299	10038
400-685	10002
687-699	10002
Waterside Plz	10010
Watts St	10013
Waverly Pl	
1-99	10003
100-131	10011
132-132	10014
133-133	10011
134-299	10014
Weehawken St	10014
West St	
1-2	10004
4-38	10004
21-47	10006
49-90	10006
140-142	10007
200-234	10282
235-299	10013
326-350	10014
352-489	10014
491-573	10014
Whinsout St	10012
White St	10013
Whitehall St	10004
Willett St	10002
William St	
1-1	10004
3-7	10004
8-8	10005
9-9	10004
10-54	10005
56-78	10005
79-83	10045
80-82	10038
84-199	10038
S William St	10004
Winerans Pl	10280
Wooster St	
1-55	10013
56-162	10012
164-168	10012
World Financial Ctr	10281
Worth St	10013
York Ave	
1100-1292	10065
1293-1311	10021
1294-1312	10065
1313-1432	10021
1433-1492	10075
1483-1483	10021
1493-1509	10075
1494-1512	10075
1511-1511	10028
1513-1656	10028
1657-1747	10128
1749-1799	10128
York St	10013

NUMBERED STREETS

Street	ZIP
1st Ave	
1-343	10003
2-346	10009
345-345	10010
445-699	10016
877-1096	10022
1097-1099	10065
1098-1100	10022
1101-1280	10065
1285-1460	10021
1461-1532	10075
1533-1537	10028
1534-1538	10075
1539-1667	10028
1668-1678	10128
1669-1679	10028
1680-1855	10128
1856-2255	10029
2256-2256	10035
2257-2257	10029
2258-2449	10035
E 1st St	
1-1	10003
74-198	10009
75-75	10003
2nd Ave	
7-13	10003
344-459	10010
460-746	10016
747-922	10017
923-1139	10022
1140-1140	10065
1141-1141	10022
1142-1311	10065
1312-1455	10021
1456-1460	10075
1457-1461	10021
1462-1537	10075
1538-1680	10028
1681-1855	10128
1856-1862	10029
1857-1863	10128
1864-2259	10029
2260-2500	10035
E 2nd St	
1-88	10003
89-97	10009
3rd Ave	
1-243	10003
244-356	10010
357-600	10016
601-605	10158
602-618	10016
619-796	10017
797-908	10022
909-909	10150
910-962	10022
964-964	10155
966-998	10022
1010-1185	10065
1186-1328	10021
1329-1409	10075
1410-1549	10028
1550-1709	10128
1710-2121	10029
2122-2122	10035
2123-2123	10029
2124-2399	10035
E 3rd St	
1-5	10003
100-399	10009
W 3rd St	10012
4th Ave	
42-48	10003
93-93	10276
95-249	10003
E 4th St	
9-133	10003
14-20	10012
22-130	10003
132-132	10009
W 4th St	
1-1	10012
153-153	10014
E 4th Walk	10009
5th Ave	
1-133	10003
2-62	10011
64-152	10011
64-64	10003
135-153	10010
155-213	10010
215-225	10010
218-334	10001
233-409	10016
350-350	10118
352-370	10001
372-396	10018
398-400	10018
402-498	10018
411-459	10016
461-517	10017
500-500	10110
508-594	10036
519-525	10175
527-549	10017
551-551	10176
553-609	10017
596-608	10020
610-638	10020
610-610	10185
611-743	10022
640-650	10019
652-666	10103
668-770	10019
745-755	10151
757-767	10153
769-769	10022
771-787	10022
788-875	10065
876-949	10021
950-990	10075
991-1059	10028
1060-1150	10128
1151-1313	10029
1314-1416	10026
1315-1415	10029
1417-2117	10035
2118-2118	10037
2119-2119	10035
2120-2367	10037
2369-2399	10037
E 5th St	
200-399	10003
500-754	10009
756-798	10009
E 6th St	
201-399	10003
400-921	10009
7th Ave	
2-22	10011
24-241	10011
243-243	10011
245-247	10001
420-440	10119
442-448	10001
577-720	10036
721-887	10019
888-900	10106
889-941	10019
7th Ave S	10014
E 7th St	
2-6	10003
90-299	10009
8th Ave	
11-19	10014
21-67	10014
68-78	10011
69-79	10014
80-278	10011
279-424	10001
421-421	10199
421-421	10116
425-483	10001
500-628	10018
625-625	10129
629-637	10018
639-789	10036
790-947	10019
950-960	10107
970-996	10019
E 8th St	
1-133	10003
200-499	10009
W 8th St	10011
9th Ave	
3-15	10014
17-29	10014
44-227	10011
228-340	10001
341-341	10199
342-448	10001
450-559	10018
560-700	10036
701-925	10019
3700-4199	10034
E 9th St	
3-17	10003
400-799	10009
W 9th St	10011
10th Ave	
1-59	10014
60-236	10011
237-239	10001
238-240	10011
241-449	10001
450-555	10018
556-685	10036
686-702	10019
687-703	10036
704-906	10019
3700-4099	10034
E 10th St	
1-1	10003
245-499	10009
W 10th St	
1-127	10011
128-399	10014
11th Ave	
2-2	10014
3-200	10011
201-201	10199
202-420	10001
421-425	10018
422-426	10001
427-534	10018
540-550	10036
663-853	10019
E 11th St	
2-8	10003
400-799	10009
W 11th St	
2-8	10011
200-399	10014
12th Ave	
1-99	10014
100-164	10011
165-239	10001
361-491	10018
500-639	10036
640-899	10019
2240-2351	10027
2352-2399	10031
E 12th St	
1-399	10003
400-731	10009
W 12th St	
2-229	10011
230-400	10014
E 13th St	
2-2	10003
4-399	10003
400-799	10009
W 13th St	
1-299	10011
300-499	10014
E 14th St	
1-334	10003
335-335	10009
336-398	10003
337-399	10003
400-899	10009
W 14th St	
2-4	10011
6-299	10011
300-599	10014
E 15th St	10003
W 15th St	10011
E 16th St	
5-7	10003
700-798	10009
W 16th St	10011
E 17th St	10003
W 17th St	10011
E 18th St	10003
W 18th St	
2-218	10011
217-217	10113
219-599	10011
220-598	10011
E 19th St	10003
W 19th St	10011
E 20th St	
2-2	10003
4-399	10003
400-698	10009
401-601	10010
W 20th St	10011
E 21st St	10010
W 21st St	
1-1	10010
100-599	10011
E 22nd St	10010
W 22nd St	
1-1	10010
100-599	10011
E 23rd St	
1-150	10010
149-149	10159
151-423	10010
152-532	10010
W 23rd St	
1-61	10010
63-99	10010
100-699	10011
E 24th St	10010
W 24th St	
6-80	10010
100-699	10011
E 25th St	10010
1-99	10010
100-599	10001
E 26th St	
7-29	10010
31-400	10010
402-498	10010
421-427	10016
W 26th St	
2-6	10010
8-58	10010
60-98	10010
100-699	10001
E 27th St	
1-399	10016
2-4	10001
6-398	10016
W 27th St	10001
W 27th Street Dr	10001
E 28th St	10016
W 28th St	10001
E 29th St	10016
W 29th St	
1-400	10001
401-401	10199
402-698	10001

409-699 10001
E 30th St 10016
W 30th St 10001
E 31st St 10016
W 31st St 10001
E 32nd St 10016
W 32nd St 10001
E 33rd St 10016
W 33rd St
1-25 10118
2-24 10001
31-31 10118
32-378 10001
201-299 10119
301-699 10001
380-380 10199
382-698 10001
E 34th St
1-134 10016
115-115 10156
135-599 10016
W 34th St
1-223 10001
2-20 10118
22-110 10001
112-122 10120
124-200 10001
202-298 10119
225-225 10122
227-297 10001
E 35th St 10016
W 35th St 10001
E 36th St 10016
W 36th St 10018
E 37th St 10016
W 37th St 10018
E 38th St 10016
W 38th St 10018
E 39th St 10016
W 39th St 10018
E 40th St 10016
W 40th St 10018
E 41st St
1-42 10017
43-53 10165
44-498 10017
55-499 10017
W 41st St
1-99 10018
100-699 10036
E 42nd St
1-53 10017
60-72 10165
74-120 10017
122-122 10168
124-498 10017
W 42nd St
5-97 10036
340-340 10108
342-698 10036
E 43rd St
2-100 10017
101-127 10170
102-398 10017
143-399 10017
W 43rd St 10036
E 44th St 10017
W 44th St 10036
E 45th St
1-3 10017
5-60 10017
61-85 10169
62-398 10017
87-399 10017
W 45th St 10036
E 46th St 10017
W 46th St 10036
E 47th St 10017
W 47th St 10036
E 48th St 10017
W 48th St
1-99 10020
6-144 10036
E 49th St 10017
W 49th St
1-1 10020
3-28 10020
30-98 10020
51-63 10112
140-699 10019
E 50th St 10022
W 50th St
3-9 10020
11-17 10020
19-143 10020
52-74 10112
136-156 10019
158-699 10019
E 51st St 10022
W 51st St
1-699 10019
2-140 10020
148-698 10019
E 52nd St
1-54 10022
55-55 10055
56-498 10022
57-499 10022
W 52nd St
2-18 10019
20-323 10019
322-322 10101
324-698 10019
325-699 10019
E 53rd St 10022
W 53rd St 10019
E 54th St 10022
W 54th St 10019
E 55th St 10022
W 55th St 10019
E 56th St 10022
W 56th St 10019
E 57th St 10022
W 57th St
2-225 10019
227-699 10019
250-250 10107
300-698 10019
E 58th St
1-139 10022
140-198 10155
141-449 10022
200-498 10022
W 58th St 10019
E 59th St 10022
W 59th St 10019
E 60th St 10022
W 60th St 10023
W 61st Dr 10023
E 61st St 10065
W 61st St 10023
E 62nd St 10065
1-299 10023
401-499 10069
E 63rd St 10065
W 63rd St
2-2 10023
400-400 10069
E 64th St 10065
1-299 10023
400-499 10069
E 65th St 10065
1-299 10023
400-499 10069
E 66th St 10065
W 66th St
2-2 10023
400-499 10069
E 67th St 10065
1-200 10023
400-499 10069
E 68th St 10065
1-199 10023
400-499 10069
E 69th St 10021
1-199 10023
400-499 10069
E 70th St 10021
W 70th St
1-399 10023
400-500 10069
E 71st St 10021
W 71st St
1-1 10023
400-499 10069
E 72nd St 10021
W 72nd St 10023
E 73rd St 10021
W 73rd St 10023
E 74th St 10021
W 74th St 10023
E 75th St 10021
W 75th St 10023
E 76th St 10021
W 76th St 10023
E 77th St
2-499 10075
500-520 10162
501-517 10075
W 77th St 10024
E 78th St 10075
W 78th St 10024
W 79st Transverse Rd 10024
E 79th St 10075
W 79th St 10024
E 80th St 10075
W 80th St 10024
E 81st St 10028
W 81st St 10024
W 81st Transverse Rd 10024
E 82nd St 10028
W 82nd St 10024
E 83rd St 10028
W 83rd St 10024
E 84th St 10028
W 84th St 10024
E 85th St 10028
W 85th St 10024
E 86th St 10028
W 86th St 10024
W 86th Transverse Rd 10024
E 87th St 10128
W 87th St 10024
E 88th St 10128
W 88th St 10024
E 89th St 10128
W 89th St 10024
E 90th St 10128
W 90th St 10024
E 91st St 10128
W 91st St 10024
E 92nd St 10128
W 92nd St 10025
E 93rd St 10128
W 93rd St 10025
E 94th St 10128
W 94th St 10025
E 95th St 10128
W 95th St 10025
E 96th St 10128
W 96th St 10025
E 97th St 10029
W 97th St 10025
E 98th St 10029
W 98th St 10025
E 99th St 10029
W 99th St 10025
E 100th St 10029
W 100th St 10025
E 101st St 10029
W 101st St 10025
E 102nd St 10029
W 102nd St 10025
E 103rd St 10029
W 103rd St 10025
E 104th St 10029
W 104th St 10025
E 105th St 10029
W 105th St 10025
E 106th St 10029
W 106th St 10025
E 107th St 10029
W 107th St 10025
E 108th St 10029
W 108th St 10025
E 109th St 10029
W 109th St 10025
E 110th St 10029
W 110th St
2-349 10026
350-398 10025
351-399 10026
400-699 10025
E 111th St 10029
1-399 10026
500-699 10025
E 112th St 10029
1-399 10026
500-699 10025
E 113th St 10029
W 113th St
100-399 10026
400-420 10025
E 114th St 10029
W 114th St
100-349 10026
351-399 10026
400-500 10025
501-599 10027
502-698 10025
601-699 10025
E 115th St 10029
W 115th St
1-399 10026
400-499 10025
501-523 10027
525-599 10027
600-699 10025
E 116th St And Fdr Dr 10029
E 116th St 10029
1-399 10026
400-699 10027
E 117th St 10035
1-399 10026
400-499 10027
E 118th St 10035
1-399 10026
400-499 10027
E 119th St 10035
1-399 10026
400-699 10027
E 120th St 10035
W 120th St 10027
E 121st St 10035
W 121st St 10027
E 122nd St 10035
W 122nd St 10027
E 123rd St 10035
W 123rd St 10027
E 124th St 10035
W 124th St 10027
E 125th St 10035
W 125th St 10027
E 126th St 10035
W 126th St 10027
E 127th St 10035
W 127th St 10027
E 128th St 10035
W 128th St 10027
E 129th St 10035
W 129th St 10027
E 130th St 10037
1-99 10037
100-699 10027
E 131st St 10037
W 131st St
1-99 10037
100-647 10027
E 132nd St 10037
1-99 10037
100-699 10027
W 133rd St
100-349 10030
350-398 10027
W 134th St
1-99 10037
100-399 10030
400-699 10031
E 135th St 10037
W 135th St
1-99 10037
100-399 10030
400-799 10031
W 136th St
1-99 10037
100-399 10030
500-699 10031
W 137th St
1-99 10037
100-399 10030
600-699 10031
E 138th St 10037
W 138th St
298A-298D 10030
1-99 10037
200-399 10030
450-699 10031
E 139th St 10037
W 139th St
1-99 10037
100-399 10030
500-699 10031
W 140th St
100-399 10030
450-699 10031
W 141st St
1-99 10037
100-399 10030
400-618 10031
620-698 10031
W 142nd St
1-99 10037
100-399 10030
451-699 10031
W 143rd St
1-99 10037
100-399 10030
451-699 10031
W 144th St
100-399 10030
413-699 10031
W 145th St
100-340 10039
341-357 10031
342-358 10039
359-700 10031
702-750 10031
W 146th St
100-164 10039
166-349 10039
400-699 10031
W 147th St
100-349 10039
400-699 10031
W 148th St
200-349 10039
400-699 10031
W 149th St
200-349 10039
400-699 10031
W 150th St
200-349 10039
400-699 10031
W 151st St
211D1-211D1 10039
100-349 10039
350-699 10031
W 152nd St
100-349 10039
400-699 10031
W 153rd St
200-349 10039
400-699 10031
W 154th St
232-232 10039
234-349 10039
400-499 10032
W 155th St
200-349 10039
400-699 10032
W 156th St 10032
W 157th St 10032
W 158th St 10032
W 159th St 10032
W 160th St 10032
W 161st St 10032
W 162nd St 10032
W 163rd St 10032
W 164th St 10032
W 165th St 10032
W 166th St 10032
W 167th St 10032
W 168th St 10032
W 169th St 10032
W 170th St 10032
W 171st St 10032
W 172nd St 10032
W 173rd St 10032
W 174th St 10033
W 175th St 10033
W 176th St 10033
W 177th St 10033
W 178th St 10033
W 179th St 10033
W 180th St 10033
W 181st St 10033
W 182nd St 10033
W 183rd St 10033
W 184th St 10033
W 185th St 10033
W 186th St 10033
W 187th St 10033
W 188th St 10040
W 189th St 10040
W 190th St 10040
W 191st St 10040
W 192nd St 10040
W 193rd St 10040
W 196th St 10040
W 201st St 10034
W 202nd St 10034
W 203rd St 10034
W 204th St 10034
W 205th St 10034
W 206th St 10034
W 207th St 10034
W 208th St 10034
W 211th St 10034
W 212th St 10034
W 213th St 10034
W 214th St 10034
W 215th St 10034
W 216th St 10034
W 217th St 10034
W 218th St 10034
W 219th St 10034
W 220th St 10034
369th Plz 10037

NEWBURGH NY

General Delivery 12550

POST OFFICE BOXES MAIN OFFICE STATIONS AND BRANCHES

Box No.s
1 - 1940 12551
2001 - 3314 12550
5000 - 5500 12551
8001 - 8005 12552
9220 - 9441 12555
9581 - 9585 12550
9603 - 9731 12555
9850 - 9850 12550
9952 - 9997 12555
10001 - 11240 12552

NAMED STREETS

Academy St 12550
Adams Rd 12550
Adonna Dr 12550
Albany Post Rd 12550
Aldendell Ct 12550
Algonquin Dr 12550
Alix Rd 12550
Allison Ave 12550
Alta Dr 12550
Ambassador Ln 12550
Amber Dr 12550
American Way 12550
Anchor Dr 12550
Anderson St 12550
Andrea Dr 12550
Angelina Aly 12550
Anita Ln 12550
Ann St 12550
Arbor Dr 12550
Archery Rd 12550
Arlington Pl 12550
Arrowhead Ct 12550
Ashley Dr 12550
Ashwood Ter 12550
Atwood Ln 12550
Austin Tyler Ct 12550
Auto Park Pl 12550
Autumn Ridge Way 12550
Avoca St 12550
Babes Ln 12550
Bainbridge Pl 12550
Baldwin Ln 12550
Balmville Ln, Rd & Ter 12550
Balsam Ln 12550
Baltsas Rd 12550
Banbury Way 12550
Bannerman View Dr 12550
Barbara Ct & Dr 12550
Barclay Mnr 12550
Barton St 12550
Bauer Ln 12550
Bay View Ter 12550
Beach St 12550
Beacon St 12550
Beaver Ct 12550
Becks Ln 12550
Beech St 12550
Beechwood Cir 12550
Belknap St 12550
Bellevue Rd 12550
Benkard Ave 12550
Bennett Rd & St 12550
Bens Way 12550
Benson Ave 12550
Berry Ln 12550
Bessie Ln 12550
Birchwood Ln 12550
Black Angus Ct 12550
Blake St 12550
Blossom Ln 12550
Blue Jay Dr 12550
Blueberry Ln 12550
Boulder Rd 12550
Brady Ave 12550
Brandywine Xing 12550
Breezy Knoll Dr 12550
Brewer Rd 12550
Briarwood Cres 12550
Bridge St 12550
Bridle Path 12550
Bright Star Dr 12550
Brighton Dr 12550
Broad St 12550
Broadway 12550
Brook Hollow Ln 12550
Brooker Dr S 12550
Brookside Ave 12550
Brookside Farms Rd 12550
Brookview Ln 12550
Bruce St 12550
Buckingham Dr 12550
Bunker Hill Rd 12550
Burning Tree Dr 12550
Bush Ave & Ln 12550
Calvin Ln 12550
Campbell St 12550
Candlestick Hill Rd 12550
Canterbury Dr 12550
Capital Ct 12550
Cardinal Ct 12550
Cargo Rd 12550
Carobene Ct 12550
Carolina Ct 12550
N Carpenter Ave 12550
Carriage Dr 12550
Carroll St 12550
Carson Ave 12550
Carter Ave & St 12550
Castle Ave & Ln 12550
Catalpa Rd 12550
Catherine St 12550

Cathy Dr 12550
Cedar Ct & St 12550
Celestial Way 12550
Center St 12550
Central Ave 12550
Centurion Ct 12550
Cerone Pl 12550
Chadsford Ln 12550
Chadwick Gdns & Pl 12550
Chambers St 12550
Champs Dr 12550
Chapel Rd 12550
Charles St 12550
Charlile Cir 12550
Chelsea View Ter 12550
Cherry Ln 12550
Chestnut Ln & St 12550
Chevy St 12550
Christie Rd 12550
Cindy Ln 12550
Circle Dr & Ln 12550
City Ter N 12550
Clarion Ct 12550
S Clark St 12550
Clinton St 12550
Cloud St 12550
Clover Ln 12550
Coach Ln 12550
Cobble Creek Dr 12550
Cochecton Tpke 12550
Cocoa Ln 12550
Colandrea Rd 12550
Colandrea Road Ext 12550
Cold Spring Ln 12550
S Colden St 12550
Colden Hill Rd 12550
Colt Pl 12550
Columbus Ave & Ln 12550
Commercial Pl 12550
Commonwealth Ave 12550
Concord St 12550
Congressional Dr 12550
Connolly Way 12550
Coranas Ln 12550
Corel Pl 12550
Coronation Path 12550
Corporate Blvd 12550
Cortland Dr 12550
Cortlandt Dr 12550
Corwin Ct 12550
Cory Ln 12550
Cottage Ave 12550
Countess Ct 12550
Country Meadow Ct 12550
Court Rd 12550
Courtney Ave 12550
Crab Apple Ct 12550
Creek Run Rd 12550
Crescent Ave 12550
Crest Rd 12550
Crestwood Ct 12550
Cronomer Hts Dr 12550
Cross St 12550
Crossroads Ct 12550
Crown Blvd 12550
Cucchiara Ln 12550
Dagny Dr 12550
Daisy Dr 12550
Dalewood Dr 12550
Dalfonso Rd 12550
Damato Dr 12550
Danskammer Rd 12550
Dapple Ter 12550
Dara Dr 12550
Dealer Dr 12550
Debra Pl 12550
Deer Run Rd 12550
Dees Way 12550
Deforest Ave 12550
Delafield Ln 12550
Delaware Rd 12550
Dene Rd 12550
Dennis Rd 12550
Devito Dr 12550
Dewey Dr 12550
Deyo Pl 12550
Diamond Ct 12550
Dickson St 12550
Disano Dr 12550
Distillery Path 12550
N & S Dix Ave 12550
Dogwood Ln & Pl 12550
Dogwood Hills Rd & Ter 12550
Dowling St 12550
Downing Ave & Way 12550
N Drury Ln 12550
Dubois St 12550
Dupont Ave 12550
Dutchess Ct 12550
Eagle Dr 12550
Eagle Height Pl 12550
Eastview Rd 12550
Echo Ln 12550
Eden Roc Rd 12550
Edgewood Dr & Ter 12550
Edward St 12550
Ellis Ave 12550
Elm St 12550
Elmhurst Ave 12550
Elmwood Pl 12550
End St 12550
Englebride Pl 12550
Enterprise Dr
  1-97 12550
  97-97 12552
  99-99 12555
  100-198 12550
Estate Blvd 12550
Eugene Dr 12550
Eunice Dr 12550
Evans Ct 12550
Express Dr 12550
Fabrizio Dr 12550
Fairview Ln 12550
Falcon Dr 12550
Fallview Dr 12550
Far Horizons Dr 12550
Farrell St 12550
Farrington St 12550
Favoriti Ave 12550
Fay St 12550
Federal St 12550
Fern Ave 12550
Fieldstone Ct 12550
Firemans Ln 12550
Firemans Lane Ext 12550
Five Oaks Dr 12550
Flamingo Dr 12550
Fleetwood Dr 12550
Flemming Dr 12550
Fletcher Dr N 12550
Floral Dr 12550
Florida Dr 12550
Forsythe Pl 12550
Fortune Dr 12550
Fostertown Dr & Rd 12550
Fowler Ave 12550
Foxwood Dr S 12550
Francis St 12550
Freedom Rd 12550
Friar Ln 12550
Front St 12550
Frozen Ridge Rd 12550
Fullerton Ave & Pl 12550
Gail Pl 12550
Gala Dr 12550
Galaxy Ln 12550
Galloway Ave 12550
Garden St 12550
Gardner St 12550
Gardnertown Rd 12550
Gardnertown Farms Rd 12550
Gargoyle Ln 12550
Gedney Way 12550
Genna Way 12550
Gida Rd 12550
Gidney Ave 12550
Gillespie Dr 12550
Glen Ln 12550
Gondolfo Dr 12550
Governor Dr 12550
Grand Ave & St 12550
Grande Vista Ct 12550
Grandview Dr 12550
Greenlawn Ave 12550
Greenwood Dr 12550
Gregory Way 12550
Greiner Rd 12550
Griener Rd 12550
Grimm Rd 12550
Grove Ct & St 12550
Gunsch Estate Dr 12550
Gusty Rd 12550
Hampton Pl 12550
Harcourt Cosman Dr 12550
Harvey Rd 12550
Hasbrouck St 12550
Hawthorne Ave 12550
Hdsn Vly Prof Plz 12550
Heather Cir 12550
Helene Ter 12550
Heming Way 12550
Hemlock Ln 12550
Henry Ave 12550
Hercules Ave 12550
Herman Ave 12550
Hibbing Way 12550
Hickory Hill Ln & Rd 12550
Hidden View Dr 12550
Hideaway Ln 12550
W High St 12550
High Point Cir 12550
Highland Ave & Ter 12550
Hill Ln & St 12550
Hill Run Rd 12550
Hillcrest Dr & Pl 12550
Hillside Ct 12550
Hilltop Ave 12550
Hinchcliffe Dr 12550
Hob St 12550
Holiday Park 12550
Hollenbeck Dr 12550
Holmes Rd 12550
Holt Ln 12550
Homewood Ave 12550
Hopeview Ct 12550
Horton Ln 12550
Howard Dr 12550
Hudson Ave 12550
Hudson Hills Dr 12550
Hudson View Dr & Ter 12550
Huff Ln 12550
Humphries Pl 12550
Hy Vue Cir, Ct & Dr 12550
Innis Ave 12550
Isis Dr 12550
Jacks Pond Rd 12550
Jamison Pl 12550
Jands Pl 12550
Jason Ct 12550
Jeanne Dr 12550
Jefwin Dr 12550
Jenny Ln 12550
Jessica Ct 12550
Jodi Dr 12550
Jodphur Ln 12550
Johanna Dr 12550
Johnes St 12550
S Johnston St 12550
Joseph X Mullins 12550
June Rd 12550
Karen Ct 12550
Katie Pl 12550
Kayla Ct 12550
Kennedy Pl 12550
Kenney Ct 12550
Kentucky Dr 12550
Kettle Ct 12550
Kim Marie Pl 12550
Kingsley Pl 12550
Knights Cir 12550
Kohl Ave 12550
Korosko Farm Rd 12550
Lafayette St 12550
Lake Dr & St 12550
Lakeside Rd 12550
Lakeview Dr 12550
Lancer Dr 12550
S Lander St 12550
Larrabee Ln 12550
Larter Ave 12550
Lattintown Rd 12550
Lauber Ln 12550
Laurie Ln 12550
Leary Ln 12550
Leeland Rd 12550
Leicht Pl 12550
Lena Ln 12550
Lenape Rd 12550
Leonard Ave 12550
Leroy Ave & Pl 12550
Leslie Rd 12550
Lester Rd 12550
Lester Clark Rd 12550
Levinson Heights Rd 12550
Lexington Dr 12550
Liberty St
  1-216 12550
  217-217 12551
  218-598 12550
  219-599 12550
Liberty Street Wh 12550
Lilac Ct 12550
Lilly St 12550
Lincoln Ter 12550
Linda Dr 12550
Linden Dr 12550
Liner Rd 12550
Little Britain Rd 12550
Little Brook Ln 12550
Little Country Rd 12550
Little Lane Rd 12550
Little Monument St 12550
Lloyd Rd 12550
Lockwood Ln 12550
Locust Ln & St 12550
Longview Dr 12550
Loscerbo Ln 12550
Lozier Ln 12550
Lutheran St 12550
Lynn Dr 12550
M And M Rd 12550
Mace Cir 12550
Madison Rose Ct 12550
Maggie Rd 12550
Magnolia Ln 12550
Maguire Way 12550
Magyar Dr 12550
Maine Ct & Dr 12550
Majestic Ct 12550
Mallard Dr 12550
Mandigo Pl 12550
Manzo Rd 12550
Maple Dr & St 12550
Maplewood Dr 12550
Marian Dr 12550
Mariners Ct 12550
Mark Ave 12550
Marlene Ct 12550
Marne Ave 12550
Mary Phyllis Ln 12550
Maryland Ct 12550
Massachusetts Dr 12550
Mattingly Way 12550
Maurice Ln 12550
Max Way 12550
Maywood Ln & Rd 12550
Mccall Pl 12550
Mccall Place Ext 12550
Mccord Dr 12550
Mcdonald St 12550
Mcdowell Pl 12550
Mcintosh Pl 12550
Mckinstry St 12550
Meadow Ave & St 12550
Meadow Hill Rd 12550
E & W Meadow Wind Ln 12550
Memorial Dr 12550
Merritt Ln 12550
Michelle Dr 12550
Midway Dr 12550
Mike Ruggerio Dr 12550
Militia Way 12550
Mill St 12550
N & S Miller Cir & St 12550
Mimosa Pl 12550
Miriam Way 12550
Mohican Rd 12550
Monarch Dr 12550
Monkey Run Rd 12550
Monroe St 12550
N Montgomery St 12550
Monument St 12550
Morley Cir 12550
Morningside Rd 12550
Morris Ave & Dr 12550
Mountainview Ave 12550
Muddle Ln 12550
Mullins Ln 12550
Nancy Ln 12550
Nelson Dr 12550
Neversink Dr 12550
New Rd & St 12550
Nicoll St 12550
Noah Pl 12550
Nob Cir & Ln 12550
Nobles Way 12550
Noel Dr 12550
North St 12550
Norton St 12550
Nott Pl 12550
Nottingham Rd 12550
O Herron Rd 12550
Oak Ln & St 12550
Oakwood Rd 12550
Odell Cir & St 12550
Ohio Dr 12550
Old Creek Rd 12550
Old Little Britain Rd 12550
Old North Plank Rd 12550
Old Pierces Rd 12550
Old Post Rd 12550
Old South Plank Rd 12550
Oliver Dr 12550
Orchard St 12550
Orchard Heights Dr 12550
Oriole Cir 12550
Orleans Rd 12550
Orr Ave 12550
Osage Ln 12550
Osprey Hill Dr 12550
Overdell Ln 12550
Overlook Dr & Pl 12550
Owens Rd 12550
Pacer Dr 12550
Paddock Pl 12550
Paffendorf Dr 12550
Palantine Ave 12550
Palomino Ter 12550
Pampas Ln 12550
Park Ave & Pl 12550
Parkview St N & S 12550
Parkwood Ln 12550
E & W Parmenter St 12550
Parr Cir 12550
Parr Lake Dr 12550
Parr Meadow Dr 12550
Pat Rd 12550
Patton Rd 12550
Paul Ave 12550
Pavillion Dr 12550
Peach Ter 12550
Penny Ln 12550
Peppermint Ln 12550
Pepsi Way 12550
Peter Ave 12550
Piccadilly Ct 12550
Pierces Rd 12550
N Pierpont Ave 12550
Pilla Dr 12550
Pine St 12550
Pine Meadow Farms Rd 12550
Pine Orchard Ln 12550
Pinnacle Blvd 12550
Plaine Ter 12550
Plank Rd 12550
Plattekill Tpke 12550
Pleasant Pl 12550
Pleasant Valley Way 12550
Pleasant View Ave 12550
Plum Ct 12550
Plymouth Rd 12550
Pomarico Dr 12550
Pommel Dr 12550
Pond Ridge Xing 12550
Pony Ter 12550
Poplar St 12550
Post Pl 12550
Potters Rdg 12550
Powder Mill Rd 12550
Powell Ave 12550
Powelton Cir & Rd 12550
Powelton Farms Rd 12550
Priand St 12550
Princess Ln 12550
Prospect St 12550
Putnam St 12550
Queens Way 12550
Racquet Rd 12550
Ramblewood Dr 12550
Ramona Rd 12550
Rayland Rd 12550
Red Oak Ter 12550
Regal Way 12550
Reggerio Rd 12550
Renwick St 12550
Revere Rd 12550
Richman Ave 12550
Ridgefield Ln 12550
Ridgeview Dr 12550
River Rd 12550
River View Ct & Pl 12550
Rivers Edge 12550
Rivers Watch 12550
Roan Ln 12550
Roberts Ln 12550
Robin Cir 12550
S Robinson Ave 12550
Rock Cut Cir & Rd 12550
Rockwood Dr 12550
Roe St 12550
Rogers Pl 12550
Roma Dr 12550
Roman Way 12550
Roosevelt Ave & Pl 12550
Rosaline Ln 12550
Route 17k 12550
Route 300 12550
Route 32 12550
Route 9w 12550
Roy Pl 12550
Royal Cir 12550
Rural Ln 12550
Russell Rd 12550
Russo Dr 12550
Rutland Ln 12550
Saddle Pl 12550
Sandalwood Dr 12550
Sara Ln 12550
Saratoga Rd 12550
Sarvis Ln 12550
Savannah Ln 12550
Scenic Dr 12550
Schullman Ln 12550
Scobie Dr 12550
Sean Ln 12550
Sequestered Rd 12550
Serenity Ln 12550
Shadowbrook Ln 12550
Shady Ln 12550
Shady Lane Ext 12550
Shelter Cv 12550
Sherman Dr 12550
Shipp St 12550
Shipwatch Dr 12550
Skyers Ln 12550
Sloane Rd 12550
Smith St 12550
South St 12550
Sparrow St 12550
Spencer Ave 12550
Spring St 12550
Spring Meadow Way 12550
Spring Square Business Park 12550
Spruce Ave 12550
Spur Ter 12550
Stacy Lee Dr 12550
Stanley Pl 12550
Stanton Rd 12550
Starrow Dr 12550
Stern Dr 12550
Stewart Ave 12550
Stewart Avenue Ext 12550
Still Hollow Rd 12550
Stillwater Ln 12550
Stirrup Dr 12550
E & W Stone St 12550
Stonegate Dr 12550
Stony Brook Ct 12550
Stony Run Rd 12550
Stonywood Dr 12550
Stori Rd 12550
Strawberry Ln 12550
W Street Rear 12550
Sulky Dr 12550
Summer Dr 12550
Summit Ridge Rd 12550
Sunday St 12550
Sunrise Dr & Ln 12550
Sunset Dr & Rd 12550
Sunset Cove Rd 12550
Surrey Pl 12550
Susan Dr 12550
Sycamore Dr 12550
Sylvan Park Dr 12550
Sylvester Ct 12550
Sylvia St 12550
Taffy Ln 12550
Taft Ave 12550
Tall Pines Dr 12550
Taylors Way 12550
Teal Ct 12550
Temple Ave 12550
Tenbrouck Ct 12550
Terry Ave 12550
Thomas Watt Dr 12550
Thompson St 12550
Three Point Pl 12550
Tighe Ave 12550
Timber Ridge Rd 12550
Tina Dr 12550
Todd Ln 12550
Toll House Ct 12550
Toms Ln 12550
Tower Rd 12550
Town Line Rd 12550
Townsend Ave 12550
Travis Ln 12550
Tree Hollow Ln 12550
Trotter Ln 12550
Tulip Ln 12550
Turkey Dr 12550
Tuskegee Rd 12550
Twin Gate Rd 12550
Ugo Dr 12550
Underhill Pl 12550
Union Ave 12550
Unity Pl 12550
Upper Ave 12550
Utopian Ct 12550
Valentine Rd 12550
Valley Ave 12550
Valley Forge Rd 12550
Valley View Dr 12550
Van Cleft Ave 12550
W Van Ness St 12550
Vanamee St 12550
Varick Homes 12550
Vermont Dr 12550
Victoria Dr 12550
Victory Ct 12550
Virginia Cir 12550
Vista Pl 12550
Walnut Ave 12550
Walsh Rd 12550
Wandering Dr 12550
Warden Cir 12550

Waring Rd 12550
Warren Rd 12550
Washington Ave, Ctr, Pl, St & Ter 12550
N & S Water St & Way 12550
Weaver Rd 12550
Wells Rd 12550
Wenmar Dr 12550
Wesley Ct 12550
West Park & St W 12550
Westbrook Rd 12550
Westwood Dr 12550
Weyants Ln 12550
Whisper Ln 12550
White St 12550
White Birch Dr 12550
White Sails Dr 12550
Whitehill Ter 12550
Wilkins St 12550
Willella Pl 12550
Willets Way 12550
S William St 12550
Williams Ave 12550
Williamsburg Ct & Dr 12550
Willow St 12550
Wilson Ave & St 12550
Winding Ln 12550
Windswept Ln 12550
Windwood Dr 12550
Windy Crest Ln 12550
Winona Ave 12550
Wintergreen Ave 12550
Wisner Ave 12550
Wood St & Ter 12550
Woodlawn Ter 12550
Yeoman Rd 12550

NUMBERED STREETS

All Street Addresses 12550

NEWCOMB NY

General Delivery 12852
General Delivery 12879

POST OFFICE BOXES MAIN OFFICE STATIONS AND BRANCHES

Box No.s
All PO Boxes 12852

NAMED STREETS

All Street Addresses 12852

NIAGARA FALLS NY

General Delivery 14302

POST OFFICE BOXES MAIN OFFICE STATIONS AND BRANCHES

Box No.s
1 - 626 14302
1 - 640 14305
1 - 620 14304
408 - 408 14303
661 - 952 14302
667 - 823 14303
721 - 778 14304
873 - 1262 14303
1000 - 1102 14302
1001 - 1120 14304
1401 - 3060 14302
2001 - 2578 14301
3001 - 3120 14304
3128 - 3255 14303
4001 - 5000 14304
8888 - 9009 14302
9002 - 9002 14304

NAMED STREETS

A St
1-99 14303
400-769 14304
3300-3399 14303
Aaron Griffin Way 14305
Acheson Dr 14303
Akshar Ct 14304
Allen Ave 14303
Amy Dr 14304
Angelo Ct 14303
Apple Ct 14304
Apple Walk 14305
Armory Pl 14301
Arrowwood Pl 14304
Ashland Ave 14301
Ashwood Dr 14304
Augustus Pl 14301
Avfuels Cir 14304
B St
1-99 14303
495-708 14304
3300-3399 14303
Baker Ave 14304
Barberry Pl 14304
Barton St 14305
Bath Ave 14305
Beckwith Ave 14304
Beech Ave 14305
Beechwood Cir 14304
Belden Pl 14303
Bell St 14305
Bellreng Dr 14304
Benjamin Dr 14304
Binkley St 14304
Birch Ave & Ct 14305
Black Creek Dr 14304
Blanchard Ave 14304
Blank Rd 14304
Blewett Ave 14304
Blue Heron Ct 14304
Bollier Ave 14304
Brandi Dr 14304
Brian Ln 14304
E Britton Dr 14304
W Britton Dr 14305
Brookhaven Dr 14304
Brookside Dr 14304
Buffalo Ave
1-4699 14303
4700-10199 14304
Builders Way 14304
Byrd Ave 14303
C St
1-99 14303
524-654 14304
3300-3399 14303
Calumet Ave 14305
Caravelle Dr 14304
Carol Ct 14304
Carrie Dr 14304
Carroll St 14305
Cayuga Dr & St 14304
Cayuga Drive Ext 14304
Cedar Ave 14301
Center St 14304
Centre Ave & Ct 14305
Champlain Ave 14304
Chapin Ave 14301
Charles Ave 14304
Chasm Ave 14305
Cherry Ln 14304
Chester Ave 14305
Chestnut Ave 14305
Chestnut Pl 14304
Chilton Ave 14301
Christi Ln 14304
Church Ave 14303
Cleveland Ave 14305
Cliff St 14305
Clifton St 14305
Cloverleaf Ct 14304
College Ave & Ter 14305
Colomba Dr 14305
Colonial Dr
6800-7799 14305
7800-8399 14304
Colvin Blvd 14304
Connecticut Ave 14305
Connecting Rd 14304
Coseglia St 14304
Council St 14304
W Creek Dr 14304
Creekside Dr 14304
Creekside Pkwy 14305
Crescent Dr 14305
Crestview Dr & Ln 14304
Crestwood Ct 14304
Crick Ct 14301
Cudaback Ave 14303
D St
1-99 14303
452-608 14304
3300-3399 14303
Danielle Dr 14304
Dariness St 14304
David Dr 14304
Dawn Dr 14304
Dean Brown Dr 14304
Debbie Dr 14304
Deborah Ln 14304
Deidre Ct 14304
Delancey Rd 14305
Delaware Ave 14305
Dell Dr 14304
Demunda Ave 14304
Depot Ave 14305
Deuro Dr 14304
Deveaux St 14305
Deveaux Woods Dr 14305
Devlin Ave 14304
Diamond Park Ln 14305
Disney Dr 14304
Divide Rd 14305
Division Ave 14305
Dogwood Pl 14304
Donna Dr 14304
Dorchester Rd 14305
Driftwood Dr 14304
Duane Ave 14305
Dudley Ave 14303
Duluth St 14305
Eagle Hts 14305
Edgewood Dr 14304
Edison Ave 14304
Effie Dr 14304
Elaine Dr 14304
E Elderberry Pl 14304
Elm Ct 14305
Elmwood Ave 14301
Elsa Pl 14304
Ely Ave 14303
Energy Blvd 14304
Ent Ave 14304
Ethel Ave 14305
Expressway Vlg 14304
F St 14303
Fairfield Ave 14305
Fairway Dr 14305
Falls St 14303
Fashion Outlet Blvd 14304
Ferchen St 14304
Ferry Ave 14301
Forest Ave 14301
Fort Ave 14303
Fox Ave 14305
Franklin Dr 14304
Frontier Ave 14304
G St 14303
Garden Ave 14305
Garfield Ave 14305
Garlow Rd 14304
Garrett Ave 14305
Gillette Ct 14305
Girard Ave 14304
Glenn St 14305
Goodyear Dr 14304
Granby Ave 14304
Grand Ave 14301
Grauer Rd 14305
Greenview Rd 14304
Greenview Ter 14305
Greenwald Ave 14304
Griffon Ave 14304
Gross Dr 14304
Grove Ave 14305
Haeberle Ave 14301
Harrison Ave 14305
Haseley Dr 14304
Hawthorne Pl 14305
Hennepin Ave 14304
Henry Ave 14304
Hermitage Rd 14305
Hickory Ln 14304
Highland Ave 14305
Hillcrest St 14303
Hird St 14304
Holly Pl 14303
Homestead Ave 14304
Hope Blvd 14305
Hudson Dr 14305
Hunt St 14304
Hyde Park Blvd
1-29 14303
31-351 14303
353-499 14303
500-1300 14301
1302-1398 14301
1400-5999 14305
S Hyde Park Blvd 14303
Independence Ave 14301
Iroquois St 14303
Isherwood Dr 14305
Jackson Dr 14304
Jacob Pl 14305
Jagow Rd 14304
James Ave 14305
Jane Dr 14304
Jayne Pl 14304
Jennifer Ct 14304
Jerauld Ave 14305
Joann Ct 14304
Joanne Cir N & S 14304
John Ave 14304
John St 14305
Johnson St 14304
Joliet Ave 14305
Jordan Dr 14304
Jordan Gdns 14305
Juron Dr 14304
Katherine Dr 14304
Kay Ellen Dr 14305
Kenneth Ct 14304
Kies Ave, Ct & St 14304
King Fisher Ln 14304
Kinross St 14304
Kirkbridge Dr 14304
Kirsch Dr 14304
Kline Rd 14304
Krug Ave 14304
Krull Pkwy 14304
Kusum Ct 14304
La Salle Ave 14301
Lafayette Ave & Cir 14305
Lake Geneva Ct 14304
Lake Mead Rd 14304
Lakeside Ct & Dr 14304
Lancelot Dr 14304
Langley St 14304
Laughlin Dr 14304
Laur Rd 14304
Laurel Rd 14304
Lawson Dr 14304
Lee Dr 14304
Lehigh Ct 14305
Lewiston Rd 14305
Liberty Ave 14305
Liberty Cir 14304
Liberty Dr 14304
Lincoln Pl & St 14305
Lindbergh Ave 14304
Linwood Ave 14305
Lisa Ln 14304
Livingston Ave 14303
Lockport Rd
2000-2199 14304
2601-2897 14305
2899-7299 14305
7700-10499 14304
Lockport St 14305
Loree Cir 14304
Loretta Dr 14304
Louisiana Ave 14305
Lozina Dr 14304
Luick Ave 14304
Luther St 14304
Mackenna Ave 14303
Macklem Ave & Ct 14305
Madison Ave 14305
Main St
100-199 14303
401-453 14301
436-451 14304
452-452 14301
454-640 14301
615-615 14302
615-615 14303
641-1399 14301
642-1398 14301
1400-2799 14305
Mallard Ct 14304
Maltondi Ave 14301
Mang Ave 14304
Manor Rd 14304
Maple Ave 14305
Marine Memorial Dr 14304
E & W Market St 14301
Maryland Ave 14305
N Mason Ct 14304
Mayflower Rd 14305
Mayle Ct 14305
Mcguire St 14304
Mckinley Ave 14305
Mckoon Ave 14305
Meadowbrook Rd 14305
Memorial Pkwy
100-499 14303
500-599 14301
Michael Ct 14305
Michigan Ave 14305
Mil Pine Plz 14304
Military Rd
880-1298 14304
1300-3399 14304
3400-4799 14305
N Military Rd 14304
S Military Rd 14304
Miller Rd 14304
Mohawk Pkwy 14304
Monroe Ave 14303
Monteagle St 14305
Mooradian Dr 14304
Morley Ave 14305
Moschel Ct 14304
Mourning Dove Ln 14304
Mueller Ct 14304
Munson Ave 14305
Nesbitt Dr 14304
Nevada Ave 14305
New Rd 14304
New Jersey Ave 14305
Niagara Ave 14305
Niagara Rd 14304
Niagara St 14303
Niagara Falls Blvd 14304
Nickis Ln 14304
Nicole Ct & Dr 14304
Niemel Dr 14304
Norman St 14305
North Ave 14305
Norwood Ave 14305
Oak Pl 14304
Olaughlin Dr 14303
Old Falls Blvd 14304
Old Falls St 14303
Olmstead St 14304
Ontario Ave 14305
Orchard Pkwy 14301
Orleans Ave 14303
Osborne Ct 14303
Osprey Ln 14304
Otis Dr 14304
Packard Ct 14301
Packard Rd
100-3198 14303
3200-4099 14303
4600-8799 14304
Panama St 14305
Park Dr 14304
Park Pl 14301
Parkview Dr 14305
Parkwood Ln 14304
Pasadena Ave 14304
Patel Dr 14304
Patricia Dr 14305
Pear Ave 14304
Penn St 14305
Pennsylvania Ave 14305
Perry Ave 14304
Pershing Ave 14304
Petroleum St 14305
Pierce Ave
700-899 14305
1100-2799 14301
Pine Ave 14301
Pinelake Dr 14304
Plakerm Ave 14305
Plaza Dr 14304
Plum Walk 14305
Point Ave 14304
Pomeroy Ave 14305
Portage Rd
100-499 14303
500-1399 14301
Porter Rd
2600-4699 14305
4900-9999 14304
Portland St 14305
Pretoria St 14305
Prospect Park & St 14303
Prospect Pointe 14303
Purple Martin Ln 14304
Quain Pl 14304
Quarry Rd 14304
Quay St 14303
Rainbow Blvd, Brg & Mall
N 14303
Ralph Ct 14304
Rankine Rd 14305
Rapids Blvd 14305
Read Ave 14304
Rebecca Dr 14304
Recovery Rd 14304
Reynolds Rd 14304
Rhode Island Ave 14305
Richmond Ave 14305
Rishan Ct 14304
River Rd 14304
W Rivershore Dr 14304
Riverside Dr 14303
Riverview Ave 14305
Robert Dr 14304
Robinson Ct 14303
Rock Dove Ln 14304
Roger Dr 14304
Rohr St 14304
Roosevelt Ave 14305
Rose Ct 14305
Roselle Ave 14305
Royal Ave 14303
Ruben Dr 14304
Sabre Park 14304
Sadlo Dr 14304
Saint Johns Pkwy 14304
Saint Joseph Rd 14304
Saint Paul St 14305
Samantha Ct 14304
Sandpiper Trl 14304
Saunders Settlement Rd
995-997 14305
999-1499 14305
1500-2145 14304
4800-5199 14305
Savannah St 14305
Sawyer Dr 14304
Schultz St 14304
Seneca Ave 14305
Seneca Pkwy 14304
Service Rd 14304
Seymour Ave 14305
Shantz Ave 14304
Sherman Ave 14305
Sherwood Ave 14301
Simmons Ave
3300-3899 14303
5600-5699 14304
Skylark Ln 14304
South Ave 14305
Spring St 14305
Sprivend St 14303
Spruce Ave 14301
Steele Cir 14304
Stephenson Ave 14304
Stoelting St 14304
Stoltz Rd 14304
Summit View Pl 14304
Sunnydale Dr 14304
Sunnyside Dr 14304
Sunset Dr 14304
Sweet Home Rd 14305
Sy Rd 14304
Sycamore Dr 14304
Sylvan Pl 14304
Tawny Dr 14304
Taylor Dr 14304
Tennessee Ave 14305
Terrace Dr 14305
Theresa Ln 14305
Thomas Loop 14304
Thompson St 14304
Thorndale Ave 14305
Thornwoods Dr 14304
Tmark Dr 14304
Tomson Ave 14304
Towhee Ct 14304
Townsend Pl 14301
Tronolone Pl 14301
Troy Ave 14304
Tuscarora Rd 14304
University Ct 14305
Utzig Dr 14304
Valle Dr 14304
Van Rensselaer Ave 14305
Vanderbilt Ave 14305
Violet Cir 14304
Virginia Ave 14305
Wagner Dr 14304
Walmore Rd 14304
Walnut Ave 14301
Ward Rd 14304
Washington St
2400-2599 14304
3900-4299 14305
Webb Pl 14303
Welch Ave 14303
Wendt Dr 14304
Weston Ave 14305
Westwood Dr 14305
Wheatfield Ave 14304
Whirlpool St
500-599 14301
601-899 14301
1401-2197 14305
2199-2699 14305
2701-2999 14305
N & S Whitham Dr 14304
Whitney Ave 14301
Wildwood Dr & Pkwy 14304
Willard Ave 14305
Williams Rd 14304
Willow Ave 14305
Willow Ln 14304
Wing Ct 14304
Witkop Ave 14304
Witmer Rd 14305
Witmer Industrial Est 14305
Woodard Ave 14305

Woodland Ave 14304
Woodland Pl 14305
Woodlawn Ave 14301
Woodside Pl 14304
Woodthrush Ct 14304
Wurl St 14304
Wyoming Ave 14305
York Rd 14304
Young St 14304
Ziblut Ct 14304
Zito Dr 14304

NUMBERED STREETS

1st Ave 14304
1st St 14303
2nd Ave 14304
2nd St
200-299 14303
400-499 14301
3rd Ave 14304
3rd St
100-399 14303
400-799 14301
4th Ave 14304
4th St
1-399 14303
400-799 14301
5th St 14303
400-599 14301
6th St 14303
400-699 14301
7th St 14301
8th St
400-799 14301
1400-1699 14305
9th St 14303
500-799 14301
2400-3499 14305
10th St 14303
500-799 14301
1600-2899 14305
11th St
1000-1399 14301
1400-2399 14305
12th St
100-499 14303
500-599 14301
13th St
100-499 14303
600-1399 14301
1400-2999 14305
14th St
200-399 14303
2300-2399 14305
15th St
200-299 14303
500-1399 14301
1400-2399 14305
16th St
400-499 14303
500-899 14301
1600-2399 14305
17th St
400-499 14303
500-1399 14301
1400-3299 14305
18th St
100-499 14303
500-1399 14301
1400-2199 14305
19th St
300-499 14303
500-1299 14301
20th St
400-499 14303
500-1199 14301
2700-3099 14305
21st St
400-499 14303
500-699 14301
2200-2999 14305
22nd St
200-499 14303
500-1399 14301
1400-2999 14305
23rd St
400-499 14303
500-699 14301
2800-3199 14305
24th St
100-499 14303
500-1399 14301
1400-2699 14305
25th St
300-499 14303
500-699 14301
26th St
400-499 14303
500-699 14301
27th St
100-499 14303
500-1399 14301
1400-2799 14305
28th St 14301
29th St
500-899 14301
2400-2599 14305
30th St
200-299 14303
500-699 14301
31st St 14301
32nd St 14303
33rd St 14301
34th St 14301
35th St 14301
36th St 14303
600-699 14301
37th St
300-399 14303
602-699 14301
38th St
300-499 14303
600-699 14301
39th St
400-499 14303
500-699 14301
47th St 14304
48th St 14305
55th St 14304
56th St 14304
57th St 14304
58th St 14304
59th St 14304
60th St 14304
61st St 14304
62nd St 14304
63rd St 14304
65th St 14304
66th St 14304
S 67th 14304
S 68th 14304
69th St 14304
70th St 14304
71st St 14304
72nd St 14304
73rd St 14304
74th St 14304
75th St 14304
76th St 14304
77th St 14304
78th St 14304
79th St 14304
80th St 14304
81st St 14304
82nd St 14304
83rd St 14304
S 84th 14304
85th St 14304
S 86th 14304
S 87th 14304
88th St 14304
89th St 14304
90th St 14304
S 91st 14304
92nd St 14304
93rd St 14304
94th St 14304
95th St 14304
96th St 14304
97th St 14304
98th St 14304
99th St 14304
100th St 14304
101st St 14304
102nd St 14304
103rd St 14304
104th St 14304

OZONE PARK NY

POST OFFICE BOXES MAIN OFFICE STATIONS AND BRANCHES

Box No.s
All PO Boxes 11417

NAMED STREETS

Albert Rd 11417
Arion Rd 11417
Atlantic Ave 11416
Belmont Ave 11417
Boss St 11417
Bristol Ave 11417
Centreville St 11417
Chicot Ct 11417
Cohancy St 11417
N Conduit Ave 11417
Crossbay Blvd 11417
Culloden Pl 11416
Desarc Rd 11417
Digby Pl 11416
Doxey Pl 11417
Drew St 11416
Dumont Ave 11417
Eckford Ave 11417
Forbell St 11416
Glenmore Ave 11417
Glerradw St 11416
Gold Rd 11417
Hawtree St 11417
Huron St 11417
Lafayette St 11417
Liberty Ave 11417
Linden Blvd 11417
Magnolia Ct 11417
Muriel Ct 11417
Old South Rd 11417
Peconic St 11417
Pitkin Ave 11417
Plattwood Ave 11417
Raleigh St 11417
Redding St 11417
Rico Pl 11417
Rockaway Blvd
8000-8098 11416
8100-9099 11416
9100-9198 11417
9200-10799 11417
Rosita Rd 11417
Silver Rd 11417
Sitka St 11417
Spritz Rd 11417
Sutter Ave 11417
Tahoe St 11417
Tridarai St 11417
Whitelaw St 11417
Woodhaven Blvd
9400-9498 11416
9529-10199 11416
10321-10399 11417
Woodhaven Ct 11416

NUMBERED STREETS

75th St
9400-9799 11416
10500-10799 11417
76th St
9400-9799 11416
10500-10799 11417
77th St
9400-10199 11416
10500-10799 11417
78th St
9400-10199 11416
10500-10598 11417
10600-10799 11417
10801-13299 11417
79th St 11417
80th St
9400-10199 11416
10500-13299 11417
81st St
9500-10299 11416
10700-13198 11417
82nd Pl 11416
82nd St
9500-9799 11416
13200-13299 11417
83rd St
9401-9697 11416
13200-13399 11417
84th St
9400-10250 11416
10501-13197 11417
85th St
9400-9799 11416
13200-13399 11417
86th St
9400-10250 11416
10500-13399 11417
87th St
9400-9799 11416
10500-13399 11417
88th St
9400-9498 11416
9500-10250 11416
10500-13400 11417
13402-13798 11417
89th St
9500-10250 11416
10300-13299 11417
90th St
9500-10200 11416
10202-10298 11416
10300-10800 11417
10802-13298 11417
91st St
9500-10200 11416
10300-10799 11417
92nd St
9500-10199 11416
10300-10498 11417
93rd St
9401-9497 11416
10300-10799 11417
94th Ave 11416
94th Pl 11417
94th St
9424-9498 11416
9500-10199 11416
10300-13799 11417
95th Ave 11416
95th Pl 11417
95th St
9400-10199 11416
10300-14999 11417
15001-15099 11417
96th Pl 11417
96th St
9400-9499 11416
10300-13800 11417
97th Ave 11416
97th St
9400-10199 11416
10300-13799 11417
98th St
9500-10199 11416
10300-10999 11417
99th Ave 11416
99th Pl 11417
99th St
9700-10199 11416
10300-10399 11417
10401-10499 11417
100th St
9401-9697 11416
9699-10199 11416
10300-10499 11417
10501-13299 11417
101st Ave 11416
101st Rd 11416
101st St
9500-10199 11416
10300-10414 11417
10416-13298 11417
102nd Ave 11416
102nd Rd 11416
102nd St
9401-9497 11416
9499-10199 11416
10300-10499 11417
103rd Ave 11417
103rd Dr 11417
103rd Rd 11417
103rd St
9500-10199 11416
10300-10799 11417
10801-10951 11417
104th St
9343-9403 11416
10300-10799 11417
105th St
9500-10199 11416
10300-13299 11417
106th Ave 11417
106th St
9301-9397 11416
10300-13299 11417
107th Ave 11417
107th St
9400-10199 11416
10300-13299 11417
108th Ave & St 11417
109th Ave 11417
133rd Ave 11417
134th Ave & Rd 11417
135th Dr & Rd 11417
149th Ave 11417
150th Rd 11417

PLATTSBURGH NY

General Delivery 12901

POST OFFICE BOXES MAIN OFFICE STATIONS AND BRANCHES

Box No.s
All PO Boxes 12901

NAMED STREETS

Abby Way 12901
Abenaki Rd 12901
S Acres Rd 12901
S Acres Main Way 12901
Ada Ct 12901
Adams Dr 12901
Addams Rd 12901
Addoms St 12901
Adirondack Ln 12901
Adirondack Hall 12901
Aiken Ct 12903
Airport Ln 12903
Alabama Ave 12903
Alana Way 12903
Alexis Ln 12901
Alexs Way 12901
Alford Blvd 12901
Algonquin Park 12901
Allen Rd & St 12901
Alpert Ln 12901
Ampersand Dr 12901
Anderson Rd 12901
Angel Ave 12901
Applewood Dr 12901
Archie Bordeau Rd 12901
Area Development Dr 12901
Arizona Ave 12903
Arkansas Ave 12903
Arnold Rd 12901
Ash St 12901
Ashley Rd 12901
Aspen Ct 12901
Autumn Dr 12901
Bailey Ave 12901
Ball St 12901
Baltimore Way 12903
Banker Rd 12901
Banks Hall 12901
Bannu Ln 12901
Barton Rd 12901
Battery St 12901
Bay Plz & Rd 12901
Beach Rd 12901
Beacon Way 12901
Beas Way 12901
Beaumont St 12901
Beekman St 12901
Bell Rd 12901
Belmont Ave 12901
Benny Blake Rd 12901
Bernards Way 12901
Big Hank Plaza Rd 12901
Birch St 12901
Birchwood Dr 12901
Blaine Rd 12901
Blair Rd 12901
Blake Rd 12901
Blew Ln 12901
Blue Heron Way 12901
Bluff Point Dr 12901
Booth Dr 12901
Bouchard Dr 12901
N Bowl Ln 12901
Bowman St 12901
Boynton Ave 12901
Bradford Rd 12901
Brand Hollow Rd 12901
Brandell Dr 12901
Brandywine Ln 12901
Breezy Point Ln 12901
Breyette Way 12901
Bridge St 12901
Brinkerhoff St 12901
Bristol Rd 12901
Broad St 12901
Broadway Rd 12901
Broderick Rd 12901
Brooks Bend Rd 12901
Brookview Dr 12901
Brown Rd 12901
Bucci Dr 12901
Buckley Rd 12901
Burke Rd 12901
Burnell Ln 12901
Bushey Blvd 12901
Butler Rd 12901
C V Way 12901
Caitlin Way 12903
Calbi Way 12901
Calkins Rd 12901
Camfield Way 12901
Camp Red Cloud Rd 12901
Can Am Dr 12901
Canestota Dr 12901
Carbide Rd 12901
Cardinal Ct 12901
Carlton Dr 12901
Carmel Dr 12901
Caroline St 12901
Carter Ct 12901
N & S Catherine St 12901
Cayuga Rd 12901
Cedar Ln & St 12901
Cedar Hedge Rd 12901
Cedar Ledge Ln 12901
Cedarwood Ln 12901
Cemetery Rd 12901
Centre Dr 12901
Champlain Dr & St 12901
Chantecler Ct 12901
Charlene Dr 12901
Charles Way 12901
Chasands Dr 12901
Chenango Rd 12901
Cherry St 12901
Christiansen Dr 12901
Circle Grv 12901
City Hall Pl 12901
Cl Stone Dr 12901
Clay Dr 12901
S Cliff Manor Dr 12901
Clifford Dr 12901
Clinton St 12901
Clinton Point Dr 12901
Club Rd 12903
Coastland Dr 12901
Cogan Ave 12901
Colby Rd 12901
College Ave 12901
Colligan Pt Rd 12901
Collins Way 12901
Colorado Ave 12903
Commodore Thomas
Macdonough Hwy 12901
Concord Ave 12901
Conifer Cir 12901
Connecticut Rd 12903
Consumer Sq 12901
Cook Ln & Rd 12901
Cooper Dr 12901
Cornelia St 12901
Couch St 12901
Country Ln 12901
W Court St 12901
Crescent Dr 12901
Crestview Dr 12901
Crete Blvd 12901
Crimson Way 12901
Cross Rd 12901
Crown Point Rd 12901
Cubb Cir 12901
Cumberland Ave 12901
Cumberland Head Rd 12901
Cusprinie Way 12901
Dale Ave 12901
Daniels Way 12901
Davies Ln 12901
Day Dr 12901
Daytona Blvd 12901
Dean Ln 12901
Debra Ln 12901
Deepdale Rd 12901
Deer Run 12901
Defredenburgh Hall 12901
Degrandpre Way 12901
Deland Way 12901
Della Dr 12901
Delord St 12901
Dennis Ave & Ln 12901
Deon Way 12901
Diana Way 12901
Dickson Point Rd 12901
Distribution Way 12901
Dock St 12901
Dogwood Ave 12901
Dorchester Dr 12901
Dormitory Dr 12903
Douglaston Dr 12901
Downs Dr 12901
Draper Ave 12901
Dubuque Way 12901
Dukette Rd 12901
Dunning Way 12901
Durand Rd & St 12901
Durkee St 12901
Dutton Ct 12901
Eddie Dr 12901
Edgewater Est 12901
Edgewood Blvd 12901
Eleanor Way 12901
Elizabeth St 12901
Elm St 12901
Emergency Services
Dr 12903
Erin Ave 12901
Estate Dr 12901
Etc Cir 12901

Ethel Way 12901
Evergreen St 12901
Everleth Dr 12901
Facteau Ave 12901
Fairway Dr 12901
Fay Ln 12901
Feathers Dr 12901
Ferris Ct 12901
Filion Way 12901
Finlay Dr 12901
Firefighters Way 12901
Firehouse Ln 12901
First St 12901
Fiske Ln 12901
Fjord Dr 12901
Flaglar Dr 12901
Flanagan Dr 12901
Fleming Way 12901
Flora Oaks Dr 12901
Florida Ave 12903
Flynn Ave 12901
Foliage Ln 12901
Fort Brown Dr 12903
Four Seasons Dr 12901
Fourth Hole Dr 12901
Fox Farm Rd 12901
Foxfire Dr 12901
Franklin Ave 12901
Fredworth Way 12901
Freeland Way 12901
Gadbois Dr 12901
Garrow Way 12901
Gary Way 12901
E Gate 12901
Gateway Dr 12901
Gebo Way 12901
Genesee Ln 12901
George St 12901
Getman Rd 12901
Gilmour Ln 12901
Glen Dr 12901
Gleneagle Dr 12901
Goff Ave 12901
Golf Course Rd 12903
Gonyo Way 12901
Goodspeed Rd 12901
Grace Ave 12901
Graham Dr 12901
Grand Isle Way 12903
Grant St 12901
Gravelly Point Dr 12901
Graves Ln 12901
Green St 12901
Green Lawn Rd 12901
Greentree Dr 12901
Gregory Ln 12901
Greta Howe Ln 12901
Grigmoore Dr 12901
Grigware Rd 12901
Gunboat Ln 12901
Gus Lapham Ln 12901
Guy Way 12901
Haley Dr 12901
Halsey Ct 12901
Hamilton St 12901
Hammond Ln 12901
Haniko Ln 12901
Hardy Rd 12901
Harlan Dr 12901
Harmony Ln 12901
Harrington Hall 12901
Harris Way 12901
Hartwell St 12901
Harvey Way 12901
Haynes Rd 12901
Hazleray Dr 12901
Healey Ave 12901
Heavenly Acres Dr 12901
Helen St 12901
Heritage Dr 12901
Heywood Way 12901
Hickory St 12901
Hidden Pines Dr 12901
W Hill Dr & Rd 12901
Hill Top Way 12901
Hillcrest Ave 12901

Hobbs Rd 12901
Holcombe Ct 12901
Holland Ave 12901
Homestead Dr 12901
Honey Dr 12901
Hood Hall 12901
Hope Dr 12901
Huntington Dr 12901
Hyde Ave 12901
Ianelli Ave 12901
Idaho Ave 12903
Imperial Ave 12901
Independence Dr 12901
Indian Bay Way 12901
Industrial Blvd 12901
Iowa St 12903
Irish Settlement Rd 12901
Iroquois St 12901
Island View Way 12901
Jane Ln 12901
Jay St 12901
Jefferson Rd 12901
Jeffrey Ln 12901
Jennifer Dr 12901
Jerry Dr 12901
Jersey Swamp Rd 12901
Johnson Ave 12901
Joshua Dr 12901
Joyce Ct 12901
Jubert Ln 12901
S Junction Rd 12901
Justin Dr 12901
Kansas Ave 12903
Kastner Rd 12901
Katherine Dr 12901
Kaycee Loop Rd 12901
Kellogg Ct 12901
Kelly Rd 12901
Kelvin Ln 12901
Kemp Ln 12901
Kennedy Ave 12901
Kensington Rd 12901
Kent Ln 12901
Kent Hall 12901
Kentucky St 12903
Kim Ct 12901
Labarge Dr 12901
Labarre St 12901
Lafayette St 12901
Lake Breeze Dr 12901
Lake Forest Dr 12903
Lake Shore Rd 12901
Lakeland Dr 12901
Lakeshore Dr 12901
Lakeside Ct 12901
Lakeview Dr 12901
Latinville Dr 12901
Latour Ave 12901
Lauradee Dr 12901
Laurel Ct 12901
Laurentian Way 12903
Layman Ln 12901
Leblanc Ln 12901
Leclair Cul De Sac 12901
Leonard Ave 12901
Lewis Ct 12901
Lexington Ave 12901
Lighthouse Rd 12901
Lincoln Ln 12901
Linda Ln 12901
Loch Ln 12901
Locklin Rd 12901
Locust St 12901
Lorraine St 12901
Louisiana Ave 12903
Lozier Pl 12901
Lts St 12901
Lynde St 12901
Lynn Ave 12901
Lyon St 12901
Lyons Rd 12901
Macdonough St 12901
Macdonough Hall 12901
Macey Ln 12901
Macomb St 12901
Macomb Hall 12901

Main Mill St 12901
Maine Rd 12903
Makara Dr 12901
Mallard Dr 12901
Manor Dr 12901
Mansfield Dr 12901
Maple St 12901
Maple Pond Dr 12901
Marcy Ln 12901
Margaret St 12901
Margaret Sanger Ln 12901
Marie Dr 12901
Marine Village Rd 12901
Marion Dr & St 12901
Mark Rd 12901
Martina Cir 12901
Maryland Rd 12903
Mason Dr 12901
Mason Hall 12901
Massachusetts St 12903
Matt Ave 12901
Matthew Way 12901
Mccarthy Dr 12901
Mcdowell Way 12901
Mcgaulley Ave 12901
Mcgee Rd 12901
Mckinley Ave 12901
Mcmartin St 12901
Meadowlark 12901
Meadowvale Rd 12901
Melody Ln 12901
Michaele Ave 12901
Middle Rd 12901
Middle Bay Rd 12901
Mildred Blvd 12901
Military Tpke 12901
Miller St 12901
Miner Rd 12901
Miranda Dr 12901
Mobile Home Dr 12901
Moffit Hall 12901
Moffitt Rd 12901
Mohawk Rd 12901
Mohican Ln 12901
Monroe Way 12901
Montana Dr 12903
Montcalm Ave 12901
Monty Rd & St 12901
Mooney Bay Dr 12901
Moreau Way 12903
Morrison Ave 12901
Mountain View Cir 12901
Museum Way 12903
Nancy Dr 12901
Nelson Rd 12901
Nepco Way 12903
Nevada Oval 12903
New St 12901
New Hampshire Rd 12903
New York Rd 12903
Newell Ave 12901
Nichols Ave 12901
Nickel St 12901
Nightengale Dr 12901
Nomad Dr 12901
North St 12901
Northern Ave 12903
Northern Pride Way 12901
Northway Ct 12901
O Connell Way 12901
Oak St 12901
Oakland Dr 12901
Ohio Rd 12903
Old Dock Rd 12901
Oliver Ct 12901
Olivetti Pl 12901
Onondaga Ln 12901
Oswego Ln 12901
Otter Crk 12901
Overlook Cir 12901
Palmer St 12901
Pardy Rd 12901
Park Ave W 12901
Patriot Dr 12901
Paula Way 12901
Pear St 12901

Pellerin Rd 12901
Penn Ave 12901
Penny Cir 12901
Pepper Ridge Dr 12901
Peru St
5300-5390 12903
5363-5389 12901
5391-5599 12901
S Peru St 12901
Peryea Dr 12901
Pike St 12901
Pine Ave & St 12901
Pine Tree Dr 12901
Pinewood Dr 12901
Pinnacle Way 12901
Plant St 12901
S Platt St 12901
Plattsburgh Ave & Plz 12901
Plattsburgh Rv Park Rd 12901
Plaza Blvd 12901
Pleasant St 12901
Pleasant Acres Rd 12901
Pleasant Ridge Rd 12901
N Point Rd 12901
Point Au Roche Rd 12901
Point Cliff Dr 12901
Point View Ter 12901
Pond St 12901
Poplar Dr 12901
Power Dam Way 12901
Pristine Dr 12901
Prospect Ave 12901
Protection Ave 12901
Pyramid Dr 12901
Quality Dr 12901
Quarry Rd 12901
Quarter Horse Ln 12901
Quinn Ln 12901
Rabideau Blvd 12901
Rainbow Vista Ln 12901
Rascoe Rd 12901
Raymond Dr 12901
Red Fox Ln 12901
Redwood St 12901
Reeves Ln 12901
Renadette Rd 12901
Renaissance Village Way 12901
Ridgeway Dr 12901
Ridgewood Dr 12901
Righi Way 12901
Riley Ave 12901
River Bend Dr 12901
Riverside Ave 12901
Robbie Way 12901
Robinson Rd & Ter 12901
Rock Rd 12901
Rockwell Rd 12901
Rocky Point St 12901
Romeo Cir 12901
Roosevelt Ter 12901
Rugar St 12901
Rugar Park Way 12901
Runway Dr 12901
Rushford Rd 12901
Rv Park Rd 12901
Rye Dr 12901
Sailly Ave 12901
Salmon River Rd 12901
Sanborn Ave 12901
Sandalwood Way 12901
Sandra Ave 12901
Santa Ln 12901
Sara Ct 12901
Saranac St 12901
Saratoga Ct 12901
Schuyler Ter 12901
Scott Way 12903
Sears Blvd 12901
Seneca Dr 12901
Sesame St 12901
Set Pt 12901
Seth Sq 12901
Shamrock Ct 12901
Sharron Ave 12901

Sheila Ave 12901
Shelburne St 12901
Sheridan Ave 12901
Sherman Pl & St N 12901
Shields Ave 12901
Shirley Ave 12901
W Shore Dr 12901
Side St 12901
Siwanoy Ln 12901
Skyway Shopping Ctr 12901
Smart Rd 12901
Smith Dr & St 12901
Smithfield Blvd 12901
Smokey Ridge Rd 12901
Snug Harbor Way 12901
Sonya Way 12901
Sorrell Ave 12901
South St 12901
Spaulding Dr 12901
Spearman Rd 12901
Spellman Rd 12901
Spit Fire Dr 12901
Spring Cir & Dr 12901
Spy Glass Way 12901
St Charles St 12901
St John Pl & St 12901
Stafford Dr & Rd 12901
Standish St 12901
Stanley Way 12901
State Route 22 12901
State Route 22b 12901
State Route 3 12901
State Route 9 12901
Steltzer Rd 12901
Stetson Ave 12901
Stone Bridge Way 12901
Stonegate Way 12901
Stratford Rd 12901
Stratton Pl 12901
Summer Dr 12901
Summer Hill Ct 12901
Sunnyside Rd 12901
Sunrise Dr 12901
Sunset Dr 12901
Superior Dr 12901
Susan Ln 12901
Tammy Ln 12901
Tanbark Dr 12901
Tara Ln 12901
Television Dr 12901
Tennessee Rd 12903
Terrace West Way 12901
Terry Ln 12901
Tetreault Dr 12901
Tiffany Way 12901
Tioga Ln 12901
Tom Miller Rd 12901
Track Side 12901
Trade Rd 12901
Trafalgar Dr 12901
Tremblay Ave 12901
Tribute Dr 12901
Trinity Pl 12901
Truman Ave 12901
Turner Ct 12901
Twin Cir 12901
Tyrell Ave 12901
Underwood Ave 12901
University Pl 12901
Us Ave
4771-4845 12901
5001-5027 12903
5029-5199 12901
Us Oval 12903
Utah Rd 12903
Valcour Blvd 12901
Valhalla Ln 12901
Valley Dr 12901
Vermont St 12901
Veterans Ln 12901
Village Dr 12901
Vintage Est 12901
Vista Dr 12901
Wall St 12901
Wallace Hill Rd 12901
Walworth St 12901

Washington Pl 12901
Washington Rd 12903
Waterhouse St 12901
Weed St 12901
Wells St 12901
Werner Schluter Way 12901
Westwood Dr 12901
Wheeling Ave 12901
Whispering Pines Rd 12901
White St 12901
Whiteface Hall 12901
Wild Goose Ln 12901
Wildwood Est 12901
William St 12901
Willow Bch 12901
Willow Dr 12903
Willow Ln 12901
Wilson Hall 12901
Windswept Ln 12901
Winter Dr 12901
Witherill Dr 12901
Wolfe Way 12901
Wood St 12901
Wood Cliff Dr 12901
Woodland Dr 12901
Woodmanor Dr 12901

POUGHKEEPSIE NY

General Delivery 12601

POST OFFICE BOXES MAIN OFFICE STATIONS AND BRANCHES

Box No.s
1 - 1389 12602
1541 - 2260 12601
2341 - 3840 12603
4600 - 6013 12602

NAMED STREETS

Abes Way 12601
Academy St 12601
Acorn Dr 12603
Adams St 12601
Adriance Ave 12601
Albany St 12601
Albany Post Rd 12601
Albert Rd 12603
Alda Dr 12603
Alden Rd 12603
Alex Way 12603
Alexander Blvd 12603
Alfred Dr 12603
Alia Ct 12603
Alice Ct 12603
Alicia Ct 12601
Allen Pl 12601
Alvin Ct 12603
Amato Dr 12601
Amber Ct 12603
Andover Ln 12601
Andrea Ct 12601
Andrea Dr 12603
Angelo Blvd 12603
Ann St 12603
Annie Ln 12603
Anthony Dr 12601
Antoinette Dr 12601
Applewood Cir 12601
Arbor Ct 12603
Arbor Hill Rd 12603
Arden Ln 12603
Argent Dr 12603
Arlington Ave 12603
Arnold Blvd 12603
Arnold Rd 12601
E Arnold Rd 12601
W Arnold Rd 12601
Artesa Dr 12603

Arthur Ln 12603
Ash Ct 12603
Aspen Ct 12603
Aspen Ter 12601
Aspen Walk 12603
Austin Ct 12603
Autumn Dr 12603
Bahret Ave 12601
Bain Ave 12601
Baker Ave 12601
Baker St
1-99 12603
101-433 12603
300-398 12601
400-434 12603
Balding Ave 12601
Baldwin Rd 12603
Balsam Sq 12601
Bancroft Rd 12601
Bank Rd 12603
Barclay St 12601
Barent Ln 12603
Barnard Ave 12601
Barnegat Rd 12601
Barnes Dr 12603
Bart Dr 12603
Bartlett St 12601
Bayberry Ln 12603
Beck Pl & Rd 12601
Bedell Rd 12603
Beechwood Ave
1-41 12601
42-42 12603
43-43 12601
44-90 12603
91-299 12601
Beechwood Park 12601
Beechwood Ter 12601
Beekman Ln 12603
Beekman St 12601
Bellas Way 12601
Bellmore Dr 12603
Belvedere Rd 12601
Bement Ave 12601
Bennett Rd 12601
Benton Rd 12603
Bermuda Blvd 12603
Bethlehem Pl 12603
Big Meadow Ln 12601
Bill Reynolds Blvd 12601
Birch Hill Dr 12603
Bircher Ave 12601
Birchwood Ter 12601
Bird Ln 12603
Birkdale Ct 12603
Biscayne Blvd 12603
Bishop Dr 12603
Boardman Rd 12603
Bobrick Rd 12601
Boces Rd 12601
Boulevard Knls 12601
Bower Rd 12603
Boxwood Ct 12601
Boynton Dr 12603
Bradley Ct 12601
Brady Pl 12601
Brentwood Dr 12603
Brett Pl 12603
Brewers Ln 12603
Brian Ct 12603
Briarcliff Ave 12603
Briarwood Dr 12601
N & S Bridge St 12601
Bridgeview Dr 12601
Bridgewater Way 12601
Bridle Ln 12603
Broadview Rd 12603
Brookland Farms Rd 12601
Brookside Ave 12601
Bruce Dr 12603
Buckingham Ave 12601
Budget Dr 12601
Burnett Blvd 12603
Bushwick Rd 12603
Buttermilk Dr 12601
Butternut Way 12601

Buttonwood Ct 12601
Cabin Way 12603
Caldwell Rd 12603
Camelot Rd 12601
Camill Dr 12603
Cannon St 12601
Cardinal Dr 12601
Carmen Dr 12603
Carnelli Ct 12603
Carol Dr 12603
Caroline Ave 12603
Carpenter Dr 12603
Carriage Hill Ln 12603
Carrington Ct 12603
Carroll St 12601
Case Ct 12603
Casper Creek Rd 12603
Casperkill Dr 12603
Castillo Ln 12601
Catharine St 12601
Cathy Rd 12603
Catskill Ave 12603
Caudie Dr 12603
Cavo Dr 12603
Cayman Ct 12603
Caywood Rd 12603
Cedar Ave 12603
Cedar Ct 12603
Cedar Ln 12601
E Cedar St 12601
W Cedar St 12601
Cedar Cliff Ln 12601
Cedar Pond Ln 12603
Cedar Valley Rd 12603
Center Ave & St 12601
Chapman Cir 12601
Charles St 12601
Cheney Dr 12601
N & S Cherry Ln & St 12601
Cherry Hill Dr 12603
Chestnut St 12601
Chestnut Ridge Rd 12603
Childrens Way 12601
Church St 12601
Circular Rd 12601
Civic Center Plz 12601
Clark St 12601
Claudia Ln 12603
Clayton Pl 12603
Cleveland Dr 12601
N & S Clinton Sq & St 12601
N & S Clover St & Way 12601
Clover Hill Dr 12603
Club Way 12603
Clubhouse Ct & Dr 12603
Coachlight Dr 12603
Cobey Ter 12601
Cochran Hill Rd 12603
Colburn Dr 12603
Colburn Dr Ext 12603
Colette Dr 12601
Coll Hollow Rd 12601
College Ave 12603
W College Ave 12601
Collegeview Ave 12603
Collins Dr 12603
Colonial Dr & Knls 12603
Columbia St 12601
Commerce St 12603
Commerce Street Ext 12603
Commons Ln 12601
Congress Ct 12603
Conklin St 12601
Cooke St 12601
Cookingham Rd 12601
Cooper Rd 12603
Cora Ln 12603
Corine Dr 12601
Corlies Ave 12601
Cortlandt Dr 12603
W Cottage Rd & St 12601
Cotton Way 12603
Cramer Rd 12603
Crannell St 12601
Cream St 12601
Creek Rd 12601
Creek Bend Rd 12603
Crescent Rd 12601
Cresthill Ln 12601
Crestwood Blvd 12603
Croft Rd 12603
Croft Hill Rd 12603
Cromwell Dr 12603
Crystal Hill Ln 12603
Cypress Ln 12601
Daisy Ln 12603
Daley Rd 12603
Dallas Dr 12603
Daniels Ct 12603
Danspence Rd 12603
Dara Ln 12601
Daria Dr 12603
Darlene Dr 12601
Darrow Pl 12603
David Ct 12603
David Dr 12601
Davies Ct & Pl 12601
Davis Ave 12603
Davis Rd 12603
Davis St 12601
De Laval Pl 12601
Dean Pl 12601
Deans Ln 12603
Debbie Ct 12601
Debra Ct 12601
Debra Hill Dr 12603
Deer Path 12601
Deer Run Rd 12603
Degarmo Pl 12601
Degarmo Rd 12603
Delafield St 12601
Delano St 12601
Delray Cir 12603
Denver Pl 12601
Diane Ct 12603
Diddell Rd 12603
Dill Ln 12601
E & W Dogwood Ct & Dr 12601
Donna Dr 12603
Donnie Pl 12603
Dorland Ave 12603
Dorliss Dr 12603
E Dorsey Ln 12601
Douglas St 12603
Downing Pl 12603
Drouilhet Ln 12603
Drum Ct 12603
Du Bois Ave 12601
Duane St 12601
Dublin Ln 12603
Durocher Ter 12603
Dutcher Pl 12601
Dutchess Ave 12601
Dutchess Tpke 12603
Dutchess Hill Rd 12601
Dwight St 12601
Eagle Ln 12601
Earl Ct 12603
Earlwood Dr & Park 12603
Eastern Pkwy 12603
Eastman Ter 12601
Easy St 12603
Eden Ter 12601
Edgar St 12603
Edgewater Rd 12603
Edgewood Dr 12603
Edwin Rd 12603
Eileen Blvd 12603
Elbern Dr 12603
Eldorado Dr 12603
Elks Ln 12601
Ellsworth Ln 12601
Elm Ct 12603
Elm Pl 12601
Elmendorf Dr 12603
Elmwood Ave 12603
Elrom Dr 12603
Emily Jane Ct 12601
Emmott Pl 12601
Empire Blvd 12603
W End Ave 12603
Erin Ct 12601
Essex Rd 12601
Estelle Rd 12601
Esterich Rd 12603
E & W Eugene Ct 12601
Evelyn Way 12603
Evergreen Ave 12601
Exeter Rd 12603
Fair Way 12603
Fair Oaks Dr 12603
Fairmont Ave 12603
Fairmont St 12601
Fairview Ave 12601
Fairview Avenue Ext 12601
Fairway Dr 12601
Falcon Ct 12603
Fallkill Ave & Pl 12601
Father Cody Dr 12601
Feller Ct & Rd 12603
Fenway Dr 12601
Fern Ln 12601
Ferris Ln
- 1-74 12601
- 75-199 12603

Field Ct 12601
Fieldstone Ct 12603
Fiji Ln 12603
Firemens Way 12603
Fitchett St & Way 12601
Flamingo Dr 12601
Flannery Ave 12601
Flower Ln 12603
Flower Hill Rd 12603
Flower Hill Road Ext 12603
Flynn Ln 12603
Forbus St
- 1-41 12601
- 42-199 12603

Forest Ave 12601
Forrest Ct & Way 12603
Foster St 12601
Fountain Pl 12603
Fountainbrook Ave 12603
Four Winds Dr 12603
Fowler Ave 12603
Fox Hl 12603
Fox Ln 12603
Fox Run 12603
Fox St 12601
Fox Ter 12603
Franklin St 12601
Frederick Dr 12603
Freedom Plains Rd 12603
Frieda Ln 12603
Friendly Ln 12603
Friendship Ln 12601
Fulton Ave 12603
Fulton Ct 12603
Fulton Grv 12601
Fulton St 12601
Gables Blvd 12603
Gale Dr 12603
Garden St 12601
Garden Street Ext 12601
Garfield Pl 12601
Garrett Pl 12603
Gaskin Rd 12601
Gate Dr & St 12601
Gentry Bnd 12603
Gerald Dr 12601
Gerry Rd 12603
Gifford Ave 12601
Glade Rd 12601
Glen Ct 12603
Glen Eagles Dr 12603
Glenwood Ave & Rd 12603
Gold Rd 12603
Golf Club Ln 12601
Grady Hill Ct 12603
N Grand Ave 12603
S Grand Ave 12603
Grand St 12601
Grant St 12601
Grapevine Pl 12603
Gray St 12603
Green St 12601
Greenbush Dr 12601
Greenfield St 12603
Greenhouse Ln 12603
Greenvale Farms Rd 12603
Greystone Ln 12601
Grove St 12601
Grubb St 12603
Gus Siko Rd 12601
Gwens Way 12601
Hagan Dr 12603
Haight Ave 12603
W Haight Ave 12603
Haight Rd 12601
Halley Ct 12601
N & S Hamilton Ct & St 12601
Hammersley Ave 12601
Hampton Rd 12603
Hankin Loop 12601
Hanscom Ave 12601
Harley Tucker Hl 12601
Harmony Cir 12603
Harrison St 12601
Hart Dr 12603
Hartstone Dr 12603
Harvard Dr 12603
Hasbrouck Dr 12603
Hatfield Ln 12603
Haviland Rd 12601
Hawk Ln 12603
Hawkins St 12601
Hawthorne Ln 12603
Hayden Ct 12603
Heathbrook Dr 12603
Helen Blvd 12603
Hemlock Rd 12603
Henderson St 12601
Henmond Blvd 12603
Hennessey Ln 12603
Hennessey Pl 12601
Henry St 12601
Hettinger Ln 12603
Hewlett Pl & Rd 12603
Hickory Ln 12603
High Ct 12603
High St 12601
High Acres Dr 12603
High Point Dr 12603
High Ridge Rd 12603
Highland Rd 12601
Hill Top Ln 12603
Hillcrest Dr 12603
Hillis Ter 12603
Hilltop Ct & Rd 12601
Hillview Cir & Dr 12603
Hinkley Pl 12601
Hoffman Ave 12603
Hoffman St 12601
Hogan Dr 12603
Holland Ct 12603
Hollow Ln 12603
Holly Ln & Walk 12603
Holmes St 12601
Homer Pl 12603
Honeymoon Ln 12603
Hook Rd 12601
Hooker Ave
- 1-164 12601
- 165-399 12603

Horizon Hill Dr 12603
Hornbeck Rd & Rdg 12603
Horseshoe Dr 12603
Howard Rd 12603
Howard St 12601
Hubbard Ln 12603
Hudson Ave 12601
Hudson Harbour Dr 12601
Hudson Heights Dr 12601
Hudson Pointe Dr 12601
Hudson View Dr 12601
Hurlihe St 12601
Husky Hill Rd 12601
Ibm Rd 12601
Idlewild Dr 12601
Indian Ln 12603
Industry St 12603
Innis Ave
- 1-198 12601
- 199-299 12603

Inwood Ave 12601
Ireland Dr 12603
Irving Ave 12601
Irwin Ct 12603
Ivy Ter 12601
Jackman Dr 12603
N & S Jackson Dr & Rd 12603
James St 12603
Jameson Ct 12603
Jamil Ct 12603
Jane St 12603
Janet Dr 12603
Jay Rd 12603
Jean Ct & Dr 12601
Jefferson Plz 12601
Jefferson Rd 12603
Jefferson St 12601
Jennifer Ct 12601
Jewett Ave 12601
Johns Blvd 12603
Jonathan Ln 12603
Jones St 12603
Judy Ter 12601
Justamere Ln 12601
Justbrand Ln 12603
Kari Blvd 12601
Keith Dr & Pl 12603
Kellerhause Dr 12603
Kelley Cir 12601
Kelsey Rd 12601
Kennedy Rd 12601
Kent Ave 12603
Kenzbrit Ct 12603
Kerr Rd 12601
Kevin Hts 12603
Kilmer Ave 12601
Kilmer Ave Ext 12601
Kim Ln 12601
Kimball Dr 12603
Kimball Rd 12601
Kimlin Ct 12603
Kinderhook Dr 12603
King Dr 12603
King St 12601
King George Rd 12603
Kingston Ave 12603
Kingwood Dr, Ln & Park 12601
Kinkead Ln 12603
Kinry Rd 12603
Kittredge Pl 12601
Knightsbridge 12603
Knolls Rd 12601
Knollwood Ln 12603
Kohlanaris Dr 12601
Krakower Dr 12601
Kristi Ln 12601
Labrador Ln 12601
Lafayette Ct 12603
Lafayette Pl 12601
Laffin Ln 12603
Lafko Dr 12603
Lagrange Ave 12603
W Lake St 12601
Lake View Ter 12601
Lakeview Ave 12601
Lakeview Ct 12603
Lakeview Rd 12603
Laney Pl 12601
Larch Ct 12603
Lauer Rd 12603
Laurel St 12601
Lawrence Rd 12601
Ledge Way 12603
Legion Rd 12601
Lent St 12601
Leonard Rd 12601
Lewis Ave 12603
Lexington Ave 12601
Liberty St 12601
Lilling Rd 12601
Lincoln Ave & Dr 12601
Linda Ct 12603
Lindbergh Pl 12603
Linden Ct & Rd 12603
Linwood Ave 12601
Little Jefferson St 12601
Little Market St 12601
Little Smith St 12601
Livingston St 12601
Lockwood Pl 12603
Locust Rd 12603
Locust Crest Ct 12603
Logans Ct 12603
Lois Ln 12603
London Close 12603
Long St 12601
Longview Rd 12603
Loockerman Ave 12601
Loren Dr 12603
Lori St 12603
Lorie Ln 12603
Lorraine Blvd 12603
Love Rd 12603
Lown Ct 12603
Ludlow Dr 12603
Lyford Ln 12601
Lynbrook Rd 12603
Lynn Rd 12603
Lyons Dr 12601
Macdonnell Hts 12603
Macghee Rd 12603
Mack Rd 12603
Maggies Way 12601
Magnolia Ln 12601
Magnolia Walk 12603
Magurno Ln 12603
Mahar Dr 12601
Main St
- 1-707 12601
- 708-718 12603
- 709-709 12601
- 720-899 12603

Mainetti Dr 12603
Maisie Ct 12601
Malmros Ter 12601
Maloney Rd 12603
Manchester Cir & Rd 12603
Mandalay Dr 12603
Manitou Ave 12603
Manor Dr & Way 12603
Mansion St
- 1-54 12601
- 55-55 12602
- 56-498 12601
- 57-399 12601

Maple Rd 12601
Maple St
- 1-500 12601
- 502-502 12601
- 510-599 12603

Maple Grove Ln 12601
Maple Street Ext 12603
Maple Winding Rd 12603
Mapleview Rd 12603
Mapleview Road Ext 12603
Marcinelli Ct 12601
Marian Ave 12601
Marie Ct 12601
Marino Rd 12601
Marist Dr 12601
Mark Ct 12603
Mark Vincent Dr 12603
Market St 12601
Marple Rd 12603
Marple Road Ext 12603
Marshall Dr 12601
W Marshall Dr 12601
Marshall Rd 12603
Marshall St 12601
Martin Dr 12603
Martin Rd 12601
Martin Ter 12603
Martis Way 12603
Marwood Dr 12601
Mary Ave 12603
Maryland Ave 12603
May Ct & St 12603
Mayapple Rd 12603
Mcalpine Dr 12601
Mcintosh Dr 12603
Mckinley Ln 12601
Meadow Ln & Rd 12603
Meadowview Dr 12603
Meier Rd 12603
Memory Ln 12603
Merrick Rd 12603
Merrimac Rd 12603
Merry Hill Rd 12603
Mews Aly 12603
Meyer Ave 12603
Michaels Ln 12603
Micort Dr 12603
Milano Dr 12603
Mildred Ave 12603
Mill St 12601
Millbank Rd 12603
Miller Pl 12601
Miller Rd 12603
Mims Path 12603
Miron Dr 12603
Misty Ridge Cir 12603
Mitchell Ave 12603
Mockingbird Ln 12601
Mollys Way 12601
Monell Ave 12603
Monitor Rd 12603
Monroe Dr 12601
Montgomery St 12601
Morehouse Rd 12603
Morgan Ave & Ct 12601
Morse St 12601
Morton St 12601
Mount Carmel Pl 12601
Mountain View Rd 12603
Muirfield Ct 12603
Mulberry Ct & Ln 12603
Muldowney Cir 12601
Musselman Dr 12601
Naples Dr 12603
Nassau Rd 12601
Needle Ln 12603
Nemes Way 12601
Neptune Rd 12601
New Hackensack Rd 12603
Nilde Ct 12603
Nina Pl 12601
Nob Hl 12603
Nobile Ln 12603
North Dr 12603
North Rd 12601
Noxon Rd 12603
Noxon St 12601
Oak Ct 12603
Oak St 12601
Oak Bend Rd 12603
Oak Crescent St 12601
Oak Grove Ln 12601
Oakdale Ave 12601
W Oakley St 12601
Oakwood Blvd 12603
Old Degarmo Rd 12603
Old Farms Rd 12603
Old Field Rd 12603
Old Manchester Rd 12603
Old Mill Dr & Rd 12603
Old Noxon Rd 12603
Old Overlook Rd 12603
Old Post Rd 12601
Old Silvermine Pl 12601
Old Smith Rd 12603
Old Spackenkill Rd 12603
Olympic Way 12603
Orchard Ln 12603
Orchard Park 12603
Orchard Pl 12601
Orchard Rd 12603
Organ Hill Rd 12603
Oriole Dr 12601
Osborne Rd 12601
Overlook Rd 12603
Overocker Rd 12603
Page Park Dr 12603

Palm Cir 12603
Palmer Ave 12601
Pam Ln 12601
Panessa Dr 12603
Panorama Ct 12603
Parasol Rdg 12603
Park Ave 12603
Park Ct 12603
Park Pl 12601
Parker Ave 12601
Parkview Ln, Pl & Ter 12603
Parkwood Blvd 12603
Parriven Rd 12603
Partners Trce 12603
Pasture Ln 12603
Pat Dr 12603
Patricia Rd 12603
Patrick Ln 12603
Patriot Ct 12603
Pavinchal Pl 12603
Peach Rd 12601
Peacock Ln 12601
Pearlbush Ln 12603
Peckham Rd 12603
Pehl Rd 12603
Pells Ct 12603
Pembroke Dr 12603
Pendell Rd 12601
Pennock Rd 12603
N & S Perry St 12601
Pershing Ave 12601
Peter Cooper Dr 12601
Peters Pl 12601
Pewter Ct 12603
Phillips Rd 12603
Philmore Dr 12603
Pilgrim Ter 12601
Pine St 12601
Pine Cone Ct 12603
Pine Echo Dr 12601
Pine Ridge Rd 12603
Pine Street Spur 12601
Pine Tree Dr 12603
Pineberry Ct 12603
Pinewood Rd 12603
Platt St 12601
Pleasant Ln 12603
Pleasant Ridge Dr 12603
Pleasant View Rd 12603
Pond Rd 12601
Pond St 12603
Pondview Ln 12603
Poplar St 12601
Potters Bnd 12601
Poughkeepsie Business
Park Dr 12603
Prestwick Ct 12603
Priscilla Ln 12603
Prospect St 12601
Pye Ln 12603
Rabbit Trail Rd 12603
Radcliff Rd 12601
Raker Rd 12603
Rambling Brook Ln 12601
N Randolph Ave 12603
S Randolph Ave 12601
Ray Blvd 12603
Raymond Ave
1-54 12603
56-60 12603
61-61 12601
63-99 12603
Reade Pl 12601
Red Cardinal Ct 12603
Red Hawk Ln 12601
Red Oaks Mill Rd 12603
Redondo Dr 12603
Regency Dr 12603
Reno Rd 12603
Reservoir Sq & St 12601
Reynolds Ave 12603
Rhobella Dr 12603
Richards Blvd 12603
Richmond Rd 12603
E Ricky Ln 12601
Ridge Rd 12603
Ridgeline Dr 12603
Ridgeview Rd 12603
Ridgewood Ter 12603
Rinaldi Blvd 12601
Ripken Ln 12601
River Point Rd 12601
Riverview Cir & Dr 12601
Robert Pl & Rd 12603
Robin Ln 12603
Robin Rd 12601
Robin Hill Dr 12601
Robinson Ln 12603
Rochambeau Ln 12601
Rochdale Rd 12603
Rock Garden Way 12603
Rockcrest Pl 12603
Rockland Rd 12601
Rockledge Rd 12601
Roland Ter 12603
Rombout Rd 12603
Rombout House Ln 12603
Rombout Ridge Rd 12603
Romca Rd 12603
Ronnie Ln 12601
Roosevelt Ave 12601
Rosalind Rd 12601
Rose Cir, Ln & St 12601
Rosedale Ct 12601
Rosewood Rd 12601
Ross Cir 12601
Rothenburgh Rd 12603
Round Hill Rd 12603
Route 376 12603
Route 44 12603
Route 9 N 12601
Rowley Rd 12601
Ruby Cir 12603
Ruppert Rd 12603
Russet Rd 12601
Ruth Rd 12601
Rymph Blvd 12601
Saddle Rock Dr 12603
Saint Anns Rd 12601
Saint Johns Pkwy 12601
Saint Josephs Ter 12603
Salem Ct 12603
Salt Point Tpke
1-505 12603
506-899 12601
Sand Dock Rd 12601
Sandi Dr 12603
Santa Anna Dr 12603
Sarasota Ln 12603
Saxon Dr 12603
Scenic Dr & Ln 12603
Scenic Hills Dr 12603
School St 12601
Schoolhouse Ln 12603
Schyler Dr 12603
Scofield Hts 12603
Scott Ct 12601
Scott Ter 12603
Seaman Rd 12601
Second Mile Dr 12601
Sedgewick Rd 12603
Seitz Ter 12603
Settlers Ct 12603
Shadow Ln 12601
Shady Tree Ln 12603
Shamrock Cir 12603
Sharon Dr 12603
Sheafe Rd 12601
Sheldon Dr 12603
Shelley Rd 12603
Sheraton Dr 12601
Sherwood Dr 12603
Sherwood Ln 12601
Short Ct 12603
Short Hill Dr 12603
Silver Ln 12603
Simone Dr 12603
Skyview Dr 12603
Slate Hill Dr 12603
Sleight Plass Rd 12603
Smith Rd 12603
Smith St 12601
Snow Ter 12601
Sommerset Dr 12603
South Ave & Rd 12601
Southview Dr 12601
Spackenkill Rd 12603
Sparrow Ln 12601
Spoor Ave 12603
Spratt Ave 12603
Spring Rd & St 12601
Spring Manor Cir 12601
Springside Ave 12603
Springside Dr 12601
Spruce St 12601
Spur Way 12603
Spy Hl 12603
Squires Gate 12603
Stanley St 12603
Stanton Ter 12603
State St 12601
Stephanie Ln 12603
Sterling Pl 12603
Steven Ct 12603
Stonehedge Ct & Dr 12603
Stout Ct 12601
Stratford Dr 12603
Strawberry Ln 12603
Streit Ave 12603
Stringham Rd 12603
Stuart Dr 12603
Styvestandt Ct & Dr 12601
Sucato Dr 12601
Sugar Maple Rd 12603
Summersweet Dr 12603
Summit Ave 12601
Sun Ln 12601
Suncrest Ct 12603
Sunfish Cove Rd 12601
Sunny Knolls Dr 12603
Sunnyside Ave 12601
Sunrise Ln 12603
Sunset Ave 12601
Sunstone Dr 12603
Superior Way 12601
Surico Dr 12601
Surrey Ln 12603
Susan Ln 12603
Susie Blvd 12603
Sutton Park Rd 12603
Swan Ct & Ln 12603
Sycamore Way 12603
Taconic St 12603
Taft Ave 12603
Tall Tree Ln 12601
Tallardy Pl 12603
Talmadge St 12601
Tamarack Hill Dr 12603
Tamidan Rd 12601
Tanglewood Ln 12603
Tay Pl 12603
Taylor Ave 12601
Terminal Rd 12601
Thames Rd 12603
Thendara Ln 12603
Thomas Ave 12603
Thompson St 12601
Thornberry Way 12603
Thorndale Ave 12603
Thornwood Dr 12603
Timberline Dr 12603
Timothy Dr 12603
Titus Rd 12603
Titus Rd Ext 12603
Titusville Ct, Hts & Rd 12603
Todd Hill Rd 12603
Toddy Ln 12603
Toms Way 12603
Toomey Dr 12603
Topaz Run 12603
Townsend Blvd 12603
Trails End 12603
Treadwell Cir 12601
Tree Top Ln 12603
Trotter Ln 12603
Troy Ln 12603
Tucker Dr 12603
Turnberry Ct 12603
Twin Hills Rd 12603
Underhill Ave 12601
Underhill Rd 12603
Union St 12601
Vaeth Rd 12603
Vail Rd 12603
Valkill Dr 12601
Valley View Dr & Rd 12603
Van Duzer Dr 12603
Van Kleeck Dr 12601
Van Siclen Dr 12601
Van Wagner Rd
1-650 12603
651-999 12601
Van Wyck Dr 12601
Vanderwater Ave 12603
Vanek Rd 12603
Vassar Rd 12603
Vassar St 12601
Vassar Lake Dr 12603
Vassar View Rd 12603
Verazzano Blvd 12601
Vernon Ter 12601
Vero Dr 12603
Vervalen Dr 12603
Verven Rd 12603
Victor Dr 12603
Victor Ln 12601
Victory Ln 12603
S View Ct 12603
Vincent Rd 12603
Violet Ave 12601
Virginia Ave 12601
Vista Dr 12601
Vista Ln 12603
Volino Dr 12603
Wagon Wheel Rd 12601
Waldorf Pl 12601
Walker Rd 12603
Walnut St 12601
Walnut Hill Rd 12603
Wantaugh Ave 12603
Washburn Dr 12603
Washington St 12601
Wasson Dr 12603
N Water St 12601
Waters Edge Rd 12601
Waterview Dr 12601
Watson Rd 12603
Wayne Dr 12601
Webster Ave 12601
Weed St 12601
Wendover Dr 12601
Wendy Dr 12603
Wennington Dr 12603
Westview Dr & Ter 12603
Westview Ter Ext 12603
Whinfield St 12601
Whipple Way 12603
N & S White St 12601
White Birch Ct 12603
Whitehall Rd 12603
Whitehouse Ave 12601
Whittier Blvd 12603
Wilbur Blvd 12603
Wilbur Ct 12601
Wild Berry Ct 12603
Wildflower Rdg 12603
Wildwood Dr 12603
Williams Rd 12603
Williams St 12601
Williams Street Ext 12601
Willow Ave 12603
Willow Bnd 12601
Willow Tree Ln 12601
Willowbrook Hts 12603
Wilmar Ter 12601
Wilmot Ter 12603
Wilson Blvd 12603
Wiltse Ln 12603
W Winding Rd 12601
Windmill Rd 12601
Windsor Ct 12601
Wing Rd 12603
Winnie Ln 12603
Winnikee Ave 12601
Wood St 12603
Woodbrook Ln 12603
Woodcliff Ave 12603
Woodland Ave 12603
S Woodlawn Ave 12601
Woodside Ter 12603
Woodview Rd 12603
Woodward Rd 12603
Woodys Way 12601
Worrall Ave 12603
Yale Ct 12603
Yates Ave & Blvd 12601
Young St 12601
Ziegler Ave 12603
Zimmer Ave 12601

QUEENS VILLAGE NY

POST OFFICE BOXES MAIN OFFICE STATIONS AND BRANCHES

Box No.s
All PO Boxes 11428

NAMED STREETS

Ashford St 11427
Bardwell Ave 11429
Bell Blvd 11427
Bellaire Pl 11429
Berichig Ave 11428
Billings St 11427
Borkel Pl 11428
Braddock Ave
22101-22119 11427
22121-22133 11427
22135-22199 11427
22200-22499 11428
22501-23599 11428
Cenchig Ave 11429
Colfax St 11429
Country Pointe Cir 11427
Cross Island Pkwy 11429
Davenport Ave 11428
Delevan St 11429
Edmore Ave 11428
Epsom Crse 11427
Fairbury Ave 11428
Francis Lewis Blvd
8605-8999 11427
9000-9499 11428
9900-11317 11429
11319-11399 11429
Grand Central Pkwy 11427
Hartland Ave 11427
Hempstead Ave 11429
Hillside Ave 11427
Hollis Ave 11429
Hollis Court Blvd
8700-8798 11427
8800-8999 11427
9000-9499 11428
Hollis Hills Ter 11427
Jamaica Ave 11428
Lyman St
8800-8899 11427
8900-8999 11428
Manor Rd 11427
Moline St
8800-8899 11427
8900-8999 11428
Monterey St 11429
Murdock Ave 11429
Musket St 11427
Nashville Blvd 11429
Peck Ave 11427
Pontiac St 11427
Range St 11427
Ransom St 11427
Robard Ln 11429
Sabre St 11427
Sawyer Ave 11427
Seward Ave 11427
Spencer Ave 11427
Springfield Blvd
8000-8999 11427
9000-9499 11428
9601-9697 11429
9699-11399 11429
Station Plz 11428
Stewart Rd 11427
Stronghurst Ave 11427
Tristric Ave 11427
Union Tpke 11427
Vanderveer St
8800-8999 11427
9000-9499 11428
Whitehall Ter 11427
Winchester Blvd
7900-8899 11427
9000-9299 11428
Witthoff Ave 11429

NUMBERED STREETS

82nd Ave 11427
85th Ave 11427
86th Ave, Dr & Rd 11427
87th Ave 11427
88th Ave & Rd 11427
89th Ave & Rd 11427
90th Ave & Ct 11428
91st Ave & Rd 11428
92nd Ave & Rd 11428
93rd Ave & Rd 11428
94th Ave, Dr & Rd 11428
95th Ave 11429
96th Ave 11429
97th Ave 11429
98th Ave 11429
99th Ave 11429
100th Ave, Dr & Rd 11429
101st Ave 11429
102nd Ave 11429
103rd Ave 11429
104th Ave & Rd 11429
105th Ave 11429
106th Ave 11429
107th Ave 11429
108th Ave 11429
109th Ave 11429
110th Ave & Rd 11429
111th Ave & Rd 11429
112th Ave & Rd 11429
113th Ave & Dr 11429
207th St
8800-8898 11427
8900-8999 11427
9000-9499 11428
9900-11399 11429
208th St
8000-8999 11427
9000-9499 11428
9900-11399 11429
209th Pl 11429
209th St
8000-8999 11427
9000-9499 11428
9900-11399 11429
210th Pl
8900-8999 11427
9000-9399 11428
210th St
8000-8999 11427
9000-9499 11428
10000-11399 11429
211th Pl
9100-9199 11428
9900-9999 11429
10001-10499 11429
211th St
8000-8999 11427
9000-9499 11428
9800-11000 11429
11002-11398 11429
212th Pl
8800-8999 11427
9000-9499 11428
10400-10499 11429
212th St
8000-8999 11427
9000-9499 11428
9800-11399 11429
213th St
8000-8999 11427
9000-9499 11428
9900-11099 11429
214th Pl 11428
214th St
8000-8999 11427
9000-9499 11428
10400-11099 11429
215th Pl
8700-8999 11427
9000-9499 11428
215th St
8000-8999 11427
9000-9499 11428
9900-11099 11429
216th St
8700-8999 11427
9000-9499 11428
9900-11099 11429
217th Ln 11429
217th Pl 11429
217th St
8000-8999 11427
9000-9499 11428
9801-9897 11429
9899-11099 11429
218th Pl
8700-8999 11427
9000-9299 11428
10200-10499 11429
218th St
8100-8999 11427
9000-9499 11428
9500-9698 11429
9700-10099 11429
219th St
8700-8999 11427
9000-9499 11428
9700-11326 11429
220th St
8900-8999 11427
9000-9499 11428
9600-10899 11429
89100-89198 11427
221st Pl
8900-8999 11427
9000-9100 11428
9102-9198 11428
221st St
8000-8999 11427
9000-9499 11428
9600-11299 11429
11301-11325 11429
222nd St
8000-8099 11427
9001-9097 11428
9099-9499 11428
9500-10999 11429
223rd St
8000-8099 11427
10000-11299 11429
224th St
9101-9197 11428
9199-9499 11428
9500-9600 11429
9602-10198 11429
225th St
9400-9498 11428
9500-10398 11429
227th St 11429
229th St 11427
230th St 11427
231st St 11427
232nd St 11427
233rd St 11427
234th St 11427
235th Ct & St 11427
236th St 11427
237th St 11427

RIDGEWOOD NY

POST OFFICE BOXES MAIN OFFICE STATIONS AND BRANCHES

Box No.s
All PO Boxes ... 11386

NAMED STREETS

Amory Ct ... 11385
Aubrey Ave ... 11385
Bleecker St ... 11385
Bunnecke Ct ... 11385
Butler Ave ... 11385
Cabot Rd ... 11385
Catalpa Ave ... 11385
Central Ave ... 11385
Centre St ... 11385
Charlotte St ... 11385
Clestans Ave ... 11385
Clover Pl ... 11385
Cody Ave ... 11385
Cooper Ave ... 11385
Cornelia St ... 11385
Covert St ... 11385
Cypress Ave ... 11385
Cypress Hills St ... 11385
Decatur St ... 11385
Dekalb Ave ... 11385
Doran Ave ... 11385
Edsall Ave ... 11385
Fairview Ave ... 11385
Flushing Ave ... 11385
Forest Ave ... 11385
Fresh Pond Rd ... 11385
Gates Ave ... 11385
George St ... 11385
Grandview Ave ... 11385
Greene Ave ... 11385
Grove St ... 11385
Hancock St ... 11385
Harman St ... 11385
Hart St ... 11385
Himrod St ... 11385
Indiana Ave ... 11385
Irving Ave ... 11385
Jefferson Ave ... 11385
Kleupfel Ct ... 11385
Linden St ... 11385
Luther Rd ... 11385
Madison St ... 11385
Margaret Pl ... 11385
Menahan St ... 11385
Metropolitan Ave ... 11385
Myrtle Ave
5400-6099 ... 11385
6060-6060 ... 11386
6100-8899 ... 11385
8901-9099 ... 11385
Norman St ... 11385
Onderdonk Ave ... 11385
Otto Rd ... 11385
Palmetto St ... 11385
Putnam Ave ... 11385
Rene Ct ... 11385
Ricard St ... 11385
Rutledge Ave ... 11385
Saint Felix Ave ... 11385
Saint Johns Rd ... 11385
Saint Nicholas Ave ... 11385
Seneca Ave ... 11385
Shaler Ave ... 11385
Stanhope St ... 11385
Starr St ... 11385
Stephen St ... 11385
Stier Pl ... 11385
Stockholm St ... 11385
Summerfield St ... 11385
Suydam St ... 11385
Tonsor St ... 11385
Traffic Ave ... 11385
Trotting Course Ln ... 11385
Troutman St ... 11385
Union Tpke ... 11385
Valentine Pl ... 11385
Weirfield St ... 11385
Willoughby Ave ... 11385
Woodbine St ... 11385
Woodhaven Blvd ... 11385
Woodward Ave ... 11385
Wyckoff Ave ... 11385

NUMBERED STREETS

All Street Addresses ... 11385

ROCHESTER NY

General Delivery ... 14692

POST OFFICE BOXES MAIN OFFICE STATIONS AND BRANCHES

Box No.s
9620 - 9620 ... 14604
10001 - 10999 ... 14610
11005 - 11537 ... 14611
12362 - 12958 ... 14612
13101 - 13900 ... 14613
14001 - 14994 ... 14614
15381 - 15818 ... 14615
16001 - 16999 ... 14616
17001 - 17969 ... 14617
18001 - 18961 ... 14618
18900 - 18950 ... 14692
19201 - 19899 ... 14619
20001 - 20960 ... 14602
22661 - 23980 ... 14692
24001 - 24998 ... 14624
25081 - 25894 ... 14625
26191 - 26970 ... 14626
30001 - 32012 ... 14603
39302 - 42111 ... 14604
60001 - 60998 ... 14606
64001 - 64980 ... 14624
67001 - 67990 ... 14617
68011 - 68015 ... 14618
77000 - 77580 ... 14617
88001 - 88174 ... 14618
90321 - 90980 ... 14609
91001 - 93358 ... 14692
270001 - 278999 ... 14627

NAMED STREETS

A Pl ... 14619
Aab St ... 14606
Abbott St ... 14606
Abbottsford Dr ... 14606
Abby Ln ... 14606
Aberdeen St ... 14619
Aberthaw Rd ... 14610
Abington Rd ... 14622
Academy Dr ... 14623
Ackerman St ... 14609
Acorn Dr ... 14625
Acorn Valley Trl ... 14624
Acton St ... 14615
Adair Dr ... 14606
Adams St ... 14608
Adarkens Dr ... 14625
Addison St ... 14606
Adeane Dr E & W ... 14624
Adela Cir ... 14624
Adelaide St ... 14606
Adele Dr ... 14616
Adeline Rd ... 14616
Adirondack St ... 14606
Admiral Park ... 14613
Adrian Rd ... 14622
Adrian St ... 14613
Adwen Pl ... 14607
Aebersold St ... 14621
Affinity Ln ... 14616
Afton St ... 14612
Agnes St ... 14621
Agnew Ct ... 14611
Ainsworth Ln ... 14624
Airinton Dr ... 14622
Airline Dr ... 14624
Airpark Dr ... 14624
Airport Way ... 14624
Ajax Rd ... 14624
Akron St ... 14609
Alaimo Dr ... 14625
Alameda St ... 14613
Alana Dr ... 14624
Albemarle St ... 14613
Albert St ... 14606
Alberta St ... 14619
Albury Dr ... 14626
Alcazar St ... 14621
Alcott Rd ... 14626
Alden Rd ... 14626
Alder Bush ... 14624
Alderbrook Trl ... 14624
Aldern Pl ... 14613
Alderwood Ln ... 14615
Aldine St ... 14619
Alecia Dr ... 14626
Aleta Dr ... 14623
Alexander Ct ... 14607
Alexander St
366A-366D ... 14607
11-13 ... 14620
15-111 ... 14620
112-112 ... 14607
113-113 ... 14620
114-300 ... 14607
302-432 ... 14607
311-319 ... 14604
321-431 ... 14607
434-450 ... 14605
452-499 ... 14605
Alexander Hall ... 14623
Alexis St ... 14609
Alfie Dr ... 14623
Alfonso Dr ... 14626
Alford St ... 14609
Alfred Ave ... 14623
Alger Dr ... 14624
Algonquin Ter ... 14611
Alhambra Dr ... 14622
Alice St ... 14611
Allandale Ave ... 14610
Allandale Dr ... 14624
Allegany Dr ... 14626
Allen Pkwy ... 14618
Allen St ... 14608
Allens Creek Rd ... 14618
Allerton St ... 14615
Alliance Ave ... 14620
Alliance Dr ... 14623
Allmeroth St ... 14620
Allwood Dr ... 14617
Alma Pl ... 14607
Almay Rd ... 14616
Almira St ... 14605
Alonzo St ... 14612
Alpha St ... 14612
Alphonse St ... 14621
Alpine Dr ... 14618
Alpine Rd ... 14612
Alpine St ... 14620
Alta Vista Dr ... 14625
Alvanar Rd ... 14606
Alvin Pl ... 14607
Alvord St ... 14609
Amador Pkwy ... 14623
Amalia Ct ... 14612
Amanda Dr ... 14624
Ambassador Dr ... 14610
Ambassador Rdg ... 14626
Amber Pl ... 14608
Amberly Cir ... 14624
Amberwood Pl ... 14626
Ambrose St ... 14608
Amerige Park ... 14617
Ames St
1-450 ... 14611
451-599 ... 14606
Amesbury Rd ... 14623
Amherst St ... 14607
Amity Aly ... 14604
Amsden Dr ... 14623
Amsterdam Rd ... 14610
W Amy Ln ... 14626
Anchor Ter ... 14617
Anderson Ave ... 14607
Andiron Ln ... 14612
Andony Ln ... 14624
Andover St ... 14615
Andrea Ln ... 14609
Andrews St ... 14604
Andrews Memorial Dr ... 14623
Andy Ln ... 14606
Angela Villa Ln ... 14626
Angelus Dr ... 14622
Angle St ... 14606
Angora Dr ... 14617
Ann Marie Dr ... 14606
Annie Ln ... 14626
Anson Pl ... 14607
Antelope Ln ... 14623
Anthony St ... 14619
Antlers Dr ... 14618
Antoinette Dr ... 14623
Antonina Ln ... 14626
Apollo Dr ... 14626
Appian Dr ... 14606
Apple Blossom Ln ... 14612
Apple Creek Ln ... 14612
Appledore Cir ... 14623
Applegrove Dr ... 14612
Appleton St ... 14611
Applewood Dr ... 14612
Aquarius Ln ... 14612
Aqueduct St ... 14614
Aragon Ave ... 14622
Arbor Dr ... 14625
Arbordale Ave ... 14610
Arborway Ln ... 14612
Arborwood Cres & Ln ... 14615
Arbutus St ... 14609
Arcadia Pkwy ... 14612
Arcampus Dr ... 14612
Arch St ... 14609
Archer Rd
1-90 ... 14624
300-399 ... 14623
Archer St ... 14613
Ardella St ... 14606
Ardmore St ... 14611
Argo Park ... 14613
Argonne St ... 14621
Argyle St ... 14607
Ariel Park ... 14621
Arklow St ... 14611
Arlidge Dr ... 14616
Arlington St ... 14607
Armbruster Rd ... 14623
Armstrong Ave ... 14617
Armstrong Rd
1-170 ... 14616
171-499 ... 14612
Arnett Blvd
1-105 ... 14611
106-1099 ... 14619
Arnold Park ... 14607
Aronica Dr ... 14623
Arrowhead Dr ... 14624
Arthur St ... 14621
Arvine Hts & Park ... 14611
Asbury St ... 14620
Ascot Dr ... 14624
Ashbourne Rd ... 14618
Ashbury Cir ... 14612
Ashford Cir ... 14626
Ashland St ... 14620
Ashley Dr ... 14620
Ashton Dr ... 14624
Ashwell Ln ... 14626
Ashwood Cir ... 14624
Ashwood Dr ... 14609
Ashwood Knl ... 14624
Asia Cir ... 14623
Aspen Dr ... 14625
Aster St ... 14615
Astor Dr ... 14610
Astronaut Dr ... 14609
Athena Dr ... 14626
Athens St ... 14621
Atkinson Ct & St ... 14608
Atlantic Ave
2-22 ... 14607
24-260 ... 14607
300-1500 ... 14609
2590-2598 ... 14625
2600-2699 ... 14625
Atlas St ... 14604
Atlee Dr ... 14626
Atwell St ... 14612
Atwood Dr ... 14606
Auburn Ave ... 14606
Audabon Cir & Ter ... 14624
Audino Ln ... 14624
Audley Way ... 14610
Audubon St ... 14610
Audubon Trl ... 14622
Augusta St ... 14605
Augustine St ... 14613
Auramar Dr ... 14609
Aurora St ... 14621
Austin Dr ... 14625
Austin St ... 14606
N & S Autumn Dr ... 14626
Autumn Chapel Way ... 14624
Autumn View Est ... 14622
Autumn Wood ... 14624
Avacado Ln ... 14606
Avalon Ct & Dr ... 14618
Avanti Dr ... 14606
Avenue A W ... 14621
Avenue B ... 14621
Avenue C ... 14621
Avenue D ... 14621
Avenue E St ... 14621
Averill Ave
1-405 ... 14620
406-799 ... 14607
Averill Ct ... 14607
Avery St ... 14606
Avery Park Ln ... 14612
Aviation Ave ... 14624
Avion Dr ... 14624
Avis St ... 14615
Avon Pl ... 14620
Avon Rd ... 14625
Avondale Park ... 14620
Avondale Rd ... 14622
Ayer St ... 14615
Azalea Rd ... 14620
Babbitt Pl ... 14608
Babcock Dr ... 14610
Bachman Rd ... 14621
Backus St ... 14608
Bacon Pl ... 14609
Baden St ... 14605
Baier Dr ... 14606
Baird St ... 14621
Bakerdale Rd ... 14616
Bakers Park ... 14617
Baldwin St ... 14609
Baleriso St ... 14605
Balestier Pl ... 14613
Balfour Dr ... 14621
Ballad Ave ... 14626
Ballantyne Rd ... 14623
Balsam St ... 14610
Balta Dr ... 14623
Bambi Ln ... 14624
Banbury Dr ... 14612
Bancroft Dr ... 14616
Banker Pl ... 14616
Bantrida Dr ... 14617
Banyan Dr ... 14616
Barbara Ln ... 14626
Barberry Ter ... 14621
Barbie Cir, Ct & Dr ... 14626
Barclay Ct ... 14612
Barclay Square Dr ... 14618
Barcrest Dr ... 14616
Bard Ln ... 14623
Bardin St ... 14615
Barker St ... 14611
Barlow Dr ... 14626
Barmont Dr ... 14626
Barn Swallow Ln ... 14624
Barnard St ... 14616
Barney Ln ... 14606
Barns Ct ... 14612
Barnum St ... 14609
Barons Rd ... 14617
Barons St
1-50 ... 14605
51-199 ... 14621
Barrett Pkwy ... 14612
Barrington Park & St ... 14607
Barrus Ln ... 14612
Barry Rd ... 14617
Bartholf Rd ... 14616
Bartlett St
1-151 ... 14608
152-299 ... 14611
Barton St
1-199 ... 14611
201-399 ... 14619
Basswood Cir ... 14615
Bastian Rd ... 14623
Bastian St ... 14621
Bateau Ter ... 14617
Battle Green Dr ... 14624
Bauer St ... 14606
Baumann St ... 14621
Bausch And Lomb Pl ... 14604
Baxter Dr ... 14626
Baxton Cir ... 14625
Bay St
1-434 ... 14605
435-1299 ... 14609
Bay Bluff Ln ... 14622
Bay Front Ln N ... 14622
Bay Front Ln S
1-699 ... 14609
3000-3199 ... 14622
Bay Knoll Rd ... 14622
Bay Point Cir ... 14622
Bay Shore Blvd
1100-1400 ... 14609
1401-2299 ... 14622
Bay View Rd ... 14609
Bay Village Dr ... 14609
Bayard Way ... 14626
Bayberry Dr ... 14609
Bayberry Ln ... 14616
Baycliff Dr ... 14609
Baycrest Dr ... 14622
Bayhill Ln ... 14609
Baylor Cir ... 14624
Baymon Dr ... 14624
Bayside Dr ... 14622
Bayton Dr ... 14622
Baywood Ter ... 14609
Beach Ave ... 14612
Beach St ... 14621
Beach Ter ... 14617
Beacon St ... 14607
Beaconsfield Rd ... 14623
Beaconview Ct ... 14617
Beahan Rd ... 14624
Beaman Rd ... 14624
Beatrice Dr ... 14625
Beatty Rd ... 14612
Beau Ln ... 14624
Beaufort St ... 14620
Beaumont Rd ... 14616
Beaver Rd ... 14624
Beaver St ... 14608
Beckwith Rd ... 14623
Beckwith Ter ... 14610
Bedford St ... 14609
Beechbrook Ln ... 14625
Beechcraft Dr ... 14606
Beechwood Dr ... 14606
Beechwood Park ... 14612
Beechwood St ... 14609
Beekman Pl ... 14620
Belcoda Dr ... 14617
Beldon Dr ... 14623
Belford Dr ... 14616
Belgard St ... 14609
Belknap St ... 14606
Bellamy Dr ... 14621
E & W Bellaqua Estates
Ct & Dr ... 14624
Belle Terre Ln ... 14626
Belleclaire Dr ... 14617
Bellehurst Dr ... 14617
Bellevue Dr ... 14620
Bellmawr Dr ... 14624
Bello Ct ... 14624
Bellwood Dr ... 14606
Bellwood Pl ... 14609
Belmanor Dr ... 14623
Belmeade Rd ... 14617
Belmont Rd ... 14612
Belmont St ... 14620
Belmore Way ... 14612
Belvedere Dr ... 14624
Belview Dr ... 14609
Belvista Dr ... 14625
W Bend Dr ... 14612
Bending Creek Rd ... 14624
Benedict Dr ... 14624
Bengal Ter ... 14610
Benjamin Ave ... 14616
Bennett Ave ... 14609
Bennington Dr ... 14616
Bennington Green Ln ... 14616
Bent Oak Rd ... 14624
Benton St ... 14620
Benwell Rd ... 14616
Berchman Dr ... 14626
Beresford Rd ... 14610
Bergen St ... 14606
Berkeley St ... 14607
Berkshire Dr ... 14626
Berkshire St ... 14607
Berlin St ... 14621
Berman St ... 14618
Bermar Park ... 14624
Bermuda Cir ... 14623
Berna Ln ... 14624
Bernard St ... 14621
Bernercrest Dr ... 14617
Bernice St ... 14615
Bernie Ln ... 14624
Berry St ... 14609
Berwick Pl ... 14612
Berwick Rd ... 14609
Berwyn St ... 14609
Bethnal Grn ... 14625
Betwood Ln ... 14612
Beverly Dr ... 14625
Beverly Hts ... 14616
Beverly St ... 14610
Bickford St ... 14606
Bidwell Ter ... 14613
Biltmore Dr ... 14617
Binnacle Pt ... 14622
Birch Cres ... 14607
Birch Ln ... 14622
Birch Hills Dr ... 14622
Birchbrook Dr ... 14623
Birchwood Dr ... 14622
Birchwood Rd ... 14606
Biredalm Rd ... 14622
Birmingham Dr ... 14618
Birr St ... 14613
Biscayne Dr ... 14612
Bishopgate Dr ... 14624
Bismark Ter ... 14621
Bittersweet Dr ... 14625
Bittner St ... 14604
Black Cedar Dr ... 14624
Black Creek Rd ... 14623
Black Duck Trl ... 14626
Black Spruce Ct ... 14616
Black Walnut Dr ... 14615
Blakeney Pl ... 14620
Blakeslee St ... 14609
Bleacker Rd ... 14609

Bleile Ter ... 14621
Bloomfield Pl ... 14620
Bloomingdale St ... 14621
Bloss St ... 14608
Blossom Cir E ... 14610
Blossom Cir W ... 14610
Blossom Rd
1-1769 ... 14610
1770-1899 ... 14625
Blue Aspen Way ... 14612
Blue Avocado Ln ... 14623
Blue Birch Dr ... 14612
Blue Grass Ln ... 14626
Blue Heron Dr ... 14624
Blue Mist Ln ... 14623
Blue Ridge Trl ... 14624
Blue Spruce Dr ... 14624
Blueberry Cres ... 14623
Bluefield Mnr ... 14612
Bly St ... 14620
Boardman St ... 14607
Bobbie Dr ... 14606
Bobrich Dr ... 14610
Boca Ave ... 14626
Bock St ... 14609
Bolding Dr ... 14623
Bond St ... 14620
Bonesteel Cir ... 14616
Bonesteel St
1-134 ... 14615
135-799 ... 14616
Boniface Dr ... 14620
Bonita Dr ... 14616
Bonnie Brae Ave ... 14618
Boothe St ... 14620
Borchard St ... 14621
Borinquen Plz ... 14605
Borrowdale Dr ... 14626
Boston St ... 14621
Boswell St ... 14611
Bott Pl ... 14605
Bouckhart Ave ... 14622
Boulevard Pkwy ... 14612
Bowman St ... 14609
Boxart St ... 14612
Boxborough Ln ... 14616
Boxwood Dr ... 14617
Boyd Dr ... 14616
Boys Club Pl ... 14608
Brad St ... 14622
Bradburn St ... 14619
Braddock Rd & St ... 14612
Bradfield St ... 14611
Bradford Rd ... 14618
Bradford St ... 14621
Bragdon Dr ... 14618
Bragdon Pl ... 14604
Bram Hall Dr ... 14626
Bram Park Pl ... 14626
Bramblewood Cir & Ln W ... 14624
Brambury Dr ... 14621
Branch Ave ... 14618
Branch St ... 14621
Branchwood Ln ... 14618
Brandon Cir ... 14612
Brandon Rd ... 14622
Brandon Woods Dr ... 14618
Brandy Brook Ln ... 14612
Brandywine Ln ... 14618
Brandywine Ter ... 14623
Branford Rd ... 14618
Brasser Dr ... 14624
Brayer St ... 14606
Brayton Rd ... 14616
Breck St ... 14609
Breckenridge Dr ... 14626
Breezeway Dr ... 14622
Bremen St ... 14621
Brentfield Cir ... 14617
Brentford Ter ... 14612
Brentwood Dr ... 14624
Brentwood St ... 14610
Bretlyn Cir ... 14618
Breton Rd ... 14622
Brett Rd ... 14609
Bretton Woods Dr ... 14618
Brewer St ... 14621
Brewerton Dr ... 14624
Brewster Ln ... 14624
Brian Dr ... 14624
Briar Cir ... 14618
Briar Ln ... 14622
Briar Hill Dr ... 14626
Briar Patch Rd ... 14618
Briar Wood Ln ... 14626
Briarcliff Rd ... 14616
Briarcliffe Rd ... 14617
Briarwood Dr ... 14617
Brick Lndg ... 14626
Bricker St ... 14609
Brickstone Cir ... 14620
Bridge View Dr ... 14615
Bridgetown Dr ... 14626
Bridgewood Dr ... 14612
Briggs St ... 14611
Bright Autumn Ln ... 14626
Bright Oaks Cir & Dr ... 14624
Brightford Heights Rd ... 14610
Brighton Park ... 14620
Brighton St ... 14607
Brighton Henrietta Town Line Rd ... 14623
Brightwoods Ln ... 14623
Brimley Mnr ... 14612
Brisbane Ln ... 14612
Bristol Ave ... 14617
Brittany Cir ... 14618
Britton Rd
1-1 ... 14612
3-136 ... 14612
137-1299 ... 14616
Broad St ... 14606
E Broad St
48-50 ... 14614
100-199 ... 14604
301-599 ... 14607
W Broad St
1-200 ... 14614
220-899 ... 14608
Broadway ... 14607
Brockley Rd ... 14609
Brockton Pl ... 14624
Brocton St ... 14612
Broderick Dr ... 14622
Broezel St ... 14613
Bronson Ct ... 14608
Bronx Dr ... 14623
Bronze Leaf Trl ... 14612
Brook Rd ... 14623
Brook Forest Path ... 14626
Brook Hill Ln ... 14625
Brook Trout Ln ... 14622
Brook Valley Dr ... 14624
Brookdale Ave ... 14619
Brookdale Park ... 14609
Brookfield Rd ... 14610
Brookhaven Ter ... 14621
Brooklawn Dr ... 14618
Brooklea Dr ... 14624
Brookline Ln ... 14616
Brooklyn St ... 14613
Brookridge Dr ... 14616
Brooks Ave
1-795 ... 14619
796-1899 ... 14624
Brookscrest Way ... 14611
Brookside Dr ... 14618
Brookview Dr ... 14617
Brookview Rd ... 14624
Brookwood Rd ... 14610
Brower Rd ... 14622
Brown Rd ... 14622
Brown St
1-499 ... 14608
500-899 ... 14611
Browncroft Blvd
1-465 ... 14609
466-600 ... 14610
601-2589 ... 14625
2591-2603 ... 14625
Browns Race ... 14614
Brownstone Ln ... 14615
Bru Mar Dr ... 14606
Brunswick St ... 14607
Brush Creek Dr ... 14612
Brush Hollow Rd ... 14626
Bryan St ... 14613
Bryn Mawr Rd ... 14624
Buck Hill Rd ... 14626
Buckingham St ... 14607
Buckland Ave ... 14618
Buckman Rd ... 14615
Bucky Dr ... 14624
Buell Dr ... 14621
Buell Rd ... 14624
Buena Pl ... 14607
Buffalo Rd
1-800 ... 14611
801-4200 ... 14624
Buffard Dr ... 14610
Bunker Hill Dr ... 14625
Buonomo St ... 14621
Burbank St ... 14621
Burben Way ... 14624
Burke Ter ... 14613
Burkedale Cres ... 14625
Burkhard Pl ... 14620
Burley Rd N ... 14612
Burling Rd ... 14616
Burlington Ave ... 14619
Burlwood Dr ... 14612
Burning Brush Dr ... 14606
Burrows Dr ... 14625
Burrows St ... 14606
Burrows Hills Dr ... 14625
Bursen Ct ... 14609
Burt Dr ... 14623
Burt St ... 14609
Burwell Rd ... 14617
Byers Ct ... 14608
Cabot Rd ... 14626
Cadillac Ave ... 14606
Cady St
1-139 ... 14608
140-201 ... 14611
Caffery Pl ... 14608
Cairn St ... 14611
Calhoun Ave ... 14606
California Dr ... 14616
Calihan Park ... 14606
Calkins Rd ... 14623
Calm Lake Cir ... 14612
Calumet St ... 14610
Calvin Rd ... 14612
Cambria Rd ... 14617
Cambridge St ... 14607
Camden St ... 14612
Camelot Dr ... 14623
Cameron St ... 14606
Cameron Hill Dr ... 14612
Camille Dr ... 14612
Camomile Ln ... 14626
Campbell Park ... 14606
Campbell St ... 14611
Campden Way ... 14610
Campus Dr ... 14623
Canal St ... 14608
Canal Hall ... 14623
Canal Landing Blvd ... 14626
Canal View Blvd ... 14623
Canal Woods ... 14626
Canary St ... 14613
Canasta Rd ... 14615
Candlelight Dr ... 14616
Candlewood Rd ... 14609
Candy Ln ... 14615
Canfield Pl ... 14607
Cannon Hill Rd ... 14624
W Canon Dr ... 14624
Canterbury Rd ... 14607
Canton St ... 14606
Canyon Trl ... 14625
Cape Cod Way ... 14623
Capri Dr ... 14624
Capron St ... 14607
Cardiana Dr ... 14612
Cardiff Park ... 14610
Cardinal Dr ... 14624
Cardogan Sq ... 14625
Caren Dr ... 14622
Carl St ... 14621
Carlee Ct ... 14616
Carleton St ... 14607
Carling Rd ... 14610
Carlisle St ... 14615
Carlsam Cir & Dr ... 14609
Carlson Rd ... 14610
Carmas Dr ... 14626
Carney Cir ... 14623
Carol Dr ... 14617
Caroline Dr ... 14624
Caroline St ... 14620
Carriage Ln ... 14617
Carriage House Ln ... 14624
Carrington Dr ... 14626
Carroll Pl ... 14620
Carry Ln ... 14609
Carter St ... 14621
Carthage Dr & St ... 14621
Carverdale Dr ... 14618
Casa Dr ... 14623
Cascade Dr ... 14614
Cascade Pl ... 14609
Case Ter ... 14609
Cashmere Ct & Ln ... 14609
Casimir Cir ... 14617
Caspar St ... 14605
Castle Park ... 14620
Castle Rd ... 14623
Castle Grove Dr ... 14612
Castlebar Rd ... 14610
Castleford Rd ... 14616
Castleman Rd ... 14620
Castleton Rd ... 14616
Castleview Dr ... 14622
Castlewood Dr ... 14624
Catalina Dr ... 14622
Catalpa Rd ... 14617
Cathaway Park ... 14610
Cattail Xing ... 14620
Cattaragus Dr ... 14623
Cavendish Pl ... 14625
Caves Pl ... 14609
Cayuga St ... 14620
Cecelia Ter ... 14622
Cedar Ln ... 14622
Cedar Ml ... 14626
Cedar Rd ... 14616
Cedar St ... 14611
Cedar Creek Trl ... 14626
Cedarfield Commons ... 14612
Cedargrove Dr ... 14617
Cedarwood Rd ... 14617
Cedarwood Ter ... 14609
Celebration Dr ... 14620
Celia Dr ... 14623
Celtic Ln ... 14626
Cennerth Rd ... 14623
Centennial St ... 14611
Center Dr ... 14609
Center Place Dr ... 14615
Centerwood Dr ... 14616
Central Ave ... 14605
Central Park
1-460 ... 14605
461-599 ... 14609
Centre Dr ... 14623
Centre Park ... 14614
Centre Ter ... 14617
Chace St ... 14606
Chad Cir ... 14616
Chadbourne Rd ... 14618
Chadwell Rd ... 14609
Chadwick Dr ... 14618
Chalet Cir ... 14618
Chalford Rd ... 14616
Chamberlain St ... 14609
Champeney Ter ... 14605
Champlain St
1-325 ... 14608
326-499 ... 14611
Chancery Ln ... 14625
Chandler St ... 14619
Chapel St ... 14609
Chapel Hill Dr ... 14617
Chapel Oaks ... 14621
Chapin St ... 14621
Charing Rd ... 14617
Charisma Dr ... 14606
Charissa Run ... 14623
Charit Way ... 14626
Charland Rd ... 14617
Charlene Dr ... 14606
Charles Ave ... 14623
Charles St ... 14608
Charlotte St ... 14607
Charlton Rd ... 14617
Charmaine Rd ... 14624
Charrington Rd ... 14609
Charter Cir ... 14606
Charters Way ... 14623
Chartwell Ct ... 14618
Charwood Cir ... 14609
Chase Sq ... 14604
Chasewood Cir ... 14618
Chateau Ln ... 14626
Chateau Sq ... 14618
Chatfield St ... 14609
Chatham Gdns ... 14605
Chautauqua Dr ... 14623
Chelmsford Ln & Rd ... 14618
Chelsea Rd ... 14617
Cheltenham Rd W ... 14612
Chemung St ... 14611
Cherry Rd
1-3 ... 14612
5-265 ... 14612
22-146 ... 14624
148-233 ... 14624
235-259 ... 14624
Cherry Creek Ln ... 14626
Cheshire Ln ... 14624
Chester Ave ... 14623
Chester St ... 14611
Chesterfield Dr ... 14612
Chesterton Rd ... 14626
Chestnut Cres ... 14624
Chestnut Dr ... 14624
Chestnut St ... 14604
N Chestnut St ... 14604
Chestnut Hill Dr ... 14617
Chestnut Ridge Rd ... 14624
Cheswell Way ... 14610
Chevalin St ... 14621
Cheviot Ln ... 14624
Chi Mar Dr ... 14624
Chicory Rdg ... 14626
Child St
1-361 ... 14611
362-699 ... 14606
Chili Ave
1-1090 ... 14611
1091-3784 ... 14624
Chili Ter ... 14619
Chili Center Coldwater Rd ... 14624
Chiltern Rd ... 14623
Chimayo Rd ... 14617
Chimney Hill Rd ... 14612
Chimney Sweep Ln ... 14612
Chinaberry Cres ... 14606
Chippendale Rd ... 14616
Chiswick Cir ... 14624
Christian Ave ... 14615
Christopher Ct ... 14606
Christyne Marie Dr ... 14626
N Church Rd ... 14612
Church St ... 14614
Churchill Dr ... 14616
Churchlea Pl ... 14611
Cider Creek Cir & Ln ... 14616
Cimarron Dr ... 14620
Cindy Ln ... 14626
Cinnabar Rd ... 14617
Circle Ct ... 14617
Circle Dr ... 14623
Circle St ... 14607
Circle Wood Rd ... 14625
Citrus Dr ... 14606
City View Dr ... 14625
Clairmount St ... 14621
Clardale Dr ... 14616
Clarence Park ... 14608
Clarington St ... 14609
Clarissa St ... 14608
Clark Ave ... 14609
Clark Park ... 14616
Clark Rd ... 14625
Clark St ... 14609
Clarkson St ... 14613
Clay Ave ... 14613
Clay Hl ... 14624
Clay Rd ... 14623
Claybourne Rd ... 14618
Claybrook St ... 14609
Clayton St ... 14612
Clearbrook Dr ... 14609
Clearview Rd ... 14616
Clearwater Cir ... 14612
Clebourne Dr ... 14625
Clematis St ... 14612
Cleon St ... 14621
Cleveland St ... 14605
Cleverdale Rd ... 14616
Cliff St ... 14608
Cliff View Dr ... 14625
Cliffmor St ... 14609
Clifford Ave
1-1495 ... 14621
1496-2399 ... 14609
Cliffordale Park ... 14609
Clifton St
1-69 ... 14608
70-199 ... 14611
Clinton Ave N
1-209 ... 14604
210-890 ... 14605
2101-2399 ... 14617
Clinton Ave S
1-181 ... 14604
183-205 ... 14604
401-1710 ... 14620
1711-2700 ... 14618
2701-3199 ... 14623
N Clinton Ave
891-2099 ... 14621
Clinton Sq ... 14604
Clintwood Ct & Dr ... 14620
Clio St ... 14612
Clove Dr ... 14625
Clover St
1-1600 ... 14610
1601-2645 ... 14618
Clover Hills Dr ... 14618
Clover Park Dr ... 14618
Clovercrest Dr ... 14618
Cloverdale Rd ... 14616
Cloverdale St ... 14612
Cloverland Dr ... 14610
Club Dr ... 14609
Club View Dr ... 14626
Coachwood Ln ... 14623
Cobb Ter ... 14620
Cobblestone Dr ... 14623
Cobbs Hill Dr ... 14610
Cobleskill Cir & Dr ... 14626
Coburg St ... 14612
Coca Cola Park ... 14605
Cohasset Dr ... 14618
Colbert Pl ... 14608
Colby St ... 14610
Cold Spring Cir ... 14624
Coldwater Cres & Rd ... 14624
Cole Ave ... 14606
Colebourne Rd ... 14609
Colebrook Dr ... 14617
Coleman Ter ... 14605
Coleridge Rd ... 14609
Colfax St ... 14606
Colgate St ... 14619
Colin St ... 14615
Collamer Dr ... 14617
College Ave ... 14607
Collenton Dr ... 14626
Collingsworth Dr ... 14625
Collingwood Dr ... 14621
Colonial Rd ... 14609
Colonial Village Rd ... 14625
Colonist Ln ... 14624
Colonnade Dr ... 14623
Colony Dr ... 14626
Colony Ln ... 14623
Colony Manor Dr ... 14623
Colony Wood Dr ... 14616
Columbia Ave
1-300 ... 14608
301-599 ... 14611
Colvin St
1-435 ... 14611
436-599 ... 14606
Colwick Rd ... 14624
Comfort St ... 14620
Commerce Dr ... 14623
Commercial St ... 14614
Commodore Pkwy ... 14625
Commons Way ... 14623
Commonwealth Rd ... 14618
Community Manor Dr ... 14623
Conant Rd ... 14623
Concord St ... 14605
Congress Ave
1-290 ... 14611
291-499 ... 14619
Conifer Ln ... 14622
Coniston Dr ... 14610
Conkey Ave
1-75 ... 14605
76-699 ... 14621
Conklin Ave ... 14609
Conmar Dr ... 14609
Conrad Dr ... 14616
Constance Way E & W ... 14612
Constitution Cir ... 14624
Continental Dr ... 14618
Cook Dr ... 14623
Cook St ... 14620
Coolidge Rd ... 14622
Cooper Rd ... 14617
Cooper St ... 14609
Copeland St ... 14609
Copley Sq ... 14626
Copley St ... 14611
Copperfield Rd ... 14615
Cor Mar Ln ... 14616
Coral Way ... 14618
Coran Cir ... 14616
Coretta Scott Xing ... 14608
Corley Dr ... 14622
Cornelia Dr ... 14606
Cornell St ... 14607
Cornhill Pl & Ter ... 14608
Cornwall Ln ... 14617
Cornwall Xing ... 14624
Corona Rd ... 14615
Coronado Dr ... 14617
Coronet Rd ... 14623
Corporate Woods ... 14623
Corrigan St ... 14612
Corwin Ave ... 14609
Corwin Rd ... 14610
Cos Grand Hts ... 14618
Cosmos Dr ... 14616
Costar St ... 14608
Costello Park ... 14608
Cotillion Ct ... 14606
Cottage St
1-225 ... 14608
226-499 ... 14611
Cottonwood Ln ... 14617
Couchman Ave ... 14617
Coulton Pl ... 14608
Council St ... 14605
Council Rock Ave ... 14610
Country Ln ... 14626
N Country Club Dr ... 14618
Country Gables Cir ... 14606
Country Place Ln ... 14612
Country Wood Lndg ... 14626
Country Woods Ln ... 14626
Countryshire Dr ... 14626

Court St
11-175 14604
177-199 14604
400-498 14607
Courtly Cir 14615
Courtright Ln 14624
Cove Dr 14617
Coventry Ave 14610
Covered Bridge Cir 14612
Coverly St 14609
Covington Rd 14617
Crab Apple Ln 14626
Cragg Rd 14616
Craig St 14611
W Craig Hill Dr 14626
Cranberry Rd 14612
Cranberry Landing Dr 14609
Cranbrooke Dr 14622
Crandon Way 14618
Cranswick Ln 14618
Cravenwood Ave 14616
Crawford St 14620
Creative Dr 14624
Creek St 14625
N Creek Xing 14612
Creek Hill Ln 14625
Creek House Dr 14626
Creek Meadow Ln 14626
Creekdale Ln 14618
Creekside Dr 14622
Creekside Ln
1-4 14624
1-1 14618
4-4 14618
6-23 14618
25-99 14618
Creekview Dr 14624
Creekview Ln 14626
Creekwood Dr 14626
Creighton Ln 14612
Crendark Dr 14626
Crerand Cir 14606
E Crest Dr 14606
W Crest Dr 14606
Crest St 14612
Crest Hill Dr 14624
Crest View Dr 14625
Crestfield Dr 14617
Crestline Rd 14618
Creston Ct 14612
Crestridge Ln 14622
Crestway Ln 14612
Crestwood Blvd 14624
Crimson Bramble Rd 14623
Crimson Woods Ct 14626
Crispin Ct 14612
Crittenden Blvd 14620
Crittenden Rd 14623
Crittenden Way 14623
Crockett Dr 14623
Crombie St 14605
Cromwell Dr 14610
Crosby Ln 14612
Crosman Ter 14620
Cross St 14609
Cross Bow Dr 14624
Cross Creek Ln 14616
Cross Gates Rd 14606
Crossfield Rd 14609
Crossroads Ln 14612
Crosswood Ct 14612
Crouch St 14609
Crown Dr 14623
Croydon Rd 14610
Crystal Ct 14606
Crystal Commons Dr 14624
Crystal Creek Dr 14612
Crystal Valley
Overlook 14623
Cuba Pl 14605
Culdorf Aly 14615
Culver Pkwy 14609
Culver Rd
1-170 14620
171-500 14607
501-2700 14609
2701-5000 14622
Culverton Dr 14609
Cumberland St
186-188 14605
216-216 14603
216-216 14604
218-298 14605
Cummings St 14609
Cunningham St 14608
Curlew St
1-100 14606
101-399 14613
Currewood Cir 14618
Currier Ln 14624
Curtice Rd 14617
Curtis St 14606
Custer St 14611
Cutler St 14621
Cutter Dr 14624
Cynthia Ln 14621
Cypress St 14620
Da Vinci Dr 14624
Dade Pkwy 14623
Daffodil Trl 14626
Daisy St 14615
Dake Ave 14617
Dake St 14605
Dakeland Rd 14617
Dakota St
1-80 14611
81-299 14606
Dalaker Dr 14624
Dale Rd 14625
Dale Rd E 14625
Dale St 14621
Daleside Rd 14617
Dalewood Dr 14625
Daley Blvd 14617
Dalia Ln 14609
Dalkeith Rd 14609
Dallas Dr 14624
Dalston Rd 14616
Damsen Rd 14612
Dana St 14606
Danbury Cir N & S 14618
Danforth Cres 14618
Danforth St 14611
Daniel Dr 14624
Danneric St 14620
Darby Cir 14626
Darien St 14611
Darlap Pl 14616
Darrington Dr 14626
Darrow St 14621
Dartford Rd 14618
Dartmouth St 14607
Darwin St 14610
Dash St 14611
Datewood Dr 14625
Daunton Dr 14624
Daus Aly 14608
Davey Cres 14624
David Ave 14620
Davis St 14605
Davy Dr 14624
Dawes Rd 14622
Dawn Dr 14617
Dawn Valley Dr 14623
Dawnhaven Dr 14624
Dawson St 14606
Day Pl 14608
Daylilly Ln 14626
Dayne St 14622
Dayton St 14621
De Mallie St 14610
Dean View Cir 14609
Dearcop Dr 14624
Deb Ellen Dr 14624
Debby Ln 14606
Deep Rock Rd 14624
Deepwood Dr 14606
Deer Run 14623
Deer Path Dr 14612
Deerfield Dr 14609
Degeorge Cir 14626
Dejonge St 14621
Del Monte St 14621
Del Rio Dr 14618
Del Rio Ln 14622
Del Verde Rd 14624
Delacorte Cir 14612
Delamaine Dr 14621
Delano St 14611
Delaware Ave 14623
Delaware St 14607
Delevan St 14605
Dellwood Cir & Rd 14616
Delmar Rd 14616
Delmar St 14606
Delray Rd 14610
Delta Ter 14617
Demeter Dr 14626
Deming St 14606
Dempsey Pl 14608
Dengler St 14611
Denise Rd
1-368 14612
370-410 14612
411-1099 14616
Denishire Dr 14624
Denning St 14607
Denonville Rdg 14625
Densmore Rd & St 14609
Denver St 14609
Depew St 14611
Dequoit Ave 14622
Deschel Dr 14626
Desmond Rd 14616
Desmond St 14615
Deville Dr 14612
Devitt Rd 14615
Devon Rd 14619
Devonshire Ct 14619
Devonshire Dr 14625
Dewain St 14615
Dewberry Dr 14622
Dewey Ave
15-17 14617
19-30 14617
32-60 14617
55-59 14608
61-63 14608
64-66 14617
65-299 14608
100-300 14608
301-1429 14613
1430-2480 14615
2481-4440 14616
4441-5299 14612
Dewitt Clinton Ln 14606
Dexter Dr 14612
Diamond Pl 14609
Diane Park 14617
Dickinson St 14621
Diem St 14620
Dierdre Dr 14617
Diplomat Way 14606
Diringer Pl 14609
Dix St 14606
Dobson Rd 14616
Dodge St 14606
Doerun Dr 14626
Doewood Ln 14606
Dogwood Gln 14625
Dogwood Ln 14622
Dohrcrest Dr 14612
Dolman Dr 14624
Dolores Dr 14626
Dominic Way 14612
Doncaster Rd 14623
Donegal Dr 14616
Donlin Dr 14624
Donlon St 14607
Donna Rd 14606
Donna Marie Cir N 14606
Doran St 14608
Dorbeth Rd 14621
Dorchester Rd 14610
Dorian Ln 14626
Dorington Rd 14609
Doris Rd 14622
Dorking Rd 14610
Dorothy Ave 14615
Dorset St 14609
Dorsetwood Dr 14612
Dorsey Rd 14616
Dorstone Rd 14624
Dortmund Cir 14624
Dorvid Rd 14617
Douglas Dr 14624
Douglas Rd 14610
Dove St 14613
Dove Tree Ln 14626
Dover Ct 14624
Dover Park 14610
Dover Rd 14617
Dowling Pl 14605
Down St 14623
Downsview Dr 14606
Dozier Ln 14622
Dr Samuel Mccree Way
1-165 14608
166-299 14611
Drake Dr 14617
Draper St 14605
Drexel Dr 14606
Drexhall Ln 14612
Drexmore Rd 14610
Driftwood Ln 14617
Driving Park Ave 14613
Druid Hill Park 14609
Drumcliff Way 14612
Drury Ln 14625
Dubelbeiss Ln 14622
Dudley St 14605
Duffern Dr 14616
Duffield Rd 14618
Dugan Pl 14612
Duke St 14609
Dumont St 14617
Dunbar St 14619
Dunbarton Dr 14618
Dunbridge Cir 14618
Duncan Dr 14612
Dundas Dr 14625
Dundee Dr 14626
Dunn St 14621
Dunn Tower Dr 14606
Dunrovin Ln 14618
Dunsmere Dr 14615
Durand Blvd & Dr 14622
Durgin St 14605
Durham St 14609
Durkar Ln 14616
Durkin Aly 14608
Durnan St 14621
Dutch Vly 14624
Dutchess Dr 14612
Dutchmans Holw 14612
Duxbury Rd 14626
Duxbury Way 14618
Dyson St 14609
Eagan Blvd 14623
Eagle St 14608
Eagle Pine Way 14623
Eagle Ridge Cir 14617
Eagle Rock Dr 14609
Earl Dr 14624
Earl St 14611
East Ave
1-370 14604
371-1210 14607
1211-3100 14610
3101-4420 14618
East Blvd 14610
East Pkwy 14617
Eastbourne Rd 14617
Eastbrooke Ln 14618
Eastgate Dr 14617
Eastland Ave 14618
Eastland Rd 14616
Eastman Ave 14615
Eastman Est 14622
Eastmoreland Dr 14620
Easton Cir 14623
Eastview Ave 14609
Eastview Commons
Rd 14624
Eastwood Trl 14622
Easy St 14625
Eaton Rd 14617
Echo St 14609
Echo Hill Dr 14609
Eddy St 14611
Eden Ln 14626
Edgebrook Ln 14617
Edgecreek Trl 14609
Edgeland St 14609
Edgemere Dr
1-5 14618
15-35 14612
37-3399 14612
Edgemont Rd 14620
Edgemoor Rd 14618
Edgerton Park 14608
Edgerton St 14607
Edgeview Ln 14618
Edgeware Rd 14624
Edgewater Ln 14617
Edgewood Ave 14618
Edgewood Park 14611
Edinburgh St 14608
Edith St 14608
Edme St 14623
Edmonds St 14607
Edmonton Rd 14609
Edside Dr 14609
Edward St 14605
Edwards Deming Dr 14606
Eglantine Rd 14616
Eiffel Pl 14621
Eileen Cir & Dr 14616
Eisenberg Pl 14620
El Centro Dr 14609
El Mar Dr 14616
El Rancho Dr 14616
Elaine Dr 14623
Elam Ln 14606
Elba St 14608
Elbert St 14609
Elder St 14606
Elderberry Cir 14625
Eldora Dr 14624
Eldorado Pl 14613
Eldridge Ave 14620
Electric Ave
1-520 14613
521-699 14615
Elgin St 14611
Elgrove Rd 14617
Elham Rd 14624
Elizabeth Pl 14605
Elk St 14615
Ellarint St 14615
Ellery Rd 14612
Ellicott St 14619
Ellington Cir 14612
Ellington Dr 14616
Ellington Rd 14616
Ellingwood Dr 14618
Ellinwood Dr 14622
Ellis Dr 14624
Ellis Pl 14612
Ellison Ave 14625
Ellison St 14609
Ellison Hills Dr 14625
Ellsinore St 14606
Elm Dr 14609
Elm Ln 14610
Elm Pl 14609
Elm St 14604
Elmcroft Rd 14609
Elmdorf Ave 14619
Elmerston Rd 14620
Elmford Rd 14606
Elmgrove Dr 14606
Elmgrove Park 14624
Elmgrove Rd
1-370 14626
371-725 14606
726-1029 14624
Elmgrove Road Ext 14624
Elmguard St 14615
Elmhurst St 14607
Elmore Dr 14606
Elmore Rd 14618
Elmridge Center Dr 14626
Elmtree Rd 14612
Elmwood Ave
1-13 14611
15-250 14611
251-2095 14620
2096-3300 14618
3301-3999 14610
Elmwood Ter 14620
Elmwood Hill Ln 14610
Elsdon St 14606
Elser Ter 14611
Elsworth Dr 14615
Elton Ave 14606
Elton St 14607
Elvira St 14606
Elwell Dr 14618
Elwood Dr 14616
Emanon St 14621
Embassy Dr 14618
Emberglow Ln 14612
Embury Rd 14625
Emerald Cir 14623
Emerald Pt 14624
Emeralda Rd 14624
Emerson Park 14606
Emerson St
1-890 14613
891-1899 14606
Emery Run 14612
Emilia Cir & Dr 14606
Emily St 14622
Emjay Ln 14612
Emmett St 14605
Emmons Dr 14618
Empire Blvd 14609
E End Way 14604
Endicar Dr 14622
Engel Pl 14620
Englert St 14605
English Rd 14616
English Station Rd 14616
English Woods 14616
Enterprise St 14619
Entress Dr 14624
Epping Way 14610
Epworth St 14611
Erath Dr 14626
Ericsson St 14610
Erie St 14608
Erie Canal Dr 14626
Erion Cres 14607
Ernestine St 14619
Ernst St 14621
Esplanade Dr 14610
Esquire Dr 14606
Essex Dr 14623
Essex St 14611
Essla Dr 14612
Estall Rd 14616
Ethel St 14608
Euclid St 14604
Euclid Building 14604
Eugene St 14606
Eva Pl 14611
Evandale Rd 14618
Evangeline St 14619
Evanwood Cir & Dr 14626
Evelyn St 14606
Eventide Ln 14617
Everclay Dr 14616
Everett Dr 14624
Everett St 14615
Evergreen Dr 14624
Evergreen Ln 14618
Evergreen St 14605
Everwild Ln 14616
Ewald Dr 14625
Ewer Ave 14622
Excel Dr 14621
Exchange Blvd
6-8 14614
10-199 14614
201-399 14608
Exchange Ct 14608
Exchange St 14608
Exeter Pl 14623
Ezio Dr 14606
Factory St 14614
Fair Pl 14609
Fair Oaks Ave 14618
Fairbanks St 14621
Fairbourne Park 14626
Fairchild Rd 14606
Faircrest Rd 14623
Fairfax Rd 14609
Fairfield Dr 14620
Fairgate St 14606
Fairhaven Rd 14610
Fairhill Dr 14618
Fairholm Dr 14624
Fairlane Dr 14626
Fairlawn Dr 14617
Fairlea Dr 14622
Fairmeadow Dr 14618
Fairmount Ave 14626
Fairmount St 14607
Fairview Ave 14619
Fairview Cres 14617
Fairview Ct 14612
Fairview Hts 14613
Fairway Dr 14612
Fairwood Cir & Dr 14623
Falcon Crest Dr 14625
Falkirk Pl 14612
Fallbrook Cir 14625
Fallenson Dr 14616
Falleson Rd 14612
Fallingwood Ter 14612
Falls St 14608
Falls View Ln 14625
Falmouth St
28-38 14615
40-199 14615
61-64 14606
Falstaff Rd 14609
Far View Hills Rd 14620
Faraday St 14610
Farbridge St 14621
Farleigh Ave 14606
Farley Rd 14621
Farm Brook Dr 14625
Farmington Rd 14609
Farnsworth Rd N & S 14623
Farnum Ln 14623
Farragut St 14611
Farrell Ter 14617
Farrington Pl 14610
Favara Cir 14609
Favor St 14608
Fawn St 14622
Fawn Hill Rd 14612
Federal St 14609
Fedex Way 14624
Felicia Ct 14612
Felix St
1-46 14608
47-99 14606
Fence St 14611
Fenton Rd 14624
Fenwick St 14608
Fern St 14606
Fern Castle Dr 14622
Fernboro Rd 14618
Ferncliffe Dr 14621
Ferndale Cres 14609
Fernwood Ave
1-280 14621
281-599 14609
Fernwood Park 14609
Ferrano St 14606
Ferris St 14609
Fessenden St 14611
Fetzner Rd 14626
Field St 14620
Fielding Rd 14626
Fieldston Ter 14610
Fieldwood Dr 14609
Fien St 14605
Fiesta Rd 14626

Fillingham Dr 14615
Fillmore St 14611
Filon Ave 14622
Finch St 14613
Finney St 14605
Fintray Pl 14607
Finucane Rd 14623
Fireglow Ln 14612
Fireside Dr 14618
Firestone Dr 14624
Fisher Rd 14624
Fishermans Cv 14626
Fitzhugh Pl S 14608
Fitzhugh St N 14614
Fitzhugh St S
1-9 14614
11-60 14614
61-399 14608
Fje Ln 14626
Flagstaff Dr 14622
Flamingo Cir & Dr 14624
Flanders Pl & St 14619
Flatt Rd 14623
Fleetwood Dr 14609
Fleming St 14612
Fleming Creek Cir 14616
Flint St
1-340 14608
341-599 14611
Flint Lock Cir 14624
Flora St 14608
Florack St 14621
Floral Dr 14617
Floralton Dr 14624
Floren Dr 14612
Florence Ave 14616
Florence St 14611
Florentine Way 14624
Florenton Rd 14617
Florida Ave 14616
Floverton St 14610
Flower St 14621
Flower City Park 14615
Flower Dale Cir & Dr 14626
Floyd Dr 14623
Flynn Rd 14612
Flynnwood Dr 14612
Fondiller Ave 14625
Fontana Ln 14612
Fonthill Park 14618
Forbes St 14611
Ford Ave 14606
Ford St 14608
Foreman Dr 14616
Forest Ave 14622
W Forest Dr 14624
Forest Glen Dr 14612
Forest Hills Rd 14625
Forest Meadow Trl 14624
Forester St 14609
Forgham Rd 14616
Forshire Ln 14623
Forsythia Dr 14624
Fort Hill Ter 14620
Fortune Ln 14626
Foster Rd 14616
Fountain St 14620
Fox Ct 14606
Fox Run 14606
Fox St 14615
Fox Hall Dr 14609
Fox Meadow Rd 14626
Foxborough Ln 14618
Foxe Commons 14624
Foxe Harrow Dr 14624
Foxshire Cir & Ln 14606
Frances St 14609
Francine Dr 14606
Frandee Ln 14626
Frank Dimino Way 14624
Frankfort St 14608
Frankland Rd 14617
Franklin Ct & St 14604
Fraser St 14609
Frear Dr 14616
Frederick Dr 14624
Frederick St 14605
Frederick Douglass St 14608
Freeland St 14606
Freemont Rd 14612
French Rd 14618
French Creek Dr 14618
French Meadow Ln 14618
Frenchwoods Cir 14618
Fresno Rd 14623
Frey St 14612
Friar Dr 14626
Friederich Park 14621
Friel Rd 14623
Fromm Pl 14605
Frondone St 14604
Frontenac Hts 14617
Frost Ave
1-350 14608
351-899 14611
Frost Meadow Trl 14612
Frostholm Dr 14624
Fuller Pl 14608
Fulton Ave
1-145 14608
146-299 14613
Furlong Rd 14623
Furlong St 14621
Furman Cres 14620
Furnace St 14614
Gable Aly 14607
Gailhaven Ct 14618
Galahad Dr 14623
Galaxy Dr 14617
Gale Ter 14610
Galena St 14612
Galusha St 14605
Galway Dr 14623
Galwood Dr 14622
Ganado Rd 14617
Garden Dr 14609
E Garden Dr 14606
W Garden Dr 14606
Garden Ln 14626
Garden St 14608
Gardham Rd 14617
Gardiner Ave 14611
Gardiner Park 14607
Garfield St 14611
Garford Rd 14622
Garland Ave 14611
Garnet St 14609
Garson Ave 14609
Gary Dr 14624
Gary Hill Dr 14624
Gas Light Ln 14610
Gates St 14606
Gates Greece Townline Rd 14606
Gates Manor Dr 14606
Gateway Cir & Rd 14624
Gatewood Ave 14624
Gawaine Ln 14623
Gayla Dr 14626
Geddes St 14606
Geiger Cir 14612
Gemini Cir 14606
Gene Dr 14624
Genesee St 14611
Genesee Park Blvd
1-130 14611
131-1301 14619
Genesee View Trl 14623
Geneva St 14621
Gennis Dr 14625
Gentry Cir 14626
Georgetown Dr 14617
Georgian Dr 14609
Georgian Court Rd 14610
Geraldine Pkwy 14624
Gerling Pl 14611
Gibbs St
1-60 14604
61-199 14605
Gilbert Dr 14609
Giles Ave 14609
Gillett Rd 14624
Gillette St 14619
Gilmore St 14605
Girard Cir 14624
Girard St 14610
Girton Pl 14607
Gladmar Dr 14622
Gladstone St 14611
Gladys St 14621
Glasgow St 14608
Glasser St 14606
Glazer Dr 14625
N Glen Dr 14626
Glen Pkwy 14609
Glen Rd 14610
Glen Cove Rise 14617
Glen Ellyn Way 14618
Glen Haven Rd 14609
Glen Iris Dr 14623
Glen Oaks Dr 14624
Glenbriar Cir & Dr 14616
Glenbrook Rd 14616
Glencross Cir 14626
Glendale Park 14613
Glenhill Dr 14618
Glenlivet Dr 14624
Glenmont Dr 14617
Glenn Holw 14622
Glenn Abbey Cir 14612
Glenora Dr & Gdns 14615
Glenridge Ln 14609
Glenside Way 14612
Glenthorne Rd 14615
Glenview Ln 14609
Glenville Dr 14606
Glenwood Ave 14613
Glide St
1-390 14611
391-1199 14606
Gloucester Cir 14623
Gnage Ln 14612
Goebel Pl 14620
Goethals Dr 14616
Gold St 14620
Golden Rd 14624
Golden Eagle Lndg 14612
Golden Fleece Dr 14623
Golden Flyer Dr 14618
Golden Oaks Way 14624
Golden Rod Ln 14623
Golfshire Dr 14626
Golfside Pkwy 14610
Goodger Park 14612
Goodman St N
1-375 14607
376-2399 14609
Goodman St S
1-600 14607
601-1199 14620
Goodway Dr S 14623
Goodwill St 14615
Gordon Dr 14626
Gordon Heights Rd 14610
Gorham St 14605
Gorsline St 14613
Gothic St 14621
Gould St 14610
Governor Ter 14609
Grace St 14605
Grafton St 14621
Graham Creek Hts 14625
Gramercy Park 14610
Granada Cir 14609
Granby St 14611
Grand Ave 14609
Grandview Ln 14612
Grandview Ter 14611
Granger Pl 14607
Grantham Rd 14609
Grape St 14608
Grassmere Park 14612
Gravely Rd 14623
Gray St 14609
Great Meadow Cir 14623
Grecian Pkwy 14626
Grecian Gardens Dr 14626
N Greece Rd 14626
Greece Center Dr 14612
Greece Ridge Center Dr 14626
Greeley St 14609
Green Acre Ln 14624
Green Ivy Cir 14623
Green Knolls Dr 14620
Green Meadow Dr 14617
Green Tree Ln 14606
Greenaway Rd 14610
Greenbriar Dr 14624
Greenbrier Ln 14623
Greendale Dr 14617
Greenfield Ln 14610
Greenfield Rd 14626
Greenhaven Rd 14617
Greenhouse Dr 14617
Greening Ct 14625
Greenlane Dr 14609
Greenlawn Dr 14622
Greenleaf Mdws 14612
Greenleaf Rd
1002A-1002C 14612
1006A-1006C 14612
1010A-1010C 14612
1014A-1014C 14612
1018A-1018C 14612
1022A-1022C 14612
1026A-1026C 14612
1030A-1030C 14612
500-998 14612
1000-1299 14612
Greenleaf St 14609
Greenside Ln 14617
Greenvale Dr 14618
Greenview Dr 14620
Greenwich Ln 14618
Greenwood St 14608
Gregory Park & St 14620
Gregory Hill Rd 14620
Greig St 14608
Grenell Dr 14624
Grenville Rd 14606
Greymere Rd 14612
Greyson Rd 14623
Greystone Ln 14618
Griffith St 14607
Grosvenor Rd 14610
S Grosvenor Rd 14618
Groton Pkwy 14623
Grove Pl & St 14605
Groveland Rd 14616
Grover St 14611
Groveview Cir 14612
Grovewood Ln 14624
Guardian Dr 14610
Guaymar Cir 14624
Guildhall Rd 14623
Guinevere Dr 14626
Haddon Rd 14626
Hagen Dr 14625
Hager Rd 14616
Hague St
1-430 14611
431-799 14606
Hale Cir 14612
Halford St 14611
Hall Aly 14608
Hall St 14609
Hall Of Justice 14614
Hallbar Rd 14626
Hallmark Rd 14625
Hallock Rd 14624
Halmore Dr 14609
Halstead St 14610
Halvern Cv 14622
Hamilton St 14620
Hamlet Ct 14624
Hamlin St 14615
Hammond St 14615
Hampden Rd 14610
Hampshire Dr 14618
Hampton Blvd 14612
Hancock St 14611
Handy St 14611
Hanford Landing Rd E 14615
Hanna Pl 14620
Hannahs Ter 14612
Harbor Hill Dr 14617
Harbor View Ter 14612
Harcourt Rd 14606
Harding Rd 14612
Hardison Rd 14617
Hardwood Ln 14616
Hargrave St 14621
Harlem St 14607
Harlow Park 14608
Harmon Pl 14620
Harmony Cir 14624
Harmony Dr 14626
Harmony Ln 14622
Harold Ave 14623
Harper St 14607
Harpington Dr 14624
Harrier Cir 14623
Harris Park 14610
Harris St 14621
Harrison St 14605
Harrison Ter 14617
Harrogate Dr 14625
Hart St 14605
Hartfeld Dr 14625
Hartford St 14605
Hartland Rd 14617
Hartom Rd 14624
Hartsdale Rd 14622
Hartsen St 14610
Hartwood Dr 14623
Harvard St
1-650 14607
651-1099 14610
Harvest Dr 14626
Harvest Hl 14624
Harvest St 14605
Harvington Dr 14617
Harway Dr 14625
Harwick Rd 14609
Harwin Dr 14623
Harwood Cir 14625
Harwood St 14620
Hastings Ln 14617
Hastings St 14613
Hathaway Rd 14617
Havelock Dr 14615
Havens Rd 14618
Havenshire Rd 14625
Havenwood Dr 14622
Haverford Ave 14609
Haviland Park 14616
Hawkins St 14605
Hawks Nest Cir 14626
Hawley St
1-260 14608
261-599 14611
Hawthorne St 14610
Hay Market Rd 14624
Hayward Ave 14609
Hazel Aly 14605
Hazel St 14623
Hazel Bark Run 14606
Hazelhurst Dr 14606
Hazelwood Ter 14609
Heantang St 14614
Hearthstone Ln 14617
Heashark Rd 14624
Heather Dr 14625
Heather Ln 14616
Heather Rdg 14626
Heather St 14610
Heather Trl 14624
Heatherstone Ln 14618
Hebard St 14605
Heberle Rd 14609
Heberton Rd 14622
Hedge St 14606
Hedgegarth Dr 14617
Heidelberg St 14609
Helen Rd 14623
Helena St 14605
Helendale Rd 14609
Helenwood Rd 14616
Hemingway Dr 14620
Hemlock Woods Ln 14615
Hempel St 14605
Henion St 14611
Henley St 14612
E Henrietta Rd
2-44 14620
46-499 14620
501-2614 14623
W Henrietta Rd 14623
Henrietta St 14620
Henry Cir 14624
Henry St 14605
Herald St 14621
Herbert St 14621
Heritage Cir & Dr 14615
Heritage Woods Ct 14615
Herkimer St 14609
Hermitage Rd 14617
Hermoso Rise 14624
Hertel St 14611
Hertford Way 14610
Hewitt St 14612
Hewlett Pkwy 14606
Hibiscus Dr 14618
Hickory Ln 14625
Hickory St 14620
Hickory Manor Dr 14606
Hickory Ridge Rd 14625
Hidden Spring Cir 14616
Hidden Valley Rd 14624
Hidden Wood Dr 14616
Hiett Rd 14626
High St 14609
W High Ter 14619
High Point Trl 14609
Highland Ave
1-1440 14620
1441-2000 14618
2001-2001 14610
2002-2002 14618
2003-2699 14610
E Highland Dr 14610
Highland Hts 14618
Highland Pkwy 14620
Highpower Rd 14623
Highview Dr 14609
Highview Ter 14624
Highwood Rd 14609
Hildegarde Rd 14626
S Hill Cir 14606
Hill Dr 14626
W Hill Est 14626
Hill Court Cir 14621
Hill Creek Ln 14626
Hill Creek Rd 14625
Hillary Dr 14624
Hillbridge Cir & Dr 14612
Hillcrest Dr 14624
Hillcrest St 14609
Hillendale St 14619
Hillhurst Ln 14617
Hillsboro Rd 14610
Hillside Ave
1-700 14610
701-999 14618
Hillswood Rd 14624
Hilltop Rd 14616
Hillview Dr 14622
Hincher St 14612
Hinchey Rd 14624
Hinkley Ln 14624
Hinsdale St 14620
Hitchcock Ln 14625
Hitree Ln 14624
Hixson St 14605
Hobart St 14611
Hobbes Ln 14624
Hoeltzer St 14605
Hoff St 14621
Hoffman Rd 14622
Hofstra Rd 14623
Hojack Park 14612
Holbrooke St 14621
Holcomb St 14612
Holcroft Rd W 14612
Holden St 14612
Holiday Rd 14623
Holland St 14605
Holleder Pkwy 14615
Hollenbeck St 14621
Holley Ridge Cir 14625
Holley Sue Ln 14626
Holli Ln 14625
Hollis St 14606
Hollister St 14605
N Hollow Rd 14626
Hollow Hill Ln 14624
Hollow Rock Trl 14612
Holloway Rd 14610
Hollybrook Rd 14623
Hollymount Rd 14617
Hollyvale Dr 14618
Hollywood Ave 14618
Hollywood Cres 14617
Hollywood St 14615
Holmes Rd 14626
Holmes St 14613
Holworthy St 14606
Holyoke St 14615
Home Pl 14611
Homer St 14610
Homestead Vw 14624
Homewood Ln 14609
Honey Bunch Ln 14609
Honeysuckle Dr 14625
Hooker St 14621
Hoover Dr 14615
Hoover Rd 14617
Hopeton Dr 14624
Hopkins St 14611
Hopper Ter 14612
Horatio Ln 14624
Horizon Dr 14625
Hortense St 14611
Howard Rd
1-495 14606
496-1500 14624
1485-1485 14611
1501-1699 14624
1502-1698 14624
Howard St 14620
Howedale Dr 14616
Howell St 14607
Howland Ave 14620
Hoyt Pl 14610
Hsbc Plz 14604
Hubbell Park 14608
Hudson Ave
1-600 14605
601-1650 14621
1651-2299 14617
Hughes Pl 14612
Humboldt St
40-92 14609
94-111 14609
112-699 14610
Hunt Holw & Pt 14624
Hunters Cv 14624
Hunters Ln 14618
Hunters Gate Dr 14606
Hunting Spg 14624
Huntington Brk 14625
Huntington Hls N 14622
Huntington Hls S 14622
Huntington Hts 14622
Huntington Mdw 14625
Huntington Park 14621
Huntington Hills Ctr 14622
Hurd Ave 14606
Hurstbourne Rd 14609
Hutchings Rd 14624
Hylan Dr 14623
Hytec Cir 14606
Ice Rose Ln 14623
Iceland Park 14611
Ida Red Ln 14626
Idle Ln 14623
Idlewood Rd 14618
Idyllwood Ln 14617
Iland Dr 14624
Illinois St 14609
Images Way 14626

Street	ZIP
Immel St	14606
Impala Dr	14609
Imperial Cir	14617
Imperial Dr	14618
Imperial Hts E	14617
Imperial Hts W	14617
Independence St	14611
Indian Grv	14624
Indian Hill Dr	14624
Indian Spring Ln	14618
Indian Trail Ave	14622
Indiana St	14609
Indigo Creek Dr	14626
Industrial St	
1-70	14614
71-199	14608
Industrial Park Cir	14624
Inglewood Dr	14619
Ingomar Dr	14612
Ingram Dr	14624
Ingress Park	14606
Initiative Dr	14624
Innovation Way	14624
Interlaken Rd	14612
International Blvd	14624
Inwood Dr	14625
Irene St	14612
Irondequoit Blvd	14609
Irondequoit St	14605
Ironstone Dr	14624
Ironwood Dr	14616
Iroquois St	14609
Irving Dr	14624
Irving Rd	14618
Irvington Rd	14620
Isabelle St	14606
Island Cottage Rd	14612
Islington Way	14610
Ivan Cmn	14624
Ivy Rdg	14617
Ivy Bridge Way	14624
Ivy Cottage Ln	14623
Jackie Cir & Dr	14612
Jacklyn Dr	14624
Jackrist Cir	14606
Jackson St	14621
Jacques St	14620
Jade Dr	14626
Jamee Ln	14606
James Cir	14616
Jamestown Ter	14615
Janes Rd	14612
Janet Ln	14606
Janice Dr	14624
Jarley Rd	14623
Jasmine Rd	14624
Jay St	
1-335	14608
336-1699	14611
Jay Scutti Blvd	14623
Jay Vee Ln	14612
Jeanmoor Rd	14616
Jefferson Ave	14611
Jefferson Rd	
2-1334	14623
1335-1335	14692
1335-1335	14602
1336-1658	14623
1337-1749	14623
Jefferson Ter	
1-100	14608
101-299	14611
Jefreelind Dr	14616
Jemison Rd	14623
Jenna Way	14623
Jennie Cir & Ln	14606
Jennifer Cir	14606
Jensen Dr	14624
Jerold St	14609
Jersey St	14609
Jersey Black Cir	14626
Jessie St	14615
Jetview Dr	14624
Jewel St	14621
Jewett St	14606
Joanne Dr	14616
Joellen Dr	14626
John St	14623
John Jay Dr	14617
Johnny Gold Ln	14626
Johnsarbor Dr E & W	14620
Johnson Rd	14616
Joli Ln	14606
Jonathan Dr	14612
Jones Ave	14608
Jonquil Ln	14612
Jordan Ave	14606
Joseph Ave	
1-590	14605
591-1199	14621
Joseph Pl	14621
Joseph C Wilson Blvd	14627
Josephine Dr	14606
Josies Ln	14616
Josons Dr	14623
Joy Ln	14617
Judson St & Ter	14611
Judy Ann Dr	14616
Juliane Dr	14624
Juliet Cres	14612
Juniper St	14610
Kafana Dr	14612
Kalyna Dr	14617
Kane Dr	14622
Kansas St	14609
Kappel Pl	14605
Karen Dr	14606
Karenlee Dr	14618
Karges Pl	14620
Karlan Dr	14617
Karnes St	14606
Karrat Dr	14622
Kartes Dr	14616
Kastner Park	14621
Kay Ave	14624
Kay Ter	14613
Kaye Park Ter	14624
Kaylin Dr	14624
Kaymar Dr	14616
Kaywood Dr	14626
Kearney Dr	14617
Keating Dr	14622
Keeler St	14621
Keller St	14609
Kellwood Dr	14617
Kelly St	14605
Kemphurst Rd	14612
Kencrest Cir & Dr	14606
Kendrick Rd	14620
Kenilworth Ter	14605
Kenmore Ln	14617
Kenmore St	14611
Kennedy Cir	14609
Kenneth Dr	14623
Kensington Ct	14612
Kensington St	14611
Kent Park	14610
Kent St	14608
Kentucky Ave	14606
Kentucky Xing	14612
Kentwood Dr	14626
Kenwick Dr	14623
Kenwood Ave	14611
Kernwood Dr	14624
Kerr Ave	14606
Kestrel St	14613
Keswick Rd	14609
Ketchum St	14621
Kettering Dr	14612
Kevin Dr	14625
Keyel Dr	14625
Keystone Dr	14625
Kilbourn Rd	14618
Killarney Dr	14616
Kilmar St	14621
Kim Ln	14626
Kimball Dr	14623
Kimbark Rd	14610
Kimberly Dr	14610
Kimberly Anne Dr	14606
Kimbrook Cir & Dr	14612
Kindares Ave	14619
Kindlewood Ln	14617
King St	14608
King Arthurs Ct	14626
Kings Hwy N	14617
Kings Hwy S	14617
Kings Ln	14617
Kings Way	14624
Kings Court Way	14617
Kings Gate N & S	14617
Kingsberry Dr	14626
Kingsboro Rd	14619
Kingsbury Ct	14618
Kingsley Rd	14612
Kingsridge Ln	14612
Kingston St	14609
Kingswood Dr	14624
Kiniry Dr	14609
Kinmont Dr	14612
Kintz St	14612
Kirby Pl	14620
Kirk Dr	14610
Kirk Rd	14612
Kirk Rd S	14612
Kirkdale Cir	14612
Kirkfield Dr	14612
Kirkland Rd	14611
Kirkstone Pass	14626
Kirkwood Rd	14612
Kislingbury St	14613
Kittling Ridge Ln	14612
Kiwanis Rd	14617
Klein St	14621
Klink Rd	14625
Klueh St	14611
Knapp Ave	14609
Knickerbocker Ave	14615
Knights Trl W	14624
Knob Rd	14626
Knoll Top Dr	14610
Knollbrook Rd	14610
Knollwood Dr	14618
Knowles Aly	14608
Knowlton Ln	14618
Kohl Dr	14616
Kohlman St	14621
Kohlwood Dr	14617
Koladyne Ave	14606
Kondolf St	14606
Kosciusko St	14621
Kramer St	14623
Kresswood Dr	14624
Kristin Dr	14624
Kron St	14619
Kuebler Dr	14624
Kuhn Rd	14612
Kyle Dr	14626
La Grange Ave	14615
La Solis Dr	14626
Labrador Dr	14616
Labrea Dr	14624
Laburnam Cres	14620
Lac De Ville Blvd	14618
Lac Kine Dr	14618
Laconia Pkwy	14618
Lacroix Court Dr	14609
Lafayette Park	14607
Lafayette Pkwy	14625
Lafayette Rd	14609
Laforce St	14621
Lagrange Ave	14613
Lake Ave	
1-499	14608
500-1384	14613
1385-1385	14615
1386-1386	14613
1387-2115	14615
2116-4799	14612
Lake Ter	14617
Lake Bluff Rd	14622
Lake Breeze Park	14622
Lake Breeze Rd	14616
Lake Front	14617
Lake Home St	14612
Lake Lea Rd	14617
Lake Meadow Dr	14612
Lake Shore Blvd	14617
Lake Shore Boulevard Ext	14617
Lake Vista Ct	14612
Lakecrest Ave	14612
Lakeland Ave	14612
Lakeport St	14612
Lakeshire Rd	14612
Lakeside Ter	14612
Lakeview Park & Ter	14613
Lakewood Dr	14616
Lalanne Rd	14623
Lambert Dr	14616
Lamberton Park	14611
Lambton Cir	14626
Lamont Pl	14609
Lamp Post Dr	14624
Lamplighter Ln	14616
Lampson St	14609
Lanark Cres	14609
Lancaster St	14615
Lancelot Ln	14623
Lancraft St	14609
Landau Dr	14606
Landing Park	14625
Landing Rd N	14625
Landing Rd S	14610
Landing St	14623
Landon Pkwy	14618
Landsdowne Ln	14618
Landstone Ter	14606
Laney Rd	14620
Lang St	14621
Langford Rd	14615
Langham St	14621
Langslow St	14620
Lansdale St	14620
Lansing Cir N	14624
Lansing Cir S	14624
Lansing St	14605
Lansmere Way	14624
Lantana Ln	14612
Lantern Ln	14623
Lanvale Park	14617
Lapham St	14615
Larch St	14612
Larchbriar Dr	14616
Laredo Dr	14624
Lark St	14613
Larkins Xing	14612
Larkspur Ln	14622
Larkwood Dr	14626
Larwood Dr	14618
Lasalle St	14606
Laser St	14621
Latona Rd	14626
Latta Rd	
1-3270	14612
3245-3245	14616
3272-3798	14612
3301-3799	14612
Lattimore Rd	14620
Lauer Cres	14605
Laura Dr	14626
Laura St	14609
Laureen Ln	14626
Laurel Ave	14624
Laurel St	14606
Laurelhurst Rd	14626
Laurelton Rd	14609
Laurelwood Dr	14626
Lavaine Way	14623
Lavender Cir	14623
Laverne Dr	14616
Lavington Dr	14626
Lawendra St	14624
Lawn St	14607
Lawndale Ter	14609
Lawnsbury Dr	14624
Lawrence St	14607
Lawson Rd	14616
Lawton St	14607
Lazy Creek Cir	14612
Le Manz Dr	14606
Le Marc Ct	14618
Leamington Cir	14626
Leander Rd	14612
Leavenworth St	14613
Lechase Dr	14606
Ledgerock Ln	14618
Ledgewood Cir & Dr	14615
Lee Pl	14608
Lee Rd	14606
Lee Circle Dr	14626
Lee Road Ext	14606
Leerie Dr	14612
Leeward Ln	14618
Lefrois St	14621
Legends Way	14612
Legion Cir	14616
Legionnaire Dr	14617
Legran Rd	14617
Lehigh Ave	14619
Leicestershire Rd	14621
Leighton Ave	14609
Lela St	14606
Leland Rd	14617
Lemon Ln	14606
N Lemoyn Ave	14612
Lenox St	14611
Lenriet St	14615
Leo Rd	14623
Leo St	14621
Leonard Rd	14616
Leopard St	14615
Leopold St	14605
Leroy St	14612
Les Harrison Dr E	14624
Leslie Pl	14609
Lester St	14623
Letchworth Ave	14626
Lettington Ave	14624
Lewis St	14605
Lexington Ave	
100-795	14613
796-1824	14606
Lexington Ct	14606
Lexington Pkwy	14624
Lianne Dr	14626
Liberty Ave	14622
Liberty Pole Way	14604
Lida Ln	14616
Lightfoot St	14623
Lighthouse St	14612
Lightwood Ln	14606
Lilac Dr	14620
Lill St	14621
Lillian Ln	14616
Lily St	14615
Lime St	14606
Lime Rock Ln	14610
Limerick Ln	14606
Lincoln Ave	14611
Lincoln St	14605
Lincoln Mills Rd	14625
Linda Dr	14616
Linden Ave	
1-199	14610
412-910	14625
Linden Park	14625
Linden St	14620
Linden Oaks	14625
Ling Rd	14612
Linnet St	14613
Linwood Pl	14607
Lion St	14615
Lisa Ann Dr	14606
Lisbet St	14623
Lisbon St	14606
Lismore Grn	14617
List Ave	14617
Litchfield St	14608
Little Creek Cir & Dr	14616
Littlewood Ln E & W	14625
Livery Way	14624
Livingston Park	14608
Lloyd St	14611
Loch Revan Hts	14617
Lochner Pl	14605
Lockwood St	14609
Locust St	14613
Locust Hill Dr	14618
Loden Ln	14623
Loderdale Rd	14624
Lodge Dr	14622
Loganberry Ln	14612
Logans Run	14626
Lois St	14606
Lomb Memorial Dr	14623
Lombard St	14606
Lombardy Cir	14612
Lone Oak Ave	14616
Lonerli St	14606
Long Acre Rd	14621
Long Meadow Dr	14621
Long Park Dr & Ln	14612
Long Pond Rd	
1-878	14612
879-1670	14626
1671-2499	14606
Long Wood Dr	14612
Longcroft Rd	14609
Longleaf Blvd	14626
Longridge Ave	14616
Longsworth Dr	14625
Longview Ter	14609
Lonran Dr	14624
Loomis St	14621
Lorenzo St	14611
Loreto Ave	14623
Lori Ln	14624
Lorimer St	14608
Loring Pl	14624
Lorraine Dr	14617
Lorraine Pl	14606
Lost Mountain Trl	14625
Louise St	14606
Love St	14611
Lowden Point Rd	14612
Lowell St	14605
Loyalist Ave	14624
Lozier St	14611
Lucena Dr	14606
Lucinda Ln	14626
Luckey St	14613
Lucrest Dr	14609
Luddington Ln	14612
Ludwig Park	14621
Luella St	14609
Lunsford Ln	14608
Luther Cir	14611
Lux St	14621
Luzerne St	14620
Lyceum St	14609
Lycoming Rd	14623
Lydia St	14612
Lyell Ave	
1-310	14608
311-2400	14606
Lyell Rd	14606
Lyellwood Pkwy	14606
Lynbrook Dr	14609
Lynchester St	14615
Lynchford Park A	14611
Lynchford Park B	14611
Lyncourt Park	14612
Lyncrest Dr	14616
Lynda Ln	14624
Lyndale Dr	14624
Lyndhurst St	14605
Lynette Dr	14616
Lynn Dr	14622
Lynnhaven Ct	14618
Lynnwood Dr	14618
Lysander Dr	14623
Mac Arthur Rd	14615
Macbeth St	14609
Macintosh Dr	14626
Macon Dr	14623
Madera Dr	14624
Madison Park N	14608
Madison Park S	14608
Madison St	14608
Madison Ter	14617
Mae Mdw	14624
Magee Ave	14613
Magnolia St	
1-230	14608
231-499	14611
Maiden Ln	
1-595	14616
596-1200	14615
1201-2166	14626
2168-2198	14626
E Main St	
1-1	14614
3-50	14614
52-98	14614
100-595	14604
596-1000	14605
1001-2399	14609
W Main St	
1-250	14614
251-609	14608
610-999	14611
Mainview Dr	14625
Majestic Way	14624
Malden St	14615
Mallard Dr	14622
Malling Dr	14621
Malm Ln	14618
Malo Ct	14612
Malone St	14621
Maltby St	14606
Malvern St	14613
Manatee Pkwy	14623
Manchester St	14621
Mandarin Dr	14626
Mandy Ln	14625
Mango Ln	14606
Manhattan Square Dr	14607
Manila St	14611
Manitou Rd	
1500-1700	14626
1702-1702	14626
2170-2309	14606
2500-2999	14624
E Manitou Rd	14612
Manitou St	14621
Mann Rd	14612
Manor Dr	14617
Manor Pkwy	14620
Manordale Ln	14623
Manse Ln	14625
Mansfield St	14606
Maple Ave	14609
Maple St	14611
Maple Knoll Dr	14626
Maple Park Hts	14625
Maple Valley Cres	14623
Mapledale St	14609
Maplehurst Rd	14617
Maplewood Ave	14613
Maplewood Dr	14615
Marble Cir & Dr	14615
Marblehead Dr	14615
Marburger St	14621
Marc Mar Cir & Trl	14606
Marcia Ln	14624
Marco Ln	14622
Mareeta Rd	14624
Margaret St	14619
Margate Dr	14616
Maria St	
1-39	14605
40-199	14621
Maricrest Dr	14616
Marie Elaina Dr	14616
Marietta St	14605
Marigold St	14615
Marilou Dr	14624
Marilyn Dr	14626
Marilyn Pkwy	14624
Marina Dr	
1-99	14617
100-110	14626
Marion St	14610
Mariposa Dr	14624
Marjorie Ct	14620
Mark St	14605
Markay Ct	14618
Marketplace Dr	14623
Markie Dr E & W	14606
Marks Hill Ln	14617
Marlands Rd	14624

Marlbank Dr ... 14612
Marlborough Rd ... 14619
Marlow St ... 14611
Marne St ... 14609
Marquette Dr ... 14618
Marsden Rd ... 14609
Marsh St ... 14619
Marshall Rd ... 14624
Marshall St ... 14607
Mart Pl ... 14606
Martin St ... 14605
Martinot Ave ... 14609
Marvin Park ... 14610
Marway Cir & Dr ... 14624
Marwood Rd
1-170 ... 14616
171-599 ... 14612
Mary Dr ... 14617
Maryknoll Park ... 14622
Maryland St ... 14613
Mascot Dr ... 14626
Mason Ave ... 14626
Mason St ... 14613
Masseth St ... 14606
Massey Dr ... 14611
Master St ... 14609
Masthead Way ... 14623
Mathew Ln ... 14626
Mathews St ... 14607
Matilda St ... 14606
Matlyn Dr ... 14624
Matthew Cir ... 14624
Maureen Dr ... 14624
Maxson St ... 14609
Maxwell Ave ... 14619
May St ... 14620
Mayberry St ... 14609
Maybrooke Rd ... 14618
Mayfair Dr ... 14617
Mayfield St ... 14609
Mayflower Dr ... 14618
Mayflower St ... 14615
Maylong Dr ... 14626
Maynard St ... 14615
Mayon Dr ... 14616
Mayville Ln ... 14617
Maywood Ave, Cir & Dr ... 14618
Mazda Ter ... 14621
Mcardle St ... 14611
Mcauley Dr ... 14610
Mccall Rd
1-99 ... 14615
100-699 ... 14616
Mcewen Rd ... 14616
Mcfarlin St ... 14605
Mcguckin St ... 14611
Mcguire Rd ... 14616
Mckee Rd ... 14611
Mckendree Dr ... 14616
Mckinley St ... 14609
Mckinster St ... 14609
Mclean St ... 14620
Mcloughlin Rd ... 14615
Mcnair Dr ... 14624
Mcnaughton St ... 14606
Mead St ... 14621
Meadow Cir ... 14609
Meadow Dr ... 14618
Meadow Ln ... 14618
Meadow Creek Cir ... 14626
Meadow Greene St ... 14612
Meadowbriar Rd ... 14616
Meadowbrook Rd ... 14620
Meadowcroft Rd ... 14609
Meadowdale Dr ... 14624
W Meadows Dr ... 14616
Meadowwood Rd ... 14616
Medallion Cir & Dr ... 14626
Medfield Dr ... 14609
Medimount Dr ... 14616
Medley Centre Pkwy ... 14622
Meech Park ... 14612
Meeting House Dr ... 14624
Meigs St
1-600 ... 14607
601-1100 ... 14620
Melody St ... 14608
Melrose St ... 14619
Melville St ... 14609
Melwood Dr ... 14626
Menard Dr ... 14616
Mendon St ... 14615
Mendota Cir & Dr ... 14626
Menlo Pl ... 14620
Mercedes Dr ... 14624
Mercer Ave ... 14606
Merchants Rd ... 14609
Mercury Dr ... 14624
Meredith Ave ... 14618
Meredith St ... 14609
Meriden St ... 14612
Meridian Centre Blvd ... 14618
Merle St ... 14605
Merlin St ... 14613
Merrick St ... 14615
Merrill St ... 14615
Merrimac St ... 14605
Merriman St ... 14607
Merrydale Dr ... 14624
Merryhill Dr ... 14625
Merton St ... 14609
Merwin Ave ... 14609
Messina St ... 14605
Methodist Hill Dr ... 14623
W Metro Park ... 14623
Metropolitan Dr ... 14620
Meyerhill Cir E & W ... 14617
Mia Ter ... 14624
Miami Dr ... 14625
Miceli Way ... 14625
Michelle Dr ... 14617
Michigan St ... 14606
Middlebrook Ln ... 14618
Middlesex Rd ... 14610
Midland Ave
1-13 ... 14621
15-299 ... 14621
20-32 ... 14620
34-37 ... 14620
39-41 ... 14620
Midtown Plz ... 14604
Midtown Tower ... 14604
Midvale Ter ... 14619
Midway Dr ... 14606
Milan St ... 14621
Milburn St ... 14607
Mildorf St ... 14609
Mile Crossing Blvd ... 14624
Milford Rd ... 14625
Milford St ... 14615
Mill Cres ... 14626
Mill Lndg ... 14626
Mill Rd ... 14626
Mill St ... 14614
Mill Hollow Xing ... 14626
Mill Pond Ln ... 14626
Mill Run Dr ... 14626
Millbank St ... 14619
Miller Ct ... 14618
Miller Ln ... 14617
Miller St
1-90 ... 14605
91-199 ... 14621
Milliner St ... 14611
Millstead Way ... 14624
Milton St ... 14619
Mimosa Dr ... 14624
Minder St ... 14615
Mineola St ... 14611
Minnesota St ... 14609
Minocqua Dr ... 14617
Minute Man Trl ... 14624
Miracle Mile Dr ... 14623
Mirage Cir ... 14626
Miramar Rd ... 14624
Mitchell Rd ... 14626
Mitchell St ... 14621
Mobile Dr ... 14616
Modelane ... 14618
Mohawk St ... 14621
Mona St ... 14609
Monaco Dr ... 14624
Monica St ... 14619
Monroe Ave
100-820 ... 14607
821-1350 ... 14620
1351-3450 ... 14618
Monroe Pkwy ... 14618
Mont Morency Cir & Dr ... 14612
Montaine Park ... 14617
Montcalm Dr ... 14617
Montclair Dr ... 14617
Monte Carlo Dr ... 14624
Monterey Pkwy ... 14618
Monteroy Rd ... 14618
Montgomery St ... 14619
Monticello Dr ... 14609
Montpelier Cir ... 14618
Montreal Pl ... 14618
Montrose St ... 14608
Montvale Ln ... 14626
Moonlanding Rd ... 14624
Moore Pl ... 14606
Moore St ... 14608
Mooring Line Dr ... 14622
Moorland Rd ... 14612
Moose St ... 14615
Moran St ... 14611
E Moreno Dr ... 14626
Morgan St ... 14611
Morncrest Dr ... 14624
Morning Glory Ln ... 14626
Morning Woods Ln ... 14625
Morningside Park ... 14607
Morningstar Dr ... 14606
Moroa Dr ... 14622
Morrie Silver Way ... 14608
Morrill St ... 14621
Morrison Ave ... 14623
Morrow Dr ... 14616
Mortimer Ave ... 14623
Mortimer St ... 14604
Morton Pl & St ... 14609
Morven Rd ... 14610
Morville Dr ... 14615
Mosley Rd ... 14616
Moulson St ... 14621
Mount Airy Dr ... 14617
Mount Hope Ave ... 14620
Mount Marcy Dr ... 14622
Mount Pleasant Park ... 14608
Mount Read Blvd
1-440 ... 14611
441-1774 ... 14606
1775-2725 ... 14615
2726-4899 ... 14616
4900-5099 ... 14612
Mount Ridge Cir ... 14616
Mount Vernon Ave ... 14620
Mountain Ln & Rd ... 14625
Mountain Ash Dr ... 14615
Mountbatten St ... 14623
Moxon Dr ... 14612
Mozart Pl ... 14605
Mudge Pl ... 14605
Muirwoods Ln ... 14622
Mulberry St ... 14620
Mule Path Cir ... 14606
Mullen Pl ... 14611
Municipal Dr ... 14609
Muriel Dr ... 14612
Murray St ... 14606
Mushroom Blvd ... 14623
Musket Ln ... 14624
Mustard St ... 14609
Myrtle St ... 14606
Myrtle Hill Park ... 14606
Mystic Ln ... 14623
Mystic Pines Cir ... 14612
Nahant Rd ... 14624
Names Rd ... 14623
Nandor Dr ... 14609
Nanette Dr ... 14626
Nantucket Rd ... 14626
Nash St ... 14605
Nassau St ... 14605
Natalie St ... 14611
Nathaniel Rochester Hall ... 14623
Navarre Rd ... 14621
Needham St ... 14615
Nellis Park ... 14608
Nelson St ... 14620
Nester St ... 14621
Netherton Rd ... 14609
Neville Ln ... 14618
New England Dr ... 14618
New Hampton Pl ... 14626
New Prince Ln ... 14624
New York St ... 14611
Newark Dr ... 14616
Newbury St
1-350 ... 14613
351-599 ... 14615
Newcastle Rd ... 14610
Newcomb Rd ... 14612
Newcomb St ... 14609
Newcrest Dr ... 14618
Newcroft Park ... 14609
Newfield Dr ... 14616
Newman Pl ... 14616
Newport Dr ... 14624
Newport Rd ... 14622
Newton Dr ... 14618
Newton Rd ... 14626
Niagara St ... 14605
Nichols St ... 14609
Nicholson St ... 14620
Nicolette Cir ... 14626
Nielson St ... 14621
Nile Dr ... 14622
Nisa Ln ... 14606
Nixon Dr ... 14622
Nob Hl ... 14617
Noel Dr ... 14606
Norcrest Dr ... 14617
Norfolk Dr ... 14624
Norfolk Pl ... 14606
Norfolk St ... 14620
Norhill Dr ... 14625
Noridge Dr ... 14622
Norlane Dr ... 14622
Norman Rd ... 14623
Norman St ... 14613
Normandale Dr ... 14624
Normandy Ave ... 14619
Norran Dr ... 14609
Norris Dr ... 14610
North Ave ... 14626
North Dr ... 14612
North St
200-939 ... 14605
940-1499 ... 14621
North Ter ... 14617
Northampton Cir ... 14612
Northampton St ... 14606
Northaven Ter ... 14621
Northbridge Dr ... 14626
Northcliffe Dr ... 14616
Northcroft Cres ... 14625
Northeast Ave ... 14621
Northern Dr ... 14623
Northern Oak Trl ... 14624
Northfield Rd ... 14617
Northgate Mnr & Rd ... 14616
Northland Ave ... 14609
Northlane Dr ... 14621
Northmore Ave ... 14606
Northumberland Rd ... 14618
Northview Ter ... 14621
Northwick Dr ... 14617
Northwind Way ... 14624
Northwood Dr ... 14612
Norton St
1-1600 ... 14621
1601-2899 ... 14609
Norton Village Ln ... 14609
Norway Dr ... 14616
Norway Spruce ... 14624
Norwich Dr ... 14624
Norwood Ave ... 14606
Norwood St ... 14607
Nory Ln ... 14606
Notre Dame Dr ... 14623
Nottingham Cir & Rd ... 14610
Nova Ln ... 14606
Nowadaga Dr ... 14617
Nunda Blvd ... 14610
Nurmi Dr ... 14616
Nursery St ... 14610
Nyby Rd ... 14624
Nye Park ... 14621
Nymark Dr ... 14626
Oak Ln ... 14610
Oak St ... 14608
Oak Bridge Way ... 14612
Oak Hill Vw ... 14611
Oakbend Ln ... 14617
Oakbriar Dr ... 14616
Oakcrest Dr ... 14617
Oakdale Dr ... 14618
Oakencen Ave ... 14613
Oakhurst Dr ... 14617
Oakland St ... 14620
Oaklawn Dr ... 14617
Oakman St ... 14605
Oakmount Dr ... 14617
Oakridge Dr ... 14617
Oakside Dr ... 14625
Oaktwist Cir ... 14624
Oakview Dr ... 14617
Oakwood Dr ... 14617
Oakwood Rd ... 14616
Oasis Ln ... 14624
Oberlin St ... 14622
Obrien St ... 14605
Ohio St ... 14609
Ok Ter ... 14621
Old Acre Ln ... 14618
Old Beahan Rd ... 14624
Old Browncroft Blvd ... 14625
Old Country Rd ... 14612
Old English Dr ... 14616
Old Hickory Trl ... 14612
Old Ivy Cir ... 14624
Old Landmark Dr ... 14618
Old Meadow Dr ... 14626
Old Mill Rd ... 14618
Old North Hl ... 14617
Old Penfield Rd ... 14625
Old Pine Ln ... 14615
Old Pond Rd ... 14625
Old Scottsville Chili Rd ... 14624
Old Stone Ln ... 14615
Old Vine Dr ... 14623
Old Well Rd ... 14626
Old Westfall Dr ... 14625
Old White Ln ... 14623
Olde Erie Trl ... 14626
Olde Harbour Trl ... 14612
Olde Post Rider Trl ... 14616
Olde Tavern Cir ... 14612
Olean St ... 14608
Oliver St ... 14607
Olivia Cir & Dr ... 14626
Olympia Dr ... 14615
Omega Dr ... 14624
Oneida St ... 14621
Oneta Rd ... 14617
Onondaga Rd ... 14621
Ontario St ... 14605
Ontario View St ... 14617
Opal Ave ... 14626
Orange St
1-100 ... 14608
101-499 ... 14611
Orange Tree Cir ... 14624
Orchard Dr ... 14618
Orchard Gln ... 14625
Orchard Rd ... 14612
Orchard St
1-190 ... 14611
191-499 ... 14606
Orchard Creek Cir & Ln ... 14612
Orchard Park Blvd ... 14609
Orchid Dr ... 14616
Oregon St ... 14605
Orenda Dr ... 14622
Oriole St ... 14613
Orland Rd ... 14622
Orlando St ... 14606
Orleans St ... 14611
Ormond St ... 14605
Orpheum St ... 14621
Osage St ... 14622
Oscar St ... 14621
Ostrom Ave ... 14606
Otis St ... 14606
W Outer Dr ... 14615
Outlook Dr ... 14622
Ovencou St ... 14611
Overbrook Ave ... 14609
Overbrook Rd
20-110 ... 14624
26-28 ... 14618
30-299 ... 14618
112-136 ... 14624
Overdale Park ... 14620
Overlook Trl ... 14612
Overview Cir ... 14623
Owaissa Dr ... 14622
Owen St ... 14615
Oxford Bnd ... 14624
Oxford St ... 14607
Packard St ... 14609
Packet Ln ... 14606
Paddington Dr ... 14624
Paddy Creek Cir ... 14615
Paddy Hill Cir & Dr ... 14616
Page Ave ... 14609
Paige St ... 14619
Paladine Rd ... 14617
Palamino Dr ... 14623
Palcham Dr ... 14618
Palisade Park ... 14620
Palleash Rd ... 14612
Palm St ... 14615
Palmer St ... 14609
Palmerston Rd ... 14618
Palo Alto Dr ... 14623
Pamda Dr ... 14617
Pamela Ln ... 14618
Panaview Dr ... 14622
Panorama Trl ... 14625
Panorama Creek Dr ... 14625
Pappert Pl ... 14620
Paragon Dr ... 14624
Paramount Ln ... 14610
Pardee Rd ... 14609
Pardee St ... 14621
Parellen St ... 14608
Park Ave
93A-93D ... 14607
1-77 ... 14606
2-14 ... 14607
16-840 ... 14607
79-177 ... 14606
179-187 ... 14606
841-1399 ... 14610
Park Cir E ... 14623
Park Cir S ... 14623
N Park Dr
2-16 ... 14612
18-238 ... 14612
280-284 ... 14609
286-599 ... 14609
Park Ln ... 14625
Park Pl ... 14625
Park Rd ... 14622
Park Point Dr ... 14623
Park View St ... 14613
Parkdale Ter ... 14615
Parkedge St ... 14606
Parker Aly ... 14607
Parker Ln ... 14617
Parker Pl ... 14608
Parkerhouse Rd ... 14623
Parkgrove Rd ... 14622
Parkington Mdws ... 14625
Parklands Dr ... 14616
Parkmere Rd ... 14617
Parkside Ave ... 14609
Parkside Cres ... 14617
Parkside Ln ... 14612
Parkview Dr ... 14625
Parkview Ter ... 14617
Parkway ... 14608
Parkwood Ave ... 14620
Parkwood Rd ... 14615
Parliament Cir ... 14616
Parma St ... 14615
Parr Cir ... 14617
Parsells Ave ... 14609
Parsons Ln ... 14610
Pasadena Dr ... 14606
Paseos Dr ... 14618
Patio Dr ... 14625
Patrician Cir & Dr N & S ... 14623
Patriot Way ... 14624
Patriots Lndg ... 14626
Patt St ... 14609
Pattonwood Dr ... 14617
Paul Rd ... 14624
Paul Road Sq ... 14624
Paula Red Ln ... 14626
Pauline Cir ... 14623
Pavilion Park & St ... 14620
Paxton Rd ... 14617
Peaceful Trl ... 14609
Peach St ... 14608
Peak Hill Dr ... 14625
Pearl St ... 14607
Pearson Ln & St ... 14612
Peart Ave ... 14622
Pearwood Rd ... 14624
Pebbleview Dr ... 14612
Peck St ... 14609
Peckham St ... 14621
Peddington Cir ... 14623
Pelham Rd ... 14610
Pemberton Rd ... 14622
Pembroke St ... 14620
Penarrow Rd ... 14618
Pendleton Hl ... 14618
Penfield Cres ... 14625
Penfield Rd
1-300 ... 14610
301-1699 ... 14625
Penhurst Rd ... 14610
Penhurst St ... 14619
Penn Ln ... 14625
Pennels Dr ... 14626
Pennsylvania Ave ... 14609
Pennwood Dr ... 14625
Penrose St ... 14612
Penview Dr ... 14625
Pepperidge Dr ... 14626
Peppermint Dr ... 14615
Perinton St ... 14615
Perkins Ave ... 14609
Perkins Rd ... 14623
Perrigo St ... 14609
Perrin Dr ... 14622
Pershing Dr ... 14609
Person Pl ... 14606
Peters Pl ... 14605
Petrel St ... 14608
Petrella Cir ... 14617
Petrossi Dr ... 14621
Petten St ... 14612
Petten Street Ext ... 14612
Pheasant Way ... 14606
Phelps Ave ... 14608
Phyllis Ln ... 14624
Piave St ... 14606
Piccadilly Sq ... 14625
Pickdale Dr ... 14626
Pickering Dr ... 14626
Pickford Dr ... 14618
Pickwick Cir & Dr ... 14618
Picturesque Dr ... 14616
Pierpont St ... 14613
Pikuet Dr ... 14624
Pilgrim Cir ... 14618
Pilot St ... 14606
Pin Oak Ln ... 14622
Pine Acres Dr ... 14618

Street	ZIP
Pine Creek Ln	14626
Pine Grove Ave	14617
Pine Knoll Dr	14624
Pine Ridge Dr	14624
Pine Tree Ln	14617
Pine Valley Dr	14626
Pinebriar Dr	14616
Pinebrook Dr	14616
Pinecliff Dr	14609
Pinecrest Dr	14617
Pinehill Dr	14622
Pinehurst Dr	14624
Pinewild Dr	14606
Pinewood Knl	14624
Pinewood Trl	14617
Pinnacle Rd	
1-154	14620
155-171	14623
156-164	14620
173-231	14623
233-235	14623
239-242	14620
243-247	14623
244-250	14620
249-251	14623
252-260	14620
253-585	14623
300-584	14623
Pinnard St	14610
Pioneer St	
1-75	14619
76-299	14611
Pioneer Hall	14623
Pippin Dr	14612
Pitkin St	14607
Pittsford St	14615
Pixley Rd	14624
Pixley Industrial Pkwy	14624
Place One Dr	14626
Placheli St	14607
Placid Pl	
2-10	14606
12-12	14606
27-29	14617
31-199	14617
Planet St	14606
Platt St	
51-120	14614
121-399	14608
Plaza Dr	14617
Pleasant Ave	14622
Pleasant St	14604
Pleasant Way	14622
Plover St	14613
Plymouth Ave N	
1-99	14614
100-999	14608
Plymouth Ave S	
1-100	14614
101-149	14608
102-150	14614
151-1165	14608
1166-1400	14611
1402-1498	14611
N Point Trl	14617
Point Pleasant Rd	14622
S Pointe Lndg	14606
Pointe Vintage Dr	14626
Polaris St	14606
Pollard Ave	14612
Pollet Pl	14626
Polo Pl	14616
Pomeroy St	14621
Pomona Dr	14616
Pond Mdw	14624
Pond View Hts	14612
Pontiac Dr	14617
Ponty Pool Cir	14616
Pool St	14606
Poolside Dr	14625
Poplar Dr	14625
Poplar St	14620
Poplar Way	14618
Poplar Garden Ln	14606
Poppy St	14617
Port View Cir	14617
Portage St	14621
Portland Ave	
1-520	14605
521-1660	14621
1661-2399	14617
Portland Ct	14621
Portland Pkwy	14621
Portsmouth Ter	14607
Post Ave	14619
Post Hill Dr	14623
Potomac St	14611
Potter St	14606
Powers Ln	14624
Pratola Pl	14612
Prescott St	14611
Presque St	14609
Preston Cir	14626
Price Ln	14608
Priem St	14607
Primrose St	14615
Prince St	
1-66	14607
67-199	14605
Prince Charles Cir	14623
Princess Dr	14623
Princeton St	14605
Priscilla St	14609
Privateers Ln	14624
Privet Way	14624
Probert St	14610
Prospect St	14608
Providence Cir	14616
Province Dr	14624
Public Market	14609
Pulaski St	14621
Pullman Ave	14615
Pumpkin Hl	14624
Purple Leaf Ln	14624
Putnam St	14605
Pyramid Ln	14624
Quail Ln	14624
Quaker Dr	14623
Qualtrough Rd	14625
Quamina Dr	14605
Quarterdeck Pl	14612
Quay Dr	14617
Queens Ln	14617
Queens St	14609
Queensberry Ln	14624
Queensboro Rd	14609
Queensway Rd	14623
Quentin Rd	14609
Quesada Dr	
1-94	14612
95-299	14616
Quinby Rd	14623
Quincy St	14609
Quinn Rd	14623
Radarick Dr	14624
Radcliffe Rd	14617
Radford Way	14612
Radio St	14621
Radnor Ln	14617
Rae Dr	14626
Raeburn Ave	14619
Rahway Ln & Rd	14606
Railroad St	14609
Rainbow Dr	14622
Raines Park	14613
Rainier St	14613
Raleigh Rd	14617
Raleigh St	14620
Ramo Dr	14606
Ramona Park	14615
Ramona St	
1-150	14613
400-400	14615
402-799	14615
Rampart St	14623
Ramsey Park	14610
Ramsgate Dr	14624
Ranch Dr	14622
Ranch Village Ln	14624
Rand St	14615
Randolph St	
1-275	14621
276-399	14609
Rangers Ct	14612
Ransford Ave	14622
Raspberry Patch Dr	14612
Raton Ave	14626
Rau St	14621
Rauber St	14605
Raven Way	14606
Raven Wood	14624
Ravenwood Ave	14619
Ravine Ave	
1-5	14613
7-499	14613
44-46	14622
50-498	14613
Rawlinson Rd	14617
Raymond Dr	14624
Raymond St	14620
Rayne Dr	14623
Red Apple Ln	14612
Red Bud Rd	14624
Red Coat Cir	14624
Red Creek Dr	14623
Red Hickory Dr	14626
Red Leaf Dr	14624
Red Oak Dr	14616
Red Plank Way	14624
Red Rock Cir & Rd	14626
Red Spruce Ln	14616
Redcedar Dr	14616
Reddick Ln	14624
Redfern Dr	14620
Redfield St	14612
Redtail Run	14612
Redwood Dr	14617
Redwood Rd	14615
Reed Park	14605
Regency Oaks Blvd	14624
Regent St	14607
Regina Dr	14606
Reginald Cir	14625
Reliance St	14621
Rellim Blvd	
1-45	14606
46-199	14624
Remington Pkwy	14623
Remington St	14621
Renaissance Dr	14626
Renay Dr	14612
Renfrew Pl	14611
Renouf Dr	14624
Rensselaer Dr	14618
Renwood St	14621
Requa St	14621
Research Blvd	14623
Reservoir Ave	14620
Resolute Cir & St	14621
Restanda St	14609
Revella St	14609
Revere Dr	14624
Revere St	14612
Rexford St	14621
Reynolds Ave	14609
Reynolds Dr	14623
Reynolds St	14608
Rhea Cres	14615
Rhinecliff Dr	14618
Rhona Pl	14620
Rialto St	14621
Riccardi Dr	14626
Richard St	14607
Richardson Rd	14623
Richland St	14609
Richmond St	14607
Richs Dugway Rd	14625
Richsquire Dr	14626
Rick Edge Cir	14609
Riddle St	14611
E Ridge Rd	
1-428	14621
425-425	14617
430-1674	14621
433-1675	14621
1676-3000	14622
W Ridge Rd	
1-1925	14615
1926-4600	14626
Ridge Ter	14626
Ridge Castle Dr	14622
Ridge Port Cir & Dr	14617
Ridgecrest Rd	14626
Ridgedale Cir	14616
Ridgeland Rd	14623
N Ridgelawn Dr	14617
Ridgelea Ct	14615
Ridgemar Rd	14615
Ridgemont Dr	14626
Ridgeview Dr	14617
Ridgeway Ave	
1-1799	14615
1800-2920	14626
2921-3199	14606
Ridgeway Ests	14626
Ridgewood Dr	14622
Ridgewood Rd	14626
Ries St	14611
Riga St	14615
Riggs Rd	14612
Rigney Ln	14612
Riley Park	14606
Ringle St	14619
Rio Blanco Rd	14624
Ripley St	14609
Ripplewood Dr	14616
Rising Pl	14607
Ritz St	14605
River Hts	14612
E River Rd	14623
River St	14612
N River St	14612
River Edge Mnr	14620
River Heights Cir	14612
River Meadow Dr	14623
River View Hts	14623
Riverbank Pl	14621
Riverferry Way	14608
Rivers Run	14623
Riverside Dr	14623
Riverside St	14613
Riverview Dr	14623
Riverview Pl	14608
Riviera Dr	14624
Robbin Cres	14624
Robin Dr	14618
Robin St	14613
Robinwood Trl	14623
Roby Dr	14618
Rochelle St	14612
Rock Beach Rd	14617
Rock Garden Est	14626
Rock Hill Rd	14618
Rockdale Trl	14612
Rocket St	14609
Rockingham St	14620
Rockland Park	14611
Rocklea Dr	14624
Rockview Ter	14606
Rockway Dr	14612
Rockwood Pl & St	14610
Rocmar Dr	14626
Rode Dr	14622
Rodenbeck Pl	14620
Rodessa Rd	14616
Rodlea Cir	14623
Rodney Ln	14625
Rogene St	14616
Rogers Ave	14606
Rogers Dr	14606
Rogers Pkwy	14617
Rohr St	14605
Rollingwood Dr	14616
Rome St	14605
Romeyn St	14608
Ronald Dr	14616
Roosevelt Rd	14618
Roosevelt St	14620
Rosalie Dr	14626
Rosalind St	14619
Rose Rd	14624
Rose Arbor Cir	14623
Rose Dust Dr	14626
Roseann Dr	14616
Rosecroft Dr	14616
Rosedale St	14620
Rosemary Dr	14621
Rosemont Cir & Dr	14617
Rosemount St	14620
Roser St	14621
Roseview Ave	14609
Rosewood Ter	14609
Roslyn St	14619
Ross St	14615
Ross Brook Dr	14625
Rossiter Rd	14620
Rossmore St	14606
Roth St	14621
Rouge Rd	14623
Round Creek Dr	14626
Round Pond Ln	14626
Rowland Pkwy	14610
Rowley Dr	14624
Rowley St	14607
Roxborough Rd	14619
Roxwood Cir & Dr	14612
Royal Oak Dr	14624
Royal View Dr	14625
Roycroft Dr	14621
Royleston Rd	14609
Ruddy Duck Ln	14626
Rudman Dr & Rd	14622
Rue De Vl	14618
Rugby Ave	14619
Ruggles St	14612
Rugraff St	14606
Rumford Rd	14626
Rumson Rd	
1-91	14612
92-1099	14616
Rundel Park	14607
Running Brook Ln	14626
Running Creek Cir	14623
Runnymede Ct & Rd	14618
Russell Ave	14622
Russell St	14607
Russett Ct	14625
Rustic St	14609
Rusty Ln	14626
Rutgers St	14607
Ruth Ter	14624
Ruth Ellen Way	14624
Rutherfield Ln	14625
Rutledge Dr	14621
Rutter St	14606
Ryan Aly	14607
Ryans Run	14624
Ryans Way	14612
Rye Rd	14626
Sable Oaks Ln	14625
Sable Ridge Ln	14612
Sachem Way	14617
Sackets Lndg	14612
Saddleback Trl	14624
Saddlehorn Dr	14626
Sagamore Cir & Dr	14617
Sager Dr	14607
Saginaw Dr	14623
Sahara Dr	14624
Saint Andrews Dr	14626
Saint Bridgets Dr	14605
Saint Casimir St	14621
Saint Clair St	14611
Saint Elias Cir	14626
Saint Jacob St	14621
Saint James St	14606
Saint Johns Dr	14626
Saint Johns Park	14612
Saint Johnsville Trl	14618
Saint Joseph St	14617
Saint Margaret Way	14625
Saint Mark Dr	14606
Saint Martins Way	14616
Saint Marys Pl	14607
Saint Patrick Dr	14623
Saint Paul Blvd	14617
Saint Paul St	
1-252	14604
253-1005	14605
1006-2000	14621
2002-2326	14621
Saint Pierre Dr	14626
Saint Regis Dr N & S	14618
Saint Rita Dr	14606
Saint Stanislaus St	14621
Salem Rd	14622
Salina St	
1-95	14611
96-199	14619
Salisbury St	14609
Salter Pl	14613
Samala Cir	14625
Samuel Way	14606
San Gabriel Dr	14610
San Marie Dr	14622
San Mateo Rd	14624
San Rafael Dr	14618
San Rose Dr	14622
Sanborn Ave	14609
Sand Pebble Dr	14624
Sandalwood Dr	14616
Sandcastle Dr	14622
Sander St	14605
Sandhurst Dr	14617
Sandoris Cir	14622
Sandra Ln	14621
Sandringham Rd	14610
Sands Rd	14624
Sandstone Dr	14616
Sandy Ln	14624
Sandymount Dr	14617
Sanfilippo Cir	14625
Sanford Pl & St	14620
Sannita Dr	14626
Sansharon Dr	14617
Santee St	
1-230	14606
231-399	14613
Santiago St	14608
Sara Minni Dr	14612
Saranac St	14621
Saratoga Ave	14608
Saredon Pl	14606
Satura Ave	14611
Sauer Pl	14620
Savannah Ct	14625
Savannah St	14607
Sawgrass Dr	14620
Sawyer Pl & St	14619
Saxton St	
1-250	14611
251-400	14606
Sayne St	14621
Scarborough Park	14625
Scenic Cir	14624
Scenic View Dr	14622
Schanck Ave	14609
Schauman Pl	14605
Scheg Ter	14624
Schell Pl	14608
Schilling Ln	14618
Schley Pl	14611
Schnackel Dr	14622
Scholfield Rd W	14617
Schoolhouse Ln	14618
Schum Ln	14609
Schwartz St	14611
Science Pkwy	14620
Scio St	
1-115	14604
116-222	14605
224-699	14605
Scotch Ln	14617
Scotch Pine Dr	14616
Scott Ln	14624
Scottcross Ln	14623
Scottsville Rd	
1-240	14611
241-1500	14624
1501-2081	14623
Scrantom St	14605
Sea View Ave	14622
Seabrook St	14621
Seacliffe Rd	14622
Seafarers Ln	14612
Seaford Dr	14617
Seager St	14620
Sean Ln	14606
Seascape Dr	14612
Sebastian Dr	14625
Sedgefield Ct	14622
Selden St	14605
Selkirk Dr	14626
Selye Ter	14613
Seminole Way	14618
Senator Keating Blvd	14618
Seneca Ave	
1-599	14621
606-2199	14617
Seneca Pkwy	14613
Seneca Rd	14622
Seneca Manor Dr	14621
Seneca Park Ave	14617
Sequoia Dr	14624
Serenity Cir	14608
Sergius Way	14612
Sesqui Dr	14624
Seth Green Dr	14621
Seth Land Dr	14617
Seville Dr	14617
Seward St	
1-575	14608
576-899	14611
Sewilo Hills Dr	14622
Seymour Rd	14609
Shadmore Dr	14626
Shadow Ln	14606
Shadowbrook Dr	14616
Shadowlawn Ct	14617
Shady Way	14616
Shady Creek Rd	14623
Shady Lane Dr	14621
Shady Pine Ln	14612
Shadywood Dr	14606
Shaemus Dr	14626
Shafer St	14609
Shaftsbury Rd	14610
Shagbark Cir	14624
Shaker Ml	14612
Shale Dr	14615
Shalimar Dr	14618
Shamrock Dr	14623
Shanbrook Dr	14612
Sharon Dr	14626
Shawnee Dr	14624
Shearado St	14621
Sheffield Rd	14617
Shelbourne Rd	14620
Sheldon Ter	14619
Shelford Rd	14609
Shell Edge Dr	14623
Shelmont Dr	14621
Shelter St	14611
Shelwood Dr	14618
Shepard Ln	14624
Shepard Rd	14624
Shepard St	14620
Shepperton Way	14626
Sheppler St	14612
Sheraton Dr	14616
Sherbrooke Ln	14624
Sherer St	14611
Sherman St	14606
Sherri Ann Ln	14626
Sherwood Ave	14619
Shetland Cir	14624
Shiloh Ct	14612
Shingle Landing Dr	14609
Shingle Mill Rd	14609
Shirewood Dr	14625
Shirley St	14610
Shirley Ter	14626
Shore Dr	14622
Shore Acres Dr	14612
Shore Vista Dr	14612
Shorecliff Dr	14612
Shoreham Dr	14618
Shoreway Dr	14612
Shorewood Dr	14617
Short St	14609
Shrubbery Ln	14624
Sibley Pl	14607
Sidney St	14609

Siebert Pl 14605
Sienna Dr 14623
Sierra Dr 14616
Sierra Rd 14624
Sigel St 14605
Silvarole Dr 14623
Silver St
1-5 14608
6-299 14611
Silver Birch Dr 14624
Silver Fox Cir 14612
Silver Oak Dr 14624
Silver Ridge Dr 14626
Silverdale Dr 14609
Silverknoll Dr 14624
Simmons St 14606
Simone Cir 14609
Simpson Rd 14617
Sisson Dr 14623
Skuse St 14605
Sky Ridge Dr 14625
Skycrest Dr 14616
Skylane Dr 14621
Skyview Dr & Ln 14625
Slater Creek Dr 14616
Sleepy Holw 14624
Sleepy Hollow Ln 14618
Small Pine Cir 14612
Smallridge Ln 14617
Smith St
100-198 14608
200-610 14608
611-899 14606
Smokewood Ln 14612
Smugglers Ln 14617
Smyles Dr 14609
Snowberry Cres 14606
Snowy Owl Rdg 14612
Snug Harbor Ct 14612
Sobieski St 14621
Sodus St 14609
Solmar Dr 14624
Somerset St 14611
Somershire Dr 14617
Somerton St 14607
Somerworth Dr 14626
Songbird Ln 14620
Sonnet Dr 14626
Sonora Pkwy 14618
Sophia Pl 14608
Sotheby Dr 14626
Sothery Pl 14624
South Ave
1-319 14604
320-1999 14620
South Dr 14612
Southampton Dr 14616
Southern Dr 14623
Southern Pkwy 14618
Southern Pine Cir 14612
Southland Dr 14623
Southridge Dr 14626
Southview Ter 14620
Southwick Ct 14623
Southwind Ct 14626
Southwind Way 14624
Southwood Ln 14618
Spanish Trl 14612
Spar Cir 14606
Sparling Dr 14616
Spartan Dr 14609
Spartan Way 14624
Spearmint Dr 14615
Spencer Rd 14609
Spencer St 14608
Spencerport Rd 14606
Spicewood Ln 14624
Spiegel Park 14621
Spier Ave 14620
Spinet Dr 14625
Spinley Ct 14626
Spring Ln 14626
Spring St 14608
Spring Creek Cir 14612
Spring Tree Ln 14612
Spring Valley Dr 14622
Springbrook Cir 14606
Springfield Ave 14609
Spruce Ave 14611
Spruce Ln 14622
Sprucewood Ln 14624
Squareview Ln 14626
E & W Squire Dr 14623
Squire Dale Ln 14612
Stace St 14612
Stafford Way 14626
Stal Mar Cir 14624
Stallion Cir 14626
Stallman Dr 14623
Standish Rd 14626
Stanfield Ter 14619
Stanford Dr 14610
Stanford Rd W 14620
Stanley St 14608
Stanridge Ct 14617
Stanton Ln 14617
Stanton St 14611
Starling St 14613
Starlite Dr 14624
Starwood Dr 14625
State St
2-300 14614
301-599 14608
Statt Rd 14624
Staudinger Pl 14621
Stebbins St 14620
Steel St 14606
Steger Pl 14622
Steko Ave 14615
Stemrose Ln 14624
Stenson St 14606
Sterling Sq 14616
Sterling St 14606
Steve Dr 14606
Stevens St 14605
Stewart Dr 14624
Stewart St 14620
Still Moon Cres 14624
Stillmeadow Dr 14624
Stillson St 14604
Stockton Ln 14625
Stone Rd
1-1281 14616
1282-1899 14615
Stone St 14604
Stone Barn Rd 14624
Stone Fence Cir & Rd 14626
Stonebriar Ln 14626
Stonecliff Dr 14616
Stonecrest Dr 14615
Stoneham Dr & Rd 14625
Stonehenge Rd 14609
Stonehill Dr 14615
Stoneleigh Ct 14618
Stoneridge Dr 14615
Stonewall Ct 14615
Stonewood Ave
1-98 14612
99-599 14616
Stonewood Park 14616
Stoney Path Ln 14626
Stoneycreek Cir & Dr 14616
Stony Point Rd 14624
Stonybrook Dr 14618
Stout St 14609
Stover Cir & Rd 14624
Stowell Dr 14616
Stranahan Park 14617
Stratford Ln 14612
Stratford Park 14611
Strathallan Park 14607
Strathmore Cir 14609
Strathmore Dr 14616
Strathmore Ln 14609
Strathmore Rd 14612
Stratton Rd 14610
Straub Rd 14626
Straub St 14613
Strawberry Hill Rd 14623
Strohm St 14612
Strollis Rd 14626
Strong St 14621
Studley St 14616
Stunz St 14609
Stutson St 14612
Suburba Ave 14617
Suburban Ct 14620
Sudbury Dr 14624
Suellen Dr 14609
Sugar Maple Dr 14615
Sullivan St 14605
Summer Ln 14626
Summer Pond Way 14624
Summer Sky Dr 14623
Summerville Dr 14617
Summit Dr 14620
Summit Circle Dr 14618
Summit Grove Park 14615
Summit Hill Dr 14612
Sumner Park 14607
Sun Valley Dr 14606
Suncrest Dr 14609
Sunderland Trl 14624
Sunflower Dr 14621
Sungrove Ln 14624
Sunny Mill Ln 14626
Sunnyside Dr 14623
Sunridge Dr 14624
Sunrise Cres 14622
Sunrise St 14615
Sunset Ct 14618
Sunset Dr 14618
Sunset Hl 14624
Sunset St 14606
Sunset Ridge Trl 14626
Sunshine St 14621
Suntru St 14605
Sunview Dr 14624
Superior Rd 14625
Superior St 14611
Superior Ter 14611
Surrey Rd 14616
Surrey Hill Way 14623
Susan Ln 14616
Susquehanna Rd 14618
Sussex Rd 14623
Suter Ter 14620
Sutorius Dr 14616
Sutters Run 14624
Sutton Pl 14620
Swan St 14604
Swansea Park 14616
Sweet Acres Dr 14612
Sweet Birch Ln 14615
Sweet Vernal Ct 14623
Sycamore St 14620
Sydenham Rd 14609
Syke St 14611
Sylvan Rd 14618
Sylvania Rd 14618
Sylvester St 14621
Sylvia Ln 14617
Sylvia Rd 14623
Symington Pl 14611
Systems Rd 14623
Tacoma St 14613
Taft Ave 14609
Tahoe Dr 14616
Tait Ave 14616
Tall Pines Dr 14616
Talnuck Dr 14612
Talon Run 14612
Talos Way 14624
Tamarack Dr 14622
Tamarack St 14612
Tameadwa Dr 14616
Tandoi Dr 14624
Tangerine Way 14606
Tanglewood Dr 14616
Tarrington Rd 14609
Tarrycrest Ln 14606
Tarrytown Dr 14624
Tarrytown Rd 14618
Tartarian Cir 14612
Tarwood Dr 14606
Tawney Pt 14626
Tay Brook Ln 14612
Taylor St 14611
Taylors Rise 14618
Teakwood Dr 14609
Tech Park Dr 14623
Technology Blvd 14626
Telco Rd 14623
Teralta St 14621
Teresa Cir 14624
Teresa St 14605
Terrace Park 14619
Terrain Dr 14618
Terry Ln 14624
Terry St 14611
Texas St 14606
Thacker St 14612
Thackery Rd 14610
Thatcher Rd 14617
Thayer St 14607
The Highlands 14622
Thendara Ln 14617
Theodore St 14621
Thistledown Dr 14617
Thomas Ave 14617
Thomas St
1-80 14605
81-199 14621
Thomas Cove Rd 14625
Thomasville Dr 14612
Thompson Rd 14623
Thorn St 14613
Thorn Apple Ln 14626
Thorncliffe Dr 14617
Thorndale Ter 14611
Thorndyke Rd 14617
Thornton Rd 14617
Thornwood Dr 14625
Thorpe Cres 14616
Thurlow Ave 14609
Thurston Ct & Rd 14619
Tiam Dr 14622
Tibbles Ln 14624
Tiernan St 14612
Tietenberg Ave 14622
Tilden St 14608
Tilstone Pl 14618
Timarron Trl 14612
Timber Oak Cir 14626
Timothy Ct 14623
Timpat Dr 14624
Timrod Dr 14617
Tindale Dr 14622
Tioga Cir & Dr 14616
Titus Ave
1-1317 14617
1318-2410 14622
Titus Ct 14617
Titus Avenue Ext 14622
Tobin Dr 14615
Tone Ter 14617
Toni Ter 14624
Toper Trl 14612
Topper Dr 14622
Torrey Pine Dr 14612
Torrington Dr 14618
Totem Trl 14617
Tottenham Rd
19-25 14609
27-199 14609
53-57 14610
59-63 14610
65-75 14610
Tower Dr 14623
Town Centre Dr 14623
Town House Cir 14616
Towngate Rd 14626
Townline Cir 14623
Townsend St 14621
Towpath Cir 14618
Towpath Ln 14618
Towpath Trl 14624
Trabold Rd S 14624
Tracy St 14607
Trade Ct 14624
Tradewind Dr 14617
Trafalgar St 14619
Trails End 14624
Trailwood Cir 14618
Transport Dr 14623
Traver Cir 14609
Traymore Rd 14609
Tree Brook Dr 14625
Tree Top Dr 14625
Treeline Dr 14612
Trelawne Dr 14622
Tremont Cir 14608
Tremont St
201-211 14608
213-500 14608
501-699 14611
Trenaman St 14621
Trento St 14606
Trevor Court Rd 14610
Treyer St 14621
Tribune Hall 14623
Trinidad St 14605
Tristram Ct 14623
Trivenco Rd 14610
Trolley Blvd & Cir 14606
Tropez Pt 14626
Troup St
1-330 14608
331-499 14611
Troutbeck Ln 14626
Troy Rd 14618
True Hickory Dr 14615
Truesdale St 14615
Trust St 14621
Tryon Est & Park 14609
Tubman Way 14608
Tufa Glen Dr 14625
Tulane Pkwy 14623
Tuliptree Ln 14617
Tully Ln 14626
Turnabout Ln 14618
Turner St 14619
Turning Leaf Ln 14612
Turpin St 14621
Turtle Rock Ln 14617
Turtlewood Trl 14626
Tuscarora Dr 14609
Twilight Dr 14617
Twin Rd 14609
Twin Beeches 14608
Twin Circle Dr 14624
Twin Oak Dr 14606
Twin Pines Ct 14616
Tyburn Way 14610
Tyler St 14621
Tyler Ter 14624
Tyringham Rd 14617
Uniman Pl 14620
Union Park 14617
Union St N
111-279 14605
280-280 14609
281-399 14605
282-398 14605
1-110 14607
S Union St
1-199 14607
2800-3099 14624
Union Pointe Dr 14624
United Way 14604
University Ave
11-200 14605
202-234 14605
236-1499 14607
1500-1999 14610
University Park 14620
Upland Dr 14617
Upper Falls Blvd 14605
Upper Valley Rd 14624
Upton Park 14607
Upton Pl 14612
Utica Pl 14608
Valencia Dr 14606
Valiant Dr 14623
Valley Cir 14622
Valley Rd 14618
Valley St 14612
Valley Brook Cir 14616
Valley Creek Rd 14624
Valley Crest Rd 14616
Valley View Cres 14617
Valley View Pl 14612
Valois St 14621
Van St 14620
Van Auker St 14608
Van Bergh Ave 14610
Van Olinda St 14621
Van Stallen St 14621
Van Voorhis Ave 14617
Vanderlin Park 14622
Vanguard Pkwy 14606
Vantage Point Dr 14624
Varden St 14609
Varian Ln 14624
Varinna Dr 14618
Vassar St 14607
Vayo St 14609
Veldor Park 14612
Velma Ln 14612
Velox St 14615
Vendome Dr N & S 14606
Veness Ave 14616
Venetia View Cir 14626
Venice Cir 14609
Ventura Rd 14624
Veredarl Dr 14618
Vermont St 14609
Vernon Pl 14618
Verona St 14608
Veronica Dr 14617
Versailles Rd 14621
Verstreet Dr 14616
Veteran St 14609
Veterans Pl 14620
Vetter St 14605
Via Costa Ct 14618
Via Rosina Ct 14618
Via Veracruz Ct 14618
Vick Park A 14607
Vick Park B 14607
Victoria Dr 14618
Victoria St 14611
Vienna St 14605
Viennawood Dr 14618
Viewcrest Dr 14609
Villa St 14606
Villa Nova Rd 14617
Village Ln 14610
Village Way 14609
Villewood Dr 14616
Vin Gate Dr 14616
Vinal Ave 14609
Vince Dr 14606
Vince Tofany Blvd 14612
Vincent St 14608
Vincor Dr 14624
Vine St 14607
Vinedale Ave 14622
Vinewood Pl 14608
Vineyard Dr 14616
Vintage Ln
400-699 14615
900-1298 14626
1301-1499 14626
Vinton Rd 14622
Violetta St 14608
Virgil Dr 14609
Virginia Ave 14619
Virginia Ln 14624
Virginia Manor Rd 14606
Viroqua Dr 14622
Visca Ln 14626
Viscount Dr 14623
Visions Cir 14626
Vista Dr 14615
Vixen Run 14625
Vixette St 14611
Vollmer Pkwy 14623
Von Deben Ln 14617
Vose St 14605
Wabash Ave 14617
Wabash St 14609
Wacona Ave 14622
Wadsworth St 14605
Wahl Rd 14609
Wainswright Cir 14626
Wait St 14605
Wakecliffe Dr 14616
Wakefield St 14621
Wakehurst Rd 14623
Walbar St 14609
Walbert Dr 14624
Walden Pl 14610
Waldo Ave 14609
Waldo St 14606
Waldorf Ave 14606
Walker St 14626
Wall St 14620
Wallace Way 14624
Walnut Park 14622
Walnut St
1-60 14611
61-199 14608
Walter Park 14611
Waltham Rd 14624
Walton St 14620
Walzer Rd 14622
Walzford Rd 14622
Wanda St 14621
Wangman St 14605
War Memorial Sq 14614
Ward St 14605
Ward Ter 14608
Warehouse St 14608
Waring Rd 14609
Warner St 14606
Warren Ave 14618
Warren St 14620
Warrenton St 14609
Warrington Dr 14618
Warsaw St 14621
Warwick Ave 14611
Washburn Park 14620
Washington Ave 14617
Washington Dr 14625
Washington St S
1-20 14614
N Washington St
2-2 14614
4-99 14614
320-346 14625
348-2199 14625
S Washington St
21-199 14608
Watch Hill Dr 14624
Watchman Ct 14624
N Water St 14604
Waterbury Ln 14625
Waterford Cir 14618
Waterview Cir 14625
Watkin Ter 14605
Waverly Pl 14608
Wayfaring Ln 14612
Wayne Dr 14626
Wayne Pl 14611
Wayside Dr 14625
Weather Wood Ln 14612
Weatherwood Ln 14624
Weaver St 14621
Webber Cir & Dr 14626
Webster Ave & Cres 14609
Webwood Cir 14626
Wedgewood Dr 14624
Wedgewood Park 14616
Weeger St 14605
Wegman Rd 14624
Wegmans Market St 14624
Weicher St 14606
Weider St 14620
Weidner Rd 14624
Weigel Aly 14621
Weiland Rd
1-645 14615
646-1499 14626
Weiland Woods Ln 14626
Weld St 14605
Weldon St 14611
Welland St 14612
Weller Dr 14617
Wellesey Knl 14624
Wellesley St 14607

Wellington Ave
1-305 14611
306-699 14619
Wellington Dr 14623
Wellington Ponds 14624
Wells St 14611
Wellsville St 14623
Welstead Pl 14613
Wembly Rd 14616
Wendell Pl 14615
Wendell St 14609
Wendhurst Dr 14616
Wendover Rd 14610
Wendy Ln 14626
Wentworth St 14611
Werner Park 14620
Wesley St 14605
West Ave 14611
West Pkwy 14616
Westage At The Hbr 14617
Westbourne Rd 14617
Westchester Ave 14609
Westerleigh Rd 14606
Westerloe Ave 14620
Western Dr 14623
Western Pine Dr 14616
Westfall Rd
2-10 14620
12-870 14620
871-2399 14618
Westfield St 14619
Westfield Commons 14625
Westgate Dr 14617
Westgate Ter 14619
Westhaven Dr 14624
Westland Ave 14618
Westmar Dr 14624
Westminster Rd 14607
Westmoreland Dr 14620
Westmount St 14615
Weston Rd 14612
Weston Rdg 14625
Westside Dr 14624
Westview Ter 14620
Westview Commons Blvd 14624
Westway Ct 14624
Westwind Dr 14624
Westwood Dr 14616
Wethersfield Rd 14624
Wetmore Park 14606
Weyl St 14621
Weymouth Dr 14625
Whalin St 14620
Wheat Hl 14624
Wheatfield Dr 14616
Wheatland St 14615
Wheeldon Dr 14616
Whelehan Cir & Dr 14616
Whipple Ln 14622
Whisper Creek Ct 14626
Whispering Pines Cir 14612
Whispering Winds Ln 14626
Whistlers Cove Ln 14612
Whitby Rd 14609
White St 14608
White Birch Cir 14624
White Fawn Run 14624
White Hall Dr 14616
White Hill Dr 14625
White Knight Ln 14623
White Oak Bnd 14624
White Oaks Dr 14616
White Rabbit Trl 14612
White Spruce Blvd 14623
White Swan Dr 14626
White Tail Rise 14622
White Village Dr 14625
Whiteford Rd 14620
Whitehouse Dr 14616
Whitestone Ln 14618
Whitewood Ln 14618
Whitlock Rd 14609
Whitman Rd 14616
Whitmore St 14620
Whitney Ln 14610
Whitney St
1-125 14611
126-399 14606
Whittier Park 14621
Whittier Rd 14624
Whittington Rd 14609
Whittlebury Dr 14612
Whittlesey St 14608
Wickerberry Ln 14626
Wicklow Dr 14617
Widman St 14605
Wilbur Ave 14606
Wilbur St 14611
Wilbur Tract Rd 14609
Wilcox St 14607
Wildbriar Rd 14623
Wilder St 14611
Wilder Ter 14612
Wildflower Dr 14623
Wildmere Rd 14617
Wildwood Dr 14616
Wilelen Rd 14624
Wilkins St 14621
Willard Ave 14620
Willhurst Dr 14606
William St 14622
William Warfield Dr 14605
Williams Rd 14626
Willis Ave 14616
Williston Rd 14616
Willite Dr 14621
Willmae Rd 14616
Willmont St 14609
Willnick Cir 14626
Willow Ave 14609
Willow St 14606
Willow Creek Ln 14622
Willow Ridge Trl 14626
Willow Weep 14623
Willow Wind Trl 14624
Willowbank Pl 14611
Willowbend Dr 14624
Willowbend Rd 14618
Willowbrook Rd 14616
Willowcrest Dr 14618
Willowdale Dr 14618
Willowen Dr 14609
Willowood Dr 14612
Wills Rd 14624
Wilmer St 14607
Wilmington St 14620
Wilmot Rd 14618
Wilshire Rd 14618
Wilson Blvd 14620
Wilson St 14605
Wilsonia Rd 14609
Wilton Ter 14619
Wimbledon Rd 14617
Winans St 14612
Winbourne Rd
1-90 14611
91-299 14619
Winchester Rd 14617
Winchester St 14615
Wind Way Cir 14624
Wind Willow Way 14624
Windemere Rd 14610
Winding Rd 14618
Winding Creek Ln 14625
Windmill Trl 14624
Windsor Park 14624
Windsor Rd 14612
Windsor St 14605
Windsorshire Dr 14624
Windwood Cir 14626
Winesap Pt 14612
Winfield Rd 14622
Wingate Dr 14624
Winhurst Dr 14618
Winona Blvd 14617
Winslow Ave 14620
Winstead Rd 14609
Winston Dr 14626
Winston Pl 14607
Winter Hazel Ct 14606
Wintergreen Way 14618
Winterroth St 14609
Winterset Dr 14625
Winthrop St 14607
Winton Pl 14623
Winton Rd S
1-465 14610
466-2299 14618
2400-3499 14623
N Winton Rd
1-600 14610
601-1899 14609
Wisconsin St 14609
Wisner Rd 14622
Wisteria Ln 14617
Witherspoon Ln 14625
Wolcott Ave 14606
Wolfert Ter 14621
Wolff St 14606
Wood Rd 14626
Wood Run 14612
Wood Cutters Cir 14612
Wood Musket Trl 14612
Wood Run Cir 14612
Wood Run Commons 14612
Wood Sorrel 14624
Woodale Dr 14616
Woodbine Ave 14619
Woodbriar Dr 14616
Woodbriar Ln 14624
Woodbridge Ct 14624
Woodbury Blvd
1-15 14604
17-21 14604
23-49 14604
51-199 14607
Woodbury Pl 14618
Woodbury St 14605
Woodcrest Dr 14625
Woodcrest Rd 14616
Woodcroft Dr 14616
Woodedge Ln 14626
Wooden Pl & St 14611
Woodford St 14621
Woodgate Ter 14625
Woodhaven Dr 14625
Woodhill Dr 14616
Woodland Cir 14622
Woodland Dr 14612
Woodland Park 14610
Woodlawn St 14607
Woodman Park 14609
Woodmill Dr 14626
Woodmont Rd 14620
Woodridge Ct 14622
Woodrow Ave 14609
Woodrow St 14606
Woodruff Gln 14624
Woodshire Ln 14606
Woodside Dr 14624
Woodside Ln 14616
Woodside Pl 14609
Woodsmeadow Ln 14623
Woodsmoke Ln 14612
Woodsong Ln 14612
Woodstock Rd 14609
Woodstone Ln 14626
Woodview Dr 14624
Woodward St 14605
Woody Ln 14625
Woolacott Rd 14617
Worcester Rd 14616
Worthington Rd 14622
Wren St 14613
Wright St 14611
Wright Ter 14605
Wyand Cres 14609
Wyatt Dr 14610
Wycombe Pl 14612
Wye Bridge Dr 14612
Wyman Dr 14622
Wyncote Ave 14609
Wyncrest Dr 14624
Wyndale Rd 14617
Wyndham Rd
5-399 14609
17-27 14612
29-151 14612
1-99 14612
Wyndover Rd 14616
Wyndshire Ln 14626
Yankee Ct 14624
Yarker Ave 14612
Yarkerdale Dr 14615
Yarmouth Rd 14610
Yates St 14609
Yolanda Dr 14624
York St 14611
Yorkshire Rd 14609
Yorktown Dr 14616
Youngs Ave 14606
Zeller Pl 14606
Zimbrich St 14621
Zimmer St 14605
Zornow Dr 14623
Zuber Rd 14622
Zygment St 14621

NUMBERED STREETS

1st St 14605
2nd Ave 14612
2nd St
3-5 14606
9-15 14617
17-73 14605
18-20 14617
22-198 14605
95-97 14606
101-199 14605
3rd Ave 14612
3rd St 14605
4th Ave 14612
4th St
1-150 14609
151-399 14605
5th Ave 14612
5th St 14605
6th Ave 14612
6th St 14605
7th Ave 14612
7th St 14609
8th St 14609

ROCKVILLE CENTRE NY

General Delivery 11571

POST OFFICE BOXES MAIN OFFICE STATIONS AND BRANCHES

Box No.s
All PO Boxes 11571

NAMED STREETS

Adams Ct 11570
Addison Pl 11570
Albany Ct 11570
Aldershott Ct 11570
Aldred Ave 11570
Allen Rd 11570
Alton Rd 11570
Amherst Ct 11570
Andover Rd 11570
Arbor Ln 11570
Arden Ct 11570
Ardsley Cir & Pl 11570
Argyle Pl 11570
Arizona Ave 11570
Arleigh Rd 11570
Arlington Ave 11570
Arrandale Rd 11570
Atkinson Rd 11570
Banbury Rd 11570
Banks Ave 11570
Baylis Rd 11570
Bedford Ave 11570
Behnke Ct 11570
Bennett St 11570
Berkshire Rd 11570
Beverly Rd 11570
Blenheim Ct & Rd 11570
Bradford Ct 11570
Bramshott Ct 11570
Brevoort Pl 11570
Briarwood Ct 11570
Broadway 11570
Brompton Rd 11570
Brouwer Ln 11570
Brower Ave 11570
Buckingham Rd 11570
Buckminster Rd 11570
Bulson Rd 11570
Burtis Ave 11570
Calais Ct 11570
California St 11570
Cambridge St 11570
Canterbury Rd 11570
Capitolian Blvd 11570
Carlisle Ct 11570
Cash Ln 11570
Cedar Ave 11570
N & S Centre Ave 11570
Chelsea Ln 11570
Chestnut St 11570
Cleveland Ave 11570
Clinton Ave 11570
Coleridge Rd 11570
College Pl 11570
Columbia Ave & Rd 11570
Combes Ave 11570
Concord St 11570
Coolidge Ave 11570
Cornell Ave 11570
Cornwell St 11570
Crocker St 11570
Cumberland St 11570
Dartmouth St 11570
Davison Pl 11570
Dekoven St 11570
Demott Ave & Pl 11570
Denton Ct 11570
Derby Rd 11570
Devon Rd 11570
Dogwood Ln 11570
Dorchester Rd 11570
Dorset Ln 11570
Dover Ct 11570
Driscoll Ave 11570
Earle Ave 11570
Edgewood Rd 11570
Essex Ln 11570
Eton Rd 11570
Fenway 11570
Fonda Rd 11570
N & S Forest Ave & Pl 11570
Forestdale Rd 11570
Fountain Ave 11570
Foxcroft Rd 11570
Front St 11570
Gateway 11570
Glenwood Rd 11570
Grand Ave 11570
Greenway 11570
Greystone Rd 11570
Hamilton Rd & St 11570
Hampshire Rd 11570
Hampton Ct 11570
Hanover Pl 11570
Hanscom Pl 11570
Hargale Ct 11570
Harrison Ave 11570
Harvard Ave 11570
Hawke Ln 11570
Hawthorne Ave 11570
Hempstead Ave 11570
Hendarad Ave 11570
Hendrickson Ave 11570
Henry St 11570
Hewitt Rd 11570
Heyward Ln 11570
Hillside Ave 11570
Hollywood Ct 11570
Holyoke Rd 11570
Howard St 11570
Huber Ct 11570
Hughes St 11570
Intervale 11570
Irving Pl 11570
Jackson Ave 11570
Jefferson Ave 11570
Judson Pl 11570
Kennedy Ave 11570
N & S Kensington Ave 11570
Kent Ct 11570
Kenwood Ct 11570
Kirkwall Ct 11570
Knollwood Rd 11570
Lafayette Ave 11570
Lakeside Dr 11570
Lakeview Ave 11570
Langdon Blvd 11570
Latimer Ct 11570
Laurel Rd 11570
Lawrence Ave & Pl 11570
Lawson Ave 11570
Lee Ave 11570
Leeds Ct 11570
Lehigh Ct 11570
Lenox Rd 11570
Leon Ct 11570
N & S Lewis Pl 11570
Lexington St 11570
Liberty Ave 11570
Lincoln Ave & Ct 11570
Linden St 11570
Linhurst Pl 11570
Loch Path 11570
Locust Ave & Ct 11570
Loel Ct 11570
N & S Long Beach Rd 11570
Madison Ave 11570
Maine Ave 11570
Major Ct 11570
Maple Ave 11570
N & S Marion Pl 11570
Marlborough Ct 11570
Marvin Ave 11570
May Ct 11570
Mc Gann Dr 11570
Mcdermott Rd 11570
Meadow Ln 11570
Meehan Ln 11570
Melton Dr E & W 11570
Merriam Ct 11570
Merrick Rd
274A-350A 11570
1-17 11570
19-275 11570
244-274 11571
276-698 11570
277-699 11570
Midfarm Rd 11570
Midwood Rd 11570
Milburn St 11570
Milford Pl 11570
Milton Ct 11570
Monroe St 11570
Montauk Ave 11570
Morris Ave 11570
Muirfield Rd 11570
Murray Ct 11570
Nassau St 11570
New York Ave 11570
Neylon Ct 11570
Norcross St 11570
Nottingham Rd 11570
Oak St 11570
Oakdale Rd 11570
Ocean Ave 11570
N Oceanside Rd 11570
Old Mill Ct 11570
Olive Ct 11570
Ongley St 11570
Ormond St 11570
Osborne Pl 11570
Overlook Ln 11570
Oxford Pl & Rd 11570
Paddock Ln 11570
N & S Park Ave, Ln & Pl 11570
Parkwood Ct 11570
Pearsall Ln 11570
Pembroke Ct 11570
Pershing Blvd 11570
Pickwick Ter 11570
Pine St 11570
Plymouth Rd 11570
Powell Ave 11570
Princeton Rd & St 11570
Purdy Ct 11570
Quealy Pl 11570
Randall Ave 11570
Raymond St 11570
Reeve Rd 11570
Reid Ave 11570
Revere St 11570
Richmond Rd 11570
River Ave 11570
Riverside Dr 11570
Rockaway Ave 11570
Rockville Ave 11570
Rockwin Rd 11570
Rodney Pl 11570
Roosevelt Pl 11570
Rose Ln 11570
Roxbury Rd 11570
Roxen Rd 11570
Royal Ct & Rd 11570
Rugby Rd 11570
Russell Pl 11570
Rutland Ave 11570
Saint James Pl 11570
Saint Marks Ave 11570
Salem Rd 11570
Schuyler Ave 11570
Scott Pl 11570
Seaman Ave 11570
Searing St 11570
Seitz Ave 11570
Shellbank Pl 11570
Shelton Ct 11570
Shepherd St 11570
Sherman Ave 11570
Sherwood Rd 11570
Smith St 11570
Southard Ave 11570
State St 11570
Stonehenge Rd 11570
Stonewell Rd 11570
Stratford Rd 11570
Strathmore Ln 11570
Sunrise Hwy 11570
Surrey Ln & Pl 11570
Sutton Pl 11570
Tamwood Ct 11570
Tanglewood Rd 11570
Tarence St 11570
Terrell Ave 11570
The Loch 11570
Thomas Rd 11570
Vanderveer Ct 11570
Varick Ct 11570
Vassar Pl 11570
Vernon Ave & Ct 11570
N & S Village Ave 11570
Vincent St 11570
Virginia Ave 11570
Voorhis Ave 11570
Wachusetts St 11570
Wallace Ct & St 11570
Walnut Ave 11570
Warwick Rd 11570
Washington St 11570
Water St 11570
Waterview Dr 11570
Waverly Pl 11570
Wellesley Rd 11570
Westminster Rd 11570
Whitby Ct 11570
Whitehall Rd 11570
Willetts Ct 11570
William St 11570

Wilson Ln ... 11570
Windermere Pl ... 11570
Windham Rd ... 11570
Winding Rd ... 11570
Windsor Ave ... 11570
E Wood Rd ... 11570
Woodbridge Rd ... 11570
Woodfield Rd ... 11570
Woodgreen Pl ... 11570
Woodland Ave ... 11570
Woods Ave & Pl ... 11570
Wright Rd ... 11570
Yale Ave & Pl ... 11570
York Ct ... 11570
Yorkshire Rd ... 11570
Yorktown St ... 11570

ROME NY

General Delivery ... 13440
General Delivery ... 13441

POST OFFICE BOXES MAIN OFFICE STATIONS AND BRANCHES

Box No.s
All PO Boxes ... 13442

NAMED STREETS

Abbe Blvd & Ln E, S & W ... 13440
Abbott Pl ... 13440
Adams St ... 13440
Albert St ... 13440
Albrecht Rd ... 13440
Amherst Dr ... 13440
Anderegg Dr ... 13440
Anken Ave & St ... 13440
Ann St ... 13440
Anthony St ... 13440
Arsenal Pl, Sq & St ... 13440
Ashland Ave ... 13440
Avenue A ... 13440
Avery Ln ... 13441
Bachman Ave ... 13440
Balsam St ... 13440
Baptiste Ave ... 13440
Bartell Ln ... 13440
Bartlett Rd ... 13440
Batavia Ave ... 13440
Bayberry Ct ... 13440
Bedford St ... 13440
Beech St ... 13440
Bel Air Dr ... 13440
Bell Rd N & S ... 13440
Belmont St ... 13440
Benedict Ave ... 13440
Bielby Rd ... 13440
Birch Ln ... 13441
Birchwood Cir ... 13440
Bishop Rd ... 13440
Bissell Ave ... 13440
Black River Blvd N & S ... 13440
Blackburn Cir ... 13440
E & W Bloomfield St ... 13440
Bomber Dr ... 13441
Bork Ave ... 13440
Bouck St ... 13440
Boyd Rd ... 13440
Bradford Dr ... 13440
Brennon Ave ... 13440
Broadway ... 13440
Brook St ... 13440
Brookley Rd ... 13441
Brooks Rd ... 13441
Brookside Dr ... 13440
Brush Ave ... 13440
Bryant Ave ... 13440
Buena Vista Dr ... 13440
Bunal Blvd & Dr ... 13440
Burhanna Rd ... 13441
Burrows Rd ... 13440
Butternut Rd ... 13440
Butts Rd ... 13440
Byrnes Ave ... 13440
Cady Rd ... 13440
Calhoun St ... 13440
Calvert St ... 13440
Camp St ... 13440
Camroden Rd ... 13440
Canal St ... 13440
Canterbury Hill Rd ... 13440
Carey St ... 13440
Carmel Dr ... 13440
Carroll St ... 13440
E & W Carter Rd ... 13440
Caswell St ... 13440
Cayuga St ... 13440
W Cedar St ... 13440
Cedarbrook Dr ... 13440
Cedarwood Dr ... 13440
Cemetery Ln & Rd ... 13440
Central Ave ... 13441
Chanute St ... 13441
Chappie James Blvd ... 13441
N & S Charles Rd & St ... 13440
Chatham St ... 13440
Cherry Dr & St ... 13440
Cherry Cove Ln ... 13440
Cherrywood Ln ... 13440
E & W Chestnut St ... 13440
Chimielewski Rd ... 13440
Church St ... 13440
Circle Dr ... 13440
Clark St ... 13440
Clinchit Rd ... 13441
Clinton Ave & St ... 13440
Cold Point Dr ... 13440
Coleman Mills Rd ... 13440
Colonel Dr ... 13440
Columbus Ave ... 13440
Concord Pl ... 13440
Cornell St ... 13440
Coronado Ln ... 13440
Cortland Ave ... 13440
Cottage St ... 13440
Country Club Dr ... 13440
County Highway 50 ... 13440
W Court St ... 13440
Craig St ... 13440
Craighurst Dr ... 13440
Crescent Dr ... 13440
Crestview Ln ... 13440
Crossgates Rd ... 13440
Croton St ... 13440
Culverton Rd ... 13440
Curtis St ... 13440
Cypress St ... 13440
Cyrus Ave ... 13440
D Angelo Ave ... 13440
Daedalian Dr ... 13441
Daily Rd ... 13440
Dale Rd ... 13440
Dart Cir ... 13441
Davidson Rd ... 13440
Davis Ave & Rd ... 13440
Dawn Dr ... 13440
Day Ave ... 13440
Dealing St ... 13440
Dean St ... 13440
Delray Dr ... 13440
Delta Ave ... 13440
Delta Dr ... 13441
Depeyster St ... 13440
Dewey Rd ... 13440
Dewitt Ln ... 13440
Dix Rd ... 13440
Dixon Dr ... 13440
E & W Dominick St ... 13440
Donald St ... 13440
Donaldson Rd ... 13441
N & S Doxtator St ... 13440
Drummond Dr ... 13440
Dry Dock Rd ... 13440
Dunham Rd ... 13440
Dunn Ave ... 13440
Dwight Dr ... 13440
East Ave ... 13440
Edgewood Dr ... 13440
Edwards Ave & Rd ... 13440
Electronic Pkwy ... 13441
Ellington Ave ... 13441
Ellsworth Rd ... 13441
Elm St ... 13440
Elmer Hill Rd ... 13440
Elsie St ... 13440
Elwood St ... 13440
E & W Embargo St ... 13440
Emerald Cir & Ln ... 13440
Emerson Ave ... 13440
W End Ln ... 13440
Erie Blvd E & W ... 13440
Essex St ... 13440
Eureka Rd ... 13440
Evans Rd ... 13440
Evening Rd ... 13440
Evergreen Dr ... 13440
Expense St ... 13440
Factory Pl ... 13440
Fairview Ln ... 13440
Fairway Ln ... 13440
Felton Ave ... 13440
Fish Hatchery Rd ... 13440
Fisk Ave ... 13440
Flower Ct ... 13440
E Floyd Ave, Pl & Rd ... 13440
Foerster Rd ... 13441
Fonda Ave ... 13440
Ford St ... 13440
Forest Ln ... 13440
Forest Ridge Dr ... 13440
Fort Stanwix Park N & S ... 13440
E & W Fox St ... 13440
Francis St ... 13440
Franklyn St ... 13440
Frederick St ... 13440
Freedom Mall ... 13440
E Front St ... 13440
Futureway ... 13441
Gansevoort Ave ... 13440
E & W Garden St ... 13440
Gardner St ... 13440
Garenewo Rd ... 13440
Gates Ave ... 13440
Geiger Rd ... 13441
Genesee Pl ... 13440
N & S George St ... 13440
Gifford Rd ... 13440
Glen Rd N & S ... 13440
Glenwood Dr ... 13440
Glur Rd ... 13440
Golf Course Rd ... 13440
Golly Rd ... 13440
Gore Rd ... 13440
Gould Pl ... 13440
Grandview Ave ... 13440
Grant Pl ... 13440
Green Tree Blvd ... 13440
Greenfield Rd ... 13440
Greenview Dr ... 13440
Greenway New London Rd ... 13440
Greenwood Mobile Trlr Park ... 13440
Griffiss Dr ... 13440
Gulf Rd ... 13440
Hager Ave ... 13440
Hall Rd ... 13440
Halpin Rd ... 13440
Hamilton St ... 13440
Hangar Rd ... 13441
Harbor Way ... 13440
Harding Blvd ... 13440
Harvard Pl ... 13440
Harvey Ave ... 13440
Hawkins Corner Rd ... 13440
Healy Ave ... 13440
Heelpath Rd ... 13440
Henderberg Rd ... 13440
Henry St ... 13440
Herkimer Ave ... 13440
Hickory St ... 13440
Highland Ave ... 13440
Hill Rd ... 13441
Hill St ... 13440
Hillcrest Dr ... 13440
Hillside Ct ... 13440
Hilson Dr ... 13440
Hoag Rd ... 13440
Hogsback Rd ... 13440
Holland Ave ... 13440
Holly St ... 13440
Holmes Rd ... 13440
Howland Ave ... 13440
Humaston Rd & St ... 13440
Humble Ln ... 13440
Huntington St ... 13440
Hurlbut Ln ... 13440
Indian Creek Ln ... 13440
Inwood Dr ... 13440
Ironwood Dr ... 13440
N & S James St ... 13440
Jane St ... 13440
Jasper St ... 13440
N & S Jay St ... 13440
Jefferson Ct & St ... 13440
Jenkins Rd ... 13440
Jervis Ave ... 13440
John St ... 13440
Karlen Rd ... 13440
Keeler Rd ... 13440
Kent St ... 13440
Kilbourn Rd ... 13440
Kingsley Ave ... 13440
Kirtland Dr ... 13441
Koenig Rd ... 13440
Kolton Dr ... 13440
Kossuth St ... 13440
Kriswood Dr & Ln ... 13440
Lakeview Dr ... 13440
Lambert Rd ... 13440
Lamphear Rd ... 13440
Langley Rd ... 13441
Laurel St ... 13440
Lawrence St ... 13440
Lee St ... 13440
Lee Fair Park ... 13440
Lee Valley Rd ... 13440
Leffingwell Ave ... 13440
Lenox St ... 13440
N & S Levitt St ... 13440
Lewicki Rd ... 13440
Lewis St ... 13440
Liberty St ... 13440
Lincoln Ave & Ln ... 13440
E & W Linden St ... 13440
Link Rd ... 13440
Lock Rd ... 13440
Locomotive Ave ... 13440
E & W Locust St ... 13440
Long Hill Rd ... 13440
Lorena Rd ... 13440
Lori Ln ... 13440
Louisa St ... 13440
Lowell Ave & Rd ... 13440
Lower Lawrence St ... 13440
Luquer St ... 13440
Lynch St ... 13440
Lyndale Dr ... 13440
Lynwood St ... 13440
Lyons St ... 13440
Macarthur Dr ... 13440
Macdill St ... 13441
Macs Pl ... 13440
N & S Madison St ... 13440
Magarchie Ln ... 13440
Maple Dr & St ... 13440
March St ... 13441
Maria Ln ... 13440
Market St ... 13441
Martin Dr & St ... 13440
Mary St ... 13440
Massena Ave ... 13440
Massock Ave ... 13440
Mather Dr ... 13441
Matthew St ... 13440
Mayberry Rd ... 13440
Mcavoy Ave ... 13440
Mckern Rd ... 13440
Mckinley Ave ... 13440
Mcrae St ... 13440
Meadow Dr ... 13440
Merrell St ... 13440
Merrick Rd ... 13440
Middle Rd ... 13440
Mill Rd & St ... 13440
Millbrook Rd ... 13440
Milles Dr ... 13440
Milton Ave ... 13440
Mobile Ave ... 13441
Mohawk Dr ... 13441
Mohawk St ... 13440
Mohawk Acres ... 13440
Monument Rd ... 13440
Moody St ... 13441
Moore Rd ... 13440
Morning Rd ... 13440
Muck Rd ... 13440
Mustang Dr ... 13440
Myrtle St ... 13440
Nassau St ... 13440
New Floyd Rd ... 13440
New London Rd ... 13440
Noble Ln ... 13440
Nock St ... 13440
North St ... 13440
Northgate Dr ... 13440
Northwinds Mnr ... 13440
Northwood Cir & Dr ... 13440
E & W Oak Dr & St ... 13440
Oakview Ter ... 13440
Oakwood St ... 13440
Obrien Rd ... 13440
Ochab Dr ... 13440
Old Floyd Rd ... 13440
Old Oneida Rd ... 13440
Olive Grove St ... 13441
Oneida St ... 13440
Oswego Rd ... 13440
Otis St ... 13441
Overhill Dr ... 13440
Oxford Ct & Rd ... 13440
Paine St ... 13441
Palmer Ave ... 13440
Panesi Ave ... 13440
Park Ave ... 13440
Park Dr ... 13440
Park St ... 13441
E Park St ... 13440
W Park St ... 13440
Park Drive Manor 1 ... 13440
Park Drive Manor 2 ... 13440
Parkway ... 13440
Parry St ... 13440
Patrick Sq ... 13441
Pazdur Blvd E ... 13440
S Pennystreet Rd ... 13440
Pepper Ave ... 13440
Perimeter Rd ... 13441
Perrin St ... 13441
Phillips Rd ... 13440
Phoenix Dr ... 13441
Pillmore Cir & Dr ... 13440
E & W Pine St ... 13440
Pinebrook Ln ... 13440
Pinecrest Dr ... 13440
Pleasant Ave & Dr ... 13440
Pond St ... 13440
Potter Rd ... 13440
Prospect St ... 13440
Rabbitt Rd ... 13440
Race St ... 13440
Railroad St ... 13440
Rapke Rd ... 13440
Ready Rd ... 13441
Reber Rd ... 13440
Revere Park ... 13440
Rickmeyer Rd ... 13440
Ridge St ... 13440
Ridge Mills Rd ... 13440
Ridgewood Dr ... 13440
Ringdahl Ct ... 13440
River Rd & St ... 13440
Riverside Dr ... 13440
Riverview Pkwy N & S ... 13440
Roberts St ... 13440
Robins St ... 13441
Rockwell St ... 13440
Rome Industrial Park ... 13440
Rome New London Rd ... 13440
Rome Oriskany Rd ... 13440
Rome Taberg Rd ... 13440
Rome Westernville Rd ... 13440
Rome Westmoreland Rd ... 13440
Roosevelt Ave ... 13440
Rose Ln ... 13440
Roser Ter ... 13440
Ruby St ... 13440
Russell Ave ... 13440
Saint Aloysius Ave ... 13440
Saint Peters Ave ... 13440
Sam St ... 13440
Sandy Cir ... 13440
Scadden Rd ... 13440
Schieferstine Rd ... 13440
School Rd ... 13440
Schuyler St ... 13440
Scott Ave ... 13440
Scott Dr ... 13441
Seifert Rd ... 13440
Selden Dr ... 13440
Selfridge St ... 13441
Seneca St ... 13440
Senn Rd ... 13440
Seville Dr ... 13440
Shady Grove Trailer Park ... 13440
Shakes Rd ... 13440
Shank Ave ... 13440
Shankenberry Ave ... 13440
Shed Rd ... 13440
Sherman Ave ... 13440
Short Hill Rd ... 13440
Sinicrope Ave ... 13440
Skinner Rd ... 13440
Sleepy Hollow Rd ... 13440
Smith Ave & Rd ... 13440
Soule Rd ... 13440
E & W South St ... 13440
Spadafora Ave ... 13440
Spring Rd & St ... 13440
Springbrook Dr ... 13440
Springhouse Rd ... 13440
Standish Rd ... 13440
Stanwix Ave & St ... 13440
Starlane Dr ... 13440
State Route 233 ... 13440
State Route 26 ... 13440
State Route 46 ... 13440
State Route 49 ... 13440
State Route 69 ... 13440
Stearns Rd ... 13440
Steuben St ... 13440
Stevens Aly & St ... 13440
Stoney Creek Rd ... 13440
Streiff Rd ... 13440
Success Dr ... 13440
Summit Ave ... 13440
Sunrise Blvd & Dr ... 13440
Sunset Dr & Ln ... 13440
Sutliff Rd ... 13440
E & W Sycamore St ... 13440
Taft Ave ... 13440
Tamarack Dr ... 13440
Tannery Rd ... 13440
Tennyson Ave ... 13440
Terrace Ct & Dr ... 13440
Teugega Point Rd ... 13440
E & W Thomas Dr, Rd & St ... 13440
Thunder Rd ... 13440
Toccolana Ave ... 13440
Tompkins Ave ... 13440
Toni Hill Rd ... 13440
Towne Dr ... 13440
Townline Rd ... 13440
Turin Rd & St ... 13440
Turner St ... 13441
Tuxedo Trailer Park ... 13440
Twin Ponds Est ... 13440
Union St ... 13440
Urbandale Pkwy ... 13440
Valentine Ave ... 13440
Van Buren Ave ... 13440
Van Tassel Ln ... 13440
Verona Mills Rd ... 13440
Victory Dr ... 13440
Vine Pl & St ... 13440
Wager Dr ... 13440
Walnut Dr & St ... 13440
Ward St ... 13440
Warner Rd ... 13440
N Washington St ... 13440
Watson St ... 13440
Watson Hollow Rd ... 13440
Webster St ... 13440
Wellesley Rd ... 13440
West St ... 13440
Westbrook Dr ... 13440
White Rd ... 13440
E Whitesboro St ... 13440
Whittier Ave ... 13440
W Willett St ... 13440
William St ... 13440
Williams Rd ... 13440
Willow Dr ... 13440
Wilson Rd ... 13440
Winchester Dr ... 13440
Winfield Cir ... 13440
Wood St ... 13440
Wood Creek Dr & Rd ... 13440
Woodland Ave ... 13440
Woodrow Ave ... 13440
Wright Dr ... 13441
E Wright St ... 13440
W Wright St ... 13440
Wright Settlement Ln & Rd ... 13440
Wuethrich Rd ... 13440
Wynn Rd ... 13440
Zingerline Rd ... 13440
Zircon Ln ... 13440

NUMBERED STREETS

All Street Addresses ... 13440

SCHENECTADY NY

POST OFFICE BOXES MAIN OFFICE STATIONS AND BRANCHES

Box No.s
All PO Boxes ... 12008

NAMED STREETS

Abbottsford Rd ... 12304
Access Pkwy ... 12302
Acorn Ct ... 12303
Acorn Dr
100-199 ... 12302
600-699 ... 12309
Acre Dr ... 12303
Adams Rd ... 12308
Adams St ... 12306
Agnes Ave ... 12303
Agostino Ave ... 12309
Air National Guard Rd ... 12302
Airport Rd ... 12302
Al Constantino Dr ... 12306
Alamo Ln ... 12304
N Alandale Ave ... 12304
Albany St
701-713 ... 12307
715-1099 ... 12307

1100-4199 12304
Albermarle Rd 12302
Albion St 12302
Alcazar Ave 12302
Alden Pl 12308
Aleda Dr 12302
Alexander Ave 12302
Alexander St
1-199 12304
400-599 12308
Alexis Ave 12309
Alflo Cir & Rd 12302
Alfred St 12304
Algonquin Rd 12309
Alheim Dr 12303
Alice St 12304
Allendale Ave 12304
Almeria Rd 12309
Alplaus Ave 12008
Altamont Ave
200-299 12304
300-1989 12303
1991-1999 12303
Alton St 12309
Alva Rd 12309
Alvey St 12304
Amanda Ln 12303
Amanda Way 12309
Amelia Dr 12309
Amelia St 12306
N & S Amherst Ave 12304
Amsterdam Ave
100-299 12302
1700-2199 12303
2201-2299 12303
Amsterdam Rd 12302
Andree Ct 12309
Angela Ct 12304
Angelina Dr 12309
Angelina Rd 12303
Angelina Ter 12303
Angelo Dr 12303
Angers Ave 12303
Anita Dr 12302
Ann Dr 12303
Anna Ct 12306
Annabelle Pl 12306
Anne Dr 12303
Anthony Dr 12303
Anthony St 12308
Anthony Way 12303
Antoinette Ct 12303
Antonia Dr
1-100 12309
102-2598 12309
1001-1099 12306
2401-2599 12309
Apeldorn Dr 12306
Appletree Ln 12309
Aqueduct Rd 12309
Arapaho Path 12302
Arbor Ave 12306
Arbor Ln 12302
Arcadian Dr 12302
Arch St 12307
Arden Rd 12302
Ardmore Ct 12309
Ardsley Pl & Rd 12308
Argo Blvd 12303
Argyle Pl 12305
Arkona Ct 12309
Arlene St 12303
Arrow St S 12304
Arrowhead Dr N & S 12302
Arthur St 12306
Ascot Ln 12309
Ash Tree Ln 12309
Ashford Ln 12309
Ashmore Ave 12309
Aster St 12306
Atateka Rd 12309
Athens St 12303
Athol Rd 12308
Augustine Ave 12306
Austin Pl 12306
Autumn Run 12306
Avenue A Ext 12308
Avenue B Ext 12308
Avenue H 12304
Avenue M 12304
Avery Pl 12307
Avon Rd 12308
Avon Crest Blvd 12309
Backus St 12307
Badgley Rd 12302
Bailey St 12303
Baker Ave E 12309
Baldwin Rd 12302
N & S Ballston Ave &
Rd 12302
Balltown Rd
400-699 12304
800-2899 12309
3200-3399 12304
Bancker Ave 12302
Baneberry Dr 12303
Banker Ave
1900-1999 12308
2301-2497 12309
2499-2599 12309
Barber Dr 12303
Barcelona Rd 12309
Barclay Pl 12309
Barhydt Rd 12302
Barney St 12307
Barrett St 12305
Barringer St 12304
Barrington Ct 12309
Barry Ln 12302
Bartlett Pl 12302
Barton Ave 12306
Barton Pl 12309
Bath St 12008
Bayberry Rd 12306
Beacon St 12302
Beaver St 12308
Becker Dr 12306
Becker St 12304
Becker Xing 12306
Bedford Rd 12308
Bee St 12306
Beech Dr 12309
Bell Ct 12303
Bellaire Dr 12302
Bellemead Ct 12309
Belleview Dr 12303
Belmont Ave
1-99 12008
1200-1500 12308
1502-1548 12308
1550-1599 12309
Belridge Rd 12309
Benedict Ave 12309
Benjamin Ln 12309
Benjamin Pl 12306
Benjamin St 12303
Bentley Rd 12309
Berg Rd 12304
Berkley Ave 12309
Berkley Rd 12302
Berkley Sq E 12302
Berkley Sq N 12302
Berkley Sq S 12302
Berkley Sq W 12302
Berkley Sq Ext 12302
Bernard St 12306
Bernard St Ext 12306
Bernice St 12303
Bertone Dr 12306
Berwyn St 12304
Betty Ln 12303
Beverly Ct 12302
Beverly St 12306
Bigelow Ave 12304
Bigwood Rd 12302
Bill Rd 12303
Birch Ln 12302
Birchknoll Dr 12302
Birchwood Dr 12303
Birchwood Ln 12309
Blatnick Way 12309
Bluebird Ln 12306
Bluff Ave 12303
Bluff Rd 12306
Bobby Ct 12309
Bogusky Ct 12306
Bolt Rd 12302
Bonner Ave 12304
Bonnyview Ln 12306
Booth Ave 12304
Bossi Ln 12303
Boston Dr 12302
Bostonian Dr 12306
Boulder Bnd 12302
Boxwood Dr 12303
Boyle Rd 12302
Bradbury St 12302
Bradford Rd 12304
Bradford St 12306
Bradintr St 12304
Bradley Blvd & St 12304
Bradt St 12306
N Brandywine Ave
2-34 12307
36-399 12307
400-1099 12308
S Brandywine Ave 12307
Breanna Dr 12304
Brendan Ln 12309
Brentwood Ln 12306
Brewer Ln 12303
Brewster St 12302
Brian Crest Ct 12306
Briar Rdg 12309
Bridge St 12303
Bridle Pathway 12303
Brier Rd 12304
Brierwood Blvd 12308
Brintowe Rd 12302
Brittany Pl 12309
Broad St
1-299 12302
1800-1999 12306
Broadway
117-197 12305
Broadway
199-800 12305
802-898 12305
1200-3099 12306
N Broadway 12305
Broadway Ctr 12305
Bromley Pl 12302
Brookhaven Dr 12309
Brookhill Dr 12309
Brookshire Dr 12309
Brookside Ave 12008
Brookside Dr 12309
Brookview Ct 12306
Brookview Dr 12303
Brookwood Dr 12302
Brower St 12303
Brown St 12304
Bruce Dr 12008
Bruce Ln 12303
Bruce St 12302
Bruno St 12306
Brunswick Pl 12303
Bryan Ave 12303
Buchanan St 12304
Buckingham Dr 12304
Budd Ter 12309
Bunker Ln 12309
Burdeck St 12306
Burnett St 12306
Business Blvd 12302
Butler St 12303
Butterfield Ave 12008
Butternut Dr 12309
Buxton St 12309
Cabernet Ct 12309
Cady Ave 12303
Caldicott Rd 12303
California Ave 12303
Cambridge Ct 12303
Cambridge Dr 12309
Cambridge Rd 12304
Cambridge Manor Dr 12302
Campbell Ave 12306
E Campbell Rd 12303
W Campbell Rd 12306
E Campbell Rd Ext 12303
Canton St 12304
Capital Blvd 12302
Cardiff Rd 12303
Careleon Rd 12303
Carlton St 12306
Carlyle Dr 12309
Carman Rd 12303
Caroline Ave 12306
Carolyn Ln 12302
Carpenter Ct 12309
Carpenter Dr
1-99 12309
2200-2299 12304
Carriage Hill Ln 12303
Carrie Ct 12309
Carrie St 12308
Cartwheel Dr 12302
Cascade Ter 12309
Cassella Rd 12303
Castine St 12309
Catalina Dr 12302
Catalpa Ct 12309
Catalyn St 12303
Catherine St
1-1 12304
1-2 12307
3-3 12304
4-98 12307
5-99 12307
100-299 12302
Catherine Woods 12309
Cayuga Ct & Rd 12309
Cedar Ct 12309
Cedar Ln 12302
Cedar St 12306
Cedarlawn Ave 12306
Center St 12302
N Center St 12305
Central Ave 12304
Central Pkwy 12309
Cephalonia Dr 12309
Chadwick Rd 12304
Chapel St 12303
Charles St
1-99 12304
400-999 12302
Charlton Rd 12302
Charter Oak Dr 12309
Cheltingham Ave 12306
Chepstow Rd 12303
Cherokee Rd 12302
Cherry Ln 12302
Cherry St 12306
Cherry Blossom Ct 12306
Chesebro Dr 12309
Cheshire Pl 12309
Chester St 12304
Chestnut Dr 12303
Chestnut Ln 12309
Chestnut St 12307
Cheyenne Rd 12302
Chinkapin Ct 12303
Chism St 12304
Chiswell Rd & St 12304
Chris Dr 12303
Chrisler Ave 12303
Christian Ct 12309
Christina Dr 12303
Christine Ln 12306
Christopher Ln 12303
Church Rd
100-1199 12302
7300-7499 12306
N Church St 12305
S Church St 12305
Churchill Sq 12309
Cimino Ln 12306
Cindy Crest Dr 12306
Circle Dr 12303
E & W Claremont Ave 12303
Clarendon St 12308
Clayton Rd & St 12304
Clement Ave 12304
Clement Rd 12303
Cleveland Ave 12306
Cliff St 12304
Clifton Park Rd 12309
Climax Ave 12304
Clinton St 12305
Clinton St Ext 12305
Close St 12307
Closson Rd 12302
Clute Crest Ln 12309
Clyde Ave 12306
Cobblestone Ct 12306
Coffee Dr 12303
Colgate Pl 12304
Colin Dr 12302
N & S College St 12305
Collins St 12302
Colonial Ave 12304
Colonial Dr
1-99 12306
5000-5099 12303
Columba Dr 12306
Columbia St 12308
Colvair Ave 12306
Comanche Trl 12309
Commerce St 12302
Commerce Park Rd 12309
Community Rd 12303
Compton Pl 12302
Concord Dr 12309
Concord St
1-100 12302
102-102 12302
2200-2299 12306
Congress St
500-1399 12303
1400-1499 12306
Coniston Rd 12304
Connor Ct 12309
Conqua Ln 12306
Consaul Rd 12304
Consaulus Ave 12306
Continental Rd 12306
Coolidge Pl 12309
Coons Rd 12303
Coplon Ave 12309
Coplon Rd 12306
Cora St 12306
Cordell Rd
1-132 12304
133-199 12303
Corlaer Ave 12304
Cornelius Ave 12309
Cornell Blvd 12302
Cornell St 12304
Corolyn Ter 12309
Coronet Ct 12309
Corporation Park 12302
Cortland Ave 12308
Cottage Row 12305
Country Rdg 12304
Country Brook Ct 12306
E Country Club Dr 12309
Country Fair Ln 12302
Country Walk Rd 12306
Country Woods Dr 12309
County Clare Ln 12309
County Line Rd 12306
Court Royale 12304
Courtside Ln 12309
Covington Ave 12304
Covington Ct 12309
Cox Ave 12306
Craig St 12307
Craigie Ave 12302
Cramer Ave
1-99 12302
600-799 12306
Cranbrook Ct 12309
Crane St
100-199 12302
500-598 12303
600-1799 12303
Cranford Pl 12306
Cranston Ave 12309
Crawford Rd 12306
Creighton Rd 12304
Crescent Rd 12309
Cresse Ave 12309
N Crest Ct 12306
Crestwood Dr 12306
Cricket Ln 12306
Crimson Oak Ct 12309
Cromer Ave 12304
Crooked St 12302
Cross Dr 12302
Crosstown Plz 12304
Crystal St 12303
Cucumber Aly 12305
Cullen Ave 12309
Culligan Rd 12302
Cumberland Pl 12302
Cunningham Ct 12309
Curry Rd
500-598 12306
600-1924 12306
1925-3099 12303
Curry Rd Ext 12303
Currybush Rd 12306
Currybush Connection 12306
Cushing Ln 12303
Cuthbert St 12302
Cutler St 12303
Cyndi Ct 12309
Cypress Dr 12302
Cypriana Ter 12306
Daggett Ter 12307
Dahlem Blvd 12309
Dahlia St 12306
Daisy Ln 12309
Dalton Dr 12308
Dalton Rd 12302
Daly Dr 12302
Danielle Dr 12303
Daniels Ave 12304
Danna Joelle Dr 12303
Danube Dr 12309
Daphne Dr 12302
Dartmouth St 12304
David Dr 12302
Davis Ter 12303
Dawn Dr
1-99 12302
300-399 12306
Dawson Rd 12302
Day Rd 12303
Day Spring Ct 12306
De Graff St 12308
Dean St 12309
Deanna Ct 12309
Dearborn Ave 12304
Debbie Dr 12306
Debbie Marie Ct 12309
Deborah Dr 12309
Debutante Mnr 12303
Decamp Ave 12309
Deer Path 12306
Deer Run 12302
Deerfield Pl 12302
Deforest Ave & St 12303
Delamont Ave 12307
Delaware Ave 12306
Delmar Ave 12306
Denise Ct 12303
Denise Dr 12309
Denison Rd 12309
Dennis Ter 12303
Denver Ave 12306
Deoham Post Dr 12303
Desmond Ave 12309
Devendorf Rd 12309
Devine St 12308
Dewitt Ave 12304
Dewitt St 12303
Dexter St 12309
Di Bella Dr 12303
Dianne Ct 12303
Division St
1-132 12304
133-133 12302
134-498 12304
135-499 12304
511-511 12302
Dobie Ln 12303
Dodge St 12306
Doherty Dr 12304
Dolan Dr 12306
Donald Ave 12304
Donald Dr 12306
Dongan Ave 12302
Dongan St 12303
Donnan Ave 12309
Doris Dr 12302
Dorothy Ln 12302
Dorsett St 12303
Dorwaldt Blvd
1400-1499 12308
1500-1799 12309
Dorwalt Ave 12309
Douglas Ct
100-199 12303
900-999 12309
Douglas Rd 12308
Dover Dr 12303
Dover Pl 12302
Dover Rd 12309
Downing St 12309
Draper Ave 12306
Driscoll Pl 12309
Droms Rd 12302
Droms Rd Ext 12302
Drott Dr 12302
Duane Ave
100-399 12307
400-499 12304
Duanesburg Rd 12306
Dublin Dr 12309
Dudley Rd 12303
Duglin Ave 12303
Dunnsville Rd 12306
Durham Ct 12309
Durham Path 12309
Durham St 12306
Dutch Meadows Ln 12302
Dynamo Ct 12309
Eagle St
1-21 12302
1-21 12307
2-98 12302
2-98 12307
23-31 12302
23-31 12307
33-99 12302
Earl Ave 12309
Earl St 12306
East St 12309
Eastern Ave 12308
Eastern Pkwy 12309
Eastholm Rd 12304
Echo Dr 12306
Edgewood Ave 12306
Edison Ave 12305
Edison Dr 12309
Edith Ln 12303
Edmel Rd 12302
Education Dr 12303
Edward Dr 12306
Edward St 12304
Elbert St 12304
Elder St 12304
Eleanor St 12306
Eleventh St 12306
Elizabeth Ct & St 12303
Ellen Ln 12302
Elliott Ave 12304
Elliott St 12302
Ellsworth Ave 12302
Elm Ln 12302
Elm St 12304
S Elm St 12304
Elmer Ave 12308
Elmlawn Ave 12306
Elmwood Dr 12302
Elmwood St 12304
Eltinge Pl 12302
Elton Ave 12309
Emmett Dr 12309
Emmett St 12307

Street	ZIP
Emmons St	12304
Empire Ave	
6200-6265	12306
6268-6299	12303
Empire Dr	12309
Englehart Dr	12302
Engleman Ave	12302
Englewood Ave	12309
Ennis Rd	12306
Erie Blvd	
100-1499	12305
1500-1898	12308
Erlynn Pl	12309
Ernie Rd	12309
Esther St	12303
Euclid Ave	12306
Eugene Dr	12303
Evans Rd	12306
Evelyn Dr	12303
Evergreen Ave	12306
Evergreen Blvd	12302
Ewa Dr	12303
Ewing Ln	12306
Exchange St	12302
Fabian Dr	12306
Faccioli Dr	12304
N & S Fagan Ave	12304
Fairfax Ave	12304
Fairlane Rd	12306
Fairlawn Pkwy	12309
Fairlee St	12306
Fairview Ave	12306
Fairway Ln	12304
Farley Pl	12302
Fasula Blvd	12303
Fawn Dr	12302
Fayette Dr	12303
Featherwood Ct	12303
Feeney Ln	12303
Fehr Ave	
1-99	12304
700-899	12309
Fenwick Ave	12304
Ferguson St	12303
Fern Ave	12306
Fern Ct	12303
Ferndale Ave	12306
Fernwood Dr	12309
Ferrara Ave	12304
Ferris Rd	12304
Ferry Rd	12309
N Ferry St	12305
S Ferry St	12305
Feuz Rd	12306
Fieldstone Dr	12304
Fiero Ave	12303
Fifteenth St	12306
Fifth St	12306
Fillmore Ave	12304
First St	12306
Fisher Rd	12306
Fisler Ave	12304
Floral Ave	12306
Florence Ave	12303
Florence St	12308
Flower Rd	12303
Flower Hill Ct	12309
Floyd St	12306
Foch Rd	12302
Ford Ave & St	12306
Fordham Ave	12306
Forest Rd	12303
Fort Hunter Rd	12303
Foster Ave	12308
Fount Rd	12304
Fourteenth St	12306
Fourth St	12306
Fox Ave	12304
Fox Hollow Rd	12309
Fox Run Dr	12303
Foxhill Dr	12309
Foxwood Dr	12303
Francis Ave	12303
Frank St	
1-399	12304
3200-3399	12306
Franklin St	
401-423	12305
425-436	12305
438-698	12305
3200-3299	12306
436-440-436-440	12305
Frantzke Ave	12309
Fred Rd	12303
Fredericks Rd	12302
Freemans Bridge Rd	12302
Front St	12305
Fuller St	12305
Fuller Station Rd	12303
Fullerton Ave	12304
Fulton Ave	12308
Furman St	12304
Gala Pl	12309
Garden Dr	12309
Garden St	12306
Garden View Dr	12303
Gardinier St	12306
Garfield Ave	12304
Gari Ln	12303
Garner Ave	12309
Garnet Ln	12302
Garrison Ave	12306
Gartholl Rd	12306
Gasner Ave	12304
Gates Dr	12306
Gay Ln	12303
Gebhardt St	12304
Genesee St	12306
Genium Plz	12304
George St	12303
George Endries Dr	12303
George Palmer Ct	12306
Georgetown Sq	12303
Georgetta Dix Plz	12307
Geraldine Ct	12306
Geraldine Pl	12309
Gerling St	12308
Germania Ave	12307
Getz Ave	12303
Ghents Rd	12306
Gibson St	12304
Gideon Trce	12302
Gifford Rd	12304
Giffords Church Rd	12306
Gillespie St	12308
Gilmore Ter	12303
Gina Marie Ct	12303
Girard Ct	12309
Glade Dr	12309
Gladstone St	12303
Gleason Rd	12302
Glen Ave	12302
Glen Ct	12306
Glen Ter	12302
Glen Eddy Dr	12309
Glenbrook Rd	12302
Glendale Pl	12303
Glendale Rd	12302
Glengary Rd	12304
Glenhill Dr	12302
Glenmeadow Ct	12309
Glenmist Ct	12306
Glenmore Dr	12309
Glenning Ln	12303
Glenridge Ct & Rd	12302
Glenview Dr	12302
W Glenville Rd	12302
Glenville St	12306
W Glenville Industrial Park	12302
Glenwood Blvd	12308
Glenwood Dr	12302
Gloria Ln	12309
Glorious Ln	12302
Gloucester Pl	12309
Godfrey Ln	12309
Goffredo Dr	12303
Goldfoot Rd	12302
Golf Ave	
1900-1999	12308
2300-2499	12309
Golf Rd	12304
Gordon Rd	12306
Gould Dr	12302
Governor Dr	12302
Governors Ln	12305
Gower Rd	12302
Grand Blvd	
1300-1300	12308
1302-1499	12308
1501-1549	12308
1551-2299	12309
Grand St	12306
Grandview Ave	12309
Grant Ave	12307
Granville Ave	12306
Gray St	12306
Greeley St	12304
Green St	12305
Greenlawn Ave	12306
Greenlawn Ct	12304
Greenpoint Ave	12303
Greens Farm Rd	12309
Greenthorne Blvd	12303
Greenway Dr	12302
Greenwood Dr	12303
E Gregg Rd	12306
Gregory Ln	12303
Grenoside Ave	
1400-1499	12308
1500-1599	12309
Greylock Ave	12304
Griffith Ln	12302
Grosvenor Sq	12308
Grove Pl	12307
Groveland Ave	12306
Guilderland Ave	12306
Gullott Dr	12306
Gurenson Ln	12309
Habel Ln	12302
Hadel Rd	12302
Haigh Ave	12304
Haigh Rd	12302
Halcyon St	12302
Halsey Dr	12304
Hamburg St	
1700-2199	12304
2231-2235	12303
2237-3099	12303
Hamilton St	
400-418	12305
420-599	12305
611-899	12307
Hamlin St	12307
Hampshire Way	12309
Hampshire Seat	12309
Hampton Ave	12309
Hanna Ct	12303
Hardin Rd	12302
Harding Blvd	12302
Harlau Dr	12302
Harlem St	12306
Harmon Rd	12302
Harold St	12306
Harris Dr	12309
Harrison Ave & St	12306
Hartland St	12309
Harvard St	12304
Harvest Dr	12302
Harwood Dr	12302
Hattie St	12308
Havenbrook Dr	12302
Haviland Dr	12302
Hawk St	
1-1	12307
2-98	12307
2-22	12302
3-19	12302
3-99	12307
Hawthorn Rd	12309
Hawthorne St	12303
Hazelwood Ave	12306
Heartland Dr	12303
Heath Ct	12309
Heather Ct & Ln	12309
Heatherington St	12302
Heckeler Dr	12302
Hedgewood Ln	12309
Hegeman St	12306
Helderberg Ave	12306
Helen Ct	12302
Helen St	12303
Helping Hand Ln	12302
Hembold Dr	12303
Hemlock Ln	12302
Hemlock St	12306
Hempshire Ct	12302
Hempstead Ct & Rd	12309
Hendrick St	12306
Hendricks St	12306
Hendrickson Ave	12309
Henry St	
1-9	12302
10-199	12304
Hereford Way	12309
Heritage Pkwy	12302
Heritage Rd	12309
Herrick Dr	12302
Hetcheltown Rd	12302
Hewett Dr	12306
Hexam Rd W	12309
Hickory Dr	12303
Hickory Ln	12302
Hickory Rd	12309
High Ave	12304
Highbridge Rd	12303
Highland Ave	12308
W Highland Dr	12303
Highland Ter	12304
Highland Park Rd	12309
Hilderbrandt Ave	12307
Hill St	12008
Hillcrest Ave	12304
Hillcrest Rd	12309
Hillcrest Vlg E	12309
Hillcrest Vlg W	12309
Hillock Ct	12302
Hillside Ave	
1-5	12308
7-901	12308
900-900	12309
902-1999	12309
Hillside Ct	12302
Hillside Dr	12302
Hilltop Rd	12309
Hillview Rd	12303
E Hite Ct	12303
Hodgson St	12305
Hoffman Ln	12306
Hoffmans Hill Rd Ext	12302
Holiday Dr	12304
Holland Rd	12303
Holly Blvd S	12302
Holly Hill Rd	12309
Hollywood Ave	12306
N & S Holmes St	12302
Homestead Ave	12304
Homestead Rd	12302
Hoosick St	12306
Hoover Rd	12309
Horizon Blvd	12306
Horstman Dr	12302
Horvath St	12303
Houlton St	12303
Howard St	12303
Howe Ave	12306
Howell St	12303
Huck Ct	12303
Hudson Ave	12306
Hudson St	
1-99	12303
500-598	12308
2000-2098	12303
Hugh St	12306
Hulett St	12307
Hummingbird Ct	12309
Huntingdon Dr	12309
Huntington Dr	12309
Huron Ct & St	12305
Huston St	12302
Hutchinson Rd	12302
Ida Ln	12303
Imperial Dr	12309
Indian Kill Rd	12302
Ingersoll Ave	12305
Inglewood Dr	12302
Inman Rd	12309
Inner Dr	12303
Insull Blvd	12306
Inwood St	12309
Inwood Ter	12303
Iovinella Ct	12306
Ireland Rd	12303
Irene St	12306
Iroquois Ln	12309
Iroquois Path	12302
Irving Rd	12302
Irving St	12308
Ives Ct	12309
Ivy Ave	12304
Jackson Ave	12304
Jackson Pl	12308
Jaclyn Dr	12303
Jade Ln	12309
Jaffrey St	12309
Jamaica Rd	12309
James St	
1-11	12302
12-12	12304
13-13	12302
14-99	12304
101-123	12302
111-111	12304
113-140	12304
125-127	12302
142-198	12304
200-399	12302
Jane Dr	12302
Jason Ln	12309
Jay	12301
Jay St	
12-26	12305
28-32	12305
34-104	12305
105-105	12302
105-105	12305
106-108	12302
106-108	12305
107-107	12302
109-113	12302
114-114	12305
115-123	12302
116-118	12302
116-118	12305
120-124	12302
122-125	12305
126-126	12302
127-127	12305
128-198	12305
129-133	12302
129-135	12305
137-137	12302
137-199	12305
200-299	12302
N Jay St	12305
Jean Pl	12303
Jeanette Dr	12306
Jeanne Dr	12303
Jefferson St	12305
Jenie Ct	12306
Jennifer Ct	12303
Jennifer Rd	12302
Jerome Ave	12306
Jerry Ave	12303
Jerry St	12304
Jessamine Ln	12303
Jesse Ct	12302
Jessica Ln	12309
Jester Ct	12304
Jewett Pl	12304
Joanne Dr	12303
John St	
1-13	12305
2-198	12302
John Alden Ln	12306
John Paul Ct	12309
Johnson Rd	12302
Jones Dr	12309
Jordan Ln	12302
Joyous Ln	12302
Judy Dr	12302
Juniper Ct	12309
Juniper Dr	12306
Juniper Ln	12303
Juracka Pkwy	12306
Kabalian Dr	12309
Kailberg Rd	12309
Kallen Ave	12304
Kalmia Dr	12302
Karenwald Ln	12309
Karl St	12306
Kathleen Dr	12302
Keator Dr	12306
Kellar Ave	12306
N & S Kelley Rd	12306
S Kellogg Ave	12304
Kelly Ln & St	12306
Kelton Ave	12304
Kendale Ave	12304
Kenmore Ave	
1-1	12304
1-3	12306
2-4	12304
5-453	12306
368-498	12306
Kensington Ct	12309
Kent Ave	12304
Kent St	12306
Kenwood Ave	12304
Kenwood St	12308
Kevin Ln	12303
Keyes Ave	12309
Kile Dr	12302
Killarney Dr	12309
Killkenny Ct	12309
Kimberly Ct	12309
Kings Ct	12303
Kings Rd	
100-799	12304
800-816	12303
818-1399	12303
1401-1499	12303
Kingston Ave	
1300-1499	12308
1501-1549	12308
1550-1599	12309
Kingswood Ct	12303
Kirvin Ln	12306
Knickerbocker Rd	12302
Knights Acres Ln	12306
Knolls Rd	12309
Knollsview Dr	12309
Knollwood Dr	12302
Knox Dr	12303
Lafayette St	12305
Lake Blvd	12304
Lake Dr	12306
Lakeview Ave	12303
Lakewood Ave	12309
Lamplighter Rd	12309
Lancashire Pl	12309
Lancaster Dr	12302
Lancaster St	12308
Landon Ter	12308
Lang St	12308
Lansing Rd N	12304
Lansing Rd S	12304
Lansing St	12303
Lark St	
2-399	12302
1200-1399	12306
Larkin St	12302
Larrabee Rd	12302
Laska Ln	12303
Lathrop Ave	12304
Lathrope Ave	12304
Laura Ln	12304
Laura St	12306
Laurel Ave & Ln	12304
Laury Ln	12302
Lawn Ave	12306
Lawndale Ave	12306
Lawnwood Ave	12304
Lea Ct	12309
Lee Ave	
1-49	12303
100-299	12304
Lee Rd	12302
Legion Dr	12303
Lenox Rd	12308
Lent Ct	12306
Leo Ave	12306
Leonard Dr	12309
Leroy St	12304
Lexington Ave & Pkwy	12309
Libby Ave	12309
Liberty Ct	12303
Liberty St	12305
Liddle Rd	12306
Lilac St	12306
Lillian Dr	12302
Lillian Rd	12303
Lincoln Ave	12307
Lincoln Dr	12302
Lincoln Hts	
2A-12A	12305
2B-10B	12305
2C-16C	12305
2D-8D	12305
2E-20E	12305
2F-8F	12305
2G-20G	12305
2H-10H	12305
1A-11A	12305
1B-9B	12305
1C-15C	12305
1D-7D	12305
1E-19E	12305
1F-7F	12305
1G-19G	12305
1H-11H	12305
Lincoln Mall	12309
Lincoln St	12302
Linda Ln	
2-4	12303
71-89	12304
91-199	12304
Lindberg Ct	12302
Linden Ct	12303
Linden St	12304
Lindsay Ave	12302
Lisa Dr & Ln	12303
Lishakill Rd	12309
S Lishakill Rd	12304
Little Hill Rd	12309
Livingston Ave	
1-11	12302
23-897	12304
899-999	12309
Lock 7 Rd	12309
Locust Ave	12307
Loeber Rd	12303
Lois Ln	12304
Lolik Ln	12302
Lomasney Ave	12308
Lombard St	12304
Londonderry Ct & Rd	12309
Lone Pine Rd	12303
Long Ave	12304
Long Meadow Ln	12306
Long Pond Dr	12306
Lorelei Ln	12302
Lori Dr	12309
Lorraine Ave	
1-299	12304
600-699	12303
Lorwood Dr	12302
Loudon Pl	12309
Louis Rd	12303
Lowell Rd	12308
Lower Broadway	12306
Lower Gregg Rd	12306
E & W Lucille Ln	12306
Lucy Rd	12303
Luigi Ct	12303
Lupe Way	12304
E Lydius St	12303
W Lydius St	
2700-2867	12306
2868-2874	12303
2876-2999	12303
Lynn Dr	12302
Lynn Plz	12309
Lynn St	12306

Lynnwood Dr 12309
Lynwood Ct 12303
Lyric St 12302
Mabel Rd 12304
Mabie Ln 12306
Macarthur Dr 12302
Macaulay Ln 12309
Mader St 12308
Madison St
1-99 12305
5100-6199 12306
Maida Ln 12306
Main Ave & St 12303
Mallards Pond Ln 12303
Manas Dr 12303
Manchester Rd 12304
Manhattan St 12308
Manor Ct 12306
Mansion Sq 12304
Mapa Ct 12309
Maple Ave
1-199 12302
900-951 12307
953-999 12307
Maple Ln 12309
Maple Ave Ext 12302
Maplecrest Ct 12309
Maplewood Ave 12303
Maplewood Dr 12302
Marcelis Ave 12302
Marcia Ct 12302
Marengo St 12306
Maria Ct 12306
Mariaville Rd 12306
Marie Ln 12303
Marie St 12304
Marilyn Dr 12302
Marilyn St 12303
Marion Ave 12303
Marion Blvd 12302
Maritime Dr 12008
Marjon Ave 12302
Market St 12302
Marlette St 12303
Marra Ln 12303
Marriott Ave 12304
Marshall Ave 12304
Marson Ave 12302
Martin St 12306
Marx St 12304
Mary Ln 12306
Mary Hadge Dr 12309
Maryland Ave 12308
Maryvale Dr 12304
Mason St 12308
Masullo Pkwy 12306
Mather Ave 12304
Maura Ln 12302
Maxon Rd 12308
Maxon Rd Ext 12308
Maxwell Dr 12309
May Ave 12303
Maybrook Dr 12302
Mayfair Dr 12302
Mayfair Rd 12309
Mayflower Dr 12306
Maywood Ave 12303
Maywood Dr 12302
Mcclellan St
1-899 12304
900-2199 12309
Mcclyman St 12307
Mcdonald Ave 12304
Mcgovern Dr 12309
Mckinley Ave 12303
Mcmichael Dr 12302
Meadow Ln 12309
Meadowview Ln 12306
Meghan Blvd 12306
Melody Ln 12309
Melrose St 12306
Memory Ln
1-5 12304
1-45 12306
2-6 12304
6-98 12306

Menga Dr 12304
Menlo Park Rd 12309
Mercer Ave 12303
Meriline Ave 12302
Merlin Dr 12309
Merritt Dr 12306
Mervin Ave 12306
Merwin Ave 12306
Michael Dr 12303
Michael Ln 12306
Michelle Ln 12309
Michelle Way 12304
Michigan Ave 12303
Middle St 12309
Midland Ave 12304
Milan Ct 12309
Miles Standish Rd 12306
Mill Ln 12305
Millard Ln 12303
Millard St 12305
Miller Ave 12303
Miller Rd 12306
Millington Rd 12309
Milton Keynes Dr 12309
Miracle Ln 12302
Mitchell Ave 12309
Mitchell Rd 12303
Mohawk Ave
1-99 12008
1-5 12302
7-7 12305
9-11 12302
13-18 12302
17-17 12305
20-698 12302
25-699 12302
Mohawk Ct 12305
Mohawk Dr 12303
Mohawk Rd 12309
Mohawk Trl 12309
Mohegan Rd 12309
Molly Ct 12309
Monarda Dr 12302
Monica Hts 12309
Monroe St 12305
Montclair Dr 12302
Montery Rd 12303
Moores Ct 12309
Morgan Ave 12309
Morgan Ct 12306
Morning Glory Way 12306
Morningside Ave 12309
Morningside Dr 12303
Morocco Ln 12304
Morris Ave 12308
Morris Rd
1-120 12304
122-138 12304
139-299 12303
Morrocco Ln 12304
Morrow Ave 12309
Morton St 12306
Mount Stuart Rd 12304
Mountainview Ave 12309
Mountainwood Dr 12302
Moyer Ave 12306
Moyston St 12307
Mullen Dr 12306
Mumford St 12307
Mykolaitis Ln 12303
Mynderse St 12307
Myron St 12309
Myrtle Ave
1-99 12304
2700-3099 12306
Nahant St 12306
Nancy Ln 12303
Napa Ct 12309
Nassau Ave & St 12304
Natalie Ct 12304
Nathaniel Dr 12303
Neal St 12302
Neil St 12306
Nelson Dr 12309
Nelson St 12306
Netherlands Blvd 12306

New Williamsburg Dr 12303
Newcastle Rd 12303
Newell Rd 12306
Newman Rd 12302
Newport Ave 12309
Nicholas Ave 12309
Nicholas Ct 12303
Nicky Dr 12306
Nimitz Rd 12304
Ninth St 12306
Niskayuna Cir 12309
Niskayuna Dr 12309
Niskayuna Rd 12309
Niskayuna St 12306
Nora Ave 12304
Norfolk Ave 12303
North Ct 12302
North St 12305
Northend Dr 12308
Northumberland Dr 12309
Northwood Ct 12309
Norwood Ave 12303
Norwood Way 12309
Notre Dame St 12306
Nott St
301-399 12305
400-1560 12308
1561-2299 12309
Nott St E 12309
Nott Ter
2-98 12308
100-199 12308
200-299 12307
Nott Terrace Hts 12308
Nottingham Mall 12309
Nutwood Ave 12304
Oak St 12306
Oak Hill Dr 12302
Oak Ridge Dr 12302
Oakdale Ave 12306
Oakdale Ct 12303
Oakhurst Dr 12302
Oakland Ave
1-99 12302
1800-1898 12308
1900-1999 12308
2100-2499 12309
Oaklawn Ave 12306
Oakleaf Dr & Hl 12303
Oakline Ct 12309
Oakmont St 12309
Oakridge Dr 12306
Oaktree Ln
1-99 12309
2000-2099 12303
2900-2999 12309
Oakwood Ave 12303
Oakwood Dr 12302
Obrien Ave 12303
Odell St 12304
Okara Dr W 12303
Old Carman Rd 12303
Old Crawford Rd 12303
Old Duanesburg Rd 12306
Old Fort Ave 12306
Old Mariaville Rd 12306
Old Mill Ln 12306
Old River Rd 12306
Old State Rd 12306
E Old State Rd 12303
W Old State Rd
2300-2747 12306
2701-2745 12303
2747-2999 12303
Old Valley Rd 12309
Olde Coach Rd 12302
Olean St 12306
Onderdonk Rd 12302
Oneida St 12308
Onondaga Rd 12309
Ontario St 12306
Opus Blvd 12306
Orchard Dr 12302
Orchard St 12303
Orchard Park Dr 12309

Oregon Ave
100-499 12304
700-999 12309
Orlinda Ave 12302
Orlyn Dr 12309
Ormond Dr 12309
Osterlitz Ave 12306
Ostrander Pl 12303
Outer Dr 12303
Overland Ave 12304
Owasco Ct 12309
Owen Rd 12303
Oxford Pl 12308
Oxford Way 12309
Paddock Cir 12306
Paige St 12307
Palazini Dr 12303
Palm Ave & St 12306
Palma Ave 12306
Palmer Ave 12309
E Palmer Ave 12303
Palmer St 12303
Pangburn Rd 12306
Pansy St 12306
Papa Pl 12303
Paradowski Rd 12302
Park Ave
1-399 12304
900-1099 12308
Park Ave W 12304
Park Ln 12302
Park Pl
1-299 12305
6000-6099 12303
Park St 12303
Parker Rd 12304
Parker St 12306
Parkers Corners Rd 12306
Parkland Ave 12302
Parklawn Ave 12306
Parkside Ave 12309
Parkview Dr 12303
Parkville Pl 12309
N & S Parkway Dr 12303
Parkwood Blvd 12308
Partridge Run 12309
Partridgeberry Ct 12303
Pashley Rd 12302
Patrick Ct 12304
Patrick Rd 12303
Pattersonville Rynex
Corners Rd 12306
Patton Dr 12303
Paul Ave 12306
Paulding St 12308
Pauline Ave 12306
Pawtucket Ave 12309
Pearl St 12303
Pearse Rd 12309
Peek St 12308
Pembroke Ct 12309
Pembroke St 12302
Penney Ln 12303
Pennsylvania Ave 12303
Perry St 12306
Pershing Dr 12302
Persimmon Dr 12303
Peter Rd 12303
Peters Ln 12309
Peyton Rd 12303
Pheasant Rdg 12309
Pheasant Walk 12303
Phillip St 12306
Phillips Rd 12306
Philomena Dr 12303
Philomena Rd 12309
Phoenix Ave 12308
Phyllis Ct 12303
Picadilly Cir 12306
Picturesque Pkwy 12303
Pine Ave
48-48 12304
100-299 12302
2300-2399 12304
Pine St 12302

E, N, S & W Pine Hill
Dr 12303
Pine Ridge Rd 12309
Pinecrest Dr 12309
Pinehaven Dr 12309
Pinehurst Pl 12304
Pinelawn Ave 12306
Pineridge Ct 12309
Pinewood Ave 12309
Pinewood Dr
1-99 12302
200-299 12303
Pinyon Dr 12303
Placid Dr 12303
Plaske Dr 12309
Platinum Ln 12303
Pleasant St 12303
Pleasantview Ave 12302
Plum St 12309
Plunkett Ave 12306
Plymouth Ave 12308
Poentic Kill Way 12306
Poersch Ct 12309
Polsin Dr 12303
Polsinelli Dr 12303
Poplar St
59-997 12306
999-1099 12306
1200-1298 12308
1300-1399 12308
Port Huron Dr 12309
Porter St 12308
Posinelli Dr 12309
Potential Pkwy 12302
Poutre Ave 12306
Praise Ln 12302
Preddice Pkwy 12302
Preisman Dr 12309
Prestige Dr 12303
Prestige Pkwy 12302
Primrose Ln 12309
Princeton St 12304
Princetown Plz & Rd 12306
Priscilla Ln 12306
Prospect St 12308
Prout Ln 12303
Providence Ave 12309
Puritan Dr 12306
Putnam Rd 12306
Putnam St 12304
Pyle Rd 12303
Quackenbush Rd 12306
Quaker Dr 12309
Quarry Ct 12302
Queen Mary Ct 12303
Queen Philomena Blvd 12304
Queens Dr 12304
Rabbetoy St 12303
Railroad St 12305
Rainbow Dr 12303
Ralmar Dr 12302
Ralph St 12304
Ramblewood Ct 12309
Randall Rd 12309
Randi Rd 12309
Randolph Rd 12308
Randomwood Dr 12303
Rankin Ave 12308
Rankin Rd 12309
N Ravine Rd 12309
Ray Ave 12304
Ray St 12309
Raymond St 12308
Rector Rd 12302
Red Coach Dr 12302
Red Oak Dr
1-99 12302
700-899 12309
Red Pine Dr 12303
Redwood Dr 12302
Regal Ave
1200-1499 12308
1500-1599 12309
Regal Ct 12302
Regent St 12309
Regina Dr 12303

Reilly Way 12309
Rembrandt Dr 12309
Remmington Rd 12303
Remsen St 12306
Rensselaer Ave 12303
Research Cir 12309
Reserve Ct 12302
Revere St 12306
Reynolds Rd 12306
N Reynolds St 12302
S Reynolds St 12302
Rice Rd 12306
Richard St 12303
Richie Ct 12309
Richland Dr 12302
Ridge Rd 12302
Ridgehill Rd 12303
Ridgewood Ln 12302
Riesling Rd 12309
Riggi Ave 12303
Risoli Ln 12306
River Rd
1-1 12305
600-1099 12306
2100-4076 12309
4078-4080 12309
River St 12305
Riverdale Ct & Rd 12309
Riverhill Blvd 12309
Riverside Ave 12302
Riverside Pl
1-299 12008
1-599 12302
Riverview Dr & Rd 12309
Roberta Rd 12303
Robin St
1-3 12306
2-4 12302
6-8 12302
7-7 12306
10-98 12302
Robins Nest 12309
Robinson Rd 12302
Robinson St 12304
Robinson St S 12304
Robinwood Ave 12306
Rocco Dr 12303
Rockland Rd 12302
Rockwood Ln 12303
Roger Hull St 12305
Roland Pl 12304
Rolling Hills Rd 12309
Roma St 12306
Romano Dr 12303
Rome Ave 12303
Ronald Pl 12303
Ronnie Ct 12306
Roosevelt Ave 12304
Roosevelt St 12306
Root Ave 12302
Rosa Rd
1-97 12308
99-410 12308
411-2399 12309
2401-2425 12309
Rose Ave 12303
Rose St 12306
Rose Ter 12309
Rosedale Way 12303
Rosehill Blvd 12309
Roselawn Ave 12306
Rosemary Dr
1-1 12302
1-2 12304
3-11 12302
3-99 12304
4-10 12302
4-10 12304
12-12 12302
18-98 12304
Rosendale Rd 12309
Rosewood Ave 12306
Rosewood St 12304
Rotary Row 12302
Rotterdam St 12306
Rotterdam Industrial
Park 12306

Rowe Rd 12309
Ruby Blvd 12302
Rudge St 12304
Rudy Chase Dr 12302
Ruffner Ct & Rd 12309
Rugby Rd
1100-1599 12308
1600-1799 12309
Runnel Dr 12304
Russell St 12304
Rutgers St 12303
Ryan Pl 12303
Sabre Dr 12306
Sacandaga Rd 12302
Saddlebrook Ln 12302
Sagemont Ct 12309
Saint Ann Dr 12309
Salem Rd 12309
Salina St 12308
Salvia Ln 12303
Samuel Ct 12306
Sandalwood Ln 12302
Sanders Ave & Rd 12302
Sandra Ct 12303
Sandra Ln 12309
Sandy Ln 12303
Sandy Crest Ct 12303
Sanford St 12304
Santa Ln 12306
Santa Fe St 12303
Santoro Rd 12306
Sara Ct 12308
Saratoga Dr & Rd 12302
Sargent Pl 12303
Sarnowski Dr 12302
Sartoli Ave 12303
Saugus St 12306
Schenectady St 12307
Schermerhorn Rd 12306
Schermerhorn St
200-299 12304
412-498 12302
Schlensker Dr 12302
Schonowee Ave 12302
School St 12304
Schuster Rd 12303
Schuyler Ave 12306
Schuyler St
1400-1700 12303
1702-1976 12303
1976-1976 12304
Schwaber Dr 12309
Scotch Ridge Rd 12306
Scott Pl 12309
Scott St 12306
Second St 12306
Seeley St 12302
Seldon St 12304
Seminole Rd 12302
Seneca Ct 12305
Seneca Rd 12309
Seneca St 12308
Serafini Dr 12303
Serif Ln 12303
Seth Ln 12302
Seventeenth St 12306
Seward Pl 12305
Shady Acres Dr 12303
Shafer St 12304
Shaker Ridge Dr 12309
Shannon Blvd 12309
Shannon Ln 12309
Shannon St 12306
Shardon Ct 12306
Shave Ct & Rd 12303
Shay St 12303
Sheffield Ave 12306
Sheffield Rd 12302
Shelbourne Ct 12309
Sheldon St 12308
Shelley Ct 12306
Shepard Ave 12304
Shereen Ct 12304
Sheridan Ave
1930-1998 12308
2200-2399 12309

Sheridan Plz 12308
Sheridan Vlg
1A-1C 12308
2A-2B 12308
3A-3C 12308
4A-4C 12308
5A-5C 12308
6A-6C 12308
7A-7B 12308
8A-8D 12308
9A-9C 12308
10A-10C 12308
11A-11C 12308
12A-12C 12308
13A-13C 12308
14A-14C 12308
15A-15C 12308
16A-16C 12308
17A-17C 12308
18A-18B 12308
19A-19C 12308
20A-20C 12308
21A-21E 12308
10D-20D 12308
9D-21D 12308
Sherman St 12303
Sherwood Rd 12303
Shirl Ln 12309
Shirley Dr 12304
Shirley Ln 12303
Shirlwood Dr 12306
Sierra Ct 12304
Silversmith Ln 12306
Simmons Ln 12302
Sir Benjamin Way 12304
Sixteenth St 12306
Sixth St 12306
Skyline Dr 12306
Skyway Dr 12302
Slater Dr 12302
Slatestone Dr 12302
Smith St 12305
Snake Hill Rd 12302
Snipe St 12306
Snowden Ave 12304
Snyder Ln 12008
Socha Ln 12302
Somerset Ln 12302
Somerset St 12304
Somerset Ter 12304
Sonya Pl 12309
South Ave
1-99 12008
500-799 12305
South Ct 12302
Southgate Dr 12304
Southwoods Ct 12306
Spawn Rd 12303
Spearhead Dr 12302
Sprague St 12307
Spring Rd 12302
Spring St 12303
Spring Blossom Ln 12306
Spring Farm Ln 12303
Spring Valley Cir 12302
Springdale Way 12306
Spruce St
1-99 12304
1000-1099 12306
Spry Ln 12303
Squire Rd 12304
St Ann St 12303
St Anna Dr 12303
St Anna Ln 12302
St Anthony Ln 12302
St Davids Ln 12309
St Francis Ln 12304
St George Pl 12304
St Jean Pl 12308
St Joseph Dr 12309
St Joseph St 12303
St Jude Ct 12302
St Jude Dr 12303
St Jude Ln 12302
St Lucille Dr 12306
St Marie St 12303
St Marks Ln 12309
St Marys Ln 12303
St Michaels Ln 12303
St Paul Ct 12304
St Stephens Ln E 12302
St Thomas Ln 12304
Stacey Crest Dr 12306
Stafford Ln 12309
Stanek Rd 12306
Stanford Ave 12304
Stanford Dr 12303
Stanford St 12308
Stanley Ln 12309
Stanley St 12307
Stanton St 12306
Stark Ave 12309
Starling Ave 12304
Starr Ave 12304
State St
1-699 12305
700-1099 12307
1100-4099 12304
4101-4199 12304
1475-1479-1475-1479 12304
1582-1584-1582-1584 12304
1592-1594-1592-1594 12304
1599-1601-1599-1601 12304
251-263-251-263 12305
State Route 158 12306
Steeple Way 12306
Steers Ave 12304
Steinmetz Homes 12304
Stephen Rd 12302
Stephens Pl 12303
Sterling Ave & Rd 12306
Steuben St 12307
Stevenson St 12308
Stone Arabia Rd 12302
Stonefield Way 12306
Stoneridge Rd 12309
Stoodley Pl 12303
Story Ave 12309
Stottle Ln 12302
Stoyka Pl 12303
Stratford Rd 12308
Strong St 12307
Stuart St 12303
Stuyvesant Dr & St 12309
Suffolk Ave 12303
Sullivan Rd 12304
Summer St 12306
Summit Ave 12307
Sumner Ave 12309
Sundew Dr 12303
Sunnyside Rd 12302
Sunrise Blvd 12306
Sunset Ln & St 12303
Surrey Rd 12302
Sussex Way 12309
Sutherland Dr 12302
Suzanne Ct & Ln 12303
Swaggertown Rd 12302
Swampscott St 12306
Swan St
1-37 12307
39-99 12307
100-299 12302
Sweetbrier Rd 12309
Sycamore Ct 12309
Sylvia Ln 12306
Tall Pines Ln 12303
Tally Ho Ct 12303
Talon Dr 12309
Tamar Dr 12309
Tamarack Ln 12309
Tansy Ct 12303
Tartan Way 12302
Taunton St 12306
Taurus Rd 12304
Taylor St
1-99 12304
3200-3299 12306
Tech Park 12302
Technology Dr 12308
Tecumseh Way 12302
Tedesco Ct 12303
Teller St 12304
N & S Ten Broeck St 12302
Ten Eyck Ave 12303
Terrace Rd 12306
Terry Ave 12303
Teviot Rd 12308
Thackery Ct 12309
Thames Dr 12309
The Plz
1201-1297 12308
1299-1499 12308
1500-2299 12309
Theodora Ave 12303
Theodore Rd 12303
Thew St 12306
Third St 12306
Thirteenth St 12306
Thompson St 12306
Tidball Rd 12306
Tieman Rd 12302
Times Cir 12306
Timmy Ct 12306
Timothy Ln
100-199 12303
1000-1099 12309
Tina Ct 12303
Tokay Ln 12309
N & S Toll St 12302
Tollgate Ln 12303
Tomahawk Trl 12302
Tony Dr 12306
Toriana Ct 12304
Torrington Ave 12306
Touareuna Rd 12302
Tower Ave 12304
Tower Dr 12306
Tower Rd 12302
Tower St 12303
Townsend Rd 12309
Traber Rd 12303
Tracy Ave 12309
Tremont Ave 12304
Trinacria Ct 12303
Trinity Ave 12306
Trottingham Dr 12309
Troy Pl 12309
Troy Schenectady Rd 12309
Tryon Ave & St 12302
Tulip St 12306
Tulip Tree Ln 12309
Turnbull St 12306
Turner Ave 12306
Turner Park Ln & Rd 12302
Twelfth St 12306
Ulster St 12308
Unadilla St 12308
Uncas Dr 12302
Union Ave 12308
Union St
1-714 12305
716-798 12305
800-1499 12308
1500-2199 12309
University Pl 12308
Upper Gregg Rd 12306
Utopia St 12304
Vale Pl 12308
Valencia Rd 12309
Valentine Dr 12303
Valerie Dr 12309
Valley Pine Dr 12303
Valleyview Ave 12306
Valleywood Dr 12302
Van Antwerp Rd 12309
Van Buren Ave 12304
Van Buren Ln 12302
Van Buren Rd 12302
Van Buren Camp Rd 12302
Van Cortland St 12303
Van Curler Ave 12308
Van Der Vere St 12303
Van Derbogart St 12308
Van Dyke Ave 12306
Van Dyke St 12304
Van Guysling Ave 12305
Van Patten Rd 12302
Van Rensselaer Dr
2100-2199 12308
2200-2299 12309
Van Ryn Ave 12304
Van Slyke Ave 12302
Van Velsen St 12303
Van Voast Ln 12302
Van Voast St 12307
Van Vranken Ave 12308
Van Winkle Ave 12302
Van Wormer Rd 12303
Van Zandt St 12304
Vassar St 12304
Veeder Ave
320-320 12305
320-320 12307
360-360 12305
Veeder St 12302
Vermont Ave 12303
Vernon Blvd & Rd 12302
Verona Ave 12308
Via Del Mar 12309
Via Del Zotto Dr 12302
Via Lino 12302
Via Maestra Dr 12302
Via Marchella 12303
Via Maria Dr 12302
Via Ponderosa 12303
Via St Gabriel 12303
Vic Ct 12303
Victoria Ct & Dr 12309
Victory Ave 12307
Viele Rd 12302
Viewland Ave 12306
Viewmont Dr 12309
Viewpointe 12306
Village Rd 12309
Vincent Ave 12306
Vincent Dr 12303
Vincenza Ln 12303
Vincenzo Dr 12309
Vine Ln 12303
Vine St 12302
Vinewood Ave 12306
Virginia Blvd 12302
Vischer Ave 12306
Vista Blvd 12306
Vista Dr 12302
Vley Rd 12302
Vley Rd Ext 12302
Vly Rd 12309
Vly Point Dr 12309
Von Roll Dr 12306
Vrooman Ave 12309
Vrooman St 12304
Wabash Ave 12306
Wagner Ave 12304
Wagner Rd 12302
Wagner St 12303
Wagon Wheel Ln 12302
Waldorf Pl 12307
Wall St 12305
Wallace Ave 12306
Wallace Rd 12304
Wallace St 12302
Walnut Ave 12306
Walnut Ln E 12309
Walnut Ln W 12309
Walnut St 12308
Walt Whitman Dr 12304
Walton Pl 12302
Wampum Dr 12302
Ward Ave 12304
Warner Rd 12309
Warren St 12305
Warwick Way 12309
Washington Ave
43A-43B 12302
1-1 12305
1-13 12302
3-14 12305
15-15 12302
15-19 12305
16-98 12305
21-25 12302
21-27 12305
29-41 12302
43-43 12305
45-53 12302
49-55 12305
57-99 12302
117-199 12305
201-299 12302
Washington Rd 12302
Washout Rd 12302
Wasil Ln 12309
Water St 12302
Waters Rd 12302
Watt St 12304
Wavell Rd 12303
Waverly Pl 12308
Wayne Rd 12303
Wayto Rd 12303
Weast Rd 12306
Weathercrest Ct & Dr 12302
Weatherwax Rd 12302
Weaver St 12305
Webster Dr 12309
Webster St 12303
Wedgewood Ave 12303
Wedgewood Hts 12306
Weir Ct 12304
Weise Rd 12302
Wellington Ave 12306
Wellington Rd 12302
Wellington Way 12309
Wells Ave 12304
Wemple Ln 12309
Wemple Rd 12306
Wemple St 12306
Wendell Ave 12308
Wendy Ct 12306
Wesley Ave 12304
West Ct 12303
N & S Westcott Rd 12306
Western Blvd 12302
Western Pkwy 12304
Westhite Ct 12303
Westholm Rd 12309
Westinghouse Pl 12306
Westminster Way 12309
Westmoreland Dr 12309
Westover Pl 12307
Westside Ave 12306
Westwood Ln 12302
Westwoods Ct 12303
Whamer Ln 12309
Wheatly Ct 12309
Whispering Pines Way 12303
White St 12308
White Birch Ct 12306
Whitehall Ct & Pl 12309
Whitmyer Dr 12309
Whitney Dr 12309
Wilber Ave 12304
Wilderness Ct 12306
Wildwood Ave
2-6 12302
3-5 12306
7-9 12302
8-10 12302
11-99 12306
Wilkins Ln 12303
Willett St 12303
William St
200-299 12303
2000-3299 12306
Williams Ave 12302
Williams St 12309
Williamsburg Dr 12303
Willow Ave 12304
Willow Dr 12303
Willow Ln 12302
Willow St 12306
Willowbrook Rd 12302
Willowcreek Ave 12304
Wilmarth St 12302
Wilson Ave 12304
Wilson Dr 12302
Wilson Rd 12302
Wilson St 12306
Wiltshire Way 12309
Windemere Ct 12309
Windermere Rd 12304
Windsor Ct 12309
Windsor Dr
1-99 12302
400-4100 12309
4102-4198 12309
Windsor Ter 12308
Windy Hill Rd 12306
Wing Ave 12303
Winne Rd 12309
Winslow Dr 12309
Winston Pl 12304
Wise Ln 12303
Witbeck Dr 12302
Wolf Hollow Rd 12302
Wood Ave 12308
Woodbridge Ave 12306
Woodcrest Dr 12302
Woodfield Dr 12309
Woodhaven Dr
100-199 12302
3100-3299 12303
Woodland Ave & Dr 12309
Woodlawn Ave 12304
Woodlawn Dr 12303
Woodlawn St 12306
Woodruff Dr 12302
Woodsfield Dr 12303
Woodside Dr 12302
Woolsey St 12303
Worcester Dr 12309
Worden Rd 12302
Worthington Rd 12303
Wren St 12302
Wright Ave 12309
Wtry Rd 12309
Wyatts Dr 12302
Wylie St 12307
Wyman St 12302
Wyoming Ave
1400-1499 12308
1500-1599 12309
Yale St 12304
Yates St 12305
Yates Vlg 12308
Yorinern Rd 12309
York Pl & Rd 12302
York Seat Rd 12309
Yorkshire Ct 12302
Yorkston St 12303
Zenner Rd 12309
Zoar Ct 12302

NUMBERED STREETS

1st Ave 12303
1st St 12008
2nd Ave 12303
2nd St 12008
3rd Ave 12303
4th Ave 12303
5th Ave 12303
6th Ave 12303
7th Ave 12303
8th Ave 12303
9th Ave 12303
10th Ave 12303
21st St 12304
22nd St 12304

SOUTHAMPTON NY

General Delivery 11969

POST OFFICE BOXES MAIN OFFICE STATIONS AND BRANCHES

Box No.s
All PO Boxes 11969

NAMED STREETS

Aberdeen Ln 11968
Adams Ln 11968
Alder Ave 11968
Aldrich Ln 11968
Andrew Ct 11968
Anns Ln 11968
Apple Rd 11968
Aqua Dr 11968
Arbutus Rd 11968
Armande St 11968
Artist Colony Ln 11968
Ashwood Ct 11968
Atterbury Rd 11968
Bailey Rd 11968
Balcomie Ln 11968
Barkers Island Rd 11968
Barnhart St 11968
Barons Ln 11968
Barrow Pl 11968
Bath House Rd 11968
Bathing Beach Rd 11968
Bauer Dr 11968
Bay Ave, Rd & St 11968
Bay View Dr, Rd & Ter N & W 11968
Bayberry Cove Ln 11968
Baywood Dr 11968
E, W & S Beach Dr & Rd 11968
Beachcomber Ln 11968
Beechwood Dr 11968
Bellows Ct & Ln 11968
Bernardine St 11968
Big Fresh Pond Rd 11968
N Bishops Ct & Ln 11968
Blackwatch Ct 11968
Boatmans Ln 11968
Bowden Sq 11968
Bowers Ln 11968
Boyesen Rd 11968
Breese Ln 11968
Briar Ln 11968
Bridies Path 11968
Broadway 11968
Broidy Ln 11968
Buckner Ln 11968
Burnett St 11968
Cameron St & Way 11968
Canoe Place Rd 11968
N Captains Neck Ln 11968
Carriage Ln 11968
Castle Hill Ct 11968
Cedar Ave, Dr & Ln 11968
Cedar Crest Rd 11968
Cedar Field Ct 11968
Cedarberry Ln 11968
Center Ave & St 11968
Channel Pond Ct 11968
Charing Way 11968
Charla Dr 11968
Cheviot Rd 11968
Chivas Ct 11968
Christopher St 11968
Clam Rd 11968
Clearview Farm Rd 11968
Club Dr 11968
Cobblefield Ln 11968
Cold Spring Ct 11968
Cold Spring Point Rd 11968
College Hills Ct 11968
Cooper Ln & St 11968
Coopers Farm Rd 11968
Coopers Neck Ln 11968
Corrigan St 11968
Country Club Dr 11968
County Road 39 11968
County Road 39a 11968
Cove Rd 11968
Cove Neck Ln 11968
Crows Nest Cir 11968
Cryder Ln 11968
Culver St 11968
Dale St 11968
David Whites Ln 11968

Davids Ct 11968
Deer Trail Rd 11968
Dellaria Ave 11968
Depot Rd 11968
Devon Pl 11968
Dewell Dr 11968
Diamon Ct 11968
Dodge St 11968
Doris Ln 11968
Dorset Rd 11968
Dory Ln 11968
Dovas Path 11968
Dover Ave 11968
Down East Ln 11968
Downs Path 11968
Duck Pond Ln 11968
Dundee Ln 11968
Dune Rd 11968
East St 11968
Eastway Dr 11968
Edge Ave 11968
Edge Of Woods Rd 11968
Edgemere Dr 11968
Edwards Ln 11968
Eel Pot Aly 11968
Eileen Dr 11968
Elm St 11968
Fair Lea Rd 11968
Fall Ct 11968
Far Pond Rd 11968
Fern Rd 11968
First Neck Ln 11968
Fish Cove Rd 11968
Flying Point Rd 11968
Fordham Rd 11968
Fords Ln 11968
Fordune Ct & Dr 11968
Forecastle Ln 11968
Forrest Dr 11968
Foster Xing 11968
Fowler St 11968
Fox Hollow Ln 11968
Fresh Pond Ln 11968
W Gate Rd 11968
Gegan Dr 11968
Gianna Ct 11968
Gin Ln 11968
Glenview Dr 11968
Gondola Gdns 11968
Great Hill Rd 11968
Great Plains Rd 11968
Greenfield Rd 11968
Greenvale Ln 11968
Grove Ave 11968
Guilfoyle St 11968
Halsey Ave, Path & St 11968
Halsey Farm Dr 11968
Halsey Neck Ln 11968
Hampton Rd & St 11968
Hannas Ct 11968
Harris Ln 11968
Harrison Ave 11968
Hartwell Ln 11968
Harvest Ln 11968
Hawthorne Rd 11968
Heady Creek Ln 11968
Hearida Rd 11968
Helens Ln 11968
Henry Rd & St 11968
Herne Pl 11968
Herrick Ln & Rd 11968
Hidden Cove Ct 11968
High St 11968
Highland Rd 11968
Highlands Dr 11968
Hildreth St 11968
S Hill St 11968
Hill Top Ave 11968
Hillcrest Ave & Ter 11968
W Hills Ct 11968
Hills Station Rd 11968
Hillside Rd 11968
Hilltop Rd 11968
Horton Ter 11968
Howell St 11968
Hubbard Ln 11968
Hunters Ln 11968
Huntting St 11968
Indian Rd 11968
Inlet Rd E 11968
Inlet View Dr 11968
Island Creek Rd 11968
Jagger Ln 11968
James St 11968
Jennings Ave & Rd 11968
Jobs Ln 11968
John St 11968
Johnny Ln 11968
Johnson Ave 11968
Jordan Ln 11968
Jule Pond Dr 11968
Juniper Ln 11968
Justan Ave 11968
Kahala Ln 11968
Kendalls Ln 11968
Kennedy Dr 11968
Kenwood Rd 11968
Kerrie Ct 11968
Kings Ln 11968
Knoll Rd 11968
Knollwood Dr 11968
Koral Dr 11968
Kraut Ln 11968
Lake Dr N 11968
Lake Side Dr 11968
Lake View Ct & Pl 11968
Landing Ln 11968
Landsdowne Ln 11968
Landsend Ln 11968
Larboard Dr 11968
Layton Ave 11968
Lee Ave 11968
Leecon Ct 11968
Leland Ln 11968
Lenape Rd 11968
Leos Ln 11968
Lewis St 11968
Library 11968
Lillian Ln 11968
Lincoln Ave 11968
Linden Ln 11968
Little Fresh Pond Rd 11968
Little Neck Rd 11968
Little Plains Rd 11968
Locust Ave 11968
Lohan Ct 11968
Lois Ln 11968
Long Springs Rd 11968
Longview Rd 11968
N & S Magee Dr & St 11968
N, S & W Main St 11968
Majors Path 11968
Maple Ave & St 11968
Margate Cir 11968
Marie Ln 11968
Mariner Dr 11968
Marylea Dr 11968
Marys Ln 11968
Maylen Dr 11968
Mcgregor Dr 11968
Meadow Ln 11968
Meadowgrass Ln 11968
Meadowmere Ln & Pl 11968
Meeting House Ln 11968
Middle Ln 11968
Middle Line Hwy 11968
Middle Pond Ln & Rd 11968
Miller Rd 11968
Millfarm Ln 11968
Millicent Dr 11968
Millstone Dr & Ln 11968
Millstone Brook Rd 11968
Milton Rd 11968
Missapoque Ave & Ct 11968
Montauk Hwy 11968
Moses Ln 11968
Mountain Laurel Ln 11968
Mullen Hill Ln 11968
Murray Ln & Pl 11968
Narrow Ln 11968
Neck Cir & Rd 11968
W Neck Point Rd 11968
New Ln 11968
Newberry Ln 11968
Nicholas Ct 11968
Norton Pl 11968
Noyack Rd 11968
Nugent St 11968
Oak Ave, Pl & St 11968
Oak Grove Rd 11968
Oak View Rd 11968
Ocean View Ave & Pkwy 11968
Oceanview Dr 11968
Ochre Ln 11968
Old Field Ln 11968
Old Fish Cove Rd 11968
Old Fort Ln 11968
Old Orchard Rd 11968
Old Sag Harbor Rd 11968
Old Town Rd & Xing 11968
Oldfield Rd 11968
Osborne Ave 11968
Osceola Ln 11968
Overlook Dr 11968
Ox Pasture Rd 11968
Park Ave 11968
Parkside Ave 11968
Parrish Rd 11968
Parrish Pond Ct & Ln 11968
Peconic Ave & Rd 11968
Peconic Bay Ave 11968
Peconic Hills Ct & Dr 11968
Peconic View Ct 11968
Pelham St 11968
Pelletreau St 11968
Petrel Rd 11968
Pheasant Ct & Ln E 11968
Pheasant Close E 11968
Phillips Ln 11968
Pierpont St 11968
Pine St 11968
Pine Tree Rd 11968
Pioneer Ln 11968
Platt Ter 11968
Pleasant Ln 11968
Pond Ln & Xing 11968
Porter Rd 11968
Post Ln, Pl & Xing 11968
Potato Field Ct & Ln 11968
Powell Ave 11968
Powers Dr 11968
Private Rd 11968
W Prospect St 11968
Pulaski Ave & St 11968
Quail Run 11968
Ragnar Ln 11968
Railroad Plz 11968
Randall Rd 11968
Raymonds Ln 11968
Raynor Rd 11968
Rebadam Ln 11968
Red Cedar Rd 11968
Reo Rd 11968
Reverend Raymond Lee Ct 11968
Ridge Rd 11968
Robinhood Ln 11968
Robins Ln 11968
Robinson Rd 11968
Rogers Ave 11968
Roman Rd 11968
Roosevelt Ave 11968
Rose Ave 11968
Rose Hill Rd 11968
Roses Grove Rd 11968
S Rosko Dr 11968
Saint Andrews Cir & Rd 11968
Sandgate Ln 11968
Sandringham Ln 11968
Sandy Hollow Rd 11968
Sanford Pl 11968
Savannah Ln N & S 11968
Scallop Pond Rd 11968
Scotch Mist Ln 11968
Scotts Rd 11968
Scotts Landing Rd 11968
Scrimshaw Dr 11968
N Sea Dr 11968
N Sea Rd
235A-235B 11968
7-180 11968
123-123 11969
181-2299 11968
182-2798 11968
N Sea Mecox Rd 11968
Seasons Ln 11968
Seaweed Rd 11968
Sebonac Rd 11968
Sebonac Inlet Rd 11968
Settlers Ln 11968
Seven Ponds Rd 11968
Seven Ponds Towd Rd 11968
Sherwood St 11968
Shinnecock Hills Rd 11968
E Shore Dr & Rd 11968
Shrubland Rd 11968
Simms St 11968
Skinner St 11968
Somerset Ave 11968
South Rd & St 11968
Southampton Hills Ct 11968
Southway Dr 11968
Spinnaker Way 11968
Spinner Rd 11968
Spring Ln 11968
Spring Pond Ln 11968
Squabble Ln 11968
Stanleys Way 11968
Stoveboat Rd 11968
Straight Path 11968
Sugar Loaf Rd 11968
Summer Dr 11968
Sunninghill Rd 11968
Swan Hill Rd 11968
Sweetbriar Rd 11968
Terrace Dr 11968
Terry Ct 11968
The Pkwy 11968
Towd Point Rd 11968
Toylsome Ln & Pl 11968
W Trail Rd 11968
Trout Ln 11968
Tuckahoe Ln & Rd 11968
Turtle Cove Dr 11968
Turtle Pond Rd 11968
Twin View Dr 11968
Underhill Dr 11968
Upland Dr 11968
Valorie Rd 11968
Van Brunt St 11968
Village Ln 11968
Wall St 11968
Walnut St 11968
Warfield Way 11968
Warren St 11968
Water Mill Towd Rd 11968
Waters Edge Rd 11968
West St 11968
Westway Dr 11968
Whalebone Landing Rd 11968
White St 11968
White Oak Ln 11968
Whites Ln 11968
Whitfield Rd 11968
Wickapogue Rd 11968
Widener Ln 11968
Wilderness Trl 11968
William Way 11968
Willis St 11968
Williz Valley Rd 11968
Willow St 11968
Wilson Rd 11968
Wiltshire St 11968
Windmill Ln 11968
Windward Way 11968
Winter Way 11968
Wireless Way 11968
Wolf Swamp Ln 11968
Woodbine Pl 11968
Woodland Ct & Dr 11968
Woodland Farm Rd 11968
Woods Ln 11968
N Wooley St 11968
Wooleys Dr 11968
Wyandanch Ln 11968

NUMBERED STREETS

All Street Addresses 11968

STATEN ISLAND NY

General Delivery 10314

POST OFFICE BOXES MAIN OFFICE STATIONS AND BRANCHES

Box No.s
1 - 680 10304
1 - 218 10307
1 - 60 10308
1 - 540 10310
1 - 252 10312
1 - 748 10314
1 - 520 10301
1 - 310 10305
1 - 320 10303
25 - 82 10309
111 - 542 10308
120 - 836 10302
241 - 300 10307
301 - 360 10312
371 - 430 10305
401 - 580 10303
601 - 658 10301
685 - 748 10303
800 - 1298 10314
981 - 999 10301
986 - 999 10312
1003 - 1060 10306
10001 - 10999 10301
20120 - 29005 10302
30001 - 39005 10303
40001 - 49002 10304
50001 - 59003 10305
60001 - 69010 10306
70001 - 79002 10307
80001 - 80542 10308
90001 - 90918 10309
100001 - 109007 10310
120001 - 129010 10312
131400 - 131919 10313
140001 - 149023 10314

NAMED STREETS

Aaron Ln 10309
Abbey Rd 10308
Abbott St 10305
Abby Pl 10301
Abingdon Ave & Ct 10308
Acacia Ave 10308
Academy Ave
101-199 10309
500-599 10307
Academy Pl 10301
Ackerman St 10308
Acorn Ct 10309
Acorn St 10306
Ada Dr
1-299 10314
301-311 10303
Ada Pl 10301
Adam Ct 10314
Adams Ave 10306
Addison Ave 10309
Adelaide Ave 10306
Adele Ct 10304
Adele St 10305
Adelphi Ave 10309
Adlai Cir 10312
Adlers Ln 10307
Admiralty Loop 10309
Adrianne Ln 10303
Adrienne Pl 10308
Agnes Pl 10305
Ainsworth Ave 10308
Akron St 10314
Alan Loop 10304
Alames Ave 10306
Alaska St 10310
Alban St 10310
Albee Ave 10312
Albert Ct 10303
Albert St 10301
Alberta Ave 10314
Albion Pl 10302
Albourne Ave 10309
Albourne Ave E 10312
Albright St 10304
Alcott St 10312
Alden Pl 10301
Alderwood Pl 10304
Alex Cir 10305
Alexander Ave 10312
Alexsandra Ct 10312
Algonkin St 10312
Allegro St 10312
Allen Ct 10310
Allen Pl 10312
Allendale Rd 10305
Allison Ave & Pl 10306
Almond St 10312
Alpine Ave 10301
Alpine Ct 10310
Altamont St 10306
Altavista Ct 10305
Alter Ave
1-200 10304
201-499 10305
Altoona Ave 10306
Alverson Ave & Loop 10309
Alvine Ave 10312
Alysia Ct 10309
Amador St 10303
Amanda Ct 10312
Amaron Ln 10307
Amazon Ct 10304
Ambassador Ln 10309
Amber St 10306
Amboy Rd
2500-3599 10306
3600-4275 10308
4276-5540 10312
5541-6939 10309
6941-6973 10309
6975-6995 10307
6997-7799 10307
Amelia Ct 10310
America Ct 10314
Amherst Ave 10306
Amity Pl 10303
Amity St 10305
Amsterdam Ave & Pl 10314
Amy Ct & Ln 10314
Anaconda St 10312
Anchor Pl 10305
Anderson Ave 10302
Anderson St 10305
Andes Pl 10314
Andrea Ct 10312
Andrea Pl 10303
Andrease St 10305
Andrews Ave 10306
Andrews St 10305
Andros Ave 10303
Androvette Ave 10312
Androvette St 10309
Anita St 10314
Anjali Loop 10314
Ann St 10302
Annadale Rd 10312
Annfield Ct 10304
Anthony St 10309
Appleby Ave 10305
Arbor Ct 10301
Arbutus Ave & Way 10312
Arc Pl 10306
Arcadia Pl 10310
Archwood Ave 10312
Arden Ave 10312
Ardmore Ave 10314
Ardsley St 10306
Area Pl 10314
Argonne St 10305
Arielle Ln 10314
Arkansas Ave 10308
Arlene St 10314
Arlington Ave 10303
Arlington Ct 10310
Arlington Pl 10303
Arlo Rd 10301
Armond St 10314
Armour Pl 10309
Armstrong Ave 10308
Arnold St 10301
Arnprior St 10302
Arrowood Ct 10309
Arthur Ave 10305
Arthur Ct 10310
Arthur Kill Rd
2-98 10306
100-199 10306
201-241 10306
242-600 10308
602-700 10308
701-747 10312
749-2015 10312
2017-2099 10312
2151-2197 10309
2199-4949 10309
5200-5204 10307
5206-5599 10307
Ascot Ave 10306
Ash Pl 10314
Ashland Ave 10309
Ashland Ave E 10312
Ashley Ln 10309
Ashton Dr 10312
Ashwood Ct 10308
Ashworth Ave 10314
Aspen Knolls Way 10312
Aspinwall St 10307
Astor Ave 10314
Athena Pl 10314
Atlantic Ave
1-199 10304
200-490 10305
Atmore Pl 10306
Auburn Ave 10314
Augusta Ave 10312
E Augusta Ave 10308
Aultman Ave 10306
Ausable Ave 10301
Austin Ave 10305
Austin Pl 10304
Avalon Ct 10303
Avenue B 10302
Averill Pl 10307
Aviston St 10306
Aviva Ct 10307
Avon Ln 10314
Avon Pl 10301
Aye Ct 10314
Aymar Ave 10301
Azalea Ct 10309
Bache Ave 10306
Bache St 10302
Baden Pl
1-49 10305
50-399 10306
Bailey Pl 10303
Baker Pl 10310
Balfour St 10305
Ballard Ave 10312
Balsam Pl 10309
Baltic Ave & St 10304
Baltimore St 10308
Bamberger Ln 10312
Bancroft Ave 10306
Bang Ter 10305
Bangor St 10314
Bank Pl 10304

Bank St 10301
Bar Ct 10309
Barb St 10312
Barbara St 10306
Barclay Ave & Cir 10312
Bard Ave
10-772 10310
773-999 10301
Baring Pl 10304
Barker St 10310
Barlow Ave
2-58 10308
60-489 10308
590-999 10312
Barnard Ave 10307
Baron Blvd 10314
Barrett Ave 10302
Barretts Ln 10310
Barrow Pl 10309
Barry Ct 10306
Barry St 10309
Bartlett Ave 10312
Barton Ave 10306
Bartow Ave 10309
Bartow St 10308
Bascom Pl 10314
Bass St 10314
Bath Ave 10305
Bathgate St 10312
Battery Rd 10305
Bay St
1-406 10301
407-899 10304
951-967 10305
969-1999 10305
Bay Ter 10306
Bay Street Lndg 10301
Bayard St 10312
Bayside Ln 10309
Bayview Ave 10309
Bayview Ln 10309
Bayview Pl 10304
Bayview Ter 10312
Beach Ave 10306
S Beach Ave 10305
Beach Rd 10312
Beach St 10304
Beachview Ave 10306
Beacon Ave & Pl 10306
Beamer Ct 10303
Bear St 10304
Beard St 10314
Beasheli Ave 10309
Bedell Ave 10307
Bedell St 10309
Bedford Ave 10306
Beebe St 10301
Beechwood Ave 10301
Beechwood Pl 10314
Beekman Cir 10312
Beekman St 10302
Beethoven St 10305
Behan Ct 10306
Belair Ln & Rd 10305
Belden St 10308
Belfast Ave 10306
Belfield Ave 10312
Bell St 10305
Bellavista Ct 10305
Bellhaven Pl 10314
Belmar Dr E & W 10314
Belmont Pl 10301
Belvedere Ct 10307
Belwood Loop 10307
Bement Ave & Ct 10310
Benedict Ave 10314
Benedict Rd 10304
Benjamin Dr & Pl 10303
Bennett Ave 10312
Bennett Pl 10312
Bennett St 10302
Bennington St 10308
Benson St 10312
Bent St 10312
Bentley Ln & St 10307
Benton Ave 10305

Benton Ct 10306
Benziger Ave 10301
Beresford Ave 10314
Berglund Ave 10314
Berkley St 10312
Berry Ave 10312
Berry Ave W 10312
Berry Ct 10309
Bertha Pl 10301
Bertram Ave 10312
Berwick Pl 10310
Berwin Ln 10310
Bethel Ave 10307
Betty Ct 10303
Beverly Ave 10301
Beverly Rd 10305
Bianca Ct 10312
Bidwell Ave 10314
Billings St 10312
Billiou St 10312
Billop Ave 10307
Bionia Ave 10305
Birch Ave 10301
Birch Ln 10312
Birch Rd 10303
Birchard Ave 10314
Bishop St 10306
Bismark Ave 10301
Blackford Ave 10302
Blackhorse Ct 10306
Blaine Ct 10310
Blaise Ct 10308
Bland Pl 10312
Bleeker Pl 10314
Block St 10306
Bloomfield Ave 10314
Bloomingdale Rd 10309
Blossom Ln 10307
Blue Heron Ct & Dr 10312
Blueberry Ln 10312
Blythe Pl 10306
Boardwalk Ave 10312
Bocce Ct 10307
Bodine St 10310
Bogert Ave 10314
Bogota St 10314
Bolivar St 10314
Bombay St 10309
Bond St 10302
Boone St 10314
Borg Ct 10302
Borman Ave 10314
Boscombe Ave 10309
Bosworth St 10310
Boulder St 10312
Boulevard St 10314
Boundary Ave 10306
Bountina Ave 10312
Bouton Ln 10312
Bovanizer St 10312
Bowden St 10306
Bowdoin St 10314
Bowen St 10304
Bower Ct 10309
Bowles Ave 10303
Bowling Green Pl 10314
Boyce Ave 10306
Boyd St 10304
Boylan St 10312
Boyle Pl & St 10306
Boynton St 10309
Brabant St 10303
Brad Ln 10314
Bradford Ave 10309
Bradley Ave & Ct 10314
Braisted Ave 10314
Brandis Ave 10312
E Brandis Ave 10308
Brandis Ln 10312
Brehaut Ave 10307
Brenton Pl 10314
Brentwood Ave 10301
Brewster St 10304
Briarcliff Rd 10305
Brick Ct 10309
Bridge Ct 10305

N Bridge St 10309
S Bridge St 10309
Bridgetown St 10314
Brielle Ave 10314
Brienna Ct 10309
Brighton Ave 10301
Brighton St 10307
Bristol Ave 10301
Britton Ave 10304
Britton St 10310
Broad St 10304
Broadway 10310
E Broadway 10306
Broken Shell Rd 10309
Brook Ave 10306
Brook St 10301
Brookfield Ave 10308
Brooks Pl 10310
Brookside Ave
2-108 10310
110-298 10314
Brookside Loop 10309
Brookspond Pl 10310
Brower Ct 10308
Brown Ave 10308
Brown Pl 10305
Brownell St 10304
Browning Ave 10314
Bruckner Ave 10303
Bruno Ln 10307
Brunswick St 10314
Bryan St 10307
Bryant Ave 10306
Bryson Ave
1-199 10302
200-499 10314
Buchanan Ave 10314
E Buchanan St 10301
W Buchanan St 10301
Buel Ave
1-99 10304
124-132 10305
134-780 10305
Buffalo St 10306
Buffington Ave 10312
Bunnell Ct 10312
Burbank Ave 10306
Burchard Ct 10312
Burden Ave 10302
Burgher Ave
1-185 10304
186-226 10305
228-425 10305
N Burgher Ave 10310
Burke Ave 10314
Burnside Ave 10302
Burton Ave 10309
Burton Ct 10306
Bush Ave 10303
Butler Ave 10307
Butler Blvd 10309
Butler Pl 10305
Butler St 10309
Butler Ter 10301
Butterworth Ave 10301
Buttonwood Rd 10304
Byrne Ave 10314
Cable Way 10303
Cabot Pl 10305
Calcagno Ct 10314
Caldera Pl 10301
Callahan Ln 10307
Callan Ave 10304
Calvanico Ln 10314
Cambria St 10305
Cambridge Ave 10314
Camden Ave 10309
Cameron Ave 10305
Campbell Ave 10310
Campus Rd 10301
Canal St 10304
Candon Ave & Ct 10309
Cannon Ave 10314
Cannon Blvd 10306
Canon Dr 10314
Canterbury Ave 10314

Canterbury Ct 10309
Canton Ave 10312
Capellan St 10312
Cardiff St 10312
Cardinal Ln 10306
Carlin St 10309
Carlton Ave 10309
Carlton Blvd 10312
Carlton Ct 10312
Carlton Pl 10301
Carly Ct 10309
Carlyle Grn 10312
Carmel Ave 10314
Carmel Ct 10304
Carnegie Ave 10314
Caro St 10314
Carol Ct 10309
Carol Pl 10303
Carolina Ct & Pl 10314
Caroline St 10310
Carolyn Ct 10309
Carpenter Ave 10314
Carreau Ave 10314
Carroll Pl 10301
Carteret St 10307
Cary Ave 10310
Cascade St 10306
Case Ave 10309
Cassidy Pl 10301
Castleton Ave
1-689 10301
690-722 10310
724-1360 10310
1362-1368 10310
1390-1440 10302
1442-1699 10302
Castor Pl 10312
W Castor Pl
1-99 10312
100-199 10309
W Caswell Ave & Ln 10314
Catherine St 10302
Catlin Ave 10304
Cattaraugus St 10301
Cayuga Ave 10301
Cebra Ave
1-30 10301
32-52 10304
54-199 10304
Cecil Ct 10303
Cedar Ave 10305
Cedar St 10304
Cedar Ter 10304
Cedar Grove Ave, Bch & Ct 10306
Cedarcliff Rd 10301
W Cedarview Ave 10306
Cedarwood Ct 10303
Celebration Ln 10304
Celtic Pl 10306
Center Pl & St 10306
Central Ave 10301
Centre Ave 10304
Challenger Dr 10312
Champlain Ave 10306
Chandler Ave 10314
Chapin Ave 10304
Charles Ave 10302
Charles Ct 10306
Charles Pl 10303
Charleston Ave 10309
Chart Loop 10309
Charter Oak Rd 10304
Chatham St 10312
Chelsea Rd 10314
Chelsea St 10307
Cherokee St 10305
Cherry Pl 10314
Cherrywood Ct 10308
Cheryl Ave 10312
Chesebrough St 10312
E Cheshire Pl 10301
Chess Loop 10306
Chester Ave 10312
Chester Pl 10304
Chesterfield Ln 10314

Chesterton Ave 10306
Chestnut Ave 10305
Chestnut Cir 10312
Chestnut St 10304
Cheves Ave 10314
Chicago Ave 10305
Chipperfield Ct 10301
Chrissy Ct 10310
Christine Ct 10312
Christopher Ln 10314
Christopher St 10303
Church Ave 10314
Church Ln 10305
Church St 10302
Churchill Ave 10309
Ciarcia Ct 10309
Circle Loop & Rd 10304
City Blvd 10301
Claire Ct 10301
Claradon Ln 10305
Clarence Pl 10306
Clarion Ct 10310
Clark Ln 10304
Clark Pl 10302
Clarke Ave 10306
Claudia Ct 10303
Clawson St 10306
Clayboard St 10306
Claypit Rd 10309
Clayton St 10305
Clearmont Ave 10309
Clermont Ave 10307
Clermont Pl 10314
Cletus St 10305
Cleveland Ave 10308
Cleveland Pl 10305
Cleveland St 10301
Cliff Ct & St 10305
Cliffside Ave 10304
Clifton Ave 10305
Clifton St 10314
Clinton Ave 10301
Clinton Ct 10301
Clinton Pl 10302
Clinton Rd 10308
Clinton St 10304
Cloister Pl 10306
Clove Rd
942A-942B 10301
112-701 10310
703-853 10310
854-998 10301
1000-1406 10301
1408-1550 10301
1796-1858 10304
1860-2075 10304
2076-2116 10305
2118-2299 10305
Clove Way 10301
Clove Lake Pl 10310
Cloverdale Ave 10308
Clovis Rd 10308
Clyde Pl 10301
Coale Ave 10314
Coast Guard Dr 10305
Cobblers Ln 10304
Coco Ct 10312
Coddington Ave 10306
Cody Pl 10312
Coldspring Ct 10304
Cole St 10309
Colfax Ave 10306
Colgate Pl 10306
Colita Ct 10307
College Ave
1-463 10314
465-519 10314
522-528 10302
530-699 10302
College Ct 10302
College Pl 10304
Collfield Ave
1-200 10302
201-799 10314
Collyer Ave 10312
Colon Ave 10308

Colon St 10312
Colonial Ct 10310
Colony Ave
65-123 10305
110-168 10306
170-399 10306
Colton St 10305
Columbia Ave 10305
Columbus Ave 10304
Columbus Pl 10314
Combs Ave 10306
Comely St 10312
Comfort Ct 10312
Commerce St 10314
Commodore Dr 10309
Comstock Ave 10314
Concord Ln & Pl 10304
Confederation Pl 10303
Conference Ct 10307
Conger St 10305
Congress St 10304
Connecticut St 10307
Connor Ave 10306
Conrad Ave 10314
Constant Ave 10314
Continental Pl 10303
Convent Ave 10309
Conyingham Ave 10301
Cooke St 10314
Coonley Ct 10303
Cooper Ave 10305
Cooper Pl 10309
Cooper Ter 10314
Copley St 10314
Copperflagg Ln 10304
Copperleaf Ter 10304
Coral Ct 10308
Corbin Ave 10308
Cordelia Ave 10309
Cornelia Ave 10312
Cornelia St 10304
Cornell Ave 10310
Cornell Pl 10304
Cornell St 10302
Cornish St 10308
Corona Ave 10306
Correll Ave
585A-585C 10309
1-199 10312
400-799 10309
Corson Ave 10301
Cortelyou Ave 10312
Cortelyou Pl 10301
Cortlandt St 10302
Coryn Ct 10312
Cottage Ave 10308
Cottage Pl 10302
Cotter Ave 10306
Cottontail Ct 10312
Cottonwood Ct 10308
Coughlan Ave 10310
Country Dr E 10314
Country Dr N 10314
Country Dr S 10314
Country Dr W 10314
Country Ln 10312
Country Woods Ln 10308
Coursen Ct & Pl 10304
Court St 10304
Courtney Loop 10305
Coventry Loop 10312
Coventry Rd 10304
Coverly Ave 10301
Coverly St 10306
Covington Cir 10312
Cowen Pl 10303
Crabbs Ln 10314
Crabtree Ave & Ln 10309
Crafton Ave 10314
Craig Ave 10307
Cranberry Ct 10309
Cranford Ave 10306
Cranford Ct 10306
Cranford St 10308
Crescent Ave 10301
Crescent Bch 10308

Crest Loop 10312
Creston Pl 10304
Creston St 10309
Crestwater Ct 10305
Crispi Ln 10308
Crist St 10305
Crittenden Pl 10302
Croak Ave 10314
Croft Ct 10306
Croft Pl 10314
Cromer St 10308
Cromwell Ave
1-187 10304
188-999 10305
Cromwell Cir 10304
Cross St 10304
Crossfield Ave 10312
Crosshill St 10301
Croton Ave 10301
Crowell Ave 10314
Crown Ave, Ct & Pl 10312
Crystal Ave
1-300 10302
301-462 10314
464-498 10314
Cuba Ave 10306
Cubberly Pl 10306
Culotta Ln 10309
Cunard Ave & Pl 10304
Currie Ave 10306
Curtis Ave 10310
Curtis Ct 10310
Curtis Pl 10301
Cypress Ave 10301
Cypress Loop 10309
Daffodil Ct 10312
Daffodil Ln 10314
Dahlia St 10312
Dakota Pl 10314
Dale Ave 10306
Daleham St 10308
Dalemere Rd 10304
Dallas St 10310
Dalton Ave 10306
Dana St 10301
Daniel Low Ter 10301
Daniella Ct 10314
Danny Ct 10314
Darcey Ave 10314
Darlington Ave
1-197 10312
199-402 10312
403-699 10309
Darnell Ln 10309
Dartmouth Loop 10306
David Pl 10303
David St 10308
Davidson Ct & St 10303
Davis Ave & Ct 10310
Dawn Ct 10307
Dawson Cir, Ct & St 10314
Dayna Dr 10305
Deal Ct 10305
Debbie St 10314
Deborah Loop 10312
Decatur Ave 10314
Decker Ave 10302
Deems Ave 10314
Deere Park Pl 10301
Degroot Pl 10310
Dehart Ave 10303
Deirdre Ct 10304
Deisius St 10312
Dekalb St 10304
Dekay St 10310
Delafield Ave
1-122 10301
124-240 10301
241-899 10310
Delafield Pl 10310
Delaware Ave
1-199 10304
200-999 10305
Delaware Pl 10314
Delaware St 10304
Delia Ct 10307

Dell Ct 10307
Dellwood Rd 10304
Delmar Ave 10312
Delmore St 10314
Delphine Ter 10305
Delray Ct 10304
Delwitt Ave 10306
Demopolis Ave 10308
Demorest Ave 10314
Denise Ct 10312
Denker Pl 10314
Denoble Ln 10301
Dent Rd 10308
Denton Pl 10314
Depew Pl 10309
Deppe Pl 10314
Derby Ct 10302
Derick Ct 10309
Deruyter Pl 10303
Deserre Ave 10312
Destiny Ct 10303
Detroit Ave 10312
Devens St 10314
Devon Loop 10314
Devon Pl 10301
Dewey Ave 10308
Dewhurst St 10314
Dexter Ave 10309
Dianas Trl 10304
Diaz Pl 10306
Diaz St 10305
Dickie Ave 10314
Dierauf St 10312
Dimarco Pl 10306
Dina Ct 10306
Dinsmore St 10314
Dintree Ln 10307
Direnzo Ct 10309
Discala Ln 10312
Disosway Pl 10310
Divine St 10304
Dix Pl 10304
Dixon Ave
  1-100 10302
  101-299 10303
  301-399 10303
Doane Ave 10308
Dobbs Pl 10301
Dockside Ln 10308
Doe Pl 10310
Dogwood Dr 10312
Dogwood Ln 10305
Dole St 10312
Dolson Pl 10303
Domain St 10314
Dominick Ln 10312
Don Ct 10312
Donald Pl 10310
Dongan Ave 10314
Dongan St 10310
Dongan Hills Ave
  1-59 10306
  61-99 10306
  100-510 10305
  512-588 10305
Donley Ave 10305
Donna Ct 10314
Dora St 10314
Dore Ct 10310
Doreen Dr 10303
Dorit Ct 10308
Dorothea Pl 10306
Dorothy St 10314
Dorval Ave & Pl 10312
Doty Ave 10305
Douglas Ave 10310
Douglas Ct 10304
Douglas Rd 10304
Dover Grn 10312
Dovetree Ln 10314
Downes Ave 10312
Downey Pl 10303
Drake Ave 10314
Draper Pl 10314
Dresden Pl 10301
Drew Ct 10309
Dreyer Ave 10314
Driggs St 10308
Driprock St 10310
Drum Rd 10305
S Drum St 10309
Drumgoole Rd E
  2-12 10312
  14-50 10312
  52-1320 10312
  1322-1872 10309
Drumgoole Rd W
  400-1630 10312
  1720-1888 10309
Dryden Ct 10302
Drysdale St 10314
Duane Ct 10301
Dublin Pl 10303
Dubois Ave 10310
Dudley Ave 10301
Duer Ave 10305
Duer Ln 10301
Dugdale St 10306
Duke Pl 10314
Dulancey Ct 10301
Dumont Ave 10305
Dunbar St 10308
Duncan Rd 10301
Duncan St 10304
Dunham St 10309
Dunhill Ave 10309
Durant Ave
  1-310 10306
  311-599 10308
  601-799 10308
Durges St 10304
Dustan St 10306
Dutchess Ave 10304
Dyson St 10304
Eadie Pl 10301
Eagan Ave 10312
Eagle Rd 10314
Eastentry Rd 10304
Eastman St 10312
Eastwood Ave 10309
Eaton Pl 10302
Ebbitts St 10306
Ebey Ln 10312
Ebony St 10306
Echo Pl 10314
Eddy St 10301
Eden Ct 10307
Edgar Pl 10304
Edgar Ter 10301
Edgegrove Ave
  1-846 10312
  847-1099 10309
Edgewater St 10305
Edgewood Rd 10308
Edinboro Rd 10306
Edison St 10306
Edith Ave 10312
N & S Edo Ct 10309
Edstone Dr 10301
Edward Ct 10314
Edward Curry Ave 10314
Edwin St 10312
Egbert Ave 10310
Egbert Pl 10305
Egmont Pl 10301
Egrit Ct 10314
El Camino Loop 10309
Elaine Ct 10304
Elbe Ave 10304
Elder Ave 10309
Eldridge Ave 10302
Eleanor Ln 10308
Eleanor Pl 10303
Eleanor St 10306
Elias Pl 10314
Elie Ct 10314
Elise Ct 10306
Elizabeth Ave 10310
Elizabeth Ct 10307
Elizabeth Pl 10309
Elizabeth St 10310
Elk Ct 10306
Elkhart St 10308
Elks Pl 10309
Ella Pl 10306
Ellicott Pl 10301
Ellington St 10304
Ellis St 10307
Ellsworth Ave 10312
Ellsworth Pl 10314
Elm Pl 10301
Elm St 10310
Elmbank St 10312
Elmhurst Ave 10301
Elmira Ave 10314
Elmira St 10306
Elmtree Ave 10306
Elmwood Ave 10308
Elmwood Park Dr 10314
Elson St 10314
Eltinge St 10304
Eltingville Blvd 10312
Elverton Ave 10308
Elvin St 10314
Elvira Ct 10306
Elwood Ave 10314
Elwood Pl 10301
Ely Ave 10312
Ely Ct 10312
Ely St 10301
Emerald Ct 10309
Emeric Ct 10303
Emerson Ave 10301
Emerson Ct 10304
Emerson Dr 10304
Emily Ct 10307
Emily Ln 10312
Emmet Ave 10306
End Pl 10312
Endor Ave 10301
Endview St 10312
Enfield Pl 10306
Engert St 10309
Englewood Ave 10309
Erastina Pl 10303
Eric Ln 10308
Erie St 10309
Erika Loop 10312
Errington Pl 10304
Erwin Ct 10306
Escanaba Ave 10308
Esmac Ct 10304
Essex Dr 10314
Estelle Pl 10309
Esther Depew St 10306
Eton Pl 10314
Eugene Pl 10312
Eugene St 10309
Eunice Pl 10303
Eva Ave 10306
Evan Pl 10312
Evans St 10314
Evelyn Pl 10305
Everett Ave & Pl 10309
Evergreen Ave
  1-89 10304
  90-999 10305
Evergreen St 10308
Everton Ave 10312
Excelsior Ave 10309
Exeter St 10308
Eylandt St 10312
Faber St 10302
Fabian St 10312
Fahy Ave 10314
Fairbanks Ave 10306
Fairfield St 10308
Fairlawn Ave & Loop 10308
Fairview Ave 10314
Fairway Ave 10304
Fairway Ln 10301
Faith Ct 10309
Falcon Ave 10306
Fancher Pl 10303
Fanning St 10314
Farailli Ave 10302
Farraday St 10314
Farragut Ave 10303
Farrell Ct 10306
Farview Pl 10304
Father Capodanno Blvd
  1-799 10305
  801-923 10305
  925-1299 10306
Fawn Ln 10306
Fayann Ln 10307
Fayette Ave 10305
Federal Pl 10303
Feldmeyers Ln 10314
Felton St 10314
Fenway Cir 10308
Ferguson Ct 10307
Fern Ave 10308
Ferndale Ave & Ct 10314
Ferry St 10302
Ferry Terminal Dr 10301
Ficarelle Dr 10309
Fiedler Ave 10301
Field St 10314
Fields Ave 10314
Fieldstone Rd 10314
Fieldway Ave 10308
Figurea Ave 10312
E Figurea Ave 10308
Filipe Ln 10308
Fillat St 10314
Fillmore Ave 10314
Fillmore Pl 10305
Fillmore St 10301
Fine Blvd 10314
Fingal St 10312
Fingerboard Rd 10305
W Fingerboard Rd
  500-900 10305
  901-957 10304
  902-958 10305
  959-1099 10304
Finlay Ave 10309
Finlay St 10307
Finley Ave 10306
Firth Rd 10314
Fisher Ave 10307
Fiske Ave 10314
Fitzgerald Ave 10308
Flagg Ct & Pl 10304
Flagship Cir 10309
Fletcher St 10305
Flint St 10306
Florence Pl 10309
Florence St 10308
Florida Ave 10305
Florida Ter 10306
Flower Ave 10309
Floyd St 10310
Foch Ave 10305
Fonda Pl 10309
Foote Ave 10301
Foothill Ct 10309
Ford Pl 10310
Forest Ave
  5-257 10301
  259-479 10301
  480-1239 10310
  1240-1638 10302
  1640-1700 10302
  1701-2700 10303
  2702-2890 10303
Forest Ct 10303
Forest Grn 10312
Forest Ln 10307
Forest Rd 10304
Forest St 10314
Forest Hill Rd 10314
Fornes Pl 10312
Forrestal Ave & Ct 10312
Fort Pl 10301
Fort Hill Cir & Park 10301
Foster Ave 10314
Foster Rd 10309
Four Corners Rd 10304
Fox Ln 10306
Fox Hill Ter 10305
Fox Hunt Ct 10301
Foxbeach Ave 10306
Foxholm St 10306
Francesca Ln 10303
Francine Ct 10306
Francine Ln 10314
Francis Pl 10304
Frank Ct 10312
Franklin Ave 10301
Franklin Ln 10306
Franklin Pl 10314
Fraser St 10314
Frean St 10304
Frederick St 10314
Freeborn St
  1-99 10305
  100-449 10306
Freedom Ave 10314
Freeman Pl 10310
Fremont Ave 10306
Front St 10304
Fuller Ct 10306
Fulton St 10304
Furman St 10312
Furness Pl 10314
Futurity Pl 10312
Gabriele Ct 10312
Gadsen Pl 10314
Gail Ct 10306
Galesville Ct 10305
Galloway Ave 10302
Galvaston Loop 10314
N & S Gannon Ave 10314
Gansevoort Blvd 10314
Garden Ct 10304
Garden St 10314
Gardenia Ln 10314
Garfield Ave 10305
Garibaldi Ave 10306
Garretson Ave
  1-170 10304
  171-187 10305
  189-999 10305
Garretson Ln
  1-29 10305
  30-98 10304
Garrison Ave 10314
Garson Ave 10305
Garth Ct 10306
Gary Ct 10314
Gary Pl 10314
Gary St 10312
Gateway Dr 10304
Gaton St 10309
Gauldy Ave 10314
Gaynor St 10309
Geldner Ave 10306
General St 10306
Genesee Ave
  1-209 10308
  262-288 10312
  290-534 10312
  536-998 10312
Genesee St 10301
Gentile Ct 10312
Geo Ct 10304
George St 10307
Georges Ln 10309
Georgia Ct 10309
Gervil St 10309
Getz Ave 10312
Geyser Dr 10312
Giacomo Ln 10310
Gianna Ct 10306
Gibson Ave 10308
Giegerich Ave & Pl 10307
Giffords Gln & Ln 10308
Gil Ct 10312
Gilbert Pl 10309
Gilbert St 10306
Giles Pl 10304
Gillard Ave 10312
Gilroy St 10309
Gina Ct 10314
Giordan Ct 10303
Girard St 10307
Gladwin St 10309
Glascoe Ave 10314
Glen Ave 10301
Glen St 10314
Glendale Ave 10304
Glenn Rd 10314
Glenwood Ave 10301
Glenwood Pl 10310
Globe Ave 10314
Gloria Ct 10302
Glover St 10308
Goethals Rd N
  600-651 10314
  653-899 10314
  915-2799 10303
S Goff Ave 10309
Gold Ave 10312
Golfview Ct 10314
Goller Pl 10314
Goodall St 10308
Goodwin Ave 10314
Gordon Pl 10301
Gordon St 10304
Gorge Rd 10304
Governor Rd 10314
Gower St 10314
Grace Ct 10301
Grace Rd 10306
Grafe St 10309
Graham Ave 10314
Graham Blvd 10305
Grand Ave 10301
Grandview Ave 10303
Grandview Ter 10308
Granite Ave 10303
Grant Pl 10306
Grant St 10301
Grantwood Ave 10312
Grasmere Ave
  1-60 10304
  61-63 10305
  65-73 10305
  75-999 10305
Grasmere Ct 10305
Grasmere Dr 10305
Graves St 10314
Gray St 10304
Grayson St 10306
Great Kills Rd 10308
Greaves Ave, Ct & Ln 10308
Greeley Ave 10306
Green St 10310
Green Valley Rd 10312
Greencroft Ave & Ln 10308
Greenfield Ave & Ct 10304
Greenleaf Ave 10310
S Greenleaf Ave 10314
Greenport St 10304
Greentree Ln 10314
Greenway Ave 10314
Greenway Dr 10301
Greenwood Ave 10301
Gregg Pl 10301
Gregory Ln 10314
Greta Pl 10301
Gridley Ave 10303
Grille Ct 10309
Grimsby St
  1-50 10305
  51-97 10306
  99-449 10306
Grissom Ave 10314
Griswold Ct 10301
Groton St 10312
Grove Ave 10302
Grove Pl 10302
Grove St 10304
Grymes Hill Rd 10301
Guilford St 10305
Guinevere Ln 10310
Gulf Ave
  200-298 10303
  600-798 10314
  2800-2890 10303
Gunton Pl 10309
Gurdon St 10314
Gurley Ave 10308
Guyon Ave 10306
Gwenn Loop 10314
Hafstrom St 10306
Hagaman Pl 10302
Hale St 10307
Hales Ave 10312
Hallister St 10309
Halpin Ave 10312
Hamden Ave 10306
Hameadis Ave 10314
Hamilton Ave 10301
Hamilton St 10304
Hamlin Pl 10302
Hammock Ln 10312
Hampton Grn 10312
Hampton Pl 10309
Hancock St 10305
Hank Pl 10309
Hannah St 10301
Hanover Ave
  1-140 10309
  142-198 10309
  200-599 10304
Harbor Ln, Loop & Rd 10303
Harbor View Ct 10301
Harbor View Pl 10305
Harbour Ct 10308
Hardin Ave 10310
Hardy Pl 10308
Hardy St 10304
Hargold Ave 10309
Harold Ave 10312
Harold St 10314
Harris Ave 10314
Harris Ln 10309
Harrison Ave 10302
Harrison Pl 10310
Harrison St 10304
Hart Ave 10310
Hart Blvd 10301
Hart Loop 10306
Hart Pl 10307
Hartford Ave 10310
Hartford St 10308
Harvard Ave 10301
Harvest Ave 10310
Harvey Ave 10314
Hasbrouck Rd 10304
Hastings Ct 10309
Hastings St 10305
Hatfield Pl 10302
Haughwout Ave 10302
Haven Ave 10306
Haven Esplanade St 10301
Havenwood Rd 10301
Hawley Ave 10312
Hawthorne Ave 10314
Hay St 10304
Haynes St 10309
Haywood St 10307
Heaney Ave 10303
Heather Ct 10303
Heberton Ave 10302
Hecker St 10307
Heenan Ave 10312
Heffernan St 10312
Heinz Ave 10308
Helena Rd 10304
Helene Ct 10309
Helios Pl 10309
Hemlock Ct, Ln & St 10309
Hempstead Ave 10306
Henderson Ave
  1-208 10301
  210-338 10301
  371-999 10310
Hendricks Ave 10301
Henning St 10314
Henry Pl 10305
Herainde Ave 10303
Hereford St 10308
Herkimer St 10301
Herrick Ave 10309
Hervey St 10309
Hett Ave 10306
Heusden St 10303
Hewitt Ave 10301

Hickory Ave 10305
Hickory Cir 10312
Hickory Ct 10309
High St 10305
Highland Ave 10301
Highland Ln 10308
Highland Rd 10308
Highmount Rd 10308
Highpoint Rd 10304
Highview Ave 10301
Hill St 10304
Hillbrook Ct & Dr 10305
Hillcrest Ave 10308
Hillcrest Ct 10305
Hillcrest St
1-213 10308
215-243 10308
244-258 10312
260-998 10312
Hillcrest Ter 10305
Hilldale Ct 10305
Hillis St 10312
Hillman Ave 10314
Hillridge Ct 10305
Hillside Ave 10304
Hillside Ter 10308
Hilltop Pl 10308
Hilltop Rd 10312
Hilltop Ter 10304
Hillview Ln & Pl 10304
Hillwood Ct 10305
Hinton St 10312
Hirsch Ln 10314
Hitchcock Ave 10306
Hoda Pl 10312
Hodges Pl 10314
Holbernt Ct 10302
Holcomb Ave 10312
Holden Blvd 10314
Holdridge Ave 10312
Holgate St 10314
Holiday Way 10314
Holland Ave 10303
Holly Ave 10308
Holly Pl 10306
Holly St 10304
Holsman Rd 10301
Holten Ave 10309
Home Ave 10305
Home Pl
1-69 10302
71-79 10314
81-199 10314
Homer St 10301
Homestead Ave 10302
Honey Ln 10307
Hooker Pl
1-160 10302
162-168 10302
200-249 10303
251-299 10303
Hooper Ave 10306
Hope Ave & Ln 10305
Hopkins Ave 10306
Hopping Ave 10307
Housman Ave 10303
Houston Ln & St 10302
Howard Ave 10301
Howard Cir 10301
Howard Ct 10310
Howe St 10310
Howton Ave 10308
Hoyt Ave 10301
Hudson Pl 10303
Hudson Rd 10305
Hudson St 10304
Huguenot Ave 10312
Hull Ave 10306
Humbert St 10305
Hunt Ln 10304
Hunter Ave 10306
Hunter Pl 10301
Hunter St 10304
Hunton St 10304
Hurlbert St 10305
Huron Pl 10301
Husson St
1-82 10305
84-100 10305
230-399 10306
Hyatt St 10301
Hygeia Pl 10304
Hylan Blvd
1-1939 10305
1941-1969 10305
1970-3299 10306
3301-3533 10306
3535-3717 10308
3719-4225 10308
4226-5219 10312
5221-5443 10312
5694-5758 10309
5760-6800 10309
6980-7423 10307
7425-7499 10307
Hylan Pl 10306
Ibsen Ave 10312
Ida Ct 10312
Idaho Ave 10309
Idlease Pl 10306
Igros Ct 10309
Ilion Pl 10306
Ilyse Ct 10306
Ilyssa Way 10312
Impala Ct 10305
Imperial Ct 10304
Ina St 10306
Indale Ave 10309
Industrial Loop 10309
Industry Rd 10314
Inez St 10309
Ingram Ave 10314
Innis St 10302
Inwood Rd 10301
Iona St 10305
Ionia Ave
1-796 10312
797-1099 10309
Iowa Pl 10314
Irene Ln 10307
Iris Ct 10309
Ironmine Dr 10304
Ironwood St 10308
Iroquois St 10305
Irving Pl 10304
Irvington St 10312
Isabella Ave 10306
Isernia Ave 10306
Islington St 10308
Ismay St 10314
Isora Pl 10306
Ithaca St 10306
Ivan Ct 10309
Ivy Ct 10309
Jackson Ave 10305
Jackson St 10304
Jacob St 10307
Jacques Ave 10306
Jaffe St 10314
Jake Ct 10304
James Pl 10305
Jamie Ct 10314
Jamie Ln 10312
Jansen Ct & St 10312
Jardine Ave 10314
Jarvis Ave 10312
Jason Ct 10306
Jasper St 10314
Jayne Ln 10307
Jeanette Ave 10312
Jefferson Ave 10306
Jefferson Blvd 10312
Jefferson St
1-200 10304
201-299 10306
Jeffrey Pl 10307
Jenna Ln 10304
Jennifer Ct 10314
Jennifer Ln 10306
Jennifer Pl 10314
Jerome Ave & Rd 10305
Jersey St 10301
Jessica Ct 10312
Jessica Ln 10309
Jewett Ave
1-9 10302
11-593 10302
594-614 10314
595-615 10302
616-999 10314
Jillian Ct 10310
Joan Pl 10314
Joel Pl 10306
Johanna Ln 10309
John St 10302
Johnson Ave 10307
Johnson Pl 10304
Johnson St 10309
Johnston Ter 10309
Jojo Ct 10307
Joline Ave & Ln 10307
Jones Pl 10310
Jones St 10314
Joseph Ave 10314
Joseph Ct 10307
Joseph Ln 10305
Josephine St 10314
Joshua Ct 10306
Journeay St 10303
Joyce Ln 10307
Joyce St 10305
Judith Ct 10305
Jules Dr 10314
Julie Ct 10314
Julieann Ct 10304
Jumel St 10308
Junction Ct 10306
Juni Ct 10314
Juniper Pl 10306
Jupiter Ln 10303
Justin Ave 10306
Kaltenmeier Ln 10305
Kansas Ave 10305
Karen Ct 10310
Katan Ave
1-479 10308
549-609 10312
611-899 10312
Katan Loop 10308
Kathleen Ct 10307
Kathy Ct 10312
Kathy Pl 10314
Kay Pl 10305
Kayla Ct 10306
Keating Pl 10314
Keating St 10309
Keats St 10308
Keegans Ln 10308
Keeley St 10305
Keiber Ct 10314
Kell Ave 10314
Kelly Blvd 10314
Kelvin Ave 10306
Kemball Ave 10314
Kenilworth Ave 10312
Kenmore St 10312
Kenneth Pl 10309
Kennington St 10308
Kensico St 10306
Kensington Ave 10305
Kent St 10306
Kenwood Ave 10312
Keppel Ave 10307
Kermit Ave 10305
Kerry Ln 10307
Keune Ct 10304
Kimberly Ln 10304
Kineradw St 10304
King St
101-209 10308
210-999 10312
King James Ct 10308
Kingdom Ave 10312
Kinghorn St 10312
Kingsbridge Ave 10314
Kingsland St 10309
Kingsley Ave 10314
Kingsley Pl 10301
Kinsey Pl 10303
Kirby Ct 10301
Kirkland Ct 10302
Kirshon Ave 10314
Kissam Ave 10306
Kissel Ave
2-242 10310
244-249 10310
251-299 10310
300-599 10301
Kiswick St 10306
Klondike Ave 10314
Knapp St 10314
Knauth Pl 10305
Knesel St 10309
Knight Loop 10306
Knox Pl 10314
Knox St 10309
Koch Blvd 10312
Kramer Ave 10309
Kramer Pl 10302
Kramer St 10305
Kreischer St 10309
Krissa Ct 10312
Kristen Ct 10304
Kruser St 10306
Kunath Ave 10309
Kyle Ct 10312
Labau Ave 10301
Laconia Ave
1-469 10305
471-519 10305
607-627 10306
629-749 10306
751-799 10306
Ladd Ave 10312
Lafayette Ave 10301
Lafayette St 10307
Laforge Ave & Pl 10302
Lagrange Pl 10302
Laguardia Ave 10314
Laguna Ln 10303
Lake Ave 10303
Lakeland Rd 10314
Lakeside Pl 10305
Lakeview Ter 10305
Lakewood Rd 10301
Lambert St 10314
Lamberts Ln 10314
Lamoka Ave
2-98 10308
100-275 10308
277-331 10308
332-699 10312
Lamont Ave
101-417 10312
419-794 10312
795-795 10309
796-796 10312
797-1099 10309
Lamped Loop 10314
Lamport Blvd 10305
Lander Ave 10314
Landis Ave 10305
Langere Pl 10305
Lansing St 10305
Larch Ct 10309
Laredo Ave 10312
Larkin St 10302
Larrison Loop 10314
Lasalle St 10303
Latham Pl 10309
Lathrop Ave
100-300 10314
301-399 10302
Latimer Ave 10314
Latourette Ln 10314
Latourette St 10309
Laurel Ave 10304
Laurie Ct 10304
Lava St 10305
Law Pl 10310
Lawn Ave 10306
Lawrence Ave 10310
Layton Ave 10301
Leason Pl 10314
Ledyard Pl 10305
Lee Ave 10307
Leeds St 10306
Leewood Loop 10304
Legate Ave 10312
Leggett Pl 10314
Legion Pl 10305
Leigh Ave 10314
Lenevar Ave 10309
Lenhart St 10307
Lennon Ct 10308
Lenzie St 10312
Leo St 10314
Leona St 10314
Leonard Ave
1-299 10314
331-399 10302
Leonello Ln 10307
Lerer Ln 10307
Leroy St 10314
Leslie Ave 10305
Lester St 10314
Letty Ct 10303
Leverett Ave
67-546 10308
547-776 10312
778-812 10312
Leverett Ct 10308
Levit Ave 10314
Lewiston St 10314
Lexa Pl 10312
Lexington Ave 10302
Lexington Ln 10308
Leyden Ave 10303
Liberty Ave
1-139 10304
141-153 10305
155-999 10305
Lighthouse Ave 10306
Lighthouse Plz 10301
Lightner Ave 10314
Lilac Ct 10303
Lillian Pl 10308
Lillie Ln 10314
Lily Pond Ave 10305
Lincoln Ave 10306
Lincoln Pl 10305
Lincoln St 10314
Linda Ave 10305
Linda Ct 10302
Linda Ln 10312
Lindbergh Ave 10306
Linden Ave 10303
Linden St 10310
Lindenwood Rd 10308
Link Rd 10304
Linton Pl 10308
Linwood Ave 10305
Lion St 10307
Lipsett Ave 10312
Lisa Ln 10312
Lisbon Pl 10306
Lisk Ave 10303
Liss St 10312
Little Clove Rd 10301
Littlefield Ave 10312
Livermore Ave
2-12 10302
14-99 10302
100-499 10314
Livingston Ave 10314
Livingston Ct 10310
Llewellyn Pl 10310
Lloyd Ct 10310
Lockman Ave, Loop & Pl 10303
Lockwood Pl 10314
Locust Ave 10306
Locust Ct 10309
Locust Pl 10308
Logan Ave 10301
Lois Pl 10301
Lombard Ct 10312
London Rd 10306
Long Pond Ln 10304
Longdale St 10314
Longfellow Ave 10301
Longview Rd
1-145 10304
146-200 10301
202-298 10301
E Loop Rd 10304
Loretto St 10307
Loring Ave 10312
Lorraine Ave 10312
Lorraine Loop 10309
Lortel Ave 10314
Lott Ln 10314
Louis St 10304
Louise Ln 10301
Louise St 10312
Lovelace Ave 10312
Lovell Ave 10314
Lowell St 10306
Lucille Ave 10309
Lucy Loop 10312
Ludlow St 10312
Ludwig Ln 10303
Ludwig St 10310
Luigi Pl 10306
Luke Ct 10306
Lulu Ct 10307
Luna Cir 10312
Lundi Ct 10314
Lundsten Ave 10309
Luten Ave 10312
Lyceum Ct 10310
Lyle Ct 10306
Lyman Ave 10305
Lyman Pl 10304
Lynbrook Ave & Ct 10309
Lynch St 10312
Lyndale Ave & Ln 10312
Lynhurst Ave 10305
Lynn Ct 10314
Lynn St 10306
Lynnhaven Pl 10310
Lyon Pl 10314
Mace St 10306
Macfarland Ave 10305
Macgregor St 10309
Macon Ave 10312
E Macon Ave 10308
Macormac Pl 10303
Mada Ave 10310
Madan Ct 10314
Madera St 10309
Madigan Pl 10304
Madison Ave 10314
Madsen Ave 10309
Magnolia Ave 10305
Maguire Ave & Ct 10309
Maiden Ln 10307
Main St 10307
Maine Ave 10314
Major Ave 10305
Malden Pl 10306
Malibu Ct 10309
Mallard Ln 10309
Mallory Ave 10305
Mallow St 10309
Malone Ave 10306
Maloney Dr 10305
Malvine Ave 10309
Manchester Dr 10312
Mandy Ct 10309
Manee Ave 10309
Manhattan St 10307
Manila Ave & Pl 10306
Manley St 10309
Mann Ave 10314
Manor Ct 10306
Manor Rd
1-200 10310
201-1599 10314
Manorville Ct 10305
Mansion Ave 10308
Manton Pl 10304
Maple Ave 10302
Maple Ct 10312
Maple Pkwy 10303
Maple Ter 10306
Mapleton Ave 10306
Maplewood Ave & Pl 10306
Maralear Ave 10305
Marble Loop 10309
Marble St 10314
Marc St 10314
Marcy Ave 10309
Maretzek Ct 10309
Margaret St 10308
Margaretta Ct 10314
Margo Loop 10301
Maria Ln 10312
Marianne St 10302
Marie St 10305
Marine Way 10306
Mariners Ln 10303
Marion Ave 10304
Marion St 10310
Marisa Cir 10309
Marisa Ct 10314
Marjorie St 10309
Mark St 10304
Market St 10310
Markham Ln 10310
Markham Pl 10314
Marne Ave 10312
Marscher Pl 10309
Marsh Ave 10314
Marshall Ave 10314
Martin Ave 10314
Martineau St 10303
Martling Ave
1-37 10310
215-299 10314
Marvin Rd 10309
Marx St 10301
Mary St 10304
Maryland Ave & Ln 10305
Mason Ave
25-197 10305
199-507 10305
509-549 10305
551-1097 10306
1099-1999 10306
Mason Blvd 10309
Mason St 10304
Massachusetts St S 10307
Mathews Ave 10310
Matthew Pl 10303
Maxi Ct 10304
May Ave 10314
May Pl 10312
Mayberry Promenade 10312
Maybury Ave 10308
Maybury Ct 10306
Mazza Ct 10312
Mcarthur Ave 10312
Mcbaine Ave 10309
Mcclean Ave 10305
Mccormick Pl 10305
Mccully Ave 10306
Mcdermott Ave 10305
Mcdivitt Ave 10314
Mcdonald St 10314
Mcgee Ln 10303
Mckee Ave 10308
Mckinley Ave 10306
Mclaughlin St 10305
Mcveigh Ave 10314
Meade Loop 10309
Meadow Ave 10304
Meadow Ct 10309
Meadow Ln 10306
Meadow Pl 10306
Meagan Loop 10307
Medford Rd 10304
Medina St 10306
Meeker St 10306
Meisner Ave 10306
Melba St 10314
Melhorn Rd 10314
Melissa St 10314
Melrose Ave 10301
Melrose Pl 10308
Melville St 10309
Melvin Ave 10314

Street	ZIP
Melyn Pl	10303
Memo St	10309
Memphis Ave	10312
Mendelsohn St	10305
Mercer Pl	10308
Mercury Ln	10314
Meredith Ave	10314
Merivale Ln	10304
Merkel Pl	10306
Merle Pl	10305
Merrick Ave	10301
Merrill Ave	10314
Merriman Ave	10314
Merrymount St	10314
Mersereau Ave	10303
Metcalfe St	10304
Metropolitan Ave	10301
Michael Ct	10308
Michael Loop	10301
Michelle Ct	10303
Michelle Ln	10306
Mickardan Ct	10304
Middle Loop Rd	10308
Midland Ave	10306
Midland Rd	10308
Midway Pl	10304
Milbank Rd	10306
Milburn St	10306
Milden Ave	10301
Mildred Ave	10314
Miles Ave	10308
Milford Ave	10301
Mill Rd	10306
Millennium Loop	10309
Miller Fld	10306
Miller St	10314
Mills Ave	10305
Millstone Ct	10314
Milton Ave	10306
Mimosa Ln	10312
Minna St	10304
Minthorne St	10301
Minturn Ave	10309
Mitchell Ln	10302
Mobile Ave	10306
Moffett St	10312
Mohn Pl	10301
Monahan Ave	10314
Monarch Ct	10314
Monroe Ave	10301
Monroe Pl	10314
Monsey Pl	10303
Mont Sec Ave	10305
Montauk Pl	10314
Montell St	10302
Monterey Ave	10312
Montgomery Ave	10301
Monticello Ter	10308
Montreal Ave	10306
Montvale Pl	10308
Moody Pl	10310
Moonlight Ct	10314
Moore St	10306
Morani St	10314
Moreland St	10306
Morgan Ln	10314
Morley Ave	10306
Morningstar Rd	10303
Morris Pl	10308
Morris St	10309
Morrison Ave	10310
Morrow St	10303
Morse Ave	10314
Morton St	10306
Mosel Ave & Loop	10304
Mosely Ave	10312
Motley Ave	10314
Mott St	10312
Mountainside Rd	10304
Mountainview Ave	10314
Mulberry Ave & Cir	10314
Muldoon Ave	10312
Muller Ave	10314
Mundy Ave	10310
Murdock Pl	10303
Murray Pl	10304
Murray St	10309
Myrna Ln	10312
Myrtle Ave	10310
Nadal Pl	10314
Nadine St	10306
Nahant St	10308
Nancy Ct	10306
Nancy Ln	10307
Narrows Rd N	
1-359	10305
401-899	10304
Narrows Rd S	
2-298	10305
400-598	10304
Nash Ct	10308
Nashville St	10307
Naso Ct	10314
Nassau Pl	10307
Nassau St	10301
Natalie Ct	10304
Nathan Ct	10309
Natick St	10306
Naughton Ave	10305
Nautilus St	10305
Navesink Pl	10306
Navigator Ct	10309
Navy Pier Ct	10304
Neal Dow Ave	10314
Neckar Ave	10304
Nedra Pl	10312
Nehring Ave	10314
Nelson Ave	10308
Neptune St	10306
Nesmythe Ter	10301
Netherland Ave	10303
Neutral Ave	10306
Nevada Ave	10306
New Ln	10305
New St	10302
New Dorp Ln & Plz	10306
New Folden Pl	10307
New York Ave	10305
New York Pl	10314
Newark Ave	10302
Newberry Ave	10304
Newton St	10312
Newvale Ave	10306
Niagara St	10301
Nicholas Ave	10302
Nicholas St	10301
Nicole Loop	10301
Nicolosi Dr & Loop	10312
Nielsen Ave	10309
Nightingale St	10306
Niles Pl	10314
Nina Ave	10314
Nippon Ave	10312
Nixon Ave	10304
Noah Ct	10303
Noel St	10312
Nome Ave	10314
Norden St	10304
Norenner Ave	10308
Norma Pl	10301
Normalee Rd	10305
Norman Pl	10309
North Ave	
1-70	10302
100-199	10314
North Dr	10305
North St	10302
Northentry Rd	10304
Northern Blvd	10301
Northfield Ave & Ct	10303
Northport Ln	10314
Northview Ct	10301
Norwalk Ave	10314
Norway Ave	10305
Norwich St	10314
Norwood Ave & Ct	10304
Nostrand Ave	10314
Notre Dame Ave	10308
Notus Ave	10312
Nugent Ave	
2-6	10305
8-669	10305
671-743	10306
745-999	10306
Nugent Ct	10306
Nugent St	10306
Nunley Ct	10304
Nunzie Ct	10303
Nutly Pl	10310
Nutwood Ct	10308
Oak Ave	10306
Oak Ct	10308
Oak Ln	10312
Oak St	10305
Oakdale Ave	10304
Oakdale St	
1-199	10308
200-382	10312
384-999	10312
Oakland Ave	10310
Oakland Ter	10304
Oakley Pl	10306
Oakville St	10314
Oakwood Ave	10301
Oban St	10312
Oberlin St	10305
Occident Ave	10304
Ocean Ave	10305
Ocean Ct	10301
Ocean Rd	10308
Ocean Ter	
1-105	10314
170-198	10301
200-799	10301
Ocean Driveway	10312
Oceanic Ave	10312
Oceanside Ave	10305
Oceanview Ave	10312
Oceanview Ln	10301
Oceanview Pl	10308
Oconnor Ave	10314
Odell Pl	10309
Oder Ave	10304
Odin St	10306
Ogden St	10312
Ogorman Ave	
1-339	10306
400-599	10308
Ohio Pl	10314
Old Farmers Ln	10304
Old Mill Rd	10306
Old Town Rd	
1-131	10304
133-219	10305
Oldfield St	10306
Olga Pl	10305
Oliver Pl	10314
Olivia Ct	10310
Olympia Blvd	
1-899	10305
901-919	10305
921-1299	10306
Oneida Ave	10301
Ontario Ave	10301
Opal Ln	10309
Opp Ct	10312
Opus Ct	10304
Orange Ave	10302
Orbit Ln	10314
Orchard Ave	10307
Orchard Ln	10312
Orchard Ln S	10312
Ordell Ave	10302
Oregon Rd	10305
Orinoco Pl	10303
Orlando St	10305
Ormond Pl	10305
Ormsby Ave	10309
Osage Ln	10312
Osborn Ave	10308
Osborne St	10312
Osgood Ave	10304
Ostrich Ct	10309
Oswald Pl	10309
Oswego St	10301
Otis Ave	10306
Ottavio Promenade	10307
Outerbridge Ave	10309
Ovas Ct	10312
Overlook Ave	10304
Overlook Dr	10304
Overlook Ter	10305
Ovis Pl	10306
Oxford Pl	10301
Oxholm Ave	10301
Pacific Ave	10312
Page Ave	
1-143	10309
200-800	10307
802-898	10307
Palisade St	10305
Palma Dr	10304
Palmer Ave	10302
Palmieri Ln	10309
Pamela Ln	10304
Paradise Pl	10307
Paris Ct	10310
Parish Ave	10314
Park Ave	10302
Park Ct	10301
Park Dr N	10314
Park Ln	10301
Park Pl	10301
Park Rd	10312
Park St	10306
Park Ter	10308
Park Hill Ave, Cir, Ct & Ln	10304
Parker St	10307
Parkinson Ave	10305
Parkview Loop	10314
Parkview Pl	10310
Parkwood Ave	10309
Parsons Pl	10301
N Path Rd	10305
Patten St	10307
Patterson Ave	
390-534	10305
536-668	10305
730-999	10306
Patty Ct	10312
Paulding Ave	10314
Pauw St	10301
Pavillion Hill Ter	10301
Paxton St	10301
Peachtree Ln	10309
Peacock Loop	10309
Peare Pl	10312
Pearl St	10304
Pearsall St	10305
Pearson St	10314
Pebble Ln	10305
Peck Ct	10306
Peel Pl	10306
Peggy Ln	10306
Pelican Cir	10306
Pelton Ave & Pl	10310
Pemberton Ave	10308
Pembrook Loop	10309
Penbroke Ave	10301
Pendale St	10306
Pendleton Pl	10301
Penn Ave	10306
Penn St	10314
Penton St	10309
Percival Pl	10309
Perine Ave	10305
Perkiomen Ave	10312
Perona Ln	10308
Perry Ave	10314
Pershing St	10305
Persimmon Ln	10314
Peru St	10314
Peter Ave	10306
Peter Ct	10304
Peter St	10314
Petersons Ln	10309
Petrus Ave	10312
Petunia Ct	10307
Pheasant Ln	10309
Phelps Pl	10301
Philip Ave	10312
Phyllis Ct	10309
Piave Ave	10305
Pickersgill Ave	10305
Piedmont Ave	10305
Pier 6	10301
Pier 7 1/2	10301
Pierce St	10304
Pierpont Pl	10314
Pike St	10301
Pilcher St	10314
Pilot Ln	10309
Pine Pl	10304
Pine St	10301
Pine Ter	10312
N Pine Ter	10312
Pinewood Ave	10306
Pitney Ave	10309
Pitt Ave	10314
Pittsville Ave	10307
Plank Rd	10314
Platinum Ave	10314
Platt St	10306
Plattsburg St	10304
Pleaderi Ave	10307
Pleasant Ct	10304
Pleasant Pl	10304
Pleasant St	10308
Pleasant Plains Ave	10309
Pleasant Valley Ave	10304
Plumtree Ln	10309
Plymouth Rd	10314
Poe Ct & St	10307
Poets Cir	10312
Poi Ct	10314
Poillon Ave	10312
Poland Pl	10314
Pommer Ave	10304
Pompey Ave	10312
Pond St	10309
Pond Way	10303
Pontiac St	10302
Poplar Ave & Ln	10309
Port Ln	10302
Port Richmond Ave	10302
Portage Ave	10314
Portland Pl	10301
Portsmouth Ave	10301
Post Ave	
700-875	10310
876-1100	10302
1102-1998	10302
Post Ln	10303
Potter Ave	10314
Pouch Ter	10305
Poultney St	10306
Powell Ln & St	10312
Prague Ct	10309
Prall Ave	10312
Pratt Ct	10312
Prescott Ave	10306
Presentation Cir	10312
President St	10314
Presley St	10308
Preston Ave	10312
Prices Ln	10314
Primrose Pl	10306
Prince Ln	10309
Prince St	10304
Princess Ln & St	10303
Princeton Ave	10306
Princeton Ln	10312
Princewood Ave	10309
Prol Pl	10312
Promenade Ave	10306
Prospect Ave	10301
Prospect Pl	10306
Prospect St	10304
Providence St	10304
Pulaski Ave	10303
Pumone Ct	10309
Purcell St	10310
Purdue Ct & St	10314
Purdy Ave	10314
Purdy Pl	10309
Purroy Pl	10301
Putnam Pl	10301
Putters Ct	10301
Pyramid Ct	10314
Quail Ln	10309
Queen St	10314
Queensdale St	10309
Quincy Ave	10305
Quinlan Ave	10314
Quinn St	10304
Quintard St	10305
Racal Ct	10314
Rachel Ct	10310
Radcliff Rd	10305
Radford St	10314
Radigan Ave	10309
Rae Ave	10312
Ragazzi Ln	10305
Railroad Ave	10305
N Railroad Ave	
1-800	10304
801-1905	10306
1907-2035	10306
2037-2193	10306
S Railroad Ave	
2-18	10305
20-118	10305
120-198	10305
800-1848	10306
1850-2162	10306
2164-2298	10306
N Railroad St	10312
S Railroad St	10312
Raily Ct	10312
Rainbow Ave	10302
E & W Raleigh Ave	10310
Ralph Ave	10312
Ralph Pl	10304
Ramapo Ave	10309
Ramble Rd	10308
Ramblewood Ave	10308
Ramona Ave	
735A-735D	10309
Ramsey Ln	10314
Ramsey Pl	10304
N Randall Ave	10301
Rankin St	10312
Raritan Ave	
1-199	10304
200-999	10305
Rathbun Ave	
1040A-1040D	10309
1-37	10312
39-749	10312
750-1099	10309
Ravenhurst Ave	10310
Ravenna St	10312
Rawson Pl	10314
Ray St	10312
Rayfield Ct	10310
Raymond Ave	10314
Raymond Pl	10310
Reading Ave	10312
E Reading Ave	10308
Rector St	10310
Red Cedar Ln	10309
Redgrave Ave	10306
Redwood Ave	10308
Redwood Loop	10309
Regal Walk	10303
Regan Ave	10310
Regent Cir	10312
Regina Ln	10312
Regis Dr	10314
Reid Ave	10305
Reiss Ln	10304
Remsen St	10304
Rene Dr	10306
Renee Pl	10314
Renfrew Pl	10303
Reno Ave	10306
Rensselaer Ave	
1-783	10312
784-1101	10309
Renwick Ave	10301
Reon Ave	10314
Retford Ave	10312
Retner St	10305
Revere Ln	10306
Revere St	10301
Reynolds Ct & St	10305
N Rhett Ave	10308
Rhine Ave	10304
Rice Ave	10314
Richard Ave	10309
Richard Ln	10314
Riche Ave	10314
Richmond Ave	
3830A-3830B	10312
874-906	10303
908-2501	10314
2503-2863	10314
2845-2845	10313
2865-2999	10314
3201-3237	10312
3239-4330	10312
4332-4998	10312
Richmond Ct	10303
Richmond Pl	10309
Richmond Rd	
551-1717	10304
1718-3718	10306
3720-3750	10306
Richmond Ter	
1-7	10301
9-600	10301
602-1048	10301
1051-1053	10310
1055-1872	10310
1873-2400	10302
2402-2438	10302
2440-2498	10303
2500-3419	10303
3421-3599	10303
Richmond Hill Rd	
1-502	10314
504-698	10314
1001-1199	10306
Richmond Valley Rd	10309
Ridge Ave	10304
Ridge Ct	10301
Ridge Loop	10304
Ridgecrest Ave	10312
Ridgefield Ave	10304
Ridgeway Ave	10314
Ridgewood Ave	10312
Ridgewood Pl	10301
Riedel Ave	10306
Riegelmann St	10302
Riga St	10306
Rigby Ave	10306
Rigimar Ct	10309
Riley Pl	10302
River Rd	10314
Rivington Ave	10314
Roanoke St	10314
Robert Ln	10301
Roberts Dr	10306
Robin Ct	10309
Robin Rd	10305
Robinson Ave	10312
Robinson Bch	10307
Rocco Ct	10310
Rochelle Pl	10312
Rochelle St	10304
Rockaway St	10307
Rockland Ave	
2-12	10306
14-15	10306
17-249	10306
599-697	10314
699-1350	10314
Rockne St	10314
Rockville Ave	10314
Rockwell Ave	10305
Rodeo Ln	10304
Roderick Ave	10305
Roe St	10310
Roff St	10304
Rogers Pl	10312
Rokeby Pl	10310
Rolling Hill Grn	10312
Roma Ave	10306
Roman Ave	10314
Roman Ct	10307
Rome Ave	10304
Romer Rd	10304

Ronald Ave 10303
Roosevelt Ave 10314
Roosevelt Ct 10314
Roosevelt St 10304
Rose Ave 10306
Rose Ct 10301
Rose Ln 10312
Rosebank Pl 10305
Rosecliff Rd 10303
Rosedale Ave 10312
Rosewood Pl 10304
Ross Ave 10306
Ross Ln 10312
Rossville Ave 10309
Roswell Ave 10314
Row Pl 10312
Rowan Ave 10306
Roxbury St 10303
Royal Oak Rd 10314
Rubenstein St 10305
Rudyard St 10306
Rugby Ave 10301
Ruggles St 10312
Rumba Pl 10312
Rumplert Ct 10302
Rumson Rd 10314
Rupert Ave 10314
Russek Dr 10312
Russell St 10308
Rustic Pl 10308
Ruth Pl 10305
Ruth St 10314
Rutherford Ct 10309
Ruxton Ave 10312
Ryan Pl 10312
Rye Ave 10312
Sable Loop 10306
Sabrina Ln 10304
Saccheri Ct 10308
Sage Ct 10302
Sagona Ct 10309
Saint Adalberts Pl 10303
Saint Albans Pl 10312
Saint Andrews Rd 10306
Saint Anthony Pl 10302
Saint Austins Pl 10310
Saint George Dr 10304
Saint George Rd 10306
Saint James Pl 10304
Saint John Ave 10314
Saint Johns Ave 10305
Saint Josephs Ave 10302
Saint Lukes Ave 10309
Saint Marks Pl 10301
Saint Marys Ave 10305
Saint Patricks Pl 10306
Saint Pauls Ave
1-198 10301
199-499 10304
Saint Stephens Pl 10306
Salamander Ct 10309
Sally Ct 10312
Salzburg Ct 10304
Samantha Ln 10309
Sampson Ave 10308
Samuel Pl 10303
Sand Ct & Ln 10305
Sandalwood Dr 10308
Sandborn St 10312
Sanders St 10303
Sandgap St 10312
Sandra Ln 10304
Sands St 10304
Sandy Ln 10307
Sandywood Ln 10309
Sanford Pl 10314
Sanford St 10307
Sanilac St 10306
Santa Monica Ln 10309
Santo Ct 10306
Sapphire Ct 10307
Sarcona Ct 10309
Satterlee St 10307
Saturn Ln 10314
Savin Ct 10304
Savo Ln 10305

Savo Loop 10309
Sawyer Ave 10314
Saxon Ave 10314
Saybrook St 10314
Scarboro Ave 10305
Scarsdale St 10308
Scenic Ln 10304
Scheffelin Ave 10306
Schindler Ct 10309
Schley Ave 10308
Schmidts Ln 10314
Schoharie St 10301
School Rd 10305
School St 10308
Schubert St 10305
Schuyler St 10301
Scott Ave 10305
Scranton Ave 10312
E Scranton Ave 10308
Scranton St 10304
Scribner Ave 10301
Scudder Ave 10309
Sea Breeze Ln 10307
Sea Gate Rd 10305
Seacrest Ave 10312
Seacrest Ln 10307
Seafoam St 10306
Seagate Ct 10305
Search Ln 10305
Seaside Ln 10305
Seaver Ave
1-80 10306
187-257 10305
259-702 10305
704-798 10305
Seaview Ave
526A-526B 10305
2-16 10304
18-184 10304
185-779 10305
781-799 10305
Seely Ln 10308
Seguine Ave 10309
Seguine Loop 10309
Seguine Pl 10312
Seidman Ave 10312
Seldin Ave 10314
Selkirk St 10309
Selvin Loop 10303
Seneca Ave 10301
Seneca Loop 10314
Seneca St 10310
Serrell Ave 10312
E Service Rd 10314
S Service Rd 10309
W Service Rd 10314
Seth Ct 10301
Seth Loop 10305
Seven Gables Rd 10304
Seward Pl 10314
Seymour Ave 10302
Shadow Ln 10306
Shadyside Ave 10309
Shafter Ave 10308
Shaina Ct 10303
Shale St 10314
Sharon Ave 10301
Sharon Ln 10309
Sharpe Ave 10302
Sharrott Ave 10309
Sharrotts Ln & Rd 10309
Shaughnessy Ln 10305
Shaw Pl 10302
Shawnee St 10301
Sheffield St 10310
Sheldon Ave
1-780 10312
781-1099 10309
Shelley Ave 10314
Shelterview Dr 10304
Shenandoah Ave 10314
Shepard Ave 10314
Sheraden Ave 10314
Sheridan Ave
1-26 10304
28-46 10304
78-98 10305
Sheridan Ct 10306
Sheridan Pl 10312
Sherman Ave 10301
Sherwood Ave 10309
Sherwood Pl 10308
Shiel Ave 10309
Shields Pl 10301
Shift Pl 10312
Shiloh St 10314
Shirley Ave 10312
Shirra Ave 10314
Shore Rd 10307
Shore Acres Rd 10305
Short Pl 10312
Shotwell Ave 10312
Sideview Ave 10314
Sierra Ct 10314
Signal Hill Rd 10301
Signs Rd 10314
Silver Ct 10301
Silver Beech Rd 10304
Silver Lake Rd 10301
Simmons Ln & Loop 10314
Simon Ct 10307
Simonson Ave 10303
Simonson Pl 10302
Sinclair Ave
1-772 10312
773-1099 10309
Singleton St 10309
Sioux St 10305
Skinner Ln 10310
Sky Ln 10304
Skyline Dr 10304
Slaight St 10302
Slater Blvd 10305
Slayton Ave 10314
Sleepy Hollow Rd 10314
Sleight Ave 10307
Sloane Ave 10306
Slosson Ave 10314
Slosson Ter 10301
Smith Ave 10314
Smith Ct 10314
Smith Pl 10302
Smith St 10305
Smith Ter 10304
Smyrna Ave 10312
Sneden Ave 10312
Snug Harbor Rd 10310
Sommer Ave 10314
Sommers Ln 10314
Sonia Ct 10309
Sophia Ln 10304
Soren St 10314
South Ave
1-718 10303
720-798 10303
900-1498 10314
1500-1900 10314
1902-2098 10314
South St 10310
Spanish Ln 10312
Sparkill Ave 10304
Spartan Ave 10303
Speedwell Ave 10314
Spencer St 10314
Sperry Pl 10312
Spirit Ln 10303
Sprague Ave & Ct 10307
Spratt Ave 10306
Spring St 10304
Springfield Ave 10314
Springhill Ave 10301
Spruce Ct 10307
Spruce Ln 10309
St Edward Ln 10304
Stacey Ln 10306
Stack Dr 10312
Stafford Ave
1-718 10312
719-999 10309
Stage Ln 10304
Stalie Ct 10309
Stanley Ave 10301

Stanley Cir 10308
Stanwich St 10304
Star Ct 10312
Starbuck St 10304
Starlight Rd 10301
Starr Ave 10310
State St 10310
Staten Island Blvd 10301
Station Ave 10309
Stebbins Ave 10310
Stecher St 10312
Steele Ave 10306
Steers St 10314
Steinway Ave 10314
Stephen Loop 10314
Stepney St 10314
Sterling Ave 10306
Stern Ct 10308
Steuben St
1-299 10304
400-645 10305
647-699 10305
Stevenson Pl 10309
Stewart Ave 10314
Stieg Ave 10308
Stobe Ave 10306
Stone Ln 10314
Stone St 10304
Stone Crest Ct 10308
Stonegate Dr 10304
Stoneham St 10306
Storer Ave 10309
Stratford Ave 10301
Stratford Ct 10314
Strauss St 10305
Strawberry Ln 10312
Stroud Ave 10312
E Stroud Ave 10308
Studio Ln 10304
Sturges St 10314
Stuyvesant Ave 10312
Stuyvesant Pl 10301
Suffolk Ave 10314
Summer St 10305
Summerfield Pl 10303
Summit Ave 10306
Summit Pl 10312
Summit Rd 10307
Summit St 10307
Sumner Ave 10314
Sumner Pl 10301
Sunfield Ave 10312
Sunnymeade Vlg 10305
Sunnyside Ter 10301
Sunrise Ter 10304
Sunset Ave 10314
Sunset Ln 10307
Sunset Hill Dr 10301
Surf Ave 10307
Surfside Plz 10307
Susan Ct 10304
Susanna Ln 10312
Sussex Ave 10314
Sutter Pl 10309
Sutton Pl 10312
Swaim Ave 10312
Swan St 10301
Sweetbrook Rd 10312
Sweetgum Ln 10314
Sweetwater Ave 10308
Swinnerton St 10307
Sycamore St
1-167 10308
168-700 10312
702-798 10312
Sydney Pl 10306
Sylva Ln 10305
Sylvan Ct 10307
Sylvan Pl 10303
Sylvaton Ter 10305
Sylvia St 10312
Tabb Pl 10302
Tacoma St 10304
Taft Ave 10301
Taft Ct 10314
Talarico Ct 10314

Talbot Pl 10304
Tallman St 10312
Tanglewood Dr 10308
Tappen Ct 10304
Targee St 10304
Tarlee Pl 10308
Tarlton St 10306
Tarring St 10306
Tarrytown Ave 10306
Tatro St 10306
Taunton St 10306
Taxter Pl 10304
Taylor Ct & St 10310
Teakwood Ct 10308
Ted Pl 10304
Teleport Dr 10311
Temple Ct 10314
Tenafly Ave & Pl 10312
Tennyson Dr
100-246 10308
248-298 10308
345-535 10312
537-999 10312
Teri Ct 10314
Terrace Ave 10309
Terrace Ct 10306
Tessa Ct 10304
Thames Ave 10301
Thayer Pl 10306
The Oval 10304
Theater Ln 10304
Thelma Ct 10304
Theresa Ln 10308
Theresa Pl 10301
Thistle Ct 10304
Thollen St 10306
Thomas Pl & St 10306
Thompson Pl 10305
Thompson St 10304
Thornycroft Ave 10312
Thurston St 10314
Tiber Pl 10301
Tides Ln 10309
Tiffany Ct 10309
Tiger Ct 10314
Tilden St 10301
Tiller Ct 10309
Tillman St 10314
Tilson Pl 10305
Timber Ridge Dr 10306
Timothy Ct 10314
Tioga St 10301
Titus Ave 10306
Toddy Ave 10314
Todt Hill Ct 10304
Todt Hill Rd
2-12 10314
14-346 10314
348-360 10314
400-1299 10304
Token St 10312
Tom Ct 10310
Tompkins Ave
1-330 10304
332-360 10305
362-1999 10305
Tompkins Cir 10301
Tompkins Ct 10310
Tompkins Pl 10304
Tompkins St 10304
Tone Ln 10305
Tonking Rd 10306
Tony Ct 10305
Topping St 10306
Topside Ln 10309
Tottenville Pl 10307
Towers Ln 10314
Townley Ave 10314
Townsend Ave 10304
Tralerin Ave 10301
Trantor Pl 10302
Travis Ave 10314
Treadwell Ave 10302
Treetz Pl 10314
Tremont Ave 10314
Trent St 10308

Trenton Ct 10309
Tricia Way 10307
Trina Ln 10309
Trinity Pl 10310
Trossach Rd 10304
Troy St 10308
Truman St 10307
Trumbull Pl 10301
Tryon Ave 10312
Tuckahoe Ave 10312
Tudor St 10308
Tulip Cir 10312
Turf Ct & Rd 10314
Turner St 10309
Tuttle St 10314
Twin Oak Dr 10304
Twombly Ave 10306
Tyler Ave 10310
Tynan St 10312
Tyndale St 10312
Tyrellan Ave 10309
Tyrrell St 10307
Tysen St 10301
Tysens Ln 10306
Uncas Ave 10309
Union Ave & Ct 10303
University Pl 10301
Upton St 10304
Urbana St 10304
Uss Arizona Ln 10305
Uss Connecticut Ct 10305
Uss Florida Ct 10305
Uss Iowa Cir 10305
Uss Missouri Ln 10305
Uss New Mexico Ct 10305
Uss North Carolina Rd 10305
Uss Tennessee Rd 10305
Utah St 10307
Utica St 10309
Utopia Ct 10304
Utter Ave 10314
Uxbridge St 10314
Vail Ave 10309
Valdemar Ave 10309
Valencia Ave 10301
Valley Rd 10304
Valleyview Pl 10314
Van St 10310
Van Allen Ave 10312
Van Brunt St 10312
Van Buren St 10301
Van Cortlandt Ave 10301
Van Duzer St
1-229 10301
230-1199 10304
Van Name Ave 10303
Van Pelt Ave 10303
Van Riper St 10302
Van Tuyl St 10301
Van Wyck Ave 10309
Vanderbilt Ave 10304
Vanessa Ln 10312
Vassar St 10314
Vaughan St 10305
Vedder Ave
1-43 10314
45-49 10314
51-199 10302
Veith Pl 10312
Veltman Ave 10302
Venice St 10304
Venus Ln 10314
Venus Pl 10312
Vera St 10305
Vermont Ave 10305
Vermont Ct 10314
Vernon Ave 10309
Verrazzano Bridge Plz 10305
Vespa Ave 10312
Veterans Rd W 10309
Victoria Rd 10312
Victory Blvd
1-1210 10301
1212-1500 10301
1502-1532 10314
1534-4499 10314

Vienna Ct 10305
Villa Ave 10302
Village Ln 10312
Villanova St 10314
Vincent Ave 10306
Vine St 10301
Vineland Ave 10312
Virginia Ave 10305
Virginia Pl 10314
Vista Ave 10304
Vista Pl 10305
Vogel Ave 10309
Vogel Ln 10314
Vogel Loop 10314
Vogel Pl 10309
Von Braun Ave 10312
Vreeland St 10302
Vulcan St 10305
Wade St 10314
Wadsworth Ave, Rd &
Ter 10305
Wagner St 10305
Waimer Pl 10312
Wainwright Ave 10312
Wakefield Ave 10314
Wakefield Rd 10312
Walbrooke Ave 10301
Walch Pl 10309
Walcott Ave 10314
Walden Ave 10306
Waldo Pl 10314
Waldron Ave 10301
Wales Pl 10310
Walker Ct 10312
Walker Dr 10303
Walker Pl 10312
Walker St
1-150 10302
152-198 10302
200-212 10303
214-499 10303
Wall St 10301
Wallace Ave 10305
Walloon St 10303
Walnut Ave 10308
Walnut Pl 10306
Walnut St 10310
Walters Ave 10301
Wandel Ave 10304
Ward Ave 10304
Wards Point Ave 10307
Wardwell Ave 10314
Waring Ave 10312
Warren St 10304
Warwick Ave 10314
Washington Ave 10314
N Washington Ave 10303
Washington Pl 10302
Watchogue Rd 10314
Water St 10304
Waterbury Ave 10309
Waterford Ct 10305
Waters Ave
1-283 10314
285-299 10314
326-332 10302
334-369 10302
Waterside Pkwy 10308
Waterside St 10306
Waterview Ct 10305
Watkins Ave 10312
Watson Ave 10314
Wave St 10304
Wavecrest St 10306
Waverly Pl 10304
Wayne St 10310
Weaver St 10312
Webster Ave 10301
Weed Ave 10306
Weiner St 10309
Weir Ln 10307
Wellbrook Ave 10314
Welles Ct 10301
Wellington Ct 10314
Wendy Dr 10312
Wenlock St 10303

Wentworth Ave ... 10305
Weser Ave ... 10304
West St ... 10310
West Ter ... 10312
Westbrook Ave ... 10303
Westbury Ave ... 10301
Westcott Blvd ... 10314
Westentry Rd ... 10304
Western Ave ... 10303
Westervelt Ave ... 10301
Westfield Ave ... 10309
Westminster Ct ... 10304
Westport Ln & St ... 10314
Westwood Ave ... 10314
Wetmore Rd ... 10301
Whalley Ave ... 10312
Wheeler Ave ... 10314
Wheeling Ave ... 10309
Whindark Ave ... 10310
Whitaker Pl ... 10304
White Pl ... 10310
White St ... 10305
White Oak Ln ... 10309
White Plains Ave ... 10305
Whitehall St ... 10306
Whitewood Ave ... 10310
Whitlock Ave ... 10304
Whitman Ave ... 10308
Whitney Ave ... 10305
Whitwell Pl ... 10304
Wiederer Pl ... 10304
Wieland Ave ... 10309
Wilbur St ... 10309
Wilcox St ... 10303
Wild Ave ... 10314
Wilder Ave ... 10306
Wildwood Ln ... 10307
Wiley Pl ... 10306
Willard Ave ... 10314
William Ave ... 10308
William St ... 10304
Willis Ave ... 10301
Willow Ave ... 10305
Willow Ln ... 10306
Willow Rd E ... 10314
Willow Rd W
- 12-146 ... 10303
- 250-544 ... 10314
- 546-899 ... 10314

Willow Pond Rd ... 10304
Willow Wood Ln ... 10308
Willowbrook Ct ... 10302
Willowbrook Rd
- 1-309 ... 10302
- 310-1299 ... 10314

Wilson Ave
- 1-299 ... 10308
- 300-999 ... 10312

Wilson St ... 10304
Wilson Ter ... 10304
Wilsonview Pl ... 10304
Wilton Ct ... 10305
Wiman Ave ... 10308
Wiman Pl ... 10305
Winant Ave ... 10309
Winant Pl ... 10309
Winant St ... 10303
Winchester Ave ... 10312
Windemere Ave ... 10306
Windermere Rd ... 10305
Windham Loop ... 10314
Winding Woods Loop ... 10307
Windmill Ct ... 10306
Windom Ave ... 10305
Windsor Ct & Rd ... 10314
Windy Hollow Way ... 10304
Winegar Ln ... 10310
Winfield Ave & St ... 10305
Wingham St ... 10305
Winham Ave ... 10306
Winslow Pl ... 10312
Winston St ... 10312
Winter Ave ... 10301
Winthrop Pl ... 10314
Wirt Ave & Ln ... 10309
Witteman Pl ... 10301

Woehrle Ave ... 10312
Wolcott Ave ... 10312
Wolkoff Ln ... 10303
Wolverine St ... 10306
Wood Ave ... 10307
Wood Ct ... 10309
Wood Ln ... 10307
Woodbine Ave ... 10314
Woodbridge Pl ... 10314
Woodcrest Rd ... 10303
Woodcutters Ln ... 10306
Wooddale Ave
- 1-99 ... 10304
- 400-500 ... 10301

Woodhaven Ave
- 1-99 ... 10301
- 100-198 ... 10304

Woodhull Ave ... 10312
Woodland Ave ... 10308
Woodlawn Ave ... 10305
Woodrose Ln ... 10309
Woodrow Rd
- 2-40 ... 10312
- 42-1120 ... 10312
- 1121-1699 ... 10309

Woodruff Ln ... 10310
Woods Of Arden Rd ... 10312
Woodside Ave ... 10304
Woodstock Ave ... 10301
Woodvale Ave & Loop ... 10309
Woodward Ave ... 10314
Woolley Ave ... 10314
Wrenn St ... 10309
Wright Ave ... 10303
Wright St ... 10304
Wycliff Ln ... 10312
Wygant Pl ... 10302
Wyona Ave ... 10314
Xenia St ... 10305
Yacht Club Cv ... 10308
Yafa Ct ... 10314
Yale St ... 10303
Yeomalt Ave ... 10312
Yeshiva Ln ... 10309
Yetman Ave ... 10307
York Ave & Ter ... 10301
Young St ... 10304
Yucca Dr ... 10312
Yukon Ave ... 10314
Zachary Ct ... 10310
Zebra Pl ... 10309
Zeck Ct ... 10314
Zephyr Ave ... 10312
Zoe St ... 10305
Zwicky Ave ... 10306

NUMBERED STREETS

1st St ... 10306
2nd Ct ... 10312
2nd St ... 10306
3rd Ct ... 10312
3rd St ... 10306
4th Ct ... 10312
4th St ... 10306
7th St ... 10306
8th St ... 10306
9th St ... 10306
10th St ... 10306

STEPHENTOWN NY

General Delivery ... 12168

POST OFFICE BOXES MAIN OFFICE STATIONS AND BRANCHES

Box No.s
All PO Boxes ... 12168

RURAL ROUTES

01 ... 12168

NAMED STREETS

Adams Rd ... 12168
Andrews Ln ... 12168
Barbara Way ... 12168
Baredarl Rd ... 12168
Beech Way ... 12168
Berkshire Way ... 12168
Bert Hager Rd ... 12168
Big Rock Way ... 12168
Black River Rd
- 1-399 ... 12169
- 1000-1098 ... 12168

Borg Rd ... 12168
Browns Rd ... 12168
Burberry Way ... 12168
Burns Rd ... 12168
Calvin Cole Rd ... 12169
Ccc Dam Rd ... 12168
Cemetery Hill Rd ... 12168
Cherry Plain Hill Rd ... 12168
N Chuckleberry Way ... 12168
Cormier Way ... 12168
County Route 5a ... 12168
Cranston Hill Rd ... 12168
E Creek Way ... 12168
Dee Rd ... 12168
East Rd ... 12168
Firehouse Way ... 12168
Firetower Rd ... 12169
Gardner Hill Rd ... 12168
Garfield Rd ... 12168
Garvin Rd ... 12168
Gentile Rd ... 12168
George Hunt Rd ... 12168
Giles Rd ... 12168
Goodrich Hollow Rd ... 12168
Gould Rd ... 12168
Grange Hall Rd ... 12168
Griffin Rd ... 12169
Gunner Hill Rd ... 12169
Hotel Rd ... 12168
Joe Ward Rd ... 12168
Jones Rd ... 12168
Knapps Rd ... 12168
Losty Rd ... 12168
Lower Hemlock Way ... 12168
Madden Rd ... 12168
Maple Way ... 12168
Mary Camp Rd ... 12168
Michelle Way ... 12168
Middle Way ... 12168
Mockler Way ... 12168
Moore Hill Rd ... 12168
Mountain View Way ... 12168
Murphy Way ... 12168
Newton Rd
- 1-199 ... 12168
- 200-399 ... 12169

Nora Way ... 12168
Oak Way ... 12168
Odell Rd ... 12168
Old Mill Rd ... 12169
Osgood Rd ... 12168
Partridge Ln ... 12168
N & S Pease Rd ... 12168
Pine Way ... 12168
Presbyterian Hill Rd ... 12168
Prescott Way ... 12169
Provost Rd ... 12168
Rhindress Way ... 12168
Robinson Hollow Way ... 12168
Round Mountain Rd ... 12168
Rutland Way ... 12168
Schendis Rd ... 12169
Schmich Rd ... 12168
Shepard Rd ... 12169
Shore Way ... 12169
Southard Rd ... 12168
Sprague Rd ... 12168
Staples Rd ... 12168
State Route 22 ... 12168
State Route 43
- 1-426 ... 12168

State Route 43
- 428-510 ... 12168
- 435-435 ... 12169
- 449-449 ... 12168
- 449-449 ... 12169
- 451-499 ... 12168
- 501-517 ... 12169
- 519-1600 ... 12169
- 1602-1698 ... 12169

S Stephentown Rd ... 12168
Sutherland Rd ... 12168
Temple Rd ... 12168
Thorton Cross Rd ... 12168
Tinley Rd ... 12169
Tom Titus Rd ... 12168
Upper Hemlock Ridge Way ... 12168
Valley View Rd ... 12168
Wemple Rd ... 12168
West Rd & St ... 12168
Whitman Rd ... 12168
Wilderness Way ... 12169
Williams Rd ... 12169
Willow Way ... 12168
Wyomanock Rd ... 12168

SYRACUSE NY

General Delivery ... 13220

POST OFFICE BOXES MAIN OFFICE STATIONS AND BRANCHES

Box No.s
C8 - C17 ... 13218
1 - 670 ... 13214
1 - 490 ... 13211
1 - 530 ... 13206
1 - 936 ... 13209
1 - 1320 ... 13201
1 - 352 ... 13212
1 - 350 ... 13207
1 - 460 ... 13205
2 - 10 ... 13218
252 - 252 ... 13202
374 - 394 ... 13212
515 - 960 ... 13205
531 - 540 ... 13211
551 - 1050 ... 13206
650 - 650 ... 13202
720 - 880 ... 13214
977 - 980 ... 13209
991 - 996 ... 13205
1239 - 1239 ... 13202
1301 - 1301 ... 13214
2000 - 2005 ... 13201
2001 - 2596 ... 13220
2337 - 2337 ... 13202
2661 - 3940 ... 13220
4567 - 4567 ... 13221
4567 - 4567 ... 13202
4690 - 4690 ... 13220
4700 - 4999 ... 13221
4878 - 4967 ... 13202
5001 - 5720 ... 13220
5259 - 5260 ... 13221
6001 - 6995 ... 13217
7001 - 7430 ... 13261
7247 - 7247 ... 13202
8001 - 8079 ... 13217
9261 - 9858 ... 13290
9631 - 9631 ... 13218
9998 - 9998 ... 13217
10001 - 10238 ... 13290
11001 - 12936 ... 13218
18202 - 13252 ... 13221
15001 - 15654 ... 13215
18001 - 18604 ... 13218
19000 - 19998 ... 13209
35001 - 37408 ... 13235
116040 - 116042 ... 13220
179998 - 179998 ... 13217

NAMED STREETS

Abbe Dr ... 13219
Abbey Rd ... 13215
Abbottsbury Ln ... 13215
Abell Ave ... 13209
Aberdeen Ter ... 13206
Academy Grn, Pl & St ... 13207
Ackerman Ave ... 13210
Acorn Path ... 13210
Adams Ave ... 13206
E Adams St
- 200-224 ... 13202
- 226-299 ... 13202
- 700-998 ... 13210
- 1000-1199 ... 13210
- 1201-1399 ... 13210

W Adams St ... 13202
Addison Dr ... 13214
Adlai Dr ... 13215
Adrian Dr ... 13212
Ahepa Cir ... 13215
Ainsley Dr ... 13210
Air Cargo Rd ... 13212
Airport Rd ... 13209
Aitchison Rd ... 13215
Alanson Rd ... 13207
Albart Dr ... 13215
Albert Rd ... 13214
Albert Ter ... 13202
Alden St ... 13210
Alexander Ave ... 13202
Alexander Dr ... 13219
Alhan Pkwy ... 13209
Alice Ave ... 13209
Alice St ... 13219
Allen Rd
- 200-1499 ... 13212
- 4300-4399 ... 13215
- 4401-4683 ... 13215

Allen St ... 13210
Alliance Bank Pkwy ... 13208
Almond St ... 13210
Alpine Dr ... 13214
Alton St ... 13215
N Alvord St ... 13208
S Alvord St
- 100-308 ... 13203
- 310-312 ... 13203
- 400-499 ... 13208

Alwyn Rd ... 13214
Amann Dr ... 13215
Amber Rd ... 13215
Ambergate Rd ... 13214
Ames Ave ... 13207
Amherst Ave ... 13205
Amidon Dr ... 13205
Amy St ... 13204
Anderson Ave
- 102-108 ... 13208
- 118-118 ... 13205
- 120-199 ... 13205

Andover Rd ... 13210
Andrews Rd ... 13214
Andrews St ... 13219
Angelou Ter ... 13202
Anne Ter ... 13212
Annetta St ... 13207
Apple St ... 13204
Aquarius Dr ... 13224
Arbor Ln ... 13214
E Arbordale Pl & Rd ... 13219
Arch St ... 13206
Archer Rd ... 13207
Arden Dr ... 13207
Ardmore Pl ... 13208
Ardmore Rd ... 13219
Ardsley Dr ... 13214
Argonne Dr ... 13207
Argyle Ave ... 13219
Aries Way ... 13209
Arlington Ave ... 13207
Arlington St ... 13209
Armitage Dr ... 13212
Armstrong Pl ... 13207
Armstrong Rd ... 13209

Arnett Ave ... 13206
Arnold Ave ... 13210
Arnts Pl ... 13208
Arsenal Dr ... 13205
Arterial Rd ... 13206
Arthur St
- 200-499 ... 13204
- 500-799 ... 13207

Ash St ... 13208
Ashdale Ave & Dr ... 13206
Ashfield Ter ... 13215
Ashford Ct ... 13211
Ashworth Pl ... 13210
Aspenwood Cir ... 13212
Aster Dr ... 13209
Atkinson Ave ... 13207
Atlantic Ave ... 13207
Audrey Dr ... 13212
Audubon Pkwy ... 13224
Augusta Dr ... 13212
Austin Ave ... 13207
Austin Dr ... 13212
Avalon Ave ... 13219
Avendong Rd ... 13209
Avery Ave ... 13204
S Avery Ave
- 101-399 ... 13204
- 400-598 ... 13219

Avery Dr ... 13212
Avoca St ... 13204
Avon Rd ... 13206
Avondale Pl ... 13210
Bacon St ... 13209
Bailer Rd ... 13215
Bailey Rd ... 13212
Bailey St ... 13209
Baird Ave ... 13206
Baker Ave ... 13205
Baker Blvd ... 13209
Baker St ... 13206
Balcomb Mill Cir ... 13215
Baldwin Ave ... 13205
Ball Cir ... 13210
Ball Rd
- 1A-1B ... 13215
- 2A-2B ... 13215
- 3A-3B ... 13215
- 5A-5B ... 13215
- 6A-6B ... 13215
- 7A-7B ... 13215
- 8A-8B ... 13215
- 9A-9B ... 13215
- 10A-10B ... 13215
- 12A-12B ... 13215
- 13A-13B ... 13215
- 18A-18B ... 13215
- 20A-20B ... 13215
- 21A-21B ... 13215
- 22A-22B ... 13215
- 23A-23B ... 13215
- 24A-24B ... 13215
- 26A-26B ... 13215
- 27A-27B ... 13215
- 28A-28B ... 13215
- 29A-29B ... 13215
- 30A-30B ... 13215
- 31A-31B ... 13215
- 32A-32B ... 13215
- 34A-34B ... 13215
- 67A-67B ... 13215
- 68A-68B ... 13215
- 69A-69B ... 13215
- 70A-70B ... 13215
- 71A-71B ... 13215
- 75A-75B ... 13215
- 76A-76B ... 13215
- 77A-77B ... 13215
- 78A-78B ... 13215
- 81A-81B ... 13215
- 82A-82B ... 13215
- 83A-83B ... 13215
- 84A-84B ... 13215
- 86A-86B ... 13215
- 94A-94B ... 13215
- 95A-95B ... 13215
- 96A-96B ... 13215
- 97A-97B ... 13215
- 100A-100B ... 13215
- 102A-102B ... 13215
- 103A-103B ... 13215
- 104A-104B ... 13215
- 105A-105B ... 13215
- 106A-106B ... 13215
- 107A-107B ... 13215
- 108A-108B ... 13215
- 109A-109B ... 13215
- 110A-110B ... 13215
- 111A-111B ... 13215
- 4-8 ... 13215
- 10-5099 ... 13215
- 5101-5111 ... 13215

Ballantyne Rd
- 100-399 ... 13205
- 617-703 ... 13207
- 705-1119 ... 13207
- 1121-1123 ... 13207

Ballard Ave ... 13205
Barclay St ... 13209
Barford Rd ... 13215
Barnes Ave ... 13207
Barrett St ... 13204
Barrington Rd ... 13214
Basin St ... 13208
Bassett St ... 13210
Baum Ave ... 13212
Baxton St ... 13212
S Bay Rd ... 13212
Beach Rd ... 13209
Beachview Ave ... 13209
Beacon Rd ... 13206
Bear Rd ... 13212
Bear St ... 13208
Bear St W ... 13204
E & W Beard Ave & Pl ... 13205
Beattie St ... 13224
Beaumont Pl ... 13214
Becker St ... 13208
N Beech St
- 101-199 ... 13210
- 200-399 ... 13203

S Beech St ... 13210
Beecher St ... 13203
Beef St ... 13215
Bel Air Dr ... 13212
E Belden Ave ... 13203
W Belden Ave ... 13204
Beley Ave ... 13211
Bellaire Pl ... 13207
Belle Ave ... 13205
Belle Ter ... 13212
Belle Isle Rd ... 13209
Belleflower Cir ... 13215
Bellevue Ave
- 100-118 ... 13204
- 120-1030 ... 13204
- 1031-1031 ... 13207
- 1032-1998 ... 13204
- 1111-1999 ... 13204
- 2000-4391 ... 13219
- 4393-4399 ... 13219

Bellevue Dr ... 13212
Bellewood Cir & Dr ... 13212
Bellshire Ln ... 13208
Belmont St ... 13211
Belmore Dr ... 13212
Bender Ave ... 13211
Benedict Ave ... 13210
Benham Ave ... 13219
Bennett Ave ... 13209
Bennington Dr ... 13205
Benoit Dr ... 13209
Berger Ave ... 13205
Bergner Rd ... 13209
Berkeley Dr ... 13210
Berkshire Ave ... 13208
Bernard Pl ... 13205
Bernard St ... 13211
Bertram Pl ... 13207
Berwick Rd N & S ... 13208
Berwyn Ave ... 13210
Bevell Ln ... 13212
Beverly Dr ... 13219
Beverly Rd ... 13207

Biltmore St 13211
Birch Rd 13209
Birchwood Rd 13212
Bishop Ave 13207
E & W Bissell St 13207
Blackstone Way 13219
Blaine St 13202
Blanchard Blvd 13209
Bloomsbury Dr 13215
Blossom Rd 13224
Blueberry Ln 13219
Boca Raton Way 13215
Boise Dr 13210
Bonnie Dr 13209
E & W Borden Ave 13205
Boss Rd 13211
Boston Rd 13211
Boston St 13206
Boulder Rd 13209
Boulevard St 13211
Bourdage Rd 13212
Box Car Ln 13219
Boxwood Ln 13206
Boyd Ave 13209
Boyden Pl 13203
Boyden St
101-105 13203
107-399 13203
400-599 13206
Boyle Dr 13215
Boysen Rd 13212
Brace St 13208
Bradbury Dr 13215
Bradford Ct 13207
Bradford Dr 13224
Bradford Ln 13224
Bradford Pkwy 13224
Bradford St 13207
Bradford Heights Rd 13224
Bradley St 13204
Brae Burn Ln 13205
Brampton Dr 13214
Brampton Rd 13205
Brandon Rd 13214
Brantford Path 13209
Brattle Rd 13203
Bray Hall 13210
Breakspear Rd 13219
Breckenridge Run 13215
Breman Ave 13211
Brendan Way 13219
Brentwood Dr 13219
Brewerton Rd
1300-1398 13208
1400-1499 13208
1501-1599 13208
1701-1797 13211
1799-2799 13211
2801-2803 13211
2804-3999 13212
Briarcliff Rd 13214
Briarledge Rd 13212
Brickyard Rd 13209
Bridge St 13209
Bridget Cir 13207
Briggs St 13208
E Brighton Ave
100-199 13205
300-699 13210
700-798 13205
800-1099 13205
W Brighton Ave
127-145 13205
147-400 13205
402-598 13205
600-800 13207
802-898 13207
Brinkerhoff Rd 13215
Bristol Pl 13210
Brittany Ln 13215
Britton Pl 13212
Broad Rd 13215
Broad St
101-297 13210
299-1199 13210
1200-1298 13224
1300-1343 13224
1345-1399 13224
Broadview Dr 13215
Brockton Ln 13214
Bronson Rd 13219
Bronson St 13205
Bronx Ave 13208
Brooke Dr 13212
Brookfield Rd 13211
Brookford Rd 13224
Brookhaven Rd 13212
Brookland Dr 13208
Brooklawn Pkwy 13211
Brooklea Dr & Pl 13207
Brookline Rd 13208
Brooks St 13209
Brookside Dr 13205
Brown Ave
100-399 13211
400-519 13208
Bruce St 13224
Brunswick Pl 13212
Bryant Ave 13204
Bryn Mawr Dr 13215
Buckingham Ave 13210
Buckley Rd 13212
Buffington Rd 13224
Bulrush Rd 13215
Bump Dr 13209
Bungalow Ter 13207
Bunker Hill Way 13207
Burdick Ave 13208
Burlingame Rd 13203
Burnet Ave
100-1299 13203
1300-3499 13206
Burnet Park Dr 13204
Burns Ave 13206
Burrstone Rd 13215
Burt St 13202
Burten St 13210
Bury Dr 13209
Bussey Rd 13215
Butler St 13210
Butterfield Cir 13212
Butternut Dr 13214
Butternut St 13208
Buxton Dr 13215
Byrne Pl 13205
Cadillac St 13208
Cadwell Pl & St 13204
Caleb Ave 13206
W Calthrop Ave 13205
Calumet Dr 13219
Calvin Rd 13207
Cam Nel Pl 13211
Cambridge Ave 13208
Cambridge St 13210
Camden Rd 13219
Camelot Cir 13219
Camelot Dr 13215
Camp Ave 13207
Campbell Rd 13211
Canal St 13210
Candee Ave 13224
Canfield Dr 13219
Caninti Dr 13212
Cannon St 13205
Canterbury Rd
100-198 13214
4100-4203 13215
4205-4207 13215
Carbon St 13208
S Carbon St 13203
Carlisle St 13208
Carlton Ave 13219
Carlton Dr
100-100 13212
102-218 13214
102-228 13212
220-398 13214
230-230 13212
301-349 13214
Carlton Rd 13207
Carnarvon Rd 13215
Carol Dr
100-102 13212
101-107 13209
109-113 13209
115-199 13209
116-116 13212
120-124 13209
Caroline Ave 13209
Carrigan Cir 13215
Case St 13209
Castle Rd 13212
W Castle St 13207
Castlebar Cir 13215
Caswell Ave 13212
Catawba St 13208
Catherine St
100-306 13212
200-200 13203
202-799 13203
308-308 13212
Caton Dr 13214
Caulfield Dr 13215
Cayuga St
100-106 13204
105-109 13209
108-499 13204
Cecilia Rd 13212
Cedar St 13210
Cedarvale Rd 13215
Cendarli Ave 13205
Centennial Dr 13207
Center St 13209
Centerville Pl 13212
Central Ave
100-199 13204
3911-4597 13215
4599-4799 13215
Century Dr 13209
E Chaffee Ave 13207
Champlin Dr 13206
Channing Pl 13205
Chapel Dr 13219
Chapman Dr 13209
Charing Rd 13214
Charlane Pkwy 13212
Charles Ave 13209
Charleston Rd 13212
Charlotte St 13204
Charmouth Dr 13207
Chatham Pl 13208
Chatham Rd 13203
Chaumont Dr 13209
Chavez Ter 13202
Cheancol Rd 13214
Chelise Hamlet Rd 13215
E, N, S & W Cheltenham Rd 13205
Chemung St 13204
Chenault Dr 13224
Cheney St 13207
Cherokee Cir 13215
Cherry Hl 13214
Cherry Rd 13219
Cherry St 13210
Cherry Valley Tpke 13215
Cherrywood Dr 13215
Chesapeake Dr 13212
Chester Dr 13208
Chester Rd 13219
Chester St 13207
Chestnut Rd & St 13212
Cheyenne Cir 13215
Chickadee Cir 13215
Chickasaw Cir 13215
Childrens Cir 13210
Chinook Dr 13210
Chippewa Cir 13215
Church Ln 13214
Church Pkwy 13212
Church St
100-104 13212
106-918 13212
199-802 13209
920-930 13212
923-7297 13212
7299-7366 13212
7368-7398 13212
Churchill Ave 13205
Cindy Ln 13215
Circle Rd
100-104 13210
101-132 13212
106-134 13210
134-198 13212
136-140 13210
Citadel Cv 13215
City Crossroads Dr 13210
City View Dr & Ter 13215
Claire Rd 13214
Clairmonte Ave 13207
Clarence Ave 13205
Clarence Dr 13212
Clarendon St 13210
Clarke St 13210
Clarton St 13212
Clayton Ave 13207
Clearview Dr
100-106 13219
100-107 13212
108-115 13219
117-199 13219
Clearview Rd 13214
Cleveland Ave 13208
Cleveland Rd 13215
Cliffside Dr 13210
Clifton Dr 13212
Clifton Pl 13206
N Clinton St
101-399 13202
500-1099 13204
S Clinton St
100-100 13261
100-100 13202
200-298 13202
300-1099 13202
Clover Rd
100-500 13219
502-798 13219
7600-7698 13212
Clover St 13204
Clover Ridge Dr 13206
Clyde Ave 13207
Cobra Ln 13211
Cody Ave 13204
Coffee Tree Ln 13212
Coffey Dr 13204
Cogswell Ave 13209
Col Eileen Collins Blvd 13212
Colburn Dr 13215
Colby Ave 13206
Coldbrook Dr 13205
Cole Rd 13215
Coleridge Ave 13204
College Pl 13210
Collier Cir 13215
N & S Collingwood Ave 13206
Collins Rd 13215
Colonial Dr 13212
Colorado Run 13215
Columbia Ave 13207
Columbus Ave
100-198 13219
101-101 13210
103-125 13219
129-129 13210
133-203 13219
200-202 13210
204-206 13210
205-206 13219
207-215 13210
208-210 13210
208-398 13219
211-299 13219
301-301 13210
303-303 13219
305-309 13210
307-311 13219
400-599 13210
E Colvin St
100-122 13205
124-300 13205
302-310 13205
400-798 13210
800-2299 13210
2301-2497 13224
2499-2799 13224
W Colvin St
100-198 13205
200-899 13205
1000-1999 13207
Commerce Blvd 13211
Commonwealth Ave 13208
Comstock Ave & Pl 13210
Conan St 13205
Concord Pl 13210
Congress Ave 13204
Conifer Dr 13205
Conklin Ave 13206
Conklin St 13209
Constellation Way N 13212
Conway Cir 13215
Cook Ave 13206
Coolidge Ave
100-199 13204
200-399 13207
Coolidge Rd 13212
Cooper Ln 13214
Copleigh Dr 13209
Copperfield Rd 13215
Cora Ave 13212
Coral Ave 13207
Corcoran Ct 13204
Cordova St 13205
Corey Rd 13219
Corliss Rd 13219
Cornell Ave 13207
E & W Corning Ave 13205
Cornish Heights Pkwy 13215
Cornwall Dr 13214
Coronado Cir 13212
Corporal Welch Rd 13215
Cortland Ave
100-232 13202
234-360 13202
362-366 13202
381-397 13205
399-599 13205
Cortland Pl 13207
Costello Ct 13204
Cotton St 13219
Coughlin Ave 13206
Country Club Dr 13215
Country View Ter 13215
Countryside Dr 13215
Court St
2-98 13208
100-3064 13208
3066-3098 13208
3100-3398 13206
3400-3404 13206
3406-3698 13206
W Court St 13204
Court Ter 13208
Court Street Rd 13206
Coventry Rd 13215
Covington Dr 13208
Cowan Ave N 13209
Cowie Ave 13206
Coykendall Ave 13204
Crabapple Ln 13219
Craddock St 13207
Crafton Ave 13207
Craig Cir 13214
Craig St 13208
Craigie St 13206
Crancou Ave 13211
Craton St 13203
Crawford Ave 13224
Crehange St 13205
Crescent Ave 13207
Cresline Dr 13206
Crested Butte Run 13215
Crestview Dr
100-299 13207
6100-6199 13212
Crestview Ter 13204
Crestwood Dr 13212
Crestwood Ln 13215
Crippen Ave & Pl 13205
Croft Cir 13215
Croly St 13224
Cross Rd 13224
Crossett St 13207
Crossover Rd 13215
Crosswalk Cir 13209
Croton Ter 13202
N Crouse Ave 13203
S Crouse Ave 13210
Croyden Ln & Rd 13224
Crysler St 13204
Crystal Dr 13212
Culbert St 13208
Cumberland Ave & Pl 13210
Cummings Ave 13208
Curtis Ave 13209
Curtis Rd 13215
Curtis St 13208
Cutler Dr 13219
Cynthia Dr 13212
Dablon Ct 13202
Daisy Dr 13209
Daisy St 13204
Dakin St 13224
Dakota St 13210
Dale St 13208
E Dale St 13206
Danbury Dr 13219
Danforth St 13208
Danforth Ter 13202
Danzig St 13206
Daphne Dr 13212
Darlington Rd E 13208
Darrow Ave 13209
David Dr 13212
Davis Rd S 13212
Davis St 13204
Dawes Ave 13205
Day Hall 13210
Daybreak Ln 13210
De Wolfe Rd 13224
Dearborn Pl 13205
Deborah Ln 13212
Deere Rd 13206
Deforest Rd 13214
Delaware St 13204
Delhi St 13203
Dell St 13210
Delmar Pl 13208
Delong Ave 13208
Delray Ave 13224
Delrose Pl 13219
Demong Dr 13214
Deon Dr 13215
Depalma Ave 13204
Derby Dr 13215
Derek Ave 13205
Destiny Usa Dr 13204
Devonshire Rd 13212
Dewberry Ln 13219
Dewey Ave 13204
Dewitt Rd 13214
Dewitt St 13203
Dewittshire Rd S 13214
Diana Ave 13210
Diane Ter 13219
Dickerson St 13202
Didama St 13224
Dillaye Ave 13206
Dippold Ave 13208
E Division St 13208
W Division St
102-198 13204
200-300 13204
302-498 13204
401-401 13290
Dixon Dr 13219
Dodge Dr 13210
Doll Pkwy 13214
Dolomite Dr 13215
Dolores Ter N & S 13212
Dolshire Dr 13212
Donald Ave 13212
Donaldson Dr 13219
Dondongs Rd 13219
Donridge Dr 13214
Dora Ave 13219
Dorchester Ave 13203
Dorchester Rd 13219
Dormar Dr 13212
Dorothy Dr 13215
Dorothy St 13203
Dorset Rd 13210
Dorwin Ave 13205
Doubletree Cir 13212
Dougal Ave 13205
Douglas St 13203
Dover Cir 13219
Downing Rd 13214
Draper Ave 13219
Driscoll Ave 13204
Drovers Ln 13214
Drumlins Ter 13224
Duane St 13207
Dubiel Ave 13209
Duchess Ln 13219
Dudley St 13204
Duke Dr 13204
Dunbarton Rd 13214
Dundee Dr 13207
Dunham Rd 13214
Dunhill Dr 13209
Dunlap Ave 13206
Dunlap Dr 13214
Dupli Park Dr 13204
Durston Ave 13203
Dwight Park Cir & Dr 13209
Dyer Ct 13210
Earl Ave 13211
East Ave
100-299 13224
4800-4899 13215
Eastbourne Dr 13206
Easterly Ter 13214
Eastern Ave 13211
Eastman Ave 13207
Eastman Rd 13212
Eastview Ave 13207
Edden Ln 13212
Eden Roc Cir 13214
Edgehill Rd 13224
Edgemere Rd & Ter 13208
Edgemont Dr 13214
Edgeware Rd 13208
Edgewood Ave 13207
Edgewood Dr 13205
Edgewood Rd 13219
Edgeworth Ave 13219
Edinger Dr 13214
Edison St 13204
Edmund Ave 13205
Edna Rd 13205
Edtim Rd 13206
Edward St 13212
N & S Edwards Ave 13206
Elaine Ave 13212
Elbow Rd 13212
Eldorado St 13206
Elgin Cir, Ct & Dr 13215
Elizabeth Dr 13212
Elizabeth St 13205
Elizabeth Blackwell St 13210
Elk St 13205
Ellen Cir 13215
Ellen St 13208
Elliott St 13204
Ellis St 13210
Elm St
100-299 13212
300-599 13203
Elmhurst Ave
2-98 13205
100-299 13207
Elmsford Rd 13214
Elmtree Ln 13219
Elmwood Ave 13207
Eloise Ter 13207
Elsner St 13203
Elton Ave 13205
Elwood Davis Rd 13212
Emeant Ave 13206

Emerson Ave 13204
Empire Ave 13207
W End Dr 13204
Enderberry Cir 13224
Endres Dr 13211
Enfield Pl 13214
Englert Ave 13208
Englewood Ave 13207
Erickson St 13206
Erie Blvd E
100-598 13202
700-1999 13210
2000-3099 13224
3100-3712 13214
3714-3798 13214
Erie Blvd W
300-302 13202
375-379 13202
400-498 13204
500-2000 13204
2002-2098 13204
Erie St 13204
Erregger Rd & Ter 13224
Essex St 13204
Ethan Allen St 13212
Ethel St 13207
Ethridge Rd 13214
Euclid Ave
101-197 13210
199-1299 13210
1300-1900 13224
1902-2498 13224
Euclid Ter 13210
Eureka St 13204
Evaleen Ave 13207
Evans Dr 13209
Evelyn Ter 13208
Everingham Ct & Rd 13205
Excalibur Dr 13215
Fabian Ln 13209
Fabius St 13204
Factory Ave 13208
Fage Ave 13205
Fairbanks Dr 13215
Fairdale Ave 13207
Fairfield Ave 13207
Fairfield Dr 13212
Fairview Ave 13203
Fairview Dr 13215
Fairway Dr 13211
Fairwood Dr
2-100 13219
101-105 13209
101-199 13219
102-106 13209
102-198 13219
Falling Leaf Trl 13212
Falso Dr 13211
Falstaff Rd 13214
Fara Dr 13215
W Farm Rd 13209
Farm Acre Rd 13210
Farmer St 13203
Farnham Rd 13219
Farrell Rd 13209
Fawn Hl 13215
Fay Rd 13219
Fay Park Dr 13212
Fayette Blvd 13224
E Fayette St
101-203 13202
205-699 13202
700-1999 13210
2000-2000 13224
2002-2799 13224
W Fayette St
101-105 13202
107-399 13202
401-997 13204
999-1999 13204
1022-1032-1022-
1032 13204
Feigel Ave 13203
Feldspar Dr 13219
Fellows Ave 13210
Fenton St 13204
Fenway Dr 13224
Fergerson Ave & Park 13212
Fern Rd 13219
Ferndale Dr 13205
Ferndale Rd 13219
Fernwood Ave 13205
Ferris Ave 13224
Fieldcrest Dr 13212
Fillmore Ave 13205
Finger Lakes Dr 13209
Fiordon Rd 13214
Firestone Dr 13206
Fiscoe Ave 13205
Fish Ave 13207
Fitch Pl & St 13204
Flaredar Ave 13207
Fletcher Ave 13207
Fletcher Dr 13212
Flint Path 13219
Floral Pkwy 13205
E & W Florence Ave 13205
Florida Rd 13211
Fobes Ave 13206
Foothill Path 13215
Ford Ave 13207
Ford Dr 13212
Fordham Rd 13203
Fordland Ave 13208
Forest Ave 13205
Forest Dr 13212
Forest Edge Dr 13215
Forest Hill Dr 13206
Forestry Dr 13210
Forman Ave 13210
Fountain St 13203
Fox Rd 13215
Foxboro Rd 13224
Franklin Ave 13209
N Franklin St
200-212 13202
214-218 13202
400-426 13204
428-500 13204
502-600 13204
S Franklin St 13202
Freeman Ave 13209
Frisbie Ct 13210
Furman St 13205
Gage Ct 13210
Gail Ln 13219
Gale Ave 13206
Gale Pl 13211
Galster Ave 13206
Game Rd 13210
Gannett Aly 13208
Garden City Dr 13211
Gardner Rd 13215
Garfield Ave & Pl 13205
Garland Rd 13219
Gary Ave 13205
Gateway Park Dr 13212
Gaynor Ave 13206
Gebhardt Ave 13208
N Geddes St 13204
S Geddes St
100-1400 13204
1402-1498 13204
1500-2299 13207
Gemini Pl 13209
Genant Dr 13204
General Irwin Blvd 13212
General Motors Dr 13206
E Genesee Pkwy 13214
E Genesee St
100-114 13202
116-602 13202
604-698 13202
700-2499 13210
2500-3199 13224
3201-3397 13214
3399-4699 13214
W Genesee St
200-498 13202
500-1999 13204
2000-2002 13219
2004-4899 13219
Genesee Park Dr 13224
George St 13212
Gerald Dr 13209
Gere Ave 13204
Gere Lock Rd 13209
Germania Ave 13219
Gertrude Ave 13209
Gertrude St
101-101 13203
101-107 13212
103-399 13203
109-142 13212
Gettman Rd 13209
Gifford Dr 13219
Gifford Pkwy 13214
Gifford St
100-112 13202
114-299 13202
300-699 13204
Gilbert Ave & St 13208
Gillespie Ave 13219
Gillis St 13209
Giminski Dr 13204
Girard Ave 13207
Glahn Ave 13205
Glass Ter 13205
E & W Glen Ave 13205
Glen Robin Dr 13215
Glencove Rd 13206
Glenfield Dr 13215
Glenview Dr 13212
Glenview Pkwy 13219
Glenwood Ave 13207
Glinden Ln 13215
Goodrich Ave 13210
Gordon Ave
101-103 13207
101-316 13211
105-327 13207
500-504 13208
506-598 13208
Gordon Pkwy 13219
Gordon Rd 13212
Gorland Ave 13224
Gould Pl 13211
Grace St 13204
Grallans Ave 13224
Grand Ave
100-199 13204
201-699 13204
1100-1333 13219
1335-1599 13219
Grandview Ave 13207
Granger Rd 13219
E Granger Rd 13219
W Granger Rd 13219
Granger St 13202
Grant Ave 13207
Grant Blvd
100-499 13206
501-797 13203
799-1299 13203
1300-3199 13208
Granville St 13206
Grape Ter 13202
Graphic Dr 13206
Grassman Ave 13208
Graston Ave 13219
Graves St 13203
Gray Ave 13203
Gray Ledge Ter 13215
Green St 13203
Green Fir Cir 13219
Green Street Anx, Ct &
Pl 13203
Greenbriar Rd 13212
Greenland Dr 13208
Greenview Ter 13215
Greenway Ave
100-199 13210
200-499 13206
Greenwood Pl 13210
Greenwood Rd 13214
Gregory Pkwy 13214
Grenfell Rd 13214
Gretchen Cir 13215
Griffin Rd 13215
Griffin St 13207
Griffiths St 13208
Grolier Rd 13215
Grove Rd 13219
Grove St
100-100 13207
100-142 13212
102-120 13207
122-126 13207
144-150 13212
Grumbach Ave 13203
Guilford Rd 13224
Haddon Rd 13214
Haddonfield Dr & Pl 13214
Haffenden Rd 13210
Hafner Dr 13212
Hafners Lndg 13212
Halcomb St 13209
Hall Ave
100-242 13205
203-205 13209
207-399 13209
244-252 13205
Halton Rd 13224
Hamden Dr 13208
Hamilton Pkwy 13214
Hamilton Rd 13212
Hamilton St 13204
Hampshire Dr 13214
Hampshire Rd 13203
E Hampton Pl 13206
Hampton Rd 13203
Hancock Dr
100-299 13207
300-398 13212
Harbor St 13204
Harding Pl 13205
Harding St 13208
Hardwicke Dr 13209
Harford Rd 13208
Harold St 13208
Harpers Ct 13214
Harriet St 13219
Harriette Ave 13210
Harrington Dr 13212
Harrington Rd 13224
Harrington St 13211
Harris Rd 13215
Harrison Pl 13202
Harrison St
201-213 13202
215-500 13202
502-598 13202
701-717 13210
719-1299 13210
Hartley St 13203
Hartson St 13204
Harvard Pl 13210
Harwood Ave 13224
Hasbrouck St 13206
Hastings Pl 13206
Hatch St 13205
Hathaway Rd 13214
Hathaway St 13208
Hatherleigh Dr & Rd 13209
Hatherly Rd 13224
Haven Hall 13210
Haverhill Dr & Pl 13214
Hawley Ave
100-198 13203
200-1499 13203
1501-1599 13203
1600-1699 13206
Hawthorne St 13210
Hayden Ave 13204
Hayes Ter 13205
Haywood Rd 13219
Hazard St 13209
Hazelhurst Ave
100-146 13212
103-599 13206
Hazelwood Ave 13224
Headson Dr 13214
Heffield Cir 13215
Heins Ave 13212
Helen St
100-198 13212
103-103 13212
104-799 13203
200-404 13212
406-408 13212
Helmi Dr 13219
Henderson Blvd 13209
Henderson Pl 13219
Henderson St 13203
Henry St 13210
Hensberry Rd 13207
Herald Pl 13202
Herbert St
101-122 13212
104-399 13208
124-128 13212
Herbst Ave 13203
Heritage Cir 13209
Herkimer St 13204
Herman Dr 13212
Herman Rd 13209
Herriman St 13204
Hertford St 13210
Herz St 13208
Hester Ave 13212
Hiawatha Blvd E 13208
Hiawatha Blvd W 13204
Hiawatha Pl 13208
Hibiscus Dr 13212
Hickman Ct 13209
Hickok Ave 13206
Hickory St 13203
Hier Ave
90-104 13212
101-101 13203
103-399 13203
High St 13208
W High Ter 13219
Highland Ave
100-128 13212
112-114 13203
116-399 13203
Highland Dr 13212
Highland Pl 13203
Highland St 13203
Highridge Dr & Pl 13215
Highview Dr 13209
Hilgert Dr 13219
Hill Ave 13211
Hillbrook Rd 13219
Hillcrest Rd
101-101 13219
101-101 13224
102-106 13219
102-112 13224
103-109 13219
105-109 13224
111-115 13219
115-115 13224
116-199 13219
Hillock Meadows Dr 13215
Hillsboro Pkwy 13214
Hillsdale Ave 13206
Hillside Ave 13219
Hillside St 13208
Hilltop Rd 13215
Hillview Ave 13207
Hillview Dr 13212
Hilmar Dr 13212
Hilton Rd 13205
Hinsdale Rd 13211
Hixson Ave 13206
Hobart Ave 13205
Hoefler St 13204
Holden St 13204
Holiday Dr 13211
Holland St 13204
Hollowcrest Rd 13219
Holly Rd 13212
Holmes Rd 13215
Holmes St 13210
Homecroft Rd 13206
Homeland Rd 13212
Homer Ave 13219
Hood Ave 13208
Hoover Dr 13205
Hope Ave 13205
Hopper Rd 13207
Horace Dr 13219
Horan Rd
112-112 13209
114-451 13209
453-515 13209
517-599 13219
Horizon Ter 13215
Hornady Dr 13209
Hornview Way 13209
Horseshoe Dr 13219
Hosmer Dr 13209
Hourigan Rd 13215
Houston Ave
100-199 13210
200-399 13224
Hovey St 13207
Howard St 13203
Howlett Hill Rd 13215
Hoytville Ave 13212
Hubbell Ave 13207
Huckleberry Ln 13219
Hudson St
104-104 13219
105-105 13204
105-105 13219
111-176 13204
178-180 13204
200-501 13207
500-500 13219
502-598 13207
503-599 13207
600-698 13219
700-1099 13219
Hughes Pl N 13210
Humbert Ave 13224
Hunt Ave
101-103 13219
105-107 13219
108-108 13207
108-108 13219
109-199 13219
110-110 13207
120-120 13219
200-598 13207
Hunter Ave 13204
Huntington Rd 13219
Huntley St 13208
Huntshill Rd 13209
Hurlburt Rd 13224
Huron Ave N 13209
Huron Ave S 13209
Huron St 13207
Hutchinson Ave 13207
Hyland Dr 13212
Ida Ave 13205
Industrial Dr 13204
Interstate Island Rd 13209
Intrepid Ln 13205
Inverness Pl 13219
Inwood Dr 13219
Iona Pl 13209
Iroquois Ave 13215
Irving Ave 13210
Isabella St 13208
Ivon Dr 13212
Ivy Ln 13219
Ivy Ridge Rd 13210
J Stanley Coyne Cir 13202
Jaclyn Dr 13205
James Ave 13209
James Dr 13215
James St
300-306 13212
308-310 13212
312-398 13212
323-397 13203
399-1699 13203
1700-3799 13206
E James St 13206
James Heath Rd 13203
Jamesville Ave 13210
Jamesville Rd 13214
Jane Dr 13219
Janet Dr 13224
Jarrett Dr 13219
Jasper Pl & St 13203
Jean Ave 13210
E & W Jefferson St 13202
Jenda Dr 13209
Jennifer Dr 13212
Jericho Dr 13210
Jerome St 13210
Jessica Dr 13212
John St
100-699 13208
109-244 13212
246-250 13212
John Glenn Blvd 13209
Jones Rd 13209
Jones St 13219
Joseph Dr 13212
Josephine Dr 13215
Josephine St
101-119 13212
104-110 13208
112-130 13208
121-127 13212
Judson St 13210
Judy Dr 13215
Julian Pl 13210
Juneway Rd 13215
Juniper Ln 13219
Jupiter Inlet Way 13215
Kandace St 13204
Kane Rd 13204
Kappesser St 13208
Kasson Rd 13215
Kayleigh Cir 13215
Kaymar Dr 13212
Kaywood Rd 13212
Keen Pl 13207
Keith Dr 13212
Kellogg St 13204
Kelsey Dr 13215
Kencrest Dr 13215
Keneriew Ave 13217
Kenlaren Cir 13212
Kenmore Ave 13205
Kenmore St 13219
Kennedy Ln 13212
E Kennedy St 13205
W Kennedy St
100-399 13205
401-499 13207
Kenneth Dr 13212
Kenruth Dr 13212
Kensington Pl & Rd 13210
Kent Pl 13219
Kenwick Dr 13208
Kenwood Ave 13208
Kenyon Dr 13209
Kevin Dr 13209
Kidd Ave 13210
Killian Dr 13224
Kimber Ave 13207
Kimber Rd 13224
Kimberly Dr E & W 13219
Kincaid Ave 13204
Kindonda Rd 13215
King Ave 13209
King St 13202
Kingsford Ter 13215
Kingsley Pl 13204
Kinne Rd 13214
Kinne St 13206
Kirk Ave 13205
Kirk Park Dr 13205
Kirkpatrick St 13208
W Kirkpatrick St 13204
Kirkwood Pl 13205
Kirsch Dr 13211
Kline St 13203
Knapp Rd 13219
Knaul St 13203
Knoll Pl 13208
Knolltop Ter 13215
Kopp Ave 13212
Kramer Dr 13207
Kratz Ave 13208
Kravec Dr 13214
Kreischer Rd 13212
Kristin Rd 13212

Kuhl Ave 13208
Kuhn Rd 13208
Lacy Pl 13208
E Lafayette Ave 13205
W Lafayette Ave
100-299 13205
301-699 13205
800-999 13207
Lafayette Rd 13205
Laforte Ave 13207
Lake Country Dr 13209
Lakeland Ave 13209
Lakeside Rd 13209
Lakeview Ave 13204
Lakeview Rd 13219
Lakewood Pines Trl 13209
Lambreth Ln 13210
Lamont Ave 13209
Lamson St 13206
Lancaster Ave & Pl 13210
Landmark Pl 13202
Landon Ave 13205
E & W Langerwood Ln 13215
Lansdowne Rd 13214
Larned St 13202
Lathrop Rd 13219
Latimer Ter 13202
Latter Dr 13205
Laura Dr 13209
E Laurel St 13203
Laursen Dr 13205
Lawdon St 13212
Lawndale Dr 13215
Lawrence Ave 13212
Lawrence Rd 13209
Lawrence Rd E 13212
Lawrence Rd W 13212
Lawrence St 13208
Lawsher Dr 13215
Lea Ln 13206
Leavenworth Ave 13204
Lee Ter 13212
Legion Dr 13212
Leighton Ave 13206
Lemoyne Ave
200-2010 13208
2012-2298 13208
2500-2502 13211
2504-2800 13211
2802-2898 13211
Lena Ter 13212
Lennox Ave 13210
Leo Ave 13206
Leon St 13205
Leonard Ave 13205
Leonard Dr 13209
Leonard St 13211
Leopold Blvd 13209
Lepage Pl 13206
Leroy Rd 13212
Leslee Ter 13219
Lewarin Dr 13212
Lewis Ave 13224
Lewis St 13204
Lewiston Dr 13210
Lexington Ave 13210
Liberty St 13204
Light Ct 13210
Lilac Ln 13209
Lilac St 13208
Lillian Ave 13206
Lime St 13224
Limehill Dr 13215
Limestone Ln 13219
Lincoln Ave 13204
Lincoln Rd 13212
Lincoln Park Dr 13203
Lind Ave 13211
Linda Dr 13215
Linda Rd 13212
Lindbergh Rd 13205
Linnie Ln 13212
Linwill Ter 13206
Lionel Ave 13209
Lisa Ln 13212
Lisi Gardens Dr 13212
Litchfield Dr 13224
Livingston Ave 13210
Lock Aly 13208
Locksley Rd 13224
Lockwood Rd 13214
Locust Ln 13219
Lodi St
200-298 13203
300-1316 13203
1318-1398 13203
1400-2799 13208
Loehr Ave 13204
Loma Ave 13208
Lombard Ave 13210
Long Acre Dr 13215
Long Branch Rd 13209
Longdon Ln 13212
Longmeadow Cir & Dr 13205
Longview Ave 13209
Lookout Cir 13209
Loomis Ave 13207
Lorenzo Dr 13206
Lorian Dr 13212
Lormik Ln 13219
N Lorraine Ave 13210
Lowe Ave 13212
N & S Lowell Ave 13204
Ludden Pkwy 13219
Luddington St 13206
Lupine Dr 13209
Lydell St 13204
Lynbrook Cir 13214
Lynch Ave 13207
Lynch St 13210
Lyncourt Dr 13208
Lynhurst Ave 13212
W Lynhurst Ave 13205
Lynmar Ln 13215
Lynn Cir 13205
Lynn Dr 13212
Lynnbrook Cir 13215
Lynnhaven Dr 13212
Lynwood Ave 13206
Mabel Rd 13209
Macdougal Pl 13207
Macgregor Ln 13215
Mackay Ave 13219
Madison St
100-120 13202
620-622 13210
624-1499 13210
Maestri Dr 13209
Magnolia St 13204
N & S Main St 13212
Mains Ave 13207
Majors Dr 13215
Makyes Rd 13215
Malcolm St 13204
Malden Rd 13211
Male Ave 13219
Malibu Hills Dr 13209
Malone Rd 13215
Malta Ln 13212
Maltbie St 13204
Malverne Dr 13208
Managers Pl 13209
E & W Manchester Rd 13219
Mancini Cir 13219
Manderson Rd 13224
Manilla St 13203
Mann Dr 13209
Manning Dr 13212
Manor Dr
100-108 13214
100-114 13212
110-161 13214
116-122 13212
163-215 13214
200-210 13212
212-298 13212
Manor Hill Dr 13215
Mansfield Rd 13219
Maple Ln 13212
Maple Rd 13219
Maple St 13210
Maple Ter 13210
Maple Grove Rd 13209
Maple Manor Dr 13212
Maplehurst Ave 13208
Maplewood Ave 13205
W Marcellus St 13204
Marcia St 13208
Margaret Dr 13209
Marguerite Ave 13207
Marian Dr
100-125 13211
102-299 13219
Marilyn Ave 13212
Marion Ave 13219
Mariposa St 13206
Maris Dr 13207
Marjorie St 13205
Mark Ave 13205
Mark Dr 13209
Markland Ave 13207
Marlborough Rd 13206
Marlett St 13207
Marly Dr 13219
Marquette St 13204
Marsden Rd 13208
Marsh Dr 13214
Marshall St 13210
Marshia Ave 13212
Martin St 13208
Martin Luther King E & W 13205
Marvin Rd 13207
Mary St
100-117 13212
101-103 13208
105-299 13208
119-125 13212
Maryland Ave 13210
Marywood Dr 13212
Mason Dr 13219
Massena St 13204
Masters Rd 13214
Mather St 13203
E & W Matson Ave 13205
Matterson Ave 13219
Matthews Ave 13209
Matthews Dr 13208
Matty Ave
100-200 13211
201-233 13211
202-898 13211
203-211 13204
301-899 13211
Maurice Ave 13207
Mautz Rd 13206
Maxwell Ave
102-102 13212
104-151 13212
114-149 13207
153-153 13212
Maxwell Ct 13207
May Ave 13207
Mayar St 13208
Mayson Ave 13219
Maywood Dr 13205
Mc Alpine St 13211
Mc Kenney Ave 13211
Mcallister Ave 13205
N Mcbride St
200-899 13203
900-1099 13208
1101-1199 13208
S Mcbride St 13202
Mcchesney Park Dr 13208
Mcclure Ave 13205
Mccormick Ave 13202
Mcdonald Rd 13215
Mckinley Ave 13205
Mclennan Ave 13205
Meade Ct 13204
Meade Rd 13206
Meadow Ln 13212
Meadow Rd 13219
Meadow Wood Dr 13212
Meadowbrook Dr
98-100 13212
102-105 13212
106-799 13210
107-115 13212
800-1800 13224
1802-1998 13224
Meays Dr 13209
Medford Rd
100-194 13211
200-399 13208
Medora Pl 13207
Melanie Cir 13212
Melbourne Ave 13224
Melrose Ave
101-101 13206
101-101 13219
103-112 13206
111-113 13219
114-118 13206
115-199 13219
200-211 13206
201-201 13219
203-211 13219
212-214 13206
217-299 13219
300-300 13206
300-300 13219
301-303 13206
301-303 13219
302-310 13206
302-398 13219
305-311 13206
311-399 13219
400-599 13206
Melrose Dr 13212
Melvin Dr 13212
Member Way 13212
Memory Ln 13212
Menlo Dr 13205
Merman Dr 13214
Merrell Rd 13219
Merrill Ln 13210
Merrill St 13208
Merriman Ave 13204
Merritt Ave 13207
Merriwether Dr 13219
Mertens Ave 13203
Merz Ave 13203
Micandrea Dr 13215
Michael Ave 13212
Michaels Ave 13208
Michaels Cir 13210
Michaels Dr 13214
Michele Dr 13219
Midland Ave
101-197 13202
199-699 13202
700-798 13205
800-3899 13205
N & S Midler Ave 13206
Midler Park Dr 13206
Milburn Dr 13207
Mildred Ave
100-100 13212
101-113 13206
115-399 13206
Miles Ave 13210
Milford Ct & Dr 13206
Millbrook Dr 13212
Millen Dr 13212
Milnor Ave 13224
Milo Ln 13219
Milton Ave
100-1099 13204
1101-1399 13204
1401-1497 13209
1499-3101 13209
3103-3203 13209
3200-3240 13219
3242-3399 13219
3401-4699 13219
Mineola Dr 13224
Minerva St 13205
Mintrenc Ave 13210
Mitchell Ave
1-97 13211
99-336 13211
103-111 13207
113-327 13207
329-499 13207
338-398 13211
500-599 13208
Mohawk Dr 13211
Mohegan St 13209
E & W Molloy Rd 13211
Monroe St 13210
Montana St 13210
Montgomery Ln 13215
Montgomery St 13202
Monticello Dr N & S 13205
Montrose Ave 13219
Moon Library 13210
Mooney Ave 13206
Moore Ave 13210
Moore Rd 13211
Morey Ave 13207
Morgan Ave 13204
Morgan Rd 13219
Morningside Ter 13210
Morton Ave 13207
Morton Rd 13214
Morton St 13204
Mosley Dr 13206
Mount Olympus Dr 13210
Mountainview Ave 13224
Mulberry Ter 13202
Munson Dr 13205
Murray Ave 13208
Myron Rd 13219
Myrtle St 13204
Nancy Dr 13212
Natures Cir 13215
Nbt Bank Pkwy 13208
Needham St 13207
Nelligan Hall 13214
Nelson St 13204
Neptune Ln 13209
Neutral Ct 13208
New St 13202
New Court Ave 13206
Newbury Hollow Ln 13210
Newcastle Rd 13219
E Newell St 13205
W Newell St
100-699 13205
700-798 13207
Newfield Rd 13214
Newport Dr 13212
Niagara Ave N 13209
Niagara Ave S 13209
Niagara St 13204
Nichols Ave 13206
Nicks Way 13209
Niven St 13224
Nixon Park Dr 13215
Noble Ave 13206
Norma Rd 13219
Norman Ave 13207
Normanor Dr 13207
North Ave 13206
Northcliffe Rd 13206
Northern Concourse 13212
Northern Lights Dr & Plz 13212
Northfield Dr 13212
Northfield Rd 13215
Northridge Rd 13214
Northrup Blvd 13209
Northway St 13224
Northwood Dr 13211
Norton Rd 13215
Norwood Ave 13206
Nottingham Rd
101-127 13210
129-599 13210
600-820 13224
November Ln 13215
Nursery Ln 13210
Oak Dr 13212
Oak Pl 13203
Oak St 13203
Oak Crest Courtyard 13219
Oak Hollow Rd 13214
Oakdale Ct & Dr 13207
Oakland St 13210
Oakley Dr 13212
Oakley Dr E 13205
Oakley Rd 13209
Oakmont Dr 13214
Oakridge Cir & Dr 13209
Oakwood Ave
100-212 13202
214-400 13202
402-498 13202
500-508 13205
510-699 13205
Oberst St 13208
Obrien Rd 13209
Occ Dr S 13215
October Dr 13215
Odessa Cir 13212
Old Homestead Rd 13215
Old Lyme Rd 13224
Old Semet Ln 13219
Old Thompson Rd 13211
Old Winding Way 13215
Oldwyck Cir 13215
Olin Dr 13219
Oliva Dr 13211
Olive St 13204
Olmstead Pl 13219
Olympus Hts 13215
Oneida St 13202
Onondaga Ave
100-199 13204
200-999 13207
Onondaga Blvd 13219
Onondaga Rd 13215
N Onondaga Rd 13219
S Onondaga Rd 13219
E Onondaga St 13202
W Onondaga St
200-499 13202
500-1799 13204
Onondaga Ter 13207
Onondaga Creek Blvd 13207
Ontario Ave 13209
Ontario St 13204
Orchard Dr E 13212
Orchard Dr W 13212
N Orchard Rd 13209
S Orchard Rd 13219
Oriskany Dr 13210
Orlando Ave 13205
Ormsby Dr 13219
Orrick Rd 13214
Orvilton Dr 13214
Orwood Pl 13208
Osceola Rd 13209
E & W Ostrander Ave 13205
Ostrom Ave 13210
Oswego St 13204
Otisco St 13204
Otto St 13205
Outlook Dr 13215
Overland Dr 13212
Overlook Dr 13207
Oxford St 13202
Pacific Ave 13207
Paddock Dr 13214
Paikin Dr 13219
Palace Ct 13212
Pallaral St 13204
Palmcrest Rd 13212
Palmer Ave
100-198 13204
103-103 13209
111-167 13204
200-399 13207
Palmer Dr 13212
Palmer Ln 13207
Palmeter Ave 13206
Paradise Cir 13209
Pardee Ave 13219
Park Ave 13204
Park Ln 13212
Park Pl 13211
Park Rd 13212
Park St
100-699 13203
701-2100 13208
2102-2298 13208
Parkside Ave 13207
Parkview Ave 13207
Parkway Dr
101-105 13207
104-104 13212
106-107 13212
109-109 13212
117-399 13207
Parkwood Pl 13219
Parrish Ln 13205
Parsons Dr 13219
Pastime Dr 13208
E Patricia Dr & Ln 13212
Patterson Ave 13219
Pattison St 13203
Paul Ave 13206
Paul Ln 13209
Peach Blossom Ave 13215
Pearl St 13203
Peat St
201-297 13210
299-399 13210
501-599 13206
Pebble Hill Cir & Rd 13214
Peck Ave 13206
Peck Rd 13209
Peck Road Ext 13209
Pegasus Cir 13209
Pelham Rd 13214
Peluso Dr 13215
Pembridge Cir 13215
Pembrook Dr 13205
Pennock St 13209
Pennsylvania Ave 13208
Penta Dr 13210
Percy St 13219
Performance Dr 13212
Peridot Dr 13219
Perry Rd 13215
Pershing Ave 13208
Peters St 13208
Phaeton Ln 13215
Pharis St 13204
Phelps Pl 13205
Phillips Rd 13214
Pickard Dr E 13211
Pickwick Rd 13214
Pierce St 13205
Piercefield Dr 13209
Pine St 13210
Pine Grove St 13210
Pine Hill Rd 13209
Pine Ridge Cir 13212
Pine Tree Dr 13212
Pitcher Ln 13212
Pittman Ln 13224
Plainfield Rd 13212
S Plarendi St 13202
Pleasant Ave 13212
W Pleasant Ave 13205
Pleasant Beach Rd 13209
Pleasant Valley Rd 13215
Pleasantview Ave 13208
Plum St 13204
Plymouth Ave 13211
Plymouth Ave S 13211
Plymouth Dr 13206
Polk St 13224
Pond Ln & St 13208
Ponderosa Dr 13215
Poole Rd 13214
Postlamp Cir 13212
Powell St 13209
Power St 13209
Presidential Cts & Plz 13202
Preston Cir 13219
Primrose Ave 13205
Primrose Ln 13212
Primrose Path 13209
Prospect Ave
200-499 13203
500-500 13208
502-504 13208
506-598 13208

Pulaski St 13204
Pumpkin Ln 13219
Putnam St 13204
Quaker Hill Rd 13224
Quartz Way 13219
Radcliffe Rd 13214
Radisson Ct 13202
Ralph Ln 13214
Ramsey Ave 13224
Randall Ave 13207
Randall Rd 13214
Randall Ter 13212
Randolph St 13205
Rann Ave 13204
Raphael Ave
100-397 13211
399-399 13211
400-499 13208
Raymond Ave 13205
E Raynor Ave
201-297 13202
299-416 13202
418-498 13202
700-798 13210
Razorback Run 13215
Rebecca St 13212
Reddick Dr 13212
Redfield Pl 13210
Redwood Dr 13212
Reed Ave 13207
Reed Rd 13202
Reese Ave 13212
Regatta Row 13209
Regency Dr 13212
Reinman Rd 13215
Remington Ave 13210
Rene Pl 13212
Renee Mdws 13215
Renwick Ave 13210
Resseguie Dr 13209
Revere Rd 13214
Rexford Rd 13212
Rich St
100-299 13204
300-500 13207
502-598 13207
Richard Rd 13215
Richardson Ave 13205
Richardson Dr 13212
Richfield Ave 13205
Richfield Blvd 13211
Richmond Ave 13204
Rider Ave 13207
Ridgecrest Dr 13212
Ridgecrest Rd 13214
Ridgeway Ave 13224
Ridgewood Dr
102-102 13212
104-214 13212
111-121 13206
123-499 13206
216-216 13212
Ridings Rd 13206
Riegel St 13206
Rigi Ave 13206
Rill Ave 13205
Rita Dr & Ln 13212
Riverdale Dr 13207
Rivoli Ave 13208
Robbins Ln 13214
Robert Dr 13210
Roberts Ave 13207
Robertson Ter 13219
Robincroft Rd 13203
Robineau Rd 13207
Robinson St
101-197 13203
199-399 13203
501-597 13206
599-699 13206
Rockford Dr 13224
Rockland Ave 13207
Rockland Dr 13212
Rockwood Pl & Rd 13215
Roe Ave 13210
Rogers Ln 13212
Rohe Rd 13215
Rolland Ter 13209
Roney Ln 13210
Roney Rd 13205
Ronnell Dr 13219
Roosevelt Ave 13210
Rose Ave 13202
Rose St 13212
Rose Lane Ter 13219
Rosebud Dr 13219
Rosemary Ln 13215
Rosemont Dr 13205
Rosewell Mdw 13214
Rosewood Cir 13212
Rosewood Rd 13209
Rosewood St 13203
Rosita St 13219
Ross Park 13208
Round Pond Rd 13212
Rowland St 13204
Roxann Ave 13212
Roxboro Cir & Rd 13211
Roxbury Rd 13206
Roxford Rd N & S 13208
Royal Crab Ave 13215
Roycroft Rd 13214
Rufus Cir 13209
Rugby Rd
100-199 13206
200-1000 13203
1002-1198 13203
Ruhamah Ave 13205
Running Ridge Rd 13212
Rushmore Dr 13215
Ruskin Ave 13207
Russell Pl 13207
Russet Ln 13209
Ruth Ave 13210
Ruth Rd 13212
Rutledge St 13219
Sabine St 13204
Sackett St 13204
Saint Anne Dr 13206
Saint John Dr 13215
Saint Louis Ave 13207
Saint Marks Ave 13204
Saint Marys Ter 13208
Salem Rd 13214
N Salina St
100-199 13202
300-499 13203
500-1799 13208
1801-1899 13208
S Salina St
100-1399 13202
1400-2199 13205
2200-2200 13207
2201-6299 13205
2300-6298 13205
Salina Meadows Pkwy 13212
Salisbury Rd 13219
Salisbury Park Dr 13224
Salt St 13203
Salt Springs Rd
101-197 13224
199-1199 13224
1200-1416 13214
1418-1699 13214
Sand Rd 13212
Sand St 13204
Sandra Dr & Ln 13212
Sandy Ln 13212
Saturn Dr 13205
Savaria Dr 13209
Sawyer St 13219
Saybrook Ln 13214
Scarboro Dr 13209
Scarlet Cir 13209
Schaffer Ave 13206
Scheanta St 13208
Schiller Ave 13203
Schneider St 13203
Schoeck Ave 13203
Schoeneck Ct 13204
School St 13204
Schuler St 13203
Schuyler St 13204
Scorpio Dr 13209
Scott Ave
96-96 13219
101-227 13219
102-102 13224
110-140 13219
198-198 13224
200-201 13224
203-299 13224
204-228 13219
206-308 13224
305-399 13219
305-799 13224
310-338 13219
310-798 13224
Scottholm Blvd & Ter 13224
Scoville Ave 13203
Searle Dr 13207
Searlwyn Rd 13205
Sedalia Cir 13224
Sedgwick Dr, Rd & St 13203
Seeley Ave 13205
Seeley Rd 13224
Semloh Dr 13219
Seneca Dr 13205
Seneca Pl 13207
Seneca St
100-105 13209
107-199 13209
200-200 13204
200-200 13209
201-299 13204
300-303 13209
305-399 13209
318-398 13204
E Seneca Tpke 13205
W Seneca Tpke
100-118 13205
120-124 13205
126-264 13205
265-799 13207
3221-5099 13215
Seneca View Dr 13209
Sequoia Dr 13215
S Service Rd 13212
Setting Sun Ter 13215
Seward St 13203
Seymour St
100-136 13202
138-199 13202
200-599 13204
601-699 13204
Shady Ln 13219
Shane Dr 13212
Shapleigh Dr 13224
Sharon Dr 13215
Sharon Rd 13209
Shaver Ave 13212
Shaw Ter 13215
Shea Rd 13215
Sheatree Ln 13212
Shelbourne Pl 13207
Sheldon Ave 13205
Sheraton Rd 13219
Sherbourne Rd 13224
Sherbrooke Cir & Rd 13214
Sherfield Dr 13209
Sheridan Pl 13206
Sheridan Rd 13215
Sherry Dr 13219
Sherwood Ave 13203
Sherwood Dr
200-299 13214
4835-4999 13215
Sherwood Ln 13212
Shirley Dr 13207
Shirley Rd 13224
Shonnard St 13204
Shop City Plz 13206
Shore Ave 13209
Shotwell Park 13206
Shrineview Dr 13219
Shuart Ave 13203
Sidman Ave 13204
Sidney St 13219
Signal Rdg 13209
Silverlace Ter 13219
Simmons Ter 13219
Simon Dr 13224
Single Dr 13212
Singleton Ave 13212
Sizzano Trl 13209
Skiff Dr 13211
Skyline Dr 13215
Skytop Rd 13210
Skytop Hall 13210
Skyview Ter 13219
Slayton Ave 13205
Sleeth Mill Cir 13212
Slindes Woods Cir 13212
Slocum Ave 13204
Slocum Hts 13210
Small Rd 13210
Smelkoff Rd 13209
Smiley Dr 13205
Smith Ln 13210
Smith Rd
100-106 13207
108-299 13207
5900-6199 13212
Smith St
100-102 13209
102-102 13224
103-116 13209
401-401 13224
403-499 13224
Snell Ter 13205
Snow Hill Dr 13215
Snowdale Dr 13209
Snyder Ave 13206
Solar St 13204
Somerset Rd 13224
South Ave
102-103 13212
105-107 13212
109-116 13209
119-129 13204
119-129 13209
126-126 13204
126-126 13209
130-130 13204
132-160 13204
162-168 13204
200-200 13209
202-204 13204
205-207 13209
208-208 13204
208-208 13209
209-209 13209
212-224 13204
226-399 13204
400-403 13209
401-401 13204
404-404 13204
404-416 13209
405-417 13209
420-498 13204
500-599 13204
600-2316 13207
2318-2598 13207
2600-4838 13215
4840-4999 13215
Southern Pine Way 13215
Southland Dr 13205
Southview Rd 13209
Spaid Ave 13210
Spaulding Ave 13205
Spencer St 13204
Spring Ln & St 13208
Springbrook Ave 13205
Springdale Cir 13224
Springfield Rd 13214
Spruce Tree Ln 13219
Stacy Pl 13207
Stadium Pl 13210
Stafford Ave 13206
Standart St 13210
Standish Dr
101-109 13212
102-115 13224
111-199 13212
116-116 13212
117-799 13224
118-798 13224
Standish Ter 13224
Stanley Dr 13219
Stanton Ave 13209
Stanton Dr 13214
Starlite Ln 13215
Stasko Dr 13209
N State St
200-699 13203
701-799 13203
800-898 13208
900-1499 13208
1501-1599 13208
511-513-511-513 13203
S State St
115-297 13202
299-1328 13202
1330-1398 13202
1400-2500 13205
2502-2598 13205
State Fair Blvd
100-556 13204
558-574 13204
575-667 13209
669-7250 13209
7252-7284 13209
Stedman St 13208
Stellium Dr 13209
Stephen Pl 13212
Sterling Ave 13207
Stetson Cir 13215
Steuben St 13208
Steven Ter 13219
Stevens Ave 13205
Stevens Pl 13210
Stevens Rd 13215
Stewart Ct 13202
Stewart Dr 13212
Stiles Rd 13209
Stinard Ave 13207
Stinson St 13209
Stockton Pl 13219
Stolp Ave 13207
Stone Ct 13204
Stonecrest Dr 13214
Stonefield Rd 13205
Stoneridge Dr 13214
Stoney Dr 13219
Stonington Cir 13215
Strand Pl 13208
Stratford St 13210
Strathmore Dr 13207
Strawflower Dr 13212
Streets Dr 13215
Strickland Dr 13215
Strong Ave 13210
Suffolk Rd 13219
Sugarwood Ln 13212
Summerfield Village
Ln 13215
Summit Ave
100-102 13209
100-102 13207
104-125 13209
104-700 13207
127-129 13209
702-798 13207
Sumner Ave 13210
Sunhill Ter 13207
Suniant St 13203
Sunnybrook Dr
100-110 13212
103-216 13219
112-206 13212
208-212 13212
Sunnycrest Rd 13206
Sunnyside Rd 13224
Sunnyside Park Rd 13214
Sunrise Dr
100-499 13205
6200-6298 13212
Sunset Ave 13208
Sunset Dr 13215
Sunset Pl 13212
Sunstruck Dr 13206
Surrey Dr 13215
Susan Dr 13212
Sutton Dr 13219
Sutton Pl 13214
Swan Ave 13206
Swansea Ave & Dr 13206
Sweeting St 13203
Sycamore Ter 13214
Syracuse St 13204
Tabitha Crk 13215
Taft Ave 13206
E Taft Rd
100-5641 13212
5640-5640 13220
5643-6349 13212
5700-6360 13212
W Taft Rd 13212
Tallmadge Rd 13212
Tallman St
400-498 13202
500-999 13204
1001-1015 13204
Tallowood Ct 13212
Tanner Rd 13215
Tarbell Rd 13206
Tarheel Run 13215
Tarolli Dr 13209
Taunton Heights Dr 13219
E & W Taylor St 13202
Teall Ave
101-197 13210
199-225 13210
227-299 13210
500-598 13206
600-2399 13206
Teall Sta 13217
Tecumseh Rd 13224
Tecumseh St 13210
Tejah Ave 13210
Temple Pl 13207
Temple St 13202
Tennyson Ave 13204
Tenterden Dr 13215
Terrace Cir 13214
Terrace Dr 13219
Terrace Rd 13210
Terraceview Rd 13214
Terry Rd 13219
Terry Rd N 13209
S Terry Rd 13219
Terry Heights Rd 13215
Terrytown Heights Dr 13219
Tex Simone Dr 13208
Thayer St 13210
Thomas Ave 13209
Thomas Rd 13214
Thompson Rd
98-312 13206
314-316 13206
318-416 13206
5501-5597 13214
5599-5899 13214
6100-6699 13206
6700-6901 13211
7200-7899 13212
Thompson Rd Spur 13212
Thunder Cloud Dr 13215
Thurber St 13210
Thurgood Ter 13202
Thurlow Dr 13205
Timber Wolf Cir 13209
Tioga St 13204
Titus Aly 13208
Toas Ave 13211
Tolbert Dr 13212
Tompkins St 13204
Topaz Trl 13219
Totman Rd 13212
Tower Ave 13206
Towers Ln 13202
Townline Rd
6501-6567 13206
6569-6581 13206
6701-6705 13211
6707-6899 13211
Townsend Pl 13208
N Townsend St
101-197 13203
199-602 13203
604-798 13203
800-1120 13208
1122-1198 13208
S Townsend St 13202
Tracy St 13204
Tradewind Cir 13212
Treeland Cir 13219
Trelign Dr 13212
Trinity Pl 13210
Trolley Barn Ln 13212
Trump St 13209
Truth Ter 13202
Tucker Rd 13215
Tuller Rd 13212
Tully St
100-198 13202
200-799 13204
Turner Ave 13219
Turnstone Cir 13219
Turquoise Trl 13219
Turtle St 13208
Tuskegee Rd 13211
Twin Elms Ln 13212
Twin Hills Dr 13207
Twin Oaks Dr 13206
Tyler Ct 13202
Tyson Pl 13206
Ulster St 13204
Underwood Way 13215
Union Ave 13203
Union Pl 13208
United Way 13202
University Ave & Pl 13210
Upland Rd 13207
Upland Circle Dr 13209
Vale St 13205
Valentine Dr 13212
Valley Dr 13207
Valley View Dr 13207
Van Buren Rd 13209
Van Buren St
200-399 13202
401-401 13210
Van Mara Dr 13212
Van Rensselaer St 13204
Van Vleck Rd 13209
Van Zandt Rd 13215
Vann St 13206
Velasko Rd
394-498 13219
500-1099 13207
4800-5100 13215
5102-5298 13215
Venus Path 13209
Verda Ave 13212
Vertex Path 13209
Vickery Rd 13212
Victoria Pl 13210
Vieau Dr 13207
Villa Maria 13212
Village Dr 13206
Village Drive Ext 13206
Vincent Dr 13211
Vincent St 13210
Vine St 13203
Vintage Rd 13215
Vip Pkwy 13211
Volney Dr 13212
Wadsworth Rd 13212
Wadsworth St
100-212 13203
214-298 13203
300-1200 13208
1202-1298 13208
Wagon Trails End 13215
Wainwright Ave 13208
Waite Ave 13204
Walberta Rd 13219
Waldorf Pkwy 13224
Walker Blvd 13209
Wall St 13204
Wally Rd 13212
Walnut Ave & Pl 13210
Walrath Rd 13205
Walsh Cir 13208

Walter Dr 13206
Walters Rd 13209
Walton Rd 13212
Walton St 13202
Warham St 13208
Waring Rd 13224
Warner Ave 13205
Warner Ct 13204
Warners Rd 13209
N & S Warren St 13202
E & W Warrington Rd 13205
Warwick Rd 13214
Washington Sq 13208
E Washington St
- 100-599 13202
- 700-900 13210
- 902-1498 13210

W Washington St 13202
Watchtower Ln 13219
E Water St
- 101-197 13202
- 199-400 13202
- 402-598 13202
- 700-998 13210
- 1000-1002 13210
- 1004-1340 13210

W Water St 13202
Waterbury Dr 13212
Watson Rd 13212
Watson St 13206
Wavel St 13206
Waverly Ave 13210
Waxwood Cir 13212
Wayland Rd 13208
Wayne St 13203
Weathervane Way 13209
Webster Ave 13205
Webster Mile Dr 13215
Websters Lndg 13202
Wedgewood Ter 13214
Weiser Ct 13202
Wellesley Rd 13207
Wellington Rd
- 1-99 13212
- 100-399 13214

Wells Ave E & W 13212
Wendell Ter 13203
Wente Ter 13207
West St 13212
N West St 13204
S West St 13202
Westbrook Hills Dr 13215
Westcott St 13210
Westfall Dr 13219
Westfall St 13209
Westholm Blvd 13219
Westlind Rd 13219
Westminster Ave 13210
Westminster Rd 13214
Westmont Rd 13219
Westmoreland Ave
- 100-198 13224
- 201-299 13224
- 300-1699 13210

Westover St 13209
Westvale Pl & Rd 13219
Westview Ave 13208
Westview Dr 13215
Westwood Ave 13211
Westwood Rd 13215
Wexford Rd 13214
Weymouth Rd 13205
Wheaton Rd 13203
Whedon Rd 13219
White Rd 13212
White St 13204
Whitestone Cir & Dr 13215
Whitmore Rd 13212
Whitney Rd 13219
Whittier Ave 13204
Whitwell Dr 13203
Wickson Rd 13219
Widewaters Pkwy 13214
Wiesner Ln 13214
Wilbert Dr 13212
N & S Wilbur Ave 13204
Wild Rose Ln 13215
Wilderness Way 13215
Wildflower Cir 13215
Wilkie Pl 13203
Wilkinson St 13204
Will Ct 13204
William St 13209
William Barry Blvd 13212
Williams St
- 100-100 13212
- 101-101 13204
- 102-221 13212
- 104-126 13204
- 223-299 13212

Willis Ave 13204
Williston Ave 13208
Willoughby Pl 13204
Willow Rd 13212
E Willow St
- 101-199 13202
- 301-497 13203
- 499-900 13203
- 902-998 13203

W Willow St 13202
Willumae Dr 13208
Wilmont Rd 13219
Wilmore Pl 13208
Wilshire Rd 13209
Wilshirl Dr 13212
Wilson Pl 13214
Wilson St 13203
Wiman Ave 13205
Winchell Dr 13209
Windemere Rd
- 100-100 13205
- 100-106 13219
- 101-299 13219
- 101-101 13205
- 108-114 13205
- 110-198 13219
- 200-204 13205
- 200-298 13219

Windham Ave 13208
Windham Dr 13224
Winding Ridge Rd 13210
Windsor Dr
- 100-399 13214
- 103-112 13212
- 114-116 13212

Windsor Dr N 13212
Windsor Pl 13210
Windwood Rd 13212
Winkworth Pkwy 13215
Winston Way 13214
Winthrop Rd 13206
Winton St 13203
Witz Dr 13212
Wolcott Ave & Ter 13207
Wolf St 13208
Wolf Hollow Rd 13219
Wood Ave 13205
Woodbine Ave 13206
Woodbriar Dr 13215
Woodbury Ave 13206
Wooded Heights Cir 13215
Woodland Ave 13205
Woodland Dr 13212
Woodland Rd 13219
Woodlawn Ter 13203
Woodruff Ave
- 100-399 13203
- 400-499 13208

Woods Ave N 13206
Woods Ave S 13206
Woods Rd
- 101-101 13212
- 103-105 13209
- 103-107 13212
- 107-1299 13209
- 109-109 13212

Woodside Dr 13224
Woodstock Way 13215
Woodstream Ter 13212
Worden Ave 13208
Worth Ave 13209
Wright Ave 13211
Wycliffe Rd 13209
Wynnfield Dr 13219
Wynthrop Rd 13209
Wyoming St 13204
Yale Ave 13219
Yenny Rd 13215
York Rd 13214
Yorkshire Blvd 13219
Young Ave 13211
Young Rd 13215

NUMBERED STREETS

1st St 13209
1st North St 13208
2nd St 13209
2nd North St 13208
3rd St 13209
4th St 13209
4th North St 13208
5th St 13209
6th St 13209
6th North St 13208
7th St 13209
7th North St 13208

TONAWANDA NY

General Delivery 14150

POST OFFICE BOXES MAIN OFFICE STATIONS AND BRANCHES

Box No.s
All PO Boxes 14151

NAMED STREETS

Adam St 14150
Alcott Ct 14150
Alexander St 14150
Alliger Dr 14150
Ames Ave 14150
Amsterdam St 14150
Amy Dr 14150
Aqua Ln 14150
Ashford Ave 14150
Avon Rd 14150
Baker Ter 14150
Balzac Ct 14150
Bannard Ave 14150
Bathurst Dr 14150
Bellah Pl 14150
Bellhurst Rd 14150
Bellinger Dr 14150
Benefield Pl 14150
Benton St 14150
Beyer Dr 14150
Blackmore St 14150
Blackstone Blvd 14150
Bonnett Ave 14150
Boswell Pl 14150
Bouck St 14150
Bradford Walk 14150
Braxmar Rd 14150
Brenton Ave 14150
Briarhurst Dr 14150
Briarlee Dr 14150
Brighton Rd 14150
Broad St 14150
Broadmoor Dr 14150
Brompton Rd 14150
Brookside Ter W 14150
Brookville Ct & Dr 14150
Broughton Ct & St 14150
Browning Ave & Cir 14150
Burnett Pl 14150
Burns Ct 14150
Burnside Dr 14150
Calhoun Pl 14150
Calvert Blvd 14150
Calvin Ct N & S 14150
Canton St 14150
Carney St 14150
Castleton Pl 14150
Catherine St 14150
Channing Pl 14150
Chapman Pl 14150
Clarence Harder Dr 14150
Clark St 14150
Cleveland Ave & Pl 14150
Clinton St 14150
Cloister Ct 14150
Cobb St 14150
Colonial Cir & Dr 14150
Colvin Blvd 14150
Colvin Boulevard Ext 14150
Colvin Woods Pkwy 14150
Commodore Ave 14150
Concord Ct 14150
Cooper Ave 14150
Cordes Dr 14150
Cornell Ct 14150
Cornwall Ave 14150
Coronet Dr 14150
Coshway Pl 14150
Countrygate Ln 14150
Court St 14150
Cowper Cir & Pl 14150
Cranbrook Rd 14150
Cranbrook Road Ext 14150
Crane Pl 14150
Creekmore Dr 14150
Creekside Dr 14150
Cresthill Ave 14150
Crestmount Ave 14150
Crestwood Ct 14150
Crowell Ct 14150
Curwood Ct 14150
Dale Dr 14150
Daniel Dr 14150
Dekalb St 14150
Delaware Ave & St 14150
Delmar Ave 14150
Delton St 14150
Desmond Ct & Dr 14150
Dexter St & Ter 14150
Dickens Ave 14150
Dolphann Dr 14150
Douglas St 14150
Drew Pl 14150
Dreyer Ave 14150
Duffy Dr 14150
Dumas Pl 14150
Dunlop Ave 14150
Dupont Ave 14150
East Ave 14150
Ebling Ave 14150
Eden Ave 14150
Edith St 14150
Edward St 14150
Eggert Rd 14150
Elgin St 14150
Ellicott Blvd & Ct 14150
Ellicott Creek Park & Rd 14150
Elm St 14150
Elmview Dr 14150
Elmwood Park E 14150
Embassy Sq 14150
Ensminger Rd 14150
Enterprise Ave 14150
Erie St 14150
Eugene St 14150
Evelyn Ct 14150
Everett Pl 14150
Evergreen Dr 14150
Exolon Dr 14150
Fairlane Ave 14150
Faragut Ave & Ct 14150
Fenwick Rd 14150
Fillmore Ave 14150
Findlay Ave 14150
Fire Tower Dr 14150
Fletcher St 14150
Floradale Ave 14150
Flyder Ave 14150
Follette Ln 14150
Forbes Ave 14150
Frances St 14150
Franklin St 14150
Frederick Ct & Rd 14150
Fremont St 14150
Fries Rd 14150
Fuller Ave 14150
Gath Ter 14150
Gibson St 14150
Glenalby Rd 14150
Glendale Dr 14150
Glenhurst Rd 14150
Glenwood Ave 14150
Gloucester Ave 14150
Grand Ave 14150
Grand Island Blvd 14150
Grant St 14150
Grayton Rd 14150
Green Ct 14150
Green Acres Rd 14150
Greendale Ave 14150
Greenfield Dr 14150
Greenhaven Ter 14150
Greenleaf Ave 14150
Greentree Rd 14150
Grove Pl, St & Ter 14150
Guenther Ave 14150
Hackett Dr 14150
Hale Ct 14150
Halladay Ln 14150
Halsey Ct 14150
Hamilton Ave 14150
Hanover St 14150
Hardy Ct 14150
Harriet St 14150
Harvington Rd 14150
Heralins Ave 14150
Heritage Ct & Rd 14150
Highland Ave 14150
E Hill Pl & St 14150
Hillcrest Rd 14150
Hinds St 14150
Holly Ln 14150
Hospitality Centre Way 14150
Howard Ln 14150
Hurst Ct 14150
Idlewood Dr 14150
Ilion St 14150
Irvington Dr 14150
Jamaica Rd 14150
James Ave & St 14150
Johnson St 14150
Joseph Dr 14150
Karen Dr 14150
Kaufman Ave 14150
Keats Ave 14150
Kenmore Ave 14150
Kerr Ave 14150
Kibler Dr 14150
Killewald Ave 14150
King St 14150
Kingsbury Ln 14150
Klinger Ave 14150
Knoche Rd 14150
Koch St 14150
Koenig Cir & Rd 14150
Kohler St 14150
Lardner Ct 14150
N & S Lawn Ct 14150
Leahy Ct 14150
Leawood Dr 14150
Lepeirs Dr 14150
Linwood Ave 14150
Longfellow Ct 14150
Longs Ave 14150
Lorelee Dr 14150
Loretta St 14150
Lorna Ln 14150
Lorna Lane Ct 14150
Luksin Dr 14150
Luzerne Rd 14150
Lynbrook Ave & Dr 14150
Main St 14150
Maldiner Ave 14150
Mallory Rd 14150
Malvern Curv 14150
W Maple St 14150
Maplegrove Ave 14150
Mapleview Dr 14150
Marian Dr 14150
Marilyn Ct 14150
Marlee Dr 14150
Mary Vista Ct 14150
Masefield Dr 14150
Mayfair Ln 14150
Mayfield Ave 14150
Mcconkey Dr 14150
Melody Ln 14150
Milens Rd 14150
Military Rd 14150
Mill St 14150
Miller Pl 14150
Millwood Dr 14150
Milton St 14150
Minerva St 14150
Mitchell Dr 14150
E Monmouth Ave 14150
Monterey Rd 14150
Moon Walk 14150
Morgan St 14150
Morrison Ave 14150
Mosher Dr 14150
Moyle Ave 14150
Mullen St 14150
Murray Ter 14150
Nadon Pl 14150
Newbury Walk 14150
Newell Ave 14150
E Niagara St 14150
Niagara Falls Blvd 14150
Niagara Shore Dr 14150
Nicholas Ct & Dr 14150
Nimitz Ct 14150
North Way 14150
Northcrest Ct 14150
Nowak St 14150
Oakview Dr 14150
Ogden Rd 14150
Ohara Rd 14150
Old Colony Ave 14150
Oriskany Dr 14150
Overbrook Ave & Pl 14150
Paradise Ln 14150
E Park Ave & Dr 14150
Parkedge Ave & Ct 14150
Parker Blvd 14150
Parkhurst Blvd 14150
Patricia Dr 14150
Patton Rd 14150
Pearce Ave 14150
Penarrow Dr 14150
Peuquet Pkwy 14150
Pilgrim Rd 14150
Pinewoods Ave 14150
Plymouth Dr 14150
Prospect Ave 14150
Pryor Ave 14150
Puritan Rd 14150
Pyle Ct 14150
Quaker Ridge Rd 14150
Queen St 14150
Queens Guard Walk 14150
Raintree Is & Pkwy 14150
Ridgedale Cir 14150
Ritchie Ave 14150
River Rd 14150
Riverview Ave & Blvd 14150
Riverwalk Pkwy 14150
Robert Gair Dr 14150
Rochelle Park 14150
Rockland Rd 14150
Rogers Ave 14150
Roosevelt St 14150
Roxley Pl 14150
Russet Pl 14150
Rye Pl 14150
Saint Amelia Dr 14150
Saint Clare Ter 14150
Sawyer Ave 14150
Schuler Ave 14150
Scott St 14150
Seymour St
- 1-95 14150
- 96-96 14151
- 97-199 14150
- 98-198 14150

Sharon Ave & Dr 14150
Shelley Ct 14150
Sheridan Dr 14150
Sheridan Parkside Dr 14150
Sherwin Dr 14150
Simson St 14150
Snug Haven Ct 14150
E Somerset Ave 14150
Somerville Ave 14150
Southcrest Ct 14150
Springfield Ave 14150
Stark St 14150
State St 14150
Steiner Ave 14150
Summit St 14150
Sunnydale Dr 14150
Sunset Ter 14150
Surrey Cir 14150
Sutley Ct 14150
Sweet Briar Ct & Rd 14150
Syracuse St 14150
Tarkington Ct 14150
Taylor Dr 14150
Thackeray Ct 14150
Thistle Ave 14150
Thoreau Ct 14150
Treadwell Rd 14150
Trumball Pl 14150
Tussing Ln 14150
Twain Ct 14150
Two Mile Creek Rd 14150
Utica St 14150
Vickers St 14150
Vicksburg Ave 14150
Vinson Ave 14150
Virginia St 14150
Wadsworth Ave & Ct 14150
Wales Ave 14150
Wall St 14150
Walpole Pl 14150
Walter Ave 14150
Warren Dr 14150
Wayside Ct 14150
Wedgewood Dr 14150
Wenonah Ter 14150
Werkley Rd 14150
Westbourne Dr 14150
Westfall Dr 14150
Westwood Dr 14150
Wheeler St 14150
Whitman Pl 14150
Whittier Pl 14150
William St 14150
Willow Dr 14150
Willowbend Rd 14150
Willowgrove Ct E, N & S 14150
Wilmington Ave 14150
Winkler Dr 14150
Woodgate Rd 14150
Woodmere Dr 14150
Woodstock Ave 14150
Woodward Ave W 14150
Wrexham Ct N & S 14150
Wynnwood Ave 14150
Yorkshire Rd 14150
Young St 14150

TROY NY

General Delivery 12180

POST OFFICE BOXES MAIN OFFICE STATIONS AND BRANCHES

Box No.s
1 - 432 12182

1 - 1750 12181
1501 - 1619 12183
1800 - 4006 12181

NAMED STREETS

Aavelord Blvd 12180
Adams St 12180
Adare Rd 12180
Ahern Ave 12180
Albany Ave 12183
Albert Dr 12182
Albert St 12180
Albia Ave 12180
Albright Ct 12180
Alder Ave 12180
Alma Ct 12180
Alsid Ct 12180
Anchor Park Way 12182
Andrew Ct 12182
Andrews Rd 12180
Angelo Dr 12180
Annie St 12180
Antonia Ct 12182
Apex Ln 12182
Appletree Ln 12180
Arbor Dr 12180
Arch St 12183
Arminghall Dr 12180
Arthur Ct 12180
Arts St 12180
Ashland Pl 12180
Ashley Way 12180
Autumn Ln 12182
Avenue A 12182
Bailey Pointe Ct 12182
Bal Harbour Dr 12182
Bald Mountain Rd 12180
Ballina St 12180
Balsam Ave 12180
Banbury Rd 12180
Bank St 12180
Banker Ave 12182
Bedford St 12180
Belair Ln 12180
Belgrade St 12182
Belle Ave 12180
Bells Ln 12180
Bellview Rd 12180
Beman Ln 12180
Bennett Rd 12182
Bentley Dr & Rd 12182
Berkeley St 12180
Berkshire Dr 12180
Betts Dr & Rd 12180
Beverly Rd 12182
Bickford Ln 12182
Big Bear Rd 12182
Billings Ave 12180
Birch Dr & St 12180
Birchkill Ln 12180
Biscayne Blvd 12182
Black Cherry Ln 12180
Blakley Ct 12180
Bleakley Ave 12182
Bleeker Ave 12180
Bleeker St 12183
Bloomingrove Dr 12180
Blue Heron Ln 12180
Bolivar Ave 12180
Bond St 12180
Bonesteel Ln 12180
Bornt Rd 12180
Boston St 12182
Bott Ln 12180
Bouton Rd 12180
Brentwood Ave 12180
Brian Ct 12182
Brick Church Rd 12180
Brickyard Rd 12182
Bridge Ave 12180
Brielle Dr 12182
Brinsmade Ter 12180
Broadview Ct & Ter 12180
Broadway
1-299 12180
301-501 12180
400-400 12181
450-598 12180
Brook St 12182
Brook Hill Dr 12180
Brookview Ave & Ln 12180
Brunswick Ave, Dr, Hls & Rd 12180
Brunswick Park Dr 12180
Bs Ln 12180
Buck Rd 12180
Buckbee Rd 12180
Bulson Rd 12180
Burden Ave 12180
Burdett Ave & Ct 12180
Burger Ln 12180
Burke Dr & St 12180
Burrett Ln 12180
Button Rd 12182
Calhoun Dr 12182
Calhoun Rd 12180
Camel Hill Rd 12180
Campbell Ave 12180
Canal Ave 12180
Cannon St 12183
Carla Ln 12180
Carlyle Ave 12180
Carolina Ave 12180
Caroline Dr 12182
Carriage Ln 12180
Carroll Pl 12180
Carroll Hill Ct 12180
Carrolls Grove Rd 12180
Catherine Ave 12180
Catherine Sweeney Apts 12180
Cedar Ave 12182
Cemetery Rd 12182
Center Ct & St 12183
Center Island Cir 12183
Centerview Dr 12180
Central Ave 12180
Centre St 12180
Cesta Ln 12180
Charl Ln 12180
Charmwood Ln 12180
Checkerberry Ln 12180
Chelsea Ct 12182
Chelton Ave 12180
Cherry Ln & St 12180
Cheryl Ct 12180
Chester Ct 12182
Christie St 12180
Church St 12180
Clarendon St 12180
Clark Ave 12180
Clearview Dr 12180
Clements Dr 12180
Cleminshaw Ave 12180
Cliff St 12180
Clinton Ave 12180
Clinton Pl 12180
Clinton St 12183
Cloverlawn Rd 12180
Cobblestone Ln 12180
Cohoes Ave 12183
Cold Springs Rd 12180
Cole Ln 12180
Colehamer Ave 12180
Colleen Rd 12180
College Ave 12180
Collins Ave 12180
N & S Colonial Hts 12180
Colvin Cir 12180
Congress St 12180
Conway Ct 12180
Cooksboro Rd 12182
Coolidge Ave 12180
Coons Rd 12180
Cooper Ave 12180
Corliss Park 12182
Cortland St 12180
Cottage St 12180
Country Way 12180
Country Garden Apts 12180
Coyote Ln 12180
Cpl William A Dickerson Pl 12180
Cragin Ave 12180
Cranston Rd 12180
Crescent Ln 12180
Crestwood Ave & Ln 12180
Crimson Cir 12180
Crockett Ave 12180
Cross St 12180
Curtis Ln 12180
Cypress St 12180
Damascus Dr 12180
Darling Rd 12180
Dartmouth St 12180
Dater Hill Rd 12180
David Ave 12180
Deana Dr 12180
Dearstyne Rd 12180
Deeb Dr 12180
Deepkill Ln 12182
Deepkill Rd
1-150 12180
151-499 12182
Deerfield Dr 12180
Defreest Ave & Dr 12180
Delamater Way 12180
Delaware Ave 12180
Delee Dr 12182
Denise Dr 12182
Denton Ln 12180
Derrick Ave 12180
Desson Ave 12180
Detroit Ave 12180
Dewey Ave 12180
Diack Pl 12182
Diamond Ave 12180
Diamond Rock Cir 12182
Diana Ln & Pl 12180
Diane Ln 12182
Division St 12180
Dixon Dr 12180
Donegal Ave 12180
Donna Rd 12182
Donna Way 12180
Dormay Ln 12182
Douw St 12180
Downey Rd 12180
Dudley Ave 12183
Dudley Hts 12180
Duncan Dr 12182
Duncan Ln 12180
Dunham St 12180
Dunleer Dr 12180
Dusenberry Ln 12180
Dusenberry Rd 12182
Eagle St 12180
Eagle Hts Rd 12180
Eagle Ridge Dr 12182
Earl St 12180
East Ave & Rd 12180
Eastover Rd
1-99 12180
100-199 12182
Easy St 12180
Eaton Rd 12180
Eddys Ln 12180
Edelman Ln 12180
Edgehill Ter 12180
Eldridge Ct 12180
Ellen Ave 12180
Ellyn Ln 12182
Elm Pl 12180
Elm St
2-6 12182
8-8 12180
10-73 12180
12-98 12182
75-99 12180
Elmgrove Ave 12180
Elmore St 12182
Elmview Rd 12180
Elmwood Dr 12180
Elsie Way 12180
Elward Rd 12180
Erie St 12180
Essex St 12180
Ethier Dr 12180
Euclid Ave & Ter 12180
Evergreen Rd 12180
Excelsior Ave 12180
Fairfield Rd 12180
Fairlawn Ln 12180
Falcon Ln 12182
Fales Ct 12180
Fallon Apts 12180
Fane Ct 12182
Farm St 12180
Farm To Market Rd 12180
Farnam Ln 12180
Farrell Rd 12180
Farrell Rd Ext 12182
Farrington Ave 12180
Farview Ave 12180
Fay Way 12180
Federal St 12180
Ferry St 12180
Fiet Ave 12180
Film Ave 12180
Fitting Ln 12180
Flensburg Dr 12180
Florence Pl 12180
Flower Rd 12180
Fogarty Rd 12182
Fonda Ave 12180
Forbes Ave 12180
Ford Ave & Rd 12180
Forest Ave 12180
Forsyth Dr 12180
Fox Hollow Rd 12180
Foxford Rd 12180
Francis St 12180
Franklin Pl 12180
Frear Ave 12180
Frear Park Vw 12180
Frederick Pl 12180
Freeman Ave 12180
Fremont Ln 12182
Front St 12180
Fulton St 12180
Garden Ct 12180
Garfield Rd 12180
Gene Ave 12180
Genesee St 12180
George St 12183
Georgian Ct 12180
Gillette Ave 12180
E & W Glen Ave & Dr 12180
Glenhaven Sq 12180
Glenkill Rd 12180
Glenmore Rd 12180
Glenwood Rd 12180
Global Vw 12180
Golden Eagle Ct 12180
Goodman Ave 12180
Grace Ct 12180
Grand St 12180
Grandview Ave, Dr & Ter 12180
Grange Rd
1-400 12180
401-451 12182
402-452 12180
453-599 12182
Granite Ln 12180
Grant Ave 12180
N Greenbush Rd 12180
Greene St 12180
Gregory Ct 12180
Griswold Ave & Hts 12180
Grove St 12180
Guiliana Cir 12180
Gurley Ave 12182
Gypsy Ln 12182
Hadden Ln 12180
Hakes Rd 12180
Hale St 12180
Haley Ln 12182
Hamilton Ave 12180
Hamilton St 12183
Hampton Place Blvd 12180
Hanover St 12180
Hansen Rd 12182
Harbinger Way 12180
Harlem St 12183
Harris Ave 12180
Harris Rd 12182
Harrison St 12180
Harvest Ln 12180
Haughney Rd 12182
Haven Ln 12182
Havermans Ave 12180
Hawthorne Ave 12180
Heather Ln 12180
Heather Ridge Rd 12180
Herrington Ln 12180
Hewitt Dr 12180
Heyden Rd 12180
Hialeah Dr 12182
Hickory Ct, Ln & St 12180
High St
1-99 12183
2-14 12180
2-14 12183
16-98 12183
16-16 12180
300-399 12182
High Meadow Rd 12180
Highland Ave & Ct 12180
Highland Acres 12180
Highpointe Dr 12182
Hilda Ct 12180
Hill Rd & St 12180
Hillcrest Ave 12180
Hillcrest St 12182
Hills Lndg 12180
Hillside Ave 12180
Hillside Rd 12182
Hilltop Ct 12182
Hilltop Rd 12180
Hillview Dr 12182
Hoosick Rd & St 12180
Hopkins Ln 12182
Hopkins St 12180
Horizon Ln 12182
Horton Ave 12180
House Ave 12180
Howard St 12180
Howe Ln 12180
Hudson Ave
1-299 12183
300-399 12182
Hudson Dr 12180
Hudson St 12180
Hughes Ave 12180
Humiston Ave 12182
Hunter Ln 12180
Hurley Rd 12182
Hutton St 12180
Hutton And 19th St 12180
Hyland Cir, Ct & Dr 12182
Ida St 12180
Indian Creek Ln 12180
E Industrial Pkwy 12180
Industrial Park Rd 12180
Ingalls Ave 12180
Inverness Dr 12180
Irish Rd 12182
Irving Pl 12180
Ives Ct 12182
Jackson Pl & St 12180
Jacob St 12180
James Ln 12182
James St 12183
Jay Ave & St 12180
Jefferson St 12180
Jesse Ct 12180
Jessica Cir 12180
John St 12183
John Snyder Rd 12180
Johnson St 12180
Jordan Rd 12180
Jordan Point Dr 12180
Joseph Ct & St 12180
Joy Ln 12180
Keefe Rd 12180
Kellogg Dr 12180
Kelly St 12180
Kemp Ave 12180
Kenworth Ave 12180
Kerry Dr 12180
Kestner Ln 12180
Keyes Ln 12180
Kiel St 12180
Killock Ave 12180
Kimberly Cir 12180
King St 12180
Kinloch Ave 12180
Kinney Ave 12180
Knollwood Dr 12180
Knowlton Ave 12182
Krieger Ln 12180
Lafayette Park & St 12183
N & S Lake Ave & Dr 12180
Lake Hills Rd 12180
Lake Shore Dr 12180
Lakeridge Dr 12180
Lakeview Ave 12180
Lakewood Pl 12180
Lance Ave 12180
Lang Rd 12180
N Langmore Ln 12180
Langstaff Ln 12180
Lann Ave 12182
Lansing Ave
1-99 12180
300-499 12182
Lansing Rd 12180
Lansing Ter 12182
Larch Ave 12180
Larix Ct 12180
Lark St 12180
Larry Ct 12182
Laundry Pl 12180
Lavin Ct 12180
Ledgestone Rd 12180
Ledgewood Dr 12180
Lee Ave 12180
Leonard Ave 12180
Leversee Rd 12182
Levi Ave 12180
Lewis St 12180
Lexington Ave 12180
Liberty Rd & St 12180
Lilac Ln 12180
Lillian Ln 12180
Lincoln Ave 12180
Linden Ave 12180
Lindsay Dr 12180
Lisa Ln 12180
Little Bear Rd 12182
Livingston St 12182
Lockrow Rd 12180
Locust Ave 12180
Log Woods Rd 12180
Long Hill Rd 12180
Lord Ave 12180
Lorenzo Dr 12180
Lori Jean Pl 12182
Loridalt Ave 12182
Loumar Ln 12182
Lower Fane Ct 12182
Lower Hudson Ave 12183
Lumax Run 12180
Luther St 12180
M St 12182
Macarthur Dr 12180
Macsherry Ct 12180
Madison Ave & St 12180
Magill Ave 12180
Main St 12180
Malone Rd 12182
Malrick Rd 12182
Mann Ave 12180
Manning Ave 12180
Manor Blvd 12180
Maple Ave & Ln 12182
Maplehurst Dr 12180
Maplewood Dr 12180
Marathon Dr 12180
Marcia Ct 12180
Marcy Ave 12180
Marion Ave 12182
Mark St 12180
Market St 12183
Marquis Ct 12180
Marshall St 12180
Marshland Ct 12180
Martin Ln 12182
Marvin Ave 12180
Mason Ln & St 12180
Massachusetts Ave 12180
Maxwell Dr 12180
Mazoway Ave 12180
Mcchesney Ave & Ct 12180
Mcchesney Ave Ext 12180
Mcclelland Ave 12180
Mckinley Ave 12180
Mcleod Rd 12180
Mcloughlin Ln 12180
Meadow Dr 12180
Meadowbrook Ln 12180
Meadowlawn Ave 12180
Meadowview Dr 12180
Mechanic St 12180
Mellon Ave 12180
Menemsha Ln 12180
Meridian Ct 12182
Merlista St 12183
Merrill Ave 12180
Meyer Ln 12182
Michael St 12180
Michele Mnr 12180
Michigan Ave 12180
Mickel Hill Rd 12180
Middle Rd 12180
Middle Hill Rd 12180
Middleburgh Ave & St 12180
Midland Rd 12180
Milky Way Rd 12182
Mill St 12180
Miller Ave & Ln 12180
Mineral Springs Rd 12182
Mitchell St 12180
Mohawk Ave 12180
Mohawk St 12183
Moneta Overlook 12182
Monroe St 12180
Montgomery St 12180
Monument Sq 12180
Moonlawn Rd 12180
Morrison Ave 12180
Morrison Manor Apts 12180
Mountain Way 12182
Mountainview Ave 12180
Mt Pleasant Ave 12180
Mt St Marys Ave 12180
Munro Ct 12180
Muriel Dr 12180
Muskrat Rd & Way 12182
Myrtle Ave 12180
N St 12182
Nadia Cir 12180
Nancy Dr 12180
Naples Ct 12180
Nassau St 12180
New Hampshire Ave 12180
New Turnpike Rd 12182
Nicholas Dr 12180
Norfolk St 12180
Norman Ln 12182
North Dr, Rd & St 12180
Northern Ct 12180
Northern Dr 12182
Northstar Dr 12180
Norton St 12180
Nott Dr 12180
Nyroy Dr 12180
O St 12182
Oak St 12180
Oak Creek Way 12180
Oak Tree Ln 12180
Oakhurst St 12182
Oakwood Ave
1-144 12180
146-162 12180
166-399 12182
Oakwood Ter 12180
Obrien Ln & Rd 12180
Odell St 12180
Oil Mill Hill Rd 12182

Old Campbell Ave 12180
Old Hickory Rd 12180
Old Siek Rd 12180
Old State Route 142 12180
Oneida Ave 12180
Oneil St 12180
Orchard Ave & Ln 12180
Orr St 12180
Osgood Ave 12183
Otsego Ave 12180
Ouimet Dr 12180
Outlook Ct 12182
Oxford Cir & Rd 12180
Packer Ave 12180
Paine St 12183
Palisade Ct 12182
Palmetto Ct 12182
Paring Rd 12180
Park Ave 12180
Park Blvd 12180
Park Dr 12180
E Park Pl 12182
W Park Pl 12182
Park St 12180
Parkview Ct 12180
Parmenter Ave 12180
Parsonage Ln 12180
Pasture Ln 12180
Patricia Dr 12180
Patriot Pl 12180
Pattison Way 12180
Patton Rd 12180
Paul Ct 12182
Paul Art Ln 12180
Pawling Ave 12180
Penny Royal Ln 12180
Peoples Ave 12180
Perry Rd 12182
Peterson Ct 12180
Petticoat Ln 12180
Pheasant Ln 12180
Phelan Ct 12180
Phillip St 12180
Pickering Ln 12180
Pine St 12183
Pine Grove Ln 12182
Pinegrove Dr 12180
Pinehurst St 12182
Pineview Ave 12180
Pinewoods Ave 12180
Piney Point Rd 12180
Plank Rd 12182
Plante Ln 12180
Pleasant St 12182
Pleasant Acres Dr 12182
Pleasantview Ave 12180
Plum Ave & Rd 12180
Plumadore Dr 12180
Poestenkill Rd 12180
Pointview Dr 12180
Polk St 12180
Pompano Dr 12182
Pond Ln 12182
Poplar Ave 12180
Powers Ln 12182
President St 12180
Prince St 12180
Project Rd 12180
Prospect Ave 12180
Prout Ave 12180
Putnam St 12180
R St 12182
Rankin Ave 12180
Ravens Ct 12180
Red Rock Rd 12182
Regatta Pl 12180
Reid Ave 12180
Rensselaer St 12180
Reynolds Rd 12180
Ribbon Candy Ln 12182
Riccardi Ln 12180
Rice Mt Pl 12182
Richfield St 12182
Richmond St 12180
Ridge Cir 12182
Ridge Dr 12180

N Ridge Est 12182
Ridge Rd 12180
Ridgewood Ave 12180
Riding Club Rd 12180
Ridler Ln 12180
Rifenberg Rd 12180
River Rd 12182
River St 12180
S River St 12180
River View Rd 12183
Riverbend Rd 12182
Robbins Ave 12180
Roberts Dr 12180
Roberts Rd 12182
Robin Ln 12180
Rock Candy Ln 12182
Rocque Ln 12180
Roosevelt Ave
1-99 12180
300-399 12182
Rose Ln 12180
Roselawn Ave 12180
Rosemary Dr 12180
Ross Tech Park 12180
Row A Way 12182
Row B Way 12182
Row D Way 12182
Row E Way 12182
Row F Way 12182
Royale Ct 12180
Russell Ct 12182
Ryan Rd 12180
Sage Ave 12180
Sage Hill Ln 12180
Sampson Ave 12180
Sandra Dr 12180
Sanford Ave 12180
Saratoga Ave & St 12183
Sausse Ave 12180
Schuyler St 12180
Scott Dr 12180
Seaforth Rd 12180
Sears Rd 12180
Seaver Way 12180
Seminole Ave 12182
Semple St 12182
Seneca St 12180
Settler Ln 12180
Seward St 12180
Seymour Ct 12180
Shafter Ave 12180
Sheldon Ave 12180
Shepherd Dr 12180
Shepherd Ln 12182
Sheridan Ave 12180
Sherman Ave 12180
Sherry Rd 12180
Shine Rd 12180
Shippey Ln 12180
Short Rd 12180
Short Essex St 12180
Skycrest Dr 12180
Skyline Dr 12180
Skyview Dr 12180
Smith Ave & Ter 12180
Smith Hill Rd 12180
Snyder Ave 12180
South Dr & St 12180
Speigletown Rd 12182
Spence St 12180
Spring Ave 12180
Spring Avenue Ext 12180
Springbrook Rd 12180
Springs Ln 12180
Springwood Mnr 12180
St Josephs St 12180
St Lukes Ave 12180
St Marys Ave 12180
St Michaels Ave 12180
St Pauls Pl 12180
St Peters Ave 12180
St Vincents Ave 12180
Stannard Ave 12180
Stanton St 12180
Starr Rd 12182
State St 12180

State Highway 2 12180
State Highway 351 12180
State Highway 7 12180
State Route 40 12182
State Route 7 12182
Sterling Ave 12180
Sterup Dr 12180
Stone Arabia Dr 12180
Stone Clay Rd 12180
Stoneledge Dr 12182
Stowe Ave 12180
Strain Ave 12180
Stratton Cir 12182
Sullivan St 12180
Summer St 12180
Summit Ave 12180
Summit Hill Way 12180
Sun Valley Rd 12182
E & W Sunnyside St 12180
Sunset Ave 12180
Sunset Ct 12180
Sunset Dr 12182
Sunset Ln 12182
Sunset Ter 12180
Sunset View Ave & Ext 12180
Swan St 12183
Sweeney Dr 12180
Sweetmilk Creek Rd 12180
Swift St 12180
Sycamore Pl 12180
Sycaway Ave 12180
Sylvan Ln 12180
Taft Ave 12180
Tague Rd 12182
Tamarac Rd 12180
Tambul Ln 12180
Tampa Ave 12182
Tarbell Ave 12180
Tate Rd 12180
Taylor Ct & Ln 12180
Terrace Dr & Pl 12180
The Knl 12180
The Crossways 12180
Thomas Ave & St 12180
Thompson St 12180
Thornton St 12180
Thurles Ct 12180
Tibbits Ave
1-199 12183
1500-3299 12180
Timberland Way 12182
Tom Phelan Pl 12180
Tower Ave 12180
Town Office Rd 12180
Tracey Ct 12180
Trenton St 12180
Trubel Pl 12180
Tucker Ave 12180
Tucker Pond Ct 12182
Turner Rd 12182
Tybush Ln 12180
Tyler St 12180
Union St 12180
Urba Ln 12180
Valleyview Ave
1-99 12180
100-199 12182
Valleyview Dr 12180
Van Buren St 12180
Van Every Ave 12180
Vandenburgh Ave & Pl 12180
Vanderheyden St 12180
Veterans Memorial Dr 12183
Victor Rd 12180
Victoria Ave 12180
Viewpoint Dr 12182
Village Dr 12180
Vista Ave & Rd 12180
Wagar Rd 12182
Waldron Ln 12180
Walker Ave 12180
Walnut St
1-9 12183
2-8 12180

10-99 12180
Walter Rd 12180
Wanda Ct 12180
Ward Hollow Rd 12180
Warren Ave 12180
Warren Ln 12182
Washington Dr, Pl & St 12180
Water St 12180
Water Plant Rd 12182
Watson Ave 12180
Wayne St 12180
Weaver Ave 12182
Wendell Ave 12180
West Ave 12180
West Rd 12180
West St 12183
Westcott Rd 12182
Westfall Ave 12180
Westlane Rd 12180
Westover Rd 12180
Westview Rd 12182
Wetsel Rd 12182
Weyrick Rd 12180
White Church Ln & Rd 12180
Whitehall St 12183
Whitman Ct 12180
Wiegner Ln 12180
Wilde Dr 12180
Wilkie Ln 12180
Willard Ave & Ln 12180
Williams Rd 12180
Williams Street Aly 12180
Willis St 12180
Willow St 12180
Willowbrook Ct & Ln 12180
Wilrose Ln 12180
Wilson Ln 12180
Windfield Ln 12180
Windsor Ave 12180
Windy Acres Rd 12180
Winnie Ave 12180
Winslow Ave 12180
Winter St 12180
Witherow Ave 12182
Woodcut Ln 12180
Woodhill Ln 12180
Woodland Rd 12180
Woodlawn Ct 12180
Woodrow Ct 12180
Woods Path 12182
Woodview Rd 12182
Woodward Ave 12180
Wool Ave 12180
Wright Lake Rd 12180
Wrpi Plz 12180
Wyck Ln 12180
Wye St 12180
Wyman Ln 12180
Wynantskill Way 12180
Yates St 12180

NUMBERED STREETS

1st Ave 12182
1st St 12180
N 1st St 12180
2nd Ave
20-246 12180
271-1099 12182
2nd St 12180
3rd Ave 12182
3rd St 12180
4th Ave
200-246 12180
247-249 12182
248-250 12180
251-899 12182
4th St 12180
5th Ave
1-245 12180
246-918 12182
919-997 12180
920-998 12182
999-2900 12180
2902-2998 12180

472-478-472-478 12182
6th Ave
1-246 12180
247-899 12182
1000-3399 12180
7th Ave
1-1 12180
3-299 12180
300-999 12182
1600-1698 12180
1700-3399 12180
8th Ave
100-199 12180
300-1199 12182
8th St 12180
9th Ave 12182
9th St 12180
10th Ave 12182
10th St 12180
11th St 12180
12th St 12180
13th St 12180
14th St 12180
15th St 12180
16th St 12180
17th St 12180
19th St 12180
21st St 12180
22nd St 12180
23rd St 12180
24th St 12180
25th St 12180
101st St 12180
102nd St 12180
103rd St 12180
104th St 12180
105th St 12180
106th St 12182
107th St 12182
108th St 12182
109th St 12182
110th St 12182
111th St 12182
112th St 12182
113th St 12182
114th St 12182
115th St 12182
116th St 12182
117th St 12182
118th St 12182
119th St 12182
120th St 12182
121st St 12182
122nd St 12182
123rd St 12182
124th St 12182
125th St 12182
126th St 12182

UNIONDALE NY

General Delivery 11553

POST OFFICE BOXES MAIN OFFICE STATIONS AND BRANCHES

Box No.s
All PO Boxes 11553

NAMED STREETS

Adams St 11553
Admiral Ln 11553
Alcyon Pl 11553
Alexander Ave 11553
Amsterdam Ave 11553
Anchor Way 11553
Arcadia Ave 11553
Ardwick Pl 11553
Argyle Ave 11553
Armond St 11553

Arthur St 11553
Ash Ct 11553
Atom Ct 11553
Avenue A 11553
Avenue B 11553
Baldwin Ct 11553
Barry Pl 11553
Beck St 11553
Bedford Ave & Ct 11553
Belmont Pl 11553
Berkley St 11553
Bira St 11553
Birch St 11553
Braxton St 11553
Brookside Ave 11553
Brown Ct 11553
California Ave 11553
Cambria St 11553
Campus St 11553
Cedar St 11553
Cewell Ave 11553
Charles Pl 11553
Charles Lindbergh Blvd 11553
Charter Ct 11553
Chester St 11553
Clare Rd 11553
Clarendon Rd 11553
Clark Pl 11553
Cleveland St 11553
Clinton Ave 11553
Coleridge Rd 11553
Colonial St 11553
Commodore Rd 11553
Compass St 11553
Cooper Ct 11553
Cornelius Ct 11553
Cornwell Ave 11553
Cottage St 11553
Cunningham Ave 11553
Cynthia Rd 11553
Dale Pl 11553
David Ct 11553
Davis Ave 11553
Decatur St 11553
Ditmas Ave 11553
Duryea Ave 11553
Earle Ovington Blvd 11553
Edgemere Ave 11553
Ellersid 11556
Elm Pl 11553
Ely Ct 11553
Emerson Pl & St 11553
Estelle Ct 11553
Fall Ave 11553
Fayette St 11553
Fenimore Ave 11553
Fisher Ave 11553
Fiske Pl 11553
Front St 11553
Fullerton Ave 11553
Galley St 11553
George Ave 11553
Gerald St 11553
Gilroy Ave 11553
Glen Curtiss Blvd 11556
Glenn Curtiss Blvd 11553
Goodrich St 11553
Grant Pl 11553
Greengrove Ave 11553
Hampton Rd 11553
Harding St 11553
Harrison St 11553
Hawthorne Ave 11553
Hempstead Blvd & Tpke 11553
Henry St 11553
Herbert Ct 11553
Hill St 11553
Hillside Ct 11553
Huntington Pl 11553
Irving Pl 11553
Ivy Pl 11553
Jaffa Ave 11553
James Pl 11553
James Doolittle Blvd 11553

Jerusalem Ave 11553
Keen Pl 11553
Knabbe Ct 11553
Krull St 11553
Laclede Ave 11553
Lafayette Ave 11553
Larboard Ct 11553
Lawrence St 11553
Lee Rd 11553
Lenox Ave 11553
Leonard Ave 11553
Leslie Ln 11553
Liberty St 11553
Lindy Pl 11553
Linwood St 11553
Locust Ave 11553
Longman Pl 11553
Lowell Rd 11553
Lynn Ct 11553
Macon Pl 11553
Manor Pkwy 11553
Maple Ave 11553
Maplegrove Ave 11553
Marc Ct 11553
Marshall Ct 11553
Martin Dr 11553
Marvin Ave 11553
Mathilda Pl 11553
Matteline St 11553
Mckenna Pl 11553
Meadowbrook Pl & Rd 11553
Menard St 11553
Merillon St 11553
Midland St 11553
Midwood St 11553
Mildred Pl 11553
Mitchell St 11553
Mize Ct 11553
Moffat Pl 11553
Myron St 11553
Nancy Ct 11553
Narrows 11553
Nassau Rd 11553
New St 11553
New Jersey Ave 11553
New York Ave 11553
Newport Rd 11553
Newton Ave 11553
Norris Ave 11553
Northern Pkwy 11553
Northgate Ct & Dr 11553
Nostrand Ave 11553
Oak St 11553
Oakley St 11553
Orbit Ln 11553
Orchard Pl 11553
Paff Ave 11553
Pamlico Ave 11553
Park Ave & Pl 11553
Pemaco Ln 11553
Pembroke St 11553
Phillip Rd 11553
Pine Pl & St 11553
Planders Ave 11553
Plymouth Ct 11553
Rochelle Ct 11553
Ruxton Pl & St 11553
Rxr Plz 11556
Saint Agnes Rd 11553
Salem Rd 11553
Smith St 11553
Southern Pkwy 11553
Spring Ave 11553
Spruce Pl 11553
Spuhler Pl 11553
Stanton Blvd 11553
Sterling St 11553
Summer Ave 11553
Susan Pl 11553
Terrace Pl 11553
Terrell Pl 11553
Terry Ct 11553
Tower Ct 11553
Trisour Ave 11553
Tulip Ct 11553
Tulsa St 11553

Union Dr 11553
Uniondale Ave 11553
Valcour Ave 11553
Van Buren St 11553
Wake St 11553
Waldorf Pl 11553
Walnut St 11553
Walter St 11553
Walton Ave 11553
Warren St 11553
Warwick St 11553
Waverly Pl 11553
Waypark Ave 11553
Webster Ave 11553
Wellelein Rd 11553
Willow St 11553
Windsor Rd 11553
Winter Ave 11553
Winthrop Dr 11553
Woodbine St 11553

NUMBERED STREETS

All Street Addresses 11553

UTICA NY

General Delivery 13504

POST OFFICE BOXES MAIN OFFICE STATIONS AND BRANCHES

Box No.s
A1 - A1 13503
1 - 1091 13503
2 - 851 13504
1601 - 2120 13503
3014 - 7777 13504
8001 - 8908 13505
9527 - 9527 13503

NAMED STREETS

Adams St 13501
Addington Pl 13501
Addison St 13502
Adirondack View Hts 13502
Adrean Ter E & W 13501
Aiken St 13502
Albany St 13501
Alda Rd 13502
Allen Rd & St 13501
Alma Ct 13502
Alyssa Cir 13502
Amy Ave 13502
Andes Ave 13502
Ann St 13502
Anna Ct 13502
Arcadia Ave 13502
Ardmore Pl 13501
Arlington Rd & Ter 13501
Armory Dr 13501
Arnold Ave 13502
Arthur St 13501
Ash St 13502
Ashland Ave 13502
Ashton Rd 13502
Ashwood Ave 13502
Aspen Dr 13502
Auburn Ave 13501
Auert Ave 13502
Augar Pl 13501
Austin Rd 13502
Avery Pl 13502
Azure Ln 13502
Bacon St 13501
Baker Ave 13501
Ballantyne Brae 13501
Bank Pl 13501
Barnes Ave 13502
Barton Ave 13502
Baxter Ave 13502
Beaton Dr 13502
Beaumond Pl 13502
Beckwith Cir & Pl 13501
Beechgrove Pl 13501
Bell Hill Rd 13502
Belle Ave 13501
Belmont Ave 13501
Bennett St 13502
Benton Ave & Cir 13501
Bette Rd 13502
Beverly Pl 13501
Beverly Rd 13502
Birchdale Rd 13502
Blandina St 13501
Bleecker St 13501
Blossom Ln 13502
Bond St 13502
Bonnie Brae 13501
Booth St 13502
Bowie Rd 13502
Boyce Ave 13501
Bradford Ave & Ln 13501
Bradley Rd 13501
Branch St 13502
Brantwood Ln & Rd 13501
Brayton Park Pl 13502
Briar Ave 13501
Briarcliff Ave 13502
Brigham Pl 13502
Brighton Pl 13501
Brinckerhoff Ave 13501
Bristol St 13502
Broad St 13501
Broadacres Rd 13502
Broadway 13502
Brody Dr 13502
Brookline Dr 13501
Brookside Ave 13501
Brown Rd 13502
Brown Gulf Rd 13502
Bryant St 13502
Buchanan Rd 13502
Buckley Rd 13501
Bull Rd 13502
Burmont Ct & Dr 13502
Burnet St 13501
Burrstone Rd 13502
Burth Pl 13502
Burton Mnr 13502
Business Park Ct & Dr 13502
Butler Ave 13502
Butterfield Ave 13501
Butternut St 13502
Calder Ave 13502
Campbell Ave 13502
Candlewood Ln 13501
Candlewyck Ln 13502
Candy Ln 13502
Capital Ave 13502
Carlile Ave 13502
Carmen Ln 13501
Caroline St 13502
Carver St 13502
Catherine St 13501
Cedarbrook Cres 13502
Centennial Cir 13502
Champlin Ave 13502
Charles St 13502
Charlotte St 13501
Chenango Rd 13502
Cherry St 13502
Chestnut St 13502
Church Rd 13502
Churchill Ave 13502
City St 13502
Claremont Ter 13501
Clark Pl 13501
Clementian St 13501
Cleveland Ave 13502
Clifford Ln 13502
Clinton Pl 13501
Collier Pl 13502
Colonial Cir 13502
Columbia St 13502
Columbus Ave 13501
Commons Rd 13502
Concord Dr 13502
Confederate Dr 13502
Conkling Ave 13501
Coolidge Rd 13502
Cooper St 13502
Copperfield St 13501
Cornelia Pl & St 13502
Cornwall Ave 13502
Cosby Rd 13502
Cosby Manor Rd 13502
Cottage Pl 13502
Country Rd 13502
Coupe Ave 13502
Court St 13502
Coventry Ave 13502
Crabapple Ave 13502
Craige Ave 13502
Crestview Dr 13502
Crestway 13501
Croissant Cir 13502
Cromwell Pl 13502
Crooked Brook Rd 13502
Cross St 13502
Crouse St 13501
Cruikshank Rd 13502
Culver Ave & Ct 13501
Cypress St 13502
Damiano Pl 13501
Daniel Ct 13502
Davis Rd W 13502
Dawes Ave & Ct 13502
Daytona St 13502
De Peyster Ave 13501
Dearborn Pl 13501
Deborah Dr 13502
Deer Trail Rd 13502
Deerfield Dr E & W 13502
Deerwood Rd 13502
Deland Dr 13502
Delaware Ave 13502
Derbyshire Pl 13501
Devereux St 13501
Dewey Ave 13501
Dewitt St 13502
Dexter Dr 13502
Dickinson St 13501
Dirleton Rd 13501
Dodge Ln 13502
Dominica Ct 13502
Domser Dr 13502
Donegal Dr 13502
Dorsey Ln 13502
Douglas Cres 13501
Downer Ave 13502
Doyle Rd 13502
Dryden Ave 13502
Dudley Ave 13501
Dunham Rd 13501
Dwight Ave 13502
Dwyer Ave 13501
Eagle St 13501
Eastwood Ave 13501
Edgewood Rd 13501
Edward St 13502
Eldorado Rd 13502
Eleanor Pl 13501
Elizabeth St 13501
Elm St 13501
Elmdale Ave 13502
Elmhurst Rd 13502
Elmwood Pl 13501
Emerson Ave 13501
Emily St 13502
Erie St 13502
Euclid Rd 13502
Evergreen Dr 13502
Faass Ave 13502
Fairfax Pl 13502
Fairview Pl 13502
Fairwood Dr 13502
Farmington Rd 13501
Farview Hts 13501
Faxton St 13501
Fay St 13502
Fern Pl 13502
Ferndale Pl 13501
Ferris Ave 13501
Fincke Ave 13502
Fineview Dr 13502
Fiore Dr 13502
Firehouse Rd 13502
Flagg Ave 13502
Floral Ct & Dr 13501
Florence St 13501
Floyd Ave & St 13502
Foery Dr 13501
Folts Ln 13502
Forest Rd 13501
Forrest St 13502
Fox Pl 13502
Francis St 13502
Franklin Sq 13502
Frederick Pl E 13502
French Rd 13502
Fulton St 13501
N Gage Rd 13502
Garden Rd 13501
Gardner St 13501
Garfield St 13502
Gates St 13502
Geer Ave 13501
Genesee Ct 13502
Genesee St
　70-2814 13502
　131-2899 13501
N Genesee St 13502
George Pl 13501
Georgetown Ave 13502
Gibson Ct & Rd 13501
Gilbert St 13501
Gillmore Vlg 13502
Gilmore Pl 13502
Girard St 13501
Glendale Pl 13502
Glenwood Rd 13501
Gold St 13501
Golden Pl 13501
Goodrich Ave 13502
Grace Rd 13502
Graham Ave & Rd 13502
Grandview Ave 13502
Grant St 13501
Grasshopper Ln 13501
Gray Ave 13502
Green St 13502
Greenview Dr 13501
Greenwood Ct 13501
Grove Pl 13501
Guelich St 13501
Haak Ave 13502
Hager St 13502
Hamilton St 13502
Hammond Ave 13501
Hampden Pl 13502
Harbor Lock Rd E & W 13502
Harbor Point Rd 13502
Harding Pl 13501
Harper St 13502
Harriet St 13501
Harrison Ave 13501
Hart St 13502
Harter Pl 13501
Hartford Pl 13502
Hawthorne Ave & Rd 13502
Hayes Pl 13501
Hazelhurst Ave 13502
Hedgewood Pl 13502
Henry St 13502
Herkimer Rd 13502
Hess Ln 13502
Hewey St 13502
Higby Rd 13501
High St 13501
Highland Ave 13502
Highview Dr 13502
Hillcrest Ave 13502
Hillcrest Manor Ct 13501
S Hills Dr 13501
Hillside Rd 13501
Hilltop Dr 13502
Hillview Dr 13501
Hilton Ave 13501
Hingham Rd 13501
Hobart St 13501
Holland Ave 13501
Hollingsworth Ave 13501
Hollister Ave 13501
Holly Dr 13502
Homestead Dr 13502
Hoover Ave 13501
Hope St 13502
Hopper St 13501
Hopson St 13502
Horatio St 13502
Hotel St 13502
Howard Ave 13501
Howe St 13501
Hubbell St 13501
Hughes St 13502
Hulser Rd 13502
Humbert Ave 13501
Huntington St 13502
Independence Sq 13502
Inman Pl 13502
Irving Pl 13501
Jacqueline Ct 13502
James St 13501
Jamestown Ave 13502
Jason St 13502
Jay St 13501
Jeanette Dr 13502
Jefferson Ave 13501
Jewett Pl 13501
Jimmy Blvd 13502
Joanne Dr 13502
John St 13501
Johns Rd 13502
Johnson Park 13501
Jones St 13502
Karen Ct 13502
Kathleen St 13501
Keck Pl 13502
Keene St 13501
Kellogg Ave 13502
Kemble St 13501
Kennedy Plz 13502
Kensington Dr 13501
Kent St 13501
Kenwood Rd 13502
Kenyon Ct 13501
Keri Ln 13502
Kernan Ave 13502
Keyes Rd 13502
Kilkenny Dr 13502
King St 13501
Kingston Rd 13502
Kiniry St 13501
Kirkland St 13502
Knapps Knolle Rd 13502
Knoll Rd 13501
Knox St 13502
Kossuth Ave 13501
Kraemer Pl 13502
Kraft Dr 13502
Lafayette St 13502
Lamb St 13502
Lansing St 13501
Lantern Ln 13502
Larchmont Ave 13502
Lathrop Pl 13501
Laura St 13501
Laurel Pl 13502
Laurelwood Dr 13502
Lawrence Ave 13502
Leah St 13501
Lee Blvd & St E 13502
Leeds St 13501
Leibel Pl 13501
Leland Ave 13502
Lenox Ave 13502
Leslie Ave 13501
Lexington Pl 13501
Liberty St 13502
Lin Rd 13501
Lincoln Ave 13502
Linda View Ln 13502
Linwood Pl 13501
Lock St 13502
Locust Dr 13502
Lomond Ct & Pl 13502
Lorraine Ave 13502
Louis St 13502
Louisa St 13501
Lowell Ave 13502
Lower Woods Rd N & S 13501
Lynch Ave 13502
Lynn Pl 13502
Lyon Pl 13502
Madison Ave 13501
Main St 13501
Mallory Rd 13502
Mandeville St 13502
Maple St 13502
Mapledale Ave 13502
Mapleton Dr 13502
Margery St 13501
Marilyn Dr 13502
Marlboro Rd 13501
Marnie St 13502
Martin St 13502
Marwood Rd 13502
Mary St 13501
Mary Elaine Dr 13502
Mason Rd & St 13501
Mather Ave 13502
Mathews Ave 13502
Maverick Ln 13502
Maynard Ave 13502
Mcbride Ave 13502
Mcgraw Rd 13502
Mcintyre Rd 13502
Mcquade Ave 13501
Mcvean St 13502
Meadow Dr 13502
Meeker Ave 13502
Melrose Ave & Pl 13502
Melvin Ct & Rd 13502
Memorial Pkwy 13501
Merriline Ave 13502
Midland Rd 13501
Mildred Ave 13502
Milgate St 13501
Miller Rd 13502
Miller St 13501
Milton Pl 13501
Minot Pl 13502
Miranda Dr 13502
Mohawk St 13501
Monaghan Ln 13502
Monroe St 13501
Monticello Pl 13502
Morris St 13501
Mortimer St 13501
Mulaney Rd 13502
Mulberry St 13502
Mummery St 13501
Narla Ln 13501
Neilson St 13501
Nellis Pl 13502
Newell St 13502
Newport Rd 13502
Ney Ave 13502
Niagara St 13501
Nichols St 13501
Nob Rd 13501
Northern Rd 13502
Northrup Dr 13502
Northwood Dr 13502
Notre Dame Ln 13502
Noyes St 13502
Oak St 13502
Oakdale Ave 13502
Obrien Ave 13502
Ogden Pl 13501
Old Burrstone Rd 13502
Old Orchard Rd 13501
Oneida St 13501
Ontario St 13501
Orchard St 13502
Oriskany St E 13501
Oriskany St W 13502
Osborne St 13501
N Oscar St 13501
Oswego St 13502
Ottillia St 13501
Park Ave 13501
E Park Ct 13501
Park Dr 13502
S Park Dr 13501
E Park Rd 13501
Parker St 13502
Parklane Dr 13502
Parkside Ct 13501
Parkview Dr 13501
Parkway Cir & Ln 13501
Patricia Ct & Ln 13501
Pauline Ave 13502
Pellettieri Ave 13501
Pierrepont Ave 13502
Pinedale Dr 13502
Pinewood Dr 13502
Pinnacle Dr 13501
Pinto Ln 13502
Pitcher St 13504
Plant St 13502
Platt St 13502
Pleasant St 13501
Plymouth Pl 13501
Poe St 13501
Pond Ln 13501
Portal Rd 13501
Potter Ave 13502
Prescott Rd 13502
Proctor Blvd 13501
Proctor View Ct & Dr 13501
Prospect St 13501
Quentin Rd 13502
Ramblewood Dr 13502
Ravine Dr 13502
Redfield Ave 13501
Redfox Cir 13502
Redwood Ave 13502
Reels Dr 13502
Regent Ct 13501
Remington Rd 13501
Residential Dr 13502
Rhoads Dr 13502
Richards Rd 13502
Richardson Ave 13502
Richmond Rd 13502
Ridge Pl & Rd 13501
Ridgecrest Rd 13502
River Rd 13502
Riverside Ctr & Dr 13502
Roberta Ln 13501
Roberts Rd & St 13502
Robin Rd
　1-99 13501
　1300-1399 13502
Rockhaven Rd 13502
Rodeo Dr 13502
Rogers Rd 13502
Roosevelt Dr 13502
Rose Pl 13502
Roseclair Ave 13502
Rosemary St 13501
Rosemont Pl 13501
Rudolph Pl 13501
Rugby Rd 13502
Russet Bush Ln 13501
Rutger Park & St 13501
Sage Ct 13501
Saint Agnes Ave 13501
Saint Anthony St 13501
Saint Jane Ave 13501
Saint Vincent St 13501
Sarah St 13502
Saratoga St 13502
School Rd 13502
Schoolcraft Rd 13501
Schoolhouse Rd 13502
Schuyler St 13502
Scott St 13501
Seneca St 13502
Servis Pl 13502
Settlers Pass 13502
Seward Ave 13502

Seymour Ave 13501
Seymour Rd 13502
Shaw St 13502
Shelly Pl 13502
Shepherd Pl 13502
Sherman Cir 13501
Sherman Ctr 13501
Sherman Dr 13501
Sherman Ln 13501
Sherman Pl 13502
Sim St 13501
Sinclair Ave 13502
Skylite Way 13502
Skyview Ln 13502
Slaytonbush Ln & Ter 13501
Smith Pl 13501
Smith Hill Rd 13502
Smithport Rd 13501
Sophia Ave 13502
South St 13501
Southgate Dr 13501
Spain Gulf Rd 13502
Spratt Pl 13502
Spring St W 13502
Springate St 13502
Spruce St 13502
Square St 13501
Stage Rd 13502
Stark St 13502
State St 13502
State Route 5 13502
State Route 8 13502
Steele Pl 13501
Steele Hill Rd 13501
Stephens Dr 13502
Sterling Dr 13502
Steuben Park 13501
Steuben Rd E 13502
Steuben St 13501
Stevens St 13502
Storrs Ave 13501
Sulzer Pl 13501
Summerset Way 13502
Summit Pl 13501
Sunlit Ter 13502
Sunny Brook Ln 13502
Sunnyside Dr 13501
Sunset Ave 13502
Sycamore Ln 13502
Sylvan Glen Rd 13501
Symonds Pl 13502
Taber Ln & Rd 13501
Tabor Pl 13502
Taft Ave 13501
Talcott Rd 13502
Tamarack St 13502
Tarbell Ter 13501
Tarlton Dr & Rd 13502
Taylor Ave 13501
The Hills Dr 13501
Theresa Ct 13502
Thieme Pl 13502
Thomas St 13501
Thorn St 13502
Thurston Blvd 13501
Tilden Ave & Ln 13501
Tilton Rd 13501
Tipperary Dr 13502
Tracy St 13502
Trenton Ave & Rd 13502
Tryon Rd 13502
Tumbleweed Dr 13502
Turner St 13501
Turnpike Rd 13502
Ty Pl 13501
Tyler Ter 13501
Union St 13501
Utica Rd 13502
Van Buren St 13501
Van Dyke Rd 13502
Van Ellis Rd 13502
Van Rensselaer Rd 13502
Van Roen Ct & Rd 13502
Van Vorst St 13501
Varick St 13502
Victoria Dr 13501
Vine Ct 13502
Wadsworth Ln E 13501
Wager St 13502
Walcott Ave 13502
Walker Rd 13502
Walker St 13501
Wall St 13501
Walnut St 13502
Ward St 13501
Warren St 13502
Washington St 13502
Wasmer St 13502
Water St 13502
Waterford Ln 13501
Watkins Ave 13502
Watson Pl 13502
Waverly Pl 13502
Weaver Ct & St 13502
Webster Ave 13501
Wells Ave, Dr & Pl 13502
Welsh Bush Rd 13501
Wesley Ave 13502
West St 13501
Westgate Dr 13502
Westminster Pl & Rd 13501
Weston Ave 13501
Wetmore St 13501
Wexford Ln 13502
Wheatley Cir 13501
Wheeler Ave 13502
White Pl 13501
White Birch Rd 13501
W Whitesboro St 13502
Wilbain Dr E & W 13502
Wilber St 13502
Wilcox St 13502
Wiley St 13502
William St 13502
Williamsburg Rd 13502
Willow Dr 13502
Windfall Rd 13502
Windsor Cir 13502
Windsor Ter 13501
Winner Ave 13502
Wisniewicz Rd 13502
Wood Ln 13502
Woodburne Dr 13502
Woodbury Dr 13502
Woodhaven Rd 13502
Woodland Vlg 13501
Woodlawn Ave E 13501
Woodlawn Ave W 13502
Woodlawn Pl 13502
Woodlawn Pl E 13502
Woodlawn Pl W 13502
Woodruff Ter 13502
Woods Rd 13502
Wurz Ave 13502
York St 13502
Young Pl 13501

NUMBERED STREETS

All Street Addresses 13501

VALLEY STREAM NY

General Delivery 11582

POST OFFICE BOXES MAIN OFFICE STATIONS AND BRANCHES

Box No.s
All PO Boxes 11582

NAMED STREETS

Addison Pl 11580
Adeline Pl 11581
Adler Pl 11580
Agnes Ct 11580
Albermarle Ave 11580
Albert Ct & Rd 11580
Alden Ave 11580
Alliance St 11580
Alsop St 11581
Alstead Rd 11580
Ambrose Ave 11580
Amherst Ave 11580
Amherst Rd 11581
Amy Ct 11581
Ann St 11580
Arcadian Ave 11580
E & W Argyle St 11580
Arkansas Dr 11580
Arley Ct 11580
Arlington Ave 11580
Ascan St 11580
Ash Ln 11581
Ash St 11580
Ashley Dr 11580
Astor Pl 11581
Aurelia Ct 11580
Austin St 11580
Avondale St 11581
Balfour St 11580
Ballard Ave 11580
Bank St 11580
Barnes Pl 11580
Barry Dr S & W 11580
Bayview Ave 11581
Bee St 11580
Beech St 11580
Bell Ct & St 11580
Benedict Ave 11580
Benson Pl 11580
Berkley St 11581
Bernard St 11580
Berry St 11580
E & W Beverly Pkwy & Pl 11580
Birch Ln 11581
Birchwood Dr N, S & W 11580
Bismark Ave 11581
Bittersweet Ln 11581
Blossom Row 11580
Boden Ave 11580
Bowe Rd 11580
Bradford Rd 11580
Brentwood Ln 11581
Bretton Rd 11580
Broadway 11580
N Brook Dr 11581
Brook Pl 11580
Brook Rd 11581
Brookfield Rd 11581
Brooklyn Ave 11581
Brookside Dr 11581
Brown St 11580
S Brush Dr 11581
Bucknell Rd 11580
Bunker Ct & Rd 11581
Burlington Pl 11580
Burt Ct 11581
Buscher Ave 11580
Caldwell Ave 11581
Caldwell Rd 11580
Cambridge St 11581
Camdike St 11580
Cameron Ln 11581
Captains Rd 11581
Carl St 11580
Carole Ct 11580
Caroline Ave 11580
Carolyn Ave 11580
E Carpenter St 11580
Carroll Ave 11580
Carstairs Rd 11581
Casper St 11580
Catalpa Ln 11581
Catherine St 11581
Cedar St 11580
Cedarhurst St 11581
Cedarlawn Blvd 11580
N Central Ave 11580
S Central Ave 11580
Central Ct 11580
Central Mall 11581
Charles Ct & St 11580
Cherry Ln & St 11581
Cherry Grove Ct 11581
E & W Chester St 11580
Chestnut Ln & St 11580
Chittendon St 11580
Clair Pl 11580
Clarendon Dr 11580
Clayton Rd 11580
Clearstream Ave 11580
Cleveland St 11580
Cliffside Ave 11581
Clinton Ave 11580
Clovelly Dr 11580
Cloverfield Rd N & S 11581
Cluett Rd 11581
Cochran Pl 11581
Cohill Rd 11580
Colfax Pl 11581
Columbine Ln 11581
Comber St 11580
Copiague St 11580
Cornwell Ave 11580
N & S Corona Ave 11580
N & S Cottage St 11580
Countisbury Ave 11580
Court St 11580
Cranford Ave 11581
Crestview Ave 11581
Crestwood Ln 11581
Cripps Ln 11581
Crowell Pl 11580
Cumberland Pl 11580
Custer St 11580
Dahlia Ln 11581
Dale Pl 11580
Damson Ln 11581
Dana Ave 11580
Daniel St 11580
Danzig Pl 11580
Darewood Ln 11581
Dartmouth St 11581
Dawson Dr 11581
Dean St 11580
Debra Pl 11581
Decker St 11580
Delmonico Pl 11581
Derby St 11581
Dewitt St 11580
Diane Pl 11581
Dianne St 11580
Dogwood Rd 11580
Dolores Dr 11581
Donald Pl 11580
E & W Dover St 11580
Downing Rd 11580
Drake St 11580
Drew St 11581
Dubois Ave 11581
Dubonnet Rd 11581
Dumont Pl 11581
Duston Rd 11581
Dutch Broadway 11580
Eagle Dr 11581
East Ave 11580
East Cir 11581
East Walk 11581
Eastwood Ln 11581
Eden Ct 11581
Edgewood Rd 11580
Edgeworth St 11581
Edlu Ct 11580
Edna Ct & Pl 11581
Edwards Blvd & Pl 11580
Elderberry Ln E 11581
Elgin Rd 11581
Elizabeth St 11580
Ella St 11580
Ellen Pl 11581
Elm St 11580
Elmont Rd 11580
Elmwood St 11581
Emerson Pl 11580
Essex Pl 11580
Ethel St 11580
Eton St 11581
E & W Euclid St 11580
S Everett St 11580
Fairfax St 11580
Fairfield St 11581
Fairmount St 11580
Fairview Ave 11581
E Fairview Ave 11580
W Fairview Ave 11580
Fanwood Ave 11581
Felton Ave 11580
E & W Fenimore St 11580
Fenwood Dr 11580
Fieldstone Ln 11581
Filbert St 11581
Finn St 11580
Fir St 11580
Firefighters Memorial Plz 11580
Firethorne Ln 11581
Flanders Dr 11581
N Fletcher Ave 11580
Flower Rd 11581
Fordham St 11581
Forest Ave & Rd 11581
Foster Ave 11580
Frances Dr 11580
S Frank St 11580
Franklin Ave 11580
N Franklin Ave 11580
S Franklin Ave
20-121 11580
107-123 11582
123-123 11580
131-179 11580
180-299 11581
Franklin Rd 11580
Fraser Pl 11581
Frederick Pl 11581
Fremont Rd 11581
Fritchie Pl 11580
Fulton Pl & St 11580
Furth Rd 11581
G St 11580
Gale Dr 11581
Garden St 11581
Garfield Ave 11580
Garland Ln 11581
E & W Gate 11580
Gates Ave 11580
S Georgia St 11580
Gibson Blvd 11581
Gilbert Pl 11581
Gladys St 11581
Glenridge Ave 11581
Gold St 11580
Goldner Ct 11580
Golf Ct & Dr 11581
Gordon Rd 11581
Gotham St 11581
Grant Dr E 11580
Green St 11580
Green Acres Mall & Rd 11581
Greenlawn Blvd 11580
Greenway Blvd 11580
Greenwood Pl 11581
Gregory St 11580
N & S Grove St 11580
Guenther Ave 11580
Haig Rd 11581
Halyard Rd 11581
Hamilton Ave & Pl 11580
Hancock Pl 11580
Harvard St 11580
Haven Ave 11580
E Hawthorne Ave 11580
W Hawthorne Ave 11580
Hawthorne Ln 11581
Heatherfield Rd 11581
Helen Ct 11581
Henderson Ave 11580
Hendrickson Ave 11580
Henrietta St 11580
N Henry St 11580
Heritage Ct 11581
Hewlett Dr 11581
Hicks St 11580
Higbie St 11580
High St 11581
Highland Rd 11580
Hillcrest Pl 11581
N Hillside Ave 11580
Hoffman St 11580
Holiday Ct 11581
Holland Ct 11580
Hollywood Ave 11581
Home St 11580
Hommell St S 11580
Hook St 11581
Hook Creek Blvd
145-145 11581
1101-13399 11580
Horton Ave & Rd 11581
Howell Rd 11580
Hudson Ave 11580
Hungry Harbor Rd 11581
Hunter Ave 11580
Idell Rd 11580
Industrial Plz 11581
Irene Ct 11580
Iris Ln 11581
Irving Pl & St 11580
Irvington St 11581
Ivanhoe Pl 11580
Ivy Pl 11580
Ixworth Rd 11580
Jackson Rd 11581
Jadwin St 11581
E & W Jamaica Ave 11580
James Ave 11580
Jane Pl 11580
Janet Pl 11581
Jasen Ave 11580
Jasmine Ln 11581
Jasper St S 11580
Jay Ct 11581
Jedwood Pl 11581
Jefferson Ave 11580
Jewel Dr 11581
Judith Ln 11580
June Ct & Pl 11581
Kallas Ct 11580
Kalmia Ln 11581
Karlston Pl 11580
Kearny Dr 11581
Keel Pl 11581
Keller St 11580
Kelly Ct 11580
Kenmore Rd 11581
Kent Rd 11580
Kilmer Ln 11581
Kulenkampf Pl 11581
Lake Dr E 11580
Lamberson St 11580
Lambeth Ln 11580
Laurel Pl 11580
Laurel Hill Dr 11581
Law St 11580
Lawn St 11580
Lawrence Ct 11581
Lee Ave 11580
Lee St 11580
Legion Pl 11581
Leonard Way 11580
Lewis St 11580
Liberty Blvd 11580
Liggett Rd 11580
E & W Lincoln Ave 11580
Linden Rd & St 11580
Littert Ave 11580
Locust St 11581
Lois Pl 11580
Longacre Ave 11581
Longview Ave 11581
Lotus Oval N & S 11581
Louise Pl 11580
Lutz Dr 11580
Lydia St 11580
Lyncrest St 11581
Lynn Dr & Pl 11580
Lynwood Dr 11580
Lyon St 11580
Mallis St 11580
Manor Rd 11580
E & W Maple St 11580
Marc Dr 11581
March Dr 11580
Margaret Dr 11580
Marjorie Ct 11581
Mark Pl 11580
Marlboro Rd 11581
Marlow Rd 11580
Marlowe Rd 11580
Martens Ave 11580
Martin Pl 11580
Mary St 11580
E Maujer St 11580
Mayfield Ln 11581
Mckeon Ave 11580
Meadow Cir 11580
Meadowbrook Ln 11580
Mehrman Ave 11580
E & W Melrose St 11580
E & W Merrick Ct & Rd 11580
Meyer Ave 11580
Michelle Pl 11581
Midvale Ln 11580
W Midway 11581
Midwood St 11580
Milburn Ct & Rd 11580
Mill Rd 11581
Miller Pl 11580
E & W Mineola Ave 11580
Miriam St 11581
Molyneaux Rd 11580
N & S Montague St 11580
Montauk St 11580
N & S Montgomery St 11580
Morgan St 11580
Morris Dr & Pkwy 11580
Motley St 11580
Mulberry Pl 11581
Munro Blvd 11581
Nancy Pl 11581
Nassau Ct 11580
Nelson Rd 11581
E New York Ave 11580
Newbold Ave 11580
Newburg Ave 11581
North Dr 11580
Nottingham Ave 11580
Nutley Pl 11581
Oak Ln & St 11581
Oakleigh Rd 11581
Ocean Ave 11580
Oceanview Ave 11581
Oliver Ave
1-199 11580
800-899 11581
1800-1866 11580
1868-1898 11580
Olsen St 11580
Orchard Pl 11580
Orleans Rd 11581
Ormonde Blvd 11580
E & W Oxford Ct & St 11580
Page Rd 11581
Palmer Pl 11580
Park Ct 11581
E Park Ct 11581
Park Dr 11580
Park Ln 11581
Park Pl 11580
N Parking 11581
Parkwold Dr E 11580
Payan Ave 11580
Pearl St 11581
Peninsula Blvd 11581
Peri Ln 11581
Pershing Ave 11581
Pershing St 11580
Peterhoff St 11580
Pflug Pl 11580
Philip Ct 11580
Pilgrim Pl 11580

Pine Ln 11581
Plainfield Ln 11581
Poplar St 11581
Prague St 11580
Prescott Ct 11581
Prescott Pl 11581
Prescott St 11580
Primrose Ln 11580
Princeton St 11580
Putnam Ave 11580
Putney Rd 11580
Radstock Ave 11580
Railroad Ave 11580
Raisig Ave 11580
Regent St 11580
Remsen Ave 11580
Remson St 11580
Restrans Rd 11581
Rica Pl 11580
Ridge Ave 11581
Ridgewood St 11580
Riva Ct 11581
Riverdale Rd 11581
Roberta St 11580
Robinson Ave 11580
Rockaway Ave
1-350 11580
352-390 11581
392-1200 11581
1202-1298 11581
Rockaway Pkwy 11580
Roeckel Ave 11580
Roland Pl 11581
Ronson Ln 11580
Roosevelt Ave 11581
Rose Ave 11580
Rosedale Rd 11581
Rottkamp St 11580
Rushfield Ln 11581
Rye Ct 11580
S St 11580
Saddle Rock Rd 11581
Saint Johns Ave 11580
E & W Saint Marks Pl 11580
Salem Rd 11580
Salem Gate 11580
Sandalwood Ave 11581
Sanford Ct 11581
Sapir St 11580
Satterie Ave 11580
Sayre Pl 11580
Scott Dr 11580
Scranton Ave 11581
Seaton Pl 11580
Seaton Gate 11580
Shaw Ave 11580
Sherbourne Rd 11580
Sheridan St 11580
Sherwood Ct & St 11581
Shine Pl 11581
Shipley Ave 11580
Sidney Pl 11581
Skidmore Pl 11581
Slabey Ave 11580
Sloan Dr E 11580
Smith St 11580
Sobro Ave 11580
South Dr 11581
Southern Dr 11580
Southern State Pkwy 11580
Southgate Dr & Rd 11581
Sprague Dr 11580
Spring Garden St 11580
Spruce Ln 11581
Stafford Rd 11580
Standish Rd 11580
State St 11580
Station Plz 11580
Stein St 11580
Stephen Pl 11580
Stewart Pl 11581
N Strathmore St 11581
Stringham Ave 11580
Stuart Ave 11580
Stuart Rd 11581
Sumpter Pl 11580
Sunnyfield Ln 11581
E Sunrise Hwy 11581
W Sunrise Hwy 11581
Sunrise Plz 11580
Sunset Rd 11580
Surrey Ln 11580
Susan Ct 11581
Sycamore Rd 11581
Sylvan Pl 11581
Talbot Ave 11581
Teneyck Ave 11580
N & S Terrace Pl 11580
Terry Pl 11580
Theodore Ct 11580
Thompson St 11580
Todd Rd 11580
Trafalgar Sq 11581
Tulip Cir 11580
Turf Rd 11581
Union St 11580
University St 11581
Val Ct 11580
Val Park Ave 11580
Valley Ln E 11581
Valley Greens Dr 11581
E & W Valley Stream Blvd 11580
Van Dam St 11581
Vanderbilt Way 11581
Verona Pl 11580
Victor St 11580
Viola St 11580
Virginia Pl 11581
Virginia St 11580
Vista Rd 11580
N & S Waldinger St 11580
Wallace Ct 11580
Warner Rd 11580
Washington Ave 11580
Waters Pl 11581
Watts Pl 11581
Wavecrest St 11581
Waverly Pl 11580
Webster St 11580
Wells Rd 11580
Wellsboro Rd 11581
West Cir & Walk 11581
Westend Ave 11580
Wheeler Ave W 11580
White St 11580
Whitehall Dr 11581
William St 11580
Willow Ln 11580
Wilson Ct, Rd & St 11581
Wilton Rd 11580
Wingate Rd 11581
Wolf Ave 11580
Wood Ln 11581
Woodcrest St 11581
Woodland Rd 11581
Woodlawn Ave 11581
Woodmere Dr 11581
Wright St 11580
Wyngate Dr E & W 11580
Zemek St 11580

NUMBERED STREETS

1st St 11581
4th St 11581
98-99 11580
5th St 11581
6th St 11581
7th St 11581

VESTAL NY

General Delivery 13850

POST OFFICE BOXES MAIN OFFICE STATIONS AND BRANCHES

Box No.s
All PO Boxes 13851

RURAL ROUTES

05 13850

NAMED STREETS

Academy Dr 13850
Acorn Dr 13850
African Rd 13850
Airborne Ave 13850
Albert Ln 13850
Aldrich Dr 13850
Alice St 13850
Almar Dr 13850
Alpine Dr 13850
Amherst Ave 13850
Anderson Rd 13850
Andrea Dr 13850
Andrews Rd 13850
Annabelle St 13850
Annetta St 13850
Ararat Dr 13850
Arbor Pl 13850
Arch Dr 13850
Arlington Ave 13850
Ash Rd 13850
Audubon Ave 13850
Avelon Dr 13850
Avondale Ct 13850
Ayres Ct 13850
Baker Hill Rd 13850
Bay St 13850
Bayberry Ln 13850
Baylor Dr 13850
Beechwood Ln 13850
Belmont Ave 13850
E Benita Blvd 13850
Birch St 13850
Brentwood Pl 13850
Briarcliff Ave 13850
Briarview Rd 13850
Bridge St 13850
Brook Hill Ave 13850
Brooklea Dr 13850
Brooks Ave 13850
Brown Rd 13850
Bunn Hill Rd 13850
Burd Dr 13850
Burris Rd 13850
Butternut Dr 13850
Cambridge Pl 13850
Cameron Ln 13850
Campus Dr 13850
Carnegie Dr 13850
Carol Ave 13850
Case Dr 13850
Castle Gardens Rd 13850
Castleman Rd 13850
Cedar St 13850
Cedarwood Dr 13850
Chalburn Rd 13850
Charles St 13850
Charleston Ave 13850
Cherry Ln 13850
Chestnut Ln 13850
E, N, S & W Circle Dr 13850
Clark St 13850
Clarkson Dr 13850
Clay St 13850
Clayton Ave 13850
Clifford Dr 13850
Clifton Blvd 13850
Clover Dr 13850
Clubhouse Rd 13850
Cole Pl 13850
Coleman St 13850
Colgate St 13850
Collins Rd 13850
Colonial Ave 13850
Commerce Rd 13850
Commercial Ave 13850
Cornell Ave 13850
Cortland Dr 13850
Costley Rd 13850
Country Club Rd 13850
E Country Gate Pl 13850
Crescent Ln 13850
Crest St 13850
Crumm Rd 13850
Culver Pkwy 13850
Dartmouth Dr 13850
David Ave 13850
Debra Dr 13850
Deerfield Pl 13850
Delano Ave 13850
Dellwood Rd 13850
Denal Way 13850
Diana Ln 13850
Dickinson Dr 13850
Dodd Rd 13850
Donna Dr 13850
Doris Ave 13850
Drexel Dr 13850
Duke Dr 13850
Earl Rd 13850
Eastland Rd 13850
Echo Rd 13850
Edgewood Rd 13850
Edward St 13850
Eldredge Dr 13850
Elizabeth St 13850
Elm St 13850
Elmhaven Dr 13850
Elmsere Pl 13850
Emerson Pl 13850
Emily Ct 13850
Ethel Pl 13850
Evergreen St 13850
Fairview Ave 13850
Ford Rd 13850
Fordham Rd 13850
Forest Ln 13850
Foster Rd 13850
Foxwood Ln 13850
Franklin Pl 13850
Frey Ave 13850
Front St 13850
Fuller Hollow Rd 13850
Galaxy Dr 13850
Garden Ln 13850
Gardner Rd 13850
Gary Dr 13850
Gates Rd 13850
George St 13850
Glenwood Rd 13850
Grand Ave 13850
Greenbriar Ct 13850
Greenlawn Rd 13850
Grippen Hill Rd 13850
Hamilton Pl 13850
Harding Ave 13850
Hartwick Ln 13850
Harvard St 13850
Harwood Dr 13850
Hawthorne St 13850
Hazel Dr 13850
Hellenic Ctr 13850
Hemlock Ln 13850
High Ave 13850
W Hill Rd 13850
Hillside Dr 13850
Hoffman Ave 13850
Hogan Rd 13850
Holbert Ave 13850
Holly Hill Rd 13850
Horan Rd 13850
Horseshoe Ln 13850
Ideal Ter 13850
Imperial Ct 13850
Imperial Woods Dr 13850
Irving Pl 13850
Jane St 13850
Jensen Rd 13850
Jodie Dr 13850
Jones Rd 13850
Juneberry Ct & Rd 13850
Kane Dr 13850
Karin Ave 13850
Katherine Ln 13850
Kathleen Dr 13850
Keenan Dr 13850
Kilmer Rd 13850
Kimble Rd 13850
King St 13850
Knapp Rd 13850
Knight Rd 13850
Lagrange St 13850
Landon Rd 13850
Lauderdale Dr 13850
Lehigh Ave 13850
Leland Ave 13850
Lennox Ave 13850
Leroy Ave 13850
Lewis St 13850
Lincoln Dr 13850
Livingston Pl 13850
Loren Ave 13850
Loretta Ln 13850
Louella St 13850
Lyndale Dr 13850
Lynnhurst Dr 13850
Lynwood Pl 13850
Madison Dr 13850
Magnolia Dr 13850
N Main St 13850
Manchester Rd 13850
Mansfield Rd 13850
Maple St 13850
Maplecrest Dr 13850
Marguerite Ct 13850
Marietta Dr 13850
Marion St 13850
Mark Ct 13850
Marlboro Pl 13850
Marshall Dr E & W 13850
Martha Rd 13850
Mary St 13850
Mason Rd 13850
Meadow Ln 13850
N & S Meadowbrook Ln 13850
Medina St 13850
Meeker Rd 13850
Melbourne St 13850
Mercer Pl 13850
Michael St 13850
Midland Rd 13850
Midvale Rd 13850
Mirador Rd 13850
Moss Rd 13850
Mountain Brook Dr 13850
Murray Hill Rd 13850
Myrtle St 13850
Nelson Rd 13850
Norris Ave 13850
North Rd 13850
Noyes Rd 13850
Oak St 13850
Oak Hollow Rd 13850
Oconnell Rd 13850
Ohara Rd 13850
Old Lane Rd 13850
Old Mill Rd 13850
Orchard St 13850
Overbrook Dr 13850
Owego Rd 13850
Oxford Pl 13850
Park Ave 13850
Parkwood Rd 13850
Pearl St 13850
Pembrooke Ln 13850
Pickwick Dr 13850
Pierce Hill Rd 13850
Pine Meadow Rd 13850
Pinebluff Dr 13850
Pinecrest Rd 13850
Plaza Dr 13850
Pleasant Dr 13850
Plough Rd 13850
Powderhouse Rd 13850
Pratt Dr 13850
Prentice Rd 13850
Princeton Dr 13850
Pumphouse Rd 13850
Purdue Dr 13850
Queensbury Ct 13850
Radcliffe Blvd 13850
Raiford Rd 13850
Rano Blvd
100-116 13850
117-117 13851
118-998 13850
119-899 13850
Rayelene Dr 13850
Red Fox Run 13850
Redwood Ln 13850
Reese Ave 13850
Rhonda Dr 13850
Richards Ave 13850
Ridge Rd 13850
Ridgehaven Dr 13850
Ridgewood Ave 13850
Rita Rd 13850
River Rd 13850
Riverside Rd 13850
Robert St 13850
Robin Ln 13850
Rock Rd 13850
Rockwell Rd 13850
Ross Hill Rd 13850
Royal St 13850
Saddlebrook Dr 13850
Salem Dr 13850
Sally Dr 13850
Sandy Dr 13850
Sarasota Ave 13850
Schubmehl Rd 13850
Sequoia Ln 13850
Seymour Rd 13850
Sheedy Rd 13850
Shippers Rd 13850
Siena Ln 13850
Skyline Dr 13850
Southwood Dr 13850
N Stage Rd 13850
Stamford Dr 13850
State Line Rd 13850
State Route 26 13850
State Route 434 13850
Stewart Rd 13850
Stonehedge Dr 13850
Stratford Dr 13850
Sunrise Pl 13850
Sunset Ave 13850
Susan Ct 13850
Sycamore St 13850
Tamarack Ln 13850
Taylor Dr 13850
Terrace Dr 13850
Tharp St 13850
Torrance Ave 13850
Tracy Creek Rd 13850
Tulane St 13850
Underwood Rd 13850
University Ct 13850
Valley Rd 13850
Vandervort Ave 13850
Verna Dr 13850
Vestal Ln, Pkwy & Rd E & W 13850
Virginia Ave 13850
Vivian Ln 13850
Wakeman Rd 13850
Walnut St 13850
Walter L Rd 13850
Warlente Rd 13850
Warren St 13850
Washington Dr 13850
Way St 13850
Westland Rd 13850
Westview Dr 13850
Wildwood Ln 13850
Willard Ave 13850
William St 13850
Willow St 13850
Winans Ave 13850
Winding Ln 13850
Winston Dr 13850
Woodberry Dr 13850
Woodgate Ln 13850
Woodlawn Dr 13850
Woods Rd 13850
Worrick Pond Rd 13850
Wright Rd 13850

NUMBERED STREETS

All Street Addresses 13850

WATERTOWN NY

General Delivery 13601

POST OFFICE BOXES MAIN OFFICE STATIONS AND BRANCHES

Box No.s
All PO Boxes 13601

NAMED STREETS

Academy Pl & St 13601
Addison St 13601
Admirals Walk 13601
Alexander St 13603
Alexandra Mdws 13601
Alexandria Ave 13601
Algonquin Ave 13601
Allen Dr & Rd 13601
Alpine Rdg 13601
Amherst St 13601
Andrew Dr 13601
Ann St 13601
Annas Way 13601
Anzio Loop 13603
Apple St 13601
Applewood Dr 13603
Arbor Dr 13601
Arcade St 13601
Archer Rd 13601
Arlington St 13601
Arsenal St 13601
Ash St 13601
Aspen Ln & St 13601
Autumn Ridge Ln 13601
Baldwin Cir 13603
Ball Ave 13601
Barben Ave 13601
Bassett St 13603
Bast Rd 13601
Bastogne Loop 13603
Bellew Ave N & S 13601
Bemis Hts 13603
Beutel Rd 13601
Bingham Ave 13601
Binsse St 13601
Birch Ln 13601
Bishop St 13601
Black River Pkwy 13601
Blount Loop 13603
Bonney Rd 13601
Boon St 13601
Boundary St 13601
Bowers Ave 13601
Boyd Pl & St 13601
Bradley St 13601
Brainard St 13601
Branche Rd 13601
Brearley Loop 13603
Breen Ave 13601
Brett St 13601
Bridge St 13601
Broadway Ave E & W 13601
Bronson St 13601
Brook Dr 13601
Brookside Drive Ext 13601
Brown Rd 13601
Buck Terminal 13601
Bugbee Dr 13601
Burchard St 13601
Burdick St 13601
Burlington St 13601
Burns Ave 13601
Butler Loop 13603
Butterfield Ave 13601
Cadwell St 13601

Cady Rd 13601
Cagwin Rd 13601
N California Ave 13601
Camp Ave 13601
Campus Dr 13601
Cardinal Ave 13603
Carr Rd 13601
Casey St 13601
Cayuga Ave 13601
Cedar Ave & St 13601
Central St 13601
Charles St 13601
Cheever Rd 13601
Cherry Tree Dr 13601
Chestnut St 13601
Chippewa St 13603
Chisholm Trl 13601
Church St 13601
Churchill Rd 13601
City Center Dr 13601
Clay St 13601
Cleveland St 13601
Clinton St 13601
Clover St 13601
Coblenz Cir 13603
Coffeen St 13601
Coffeen Street Rd 13601
Coleman Ave 13601
College Hts 13601
Colonial Manor Rd 13601
N Colorado Ave 13601
Columbia St 13601
Combs Rd 13601
Commerce Park Dr E 13601
Concrete Dr 13601
Conde Ln 13601
Conger Ave 13601
Constitution Ave 13603
Contessa Ln 13601
Converse Dr & Ln 13601
Cook Rd 13601
Cooper St 13601
Corey Rd 13601
Cornwell Ln 13601
Cosgrove St 13601
Cottontail Dr 13601
County Route 155 13601
County Route 156 13601
County Route 159 13601
County Route 16 13601
County Route 161 13601
County Route 162 13601
County Route 165 13601
County Route 190 13601
County Route 200 13601
County Route 32 13601
County Route 49 13601
County Route 53 13601
County Route 55 13601
County Route 62 13601
County Route 63 13601
County Route 64 13601
County Route 65 13601
County Route 66 13601
County Route 67 13601
County Route 68 13601
Court St 13601
Cramer Rd 13601
Cranberry Dr 13603
Crane Ln 13601
Creekwood Dr 13601
Cronk Rd 13601
Cross Rd & St 13601
Cullen Dr 13601
Curtis St 13601
Dartmouth St 13601
Davidson St 13601
Dayton Loop 13603
Deer Run Rd 13601
Deerfield Dr 13603
Desoto Dr 13603
Diane Dr 13601
Dickinson Loop 13603
Dimmick St 13601
E & W Division St 13601
Doney Dr 13601
Dorsey St 13601
Duffy Loop 13603
Earl St 13601
East Ave & St 13601
Eastern Blvd 13601
Echo Dr 13601
Eddy St 13601
Edgewood Dr 13603
Edmund St 13601
Edsel St 13603
Eimicke Dr & Pl 13601
Elm St 13601
Elmore Ln 13601
Ely St 13601
Emerson Pl & St 13601
Emmett St 13601
Engine St 13601
Erie St 13601
Eveleigh Rd 13601
Exchange St 13601
Fabco Rd 13601
Factory Sq & St 13601
Faichney Dr 13601
Fairbanks St 13601
Fairmont Ave 13601
Fairview St 13601
Falcon Dr 13603
Farwell St 13601
Fassett St 13601
Ferguson Ave 13601
Few Loop 13603
Fields Rd 13601
Fisher Cir & Rd 13601
Fitzsimmons Loop 13603
Floral Dr 13601
Flower Ave & St 13601
Forest Dr
99101A-99101B 13603
Forsythe Loop 13603
Fox Rd 13601
Fox Ridge Rd 13601
Fralick Rd 13601
Francis St 13601
Franklin St 13601
Freeman Creek Rd 13601
Frontenac St 13601
Gaffney Dr 13601
Gale St 13601
Galtongs St 13601
Gardner Dr 13601
Garrison Dr 13603
Gates St 13603
General Brown Loop 13603
General Grant St 13603
General Patton St 13603
General Pike Loop 13603
Gilbert St 13601
Gill St 13601
Gillette Rd 13601
Gillman Loop 13603
Girard Ave 13601
Glen Ave & St 13601
Goodale St 13601
Gotham Rd & St 13601
Gould Rd 13601
Grace Loop 13603
Graham Rd 13601
Grant St 13601
Gray Wolf Dr 13603
Green St 13601
Greensview Dr 13601
Griffin St 13601
Grove St 13601
Hadcock Rd 13601
Haley St 13601
Hamilton Loop 13603
Hamlin St 13601
Hamp Rd 13601
Hancock St 13601
Haney St 13601
Harewood Ave 13601
Harris Dr 13601
Harrison St 13601
Harvard St 13601
Harvest Blvd 13603
Haven St 13601
Hazelhurst Ave 13601
Heather Acres Dr 13601
Herbrecht Rd 13601
W Hewitt St 13601
Hickory Dr 13603
Hickory Ln 13601
Hickox Rd 13601
High St 13601
Highland Ave 13601
Highland Dr 13603
Hillcrest Ave 13601
Hillside Dr 13601
Hinds Rd 13601
E & W Hoard St 13601
Holcomb St 13601
Holdenbury Dr 13603
Holly St 13601
Howk St 13601
Hubbard Rd 13601
Hudson Ln 13603
Hungerford St 13601
Hunt St 13601
Hunter Loop 13603
Huntington St 13601
Huron St 13601
N & S Hycliff Dr 13601
N & S Indiana Ave 13601
Indigo Way 13603
Industrial Blvd 13601
Iris Ave 13603
Iroquois Ave E & W 13601
Ives St 13601
Ives Street Ext 13601
J B Wise Pl 13601
Jackson Loop 13603
Jacobs Rd 13601
James St 13603
Jefferson St 13601
Jefferson County Dr 13603
Jericho Rd 13601
Jewell Dr 13601
Juniper Way 13603
Katherine St 13601
Katie Ln 13601
Keyes Ave 13601
Kieff Dr 13601
King Loop 13603
Knickerbocker Dr 13601
Knowlesville Rd 13601
Knowlton Ave 13601
Kristina Park 13601
La Martina Dr 13601
Lachenauer Dr 13601
Lafave Rd 13601
Lane Rd 13601
Langdon Dr 13603
Lansing St 13601
Larlera Loop 13603
Lawler Dr 13601
Lawrence St 13601
Lee St 13601
Leon Ave 13601
Leray Dr 13603
Leray St 13601
Lewis Ave 13603
N Lewis Ave
8401A-8401E 13603
8403A-8403D 13603
8406A-8406E 13603
8407A-8407D 13603
8408A-8408E 13603
8409A-8409E 13603
8411A-8411D 13603
8412A-8412E 13603
8413A-8413D 13603
8414A-8414D 13603
8415A-8415E 13603
8417A-8417D 13603
8419A-8419D 13603
8420A-8420E 13603
8421A-8421D 13603
8423A-8423D 13603
8425A-8425D 13603
8427A-8427E 13603
8428A-8428D 13603
8429A-8429C 13603
8430A-8430E 13603
8431A-8431E 13603
8432A-8432D 13603
8433A-8433C 13603
8434A-8434E 13603
8435A-8435E 13603
8429D-8433D 13603
8405A-8405E 13603
8491-8499 13603
S Lewis Ave
8201A-8201B 13603
8203A-8203B 13603
8205A-8205B 13603
8207A-8207B 13603
8209A-8209B 13603
8211A-8211E 13603
8212A-8212B 13603
8213A-8213B 13603
8214A-8214D 13603
8215A-8215E 13603
8217A-8217E 13603
8218A-8218B 13603
8220A-8220B 13603
8222A-8222B 13603
8224A-8224B 13603
8226A-8226B 13603
8228A-8228B 13603
8230A-8230B 13603
8232A-8232B 13603
8234A-8234B 13603
8236A-8236B 13603
Lewis St 13601
Liberty Ave 13601
Lillian St 13601
Lincoln St 13601
Little Tree Dr 13601
Littlefield Dr 13601
Livingston Way 13603
Lloyd Rd 13601
Logan St 13601
Loomus Dr 13601
E & W Lynde St 13601
Madison Ave 13601
Madison Barracks St 13603
Main Ave 13601
Main St
6161A-6161B 13603
6305A-6305B 13603
6307A-6307B 13603
2-598 13601
600-736 13601
738-898 13601
6149-6306 13603
6308-8898 13603
E Main St 13601
W Main St 13601
Maple Ave 13601
Maple View Pl 13603
Marble St 13601
Marie Ln 13601
Marra Dr 13601
Martin Rd & St 13601
Massey St 13601
Maywood Ter 13601
Mcclelland St 13601
Mchenry Loop 13603
Meade St 13601
N & S Meadow Ave, Ln & St 13601
Meadow Wood Dr 13603
Mechanic St 13601
Meriline Ave 13601
Micek Rd 13601
N Michigan Ave & St 13601
Middle Rd 13601
Middle Lewis Ave 13603
Mifflin Loop 13603
Military Rd 13601
Mill St 13601
Miller Rd 13601
Moffett St 13601
Mohawk St 13601
Monarch Dr 13603
Monroe Ave 13601
Moore Ave 13601
Morgan St 13603
Morrison Ave & St 13601
Morse Ln 13601
Moulton St 13601
Mountain View Dr 13603
Mulberry Ave 13603
W Mullin St 13601
Mundy St 13601
Murrock Cir & Rd 13601
Mustard Rd 13601
Myrtle Ave 13601
Nancy Rd 13603
Nellis St 13601
New York Ave 13601
Newell St 13601
Newman Dr 13601
North St 13601
Northern Blvd 13603
Oak St 13601
Oak Pointe Ln 13601
Ohio St 13601
Old Rices Rd 13601
Old Rome Rd 13601
Olive St 13601
Olmstead Dr 13601
Omaha St 13603
Ontario Dr N & S 13601
Orchard Dr 13603
Osprey Loop 13603
Overlook Dr 13601
Overlook Pl 13603
Overton Dr 13601
Packard Dr 13603
Paddock Arc & St 13601
Palmer St 13601
Pamelia Ave 13601
Park Ave, Dr, Pl & St E & W 13601
Parker Rd & St 13601
Patricia Dr 13601
Pawling St 13601
N & S Pearl Ave & St 13601
Perch Lake Rd 13601
Pheasant Run 13601
Phelps St 13601
Pine St 13601
Pinehurst Dr 13603
Pinkney Dr 13603
Pioneer Plaza Dr 13601
Plaza Dr 13601
N & S Pleasant St 13601
Plum Ave 13601
Polk St 13601
Poplar St 13601
Portage St 13601
Porter Rd 13601
Pratt St 13601
W Prospect St 13601
Public Sq 13601
Rail Dr 13601
Railroad St 13601
Rainsford St 13601
Rambler Way 13603
Rand Dr 13601
Reasoner Rd 13601
Reasoner Road Ext 13601
Redwood Ln 13601
Reed Rd 13601
Reeves St 13601
Remington St 13601
Rexford Pl 13601
Reylea St 13601
Rich Rd 13601
Richards Dr 13601
Ridge Rd 13601
Ridgeview Rd 13601
Riggs Ave 13601
Riverbend Dr E & W 13601
Riverglade Dr 13601
Rosedale St 13601
N & S Rutland Pl & St 13601
Saint Mary St 13601
Salerno Rd 13603
Salina St 13601
Salisbury St 13601
Salmon Run Mall Loop & Rd 13601
Sams Dr 13601
Sand St 13601
Sandpiper Dr 13603
Sandy Creek Rd 13603
Sandy Creek Valley Rd 13601
Saratoga Rd 13603
Sawdy Rd 13601
Schley Dr 13601
Scio St 13601
Scotch Pine Dr 13603
Seneca St 13601
Seward St 13601
Seymour St 13601
Shepard St 13601
Sheridan St 13601
Sherman St 13601
Sill St 13601
Slate Rd 13601
Slater Rd 13601
Smallwood Ct 13603
Smith St 13601
Snell St 13601
Spencer Rd 13601
Spindle Ln 13601
Spraight Loop 13603
Spring Ave 13601
Spring Valley Dr 13601
Spruce Cres 13601
St Vith Way 13603
Starbuck Ave 13601
State Pl & St 13601
State Route 12 13601
State Route 126 13601
State Route 12f 13601
State Route 180 13601
State Route 232 13601
State Route 283 13601
State Route 3 13601
State Route 342 13601
State Route 37 13601
Sterling Pl & St 13601
Stone Cir & St 13601
Stuart St 13601
Summer St 13601
Summit Dr 13601
Sunset Rdg 13601
Superior St 13601
Swan Rd & St 13601
Sweet St 13601
Switzer Rd 13601
Sycamore Dr 13603
Sycamore Way 13601
Tall Timber Trl 13601
Teal Dr 13601
Temple St 13601
W Ten Eyck St 13601
Thompson Blvd, Park & St 13601
Tilden St 13601
Timberline Dr 13603
Towne Center Dr 13601
Trillium Ave 13603
Twin Oaks Dr 13601
Union St 13601
Us Route 11 13601
Utah St 13603
Vaadi Rd 13601
Van Allen Rd N & S 13601
Vanduzee St 13601
Victory Ln 13601
Vincent Ln 13603
Waite Ave 13601
Walker Ave 13601
Waltham St 13601
Ward St 13601
Warren St 13601
Washington Loop 13603
Water St 13601
Waterman Dr & Rd 13601
Waterview Pl 13603
Wayside Dr 13601
Wealtha Ave 13601
Weaver Rd 13601
Weldon Dr 13601
West St 13601
Westbury Ct 13603
Westminster Rd 13601
White Rd 13601
Whitesville Rd 13601
Wight Dr 13601
Wildwood Dr 13603
William St 13601
William T Field Dr 13601
Williamson Loop 13603
Willow Dr 13603
Willow St 13601
Willowbrook Dr 13601
Winslow St 13601
Winterhaven Dr 13603
Winthrop St 13601
Woodard Rd 13601
Woodberry Ln 13603
Woodcrest Ln 13603
Woodland Dr
11720A-11720B 13603
Woodlawn Ave 13601
W Woodruff St 13601
Woodruff Settlement Rd 13601
Woodside Dr 13601
Wright Dr 13601
Wyoming Ave 13601
York St 13603
Youngs Rd 13601

WEST BABYLON NY

General Delivery 11704

POST OFFICE BOXES MAIN OFFICE STATIONS AND BRANCHES

Box No.s
1001 - 1960 11704
5001 - 5638 11707
9003 - 9996 11704

NAMED STREETS

All Street Addresses 11704

NUMBERED STREETS

All Street Addresses 11704

WEST POINT NY

General Delivery 10996

POST OFFICE BOXES MAIN OFFICE STATIONS AND BRANCHES

Box No.s
1 - 5000 10997
1 - 8000 10996
9998 - 9998 10997

NAMED STREETS

All Street Addresses 10996

WHITE PLAINS NY

General Delivery 10602

POST OFFICE BOXES MAIN OFFICE STATIONS AND BRANCHES

Box No.s
1 - 1310 10602

1 - 640 10603
1 - 356 10605
70 - 70 10610
800 - 905 10603
1401 - 8420 10602
9070 - 9997 10610
9998 - 9998 10602

NAMED STREETS

Abbey Dr 10604
Abbeyville Ln 10607
Adams Pl 10603
Adrienne Pl 10605
Aiken Way 10607
Alan Pl 10607
Albemarle Rd 10605
Albro Ln 10603
Alex Dr 10605
Alexander Ave 10606
Allan Dr 10605
Allegra Ct 10603
Amanda Ct 10607
Amherst Pl 10601
Amity Ct 10603
Amy Pl 10605
Antony Rd 10605
Appletree Close 10603
Aqueduct Rd 10606
Arborwood Ln 10603
Archer Ave 10603
Arthur Ln 10603
Audrey Ln 10605
Augusta Pl 10603
Augustine Rd 10603
Avondale Rd 10605
Balmoral Cres & Ln 10607
Bank St 10606
Barker Ave 10601
Barksdale Rd 10607
Barnwell Dr 10607
Barton Rd 10605
Battle Ave 10606
Baylor Cir 10605
Bayne Pl 10605
Beal Pl 10603
Beaufort St 10607
Beech St 10603
Beech St W 10604
Belding Ave 10603
Bellwood Rd 10603
Belmont St 10605
Belway Pl 10601
Benedict Ave 10603
Benedict Rd 10607
Beverly Rd 10605
Biltom Rd 10607
Birch St 10604
Birch St W 10607
Birchwood Rd 10605
Bird Pl 10605
Blackthorn Ln 10606
Bloomingdale Rd 10605
Bogert Ave 10606
Bolton Ave 10605
Bond St 10603
Bonnie Briar Rd 10607
Borneman Pl 10606
Bowbell Rd 10607
Brad Ln 10605
Bradford Ave 10603
Bradley Ave 10607
Brady Pl 10606
Branch Brook Rd 10605
Brandywine Dr 10605
Brentwood Ave 10605
Briga Ln 10605
Broad Pkwy 10601
Broad St 10603
Broadview Ave 10607
N Broadway
1-43 10601
44-58 10603
45-59 10601
60-1299 10603
S Broadway
1-96 10601
98-102 10601
104-199 10605
153-155-153-155 10605
7-11-7-11 10601
Brockway Pl 10601
Brook Hills Cir 10605
Brookdale Ave 10603
Bryant Ave & Cres 10605
Buckout Rd 10604
Buena Vista Dr 10603
Burling Ave 10605
Bursley Pl 10605
Byron Ave
1-5 10605
6-99 10606
Calvin Ct 10603
Cambridge Ave 10605
Camelot Ct 10603
Canfield Ave 10601
Canterbury Rd 10607
Carhart Ave 10605
Carlton St 10607
Carriage Way 10605
Carriage Hill Rd 10604
Carrigan Ave 10605
Castle Brooke Rd 10604
Castle Heights Pl 10603
Cedarwood Rd 10605
Central Ave 10606
Charles St 10606
Charlotte St 10606
Chase Ave 10606
Chatham Pl 10605
Chatterton Ave & Pkwy 10606
S Chelsea Rd 10603
Chesley Rd 10605
Chester Ave 10601
Chester Pl 10607
Chestnut Hill Ave 10606
Church Ct 10603
Church St
1-103 10601
1-99 10603
104-104 10603
105-187 10601
106-188 10601
189-399 10603
City Pl 10601
Clarion Dr 10603
Classic Ct 10603
Cleveland St 10606
Clifton Ln 10605
Clinton St 10605
Clove Rd 10603
Cloverdale Ave 10603
Cloverwood Rd 10605
Club Pointe Dr 10605
Cobb Ave 10606
Cobblefield Ln & Rd 10605
Colden Ave 10606
Collyer Pl 10605
Colonial Rd 10605
Colorado Ave 10607
Commerce St 10605
Concord Ave 10606
Coolidge Ave 10606
Cooper Rd 10603
Copper Beech Cir 10605
Coralyn Ave 10605
Cottage Pl 10601
Cottonwood Ln 10605
Country Club Dr 10607
County Center Rd
1-7 10607
9-99 10607
101-197 10603
199-399 10603
Court St 10601
Crane Ave 10603
Craven Ln 10605
Crescent Pl 10606
Crest Dr 10607
Cromwell Pl 10601
Cross St 10606
Cummings Ave N 10603
Cushman Rd 10606
Custis Ave 10603
Dale St 10605
Daniels Pl 10604
Darby Ct 10605
Dartmouth Ter 10607
David Ter 10603
Davis Ave
1-26 10601
27-27 10605
29-299 10605
Dekalb Ave 10605
Dellwood Rd 10605
Denim Pl 10603
Dennison St 10606
Depot Plz 10606
Devonshire Dr 10605
Dobbs Ferry Rd 10607
Don Ln 10607
Downing Dr E & W 10607
Doyer Ave 10605
Dr Martin Luther King Blvd 10601
Drake Ln 10607
Dreier Ln 10605
Drisler Ave 10607
Duell Rd 10603
Dunderave Rd 10603
Dunlap Way 10603
Dupont Ave 10605
Durham Rd
4-6 10607
8-52 10607
10-30 10605
32-32 10605
54-54 10607
61-67 10607
70-72 10607
Dusenbury Pl 10601
Eagle Ct 10605
Earlwoode Dr 10606
Eastdale Rd 10605
Easthaven Ln 10605
Easton Ave 10605
Eastview Ave 10601
Eden Ct 10603
Edgepark Rd 10603
Edgewold Rd 10607
Edgewood St 10605
Edna St 10606
Eldorado Ct 10603
Ellis Dr 10605
Elm St 10603
Elmwood Rd 10605
Emmalon Ave & Cir 10603
Ethelridge Rd 10605
Ethelton Rd 10603
Evarts Ave 10607
Fair St 10607
Fairfield St 10606
Fairview Ave 10603
Fairway Dr 10605
Fernwood Rd 10605
Ferris Ave
1-35 10601
36-299 10603
264-264 10601
Festival Ct 10603
Fillmore Pl 10606
Finmor Dr 10607
Fisher Ave
60-99 10606
100-100 10602
101-399 10606
102-398 10606
Fisher Ct 10601
Fisher Ln 10603
Florence Ave 10607
Francine Ct 10607
Franklin Ave 10601
Freedom Rd S 10603
Friendship Ct 10603
Fulton St 10606
Gabriel Ct 10605
Gala Ct 10603
Garden St 10607
Gedney Cir, Ter & Way 10605
Gedney Esplanade 10605
Gedney Park Dr 10605
Gene Pl 10605
General Heath Ave 10603
Gentreld Rd 10603
Geyser Pl 10607
Gibson Ave 10607
Glenbrooke Dr 10605
Glendon Cir 10605
Glenn St 10603
Golden Pond Rd 10604
Goodwin Ave 10607
Granada Cres 10603
Grand St 10601
W Grand St 10607
Grandview Ave 10605
Grant Ave 10603
Grant Way 10607
Grassland Rd 10603
Greenacres Ave 10606
Greenacres Ln 10607
Greenacres Way 10606
Greenburgh Commons Way 10603
Greene Ln 10605
Greenridge Ave 10605
Greenvale Cir 10607
Greenwood Ln 10607
Griffin Pl 10603
Grove Rd 10603
Haarlem Ave 10603
Hadden Ave 10601
Hale Ave
1-63 10601
65-67 10601
69-99 10601
100-299 10605
Hall Ave
1-7 10603
8-1700 10604
Hamilton Ave 10601
N Hampton Dr 10603
Hampton Ter 10607
Harding Ave 10606
Harmon St 10606
Harrison Pl 10603
Hartford Ln 10603
Hartsdale Ave
1-99 10605
100-299 10606
W Hartsdale Rd 10607
Harvard Ct 10605
Harwood Ave 10603
Hathaway Ln 10605
Haviland Ln 10605
Hawley St 10606
Hawthorne St 10603
Hazelton Dr 10605
Heather Ln 10605
Heatherbloom Rd 10605
Heirloom Ct 10603
Helena Ave 10605
Hemlock Cir 10605
Herbert Ave 10606
Hewitt Ave 10605
Highland Ave 10606
Highview Pl 10604
Hillair Cir & Ct 10605
Hillandale Ave E 10603
Hillcrest Ave 10607
Hilldale Pl 10604
Hillside Ave
11-26 10601
100-652 10603
177-177 10607
179-799 10603
Hillside Ave S 10607
Hillside Ter 10601
Hillside Close 10603
Hilltop Ln 10607
Holbrooke Rd 10605
Holland Ave 10603
Home St 10606
Homeside Ln 10605
Horton Mill Rd 10604
Hotel Dr 10605
Howard Ave 10606
Hubbard Dr 10605
Hunt Pl 10606
Hunter Rd 10603
Hunting Ridge Rd 10605
Idlewood Rd 10605
Independence St 10606
Indian Trl 10603
Ingleside Ln 10605
Intervale Ave 10603
Intervale St 10606
Inverness Ct 10605
Irving Pl 10606
Ivy Pl 10605
Jackson Ave 10606
Jackson Pl 10603
Jared Dr 10605
Jay Ct 10607
Jefferson Ave 10606
Jefferson Pl 10603
Jeffrey Way 10607
Jennings Rd 10605
Joan Ave 10607
Jones Pl 10606
June Ct 10605
Juniper Hill Rd 10607
Kass Rd 10605
Kathwood Rd 10607
Kenneth Rd 10605
N Kensico Ave
1-59 10603
60-299 10604
S Kensico Ave 10601
Kensico Knoll Pl 10603
Kent Rd 10603
Kirby Ter 10603
Knollwood Rd
75-97 10607
99-305 10607
306-1199 10603
Lafayette Ave 10603
Lafayette St 10606
N Lake Cir 10605
Lake St
1-7 10603
9-48 10603
49-89 10604
50-90 10603
91-148 10604
150-198 10604
Lakeview Dr N 10603
Lambert Rd 10605
Lana Cir 10603
Landers Rd 10607
Landers Manor Rd 10607
Landmark Ct 10603
Larindis Ave 10605
Lark Ave 10607
Lark Pl 10605
Laurel Rd 10605
Lawrence Ave, Ct & Dr 10603
Leather Stocking Ln 10603
Lee Ave 10606
Legacy Cir 10603
Legend Cir 10603
Leir Ct 10605
Leith Pl 10605
Lenox Ave 10603
Lenroc Dr 10607
Lester Pl 10606
N Lexington Ave 10601
S Lexington Ave
182A-182B 10606
2-598 10606
77-233 10601
235-599 10606
Liberty St 10606
Limerick Ct 10603
Lincoln Ave 10606
Lincoln Pl 10603
Linda Ave 10605
Linwood Pl 10606
Literiew Rd 10607
Little Ln 10605
Little John Pl 10605
Livingston Ave 10605
Locust Ave 10605
Longdale Ave 10607
Longview Ave
1-12 10601
13-199 10605
Lynton Pl 10606
Lyon Pl 10601
Macy Ave 10605
Madison Pl 10603
Main St
50-59 10606
81-97 10601
99-446 10601
448-480 10601
Mamaroneck Ave
1-215 10601
216-216 10605
218-1999 10605
Manhattan Ave
1-61 10607
62-62 10603
63-63 10607
64-199 10603
Manitou Trl 10603
Manor Ave 10605
Manor Dr 10603
N Manor Dr 10603
S Manor Dr 10603
Manor Pl 10605
Mansfield Rd 10605
Maple Ave
1-49 10605
2-48 10601
50-199 10601
200-299 10606
E Maple Ave 10601
Maple St 10603
Maplemoor Ln 10605
Marlette Pl 10605
Martha Ln 10607
Martine Ave
1-49 10606
51-97 10601
99-191 10601
170-170 10602
192-398 10601
193-299 10601
Maryton Rd 10603
Mason St 10607
Mayfair Way 10603
Mcbride Ave 10603
Mcdougal Dr 10603
Mcguiness Ln 10605
Mckinley Ave 10606
Mclean Ave 10607
Meadow Way 10605
Meadowbrook Rd 10605
Meda Pl 10605
Merritt Ave 10606
Merritt Ave W 10607
Midchester Ave 10606
Middale Rd 10605
Middle Rd 10605
Midland Ave 10606
Midway Rd 10607
Miles Ave
1-69 10605
70-199 10606
Mileview Ave 10606
Milford Dr 10606
Milford Close 10606
Miller Ter 10607
Minerva Pl 10601
Mistanta Ave 10601
Mitchell Pl 10601
Mitchie Dr 10606
Mohawk Trl 10603
Monroe Dr 10605
Monroe Pl 10603
Montana Pl 10607
Montross St 10603
Morgan Pl 10605
Morningside Ave & Pl 10603
Mortimer Ter 10607
Morton Pl 10603
Moss Run 10605
Mount Morris Ave 10604
Mulberry Ln 10605
Murchison Pl 10605
Myrtle St 10606
Nethermont Ave 10603
New St 10607
New York Ave S 10606
Newcomb Pl 10606
Nikki Dr 10605
Nina Ln 10605
Normandy Rd 10603
North Rd 10603
North St 10605
Northdale Rd 10605
Northview Pl 10603
Nosband Ave 10605
Nutgrove St 10606
Oak St
1-34 10603
35-37 10607
36-38 10603
39-99 10607
Oak St N 10603
Oakley Ave 10601
Oakley Rd 10606
Oakridge Rd 10607
Oakwood Ave 10605
Odell Ave 10606
Ogden Ave 10605
Old Rd 10607
Old Farm Cir 10605
Old Kensico Rd
210-313 10607
314-799 10603
Old Knollwood Rd 10607
Old Mamaroneck Rd 10605
Old Tarrytown Rd 10603
Oliver Ave 10603
Orawaupum St 10606
Orchard Dr 10603
Orchard Pkwy 10606
Orchard Pl 10603
Orchard St
1-9 10607
31-35 10603
100-299 10604
Osborne St 10606
Otis Ave 10603
Ovation Ct 10603
Overlook Ct 10603
Overlook Rd 10605
Overlook Rd N 10603
Oxford Rd 10605
Paddock Rd 10605
Palisade Ave 10607
Palmer Ave 10603
Park Ave 10603
Park Ave W 10607
Park Cir 10603
Park Rd 10606
Park Ter 10603
Park Ridge Ln 10603
Parkview Ct 10603
Parkway Homes Rd 10603
Partridge Rd 10605
Patricia Ln 10605
Paulding St 10601
Pebble Beach Ln 10605
Pepperidge Ln 10605
Perry Ave 10603
Persimmon Ln 10605
Pilgrim Rd 10605
Pin Oak Ln 10606
Pinebrook Dr 10605
Pineridge Rd 10603
Pinewood Cir 10603
Pinewood Dr 10603
Pinewood Rd 10605
Piper Ct 10607
Platt Pl 10603
Pleasant Ave 10605

Street	ZIP
Plymouth Pl	10605
Plymouth Rd	10603
Polk Pl	10603
Pomander Dr	10607
Pondcrest Ln	10607
Pondside Dr	10607
Poplar St	10607
E Post Rd	10601
W Post Rd	10606
Prescott Ave	
1-32	10606
33-199	10605
Preserve Ct	10607
Primrose Ave W	10607
Primrose Ct	10603
Primrose St	10606
Proakers Ave	10606
Prospect Ave	10607
W Prospect Ave	10607
Prospect St	
1-46	10605
47-199	10606
Prospect St W	10607
Purdy Ave	10605
Putnam Ave	10606
Quarropas St	10601
Quinby Ave	10606
Quincy Ln	10605
Quintard Pl	10607
Railside Ave	10605
Ralph Ave	10606
Randolph Rd	10607
Rathbun Ave	10606
Redwood Rd	10605
Renaissance Sq	10601
Reservoir Rd	10603
Reunion Rd	10603
Reverie Ct	10603
Reynal Rd	10605
Ria Dr	10605
Richards St	10603
Richbell Rd	10605
Ridgeview Ave	10606
Ridgeway Cir	10605
Rita Ln	10607
Ritchey Pl	10605
Riverdale Ave	10607
Robert Ln	10607
Roberta Pl	10603
Robertson Ave	10606
Robinhood Rd	10605
Rock Cliff Pl	10603
Rockingchair Rd	10607
Rockledge Ave	10601
Rockledge Rd	10603
Roger Pl	10605
Roland Ave	10603
Roland Dr	10605
Rolling Ridge Rd	10605
Rollingfield Rd	10605
Romar Ave	10605
Roosevelt St	10606
Rosa Dr	10607
Rose St	10605
Rosedale Ave	10605
Rosemont Blvd	10607
Rosewood Rd	10605
Ross St	10603
Russell St	
1-130	10606
131-131	10607
132-132	10606
133-199	10607
Rutherford Ave	10605
Sage Ct	10605
Saint Marys Pl	10603
Salem Pl	10605
Salem Rd	10603
Sammis Ln	10605
Saratoga Rd	10607
Saw Mill River Rd	10607
Saxon Woods Rd	10605
Saxon Woods Pk Dr	10605
School St	10606
Schuyler Pl	10605
Sciortino Pl	10607
Scott Cir	10606
Seneca Ave	10603
Seton Way	10605
Seymour Pl	10605
Shapham Pl	10605
Shatterhand Close	10603
Sherill Ct	10605
Sherman Ave	
1-30	10605
45-199	10607
Shirley Ln	10607
Sky Meadow Pl	10607
Smallwood Pl	10603
Smith Ave	10605
Sonny Trl	10605
Soundview Ave & Cir	10606
South Rd	10603
Southdale Rd	10605
Southminster Dr	10604
Southwood Pl	10607
Sparrow Cir	10605
Springdale Ave	10604
Spruce Dr	10605
Spruce Rdg	10604
Stadium Rd	10607
Stafford Pl	10604
Stanley Rd	10605
Sterling Ave	10606
Stevens St	10606
Stewart Pl	10603
Stone Ave	10603
Stonegate Ct	10605
Stoneham Pl	10607
Stonewall Cir	10607
Stratford Ave	10605
Stratford Rd	10603
Stuart Way	10607
Summit Ave	10606
Summit St	10607
Sunset Dr	10604
Surrey Way	10607
Surrey Close	10607
Susan Ct	10605
Sybil St	10606
Sycamore Ln	10605
Sylvan Rd	10605
Tarryhill Way	10603
Tarrytown Rd	10607
Teillaud St	10607
Teramar Way	
1-15	10607
1-1	10605
2-16	10607
2-4	10605
5-6	10605
Terrace Ave	10603
Terrace St	10607
Thelma Pl	10605
Thomas Way	10607
Thompson Ave	10603
Thorncliffe Ln	10603
Tibbits Ave	10606
Tomahawk Dr	10603
Tompkins Ave	10603
Topland Rd	10605
Totem Pole Pl	10603
Tournament Dr	10605
Tradition Ct	10603
Traverse St	10606
Trenton Ave	10606
Twin Pond Ln	10607
Tyler Pl	10603
Valhalla Ave & Pl	10603
Valimar Blvd	10603
Van Buren Pl	10603
Van Wart Ave	10606
Vermont Ave	10606
Victory Ct	10603
View St	10607
Vintage Ct	10603
Virginia Rd	10603
Waldo Ave	10606
Wallace Pl	10606
Waller Ave	
1-43	10601
44-198	10605
Walnut Ct	10605
Walnut St	10607
Walton Ave	10606
Walworth Ave & Ter	10606
Wardman St	10603
Warren Ave	
1-137	10607
138-299	10603
Warren St	10603
Washington Ave	10603
Water St	10601
Wayne Ave	10606
Wayne Way	10607
Wayside Dr	10607
Wellford Rd	10607
Wellington Ter	10607
West St	10605
Westchester Ave	
2-6	10601
8-203	10601
1000-1030	10610
Westchester View Ln	10607
Westfield Cir, Ln & Rd	10605
Westhaven Ln	10605
Westhelp Dr	10603
Westminster Dr	10604
Westmoreland Ave	10606
Westview Ave	10603
Westway	10605
White House Rd	10607
Whitewood Rd	
1-99	10603
1-99	10605
Whitney St	10606
Whittington Rd	10607
William St	10601
Willowbrook Rd	10605
Willows Ln	10605
Wilmont Ave	10605
Wilshire Dr	10605
Wilson St	10606
Wimbledon Ct	10607
Winding Ridge Rd	10603
Windom St	10607
Windsor Ter	10601
Windward Ave	10605
Winnetou Rd	10603
Winslow Rd	10606
Winthrop Ave	10606
Woodbrook Rd	10605
Woodhampton Dr	10603
Woodhollow Rd	10605
Woodland Pl	10606
Woodland Hills Rd	10603
Woodlands Ave & Ln	10607
Woodrow Pl	10606
Woods Way	10605
Worthington Rd & Ter	10607
Wyanoke St	10606
Wyndham Close	10605
Wyndover Rd	10603
Wyndover Woods Ln	10603
Wyoming Ave	10607
Yellowstone Ave	10607
York St	10607
Yosemite Ave	10607

NUMBERED STREETS

Street	ZIP
All Street Addresses	10606

YONKERS NY

Street	ZIP
General Delivery	10702

POST OFFICE BOXES MAIN OFFICE STATIONS AND BRANCHES

Box No.s	ZIP
1 - 730	10702
1 - 360	10705
1 - 460	10710
1 - 1308	10704
1 - 1320	10703
401 - 680	10705
501 - 778	10710
801 - 830	10705
805 - 1498	10702
1401 - 1890	10704
2000 - 3333	10703
7000 - 7050	10710
9998 - 9998	10702

NAMED STREETS

Street	ZIP
Abbey Pl	10701
Abbott St	10703
Abeel St	10705
Abner Pl	10704
Adams Pl	10703
Agar St	10701
Agawam N & S	10704
Alan B Shepard Jr Pl	10705
Albemarle Pl	10701
Alden Ave	10710
Alder St	
1-80	10701
81-199	10705
Alexander Ave	10704
Alexander Pl	10704
Alexander St	10701
Algonquin Rd	10710
Alida St	10704
Allen Ave N	10704
Allendale Rd	10710
Alpine Rd	10710
Alta Ave	10705
Alta Pl	10710
Alta Vista Dr	10710
Altamont Pl	10704
Altonwood Pl	10710
Amackassin Ter	10703
Amberson Ave	10705
Ambrose Pl	10701
Amherst Dr	10710
Andover Rd	10710
Annmarie Pl	10703
Annsville Trl	10703
Aqueduct Ave	10704
Aqueduct Pl	10701
Arbor St	10701
Arcadia Pl	10710
Archer Ave	10710
Archer St	10701
Arden Pl	10701
Argyle Ter	10701
Arlington St	10710
Armonk Ave	10710
Armstrong Ave	10701
Arthur Pl & St	10701
Ascot Rd	10710
Ash St	10701
Ashburton Ave & Pl	10701
Ashford Pl	10701
Ashton Rd	10705
Astor Pl	10705
Austin Ave	10710
Autumn Cir	10703
Avon Pl	10701
Avondale Rd	10710
Axminster St	10701
Ayton Ln	10710
Babcock Pl	10701
Bacon Pl	10710
Bainbridge Ct	10710
Bainton St	10704
Bajart Pl	10705
Baldwin Pl	10701
Balint Dr	10710
Ball Ave	10701
Barlow St	10704
Barney St	10710
Barton Rd	10701
Bashford St	10701
Bayley Ave	10705
Beacon St	10701
Beaumont Cir	10710
Bedford Pl	10710
Beech St	10701
Beech Ter	10705
Beechwood Ter	10705
Belden Ave	10704
Belknap Ave	10710
Bell Pl	10701
Bellevue Ave & Pl	10703
Belmont Ave	10704
Belmont Pl	10701
Belmont Ter	10703
Belvedere Dr	10705
Bennett Ave	10701
Berkeley Ave	10705
Berkshire Rd	10710
Berleari Ave	10701
Beverly Rd	10710
Biltmore Ave	10710
Birch Rd	10705
Bishop Wm J Walls Pl	10701
Blackford Ave	10704
Bobolink Pl & Rd	10701
Bolmer Ave	10703
Bonnie Briar Rd	10710
Boone St	10704
Borcher Ave	10704
Boulder Pl	10705
Boxwood Rd	10710
Bradford Blvd	10710
Braintree Ln	10710
Brandon Rd	10704
Brandt Ter	10710
Breglia St	10704
Bretton Rd	10710
Brewster Ave	10701
Briar Hill Dr	10710
Bridge St	10705
Briggs Ave	10701
Bright Pl	10705
Bristol Pl	10710
N Broadway	10701
S Broadway	
434A-434B	10705
S Broadway	
1-187	10701
188-192	10705
189-193	10701
194-199	10705
200-200	10701
201-699	10705
202-698	10705
Bronx Ter	10704
Bronx River Rd	10704
Brook St	10701
Brookdale Dr	10710
Browning Ave	10704
Bruce Ave	10705
Bryant Rd	
1-40	10705
41-47	10701
42-46	10705
49-99	10701
Bryn Mawr Pl & Ter	10701
Brynwood Rd	10701
Buckingham Rd	10701
Buena Vista Ave	10701
Burbank St	10710
Burhans Ave	10701
Burtis Ave	10701
Bushey Ave	10710
Butler Pl	10710
Byrd Pl	10710
Byron Ave & Pl	10704
Calmet Pl	10704
Calvi Ln	10701
Campion Pl	10701
Candlewood Dr	10710
Canfield Ave	10710
Canterbury Rd	10704
Cantitoe Rd	10710
Canyon Cir	10705
Carlisle Pl	10701
Carlton Ave	10710
Caroline Ave	10705
Carroll St	10705
Carver Ter	10710
Caryl Ave	10705
Cascade Ter	10703
Catskill Ave	10704
Cayuga Rd	10710
Cecil Crest Rd	10701
Cedar Pl	10705
Cedar St	10701
Celli Pl	10701
Cenchenc Rd	10710
Central Park Ave	
1-65	10705
66-1299	10704
1300-2799	10710
Centre St	10701
Cerone Ave	10704
Cerrato Ln	10701
Chamberlain Ave	10704
Chanfrue Pl	10703
Charles Pl	10704
Charlotte St	10710
Chase Ave	10703
Chatham Ter	10710
Chelsea Pl	10710
Cherokee Rd	10710
Cherrywood Rd	10710
Cherwing Rd	10701
Cheshire Ln	10710
Chester Dr	10710
Chester Pl	10704
Chestnut St	10701
Chippewa Rd	10710
Churchill Ave	10704
Clarendon Ave	10701
Clark St	10704
Clayton Pl	10704
Clement St	10710
Cleveland Pl	10710
Cliff Ave	10705
Cliff St	10701
Cliffside Dr	10710
Clifton Ave	10705
Clinton Pl & St	10701
Clover St	10703
Clubway Cir	10710
Clunie Ave	10703
Cochrane Ter	10710
Cole St	10710
Colgate Ave	10703
Colin St	10701
College Pl	10704
Colonel Ct	10710
Colonial Pkwy N	10710
Columbus Pl	10701
Concord Rd	10710
Constant Ave	10701
Convent Ave & Pl	10703
Conway Ter	10710
Cook Ave	10701
Coolidge Ave	10701
Cooper St	10704
Copcutt Ln	10701
Corbalis Pl	10703
Corley St	10701
Cornell Ave	10705
Coronet Rd	10710
Corporate Blvd	10701
Corporate Blvd S	10701
Corporate Dr	
1-99	10710
100-198	10701
Cortlandville Ln	10705
Cottage Gdns	10701
Courter Ave	10705
Courtney Pl	10704
Covington Rd	10710
Cowdrey St	10701
Cowles Ave	10704
Cox Ave	10704
Coyle Pl	10705
Crawford St	10705
Crescent Pl	10704
Cresthill Rd	10710
Crestmont Ave	10704
Crestvale Ter	10710
Cricklewood N & S	10704
Crisfield St	10710
Cromwell Pl	10701
Cross County Ctr & Mall	10704
Cross Hill Ave	10703
Croton Ter	10701
Crotty Ave	10704
Croydon Rd	10710
Culver St	10705
Cumberland Dr	10704
Curran Ct	10710
Currans Ln	10701
Curtis Ln	10710
Custer Ave	10701
Cypress St	10704
Dalton Rd	10701
Damon Ln	10705
Danby Pl	10710
Dartmouth Ave	10701
Davenport Rd	10710
David Ln	10701
Dearborne St	10710
Deerfoot Ln	10710
Dehaven Dr	10703
Delano Ave W	10704
Delavan Ter	10703
Delaware Rd	10710
Delia Ct	10710
Demartino Ave	10703
Depew Ave	10710
S Devoe Ave	10705
Dexter Rd	10710
Dickinson Ave	10703
Dock St	10701
Dogwood Ln	10701
Donald Ct	10710
Donnybrook Pl	10710
Dorchester Dr	10710
Douglas Ave	10703
Dover Ln	10710
Downing St	10705
Drake Pl	10710
Dudley Pl	10703
Dudley St	10701
Dugan Ln	10710
Dunbar St	10710
Dunston Ave	10701
Dunwoodie St	10704
Durst Pl	10704
East Dr	10704
Eastman Pl	10701
Eastview Ave	10703
Eastwind Rd	10710
Edgecliff Ter	10705
Edgecomb Pl	10710
Edgewood Ave	10704
Edison Ave	10710
Edwards Pl	10703
Eisenhower Dr	10710
Elaine Ter	10701
Eldridge Ave	10701
Electra Ln	10704
Elicar Ter	10701
Elinor Pl	10705
Elissa Ln	10710
Elizabeth Pl	10703
Elliott Ave	10705
Ellsworth Ave	10705
Elm St	10701
Emerald Pl & St	10703
Emerson St	10704
Emmett Pl	10703
Empire St	10704
Engine Pl	10701
Enterprise Blvd	10701
Entrance Ct	10710
Etville Ave	10703
Euclid Ave	10705
Executive Blvd & Plz	10701
Fairfield Pl & Rd	10705
Fairmount Ave	10701
Fairview St	10703
Falmouth Rd	10710
Fanshaw Ave	10705
Farkento Ave	10704
Farquhar Ave	10701
Farrell Pl N & S	10701

Street	ZIP
Father Finian Sullivan Dr	10703
Federal St	10705
Fegan St	10701
Fennimore Ave	10701
Fenway N & S	10704
Fern Ter	10701
Fernbrook St	10705
Ferndale St	10701
Fero St	10701
Fillmore St	10701
First St	10704
Fitzgerald St	10710
Flagg St	10703
Floral Ln	10703
Florence St	10704
Forest Ave	10705
Forman St	10703
E Fort Hill Ave & Rd	10710
Fortfield Ave	10701
Fowler Ave	10701
Fox Ave	10704
Fox Ter	10701
Francis Ter	10704
Franklin Ave	10705
Frazier Pl	10704
Frederic Pl & St	10703
French Ter	10704
Frey Ave	10704
Frum Ave	10704
Fullerton Ave	10704
Gaffney Pl	10704
Gail Rd	10710
Gailmore Dr	10710
Garfield St	10701
Garmany Pl	10710
Gateway Rd	10703
Gavin St	10701
Gerri Ln	10703
Gibson Pl	10705
Gilbert Pl	10701
Gladstone Pl	10703
Glearent Ave	10703
Gleeson Pl	10704
Glen Rd	10704
Glenbrook Ave	10705
Glenhill Ave	10701
Glenwood Ave	
1-128	10701
129-300	10703
302-398	10703
76-74-76-74	10701
Glenwood Gdns	10701
Glover Ave	10704
Gold St	10701
Gordon St	10701
Gramatan Dr	10701
Gramercy Ave	10701
Grandview Blvd	10710
Graner Pl	10703
Grange Ave	10710
Granite Pl	10701
Grant St	10704
Grant Pk Dr	10703
Grapanche St	10701
E Grassy Sprain Rd	10710
Gray Pl	10705
Gray Oaks Ave	10710
Greene Pl	10701
Greenvale Ave	10703
Greenwood Rd	10701
Greystone Pl & Ter	10701
Griffith Ave	10710
Grosbeak Rd	10701
Groshon Ave	10701
Grove St & Ter	10701
Guion St	10701
Gunther Ave	10704
Halcyon Pl	10701
Hall Pl	10705
Halladay Ave	10701
Halley St	10704
Halsey Rd	10710
Halstead Ave	10704
Hamilton Ave	10705
Hampton Ave	10710
Hancock Ave	10705
Harding Ave	10704
Hardy Pl	10703
Harmony Park	10701
Harriman Ave	10701
Harrison Ave	10705
Hart Ave	10704
Harty St	10701
Harvard Ave	10710
Hawley Ter	10701
Hawthorne Ave	
2-2	10701
4-157	10701
158-499	10705
Hawthorne Pl	10705
Hayward St	10704
Hazelton Rd	10710
Hearst St	10703
Hearthstone Rd	10710
Heathcote Rd	10710
Heights Dr	10710
Helena Ave	10710
Hemlock Rd	10705
Henderson Ave	10704
Henrietta St	10701
Henry St	10701
Herald St	10704
Herbert Pl	10704
Herriot Pl & St	10701
Herrmann Pl	10710
High St	10703
Highland Ave & Pl	10705
Highview Ter	10705
Hildreth Pl	10704
Hill Ter	10701
Hillbright Ter	10703
Hillcrest Ave	10705
Hillside Ave	10703
Hillside Dr	10705
Hilltop Acres	10704
Hillview Ave	10704
Hillwood Pl	10710
Hiscock Pl	10704
Holbrook Ave	10710
Holls Ter N	10701
Holly St	10704
Hollywood Ave	10707
Holmes St	10704
Homecrest Ave & Oval	10703
Homesite Pkwy	10701
Homewood Ave	10701
Hoover Rd	10710
Horatio St	10710
Howard Pl	10701
Huber Pl	10704
Hudson St & Ter	10701
Hudson View Dr	10701
Hudsonview Ter	10701
Hughes Ter	10701
Hunt Ave	10710
Hunter Ave	10704
Huntington Dr	10704
Hunts Bridge Rd	10704
Huron Rd	10710
Hyatt Ave & Pl	10704
Ingram St	10701
Intervale Pl	10705
Inwood St	10704
Iroquois Rd	10710
Ivanhoe Pl	10710
Ivy Pl	10701
Jackson St	10701
Jefferson St	10701
Jennifer Ln & Pl	10710
Jervis Rd	10705
Jessamine Ave	10701
Jfk Memorial Dr	10701
Joan Dr	10704
Jody Ln	10701
John St	10701
Jones Pl & St	10703
Jost Pl	10704
June St	10710
Kathwood Rd	10710
Kathy Ln	10701
Kendon Pl	10710
Kenilworth Rd	10701
Kenmore St	10710
Kettell Ave	10704
Keystone Rd	10710
Kimball Ave & Ter	10704
Kincaid Dr	10710
King Ave	10704
King St	10703
Kingman Ter	10701
Kingsley Dr	10710
Kingston Ave	10701
Kinross Pl	10703
Kipling Rd	10710
Kneeland Ave	
1-325	10705
326-499	10704
Knollwood Rd	10701
Knowles St	10705
Lafayette Pl	10701
Lake Ave	
1-214	10703
215-300	10701
302-398	10701
Lakeside Dr	10705
Lakeview Ave	10710
Lamar Pl	10710
Lamartine Ave & Ter	10701
Lanark Rd	10705
Landis Pl	10704
Landscape Ave & Pl	10705
Lane St	10701
Larkin Ctr & Plz	10701
Larkspur Ln	10704
Larrimore Rd	10710
Larry Pl	10701
Lasalle Dr	10710
Lattin Dr	10705
Laurel Pl	10704
Lawrence Pl	10701
Lawrence St	10705
Lawton St	10705
Lee Ave	10705
Lefferts Rd	10705
Lehman Ter	10705
Leighton Ave	10705
Lembo Dr	10710
Lennon Ave	10701
Leona Dr	10710
Leonard Pl	10704
Leroy Ave & Pl	10705
Lewis Ave	10703
Lewis Pkwy	10705
Lewis Pl	10703
Lewis St	10703
Lincoln Ave	10704
Lincoln Ter	10701
Linda Ln	10710
Linden St	10701
Lindsey St	10704
Linn Ave & Pl	10705
Linwick Pl	10704
Little John Pl	10704
Livingston Ave	10705
Lockwood Ave	10701
Locust Hill Ave	10701
Longmeadow Rd	10704
Longspur Rd	10710
Longvue Ter	10710
Loomis Ave	10704
Loring Ave	10704
Lorri Ln	10710
Loudoun St	10705
Lowell St	10701
Ludlow St	10705
Lusk Ave	10704
Madeline Pkwy	10705
Madison Ave	10701
Main St	
1-98	10701
79-81-79-81	10702
W Mall Walk	10704
Manchester Rd	10710
Mangrove Rd	10701
Manning Ave	10701
Manor Dr	10710
Manor House Sq	10701
Mansion Ave	10704
Maple Pl	10704
Maple St	10701
Marco Ave	10704
Maria Ln	10710
Marion Ave	10710
Marion Pl	10705
Market Pl	10701
Market St	10710
Marlboro Ln	10710
Marlborough Rd	10701
Marshall Rd	10705
Marston Pl	10704
Martha Ave	10704
Martin Rd	10701
Marwood Ln	10701
Mary Lou Ave	10703
Massitoa Rd	10710
May St	10710
Mayfair Rd	10710
Mayflower Dr	10710
Mccollum Pl	10704
Mcfadden Cir	10701
Mckinley Ave	10704
Mclean Ave	
1-659	10705
660-1099	10704
619-621-619-621	10705
Mcmahon Ave	10704
Meadowbrook Pl	10703
Melrose Ave	10710
Merrick Close	10710
Meyer Ave	10704
Middleboro Dr	10710
Middlesex Ln	10710
Midland Ave	
1-250	10705
251-1306	10704
1308-1308	10704
Midland Ter	
1-45	10705
46-67	10704
69-139	10704
Midwood Ave	10701
Mildred St	10704
Mile Square Pl	10704
Mile Square Rd	
1-599	10701
600-1199	10704
Mill St	10701
Minerva Dr	10710
Minetta Pl	10710
Minnewaska Rd	10710
Mitchell Ave	10701
Mohawk Rd	10710
Monroe Pl	10705
Monroe St	10710
Monsignor Lings Ln	10701
Montague Pl & St	10703
Montclair Pl & Rd	10710
Monterey Pl	10710
Montgomery Ave	10701
Montrose Rd	10710
Mooney Pl	10701
Moquette Row N & S	10703
Morgan St	10701
Morningside Ave & Pl	10703
Morris Cres, Pl & St	10705
Morsemere Ave	10703
Morsemere Pl	10701
Morsemere Ter	10703
Mostyn St	10701
Moultrie Ave	10710
Mount Carmel Pl	10701
Mount Pleasant Rd	10703
Mountaindale Rd	10710
Mulberry St	10701
Mulford Gdns	10703
Munn Pl	10704
Murray Ave	10704
Myrtle St	10703
Nassau Rd	10710
Nelson St	10704
Nepera Pl	10703
Nepperhan Ave	
1-352	10701
354-588	10701
501-587	10703
589-1600	10703
1602-1698	10703
New Ave & Pl	10704
New Main St	10701
New School St	10701
Newkirk Rd	10710
Newport Rd	10710
N & S Nichols Ave	10701
Nile St	10704
Nimitz Pl & Rd	10710
Nolan Ave	10704
Normandy Rd	10701
North Dr	10704
Northfield St	10701
Northrop Ave	10710
Northview Pl & Ter	10703
Northwind Rd	10710
Norwood Rd	10710
Nostrand Pl	10701
Oak St	10701
Oakland Ave	10710
Odell Ave	
1-160	10701
162-500	10703
501-507	10710
502-508	10703
509-699	10710
Odell Plz	
1-99	10701
7-7	10703
Odell Ter	10701
Old Jerome Ave	10704
Old Nepperhan Ave	10703
Oliver Ave	10701
Oneida St	10703
Onondaga St	10704
Orchard Pl & St	10703
Orient St	10704
Oriole Rd	10701
Osmun Pl	10701
Otis Dr & Ln	10710
Otsego Rd	10710
Otsego St	10704
Outlook Ave	10710
Oval Ct	10710
Overcliff St	10705
Overhill Pl	10704
Overlook Ter	10701
Oxford Ave	10710
Page Ave	10704
Palisade Ave	
1-184	10701
185-899	10703
Palmer Rd	10701
Park Ave	10703
Park Avenue Ter	10703
Park Hill Ave	
1-142	10701
144-150	10701
151-499	10705
30-32-30-32	10701
Park Hill Pl	10705
Park Hill Ter	10705
Park View Ave	10710
Parkway E	10701
Parkway N	10704
Parsons St	10701
Patmore Ave	10710
Patricia Pl	10704
Patti Ln	10701
Patton Dr	10710
Paula Ave	10704
Pearl St	10701
Pelton St	10705
Pembrook Dr	10710
Perelans Ave	10705
Pershing Ave	10705
Philipse Pl & Rd	10701
Pier St	10705
Pier Pointe St	10701
Pietro Dr	10710
Pilgrim Ave	10710
Pine St	10701
Plymouth Ave	10710
Pocono Ave	10701
Point St	10701
Pomona Ave	10703
Pond Rd	10701
Pondview Ln	10710
Poplar St	10701
Porach St	10701
Portland Pl	10703
Post St	10705
Potomac St	10710
Prescott St	10701
Primrose Ave	10710
Princeton Ave	10710
Prior Pl	10710
Priscilla Ave	10710
Prospect Dr	10705
Prospect St	10701
Prospect Ter	10705
Providence Ave	10710
Pulsifer Ave	10701
Puritan Ave	10710
Purser Pl	10705
Putnam Ave	10705
Queens Dr	10701
Quentin Charlton Ter	10705
Quincy Ln	10710
Quincy Pl	10701
Radford Pl	10701
Radford St	10705
Railroad Ave & Pl	10710
Ramsey Ave	10701
Randolph St	10705
Ravenswood Rd	10710
Ravine Ave	10701
Raybrook Pl & Rd	10704
Raymond Pl	10704
Reade St	10703
Regent Pl	10710
Regina Pl	10703
Remsen Cir & Rd	10710
Rex Pl	10704
Richfield Ave	10704
Richmond Pl	10701
Rider Ave	10710
Ridge Ave	10703
Ridge Dr	10705
Ridge Rd	10705
Ridge Hill Blvd, Ln & Rd	10710
Ridgeland Rd	10710
Ridgeview Ave	10710
Ridgewood Ave	10704
Rigby St	10704
Ritchie Dr	10705
Ritters Ln	10703
River Pl	10703
Riverdale Ave	
1-168	10701
169-599	10705
Riverview Pl	10701
Roanoke St	10710
Robbins Pl	10705
Roberts Ave	10703
Roberts Ln	10701
Robley St	10704
Rock Ln	10701
Rock Pl	10705
Rockland Ave	10705
Rockledge Pl	10705
Rockne Rd	10701
Rollins St	10705
Romaine Ave	10705
Romano Ln	10701
Roosevelt St	10701
Rose Ln	10705
Rosedale Rd	10710
Rosehill Ter	10703
Rossiter Ave	10701
Roundhill Dr	10710
Roundtop Rd	10710
Roxbury Dr E	10710
Royal St	10704
Rudolph Ter	10701
Rugby Rd	10710
Rumsey Ave	10701
Rumsey Rd	
1-244	10705
245-245	10701
246-398	10705
247-399	10705
Runyon Ave	10710
Rushby Way	10701
Ryder Pl	10704
Sadore Ln	10710
Saint Andrews Pl	10705
Saint Barnabas Pl	10704
Saint Casimir Ave	10701
Saint George Pkwy	10710
Saint James Ter	10704
Saint Johns Ave	10704
Saint Josephs Ave	10703
Saint Marks Pl	10704
Saint Marys St	10701
Salem Way	10710
Salisbury Rd	10710
Sanford St	10705
E Sanford St	10704
Saratoga Ave	10705
Sauanna Pl	10710
Saw Mill River Rd	
1-599	10701
600-1399	10710
1401-1499	10710
484-486-484-486	10701
99-101-99-101	10701
Scenic Ln	10710
School St	10701
Schroeder St	10701
Scott Ave	10704
Scramble Way	10710
Second St	10710
Secor Pl	10704
Sedgwick Ave	10705
Seminary Ave	10704
Seneca Ave	10710
Serena Ln	10703
Seymour St	10701
Sharon Way	10710
Shawnee Ave	10710
Shelburne Rd	10710
Shelley Ave	10701
Sherman Ave	10705
Sherwood Ave & Ter	10704
Shipman Ave	10704
Shonnard Pl	10703
Shonnard Ter	10701
Shoreview Dr	10710
Sidehill Ln	10710
Simpson Pl	10710
Skywood Ct	10710
Slater Ave	10710
Smart Ave	10704
Somerset Dr	10710
Sommerville Pl	10703
Soundview Ave	10704
South Cir	10703
South Dr	10704
Speedling Pl	10703
Spencer Pl	10705
Sprain Pl	10701
Sprain Rd	10710
Spring Rd	10705
Springer Ave	10704
Spruce St	10701
Squire Ave	10703
St Jude Pl	10703
Standish Ave	10710
Stanley Ave & Pl	10705
Staunton St	10704
Sterling Ave	10704
Stevens Ave	10704
Stew Leonard Dr	10710
Stewart Pl	10701
Stillwell Ave	10704
Stockbridge Rd	10710
Stokes Rd	10710
Stone Ave	10701
Storey Ln	10710
Stratton St S	10701
Sudbury Dr & Pl	10710

Suffolk Trl 10710
Summerfield St 10701
Summit St 10701
Sumner Ave 10704
Sunlight Hl 10704
Sunny Slope Ter 10703
Sunnyside Dr 10705
Sunrise Ter 10703
Sunset Dr 10704
Surrey Ln 10710
Sutton Oval 10701
Suydam Pl 10701
Sweetfield Cir 10704
Taft Ave 10704
Tall Tulip Ln 10710
Teresa Ave 10704
The Crossway 10701
Thomas Pl 10701
Thurman St 10701
Thurton Pl 10704
Tibbetts Rd 10705
Tioga Ave 10704
Tocco Pl 10704
Tompkins Ave
1-99 10710
198-299 10703
Toni Ln 10710
Torre Pl 10703
Touissant Ave 10710
Tower Pl 10703
Trausneck Pl 10703
Travers Ave 10705
Treadwell Pl 10710
Trenchard St 10704
Trinity St 10701
Troy Ln 10701
Truesdale Pl 10705
Truman Ave 10703
Tuckahoe Rd 10710
Tudor Ln 10701
Turner St 10704
Tybee Pl 10710
Tyndale Pl 10701
Tyndall Ave 10710
Umberto Pl 10701
Undercliff St 10705
Underhill St 10710
Union Pl 10701
University Ave 10704
Upland Ave & Pl 10703
Upper Mall Walk 10704
Urban Pl 10701
Valdale Ave 10705
Valentine Ln 10705
Valentine St 10704
Valerie Dr 10703
Valley Ave 10703
Valley Rd 10705
Valley Close 10705
Valley View Dr 10710
Van Buren St 10701
Van Cortlandt Park
Ave 10705
Van Cortlandt Pk Ave .. 10701
Van Der Donck St 10701
Vark St 10701
Veltri Ln 10704
Vernon Ave & Pl 10704
Verona Ave 10710
Vesta Pl 10703
Via Trenta Ct 10710
Victor St 10701
Victoria Ln 10701
Villa Ave 10704
Vineyard Ave 10703
Virginia Pl 10703
Virginia St 10704
Volz Pl 10701
Voss Ave 10703
Vredenburgh Ave 10704
Wainwright Ave 10710
Wakefield Ave 10704
Wallace Pkwy 10705
Walnut St 10701
Walsh Rd 10701
Warburton Ave 10701
Waring Pl 10703
Waring Row 10701
Wasylenko Ln 10701
Water Grant St 10701
S Waverly Pl & St 10701
Wc Handy Pl 10710
Webb Pl 10710
Webster Ave 10701
Wellesley Ave 10705
Wells Ave 10701
Wells Park Dr 10705
Wendel Pl 10701
Wendover Rd
1-329 10705
330-338 10704
331-339 10705
340-399 10704
West Dr 10704
Westerly St 10704
Western Ave 10705
Westminster Dr 10710
Westmoreland Dr 10704
Westwind Rd 10710
Westwood Rd 10710
Whelan Pl 10703
Whitman Rd 10710
Whittier Ave 10704
Wicker St 10701
Wickes Ave 10701
Wilbur St 10704
Wilcox Ave 10705
William St 10701
Willow Pl & St 10701
Winans Dr 10701
Winchester Ave & Dr ... 10710
Windermere Dr 10710
Windsor Ter 10701
Winfred Ave 10704
Wingate Pl & Rd 10705
Winnebago Rd 10710
Winston Pl 10701
Winthrop Ave 10710
Winton Pl 10710
Wolffe St 10705
Woodbine St 10704
Woodland Ave 10703
Woodland Ter 10701
Woodlawn Ave 10704
Woodrow Ave & Dr 10710
Woodstock St 10701
Woodworth Ave 10701
Woodycrest Ave 10701
Worth St 10701
Wright Pl 10704
Xavier Dr 10704
Yonkers Ave
1-399 10701
400-1299 10704
Yonkers Ter 10704
Yorkshire Pl 10701
Young Ave 10710

NUMBERED STREETS

All Street Addresses 10704

North Carolina

People QuickFacts	North Carolina	USA
Population, 2013 estimate	9,848,060	316,128,839
Population, 2010 (April 1) estimates base	9,535,471	308,747,716
Population, percent change, April 1, 2010 to July 1, 2013	3.3%	2.4%
Population, 2010	9,535,483	308,745,538
Persons under 5 years, percent, 2013	6.2%	6.3%
Persons under 18 years, percent, 2013	23.2%	23.3%
Persons 65 years and over, percent, 2013	14.3%	14.1%
Female persons, percent, 2013	51.3%	50.8%
White alone, percent, 2013 (a)	71.7%	77.7%
Black or African American alone, percent, 2013 (a)	22.0%	13.2%
American Indian and Alaska Native alone, percent, 2013 (a)	1.6%	1.2%
Asian alone, percent, 2013 (a)	2.6%	5.3%
Native Hawaiian and Other Pacific Islander alone, percent, 2013 (a)	0.1%	0.2%
Two or More Races, percent, 2013	2.0%	2.4%
Hispanic or Latino, percent, 2013 (b)	8.9%	17.1%
White alone, not Hispanic or Latino, percent, 2013	64.4%	62.6%
Living in same house 1 year & over, percent, 2008-2012	84.4%	84.8%
Foreign born persons, percent, 2008-2012	7.5%	12.9%
Language other than English spoken at home, pct age 5+, 2008-2012	10.8%	20.5%
High school graduate or higher, percent of persons age 25+, 2008-2012	84.5%	85.7%
Bachelor's degree or higher, percent of persons age 25+, 2008-2012	26.8%	28.5%
Veterans, 2008-2012	738,926	21,853,912
Mean travel time to work (minutes), workers age 16+, 2008-2012	23.5	25.4
Housing units, 2013	4,394,261	132,802,859
Homeownership rate, 2008-2012	67.1%	65.5%
Housing units in multi-unit structures, percent, 2008-2012	17.1%	25.9%
Median value of owner-occupied housing units, 2008-2012	$153,600	$181,400
Households, 2008-2012	3,693,221	115,226,802
Persons per household, 2008-2012	2.51	2.61
Per capita money income in past 12 months (2012 dollars), 2008-2012	$25,285	$28,051
Median household income, 2008-2012	$46,450	$53,046
Persons below poverty level, percent, 2008-2012	16.8%	14.9%

Business QuickFacts	North Carolina	USA
Private nonfarm establishments, 2012	217,404	7,431,808
Private nonfarm employment, 2012	3,352,151	115,938,468
Private nonfarm employment, percent change, 2011-2012	2.1%	2.2%
Nonemployer establishments, 2012	669,501	22,735,915
Total number of firms, 2007	798,791	27,092,908
Black-owned firms, percent, 2007	10.5%	7.1%
American Indian- and Alaska Native-owned firms, percent, 2007	1.0%	0.9%
Asian-owned firms, percent, 2007	2.5%	5.7%
Native Hawaiian and Other Pacific Islander-owned firms, percent, 2007	0.1%	0.1%
Hispanic-owned firms, percent, 2007	2.7%	8.3%
Women-owned firms, percent, 2007	28.2%	28.8%
Manufacturers shipments, 2007 ($1000)	205,867,299	5,319,456,312
Merchant wholesaler sales, 2007 ($1000)	88,795,885	4,174,286,516
Retail sales, 2007 ($1000)	114,578,173	3,917,663,456
Retail sales per capita, 2007	$12,641	$12,990
Accommodation and food services sales, 2007 ($1000)	16,126,939	613,795,732
Building permits, 2012	48,692	829,658

Geography QuickFacts	North Carolina	USA
Land area in square miles, 2010	48,617.91	3,531,905.43
Persons per square mile, 2010	196.1	87.4
FIPS Code	37	

(a) Includes persons reporting only one race.
(b) Hispanics may be of any race, so also are included in applicable race categories.
FN: Footnote on this item for this area in place of data
NA: Not available
D: Suppressed to avoid disclosure of confidential information
X: Not applicable
S: Suppressed; does not meet publication standards
Z: Value greater than zero but less than half unit of measure shown
F: Fewer than 100 firms
Source: US Census Bureau State & County QuickFacts

North Carolina

3 DIGIT ZIP CODE MAP

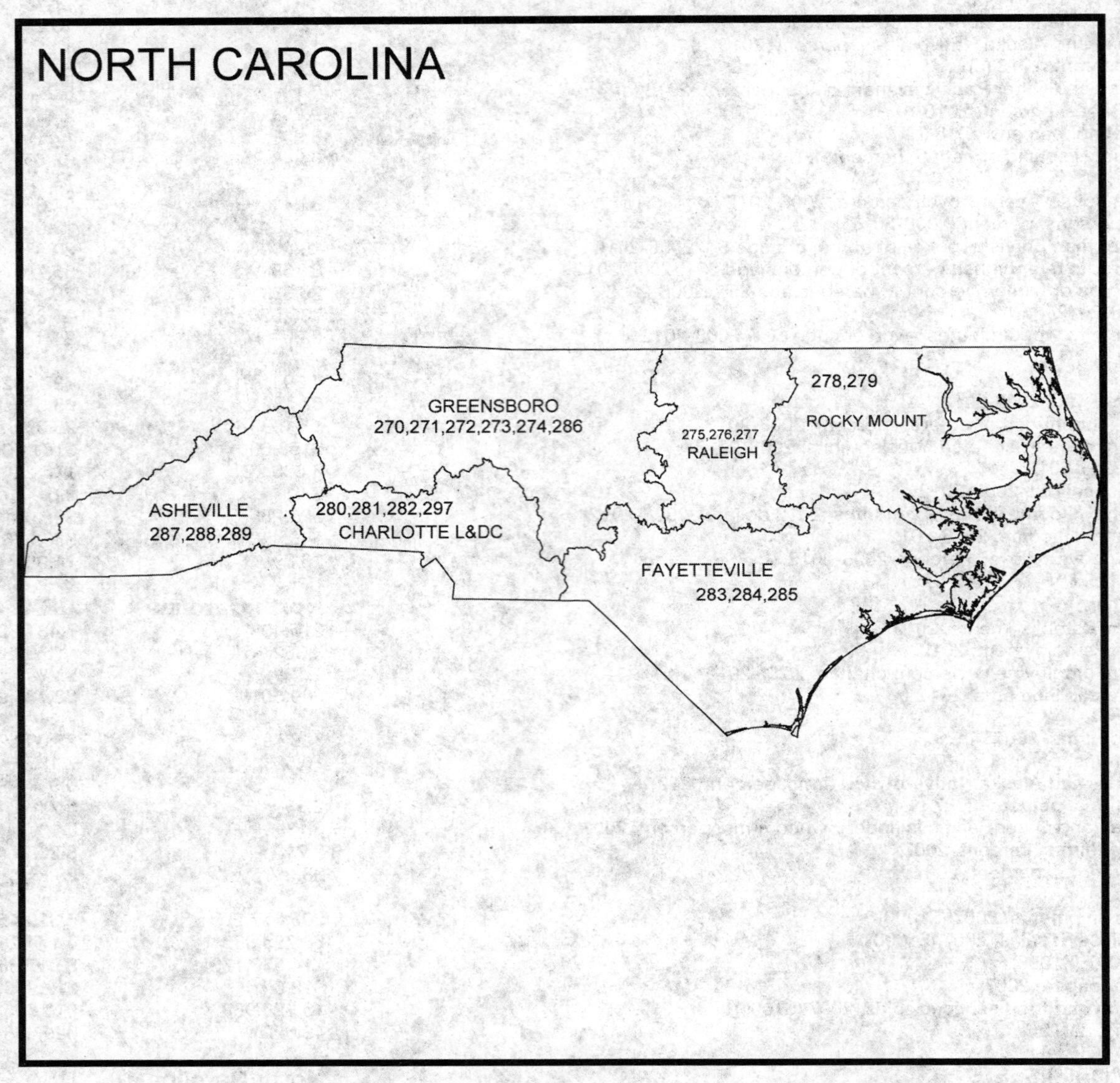

North Carolina

(Abbreviation: NC)

Post Office, County — ZIP Code

Places with more than one ZIP code are listed in capital letters, See pages indicated.

Aberdeen, Moore 28315
Advance, Davie 27006
Ahoskie, Hertford 27910
Alamance, Alamance 27201
ALBEMARLE, Stanly (See Page 2737)
Albertson, Duplin 28508
Alexander, Buncombe 28701
Alexander Mills, Rutherford 28043
Alexis, Gaston 28006
Alliance, Pamlico 28509
Almond, Swain 28702
Altamahaw, Alamance 27202
Amf Greensboro, Guilford 27425
Andrews, Cherokee 28901
Angier, Harnett 27501
Ansonville, Anson 28007
APEX, Wake (See Page 2737)
Aquone, Cherokee 28781
Arapahoe, Pamlico 28510
Ararat, Surry 27007
Archdale, Guilford 27263
Arden, Buncombe 28704
Ash, Brunswick 28420
ASHEBORO, Randolph (See Page 2739)
ASHEVILLE, Buncombe (See Page 2742)
Askewville, Bertie 27983
Atkinson, Pender 28421
Atlantic, Carteret 28511
Atlantic Beach, Carteret 28512
Aulander, Bertie 27805
Aurora, Beaufort 27806
Autryville, Sampson 28318
Avon, Dare 27915
Ayden, Pitt 28513
Aydlett, Currituck 27916
Badin, Stanly 28009
Badin Lake, Stanly 28127
Bahama, Durham 27503
Bailey, Nash 27807
Bakersville, Mitchell 28705
Bald Head Island, Brunswick 28461
Balsam, Jackson 28707
Balsam Grove, Transylvania 28708
Banner Elk, Avery 28604
Banner Elk, Watauga 28691
Barber, Rowan 27013
Barco, Currituck 27917
Barium Springs, Iredell 28010
Barnardsville, Buncombe 28709
Barnesville, Robeson 28319
Bat Cave, Henderson 28710
Bath, Beaufort 27808
Battleboro, Edgecombe 27809
Bayboro, Pamlico 28515
Bear Creek, Chatham 27207
Bear Grass, Martin 27892
Beargrass, Martin 27892
Beaufort, Carteret 28516
Beech Mountain, Avery 28604
Belews Creek, Forsyth 27009
Belhaven, Beaufort 27810
Bellarthur, Pitt 27811
Belmont, Gaston 28012
Belvidere, Perquimans 27919
Belville, Brunswick 28451
Bennett, Chatham 27208
Benson, Johnston 27504
Bermuda Run, Davie 27006
Bessemer City, Gaston 28016
Bethania, Forsyth 27010
Bethel, Pitt 27812
Beulaville, Duplin 28518
Biltmore Forest, Buncombe 28803
Biltmore Lake, Buncombe 28715
Biscoe, Montgomery 27209
Black Creek, Wilson 27813
Black Mountain, Buncombe 28711
Bladenboro, Bladen 28320
Blanch, Caswell 27212
Blounts Creek, Beaufort 27814
Blowing Rock, Watauga 28605
Boardman, Columbus 28438
Boger City, Lincoln 28092
Bogue, Carteret 28570
Boiling Spring Lakes, Brunswick 28461
Boiling Springs, Cleveland 28017
Bolivia, Brunswick 28422
Bolton, Columbus 28423
Bonlee, Chatham 27213
Boomer, Wilkes 28606
Boone, Watauga 28607
Boonville, Yadkin 27011
Bostic, Rutherford 28018
Bowdens, Duplin 28398
Brasstown, Clay 28902
Brentwood (See Raleigh)
Brevard, Transylvania 28712
Bridgeton, Craven 28519
Broadway, Lee 27505
Browns Summit, Guilford 27214
Brunswick, Columbus 28424
Bryson City, Swain 28713
Buffalo Lake, Lee 27330
Buies Creek, Harnett 27506
Bullock, Granville 27507
Bunn, Franklin 27508
Bunnlevel, Harnett 28323
Burgaw, Pender 28425
BURLINGTON, Alamance (See Page 2747)
Burnsville, Yancey 28714
Butner, Granville 27509
Butters, Bladen 28320
Buxton, Dare 27920
Bynum, Chatham 27228
Cajahs Mountain, Caldwell 28645
Calabash, Brunswick 28467
Calypso, Duplin 28325
Camden, Camden 27921
Cameron, Harnett 28326
CAMP LEJEUNE, Onslow (See Page 2750)
Candler, Buncombe 28715
Candor, Montgomery 27229
Canton, Haywood 28716
Cape Carteret, Onslow 28584
Cape Fear, New Hanover 28401
Caroleen, Rutherford 28019
Carolina Beach, New Hanover 28428
Carolina Shores, Brunswick 28467
Carrboro, Orange 27510
Carthage, Moore 28327
CARY, Wake (See Page 2750)
Casar, Cleveland 28020
Cashiers, Jackson 28717
Castalia, Nash 27816
Castle Hayne, New Hanover 28429
Caswell Beach, Brunswick 28465
Catawba, Catawba 28609
Cedar Falls, Randolph 27230
Cedar Grove, Orange 27231
Cedar Island, Carteret 28520
Cedar Mountain, Transylvania 28718
Cedar Point, Onslow 28584
Cedar Rock, Caldwell 28645
Centerville, Franklin 27549
Cerro Gordo, Columbus 28430
Chadbourn, Columbus 28431
CHAPEL HILL, Orange (See Page 2755)
CHARLOTTE, Mecklenburg (See Page 2759)
Cherokee, Swain 28719
Cherry Point, Craven 28533
Cherryville, Gaston 28021
Chimney Rock, Rutherford 28720
China Grove, Rowan 28023
Chinquapin, Duplin 28521
Chocowinity, Beaufort 27817
Claremont, Catawba 28610
Clarendon, Columbus 28432
Clarkton, Bladen 28433
CLAYTON, Johnston (See Page 2781)
Clemmons, Forsyth 27012
Cleveland, Rowan 27013
Cliffside, Rutherford 28024
Climax, Guilford 27233
CLINTON, Sampson (See Page 2784)
Clyde, Haywood 28721
Coats, Harnett 27521
Cofield, Hertford 27922
Coinjock, Currituck 27923
Colerain, Bertie 27924
Coleridge, Randolph 27316
Colfax, Guilford 27235
Collettsville, Caldwell 28611
Colon, Lee 27330
Columbia, Tyrrell 27925
Columbus, Polk 28722
Comfort, Jones 28522
Como, Hertford 27818
CONCORD, Cabarrus (See Page 2784)
Conetoe, Edgecombe 27819
Connelly Springs, Burke 28612
Conover, Catawba 28613
Conway, Northampton 27820
Cooleemee, Davie 27014
Corapeake, Gates 27926
Cordova, Richmond 28330
Cornelius, Mecklenburg 28031
Corolla, Currituck 27927
Council, Bladen 28434
Cove City, Craven 28523
Cramerton, Gaston 28032
Creedmoor, Granville 27522
Creston, Ashe 28615
Creswell, Washington 27928
Crossnore, Avery 28616
Crouse, Lincoln 28033
Crumpler, Ashe 28617
Culberson, Cherokee 28903
Cullowhee, Jackson 28723
Cumberland, Cumberland 28331
Cumnock, Lee 27237
Currie, Pender 28435
Currituck, Currituck 27929
Dallas, Gaston 28034
Dana, Henderson 28724
Danbury, Stokes 27016
DAVIDSON, Mecklenburg (See Page 2787)
Davis, Carteret 28524
Deep Gap, Watauga 28618
Deep Run, Lenoir 28525
Delco, Columbus 28436
Denton, Davidson 27239
Denver, Lincoln 28037
Dillsboro, Jackson 28725
Dobson, Surry 27017
Dover, Craven 28526
Drexel, Burke 28619
Dublin, Bladen 28332
Duck, Dare 27949
Dudley, Wayne 28333
DUNN, Harnett (See Page 2787)
Durants Neck, Perquimans 27930
Durants Neck, Perquimans 27944
DURHAM, Durham (See Page 2787)
E Fayetteville, Cumberland 28301
Eagle Rock, Wake 27591
Eagle Springs, Moore 27242
Earl, Cleveland 28038
East Arcadia, Columbus 28456
East Bend, Yadkin 27018
East Fayetteville, Cumberland 28301
East Flat Rock, Henderson 28726
East Lake, Dare 27953
East Spencer, Rowan 28039
Eastover, Cumberland 28312
EDEN, Rockingham (See Page 2795)
Edenton, Chowan 27932
Edneyville, Henderson 28727
Edward, Beaufort 27821
Efland, Orange 27243
ELIZABETH CITY, Pasquotank (See Page 2796)
Elizabethtown, Bladen 28337
Elk Park, Avery 28622
Elkin, Surry 28621
Ellenboro, Rutherford 28040
Ellerbe, Richmond 28338
Elm City, Wilson 27822
Elon, Alamance 27244
Elon College, Alamance 27244
Emerald Isle, Carteret 28594
Enfield, Halifax 27823
Engelhard, Hyde 27824
Enka, Buncombe 28728
Ennice, Alleghany 28623
Eno Valley, Durham 27712
Ernul, Craven 28527
Erwin, Harnett 28339
Ether, Montgomery 27247
Etowah, Henderson 28729
Eure, Gates 27935
Eureka, Wayne 27830
Everetts, Martin 27825
Evergreen, Columbus 28438
Fair Bluff, Columbus 28439
Fairfield, Hyde 27826
Fairmont, Robeson 28340
Fairview, Buncombe 28730
Faison, Duplin 28341
Faith, Rowan 28041
Falcon, Cumberland 28342
Falkland, Pitt 27827
Fallston, Cleveland 28042
Farmville, Pitt 27828
FAYETTEVILLE, Cumberland (See Page 2798)
Fearrington Village, Chatham 27312
Ferguson, Wilkes 28624
Flat Rock, Henderson 28731
Fleetwood, Ashe 28626
Fletcher, Henderson 28732
Fontana Dam, Graham 28733
Forest City, Rutherford 28043
Fort Bragg, Cumberland 28307
Fountain, Pitt 27829
Four Oaks, Johnston 27524
Foxfire Village, Moore 27281
Frank, Avery 28657
FRANKLIN, Macon (See Page 2807)
Franklinton, Franklin 27525
Franklinville, Randolph 27248
Fremont, Wayne 27830
Frisco, Dare 27936
Fuquay Varina, Wake 27526
Garland, Sampson 28441
Garner, Wake 27529
Garysburg, Northampton 27831
Gaston, Northampton 27832
GASTONIA, Gaston (See Page 2810)
Gates, Gates 27937
Gatesville, Gates 27938
George, Northampton 27897
Germanton, Stokes 27019
Gerton, Henderson 28735
Gibson, Scotland 28343
Gibsonville, Guilford 27249
Glade Valley, Alleghany 28627
Glen Alpine, Burke 28628
Glen Raven, Alamance 27215
Glendale Springs, Ashe 28629
Glendon, Moore 27325
Glenville, Jackson 28736
Glenwood, Mcdowell 28737
Gloucester, Carteret 28528
Godwin, Sampson 28344
Gold Hill, Rowan 28071
Golden Valley, Rutherford 28018
GOLDSBORO, Wayne (See Page 2814)
Goldston, Chatham 27252
Graham, Alamance 27253
Grandy, Currituck 27939
Granite Falls, Caldwell 28630
Granite Quarry, Rowan 28072
Grantsboro, Pamlico 28529
Grassy Creek, Ashe 28631
Green Level, Alamance 27217
Green Mountain, Yancey 28740
Greenevers, Duplin 28458
GREENSBORO, Guilford (See Page 2817)
GREENVILLE, Pitt (See Page 2825)
Grifton, Pitt 28530
Grimesland, Pitt 27837
Grover, Cleveland 28073
Gulf, Chatham 27256
Gumberry, Northampton 27831
Halifax, Halifax 27839
Hallsboro, Columbus 28442
Hamilton, Martin 27840
Hamlet, Richmond 28345
Hampstead, Pender 28443
Hamptonville, Yadkin 27020
Harbinger, Currituck 27941
Harkers Island, Carteret 28531
Harmony, Iredell 28634
Harrells, Sampson 28444
Harrellsville, Hertford 27942
Harris, Rutherford 28074
Harrisburg, Cabarrus 28075
Hassell, Martin 27841
Hatteras, Dare 27943
Havelock, Craven 28532
Havelock, Craven 28533
Haw River, Alamance 27258
Hayesville, Clay 28904
Hays, Wilkes 28635
Hazelwood, Haywood 28738
Hazelwood, Haywood 28786
HENDERSON, Vance (See Page 2829)
HENDERSONVILLE, Henderson (See Page 2831)
Henrico, Northampton 27842
Henrietta, Rutherford 28076
Hertford, Perquimans 27930
Hertford, Perquimans 27944
HICKORY, Catawba (See Page 2836)
Hiddenite, Alexander 28636
HIGH POINT, Guilford (See Page 2839)
High Shoals, Gaston 28077
Highfalls, Moore 27259
Highlands, Macon 28741
Hildebran, Burke 28637
Hillsborough, Orange 27278
Hobbsville, Gates 27946
Hobgood, Halifax 27843
Hobucken, Pamlico 28537
Hoffman, Richmond 28347
Holden Beach, Brunswick 28462
Hollister, Halifax 27844
Holly Ridge, Onslow 28445
Holly Springs, Wake 27540
Hookerton, Greene 28538
Hope Mills, Cumberland 28348
Horse Shoe, Henderson 28742
Hot Springs, Madison 28743
Hubert, Onslow 28539
Hudson, Caldwell 28638
HUNTERSVILLE, Mecklenburg (See Page 2843)
Hurdle Mills, Person 27541
Husk, Ashe 28643
Icard, Burke 28666
Indian Beach, Carteret 28512
Indian Trail, Union 28079
Ingold, Sampson 28441
Iron Station, Lincoln 28080
Ivanhoe, Sampson 28447
Jackson, Northampton 27845
Jackson Springs, Moore 27281
JACKSONVILLE, Onslow (See Page 2845)
Jamestown, Guilford 27282
Jamesville, Martin 27846
Jarvisburg, Currituck 27947
Jefferson, Ashe 28640
Jonas Ridge, Burke 28641
Jonesville, Yadkin 28642
Julian, Guilford 27283
KANNAPOLIS, Cabarrus (See Page 2848)
Kelford, Bertie 27847
Kelly, Bladen 28448
Kenansville, Duplin 28349
Kenly, Johnston 27542
KERNERSVILLE, Forsyth (See Page 2850)
Kill Devil Hills, Dare 27948
King, Stokes 27021
Kings Mountain, Cleveland 28086
Kingstown, Cleveland 28150
KINSTON, Lenoir (See Page 2852)
Kipling, Harnett 27543
Kittrell, Vance 27544
Kitty Hawk, Dare 27949
Knightdale, Wake 27545
Knotts Island, Currituck 27950
Kure Beach, New Hanover 28449
La Grange, Lenoir 28551
Lake Junaluska, Haywood 28745
Lake Lure, Rutherford 28746
Lake Park, Union 28079
Lake Santeetlah, Graham 28771
Lake Toxaway, Transylvania 28747
Lake Waccamaw, Columbus 28450
Lakeview, Moore 28350
Landis, Rowan 28088
Lansing, Ashe 28643
Lasker, Northampton 27845
Lattimore, Cleveland 28089
Laurel Hill, Scotland 28351
Laurel Park, Henderson 28739
Laurel Springs, Alleghany 28644
LAURINBURG, Scotland (See Page 2854)
Lawndale, Cleveland 28090
Lawsonville, Stokes 27022
Leasburg, Caswell 27291
Leggett, Edgecombe 27886
Leicester, Buncombe 28748
Leland, Brunswick 28451
Lemon Springs, Lee 28355
Lenoir, Caldwell 28633
Lewiston Woodville, Bertie 27849
Lewisville, Forsyth 27023
LEXINGTON, Davidson (See Page 2855)
Liberty, Randolph 27298
Lilesville, Anson 28091
Lillington, Harnett 27546
LINCOLNTON, Lincoln (See Page 2859)
Linden, Cumberland 28356
Linville, Avery 28646
Linville Falls, Burke 28647
Linwood, Davidson 27299
Little Switzerland, Mcdowell 28749
Littleton, Halifax 27850
Locust, Stanly 28097
Longisland, Catawba 28609
Longwood, Brunswick 28452
Louisburg, Franklin 27549
Lowell, Gaston 28098
Lowgap, Surry 27024
Lowland, Pamlico 28552
Lucama, Wilson 27851
Lumber Bridge, Robeson 28357

LUMBERTON, Robeson
(See Page 2861)
Lynn, Polk 28750
Macclesfield, Edgecombe 27852
Macon, Warren 27551
Madison, Rockingham 27025
Maggie Valley, Haywood 28751
Magnolia, Duplin 28453
Maiden, Catawba 28650
Mamers, Harnett 27552
Manns Harbor, Dare 27953
Manson, Vance 27553
Manteo, Dare 27954
Maple, Currituck 27956
Maple Hill, Pender 28454
Marble, Cherokee 28905
Margarettsville, Northampton . 27853
Marietta, Robeson 28362
Marion, Mcdowell 28737
Marion, Mcdowell 28752
Mars Hill, Madison 28754
Marshall, Madison 28753
Marshallberg, Carteret 28553
Marshville, Union 28103
Marston, Richmond 28363
Marvin, Union 28173
MATTHEWS, Union
(See Page 2863)
Maury, Greene 28554
Maxton, Robeson 28364
Mayodan, Rockingham 27027
Maysville, Jones 28555
Mc Adenville, Gaston 28101
Mc Farlan, Anson 28102
Mc Grady, Wilkes 28649
Mc Leansville, Guilford 27301
Mccutcheon Field, Onslow ... 28545
Mebane, Alamance 27302
Merritt, Pamlico 28556
Merry Hill, Bertie 27957
Mesic, Pamlico 28515
Micaville, Yancey 28755
Micro, Johnston 27555
Middleburg, Vance 27556
Middlesex, Nash 27557
Midland, Cabarrus 28107
Midway Park, Onslow 28544
Mill Spring, Polk 28756
Millers Creek, Wilkes 28651
Mills River, Henderson 28732
Mills River, Henderson 28759
Milton, Caswell 27305
Milwaukee, Northampton 27820
Mineral Springs, Union 28108
Minneapolis, Avery 28652
Minnesott Beach, Pamlico 28510
Mint Hill, Mecklenburg 28227
Misenheimer, Stanly 28109
Mocksville, Davie 27028
Momeyer, Nash 27856
Moncure, Chatham 27559
MONROE, Union
(See Page 2865)
Montezuma, Avery 28653
Montreat, Buncombe 28757
Mooresboro, Cleveland 28114
MOORESVILLE, Iredell
(See Page 2868)
Moravian Falls, Wilkes 28654
Morehead City, Carteret 28557
MORGANTON, Burke
(See Page 2871)
Morrisville, Wake 27560
Morven, Anson 28119
Mount Airy, Surry 27030
Mount Airy, Surry 27031
Mount Gilead, Montgomery ... 27306
Mount Holly, Gaston 28120
Mount Mourne, Iredell 28123
Mount Olive, Wayne 28365
Mount Pleasant, Cabarrus 28124
Mount Ulla, Rowan 28125
Mountain Home, Henderson .. 28758
Moyock, Currituck 27958
Mt Holly, Gaston 28120
Murfreesboro, Hertford 27855
Murphy, Cherokee 28906
N Topsail Beach, Onslow 28460
Nags Head, Dare 27959
Nakina, Columbus 28455
Naples, Henderson 28760
Nashville, Nash 27856
Navassa, Brunswick 28451
Nebo, Mcdowell 28761
NEW BERN, Craven
(See Page 2871)
New Hill, Wake 27562
New London, Stanly 28127
Newell, Mecklenburg 28126
Newland, Avery 28657
Newport, Carteret 28570
Newton, Catawba 28658
Newton Grove, Sampson 28366
Norlina, Warren 27563
Norman, Richmond 28367
North Wilkesboro, Wilkes 28659
Northwest, Brunswick 28451
Norwood, Stanly 28128
Oak City, Martin 27857
Oak Island, Brunswick 28465
Oak Ridge, Guilford 27310
Oakboro, Stanly 28129
Ocean Isle Beach,
Brunswick 28469
Ocracoke, Hyde 27960
Old Fort, Mcdowell 28762
Olin, Iredell 28660
Olivia, Harnett 28368
Oriental, Pamlico 28571
Orrum, Robeson 28369
Otto, Macon 28763
Oxford, Granville 27565
Pantego, Beaufort 27860
Parkton, Robeson 28371
Parmele, Martin 27861
Patterson, Caldwell 28661
Paw Creek, Mecklenburg 28130
Peachland, Anson 28133
Peletier, Onslow 28584
Pelham, Caswell 27311
Pembroke, Robeson 28372
Pendleton, Northampton 27862
Penland, Mitchell 28765
Penrose, Transylvania 28766
Pfafftown, Forsyth 27040
Pikeville, Wayne 27863
Pilot Mountain, Surry 27041
Pine Hall, Stokes 27042
Pine Knoll Shores, Carteret .. 28512
Pine Level, Johnston 27568
Pinebluff, Moore 28373
PINEHURST, Moore
(See Page 2874)
Pineola, Avery 28662
Pinetops, Edgecombe 27864
Pinetown, Beaufort 27865
Pineville, Mecklenburg 28134
Piney Creek, Alleghany 28663
Pink Hill, Lenoir 28572
Pinnacle, Stokes 27043
Pisgah Forest, Transylvania .. 28768
Pittsboro, Chatham 27228
Pittsboro, Chatham 27312
Pleasant Garden, Guilford 27313
Pleasant Hill, Northampton 27866
Plumtree, Avery 28664
Plymouth, Washington 27962
Point Harbor, Currituck 27964
Polkton, Anson 28135
Polkville, Cleveland 28136
Pollocksville, Jones 28573
Pope Army Airfield,
Cumberland 28308
Poplar Branch, Currituck 27965
Potecasi, Northampton 27867
Powells Point, Currituck 27966
Powellsville, Bertie 27967
Princeton, Johnston 27569
Princeville, Edgecombe 27886
Proctorville, Robeson 28375
Prospect Hill, Caswell 27314
Providence, Caswell 27315
Purlear, Wilkes 28665
Raeford, Hoke 28376
RALEIGH, Wake
(See Page 2875)
Ramseur, Randolph 27316
Randleman, Randolph 27317
Raynham, Robeson 28383
Red Cross, Stanly 28129
Red Oak, Nash 27868
Red Springs, Robeson 28377
REIDSVILLE, Rockingham
(See Page 2892)
Rennert, Robeson 28386
Research Triangle Park,
Durham 27709
Rex, Robeson 28378
Rhodhiss, Caldwell 28667
Rich Square, Northampton 27869
Richfield, Stanly 28137
Richlands, Onslow 28574
Ridgecrest, Buncombe 28770
Ridgeway, Warren 27570
Riegelwood, Columbus 28456
Roanoke Rapids, Halifax 27870
Roanoke Rapids Air Force
Sta, Halifax 27870
Roaring Gap, Alleghany 28668
Roaring River, Wilkes 28669
Robbins, Moore 27325
Robbinsville, Graham 28771
Robersonville, Martin 27871
ROCKINGHAM, Richmond
(See Page 2892)
Rockwell, Rowan 28138
ROCKY MOUNT, Edgecombe
(See Page 2893)
Rocky Point, Pender 28457
Rodanthe, Dare 27968
Roduco, Gates 27969
Rolesville, Wake 27571
Ronda, Wilkes 28670
Roper, Washington 27970
Rose Hill, Duplin 28458
Roseboro, Sampson 28382
Rosman, Transylvania 28772
Rougemont, Durham 27572
Rowland, Robeson 28383
ROXBORO, Person
(See Page 2896)
Roxobel, Bertie 27872
Ruffin, Rockingham 27326
Rutherford College, Burke 28671
Rutherfordton, Rutherford 28139
Rutherfrd Col, Burke 28671
Saint Helena, Pender 28425
Saint James, Brunswick 28461
Saint Pauls, Robeson 28384
Salemburg, Sampson 28385
SALISBURY, Rowan
(See Page 2898)
Salter Path, Carteret 28575
Saluda, Polk 28773
Salvo, Dare 27972
Sandy Ridge, Stokes 27046
Sandyfield, Columbus 28456
SANFORD, Lee
(See Page 2901)
Sapphire, Transylvania 28774
Saratoga, Wilson 27873
Sawmills, Caldwell 28630
Saxapahaw, Alamance 27340
Scaly Mountain, Macon 28775
Scotland Neck, Halifax 27874
Scotts, Iredell 28699
Scottville, Ashe 28672
Scranton, Hyde 27875
Seaboard, Northampton 27876
Seagrove, Randolph 27341
Sealevel, Carteret 28577
Sealevel, Carteret 28581
Sedalia, Guilford 27342
Selma, Johnston 27576
Semora, Person 27343
Seven Devils, Avery 28604
Seven Lakes, Moore 27376
Seven Springs, Wayne 28578
Severn, Northampton 27877
Seymour Johnson A F B,
Wayne 27531
Seymour Johnson Afb,
Wayne 27531
SHALLOTTE, Brunswick
(See Page 2904)
Shannon, Robeson 28386
Shannon Plaza, Durham 27707
Sharpsburg, Nash 27878
Shawboro, Currituck 27973
SHELBY, Cleveland
(See Page 2905)
Sherrills Ford, Catawba 28673
Shiloh, Camden 27974
Siler City, Chatham 27344
Siloam, Surry 27047
Simpson, Pitt 27879
Sims, Wilson 27880
Skyland, Buncombe 28776
Smithfield, Johnston 27577
Smyrna, Carteret 28579
Sneads Ferry, Onslow 28460
Snow Camp, Alamance 27349
Snow Hill, Greene 28580
Sophia, Randolph 27350
South Brunswick, Brunswick ... 28470
South Mills, Camden 27976
SOUTHERN PINES, Moore
(See Page 2908)
Southern Shores, Dare 27949
Southmont, Davidson 27351
Southport, Brunswick 28461
Sparta, Alleghany 28675
Speed, Edgecombe 27881
Spencer, Rowan 28159
Spindale, Rutherford 28160
Spring Hope, Nash 27882
Spring Lake, Cumberland 28390
Spruce Pine, Mitchell 28777
Stacy, Carteret 28581
Staley, Randolph 27355
Stallings, Union 28104
Stanfield, Stanly 28163
Stanley, Gaston 28164
Stantonsburg, Wilson 27883
Star, Montgomery 27356
State Road, Surry 28676
STATESVILLE, Iredell
(See Page 2909)
Stedman, Cumberland 28391
Stella, Carteret 28582
Stem, Granville 27581
Stokes, Pitt 27884
Stokesdale, Guilford 27357
Stoneville, Rockingham 27048
Stonewall, Pamlico 28583
Stony Point, Alexander 28678
Stovall, Granville 27582
Stumpy Point, Dare 27978
Sugar Grove, Watauga 28679
Sugar Mountain, Avery 28604
Summerfield, Guilford 27358
Sunbury, Gates 27979
Sunset Beach, Brunswick 28468
Supply, Brunswick 28462
Surf City, Onslow 28445
Swannanoa, Buncombe 28778
Swanquarter, Hyde 27885
Swansboro, Onslow 28584
Swepsonville, Alamance 27359
Sylva, Jackson 28779
Tabor City, Columbus 28463
Tapoco, Graham 28771
Tar Heel, Bladen 28392
Tarawa Terrace, Onslow 28543
Tarboro, Edgecombe 27886
Taylorsville, Alexander 28681
Teachey, Duplin 28464
Terrell, Catawba 28682
THOMASVILLE, Davidson
(See Page 2913)
Thurmond, Wilkes 28683
Tillery, Halifax 27887
Timberlake, Person 27583
Toast, Surry 27049
Tobaccoville, Forsyth 27050
Todd, Ashe 28684
Topsail Beach, Onslow 28445
Topton, Cherokee 28781
Townsville, Vance 27584
Traphill, Wilkes 28685
Trent Woods, Craven 28562
Trenton, Jones 28585
Trinity, Randolph 27370
Triplett, Watauga 28618
Troutman, Iredell 28166
Troy, Montgomery 27371
Tryon, Polk 28782
Tuckasegee, Jackson 28783
Turkey, Sampson 28393
Turnersburg, Iredell 28688
Tuxedo, Henderson 28784
Tyner, Chowan 27980
Union Grove, Iredell 28689
Union Mills, Rutherford 28167
Unionville, Union 28110
Valdese, Burke 28690
Vale, Lincoln 28168
Valle Crucis, Watauga 28691
Vanceboro, Craven 28586
Vandemere, Pamlico 28587
Vass, Moore 28394
Vaughan, Warren 27586
Vilas, Watauga 28692
Waco, Cleveland 28169
Wade, Cumberland 28395
Wadesboro, Anson 28170
Wagram, Scotland 28396
WAKE FOREST, Wake
(See Page 2913)
Walkertown, Forsyth 27051
Wallace, Duplin 28466
Wallburg, Davidson 27373
Walnut Cove, Stokes 27052
Walstonburg, Greene 27888
Wanchese, Dare 27981
Warne, Clay 28909
Warrensville, Ashe 28693
Warrenton, Warren 27589
Warsaw, Duplin 28398
Washington, Beaufort 27889
Watha, Pender 28478
Waves, Dare 27982
Waxhaw, Union 28173
WAYNESVILLE, Haywood
(See Page 2915)
Weaverville, Buncombe 28787
Webster, Jackson 28788
Weddington, Union 28104
Welcome, Davidson 27374
Weldon, Halifax 27890
Wendell, Wake 27591
Wentworth, Rockingham 27375
Wesley Chapel, Union 28104
Wesleyan College, Nash 27804
West End, Moore 27376
West Jefferson, Ashe 28694
Westfield, Surry 27053
Whispering Pines, Moore 28327
Whitakers, Nash 27891
White Oak, Bladen 28399
White Plains, Surry 27031
Whitehead, Alleghany 28675
Whiteville, Columbus 28472
Whitsett, Guilford 27377
Whittier, Jackson 28789
Wilbar, Wilkes 28651
Wilkesboro, Wilkes 28697
Willard, Pender 28478
Williamston, Martin 27892
Williston, Carteret 28579
Williston, Carteret 28589
Willow Spring, Wake 27592
WILMINGTON, New Hanover
(See Page 2919)
WILSON, Wilson
(See Page 2925)
Wilsons Mills, Johnston 27593
Windsor, Bertie 27983
Winfall, Perquimans 27985
Wingate, Union 28174
Winnabow, Brunswick 28479
WINSTON SALEM, Forsyth
(See Page 2927)
Winterville, Pitt 28590
Winton, Hertford 27986
Wise, Warren 27594
Woodfin, Buncombe 28804
Woodland, Northampton 27897
Woodleaf, Rowan 27054
Wrightsville Beach, New
Hanover 28480
Yadkinville, Yadkin 27055
Yanceyville, Caswell 27379
Youngsville, Franklin 27596
Zebulon, Wake 27597
Zionville, Watauga 28698
Zirconia, Henderson 28790

ALBEMARLE NC

General Delivery 28001

POST OFFICE BOXES MAIN OFFICE STATIONS AND BRANCHES

Box No.s
1 - 3274 28002
9998 - 9998 28001

NAMED STREETS

All Street Addresses 28001

NUMBERED STREETS

N & S 1st Ave & St 28001
2nd Ave 28001
N 2nd St 28001
S 2nd St
100-399 28001
320-320 28002
400-1098 28001
401-1099 28001
N & S 3rd Ave & St 28001
N & S 4th 28001
N & S 5th 28001
N 6th St 28001
N 7th Ave & St 28001
N 8th St 28001
N 9th St 28001
N 10th St 28001
N 11th St 28001

APEX NC

General Delivery 27502

POST OFFICE BOXES MAIN OFFICE STATIONS AND BRANCHES

Box No.s
All PO Boxes 27502

RURAL ROUTES

02, 03 27523

NAMED STREETS

W Abberley Ln 27502
Abbey Oak Ln 27502
Abby Knoll Dr 27502
Abraham Cir 27502
Abruzzo Dr 27502
Acorn Hill Ln 27502
Ada St 27502
Air Park Dr 27523
Akebia Way 27539
Aladdin Cir 27502
Alba Trl 27502
Albertson Pl 27502
Albritton Pl 27502
Alden Mist Ct 27539
Aldenwood Pl 27539
Alderny Dr 27502
Alderwood Ct 27502
Alice Ct 27502
N & S Alodie Ct 27502
Alphabet Rd 27523
Alpharetta Trl 27539
Alphawood Dr 27539
Alsace Dr 27502
Alston Rd 27523
Alstonville Rd 27523
Altair Cir 27502
Ambergate Sta 27502
American Ct 27523
American Way 27502
Anora Dr 27502
Anterbury Dr 27502
Antler Ct 27502
Apache Ln 27502
Apex Barbecue Rd 27502
Apex Peakway 27502
Apostle Dr 27502
Appaloosa Trl 27523
Appamattox Rd 27539
Apple Branch Ct 27539
Applecross Cir 27539
Applethorn Dr 27502
Arbor Valley Ln 27502
Argus Ct 27502
Arrowhead Dr 27539
Art Farm Rd 27502
Arthur Pierce Rd 27539
Ashbark Ct 27502
Ashley Rd 27539
Ashley Downs Dr 27502
Ashmill Ct 27539
Assurance Ln 27523
Aston Woods Ct 27523
Astor Valley Cir 27539
Atando Ct 27502
Atkinson Ct 27502
Autumnwood Cir 27502
Averroe Dr 27502
Avery Le Cir 27502
Aviary Cir 27539
Avoncroft Ct 27502
Avonlea Ct 27502
Ayden Mill Rd 27539
Babel Ct 27502
Baberton Dr 27502
Baffins Bay Path 27523
Bakers Aly 27539
Bally Shannon Way 27539
Ballytore Dr 27539
Bamburgh Ln 27539
Banstead Ct 27539
Banview Ln 27539
Barbee Rd 27523
Barnside Ln 27539
Barrow Nook Ct 27502
Basildon Ct 27539
Baslow Dr 27539
Batchelor Rd 27523
Batsonwood Pl 27539
Battery Bee Ln 27523
Battery Wagner Dr 27523
Battlewood Rd 27523
Baucom St 27502
Bay Bouquet Ln 27523
Baybark Cir 27539
Baysdale Ln 27523
Beaudet Ln 27523
Beaver Trl 27502
Beaver Creek Rd 27502
Beaver Creek Commons Dr 27502
Beckwith Farm Rd 27523
Becton Ct 27539
Bedford Ridge Dr 27539
Beech Hollow Pl 27502
E & W Beechmont Cir 27502
Beechtree Ct 27523
N & S Bell Haven St 27539
Bellagio Dr 27539
Bells Chapel Rd 27523
Bells Lake Rd 27539
Bells Pointe Ct 27539
Belnap Dr 27539
Benoit Pl 27502
Bentgrass Ct 27539
Bergen Ave 27502
Beringer Pl 27502
Berrygarden Ct 27502
Bexley Hills Bnd 27502
Big Leaf Loop 27502
Bingley Ct 27539
Bird Crk 27523
Birkenhead Ct 27539
Bizzell Ct 27539
Black Forest Dr 27539
Black Oak Ct 27502
Black Willow Dr 27523
Blackburn Rd 27502
Bladestone Ct 27502
Blanchard St 27502
Blaney Franks Rd 27539
Blaston Ct 27502
Blazing Trail Dr 27502
Bleasdale Ct 27539
Blossom Bay Ln 27523
Blue Horizon Dr 27539
Blue Needle Ln 27539
Blue Thorn Dr 27539
Blushing Rose Way 27502
Bob Horton Rd 27523
Bobbitt Rd 27539
Bodeswell Ln 27502
Bodwin Ln 27502
Bonhill Ct 27502
Bostian Dr 27539
Bouldercrest Ct 27539
Bountiful Ln 27539
Bountywood Dr 27539
Boxwood Ln 27502
Brad Ct 27502
Bramhall Ct 27502
Branch Creek Way 27539
Branch Line Ln 27502
Brandenton Way 27502
Brandon Crest Dr 27539
Branston Way 27539
Brantley Dr 27539
Branum Ct 27523
Brashear Ct 27523
Brasstown Ln 27502
Bray Ct 27502
Braywood Ct 27539
Breezemere Ct 27502
Brently Dr 27539
Briarberry Ct 27502
Briarcliff St 27502
Briarfield Dr 27502
Briarhurst Way 27539
Brickstone Dr 27502
Bridgeham Way 27502
Brierridge Dr 27502
Brighton Bluff Dr 27539
Brighton Forest Dr 27539
Brighton Ridge Dr 27539
Bristers Spring Way 27523
Bristol Blue St 27502
Brittany Point Ct 27502
Brittingham Loop 27502
Brittley Way 27502
Broadstone Way 27502
Broadwing Way 27539
Broken Yolk Trl 27523
Brook Cross Dr 27539
Brookewater Pl 27539
Brooklyn Rd 27502
Bryan Dr 27502
Bryant Pond Ln 27502
Brycker Ct 27502
Bryn Mawr Ct 27502
Buckhaven Ct 27502
Buckingham Way 27502
Buckskin Ln 27539
Buckwood Dr 27539
Buddy Dr 27502
Buffkin Ct 27539
Bull Run Dr 27539
Bullfinch Ln 27523
Bullhead Rd 27502
Bullock Ct 27502
Bungalow Park Dr 27502
Burgess Rd 27523
Burgess Hill Ct 27539
Burham Ct 27502
Burma Dr 27539
Burnside Dr 27539
Burnt Hickory Ct 27502
Burnt Pine Ct 27502
Butterbiggins Ln 27539
Butterfinger Ln 27502
Buttermilk Way 27502
Buttonquail Dr 27539
Buxton Wood Pl 27539
Byrdshire Ln 27502
C Kelly Farm Rd 27523
Cabana Dr 27539
Cabin Wood Ct 27502
Caboose Trl 27502
Cairphilly Castle Ct 27502
Caley Rd 27502
Caley Wilson Rd 27523
Calico Dr 27523
Callowhill Ct 27539
Camberley Dr 27502
Cambridge Hall Loop 27539
Cambridge Village Loop 27502
Camden Town Pl 27502
Cameron Glen Dr 27502
Cameron Valley Ct 27502
Cameron Woods Dr 27523
Camp Branch Ln 27502
Campground Rd 27523
Campione Way 27502
Candun Dr 27523
Cannonford Ct 27502
Canonicus Ct 27523
Canopy Woods Dr 27539
Canterbury Brook Ln 27502
Canterwood Dr 27539
Cantrell Ln 27502
Canyon Creek Way 27523
Capitata Xing 27502
Capri Dr 27539
Capulin Crest Dr 27539
Cardinal Blvd & St 27502
Care Free Cv 27523
Cargill Ln 27523
Caristonia Way 27502
Carlotta Ct 27539
Carolina Bell Rd 27523
Carriage Ridge Way 27502
Carriagehouse Ct 27539
N & S Carroll St 27502
Carsona Ct 27502
Carvers Creek Ln 27502
Cary Ct 27539
Cary Oaks Dr 27539
Cash St 27502
Cash Hill Dr 27523
Cassowary Ln 27523
Castelaine Cir 27502
Castleberry Rd 27523
Castlebridge Ct 27502
Castleburg Dr 27523
Caterpillar Dr 27539
Cateswood Ct 27539
Catherine Pl 27539
Catlette St 27523
Catskill Ct 27523
Cavatina Ct 27539
Cedar Glen Ct 27539
Cedar Trail Ln 27502
Cedar Twig Ct 27502
Cedar Wynd Dr 27502
Celandine Dr 27502
Celestine Pl 27502
Centennial Ct 27523
Center St 27502
Center Heights Ct 27502
Center Park Way 27502
Chanticlair Dr 27502
Chantilly Ct 27502
Chapel Glen Dr 27502
Chapel Ridge Rd 27502
Chapel Valley Ln 27502
Chapel View Dr 27523
Chapel View Ln 27502
Charington Ct 27502
Charlbert Ct 27539
Charlion Downs Ln 27502
Charred Oak Cir 27502
Chaswold Ct 27539
E & W Chatham St 27502
Chaumont Dr 27539
Checker Ct 27502
Chedington Dr 27502
Chenworth Dr 27502
Cherokee Ct 27502
Cherokee Sunset Rd 27502
Cherrystone Ln 27539
Chessie Sta 27502
Chestnut St 27502
Chickadee Ln 27502
Chickamauga Dr 27539
Chickering Ct 27502
Chilcott Ln 27502
Chimney Hill Dr 27502
Chimney Rock Ct 27502
Choplinshire Way 27539
Churchill Falls Pl 27539
Churchwood Dr 27502
Cicada Pl 27539
Circeo Ct 27502
Circle Dr 27539
Citrus Hill Dr 27502
Clarice Ln 27502
Claridge Ct 27539
Clark Farm Rd 27502
Classic Rd 27539
Claude Laurel Dr 27523
Clubhouse Ln 27523
Clyde Dr 27539
Clyde Farrell Rd 27523
N & S Coalport Dr 27502
Cockle Burr Dr 27539
Colby Chase Dr 27539
Colehurst Cres 27502
Colonial Oaks Dr 27539
Colony Woods Dr 27523
Combine Cir 27502
Commerce St 27502
Commodore Dr 27502
Concerto Ct 27539
Cone Ave 27502
Constitution Ct 27523
Cooke St 27502
Cookie Hill Ln 27523
Copeland Rd & St 27523
Copper Ridge Ct 27502
Coppercoin Ct 27502
Copperhead Rd 27539
Coralberry Cir 27539
Cordell Pl 27502
Coriander Ct 27539
Cornerstone Ridge Dr 27539
Correnna St 27502
Corsham Dr 27502
Cortland Dr 27539
Country Estates Mhp 27523
Country Glen Ct 27502
Country Valley Ct 27502
Covington Trce 27502
Covington Hill Way 27502
Craig Dr 27539
Cranswick Pl 27523
Cranwell Ct 27502
Creek Glen Way 27502
Creekbird Rd 27523
Creekside Hills Dr 27502
Creekside Landing Dr 27502
Creekwood Bluffs Ct 27539
Cregler Dr 27502
Crestwood Ct 27539
Crocketts Ct 27502
Crooked Brook Trl 27539
Cross Country Ln 27502
Crossvine Ct 27539
Crosswinds Rd 27523
Crosswinds Campground 27523
Crown Pointe Blvd 27502
Cuddington Ct 27502
Culvert St 27502
Cumberland Gap Ct 27523
Cunningham St 27502
Curley Maple Ct 27502
Cypress View Way 27502
Dalgarven Dr 27502
Daresbury Dr 27502
Darewood Ct 27539
Darley Dale Loop 27502
Davis Dr 27523
Dawn Ridge Ct 27523
Day Lily Ln 27539
Daysprings Ct 27539
Dayton Ridge Dr 27539
E Deer Run 27523
Deer Meadow Dr 27539
Deer Path Rd 27539
Deerborn Dr 27539
Deerfield Rd 27523
Delmayne Dr 27502
Democracy Ct & Pl 27523
Denman Dr 27539
Derry Down Ln 27539
Deveron Ct 27523
Devonhurst Ct 27502
Dezola St 27539
Dial Dr 27523
Diesel Path 27523
Dinsorette Ln 27539
Dirt Rd 27539
Doe Ct 27523
Doe Ln 27539
Doemont Dr 27539
Doeskin Dr 27539
Dogwood Ln 27502
Dotson Way 27523
Double Helix Rd 27523
Double Spring Ct 27502
Dove Forest Ln 27539
Doves Haven Dr 27539
Downing Pl 27502
Drexel Hill Ct 27539
Driskill Ct 27502
Drumlin Dr 27502
Dry Creek Ct 27523
Dual Parks Rd 27502
Dumont Ct 27523
Duncroft Ct 27502
Dunn Ridge Ln 27502
Dunvegan Ct 27502
Dunwick Ct 27523
Durnford Dr 27539
Dutch Elm Dr 27539
Eagles Watch Ct 27502
Earl Goodwin Rd 27523
Earnest Jones Rd 27523
Earth Dr 27539
Eastham Dr 27502
Eastleigh Ct 27502
Eastridge Dr 27539
Eastview St 27502
Ebenezer Rd 27502
Echo Creek Pl 27539
Echo Glen Ln 27523
Eddie Creek Dr 27539
Edinburgh Downs Ln 27502
Edwards Dr 27539
Eisenhower Dr 27539
Elbury Dr 27502
Elderberry Ln 27539
Eldon Ln 27502
Elizabeth Ln 27523
N & S Ellington St 27502
Ellinwood Dr 27539
N & S Elm St 27502
Elmstead Ct 27502
Elmswick Ct 27539
Energy Dr 27502
Englewood Dr 27539
Erlwood Ct 27502
Essie Dr 27523
Estate Dr 27502
Evans Rd 27502
Evening Star Dr 27502
Evening Storm Pl 27539
Ever After Ln 27523
Everard Ct 27539
Evian Ct 27502
Eyam Hall Ln 27502
Fair Haven St 27539
Fair Oaks Ln 27502
Fair Spring Ct 27502
Fair Weather Ct 27523
Fairdale Ct 27502
Fairfax Woods Dr 27502
Fairview Rd 27502
Fairview St 27539
Fairview Ridge Ln 27539
Faith St 27539
Fallen Oak Dr 27502
Fallon Ct 27502
Family Circle Rd 27539
Fantail Ln 27523
Fanwood Ct 27502
Fargale Ln 27539
Farmpond Rd 27523
Farrells Crk 27523
Farrington Rd 27523
E Farthold Aly 27539
Fawnview Ct 27539
Feathercrest Ln 27539
Felder Ave 27539
Feldon River Ct 27539
Fern Berry Ct 27502
Fern Valley Ln 27523
E Ferrell Rd W 27523
Ferrington Ct 27539
Ferson Rd 27523
Field Glow Ln 27539
Firenza Dr 27502
Fitchburg Ct 27523
Fletcher Mill Ct 27539
Flint Valley Ln 27502
Flints Pond Cir 27523
Flippin Way 27539
Floresta Dr 27539
Flying Hawk Rd 27523
Folkner Trl 27523
Foraker St 27539
Fordcrest Dr 27502
Forest Grove Dr 27502
Forestcrest Ct 27502
Forester Ln 27539
Forget Me Not Rd 27523
Formal Pl 27502
Forrymast Trl 27539
Forthview Way 27502
Fox Shadow Dr 27502
Fox Terrace Dr 27502
Foy Glen Ct 27539
Franconia Way 27502
Frenchurch Way 27502
Friendship Rd
3000-3799 27502
3800-4799 27539
Frissell Ave 27502
Frontenac Ct 27539
Fullcrest Way 27539
Gablefield Ln 27502
Gables Gate Ct 27539
Galant Fox Ct 27539
Galimore Way 27502
Gallent Hedge Trl 27539
Garden Gate Pl 27502
Garden Oaks Ln 27539
Garden Plaza Way 27502
Garden Side Way 27502
Garden Spot Path 27539
Gardner Rd 27523
Garrity Ct 27502
Gatewood Falls Ct 27539
Geiger Cir 27539
Geoffrey Ct 27539
George Pl 27502
Germaine St 27502
Gigantea Ln 27502
Gilby Rd 27502
Gilchrist Ln 27539
Gillingham Dr 27539
Glade Hill Dr 27539
Glashields Way 27539
Glaston Ct 27502
Glastonbury Rd 27539
Glen Arbor Dr 27539
Glen Cairn Ct 27502
Glen Summitt Ct 27502
Glendale Dr 27539
Glenrothes Cv 27539
Glenshire Ct 27502
Glentanner Ct 27502
Glenwell Ct 27539

Golden Plover Dr 27502
Golden Ridge Ct 27502
Goldenview Ct 27539
Goldfinch Ln 27523
Goldleaf Ct 27539
Goldspot Ct 27502
Good Shepherd Way 27523
Goodwin Rd 27523
Goodworth Dr 27539
Goolsby Ct 27539
Gopher Ln 27502
Graham Newton Rd 27539
Grand Barton Ct 27502
Grand Central Sta 27502
Grand Helton Ct 27502
Grand Pine Pl 27539
Grandbridge Dr 27539
Grande Chateau Ln 27502
Grande Maison Dr 27502
Grappenhall Dr 27502
Grassview Ct 27502
Grassy Point Rd 27502
Grassy Ridge Ct 27502
Graybark Ct 27502
Grayling Dr 27539
Grayson Jenkins Rd 27523
Graystar Rd 27502
Grazing Meadows Ct 27502
Great Northern Sta 27502
Green Ford Ln 27502
Green Glen Way 27502
Green Grass Ct 27502
Green Hickory Ct 27523
Green Level Rd 27523
Green Level Church
Rd 27523
Green Level West Rd 27523
Green Passage Ln 27502
Greendale Ct 27502
Greenlea Dr 27523
Greenleaf St 27502
Grenoch Valley Ln 27539
Gretna Ln 27539
Greycrest Ct 27539
Greyhawk Pl 27539
Greymoss Ln 27539
Grindstone Dr 27502
Grouse Trl 27502
Grove St 27502
Gullane Ct 27502
Gumdrop Path 27502
Gumleaf Dr 27539
Haddon Hall Dr 27502
Halsmer Ct 27502
Hambridge Ct 27502
Hammerstone Way 27539
Hampstead Heath Ln 27502
Handel Ln 27502
Handhewn St 27502
Hanson Walk Ln 27539
Happy Days Ct 27502
Harbor Haven Dr 27502
Hardenridge Ct 27539
Hardwood Dr 27539
Harriat Dr 27539
Hartwood Ct 27539
Harvestwood Dr 27539
Harwood St 27502
Hasbrouck Dr 27523
Hattie Rd 27523
Haughton Green Ct 27502
Havelock Ct 27539
Haventree Ct 27502
Hawks Nest Way 27502
Hawks Ridge Ct 27539
Hawkscrest Ct 27502
Haybarn Ct 27502
Haywards Heath Ln 27502
Hazelhurst Cir 27502
Healthplex Way 27502
Hearn Ct 27539
Hearthside Ct 27502
Heathcote Ln 27502
Heatherwood Dr 27502
Heathwood Dairy Rd 27502
Heavy Weight Dr 27539
Hedera Way 27539
Hemlock Hills Ln 27539
Henderson Rd 27539
Henniker St 27523
Henson Pl 27502
Herbert St 27502
Heritage Dr 27523
Heritage Creek Dr 27539
Heritage Meadows Ln 27539
Heritage Village Ln 27502
Herndon Ln 27539
Hester Rd 27502
Hibiscus Ct 27523
Hickory Bottom Ct 27502
Hickory Hill Ln 27523
Hickory Valley Ct 27502
Hickory View Ln 27502
Hidden Stream Dr 27539
Hidwell Pl 27539
High Holborn Ct 27502
High Lonesome Ln 27539
High Ramble Ln 27502
Highland Rd 27523
Highland Creek Dr 27539
Highland Mist Cir 27539
Hill Hollow Way 27523
Hillantrae Ln 27502
Hillcrest Rd 27502
Hillcroft Ct 27502
Hillsford Ln 27502
Hilltop Farms Rd 27502
Hilt Ct 27502
Himalaya Way 27502
Hinman Ln 27539
Hinton St 27502
Historic District Ln 27502
Hoboken Ct 27502
Hogan Farm Rd 27523
Holland Rd 27502
Holland Chapel Rd 27523
Holleman St 27502
Holly St 27502
Holly Brook Dr 27539
Holly Run Rd 27539
Holly Springs Rd 27539
Holly Springs New Hill
Rd 27539
Holly Stream Ct 27539
Hollyhock Ln 27539
Holt Rd 27523
Holtridge Dr 27523
Homegate Cir 27502
Homeplace Dr 27539
Homeport Cir 27539
Homesong Way 27502
Homestead Ct 27523
Homestead Park Dr 27502
Hope Hill Ln 27502
Horsham Way 27502
Horton Pond Rd 27523
Hortons Trailer Park 27523
Housatonic Ct 27523
Howell Rd 27523
Hudson Ave 27502
N & S Hughes St 27502
Humie Olive Rd 27502
Hundleby Dr 27539
Huntcliff Ct 27539
Hunter St 27502
Hurdover Rd 27539
Huskfield Ct 27539
Indian Trl 27502
Indian Creek Ln 27523
Inglenook Pl 27502
Ingraham Dr 27502
Inkberry Ct 27539
Interior Ct 27502
Investment Blvd 27502
Ironcreek Pl 27539
Irongate Dr 27502
Ironsides Ln 27523
Iveysprings Ct 27539
Ivory Bluff Trl 27539
Ivy Glen Dr 27502
J B Morgan Rd 27523
Jacks Dr 27502
Jacobs Creek Ln 27523
James St 27502
James Ext St 27502
James Mill Ct 27539
Jamie Lynn Ln 27523
Jamison Park Dr 27539
Jamison Woods Ln 27539
Jehon Ct 27502
Jenks Rd 27523
Jenks Carpenter Rd 27523
Jerimouth Dr 27502
Jernigan Dr 27539
Jerryanne Ct 27523
Jersey City Pl 27523
Jessie Dr 27539
John Horton Rd 27523
Johnson Pond Rd 27539
Jones St 27502
Jones Family Rd 27539
Jordan Lake Commons
Dr 27523
Joslyn Ridge Ct 27502
Jovel Ct 27539
Kearse Rd 27539
Keith St 27502
Kellerhis Dr 27502
Kelly Ct 27539
Kelly Rd
1000-1199 27523
1200-2699 27502
Kelly Brook Ct 27502
Kelly Glen Dr 27502
Kelly Point Ct 27502
Kelly West Dr 27502
Kellyridge Dr 27502
Kelvington Pl 27502
Kenneil Ct 27502
Kenneth Ridge Ct 27523
Kentbury Ln 27502
Kentshire Pl 27523
Keokuk Ct 27523
Keppoch Ct 27502
Kiftsgate Ln 27502
Kildaire Farm Rd 27539
Kildalton Pl 27539
Kildee Ct 27539
King David Ct 27539
Kingfield Dr 27539
Kings Castle Dr 27502
Kings Pine Ln 27539
Kings View Trl 27502
Kingsway Dr 27502
Kinship Ln 27502
Kissena Ln 27502
Knightsborough Way 27502
Knightshire Dr 27539
Knollcreek Dr 27539
Knollwood Dr 27539
Knottsberry Way 27539
Kylesku Ct 27502
Lacuna Woods Ln 27539
E & W Lady Diana Ct 27502
W Lake Rd 27539
Lake Farm Rd 27523
Lake Marsha Ct 27523
Lake Meadow Dr 27502
Lake Pine Dr 27502
Lake Song Cir 27539
Lakeview Dr 27502
Lambton Wood Dr 27539
Lamm Dr 27502
Lanewood Way 27502
Langshire Ct 27502
Langston Cir 27539
Lansbrooke Ln 27502
Lantern Light Ct 27539
Larboard Dr 27502
Larkhaven Pl 27539
Latheron Ct 27502
Laura Duncan Rd
400-1799 27502
1800-2499 27523
Laura Margaret Ln 27523
Laura Village Rd 27523
Laurel Berry Ct 27502
Laurel Springs Way 27523
Lavinnia Ln 27539
Lawdraker Rd 27539
Lawson Ln 27502
Layton Ridge Dr 27539
Lazio Ln 27502
Lazy Days Ct 27502
Lees Locke Ln 27539
Leicester Ct 27539
Lemon Drop Cir 27502
Les Arbres Dr 27539
Les Paul Ln 27539
Lethaby Ct 27502
Lett Rd 27539
Levering Mill Rd 27539
Lewter Shop Rd 27523
Lexham Ct 27539
Lexington Farm Rd 27502
Lexington Pointe Ln 27502
Lexington Ridge Ln 27502
Lianfair Ln 27539
Licorice Dr 27502
Lilyford Ln 27502
Lindell Dr 27539
Lindfield Ct 27502
Linwood St 27502
Linwood Apartments 27502
Little White Pine Ct 27539
Littleman Ln 27539
Litton St 27502
Lockley Rd 27539
Locust Grove Dr 27539
Log Barn Ln 27523
Logans Call Ct 27539
Loganwood Dr 27523
Lone Oak Ln 27502
Long Gate Way 27502
Longton Hall Ct 27502
Lorbacher Rd 27539
Lorry Ln 27539
Lower Creek Ct 27539
Lucky Dr 27539
Lucy Lee Ln 27539
Lufkin Rd 27539
Luther Rd 27523
Lylebourne Ct 27502
Lynch St 27502
Lyndenbury Dr 27502
Lynnford Dr 27539
Lynnhaven Dr 27539
M T Holland Rd 27523
Madison Hill Ct 27502
Magdala Pl 27502
Magnolia Breeze Ct 27502
Mandavilla Way 27539
Manderston Ln 27502
Manns Loop Rd 27539
Mannsfield Ct 27539
Manter Ln 27523
Maple Ave 27502
Maple Bottom Dr 27539
Maple Creek Ct 27502
Maple Crest Ct 27502
Maple Shade Ln 27502
Maple Springs Dr 27523
Maplechase Ln 27539
Maplegreen Ln 27502
Marazzi Trl 27502
Marco Dr 27502
Mark Weaver Ln 27502
Marker Dr 27502
Markham Ln 27523
Markham St 27502
Markham Plantation 27523
Maroni Dr 27502
Marquis Ct 27502
Marston Ct 27502
Marthas Chapel Rd 27523
Mashpee Ln 27539
N & S Mason St 27502
Matlock Ct 27539
Matney Ln 27502
Maubrey Ct 27502
Maxton Crest Dr 27539
Maya Ct 27502
Mayfield Dr 27539
Mccoy Rd 27523
Mckenzie Meadow Ln 27539
Mcqueens Dr 27523
Meadow Beauty Dr 27539
Meadow Gate Dr 27502
Meadow Lake Dr 27539
Meadowhaven Dr 27539
Meadowrock Ln 27502
Meadowview Ct 27539
Megwood Ct 27539
Melbry Ct 27502
Mellonsbury Dr 27502
Menteith Ct 27502
Merchant Dr 27523
Merion Station Dr 27539
Merrimac Dr 27539
Metro Sta 27502
Meyerswood Dr 27539
Mica Lamp Ct 27502
Middle Creek Park
Ave 27539
Midstream Ct 27539
Midsummer Ln 27502
Milano Ave 27502
Milk Paint Aly 27502
Milky Way Dr 27502
Mill Hopper Ln 27502
Millens Bay Ct 27539
Millyork Ct 27539
Minnifer Ct 27539
Misty Hollow Ln 27502
Misty Lake St 27539
Misty Water Ct 27502
Mockingbird Ct 27523
Mockingbird Ln 27502
Modest Way 27502
Monaco Ter 27502
Monarch Birch Dr 27539
Mondavi Pl 27502
Moneta Ln 27539
Monitor Ct 27539
Monte Ter 27502
Montvale Ct 27502
E & W Moore St 27502
Morecambe Way 27539
Moretz Ct 27502
Morning Dew Ln 27539
Morning Mist Ct 27539
Morrisville Pkwy 27523
Mosley Ave 27539
Moss Mountain Ln 27539
Mosstree Dr 27502
Mossy Glade Cir 27502
Mossy Rock Way 27539
Mostyn Ln 27502
Moulin Way 27523
Mount Pisgah Church
Rd 27523
Mount Zion Church Rd 27502
Mountain Ct 27502
Mountainbrook Rd 27539
Mutch Dr 27502
Myrtle Grove Ln 27502
Myrtle View Ct 27502
Napa Pl 27502
Napleton Cir 27502
Napoli Dr 27502
Narnia Dr 27539
Nasturtium Way 27502
Nc Highway 55 W
800-1399 27502
Nc Highway 55 W
1400-1799 27523
Nc Highway 751 27523
Needle Pine Dr 27539
Nellie Rd 27539
Neodak Rd 27523
Ness Dr 27539
New Brighton Dr 27539
New Chester Ct 27502
New Dover Rd 27539
New Haven St 27539
New Hill Olive Chapel
Rd 27502
New Hope Church Rd 27523
New Oxford Dr 27539
New Timber Path 27502
New Yarmouth Way 27502
Newberry Grove Dr 27539
Newbury Park Way 27539
Newcomb St 27539
Newington Way 27502
No Record St
99-99 27523
199-199 27539
North St 27502
Norwood Ln 27502
Nottinghill Walk 27502
Nutting Ln 27523
Oak St 27502
Oak Bark Dr 27539
Oak Branch Dr 27539
Oak Fork Dr 27539
Oak Hill Dr 27523
Oak Park Dr 27539
Oak Pine Dr 27502
Oak Stream Ln 27523
Oak Tree Dr 27539
Oaken Pl 27539
Oakgate Ct 27502
Oakland Dr 27539
Oakley Woods Ln 27539
Oakwell Ct 27502
Obridge Ct 27502
October Glory Ln 27539
Old Byre Way 27502
Old Carriage Ct 27502
Old Cask Way 27502
Old Center St 27539
Old Compton Pl 27502
Old Grove Ln 27502
Old Hill Ct 27502
Old Holly Springs Apex
Rd
2700-2899 27502
2900-4599 27539
Old Holly Tree Ct 27502
Old House Ct 27502
Old Ivey Rd 27523
Old Jenks Rd 27523
Old Kestrel Dr 27523
Old London Way 27523
Old Mill Village Dr 27502
Old Raleigh Rd 27502
Old Smithfield Rd 27539
Old Sorrell Rd 27539
Old Sturbridge Dr 27539
Old Us 1 Hwy 27502
Old White Oak Church
Rd 27523
Olde Thompson Creek
Rd 27523
Olde Walker Mill Rd 27502
Olive St 27502
Olive Chapel Rd 27502
Olive Chapel Road
Ext 27502
Olive Dairy Rd 27502
Olive Farm Rd 27502
Olives Chapel Rd 27502
Optimist Farm Rd 27539
Orchard Crest Ct 27539
Orchard Knoll Dr 27539
Orchard Point Ct 27539
Orchard Villas Ave 27502
Orchestra Ct 27539
Overby Rd 27539
Overcliff Dr 27502
Oxford Green Dr 27539
Paddock Dr 27523
Padstone Dr 27502
Painted Creek Way 27539
Palace Ct 27502
Palermo Ct 27539
Paradox Ct 27523
Park Summit Blvd 27523
Parkers Creek Rd 27523
Parkers Creek Beach
Rd 27523
Parkerson Ln 27502
Parkfield Dr 27502
Parliament Pl 27502
Parsifal Pl 27502
Passaic Way 27523
Pastro Ct 27502
Patapsco Dr 27523
Pate St 27502
Patrick Place Dr 27539
Patriot Way 27523
Patterson Grove Rd 27502
Paynes Ct 27539
Peabody Pl 27523
Peace Haven Pl 27502
Peach Blossom Ln 27539
Peachstone Ct 27539
Peak Ct 27539
Pearson St 27502
Pearson Farms Rd 27502
Pemberton Hill Rd 27502
Pendula Path 27502
Pennington Way 27502
Pennino Way 27502
Pepper Bush Ct 27502
Percussion Dr 27539
Perney Ct 27539
Perry Rd 27502
Perry Farms Dr 27502
Perrymount Ct 27502
Persimmon Pl 27523
Piazzo Ct 27502
Pierce Olive Rd 27539
Pierre Pl 27502
Pikeview Ln 27502
Pilot Mountain Ct 27502
Pilsley Rd 27539
Pine Cut Ln 27502
Pine Knob Ct 27502
Pine Mill Ln 27502
Pine Nut Ln 27502
Pine Rail Ln 27523
Pine Tag Ct 27502
Pinedale Rd 27523
Pinefield Rd 27523
Pineslope Dr 27539
Pinewood Dr 27502
Piney Branch Dr 27539
Piney Woods Ln 27502
Pink Cherokee Ct 27502
Pinkerton Pl 27539
Pizzo Pt 27502
Placid Creek Ln 27539
Pleasant Plains Rd 27502
Pleasant View Dr 27539
Poets Corner Ct 27523
Poets Glade Dr 27523
S Pointe Dr 27539
Pond View Ct 27523
Pony Soldier Dr 27539
Poplar Ln 27523
Porchaven Ln 27539
Porchside Dr 27502
Port Haven Dr 27502
Portobello Rd 27502
Portwind Ln 27539
Post Rail Ln 27502
Powell Hatley Dr 27523
Powell Meadow Ct 27539
Preatonwood Dr 27539
Presenteer Trl 27539
Preservation Ln 27502
Pricewood Ln 27502
Princes Dead End Rd 27502
Pristine Water Dr 27539
Production Dr 27539
Proper Ct 27502
Providence Green Ln 27502
Public Dr 27502
Purple Glory Dr 27502
Quail Cir 27502
Quail Ridge Dr 27523
Queen City Cres 27523
Quisisana Rd 27502
Rabbit Walk Ln 27523
Ragan Rd 27502
Rainesview Ln 27502
Ramblewood Dr 27523
Ranger Pl 27502
Rapp Ln 27502
Rayanne Ct 27502

Rays Dr 27523
Reams Ct 27523
Red Barn Way 27502
Red Cedar Way 27523
Red Deer Ct 27502
Red Maple Ct 27523
Red Rock Dr 27539
Red Sage Ct 27502
Red Sunset Dr 27502
Red Twig Rd 27502
Redwater Branch Ct 27502
Reedy Ct 27502
Reliance Ave 27539
Restonwood Dr 27539
Restoration Way 27502
Reunion Arbor Ln 27539
Reunion Creek Pkwy 27539
Reunion Meadows Ln 27539
Reunion Park Dr 27539
Reunion Pine Dr 27539
Reunion Plaza Rd 27539
Reunion Ridge Way 27539
Reunion Woods Trl 27539
Rexhill Ct 27502
Rhodes Rd 27539
Rhythm Dr 27539
Richardson Rd 27502
Ridge Lake Dr 27539
Ridgeback Rd 27523
Ridgepine Dr 27502
Righters Mill Way 27539
Riley Oaks Ln 27539
Ringgold Dr 27539
River Cir 27502
River Dee Ct 27502
River Falls Dr 27539
Rock Island Dr 27502
Rocklyn Ln 27502
Rocky Rd 27523
Rocky Mountain Way 27502
Rolling Knoll Rd 27523
Rollsby Ct 27539
Roosondall Ct 27523
Rosabella Ln 27502
Rose Laurel Ct 27523
Rosiere Dr 27539
Roswellcrest Ct 27539
Rothwood Way 27502
Royal Hunt Ct 27502
Royal Red Trl 27502
Royce Webster Dr 27523
Runells Ln 27539
Rushden Way 27502
Rushing Breeze Ct 27502
Rushing Wind Way 27502
Rustic Mill Dr 27539
Rustic Pine Ct 27502
Saddle River Rd 27502
Saint Edmunds Ln 27539
Saint Emilion Ct 27502
E & W Saint Helena Pl 27502
E & W Saint Julian Pl 27502
Salem Dr 27539
N Salem St
100-1599 27502
1600-2399 27523
S Salem St 27502
Salem Church Rd 27523
Salem Towne Ct 27502
Salem Village Dr 27502
Samara St 27502
Sammons Ct 27539
Sanair Ct 27502
Sanbour Dr 27502
Sancroft Dr 27539
Sandy Hills Ct 27523
Santa Rosa Dr 27502
Sardinia Ln 27502
Sassacus Ln 27523
Satinwood Dr 27502
Satori Way 27539
Saunders St 27502
Savoy Way 27502
Sawcut Ln 27502
Sawyers Mill Dr 27539
Schieffelin Rd 27502
Scissortail Ln 27523
Scotts Ridge Trl 27502
Sea Biscuit Ln 27539
Seaboard St 27502
Seaforth Beach Rd 27523
Seagram St 27502
Seagroves Ct 27502
Sears Place Dr 27523
Secluded Acres Rd 27523
Sedona Pl 27539
Senoma Pl 27502
Senter Farm Rd 27539
Sentimental Ln 27539
Serene Forest Dr 27539
Serenity Trl 27523
Settlement Dr 27523
Sexton Rd 27523
Shackleton Rd 27502
Shad Ln 27523
Shadow Mist Ct 27539
Shady Lane Cir 27523
Shady Ridge Ct 27502
Shalon Ct 27502
Shannon Cir 27539
Sharp Top Trl 27502
Shawcroft Ct 27502
Sheffield St 27539
Shell Point Way 27523
Shelter Haven Dr 27502
Shepherds Glade Dr 27523
Shepherds Vineyard Dr 27502
Shining Star Ct 27502
Shoofly Path 27502
Shopton Dr 27502
Short St 27502
Shumard Oak Ln 27539
Silky Dogwood Trl 27502
Silver Bend Dr 27539
Silver Branch Ct 27539
Silver Stirrup Ln 27502
Simca Ct 27502
Simonton Ct 27539
Sir Brennan Ct 27523
Skinny Pine Ct 27502
Sky Meadow Dr 27539
Slayton Dr 27539
Sleepy Valley Rd 27523
Smith Rd 27539
Smokewood Dr 27502
Snafflebit Ln 27502
Snowdrop Ct 27502
Soaring Hawk Pl 27539
Solandra Ln 27539
Songbird Ct 27523
Southmoor Ct 27502
Southwinds Run 27502
Sparta Ln 27502
Speckled Alder Ct 27523
Splitrock Trl 27539
Spotter Dr 27502
Spring St 27539
Spring Arbor Ct 27502
Spring Dove Ln 27539
Spring Fern Ct 27502
Spring Gate Ct 27502
Springmill Ct 27502
Springtime Dr 27539
Spurwood Ct 27502
Squaw Walden Ln 27523
Stanwood Dr 27502
Star Flower Ct 27539
Starita Ct 27502
State Park Rd 27523
Steam Ridge Ct 27523
Steele Creek Ct 27502
Steeple Chase Bnd 27502
Stenness Ct 27502
Stephenson Rd 27539
Sterling Silver Dr 27502
E & W Sterlington Pl 27502
Steven Cir 27539
Stick Barn Ln 27502
E Stone Rd 27523
Stone Point Ln 27523
Stonecreek Dr 27539
Storemont Way 27539
Strawthorne Ct 27502
Straywhite Ave 27539
Striped Maple Ct 27539
Sugargrove Ct 27539
Sugarland Dr 27502
Summer Brook Dr 27539
Summer Days Ct 27502
Summer Oaks Dr 27539
Summer Ridge Ct 27539
Summer Stars St 27502
Summercrest Dr 27539
Summit Lake Dr 27523
Suncliffe Ct 27539
Sunlake Farms Rd 27539
Sunny Brae Ct 27502
Sunny Creek Ln 27502
Sunrise Ave 27539
Sunset Ave 27502
Sunset Fairways Dr 27539
Sunset Lake Rd 27539
Sunset Meadows Dr 27523
Sunset Pointe Dr 27539
Sunshine Crest Ct 27539
Sunshine Valley Ln 27539
Surry Dale Ct 27502
Surry Ridge Cir 27502
Sutton Glen Dr 27523
Swandon Ct 27502
Sweet Laurel Ln 27523
Sweet Tart Ln 27502
Sweetgum Dr 27539
Sweetwater Red Ct 27502
Swift Wind Pl 27539
Sworton Ct 27502
Sycamore St 27502
T D Ln 27539
Talicud Trl 27539
Talisker Ct 27502
Tamora Ct 27502
Tartarian Trl 27502
Tavernier Ct 27539
Taywood Way 27502
Tear Drop Cir 27539
Technology Dr 27539
Telford Ln 27502
Templeton St 27502
Templeton Gap Dr 27523
Ten Ten Rd 27539
Tender Dr 27539
Tendy Ln 27502
Terasina Ct 27502
Terrace Green Ln 27502
Terrene Dr 27539
Terric Summit Ln 27502
Teulon Way 27502
Tewdsbury Ct 27502
Thane Ct 27539
Thistle Top Trl 27502
Thomas Cash Rd 27523
Thompson Rd 27523
Thompson St 27502
Thorn Hollow Dr 27523
Thorncrest Dr 27539
Thorncroft Ln 27502
Thorngate Rd 27502
Thriftwood Dr 27539
Thurrock Dr 27539
Tice Hurst Ln 27502
Tiemouse Ln 27523
Tiltonshire Ln 27539
Timber Cut Ln 27502
Timberlea Ct 27502
Timken Forest Dr 27502
Timpani Trl 27539
Tingen Rd 27502
Toad Hollow Trl 27502
Tobacco Farm Dr 27502
Tobacco Leaf Ln 27502
Todd Ln 27523
Tody Goodwin Rd 27502
Tordelo Pl 27502
Torrence Dr 27502
Tortoise Shell Dr 27523
Tosca Trl 27502
Towhee Dr 27502
Town Home Dr 27502
Town Side Dr 27502
Tracey Creek Ct 27502
Trackmire Ln 27539
Trafford Ct 27502
Trafford Park Ct 27502
Transit Trl 27502
Tranter Dr 27502
Tree Haven Dr 27539
Treetop View Ln 27539
Treewood Ln 27539
Treviso Ln 27502
Treys Ct 27539
Tribayne Ct 27502
Tribble Gate Ct 27502
Troyer Pl 27502
Truelove Dr 27539
Tucker Dr 27539
Tuffeto Trce 27502
N & S Tunstall Ave 27502
Turnbuckle Ct 27539
Turner Dr 27539
Turner Trailer Park 27539
Turtle Creek Farm Rd 27523
Twelve Oaks Ln 27502
Twig Ct 27539
Twin Circle Ct 27502
Twin Creek Rd 27523
Two Pond Ln 27523
Tyne River Ct 27539
Umbria Ct 27502
Upchurch St 27502
Urbino Ct 27502
Us 64 Hwy E & W 27523
Valley Hill Ct 27539
Valley Rush Dr 27502
Van Gogh Ln 27539
Vanclaybon Rd 27523
Vandam Dr 27539
Vatersay Dr 27502
Vaudry Ct 27502
Vauxhall Dr 27502
Veneto Pl 27502
Venezia Way 27502
Verde Rd 27523
Versa Ct 27502
Vetta Cv 27502
Victorian Grace Ln 27539
Victory Pine Ln 27539
Village Commons Ln 27502
Village Loop Dr 27502
Villagio Dr 27502
Vincendo Rd 27502
Vintage Grove Ln 27502
Vintage Hill Cir 27502
Virginia Pine Ln 27539
Viscount Ln 27539
Vision Dr 27523
Waddell Ct 27502
Walden Rd 27502
Walden Creek Dr 27523
Walden Glade Run 27523
Walden Meadow Dr 27523
Walden Woods Dr 27523
Walnut Hill Ct 27502
Wandering Swan Ln 27502
Wandle Ln 27502
Wanstraw Way 27539
Warm Wood Ln 27539
Wasdell Way 27523
Waterclose Ct 27502
Waterdale Ct 27502
Waterford Green Dr 27502
Waterland Dr 27502
Watersglen Dr 27502
Waterton Ln 27502
Watertree Ln 27502
Waynesmill Dr 27539
Weaver Crossing Rd 27502
Weaver Hill Dr 27502
Wedge Porr Ct 27539
Weehawken Pl 27523
Weeping Oak Ct 27539
N & S Wellonsburg Pl 27502
Wellstone Cir 27502
Wendhurst Ct 27502
Wesley Ct 27539
Wesley Ridge Dr 27539
West St 27502
Westbury Hill Ln 27539
Westford Way 27539
Westleigh Ct 27539
Westwood Ln 27539
Wexleigh St 27502
Whippowill Ct 27502
Whispering Wind Dr 27539
Whistle Call Run 27539
Whistleberry Ct 27539
Whistling Quail Run 27502
Whiston Dr 27502
White Cloud Cir 27502
White Dogwood Rd 27502
White Kousa Pl 27502
White Magnolia Ct 27502
White Oak Church Rd 27523
White Oak Creek Dr 27523
White Pond Ct 27523
White Swan Ct 27539
White Trillium Ln 27539
Whitehart Ln 27539
Whitetail Dr 27539
Wickham Ridge Rd 27539
Wicksteed Ct 27502
Wild Apple Ct 27523
Wild Cherry Dr 27523
Wild Sonnet Ct 27502
E Williams St
100-1399 27502
1400-2399 27539
W Williams St
100-1299 27502
1400-1400 27523
1402-1799 27523
Willow Branch Ct 27502
Willow Knoll Ct 27502
Willow Trace Ct 27539
Willowdale Ct 27539
Willowleaf Way 27502
Wimberly Rd 27523
Windcap Dr 27539
Windcrest Dr 27502
Windermere Lake Ct 27502
Winding Way 27502
Winding Creek Rd 27502
Winding Oak Way 27539
E Windiste Blvd 27523
Windscape Dr 27539
Windsong Cir 27539
Windy Rd 27502
Windy Creek Ln 27502
Wine Berry Rd 27523
Winecott Dr 27502
Wingspan Ct 27539
Winpost Ln 27502
Winter Hill Dr 27502
Winterview Pl 27539
Wirks Worth Cir 27502
Wisteria Ln 27523
Witheridge Ct 27502
Wizard Ln 27523
Wolfs Bane Dr 27539
Woodbriar St 27502
Wooded Lake Dr 27523
Woodfield Dead End Rd 27539
Woodgate Ln 27502
Woodlands Creek Way 27502
Woodleaf Ln 27539
Woodmill Run 27539
Woods Creek Rd 27539
Woodsaw Xing 27502
Woolard Way 27502
Wrenn St 27502
Wrenn Meadow Ct 27539
Wrenns Nest Dr 27539
Wrennstone Ct 27539
Wrong Way 27523
Wyckford Pl 27539
Wyndridge Dr 27539
Xanthacarpa Ct 27502
Yatesdale Ct 27502
Yellow Jasmine Path 27502
Yellow Rainbow Ct 27502
N York Ct 27502
Yorkmont Ct 27502
Zeno Rd 27502

NUMBERED STREETS

All Street Addresses 27502

ASHEBORO NC

General Delivery 27203

POST OFFICE BOXES MAIN OFFICE STATIONS AND BRANCHES

Box No.s
1 - 10002 27204
77703001 - 77703043 27203
77705001 - 77705043 27205

RURAL ROUTES

01, 02, 03, 04, 05, 06, 07, 08, 10, 11, 12 27205

NAMED STREETS

Abby Ln 27205
Abner Rd 27205
E & W Academy St 27203
Akins St 27205
Albemarle Rd
500-999 27203
1000-1199 27205
Alexander Ct 27205
Allen Ct 27205
E & W Allred St 27203
Amelia Ct 27203
Amity Rd 27203
Anchor Dr 27205
Andrew Hunter Rd 27203
Andrews St 27205
Anns Ct 27205
Anthony Ct 27205
Appaloosa Trl 27205
Apple Tree Rd 27205
Applegate Ln 27205
April Ln 27205
Arabian Dr 27205
Archie Newsom Rd 27205
Arlington Dr 27205
Arlington Drive Ext 27205
Armfield Ave 27203
Arnold St 27203
Arrowstone Dr 27205
Arrowwood Rd 27205
Art Bryan Dr 27203
Arthur St 27203
Ashdol St 27203
Asheboro Country Club Rd 27205
N Asheboro School Rd 27203
Ashebrook View Ln 27205
Ashewood Cir 27203
Ashley St 27203
Ashmont Ct 27205
Ashworth Rd 27205
Ashworth Road Ext 27205
Ashworth View Dr 27205
Aspen Ct 27205
Asteroid Rd 27205
Atlantic Ave 27205
Auman Ave 27205
Auman Clay Rd 27205
Autumn Ln 27205
Autumn Wood Ln 27205
Avanti Dr 27205
Avondale Ave 27203
Aycock St 27203
B B Trl 27205
Bachelor Creek Rd 27205
Back Creek Ct, Rd & Ter 27205
Back Creek Church Rd 27205
Bailey Rd 27205
E Bailey St 27203
W Bailey St 27203
E & W Balfour Ave 27203
Balsam St 27205
Bank St 27203
Barber Dr 27203
Barberry Ct 27205
Bay Leaf Ct 27203
Beane St 27205
Beane Country Rd 27205
E & W Beasley St 27203
Beaver Brook Ln 27205
Beech Tree Pl 27203
Beechwood Ct & Dr 27205
Bell Simmons Rd 27205
Ben Lambeth Rd 27205
Bennett St 27203
Bennett Farm Rd 27205
Benson Fox Dr 27205
Berkley Ln & Pl 27205
Berrie Pl 27205
Bessie Bell Rd 27205
Bethel Friends Rd 27205
Bethel Lucas Rd 27205
Betts St 27203
Betty Mcgee Dr 27205
Big Country Dr 27205
Billy Cranford Ln 27205
Billy Walker Rd 27205
Bingham Loflin Rd 27205
Bird Song Trl 27205
Birdie Pl 27205
Birkhead St 27203
Black Mountain Rd 27205
Bluebill Ln 27205
Bluebird Ln 27205
Bob Kivett Rd 27205
Bobby Moran Dr 27205
Bogey Ln 27205
Boling Rd 27203
Bondurant Rd 27205
Bonita Ln & St 27205
Booker T Washington Ave 27203
Boone Farm Rd 27205
Bossong Dr 27205
Boyd Ave 27205
Boyles Dr 27205
Brady Ave 27203
Branchwater Rd 27205
Branchwood Rd 27205
Brantley Dr 27205
Brassie Ct 27205
Bray Blvd 27205
Breckenwood Ct 27203
Breeze Hill Rd 27203
Breeze Way Ct 27203
Brentwood Ct 27203
Brevard Dr 27205
Brewer St 27203
Briarcliff Dr 27205
Bright Star Ln 27205
Briles Dr 27205
Britt Ave 27203
Brittain St 27203
Broad Oaks St 27203
Brook Dr 27205
Brookdale Dr 27205
Brookdale Rd 27203
Brookside Ct 27203
Brookside Dr 27205
Brookway Rd 27205
Brookwood Dr 27203
Browers Chapel Rd 27205
Brown Trl 27205
Brownmire Dr 27205
Brownstone Hills Dr 27205

Brubaker Rd 27205
Buckford Rd 27205
Buffalo Ford Rd 27205
Bugatti Ave 27205
Bullins Ln 27205
Bunting Rd 27205
Bur Mill Rd 27203
Burgess St 27203
Burney Rd 27205
Burns St 27203
Burns Farm Rd 27205
Cable Creek Rd 27205
Callicut St 27203
Callicutt Henley Rd 27205
Camden Ct 27203
Camelot Dr 27203
Cameron Cir, Dr & Pl 27205
Candlebrook Dr 27205
Cane Mill Rd 27205
Cannon Ct 27205
Cannon Heights Dr 27205
Canoy Dr 27203
Canterbury Trl 27205
Caraway Mountain Rd 27205
Cardinal St 27205
Carl Dr 27203
Carolina Ave 27203
Carowood Dr 27205
Carriage Ln 27205
Carriage Way Rd 27205
Carson Rd 27203
Cascade Ave 27203
Caspn Dr 27203
Cedar Rd 27203
Cedar Bird Trl 27205
Cedar Creek Dr & Rd 27205
Cedar Falls Rd 27203
Cedar Grove Rd 27205
Cedar Grove Drive Ext 27205
Cedar Lodge Rd 27205
Cedar Rock Mountain Rd 27205
Cedar Wood Pl 27203
Cedarwood Ct 27205
Celeste Ln 27203
Center St 27203
Center Cross Church Rd 27205
E & W Central Ave 27203
Central Falls Rd 27203
E Chamberlin Dr 27205
Champagne Dr 27203
Chaney Rd 27205
Chapel Gate Ln 27205
Charles Ave 27205
Charlotte Church Rd 27205
Charmin Dr 27205
Chartier Ct 27205
Cheddington Dr 27203
Cherokee St 27203
N & S Cherry St 27203
Cheshire Pl 27205
Chestnut St 27203
Cheyenne Cir 27205
Chickadee Cir 27203
N & S Church St 27203
Circle B Dr 27205
City Lake Rd 27205
City View St 27203
Clapp Dr 27205
Clarendon Rd 27205
Clay St 27203
Clearview Dr 27205
Clearwater Ct 27205
Clegg Ave 27203
Cleon St 27205
Cleveland St 27205
Cliff Rd
200-1299 27203
1300-1499 27205
Cliffwood Dr 27205
Clover St 27203
Cloverfield Rd 27205
N Club Dr 27205
Club View Dr 27205
Clyde King Rd 27205
Cole Mountain Rd 27205
Coleridge Rd 27203
Colonial Dr 27205
Colony Rd 27205
Commerce Pl 27203
Connector Rd 27205
Cool Springs Rd 27203
Coolers Knob Trl 27205
Cooper Rd 27205
Cooper St 27203
Copperhead Rd 27205
Copples Rd 27205
Copples Road Ext 27205
Cordie Dr 27205
Cornell St 27203
Cortez Rd 27205
Corvette Ave 27205
Corwith Ave & St 27205
Country Ln
2200-2398 27203
2201-2399 27205
Country Trl 27205
Country Club Dr 27205
Country Place Rd 27203
Countryside Ct 27205
Countryside Acres Dr 27205
Covenant Mountain Rd 27203
Coventry Pl 27203
Cox Ave 27205
N Cox St 27203
S Cox St 27203
Cox Brothers Rd 27205
Cox Mill Rd 27205
Coxemoor Pl 27205
Coy Stella Trl 27205
Cracklin Dr 27203
Craig St 27205
Cranbrook Cir & Way 27205
Cranford St 27203
Craven Dr 27203
Craven Ln 27205
S Creek Ct 27205
Creekridge Dr 27205
Creeks Crossing Rd 27205
Creekside Dr 27203
Creekway Rdg 27205
Cresent Dr 27203
Crestview St 27205
Crestview Church Rd 27205
Crestwood Ln 27205
Cristy Cir 27205
Croomcrest Rd 27205
Cross St 27203
Cross Creek Rd 27205
Crowne Park Ave 27203
Crystal Wood Rd 27205
Curry Dr 27205
Cypress Dr 27205
D And J Mhp 27205
Dairy St 27203
Daisy Rd 27203
Daniel Rd 27205
Danny Bell Rd 27205
Danwood St 27205
Darkento St 27203
Daves Mountain Ct 27205
Davidson Rd 27205
Davidson Country Ln 27205
Davis St 27203
Dawson Miller Rd 27205
Deer Horn Ct 27205
Deer Ridge Rd 27205
Deer Run Ln 27205
Deer Track Rd 27205
Deerberry Ct 27205
Deerhorn Ct 27205
Dellwood Ave 27203
Dennis St 27203
Dewey Rd 27203
Dinah Rd 27203
Dinah Road Ext 27205
E Dixie Dr 27203
W Dixie Dr
400-1099 27205
1100-1299 27203
1300-1899 27205
Dixon Ave & St 27205
Dogwood St & Trl 27205
Donna Rd 27205
Dooley Dr 27203
Doris Acres St 27205
E Dorsett Ave 27203
Dot Dr 27205
Doul Mountain Rd 27205
Dover St 27203
Draper St 27203
Drum St 27205
Dublin Rd 27203
Dublin Square Rd 27203
Duck Pond Ln 27205
Dumont St 27203
Dunbar St 27203
Dunbar Bridge Rd 27205
Dundee St 27205
Dunlap St 27203
Dunwoody Ct 27203
Dusty Path Dr 27205
Dynasty Dr 27205
Eagles Field Rd 27205
Earl Brown Rd 27205
Earnhardt Rd 27205
East Dr 27205
East St 27203
Easton Ext 27205
Eastview Dr 27203
Eastwood Dr 27205
Echo Rdg 27205
Eckerd St 27203
Edge Ct 27205
Edgewood Cir & Rd 27205
Edgewood View Dr 27205
Edna St 27203
Elbert Brady Rd 27205
Elderberry Ct 27205
Eldorado Rd 27205
N & S Elm St 27203
Elwood Stout St 27205
Emerald Rock Rd 27205
Emerald Rock Road Ext 27205
Emerson Dr 27205
Emmanuel Church Rd 27205
Englewood Dr 27203
English St 27203
Enterprise St 27203
Enzo Ln 27205
Ernest Rd 27203
Ethan Ct 27203
Ethan Springs Rd 27205
Eton Ave 27203
Executive Way 27203
Fairfax Ct 27203
Fairfield St 27203
Fairview Farm Rd 27205
Fairway Rd 27205
Fairwood Trl 27205
Faith Meadows Ln 27205
Falcon Hills Dr 27205
Falling Oak Rd 27205
Farlow Lake Ct 27205
Farmer Rd 27203
Farmwood Ln 27205
Farr St 27203
Fawn Dr 27205
N Fayetteville St 27203
S Fayetteville St
1-1399 27203
1400-3099 27205
Fermer Rd 27203
Fern Dr 27203
Ferrari Dr 27205
Fesmire St 27205
Fiddlers Creek Rd 27205
Fieldcrest Ct 27205
Filler Rd 27205
Filler Road Ext 27205
Finchley Ct 27203
Fireside Ct 27205
First St 27205
Fisher Cir 27205
Fleta Brown Rd 27205
Flint St 27203
Floyd Dr 27205
Foggy Mountain Rd 27205
Foothills Dr 27205
Forest Ln 27205
Forest Brook Cir 27203
Forest Hills Dr 27205
Forest Lake Dr 27205
Forest Oaks Dr 27205
Forest Park Dr 27203
Forest Valley Dr 27205
W Fork Dr 27205
Foster St 27203
Foust Dr 27205
Foust St 27203
Fox Dr 27205
Fox Ridge Rd 27205
Fox Run Dr 27205
Foxburrow Rd 27205
Foxfire Rd 27205
Foxworth Rd 27203
Francis St 27203
Frank Rd 27205
Frank Lamb Dr 27205
Frankie Trl 27205
Franks St 27203
Frankton Ct 27205
Frazier St 27203
Fredrick St 27205
Freedom Dr 27203
Freedom Trl 27205
Freedom State St 27205
Friendly Cir 27205
Friendly Rd 27203
Friendly Acres Rd 27205
Friendship Rd 27205
Frye Farms Rd 27205
Fulton Rd 27205
Galway Pl 27203
Gant St 27203
Gardengate Rd 27205
Gardiner Rd 27203
Garner Farm Rd 27205
Garren Town Rd 27205
W Gate Rd 27205
Gearren St 27205
Geffen Ln 27205
Gentry Acres Rd 27205
Giles Chapel Rd 27205
Glade Rd 27205
Glen Cir 27203
Glendale Dr 27205
Glenn Dr 27205
Glenn Country Rd 27205
Glenwood Rd 27203
Glovinia St 27203
Gold Hill Rd 27203
Golda Ave 27203
Golden Meadow Rd 27205
Good Luck Rd 27205
Gopher Woods Rd 27205
Gospel Chapel Dr 27205
Graceland Dr 27205
Grady Williams Dr 27205
Grange Hall Rd 27205
Grantville Ln 27205
Gray Owl Rd 27205
Green Farm Rd 27205
Green Mountain Dr 27205
Green Valley Rd 27205
Greenbrush Rd 27205
Greencastle Rd 27205
Greene Oak Rd 27205
Greenfield St 27203
Greenlawn Dr 27203
Greenleaf Acres Dr 27205
Greenmont Dr 27205
Greensboro St 27203
Greentree Ct 27205
Greenvale Rd 27203
Greenview Dr 27205
Greenwood Rd 27203
Gregory Ct 27205
Grey Rabbit Run 27205
Greystone Rd 27203
Gumtree Rd 27205
Halifax St 27205
Hall Dr 27205
Hamilton St 27205
Hamlin St 27203
Hammer Ave 27203
Hampton Ct 27205
Hampton Rd 27203
Hannah Dr 27205
Hanner Hill Rd 27205
Hanover Ct 27203
Happy Ln 27205
Happy Hollow Rd 27205
Hardwood Trl 27205
Harmony Trl 27205
Harper Rd 27205
Harris Family Ln 27205
Harrison St 27203
Harvell Rd & St 27205
Harvell Street Ext 27205
Harvest Cir 27203
Hasty St 27203
Hawk Watch Rd 27205
Hawthorne Dr 27205
Hayes Dr 27205
Hayfield Dr 27205
Hazelwood St 27205
Heather Ct 27203
Heather Glenn Pl 27205
Hemlock Dr 27205
Henley Dr 27205
Henley Country Rd 27203
Henry Rd 27205
Henry Parrish Rd 27205
Henson Rd 27203
Heritage Ct 27203
Hickory Dr 27205
Hickory Creek Trl 27205
Hickory Forest Dr 27203
Hidden Ct 27205
N & S High St 27203
High Meadow Dr 27205
High Pine Church Rd 27205
Highland Ct & St 27203
Highlands Ln 27205
Highridge St 27205
Hight St 27203
Highwood Dr 27205
Hill St 27203
Hillary Ct 27205
Hillbrook Dr 27205
Hillcrest Cir 27203
Hillsdale Ct 27205
Hillsdale Dr 27203
Hilltop Church Rd 27205
Hillview St 27205
Hilton Trl 27205
Hinshaw St 27203
Holland St 27203
Hollings Rd 27205
Holly Dr 27205
Holly St 27203
Home Ave 27203
Homeplace Trl 27205
Honey Locust Rd 27205
Honeysuckle Rd 27203
Honeysuckle Rdg 27205
Hoover St 27203
Hoover Hill Rd 27205
Hopewell St 27203
Hopewell Friends Rd 27205
Horse Canyon Rd 27205
Horse Carriage Ln 27205
Horse Mountain Dr 27205
Howard Ave 27203
Howard Auman Rd 27205
Howard Auman Road Ext 27205
Hoyle Dr 27205
Hub Morris Rd 27205
Hudson Ln 27205
Hughes St 27203
Humble St 27203
Humble Hollow Dr 27203
Hunt Master Trl 27205
Hunter Ct 27205
Ideal Dr 27203
Idlebrook Trl 27205
Idlewood Dr 27205
Independence Ave 27205
Independence Dr 27203
Indian Ct 27205
Indian Paint Trl 27205
Indian Springs Rd 27205
Indian Wells Loop 27205
Indigo Trl 27205
Industrial Park Ave 27205
Ingram Dr 27203
Inwood Rd 27205
Iron Loop Dr 27205
Iron Mountain Rd 27205
Iron Mountain View Rd 27205
Itasca Ct 27203
James St 27203
Janice Acres St 27205
Jarrell Dr 27205
Jarvis Miller Rd 27205
Jason Hoover Rd 27205
Jefferson St 27205
Jennifer Dr 27205
Jennifer View Dr 27205
Jennings Country Dr 27205
Jericho Butler Dr 27205
Jerico Rd 27205
Jerry Hughes St 27205
Jim Lewallen Rd 27205
Joe Farlow Rd 27205
Johnnys Way Rd 27203
Johns Ridge Dr 27205
Jones Rd 27205
Jones St 27203
Jones Country Trl 27205
Jordan Ave & St 27203
Joyce St 27203
Juniper Ct 27203
Karla Dr 27205
Keeling St 27205
Kelly Ave 27203
Kelly Cir 27203
Kemp Blvd 27203
Kemp Mill Rd 27205
Ken Lee Ct 27205
Kenmore Dr 27203
Kennedy Country Dr 27205
Kennelwood Dr 27203
Kermit Hunt Rd 27205
Kerry St 27203
Keyauee Dr 27205
Keyauwee Ridge Rd 27205
Keystone Dr 27203
Kidd Dr 27203
Kildare Rd 27203
Kilowatt Dr 27205
Kimberly Dr 27205
Kindley Rd 27205
Kindley Farm Rd 27205
Kindley Farm Road Ext 27205
King Ct 27203
King Mtn Rd 27205
King View Rd 27205
Kingdom Hall Church Rd 27205
Kingsway Rd 27203
E & W Kivett St 27203
N, S & W Lake Dr 27205
Lake Country Dr 27205
Lake Country Drive Ext 27205
Lake Lucas Rd 27205
Lake Park Rd 27205
Lakecrest Rd 27203
Lakeview Rd 27203
Lamar Dr 27203
Lamb Country Rd 27205
Lambert Dr 27205
Lambert Mine St 27205
Landis Ct 27203
Lanier Ave 27203
Lanier Rd 27205
Lansdowne Ln & Rd 27205
Lansdowne Lakes Ln 27203
Lantern Dr 27205
Lassiter Ln 27205
Lassiter Mill Rd 27205
Latham Harvell Rd 27205
Laura Ct 27205
Lauralwood Pl 27205
Laurel Dr 27205
Lawrence Dr 27205
Lawrence Heights Ave 27205
Lazell Ave 27205
Ledwell Rd 27205
Lee St 27203
Lee Valley Rd 27205
Legend Dr 27205
Leo Cranford Rd 27205
Leslie St 27205
Lester Russell Dr 27205
Levance St 27203
Lewallen Rd 27205
Lewis St 27203
Lewis Country Dr 27205
Lewis Thomas Rd 27205
Lexington Pl & Rd 27205
Lexington Commons Dr 27205
Liberty Cir 27205
Liberty St 27203
Liberty Circle Ext 27205
Lincoln Ave 27205
Linda Ln 27205
Lindale Dr 27205
Lindley Ave 27203
Lindsey Ave 27203
Lineberry St 27203
Linnie Ct 27205
Lions Rest Rd 27205
Lisbon Rd 27205
Little Gate Dr 27203
Little Lakes Trl 27205
Little River Rd 27205
Lloyd St 27205
Loach St 27203
Locust Mountain Trl 27205
Loe Fall Ave 27205
Loflin Pond Rd 27203
Lord Randolph Cir 27205
Lotus Ln 27205
Lowdermilk Rd 27205
Lowe Country Rd 27205
Lucas Dr 27205
Luck Rd 27205
Lucy Ln 27205
Ludlum Ln 27205
Luther Country Ln 27205
Luxury Ln 27205
Macarthur St 27203
Mack Rd 27205
Mackie Ave 27205
Macon St 27203
Madison Cir 27203
N & S Main St 27203
Mandover Ct 27205
Maness Coble Dr 27205
Manor Cir 27205
Manorview Rd 27205
Maple Ave 27203
Maple Hill Ct 27205
Maple Ridge Rd 27205
Marathon Dr 27205
Marigold Ln 27205
Mark Ave 27205
Marmaduke Cir 27203
Marshall Ln 27205
Martin Hill Ave 27205
Martin Luther King Jr Dr 27203
Masons Dr 27205
Maurine Dr 27205
Mayberry Ln 27205
Mcalister St 27203
Mccranford Rd 27205
N Mccrary St
100-199 27203
300-899 27205
S Mccrary St 27203
Mcdaniel Dr & Rd 27205
Mcdermott St 27205

Mcdowell Rd 27205
Mcdowell Country Trl 27203
Mcknight St 27203
Mclaren Ln 27205
Mclaurin Dr 27203
Mcmasters St 27203
Mcneal St 27203
Mcpherson St 27203
Meadow Rd 27205
Meadow Ridge Ct 27205
Meadowbrook Rd 27203
Meadowbrookrd Ext 27203
Meadowlands Dr 27205
Mechanic Rd 27205
Medfield Cir 27205
Memorial St 27203
Memory Ln 27203
Meredith Ct 27205
Meredith Country Rd 27205
Middleton Cir 27205
Midway Acres Rd 27205
Milbrook Dr 27205
Miles Moffitt Rd 27205
Mill Creek Rdg 27205
Miller Rd 27205
W Miller St 27203
Miller Country Dr 27205
Miller Road Ext 27205
Millie Ln 27205
Millikan Dr 27203
Min Lee Dr 27205
E & W Mine St 27205
Moffitt Rd 27205
Moffitt Road Ext 27205
Monarch Ln 27205
Monroe Ave 27205
Montclair Ct 27205
Monterey Rd 27205
Montley View Dr 27205
Moody St 27203
Moonlight Meadow Rd 27205
Moore Rd 27205
Moran Dr 27205
Morgan Ave 27205
Morgan Country Rd 27203
Morton Ave 27205
Mount Cross St 27203
Mount Lebanon Rd 27205
Mount Shepherd Rd 27205
Mount Shepherd Road
Ext 27205
Mount Sheppard Trailer
Park 27205
Mount Tabor Church
Rd 27205
Mountain Ln, Rd &
Ter 27205
Mountain Brook Rd 27205
Mountain Brook Road
Ext 27205
Mountain Creek Rd 27205
Mountain Lake Rd 27205
Mountain Laurel Ln 27205
Mountain Meadow Dr 27205
Mountain Oak View Dr 27205
Mountain Of Faith Rd 27205
Mountain Top Dr 27203
Mountain Valley Dr &
Pl 27205
Mountain View Dr &
Rd 27205
Mountain View Church
Rd 27205
Mt Shepherd Rd 27205
Muriel Ln 27205
Myrtle St 27205
Nassau Trl 27205
Nathans Trl 27205
Nc Highway 134 27205
Nc Highway 42 N 27203
Nc Highway 42 S 27205
Nc Highway 49 S 27205
Neely Dr & Rd 27205
New Century Dr 27205
New Hope Church Rd 27205
Newbern Ave 27205

Newell St 27203
Nighthawk Rd 27205
No Record 27205
Nolen Ave 27205
Nolen Avenue Ext 27205
Norman St 27205
North St 27203
Northampton Dr
400-499 27205
500-699 27203
Northmont Dr 27205
Northmont Lake Dr 27205
Northpointe Dr 27205
Northridge Dr 27205
Northshore Dr 27203
Northside Ter 27203
Northview Dr 27205
Northwood Dr 27203
Norwood Ln 27205
Nottingham St 27203
Oak Dr 27205
Oak Bend Dr 27203
Oak Grove Church Rd 27205
Oak Hollow Dr 27205
Oak Leaf Rd 27205
Oak Tree Rd 27205
Oak View Ln 27205
Oakdale Dr 27205
Oakdale St 27203
N Oakdale St 27205
Oakgrove Rd 27205
Oakhurst Dr & Rd 27205
Oakland Ave 27203
Oakmont Dr 27205
Oakwood Acres Rd 27205
Occoneechee St 27203
Odat Trl 27205
Old Asheboro Rd 27205
Old Asheboro Road
Ext 27205
Old Buffalo Ford Rd 27205
Old Cedar Falls Rd 27203
Old Cox Rd 27203
Old Depot Dr 27205
Old Farmer Rd
1100-1199 27203
1200-2499 27205
Old Forest Ct 27205
Old Humble Mill Rd 27205
Old Lexington Rd 27205
Old Liberty Rd 27203
Old Mill Rd 27205
Old Mill Ford Trl 27205
Old Nc Highway 13 27205
Old Nc Highway 49 27205
Old Plank Rd 27205
Old Road Dr 27205
Old Spruce Dr 27203
Old Stagecoach Rd 27205
Old State Hwy 27205
Old Troy Rd 27205
Old Uwharrie Rd 27205
Olde Main Terrace Dr 27203
Olde Towne Pkwy 27205
Orlendo Dr 27203
Osborn Mill Rd 27205
Osprey Dr 27205
Otis Rd 27203
Paige Ct 27205
Painter Rd 27205
Palomino Dr 27205
Panther Creek Rd 27205
Panther Mountain Rd 27205
Park Dr 27205
N Park Dr 27205
S Park Dr 27205
N Park St 27203
S Park St
100-1100 27203
1101-1197 27205
1102-1198 27203
1199-1200 27205
1201-1299 27203
1202-1398 27205
1301-1399 27205
1400-1499 27203

Parker Dr 27205
Parkside Dr 27203
Parkview St 27203
Pastureview Rd 27205
Patriot Woods Dr 27205
Patton Ave 27203
N Patton Ave
100-199 27205
400-499 27203
Peachtree St 27203
Pebble Rdg 27203
Pennsylvania Ave 27203
Pennwood Dr 27203
Pentecostal Church
Rd 27203
Pepperidge Rd 27205
Perry St 27205
Pershing St 27203
Phillips Country Trl 27205
Piedmont St 27203
Pilot Ct 27205
Pilot Mountain Rd 27205
Pilots View Rd 27205
Pine Ct, Ln & St 27205
Pine Creek Rdg 27205
Pine Grove Dr 27205
Pine Hill Rd 27205
Pine Knoll Ct 27203
Pine Lakes Dr 27205
Pine Needles Dr 27205
Pine Ridge Rd 27205
Pine Top Ln 27205
Pineview Rd & St 27203
Pinewood Rd 27205
Pinewood Forest Dr 27205
Pisgah Rd 27205
Pisgah Church Rd 27205
Pisgah Covered Bridge
Rd 27205
Plantation Cir 27205
Pleasant St 27203
Pleasant Cross Rd 27203
Plummer St 27203
Polo Crowne Ave 27203
Pond Side Dr 27205
Ponderosa Heights Pl 27205
Poole Town Rd 27205
Poplar St 27203
Poplar Forest Ln 27205
Porsche Way 27205
Portage Pkwy 27205
Powhatan Ave 27203
Prairie Trl 27205
E & W Presnell St 27203
Princeton Ct 27205
E & W Pritchard St 27203
Q Rd 27205
Quail Roost Dr 27205
Quaker Dr 27203
Queens Rd 27203
Queens Meadow Ct 27205
Quentin Dr 27205
R H Dr 27205
Ragsdale Rd 27203
Railroad St 27203
Rainbow Dr 27203
Rainbow Loop 27205
Rambling Rd 27205
Randall St 27203
N & S Randolph Ave &
Mall 27203
Randolph Tabernacle
Rd 27203
Ravenwood Dr 27205
Ray St 27205
Rayburn St 27203
Red Fox Trl 27205
Redding Rd 27203
Redwood Dr 27205
Reeder Rd 27205
Reeder Road Ext 27205
Reflection Ln 27205
Register St 27205
Revelle Trl 27205
Rice Dr 27205
Rich Ave 27203

Rich Country Dr 27205
Richards Cir 27205
Richland Pl 27205
Richland Park Dr 27205
Ridge St 27205
Ridgeback Rd 27205
Ridgecrest Ln 27205
Ridgecrest Rd 27203
Ridges Mountain Rd &
Trl 27205
Ridgeway Cir & Dr 27205
Ridgewood Cir 27205
Rilla St 27205
E & W River Ct &
Run 27205
River Estates Dr 27205
E River Run Dr & Ext 27205
Roadrunner Dr 27205
Robbins Cir 27205
Robbins St 27203
Robins Nest 27203
Rock Crusher Rd 27203
Rock Quarry Rd 27203
Rock Spring Rd 27205
Rock Wrenn Trl 27205
Rockcliff Ct & Ter 27205
Rocklane Dr 27205
N Rockridge Rd 27205
Rockwood Rd 27205
Rocky Ln 27205
Rocky Knoll Rd 27205
Rocky Knoll Road Ext 27205
Rocky Top Cir 27205
Rocwood Dr 27205
Roland Ln 27205
Rolling Rd 27205
Rolls Ln 27205
Roman Rd 27205
Roosevelt Rd 27205
Rose Ave 27205
Rose Ln 27205
Rose Garden Trl 27205
Rose Hill Rd 27205
Rose Lane Rd 27205
Roseboro Dr 27203
Rosemont Rd 27203
Ross St 27203
Ross Harris Rd 27205
Royce Ln 27205
Running Cedar Rd 27205
Rush Mountain Road
Ext 27205
Rushwood St 27205
Russell St 27205
Saddlewood Ct 27203
Salem Ct 27205
E Salisbury St
100-999 27203
1000-1099 27205
1100-1899 27203
W Salisbury St 27203
Salmons Dr 27205
Sam Jackson Rd 27205
Sandtrap Ln 27205
Sanford St 27203
Saunders Dr 27203
Saunders Trl 27205
Savannah Dr 27205
Sawyersville Rd 27205
Scaleybark Ln 27205
Scarboro St 27203
Scenic Dr 27203
Scenic Point Dr 27205
Science Hill Rd 27205
Scott Farm Rd 27205
Scott Mcdowell Dr 27205
Scott Mountain Rd 27205
Scott Mountain Road
Ext 27205
Seadelin Rd 27205
Seagrove Plank Rd 27205
Seminole Dr 27205
Sequoia Ave 27205
Sewell Dr 27203
Shady Dr 27205
Shady Knoll Dr 27205

Shady Williams Dr 27205
Shambley Rd S 27205
Shamrock Rd
100-1299 27203
1300-1699 27205
Shana Ln
1000-1099 27203
1100-1299 27205
Shannon Rd 27203
Sharon Ave 27203
Sharron Dr 27205
Shaw St 27205
Sheffield St 27203
Shepherds Way 27205
Sheridan Dr 27205
Sherwood Ave & Rd 27205
Sherwood Oaks Dr 27205
Silver Ave 27203
Simpson Ave 27203
Skeen View Rd 27205
Sky Dr 27205
Skycrest Country Rd 27205
Skyline Dr 27205
Slate Ave 27205
Slick Rock Mountain
Rd 27205
Smyrna Grove Dr 27205
Snowdon Ct 27203
Sohomey Dr 27205
Sonora Dr 27205
Sourwood Dr 27205
Southmont Dr 27205
Southmont Heights
Ave 27205
Southway Rd 27205
Southwood Dr 27205
Spanish Dr & Ln 27205
Sparrow Trl 27205
Spearmint Dr 27205
Spencer Ave 27203
Spencer Meadow Rd 27205
Spero Rd
900-1099 27203
1100-2199 27205
Spinks Rd 27205
Spinks St 27203
Spoons Chapel Rd 27205
Spoons Chapel Church
Rd 27205
Spring Dr 27205
Spring St 27203
Spring Forest Rd 27205
Spring Garden St 27203
Spring Valley Rd 27205
Spring Village Dr 27205
Springdale Dr & Ln 27205
Springwood Rd 27205
Squirrel Creek Rd 27205
Squirrel Den Rd 27205
Squirrel Hollow Ln 27205
Stable Brook Rd 27205
Staleys Farm Rd 27205
Stallion Trl 27205
Star Gazer Dr 27205
Starr Ct 27205
Steele St 27203
Steppingstone Ln 27205
Sterling St 27203
Stone Bridge Rd 27205
Stone Country Ln 27205
Stone Haven Dr 27203
Stonecrest Ct 27205
Stoney Creek Dr 27205
Stout Farm Rd 27205
Stowe Ave 27203
Straight St 27203
Stratford Way 27205
Stream Watch Trl 27205
E & W Strider St 27203
Strieby Church Rd 27205
Strieby Church Road
Ext 27205
Stutts Rd 27205
Summit Ave 27203
Sunbeam Ct 27205
Sunburst Rd 27205

Sunflower Dr 27203
Sunny Ln 27205
Sunrise Ave 27203
Sunset Ave
100-1099 27203
1200-1599 27205
Sunset Dr 27205
Sunset Dr N 27205
Sweetwater Trl 27205
Sykes Farm Rd 27205
Sylvan Dr
200-299 27205
2400-2499 27203
Sylvan Way 27205
Sylvan Woods Dr 27205
Tabernacle School Rd 27205
Tabor Ct 27203
E & W Taft Ave 27203
Tall Pine St 27205
Tall Pine Street Ext 27205
Talmer Wright Rd 27205
Tamworth Rd 27203
Tanglewood Ln 27205
Tar Heel Trl 27205
Taylor Dr 27203
Taylors Creek Dr 27205
Telephone Ave 27205
Teresa Way 27205
Terry Ave 27203
Thayer Dr 27205
Third St 27205
Thomas St 27203
Thornburg Rd 27205
Thornburg Farm Trl 27205
Thornsdale Dr 27203
Thoroughbred Rd 27205
Three B Rd 27205
Tiger Flower Rd 27205
Timbal Ct 27205
Timberlane 27205
Timberwolf Trl 27205
Tipton Dr 27203
Toms Creek Rd 27205
Tonys Way 27203
Topaz Dr 27205
Tory Ln 27205
Tot Hill Trl 27205
Tot Hill Farm Rd 27205
Traci St 27203
Trade St 27203
Tranquil Ln 27205
Transfer Station Pl 27203
Tree House Ln 27205
Tremont Dr 27203
Trogdon St 27205
Trogdon Hill Rd 27205
Trogdon Pond Rd 27203
Trollinger Rd 27205
Trotter Ln & Rd 27205
Tryon St 27203
Tucker St 27203
Tudor Dr 27205
Turner St 27203
Turning Oaks Trl 27205
Twain Dr 27203
Twelve Tree Rd 27205
Twin Creek Rd 27205
Twin Crystal Trl 27205
Twin Flower Rd 27205
Ulah Ct 27205
Underwood St 27203
Union Church Rd 27205
Us 220 Byp 27203
Us Highway 220 S 27205
Us Highway 220 Bus
N 27203
Us Highway 220 Bus
S 27205
Us Highway 64 E 27203
Us Highway 64 W 27205
Uwharrie St 27203
Valewood Dr 27205
Valley Rd 27203
Valley Dale Ln 27203
Valley Grove Rd 27205
Vance St 27203

Vancroft St 27205
Vernon St 27203
Vesper Trl 27205
Vestal Creek Ct 27205
Veterans Loop Rd 27205
Viewmont Ct & Dr 27205
Vincent Dr 27203
Viper Ln 27205
Virgil Hill Rd 27205
Virginia Ave 27203
Virginia Acres Dr 27205
Vision Dr 27203
Vista Pkwy
200-499 27205
500-699 27203
Voncannon Farm Rd 27205
E & W Wainman Ave 27203
Waketa Dr 27203
Walden Rd 27205
E Walker Ave 27203
W Walker Ave 27203
Walker Cir 27205
Walker Dr 27205
Walker Rd 27205
Walker Country Ln 27205
Walnut Dr 27205
Walnut St 27203
Walnut Creek Ln 27205
Walter Saunders Dr 27203
Walton Ct 27203
E & W Ward St 27203
Ward Valley Dr 27203
Washington Ave 27203
Watercrest Trl 27205
Waterside Dr 27203
Watkins St 27203
Wayne Rd 27205
Waynick Meadow Rd 27205
Wedge Pl 27205
Wedgewood Forest Dr 27205
Wellington Pl 27205
Wells Cir 27203
Wesley Ct 27203
West St 27205
Westbury Dr 27205
Westchapel Rd 27205
Westgate Rd 27205
Westminster Ct 27205
Westminster Dr 27203
Westmont Cir, Ct & Dr 27205
Westover Ter 27205
Westside Cir 27205
Westview St 27205
Westwood Ave & Dr 27205
Whale Tail Rd 27205
Whippoorwill Dr 27205
Whitaker Rd 27205
White Oak St 27203
White Pines Ln 27205
Whitley St 27205
Whitley Country Rd 27205
Wildflower Ct 27205
Wildwood Ln 27205
William Ave 27203
William Dr 27205
Williams Farm Rd 27205
Willow Rd 27203
Willow Creek Ct 27203
Willow Downs Ct 27205
Willow Grove Trl 27205
Willow Lake Rd 27203
Willow Wood Rd 27205
Willow Wright Trl 27205
Wilson Dr, Ln & St 27205
Winchester Heights Dr 27205
Windermere Ct 27203
Windflower Ln 27205
Winding Woods Ln 27205
Windriver Rd 27205
Windsor Dr & Trl 27205
Winnetka Ct 27205
Winslow Ave 27205
Winter St 27203
Wood Bluff Trl 27205
Woodale Dr 27205
Woodberry St 27203

Woodcrest Dr 27205
Woodcrest Rd 27203
Woodell Country Rd 27205
Woodfern Rd 27205
Woodfield Scout Trl 27205
Woodglo Dr 27205
Woodhaven Dr 27205
Woodland Cir 27203
Woodland Dr 27205
Woodland Trl 27203
Woodland View Pl 27205
Woodlane Ct 27205
Woodlawn St 27203
Woodmint Rd 27205
Woodridge Dr 27205
Woods Stream Ln 27205
Woodside Pl 27205
Worth St 27203
Wow Rd 27203
Wrennwood Ct 27203
Yancey Ave 27203
Yesteroaks Ct 27205
York St 27203
Yorkmont Ct 27203
Yorktown Ln 27203
Young Rd 27205
Yzex St 27203
Zoo Pkwy 27205

ASHEVILLE NC

General Delivery 28802

POST OFFICE BOXES MAIN OFFICE STATIONS AND BRANCHES

Box No.s
1 - 3338 28802
5001 - 5980 28813
6001 - 6959 28816
7001 - 7674 28802
8001 - 8998 28814
9000 - 9998 28815
9998 - 9998 28813
10000 - 10000 28816
10171 - 10515 28806
15001 - 15978 28813
16001 - 17958 28816
18001 - 18960 28814
19001 - 19969 28815
20001 - 20002 28802
25001 - 26078 28813
28802 - 28802 28802
28804 - 28804 28804
28813 - 28813 28813
28815 - 28815 28815
30000 - 30000 28802

NAMED STREETS

Abbey Cir 28805
Abingdon Way 28804
Academy St 28803
Acadia Dr 28806
Ace Dr 28803
Acorn Rd 28804
Acton Cir 28806
Adams St 28801
Adams Hill Rd 28806
Adamswood Rd 28803
Addison Ct 28806
Aden Ln 28801
Aiken Rd 28804
Alabama Ave 28806
Albemarle Pl & Rd 28801
Alclare Ct & Dr 28804
Aldersgate Cir 28803
Alex Dr 28805
Alex Breeze Way 28806
Alexander Dr
2-98 28801
600-699 28805
Alexander Chapel Dr 28804
Alfa Vw 28804
Alissas Little Way 28806
All Souls Cres 28803
Allen Ave 28803
Allen St 28806
Allen Hill Dr 28805
Allesarn Rd 28804
Alliance Ct 28806
Allison Ct 28805
Allison Lee Loop 28803
Almond Glen Dr 28806
Alpine Ct & Way 28805
Alpine Ridge Dr 28803
Als Rdg 28804
Alsatian Ln 28805
Altamont Vw 28804
Altamont Ridge Dr 28806
Amanda Dr 28804
Amanda Gail 28806
Amangela Dr 28806
Amazing Grace Ln 28804
Amber Ln 28803
Ambler Rd 28805
Amboy Rd 28806
American Way 28806
Amherst Rd 28803
Anders Dr 28806
Andway Dr 28806
Andy Angie Cir 28806
Angel Cir 28803
Angelus Cir 28805
Angle St 28803
Angler Trl 28803
Angus Ln 28805
N & S Ann St 28801
Annandale Ave 28801
Annie Ln 28805
Annie St 28806
Antebellum Dr 28806
Antique Ln 28806
Antler Hill Rd 28803
Apache Trl 28805
Apogee Dr 28806
Apostolic Way 28805
Appalachian Way 28806
Appalachian Village Rd 28804
Appeldoorn Cir 28803
Apple Ln 28804
Apple Blossom Ln 28806
Apple Cider Ln 28806
Apple Tree Way 28805
Applewood Dr 28805
Approach Rd 28803
Arbor Ln 28805
Arbor St 28806
Arbor Meadow Ln 28805
Arbor Ridge Trl 28806
Arboretum Rd 28803
Arborvale Rd 28801
Arbutus Rd 28805
Archery Rd 28806
Archwood Ct & Dr 28806
Arco Rd 28805
Arctic Rd 28806
Arden Rd 28803
Ardmion Park 28801
E Ardmore Pl & St 28803
Ardoyne Rd 28804
Argyle Ln 28806
Arlington St 28801
Arnold Rd 28805
Arrow Pl 28805
Arrowhead Ln 28806
Arrowood Rd 28806
Arthur Rd 28806
Arwood Ln 28804
Asbury Rd 28804
Ascension Ct & Dr 28806
Ascot Cir 28803
Ascot Point Cir 28803
Asheland Ave 28801
Asheville School Rd 28806
Asheville Springs Cir 28806
Ashley Cir & Rd 28805
Ashmont Dr 28806
Ashwood Dr & Ln 28803
Aspen Ct 28806
Aspen Way 28803
Aston St 28801
Atherton Way 28803
Atkinson St 28801
Atlanta Ave 28806
Atlas Ct 28806
Attaberry Ct 28805
Auburndale Dr 28806
Audrey Ln 28806
Audubon Dr 28804
Aurora Dr 28805
Aurora Vista Dr 28806
Austin Ave 28801
Austin Dr 28805
Autumn Ridge Ln 28803
Autumn Rush Ln 28806
Avery Ln 28805
Avon Ave 28806
E Avon Pkwy 28804
W Avon Pkwy 28804
Avon Rd 28805
Avondale Rd 28803
Avondale Heights Rd 28803
Avondale Ridge Rd 28803
Azalea Dr 28805
Azalea Rd E 28805
Azalea St 28803
Azalea Ter 28803
Aztec Ln 28806
Azure Sage Way 28806
Baboos Pl 28806
Bailey Rd 28806
Bailey Hill Ln 28805
Baird Aly 28804
Baird Ln 28804
Baird St 28801
Baird Cove Ln & Rd 28804
E & W Baird Mountain Rd 28804
Baity Dr 28806
Baker Ave, Dr, Pl & Rd 28806
Bald Eagle Ln 28805
Baldwin St 28803
Ballantree Dr 28803
Balm Grove Ave 28806
Balsam Ave 28806
Bamwood Dr 28804
Banbury Cross St 28801
Bancroft Trl 28804
Baneberry Ct 28803
Banjo Way 28804
Banks Ave 28801
Bannister Dr 28804
Barbee Cir 28806
Barbetta Dr 28806
Barcliff Ln 28805
Barcroft Trl 28805
Barebridge Hls 28804
Barfield Ave 28801
Barger Rd 28803
Barn Owl Rd 28806
Barnard Ave 28804
Barnes Rd 28803
Barnwood Dr 28804
Barrett Ln 28803
Barrington Dr 28803
Barry Pl 28806
Bartlett St 28801
Bartlett Mountain Rd 28805
Barton Rd 28804
Bartrams Walk Dr 28804
Bassett Rd 28804
Bassett Rd Ext 28804
Baton Ln 28803
Battery Park Ave 28801
Battle Rd 28803
Battle Sq 28801
Baxter St 28801
Bay St 28801
Beadle Ln 28803
Beagle Run 28804
Beam Bnd 28806
N & S Bear Creek Dr, Ln, Pl & Rd 28806
Bear Den Rd 28805
Bear Knoll Dr 28805
Bear Left 28805
Bear Mountain Rd 28804
Bear Path Rd 28805
Bear Woods Trl 28805
Bearberry Ln 28803
Bearden Ave 28801
Beaucatcher Rd 28805
S Beaumont St 28801
Beaver Dr 28804
Beaver Creek Ln 28804
Beaver Lake Hts 28804
Beaver Point Park 28804
Beaver Ridge Rd 28804
Beaver Valley Rd 28804
Beaverbrook Ct & Rd 28804
Beaverdam Ct & Rd 28804
Beaverdam Knoll Rd 28804
Beck Dr 28806
Bedford Ln 28803
Bee Ridge Rd 28803
Beech Hill St 28801
Beech Tree Ln 28804
Beechwood Rd 28805
Bees Mountain Dr 28804
Begonia Gdn 28806
Bell Rd 28805
Bella Way 28803
Belleair Rd 28806
Bellevue Rd 28803
Bellhaven Rd 28805
Belmont Ave 28806
Belvedere Rd 28803
Ben Franklin Ln 28805
Ben Lippen Rd 28806
Ben Lippen School Rd 28806
Ben Nevis Ct 28803
Bennington Ct 28803
Benson Dr & Rd 28806
Bent Creek Preserve Rd 28806
Bent Creek Ranch Rd 28806
Bent Oak Ln 28803
Bent Tree Dr 28803
Bent Tree Rd 28804
Berachah Valley Pl 28805
Beri Cir, Ct, Dr & Sq 28806
Berkshire 28805
Bermuda Sand Dr 28806
Berry Hill Rd 28806
Beth Ln 28806
Beth Hill Ct 28806
Bethany Woods Dr 28805
Bethel Dr 28803
Bethesda Rd 28805
Betsy Ross Ln 28805
Beulah Ln 28806
Beverly Rd 28805
Beverly Rd W 28806
Bevlyn Dr 28803
Bible Belt Way 28803
Bideford Row 28803
Big Bear Trl 28803
Big Ben Dr 28806
Big Level Dr 28804
Big Rock Rd 28806
Big Spring Dr 28804
Billiard Ln 28806
Bills Dr 28803
Biltmore Ave
39A-39D 28801
1-599 28801
601-613 28801
615-659 28803
661-799 28803
801-899 28803
Biltmore Plz 28803
Biltmore Estates Dr 28803
Bingham Rd 28806
Birch Pl & St 28801
Birch Forest Ln 28803
Birchwood Ln 28805
Birds Eyeview Dr 28806
Bittersweet Ln 28805
Black St 28801
Black Gum Dr 28805
Black Locust Dr 28804
Black Oak Dr 28804
Blackberry Ln 28804
Blackstone Ave 28804
Blackwood Rd 28804
Blair St 28801
Blake St 28801
Blake Mountain Cir 28803
Blakewood Ct 28803
Blalock Ave 28803
Blanton St 28801
Bleachery Blvd
100-199 28805
1200-1299 28803
Bloom Ln 28805
Blue Ridge Ave 28806
Blue Ridge Vis 28805
Blue Ridge Acres Rd 28806
Blueberry Rdg 28804
Blueberry Hill Rd 28804
Bluebird Rdg 28804
Bluebonnet Pl 28806
Bluebriar Rd 28804
Bob Barnwell Rd 28803
Bobby Ln 28804
Boddington Ct 28803
Bohemian Ln 28805
Bond St 28801
Bondo Rd 28803
Bonita Cir 28806
Booker Ave & St 28803
Boone St 28806
Bordeau Pl 28801
Boris St 28806
Bostic Pl 28803
Boston Way 28803
Botany Ct & Dr 28805
Botany View Ct 28805
Botany View Ct Ext 28805
Boulder Way 28803
Boulder Creek Way 28805
Bourne Ln 28803
Bowling Park Rd 28803
Bowman Dr 28806
Boyd Ave 28806
Brad St 28803
Braddock Way 28803
Bradford Pear Ln 28804
Bradhall Dr 28806
Bradley St 28806
N & S Braeside Cir, Ct & Ln 28803
Bramlet Ct & St 28806
Brandi Dr 28806
Brandywine Ln 28805
Branning St 28806
Breakers Ln 28806
Breckenridge Pkwy 28804
Breezeway Dr 28803
Breezy Glenn Ct 28805
Brennan Brook Dr 28806
Brent Knl 28805
Brentwood Dr 28806
Brevard Rd
1-19 28806
21-590 28806
591-591 28810
592-1898 28806
593-1899 28806
Breyerton Ct 28804
Briar Knoll Ct 28803
Briarcliff 28804
Briarcliff Dr 28803
Briarcliff Ln 28806
Briarcliff Ter 28806
Briarwood Rd 28804
Brickyard Ct, Dr, Pl & Rd 28806
Bridgeman Dr 28803
Bridle Path Rd 28804
Briggs Rd 28805
Brinkley Dr 28806
Brisco Dr 28803
Bristol Pl 28803
Britt Dr 28805
Broad St 28801
Broadview Ave & Dr 28803
Broadway St
1-464 28801
466-498 28801
701-797 28804
799-899 28804
Brody Trl 28804
Brook Dr 28805
Brook St 28803
Brook Ter 28805
Brookcliff Dr 28804
Brookdale Rd 28804
Brookgreen Pl 28804
Brooklawn Chase 28803
Brooklet St 28801
Brookline Dr 28803
Brooklyn Ln & Rd 28803
Brookshire Ext 28803
Brookshire Pl 28806
Brookshire St 28803
Brookside Dr 28806
Brookside Rd 28803
Brookwood Ct & Rd 28804
Brotherton Ave 28806
Brown Ave 28804
Brown Rd 28806
Browndale Rd 28805
Brownstone Dr 28806
Browntown Rd 28803
Brownwood Ave 28806
Bruce Dr 28806
Brucemont Cir & Pl 28806
Brushwood Rd 28804
Bryant St 28806
Bryson St 28803
Buchanan Ave 28801
Buchanan Pl 28801
Buchanan Rd 28803
Buck Acres Dr 28806
Buck Cove Ter 28805
Buckhorn Branch Rd 28806
Buckingham Ct 28803
Bucks Hill Dr 28806
Bucks Park Dr 28806
Buckshot Ridge Dr 28804
Buckstone Pl 28805
Buckthorn Ln 28803
Buena Vista Rd 28803
Buffalo St 28806
Buffalo Trl 28805
Bulb Glen Dr 28806
Bull Creek Rd 28805
Bull Mountain Rd 28805
Bulldog Dr 28801
Bumble Bee Gdns & Ln 28806
Bump Rd 28805
W Buncombe School Rd 28806
Bungalow Way 28804
Burk St 28806
Burleson Rd 28805
Burlwood Ct 28804
Burnside Dr 28803
Burton St 28806
Busbee Rd 28803
Busbee Knoll Rd 28803
Busbee Mountain Rd 28803
Busbee View Rd 28803
Buttonwood Ct 28806
Buxton Ave 28801
Byrdcliffe Ln 28805
Cabelle Pl 28806
Cable Cv 28804
Cady Ct 28803
Caledonia Rd 28803
Cambridge Rd 28804
Camby St 28801
Camden Ave 28804
Camelia Ln 28806
Cameron St 28801
Camp Allis Rd 28805
Campbell Cir 28803
Campground Rd 28805
Canary Ct 28806
Candler Knob Rd 28806
Candlestick Ln 28803
Cane St 28806
Canoe Ln 28804
Canteberi Ct 28806
Canterbury Rd
1-99 28805
2-4 28801
6-98 28805
1-3 28801
Canterfield Dr 28803
Cantrell Dr 28804
Caper Trl 28806
Capps Rd 28804
Cardigan Cir 28805
N Cardinal Dr 28806
Cardinal Crest Ln 28805
Cardinal Ridge Dr 28805
Carey Ln 28804
Caribou Rd 28803
Carjen Ave 28804
Carl Alwin Pl 28803
Carlton Pl 28806
Carlyle Way 28803
Carolina Ln 28801
Carraway Ct 28804
Carrier Pl & St 28806
Carroll Ave 28801
Carson Creek Dr 28803
Carter St 28801
Carter Cove Rd 28804
Carver Ct 28803
Carvers Creek Dr 28806
Cary Ln 28804
Case Rd 28806
Case Creek Ln 28806
Caspian Way 28806
Casselberry Rd 28806
Cassidy Ln 28803
Castanea Mountain Dr 28803
Casteel Ln 28803
Castle St 28803
Castleknock Dr 28803
Castlerock Dr 28806
Catalina Ct 28806
Catamount Trce 28806
Catawba St 28801
Cauble St 28801
W Cedar Ln 28806
Cedar St 28803
Cedar Trl 28803
Cedar Chine 28803
Cedar Crest Dr 28803
Cedar Farm Rd 28803
Cedar Forest Trl 28803
Cedar Hill Cir 28806
Cedar Hill Dr 28803
Cedar Hill Rd 28806
Cedar Knoll Pl & Rd 28806
Cedar Mountain Rd 28803
Cedar Ridge Dr
1-12 28806
100-199 28803
Cedar Summit Rd 28803
Cedarcliff Cir & Rd 28803
Cedarview Dr 28803
Cedarwood Ct, Dr, Ln, Rd, Ter, Trl & Vly 28803
Celebration Pl 28806
Celia Pl 28801
Center St 28803
Central Ave 28801
Central Ave W 28806
Centre Park Dr 28805
Century Blvd 28803
Cessna Way 28806
Chadwick Wade Dr 28804
Chamberlain Dr 28806
Chamblee Rdg 28805
Chambwood Park 28804
Chance Cv 28806
Chapel Cir & Rd 28803
Chapel Hill Church Rd 28803

Chapel Park Pl & Rd 28803
Chapman Dr 28805
Chapman Drive Ext 28805
Charland Frst 28803
Charles St 28801
Charles Lance Pl 28806
Charles Ridge Rd 28805
Charlie Authur Ln 28806
Charlotte Hwy 28803
Charlotte St 28801
S Charlotte St 28801
Charlyn Dr 28803
Charter Gln 28804
Chateau Pl 28805
Chatham Rd 28804
Chauncey Cir 28803
Cheerio Ln 28803
Cherokee Rd
1-7 28801
8-50 28806
16-58 28801
60-70 28801
71-101 28806
72-160 28801
162-500 28804
Cherry Ln 28804
Cherry St 28801
Cherry Grove Ln & Rd 28805
Cherry Meadows Way 28806
Cherry Willow Ln 28804
Chesten Mountain Dr 28803
Chester Pl 28806
E Chestnut St 28801
W Chestnut St 28801
Chestnut Ter 28803
Chestnut Mountain Ln & Rdg 28803
W Chestnut Ridge Ave 28804
Cheyenne Ct 28803
Chicadee Ln 28806
Chicken Aly 28801
Chicory Ln 28803
Chiles Ave 28803
Chimney Crest Dr 28806
Chipmunk Cove Rd 28804
Choctaw St 28801
Choo Choo Ln 28806
Chowder Cove Rd 28805
Christina Ct 28806
Christopher Ln 28804
Chunns Cove Rd & Trl 28805
Chunns View Dr 28805
Church Rd 28804
Church St 28801
Churchill St 28801
Cimarron Dr 28803
Circle St 28801
Cisco Rd 28805
City Homes Pl 28806
W City View Dr 28804
Clairmont Ave 28804
Clarence Ct 28806
Clarendon Ave 28804
Clarendon Rd 28806
Clark Branch Rd 28806
Clarke Rd 28805
Classic Dr 28805
Claude Dr 28806
Claxton Pl 28801
Clay St 28806
Clayton Ave 28806
Clayton St 28801
Clear Vista Cir, Dr & Ln 28805
Clearbrook Rd 28805
Clearbrook Xing 28803
Clearspring Dr 28803
Clearview Ter 28804
Cleftridge Ct 28803
Clement Dr & Pl 28805
Clement Cove Rd 28806
Clemmons St 28801
Clemson Ct 28806
Cleveland Ave 28803
Cliffside Ct 28803
Cliffview Ct & Dr 28803
Clifton Ave 28806
Clifton Pl 28804
Climbing Aster Way 28806
Clingman Ave & Pl 28801
Clingman Avenue Ext 28801
Clinton Ave 28806
Cloister Cv 28804
Clove Bud Rd 28803
Clovelly Way 28803
Cloverleaf Ln 28803
Cloyes St 28806
Club St 28801
Club Knoll Rd 28804
Club View Rd 28804
Clubhouse Ct 28803
Clubside Dr 28804
Clubwood Ct 28803
Clyde St 28801
Cm Doan Ln 28806
Coach Ct 28806
Coach Crest Dr 28806
Coachmans Ct & Trl 28803
Cobble Dr 28804
Cobblestone Path 28804
Coffey Cir & Pl 28806
Cogswood Rd 28804
Cokesbury Ln 28803
Cole St 28803
Coleman Ave 28801
Coleys Cir 28806
College Pl & St 28801
Collier Ave 28801
Collins Mountain Dr 28804
Colonial Pl 28804
Columbine Rd 28803
Commerce St 28801
Community St 28804
Company St 28804
Compton Dr 28806
Concord Pl & Rd 28803
Concord Knoll Ln 28803
Conestee Pl & St 28801
Congress St 28801
Conifer Ct 28803
Cooper Blvd 28806
Coopers Hawk Dr 28803
Copper Leaf Ln 28803
Copperwood Dr 28803
Cordell Pl 28803
Cordial Ct 28803
Cordova St 28806
Cornelia St 28801
Cornell St 28803
Cortland Way 28806
Cottage Ct 28801
Cottage Dr 28805
Cottage St 28804
Cottage Cove Ln 28803
Cottontail Rd 28805
Country Club Ln, Rd & Trl 28804
Country Gardens Ln 28806
Country Meadows Dr 28806
Country Mountain Rd 28803
Country Spring Dr 28804
Countryside Dr & Ln 28804
Court Plz 28801
Court View Ln 28806
Courtland Ave & Pl 28801
Courtney St 28806
Covan Cv 28803
Cove View Ln 28805
Coventry Cir 28806
Covered Bridge Ln 28804
Covewood Ln, Rd & Trl 28805
Covington St 28806
Cowan Rd 28806
Cowan Cove Pl & Rd 28806
Coxe Ave
1-40 28801
33-33 28802
41-299 28801
42-198 28801
Crabapple Ln 28804
Craft Dr 28806
Craftsman Cir 28805
Craftsman View Dr 28804
Craggy Ave 28806
Craggy Cir 28803
Craig Cir 28805
Crandon Ct 28804
Cranesway Dr 28806
Cranford Rd 28806
Craven St 28806
Crayton Rd 28803
Crayton Creek Way 28803
Creasman Pl 28806
Credg Rd 28805
Creek Dr 28805
Creek View Dr 28806
Creekside Ct 28803
Creekside Dr 28804
Creekside Ln 28803
Creekside Way 28804
Creekside View Dr 28804
Creekwood Rd 28806
Crescent Ln 28804
Crescent St
1-99 28801
6-30 28804
32-98 28801
N Crescent St 28801
Crest Ave 28803
Crest Knoll Rd 28806
Crestfield Ave 28804
Crestland Rd 28803
Crestmont Ave 28806
Crestridge Dr 28803
Crestview Ct 28806
Crestview St 28803
Crestwood Ln & Rd 28804
Cricket Ln 28804
Cricket Crossing Ct 28804
Cricklewood Sq 28804
Crimson Clover Path 28806
Cris Ln 28806
Crispin Ct 28803
Crockett Ave 28805
Crocus Ln 28803
Crofoot Trl 28804
Crooked Crk & Dr 28803
Crooked Creek Dr 28804
Cross Pl & St 28801
Crossroad Ct 28806
Croton Ct 28803
Crowell Rd 28806
Crowell Square Ct 28806
Crowfields Dr & Ln 28803
Crown St 28806
Crown Point Dr 28803
Crowningway Dr 28804
Crystal Country Way 28804
Crystal June Ln 28803
Cub Pl & Rd 28806
Cuddly Rd 28805
Cullowhee St 28801
Culvern St 28804
Cumberland Ave, Cir & Pl 28801
Cummins Rd 28805
Curci Dr 28803
Curtis Dr 28804
Curve St 28801
Cutlers Grn 28805
Cynthia Dr 28804
Cypress Dr 28803
Daffodil Dr 28806
Dailey Dr 28801
Dairty Ct 28806
Dairy Rd 28803
Dairy Gap Rd 28804
Daisy Ln 28806
Daisy Hill Rd 28805
Dale St 28806
Dalea Dr 28805
Dallas St 28806
Dalton St 28803
Dancing Trees Dr 28803
Daniel Rd 28806
Daniel Brooke Dr 28806
Danner Ln 28806
Danville Pl 28801
Darcus Ln 28806
Darcy Ln 28804
Dartmouth St 28806
Davenport Pl & Rd 28806
David Ct 28806
Davida Dr 28806
Davidson Dr 28801
Davidson Rd 28803
Davidson St 28806
Davis Dr 28806
Davlyn Dr 28806
Dawnwood Cir 28803
Dawson Pl 28803
Dawson Steele Ct 28803
Daybreak Ln 28805
Dayflower Dr 28803
Dayspring Dr 28803
Daystar Ln 28806
Dayton Rd 28804
Deanwood Cir 28803
Dearborn St 28803
Deaver Dr & St 28806
Deaver Park Cir & Rd 28806
Deavermont Cir 28806
Deaverview Pl & Rd 28806
Debra Ln 28806
Decker Dr 28803
Deer Run 28805
Deer Park Rd 28803
Deer Run Ct & Dr 28803
Deerfield Rd 28803
Deerhaven Ln 28803
Deerlake Dr 28803
Deerview Ln 28804
Deerwood Dr 28805
Delano Rd 28805
Delaware Ave, Pl & Ter 28806
Delchester Ln 28803
Deleuil Dr 28806
Dell St 28806
Dellwood St 28806
Delta Loop 28806
Denali Dr 28806
Dennie Hill Rd 28806
Deno Dr 28806
Departure Dr 28804
Depot St 28801
Desota St 28806
Desperate Ln 28806
Desperation Ln 28806
Destination Dr 28806
Detroit Pl 28806
Deva Glen Rd 28804
Devereux Ln 28806
Devon Ln 28803
Devonshire Pl 28803
Dewey Crst 28806
Dexter Way 28804
Dexter Mcconnell Dr 28806
Deymac Dr 28806
Dianthus Dr 28803
Dickerson Ln 28804
Digges Rd 28805
Dillard Dr 28806
Dillingham Cir & Rd 28805
Dingle Creek Ln 28803
Dirt Rd 28805
Distant View Dr 28803
Dix Creek Chapel Rd 28806
Dockery Dr 28806
Doctors Dr & Park 28801
Dodge St 28803
Dog Patch Trl 28806
Dogwood Ct 28805
Dogwood Grv 28805
Dogwood Knl 28805
Dogwood Ln 28803
Dogwood Rd
1-1 28804
3-6 28804
4-82 28806
8-40 28804
29-77 28804
83-199 28806
84-98 28806
N Dogwood Rd 28804
Dogwood Hollow Ln 28804
Dominic Ln 28805
Domino Ln 28806
Donna Dr 28801
Donna Lynn Rd 28804
Donnybrook Ct & Dr 28806
Dorchester Ave 28806
Dortch Ave 28801
Double Oaks Dr 28805
Doubles Aly 28803
Douglas Pl 28803
Douglas Rd 28806
Dove Rd 28806
Dove Haven Dr 28804
Dove Tree Ln 28806
Dover St 28804
Downing St 28806
Dragon Ln 28806
Drake St 28806
Dreamland Ct 28803
Drifter Trl 28805
Driftwood Ct 28805
Druid Dr 28806
Dry Ferry Rd 28806
Dry Ridge Rd 28804
Dryman Mountain Rd 28806
Dryman Valley Rd 28804
Duchess Ln 28806
Duckers Vw 28805
Dudley Baker Ct 28803
Duke St 28803
Dundee St 28801
Dunkirk Rd 28803
Dunn St 28806
Dunwell Ave 28806
Dunwood Rd 28804
Durham St 28806
Durwood Dr 28804
Dutchman Ln 28803
Dysart St 28806
Eagle St 28801
Eagle Ridge Dr & Trl 28803
Eaglebear Dr 28806
Eagles Nest Ln 28806
East Ln 28801
East St 28803
Eastmoor Dr 28805
Eastover Dr 28806
Eastview Ave 28803
Eastview Cir 28806
Eastway St 28804
Eastwood Rd 28803
Easy Living Ln 28806
Echo Ln 28806
Eclipse Dr 28804
Ector St 28806
Edbar St 28803
Edgar St 28806
Edgedale Dr 28804
Edgehill Ave 28801
Edgelawn Rd 28804
Edgemont Rd 28801
Edgewater Ln 28804
Edgewood Rd 28804
Edgewood Rd E 28805
Edgewood Rd S 28803
Edgewood Road Ext 28803
Edwards St 28806
Edwin Pl 28801
Elderberry Ln 28805
Eliada Home Rd 28806
Elizabeth Pl & St 28801
Elk Trl 28804
Elk Mountain Pl, Rd & Rdg 28804
Elk Mountain Scenic Hwy 28804
Elk Park Dr 28804
Elk Ridge Dr 28804
Elkdale Dr 28804
Elkin St 28806
Elkmont Dr, Pl & Ter 28804
Elkwood Ave 28804
Ellege Ln 28806
Ellenwood Dr 28804
Ellicott Ln 28803
Ellington Dr 28804
Elliott St 28803
Elly Ln 28803
Elm Dr 28805
Elm St 28801
Elmore St 28804
Elmwood Ln 28803
Elmwood Pl 28804
Eloise St 28801
Emma Rd 28806
Emma Hills Dr 28806
Emmaus Rd 28805
Emory Pl & Rd 28806
E End Pl 28801
W End Way 28806
English Hills Dr 28804
English Holly Ct 28806
English Ivy Rd 28806
Eola Ave 28806
Erskine Ave & St 28801
Erwin Dr 28806
Erwin Hills Rd 28806
Estelle Park Dr 28806
Estes Ct 28806
Euclid Blvd 28806
E Euclid Pkwy 28804
W Euclid Pkwy 28804
Eva Cir 28806
Eve Ct & Dr 28806
Evelake Dr 28806
Evelyn Pl 28801
Evelyn Acres Anx, Arc & Dr 28806
Evergreen Ave 28806
Evergreen Ln 28801
Executive Park 28801
Expo St 28806
Ezelle St 28806
Faculty Dr 28806
Faircrest Rd 28804
Fairfax Ave 28806
Fairhaven Ct 28803
Fairmont Rd 28804
Fairsted Dr 28803
Fairview Ave, Rd & St 28803
Fairview Oaks Ln 28803
Fairway Dr 28805
Fairway Pl 28803
Fairway Rd 28804
Fairyland Dr 28805
Faith Dr 28806
Fall Mountain Rd 28803
Fall Pippin Ln 28803
Fallen Spruce Dr 28806
Falling Leaf Ln 28803
Family Ln 28806
Far Horizons Ln 28803
Farida Dr 28804
Farleigh St 28803
Farm Rd 28804
Farm St 28806
E & W Farm Creek Dr 28806
Farnwood Ave 28804
Fast Break Ln 28804
Faulkner Ave 28805
Fawn Dr 28803
Fayetteville St 28806
Feather Dr 28805
Federal Aly 28801
Fen Way 28803
Fender Valley Rd 28804
Fenner Ave 28804
Ferguson Dr 28806
Fern St 28803
Fern Cove Rd 28804
Fern Creek Ln 28804
Fern Glade Rd 28804
Fernbrook Pl 28804
Ferncliff Dr 28805
Fernlawn Rd 28805
Fernstone Rd 28804
Fernwood Ave 28806
Fernwood Park 28803
Ferry Rd 28806
Festiva Ln 28804
Fieldcrest Cir, Ct & Pl 28806
Fielding St 28803
Finalee Ave 28803
Fir Tree Ln 28803
Firethorne Dr 28804
Firwood Ct 28804
Fisher Ln 28804
Fiver Ln 28803
Flamingo Ln 28806
Flaxen Ln 28803
Fleming Ct 28803
Flight Quest Dr 28806
Flint St 28801
Flora Rosa Trl 28803
Florham Pl 28806
Florida Ave & Pl 28806
Flower Garden Rd 28805
Flowering Cherry Dr 28805
Flowering Plum Dr 28806
Floyd Dr 28803
Floyds Chapel Ln 28806
Fluttering Elm Ln 28804
Flynn Branch Rd 28804
Foggy Hollow Trl 28806
Fontaine Dr 28804
Foothills Rd 28804
Ford St 28806
Fordbrook Rd 28806
Fore Rd 28806
Fore Way 28805
Forehand Loop 28803
Forest Ln 28805
N Forest Ln 28804
Forest Rd 28803
E Forest Rd 28803
Forest St 28803
Forest Edge Dr 28806
Forest Glen Trl 28805
Forest Hill Dr 28803
Forest Lake Dr 28803
Forest Park Ln 28803
Forest Ridge Dr 28806
Forest Run Dr 28803
Forest Spring Dr 28804
Forest View Dr 28804
Forestdale Dr 28803
Forever Friend Ln 28806
Forevermore Ln 28803
Forsythe St 28801
Fortunate Dr 28806
Foster Estate Dr 28806
Four Wheel Dr 28806
Fox Dr 28803
Fox Rd 28804
Fox Chase Rd 28804
Fox Den Rd 28805
Fox Lair Ct 28805
Fox Ridge Rd 28804
Foxcroft Dr 28806
Foxfire Dr 28803
Foxglove Ct 28805
Foxjump Field Dr 28805
Foxwood Dr 28804
Frady Ln 28803
Frances St 28806
Frank Paul Pl 28803
Frankie Ln 28804
Franklin Trace Dr 28804
Frederick St 28801
Frederick Law Olmsted Way 28806
Freedom Ln 28803
Fremont Rd 28806
N & S French Broad Ave 28801
French Willow Dr 28804
Freno Dr 28803
Friendly Cir, Holw, Ln & Way 28806
Frill Hill Dr 28806
Frisbee Rd 28806
Frith Dr 28803
Front St 28804

Frontier Ct 28805
Frosty Ln 28806
Fuller Ln 28805
Fulton St 28801
Furman Ave & Ct 28801
Fury Dr 28806
Future Dr 28803
Gabrielle Ln 28805
Gaia Ln 28806
Gaines Ave 28803
Gala Dr 28803
Galahad Pl 28806
Galax Ave 28806
Galloway Dr 28803
Gamblers Run 28806
Garden Cir 28806
Garden Rd 28804
Garden Ter 28804
Gardenwood Dr & Ln 28803
Gardner Dr 28803
Garfield St 28803
Garland Dr 28804
Gash Farm Rd 28805
Gashes Creek Rd
1-299 28805
300-399 28803
Gaston St 28801
Gaston Mountain Rd 28806
Gatehouse Ct 28803
Gatewood Rd 28806
Gawain St 28806
Gay St 28801
Gelding Ln 28806
Gentlebreeze Ln 28805
George Washington
Carver Ave 28801
Georgia Ave
1-99 28806
2-98 28804
Georgia Hill Dr 28806
Gerber Rd 28803
Gertrude Pl 28801
Gibson Rd 28804
Gilbert St 28804
Gill St 28806
Gilliam Pl 28801
Gilligans Aly 28805
Gillis Rd 28806
Gilmore Dr 28803
Ginell Cir 28804
Gins Run 28803
Girdwood St 28801
Glade Cove Rd 28804
Gladstone Rd 28805
Glen Cable Rd 28805
Glen Falls Rd 28804
Glen Woods Ct 28803
Glendale Ave 28803
Glendale Rd 28804
Glenview Rd 28804
Glenway Dr 28804
Glimmer Dr 28806
Gobblers Knob 28806
Golden Hawk Trl 28805
Golden Tree Ln 28806
Goldfinch Ln 28803
Goldview Dr & Rd 28804
Golf St 28801
Golf View Rd 28804
Good Intentions Rd 28806
Goodman Rd 28804
Goodwill St 28806
Gorman Bridge Rd
1-299 28804
300-1799 28806
Gosnell Rd 28804
Governors Ct 28805
Governors Dr 28804
Governors Way 28804
Governors View Rd 28805
Grace Ave 28804
Gracelyn Rd 28804
Gracious Ln 28803
Grady Parris Ln 28806
Grady Ridge Dr 28806
Graham Ln 28803

Graham Rd 28805
Grail St 28801
Granada St 28806
Granby St 28801
Grand Kids Dr 28806
Grandview Cir 28806
Grandview Ct 28806
Grandview Dr 28806
Grandview Pl 28805
Grandview Rd 28806
Grant St 28803
Grapevine Ln 28806
Graphic Ln 28806
Grassy Rd 28805
Grassy Glen Ln 28804
Grassy Park Dr 28805
Grassy Ridge Rd 28805
Gray Ct 28806
Gray St 28801
Gray Eagle Dr 28805
Graystone Rd 28804
Greeley St 28806
Green St 28801
Green Gorge Trl 28804
Green Hill Ave 28806
Green Oak Rd 28804
Green Tractor Ln 28806
Green Tree Ln 28805
Green Valley Ct, Rd &
Ter 28806
Greenbriar Ct & Rd 28805
Greenleaf Cir 28804
Greenleaf Circle Ext 28804
Greenlee Ave 28801
Greenmont Dr 28803
Greenwood Ave 28806
Greenwood Pl 28803
Greenwood Rd 28803
Gretchen Ln 28806
Grey River Run 28804
N & S Griffing Blvd &
Cir 28804
Grindstaff Dr 28803
Grove Park 28804
Grove St
1-3 28804
2-2 28801
4-68 28801
S Grove St 28801
Grove Knoll Ct 28805
Grovewood Rd 28804
Gudger St 28801
Guess Ct 28806
Guinevere Ct 28806
Guthrie Ln 28805
Hack Rhodes Dr 28806
W Haith Dr 28801
Hall Sayles Dr 28803
Hallmark Ln 28806
Hamby Dr 28803
Hamilton St 28801
Hamlin Cir 28806
Hampden Rd 28805
Hampshire Cir 28804
Hampstead Rd 28804
Hampton St 28803
Hampton Parish 28805
Hank Cir 28806
Hannah Dr 28804
Hanover St 28806
Hansel Ave 28806
Happy Crow Ln 28805
Happy Valley Rd 28806
Harbinger Way 28803
Harbor Ln 28803
Hare Rdg 28803
Harkridge Rd 28804
Harmon Cir 28803
Harmony Ln 28803
Harnett St 28806
Harris Ave 28806
Harris Rd 28803
Harris St 28803
Harrisland Dr 28806
Harrison St 28801
Hartle Dr 28803

Harvard Pl 28806
Hasbrook Ln 28804
Hat Creek Dr 28806
S Haven Rd 28804
Haw Creek Cir, Ln &
Trce 28805
Haw Creek Mews Dr &
Pl 28805
Hawk Rdg 28804
Hawk View Dr 28804
Hawkins Ln 28806
Hawthorne Dr 28805
E Hawthorne Dr 28805
Hawthorne Ln 28801
Hayes Green Rd 28806
Haywood Rd 28806
Haywood St 28801
W Haywood St 28801
Haywood Ter 28806
Hazel Hill St 28803
Hazel Mill Rd 28806
Hazelnut Dr 28806
Hazelwood Rd 28806
Hazzard St 28801
Heart Dr 28806
Hearthstone Dr 28803
Heartwood Cir 28806
Heath Ridge Rd 28806
Heathbrook Cir 28803
Heather Ct 28804
Heather Dr 28806
Heather Pl 28803
Heavens Above 28806
Heavens View Dr 28803
Hedgerose Ct 28805
Hedgewood Ct 28804
Helton Dr 28803
Hemlock Dr
1-99 28803
8-22 28806
Hemlock Ln 28803
Hemlock Rd 28803
Hemphill Rd 28803
Hemphill Knob Rd 28803
Hemphill Knoll Rd 28803
Hendersonville Rd
1-799 28803
780-780 28813
800-2002 28803
801-2099 28803
Hendrix St 28806
Henrietta St 28801
Hensley Dr
1-99 28805
1-99 28806
2-98 28805
2-98 28806
Hensley Hill Ln 28806
Heradiso Rd 28804
Heritage Dr 28806
Herman Ave 28803
Herman St 28801
Herman Avenue Ext 28803
Herringbone Dr 28806
Herron Ave 28806
Hessen Rd 28804
Hi Alta Ave 28806
Hiawassee St 28801
Hiawatha Ct 28806
Hibernia St 28801
Hibiscus Ln 28803
Hibriten Dr 28801
Hickman Rd 28803
Hickory Dr 28806
Hickory Ln
1-99 28804
300-999 28805
Hickory St 28804
Hickory Ter 28806
Hickory Forest Rd 28805
Hickory Tree Rd 28805
Hicks Mckinney Rd 28806
Hidden Acres Dr 28806
Hidden Brook Ln 28806
Hidden Cabins Ln 28804
Hidden Falls Dr 28804

Hidden Springs Dr 28804
High St 28804
High Court Entrance 28806
High Meadow Rd 28803
High Oaks Dr & Est 28806
High Top Ln 28803
Highbridge Xing 28803
Highland Pl 28804
Highland St 28801
Highland Center Blvd 28806
Highland Grove Rd 28806
Highlander Rd 28804
Hildebrand St 28801
Hill St 28801
Hillary Dr 28804
Hillbilly Way 28805
Hillcreek Dr 28804
Hillcrest Dr 28806
Hillcrest Rd 28804
Hilldale Rd 28803
Hillendale Rd 28805
Hilliard Ave 28801
Hillside St 28801
Hillside Ter 28806
Hillside Walk 28801
Hillside Mobile Hm Pk 28803
Hilltop Rd 28803
Hilltopia Rd 28805
Hillview Cir & Rd 28805
Hitching Post Ln 28806
Hogan View Dr 28804
Holcombe Dr 28806
Holcombe Ridge Dr 28806
N Holland St 28801
Holland Mountain Vw 28804
Hollifield Rd 28804
Holly Dr 28805
Holly Ln 28806
Holly St 28806
Holly Arbor Ln 28803
Holly Hill Ct 28806
Holly Hill Dr 28806
Holly Hill Rd 28803
Hollybrook Dr 28803
Hollyridge Dr 28803
Hollywood St 28801
Holmwood Rd 28801
Holt Ln 28803
Homeway Rd 28806
Homewood Dr 28803
Hominy Creek Rd 28806
Honey Dr 28805
Honeysuckle Ln 28806
Hope Cir & Ln 28804
Hopedale Cir 28806
Horizon Hill Pl & Rd 28804
Hornot Cir 28806
Hospital Dr 28801
Houghton Pl 28806
House Ln 28806
Houser Rd 28803
Houston Cir, Pl & St 28801
Howard St 28806
Howard Row Pl 28805
Howland Rd 28804
Howling Wolf Ct 28804
Hoyle Ln 28804
Hubbard Ave 28806
Hudson St 28806
Huffman Rd 28806
Hughes Trl 28806
Humble Hl 28805
Hummingbird Ln 28806
Hunt Hill Pl 28801
Hunters Way 28804
Hunters Ridge Dr 28803
Huntinggreen Dr 28804
Huntington Rd 28805
Huntington St 28801
Huntington Chase Dr 28805
Huntley Dr 28803
Huntsman Pl 28803
Husky Ln 28805
Hy Vu Dr 28804
Hyacinth Ln 28805
Hyannis Dr 28804

Hyde Park Dr 28806
Ian River Dr 28806
Idle Hour Dr 28806
Idlewood Dr 28806
Impala Trl 28806
Imperial Ct 28803
In God We Trust Dr 28806
Independence Blvd 28805
Indian Pl 28805
Indian Trl 28803
Indian Falls Est & Rd 28803
Indian Knob Rd 28803
Indian Ridge Rd 28803
Indian Wells Rd 28803
E Indiana Ave 28806
Ingle Rd 28804
Inglewood Ave 28806
Inglewood Dr 28805
Inglewood Rd 28804
Innsbrook Rd 28804
Integrity Dr 28804
Interstate Blvd 28806
Iona Cir 28806
Iris St 28803
Irving St 28804
Irwin Dr 28803
Ivanhoe Ave 28806
Ivington Cir 28803
Ivy St 28806
Ivy St N 28804
J Keever Cv 28803
Jack Nelson Dr 28806
Jackson Park Ln 28804
Jackson View Rd 28806
Jacob Ln 28806
Jaks Ridge Dr 28805
Jamie Hill Dr 28806
Jan Dr 28803
Jane St 28801
Jane Mountain Trl 28803
Janice Dr 28803
Jarnaul Ave 28804
Jarrett St 28806
Jasmine Ln 28803
Jason St 28801
Jean Dr 28803
Jeff Dr 28806
Jefferson Cir 28805
Jefferson Dr 28801
Jeffress Ave 28803
Jen June Ln 28806
Jennifer Ln 28803
Jenny St 28806
Jesse Ln 28806
Jett Ct 28806
Joan Way 28806
Joes Dr 28806
Joglen Dr 28804
John St 28801
Johns St 28806
Johnson Dr & Rd 28804
Johnston Blvd 28806
Johnston School Rd 28806
Jones St 28804
Jones Cove Rd 28805
Jones Hillock Dr 28805
Jonestown Rd 28804
Jordan St 28801
Jordans Star Way 28806
Joseph Dr 28803
Josie Ln 28804
Joyner Ave 28806
Julia St 28801
Julianne Pl 28805
June Sayles Rd 28803
Juno Dr 28806
Kalmia Dr 28804
Kanupp Knl 28803
Karen Pl 28806
Katherine Pl 28801
Katies Ridge Dr 28804
Katra Ln 28805
Keasler Cir & Rd 28805
Keebler Rd 28803
Keenan Rd 28805
Keeping Kyle Xing 28804

Keever Rd 28803
Kelly Dr 28806
Kemon Dr 28806
Kenai Dr 28806
Kendall St 28806
Kenilwood Pl 28803
Kenilworth Knls 28805
Kenilworth Rd
1-328 28803
329-599 28805
Kenmore St 28803
Kensington Dr 28805
Kensington Pl 28803
N Kensington Rd 28804
W Kensington Rd 28804
Kent Pl 28804
Kent St 28803
Kentmere Ln 28803
Kenton Ln 28803
Kentucky Dr 28806
Kenwood St 28806
Keswick Dr 28803
Kevin Ct 28806
Keystone Dr 28806
Keystone Drive Ext 28806
Kids Town Rd 28806
Kildare Pl 28806
Kilkenny Dr 28806
Killian Ln & Rd 28804
Kilpatrick Crst 28806
Kimberly Ave 28804
Kimberly Knoll Rd 28804
King St 28804
King Arthur Pl 28806
Kingbird Ln 28803
Kingfisher Ln 28806
Kingie Dr 28805
Kings Rdg 28804
Kingsgate Rd 28805
Kingwood Pl 28804
Kirby Pl & Rd 28806
Kirkland Dr 28805
Kirkman Rd 28805
Kirkwood Dr 28805
Kitchen Pl 28803
Klein St 28805
Klondyke Ave & Pl 28801
Knauth Rd 28805
Knob St 28801
Knob Hill Rd 28806
Knoll Ridge Dr 28804
Knollview Dr 28806
Knollway Ct 28806
Knollwood Pl 28804
Knoxville Pl 28801
Koala Ct 28806
Kodiak Ct 28806
Kuykendall Rd 28805
Kuykendall Branch Rd 28804
Kyles Ct 28806
La Mancha Dr 28805
La Rue St 28806
Lacey Ln 28806
Lackey Ln 28804
Lady Huntingdon Ln 28803
Lafayette Ave 28805
Lafayette Dr 28806
Lake Town Ln 28804
Lakeshore Dr & Ln 28804
Lakeshore Drive Ext 28804
Lakeside Dr 28806
Lakeview Rd & Ter 28804
Lakeview Acres Dr 28806
Lakewood Dr & Pkwy 28803
Lamar Ave 28803
Lamb Ave 28806
Lambeth Dr 28803
Lance Ln 28806
Lance Rd 28803
Lancelot Ln 28806
Landis Ct 28806
Landsdowne Ct 28803
Lane Ave 28806
Langwell Ave 28806
Lanning Ave 28806
Lanvale Ave 28806

E Larchmont Rd 28804
Largo Ln 28806
Lariat Trl 28804
Larkspur Ct 28805
Larlyn Ln 28804
Larry James Dr 28805
Latrobe St 28801
Latta St 28801
Laurel Ave 28804
Laurel Ln 28805
Laurel Loop 28806
Laurel Ter 28804
Laurel Trl 28803
Laurel Creek Dr 28803
Laurel Place Dr 28803
Laurel Ridge Rd 28805
Laurel Summit Dr 28803
Laurel Valley Dr 28805
Laurelton Ln 28803
Laurie Ln 28806
Lawndale Ave 28806
Lawrence Pl 28801
Lawson Ln 28806
Lawterdale Rd 28804
Lawterdale Circle
Number One 28804
Lawterdale Circle
Number Two 28804
Lawyers Walk 28801
Le An Hurst Rd 28803
Le Vista Ln 28806
Leannas Way 28805
Ledain Ln 28806
Ledford Dr 28806
Lee Ave 28804
Lee St 28803
Lee St N 28801
Leel Dr 28805
Lees Creek Rd 28806
Legacy Oaks Pl 28803
Leila Ln 28806
Leisure Loop 28804
Leisure Mountain Rd 28804
Leita Ln 28806
Lela Johnson Ln 28803
Lemon Tree Ln 28806
Lena Ln 28806
Lennox Ct & St 28801
Lenoir St 28803
Leroy Hill Ln 28806
N & S Leslie Ln 28805
Leucothoe Ln 28803
Levy Ln 28805
N & S Lexington Ave 28801
Liberty St 28803
N Liberty St 28801
S Liberty St 28801
W Liberty St 28801
Liberty Oak Dr 28804
Lilac St 28806
Lillian Ln 28806
Lily Ln 28806
Lincoln Ave 28803
W Lincoln Ave 28801
Lincoln Park Ext 28803
Linda Ln 28803
Linda Vista Dr 28806
Linden Ave 28801
Lindsey Rd 28805
Line House Rd 28803
Lionel Pl 28806
Lipton Grv 28805
Little Bear Ln 28804
Little Billy Ln 28803
Little Cedar Ct 28805
Little Forest Dr 28806
Little Jones Mtn 28805
Little Knob Rd 28803
Livingston St 28801
Lockley Ave 28804
Lockwood Ln 28806
Locust Ave 28804
Locust Cir 28806
Locust St 28803
Lodge St 28803
Logan Ave & Cir 28806

Logan Hill Ln 28803
London Rd 28803
Lone Pine Rd 28803
Long St 28804
Long Winding Rd 28805
Longview Rd 28806
Longwood Ln 28806
W Looking Glass Ln 28805
Lookout Dr 28804
Lookout Rd 28804
Lookout Rd E 28805
Loomis Ave 28803
Looney Creek Ln 28806
Lora Ln 28803
Lorena Dr 28806
Lorenz Ln 28806
Lornelle Pl 28804
Lorraine Ave 28804
Lost Mountain Ln 28805
Lotus Pl 28804
N Louisiana Ave 28806
Louisville Pl 28806
Love It Ln 28806
Lovely Ln 28803
Lovers Loop Rd 28803
Lowe Ave 28803
Lowell St 28803
Lower Barton Rd 28804
Lower Bend Rd 28805
Lower Bucks Dr 28806
Lower Grassy Branch Rd 28805
Lower Stradley Mountain Rd 28806
Lucerne Ave 28806
Lucille Dr 28805
Lucky Ln 28804
Lufty Ave 28806
Lunsford Rd 28805
Lupine Loop 28805
Luther St 28806
Lydia Ln 28806
Lyman St 28801
Lyme Ct 28803
Lynmar Ave 28804
Lynn Cove Rd 28804
Lynndale Ave 28806
Lynnstone Ct 28805
Lynwood Cir 28806
Lynwood Ct 28806
Lynwood Rd 28804
Macallan Ln 28805
Macces Ln 28806
Mace Ave 28806
Macedonia Dr & Rd 28804
Macks View Dr 28806
Macon Ave
1-173 28801
174-299 28804
173 1/2-173 1/2 28801
Madeline Ave 28806
Madison Ave & St 28801
Magma Ct 28806
Magnolia Ave 28801
Magnolia Way 28806
Magnolia Farms Dr 28806
Magnolia Hill Ct 28806
Magnolia Valley Ct 28806
Magnum Way 28803
Main St 28803
Majestic Ave 28806
Majestic Mtn Dr 28805
Mallard Dr 28806
Manetta Rd 28804
Maney Ave 28804
Manila Pl & St 28806
Mann Dr & Rd 28805
Manor Ridge Dr 28804
Maple Dr 28805
W Maple Dr 28805
Maple St 28806
Maple Crescent St 28806
Maple Leaf Ct 28803
Maple Ridge Ln 28806
Maple Springs Rd 28805
Maplewood Dr 28806

Maplewood Pkwy 28804
Maplewood Rd 28804
Marbil Ln 28805
Marble Way 28806
Mardell Cir 28806
Margaret Ln 28805
Marietta St 28803
Marigold St 28803
Marion Gaddy Rd 28806
Marjorie St 28801
Mark Twain Rd 28805
N & S Market St 28801
Marlborough Dr 28805
Marlborough Rd 28804
Marlowe Dr 28801
Marlwood Ct 28804
Marne Rd 28803
Mars Dr 28804
Martel Ln 28804
Martel Mill Vlg 28804
Marthas Way 28806
Martin Ave 28806
Martin Luther King Jr Dr 28801
Martindale Rd 28804
Mary Wendy Rd 28804
Massey Rd 28804
Masters Ln 28806
Maude Ave 28803
Max St 28801
Maxwell Rd 28805
Maxwell St 28801
Mayberry Dr 28804
Mayfair Dr 28806
Mayfield Rd 28804
Mayflower Dr 28804
Mayo Dr 28806
Maywood Rd 28804
Mcarthur Ln 28803
Mcclain St 28803
Mccormick Pl 28801
Mcdade St 28806
Mcdowell St
1-199 28801
209-297 28803
299-599 28803
Mcfalls Rd 28805
Mcglamery Ln 28806
Mcilwain Rd 28806
Mcintosh Rd 28806
Mcintyre Dr 28803
Mckinney Dr 28806
Mckinney Pl 28806
Mckinney Rd
1-99 28805
7-96 28806
100-162 28805
100-498 28806
101-161 28805
101-499 28806
Mckinney Lane Dr 28806
Mckinnish Cove Dr & Rd 28806
Mcpherson St 28804
Mctindal Cir 28803
Meadow Rd 28803
Meadow Run 28806
Meadow Lake Rd 28803
Meadow Ridge Dr 28804
Meadow Run Ext 28806
Meadow Village Ln 28803
Meadow Vista Ct 28803
Meadowbrook Ave 28806
Meadowlark Rd 28805
Meadowood Mhp Dr 28806
Meadowview Rd 28804
Meandering Trl 28806
Medical Park Dr 28803
Melbourne Pl 28801
Melissa Ct 28806
Melnick Ter 28803
Melody Ln 28803
Melody Rose Ln 28804
Melrose Ave 28804
Melton Dr 28805
Memory Ln 28805

Merchant St 28803
Mercy Ridge Rd 28804
Merion Ct & Dr 28806
Merlin Way 28806
Merrills Chase 28803
Merrills Cove Rd 28803
Merrills Ridge Rd 28803
Merrimon Ave
1-399 28801
400-790 28804
725-725 28814
791-1499 28804
792-1498 28804
N Merrimon Ave 28804
Merrimon Pl 28801
Merrit St 28801
Merritt Dr 28806
Metcalf St 28806
Metz Dr 28806
Meyers Ave 28806
Mezzo Cv 28804
Mica Mine Rdg 28806
Michael St 28801
Michigan Ave 28806
Mid Court Dr 28804
Middle Grassy Branch Rd 28805
Middlebrook Rd 28805
Middlemont Ave 28806
Midland Dr 28804
Midway Dr 28804
Midwood Dr 28804
Mildred Ave 28806
Mill Rd 28805
Mill Creek Loop 28806
Mill Stone Dr 28803
Millbrook Rd 28806
Miller Ln 28803
Miller Rd E 28805
Miller Rd S 28803
W Miller Rd 28806
Miller St 28801
Miller Branch Rd 28805
Mills Pl 28804
Mills Gap Rd 28803
Mimosa Cir 28805
Mimosa Dr 28806
Mimosa Ln 28806
Mineral Springs Rd 28805
Mint Ln 28806
Minuteman Dr 28806
Miracle Dr 28803
Miramar Dr 28806
Mirehouse Run 28803
Misty Day Ct 28806
Misty Morning Rd 28805
Mitchell Ave 28806
Mockingbird Cir & Ln 28806
Moffitt Rd 28805
Moffitt Branch Rd 28805
Moffitt Hill Dr 28805
Monroe Pl 28801
Montana Ave & Cir 28806
Monte Vista Rd 28806
Montford Ave 28801
Montford Park Pl 28801
Montgomery St 28806
Montrose Ave 28804
Montview Dr 28801
Monty St 28806
Moody Rd 28806
Moon Shadow Ln 28805
Moore Ave 28806
Moore St 28804
Moorecrest Rd 28806
Mooseheart Ln 28806
Morance Ave 28804
Moreview Dr 28803
Morgan Ave 28801
Morgan Ridge Ln 28806
Moriah Ln 28803
Morning Dew Dr 28804
Morning Fog Way 28804
Morning Glory Dr 28805
Morning Mist Ln 28805
Morningside Ct & Dr 28806

Morris Pl, Rd & St 28806
Morrow Farm Rd 28804
Morse Dr 28806
Moss Garden Rd 28803
Moss Pink Pl 28806
Mossy Log Ln 28806
Mossy Stone Way 28806
Mostert Dr 28804
Mount Carmel Dr, Pl & Rd 28806
Mount Carmel Trlr Pk Rd 28806
Mount Clare Ave & Pl 28801
Mount Olive Dr, Ln & Ter 28804
Mount Olive Church Rd 28804
Mount Vernon Aly, Cir & Pl 28804
Mountain St 28801
Mountain Ter 28806
E Mountain Way 28805
Mountain Breeze Trl 28803
Mountain Chateau Ln 28804
Mountain Glen Dr 28804
Mountain Haven Dr 28803
Mountain Laurel 28805
Mountain Ridge Dr & Ln 28803
Mountain Site Ln 28803
Mountain Site Ln Ext 28803
Mountain Song Ln 28806
Mountain Spirit Dr 28805
Mountain View Rd 28805
Mountain Vista Dr 28804
Mountainbrook Rd 28805
Mountainview Rd 28806
Mulberry St 28804
Mulberry Hill Dr 28806
Mulder Dr 28805
Mulvaney St 28803
Munn Dr 28805
Murdock Ave
1-100 28801
102-154 28801
155-181 28804
183-399 28804
Murray Ln 28806
Muse Dr 28806
Musterfield Dr 28805
Myra Pl 28806
Myrtle St 28801
Mystic Mountain Rd 28803
Nacrosta Acres 28805
Nanas Branch Rd 28806
Nancy St 28806
Nantahala St 28801
Naomi Dr 28806
Naples Rd 28804
Narbeth Rd 28806
Naylor Rd 28806
Nebraska St 28806
Nelon Rd 28804
Neptune Dr 28804
Nesmith Ln 28804
Nethermead Dr 28803
Nevada Ave 28806
New St 28804
New Castle Ct 28803
New Cross N & S 28805
New Haw Creek Rd 28805
New Hope Rd 28804
New Jersey Ave 28806
New Leicester Hwy 28806
New Walnut St 28804
Newbern Ave 28803
Newbridge Pkwy 28804
Newfound Rd 28806
Newstock Rd 28804
Niagra Dr 28806
Nicholas Dr 28803
Nichols Hill Dr 28804
Nichols Hill Drive Ext 28804
Nicky Ln 28803
Night Frost Ln 28806
Nil Giri Dr 28803

Nina St 28804
Ninebark Ct 28806
Nix Dr 28804
Nixon Ter 28805
Noble St 28806
Nodding Ln 28803
Nomad Cir 28806
Nordic Trl 28804
Norfolk St 28803
Norman Dr 28806
Norman Austin Dr 28804
Normandy Rd 28803
North Rd 28804
North St 28801
Northbrook Pl 28804
Northington Dr 28805
Northside Dr & Ter 28804
Northview St 28801
Northwood Rd 28804
Norton Dr 28804
Norwich Dr 28803
Norwood Ave 28804
Nova Ln 28805
Nunez Dr 28806
Oak Ln 28801
Oak Pl 28803
Oak Plz 28801
Oak St 28801
W Oak St 28806
Oak Crescent Dr 28806
N & S Oak Forest Ct & Dr 28803
Oak Hill Cir & Dr 28806
Oak Hollow Ct & Dr 28805
Oak Knoll Rd 28804
Oak Lodge Rd 28806
Oak Park Rd 28801
Oak Ridge Rd 28805
Oak Terrace Dr & Rd 28806
Oakbrook Dr 28806
Oakcrest Dr & Pl 28806
Oaken Ct 28803
Oakhaven Ter 28803
Oakland Rd 28801
Oaklawn Ave 28804
Oakley Pl 28806
Oakley Rd 28803
Oakley Dogwood Dr 28803
Oakley School Rd 28803
Oakmont Ter 28806
Oakmoss Ln 28806
Oaks Cir & Dr 28806
Oakview Rd 28803
E Oakview Rd 28806
W Oakview Rd 28806
Oakview Park Rd 28803
Oakwilde Dr 28803
Oakwood St 28806
Obrians Way 28803
Ocala St 28801
Ocasey Rd 28806
Ocaso Dr 28806
Ocenchar Rd 28806
Odd Bits Ln 28806
Odonald Rd 28806
Offshore Dr 28805
Ohenry Ave 28801
Old 74 28803
Old Asheland Ave 28801
Old Beaverdam Rd 28804
Old Brevard Rd 28806
Old Burnsville Hill Rd 28804
Old Camby Rd 28805
Old Charlotte Hwy 28803
Old Chunns Cove Rd 28805
Old Coggins Pl 28805
Old County Home Rd 28806
Old Dairy Gap Rd 28804
Old Elk Mountain Rd 28804
Old Fairview Rd 28803
Old Farm School Rd 28805
Old Forest Rd 28803
Old Greenwood Rd 28803
Old Haw Creek Rd 28805
Old Haywood Rd 28806
Old Highway 20 Rd 28806

Old Home Rd 28804
Old Huffman Holw 28806
Old Leicester Hwy
1-299 28804
300-1699 28806
Old Leicester Rd 28804
Old Logging Rd 28804
Old Lyman St 28801
Old Marshall Hwy 28804
Old Olivette Rd 28804
Old Parham Rd 28806
Old Ridge Rd 28803
Old Rymer Dr & Rd 28806
Old Sardis Road Cir 28806
Old Starnes Cove Rd 28806
Old Stone Gate Pl 28804
Old Toll Rd 28804
Old Weaverville Rd 28804
Old Weaverville Road Ext 28804
Old West Chapel Rd 28803
Old Wolfe Rd 28805
Olde Cottage Ln 28803
Olde Eastwood Village Blvd 28803
Olive St 28801
Olivette Rd 28804
Olivewood Dr 28805
Olmsted Cir & Dr 28803
Olney Rd 28806
Ona Berry Ln 28803
Onteora Blvd 28803
Onteora Oaks Dr 28803
Ora St 28801
Orange St 28801
Orchard Pl, Rd & St 28801
Orchard Ridge Dr 28804
Orchid Ln 28803
Oregon Ave 28806
Orion Way 28806
Ormond Ave 28806
Orwell Ave 28806
Osborne Rd 28804
Osborne St 28806
Oteen Church Rd 28805
Oteen Park Pl 28805
Otis St 28801
Otis Campbell Rd 28806
Ottari Rd 28804
Overbrook Pl & Rd 28805
Overland Industrial Blvd 28806
Overlook Cir, Ct, Pl & Rd 28803
Overton Way 28803
Owen Hollow Rd 28806
Owenby Rd 28804
Owenby Cove Rd 28803
Owens Bell Ln 28801
Oxford Ct 28804
Ozark Spring Ln 28805
Pacifico Dr 28806
N, S, SW & W Pack Sq 28801
Pacoda Ct & St 28806
Page Ave 28801
Paisley Dr 28806
Palm Ct 28806
Palmer Ln 28804
Palmer St 28801
Panda St 28805
Panola St 28801
Panorama Ct & Dr 28806
Paper Birch Ave 28806
Paramount Ln 28801
Parham Hill Rd 28804
Park Ave 28803
Park Ave N 28801
Park Rd 28803
Park Sq 28801
Park Lane Ave 28806
Park Ridge Ct 28803
Parker Rd
1-99 28803
100-399 28805
Parkman Pl 28806

Parkside Pl 28804
Parkview Dr 28805
Parkview Dr Ext 28805
Parkway Ct 28803
Parkway Dr 28806
Parkway Loop 28803
Parkway Creek Dr 28803
Parkway Vista Dr 28805
Parkwood Ave
1-99 28804
1300-1399 28806
Parsonage Dr 28804
Parton Dr 28804
Pasture Vw 28806
Path Finder Trl 28806
Patina Trl 28806
Patriots Dr 28805
Patterson Dr 28806
Patti Ln 28804
Patton Ave
2-16 28801
18-250 28801
252-260 28801
600-1301 28806
1302-1302 28816
1303-1799 28806
1304-1698 28806
Patton Cir 28804
Patton Pl 28805
Patton Mountain Rd 28804
Patton Woods Pl 28804
Paul Williams Rd 28803
Paynes Way 28801
Peace St 28806
Peace Haven Dr 28806
Peach St 28806
Peach Knob Dr 28804
Peachtree Rd 28803
Pearl St 28801
Pearson Dr 28801
Pearson Bridge Rd 28806
Pebble Creek Dr 28803
Pebblebrook Ln 28803
Peek Ridge Ln 28806
Peeler Dr 28803
Pelham Rd 28803
Pelzer St 28804
Penley Ave 28804
Pennsylvania Ave & Pl 28806
Penny Ln 28805
Pentland Hills Dr 28806
Peppercorn Ln 28805
Peppermill Dr 28804
Percivale Ct 28806
Perdue Pl 28806
Peregrine Ln 28804
Periwinkle Dr 28804
N Pershing Rd 28805
Persimmon Ln 28805
Petunia Ln 28803
Pheasant Dr 28803
Pheasant Ridge Dr 28804
Phifer St 28801
Phillip Justin Dr 28805
Picadilly Ln 28806
Pickard Pl 28803
Pickwick Rd 28803
Piedmont Rd 28804
Piercy St 28806
Pinchot Dr 28803
Pindari Rdg 28804
Pine Ln 28806
Pine Rd 28805
Pine St 28801
Pine Acre Blvd 28804
Pine Burr Rd 28806
Pine Cone Dr 28805
Pine Cove Rd 28804
Pine Grove Ave 28801
Pine Knoll Dr & St 28806
Pine Meadow Dr 28804
Pine Ridge Rd
1-15 28804
11-21 28805
16-76 28804
20-40 28805

39-43 28804
Pine Spring Dr 28805
Pine Tops Dr 28804
Pine Tree Cir & Rd 28804
Pine Valley Ln 28805
Pinebrook Rd 28804
Pinebrook Club Dr 28804
Pinecrest Dr 28803
Pinecroft Pl & Rd 28804
Pinedale Ln & Rd 28805
Pinehurst Ct & Rd 28805
Pinellas Ave 28806
Pineview Rd 28804
Pineview St 28806
Pinewood Pl 28806
Pinewood Rd 28805
Pinewood St 28804
Piney Hill Rd 28804
Piney Mountain Dr 28805
Piney Park Rd 28806
Pinnacle Pt 28805
Pinnacle View Rd 28803
Pinners Ln 28803
Pinners Cove Rd 28803
Pioneer Dr & Trl 28805
Pisgah Pkwy 28806
Pisgah View Ave 28803
Pisgah View Ct 28806
Pisgah View Rd 28806
S Plains Dr 28803
Plantation Dr 28806
Plateau Rd 28805
Pleasant Run 28806
Pleasant Hill Dr 28804
Pleasant Ridge Dr 28805
Plemmons St 28806
Plymouth Cir & Ct 28803
S Point Dr 28804
Point Bluff Dr 28804
W Pointe Dr 28806
Points West Dr 28804
Pole Barn Dr 28806
Pole Creasman Rd 28806
Polly Way 28806
Pond Ln 28804
Pond Rd 28806
Pond Road Cir 28806
Pondberry Ct 28806
Poplar Ln 28804
Poplar Creek Dr 28805
Poplor Run Cir 28804
Poppas Way 28806
Popple Dr 28806
Poppy Ln 28803
Pops Way 28806
E Porter Rd & St 28803
Porters Cove Rd 28805
Portway Ln 28803
Possum Trot Rd 28806
Post Rd 28806
Pounders Dr 28804
Powder Ridge Dr 28803
Powell St 28806
Powers Dr 28806
Powers Rd 28804
Prairie Path 28805
Pressley Ct & Rd 28805
Price Rd 28805
Prickly Juniper Trl 28806
Primrose Ln
1-99 28805
500-599 28806
Prince William Rd 28804
Princeton Dr 28806
Proctor Dr 28803
Prospect St 28804
Providence Rd 28806
Pruitt St 28806
Puckett Rd 28806
Puffin Ln 28804
Pyrite Way 28806
Quail Holw 28804
Quail Cove Rd 28804
Queen Bee Trl 28806
Quiet Acres Dr 28805
Quigley Dr 28806
Quinn Ct 28805
R Morton Ln 28806
Rabbit Run 28805
Race Path Way 28806
Racquet Club Rd 28803
Radford Ln 28805
Rainbow Hill Dr 28803
Rajo Rd 28803
N & W Raleigh Ave &
Rd 28803
Ralph St 28801
Ramble Way 28803
Ramble On Rd 28806
Rambling Ridge Rd 28804
Ramey Hill Dr 28806
Ramoth Rd 28804
Ramsey Rd 28806
Randall St 28801
Ranger Dr 28805
Rankin Ave 28801
W Rash Rd 28806
Rathburn Pl 28806
Rathfarnham Cir & Rd 28803
Ratt Man Ln 28803
Raven Ridge Ln 28805
Raven Rock Dr 28806
Ravencroft Ln 28803
Ravenna St 28803
Ravenscroft Dr 28801
Ravine Ext & Rd 28804
Rebel Dr 28805
Rector St 28801
Red Cedar Ln 28803
Red Fox Cir 28803
Red Oak Dr 28804
Red Oak Ter 28803
Red Roof Ln 28804
Red Tail Ridge Rd 28806
Redbo Ln 28806
Reddick Rd 28805
Redfern St 28806
Redtail Hawk Ln 28804
Redwing Ln 28805
Redwood Rd 28804
Reed Rd 28805
Reed St
1-899 28803
1000-1099 28804
Reedy Creek Ln 28804
Reemes Rd 28806
Reese Rd 28805
Reese St 28804
Regan Ln 28806
Regent Park Blvd 28806
Reister Ln 28806
Relic Ln 28804
Remington Dr 28806
Renee Rd 28806
Reservoir Rd 28803
Resort Dr 28806
Restaurant Ct 28805
Reuben Rd 28804
Revonda Dr 28804
Rex Dr 28806
Reynolda Dr 28803
Reynolds Hts 28804
Reynolds Pl 28804
Reynolds Rd 28806
Reynolds Mountain
Blvd 28804
Reynolds School Rd 28803
Rhodes Cemetary Dr 28806
Rhododendron Cir, Dr, Pl
& Trl 28805
Rhudy Rd 28806
Rice Mdws 28804
Rice Rd 28806
Rice Branch Rd 28804
Riceville Rd 28805
Rich St 28806
Rich Hill Rd 28804
Richard St 28803
Richie St 28801
Richland St 28806
Richmond Ave 28806
Richmond Hill Dr &
Rd 28806
Riddle Ln 28806
Ridge Ave 28803
N Ridge Dr 28804
Ridge Rd
1-99 28806
36-56 28803
58-61 28803
63-99 28803
800-899 28806
Ridge St 28801
Ridge Ter 28804
Ridge Cross Rd 28805
Ridge Runner Ln 28806
Ridge View Dr 28803
Ridgecrest Rd 28803
Ridgefield Blvd 28806
Ridgefield Ct 28806
Ridgefield Pl 28803
Ridgehaven Dr 28804
Ridgeland Ln 28805
Ridgelawn Rd 28806
Ridgeview Dr 28804
Ridgeview Way 28803
Ridgeway Ave & Dr 28806
Ridgewood Pl 28804
Rise Village Ln 28806
River Hills Rd 28805
River Knoll Dr 28805
River Link Ln 28806
River Mead Ct 28804
River Ridge Dr 28803
River Stone Trl 28805
River Walk Dr 28804
Riverbend Dr 28805
Rivers Edge Rd 28805
Riverside Dr
1-700 28801
702-898 28801
800-3199 28804
Riverview Dr 28806
Riverview Pkwy 28805
Riverview Church Rd 28806
Robert Clayton Dr 28805
Roberts Rd
1-99 28803
200-1999 28806
Roberts St 28801
Robin Ln 28806
Robindale Ave 28801
Robinhood Rd 28804
Robinson Ave 28803
Robinson Creek Rd 28803
Robinson Valley Dr 28806
Robinwood Ave 28806
Rock Hill Cir, Ln, Pl &
Rd 28803
Rock Hill Road Ext 28803
Rockcliff Pl 28801
Rocket Dr 28803
Rockhold Dr 28804
Rocking Porch Ln, Rd &
Rdg 28805
Rocky Point Cir 28803
Rocky Ridge Rd 28806
Rocky Slope Rd 28804
Rodgers Pl 28806
Roebling Cir 28803
Rogers Acres Dr 28804
Rollie Ln 28806
Rolling Ter 28805
Rolling Hills Dr 28806
Rolling Oaks Dr 28806
Rolling View Dr 28805
Rollingwood Rd 28805
Ronsanne Pkwy 28804
Roosevelt St 28801
Roost Ln 28803
Roosters Trl 28806
Rose St 28806
Rose St W 28803
Rose Hill Rd 28803
Rose Petal Ln 28806
Rosebay Ln 28803
W Rosecrest Ct & St 28804
Rosefield Dr 28805
Rosemary Rd 28806
Rosemont Ct 28803
Rosewood Ave 28801
Ross Creek Dr 28805
Rosscraggon Dr & Rd 28803
Rotary Dr 28803
Rotunda Cir 28806
Rough Point Ct 28806
Round Oak Rd 28804
Round Top Rd 28803
Roundabout Way 28805
Rufus Ridge Ln 28804
Rugby Way 28804
Rumbough Pl 28806
Running Ridge Rd 28804
Ruslans Dr 28806
Russell St 28806
Russet Ln 28803
Rustling Oaks Ln 28805
Rutherford Rd 28803
Rylee Rdg 28805
Sabian Ct 28806
Saddleback Ct 28803
Sagamore Ln 28806
Sagebrush Cir 28803
Sahalee Dr 28804
Saint Albans Ct 28803
Saint Augustine Pl 28805
Saint Charles Ct 28803
Saint Charles Pl 28804
Saint Davids Ct 28803
Saint Dunstans Cir &
Rd 28803
Saint Giles Pl 28803
Saint Marys Ln 28803
Saint Paul St 28803
Salem Ave 28804
Sales Farm Dr 28803
Salisbury Dr 28803
Salola St 28806
Saluda St 28806
Samayoa Pl 28806
Sambo Ln 28806
Sand Hill Ct, Ln & Rd 28806
Sand Hill School Rd 28806
Sandhurst Dr 28806
Sandon Cir & Dr 28804
Sandra Dr 28803
Santee St 28801
Sara St 28801
Saratoga St 28806
Sardis Dr & Rd 28806
Sareva Pl 28804
Sarge Ln 28806
Sassafras St 28801
Sassy Ln 28805
Saunooke Rd 28805
Savannah Woods Ct 28806
Sawmill Rd 28803
Sawyer Ave 28801
Sawyer Rd 28806
Sayles Rd 28803
Scarlet Oak Ln 28803
Scenic Dr 28805
Scenic View Knls 28804
Schenck Pkwy 28803
School Rd 28806
School Rd E 28803
Science Of Mind Way 28806
Scott St 28801
Scott Mountain Rd 28806
Scottish Cir 28803
Scottlynn Ct & Dr 28806
Scottsdale Dr 28806
Sculley Dr 28805
Season Ln 28805
Secluded Forest Dr 28804
Secluded Vista Dr 28803
Seedling Grv 28806
Selwyn Pl & Rd 28806
Seminole St 28803
Senator Reynolds Rd 28804
Serendipity Trl 28804
Serenity Hill Ct 28803
Serviceberry Cir 28803
Sevan Ct 28806
Seven Oaks Rd 28806
Sevier St 28804
Shackleford Ct & Dr 28806
Shadow Dr 28804
Shadow Creek Ln 28806
Shadow Oaks Dr 28806
Shadowbrook Dr 28805
Shadowlawn Dr 28806
Shady Cir 28805
Shady Cove Ln 28804
Shady Grove Ln 28804
Shady Lane Dr 28805
Shady Oak Dr 28803
Shady Park Ln 28804
Shady Pines Dr 28805
Shady Ridge Ln 28805
Shadywood Cir 28803
Shagbark Dr 28806
Shakedown St 28803
Shaker Ct 28805
Shamby Dr 28806
Shamrock Dr 28803
Shannon Dr 28803
Sharon Rd 28804
Shawnee Trl 28805
Sheffield Cir 28803
Shelburne Dr & Rd 28806
Shelby Dr 28803
Shelby Rd 28806
Shelter Cv 28803
Shelwood Cir 28804
Shenandoah Rd 28805
Sheppard Dr 28806
Sherdover Estates Dr 28806
Sheridan Rd 28803
Sherwood Rd
1-10 28805
11-99 28803
101-199 28803
Shiloh Rd 28803
Shirey Dr 28806
Shooting Range Ln 28803
Shope Rd 28805
Shope Creek Rd 28805
Shope Creek Estates
Dr 28805
E Shore Dr 28805
Shorewood Dr 28804
Short St 28801
Short Breezeway Dr 28803
Short Coxe Ave 28801
Short Flint St 28801
Short Ivy St 28806
Short Log Rd 28804
Short Madison Ave 28801
Short Michigan Ave 28806
Short Shiloh Rd 28803
Short Tremont St 28806
Short Vine St 28804
Shortia Ln 28803
Shovel Head Dr 28803
Shunka Dr 28806
Sienna Dr 28806
Siesta Ln 28806
Silent Pl 28806
Siler Ln 28803
Silk Tree Ln 28803
Silo Dr 28806
Silo View Ct 28804
Silver Ter 28804
Silver Dollar Ln 28804
Silver Long Rd 28806
Silver Springs Dr 28803
Silverling Dr 28806
Silverrod Ln 28803
Silverstone Dr 28805
Simpson St 28803
Simpson Hollow Rd 28803
Sivart Way 28806
Skipstone Rd 28803
Skycliff Dr 28804
Skyhawk Ln 28806
Skyland Cir 28804
E Skyland Cir 28804
W Skyland Cir 28804
Skyland Ter 28806
Skyland Office Park 28803
Skyline Ter 28806
Skyloft Dr 28801
Skylyn Ct 28806
Skyview Cir 28804
Skyview Ct 28803
Skyview Dr 28804
Skyview Pl 28804
Skyview Ter 28806
Skyview Park Dr 28805
Slackers Ln 28806
Sleepy Hollow Dr 28805
Slosman Dr 28806
Small Mountain Dr 28805
Smart Rd 28806
Smile Ave 28806
Smith Rd 28806
Smith Graveyard Rd 28806
Smokey Rd 28803
Smokey Park Hwy 28806
Smooth Rock Trl 28803
Snap Dragon Ct 28804
Sneaking Creek Ln 28805
Snelson Dr 28806
Snelson Ln 28805
Snow Cap Ct 28805
Snow Shoe Dr 28803
Snow White Dr 28806
Snowberry Rd 28806
Snowbird Dr 28804
Snyder Dr 28804
So So Way 28806
Soco St 28801
E, N & W Sondley Dr &
Pkwy S 28805
Sondley Woods Pl 28805
Sonnet Ln 28804
Sorrel Ct 28803
Sourwood Ln E 28805
South Ln 28804
Southern St 28801
Southside Ave 28801
Southside Village Dr 28803
Southwood Rd 28803
Spanish Oaks 28804
Spartan Ave 28806
Spears Ave 28801
Speckled Hen Ln 28805
Spike Way 28806
Spinet St 28806
Spirit Trl 28805
Spivey Pl 28806
Spivey Mountain Rd 28806
Split Oak Trl 28804
Split Rail Dr 28806
Spooks Branch Ext &
Rd 28804
Spooks Mill Cv 28804
Spreading Oak Ln 28806
Spring Dr 28806
Spring Cove Rd & Ter 28804
Spring Creek Trl 28806
Spring Forest Cir 28803
Spring Glen Rd 28804
Spring Hill Dr 28804
Spring Hollow Cir 28805
Spring Park Rd 28805
Springbrook Rd 28804
Springdale Ave 28803
Springdale Rd
1-99 28805
2-8 28803
10-12 28805
14-20 28803
22-98 28805
Springlawn Way 28805
Springmill Dr 28806
Springside Dr 28806
Springside Park 28803
Springside Rd 28803
Springvale Ave 28803
Springwood Dr 28805
Sprinkle St 28806
Spruce Dr 28805
N Spruce St 28801
S Spruce St 28801
Spruce Hill Ct & Ln 28805
Spruce Shade Ct 28803
Spy Glass Ln 28805
Squirrel Hill Rd 28804
Staak Dr 28803
Stage Ln 28801
Stamford St 28803
Stancliff Dr 28803
Standing Woods Dr 28804
Starmount Dr 28806
Starnes Ave 28801
E Starnes Cove Ct, Dr,
Pl & Rd 28806
State St 28806
Steele Ave 28803
Steeplechase Ct 28803
Steeplecross Ct 28806
Stegall Ln 28805
Stephanie Ln 28805
Stephenson Ln 28805
Sterling St 28803
Sterling Roberts Way 28801
Stevens Ln 28805
Stevens St 28803
Stevens Hill Rd 28805
Stewart St 28806
Stillview Dr 28804
Stillwell Dr 28804
Stockbridge Pl 28805
Stockwood Ln & Rd 28803
Stockwood Road Ext 28803
Stokes Dr 28805
Stone Cliff Dr 28803
Stone Cottage Rd 28806
Stone River Dr 28804
Stonebridge Dr 28805
Stonecrest Dr 28803
Stoner Rd 28803
Stoneridge Blvd 28804
Stones Throw Ln 28803
Stoney Hill Ct 28804
Stoney River Path 28804
Stony Rdg 28804
Stormy Ridge Dr 28806
Stradley Mountain Rd 28806
Stradwood Pl 28804
Stratford Dr & Rd 28804
Stratus Ln 28803
Strawbridge Ct 28803
Strawflower Ln 28806
W Street Ext 28801
Stuart Cir 28804
Stuyvesant Cres & Rd 28803
Success Ave 28806
Sugar Maple Ln 28805
Sulphur Springs Rd 28806
Summer St 28804
Summer Hill Dr 28804
Summerglen Ct & Dr 28806
Summerlin Dr 28806
Summershade Ct 28806
Summersweet Ln 28803
Summit Ave & St 28803
Summit Tower Cir 28804
Sumner Pl 28804
Sun Haven Dr 28806
Sun Hill Rd 28806
Sunbird Ln 28805
Sundown Dr 28803
Sunny Ridge Dr 28804
Sunnybrook Dr 28805
Sunnycrest Dr 28805
Sunnyside Ln 28804
Sunnyview Ter 28806
Sunridge Rd 28806
Sunrise Dr 28806
Sunrise Smt 28804
Sunset Dr
1-99 28804
1-99 28806
2-98 28804
2-98 28806
100-599 28804
Sunset Ln 28804
Sunset Pkwy 28801

Street	ZIP
Sunset Smt	28804
Sunset Ter	28801
Sunset Trl	28804
Sunset Vw	28804
Sunset Walk	28804
Sunset Hills Ct, Dr & Ln	28803
Sunwashed Way	28803
Surrey Run	28803
Surrey Green Dr	28806
Swan St	28803
Swan Hill Ln	28805
Swanger Rd	28805
Swanna View Dr	28805
Swannanoa Ave	28806
Swannanoa River Rd	
1-99	28803
1-49	28805
2-98	28803
50-998	28805
51-999	28805
Sweet Gum Dr	28805
Sweet Spire Rdg	28804
Sweetbriar Ct	28803
Sweeten Way	28803
Sweeten Creek Rd & Xing	28803
Sweeten Creek Industrial Park	28803
Sweetwater Dr	28806
Swift St	28804
Swindale St	28801
Sycamore St	28804
Sycamore Tree Crk	28806
Sydney Ln	28806
Sylvan Ave	28801
Syrlin St	28804
Tacoma Cir, Pl & St	28801
Taft Ave	28803
Tahkieostie Trl	28806
Tahkioestie Dr	28801
Talmadge Ct & St	28806
Tamarac Cir	28806
Tamarac Trl	28803
Tampa Ave	28806
Tanbark Meadow Ln	28805
Tanglewood Dr	28806
Tap Dr	28803
Tara Dr	28806
Tarpon Ave	28806
Tasha Ln	28806
Tate Dr	28806
Tater Trl	28806
Tattle Branch Cir	28805
Taylor St	28804
Teakwood Pl	28806
Technology Dr	28803
Teems Ln	28805
Telfare Ln	28803
Temple Ave	28804
Tennant Ln	28805
Tequila Trl	28806
Terrace Ct	28804
Terrace Rd	28801
Terraine Ln	28806
Terre Trl	28804
Terri Dr	28804
Texas St	28806
Thad Bradley Rd	28806
The Cir	28801
Thetford St	28803
Thistle Knoll Ct	28803
Thomas St	28806
Thomas Lee Dr	28805
Thomas Wolfe Plz	28801
Thompson Rd	28806
Thompson St	28803
Thorn Ridge Dr	28803
Thorny Rdg	28805
Three Oaks Dr	28804
Thurland Ave	28803
Tiffany Ln	28804
Timber Ct	28803
Timber Dr	28804
Timber Ln	
1-99	28806
600-1002	28804
Timber Pl	28804
Timber Trl	28804
Timber Moss Dr	28804
Timber Wolf Ct	28804
Timberlake Dr	28803
Timberwood Dr	28806
Timothy St	28801
Timson Rd	28803
Tingle Aly	28801
Tipperary Dr	28806
Titan Dr	28806
Tiverton Ln	28803
Tivoli Dr	28806
Toad Dr	28806
Toadshade Ln	28805
Toby Dr	28806
Top Notch Ln	28806
Touchstone Rd	28805
Town Mountain Rd	
1-20	28801
21-2999	28804
Town Square Blvd	28803
Townview Dr	28806
Toxaway St	28806
Trade St	28801
Tradewind Dr	28806
Trafalgar Cir	28805
Trailridge Rd	28804
Trappers Run Dr	28805
Tre Ln	28806
Tread Way	28806
Treetop Rd	28804
Treetops Ln	28803
Trellis Ct	28806
Tremont St	28806
Trevors Trl	28806
Trexler Rd	28806
Trey Bourne Dr	28804
Tried St	28803
Trillium Ct	28805
Trinity Ct	28805
Trinity Chapel Rd	28805
Trio Ln	28803
Triple H Dr	28806
Tristen Dr	28806
Trojan St	28804
Trotter Pl	28806
Trotter Run	28803
Trotters Cir	28803
Trout Lily Gln	28805
Truckers Pl	28805
True Faith Dr	28806
Trumpet Ln	28803
Trust Hvn	28804
Tryon St	28806
Tryst Dr	28805
Tsali Trl	28804
Tsuga Rise	28805
Tuckaway Dr	28803
Tumbleweed Trl	28806
Tunnel Rd	
1-1172	28805
1141-1141	28815
1173-1799	28805
1174-1798	28805
1070-1-1070-4	28805
S Tunnel Rd	28805
Turbyfill Ln	28806
Turtle Creek Dr	28803
Turtledove Trl	28805
Tuskeegee St	28801
Twin Oaks Dr	28806
Twins Ln	28806
Tylers Cookie Ln	28806
Udell Cir, Ct & Pl	28806
Unadilla Aly & Ave	28803
Unaka Ave	28803
Uncle Dr	28806
Unicorn Farm Rd	28805
Union St	28804
University Hts	28804
Upland Rd	28804
Upper Beverly Rd	28805
Upper Grassy Br Rd	28805
Upper Grassy Branch Ext	28805
Upper Herron Cove Rd	28804
Upper Moffitt Rd	28805
Upper Sondley Dr	28805
Utopia Rd	28805
Vail Ct	28806
Valle Vista Dr	28804
Valley Ln	28804
Valley St	28801
Valley Creek Dr	28803
Valley Park Rd	28804
Valley Springs Rd	28803
Valley View Rd	28803
Valleywood Ct	28803
Vance Crescent Ext & St	28806
Vance Gap Rd	
1-59	28805
61-62	28804
63-199	28805
200-250	28804
252-398	28804
259-299	28805
301-399	28804
Vandalia Ave	28806
Vanderbilt Pl	28801
Vanderbilt Rd	28803
Vanderbilt Ter	28806
Vanderbilt Park Dr	28803
Vaux Ct	28803
Velvet Ridge Ln	28806
Venus Dr	28804
Veranda Trl	28803
Verano Ct	28806
Verde Dr	28806
Verde Vista Cir	28805
Verlestr Rd	28803
Vermont Ave, Ct & Ext	28806
Vernell Ave	28801
Verona Dr	28806
Veronica Ln	28801
Versant Dr	28804
Vester Ct	28803
Veterans Dr	28805
Viburnum Ln	28803
Victoria Rd	28801
Victory Ln	28804
View St	
1-3	28803
1-24	28804
26-26	28804
100-1299	28806
View Crest Ln	28806
W Viewmont Dr	28806
Viewpointe Ln	28806
Vifania Ln	28806
Village Dr & Ln	28803
Village Creek Dr	28806
Village East Ct	28805
Village Pointe Ln	28803
Villas Ct	28806
Villemagne Dr	28804
Vine St	28804
Vinewood Cir	28806
Vineyard Blvd	28805
Vineyard Pl	28804
Violet Hill Cir	28805
Virginia Ave	28806
Vista St	28803
Vista View Dr	28803
Vivian Ave	28801
Volvo Dr	28803
Von Ruck Ct & Ter	28801
Wagner Branch Rd	28806
Wagon Rd	28805
Wake Robin Way	28805
Wakefield Dr	28803
Walden Ridge Dr	28803
Wales St	28803
Wall St	28801
Wallen Dr	28806
Walnut Ln	28804
E Walnut St	28801
W Walnut St	28801
Walnut Grove Ln	28806
Walnut Springs Dr	28804
Walnut Tree Rdg	28806
Walsh Trace Dr	28803
Walter Lees Pl	28804
Walter Morgan Dr	28803
Walton St	28801
Wamboldt Ave	28806
E Waneta St	28801
Wanoca Ave	28803
Warren Ave	28803
Warren Haynes Dr	28806
Warwick Pl	28804
Warwick Rd	28803
Washington Ave	28804
Washington Rd	28801
Watauga Pl & St	28801
Water St	28801
Water Rock Ter	28806
Waterford Ct	28806
Waters Rd	28805
Waterside Dr	28804
Waverly Ct	28805
Waverly Rd	28803
Waynesville Ave	28806
Wayside Rd	28805
Weaver St	28801
Weaver Hill Rd	28805
Weaverville Rd	28804
Webb Cove Rd	28804
Webb Springs Rd	28804
Wedgefield Dr & Pl	28806
Wedgewood Ln	28803
Weeping Willow Ln	28804
Weiss Ct & Rd	28806
Wellen Way	28803
Wellington Dr	28804
Wellington St	28806
Wells Ave	28806
Wellstone Ln	28803
Welwyn Ln	28805
Wembley Rd	28804
Wendover Rd	28806
Wendy Ln	28805
Wentworth Ave	28803
Wesley Dr	28803
Wesley Branch Rd	28806
West St	28801
Westall Ave & Dr	28804
Westchester Dr	28803
Westforest Ln	28806
Westgate Pkwy & Rd	28806
Westhaven Dr	28804
Westminster Dr	28804
Westmont Dr	28806
Westmore Dr	28806
Weston Pl & Way	28803
Weston Heights Dr & Pl	28803
Westover Aly & Dr	28801
Westridge Ct	28806
Westridge Dr	28803
Westside Dr	28806
Westview Ave	28803
Westview Ln	28803
Westview Rd	28804
Westwood Dr	28806
Westwood Pl	28806
Westwood Rd	
1-11	28803
2-18	28803
2-4	28804
5-16	28804
13-19	28803
18-198	28804
101-199	28804
Wexford Way	28805
Whipoorwill Hl	28804
Whisper Creek Ln	28804
Whispering Hill Dr	28804
Whispering Pines Dr	28803
Whispering Rock Ln	28803
Whispering Woods Dr	28804
White Ave	28803
White Ash Dr E	28803
White Fawn Dr	28801
White Oak Rd	28803
White Oak Gap Rd	28803
White Pine Ct & Dr	28805
White Rose Ln	28804
Whitney Dr	28806
Whitson Rd	28805
Wicklow Dr	28806
Wilbar Ave	28801
Wilburn Pl & Rd	28806
Wild Cherry Ln & Rd	28804
Wild Fern Ln	28806
Wild Orchid Ln	28805
Wilde Brook Dr	28806
Wilderness Rd	28804
Wilderness Cove Rd	28804
S Wildflower Ln & Rd	28804
Wildwood Ave	28804
Wildwood Acres Rd	28806
Wiley Dr	28804
Wilhide Rd	28805
William Warren Dr	28806
Williams St	28803
Williamsburg Pl	28803
Willis Rd	28806
Willoughby Run Dr	28803
Willow Ct	28805
Willow Rd	28804
N & S Willow Brook Dr	28806
Willow Creek Dr	28803
Willow Lake Dr	28805
Willow Oak Dr	28805
Willow Pond Ln	28806
Willow Tree Run	28803
Willowbrook Rd	28805
Willowick Dr	28803
Wilmary Ln	28803
Wilmington Rd	28803
Wilmington St	28806
Wilshire Dr	28806
Wilson Aly	28801
Wilson Rd	28806
Wilson St	28803
Wilson Creek Dr	28803
Wilson Watts Dr	28805
Winchester Pl	28806
Wind Ridge St	28806
Wind Whisper Dr	28804
Windcliff Dr	28803
Windflower Ct	28805
Windgate Pl	28805
Winding Rd	28803
Windover Dr	28803
Windrow Dr	28805
Windsor Dr	28803
Windsor Rd	28804
Windstone Dr	28804
Windswept Dr	28801
Windward Dr	28803
Windwhisper Dr	28804
Windy Gap Rd	28804
Windy Hills Rd	28806
Windy Hollow Rd	28806
Windy Ridge Trl	28804
Wineberry Ln	28803
Winery Rd	28803
Wingfield Way	28806
Winnfred St	28806
Winston Ave	28803
Winter Woods Dr	28806
Winters Edge Ln	28803
Winterview Dr	28803
Winterwind Dr	28803
Winthrop Rd	28806
Wishes Ln	28804
Wisteria Ct	28806
Wisteria Dr	28804
Wolf Rd	28805
Wolf Cry Ln	28803
Wolfe Bridge Ln	28804
Wolfe Cove Rd	28804
Wolfe Park Cir	28804
Wondu View Ct	28806
Wood Aly & Ave	28803
Wood Duck Ln	28806
Wood Hill Dr	28804
Woodberry Ln	28806
Woodbine Rd	28804
Woodbury Rd	28804
Woodcrest Pl & Rd	28804
Woodfield Dr	28803
Woodfin Ave	28804
N Woodfin Ave	28804
Woodfin Pl	28801
Woodfin St	28801
Woodgate Rd	28806
Woodhaven Pl & Rd	28805
Woodland Ct	28805
Woodland Dr	28806
Woodland Knls	28804
Woodland Rd	28804
Woodland Rd W	28806
Woodland Rdg	28804
Woodland Ter	28806
Woodland Hills Rd	28804
Woodlawn Ave	28801
Woodlea Ct	28806
Woodley Ave	28804
Woodlink Rd	28801
Woodmont Dr	28806
Woodpeck Ridge Ln	28806
Woodridge Ln	28806
Woodrow Ave & Pl	28801
Woodsedge Dr	28803
Woodside Pl	28801
Woodsong Dr	28803
Woodstream Ln	28803
Woodvale Ave	28804
Woodvine Rd	28803
S Woodward Ave	28804
Woodwind Ter	28806
Woody Ln	28804
Woody Glen Rd	28805
Worley Pl	28806
Wren Ln	28806
Wren Way Dr	28803
Wright Rd	28804
Wt Weaver Blvd	28804
Wyatt St	28803
Wykle Rd	28805
Wynn St	28801
Wynne Dr	28806
Wyntree Dr	28803
Wyoming Rd	28803
Wyoming Road Ext	28803
Xanadu Dr	28806
Yale St	28806
Yarrow Pl	28801
Yellowood Ln	28803
Yorkminster Loop	28803
Yorkshire St	28803
Yosimite Trl	28806
Young St	28801
Young Rock Rd	28806
Youngs Mountain Rd	28805
Zachary Ridge Rd	28804
Zander Way	28805
Zane Ln	28805
Zephyr Dr	28806
Zia Ln	28803
Zillicoa St	28801
Zoe Ln	28803

NUMBERED STREETS

Street	ZIP
1st St	28803
2nd St	28803
3rd St	28804
15-199	28803
4th St	28803
4th Street Ext	28804
5th Ave	28806
5th St	28804
6th St	28804
20th St	28806

BURLINGTON NC

General Delivery	27215

POST OFFICE BOXES MAIN OFFICE STATIONS AND BRANCHES

Box No.s	ZIP
P501 - P501	27216
1 - 2958	27216
3001 - 4386	27215
5001 - 9023	27216
9996 - 9998	27215
9998 - 13400	27216

NAMED STREETS

Street	ZIP
Aaron St	27215
Aarons Way	27217
Abernathy Trl	27215
Abingdon Pl	27215
Abner Fitch Rd	27217
Acorn St	27215
Ada St	27217
Adair Ln	27215
E Adams Ct	27215
Adams St	27217
Adams Way	27215
Adder Ridge Ln	27217
Aglish Ct	27215
Airpark Rd	27215
Airport Loop	27215
Alamance Rd	27215
Alamance Baptist Churc Loop	27215
Albany St	27215
Albert St	27217
Albert Jeffries Rd	27217
Albright Ave	27215
Alden St	27217
Alder St	27217
Ale Dr	27217
Alex Faye Dr	27217
Allendale Dr	27215
Allison Ct	27215
Alma Ln	27215
Altamahaw Union Ridge Rd	27217
Alyece Ct	27215
Alzora Ct	27215
Amberley Ct	27215
American Dr	27217
Amesbury Ct	27215
Amherst Ave & Ct	27215
Amick St	
1800-1899	27217
2200-2299	27215
Anders Ct & Way	27217
Anderson Rd	27217
Andrea Ln	27215
Angel Falls Dr	27215
Angier Trl	27217
Anita Ct	27215
Ann Elizabeth Dr	27215
Anthony Ct	27215
Anthony Ct S	27215
Anthony Rd	27215
N Anthony St	27217
S Anthony St	27215
Antioch Church Rd	27215
Apple St	27217
Apple Blossom Ln	27217
Aquinas Ct	27215
Arbor Dr	27215
Archer St	27215
Arden St	27215
Ardmore St	27215
Argyle Trl	27215
Arlington Ave	27215
Armfield Ave	27215
Arrow Ln	27215
Asbury Ct	27215
Ashe Dr	27215

Ashe St 27217
N & S Ashland Dr 27217
Ashley Pl 27215
Ashley Ridge Dr 27215
Ashton Park Ln 27215
Askew St 27215
Attica St 27217
Atwater Rd 27217
Atwater St 27215
Atway Loop 27215
Atwood Dr 27215
Auburn Dr 27215
Audrey Ln 27217
Aunt Marys Rd 27217
Austin St 27217
Ava St 27215
N & S Aviation Dr 27215
Aviemore Run 27215
Avon Ave 27215
Avondale Dr 27217
Aycock Ave 27215
Azalea Cir 27215
Baker St 27217
Baker Bell Farm Rd 27217
Baker Farm Rd 27217
Bakersfield Trl 27215
Baldwin Rd 27217
Barbee St 27217
Barber Foster Rd 27217
Barclay Ln 27217
Bard Ct 27215
Barham St 27215
Barnes St 27217
Barnwell Blvd 27217
Barts St 27217
Basil Holt Rd 27217
Basin Creek Rd 27217
Battlefield Rd 27215
Bayberry Ct 27215
Baynes Rd 27217
Baynes Road Ext 27217
Bearberry Trl 27217
N & S Beaumont Ave & Ct 27217
Beaver Creek Rd 27215
Beaver Hills Dr 27215
Bedford Ct & St 27215
Beech Ct & Dr 27217
Beechwood Trl 27217
Bell St 27215
Bellemont Ln 27215
Bellemont Alamance Rd 27215
Bellemont Mount Hermon Rd 27215
Bellvue St 27217
Belmont St 27215
Ben Harvey Trl 27217
Benjamin Ct 27215
Bennett St 27217
Bentley Ln 27217
Berkley Rd 27217
Berkshire Rd 27215
Berrysteed Ct 27215
Berwick Dr 27215
Bethel St 27217
Bethel Methodist Ch Rd 27217
Bettys Trl 27215
Bh Harvey Trl 27217
Bidney Dr 27215
Bigelow St 27217
Bill Aldridge Rd 27217
Bill Allred Ln 27215
Billingham Dr 27215
Billy Holt Trl 27215
Biltmore St 27215
Birch Ct 27217
Birch Dr 27217
Birch Ln 27215
Birchwood Dr 27217
Black Bear Cv 27215
Black Elk Ct 27215
Black Walnut Ct 27217
Blackwater Ct 27215
Blackwell Rd 27217
Blanchard Rd 27217
Blanche Dr 27215
Bland Blvd 27217
Blue Moon Trl 27217
Blueboy Trl 27215
Bob Rainey Trl 27217
Bob Shepherd Dr 27215
Bonnar Bridge Pkwy & Rd 27215
Bonnie Ln 27215
Bonnie Loch Dr 27215
Boone Ln 27217
Boone Rd 27217
Boone St 27215
Boone Station Dr 27215
Border St
100-299 27215
1100-1299 27217
Border Lake Trl 27217
Boston Dr 27215
Bow Ct 27215
Bowman Ave 27217
Boyd Wright Rd 27215
Bradbury Dr 27215
Bradford Ct 27215
Bradley St 27215
Brafford Ln 27217
Brandon Ln 27217
Brandy Ln 27217
Brassfield Dr 27217
Brent Ct 27215
Brentwood Dr 27215
Briarcliff Rd 27215
Briarwood Dr 27215
Brick Church Rd 27215
Bridges St 27215
Bridgewater Dr 27217
Brigham Dr 27215
Brightwood Dr 27217
Bristol Ct 27215
Brittney Ln 27215
N Broad St 27217
S Broad St 27215
Broadview Dr 27217
Brompton Ct 27215
Brook Hills Ct & St 27217
Brookline Dr 27217
Brooklyn St 27217
Brooks St 27215
Brookside Dr 27217
Brookstone Dr 27215
Brookwood Ave 27215
Brown Ave 27215
Brown Bear Dr 27215
Brown Lovell Ln 27217
Bryan St 27215
Brycewood Ct & Dr 27215
Buckeye Ct 27215
E & W Buckhill Rd 27215
Buckingham Ct & Rd 27217
Buckner St 27217
Buckthorn Trl 27217
Burch Bridge Rd 27217
Burch Run Dr 27217
Burlingate Pl 27215
Burlington Rd 27215
Burlington Square Mall 27215
Buttermilk Dr 27217
Buttermilk Hills Rd 27217
Buxton Way 27215
Byrd Rd 27217
Byrds Sawmill Rd 27217
Cabin Rd 27215
Cadiz St 27215
Cairn Cir 27217
Cale Dr 27215
Callie Ln 27215
Calvin Ct 27215
Cambridge Rd 27215
Camden St 27217
Cameron St 27215
Camp Rd 27217
Canterbury Dr 27215
Cappoquin Way 27215
Caprice Ln 27215
Capstone Ct 27217
Carden St 27215
Cardinal Ln 27215
Cardwell Dr 27215
Carl Madren Rd 27217
Carla Ct 27217
Carlton Ave 27217
Carolina Ave 27215
Carolina Rd 27217
Carolina Mill Rd 27217
Carriage Loop 27217
Carriage Pl 27215
Carriage Way 27215
Carrick Dr 27215
Carrie Ct 27215
Carson Farms Dr E & W 27215
Carson Woods Dr 27215
Carter Rd 27217
Carver St 27217
Cary St 27215
Cascade Dr 27217
Cashell Ct 27215
Caswell St 27217
Cates Ave 27215
Cates Loop Rd 27217
Catherine Dr & Ln 27215
Catlin St 27217
Cedar Ave 27217
S Cedar Rd 27215
Cedar Ridge Dr 27217
Cedarwood Dr 27215
Celina St 27217
Center Ave 27215
Central Ave & Dr 27215
Century Ct 27215
Cesnna Dr 27215
Chandler Ave, Ct & St 27217
Channing Ct 27215
Chapel Hill Rd 27215
Charley Ln 27215
Charlie Ingle Ln 27215
Charlotte Ln 27215
Chase St 27217
Chaucer Ct 27215
Cheekpoint Pl 27215
Chelsea Cir 27217
Cherry Ct & Dr 27215
Chestnut St 27217
Cheyenne Dr 27217
Choyce St 27217
Christopher Dr 27217
Christys Ln 27217
Chucks Ct 27215
N Church St 27217
S Church St 27215
Churchill Dr 27215
Circle Dr 27215
Clapp Mill Rd 27215
Clarendon Rd 27215
Claude Simpson Rd 27217
Clay Ct & St 27215
Clearwater Way 27215
Cleveland Ave
300-499 27215
900-1499 27217
Cleveland Ct 27215
Climax St 27217
Clover Ct 27217
Cloverdale St 27217
Clyde St 27217
Clyde Thompson Trl 27217
Coachlight Trl 27215
N & S Cobb Ave 27217
Cobblestone Ct 27215
Cobbside Dr 27215
Coble St 27215
Colby Ct 27215
Coleman Rd 27217
Coley Ct 27217
Collins Dr 27215
Collinwood Dr 27215
Colonial Dr 27215
Colt Trl 27217
Columbia Ave 27217
Columbine Ln 27215
Combs St 27215
Commerce Pl 27215
Comrie Ln 27215
Comstock Rd 27215
Conners Ct 27215
Convenient Trl 27217
Cooke St 27215
Coppergate Trl 27215
Corbett Rd 27217
Cornerstone Dr 27215
Cornwallis Dr 27215
Corporation Pkwy 27215
N & S Cosby Ct 27217
Cottage Pl 27217
Country Club Dr 27215
Country Hill Ln 27217
Courtland Ter 27217
Coventry Pl 27215
Coveside Trl 27217
Covey Trl 27217
Coy St 27215
Craig St 27215
Crater St 27217
Creekview Ct 27217
Crescent Ave 27217
Crestview Dr 27217
Crestwell Dr 27215
Crestwood Ct & Dr 27215
Crosby Dr 27215
Cross St 27217
Cross Country Ln 27217
Cross Creek Ln 27217
Cross Ridge Ct 27217
Crossridge Dr 27217
Crouse Ln 27215
Crumpton Trl 27217
Crystal Skye Ct 27215
Cullen Ct 27215
Curry Ln 27217
Dailey St 27217
Dailey Store Rd 27217
N & S Dale Ct 27215
Dalkins Ct 27215
Danbrook Rd 27215
Dandora Rd 27217
Danford Rd 27215
Danieley Water Wheel Rd 27217
Dare St 27217
Darrell Davis Rd 27217
David Moore Rd 27217
E & W Davis St 27215
Day Ave 27217
Dc Oakley Rd 27217
Dean Coleman Rd 27215
Dee St 27215
Deep Creek Church Rd 27217
Deepwoods Dr 27215
Deer Ln 27215
Deer Run Trl 27217
Deerfield Dr 27215
Delaine Dr 27215
Delaney Ct & Dr 27215
Delaware Ave 27217
Denise Dr 27215
Dennis Dr 27215
Devonshire Ct & Ln 27215
Diana Cir 27215
Dickey Rd 27217
Dickey Mill Rd 27217
Dillard Cir & St 27215
Dixie St 27217
Dixon Dr & Ln 27217
Dixon Swimming Pool Rd 27217
Doctor Floyd Scott Ln 27217
Dodson Rd 27215
Dogwood Dr 27215
Dogwood Ln 27215
Dogwood Rd 27215
Dogwood St 27215
Doncaster Ln 27217
Donnelly Ct 27215
Donovan St 27215
Doolin St 27215
Doral Ct 27215
Doris Dr 27217
Dorsett St 27215
Dothan Ave 27217
Dover Ave 27217
Downing Ct & Dr 27215
Dr Pickett Rd 27215
Dresden Dr 27217
Dry Creek Ln 27217
Dublin Ct 27215
Dudley St 27217
Duggins Dr 27217
Dunbar Pl 27215
Dunleigh Dr 27215
Dunlevy Ct 27215
Dunmore Dr 27215
Durham St 27217
Durham Meadows Ct & Dr 27217
Durham Street Ext 27217
Earl Kimber Rd 27217
Eastwood Ct 27215
Eb Tate Rd 27217
Eddy Ct 27215
Eden St 27215
Edgewood Ave & Ct 27215
Edinburgh Ct & Dr 27215
Edith St 27215
Elder Ct, Ln & Way 27215
Eldermont St 27215
Elderwood Ln 27215
Eldorado St 27217
Elizabeth Ave & St 27217
Elk Ct, Dr & St 27215
Elkdemont Ct 27217
Eller Dr 27217
Ellis Jeffries Rd 27217
Elm Ct & St 27217
Elmdale Rd 27215
Elmira St 27217
Elva Dr 27217
Elvira Trl 27217
Elwood Ct & St 27217
Engleman Ave & Ct 27215
English Ct 27215
Enoch St 27217
Eric Ln 27215
Erwin Ave 27217
Ethan Pointe Dr 27215
Ethans Way 27215
Euliss Rd 27215
Evans St 27217
Everett St 27215
Evergreen Ave 27217
Evergreen Ln 27215
Fair St 27217
Fairfax Dr 27217
Fairfield Dr & St 27215
Fairland Ct 27215
Fairview Dr 27215
Fairview St
100-199 27217
1600-1899 27215
N & S Fairway Dr 27215
Falkirk Dr 27215
Farm House Trl 27215
Farmview 27215
Farmview Dr 27215
Farningham Ln 27215
Faucette Ave 27215
Faucette Ln 27217
Faucette Rd 27215
Faucette St 27215
Faulkner Dr 27215
Fay Ct 27217
Faye Dr 27217
Ferguson Rd 27217
Fern Glen Dr 27215
Ferndale Dr 27215
Fernway Dr 27215
Fernwood Ter 27217
Field Pine Ct 27217
Fieldstone Dr 27215
Finnsbury Dr 27217
Firethorn Trl 27215
N Fisher St 27217
S Fisher St 27215
Fitch Rd & St 27217
Fix St 27215
N Flanner St 27217
S Flanner St 27215
Fleeman Ln 27217
Fleet Isley Trl 27215
Fleming Graham Rd 27217
Flint St 27215
Flora Ave 27217
Florence Rd & St 27217
Floyd St 27215
Floyd Scott Ln 27217
Flushing St 27215
N & S Fonville Rd & St 27217
Forbes Way 27215
Ford St 27217
Forest Dr 27215
NW Forestdale Dr 27215
Foster Ln 27215
Foster St 27217
Fountain Pl 27215
Fowler Trl 27217
Fox Run Rd 27215
Foxfire Ln 27217
Foxton Ln 27215
Foy Jane Trl 27217
Frank Holt Dr 27215
Franklin Ct & St 27215
Freedom Dr 27215
Freeland Trl 27217
Friendly Rd 27217
Friendship Patterson Mill Rd 27215
Friendship Rock Creek Rd 27215
E & W Front St 27215
Fulton St 27217
Fuqua Ln 27217
Gairloch Trce 27215
Garden Cir 27217
Garden Ct 27215
Garden Rd 27215
Gardner Holt Rd 27215
Garfield Rd 27215
Garrett House Trl 27215
Gattis St & Trl 27217
Gentry Ln 27217
George Trl 27217
George Miles Rd 27217
Georgia Ave 27217
Gerringer Rd 27217
Gerringer Mill Rd 27217
Gilchrist Dr 27215
Gilmer St 27215
Glade Ct 27217
Glen Oaks Rd 27217
Glen Raven Rd 27217
Glencoe St 27217
Glendale Ave 27215
Glenkirk Dr 27215
Glenn St 27217
Glenndale Ln 27215
Glenview Ln 27215
Glenwood Ave 27215
Glidewell Dr 27215
Goldfinch Trl 27217
Gordon St 27217
Gorrell St 27215
Grace Ave 27217
Gracewood Ct 27217
Graham St 27217
N & S Graham Hopedale Rd 27217
Grand Oaks Blvd 27215
Grandmere Dr 27215
Granville St 27215
Grassy Ln 27215
Graves St 27217
Gray St 27217
Green St 27217
Green Level Loop 27217
Green Level Church Rd 27217
Green Valley Blvd 27217
Greenbriar St 27215
Greenfern Ct 27215
Greentree Rd 27217
Greenway St 27217
Greenwood Dr 27217
Greenwood St 27217
Greenwood Ter 27215
Greeson Ln 27215
Gregson Ct 27215
W Grey Gables Dr 27215
Grimes St 27217
Ground Hog Trace Dr 27215
Grove Park Dr 27215
Grover Ln 27217
Gun Dr 27215
Gunn Ln & St 27217
N & S Gurney Ct & St 27215
Gwyn Rd 27217
E Haggard Ave 27217
Hahn Rd 27215
Hale Ct & St 27217
Hall Ave 27217
Hallie Long Ln 27217
Hamilton Rd & St 27217
Hampton Ct 27217
Hancock St 27217
E & W Hanford Rd 27215
Hangar Rd 27215
Hanner Rd 27217
Hanover Rd 27217
Hansel Trce 27215
Harden St 27215
Harper Trl 27215
Harrell St 27217
Harriet Dr 27215
Harris Dr 27217
Harris Rd 27215
Harris St 27217
Harrison Ct & Dr 27215
Harry Ct 27215
Harvey Dr 27217
Hassell Corbett Rd 27217
Hatch St 27217
Hatchery Rd 27215
Haw River Hopedale Rd 27217
Hawkins St 27217
Hawthorne Ln 27215
Haynes St 27215
Hazel Dr 27217
Hazel Rd 27215
Headrick Dr 27217
Heather Rd 27215
Hedge St 27217
Henry Dr & Rd 27215
Herbin Hts 27215
W Heritage Dr & Ln 27215
Herman Blue Ct 27217
Hermitage Rd 27215
Herron Rd 27215
Hester Rd 27217
Hiawatha Ct & Pl 27217
Hickory Ave 27215
Hickory Ln 27217
Hickory Hill Rd 27215
Hickory Nut Pt 27217
Hidden Creek Pt 27215
Hiddenwood Ln 27215
High St 27215
Highland Ave 27217
Highview St 27215
Hill St 27217
Hillcrest Ave 27215
Hilldale 27217
Hilldale Dr 27215
Hillford Dr 27217
Hillside Dr
1-99 27217
100-199 27215
300-399 27217
Hilltop Rd 27217
Hilton Rd 27217
Hodges Rd 27217
Hoffman Pl 27215
Holland Ave 27217
Hollars St 27217
Holly Ct & St 27217

Street	ZIP
Holly Brook Dr	27217
Holly Hill Ln, Mall & St	27215
Hollywood Dr	27217
E & W Holt St	27217
Holt Cross Rd	27215
Holts Store Rd	27215
Home Ct	27217
Homewood Ave	27217
Hood St	27217
Hooker St	27217
Hoover Dr	27217
Horner Ct	27215
Hoskins Cir, Ct & Rd	27215
Howard St	27217
Howle Dr	27215
Huffines Dr & Rd	27217
Huffman Ct, Dr & Ln	27215
Huffman Mill Rd	27215
Hughes Ct	27217
E Hughes Mill Rd	27217
Hunt St	27217
Huntington Ct & Rd	27215
Huntley Way	27215
Hutchins Rd	27217
Hutchinson Ct	27215
Hyde St	27217
Ian Ct	27215
Idlewild Ave	27217
Indian Springs Rd	27217
Indian Valley Dr	27217
Indian Village Trl	27217
S Industrial Dr	27215
Industry Dr	27215
Inge Rd	27215
Ingle Ct & St	27215
Ingle Dairy Rd	27215
Ingle Farm Rd	27215
Ingle View Ct	27215
Inglewood Dr & Rd	27215
International Rd	27215
N & S Ireland St	27217
Isley Ln	27215
Isley Pl	27215
Isley Rd	27217
Isley St	27215
Isley School Rd	27215
J Duke Roney Trl	27217
Ja Sharpe Rd	27215
Jackson St	27217
Jacob Dixon Trl	27217
Jacobs Trl	27215
James Dr & St	27217
James Boswell Rd	27217
Jamestown Ct	27215
Jane St	27217
Java Ln	27215
Jefferson St	27215
Jeffries St	27217
Jeffries Cross Rd	27217
Jeffries Graham Trl	27217
Jerkins St	27217
Jim Barnwell Rd	27217
Jim King Rd	27217
Joe Mitchell Rd	27217
John Lewis Rd	27217
Johnson Ln	27217
Johnson Rd	27217
Johnson St	27215
Jon Hus Ct	27215
Jones St	27217
W Jones Ter	27215
Jons Forest Ln & Trl	27217
Jordan Creek Dr	27215
Jordan Meadows Dr	27215
Joseph St	27215
Jount Ct	27215
Joy Dr	27215
Joyce Ct	27217
Joyful Way	27215
Judy Ln	27217
Juniper Dr	27215
Justin Ct	27217
Juston Dr	27217
Jw Graves Rd	27217
Kayo Trl	27217
Keck Dr	27215
Keepee Trl	27215
Kellam Ct	27215
Kellie Lee Ln	27215
Kelso Ln	27215
Ken Ross Dr	27215
Kendele Ct	27215
Kennedy Ct	27217
Kennedy Rd	27215
Kensington Pl	27215
Kent St	27217
Kenwood Dr	27215
Keogh St	27215
Kerney Dr	27215
Kernodle Dr	27215
Kerrs Chapel Rd	27217
Keswick Dr	27215
Key St	27217
Kidd Dr	27217
Kilby St	27215
Kilroy St	27215
Kimber Rd	27217
Kimberly Rd	27215
E & W Kime St	27215
Kimesville Rd	27215
Kimsville Rd	27215
Kincade Dr	27215
King St	27217
King Family Trl	27217
Kingsbury Ct	27215
Kinley	27215
Kinnan Dr	27217
Kirkpatrick Rd	27215
Kirkwood Dr	27215
E & W Kitchin St	27215
Kivett St	27215
Knoll Ridge Rd	27217
Knollwood Dr	27217
Knox Ct	27215
Koury Dr	27215
Lab Ln	27217
Lacy St	27215
Lael Forest Trl	27215
Lake Dr	27217
E Lake Dr	27215
W Lake Dr	27215
Lake Cammack Ct	27217
Lake Point Trl	27215
Lakeshore Ln	27217
Lakeside Ave	27215
Lakeview Ave	27215
Lakeview Dr	
100-499	27215
501-599	27215
1600-2099	27217
Lakeview Ter	27215
Lakewood Ct	27215
Landon Ct	27217
Lane St	27217
Lanier Ct	27217
Larry St	27217
Lauder Ln	27215
Laurel Hill Dr	27215
Laurel Meadow Ct	27215
Lavista Dr	27215
Layell Dr	27215
Lear Dr	27215
Lee Dr	27215
Lee St	27217
Lena Ct	27217
Lenora St	27217
Lenore Dr	27215
Lenox Pl	27215
Leonard Ct	27217
Lester Ct	27215
Lester Dr	27215
Lewis Dr	27215
Lewis Rd	27217
S Lexington Ave	27215
Liberty Dr	27215
Liggins Ct	27217
Limerick Dr	27215
Lincoln St	27217
Lindale St	27215
Lindsey St	27217
Little Robert Dr	27215
Littlejohn Ct & Ln	27217
Loch Ridge Pkwy	27215
Lochmaddy Dr	27215
Lochshire Dr	27215
Lockesley Ln	27217
Loetta Trl	27217
N Logan St	27215
S Logan St	27215
Logan Street Ext	27215
Londonberry Ct	27215
Lone Oak Rd	27217
Long Ave	27217
Long St	
1100-1199	27217
1200-1499	27215
Long Oak Rd	27217
Longpine Rd	27215
Longshadow Ct & Dr	27217
Longview Dr	27215
Loop Rd	27217
Louis St	27217
Louis Graham Rd	27217
Lowder Rd	27217
Lowe Blvd	27217
Lowell Dr	27217
Lower Hopedale Rd	27217
Loy Ln	27215
Loy St	27217
Loyola Ct	27215
Luck Stone Rd	27217
Luggins Ct	27217
Lunsford Dr	27217
Luther Ct	27215
Lynn Dr	27215
Lynnwood Dr	27215
Mableton Dr	27217
Macarthur Ln	27217
Macdougall Dr	27215
Macgregor Dr	27217
Macleod St	27215
Macon St	27217
Madison St	27217
Magnolia Ln	27217
N Main St	27217
S Main St	27215
Majesty Dr	27217
Malone Ct & Rd	27215
Manchester Ln	27215
Manley Trl	27217
Mansfield Rd	27217
Maple Ave	
100-406	27215
405-405	27216
407-3899	27215
408-3898	27215
Maple Ridge Ct & Dr	27217
Mapleview Ln	27217
Margaret Ln	27217
Marion Ct	27215
Mark Dr	27217
E Market St	27217
Markham St	27217
Markwood Rd	27217
Marlborough Rd	27215
Marlow Dr	27215
Martin St	27217
Maryland Ave	27217
Massey St	27217
Mather Ct	27215
Matherly Trl	27217
Mathis Trl	27217
N & S Maury Arch	27215
May Ct & Dr	27215
Mayberry Ln	27215
Mccauley Rd	27217
Mccray Ct, Dr & Rd	27217
Mccuiston Dr	27215
Mcdade Rd	27215
Mcgrew Dr	27215
Mckinney St	27217
Mclone Rd	27215
Mcpherson Rd	27215
Meadow Ridge Ln	27217
Meadowbrook Dr	27215
Meadowlark Ct	27215
Meadowood Dr	27215
Meadowtop Cir	27217
N Mebane St	27217
S Mebane St	27215
Mebane Rogers Rd	27217
Meeting Ground Rd	27217
Melmark Dr	27217
Melody Ln	27215
Melrose Dr	27217
Memorial Dr	27215
Meridian St	27217
Merlin Ct	27215
Merritt Trl	27217
Miami Ave	27215
Michel St	27217
Michelle Dr	27217
Midland Ct	27215
Mill Race Rd	27217
Miller St	27215
W Millstone Pl & Rd	27215
Milton Holt Ln	27215
Mine Creek Rd	27217
Mirror Lake Dr	27215
Mistletoe Dr	27217
Mitchell Ct, Ln & St	27217
Mobile Manor Rd	27217
Monroe Holt Rd	27215
Montclair Dr	27217
Montgomery St	27217
Monticello Ct	27215
Moorgate Ct	27215
Moorland Ct	27215
Moran St	27215
E & W Morehead St	27215
Morgan Ter	27217
Morgan Glen Dr	27217
Morgan Hill Trl	27217
Morgan Leigh Ct	27217
Morgantown Rd & St	27217
Morningside Ct & Dr	27217
Morton Dr	27217
Moser Ln	27215
Moss Miles Rd	27217
Motley St	27217
Mount Hermon Rock Crk Rd	27215
Mount Pleasant Church Rd	27215
Mount Vernon Church Rd	27217
Mountain View Rd	27215
Mountain View Trl	27217
Mountainside Ln	27217
Mrs Blanchard Rd	27215
Muhlenberg Ct	27215
Murray St	27217
Muskrat Trl	27215
Nance St	27217
N & S Nc Highway 119 Anx	27217
N Nc Highway 49	27217
S Nc Highway 49	27215
Nc Highway 61 S	27215
Nc Highway 62 E	27215
N Nc Highway 62	27217
S Nc Highway 62	
3200-6799	27215
S Nc Highway 62	
9700-12999	27217
N Nc Highway 87	27217
Neals Hls	27217
Neals Hills Rd	27217
Neese Ct & Dr	27215
New St	27217
New Hill St	27217
New Jersey Ave	27217
New Oak Trl	27217
New Street Flds	27215
New York Ave	27215
Newbern Ct	27215
Newcastle Dr	27215
Newsome Ct	27217
Nike Dr	27217
Nire Valley Dr	27215
No Record	27217
Normandy Dr	27215
Norris Trl	27217
North Ave	27217
Northern Bnd	27217
Northside Dr	27217
Nottingham Ln	27215
Nottoway Ter	27215
Nova Ln	27215
Oak Cir	27217
Oak St	27215
Oakbury Rd	27215
Oakcrest Ct	27217
Oakdale Ct	27217
Oakland Dr	27215
Oakley Farm Rd	27217
Oakridge Ct	27217
Oakwood Dr	27215
Odell King Rd	27217
Oklahoma Ave	27217
Old Alamance Rd	27215
E & W Old Glencoe Rd	27217
Old Nc Highway 62	27217
Old Orchard Ln	27217
Old Saint Marks Church Rd	27215
Old Stoney Mountain Rd	27217
Old Trail Rd	27215
Olive Dr	27215
Oliver Ln	27217
Olmstead Dr	27215
Oneal St	27215
Orbert St	27217
Orice St	27215
Osborne Dr	27215
Oscar Bailey Rd	27217
Otter Ct	27215
Otter Creek Trl	27215
Otway St	27215
Overbrook Rd & Ter	27215
Overhill Dr	27217
Overlook Ct	27215
Overman Dr	27215
Oxford Ln	27215
Pa Will Trl	27217
Pace Landing Trl	27217
Pagetown Rd	27217
Paige Dr	27215
Palmer St	27217
Paris St	27215
Park Ave & Rd	27217
Park Road Ext	27215
Parker St	27217
Parkside Dr	27215
Parkview Dr	27215
Parkwood St	27215
Parrish St	27215
Paschal Rd	27217
Passavant Ct	27215
Patillo Church Rd	27217
Patsy Trl	27215
Peace Ln	27215
Peachtree St	27215
Pebblestone Trl	27215
Peele St	27215
Peeler St	27215
Penland Dr	27217
Pennlawn Trl	27217
Pennsylvania Ave	27215
Pepperidge St	27215
Perry Cir	27217
Perrys Mobile Home Park Dr	27217
Phillips St	27217
Picketts Trl	27215
Pickwood Dr	27215
Piedmont Way	27217
N Pierce Ave	27215
Pine St	
400-699	27217
900-999	27215
Pine Grove Dr	27215
Pine Knoll Ter	27217
Pine Ridge Ct, Ln & Trl	27217
Pine Trail Rd	27215
Pinebrook Dr	27217
Pinecrest St	27215
Pinecroft Dr	27217
Pineview Dr	27215
Pineway Dr	27215
Pinewood Trce	27215
Pinnix Rd	27217
Piper Ln	27215
Plaid St	27215
Plantation Dr	27215
Plarinda Dr	27215
Plaza Dr	
600-899	27217
1200-1399	27215
Pleasant Brook Way	27217
Pleasant Grove Un Sch Rd	27217
Pleasant Woods Ct	27217
Plum St	27215
Plymouth St	27217
Polk St	27217
Pollard Ave W	27217
Pond Rd	27215
Porter G Simmons	27217
Porter Sharpe Rd	27215
Porterfield Dr	27217
Portsmouth Ct	27215
Powell Rd & Trl	27217
Power St	27217
Preacher Hayes Rd	27217
Preston St	27217
Pride Ave	27217
Professional Park Dr	27215
Pruitt Rd & Trl	27217
Quad Ct	27215
Quail Run Ln	27215
Quaker Lake Trl	27217
Quality Dr	27217
Queen Ann St	27217
Quintas Ave	27215
R Dean Coleman Rd	27215
Raccoon Run Dr	27215
Race Track Rd	27215
Rader Ct & St	27215
Radiance Dr	27215
Rae Dr	27215
Railroad St	27217
Rainbow Ave	27215
Rainey St	27217
Ramada Rd	27215
Random Ct & Ln	27215
Rascoe Rd	27217
Rascoe Dameron Rd	27217
Rauhut St	27217
Ravenwood Trl	27217
Ray St	27217
Ray Massey Trl	27217
Rayon St	27217
Reavis Ln	27215
Rebecca Ct	27217
Red Shepherd Dr	27215
Red Wolf Way	27215
Redell Dr	27217
Regency Ct & Dr	27215
Regent Park Ln	27217
Regulator Dr	27215
Reichert Trl	27215
Rendall Ct & St	27215
Reynolds Dairy Rd	27215
Richards Ave	27215
Richmond Ave	27217
Ridge Ct	27215
W Ridge Ct	27215
S Ridge Rd	27217
Ridgecrest Ave	27215
Ridgeside Ct	27215
Ridgeway Dr	27217
Ridgewood Ct	27215
Rileys Trl	27215
River Rd	27217
River Hills Ln	27217
Riverside Dr	27217
Riverview Dr	27217
Riverwood Trl	27217
Rob Shephard Dr	27215
Robert L Brooks Ln	27215
Roberta Dr	27217
Roberts Rd	27217
Robertson St	27217
Robin Hood Dr	27217
Rock Hill Rd	27215
Rocklane Dr	27215
Rockledge Dr	27217
Rockwood Ave	27215
Rocky Cliff Trl	27215
Roger St	27217
Rolling Rd	27217
Rolling Hills Rd	27217
Rolling Meadow Ct & Ln	27217
Rollingwood Dr W	27217
Rollingwood Rd	27215
Rone Rd	27217
Roney Lineberry Rd	27217
S Rosa Ct	27215
Rose Ct	27217
Rosemary Dr	27215
Rosenwald St	27217
Roslyn Dr	27215
Ross St	27217
Ross Acres Road 1	27217
Ross Acres Road 2	27217
Rosswood Dr	27215
Routh Rd	27217
Royster Woods Trl	27217
Rudd St	27217
E & W Ruffin St	27217
Rural Retreat Rd	27215
Russell Mcpherson Rd	27215
Saconn Dr	27215
Saddle Club Ln	27217
Saddle Club Rd	27215
Saige Ct	27217
Saint George Ct	27215
N & S Saint John St	27217
Saint Marks Church Rd	27215
Saint Regis Dr	27217
Saintsbury Dr	27215
Salvet St	27215
Sam Gwynn Ct	27217
Samara Dr	27215
Sandpiper Trl	27217
Sandrock Dr	27217
Sandy Cross Rd	27217
Sans Mill Rd	27217
Sarah Rhyne Rd	27217
Sartin Rd	27217
Saunders Rd	27217
Sawmill Rd	27217
School St	27215
Scott St	27215
Seabury Ct	27215
Sedgefield St	27215
Sellars St	27217
N & S Sellars Mill Rd	27217
Serenity Dr	27215
Seton Ct	27215
Setter Dr	27217
Shadowbrook Ct & Dr	27215
Shady Dr	27215
Shady Ln	27217
Shadylawn Dr	27215
Shamrock Dr	27215
Shaniqua Dr	27217
Shanks St	27217
Shannon Dr	27215
Sharp Shooter Rd	27217
Sharpe Rd	27217
Sharpe Shooters Rd	27217
Shaw St	27217
Shawnee Dr	27215
Sheffield Ct	27215
Shelburne Ct	27215
Shepherd Ct	27215
Shepherd Dr	27215
Shepherd St	27217
Sherard Trl	27215
Sherri Dr	27217
Sherry Dr	27215
Sherwood Dr	27215
Shiniqua Dr	27217
Shirley Dr	27215
Shoe Rd	27215

Shoffner St 27215
Shoffners Loop 27217
Shonnette Dr 27217
Short St 27217
Sidney Ave 27217
Sidney Albright Trl 27215
Silverlake Dr 27215
Simmons Ct 27215
E & W Simpson Rd 27217
Sinclair Trce 27215
Sky View Ln 27215
Small Ct 27215
Smelly Ln 27217
Smith Rd 27215
Smith St 27217
Smith Bullis Ln 27215
Snow Ct 27215
Snug Harbor Rd 27217
Sodbuster Dr 27217
Somers Ave 27215
Somerton Pl 27215
Southern High School Rd 27215
Southern Moore Trl 27215
Spanish Oak Hill Rd 27215
Spence Ct & St 27217
Spoon Dr 27217
Spring Loop 27217
Spring Rd 27217
S Spring St 27215
Spring Valley Dr 27217
Springbrook Dr 27215
Springdale Dr 27215
Springfield Ct 27215
Springhill Dr 27217
Springview Ct 27215
Springwood Dr 27215
Springwood Church Rd 27215
Spruce Ln & St 27217
Squaw Valley Trl 27215
Sr Allred Rd 27217
Stafford St 27217
Stagg St 27217
Stainback Rd 27217
Staley St 27217
Stanfield Rd 27217
Stanley Dr 27215
Stella Ln 27217
Sterling Ct 27215
Stockard St 27217
Stokes St 27215
Stone St 27215
Stonecrest Dr 27215
Stonewall Ave 27217
Stonewall Springs Rd 27217
Stonewyck Dr 27215
Stoney Creek Church Rd 27217
Stoney Creek Mountain Rd 27217
Stoney Mountain Rd 27217
Stoneybrook Ct 27215
Storey St 27217
Stout St 27215
Strader Dr 27215
Stratford Ct 27215
Stratford Rd 27217
Stratford Oaks Ct 27215
Stuart Ct 27215
Sturbridge Ct 27215
Styles Thompson Dr 27217
Suanne Ln 27215
Sudie Dr 27217
Sullivan Park Cir 27215
Sumac Ln 27215
Summersville Pl 27215
E & W Summit Ave 27215
Sumner Ln 27217
Sumpter St 27217
Sundance Dr 27215
Sunflower Ct 27217
Sunnybrook Dr 27215
Sunset Dr & Hls 27215
Sunset Breeze Ln 27217
Sunset Meadows Trl 27217

Surich Dr 27215
Sutton Pl 27215
Swann Rd 27217
Sweetbay Cir 27215
Sycamore Dr 27217
Sykes St 27215
Tan Ct 27215
Tanbark Ct 27215
Tangle Ridge Trl 27217
Tanner Ct 27215
Tapscott Ln 27217
Tara Ln 27217
W Tarboro St 27215
Tarleton Ave 27215
Tarpley St 27215
Tartan Ln 27215
Tate Dr 27215
Tate St 27217
Taylor Ct & St 27217
Teal Ct 27215
Tee Time Ave 27215
Terrace Dr 27215
Terry Smith Trl 27217
Texas Ave 27217
Thaxton Trl 27215
Thistle Dr 27217
Thistle Downs Dr 27215
W Thomas St & Way 27215
Thomas Arlendo Dr 27215
Thomas Haith Ln 27217
Thompson St 27215
Tiki Ln 27215
Tillman St 27217
Timber Trl 27215
Tom Barnwell Trl 27217
Tower Dr 27215
Tracy Dr 27217
W Trade St 27217
Trail Eight 27215
Trail Five 27215
Trail Four 27215
Trail One 27215
Trail Six 27215
Trail Three 27215
Trail Two 27215
Travis Ln 27217
Tremont Dr 27215
Tremore Club Dr 27215
Tribek Ct & Dr 27215
Trilek Ct 27215
Troendly St 27217
Trollinger St 27215
Trollingwood Rd 27217
Troxler Rd 27215
Truitt Dr 27215
Tryon St 27217
Tuck Dr 27215
Tucker St 27215
Tucker Street Ext 27215
Turner St 27217
Turrentine St 27215
Tweed Ln 27215
Tyler View Ct 27215
Tyndall Dr 27215
Union Ave 27217
Union Ridge Rd 27217
Union Ridge Road Ext 27217
University Dr 27215
Valeria Ct 27215
Valleydale Dr 27215
Valleywood Ct 27217
Van Dr 27215
Vance St 27217
Vanderford St 27215
Vaughn Ln & Rd 27217
Venie St 27215
Veterans Dr 27215
Victoria Falls Dr 27215
W View Dr 27215
Viewcrest Ct 27215
Village Ct 27215
Vine St 27217
Vinings Dr 27217
Vinson Rd 27217
Vintani Rd 27215
Viola Dr 27215

Violet Ct 27217
Virginia Ave 27217
Vista Knoll Dr 27215
Von Bora Ct 27215
Wade St 27217
Wade Coble Dr 27215
Wagner Dr 27215
Walden Ln 27215
Wales Ct 27215
Walker Ave 27215
Wallace St 27217
Walnut St 27217
Waltham Blvd 27215
Warren Farm Dr 27217
Warwick Ct & Dr 27215
Washington St 27215
Waterford Pl 27215
Watermill Dr 27215
Watkins Rd 27215
Watson Dr 27217
Watt Dr 27215
Waverly Way 27215
Wayne Trl 27217
E & W Webb Ave 27217
Welch St 27217
Weldon Cobb Trl 27215
Wellington Rd 27217
Wesley Ct 27215
Westbrook Ave, Ct & Dr 27215
Westchester Dr 27217
W Westgate Dr 27215
Westhampton Ct & Dr 27215
Westmont Dr 27217
Westmoreland Ct & Dr 27217
Weston Ct 27215
Westover Ter 27215
Westridge Ct & Dr 27215
Westview Dr 27217
Westview Ter 27215
Westwood Rd 27217
Wexford Pl 27215
Wheeler Bridge Rd 27215
Whispering Wind Rd 27217
White Oak Dr 27215
White Rock Ln 27215
White Swan Dr 27217
Whitefield Ct 27215
Whites Kennel Rd 27215
Whitesell Dr & Rd 27215
Whitesell Farm Ln 27215
Whitney Burche Trl 27217
Whitsett St
1200-1240 27217
1241-1297 27215
1242-1298 27217
1299-2299 27215
Whitsett Park Rd 27215
Whitt Ave 27215
Wicker St 27217
Wickham St 27215
Wicklow Dr 27215
Widow Foster Rd 27217
Wiggins St 27215
Wildwood Ln 27215
Wilkins Rd & St 27217
William Allen Rd 27217
William Penn Ct 27215
Williams St 27217
Williams Mill Rd 27215
Williamson Ave 27215
Williamson St
100-499 27215
1100-1299 27217
Willie Pace Rd 27217
Willie Spoon Ln 27217
Willoughby Ct 27215
Willoughby Rd 27217
Willow Ave 27215
Willow Lake Rd 27217
Willow Oak Dr 27215
Willow Spring Ln 27215
E & W Willowbrook Dr 27215
Wilmington St 27215
Wilson Dr 27215
Wiltshire Dr 27217

Wimbledon Cir 27215
Windfield Ridge Dr 27215
Windham Ave 27217
Winding Trl 27217
Winding Trail Ct 27217
Windsor St 27217
Windy Knoll Dr 27215
Winston Dr 27215
Winterbell Dr 27215
Wisteria Ct 27217
Wood Ave 27215
Wood Thrush Ln 27217
Woodbrier Ln 27215
Woodbrooke Dr 27217
Woodbury Ct & Dr 27217
Woodhaven Dr 27217
Woodhue Dr 27215
Woodland Ave 27215
Woodleigh Ave 27217
Woodridge Ct & Rd 27215
Woods End Trl 27217
Woody Ln 27215
N Worth St 27217
S Worth St 27215
Wr Ln 27217
Wrenn St 27215
Wyatt Ln & Rd 27217
Wycliff Ct 27215
Wynnwood Dr 27217
Yamota Rd 27217
York Ct, Pl & Rd 27215
Yorktowne Ct 27215
Young St 27215
Yount Ct 27215
Zimmerman Trl 27217
Zwingli Ct 27215

NUMBERED STREETS

All Street Addresses 27215

CAMP LEJEUNE NC

POST OFFICE BOXES MAIN OFFICE STATIONS AND BRANCHES

Box No.s
All PO Boxes 28547

NAMED STREETS

A St 28542
Alabama Ave 28547
Alaska Ct 28547
Arizona St 28547
Arkansas St 28547
Ash St 28547
Barnett Way 28547
Barrow St 28547
Bestwick Ave 28547
Bevin St 28547
Bicentennial Ave 28547
Birch St 28547
Blackwood Rd 28547
Brewster Blvd 28547
California St 28547
Carolina Ct & St 28547
Cates Way 28547
Chapman Dr 28547
Colorado Ave 28547
Connecticut St 28547
Cooper St 28547
Cukela Ave & Ct 28547
D St 28542
Dailey Ln 28547
Dantrins St 28547
Delaware Ave 28547
Dewey St 28547
E St 28547
East Rd 28547
Eden St 28547

Elliott Ct 28547
F St 28547
Florida Ave & St 28547
French Crk 28542
Fuller Ave 28547
G St 28547
Georgia St 28547
Greene St 28547
Harvey St 28547
Hawaii St 28547
Hill Plz 28547
Holcomb Blvd 28547
Idaho Ct 28547
Illinois St 28547
Indiana St 28547
Iowa Ct 28547
Jackson St 28547
Jones St 28547
Julian C Smith Dr 28547
Kansas Ct 28547
Kent Rd 28547
Kentucky Ct 28547
Louis Rd 28547
Louisiana St 28547
Lucy Brewer Ave 28547
Maine Ct 28547
Maryland Ave 28547
Massachusetts Ct 28547
Mcb Camp Lejeune 28542
Mchugh Blvd 28547
Michael Rd 28547
Michigan Ave, Ct & St 28547
Minnesota Ct 28547
Mississippi St 28547
Molly Pitcher Rd 28547
Montana St 28547
Montford Landing Rd 28542
N St 28547
Nebraska Ct 28547
Nevada Ct 28547
Neville Cv 28547
New Mexico St 28547
Ohio Ct 28547
Oklahoma Ct 28547
Onslow Dr 28547
Oregon St 28547
Pate Ct 28547
Pender St 28547
Peridger 28542
Poe Rd 28542
Post Ln 28547
Psc 28542
Puckett Dr 28547
Recovery Way 28547
Saint Mary Dr 28547
Service Rd 28547
Seth Williams Blvd 28547
Shepard Ct 28547
Shoup Ln 28547
Stone St 28547
Surgeons Row 28547
Sweet Ln 28547
Texas Ct 28547
Timmerman Ave & Pl 28547
Utah St 28547
Vermont Ct 28547
Virginia St 28547
Virginia Dare Dr 28547
Washington St 28547
Wavell St 28547
West Rd 28547
Winston Rd 28547

CARY NC

General Delivery 27511

POST OFFICE BOXES MAIN OFFICE STATIONS AND BRANCHES

Box No.s
1 - 2212 27512
3001 - 4996 27519
5001 - 5900 27512
6001 - 6060 27519
8000 - 9998 27512

RURAL ROUTES

42 27518
62 27519

NAMED STREETS

Abbey Ln 27511
Abbey Hall Way 27513
Abbey View Way 27519
Abbots Glen Ct 27511
Abbott Ln 27513
Abercom Ct 27519
Abernathy Ct 27511
Aberson Ct 27519
Abingdon Ct 27513
Aborfield Ct 27513
Abram Dr 27511
Absher Ct 27519
N Academy St
100-199 27511
200-699 27513
S Academy St
100-200 27511
201-205 27519
202-398 27511
207-399 27511
Academy View Ct 27513
Acadia Ct 27513
Accolade Dr 27513
Ackworth Ct 27519
W Acres Cres 27519
Adams St 27513
Adela Ct 27519
Advent Ct 27518
Adventure Trl 27513
Aeroglide Dr 27511
Affinity Ln 27519
Affirmed Way 27519
Afton Meadow Ln 27518
Agassi Ct 27511
Agricola Ave 27519
Airlie Ct 27513
Aisling Ct 27513
Akiry Ct 27511
Albert Ct 27513
Albion Pl 27519
Alden Bridge Dr 27519
Alden Village Ct 27519
Alder Ln 27518
Aldersbrook Ct 27519
Alexan Dr 27519
Alicary Ct 27511
Alidade Ct 27513
Allen Lewis Dr 27513
Allenhurst Pl 27518
Allforth Pl 27519
Alliance Cir 27519
Allison Way 27511
Alma Dr 27511
Almaden Way 27518
Alston Ave 27519
Alston Village Ln 27519
Altarbrook Dr 27519
Ambassador St 27513
Amber Creek Cir 27513
Amberglow Pl 27513
Ambermore Pl 27519
Ambiance Ln 27518
Amblewood Dr 27511
Ambrose Park Ln 27518
Amesbury Ln 27511
Amiable Loop 27519
Ampad Ct 27513
Anamoor Dr 27513
Anderson Ct 27511
Angelica Cir 27518
Anglers Cv 27513
Angora Ct 27513
Angus Ct 27511

Anita Way 27513
Ann St 27511
Anna Lake Ln 27513
Annagrey Cir 27513
Annandale Dr 27511
Anniston Ct 27519
Ansley Walk Ln 27518
Antler Point Dr 27513
Antrim Meadow Ln 27519
Anvil Ct 27513
Apex Morrisville Rd 27519
Applecross Dr 27511
Appledown Dr 27513
Appletree Ln 27513
Appomattox Rd 27513
April Bloom Ln 27519
Arabella Ct 27518
Arbor Way 27513
Arbor Brook Dr 27519
Arbor View Dr 27519
Arbordale Ct 27518
Arboretum Trce 27518
Arbuckle Ln 27511
Arden Crest Ct 27513
Aridith Ct 27511
Arlat Ln 27519
Arlington Rdg 27513
Armfield Ct 27519
Armour St 27518
Arrow Head Way 27513
Arrow Leaf Cir 27519
Arrundale Dr 27511
Art Cir 27511
Arvada Dr 27519
Arvind Oaks Cir 27519
Arvo Ln 27513
Asbill Ct 27518
Ashdown Forest Ln 27519
Ashe Ave 27511
Ashford Ln 27511
Ashley Dr 27513
Ashley Brook Ct 27513
Ashley Glen Dr 27513
Ashley Rose Dr 27519
Ashley Springs Ct 27513
Ashmore Dr 27519
Ashton Pl 27511
Ashtree Ct 27519
Ashville Ave 27518
Ashwick Ct 27513
Ashwyn Ct 27518
Askham Dr 27511
Aspen Hollow Ct 27518
Assembly Ct 27511
Astor Ct 27518
N & S Atley Ln 27513
Atterbury Ln 27518
Attmore Way 27519
Audreystone Dr 27518
Audubon Parc Dr 27518
Augustine Trl 27518
Austin Ave 27511
Austin Pond Dr 27519
Auto Mall Dr 27511
Auto Park Blvd 27511
Autumn Cir 27518
Autumngate Dr 27518
Autumnstone Way 27519
Avella Ct 27519
Avenue Of The Est 27518
Avery Cir 27511
Awesome St 27511
Ayelsford Dr 27518
Aylestone Dr 27519
Ayr Ct 27511
Backbay Dr 27513
Badin Lake Ct 27519
Baines Ct 27511
Bald Eagle Ln 27518
Baliji Pl 27513
Ballad Creek Ct 27519
Ballatore Ct 27519
Balmoral Dr 27511
Balsamwood Ct 27513
Balwins Gate 27511
Balzac Ct 27511

Bancroft Brook Dr 27519
Bankhead Dr 27519
Banks Knoll Dr 27519
Bannerman Ln 27519
Banningford Rd 27518
Banyon Grove Loop 27513
Banyon Tree Ln 27513
Barbary Ct 27511
Barbosa Ln 27518
Barcelona Ct 27513
Barcladine Ct 27511
Barclay Valley Dr 27519
Barcliff Ter 27518
Bardsey Ct 27513
Bargate Dr 27511
Barnbridge Ct 27519
Barnes St 27511
Barnes Spring Ct 27519
Barnet Ridge Ct 27519
Barningham Ct 27519
Barometer Ln 27513
Barons Glenn Way 27513
Barret Manor Ct 27513
Barrett Woods Ct 27513
Barriedale Cir 27519
Barron Ct 27511
Barthel Dr 27513
Bartica Ct 27519
Bass Ct 27513
Bass Pro Ln 27513
Bastille Ct 27511
Bathgate Ln 27513
Battenburg Ct 27519
Battersea Park Cir 27513
Battery Point Pl 27513
Battery Walk Ln 27519
Baucom Grove Ct 27519
Bay Dr 27511
Bay Willow Ct 27519
Baybrook Ct 27518
Bayliss Ct 27519
Bayoak Dr 27513
Bayreuth Pl 27513
Beachers Brook Ln 27511
Beacon Cove Dr 27511
Beacon Falls Ct 27519
Beacon Hollow Pl 27519
Bear Oak Ln 27519
Beasley Ct 27513
Beaujolais Ct 27511
Beaver Dam Rd 27519
Beaver Pine Way 27511
Bebington Dr 27513
N & S Becket St 27513
Beckford Rd 27518
Beckingham Loop 27519
Bedbrook Ct 27519
Beech St 27513
Beech Forest Ct 27513
Beech Slope Way 27518
Beechtree Dr 27513
Beeley Ct 27519
Beeston Ct 27519
Belclaire Ct 27513
Belhaven Rd 27513
Bell Arbor Ct 27519
Bell Arthur Dr 27519
Bell Vista Dr 27513
Bellamy Ct 27511
Belle Isle Ct 27513
Belles Landing Ct 27519
Bellshill Ct 27513
Belmont View Loop 27519
Beloit Ct 27511
Belrose Dr 27513
Benedetti Ct 27513
Benedum Pl 27518
N Benson Ct 27513
Bentbrook Ct 27519
Bentbury Way 27518
Benttree Forest Dr 27519
Benwell Ct 27519
Beowulf Ln 27519
Beraneak Ln 27519
Bergeron Way 27519
Bergstrand Ct 27513

Bern St 27511
Berry Chase Way 27519
Berry Rose Way 27518
Berrybrook Ct 27519
Bert Ct 27511
Bervie Ct 27511
Berwick Valley Ln 27513
Bethabara Ln 27513
Bethelview Ct 27519
Bethenia Pl 27511
Betsworth Ct 27513
Bevington Hill Ct 27513
Bexhill Dr 27518
Bexley Bluff Ln 27513
Bickerton Ct 27519
Bideford Pl 27513
Big Rock Ct 27513
Bigelow Rd 27519
Bighorn Cir 27513
Billingrath Turn Ln 27519
Billington Ct 27519
Birch Cir 27511
Birch Glen Ct 27513
Birdwood Ct 27519
Birk Bluff Ct 27518
Birkhaven Dr 27518
Birklands Dr 27518
Birstall Dr 27519
Biscayne Cir 27513
Bishop Ct 27513
Bishop Brook Ct 27519
Bittercress Ct 27518
Black Angus Run 27513
Black Bear Ct 27513
Blackbird Ct 27511
Blackfriars Loop 27519
Blackheath Ct 27513
Blackmar St 27519
Blackshoals Dr 27511
Blooming Forest Pl 27518
Bloomingdale Dr 27511
Bloomsbury Pl 27519
Blossom Grove Dr 27519
Blowingrock Ln 27518
Blue Boar Ct 27519
Blue Jack Oak Dr 27519
Blueberry Woods Ln 27518
Bluff Oak Dr 27519
Blythewood Ct 27513
Bog Hill Ln 27519
Bogue Ct 27511
Boldleaf Ct 27513
Bolton Grant Dr 27519
Boltstone Ct 27513
Bond Lake Dr 27513
Bonnell Ct 27511
Bonner Ct 27511
Bonniewood Dr 27518
Boone Ridge Ln 27519
Bordeaux Ln 27511
Borotra Ct 27511
Boscawen Ln 27519
Bosswood Ct 27518
Bosworth Pl 27519
Boulderstone Way 27519
E & W Boundary St 27513
Bourke Pl 27511
Bourne Wood Dr 27518
Bowcastle Ct 27518
Bowden St 27513
Bowers Ln 27519
Boxwood Ct 27511
Boyd St 27513
Bradford Green Sq 27519
Bradford View Dr 27519
Bradhurst Pl 27519
Bradshire Ct 27513
Bradwyck Dr 27513
Brady Ct 27511
Braebrook Way 27519
Braelands Dr 27518
Braemar Ct 27511
Braeside Ct 27519
Braintree Ct 27513
Bramante Pl 27518
Brampton Ln 27513

Branch Hollow Dr 27519
Branchway Rd 27519
Branniff Dr 27513
Brannigan Pl 27511
Branning Ct 27519
Brant Point Pl 27513
Branton Dr 27519
Brass Ring Ct 27513
Braswell Brook Ct 27513
Brave River Ct 27519
Breakers Pl 27511
Brechin Ct 27518
Breckenwood Dr 27513
Brendan Choice 27511
Breyman Ct 27518
Briarcliff Ln 27511
Briarcreek Ct 27513
Briardale Ave 27519
Briargate Terrace Ln 27519
Bridewell Ct 27518
Bridgegate Dr 27519
Bridgemill Way 27519
Bridgepath Dr 27513
Bridgeway Ct 27511
E & W Bridgford Dr 27518
Bridle Boast Rd 27519
Bridle Creek Dr 27513
Bridlebit Ct 27513
Brigh Stone Dr 27513
Bright Angel Dr 27513
Bright Beginning Way 27519
Bright Sand Ct 27513
Brightleaf Ct 27513
Brimmer Ct 27518
Brisbane Woods Way 27518
Bristol Bay Ct 27513
Bristol Hill Ct 27513
Brittany Pl 27511
Broadford Dr 27511
Broadgait Brae Rd 27519
Broderick Pl 27519
Brodick Ct 27511
Brodie Lloyd Ct 27519
Brogan Pl 27511
Broken Bow Ct 27513
Brokenshire St 27519
Bromfield Way 27519
Bronte Ln 27513
Bronzewood Ct 27518
Brook Arbor Dr 27519
Brook Creek Dr 27519
Brook Fryar St 27519
Brook Hollow Ct 27513
Brookbank Hill Pl 27519
Brookcliff Ln 27511
Brookesby Ct 27519
Brookgreen Dr 27511
Brookhill Way 27519
Brookridge Dr 27518
Brooks Park Ln 27519
Brooksville Ct 27519
Broward Ln 27519
Brownfield Ct 27511
Bruce Dr 27511
Brunson Ct 27511
Brunswick Pl 27513
Brush Stream Dr 27511
Bryce Pl 27511
Buckden Pl 27518
Buckhurst Dr 27513
Buckingham Ct 27511
Buckland Mills Ct 27513
Buena Vista Dr 27513
Buffwood Ct 27518
Bulon Dr 27518
Burbage Cir 27519
Burghead Ct 27511
Burgwin Wright Way 27519
Burlingame Way 27513
Burnaby Ct 27519
Burnley Dr 27511
Burrus Hall Cir 27519
Burwick Rd 27511
Butterwood Ct 27511
Buxton Grant Dr 27519
Byrams Ford Dr 27513

Byrd Hill Ct 27519
Byrum St 27511
Cabernet Cir 27511
Cabin Cove Rd 27519
Cagle Shoals Pl 27519
Caitboo Ave 27518
Cakebread Ct 27519
Calebra Way 27519
Callan Park Ln 27511
Callandale Ave 27518
Callay Hill Way 27519
Callum Pl 27519
Calm Ct 27519
Calm Winds Ct 27513
Calton Hill Ct 27511
Cambay Ct 27513
Cambrian Way 27511
Camden Branch Dr 27518
E & W Camden Forest Dr 27518
Camden Yards Way 27519
Cameron Ct 27511
Cameron Pond Dr 27519
Camise Ln 27518
Canberra Ct 27513
Candace Pl 27513
Candia Ln 27519
Candle Tea Ct 27513
Candy Apple Ct 27513
Candytuff Ct 27513
Caniff Ln 27519
Canon Gate Dr 27518
E & W Canopy Oak Ct 27513
Canterfield Rd 27513
Canterstone Ct 27518
Canton Chase Ct 27513
Canty Ct 27511
Canyon Run 27513
Cape Cod Dr 27511
Capistrane Dr 27519
Capriole Ln 27519
Caraway Ln 27519
Carbe Ct 27519
Carbon Hill Ct 27519
Carla Ct 27513
Carlton Commons Ln 27519
Carluke Ct 27511
Carmel Ct 27511
Carmichael Ct 27511
E & W Carnaby Ct 27513
Carnoustie Cir 27511
Carolina Sky Pl 27519
Carolyn Ct 27511
Carostone Ct 27513
Carpenter Brook Dr 27519
Carpenter Creek Pl 27519
Carpenter Fire Station Rd 27519
Carpenter Glenn Dr 27519
Carpenter Town Ln 27519
Carpenter Upchurch Rd 27519
Carramore Ave 27519
Carriage Ln 27511
Carric Bend Ct 27519
Carriole Ct 27513
Carrousel Ln 27513
Carswell Ln 27519
Cartecay Dr 27519
Carterwood Ct 27519
Carvers Gap Ct 27519
NW Cary Pkwy 27513
SE Cary Pkwy
100-799 27511
900-998 27518
1000-1199 27518
SW Cary Pkwy
100-2399 27511
2400-3699 27513
3701-4899 27519
Cary St 27513
Cary Glen Blvd 27519
Cary Pines Dr 27513
Cary Reserve Dr 27519
Cary Towne Blvd 27511

Carywood Dr 27513
Casablanca Ct 27519
Cascade Pointe Ln 27513
Casey Brook Ct 27519
Cashie Ct 27519
Cass Ct 27511
Cassidy Ct 27511
Castalia Dr 27513
Castle Bay Ct 27511
Castle Garden St 27513
Castle Hayne Dr 27519
Castlebury Creek Ct 27519
Castlefern Dr 27513
Castlemaine Ct 27519
Castlewood Ct & Dr 27511
Catchpenny Ct 27519
Cathedral Way 27513
Catherwood Pl 27518
Catiboo Dr 27518
Catlin Rd 27519
Cavendish Dr 27513
Caviston Way 27519
Caymus Ct 27519
E Cedar St 27511
Cedar Cliff Ct 27518
Cedar Creek Dr 27513
Cedarpost Dr 27513
Center Ct 27511
Center Pointe Dr 27513
Centerville Ct 27513
Centre Green Way 27513
Centrewest Ct 27513
Chadmore Dr 27518
E & W Chalfont Way 27513
Chalk Maple Dr 27519
Chalk Meadow Dr 27519
Chalkwell Ct 27519
Chalmette Ct 27513
Chalon Dr 27511
Chamness Dr 27513
Champion Dr 27511
Champions Point Way 27513
Champlain Ct 27519
Chancellors Ridge Ct 27513
Chandler Grant Dr 27519
Channing Pl 27519
Chaparral Ct 27513
Chapel Creek Ct 27513
Chapel Hill Rd 27513
Chapelwood Way 27518
Chaps Ct 27513
Chardonnay Ln 27511
E & W Charing Cross 27513
Chariot Ct 27519
Charlemagne Ct 27511
Charles Ct 27511
Charleville Ct 27519
Charlie Gaddy Ln 27511
Charlies Way 27519
Charmwood Ct 27518
Charolais Trl 27513
Charter Ct 27511
Charter Oaks Cir 27511
Chasbrier Ct 27518
Chatburn Cir 27513
Chateau Pl 27511
Chatfield Ct 27513
E Chatham St 27511
W Chatham St
1000-1179 27511
1180-1799 27513
Chatham Woods Dr 27511
Chatsworth St 27513
Chattel Close 27513
Chelmsford Ct 27518
Cherry Grove Dr 27519
Cherry Hill Ln 27518
Chertsey Ct 27519
Cherwell Dr 27513
Chesapeake Ln 27511
Chessington Ct 27513
Chessridge Way 27519
Chessway Dr 27519
Chesterfield Dr 27513
Chestnut St 27511
Chestone Ct 27513

Cheswick Pl 27511
Cheverly Dr 27511
Chevis Dr 27513
Chevron Cir 27513
Chickory Castle Way 27519
Chicory St 27519
Chime Ct 27519
Chimney Rise Dr 27511
Chimo Ct 27513
Chinqua Pine Dr 27519
Chip Cir 27513
Chiselhurst Way 27513
Chisholm Ct 27511
Choptank Ct 27513
Chris Ct 27511
Christenbury Ln 27511
Christian Creek Pl 27519
Christofle Ln 27511
Christow Ct 27519
Chula Vista Ct 27513
Church Rd 27513
Churchview St 27513
Cibola Dr 27513
Cimmaron Ct 27511
Cindy St 27511
E & W Circle Dr 27511
Circle On The Grn 27519
Citadel Creek Ln 27519
Citreon Ct 27511
Citrus Pl 27519
City Walls St 27513
Clancy Cir 27511
Clare Ct 27511
Clarenbridge Dr 27519
E & W Clarksville Ct 27513
Clay St 27511
Clear River Pl 27519
Clear Sky Ct 27513
Clearcreek Ct 27513
Clearport Dr 27519
Clendenen Ct 27513
Climbing Ivy Ct 27511
Climbing Rose Turn 27518
Clingstone Ct 27519
Clinton Ct 27511
Cloud Crossing Cir 27513
Clubstone Ln 27518
Clyde Bank Ct 27511
Clydesdale Ct 27513
Coalburn Pl 27511
Coatbridge Cir 27511
Cobalt Dr 27513
Cochet Ct 27511
Cockleshell Ct 27513
Coconut Mews 27513
Coffin Bay Ct 27519
Colchis Ct 27513
Cole Ct 27511
Cole Canyon Ct 27513
Cole Crest Ct 27513
Cole Stream Ct 27513
Cole Valley Dr 27513
Colen Ct 27511
Colinsburgh Ct 27518
Collamer Dr 27519
Colleen Cir 27519
Collier Pl 27513
Collin Creek Ln 27513
Collington Dr 27511
Collins Rd 27519
Colonades Way 27518
Colonial Townes Ct 27511
Colora Ct 27513
Colt Bridge Ct 27519
Coltsgate Dr 27518
Columbus Ave 27518
Commons Hill Dr 27519
Commons Walk Cir 27519
Commonwealth Ct 27511
Comrie Pl 27518
Conagra Ct 27519
Concannon Ct 27511
Coniston Ct 27511
Connelly Springs Pl 27519
Connemara Dr 27519
Connors Cir 27511

Considine Ct 27519
Contessa Dr 27513
Convention Dr 27511
Conway Ct 27513
Coogee Ln 27513
Coorsdale Dr 27511
Copper Green St 27513
Copper Hill Dr 27518
Copperleaf Pl 27519
Copperstone Ln 27518
Coral Ct 27511
Coral Vine Ter 27518
Cordova Ct 27518
Corgy Dr 27513
N & S Corncrib Ct 27513
Cornerstone Dr 27519
Corning Rd 27518
E & W Cornwall Rd 27511
Cornwall View Ct 27511
Coronado Way 27511
Corral Ct 27513
Corrigan Way 27519
Corsica Ln 27511
N & S Coslett Ct 27513
Cottsmore Ct 27519
Cougar Ct 27513
Council Gap Ct 27513
Country Ct 27511
Country Ln 27513
Countryside Ln 27518
Courts Garden Way 27513
Cove Creek Dr 27519
Coventry Ln 27511
Covewood Ct 27513
Covington Square Dr 27513
Cowley Rd 27518
Cozy Oak Ave 27519
Crabtree Crossing Pkwy 27513
Crafton Park Ln 27519
Crampton Grove Way 27519
Cranborne Ln 27519
Cransley Meadow Ln 27519
Craven Hill Ct 27518
Creek Park Dr 27513
Creekbury Ct 27519
Creekstone Ln 27511
Creekwatch Ln 27513
Creighton Ct 27511
Crescent Grn 27518
Crescent Arbor Ln 27518
Crescent Commons Dr 27518
Crest Rd 27513
Crestpoint Ct 27513
Crestridge Ct 27513
Creststone Dr 27519
Crestview Ct 27518
Crickentree Dr 27518
Cricket Ln 27518
Cricket Hill Ln 27513
Cricketfield Ln 27518
Cricketgrass Dr 27513
Crigan Bluff Dr 27513
Crilly Ln 27518
Crimmons Cir 27511
Croatan Cir 27513
Cromwell Ct 27513
Crooked Pine Dr 27519
Cross Keys Ct 27511
Cross Mountain Ct 27519
Crossmore Dr 27519
Crossroads Blvd 27518
Crossroads Manor Ct 27518
Crosswaite Way 27518
Crosswind Dr 27513
Crown Ct 27511
Crown Forest Ct 27518
Croydon Glen Ct 27519
Crystal Ct 27513
Crystal Brook Ln 27513
Culcross Ct 27513
Culpepper Hill Ct 27513
Cumberland Green Dr 27513
Cumulus Ct 27513
Cunningham Ct 27511
Cupola Chase Way 27519

Curson Ct 27513
Cuscowilla Dr 27511
Custer Trl 27513
Cutty Ct 27518
Cuvasion Ct 27519
Cypress Cir 27511
Cypress Creek Ct 27519
Dabney Rd 27511
Dagenham Ln 27518
Dahlia Pl 27511
Daleshire Dr 27519
Dalmeny Dr 27513
Dalrymple Ln 27511
Dancers Pointe Ln 27518
Danforth Dr 27511
Dannor Ct 27511
Dansk Ct 27511
Danton Dr 27518
Darby Gale Dr 27518
Darbytown Pl 27513
Dark Oak Dr 27513
Darlena Ct 27511
Darlington Oak Dr 27519
Darrington Dr 27513
Davenbury Way 27513
Davidson Point Rd 27513
Davis Dr 27519
Davis Grove Cir 27519
Daybreak Bluff Dr 27519
Deanscroft Ct 27518
Debra Dr 27511
Debrock Ct 27519
Dechlan Ln 27513
Declair Ct 27513
Decourley Ln 27513
Decree Pl 27519
Deep Gap Run 27519
Deer Isle Ct 27519
Deer Park Ln 27518
Deer Valley Dr 27519
Deerfield Dr 27511
Deerwalk Ct 27513
Degas Ct 27511
Del Mar Oaks Dr 27519
Del Rio Dr 27519
Del Webb Ave 27519
Delba Ct 27519
Delchester Ct 27513
Delmar Rd 27511
Delta Ct 27513
Delta Downs Dr 27519
Denham Walk Ct 27518
Dennison Ln 27519
Deodora Ct 27513
Desert Tree Ct 27519
Deshire Mist Ln 27519
N & S Devimy Ct 27511
Devine Way 27511
Devon Ave 27511
Devonbrook Ln 27518
Devonhall Ln 27518
Dewberry Ct 27518
Dewitt Ct 27513
Dillard Dr 27518
Dilworth Ct 27513
Dirkson Ct 27511
Disraeli Dr 27513
Dittfield Pl 27519
Divot Ln 27513
Dixieland Trl 27519
N Dixon Ave 27513
S Dixon Ave 27511
Dockside Pl 27511
Doctrine Way 27519
Dogwood St 27511
Dometh Ct 27519
Dominion Hill Dr 27519
Donaldson Ct & Dr 27511
Donna Pl 27513
Dorchester Pines Ct 27511
Doric Ct 27519
Dorothy Dr 27511
Dorset Dr 27511
Douty Ct 27519
Dove Cottage Ln 27519
Dovershire Ct 27513
Dowell Dr 27511
Dowington Ln 27519
Down East Pl 27519
Downing Forest Pl 27519
Downing Glen Dr 27519
Doylin Dr 27511
Drakeford Dr 27513
Drakewood Pl 27518
N & S Drawbridge Ln 27513
Draymore Way 27519
Dresden Meadow Ct 27519
Drexelbrook Ct 27519
Drummond Pl 27511
Dry Ave 27511
Drysdale Ct 27511
Drystack Way 27519
Drywood Pl 27513
Dub Ct 27511
Dublin Woods Dr 27513
Duck Mill Cir 27519
Duckhead Pt 27518
Duckwood Ln 27518
Duden Ct 27513
Duke St 27511
Dumbarton Ct 27511
Dumbledore Ct 27519
Dumnonia Ct 27513
Dunbar Ct 27511
Dunblane Ct 27511
Duncan Hill Ct 27518
Duncan Vale Way 27511
Duncansby Ct 27511
Dundalk Way 27511
Dundee Ct 27511
Dunedin Ct 27511
Dungarven Loop 27513
Dunhagan Pl 27511
Dunnellon Ln 27519
Dunnet Ct 27511
Dunsford Pl 27511
E Durham Rd
100-330 27513
331-399 27511
W Durham Rd 27513
Durington Pl 27518
Dursley Way 27519
Duryer Ct 27511
Dutchess Dr 27513
W Dutton Ct 27513
E & W Dynasty Dr 27513
Eagle Ct 27511
Eagle Meadow Ct 27519
Eagle Swoop Ct 27513
Eagles Nest Ct 27513
Eaglesham Way 27513
Earhart Cir 27511
Earl Dr 27511
Earnscliff Ct 27519
Easton Grey Loop 27519
Eaton Pl 27513
Echo Pass Ct 27513
Echowood Ln 27518
Ecklin Ln 27519
Eclipse Dr 27518
Ed Simmons Ct 27511
Edenhurst Ave 27513
Edgehill Pkwy 27513
Edgemore Ave 27519
Edinburgh Dr 27511
Edinburgh South Dr 27511
Edmonton Ct 27518
Elan Hall Rd 27519
Elderberry Hill Ct 27513
Eldridge Loop 27519
Electra Dr 27513
Elgin Ct 27511
Elkton Green Ct 27519
Ellsworth Pl 27511
Ellynn Dr 27511
Elm St 27511
Elmview Dr 27519
Elstow Ct 27519
Elverson Pl 27519
Emerald Downs Rd 27519
S Emerrall Trl 27518
Emery Gayle Ln 27519
Emile Zola Dr 27511
Empire Cir 27513
Empress Ln 27513
Endeavor Way 27513
Endhaven Pl 27519
Enfield Grant Ct 27519
Enfield Hill Dr 27519
Enfield Ridge Dr 27519
English Cottage Ln 27518
Ennis Creek Ln 27513
Environmental Way 27519
Epping Way 27511
Equestrian Ct 27513
Erskine Ct 27511
Escher Ln 27511
Escott Ct 27518
Esk Ct 27511
Espirit Ct 27519
Esplanade Ct 27511
Esquire Ln 27513
Essex Forest Dr 27518
Estes Ct 27511
Ethans Glen Ct 27513
Eton Hall Ln 27519
Euphoria Cir 27519
Evans Rd 27513
Evans Estates Dr 27513
Evans Farm Rd 27519
Evanshire Dr 27513
Evanvale Ct 27518
Evert Dr 27511
Excalibur Ct 27513
Executive Cir 27511
Exeter Ct 27511
Eyemouth Ct 27513
Faculty Ave 27511
Fairbanks Rd 27513
Fairchild Downs Pl 27518
Faircloud Ct 27513
Fairfax Ln 27513
Fairfield Ln 27511
Fairgreen Way 27511
Fairgrove Way 27511
Fairlane Rd 27511
Fairview Rd 27511
Fairway Valley Ct 27513
Fairwinds Dr 27518
Falcone Pkwy 27511
Falkirk Ct 27511
Fallen Acorn Cir 27519
Fallen Cedar Ln 27513
Fallen Elm Ave 27513
Fallsworth Dr 27513
Faraday Ct 27518
Farm Brook Dr 27518
Farmington Woods Dr 27511
Farmstead Dr 27511
Farren Ct 27511
Farrow Glen Loop 27519
Fawley Ct 27519
Fawn Ct 27513
Felspar Way 27518
Fenmore Pl 27519
Fentress Ct 27519
N & S Fern Abbey Ln 27518
Fern Bluff Way 27518
Fern Meadow Dr 27513
Fern Ridge Dr 27518
Ferncrest Ct 27519
Ferncroft Ct 27519
Fernglen Pl 27511
Fernlea Ct 27511
Fernwood Cir 27511
Ferrell St 27513
Ferris Wheel Ct 27513
Fetzer Ct 27513
Field St 27513
Fieldbrook Ct 27519
Fifemoor Ct 27518
Fifer Ct 27511
Filtrona Ct 27519
Finnbar Dr 27519
Finnway Ln 27519
Finsbury Fields Ct 27519
Firetree Ln 27513
Firth Glen Dr 27519
Fishers Creek Ct 27513
Flemington Ct 27518
Fletcher Ct 27511
Flintlock Ct 27513
Flora Mcdonald Ln 27511
Flora Springs Dr 27519
Fly Bridge Dr 27519
Flying Hills Cir 27513
Flying Leaf Ct 27513
Foilage Cir 27518
Foliage Cir 27518
Folklore Way 27519
Footbridge Pl 27519
Foresight Dr 27519
Forest Brook Dr 27519
Forest Edge Dr 27518
Forest Green Dr 27511
Forest Hills Ct 27511
Forest Run Pl 27518
Forest Wind Way 27513
Fort Worth Ct 27519
Foscoe Ln 27513
Fountain Brook Cir 27511
Fountain Wynd Ct 27519
Fox Ct 27513
Fox Briar Ln 27518
Fox Den Ct 27513
Fox Horn Run 27511
Fox Squirrel Ct 27518
Fox View Pl 27511
Foxcrest Ct 27513
Foxdale Grant Ct 27519
Foxdale Ridge Dr 27519
Frances Green Ln 27519
Francisca Ln 27511
Frank Page Dr 27511
Franklin Chase Ct 27518
Franklin Heights Rd 27518
Franklin Hills Pt 27519
Franklin Manor Ln 27519
Franks Creek Dr 27518
Freeport Dr 27519
Frehold Ct 27519
Frenchmans Bluff Dr 27513
Fresno Pl 27513
Fringe Tree Ct 27519
Frohlich Dr 27513
Front Ridge Dr 27519
Frontgate Dr 27519
Frontier Ct 27513
Frostwood Dr 27518
Fryar Creek Dr 27519
Fryars Frontier Trl 27519
Futrell Dr 27519
Fyfe Ct 27511
Gables Point Way 27513
Gallberry Dr 27519
Gallop Rd 27513
Galsworthy St 27518
Galveston Ct 27513
Gambardelli Ct 27519
Garendon Dr 27519
Gatehouse Dr 27511
Gatepost Ln 27513
Gatestone Ct 27518
Gathering Park Cir 27519
Gayle Cir 27513
Gearrland Ln 27518
Geddy House Ln 27519
Gentlewoods Dr 27518
Georgian Hills Dr 27519
E & W Gerrell Ct 27511
Gettysburg Dr 27513
Gibson Creek Pl 27519
Gifford Ct 27511
Gillespie Ct 27513
Gillinder Pl 27519
Gilmanton Rd 27519
Ginger Wood Ln 27518
Gingergate Dr 27519
Giovanni Ct 27518
Gisborne Ct 27519
Giverny Pl 27513
Glade Park Rd 27518
Glasgow Rd 27511
Glebe Way 27519
Glen Abbey Dr 27513
Glen Alpine Cir 27513
Glen Bonnie Ln 27511
Glen Echo Ln 27518
Glen Hearth Ct 27518
Glen Mavis Ct 27518
Glenaire Cir 27511
Glenbrae Ct 27518
Glenbuckley Rd 27511
Glendale Dr 27511
Glendon Way 27519
Glengarry Dr 27511
Glenhigh Ct 27511
Glenhope Ct 27511
Glenmore Rd 27519
Glenolden Ct 27513
Glenrose Ln 27518
Glensford Way 27513
Glenstone Ln 27518
Gold Meadow Dr 27513
Gold Point Dr 27519
Golden Harvest Loop 27519
Goldenrod Dr 27513
Goldenthal Ct 27519
Goldwood Ct 27513
Good Hope Church
Rd 27519
Good Wood Cir 27513
Gooseneck Dr 27513
Gordon St 27511
Gorecki Pl 27513
Gorge Ct 27518
Gosling Way 27519
Govan Ln 27511
Grace Hodge Dr 27519
Gracewood Ct 27513
Grahamwood Ct 27519
Granby Ct 27511
Grande Classic Way 27513
Grande Harmony Pl 27513
Grande Heights Dr 27513
Grande Meadow Way 27513
Grande Sky Ct 27519
Grande Valley Cir 27513
Grandtree Ct 27519
Grannon Ct 27519
Grant Forest Ln 27519
Gravel Brook Ct 27519
Gray St 27513
Gray Mares Ln 27518
Gray Owl Garth 27511
Graywick Way 27513
Great Lake Dr 27519
Great Point Pl 27513
Green Alder Ct 27519
E & W Green Forest
Dr 27518
Green Hope School
Rd 27519
Green Level Rd 27513
Green Level Church
Rd 27519
Green Level Mh Park 27519
Green Level To Durham
Rd 27519
Green Level West Rd 27519
Green Park Ln 27518
Greenfield Knoll Dr 27519
Greengate Ct 27511
Greenhaven Ln 27518
Greenmont Ln 27511
Greenock Ct 27511
Greenstone Ln 27518
Greensview Dr 27518
Greenway Overlook 27518
Greenwood Cir & Dr 27511
Gregory Dr 27513
Gregory Manor Ct 27518
Gregson Dr 27511
Grendon Pl 27519
Grey Bridge Row 27513
Grey Fox Ct 27511
Grey Horse Dr 27513
Greycliff Ct 27518
Greyfriars Ln 27518
Greygate Pl 27518
Greyhorne Way 27519
Greymist Ln 27518
Greystone Crest Way 27519
Griffis St 27511
Grimstead Cir 27511
Grisdale Ln 27513
Grist Valley Ln 27518
Grogans Mill Dr 27519
Grove Club Ln 27513
Grove Hall Ct 27513
Gucci Dr 27518
Guernsey Trl 27518
Gwinnett Pl 27518
Hab Tower Pl 27513
Haddington Dr 27511
Haddonfield Ln 27513
Hadley Creek Dr 27519
Hafton Ct 27518
Hagan Ct 27511
Halcyon Meadow Dr 27519
Halesworth Dr 27511
Haley House Ln 27519
Halls Mill Dr 27519
Halpen Dr 27513
Hamilton Ct 27511
Hamilton Hedge Pl 27519
Hampshire Ct 27511
Hampton Lee Ct 27513
Hampton Valley Rd 27511
Hanahan Ct 27513
Haniman Park Dr 27513
Hanover Pl 27511
Harbin Ridge Ct 27519
Harbor Creek Dr 27511
Hardaway Ct 27513
Hardenbrook Ct 27519
Harlon Dr 27511
Harmony Hill Ln 27513
Harris Ct 27511
N Harrison Ave
100-199 27511
200-2199 27513
S Harrison Ave 27511
Harrison Oaks Blvd 27513
Harsworth Dr 27519
Harvest Creek Pl 27518
Harvest Row Ct 27513
Hassellwood Dr 27518
Hastings Pl 27511
Havensite Ct 27513
Havers Dr 27518
Haversham Ct 27513
Haverstock Ct 27513
Hawk Tree Ln 27518
Hawks Nest Ct 27513
Hawksong Pl 27518
Haywood Hall Ln 27519
Headlands Ln 27518
S Hearanne Dr 27519
Heart Pine Dr 27518
Heartsbourne Pl 27513
Heater Dr 27511
Heathers Gln 27511
Heathmere Ct 27518
Heathmoor Ln 27513
Heathridge Ln 27513
Hebride Ct 27513
Heck Andrews Way 27519
Hedgerow Ct 27513
Hedgewood Ct 27519
Hedspeth Ln 27519
Hedwig Ct 27518
Heidinger Dr 27511
Helmsdale Dr 27511
Hemingford Grey Ct 27518
Hemlock St 27513
Hempstead Ct 27513
Hendricks Rd 27519
Hennigan Dr 27519
Heralds Way 27519
Hereford Ln 27518
Heritage Ct 27513
Heritage Pines Dr 27519
Hertfordshire Ct 27511
Hesler Ct 27519
Hewespoint Ct 27519
Hiawatha Ct 27513
Hickory St
200-299 27511
400-499 27513
Hickorywood Blvd 27519
Hidden Bluff Ln 27513
Hidden Oaks Dr 27513
Hidden Quail Ct 27519
Hidden Rock Ct 27513
Hidden Springs Rd 27513
High Country Dr 27513
High House Rd
100-199 27511
200-1799 27513
1900-2499 27519
High Meadow Dr 27511
High Pine Ct 27513
High Slope Dr 27518
Highclere Ln 27518
Highcroft Dr 27519
Highfalls Ct 27519
Highfield Ave 27519
Highgate Oak Dr 27519
Highland Trl 27511
Highland Commons Ct 27511
Highland Manor Pl 27511
Highland Village Dr 27511
Highlands Bluffs Dr 27518
Highlands Lake Dr 27518
Highloch Ct 27511
Highstone Rd 27519
Highwood Pines Pl 27519
Hilary Pl 27513
Hilda Grace Ln 27519
W Hill Dr 27519
Hill Rise Pl 27519
Hilliard Ln 27519
Hilliard Forest Dr 27519
Hillsboro St 27513
Hillsdale Ct 27511
Hilltop View St 27513
Hillview Dr 27511
Hilsdorf Ct 27513
Hindsight Dr 27519
Hobblebrook Ct 27518
Hofman Ct 27519
Hogans Valley Way 27513
Holland Bend Dr 27519
Hollingsworth Ct 27513
Holloway St 27513
Hollowoak Ct 27513
Hollowridge Ct 27519
Holly Cir 27511
Holly Hill Ct 27511
Hollycliff Ln 27518
Holmhurst Ct 27519
Holsten Bank Way 27519
Holt Rd 27519
Holt St 27511
Holtz Ln 27511
Homestead Dr 27513
Honeysuckle Ln 27513
Honeywood Ct 27518
Hopewell Downs Ln 27519
Horatio Ct 27519
Hornchurch Loop 27519
Horne Creek Ct 27519
Horsepond Ct 27513
Hortons Creek Rd 27519
Hosta Lily Ct 27513
Houndschase Run 27513
Hounslow Ct 27518
Houston Cir 27513
Howard Rd 27519
Howard Grove Pkwy 27519
Howland Ave 27513
Hoy Ct 27511
Hudson Ct 27511
Huger Ln 27513
Hunter St 27511
Hunter Park Ct 27511
Hunters Xing 27518
Hunters Point Way 27511
Hunting Chase 27513
Huntington Cir 27513
Huntington Wood Ct 27519

Huntly Ct 27511
Huntsmoor Ln 27513
Huntsworth Pl 27513
Huntwood Ln 27511
Hyde Park Ct 27513
Hydon Dawn Ln 27518
Illicium Ct 27518
Imperial Rd 27511
Indian Elm Ln 27519
Indian Wells Rd 27519
Indigo Dr 27513
Indigo Ridge Pl 27519
Innisbrook Ct 27513
Inverleigh Dr 27513
Inverness Ct 27511
Iowa Ln 27511
Iron Hill Dr 27519
Iverton Ln 27519
Ivy Ln 27511
Ivy Tree Pl 27519
Ivyshaw Rd 27519
Ivywood Ln 27518
Jade Hill Dr 27519
N & S Jaguar Ct 27513
Jamerson Rd 27519
James Jackson Ave 27513
James River Rd 27511
Jamestown Ct 27511
Jamie Ct 27511
Janey Brook Ct 27519
Jaslie Dr 27518
Jason Ct 27511
Java Ct 27519
Javelin Ct 27513
Jefferson Dr 27511
Jenks Rd 27519
Jenks Carpenter Rd 27519
Jerry Dr 27511
Jersey Ridge Rd 27518
Jesnick Ln 27513
Jessfield Pl 27519
Jewel Creek Dr 27519
Jo Anne Cir 27513
Jockey Club Cir 27519
Jodhpur Dr 27513
Joel Ct 27513
John Deere Run 27513
E & W Johnson St 27513
Joliesse Ln 27519
N & S Jones St 27511
Jones Franklin Rd 27518
Joppa Ct 27513
Jordan Creek Dr 27519
Joseph Pond Ln 27519
Joshua Glen Ln 27519
Joshua Tree Ct 27519
Joust Ct 27513
E & W Jules Verne
Way 27511
Juliet Cir 27513
Kaladar Ct 27513
Kalida Ct 27513
Kalmia Ln 27518
Kamprath Pl 27519
Karen Ct 27511
Karpen Ln 27519
Katahdin Way 27519
Kathryn St 27511
Katie Ln 27519
Katy Stella Dr 27519
Kazmann Ct 27513
Kc Farm Rd 27519
Keating Pl 27518
Keaton Ridge Ct 27519
Keener St 27511
Keeton Ln 27511
Keisler Dr 27518
Keith Ct & Dr 27511
Keithwood Ln 27511
Kelekent Ln 27518
Kelly Springs Ct 27519
Kelso Ct 27511
Kelty Ct 27511
Kemper Ln 27518
Kempmill Ct 27519
Kempthorne Rd 27519
Kempwood Dr 27513
Kenbridge Ln 27511
Kendleton Pl 27518
Kendlewick Dr 27511
Kenmure Ct 27511
Kennicott Ave 27513
Kennondale Ct 27519
Kensbury Cir 27513
Kensington Dr 27511
Kensington Hill Way 27518
Kensley Haven Ct 27519
Kent Dr 27511
Kerrwood Ln 27513
Ketrick Ct 27519
Kettering Ln 27511
Kettlebridge Dr 27511
Kettlewell Ct 27519
Kevin Way 27511
Key West Mews 27513
Keystone Dr 27513
Kiawah Dr 27513
Kiernan Choice 27511
Kilarney Dr 27511
Kilarney Ridge Loop 27511
Kilbreck Dr 27511
Kildaire Farm Rd
200-1799 27511
1801-1897 27518
1899-3899 27518
Kildaire Woods Dr 27511
Kildonan Pl 27511
Killam Ct 27513
Killearn Mill Ct 27513
Killingsworth Dr 27518
Kilmayne Dr 27511
Kilmorack Dr 27511
Kilmory Dr 27511
Kimbolton Dr 27511
Kindletree Ct 27513
Kindred Way 27513
Kinellan Ln 27519
King St 27513
King Charles Ln 27511
King Edward Ct 27511
King George Loop 27511
King Henry Ct 27511
King James Ct 27513
Kings Arm Way 27518
Kings Fork Rd 27511
Kingsclere Dr 27511
Kingsford Dr 27518
Kingsmill Rd 27511
Kingston Grove Dr 27519
Kingston Ridge Rd 27511
Kingswood Dr 27513
Kingussie Ct 27511
Kinnaird Ln 27511
Kinsey Cir 27511
Kirkcaldy Rd 27511
W Kirkfield Dr 27518
Kirkshire Cir 27511
Kirkwall Pl 27511
Knight Ave 27511
N & S Knightsbridge
Rd 27513
Knotts Valley Ln 27519
Korbel Pl 27513
Kornegay Pl 27513
Koster Hill Pl 27518
Kramer Ct 27511
Kristin Ct 27513
Kronos Ln 27513
Kyle St 27511
Kylemore Cir 27513
Kylie Savannah Ct 27511
La Quinta Ct 27518
Laconia Woods Pl 27519
Lacoste Ln 27511
Lake Dr 27513
N Lake St 27511
S Lake St 27511
Lake Brandt Dr 27519
Lake Cliff Ct 27513
Lake Grove Blvd 27519
Lake Hickory Ct 27519
Lake Hollow Cir 27513
Lake Norman Dr 27519
Lake Pine Dr 27511
Lake Tillery Dr 27519
Lakeleaf Ct 27518
Lakeside Lofts Cir 27513
Lakeside View Ct 27513
Lakewater Dr 27511
Lakeway Ct 27511
Lalex Rd 27519
Lamarack Way 27518
Lamlash Ln 27511
Lanark Ct 27511
Lancer Dr 27519
Landing Ln 27511
Landsdowne Ct 27519
Landser Ct 27519
Landuff Ct 27519
Lane Dr 27511
Langdale Pl 27513
Langford Valley Way 27513
Langston Mill Ct 27518
Langston Pond Rd 27518
Lanigan Pl 27513
Lantana Cir 27513
Lantern Green Ct 27518
Lantern Ridge Ln 27519
Lapis Ln 27519
Laramie Ct 27513
Large Oaks Dr 27518
Larkhall Ct 27511
Larkspur Ln 27513
Larkwood Ln 27518
Lasky Ct 27511
Lathbury Landing Way 27513
Laughridge Dr 27511
Laura Duncan Rd 27513
Laurel Branch Dr 27513
Laurel Garden Way 27513
Laurel Hollow Pl 27513
Laurel Oak Ct 27519
Laurel Park Pl 27511
Laurel Wreath Ln 27519
Laurelwood Ln 27518
E & W Laurenbrook
Ct 27518
Laurie Ln 27513
Lavender Ct 27513
Laver Dr 27511
Lavewood Ln 27518
Lawnwood Ct 27519
Lawrence Rd 27511
Lazy Dee Dr 27519
Leblanc Ct 27513
Leckford Way 27513
Ledgestone Way 27519
Ledsome Ln 27511
Lee Cir 27511
Leeward Ct 27511
Legacy Village Dr 27518
Legault Dr 27513
Legend Oaks Ct 27513
Leinbach Ct 27513
Leisure Ct 27511
Leith Meadow Ct 27511
Lelcester Ct 27519
Lendl Ct 27511
Leonard Christian Rd 27519
Level Ridge Dr 27519
Lewey Dr 27519
Lewey Brook Dr 27519
Lewey Stone Ct 27519
Lewiston Ct 27513
Lexington Ct 27511
Liberty Cliff Dr 27519
Lifeson Way 27519
Lighthouse Way 27511
Lilly Atkins Rd 27518
Lily Creek Dr 27518
Lime Creek Ct 27519
Linda Ct & Dr 27513
Lindemans Dr 27519
Linden Park Ln 27519
Lindenthal Ct 27513
Lindsey Ave 27519
Linecrest Ct 27518
Links End Dr 27513
Linton Ct 27511
Linton Banks Pl 27513
Linville Gorge Way 27519
Linville River Rd 27511
Lions Gate Dr 27518
Lions Mouth Ct 27518
Lipford Dr 27519
Lippershey Ct 27513
Listening Ridge Ln 27519
Listokin Ct 27519
Littleford Ln 27519
Lively Ct E & W 27511
Livingstone Dr 27513
Loch Bend Ln 27518
Loch Cove Ln 27518
Loch Haven Ln 27518
Loch Highlands Dr 27518
Loch Lomond Cir 27511
Loch Pointe Dr 27518
Loch Ryan Way 27513
Loch Stone Ln 27518
Loch Vale Ln 27518
Lochberry Ln 27518
Lochcarron Ln 27511
Lochfield Dr 27518
Lochinvar Ct 27511
W Lochmere Dr 27518
Lochmere Forest Dr 27518
Lochness Ln 27511
Lochside Dr 27518
Lochview Dr 27518
Lochwood East Dr 27518
Lochwood West Dr 27518
Lockheed Cir 27513
Logan Cir 27511
Lomond Ln 27518
London Plain Ct 27513
Lone Eagle Ct 27513
Lone Star Way 27519
Lonesome Pine Dr 27513
Long Shadow Ln 27518
Longbridge Dr 27518
Longchamp Ln 27519
Longhurst Ct 27519
Longleaf Pl 27518
Longstock Ct 27513
Lord Dr 27511
Lord Byron Ct 27513
Lord Levens Ln 27519
Lost Tree Ln 27513
Louben Valley Ct 27513
Louis Stephens Dr 27519
Love Valley Dr 27519
Lucent Ln 27518
Lucia Ln 27519
Ludgate Ct 27519
Ludington Ct 27513
Ludlow Ct 27513
Ludstone Ct 27513
Luke Meadow Ln 27519
Lulworth Ct 27519
Lutterworth Ct 27519
Luxon Pl 27513
Lyerly Ln 27511
Lyncroft Ln 27519
Lynden Valley Ct 27519
Lynn Ct 27511
Lyric Ct 27519
Mabley Pl 27519
Macalyson Ct 27511
Macarthur Dr 27513
Macclamrock Ct 27518
Macduff Ct 27511
Macedonia Rd 27518
Macedonia Lake Dr 27518
Macgregor Pines Dr 27511
Mackenan Dr 27511
Maclaurin St 27518
Macon Dr 27511
Madison Ave 27513
Madison Grove Pl 27519
Madison Square Ln 27513
Madondel Dr 27513
Madrigal Ct 27513
Magalloway Dr 27519
Magerton Ct 27511
Magnolia Dr 27513
Magnolia Birch Ct 27519
Magnolia Bloom Ct 27519
Magnolia Song Ct 27519
Magnolia Tree Ct 27518
Magnolia Woods Dr 27518
Mainsail Dr 27511
Majnun Ln 27513
Makefield Ct 27519
Malcolm Valley Pl 27511
Maldon Dr 27513
Maltland Dr 27518
Manassas Gap Pl 27519
Manchester Dr 27511
Mancino Ct 27519
Manhattan Ct 27511
Manifest Pl 27519
Manor Garden Way 27513
Mantra Ct 27513
Maple Ave 27511
Maple St 27513
Maple Hill Dr 27519
Marble Falls Way 27519
Marble Glow Ct 27519
Marble House Ct 27519
Marblecreek Ln 27519
Marbury Ct 27513
Mardonie Reach Ln 27519
Marigold Ridge Dr 27513
W Marilyn Cir 27513
Mariposa Dr 27513
Marjorie Dr 27511
Marksmans Way 27519
Maroubra Loop 27513
Marquette Dr 27513
Marsalis Way 27519
Marsburg Ln 27519
Marsden Ct 27518
Marseille Pl 27511
Marsena Ln 27513
Marshfield Pl 27513
Martin Tavern Rd 27513
Martina Ct 27511
Martinique Pl 27511
Martins Point Pl 27519
Marvista Ct 27518
Master Ct 27513
Matheson Pl 27511
Matilda Pl 27513
Matrix Dr 27513
Maude Ct 27519
Maumee Ct 27513
Maury Odell Pl 27513
Maximillian Ct 27513
Maybole Ct 27511
Mayfair St 27513
NE Maynard Rd 27513
NW Maynard Rd 27513
SE Maynard Rd 27511
SW Maynard Rd
100-1099 27511
1100-1199 27513
Maynard Creek Ct 27513
Maynard Crossing Ct 27513
Maynard Summit Way 27511
Mayodan Dr 27511
Mccartney Ct 27513
Mccloud Ct 27511
Mcconnell Ln 27519
Mccorquodale Ct 27513
Mccoy Ct 27511
Mccrimmon Pkwy 27519
Mcdole Cir 27511
Mcintire Ln 27513
Mcintosh Ct 27511
Mckirkland Ct 27511
N & S Mclean Ct 27513
Mcrae Rd 27519
Mcwaine Ln 27513
Meadow Dr 27511
Meadowglades Ln 27518
Meadowstone Ct 27513
Meadowvale Cir 27519
Medallion Cir 27513
Medcon Ct 27511
Medici Ct 27518
Medlin Dr 27511
Meeting St 27518
Megan Ct 27511
Melanie Ln 27511
Melling Pl 27519
Mellon Ct 27511
Melody Ln 27513
Melvin Jackson Dr 27519
Mentmore Pl 27519
Mercer Grant Dr 27519
Mereworth Pl 27513
Merida Cir 27519
Merlot Ct 27518
Merowe Ct 27513
Merriwood Dr 27511
Merry Hill Dr 27518
Mesquite Ridge Pl 27519
Methven Grove Dr 27519
Metlife Way 27513
Mica Leaf Pl 27519
Michelangelo Way 27518
Michelin Pl 27511
Michigan Ave 27519
Mickey Ln 27513
Middlefield Hill Ct 27519
Middleton Ave 27513
Midenhall Way 27513
Milford Ct 27511
Mill Gate Ln 27519
Millercrest Ln 27519
Millers Creek Dr 27519
Milley Brook Ct 27519
Millhous Dr 27513
Mills Rd 27519
Mills Park Dr 27519
Millsfield Dr 27519
Millsford Hill Pl 27518
Mint Ct 27513
Mint Hill Dr 27519
Mintawood Ct 27519
Minton Valley Ln 27519
Minute Man Dr 27513
Miramar Ct 27513
Mirror Lake Ct 27513
Miss Georgia Ct 27511
Misty Ct 27513
Misty Rise Dr 27519
Misty Springs Ct 27519
Mistymoor Pl 27513
Mittglen Ln 27518
Mixboro Dr 27519
Mixedwood Ct 27518
Mockingbird Ln 27511
Modena Dr 27513
Molly Ct 27511
Monarch Way 27518
Mont De Sion Dr 27513
Montauk Point Pl 27513
Montelena Pl 27513
Montford Hall Ct 27519
Montibello Dr 27513
N & S Montreal Ct 27511
Montville Valley Ct 27519
Monument View Ln 27519
Moravia Ln 27513
Moray Ct 27511
Moreland Ct 27518
Morganford Pl 27518
Morgans Corner Run 27519
Morninghills Ct 27518
Morningside Dr 27513
Morris Branch Ct 27519
Morris Dale Ln 27519
Morrisville Pkwy 27519
Morrisville Carpenter
Rd 27519
Morrow Mountain Dr 27513
Moss Rose Ct 27518
Mosswood Ln 27511
Mount Eden Pl 27518
Mount Pisgah Way 27519
Mount Rogers Cir 27519
Mountain Maple Dr 27519
Mountain Pine Dr 27519
Mountain Vista Ln 27519
Mountbery Ct 27518
Muir Brook Pl 27519
Muir Woods Dr 27513
Murdock Creek Ct 27519
Murphy Dr 27513
Murray Glen Dr 27519
Muscadine Ct 27513
Muses Ct 27513
Musgrove Cir 27518
Musselburgh Dr 27518
Myers Farm Ct 27519
Myrtle Oak Dr 27519
Nanny Reams Ln 27519
Nantucket Dr 27513
Naperville Dr 27519
Napoleon Ct 27511
Natchez Ct 27519
Nathaniel Ct 27511
Nc 55 Hwy 27519
Needle Park Dr 27513
Neilson Ct 27511
Nevins Pl 27519
New Bingham Ct 27513
New Boca Way 27518
New Britain Ct 27511
New Castle Ct 27511
New Deer Ln 27518
New Edition Ct 27511
New Holland Pl 27519
New Hope Church Rd 27519
New Kent Pl 27511
New Londondale Dr 27513
New Milford Rd 27519
New Rail Dr 27513
New Waverly Pl 27518
Newington Hills Way 27513
Newport Cir 27511
Newstead Way 27519
Newton Grove Rd 27519
Niles St 27511
Nimbus Ct 27513
No Record St
199-199 27513
299-299 27519
Noel Ann Ct 27511
Norcross Pl 27513
Norham Dr 27513
Noritake Dr 27513
Normancrest Ct 27519
Normandale Dr 27513
Normandy St 27511
Northampton Dr 27513
Northcote Dr 27519
Northington Pl 27513
Northlands Dr 27519
Northstar Ct 27513
Northwoods Dr 27513
Northwoods Village Dr 27513
Norwell Blvd 27513
Nottely Pl 27519
Nottingham Cir, Ct &
Dr 27511
Nowell Creek Ct 27511
Nugent Dr 27519
Oak St
100-199 27519
600-699 27511
Oak Harbor Ln 27519
Oak Hill Loop 27513
Oak Island Dr 27513
Oak Ridge Dr 27519
Oakley Ct 27511
Oakmist Dr 27513
Oakpond Ct 27513
Oakridge Rd 27511
Oalry Dr 27511
Oberon Ct 27513
Ocala Ct 27513
Ocean Spray Dr 27519
Oceana Pl 27513
Oceanside Ln 27519
Oconee Ct 27513
Odessa Cir 27513
Ohara Ct 27513
Okehampton Ct 27518
Okelly Ln 27511
Okelly Chapel Rd 27519

Old Apex Rd
400-699 27511
700-1699 27513
Old Bridge Ln 27518
Old Dock Trl 27519
Old London Way 27513
Old Place Rd 27519
Old Pros Way 27513
Old Raleigh Rd 27511
Old Reedy Creek Rd 27513
Old Rockhampton Ln 27513
Olde Alphe Cir 27519
Olde Carpenter Way 27519
Olde Tree Dr 27518
Olde Weatherstone Way 27513
Oldham Forest Xing 27513
Olive Pl 27511
Ollivander Dr 27519
Olson St 27511
Olympic Dr 27513
Onyx Creek Dr 27518
Opera Ct 27519
Orangewood Ct 27519
Orbison Dr 27519
Orchard Park Dr 27513
Oregon Cir 27511
Orilla Ct 27513
Orion Ct 27513
Ormsby Ct 27519
Ortons Point Pl 27513
Orum Dr 27513
Oscar Ln 27513
Otmoor Ln 27519
Otter Dr 27513
Otter Cliff Way 27519
Otterbein Ct 27513
Ottermont Ct 27513
Overcup Oak Ln 27519
Overview Ln 27511
Owltown Rd 27519
Oxcroft St 27519
Oxford Pl 27511
Oxford Creek Rd 27519
Oxford Mill Ct 27518
Oxon Ct 27511
Oxpen Ct 27513
Oxpens Rd 27513
Oxyard Way 27519
Oyster Bay Ct 27513
Ozone Ct 27513
Pacoval Pl 27513
Paddy Rock Ct 27518
Padgett Ct 27518
Padgham Ln 27518
Page St 27511
Pahlmeyer Pl 27519
Painted Fall Way 27513
Painted Turtle Ln 27519
Palace Grn 27518
Paladin Pl 27513
Palaver Ln 27519
Palmer Pl 27511
Palmer Meadow Ct 27513
Palmetto Dr 27511
Palmwood Ct 27519
Pamlico Dr 27511
Pande Cir 27511
Panorama Park Pl 27519
Panorama View Loop 27519
Panoramic Ct 27519
Paper Chase Ct 27519
Parable Way 27519
Parchment Ct 27518
Parish House Rd 27513
E & W Park St 27511
Park James Way 27518
Park Oaks Ct 27519
Park Valley Ln 27519
Park Village Dr 27519
Park York Ln 27519
Parkarbor Ln 27519
Parkbow Ct 27519
Parkbranch Ln 27519
Parkbrook Cir 27519
Parkcanyon Ln 27519
Parkcrest Dr 27519
Parkgate Dr 27519
Parkgrove Ct 27519
Parkhollow Ct 27519
Parkknoll Ln 27519
Parkleaf Cir 27519
Parkman Grant Dr 27519
Parkmeadow Dr 27519
Parkmist Cir 27519
Parkmount Cir 27519
Parkrise Ct 27519
Parkroyale Ln 27519
Parkspring Ct 27519
Parkthrough St 27511
Parkton Ct 27511
Parktop Dr 27513
Parktree Ct 27519
Parkview Cir 27511
Parkvine Cir 27519
Parkwalk Ct 27519
Parkway Office Ct 27518
Parkwhisper Ct 27519
Parkwind Ct 27519
Parmalee Ct 27519
Parson Woods Ln 27518
Parsons Ln 27511
Partheni Ct 27519
Passport Way 27513
Pat Dr 27511
Patrick Cir 27511
Peach Orchard Pl 27519
Peachland Dr 27519
Peachtree Point Ct 27513
Pebble Creek Dr 27511
Pebble Loch Ln 27518
Pebble Ridge Farms Ct 27513
Peckskill Ct 27519
Peg St 27511
Pellinore Ct 27513
Peltier Dr 27519
Penchant Ct 27513
Pendren Pl 27513
Penland Ct 27519
Pennsbury Ct 27513
Penny Ln 27511
Penny Rd 27518
Penrose Valley Cir 27518
Penwood Dr 27511
Peranna Pl 27518
Perth Ct 27511
Petty Farm Rd 27519
Phacelia Way 27518
Phauff Ct 27513
Phillips Medical Way 27519
Picardy Village Pl 27511
Pickering Pl 27513
Pickett Ln 27511
Pickett Branch Rd 27519
Picturesque Ln 27519
Piermont Dr 27519
Piershill Ln 27519
Pierside Dr 27519
Pindos Dr 27519
Pine St 27511
Pine Island Dr 27513
Pine Stroll Dr 27513
Pinedale Springs Way 27511
Pinehill Way 27513
Pineland Dr 27511
Pinestone Ct 27519
Pinetuck Ct 27513
Piney Gap Dr 27519
Piney Plains Rd 27518
Pink Acres St 27518
Pinnacle Dr 27518
Pinner Weald Way 27513
Pioneer Ct 27511
Piper Stream Cir 27519
Piperwood Dr 27518
Placid Pl 27518
Planetree Ln 27511
Plantation Dr 27511
Planters Wood Ln 27518
Playford Ln 27519
Pleasants Ave 27511
Plum Branch Dr 27519
Plumtree Way 27518
Plyersmill Rd 27519
Pocono Ln 27513
Point Comfort Ln 27519
Point Harbor Dr 27519
Pointe Crest Ct 27513
Pointer Creek Ct 27519
Polk St 27511
Polperro Dr 27513
Pond St 27511
Pond Bluff Way 27513
Pond Glen Way 27519
Pond Village Ln 27518
Pony Club Cir 27519
Poplar St 27511
Poplar Branch Ln 27519
Poplar Knoll Ct 27519
Poplin Ct 27519
Poppleford Pl 27518
Portnoch Ct 27511
Portrait Dr 27513
Portstewart Dr 27519
Potomac Grove Pl 27519
Potterstone Glen Way 27519
Powder Mill Ct 27518
Powers Ferry Rd 27519
Prairie Meadows Ct 27519
Praxis Way 27519
Precept Way 27519
Presidents Walk Ln 27519
Preston Arbor Ln 27513
Preston Executive Dr 27513
Preston Grove Ave 27513
Preston Oaks Ln 27513
Preston Pines Dr 27519
Preston Ridge Ct 27513
Preston Village Way 27519
Prestonwood Pkwy 27513
Prestwick Pl 27511
Primrose Ln 27511
Prince St 27511
Prince Albert Ln 27511
Prince Farm Rd 27519
Prince Oliver Pl 27519
Prince William Ln 27511
Proctor Woods Ln 27518
Promontory Point Dr 27513
Pueblo Ridge Pl 27519
Purple Sage Ct 27513
Putnam Ln 27519
Quade Dr 27513
Quaid Dr 27513
Quaker Dell Ln 27519
Quality Ln 27513
Quarrystone Cir 27519
Quarter Path 27518
Quartermaine Ct 27513
Quartz Crystal Pl 27519
Queen Elizabeth Dr 27513
Queens Knoll Ct 27513
Queensdale Dr 27519
Queensferry Rd 27511
Quid Ct 27513
Quincy Ct 27511
Rainbow Ct 27511
Rainmist Cir 27513
Raleigh Rd 27513
Ralph Dr 27511
Rams Loop 27519
Ramsey Ct 27511
Ramsey Grant Dr 27519
Ramsey Hill Dr 27519
Ranchero Ct 27513
Randolph Ct 27511
Raphael Dr 27511
Rapid Falls Rd 27519
Rapport Dr 27519
Rattle Snap Ct 27519
Ravendale Pl 27513
Ravenhollow Ct 27518
Ravenna Way 27513
Ravenstone Dr 27518
Rawhide Ct 27513
Realtors Way 27513
Rebecca Cir 27518
Red Bud Ct 27513
Red Field St 27513
Red Stone Ct 27513
Red Top Hills Ct 27513
Redbud Cir 27519
Redfern Dr 27518
Redgate Dr 27513
Reed St 27511
Reedhaven Dr 27513
Reedy Branch Pl 27518
Reedy Creek Rd 27513
Reedy Creek Church Rd 27513
Reeve Hall Dr 27519
Regal Pine Ct 27518
Regency Pkwy 27518
Regency Pl 27511
Regency Forest Dr 27518
Reinhold Ln 27513
Remington Oaks Cir 27519
Renaissance Park Pl 27513
Renoir Ct 27511
Rensford Pl 27513
Renshaw Ct 27518
Repton Ct 27519
Resident Cir 27519
Residents Club Dr 27519
Retford Grant Ct 27519
Reton Ct 27513
Revere Crossing Ln 27519
Revere Forest Ct 27519
Rexford Ln 27518
Rhapsody Ct 27519
Ribbon Ln 27518
Rice Ranch Way 27518
Richard Dr 27513
Richelieu Dr 27518
Richmond Ct 27511
Ridge Hollow Ct 27513
Ridge View Dr 27511
Ridgecrest Rd 27511
Ridgefield Dr 27519
Ridgemont Hill Rd 27513
Ridgepath Way 27511
Riesling Pl 27511
Riggins Mill Rd 27519
Riggsbee Farm Dr 27519
Rigside Pl 27511
Rina Ct 27518
Ringleaf Ct 27513
Riparian Way 27519
Ripley Ct 27513
Ripplewater Ln 27518
Riva Trace Dr 27513
River Bottom Rd 27519
River Pine Dr 27519
River Song Pl 27519
Rivergreen Ct 27518
Riversville Ct 27519
Riverton Pl 27511
Riverwalk Cir 27511
Roanoke Dr 27513
Robbins Reef Way 27513
Robert St 27511
Roberts Rd 27519
Rochelle Rd 27513
Rock Creek Ln 27511
Rock Pointe Ln 27513
Rockhaven Ct 27518
Rockland Cir 27519
Rockland Ridge Dr 27519
Rockport Ridge Way 27519
Rockspray Ct 27513
Rocky Hill Ln 27519
Rodwell Ct 27518
Roebling Ln 27513
Roland Glen Rd 27519
Rolling Springs Dr 27519
Romaine Ct 27513
Ronaldsby Dr 27511
Roni Ct 27519
Ronsard Ln 27511
Rosaler Ct 27519
Rose St 27511
Rose Point Dr 27518
Rose Sky Ct 27513
Rose Valley Woods Dr 27513
Rosebrooks Dr 27513
Rosecommon Ln 27511
Rosecrans Ct 27518
Rosedown Dr 27513
Rosenberry Hills Dr 27513
Rosepine Dr 27519
Rosewall Ln 27511
Ross St 27511
Rossellini Pl 27518
Rosswood Pl 27513
Rothes Rd 27511
Rothschild Pl 27511
Roundtop Rd 27519
Roundtree Ct 27513
Rowley Ct 27519
Royal Berry Ct 27511
Royal Birkdale Dr 27518
Royal Club Dr 27513
Royal Glen Dr 27518
Royal Tower Way 27513
Royce Dr 27518
Rozelle Valley Ln 27519
Rubin Ct 27511
Running Creek Rd 27518
Rushingwater Dr 27513
Russo Valley Dr 27519
Rustic Ridge Rd 27511
Rustic Wood Ln 27518
Ruth St 27511
Rutherglen Dr 27511
Ryan Rd 27511
Rye Ridge Rd 27519
Ryehill Dr 27519
Sabino Dr 27519
Sabiston Ct 27519
Sable Ct 27513
Saddlehorn Ct 27513
Sage Commons Way 27513
Saint Andrews Ln 27511
Saint Brides Ct 27518
Saint Charles Pl 27513
Saint Lazare Dr 27513
Saint Lenville Dr 27518
Salem Ct 27511
Salford Ct 27513
Saltoun Ct 27511
Samuel Cary Dr 27511
Sand Dollar Rd 27519
Sand Pine Dr 27519
Sandy Creek Ct 27519
Sandy Hook Way 27513
Sandy Whispers Pl 27519
Sanger Dr 27519
Santa Fe Trl 27519
Santorini Dr 27519
Sarabande Dr 27513
Sarazen Meadow Way 27513
Sas Campus Dr 27513
Saunders Grove Ln 27519
Savannah Cir 27511
Sawgrass Hill Ct 27519
Scarlet Petal Ln 27519
Scarlet Sky Way 27518
Schaffer Close 27518
Schooner Dr 27519
Schubauer Dr 27513
Scots Cove Ln 27518
Scots Fir Ln 27518
Scott Pl 27511
Scotwinds Ct 27518
Sea Glass Ct 27519
Sea Salt Ct 27519
Seabreeze Ct 27513
Seabrook Ave 27511
Seahorse Ct 27519
Sealine Dr 27519
Sears Farm Rd 27519
Searstone Dr 27513
Seattle Slew Ln 27519
Sedgebrook Dr 27511
Sedgefield Park Ln 27519
Sedgemoor Dr 27513
Sedgman Ct 27511
Selkirk Ct 27511
Selly Manor Ct 27518
Selwood Pl 27519
Selwyn Ln 27511
Sentinel Ferry Ln 27519
Sequoia Ct 27513
Serence Ct 27518
Seth Ct 27511
Settlers Cir 27513
Sevenstone Dr 27513
Severn Ct 27511
Seymour Pl 27519
Seymour Creek Dr 27519
Shadow Bend Ln 27518
Shady Ct 27513
Shady Creek Trl 27513
Shady Meadow Cir 27513
Shaftsberry Ct 27513
Shale Gray Ct 27519
Shannon Oaks Cir 27511
Sheldon Dr 27513
Shepton Dr 27519
Shergold St 27519
Sherringham Ct 27519
Sherwood Ct 27511
Sherwood Forest Pl 27519
Shillings Chase Dr 27518
Shincliffe Ct 27511
Shirley Dr 27511
Shotts Ct 27511
Shriver Ct 27511
Shurling Pl 27519
Sienna Hill Pl 27519
Silk Hope Dr 27519
Silk Leaf Ct 27518
Silo Ct 27513
Siltstone Pl 27519
Silver Fox Ct 27511
Silver Lining Ln 27513
Silver Stream Ln 27519
Silverado Trl 27519
Silverberry Ct 27513
Silverbow Ct 27519
Silverbrook Dr 27513
Silvercliff Trl 27513
Silvergrove Dr 27513
Silverridge Ct 27513
Silverrock Ct 27513
Silverton Ct 27519
Silverwood Ln 27518
Simbury Glen Ct 27519
Sir James Ct 27513
Sir Walker Ln 27519
Skipwyth Cir 27513
Skye Ln 27518
E & W Skyhawk Dr 27513
Skyros Loop 27519
Slate Blue Pl 27519
Slate Creek Pl 27519
Sloan Dr 27511
Small Creek Ln 27518
Smallwood Ct 27513
Sminered Dr 27511
Smiths Knoll Ct 27513
Smokehouse Ln 27513
Smokemont Dr 27513
Snap Turtle Dr 27519
Snapdragon Ct 27513
Snow Camp Dr 27519
Snowy Egret Trl 27518
Snowy Owl Ln 27518
Soccer Park Dr 27511
Solitude Way 27518
Solstice Cir 27513
Solway Ct 27511
Somersby Ct 27519
Sonoma Valley Dr 27518
Sorrell St 27513
Southbank Dr 27518
Southglen Dr 27518
Southhill Dr 27513
Southmoor Oaks Ct 27518
Southwick Ct 27513
Southwold Dr 27519
Spartacus Ct 27518
Spector Ct 27518
Spencer Crest Ct 27513
Spindle Creek Ct 27519
Spinnaker Ct 27519
Spivey Ct 27513
Spring St 27511
Spring Bud Dr 27513
Spring Cove Dr 27511
Spring Green Rd 27519
Spring Hollow Ln 27518
Spring Needle Ct 27513
Spring Ridge Rd 27518
Springberry Ct 27518
Springbrook Pl 27518
Springfork Dr 27513
E & W Springhill Ct 27511
Springland Ct 27519
Springset Dr 27513
Springwater Ct 27513
Springwell Cir 27511
Spruce St 27513
Squire Ct 27511
Stablegate Dr 27513
Stafford Brook Ln 27519
Stags Leap Ct 27519
Stagville Ct 27519
Stamford Dr 27513
Stanley Ct 27513
Stanopal Dr 27511
Stansbury Ct 27518
Stanza Ct 27519
Star Ln 27513
Star Thistle Ln 27513
Starcross Ct 27519
Starden Brook Ct 27519
Steel Trap Ct 27513
Steep Bank Dr 27518
Stephanie Dr 27511
Stephens Rd 27518
Sterling Ridge Way 27519
Sterlingdaire Dr 27511
Stillman Creek Dr 27519
Stokesay Ct 27513
Stone St 27511
Stone Cove Ln 27519
Stone Ferris Ct 27519
Stonebanks Loop 27518
Stonebend Loop 27518
Stonebridge Rd 27518
Stonecrest View Ln 27519
Stonecroft Ln 27519
Stoneford Ct 27513
Stonehollow Ct 27513
Stoneleigh Dr 27511
Stonewater Glen Ln 27519
Stony Point Ln 27511
Storm Ct 27513
Stourbridge Cir 27511
Stowage Dr 27519
Strass Ct 27511
Strath Ln 27518
Strathburgh Ln 27518
Strathorn Dr 27519
Streamview Dr 27519
Strendal Dr 27519
Stromer Dr 27513
Sturdivant Dr 27511
Sudbury Dr 27513
Suffolk Ct 27511
Sugar Hill Pl 27519
Summer Harvest Ct 27519
Summer Lakes Dr 27513
Summerglow Ct 27513
Summerhouse Rd 27519
Summertime Pl 27511
Summerview Ln 27518
Summerwalk Ct 27518
Summerwinds Dr 27518
Summey Ct 27513
Sumter Ct 27519
Sundew Ln 27518
Sunrise Rd 27513
Sunstone Dr 27519
Surrey Ct 27511
Sussex Ln 27511
Suterland Rd 27511
Swallow Hill Ct 27513
Swan Quarter Dr 27519
Swannanoa Cir 27513

Swansboro Dr 27519
Sweetspire Way 27513
Swift Commons Ln 27513
Swiftside Dr 27518
Swiftwater Ct 27513
Swiss Lake Dr 27513
Swiss Stone Ct 27513
Swordgate Dr 27513
Sycamore St 27513
Sykes St 27519
Sylvan Grove Dr 27518
Sylvia Ln 27511
Symphony Ct 27518
Tabula Pl 27513
Tack Ct 27513
Tain Ct 27511
Talking Rock Dr 27519
Talloway Dr 27511
Talon Dr 27518
Talton Ridge Dr 27519
Tamarak Wood Ct 27519
N & S Tamilynn Cir 27513
Tamworth Hill Ln 27519
Tanglewood Dr 27511
Tapestry Ter 27511
Tarbert Ct & Dr 27511
Tarlow Ct 27513
Tasman Ct 27513
Tassle Branch Way 27513
Tate St 27511
Tattenhall Dr 27518
Tavernelle Pl 27519
Tawny Ridge Ln 27513
Taylor Ct 27511
Taylors Pond Dr 27513
Tayport Ct 27511
Teaberry Ct 27519
Teaching Dr 27519
Tealight Ln 27513
Team Hendrick Way 27511
Teatree Ct 27513
Telia Pt 27513
Tellico Pl 27519
Telmew Ct 27518
Temple Gate Dr 27518
Templeton St 27511
Ten Ten Rd 27518
Tenbury Wells Dr 27518
W Terminal Blvd 27519
Terrace Dr 27511
Terrace Wood Ct 27511
Terrastone Pl 27519
Thamesford Way 27513
Thensia Ct 27513
Thistle Briar Pl 27511
Thomaston Hill Ct 27519
Thoresby Ct 27519
Thorncliff Cir 27513
Thornewood Dr 27518
Thornhurt Dr 27513
Thornton Grant Ct 27519
Thresher Ct 27513
Tibbetts Rock Dr 27513
Ticonderoga Rd 27519
Tiercel Ct 27518
Timber Hitch Rd 27513
Timber Mist Ct 27519
Timber View Ln 27511
Todd St 27511
Tolliver Ct 27511
Tomkins Loop 27519
Toms Creek Rd 27519
Topsail Ct 27511
Torcastle Cir 27513
Torrey Pines Dr 27513
Tower Hamlet Dr 27518
Towerview Ct 27513
Town Creek Dr 27519
Towne Village Dr 27513
Townsend Ct 27518
Township Arbor Rd 27518
Trackers Rd 27513
Tracy Ct 27513
Trafalgar Ln 27513
Trail Bend Ct 27513
Trailing Fig Ct 27513

Trailing Oak 27513
Trailview Dr 27513
Tranquil Dr 27519
Tranquil Sound Dr 27519
Transom View Way 27519
Trappers Run Dr 27513
Trappers Sack Rd 27513
Travertine Dr 27519
Travilah Oaks Ln 27518
Travis Park 27511
Treadwell Ct 27513
Treborman Ct 27519
Trelawney Ln 27519
Trellis Grn 27518
Trembath Ln 27519
Trent Woods Way 27519
Tresa Brook Ct 27519
Triangle Trade Dr 27513
Trident Ct 27518
Triland Way 27518
Trillingham Ln 27513
Trimble Ave 27511
Trimman Pl 27519
Trolleystone Ct 27519
Troon Ct 27511
Troon Village Ln 27511
Tropez Ln 27511
Troycott Pl 27519
Trumbley Ct 27519
Tryon Rd
5801-5997 27518
5999-6900 27518
6902-7398 27518
7201-7299 27511
7301-7399 27518
Tryon Manor Dr 27518
Tryon Towne Cir 27518
Tryon Village Dr 27518
Tryon Woods Dr 27518
Tulliallan Ln 27511
Turk House Ln 27519
Turnberry Ln 27518
Turner Creek Rd 27519
Turquoise Creek Dr 27513
Tussled Ivy Way 27513
Tutbury Pl 27519
Tweed Cir 27511
Twilight Ct 27513
Twin Oaks Pl 27511
Two Creeks Rd 27511
Twyla Rd 27519
Tynemouth Dr 27513
Umstead Hollow Pl 27513
Unaka Ct 27519
Underwood Arbor Pl 27518
Union St 27511
Union Jack Ln 27513
Union Mills Way 27519
Unison Ct 27519
Unity Pl 27518
Upchurch Dead End Rd 27519
Upchurch Farm Ln 27519
Upchurch Meadow Rd 27519
Uplands Creek Dr 27519
Upper Valley Ct 27518
Uprock Dr 27519
Urban Dr 27511
Uxbridge Ct 27513
Valenta Ct 27513
Valley Woods Ln 27513
Valleystone Dr 27519
Vallonia Dr 27519
Vandalia Dr 27519
Vashon Ct 27513
Ve Theyl Ln 27513
Venetian Ct 27518
Ventnor Pl 27519
Vermel Ct 27513
Versailles Dr 27511
Vickie Dr 27511
Vicksburg Dr 27513
Victor Hugo Dr 27511
Victoria Station Ct 27518
Village Cross Way 27518
Village Greenway 27511

Village Orchard Rd 27519
Vinca Cir 27513
Vinecrest Ct 27518
Vineyard Ln 27513
Virens Dr 27511
Virginia Pl 27513
Vishay Ct 27519
Vista Green Ct 27513
Vista Rose Ct 27513
Vyne Ct 27519
Wabash Cir 27513
Wackena Rd 27519
Waco St 27511
Wade Dr 27519
Wade Green Pl 27519
Wadsworth Ct 27519
Wagon Trail Dr 27513
Wake Robin Ln 27519
Wakehurst Dr 27519
Walcott Way 27519
Waldenbrook Ct 27513
Waldo St 27511
Waldo Rood Blvd 27519
Walford Way 27519
N & S Walker St 27511
Walker Stone Dr 27513
Wallsburg Ct 27518
Walmsley Ct 27519
Walnut St
100-1799 27511
1800-2999 27518
Walshingham Ln 27513
Wapner Ct 27519
War Admiral Ct 27519
Ward St 27511
Warley Cir 27513
Warlick Green Ln 27519
Warren Ave 27511
Warson Ct 27519
Warwick Hills Ct 27518
Washington St 27511
Water Hickory Dr 27519
Water Leaf Ln 27518
Waterfall Ct 27513
Waterford Forest Cir 27513
Waterford Lake Dr 27519
Waterloo Station Dr 27513
Waverly Hills Dr 27519
Wax Myrtle Ct 27513
Waxwood Ln 27518
Wayfield Ln 27518
Waylan Hills Dr 27519
Weather Ridge Ln 27513
Weatherbrook Way 27513
Weatherly Pl 27518
Weavers Ridge Dr 27519
Webb St 27511
Webster St 27511
Wedgemere St 27519
Wedonia Dr 27519
Wee Loch Dr 27511
Weeping Beech Way 27518
Weeping Tree Dr 27513
Weingarten Pl 27519
Welchdale Ct 27513
Wellbrook Station Rd 27519
Wellesley Trade Ln 27519
Wellington Ln 27511
Wellington Ridge Loop 27518
Wendy Ct 27511
Wentbridge Rd 27519
N West St 27513
S West St 27511
Westbank Ct 27513
Westbourne Ct 27519
Westfalen Dr 27519
Westhigh St 27513
Weston Pkwy 27513
Weston Estates Way 27513
Weston Green Loop 27513
Weston Oaks Ct 27513
Westongate Way 27513
Westover Hills Dr 27513
Westport Dr 27511
Westside Ct 27511
Westview Cove Ln 27513

Westwind Ct 27511
Wethersfield Dr 27513
Wexwood Ct 27519
Weycroft Ave 27519
Weycroft Grant Dr 27519
Weycroft Ridge Dr 27519
Wheatley Way 27513
Wheatsbury Dr 27513
Wheelwright Pl 27519
Whirlaway Ct 27519
Whisper Creek Ct 27513
Whisper Rock Trl 27519
Whispering Pines Ct 27511
Whisperwood Dr 27518
Whitborn Ct 27511
Whitby Ct 27511
Whitcomb Ln 27518
White Bloom Ln 27519
White Bluff Ln 27513
White Lake Ct 27519
White Lily Ct 27519
White Oak Dr 27513
White Sands Dr 27513
White Sedge Dr 27513
Whiteberry Dr 27519
Whitebridge Dr 27519
Whitehall Way 27511
Whitehaven Ln 27519
Whitemark Ln 27511
Whitlock Ln 27513
Whittlewood Dr 27513
Whittshire Ct 27513
Wickham Pl 27513
Wicklow Ct & Dr 27511
Widdington Ln 27519
Widecombe Ct 27513
Widen Ct 27511
Wigan Cir 27513
Wightman Ct 27511
Wilander Dr 27511
Wild Brook Ct 27519
Wild Weasel Way 27513
Wilkinson Ave 27513
Willenhall Ct 27519
Willesden Dr 27513
William Henry Way 27519
Williams St 27511
Willoughby Ln 27513
Willow St 27511
Willow Thicket Ct 27519
Willowbrook Dr 27511
Willowmere Ct 27513
Willowmist Ct 27519
Wilshire Dr 27511
Wilson Rd 27513
Wimbledon Ct 27511
E Wind Ln 27518
Windance Ct 27518
Windbyrne Dr 27513
Windfall Ct 27513
Winding Pine Trl 27519
Winding Ridge Dr 27518
Windrock Ln 27518
Windspring Ct 27518
Windstream Way 27518
Windswept Ln 27518
Windvale Ct 27518
Windward Ct 27513
Windwick Ct 27518
Windy Peak Loop 27519
Windy Point Ln 27518
Windy Rush Ln 27518
Wineleaf Ln 27518
Winfair Dr 27513
Winfred Dell Ln 27511
Winners Cir 27511
Winslow Ct 27513
Winstead Dr 27513
Winston Hill Dr 27513
Winterborne Dr 27519
Winterbrook Ct 27518
Wintermist Dr 27513
Winwood Dr 27511
Wisdom Dr 27519
Wishaw Ct 27511
Witham Park Ct 27518

Withwyndle Ct 27518
Wittenberg Dr 27519
Wittenham Dr 27519
Wohler Ct 27513
Wollston Ct 27519
Wolverine Rd 27513
Wood St 27513
Wood Forest Dr 27519
Wood Hollow Dr 27513
Wood Lily Ln 27518
Wood Sorrel Way 27518
Woodarbor Cir 27513
Woodbury Ct 27511
Woodcreek Dr 27511
Wooded Hill Way 27519
Woodfield Lake Rd 27518
Woodglen Dr 27518
Woodgrove Ln 27518
Woodham Cir 27513
Woodhue Ln 27518
Woodington Ct 27518
Woodland Ct 27511
Woodland Dr 27513
Woodland Pond Dr 27513
Woodland Ridge Ct 27519
Woodruff Ct 27518
Woodsage Way 27518
N & S Woodshed Ct 27513
Woodside Glen Pl 27519
Woodstar Dr 27513
Woodstream Dr 27518
Woodtrail Ln 27518
Woodway Bluff Cir 27513
Woodwinds Industrial Ct 27511
Wordsmith Ct 27518
Wrenhaven Way 27518
Wrenn Dr
100-148 27511
100-198 27512
101-103 27511
101-199 27512
107-147 27511
149-299 27511
W Wyatts Pond Ln 27513
Wybel Ln 27513
Yates Store Rd 27519
Yellow Birch Dr 27519
Yellowfield Way 27518
Yeovil Way 27513
Ymca Dr 27513
York St 27511
Yorkhill Dr 27513
Yorkshire Dr 27511
Youngsford Ct 27513
Yubinaranda Cir 27511
Zev Summit Ln 27511
Zumbach Way 27513

CHAPEL HILL NC

General Delivery 27514

POST OFFICE BOXES MAIN OFFICE STATIONS AND BRANCHES

Box No.s
1 - 1371 27514
470 - 8895 27515
8840 - 8840 27516
9001 - 10340 27515
16001 - 17314 27516

RURAL ROUTES

02 27514
03, 04, 05, 10, 11, 14, 15, 16, 19 27516
13, 18 27517

NAMED STREETS

Abbey Rd 27516
Aberdeen Dr 27516
Abernathy Dr 27517
Adair St 27514
Adams Way 27516
Adelaide Walters St 27517
Adirondack Way 27517
Adrians Pl 27514
Akin Trl 27516
Alaska Ln 27517
Albany Pt 27517
Albert Rd 27516
Alder Pl 27517
Alderman Dorm 27514
Aldershot Ct 27517
Aldridge Trl 27514
Alexander 27517
Alexander Dr 27514
Alexander Dorm 27514
Alice Ingram Cir 27517
Allard Rd 27514
Alston Dr 27516
Alta Ct 27514
Amazing Grace Ln 27516
Amber Wood Run 27516
Amberidge Dr 27514
Amesbury Dr 27514
Amity Ct 27516
Amy Ln 27516
Andrews Ln 27516
Andys Ln 27516
Angel Way 27516
Angier Dr 27514
Anglese Ct 27516
Ann Ln 27516
Anna Belle Dr 27517
Annabelle Ln 27516
Antler Point Rd 27516
Apple St 27514
Araya Ln 27516
Arbor Creek Ct 27516
Arbor Lea 27517
Arboretum Dr 27517
Arborgate Cir 27514
Arbutus Pl 27517
Arcadia Ln 27514
Archdale 27517
Arlen Park Dr 27516
Arlington St 27514
Arnolds Woods Rd 27516
Arrowhead Rd 27514
Ascot Pl 27517
Ashe Pl 27517
Ashley Ct 27514
Ashley Forest Rd 27514
Aster Pl 27516
Atterbury St 27516
Audley Ln 27517
Audubon Rd 27514
Autumn Dr 27516
Autumn Ln 27516
Autumn Way 27517
Avalon Ct 27514
Avas Loop 27516
Avery 27517
Avery Dorm 27514
Aycock 27517
Aycock Dorm 27514
Azalea Dr & Pl 27517
Baity Hill Dr 27514
Baldwins Ford Rd 27516
Balmoral Pl 27516
Balsam Ct 27514
Balthrope Pl 27517
Banbury Ln 27517
Banks Dr 27514
Banstead Pl 27517
Barbara Ct 27514
W Barbee Chapel Rd 27517
Barclay Rd 27516
Barefoot Dr 27517
Barksdale Dr 27516
Barn Dr 27517
Barnes Dr 27517
Barnhardt Ct 27517
Barnhill Pl 27514
Barrington Hill Rd 27516

Barton Ln 27516
Bartram Dr 27517
Baskerville Cir 27517
Basnight Ln 27516
Basswood Ct 27514
Battle Ln 27514
Baxter 27517
Bay Colony Ct 27517
Bayberry Dr 27517
Baynes Ct 27517
Bayswater Pl 27517
Bayview Dr 27516
Baywood Pl 27516
Bear Tree Crk 27517
Bearkling Pl 27517
Beaver Dam Ct 27514
Beaver Dam Rd 27517
Beech Rd 27517
Beecham Way 27517
Beechgrove Ln 27516
Beechridge Ct 27517
Beechtree Ct 27514
Beechwood Cv & Ln 27516
Belfair Way 27517
Bell Cir 27516
Bell Flower Ct 27516
Belmont St 27517
Benbury 27517
Benjamin Dr 27516
Bennett Rd 27517
Bennett Mountain Trce 27516
Bennett Orchard Trl 27516
Bennett Ridge Rd 27516
Bennington Dr 27516
Bent Tree Ln 27516
Benwall Ct 27516
Benwick Ct 27517
Beringer Pl 27516
Berkley Rd 27517
Bernard St 27514
Berry Andrews Rd 27516
Berry Patch Ln 27514
Bethel Hickory Grove Church Rd 27516
Bethlehem Ln 27514
Bickett 27517
Big Branch Rd 27516
Big Meadows Pl 27514
Big Rock Dr 27517
Big Still Rd 27516
Big Woods Rd 27517
Billabong Ln 27516
Billie Holiday Ct 27514
Birch Cir 27517
Birchcrest Pl 27516
Birnamwood Dr 27516
Black Oak Pl 27517
Black Tie Ln 27514
Black Trumpet Rd 27517
Blackberry Cv 27517
Blackcherry Ln 27514
Blacknell Dr 27517
Blackwood Mountain Rd 27516
Blakely Dr 27517
Blissenbach Ln 27516
Bloomsbury Ct 27517
Blue Granite Ct 27514
Blueberry Ln 27516
Bluefield Rd 27517
Bluestone Ct 27514
Bluff Trl 27516
Bobcat Rd 27516
Bolin Hts 27514
Bolin Brook Farm Rd 27516
Bolinas Ct & Way 27517
Bolinwood Dr 27514
Bolton Pl 27516
Bonsail Pl 27514
Booker Creek Rd 27514
Booth Rd 27516
Boothe Hill Rd 27517
Bordeaux Ct 27517
Bost 27517
Botanical Way 27517
Boulder Ln 27514

Street	ZIP
Boulder Bluff Trl	27516
N & S Boundary St	27514
Bowden Rd	27516
Bowling Creek Rd	27514
Boxwood Pl	27517
Boyd	27517
Brace Ln	27516
Bracken Ln	27516
Bradford Pl	27517
Bradley Rd	27516
Bragg	27517
Branch	27517
Branch St	27516
Brandon Rd	27517
Brandywine Rd	27516
Brannon Ct	27516
Branson St	27514
Braswell Ct, Pl & Rd	27516
Breckenridge Pl	27514
Brenda Ct	27516
Brendan Ct	27516
Brewington Ln	27516
Briar Chapel Pkwy	27516
Briar Patch Ln	27516
Briarbridge Ln	27516
Briarbridge Valley Rd	27516
Bridgeton Pl	27514
Bridgewater Ct	27517
Bridle Run	27514
Bridle Spur	27516
Brigham Rd	27517
Bright Sun Pl	27516
Brighton Ct	27516
Brights Way	27516
Brightside Dr	27516
Brightwood Pl	27516
Brisbane Dr	27514
Bristol Dr	27516
Britt	27517
Britt Ct	27514
Brittany Ln	27517
Britton Dr	27516
Broad Leaf Ct	27517
Broadwell Rd	27516
Brogden	27517
Brookberry Cir	27517
Brookfield Dr	27516
Brookford Ct	27516
Brookgreen Dr	27516
Brookhollow Ln	27517
Brooks St	27516
Brookside Dr	27516
Brookstone Ct	27514
Brookview Dr	27514
Broughton	27517
Brown Bear	27517
Bruin Trl	27516
Brunswick Ct	27516
Bruton Dr	27516
Buck Taylor Trl	27516
Buckeye Ln	27516
Buckner Ln	27517
Buena Vista Way	27514
Bugle Ct	27516
Bumphus Rd	27514
Burlage Cir	27514
Burlwood Pl	27516
Burning Tree Dr	27517
Burns Pl	27516
Burnwood Ct	27514
Burnwood Pl	27517
Burrington	27517
Burris Pl	27516
Burton	27517
Bush Creek Ln	27517
Butler Ct	27514
Butler Rd	27516
Butler Glen Dr	27516
Butterfield Ct	27516
Butterfly Ct	27517
Butternut Dr	27514
Buttons Rd	27514
Buxton Ct	27514
Bynum St	27516
Bypass Ln	27517
Bywater Way	27516
Cabernet Dr	27516
Cabin Ln	27517
Caitlin Ct	27516
Cala Lily Ct	27516
Calderon Dr	27516
Caldwell Ext & St	27516
Callard Run	27514
Calm Winds Ct	27517
Calwell Creek Dr	27517
Camden Ln	27516
S Camellia St	27516
E Cameron Ave	27514
W Cameron Ave	27516
Cameron Ct	27516
Cameron Glen Dr	27516
Camille Ct	27516
Camp Cir	27514
Campbell Ln	27514
Cane Valley Ct & Ln	27516
Cannamann Rd	27516
Canopy Ln	27516
Canterbury Ln	27517
Canton Ct	27516
Caprea Ct	27514
Cardiff Pl	27516
Cardinal Ln	27516
Carefree Way	27516
Carl Dr	27516
Carl Durham Rd	27516
Carlton Dr	27516
Carmichael St	27514
Carmichael Dorm	27514
Carmine Ct	27514
Carolina Ave	27514
Carolina Mdws	27517
Carolina Forest Ct & Rd	27516
Carolina Meadows Villa	27517
Carr	27517
Carr St	27516
Carriage Cir	27514
Carriage Way	27517
Carrie Rd	27516
Carson Rd	27517
Carter Walk Way	27516
Carteret	27517
Carver St	27516
Cary	27517
Cascade Dr	27514
Cassidy Ln	27516
Caswell Rd	27514
Catawba Ct	27514
Cates Farm Rd	27516
Catesby Ln	27514
Cattail Ln	27516
Catullo Run	27516
Cedar Ct	27516
Cedar Pass	27514
Cedar St	27514
Cedar Vlg	27516
Cedar Berry Ln	27517
Cedar Breeze Ln	27517
Cedar Brook Way	27516
Cedar Club Cir	27517
Cedar Falls Rd	27514
Cedar Fork Trl	27514
Cedar Hills Cir & Dr	27514
Cedar Lake Rd	27516
Cedar Meadows Ln	27517
Cedar Pond Ln	27517
Cedar Run Ln	27516
Cedar Springs Ln	27516
Cedar Terrace Rd	27516
Cedar Village Rd	27516
Cedarwood Ct	27514
Cedronella Dr	27514
Celastrus Dr	27514
Celeste Cir	27517
Celtic Cir	27516
Central St	27517
Channing Ln	27516
Chapel St	27516
Chapel Hill Creamery Rd	27516
Charles Ln	27516
Charlesberry Cir & Ln	27517
Charleston Ln	27517
Charlock Ct	27514
Charrington Pl	27517
Chase Ave	27514
Chase Park Rd	27516
Chateau Pl	27516
Chatham Dr	27516
Chatham Ln	27514
N Chatham Pkwy	27517
Chatham Downs	27517
Chedworth Ct	27517
Cheekiboy Ln	27516
Cherokee Cir	27514
Cherokee Dr	27517
Cherry	27517
Cherry Laurel Ln	27516
Cherrywood Cir	27514
Chesapeake Way	27516
Chesley Ct & Ln	27514
Chestnut Ln	27514
Chestnut Rd	27517
Chestnut Way	27516
Chicory Ln	27516
Chimeneas Pl	27517
Chinaberry Crse	27516
Chippoaks Dr	27514
Christine Ct	27516
Christopher Dr	27517
Christopher Rd	27514
S Christopher Rd	27514
Church St	27516
Churchill Dr	27517
Circadian Way	27516
N & S Circle Dr	27516
Circle Park Pl	27517
Clarence Dr	27516
Claris Ct	27514
Clark Ct & Rd	27516
Claymore Rd	27516
Clayton Rd	27514
Clearwater Farm Trl	27517
Clearwater Lake Rd	27517
Cleland Dr	27517
Cliffdale Rd	27516
Cliffside Dr	27516
Cloister Ct	27514
Clover Dr	27517
Club Dr	27517
Clyde Rd	27516
Coach Way	27516
Cobb Ter	27514
Cobb Dorm	27514
Cobble Ridge Dr	27516
Cobblestone Ct	27514
Cobblestone Dr	27516
Cobblestone Pl	27516
Coggins Mine Ct	27517
Coker Dr & Ln	27517
Colburn Pt	27516
Colby Pl	27517
Colchester Ct	27517
Cole Dr	27517
Cole Pl	27517
Cole St	27516
Cole Plaza Dr	27517
Colfax Dr	27516
Colleen Ln	27516
Collins Creek Ct & Dr	27516
Collins Mountain Ct & Rd	27516
Collinson Dr	27514
Collums Rd	27516
Colony Ct	27516
Colony Woods Dr	27517
Columbia Pl E	27516
Columbia Pl W	27516
N Columbia St	
100-299	27514
300-999	27516
S Columbia St	27514
Columbia Place Dr	27516
Commons Way	27516
Concord Dr	27516
Concordia Ct	27514
Coneflower Ct	27517
Conner Dr	27514
Connor Dorm	27514
Continental Trailer Park	27517
Cool Spring Dr	27514
Coolidge St	27516
Cooper St	27517
Cooper Glen Pl	27517
Copeland Rd	27516
Copeland Way	27517
Copper Beech Ct	27517
Copper Lantern Dr	27516
Copperline Dr	27516
Corbin Hill Cir	27514
Cornerstone Rd	27516
Cosgrove Ave	27514
Cottage Ln	27514
Cotton St	27516
Cottonwood Ct	27514
Couch Rd	27514
Couer Du Bois Ln	27516
Council	27517
Council Ln	27516
Country Rd	27514
Country Club Rd	27514
Courtney Ln	27516
Covington Dr	27514
Cra Mer Ln	27516
Crabapple Ln	27514
Craborchard Pl	27514
Crabtree Dr	27516
N Crabtree Knls	27514
S Crabtree Knls	27514
Crabtree Ln	27516
Craig	27517
Craig St	27516
Craig Hill Ln	27516
Craige N	27514
Craige Dorm	27514
Crane Meadow Pl	27514
Cranebridge Pl	27517
Crawford Dairy Rd	27516
Creek Ridge Ln	27514
Creek Run Ct	27514
Creek Wood Dr	27514
Creeks Edge	27516
Creekside Ln	27514
Creekstone Dr	27516
Creel St	27516
Crescent Dr	27516
Crescent Ridge Dr	27516
Crest Dr	27516
Crestwood Cir	27516
Crestwood Ln	27517
Crew	27517
Critz Dr	27516
Crofton Springs Pl	27516
Croom Ct	27514
Cross Creek Ct	27517
Cross Creek Dr	27514
Crossland Rd	27517
Crow Holw	27514
Crowther Ct	27514
Crystal Cv	27517
Crystal Springs Ct	27516
Cub Creek Rd	27517
Culbreth Cir & Rd	27516
Culbreth Park Dr	27516
Culp Hill Dr	27517
Cumberland Rd	27514
Curlew Dr	27517
Currie	27517
Curtis Rd	27514
Cynthia Dr	27514
Cypress Rd	27517
D M Dr	27516
Dailwood Ln	27516
Daimler Dr	27516
Dairy Ct	27516
Dairy Glen Rd	27516
Dairyland Rd	27516
Daisy Ln	27516
Daley Rd	27514
Dalton Dr	27517
Damascus Church Rd	27516
Daniel	27517
Danning Dr	27516
Daphne Ct	27516
Darcy Ln	27516
Dark Forest Dr	27516
Darlin Cir	27514
Dartford Ct	27517
Dartmouth Ct	27516
Daventry Ct	27517
David Miller Ct	27517
David Stone Dr	27517
Davie	27517
Davie Cir	27514
Davie Ln	27514
Davis Love Dr	27517
Dawes St	27516
Dawson Rd	27516
Dee St	27517
Deepwood Rd	27514
Deer Path	27516
Deer Ridge Dr	27516
Deerfield Trl	27516
Deerwood Ct	27517
Defoe Ct	27517
Delberts Pond Rd	27514
Della St	27516
Dellocks Rd	27514
Deming Rd	27514
Derby Ln	27514
Deseret Ln	27516
Diana Del Silva Ct	27516
Dickens Ct	27514
Dickerson Ct	27514
Diggs Ln	27517
Dixie Dr & Ln	27514
Dixie Garden Dr	27516
Doar Rd	27514
Dobbins Dr	27514
Dobbs	27517
Dodsons Crossroads	27516
Dogwood Dr	27516
Dogwood Knl	27517
Dogwood Acres Dr	27516
Dollar Rd	27516
Donegal Dr	27517
Dorset Pt	27516
Doug Clark Ln	27516
Douglas Rd	27517
Downing Ct	27516
Dragonfly Trl	27517
Drayton Ct	27516
Drew Ln	27516
Drew Hill Ln	27514
Driskel Ct	27517
Dromoland Rd	27516
Droughton Ct	27517
Drummond	27517
Dublin Rd	27516
Dubose Home Ln	27517
Duchess Ln	27516
Duck Pond Trl	27514
Dudley	27517
N & S Duelling Oaks Dr	27517
Duffys Way	27516
Dunbrook Dr	27517
Duncan Ct	27514
Dundalk Dr	27517
Dunmore Pl	27517
Durant St	27517
Dutchess Ln	27517
Eagle Dr	27517
Eagle Rock Ct	27516
East Dr	27516
Eastbrook Dr	27516
Eastchurch	27517
Eastgreen Dr	27516
Eastowne Dr	27514
Eastridge Pl	27516
Eastwind Pl	27517
Eastwood Rd	27514
Eastwood Lake Rd	27514
Easy St	27516
Echo St	27517
Eco Dr	27516
Eden Ln	27517
Edgar St	27516
Edgehill Pl	27516
Edgestone Pl	27517
Edgewater Cir	27516
Edgewood Rd	27517
Edisto Ct	27514
Edmister Ln	27516
Edwards Dr & St	27516
Edwards Ridge Rd	27517
Ehringhaus	27517
Ehringhaus S	27514
Ehringhaus Dr	27514
Ehringhaus Dorm	27514
Elcombe Ct	27517
Elderberry Dr	27517
Elizabeth St	27514
Elkins Ln	27516
Ellen Pl	27514
N & S Elliott Rd	27514
Ellsworth Ct	27517
Ellsworth Pl	27516
E & W Elm Cir	27517
Elm Grove Ln	27516
Elmdale Dr	27517
Elmstead Pl	27517
Elmwood Cir	27514
Elva Ln	27516
Emerald Crest Pt	27516
Emerson Dr	27514
Emerywood Pl	27516
Emily Ln	27516
Emily Rd	27514
Emory Dr	27517
Endor Dr	27516
Englewood Dr	27514
Environ Way	27517
Ephesus Church Rd	27517
Erwin Rd	27514
Essex Dr	27514
Essex Ln	27517
N Estes Dr	27514
S Estes Dr	
100-126	27514
125-125	27515
127-299	27514
128-298	27514
Estes Drive Ext	27516
S Estes Drive Ext	27517
Esther Dr	27516
Ethel Jean Ln	27516
Eubanks Rd	27516
Europa Dr	27517
Everard	27517
Everett Dorm	27514
Evergreen Ln	27514
Excell Dr	27516
Fair Oaks Rd	27516
Fairfield Ct	27516
Fairfield Dr	27517
Fairlane St	27517
Fairoaks Cir	27516
Faison Rd	27517
Falconbridge Rd	27517
Falkner Dr	27517
Fallen Log	27516
Fallen Oak Ln	27516
Fallenwood Ln	27516
Falling Cedars Dr	27516
Falls Dr	27514
Falmouth Ct	27517
Familiar Way	27516
Fan Branch Ln	27516
Farm House Dr	27516
Farmington Dr	27517
Farmstead Dr	27516
S Farnleigh Dr	27517
Farrington Dr	27514
Farrington Rd	27517
Farrington Mill Rd	27517
Farrington Point Rd	27517
Fawn Ridge Rd	27516
Fellowship Dr	27517
Fells Way	27516
Fenton Pl	27517
Ferguson Rd	27516
Fern Ln	27514
Fern Creek Ln	27516
Fernwood Ct & Ln	27516
Ferrell Rd	27517
N & S Fields Cir	27516
Fieldstone Ct	27514
Finley Forest Cir & Dr	27517
Finley Golf Course Rd	27517
Fireside Dr	27517
Five Forks Rd	27516
Flagstone Ct	27517
Flemington Rd	27517
Floral Dr	27516
Forbush Mountain Dr	27514
Ford Rd	27516
Fordham Blvd	27514
Forest Dr & Gln	27517
Forest Creek Rd	27514
Forest Hill Rd	27514
Forest Knoll Dr	27516
Forest Oaks Dr	27514
Forest Ridge Dr	27514
Forked Pine Ct	27517
Forsyth Dr	27517
Forsythia Ct	27517
Founders Ridge Dr	27517
Fountain	27517
Fountain Ridge Rd	27517
Fowle	27517
Fox Run	27516
Foxboro Ct	27516
Foxfire Dr	27516
Foxglen Ct	27516
Foxhall Pl	27517
Foxlair Rd	27516
Foxridge Ct & Rd	27514
Foxwood Dr	27514
Foxwood Farm Trl	27516
Frances St	27517
Frankie Boy Ln	27516
Franklin Pl	27514
Franklin Rdg	27517
Franklin Sq	27514
E Franklin St	27514
W Franklin St	27516
Fraternity Ct	27516
Freeland Trailer Park	27514
Friar Ln	27517
Friday Ln	27514
Friday Center Dr	27517
Friendly Ln	27514
Gait Way	27516
Galax Ct	27516
Galilean Trl	27516
Gallup Rd	27517
Galway Dr	27517
Garden St	27517
Garden Gate Dr	27516
Gardner Cir	27516
Gates Ln	27516
Gattis	27517
Gemena Rd	27516
Genesis Rd	27516
Genestu Dr	27516
Gentle Winds Dr	27517
George Cir	27514
Gibbon Dr	27516
Gibbs	27517
Gilmore Rd	27516
Gimghoul Rd	27514
Ginger Rd	27514
Ginkgo Trl	27516
Glade St	27516
Glandon Dr	27514
Glen Ln	27514
Glen Eden Ct	27516
Glen Forest Dr	27517
Glen Haven Dr	27516
Glen Lennox Shop Ctr	27517
Glen Ridge Dr	27516
Glenburnie St	27514
Glencrest Pl	27514
Glendale Dr	27514
Glenhill Ln	27514
Glenmore Rd	27516
Glenn Glade	27517
Glenview Pl	27514
Glenwood Dr	27514

Gloucester Ct 27516
Glynmorgan Way 27516
Gold Mine Loop & Rd 27516
Golden Heather 27517
Golden Pond Rd 27516
Golfers Ridge Ct 27517
Gomains Ave 27516
Gone Fishin Rd 27516
Gooseneck Rd 27514
Gore St 27516
Governors Dr 27517
Grace Ave 27517
Gracewood Pl 27516
Gracie Cir 27516
Grady 27517
Graham 27517
N Graham St 27516
S Graham St 27516
Graham Dorm 27514
Grainger Ln 27514
Granger Rd 27516
Granite Mill Blvd 27516
Granite Ridge Rd 27516
Grant St 27516
Granville Rd 27514
Granville Towers Ln E 27514
Grassy Creek Way 27517
Gray Bluff Trl 27517
Graylyn Dr 27516
Graystone Dr & Ln 27514
Great Oaks Pl 27517
Great Ridge Pkwy 27516
Green Cedar Ln 27517
Green Hill Dr 27514
N & S Green Tree Trl 27516
Green Willow Ct 27514
Greenbriar Ct & Sta 27516
Greene St 27516
Greenfield Rd 27516
Greenleaf Dr 27516
Greenmeadow Ln 27514
N Greensboro St 27516
Greentree Trl 27516
Greenview Dr 27516
Greenwood Ln & Rd 27514
Greenwood Road Ext 27514
Grey Squirrel Ct 27517
Grier 27517
Grimes Dorm 27514
Gristmill Ln 27514
Groomsbridge Ct 27516
Grove St 27517
Grovewood Ln 27516
Gunston Ct 27514
Gurnsey Trl 27517
Habitat Cir 27516
Hackney Rd 27516
Haddon Hall Cir 27517
Hairston Rd 27516
Halenewo Rd 27517
Halerner Rd 27516
Hales Wood Rd 27517
Half Dollar Rd 27516
Half Moon Pt 27514
Halifax Rd 27514
S Hamilton Rd 27517
Hammock Bnd 27517
Hampshire Pl 27516
Hampton Ct 27514
Hampton Hill Pl 27517
Hancock Pl 27517
Hanford Rd 27516
Hanft Knls 27514
Hanover Pl 27516
Hansen Creek Rd 27516
Hanser Ct 27516
Hardin Cir 27516
Hardwick Pl 27516
Harlow Bnd 27516
Harrington Hts 27517
Harrington Pt 27516
Harrison Ct 27516
Hartig St 27516
Harvey 27517
Harward Ln 27516
Hasell 27517
Hatch Rd 27516
Hathaway Ln 27514
N Haven Dr 27516
N & S Hawick Ct 27516
Hawk Ridge Rd 27516
Hawkins 27517
Hawksbill Pl 27514
Hawthorn Pl 27517
Hawthorne Ln 27517
Hayden Pond Ln 27517
Hayes Rd 27517
Hayworth Dr 27517
Hazelnut Ct 27516
Hearthstone Ln 27516
Heartwood Dr 27516
Heath Rd 27517
Heather Ct 27517
Heatherwood Dr 27516
Hebrides Dr 27517
Heels Dr 27516
Helmsdale Dr 27517
Hemler Dr 27517
Hemlock Dr 27517
Henderson St 27514
Henley Dr & Rd 27517
Henry Ct 27516
N & S Heritage Cir & Loop 27516
Herndon Woods Rd 27516
Heron Pond Dr 27517
Hibbard Dr 27514
Hickory Dr 27517
Hickory Forest Rd 27516
Hidden Acres Ln 27516
Hidden Oaks Dr 27517
Hidden Valley Dr 27516
Hideaway Dr 27516
High Hickory Rd 27516
High Meadow Rd 27514
High School Rd 27516
Highgrove Dr 27516
Highland Cir 27517
Highland Dr 27514
Highland Dr N 27517
Highland Dr S 27517
Highland Trl 27516
Highland Woods Rd 27517
Highstream Pl 27516
Highview Dr 27517
Hill Dr & St 27514
Hill Creek Blvd 27516
Hillcrest Cir & Rd 27514
Hillsborough Rd 27516
Hillsborough St 27514
Hillside Dr & Pl 27517
Hillspring Ln 27516
Hilltop St 27516
Hillview Rd 27514
Hinton Rd 27517
Hinton James Dr 27514
Hodges 27517
Hoey 27517
Hogan Glen Ct 27516
Hogan Ridge Ct 27516
Hogan Woods Cir 27516
Holden 27517
Holland Dr 27514
Hollow Ct 27516
Hollow Oaks Dr 27516
Holloway Ln 27514
Hollowood Ct 27514
Holly Cir 27514
Holly Ln 27517
Holly Creek Ln 27516
Holly Hill Rd 27516
Holly Ridge Rd 27516
Holman Ln 27516
Holmes 27517
Holt 27517
Homeplace Dr 27517
Homer Ruffin Rd 27516
Homestead Rd 27516
Homewood Dr 27514
Honeypot Ln 27517
Honeysuckle Ct & Rd 27514
Hooper Ln 27514
Hoot Owl Ln 27514
Hotelling Ct 27514
N & S Hound Ct 27516
Houston Rd 27514
Howard Hill Rd 27516
Howell Ln & St 27514
Hubert Herndon Rd 27516
Hudson Rd 27517
Hummingbird Hill Rd 27517
Hunter Hill Pl 27517
Hunter Hill Rd 27516
Hunters Way 27517
Hunters Ridge Rd 27517
Huntingridge Rd 27517
Huntington Dr 27514
Huntsman Ct 27516
Huters Way 27517
Hyde 27517
Indian Camp Rd 27516
Indian Springs Rd 27514
Indian Trail Rd 27514
Indigo Trl 27516
Inverness Way 27516
Iredell 27517
Iris Ln 27514
Iron Mountain Rd 27517
Ironwood Pl 27514
Ironwoods Dr 27516
Irvin Cir 27514
Isley St 27516
Ives Ct 27514
Ivey Rd 27516
Ivy Ct 27516
Ivy Brook Ln 27516
J D Ct 27516
J Villa Dr 27516
Jack Bennett Rd 27517
Jack Gates Cir 27516
Jackie Robinson St 27517
Jackson Cir 27514
James N 27514
James Dorm 27514
Jamestowne Pl 27517
Jarvis 27517
Jason Gln 27516
Jay St 27516
Jay Thomas Dr 27517
Jean Ct 27514
Jefferson Choice 27516
Jeremiah Dr 27517
Jewell Dr 27516
Jo Mac Rd 27516
Joels Way 27517
Joes Dr 27517
Johns Woods Rd 27516
Johnson Ln & St 27516
Johnson Mobile Home Park 27516
Jolyn Pl 27517
Jonan Ct 27516
Jones St 27514
Jones Branch Rd 27517
Jones Creek Pl 27516
Jones Ferry Rd 27516
Jordan Hls 27517
Jordan Lake Mh Park 27517
Joyner Dorm 27514
Jubilee Dr 27516
Juliette Ct 27516
Juniper Pl 27514
Justice St 27516
Justin Pl 27514
Karen Woods Rd 27516
Karin Ct 27514
Keith Ct & Ln 27516
Kelly Ct 27516
Kenan St 27516
Kenan Dorm 27514
Kendall Dr 27517
Kenilworth Pl 27516
Kenmore Rd 27514
Kennebec Dr 27517
Kensington Dr 27514
Kepley Rd 27517
Kestrel Keep Ln 27516
Kildaire Rd 27516
Kileway Dr 27517
Kiley St 27516
Kilkenny Dr 27517
Killington Ct 27517
Kimbolton Pl 27516
Kinetic Way 27516
King Cir 27516
Kings Mill Rd 27517
Kings Mountain Ct 27516
Kingsbury Dr 27514
Kingston Ct & Dr 27514
Kingswood Dr & Ln 27517
Kingswood Apts 27516
Kinsale Dr 27517
Kirkwood Dr 27514
Kit Ln 27516
Kitchin 27517
Knob Ct 27517
Knolls St 27516
Knollwood Dr 27514
Knotty Pine Dr 27517
Knox Way 27517
Korinna Pl 27516
Kornegay Pl 27514
Kousa Trl 27516
Kristie Ln 27516
Labrador Ln 27516
Lacock Rd 27516
Lacrosse Pl 27517
Lady Bug Ln 27516
Lady Di Dr 27516
Laine Rd 27516
Lair Ct 27516
Lake Ct 27516
Lake Ellen Dr 27514
Lake Hogan Ln 27516
Lake Hogan Farm Rd 27516
Lake Manor Rd 27516
Lake Ridge Pl 27516
Lake Valley Trl 27517
Lake Village Trailer Park 27516
N & S Lakeshore Ct, Dr & Ln 27514
Lakeview Trailer Park 27514
Lamont Ct 27517
Lanark Rd 27517
Lancaster Dr 27517
Lance St 27514
Landerwood Ln 27517
Landing Dr 27514
Lanier Dr 27517
Lapin Ln 27516
Lariat Ln 27517
Lark Cir 27517
Larkins 27517
Lashley Rd 27516
Lassens Trl 27516
Lategan Ln 27516
Laura May Ln 27517
Laurel Hill Cir & Rd 27514
Laurel Hill Road Ext 27514
Laurel Springs Dr 27516
Laurens Way 27516
Lavenia Ln 27516
Lea Ct 27516
Leak Ln 27516
Leasar Ct 27516
Leclair St 27517
Ledge Ln 27514
Legacy Ter 27516
Legacy Falls Dr N & S 27517
Legend Oaks Dr 27517
Legends Way 27516
Legion Rd 27517
Legion Road Ext 27517
Leslie Dr 27516
Less Traveled Rd 27514
Leta Dr 27516
Lewis Rd 27514
Lewis Dorm 27514
Lexes Trl 27516
Lexington Cir & Dr 27516
Library Dr 27514
Lil Marcia Ln 27516
Lil Nia Ln 27516
Lina Mae Ln 27516
Lincoln Ln 27516
Lindas Mdws 27516
Linden Rd 27517
Lindsey St 27516
Link Rd 27516
Linnaeus Pl 27514
Litchford Rd 27514
Little St 27517
Little Bend Ct 27517
Little Branch Trl 27517
Little Creek Farm Rd 27516
Little Spring Rd 27516
Littlejohn Rd 27517
Livingston Pl 27516
Lizzie Ln 27516
Loblolly Ln 27516
Lochlaven Ln 27516
Locust Ct 27516
Lombard Dr 27517
Lone Pine Rd 27514
Lonebrook Dr 27516
Long 27517
Long Meadows Rd 27516
Longleaf Dr 27517
E & W Longview St 27516
Longwood Dr & Pl 27514
Louis Armstrong Ct 27514
Lovingood Ln 27516
Lucas Ln 27516
Lucas Farm Ln 27516
Lucille Ln 27516
Lucky Ln 27517
Lucy Ln 27516
Ludwell 27517
Luna Ln 27517
Lynn Rd 27517
Lynwood Pl 27517
Lyons Rd 27514
Lystra Hls, Ln & Rd 27517
Lystra Estates Dr 27517
Lystra Hills Ln 27517
Lystra Preserve Dr 27517
Macrae Ct 27516
Maddry Ct 27516
Madera Ln 27517
Madison Womble Rd 27517
Mafolie Ct 27514
Magnolia Ct 27516
Main St 27516
Majestic Ct 27517
Mallard Ct 27517
Mallette St 27516
Manchester Pl 27516
Mangum Ct 27517
Mangum Dorm 27514
Manly St 27517
Manly Dorm 27514
Manning Dr 27514
Manns Ct 27516
Manns Chapel Rd 27516
Manor Dr 27516
Manor Hill Ct 27516
Manora Ln 27516
Map Ridge Rd 27516
Maple Dr 27514
Maple Ridge Dr 27516
Marcus Rd 27514
Margaret Pl 27516
Margaret Daniel Ln 27516
Mariakakis Plz 27514
Marigold Ct 27516
Marilyn Ln 27514
Marin Dr & Pl 27516
Marion Way 27516
Marions Ford Rd 27516
Market St 27516
Markham Ct & Dr 27514
Marks Ln 27516
Marlon Dr 27517
Marriott Way 27517
Martha Ln 27514
Martin Luther King Jr Blvd 27514
Martin Luther King Jr St 27517
Marvin Edwards Ln 27517
Mary Charles Ln 27516
Mason St 27516
Mason Farm Pl & Rd 27514
Maxeben Way 27516
Maxwell Rd 27517
May Ct 27514
Mayberry Ct 27514
Maynard Farm Rd 27516
Mayse Dr 27514
Maywood Way 27516
Mccauley Ln 27516
Mccauley St
100-598 27516
101-101 27514
103-599 27516
Mcdade St 27516
Mcghee Rd 27517
Mcgowan Ln 27516
Mcgregor Dr 27514
Mcgregor Woods Rd 27517
Mciver Dorm 27514
Mclean 27517
Mclennans Farm Rd 27516
Mcmasters St 27516
Meacham Rd 27516
Meadow Ln
1-399 27517
1200-1699 27516
Meadow Run 27517
Meadow Crest Dr 27516
Meadow Greer Rd 27516
Meadow Ridge Ln
1-899 27517
8500-8799 27516
Meadow Run Ct 27516
Meadow Sweet Ln 27516
Meadowbrook Dr 27514
Meadowmont Ln 27517
Meadowmont Village Cir 27517
Meadowoods Trl 27516
Meares Rd 27514
Meeting St 27516
Meg Wag Ln 27514
Mel Oak Dr & Trl 27516
Melanie Ct 27514
Melrose Pl 27516
Melville Loop 27514
Mendel Dr 27514
Mercedes Dr 27516
Merin Rd 27516
Merritt Dr 27517
N & S Merritt Mill Rd 27516
Michaels Way 27516
Michaux Rd 27514
Middlebrook Ct 27514
Midstream Ct 27517
Mijos Ln 27514
Mike Lashley Ln 27516
Mill Hill Ln 27517
Mill Race Dr 27514
Mill Ridge Ln 27514
Mill Run Dr 27514
Mill Valley Rd 27516
Millbrae Ln 27514
Miller 27517
Millhouse Rd 27516
Millikan Rd 27516
Millingport Ct 27517
Millwood Ct 27514
Milton Ave 27514
Mimosa Dr 27514
Mint Springs Rd 27514
Miramar Pl 27517
Misty Woods Cir 27514
Mitchell Ln 27516
Mocker Nut Ln 27517
Monroe St 27516
Montclair Way 27516
Monterey Valley Dr 27516
Monxton Ct 27517
Moonlight Dr 27516
Moonridge Rd 27516
Morehead 27517
Morgan Bend Ct 27517
Morgan Bluff Ln 27517
Morgan Creek Ln & Rd 27517
Morgan Oaks Dr 27516
Morgans End Way 27516
Morganscliff Ct 27517
Moring 27517
Morning Ridge Ln 27516
Morrison S 27514
Morrison Dorm 27514
Morrow Farm Ln 27516
Morrow Mill Rd 27516
Morton Rd 27517
Moseley 27517
Mossbark Ln 27514
Mosswood Ct 27516
Mossy Rock Rd 27516
Mount Bolus Rd 27514
Mount Carmel Church Rd 27517
Mount Sinai Rd 27514
Mountain Dr 27516
Mountain Creek Rd 27516
Mountain Heather 27517
Mountain Laurel 27517
Mountain View Rd 27516
Mountside Dr 27516
Mourning Dove Trl 27517
Muir Ln 27514
Mulberry Ln 27516
Mulligan Dr 27517
Mullin Ct 27514
Municipal Dr 27516
Murray Ln 27517
Napa Valley Way 27516
Nash 27517
Natalie Ave 27516
Nature Trl 27517
W Nc Highway 54 Byp W 27516
Nc Highway 86 27514
Nellie Gray Ct 27516
Nelson Hwy 27517
Neville Rd 27516
New Castle Dr & Pl 27517
New Cooper Sq 27517
New Hope Dr 27514
New Hope Trce 27516
New Hope Church Rd
100-1799 27516
1900-3299 27514
New Jericho Rd 27516
New Light Trl 27516
New Parkside Dr 27516
New Rhododendron 27517
New Rise Ct 27516
New Stateside Dr 27516
Newberry Ln 27516
Newell St 27516
E & W Newman Rd 27517
Niagra Dr 27517
Night Heron 27517
Nightmare Ln 27516
Nine Gates Rd 27516
No Record St
199-199 27516
299-299 27517
Noble St 27516
Nodding Oak 27516
Nolen Ln 27516
North St 27516
Northern Park Dr 27516
Northfield Dr 27516
Northridge Ln 27514
Northside Dr 27516
Northwood Dr 27516
Norwood Rd 27516
Nottingham Dr & Ln 27517
Nunn Ln & St 27516
Nuttal Pl 27514
Nuttree Ln 27516
Oak Is 27516
Oak Crest Dr 27516
Oak Forest Rd 27516
Oak Glen Pl 27516
Oak Hill Rd 27514

Street	ZIP
Oak Hollow Rd	27516
Oak Leaf Dr & Ln	27516
Oak Park Dr	27517
Oak Tree Dr	27517
Oakland Ln	27516
Oakley Farm Rd	27517
Oakleys Peak	27516
Oakridge Ln	27517
Oakstone Dr	27514
Oakwood Dr	27517
Oasis Dr	27516
Ocoee Falls Dr	27517
Oconee Ct	27516
October Woods Rd	27516
Odaniel Trl	27516
Oday Dr	27516
Ohagan Way	27516
Old Barn Ln	27517
Old Bridge Ln	27517
Old Cooper Sq	27517
Old Durham Rd	27517
Old East Dorm	27514
Old Farrington Rd	27517
S Old Fayetteville Rd	27516
Old Field Dr	27514
Old Forest Creek Dr	27514
Old Franklin Grove Dr	27514
Old Greensboro Rd	27516
Old Hope Valley Farm Rd	27517
Old Lambsville Rd	27516
Old Larkspur Way	27516
Old Legacy Ln	27516
Old Lystra Rd	27517
Old Markham Pl	27514
Old Mason Farm Rd	27517
Old Mill Rd	27514
Old Nc 86	27516
Old Nc Highway 10	27514
Old Orchard Rd	27517
E Old Oxford Rd	27514
Old Pineview Rd	27516
Old Pittsboro Rd	27516
Old Post Rd	27517
Old Rocky Ridge Rd	27514
Old Sawmill Rd	27516
Old School Rd	27516
Old Spring Rd	27516
Old Stable Ct	27514
Old Sterling Dr	27514
Old Stonehouse Rd	27516
Old University Station Rd	27514
Old West Dorm	27514
Old Wilder Ln	27517
Oldham Pl	27516
Oliver Ln	27516
Oosting Dr	27514
Opus Way	27516
Orange Chapel Clover Garden Rd	27516
Orange Grove Rd	27516
Orchard Ln	27514
Orchard Vly	27517
Orchard Vw	27517
Orlando Pl	27516
Oteys Rd	
500-599	27514
600-699	27517
Outrider Trce	27516
Oval Park Pl	27517
Overlake Dr	27516
Overland Dr	27517
Overland Psge	27516
Overlook Pt	27514
Owen	27517
Owen Towne Rd	27516
Owens Ct	27514
Oxbow Crossing Rd	27516
Oxford Ct	27516
Oxford Hills Dr & Pl	27514
Oxfordshire Ln	27517
Paddington Pl	27517
Page Xing	27517
Painted Turtle Ln	27516
Palafox Dr	27516
Palmyra Pl	27514
Palomar Pt	27516
Parchemin Trl	27516
S Park Dr	27517
Park Pl	27514
Park Rd	27516
Park And Stay Trailer Park	27517
Park Bluff Dr N	27517
Parker Rd	27517
Parker Dorm	27514
Parkridge Ave	27517
Parkside Cir & Dr	27516
Parkview Cres	27516
Parrish Rd	27516
Partin St	27514
Partin Farm Trl	27516
Partridge Run	27516
Partridgeberry Rd	27516
Pathway Ct & Dr	27516
Patterson Dr & Pl	27516
Patton Pl	27517
Paul Hardin Dr	27514
Pauline Dr	27514
Peace St	27517
Peaceful Pl	27517
Peakview Pl	27517
Pearl Ln	27517
Pebble Ct	27516
Pebble Springs Rd	27514
Peeler Creek Ln	27516
Penick Ln	27516
Penny Ln	27514
Pepper Pl	27516
Perdue Dr	27517
Performance Way	27517
Perkins Dr	27514
Perry Creek Dr	27514
Pharr	27517
Philpott Dr	27517
Phils Creek Rd	27516
Phils Ridge Rd	27516
Phoenix Dr	27516
Pickard Ln	27514
Pickards Meadow Rd	27516
Pin Oak Ct	27517
Pinchot Ln	27514
Pine Ln	27514
Pine Acres Rd	27516
Pine Bluff Trl	27516
Pine Hill Dr	27514
Pine Tree Ln	27514
Pinegate Cir	27514
Pinehurst Dr	27517
Pineview Ct, Dr & Rd	27516
Pinewood Dr	27517
Piney Mountain Rd	27514
Pinoak Ct	27514
Pioneer Path	27517
Pitch Pine Ln	27514
Pittsboro St	27516
Plant Rd	27514
Plaza Dr	27517
Plaza Drive Ext	27517
Plum Ln	27517
Plumtree Ln	27517
Poinsett Dr	27517
Point Prospect Pl	27514
Pokeberry Bend Dr	27516
Polks Pl & Trl	27516
Polks Landing Rd	27516
Poplar St	27516
Porter	27517
Porter Pl	27514
Portsmith Pl	27516
Possum Pl	27516
Powder Mill Rd	27514
Powell St	27516
Poythress Rd	27516
Presque Isle Ln	27514
Preston Spring Ln	27516
Prestwick Rd	27517
Price Creek Rd	27516
Priestly Creek Dr	27514
Princeton Rd	27516
Priscilla Ln	27516
Pritchard Ave	27516
Pritchard Avenue Ext	27516
Providence Rd	27514
Providence Glen Dr	27514
Public Works Dr	27516
Pulpit Hill Rd	27516
Puma Ln	27516
Pump House Loop	27517
Purefoy Dr	27516
Purefoy Rd	27514
Purple Sage Ln	27516
Purtnear Ln	27514
Pussycat Ln	27516
Quadrangle Dr	27517
Quail Hill Ct	27514
Quailview Dr	27516
Quarry Pl	27517
Quinn Ct	27516
Ragtime Rd	27516
Rain Lily Trl	27516
Rain Tree Ln	27516
Raintree Bnd	27517
Raleigh Rd	
500-999	27514
1000-1098	27517
1001-1099	27514
1100-2399	27517
Raleigh St	27514
Ranch Rd	27516
Randolph Ct	27516
Ransom St	27516
Ray Rd	27516
Reade Rd	27516
Reagan Mead Ln	27516
Reaves Dr	27516
Red Bud Ln & Rd	27514
Red Cedar Pl	27514
Red Drum Rd	27516
Red Pine Rd	27516
Redfoot Run Rd	27516
Reeves Rd	27516
Regent Pl	27514
Reid	27517
Rex Rd	27516
Reynard Rd	27516
Reynolds Ct	27517
Rhododendron Ct & Dr	27517
Rice	27517
Richardson Ln	27516
Richland Ct	27516
Ridge Ln	27514
Ridge Rd	27514
Ridge Trl	27516
Ridge Springs Dr	27516
Ridge Top Dr	27516
Ridge View Ln	27516
Ridgecrest Dr	27514
Ridgefield Dr & Rd	27517
Ridgeway Rd	27517
Ridgewood Ln	27514
Ridgewood Rd	27516
Riggsbee Rd	27514
Rigsbee Rd	27514
Ritchie Rd	27516
River Birch Ln	27514
Roark Hoey Loop	27517
Robbins St	27517
N & S Roberson St	27516
Robin Rd	27516
Rochelle Dr	27517
Rock Creek Rd	27514
Rock Garden Rd	27516
Rock Hill Dr	27517
Rocky Knls	27516
Rodney Ln	27517
Rogers Rd	27516
Rogerson Dr	27517
Rolling Rd	27514
Rolling Meadows Ln	27517
Rollingwood Rd	27516
Roosevelt Dr	27514
Roper Ln	27517
Rose Ln	27514
Rosebud Ln	27517
E Rosemary St	27514
W Rosemary St	27516
Rosewood Ct	27514
Rossburn Way	27516
Rosswood Rd	27516
Roundhill Rd	27514
Roundtree Rd	27514
Rowan	27517
Rowe Rd	27516
Ruffed Grouse	27517
Ruffin Dorm	27514
Ruffins	27517
Running Cedar Dr & Rd	27517
Running Deer Trl	27517
Running Green Rd	27514
Rusch Rd	27516
Ruskin Dr	27516
Russell	27517
Russells Ford Rd	27516
Rutgers Pl	27517
Sabre Ct	27516
Saddle Ridge Rd	27514
Sage Rd	27514
Sagebrush Rd	27516
Saint Andrews Ln & Pl	27517
Saint Ayers Way	27517
Saint James Pl	27514
Saint Louis Pl	27516
Saint Thomas Dr	27517
Salem Ln	27516
Salix St	27516
Saluda Ct	27514
Sam Jones Rd	27517
San Juan Ct & Dr	27514
San Mateo Pl	27514
San Miguel Pl	27514
San Sophia Dr	27514
Sandberg Ln	27516
Sandcreek Ct	27517
Sandy Rdg	27516
Sandy Creek Trl	27514
Sandy Ridge Rd	27516
Saratoga Trl	27516
Sarita Ln	27516
Saunders	27517
Savannah Ter	27516
Saxapahaw Run	27516
Scarlet Oak Ln	27516
Scarlett Dr	27517
Scenic View Ln	27516
Schnibben Pl	27517
School Ln	27516
Schultz St	27514
Scott	27517
Scott Ln	27514
Seawell School Rd	27516
Sedgefield Dr	27514
Sedgewood Rd	27516
Seminole Dr	27514
Senlac Rd	27514
N Serenity Hill Cir	27516
Serrano Way	27517
Sertoma Rd	27516
Sesame Rd	27516
Settle	27517
Severin St	27516
Shadow Ridge Pl	27516
Shadowood Dr	27514
Shady Ln	27517
Shady Creek Dr	27517
Shady Lawn Ct & Rd	27514
Shady Lawn Road Ext	27514
Shady Nook Ct	27517
Shagbark Ct	27517
Shalestone	27516
Shallowford Ln	27517
Shannon Dr	27516
Sharon Rd	27517
Sharp St	27516
Sheffield Cir	27517
Shepherd Ln	27514
Shirley Ct	27514
Shoccoree Ridge Dr	27516
Short St	
100-199	27517
200-299	27516
Shotts Farm Rd	27516
Sidney Green St	27516
Sierra Dr	27514
Silers Fen Ct	27517
Silo Dr	27514
Silver Birch Ct	27517
Silver Cedar Ct & Ln	27514
Silver Creek Trl	27514
Silver Glade	27514
Simerville Rd	27517
Sir Richard Ln	27517
Skipper Bowles Dr	27514
Skye Dr	27516
Sleepy Holw	27517
Sleepy Hollow Rd	27517
Small Pond Rd	27517
Smith Ave	27516
Smith Level Rd	27516
Sneeden Rd	27517
Snipes Farm Rd	27516
Solitude Pt	27516
Somerset Dr	27514
Somersview Dr	27514
Songbird Ln	27514
Sonoma Way	27516
Sothel	27517
Sourwood Cir & Dr	27517
South Rd	27514
Southern Dr & Trl	27516
Southern Green Pl & Way	27517
Southwoods Dr	27517
Spaight	27517
Sparrow Trl	27514
Sparrow Apartments	27517
Sparrow Run Ln	27517
Spencer Ct	27517
Spencer Dorm	27514
Spicewood Pl	27514
Spring Ln	
1-199	27517
200-299	27516
Spring Dell Ln	27517
Spring House Ln	27516
Spring Meadow Dr	27517
Spring Vista Ct	27516
Springberry Ln	27517
Springdale Way	27517
Springhill Forest Pl & Rd	27516
Springview Trl	27517
Spruce St	27517
Sprunt St	27517
Stacy Dorm	27514
Stadium Dr	27514
Staffield Ln	27516
Stag Trl	27516
Stagecoach Rd	27514
Stallings Rd	27516
Stancell Dr	27517
Standing Rock Rd	27516
Standish Dr	27517
Stanford Rd	27516
Stanley	27517
Stansbury Rd	27516
Starns Ridge Rd	27516
Stateside Dr	27514
Stayman Cir	27514
Stedman	27517
Steeple Chase Ln	27517
Steeplechase Rd	27514
Stephens	27517
Stephens St	27516
Sterling Bridge Rd	27516
Stewart Ln	27514
Still Crossing Rd	27516
W Stinson St	27516
Stokes	27517
Stone Brk	27514
Stone Creek Ct	27514
Stonegate Dr	27516
Stonehill Ct & Rd	27516
Stoneridge Dr & Pl	27514
Stones Throw	27516
Stoney Creek Way	27517
Stoneybrook Rd	27516
Stoneycreek Rd	27514
Stony Branch Trl	27516
Stony Hill Rd	27516
Storybook Farm Ln	27516
Stratford Dr	27516
Strawberry Patch	27516
Strowd Ln	27516
Sturbridge Ln	27516
Sudbury Ln	27516
Suffolk Pl	27516
Sugar Spring Rd	27516
Sugarberry Rd	27514
Sully Ct	27514
Summerfield Crossing Rd	27514
Summergate Cir	27516
Summerlin Dr	27514
Summersweet Ln	27516
Summerwalk Cir	27517
Summerwind	27516
Sun Forest Way	27517
Sundance Pl	27514
Sunnyside Ct	27516
Sunrise Ln	27516
Sunrise Rd	27514
Sunset Dr	27516
Sunset Creek Cir	27516
Sunset Ridge Ln	27516
Surry Rd	27514
Sutton Pl	27514
Swain	27517
Swan Lake Ct	27517
Swansea Ln	27516
Swaying Trees Ct	27517
Sweetbriar Ln	27514
Sweetbush Rd	27516
Sweeten Creek Rd	27514
Swift Run	27514
Sycamore Dr	27514
Sykes St	27516
Sylvan Way	27516
Sylvan Cove Trl	27516
Syston Ct	27517
Tabardry Mill Prt	27516
Tabscott Ln	27514
Tadley Dr	27514
Talbryn Way	27516
Tall Oaks Rd	27516
Tallyho Trl	27516
Tamalpais Pt	27514
Tamarack Cir	27517
Tanager Ln	27517
Tanyard Ct	27517
Tarwick Ave	27516
Taylor St	27514
Taylor Hall Pl	27517
Teagan Ct	27516
Teague Dorm	27514
Tecumseh Path	27516
Teer Rd	27516
Telluride Trl	27514
Tendril Ln	27516
Tenney Cir	27514
Terrace View Dr	27516
Terrell Wood Ln	27516
Tharrington Dr	27516
The Gln	27514
The Holw	27516
The Courtyard	27516
The Glades	27517
The Preserve Trl	27517
Thetford Ct	27516
Thomas Berry Way	27516
Thorncroft Pl	27517
Thornwood Rd	27517
Tidwell Rd	27516
Tilbury Ct	27517
Tilghman Cir	27514
Tilleys Branch Rd	27516
Tilleys Farm Rd	27516
Timber Ln	27516
Timber Hollow Ct	27514
Timberhill Pl	27514
Timberidge Ct	27516
Timberidge Trailer Park	27516
Timberlyne Ct & Rd	27514
Timothy Ln	27516
Tinkerbell Rd	27517
Tobacco Farm Way	27516
Torrey Pines Pl	27517
Totten Pl	27514
Tottenham Ln	27517
Toucan Dr	27516
Tower Hl	27517
Tower Apartments	27516
Towne Ridge Ln	27516
Townhouse Apartments	27514
Toynbee Pl	27514
Tradescant Dr	27517
Traditional Way	27516
Trailwood Ct	27516
Tramore Dr	27516
Travis Ct	27516
Treetop Pl	27517
Trellis Ct	27516
Tremont Cir	27516
Trenton Rd	27517
Treywood Ln	27516
Trice Atwater Rd	27516
Trillium Pl	27517
Trinity Ct	27516
Trinkus Mnr	27514
Triple Crown Dr	27516
Tripp Rd	27516
Tripp Farm Rd	27516
Trout Lilly Ln	27516
Tryon Ct	27517
Tuckers Pond Dr	27516
Tupelo Ln	27514
Turkey Farm Rd	27514
Turnage Rd	27517
Turnberry Ln	27517
Turner	27517
Turtle Point Bnd	27516
Turtleback Crossing Dr	27516
Turvey Ct	27514
Tweed Pl	27517
Twilight Ln	27517
Twin Elms	27516
Twin Streams Rd	27516
Twisted Oak Dr	27516
Ukiah Ln	27514
Umbrio Ln	27517
Umstead	27517
Umstead Dr	27516
Union Grove Rd	27516
Union Grove Church Rd	27516
W University Dr	27516
University Lake Rd	27516
University Of Nc	27514
University Station Rd	27514
Unwin Pl	27516
Us 15 501 N & S	27517
Vail Dr	27517
Valen Ct	27516
Valentine Ln	27516
Valinda Dr	27514
Valley Pl	27516
Valley Meadow Dr	27516
Valley Park Dr	27514
Vallie Hi Ln	27516
Van Doren Pl	27517
Vance Knls	27517
Vance St	27516
Vauxhall Pl	27517
Velma Rd	27514
Vernon Dr	27516
Vernon Hills Ct	27514
Vickers Rd	27517
Victory Park Dr	27517
Vilcom Center Dr	27514
Village Dr	27516
Village Ln	27514
Village Crossing Dr	27517
Village Gate Dr	27514
Village Park Dr	27517
Vintage Dr	27516
Virginia Dr	27514
Vitex St	27516

Wabash Rd 27516
Walden Pl 27516
Walkabout Way 27516
Walker 27517
Walnut St 27517
Walnut Branch Rd 27516
Walnut Cove Rd 27516
Walser 27517
Waltham Pl 27517
Wannie And Wade Rd 27516
Ward 27517
Ward St 27516
Warren Ct 27516
Waterford Pl 27517
Watson Rd 27516
Watts Apartments 27517
Wave Rd 27517
Waverly Forest Ln 27516
Wayfarer Ct 27514
Wb Cheek Dr 27517
Weatherstone Dr 27514
Weaver Rd 27514
Weaver Dairy Rd
1-1130 27514
1129-1129 27516
1131-1199 27514
1132-1198 27514
Weaver Dairy Road Ext 27516
Weaver Mine Trl 27517
Webb 27517
Wedgewood Ct & Rd 27514
Weeping Cherry Ct 27514
Weiner St 27516
Welcome Dr 27516
Weldon Dr N & S 27516
Wellesley Pl 27517
Wellington Dr 27514
Wells Ct 27514
Wendell Rd 27517
Wentworth St 27516
Wesley Ct & Dr 27516
Westbury Ct & Dr 27516
Westchester Pl 27514
Western Trl 27516
Westgreen Dr 27516
Westhampton Way 27516
Westminster Dr 27514
Weston Ln 27516
Westover Ct 27514
Westside Dr 27516
Westwood Dr 27516
Weybridge Pl 27517
Weyer Dr 27516
Weymouth Pl 27516
Wheelwright Cmn 27516
Whippoorwill Ln 27517
Whirlaway Ln 27516
Whisper Ln 27514
Whispering Oak Ct 27516
Whispering Pines Ct 27517
Whispering Pines Mhp 27517
Whistling Tree 27514
Whitaker St 27516
White Cross Rd 27516
White Oak Trl 27516
White Oak Way 27514
White Pine Way 27516
White Plains Rd 27517
White Rock Church Rd 27517
Whitehead Cir & Rd 27514
Whitehead Dorm 27514
Whitfield Rd 27514
Whitley Dr 27517
Whitmore Cir 27516
Whitney Ln 27516
Wicker Dr 27517
Wicklow Pl 27517
Wild Azalea Ln 27516
Wild Ginger Rdg 27517
Wild Iris Ln 27514
Wild Primrose Ln 27514
Wild Turkey Trl 27516
Wildcat Ln 27516
Wildcat Creek Rd 27516

Wilder Pl 27514
Wilder Rdg 27517
Wildwind Dr 27516
Wildwood Dr 27517
Wilkinson 27517
Wilkinson Creek Ln 27516
Williams Cir 27516
Williamson Dr 27514
Willie Boldin Rd 27516
Willis Rd 27516
Willow Dr
800-1022 27514
1023-1399 27517
1700-1799 27514
Willow Ter 27514
Willow Way 27516
Willow Blair Pl 27516
Willowbend Dr 27517
Willowspring Pl 27517
Wilson Rd & St 27516
Wilson Creek Rd 27516
Windfall Creek Dr 27517
Windhover Dr & Pl 27514
Winding Creek Ln 27516
Windorah Pl 27517
Windsor Cir, Pl & Rd 27516
Windy Hill Rd 27514
Windy Knoll Cir 27516
Windy Ridge Rd 27517
Winged Elm Ln 27514
Winkler Way 27516
Winks Way 27516
E & W Winmore Ave 27516
Winningham Rd 27516
Winslow Pl 27517
Winsome Ln 27516
Winston Pl 27514
Winston Dorm 27514
Winston Ridge Dr 27516
Winter Dr & Gdn 27517
Winterberry Dr 27514
Winterberry Way 27516
Wisteria Dr 27514
Wolfs Ct & Trl 27516
Wood Cir 27514
Wood Creek Ct 27516
Wood Duck Ct 27517
Wood Laurel Ln 27517
Wood Sage Dr 27516
Woodbend Ct 27516
Woodbine Dr 27517
Woodbridge Dr 27516
Woodbridge Ln 27514
Woodcrest Dr 27516
Woodcrest Trailer Park 27516
Woodgate Dr 27516
Woodglen Ln 27516
Woodhaven Rd 27514
Woodkirk Ln 27514
Woodland Ave 27516
Woodland Path 27517
Woodland Grove Ln 27516
Woodleaf Dr 27516
Woodlot Rdg 27516
Woodmark Ct 27514
Woodshire Ln 27514
Woodside Trl 27517
Woodward Way 27516
Worsham Dr 27516
Worth 27517
Wrenn Pl 27516
Wyndham Dr 27516
Wyrick St 27516
Wysteria Way 27514
Yale Ln 27517
Yates Motor Company Aly 27516
Yeargen Pl 27516
Yellow Brick Rd 27516
York Pl 27517
Yorkshire Ln 27516
Yorktown Ct & Dr 27516
Yukon Ln 27514
Zapata Ln 27517
Zeiger Ln 27516
Zephyr Dr 27517

CHARLOTTE NC

General Delivery 28204

POST OFFICE BOXES MAIN OFFICE STATIONS AND BRANCHES

Box No.s
DX - DX 28220
CEC - CEC 28220
1000 - 1404 28201
2200 - 3140 28241
3800 - 3810 28227
5001 - 5674 28299
6000 - 6304 28207
7001 - 7950 28241
8000 - 8080 28262
8500 - 8500 28271
8600 - 8600 28224
9001 - 9453 28299
9225 - 9309 28241
9480 - 9991 28299
11001 - 12953 28220
16001 - 16958 28297
18002 - 18972 28218
19001 - 19994 28219
20006 - 20455 28202
23001 - 23898 28227
25001 - 25972 28229
26001 - 27020 28221
28201 - 28201 28201
28241 - 28241 28241
28260 - 28260 28260
28271 - 28271 28271
29001 - 29782 28229
30001 - 30894 28230
31001 - 31894 28231
32001 - 32896 28232
33000 - 33896 28233
34001 - 34799 28234
35001 - 35698 28235
36000 - 36964 28236
37001 - 37998 28237
38001 - 39529 28278
42001 - 44674 28215
49000 - 49795 28277
60002 - 60998 28260
65000 - 65721 28265
67001 - 67296 28226
70098 - 71107 28272
75000 - 75999 28275
77001 - 79386 28271
189001 - 189118 28218
190001 - 195003 28219
217001 - 217300 28221
220001 - 222202 28222
240001 - 242948 28224
410001 - 411832 28241
470001 - 475340 28247
480001 - 482000 28269
560001 - 564300 28256
601008 - 603100 28260
620001 - 622818 28262
667301 - 669874 28266
680001 - 681976 28216
690001 - 691794 28227
751000 - 752195 28275
790001 - 792850 28206

NAMED STREETS

A Ave 28216
Aaa Dr 28212
Aaronda Ct 28213
Abbey Pl 28209
Abbey Brook Ct 28216
Abbey Court Dr 28278
Abbey Hill Ln 28210
Abbeydale Dr 28205
Abbots Bridge Rd 28277
Abbotsbury Ct 28277
Abbotsford Ct 28270
Abbotsinch Ct 28269

Abbotswood Dr 28226
Abbott St 28203
Abbotts Glen Dr 28212
Abbottsgate Ln 28269
Abbywood Ln 28269
Abeline Rd 28217
Abelwood Rd 28216
Abenaki Dr 28214
Abercorn Ln 28227
Abercromby St 28213
Aberdale Way 28273
Aberdeen St 28208
Aberdeen Glen Pl 28214
Aberdeen Wood Ct 28226
Aberdun Ct 28215
Aberglen Dr 28262
Abernathy Rd 28216
Abigail Glen Dr 28212
Abingdon Rd 28211
Abiza Dr 28213
Able Glen Ct 28214
Abner Ln 28269
Abney Ct 28227
Abode Lilly Ln 28227
Abrell Walk Ct 28226
Abson Ct 28215
Acacia Ridge Ct 28269
Academy St 28205
Acadian Woods Dr 28227
Accent Ct 28214
Accrington Ct 28227
Acorn St 28205
Acorn Creek Ln 28269
Acorn Forest Ln 28269
Acorn Oaks Rd 28215
Acorn Valley Ct 28214
Acqui Pl 28277
Acquinas Pl 28210
Acre Hill Ct 28277
Acton Ct 28227
Ada Ct 28213
Adair Manor Ct 28277
Adaire Cir 28227
Adams Dr 28215
Adare Mews Rd 28217
Addington Ct 28277
Addison Dr 28211
Adel Ln 28269
Adelaide Ct 28213
Adison Gray Ln 28270
Adkins Ct 28205
Adlin Ave 28262
Admiral Ave 28205
Adobe Rd 28277
Adonis Ct 28213
Adrian Ct 28270
Adriatic Dr 28227
Advocator Ln 28216
Aerial Ct 28213
Afternoon Ct 28216
Afton Ln 28208
Agava Ln 28215
Ainsdale Rd 28226
Ainslie Ct 28269
Ainslie Downs St 28273
Ainsworth St 28216
Aintree Rd 28215
Air Park Rd W 28214
Air Ramp Rd 28214
Airlie St 28205
Airline St 28208
Airport Dr 28208
Airport Center Pkwy 28208
Airways Dr 28269
Akram Ct 28215
Alabama Ave 28216
Alabarda Ln 28273
Alabaster Ct 28269
Alamance Dr 28227
Alamore Ct 28208
Alanbrook Rd 28215
Alanby Ln 28270
Alanhurst Pl 28217
Alba Ct 28269
Albaneen Ct 28215
Albany Ln 28205

Albemarle Rd
4700-5199 28205
5200-6500 28212
6501-6899 28212
6501-6501 28229
6502-6898 28212
6900-15399 28227
10300-11198 28227
11200-12300 28227
12302-13298 28227
Alberson Ct 28217
Albertine Dr 28269
Alberto St 28207
Albion Ln 28278
Albright Ave 28212
Albury Walk Ln 28277
Alcea St 28214
Alcove Ct 28210
Aldeborough Ln 28270
Alden Glen Dr 28269
Alden Oaks Ln 28270
Alder Ct 28215
Alderbrook Ln 28270
Aldergate Ct 28210
Aldergrove Rd 28270
Alderknoll Ct 28216
Alderman Ln 28277
Alderpoint Ln 28262
Aldersgate Ave 28213
Aldershot Ct 28211
Alderson Dr 28269
Alderwood Ln 28215
Aldworth Ln 28226
Aldwych Way 28216
Alexa Rd 28277
Alexander Rd
2300-2999 28262
6400-8199 28270
N Alexander St
200-799 28202
900-1199 28206
1300-3499 28205
Alexander Glen Dr 28262
Alexander Hall Dr 28270
Alexander Martin Ave 28277
Alexander Mill Dr 28277
Alexander Park Dr 28206
Alexander Pointe Dr 28262
Alexander Valley Dr 28270
Alexandra Alley Dr 28210
Alexandria Ln 28270
Alexis Dr 28227
Alexis Dawne Ln 28214
Alfred St 28211
Alice Ave 28208
Alice Mcginn Dr 28277
Alicia Brittany Ln 28212
Alijon Ct 28278
All Saints Ln 28226
Alleghany St 28208
Allegiance Dr 28217
Allegro Ct 28270
Allen Rd E 28269
Allen Rd S 28269
Allen St 28205
Allen A Brown Rd 28269
Allen Black Rd 28227
Allen Jay Dr 28216
Allen Munn Ln 28227
Allen Station Dr 28227
Allenbrook Dr 28208
Allendale Pl 28211
Allenstown Dr 28215
Allenton Trails Ln 28212
Allenwick Cir 28227
Allenwood Rd 28270
Allerton Way 28213
Allforth Ln 28277
Allison Ave 28226
Allison Ln 28277
Allison Ashworth Ct 28217
Allison Forest Trl 28278
Allison Woods Dr 28277
Allister Dr 28227
Allness Glen Ln 28269
Alloway Ln 28278

Allucin Dr 28278
Allwood Dr 28217
Allyson Park Dr 28277
Alma Ct 28206
Alma Blount Blvd 28277
Almond Rd 28227
Almond Hills Dr 28262
Almora Dr 28216
Alnwick Ct 28262
Aloysia Ln 28269
Alpha St 28205
Alpha Mill Ln 28206
Alpine Cir 28270
Alpine Ln 28269
Alpine Forest Ct 28270
Alrick Pl 28217
Alsace Dr 28278
Alston Hill Dr 28214
Altacrest Pl 28217
Altliff Ct 28213
Altomonte Ave 28227
Altondale Ave 28207
Alvanley Hills Ct 28262
Alvarado Way 28277
Alvin Woods Dr 28214
Alwyn Ct 28269
Alydar Ct 28216
Alydar Commons Ln 28278
Alyssa Faith Ct 28278
Amadeus Dr 28227
Amado St 28215
Amanda Nichole Ct 28212
Amaranthus Ct 28269
Amarillo Dr 28262
Amarone Dr 28277
Amay James Ave 28208
Ambassador St 28208
Amber Dr 28208
Amber Creste Ln 28212
Amber Glen Dr 28269
Amber Leigh Way Dr 28269
Amber Meadows Dr 28269
Amber Mist Ln 28211
Amber View Ct 28216
Amberglades Ln 28215
Amberhill Ln 28216
Amberly Ln 28213
Amberton Ln 28226
Amberway Ct 28269
Amberwood Ct 28226
Amble Dr 28206
Ambleside Dr 28216
Amboy Ct 28205
Ambridge Dr 28216
Ambrosia St 28278
Ame Ln 28269
Amelia Dr 28212
Ameria Rd 28215
Americana Ave 28215
Amerigo St 28208
Ameron Dr 28206
Ames Hollow Rd 28216
Amesbury Ave 28205
Amesbury Hill Dr 28269
Amethyst St 28277
Amherst Pl 28204
Amherst Glen Dr 28213
Amherst Trail Dr 28226
Amherst Villa Ct 28273
Amity Ct 28215
Amity Pl 28212
Amity Garden Ct 28205
Amity Pointe Rd 28215
Amity Springs Dr 28212
Amontillado Dr 28277
Amos Hoard Rd 28214
Amos Smith Rd 28214
Amrita Ct 28211
Amur Ct 28262
Amy Dr 28213
Amyington Dr 28226
Anastasia Ct 28216
Ancient Oak Ln 28277
Anderson Rd 28269
Anderson St 28205
Andi Kathryn Ct 28214

Andora Dr 28227
Andover Rd 28211
Andover Creek Dr 28210
Andover Woods Dr 28210
Andrea Way 28277
Andrew Carnegie Blvd 28262
Andrew Colten Ct 28214
Andrew James Dr 28216
Andrew Thomas Dr 28269
Andrew Ward Ave 28216
Andrews Links St 28277
Andrill Ter 28216
Andros Ln 28215
Anduin Falls Dr 28269
Anette Ave 28227
Angel Way Ct 28214
Angela Marie Ct 28215
Angelica Ln 28277
Anglesey Ct 28278
Angwin Pl 28262
Anita Ct 28208
Ankeny Ct 28269
Ann Arbor Pl 28227
Ann Baker Ct 28217
Ann Elizabeth Dr 28213
Ann Franklin Ct 28216
Ann Marie Dr 28217
Ann Smith Ln 28278
Anna Garrison Rd 28206
Anna Jordan Dr 28213
Anna Rose Rd 28273
Annabel Lee Ln 28277
Annahill Ct 28277
Annaleis Ct 28227
Annalexa Ln 28277
Annalong Rd 28278
Annan Ct 28277
Annandale Dr 28269
Annbick Ln 28269
Anne St 28205
Anne Brower Rd 28213
Anne Crossing Rd 28277
Annerly Ct 28226
Annie Acres Ln 28277
Annie Oakley Trl 28227
Annisa Ct 28208
Annlin Ave 28209
Annsdale Ln 28273
Ansel Ln 28216
Ansley Ct 28211
Ansley Falls Dr 28217
Ansley Garden Dr 28217
Ansley Walk Ln 28277
Anson St 28209
Ansted Way Ct 28273
Antebellum Dr 28273
Antelope Ln 28269
Anthem Ct 28205
Anthony Cir 28211
Anthony Mark Moore Ln 28216
Antlers Ln 28210
Antrim Ct 28217
Anvil Ln 28270
Anzack Ln 28269
Apalachin Dr 28212
Apleby Ln 28277
Appaloosa Ln 28215
Appaloosa Way Ln 28216
Apple Blossom Ct 28227
Apple Creek Dr 28227
Apple Dove Ct 28214
Apple Glen Ln 28269
Apple Mint Ct 28227
Apple Pie Ct 28227
Apple Twig Dr 28270
Apple Way Ct 28227
Appleberry Ln 28214
Applecross Ln 28215
Appledale Dr 28262
Applegate Rd 28209
Appleton Ct 28210
Applevalley Ct 28269
Applewood Ln 28227
Appley Mead Ln 28269
Appling Ln 28278

April Ln 28215
April Day Ln 28226
April Ridge Ln 28215
Aqua Ct 28215
Aqua Chem Dr 28208
Aqueduct Ct 28216
Aquitaine St 28277
Arabella Dr 28273
Arabian Mews Ln 28278
Aragorn Ln 28212
Aragorn Ln NW 28269
Aransas Rd 28214
Arapaho Dr 28214
Arbor Ln 28209
Arbor Creek Dr 28269
Arbor Crest Ct 28262
Arbor Day Ct 28269
Arbor Glen Ln 28210
Arbor Grove Ln 28277
Arbor Meadows Ct 28269
Arbor Pointe Dr 28210
Arbor Ridge Dr 28273
Arbor Spring Dr 28269
Arbor Trace Dr 28273
Arbor Trail Ct 28277
Arbor Tree Ln 28273
Arbor Vista Dr 28262
Arbordale Ave 28215
Arboretum Dr 28270
Arboretum Vw 28226
Arborgate Dr 28273
Arborhill Rd 28270
Arborloft Ct 28270
E & W Arbors Dr 28262
Arborview Ct 28269
Arborway 28211
Arborwood Ct 28226
Arborwood Dr 28208
Arbourgate Meadows
Ln 28277
Arbroath Ct 28278
Arcadia Ave 28209
Archdale Dr
200-1399 28217
1400-3499 28210
Archer Ave 28217
Archgate Ct 28273
Archibald Ct 28277
Arching Oak Ln 28212
Arco Corporate Dr 28273
Arcola Ln 28277
Ardberry Pl 28211
Arden St 28206
Arden Gate Ln 28262
Ardenetti Ct 28227
Ardenwoods Dr 28215
Ardley Manor Dr 28227
Ardley Park Way 28227
Ardley Place Cir 28227
Ardmore Rd 28209
Ardrey Crest Dr 28277
Ardrey Kell Rd 28277
Ardrey Stead Ct 28277
Ardrey Woods Dr 28277
Ardsley Rd 28207
Ardwyck Pl 28277
Arginion Ln 28262
Argonaut Dr 28210
E & W Argyle Dr 28213
Aria Ct 28215
Arista Ct 28214
Arklow Rd 28269
Arlandes Dr 28278
Arleta Cir 28277
Arley Hall Ct 28262
Arlington Ave 28203
Arlington Church Rd 28227
Arlington Hills Dr 28227
Arlington Oaks Dr 28227
Arlyn Cir 28213
Armitage Dr 28269
Armorcrest Ln 28277
Armory Dr 28204
Armour Dr 28206
Armour Ridge Dr 28273
Arnold Dr 28205
Aronomink Dr 28210
Arosa Ave 28203
Arrington Heights Pl 28278
Arrington Manor Pl 28277
Arroll Ct 28213
Arrow Ln 28227
Arrow Pine Dr 28273
Arrowcreek Dr 28273
Arrowgrass Way 28278
Arrowhawk Dr 28217
E & W Arrowhead Dr 28213
E Arrowood Rd 28217
W Arrowood Rd
100-2299 28217
2500-3999 28273
Arrowpoint Blvd & Ln 28273
Arrowridge Blvd S 28273
Arrowsmith Ln 28270
Arroyo Dr 28227
Arsenal Ct 28273
Artesa Ct 28214
Artesa Mill Ln 28214
Artesian Ct 28270
Artists Way 28205
Artwin Rd 28213
Artwood Ln 28217
Arty Ave 28208
Arundel Dr 28209
Arve Pl 28227
Arvin Dr 28269
Arvind Oaks Ct 28277
Arwen Rd 28214
Asbury Ave 28206
Asbury Hall Ct 28209
Ascoli Pl 28277
Ascot Dr 28215
Ash Cove Ln 28269
Ashbluff Ct 28216
Ashbourne Ln 28227
Ashbourne Hall Rd 28277
Ashbrook Pl 28209
Ashburton Dr 28216
Ashby St 28206
Ashcliff Ln 28270
Ashcraft Ln 28209
Ashcrest Dr 28217
Ashdale Pl 28215
Ashe Ct 28215
Asheby Dr 28213
Asheford Woods Ln 28278
Asheley Glen Dr 28227
Asher Ct 28215
Asherton Dr 28226
Asheton Creek Dr 28273
Asheville Pl 28203
Ashfield Ct 28226
Ashford St 28214
Ashford Crest Ln 28226
Ashford Leigh Ct 28269
Ashgrove Ln 28270
Ashland Ave 28205
Ashleigh Oaks Ct 28273
Ashley Cir & Rd 28208
Ashley Hall Dr 28227
Ashley Hill Ct 28262
Ashley Lake Ct 28262
Ashley Meadow Dr 28213
Ashley Park Ln 28210
Ashley View Dr 28213
Ashleytown Ln 28270
Ashlight Dr 28278
Ashlyn Chase Ct 28277
Ashlyn Elizabeth Ct 28214
Ashmeade Rd 28211
Ashmont Pl 28269
Ashmore Dr 28212
Ashridge Dr 28226
Ashton Dr 28210
Ashton Gate Dr 28270
Ashton Oaks Dr 28278
Ashwood Dr 28215
Ashworth Rd 28211
Ashwyn Dr 28211
Aspen Ct
4700-4899 28210
8100-8699 28227
Aspen Bend Ct 28277
Aspen Hills Ln 28277
Aspendale Ln 28212
Aspinwall Dr 28216
Assembly Brooke Dr 28214
Associates Ln 28217
Aster Dr 28227
Asterwind Ct 28277
Aston Mill Pl 28273
Astonboro Dr 28216
Astor Ln 28208
Astor Hall Dr 28277
Astoria Dr 28262
Atando Ave 28206
Atchinson Dr 28227
Athenian Ct 28262
Athens Pl 28205
Atherton St 28203
Atherton Heights Ln 28203
Atkins Circle Dr 28277
Atkins Ridge Dr 28213
Atkinson Dr 28214
Atlantique Ct 28213
Atlas Dr 28269
Atlas Cedar Dr 28215
Atleigh Ct 28226
Atmore St 28205
Attaberry Dr 28205
Attwood Ct 28217
Atwater Ln 28269
Atwell Ct 28211
Aubrac Ln 28213
Aubreywood Dr 28214
Auburn Ave 28209
Auburn Hill Ln 28269
Auburn Top Ln 28277
Auburn Whisper Ln 28227
Auburndale Rd 28205
Audrey St 28215
Audrey Lake Dr 28213
Audubon Rd 28211
August Ln 28227
Augusta St 28216
Augustine Way 28270
Augustine Hill Ln 28227
Aullcin Ct 28278
Aulton Link Ct 28269
Austin Ct 28227
Austin Dr 28213
Austin Dekota Dr 28269
Austin Knoll Ct 28269
Austin Ridge Ln 28214
Austin Samuel Pl 28214
Auston Crossing Dr 28216
Austringer Pl 28278
Auten Ave 28269
Auten Rd 28216
Auten St 28208
Autumn Ct 28209
Autumn Applause Dr 28277
Autumn Blaze Dr 28278
Autumn Creek Ct 28278
Autumn End Cir 28212
Autumn Gate Ln 28216
Autumn Gold Ct 28278
Autumn Harvest Ln 28269
Autumn Lake Ct 28213
Autumn Leaf Ln 28277
Autumn Moss Ct 28277
Autumn Oak Dr 28269
Autumn Rain Ln 28209
Autumn Ridge Dr 28269
Autumn Trail Dr 28213
Autumnwood Ln 28213
Avalon Ave 28208
Avalon Forest Ln 28269
Avalon Loop Rd 28269
Avaly Ln 28277
Avant St 28204
Avatar Dr 28215
Avebury Dr 28213
Avelon Valley Dr 28277
Aven Creek Ct 28273
Avening Ct 28215
Avensong Crossing Dr 28215
Aventide Ln 28215
Avery Ct 28215
Avery Meadows Dr 28216
Aviary Hill Way 28214
Avignon Ln 28226
Avila Ct 28278
Avon Farm Ln 28269
Avoncliff Dr 28270
Avondale Ave 28210
Avonhurst Ln 28269
Avonlea Ct 28269
Avonwood Ln 28270
Axar Rd 28208
Axis Ct 28273
Axminster Ct 28210
Axson Ln 28278
Aycock Ln 28209
Ayers Orchard Way 28227
Aylesbury Ln 28227
Aylesford Rd 28211
Aynrand Ct 28269
Ayrshire Pl 28210
Ayrshire Glen Pl 28273
Ayrsley Town Blvd 28273
Ayscough Rd 28211
Azalea Ln 28206
Azalea Hills Dr 28262
Azure Valley Pl 28269
B Ave 28216
Babbitt Way 28216
Baberton Ct 28269
Bacardi Ct 28277
Back Acre Dr 28213
Back Bay Ct 28212
Back Creek Dr 28213
Back Creek Church
Rd 28213
Back Ridge Rd 28277
Backwater Dr 28214
Bacon Ave 28208
Badenoch Ct 28217
Badger Ct 28206
Baffin Ct 28269
Bagby Ln 28208
Baggins Ln 28269
Bagley Ln 28227
Baileywick Rd 28277
Bain Farm Rd 28227
Bain School Rd 28227
Bainbridge Rd 28212
Bainview Dr 28227
Baker Dr 28210
Bakewell Ct 28270
Balancing Rock Ct 28262
Balata Ct 28269
Balbriggan Ct 28262
Balch Manor Ct 28277
Balcorn Pl 28214
Bald Eagle Dr 28215
Bald Ridge Dr 28227
Baldwin Ave 28204
Baldwin Hall Dr 28277
Balenie Trace Ln 28277
Bales Ln 28227
Baleville Dr 28227
Balfour Ln 28216
Balgreen Ct 28212
Ballantray Pl 28269
Ballantyne Commons
Pkwy 28277
Ballantyne Corporate
Pl 28277
Ballantyne Country Club
Dr 28277
Ballantyne Crossing
Ave 28277
Ballantyne Forest Dr 28277
Ballantyne Glen Way 28277
Ballantyne Lake Rd 28277
Ballantyne Meadows
Dr 28277
Ballantyne Medical Pl 28277
Ballantyne Trace Ct 28277
Ballantyne Village Way 28277
Ballanvilla Dr 28277
Ballencourt Ln 28226
Ballentyne Ct 28210
Ballina Way 28214
Ballinard Ln 28277
Ballinderry Dr 28273
Ballinger Ln 28277
Ballston Ct 28269
Ballwood Ct 28227
Bally Duff Ln 28262
Ballybay Dr 28278
Ballyclare Ct 28213
Ballyhack Ct 28273
Ballyshannon Ln 28278
Balmoral Cir 28210
Balmoral Park Dr 28277
Balsam Ter 28214
Balsam Bay Rd 28227
Balsam Fir Dr 28212
Balsam Fir Ln 28215
Balsam Tree Dr 28269
Baltimore Ave 28203
Baltinglass Ct 28273
Baltray Rd 28278
N Baltusrol Ln 28210
Balvenie Ct 28215
Bambi Ct 28269
Bamburgh Ct 28216
Banard St 28277
Banbury Dr 28216
Bancroft St 28206
Bandy Dr
6200-6299 28227
6300-6399 28215
Banfield Pl 28226
Banfshire Rd 28215
Bangor Rd 28217
Baniff Cir 28277
W Bank Dr 28214
Bank St 28203
Bankhead Rd 28278
Bankston Pl 28215
Bankwood Dr 28211
Banner Elk Dr 28216
Bannington Rd 28226
Bannister Pl 28213
Bannock Dr 28277
Bannock Glen Dr 28212
Bannockburn Pl 28211
Banteer Rd 28270
Bantry Ln 28262
Banwell Ln 28269
Banyan Ct 28215
Bar Harbor Ln 28210
Baraway Dr 28227
Barbee Dr 28269
Barberry Ct 28211
Barcan Ct 28210
Barclay Downs Dr
3500-3598 28209
3600-4499 28209
4700-4799 28210
Barclay Forest Dr 28213
Barclay Woods Ct 28226
Barcliff Dr 28212
Barcroft Ln 28216
E Barden Rd 28226
Bardot Dr 28216
Bardstown Rd 28226
Bareback Dr 28214
Barefoot Forest Dr 28269
Barfield Dr 28217
Bark Mead Dr 28273
Barkley Rd 28209
Barkridge Rd 28227
Barksdale Cir 28270
Barley Ln 28216
Barlowe Rd 28208
Barmettler Dr 28211
Barn Board Ln 28262
Barn Stone Dr 28227
Barnard St 28227
Barncliff Rd 28227
Barney Dr 28227
Barnhill Dr 28205
Barnsdale Ln 28227
Barnside Ln 28216
Barnsley Pl 28209
Barnview Ct 28269
Baroda Ln 28269
Baronia Pl 28277
Barons Court Rd 28213
Baronwood Ln 28214
Barossa Valley St 28277
Barr Dr 28212
Barrands Ln 28278
Barrelli Ct 28277
Barrette Pl 28277
Barringer Dr
2000-2298 28208
2300-2700 28208
2702-2998 28208
3000-4399 28217
Barrington Dr 28215
Barrister Way 28216
Barroso Ln 28213
Barry Dr 28214
Barry St 28205
Barry Oak Cir 28214
Barry Whitaker Pl 28227
Barrymore Dr 28213
Barson Ln 28269
Bartlett Rd 28227
Bartling Rd 28209
Barton Creek Dr 28262
Barvas St 28262
Barwen Ct 28262
Barwick Rd 28211
Bascale Ln 28227
Bascom St 28205
Basel Pl 28227
Baseline Rd 28262
Basin St 28203
Bask Ct 28227
Baskerville Ave 28269
Bass Ln 28270
Bastia St 28277
Bastille Dr 28278
Batavia Ln 28213
Bath Abbey Ct 28278
Bathurst Dr 28227
Batten Ct 28227
Battery Pl 28273
Battle Ct 28215
Battle Creek Ct 28269
Baucom Rd 28269
Baucom St 28216
Baxter St
800-899 28202
900-1999 28204
Baxter Caldwell Dr 28213
Baxter Harris St 28206
Bay St
1700-1999 28204
2000-2699 28205
Bay Hill Club Dr 28277
Bay Ivy Ct 28227
Bay Pines Ct 28269
Bay Tree Way 28277
Bayberry Dr 28209
Baybrook Ln 28277
Baylor Dr 28210
Baylor Way Ct 28215
Bayse Ct 28273
Baystock Rd 28208
Bayswater Ln 28212
Bayview Pkwy 28216
Baywood Ct 28215
Beachmont Ave 28208
Beacon St 28205
Beacon Forest Dr 28270
Beacon Hill Ln 28270
Beacon Ridge Rd 28210
Beaconsfield Rd 28214
Beagle Ln 28216
Beagle Club Rd 28214
Beaker Ct 28269
Beal St 28211
Bealer Rd 28208
Beam Rd 28217
Beam Lake Dr 28216
Beaman Ave 28273
Beamish Pl 28227
Bear St 28214
Bear Brook Dr 28214
Bear Grass Ln 28227
Bear Mountain Rd 28214
Beard Rd 28269
Beardsley Dr 28269
Bearmore Dr 28211
Bearoak Ln 28269
Bearsden Ct 28217
Bearsfoot Ln 28227
Bearwallow Ct 28213
Bearwood Ave 28205
Beasley Ln 28206
Beatties Ford Rd
100-2126 28216
2127-8599 28216
2127-2127 28297
2128-8598 28216
Beatty Dr 28214
Beau Riley Rd 28277
Beaucatcher Ln 28270
Beaufort Cir 28227
Beaugard Dr 28208
Beaumont Ave 28204
Beauvista Dr 28269
Beauwyck Ct 28211
Beaux St 28208
Beaver Brook Way 28277
Beaver Creek Dr 28269
Beaver Dam Ln 28227
Beaver Hollow Ct 28269
Beckenham Dr 28227
Becket Ridge Rd 28270
Beckett Ct 28211
Beckford Dr 28226
Beckham Ct 28211
Beckhaven Ln 28216
Beckley Pl 28227
Beckwith Pl 28205
Becton Park Dr 28227
Beddingfield Dr 28278
Bedford Rd 28214
Bedford Green Ln 28215
Bedfordshire Dr 28226
Bedlington Dr NW 28269
Bedlington Rd 28278
Bedrock Rd 28270
Bee Tree Cir 28270
Beech Cove Ln 28269
Beech Crest Pl 28269
Beech Mint Dr 28227
Beech Nut Rd 28208
Beechbrooke Rd 28227
Beechdale Dr 28212
Beecher Dr 28215
Beechgrove Ct 28212
Beechknoll Ct 28212
Beechtree Ct 28210
Beechway Cir 28213
Beechwood Ter 28226
Beeding St 28278
Beencenc Rd 28214
Beeswood Dr 28277
Begonia Dr 28215
Beith Ct 28269
Belcamp Ln 28215
Belcaro Ln 28273
Belcher Ln 28226
Belchester Cir 28215
Belcross Dr 28205
Beldegreen Ct 28216
Beldelac Ave 28205
Belfast Dr 28208
Belford Ct 28226
Belgrave Pl 28203
Belicourt Dr 28277
Belknap Rd 28211
Bell Glen Ct 28269
Bella Ct 28210
Bella Marche Dr 28227
Bella Reese Rd 28277
Bella Vista Ct 28216
Bellaire Dr 28216
Bellaire Ridge Dr 28277
Belle Bragg Way 28214
Belle Oaks Dr 28217
Belle Plaine Dr 28215
Belle Terre Ave 28205

Belle Vernon Ave 28210
Bellechasse St 28210
Bellefonte Dr 28206
Bellegarde Dr 28277
Belleglade Trl 28227
Bellegrove Pl 28270
Bellemeade Ln 28270
Bellerive Ct 28277
Bellevue Ln 28226
Bellfield Pl 28270
Bellflower Ln 28227
Bellhaven Blvd
3300-8499 28216
8500-10199 28214
Bellhaven Cir 28214
Bellhaven Walk Ct 28277
Bellingham Ln 28215
Bellmore Ct 28269
Bellows Ln 28270
Bellows Pl 28227
Bells Knox Rd 28214
Bells Mill Dr 28269
Bellville Ct 28269
Bellwood Ln 28270
Belmar Place Rd 28269
Belmeade Dr 28214
Belmeade Green Dr 28214
Belmont Ave
401-497 28206
499-699 28206
800-1299 28205
Belmont Run Ln 28213
Belmont Stables Dr 28216
Belmont Stakes Ln 28278
Belmont Walk Way 28277
Belmorrow Dr 28214
Belquin Ct 28212
Belrose Ln 28209
Belshire Ln 28205
Belstead Brook Ct 28216
Belton St 28209
Beltway Blvd 28214
Belvedere Ave 28205
Belvoir Ct 28270
Bembridge Ct 28269
Ben Craig Dr 28262
Ben Franklin Ct 28277
Ben Livingston Rd 28214
Benard Ave 28206
Benbow Ln 28214
S Bend Ln 28277
Benderloch Dr 28277
Bending Birch Pl 28206
Bending Branch Rd 28227
Benfield Rd 28269
Bengali Cir 28213
Benita Dr 28212
Benjamin St 28203
Bennett St 28213
Bennett Neely Ln 28269
Bennett Woods Ct 28216
Bennettsville Ln 28262
Benning St 28216
Benning Wood Dr 28270
Bennington Pl 28211
Benridge Ln 28226
Bent Branch Rd 28226
Bent Creek Cir 28227
Bent Leaf Ct 28216
Bent Oak Rd 28226
Bent Pine Cir 28270
Bent Tree Ct 28212
Bent Twig Ct 28226
Bentgrass Ct 28227
Bentgrass Run Dr 28269
Benthaven Ln 28269
Bentley Pl 28205
Bentley Oaks Ln 28270
Benton Pl 28277
Bentridge Dr 28226
Bentway Dr 28226
Benziger Ct 28214
Bere Island Dr 28278
Berea Ct 28226
Beresford Rd 28211
Beretania Cir 28211

Berewick Commons
Pkwy 28278
Bergen Ct 28210
Beritstrasse Ct 28277
Berkeley Ave
600-1299 28203
1300-1399 28204
Berkeley Creek Ln 28277
Berkeley Estates Dr 28277
Berkeley Forest Ln 28277
Berkeley Greene Dr 28277
Berkeley Hill Dr 28262
Berkeley Park Ct 28277
Berkeley Pines Ln 28277
Berkeley Place Dr 28262
Berkeley Pond Dr 28277
Berkeley View Cir 28277
Berkeley Woods Ln 28277
Berkshire Rd 28209
Bernardy Ln 28269
Bernbrook Shadow Ln 28269
Bernbrooke Ct 28270
Berneway Dr 28227
Berolina Ln 28226
Berry Creek Rd 28214
Berry Miller Ct 28262
Berry Ridge Rd 28270
Berry Tree Ct 28216
Berrybrook Ln 28269
Berrybush Ct 28269
Berryhill Dr 28214
Berryhill Rd 28208
Berrypatch Ct 28211
Bershire Ln 28262
Bertha Dr 28262
Bertonley Ave 28211
Berwick Rd 28269
Bessant Ct 28262
Bessbrook Rd 28278
Bessie Ct 28213
Bethany Pl 28212
Bethany Brook Ln 28273
Bethel Rd 28208
Bethesda Ct 28226
Betsy Dr 28211
Betsy Ross Ct 28277
Betterton Ln 28269
Beverly Cir 28270
Beverly Dr 28207
Beverly Crest Blvd 28270
Beverly Springs Dr 28270
Beverwyck Rd 28211
Bevington Pl 28277
Bevington Brook Ln 28277
Bevington Hollow Cir 28277
Bevington Oaks Ct 28277
Bevington Ridge Rd 28277
Bevington Woods Ln 28277
Bevis Dr 28209
Bexley Pl 28227
Bexton St 28273
Bianca Ct 28214
Bibury Ln 28211
Bickham Ln 28269
Bickleigh Pl 28215
Biddstone Ct 28226
Biden Ct 28212
Biederbeck Dr 28212
Biemann Valley Dr 28227
Bienville Pl 28270
Biesterfield Dr 28216
Big Bass Ct 28214
Big Bear Dr 28278
Big Cone Pl 28210
Big Horn Cir 28214
Big Leaf Dr 28262
Big Oak Dr 28210
Big Oak Ln 28227
Big River Rd 28216
Billingham Dr 28269
Billings Park Dr 28213
Billingsley Rd 28211
Billingsville School Ct 28214
Billy Graham Pkwy 28201
Billy Smith Ln 28227
Bilmark Ave 28213

Biltmore Dr 28207
Binford Ct 28212
Binfords Ridge Rd 28226
Bingham Dr 28213
Birch Ct 28205
Birch Heights Ct 28213
Birch Knoll Ct 28213
Birch Leaf Ct 28215
Birchbark Ln 28227
Birchcrest Dr 28205
Birchcroft Ln 28269
Birchfield Ct 28277
Birchhill Rd 28227
Birchhollow Dr 28215
Birchley Cir 28213
Birchstone Ln 28269
Birchwood Dr 28214
Bird Watch Ln 28214
Birdie Ct 28227
Birdsong Ln 28214
Birdwell Ct 28269
Birkdale Dr 28208
Birkdale Valley Dr 28277
Birkwood Ct 28278
Birling Rd 28278
Birmingham Dr 28210
Birnamwood Ln 28278
Birnen Dr 28210
Bisaner St 28269
Biscayne Dr 28205
Biscoe Way Ln 28262
Bishar Ln 28277
Bishop Dr 28217
Bishop Crest Ln 28277
Bishop Madison Ln 28216
Bishopton Pl 28216
Bismark Pl 28211
Bitter Creek Dr 28214
Bitterbush Ct 28269
Bitterroot Ct 28269
Bittersweet Ln 28270
Bittinger Ct 28216
Black Ave 28216
Black Bear Ct 28214
Black Cherry Dr 28262
Black Chestnut Pl 28278
Black Diamond Ct 28216
Black Dog Ln 28214
Black Duck Ct 28273
Black Fox Ct 28269
Black Heath Cir 28214
Black Kettle Dr 28213
Black Maple Ave 28269
Black Satchel Rd 28216
Black Sycamore Dr 28226
Black Trail Ct 28269
Black Walnut Ln 28262
Black Watch Ct 28277
Blackberry Cir 28209
Blackberry Ridge Ln 28208
Blackbird Ct 28269
Blackbird Hill Ln 28227
Blackbridge Ln 28213
Blackburn Ct 28209
Blackfriars Ct 28278
Blackhawk Rd 28213
Blackhorse Ln 28210
Blackjack Ln 28213
Blackmon St 28208
Blackmuir Wood Cir 28270
Blackthorne Ln 28209
Blacktree Ln 28226
Blackwood Ave 28205
Bladworth Ct 28277
Blair Rd 28227
Blair House Ct 28270
Blairbeth St 28277
Blairhill Rd 28217
Blairmore Dr 28211
Blairtree Ct 28227
Blake A Dare Rd 28269
Blake Port Ct 28270
Blakeford Ln 28226
Blakeney Dr 28277
Blakeney Centre Dr 28277
Blakeney Greens Blvd 28277

Blakeney Heath Rd 28277
Blakeney Park Dr 28277
Blakeney Preserve Dr 28277
Blakeney Professional
Dr 28277
Blakewood Dr 28277
Blalock Ave 28210
Blanbeth St 28277
E & W Bland St 28203
Blandford Dr 28262
Blandwood Dr 28217
Blasdell Ct 28269
Blaydes Ct 28226
Blaydon Dr 28227
Blaze Manor Ln 28215
Blazeprince Dr 28215
Blazer Dr 28216
Bleckley Ct 28270
Bleeker St 28215
Blendwood Dr 28215
Blenheim Rd 28208
Blessing St 28208
Blithe Low Pl 28273
Block House Ct 28277
Blockade Ct 28226
Bloomdale Dr 28211
Bloomfield Dr 28277
Bloomsbury Pl 28226
Blossoming Ct 28273
Blowing Rock Way 28210
Blue Ash Ln 28215
Blue Aster Ln 28269
Blue Bell Ln 28270
Blue Blossom Rd 28277
Blue Bridge Ct 28214
Blue Cedar Ln 28277
Blue Finch Ln 28269
Blue Grove Rd 28277
Blue Hampton Ln 28213
Blue Heron Dr 28226
Blue Jasper Rd 28277
Blue Jay Ln 28227
Blue Junction Rd 28277
Blue Lilac Ln 28269
Blue Mist Cir 28262
Blue Moss Ct 28214
Blue Mountain Ln 28262
Blue Oaks Ct 28214
Blue Ridge Cir 28270
Blue Rock Dr 28213
Blue Sky Ln 28269
Blue Spruce Ln 28227
Blue Tick Ct 28269
Blue Topaz Ct 28216
Blue Willow Ln 28227
Blueberry Ln 28226
Blueberry Hollow Pl 28208
Blueberry Patch Ln 28208
Bluebird Dr 28226
Bluebonnet Rd 28212
Bluefield St 28273
Bluegill Rd 28216
Bluesage Cir 28270
Blueshot Ct 28273
Bluestar Ln 28226
Bluestem Ln 28277
Bluestone Ct 28212
Bluewing Teal Ct 28273
Bluff Ct 28206
Bluff Wood Cv 28212
Bluffton Ridge Dr 28278
Blushing Star Ct 28215
S Blvd 28203
Blythe Blvd 28203
Blythe Ridge Ct 28213
Blythedale Dr 28213
Blythwood Ln 28227
Boars Head Ct 28214
Boaz Ct 28211
Bob Beatty Rd 28269
Bob White Ct 28213
Bobby Ln 28211
Bobcat Pl 28269
Bobhouse Dr 28277
Bobolink Ln 28226
Bobterry Ct 28216

Bodenham Ct 28215
Bodgit Ln 28215
Bodkin Ct 28215
Bogart Dr 28262
Boham Ct 28277
Bolingbrook Ln 28273
Bolling Rd 28207
Bolton Ct 28269
Bomar Dr 28216
Bon Rea Dr 28226
Bonaire Dr 28208
Bonavie Cir 28215
Bond St 28208
Bondale Pl 28216
Bondhaven Dr 28215
Bonita Ln 28262
Bonita Vista Ln 28227
Bonlyn Dr 28227
Bonner Bridge Ct 28273
Bonneville Dr 28205
Bonnie Ln 28213
Bonnie Blue Ln 28273
Bonnie Briar Cir 28277
Bonnie Butler Way 28270
Bonnie Cone Ln 28262
Bonnybridge Ct 28278
Bonnybrook Ln 28212
Bonnyrigg Ct 28270
Bonroi Ave 28213
Bonwood Dr 28211
Bookbinders Ln 28270
Booker Ave 28216
Bookwalter Ct 28277
Boomerang Way 28269
Boone St 28216
Borchetta Dr 28277
Bordeaux St 28277
Border Dr 28208
Bosham Ln 28270
Bosswell Rd 28215
Bost St 28208
Boston Ave 28212
Botany St 28216
Bottlebrush Pl 28277
Boudins Ln 28278
Boulder Ln 28269
Boulder Creek Dr 28273
Boulware Ct 28277
Bournewood Ln 28226
Bourton House Dr 28211
Bow Rd 28217
Bowery Ct 28215
Bowman Rd 28217
Bowsby Ct 28215
Bowstring Ct 28214
Box Car Ct 28227
Boxelder Ln 28262
Boxer Ln 28269
Boxford Ct 28215
Boxmeer Dr 28269
Boxwood Ln 28210
Boyce Rd 28211
Boyd St 28208
Boyd Cove Ln 28278
Boyer St 28208
Boykin Spaniel Rd 28277
Boylston Dr 28216
Boysenberry Ct 28216
Brace Rd 28211
Bracebridge Ct 28278
Brachetto Pl 28277
Brachnell View Dr 28269
Bracken House Ln 28277
N Brackenbury Ln 28270
Brackenview Ct 28214
Bradbury Dr 28209
Braddock Ln 28277
Braden Dr 28216
Bradenbury Ct 28215
Bradenton Dr 28210
Bradford Dr 28208
Bradford Lake Ln 28269
Bradford Woods Dr 28209
Bradgate Rd 28217
Bradley Ct 28227
Bradley Russell Ct 28214

Bradlow Ct 28210
Bradstock Ln 28226
Bradstreet Commons
Way 28215
Bradwell Dr 28269
Brady Dr 28269
Braeburn Rd 28211
Braemar Ter 28210
Braeside Ct 28270
Braewick Pl 28227
Braewood Pl 28226
Bragg St 28273
Brahman Meadows Ln 28273
Braid Hills Dr 28277
Braids Bend Ct 28269
Bralers Dr 28269
Bramble Pl 28208
Bramble Ridge Ct 28215
Brambleton Ct 28277
Bramblewood Dr 28217
Bramlet Rd 28205
Brampton Dr 28215
Bramwyck Dr 28210
Branch St 28215
Branch Bend Ln 28273
Branch Hill Cir 28213
Branch Way Ct 28273
Branchview Dr 28217
Branchwater Ave 28277
Brancusi Ct 28215
Brandemere Ct 28210
Brandenburg Ct 28210
Brandermill Pl 28226
Brandie Glen Rd 28269
Brandon Cir 28211
Brandon Rd 28207
Brandon Brook Dr 28277
Brandon Manor Ln 28211
Brandon Trail Dr 28213
Brandonwood Ct 28226
Brandy Ridge Ln 28269
Brandybuck Dr & Ln 28269
Brandywine Rd 28209
Brangus Ln 28227
Brannock Hills Dr 28278
Branscomb Dr 28262
Branson Ct 28210
Brantford Dr 28210
Brantham Ct 28211
Branthurst Dr 28269
Brantley Dr 28214
Brass Bell Ct 28227
Brass Eagle Ln 28210
Brassy Creek Ln 28269
Bratcher Ave 28216
Brathay Ct 28269
Brattleboro Ct 28217
Bratton Pl 28277
Braveheart Ln 28216
Brawer Farm Dr 28269
Brawley Ln 28215
Braxfield Dr 28217
Braxton Dr 28226
Bray Dr 28214
Brazos St 28214
Breamore Dr 28270
Brechin Dr 28277
Breckfield Ct 28278
Bredon Dr 28226
Breeders Cup Cir 28215
Breezehill Ln 28262
Breezewood Dr 28262
Breezy Knoll Ct 28210
Breezy Morn Ln 28269
Breezy Trail Ln 28216
Breitling Grove Pl 28212
Brem Ln 28277
Bremer Ct 28210
Bremerton Ct 28227
Brenda Ct 28269
Brenda Ann Rd 28214
Brendon Patrick Ct 28262
Brenly Ct 28269
Brenock Ln 28269
Brent Hall Ct 28270
Brentford Dr 28210

Brentmoor Dr 28262
Brentwood Pl 28208
Breton Rd 28214
Brett Ct 28216
Breuster Dr 28210
Brevard Ct 28202
N Brevard St
300-799 28202
900-2399 28206
2400-2899 28205
S Brevard St 28202
Brevera Cir 28213
Brewer Dr 28208
Brewster St 28216
Brewton Dr 28206
Briabend Dr 28209
Brian William Rd 28212
Brianna Way 28217
Brianton Pl 28226
Brianwood Ct 28269
Briar Creek Rd 28205
Briar Oak Ct 28226
Briar Ridge Dr 28270
Briar Rose Ct 28269
Briarberry Ct 28270
Briarcliff Pl 28207
Briarcrest Ct & Dr NW 28269
Briardale Dr 28212
Briarfield Dr 28205
Briargrove Dr 28215
Briarhill Dr 28215
Briarhurst Pl 28227
Briarly Ct 28210
Briarpatch Ln 28211
Briarthorne Dr 28269
Briarwick Ln 28277
Briarwood Dr 28215
Brice St 28208
Brick Church Ct 28277
Brick Dust Way 28269
Bricker Dr 28273
Brickleberry Ln 28262
Brickstone Dr 28227
Brickyard Rd 28214
Bridal Veil Dr 28217
Briddle Hall Ct 28214
Brideswell Ln 28278
S Bridge Cir 28273
Bridge Creek Way 28277
Bridgehampton Dr 28262
Bridgehampton Club
Dr 28277
Bridgemount Ave 28277
Bridgepath Trl 28269
Bridgeport Dr 28215
Bridger Ct 28211
Bridgeview Ln 28277
Bridgeville Ln 28262
Bridgewalk Dr 28277
Bridgewater Ln 28227
Bridgewood Ln 28226
Bridle Ct 28216
Bridle Brook Way 28270
Bridle Ridge Ln 28269
Bridle Stone Ct 28273
Bridlepath Ln 28211
Bridlespur Ln 28210
Bridlewood Ln 28215
Brief Rd 28227
Brigadier Ln 28227
Briggs Dr 28269
Bright Rd 28214
Bright Angel Ct 28277
Brightfalls Way 28213
Brighthaven Ln 28214
Brightleaf Pl 28269
Brighton Pl
1100-1199 28205
14700-15199 28227
Brighton Brook Dr 28212
Brighton Park Dr 28227
Brightstar Valley Rd 28227
Brightstone Ct 28277
Brigmore Dr 28226
Brigstock Ct 28269
Brim St 28214

Brimberry Ct 28216
Brimwood Ter 28214
Brinsdale Ct 28227
Brinton Pl 28226
Brisbane Ct 28215
Bristle Ln 28214
Bristle Creek Ct 28214
Bristle Toe Ln 28277
Bristlecone Ct 28227
Bristley Rd 28227
Bristol Dr 28208
Bristol Ford Pl 28215
Bristol Place Ct 28226
Brite And Earley Rd 28214
British Gardens Ln 28277
Brittany Ct 28270
Brittany Oaks Dr 28277
Brittmore Ct 28227
Brittni Dayle Dr 28214
Britton Wood Pl 28278
Brixham Hill Ave 28277
Brixton Ct 28205
Broad St 28210
Broad Creek Ct 28262
Broad Hollow Dr 28226
Broad Oak Dr 28273
Broad Ridge Ct 28269
Broadfield Rd 28226
Broadford Ct 28277
Broadleaf Pl 28226
Broadmoor Dr 28209
Broadview Dr 28217
Broadwater Ln 28273
Broadwick St 28213
Broadwing Pl 28278
Brock Run 28269
Brockbank Rd 28209
Brockhampton Ct 28269
Brocklehurst Ln 28215
Brockley Ct 28215
Brockton Ln 28226
Brogan Dr 28214
Broken Arrow Ct 28227
Broken Branch Rd 28213
Broken Oak Ln 28226
Broken Pebble Ln 28227
Broken Pine Ln 28269
Broken Saddle Ln 28226
Broken Stone Ct 28214
Broken Woods Rd 28278
Bromley Rd 28207
Brompton Ln 28269
Bromwich Rd 28208
Bronwin St 28273
Bronze Pike Dr 28273
Brook Rd 28205
Brook Canyon Dr 28212
Brook Crossing Ct 28212
Brook Falls Ct 28269
Brook Farm Ln 28214
Brook Forest Ln 28211
Brook Hollow Rd 28270
Brook Meadow Pl 28214
Brookbury Ct 28226
Brookchase Ln 28205
Brookcrest Dr 28210
Brookdale Ave 28210
Brookdale Dr 28215
Brooke Nicole Pl 28213
Brookfield Dr 28210
Brookfield Pl 28270
Brookfield Pointe Dr 28216
Brookford St 28273
Brookgreen Dr 28227
Brookhaven Rd 28210
Brookhill Rd 28203
Brookhurst Dr 28205
Brookings Dr 28269
Brooklain Dr 28214
Brooklet Ln 28212
Brookmeade Dr 28226
Brookmere Ln 28214
Brookmont Pl 28210
Brooknell Ter 28270
Brookridge Ln 28211
Brookrun Dr 28209

Brooks Knoll Ln 28227
Brooks Mill Rd 28227
Brooksedge Dr 28216
Brookshire Blvd 28216
Brookside Ave 28203
Brookside Ln 28262
Brookstead Dr 28215
Brookstead Meadow
Ct 28215
Brooksvale St 28208
Brooktree Dr 28208
Brookview Dr 28205
Brookway Dr 28208
Brookwood Rd
2100-2299 28211
3700-4699 28215
Brookwood Valley Ln 28227
Broomsage Ln 28217
Brossa Valley St 28277
Brotherly Ln 28278
Brown Bark Ter 28226
Brown Grier Rd 28273
Brown Oak Ct 28227
Browne Rd 28269
Brownes Creek Rd 28269
Brownes Ferry Rd 28269
Brownes Pond Ln 28277
Brownestone View Dr 28269
Brownfield Trail Ct 28273
Browning Ave 28205
Browns Ave 28208
Brownstone St 28216
Bruff Ct 28270
Brumit Ln 28269
Brunning Glen Ct 28215
N Bruns Ave 28216
S Bruns Ave 28208
Brunswick Ave 28207
Bruntsfield Pl 28277
Brush Creek Ln 28227
Brushwood Dr 28262
Brushy Ln 28270
Bryan Furr Dr 28216
Bryanstone Ct 28226
Bryant St 28208
Bryant Farms Rd 28277
Bryant Field Cir 28277
Bryant Meadows Dr 28278
Bryn Athyn Ct 28269
Brynfield Dr 28277
Brynhurst Dr 28210
Brynmar Dr 28270
Brynwood Dr 28226
Bryony Ct 28277
Bryson Ct 28211
Bryson Bend Dr 28277
Bubbling Branch Ln 28273
Bubbling Brook Ct 28278
Buccaneer Rd 28227
Buchanan St 28203
Buchanan Brake Ln 28277
Buchannon Corner Dr 28213
Buck Ct 28269
Buckeye Ln 28270
Buckfield Pl 28277
Buckhaven Ct 28227
Buckhead Ct 28211
Buckhorn St 28216
Buckie Ct 28278
Buckingham Dr 28209
Buckland Rd 28278
Bucklebury Ct 28269
Buckleigh Dr 28215
Buckminister Ct 28269
Bucknell Ave 28207
Buckskin Ln 28227
Buckspring Ln 28269
Buckstone Ln 28277
Buckthorne Ridge Ln 28278
Buckvalley Dr 28214
Budding Ct 28227
Buddy Holly Rd 28216
Buena Vista Ave 28205
Buene Aire Dr 28227
Buffalo Valley Dr 28214
Buffton Ct 28277

Buggy Horse Rd 28277
Bugle Ct 28273
Buick Dr 28212
Bullard St 28208
Bulle Rock Ct 28216
Bullock Dr 28214
Bullock Greenway
Blvd 28277
Bumpious Ct 28273
Bunch Walnuts Rd 28278
Bunche Dr 28205
Bunclody Dr 28213
Bundy Cir 28211
Bungalow Rd 28208
Bunker Hill Cir 28210
Bunnyfriend Rd 28262
Bunting Ln 28227
Bur Oak Dr 28214
Burbank Dr 28216
Burch Dr 28269
Burch Shire Rd 28269
Buren Ave 28208
Burgandy Dr 28262
Burgate Dr 28215
Burgess Dr 28208
Burgin St 28205
Burkandt Rd 28227
Burke Dr 28208
Burkhard Way 28226
Burkholder Rd 28214
Burkland Dr 28205
Burkston Rd 28269
Burleigh St 28211
Burleson Dr 28215
Burlwood Rd 28211
Burma Dr 28214
Burmester Ln 28227
Burmith Ave 28269
Burnaby Ct 28269
Burner Dr 28205
Burnette Ave 28208
Burning Bush Ct 28227
Burning Oak Ln 28216
Burning Tree Dr 28277
Burnley Rd 28210
Burnside Ln 28277
Burnt Hickory Dr 28278
Burnt Leather Ln 28277
Burnt Mill Rd 28210
Burnt Umber Dr 28215
Burntwood Ct 28227
Burnwick Ct 28213
Burr Oak Ln 28278
Burroughs St 28213
Burton St 28206
Burtonwood Cir 28212
Burwash Ct 28277
Bush Mill Ln 28270
Bushy Creek Dr 28216
Bushy Pine Ct 28273
Business Ln 28227
Business Center Dr 28214
Bustlehead Ct 28262
Butler Rd 28208
Butner Trail Ln 28269
Butterfly Ln 28269
Buttermere Pl 28213
Butternut Ct 28203
Butterwick Ln 28212
Button Bush Ct 28216
Button Pointe Ct 28216
Buttonwood Ct 28215
Bydand Ct 28215
Byerly Ct 28209
Byrchmont Pl 28210
Byrnes St 28205
Byrum Dr 28217
Byrum St 28216
Byswick Pl 28270
Byway Rd 28214
Bywood Ln 28209
C Ave 28216
Cabarrus Rd 28227
Cabe Ln 28214
Cabell Way 28211
Cabell View Ct 28277

Cabin Creek Ct 28269
Caboose Ct 28226
Cabot Cir 28226
Cabot Hill Ct 28213
Cabotwood Ln 28212
Cactus Valley Rd 28277
Cadagon Ct 28270
Cadbury Ct 28277
Caddy Ct 28278
Caden Lee Way 28273
Cadence Ct 28273
Cadencia Ct 28262
Cades Cove Dr 28273
Cadmium Ct 28215
Cafferty Cir 28215
Cagle Dr 28227
Cagney St 28262
Cahill Ln 28277
Cairns Mill Ct 28269
Cairnsmore Pl 28227
Calais Pl 28211
Caldwell Rd 28213
N Caldwell St
200-799 28202
900-1799 28206
S Caldwell St
200-599 28202
1000-1299 28203
Caldwell Forest Dr 28213
Caldwell Ridge Pkwy 28213
Caldwell Williams Rd 28216
Caledonian Ln 28273
Caleo Cir 28270
Calgary Dr 28215
Calibre Crossing Dr 28227
Calico Ct 28212
Calico Crossing Dr 28273
Caliterra Dr 28227
Callabridge Ct 28216
Callahan St 28206
Callahan Mill Dr 28213
Callander Ct 28277
Callender Ln 28269
Calley Glenn Ln 28226
Calliope Ct 28227
Callison Ct 28215
Callow Forest Dr 28273
Calloway Dr 28277
Calloway Glen Dr 28273
Calpella Ct 28262
Calton Ln 28214
Calumet Pl 28210
Calverie Ct 28278
Calvert St 28208
Calvine Ave 28206
E & W Cama St 28217
Camalier Ln 28273
Camargo Ct 28277
Camaross Dr 28270
Cambellton Dr 28269
Camberwell Rd 28227
Camborne Pl 28210
Cambria Rd 28210
Cambridge Rd 28209
Cambridge Bay Dr 28269
Cambridge Beltway Dr 28273
Cambridge Commons
Dr 28215
Cambridge Crescent
Dr 28226
Cambridge Green Dr 28277
Cambridge Hill Ln 28270
Cambridge Woods Ct 28277
Camden Rd 28203
Camden Creek Ln 28273
Camden Meadow Dr 28273
Camden Park Pl 28210
Camden Trail Ct 28277
Camelback Cir 28226
Camellia Ln 28277
Camelot Dr 28270
Cameo Ct 28270
Cameron Ave 28204
Cameron Forest Ln 28210
Cameron Glen Dr 28210
Cameron Oaks Dr 28211

Cameron Spring Rd 28214
Cameron Valley Pkwy
4500-4599 28211
4800-4999 28210
Cameron Walk Ct 28217
Cameron Wood Dr 28210
Camfield St 28277
Camilla Dr 28226
Camp Greene St 28208
Camp Stewart Rd 28215
Camp Verde Ln 28277
Campbell Dr 28205
Campbell Burn Ct 28212
Campbell Creek Ln 28212
Campbell Hall Ct 28277
Campion Ct 28213
Campus St 28216
Campus Edge Cir 28262
Campus Pointe Ct 28262
Campus Walk Ln 28262
Camrose Dr 28215
Canary Ct 28269
Canberra Pl 28227
Canbury Ct 28269
Cancun Way 28227
Candis Dr 28212
Candle Ct 28211
Candle Leaf Ct 28269
Candleberry Ct 28210
Candlehill Dr 28227
Candlelight Ct 28226
Candler Ln 28217
Candlestick Ct 28273
Candlewood Dr 28210
Candlewyck Ln 28226
Candystick Ln 28213
Candytuff Ln 28278
Cane Ct
3800-3899 28278
7100-7199 28226
Cane Crossing Rd 28277
Cane Field Dr 28273
Canfield Hill Ct 28270
Canipe Dr 28269
Canipe Farm Ct 28269
Canmore St 28277
Cannarti Dr 28273
Cannes St 28277
Cannings Ln 28262
Cannon Ave 28269
Cannon Creek Ln 28216
Cannonball Dr 28213
Cannongate Dr 28227
Canoebrook Rd 28210
Canopy Ln 28269
Canso Ct 28269
Canter Dr 28227
Canter Post Dr 28216
Canterbrook Dr 28269
N & S Canterbury Rd 28211
Canterbury Hill Cir 28211
Canterway Dr 28227
Canterwood Dr 28213
Cantey Pl 28211
Cantle Dr 28216
Canton Pl 28206
Cantwell St 28208
Canvasback Dr 28273
Canyon Dr 28262
N Canyon Rd 28214
Canyon Trl 28270
Canyon Creek Ln 28216
Cape Ferry Ct 28277
Capitol Dr 28208
Capon Springs Ln 28227
Capps Rd 28278
Capps Hill Dr 28216
Capps Hill Mine Rd 28216
Capps Hollow Dr 28216
Capra Ct 28214
Capricorn Ln 28277
Caprington Ave 28262
Caprock Ct 28213
Capstone Ct 28215
Captain Ardrey Rd 28277
Captain Jack Cir 28215

Captain John Ln 28273
Captain Neal Ln 28273
Capworth Ln 28273
Caracara Ct 28278
Caradon Dr 28227
Caragana Ct 28277
Caranna Ct 28277
Carastan Dr 28216
Caravel Ct 28215
Caraway Woods Ct 28277
Carberry Ct 28226
Card St 28205
Cardamon Ct 28273
Carden Dr 28227
Carderock Ct 28214
Cardiff Ave 28205
Cardigan Ave 28215
Cardinal Dr 28205
Cardinal Glen Ct 28269
Cardinal Point Rd 28269
Cardinal Ridge Ct 28270
Cardinals Nest Dr 28269
Cardington Ct 28216
Carelock Cir 28215
Carey Ct 28210
Carfax Dr 28216
Caribou Ct 28273
Carillon Way 28270
Carisbrook Ln 28277
Carlanda Cir 28209
Carleen Way Dr 28213
Carlesbrooke Ter 28270
Carleto Ct 28214
Carlingford Ct 28208
Carlota Ct 28269
Carlotta St 28208
Carlow Hills Pl 28278
Carlsbad Rd 28270
Carlton Ave 28203
Carlton Woods Ln 28278
Carly Ln 28227
Carlyle Dr 28208
Carmathen Rd 28269
Carmel Rd
1400-5999 28226
6001-8699 28226
6300-8698 28226
6300-6300 28247
Carmel Acres Dr 28226
Carmel Chace Dr 28226
Carmel Club Dr 28226
Carmel Commons
Blvd 28226
Carmel Crossing Rd 28226
Carmel Estates Rd 28226
Carmel Executive Park
Dr 28226
Carmel Forest Dr 28226
Carmel Hills Dr 28226
Carmel Lakes Dr 28226
Carmel Oaks Ct 28226
Carmel Park Dr & Ln 28226
Carmel Ridge Rd 28226
Carmel Station Ave 28226
Carmel Valley Rd 28226
Carmel Vista Ln 28226
Carmenet Ln 28214
Carmine St 28206
Carmody Ct 28277
Carnbrook Pl 28212
Carnegie Blvd 28209
Carneros Creek Rd 28214
Carnfeld Ln 28215
Carnival St 28262
Carnoustie Ln 28210
Carnsore Ct 28214
Carob Tree Ln 28215
Carol Ave 28208
Carol Ann Dr 28215
Carol Leigh Dr 28213
Carole Ln 28214
Carolina Ave 28208
Carolina Academy Rd 28277
Carolina Crossing Dr 28273
Carolina Forest Ct 28273
Carolina Laurel Ct 28215

Carolina Lily Ln 28262
Carolina Oak Cir 28273
Carolina Rose Ter 28215
Caroline Whitney Cir 28212
Carolyn Dr 28205
Carolyn Ln 28213
Caronia St 28208
Carosan Ln 28270
Carothers St 28216
Carousel Dr 28212
Caroway St 28262
Carowill Cir 28209
Carowinds Blvd 28273
Carpentaria Ct 28215
Carpenter Dr 28226
Carpenter Cabin Dr 28216
Carpet St 28273
Carradale Way 28278
Carrbridge Ln 28226
Carriage Drive Cir 28205
Carriage Hill Pl 28262
Carriage Lake Dr 28273
Carriage Oaks Dr 28262
Carriagehouse Ln 28226
Carriageway Ln 28227
Carrie Ln 28227
Carrier Dr 28216
Carrington Ct 28208
Carrington Dr 28214
Carrington Hill Dr 28214
Carrington Oaks Dr 28273
Carrollton Ln 28210
Carrolwood Dr 28217
Carronbridge Ln 28216
Carrot Patch Dr 28216
Carrowmore Pl 28208
Carsdale Pl 28210
E & W Carson Blvd 28203
Carson Whitley Ave 28277
Carsons Pond Rd 28226
Carstairs St 28213
Carswell Ln 28277
Carter Ave 28206
Carter Creek Dr 28227
Carteret St 28205
Cartesian Dr 28214
Cartgate Ln 28273
Cartier Way 28208
Cartness Pl 28226
Cartwright Pl 28208
Carved Oak Cir 28227
Carved Tree Ln 28262
Carver Blvd & Pl 28269
Carver Cove Ln 28208
Carver Falls Rd 28214
Carver Pond Rd 28269
Carving Tree Dr 28227
Cary Ridge Dr 28277
Carya Pond Ln 28212
Carysbrook Ln 28217
Casa Ct 28215
Casa Lake Dr 28215
Casa Loma St 28269
Casa Lynda Ln 28215
Casa Nuestra Dr 28214
Cascade Cir 28211
Cascade Pointe Blvd 28208
Caselton Ct NW 28269
Cashel Ct 28270
Casino Dr 28216
Caslon Ct 28270
Casper Dr 28214
Cassamia Pl 28211
Cassamia Glen Cir 28211
Cassington Ct 28273
Cassio Ct 28227
Castellaine Dr 28226
Castello Ln 28269
Castle Ct 28213
Castle Abbey Ln 28277
Castle Garden Ln 28215
Castle Pine Ct 28226
Castle Ridge Ct 28269
Castle Terrace Ct 28215
Castle Watch Ave 28277
Castlebar Rd 28270

Street	ZIP
Castlebay Dr	28277
Castleberry Ct	28209
Castlecomer Dr	28262
Castlecove Rd	28278
Castleford Dr	28227
Castlegate Dr	28226
Castleglen Ct	28269
Castlehayne Ct	28215
Castlekeep Rd	28226
Castlemaine Dr	28269
Castlerock Dr	28215
Castlestone Dr	28227
Castleton Rd	28211
Castletown House Dr	28273
Castlewood Rd	28209
Castlewynd Ct	28212
Casual Corner Ln	28227
N & S Caswell Rd	28204
Catalina Ave	28206
Catalina Ln	28216
Catawba Ave	28205
Cates St	28202
Catfish Dr	28214
Cathedral Way	28278
W Catherine St	28203
Catherine Miller Dr	28273
Catherine Simmons Ave	28216
Catherines Mine Cir	28277
Cathey Rd	28214
Cattail Ct	28215
Caudell Pl	28215
Causeway Dr	28227
Cavaletti Pl	28227
Cavalier Ct	28205
Cavan Ct	28270
Cavanshire Trl	28278
Cave Creek Ct	28213
Cavendish Ct	28211
Cavett Ct	28269
Cavonnier Ln	28216
Cayenne Dr	28214
Cayman Way	28217
Caymus Dr	28269
S Cecil St	28204
Cecilia Ln	28273
Cedar Ln	28226
N Cedar St	28202
S Cedar St	
200-799	28202
800-1099	28208
Cedar Bird Ln	28270
Cedar Bluff Ln	28227
Cedar Circle Dr	28210
Cedar Cliff Dr	28216
Cedar Cove Ct	28270
Cedar Creek Ln	28210
Cedar Crest Ct	28226
Cedar Croft Dr	
6100-6399	28226
6400-6599	28270
Cedar Crossings Dr	28273
Cedar Farm Rd	28278
Cedar Glen Dr	28212
Cedar Grove Rd	28227
Cedar Hill Dr	28273
Cedar Lake Ct	28226
Cedar Point Ln	28210
Cedar Post Ln	28215
Cedar Rock Dr	28273
Cedar Rose Ln	28217
Cedar Run Way	28273
Cedar Springs Rd	28212
Cedar Stone Trl	28277
Cedar Trail Ln	28210
Cedar Tree Ln	28227
Cedar View Rd	28226
Cedar Walk Ln	28277
Cedarbrook Dr	28215
Cedarcreek Dr	28215
Cedardale Ridge Ct	28269
Cedarfield Rd	28227
Cedarforest Dr	28226
Cedarhurst Dr	28269
Cedarknoll Ct	28270
Cedarmint Dr	28227
Cedars East Ct	28212
Cedarvale Rd	28214
Cedarwild Rd	28212
Cedarwood Ln	28212
Celandine Ct	28213
Celbridge Ct	28270
Celebration Rd	28278
Celeste Ct	28270
Celia Ave	28216
Cello Ct	28215
Celosia Dr	28262
Celtic Ct	28277
Cemetary St	28216
Cemetery St	28216
Cemkey Way Ct	28269
Centennial Dr	28213
Center Lake Dr	28216
Center Park Dr	28217
Centerfield Dr	28214
Centergrove Ln	28214
Centerline Dr	28278
Central Ave	
5559A-5559B	28212
600-1299	28204
1300-5199	28205
5200-5799	28212
Central Dr	28227
Central Pacific Ave	28210
Centre St	28216
Century Pl	28206
Century Oaks Ln	28262
Cerise Dr	28269
Cessna Rd	28208
Chaceview Ct	28269
Chadburn Ln	28215
Chadfort Ln	28226
Chadmore Dr	28270
Chadmore South Dr	28270
Chadsford Pl	28211
Chadsworth Ct	28269
Chadwell Ln	28269
Chadwick Pl	28226
Chadwyck Farms Dr	28226
Chagall Ct	28205
Chalcome Ct	28210
Chalcroft Ct	28227
Chalet Ln	28278
Chalfont Ct	28262
Chalgrove Ln	28216
Chalk Hill Ln	28214
Chalkstone Rd	28216
Challenger Dr	28213
Challis Farm Rd	28226
Challis Hill Ln	28226
Challis View Ln	28226
Challisford Ln	28226
Chalmers St	28217
Chalyce Ln	28270
Chamberlain Ave	28208
Chamberlain Rd	28277
Chamberlain Hall Ct	28277
Chambray Ln	28278
Chambwood Dr	28205
Chameroy Ct	28270
Champaign St	28210
Champions Crest Dr	28269
Chancellor Park Dr	28213
Chancellors Pl	28213
Chandler Pl	28211
Chandler Haven Dr	28269
Chandonwood Ct	28226
Chandworth Rd	28210
Channing Ct	28215
Chansonette Ct	28213
Chanticleer Ct	28214
Chantilly Ln	28205
Chantress Ln	28215
Chapeclane Rd	28278
Chapel Creek Ct	28226
Chapel Crossing Ct	28269
Chapel Ridge Rd	28269
Chapelton Dr	28214
Chaplin Ln	28211
Chapman St	28216
Chapparall Ln	28215
Chapparall View Ln	28215
Chapultepec Rd	28210
Char Meck Ln	28205
Charbray Ln	28213
Charcon Ct	28213
Charette Ct	28215
Charidge Ln	28262
Charing Pl	28211
Charing Grove Ln	28273
Charles Ave	28205
Charles Crawford Dr	28269
Charles Patrick Ct	28214
Charleston Dr	28212
Charleston Place Ln	28212
Charlestowne Manor Dr	28211
Charlie Hipp Rd	28214
Charlotte Dr	28203
Charlotte Park Dr	28217
Charlotte View Dr	28277
Charlottetowne Ave	28204
Charlton Ln	28210
Charmal Pl	28226
Charmapeg Ave	28211
Charminster Ct	28269
Charnay Ter	28226
Charndon Village Ct	28211
Charnell Ln	28216
Charnwood Ct	28277
Charolais Ln	28213
Charred Pine Cir	28227
Charter Pl	28211
Charter Brook Dr	28270
Charter Hills Rd	28277
Charter Oak Ln	28226
Charterhall Ln	28215
Chartwell Ln	28212
N & S Chase St	28207
Chaser Ridge Ct	28216
Chasewater Dr	28277
Chasewind Dr	28269
Chasewood Dr	28212
Chastain Ave	28217
Chastain Parc Dr	28216
Chastain Walk Dr	28216
Chatfield Dr	28278
Chatford Ln	28210
Chatham Ave	28205
Chatham Oaks Trl	28210
Chatham Ridge Cir	28273
Chatsworth Ct	28277
Chattanooga Ln	28227
Chattaroy Dr	28214
Chatterbird Ct	28226
Chaucer Dr	28210
Chaumont Ln	28277
Chausley Ct	28211
Chavel Ln	28269
Cheddington Dr	28211
Chedworth Dr	28210
Cheleys Ridge Ln	28270
Chelmsford Rd	28211
Chelsea Dr	28209
Chelsea Bay Dr	28278
Chelsea Garden Ct	28213
Chelsea Jade Ln	28269
Chelsea Place Ct	28211
Cheltenham Rd	28211
Chelton Oaks Dr	28214
Chelton Ridge Ln	28277
Chelveston Dr	28208
Chelwood Pl	28217
Chenango Dr	28212
Chencom Dr	28208
Chepstow Ct	28262
Cherokee Pl & Rd	28207
Cherring Ln	28262
Cherry St	28204
Cherry Bluff Ct	28216
Cherry Tree Ln	28270
Cherry Tripp Dr	28212
Cherry Wood Ln	28217
Cherrybrook Dr	28227
Cherrycrest Ln	28217
Cheryl Anne Pl	28262
Chesapeake Dr	28216
Chesham Dr	28227
Cheshire Ave	28208
Chesley Dr	28277
Chessel Pl	28226
Chester Ln	28273
Chesterbrook Ln	28273
Chesterfield Ave	28205
Chestnut Ave	28205
Chestnut Glen Ct	28215
Chestnut Grove Ln	28210
Chestnut Knoll Ln	28269
Chestnut Lake Dr	28227
Chestnut Oak Ln	28215
Chestnut Ridge Dr	28215
Cheston Pl	28211
Cheval Pl	28205
Chevington Rd	28226
Cheviot Rd	28269
Cheviott Hill Ln	28213
Chevis Ct	28277
Chevron Dr	28211
Chewink Ct	28227
Cheyenne Dr	28262
Chianti Dr	28277
Chicago Ave	28203
Chickadee Dr	28269
Chicopee Dr	28227
Chicory Dr	28213
Chidester Ct	28277
Chidley Dr	28269
Chiefly Ct	28212
Chieftain Dr	28216
Chigger Cir	28227
Chilcomb Ct	28262
Chilford Ct	28213
Chilham Pl	28226
Chillingworth Ln	28211
Chillmark Rd	28226
Chiltern Hills Trl	28215
Chilton Pl	28207
Chilvary Dr	28277
Chimney Corner Ct	28210
Chimney Ridge Trl	28269
Chimney Rock Ct	28262
Chimney Springs Pl	28269
Chinaberry Ct	28269
Chinabrook Ct	28270
Chinchester Ln	28270
Chinemist Ct	28269
Chinley Ct	28226
Chinquapin Ct	28269
Chipley Ave	28205
Chipola Dr	28215
Chippendale Rd	28205
Chippenham Ln	28277
Chipstead Ln	28277
Chipstone Rd	28262
Chisholm Ct	28216
Chislehurst Rd	28227
Chiswell Ct	28269
Chiswick Ct	28226
Chiswick Rd	28211
Chital Rd	28273
Choate Cir	28273
Chollywood Dr	28211
Choppy Wood Cir	28226
Chorale Ct	28270
Chowning Tavern Ln	28262
Choyce Ave & Cir	28217
Chretien Point Dr	28270
Chrisbry Ln	28215
Christenbury Rd	28269
Christenbury Hills Ln	28269
Christensens Ct	28270
Christian Scott Ln	28214
Christian Tyler Ct	28278
Christie Ln	28217
Christie St	28208
Christina Marie Ct	28213
Christmas Ct	28216
Christopher Pl	28226
Chrudan Dr	28262
Chuck Hollow Ln	28277
Chuck Wagon Ct	28262
Chuckwood Dr	28227
Church St	28227
N Church St	
200-799	28202
800-2199	28206
S Church St	
200-599	28202
1000-1599	28203
Churchfield Ln	28277
Churchill Dr	28269
Churchill Rd	28211
Churchill Downs Ct	28211
Churchill Park Ct	28210
Churchton Pl	28277
Ciera Nichole Ct	28214
Cigar Ct	28273
Cilantro Way	28214
Cimarron Hills Ln	28278
Cinderella Rd	28213
Cindy Ln	
2100-2299	28216
2500-3199	28269
Cindy Creek Ln	28216
Cindy Park Dr	28216
Cindy Woods Ln	28216
Cinnabay Dr	28216
Cinnamon Cir	28227
Cinnamon Field Rd	28273
Cinnamon Teal Dr	28269
Circle Ave	28207
Circle Dr	28262
Circle Tree Ln	28277
Circlegreen Dr	28273
Circles End	28226
Circlewood Dr	28211
Ciscayne Pl	28211
Citadel Pl	28269
Citiside Dr	28215
City View Dr	28212
Clackwyck Ln	28262
Claiborne Woods Rd	28216
Clairemore Pl	28216
Clairmont Grove Ct	28277
Clancy Pl	28227
Clanton Rd	
100-1299	28217
1400-1699	28208
Clardy Ct	28205
Clare Olivia Dr	28269
Claremont Rd	28214
Clarence St	28216
Clarencefield Dr	28216
Clarendon Rd	28211
Clarice Ave	28204
Claridge Ln	28209
Clark Blvd	28262
Clark St	28205
Clarke Creek Pkwy	28269
Clarke Ridge Ct	28269
N Clarkson St	28202
S Clarkson St	
200-399	28202
900-1599	28208
Clarkson Green St	28202
Clarkson Mill Ct	28202
Clarmont Grove Ct	28277
Classic Dr	28262
Claude Freeman Dr	28262
Clavell Ln	28210
Clavemorr Castle Ct	28277
Clavemorr Glenn Ct	28226
Clawson Ct	28209
Clay Ave	28208
Clay Bank Dr	28227
Claybrooke Dr	28262
Claybury Ct	28227
Clayfield Ct	28209
Clayford Rdg	28215
Claymont Dr	28227
Claysparrow Rd	28278
Clayton Dr	28203
Clear Creek Commerce Dr	28227
Clear Crossing Ln	28227
Clear Day Ct	28269
Clear Meadow Ln	28227
Clear Springs Ct	28214
Clear Stream Ct	28269
Clearmont Ave	28212
Clearvale Dr	28227
Clearview Dr	28216
Clearwater Rd	28217
Clearwood Ln	28214
Clematis Dr	28211
Clement Ave	
300-799	28204
1100-1299	28205
Clementine Ct	28277
Clems Branch Dr	28277
Clemson Ave	28205
Clendon Ct	28216
Cleopatra Dr	28213
Cleve Brown Rd	28269
Cleveland Ave	28203
Cliff Cameron Dr	28269
Cliffrose Way	28216
Cliffs Inn Cir	28214
Cliffside Dr	28270
Cliffvale Ct	28269
S Cliffwood Pl	28203
Clifton St	28216
Clingman Ln	28214
Clint Ln	28213
Clinton Dr	28216
Clintwood Dr	28213
Clippard Ct	28216
Cloister Dr	28211
Cloisters Club Ln	28278
Clonmel Pl	28262
Clooney Ln	28262
Clos Du Val Rd	28214
Closeburn Rd	28210
N Cloudman St	28216
S Cloudman St	28208
Cloughy Cir	28212
Cloven Pl	28273
Clover Rd	28211
Clover Bottom Dr	28227
Clover Gap Dr	28214
Clover Hill Ln	28215
Clover Hitch Dr	28215
Cloverdale Ave	28212
Cloverfield Rd	28211
Cloverleaf Ct	28277
Cloverside Ln	28269
Cloverwood Ct	28270
Cloyne Ct	28213
Club Rd	28205
Club Car Ct	28227
Club Champion Ln	28227
Club Creek Ln	28277
Club Field Ct	28227
Club Trophy Ln	28227
Clubhouse Ct	28227
Clubhouse View Ln	28227
Clyde Dr	28208
Clydesdale Ter	28208
Clymer Ct	28269
Coach Hill Ln	28212
Coachford Ct	28270
Coaching Inn Ct	28270
Coachlight Cir	28262
Coachman Cir	28277
Coachwood Ct	28216
Coatbridge Dr	28269
Coatbridge Ln	28212
Coates Ct	28213
Cobble Glen Way	28269
Cobbler Patch Ct	28278
Cobbleridge Dr	28215
Cobblestone Ct	28217
Cobden Ln	28216
Coble Ave	28215
Coble Rd	28227
Coburg Ave	28215
Coburn Ct	28277
Coca Cola Plz	28211
Cochran Pl	28205
Cochran Farm Ln	28269
Cochran Ridge Ave	28213
Cochrane Dr	28269
Coddington Pl	28211
Coddington Ridge Dr	28214
Cody Pl	28277
Coffee Tree Ct	28215
Coffeeberry Ln	28227
Coffey Creek Dr	28273
Coffey Point Dr	28217
Coker Ave	28208
Colby Ct	28226
Colchester Pl	28210
Cold Harbor Dr	28214
Cold Springs Rd	28215
Cold Water Ln	28212
Coldstream Ln	28205
Cole Mill Rd	28270
Colebrook Rd	28215
Coleman Dr	28215
Coleridge Ct	28269
Coleshire Ct	28269
Coley View Ct	28226
Colfax St	28216
Colgate Cir	28214
Colin Creek Ln	28214
Colin James Way	28273
Coliseum Dr	28205
Coliseum Centre Dr	28217
N College St	
100-699	28202
800-999	28206
S College St	
100-200	28202
201-201	28244
202-698	28202
203-699	28202
1200-1399	28203
College View Ln	28262
Collegiate Ave	28262
Colleton Pl	28270
Colleton River Ln	28278
Colley Ford Ln	28273
Collier Ct	28205
Collingdale Pl	28210
Collingham Dr	28273
Collingwood Dr	28209
Collins St	28269
Collins Aikman Dr	28262
Colmar Ln	28270
N & S Colonial Ave	28207
Colonial Country Ln	28277
Colonial Rea Ct	28226
Colonist Dr	28216
Colonnade Dr	28205
Colony Rd	
2100-2300	28209
2302-2498	28209
2800-4099	28211
4600-7899	28226
Colony Acres Dr	28217
Colony Crossing Dr	28226
Colony Grove Ln	28277
Colony Hill Dr	28214
Colony Line Ct	28210
Colony Oaks Dr	28277
Colony Parkway Dr	28211
Colony Woods Dr	28277
Colorado Ave	28206
Colston Ct	28210
Coltart Ct	28262
Coltsgate Rd	28211
Coltswood Ct	28211
Columbia Crest Ct	28270
Columbine Cir	28211
Columbine Ct	28226
Columbus Cir	28208
Colvard Cir	28269
Colvard Park Way	28269
Colville Rd	28207
Colwick Rd	28211
Colwyn Pl	28211
Comfrey Ct	28213
Comiskey Ave	28273
Commack Dr	28216
S Commerce Blvd	28273
Commerce St	28203
Commercial Ave	28205
Commons Creek Dr	28277
Commons Crossing Dr	28277
Commons East Dr	28277
Commonwealth Ave	28205

Community Cir 28215
N Community House Rd 28277
Compatible Way 28262
Compton Ct 28270
Comstock Dr 28217
Concordia Ave 28206
Condon St 28216
Condor Cir 28269
Condover Pl 28270
Coneflower Dr 28213
Conestoga Dr 28270
Conference Dr 28212
Congregation Dr 28278
Congress St 28209
Congressional Club Dr 28277
Conifer Cir 28213
Coniston Pl 28207
Conklin Pl 28212
Conlan Cir 28277
Connan Ln 28226
Connecticut Ave 28205
Connecting Rd 28209
Connell Rd 28227
Connell Green Dr 28213
Connell Mill Ln 28227
Connelly Cir 28208
Conner Ct 28227
Conner Ridge Ln 28269
Connery Ct 28269
Connestee Ct 28269
Connor Blvd 28226
Conservatory Ln 28210
Constable Ct 28209
Constitution Ln 28210
Constitution Hall Dr 28277
Contemporary Pl 28217
Continental Blvd 28273
Conway Ave 28209
Cooks Way Dr 28216
Cool Springs Ln 28226
Cool Water Ct 28215
Coolbrook Ct 28217
Coolidge Dr 28216
Cooper Dr 28210
Cooper Ln 28217
Cooper Run Ln 28269
Coopers Ridge Ln 28269
Coopersdale Rd 28273
Copenhagen Ln 28216
Copernicus Cir 28226
Coppala Dr 28216
Copper Way 28277
Copper Beech Trce 28273
Copper Creek Ct 28227
Copper Hill Ln 28269
Copper Leaf Ln 28277
Copper Mountain Blvd 28277
Copper Ridge Trl 28273
Copper Top Ct 28214
Copperleaf Commons Ct 28277
Coppermine Ln 28269
Copperplate Rd 28262
Cora St 28216
Coral Ridge Dr 28227
Coral Rose Rd 28277
Coral Valley Rd 28214
Coralbell Ln 28213
Coram Pl 28213
Corbett St 28208
Corbett Square Ln 28214
Corbin Ln 28277
Cord Wood Cir 28227
Cordage St 28273
Corder Dr 28212
Coreopsis Rd 28213
Corey Common Ave 28216
Corey Commons Ave 28216
Coriander Ct 28215
Corinth Ct 28227
Corinthian Pl 28211
Coriolanus Ct 28227
Cork Water Pl 28226
Corkstone Dr 28227
Corktree Ct 28212
Corliss Ave 28277
Cormwell Ln 28217
Cornelia Dr 28269
Cornelius St 28206
Cornell Ave 28211
Corner Ct 28269
Cornerstone Dr 28269
Cornerwood Ln 28211
Cornflower Cir 28212
Cornflower Commons Dr 28227
Cornielle Ln 28216
Cornish Pl 28210
Cornus Ln 28273
Cornwall St 28205
Cornwallis Ln 28270
Cornwallis Camp Dr 28226
Corolla Ln 28277
Coronado Dr 28212
Coronation Blvd 28227
Coronet Way 28208
Corporate Center Dr 28226
Corporation Cir 28216
Corradale Rd 28278
Corriente Ct 28213
Corrigan Ct 28277
Corrine Ct 28270
Corry Dr 28215
Corrystone Dr 28277
Corsair Ct 28278
Cortelyou Rd 28211
Cortez Trl 28227
Cortland Rd E & W 28209
Corton Dr 28203
Corvus Ct 28216
Corwin Dr 28213
Cory Bret Ln 28278
Cosby Pl 28205
Cosmos Way 28227
Costigan Ln 28277
Cota Ct 28262
Cotillion Ave 28210
Cotswold Ct 28213
Cottage Pl 28207
Cottage Cove Ln 28215
Cottage Oaks Dr 28269
Cottageville Ln 28208
Cottingham Ln 28211
Cotton Creek Dr 28226
Cotton Gum Rd 28227
Cotton Planter Ln 28270
Cotton Press Rd 28277
Cotton Stand Rd 28277
Cottontail Ct 28270
Cottonwood St 28206
Cottonwood Park Dr 28214
Cougar Ln 28269
Cougar Hill Ct 28216
Coulee Pl 28217
Couloak Dr 28216
Coulport Ln 28215
Coulter Xing 28213
Coulwood Dr 28214
Coulwood Oak Ln 28214
Count Fleet Ln 28215
Country Ln
4100-4799 28270
10200-10599 28214
Country Barn Ct 28273
Country Club Dr & Ln 28205
Country Oaks Rd 28227
Country Ridge Rd 28226
Country View Ct 28211
Country Walk Dr 28212
Country Woods Dr 28227
Countrymens Ct 28210
Countryside Dr 28213
Counts Pl 28277
County Donegal Ct 28277
County Downs Ln 28270
County Louth Ct 28277
N Course Dr 28277
Court Dr 28211
Courtland Dr 28212
Courtney Commons Ln 28217
Courtney Creek Dr 28217
Courtney Landing Dr 28217
Courtney Meadows Ln 28217
Courtney Oaks Rd 28217
Courtney Park Rd 28217
Courtney Ridge Ln 28217
Courtside Ln 28270
Courtview Dr 28226
Cove Point Dr 28278
Cove Ridge Ln 28212
Covecreek Dr 28215
Covedale Dr 28270
Covelo Ct 28262
Coventry Rd 28211
Coventry Commons Dr 28227
Coventry Court Ln 28277
Coventry Ridge Ct 28216
Coventry Row Ct 28270
Covered Bridge Ln 28210
Coves Edge Ln 28278
Coves End Ct 28269
Covewood Ct 28270
Covey Chase Dr 28210
Covey Hollow Ct 28210
Covey Rise Ct 28226
Covington Ct 28277
Covington Oaks Dr 28205
Covingtonwood Dr 28214
Cow Hollow Dr 28226
Cowboy Ln 28216
Cowles Rd 28208
Coxe Ave 28208
Coxville Dr 28214
Coxwood Ct 28227
Coy Ct 28216
Coyle Cir 28277
Coyote Ln 28277
Coyote Creek Ct 28278
Cozen Way 28215
Cozumel St 28227
Cozy Cove Rd 28278
Cpcc West Campus Dr 28208
Crab Orchard Ct 28212
Crabapple Tree Ln 28214
Craddock Ave 28208
E Cradwash Rd 28209
Craftsbury Dr 28215
Craftsman Ln 28204
Cragland Ct 28269
Craig Ave 28211
Craig St 28214
E & W Craighead Rd 28206
Craighill Ln 28278
Craigholm Ct 28262
Craigmore Dr 28226
Craigmoss Ln 28278
Craigwood Dr
4500-4799 28215
4800-5099 28212
Crail Ct 28269
Cranberry Nook Ct 28269
Cranberry Woods Ct 28208
Cranborne Chase Ct 28210
Cranbourn Ct 28215
Cranbrook Ln 28207
Crandon Dr 28216
Crane Point Dr 28227
Cranfield Ln 28277
Cranford Dr 28209
Cranston Ct 28277
Cranswick Pl 28227
Crape Myrtle Ln 28216
Crater St 28205
Craven Hill Dr 28216
Cravenridge Dr 28217
Crawford Dr 28216
Crawford Brook Ln 28269
Crayton Dr 28269
Credenza Rd 28208
S Creek Rd 28277
Creek Bend Dr 28277
Creek Breeze Rd 28269
Creek Dale Ln 28277
Creek Park Dr 28262
Creek Turn Dr 28278
Creek Valley Dr 28270
Creekbed Ln 28210
Creekridge Rd 28212
Creekside Park Rd 28277
Creekstone Pl 28213
Creektree Ct 28278
Creekview Ct 28214
Creekwood Quorum Dr 28212
Creemore Dr 28213
Creeping Flora Ln 28216
Creighton Dr 28205
Crenshaw Ct 28216
Creola Rd
5800-6299 28270
6300-6499 28226
Crescent Ave 28207
Crescent Day Ct 28212
Crescent Executive Dr 28217
Crescent Ridge Dr 28269
Crescent Run Ct 28277
Crescent Springs Dr 28273
Crescent View Dr 28269
Cressa Ct 28273
Cressida Dr 28210
Cressingham Ct 28227
Crest Cove Rd 28278
Cresta Ct 28269
Crestbrook Dr 28211
Crestdale Dr 28216
Crestfield Dr 28269
Cresthill Dr
3000-3199 28212
11300-11699 28227
Crestland Ave 28269
Crestmere St 28208
Crestmont Dr 28205
Creston Cir 28214
Crestridge Dr 28217
Crestshire Rd 28227
Crestside Ln 28227
Crestview Ct 28262
Crestview Dr 28216
Crestway Cir 28216
Crestwick Ct 28269
Crestwood Dr
5800-5999 28216
10100-10599 28277
Creswell Ct 28215
Cricket Glen Ct 28226
Cricket Lake Dr 28277
Cricket Place Cir 28214
Cricketeer Dr 28216
Cricketfield Ct 28277
Cricketwood Ln 28215
Cricklade Dr 28262
Cricklewood Ln 28212
N Crigler St 28216
S Crigler St 28208
Crimson Sargent Dr 28213
Cringle Ct 28226
Cripple Creek Ln 28277
Crisfield Rd 28269
Crisman St 28208
Crisp Wood Ln 28269
Crispin Ave 28208
Cristina Ct 28270
Crociani Dr 28277
Crockett Ln 28270
Crocus Ct 28217
Croft Haven Dr 28269
Croft Mill Ln 28226
Crofton Ct 28205
Crofton Springs Dr 28269
Cromarty Ln 28227
Cromer St 28208
Crompton St 28273
Cromwell Ct 28205
Crooked Branch Ln 28278
Crooked Creek Dr 28214
Crooked Oak Ln 28226
Crooked Pine Ct 28215
Crosby Rd 28211
Cross St 28269
Cross Beam Dr 28217
Cross Country Rd 28270
Cross Creek Ln 28212
Cross Field Ln 28226
Cross Roads Pl 28208
Cross Tie Ct 28227
Cross Winds Rd 28227
Crossbow Ct 28216
Crosscut Dr 28214
Crossgate Rd 28226
Crosshaven Dr 28278
Crosshill Ct 28277
Crossing King Dr 28212
Crosspoint Center Ln 28269
Crossridge Rd 28214
Crosstimbers Dr 28215
Crossview Ln 28226
Crossvine Ln 28215
Crosswood Ct 28215
Crowder Ct 28210
Crowflock Ct 28226
Crowley Ct 28277
Crown Ct 28211
Crown Centre Dr 28227
Crown Colony Dr 28270
Crown Crescent Ct 28227
Crown Harbor Dr 28278
Crown Hill Dr 28227
Crown View Dr 28227
Crownfield Ln 28212
Crownpoint Executive Dr 28227
Crownsgate Ct 28207
Crownvista Dr 28269
Crows Nest Ln 28226
Croydon Rd
2200-2399 28207
2400-2699 28209
Cruden Bay Way 28277
Crump Hill Ct 28227
Crutchfield Pl 28213
Crystal Rd 28205
Crystal Arms Way 28269
Crystal Crest Way 28269
Crystal Downs Ln 28278
Crystal Erica Ln 28214
Crystal Leaf Pl 28269
Crystal Pointe Dr 28215
Csx Way 28214
Cub Creek Ln 28216
Cullen Ct 28278
Cullendale Ct 28262
Cullingford Ln 28216
Cullman Ave 28206
Culloden Ct 28214
Culloden More Ct 28217
Culpepper Ct 28278
Culross Ln 28278
Cumberland Ave 28203
Cumberland Dr 28227
Cumberland Cove Dr 28273
Cumnor Ln 28277
Cunningham Dr 28208
Cunningham Park Ct 28269
Cupped Oak Ct 28213
Cureton Pl 28217
Curico Ln 28227
Curlee Ct 28277
Curraghmore Rd 28210
Currier Rd 28215
Currituck Dr 28210
Currywood Pl 28227
Curt Walton Ave 28269
Curtiswood Dr 28213
Cushing Dr 28216
Cushman St 28206
Custer St 28216
Cutchin Dr 28210
Cutler Pl 28205
Cutshaw Ct 28215
Cypress Ct 28277
Cypress Club Dr 28210
Cypress Creek Ln 28210
Cypress Forest Dr 28216
Cypress Park Ln 28273
Cypress Pond Dr 28269
Cypress Ridge Dr 28262
Cypress Tree Ln 28215
Cypress View Dr 28262
Cyrus Dr 28205
D Ducks Ln 28273
Dabney Dr 28262
Dabney Vigor Dr 28209
Dacavin Dr 28226
Dade St 28205
Daerwood Pl 28215
Daffodil Dr 28269
Dahlia Dr 28213
Dahlia Blossom Dr 28226
Dairus Kay Ct 28273
Dairy Ct 28277
Dairy Farm Ln 28209
Daisy Bee Ct 28216
Daisy Moore Ln
2500-2598 28206
2500-2598 28216
2501-2599 28206
Daisyfield Dr 28269
N Dakota St 28216
Dalbeth St 28213
Dale Ave
600-1299 28216
6200-6499 28212
Dalebrook Dr 28216
Dalecrest Dr 28269
Dalehurst Dr 28205
Dalesford Dr 28205
Daleview Dr 28214
Dallas Ave 28205
Dalmeny House Ln 28215
Dalmoor Dr 28212
Dalphon Jones Dr 28213
Dalston Ln 28210
Dalton Ave 28206
Daltrey Ln 28277
Daly Way 28216
Damascus St 28213
Damask Dr 28206
Damson Plum Ln 28215
Dan Caudle Rd 28273
Dan Maples Dr 28277
Dana Ct 28212
Danbrooke Park Dr 28227
Danbury St 28211
Dancing Wind Rd 28277
Danforth Ln 28208
Daniel Ln 28214
Daniel St 28205
Daniel Dwayne Dr 28214
Daniel Place Dr 28213
Danielle Christina Ct 28216
Danlow Pl 28208
Dannelly Park Dr 28269
Dannyn Grove Ct 28214
Danson Dr 28277
Dantrey Pl 28208
Danube Dr 28227
Danvers Dr 28213
Daphne Dr 28269
Dapple Ct 28215
Dapple Grey Ln 28213
Darbrook Dr 28205
Darby Ave 28216
Darby Chase Dr 28277
Darbyshire Pl 28216
Darbywine Dr 28216
Darcy Hopkins Dr 28277
Darden Ct 28211
Dare Dr 28206
Darerca Ct 28216
Daresby Ct 28226
Daria Ct 28269
Darius Ct 28227
Dark Star Ct 28278
Darnell Dr 28214
Darnley Pl 28226
Darrow Ln 28217
Dartford Ln 28227
Dartington Ridge Ln 28262
Dartmoor Pl 28227
Dartmouth Ct NW 28269
Dartmouth Pl 28207
Darventry Ct 28226
Darwick St 28216
Darwin Cir 28209
Dashiel Dr 28262
Datha Ave 28269
Daufuskie Dr 28278
Dauphine Dr 28216
Davant Ln 28209
Dave Thomas Ln 28214
Davenport St 28208
Daventry Pl 28215
David Ave 28214
David Cox Rd 28269
David Earl Dr 28213
David Jennings Ave 28213
David Lee Ln 28227
David Taylor Dr 28262
David Wellman Rd 28215
N Davidson St
300-799 28202
900-1799 28206
1800-3899 28205
S Davidson St 28202
Davinci Ln 28226
Davis Ave 28208
Davis Dr 28270
Davis Ln 28269
Davis Rd 28227
Davis Crossing Ct 28269
Davis Forest Ln 28262
Davis Lake Pkwy 28269
Davis Meadows Dr 28216
Davis Ridge Dr 28269
Davis Trace Dr 28227
Daviswood Ct 28270
Dawn Cir 28213
Dawnalia Dr 28208
Dawndeer Ln 28212
Dawnhurst Ln 28214
Dawnmist Ln 28269
Dawnridge Dr 28226
Dawnshire Ave 28216
Dawnview Pl 28208
Dawnwood Dr 28212
Dawson Ave 28216
Day Lilly Ln 28216
Dayan Dr 28216
Dayberry Ln 28227
Daybreak Dr 28269
Dayspring Dr 28227
Daytona Ave 28214
Deacon Ave 28204
Dean St 28216
Deanna Ln 28217
Deanscroft Dr 28226
Deanwood Pl 28217
Dearborn Ave 28206
Dearmon Dr 28205
Dearmon Rd 28269
Dearview Ln 28269
Deason Ct 28205
Deaton Hill Dr 28269
Deberry Ct 28213
Deborah St 28270
Decapolis Dr 28215
Decatur Ct 28213
Deckford Pl 28211
Dedmon Dr 28216
Deep Forest Ln 28214
Deep Gap Ct 28217
Deep Hollow Ct 28226
Deep Meadow Ln 28210
Deepwood Dr 28226
Deer St 28214
Deer Brook Ln 28210
Deer Chase Ln 28262
Deer Cross Trl 28269
Deer Falls Ln 28226
Deer Hollow Ct 28226
Deer Ridge Ln 28277
Deer Run Ct 28273
Deer Spring Ln 28210
Deer Stand Ct 28214
Deer Track Ct 28227
Deer Trail Ln 28273
Deer Walk Ave 28270
Deerfield Pl 28209
Deergreen Ln 28262

Deerhorn Ct 28227
Deering Dr 28210
Deermont Ct 28211
Deerpark Ln 28277
Deerpath Ct 28262
Deerton Rd 28269
Deerwood Rd 28214
Degrasse Dr 28269
Dehavilland Dr 28278
Deherradora Ave 28208
Dekalb Pl 28262
Del Rio Rd 28277
Delamere Ln 28269
Delander Ln 28214
Delane Ave 28211
Delaware Dr 28215
Delberry Ln 28277
Delchester Dr 28210
Delgany Dr 28215
Delham Dr 28215
Deliah Ln 28215
Delisa Dr 28214
Delivau Dr 28215
Della Dr 28217
Dellfield Way 28269
Dellinger Cir & Dr 28269
Dellwood Ave 28209
Delmahoy Dr 28277
Delmar Ln 28217
Deloach Ct 28270
Delores Ferguson Ln 28277
Delpond Ln 28226
Delprado Cir 28216
Delrose Ln 28216
Delshire Ln 28273
Delsing Ct 28214
Delta Ln 28215
Delta Crossing Ln 28212
Delta Lake Dr 28215
Deluca Dr 28215
Dembrigh Ln 28262
Demeter Ln 28262
Demill Ln 28215
Demington Ln 28269
Democracy Dr 28212
Denali Ln 28216
Denbigh Dr 28226
Denbur Dr 28215
Denmark Rd 28273
Denmeade Dr 28269
Denning Pl 28227
Dennington Grove Ln 28277
Dennis Ct 28213
Dennis Rd 28227
Denon Hills Dr 28212
Densmore Dr 28205
Denson Pl 28215
Dent Ct 28210
Denver Ave 28208
Denview Ln 28208
Deodora Cedar Ln 28215
Depaul Ct 28216
Derby Farm Ln 28278
Derby Meadows Ct 28216
Derbyshire Dr 28270
Derek Christopher Ct 28214
Derita Ave
2401-2599 28269
2505-2505 28221
2505-2999 28269
Derita Woods Ct 28269
Derry Dr 28262
Derry Hill Pl 28277
Derrydowne Dr 28213
Derryfield Dr 28213
Derryrush Dr 28213
Deruyter Cir 28269
Dervish Ln 28269
Derwent Ct 28278
Deshler Ct 28273
Deshler Morris Ln 28216
Desire St 28262
Desmond Pl 28210
Despa Dr 28227
Destin Ln 28277
Devas Ct 28269
Deveron Dr 28211
Devon Dr 28209
S Devon St 28213
Devon Croft Ln 28269
Devonbridge Ln 28269
Devongate Ln 28269
Devonhill Ln 28269
Devonwood Ln 28214
Dewberry Ln 28278
Dewberry Ter 28208
Dewey Dr 28214
Dewitt Ln 28217
Dewmorn Pl 28269
Dewolfe St 28208
Dewy Morn Dr 28216
Dexter St 28209
Dexter Lemmond Ct 28227
Diablo Ct 28215
Diadem Ct 28273
Diamond Creek Cir 28273
Diamond Grove Ln 28208
Diamond Summit Ct 28278
Diana Dr 28203
Dianne Dr 28215
Dianthus Ct 28277
Dickens Ave 28208
Dickie Ross Rd 28277
Dickinson Pl 28207
Dickson Ln 28262
Dietrich Ln 28262
Digital Dr 28262
Dillard Ridge Dr 28216
Dillard Valley Rd 28214
Dilling Farm Rd 28214
Dillion Ct 28277
Dilworth Rd 28203
Dilworth Crescent Row 28203
Dilworth Heights Ln 28209
Dilworth Mews Ct 28203
Dinadan Dr 28217
Dingess Rd 28273
Dinglewood Ave 28205
Dinkins Coach Pl 28277
Dion Ave 28212
Dipali Ct 28214
Diploma Dr 28262
Diplomat Ln 28210
Discovery Ln 28216
Display Dr 28273
Distribution St 28203
Distribution Center Dr 28269
District Dr 28213
Division St 28205
W Dixie Dr & Rd 28278
Dixie Ann Dr 28262
Dixie Glen Dr 28277
Dixie Hills Dr 28277
Dixie River Rd 28278
Dixon St 28216
Dixter Ln 28211
Dobbs Ct 28277
Doblinway Dr 28215
Dobson Dr 28213
Doby Springs Dr 28262
Docia Crossing Rd 28269
Dock View Ln 28278
Dockery Dr 28209
Dockside Dr 28227
Dodge Ave 28208
Doe Ct 28277
Doe Run Rd 28277
Doggett St 28203
Dogwood Ave 28206
Dogwood Cir 28208
Dogwood Dr 28215
Dogwood Pl 28212
Dogwood Ridge Dr 28227
Dolat Ct 28214
Dolcetto Way 28277
Dollar Cir 28270
Dolley Todd Dr 28216
Dolly Todd Dr 28216
Dollyshore Pl 28215
Dolphin Ln 28215
Dominion Pl 28277
Dominion Crest Dr 28269
Dominion Green Dr 28269
Dominion Village Dr 28269
Domino Ct 28205
Don Lochman Ln 28277
Donald Ross Rd 28208
Donatello Ave 28205
Doncaster Dr 28211
Donegal Dr 28212
Donet Terrace Dr 28215
Donlee Dr 28216
Donna Ave 28205
Donna Dr 28213
Donna Ve Ln 28277
Donnefield Dr 28227
Donnegal Farm Rd 28270
Donnel Ct 28273
Donnellson Common
Ct 28216
Donnington Dr 28277
Donnybrook Pl 28205
Donovan Pl 28215
Dooley Dr 28227
Dora Dr 28215
Dorcas Ln 28278
Dorchester Pl 28209
Doris Ave 28205
Doris Ray Ct 28216
Dorn Cir 28212
Dornier Ct 28278
Dorothy Dr 28203
Dorshire Ct 28269
Dorton St 28213
Doster Ave 28277
N Dotger Ave
100-299 28207
300-499 28204
S Dotger Ave 28207
Dotts Ct 28226
Double Cedar Dr 28214
Double Creek Crossing
Dr 28269
Double Eagle Gate
Way 28210
Double Lakes Dr 28212
Double Oaks Rd 28206
Double Rein Rd 28215
Double Springs Ct 28262
Doubletree Dr 28227
Doug Mayes Pl 28262
Dougherty Dr 28213
Doughton Ln 28217
Douglas Dr 28217
Dove Dr 28214
Dove Cottage Dr 28226
Dove Meadow Dr 28278
Dove Stand Ln 28226
Dove Tree Ln 28213
Dovecote Ct 28210
Dovefield Rd 28277
Dovehunt Pl 28277
Dover Ave 28209
Dover Downs Dr 28216
Doverdale Ln 28217
Doverhill Pl 28262
Doveridge St 28273
Dovershire Rd 28270
Doverstone Ct 28208
Doves Canyon Ln 28278
Doves Nest Cir 28226
Doves Roost Ct 28211
Dovetail Ct 28227
Dovewood Dr 28226
Dow Rd 28269
Dowgate Dr 28208
Dowington Dr 28277
Dowling Dr 28205
Downfield Wood Dr 28269
Downing St 28205
Downing Creek Dr 28269
Downpatrick Pl 28262
Downs Ave 28205
S Downs Trl 28215
Downy Birch Rd 28227
Doyle Dr 28216
Dr Carver Rd 28208
Dragonfly Ln 28277
Drains Bay Ct 28214
Drake Watch Ln 28262
Drakes Crossing Dr 28262
Drakestone Ct 28226
Drakeview Ct 28270
Draper Ave 28205
Drawbridge Dr 28215
Draycott Ave 28213
Drayton Hall Ln 28270
Dresden Dr E & W 28205
Dressage Blvd 28227
Drexel Pl 28209
Drexel Bay Ln 28227
Drexmore Ave 28209
Drifter Dr 28227
Driftwood Dr 28205
Driftwood Commons
Ct 28227
Driscoll Ct 28269
Driwood Ct 28269
Druid Cir 28206
Drum St 28208
Drummond Ave 28205
Drury Dr 28206
Dry Brook Rd 28269
Dryden Ln 28210
Dubarry St 28211
Dublin Rd 28208
Dubois Ct 28208
Duchamp Dr 28215
Duck Pond Ct 28277
Duckett Ct 28273
Duckhorn Dr 28277
Ducksbill Dr 28277
Duckwood Ln 28215
Duckworth Ave 28208
Dudley Dr 28205
Due West Dr 28278
Duffin Dr 28215
Dugan Dr 28270
Duiske Abby Ct 28273
Duke Lancaster Dr 28277
Dulin Creek Blvd 28215
Duluth Park Dr 28277
Dulverton Dr 28226
Dumbarton Dr 28210
Dumbarton Pl 28211
Dumont Ln 28269
Dunaire Dr 28205
Dunart Ct 28212
Dunavant St 28203
Dunaverty Pl 28277
Dunbar St 28208
W Dunbar St 28203
Dunberry Ct 28214
Dunblane Ct NW 28269
Dunbritton Ln 28277
Dunbrody Ln 28273
Dunbrook Ln 28217
Duncan Ave 28205
Duncan Gardens Dr 28206
Duncourtney Ln 28277
Duncroft Ln 28215
Dundalk Rd 28270
Dundarrach Ln 28277
Dundeen St 28216
Dunedin Ln 28270
Dunes Ct 28226
Dunfield Ct 28269
Dunford St 28277
Dungannon Ct 28278
Dungarvon Ct 28262
Dunhill Dr 28205
Dunkirk Dr 28203
Dunlanwood Cir 28226
Dunlavin Way 28205
Dunleigh Dr 28214
Dunmoor Valley Ct 28226
Dunmurry Ln 28217
Dunn Ave 28205
Dunn Commons Pkwy 28216
Dunnington Ct 28216
Dunoon Ln 28269
Dunrobin Ln 28226
Dunsinane Dr 28227
Dunslow Ct 28269
Dunstaff Rd 28269
Dunstan Ct 28215
Dunwick Pl 28226
Dunwoody Dr 28215
Dupont Dr 28217
Dupplin Castle Ct 28277
Dupree St 28208
Durant Blvd 28277
Durham Ln 28269
Durmast Ct 28227
Durness Dr 28278
Durrango Ct 28278
Durston Ct 28269
Dusky Pine Dr 28215
Dusty Cedar Ct 28269
Dusty Saddle Rd 28277
Dusty Trail Rd 28269
Dutchess St 28269
Duvall Meadow Ln 28216
Duvalla Ave 28209
Duxbury Ct 28227
Duxford Ln 28269
S Dwelle St 28208
Dwight St 28212
Dwight Evans Rd 28217
Dwightware Blvd 28227
Dylan Shane Ln 28214
Eagerlis Rd 28278
Eagle Ct 28277
Eagle Gln 28210
Eagle Chase Dr 28216
Eagle Claw Ct 28227
Eagle Creek Dr 28269
Eagle Feathers Dr 28214
Eagle Lake Dr 28217
Eagle Peak Dr 28214
Eagle Ridge Dr 28214
Eagle Rock Ln 28214
Eaglebrook Dr 28227
Eaglecrest Rd 28212
Eagles Field Ct 28269
Eagles Landing Dr 28214
Eagles Point Ct 28277
Eagleview Dr 28278
Eaglewind Dr 28212
Eaglewood Ave 28212
Eaker Ct 28215
Eargle Rd 28269
Earlham Ct 28277
Earlswood Dr 28269
Early Ct 28205
Early Bird Way 28227
Early Flight Dr 28262
Early Meadow Way 28227
Early Mist Ln 28269
Earney Dr 28214
Earthenware Dr 28269
Easen Ct 28211
East Blvd 28203
Eastbourne Rd 28227
Eastbrook Rd 28215
Eastburn Rd 28210
Eastcrest Dr 28205
Easter Ln 28208
Eastfield Park Dr 28269
Eastfield Village Ln 28269
Eastham Ln 28209
Easthampton Cir 28277
Easthaven Dr 28212
Eastland Ct 28212
Easton Pl 28212
Easton Grey Ln 28277
Eastover Rd 28207
Eastover Hills Ct 28211
Eastover Ridge Dr 28211
Eastover Woods Cir 28207
Eastport Rd 28205
Eastshire Ct 28226
Eastview Dr 28211
Eastway Dr
100-399 28213
400-4399 28205
Eastwind Dr 28273
Eastwood Dr 28205
Eastwych Ct 28226
Eastwycke Place Dr 28215
Easy St 28269
Easywater Ln 28278
Eaton Cir 28208
Eaton Rd 28205
Eatonton St 28208
Eaves Ln 28215
Ebara Ln 28213
Ebb Pl 28210
Eben Dr 28269
Ebley Ln 28227
Ebony Rd 28216
Ebullient St 28278
Echo Ln 28227
Echo Cove Ln 28273
Echo Forest Dr 28270
Echo Glen Rd 28213
Echodale Dr 28217
Ed Brown Rd 28273
Ed Reid St 28216
Eddings Dr 28270
Eddington St 28208
S Eddleman St 28208
Eddystone Dr 28270
Eden Hall Ct 28277
Edenbridge Ln 28226
Edenderry Dr 28270
Edenton Rd 28211
Edenwood Pl 28212
Edge Lake Dr 28217
Edgegreen Dr 28217
Edgehill Rd N & S 28207
Edgemont Rd 28211
Edgemore Ct 28270
Edgepine Dr 28269
Edgerly Ct 28214
Edgerton Dr 28213
Edgevale Dr 28216
Edgewater Dr 28210
Edgewater Forest Ln 28278
Edgeweir Ct 28269
Edgewood Rd 28208
Edgewood Grove Trl 28226
Edgeworth Ct 28213
Edinborough Dr 28216
Edinburgh Ln
900-998 28209
9800-9899 28269
Edindale Dr 28277
Edinmeadow Ln 28269
Edison St 28206
Edmonton Pl 28269
Edmore Blvd 28216
Edsdale Pl 28216
Edsel Pl 28205
Edsel Laney Dr 28216
Education Way 28262
Edward St 28213
Edwards Pl 28227
Edwin Jones Dr 28269
Effingham Rd 28208
Egan Way 28277
Egerton Dr 28277
Eglinton Toll Ct 28213
Egret Ln 28227
Egrets Point Dr 28278
El Campo Ct 28277
El Greco Ct 28226
El Molino Dr 28214
El Mundo St 28216
El Verano Cir 28210
Elam Ct 28213
Elberon Ct 28269
Elcar Dr 28214
Elder Ave 28205
Elderbank Dr 28216
Elderslie Dr 28269
Elderwood Ln 28214
Eldon Dr 28277
Eldorado Ave 28262
Eleanor Dr
4700-4999 28208
9200-9499 28214
Electra Ln 28212
Elementary View Dr 28269
Elena Dr 28278
Elendil Ln 28269
Elessar Pl 28212
Elfreda Rd 28270
Elgin Dr 28214
Elgywood Ln 28213
Eli St 28204
Eli Whitney Ct 28227
Elise Marie Dr 28214
Elizabeth Ave 28204
Elizabeth Rd 28269
Elizabeth Crest Ln 28277
Elizabeth Glen Dr 28270
Elizabeth Madison Ct 28277
Elizabeth Oaks Ave 28216
Elizabeth Townes Ln 28277
Elk Dr 28213
Elk Creek Ct 28214
Elkhorn Dr 28278
Elkin Ln 28205
Elkington Ln 28227
Elkmont Pl 28208
Elkston Dr 28210
Elkwood Cir 28205
Ella St 28206
Ella Jane Ln 28273
Ellen Ave
2300-2398 28208
2400-2499 28208
2501-2599 28208
3600-3699 28205
Ellencroft Ln 28215
Ellendale Dr 28217
Ellenwood Pl 28217
Ellesmere Ct 28227
Ellie Ln 28208
Ellingsworth Ln 28214
Ellington St 28211
Ellington Farm Ln 28227
Ellington Park Dr 28277
Elliot St 28202
Elliott Dr, Rd & St 28216
Ellis St 28216
Ellison St 28204
Ellisway Rd 28216
Ellsworth Rd 28211
Elm Ln
8800-8999 28226
9600-11999 28277
Elm St 28206
Elm Bend Dr 28273
Elm Cove Ln 28269
Elm Creek Ln 28277
Elm Field Ct 28227
Elm Forest Dr 28212
Elm Hill Ct 28217
Elm Tree Ln 28227
Elmdale Ct 28206
Elmhurst Rd 28209
Elmin St 28208
Elmstone Dr 28277
Elmwood Cir 28214
Elon St 28208
Elphin Ct 28270
Elrod Ln 28277
Elrond Dr NW 28269
Elrose Pl 28277
Elsberry Ln 28213
Elsenham Ln 28269
Elsie Caldwell Ln 28213
Elsinore Pl 28227
Elstree Dr 28226
Elswick Ln 28214
Elton Pl 28208
Elven Ln 28269
Elverson Dr 28277
Elvis Dr 28215
Elwood Dr 28227
Elyse Manor Ct 28214
Elysian Fields St 28262
Emden Ct 28213
Emerald Branch Ln 28273
Emerald Cove Dr 28262
Emerald Dunes Dr 28278
Emerald Fern Way 28214
Emerald Meadow Ln 28273
Emerald Point Dr 28278
Emerson Ave 28204

Emerywood Dr 28210
Emily Ln 28216
Emily Hope Dr 28214
Emma Lynn Ct 28269
Emmanuel Dr 28216
Emmons Ln 28212
Emmy Ln 28226
Emory Ln 28211
Empire Woods Ct 28277
Empress Ct 28227
Emstead Ct 28210
Emsworth Ln 28277
Enchantment Cove Ln 28216
Enclave Pl 28277
E End St 28208
Endd Ct 28214
Enderly Rd 28208
Endhaven Ln 28277
Endicott Ct 28205
Endolwood Dr 28215
Endwell Dr 28212
Eneida Sue Dr 28214
Enfield Rd 28205
Engineer Ln 28227
England St 28273
Englefield Way 28226
Englehardt St 28216
English Dr 28216
English Elm Ct 28277
English Garden Dr 28226
English Hills Dr 28212
English Ivy Ln 28227
English Meadows Ln 28226
English Oak Ln 28278
English Saddle Ln 28273
English Setter Way 28269
English Sparrow Ln 28210
English Tudor Ln 28211
English Walnut Ln 28215
Enoch Dr 28269
Enslow Pl 28216
Enterprise Dr 28206
Entrance Dr 28273
Entwhistle Ct 28226
Enwood Dr 28214
Equipment Dr
4300-5199 28269
5201-6399 28262
Equitable Pl 28213
Erica Ct 28227
Erickson Rd 28205
Erie St 28216
Erin Ct 28210
Erin Taylor Ln 28206
Erinbrook Ln 28215
Erinshire Rd 28211
Ernest Russell Ct 28269
Ernie Dr 28269
Errington Ln 28227
Erskine Dr 28205
Erwin Rd 28273
Erwin Ridge Ave 28213
Erwin Trace Dr 28213
Escaflowne Ave 28216
Esherwood Ln 28270
Esmeralda Dr 28269
Esplanade St 28262
Essen Ln 28210
Essex St 28205
Essex Fells Dr 28277
Essex Hall Dr 28277
Essington Dr 28270
Estates Ave 28209
Estelle St 28216
Esther Ln 28214
Ethan Ct 28226
Ethel Ct 28214
Ethel Guest Ln 28206
Ethereal Ln 28226
Etherton Ct 28216
Ettrick Pl 28278
Euclid Ave 28203
Eudora Rd 28277
Euler Way 28214
Eureka St 28206
Eurostar Dr 28213
Eustis Pl 28214
Euston Ct 28227
Evangelion Ct 28216
Evans Rd 28227
Evanshire Dr 28216
Evanton Loch Rd 28278
Evelyn Ave 28213
Evening Flight Ln 28262
Eveningside Dr 28206
Eveningwood Ct 28226
Eventine Ct 28214
Everclear Ct 28216
Everett Dr 28214
Everett Pl 28205
Evergreen Dr 28208
Evergreen Hollow Dr 28269
Evergreen Terrace Dr 28277
Everidge Pl 28227
Evermoore Ct 28226
Eversfield Ln 28269
Everton Dr 28273
Ewen Cir 28269
Ewert Cut Ln 28269
Ewing Ave 28203
Exbury Ct 28269
Exchange St 28208
Executive Cir 28212
Executive St
2200-2399 28208
2318-2318 28266
2400-2498 28208
2401-2499 28208
Executive Center Dr 28212
Exeter Rd 28211
E Exmore St 28217
Express Dr
4800-4899 28208
4800-4800 28219
Faber St 28208
Fabyan Ln 28262
Fagan Way 28216
Fair St 28208
Fair Grounds Park Dr 28269
Fair Grove Ln 28212
Fair Lawn Rd 28215
Fair Springs Rd 28227
Fair Valley Dr 28226
Fair Wind Ln 28212
Fairbanks Rd 28210
Fairbluff Pl 28209
Fairbourne Ct 28269
Fairbridge Rd 28277
Fairbrook Dr 28216
Fairchase Ave 28269
Fairchild Ln 28277
Faircreek Ct 28269
Faircrest Dr 28210
Faires Rd 28215
Faires Farm Rd 28213
Fairfax Dr 28209
Fairglen Rd 28269
Fairgreen Dr 28217
Fairground Ave 28208
Fairhaven Dr 28213
Fairhaven St 28208
Fairheath Rd 28210
Fairhill Pl 28270
Fairhope Ct 28277
Fairington Oaks Dr 28227
Fairlane Dr 28214
Fairlawn Crescent Ct 28226
Fairlea Dr 28269
Fairmarket Pl 28215
Fairmead Dr 28269
Fairmeadows Dr 28269
Fairmont St 28216
Fairplains Ct 28278
Fairstone Ave 28269
Fairview Rd
5500-5899 28209
5900-6899 28210
6901-6999 28210
7600-8899 28226
7900-10999 28227
Fairview Oak Ln 28211
Fairvista Dr 28269
Fairway Downs Ct 28277
Fairway Mist Ct 28227
Fairway Point Dr 28269
Fairway Ridge Rd 28277
Fairway Row Ln 28277
Fairway View Dr 28277
Fairway Vista Dr 28226
Fairwood Ave 28203
Faison Ave 28205
Faith St 28227
Falcon St 28211
Falconcrest Dr 28269
Falconer Pl 28278
Falconhurst Dr 28216
Falconry Way 28278
Falconwood Ct 28227
Falkirk Pl 28270
Fall Ct 28212
Fallbrook Dr 28226
Fallen Spruce Ct 28227
Fallen Tree Ct 28262
Falling Leaves Dr 28277
Falling Meadows Ln 28273
Falling Rock Ct 28213
Falling Stream Dr 28214
Falling Tree Ct 28273
Fallingswood Ct 28217
Fallon Ct 28226
Fallon Farm Rd 28278
Fallon Trace Ave 28277
Fallow Ln 28273
Falls Branch Ln 28214
Falls Church Rd 28270
Falls Creek Ln 28209
Falls Lake Dr 28270
Falls Ridge Ln 28269
Fallsdale Dr 28214
Fallston Ct 28208
Fallview Dr 28278
Falmouth Ln 28269
Falmouth Rd 28205
Falstaff Dr 28227
Fannie Cir 28205
Fanning Manor Ct 28277
Far West Dr 28269
Faraday St 28208
Faringford Ct 28262
Farley St 28205
Farlow Rd 28269
Farm Gate Dr 28215
Farm Oak Dr 28227
Farm Pond Ln 28212
Farm Tree Ln 28209
Farmbrook Dr 28210
Farmchase Ct 28277
Farmcrest Dr 28206
Farmer St 28208
Farmfield Ln 28213
Farmhurst Dr 28217
Farmingdale Dr 28212
Farmington Ln 28205
Farmlake Dr 28227
Farmland Rd 28226
Farmleigh Ave 28273
Farmstead Dr 28227
Farmview Rd 28205
Farmway Pl 28215
Farmwood Ct 28214
Farnsfield Ct 28270
Farnsworth Ln 28215
Farrhill Rd 28214
Farrington Ln 28227
Farrior Dr 28215
Farris Wheel Ct 28269
Farthington Cir 28217
Fatima Pl 28227
Faulconbridge Rd 28227
Faulkner Pl 28211
Fawn Crossing Ct 28215
Fawn Ridge Ct 28226
Fawn View Dr 28216
Fawnbrook Ln 28217
Fawndale Dr 28269
Fazenda Dr 28214
Feather Ln 28212
Feather Bend Ct 28269
Featherbrook Rd 28262
Feathers Pl 28213
Featherstone Dr 28213
Feeny Ct 28278
Feld Farm Ln 28210
Feldbank Dr 28216
Felicity Ct 28277
Felizzano Pl 28277
Fellows Ln 28215
Fellowship Dr 28262
Fellsway Rd 28209
Felton Ct 28277
Fenceline Dr 28278
Fenning Dr 28227
Fenton Pl 28207
Fenway Dr 28273
Fenwick Ct 28209
Ferguson Ct 28205
Ferguson Rd 28227
Ferguson Forest Dr 28273
Fern Ave 28208
Fern Glen Ct 28227
Fern Springs Ct 28227
Fern Valley Dr 28216
Fernbank Dr 28226
Fernbrook Rd 28208
Ferncliff Rd 28211
Ferndale Pl 28215
Fernhill Dr 28217
Fernhurst Ln 28277
Fernleaf Ct 28215
Fernledge Ct 28269
Fernmoss Ct 28269
Fernside Dr 28227
Fernspray Rd 28215
Fernstone Cir 28227
Fernwood Dr 28211
Ferrell Ave 28216
Ferrell Commons Rd 28269
Ferrum Ln 28278
Ferzon Ln 28227
Fesbrook Ct 28270
Fescue Ct 28216
Festiva Ct 28273
Fetlock Ct 28216
Ficus Tree Ln 28215
Fiddleleaf Ct 28215
Fiddlers Roof Ln 28277
Field Dove Ct 28210
Field Maple Ln 28270
Fieldbrook Pl 28209
Fieldcrest Rd 28217
Fieldcroft Dr 28277
Fieldgate Dr 28277
Fielding Ave 28211
Fielding Rd 28214
Fieldlark Ln 28227
Fieldpointe Ln 28210
Fieldridge Rd 28214
Fieldstone Ct 28269
Fieldvale Pl 28217
Fieldview Rd 28211
Fieldwood Rd 28227
Fifendrum Ln 28216
Fig Ln 28215
Filbert Ln 28215
Fillian Ln 28269
Fillmore Ave 28203
Filly Rd 28227
Filson Ct 28214
Finborough Ct 28214
Fincastle Ct 28215
Fincher Blvd 28269
Finchley Dr 28215
Findon Pl 28215
Finley Ln 28227
Finley Pl 28210
Finn Ln 28262
Finn Hall Ave 28216
Finsbury Pl 28211
Fiorentina St 28277
Fir Knoll Rd 28227
Fircrest Dr 28217
Fire Tree Ln 28227
Firefighter Pl 28204
Firefly Ln 28215
Firelight Ln 28212
Firenza Cir 28273
Fireside Dr 28213
Fireside Ln 28215
Firespike Rd 28277
Firestone Dr 28216
Firestreak Dr 28216
Firethorne Rd 28205
First St 28208
First Bloom Rd 28277
First Flight Dr 28208
First Run Ct 28215
First Ward Ct 28202
Firwood Ln 28209
Fishers Farm Ln 28277
Fishers Pond Dr 28277
Fitchburg Ct 28214
Fitzgerald Ave 28213
Fitzroy Ln 28277
Fitzwilliams Ln 28270
Five Cedars Rd 28226
Five Knolls Dr 28226
Five Oaks Ct 28227
Flagler Ln 28216
Flagstaff Dr 28210
Flagstop Ct 28226
Flakenta Dr 28213
Flamingo Ave 28205
Flanders St 28277
Flarenti Ave 28203
Flat Creek Dr 28277
Flat Iron Rd 28226
Flat River Dr 28262
Flat Rock Dr 28214
Flat Stone Rd 28213
Flaxseed Ln 28216
Flaxton Dr 28227
Fleetwood Dr 28208
Fleming St 28208
Flennigan Way 28277
Fletcher Cir 28226
Flint St 28216
Flint Glenn Ln 28262
Flintgrove Rd 28226
Flintridge Dr 28212
Flintrock Rd 28214
Flintrock Falls Ln 28278
Flintshire Rd 28227
Flintwood Ln 28226
Flodden Field Ct 28217
Floral Ave 28203
Floral Grove Ln 28216
Floral Hall Dr 28277
Florence Ave 28212
Florida Ave 28205
Floufisher Ct 28277
Flowe Dr 28213
Flowerfield Rd 28210
Flowering Dogwood Ln 28270
Flowers Ct 28215
Flowing Brook Ct 28273
Floyd Smith Office Park
Dr 28262
Flushing Ct 28215
Flying Eagle Ln 28278
Flying Scotsman Dr 28213
Flynwood Dr 28205
Foal Ct 28227
Foggy Bank Ln 28214
Foggy Meadow Rd 28269
Fokker Pl 28278
Folger Dr
6400-7399 28270
7400-7599 28226
Folio Club Dr 28277
Folkston Dr 28205
Folly Ct 28273
Folly Gate Ct 28262
Fontaine Ct 28270
Fontana Ave 28206
Fonthill Ln 28210
Forbes Dr 28277
E Ford Rd 28205
S Ford Rd 28214
Ford St 28216
Fordham Rd 28208
Fordwood Dr 28208
Fordyce Ct 28269
Forest Dr
2000-2899 28211
9500-10299 28216
Forest Dr E 28211
Forest Cross Dr 28216
Forest Gate Ln 28270
Forest Glen Rd 28212
Forest Green Dr 28227
Forest Grove Ct 28269
Forest Hills Dr 28226
Forest Home Rd 28278
Forest Knoll Dr 28215
Forest Landing Dr 28213
Forest Manor Ct 28215
Forest Mist Way 28273
Forest Mountain Ct 28227
Forest Oak Dr 28209
Forest Park Dr 28209
Forest Path Dr 28269
Forest Pine Dr 28273
Forest Point Blvd
7100-7899 28217
7900-8399 28273
Forest Point Cir 28273
Forest Pond Dr 28262
Forest Run Ln 28277
Forest Side Ln 28213
Forest Stream Ct 28213
Forest View Ln 28213
Forest Way Dr 28212
Forestbrook Dr 28208
Forestdale Dr 28227
Forestridge Commons
Dr 28269
Forestrock Dr 28269
Forestwinds Ln 28216
Forrest Rader Dr 28227
Forsyth Hall Dr 28273
Forsyth Park Dr 28273
Forsythia Cir 28208
Fort St 28205
Fortbridge Ln 28277
Fortescue Dr 28213
Fortrose Ln 28277
Fortune St 28205
Fortunes Ridge Trl 28269
Forty Niner Ave 28262
Forwood Ct 28215
Foster Ave 28203
Foster Brook Dr 28216
Founders Cir 28211
Founders Club Ct 28269
Fountain Ln 28278
Fountain Vw 28203
Fountaingrass Ln 28269
Fountaingrove Dr 28262
Fountainhill Ridge Rd 28226
Four Acre Ct 28210
Four Farms Rd 28215
Four Mile Creek Rd 28277
Four Seasons Ln 28212
Four Sisters Ln 28215
Four Winds Dr 28212
Fowler Ct 28216
Fowler Farm Rd 28227
Fowler Springs Ln 28212
S Fox St 28204
Fox Brook Ln 28211
Fox Chapel Ln 28270
Fox Chase Ln 28269
Fox Cove Dr 28273
Fox Crossing Dr 28216
Fox Den Trl 28214
Fox Glen Rd 28269
Fox Hill Dr 28269
Fox Hollow Rd 28227
Fox Hound Ct 28212
Fox Hunt Rd 28212
Fox Meade Ln 28215
Fox Mill Ln 28277
Fox Point Dr 28269
Fox Run Dr 28212
Fox Sparrow Ln 28278
Fox Swamp Rd 28215
Fox Thorne Dr 28216
Fox Trot Dr 28269
Fox Valley Rd 28278
Foxborough Rd 28213
Foxbriar Trl 28269
Foxcrest Dr 28227
Foxcroft Ln 28213
Foxcroft Rd 28211
Foxcroft Woods Ln 28211
Foxdale Ct 28277
Foxden Ct 28227
Foxfire Rd 28270
Foxford Pl 28215
Foxglove Dr 28226
Foxhall Dr 28210
Foxhaven Dr 28277
Foxmoor Dr 28226
Foxridge Rd 28226
Foxwood Rd 28226
Foxworth Dr 28226
Foxx Oak Pl 28210
Frances Glen Dr 28213
Frances Irene Dr 28215
Frances Park Dr 28213
Francis Marion Ct 28277
Frank Dr 28215
Frank Grier Rd 28215
Frank Little Ct 28269
Frank Vance Rd 28216
Frank Wiley Ln 28278
Franklin Ave 28206
Franklin Springs Cir 28217
Franklin Square Rd 28213
Franklin Thomas Pl 28214
Franzia Ct 28269
Frazier Ave 28216
Fred Gutt Dr 28270
Fred Herron Ct 28215
Frederick Pl 28210
Free Ct 28216
Free Bird Ave 28216
Free Throw Ln 28217
Freedom Dr
1400-5299 28208
5400-6899 28214
Freeland Ln 28217
Freestone Dr 28216
French St 28216
French Woods Rd 28269
Frenchman St 28262
Frescoe Ct 28277
Fresh Wind Ave 28212
Freshwell Rd 28273
Frew Rd 28206
Friar St 28208
Friar Tuck Ln 28227
Friendly Pl 28213
Fringe Tree Dr 28227
Frog Hopper Ln 28213
Frogs Leap Ct 28277
Frohock Pl 28277
Fromby Ct 28211
Frontenac Ave 28215
Frosch Rd 28278
Frostmoor Pl 28269
Frostwood Pl 28215
Frosty Ln 28216
Fruehauf Dr 28273
Fruitland Rd 28277
Fruitwood Dr 28214
Frye Pl 28269
Fugate Ave 28205
Fuller Pl 28277
Fuller Ridge Cir 28270
Fullerton Ct 28214
Fulton Ave 28205
Fultram Ln 28227
Furlong Trl 28269
Furman Pl 28210
Furrier Dr 28270
Furrow Dr 28270
Fuschia Ct 28215
Gable Rd 28273
Gablestone Way 28207
Gadwall Ct 28273
Gaelic Pl 28227

Gailes Dr 28278
Gainesborough Rd 28205
Gainsford Ct 28210
Gait Dr 28227
Galardia Rd 28215
Galax Dr 28213
Galaxie Rd 28214
Galena Ct 28212
Galena View Dr 28269
Galesburg St 28216
Gallagher St 28208
Gallant Ln 28273
Gallant Fox Way 28277
Gallatin Ln 28213
Galleria Blvd 28270
Galleria Club Ln 28270
Galleria Court Dr 28270
Gallery Pointe Ln 28269
Galloway Rd 28262
Gallowgate Ln 28213
Galty Ln 28270
Galway Dr 28215
Gambia St 28208
Gamesford Dr 28277
Gammon Rd 28269
Gamton Ct 28226
Gander Dr 28277
Gandolf Ct 28213
Gannett Dr 28214
Ganso Ln 28214
Ganymede Pl 28227
Garamond Ct 28270
Garamond Wood Dr 28278
Garbow Ct 28270
Garden Ter 28203
Garden Club Ln 28210
Garden District Dr 28202
Garden Gate Ct 28212
Garden Grove Ln 28269
Garden Oaks Ln 28273
Garden Terrace Ct 28210
Garden Trace Ct 28216
Garden Walk Ln 28216
Gardendale Ct 28269
Gardenia St 28215
Gardenside Ln 28278
N Gardner Ave 28216
S Gardner Ave 28208
Gardner Ln 28270
Gardner Pond Ct 28270
Garfield St 28208
Garganey Ct 28269
Garibaldi Ave 28208
Garland Ct 28277
Garman Hill Dr 28214
Garmoyle St 28277
Garnet Field Ct 28269
Garnette Pl 28216
Garrett Grigg Rd 28262
Garringer Pl 28208
Garris Rd 28209
Garrison Dr 28269
Garrison Rd
900-1599 28262
9000-10899 28278
Garrison St 28205
Garrison Watch Ave 28277
Garst Dr 28214
Garth Wood Rd 28273
Garvin Dr 28269
Garvis Dr 28269
Gaskill Ct 28269
Gaston St 28208
Gate Post Rd 28211
Gatehouse Ct 28277
Gatekeeper Ln 28227
Gates Dr 28227
Gatesmills Ave 28213
Gatesville Ln 28270
Gateway Blvd 28208
Gatewood Dr 28208
Gatewood Oaks Dr 28210
Gathering Ct 28278
Gatwick Ct 28215
Gauley Cir 28273
Gayle Ave 28212
Gaynelle Dr 28215
Gaynor Rd 28211
Gaywind Dr 28226
Gaywood Dr 28273
Gearus Dr 28227
Gel Garry Pl 28215
Gelbray Ct 28213
Gelding Dr 28215
Gelligum Dr 28277
Gemstone Ct 28269
Gemway Dr 28216
Gene Ave 28205
Gene Downs Rd 28262
General Dr 28273
General Commerce Dr 28213
General Industrial Dr 28213
General Pershing Dr 28209
Generations St 28278
Genesis Park Pl 28206
Geneva Ct 28209
Genevieve Ct 28270
Genoa Ln 28262
Gentle Breeze Dr 28273
Gentle Stream Ln 28214
Gentry Pl 28210
Geoffrey Ct 28213
George St 28208
George Wythe Ct 28277
Georgeanne Ct 28217
Georgetown Dr 28213
Georgia Ave 28205
Georgian Hall Dr 28277
Gera Emma Dr 28215
Gerald Dr 28217
Gerald Lee Ct 28270
Geraldine Powe Dr 28206
Geranium Ln 28215
Germaine Ter 28226
Gerren Ct 28217
Gesco St 28208
Getalong Rd 28213
Getaway Ln 28215
Gibbon Rd 28269
Gibbon Terrace Ct 28269
Gibbons Link Rd 28269
Gidleigh Ct 28216
Gifford Park Ct 28215
Gilbert St 28216
Gilead St 28217
Gillespie Ct 28205
Gillman Ct 28269
Gilmore Dr 28209
Gilston Ct 28273
Ginger Ln 28213
Ginger Spice Ln 28227
Ginhouse Ln 28277
Ginkgo Ln 28215
Ginovanni Way 28227
Girard Ct 28212
Girl Scout Rd 28278
Giverny Dr 28226
Gladden Ct 28227
Glade Hill Rd 28270
Glade Spring Ln 28216
Gladstone Ln 28205
Gladwood Ln 28269
Gladwyne Pl 28269
Glaetzer Ln 28270
Glamorgan Ct 28269
Glanworth Ct 28213
Glasgow Rd 28214
Glasgow Green Ln 28213
Glass Mountain Ct 28277
Glassport Ln 28210
Glaston Ln 28262
Glastonbury Ct 28270
Glaze Ct 28269
Glazer Valley Ct 28214
Glen Ter 28211
Glen Abbey Dr 28278
Glen Brook Dr 28215
Glen Brook Ln 28269
Glen Cove Dr 28269
Glen Eden Ct 28227
Glen Ellyn Ct 28213
Glen Forest Dr 28226
Glen Hollow Ct 28273
Glen Hope Ln 28269
Glen Laurel Way 28210
Glen Manor Dr 28269
Glen Myrtle Ave 28262
Glen Oaks Rd 28270
Glen Olden Rd 28269
Glen Robin Ct 28205
Glen Shadow Ln 28212
Glen Shira Ct 28208
Glen Summit Dr 28270
Glenbrier Dr 28212
Glenburn Ln 28278
Glencairn Ct 28269
Glencannon Dr 28227
Glencroft Rd 28227
Glencurry Dr 28214
Glendale Rd 28209
Glendale Chase Ct 28217
Glendevon Ct 28273
Glendock Ct 28269
Glendon Hall Ln 28262
Glendora Dr 28212
Glenduff Pl 28278
Gleneagles Rd 28210
Glenelm Ct 28212
Glenfall Ave 28210
Glenfiddich Dr 28215
Glenfinnan Dr 28277
Glenford Pl 28278
Glenham Dr 28210
Glenhaven Dr 28214
Glenhill Ct 28208
Glenkirk Rd 28210
Glenlake Dr 28208
Glenlea Park 28216
Glenlea Commons Dr 28216
Glenlea Vista Ct 28216
Glenlea Walk Ln 28216
Glenleaf Ct 28270
Glenlivet Ct 28278
Glenlockhart Ln 28273
Glenluce Ave 28213
Glenmac Rd 28215
Glenmont Dr 28227
Glenmoor Dr 28214
Glenmore Garden Dr 28270
Glenn St 28205
Glenn Abbey Way 28277
Glenn Teague Rd 28216
Glenolden Dr 28269
Glenover Cir 28269
Glenridge Rd 28211
Glenrock Dr 28217
Glenshire Ct 28269
Glenstar Ter 28205
Glenstone Ct 28269
Glenview Ct 28215
Glenville Ave 28215
Glenwater Dr 28262
Glenway Ct 28226
Glenwood Dr 28208
Glisson Ct 28210
Globe Ct 28205
Gloman Ct 28227
Glory St 28206
Glory Meadow Ct 28278
Gloryland Ave 28213
Glouchester Cir 28226
Glowing Star Dr 28215
Gloxinia Rd 28215
Glynmoor Lakes Dr 28277
Godley Ln 28216
Godsey Wood Dr 28213
Goff St 28208
Goff House Ct 28214
Gold Dust Ct 28269
Gold Medal Cir 28278
Gold Mine Ct 28227
Gold Nugget Ct 28216
Gold Pan Rd 28215
Gold Rush Blvd 28262
Gold Wagon Ln 28227
Gold Worthy Ct 28212
Golden Dr 28216
Golden Apple Ct 28215
Golden Dale Ln 28262
Golden Eagle Ln 28227
Golden Glow Ct 28212
Golden Heights Ct 28214
Golden Leaf Ct 28277
Golden Maple Ln 28215
Golden Oak Ct 28216
Golden Pond Dr 28269
Golden Rain Ct 28277
Golden Ridge Ln 28208
Golden River Ln 28277
Golden Rose Ln 28216
Golden Spike Dr 28227
Golden Sun Ct 28278
Golden View Dr 28278
Goldenblush Cir 28269
Goldeneye Dr 28216
Goldenfield Dr 28269
Goldenrod Ln 28227
Goldenwillow Dr 28215
Goldfields Dr 28227
Goldfinch Rd 28227
Goldsmith Ct 28215
Goldsmith Ln 28227
Goldstaff Ln 28273
Goldstone Ln 28211
Golf Acres Dr 28208
Golf Course Ln 28208
Golf Links Dr N
11000-11034 28277
11035-11035 28271
11035-11399 28277
11036-11398 28277
Golf Ridge Dr 28277
Golfview Ct 28227
Golspie Ct 28277
Gondola Ave 28213
Goneaway Rd 28210
Goodall Ct 28227
Goodloe Dr 28262
Goodman Rd
1000-1299 28214
5700-5798 28278
5800-5899 28278
Goodrich Dr 28273
Goodwin Ave 28205
Goose Ct 28277
Goose Landing Dr 28269
Gooseberry Rd 28208
Goosedown Ct 28216
Goosefoot St 28277
Gordon St 28205
Gordon Walters Dr 28213
Gordonvale Pl 28226
Gore St 28214
Gorham Dr 28226
Gorham Gate Dr 28269
Gosford Pl 28277
Goshawk Ln 28216
Goshen Ln 28270
Goshen Pl 28211
Gosling Terrace Rd 28262
Gosnell Dr 28227
Gossett Ave 28208
Gossomer Bay Dr 28270
Gothic Ct 28210
Governor Morrison St 28211
Governors Ln 28211
Governors Row 28277
Governors Club Ct 28278
Governors Hill Ln 28211
Gower Ct 28278
Grabill Dr 28269
Graburn Rd 28226
Graburns Ford Dr 28269
Grace Ln 28262
Grace St
1000-1799 28205
1800-2099 28204
Grace Meadow Ln 28214
Gracie Way 28204
Graduate Ln 28262
Grafton Dr 28215
Grafton Pl 28212
N Graham St
200-799 28202
800-4499 28206
4700-5799 28269
S Graham St
300-499 28202
1100-1399 28203
Graham Meadow Dr 28213
Graham Park Dr 28273
Grahamson Ln 28269
Grahamwood Pl 28277
Grain Mill Ln 28214
Granada Dr 28226
Granard Ln 28269
Granby Cir 28217
Grand Canal Way 28270
Grand Fir Rd 28227
Grand Junction Rd 28227
Grand Lake Dr 28208
Grand Oak Dr 28277
Grand Palisades Pkwy 28278
Grand Teton Dr 28269
Grand Traverse Dr 28278
Grande Heights Dr 28269
Grandeur Rd 28269
Grandfathers Ln 28226
Grandiflora Dr 28278
Grandin Rd 28208
Grandview Ridge Dr 28215
Granger Ave 28208
Granite St 28273
Granite Creek Ln 28269
Granite Trail Ln 28214
Granstark Ct 28216
Grant St 28208
Grantchester Cir 28262
Grantham Ln 28262
Grantwood Pl 28273
Granville Rd 28207
Grapetree Ct 28215
Grapevine Dr 28217
Grapeyard Ct 28273
Graphic Ct 28206
Grasmere Dr 28270
Grass Dr 28216
Grass Field Rd 28213
Grass Hollow Ct 28216
Grass Meadows Ct 28216
Grass Ridge Dr 28216
Grass Run Ct 28216
Grasset Ave 28269
Grasshopper Ln 28278
Grasslands Ct 28273
Grassy Crops Rd 28277
Grassy Knob Ct 28273
Grassy Patch Ln 28216
Grassy Plain Ct 28214
Gray Dr 28213
Gray Birch Ct 28215
Gray Dove Ct 28216
Gray Feather Dr 28262
Gray Gate Ln 28210
Gray Ghost Ct 28278
Gray Moss Rd 28270
Gray Willow Rd 28227
Graybark Ave 28205
Graybeard Ct 28226
Grayling Ct 28227
Graymist Dr 28215
Graymont Dr 28217
Graypark Dr 28269
Grays Creek Ln 28214
Grays Ridge Dr 28269
Graywell Ln 28277
Great Bear Ct 28269
Great Future Dr 28277
Great Laurel Rd 28227
Great Oaks Ln 28270
Great Wagon Rd 28215
Greatford Ct 28215
Green St 28214
Green Apple Dr 28215
Green Cane Dr 28277
Green Clover Dr 28269
Green Fairway Dr 28215
Green Forest Dr 28212
Green Gable Ct 28270
Green Grass Rd 28227
Green Hedge Ave 28269
Green Heron Ct 28278
Green Hill Rd 28278
Green Ivy Ln 28217
Green Lea Ct 28273
Green Meadow Dr 28269
Green Moss Ln 28208
Green Mountain Rd 28278
Green Needles Ct 28217
Green Oaks Ln 28205
Green Park Cir 28217
Green Pasture Rd 28269
Green Rea Rd 28226
Green Ridge Dr 28217
Green Tee Ln 28277
Green Trail Ln 28204
Green Turtle Dr 28210
Green Vista Ct 28212
Green Willow Ln 28226
Greenbank Ct 28214
Greenbriar Rd 28209
Greenbriar Hills
Plantation Rd 28277
Greenbrook Dr 28205
Greencastle Dr 28210
Greencove Dr 28270
Greencreek Dr 28273
Greencrest Dr 28205
Greene St 28269
Greenfield Dr 28270
Greenfield Commons
Dr 28226
Greenfinch Dr 28278
Greenford Ct 28277
Greengate Ln 28211
Greenhaven Ln 28205
Greenhead View Rd 28262
Greenhill Dr 28217
Greenhill St 28214
Greenhurst Dr 28214
Greenland Ave 28208
Greenlawn Hills Ct 28213
Greenleaf Ave 28202
Greenloch Ct 28269
Greenock Ridge Ct 28269
Greenook Ct 28217
Greensboro St 28206
Greenside Ct 28277
Greenspire Ct 28262
Greentree Dr 28211
Greenvale Ln 28277
Greenview Pl 28208
Greenview Terrace Ct 28277
Greenware Trl 28269
Greenway Ave 28204
Greenway Bend Dr 28226
Greenway Crescent Ln 28204
Greenway Industrial Dr 28273
Greenway View Ct 28278
Greenway Village Dr 28269
Greenway Vista Ln 28216
Greenwich Rd 28211
Greenwing Ct 28273
Greenwood Clfs 28204
Greenwood Ct 28215
Greenwood Dr 28217
N Gregg St 28216
S Gregg St 28208
Gregory Pl 28227
Grenada Dr 28227
Grenelefe Village Rd 28269
Gresham Pl 28211
Gretna Green Dr 28217
Grey Coat Ct 28273
Grey Dogwood Ct 28269
Grey Squirrel Ct 28277
Grey Timbers Ct 28227
Greyabby Ct 28270
Greybriar Forest Ln 28278
Greycrest Dr 28278
Greycroft Ct 28277
Greyhound Dr 28269
Greyleaf Pl 28210
Greylock Ct 28213
Greylock Ridge Rd 28269
Greylyn Dr 28226
Greymore Ct 28277
Greymouth Rd 28262
Greyson Heights Dr 28277
Greyson Ridge Dr 28277
Greystone Rd 28209
Greywood Dr 28212
Grice Ct 28210
Gricklade Dr 28262
Grier Ave 28216
Grier Rd
7300-7799 28213
8300-8999 28215
Grier Farm Ln 28270
Grier Springs Ln 28213
Griers Fork Dr 28273
Griers Grove Rd 28216
Griers Pasture Dr 28278
Grierton Ct 28205
Grierview Ln 28213
Griffith Rd 28217
Griffith St 28203
Grimes St 28206
Grimmersborough Ln 28270
Gristmill Ln 28227
Grobie Way 28216
Grosbeak Ln 28269
Grosner Pl 28211
Grosse Pointe Ln 28227
Groth Ct 28277
Grove Rd 28216
Grove St
1000-1099 28202
4200-4399 28269
Grove Creek Ln 28273
Grove Crest Ln 28262
Grove Hall Ave 28227
Grove Hill Dr 28262
Grove Park Blvd 28215
Grove Point Rd 28277
Grove Side Ln 28262
Groveton Ct 28269
Groveview Ct 28269
Grovewood Dr 28208
Gruenewald Ln 28210
Guadalupe Ln 28214
Guardhouse Ct 28262
Guenoc Ct 28270
Guernsey Ct 28213
Guest House Ct 28270
Guildbrook Rd 28226
Guildcrest Ln 28213
Guildhall Ln 28213
Guilford Rd 28209
Guinevere Dr 28277
Gulf Dr 28208
Gullane Ct 28277
Gum St 28208
Gum Branch Rd 28214
Gum Tree Ln 28214
Gunn St 28216
Gunners Ct 28270
Gunnison Ln 28277
Gunpowder Point Dr 28277
Gunston Ct 28226
Gustar Ct 28212
Gusty Ct 28208
Guyandotte Pl 28212
Gwaltney Pl 28277
Gwynne Ave 28205
Gwynne Hill Rd 28215
Habersham Dr 28209
Habersham Pointe Cir 28226
Habina Ct 28215
Hackberry Ln 28226
Hackberry Creek Trl 28269
Hackberry Grove Cir 28269
Hackett Ln 28269
Hackney Ct 28215
Haddington Dr 28215
Haddington Dr NW 28269
Haddonfield Pl 28277
Haddonshire Ln 28270
Hadleigh Pl 28210
Hadley Green Ct 28210
Hadlow Ct 28278
Hadrian Way 28211

Street	ZIP
Hadrians Walk Ct	28227
Hadstone Ln	28215
Hagen Ct	28262
Hager Dr	28208
Hagerstone Way	28216
Hagler Dr	28269
Haines St	28216
Haines Mill Rd	28273
Halcott Ln	28269
Halesworth Dr	28211
Half Dome Dr	28269
Half Halt Ave	28227
Halford Pl	28211
Halkirk Manor Ln	28278
Hall Ave	28205
S Hall Dr	28270
Hallam Ct	28269
Halliwell St	28262
Halsey St	28208
Halstead Dr	28209
Halter Dr	28278
Halton Park Dr	28262
Hamel St	28215
Hamilton Cir	28216
Hamilton Dr	28216
Hamilton Rd	
11900-13199	28273
13300-13799	28278
Hamilton St	28206
Hamilton Crossings Dr	28214
Hamilton Forest Dr	28216
Hamilton Green Dr	28273
Hamilton Jones Dr	28215
Hamilton Mill Rd	28270
Hamilton Oaks Dr	28216
Hamilton Place Dr	28273
Hamilton Russell Ln	28269
Hammer Mill Ct	28270
Hammersmith Ct	28262
Hammett St	28205
Hammock Creek Pl	28278
Hammond Dr	28215
Hammonds St	28214
Hamorton Pl	28205
Hamory Dr	28212
Hampshire Pl	28205
Hampshire Woods Ct	28277
Hampton Ave	28207
N Hampton Dr	28227
S Hampton Dr	28227
Hampton Church Rd	28262
Hampton Gardens Ln	28209
Hampton Manor Dr	28226
Hampton Oaks Ln	28270
Hampton Place Dr	28269
Hampton View Ct	28213
Hampton Way Dr	28213
Hampton Woods Ct	28277
Hamptonridge Dr	28210
Hamptons Landing Rd	28277
Hanberry Blvd	28213
Hancock Ter	28205
Handley Pl	28226
Hanes Bee Ln	28278
Hanford Ct	28217
Hangar Rd	28208
Hanging Ivy Dr	28215
Hanging Moss Trl	28227
Hankins Rd	28269
Hanlin Ct	28277
Hanloch Ct	28262
Hanna Ct	28212
Hannah Alexander Ln	28227
Hannah Rae Ct	28214
Hannibal Ct	28214
Hannon Rd	28227
Hanover St	28205
Hanover Glen Rd	28210
Hanover Hills St	28277
Hanover Hollow Dr	28210
Hanover Ridge Ct	28210
Hanover South Trl	28210
Hanover Woods Pl	28210
Hansard Dr	28214
Hansbury Dr	28216
Hanson Dr	28207
Hanson Rd	28273
Hanway Ct	28273
Hanworth Trace Dr	28277
Happy Hollow Dr	28227
Happy Valley Dr	28270
Harbinger Ct	28205
Harbor Dr	28214
Harbor Estate Rd	28278
Harbor Oaks Ln	28278
Harbor View Rd	28278
Harburn Forest Dr	28269
Harcombe Dr	28277
Harcourt Ln	28212
Hardee Cove Ct	28227
Harding Pl	28204
Hardison Rd	28226
Hardwick Rd	28211
Hardwood Watch Ct	28277
Hargett Ct	28211
Hargrove Ave	28208
Harland St	28216
Harlee Ave	28208
Harlequin Dr	28273
Harlington Ln	28270
Harmonious St	28278
Harmony Bridge Pl	28216
Harmony Glen Ct	28273
Harpendon Ln	28273
Harpley Ct	28215
Harps Mill Ct	28270
Harri Ann Dr	28227
Harrier Rd	28216
Harriett Ave	28216
Harrill St	28205
Harringham Ln	28269
Harrington Woods Rd	28269
Harris Rd	28211
Harris Corners Pkwy	28269
Harris Cove Dr	28269
Harris Glen Dr	28269
Harris Grove Ln	28212
Harris Hill Ln	28269
Harris Houston Rd	28262
Harris Mill Ln	28262
Harris Oak Blvd	28269
Harris Park Blvd	28227
Harris Pointe Dr	28269
Harris Pond Dr	28269
Harris Ridge Dr	28269
Harris Station Blvd	28213
Harris Technology	
Blvd	28269
Harris Trace Ct	28227
Harris Woods Blvd	28269
Harrisburg Rd	
6200-6899	28227
6900-11599	28215
Harrison Rd	28270
Harrison St	28208
Harrison Steel Dr	28277
Harrisons Crossing	
Ave	28277
Harrisonwoods Pl	28270
Harrow Pl	28205
Harrowfield Rd	28226
Harsworth Ln	28277
Hart Rd	28214
Harte Cir	28216
Hartfield Downs Dr	28269
Hartford Ave	28209
Hartland Cir	28205
Hartley St	28206
Hartley Hills Dr	28213
Hartmill Ct	28226
Hartness Ave	28211
Hartsell Pl	28215
Hartwell Farm Dr	28278
Hartwicke Pl	28270
Harvard Pl	28207
Harvest Ln	28210
Harvest Hill Dr	28212
Harvest Time Ct	28278
Harvey St	28206
Harvey Walker Ln	28278
Harwick Pl	28211
Harwood Ln	28214
Harwood Cove Ct	28214
Harwood Hills Ln	28214
Harwyn Dr	28215
Hashem Dr	28208
Hassell Pl	28209
Hastings Dr	28207
Hastings Mill Ln	28277
Hateras Ave	28216
Hatfield Rd	28278
Hathaway St	28211
Hathaway Hills Dr	28214
Hatherly Rd	28209
Hathshire Dr	28262
Hatley Pl	28277
Hatter Ridge Ter	28214
Hattie Little St	28269
Hatton Ct	28277
Hatton Cross Dr	28278
Hatwynn Rd	28269
Havasu St	28273
Havel Ct	28211
Havelock Ave	28208
Haven Dr	28209
Haven Ridge Ln	28215
Havencrest Ave	28211
Havenlock Pl	28215
Havenwood Rd	28205
Haverford Pl	28209
Haverhill Dr	28209
Haversham Ct	28216
Haverstick Pl	28226
Haverstraw Ct	28212
Havilon Ct	28211
Hawaii Dr	28216
Hawfield Rd	28214
Hawfield Farms Rd	28277
Hawfield Way Dr	28277
Hawfield Woods Ln	28277
Hawick Ct	28278
Hawick Valley Ln	28277
Hawk Crest Ct	28270
Hawk Roost Ct	28214
Hawk Shadow Ln	28277
Hawkbill Pl	28278
Hawkeye Dr	28273
Hawkins Pl	28269
Hawkins St	28203
Hawkins Meadow Ct	28213
Hawks Moor Ct	28262
Hawksnest Dr	28269
Hawkstand Ln	28210
Hawkwood Ln	28277
Hawley St	28214
Haws Run Ct	28277
Hawthorne Dr	28227
Hawthorne Ln	
100-999	28204
1000-1799	28205
Hawthorne Bridge Ct	28204
Haxley Ln	28278
Hay Meadow Dr	28227
Haybridge Rd	28269
Haybrook Ln	28262
Haycox St	28216
Hayden Dr	28269
Hayes Ct	28205
Hayfield Rd	28213
Haying Pl	28227
Hayling Rd	28226
Hayloft Cir	28226
Haymarket Rd	28214
Haymow Ct	28270
Haynes Hall Pl	28270
Haywain Ct	28213
Haywood Ct	28205
Hazel St	28208
Hazelcroft Ln	28269
Hazelhurst Ave	28211
Hazelnut Cir	28212
Hazelton Dr	28210
Hazelview Dr	28277
Hazlitt Ct	28269
Hazy Valley Ct	28269
Headford Rd	28277
Headquarters Farm Rd	28262
Hearst Ct	28269
Hearthstone Ct	28211
Heartleaf Rd	28227
Heartwood Ln	28227
Heath Glen Dr	28227
Heath Lake Dr	28227
Heath Ridge Ct	28210
Heath Valley Rd	28210
Heathcliff St	28208
Heathcott Cir	28262
Heathcrest Ct	28269
Heathcroft Ct	28269
Heather Ln	28209
Heather Glen Ln	28208
Heather Nicole Ln	28227
Heather Ridge Ct	28226
Heather View Ct	28216
Heatherbrook Ave	28213
Heatherdale Ct	28212
Heatherford Dr	28226
Heathergate Ln	28227
Heatherly Ct	28277
Heathermoor Ct	28209
Heathers Mist Ave	28213
Heatherton Pl	28270
Heatherwood Ln	28227
Heathfield Ct	28215
Heathgate Rd	28226
Heathmoor Ln	28211
Heathstead Pl	28210
Heathstone Ln	28210
Heathway Dr	28213
Heathwood Rd	28211
Heavy Equipment School	
Rd	28214
E Hebron St	28273
Hebron Commerce Dr	28273
Hedder Ct	28210
Hedge Maple Rd	28269
Hedgecrest Pl	28269
Hedgelawn Dr	28262
Hedgemore Dr	28209
Hedgerow Ct	28209
Hedgerow Park Rd	28277
Hedgeway Dr	28278
Hedgewyck Pl	28211
Hedingham Ct	28269
Hedley Way	28210
Heflin St	28205
Heiden Dr	28227
Heidleburg Ln	28210
Heil Pl	28216
Heirloom Cir	28277
Hekate Dr	28227
Helen Harper Ct	28216
Helena Cir	28227
Helena St	28208
Helios Ln	28262
Hellebore Rd	28213
Helms Rd	28214
Helmsdale Ave	28212
Helmsley Ct	28273
Helper Dr	28215
Heman Dr	28269
Hemby Pl	28270
Hemby Woods Dr	28262
Hemingford Ct	28277
Hemlock St	28203
Hemphill St	28208
Hempstead Pl	28207
Hemsworth Ter	28227
Henbane Ct	28213
Henderson Cir & Rd	28269
Henderson Oaks Dr	28269
Henderson Valley Ln	28269
Hendricks Chapel Ln	28216
Hendry Rd	28269
Henery Tuckers Ct	28270
Henley Pl	28207
Hennessy Pl	28210
Hennigan Place Ln	28214
Henry David Ct	28214
Henry Thoreau Rd	28214
Henshaw Rd	28209
Henslowe Ln	28262
Herb House Ct	28227
Herbert Flowe Rd	28227
Herbert Spaugh Ln	28208
Herdon Ct	28277
Here At Last Ln	28278
Hereford St	28213
Heriot Ave	28217
Heriot Field Dr	28278
Heritage Pl	28210
Heritage Hills Ln	28269
Heritage Lake Dr	28262
Heritage Pointe Rd	28262
Heritage Woods Pl	28269
Hermance Dr	28278
Hermiston St	28278
Hermit Thrush Ln	28278
Hermitage Ct & Rd	28207
Hermsley Rd	28278
Heron Cove Ct NW	28269
Heron Glen Dr	28269
Heron Point Pl	28278
Herons Pond Ct	28215
Heronwood Ln	28227
Herrin Ave	28205
Herring Gull Way	28278
Hershey St	28213
Hertford Rd	28207
Hesperus Ct	28216
Hethersett Ln	28227
Hewitt Dr	28269
Hewitt Associates Dr	28262
Hey Rock Ct	28269
Heydon Hall Cir	28210
Heysham Ln	28269
Heywood Ave	28208
Hezekiah Pl	28215
Hibiscus Cir	28273
Hickok Ct	28270
Hickory Dr	28215
Hickory Ln	
2300-2399	28206
5200-5399	28216
Hickory Bluff Ct	28208
Hickory Cove Ln	28269
Hickory Creek Rd	28214
Hickory Forest Dr	28277
Hickory Grove Rd	28215
Hickory Hollow Ln	28227
Hickory Knoll Ln	28227
Hickory Nut St	28205
Hickory Ridge Ln	28227
Hickory Stick Pl	28277
Hickory Trace Dr	28227
Hickory Trail Ln	28277
Hickory Tree Ln	28277
Hickory Valley Ct	28212
Hickory View Ln	28278
Hidden Ct	28214
Hidden Creek Dr	28214
Hidden Forest Dr	28213
Hidden Glen Dr	28273
Hidden Grove Trl	28215
Hidden Hills Ln	28227
Hidden Meadow Ln	28269
Hidden Ridge Ln	28216
Hidden Stream Ct	28213
Hidden Valley Rd	28213
Hidden View Dr	28227
Hiddenbrook Dr	28205
Hideaway Rd	28278
High St	28211
High Bluff Ct	28278
High Chase Ln	28273
High Creek Ct	28277
High Falls Ln	28262
High Glen Dr	28269
High Hamptons Dr	28210
High Laurel Ln	28269
High Meadow Ln	28217
High Oaks Ln	28277
High Point Ct	28278
High Ridge Rd	28270
High Valley Ln	28269
High Winds Ln	28208
Highbanks Ct	28212
Highbrook Dr	28212
Highbury Ln	28213
Highcrest St	28277
Highcroft Ln	28269
Highfield Ct	28216
Highflyer Woods Ln	28278
Highgrove St	28277
Highlake Dr	28215
Highland Ave	
4300-4499	28269
6300-6499	28215
Highland St	28208
Highland Castle Way	28270
Highland Commons	
Rd	28269
Highland Creek Pkwy	28269
Highland Forest Dr	28270
Highland Glen Dr	28269
Highland Meadow Rd	28273
Highland Mist Ln	28215
Highland Park Dr	28269
Highland Ridge Ln	28216
Highland Shoppes Dr	28269
Highland View Ln	28214
Highlander Ct	28269
Highlands Crossing Dr	28277
Highlawn Dr	28212
Highroad Dr	28262
Highstream Ct	28269
Hightimbers Ct	28215
Hightower Ct	28227
Highview Rd	28210
Highwood Pl	28210
Highworth Dr & Ln	28214
Hilary Cir	28217
Hilbriar Ct	28215
Hilda Ct	28226
Hildebrand St	28216
Hildreth Ct	28226
N Hill Cir	28213
Hill Rd	28210
W Hill St	
600-699	28202
800-999	28208
Hill Point Ct	28262
S Hill View Dr	28210
Hillandale Dr	28270
Hillary Pl	28270
Hillbourn Dr	28212
Hillbrook Dr	28226
Hillcrest St	28206
Hilldale Way	28226
Hilliard Dr	28205
Hillingdon Rd	28226
Hillmont Dr	28226
Hillock Ct	28215
Hillsboro Ave	28213
Hillsdale Ave	28209
Hillside Ave	28209
Hillside Dr	28227
Hillside Ln	28226
Hillstone Ct	28273
Hillswick Dr	28215
Hilltop Cir	28269
Hillwood Ct	28210
Hilo Dr	28206
Hilton Dr	28214
Himel St	28215
Hinsdale St	28210
Hinsley Ln	28227
Hipp Rd	28216
Hiram St	28208
Hirsch Dr	28277
Hitchcock Ln	28262
Hitchgate Dr	28227
Hitching Post Ln	28212
Hive Dr	28217
Hobart Ct	28209
Hobbitshire Ln	28269
Hobbs St	28206
Hobbs Creek Ln	28213
Hobbs Hill Dr	
4400-4599	28215
4600-4999	28212
Hobby Ct	28213
Hodge Ln	28227
Hodgson Rd	28211
Hoffman Ct	28269
Hofstra Ct	28227
Hogan Ct	28270
Hogans Bluff Ln	28227
Hogans Way Ct	28269
Holabird Ln	28208
Holbert Cir	28269
Holbrook Dr	
4400-4599	28205
4600-4899	28212
Holbrook Square Ct	28216
Holburn Ct	28227
Holcombe Ave	28208
Holden Ct	28277
Holding St	28227
Holgate Hill Dr	28227
Holiday Dr	28215
Holland Ave	28206
Holland Park Ln	28277
Holliford Ct	28215
Hollirose Dr	28227
Hollis Rd	28209
Holliswood Ct	28217
Hollow Dr	28212
Hollow Creek Cir	28262
Hollow Glen Pl	28226
Hollow Maple Dr	28216
Hollow Oak Dr	28227
Hollow Ridge Ln	28269
Hollow Tree Ct	28226
Holloway St	28213
Hollowood St	28216
Holly Ln	28270
Holly St	28216
Holly Creek Ct	28216
Holly Fern Cir	28211
Holly Grove Ct	28227
Holly Hill Rd	28227
Holly Hill Farm Rd	28277
Holly Knoll Dr	28227
Holly Lee Dr	28212
Holly Oak Ln	28215
Holly Park Dr	28214
Holly Ridge Blvd	28216
Holly Tree Dr	28215
Holly Tree Ln	28216
Holly Vista Ave	28269
Hollyberry Dr	28227
Hollybrook Dr	28277
Hollybrook Ln	28227
Hollyburgh Ter	28215
Hollybush Ln	28277
Hollyday Ct	28210
Hollyheath Ln	28209
Hollyhouse Dr	28215
Hollystone Ln	28215
Hollywood St	
800-999	28211
7500-7699	28269
Holm Oak Pl	28262
Holmes Dr	28209
Holroyd Ct	28211
Holston Ct	28215
Holt St	28205
Holton Ave	28208
Holyoke Ln	28226
Home Place Ln	28227
Homecoming Way	28278
Homestead Pl	28277
Homestead Glen Blvd	28214
Homewood Dr	28262
Homewood Pl	28217
Hondures Dr	28206
Honegger Dr	28211
Honey Bee Cir	28226
Honey Creek Ln	28270
Honey Fig Rd	28277
Honey Flower Pl	28214
Honey Hill Ln	28273
Honey Hurst Ln	28212
Honeycomb Cir	28277
Honeynut Dr	28277
Honeysuckle Ln	28212
Honeywood Ave	28216
Honor Guard Ave	28277
Honors Ct	28210
Hood Dr	28213
Hood Rd	28215

Hood Bend Ct 28273
Hoodridge Ln 28227
Hooksett Ct 28217
Hookston Ln 28273
Hooper Ct 28212
Hoover Cir 28214
Hoover Dr 28269
Hoover St 28208
Hope Valley Ln 28213
Hopecrest Dr 28210
Hopedale Ave 28207
Hopeful Ct 28214
Hopeton Rd 28210
Hopewood Ln 28216
Hopkins St 28269
Horace St 28208
Horace Mann Rd 28269
Horadeli Dr 28212
Horizon Cir 28215
Hornbeam Ct 28269
Horne Dr 28206
Hornell Pl 28270
Hornet Dr 28216
Hornwood Ct 28215
Horse Chestnut Ln 28277
Horse Pasture Ln 28269
Horsecroft Ct 28277
Horseplay Ct 28277
Horseshoe Ln 28208
Horseshoe Bend Dr 28215
Horsham Ct 28277
Horton Ct 28210
Horton Rd 28278
Hoskins Rd 28208
N Hoskins Rd 28216
S Hoskins Rd 28208
Hoskins Avenue Dr 28208
Hoskins Mill Ln 28208
Hoskins Ridge Ln 28216
Hosta Dr 28269
Hoste Way Ln 28216
Hough Rd
3900-4199 28209
14800-14999 28227
Hough St 28214
Houldsworth Dr 28213
Houndstooth Dr 28227
Hounslow Ln 28213
Houston St 28214
Houston Branch Rd 28270
Houston Heights Rd 28262
Houston Ridge Rd 28277
Hove Rd 28227
Hovis Rd
4200-5499 28208
5500-5699 28216
Howard Cir 28214
Howard St 28269
Howell Ct 28277
Howell Center Dr 28227
Howerton Ct 28270
Howie Cir 28205
Howland Ln 28226
Howt Galvin Way 28214
Hoyle Dr 28227
Hoyt Ct 28210
Hubbard Rd 28269
Hubbard Falls Dr 28269
Hubbard Point Dr 28269
Hubbard Woods Rd 28269
Huckleberry Rd 28210
Hucks Rd 28269
Hudson St 28205
Hudson Graham Ln 28216
Hugh Caldwell Rd 28214
Hugh Forest Rd 28270
Hughes Dr 28213
Hugue Way 28214
Hulston Ct 28211
Humber Ct 28215
Humberview Ln 28270
Humboldt Dr 28277
Hummingbird Ln 28212
Humphrey St 28208
Hundred Oaks Dr 28217
Hungerford Pl 28207
Hunslet Cir 28206
Hunt Glenn Ct 28216
Hunt Stand Ln 28226
Huntcliff Dr 28226
Huntdale Ct 28212
Hunter Ave 28262
Hunter Ln 28211
Hunter Crest Ln 28209
Hunter Forest Ct 28213
Hunter Green Ln 28227
Hunter Hill Ln 28216
Hunter Oaks Ln 28213
Hunter Pine Ln 28270
Hunter Ridge Dr 28226
Hunter Trail Ln 28226
Hunters Trce 28262
Hunters Creek Ct 28269
Hunters Crossing Ln 28215
Hunters Glen Dr 28214
Hunters Landing Dr 28273
Hunters Pointe Ct 28269
Hunters Spring Dr 28269
Hunters Trace Ct 28262
Hunters Whip Ct 28269
Huntfield Dr 28270
Hunting Birds Ln 28278
Hunting Ridge Ln 28212
Hunting Wood Ct 28216
Huntington Meadow Ln 28273
Huntington Park Dr 28211
Huntingtowne Farms Ln 28210
Huntland Ct 28277
Huntley Pl 28207
Huntley Rd 28227
Huntlynn Rd 28214
Huntman Way 28226
Huntmeadow Dr 28269
Hunts End Ct 28214
Huntscroft Ln 28226
Huntsham Rd 28227
Huntsmaster Dr 28277
Huntsmoor Dr 28217
Huntwell Commons Ln 28226
Huntwood Dr 28214
Hurstbourne Green Dr 28277
Hurston Cir 28208
Hutchinson Ln 28216
Hutchison Mcdonald Rd 28269
Huxley Rd 28277
Huyton Ct 28215
Hyacinth Ct 28215
Hyde Glen Ct 28262
Hyde Park Dr 28216
Hyde Pointe Ct 28262
Hydes Way 28262
Hyndman Ct 28214
Hyperion Ct 28216
Hyperion Hills Ln 28278
I K Beatty St 28214
Iberville St 28270
Ibis Ct 28205
Ibm Dr 28262
Icon Way 28216
Ideal Way 28203
Idle Wheels St 28215
Idlebrook Dr 28212
Idlewild Rd
6100-7999 28212
8000-9532 28227
9533-9597 28227
9534-9598 28227
9599-9799 28227
4900-5399 28227
Idlewild Brook Ln 28212
Idlewood Cir 28209
Ikarios Dr 28227
Ikea Blvd 28262
Ilana Ct 28204
Ilex Ct 28211
Ilford St 28215
Illoria Dr 28273
Impala Ln 28216
Impatien Dr 28215
Imperial Ct 28273
Imperial Oak Ln 28273
E Independence Blvd
100-1199 28204
1200-4599 28205
4600-6799 28212
6800-8899 28227
S Independence Blvd 28204
India Wilkes Pl 28270
Indian Ln 28213
Indian Hills Ln 28278
Indian Meadows Ln 28210
Indian Ridge Ln 28214
Indian Rock Rd 28270
Indian Trail Rd 28227
Indica Ct 28213
Indigo Row 28277
Industrial Center Cir 28213
Ingelow Ln 28226
Ingle St 28216
Inglehurst Dr 28273
Ingleside Dr 28210
Ingleton Ct 28269
Ingraham Pl 28270
Inlet Pointe Ct 28216
Innes Ct 28277
Innisfree Pl 28226
Innsbrook Rd 28226
Insdale Ct 28269
Insley Ct 28210
Interface Ln 28262
Intermilan Way 28277
International Dr 28270
International Airport Dr 28208
Interstate St 28208
N Interstate 85 Service Rd
2200-5298 28206
4301-5099 28269
5201-6497 28262
6499-7099 28262
S Interstate 85 Service Rd
200-4199 28208
4200-4299 28214
4301-6699 28214
Interstate North Dr 28206
Interurban Ave 28208
Inverary Pl 28226
Inverness Rd 28209
Invershiel Ct 28227
Inwood Dr 28209
Iola Dr 28269
Ira Flowe Rd 28227
Irby Dr 28209
Iredell Dr 28269
Iris Dr 28205
Irish Ln 28214
Irma St 28216
Iron Brigade Ln 28269
Iron Gate Ln 28212
Iron Horse Ct 28227
Iron Stone Ct 28227
Ironkettle Rd 28270
Ironside Ave 28203
Ironwood St 28206
Irving Dr 28216
Irvington Dr 28205
N Irwin Ave 28202
S Irwin Ave 28202
Irwin Rd 28215
Irwin Valley Ct 28269
Irwin Wood Ln 28269
Isaac Dr 28216
Isaac Hunter Dr 28214
Isabel Ct 28211
Isabella Pl 28227
Isenhour St 28206
Island Cove Ln 28216
Island Lake Dr 28214
Island Park Cir 28262
Island Point Rd 28278
Isleworth Ave 28203
Isthmus Ct 28215
Ivanhoe Pl 28205
Iverify Dr 28217
Iverleigh Trl 28270
Iverson Way 28203
Ivey Dr 28205
Ivey Chase Ln 28277
Ivey Creek Dr 28273
Ivory Ct 28215
Ivory Palm Dr 28227
Ivy Brook Ct 28269
Ivy Falls Ct 28226
Ivy Hollow Dr 28227
Ivy Meadow Dr 28213
Ivy Ridge Pl 28269
Ivy Run Ct 28270
Ivydale Dr 28212
Ivygate Ln 28226
Ivystone Ct 28277
J Julian Ln 28208
J M Keynes Dr 28262
J N Pease Pl 28262
Jack Russell Ct 28269
Jackson Ave 28204
Jackson Dr 28269
Jackson Pond Dr 28273
Jacob Martin Dr 28269
Jacobs Ln 28204
Jacobs Creek Dr 28270
Jacobs Fork Ln 28273
Jacquelyn Ct 28273
Jade St 28277
Jade Glen Dr 28262
Jakes Ln 28208
Jakobson Dr 28215
Jaldena Dr 28227
James Rd 28215
James St
1000-1299 28216
2800-2899 28208
5500-5799 28216
James Blakeney Ave 28277
James Drew Ct 28270
James Jack Ln 28277
James Madison Ct 28277
James Richard Dr 28277
James Valley Ct 28270
Jameston Dr 28209
Jamison Ln 28269
Jamison Place Ct 28227
Jane Ave 28269
Jansen Ridge Way 28278
Jardin Way 28215
Jardiniere Ct 28226
Jarmon Ct 28213
Jarrell Ct 28211
Jaslie Ln 28227
Jasmin May Dr 28226
Jason Ave 28208
Jaspar Crest Ln 28269
Javitz Rd 28216
Jay St 28208
Jean Grimes Dr 28269
Jeanette Cir 28213
Jeans Ct 28214
Jeff St 28205
Jeff Adams Dr 28206
Jefferson Dr 28270
Jefferson Colony Rd 28227
Jefferson Davis St 28206
Jeffrey Bryan Dr 28213
Jem Ct 28226
Jena Ct 28210
Jenkins Ave 28211
Jenkins Dr 28212
Jenna Marie Ln 28210
Jennie Linn Dr 28215
Jennings St 28216
Jenny Ann Dr 28216
Jensen St 28205
Jepson Ct 28214
Jeremiah Blvd 28262
Jericho Ln 28270
Jerilyn Dr 28212
Jerpoint Abby Dr 28273
Jersey Ln 28209
Jessamine Ln 28214
Jessica Pl 28269
Jessica Leigh Ln 28269
Jessie St 28206
Jester Ln 28211
Jewelflower Rd 28227
Jim Harper Ln 28227
Jimmy Oehler Rd 28269
Joannas Ct 28214
Jocelyn Ln 28269
Jockeys Ridge Dr 28277
Jodhpur Ct 28212
Joe St 28206
Joe Morrison Ln 28214
Joe Whitener Rd 28213
Joel Turner Dr 28216
John Adams Rd 28262
John Beck Dr 28273
John Bostar Ln 28215
John Crosland Jr Dr 28208
John Gladden Rd 28214
John J Delaney Dr 28277
John K Hall Way 28277
John Kirk Dr 28262
John Mccarroll Ave 28216
John Mcgraw Ln 28214
John Penn Cir 28215
John Price Rd 28273
John Redford Rd 28262
John Russell Rd
9300-9699 28215
9700-11099 28213
Johnnette Dr 28212
Johnny Cake Ln 28226
Johnny Reb Ln 28273
Johns Towne Dr 28210
Johnson Rd & St 28206
Johnson And Wales Way 28202
Johnson Creek Rd 28215
Johnston Rd
10100-10298 28210
10600-11999 28226
12100-16599 28277
Johnston Mill Ct 28269
Johnston Oehler Rd 28269
Johoy Dr 28216
Joli Cheval Ln 28227
Joliette Ln 28277
Jonas Creek Way 28277
Jonathans Ridge Rd 28227
Jones St 28208
Jones Crossing Rd 28277
Jones Ridge Dr 28226
Jonquil St 28211
Jordan Pl 28205
Jordan Rae Ln 28277
Jordans Pond Ln 28214
Jordanus Ct 28277
Jordi Way 28213
Joseph Clark Rd 28273
Joseph Hewes Ct 28212
Joseph Howard Ct 28214
Josephine Ct 28205
Josh Birmingham Pkwy 28208
Joshua Ln 28217
Joshua Cain Rd 28213
Joshua Tree Ct 28227
Josie St 28213
Journey Ct 28205
Jousting Ct 28277
Joy Ln 28217
Joy St 28208
Joyce Dr 28215
Joyce Kilmer Dr 28213
Joyceton St 28208
Joyeland Cir 28214
Judal Ln 28269
Judas Tree Ln 28227
Judith Ct 28211
Judson Ave 28208
Julep Ln 28273
Jules Ct 28226
Julia Ave 28206
Julia Lee Ct 28216
Julia Maulden Pl 28206
Julian Price Pl 28208
Juliette Low Ln 28227
Julliard Dr 28227
Jumper Dr 28227
Junction Ct 28215
June Dr 28205
June Furr Rd 28216
Juneberry Ct 28216
Junipeous Dr 28269
Juniper Dr 28269
Juniper Trace Dr 28277
Juniper Tree St 28215
Juniperus Dr 28269
Jupiter Ln 28213
Jupiter Hills Ct 28277
Jura Dr 28227
Justice Ave 28206
Justin Ct 28216
Justin Elie Ct 28213
Justins Forest Dr 28212
Juventus St 28277
Jw Clay Blvd 28262
Kadey Dr 28208
Kalabash Rd 28278
Kaladar Ct 28216
Kalamath Glen Ct 28215
Kalis Pl 28262
Kalispell Ln 28269
Kallam Ct 28215
Kalynne St 28208
Kanfer Ct 28226
Kanimbla Dr 28214
Kanturk Ct 28213
Kapheim Ct 28273
Kapplewood Ct 28226
Karam Ln 28215
Karen Ct 28205
Karen Graham Ct 28278
Karendale Ave 28208
Karenstone Dr 28215
Karina Falls Ct 28273
Karnak Ct 28216
Karylsturn Ct 28269
Katelyn Dr 28269
Katherine Kiker Rd 28213
Kathleen Ct 28217
Kathryn Blair Ln 28226
Katie Creek Ct 28213
Katonah Ave 28208
Katrine Ct 28208
Katy Flyer Ave 28210
Kavan Hunter Dr 28214
Kavanaugh Dr 28205
Kay St 28216
Kaybird Ln 28270
Kayce Ln 28213
Kayla Ln 28215
Kayron Dr 28269
Keara Way 28270
Kearney Ct 28273
Keaton Ave 28269
Keats Ave 28212
Keble Dr 28269
Kee Ct 28203
Keegan Way 28270
Keeling Pl 28210
Keels Ct 28269
Keeneland Ln 28216
Keener Creek Rd 28216
Keener Ridge Rd 28216
Keeter Dr 28214
Kegsworth Dr 28273
Keith Dr 28269
Keithcastle Ct 28210
Keithwood Pl 28269
Kelburn Ln 28278
Kelden Walker Ln 28269
Kelford Ln 28270
Kellen Way 28210
Keller Ave 28216
Kellington Ct 28273
Kelly Rd 28216
Kelly St 28205
Kelly Grange Pl 28226
Kelly Woods Ln 28277
Kelsey Dr 28215
Kelsey Emma Ct 28269
Kelsey Woods Ct 28212
Kelso Ct 28278
Kelston Pl 28212
Keltic Cove Dr 28227
Kelvin Park Cir 28216
Kelway Ave 28210
Kelyn Hills Dr 28278
Kem Arbor Way 28227
Kemp St 28213
Kemp Mundy Ln 28216
Kemper Ln 28227
Kempsford Dr 28262
Kempshott Ct 28273
Kempton Pl 28208
Kemptown Square Sq N & S 28227
Ken Hoffman Dr 28262
Kenbrooke Dr 28262
Kendale Ct 28216
Kendall Dr
2400-2799 28216
9100-9699 28214
Kendalton Meadow Dr 28227
Kendan Knoll Dr 28262
Kenderly Ct 28277
Kendra Ct 28277
Kendrick Ave 28269
Kendrick Dr 28214
Kendrick Cross Rd 28273
Kenhill Dr 28208
Kenilworth Ave
600-1299 28204
1300-2199 28203
Kenlauren Ter 28210
Kenley Ln 28217
Kenlough Dr 28209
Kenmont Dr 28269
Kenmore Ave 28204
Kennard Dr 28216
Kennedy St 28206
Kennel Ln 28277
Kennerly Cove Ct 28269
Kennesaw Dr 28216
Kenneth Ln 28227
Kenneth Glenn Dr 28213
Kenneth Oren Dr 28213
Kennetuck Ct 28273
Kennewick Rd 28216
Kenninghall Ct 28269
Kennington Ct 28270
Kennon St 28205
Kennsington Hill Ct 28216
Kensal Ct 28211
Kensal Green Dr 28278
Kensett Ave 28214
Kensington Dr 28205
Kensington Gardens Ct 28277
Kensington Palace Ln 28277
Kensington Station Pkwy 28210
Kenstead Cir 28214
Kensworth Ct 28277
Kent Village Dr 28269
Kentberry Dr 28214
Kentbrook Dr 28213
Kentdale Ct 28270
Kentland Ln 28210
Kentshire Ln 28215
Kentucky Ave 28216
Kentucky Derby Dr 28215
Kentucky Home Ln 28278
Kenwood Ave 28205
Kenyon Ct 28211
Kern St 28208
Kerr Ln 28216
Kerry Ln 28215
Kerry Glen Ln 28226
Kerrybrook Cir 28214
Kersey Ct 28213
Kersey Glen Ln 28216
Kersfield Pl 28227
Kessler Dr 28277
Kestral Ridge Dr 28269
Kestrel Ct 28269
Keswick Ave 28206
Kettering Dr 28226

Street	ZIP
Kettlewell Ln	28277
Kevin Ct	28205
Kevin Henry Pl	28277
Kew Ter	28215
Kew Gardens Ln	28277
Key St W	28208
Key Ridge Ct	28216
Keystone Ct	28210
Keyway Blvd	28215
Kibworth Ln	28273
Kidd Ln	28216
Kieldon Ct	28277
Kiev Dr	28216
Kiftsgate Ct	28226
Kiker Cir	28214
Kilberry Ln	28277
Kilborne Dr	28205
Kilbridge Woods Ct	28262
Kilchurn Ct	28277
Kilcullen Dr	28270
Kildare Dr	28215
Kiley Ln	28216
Kilgo Way	28205
Killarney Pl	28262
Killashee Ct	28213
Killian Ridge Ct	28227
Killingdeer Ln	28226
Kilmarsh Ct	28262
Kilmartin Ln	28269
Kilmonack Ln	28270
Kilmory Ter	28210
Kilpatrick Ln	28277
Kilpeck Ct	28278
Kilrush Dr	28214
Kilsyth St	28278
Kilty Ct	28269
Kim Dr	28214
Kimberly Rd	28208
Kimberton Dr	28270
Kimblewyck Ln	28226
Kimmel Ln	28216
Kimmerly Creek Dr	28215
Kimmerly Glen Ln	28215
Kimmerly Woods Dr	28215
Kimmswick Rd	28214
Kimrod Ln	28270
Kimwood Pl	28205
Kincaid Ct	28277
Kincross Ln	28277
Kinderway Ave	28214
Kindletree Rd	28210
Kindling Ct	28227
King Rd	28215
King Arthur Dr	28277
King Edward Rd	28211
King Eider Dr	28273
King George Dr	28213
King Louis Ct	28277
King Owen Ct	28211
King Richard Ct	28227
Kingbird Ct	28215
Kingfisher Dr	28226
Kinghurst Dr	
5800-6099	28227
6100-6899	28216
Kinglet Ln	28269
Kingman Dr	28217
N Kings Dr	28204
S Kings Dr	
100-999	28204
1000-1399	28207
Kings Canyon Dr	28210
Kings Carriage Ln	28278
Kings Castle Ct	28277
Kings Creek Dr	28273
Kings Falls Dr	28210
S Kings Parade Blvd	28273
Kings Ridge Dr	28217
Kingsbury Dr	28205
Kingscote Cir	28226
Kingscross Dr	28211
Kingsdown Ave	28270
Kingsford Dr	28217
Kingsgate Pl	28211
Kingsland Ct	28269
Kingsley Dr	28270
Kingsley View Dr	28277
Kingsmeade Ct	28226
Kingsmill Ter	28270
Kingsnorth Rd	28269
Kingspark Dr	28208
E & W Kingston Ave	28203
Kingston Forest Dr	28277
Kingston Place Dr	28277
Kingstree Dr	28210
Kingsway Cir	28214
Kingswood Rd	28226
Kingville Dr	28213
Kinley Commons Ln	28278
Kinnairds St	28278
Kinnegal Ln	28278
Kinsale Ln	28215
Kinsley Marie Ln	28215
Kinsmore Ln	28269
Kinston Ridge Pl	28273
Kinvara Ct	28270
Kipling Dr	28212
Kipperly Ct	28270
Kirby Dr	28214
Kirby Mews Ct	28277
Kirchenbaum Dr	28210
Kirk Pl	28227
Kirk Farm Ln	28213
Kirkcaldy Ln	28227
Kirkdale Ct	28208
Kirkfield Ct	28209
Kirkgard Trl	28269
Kirkgate Ln	28215
Kirkhom Ct	28277
Kirkland Ave	28208
Kirkley Ct	28277
Kirkley Glen Ln	28215
Kirkley View Ct	28277
Kirkmont Dr	28269
Kirkpatrick Rd	28211
Kirkstall Ct	28226
Kirkstone Ct	28216
Kirkview Ln	28213
Kirkville Ln	28216
Kirkwich Ct	28277
Kirkwood Ave	28203
Kirkwynd Commons Dr	28278
Kirsten Nicole Rd	28278
Kirt Ct	28213
Kirwan Ct	28216
Kishorn Ct	28215
Kiska Ct	28214
Kismet Dr	28214
Kissimmee Ln	28227
Kistler Ave	28205
Kitley Pl	28210
Kittansett Dr	28262
Kittredge Rd	28227
Kitty Dr	28216
Klondike Ln	28216
Knapdale Ln	28226
Kneighton Ln	28262
Knell Dr	28212
Knickerbocker Dr	28212
Knight Ct	28217
Knight Castle Dr	28277
Knight Crest Ct	28210
Knights Bridge Rd	28210
Knightsdale Dr	28277
Knightsgate Ct	28269
Knightswood Dr	28226
Knob Hill Ct	28210
Knob Oak Ln	28211
Knoll Ridge Ct	28208
Knollbrook Dr	28270
Knollcrest Dr	28208
Knollgate Dr	28212
Knollwood Cir	28213
Knollwood Ct W	28213
E Knollwood Ct	28213
Knollwood Rd	28211
Knothole Ln	28214
Knotty Pine Cir	28227
Knowledge Cir	28277
Knowlesly Rd	28227
Knox Farm Rd	28278
Kobuk Ln	28269
Kodiak Ct	28215
Kody Marie Ct	28210
Kohler Ave	28206
Konsler Dr	28214
Kool Springs Dr	28227
Korniv Dr	28216
Korp Rd	28216
Kotlik Dr	28269
Kotz Ct	28269
Kousa Pl	28278
Kraus Glen Dr	28214
Krefeld Dr	28227
Krefeld Glen Dr	28227
Kris Ln	28214
Krishna Ln	28277
Krislyn Woods Pl	28278
Kristens Mare Dr	28277
Kronos Pl	28210
Krupa Ct	28205
Kuck Rd	28227
Kuralt House Ct	28210
Kurt Ct	28209
Kuykendall Rd	28270
Kylemore Ct	28210
Kyliglen Ln	28216
Kyndall Walk Way	28269
Kyrene Rd	28277
L D Parker Dr	28206
La Brea Dr	28216
La Crema Dr	28214
La Gorce Dr	28226
La Maison Dr	28226
Labeau Ave	28277
Laborde Ave	28269
Laburn Ave	28214
Laburnum Ave	28205
Lacewood Pl	28270
Lacie Ln	28211
Lacoste Ct	28226
Lacroix St	28277
Lada Ln	28227
Ladbroke Ct	28278
Ladley Ct	28226
Ladonia Ct	28277
Ladora Dr	28262
Lady Ann Ct	28216
Lady Bank Dr	28269
Lady Candice Ln	28270
Lady Fern Cir	28211
Lady Grace Ln	28270
Lady Liberty Ln	28217
Lafayette Ave	28203
Lafite St	28277
Lago Vista Ct	28277
Lagrande Dr	28269
Lahaina Ln	28278
Lahinch Ct	28277
Lailwood Cir	28227
Laine Rd	28214
Lake Ave	28208
Lake Dr	
1500-2099	28214
2900-3399	28269
6300-6599	28215
Lake Rd	
3301-3397	28269
3399-4599	28269
5900-6899	28227
E Lake Rd	28215
Lake Challis Ln	28226
Lake Crossing Dr	28278
Lake Erie Ln	28273
Lake Forest Rd E	28227
Lake Leslie Ln	28270
Lake Providence Ln	28277
Lake Ridge Rd	28278
Lake Spring Ave	28216
Lake Way Dr	28214
N & S Lakebrook Rd	28214
Lakecrest Dr	28215
Lakedell Dr	28215
Lakefill Rd	28212
Lakefront Dr	28278
Lakehill Rd	28214
Lakehouse Ln	28210
Lakeland Dr	28214
Lakemist Dr	28217
Lakepoint Forest Dr	28278
Lakeridge Commons Dr	28269
S Lakes Dr	28273
Lakeside Dr	
3300-4199	28270
6600-7399	28215
E Lakeside Dr	28215
N Lakeside Dr	28215
Lakeview Dr	28270
Lakeview Ln	28214
Lakeview Rd	
4400-5499	28216
5500-6699	28269
Lakeview St	28208
Lakeview Ridge Dr	28278
Lakewood Ave	28208
Lakewood Edge Dr	28269
Lakota Ct	28269
Lalex Ln	28209
Lamar Ave	28204
Lambert Bridge Dr	28270
Lambeth Dr	28213
Lambrook Ct	28269
Lamina Ct	28227
Lammers Ln	28226
Lamoille Ln	28278
Lamond Pt	28278
Lamont Dr	28210
Lampasas Ln	28214
Lampkin Way	28269
Lampkin Park Dr	28269
Lamplighter Pl	28217
Lampmeade Ln	28273
Lanaken Dr	28216
Lanark Ct	28217
Lancashire Dr	28227
Lancaster Hwy	28277
Lancaster Park Dr	28277
Lancelot Dr	28270
Lancer Dr	28226
Lancewood Pl	28214
Lancken Dr	28277
Land Grant Rd	28217
Landen Dr	28277
Lander St	28208
Landerwood Dr	28210
Landing Green Dr	28277
Landing Place Ln	28277
Landing View Ln	28226
Landis Ave	28205
Landmark Dr	28270
Landon St	28215
Landover Rd	28278
Lands End	28278
Landsburg Ln	28210
E Lane Dr	28212
Lanecrest Dr	28215
Lanewood Pl	28208
Langden Gate Dr	28273
Langford Ct	28227
Langham Ct	28269
Langhorne Ave	28205
Langley Cir & Rd	28215
Langley Mill Ct	28215
Langston Dr	28278
Langston Mill Rd	28216
Langtree Ln	28227
Langwell Ln	28278
Lanier Ave	28205
Lanier Islands Cir	28273
Lanigan St	28277
Lannier Falls Ln	28270
Lansbury Ct	28226
Lansdale Dr	28205
Lansdowne Rd	28270
Lansford Rd	28277
Lanshire Ct	28262
Lansing Dr	28270
Lantana Ave	
5300-5399	28205
5400-5799	28212
Lantern Ct	28227
Lantern Walk Cir	28277
Lanterntree Ln	28215
Lanzerac Manor Dr	28269
W Laporte Dr	28216
Larch St	28203
Larchmont Ave	28215
Larchmont Cir	28214
Larewood Dr	28215
Large Oak Ln	28227
Larimer Ln	28262
Larix Dr	28273
Larkfield Ln	28210
Larkhall Ln	28211
Larkhaven Rd	28216
Larkhaven Village Dr	28215
Larkhull Dr	28216
Larkin Pl	28211
Larkmead Forest Dr	28269
Larkmoore Ct	28208
Larkridge Ct	28226
Larkspur Ln	28205
Larkston Dr	28226
Larne Cir	28214
Larochelle Ln	28226
Larrisa Ct	28226
Larry Dr	28214
Larson Ln	28270
Larwill Ln	28216
Lasalle St	28216
Lassen Ct	28214
Lassen Bay Pl	28215
Lassiter Ln	28213
Latchington Ct	28227
Latham Pl	28216
Latherton Ln	28278
Lathrop Ln	28211
Latrobe Dr	28211
Latta Ave	28214
Lattice Ct	28269
Lattimore Ave & St	28203
Lauder Ct	28278
Laura Dr	28212
N Laurel Ave	
100-260	28207
300-499	28204
S Laurel Ave	28207
Laurel Crest Ct	28269
Laurel Grove Ln	28226
Laurel Hill Ln	28217
Laurel Lake Ln	28277
Laurel Mill Dr	28262
Laurel Park Ln	28270
Laurel Pond Ln	28262
Laurel Ridge Trl	28269
Laurel Run Dr	28269
Laurel Springs Ct	28227
Laurel Trace Dr	28273
Laurel Twig Ct	28215
Laurel Valley Rd	28273
Laurel View Dr	28273
Laurel Walk Ct	28277
Laurelwood Cir	28214
Lauren Elizabeth Ct	28214
Lauren Glen Rd	28226
Lauren Kay Ct	28216
Lauren Village Dr	28213
Laurenfield Dr	28269
Laurenhurst Ln	28270
Laurens Ridge Rd	28273
Lauriston Pl	28227
Laurium Rd	28226
Lavender Cir	28262
Lavender Trace Ct	28273
Lavern St	28215
Lavershire Ct	28262
Laveta Ln	28269
Lavista Way	28277
Lavon Ct	28213
Lawing Rd	28216
Lawing St	28214
Lawing School Rd	28214
Lawkins Ln	28270
Lawndale Rd	28209
Lawnmeadow Dr	28216
Lawrence Farm Ln	28278
Lawrence Gray Rd	28262
Lawrence Orr Rd	28212
Lawry Run Dr	28273
Lawson Ln	28215
Lawton Rd	28216
Lawton Bluff Rd	28226
Lawyers Rd	28227
Lawyers Glen Dr	28227
Lawyers Station Dr	28227
Laxton Ct	28270
Layla Dr	28216
Laysan Teal Ln	28262
Layton Ridge Ln	28214
Lazio Ln	28277
Lazy Dr	28215
Lazy Branch Rd	28270
Lazy Creek Ln	28213
Lazy Day Ln	28269
Lazy Oak Ln	28273
Lazy Willow Ln	28273
Lea Wood Ln	28227
Leacroft Ct	28226
Leadenhall Ln	28262
Leaf Ct	28214
Leaf Arbor Ln	28277
Leafcrest Ln	28210
Leafmore Dr	28213
Leaford Ct	28227
Leah Meadow Ln	28227
Leake St	28208
Leamington Ln	28226
Leaning Pine Ln	28215
Leaning Tree Dr	28213
Learning Ln	28277
Leaside Ln	28209
Leatherwood Ct	28227
Leaves Ln	28213
Leawood Run Ct	28269
Leazer Ct	28277
Lebanon Dr	28273
Lebanon Rd	28227
Lebaron St	28270
Lederer Ave	28277
Ledger Ct	28277
Ledgestone Pl	28227
Ledgewood Ln	28203
Ledson Ct	28214
Lee Dr & St	28214
Lee Manor Ln	28277
Lee Marie Ln	28269
Lee Rea Rd	28226
Leecrest Dr	28214
Leeds Dr	28205
Leeper Dr	28277
Lees Court St	28211
Lees Crossing Dr	28213
Leesburg Rd	28215
Leeson Ln	28270
Legacy Cir	28277
Legacy Lake Ln	28269
Legacy Park Dr	28269
Legacy Walk Ln	28213
Legare Ct	28210
Legato Ln	28269
Legend Creek Ln	28227
Legette Ct	28277
Leghorn Ct	28215
Legolas Ln	28269
Legranger Rd	28262
Leharne Dr	28270
Leicester Ct	28277
Leigh Ave	28205
Leigh Cir	28216
Leigh Glen Cir	28269
Leinster Dr	28277
Leipzig Dr	28210
Leisure Garden Ln	28227
Leith Way	28278
Leitrim Ct	28277
Lela Ave	28208
Lela Gardens Way	28227
Leland St	28214
Lemington Dr	28227
Lemmond Acres Dr	28227
Lemon Tree Ln	28211
Lemongrass Ln	28214
Lemsford Way	28215
Lence Ct	28269
Lenhart Dr	28226
Lennox Ave	28203
Lennox Square Rd	28210
Lennoxshire Ln	28210
Lennoxshire Square Ct	28210
Lenox Hill Pl	28269
Lenox Pointe Dr	28273
Lenswood Ct	28214
Lenten Rose Ct	28277
Leolillie Ln	28216
Leonardslee Ct	28226
Leonine Ct	28269
Leopold Pl	28215
Leota Dr	28206
Leroy St	28205
Leslie Dr	28269
Lester St	28208
Lester Hill Ct	28269
Lethco Way	28277
Level Creek Ln	28214
Levisey Ln	28269
Levy Way	28205
Lewhaven Dr	28208
Lewis Carroll Ct	28213
Lewisburg St	28216
Lewiston Ave	28208
Lex Dr	28262
Lexham Ln	28277
Lexington Ave	28203
Lexington Cir	28213
Lexington Approach Dr	28262
Leyton Pl	28227
Liatris Ln	28213
Liberton Ct	28216
Liberty Bell Ct	28269
Liberty Hall Pl	28277
Liberty Hill Dr	28227
Liberty Pointe Ln	28214
Libeth St	28205
W Liddell St	28206
Lido Ave	28211
Lifeline Ln	28278
Lifford Dr	28214
Liggett St	28208
Lightspun Ln	28216
Ligon Ct	28213
Ligustrum St	28206
Lila Wood Cir	28209
Lilac Rd	28209
Lillian Way	28226
Lilliesleaf Glenn Ln	28277
Lillington Ave	28204
Lilly Mill Rd	28210
Lilly Pond Ct	28273
Lillyshire Pl	28213
Lily Pad Ct	28262
Lilybet Ln	28278
Lima Ave	28208
Limehurst Pl	28278
Limerick Dr	28270
Limey Ct	28270
Lina Ardrey Ln	28277
Linalda Ct	28214
Lincoln St	28203
Lincoln Heights Ct	28216
Lincrest Pl	28211
Linda Ln	28211
Linda Lake Ct & Dr	28215
Linda Lou Ct	28213
Linda Vista Ln	28216
Lindahl Ln	28277
Lindbergh St	28208
Linden Berry Ln	28269
Linden Forest Ln	28270
Linden Ridge Ln	28216
Linden Tree Ln	28277
Lindfield Ct	28227
Lindhall Ct	28209
Lindrick Ln	28277
Lindstrom Dr	28226
Lineredg Rd	28216
Linganore Pl	28203
Links Dr	28277
Linkside Ct	28277
Linkwood Pl	28208
Linsbury Ct	28213
Linville Forest Ct	28211

N Linwood Ave 28216
S Linwood Ave 28208
Lion Cub Ln 28273
Lioness St 28273
Lions Mane St 28273
Lions Paw St 28273
Lions Pride Ct 28273
Lionstone Dr 28262
Lippards Hunt Ct 28277
Lipton Ln 28227
Lisa Cir 28215
Lisa Carole Dr 28214
Lisbon Ln 28269
Lisha Ln 28277
Liska Ct 28227
Lismore Valley Ln 28226
Lismorre Castle Ct 28273
Lissadell Cir 28277
Lissom Ln 28217
Litchfield Rd 28211
Little Ave 28226
Little Abbey Ln 28278
Little Brim Ln 28214
Little Brook Ln 28226
Little Buggy Ln 28273
Little Cove Rd 28270
Little Creek Rd 28227
Little Fox Ln 28227
Little Gem Ln 28278
Little Hampton Pl 28215
Little Hope Rd 28209
Little Moser Ln 28227
Little Rock Rd 28214
Little Stoney Ct 28269
Little Whiteoak Rd 28215
Littlefield Rd 28214
Littlefield St 28211
Littlejohn Ct 28227
Littleleaf Dr 28215
Littleton Ct 28227
Live Oak Dr 28227
Livengood Ln 28269
Livermore Ln 28227
Livingston Dr 28211
Livingston Mill Rd 28273
Livingstone Falls Dr 28217
Llewellyn Pl 28207
Lobilia Ln 28214
Loblolly Ln 28210
Lobo Ln 28216
Loch Ln 28226
Loch Arbor Ln 28227
Loch Glen Way 28278
Loch Lomond Dr 28278
Loch Loyal Dr 28273
Loch Stone Ct 28210
Lochfoot Dr 28278
Lochinvar Dr 28227
Lochlain Dr 28217
Lochleven St 28208
Lochness Ln 28208
Lochridge Rd 28209
Lochway Ln 28269
Lockerbie Ln 28215
Lockhart Dr 28203
Lockhorn Ct 28227
Lockley Dr 28207
Lockman Ln 28269
Lockmont Dr 28212
Lodestone Rd 28215
Lodge South Cir 28217
Lodgepole Pl 28210
Log Cabin Rd 28213
Logan Ct 28210
Logan Grove Rd 28227
Loganberry Trl 28262
Loganville Dr 28269
Logging Pl 28227
Logie Ave 28205
Loire Valley St 28277
Lola Ave 28205
Loma Ln 28205
Loma Linda Ln 28270
Lomax Ave 28211
Lomax Ridge Dr 28216
Lombardy Cir 28203
Lomond Ave 28206
London Cir 28270
Londonderry Rd 28210
Londonshire Dr 28216
Londontowne Dr 28226
Lone Oak Ct 28270
Lone Star Cir 28226
Lone Tree Ct 28269
Lonesome Oak Cir 28278
Long Ave 28212
Long Rd 28227
Long Cove Dr 28277
Long Creek Pkwy 28214
Long Creek Club Dr 28216
Long Creek Fairway
Dr 28216
Long Creek Green Dr 28216
Long Creek Park Dr 28269
Long Creek Tee Ct 28216
Long Forest Dr 28269
Long Grass Ct 28216
Long Hill Dr 28214
Long Meadow Rd 28210
Long Needles Dr 28277
Long Nook Ln 28277
Long Paw Ln 28214
Long Pine Dr 28227
Long Ridge Ln 28214
Long Run Ln 28216
Long Talon Way 28278
Long Valley Dr 28273
Long Valley Rd 28270
Longacre Dr 28214
Longbow Rd 28211
Longbriar Dr 28212
Longbrook Dr 28270
Longdale Dr 28217
Longfellow St 28205
Longfield Cir 28270
Longford Ct 28210
Longhedge Ln 28273
Longleaf Dr 28210
Longmont Dr 28277
Longnor St 28214
Longstone Ln 28277
Longstraw Rd 28227
Longtree Ln 28227
Longvale Ln 28214
Longview Dr 28214
Longview Club Ln 28216
Longwood Dr 28209
Looking Glass Ln 28269
Lookout Ln 28205
Lookout Point Dr 28269
Lorden Ave 28213
Lorelei Pl 28227
Lorene Ave 28209
Loretta Pl 28215
Lori Ln 28226
Loring Ln 28227
Lorna St 28205
Loropetalum Rd 28215
Lorraine Dr 28270
Lorwind Ct 28262
Lost Boy Ct 28213
Lost Oak Rd 28270
Lost Tree Ln 28226
Lothar Ridge Ln 28216
Lottie Ln 28262
Loudoun Ln 28262
Loughlin Ln 28273
Louglen Cir 28212
Louis Rose Pl 28262
Louisburg Square Ln 28210
Louise Ave
400-999 28204
1000-1499 28205
Louisiana Ave 28208
Lourdes Ct 28277
Louvaine Dr 28227
Love Ave 28205
Love Ridge Ln 28213
Loveden Ct 28215
Lovett Cir 28210
Lovvorn Ln 28214
Low Meadow Ct 28277
Lowen Rd 28269
Lower Shoal Creek Ct 28277
Lowwoods Cir 28214
Loxton Cir 28214
Loyalist St 28216
Loyola Ct 28227
Lubbock Pl 28215
Lucas Ln 28213
Lucca Ct 28227
Lucena St 28206
Lucern Ct 28277
Luckwood Ct 28227
Lucky Horseshoe Ln 28277
Lucky Penny St 28208
Lucy Jane Ln 28270
Ludell Ln 28215
Ludi Mae Ct 28227
Ludlow Dr 28216
Ludwell Branch Ct 28277
Ludwig Dr 28215
Luke Crossing Dr 28226
Lukes Dr 28216
Lumarka Dr 28212
Lumber Ln 28214
Lumina Ave 28208
Lumley Dr 28277
Lumsden Rd 28262
Lundale Ct 28273
Lundin Links Ln 28277
Lundy Ln 28214
Lunenberg Ln 28278
Lunsford Pl 28205
Luray Ave 28278
Lusby Ct 28269
Luscombe Farm Rd 28278
Lusterleaf Holly Rd 28227
Lustre Rd 28215
Luther St 28204
Luthers Rock Ct 28270
Lutomma Cir 28270
Luton Ct 28262
Lutzen Way Ct 28270
Lydia Ave 28205
Lyerly Dr 28215
Lyford Ct 28227
Lyles Ct 28213
Lyleton Ln 28269
Lyme Brook Ln 28206
Lymington Ct 28227
Lynbridge Dr
1900-2499 28270
2500-2699 28226
Lynbrook Dr 28211
Lynchester Pl 28216
Lyndale Pl 28210
Lynderwood Ct 28273
Lyndhurst Ave 28203
Lyndonville Dr 28277
Lynette Ct 28217
Lynfield Dr 28212
Lynford Dr 28215
Lynhaven St 28205
Lynmont Dr 28212
Lynn Ave 28226
Lynn St 28208
Lynn Lee Cir 28269
Lynn Parker Ln 28278
Lynnewood Glen Dr 28269
Lynnville Ave 28205
Lynnwood Dr 28209
Lynrose Ct 28226
Lynton Blvd 28227
Lynway Dr 28203
Lynworth Pl 28212
Lyon Ct 28205
Lystra Ln 28262
Lytham Dr 28210
Lyttleton Dr 28211
M St 28204
Mabe Dr 28216
Mable Hubbard Dr 28208
Mable Way Dr 28226
Macandrew Dr 28226
Macanthra Dr 28213
Macdara Glenn Ct 28226
Macfarlane Blvd 28262
Macgregor Ln 28278
Machrie Ct 28269
Macie St 28217
Mack St 28214
Mackenzie Ct 28227
Mackinac St 28269
Macon St 28208
Macquarie Ln 28227
Macvean Ln 28208
Maddox Ct 28269
Madeline Meadow Dr 28217
Madinchi Rd 28226
Madison Ave 28216
Madison Dare St 28214
Madison Hill Ct 28273
Madison Oaks Ct 28226
Madison Park Dr 28269
Madison Square Pl 28216
Madras Ln 28211
Madrid St 28216
Madrigal Ln 28214
Magdalena Ct 28226
Magennis Grove Ct 28216
Magenta Ln 28262
Maggie Ln 28210
Maggie Laney Dr 28216
Maggiucci Pl 28227
Maglev Ln 28213
Magnasco Ln 28208
Magnolia Ave 28203
Magnolia Bridge Rd 28210
Magnolia Creek Ct 28270
Magnolia Heights Ct 28270
Magnolia Hill Dr 28205
Magnolia Tree Ln 28215
Magnolia Woods Ln 28277
Mahogany Dr 28227
Mahogany Woods Dr 28210
Mahonia St 28277
Mahopac St 28208
Maid Marion Ln 28227
Maidenhair Ct 28215
Main Dr 28262
Main St 28204
Mainline Blvd 28203
Maitland Ln 28215
Majestic Meadow Dr 28216
Majestic Oak Dr 28278
Major St 28208
Malagant Ln 28213
Malcolm Ln 28213
Malibu Dr 28215
Malinced Rd 28207
Mallaranny Rd 28278
Mallard Dr 28269
Mallard Dr S 28227
Mallard Cove Ct 28269
Mallard Creek Rd 28262
E & W Mallard Creek
Church Rd 28262
Mallard Crossing Dr 28262
Mallard Forest Dr 28269
Mallard Glen Dr 28262
Mallard Green Pl 28262
Mallard Grove Rd 28269
Mallard Highlands Dr 28262
Mallard Hill Dr 28269
Mallard Lake Rd 28262
Mallard Landing Rd 28278
Mallard Park Dr
6500-6699 28269
6700-6799 28262
Mallard Pine Ct 28262
Mallard Ridge Dr 28269
Mallard Roost Rd 28262
Mallard View Ln 28269
Mallard Way Dr 28216
Mallard Woods Pl 28262
Mallen Dr 28212
Mallory St 28205
Mallory Taylor Ln 28216
Mallow Pl 28270
Malta Pl 28215
Malvern Rd 28207
Malvina Ln 28216
Mammoth Oaks Dr &
Ln 28270
Mamolake Rd 28270
Manbey Ct 28269
Manchester Dr 28217
Manchester Ln 28227
Mandarin Blvd 28205
Manderly Dr 28214
Mandolin Ct 28227
Mandy Place Ct 28216
Manes Ct 28208
Manford Ct 28217
Mangla Dr 28214
Manhasset Rd 28209
Manheim Ct 28226
Manitoba Ln 28277
Manley St 28216
Manning Dr 28209
Manning Rd 28269
Mannington Dr 28270
Manor Rd 28209
Manor House Dr 28270
Manor Mill Rd 28226
Mansfield Ave 28211
Mantario Dr 28269
Manteo Ct 28208
Mantle Ct 28205
Manzanita Dr 28227
Maple Dr & St 28269
Maple Cove Ln 28269
Maple Forest Ct 28270
Maple Glenn Ln 28226
Maple Haven Ct 28227
Maple Hollow Ln 28227
Maple Knoll Ave 28212
Maple Park Ln 28269
Maple Shade Ln 28270
Maple Spring Dr 28278
Maple Sugar Pl 28210
Maple Tree Ct 28214
Maple Valley Pl 28210
Maplebrook Ln 28227
Maplecrest Dr 28212
Maplegrove Dr 28216
Maplehurst Dr 28277
Mapleleaf Ln 28208
Mapleridge Dr 28210
Mapleton Rd 28273
Maplewood Ln 28227
Mar Vista Cir 28209
Marathon Hill Rd 28269
Marbetta Ln 28215
Marble St 28208
Marble Hill Dr 28262
Marblerock Ct 28215
Marbury Rd 28269
Marcel Ln 28226
Marcella Dr 28277
Marchand Ln 28262
Marching Duck Dr 28210
Marcus Ct 28213
Marden Ct 28215
Maremont Ct 28270
Marengo Cir 28216
Marett Ct 28269
Margaret Ln 28214
Margaret Belle Ln 28213
Margaret Brown St 28202
Margaret Kelly Ct 28216
Margaret Turner Rd 28216
Margate Ave 28205
Margellina Dr 28210
Margie Ann Dr 28213
Margo Dr 28214
Marguerite Ave 28205
Maria Christina Ln 28214
Maria Ester Ct 28277
Mariannes Ridge Rd 28273
Maribel Ave 28216
Maricopa Rd 28277
Maricopa Ridge Ln 28270
Marie Roget Way 28277
Marietta St
900-1299 28214
3300-3399 28208
Marigold Pl 28269
Marin Dr 28215
Mariners Watch Ct 28278
Marino Ct 28212
Marionwood Dr 28269
Maris Ct 28210
Marita Dr 28214
Mark Twain Rd 28213
Market St 28215
Market House Ln 28227
Markham Ct 28205
Markham Woods Ct 28214
Markland Dr 28208
Markswood Rd 28278
Markus Dr 28227
Markway Dr 28215
Markworth Rd 28210
Marlborough Rd 28208
Marlbrook Dr 28212
Marlene St 28208
Marlette Dr 28214
Marley Cir 28214
Marley Walk Ln 28277
Marlowe Ave 28208
Marlstone Ln 28215
Marlwood Cir 28227
Marlwood Ter 28209
Marlynn Dr 28262
Marmac Rd 28208
Marmion Rd 28208
Marmot Point Ln 28270
Marney Ave 28205
Marryat Ct 28211
Marsailles Ct 28277
Marsena Ct 28213
Marsh Rd 28209
Marsh Walk Ct 28270
Marsh Wren Ct 28278
Marshall Ave 28208
Marshall Pl 28203
Marshall Acres Dr 28214
Marshall Air Dr 28217
Marshall Valley Ct 28227
Marshbank Ln 28269
Marston Ct 28215
Martele Dr 28227
Martha Ellen Ln 28213
Marthas Ridge Dr
4500-4599 28215
4600-4799 28212
Martin St 28216
Martin Lake Rd 28227
E & W Martin Luther
King Blvd 28202
Martindale Ln 28216
Marvin Rd
3400-3899 28211
15200-17999 28277
Marvin Smith Rd 28208
Marwick Rd 28278
Mary Alexander Pl &
Rd 28262
Mary Ann Dr 28214
Mary Blair Ln 28214
Mary Charlotte Dr 28262
Mary Crest Ln 28227
Mary Jo Helms Dr 28215
Mary Juan Ln 28213
Mary Marie Ct 28278
Maryanna Ct 28213
Maryfield Ln 28277
Maryhurst Ln 28226
Maryland Ave 28209
Masheadi Dr 28217
Mason Cir 28205
Mason Dr 28269
Mason Mill Pl 28273
Mason Oaks Ct 28211
Masonic Dr 28205
Massey Ct 28213
Masters Ct 28226
Masterton Rd 28262
Matador Ln 28209
Matarese Ct 28213
Mather Green Ave 28203
Matheson Ave
100-199 28206
500-2199 28205
Mathis Dr 28208
Matisse Ln 28215
Matlea Ct 28215
Mattforest Cir 28277
Matthew Martin Ln 28216
Matthews Mint Hill Rd 28227
Mattia Ct 28270
Mattie Ct 28213
Mattingridge Dr 28270
Mattingwood Dr 28270
Mattoon St 28216
Mattox Ct 28216
Mattson Pl 28277
Maureen Dr 28205
Maury St 28208
Max Meadows Dr 28227
Maxam Ct 28273
Maxwell Ariel Ln 28205
May St 28217
May River Ln 28278
Mayapple Ln 28269
Maybank Dr 28211
Mayberry Ln 28212
Maycroft Dr 28262
Mayer House Ct 28214
Mayerling Dr 28227
Mayfair Ave 28208
Mayfield Ave 28209
Mayfield Terrace Dr 28216
Mayflower Rd 28208
Mayhew Country Dr 28227
Mayhew Forrest Ln 28227
Mayhurst Ct 28213
Maylandia Rd 28269
Maylin Ln 28210
Maynard Rd 28270
Maypole Ct 28205
Mayridge Dr 28215
Mays Chapel Ln 28270
Mayspring Pl 28269
Maytell Ct 28277
Mayview Dr 28205
Maywood Dr 28205
Mazen Ct 28215
Mcadam Way 28269
Mcaden St 28205
Mcafferty Ct 28277
Mcallister Dr 28216
Mcallister Park Dr 28277
Mcalpine Dr 28217
Mcalpine Ln 28212
Mcalpine Cove Ct 28270
Mcalpine Farm Rd 28226
Mcalpine Glen Dr 28227
Mcalpine Overlook Ct 28226
Mcalpine Park Dr 28211
Mcalpine Valley Ct 28277
Mcalwaine Preserve
Ave 28277
Mcalway Rd
100-1100 28211
1102-1198 28211
1200-1299 28205
Mcarthur Ave 28206
Mcbride St 28215
Mccall St 28206
Mccallum Ct 28226
Mccarron Way 28215
Mccartney Way 28216
Mcchesney Dr 28269
Mcclelland Ct 28206
Mcclintock Rd 28205
Mcclure Cir, Dr & Rd 28216
Mcclure Bridge Rd 28277
Mcclure Manor Dr 28277
E Mccollough Dr 28262
Mccomb Manor Ct 28277
Mccombs St 28208
Mccord St 28216
Mccorkle Rd
1000-1699 28214
9200-9299 28215
Mccullers Ct 28277
Mccullough Dr 28262
Mccurdy Trl 28269

Street	ZIP
Mcdaniel Ln	28213
Mcdonald Ave	28203
Mcdonald Dr	28216
Mcdonald Rd	28214
Mcdonald St	28216
N Mcdowell St	
100-200	28204
201-201	28202
201-599	28204
201-201	28230
201-201	28231
201-201	28232
201-201	28233
201-201	28234
201-201	28235
201-201	28236
201-201	28237
202-598	28204
1300-3499	28205
S Mcdowell St	28204
Mcdowell Farms Dr	28217
Mcduff Ter	28215
Mcewen Pl	28227
Mcewen Lake Ln	28227
Mcgarry Trl	28214
Mcgill St	28213
Mcginn Pl	28277
Mcginn Grove Dr	28216
Mcginns Trace Ct	28277
Mcgloughlin Way Ct	28273
Mcgoogan Ln	28277
Mcgrath Dr	28269
Mcgregor Dr	28227
Mcilroy Rd	28212
Mcintyre Ave	28216
Mcintyre Ridge Dr	28216
Mckay Rd	28269
Mckee Rd	
2400-4799	28270
16700-18399	28278
Mckee Forest Ct	28216
Mckelvey St	28215
Mckemey Pl	28277
Mckendree Way	28269
Mckenna Ct	28212
Mckenzie Creek Dr	28270
Mckinley Dr	28208
Mcknitt Ln	28277
Mclaughlin Dr	28212
Mclaughlin Ln	28269
Mclean Rd	28213
Mcleary Cir	28277
Mcmahan Dr	28226
Mcmanus Dr	28205
Mcmillan St	28205
Mcmullen Creek Pkwy	28226
Mcnair Rd	28212
Mcneil Paper Ct	28214
Mcninch St	
300-599	28202
600-899	28208
Mcpherson Dr	28226
Mcquay St	28208
Mcrae St	28204
Mcrorie Rd	28216
Mctaggart Ln	28269
Mcteal Pl	28262
Mcwhirter Rd	28227
Meacham St	28203
Meade Ct	28211
Meade Glen Ct	28273
Meadecroft Rd	28214
Meadhaven Dr	28273
Meadow Ln	28205
Meadow Bank Ln	28262
Meadow Bluff Dr	28226
Meadow Bottom Rd	28277
Meadow Glen Dr	28227
Meadow Green Dr	28269
Meadow Grove Way	28216
Meadow Haven Ln	28270
Meadow Hill Dr	28212
Meadow Hollow Dr	28227
Meadow Knoll Dr	28269
Meadow Lakes Dr	28210
Meadow Oak Dr	28208
Meadow Post Ln	28269
Meadow Rose Ln	28215
Meadow Run Ln	28277
Meadow Stone Ct	28273
Meadow Vista Rd	28213
Meadowbrook Rd	28211
Meadowcliff Dr	28215
Meadowcrest Ln	28226
Meadowcroft Ct	28215
Meadowdale Ln	
7300-8099	28212
8100-8299	28227
Meadowfield Rd	28215
Meadowind Cir	28226
Meadowland Dr	28215
Meadowlark Ln	28210
Meadowlark Landing Dr	28216
Meadowmead Ct	28273
Meadowmont Dr	28269
Meadowmont View Dr	28269
Meadowood Ln	28211
Meadowridge Dr	28226
Meadowview Ln	28270
Meadowview Hills Dr	28269
Meadston Ln	28210
Means Ct	28278
Mearn Rd	28216
Mebane Dr	28213
Mecklenburg Ave	28205
Mecklenburg Shrine Clb Rd	28215
Medallion Dr	28205
Medearis Dr	28211
Medford Dr	28205
Medical Plaza Dr	28262
Medinah Ct	28210
Medlock Ln	28277
Medoc Mountain Dr	28270
Meeting St	28210
Meffert Ln	28214
Meg Meadow Dr	28227
Megan Ln	28226
Megington Dr	28226
Megwood Dr	28277
Melanie Ct	28205
Melanie Thompson Dr	28213
Melba Dr	28212
Melbourne Ct	28209
Melchor Ave	28211
Melissa Ln	28227
Mellow Dr	28213
Mellwood Dr	28214
Melody Ln	
6600-6899	28215
7100-7299	28214
Melshire Ln	28269
Melstrand Way	28269
Melynda Rd	28208
Memphian Ct	28210
Mendenhall Ct	28211
Mendham Dr	28215
Mendora Dr	28215
Mentmore Ct	28216
Mentone Ln	28269
Mercury St	28205
Meredith Ave	28208
Mereview Ct	28210
Merganzer Ct	28273
Meridale Crossing Dr	28269
Meridian Dr	28216
Merimac Dr	28273
Meringue Pl	28270
Merion Hills Ct	28269
Merlane Dr	28206
Merlin Meadows Ct	28277
Merlot Ln	28269
Mermans Rd	28270
Merridale Dr	28214
Merrie Rose Ave	28213
Merrifield Rd	28211
Merrill Pl	28216
Merrily Ln	28214
Merrimack Ct	28210
Merriman Ave	28203
Merriweather Dr	28273
Merry Mount Dr	28226
Merry Oaks Rd	28205
Merryvale Ln	28214
Merryvale Forrest Dr	28214
Merrywood Rd	28210
Merseyside Ct	28213
Mersham Ct	28269
Mersington Ln	28277
Merton Woods Ln	28273
Merve Pl	28203
Merwick Cir	28211
Mesa Verde Rd	28277
Messian Ct	28210
Metaghan Ct	28278
Metals Dr	28206
Metheney Dr	28227
Metroliner Ct	28213
Metromont Pkwy	28269
Metromont Industrial Blvd	28269
Metroon Dr	28227
Metropolitan Ave	28204
Metter St	28270
Metts Rd	28214
Miami Cir	28216
Michael Dr	28215
Michael Baker Pl	28209
Michael Crossing Dr	28213
Michael Lynn Rd	28278
Michael Shane Ct	28278
Michael Wylie Dr	28217
Michaels Landing Dr	28262
Michaw Ct	28269
Michelangelo Ct	28226
Michelle Linnea Dr	28262
Michendo Dr	28277
Michigan Ave	28215
Mickleton Rd	28226
Microsoft Way	28273
Middle Acres Rd	28213
Middle Stream Rd	28213
Middlebridge Ln	28270
Middleburg Dr	28212
Middlebury Pl	28212
Middleton Dr	28207
Midfield Dr	28206
Midland Ave	28208
Midlothian Ct	28217
Midsomer Rd	28214
Midvale Ter	28215
Midwood Pl	28205
Milan Rd E	28216
Milbrook Rd	28211
Milburn Ct	28214
Miles Ct	28216
Milford Rd	28210
Milhaven Ln	28269
Milhof Ct	28269
Mill Rd	28216
Mill Cove Cir	28262
Mill Creek Ln	28209
Mill Pond Rd	28226
Mill Race Rd	28270
Mill River Ln	28273
Mill Run Dr	28209
Mill Stream Ct	28209
Millbridge Dr	28208
Millbrook Rd	28211
Millbury Ct	28211
Miller St	28203
Millers Creek Ln	28278
Millerton Ave	28208
Millie Ln	28205
Millingden Ct	28277
Millingport Pl	28273
Millsford Ct	28277
Millside Dr	28215
Millstone Ln	28270
Millstream Ridge Dr	28269
Millview Trace Ln	28227
Millwood Cir	28214
Millwood Ln	28270
Millwright Ln	28277
Milport Pl	28215
Milstead Ct	28215
Milton Rd	28215
Milton Hall Pl	28270
Milton Morris Dr	28227
Mimosa Ave	28205
Mimosa Ridge Ct	28208
Mina Ct	28277
Mineral Ridge Way	28269
Mineral Springs Rd	28262
Minewood Ave	28227
Minglewood Dr	28262
Mingus Rd	28216
Mingus Cabin Ln	28214
Minitree Ln	28214
Minnesota Rd	28208
Minnie Lemmond Ln	28227
Minstone Dr	28227
Mint St	28214
S Mint St	
201-297	28202
299-899	28202
1000-1999	28203
Mint Forest Dr	28227
Mint Hill Village Ln	28227
Mint Thistle Ct	28269
Mintbrook Dr	28227
Mintleaf Dr	28269
Mintridge Rd	28227
Mintstone Dr	28227
Mintvale Dr	28269
Mintwood Dr	28227
Mintworth Ave	28227
Minuet Ln	28217
Minuteman Way	28208
Mirabeau Ln	28226
Mirabell Rd	28226
Miranda Rd	28216
Miriam Dr	28205
Mirow Pl	28270
Mirror Lake Dr	28226
Misenheimer Rd	28215
Mission Pl	28210
Mission Hills Rd	28227
Mistletoe Dr	28273
Mistral Way	28208
Misty Ln	28269
Misty Arbor Way	28269
Misty Brook Ln	28273
Misty Creek Dr	28269
Misty Dawn Ln	28270
Misty Dew Ct	28273
Misty Eve Ln	28213
Misty Hill Ln	28270
Misty Lake Dr	28212
Misty Morn Dr	28215
Misty Morning Dr	28212
Misty Moss Ct	28227
Misty Oaks Dr	28269
Misty Pine Ct	28215
Misty Pine Ln	28217
Misty Ridge Ln	28277
Misty Rose Ln	28216
Misty Vale Rd	28214
Misty Valley Ct	28226
Misty View Ct	28215
Misty Way Ln	28212
Misty Wood Dr	28269
Mitchell Glen Dr	28277
Mitchell Grant Way	28213
Mitchell Hollow Rd	28277
Mitzi Deborah Ln	28269
Moberly Ct	28277
Mobile Dr	28269
Mobile Ln	28215
Moccasin Ct	28214
Mock Orange Dr	28277
Mock Robin Ln	28212
Mockingbird Ln	28209
Modern Way	28217
Mohawk Ct	28215
Mohigan St	28205
Molly Elizabeth Ln	28269
Mollys Pl	28212
Mona Dr	28206
Monarch Dr	28214
Monarch Birch Ln	28215
Monarda Ct	28216
Moncure Dr	28209
Monet Ter	28226
Monferrato Way	28277
Monfreya Ct	28212
Monique Ln	28210
Monmouth Dr	28269
Monogramm Ln	28227
Monroe Rd	
3300A-3300Z	28205
2700-5399	28205
5400-8899	28212
8900-9900	28270
9902-10098	28270
Mont Blanc Dr	28227
Mont Carmel Ln	28217
Montague St	28205
Montana Dr	28216
Montauk Dr	28227
Montbrook Dr	28214
Montcalm St	28208
Montclair Ave	28211
Montcrest Dr	28217
Montecastillo Pl	28278
Montego Dr	28215
Monteiane Dr	28270
Monteith Dr	28213
Montelena Dr	28214
Monterey St	28216
Montezuma Trl	28227
Montford Dr	28209
Montgomery St	28216
Montgomery Gardens Dr	28216
Montibello Dr	28226
Monticello Ter	28204
Montpelier Rd	28210
Montreat St	28206
Montrose Ct	28207
Montrose Dr NW	28269
Montrose St	28205
Montvale Ct	28226
Monument St	28208
Moody Rd	28215
Moondance Ln	28214
Moonlight Ln	28269
Moonridge Dr	28226
Moorebrook Dr	28214
Mooreland Farms Rd	28226
Moores Chapel Loop & Rd	28214
Moores Glen Dr	28209
Moores Park Dr	28214
Moorgate Rd	28214
Moorhen Dr	28216
Moorland Dr	28226
Moose Ln	28269
Morablin Dr	28277
Moran Ln	28277
Moravian Ln	28207
Moray Ct	28211
Mordred Ln	28277
Morehead Rd	28262
E Morehead St	
100-899	28202
900-1499	28204
1500-1699	28207
W Morehead St	
100-499	28202
500-2399	28208
2401-2499	28208
Morehead Medical Dr	28204
Morehead Square Dr	28203
Moreland St	28208
Moretz Ave	28206
Morgan St	28208
Morgan Creek Dr	28273
Morgan Downs Ct	28270
Morgan Glenn Dr	28227
Morgan Lee Ave	28213
Morgan Run Ct	28216
Morgan Valley Ln	28270
Morgana Ct	28277
Morganford Rd	28211
Morgense Pl	28212
Morington Ln	28227
Morning Dr	28208
Morning Breeze Ln	28208
Morning Creek Ln	28214
Morning Dew Ct	28269
Morning Glory Dr	28262
Morning Mist Ln	28273
Morninglow Ct	28212
Morningside Dr	28205
Morningside Rd	28214
Morningsong Ln	28269
Morningstar Place Dr	28262
Mornington Dr	28227
Morningview Ct	28269
Morris St	28202
Morris Estate Dr	28262
Morris Farm Ln	28227
Morris Field Dr	28208
Morris Park Dr	28227
Morris Pond Dr	28227
Morrisette Ct	28277
Morrison Blvd	28211
Morrocroft Ln	28211
Morrocroft Farms Ln	28211
Morrowick Rd	28226
Morrowick Circle Dr	28226
Morrowood Ln	28216
Morsey Ct	28269
Morson St	28208
Mortemer Ln	28262
Morton St	28208
Mortonhall Rd	28215
Morven Ln	28270
Mosby Ln	28273
Moscato Ct	28277
Moss Rd	28273
Moss Bank Ct	28262
Moss Cove Ct	28227
Moss Glen Ct	28269
Moss Lake Rd	28214
Moss Mill Ln	28277
Moss Point Dr	28277
Moss Spring Rd	28270
Moss Stream Ln	28214
Mossborough Ct	28227
Mossburg Ct	28214
Mossburn Rd	28262
Mosscroft Ln	28215
Mossdale Ln	28278
Mosstree Cir	28215
Mosswood Ct	28227
Mossy Bank Pl	28269
Mossycup Dr	28215
Motor Sport Ln	28269
Mottisfont Abbey Ln	28226
Moulton Ct	28213
Moultrie St	28209
Mount Clare Ln	28210
Mount Holly Rd	28214
Mount Olive Church Rd	28278
Mount Royal Ln	28210
Mountain Aire Cir	28214
Mountain Apple Dr	28227
Mountain Breeze Ct	28210
Mountain Cove Dr	28216
Mountain Crest Cir	28216
Mountain Flower Ct	28214
Mountain Island Dr	28214
Mountain Island Brook Ln	28214
Mountain Island Promenade Dr	28216
Mountain Ivy Ct	28210
Mountain Lake Cv	28216
Mountain Laurel Ln	28269
Mountain Park Dr	28214
Mountain Pine Dr	28214
Mountain Point Ln	28216
Mountain Quail Dr	28216
Mountain Springs Dr	28278
Mountain Trail Dr	28214
Mountainbrook Rd	28210
Mountainside Ln	28278
Mountainview Dr	28270
Mountainwater Dr	28262
Mounting Rock Rd	28217
Mourning Dove Ln	28269
Mozart Ct	28269
Mt Holly Hntrsvl Rd	28216
Mt Holly Huntersville Rd	28214
Mt Isle Harbor Dr	28214
Mt Kisco Dr	28213
Mt Mansfield Rd	28278
Mt Misco Dr	28213
Mt Vernon Ave	28203
Mulberry Ave	28216
Mulberry Church Rd	28208
Mulberry Grove Rd	28227
Mulberry Pond Dr	28208
Mulhouse Ct	28226
Mullens Ford Rd	28226
Mullis Rd	28215
Mullis Forest Ct	28227
Mumford Ln	28213
Munday Ct	28270
Munsee St	28213
Munsing Dr	28269
Munson Hill Rd	28278
Murdock Rd	28205
Murfield Ct	28278
Murphey Trail Ln	28277
Murphy Hill Pl	28214
Murray St	28269
Murray Grey Ln	28273
Murrayhill Rd	
4100-4899	28209
4900-5899	28210
Muscadine Ln	28214
Museum Dr	28207
Musket Ln	28273
Muskogee Dr	28212
Musselburg Ct	28277
Myerly Pl	28211
N Myers St	
100-699	28202
1000-1199	28206
2800-3199	28205
Myers Hunter Ln	28270
Myers Mill Ln	28277
Myers Park Dr	28207
Myra Way	28215
Myrica Ln	28213
Myrtle Ave	28203
Myrtle Lynn Ct	28213
Mystic Ln	28227
Nada Park Cir	28269
Nadies Ct	28214
Nance Rd	28214
Nance Cove Rd	28214
Nancy Dr	28211
Nancy Creek Rd	28270
Nancy Marie Ct	28213
Nancy Ruth Ln	28227
Nandina St	28205
Nannyberry Ln	28273
Nantuckett Ln	28270
Napa Ridge Ct	28277
Napton Ct	28213
Narayan St	28227
Nash Ave	28213
Nassau Blvd	28205
Nathan Dr	28269
Nathanael Greene Ln	28227
Nathaniel Russell Ln	28227
Natick Dr	28214
Nations Dr	28217
Nations Crossing Rd	28217
Nations Ford Rd	
5100-8999	28217
9000-10799	28273
Nature Pl	28214
Nature Walk Dr	28212
Naturewood Ct	28214
Nc Music Factory Blvd	28206
Neal Dr	28213
Neal Rd	28262
Nealwood Ln	28277
Ned Ct	28273
Needham Dr	28270
Needlepoint Rd	28215
Neely St	28205
Neely Glen Dr	28278
Nelson Ave	28216

Nelson Rd 28227
Neon Ln 28270
Nesbitt Dr 28208
Ness Ct 28208
Nesslaw Dr 28227
Nestar Pl 28273
Nesting Ct 28214
Nestle Way 28211
Netherfield Ct 28277
Netherhall Dr 28269
Netherton Ln 28269
Netherwood Dr 28210
Nettle Dr 28216
Nettlewood Ln 28277
Network Ln 28262
Neuhoff Ln 28269
Nevada Blvd 28273
Nevermore Way 28277
Nevin Rd
3300-5699 28269
6100-6699 28262
Nevin Brook Rd 28269
Nevin Glen Dr 28269
Nevin Place Dr 28269
New Abbey Pl 28273
New Bern St 28203
New Bern Station Ct 28209
New Colony Dr 28273
New Day Ct 28215
New England St 28269
New Fashion Way 28278
New Garden Ct 28215
New Hamlin Way 28210
New Hampshire Dr 28227
New Hope Rd 28203
New House Dr 28269
New Life Rd 28216
New Mark Ave 28278
New Mill Way 28278
New Pineola Rd 28208
New Providence Ln 28277
New Renaissance Way 28208
New Sheldon Dr 28214
New Steam Ln 28216
Newbary Ct NW 28269
Newberry St 28208
Newberry Park Ln 28277
Newbridge Rd 28278
Newcastle St 28216
Newchurch Cir 28269
Newcombe Ct 28277
Newell Ave 28205
Newell Rd 28278
Newell Acres Dr 28215
Newell Baptist Church Rd 28213
Newell Farm Rd 28213
Newell Hickory Grove Rd
7800-7899 28213
9400-9599 28215
9700-10299 28213
Newell View Ln 28213
Newfane Rd 28269
Newfield St 28216
Newfound Hollow Dr 28214
Newfoundland Ct 28214
Newgard Ct 28269
Newgate Ct 28226
Newgrass Ln 28227
Newhall Rd 28270
Newhart Rd 28214
Newington Ct 28227
Newland Rd 28216
Newlands Corner Ln 28277
Newmans Ln 28270
Newmans Ridge Ct 28270
Newry Ct 28270
Newton Ln 28277
Newtonmore Dr 28278
Ney Manor Way 28277
Niagara Cir 28214
Niccoline Ln 28214
Nicholas Ave 28269
Nickelridge Ct 28273
Nickleby Ct 28210

Nicks Tavern Rd 28215
Nicole Cir 28277
Nicole Ln 28269
Nicole Eileen Ln 28216
Nicolet Glen Dr 28215
Nicolette Ct 28215
Nigel Ct 28213
Night Heron Ln 28211
Nightingale Ln 28226
Nightshade Oaks Dr 28227
Nijinsky Ct 28216
Nikki Cole Dr 28215
Nimue Ct 28277
Nine Eagles Ln 28278
Nine Iron Ct 28277
Ninebark Trl 28278
Ninth Fairway Ln 28227
Nobility Ct 28269
Nobles Ave 28208
Noda Blvd 28205
Noel Pl 28208
Noland Woods Dr 28277
Nolen Ln 28277
Nolen Park Ln 28209
Nolesgate Rd 28215
Nolet Ct 28215
Nolley Ct 28270
Noras Path Rd 28226
Norchester Ct 28227
Norcroft Dr 28269
Norcross Pl 28205
Norfolk Ave 28203
Norkett Dr 28215
Norland Rd 28205
Norlington Ct 28273
Norma St 28208
Normancrest Ct 28270
Normandin Ct 28216
Normandy Rd 28209
Normans Landing Dr 28273
Norris Ave 28206
North Ave 28208
Northampton Dr 28210
Northaven Dr 28206
Northbend Dr 28262
Northbrook Dr 28216
Northbury Ln 28226
Northchase Dr 28213
Northcliff Dr 28216
Northcrest Dr 28206
Northerly Rd 28206
Northern Red Oak Dr 28227
Northgate Ave 28209
Northgate Trail Dr 28215
Northlake Ct 28216
Northlake Auto Plaza Blvd 28269
Northlake Centre Pkwy 28216
Northlake Commons Blvd 28216
Northlake Mall Dr 28216
Northmore St 28205
Northpark Blvd 28216
Northpointe Industrial Blvd 28216
Northpointeindustrial Blvd 28216
Northridge Dr 28269
Northridge Village Dr 28213
Northside Rd 28269
Northsprings Dr 28277
Northstream Dr 28208
Northway Dr 28208
Northwood Dr 28216
Northwoods Business Pkwy 28269
Northwoods Forest Dr 28214
Norton Rd 28207
Norway Ct 28269
Norway Spruce Ct 28262
Norwell Pl 28205
Norwich Pl 28208
Norwich Rd 28227
Norwood Dr 28208
Notchview Ct 28210
Notebook Trl 28214

Nottaway Place Dr 28227
Nottingham Dr 28211
Nottinghill Ln 28269
Nottoway Dr 28213
Novella Dr 28215
Nugget Ct 28262
Nugget Hill Rd 28227
Numenore Dr 28269
Nutcracker Pl 28212
Nuthatch Ct 28277
Nutmeg Ln 28227
Nyewood Ct 28269
O Casey Ln 28213
O Hara Dr 28273
Oak Dr
4300-4899 28269
5400-5799 28216
5800-7199 28227
Oak Dr NE 28269
Oak Ln 28213
Oak St
400-899 28214
1500-1899 28269
6200-6299 28208
11600-11899 28269
Oak Arbor Ln 28205
Oak Bend Ct 28215
Oak Canyon Ln 28227
Oak Cove Ln 28269
Oak Creek Dr 28270
Oak Embers Ct 28278
Oak Forest Dr 28215
Oak Gate Dr 28210
Oak Glen Ln 28277
Oak Grove Rd 28205
Oak Hill Rd 28227
Oak Hill Village Ln 28217
Oak Hollow Dr 28227
Oak Knoll Ln 28214
Oak Lake Blvd 28208
Oak Leigh Dr 28262
Oak Meadow Ct 28210
Oak Mint Dr 28227
Oak Pasture Ln 28269
Oak Pond Cir 28277
Oak Run Dr 28210
Oak Trail Ln 28216
Oak Valley Ln 28205
Oakbark Ln 28226
Oakbluff Cir 28216
Oakboro Ln 28214
Oakbriar Ln 28273
Oakbrook Dr 28210
Oakburn Dr 28269
Oakcrest Pl 28209
Oakcrest Green Dr 28217
Oakdale Rd 28216
Oakdale Commons Ct 28216
Oakdale Creek Ln 28216
Oakdale Green Dr 28216
Oakdale Meadows Ct 28227
Oakdale Pasture Dr 28216
Oakdale Woods Dr 28216
Oaken Rail Ln 28216
Oakhaven Dr 28273
Oakland Ave 28204
Oakland Hills Pl 28277
Oaklawn Ave
800-1499 28206
1500-2199 28216
Oakley Ln 28270
Oakmeade Dr 28270
Oakmont Ave 28205
Oakridge Dr 28216
Oakshire Cir 28214
Oakside Ct 28210
Oakspring Ct 28273
Oakstone Pl 28210
Oakthorpe Dr 28277
Oakton Glen Ct 28262
Oakton Hunt Dr 28262
Oakview Ln 28226
Oakwielde Ct 28227
Oakwinds Ct 28269
Oakwood Ave
3400-3799 28205

7400-7499 28227
Oakwood Dr 28269
Oakwood Ln 28215
Oakwood Rd 28269
Oakwood Creek Ln 28262
Oasis Ln 28214
Oban Passage Dr 28273
Oberbeck Ln 28210
Oberland Pl 28227
Oberlin Ln 28262
Oberwald Pl 28227
Oberwood Dr 28270
Obrien Ct 28269
Ocala Rd 28269
Occum Pl 28277
Ochre Dr 28215
Ockeechobee Ct 28227
Oconee Ln 28213
Ocracoke St 28208
October Ct 28208
Odell Heights Dr & Way 28227
Odell School Rd 28262
Odessa Ave & Ln 28216
Odum Ave 28216
Office Park Dr 28273
Ogden Pl 28213
Oglethorpe Pl 28209
Oglukian Rd 28226
Ohaus Ct 28216
Okeefe Ct 28215
Olando St 28206
Old Ardrey Kell Rd 28277
Old Ash Ct 28216
Old Barn Rd 28270
Old Bell Rd 28270
Old Belmeade Dr 28214
Old Brassle Dr 28227
Old Bridge Ln 28269
Old Carolina Dr 28214
Old Cedar Ln 28215
Old Chapel Ln 28210
Old Closeburn Ct 28210
Old Coach Rd 28215
Old Concord Rd 28213
Old Corral St 28277
Old Course Dr 28277
Old Dairy Ln 28211
Old Dowd Rd
5000-6299 28208
6300-10299 28214
Old Farm Rd 28226
Old Forester Ln 28214
Old Forge Dr 28226
Old Fox Trl 28269
Old Fox Hunt Ln 28227
Old Gold Mine Ct 28227
Old Goose Ln 28262
Old Hebron Rd 28273
Old Hickory Ct 28227
Old Holland Rd 28262
Old Iron Ln 28215
Old Ironside Dr 28213
Old Lantern Way 28212
Old Lawyers Rd 28227
Old Magnolia Ln 28227
Old Maple Cir 28278
Old Meadow Rd 28227
Old Moores Chapel Rd 28214
Old Mount Holly Rd
5700-6499 28208
6501-6997 28214
6999-8199 28214
Old Nations Ford Rd 28273
Old North Ct 28270
Old Oak Ln 28227
Old Orchard Ln 28226
Old Persimmon Dr 28227
Old Pineville Rd 28217
Old Plank Rd 28216
Old Plantation Ln 28226
Old Post Rd 28212
Old Potters Rd 28269
Old Prairie Rd 28277

Old Providence Ln & Rd 28226
Old Reid Rd 28210
Old Robinson Trl 28262
Old Saybrook Ct 28211
Old Silo Dr 28216
Old South Ct 28277
Old Spice Ln 28277
Old Statesville Rd
4300-4599 28206
6400-10999 28269
Old Steele Creek Rd 28208
Old Steine Rd 28269
Old Stone Rd 28226
Old Stone Xing 28213
Old Stone Crossing Dr 28213
Old Stoney Creek Ct 28269
Old Sugar Creek Rd 28269
Old Surry Ln 28277
Old Tayport Pl 28277
Old Timber Rd 28269
Old Towne Ct 28217
Old Tree Ln 28216
Old Vine Ct 28214
Old Wagon Rd 28269
Old Watt Ln 28273
Old Wayside Rd 28277
Old Well St 28212
Old Well House Rd 28226
Old Wicke Ln 28208
Old Willow Rd 28269
Old Woods Rd 28209
Oldbriar Ln 28216
Oldcorn Ln 28262
Olde Chantilly Ct 28205
Olde English Dr 28216
Olde Irongate Ln 28227
Olde Ivy Way 28262
Olde Justin Pl 28262
Olde Mill Stream Ct 28277
Olde Saint Andrews Ct 28277
Olde Savannah Rd 28227
Olde Stonegate Ln 28227
Olde Sycamore Dr 28227
Olde Troon Dr 28277
Olde Turnbury Ct 28277
Olde White Ln 28226
Olde Whitehall Rd 28273
Oldecastle Ct 28277
Oldehurst Pl 28262
Olden Ct 28262
Oldenburg Dr 28210
Oldenway Dr 28269
Oldfield Rd 28226
Oldham Pl 28227
Oldridge Ct 28226
Ole Roam Ct 28227
Oleander Dr 28278
Oleander Hill Ct 28214
Olinda St 28215
Oline Pl 28212
Oliva Diane Ln 28216
Olivet Dr 28227
Olivia Ln 28277
Olivia Catherine Way 28213
Olivia View Ct 28210
Olmsted Dr 28262
Olmsted Park Pl 28203
Olney St 28208
Olsen Ln 28213
Olympic St 28273
Olympic Club Dr 28277
Olympus Dr 28214
One Woodlake Ct 28215
Oneida Rd 28269
Onslow Dr 28205
Ontario Pl 28269
Onyx St 28216
Opal St 28208
Opal Crest Dr 28227
Open Book Ln 28270
Open Field Ln 28226
Optimist Ln 28205
Opus Ln 28214
Orange St 28205

Orange Tree Ct 28215
Oransay Way 28278
Oratorio Pl 28270
Orchard Cir 28217
E Orchard Ln 28210
Orchard Grass Ct 28278
Orchard Lake Dr 28270
Orchard Ridge Dr 28227
Orchard Stone Run 28277
Orchard Trace Ln 28213
Orchenco Dr 28262
Orchid Pl 28277
Orchid Blossom Ln 28214
Orchid Hill Ln 28277
Ordermore Ave 28203
Ordway Ct 28270
Oregon St 28208
Oregon Oak Ct 28227
Oren Thompson Rd 28213
Orient Rd 28211
Oriole Pl 28269
Oriole St 28203
Orkney Ct 28278
Ormand Ct 28209
Ormeau Dr 28277
Ormsby Ct 28211
Orofino Ct 28269
Oroville Ct 28214
Orr Rd 28213
Orr St 28269
Orr Industrial Ct 28213
Orren Ct 28217
Orrview Dr 28227
Orton St 28208
Orvis St 28216
Orwin Manor Ln 28216
Osage Cir 28269
Osborne Ave 28204
Osceola Ln 28269
Oshanta Ct 28270
Osmond St 28208
Osprey Dr 28226
Osprey Knoll Dr 28269
Osprey Watch Ct 28227
Osterley Ct 28278
Oswald Ln 28277
Oswego Ct 28226
Othello Pl 28227
Ottawa Ln 28227
Otter Creek Dr 28277
Otterdale Ct 28277
Ottington Pl 28262
Otts St 28205
Otwell Ct 28216
Out Of Bounds Dr 28210
Outer Bridge Ln 28270
Outwell Rd 28278
Overbrook Ter 28214
Overcup Ln 28273
Overhill Rd 28211
Overland Ct 28227
Overland Park Ln 28262
Overlay Ct 28216
Overlook Trl 28212
Overlook Cove Rd 28216
Overlook Mountain Dr 28216
Overstone Ct 28277
Ovington Cir 28226
Owen Blvd 28213
Owenby Ct 28270
Owl Nest Ln 28277
Owls Perch Dr 28278
Oxer Rd 28227
Oxford Pl 28207
Oxford Commons Dr 28277
Oxford Crescent Ct 28226
Oxford Hill Ct 28269
Oxford Landing Ln 28270
Oxford Woods Ct 28277
Oxwynn Ln 28270
Paces Ferry Ln 28226
Paces Glen Ave 28212
Paces Oaks Blvd 28213
Pachino Way 28277
Pacific St 28208
Pacific Echo Dr 28277

Padderborn Ct 28215
Paddington Ct 28277
Paddle Oak Rd 28227
Paddock Cir 28209
Padget Parrish Ct 28270
Padstow Ct 28215
Page Ct 28270
Page Mill Ln 28270
Pahlmeyer Ln 28277
Pahokee Dr 28227
Painted Fern Ct 28269
Painted Pony Ct 28269
Painted Tree Rd 28226
Painter Pl 28212
Paisley Dr 28269
Paisley Pl 28208
Palace Dr 28211
Palatine Ln 28214
Pale Hickory Ln 28215
Pale Moss Ln 28269
Paleface Pl 28214
Palestrina Rd 28215
Palladium Pl 28269
Pallisers Ter 28210
Palm Ave 28205
Palm Breeze Ln 28208
Palmer Dr 28212
W Palmer St
300-599 28203
1000-1099 28208
Palmer Plaza Ln 28211
Palmerfield Dr 28227
Palmetto Ct 28227
Palmutum Pl 28269
Palo Alto Ln 28227
Palomar Mountain Dr 28278
Palomino Ct 28216
Paloverde Ln 28227
Palustris Ct 28269
Pamela Dr 28216
Pamela Lorraine Dr 28213
Pamlico St 28205
Pampas Cir 28226
Pandora Ct 28212
Pangborn Pl 28278
Pangle Dr 28217
Panglemont Dr 28269
Pansley Dr 28226
Panther Pl 28269
Panthersville Dr 28269
Papa Joe Hendrick Blvd 28262
Paper Birch Dr 28215
Paper Tree Rd 28227
Paper Whites Pl 28269
Paperbark Cir 28277
Par Cove Ln 28277
Paradise Ridge Rd 28277
Paragon Dr 28273
Parasol Tree Pl 28278
Pargo Rd 28216
Parham Pl 28270
Parish Ln 28226
E Park Ave 28203
W Park Ave 28203
Park Dr 28204
Park Ln 28214
Park Ln W 28214
Park Rd
1600-2599 28203
2600-2698 28209
2700-4118 28209
4117-4117 28220
4119-5499 28209
4120-5498 28209
5600-6398 28210
6400-10799 28210
10900-12199 28226
Park Walk E 28269
Park Walk W 28269
Park Cedar Dr 28210
Park Charlotte Blvd 28273
Park Creek Dr 28262
Park Crossing Dr 28210
Park Fairfax Dr 28208
Park Hickory Dr 28227

Park Hill Rd 28277
Park Phillips Ct 28210
Park Place Dr 28262
Park Pond Dr 28262
Park Sharon Ct 28210
Park Slope Dr 28209
Park South Dr 28210
Park South Station Blvd 28210
Park Springs Ct 28210
Park Vista Cir 28226
Park West Dr 28209
Park Willow Dr 28210
Parkaire Ln 28217
Parkay Pl 28214
Parkchester Dr 28277
Parkdale Dr 28208
Parker Dr 28208
Parker St 28216
Parker Green Trl 28269
Parkers Crossing Dr 28215
Parkhighland Ct 28273
Parkhouse Ln 28269
Parkhurst Ln 28227
Parkland Cir 28227
Parkleigh Dr 28262
Parkmont Dr 28208
Parkridge Dr 28214
Parks Farm Ln 28277
Parkside Dr 28208
Parkside Terrace Ln 28202
Parkstone Dr 28210
Parkton Rd 28215
Parkway Ave 28208
Parkway Plaza Blvd 28217
Parkwood Ave
100-599 28206
600-1699 28205
Parkwood Dr 28214
Parliament Ct 28216
Parlor Rd 28277
Parnie Ct 28213
Parsifal Ln 28213
Parson St 28205
Parthenon Ct 28262
Partia Ln 28262
Parting Brook Ct 28210
Partridge Cir 28212
Partridge Cross Ln 28214
Partridgeberry Dr 28213
Parview Dr N & S 28226
Paschall Rd 28278
Passeres Ct 28215
Passour Ridge Ln 28269
Pastern Ct 28216
Pasture Ln 28215
Pasture View Ct 28269
Patch Ave 28206
Patchwork Cir 28270
Pathfinder Ct 28214
Patio Ct 28205
Patric Alan Ct 28216
Patricia Ave 28205
Patricia Ann Ln 28269
Patricia Ryan Dr 28216
Patrick Pl 28210
Patrick Henry Ln 28277
Patriot Dr 28227
Patriots Hill Rd 28227
Patriots Point Ln 28214
Patterson St 28205
Patton Ave 28216
Patton Dr 28214
Patton St 28269
Patton Ridge Ct 28269
Pattonsburg Dr 28213
Paul Buck Blvd 28217
Paul Schadt Ln 28227
Paula Cir & Ct 28216
Pauline Ln 28216
Paulston Rd 28277
Pavilion Blvd 28262
Paw Creek Rd 28214
Pawley Dr 28214
Pawleys Plantation Ln 28278
Pawnee Dr 28214
Pawpaw Ln 28269
Pawtuckett Rd 28214
Paxton Ct 28213
Paxton Run Rd 28277
Peacan Flats Dr 28278
Peace St 28215
Peaceful Glen Rd 28273
Peaceful Way Dr 28206
Peacehaven Dr 28214
Peach St 28269
Peach Bottom Ln 28205
Peach Grove Ln 28277
Peach Orchard Rd 28215
Peach Park Ln 28216
Peach Place Ln 28216
Peachcrest Rd 28216
Peachcroft Rd 28216
Peachtree Dr S 28217
Peachtree Rd 28216
Peachwood Dr 28216
Peacock Ln 28215
Peakwood Ct 28269
Pear Tree Rd 28216
Pearl St 28262
Pearl Crescent Dr 28216
Peary Ct 28211
Pebble St 28206
Pebble Creek Way 28269
Pebble Pond Dr 28226
Pebblebrook Dr 28208
Pebbleford Ct 28262
Pebbleridge Dr 28212
Pebblestone Dr 28212
Pebworth Ct 28227
Pecan Ave
400-699 28204
800-1799 28205
Pecan Cove Ln 28269
Pecan Meadow Ct 28278
Pecanbluff Ct 28216
Pecanwood Rd 28214
Peckham Rye Rd 28227
Peco Rd 28277
Pecota Ln 28216
Pedigree Ln 28269
Pedlar Mills Rd 28278
Peggy Ln 28227
Pegram St 28205
Pelham Ln 28211
Pelican Ct 28227
Pella Rd 28211
Pelligrini St 28208
Pellyn Farm Ct 28226
Pelorus Ln 28269
Pelton St 28217
Pemberton Dr 28210
Pembroke Ave 28207
Pembry Links Cir 28277
Pembury Ln 28210
Pemswood St 28277
Pencade Ln 28215
Pence Rd 28215
Pence Grove Rd 28215
Pence Pond Ln 28227
Pencoyd Ln 28210
Pendale Rd 28210
Pendennis Ln 28210
Pender Pl 28209
Pendleton Ave 28210
Pendock Ct 28226
Pengelly Ct 28212
Peninsula Ln 28273
Penman St 28203
Penmarric Ct 28270
Penmore Ln 28269
Penn Ln 28212
Penn St 28203
Pennacook Dr 28214
Pennant Pl 28212
Penninger Cir 28262
Pennsylvania Ave 28216
Pennwood Ln 28215
Penny Way 28213
Penny Point Pl 28212
Pennycross Ln 28216
Penrose Ln 28217
Pensfold Dr 28269
Pensford Ln 28270
Penshurst Trce 28210
Penstemons Dr 28215
Pentreath Ln 28210
Penway Ct 28209
Pepper Ann Ln 28216
Pepper Bush Ln 28212
Pepperbush Ct 28262
Peppercorn Ln 28205
Pepperdine Dr 28226
Pepperdine Ridge Ct 28226
Pepperhill Rd 28212
Pepperidge Dr 28226
Peppermint Ln 28215
Pepperpike Way 28213
Pepperstone Ln 28269
Peppertree Ln 28277
Pepperwich Pl 28277
Peranna Pl 28211
Percussion Ct 28270
Percy Ct 28277
Perdido St 28262
Peregrine Ct 28269
Perennial Terrace Dr 28206
Performance Rd 28214
Pergola Pl 28213
Pergola View Ct 28213
Perimeter Pkwy 28216
Perimeter St W 28214
Perimeter Pointe Pkwy 28208
Perimeter Station Dr 28216
Perimeter West Dr 28214
Perimeter Woods Dr 28216
Periwinkle Ct 28269
Perkins Rd 28269
Pernell Ln 28213
Perrin Pl 28207
Perry Ct 28211
Perry June Ave 28213
Persimmon Creek Dr 28227
Persimmon Tree Dr 28273
Perth Ct 28215
Perugia Way 28273
Pesca Ln 28213
Petal Ct 28227
Pete Brown Rd 28269
Peterborough Ln 28270
E & W Peterson Dr 28217
Petrea Ln 28227
Peverell Ln 28270
Pewsbury Rd 28210
Pewter Ln 28270
Peyton Ct 28262
Peyton Randolph Dr 28277
Pharr St 28262
Pheasant Ln 28277
Pheasant Chase Ln 28216
Pheasant Glen Rd 28214
Phil Aull Pl 28207
Phil Oneil Dr 28215
Philadelphia Ct 28216
Philemon Ave 28206
Philips Spring Ct 28227
Phillip Davis Dr 28217
Phillips Ave 28208
Phillips St 28269
Phillips Fairway Dr 28216
Phillips Gate Dr 28210
Phillips Place Ct 28210
Phlox Ct 28213
Phoenix Pl 28211
Phone Valley Dr 28278
Phyliss Ln 28227
Piaffe Ave 28227
Picardy Pl 28209
Picasso Ct 28205
Piccadilly Dr 28211
Piccone Brook Ln 28216
Pickens Ct 28205
Pickerel Ln 28213
Pickering Dr 28213
Pickering Grove Ln 28216
Pickett Ct 28226
Pickway Dr 28269
Pickwick Ln 28211
Piedmont St 28204
Piedmont Hills Pl 28217
Piedmont Row Dr 28210
Piedmont Row Dr S
6000-6058 28210
6060-6060 28287
6061-6099 28210
Pierce St 28203
Piercy Woods Ct 28269
Pierpoint Dr 28269
Pierson Dr 28205
Pike Rd 28262
Pilcher Dr 28278
Pima Cotton Dr 28226
Pimilico Trace Ln 28216
Pimlico Dr 28273
Pimpernel Rd 28213
Pin Hook Rd 28215
Pin Oak Cir 28212
Pin Oak Ct 28226
Pin Oak Acres Way 28277
Pinaceal Ct 28215
Pinafore Dr 28212
Pinckney Ave 28205
Pine Cir 28215
Pine Dr 28269
Pine St 28269
N Pine St
200-699 28202
2100-2699 28206
Pine Trl 28227
Pine Bluff Cir 28214
Pine Branch Ct 28269
Pine Cape Dr 28214
Pine Chapel Dr 28273
Pine Creek Dr 28270
Pine Field Ct 28227
Pine Forest Rd 28214
Pine Glen Ct 28273
Pine Grove Ave 28227
Pine Grove Cir 28206
Pine Harbor Rd 28278
N Pine Hill Ln 28215
Pine Hill Rd 28227
Pine Hollow Dr 28212
Pine Island Dr 28214
Pine Lake Ln 28227
Pine Meadow Dr 28269
Pine Mountain Rd 28214
Pine Needle Trl 28227
Pine Oaks Dr 28217
Pine Ridge Rd 28226
Pine Terrace Ct 28273
Pine Thicket Ct 28226
Pine Tree Cir 28278
Pine Tree Dr 28270
Pine Valley Rd 28210
Pine Valley Club Dr 28277
Pinebark Ct 28212
Pineborough Rd 28212
Pinebrook Cir & Dr 28208
Pineburr Ct & Rd 28211
Pinecrest Ave 28205
Pinedale Ln 28214
Pinehaven Ct 28215
Pinehurst Pl 28209
Pineland Pl 28277
Pineleaf Dr 28269
Pinemont Ln 28212
Pinenoll Ln 28215
Pineshadow Dr 28262
Pinestream Dr
2500-2599 28216
4400-4499 28227
Pinetta Ln 28262
Pineview Rd 28211
Pineville Matthews Rd
1500-2899 28270
3000-8999 28226
Pineville Point Ave 28217
Pinewood Ave 28214
Pinewood Cir
1800-2299 28211
7500-7999 28227
Pinewood Dr 28269
Pinewood Ln 28269
Piney Creek Ct 28215
Piney Grove Rd 28212
Piney Path Rd 28212
Pink Dogwood Ln 28262
Pinnacle Dr 28262
Pinnacle Point Ln 28216
Pinoca Rd 28208
Pinstripe Ln 28227
Pinta Ct 28227
Pintail Pl 28269
Pintail Landing Ln 28278
Pinto Pl 28213
Pinyon Pine Ln 28215
Pioneer Ave 28273
Pioneer Ct 28227
Piper Ln 28208
Piper Glen Dr 28277
Piper Point Ln 28277
Piper Station Dr 28277
Pipestone Ln 28269
Pirates Pl 28216
Pirates Cove Ct 28227
Pisgah Way 28217
Pital Ct 28214
Pitchfork Ln 28227
Pitts Dr 28216
Pitty Pat Ct 28273
Placer Maple Ln 28269
Placid Pl 28211
Placid Lake Dr 28214
Plainfield Dr 28215
Plainview Rd 28208
Plainwood Dr 28216
Plantain Ct 28213
Plantation Pl 28209
Plantation Rd 28270
Plantation Falls Ln 28227
Plantation Park Blvd 28277
Plantation Ridge Rd 28214
Plantation Woods Dr 28278
Planters Pl 28216
Planters Estates Dr 28278
Planters Knob Ln 28273
Planters Knoll Ct 28227
Planters Ridge Rd 28270
Planters Row Dr 28278
Planters View Dr 28278
Planters Walk Ct 28210
Planters Watch Dr 28278
Planters Wood Ln 28262
Plashet Ln 28227
Plato Cir 28208
Playfair Ln 28277
Plaza Ln 28215
Plaza Meadow Dr 28215
Plaza Park Dr 28215
Plaza Road Ext 28215
Plaza Walk Dr 28215
Pleasant Dr 28211
Pleasant Dale Dr 28214
Pleasant Grove Rd 28216
Pleasant Hill Rd 28278
Pleasant Oaks Cir 28216
Pleasant Ridge Rd 28215
Pleasant View Ln 28227
Pleasant Way Ln 28273
Pleasant Wyatt Pl 28277
Plott Rd 28215
Plough Dr 28227
Plover Dr 28269
Plowdon Ct 28215
Plowstone Ct 28278
Plum St 28269
Plum Arbor Way 28209
Plum Creek Ln 28210
Plum Nearly Ln 28211
Plumcrest Dr 28216
Plumgrove Ct 28210
Plumleaf Dr 28213
Plumstead Rd 28216
Plymouth Ave 28206
Plymouth St 28217
Pochard Ct 28269
Poe Ct 28277
Poindexter Cir 28209
Poindexter Dr
100-199 28203
200-1099 28209
Poinsett St 28206
S Point Blvd 28273
S Point Dr 28277
Point Comfort Ln 28226
Point Lake Dr 28227
Point Lookout Rd 28278
Point O Woods Dr 28216
Point South Dr 28273
W Pointe Dr 28214
Pointed Leaf Ct 28213
Pointer Ridge Dr 28214
Pointview Pl 28269
Polara St 28270
Polk St 28206
Polk And White Rd 28269
Pollard Ct 28270
Pollys Garden Cir 28213
Polo Gate Blvd 28216
Polo Ridge Ct 28210
Pomerane Pl 28277
Pomfret Ln 28211
Pompano Dr 28216
Pond Meadow Ct 28213
Pond Valley Ct 28269
Pond Vista Ct 28216
Pondella Dr 28213
Ponderosa Pine Ln 28215
Ponders End Ln 28213
Pondridge Ct 28269
Pondside Ln 28213
Pondview Ln 28210
Pontchatrain Ave 28273
Pontifex Ct 28211
Pony Ct 28213
Ponytail Ln 28227
Poolside Ln 28208
Pope Farm Rd 28269
N Poplar St
100-799 28202
900-2899 28206
S Poplar St 28202
Poplar Forest Dr 28278
Poplar Grove Dr 28269
Poplar Hill Rd 28270
Poplar Springs Dr 28269
Poplarcrest Ln 28214
Poppleton Ct 28273
Poppy Hills Ln 28226
Porta Ferry Dr 28213
Portburn Rd 28211
Porter St 28208
Porter Creek Rd 28262
Porter Place Ct 28278
Porterfield Rd 28226
Portia Pl 28227
Portland Ave 28207
Portland Rose Ln 28210
Portmarnock Ct 28277
Portobello Way 28273
Portola Ct 28269
Portrush Ln 28273
Portside Ct 28278
Portstewart Ln 28270
Possum Trot Ln 28215
Post Canyon Ln 28213
Post Oak Rd 28270
Post Ridge Ct 28226
Postage Due 28205
Potenza Dr 28262
Potomac Blvd 28216
Potomac Ct 28211
Potpourri Pl 28215
Potters Glen Rd 28269
Pound Hill Ln 28277
Powatan Ct 28269
Powder Horn Rd 28212
Powder Mill Pl 28277
Powell Rd 28215
Pozzi Rd 28216
Prails Mill Ln 28262
Prairie Ln 28214
Prairie Falcon Ln 28278
Prairie Glen St 28278
Prairie Ridge Ln 28213
Prairie Valley Dr 28269
Prairiegrouse Ct 28214
Pralerm Rd 28211
Preakness Ct 28273
Preakness Stakes Ln 28215
Premier Dr 28277
Prentice Pl 28210
Presco Ct 28262
Prescott Ct 28269
Prescott Hill Ave 28277
Prescott Pond Ln 28270
Preservation Ln 28278
Preservation Park Dr 28214
Preservation Pointe Dr 28216
Preserve Pl 28211
Presidential Ln 28262
Presidents Ct 28217
Presmann Ct 28269
Presnell Pl 28273
Pressley Rd
500-1499 28217
8000-8199 28216
Prestbury Blvd 28216
Prestigious Ln 28269
Prestmoor Ct 28262
Preston Ct 28215
Preston Ln 28270
Prestwick Ln 28212
Prett Ct 28270
Price Ln 28217
Prideland Ct 28273
Prim Rose St 28208
Primm Rd 28216
Prince St 28216
Prince Charles St 28213
Prince Edward Ln 28277
Prince George Rd 28210
Prince Hall Ave 28206
Prince Williams Ln 28270
Princess Pl 28208
Princess St 28269
Princess Ann Dr 28212
Princeton Ave
1100-1999 28209
2000-2199 28207
Princeton Commons Dr 28277
Princeton Village Dr 28277
Prindle Lake Dr 28227
Print Ct 28214
Priory Ct 28262
Pritchard St 28208
Pro Am Dr 28211
Progress Ln 28205
Pronterm Rd 28227
Prospect Dr 28213
Prospector Ln 28227
Prosperity Ct 28269
Prosperity Church Rd 28269
Prosperity Commons Dr 28269
Prosperity Park Dr 28269
Prosperity Point Ln 28269
Prosperity Ridge Rd 28269
Prosperity View Dr 28269
Prosser Way 28216
Provand Ct 28278
Provence Ln 28277
Provence Village Ln 28226
Providence Dr 28211
E Providence Dr 28270
Providence Ln W 28226
Providence Rd
100-1799 28207
1800-4399 28211
4400-5299 28226
5300-5399 28277
5301-5339 28226
5400-6700 28226
6702-7898 28226
7501-7599 28270
7900-12299 28277
Providence Rd W 28277
Providence Arbours Dr 28270
Providence Branch Ln 28270

Providence Canyon Dr 28270
Providence Church Ln 28277
Providence Colony Dr 28277
Providence Country Club Dr 28277
Providence Court Ln 28270
Providence Creek Ln 28270
Providence Crest Ln 28270
Providence Estates Ct 28270
Providence Forest Ln 28270
Providence Glen Rd 28270
Providence Green Ct 28277
Providence Grove Ln 28270
Providence Manor Rd 28270
Providence Park Dr 28270
Providence Pine Ln 28270
Providence Plantation Ln 28270
Providence Spring Ln 28270
Providence Square Dr 28270
Providence Trail Ln 28270
Providence View Ln 28270
Provincetowne Dr 28277
Pruitt St 28208
Pryor St 28208
Puddingstone Cv 28210
Puddle Duck Rd 28262
Pueblo Ln 28227
Pullengreen Dr 28277
Pump Station Rd 28216
Pumpkin Way Dr 28227
Purple Bloom Ln 28262
Purple Dawn Dr 28213
Purple Finch Ct 28269
Purple Thistle Ln 28215
Purser Dr 28215
Purslane Ct 28213
Pytchley Ln 28273
Quail Dr 28269
Quail St 28214
Quail Acres Rd 28277
Quail Canyon Dr 28226
Quail Chase Ct 28277
Quail Field Dr 28227
Quail Forest Dr 28226
Quail Glenn Ct 28226
Quail Hill Rd 28210
Quail Hollow Rd 28210
Quail Hunt Ln 28226
Quail Lake Dr 28210
Quail Meadow Ln 28210
Quail Park Dr
6900-7799 28227
7600-7799 28210
Quail Ridge Dr
4300-5399 28227
7000-7499 28226
Quail View Rd 28226
Quail Wood Dr 28226
Quailrush Rd 28226
Quaking Grass Ct 28217
Quality Dr
10800-10999 28278
10926-10926 28241
11000-11098 28278
11001-11099 28278
11100-11199 28273
Quarry Rd 28212
Quarterbridge Ln 28262
Quarterhorse Ct 28215
Quarters Ln 28227
Queary Ct 28277
Queen Anne Rd 28217
Queen Charlottes Ct 28211
Queen City Dr 28208
Queens Rd
100-399 28204
400-1999 28207
2000-2399 28207
1000-2199 28207
Queens Carriage Pl 28278
Queens Harbor Rd 28278
Queens Oaks Ct 28210
Queensberry Dr 28226
Queensborough Ct 28216
Queensbridge Rd 28213
Queensbury Ct 28269
Queensgate Ln 28214
Queensland Dr 28270
Queensmead Cir 28273
Queenswater Ln 28273
Quentin St 28216
Quiet Bay Ct 28278
Quiet Cove Ct 28215
Quiet Creek Cir 28213
Quiet Pine Ct 28273
Quiet Stream Ct 28273
Quiet Water Pl 28214
Quiet Wood Ct 28277
Quilting Bee Ln 28216
Quincy St 28203
Quinn Dr 28269
Quintrell Dr 28277
Quixley Ln 28273
Rabbit Ridge Rd 28270
Rabbits Foot Ln 28217
Rachel St 28206
Rachelwood Dr 28273
Racine Ave 28269
Racquet Wood Ct 28226
Radbourne Blvd 28269
Radcliffe Ave 28207
Raddington Ln 28269
Radford Ave 28217
Radio Rd 28216
Radley Ct 28208
Radner Ln 28277
Radrick Ln 28262
Raeburn Ln 28227
Ragan Elizabeth Ct 28278
Rail Crossing Ln 28209
Rain Ct 28214
Rain Creek Way 28262
Rainbarrel Rd 28278
Rainbow Cir 28206
Rainbow Dr 28227
Rainbow Forest Dr 28277
Raindance Cir 28214
Rainman Way 28227
Rainsong Ct 28210
Raintree Ln 28277
Raisin Tree Ln 28215
Raj Ct 28227
Raku Ct 28269
Raleigh St
3800-4099 28206
4200-4399 28213
Rally Dr 28277
Rama Rd
400-1599 28211
1900-2399 28212
Ramath Dr 28211
Ramblelake Rd 28273
Ramblewood Ln 28210
Rambling Rose Dr 28212
Ramhorne Ct 28210
Ramona St 28208
Rampart St 28203
N Ramsey St 28216
S Ramsey St 28208
Ramsgate Rd 28270
Ranburne Rd 28227
Ranch Rd 28208
Ranchview Ln 28216
Ranchwood Dr 28217
Rancliffe Ct 28269
Randall St 28205
Randolph Rd
1900-2799 28207
2800-5699 28211
5700-5799 28270
Randolph Oaks Ct 28211
Random Pl 28215
Randstone Ct 28211
Randy Dr 28215
Raney Way 28205
Ranier Ave 28204
Rankin Pl 28277
Ranleigh Ln 28273
Ranlo Ave 28204
Rapallo Way 28277
Raphael Pl 28205
Rapid Springs Ct 28262
Rappahanock Rd 28215
Raptor Ct 28278
Raspberry Knoll Dr 28208
Rathangan Dr 28273
Rathburn Ln 28277
Rathlin Ct 28270
Rattersly Ct 28277
Rau Ct 28215
Ravanna Dr 28213
Raven Pl 28210
Raven Glen Ct 28212
Raven Park Dr 28216
Raven Rock Ct 28270
Raven Top Dr 28227
Ravencliff Dr 28226
Ravencrest Dr 28269
Ravencroft Dr 28208
Ravendale Dr 28216
Ravenglass Ln 28227
Ravenridge Ct 28216
Ravenswood Rd 28216
Ravenwing Dr 28262
Rawald Dr 28212
Raya Ct 28204
Rayecliff Ln 28214
Raymond Pl 28205
Rayners Hill Dr 28277
Raynham Dr 28262
Raynor Rd 28277
Rayon St 28216
Raysmoor Dr 28216
Rea Rd
2500-5599 28226
5800-6299 28277
6301-10699 28277
6400-6498 28226
6400-10698 28277
Rea Croft Dr 28226
Rea Forest Dr 28226
Reafield Dr 28226
Reagan Dr 28206
Realtree Ln 28214
Reames Rd
6400-9299 28216
10600-11899 28269
Reavencrest Park Dr 28277
Rebecca Ave 28208
Rebecca Bailey Dr 28262
Rebecca Run Dr 28269
Rebel Dr 28210
Rebus Rd 28227
Red Barn Ln 28210
Red Berry Ct 28213
Red Birch Dr 28262
Red Bird Trl 28226
Red Blossom Way 28277
Red Bluff Ct 28269
Red Branch Ln 28226
Red Buckboard Ln 28278
Red Bud Cir 28214
Red Cap Ln 28270
Red Carriage Ln 28212
Red Cedar Ln 28226
Red Clay Ln 28269
Red Clover Ln 28269
Red Cow Rd 28277
Red Crest Ln 28262
Red Cypress Ct 28216
Red Feather Dr 28277
Red Fez Club Rd 28278
Red Finch Ln 28214
Red Fox Trl 28211
Red Hickory Ln 28273
Red Hill Rd 28216
Red Holly Ct 28215
Red Leaf Dr 28215
Red Lion Rd 28211
Red Maple Dr 28277
Red Mulberry Way 28273
Red Oak Blvd 28217
Red Oak Ln 28226
Red Osier Ct 28270
Red Pine Ct 28262
Red Roan Pl 28215
Red Robin Ln 28214
Red Rock Rd 28270
Red Roof Dr 28217
Red Rose Ct 28269
Red Rust Ln 28277
Red Setter Ln 28227
Red Shed Ln 28269
Red Snow Ct 28215
Red Spruce Dr 28215
Red Squirrel Trl 28215
Red Tail Ct 28269
Red Tallen Ct 28214
Red Twig Dr 28213
Red Vulcan Ct 28213
Red Water Rd 28277
Red Wine Ct 28273
Redbridge Trl 28269
Redbud Dr 28227
Redbud St 28216
Redbud Tree Ct 28273
Redcoat Dr 28211
Redding Rd 28216
Redding Glen Ave 28216
Reddman Rd 28212
Redfern Ct 28212
Redfield Dr 28270
Redgrave Ln 28227
Redmond Trace Rd 28277
Redspire Dr 28278
Redstart Ct 28269
Redstone Mountain Ln 28277
Redstone View Dr 28269
Redstones Rd 28212
Redwood Ave 28205
Redwood Valley Ln 28277
Reece Rd 28209
Reedham Ct 28208
Reedmont Ln 28269
Reedy Creek Rd 28215
Reefton Rd 28262
Reese Furr Dr 28216
Reeves Ct 28208
Reeves St 28269
Regal Ct 28269
S Regal Ln 28210
Regal Estate Ln 28212
Regal Oaks Dr 28212
Regalview Ct 28278
Regatta Ln 28227
Regehr Ave 28214
Regena Ln 28278
Regency Dr 28211
Regent Park Ln 28210
Regent Ridge Ln 28278
Regncy Ex Pk Dr 28217
Rego St 28216
Reid Ave 28208
Reid Alexander Ln 28227
Reid Brook Ln 28208
Reid Meadows Dr 28208
Reid Oaks Dr 28208
Reid Park Ln 28208
Reigate Rd 28262
Reinbeck Dr 28269
Reindeer Way Ln 28216
Reliance St 28208
Rembert Ct 28206
Rembrandt Cir 28211
Remford Ct 28215
Remick Ct 28214
Remington St 28216
Reminisce Ln 28278
Remount Rd
100-600 28203
602-998 28203
1000-1198 28208
1200-2499 28208
Remus Rd 28203
Rena Mae Ln 28227
Renaissance Ct 28226
Renaissance Ridge Rd 28217
Renard Ridge Rd 28212
Renda Ct 28215
Renee Dr 28216
Renee Savannah Ln 28216
Renfrow Ln 28270
Reniston Dr 28210
Renner St 28216
Rennes St 28277
Reno Ave 28216
Renoir Ct 28215
Rensford Ave 28207
S Rensselaer Ave & Pl 28203
Rental Car Rd 28214
Renwick Rd 28211
Research Dr 28262
Resolves Ln 28277
Reston Rd 28278
Retana Dr 28270
Retriever Way 28269
Reunion St 28278
Revlock Ct 28226
Revlon Pl 28212
Revolution Ct 28262
Rexford Rd 28211
Rexwood Pl 28210
Reynard Ln 28215
Reynolds Dr 28209
Rhett Ct 28273
Rhett Butler Pl 28270
Rhian Brook Ln 28216
Rhinehill Rd 28278
Rhodes Ave 28210
Rhododendron Ct 28205
Rhone Dr 28226
Rhone Valley Dr 28278
Rhygate Cir 28226
Rhyne Rd 28214
Rhyne Station Rd 28214
Rialto Ct 28214
Riana Way 28214
Ribble Ct 28215
Ribbonwalk Trl 28269
Rice Mill Ln 28227
Rice Planters Rd 28273
Riceland Pl 28216
Ricewell Rd 28226
Rich Ln 28216
Richard Pl 28216
Richard St 28208
Richard Barry Dr 28270
Richard Rozzelle Dr 28214
Richardson Dr 28211
Richardson Park Ct 28269
Richfield Ln
6200-6348 28269
9800-9899 28215
Richland Dr
900-1399 28211
1400-1699 28205
Richmond Pl 28209
Richmond Rd 28227
Richmond Hill Ct 28277
Richmond Park Ave 28277
Richport Dr 28277
Richway Ct 28216
Riddings Ct 28269
Rider Wood Ln 28278
Ridge Ave 28208
N Ridge Ct 28215
Ridge Dr 28269
S Ridge Dr 28273
Ridge Rd 28269
Ridge Acres Rd 28214
Ridge Cliff Dr 28269
Ridge Cove Cir 28273
Ridge Creek Dr 28273
Ridge Haven Ln 28277
Ridge Lane Rd 28262
Ridge Oak Dr 28273
Ridge Path Ln 28269
Ridge Peak Ct 28269
Ridge Point Ct 28212
Ridgebrook Dr 28210
Ridgecrest Ave 28211
Ridgedale Ct 28206
Ridgefield Dr 28269
Ridgeforest Dr 28277
Ridgeley Dr 28208
Ridgeline Ln 28269
Ridgeloch Pl 28226
Ridgemont Ave 28208
Ridgemore Dr 28277
Ridgetop Trl 28215
Ridgevalley Dr 28208
Ridgeview Commons Dr 28269
Ridgeway Ave 28204
Ridgeway Park Dr 28277
Ridgewell Ct 28215
Ridgewood Ave 28209
Riding Hill Ave 28213
Riding Trail Rd 28212
Riesling Ct 28277
Riesman Ln 28210
Rigsby Rd 28273
Riley Ave 28269
Riley Woods Ln 28269
Rileys Ridge Rd 28226
Rillet Ct 28269
Rim Rock Ct 28278
Rimerton Dr 28226
Rimrock Canyon Dr 28226
Rindle Ct 28269
Rinehart Ct 28270
Ringed Teal Rd 28262
Ringneck Rd 28216
Ringtail Ln 28216
Ringwood St 28208
Rio Grande Ln 28227
Ripple Way 28262
Risburg Ln 28262
Riseley Ln 28270
Rising Meadow Rd 28277
Rising Oak Dr 28206
Rising Sun Ter 28227
Ritch Ave 28206
Rittenhouse Cir 28270
Ritter Dr 28270
Riva Ridge Ct 28216
Rivendell Ln
4100-4299 28227
8700-10299 28269
River Cir 28216
River Bluff Ct 28214
River Cabin Ln 28278
River Falls Dr 28215
River Hills Ct 28214
River Hollow Ct 28214
River Lure Blvd 28278
River Oaks Ln 28226
River Ridge Rd 28226
River Rock Ct 28214
River Shore Dr 28278
River Valley Ct 28227
River Walk Way 28214
Riverbend Rd 28210
Riverbirch Dr 28210
Riverdale Dr 28273
Riverdowns Ct 28278
Riverfront Dr 28216
Rivergate Pkwy 28273
Rivergreen Ln 28227
Riverhaven Dr 28214
Riverine Dr 28216
Riverpointe Dr 28278
Riverside Dr 28214
Riverstone Way 28277
Riverton Ct 28227
Riverview Dr 28216
Riverwood Rd 28270
Riviere Dr 28211
Roadway St 28208
Roaming Path Ct 28214
Roanoke Ave 28205
Rob Roy Ct 28208
Robanna Ct 28214
Robbie Cir 28278
Robert Burns Ct 28213
Robert Frost Ln 28213
Robertson Ave 28208
Robeson Creek Dr 28270
Robin Ln 28269
Robin Rd 28211
Robin Crest Rd 28226
Robin Hill Dr 28210
Robin Hollow Dr 28227
Robin Terry Ct 28208
Robinhood Cir 28227
Robinhood Rd 28211
Robins Nest Ln 28269
Robinson Cir 28206
Robinson Church Rd 28215
Robinson Forest Dr 28277
Robinson Meadow Ct 28277
Robinson Rock Ct 28277
Robinwood Dr
4000-4299 28212
5000-5299 28215
Robley Tate Ct 28270
Robmont Rd 28270
Robsart Ct 28277
Robur Ct 28269
Robyns Glen Dr 28269
Rocbridge Ln 28208
Rocester Dr 28215
Rocha Ct 28215
Roche Ln 28216
Rochelle Ln 28208
Rock Canyon Dr 28226
Rock Creek Dr 28226
Rock Dove Ct 28277
Rock Gap Rd 28278
Rock Hollow Dr 28212
Rock Island Rd 28278
Rock Knoll Dr 28214
Rock Point Rd 28270
Rock Springs Rd 28226
Rock Stream Dr 28269
Rockabill Ln 28278
Rockaway Ct 28217
Rockbrook Dr 28211
Rockcastle Dr 28273
Rockcliff Ct 28210
Rockefeller Ln 28210
Rocket Ln 28213
Rockfern Rd 28217
Rockford Ct 28209
Rockhaven Dr 28216
Rockhill Ln 28277
Rocklake Dr 28214
Rockland Dr 28213
Rockledge Dr 28210
Rocklyn Pl 28209
Rockmeadow Dr 28216
Rockmoor Ridge Rd 28215
Rockmore Ln 28226
Rockshire Dr 28227
Rockspray Ct 28215
Rockview Ct 28226
Rockway Dr 28205
Rockwell Blvd W 28269
Rockwell Church Rd 28269
Rockwood Dr 28214
Rockwood Rd
4000-4399 28214
4900-5599 28216
9800-10499 28215
Rockwood Forest Ln 28212
Rocky Rd 28215
Rocky Brook Ct 28269
Rocky Falls Rd 28211
Rocky Ford Club Rd 28269
Rocky Gap Ln 28278
Rocky Glen Ln 28214
Rocky Knoll Dr 28210
Rocky Mount Ct 28214
Rocky Ridge Dr 28217
Rocky River Rd
1600-2699 28213
2800-9899 28215
Rocky River Rd W 28213
Rocky River Church Rd 28215
Rocky Spring Ct 28262
Rocky Trace Way 28273
Rocky Trail Ct 28270
Rodey Ave 28206
Rodman St 28205
Roe Buck Meadow Ln 28278
Rogalla Dr 28277
Rogers St 28208
Roland St 28205
Rolette Ct 28216

Street	ZIP
Rolling Acres Rd	28213
Rolling Creek Ct	28270
Rolling Fields Rd	28227
Rolling Glen Ct	28214
Rolling Hill Dr	28213
Rolling Hill Rd	28227
Rolling Oak Ln	28227
Rolling Rock Ct	28215
Rolling Sky Dr	28273
Rolling Stone Ave	28216
Rolling Wheels	28215
Rollingbrook Dr	28217
Rollingridge Dr	28211
Rollingwood Dr	28217
Rollins Ave	28205
Rolston Dr	28207
Romana Red Ln	28213
Romany Rd	28203
Romare Bearden Dr	28208
Rome Ct	28209
Ron Allen Ct	28227
Ronald St	28216
Ronda Ave	28211
Rook Rd	28216
Ropemakers Ct	28227
Ropley Ct	28211
Rosa Parks Pl	28216
Rosada Dr	28213
Rosapenny Rd	28278
Rosberg Ln	28216
Rose St	28208
Rose Creek Ct	28262
Rose Garden Ter	28204
Rose Lake Dr	28217
Rose Meadow Ln	28277
Rose Point Ln	28216
Rose Ridge Pl	28217
Rose Terrace Ct	28215
Rose Thorn Pl	28217
Rose Valley Dr	28210
Rose Vine Pl	28217
Rosebank Ln	28226
Rosebay Ct	28210
Roseberry Ct	28277
Rosebriar Ln	28277
Rosecliff Dr	28277
Rosecran Dr	28215
Rosecrest Dr	28210
Rosecroft Dr	28215
Rosefield Ct	28215
Rosegate Ln	28270
Rosehall Dr	28227
Rosehaven Dr	28205
Rosehedge Ln	28205
Rosehill Dr	28212
Roseland Ave	28277
Roselawn Pl	28211
Rosemallow Rd	28213
Rosemary Ln	28210
Rosemede Dr	28227
Rosemont St	28208
Rosena Dr	28227
Roseton Ln	28277
Rosetree Ct	28213
Rosetta St	28216
Roseview Ln	28205
Rosewater Ct	28226
Rosewood Cir	28211
Rosewood Park Ln	28262
Roslyn Ave	28208
Ross Ave	28208
Ross Moore Ave	28205
Rosslare Villas Ct	28226
Roswell Ave	
2000-2399	28207
2400-2799	28209
Rosy Billed Dr	28262
Rosy Mound Ln	28216
Rotary Dr	28269
Roth House Rd	28278
Rothchild Dr	28270
Rothe House Rd	28273
Rotherby Ct	28215
Rotherfield Ct	28277
Rotherham Ln	28216
Rothesay Dr	28277
Rothman Ln	28215
Rothmore St	28215
Rothmore View Ct	28215
Rothmullan Dr	28262
Rothwell Dr	28227
Rothwood Dr	28211
Rotunda Rd	28226
Rouda Ln	28269
Rougemont Ln	28277
Round Hill Rd	28211
Round Oak Rd	28210
Round Rock Rd	28277
Roundabout Ln	28210
Roundhouse Cir	28227
Roundhouse Ln	28226
Rounding Run Rd	28277
Roundleaf Dr	28213
Roundstone Way	28216
Roundtable Ct	28277
Rountree Rd	28217
Rousay Rd	28278
Rowan St	28208
Rowan Way	28214
Rowe Ct	28278
Roxanna Ct	28214
Roxborough Rd	28211
Roxborough Pkwy Dr	28211
Roxbury Ct	28214
Roxfield Ln	28215
Roxton Ct	28208
Roy St	28208
Roya Pl	28213
Royal Ct	28202
Royal Aberdeen Ct	28277
Royal Birkdale Ct	28277
Royal Bluff Dr	28269
Royal Castle Ct	28277
Royal Celadon Way	28269
Royal Crest Dr	28210
Royal Dornoch Ct	28277
Royal Fern Ln	28215
Royal Gorge Ave	28210
Royal Highlands Ct	28277
Royal Lytham Ct	28277
Royal Oak Rd	28278
Royal Point Dr	28273
Royal Portrush Dr	28277
Royal Ridge Ln	28212
Royal Scot Ln	28227
Royal Tree Ct	28216
Royal Troon Ct	28277
Royal Winchester Dr	28277
Royal York Ave	28210
Royalwood Ln	28273
Royce Ct	28277
Royce Hall Ln	28269
Royden Pl	28226
Royston Rd	28208
Rozumny Dr	28216
Rozwood Dr	28216
Rozzelles Ferry Rd	
1800-3099	28208
3101-3199	28208
3200-5299	28216
5300-11699	28214
Rozzelles Landing Dr	28214
Rozzells Cir	28208
Rua Cir	28215
Rubin Lura Ct	28269
Rubine St	28208
Ruby St	28208
Ruby Hill Pl	28278
Ruby Valley Rd	28277
Rucker Cliff Dr	28214
Rudd Ct	28216
Ruddy Ct	28273
Rudence Ct	28278
Rudolph Rd	28216
Rudolph Dadey Dr	28277
Rudwick Ln	28226
Rugby Ln	28226
Rugged Stone Way	28227
Rugosa Ct	28273
Rumney Ct	28216
Rumple Rd	28262
Rumson Ct	28213
Rumstone Ln	28262
Runaway Bay Dr	28212
Running Brook Rd	28214
Running Deer Rd	28214
Running Rapids Rd	28214
Running Ridge Rd	28226
Running Wood Ln	28215
Runnymede Ln	
1400-1999	28211
2101-2397	28209
2399-2599	28209
Runswyck Ct	28269
Rupert Ln	28215
Rush Ave	28208
Rush Wind Dr	28206
Rushmore Dr	28277
Ruskin Dr	28209
Russborough Ct	28273
Russell Ave	28216
Russell Rd	28262
Russet Pl	28227
Russet Oak Ln	28277
Russian River Pl	28277
Rust Wood Pl	28227
Rustic Ln	28210
Rustic Ridge Ct	
2600-2699	28270
7300-7399	28226
Rustic View Ct	28216
Rustlewood Ln	28226
Rusty Ct	28227
Rusty Plow Ct	28216
Rutgers Ave	28206
Ruth Dr	28215
Ruth Ferrell Ct	28269
Ruth Haven Dr	28227
Ruth Polk Ct	28269
Rutherford Dr	28210
Rutherglen Ct	28213
Rutland Dr	28217
Rutledge Ave	28211
Ruxton Ct	28214
Ryan Ct	28214
Ryan Courtney Sq	28227
Ryan Jay Dr	28269
Ryan Michael Ct	28262
Ryder Ave	28226
Rye Mill Ct	28277
Ryerson Ct	28213
Sabella Ln	28216
Sable Cap Rd	28227
Sablewood Dr	28205
Sabrina Ct	28210
Sackett Way	28269
Saddle Oak Ct	28262
Saddle Pace Ln	28269
Saddle Point Rd	28212
Saddle Ridge Rd	28212
Saddle Run Trl	28269
Saddle Trail Ln	28269
Saddleback Ct	28210
Saddlebrook Ct	28226
Saddlebury Ln	28226
Saddlehorse Ln	28215
Saddleview Ct	28215
Saddlewood Ln	28227
Sadler Rd	28278
Sadler Glen Dr	28214
Saffir Ct	28227
Safflower Cir	28262
Saffron Ct	28215
Sagamore Rd	28209
Sage Ave	28216
Sage Hills Dr	28277
Sage Thrasher Ln	28278
Sagekirk Ct	28278
Sagestone Ct	28262
Saguaro Ct	28269
Sahalee Ln	28216
Saint Andrews Ln	28205
Saint Andrews Homes Pl	28205
Saint Anne Pl	28213
Saint Audrey Pl	28269
Saint Bernard Way	28269
Saint Charles Ln	28278
Saint Christopher Ct	28277
Saint Evans Rd	28214
Saint George St	28205
Saint Germaine Ln	28210
Saint James Pl	28205
Saint John Ln	28210
Saint Julien St	28205
Saint Lawrence Ave	28227
Saint Lucia Ln	28277
Saint Luke St	28216
Saint Mark St	28216
Saint Mary Ave	28205
Saint Pierre Ln	28277
Saint Stephen Ln	28210
Saint Thomas Ln	28277
Saint Timms Ct	28226
Saint Vardell Ln	28217
Saint Vincent Ln	28277
Sainte Rose Ln	28226
Saintfield Pl	28270
Saintsbury Pl	28270
Salamander Ct	28215
Salamander Run Ln	28215
Salem Dr	28209
Salem Church Rd	28216
Salem Glen Ct	28278
Salinger Way	28215
Sally Ln	28227
Salome Church Rd	28262
Salt Box Ct	28277
Salute Blvd	28227
Salvia St	28277
Salvistrin St	28214
Sam Dee Rd	28215
Sam Drenan Rd	28205
Sam Neely Rd	
12200-12499	28278
12800-12999	28273
Sam Roper Dr	28269
Sam Wilson Rd	28214
Samara Ct	28269
Samlen Ln	28214
Sampson St	28208
Samuel St	28206
Samuel Guilford Ct	28270
Samuel Neel Rd	28278
San Francisco Cir	28216
San Gabriel Ave	28214
San Luis Ln	28227
San Marco Dr	28227
San Marcos St	28214
San Paolo Ln	28277
San Rey Ct	28215
San Saba St	28214
Sand Hills Ct	28215
Sandboar St	28215
Sandburg Ave	28213
Sanders Ave	28216
Sanders Creek Ct	28269
Sanderson Ln	28226
Sandhurst Dr	28205
Sandleheath Ct	28277
Sandlewood Rd	28205
Sandman Ln	28216
Sandpines Ln	28262
Sandpiper Dr	28277
Sandridge Rd	28210
Sandringham Pl	28262
Sandstone Rd	28277
Sandtrap Ln	28226
Sandy Ave	28213
Sandy Glen Ct	28212
Sandy Hook Ct	28214
Sandy Porter Rd	28273
Sandy River Ln	28273
Sandy Spring Ln	28213
Sandyway Ln	28273
Sanford Ln	28211
Sanibel Dr	28227
Sanridge Wind Ln	28262
Sansberry Rd	28262
Santa Cruz Trl	28227
Santa Fe Ln	28227
Santa Lucia Dr	28277
Santa Maria Ln	28227
Santee St	28208
Santeelah Ct	28217
Santell Ln	28214
Santorini Ln	28277
Sapona Ct	28277
Saquache Dr	28269
Sarah Dr	28217
Sarah Elizabeth Ln	28277
Sarah Hall Ln	28270
Sarah Marks Ave	28203
Sarandon Ct	28215
Saranita Ln	28278
Saratoga Dr	28208
Sardis Ln	28270
Sardis Rd	28270
Sardis Rd N	
100-2000	28270
2001-2099	28227
2001-2099	28270
2002-2098	28270
2100-2699	28227
Sardis Cove Dr	28270
Sardis Creek Ln	28270
Sardis Crossing Dr	28270
Sardis Forest Dr	28270
Sardis Green Ct	28270
Sardis Oaks Rd	28270
Sardis View Ln	28270
N Sardis View Ln	28270
Sardis View Rd	28211
Sardiscroft Rd	28270
Sardony Ln	28213
Sarena Pl	28208
Sargeant Dr	28217
Sarnia Pl	28269
Sassafras Ln	28278
Satterfield Ct	28215
Satterwythe Ln	28215
Saucalito Ct	28215
Saunton Ct	28277
Savannah Club Dr	28273
Savannah Creek Dr	28273
Savannah Garden Dr	28273
Savannah Springs Dr	28269
Saw Mill Rd	28278
Sawgrass Ct	28226
Sawgrass Ridge Pl	28269
Sawleaf Ct	28215
Sawmill Trace Dr	28213
Sawtooth Ct	28227
Sawyer Dr	28213
Saxonbury Way	28269
Saybrook Ct	28227
Sayre Rd	28209
Scaleybark Rd	28209
Scarcliff Ln	28277
Scarlet Cir	28273
Scarlet Crest Ct	28227
Scarlet Oak Ln	28226
Scarlet Runner Dr	28215
Scarlet Sage Dr	28215
Scarlet Tanager Dr	28278
Scarsdale Dr	28227
Scholastic Dr	28277
Scholtz Rd	28217
School St	28205
School House Ln	28226
Schooner Ln	28270
Schooner Bay Ln	28215
Schubert Pl	28227
Scofield Rd	28209
Scone Palace Ct	28278
Scorpio Ln	28227
Scotch Heather Way	28277
Scotch Moss Ct	28269
Scotch Pine Cir	28262
Scothurst Ln	28277
Scotland Ave	28207
Scotland Hall Ct	28277
Scotland Ridge Rd	28211
Scotney Bluff Ave	28273
Scots Bluff Dr	28227
Scott Ave	
1300-1399	28204
1400-2199	28203
2201-2299	28203
Scott Creek Dr	28213
Scott Futrell Dr	
1801-4199	28208
4301-4399	28214
Scott Gate Ct	28277
Scottie Pl	28217
Scottish Kilt Ct	28277
Scottridge Dr	28217
Scotts Elm Ct	28215
Scottsbrook Dr	28213
Scottsburg Ct	28227
Scottsdale Rd	28217
Scottsman Trace Dr	28273
Scottsmoor Dr	28214
Scottview Dr	28214
Scottwood Ter	28212
Scourie Ln	28277
Scrimshaw Ln	28215
Scuppernong Ct	28215
Seaboard St	28206
Seabrook Dr	28208
Seacroft Rd	28210
Seaforth Dr	28205
Sealey Ct	28277
Seaman Dr	28217
Seamill Rd	28278
Sean Ridge Ln	28277
Sears Ct	28205
Sears Rd	28214
Seascape Ln	28278
Season Grove Ln	28216
Seasons Ct	28269
Seaton Dr	28227
Seattle Slew Ct	28215
Sebastiani Dr	28214
Sebrena Pl	28211
Sebring Cir	28215
Second St	28208
Secret Cove Ct	28227
Secret Garden Ln	28214
Secretariat Dr	28216
Section View Ln	28278
Sedgeburn Dr	28278
Sedgefield Rd	28209
Sedgemoor Ln	28277
Sedgewich Ln	28277
Sedgewood Cir	28211
Sedgewood Forest Ln	28211
Sedgewood Lake Dr	28211
Sedgewood Place Ct	28211
Sedley Rd	28211
Seedling Ln	28214
Segundo Ln	28278
Seifert Cir	28205
Seigle Ave	
600-899	28204
900-1899	28205
Seigle Point Ave & Dr	28204
Sela Ct	28227
Selari Ct	28216
Seldon Dr	28216
Selkirk Pl	28270
Selkirkshire Rd	28278
Sellars Ct	28211
Selsey Pl	28277
Selwyn Ave	
1900-2399	28207
2400-3999	28209
Selwyn Farms Ln	28209
Selwyn Oaks Ct	28209
Selwyn Place Rd	28209
Seminole Ct	28210
Seneca Pl	
100-1299	28210
1300-1599	28209
Seney Dr	28214
Senior Dr	28216
Senter Ct	28277
Sentinel Cir	28210
Sentinel Oak Ln	28214
Sentinel Post Rd	28226
Sentry Post Rd	28208
September Ln	28208
Sequoia Pl	28217
Sequoia Grove Ln	28214
Sequoia Red Ln	28226
Serape Rd	28277
Serenade Ct	28215
Serendipity Ln	28277
Serene Ln	28216
Serenity Way	28269
Service St	28206
Sessile Oak Ln	28270
Seth Thomas Rd	28210
Seths Dr	28269
Seton House Ln	28277
Setter Trace Ln	28216
Settlemyer Ct	28212
Settlers Ln	28202
Settlers Bridge Ct	28214
Settlers Path Ln	28278
Settlers Trail Ct	28278
Seven Eagles Rd	28210
Seven Oaks Dr	28215
Severn Ave	28210
Sevilla Ct	28226
Seward Pl	28211
Sewickley Dr	28209
Seymour Dr	28208
Shackleford Ter	28227
Shad Ct	28208
Shadbrush Ct	28215
Shade Valley Rd	28205
Shaded Ct	28273
Shademaster Pl	28278
Shadow Ln	28214
Shadow Cove Ln	28216
Shadow Creek Rd	28226
Shadow Grove Cir	28277
Shadow Lawn Rd	28269
Shadow Moss Ct	28227
Shadow Oaks Dr	28269
Shadow Pine Dr	28269
Shadow Pond Ln	28226
Shadow Ridge Ln	28273
Shadow Rock Ct	28270
Shadow Vista Ct	28227
Shadowbrook Ln	28211
Shadowcrest Dr	28217
Shadowlake Dr	28226
Shadowood Ln	28273
Shadowstone Dr	28270
Shady Cir	28216
Shady Ln	
2900-2999	28208
7400-7799	28215
Shady Bark Ct	28227
Shady Bluff Dr	28211
Shady Creek Rd	28216
Shady Grove Ln	28217
Shady Oak Ct	28227
Shady Oak Trl	28210
Shady Pine Ct	28214
Shady Reach Ln	28214
Shady Rest Ln	28214
Shadycroft Cir	28226
Shadyside Ct	28269
Shadyview Dr	28210
Shaffer Valley Way	28273
Shaffhausen Pl	28227
Shafter Ct	28214
Shaftesbury Ln & Rd	28270
Shagbark Ln	28226
Shaker Dr	28210
Shalimar Dr	28216
Shallow Oak Ct	28269
Shallow Pond Rd	28278
Shallow Well Dr	28278
Shallowood Ln	28277
Shalom Dr	28216
Shamrock Dr	
1300-2999	28205
3000-4799	28215
Shanagarry Dr	28278
Shandon Cir	28226
Shandon Way Ln	28262
Shane Ln	28214
Shanghai Links Pl	28278
Shannon Green Dr	28213
Shannon Park Ln	28273
Shannon Willow Rd	28226
Shannonhouse Dr	28215
Shannopin Dr	28270

Street	ZIP
Shanon Darby Ln	28214
Sharon Ave	28211
Sharon Ln	28211
Sharon Pkwy	28211
Sharon Rd	
2000-2331	28207
2332-4699	28211
4700-6999	28210
7001-8999	28210
Sharon Rd W	28210
Sharon Acres Rd	28210
N Sharon Amity Rd	
100-1599	28211
1600-4999	28205
5000-5198	28215
5200-5899	28215
S Sharon Amity Rd	28211
Sharon Chase Dr	28215
Sharon Commons Ln	28210
Sharon Forest Dr	28212
Sharon Hills Rd	28210
Sharon Lakes Rd	28210
Sharon Oaks Ln	28210
Sharon Pointe Rd	28215
Sharon View Rd	
2800-3799	28210
3800-6099	28226
Sharon Woods Ln	28210
Sharonbrook Dr	28210
Sharpe Rd	28227
Sharpes Cir	28214
Sharpthorne Pl	28270
Sharview Cir	28217
Sharyn Dr	28214
Shasta Ln	28211
Shasta Hill Ct	28211
Shaver Dr	28277
Shawnee Dr	28209
Shea Ln	28227
Sheets Cir	28214
Sheffield Dr	28205
Sheffield Crescent Ct	28226
Sheffield Park Ave	28211
Sheffingdell Dr	28226
Shelburne Pl	28227
Shelden Ct	28227
Shelley Ave	28269
Shelley Terrace Ln	28212
Shellnutt Ln	28209
Shellview Ln	28214
Shelly Pines Dr	28262
Shelly Terrance Ln	28212
Shelter Cove Ln	28216
Shelter Rock Ct	28214
Shelton St	28270
Sheltonham Way	28216
Shenandoah Ave	28205
Shenandoah Cir	28215
Shenandoah Pl	28215
Shenington Pl	28216
Shepherdleas Ln	28277
Shepley Ct	28226
Sheppard Ct	28211
Sherbourne Dr	28210
Sherbrooke Dr	28210
Sheridan Dr	28205
Sheringham Way	28227
Sherington Way	28227
Sherman Dr	28273
Sherrill St	28208
Sherwood Ave	28207
Sherwood Forest Dr	28226
Sheryl Cir	28217
Shetland Ln	28278
Shillington Pl	28210
Shiloh Ridge Ln	28212
Shimmering Lake Dr	28214
Shindary Ave	28206
Shingle Oak Rd	28227
Shining Oak Ln	28269
Shining Rock Ct	28277
Shinkansen Dr	28213
Shinnecock Hill Ln	28277
Shiny Meadow Ln	28215
Ship St	28269
Shipwright Ln	28215
Shiras Ct	28273
Shire Dr	28216
Shiredale Ln	28212
Shirhall St	28214
Shirley Dr	28214
Shitert Dr	28273
Shoal Brook Ct	28277
Shoal Creek Ct	28277
Shocco Ln	28215
Shoemaker Ct	28270
Shopton Rd	
1500-4499	28217
5000-5699	28278
Shopton Rd W	28278
Shore Ln	28277
Shore Haven Ct	28269
Shoreham Dr	28211
Shoreline Dr	28214
Shorewood Dr	28277
Short Hills Dr	28217
Short Line Ct	28210
Shorthorn St	28213
Shortleaf Pine Ct	28215
Shoshone Ct	28214
Shoup Ct	28216
Shropshire Ter	28215
Shuffletown Dr	28214
Shufford Ct	28277
Shuman Ln	28269
Shumard Oak Ln	28226
Shutterfly Rd	28217
Sickles Dr	28273
Sid Crane Dr	28216
Sidney Cir	28269
Sidney Crest Ave	28213
Sidras Ct	28270
Siemens Ave	28273
Sienna Dr	28215
Sierra Dr	28216
Sierra Woods Ct	28216
Signer Rd	28278
Sikes Pl	28277
Silabert Ave	28205
Silas Ave	28206
Silas Ed Ln	28227
Silchester Ln	28215
Silkstream Ln	28262
Silkwood Ct	28226
Sills Ct	28215
Silo Ln	28226
Silvaire Farm Rd	28278
Silver Ct	28217
Silver Arrow Dr	28273
Silver Bell Dr	28211
Silver Birch Dr	28269
Silver Charm Ct	28215
Silver Coach Ln	28273
Silver Crescent Dr	28273
Silver Dart Pl	28278
Silver Eagle Dr	28214
Silver Falls Way	28227
Silver Fox Rd	28270
Silver Garden Ln	28216
Silver Glen Ln	28262
Silver Lake Ct	28277
Silver Maple Ln	28227
Silver Ore Ln	28216
Silver Pheasant Dr	28226
Silver Pine Dr	28277
Silver Pond Ct	28210
Silver Spur Ct	28273
Silver Star Ln	28210
Silver Stream Rd	28226
Silver Valley Dr	28215
Silverado Ln	28277
Silverberry Ct	28214
Silvercrest Dr	28215
Silverfern Ln	28277
Silverfield Ln	28215
Silverleaf Rd	28217
Silvermere Way	28269
Silveroak Ln	28277
Silversmith Ln	28270
Silversword Dr	28213
Silverthorn Dr	28273
Silverton Dr	28215
Silverwood Ln	28215
Simbrah Way	28273
Simca St	28216
Simmon Tree Rd	28270
Simmons St	28208
Simonton Dr	28269
Simpson Dr	28205
Simpson Rd	28216
Simpson St	28262
Simsbury Rd	28226
Sinclair St	28208
Singing Cove Ct	28273
Singing Hills Ct	28269
Singing Oak Ct	28269
Singingpine Rd	28214
Singingwood Ln	28226
Singleleaf Ln	28278
Singletary Ln	28227
Singletree Rd	28227
Sipes Ln	28269
Sir Anthony Dr	28262
Sir Barton Ct	28215
Sir Charles Pl	28277
Sir Francis Drake Dr	28277
Sir Lionel Ct	28277
Sir Winstons Pl	28211
Sirona Dr	28273
Sirus Ln	28208
Sitka Ct	28227
Six Point Ln	28269
Sj Lawrence Rd	28273
Skip Stone Dr	28214
Skipper Ct	28227
Skipton Ln	28277
Skipwith Pl	28217
Sky Dr	28226
Skycrest Dr	28269
Skycrest Ln	28217
Skyland Ave	28205
Skylark Ct	28210
Skyline Dr	28269
Skyline View Way	28204
Skylla Ln	28262
Skymaster Ct	28278
Skyview Rd	28208
Slade Castle Ct	28273
Slagle Dr	28215
Slalom Hill Rd	28278
Slater Rd	28216
Slater Ridge Dr	28216
Slater Springs Dr	28216
Slatewood Rd	28212
Slaton Rd	28217
Sledge Rd	28278
Sleepy Hollow Rd	28217
Sleigh Bell Ln	28216
Slickrock Cir	28215
Slippery Creek Ln	28227
Sloan Dr	28208
Sloan St	28209
Sloane Square Way	28211
W Slope Ln	28209
Sloping Oaks Rd	28212
Small Ave	28269
N Smallwood Pl	28216
S Smallwood Pl	28208
Smart Ln	28277
Smith Dr	28214
Smith Ln	28208
Smith Rd	28273
N Smith St	28202
Smith Boyd Rd	28273
Smith Corners Blvd	28269
Smithfield Dr	28270
Smithfield Church Rd	28210
Smithton Ln	28213
Smithwood Ct	28269
Smoke House Dr	28270
Smoke Mont Dr	28273
Smoke Ridge Ct	28210
Smoke Tree Ln	28226
Smokehollow Rd	28227
Smokerise Hill Dr	28277
Smooth Path Dr	28214
Smooth Rock Ct	28210
Smoothstone Ln	28214
Smugglers Ct	28216
Smythe Forest Dr	28214
Snapfinger Dr	28277
Snooze Ln	28227
Snow Ln	28227
Snow Bird Ln	28227
Snow Creek Ln	28273
Snow Hill Ct	28269
Snow Ridge Ln	28278
Snow White Ln	28213
Snowbell Ct	28215
Snowbird Ct	28227
Snowcrest Ct	28212
Snowden Ln	28270
Snowdrop Dr	28215
Snowflake Ct	28215
Snug Harbor Rd	28278
Soapstone Dr	28269
Soaring Eagle Ln	28227
Soaringfree Ln	28226
Sobeck Ln	28269
Socata Way	28269
Social Cir	28216
Society St	28277
Sofia Ln	28262
Sofley Rd	28206
Softwind Dr	28273
Softwood Ct	28273
Solace Ct	28269
Solano Dr	28262
Solar Way	28278
Soldier Rd	28278
Solectron Dr	28262
Solemn Point Ln	28216
Solitude Ct	28227
Solomon St	28216
Solway Ln	28269
Somerdale Ln	28205
Somerset Dr	28209
Somerset Springs Dr	28262
Somersworth Dr	28215
Sonata Pl	28211
Song Sparrow Ln	28269
Sonoma Ln	28278
Sonoma Valley Dr	28214
Sonora Ln	28208
Sorrel Ct	28278
Sorrel Ridge Dr	28227
Sorrento Ct	28269
South Blvd	
1100-2599	28203
2600-4699	28209
4700-6300	28217
6241-6241	28224
6301-7099	28217
6302-7098	28217
7100-9999	28273
Southampton Rd	28217
Southampton Commons Dr	28277
Southampton Ridge Dr	28227
Southbourne Rd	28273
Southbridge Forest Dr	28273
Southbrook Dr	28277
Southby Ct	28270
Southend Dr	28203
Southern Garden Ln	28278
Southern Oak Ct	28214
Southern Pine Blvd	28273
Southern Sugar Dr	28262
Southfield Dr	28273
Southgate Dr	28205
Southgate Commons Dr	28277
Southminster Ln	28216
Southmoor Oaks Ct	28277
Southpark Ln	28210
Southridge Ct	28226
Southside Dr	28217
Southstream Blvd	28217
Southwest Blvd	28216
Southwind Dr	28216
Southwold Dr	28217
Southwood Ave	28203
Southwood Dr	28216
Southwood Oaks Ln	28212
Spalding Pl	28226
Spandril Ln	28215
Spanish Moss Ln	28262
Spanish Oak Rd	28227
Spanish Quarter Cir	28205
Sparkling Brook Ct	28214
Sparrow Springs Ln	28214
Sparrow Valley Way	28214
Sparrowridge Ct	28278
Sparta Ave	28208
Spearmint Dr	28227
Spector Dr	28269
Speedwell Ct	28213
Spencer St	28205
Speyside Ct	28215
Spice Hollow Ct	28277
Spicebush Ct	28215
Spicewood Dr	28227
Spin Drift Ct	28269
Spindle St	28206
Spindletop Pl	28277
Spirea Ct	28215
Spirit Bound Way	28273
Splashwood Ct	28227
Split Oak Dr	28227
Split Pine Ct	28273
Split Rail Ln	28227
Splitrock Ln	28214
Sprague Ave	28205
Spratt St	28206
Spreading Oak Ln	
11400-11599	28226
15000-15099	28278
Spreco Ln	28214
Spring Ln	28213
Spring St	28206
Spring Branch Ct	28227
Spring Camp Way	28277
Spring Creek Ln	28273
Spring Crest Ct	28269
Spring Fall Ct	28213
Spring Fancy Ln	28277
Spring Forest Dr	28208
Spring Frost Ct	28278
Spring Garden Ln	28213
Spring Glen Ave	28212
Spring Harvest Dr	28227
Spring Hollow Way	28277
Spring Lake Dr	28212
Spring Laurel Dr	28215
Spring Lee Ct	28269
Spring Meadow Dr	28227
Spring Morning Ln	28227
Spring Oak Dr	28208
Spring Park Dr	28269
Spring Rain Ct	28278
Spring Ridge Ln	28215
Spring Terrace Ln	28269
Spring Trace Dr	28269
Spring Valley Rd	28210
Springbank Ln	28226
Springbeauty Dr	28227
Springbrook Rd	28217
Springdale Ave	
1600-2337	28203
2339-2399	28203
5300-5499	28227
Springfield Dr	28212
Springfield Gardens Dr	28227
Springfield Valley Rd	28214
Springflower Ct	28262
Springhaven Dr	28269
Springhead Ln	28215
Springhill Rd	28214
Springholm Dr	28278
Springhouse Ln	28211
Springmist Dr	28262
Springmont Ln	28208
Springpoint Ln	28278
Springs Dr	28226
Springs Farm Ln	28226
Springs Mill Rd	28277
Springs Village Ln	28226
Springset Dr	28212
Springside Ln	28226
Springview Rd	28213
Springway Dr	28205
Springwood Ln	28210
Sprinkle Ln	28273
Spruce St	28203
Spruce Knob Ln	28214
Spruce Mountain Rd	28214
Spruce Peak Rd	28278
Spruce Pine Pl	28210
Sprucewood Rd	28278
Spur Ranch Rd	28277
Spurs Ranch Rd	28277
Spurwig Ct	28278
Spyglass Pl	28214
Squire Dr	28211
Squirrel Hill Rd	28213
Squirrel Hollow Ln	28270
Squirrel Nest Ln	28227
Squirrel Trail Ln	28269
Squirrels Foot Ct	28217
Sretaw Dr	28210
St Clair Dr	28270
St Croix Ln	28277
St Frances Dr	28269
St Ives Pl	28211
St John St	28216
St Johns Church Rd	28215
St Michaels Ln	28227
St Moritz Ln	28226
St Paul St	28216
Stable Ct	28216
Staccato St	28270
Stacy Blvd	28209
Stafford Cir	28211
Stafford Dr	28208
Stafford Rd	28215
Stafford Oaks Ave	28213
Staffordshire Ln	28213
Stags Leap Ct	28277
Stainsby Ln	28273
Stallion Ct	28215
Stallions Glen Ln	28277
Stallworth Dr	28226
Stamey Cir	28209
Stanborough Ct	28262
Stancill Pl	28205
Standing Stone Ct	28210
Standing Wood Ct	28227
Standish Pl	28216
Stanette Dr	28277
Stanfield Dr	28210
Stanford Pl	28207
Stanley Ave	28205
Stanton Green Ct	28277
Stanwyck Ct	28211
Stapleton Ln	28270
Star Hill Ln	28214
Starbrook Dr	28210
Starcrest Dr	28210
Stardust Dr	
4300-4599	28269
5600-5699	28216
Starflower Dr	28215
Stargard Ct	28270
Stargaze Ln	28269
Stargrass Ct	28213
Starhaven Dr	28215
Starita Rd	
1500-2099	28206
2300-2899	28269
Starkwood Dr	28212
Starling Ct	28213
Starlite Pl	28210
Starmount Ave	28269
Starmount Cove Ln	28210
Starnes Rd	28214
Starnes Randall Rd	28215
Starr Neely Rd	28273
Starvalley Dr	28210
Starwood Ave & Dr	28215
State St	28208
Stateline Rd	28273
Stately Oak Ln	28227
Statesman Dr	28227
Statesville Ave	28206
Statesville Rd	28269
Stedwick Pl	28211
Steed Ct	28269
Steel Gardens Blvd	28205
Steel Yard Ct	28205
Steele Creek Rd	
6800-8399	28217
8400-12899	28273
12900-12998	28278
12901-13799	28273
13000-13798	28273
13800-13899	28278
13900-16499	28273
Steele Creek Place Dr	28273
Steele Meadow Rd	28273
Steele Oaks Dr	28273
Steele Trace Ct	28278
Steeleberry Dr	28217
W Steeleberry Dr	28278
Steelechase Dr	28273
Steelecroft Pkwy	28278
Steelecroft Farm Ln	28278
Steelewood Pl	28269
Steeplechase Rd	28226
Steepleglen Ct	28269
Steepleton Way	28215
Stegall St	28217
Steinbeck Ct	28216
Steiner Pl	28211
Stella Dr	28262
Stem Ct	28227
Stephanie St	28212
Stephen Thompson Ln	28213
Stephendale Dr	28273
Stephens Farm Ln	28269
Stephenson Ct	28277
Stepping Stone Dr	28215
Sterling Ct	28215
Sterling Rd	28209
Sterling Haven Rd	28215
Sterling Magnolia Ct N & S	28211
Sterncrest Pl	28210
Stetson Dr	28262
Stettler View Rd	28210
Steve Chapman Dr	28217
Steven Lorimer Ln	28209
Stevensville Ln	28277
Stewart Creek Blvd	28216
Stewart Ridge St	28277
Stewart Spring Ln	28216
Stewarton Ln	28269
Stewarts Bend Ln	28277
Stewarts Crossing Dr	28215
Still Pond Ct	28214
Stillgreen Ln	28214
Stillmeadow Dr	28277
Stillwater Ln	28227
Stilwell Oaks Cir	28212
Stinson Glen Ln	28214
Stirling Trace Ct	28277
Stirlingshire Ct	28278
Stirrup Ct	28215
Stirrup Ridge Ln	28270
Stockbridge Dr	28210
Stockholm Ct	28273
Stockport Pl	28273
Stocktie Rd	28210
Stockwell Ct	28270
Stockwood Dr	28212
Stoddart Ln	28226
Stokes Ave	28210
Stone Ct	28226
Stone Abbey Pl	28215
Stone Arbor Way	28273
Stone Bluff Ct	28214
Stone Borough Dr	28277
Stone Bunker Dr	28227
Stone Canyon Ln	28227
Stone Creek Ct	28227
Stone Creek Dr	28211
Stone Mountain Ct	28262
Stone Orchard Pl	28209
Stone Park Dr	28269
Stone Porch Rd	28277
Stone Post Rd	28217
Stone Trail Rd	28213
Stonebriar Dr	28277

Stonebridge Ln 28211
Stonebridge Way 28227
Stonebrook Ct 28269
Stonecrest Dr 28212
Stonecroft Park Dr 28226
Stonecrop Ct 28210
Stonedale Ct 28216
Stoneface Rd 28214
Stonefield Dr 28269
Stonefort Ct 28216
Stonegate Dr 28216
Stoneglen Path 28269
Stonegrove Ln 28273
Stonehaven Dr 28215
Stonehenge Ln 28216
Stonehill Ct 28213
Stonehurst Dr 28214
Stoneleigh Ln 28277
Stoneman Pl 28217
Stonemark Dr 28277
Stonemarsh Ct 28269
Stonemill Ct 28226
Stonepath Ln 28277
Stoneridge Rd 28226
Stones Landing St 28278
Stonesthrow Ct 28226
E Stonewall St 28202
Stonewood Dr 28210
Stoney Branch Dr 28216
Stoney Corner Ln 28210
Stoney Creek Ln 28262
Stoney Garden Dr 28269
Stoney Glen Dr 28227
Stoney Hill Ln 28277
Stoney Meadow Dr 28227
Stoney Place Ct 28262
Stoney Point Ln 28210
Stoney Pond Ln 28227
Stoney Ridge Trl 28210
Stoney Run Ct 28269
Stoney Trace Dr 28227
Stoney Valley Ct 28269
Stoneybrook Rd 28205
Stoneykirk Ln 28269
Stoneyridge Dr 28214
Stonier Ct 28226
Stonington Ln 28227
Stony Path Dr 28214
Stonyford Pl 28216
Storehouse Rd 28227
Stornoway Ct 28227
Stourbridge Lion Dr 28213
Stourton Ln 28226
Stowe Ln 28262
Stowe Acres Dr 28262
Stowe Derby Dr 28278
Stowmarket Pl 28216
Stoxmeade Dr 28227
Stradbrook Dr 28210
Strangford Ave 28215
Stratford Ave 28205
Stratford Hall Ct 28227
Stratford Park Ct 28210
Strathmoor Dr 28277
Strawberry Ln 28277
Strawberry Hill Dr 28211
Strawberry Patch St 28208
Strawberry Point Dr 28215
Stream Bank Dr 28269
Stream Ridge Dr 28269
Streamside Dr 28212
Streatham Ln 28262
Streator Ct 28216
Strickland Ct 28277
Strider Dr 28212
Stringfellow Ln 28278
Stripes Ct 28217
Strollaway Rd 28278
Stromley Dr 28262
Stronvar House Ln 28277
Stroud Park Ct 28206
Stuart Andrew Blvd 28217
Stuarts Draft Ct 28278
Studley Rd 28212
Studman Branch Ave 28278
Sturbridge Dr 28214

Sturkie Ct 28277
Subira Ln 28215
Suburban Dr 28269
Sudbury Rd 28205
Suffield Ct 28269
Suffolk Pl 28211
E Sugar Creek Rd
100-699 28213
700-1699 28205
W Sugar Creek Rd
100-1299 28213
1300-2899 28262
2901-3099 28262
3200-7499 28269
Sugar Hollow Dr 28214
Sugar Loaf Ct 28210
Sugar Maple Ln 28215
Sugar Mill Rd 28210
Sugar Oats Ln 28213
Sugarberry Dr 28269
Sugarbush Dr 28214
Sugarcane Ct 28227
Sugarstone Ln 28269
Sugarwood Dr 28226
Sulkirk Rd 28210
Sulky Plough Rd 28277
Sulleyfield Pl 28273
Sullins Rd 28214
Sullivan Dr 28215
Sullivan Ridge Dr 28277
Sullivans Trace Dr 28217
Sulstone Ln 28210
Sultana Cir 28227
Sumac Dr 28211
Summer Pl 28213
Summer Breeze Ct 28277
Summer Club Rd 28277
Summer Coach Dr 28216
Summer Creek Ln 28269
Summer Darby Ln 28270
Summer Gate Dr 28226
Summer House Ct 28210
Summer Meadow Ct 28216
Summer Oaks Dr 28212
Summer Valley Ct 28269
Summerberry Ct 28277
Summercrest Ct 28269
Summercroft Ln 28269
Summerford Dr 28269
Summerglen Cir 28227
Summergold Way 28269
Summerhill Dr 28212
Summerhill Ridge Dr 28226
Summerlake Rd 28226
Summerlea Dr 28214
Summerlin Pl 28226
Summermore Dr 28270
Summerour Pl 28214
Summerpond Ct 28226
Summerston Pl 28277
Summertree Ln
6200-6299 28226
6400-6599 28270
Summerville Rd 28214
Summerwood Ln 28270
Summey Ave 28205
N Summit Ave 28216
S Summit Ave 28208
W Summit Ave 28203
Summit Commons Blvd 28277
Summit Greenway Ct 28208
Summit Hills Dr 28214
Summit Walk Dr 28270
Summitt Tree Ct 28277
Sumner Green Ave 28203
Sumner Hall Ln 28226
Sumter Ave 28208
Sun Meadow Ln 28214
Sun Mist Ln 28210
Sun Ray Ct 28212
Sun Valley Ln 28226
Sunbeam Ln 28269
Sunbow Ln 28277
Sunbridge Ct 28269
Sunburst Ln 28213

Sunbury Ln 28211
Sunchaser Ln 28210
Suncrest Ct 28215
Sundance Ct 28277
Sundance Meadow Ct 28278
Sunderland Pl 28211
Sundew Ct 28215
Sundial Ln 28206
Sundown Ln 28226
Sunfield Dr 28215
Sunflower Rd 28227
Sunflower Valley Dr 28278
Sunglow Ct 28212
Sunhaven Ct 28262
Suninghurst Ln 28277
Sunlea Ln 28212
Sunlit Ln 28273
Sunman Rd 28216
Sunningdale Ct 28226
Sunningdale Dr 28277
Sunninghill Park Rd 28277
Sunny Glen Way 28278
Sunnybrook Dr 28210
Sunnycrest Ln 28217
Sunnyfield Ct 28215
Sunnymede Ln 28209
Sunnyside Ave 28204
Sunnyvale Ln 28210
Sunnywood Ln 28270
Sunpath Cir 28269
Sunridge Ln 28215
Sunrise Ct 28212
Sunrise View Dr 28278
Sunset Blvd 28269
Sunset Cir 28216
Sunset Dr
2700-3299 28209
4300-7899 28227
Sunset Rd
1100-4699 28216
4801-4897 28269
4899-5399 28269
Sunset Chase Ln 28212
Sunset Greens Dr 28216
Sunset Hill Rd 28227
Sunset Oaks Dr 28216
Sunset Ridge Ct 28269
Sunset Village Dr 28216
Sunstar Ct 28226
Sunstone Dr 28269
Sunswept Ln 28226
Suntrace Way 28269
Sunview Dr 28210
Sunwalk Ct 28269
Sunway Dr 28227
Superior St 28273
Surface Hill Rd 28227
Surrey Rd 28227
Surreyhill Ct 28270
Surreywood Pl 28270
Surry Ct 28227
Surry Ridge Ct 28210
Susan Dr 28215
Susan St 28208
Susanna Dr 28214
Sussex Ave 28210
Sussex Sq N 28227
Sussex Sq S 28227
Suther Rd 28213
Sutherby Dr 28277
Sutherlin Forest Ct 28215
Sutter Creek Ln 28227
Sutters Hill Ct 28269
Suttle Ave 28208
Sutton Dr 28216
Sutton Springs Rd 28226
Suttonview Dr 28269
Swallow Ln 28273
Swallow Tail Ln 28269
Swan Dr 28216
Swan Lake Ln 28277
Swan Meadow Ln 28226
Swanee Ln 28273
Swank Pl 28216
Swann Branch Dr 28273
Swanquarter Dr 28262

Swans Run Rd 28226
Swansong Ln 28213
Swanston Dr 28269
Swayers Mill Rd 28262
Swearngan Rd 28216
Swearngan Ridge Ct 28216
Sweden Rd 28273
Swedish Ivy Ln 28227
Sweet Bing Ct 28262
Sweet Cedar Ln 28210
Sweet Fern Way 28273
Sweet Flag Ct 28262
Sweet Grove Ct 28269
Sweet Oak Ct 28210
Sweet Plum Dr 28215
Sweet Rose Ct 28269
Sweet Sage Ln 28227
Sweetbriar St 28205
Sweetbriar Ridge Dr 28269
Sweetfield Dr 28269
Sweetgrass Ln 28226
Sweetgum Ln 28211
Sweethoney Cir 28227
Sweetleaf Pl 28278
Sweetspire Rd 28215
Sweetwater Ct 28227
Swift Arrow Ln 28214
Swindon Ct 28215
Swinford Pl 28270
Swing Ln 28226
Swinstead Pl 28227
Swiss Holw 28227
Swordgate Dr 28226
Sycaberry Ln 28227
N & S Sycamore St 28202
Sycamore Berry Ct 28227
Sycamore Club Dr 28227
Sycamore Creek Ct 28227
Sycamore Creek Dr 28273
Sycamore Green Pl 28202
Sycamore Grove Ct 28227
Sycamore Hill Ln 28277
Sydenham Ct 28277
Sydney Dr 28270
Sydney Overlook Ln 28269
Sylvan Dr 28269
Sylvan Oak Way 28273
Sylvania Ave 28206
Sylvia Ct 28205
Symphony Rd 28216
Symphony Woods Dr 28269
Syracuse Dr 28216
Sythe Ct 28226
Tabcat Ct 28273
Table Rock Rd 28226
Tabor Ln 28211
Tacoma St 28208
Taftnale Ct 28214
Taggart Creek Rd 28208
Taggert Ct 28215
Taggert Trail Dr 28273
Tahoe Dr 28273
Taimi Dr 28214
Takeridge Ct 28277
Talbany Pl 28215
Talbert Paige Ct 28277
Talcott Dr 28227
Taliesin Ct 28204
Tall Cedar Ct 28273
Tall Meadow Rd 28214
Tall Oak Pl 28226
Tall Oaks Trl 28210
Tall Tree Ln 28214
Tallard Ln 28270
Tallia Ct 28269
Tallu Rd 28269
Tallwood Ct 28216
Tally Ho Ct 28212
Talmage Ct 28211
Talus Trace Ln 28215
Talwyn Ct 28269
Tamalpais Ct 28215
Tamarack Dr 28278
Tamarron Dr 28277
Tamerlane 28205
Tamora Dr 28227

Tamworth Dr 28210
Tanager Ln 28269
Tanager Park Dr 28269
Tanbridge Rd 28226
Tangle Dr 28211
Tanglebriar Dr 28208
Tanglebrook Ln 28216
Tanglewood Ln 28211
Tangley Ct NW 28269
Tannehill Ct 28226
Tanner Hl 28227
Tanneron Pl 28226
Tanners Ct 28262
Tansy Dr 28214
Tantilla Cir 28215
Tanton Ln 28273
Tanyard Ln 28217
Taos Ct 28277
Tapestry Ct 28262
Tapestry Woods Ct 28273
Tappan Pl 28205
Tapperty Cir 28226
Tar Heel Rd 28208
Tara Dr 28211
Tara Ln 28213
Tara Glenn Ct 28277
Tara Oaks Dr 28227
Tara Pines Ct 28270
Taragate Dr 28273
Taralyn Meadows Dr 28214
Taranasay Ct 28269
Taras Ridge Ln 28214
Tarby Ct 28269
Tarentaise Pl 28273
Tarland Ln 28269
Tarleton Twins Ter 28270
Tarpan Ct 28216
Tarpway Rd 28269
Tarrington Ave 28205
Tarrymore Pl 28270
Tarrywood Ln 28205
Tartan Ct 28212
Tartan Green Ct 28227
Tartarian Ct 28215
Tasse Pl 28262
Tate St 28216
Tattersall Dr 28210
Tatum Rd 28214
Taurus Dr 28205
Tauten Ct 28269
Tavernay Pkwy 28262
Tayland Cellers St 28277
Taylor Ave 28216
Taylor Ridge Ln 28273
Taylorford Pl 28277
Taymouth Ln 28269
Tayport Dr 28278
Tea Rose Ln 28262
Teaberry Ct 28227
Teague Ln 28215
Teakwood Dr 28217
Teal Point Dr 28205
Tealridge Ln 28277
Teaneck Pl 28215
Teasdale Ln 28277
Technology Dr 28262
Teddington Dr 28214
Tedorill Ln 28226
Teeter Dr 28215
Television Pl 28205
Telfair Rd 28210
Telfair Meadow Dr 28227
Telford Pl 28205
Telscombe Ct 28273
Tema Cir 28214
Tempest Pl 28216
Temple Ln 28205
Templeton Ave 28203
Tempo St 28278
Tempsford Ln 28210
Ten Trees Ln 28269
Tenby Ct 28226
Tench St 28214
Tendring Ct 28215
Tenencia Ct 28277
Tenille Pl 28227

Tennessee Ave 28216
Tennille Ct 28212
Tennyson Dr 28208
Tensbury Ct 28210
Teresa Ave 28214
Teresa Ln 28216
Teresa Jill Dr 28213
Terianti Dr 28215
Terissa Dr 28214
Terminal St 28208
Termini Dr 28262
Terra Cotta Dr 28215
Terra Linda Ln 28215
Terrace Dr 28211
Terrace View Ct 28269
Terrebonne Ct 28210
Terrence Pl 28209
Terrick Ct 28273
Terrier Way 28269
Terry Ln 28215
Terrybrook Ln 28205
Terryglass Ln 28278
Tesh Ct 28269
Tessava Ct 28210
Tessera Dr 28214
Teton Trl 28269
Teversham Ln 28210
Tew Ct 28270
Tewkesbury Rd 28269
Texas Ct 28208
Texland Blvd 28273
Textile Way
1900-1998 28208
2900-2999 28205
Thackery Ln 28205
Thackmore Ln 28213
Thalia Dr 28262
Thamesmead Ln 28227
Thatcher Ct 28262
Thatcher Hall Ct 28277
Thaxton Pl 28226
Thayer Rd 28214
The Grn 28277
The Plz
1100-1234 28205
1233-1233 28299
1233-1233 28207
1235-4399 28205
1236-4398 28205
4400-8199 28215
Thelema Ln 28269
Thelo Dr 28212
Thera Dr 28206
Theran Ln 28278
Thermal Rd
1400-1499 28212
6100-7499 28211
Thetford Ct 28211
Thicket Ct 28273
Thistle Ct 28211
Thistle Bloom Ct 28269
Thistle Field Ln 28273
Thistledown Ct 28269
Thistlewood Cir 28273
Thomas Ave 28205
Thomas Rd 28278
Thomas Payne Cir 28277
Thomas Ridge Dr 28269
Thomasboro Dr 28208
Thomashire Ct 28262
Thomasson Place Cir 28213
Thompson Ave 28227
Thompson Rd
5500-5899 28216
13600-16599 28227
Thompson St 28216
Thompson Brook Ln 28212
Thompson Farm Ln 28278
Thompson Greens Ln 28212
Thompson Place Dr 28227
Thoreau Ct 28214
Thorn Blade Dr 28270
Thorn Bluff Rd 28214
Thorn Hill Ln 28208
Thorn Tree Ct 28210
Thornbird Dr 28227

Thornbriar Ct 28277
Thornbrook Pl 28269
Thornbush Ct 28270
Thorncliff Dr 28210
Thorncrest Rd 28277
Thorncrown St 28214
Thornfield Rd
2100-2299 28217
2400-2599 28273
Thornhaven Ct 28212
Thornhill Club Dr 28277
Thornridge Rd 28226
Thornton Rd 28208
Thornton Oaks Ct 28270
Thornwood Rd 28213
Thorpe Ct 28270
Thorson Hill Ct 28212
Thousand Oaks Ct 28227
Threatt Woods Dr 28277
Three Lakes Dr 28277
Three Rivers Ct 28273
Three Sisters Ln 28227
Three Vistas Ct 28277
Thrift Rd 28208
Thriftwood Dr 28208
Thurles Ct 28270
Thurmond Pl 28205
Thurmont Ct 28277
Thyme Ct 28214
Tiara Ln 28212
Tibble Creek Way 28227
Tiburon Cir 28215
Tichborne Rd 28278
Ticino Ln 28227
Tiergarten Ln 28210
Tiffani Ln 28210
Tiffany Crest Ct 28227
Tiffany Rose Pl 28206
Tifton Rd 28226
Tifton Grass Ln 28269
Tiger Ln 28262
Tiger Lily Ln 28215
Tigerton Ln 28269
Tigress Ct 28273
Tilbury Ct 28212
Tilden Rd 28214
Tileston Ct 28270
Tillery Dr 28226
Tillman Rd 28208
Timahoe Ln 28278
Timber Ln 28270
Timber Commons Ln 28212
Timber Creek Ct 28227
Timber Crossing Rd 28213
Timber Falls Ct 28273
Timber Hill Ct 28226
Timber Hollow Dr 28205
Timber Lake Dr 28227
Timber Oaks Ln 28212
Timber Ridge Dr 28227
Timber Ridge Rd 28213
Timber Springs Dr 28212
Timberbluff Dr 28216
Timberbrook Dr 28208
Timbercrest Cir 28226
Timberline Rd 28210
Timberneck Ct 28277
Timbertop Ln 28215
Timberway Dr 28213
Timblin Ct 28277
Timeplanner Dr 28206
Timmons Ct 28227
Timothy Ct 28277
Tindle Hill Ln 28216
Tinkerbell Ln 28210
Tinkerton Ct 28227
Tinnahinch Rd 28278
Tinnin Ave 28206
Tioga Ln 28273
Tippah Ave 28205
Tippah Park Ct 28205
Tipperary Pl 28215
Tipperlinn Way 28278
Tipton Dr 28206
Tirano Ct 28216
Tirling Ct 28215

Titleist Dr 28277
Tiverton Pl 28215
Tivoli Ct 28211
Toal St 28206
Toano Rd 28215
Tobin Ct 28211
Toby Ct 28213
E Todd Ln 28208
W Todd Ln 28208
Todd Rd
300-399 28208
8300-8599 28214
8601-8699 28214
Toddington Ln 28270
Toddville Rd 28214
Toddway Ln 28214
Tolland Ln 28277
Tolleson Ave 28277
Tolliver Dr 28277
Toluca Pl 28208
Tom Castain Ln 28226
Tom Hunter Rd 28213
Tom Query Rd 28213
Tom Sadler Rd 28214
Tom Short Rd 28277
Tomahawk Ln 28214
Tomlin Green Ln 28277
Tompkins Rd 28227
Tomsie Efird Ln 28269
Tonawanda Dr 28277
Tony Ct 28214
Toomey Ave 28203
Top Seed Ct 28226
Topeka Dr 28227
Topping Pl 28209
Topsail Ct 28212
Topsfield Rd 28211
Tor Dr 28269
Torchbearer Ln 28278
Toringdon Way 28277
Torphin Ct 28269
Torrelle Dr 28277
Torrence St 28269
N Torrence St 28204
S Torrence St 28204
Torrence Branch Rd 28278
Torrence Grove Church Rd 28213
Torrey Pines Ct 28226
Torrington Ln 28262
Torry Pines Dr 28227
Tortola Rd 28214
Tory Pl 28215
Toscana Ln 28278
Toscana Way 28273
Tottenham Rd 28226
Totteridge Dr 28277
Touch Me Not Ln 28216
Touchstone Ln 28227
Touchwood Dr 28227
Toullousse St 28277
Tower Ct 28209
Tower Point Dr 28227
Towering Pine Dr 28269
Towering Pine Way 28208
Towhee Ct 28269
Towill Pl 28211
Town And Country Dr 28226
Townes Rd 28209
Townsbury Pl 28215
Townsend Ave 28205
Township Rd 28273
Towton Ct 28262
Toxaway Ln 28269
Trace Chain Ln 28278
Tracewood Ct 28215
Tracy Ave 28214
Tracy Dr 28217
Tracy Glenn Ct 28269
Tradd Ct 28210
E Trade St 28202
W Trade St
100-1099 28202
1400-2299 28216
2500-3100 28208
3102-3198 28208

Trade Park Ct 28217
Tradewinds Ln 28226
Trading Path Way 28277
Tradition View Dr 28269
Traditional Ln 28211
Traherne Ct 28213
Trail View Dr 28226
Trailer Dr 28269
Trailhead Ct 28227
Trailing Rock Dr 28214
Trailmoor Rd 28278
Trailwater Rd 28278
Tralee Pl 28262
Trammel Ln 28227
Tranquil Ave 28209
Tranquil Point Way 28215
Tranquillity Dr 28216
Transport Dr 28269
Tranters Creek Ln 28273
Trapper Ct 28270
Trappers Creek Ct 28270
Travelers Ct 28226
Travers Run Dr 28215
Travis Ave 28204
Travis Floyd Ln 28214
Travis Gulch Dr 28277
Travis Reid Ln 28227
Traymore Ln 28278
Tree Canopy Rd 28277
Tree Haven Dr 28270
Treebark Dr 28226
Treebranch Dr 28216
Treefrog Ct 28262
Treeline Pl 28215
Treetop Ct 28212
Trefoil Dr 28226
Trehurst Ct 28269
Trellis Pointe Blvd 28227
Tremaine Ct 28227
Trembeth Dr 28205
E & W Tremont Ave 28203
Tremont Place Rd 28227
Trent St 28209
Trentle Ct 28211
Trenton Pl 28226
Trentsby Pl 28216
Trentwood Pl 28216
Tresanton Dr 28210
Trescott Ct 28212
Tresevant Ave 28208
Tresham Ct 28215
Tressel Ln 28227
Trevor Ct 28270
Trexler Ave 28269
Trey View Ct 28227
Treyburn Dr 28216
Treyford Ln 28270
Treymore Ln 28262
Triangle Dr 28208
Triangle Park Rd 28277
Tribal Dr 28214
Tribecca St 28270
Tribune Dr 28214
Trickling Water Ct 28273
Triece Ln 28215
Trillium Ln 28211
Trillium Fields Dr 28269
Trimbach Way 28269
Trimmings Ct 28226
Trinity Rd 28216
Triple J Ct 28227
Triple Oak Rd 28277
Tripp Pl 28277
Tripper Ln 28226
Tristan Ct 28213
Tritton Pl 28227
Triveny Rd 28226
Troika Ct 28277
Trojan Dr 28278
Troon Ln 28214
Tross St 28205
Trossacks Ct 28212
Trotter Rd 28216
Trotters Ridge Rd 28227
Trout Ln 28214
Trowbridge Ct 28270

Trudie Ln 28227
Truelight Church Rd 28227
Truesdale Pl 28277
Truewood Dr 28227
Trull St 28216
Truman Rd 28205
Trumble Ln 28262
Truscott Rd 28226
Tryclan Dr 28217
S Tryon 28285
N Tryon St
100-798 28202
101-101 28246
103-799 28202
800-4299 28206
4300-6701 28213
6700-6700 28256
6702-7098 28213
6703-7099 28213
7100-7399 28262
7400-7498 28213
7400-12298 28262
7401-12299 28262
S Tryon St
101-101 28280
103-299 28202
112-112 28284
114-210 28202
212-212 28281
214-998 28202
301-301 28282
303-999 28202
1000-2999 28203
3000-7799 28217
7800-12899 28273
12900-15500 28278
15502-15598 28278
Trysting Rd 28227
Tuckalake Dr 28215
Tuckaseegee Rd
700-6099 28208
6100-8100 28214
8102-8498 28214
Tucker St 28269
Tucker Crossing Ln 28273
Tuckerbunn Dr 28270
Tuckers Glen Ln 28216
Tuckton Ct 28262
Tuffy Ln 28278
Tufnell Ct 28262
Tufton Ct 28215
Tufton Brae Ct 28226
Tufts Dr 28227
Tulane St 28205
Tulip Hill Dr 28270
Tulip Point Ct 28213
Tulip Tree Ln 28273
Tullamore Ln 28269
Tullamore Park Cir 28226
Tulloch Rd 28278
Tullock Creek Dr 28269
Tully House Ct 28277
Tumbleweed Ct 28208
Tunnel Rd 28208
Tunston Ln 28269
Tupelo Ln 28269
Turkey Hill Rd 28277
Turkey Oak Dr 28227
Turkey Point Dr 28214
Turley Ridge Ln 28273
Turmeric Ct 28215
Turn Stone Ct 28226
Turnabout Pl 28269
Turnberry Ln 28210
Turnbridge Rd 28226
N Turner Ave 28216
S Turner Ave 28208
Turney Rd 28269
Turning Hawk Rd 28277
Turning Leaf Ct 28262
Turning Oak Dr 28208
Turning Point Ln 28277
Turning Stick Ct 28213
Turning Wheel Dr 28214
Turquoise Dr 28215
Turtle Creek Ln 28273
Turtle Cross Ln 28269

Turtle Neck Ln 28227
Turtle Point Rd
2000-2299 28262
16500-17099 28278
Turtle Rock Ct 28277
Turtleback Ct 28269
Tuskan Dr 28270
Tutor St 28227
Tuttle Bee Ct 28273
Tuxedo Ct 28211
Tweed Rd 28278
Tweedsmuir Glen Ln 28215
Twelve Oaks Pl 28270
Twelvestone Ct 28269
Twickingham Ct 28212
Twiford Pl 28207
Twilight Dr 28227
Twilight Rd 28210
Twilight Hill Ct 28277
Twillingate Dr 28215
Twin Dr & Ln 28269
Twin Ash Ct 28214
Twin Brook Dr
1700-1799 28208
5400-6099 28269
Twin Creek Dr 28262
Twin Eagles Ct 28278
Twin Falls Ct 28227
Twin Lakes Pkwy 28269
Twin Oaks Pl 28212
Twin Ridge Dr 28210
Twined Creek Ln 28227
Twinfield Dr 28216
Twinleaf Ct 28227
Twisted Bark Ln 28213
Twisted Oaks Rd 28212
Twisted Pine Dr 28269
Two Moons Dr 28212
Twynham Ln 28226
Tyler Brook Ln 28227
Tyler Finley Way 28269
Tyler Trail Ct 28262
Tyndale Ave 28210
Tyne Ct 28210
Tyner St 28262
Tyng Way 28211
Tynwald Ct 28278
Tynwald Ln 28227
Tyrone Dr 28215
Tyson St 28209
Tyvola Dr 28210
Tyvola Rd
400-1199 28217
1300-2300 28210
2302-3198 28210
W Tyvola Rd
100-2899 28217
3801-3897 28208
3899-4699 28208
Tyvola Centre Dr 28217
Tyvola Glen Cir 28217
Umar Ct 28215
Umbrella Ln 28278
Umstead St 28205
Unaka Ave 28205
Underwood Ave 28213
Uninchen Dr 28210
Union St 28205
Union Pacific Ave 28210
Union School Rd 28262
Union Station Ct 28210
University Dr 28209
University Center Blvd 28262
University Church Dr 28216
University City Blvd 28213
University Commercial Pl 28213
University East Dr 28213
University Exec Park Dr 28262
University Heights Ln 28213
University Park Ln 28213
University Pointe Blvd 28262
University Station Cir 28269
University Terrace Dr 28262
University Village Blvd 28262

Univrsty Rdge Dr 28213
Univrsty Wlk Cir 28213
Upas Ln 28227
Uphill Ct 28269
Upper Asbury Ave 28206
Uppergate Ln 28215
Upsall Ct 28215
Urban Pl 28209
Urbana Dr 28214
Us Highway 29 28262
Uxbridge Woods Ct 28205
Vagabond Rd 28227
Vail Ave 28207
Valcourt Rd 28216
Valencia Ter
2000-2700 28226
2702-2798 28226
2800-3299 28211
Valendra Dr 28215
Valentine Ln 28270
Valerian Ct 28213
Valerie Dr 28216
Valeview Ln 28269
Valewood Ct 28210
Valhalla Ct 28269
N Valley Ct 28273
Valley Rd 28270
Valley Forge Rd 28210
Valley Grove Rd 28227
Valley Haven Dr 28211
Valley Oak St 28277
Valley Ridge Rd 28214
Valley Spring Dr 28277
Valley Stream Rd 28209
Valleybrook Rd 28270
Valleydale Rd 28214
Valleymoon Ln 28214
Valleyview Dr
2300-2499 28215
2500-2699 28212
4601-4699 28215
Valleywood Pl 28216
Valmere Dr 28227
Valrose Dr 28216
Van Ave 28269
Van Buren Ave 28216
Van De Rohe Dr 28215
Van Dyke Dr 28213
Van Every St 28205
Vance Rd 28216
Vance Davis Dr 28269
Vancouver Dr 28213
Vandalia Dr 28212
Vanderbilt Rd 28206
Vanderbrook Rd 28215
Vanderhorn Ln 28226
Vane Ct 28206
Vanhoy Ln 28269
Vanizer St 28208
Vantage Pl 28216
Vardall Ct 28226
Varden Ct 28208
Variety Ln 28278
Varsity Ln 28262
Varsovie Ct 28278
Vasser Pl 28216
Vaughan Dr 28273
Vauxhall Ct 28226
Veckman Ct 28269
Venado St 28215
Vendue Pl 28226
Ventana Ct 28277
Ventner Ct 28214
Ventosa Dr 28205
Ventura Ave 28216
Ventura Way Dr 28213
Vera Ct 28217
Vera Jones Ln 28213
Veramonte Ct 28227
Verbena St 28217
Verdant Ct 28273
Verdas Path 28227
Verde Ct 28215
Verde Creek Rd 28214
Verdugo Dr 28277
Verdun Dr 28210

Verese Ct 28216
Vermel Ct 28216
Vermilion Dr 28215
Vernazza Pl 28277
Vernedale Rd 28212
Vernedale Glen Dr 28212
Verney Ln 28226
Vernon Dr 28211
Vernon Wood Ln 28262
Verns Ave 28214
Vero Ln 28215
Veronica Dr 28215
Versage Dr 28227
Versailles Ln 28277
Vescova Ct 28212
Vestal Pl 28212
Vestry Pl 28270
Via Del Compo Rd 28227
Via Romano Dr 28270
Via Siena Dr 28227
Via Sorrento Dr 28277
Viburnum Ct 28215
Viburnum Way Ct 28208
Viceregal Ct 28216
Vickery Dr 28215
Vicksburg Rd 28227
N & S Vicksburg Park Ct 28210
Victoria Ave
100-299 28202
4800-5699 28269
Victoria Mill Ct 28277
Victorian Pl 28203
Victory Ln 28269
Vidal Ln 28226
View Way Dr 28215
Viewmont Dr 28215
Vilandry Way 28273
Villa Ct 28211
Villa Trace Pl 28277
Village Ct 28203
Village Brook Dr 28210
Village Glen Ln 28269
Village Green Dr 28215
Village Lake Dr 28212
Village Pond Dr 28278
Villalonga Ln 28277
Vilma St 28208
Vinca Cir 28213
Vincent Ln 28210
Vine Cliff Ln 28214
Vineleaf Ln 28216
Vinetta Ct 28215
Vinewood Pl 28205
Vineyard Ln 28210
Vineyard Row 28227
Vining Ct 28216
Vinnies Way 28214
Vino Ct 28214
Vinoy Blvd 28262
Vintage Ln 28226
Vinton St 28216
Vinton Ridge Ct 28214
Viola Dr 28215
Violet Dr 28205
Vireo Ct 28269
Virginia Ave 28205
Virginia Cir 28214
Virginia Dare Cir 28277
Virginian Ln 28226
Virkler Dr 28273
Viscount Ln 28269
Vision Dr 28203
Vista Dr 28212
Vista Canyon Dr 28226
Vista Grande Cir 28226
Vista Haven Dr 28226
Vista Verde Ct 28273
Vlosi Dr 28226
Voeltz Dr 28269
Vogel Ct 28206
Volunteer Ct 28213
Volusia Ct 28262
Von Thuringer Ct 28210
Voncannon Dr 28216
Voyager Rd 28214

E W T Harris Blvd
100-899 28262
900-2999 28213
3900-7099 28215
7100-9999 28227
10100-11399 28212
W W T Harris Blvd
100-1999 28262
2200-7099 28269
7800-8499 28216
Wabash Ave 28208
Wabeek Ct 28278
Waco St 28204
Waddell St 28216
Wade Ardrey Rd 28277
Wade E Morgan Rd 28269
Wadebridge Cv 28210
Wading Ln 28215
Wadsworth Pl 28206
Waggoneer Cir 28270
Waggoners Glen Ln 28226
Wagon Oak Rd 28212
Wagon Wheel Ct 28277
Wagonford Ln 28273
Waightstill Way 28277
Wainwright Ave 28206
Wake Dr 28269
Wake St 28216
Wakefield Dr 28209
Wakehurst Rd 28226
Wakeley Ct 28208
Wakerobin Ln 28213
Walcourt Valley Pl 28270
Walden Ct 28210
Walden Ponds Rd 28214
Walden Ridge Dr 28216
Walden Station Dr 28262
Waldon Rd 28214
Waldon Park Ln 28214
Wales Ave 28209
Wales St 28269
Walford Dr 28208
Walker Rd 28211
Walker Branch Rd 28273
Walkers Cove Trl 28214
Walkers Creek Dr 28273
Walkers Crossing Dr 28273
Walkers Down Ct 28273
Walkers Ferry Rd
8500-9999 28214
10000-10899 28278
Walkers Glen Ct 28273
Walkers Meadow Ln 28273
Walking Horse Ln 28215
Walking Path Ln 28213
Walking Stick Dr 28278
Wallace Ave, Ln & Rd 28212
Wallace Cabin Dr 28212
Wallace Creek Ln 28212
Wallace Glen Dr 28212
Wallace Neel Rd 28278
Wallace Ridge Dr 28269
Wallace View Ct 28212
Walland Ln 28273
Waller Way 28210
Walney Ct 28215
Walnut Ave 28208
Walnut Cove Dr 28227
Walnut Creek Ln 28227
Walnut Grove Ln 28227
Walnut Hill Dr 28278
Walnut Park Dr 28262
Walnut Ridge Ct 28217
Walnut Springs Dr 28277
Walnut View Dr 28208
Walnut Wood Dr 28227
Walsh Blvd 28226
Walsham Dr 28277
Walston Ln 28211
Walter St 28208
Walter Nelson Rd 28227
Walterboro Rd 28227
Walthall Ct 28210
Waltham Ct 28269
Waltham Ln 28270
Waltham Pl 28227

Walton Rd 28208
Walton Heath Ln 28277
Wamac Ct 28214
Wamath Dr 28210
Wanamassa Dr 28269
Wandering Brook Dr 28273
Wandering Creek Dr 28216
Wandering Creek Way 28227
Wandering Way Dr 28226
Wanderview Ln 28214
Waneden Ln 28278
Wannamaker Ln 28226
Wapiti Ct 28273
War Eagle Ln 28214
War Emblem Ct 28216
Warbler Ct 28210
Warbler Wood Ct 28269
Warburton Rd 28211
Ware Rd 28212
Wareham Ct 28207
Warehouse Rd 28227
Warewhip Ln 28210
Waring Pl 28277
Warm Springs Ct 28278
Warp St 28205
Warren Rd 28278
Warren Burgess Ln 28205
Warrington Dr 28211
Warwick Cir 28210
Warwick Castle Way 28277
Warwick Crest Ln 28215
Warwickshire Ln 28270
Washburn Ave 28205
Washington Ave 28216
Washington Blvd 28262
Washington Pl 28269
Washoe Pine Ln 28215
Watauga Ave 28208
Watch Hill Ct 28210
Water Ct 28269
Water Haven Ln 28262
Water Mill Ct 28215
Water Oak Rd 28211
Water Ridge Pkwy 28217
Water Walk Ln 28208
Water Wheel Ct 28209
Waterbrook Ln 28277
Waterbury Dr 28209
Watercrest Rd 28210
Waterelm Ln 28269
Waterfall Pl 28278
Waterflower Ln 28262
Waterford Dr 28226
Waterford Creek Ln 28212
Waterford Crest Dr 28226
Waterford Glen Loop 28226
Waterford Hills Dr 28269
Waterford Knoll Dr 28226
Waterford Lakes Dr 28210
Waterford Ridge Dr 28212
Waterford Square Dr 28226
Waterford Tide Loop 28226
Waterford Valley Cir 28269
Waterfowl Ln 28262
Watergate Rd 28270
Waterlily Ln 28262
Waterloo Dr 28269
Waterlyn Dr 28278
Waterlyn Club Dr 28278
Waterman Ave 28205
Watermelon Ln 28278
Watermoss Ln 28262
Waterplace Ln 28273
Waterrock Rd 28214
Waters Point Ct 28277
Waters Trail Dr 28216
Waters Vista Cir 28213
Waterside Dr 28278
Watersreach Ln 28277
Waterstone Ln 28262
Watersway Ct 28214
Waterthrush Pl 28278
Waterton Leas Ct 28269
Watertrace Dr 28278
Watlington Dr 28270
Watson Dr 28208
Watts Dr 28216
Watts Bluff Dr 28213
Wattsdale Ave 28216
Waverly Ave 28203
Waverly Hall Dr 28211
Waverly Lynn Ln 28269
Waverlyglen Ct 28269
Waxahachie Ave 28214
Waxberry Dr 28277
Waxwind Ln 28226
S Way Rd 28215
Waybridge Ln 28210
Waycross Dr 28214
Wayland Dr 28277
Waymart Ln 28278
Wayside Ct 28269
Waywood Ct 28273
Weakly Ct 28212
Wealdstone Ct 28227
Wearn Ct 28206
Weathersford Pl 28213
Weathersford Rd 28227
Weatherstone Cir 28278
Weaver Mill Ln 28226
Weavers Glenn Pl 28262
Weber Ct 28211
Webster Pl 28209
Weddington Ave 28204
Wedge Ct 28277
Wedgedale Dr 28210
Wedgefield Dr 28208
Wedgewood Dr 28210
Wedgewood Commons
Dr 28277
Wednesbury Blvd 28262
Wedron Ct 28216
Weeping Fig Ln 28215
Wegon Ln 28216
Weighmont Ct 28227
Weirton Pl 28226
Welbeck Ct 28215
Welch Pl 28216
Weldon Ave 28205
Welford Rd 28211
Welker St 28204
Well Rd 28227
Well Spring Dr 28262
Welland Trl 28215
Wellesley Ave
1700-1899 28209
2000-2499 28207
Wellhouse Ct 28210
Welling Ave 28208
Wellingford St 28213
Wellington Ct 28211
Wells St 28206
Wellshire Commons
Cir 28277
Wellston Dr 28210
Wellwood Cir 28212
Welwyn Ln 28210
Wembley Ct 28213
Wembley Dr 28205
Wenda Pl 28212
N Wendover Rd
100-922 28211
921-921 28222
923-1299 28211
924-1298 28211
1300-1799 28205
S Wendover Rd 28211
Wendover Heights Cir 28211
Wendover Hill Ct 28211
Wendover Park Ln 28211
Wendwood Ln 28211
Wenlock Cir 28270
Wensley Dr 28210
Wentwater St 28213
Wentworth Pl 28209
Weona Ave 28209
Werburgh St 28209
Wertz Dr 28214
Wesbrook Dr 28214
Wesconnett Dr 28214
Wesley Ave 28205
Wesley Alan Ln 28213
Wesley Heights Way 28208
Wesleyan Ct 28227
Wessix Pl 28226
Wessynton Dr 28226
West Ave 28208
West Blvd
100-899 28203
1100-5799 28208
Westbend Dr 28262
Westbourne Dr 28216
Westbrook Dr
301-797 28202
799-1099 28202
1800-1899 28208
Westbury Rd 28211
Westbury Glen Ct 28262
Westbury Lake Dr 28269
Westbury Woods Dr 28277
Westchester Blvd 28205
Westcliff Dr 28208
Westcott Ter 28270
Westcreek Ct 28227
Westcrest Dr 28208
Westdale Dr 28208
Westerly Hills Dr 28208
Western Gailes Way 28270
Westerwood Dr 28214
Westerwood Village Dr 28214
Westfalen Ct 28216
Westfield Rd
2300-2499 28207
2500-2698 28209
2700-3299 28209
Westgarth Ave 28277
Westgate Ln 28208
Westgrove Dr 28208
Westhall Dr 28278
Westham Ridge Rd 28217
Westhampton Dr 28208
Westhope St 28216
E Westinghouse Blvd 28273
E Westinghouse
Commons Dr 28273
Westlake Dr 28273
Westmill Ln 28277
Westminster Pl 28207
Westmont Dr 28217
Westmoreland Ave 28205
Westnedge Dr 28226
Westoak Dr 28217
Weston St 28209
Weston Woods Ln 28216
Westover St 28205
Westpark Dr 28217
Westport Rd 28208
Westray Ct 28269
Westridge Dr 28208
Weststone Dr 28208
Westway Dr 28208
Westwinds Ct 28214
Westwood Ave 28203
Westwood Pointe Dr 28273
Wet Stone Way 28208
Wetherburn Ln 28262
Wetstone Way 28208
Wexford Ct 28210
Wexford Dr 28227
Wexford Meadows Ln 28262
Weyland Ave 28208
Weymouth Ln 28270
Whaleys Ct 28273
Wharton Ln 28270
Wheat Meadow Ln 28270
Wheat Ridge Rd 28277
Wheatfield Rd 28277
Wheatley Ave 28205
Wheaton Pl N & S 28211
Wheatside Dr 28262
Wheeler Dr 28211
Wheelock Rd 28211
Whetstone Ct 28226
Whiffletree Rd 28210
Whilden Ct 28211
Whippet Ridge Ct 28217
Whipple Pl 28215
Whipps Cross Ct 28277
Whisnant St 28206
Whisper Trl 28214
Whisper Creek Dr 28277
Whisperfield Ln 28215
Whispering Way 28212
Whispering Brook Ct 28216
Whispering Cove Ct 28214
Whispering Falls Ave 28227
Whispering Forest Dr 28270
Whispering Leaf Ct 28227
Whispering Oaks Dr 28213
Whispering Oaks Ln 28273
Whispering Pines Dr &
Ln 28217
Whispering Willow Ct 28210
Whispering Wind Dr 28277
Whisperwood Pl 28226
Whistlers Chase Dr 28269
Whistlers Knoll Ct 28227
Whistlestop Rd 28210
Whistlewood Ln 28208
Whistley Green Dr 28269
Whistling Duck Ct 28273
Whistling Oak Ct 28269
Whistling Swan Rd 28278
Whiston Grove Ct 28215
Whitby Ln 28211
Whitcomb St 28269
White Ash Ct 28227
White Aspen Pl 28269
White Barn Ct 28273
White Cascade Dr 28269
White Cedar Ct 28213
White Cliffs Dr 28227
White Dove Ct 28277
White Elm Ln 28273
White Feather Ln 28214
White Fish Ln 28214
White Frost Rd 28277
White Hemlock Ln 28270
White Horse Ln 28270
White Mist Ln 28269
White Moon Ct 28213
White Oak Rd 28210
White Pine Ln 28262
White Pine Rd 28215
White Plains Rd 28213
White Rapids Rd 28214
White Rock Ct 28269
White Stag Dr 28269
White Water Falls Dr 28217
White Willow Rd 28273
Whitebark Ct 28262
Whitebridge Ln 28262
Whiteburn Ct 28278
Whitecastle Ct 28277
Whitegate Ln 28269
Whitehall Dr 28208
Whitehall Estates Dr 28273
Whitehall Executive
Center Dr 28273
Whitehall Park Dr 28273
Whitehaven Ave 28208
Whitehawk Hill Rd 28227
Whitehill Dr 28269
Whitehurst Rd 28217
Whitekirk Pl 28277
Whitemarsh Ct 28210
Whitesail Dr 28278
Whitestone Rd 28270
Whitetail Ct 28269
Whitethorn Dr 28277
Whitewater Dr 28214
Whitewater Center
Pkwy 28214
Whitewood Trl 28269
Whitfield Ridge Dr 28277
Whitford Ln 28210
Whithorn Way 28278
Whiting Ave 28205
Whitingham Dr 28215
Whitley Ln 28215
Whitley Moore St 28273
Whitlock Dr 28214
Whitlock Crossing Ct 28273
Whitmire Ln 28227
Whitmore Pond Ln 28270
Whitney Hill Rd 28226
Whitside Ln 28214
Whittel Pl 28216
Whittersham Dr 28262
Whittier Pl 28212
Whittington St 28206
Whittlington Dr 28215
Whitwell Ct 28226
Whitworth Way 28270
Wicked Oak Ln 28216
Wicker Dr 28210
Wickersham Rd 28211
Wickford Pl 28203
Wickham Ln 28208
Wicklow Pl 28205
Wicklow Brook Ct 28277
Wickville Dr 28215
Widgeon Ct 28273
Wigwam Dr 28214
Wilann Dr 28215
Wilbanks Dr 28278
Wilbrown Cir 28217
Wilburn Ct 28277
Wilburn Park Ct 28262
Wilburn Park Ln NW 28269
Wilby Dr 28270
Wilby Hollow Dr 28270
Wilcox St 28203
Wild Azalea Ln 28277
Wild Dogwood Ct 28273
Wild Dove Ln 28277
Wild Duck Ct 28262
Wild Elm Rd 28277
Wild Garden Ct 28269
Wild Heather Ct 28273
Wild Holly Ln 28226
Wild Lark Ct 28210
Wild Meadow Trl 28227
Wild Nursery Ct 28215
Wild Oak Ct 28216
Wild Orchid Ct 28262
Wild Partridge Rd 28226
Wild Rose Ln 28269
Wild Strawberry Dr 28215
Wild Turkey Ln 28214
Wild Willow Ln 28277
Wildberry Ct 28262
Wildbracken Ct 28210
Wildburne Ct 28262
Wilderness Trail Dr 28214
Wildflower Ct 28227
Wildhoney Ln 28227
Wildleaf Ct 28212
Wildlife Rd
1600-2899 28214
10200-12399 28278
Wildwood Ave 28208
Wildwood Dr 28214
Wildwood Muse Ct 28273
Wilford Ct 28277
Wilgrove Mint Hill Rd 28227
Wilgrove Pond Pl 28227
Wilgrove Way Dr 28213
Wilhelmina Ave 28205
Wilkins Terrace Dr 28269
Wilkinson Blvd
1900-6099 28208
6100-9799 28214
Wilklee Dr 28277
Will Hollow Ln 28227
Willamette Valley Dr 28215
Willard St 28208
Willard Farrow Dr 28215
Willesden Ln 28277
Willetta Dr 28217
Willhaven Dr 28211
Willhill Rd 28227
William Caldwell Ave 28213
William Davie Ln 28277
William Ficklen Dr 28269
William Harry Ct 28211
William Harvey Ct 28278
William Penn Ln 28277
William Porter Rd 28277
William Reynolds Dr 28215
William Stowe Dr 28262
William Walker Ct 28278
William Wylie Dr 28215
Williams Rd
6000-6699 28215
10100-11299 28227
11300-11999 28227
Williams Glenn Rd 28273
Williams Pond Ln 28277
Williamsgate Ln 28215
Williamson St 28208
Willie Worrell Dr 28215
Willilyn Ln 28214
Willis St 28204
Willoughby St 28207
Willoughby Run Dr 28277
Willow St 28208
Willow Bark Ct 28210
Willow Bend Cir 28210
Willow Bend Ln 28227
Willow Branch Rd 28227
Willow Bridge Ct 28216
Willow Creek Dr 28270
Willow Crest Dr 28214
Willow Croft Ct 28226
Willow Crossing Dr 28210
Willow Falls Rd 28215
Willow Gate Ln 28215
Willow Green Pl 28206
Willow Haven Ln 28262
Willow Manor Rd 28209
Willow Meadow Ln 28277
Willow Oak Rd 28209
Willow Park Dr 28205
Willow Point Dr 28277
Willow Ridge Rd 28210
Willow Rock Dr 28277
Willow Run Dr 28277
Willow Run Rd 28210
Willow Spring Rd 28215
Willow Tree Ln 28277
Willow Valley Ct 28273
Willowbrae Rd 28226
Willowglen Trl 28215
Willowhurst Ct 28210
Willowick Ct 28226
Willowlake Ct 28227
Willowood Dr 28210
Willows Pond Ct 28277
Willows Wisp Dr 28277
Wills Way 28227
Wilma Lee Ct 28208
Wilmar Blvd 28273
Wilmette Ct 28210
Wilmore Dr 28203
Wilmore Walk Dr 28203
Wilora Lake Rd
5300-5399 28205
5400-6399 28212
Wilora Landing Rd 28212
Wilsham Ct 28226
Wilshire Pl 28205
Wilson Ave 28208
Wilson Dr 28270
Wilson Ln 28206
Wilson St 28213
Wilson Glen Dr 28214
Wilson Grove Rd 28227
Wilson Hall Dr 28277
Wilson Heights Ave 28216
Wilson Ridge Ln 28227
Wilson Woods Dr 28227
Wilton Pl 28227
Wilton Gate Dr 28262
Wiltshire Ln 28262
Wiltshire Manor Dr 28278
Wiltshire Ridge Rd 28269
Wimbledon Rd 28209
Wimbleton Ct 28226
Win Hollow Ct 28215
Winburn Ln 28226
Winchelsea Dr 28212
Winchester St 28208
N Wind Pl 28210
Wind Chime Ct 28208
Wind Flower Ln 28210
Wind Ridge Dr 28277
Windbluff Dr 28277
Windchase Ln 28269
Windemere Ln 28211
Windfern Ct 28226
Windgrove Dr 28273
Windham Pl 28205
Winding Branch Ct 28216
Winding Brook Rd 28226
Winding Canyon Dr 28214
Winding Cedar Trl 28212
Winding Creek Ln 28226
Winding Jordan Ln 28269
Winding Oak Dr 28270
Winding Path Way 28204
Winding River Dr 28214
Winding Way Rd 28226
Winding Wood Ln 28209
Windlock Dr 28270
Windmill Pl 28226
Windrift Rd 28215
Winds Crossing Dr 28273
Windshire Ln 28273
Windsong Dr 28273
Windsor Ave 28209
Windsor Ct 28273
Windsor Dr 28209
Windsor Castle Ln 28277
Windsor Crescent Ct 28226
Windsor Gate Ln 28215
Windsor Ridge Dr 28277
Windstream Ct 28210
Windswept Dr 28226
Windtree Ln 28215
Windus Ct 28273
Windward Cv 28278
Windwood Cir 28226
Windy Creek Dr 28262
Windy Grove Rd 28278
Windy Knoll Ln 28227
Windy Meadow Ln 28269
Windy Ridge Rd 28270
Windy Rock Way 28273
Windy Valley Dr 28208
Windy Wood Ct 28273
Windygap Rd 28278
Windyrush Rd 28226
Winedale Ln 28205
Winery Ln 28227
Winfield Dr 28205
Winford Ln 28262
Wingate Ave 28208
Wingate Dr 28214
Wingdale Dr 28213
Winged Bourne 28210
Winged Elm Ct 28212
Winged Teal Rd
14100-14299 28273
14300-14599 28278
Winged Trail Ct 28277
Wingedfoot Rd 28226
Winget Rd 28278
Winget Pond Rd 28278
Wingfield Ln 28227
Wingfield Pl 28210
Winghaven Dr NW 28269
Winghaven Ln 28210
Wingmont Dr 28269
Wingrave Dr 28270
Wingstone Ln 28262
Winners Cir 28215
Winnifred St 28203
Winnington Cir 28226
Winnipeg Cir 28210
Winona St 28203
Winpole Ln 28273
Winsford Ct 28226
Winsland Ln 28277
Winslet Dr 28277
Winslow Dr 28269
Winslow Green Dr 28210
Winslow Hills Dr 28278
Winsted Ct 28262
Winston Dr 28205
Winston St 28206
Winston Hall Ct 28277

Winston Oaks Ct 28213
Winter St 28205
Winter Elm Ln 28227
Winter Hazel Rd 28278
Winter Heath Way 28227
Winter Moss Ct 28227
Winter Oaks Ln 28210
Winter Park Ct 28216
Winter Pine Ln 28269
Winter View Ct 28269
Winterberry Pl 28210
Winterbourne Ct 28277
Wintercrest Ln 28209
Winterfield Pl 28205
Wintergreen Dr 28211
Winterhaven Dr 28212
Winterset Dr 28270
Wintersweet Ln 28277
Winterwind Ct 28213
Winterwood Pl 28215
Winthorp Ridge Rd 28270
Winthrop Ave 28203
Winthrop Chase Dr 28212
Winyah Bay Ln 28278
Wisbech Ct 28215
Wiseman Dr 28227
Wishing Well Ln 28270
Wisley Blvd 28226
Wismar Ct 28270
Wister Pl 28210
Wisteria Dr 28210
Witham Ct 28270
Witham Psge 28215
Wither Steele Ct 28273
Withers Rd 28278
Withers Cove Rd 28278
Withers Cove Park Dr 28278
Withers Mill Dr 28278
Withershinn Dr 28262
Wittstock Dr 28210
Woburn Rd 28277
Woffington Ct 28273
Wolf Creek Trl 28269
Wolf Den Ln 28277
Wolf Run Dr 28277
Wolf Trap Ct 28210
Wolfberry St 28206
Wolfe St 28205
Wolfe Ridge Rd 28210
Wolverine Ct 28213
Wondering Oak Ln 28269
Wonderland Ct 28215
Wonderwood Dr 28211
Wood Ct 28277
Wood Beam Ct 28227
Wood Branch Dr 28273
Wood Dale Ter 28203
Wood Duck Crossing Dr 28278
Wood Edge Ct 28227
Wood Lake Ct 28210
Wood Meadow Dr 28227
Wood Ridge Dr 28277
Wood Valley Ln 28270
Wood Vista Dr 28216
Wood Warbler Dr 28278
Woodard St 28269
Woodbend Dr 28212
Woodberry Rd 28212
Woodberry Trail Ln 28262
Woodbine Ln 28210
Woodbourne Ln 28273
Woodbriar Trl 28205
Woodbridge Rd 28227
Woodbridge Valley Cir 28227
Woodbrook Ln 28211
Woodchuck Rd 28270
Woodcliff Ct 28277
Woodcock Ln 28216
Woodcreek Dr 28226
Woodcrest Ave 28203
Woodcroft Ct 28213
Wooden Peg Ct 28273
Wooden Rail Ln 28227
Woodend Ct 28277
Woodfield Dr 28215
Woodfire Rd 28269
Woodford Bridge Dr 28216
Woodfox Dr 28277
Woodgate Ln 28226
Woodglen Ln 28226
Woodgreen Ter 28205
Woodhaven Rd 28211
Woodhill Ln 28205
Woodhill Manor Ct 28215
Woodhollow Rd 28227
Woodhurst Ln 28227
Woodington Ln 28214
Woodknoll Dr 28217
Woodland Ave 28227
Woodland Cir 28216
Woodland Dr 28205
Woodland Ln 28214
Woodland Commons Dr 28269
Woodland Cove Ct 28216
Woodland Farm Dr 28215
Woodland Hills Rd 28269
Woodland Park Ln 28214
Woodland Ridge Ln 28278
Woodland Watch Ct 28277
Woodlands Pointe Dr 28216
Woodlark Ln 28211
E Woodlawn Rd
100-399 28217
400-1999 28209
2001-2099 28209
W Woodlawn Rd 28217
Woodleaf Rd 28205
Woodleigh Oaks Dr 28226
Woodlynn Dr 28214
Woodman Ave 28216
Woodmere Crossing Ln 28226
Woodmere Trace Dr 28277
Woodmont Pl 28211
Woodnotch Ct 28269
Woodpark Blvd 28206
Woodrdg Ctr Dr 28217
Woodriver Ln 28277
Woodrock Ct 28214
Woodrose Ct 28262
Woodruff Pl 28208
Woods Corner Ct 28277
Woods End Ln 28277
Woodscape Dr 28212
Woodsedge Dr 28216
Woodshed Cir 28270
Woodship Ct 28214
Woodshire Dr 28208
Woodside Ave 28205
Woodsman Ct 28213
Woodsong Ct 28226
Woodsorrel Ln 28213
Woodstock Dr 28210
Woodstone Dr 28269
Woodstream Dr 28210
Woodthorn Pl 28226
Woodthrush Dr 28227
Woodtop Ct 28214
Woodvale Pl 28208
Woodvalley Dr 28216
Woodview Cir 28277
Woodward Ave 28206
Woodwardia Dr 28210
Woodway Pl 28208
Woodwedge Dr 28227
Woodwind St 28213
Woody Glen Pl 28215
Woody Grove Ln 28210
Woody Point Rd 28278
Woody Ridge Rd 28273
Woolcott Ave 28213
Woolwine Rd 28278
Worcaster Pl 28211
Wordsworth Ln 28211
Worley Dr 28215
Worsley Ln 28269
Worstel Ln 28277
Worth Pl 28216
Worthford Ct 28226
E & W Worthington Ave 28203
Worthley Ct 28211
Wrangell Ln 28214
Wrangler Ln 28213
Wrangler Trail Way 28277
Wrayhill Dr 28262
Wren Creek Dr 28269
Wrenfield Ct 28277
Wrens Nest Ln 28269
Wrentree Dr 28210
Wrenwood Ln 28211
Wrenwood Pond Ct 28211
Wrexham Ct 28269
Wright Ave 28211
Wrights Ferry Rd 28278
Wrigley Dr 28273
Wriston Pl 28209
Ws Lee Ct 28277
Wyalong Dr 28227
Wyanoke Ave 28205
Wyche Ln 28273
Wycliff Pl 28210
Wycombe Ct 28226
Wylam Dilly Ct 28213
Wylie Meadow Ln 28269
Wyman Ln 28226
Wymering Rd 28213
Wynborough Ln 28269
Wynbrook Way 28269
Wyncliff Ct 28207
Wyndale Ter 28214
Wyndbend Ln 28227
Wyndcrofte Pl 28209
Wyndfield Ln 28270
Wyndham Chase Ln 28277
Wyndham Forest Dr 28277
Wyndham Hill Dr 28269
Wyndham Oaks Dr 28277
Wyndham Pointe Dr 28213
Wynfaire Ln 28210
Wynhollow Downs Ln 28277
Wynington Dr 28226
Wynmore Pl 28208
Wynyates Ln 28270
Wyoming Ave 28273
Wyre Forest Ct 28270
Wythe House Ct 28270
Yachtsman Harbor Dr 28278
Yadkin Ave 28205
Yager Creek Dr 28273
Yahtzee Ln 28208
Yale Pl 28209
Yancey Rd 28217
Yandem Ct 28269
Yardley Pl 28212
Yarmouth Rd 28227
Yarrow Rd 28213
Yates Ct 28215
Yateswood Dr 28212
Yaupon Rd 28215
Yearwood Ln 28214
Yellow Oak Rd 28227
Yellow Pine Ct 28277
Yellow Rose Ln 28269
Yellow Spaniel Ct 28269
Yellow Tail Ct 28270
Yellowood Rd 28210
Yellowstone Dr 28208
Yellowstone Springs Ln 28273
Yeoman Rd 28217
Yerton Ct 28213
Yoradins Ave 28204
E Yorensou St 28202
York Rd
12800-12899 28273
13000-13998 28278
14000-16399 28278
York Center Dr 28273
York Crossing Dr 28273
Yorkdale Dr
700-1399 28217
2300-2599 28273
Yorkford Dr 28269
Yorkhills Dr 28217
Yorkmont Rd
700-2499 28217
2600-4799 28208
Yorkmont Ridge Ln 28217
Yorkridge Dr 28273
Yorkshire Dr 28217
Yorktowne Dr 28226
Yorkview Ct 28270
Yorkville Ct 28273
Yoruk Forest Ln 28211
Young Fawn Ct 28278
Young Poplar Pl 28277
Youngblood Rd 28278
Youngblood St 28203
Yuma St 28213
Yvonne Ln 28216
Zackery Ave 28277
Zeb Morris Way 28227
Zebulon Ave 28208
Zelkova Ln 28277
Zephyr Ln 28209
Zermatt Ln 28226
Ziegler Ln 28269
Zion Ct 28209
Zion Renaissance Ln 28269
Zircon St 28205
Zoar Rd 28278
Zorich Dr 28227

NUMBERED STREETS

E 1st St
100-199 28202
1300-1399 28204
W 1st St 28202
W 2nd St 28208
3rd St 28208
E 3rd St
200-299 28202
1100-1899 28204
W 3rd St 28202
E 4th St
400-899 28202
900-1899 28204
W 4th St
100-198 28202
200-999 28202
1301-1397 28208
1399-1500 28208
1502-1698 28208
E 5th St
100-799 28202
1400-2699 28204
W 5th St 28202
E 6th St 28202
300-1099 28202
1300-1399 28216
E 7th St
100-899 28202
900-2699 28204
W 7th St 28202
E 8th St
100-899 28202
900-2399 28204
W 8th St 28202
E 9th St
100-799 28202
1900-2199 28204
W 9th St 28202
E 10th St
600-799 28202
1000-1499 28204
W 10th St 28202
E & W 11th 28206
E & W 12th 28206
E 13th St 28206
E 15th St 28206
800-1199 28205
E 16th St
200-699 28206
800-1299 28205
E 17th St
400-499 28206
700-1199 28205
E 18th St
400-599 28206
600-1199 28205
E 19th St
400-599 28206
600-1199 28205
E 20th St 28205
E 21st St 28206
E 22nd St 28206
E & W 23rd 28206
E 24th St 28205
W 24th St 28206
E 25th St
400-499 28206
500-799 28205
W 25th St 28206
E 26th St 28205
W 26th St 28206
E 27th St
100-399 28206
600-699 28205
W 27th St 28206
E 28th St
100-299 28206
400-799 28205
W 28th St 28206
W 29th St 28206
W 30th St 28206
W 31st St 28206
E 32nd St 28205
W 32nd St 28206
E 33rd St 28205
E 34th St 28205
E 35th St 28205
E 36th St 28206
400-1299 28205
E 37th St 28205
77 Center Dr 28217

CLAYTON NC

General Delivery 27520

POST OFFICE BOXES MAIN OFFICE STATIONS AND BRANCHES

Box No.s
All PO Boxes 27528

RURAL ROUTES

01, 03, 04, 05, 07 27520
02, 06 27527

NAMED STREETS

Abbington Ct 27527
Abram Way 27520
Academy Ln 27520
Adams Ct 27520
Agin Court Pl 27520
Ainsley Ct 27527
Airport Industrial Dr 27520
Alamo Ct 27527
Alan Ln 27520
Albemarle Dr 27527
Alder Ln 27520
Aleah Ct 27520
Alecia Ct 27527
E & W Alex Dr 27520
Allen Rd 27520
Allison Way 27527
Alpine Way 27527
Altavista Ct 27520
Alto Ct 27520
Amelia Rd 27520
Amelia Church Rd 27520
Amelia Station Way 27520
Amesbury Ln 27520
Amos St 27520
Amsterdam Dr 27527
Amy Dr 27520
Anderby Dr 27527
Andrea Dr 27527
Andrews St 27520
Angela Ct 27520
Angus Ct 27520
Anna Dr & Pl 27520
Annandale Dr 27520
Annie V Dr 27520
Antler Dr 27527
Apache Dr 27527
Apple Ct 27527
Applecross Dr 27520
Applewood Dr 27520
April Dr 27520
Arabella Ln 27520
Arch Oak Ct 27527
Archer Lodge Rd 27527
Ariel Ct 27520
Arlington Dr 27520
Armour Ct 27527
Arrowwood Cir 27520
Arthur Dr 27520
Ashby Dr 27527
Ashe Meadow Ln 27527
Ashebury Dr 27527
N & S Ashlyn Dr 27527
Ashton Ct 27527
Aspen Cir 27520
Astor St 27520
Athletic Club Blvd 27527
Athol Ct 27527
Atkinson St 27520
Auburn Ct 27520
Austin Farm Ln 27520
Austin Pond Rd 27520
Autumn Ct & Ln 27520
Avenel Ln 27527
Averasboro Dr 27520
Avery Farm Ln 27520
Aviary Ct 27520
Avocet Ln 27520
Avondale Dr 27520
Aycock Ct 27527
Ayden Dr 27520
Aynor Cir 27520
Bahama Ct 27520
Bailywick Dr 27527
Bald Dr 27520
Ballot Rd 27520
Balmoral St 27520
Baltasrol Ct 27520
Barbara Dr 27520
Barber Mill Rd 27520
Barbour St 27520
Barclay Ln 27520
W Barnes St 27520
Barnes Ridge Dr 27520
Barrowby Dr 27527
Bayberry Ct 27520
Bayleaf Cir 27527
Bayliner Ct 27520
Beaver Dr 27527
Beckwith Ave 27527
Bed Rock Dr 27520
Bedford Ln 27520
Bee Ln 27520
Beechleaf Ct 27520
Belhaven Dr 27520
Belk Ct 27520
Bella Casa Way 27527
Bellagio Ct 27527
N & S Bellaire Ct 27527
Bellefield Ln 27527
Bennent Dr 27520
Bennett Pl 27527
Benning Cir 27527
Bennington Dr 27520
Benningwood Ct 27520
Benny Rd 27520
Bent Branch Loop 27527
Bent Creek Ct 27527
Bentley Way 27527
Benttree Dr 27520
Bentwood Ln 27520
Bergamont Cir 27520
Berkeley Ct 27520
Bertram Dr 27520
Berwick Pl 27520
Bess Dr 27520
Best Wood Dr 27520
Betsy Ct 27520
Bevington Ct 27520
Bexley Way 27527
Big Pine Rd 27520
Billington Ct 27520
Bilston Dr 27520
Biltmore Dr 27520
Birch Ln 27520
Birchwood Ct 27520
Birkdale Dr 27527
Black Forest Dr 27527
Blackmon Farms Ln 27527
Blackthorne Ct 27520
Blanchard St 27520
E & W Blanche St 27520
Bleeker Dr 27527
Blount Creek Est 27520
Blue Pond Rd 27520
Blue Slate Ln 27520
Bluebell Ct 27520
Bobbitt Rd 27520
S Boling St 27520
Booker Ct 27520
Boswell Ln 27527
Boulder Dr 27520
Box Grove Ct 27527
Bradborne Cir 27527
Bradford Cir 27527
Bradford Pl 27520
Bradshaw Way 27527
Brady Dr 27520
Braemar Cir 27520
Bragg Ct 27527
Brampton Cir 27527
Branch Ct 27520
Branding Iron Dr 27520
Brandon Dr 27520
Brandywood Dr 27520
Breeze Ln 27520
Breezewood Ln 27520
Breland Dr 27520
Brenda Ct 27520
Briarwood Cir & Dr 27520
Bridge Ct 27527
Bridge Ln 27520
Bridgeport Cir 27527
Bridgham Pl 27527
Brigadoon Dr 27520
Bright Leaf Dr 27520
Brigsley Cir 27527
Brindley Cir 27520
Bristol Cir 27527
Brittany Dr 27520
Broadmoor Way 27520
Brook St 27520
Brook Valley Dr 27520
Brookberry Ln 27527
Brookgreen Dr 27527
Brookhaven Dr 27527
Brookhill Dr 27520
Brookline Ct 27527
Brookmont Dr 27527
Brooksby Ct 27527
Brookview Ct 27520
Broomhill Ct 27527
E Browning Ct 27520
Brylee Ln 27520
Buchanan Ln 27527
Buckhorn Ln 27527
Buckleigh Dr 27527
Buckskin Dr 27520
Buffalo Rd 27527
Butternut Ln 27520
Buttonwood Ln 27520
Byrd Dr & Rd 27527
Cabernet Ct 27520
Cabin Bar Dr 27520
Cabin Branch Rd 27520
Calabria Ct 27527
Caledonia Ln 27520
Callie Ct 27527
Cambridge Ct 27520
Cambridge Elm Dr 27520

Camel St 27520
Cameo Ct 27527
Cameron Way 27520
Campen Ct 27527
Canadian Ln 27520
Canady St 27520
Candlewood Dr 27520
Canterbury Rd 27520
Canvasback Ln 27520
Canyon Rd 27520
Cape Ct 27520
Cardinal Ct & Dr 27520
Cardinal Acres 27520
Caribou Ln 27527
Carlisle Ct 27520
Carlton St 27520
Carmen Ln 27520
Carol Dr 27520
Caroline Ct 27520
Carrie Dr 27527
Carter St 27520
Casey Rd 27520
Cassidy Ct 27520
Castello Way 27527
Castleberry Rd 27527
Castlewood Dr 27520
Catria Ct 27527
Ccc Dr 27520
Cedar Ct 27520
Cedar Brook Ct 27520
Cedar Grove Ct 27527
Cedardale Ct 27520
Cedarwood Ct 27520
Central St 27520
Chadford Pl 27520
Chalmers Dr 27520
Chamberlain Dr 27527
Champion St 27520
Chanticleer Cir 27527
Chapel Dr 27520
Chardonney Dr 27520
Charles St 27520
Charleston Dr 27527
Charlie Ln 27520
Charlotte Ct 27520
Charter Oak Dr 27520
Chase St 27520
Chatham Ct 27527
Cheltenham Dr 27520
Cherokee Dr 27527
Cherry Ct 27520
Cherry Bark Loop 27527
Cherry Laurel Dr 27527
Chesney Ct 27527
Chesterfield Ct 27520
Chestertown Ct 27527
Chestnut Dr 27520
Chickasaw Cir 27527
Chippenham Ct 27520
Christenbury Ln 27527
Christian St 27527
Christopher Dr 27520
Christy Cir 27520
N & S Church St 27520
Churchill Downs Dr 27520
Cimarron Cir 27527
Cindy Ln 27520
Cirrus Dr 27520
City Rd 27520
Claim Rd 27520
Claire Dr 27520
Clark Pond Rd 27527
Clay St 27520
Claymore Dr 27527
W Clayton Park 27520
Clayton St 27527
Clayton Commerce Ctr 27520
Clayton Pointe Dr 27520
Clearwater Ct 27520
Clemmons Dr 27520
Cleveland Rd 27520
Cleveland Fire Rd 27520
Cliffside Cir 27527
Cloverdale Dr 27520
Coachman Ct 27520
Cobblestone Ct 27520

Cobey Ct 27520
Cole Rd 27520
Collinsworth Dr 27527
Colonial Dr 27527
Colony Cir & Rdg 27520
Colt Cir 27520
Commodore St 27520
Compressor Dr 27520
Compton St 27520
Concord Ct 27520
Cone Cir 27520
Conner Dr 27520
Contender Dr 27520
Contessa Ct 27520
Cooper St 27520
Cooper Branch Rd 27520
Corbett Rd 27520
Coriander Ln 27527
Correy Pl 27520
Cortland Cir 27520
Corvina Dr 27520
Costa Ct 27527
Cottage Dr 27527
E & W Cotton Gin Dr 27527
Cottonwood Cir 27527
Cottonwood Dr 27520
Cottsworth Ct 27527
Country Ln 27520
Country Hollow Ln 27520
Country Trails Dr 27520
Cove Cir 27520
E & W Coventry Ct 27527
Covered Ct 27527
Covered Bridge Rd
1-1199 27520
2601-2697 27520
2699-6799 27527
Covert Dr 27527
Covey Ln 27520
Covington Ct 27527
Coxwoods Rd 27520
Crabapple Ln 27527
Cranberry Ct 27520
Creekbend Cir 27527
Creekside Ct & Dr 27520
Creekview Cir & Dr 27520
Crenshaw Ct 27527
Crescent Dr 27520
Crest Cir 27520
Crestdale Dr 27520
Cricket Hollow Run 27520
Crissie Ct 27527
Crooked Creek Rd 27520
Crossdale Ct 27520
Cruz Jeffries Rd 27520
Crystal Creek Dr 27527
Cunningham Ln 27527
Cypress Ct 27520
Daffodil Ln 27527
Dailwill Rd 27520
Dairy Rd 27520
Damon St 27520
Dancing Shoes Ct 27520
Darfield Ct 27520
David Ln 27520
Dawson Dr 27527
Day Flower Dr 27527
Dean Ave 27520
Debbar Dr 27520
Debbie Dr 27527
Deep Canyon Dr 27520
Deep Creek Dr 27520
Deep Forest Ln 27520
Deer Run 27520
Deer Trl 27527
Deer Crossing Ln 27520
Deer Flag Ln 27527
Deer Trace Ln 27520
Deer Woods Ct 27527
Deerfield Dr & Trl 27527
Denby Cir 27527
Dennis Way 27520
Dewberry Ct 27520
Diamond Creek Dr 27520
Dixie Ct 27520
N Dodd St 27520

Doe Ln 27527
Dogwood Ave & Rdg 27520
Dogwood Forest Ln 27520
Domenica Way 27527
Dongola St 27520
Donna Ct 27520
Donzi Ct 27520
Dorothy Dr 27520
Dory Ln 27520
Dove Ct 27520
Dove Ln 27527
Dove Pointe Ln 27520
Drayton St 27527
Drew Ct 27520
Drexel Ct 27520
Duba Dr 27520
Duck Pond Ln 27520
Duffy St 27527
Dulwich Way 27527
Duncan Ct 27527
Dunley Cir 27527
Dunmore Dr 27527
Dunoon Ct 27520
Dupree Ct 27527
Durant Rd 27527
S Durham St 27520
Eagle Pointe Ln 27520
Eagle Rock Pl 27520
Eason Dr 27520
Eastwood Dr 27520
Eddlestone Ct 27520
Edgewater Dr 27520
Edinburgh Pl 27527
Egret Ct 27520
Eight Js Ln 27520
Elaine Dr 27520
Elizabeth Ct 27520
Ellas Ln 27520
Ellen Cir 27527
S Ellington St 27520
Elmsly Cir 27527
Elmwood Ln 27520
Elway Dr 27527
Emmett Crest Ct 27520
Enchanted Trl 27520
Englewood Dr 27520
English Oak Ln 27520
Enterprise Dr 27520
Equine Ln 27520
Essex Ln N & S 27520
Eton Ct 27520
Eunice Dr 27520
Evan Ct 27520
Evening Ln 27527
Everette Ave 27520
Evergreen Cir 27520
Executive Dr 27520
Exide Dr 27520
Faircloth Ct 27520
Faire Ln 27527
Fairmont Dr 27520
Fairway Dr 27520
Falcon Ct 27520
Falcon Pointe Ln 27520
Faldo Rdg 27527
Falling Creek Ct 27520
Falling Oak Ct 27520
Falls Dr 27527
Falmouth Ct 27527
Family 27527
N Farm Dr 27527
Farmington Dr 27520
Farrington Dr 27520
Fawn Ln 27527
N & S Fayetteville St 27520
Feather Dr 27520
Feather Falls Ct 27527
Feeney Ct 27520
Feezor Ct 27520
Felicia Ct 27520
Ferndale Ct 27527
Fernwood Dr 27520
Fieldstone Dr & Ln 27520
Fig Berry St 27527
Finley Ct 27527
Fire Brand Dr 27520

Fire Department Rd 27527
Fire Rescue Dr 27520
Fireweed Pl 27527
First Light Trl 27527
Fisher St 27520
Flamingo Dr 27520
Fletcher Rd 27527
Florence Dr 27527
Flowers Pkwy 27527
Flowers Crest Way 27527
Flowers Crossroads
Way 27527
Fogleglen Dr 27520
Folden Dr 27520
Fontana Dr 27527
Forest Dr 27520
Forest Oaks Dr 27527
Fort Dr 27520
Fort Boone Ct 27527
Forty Niners Rd 27520
Fountain Dr 27520
Fox Den 27527
Fox Hollow Dr 27527
Fox Hunt Ln 27527
Fox Ridge Rd 27527
Foxfire Ln 27527
Francis Dr 27527
Frazier Dr 27527
Fringe Tree Ln 27520
E Front St
100-198 27520
200-300 27520
302-604 27520
604-604 27528
606-898 27520
W Front St 27520
Gadwall Ln 27520
Gallop Dr 27520
E Garner Rd 27520
Garnet Ln 27520
Garrison Ave 27520
Gasper Ct 27527
Gateway Dr 27520
Gathering Dr 27527
N & S Gattis Dr 27527
Gatwick Ct 27520
Gehrig Ln 27527
Genoa Ln 27527
George Wilton Dr 27520
Georgetowne Dr 27520
Geranium Way 27527
Gibson Ln 27527
Glasgow Dr 27520
Glen Forest Dr 27520
Glen Laurel Rd 27527
Gleneden Dr 27520
Glengariff Ln 27527
Glenn St 27520
Glory Ridge Way 27520
Gold Digger Rd 27520
Golden Curls Ct 27520
Golden Nugget Dr 27520
Goldthread Ave 27527
Gordon Rd & St 27520
Government Rd 27520
Grace Meadows Dr 27520
Gracie Ln 27520
Grand Manor Ct 27527
Grande Overlook Dr 27527
Granite Ln 27520
Granny Farm Rd 27520
Grant Ln & St 27520
Granton Ct 27520
Grantwood Dr 27527
Grayson Pl 27520
Great View Ct 27527
Green Ln 27520
Green Park 27520
Green Path 27527
Green Way Dr 27520
Green Willows Dr 27527
Greenbrier Ct 27527
Greenfield Ln 27527
Greenlyn Dr 27527
Greenwood Dr 27520
Gregory Dr 27520

Greybridge Ct 27520
Greystone Cir 27520
Grill Rd 27520
Groundsel Pl 27527
Grouse Ct 27520
Grove St 27520
Grovewood Dr 27520
Gulley Dr 27520
Guy Rd 27520
Hackney Trl 27527
Hadley Ln 27527
N & S Hadrian Ct 27520
Hamby St 27520
Hanlith Ct 27527
Happy Trails Rd 27520
Hardaway Pt 27527
Hardee Ln & St 27520
Harding Dr 27527
Hardwood Ridge Ct 27520
Harmony Ct 27520
Harrison Rd 27527
Harvest Ct 27520
Harvest Mill Ln 27520
Harvest Moon Dr 27527
Hastings Dr 27527
Hatteras Ct 27520
Hawkesburg Dr 27527
Hawthorn Dr 27520
Hay Field Dr 27520
Haywood Ln 27520
Hazel St 27527
Heart Wood Ct 27527
Heather Downs Ln 27520
Heathwood Dr 27527
Hedgerow Ln 27527
Hein Dr 27520
Helen Jean Ct 27527
Helena Ln 27527
Hemlock Cir & Pl 27520
Hemlock Green Ln 27527
Hemmingway Ct 27520
Henry Ct 27520
Hereford Dr 27520
Herndon Ct 27520
Hibiscus Dr 27527
Hickory Dr & St 27520
Hickory Ridge Ln 27520
Hidden Acres Dr 27527
Hidden Valley Dr 27527
High Chaparral Dr 27527
Hill Row Ln 27520
Hill Shore Ln 27527
Hillcrest Cir & Ln 27520
Hillsdale Dr 27527
Hind Dr 27527
Hinton Ct 27527
E Hinton St 27520
W Hinton St 27520
Hobbs St 27520
Hocutt Dr 27520
Hocutt Farm Dr 27527
Hogan Cir 27527
Hogans Way 27520
Holder Cir 27527
Holding St 27520
Holly Cir 27527
Holly Ct 27520
Holly Point Pl 27520
Hollyridge Ct 27527
Home Trace Cir 27520
Homestead Way 27527
Honeybee Trce 27520
Honeysuckle Ct 27527
Hood Farm Rd 27520
Hope Ln 27527
Horatio Ct 27520
E & W Horne St 27520
Horsemans Ridge Dr 27520
Horseshoe Ln 27520
Houston Ln 27527
Huntclub Dr 27520
Hunter Way 27520
Hunters Pt 27520
Hunters Ridge Dr 27527
Hunting Lodge Rd 27520
Huntsbridge Dr 27520

Hutson Ln 27527
Hyde Park Cir 27520
Icana Poole Rd 27520
Idlewood Ln 27527
Imperial Dr 27527
Impressive Ln 27520
Indian Camp Rd 27520
Innsbruck Dr 27527
Iris St 27520
Irondale Dr 27520
Ironwood Ln 27520
Irvan St 27520
Isabella Ct 27527
Ivy Dr 27527
Jack Rd 27520
Jacobs Ct 27527
James Pl 27520
James Land Dr 27520
Jasmine Dr 27527
Jasper Dr 27520
Javelin Ct 27520
Jeffrey Dr 27527
Jennifer Dr 27520
Jenny Cir 27520
Jessica Dr 27520
Joel Ct 27520
John St 27520
Johnson Dr 27520
Johnson Estate Rd 27520
Johnston Way 27520
Jonas Cir 27527
Jones Cir 27520
Josiah Dr 27527
Joy Dr 27520
Joyner St 27520
Jubilee Ct 27527
Julian Ln 27527
Juneberry Pl 27527
Juniper Dr 27520
Justin Ct 27520
Kapok Ct 27520
Karen Dr 27520
Kate Hill Ln 27527
Katie Dr 27520
Kay Cir 27520
Keller Dr 27520
Kelly Ln 27520
Kelsey Ct 27520
Kendall Dr 27520
Kenilworth St 27527
Kenmore Dr 27520
Kennel Ln 27520
Kensington Ct 27527
Kentucky Dr 27527
Kentucky Derby Dr 27520
Kerriann Ln 27520
Kershaw Ln 27520
Keswick Ln 27520
Kevin Ct 27520
Kilbride Way 27520
Kildaire Ct 27520
N Kildee St 27520
Kilgo St 27520
Killarney Ln 27520
Killington Dr 27520
Kimberly Ln 27520
Kings Canyon Ct 27527
Kingsbury Ct 27527
Kingsmill Ln 27527
Kingston Ct 27527
Kintyre Dr 27520
Kirkland Ct 27527
Knights Bridge Dr 27520
Knollwood Pl 27527
Kollinova Dr 27520
Korat Ln 27520
Kramer Path 27527
Kristen Ct 27527
Kylemore Pl 27520
La Varra Dr 27520
Ladonna Ln 27520
Lafoy Dr 27527
Lake Dr 27520
Lake Point Dr 27527
Lakemont St 27520
Lakeside Dr 27520

Lakeview Dr 27520
S Landing Dr 27520
Lantana Cir 27520
Lark Ct 27520
Larson Ct 27520
Lassiter Farms Ln 27520
Lauderdale Trl 27527
Laurel Ridge Dr 27520
Lawhorn Dr 27520
Leah Cir & Dr 27520
Leather Oak Trl 27520
N & S Ledford Dr 27520
Lee Ct, Rd & St 27520
Lee Forest Ct 27520
Leeway Ct 27520
Legare Ct 27520
Lena Dr 27520
Lennox Dr 27520
Liberty Ln 27520
Lightfoot Dr 27520
Lillian Dr 27520
Lily Xing 27527
Limeberry Ct 27520
Lindsay Ct 27520
Lins Pl 27520
Linwood Ln 27527
Lisann Ct 27520
Little Creek Church
Rd 27520
Livingston Pl 27520
Loblolly Cir 27520
Loblolly Ct 27527
Loch Lomond Dr 27520
Lockberry Ct 27520
Locket Dr 27520
Lockfield Dr 27520
Lockwood Dr 27527
Lois Ln 27520
N & S Lombard St 27520
Long Cove Ct 27527
Long Needle Dr 27520
Loop Rd 27527
Lopez Ln 27527
Louise Ln 27520
Lucy Ct 27527
Luther Ct 27520
Lynn Dr 27520
Lynshire Ave 27527
Macbeth Cir 27527
Macon Ct 27527
Madeleine Dr 27527
Magnolia Cir 27527
Magnolia Ct 27527
E & W Main St 27520
Majestic Ln 27520
Malcolm Dr 27520
Manchester Trl 27527
Mandarin Loop 27520
Manning Dr 27527
Manor Dr 27520
Mantle Dr 27527
Maple Ridge Dr 27527
Marcellus Way 27527
Marino Pl 27527
Mariposa Ln 27527
Marlowe Ct 27520
Marrian Dr 27520
Marsala Dr 27527
Marsh Ct 27520
Marshlane Way 27527
Mary Ellen Way 27520
Mary Leigh Ct 27520
Mary Sandra Pl 27520
Matthews Cir & Rd 27520
Mattingly Ln 27527
Maude Ln 27520
Mayfair Ct 27520
Mayflower Way 27527
Maylon Ln 27520
Mccarthy Dr 27527
Mccullers St 27520
Mcdougle Ln 27520
Mcgirt Ct 27520
Mcguire Ln 27527
Mckenzie Cir 27520
Mckinnon Dr 27520

Mclemore Rd 27520
Mcnichol Ct 27520
Meadow Ct, Ln & Run 27520
Meadow Creek Dr 27520
Meadow Loop Dr 27527
Meadowland Dr 27520
Meadowlark Ct 27520
Mechanical Dr 27520
Medical Park Pl 27520
Medina Ct 27527
Medlin Rd 27527
Melanie Ct 27520
Melissa Ct 27520
Melville Ln 27527
Mercantile Ct 27520
Merganser Ct 27520
Merlot Ct 27520
Mesa Ct 27527
Meta Dr 27520
Mial St 27520
Michael Way 27520
E Midalest Ave E 27527
Middlecrest Way 27527
Middleton St 27520
E & W Milan Ct 27527
Mill Cir 27527
Mill St 27520
Mill Creek Dr 27527
Millstone Dr 27527
Millwood Dr 27527
Mimosa St 27520
Miracle Way 27520
E Miravista Ct 27527
Missy Ln 27520
Mitchell Ave & St 27520
Mocha Ln 27520
Mohawk Trl 27527
Mohican Trl 27527
Monroe Rd 27520
Monticello Pl 27520
Montpelier Ln 27527
Moore St 27520
Moorgate Ct 27520
Morning Chase Ln 27527
Morning Dove Ct 27527
Moser Pl 27520
E & W Moss Creek Dr 27520
Motorcycle Rd 27527
Moultrie Ct 27527
Mount Moriah Dr 27520
Mount Vernon Dr 27520
Mountain Laurel Dr 27527
Mueller Dr 27520
Muirfield Ln 27527
Mulberry Rd 27520
S Murphrey Rd 27527
Murphy Dr 27527
Myrtle Ln 27520
Namath Ct 27527
Nancy Ct 27520
Naples Ln 27527
Narcissus Ct 27527
Nassau Ct 27520
Nathan Dr 27520
Nathaniel Dr 27520
Nc Highway 42 E 27527
Nc Highway 42 W 27520
Nelson Ct 27520
Nelson Ln 27527
Neuse Colony Dr 27527
Neuse Landing Dr 27527
Neuse Ridge Dr 27527
Neuse River Pkwy 27527
New St 27520
New Castle Ct 27520
Nickel Dr 27520
Nicklaus Way 27520
N & S Nikol Way 27520
No Record St 27527
Nolan Cir 27520
Normandy Dr 27527
Norris Rd 27520
Northcliff Ct 27527
Northfort Dr 27527
Norwich Dr 27520
Norwood Dr 27527

Oak St & Trl 27520
Oak Alley Trl 27527
Oak Creek Dr 27520
Oak Hollow Ct 27527
Oak Run Dr 27520
Oak Vine Cir 27527
Oakdale Ave 27520
Oakfield Ter 27520
Oakmont Ct 27527
Oakton Dr 27520
Oakwood Cir 27520
Oglethorpe Ave 27527
Ohara Dr & St 27520
Old Nc Highway 42 E 27527
Old Ranch Rd 27520
Old Us 70 Hwy W 27520
Old Yogi Ln 27520
Old York Cir 27527
Oleander Dr 27527
W Olive Rd 27520
Olive Tree Ln 27520
Oliver Ct 27520
N & S Oneil St 27520
N Oneil Street Ext 27520
Opal Ln 27520
N & S Orchard Dr 27520
Orton Rd 27520
Outcrop Ct 27520
Oxford Ct 27520
Page St 27520
Paisley Ct 27527
Palmer Ct 27527
Palmer Dr 27527
Pamela Ln 27527
Paraggi Ct 27527
Park Dr & Pl 27520
Parkdale Ln 27520
Parker St 27527
Parkridge Dr 27527
Parkside Village Dr 27520
Parque De Sarah Pl 27527
Parrish Dr 27520
Pay Day Ln 27520
Payton Dr 27527
Peace Ln 27527
Peach Blossom Ct 27527
Peachtree Ln 27527
Pear Tree Ln 27520
Pearson Pl 27527
Pebble Dr 27520
Pebblebrook Cir 27527
Pecan Cir 27520
Pecan Ln 27527
Peele Rd 27520
Peninsula Ct 27527
Penninah Ct 27527
Penny Ln & St 27520
Pepperstone Ct 27520
Percy Dr 27520
Perlmutter Ct 27527
Persano Ln 27520
Persimmon Cir 27527
Pet Rock Ct 27527
Pheasant Dr 27520
Piccadilly Ct 27527
Pine Ln & Trl 27520
Pine Bark Ln 27520
Pine Hollow Dr 27520
Pine Knoll Dr 27520
Pinecone Pl 27527
Pinecroft Dr & Pl 27520
Pineland Ave 27527
Pineville Blvd 27527
Pinewinds Ct 27520
Pinnacle Pt 27527
Pintail Ln 27520
Plantation Ct 27527
Plantation Dr 27527
Plantation Rd 27527
Plaza De Luke Sq 27527
Plott Hound Dr 27520
Plum Ln 27527
Plymouth Dr 27520
Pocahontas Trl 27527
Point Ln 27527
Polenta Rd 27520

Polly Pl 27520
Pond Ave 27527
Pond St 27520
Ponderosa Dr 27520
Pondfield Ct 27527
Pony Farm Rd 27520
Pope Ct 27520
Poplar Dr 27520
Port O Pnes 27520
Portofino Dr 27527
Post Oak Ct 27527
Potted Plant Ct 27520
Powell Dr 27520
Powhatan Rd
1-3699 27527
3700-4199 27520
Preakness Dr 27527
Prestwick Dr 27527
Pricket Ln 27527
Primrose Ln 27520
Pritchard Rd 27527
Privenne Rd 27520
Pryzwansky Dr 27520
Pungo Ct 27520
Pursuit Ct 27520
Quail Ct & Trl 27520
Quail Roost 27527
Queen Ann Dr 27527
Queens Ferry Ln 27520
Raccoon Run 27527
Rachels Way 27520
Radcliffe Ct 27527
Rainbow Canyon Dr 27527
Raintree Dr 27527
Rainwater Ct 27520
Raleigh Rd 27520
Ramblewood Dr 27520
Ranch Rd 27520
Randolph Dr 27520
Rapallo Ct 27527
Raven Hill Ct 27520
Raymond Dr 27527
Red Clover Pl 27520
Red Leaf Trl 27527
Red Oak Ln 27520
Red Star Ln 27520
Redbay Ln 27520
Redbud Dr 27520
Redwood Ct 27520
Reeder Branch Dr 27520
Regency Park Dr 27520
Regent Ct 27527
Regulator Dr 27520
Remington Dr 27520
Richmond Dr 27527
Ridge Cir, Ct, Dr & Rd 27520
Ridge Way Ln 27520
Ridgecrest Dr 27520
E & W Ridgeview Dr 27520
Riley Pl 27520
River Dell Rd 27520
River Dell Townes
Ave 27520
River Hills Dr 27527
River Knoll Dr 27520
River Oak Dr 27520
River Oaks 27520
River Rock Ct 27527
Riverbend Dr 27520
Riverbirch Way 27527
Riverdale Rd 27527
Riverglade Dr 27527
Riverstone Dr 27527
Riverview Dr 27520
Riverwood Dr 27520
Roanoke Way 27527
N & S Robertson St 27520
Robin Ln 27520
Rock Cir 27520
Rock Pillar Rd 27520
Rockport Dr 27520
Rockrose Ave 27527
Rocky Pl 27520
Rocky Branch Rd 27520
Roe Ln 27520
Rolling Meadows Dr 27527

Roosevelt Ave 27520
Roscommon Ln 27520
Rose St 27520
Rosebay Ln 27527
Rosemary St 27520
Roundtree Ct 27520
Rowan Dr 27520
Rubert Ave 27520
Rudy Dr 27520
Rudy Ln 27527
Rufus Ln 27527
Ryans Ln 27520
Ryland Dr 27520
Ryley Pl 27520
Saddlebrook Dr 27527
Sadisco Rd 27520
Sailfish Ct 27520
Saint Ives Ct 27520
Saint James Ct 27520
Saint Jiles Dr 27520
Saint Lawrence Way 27520
Saint Martin Way 27527
Salerno Dr 27527
Sandecker Ct 27520
Sandlebrook Dr 27520
Sandy Bottom Ct 27520
Sandy Branch Ln 27527
Sandy Creek Dr 27527
Sandy Ridge Dr E &
W 27520
Sanidine Ln 27527
Santa Gertrudis Dr 27520
Sapphire Ct 27520
Sara Ln 27527
Saratoga Ln 27520
Sarazen Dr 27527
Sardinia Ln 27527
Sassafras Ln 27527
Satinwood Dr 27520
Savannah Ln 27527
Sawtooth Oak Trl 27520
Saxon Ct 27527
Scarlet Oak Run 27520
E School Rd 27527
Scotch Bonnet Rdg 27520
Scott Ct 27527
Scuppernong Way 27520
Sequoia Dr 27527
Serenia Cir 27527
Ses Dr 27520
Seths Way 27527
Setter Pt 27520
Seven Oaks Dr 27520
Shad Boat Ln 27520
Shady Ln 27520
Shady Meadow Ln 27520
Shannon Dr 27520
Shapiro Ct 27527
Sharpstone Ln 27527
Shauna Cir 27520
Shelburne Dr 27527
Shelby Ct 27527
Shelton Ct 27527
Sherwood Dr 27527
Shields Ct 27520
Short Johnson Rd 27520
Shotwell Rd 27520
Sicily Dr 27527
Siena Way 27527
Sierra Ridge Dr 27527
Sierre Ln 27527
Silkgrass Way 27527
Silver Creek Dr 27527
Sioux Ln 27520
Skye Cir 27520
Skygrove Dr 27527
Skylor Dr 27520
Slate Top Rd 27520
Slateford Dr 27520
Sleepy Creek Dr 27520
Smart Ct 27520
N & S Smith Dr & St 27520
Smiths Creek Dr 27520
E & W Smoketree Ct 27527
Snead Dr 27527
Softwind Dr 27520

Somers Ln 27527
Sommerset Dr 27520
Sonny Rd 27520
Southerland Rd 27527
Southmead Dr 27527
Southmont St 27527
Southwick Ave 27527
Spalding Ln 27527
Spaniel Ln 27520
Spanish Oak Way 27520
Spearhead Pl 27520
Spring Valley Dr 27520
Spring Watering Hole
Dr 27520
Springbrook Ave 27520
Springfield Ct 27527
Springwood Pl 27520
Stafford Cir 27527
E & W Stallings St 27520
Standing Oaks Ln 27527
Stansbury Ln 27527
Starbright Ln 27527
Stargrass Ave 27527
Starling St 27520
Starmont Dr 27527
Starmount Rd 27520
State Ave 27520
Stauffer Ct 27520
Steel Bridge Rd 27520
Steeler Ln 27527
Stephanie Ln 27520
Sterling Dr 27527
Stewart Ln 27527
N Stewart St 27520
Stewarts Knob Dr 27527
Stillwood Ct 27520
Stone Ln & Pl 27520
Stonebrook Dr 27520
Stonehenge Dr 27520
Stonewood Ct 27520
Stoney Creek Dr 27520
Stratus Ln 27520
Streamwood Way 27527
Strickland Rd 27520
Sturbridge Dr 27520
Stylish Sierra Dr 27520
Sugarberry Ln 27520
Sugarfield Ln 27527
Sumac Ct 27520
Summer Place Ct 27527
Summerbrooke Ct 27520
Summerfield Cir 27527
Summerglow Ct 27527
Summerset Ct 27527
Summerwinds Cir &
Ct 27520
Summerwood Dr 27520
Summit St 27520
Summit Overlook Dr 27527
Sundew Ct 27527
Sunflower Way 27527
Sunny Way 27520
Sunnyview Ln 27520
Sunray Dr 27520
Sunset Ct & Ln 27520
Sunset Pointe Dr 27520
Surrey Ct 27520
Swann Trl 27527
Sweet Gum Pl 27520
Sweetbay Ct 27527
Sweetbriar Ct 27520
Swift Creek Dr & Rd 27520
Syphrona Cir 27527
T R Dr 27520
Tall Oak Ct 27520
Tall Pines Ln 27520
Talmadge Farm Dr 27527
Tamarind Ct 27527
Tanglewood Dr 27527
Tanners Way 27527
Tara Dr 27520
Tarkenton Ct 27527
Tavistock Ct 27520
Tayside Pl & St 27520
Teasel Ct 27527
N Tech Dr 27520

S Tech Park Ln 27520
Tew Ct 27520
Texas Cattle Dr 27520
Thomas Dr 27520
Thornbury St 27527
Thorndale Ct 27527
Thornhill Ct 27520
Thornwood Ct 27520
Tiffany Ct 27520
Timber Ln 27520
Timber Croft Dr 27520
Timberline Ct 27520
Timothy Rdg 27520
Tobacco Ln 27520
Tomahawk Dr 27520
Torino Ave 27527
Torrey Pines Dr 27527
Town Centre Blvd 27520
Townsend Dr 27527
Tracy Dr 27520
Tradd Ct 27520
E & W Trafalgar Ct 27520
Trailing Oak Trl 27527
Trailwood Dr 27520
Tram Ln 27520
Trantham Trl 27527
Trawick Pl 27520
Treetop Ct 27527
Treewood Ln 27527
Trellis Ct 27520
Trenburg Pl 27520
Trestlewood Ln 27520
Trevor Rdg 27527
Treymore Dr 27520
Trillium Way 27527
Triple Crown Cir 27527
Triton Ct 27520
Trotters Run 27520
Troy Dr 27520
Tulip St 27520
Turnberry Ln 27527
Tuscarora Ln 27520
Twin Acres Rd 27520
Twin Leaf Cir 27520
Twin Pines Ct 27527
N & S Two Does Ct, Dr
& Ln 27520
E & W Umbria Ct 27527
Umstead Dr 27520
Us 70 Bus Hwy W 27520
Us 70 Business Hwy
W 27520
Us Highway 70 E & W 27520
Us Highway 70a E 27520
Uzzle Industrial Dr 27520
Valentino Ct 27527
Valley Ct & Dr 27520
Valley Creek Dr 27527
Valleycastle Ct 27520
Valleyfield Dr 27527
Ventasso Dr 27527
Ventura Dr 27527
Vercelli Dr 27527
Verrazano Pl 27520
Vetriana Way 27527
Vi Ln 27520
Vine Hill Ct 27520
Vinson Ct 27520
Vinson Rd 27527
Vinson Ridge Ln 27527
Vintage Ct 27520
Vinyard Dr 27520
Virginia St 27520
Virginia Pine Dr 27520
Vista Ct 27527
Wahoo Dr 27520
Walden Way 27527
Walford Park 27520
E & W Walker Woods
Ln 27527
Wall St 27520
Walnut Creek Dr 27520
Walthom Dr 27520
Warren St 27520
Warrick Pl 27527
Warwick Ct 27520

Washington St 27520
Waterfield Dr 27527
Waterford Dr 27520
Waterleaf Pl 27527
Waterside Ct 27527
Watkins Rd 27520
Watrus Dr 27527
Watson Cir 27527
Watsons Mill Ln 27527
Waverly Dr 27527
Waymon Way 27520
Weathersby Ln 27520
Wedgewood Pl 27527
Weldon Dr 27520
Wellspring Cir 27527
Wembley Dr 27527
Wembury Dr 27527
Wensley Ct 27527
West St 27520
Westbrook Ln 27520
Westchase Dr 27527
Westcliff Ct 27527
Westcote Ln 27527
Westfield Ct 27527
Westgrove Pt 27520
Westminster Dr 27520
Westwinds Ct 27520
Westwood Pl 27520
Wexford Dr 27520
Wheatfield Ln 27527
Wheeler Ct 27527
Whisper Wind Rd 27520
Whispering Pines Dr 27520
E & W Whitaker St 27520
White Oak Cir & Ct 27520
White Pine Dr 27527
Whitehall Ct 27520
Whitetail Ln 27527
Wick Ct 27520
Widespan Dr 27520
Wigeon Ln 27520
Wild Wing Ct 27520
Wildberry Ct 27520
N & S Wilders Ridge
Way 27527
Wilders Woods Grove
Ln 27527
Wildwood Dr 27520
Will Ct 27520
William Ln 27520
Willie Farm Ln 27520
Willow Dr 27520
Willow Bend Ct 27527
Willow Branch Ln 27527
Willow Hill Ln 27520
Willow Oak Trl 27520
Willowbrook Cir 27527
Willowtree Ln 27520
Wilshire Way 27520
E Wilson St 27520
Wilson Jones Rd 27520
Wilsons Mills Rd 27520
Wiltshire Dr 27527
Wimbledon Ct 27520
Winchester Pl 27520
Windgate Dr 27527
Windham Way 27520
Winding Oak Way 27520
Winding Wood Dr 27520
Windless Trl 27527
Windsor Ct 27520
Windsor Green Dr 27527
Windwood Ct 27527
Winslow Ln 27527
Winston Rd 27520
Winston Pointe Dr 27520
Winterberry St 27527
Wise Rd 27520
Wishbone Cir 27520
Wisteria Dr 27527
Wolverton Dr 27527
Wood Bend Ct 27520
Wood Duck Ln 27520
Wood Stork Ct 27520
Woodberry Dr 27527
Woodbriar St 27520

Woodcreek Ln 27520
Woodcrest Dr 27520
Woodglen Dr 27527
Woodlawn Way 27520
Woodmere Dr 27520
Woodridge Ct 27520
Woods Manor Ln 27527
Woodside Dr 27520
Woodson Dr 27527
S Woodstone Dr 27527
Worth Dr 27527
Worthington Ct 27527
Wren Ln 27520
Wright Ln 27527
Wylie Ct 27527
Wyndfall Ln 27527
Wynfield Dr 27520
Wynston Way 27520
Yale Ct 27520
Yarmouth Dr 27520
Yates Dr 27520
Yellow Daisy Pl 27527
Yellow Ribbons Ct 27520
York Ln 27527
Yorkbury Dr 27527
Yorkshire Dr 27520

NUMBERED STREETS

All Street Addresses 27520

CLINTON NC

General Delivery 28328

POST OFFICE BOXES MAIN OFFICE STATIONS AND BRANCHES

Box No.s
1 - 3700 28329
28328 - 28328 28328

RURAL ROUTES

04 28328

NAMED STREETS

All Street Addresses 28328

NUMBERED STREETS

All Street Addresses 28328

CONCORD NC

General Delivery 28025

POST OFFICE BOXES MAIN OFFICE STATIONS AND BRANCHES

Box No.s
1 - 2136 28026
2801 - 3435 28025
5001 - 9998 28027

NAMED STREETS

Aarick Ln 28027
Aaron Pl NW 28027
Aaron Rd 28025
Abbey Ln SE 28025
Abbey Ridge Pl NW 28027
Abercorn St NW 28027
Aberdeen Ct NW 28027
Abilene Rd 28025
Abington Ct & Dr 28025
Abshire Ln 28025
Academy Ave NW 28025
Accent Ave SE 28025
Acorn Cir 28025
Action Dr NW 28027
Adams St NE 28025
Adams Creek Ct & Dr 28025
Adamshire Ave 28025
Admiral Ave SW 28027
Aershire Ct 28025
Afterglow Ave 28025
Afton Run St 28027
Akins Dr NW 28027
Alamance Dr NW 28027
Alamo Ct SW 28027
Albany Dr NW 28027
Alberta Ct SW 28027
Alderman Rd 28025
Aldridge Pl NW 28027
Aldridge Farm Rd 28025
Alexander Rd 28027
Alexander St NW 28025
Alexia Ct NW 28027
Alexis Ct SW 28027
Alister Ave SW 28027
Alleghany St NW 28027
Allen Dr NW 28027
Allendale Ct 28025
Alliance Ave SW 28027
Allison St NW 28025
Allison Mews Pl NW 28027
Almeda Pl NW 28027
Almond Dr 28025
Alpha Ct SW 28027
Alstead Ct NW 28027
Alston Pl NW 28025
Altacrest Dr 28027
Alvadero Ct 28025
Amalia St NE 28025
Amarillo Dr SW 28027
Amber Ct SW 28025
Amber Ridge Rd NW 28027
Amberdeen Ct 28025
Ambergate Pl NW 28027
American Ave NE 28025
Amhurst St SW 28025
Amigo Dr 28025
Amity Ave SW 28025
Amsbury Rd 28025
Amy Ln NW 28027
Andover St NW 28027
Andrews St NW 28027
Ann St NW 28025
Annette Dr 28027
Ansley Ct 28027
Antietam Pl SW 28027
Antonio Ct NW 28027
Apple Tree Pl NW 28027
Applegate Dr 28027
Appleton Hollow Ave NW 28027
April Ct SW 28027
Arbor Knl & St NE 28025
Arbor Commons Ln 28027
Arbor Oaks Cir 28025
Archdale Dr 28027
Archibald Rd 28025
Arizona Pl NW 28027
Arlee Cir SW 28025
Arlington Ave SE 28025
Armentrout Dr 28025
Armstrong Rd 28025
Arrowhead Dr SE 28025
Artdale Rd SW 28027
Ash Ave NW 28025
Ashdale Ct 28027
Ashebrook Dr 28025
Asheford Green Ave NW 28027
Asherton Pl NW 28027
Ashford Dr 28027
Ashley Dr 28025
Ashley Green Ct NW 28027
Ashlyn Dr SE 28025
Ashton Ct SW 28027
Aspen Ln & Way NW 28027
Aspen Ridge Ln NW 28027
Astonshire Ln 28027
Astoria Ln NW 28027
Atando Rd 28025
Atwater Dr 28025
Aubrey Way 28027
Audley End Ct NW 28027
Audubon Ln 28025
Aundria Ln NW 28027
Aurora Dr 28025
Autumn Ln 28025
Autumn Fire Ave NW 28027
Autumn Knoll Pl NW 28027
Avery Ct 28025
Avian Pl 28025
Aviation Blvd & Cir NW 28027
Avon Ct NW 28027
Avondale Pl 28027
Axton Pl NW 28027
Aycock St NE 28025
Azalea Rd 28025
Aztec Dr 28025
Babbling Brook Ln 28025
Backwoods Pond Ln 28025
Baileys Lake Rd NW 28027
Bainbridge Dr NE 28025
Ballard St NW 28027
Baltic Ave NW 28027
Bampton Dr 28027
Banbury Ln 28025
Banyon Ct NW 28027
Baptist Ln 28025
Barbee Rd SW 28027
Barber St NW 28027
Barclay Ct SE 28025
Bardwell Ave NW 28027
Barefoot Ln 28025
Barfield St 28027
Barley St SW 28027
Barnett Rd 28027
Barnfield Rd 28025
Barnhardt Ave NW 28027
Barnhardt Rd NW 28027
Barossa Valley Dr NW 28027
Barr Rd 28027
Barrier Rd 28025
Barrier Georgeville Rd 28025
Barrington Pl NW 28027
Barrow Ave NE 28025
Barrowcliffe Dr NW 28027
Bartram Ave 28025
Basswood Dr 28025
Baucom Rd 28025
Baxter Pl SE 28025
Bay Ave & Ct 28025
Bay Meadows Ave NW 28027
Bayberry Trl 28027
Bayfield Pkwy 28027
Baystone Pl 28025
Baytree Ct SW 28027
Beacon St NW 28027
Beacon Hill Ct 28025
Beacontree Ct NW 28027
Beak Blvd 28025
Beans Way NW 28027
Beard Rd 28027
Beavers Cove Ln NW 28027
Beckette Ct NW 28027
Beckwick Ln 28025
Bedford Pl NW 28027
Beech St NW 28025
Beechwood Ave 28025
Bell St SW 28025
Bellamy Pl NW 28027
Bellhaven Pl NW 28027
Bellhook Pl NW 28027
Bellingham Dr NW 28027
Belmont Ct NW 28027
Belt Rd 28027
Belvedere Dr NW 28027
Benjamin Walker Ln 28027
Bennington Dr NW 28027
Bensalem Ln 28027
Bent Branch Dr SW 28025
Bent Creek Dr SW 28027
Bent Oak Trl 28027
Bentley Pl SW 28027
Benton Chase St NW 28027
Bentridge Dr NW 28027
Berkeley Pl 28027
Bermuda Ct NW 28027
Berry Hill Ct 28025
Berwick Ct NW 28027
Besor Pl NW 28027
Bethany Ct NW 28027
Bethel Church Rd 28025
Beverly Dr NE 28025
Bexley Village Dr 28027
Biggers Rd 28025
Bill St NW 28025
Biltmore Dr 28025
Bingham Dr NW 28027
Birch Ave SE 28025
Birchfield Ln NW 28027
Birchwood Trl NE 28025
Birdie Way Ct 28025
Birdsong Rd 28025
Birmingham Ave NW 28027
Birnamwood Dr 28025
Biscayne Dr 28027
Bishop Ln 28025
Bison Ct 28025
Blackberry Trl 28027
Blackstone Ct NW 28027
Blackvine Dr 28025
Blackwelder Dr 28025
Blackwelder Rd 28025
Blake Dr 28025
Blake Brook Dr 28025
Blanchette Ct 28025
Blandwood Dr 28025
Bleachery Ct NW 28025
Blenheim Ct NE 28025
Blossom Dr 28025
Blue Bird Pl 28025
Blue Ridge Dr 28027
Blue Sky Dr 28027
Bluebill Dr 28025
Bluff Ave SW 28027
Blume Ave SE & SW 28025
Boger Ct SW 28027
Bogle Dr 28027
Bonanza Dr 28025
Bondale Rd 28025
Bonnie St SE 28025
Bonwood Dr 28025
Booker Dr SW 28025
Boones Farm Rd 28027
Border Pl NW 28027
Bost Ave SW 28027
Bost Cutoff Rd 28025
Bostwood Ln 28025
Boswell Ct NW 28027
Botanical Ct NW 28027
Botany Dr 28027
Boulder Dr 28025
Boxcar Ln 28025
Boxwood Dr 28027
Boyden Pl NW 28027
Boyington Ct 28025
Brackley Pl NW 28027
Bradford Rd NW 28027
Bradley St 28025
Braeburn Rd NW 28027
Brafford Dr 28025
Bramblewood Ct SE 28025
Branch Dr SW 28027
Branchview Dr 28025
Branchwood Cir NE 28025
Brandon Cir 28025
Brandon Chase Ln 28025
Branson Rd NW 28027
Braughton Ave 28025
Bravery Pl SW 28027
Braxton Dr 28025
Breakwood Dr 28025
Breezy Ln 28025
Briarwood Pl SE 28025
Brice Pl SW 28027
Brickstone Cir 28025
Brickyard Tarrace Ct 28027
Brickyard Terrace Ct 28027
Bridlewood Pl NE 28025
Brigadoon Ct 28025
Bright Orchid Ave 28025
Brighton Ct NW 28027
Brightwood Ct SW 28025
Bristol Pl NW 28027
Broad Dr SW 28025
Broadleaf Dr 28027
Broadstairs Dr 28025
Brockton Ct NW 28027
Broderick St NW 28027
Brook Ave SE 28025
Brook Valley Ct NE 28025
Brookcliff Pl NW 28027
Brookgreen Pl NW 28027
Brooknell Ct NW 28027
Brookstone Dr NW 28027
Brookville Ave SW 28027
Brookwood Ave NE & NW 28025
Brown St SW 28027
Brown Lee Dr SW 28025
Brownwood Ln NW 28027
Brumley Ave NE 28025
Brunting Ln SW 28025
Brusharbor Rd 28025
Bruton Dr NW 28027
Bruton Smith Blvd 28027
Buck Pl NW 28025
Buckboard Cir 28025
Buckleigh Ct NW 28027
Buffalo Ave NW 28025
Buffalo Hills Dr 28025
Buffinton Ct NW 28027
Buford St NW 28025
Bull Run St 28027
Bullfrog Pl 28025
Bunker Grass Ln SW 28027
Burck Dr NW 28027
Burford Ln NW 28027
Burlwood Rd 28025
Burning Embers Ln 28025
Burrage Rd NE 28025
Burrell Ave NW 28027
Burris Ct & Ln SW 28027
Business Blvd NW 28027
Byfield Dr 28025
Byjo St 28027
Byrd Ct NW 28025
Cabarrus Ave E 28025
Cabarrus Ave W
1-337 28025
428-498 28027
500-799 28027
NW Cabarrus Dr 28027
Cadre Cir 28025
Caldwell Dr SE 28025
Calgary Pl NW 28027
Calloway Ave NW 28027
Cambridge Ct NE 28025
Cambridge Heights Pl NW 28027
Cambrook Ct 28027
Camden Ct NW 28027
Camden Town Dr NW 28027
Cameo Ct NW 28027
Cameron Ave NE 28025
Camilla Pl SE 28025
Campus Dr SW 28025
Camrose Cir & Ct NE 28025
Candle Ct NW 28027
Candlestick Ct SW 28025
Candlewood Dr NW 28027
Cannon Ave NW 28027
Canter Ct NW 28027
Canton Dr 28027
Canvasback Ct SE 28025
Capella Ave NW 28027
Capstone Ave 28025
Caralea Valley Dr NW 28027
Cardinal Pl SW 28027
Carly Ct 28025
Carlyle Dr NW 28027
Caro Mar Pl NW 28027
Carol Ct 28025
Carolando Dr SW 28027
Carolina Ave & Ct 28025
Carolina Pointe Ct SW 28027
Carolyn Dr SE 28025
Carpenter Ct NW 28027
Carriage Ave SW 28027
Carrie Ct 28027
Carrington Ct SW 28027
Carter Ct NW 28027
Carver Ave SW 28025
Cascade Dr NW 28027
Cashion Ct NW 28027
Castle Rd 28027
Castle Rock Ct 28025
Castlewood St NE 28025
Cates Ct NW 28027
Cavalier Ct NW 28027
Cayon Ct NW 28027
Cedar Dr NW 28025
Cedar Ridge Ln 28025
Cedar Springs Dr SW 28027
Cedarbrook Ln SW 28027
Cedarfield Ct NW 28027
Cedarwood Pl SE 28025
Celtic Dr NW 28027
Centennial Ct SW 28025
Centergrove Rd 28025
Central Dr NW 28027
Central Cabarrus Dr 28025
Central Heights Dr SW 28025
Cessna Rd 28027
Chadbourne Ave NW 28027
Chadbury Dr NW 28027
Chadmore Ln NW 28027
Chadwick Dr 28025
Chalice St SW 28027
Chalmers Ct NW 28027
Champion Ln SW 28025
Chandler Ave NW 28027
Chanel Ct 28025
Channing Cir NW 28027
Chapel Creek Rd SW 28025
Chapwin Cir NW 28027
Charing Pl SW 28025
Charmwood Ct NW 28027
Charter Ct SE 28025
Chartwell Ct 28025
Chase Ct 28027
Chase Prairie Ave NW 28027
Chastain Ave 28025
Chatfield Ln SW 28027
Chatham Ct NW 28027
Chatham Oaks Dr 28027
Chatsworth Ct NW 28027
Chaucer Pl NW 28027
Chedworth Ct 28025
Chelsea Dr 28025
Chelwood Dr NW 28027
Cherith Ct NW 28027
Cherokee Dr SE 28025
Cherry Ln NW 28027
Cherrycrest Ct 28025
Chesney St NW 28027
Chestnut Dr SW 28025
Cheswick Ave 28025
Chevaron Dr 28025
Chinaberry Ln 28027
Christenbury Pkwy & Rd 28027
Christenbury Hall Ct & Dr 28027
Christianna Ct NW 28027
Christopher Rd 28025
Church St N 28025
Cindy Ln 28025
Circle Dr NE 28025
Circle R Rd 28025
Clara Cir 28025
Claramont Dr SW 28027
Clarence Jordan Ct 28027
Claridge Rd 28027
Clarkes Meadow Dr NW 28027
Clarkes View Pl NW 28027
Claw Ct 28025
Claymont St SE 28025
Clearview Ct SE 28025
Clearwater Dr NW 28027
Cleary Ct NW 28027
Cliff Haven Dr 28025
Cliffdale Dr 28025
Clifftonville Ave SW 28025
Cliffwood St NW 28027
Cline Ct SW 28025
Cline St 28027
Cline School Rd 28025
Clintwood Dr NW 28027
Cliveden Ave NW 28027
Clivenden Ave NW 28027
Cloister Ct NW 28027
Clover Rd NW 28027
Cloverhill Pl NW 28027
Club View Dr 28025
Coach House Pl NW 28027
Coast Laurel Ave NW 28027
Cobblestone Ln NW 28027
Cochran Rd SW 28027
Cochran Farm Rd SW 28027
Cochran Park Rd NW 28027
Coddle Creek Dr 28027
Coddle Market Dr NW 28027
Cold Creek Farms Rd 28025
Cold Springs Rd 28025
Coldwater Ct SE 28025
Coleman Cir NW 28027
Coley St SW 28027
Colfax Dr SE 28025
College Cir SW 28027
Collingswood Dr NW 28027
Colonial Ave SE 28025
Colorado Dr NW 28027
Colwick Ct NW 28027
Commerce Dr 28025
Commercial Park Dr SW 28027
Commons Park Cir NW 28027
Compton Ct NW 28027
Concord Pkwy N
200-1199 28027
1200-1599 28025
1601-1699 28025
Concord Pkwy S 28027
Concord Chase Cir 28025
Concord Commons Pl SW 28027
Concord Farm Rd 28027
Concord Lake Rd 28025
Concord Mills Blvd 28027
Concord Pointe Ln SW 28027
Concord Speedway Dr 28025
Confederate Dr SW 28027
Conifer Pl 28025
Continental Dr 28025
Cook St NW 28025
Copeland Rd 28025
Copperfield Blvd NE 28025
Coral St SW 28027
Coral Bells Ct NW 28027
Corban Ave SE & SW 28025
Corey Ave SW 28025
Corina Rd 28025
Corl Rd 28027
Cornwall Ct NW 28027
Corporate Dr NW 28027
Cottingham Pl NE 28025
Cottontail Ln SE 28025
Cottonwood Trl 28027
Coulwood Cir 28027
Country Barn Dr 28025
Country Club Dr NE 28025
Country Home Rd 28025
Country View Rd 28025
Countrywood Pl SE 28025
Courage Ct SW 28027
Courtney Ct & St 28025

Cove Creek Pl SE 28025
Covington Dr NW 28027
Cox Mill Rd 28027
Cozart Ct SW 28025
Crab Tree Ct SW 28025
Craig Ave 28027
Craigmont Ln NW 28027
Crane Ct 28025
Cranford Pl SW 28025
Craven Ln 28025
Creek Trl SE 28025
Creekside Dr SE 28025
Creeping Turtle Dr 28025
Cress Rd 28025
Cress Farm Rd 28027
Cresthaven Ct NW 28027
Crestmont Dr SE 28025
Crestside Dr SE 28025
Crestview Dr 28027
Creswell Dr NE 28025
Crisco Rd S 28027
Cross Ave SW 28027
Crossbow Cir NW 28027
Crosspointe Dr NE 28025
Crossroads Pl 28025
Crowell Dr NW & SW 28025
Crown Point Cir NW 28025
Crystal Cove Pl SW 28025
Crystalwood Ct NW 28027
Cub Run Dr 28027
Culloden Ct 28027
Cumberland Ct SW 28025
Curtland Pl NW 28027
Cy Cir 28025
Cypress St SW 28025
Daffodil Ln 28025
Dairy Farm Rd 28025
Dakeita Cir 28025
Daley Cir 28025
Dalton Ct NW 28027
Dana Ct 28027
Danbrooke Dr 28025
Danbury Circle Dr NW 28027
Danielle Downs Ct SE 28025
Darby Creek Ave NW 28027
Darcy Ct 28025
Dartmoor Ave NW 28027
Dartwood Dr NW 28027
Darwin Trl NW 28027
Datsun Ave 28027
David Fudge Pl NW 28027
Davidson Dr NW 28025
Davidson Hwy 28027
Davis St SW 28025
Dawn Ridge Pl SW 28027
Dayvault St SW 28025
Dc Dr 28025
Deacon Ct SW 28025
Deal St SE 28025
Dearborn Pl NW 28027
Debra Cir SW 28025
Deep Cove Dr NW 28027
Deepwood Pl NW 28027
Deerfield Dr NW 28027
Deerwood Pl NW 28027
Delaney Dr 28027
Dellwood Ct SE 28025
Delrae Cir 28027
Denise Cir SW 28025
Dennbriar Dr NW 28027
Derby Ln NW 28027
Derita Rd 28027
Desert Willow Ct NW 28027
Dessie Ct 28025
Devereaux Ct NE 28025
Deveron Pl NE 28025
Devonshire Dr 28027
Dewitt Ct & Dr NW 28027
Dickens Pl NE 28025
Dileen Dr 28025
Division St SW 28027
Dockside Ln NW 28027
Doe St 28025
Dogwood Park 28027
Dogwood St SE 28025
Dolly St NW 28027

Doncastle Ct 28025
Donelea Ln NW 28027
Donna Dale Ave SE 28025
Donnington Ln NW 28027
Doris Ct SE 28025
Dorland Ave SW 28025
Dorsett Ct NW 28027
Double Eagle St SW 28027
Douglas Ave NW 28027
Dove Ave SW 28025
Dove Point Dr SW 28025
Down Patrick Ln NW 28027
Downing Ct SE 28025
Dr Floyd Rd 28025
Drake Mill Ln SW 28025
Drakestone Rd 28027
Drayton Ln 28027
Dresden Pl SW 28025
Drummond Dr NW 28027
Duck Point Dr 28025
Duckhorn St NW 28027
Dulin Dr SW 28027
Dumbarton St NW 28027
Dunberry Pl SW 28025
Dunhill Ln SW 28025
Dunkirk Dr 28027
Dunloe Ct 28025
Dunmore Ct SW 28027
Durham Ct NW 28027
Dusty Ln NW 28027
Duval St NW 28025
Dylan Pl NW 28027
Eagle View Pl NW 28027
Eaglebrook Dr 28027
Eagles Glen Ct SW 28027
Earl Ave NE 28025
Eastbrook Ave NE 28025
Eastcliff Dr SE 28025
Eastover Cir & Dr 28025
Eastridge Ct 28025
Eastside Dr SW 28025
Easy St 28027
Eden St NW 28027
Edenbury Dr 28027
Edenton St NW 28027
Edgefield Rd 28025
Edgepine Ln NW 28027
Edgewater Dr NW 28027
Edgewood Ave & Cir 28025
Edison Square Dr NW 28027
Edna Dr 28027
Edward Ave SW 28025
Eisenhower Pl NW 28027
Elaine Pl NW 28025
Elatia Cir 28025
Elgin Ct & Dr 28025
Elizabeth St SW 28025
Elizabeth Lee Dr NW 28027
Elkwood Ct 28025
Ella St NW 28027
Ellie Ct 28025
Ellington St NW 28027
Elm Ave NW 28025
Elmhurst Ln 28025
Elsfield Ave NW 28027
Emerald Dr 28025
Emery Ave NW 28027
Emory Ln NW 28027
Enclave Cir 28027
Endecott Ct NW 28027
Englewood St NE 28025
English Ct NW 28027
Enterprise Dr NW 28027
Epworth St NW 28027
Equestrian Rd 28027
Erickson Ct 28025
Erinbrook Dr 28025
Ervin Ave NW 28025
Eschol Ln NW 28027
Essex Dr 28025
Estridge Ln 28027
Ethel Ln 28027
Eucalyptus Ct NW 28027
Euclid Ave NW 28027
Eudy Dr NW 28027
Eugene Pl SW 28025

Eva Dr NW 28027
Evans St NW 28027
Evanston St NW 28027
Evelyn Dr 28025
Everette Dr 28027
Eversham Dr NW 28027
Exchange St NW 28027
Executive Park Dr 28025
Faggart Ave NW 28027
Fair Oaks Pl NW 28027
Fairbanks Dr NW 28027
Fairbluff Rd 28025
Fairington Dr NW 28027
Fairmead Dr 28025
Fairport Dr SE 28025
Fairview Ct SW 28025
Fairway Ridge Dr NW 28027
Fairwoods Dr NW 28027
Faith Dr SW 28025
Faith Trl 28025
Falcon Dr 28025
Falcon Chase Dr SW 28027
Fallbrook Pl NW 28027
Falling Leaf Dr NW 28027
Fallwood Dr SE 28025
Famous Dr 28025
Faraway Cir 28025
Fargo Dr SW 28027
Farm Branch Dr SW 28027
Farm Lake Dr SW 28027
Farm Pond Rd 28025
Farmer St 28027
Farmers Glade Pl NW 28027
Farmington Ct 28025
Farmwood Blvd SW 28027
Fauna Ave NW 28027
Fawn Cir SW 28025
Fawn Ridge Rd NW 28027
Fawnbrook Ave SW 28027
Feather St 28025
Fenix Dr SW 28027
Fenton Dr 28027
Fenwick Pl 28025
Fern Ave SW 28025
Fern Dancer Ct 28027
Ferncliff Dr NW 28027
Fescue Pl SW 28027
Fetzer Ave NW 28027
Fieldcrest Cir NW 28027
Fieldstone Dr 28027
Finger Lake Dr 28027
Fink Ave NW 28027
Finley Pl NW 28027
Firebrick Ln SW 28025
Firecrest St SE 28025
Firelight Ct SW 28027
Firethorne Ave SW 28027
Firethorne Ln 28025
First Turn Ct SW 28025
Fisher St 28027
Fisher Farm Ln NW 28027
Fishermans Dr NW 28027
Fisk St NW 28027
Fitzgerald St NW 28025
Flannery Pl NW 28027
Fleetwood Dr SW 28027
Fletcher Ct SW 28025
Flicker St 28027
Flint Ridge Dr 28025
Flora Ave NW 28027
Florence St NW 28027
Flowe St NW 28027
Flowe Farm Rd 28025
Flower Bonnet Ave NW 28027
Flowerfield Dr 28025
Flowes Store Rd E 28025
Flynwood Pl SW 28027
Fontana Ct SW 28025
Foothills Ln 28025
Footsie Ln 28025
Forest St NW 28025
Forest Cliff Ct NE 28025
Forestdale St 28025
Forrest Ridge Dr NW 28027
Forsythe Ln 28025

Fortune Ave NW 28027
Fossil Ln SW 28025
Fountainview Ave 28025
Four Winds Ct SW 28027
Fowler Rd 28025
Fox St SW 28025
Fox Meadow Ct 28025
Foxford Dr 28025
Foxrun Cir SE 28025
Foxwood Dr SE 28025
Frankfurt Dr 28025
Franklin Ave NW 28025
Franklin Tree Dr NW 28027
Freedom St SW 28025
Freeman Rd 28025
Freeze Ave NW 28025
Fresh Water Ct 28027
Friendly Ave 28027
Fringewood Dr 28025
Friskie Ln 28027
Frostwood Ln 28025
Fryling Ave SW 28025
Fulton Ct 28025
Furr Ave NW 28027
Gable Oaks Ln NW 28027
Gail Ln 28027
Gainesway Ct NW 28027
Gaither Pl NW 28027
Galloway Ln SW 28025
Gambel Dr NW 28027
Garden Ter 28025
Garrett Dr SW 28027
Garrison Ct SW 28025
Garrison Inn Ct NW 28027
Garver Cir 28027
Gasser Dr SW 28027
Gatehouse Ct NW 28027
NE Gateway Ct NE 28025
Gateway Ln NW 28027
Gatsby Pl NW 28027
Gaylan Ct SW 28027
Gaywood Dr 28025
Geary St NW 28027
Gene Ct SE 28025
Geneva Dr 28025
Gentry Rd 28027
George Bay Ct 28027
George W Liles Pkwy NW 28027
Georgetown Dr NW 28027
Georgia St NW & SW 28025
Gerry Ct 28025
Gettysburg Dr NW 28027
Gibson Dr NW 28025
Giverny Ct NW 28027
Gladden Pl NW 28027
Glen Eagles Ln SW 28027
Glen Haven Dr SW 28027
Glen Laurel Dr 28025
Glen Rae St SW 28025
Glendale Ave SE 28025
Glenmoor Ct 28027
Glenn St NW 28027
Glenn Afton Blvd 28025
Glenwood Dr SW 28025
Glouster Ct 28025
Goar St SW 28025
Gold St NW & SW 28025
Gold Hill Rd 28025
Gold Rush Dr 28025
Golden Desert Ct NE 28027
Golden Eye Dr 28025
Golding Dr 28027
Goldmoor Dr NE 28025
Golf Ball Cir 28025
Goodman Cir NE 28025
Goodman Rd 28027
Goodson Pl SW 28027
Goosefoot Ct NW 28027
Governors Pointe Ct NE 28025
Grace Ave NW 28027
Graham Dr SW 28025
Granada Dr SW 28027
Grand Canyon Rd NW 28027
Grand National Ln SW 28027

Grand Oaks St NW 28027
Grand Summit Blvd 28027
Grandhaven Dr 28027
Grandview Dr NE 28025
Grantwood Ave NW 28027
Gratton Dr NE 28025
Graystone Ct 28025
Greathorn Ln 28027
Green Dr & St 28027
Green Acres Cir 28025
Green Haven Ct 28025
Greenbriar Rd 28025
Greenfield Cir & Dr NW 28027
Greenside Dr NW 28027
Greenwood Dr SW 28027
Gretel Ave NW 28027
Greygate St SW 28027
Greyson Ct NW 28027
Greystone Dr SW 28027
Grier Ave SW 28025
Griffin Cir 28025
Griffins Gate Dr SW 28025
Grist Mill Dr SW 28025
Griswell Dr NW 28027
Groff St NW 28027
Grossbeak Cir 28025
Grouse Dr 28025
Grove Ave NW 28025
Grove Creek Pond Dr SW 28027
Guilford Ct NW 28027
Gurley Dr NW 28027
Guy Ave NW 28025
Gwyn Ct NW 28027
Habersham Ct NW 28027
Hackberry Ln SW 28027
Haestad Ct 28025
Hahn Blvd, Pl & St 28025
Hall Ave NW 28027
Hallstead St 28025
Halton Crossing Dr SW 28027
Halyburton St NE 28025
Hamberton Ct NW 28027
Hamby Branch Rd 28025
Hamilton Dr NE 28025
Hampton Chase Dr SW 28027
Hampton Forrest Dr 28027
Hanford Pl NW 28027
Hania Dr SW 28027
Hanna Ct NW 28027
Hanover Dr NW 28027
Hansom Ln NW 28027
Hanwell Ln NW 28027
Harbor Dr 28025
Hardwicke Pl NW 28027
Hardwood Ln 28027
Harold Pl SW 28025
Harold Goodman Cir SW 28025
Harp Dr SW 28027
Harris Rd 28027
Harris St NW 28027
Harrison Dr NW 28027
Hartman Pl NW 28027
Hartsell School Rd SW 28027
Harvell Dr 28025
Harvest Pond Dr NW 28027
Hathwyck Ct NW 28027
Hatley Cir NE 28025
Havenbrook Way NW 28027
Havencrest Ct NW 28027
Haverford Rd NW 28027
Hawick Commons Dr 28027
Hawks Nest Dr 28027
Hawthorne St SW 28027
Hayden Way 28025
Hazelmere St NW 28027
Hearth Ln SW 28025
Hearthstone Ct NW 28027
Heathcliff Rd 28025
Heather Ln 28025
Heatherwood Ct NW 28027

Hedgemore Ct NW 28027
Heglar Rd 28025
Heidelberg Dr 28025
Helen Dr NW 28027
Helmsley Ct 28027
Hemlock St SW 28025
Hemmings Pl NW 28027
Hempstead Ct 28025
Hendrix Ct 28025
Henslee Pl 28025
Heritage Farm Ave NW 28027
Hermitage Dr SE 28025
Heron Ln 28025
Heron Point Pl SW 28025
Herrons Nest Pl NW 28027
Hertling Dr NW 28027
Hess Rd 28025
Hickory Ave & St SW 28027
Hickory Grove Dr SW 28027
Hickory Nut Trl 28027
Hidden Oaks Dr SE 28025
Hidden Park Dr 28025
Hidden Valley Dr 28027
High Ave SW 28025
High Meadows Dr 28025
High Ridge Ln 28027
Highgrove Pl 28027
Highland Ave & St SW 28027
Highlander Ct 28025
Highway 200 28025
Highway 29 N 28025
Highway 49 N 28025
Highway 49 S
1-799 28025
Highway 49 S
1000-2199 28027
Highway 601 Byp S 28025
Highway 73 E 28025
Hildreth Ct 28025
Hillandale Pl & St 28025
Hillcrest Ave SE 28025
Hilliard Ln 28025
Hillsdell Dr 28027
Hillshire Ct 28027
Hillside Ave SW 28025
Hilltop Ave SW 28025
Historic Springs Dr 28025
Hogan Ct 28025
Holburn St SW 28025
Holden Ave 28025
Hollows Glen Ct SW 28027
Holly Hills Ct NW 28027
Holmes Ct 28027
Holshouser Rd 28027
Homecliff Dr 28025
Homer Ave NW 28025
Homerine St NE 28025
Homestead Pl 28025
Honduras St NW 28027
Honeycutt Dr SE 28025
Hooper Dr SW 28027
Hoover Ave NE 28025
Hopkins St 28027
Horizon Ct NW 28027
Hornets Nest Ct 28027
Houston St NE 28025
Howerton Ave NW 28027
Huckleberry Trl 28027
Hudwall Rd 28025
Huie St NW 28027
Hunteroak Dr 28027
Hunters Trace Dr 28027
Huntingwood Pl NE 28025
Huntley Pl SW 28027
Hyde Park Dr NE 28025
Hydrangea Cir NW 28027
Ichabod Cir 28025
Idaho Ln NW 28027
Ideal Dr SE 28025
Idlewild Dr 28027
Ikerd Dr SE 28025
Indian Beech Ave NW 28027
Industrial Ct 28025
Ingleside Dr SE 28025

International Dr NW 28027
Inverness Pl NW 28027
Irish Potato Rd 28025
Irish Woods Dr 28025
Isaac St 28027
Island Point Dr NW 28027
Island View Dr 28025
Israel Dr 28025
Ithaca Dr 28025
Ives St NW 28027
Ivey St NW 28025
Ivey Cline Rd 28027
Iveywood Pl NW 28027
Ivy Grove Ct NW 28027
Ivy Walk Ct NW 28027
Ivydale Ave SW 28027
Jabbok Pl NW 28027
Jackson Ter SW 28027
Jaf Dr 28025
James St SW 28025
Jameson Dr NW 28027
Jamestown Rd 28027
Janrose Ct NW 28027
Jarvis Cir 28027
Jason Dr 28025
Jeff Yates St SW 28027
Jefferson Ave NE 28025
Jensen Ln 28025
Jerman Dr 28025
Jerod Ct 28025
Jessica Ln 28025
Jim Johnson Rd 28027
Jim Kiser Rd 28025
Joe Bost Rd 28025
John Furr Rd 28025
John Galt Way NW 28027
John Q Hammons Dr NW 28027
John White Rd 28025
Johnson St SW 28027
Johnston St 28027
Johnston Farm Rd 28027
Jones Ave NW 28025
Josephine Ln SW 28027
Journey St SW 28025
Joyner Rd 28025
Juanita Dr NW & SW 28027
Jubilee Ct 28027
Judge Pl NW 28027
Juniper Pl SE 28025
Juniper Grove Ct SW 28027
Kannapolis Hwy
1900-2449 28027
2450-2499 28025
Kannapolis Pkwy 28027
Karen Ave SE 28025
Kathryn Dr SE 28025
Kathy Dr 28025
Katrina Ave 28025
Kay Pl SE 28025
Kay Bird Ln 28027
Keenan Dr SE 28025
Keeneland Pl SW 28027
Kellybrook Dr 28025
Kendale Ave NW 28027
Kendra Dr SW 28025
Kenilworth Ct NW 28027
Kenton Glenn Ct NW 28027
Kentucky Ave SW 28025
Kepley Rd NW 28027
Kerr St NW 28025
Kesler Ave NW 28027
Keystone Ct NW 28027
Kidd Ct NE 28025
Kildare Dr 28025
Kim St SW 28027
Kimberly Ln 28025
Kindling Pl SW 28025
Kindred Cir NW 28027
King Fredrick Ln SW 28027
Kingfield Dr SW 28027
Kings Creek Ct NE 28025
Kings Crossing Dr NW 28027
Kingsport Dr NE 28025
Kinsley Ave NW 28027
Kintyre Ct NW 28027

Kirkland Ct 28025
Kirkwood Dr 28025
Kiser Rd SW 28025
Kiser Woods Dr SW 28025
Kison Ct NW 28027
Kite Ct 28025
Kiwi Ct 28025
Kluttz Ct & Rd SW 28025
Knightbridge Dr 28025
Knoll Ct SE 28025
Knollcrest Dr NE 28025
Krimminger Ave SE 28025
Kye Dr NW 28027
La Forest Ln 28025
Lacewood Ct 28025
Lacoma Ln 28025
Laguna Ave NW 28027
Lahana Rd & St NW & SW 28027
Lake Concord Rd NE 28025
Lake Lynn Rd 28025
Lake Spring Ave NW 28027
Lakeland Rd 28027
Lakepoint Ct 28025
Lakeshore Pl NW 28027
Lakeside Dr SW 28027
Lakewood Ct NW 28027
Lamar Rd 28025
Lampshire Dr NW 28027
Lancashire Way 28025
Lancaster St NW 28027
Lancelot Cir NE 28025
Lancer Ct NW 28027
Landale Ct NW 28027
Lands End Ct SW 28027
Laney St 28027
Langford Ave NW 28027
Langley Dr SE 28025
Langshire Ct NW 28027
Lansfaire Ave NW 28027
Lansing St NW 28027
Lanstone Ct SW 28027
Laramie Rd SW 28027
Laraway Ct NW 28027
Larchlea Pl 28025
Lark Ct SW 28027
Larkhaven Ave SW 28027
Larkview Dr SW 28027
Laurel St NW 28027
Laurel Bay St NW 28027
Laurelview Dr NW 28027
Laurelwind Pl SW 28027
Laurelwood Ct 28025
Lauren Glen St NW 28027
Laurens Dr 28027
Laurie Ave NW 28027
Laverne Dr SW 28027
Lawings Dr SW 28027
Lawndale Ave & Pl 28025
Lazy Ridge Ln 28025
Le Phillip Ct NE 28025
Leafmore St 28027
Leah Ct NW 28027
Lecline Cir & Dr 28025
Ledbury Ct NW 28027
Lee Ct SW 28027
Lee Ann Dr NE 28025
Lefler St 28025
Legend St SW 28027
Leighton Dr SW 28027
Lemley Rd NW 28027
Lemming Dr 28025
Lemmon Ave NW 28027
Lemon Tree Ln SW 28025
Lempster Dr NW 28027
Lenhaven St 28025
Lenmore Ct & Dr 28025
Lenox Ave SE 28025
Leo Rd NW 28027
Leverwood Ave NW 28027
Lexford Ct 28025
Lexington Pl NW 28027
Liberty Dr SW 28027
Liberty Ridge Rd 28025
Lily Green Ct NW 28027
Lincoln St SW 28025
Linda Wood Ln 28025
Linden Ave SW 28027
Lindler Dr 28027
Linker Ave NW 28027
Lisa Dr 28025
Liske Ave NW 28027
Litaker Ln 28025
Litchfield Pl NW 28027
Little Creek Ln NW 28027
Little Falls Dr 28025
Littleton Dr 28025
Livingston Dr NE 28025
Livingstone Ct NE 28025
Lizzie Ct NW 28027
Lloyd Pl NW 28027
Lloyd Garmon Ln 28025
Loblolly Ct SW 28027
Loch Lomond Cir 28025
Lockhart Pl NW 28027
Lockwood Rd 28027
Locust St NW 28025
Lofton Ct 28025
Logan Ave SW 28025
Lolabridge St NW 28027
Lomax Ct SE 28025
Londonderry Ct NW 28027
Long Ave NE 28025
Long Leaf Ct 28025
Longwood Dr SW 28027
Lonnie Bascom Cir 28025
Lorain Ave NW 28027
Lore St SW 28025
Louise Dr SE 28025
Love St SW 28027
Lowe Ave NW 28027
Lower Rocky River Rd 28025
Lucky Dr NW 28027
Lucy Ave NW 28027
Ludwig Ave 28027
Lyerly Ridge Rd NW 28027
Lyla Ave 28027
Lyles Ln NW 28027
Lynchburg Dr 28027
Lynn Dr 28025
Lynnwood Dr 28025
Lynwood Dr NW 28027
Lyons Blvd 28025
Lyric Ave NW 28027
Macedonia Church Rd 28027
Mackenzie Ct SW 28027
Maderia Dr NW 28027
Madison Ave NE 28025
Madres Ct 28025
Magnolia St NW 28025
Magnolia Crossing Cir NW 28027
Mahan St SW 28025
Mahland Ct NW 28025
Mahogany Pl SW 28025
Maid Marian Ln 28027
Maiden Ln SW 28025
S Main St SW 28025
Majestic Ct SE 28025
Mall Dr 28025
Mallard Dr 28025
Malvern Dr SW 28025
Mammoth Oaks Dr 28025
Manassas Dr 28027
Manatee Dr 28027
Mandalay Pl SW 28027
Manor Ave SW 28025
Manor Oak Pl NW 28027
Manor View Dr NW 28027
Manston Pl SW 28025
Manteo Dr 28027
Maple Ave NW 28027
Maple Bluff Ln 28025
Maple Grove Ln NW 28027
Marasol Ln 28027
Marble St SE 28025
Margate St SW 28025
Marietta Pl NW 28025
Marilyn Ct 28025
Mark Dr 28025
Market St SW 28025
Marlboro Dr SW 28027
Marlow Dr 28027
Marmot Pl 28025
Marquette St NW 28027
Marsh Ave NE & NW 28025
Marshall Dr 28027
Marshdale Ave SW 28025
Martin St NE 28025
Mary Cir 28025
Matchstick Pl SW 28025
May St NE 28025
Maybrook Ct SW 28027
Mayfield Ct NW 28027
Mba Ct 28025
Mcanulty Rd 28025
Mcarthur Ave SE 28025
Mccachern Blvd SE
1-67 28025
66-66 28026
68-98 28025
69-99 28025
Mccamie Hill Pl 28025
Mcclenny Dr 28027
Mccoppin Ct NE 28025
Mccready St NE 28025
Mccurdy St NW 28027
Mcdonald St NW 28027
Mcgill Ave NW
1-275 28025
277-299 28025
300-499 28027
Mcginnes Pl NW 28027
Mcgregor Dr NE 28025
Mckinnon Ave NE 28025
Mclaren Ct NW 28027
Meadow Ave NE 28025
Meadow Bluff Ct NW 28027
Meadow Embers Dr 28025
Meadow Oaks Dr 28025
Meadow Ridge Ct & Dr 28027
Meadowbrook Ln SW 28027
Meadowlark Cir & Ln 28025
Meadowview Ave SW 28027
Means Ave SE 28025
Medford Dr NW 28027
Medical Park Dr 28025
Meeting St 28025
Meidas Ct NW 28027
Melanie Ct 28025
Melba Ave SW 28025
Melchor Ct SW 28025
Melody Ct 28025
Melrose Dr SW 28025
Memorial Blvd 28025
Memory Ln 28025
Meredith Ct 28025
Meridian Ct SW 28025
Merle Rd 28025
Merrymount Ct 28025
Mexico Rd 28025
Miami Ln 28025
Miami Church Rd 28025
Michael Ave 28025
Middlecrest Dr NW 28027
Midpines Dr 28025
Milford Ct NW 28025
Mill Bluffs Ln 28025
Mill Ruins Ave SW 28025
Mill Wright Rd 28025
Millard Fuller Way 28025
Millbrook Ct 28025
Miller Ave SW 28025
Millet St SW 28027
Millpond Way 28027
Mills Ave NW 28027
Mills Cir 28025
Milltown Ct SW 28025
Milo Ave SW 28025
Milton Ave NE 28025
Mine Springs Rd 28025
Miramar St NE 28025
Mirawood Trl NE 28025
Misenheimer Dr NW
200-319 28025
320-399 28027
Missy Cir NW 28027
Mistletoe Ridge Pl NW 28027
Misty Forest Pl NW 28027
Mistywood Ln 28027
Mobile Trail Dr 28027
Mona Ave NE 28025
Monarch Ct SW 28027
Monitor Ct 28027
Monroe Ct NW 28027
Monta Dr 28025
Montana Cir NW 28027
Monterosa Rd 28025
Montford Ave NW 28027
Montgrove Pl NW 28027
Monticello Dr NW 28027
Moonlight Drive Trl SW 28025
Moonstone Dr 28025
Moore Dr & Pl 28025
Mooresville Rd 28027
Moose Lodge Rd 28025
Moray Ct NW 28027
Morehead Rd 28027
Moreland Wood Trl NW 28027
Morgan Pl SW 28025
Morning Dew Dr 28025
Morning Pond Ln 28025
Morris Burn Dr SW 28027
Morris Glen Dr SW 28027
Morrison Rd 28025
Morrow Ct NE 28025
Morton Ave 28025
Moss Dr 28027
Moss Farms Rd NW 28027
Moss Plantation Ave NW 28027
Motorsports Dr SW 28027
Mott Shue Dr SW 28027
Mount Olive Rd 28025
Mount Olivet Rd 28025
Mount Pleasant Rd N & S 28025
Mountain Laurel Ave NW 28027
Mountaineer Ln 28025
Mountcrest Cir NW 28027
Mountview Ct SE 28025
Mrn Dr NW 28027
Muir Ct NW 28027
Mulberry Rd 28025
Munsen Rd 28025
Muse Ct NW 28027
Muskratt Pl SE 28025
Myint Ln NW 28027
Myrtle Ave SW 28025
Nannyberry Ln 28025
Napa St NW 28027
Nash Ave 28025
Navajo Trl 28027
Navion Pl 28025
Nc Highway 73 E 28025
Neisler Rd 28025
Nesbitt Rd 28027
New Castle Ct NE 28025
New Gate Ct NW 28027
New Haven St NW 28027
Newburg Pl SW 28027
Newell St NW 28025
Newhall St 28025
Newton Dr 28027
Nicholas Pl NW 28027
No Mans Ave 28027
Nolen Ave NW 28027
Norfleet St 28025
Norma Dr 28025
Norman Pt 28025
Northchase Dr 28027
Northgate Blvd NE 28025
Northwinds Dr NW 28027
Norwood Rd 28027
Nuthatch Ln 28025
Oak Dr SW 28027
Oak Haven Pl NW 28027
Oak Pond Pl NW 28027
Oak Trail Cir 28025
Oakdale Ave SW 28027
Oakland Ave SE & SW 28025
Oakview Dr SW 28027
Oakwood Ave 28027
Obeds Ln NW 28027
Obrien Pl SW 28025
Octavia St 28025
Odell Cir 28027
Odell Dr NW 28025
Odell Place Dr 28027
Odell School Rd 28027
Office Dr SW 28027
Old Airport Rd 28025
Old Ashworth Ln NW 28027
Old Cedarwood Dr NW 28027
Old Charlotte Rd SW 28027
Old Davidson Pl NW 28027
Old Farm Rd SE 28025
Old Glory Dr 28025
Old Greylyn Ct NW 28027
Old Harmony Dr NW 28027
Old Lake Lynn Rd 28025
Old Macedonia Ct 28027
Old Monroe Cir 28025
Old Plantation Dr SW 28027
Old Salisbury Concord Rd 28025
Old Sapp Rd 28025
Old South Ct SW 28027
Old Speedway Dr NW 28027
Old State St SW 28027
Old Wagon Wheel Ln 28025
Olde Creek Trl 28025
Olde North Church Rd 28025
Olive Hill Ave NW 28027
Ophela Ct SW 28027
Optimist Club Dr 28025
Opus Ct 28027
Orchard Pl NE 28025
Oriole Ln 28025
Orphanage Cir & Rd 28027
Osprey Ct SE 28025
Oulten St 28027
Overbrook Dr NE 28025
Overcash Rd 28027
Owens Ct NW 28027
Owl Creek Ln 28027
Oxford Ct 28025
Paddington Dr SW 28025
Paddle Pl NW 28027
Palafox Dr 28027
Palaside Dr NE 28025
Palmer Ave SW 28027
Pamela St NE 28025
Pamlico Pl NW 28027
Panthers Den Ct 28027
Papa Pl 28027
Parade Ln SW 28025
Parallel Ct NW 28025
Park Dr SW 28027
Park St SW 28025
Park Grove Pl NW 28027
Parkmont Rd 28027
Parks Lafferty Rd 28025
Parksie Ct SW 28027
Parkview Ct SW 28025
Parkway Ave NW 28027
Parkwood Dr NW 28027
Parrish Pl SW 28027
Partridge Bluff Dr NE 28025
Pascal Ct NW 28027
Patee Ln 28027
Patience Dr 28025
Patricia Dr NW 28025
Patrick Ave SW 28025
Patrick Henry Dr NW 28027
Patriot Ct NE 28025
Patriot Plantation Blvd 28027
Patriots Place Dr 28025
Patterson Ave SE 28025
Patton Ct SE 28025
Peachtree Ave NW 28025
Pearl Ave SW 28027
Pebble Ave SW 28027
Pebble Creek Dr 28025
Pebble Stone Ct NW 28027
Pebblebrook Cir SW 28027
Pecan Ave & Ct 28025
Peigler St NW 28027
Pembrook Dr 28025
Penelope Pl NE 28025
Penninger Rd 28025
Pennington Pl NW 28027
Penny Ln 28025
Penrod Dr SW 28027
Peoples Ct 28025
Pepperidge Ave NW 28027
Peppertree Ave 28027
Perennial Dr NW 28027
Performance Dr SW 28027
Perry St 28027
Perth Ct 28027
Petersburg Dr 28027
Peyton Ct NW 28027
Pharr Dr SW 28027
Pheasant Dr 28025
Phifer Ave NW 28025
Phil Ln 28027
Phoenix Cir 28025
Pickney Ct 28025
Pier Point Ct NW 28027
Pine St NW 28025
Pine Bough Ln 28027
Pine Circle Dr NW 28027
Pine Grove Church Rd 28025
Pine Trail Ln 28025
Pinecrest Dr SW 28027
Pineridge Pl & St 28025
Pinetree Ave SW 28027
Piney Ct 28025
Piney Church Rd 28025
Piney Pointe Rd 28025
Pintail Dr 28025
Pioneer Mill Rd 28025
Piper Ct 28025
Pit Rd S 28027
Pit Stop Ct NW 28027
Pitts School Rd 28027
Plantation Rd NW 28027
Pleasant Dr 28025
Pleasant Hill Dr 28025
Pless St NW 28027
Plott Dr SW 28025
Point View Ct 28025
Pointe Andrews Dr 28025
Pointer Ct SE 28025
Pokeberry Trl 28027
Pond Landing Ct 28025
Ponderosa Ln 28025
Pondview Ct 28025
Poole Pl NW 28027
Poplar St SW 28027
Poplar Crossing Dr NW 28027
Poplar Tent Rd 28027
Poplar Woods Dr 28027
Porter St NW 28027
Porters Ct 28025
Post Oak Ave SW 28025
Potomac Dr NW 28027
Potter Ridge Rd 28025
Pounds Ave SW 28025
Powder St NW & SW 28025
Powerhouse Ct 28027
Preadtor Dr 28025
Preakness Ct NW 28027
Prescott Pl NW 28027
Pressley Downs Dr SE 28025
Prestbury Rd NW 28027
Prestwick Ct NW 28027
Prey Ln 28025
Primrose Ln NW 28027
Prince Cir 28025
Princess Ave SW 28025
Prior Dr NW 28027
Progress Pl 28025
Propston St NW 28025
Providence Ct NW 28027
Province Dr NW 28027
Pulaski Dr SW 28027
Pullman St SW 28025
Quail Dr NW 28027
Quarry View Dr NW 28027
Quay Rd 28027
Quebec Ct 28027
Queens Dr SW 28025
Quiet Cv 28027
Quiet Stream Dr 28025
Rabon St SE 28025
Racers Aly 28027
Raceway Dr SW 28027
Radcliff Pl NW 28027
Railroad Dr NW 28025
Railway Pl SW 28025
Rainbow St SW 28025
Raintree Cir 28027
Raleigh St NW 28027
Rama Wood Dr SE 28025
Ramdin Ct NW 28027
Ramsgate Dr SW 28025
Ranchway Dr SW 28027
Randall Ct 28025
Rankin Rd 28027
Rathlin Ct NW 28027
Ravenscroft Ln NW 28027
Ravenswood Rd NE 28025
Ravine Cir SE 28025
Rawhide Ct NW 28027
Ray Linker Rd 28025
Ray Suggs Pl NW 28027
Red Bird Cir 28025
Red Cedar Pl NW 28027
Red Fox Ln 28025
Red Maple Dr NW 28027
Red Tip Dr SE 28025
Redbud Pl NW 28027
Redmond Ct NW 28027
Reed St NE 28025
Regal Cir 28025
Rembrandt Dr SW 28027
Remington Ln NW 28027
Renfrew Dr 28027
Republic Ct NW 28027
Reservoir Pl 28025
Retreat Dr 28025
Retriever Ct SE 28025
Revolutionary Dr NW 28027
Rheo Ct NW 28027
Rich Pl NE 28025
Ridenhour Ct SE 28025
Riders Glen Ct 28027
Ridge Ave, Ct & Rd 28025
Ridge Crossing Ct NW 28027
Ridgewood Dr 28027
Riding Trail Ln 28027
Rimer Rd 28025
Rinehardt Rd 28025
Ring Ave SW 28025
Ringtail Ct 28025
Rippling Stream Dr NW 28027
Rivendell Ln NW 28027
River Bend Rd 28025
River Birch Dr SE 28025
River Oaks Dr NW 28027
Riverglen Dr NW 28027
Riverwalk Dr NW 28027
Robbins St SW 28025
Roberta Rd SW 28027
Roberta Church Rd SW 28027
Roberta Farms Ct SW 28027
Roberta Meadows Ct 28027
Roberta Woods Dr SW 28027
Robins Nest Rd 28027
Robinson Dr SW 28027
Rock Bass Ct 28025
Rock Hill Church Rd NW 28027
Rockcreek Ct 28025
Rockcrest Ct 28027
Rockingham Ct SW 28025
Rockland Cir SW 28027
Rocky Meadows Ln 28025

Rocky River Rd
4400-4999 28027
5001-5001 28027
5002-7999 28025
Rocky Shoals Pl 28025
Rocky Spring Ct NW ... 28027
Rocky Trace Ct NW 28027
Roland Ave 28027
Rolling Hills Ct 28025
Rollingwood Dr SE 28025
Rone Ave SW 28025
Rose Ct NW 28027
Roseberry Pl 28025
Rosedale Dr SW 28027
Rosegaye Ave SW 28025
Rosehaven Ct SE 28025
Rosehill Ct SW 28025
Rosemont Ave SE 28025
Ross Lee Dr 28025
Roswell Ct NW 28027
Rothmoor Dr NE 28025
Roundcliff Dr 28025
Roush Pl NW 28027
Roxanne Ct NW 28027
Ruben Linker Rd NW ... 28027
Rubens Rd SW 28027
Ruff Rd 28025
Runneymede St SW 28027
Running Deer Dr 28025
Rural Dr NW 28027
Rustic Ln NW 28027
Rutherford Dr SW 28025
Rutledge Ave SW 28025
Ryan St NW 28027
Sable Ct 28025
Saddlewood Cir SW 28025
Sagebrush Cir 28025
Sagewood Pl SW 28025
Sahara St 28025
Saint Adriens Way 28025
Saint Andrews Cir NW . 28027
Saint Andrews Pl 28025
Saint Annes Ct NW 28027
Saint Catherines Ct 28025
Saint Charles Ave NE .. 28025
Saint James St NW 28025
Saint Johns Ave NW ... 28025
Saint Johns Church
Rd 28025
Saint Mary Ave NW 28025
Salem St SW 28025
Samuel Adams Cir
SW 28027
Sanctuary Ridge Dr 28025
Sandburg Dr 28027
Sandlewood Ln 28025
Sandringham Pl 28025
Sandstone Ct 28025
Sandusky Blvd 28027
Sandy Ln SW 28027
Sandy Bottom Dr NW .. 28027
Sandy Point Dr SW 28025
Sapp Rd 28025
Sarah Dr NW 28027
Satchel Ln 28027
Saxon Ct 28027
Scalybark Trl 28027
Scenic Dr NE 28025
Scenic Pine Ln 28025
Schad Ct SW 28025
Schulmann Pl SW 28025
Scotia Ave NW 28027
Scott St SW 28025
Scott Padgett Pkwy
NW 28027
Scottland Dr 28025
Search Dr 28025
Sebastian Way 28025
Sebring Ct SW 28025
Sedgefield St SW 28025
Sedgewick Dr SW 28027
Seminole Ave SE 28025
September Ct SW 28025
Serenade Ave NW 28027
Setter Ct & Ln 28025
Seven Eagles Ct SW ... 28027

Shadow Dr NW 28027
Shadow Brook Ct NW .. 28027
Shadow Creek St NW .. 28027
Shadowcrest Dr SW 28027
Shadowridge Pl NW 28027
Shady Bluff Ct 28025
Shady Lane Ave 28027
Shalimar Dr 28025
Shamrock St NE 28025
Shanaclear Ave 28027
Shankle St 28027
Shannon Dr SW 28025
Shasta St NW 28027
Shea St 28025
Shearwater Ave NW 28027
Shellbark Dr 28025
Shelter Wood Ct SE 28025
Shelton Rd NW 28027
Shenandoah Dr SW 28027
Shepard Ave SE 28025
Sheridan Dr 28027
Sherwin Ln 28025
Sherwood Ct NW 28027
Shetland Pl NW 28027
Shields Dr NW 28027
Shimpock Rd 28027
Shinn St SE 28025
Shoreview Dr 28027
Short St SW 28027
Shrader St NW 28027
Shumacher Ave NW 28027
Sidesmur Ct NE 28025
Siesta Ct 28027
Sign Dr NW 28027
Signal Ct SW 28025
Silver Fox Dr 28027
Silver Oak Ter NE 28025
Simplicity Rd 28025
Simpson Dr NE 28025
Sinai Pl NW 28027
Sir Raleigh Dr 28025
Skidaway St NW 28027
Skipping Stone Ln NW . 28027
Skipwith St SW 28025
Sloop Arthur Dr 28027
Small Ave NW 28027
Snyder Ct NE 28025
Softwind Ln 28025
Somerled Ct 28027
Somerset Ct NW 28027
Songwood Rd 28025
Soothing Ct Pl NW 28027
Sossamon Ln NW 28027
Southampton Dr NW ... 28027
Southberry Pl NW 28027
Southcircle Dr NW 28027
Southern Chase Ct
SW 28025
Southern Oak Ave
NW 28027
Southwind Ct SW 28025
Spaniel Dr SE 28025
Sparta St NW 28027
Speedrail Ct 28025
Speedway Pl NW 28025
Spencer Ave NW 28025
Splicewood Dr SW 28027
Sportsman Dr 28027
Spradley Ct NW 28027
Spring St NW & SW 28025
Spring Gate Ct 28025
Springbrook Ave NE 28025
Springfield Dr NW 28027
Springview Ct NW 28027
Spruce Ave 28027
Spruce Pl SE 28025
Sprucewood Pl NW 28027
Spur Ln 28027
Stable Rd 28027
Stacybrook Dr SE 28025
Stafford Farm Rd 28025
Stagecoach Rd NW 28027
Stallings Rd 28025
Standish Way NW 28027
Stanley Dr 28027
Stardust Pl NW 28027

Starlight Dr 28027
Starmount Park Blvd ... 28027
Station Ln SW 28025
Staton Pl NW 28027
Sternbridge Dr 28025
Stewart St NW 28027
Still Oaks Ct NW 28027
Stillwater Ct NW 28027
Stirewalt Rd 28027
Stirrup Pl NW 28027
Stockton Ave NW 28027
Stone Ave SW 28027
Stone Pile Dr SW 28025
Stonecrest Cir SW 28027
Stonefield St SW 28027
Stonehaven Ct SW 28027
Stoneridge Ct 28025
Stones Throw Dr 28025
Stonewall Cir SW 28027
Stoney Ln NW 28027
Stoney Creek Dr NW ... 28027
Storybook Ave NW 28027
Stough Rd SW 28027
Stricker Ave NW 28027
Strickland Pl 28027
Sturbridge Ln 28025
Suburban Ave NE 28025
Suffield Ln 28025
Summerford Ct NW 28027
Summerhill Ct NW 28027
Summerlake Dr SW 28025
Summers Glen Dr NW . 28027
Summerwind Ct SW 28027
Summit Ct SE 28025
Sumner Ave NW 28027
Sunberry Ln NW 28027
Sunchase Ct NW 28025
Suncrest Ter NW 28027
Sundale Ave NW 28027
Sundance Dr 28027
Sunderland Rd SW 28027
Sunnyside Dr SE 28025
Sunrise Pl SE 28025
Sunset Dr SE 28025
Sunshine Ln 28027
Sunview Dr NW 28027
Supply Ct NW 28027
Surrey Trace Ct NW 28027
Surry Trace Cir NW 28027
Susie Brumley Pl NW .. 28027
Suther Rd 28025
Sutherland Pl NW 28027
Sutro Forest Dr NW 28027
Sutters Rd 28027
Swallow Dr 28025
Swan Dr 28027
Swaringen Dr 28025
Swaying Oaks Ct 28025
Sweet Bay Ct & Ln 28027
Sweet Shrub Ct NW 28027
Swink St SW 28027
Sybbie St 28027
Sycamore Ave SW 28025
Sycamore St 28027
Sycamore Ridge Rd
NE 28025
Sylvan St SW 28025
Tabitha Ln 28025
Tala Dr SW 28027
Talledaga Ln SW 28025
Tallowtree Ln 28025
Tamarac Ct 28025
Tanglewood Dr NE 28025
Tania Ct 28025
Tarlton Pl NW 28025
Tarrymore Ln SW 28027
Tartan Ln NW 28027
Tasseys Pl SW 28027
Tater Ridge Rd 28025
Taunton Ct NW 28027
Taylor Ct NW 28027
Taylor Glen Ln NW 28027
Teal Ct NW 28027
Tealstone Ct 28025
Templeton Ave 28025
Tenneyson Ct NW 28027

Terminal Ct NW 28027
Terrytown St 28025
Tetbury Ave NE 28025
Thanet St SW 28025
Thistle Brook Dr 28027
Thompson Dr 28025
Thorndale Rd 28025
Thoroughbred Pl NW ... 28027
Three Sisters Ln 28027
Thunder Rd 28027
Thunderbolt Rd 28025
Tidmarsh Ct NW 28027
Tiffany St NW 28027
Tilley Rd 28025
Timber Pl SE 28025
Timber Falls Pl NW 28027
Timothy Dr 28025
Todd Dr NE & NW 28025
Tom Morris Ln SW 28027
Tom Reid Rd 28025
Torrington Ln NW 28027
Touch Me Not Ln 28025
Tournament Dr SW 28025
Tower Cir NW 28027
Towncreek Pl 28025
Trade St NW 28027
Tradewind Ln 28025
Trail Rd 28027
Tramacera Ct NW 28027
Tranquility Ave NW 28027
Trantham Dr SW 28027
Traton Cir 28025
Travis Ln NW 28027
Treasure Dr & Pl 28025
Treeline Dr 28027
Tremont Ave NW 28027
Trestle Ct SW 28025
Treva Anne Dr SW 28025
Tribune Ave SW 28027
Trillium St NW 28027
Trimble Cir NW 28027
Trinity Church Dr &
Rd 28027
Triple Crown Dr SW 28027
Tripolis St SE 28025
Tripp Ter NW 28027
Trippett St NW 28027
Triumph Dr SW 28027
Troon Dr SW 28027
Trotwood St NE 28025
Troxler Cir NW 28027
Tudor Ct 28025
Tufton Pl NW 28027
Tulake Dr 28027
Tulip Ave SW 28025
Tulsa Ct NW 28027
Turnberry Ct SW 28027
Turning Leaf St NW 28027
Turning Point Ln 28027
Turnridge Ct NW 28027
Tweed Ct NW 28027
Twelve Oaks Rd 28025
Twilight Dr 28025
Twin Oaks Ct 28027
Twinfield Dr 28025
Twinkle Dr 28025
Tybee Ct SW 28027
Tyndall Dr NW 28027
Tyne Castle Ct 28025
Union St N & S 28025
Union Bay Ct SE 28025
Union Cemetery Rd
SW 28027
Unity Ln NW 28027
Untz Rd 28027
Urban Dr NW 28027
Us Highway 601 S
200-299 28027
Us Highway 601 S
3100-7999 28025
Us Highway 601 Byp ... 28027
Valencia Ave NW 28027
Valiant Ave SW 28027
Valley St NW & SW 28025
Valley Brook Ln SE 28025
Valley Glenn Ct NW 28027

Valley Trail Ct 28025
Van Gogh Dr SW 28027
Van Tassel Dr 28025
Vance Dr NE 28025
Vanderburg Dr S 28025
Vanderhorst Dr 28025
Vee Ave SW 28025
Vega St NW 28027
Veitor Ave NW 28027
Verble Pl SW 28027
Verde View Ct 28027
Vericham Rd 28027
Vern Ct 28025
Vernette Ct 28025
Veterans Ave 28025
Victory Ln SW 28027
Viking Pl SW 28025
Village Dr NW 28027
Vinehaven Dr NE 28025
Vinning St NW 28027
Violet Ter NW 28027
Violet Cannon Dr NW .. 28027
Virginia St SE 28025
Vista Pl NW 28027
Wabash Ln 28027
Wago Ln 28027
Wagonwheel Ln 28025
Wakefield Dr 28027
Wakemeadow Pl NW ... 28027
Waldelde Rd 28025
Walden Ln 28027
Waldens Pond Trwy 28025
Wales Ct NW 28027
Walkers Glen Dr NW ... 28027
Walnut Ave NW 28027
Walnut Crest Ct NE 28025
Walsh Dr NW 28027
Walter Dr NW 28027
Ward Ave 28025
Warren St NE 28025
Warren C Coleman Blvd
N 28027
Warren Coleman Blvd .. 28025
Washington Ln SE 28025
Water St NW 28027
Water Valley Ct NW 28027
Watercrest Dr NW 28027
Waterford Dr NW 28027
Wateroak Dr 28027
Waterstone Pl SW 28027
Waterview Dr NW 28027
Waterwheel St SW 28025
Watson Dr 28025
Watson Mills St NW 28027
Watts Ave 28025
Waverly Ct NE 28025
Wayne Ct SE 28025
Weatherstone Pl 28025
Webb Rd 28025
Weddington Rd NW 28027
Weddington Road Ext .. 28027
Weddington Woods St
NW 28027
Wedgewood Cir NE 28025
Weejuns Dr 28025
Weeping Willow Dr
NW 28027
Weldon Cir NW 28027
Wellbourne Ct NW 28027
Wellington Chase Dr ... 28027
Wellspring Ct NW 28027
Wendover Rd NW 28027
Wendy Ln 28027
Wensil St NW 28025
Wentworth Dr NE 28025
Wessex Dr NE 28025
West Ave SW 28027
Westfield Ave NW 28027
Westminster Dr 28027
Westmoreland Dr NW .. 28027
Weston Point Pl 28025
Westridge Ln SW 28027
Westview Rd 28025
Westwinds Blvd NW 28027
Wexford Pl NW 28027
Weyburn Dr NW 28027

Wheat Dr SW 28027
Wheatfield Pl 28025
Wheaton Way NW 28027
Wheeler Rd 28025
Whippoorwill Ln 28025
Whispering Pines Dr 28025
White St NW & SW 28027
Whitewater Way NW ... 28027
Whitman Dr NW 28027
Whitmire Ln SW 28027
Whitney Pl NW 28027
Widespread Ave NW ... 28027
Wightman Oaks Ct 28027
Wild Turkey Ln 28025
Wilder Rd 28025
Wilhelm Pl NE 28025
Wilkinson Ct SE 28025
Willetta Pl NW 28027
William Evans Pl NW ... 28027
Williamsburg Ct & Dr ... 28025
Williamsport Dr NW 28027
Willis Park Cir 28027
Willow Ln NW 28025
Willow Grove Ln 28025
Willowbreeze Ct SW 28025
Willowbrook Dr NW 28027
Wilmar St NW 28025
Wilshire Ave SW
1-23 28025
25-611 28025
612-799 28027
Wilshire Ct 28025
Wilson St NE 28025
Wimbledon St 28025
Winborne Ave SW 28025
Winchester Dr & Rd 28027
Wind Song Ct 28025
Windjammer Ct SW 28027
Windrose Ln SW 28025
Windsor Pl NE 28025
Windswept Rd SW 28027
Windward Ct NW 28027
Windy Rd 28027
Winecoff Ave NE 28025
Winecoff Ave NW
1-49 28025
51-233 28025
234-499 28027
Winecoff School Rd 28027
Winecoff Woods Dr
NW 28027
Winfield Blvd SE 28025
Wingard Rd 28025
Wingate Way NW 28027
Wingrave St NW 28027
Winners Cir SW 28025
Winslow Ave NW 28027
Winston Dr NW 28027
Winter Garden Dr 28025
Winterberry Ct NW 28027
Wintercrest Dr 28025
Winthrop Dr 28025
Wishon Rd 28025
Woburn Alley Dr NW ... 28027
Wolfmeadow Dr SW 28027
Wood Duck Ct NW 28027
Woodbrook Pl NE 28025
Woodbury Ter NW 28027
Woodcrest Dr SW 28027
Woodend Dr SE 28025
Woodhaven Pl NW 28027
Woodland Cir & Dr 28025
Woodlawn Ave SW 28025
Woodridge Ct NW 28027
Woodsdale Pl SE 28025
Woodway Dr 28025
Woody Ct SW 28025
Worthington Ct NE 28025
Wrangler Dr SW 28027
Wrenfield Ln 28025
Wycliff Ct NW 28027
Wyndham Pl NE 28025
Wynnbrook Way 28027
Wyoming Dr NW 28027
Wyth Ct SW 28025
Yates Mill Dr SW 28027

Yellow Poplar Ln 28025
Yellowstone Ct 28025
Yesteryear Trl 28027
Yorke St NW 28027
Yorkshire Pl NW 28027
Yorktown St NW 28025
Young Ave, Cir, Ct & Pl
SW 28025
Yvonne Dr SW 28027
Zebulon Ave SW 28027
Zephyr Dr NW 28027
Zered Pl NW 28027
Zion Church Rd E 28025

NUMBERED STREETS

All Street Addresses 28027

DAVIDSON NC

General Delivery 28036

POST OFFICE BOXES MAIN OFFICE STATIONS AND BRANCHES

Box No.s
1 - 4840 28036
5001 - 8990 28035
9998 - 9998 28036

NAMED STREETS

All Street Addresses 28036

DUNN NC

General Delivery 28334

POST OFFICE BOXES MAIN OFFICE STATIONS AND BRANCHES

Box No.s
1 - 4192 28335
28334 - 28334 28334

RURAL ROUTES

01, 02, 04, 07, 09, 11 .. 28334

NAMED STREETS

All Street Addresses 28334

NUMBERED STREETS

All Street Addresses 28334

DURHAM NC

General Delivery 27702

POST OFFICE BOXES MAIN OFFICE STATIONS AND BRANCHES

Box No.s
2252A - 2252A 27702
2291A - 2291A 27702
1 - 2332 27702
2401 - 3299 27715
3030 - 3030 27703

3301 - 9998 27702
9998 - 9998 27715
9998 - 9998 27717
9998 - 9998 27722
11001 - 11998 27703
12001 - 14999 27709
15000 - 16280 27704
17969 - 17976 27715
18001 - 20041 27707
21001 - 21398 27703
25001 - 30111 27702
50520 - 52740 27717
61000 - 62666 27715
71011 - 75002 27722
110001 - 113706 27709

RURAL ROUTES

04, 06, 13 27703
05 27704
01, 02 27705
07 27707
08, 09, 17, 19 27712
03 27713

NAMED STREETS

Aaron Cir 27713
Abbey Pl 27707
Abbotsford Ct 27712
Abbott Ln 27703
Abelia Ct 27704
Abercromby Dr 27713
Aberdeen Dr 27704
Abingdon Way 27713
Abron Dr 27713
Academia Ct 27713
Academy Rd 27707
Academy Ridge Dr 27705
Acadia St
1400-1699 27701
2400-2699 27704
Accura Ct 27712
Acker Ave 27704
Acorn Ct 27713
Acornridge Ct 27707
N & S Adams St 27703
Addison Ct 27712
Adell Way 27703
Ader St 27704
Adler Ct 27703
Adlett Ln 27703
Admiral Ln 27705
Adventure Trl 27703
Afton Pl 27703
Aiken Ave 27704
Ainsley Ct 27713
Ainsworth Ct 27713
Akal Ct 27713
Akron Ave 27713
Al Acqua Dr 27707
Alabama Ave 27705
Alameda St 27704
Alamo Ct 27705
Alba Ln 27707
Albany St 27705
Albemarle St 27701
Alben St 27713
Albert Ct 27713
Albritton Dr 27705
Albury Pl 27712
Alcona Ave 27703
Alcott St 27701
Alderbrook Ln 27713
Alderman Ln 27705
Aldersgate Ct 27705
Alexan Dr 27707
Alexander Ave 27705
Alexis Ct 27703
Alfred St 27713
Alhambra Ct 27703
Alicia Ct 27704
Alleghany St 27705
Allen Moore Ct 27703
Allendown Dr 27713
Allgood St 27704
Allister Rd 27703
Alma St 27703
Alman Dr 27705
Alnick Ct 27712
Alpha Dr 27703
Alpine Rd 27707
Alsey Pl 27707
N Alston Ave 27701
S Alston Ave
100-1399 27701
1400-2399 27707
2400-6799 27713
Altmont Ct 27705
E & W Alton St 27707
Altrada Dr 27712
Alumni Ave 27713
Alumwood Pl 27705
Alyea Ct 27703
Amador Pl 27712
Aman Ct 27713
Amanda Rd 27713
Amarillo Rose Ln 27712
Amaryllis Ln 27712
Amayo Ct 27713
Ambassador Dr 27703
Amber Pl 27701
Amber Stone Way 27704
Amberglen Ct 27712
Amberly Dr 27704
Amberwood Dr 27705
Ambridge St 27704
American Dr 27705
Amesbury Ln 27707
Amhurst Rd 27713
Anacosta St 27707
Ancient Oak Ct 27704
Ancroft Ave 27713
Anderson St
201-297 27705
299-1299 27705
1300-1699 27707
Andi Ct 27713
Andover Rd 27712
Andrews Rd 27705
Andrews Chapel Rd 27703
Anele Rd 27712
N & S Angela Cir & Way 27703
Angier Ave
800-1499 27701
1500-4799 27703
Angus Rd 27705
Anita St 27701
Annandale Rd 27705
Annapolis Ct 27705
Anson St 27703
Anthony Dr 27705
Antioch Ct 27703
Antler Point Dr 27713
Apex Hwy 27713
Apex St 27707
Apollo St 27704
Appleblossom Ct 27707
Applecross Ct 27713
Appleton Pl 27705
Applewood Sq 27713
Appling Way 27703
Arbor St 27701
Arborfield Ln 27713
Archdale Dr 27707
Arcola Ln 27705
Arden Ln 27703
Ardmore Dr 27713
Ardsley Dr 27704
Argonaut Dr 27705
Argonne Dr 27704
Arlene St 27704
Arlington St 27707
Armitage Dr 27703
Arnette Ave
600-999 27701
1000-1499 27707
Arnold Rd 27707
Arrington St 27707
Arrowhead Dr 27705
Arrowwood Ct 27712
Artelia Dr 27703
Arthur Ln 27705
Arthurs Way 27705
Artis Ln 27703
Arvin Rd 27704
Asbury Ct 27703
Ascott Way 27713
Ashburn Ln 27703
Ashe St 27703
Ashe Ridge Ln 27703
Ashford Ln 27713
Ashland Dr 27705
Ashley St 27704
Ashmont Ln 27713
Ashton Gln 27703
Ashton Pl 27701
Ashwood Sq 27713
Ashworth Dr 27707
Aspen Ct 27707
Aster Dr 27705
Astor Ct 27705
Athens Ave 27707
Atka Ct 27703
Atkins Heights Blvd 27713
Atlantic St 27707
Atlas St 27705
Atterbury Ln 27712
Atwood Ct 27703
Auburn St 27705
Auburn Square Dr 27713
Auburn Village Dr 27713
Auburndale Dr 27713
Aucuba Ct 27704
Audrey Dr 27703
Audubon Lake Dr 27713
Augusta Dr 27707
Aurora Ct 27713
Austin Ct 27707
Auto Dr 27707
Auto Park Dr 27707
Autrey Mill Cir 27703
Autumn Dr 27712
Autumn Leaf Ln 27704
Autumn Ridge Dr 27712
Autumn Woods Dr 27713
Avalon Rd 27704
Avery St 27707
Avett Dr 27703
Avon Rd 27707
Avon Brook Ln 27705
Avon Lake Dr 27713
Avondale Dr
1200-1999 27701
2000-2299 27704
Avonlea Ct 27713
Ayers Pl 27703
Azalea Dr 27703
Azzi Ct 27703
Baccalaureate Blvd 27713
Bacon St
500-1099 27703
1200-1599 27707
Bagpipe Ln 27712
Bailey St 27703
Bainbridge Dr 27713
Bair Cir 27704
Baird St 27712
Baker St 27713
Bakers Mill Rd 27707
Baldwin Dr 27712
Balfour E & W 27713
Ballard Ct 27712
Bally Castle Dr 27713
Balmoray Ct 27707
Baltic Ave 27707
Banbury Way 27707
Bancroft Dr 27705
Bandock Dr 27703
Banner St 27704
Banneret Pl 27713
Baptist Rd
100-1702 27704
1703-3599 27703
Barbary St 27707
Barbee Rd 27713
Barcelona Ave 27707
Barclay Rd 27712
Bardeck Dr 27712
Barenwood Cir 27704
Barkridge Ct 27713
Barkwood Ct 27713
Barley Cir 27707
Barliff Pl 27712
Barn View Pl 27705
Barnhill St 27707
Barnsdale Ct 27713
Baronet Ct 27713
Barratts Chapel Ct 27705
Barrett Pl 27713
Barringer Pl 27705
Barrington Pl 27705
Barrington Overlook Dr 27703
Barry St 27704
Barrymore Ave 27705
Bartlett Dr 27705
Barton St 27707
Barwick Dr 27704
Barwinds Cir 27713
Basil Dr 27713
Basset Hall Dr 27713
Bates St 27712
Bay St 27701
Bay Bush Ct 27712
Bay Meadows Ln 27705
Bay Point Dr 27713
Bay Ridge Ct 27713
Bayard Rd 27703
E & W Bayberry Ct 27713
Bayleaf Dr 27712
Baylor St 27703
Baytree Ct 27705
Beacon Pl 27703
Beacon Hill Ln 27705
Beamon St 27707
Beasley Ave 27703
Beaufort Ct 27713
Beaumont Dr 27707
Beaver Pl 27705
Beaver Creek Ln 27703
Beaver Dam Run 27703
Beck Rd 27704
Beckett St 27712
Beckford Pl 27705
Beckham Pl 27703
Becton Cir 27712
Bedford St 27707
Bee Hill Pl 27705
Beebe Dr 27713
Beech Trl 27705
Beech Bluff Ln 27705
Beech Grove Dr 27705
Beech Slope Way 27713
Beechnut Ln 27707
Beechtree Ct 27713
Beechwood Dr 27707
Belden Dr 27703
Belfort St 27701
Belgrave Pl 27707
Belgreen Rd 27713
Belk St 27712
Bell St 27707
Belleflower Dr 27703
Bellenden Dr 27713
Bellevue Ave 27705
Bellmeade Bay Dr 27703
Bellmore Ct 27703
Belmont Dr 27703
Belt St 27701
Beltre Ct 27705
Belvin Ave 27704
Ben Bow Dr 27704
Ben Franklin Blvd 27704
S Bend Dr 27713
Benefactor Ln 27705
Bengel Dr 27703
N & S Benjamine St 27703
Bennett Ct 27701
Bennett Memorial Rd 27705
Benning St 27703
Bennington Pkwy 27713
Bennington Park Dr 27703
Benny Ross Rd 27703
Bent Branch Ct 27704
Bent Oak Ct & Dr 27705
Bent Pine Ct 27705
Bentgrass Ln 27705
Bentley Dr 27707
Bentwood Pl 27703
Berg Pl 27712
Bergman Rd 27705
Berini Dr 27705
Berkeley St 27705
Bermouth Ct 27705
Bermuda Ct 27703
Bermuda Green Dr 27703
Bernard Cir 27705
Bernard Dr 27703
Bernice St 27703
Berry Ct 27703
Berry Bush Pl 27705
Berry Farm Rd 27713
N & S Berrymeadow Ln 27703
Bertland Ave 27705
Berwick Ct 27707
Berwyn Ave 27704
Bess Ct 27707
Bessemer Pl 27712
Beta Rd 27703
Bethany Pl 27712
Bethesda Ave 27703
Bettie Ln 27707
Bevel Ct 27704
Beverly Dr 27707
Bevington Ln 27703
Bexley Ave 27707
Biddle Ct 27705
Big Bluff Pl 27712
Big Fork Rd 27712
Big Leaf Way 27704
Big Oak Ct & Dr 27705
Big Twig Ln 27703
Bigstone Dr 27703
Biltmore Pl 27712
Bingham St 27703
Birch Dr 27712
Birch Run Dr 27712
Birchcrest Ct 27713
Birchwood Park 27713
Birds Nest Ct 27703
Birkdale Ct 27713
Birmi Dr 27713
Birmingham Ave 27704
Birnham Ln 27707
Biscayne Rd 27707
Bishopstone Dr 27705
Bitter Root Dr 27705
Bittersweet Dr 27705
Bivins Rd 27712
Bivins St 27707
Black Boulder Trl 27712
Blackberry Ln 27712
Blackford Ct 27712
N Blacknall St 27703
S Blacknall St
100-199 27703
200-299 27701
Blacksmith Cir 27707
Blackstone Dr 27712
Blackwell St 27701
Bladenboro Ct 27713
Blair St 27704
Blake Ct 27712
Blakeford Dr 27713
Blanchard Rd 27713
Bland Spring Pl 27713
Bloem Ct 27707
Blossomwood Dr 27703
Blount St 27707
Blue Bottle Ln 27705
Blue Crest Ln 27705
Blue Dog Ln 27705
Blue Grass Rd 27703
Blue Hill Ln 27703
Blue Iris Ln 27703
Blue Ridge Ct 27703
Blue Spruce Dr 27712
Blue Violet Way 27713
Bluebell Ct 27713
Bluebird Ct 27713
Bluebird Trl 27705
Bluestone Rd 27713
Bluffs Ln 27712
Bluffside Ct 27712
Boardman Ct 27705
Bob Wilkes Ct 27703
Bobby Parker Pl 27703
Bobcat Ct 27713
Bobs Ln 27704
Bogarde St 27705
Bogie Ct 27705
Bolter Ct 27704
Bolton St 27705
Bombay Dr 27703
Bon Air Ave 27704
Bonaparte Way 27707
Bond St 27707
Bonham Ct 27703
Bonhill Dr 27712
Bonnie Dr 27712
Bonnie Brae Rd 27703
Bonsell Pl 27707
Booker Ave 27713
Boone St 27703
Booth Meadow Ln 27713
Boswell St 27703
Bougainvillea Ct 27713
Boulder Rd 27713
Bounty Ln 27713
Bowen St 27703
Bowler Dr 27703
Bowling Creek Way 27712
Boxley Ct 27704
Boxwood Dr 27713
Boyce Mill Rd 27703
Boylan Rd 27712
Bracada Dr 27705
Braddock Cir 27713
Braden Ct & Dr 27713
Bradford Cir 27713
Bradley Cir 27713
Brafferton Ct 27713
Bragg Rd 27704
Braine Ct 27703
Bramble Dr 27712
Brambury Xing 27704
Bramerton Ct 27705
Branchview Dr 27713
Branchwood Dr 27705
Brandermill Dr 27713
Brandon Rd 27713
Brandywine Ct 27705
Brant St 27707
Brassy Creek Ave 27712
Bravehart Ct 27713
Braxton St 27701
Brecknock St 27705
Breedlove Ave 27703
Brenda Ct 27712
Brenmar Ct & Ln 27713
Brenrose Cir 27705
Brentwood Rd 27713
Breslin Trl 27712
Breton Pl 27707
Brevard Ct 27713
Brewington Pl 27712
Briana Dr 27712
Briarcliff Rd 27707
Briardale Ln & Rd 27712
Briarfield Ct 27713
Briarhaven Dr 27703
Briarwick Ct 27713
Briarwood Ct 27713
Brickstone Pl 27712
Bridgefield Pl 27705
Bridgeman Ct 27703
Bridgeport Dr 27713
Bridgewood Dr 27713
Bridle Pl 27704
Bridlewood Rd 27704
E Bridlewood Trl 27713
W Bridlewood Trl 27713
Brier Crossings Loop 27703
Brigadoon Dr 27705
N & S Briggs Ave 27703
Brightfield Ln 27712
Brightleaf Ct 27713
Brighton Rd 27707
Brightwood Ln 27703
Brimmer St 27703
Bristlewood Dr 27703
Bristol Rd 27707
E & W Britania Ave 27704
Britney Ct 27713
Britt St 27705
Brixton Ln 27707
Broach Rd 27703
Broad St
600-2199 27705
2200-2999 27704
Broadfield Ct 27712
Broadway St 27701
Brockwell Rd 27705
Brocton Pl 27712
Brodie St 27703
Bronze Leaf Pl 27705
Brook Ln 27712
Brook Chase Ln 27705
Brookhaven Dr 27707
Brooklane Dr 27712
Brooks Rd 27703
Brookshire Rd 27707
Brookside Pl 27705
Brookstone Dr 27713
Brookview St 27713
Brookwood Ct 27712
Brookwood Dr 27707
Broomfield Ter 27705
Broomsedge Way 27712
Broomstraw Ct 27704
Brotherly Ct 27713
Broughton Dr 27704
Brower Cir 27705
Brown Ave 27705
Brown St 27713
Brown Bark Ct 27712
Brown Lee Pl 27707
Bruce St 27703
Brunson Rd 27703
Brunswick Ct 27705
Bruton Rd 27705
Bryan Pl 27712
Bryant St 27703
Brye St 27703
Bryncastle Ct 27707
Brynhurst Ct 27713
Brynwood Ave 27713
N Buchanan Blvd
100-798 27701
800-1199 27701
1201-1299 27701
1800-1899 27705
S Buchanan Blvd 27701
Buchanan Dr 27707
Buck Crossing Dr 27713
Buckhead Ct 27703
Buckingham Rd 27707
Buffalo Way 27704
Bullock Ln 27713
Bullock Rd 27704
Bundy Ave 27704
Bungalow Ave 27703
Bunker Hill Pl 27705
Bunn Ter 27703
Burbank Cir 27713
Burch Ave 27701
Burgess Ln 27707
Burgundy Rd 27712
Burke St 27707
Burlington Ave 27707
Burnette St 27707
Burnley Ct 27707
Burrell Rd 27703
Burton Rd 27704
Burwell Ct 27705
Butler Ave 27705
Butler Rd 27703
Butler St 27707
Butner St 27704

Butterfly Ln 27707
Butternut Rd 27707
Butterwick Pl 27705
Buttonbush Dr 27712
Buttonwood Ct 27713
Buxbury Ln 27713
Buxton St 27713
Byerly Ct 27713
Bynum St 27705
Byrd Rd 27705
W Bywood Dr 27712
C View Rd 27713
Cabe Ford Rd 27705
Cabes Mill Rd 27705
Cabin Branch Dr 27712
Cabin Creek Rd 27712
Cadillac Ave 27704
Cain Rd 27712
Cairn Ct 27705
Calais Dr 27712
Calaveras Ct 27713
Calibre Park Dr 27707
Caliper Way 27713
Callahan Cir 27703
Callandale Ln 27703
Callaway Ct 27704
Calle Luna Ct 27707
Callista Ct 27707
Calumet Dr 27704
Calvander Ct 27704
Calvert Pl 27701
Calvin St 27701
Camberly Dr 27704
Camberwell Ct 27707
Cambian Pl 27704
Cambridge Rd
3400-3599 27707
3700-3899 27705
Camden Ave
800-1300 27701
1302-1398 27701
1400-2199 27704
Camellia Dr 27705
Camelot Ct 27705
Cameron Blvd 27705
Cameroons Pl 27703
Cammie St 27705
Campus Dr 27705
Campus Walk Ave 27705
Cana St 27707
Canadian Ct 27713
Canal St 27701
Canary Ct 27713
Candlelight Ct 27707
Candlewick Way 27704
Candlewood Pl 27704
Candytuft Ln 27713
Cannada Ave 27704
Cannon Dr 27705
Cansler Dr 27712
Canter Pl 27712
Canter Ridge Ct 27704
Canton Dr 27703
Capitol St 27704
Capitola Dr 27713
Capps St 27707
Capri Ter 27703
Captains Ct 27712
Capul Dr 27703
Carden Ln 27703
Cardens Creek Dr 27712
Cardinal Dr 27707
Cardinal Lake Dr 27704
Cardriff Pl 27712
Carey Pl 27712
Caribou Xing 27713
Carlion Ct 27713
Carlisle Dr 27707
Carlton Ave 27701
Carlton Crossing Dr 27713
Carmel Ln 27713
Carmen Ln 27707
Carnation Dr 27703
Carolina Ave 27705
Carolina Cir 27707
Caroline Dr 27705
Carolwood Ln 27713
Carolyn Dr 27703
Carpenter Rd 27704
Carpenter Fletcher Rd 27713
Carpenter Pond Rd 27703
Carr Rd 27703
Carramore Ln 27705
Carrickfergus Ct 27713
Carroll Aly 27701
Carroll St
600-999 27701
1000-1499 27707
Carson Cir 27705
Carter Ave 27703
Carthage Ct 27703
Cartman Dr 27704
Carved Oak Dr 27707
Carver St
500-999 27704
2000-4099 27705
4100-4199 27712
E Carver St 27704
W Carver St 27704
Carylynn Ct 27703
Carywood Dr 27703
Casa St 27704
Casabelle Ct 27713
Cascade Falls Ln 27713
Cascadilla St 27704
Case St 27705
Cash Rd 27703
Cashitat St 27707
Caspian Ct 27713
Cassandra Dr 27712
Cassington Ln 27705
Castell Dr 27713
Castlebar Ln 27713
Castlebay Rd 27703
Castlerock Dr 27713
Castlewell Pl 27703
Castlewood Dr 27713
Caswell Pl 27705
Cat Tail Ct 27703
Catalina St 27713
Catalpa Dr 27704
Catamount Ct 27704
Catawba Dr 27704
Cathy Dr 27703
Catskill Ct 27713
Cauldwell Ln 27705
Caverstone Ln 27713
Caviness Rd 27704
Cayman Ct 27703
Cecil St 27707
Cedar St & Ter 27707
Cedar Bluff Ct 27704
Cedar Creek Dr 27705
Cedar Elm Rd 27713
Cedar Glen Dr 27713
Cedar Grove Dr 27703
Cedar Hill Dr 27713
Cedar Ridge Way 27705
Cedarwood Dr 27707
Celtic Dr 27703
Centennial Dr 27712
Center St 27704
Centerville Ln 27713
Centerway Dr 27705
Central Park Dr 27703
Century Oaks Dr 27713
Chadbourne Dr 27703
Chadron Rd 27713
Chadwick Pl 27704
Chalcedony Ct 27703
Chalice St 27705
Chalk Level Rd 27704
Chalmers St 27707
Chamberlin Ave 27704
Chamfer Pl 27704
Champaign Dr 27707
Champions Pointe Dr 27712
Chance Rd 27703
Chancellors Ridge Dr 27713
Chancery Pl 27707
Chandellay Dr 27705
Chandler Rd 27703
E & W Channing Ave 27704
Chanter Ct 27705
Chanticleer Dr 27713
Chantilly Pl 27707
Chapel Hill Rd
1500-1599 27701
1700-2999 27707
E Chapel Hill St
100-324 27701
323-323 27702
325-599 27701
326-598 27701
W Chapel Hill St 27701
Chapel Hill Nelson
Hwy 27709
Chapin St 27707
Chapparal Dr 27713
Charing Pl 27713
Charlana Dr 27712
Charles St 27707
Charleston Dr 27712
Charlestown Rd 27703
Charlotte St 27705
Chartwell Ct 27703
Chase St 27707
Chasewood Ct 27703
Chateau Rd 27704
Chatham Pl 27701
Chatham Glen Dr 27713
Chatsworth Way 27713
Chattleton Ct 27712
Chatton Pl 27705
Chaucer Dr 27705
Chautauqua Ave 27707
Checkerberry Ln 27703
Cheek Rd 27704
Chelan Ct 27713
Chelmsford Dr 27705
Chelsea Cir 27707
Chenault Pl 27707
Cher Dr 27713
Cherokee Ct 27712
Cherry Dr 27707
Cherry Grv 27703
Cherry Blossom Cir 27713
Cherry Blossom Dr 27703
Cherry Creek Dr 27703
Cherry Creek Ln 27705
Cherrybark Dr 27704
Cherrycrest Dr 27704
Cheryl Ave 27712
Chesapeake Ave 27712
Chesden Dr 27713
Cheselden Dr 27713
Cheshire Ct 27705
Cheshire Bridge Rd 27712
Chesley Ln 27713
Chester St 27701
Chester Springs Rd 27707
Chestnut St 27707
Chestnut Bluffs Ln 27713
Cheswick Pl 27707
Cheviot Ave 27707
Chevoit Ct 27712
Chicago St 27707
Chickasaw Rd 27703
Chicopee Trl 27707
Chimney Ridge Pl 27713
Chimney Stone Rd 27704
Chimney Top Ct 27705
Chin Page Rd 27703
China Doll Ct 27713
Chintelly Ct 27703
Chipley Ct 27703
Chippenham Rd 27707
Chippers Way 27705
Chiswell Ct 27705
Chivalry Dr 27703
Chorley Rd 27703
Chowan Ave 27713
Chownings St 27713
Christian Ave 27705
Christie Ln 27713
Christopher Ct 27704
N Church St 27701
Churchill Cir 27707
Churchland Ct 27707
Churchwell Ct 27713
Chutney Dr 27712
Cibola Ct 27713
Cilantro Ct 27713
Cinnamon Dr 27707
Circle Dr 27705
Cisco St 27707
Citation Cir 27704
Citation Dr 27713
Citrine Ct 27703
City Hall Plz 27701
Claire Ct 27713
Clancey Ct 27712
Clare Ct 27713
Claremore Dr 27712
Clarendon St 27705
Clarion Dr 27705
Clark St 27701
Clark Lake Rd 27707
Clarksdale Ln 27713
Clausun Dr 27713
Clay St 27703
Clayton Rd 27703
Clearbrook Ct 27703
Clearfield Dr 27703
Clearview Ln 27713
Clearwater Dr 27707
Clematis Ln 27707
Clements Dr 27704
Clermont Rd 27713
Cleveland St 27701
Cliff St 27707
Clifford Dr 27704
Cliffside Dr 27704
Clinton Rd 27703
Clover Pl 27705
Clover Hill Pl 27712
Cloverdale Dr 27703
E Club Blvd 27704
W Club Blvd
100-499 27704
600-1299 27701
1300-2599 27705
Club House St 27712
Clubstone Ct 27713
Clyde Ct 27712
Coach Ter 27713
Coachmans Way 27705
Cobb St
500-599 27701
600-1099 27707
Cobble Pl 27712
Cobble Creek Ct 27712
Cobble Glen Ct 27713
Cobble Ridge Ln 27713
Cobbleridge Ct 27713
Cobblestone Pl 27707
Cobscook Dr 27707
Cody St 27703
Cofield Cir 27707
Cohnwood Dr 27705
Coke Ct 27705
Colbury Ct 27713
Colchester St 27707
Colclough Ave 27704
Cole St 27701
Cole Mill Rd
1100-1699 27705
1700-4199 27712
4400-6199 27705
Cole Pond Dr 27705
Colewood Dr 27705
Coley Rd 27703
Colfax St 27701
Colgate St 27704
Colindale Ct 27704
Collander Dr 27707
College Ave 27713
Collegiate Cir 27713
Collier Dr 27707
Collins Dr 27712
Collinswood Ct 27703
Colonial St 27701
Colonial Heights Dr 27704
Colony Pl & Rd 27705
Colorado Ave 27707
Colton Ct 27713
Columbia Ave 27707
Colvard Farms Rd 27713
Colvard Park Dr 27713
Colville Rd 27707
Comet Ct 27705
Comfort Ln 27705
Commerce St 27701
Commons Blvd 27704
Commonwealth St 27703
Communications Dr 27704
Community Dr 27705
Community Center Rd 27705
Compton Pl 27707
Comptonfield Dr 27703
Concord St 27707
Conder Pl 27703
Cone Ave 27704
Conestoga Dr 27705
Conifer Ct 27712
Conifer Glen Ln 27705
Conklin Dr 27713
Conover Rd 27703
Constance Ave 27704
Constance Spry Way 27713
Constitution Dr 27705
Consultant Pl 27707
Continental Dr 27712
Converse Rd 27703
Conway Dr 27713
Conyers Ave 27701
Cook Rd 27713
Cooksbury Dr 27704
Cool Springs Rd 27713
Coolidge Pl 27705
Cooper St 27703
Copley Mountain Dr 27705
Copper Creek Dr 27713
Copper Hill Ct 27713
Copper Leaf Pkwy 27703
Copper Ridge Dr 27707
Coral Dr 27713
Coralbell Ct 27703
Corby Ln 27705
N & S Corcoran St 27701
Cordoba St 27704
Coriander Ct 27713
Corinth Ln 27704
Corktree Ct 27712
Cornell St 27707
Corning Ct 27705
Cornstalk Ct 27703
Cornwall Rd 27707
Cornwallis Ct 27707
Cornwallis Rd 27709
E Cornwallis Rd
100-599 27707
1100-2699 27713
W Cornwallis Rd
100-999 27707
1100-5699 27705
Corona St 27707
Coronado Ln 27713
E & W Corporation St 27701
Corrida Ave 27704
Cortez Dr 27703
Cortona Dr 27707
Costin Ct 27713
Cotherstone Dr 27712
Cotswold Pl 27707
Cottage Ln 27713
Cottage Woods Ct 27713
Cottendale Dr 27703
Cottonseed Way 27703
Cottonwood Dr
3400-3799 27707
3800-4199 27705
Couch Mountain Rd 27705
Cougar Ct 27705
Country Ln 27713
Country Club Dr 27712
Country Lane Dr 27705
Courtland Dr 27707
Courtney Creek Blvd 27713
Cove Hollow Dr 27703
Coventry Rd 27707
Covewood Ct 27713
Covey Ct 27712
Covington Ln 27712
Cox Ave 27701
Cozart Rd 27703
Cozart St 27704
Crabapple Rd 27712
Crabtree Ave 27704
Crafton St 27703
Craig Rd 27712
Crail Ct 27712
Cranbrook Ct 27713
Crane St 27703
Cranford Rd 27705
Craven St 27704
Crawford Ct 27703
Creech Rd 27704
NE Creek Pkwy 27713
Creeks Edge Ct 27713
Creekside Cv 27712
Creekstone Dr 27703
Creekview Ln 27705
Creekwood Trl 27705
Creighton Hall Way 27703
Crenshaw Ln 27713
Crepe Myrtle Pl 27705
Crescent Hill Ct 27704
Crest St 27705
Crestbury Ct 27713
Crestmont Ct 27703
Crestview Dr 27712
Crete St 27707
Crichton Ln 27713
Cricket Ln 27707
Cricket Ground 27707
Crievewood Dr 27712
Crimson Dr 27713
Crimson Clover Ct 27704
Crimson Creek Dr 27713
Crimson Oak Dr 27713
Croasdaile Dr 27705
Croasdaile Farm Pkwy 27705
Cromwell Rd 27705
Crooked Creek Ln &
Pkwy 27713
Crosby Rd 27704
Cross St 27701
Cross Timbers Dr 27713
Crossing Dr 27703
Crossview Ln 27703
Crosswind Ave 27707
Crosswood Dr 27703
Crowell St 27707
Crown Hill Dr 27707
Croydon Pl 27713
Crutchfield St 27704
Crystal Ct 27705
Crystal Creek Dr 27712
Crystal Lake Rd 27705
Crystal Oaks Ct 27707
Cub Creek Rd 27704
Cullowee Ct 27713
Culpepper Ct 27712
Cultivar Ln 27713
Cumberland Dr 27705
Current Ln 27712
Curriculum Ct 27713
Currin Rd 27703
Curtis St 27707
Curtis Bane Rd 27705
Cushman St 27703
Custer Cir 27713
Cynthia Ct & Dr 27704
Cypress Ct 27707
Da Vinci St 27704
Dacian Ave 27701
Daffodil Ln 27712
Daile Ct 27712
Dairy Rd 27703
Dairy Pond Pl 27705
Daisy Dr 27713
Dakota St 27707
Dale St 27701
Dalidary Ct 27703
Dallas St 27707
Dalton Ct 27705
Daly Ct 27705
Damsel Way 27704
Dana Ct 27712
Danbury Dr 27703
Dandy Dr 27704
Dandywood Ln 27713
Daneborg Rd 27703
Danesfield Ct 27707
Danforth Pl 27712
Daniel Rd 27703
Dansey Cir 27713
Danube Ln 27704
Danziger Dr 27707
Darby Rd 27707
Darby Glen Ln 27713
Dardanelle Ln 27713
Darden Pl 27712
Dare Run 27705
Darian Way 27713
Dark Cir 27707
Darrow Rd 27704
Dartmouth Dr 27705
Darwin Rd 27707
Dauphine Pl 27707
Dave Smith Rd 27703
David St 27704
Davidson Ave 27704
Davie Dr 27704
Davis Dr 27709
Davisson Dr 27705
Dawkins St 27707
Dawn Trl 27712
Dawson Ct 27703
Day Lily Dr 27705
Dayton St 27701
Dean St 27707
Dearborn Dr 27704
Deas Dr 27705
Deblyn Ct 27713
Debonair Cir 27705
Debra Dr 27704
Dedmon Ct 27713
Deep Forest Dr 27713
Deep Wood Cir 27707
Deer Run 27704
Deer Chase Ln 27705
Deer Nest Ln 27705
Deerchase Wynd 27712
Deerfield Ave 27712
Deerview Trl 27712
Deerwood Ct 27712
Deerwood Ln 27705
Degaulle Pl 27707
Dekalb St 27705
Del Webb Arbors Dr 27703
E & W Delafield Ave 27704
Delano St 27703
Delaware Ave 27705
Delbert Ave 27704
Delchester Ct 27713
Dello St 27712
Dellwood Dr 27705
Delmar Dr 27703
Delray St 27713
Demerius St 27701
Demille St 27704
Denada Path 27707
Denfield St 27704
Denise St 27704
Densbury Ct 27713
Denton St 27713
Denver Ave 27704
Denwood Ln 27705
Derby Ct 27707
Derbyshire Pl 27713
Destrier Dr 27703
Development Dr 27709
Devereaux Ln 27712
Devlin Pl 27707
Devon Rd 27707
Dewitt St 27705
Dexter St 27701
Dezern Pl 27705
Dial Dr 27713
Diamond Ct 27703

Diamond Ln 27704
Diamond Head Dr 27705
Diane St 27704
Dickens Ln 27703
Dickson Mill Rd 27705
Digby Pl 27705
Dilbagh Dr 27703
N & S Dillard St 27701
Dinara Dr 27705
Dinsmore Ln 27704
Diploma Dr 27713
Discovery Way 27703
Dixon Rd 27707
Dobbins Dr 27707
Dobbs Pl 27707
Doc Nichols Rd 27703
Dodge Rd 27704
Dodson St 27703
Dodsworth Ct 27705
Dogwood Rd 27705
Dollar Ave 27701
Dolwick Dr 27713
Dominion St 27704
Donlee Dr 27712
Donnelly Ct 27713
Donnigale Ave 27705
Donnybrook Ct 27713
Donphil Rd 27712
Dorothy Dr 27701
Dorset Pl 27713
Doubleday Pl 27705
Douglas St 27705
Dove Creek Rd 27705
Dover Rd 27707
Dover Ridge Ln 27712
Dovershire Pkwy 27704
Dovetail Dr 27704
Dowd St 27701
Downing St 27705
Doyle Rd 27712
Draebury Ln 27713
Drake Ave 27705
Drakesway Ct 27713
Draper St 27704
Drayton Ct 27712
Dresden Dr 27707
Drew St 27701
Drewry St 27703
Drexall Ave 27704
Driftwood Dr 27707
N Driver St
100-899 27703
900-1399 27701
S Driver St 27703
Drucilla Ct 27705
Druid Pl 27707
Drummond Ct 27713
Dry Creek Rd 27707
Dryden Ln 27713
Drye Ln 27713
Drysdale Ct 27713
Duane St 27703
Dubarry Ct 27705
Dublin St 27704
Dubonnet Pl 27704
Duck Pond Ct 27703
Dude Ranch Rd 27704
Dudley Cir 27703
Duffers Pl 27705
N Duke St
101-197 27701
199-1699 27701
2000-4099 27704
S Duke St
100-899 27701
900-1199 27707
Duke Forest Park Ln 27705
Duke Homestead Rd
2600-3299 27705
3300-3699 27704
Duke Of Gloucester Cir 27713
Duke University Rd
1500-1700 27701
1702-1998 27701
2200-2300 27705
2302-2398 27705
Dula St 27705
Dulaire Dr 27713
Duluth St 27705
Dunbar St 27701
Duncan St 27707
Dundee Ct 27712
Dunhill Dr 27713
Dunkeld Way 27705
Dunn Ave 27713
Dunnagan Dr 27705
Dunnhaven Ct 27712
Dunsinane Dr 27707
Dunstan Ave 27707
Dupont Cir & Dr 27705
Dupree St
400-499 27707
501-597 27701
599-999 27701
Durante Pl 27704
Durbin Pl 27705
Durham Dr & Rd 27707
Durham Chapel Hill Blvd 27707
Dutchess Ln 27707
Duval St 27703
Duxbury Ct 27707
Duxford Ct 27703
Dwire Pl 27705
Eagle Dr 27712
Eagle Lodge Ln 27703
Eagle Ridge Ct 27713
Eagle View Dr 27713
Eagles Nest Dr 27712
Eaker Dr 27712
Eakes Dr 27704
Earl Rd 27712
Easley St 27705
Eastcrest Ct 27713
Eastis Dr 27705
Eastman Dr 27705
Eastway Ave 27703
Eastwood Dr
1800-1999 27713
2000-2299 27703
Eatondale Rd 27704
Ebon Rd 27713
Echo Rd 27707
Ed Cook Rd 27703
Eddy Trl 27703
Edenberry Dr 27713
Edenton Ln 27707
Edgar St 27701
Edgebrook Cir 27703
Edgemont Dr 27704
Edgemont Ln 27701
Edgerton Dr 27703
Edgevale Rd 27701
Edgewater St 27705
Edgewood Dr 27713
E Edgewood Dr 27704
W Edgewood Dr 27704
Edinborough Dr 27703
Edison Ln 27712
Edith St 27705
Edmund St 27705
Edsel Rd 27712
Education Ave 27713
Edward St 27701
Edwin Ave 27705
Elaine Cir 27703
Elam Ct 27705
Elba St 27705
Elder St 27705
Elderberry Ct 27703
Elf St 27705
Elgin St 27704
N & S Elizabeth St 27701
Elk Ridge Rd 27712
Elk River Dr 27704
Ellen St 27705
E Ellerbee St 27704
Ellington St 27704
Elliott St 27701
Ellis Rd 27703
Ellisfield Dr 27705
Ellison Dr 27713
N & S Elm St 27701
Elm Tree Ct 27703
Elmira Ave 27707
Elmo St 27701
Elmridge Ct 27713
Elmset Ln 27713
Elmwood Ave 27707
Ember Dr 27703
Emerald Cir 27713
Emerald Forest Dr 27713
Emerald Pond Ln 27705
Emeraldwood Dr 27705
Emerson Pl 27707
Emily St 27704
Emily Bane Rd 27705
Emmy Ln 27712
Emoryfield Pl 27704
Emperor Blvd 27703
E End Ave 27703
Endor Ln 27704
Enesco Cir 27703
Enfield Dr 27703
N & S Engels Cir 27703
Englert Dr 27713
Englewood Ave
300-1299 27701
1300-2699 27705
English Ivy Dr 27703
Eno River Dr 27704
Eno Woods Trl 27712
E & W Enterprise St 27707
Enzo Ct 27713
Ephesus Church Rd 27707
Epperson Dr 27712
Epping Ct 27703
Epworth Pl 27707
Erie St 27707
Erlwood Way 27704
Ernest Pl 27707
Erwin Rd
400-899 27707
1601-1997 27705
1999-4899 27705
4900-5199 27707
Essex Rd 27704
Estelle Ct 27704
Esterbrook Ct 27703
Estes St 27701
Esther Dr 27703
Eton Rd 27707
Etta Rd 27705
Eubanks Rd 27707
Euclid Rd 27713
Eugene St 27701
Eva St
600-999 27701
1100-1299 27703
Evans St 27705
Evanshire Ln 27713
Evanston Ave 27703
Evanwald Ct 27703
Evelyn St 27701
Everett Pl 27701
Evergreen St
1200-1399 27701
1401-1499 27701
1500-1899 27703
Exchange Pl 27713
Exeter Way 27707
N Exeter Way 27703
Exum St 27701
Faber St
200-299 27704
1400-1499 27705
Facade St 27707
Fairbanks Cir 27705
Faircroft Ct 27703
Fairfax Rd 27701
Fairfield Rd 27704
Fairgreen Pl 27705
Fairlawn Rd 27705
Fairmont St 27713
Fairntosh Pl 27712
Fairoaks Rd 27712
Fairstone Ct 27713
Fairview St 27707
Fairway Ln 27712
Fairwoods Dr 27712
Faison Rd 27705
Faith Dr 27704
Falcon Nest Ct 27713
Faleania Dr 27713
Falkirk Dr 27712
Fall Cir 27713
Fallen Oak Ct 27713
Fallenwood Ave 27713
Falling Star Way 27704
Falling Water Dr 27713
Falls Lake Rd 27703
Falls Pointe Dr 27713
Falls Village Ln 27703
Fallsworth Dr 27705
Fanning Way 27704
Fargo St 27707
Farintosh Valley Ln 27703
Farm Rd 27713
Farm Gate Ave 27705
Farm House Ln 27703
Farmwood Rd 27704
Farntosh Valley Ln 27703
Farrington Rd 27707
Farthing St 27704
Fashion Pl 27705
Faucette Ave 27704
Fawn Ave 27705
Fay St
1300-1699 27701
1800-2499 27704
Fayetteville Rd 27713
Fayetteville St
600-1199 27701
1200-3799 27707
3800-4699 27713
2410-2-2410-2 27707
Featherglen Ct 27703
Feldspar Way 27703
Felicia St 27704
Fellowship Dr 27704
Fenimore St 27703
Fentress Ct 27713
Fenwick Pkwy 27713
Ferguson E & W 27713
Fern St 27701
Fernando St 27703
Fernbrook Rd 27703
Ferncrest Dr 27705
Fernway Ave 27701
Fernwood Ct 27713
Ferrand Dr 27705
Ferrell Rd 27704
Ferriday Dr 27713
Ferris Rd 27704
Few Cir 27705
Fews Ford Ln 27712
Ficklin Ct 27712
Fidelity Dr 27703
Fieldcrest Ct 27713
Fielding Ct 27703
Fieldstone Pl 27704
Fiesta Rd 27703
Finley St 27705
Finsbury St 27703
Fircrest Ct 27703
Fire Rock Pl 27703
Firethorn Ct 27712
Firth Rd 27704
Fisher Pl 27707
Fiske St 27703
Fitzford Ct 27712
Fitzgerald Ave 27707
Five Oaks Dr 27707
Flagstaff Ct 27713
Flagstone Way 27712
Flamingo Rd 27705
Flanders Dr 27703
Flatford Ct 27704
Fleetwood St 27701
Fleming Dr
100-399 27712
900-999 27705
Fletchers Chapel Rd
1600-2099 27703
2100-2599 27704
Flint Ln 27713
Flintlock Ln 27704
Flowering Apricot Dr 27703
Floyd Dr 27704
Folkston Dr 27704
Folleto Ct 27703
Folsom Ln 27705
Fontana Ct 27713
Ford Ln 27704
Fordice Ct 27712
Forest Rd 27705
Forest At Duke Dr 27705
Forest Creek Dr 27713
Forest Edge Trl 27705
Forest Glen Dr 27713
Forest Green Dr 27705
Forest Grove Ct 27703
E & W Forest Hills Blvd & Plz 27707
Forest Oaks Dr 27705
Forest Ridge Dr 27713
Forest Ridge Pl 27705
Forest View Pl 27713
Forestview St 27707
Forestwood Dr 27707
Forge Rd 27713
Forierl Dr 27712
Formosa Ave 27707
Forrestal Dr 27703
Forrestdale Dr 27712
Forrester St 27704
Forsythia Ct 27705
Fortunes Ridge Dr 27713
Foster St 27701
Founders Cir 27703
Fountain St 27703
Fountain View Ln 27705
Four Seasons Dr 27707
Foushee St 27704
Fox Dr 27712
Fox Chase Ln 27713
Fox Run Ct 27705
Foxcroft Ln 27713
Foxhunt Dr 27712
Foxlair Ct 27712
Foxridge Cres 27703
Foxwood Pl 27705
Framer Ln 27704
Francis St 27707
Franklin St 27701
Frasier St 27704
Freedom Lake Dr 27704
Freeman Rd 27703
Freemont Rd 27705
Frenchmans Creek Dr 27713
Freshman Dr 27713
Friends School Rd 27705
Friendship Rd 27705
Frinton Pl 27704
Front St 27705
Frontier Way 27713
Fuller St 27701
Fulton St 27705
Furman Ln 27712
Gable Ct 27704
Gable Ridge Dr 27713
Gablefield Ln 27713
Gaithers Pointe Dr 27713
Galax Ln 27703
Galaxy Ct 27705
Galena Ct 27704
Galverston Dr 27712
Gamble Ct 27712
Gandhi Dr 27703
Ganesh Pl 27705
Gann St 27701
Ganyard Farm Way 27703
Garber Ct 27705
Garcia Ave 27704
Garden Hills Ct 27712
Gardenia Ct 27705
Gardenview Pl 27713
Garland St 27705
Garretson Ct 27705
Garrett Dr 27705
Garrett Rd 27707
Gary St 27703
Gasper Ct 27713
Gaston Ave 27707
Gaston Manor Dr 27703
Gate Hill Rd 27705
Gatehouse Ln 27707
Gatesway Ct 27707
Gateview Ct 27703
Gatewood Dr 27712
Gathering Pl 27713
Gatlin Ct 27707
Gattis St 27701
Gearwood Ave 27701
Gebel Ln 27705
E Geer St
100-799 27701
800-4399 27704
W Geer St 27701
Genchand Rd 27703
Genesee Dr 27712
Geneva Ct & Dr 27713
Genlee Ct & Dr 27704
Gentry Dr 27705
Geoffrey Rd 27712
George King Rd 27707
George Watts Hill Dr 27709
Georgetown Ct 27705
Georgia Ave 27705
Geranium St 27704
Gerard St 27701
Gibson Rd 27703
Gilbert St 27701
Gillette Ave 27701
Gilman St 27703
Gilmore Ave 27707
Gin St 27705
Ginger Hill Ln 27703
Gingerberry Dr 27713
Gingerwood Ln 27713
Glade Aster Dr 27704
Glade Crest Way 27704
Gladstone Dr 27703
Glaive Cir & Dr 27703
Glasgow St 27705
Glasson St 27705
E & W Gleewood Pl 27713
Glen Eden Rd 27713
Glen Falls Ln 27713
Glen Hollow Dr 27705
Glenbrittle Dr 27704
Glenbrook Dr 27704
Glenburnie Ln 27704
Glenco Rd 27703
Glenda Rd 27704
Glendale Ave
800-2099 27701
2100-3099 27704
Glendarion Dr 27713
Gleneagles Pl 27712
Glengary Ct 27707
Glenmore Dr 27707
Glenn Rd 27704
Glenn Glade Dr 27712
Glenn School Rd 27704
Glennstone Dr 27704
Glenoaks Dr 27712
Glenrose Dr 27703
Glenview Ln 27703
Glenwood Ave 27703
Glenwood Dr 27705
Glidewell Ct 27707
Gloria Ave 27701
Glossy Leaf Pl 27712
Gloucester Ct 27713
Glover Rd 27703
Golden Dr 27705
Golden Belt Pkwy 27703
Golden Crest Dr 27704
Golden Eagle Dr 27704
Golden Heather Dr 27712
Golden Meadow Ct 27704
Goldendale Dr 27703
Goldenrod Pl 27705
Goldenview Ct 27713
Goldflower Dr 27713
Goldmist Ln 27713
Goldston Ave 27712
N Goley St 27703
S Goley St
100-199 27703
200-299 27701
Golf St 27705
Gooch Rd 27704
Goochland Dr 27703
Goodwin Rd 27712
Goodyear Cir 27713
Gordon St 27701
Gordon Thomas Dr 27705
Gorham Pl 27705
Gorman Church Rd 27704
Govan Dr 27705
Governors Pl 27705
Grace Ln 27701
Graceview Way 27705
Graduate Ct 27713
Grady Dr 27712
Grady Ln 27705
Grafton Ct 27713
Grammercy Pl 27704
Granada Dr 27703
Granbury Dr 27713
Granby St 27701
Grand Lillie Dr 27712
Grand Mesa Dr 27713
Grandale Dr 27713
Grande Oaks Rd 27712
Grandhaven Dr 27713
Grandimere Ct 27703
Grandover Dr 27713
Grandview Dr 27703
Grandview Forest Dr 27713
Grandwood Cir 27712
Granite Pl 27713
Grannys Acres 27713
Grant St 27701
Grantham St 27703
Granville Cir 27705
Grapevine Trl 27707
Grassy Creek Cir 27703
Grassy Glen Cv 27712
Gray Ave 27701
Gray Bluff Pl 27705
Gray Fox Ct 27713
Great Bend Dr 27704
Great Oak Ct 27713
Green St
300-1299 27701
1300-2599 27705
Green Lane Dr 27712
Green Mill Ln 27707
Green Oak Dr 27712
Green Springs Ct 27713
Green Valley Ln 27705
Greenbay Dr 27712
Greenbriar Dr 27705
Greenbriar Rd 27701
Greenfield Ct 27705
Greenglen Dr 27705
Greenhaven Dr 27704
Greenleaf St 27701
Greens At Pleasant 27705
Greens Hollow Ln 27713
Greenside Ct 27707
Greenview Dr 27713
Greenway Cir 27705
Greenwich Pl 27705
Greenwood Dr 27704
Greers Ferry Ct 27713
N & S Gregson St 27701
Gresham Ave 27704
Gretmar Dr 27705
Grey Elm Trl 27713
Greyfield Blvd 27713
Greylee Dr 27712
Greymist Dr 27713
Greyson Dr 27703
Greystone Ct 27713
Greystone Dr 27703
Griffith Pl 27703

- Grifton Pl 27704
- Grimes Ave 27703
- Grist Mill Ln 27712
- Grosbeak Ln 27713
- Grosmont Ct 27704
- Groucho Rd 27705
- Grouse Ct 27704
- Grove Park Rd 27705
- Grove Ridge Dr 27703
- Guardian Dr 27703
- Guernsdel St 27705
- Guess Rd
  - 1201-1397 27701
  - 1399-1799 27701
  - 1800-4099 27705
  - 4100-6699 27712
- Guilder Cv 27713
- Guilford Pl 27713
- Guinevere Ct 27712
- Gulf St 27703
- Gunston Ln 27703
- Gunter St 27707
- Gurley St 27701
- Gus Rd 27703
- N & S Guthrie Ave 27703
- Guy Walker Way 27703
- Gwendolyn Cir 27703
- Hackberry Ln 27705
- Hackney Ln 27703
- Haddington Dr 27712
- Haddon Rd 27705
- Hadley Ln 27713
- Hadrian Dr 27703
- Haggis Ct 27705
- Hale St 27705
- Haledon Cir 27713
- Halifax Ln 27701
- Hall Rd 27704
- Hallbrook Ct 27712
- Halley St 27707
- Hallmark Rd 27712
- Halsey Pl 27707
- Halyard Ct 27713
- Hamilton Ave 27703
- Hamilton Way 27713
- Hamilton Green Dr 27703
- Hamlin Rd 27704
- Hamlin St 27701
- E Hammond St 27704
- Hampshire Ct 27713
- Hampstead Village Dr 27703
- Hamstead Ct 27707
- Hancock St 27704
- Hanes Dr 27709
- Hanford Rd 27703
- Hannah Ct 27713
- Hanover St 27701
- Hanska Ct 27713
- Hanson Rd 27713
- N & S Hardee St 27703
- Hardwick Ct & Dr 27713
- Hargrove St 27701
- Harkness Cir 27705
- Harmony Rd 27713
- Harnett St 27703
- Harold Dr 27712
- Harold Keen Ct 27703
- Harper Pl 27701
- Harrier Ct 27713
- Harrigan Ct 27705
- Harriman Rd 27705
- Harrington Pl 27713
- Hart St 27703
- Hartford Ct 27707
- Hartley Pl 27707
- Harvard Ave 27703
- Harvest Rd 27704
- Harvest Oaks Ln 27703
- Harvey Pl 27705
- Harwood Ct 27713
- Hastings Sq 27707
- Hathaway Rd 27707
- Hatteras Ln 27713
- Haulton Ct 27705
- W Haven Dr & Pl 27705
- Haven Hollow Way 27713
- Havenhill Dr 27712
- Haventree Rd 27713
- Haverford St 27705
- Hawaii Ct 27713
- Hawick Ln 27704
- Hawkins St 27703
- Hawthorne Dr 27712
- Hay Sedge Ct 27705
- Haycox Ct 27713
- Hayfield Dr 27705
- Hayride Pl 27703
- Hayti Ln 27701
- Hayward Rd 27705
- Haywood Ct 27705
- Hazel St 27701
- Hazelwood Dr 27703
- Hazen Ct 27712
- Hearthside St 27707
- Hearthwood Cir 27713
- Heath Pl 27705
- Heather Pl 27707
- Heather Glen Rd 27712
- Heather Ridge Ct 27712
- Heatherford Ct 27704
- Heatherstone Ct 27703
- Heatherwood Ln 27713
- Hebron Rd 27704
- Hedfield Way 27713
- Hedgerow Ln 27705
- Hedgerow Pl 27704
- Heidelberg St 27704
- Hellen Ct 27704
- Hemlock Ave 27707
- Hemlock Dr 27705
- Hemlock Hill Dr 27703
- Hemming Way 27713
- Hemmingwood Dr 27713
- Hemsworth St 27707
- Henderson St 27701
- Hendricks Ct 27707
- Henner Pl 27713
- Henningson Way 27705
- Herbert St 27703
- Hereford Rd 27704
- Heritage Dr 27712
- Hermine St 27705
- Hermitage Ct 27707
- Hermitage Court Dr 27707
- Herndon Rd 27713
- Herrick Pl 27707
- Herring Blvd 27704
- Hertford Pl 27703
- Hester Rd 27703
- Hibiscus St 27701
- Hickory St 27701
- Hickory Glen Ln 27703
- Hickory Grove Rd 27703
- Hickory Hollow Rd 27705
- Hickory Nut Dr 27703
- Hickory Trace Ln 27713
- Hickorywood Sq 27713
- Hicks St 27705
- Hico Way 27703
- Hidcote Cir 27713
- Hidden Hollow Dr 27703
- Hidden Meadow Ct 27704
- Hidden Ridge Ct 27707
- Hidden Springs Dr 27703
- Hidden Treasure Dr 27712
- Hiddenbrook Dr 27703
- Hideaway Ln 27712
- Higbee St 27704
- High St 27707
- High Fox Dr 27703
- High Meadow Rd 27712
- High Ridge Dr 27707
- High Rock Ct 27713
- Higher Learning Dr 27713
- Highgate Dr 27713
- Highgrove Ln 27713
- Highland Ave 27704
- N Highland Dr 27712
- Highland Ridge Ct 27712
- Highplains Rd 27713
- Hill St 27707
- Hillandale Rd 27705
- Hillcrest Dr 27705
- Hillgrand Dr 27705
- Hillock Pl 27712
- W Hills Dr 27705
- Hillsborough Rd 27705
- Hillside Ave 27707
- Hilltop Dr 27703
- Hillview Dr 27703
- Hilton Ave 27707
- Hinesley Rd 27703
- Hinson Dr 27704
- Hitchcock Dr 27705
- Hitching Rack Ct 27713
- Hock Parc 27704
- Hocutt Rd 27703
- Holbrook St 27704
- Holder Rd 27703
- Holland St 27701
- Holland Street Mall 27701
- Holloman Rd 27703
- Hollow Oak Dr 27713
- Hollow Rock Rd 27707
- Holloway St
  - 200-1399 27701
  - 1400-3699 27703
- Holly Ln 27712
- Holly Berry Ln 27703
- Holly Blossom Dr 27703
- Holly Grove Way 27713
- Holly Heights Rd 27704
- Holly Hill Dr 27713
- Hollyhock Ct 27713
- Hollyridge Dr 27712
- Hollywood St 27701
- N Holman St
  - 1-99 27703
  - 100-199 27701
  - 200-399 27703
- S Holman St 27701
- Holmes Cir 27713
- Holston Dr 27704
- Holt School Rd 27704
- Home Rd 27704
- Home Croft Ct 27703
- Homeland Ave 27707
- Homer St 27707
- Homestead Ct 27713
- Homewood Ave 27707
- Honeycutt Dr 27707
- Honeysuckle Ln 27703
- Honor Dr 27707
- Hood St 27701
- N & S Hoover Hl & Rd 27703
- Hope Ave 27707
- Hope Valley Rd 27707
- Hopedale Ave 27707
- Hopewell Dr 27705
- Hopkins St 27701
- Hoppers Dr 27704
- Hopson Rd 27703
- Horizon Cir 27712
- Horizon Pl 27705
- Hornbuckle Pl 27707
- Horsebarn Dr 27705
- Horseshoe Cir 27712
- Horseshoe Rd 27703
- Horton Rd
  - 500-1499 27704
  - 1500-1599 27705
- Hounds Chase Dr 27703
- House Ave 27707
- Houston Rdg 27713
- Hoverhill St 27703
- Howard St 27704
- Howe St 27705
- Howlett Pl 27703
- Hoyle St 27704
- Huckleberry Ct 27713
- Hudson Ave
  - 1000-1199 27704
  - 1300-1499 27705
- E Hudson Ave 27704
- Hugo St 27704
- Hull Ave 27705
- Hulon Dr 27705
- Hummingbird Ln 27712
- Humphrey St 27701
- Hunt St 27701
- Hunter Dr 27712
- Hunters Ln 27713
- Hunters Green Ct 27712
- Hunters Ridge Trl 27707
- Hunting Chase 27713
- Huntington Ave 27707
- Huntscroft Ct 27713
- Huntsman Dr 27713
- Hurdle Ct 27713
- Hurley Rd
  - 600-699 27703
  - 700-899 27704
- Huron St 27707
- Hursey St 27703
- Huse St 27707
- Husketh Dr 27703
- Huxey Glenn Ct 27703
- N Hyde Park Ave
  - 100-899 27703
  - 900-1599 27701
- S Hyde Park Ave 27703
- Icon Ct 27703
- Ida St 27705
- Idlewood Dr 27703
- Imperial Dr 27712
- Independence Ave 27703
- Indian Trl 27705
- Indian Head Ct 27703
- Indiana Ave 27705
- N & S Indiancreek Pl 27703
- Indigo Dr 27705
- Indigo Creek Trl 27712
- Indonger St 27701
- Industrial Dr 27704
- Industry Ln 27713
- Inez Ct 27713
- Infinity Ln 27705
- Infinity Rd 27712
- Inglenook Rd 27707
- Ingram Ct 27713
- Inlet Ave 27704
- Innisfree Dr 27707
- Innovation Dr 27709
- Intercross Rd 27704
- Intermere Rd 27704
- Intern Way 27713
- International Dr 27712
- Interpike Rd 27704
- Interstate 85 W 27705
- Interworth Dr 27704
- Intrepid Ct 27703
- Intuition Cir 27705
- Inverness Dr 27712
- Inwood Dr 27705
- Ipswich Ct 27705
- Iredell St 27705
- Iron Tree Ct 27712
- Irving Way 27703
- Isaacs Way 27713
- Isenhour St 27713
- Ithaca St 27707
- Ivey Wood Ln 27703
- Ivy St 27701
- Ivy Creek Blvd 27707
- Ivy Meadow Ln 27707
- E Jackie Robinson Dr 27701
- Jackson Rd 27705
- Jackson St 27701
- Jacob St 27701
- Jadewood Ct 27705
- Jamaica Pl 27713
- James St 27707
- James Ross Rd 27713
- Jan Ct 27707
- Jane Ln 27703
- Janet St 27707
- Jarvis Ct 27703
- Jasmine Pl 27712
- Jason Ct 27705
- Jean Ave 27707
- Jefferson Dr 27712
- Jeffries Rd 27704
- Jenee Ln 27703
- Jennel Way 27707
- Jennifer Dr 27705
- Jennings Ln 27713
- Jerome Rd 27713
- Jersey Ave 27707
- Jesmond St 27707
- Jessica Ct 27704
- Jester Rd 27713
- Jewel Flower Pl 27705
- Jigsaw Dr 27704
- Jim Lyon Rd 27704
- Jimmy Rogers Rd 27704
- Joci Ct 27704
- Joel Ct 27703
- Johnson Mill Rd 27712
- Johnstone Ct 27712
- Jomali Dr 27705
- Jonathan Cir 27707
- Jones Cir 27703
- Jonquil St 27712
- Joplin St 27703
- N & S Joyland Ave 27703
- Joyner Rd 27704
- Jrk Dr 27705
- Jua Vly 27707
- Jubilee Ln 27707
- Judy Ln 27703
- Julian Carr St 27701
- Juliette Dr 27713
- Junction Rd
  - 100-899 27703
  - 900-1499 27704
- Juniper St
  - 800-1399 27701
  - 1400-1699 27703
- Jupiter Hills Ct 27712
- Justice St 27704
- Justin Ct 27705
- Kaitlin Dr 27713
- Kamis St 27707
- Kandes Ct 27713
- Kanewood Dr 27707
- Kangaroo Dr
  - 3500-3521 27705
  - 3520-3520 27715
  - 3522-3698 27705
  - 3523-3699 27705
- Kaplan Ct 27703
- Kara Pl 27712
- Karigan Ct 27703
- Kate St 27703
- Katie Ln 27705
- Keeneland Ct 27713
- Keith St
  - 500-599 27703
  - 2800-2899 27704
- Kellom Ct 27713
- Kelly Aly 27701
- Kelly Dr 27707
- Kelvin Dr 27712
- Kemmont Dr 27713
- Kemp Rd 27703
- Kenan Rd 27704
- Kendall Dr 27703
- Kendall Ridge Ct 27703
- Kendrick Cir 27703
- Kendridge Dr 27712
- Kenmore Rd 27705
- Kent St
  - 700-899 27701
  - 1000-1799 27707
- Kent Lake Dr 27713
- Kentington Dr 27713
- Kenwood Rd 27712
- Keohane Dr 27705
- Kerley Rd 27705
- Kerr Ct 27713
- Kerrigan Ct 27703
- Kersey Ct 27713
- Kestrel Dr 27713
- Kestrel Heights Ct 27703
- Keswick Ct 27713
- Kettering Dr 27713
- Kettle Creek Rd 27705
- Kevin Ct 27713
- Keystone Pl 27704
- Khalsa Ct 27713
- Kilarney Dr 27703
- Kilary Dr 27713
- Kilbreth Ave 27713
- Kilburn Ln 27704
- Kildrummy Ct & Dr 27705
- Kilgo Dr 27705
- Kilkenny Ct 27713
- Kilmer Ter 27703
- Kilt Way 27712
- Kiltshire Rd 27712
- Kimball Dr
  - 800-1099 27705
  - 1100-1199 27712
- Kimberly Dr 27707
- Kimbrough Ct 27703
- Kinard Rd 27703
- Kincaid Ct 27703
- Kindlewood Dr 27703
- King St 27703
- King Charles Rd 27707
- Kingdom Way 27704
- Kingfisher Way 27713
- Kinglet Ct 27713
- Kings Cross Ln 27713
- Kings Grant Ct 27703
- Kings Mount Ct 27713
- Kingsbury Dr 27712
- Kingsley Woods Dr 27703
- Kingston Ave 27704
- Kingston Mill Ct 27701
- Kinlock Dr 27712
- Kinney Glen Ct 27713
- Kinross Ct 27712
- Kinsey Ct 27705
- Kipling Way 27713
- Kirby St 27713
- Kirk Rd 27705
- Kirkland Run 27713
- Kirkwood Dr 27705
- Kismet Dr 27705
- Kiss Dr 27704
- Kissimee Ct 27713
- Kit Creek Rd 27709
- Kitchner Ct 27705
- Kith Pl 27712
- Kitty Hawk Ct 27703
- Klein Dr 27705
- Knight Dr
  - 600-999 27712
  - 5600-6199 27705
- Knights Arm Dr 27707
- Knightsbridge Ct 27707
- Knightwood Dr 27703
- Knob Ct 27703
- Knobhill Rd 27704
- Knoll Cir 27713
- Knollwood Dr 27712
- Knothole Ln 27704
- Knox Cir 27701
- E Knox St 27701
- W Knox St
  - 101-197 27701
  - 199-1299 27701
  - 1300-2799 27705
- Koback Dr 27712
- Kobold Ln 27707
- Kramer Pl 27703
- Kristen Marie Ln 27713
- Kristy Pl 27703
- Kulbir Ct 27713
- Laboratory Dr 27709
- Lacebark Ln 27713
- Lacy Rd 27713
- Ladd Dr 27712
- Lady Aster Ct 27712
- Lady Banks Dr 27703
- Lady Slipper Ln 27704
- Lafayette St 27707
- Lake Dr 27704
- Lake Cook Dr 27713
- Lake Elton Rd 27713
- Lake Hill Dr 27713
- Lake Valley Ln 27703
- Lake Village Dr 27713
- Lake Vista Dr 27712
- Lakedale Dr 27713
- Lakehurst Ct 27713
- Lakeland St 27701
- Lakemist Cir 27713
- Lakemont Cir 27703
- Lakeridge Cv 27703
- Lakeshore Dr 27713
- Lakeside Dr & Ln 27712
- E Lakeview Dr 27707
- W Lakeview Dr 27707
- Lakeview Rd 27712
- E & W Lakewood Ave 27707
- Lamar St 27705
- Lamb Ct 27712
- Lambeth Cir 27705
- Lamond Ave 27701
- Lancaster St 27701
- Landis Dr 27705
- Landmark Pl 27705
- Landon St 27703
- Landon Farms Ln 27704
- Landover Ct 27713
- Landreth Ct 27713
- Landsbury Dr 27707
- Lane St 27707
- Lanecrest Pl 27705
- Lang St 27703
- Langford Ter 27713
- Lanier Pl 27705
- Lanier Valley Dr 27703
- Lansdowne Dr 27712
- Lansgate Ct 27713
- Lansing Ave 27713
- Lantern Pl 27707
- Lantern View Ln 27703
- Larch Ct 27703
- Larchmont Rd 27707
- Larchwood Dr 27713
- Lark Ln 27712
- Larkin St 27703
- Larkspur Cir 27713
- Larmack Ct 27713
- N & S Lasalle St 27705
- Lassiter St 27707
- Lassiter Homestead Rd 27713
- Lathrop St 27703
- Latta Cir 27712
- Latta Rd 27712
- Latta St 27701
- Lattimore Ln 27713
- Laurel Ave 27701
- Laurel Dr 27703
- Laurel Creek Way 27712
- Laurel Crest Dr 27712
- Laurel Leaf Ct 27703
- Laurel Meadows Dr 27704
- Laurel Mist Way 27703
- Laurel Oaks Dr 27713
- Laurel Ridge Rd 27705
- Laurel Springs Dr 27713
- Lauren Ln 27704
- Laurent Dr 27712
- Laurston Ct 27712
- E & W Lavender Ave 27704
- Lawndale Ave 27705
- E Lawson St
  - 1-99 27701
  - 100-499 27707
  - 601-897 27701
  - 899-1399 27701
  - 1400-1799 27703
- W Lawson St 27707
- Laymans Chapel Rd 27704
- Lazyriver Dr & Ln 27712
- Lazywood Ln 27712
- Leacroft Way 27703
- Leader Ln 27703
- League Way 27705
- Leah Ln 27712
- Leapale Ln 27713
- Learned Pl 27705
- Leathers Ct 27705
- Lebanon Cir 27712
- Ledford Ct 27713
- Ledgerock Way 27703

Lednum St 27705
Lee St 27701
Leesville Rd 27703
Leeward Ct 27713
Legacy Ln 27713
Legion Ave 27707
Leigh Farm Rd 27707
Leitzel Ct 27713
Lemay St 27713
Lemon Dr 27703
Lemongrass Ln 27713
Lenox Ln 27703
Leon St
700-1099 27704
1100-1100 27705
1101-1101 27704
1102-1499 27705
Leonard Dr 27703
Leonardo Dr 27713
Lewis St 27705
Lexham Ct 27713
Lexi Ln 27705
Lexington St 27707
Leyburn Pl 27705
Liberty St
300-999 27701
1000-2199 27703
Libson St 27703
Lick Creek Ln 27703
Liddington Dr 27705
Liggett St 27701
Light St 27704
Lightfoot Dr 27703
Lightwood St 27703
Lillie Dr 27712
Lillington Dr 27704
E & W Lilyfield Ct 27703
Lime St 27704
Limerick Ln 27713
Lin Tilley Rd 27712
Lincoln St
1200-1699 27701
2200-2699 27707
Lincolnshire Ct 27712
Lindbergh St 27704
Linden Rd & Ter 27705
Linden Oaks Ave 27713
Lindenshire Dr 27705
Lindley Dr 27703
Lindmont Ave 27704
Linfield Dr 27701
Linganore Pl 27707
Links Cir 27707
Linkside Ct 27703
Linville Ct 27703
Linwood Ave
300-499 27707
501-697 27701
699-1299 27701
Lions Ct 27704
Lipscomb Dr 27712
Litchfield Ct 27707
Litho Way 27703
Little Acres Dr 27713
Little Creek Rd 27713
Little Rogers Rd 27704
Little Springs Ln 27707
Little Stone Cir 27703
Little Valley Ct 27704
Littleleaf Ln 27713
Littlewood Ln 27707
Live Oak Cir 27703
Live Oak Trl 27705
Livingstone Pl 27707
Loblolly Ct
1-99 27712
5600-5699 27705
Loblolly Dr 27712
Loch Ness Ct 27705
Lochaven Dr 27712
Lochinvar Dr 27705
Lochnora Pkwy 27705
S Lochridge Dr 27713
Lockridge Rd 27705
Lockwood Dr 27712
Locust Dr 27703

Lodestone Dr 27703
Lodge St 27707
Loftin Dr 27704
Logan St 27704
Loganbury Dr 27713
Logger Ct 27713
Logging Trl 27707
Lombard Ave 27705
London Cir 27701
Lone Tree Ct 27713
Long St 27703
Long Crescent Dr 27712
Long Leaf Dr 27712
Long Ridge Rd 27703
Long Shadow Pl 27713
Longford Ct 27713
Longmont Dr 27703
Longview Trl 27703
Longwood Dr 27713
Lopez Rd 27703
Lorain Ave 27704
Lorelei Ct 27713
Lost Ln 27713
Lost Tree Ct 27703
Louis Stephens Dr 27709
Louise Cir 27705
Love Dr 27704
Lovette Rd 27703
Lowry Ave 27701
Loyal Ave & Pl 27713
Lucas Dr 27713
Lucerne Ln 27707
Lucknam Ln 27707
Ludgate Dr 27713
Ludwell Pl 27705
Lullwater Ct 27703
Lumley Rd 27703
Luna Ln 27705
Lunsford Dr 27705
Lure Ct 27713
Luther Rd 27712
Lutz Ln 27703
Lyckan Pkwy 27707
Lydias Way 27713
Lyle Ct 27704
Lynbrook Cir 27712
E & W Lynch St 27701
Lynley Rd 27703
Lynn Ct & Rd 27703
Lynn Forest Dr 27713
Lynnwood Valley Ct 27703
Lyon St 27701
Lyon Farm Dr 27713
Lyon Tree Ln 27713
Lyric St 27701
Lytham Ln 27707
Macgregor Ct 27705
Mackenzie Ct 27713
Macon St 27701
Macwood Dr 27712
Madden Ave 27712
Madeira Ct 27713
Madison St 27701
Madrid Ln 27704
Maere Ct 27712
Magna Dr 27703
Magnolia Dr 27707
Magnolia Oak Pl 27703
Magnolia Tree Ln 27703
Mahala Dr 27704
Mahone St 27713
Maida Vale Ct 27707
Maidenhair Ct 27703
E Main St
100-1299 27701
1300-3099 27703
W Main St
100-1199 27701
1201-1299 27701
1800-1998 27705
2000-2100 27705
2102-2998 27705
Majestic Dr 27707
Malbry Pl 27704
Malik Dr 27703
Mallard Ave 27701

Mallory Ln 27713
Malvern Rd 27707
Manchester Dr 27707
Mandel Rd 27712
Mandy Ct 27707
Manford Dr 27707
N & S Mangum St 27701
Manning Pl 27701
Manning Way 27703
Mannix Rd 27704
Mansfield Ave 27703
Manson Pl 27703
Manteo St 27701
Maple Rdg 27704
N Maple St 27703
S Maple St 27703
Maple Leaf Dr 27705
Maplewood Ave 27701
Maplewood Dr 27704
Marble Dr 27713
Marbrey Dr 27703
Marcella Ct 27707
Marchmont Ct 27705
Marena Pl 27707
Margaret Ave 27705
Marigold Pl 27705
Marilee Glen Ct 27705
Marion Ave 27705
Marist Ct 27713
Market St 27701
E Markham Ave 27701
W Markham Ave
100-1200 27701
1202-1298 27701
1300-1798 27705
1800-1999 27705
Marlborough Way 27713
Marlin Dr 27703
Marlowe Dr 27705
Marly Dr 27703
Marne Ave 27704
Maroon Dr 27713
Marquis Dr 27704
Mars Ct 27703
Marsh Ct 27704
Marsh Landing Ct 27703
Marshall Way 27705
Martha St 27707
Martin St 27704
Martin Luther King Pkwy
100-1000 27713
1002-1098 27713
1100-1899 27707
Martry Rd 27713
Marvin Dr 27707
Mary Martin Rd 27703
Marydell Ln 27707
Maryland Ave 27705
Marywood Dr 27712
Mason Rd 27712
Masondale Ave 27707
Massey Ave 27701
Massey Chapel Rd 27713
Mathison St 27701
Matilene Ave 27707
Matterhorn Dr 27713
Matthews Rd 27712
Mattie Ct 27704
Maxwell Ave 27701
May Rd 27703
Mayapple Pl 27705
Maybank Ct 27713
Mayfair St 27707
Mayfield Cir 27705
Mayflower Ct 27703
Maymount Dr 27703
E & W Maynard Ave 27704
Mayo St 27704
Mayruth Dr 27713
Mcbenson Pl 27705
Mccallie Ave 27704
Mccarthy Ct 27712
Mccool Ct 27703
Mccormick Rd 27713
Mcdermott Dr 27705
Mcdowell Rd 27705

Mcfarland Rd 27707
Mcgehee St 27707
Mcgill Pl 27701
Mckinley St 27705
Mckittrick Ln 27712
Mclamb Dr 27703
Mclaurin Ave 27707
Mcnair St 27707
Mcneil Ln 27703
Mcqueen Dr 27705
Meade Ln 27707
Meadhall Ct 27713
Meadow Dr 27713
Meadow Rd 27705
Meadow Lark Pl 27712
Meadowbrook Dr 27712
Meadowcrest Dr 27703
Meadowrun Dr 27707
Meadston Dr 27712
Mebane Ln 27703
Medallion Dr 27704
Medearis Ct 27707
Medford Rd 27705
Medical Park Dr 27704
Medina St 27707
Meeting St 27705
Meeting House Ln 27707
Melanie St 27704
Melbourne St 27703
Mellon Ct 27704
Mellwood Dr 27712
Melody Cir 27707
Melrose Ave 27704
Melstone Turn 27707
Memorial St 27701
Memory Ln 27712
Memphis St 27707
Mercia Cir 27703
Mercury Ct 27703
Meredith Dr 27713
Meridian Pkwy 27713
Meriwether Dr 27704
Merrick St 27701
Merrimac St 27707
Methodist St 27703
N Miami Blvd
600-1499 27703
1500-1799 27701
S Miami Blvd 27703
Michael Dr 27704
Mickey Cir 27712
Middle St 27703
Middlebrook Ct & Dr 27705
Middlebury Ct 27713
Middlesborough Ct 27705
Middleton Ave 27705
Middleton Rd 27713
Midgette Pl 27703
Midland Ter 27704
Midpines Ct 27713
Midway Ave 27703
Milan St 27704
Milford Ln 27713
Mill Ct 27713
Mill St 27704
Mill Haven Ct 27713
Miller Ct & Dr 27704
Millspring Dr 27705
Millstone Dr 27713
Milner Pl 27703
Milton Rd
100-312 27712
311-311 27722
314-2298 27712
401-2299 27712
Mimosa Dr 27713
Mimosa St 27703
Mine Bluff Ct 27713
N & S Mineral Springs
Rd 27703
Minerva Ave 27701
Minnestott Way 27704
Mint Hill Ct 27703
Minuteman Ct 27705
Miosha St 27701
Miramont Dr 27712

Mirando Pl 27707
Miriam Cir 27704
Missell Ave 27713
Mist Lake Dr 27704
Mistletoe Ln 27703
Misty Creek Ct 27705
Misty Morning Ct 27712
Misty Pine Ave 27704
Misty Pond Ct 27713
Misty Ridge Rd 27712
Mockingbird Ln 27703
Mohawk Trl 27707
Mohegan Dr 27712
Moline St 27707
Monaco Ct 27713
Monarch Way 27713
Moneta Way 27703
Monk Rd 27704
Monmouth Ave 27701
Monroe Ave 27707
Mont Haven Dr 27712
Montana Way 27707
Montauk Pl 27713
Montcastle Ct 27705
Montclair Cir 27713
Montcrest Dr 27713
Monteith Ct 27713
Monterey Ln 27713
Monterrey Creek Dr 27713
Montford Rd 27705
Montgomery St 27705
Montibillo Pkwy 27713
Monticello Ave 27707
Montrose Dr 27707
Montvale Dr 27705
Moon Valley Ln 27705
Moonlight Ct 27703
Moonstone Ct 27703
Moore Dr 27709
Moore Pl 27701
Moorefield Ct 27705
Moores Creek Rd 27705
Moorgate Ave 27704
Mooring Ct 27703
Moortown Ct 27713
Morcroft Ln 27705
Mordecai St 27705
Morehead Ave 27707
Morehead Hill Ct 27703
Moreland Ave 27707
E & W Morgan St 27701
Morgans Ridge Ln 27707
Moriah Hill Rd 27707
Morning Glory Ave
1-99 27703
900-998 27701
1000-1299 27701
1300-1599 27703
Morning Sun St 27713
Morning View Ct 27703
Mornings Way 27712
Morningside Dr 27713
Morningview Dr 27703
Morreene Rd 27705
Morrell Ln 27713
Morris St 27701
Morristown Cir 27705
Morse Cir 27713
Mortise Ct 27704
Morton Dr 27704
Morven Pl 27701
Moss Creek Ct 27712
Moss Grove Ln 27703
Moss Spring Ct 27712
Mossdale Ave 27707
Mount Hermon Church
Rd 27705
Mount Level Rd 27704
Mount Moriah Rd 27707
Mount Sinai Rd 27705
Mountain Brook Cir 27704
Mountain Island Dr 27713
Mountain Lake Ct 27713
Mountainview Ave 27705
Mozelle St 27703
Mt Evans Dr 27705

Muirfield Ct 27712
Mulberry Ct 27713
Muldee St 27703
Murphy St 27701
Murphy School Rd 27705
E & W Murray Ave 27704
Murray Hill Dr 27712
Muscadine Ct 27703
Musket Ln 27705
Mustang Ct 27705
Mutual Ct & Dr 27707
Myers St 27707
Myers Park Dr 27705
Myra St 27707
Myra Glen Pl 27707
Myrtlewood Dr 27705
Mystic Dr 27712
Nadeau Ct 27704
Nancy St 27701
Nancy Rhodes Dr 27712
Nantahala Dr 27713
Nantuckett Ave 27703
Naples Pl 27703
Nash St 27707
Natchez Way 27712
Nation Ave 27707
E Nc Highway 54 27713
W Nc Highway 54
100-799 27713
W Nc Highway 54
1100-1699 27707
Nc Highway 55
1600-2499 27707
4600-6599 27713
Nc Highway 751
6700-6999 27713
7000-7036 27707
7037-7099 27713
7100-7122 27707
7124-7198 27707
7129-7197 27713
7199-7201 27713
7202-7298 27707
7203-9999 27713
7300-9998 27713
Nc Hwy 55 27713
Neal Rd 27705
Nebo St 27707
Neff St 27705
Nellowood St 27704
Nelson St 27707
Neptune Ct 27712
Nethers Ct 27704
Nettie Stanley Rd 27705
Neville St 27701
New Bedford Ct 27704
New Bern Pl 27707
New Haven Dr 27703
New Hope Commons
Dr 27707
New Hope Commons
Boulevard Ext 27707
New Leaf Ln 27705
New Millennium Way 27709
Newberry Ln 27703
Newby Dr 27704
Newcastle Rd 27704
Newell St 27705
Newgate Ct 27713
Newhall Rd 27713
Newkirk St 27703
Newland Pl 27703
Newman St 27701
Newport Dr 27705
Newquay St 27705
Newsom St 27704
Newton Dr 27707
Newtown Ct 27713
Nichols Farm Dr 27703
Nickel Creek Cir 27713
Nicklaus Dr 27705
Nightfall Ct 27713
Nimitz Ave 27713
S Nipper Ct 27704
Nita Ln 27712
Nixon St 27707

No Record St
99-99 27704
199-199 27707
299-299 27713
Noah Dr 27703
Nob Hill Rd 27704
Nobel Dr 27703
Noorin Ct 27713
Norcross Rd 27713
Normandy St 27707
North St 27701
Northampton Rd 27707
Northbury Cir 27712
Northcliff Dr 27712
Northcreek Dr 27707
Northern Durham
Pkwy 27703
Northern Way Ct 27712
Northgate St 27704
Northgate Shopping
Ctr 27701
Northlake Dr 27703
Northwood Cir 27701
Northwood Hills Ave 27704
Norton St 27701
Norway Spruce Dr 27703
Norwich Way 27707
Norwood Ave 27707
Nottaway Rd 27707
Novaglen Rd 27712
November Dr 27712
Nutmeg Ct 27713
Nuttree Way 27713
Oak Dr 27707
E Oak Dr
800-1099 27705
1100-1100 27712
1102-1299 27712
N Oak Ln 27712
Oak Grove Pkwy 27703
Oak Hill Dr 27712
Oak Park Dr 27703
N Oak Ridge Blvd 27707
Oakbrook Dr 27713
Oakchest Ct 27703
Oakland Ave 27705
Oakmont Ave 27713
Oakside Ct 27703
Oakview St
100-199 27713
3900-4099 27703
Oakwind Ct 27713
Oakwood Ave 27701
Oberlin Dr 27705
Obie Dr 27713
Obsidian Way 27703
Ocean Ct 27704
Octavia Ct 27705
October Dr 27703
Odell St 27703
Odyssey Dr 27713
Ogburn Ct 27705
Okeefe Ct 27712
Okelly Chapel Rd 27713
Old Autumnwood Dr 27705
Old Barn Ave 27704
Old Chapel Hill Rd 27707
Old Cole Mill Rd 27712
Old Cornwallis Rd 27713
Old Durham Rd 27707
Old Farm Rd 27704
Old Fayetteville St 27701
Old Fish Dam Rd 27704
Old Forge Cir 27712
Old Fox Trl 27713
Old Harness Pl 27704
Old Hillsborough Rd 27705
Old Home Place Ln 27713
Old Hope Creek Path 27707
Old Kemp Rd 27703
Old Maple Ln 27713
Old Nc 10 27705
Old Oak Ct 27705
Old Orchard Ave 27704
Old Oxford Rd
200-2499 27704

2700-2798 27712
2800-5899 27712
Old Page Rd 27703
Old Stony Way 27705
Old Sugar Rd 27707
Old Towne Pl 27713
Old Trail Dr 27712
Old Well St 27704
Olde Coach Rd 27707
Olde Union Ct 27703
Oldelara 27709
Oleander Dr 27703
Olive Pl 27704
Olive Branch Rd 27703
Olivene Dr 27703
Oliver Ln 27713
Olivia Ct 27704
Olney Dr 27705
Olson Dr 27712
Olympic Dr 27704
Om Ct 27703
Omah St 27705
Omega Rd 27712
Omer Ln 27703
Oneida Ave 27703
Oneluska Dr 27705
Onslow St 27705
Ontario Ct 27713
Onyx Ct 27703
Opal Ct 27703
Open Air Camp Rd 27712
Operations Dr 27705
Ora Ave 27704
Oran Ave 27704
Orange St 27701
Orangewood Dr 27705
Orchard Dr 27713
Orchard Way 27704
Orchard Oriole Ln 27713
Orchid Ct 27713
Oregon St 27705
Orient St 27701
Orindo Dr 27713
Oriole Dr 27707
Oriskony Way 27703
Orvieto Way 27707
Osage Pl 27712
Osborne Pl 27705
Osprey Pl 27712
Other Duck Ln 27705
Otis St 27707
Ottawa Ave 27701
Otter Run 27705
Otters Run 27712
Oval Dr 27705
Overby Dr 27713
Overhill Ter 27707
Overland Dr 27704
Overlook Ave 27712
Owen St 27703
Owls Wood Ln 27705
Oxboro Cir 27713
Oxford Dr 27707
Oxmoor Dr 27703
Ozark Ct 27713
Pace St 27705
Paces Ferry Dr 27712
Pacific Ave 27704
Packard St 27704
Padstow Ct 27704
Page Rd 27703
Page Creek Ln 27703
Page Point Cir 27703
Page Road Ext 27703
Pageford Dr 27703
Pagemore Ct & Ln 27703
Paladin Ct 27713
Palmer St 27707
Palmetto Cir 27703
Palomino Ln 27712
Pamela Dr 27704
Pamlico St 27701
Panama Ter 27713
Panamint Dr 27705
Panoramic Dr 27703
Panther Creek Ct &
Pkwy 27704
Panthers Run Dr 27713
Panzer Pl 27713
Paper Birch Ln 27705
Paperbark Ct 27713
Par Pl 27705
Paradise Pl 27705
Paragon Cir 27712
Park Ave
500-899 27703
900-1299 27701
Park Dr 27709
Park Pl 27712
Park Plz 27709
Park Forty Plz 27713
Park Glen Pl 27713
Park Overlook Dr 27712
Park Ridge Rd 27713
Parker St 27701
Parkhaven Pl 27712
Parkridge Ct 27705
Parkside Dr 27707
Parkview Dr 27712
Parliament Ct 27703
Parquet St 27707
E & W Parrish St 27701
Parson Chase 27713
Parsons Green Ct 27704
Parthenia Dr 27705
Partridge St 27704
Pascal Way 27705
Paschall Dr 27705
Pathwood Ln 27705
Patriot Cir 27704
Patriot Dr 27703
Patterson Rd
100-2799 27704
5400-5499 27705
Pattersons Mill Rd 27703
Paul Rd 27704
Pauli Murray Pl 27701
Paulwood Ct 27704
Pavillion Pl 27707
Pawnee Ct 27712
E Peabody St
300-1199 27701
1900-2199 27703
W Peabody St 27701
Peace St 27701
Peachtree Pl 27701
Peachway Ct & Dr 27705
Pear Tree Ln 27703
Pearce Pl 27712
Pearl St 27701
Pearl Knoll Cir 27703
Pearson Dr 27713
Pebble Way 27703
Pebble Creek Xing 27713
Pebblestone Dr 27703
Pecan Pl 27704
Pedder Ct 27713
Pedestal Rock Ln 27712
Pegram Ct 27703
Pekoe Ave 27707
Pelham Rd 27713
Pembroke Dr 27704
Pencade Ln 27713
Pendergrass St 27704
Pendleton Ct 27713
Penhurst Ct 27713
Penley Ct 27713
Penn Dr 27703
Pennington Pl 27707
Pennock Rd 27703
Pennsylvania Ave 27705
Pennypacker Ln 27703
Penrith Dr 27713
Penrod Rd 27703
Penzance St 27704
Peppercorn St 27704
Peppertree St 27705
Perennial Dr 27705
Perfect Moment Dr 27713
Peridot Pl 27703
Perigrine Way 27703
Periwinkle Ct 27703
Perkins Rd 27705
Perriwinkle Pl 27713
Perry St 27705
Pershing St 27705
Persimmon Ct 27712
Person St 27703
Perth Pl 27712
Pervis Rd 27704
Petersburg Pl 27703
E Pettigrew St
1-1599 27701
1600-2999 27703
W Pettigrew St
101-197 27701
199-599 27701
1201-1297 27705
1299-2999 27705
Peyton Ave 27703
Phauff Ct 27703
Phillips Way E & W 27713
Piccadilly Ct 27713
Pickard Pl 27703
Pickett Rd 27705
Pickford Pl 27703
Pickran Cir 27705
Pickwick Trl 27704
E & W Piedmont Ave 27707
Piedmont Forest Ct 27703
Pierre Pl 27704
Pike St 27707
Pilling Pl 27707
E & W Pilot St 27707
Pilton Pl 27705
Pin Oak Dr 27707
Pinafore Dr 27705
Pine Way 27712
Pine Bark Trl 27705
Pine Cone Dr 27707
Pine Cone Ln 27705
Pine Glen Trl 27713
Pine Hill Rd 27707
Pine Needle Ct 27705
Pine Top Pl 27705
Pine Trail Dr 27712
Pine Valley Dr 27712
Pinebrook Dr 27713
Pineburr Pl 27703
Pinecrest Rd 27705
Pinedale Dr 27705
Pineland Ave 27704
Pinestraw Way 27713
Pinetree Ct 27705
Pineview Cir 27705
Pineview Rd 27707
Pinewood Ct 27713
Pinewood Dr 27705
Piney Bluff Ct 27705
Piney Creek Ln 27705
Piney Hollow Ct 27705
Piney Park Ln 27713
Piney Ridge Ct 27712
Pinnacle Rd 27705
Pinyon Pl 27707
Piper St 27704
Piperwood Ct 27713
Pittard Sears Rd 27713
Pittsford Pl 27707
Placid Ct 27713
Plano Dr 27703
Plantation Dr 27712
Planters Ct 27712
Play Gate Ln 27703
Pleasant Dr 27703
Pleasant Green Rd 27705
Pleasant Hill Dr 27712
Pleasant View Rd 27705
Plowlan Pl 27707
N Plum St 27703
S Plum St
100-599 27703
700-1099 27701
Plumas Dr 27705
Plummer Pl 27703
Plumtree Ct 27703
Plymouth Rd 27707
Pocono Dr 27705
Poinciana Dr 27707
E Pointe Dr 27712
N Pointe Dr 27705
Pointe Pl 27712
Pointe View Ct 27713
Pommel Ln 27703
Pomona Dr 27707
Pond View Ct 27705
Ponderosa Dr 27705
Ponderosa Ln 27712
Pondview Ln 27712
Pope Rd 27707
Poplar St 27703
Poppy Trl 27713
Porchlight Ct 27707
Porter Cir 27704
Porters Glen Pl 27713
Portico Ln 27703
Portofino Pl 27707
Portsmouth St 27704
Post Ave 27703
Post Oak Rd 27705
N & S Poston Ct 27705
Potter St 27701
Powder Springs Pl 27712
Powderhill Pl 27707
Powe St 27705
Powell Dr 27703
Powers Ln 27712
Prairie View Ct 27703
Pratt St 27705
Preakness Dr 27713
Prentiss Pl 27707
Prescott Dr 27712
Presidential Dr 27703
Presidents Dr 27704
Preston Ave 27705
Preston Ct 27703
Prestwick Pl 27705
Price Ave
300-499 27707
500-999 27701
Primitive St 27701
Primrose Pl 27707
Prince St 27707
Princess Ann Dr 27703
Princeton Ave 27707
Prioress Dr 27712
Prison Camp Rd 27705
Pritchard Pl 27707
Proctor St 27707
Professor Pl 27713
Prologue Rd 27712
Promenade Ct 27713
Prospect Pkwy 27703
Prospectus Dr 27713
Providence Ct 27705
Providence Ridge Ln 27713
Prudence St 27704
Puller Ct 27707
Pulley Pl 27707
Pump Station Ln 27712
Pumpkin Pl 27703
Putnam Ln 27713
Putters Ct 27703
Pycroft Ct 27703
Pyrite Pl 27703
Quail Dr 27703
Quail Hunt Cir 27712
Quail Ridge Rd 27705
Quartz Dr 27703
Quebec Dr 27705
N Queen St 27701
Queen Ferry Ct 27712
Queensbury Cir 27713
Queensland Ct 27712
Quiet Woods Pl 27712
Quincemoor Rd 27712
Quincy St 27703
Quintin Pl 27705
Rabbits Glen Ter 27713
Racine St 27707
Rada Dr 27703
Radcliff Cir 27713
Radley Pl 27705
Railroad St 27701
Rainbow Way 27707
Raindrop Cir 27712
Rainmaker Dr 27704
Raintree Rd 27712
Raj Dr 27703
Ramblegate Ln 27705
Ramblewood Ave 27713
Ramcat Rd 27713
Ramseur St 27701
Ranbir Dr 27713
Randall Rd 27707
Randolph Pl 27703
Randolph Rd 27705
Rapids Ln 27705
Rastille Ln 27712
Ratcale Ln 27705
Rathie Dr 27703
Rattan Bay Ct 27713
Raven St 27704
Ravenstone Ln 27703
Ravenswood Pl 27713
Rawdon Dr 27713
Raynor St 27703
Reams Pl 27703
Reams Run Rd 27713
Red Ash Cir 27704
Red Bird Dr 27704
Red Bluff Ct 27713
Red Carriage Ave 27704
Red Cedar Cir 27712
Red Coach Rd 27712
Red Crest Ln 27704
Red Elm Dr 27713
Red Feather Ct 27704
Red Hat Ln 27713
Red Mill Rd
3400-6999 27704
8300-8399 27712
Red Oak Ave 27707
Red Sage Ct 27703
Red Spring Ct 27703
Red Sunset Ln 27703
Redbud Ct 27713
Redding Ln 27712
Redear Pl 27703
Redfern Way 27707
Redgate Dr 27703
Redmond Dr 27712
Redstone Ct 27703
Redwood Rd 27704
Reed Ct 27703
Reedy Way 27703
Rees Ln 27705
Reese Rd 27712
Reflection Way 27713
Regan Ct 27703
Regency Dr 27713
Regent Rd 27707
Regiment Way 27705
Regis Ave 27705
Reichard St 27705
Reid Dr 27705
Reigal Wood Rd 27712
Reliance Rd 27703
Reliant Pl 27712
Remington Cir 27705
Renaissance Pkwy 27713
Rencher Ct 27703
Renee Dr 27705
Renfrew Dr 27705
Renovators Pl 27704
Reservoir St 27703
Residence Inn Blvd 27713
Reta Rd 27704
Revere Rd 27713
Rexing Ct 27713
Reynolda Cir 27712
Reynolds Ave & Ct 27707
Rhew Dr 27704
Rhododendron Dr 27712
Rhygate Ct 27713
Rhyn Ct 27704
Riceland Dr 27705
Richardson Cir 27713
Richsand St 27705
Richwood Rd 27705
Ricon Pl 27703
Riddle Rd
1200-2199 27713
2300-2699 27703
Ridge Pl & Rd 27705
Ridge Wood St 27713
Ridgecrest Cir 27712
Ridgestone Pkwy 27712
Ridgeview Rd 27712
Ridgeway Ave 27701
Rigsbee Ave 27701
Riley Dr 27704
Ringwood Ct 27713
Rio Grande Ct 27703
Ripley St 27707
Rippling Stream Rd 27704
Rita Ct 27713
Ritten Ct 27712
River Birch Rd 27705
River Rock Dr 27704
River Run Rd 27712
Riverbark Ln 27703
Riverbend Dr 27705
N & S Riverdale Dr 27712
Riverland Farm Ct 27703
Rivermont Rd 27712
Riverside Dr 27704
Riverwalk Ter 27704
Roane St 27704
Roanoke St 27704
Robbins Rd 27703
Roberson St 27703
Robinhood Rd 27701
Robinwood Rd 27713
Rochambeau Ct 27704
Rochelle St 27703
Rochester St 27704
Rock St 27707
Rock Cottage Ct 27707
Rockford Rd 27713
Rockhouse Ct 27713
Rockport Dr 27703
Rockwall Garden Way 27713
E & W Rockway St 27704
Rockwood Cir 27707
Rocky Creek Dr 27704
Rocky Point Ln 27712
Rocky Springs Rd 27705
Rockywalk Ct 27713
Rodeo Dr 27704
Rodham Rd 27703
Rodolphe St 27712
Rogers Rd 27703
Rolling Hill Rd 27705
Rolling Meadows Dr 27703
Rolling Pines Ave 27703
Rollingview Ct 27713
Rollingwood Dr 27713
Rome Ave 27701
Rondelay Dr 27703
Roney St 27701
Roosevelt St 27707
Rosaline Ln 27713
Rose Rd 27712
Rose Bay Ct 27713
Rose Brook Dr 27713
Rose Garden Ln 27707
Rose Of Sharon Rd 27712
Rose Petal Dr 27705
Rosebriar Dr 27705
Rosebud Ln 27704
Rosedale Ave 27707
Rosedale Creek Dr 27703
Rosedawn Ct 27703
Rosedown Ct 27703
Rosehill Ave 27705
Roseland Ave 27712
Rosemary Ave 27705
Rosemeade Pl 27712
Rosemont Dr & Pkwy 27713
Rosetta Dr 27701
Rosewood Dr 27705
Rosewood St 27701
Roslyn Rd 27712
Ross Ln 27713
Ross Rd 27703
Rossford Ln 27713
Roswell Ct 27707
Rothbury Dr 27712
Rother Ln 27707
Round Rock Blvd 27703
Round Spring Ln 27712
Rowemont Dr 27705
Rowena Ave 27703
N Roxboro Rd 27712
N Roxboro St
100-1800 27701
1802-1898 27701
1900-5199 27704
S Roxboro St
200-499 27701
501-599 27701
600-2999 27707
3800-5899 27713
Royal Dr 27704
Royal Oaks Dr 27712
Royal Sunset Dr 27713
Roycroft Dr 27703
Ruby St 27704
Ruby Ridge Rd 27703
Ruffin St
1200-1899 27701
1900-2199 27704
Rufus Dr 27705
Rugby Rd 27707
Ruggles St 27704
Running Brook Ct 27713
Running Cedar Trl 27712
Running Fox Ln 27703
Ruritan Rd 27703
Rush Ct 27713
Ruskins Ave 27704
Russell Rd 27712
Russet Ct 27712
Rustic Wood Ln 27713
Rustica Dr 27713
Ruth St 27704
Rutherford St 27705
Rutledge Ave 27704
Ryan St 27704
Ryefield Dr 27713
Sabre Ct 27713
Saddle Dr 27712
Saddle Creek Ln 27703
Saddle Ridge Ave 27704
Saddlewood Ct 27713
Sadie Scarlett Ln 27705
Safeway St 27705
Sagar Ct 27703
Sagebrush Ln 27703
Sagerview Way 27713
Sagewood Pl 27705
Saint Albans Ct 27712
Saint Andrews Ct 27707
Saint Clair Pl 27712
Saint James Ct 27713
Saint John Dr 27703
Saint Marks Rd 27707
Saint Paul St 27704
Saint Thomas Dr 27705
Salem St 27703
Salix Dr 27713
Salmon River Dr 27705
Salvone Ct 27703
Salwood Ln 27712
Salzburg Ct 27704
Sameer Ct 27703
Samoa Ct 27705
San Marcos Ave 27703
San Rimini Way 27707
Sana Ct 27713
Sanderling Ct 27713
Sanders Ave 27703
Sanderson Dr 27704
Sandhill Ln 27713
Sandhurst Ct 27712
Sandlewood Dr 27712
Sandstone Dr 27713
Sandstone Ridge Ct &
Dr 27713
Sandy Bluff Ct 27703

Sandy Creek Dr 27705
Sandy Ridge Ln 27705
Sandybrook Ct 27703
Sangre De Cristo Dr 27705
Santee Rd 27704
Sapphire Dr 27703
Sarah Ave 27707
Saratoga Dr 27704
Sargent Pl 27707
Sassafras Hill St 27712
Sater St 27703
Saturn Ct 27703
Savannah Ave 27707
Savannah Place Dr 27713
Savi Ct 27713
Sawmill Ln 27712
Sawmill Creek Pkwy 27712
Sawyer St 27707
Saxford Pl 27713
Saxony Dr 27707
Sayward Dr 27707
Scalybark Rd 27712
Scaresdale Pl 27707
Scarlet Oak Ct 27712
Scarlet Sage Dr 27704
Scenic Ct 27713
Scheer Ave 27703
Scholastic Cir 27713
Scoggins St 27703
Scotland Pl 27705
Scotney Cir 27713
Scots Pine Xing 27713
Scott Pl 27705
Scott King Rd 27713
Scottish Ln 27707
Scottsdale St 27712
Scottybrook Ct 27703
Scout Dr 27707
Scranton Pl 27713
Scuppernong Ln 27703
Scythe Ct 27705
Seaforth Dr 27713
Seagrove Ct 27703
Sean Francis Way 27713
Seaton Rd 27713
Seawell Ct 27703
Sedgefield St 27705
Sedgewood Ct 27713
Sedley Pl 27705
Sedwick Rd W 27713
E & W Seeman St 27701
Selby Ave 27713
Selkirk St 27707
E & W Seminary St 27701
Senior Ave 27713
September Dr 27703
Sequoia Ct 27707
Serenity Ct 27704
Seterra Bnd 27712
Settlement Dr 27713
Settlers Mill Ln 27713
Seven Oaks Rd 27704
Severn Grove Dr 27703
Severna Ct 27704
Sevier St 27705
Seville Ct 27703
Shadebush Dr 27712
Shadow Creek Ct 27712
Shadow Hawk Dr 27713
Shadow Moss Pl 27705
Shady Ln 27712
Shady Bluff St 27704
Shady Creek Dr 27713
Shady Grove Rd 27703
Shady Grove Church Rd 27703
Shady Point Ct 27703
Shady Ridge Ct 27713
Shady Side Ln 27713
Shady Spring Pl 27713
Shaftsbury St
 2700-3599 27704
 3600-3799 27705
 3800-3899 27704
Shagbark Dr 27703
Shakori Trl 27707
Shalimar Dr 27713
Shamrock Rd 27713
Shannas Way 27713
Shannon Rd
 3000-3799 27707
 3710-3710 27717
Shantercliff Pl 27712
Shari Ct 27704
Sharpstone Ln 27703
Shasta Ct 27713
Shaw Rd 27704
Shawnee St 27701
Shay Dr 27704
Shearwater Dr 27713
Shelburn Ct 27712
Shellbrook Ct 27703
Shelly Pl 27707
Shelter Cv 27713
Shelton Ave 27707
Shenandoah Ave 27704
Shepard Springs Ct 27713
Shepherd St
 600-999 27701
 1000-1499 27707
Sherbon Dr 27707
Sherbrooke Dr 27712
Sheridan Dr 27707
Sherman Ave 27707
Sherron Rd 27703
Sherwood Dr 27705
Shields Ct 27713
Shiley Dr 27704
Shiloh Dr 27703
Shirley St 27705
Shirley Caesar Ct 27701
Shiva Ct 27703
Shoccoree Dr 27705
E Shoreham St 27707
Shoreline Cv 27703
Shrewsbury St 27707
Shropshire Pl 27707
Sibling Pine Dr 27705
Sidbrook Ct 27704
Sidepark St 27703
Sidneys Way 27703
Siena St 27712
Sierra Ct 27704
Signet Dr 27704
Silhouette Dr 27713
Silicon Dr 27703
Silk Tree Ln 27713
Silkwood Dr 27713
Silver Maple Ct 27705
Silver Pine Ct 27713
Silver Star Dr 27713
Silverbell Ct 27713
Silverbush Ct 27707
Silverton Ct 27713
Silverwood Ct 27713
Sima Ave 27703
Sima St 27701
Simmons St 27701
Sinclair Cir 27705
Singing Woods Pl 27712
Sinnott Cir 27713
Sir Gawain Way 27713
Six Gables Rd 27712
Six Mills Ct 27713
Skipwith Ct 27707
Sky Lane Dr 27704
Skybrook Ln 27703
Skylark Way 27712
Skyler Ln 27705
Skyline Dr 27712
Slate Ct 27703
Slater Rd 27703
Slateworth Dr 27703
Slaytenbush Ln 27703
Sleepy Creek Dr 27713
Sloan St 27701
Smith Dr 27712
Smokeridge Ct 27713
Smoketree Ct 27712
Smoky River Ct 27704
Snow Crest Trl 27707
Snow Hill Dr & Rd 27712
Snow Valley Rd 27712
Snowmass Way 27713
Snyder St 27703
So Hi Dr 27703
Softree Ln 27712
Solitude Way 27713
Solo Cv 27713
Solterra Way 27705
Somerdale Dr 27713
Somerknoll Dr 27713
Somerset Dr 27707
Sonnett Pl 27712
Sophomore Ct 27713
Sourwood Rd 27712
South St 27707
Southampton Pl 27705
Southerland St 27703
Southern Ave 27713
Southern Dr 27703
Southgate St 27703
Southpark Dr 27713
Southpoint Auto Park Blvd 27713
Southpoint Crossing Dr 27713
Southshore Pkwy 27703
Southview Rd 27703
Southwest Dr 27713
Southwood Dr 27707
Sovereign St 27705
Sowell St 27701
Sparella St 27703
Sparger Rd 27705
Sparger Springs Ln 27705
Sparwood Dr 27705
Spaulding St 27701
Spears Ln 27713
Spector St 27704
Spencer St 27705
Spicebush Ct 27712
Spicers Ct 27705
Spicewood Ct 27703
Spindlewood Ct 27703
Spinnaker Ct 27703
Spiralwood Pl 27703
Split Rail Pl 27712
Spreading Oak Ct 27713
Spring St 27703
Spring Blossom Ln 27705
Spring Creek Dr
 1900-2099 27704
 4200-4299 27705
Spring Garden Dr 27713
Spring Glen Ct 27703
Spring Lake Ct 27713
Spring Meadow Dr 27713
Spring Valley Ln 27713
Spring Water Ln 27712
Springdale Dr 27707
Springhouse Pl 27705
Springmoor Ln 27713
Springstop Ln 27705
Springtree Cir 27712
Springview Ln & Trl 27705
Spruce St
 500-899 27703
 900-998 27701
 1000-1299 27701
Spruce Knob Ct 27705
Spruce Pine Trl 27705
Sprucewood Dr 27707
Sprunt Ave 27705
Squirrel Hollow Ln 27713
St Elias Dr 27705
Stacey Glen Ct 27705
Stacy Dr 27712
Stadium Dr
 400-1399 27704
 1900-2199 27705
 2200-2999 27704
Stafford Dr 27705
Stage Rd 27703
Stagecoach Rd 27713
Staley Pl 27705
Stallings Rd 27703
Stan Wright Ct 27703
Stanford Dr 27707
Stanley Rd 27704
Stanwood St 27703
Starcross Ln 27713
Stardust Ct & Dr 27712
Starlight Dr 27707
Starling Ln 27713
Starmont Dr 27705
Starwood Ln 27712
State St 27704
Station Rd 27705
Statler Dr 27703
Stedman St 27704
Stedwick Pl 27712
Steele St 27707
Steeple Chase Ct 27713
Stennis Way 27703
Stephen Scarlett Ln 27705
Stephens Dr 27703
Stephens Ln 27712
Stephenson St 27704
Stepney Ct 27713
Stepping Stone Dr 27713
Stepping Stone Ln 27705
Sterling Dr 27712
Sterling Ridge Ln 27707
Still Pond Ct 27713
Stillhouse Pl 27704
Stillview Dr 27712
Stillwater Park 27707
Stinhurst Dr 27713
Stirrup Ln 27703
Stirrup Creek Dr 27703
Stockbridge Ct 27705
Stockton Way 27707
Stokes St 27701
Stone Rd 27703
Stone Fence Ct 27704
Stone Hill Ct 27704
Stone Lion Dr 27703
Stone Mill Pl 27712
Stone Park Ct 27703
Stone Village Ct 27704
Stonebridge Dr 27712
Stonegate Dr 27705
Stoneglen Ct 27712
Stonehedge Ave 27707
Stonehouse Ct 27713
Stoneleigh Ct 27703
Stonelick Dr 27703
Stoneridge Cir, Pl & Rd 27705
Stones Throw Ln 27713
Stonewall Way 27704
Stoney Dr 27703
Stoney Creek Cir 27703
Stoney Knoll Dr 27713
Stoneybrook Dr 27705
Stradbrooke Ct 27705
Strangford Ln 27713
Straninc Rd 27705
Stratford Rd 27707
Stratford Lakes Dr 27713
Stratton Way 27704
Strauss Dr 27703
Strawberry Ln 27712
Strawberry Ridge Ln 27713
Streamley Ct 27705
Streamview Ct 27713
Strebor St 27705
Striding Ridge Ct 27713
Stroller Ave 27705
Strolling Way 27707
Strowd Ct 27703
Stuart Dr 27707
Student Pl 27713
Sturbridge Dr 27713
Sturdivant Rd 27705
Suda Dr 27703
Sudbury Rd 27704
Sudley Ct 27712
Sue Ann Ct 27704
Suffolk St 27707
Sugar Creek Ct 27713
Sugar Grove Ct 27703
Sugar Maple Ct 27703
Sugar Pine Ln 27705
Sugar Pine Trl 27713
Sugar Tree Pl 27713
Sugarwood Pl 27705
Suitt Rd 27703
Sullivan St 27701
Summer Breeze Dr 27704
Summer Ridge Ct 27712
Summer Rose Ln 27703
Summer Storm Dr 27704
Summerfield Dr 27712
Summerglen Ct 27713
Summerlin Rd 27704
Summertime Ct 27707
Summerville Ln 27712
Summit St 27707
Summit Ridge Dr 27712
Sun Dried Ct 27704
Sun Valley Dr 27707
Suncrest Ct 27703
Sundance Cir 27713
Sundial Cir 27704
Sunflower Ct 27713
Sunlight Dr 27707
Sunningdale Way 27707
Sunny Ct 27705
Sunny Oaks Pl 27712
Sunny Ridge Dr 27705
Sunnyside Dr 27705
Sunrise Pl 27705
Sunset Ave 27705
Sunstone Dr 27712
Superior Ct 27713
Surles Ct 27703
Surrey Ln & Rd 27707
Surrey Green Ln 27707
Susanna Dr 27705
Sutherland Ct 27712
Sutteridge Ct 27713
Sutton Pl 27703
Swabia Ct 27713
Swallows Ridge Ct 27713
Swan St 27701
Swanns Mill Dr 27704
Swansea St 27707
Swarthmore Rd 27707
Sweeney Dr 27705
Sweet Clover Ct 27703
Sweet Gale Dr 27704
Sweet Gum Ct 27703
Sweetbay Ct 27704
Sweetberry Cir 27703
Sweetbriar Rd 27704
Swift Ave
 100-499 27705
 600-699 27701
Swift Creek Xing 27713
Swiftstone Ct 27713
Swindell Ct 27703
Swing Rd 27704
Swink Ln 27705
Sybil Dr 27703
Sycamore Dr 27703
Sycamore St 27707
Sycamore Shoals Rd 27705
Sydenham Rd 27713
Sylvan Rd 27701
Sylvias Ct 27703
Synnotts Pl 27705
Syracuse Pl 27704
Tabernacle Ct 27703
Tacoma Ct 27712
Taft St 27703
Tahoe Dr 27713
Talcott Dr 27705
Tall Leaf Trl 27712
Tall Oaks Dr 27713
Tampa Ave 27705
Tanager Trl 27707
Tanglewood Dr 27705
Tannenbaum St 27705
Tanners Mill Dr 27703
Tapestry Ter 27713
Taproot Ln 27705
Tarawa Ter 27705
Tarik Dr 27707
Tarleton E & W 27713
Tarra Pl 27707
Tarrywood Ct 27703
Tartan Ct 27705
Tattersall Dr 27713
Tatum Dr 27703
Taulton Ct 27705
Tavern Pl 27707
Tavistock Dr 27712
Taylor St
 1-99 27703
 800-1213 27701
 1230-2499 27703
Taylor Ridge Dr 27703
Teague Pl 27707
Teahouse Ct 27707
Teakwood Ct 27713
Technology Dr 27704
Teel Dr 27704
Teermark Ln 27703
Teknika Pkwy 27712
Temple Ln 27713
Ten Springs Ln 27705
Tennessee Rd 27704
Tennwood Ct 27712
Tennyson Pl 27704
Tenure Cir 27713
Terry Rd 27712
Tetley Pl 27712
Tetons Ct 27703
Texanna Cir 27713
Thackery Pl 27707
Thames Ave 27704
Thaxton St 27701
The Vlg 27703
Thebes Pl 27703
Thelma St 27704
Thensia Ct 27703
Theodore Ln 27703
Theresa St 27707
Thetford Rd 27707
Third Fork Rd 27707
Thistlecone Way 27707
Thistlerock Ln 27703
Thompson Rd 27704
Thompsonville Ct 27713
Thoreau Dr 27703
Thorn Brook Ct 27703
Thornblade Ct 27712
Thorne St 27704
Thorne Ridge Dr 27713
Thorngate Rd 27703
Thornwood Dr 27703
Thorton Ct 27703
Three Diamond Ln 27704
Thunder Rd 27712
Tiffany Pl 27705
Timber Pl 27704
Timber Ridge Dr 27713
Timber Wolf Dr 27713
Timbercreek Ct 27712
Timberly Dr 27707
Timbermill Ln 27713
Timmons Dr 27713
Timothy Ave 27707
Timpson Ave 27703
Tin Barn Pl 27705
Tinsbury Pl 27713
Tipi Ln 27705
Tippecanoe Ct 27713
Tipperary Ct 27713
Tisdale St 27705
Tobacco Rd 27704
Tobler Ct 27704
Toby St 27701
Tocuvan Pl 27705
Todd St 27704
Token House Rd 27703
Tolson Dr 27703
Tom Clark Rd 27704
Tom Cook Dr 27705
Tom Wilkinson Rd 27712
Tomahawk Trl 27712
Tommy Wells Dr 27704
Toms Rock Pl 27704
Tonbridge Way 27707
Topaz Ct 27703
Topaz Jewel Ct 27713
Topeka Ct 27713
Toroella St 27704
Torredge Rd 27712
Torrey Heights Ln 27703
Torrey Pine Ln 27713
Touchstone Dr 27713
Tower Blvd 27707
Townsend St 27704
Tracy Trl 27712
Trading Path 27712
Trafalgar Pl 27707
Trail Twenty Three 27707
Trail View Ln 27713
Trail Wood Dr 27705
Trails End Rd 27712
Tralea Dr 27707
Tranquil Rd 27713
Trapp Hill Pl 27705
Trappers Ct 27712
Travertine Ln 27703
Travis Cir 27713
Trawick Ct 27713
Trawick Pl 27712
Treeline Dr 27705
Treetop Rdg 27705
Tremont Dr 27705
Trent Dr 27705
Trentwood Ct 27703
Trescott Dr 27703
Tressel Way 27707
Treviso Pl 27707
Trevor Cir 27705
Treyburn Point Dr 27712
Triangle Dr 27709
S Tricenter Blvd 27713
Trident Pl 27707
Trillium Ct 27712
Trimble Ct 27705
E Trinity Ave
 100-198 27701
 200-599 27701
 800-999 27704
W Trinity Ave 27701
Trinity Rd 27703
Trinness Dr 27707
Tripoli Dr 27713
Troon Ln 27712
Trotter Ridge Rd 27707
Troy St 27703
Troys Mountain Ln 27705
Truce St 27703
Truman St 27701
Trump Ct 27703
Truss Way 27704
Trustee St 27713
Tryon Rd 27705
Tuckawanna Ave 27703
Tucker St 27701
Tudor Pl 27713
Tuftin Dr 27703
Tuggle St 27713
Tulip Poplar Cir 27704
Tulip Tree Ct 27712
Tumlin Ct 27703
Turkey Farm Rd 27705
Turmeric Ln 27713
Turnberry Cir & Ct 27712
Turner Rd 27703
Turning Leaf Ln 27712
Turquoise Dr 27703
Turrentine St 27704
Tuscany St 27712
Tw Alexander Dr
 1-199 27709
 1600-1799 27703
 1904-1912 27709
Twin Creeks Ct 27703
Twin Mountain Rd 27705
Twin Oaks Dr 27712
Twin Pines Ln 27705
Twinleaf Pl 27705
Twisted Oak Pl 27705
Tyler Ct 27701
Tyndrum Dr 27705

Tyne Dr ... 27703
Tyonek Dr ... 27703
Umstead Rd ... 27712
E Umstead St
100-499 ... 27707
500-699 ... 27701
W Umstead St ... 27707
Underwood Ave ... 27701
Union Grove Rd ... 27703
United Dr ... 27713
University Dr ... 27707
University Station Rd ... 27705
Upchurch Cir ... 27705
Upchurch Farm Rd ... 27713
Upton Ct ... 27713
Urban Ave ... 27701
E Us 70 Hwy ... 27703
Us 70 Service Rd ... 27703
Us Highway 15 501
Byp ... 27705
Us Highway 70 W ... 27705
Us Highway 751 ... 27705
Usher St ... 27704
Uzzle St ... 27713
Vair St ... 27703
Vale St ... 27703
Valetta Rd ... 27712
Valley Dr ... 27704
Valley Run ... 27707
Valley Forge Rd ... 27705
Valley Mede Dr ... 27713
Valley Ridge Dr ... 27713
Valley Springs Rd ... 27712
Valleydale Dr ... 27703
Valleyshire Rd ... 27707
Valmet Dr ... 27703
Van Dr ... 27703
Vandalia Pl ... 27712
Vanderbilt Ct ... 27705
Vandora Pl ... 27705
Vanguard Ct & Pl ... 27713
Vantage Ct ... 27712
Variform Dr ... 27712
Varina Dr ... 27704
Venetia Cv ... 27703
Ventana Ct ... 27712
Ventoria Rd ... 27712
Ventura Dr ... 27712
Venus Dr ... 27703
Vermel Ct ... 27703
Vermillion Dr ... 27713
Versailles St ... 27704
Vesson Ave ... 27707
Vestavia Dr ... 27704
Vestrial Ln ... 27703
Vickers Ave
700-999 ... 27701
1000-1499 ... 27707
Vickery Hill Ct ... 27703
Vicksburg Ln ... 27712
Victor Ave ... 27707
Victoria Dr ... 27713
Victorian Oaks Dr ... 27713
Victory Blvd ... 27705
Viking Dr ... 27703
Villa Dr ... 27712
Village Circle Way ... 27713
Vine St ... 27703
Vineyard St ... 27707
Vinson Pl ... 27705
Vintage Hill Ct, Dr &
Pkwy ... 27712
Vintage Holly Dr ... 27703
Violet St ... 27701
Virgie Rd & St ... 27705
Virgil Rd ... 27703
Virginia Ave ... 27705
Virginia Dare Ct ... 27705
Vista St ... 27701
Vistawood Way ... 27713
Vivaldi Dr ... 27712
Vivian St ... 27701
Voyager Pl ... 27712
Wa Wa Ave ... 27707
Wabash St ... 27701
Waconda Ct ... 27713

Waddell Ct ... 27703
Wade Dr ... 27712
Wade Rd ... 27705
Wadesboro St ... 27703
Wadsworth Ave ... 27707
Wagon Ct ... 27707
Wagoner St ... 27705
Wainwright Ct ... 27712
Wake Pl ... 27701
Wake Rd ... 27713
Wake Forest Rd ... 27703
Wakerobin Pl ... 27712
Walcott Ln ... 27712
Walkenwood Ct ... 27713
Walker St ... 27701
Wall St ... 27701
Wallace St ... 27707
Wallace Smith Dr ... 27703
Wallingford Pl ... 27707
Walnut St ... 27705
Walnut Cove Dr ... 27713
Walsenburg Dr ... 27712
Walton St ... 27703
Waltz Rd ... 27704
Wanda Ridge Dr ... 27712
Wanderlust Ln ... 27712
Warbler Ln ... 27712
Ward St ... 27707
Ware Creek Ct ... 27713
Waring St ... 27704
Warner St ... 27705
Warren St ... 27704
Washington St
501-697 ... 27701
699-1899 ... 27701
1900-2099 ... 27704
Watauga Ct ... 27713
Water Garden Way ... 27713
Water Stone Ct ... 27705
Waterbury Dr ... 27707
Wateredge Dr ... 27707
Wateree Dr ... 27713
Waterford Valley Dr ... 27713
Wateroaks Ct ... 27703
N Waters Edge Dr ... 27703
Waterview Ct ... 27703
Watkins Rd ... 27707
Watson Rd ... 27704
Watts St ... 27701
Wavecrest Ct ... 27713
Waverly Pl ... 27713
Waxhaw Dr ... 27712
Waycross Rd ... 27704
Wayfield Ave ... 27713
Wayne Cir ... 27707
Wayne Dr ... 27704
Wayne St ... 27713
Wayside Pl ... 27705
Waystone Pl ... 27703
Wayward Dr ... 27703
Weather St ... 27703
Weather Hill Cir ... 27705
Weatherby Dr ... 27703
Weathergreen Ct ... 27713
Weatherly Dr ... 27703
Weathersfield Dr ... 27713
Weathervane Dr ... 27703
E & W Weaver St ... 27707
Weaver Dairy Rd ... 27707
Webb Cir ... 27705
Webster Ct ... 27705
Weck Dr ... 27709
Wedgedale Ave ... 27703
Wedgewood Ln ... 27713
Weeping St ... 27704
Weeping Beech Way ... 27713
Weeping Willow Dr ... 27704
Welch Pl ... 27707
Welcome Cir & Dr ... 27705
Weldon Ter ... 27703
Weldon Ridge Ct ... 27705
Welkin Ct ... 27713
Wellingham Dr ... 27713
Wellington Dr ... 27704
Wellons Dr ... 27703
Wells St ... 27707

Wembley Ct ... 27705
Wendover Ct & Ln ... 27713
Wendy Way ... 27712
Wenham Dr ... 27703
Wenonah Way ... 27713
Wensley Dr ... 27712
Wentworth Dr ... 27707
Wentz Dr & Rd ... 27703
Wescott Pl ... 27712
Wesker Cir ... 27703
Wesleywood Dr ... 27707
Weslyn Trace Dr ... 27703
West Ave ... 27704
E West Fwy ... 27701
Westbury Pl ... 27707
Westchester Rd ... 27707
Westcrest St ... 27707
Western Byp ... 27705
Western Park Pl ... 27705
Westfield Dr ... 27705
Westgate Dr ... 27707
Westglen Rd ... 27705
Westgrove Ct ... 27703
Westminster Ave ... 27704
Weston Downs Dr ... 27707
Westover Rd ... 27707
Westpark Dr ... 27713
Westridge Dr ... 27713
Westwood Dr ... 27707
Wetherburn Pl ... 27703
Wexford Dr ... 27713
Weyburn Rd ... 27704
Weymouth St ... 27707
Wg Scarlett Dr ... 27705
Wheat Grain St ... 27704
Wheat Mill Rd ... 27704
Wheaton Rd ... 27704
Wheatstone Ct ... 27712
Wheeling Cir ... 27713
Wheels Hill Rd ... 27705
Whetstone Ct ... 27703
Whilden Dr ... 27713
Whippoorwill St ... 27704
Whispering Meadow
Ln ... 27712
Whispering Oak Ln ... 27704
Whispering Pines Cir ... 27705
Whisperwood Dr ... 27713
Whistler Woods Ct ... 27703
Whitaker Rd ... 27707
Whitburn Pl ... 27705
Whitby Ct ... 27703
Whitcomb St ... 27701
White Ash Dr ... 27712
White Cliff Ln ... 27712
White Dove Rd ... 27703
White Oak Ave & Dr ... 27707
White Pine Dr ... 27705
White Run Ct ... 27712
White Spruce Ct ... 27703
White Willow Ct ... 27703
Whitehall ... 27707
Whitfield Rd
100-199 ... 27705
4400-5599 ... 27707
Whitley Dr ... 27707
Whitmore Ln ... 27707
Whitney Ln ... 27713
Whitt Rd ... 27712
Whittier Way ... 27712
Wicker Ct ... 27712
Wickersham Dr ... 27713
Wicklow Ln ... 27713
Wiggins St ... 27704
Wilbon St ... 27704
Wild Goose Cir ... 27712
Wild Harvest Ct ... 27712
Wild Meadow Dr ... 27705
Wild Sage Way ... 27703
Wildberry Ln ... 27705
Wilderness Rd ... 27712
Wildrose Dr ... 27704
Wildwood Dr ... 27712
Wiley Ave ... 27704
Wilhelm Dr ... 27705
Wilkerson Ave ... 27701

Wilkins Dr ... 27705
Willa Way ... 27703
Willard St ... 27701
Willbea Rd ... 27705
Willett Rd ... 27705
William Penn Plz ... 27704
William Vickers Ave ... 27701
Williams Way ... 27704
Williamsburg Rd ... 27707
Williamsburg Way ... 27713
Willis Ct ... 27704
Willoughby Ct ... 27713
Willow Dr ... 27712
Willow Bridge Dr ... 27707
Willow Creek Cir ... 27705
Willow Oak Ct ... 27705
Willow Point Ct ... 27703
Willow Springs Rd ... 27703
Willowbrook Dr ... 27703
Willowcrest Rd ... 27703
Willowdale Dr ... 27707
N Willowhaven Dr ... 27712
Wilma Dr ... 27712
Wilshire Dr ... 27707
Wilson Rd ... 27712
Wilson St ... 27705
W Wilson St ... 27705
Wiltshire Pl ... 27713
Winburn Ave ... 27704
Winchester Ct ... 27707
Windcourt Pl ... 27713
Windcrest Rd ... 27713
Windermere Dr ... 27712
Winders Ln ... 27712
Windflower Pl ... 27705
Windgate Dr ... 27705
Winding Way ... 27707
Winding Arch Dr ... 27713
Winding Creek Cir ... 27705
Winding Ridge Rd ... 27713
Windlestraw Dr ... 27713
Windover Dr ... 27712
Windrow Pl ... 27705
Windrush Ln ... 27703
Windsong Ln ... 27713
Windsor Way ... 27707
Windsor Glen Dr ... 27703
Windy Hill Rd ... 27703
Windyrush Ct ... 27703
Wineberry Dr ... 27713
Winfield Dr ... 27707
Winged Elm Ln ... 27705
Winkler Rd ... 27712
Winnabow Ct ... 27703
Winners Cir ... 27713
Winrock Pl ... 27705
Winston Rd ... 27704
Winterberry Ridge Dr ... 27713
Winterfield Pl ... 27705
Wintergreen Pl ... 27707
Winthrop Ct ... 27707
Winton Rd ... 27707
Winward Pointe Dr ... 27703
Wise Pl ... 27707
Wishart St ... 27704
Wisteria Ave ... 27704
Withers Ct ... 27701
Witherspoon Blvd ... 27707
Wittenberg Way ... 27704
Wofford Rd ... 27707
Wolfpack Ln ... 27704
Womack Dr ... 27712
Womble Cir ... 27705
Wood Chapel Ln ... 27703
Wood Cottage Ct ... 27707
Wood Duck Ct ... 27713
Wood Haven Dr ... 27712
Wood Lily Ct ... 27713
Wood Meadow Ln ... 27703
Wood Valley Ct ... 27713
Woodbark Ln ... 27703
Woodberry Rd ... 27707
Woodbine Ct ... 27705
Woodbriar Ct ... 27707
Woodburn Rd ... 27705
Woodcliff Cir ... 27712

Woodcreek Ct ... 27713
N & S Woodcrest St ... 27703
E & W Woodcroft
Pkwy ... 27713
Woodford E & W ... 27713
Woodgate Ct ... 27713
Woodgreen Dr ... 27704
Woodgrove St ... 27703
Woodhall Ln ... 27712
Woodhill Ct ... 27713
Woodlake Dr ... 27713
Woodland Dr ... 27701
Woodland Park Rd ... 27703
Woodlea St ... 27704
Woodmont Dr ... 27705
E & W Woodridge Dr ... 27707
W Woodrow St ... 27705
Woods St ... 27703
Woodsage Ln ... 27713
Woodsdale Dr ... 27703
Woodsey Ct ... 27703
Woodside Park Ln ... 27704
Woodsprite Ct ... 27703
Woodstock Rd ... 27705
Woodtrellis Ct ... 27703
Woodview Dr ... 27704
Woodward Ln ... 27713
Woodway Club Dr ... 27713
Woodway Park Dr ... 27713
Woodwinds Dr ... 27713
Wooten Ct ... 27703
Worcester Pl ... 27707
Worland Dr ... 27712
Worth St ... 27701
Wortham St ... 27705
Wortley Dr ... 27713
Wrenn Rd
1000-1399 ... 27703
4000-4299 ... 27705
Wrenwood Ct ... 27703
Wright Hill Dr ... 27712
Wrightwood Ave ... 27705
N & S Wycliff Dr ... 27703
Wyeth Ave ... 27707
Wyldewood Rd ... 27704
Wyman Pl ... 27707
Wyndham Ln & Pl ... 27705
Wynfair Dr ... 27713
Wynford Dr & Pl ... 27707
Wynmore Dr ... 27713
Wynne Rd ... 27713
Wyntercrest Ln ... 27713
Wythebrook Ln ... 27713
Yadkin St ... 27703
Yancey St ... 27701
Yardley Ter ... 27707
Yarmouth Pl ... 27707
Yarrow Dr ... 27703
Yates Rd ... 27703
Yearby Ave ... 27705
Yellowood Ct ... 27705
Yellowood Ln ... 27712
Yellowstone Dr ... 27713
Yonder Trl ... 27705
Yorennes Rd ... 27704
York Ct ... 27705
York Woods Pl ... 27705
Yorkdale Ct ... 27707
Yorkfield Ct ... 27713
Yorkshire Dr ... 27705
Yorktown Ave ... 27713
Yosemite Cir ... 27713
Young St ... 27703
Zelko Ct ... 27705
Zenith Pl ... 27705
Zepher Pl ... 27713
Zero Rd ... 27705
Zumwalt Ct ... 27703

NUMBERED STREETS

All Street Addresses ... 27705

EDEN NC

General Delivery ... 27288

POST OFFICE BOXES MAIN OFFICE STATIONS AND BRANCHES

Box No.s
1 - 5248 ... 27289
9998 - 9998 ... 27288
9998 - 9998 ... 27289

RURAL ROUTES

01, 02, 03 ... 27288

NAMED STREETS

Aaron Ln ... 27288
Adams St ... 27288
E & W Aiken Rd ... 27288
Alpine Ct ... 27288
Amanda Ln ... 27288
Amelia Ct ... 27288
Anderson Rd & St ... 27288
E & W Arbor Ln ... 27288
Armfield St ... 27288
Ash St ... 27288
Ashby St ... 27288
Ashley Loop ... 27288
Ashton Cir ... 27288
Audubon Rd ... 27288
Avery Dr ... 27288
Ayden Rd ... 27288
Azalea Rd ... 27288
B St ... 27288
B Austin Dr ... 27288
Barnes Rd ... 27288
Barnett St ... 27288
Bay St ... 27288
Bear Slide Ct ... 27288
Beaver Run ... 27288
Beck Rd ... 27288
Beddingfield Rd ... 27288
Bedford Dr ... 27288
Beech St ... 27288
Beech Tree Ct ... 27288
Beechwood Ln ... 27288
Beeson Rd S ... 27288
Belmont Ct ... 27288
Benjamin Rd ... 27288
Benson Rd ... 27288
Bent Grass Ln ... 27288
Bermuda Dr ... 27288
N & S Bethel St ... 27288
Bethlehem Church Rd ... 27288
Bettie Ln ... 27288
Billie Harris St ... 27288
Birch Rd ... 27288
Black Bottom Rd ... 27288
Blackstock St ... 27288
Blue Creek Rd ... 27288
Boone Rd ... 27288
Boxwood Rd ... 27288
Boyd St ... 27288
Boyles Cir ... 27288
Bradford St ... 27288
Brammer Rd ... 27288
Branch Rd & St ... 27288
Brandywine Dr ... 27288
Brenda Ct S ... 27288
Brentwood Rd ... 27288
Briarwood Dr & Trl ... 27288
N Bridge St ... 27288
Brightwood Ct & Rd ... 27288
Brookside Dr ... 27288
Bryant St ... 27288
Buchannan St ... 27288
Buck Ln & Rd ... 27288
Bull Run Dr ... 27288
Burton St ... 27288
Business Park Dr ... 27288
Butler Rd ... 27288

Buttercup Rd ... 27288
N & S Byrd St ... 27288
C St ... 27288
Caleb Ln & St ... 27288
Camellia Ln ... 27288
Carolina Ave ... 27288
Caroline Ln ... 27288
Carolyn Ct ... 27288
Carpenter Rd ... 27288
Carpet Ln ... 27288
Carrie Ln ... 27288
Carrington Ln ... 27288
Carroll St ... 27288
Carter Dr & St ... 27288
Cascade Ave ... 27288
Caudle Ln ... 27288
Cedar Ln & St ... 27288
Cedar Falls Ln ... 27288
Cedarwood Dr ... 27288
N & S Center Ct & St ... 27288
Center Church Rd ... 27288
Central Ave ... 27288
Charlie St ... 27288
Chatham Ct & Ln ... 27288
Cherry St ... 27288
Chestnut St ... 27288
Childrens Ln ... 27288
Chumney Loop ... 27288
Church St ... 27288
Cicero Trl ... 27288
Circle Dr & Loop ... 27288
Clark St ... 27288
Clarkway Ave ... 27288
Clay Dr ... 27288
Clearview Rd ... 27288
Clifton St ... 27288
Clover Ct ... 27288
Cochran Farm Rd ... 27288
Coleman St ... 27288
College St ... 27288
College Village Dr ... 27288
Commerce Dr ... 27288
Conover Dr ... 27288
Coolidge Dr ... 27288
Copper Dr ... 27288
Cornet Dr ... 27288
Cottage Ln ... 27288
Country Ln ... 27288
Country Club Dr ... 27288
Country Lane Cir ... 27288
Country Side Dr ... 27288
Country View Ln ... 27288
Countryside Dr ... 27288
Cox St ... 27288
Creekridge Dr ... 27288
Cricket Rd ... 27288
Crouch Rd ... 27288
Cypress Hill Dr ... 27288
D St ... 27288
Dacur St ... 27288
Daisy Ct & Rd ... 27288
Dallas Rd & St ... 27288
Dameron St ... 27288
Dan River Church Rd ... 27288
Daniel Adkins St ... 27288
David Dr ... 27288
Davis St ... 27288
Decatur St ... 27288
Deer Path ... 27288
Delaware Ave ... 27288
Della Dr ... 27288
Denson Rd ... 27288
Deshazo St ... 27288
Destafano Rd ... 27288
Devonway St ... 27288
Dillard Ct ... 27288
Dishmon Loop ... 27288
Dixon Rd ... 27288
Dodge St ... 27288
Dogwood Dr & Ln ... 27288
Draper Ln ... 27288
Drumheller Ct ... 27288
Dumaine St ... 27288
Dunn St ... 27288
Dusty Ln ... 27288
Dyer St ... 27288

Early Ave 27288
Easley Rd 27288
Eastern St 27288
Eden Rd 27288
N & S Edgewood Rd 27288
Eisenhower Ct 27288
Elam Ave 27288
Ellerbe Ct 27288
Ellett Ave 27288
Elm St 27288
Empire Dr 27288
Enright St 27288
Entrance Ct 27288
Equine Trl S 27288
Estes Farm Trl 27288
Evergreen Ct 27288
Ewell St 27288
Fagg Dr 27288
Fairmont Dr 27288
Fairway Dr 27288
Farrell St 27288
Fawn Rd 27288
N Fieldcrest Rd 27288
Fields St 27288
Fireman Club Rd 27288
Fisher St 27288
Fisher Hill Rd 27288
Floyd Rd 27288
Floyds Cir 27288
Flynn St 27288
Forbes St 27288
Ford St 27288
Forest Rd 27288
Fourth Ave 27288
Fox Run 27288
Fraker Pl 27288
Frank Cherry St 27288
Franklin Dr 27288
French St 27288
Friendly Rd 27288
Front St 27288
Galloway St 27288
Gant Rd 27288
Garden Rd 27288
Garrett Rd 27288
Gayle Ave 27288
Geneva Dr 27288
George St 27288
Georgia Ave 27288
Gilley Rd 27288
Ginny Rd 27288
Givens St 27288
Glencove Dr 27288
Glendale Cir & Dr 27288
Gleneagle Dr 27288
Glenmoor Dr 27288
Glenn St 27288
Glenoak Dr 27288
Glenridge Dr 27288
Glenrobin Dr 27288
Glenwood Rd 27288
Gloria Dr 27288
Glovenia St 27288
Gordon St 27288
Gracewood Dr 27288
Gracie St 27288
Grand Oaks Dr 27288
Grant St 27288
Green St 27288
Green Knolls Dr 27288
Greentree Trl 27288
Greenway Dr 27288
Greenwood St 27288
Gresham St 27288
Grogan St 27288
W Grove St 27288
Gusler Dr 27288
S Hairston St 27288
Haizlip St 27288
N & S Hale St 27288
Haled St 27288
Hall Ln 27288
N & S Hamilton St 27288
Hamlin St 27288
Hampton Rd & St 27288
Harmon Dr 27288
Harrington Hwy 27288
E & W Harris Pl & St 27288
Harrison Rd & St 27288
Harry Akers St 27288
Harvey St 27288
Hay St 27288
Haywood St 27288
Hazel Ln 27288
Heather Ct 27288
Henderson Rd 27288
Henry St 27288
Heritage Rd 27288
Hickory St 27288
Hidden Valley Dr 27288
N & S High St 27288
Highland Ave & Dr 27288
Highland Park Dr 27288
Hill St 27288
Hillcrest Dr 27288
Hillside Dr 27288
Hilltop Ln 27288
Hodges St 27288
Holland Rd & St 27288
Holliman Dr 27288
Hollingsworth St 27288
Holly Rd & St 27288
Hoover Rd 27288
Hopkins Ct 27288
Hopper Ln 27288
Howe St 27288
Hubbard St 27288
Hudson St 27288
N & S Hundley Dr 27288
Hunter St 27288
Hurd Ave 27288
Hurst St 27288
Hylton St 27288
Ike Dr 27288
Indian Trl 27288
Indian Ridge Ct 27288
Industrial Dr 27288
Irving Ave 27288
Jackson St 27288
James Cir & St 27288
Jane Ct 27288
Jarrell Farm Rd 27288
Jarrett St 27288
Jay St 27288
Jefferson St 27288
John St 27288
N & S Johnston St 27288
Jones St 27288
Josephine Rd 27288
Joyce Ct 27288
Judy Rd 27288
Jumper Rd 27288
Kallam Ct 27288
Karen Dr 27288
Kathy Dr 27288
Kemp St 27288
Kendall St 27288
N & S Kennedy St 27288
E & W Kings Dr & Hwy 27288
Kingston Rd 27288
Kirkwood Ct & Dr 27288
Klyce St 27288
Knight St 27288
Knollwood Dr 27288
Knott St 27288
Kuder St 27288
W Lake Dr, Rd & St 27288
Lake Forest Ct 27288
Lakecrest Rd 27288
Lakewood Rd 27288
Lambert Dr 27288
Land St 27288
Landfall Dr 27288
Landfill Rd 27288
Lane Rd 27288
Lark Rd 27288
Lattimore Rd 27288
Laurel Wood Dr 27288
Laurell Dr 27288
Lavender Dr 27288
Lawrence St 27288
Lawson St 27288
Lee St 27288
Leffew Dr 27288
Legrande Dr 27288
Lennox Dr 27288
Lenoir Dr 27288
Lewis St 27288
Lincoln St 27288
S Linden Dr 27288
Lindsay Dr 27288
Lisa St 27288
Lloyd St 27288
Loftus St 27288
Londis St 27288
London Rd 27288
Long Rd & St 27288
Longhook Rd 27288
Longwood Dr 27288
Louise Ave & Ct 27288
Lynrock St 27288
Mabes Rd 27288
Mable St 27288
S Madison St 27288
Main St 27288
Malibu St 27288
Manley St 27288
Manning St 27288
Maple Ln, Rd & St 27288
Maplewood Dr 27288
Marion Ridge Dr & Ln 27288
Marshall St 27288
Martin St 27288
Martinwood Rd 27288
Maryland Ave 27288
Matrimony Rd 27288
Matthews St 27288
May St 27288
Mcconnell Ave 27288
Mcdaniel Rd 27288
E & W Meadow Rd 27288
Meadowgreen Village Dr 27288
Meadowood Rd 27288
Meadowview Ln 27288
Mebane St 27288
Mebane Bridge Rd 27288
Meeks Rd 27288
Meredith Ct 27288
Merriman St 27288
Michelle Ln 27288
Miles St 27288
Mill Ave 27288
Millbrook Dr 27288
Miller Ct 27288
Millner St 27288
Mimosa Trl 27288
Moir St 27288
Moir Mill Rd 27288
Moncure St 27288
Monroe St 27288
Monticello St 27288
E & W Moore St 27288
Morehead St 27288
Morgan Rd 27288
Mountain Valley Dr 27288
Mt Laurel Trl 27288
Murphy Ln 27288
Murray Dr 27288
Nance St 27288
Nantucket Dr 27288
Nature Ln 27288
Nc Highway 135 27288
Nc Highway 14 27288
Nc Highway 700 27288
Nc Highway 770 27288
Nc Highway 87 N & S 27288
N & S New St 27288
New Fagge Rd 27288
Norman Dr 27288
North St 27288
Northridge Dr 27288
Nova Dr 27288
Oak St 27288
Oak Forest Acres Dr 27288
Oak Ridge Dr 27288
N & S Oakland Ave & St 27288
Oakwood Dr 27288
Odle Ln 27288
Old Heritage Rd 27288
Old Nc Highway 87 27288
Oleander Dr 27288
Orchard Dr 27288
Orrell St 27288
Osborne Cir & St 27288
Overby St 27288
Overlook Ave 27288
Owl Rd 27288
Palmer Ct 27288
Panther Ln 27288
S Park Ave, Cir, Rd & Ter 27288
Parker Rd 27288
Patrick St 27288
Patterson St 27288
Peach Rd 27288
Periwinkle Rd 27288
Person St 27288
Pervie Bolick St 27288
Pete Dr 27288
Peter Hill St 27288
Phillips St 27288
Piedmont St 27288
N Pierce St
100-333 27288
332-332 27289
334-398 27288
335-399 27288
S Pierce St 27288
Pine Ln & Rd 27288
Pine Crest Dr 27288
Pine Knot 27288
Pine View Rd 27288
Pinewood Pl 27288
Piney Fork Church Rd 27288
Pitcher Ave 27288
Plantation Rd 27288
N Polk St 27288
Portsmouth Dr 27288
Powell Dr 27288
Pratt Rd 27288
Preston St 27288
Price Rd & St 27288
Price Grange Rd 27288
N & S Primitive St 27288
Prospect St 27288
Quesinberry Rd 27288
Rainey Ct 27288
Rakes St 27288
Ray St 27288
Red Cedar Ln 27288
Red Clay Rd 27288
Redbud Rd 27288
Redwood Rd 27288
Reservoir St 27288
Reuben Rd 27288
Reynolds St 27288
Rhodes Rd 27288
N & S Rickman St 27288
Ridge Ave & St 27288
Ridgeland Ave 27288
River Chase Dr 27288
River Ridge Rd 27288
Rivercrest Dr 27288
Riverside Cir & Dr 27288
Riverview St 27288
Roach Creek Rd 27288
Rob Tom Rd 27288
Roberts Rd & St 27288
Robin Rd 27288
Robindell Ct 27288
Roosevelt St 27288
Rose St 27288
Rosewood Ln 27288
Round Hill Rd 27288
Round House Rd 27288
Royal Rd 27288
Sanderlyn Ct 27288
Scott St 27288
Scotts Dr 27288
Seagraves Dr 27288
Seymour Ct 27288
Shady Grove Rd 27288
Shamrock Ct & Rd 27288
Shannon Dr & Ln 27288
Sharpe Ave 27288
Shawn St 27288
Shedd St 27288
Sheila Dr 27288
Sherwood Ct 27288
Shively Dr 27288
Short Morgan St 27288
Short Union St 27288
Silver Leaf Trl 27288
Simmons Rd 27288
Simpson St 27288
Skyline Cir 27288
Slaydon Rd 27288
Slayton St 27288
Smith St 27288
Smith Acres Rd 27288
Snody Dr 27288
South Ave 27288
Southwood Dr 27288
Spangler Farm Rd 27288
Sparrow Rd 27288
Spring St 27288
Springwood Dr 27288
Spruce St 27288
E & W Stadium Dr 27288
Stancliff Ct 27288
Stanton St 27288
Steeple Rd 27288
Stegall St 27288
Stephens St 27288
Stoneybrook Dr 27288
Stovall Loop & St 27288
Stratford Rd 27288
Straws Trl 27288
Strutton Ln 27288
Stuart St 27288
Summit Loop & Rd 27288
Sundance Trl 27288
Sunrise Rd 27288
Sunset Dr 27288
Sycamore Ct 27288
T Bird Ln 27288
Taft St 27288
Tanglebrook Trl 27288
Tate Vernon Ln 27288
Taylor St 27288
Teaberry Loop 27288
Tellowee Rd 27288
Teresa Dr 27288
The Blvd 27288
Thomas St 27288
Thomas Estates Rd 27288
Thompson St 27288
Thornton St 27288
Tolbert St 27288
Town Creek Rd 27288
Trogdon Dr 27288
Trollinger Ct 27288
Truman St 27288
Tulloch St 27288
Turner St 27288
Twila Ln 27288
Twin Lakes Dr 27288
Tyner Pl 27288
Union St 27288
Valley Dr & Trl 27288
N & S Van Buren Rd 27288
Vaughn St 27288
Victor St 27288
Viking Dr 27288
Village Dr 27288
Vine St 27288
Vinson St 27288
Vintage Rd 27288
Virginia St 27288
Von Ruck Rd 27288
Walker Hl 27288
Wall St 27288
Walnut St 27288
Walter Chambers St 27288
Ward Rd 27288
Ware St 27288
Warehouse St 27288
E & W Warren Ave & Rd 27288
Washburn Ave 27288
Washington St 27288
Water St 27288
Weaver St 27288
Wedgewood Ct 27288
Weeping Willow Way 27288
West Ave 27288
Westerly Park Rd 27288
Westfield Rd 27288
Westwood Dr 27288
White Oak Ct 27288
Wildflower Ln 27288
Williams St 27288
Willow St 27288
Wilshire Dr 27288
Wilson St 27288
Wimbish Rd 27288
Windmill Dr 27288
Windy Rd 27288
Wood Rd 27288
Woodhaven Dr 27288
Woodland Dr 27288
Woodpecker Rd 27288
Woodrow Ave 27288
Woods St 27288
Woodstock Rd 27288
Woodview Dr 27288
Wrights Trl 27288
Yount Rd 27288

NUMBERED STREETS

All Street Addresses 27288

ELIZABETH CITY NC

General Delivery 27909

POST OFFICE BOXES MAIN OFFICE STATIONS AND BRANCHES

Box No.s
1 - 794 27907
1001 - 9998 27906

RURAL ROUTES

01, 02, 03, 04, 05, 06, 07, 08, 09, 11 27909

NAMED STREETS

A St 27909
Academy Ct 27909
Adams St 27909
Adams Creek Rd 27909
S Adams Landing Rd 27909
E & W Adelaide Ct 27909
Agape Way 27909
Agawam St 27909
Airship Rd 27909
Albatross St 27909
Albemarle Dr 27909
Alexander Ct 27909
Aline Dr 27909
Allen Ave 27909
Alton St 27909
Amber Dr 27909
Amstel Ct 27909
Anderson St 27909
Anne St 27909
Apollo Ct 27909
Arbutus St 27909
Asbury Ln 27909
N & S Ashe St 27909
Ashley Dr 27909
Ashton Ave & Dr 27909
Austin Lee Cir 27909
Aydlett Cir & Dr 27909
Azalea Trl 27909
B St 27909
Bailey St 27909
Ball Rd & St 27909
Ballast Ct 27909
Bank St 27909
Banks Rd 27909
Barnhill Rd 27909
Bart James Rd 27909
Bartlett Ave 27909
Bateman Dr 27909
Baxter St 27909
Bayberry Dr 27909
Bayshore Dr 27909
Bayside Rd 27909
Beanway St 27909
Beau Pkwy 27909
Becca Dr 27909
Beech St 27909
Beechwood Ave 27909
Bell St 27909
Berea Church Rd 27909
Berkley Trailer Court Rd 27909
Betty Dr 27909
Beverly Dr 27909
Bias St 27909
Big Daddy Pkwy 27909
Bigfoot Trl 27909
Binnacle Ct 27909
Birdie Ln 27909
Bishop Ct 27909
Black Walnut Dr 27909
Blackbeard Dr 27909
Blackstock Ct 27909
Blimp View Dr 27909
Blindman Rd 27909
Blount Rd 27909
Blue Bonnet St 27909
Bluebird Dr 27909
Bluff Point Rd 27909
Bobwhite Dr 27909
Body Rd 27909
Bogues Beach Ln 27909
Bonner Dr 27909
Bonney St 27909
Boston Ave 27909
Bradley Dr 27909
Brant Ct 27909
Brantwood Dr 27909
Brantwood Trailer Park 27909
Bray St 27909
Breezewood Dr 27909
Briarwood Rd 27909
Brick House Ln 27909
Brickhouse Pt & Rd 27909
Brickhouse Point Rd 27909
Brite Ave 27909
E & W Broad St 27909
Broadview Cir 27909
Brock Ridge Run 27909
Brookridge Dr 27909
Brooks Ave 27909
Broomfield Trl 27909
Brothers Dr & Ln 27909
Brothers Acres 27909
Brown St 27909
Bruce Dr 27909
Brumsey Dr 27909
Bunnell Ave 27909
E & W Burgess St 27909
Burke St 27909
Burkley Mobile Est 27909
Burlington Dr 27909
Butlers Ln 27909
Byrd St 27909
Byron Ct 27909
Byrum St 27909
C St 27909
Caddy Dr 27909
Cahoon Ln 27909
Cale St 27909
Calvert St 27909
Camden Ave & Cswy 27909

Camellia Dr 27909
Camelot Ct 27909
Cameron Dr 27909
Campground Rd 27909
Capital Trce 27909
Captains Ct 27909
Cardinal Ct & Way 27909
Cardwell St 27909
Carolina Ave 27909
Carter Rd 27909
Cartwright Rd 27909
Carver St 27909
Casey St 27909
Castle Ct 27909
Catilina Ave 27909
Cayuse Way 27909
Cedar St 27909
Cedar Point Cir 27909
Celeste St 27909
Center St 27909
Center Cross Dr 27909
Chadburn Ave 27909
Chalk St 27909
Chances Ln 27909
Chancey Dr 27909
Chappell Gardens Dr 27909
Charlene Dr 27909
Charles St 27909
Charlotte St 27909
Cherokee Park Rd 27909
Cherry Glade Rd 27909
Chesson St 27909
Chesterfield Dr 27909
Chestnut Dr & St 27909
Chicken Corner Rd 27909
Chip Dr 27909
Christie Cir 27909
E & W Church St 27909
Circus Rd 27909
W City Dr 27909
City Center Blvd 27909
Clancey Ct 27909
Claremont Ct 27909
Clay Ct 27909
Climbing Vine Run 27909
Clubhouse 27909
N & S Cobb St 27909
Cody St 27909
Cohoon St 27909
College St 27909
E & W Colonial Ave 27909
Commander Rd 27909
Commerce Dr 27909
Commercial Blvd 27909
Commissary Rd 27909
Compass Dr 27909
Consolidated Rd 27909
Continental Dr & Plz 27909
Cooke St 27909
Cooper St 27909
Coopers Ln 27909
Copeland Dr 27909
Coppersmith Rd 27909
Corporate Dr 27909
Corsair Cir 27909
Cosmo Dr 27909
Country Club Dr 27909
County St 27909
Courthouse Ln 27909
Crawford St 27909
Creek Ct & Rd 27909
Creekside Ln 27909
Crescent Dr 27909
Crocker Hill Rd 27909
Crooked Run Rd 27909
Crossbow Ct 27909
Crosswinds Dr 27909
Crystal Lake Dr 27909
Culpepper Ln & St 27909
Cutter Ln 27909
E & W Cypress St 27909
Dan And Mary St 27909
Dance St 27909
Dances Bay Rd & Trl 27909
Danielle 27909
Darian Dr 27909

Davis Ave & Rd 27909
Davis Bay Rd 27909
Dawson St 27909
Debry St 27909
Deer Run 27909
Delaware Ave 27909
Delia Dr 27909
Dellaire Dr 27909
Dennis Dr 27909
Dockside Rd 27909
Doewood Ct 27909
Dogwood Trl 27909
Don Dr 27909
Doris Dr 27909
Dorri Dr 27909
Doublebridge Rd 27909
Dramtree Dr 27909
Driftwood Dr 27909
Drummond Dr 27909
Dry Ridge Rd 27909
Duchess Ln 27909
Duke St 27909
Dukes Ct 27909
Dunstan Ln 27909
Durant Dr 27909
N & S Dyer St 27909
Eagle Ln 27909
Eason Ln 27909
East St 27909
Eastway St 27909
Edge St 27909
Edgewood Ct & Dr 27909
Edith Ln 27909
Edrieann Dr 27909
Egan Ln 27909
Egret Ct 27909
E Ehringhaus St 27909
W Ehringhaus St
- 100-1000 27909
- 1001-1001 27906
- 1001-1899 27909
- 1001-1001 27907
- 1002-1898 27909

Eichler Ln 27909
Elbert 27909
Elcinoco Dr 27909
Elder St 27909
Eleuthera Way 27909
E & W Elizabeth St 27909
Elizabeth Manor Dr 27909
N & S Elliott St 27909
Elmwood Ct 27909
Elsie Ct 27909
Emerald Lake Cir 27909
Emily St 27909
Enchanted Way 27909
Enfield Ct 27909
English Row 27909
Enterprise Dr 27909
Esclip Rd 27909
Esquire Ln 27909
Etheridge St 27909
Everett Dr 27909
Evergreen Dr 27909
Excalibur Ct 27909
S Executive Dr 27909
Eyrie Ln 27909
Factory St 27909
Fair St 27909
Fair Wind Ct 27909
Fairfax Ave 27909
Fairground Rd 27909
Fairlead Dr 27909
Fairway Ter 27909
Farm Dr 27909
E & W Fearing Ave & St 27909
Ferry Rd 27909
Firetower Rd 27909
Fleetwood St 27909
Fletcher Dr 27909
Flint Trl 27909
Flora St 27909
Florida Rd 27909
Folley Rd 27909

Forbes Mobile Home Park 27909
Foreman Bundy Rd 27909
Forest Cir 27909
Forest Hill Cir 27909
Forest Park Rd 27909
Forrest Dr 27909
Forrest Skipper Dr 27909
Fort Bragg Dr 27909
Foxboro Dr 27909
Francis St 27909
Franklin St 27909
Frog Island Rd & Spur 27909
Galera Ct 27909
Garden St 27909
Gardner Point Dr 27909
Gaston Dr 27909
Gaulberry Rd 27909
Gemini Dr 27909
Gene St 27909
George St 27909
George Wood Dr 27909
Gibson Ln 27909
Glade Rd & St 27909
Glendale Ave 27909
Golfclub Dr 27909
Goodwin Ave 27909
Gosnold Ave 27909
Gospel Rdg 27909
Grace Dr 27909
Gradner Pt 27909
Grady St 27909
Grandview Dr 27909
Graves Ave & St 27909
Green Run Ct 27909
Greenleaf St 27909
Gregory St 27909
E & W Grice St 27909
N & S Griffin St 27909
Griffin Swamp Rd 27909
Griggs St 27909
Grove St 27909
Gulfstream Dr 27909
Gum Bridge Rd 27909
Hackney Ct 27909
Haley Point Rd 27909
Halls Creek Rd 27909
Halstead Blvd 27909
Ham Overman Rd 27909
Hammer Rd 27909
Hampton Dr 27909
Hanover St 27909
Harbor Bay Dr 27909
Harding St 27909
Hariot Dr 27909
Harney St 27909
Harrell St 27909
Harrier Ct 27909
Harrington Trailer Park 27909
Harris Dr & Rd 27909
Harvest Point Rd 27909
Harvey St 27909
Hassell Rd 27909
Hastings Ln 27909
Hathaway Dr 27909
Hawthorne Dr 27909
Hemlock St 27909
Hercules Ct 27909
E & W Heron Ct 27909
Herrington Rd 27909
Herrington Village Apartment 27909
Hersey Sawyer Rd 27909
Hewitt Dr 27909
Hickory Dr 27909
Highland Ave 27909
Hills Ave 27909
Hines Ave 27909
Hobbs Ln 27909
Hobbs Landing Rd 27909
Hockmeyer Dr 27909
Hoffler St 27909
Hoggard St 27909
Holly Dr & St 27909
Homestead Vlg 27909
Honeysuckle St 27909

Hope Ct 27909
Hopkins Dr 27909
Horner St 27909
Horseshoe Rd 27909
N & S Hughes Blvd 27909
Hull Dr 27909
Hummingbird Way 27909
Hunnicutt Ave 27909
Hunter St 27909
Hunters Trl E & W 27909
Hyman Cir 27909
Ibis Way 27909
Ida Acres 27909
Impact Dr 27909
S Inaqua Ct 27909
Indian Woods Rd 27909
Inlet Dr 27909
Interpath Pkwy 27909
Ivy Trce 27909
Jackson Dr 27909
James Cir 27909
Jane Ln 27909
Jason Dr 27909
Jefferson St 27909
Jennifer Dr 27909
Jennings Dr 27909
Jessica St 27909
Jessup St 27909
Jester Ct 27909
Joanna Dr 27909
John White Rd 27909
Johnson Rd 27909
Jones Ave & Dr 27909
Jordan Plz & St 27909
Joyce Dr 27909
Julia Ct 27909
Juniper Lndg & St 27909
Kaitlyn Way 27909
Kathryn Ct 27909
Katies Trl 27909
Kayla Ct 27909
Keith Dr 27909
Kelly Dr 27909
Kelsey Rd 27909
Kevin Dr 27909
Kimberly Ct 27909
King St 27909
King Arthur Ct 27909
Kingswood Blvd 27909
Kitty Hawk Ln 27909
Kiwi Ct 27909
Knobbs Creek Dr 27909
Kris Dr 27909
Kristin St 27909
Kylers Way 27909
L And M Dr 27909
Lady Frances 27909
Lady Patricia Dr 27909
Lafayette Ave 27909
Lakeside Dr 27909
Lambs Grove Rd 27909
Lambsberry Cir 27909
Lance Dr 27909
Landfill Rd 27909
Lands End Dr 27909
Lane Dr & St 27909
Lannon Ln 27909
Lark St 27909
Lassiter St 27909
Laura Lee St 27909
Laurel Ave 27909
Lee Cir 27909
Leigh Farm Rd 27909
Lejune Ct 27909
Lessie Ln 27909
Letitia Dr 27909
Lexington Dr 27909
Liberator St 27909
Lighthouse Dr 27909
Lincoln St 27909
Lindsey 27909
Linwood Dr 27909
Lions Club Rd 27909
Lisas Way 27909
Lister Chase 27909
Little River Dr 27909

Little River Retreat 27909
Lobell Ln 27909
Locust St 27909
Long Ln 27909
Long Point Dr 27909
Loop Rd 27909
Louisa St 27909
Lovers Ln 27909
Lowe St 27909
Lowry St 27909
Ludford Rd 27909
Lula Meads Rd 27909
Lunn Dr 27909
Lynchs Corner Rd 27909
Lynette Dr 27909
Lynn Dr 27909
Mac Dr 27909
Macey Jo Ct 27909
Mackey Dr 27909
Madeline Ln 27909
Madison Ave 27909
Madrin St 27909
Maggie Ln 27909
Magnolia St 27909
Maidens Ct 27909
E & W Main St 27909
W Main Street Ext 27909
Majesty Ct 27909
Mallard Dr 27909
Manns Trailer Park 27909
Mansfield Trailer Park 27909
Maple St 27909
Maplewood Ave 27909
Marantha Pl 27909
Margaret Dr 27909
Marian Ave 27909
Mariner Ct 27909
Marlin St 27909
Marr Ave 27909
Martha Dr 27909
S Martin St 27909
N Martin L King Dr 27909
Martin Luther King Jr Dr 27909
Maryland Ave 27909
Massachusetts Ave 27909
Matthews Dr 27909
N Mcarthur St 27909
N & S Mcmorrine St 27909
N Mcpherson St & Xing 27909
Mcphersons Trailer Park 27909
Meadow Dr 27909
Meadowlark Ln 27909
Meads St 27909
Meads Pool Rd 27909
Meadstown Rd 27909
Medical Dr 27909
Meekins St 27909
Megan Dr 27909
Melonie Dr 27909
Merriwood Ave 27909
Methodist Church Rd 27909
Mia Ct 27909
Midgett Dr 27909
Mill St 27909
Mill End Ct 27909
Millbrooke Cir 27909
Miller Ln 27909
Millpond Rd 27909
Mimosa Ln 27909
Mitchell Dr 27909
Mockingbird Dr 27909
Moonlight Trl 27909
Moonlight Bay Trailer Ct 27909
Moore St 27909
Morgan Rd & St 27909
Morgans Corner Rd 27909
Morrisette Ave 27909
Mosley St 27909
Mount Herman Dr & Rd 27909
Mount Hermon Church Rd 27909

Nance Ct 27909
Nancy Dr 27909
Native Dancer Ct 27909
Nelson St 27909
New Rd 27909
New Jersey Ave 27909
New York Ave 27909
Newby St 27909
Newland Rd 27909
Newport Ave 27909
Nicholas Ct 27909
Nixonton Loop & Rd 27909
Noble Ct 27909
Norma Dr 27909
Normal Ave 27909
North St 27909
Northbanks Rd 27909
Northside Park & Rd 27909
Northway St 27909
Nuggett Trl 27909
Oak Dr 27909
Oak Grove Ave 27909
Oak Stump Rd 27909
Oakdale Dr 27909
Oakview Dr 27909
Oakwood Ln 27909
Ocean Hwy 27909
Oconnor Ln 27909
Okisko Rd 27909
Old Foreman Bundy Rd 27909
Old Halls Creek Rd 27909
Old Hertford Hwy 27909
Old Mcdonald Rd 27909
Old Oak Rd 27909
Old Okisko Rd 27909
Old Us 17 27909
Olde Lebanon Trl 27909
Olivet Cir 27909
Orchard Dr 27909
Osprey Ct & Cv 27909
Overman Cir 27909
Owens Dr 27909
Ownley Rd 27909
Pailin Creek Rd 27909
Palliser Ct 27909
Palmer Dr 27909
Palomino Ct 27909
Panama St 27909
Park Dr & St 27909
Park Circle Rd 27909
Park Circle East Rd 27909
Parker Ln 27909
Parkview Dr 27909
Parsonage St 27909
Pasquotank Station Rd 27909
Patrick Way 27909
Paxton St 27909
Pearl St 27909
Peartree Rd 27909
Pecan Ct 27909
Pelican St 27909
Pelican Pointe Dr 27909
Pendleton Ln 27909
E Penny Dr 27909
Perkins Ln 27909
Perquimans Ave 27909
Perry St 27909
Persse St 27909
Perth Dr 27909
Phaeson Pl 27909
Pierces Trailer Park 27909
Pike Dr 27909
Pine St 27909
Pinelake Dr 27909
Pineshore Rd 27909
Pineview Dr 27909
Pinewood Ave 27909
Pintail Cres 27909
Pirates Trl 27909
Pitts Chapel Rd 27909
Plantation Dr 27909
Planters Run 27909
Pleasant Dr 27909
N & S Poindexter St 27909

Pointe Vista Dr 27909
N & S Pool St 27909
Poplar Dr 27909
Possum Quarter Rd 27909
Pot O Gold Trl 27909
Powell Ct 27909
Powers Dr 27909
Preyer Ave 27909
Price St 27909
Prince George Cir 27909
Prince William Dr 27909
Princess Anne Cir 27909
Prindary Rd 27909
Pritchard Rd & St 27909
Pritchards Trailer Park 27909
Providence Rd 27909
Quail Run 27909
Quaker Dr 27909
Queen St 27909
Queenswood Blvd 27909
Rabbits Trl 27909
Rachel Dr 27909
Railroad Ave 27909
Raintree Run 27909
Raleigh St 27909
Ramsey Rd 27909
Ranch Dr 27909
Raven Way 27909
Ray St 27909
Rebellion Point Rd 27909
Red Cedar Run 27909
Red Gate Dr 27909
Reedy Creek Dr 27909
Reid Dr 27909
Renaissance Cir 27909
Rhode Island Ave 27909
Rhonda Rd 27909
E Rich Blvd 27909
Richardson St 27909
Ricochet Ct 27909
Riddick Rd 27909
Ridgefield Dr 27909
Ridley St 27909
Riley Dr 27909
Rileys Way 27909
River Rd 27909
Rivers Edge Cir 27909
Rivers Retreat Way 27909
Rivershore Rd 27909
Riverside Ave 27909
N & S Road St 27909
Roanoke Ave 27909
Robbins Ave 27909
Robinson St 27909
Rochelle Dr 27909
Rolling Acres Dr 27909
Rookery Run 27909
Roscoe Dr 27909
Rosebud Ave 27909
Rosecroft Dr 27909
Rosedale Dr 27909
Rosewood Ave 27909
Roundtree Dr 27909
Russell Ln 27909
Saint Judes Is 27909
Salem Dr 27909
Salem Church Rd 27909
Sam Davis Dr 27909
Sample Dr 27909
Sandfiddler Dr 27909
Sandpiper Dr 27909
Sandy Rd 27909
Sanford Dr 27909
Saunders Dr 27909
Savin Rd 27909
Sawmill Rd 27909
Sawyer Dr, Rd & St 27909
Sawyer Trailer Park 27909
School House Rd 27909
Schwarzkopf Dr 27909
Scotland Dr 27909
Scott Rd 27909
Scott Land Dr 27909
Scotts Ln 27909
Seagull Dr 27909
Seaview Dr 27909

Selby Rd 27909
Selden St 27909
Sexton Rd 27909
Shadneck Rd 27909
Shadowwood St 27909
Shady Dr 27909
Shanna Dr 27909
Shannon St 27909
Shard Trl 27909
Shellie Dr 27909
Shepard St 27909
Shillingtown Rd 27909
Shiloh St 27909
Shirley St 27909
Simeon Ct 27909
Simpson St 27909
Simpson Ditch Rd 27909
Small Dr 27909
Smalls Acres 27909
Smalls Trailer Park 27909
Soundneck Rd 27909
South St 27909
Southern Ave 27909
Southgate Mall 27909
Southway St 27909
Speed St 27909
Spellman St 27909
Spence Dr 27909
Spindrift Trl 27909
Spoonbill Loop 27909
Springvale St 27909
Spruce St 27909
Spruill Dr 27909
Spud Dr 27909
Stacie Dr 27909
Stafford Rd 27909
Stalling Ct 27909
Starboard Ct 27909
Stedman Ln E 27909
Stevensons Trailer Park 27909
Stone St 27909
Strawberry Acres Dr 27909
Sudie Cir 27909
Sulidae Ct 27909
Summerfield St 27909
Sun Gro Dr 27909
Sundown Dr 27909
Sunny Acres Dr 27909
Sunrise Trl 27909
Sunset Cir 27909
Sutton Dr 27909
Sycamore Ln 27909
Sydney Way 27909
Sylvan Ct 27909
T Com Dr 27909
Tadmore Rd 27909
Tanglewood Dr & Pkwy 27909
Tanners Ct 27909
Tarheel Ct 27909
Tatem Ln 27909
Taylors Ln 27909
Teal Trce 27909
Temple Rd 27909
Terrace Way 27909
Terrilynn Way 27909
Terry St 27909
Thunder Rd 27909
Tiara Ct 27909
Tideland Dr 27909
Tidewater Way 27909
Tiff Ln 27909
Timber Trl 27909
Timmerman Dr 27909
Timothy Dr 27909
Tonto Ct 27909
Toxey Rd 27909
Toxeys Trailer Park 27909
Traci Dr 27909
Travis Dr 27909
Triad Vlg 27909
Trinkaloe Rd 27909
Troy Dr 27909
Tucker Ln 27909
Turners Ave 27909
Turnpike Rd 27909
Tuscarora Ave 27909
Tuxey Rd 27909
Twiford Rd 27909
Ulster Dr 27909
Uncle Buddy Dr 27909
Union St 27909
Union Chapel Rd 27909
Upriver Rd 27909
Us Highway 158 S 27909
Us Highway 17 S 27909
Vickie Dr 27909
Villa Dr 27909
Village Dr 27909
Vine St 27909
Vineyard Ct 27909
Virginia St 27909
Wades Point Rd 27909
Walker Ave 27909
Walnut St 27909
Walston St 27909
E & W Ward St 27909
Warden St 27909
Wareham St 27909
Warren Way 27909
Washington St 27909
N & S Water St 27909
Water Crest Cir 27909
Waterside Dr 27909
Weeks Dr & St 27909
Weeksville Rd 27909
Wellfield Rd 27909
Wesley Dr 27909
Westover St 27909
Westway St 27909
Westwood Dr 27909
Wet Patch Rd 27909
Whipple Ave 27909
White St 27909
Whitehurst Rd & St 27909
Widgeon Ct 27909
Wiley Dr 27909
William Dr 27909
E, N, S & W Williams Cir 27909
Willis Dr 27909
Willow St & Way 27909
Wills Rd 27909
Wilson St 27909
Wilsons Trailer Park 27909
Winborne Loop 27909
Windermere Dr 27909
Windfield Dr 27909
Windsor Ct 27909
Windwood Dr 27909
Winslow Rd & St 27909
Winston St 27909
Witherspoon St 27909
Wood St 27909
Wood Duck Way 27909
Woodruff Ave 27909
Wright St 27909
York St 27909
Zack Cir 27909

NUMBERED STREETS

All Street Addresses 27909

FAYETTEVILLE NC

General Delivery 28302

POST OFFICE BOXES MAIN OFFICE STATIONS AND BRANCHES

Box No.s
B - J 28302
1 - 7000 28302
8001 - 10019 28311
11001 - 11116 28303
12001 - 13121 28311
14001 - 20116 28301
25001 - 28358 28314
28301 - 28301 28301
28302 - 28302 28302
28303 - 28303 28303
28304 - 28304 28304
28305 - 28305 28305
28306 - 28306 28306
28309 - 28309 28309
35001 - 36396 28303
40101 - 44154 28309
53001 - 58618 28305
64001 - 65578 28306
87001 - 88114 28304
99301 - 99997 28302
153400 - 153400 28301

RURAL ROUTES

21 28304
03, 12, 20, 34, 37 28306
10, 32, 39 28311
48, 55 28312

NAMED STREETS

A B Carter Rd 28312
A B Smith Rd 28312
Abasco St 28312
Abbey Ln 28311
Abbey Forde Dr 28311
Abbeydale Ln 28304
Abbott Ln 28312
Abbotts Landing Cir 28314
Abbotts Park Rd 28311
Abbottswood Dr 28301
Abco Ln 28312
Abercarn Way 28311
Abercrombie Ct 28312
Aberdeen Pl 28303
Abernathy Dr 28311
Abigail Rd 28312
Abilene Rd 28303
Abington St 28314
Abraham Ave 28312
Abram St 28312
Abrams St 28311
Acacia Cir & Dr 28314
Accord Rd 28312
Acoma Ct 28312
Acorn St 28303
Acus Ct 28303
Adair St 28303
Adam St 28301
Adams Lake Dr 28304
Addie Ln 28306
Addingham Ct 28304
Addison St 28314
Aden Pl 28306
Adger Ct 28314
Adkins Hill Dr 28306
Admiral Dr 28303
Adobe Ct 28303
Adolphus Dr 28314
Adrian Dr 28314
Afton Ln 28306
Aftonshire St 28304
Agate St 28311
Aglow Dr 28312
Agnes Scott Ct 28311
Agway St 28312
Aimsworth Ct 28304
Ainsley St 28314
Airedale Ct 28311
Airline Dr 28306
Airport Rd 28306
Ajuga Pl 28314
Ake St 28306
Akins Dr 28311
Al Ray Rd 28312
Alabama Ln 28306
Alabaster Way 28314
Alagon Ct 28314
Alamance Rd 28304
Alameda Dr 28304
Alan St 28314
Albany St 28301
Albatross Rd 28312
Albemarle Dr 28311
Alberry Pl 28304
Albert St 28301
Albertha Ln 28312
Albertson Ln 28312
Alco Cir 28311
Aldbury Ct 28306
Alden Dr & St 28304
Alder Rd 28304
Alderman Rd 28306
Aldwych Pl 28304
Ale Ct 28314
Alexander St 28301
Alexandra Park Dr 28311
Alexis Dr 28312
Alforodo St 28306
Alfred St 28301
Alice St 28312
All Saints Dr 28314
Alleghany Rd 28304
Allegiance Ave 28312
Allonby Rd 28314
Alloway Pl 28303
Allsbrook Dr 28301
Allwood Dr 28303
Ally Rayven Dr 28306
Alma St 28303
Almond Rd 28306
Aloha Dr 28311
Aloine Ln 28306
Alpha Dr 28303
Alphin St 28312
Alpine St 28311
Alson Rd 28314
Altgero Ave 28306
Altitude Dr 28312
Alva Cir 28311
Alvin St 28304
Amanda Cir 28304
Amarillo Dr 28314
Amber Dr 28311
Amber Gate Path 28314
Amberhill Ct 28311
Amberjack Rd 28306
Amberly Way Dr 28303
Ambition Rd 28306
Amboy Dr 28303
Ambrose Pl 28314
Amelia Dr 28304
Americus Dr 28312
Ames St 28301
Amesbury Rd 28311
Amethyst Ct 28311
Amherst Dr 28306
Amigo Dr 28305
Amish Dr 28314
Ammie Horne Way 28312
Amoora Dr 28304
Amour Dr 28306
Ampco St 28303
Amstead Ave 28314
Amye St 28301
Anarine Rd 28303
Ancestry Dr 28304
Ancient Ct 28312
Ancoda Dr 28304
N Ancon Dr 28304
Anderson St 28301
Andes Ct 28304
Andover Rd 28311
Andrea Ct 28314
Andrews Rd 28311
Andros Dr 28314
Andy St 28303
Angel Dr 28306
Angel Oak Dr 28314
Angelia M St 28312
Angie Dr 28311
Angle Dr 28304
Anglian Dr 28311
Angus Ct 28312
Anhinga Ct 28306
Anita Rd 28303
Ann St 28301
Anona Dr 28314
Anson Dr 28311
Antelope St 28312
Anthem Ln 28311
Antique Ct 28312
Antoinette Cir 28312
Antura Dr 28314
Apache St 28303
Appalachin Dr 28311
Appamattox Ct 28305
Apple Tree Ln 28312
Applebury Ln 28306
Applecross Ave 28304
Applegate Rd 28306
Appleton Ct 28306
Applewhite Rd 28304
Applewood Ln 28303
Approved Dr 28306
Apricot Ct 28311
April Dr 28314
Apsley Ct 28304
Aquatica Ln 28312
Aquinas Ave 28311
Arailia Dr 28314
Aramid Rd 28311
Arapahoe Ct 28304
Arberdale Dr 28304
Arbor Rd 28311
Arbor Grove Ct & Ln 28306
Arboretum Pl 28303
Arbutus Trl 28311
Arcadia Ct 28311
Arch St 28301
Archcrest Ct 28304
Archdale Rd 28311
Arden Ct 28314
Ardenwoods Dr 28306
Ardfern Pl 28306
Ardmore Dr 28312
Argentine Cir 28306
Argon Ave 28311
Argosy Ct 28304
Argyll Rd 28303
Ariel Ct 28306
Aristocrat Ln 28306
Arizona Ct 28304
Arlington Ave 28303
Armadillo Dr 28311
Armatha Estate Pl 28306
Armour Ave 28306
Armstrong St 28301
Arnish Ct 28306
Arran Cir 28304
Arrondale Ct & Dr 28311
Arrow Ridge Way 28304
Arrowood Rd 28311
Arsenal Ave 28305
Artemis Dr 28311
Artesian Ct 28304
Arthington St 28311
Arthur St 28301
Arundel Ct 28311
Asbury Rd 28312
Ascot Ave 28303
Ashboro St
600-899 28311
3000-3399 28306
Ashbrook Rd 28314
Ashburton Dr 28301
Ashdown Pl 28311
Ashe St 28306
Ashfield Dr 28311
Ashford Ave 28305
Ashgrove Dr 28311
Ashleman Dr 28314
Ashley St 28305
Ashridge Dr 28304
Ashton Rd 28304
Ashwood Cir 28303
Aspen Cir 28304
Aspen Ct 28314
Assembly Ct 28306
Assurian Ct 28306
Aster Ct 28311
Astron Ln 28314
Athens Ave 28301
Atlantic Ave 28306
Atmore Dr 28314
Attica Dr 28312
Attonbury Ln 28312
Attorney Dr 28304
Atwell Dr 28314
Atwick Dr 28304
Auburn Dr & St 28306
Auburndale Ln 28314
Auckland Ct 28306
Audrey Ct 28303
August Dr & Pl 28314
Augusta Dr 28305
Aultroy Dr 28306
Aura Rd 28311
Austin Dr 28311
Austin West Rd 28312
Australia Dr 28306
Autumn Dr 28311
Avalon Dr 28303
Avant Ferry Ct 28306
Averton Ct 28314
Avery Rd 28312
Aviation Pkwy 28306
Avila Dr 28314
Avon St 28304
Avon Dale St 28306
Avoncroft Dr 28306
Ayrshire Ct 28311
Ayton Pl 28304
Azalea Dr 28301
Azalea Bluff Dr 28301
Aztek Pl 28314
B St 28301
Babcock Ct 28314
Bac Ct 28314
Bacarro Pl 28314
Back St 28306
Backbay Rd 28306
Badger Ct 28303
Badin Ct 28314
Badin Lake Ln 28314
Bagdad Rd 28306
Bagpipe Ct 28312
Bahama Loop 28314
Bahia Loop 28314
Bailey Ct 28314
Bailey St 28306
Bailey Lake Rd 28304
Bain Dr 28301
Bainbridge Ct 28301
Baird Rd 28312
Baj Dr 28312
Baker St 28303
Bakers Mill Rd 28306
Balaam Rd 28306
Balancer Dr 28306
Balboa St 28306
Bald Cypress Ct 28304
Bald Mountain Dr 28311
Baldoon Dr 28314
Balfour Pl 28311
Ballpark Rd 28312
Balmoral Dr 28304
Bamgoo St 28314
Bammel Dr 28306
Banbury Ct & Dr 28304
Bancroft Ave 28301
Bandera Dr 28303
Bandore Cir 28312
Bandy Cir 28306
Bangle St 28306
Bangor Ct 28314
S Bank Ct 28306
Bankers Dr 28311
Bankhead Dr 28306
Bankside Dr 28311
Banner Elk Dr 28304
Bannerman Ct 28314
Bantam St 28306
Banyan Rd 28304
Barber Ave 28303
Barbershop Dr 28312
Barbour Ct 28301
Barbour Lake Rd 28306
Barcelona Dr 28303
Bardolino Dr 28306
Bardstown Ct 28304
Barefoot Rd 28306
Barfield Dr 28314
Bargain St 28303
Bargemaster Dr 28306
Barges Ln 28301
Barkley Dr 28303
Barksdale Rd 28301
Barley Hill Ct 28314
Barlow Ave 28306
Barn Hart Rd 28306
Barn Owl Dr 28306
Barnabus Cir 28304
Barnby Pl 28306
Barnes St 28306
Barnwell Pl 28303
Barrett St 28306
Barrington Cir 28303
Barrington Cross 28303
Barron Way 28311
Barry Dr 28314
Bartlet Glen Ln 28306
Bartlett Ct 28314
Bartons Landing Pl 28314
Bartow Dr 28301
Barwick Dr 28304
Barwin Dr 28304
Basewood St 28311
Bashford Ct 28304
Bashlot Pl 28303
Basin Dr 28304
Basking Ridge Dr 28314
Bass Dr 28314
Bass Hill Ln 28312
Bassman Ln 28314
Bat Cave Dr 28312
Bateman Ct 28303
Batesfield Dr 28311
Bath Ln 28314
Bathgate Ct 28312
Battery Ct 28306
Battle Rd 28314
Bavaria Pl 28314
Baxley St 28306
Baxter St 28311
Bay Forest Dr 28312
Bayberry Ct 28314
Bayfield Loop 28314
Bayham Ct 28304
Bayleaf Dr 28304
Baylor Dr 28306
Baysden Ct 28303
Bayshore Dr 28311
Bayside Dr 28306
Baystone Rd 28314
Bayview Dr 28305
Baywater Dr 28304
Baywood Rd 28312
Baywood Point Dr 28312
Beacon St 28311
Beaconfield Dr 28311
Beagle Dr & Run 28311
Bear Creek Cir 28304
Bear Grass St 28314
Beard Rd 28312
Bears Den Way 28312
Beatrice Rd 28312
Beaubien Dr 28306
Beaufort Dr 28304
Beaumont Rd 28304
Beaver Creek Dr 28303
Beaver Lake Rd 28306
Beaver Run Dr 28314
Beaverlodge Ct 28311
Beaverpond Ct 28311
Beaverstone Dr 28314
Beckett Ct 28306
Beckford Ln 28304
Beckham Pl 28304
Bedell Pl 28314
Bedford Rd 28303
Bedfordshire Pl 28312
Bedloe St 28304

Bedrock Dr 28303
Bee Hive Dr 28312
Beebe Estate Cir 28314
Beech St 28303
Beechnut Ct 28311
Beechridge Rd 28312
Bees Ferry Dr 28306
Begonia Dr 28314
Bel Aire St 28306
Belews Creek Ln 28312
Belfast Ct 28304
Belford Rd 28314
Belgian Ave 28306
Belhaven Rd 28306
Bell Arthur Ln 28312
Bella Vista Cir 28311
Belle Terre Ct 28304
Bellemeade Rd 28303
Bellflower St 28314
Bellingham Way 28312
Bellview Dr 28303
Bellwood Ct 28314
Belmont Ave & Cir 28305
Belridge Dr 28306
Belt Blvd 28301
Belvedere Ave 28305
Ben Mcnatt Rd 28312
Bending Birch Ln 28304
Bendix Pl 28304
Benevente Loop 28314
Benjamin St 28311
Bennett Dr 28301
Bennington Rd 28303
Benny St 28306
Benson Pl 28306
Bent Grass Dr 28312
W Bent Grass Dr 28312
Bent Grass Pl 28306
Bent Pine Dr 28304
Bent Tree Dr 28314
Benton Dr 28311
Bentridge Ln 28304
Berger Dr 28304
Beringer Dr 28306
Berkley Pl 28304
Berkley Hall Way 28303
Berkshire Rd 28304
Berma Ct 28303
Bernadine St 28311
Berriedale Dr 28304
Bertram Dr & Pl 28314
Berwick Dr 28314
Berwyn Cross 28311
Besly Ct 28304
Bessemer Cir 28301
Beswick Ct 28306
Beta St 28304
Bethesda Ct 28303
Bethpage Ln 28311
Bethune Dr 28311
Bethune St 28305
Betts Dr 28311
Beuer Dr 28314
Beulah Rd 28311
Beverly Dr 28314
Bevil St 28301
Bexley Ct 28312
Bianca Ct 28314
Bibar Rd 28304
Bibb Ct 28314
Bickett St 28303
Bienville Dr 28311
Big Wood Rd 28314
Bighorn Dr 28303
Bill Dr 28306
Bill Hall Rd 28306
Billingsford Cir 28311
Biltmore Dr 28304
Bimbo Dr 28304
Bimini Pl 28314
Bingham Dr & Pl 28304
Birch Rd 28304
Birchcreft Dr 28304
Birchfield Ct 28306
Birchmere Way 28312
Birchwood Way 28314
Birdsong Ln 28303
Birkdale Ct 28303
Birkhoff Ln 28304
Birmingham Dr 28306
Birnam Dr 28305
Biscayne Dr 28301
Bishopgate Pl 28304
Bismark Ct 28304
Bitterroot Ct 28314
Bittersweet Dr 28306
Biway Cir 28311
Bixley Dr 28303
Black Creek Ct 28311
Black Tower Ct 28306
Blackberry Ct 28311
Blackbird Dr 28314
Blackford Rd 28314
Blackfriars Rd 28304
Blackjack Rd 28314
Blackman Rd 28312
Blackwater Ct 28306
Blackwell St 28312
Bladen Cir 28312
W Bladen Union Church Rd 28306
Blairmore Pl 28314
Blairwood Dr 28304
Blake St 28301
Blan St 28311
Blandford Pl 28311
Blankshire Rd 28314
Blanton Rd 28303
Blantyre Way 28306
Blayne Dr 28303
Blaze Ct 28314
Blockade Runner Dr 28306
Bloom Ave 28304
Bloomfield Dr 28311
Bloomingdale Ct 28303
Bloomsbury Dr 28306
Blossom Rd 28306
Blount St 28301
Blue St 28301
Blue Heron Ct 28314
Blue Jay Ct 28306
Blue Spring Rd 28304
Blue Teal Ct 28304
Blue Tick St 28311
Blue Wren Dr 28312
Bluebell Ct 28311
Blueberry Pl 28301
Bluebird Ln 28311
Bluebush Dr 28312
Bluegill Ct 28306
Bluejay Ct 28304
Blueridge Rd 28303
Bluestone Ln 28311
Bluewater Dr 28306
Bluewater Pl 28311
Bluff St 28311
Bluffside Dr 28312
Bluffview Dr 28314
Blythewood Ln 28311
Boahn Dr & St 28306
Boars Head Ct 28311
Boat Landing Dr 28306
Bob St 28303
Bob White Ct 28303
Bobbie St 28306
Bobby Jones Dr 28312
Bobcat Rd 28306
Bobolink Ct 28306
Bogie Island Rd 28312
Boise Ct 28306
Bolin Ct 28303
Bolivia St 28306
Bolla Dr 28306
Bolt Rock Way 28306
Bolton St 28306
Bombay Dr 28312
Bonanza Dr 28303
Bonaventure Ct 28314
Bond Ct 28314
Bone Creek Cir & Dr 28314
Bonfield Dr 28312
Boniface Ct 28306
Bonita Ct 28314
Bonlee Rd 28306
Bonney Ln 28306
Bonnie St 28303
Bonnie Bell Ln 28314
Bonnington Ct 28312
Bonwood St 28312
Boone Trl 28306
Boone Trail Ext 28304
Boots Ln 28311
Bordeaux Park Dr 28306
Boros Dr 28303
Borthwick Dr 28306
Bosden Pl 28314
Boss Dr 28303
Bostian Dr 28304
Bostic Ct 28314
Bostick Dr 28314
Boswell Ct 28303
Botany Ct 28303
Boulder Ln 28311
Boundary Ln 28301
Bovill Ct 28314
Bow St 28301
Bowden Rd 28311
Bowling Green Dr 28304
Bowman Ct 28304
Boxley Ct 28306
Boxwood Ln 28311
Boyer Ct 28304
Boykin Rd 28312
Boylan St 28306
Boynton Dr 28306
Bozeman Loop 28303
Bracebridge Ct 28306
Braddock Dr 28301
Braddy Rd 28306
Bradford Ave 28301
Bradley St 28311
Braehead St 28306
Braemar Pl 28314
Bragg Blvd
100-1699 28301
1700-6499 28303
Brainerd Ave 28301
Bramblewood Ct 28314
Bramcote Ln 28312
Branchwood Cir 28314
Brandermill Rd 28314
Brandon Ct 28311
Brandts Ln 28301
Brandy Ln 28306
Brandywine Ct 28304
Brannan Way 28314
Branson St 28305
Brass Ct 28311
Brasswood Dr 28314
Bravery Ln 28301
Bravo Dr 28311
Brawley Ave 28314
Braxton Blvd 28311
Braxton Edge Rd 28312
Braybrooke Pl 28314
Bream Pl 28306
Brechin Rd 28303
Breckinridge St 28311
Brecknock Ct 28311
Breece St & Trl 28312
Breezewood Ave 28303
Bremer St 28303
Brenda Dr 28311
Brennan Cir 28312
Brentford Dr 28306
Brentwood Dr 28304
Brett Ct 28305
Brevard Ct 28311
Brewer St 28301
Brewster Dr & Pl 28303
Briar Cir 28306
Briarcliff Dr 28305
Briarcreek Pl 28304
Briargate Ln 28314
Briarwood Ln 28303
Brick Spring Rd 28312
Brickyard Dr 28306
Bridgeman Dr 28303
Bridger St 28301
Bridgeton Way 28312
Bridgette St 28314
Bridgeview Dr 28306
Bridle St 28306
Brigadoon Ln 28305
Bright Ct 28303
Bright View St 28314
Brighton Rd
800-999 28314
907-907 28309
Brightwood Dr 28303
Brinkley St 28301
Brisbane Ct 28314
Brisby Ct 28303
Bristlecone Rd 28311
Bristol Dr 28314
Briton Cir & Ct 28314
Brittany Pl 28314
N & S Broad St 28301
Broad Muskeg Rd 28312
Broadell Dr 28301
Broadfoot Ave 28305
Broadhill Ln 28311
Broadman Ave 28304
Broadmore Dr 28314
Broadview Dr 28301
Brockwood St 28314
Brocton Dr 28303
Brody Dr 28306
Brokenhurst Ct 28311
Bromley Dr 28303
Bromsworth Trl 28311
Bromwich Ct 28306
Bronco Ln 28303
Bronwyn St 28314
Brook St 28305
Brook Run Dr 28306
Brookberry Ct 28306
Brookcliff Rd 28304
Brookcrossing Dr 28306
Brookemere Pl 28304
Brookfield Rd 28303
Brookford Ct 28314
Brookgreen Dr 28304
Brookhaven Dr 28303
Brookhollow Dr 28314
Brookridge Dr 28314
Brookshire St 28314
Brookside Ave 28305
Brookstone Ln 28314
Brookwood Ave 28301
Broomfield Ct 28311
Broomsgrove Dr 28306
Brougham Rd 28311
Brown Rd 28306
Brown Pelican Ct 28306
Brownlee Dr 28304
Browns Ln 28301
Brownwood Ct 28303
Broyhill Rd 28314
Brucemount Pl 28304
Bruner St 28301
Brunson Rd 28312
Brunswick Rd 28303
Brush Crk 28314
Brushy Hill Rd 28306
Brussels Ct 28304
Bryan St 28305
Bryanstone Way 28314
Bryce Creek Ln 28303
Bryn Mawr Dr 28304
Bubble Creek Ct 28311
Buck Ct 28311
Buck Creek Ct 28304
Buckfast Ct 28311
Buckhead Rd 28303
Buckhorn Rd 28304
Buckingham Ave 28301
Buckland Dr 28312
Bucknell Rd 28304
Buckner St 28312
Buckskin Dr 28306
Bucktail Rd 28311
Buddingbrook Dr 28304
Buddy Cir 28314
Buena Vista Dr 28311
Buffalo St 28303
Buffaloberry Pl 28304
Bugle Call Dr 28314
Buhman Dr 28314
Buie Ct
300-399 28314
400-499 28304
Builders Blvd 28301
Bull Run St 28304
Bulla Pl 28303
Bullard Cir 28311
Bullard Ct 28312
Bullard St 28301
Bullock St 28301
Bulova Pl 28311
Bun Brady Rd 28312
Bunce Rd 28314
Bundy Ct 28314
Bunk House Pl 28314
Bunker Hill Rd 28314
Burbank St 28306
Burberry Dr 28306
Bureau Dr 28312
Burford Ct 28314
Burgaw Dr 28306
Burgenfield Dr 28314
Burgess St 28301
Burgoyne Ct & Dr 28314
Burke Ln 28306
Burleigh Pl 28311
Burleson Ct 28304
Burlington Dr 28312
Burlwood Ct 28303
Burnett Ave 28306
Burnettown Ave 28306
Burning Tree Ct 28306
Burns St 28301
Burnside Pl 28311
Burton Dr 28306
Burwell Dr 28314
Butler Rd 28301
Butler Nursery Rd 28306
Butter Branch Dr 28311
Butterfly Ct 28306
Buttermere Dr 28314
Butternut Dr 28304
Butterwood Cir 28314
Buttonwood Ave 28314
Buxton Blvd 28301
Byford Ct 28314
Byrd St 28301
N & S C St 28301
Cabana Dr 28306
Cabretto Cir 28306
Cabrini Ct 28312
Cactus Ct 28303
Cade Hill Ave 28312
Cadenza Loop 28312
Cadmium Ct 28311
Cadney Ct 28314
Cage St 28306
Cagle Ct 28304
Cain Rd 28303
Caisson Dr 28311
Caithness Dr 28306
Calamar Dr 28314
Calamint Ln 28305
Calcium Rd 28312
Calcutt St 28305
Caldera Pl 28304
Caldwell St 28301
Caleb Dr 28312
Caledonia Cir 28301
California Dr 28304
Calista Cir 28304
Calla Cir 28303
Callahan Cir 28314
Callery Knoll Ct 28306
Callie Rd 28312
Calver Ct 28311
Calvin Cir 28303
Calvin Willis Ln 28306
Camberly Dr 28306
Cambridge St 28303
Cambridge Arms 28303
Camden Rd 28306
Camden Road Ext 28306
Camel Back Rd 28306
Camellia Dr 28303
Camelot Dr 28304
Cameo Ct 28311
Cameron Rd 28306
Cameron Woods Ln 28306
Camomile Dr 28306
Camp Tom Upchurch Rd 28306
Campbell Ave, St & Ter 28301
Campground Rd 28314
Camrose Ct 28304
Camson Rd 28306
Canady St 28306
Canary Dr 28314
Candleberry Ct 28301
Candlelight Dr 28311
Candlenut Dr 28312
Candlewick Ct 28306
Candlewood Dr 28314
Candytuft St 28311
Canford Ln 28304
Canmorre Ct 28306
Cannon St 28303
Canopy Ln 28305
Canterbury Rd 28304
Canton St 28312
Cantrell Ct 28314
Canvasback Dr 28304
Canyon Ct 28303
Canyon Crest Cir 28314
Canyonland Ct 28303
Cape Ct 28304
Cape Center Dr 28304
Cape Fear Ave 28303
Cape Fear Trl 28311
Cape Point Dr 28312
Capeharbor Ct 28314
Capitol Pear Ln 28301
Capri St 28301
Capstan Dr 28306
Captains Pl 28311
Captivating Ct 28314
Caramel Dr 28306
Carbine St 28306
Carbonton St 28301
Cardale Dr 28306
Cardiff Dr 28304
Cardigan Ct 28303
Cardinal Cir 28312
Careygate Ct 28304
Carfew Ct 28312
Caribou Ct 28314
Carl Steiner Rd 28311
Carlo Rossi Dr 28306
Carlos Ave 28306
Carloway Dr & Pl 28304
Carlson Bay Cir 28314
Carlton Pl 28311
Carnegie Dr 28311
Carnforth Ct 28304
Carnsmore Dr 28304
Carol St
600-699 28312
800-899 28303
Carolee Ct 28314
Carolina Ave
800-999 28301
5700-5799 28306
Carolina Wren Dr 28312
Carolyn Ct 28304
Carpet Grass Pl 28306
Carriage Ln 28305
Carriage Rd 28312
Carrington Pl 28314
Carroll Ave 28311
Carrollburg Dr 28303
Carson Ct & Dr 28303
Carter Baron Pl 28304
Carteret Pl 28311
Carthage Dr 28301
Cartman Dr 28314
Cartwright Dr 28303
Carula Ln 28304
Carver St 28301
Carver Falls Rd 28311
Carver Oaks Dr 28311
Carver Pine Loop 28311
Cascade St 28301
Cashiers Ln 28311
Cashwell St 28301
Caskey Dr & Rd 28311
Casper Ct 28303
Caspian Ct 28304
Cassell Dr 28311
Cassidy Ct 28303
Casting Ct 28314
Castle Falls Cir 28314
Castle Hayne Rd 28303
Castle Rising Rd 28314
Castle Rock Dr 28304
Castlebar Dr 28311
Castlebay Ct 28303
Castlefield Ln 28306
Catalina Rd 28306
Catalpa Rd 28304
Catawba St 28303
Caterwaul Ln 28312
Catfish Rd 28306
Catherine Dr 28306
Catman Dr 28312
Cattail Cir 28312
Cattesmore Rd 28311
Caveson Ct 28311
Caviness St 28314
Cawdor Dr 28304
Cay Ct 28314
Cayman Dr 28306
Cecil St 28312
Cedar St 28312
Cedar Brook Cir 28304
Cedar Chest Ct 28314
Cedar Creek Rd 28312
Cedar Crossing Rd 28304
Cedar Glen Dr 28314
Cedar Hill Dr 28312
Cedric St 28303
Cellner Dr 28314
Celtic Dr 28306
Cemdil Dr 28312
Center St
1000-1199 28306
1500-1599 28311
1900-2099 28306
Central Dr 28301
Century Cir 28306
Century Oaks Dr 28314
Chad Pl 28314
Chadborne Dr 28312
Chadwick Rd 28301
Chagford Ln 28306
Chagrin Rd 28311
Chalmers Ct 28311
Chambercomb Ct 28303
Chambersburg Rd 28314
Chamblee Dr 28306
Chambrian Dr 28314
Champs Ct 28306
Chance St 28301
Chandler St 28303
Channing Dr 28303
Chantelle Dr 28306
Chanticleer Ct 28306
Chapel Ln 28314
Chapman St 28306
Charbonneau Ct 28304
Charger Ct 28306
Charity Ln 28304
Charles Ave 28311
Charles Ct 28311
Charles St 28306
Charles Thigpen Dr 28306
Charleston Pl 28303
Charlie Dr 28311
Charlotte Dr 28305
Charmain St 28311
Charring Cross Ln 28314
Chartley Dr 28304
Chase St 28301

Chasewater Rd 28306
Chason Ridge Dr 28314
Chatham St 28301
Cheer Ln 28301
Chelsea Rd 28314
Cheltenham Rd 28304
Chene St 28306
Cheraw St 28306
Cherokee Dr 28303
Cherry Ln 28304
Cherry Hill Ln 28312
Cherry Laurel Dr 28314
Cherry Plum Dr 28306
Cherry Point Dr 28306
Cherrystone Rd 28311
Chesaning Pl 28311
Chesapeake Pl & Rd 28311
Cheshire Ct 28314
Chester Cir 28303
Chester Lake Pl 28301
Chesterbrook Dr 28314
Chesterfield Dr 28305
Chestnut St 28301
Chestnut Wood Dr 28314
Cheswick Pl 28306
Chevy Chase St 28306
Chewton Ct 28314
Cheyenne St 28303
Chicago Dr 28306
Chickadee St 28306
Chickasaw St 28303
Chickenfoot Rd 28306
Childers Dr 28304
Chillingworth Dr 28306
Chilton Dr 28314
Chimney Brook Rd 28312
Chimney Swift Dr 28306
Chinaberry Dr 28306
Chinas Ct 28314
Chinoak Dr 28314
Chippendale Ct 28306
Chippenham St 28312
Chipper St 28312
Chipstead Dr 28312
Chisholm Trl 28303
Chislehurst St 28312
Chloe Dr 28301
Christian St 28312
Christina St 28314
Christmas Berry Ct 28312
Christopher Way 28303
Chromium Ct 28311
Church St
1400-1499 28301
3100-3199 28312
6200-6399 28311
N & S Churchill Dr 28303
Cicada St 28306
Cimarron Dr 28303
Cinder Ln 28312
Cinder Hill Ct 28306
Cindy Dr 28314
Cinnamon Creek Cir 28314
Circle Ct 28301
W Circle Ct 28301
Circle Dr 28305
Circle Point Ct 28306
Cisco Ct 28303
Cissna Dr 28303
Citadel Pl 28306
Cityview Ln 28301
Cl Tart Cir 28314
Clairborne Dr 28314
Claremont Ave 28305
Clarence Dr 28311
Clarendon St 28305
Clark St 28305
Clark West Rd 28312
Clarkville Ct 28306
Classic Rd 28306
Claude St 28303
Claude Lee Rd 28306
Claudia Way 28312
Clayton Dr 28311
Clean Sweep Ln 28311
Clear Branch Rd 28311

Clear Pines Ct 28304
Clear Spring Dr 28314
Clearwater Dr 28311
Clematis St 28304
Clemson Dr 28306
Cleo Pl 28306
Cleve St 28303
Cleveland Ave 28312
Cliff Swallow Dr 28306
Cliffbourne Dr 28303
Cliffdale Ct 28314
Cliffdale Rd
200-4299 28303
4300-9499 28314
9500-9699 28304
Clifford Ave 28314
Cliffside Dr 28303
Climbing Tree Ln 28306
Clinchfield Dr 28304
Clinton Rd
1300-4944 28312
4946-4998 28312
5201-7597 28314
7599-8999 28314
Cloister Ct 28314
Clovelly St 28312
Cloverfield Ln 28312
Cloverhill Pl 28311
Club Cir 28305
Cluny Dr 28303
Clyde St 28303
Clyne St 28311
Coachmans Way 28303
Coachway Dr 28306
Coathill St 28314
Cobbelstone Dr 28311
Cobblestone Pl 28304
Cobra Dr 28303
Coburn St 28312
W Cochran Ave 28301
Cocoanut Ct 28314
Coffman St 28306
Cogdell Rd 28312
Coinjock Cir 28304
Cokefield Dr 28306
Coker St 28311
Colby Ct 28314
Cold Harbor Ct & Dr 28304
Coldwater Dr 28312
Coleman Rd 28312
Coleridge Dr 28304
Coley Dr 28301
Colgate Dr 28304
Colinwood Dr 28303
Coliseum Dr 28306
College St 28301
College Center Dr 28311
Collins St 28303
Colonial Dr 28301
Colonial Park Dr 28311
Colony Dr 28301
Colton Dr 28303
Colts Pride Dr 28312
Columbia Dr 28304
Columbine Rd 28306
Comanche St 28303
Comet Cir 28314
Comfey Ct 28301
Commerce St 28305
Commission Dr 28301
Commonwealth Ave 28301
Community Dr 28312
Companion Ct 28306
Compton Pl 28304
Comstock Ct 28303
Conaway Dr 28314
Concho Ct 28303
Concord Dr 28311
Condor Ct 28306
Cone Cir 28306
Conestoga Dr 28314
Confidence Ct 28301
Congenial Ct 28314
Conifer Dr 28314
Connection Dr 28311
Connie St 28306

Conover Dr 28304
Conrad Ct 28312
Conservation Ct 28314
Constitution Dr 28301
Contentment Ct 28314
Control Tower Rd 28306
Converse Ave & Ct 28303
Cookville Ct 28306
Cool Shade Dr 28303
N & S Cool Spring St 28301
Coolee Cir 28311
Coolidge St 28311
Cooper Rd 28311
Cooper St
1-199 28306
4400-4599 28312
Cope St 28306
Copenhagen Dr 28301
Cora Lee Dr 28303
Corado Cir 28304
Coral Ct 28311
Corapeake Dr 28312
Cordelia Ct 28306
Cordial Loop 28314
Cordoba Ct 28314
Cornell Dr 28306
Cornfield Ave 28314
Corning Pl 28314
Cornish St 28314
Cornstalk Dr 28306
Coronada Pkwy 28306
Coronation Dr 28311
Corporate Rd 28306
Corporation Dr 28306
Corrinna St 28301
Corsegan Rd 28306
Cory Cir 28312
Cosgrove Dr 28306
Cosmo Dr 28304
Cossack Ln 28306
Cotoneastern Ct 28306
Cottage Way 28311
Cottingham Ct 28304
Cotton Top Pl 28314
Cotton Valley Dr 28314
Cottonbelt Way 28314
Cottonwood Ave 28314
Cottonwood Dr 28304
Council Rd 28306
Council St 28301
Country Club Dr 28301
Country Cove Ln 28312
Country Living Ln 28312
Country Side Trailer Park 28304
Countryside Dr
3000-3199 28312
6400-6599 28311
County Line Rd 28306
Courtney St 28301
Courtshire Ct 28303
Courtyard Ln 28303
Cove Creek Pl 28311
Cove Crest Cir 28314
Coventry Rd 28304
Covenwood Dr 28303
Coverly Sq 28303
Covey Dr 28314
Covington Dr 28306
Cowan St 28306
Cowboy Dr 28306
Cowles St 28303
Cozy Branch Rd 28314
Crabapple Cir 28303
Crabtree Ct 28304
Crabwalk Ct 28306
Craft St 28311
Craiglaw Dr 28306
Crain Ct 28306
E & W Cramer Dr 28306
E & W Cranberry Ct 28306
Cranbrook Dr 28301
Cranford Ct 28303
Cranton Cir 28304
Craven St 28306
Crawford St 28301

Crayton Cir 28314
Creed St 28303
Creek Meadows Pl 28304
Creek Path Pl 28311
Creek Side Run 28303
Creekbottom Trl 28312
Creekdew Ct 28306
Crescent Ave 28305
Crescent Commons Way 28314
Cressida Dr 28311
Crest St 28306
Creston Cir 28314
Crestridge Ct 28306
Crestview Dr 28304
Crestwood Ave 28304
Cricket Rd 28306
Crinoline Dr 28306
Cripplecreek Ct 28306
Criss Dr 28303
Crittercreek Rd 28306
Cromwell Ave 28311
Crooked Creek Ct 28301
Cross St 28306
Cross Anchor Dr 28312
Cross Bow Ct 28314
Cross Creek Mall 28303
Cross Creek St 28301
Cross Pointe Ct & Dr 28314
Crossbend Ct 28314
Crosshill St 28312
Crossway Dr 28304
Crowfield Ct 28311
Crown Ave 28303
Crown Ridge Ct 28314
Crows Nest Dr 28306
Croydon Ave 28311
Crystal Dr 28311
Crystal Springs Dr & Rd 28306
Crystobal Rd 28311
Cude St 28306
Cuffley Dr 28314
Culbreth Dr & Rd 28312
Cullen Dr 28304
Culpepper Ln 28304
Cumberland Dr 28311
Cumberland Rd 28306
Cumberland St 28301
Cumberland Bay Dr 28306
Cumberland Creek Dr 28306
Cumberland Gap Dr 28306
Cumbrian Ct 28314
Cunningham St 28303
Currie St 28301
Currin St 28311
Curry Ford Dr 28314
Cushing Dr 28311
Custer Ave 28312
Cutchen Ln 28314
Cypress Rd 28304
Cypress Trace Dr 28314
Daharan Dr 28314
Dahlgren Ave 28314
Dairy Dr 28304
Daisy Ln 28303
Dakota Ct 28303
Dale Dr 28303
Dalehead Ct 28306
Dallas St 28306
Dalmore Dr 28311
Dalton Rd 28314
Damascus Rd 28303
Dan St 28303
Dana Way 28314
Danbury Rd 28311
Dancy St 28301
Dandelion Ln 28306
Dandridge Dr 28303
Dandy Loop Rd 28314
Danforth Pl 28303
Daniels St 28312
Danish Dr 28303
Dante Ln 28314
Danville Dr 28311
Danzante Pl 28306

Daphne Cir 28304
Dapplegray Dr 28306
Darby St 28306
Darien Dr 28304
Dark Branch Rd 28304
Darlington Dr 28311
Darnell St 28314
Darrock Ct 28311
E & W Darrow Dr 28304
Dartmouth Dr 28304
Dartmund Pl 28314
Darvel Ave 28304
Dasher Ln 28306
Dashland Dr 28303
Data Ct 28311
Daughtridge Dr 28311
David St 28304
David J Rd 28312
Davidson Dr 28306
Davie St 28301
Davis Ct 28305
Davis St
100-499 28305
1300-1399 28311
Davis Bynum Dr 28306
Dawnview Pl 28304
Dawnwood Ct & Dr 28311
Day Ct 28314
Daybrook Ct 28314
Daylilly Dr 28314
Dayspring Dr 28314
Daytona Rd 28311
De Koven Dr 28306
De Paul Dr 28311
Deadwyler Dr 28311
Deal St 28306
Deanscroft Pl 28314
Debbie St 28314
Decatur Dr & Pl 28303
December Dr 28314
Decent Rd 28312
Decillion Rd 28312
Decor St 28304
Dedication Dr 28306
Deep Channel Ct 28306
Deep Creek Rd 28312
Deep Hollow Ct 28311
Deep Swamp Ln 28314
Deepwater Ct 28306
Deer Hill Rd 28314
Deer Lakes Rd 28311
Deercreek Ct 28311
Deerhorn Ct 28314
Deerpath Dr 28311
Deertrot Dr 28314
Deerwood Dr 28303
Dees St 28306
Dehavilland Dr 28311
Deland Ave 28303
Delaware Dr 28304
Delbert Dr 28306
Delco St 28311
Delcross St 28306
Delightful Ct 28314
Delina St 28311
Delliert Ct 28303
Dellwood Dr 28304
Delmar St 28304
Delona Gdns 28301
Delta Dr 28304
Demarest Ct 28311
Denada Ct 28303
Denham Ct 28304
Denise Pl 28314
Denison Pl 28314
Dennis Harold Simmons Rd 28312
Dental Ln 28314
Denton Ct 28306
Denver Dr 28304
Departure Ln 28312
Derbyshire Rd 28314
Derc Rd 28306
Derose Ct & Dr 28311
Derrydowne Ct 28304
Des Planes Ave 28306

Desert Cove Cir 28312
Deslan St 28306
Desmond Dr 28314
Dessa Ree Ln 28314
Destiny Dr 28312
Devane St 28305
Devers St 28303
Devlin Dr 28303
Devoe Ave 28314
Devonshire Dr 28304
Devonwood Sq 28314
Dewop Dr 28306
Dewsberry Dr 28304
Dexter Ln 28314
Diamond Rd 28311
Diamond Point Trl 28311
Diane St 28306
Diascond Dr 28306
Dick St 28301
Didsbury Cir 28306
Digby Ct 28306
Dillon Dr 28306
Dinmont Cir 28306
Dinsmore Dr 28306
Diplomat Dr 28304
Dipper Dr 28306
Distinct Cir 28314
Distribution Dr 28311
Diver St 28306
Division Pl 28312
Divot Pl 28312
Dixie Trl 28306
Dixon Dr 28305
Dobbin Ave 28305
Dobbin Holmes Rd 28312
Dobson Dr 28311
Doc Bennett Rd 28306
Docia Cir 28314
Dock St 28306
Dockridge Ct 28304
Dockside Dr 28304
Dockvale Dr 28306
Dockwood Ct 28306
Documentary Dr 28306
Doda Dr 28306
Dodge Ct & Dr 28303
Doe Run Dr 28311
Doggitty Dr 28306
Dogtrot Ct 28311
Dogwood St 28301
Doland Ct 28306
Dolittle Rd 28306
Doll St 28303
Domain Dr 28311
Dominion Rd 28306
Domino Dr 28306
Don St 28306
Donabell Dr 28306
Donaldson St 28301
Doncaster Dr 28304
Donna St 28306
Donny Brook Ct 28314
Donovan St 28301
Donray Dr 28303
Doonvalley Dr 28306
Dorado Cir 28304
N & S Dorchester Pl 28314
Dorenchi Rd 28306
Dorian Rd 28306
Dormy Cir 28314
Dornoch Dr 28303
Dorset Ave 28303
Dorsey Pl 28306
Dorsey St 28314
Dothan Dr 28306
Double J 28312
Double Oaks Dr 28306
Dougkirk Ct 28304
Douglas St 28312
Dove Hunter Cir 28306
Dovenby Ct 28306
Dover Ct 28304
Dovetail Dr 28314
Dow Ct 28314
S Dowfield Dr 28311
Dowless Dr 28311

Downing Rd & St 28312
Downs Pl 28306
Doyle Ct 28304
Dragonfly Dr 28306
Dragonhead Rd 28311
Dragoon Rd 28306
Drake St 28301
Drakestone Ct 28301
Draper Rd 28312
Draughon Rd 28312
Draughone Ave 28306
Draycott Rd 28311
Drayton Rd 28303
Drew Ct 28311
Driftstone Cir 28311
Driftwood Dr 28306
Druid St 28301
Druid Cross Rd 28314
Drury Ln 28303
Dublin Ct 28314
Duchess Dr 28304
Duck Ct 28314
Duck Pl 28306
Dude Ct 28303
Dudley Dr 28314
Dudley Rd 28312
Dudwright Ct 28306
Duff Ct 28303
Duggins Way 28312
Duke St
100-299 28304
3300-3399 28306
Dullcrest Ln 28312
Dumbarton Rd 28306
Dumfries Dr 28306
Dumont Pl 28303
Dunbane Ct 28311
Dunbar Dr 28303
Dunblane Way 28311
Dunbridge Dr 28314
Dunbrook Ct 28312
Duncan St 28303
Duncastle Rd 28314
Dundee Rd 28303
Dundennon Dr 28306
Dundle Rd 28306
Dunebuggy Ln 28306
Dunham Dr 28304
Dunholme Dr 28304
Dunkirk Ct 28306
Dunleith Pl 28311
Dunloe Ct 28311
Dunmore Rd 28303
Dunn Rd 28312
Dunvegan St 28311
Dunwoody Dr 28306
Duplinwood Rd 28311
Dupont St 28301
Durango Ct 28304
Durant Dr 28304
Durden Ln 28303
Durham St 28301
Durness Ct 28306
Duroc Ct 28314
Durwood Dr 28311
Duval Dr 28304
Dwain Dr 28305
Dwelle Dr 28306
Dwight Cir 28311
Dwirewood Dr 28303
Dyke St 28306
Dysart Pl 28314
Eagle Ct 28304
Eagle St 28306
Eagle Crest Ln 28306
Eagle Pass Cir 28304
Eaglechase Dr 28314
Earl St 28303
Early St 28311
Easley Ln 28303
Eastcliff Ct 28304
Eastdale Dr 28311
N Eastern Blvd 28301
S Eastern Blvd
511A-511B 28301
100-899 28301

900-2699 28306
Eastgate St 28312
Easthampton Ct & Rd 28314
Eastman Rd 28314
Eastover St 28312
Eastwood Ave 28301
Eaton St 28301
Eau Gallie Dr 28311
Eccles Dr 28301
Echo Ln 28303
Eclipse Dr 28311
Ecru Ct 28314
Eddies Ln 28311
Edelweiss Pl 28306
Eden Rd 28306
Eden Cross St 28303
Edenwood Dr 28303
Ederton Ct 28304
Edgar St 28301
Edgecombe Ave 28301
Edgedale Dr 28304
Edgehill Rd 28314
Edgeside Ct 28303
Edgeware Ct 28314
N & S Edgewater Dr 28303
Edgeway Loop 28314
Edgewood St 28306
Edinburgh Dr 28303
Edmeston Dr 28311
Edmonton Rd 28304
Edna St 28311
Edward St 28301
Edwards St 28312
Edwinstowe Ave 28311
Egret Ct 28303
Egypt Rd 28314
Eichelberger Dr 28303
Elba St 28312
Elcar Dr 28306
Elcona St 28311
Elcone Dr 28306
Elder Ln 28304
Elderberry Dr 28311
Eldorado Rd 28306
Eldridge St 28301
Eleanor Ave 28312
Electra Ct 28304
Elementary Dr 28301
Elijah B Pl 28306
Elizabeth Dr 28304
Elk Ct 28301
Elkdale Ln 28311
Elkhorn Dr 28314
Elkins St 28304
Elkton Ct 28304
Ella Mae Dr 28314
Ellen Ln 28306
Ellenbrook Dr 28312
Ellerslie Dr 28303
Ellesmere Dr 28311
Ellie Ave 28314
Ellington St 28305
Elliot Bridge Rd 28311
Elliot Farm Rd 28311
Elliotte Cir 28301
Ellipse Cir 28306
Ellis St
700-899 28301
900-1099 28305
Ellis Jackson Rd 28306
Ellsworth Dr 28304
Elm St
1043A-1043B 28303
Elmhurst Dr 28304
Elms Thorpe Dr 28312
Eloise St 28311
Elon St 28306
Elsie Cir 28312
Elstree Pl 28314
Elton Dr 28306
Elvira St 28303
Elwood Dr 28306
Embassy Ct 28306
Ember Heart Ln 28312
Emeline Ave 28303
Emerald Dr 28311
Emerson Ave 28306
Emerywood Rd 28312
Emily St 28301
Emory Ct 28311
Empire Ct 28306
Empress Ln 28304
Enchanting Ct 28314
Enclave Dr 28301
Encore St 28312
End Pl 28314
Endsleigh Ct 28311
Enfield Dr 28303
England Dr 28306
Englewood Dr 28312
English Ct 28314
English Oaks Dr 28314
English Saddle Dr 28314
Enloe St 28306
Enniskillen Rd 28312
Enoch Ave 28301
Enterprise Ave 28306
Enthorpe Ct 28306
Ephraim Dr 28312
Epps Rd 28306
Erie Dr 28311
Ernest St 28301
Ervin Alston Rd 28306
Escapade Dr 28306
Essex Pl 28301
Essie Davis Rd 28306
Esther Ln 28312
Ethelored St 28303
Etta St 28311
Eucalyptus Rd 28304
Eufaula St 28301
Eugene St 28306
Eunice Dr
200-300 28311
302-398 28311
7500-7799 28306
Eureka Ave 28311
Eutaw Vlg N 28303
Evans Dairy Rd 28312
Evans Harris Ln 28311
Evanston St 28314
Everena Dr 28301
Everglade Dr 28303
Everitte St 28306
Everton Dr 28306
Ewe Ct 28314
Ewing Dr 28304
Exchange Pl 28311
Executive Pl 28305
Exeter Ln 28314
Expo St 28311
Ezras Ct 28304
Faber St 28304
Facility Dr 28301
Fagins Way 28304
Fair St 28306
Fair Oaks Dr 28311
Faircloth St 28312
Fairfax Ave & Pl 28303
Fairfield Rd 28303
Fairforest Dr 28304
Fairgrove Ct 28312
Fairington Ln 28305
Fairmont Ct 28304
Fairpoint Dr 28314
Fairvale Dr 28303
Fairview St 28312
Fairway Dr 28305
Fairwinds Ln 28306
Fairwood Ct 28305
Faison Ave 28304
Faith Dr 28314
Falcon Crest Cir 28304
Falcon Villiage Sh Ctr 28304
Falkirk Dr 28304
Falkland Ct 28311
Falkner Pl 28303
Fallberry Dr 28306
Falling Creek Ln 28304
Falling Tree Rd 28306
Falling View Ct 28306
Fallingwood Rd 28311
Fallow Run 28312
Falls Church Ct 28311
Fallstaff Dr 28306
Falmont Pl 28314
Fame Ln 28306
Family St 28314
Family Lodge Dr 28303
Fanning Cir 28314
Faraday Pl 28303
Fargo Dr
1800-1999 28304
2000-2199 28306
Farley Pl 28303
Farm Circle Rd 28306
Farmall Dr 28306
Farmbrook Rd 28303
Farmers Rd 28311
Farmington St 28314
Farmview Dr 28311
Farthing Ct 28303
Farwell Dr 28304
Fashion Ln 28304
Fawn Ct & Rd 28303
Fay Hart Rd 28306
Fayette Ave 28301
Fayetteville Rd 28304
Feathercombe Ct 28306
Feldspar Ln 28314
Felix Ct 28314
Fen Ct 28314
Fenmark Pl 28314
Fenwick Pl 28303
Fergueson Dr 28311
Ferncliff Ct 28314
Ferncreek Dr & Pl 28314
Ferndale Ln 28306
Ferndell Dr 28314
Fernfield Rd 28306
Fernwood Dr 28311
Ferrand Dr 28306
Ferrell Ave 28312
Ferrell Dr 28303
Ferris St 28306
Festus Ave 28303
Fieldcrest Dr 28303
Fields Rd 28312
Fife St 28311
Fig Ct 28305
Fillyaw Rd 28303
Filter Plant Dr 28301
Final Approach Dr 28312
Finch Rd 28306
Finnegan St 28303
Fire Wood Ct 28314
Firefly St 28306
Firethorn Dr 28311
Fisher Rd 28304
Fisher St 28301
Fishing Hole Trl 28314
Fishing Pier Rd 28306
Fiske Dr 28311
Fitzgerald Pl 28311
Five Sisters Ct 28311
Fl Mcdaniel Rd 28312
Flagstone Ct 28303
Flamingo Dr 28306
Flanagan Pl 28304
Flat Rock Dr 28311
Flea Hill Rd 28312
Fledger St 28305
Fleetwood Dr 28305
Fleishman St 28303
Fleming St 28311
Fletcher Ave 28303
Fleur Dr 28306
Flint Dr 28304
Flint Mill Ct 28306
Flintcastle Rd 28314
Flintlock Ct 28304
Flintshire Rd 28304
Flintwood Rd 28314
Floras Ln 28311
Florida Dr
3200-3399 28301
3400-3499 28311
Florida Drive Ext 28311
Flowering Bradford
Way 28306
Flying Cloud Ln 28314
Foch St 28306
Fogarty Dr 28311
Folger St 28314
Folkstone Cir 28306
Fontana St 28301
Footbridge Ln 28306
Foothill Ln 28311
Ford Ln 28312
Fordham Dr & Rd 28304
N Forest Dr 28303
Forest Rd 28305
Forest Creek Dr 28303
Forest Gump Dr 28304
Forest Hills Dr 28303
Forest Lake Rd 28305
Forest Lodge Dr 28306
Forest Oak Dr 28304
Forestview Dr 28304
Fork Rd 28314
Formosa Ct 28306
Forse House Cir 28306
Forsythe St
1-99 28304
100-499 28303
500-599 28304
Forsythia Dr 28306
Fort Bragg Rd
1200-1699 28305
1700-3399 28303
Fort Worth 28312
Fortress Ln 28306
Foster Dr 28311
Foster Gwin Ln 28304
Foundation Ln 28301
Fountain Grove Cir 28304
Fountainhead Ln 28301
Four Ply Ln 28311
Four Wood Dr 28312
Fourhorse Ct 28311
Fourseasons Rd 28311
Fox Ct 28314
Fox Fern Dr 28314
Fox Grove Cir 28304
Foxberry Rd 28314
Foxcroft Dr 28311
Foxdenton Pl 28303
Foxfire Rd 28303
Foxglenn Dr 28314
Foxhall Rd 28303
Foxhill Pl 28314
Foxhound Ct 28314
Foxhunt Ln 28314
Foxlair Dr 28311
Foxlake Dr 28314
Foxton Ct 28304
Foxtrail Dr 28311
Foxtrot Dr 28303
Francis Dr & St 28306
Franciscan Dr 28306
Frank St 28306
Frank Welsh Rd 28306
Frankfort Cir 28303
Frankie Ave 28304
Franklin St 28301
Franzia Dr 28306
Fraser Dr 28303
Frease Rd 28312
Fred Cates Ave 28304
Fredonia Dr 28311
Fredrick Dr 28314
Freeman St 28301
Freeport Rd 28303
Fremont Cir 28311
Frenchorn Ln 28314
Fresno Dr 28303
Friar Ave 28304
Friendly Rd 28304
Frink St 28301
Frontera Pl 28306
W Frontier Ave 28312
Frostwood Pl 28304
Fruitwood Ct 28311
Fuji Dr 28303
Fulham Rd 28311
Fuller St 28305
Fulton St 28312
Furlong Pl 28312
Furman Dr 28304
Furnish Dr 28304
Future St 28304
Gables Ct 28301
Gables Dr
1000-3399 28301
3400-3699 28311
Gaddis Dr 28306
Gaddy Ave 28301
Gaelic Dr 28306
Gaffsail Dr 28301
Gainey Rd 28306
Gairloch Dr 28304
Galatia Church Rd 28304
Galax Dr 28304
Galena Rd 28314
Gallant Ridge Dr 28314
Gallberry Ln 28312
Galleria Dr 28303
Galloway Dr 28303
Gallup Dr 28304
Galvants Ferry Ln 28306
Galveston Dr 28303
Gambrills Ct 28304
Gamewell Cir 28312
Garden Ct 28311
Garden Grove Ln 28303
Gardenia Ave 28311
Gardenwood Ct 28314
Gardner St 28311
Garfield Dr 28303
Garland Dr 28314
Garner St 28311
Garnet Dr 28311
Garrett St 28303
Garvin St 28306
Gary St 28311
Gaston Ct 28314
Gaston Village Ln 28312
Gate Post Ct 28314
Gateway Dr 28306
Gatewood Dr 28304
Gatwick Rd 28311
Gavins St 28303
Gayron Dr 28311
Gaza Cir 28314
Gazella Cir 28303
Geiberger Dr 28303
Gem Ct 28314
Gemini Dr 28303
General Lee Ave 28305
Geneva Ct 28306
Genoe Dr 28312
Gentle Bend Way 28314
Gentle Breeze Ct 28306
Gentry St 28301
George Dr 28314
George St 28301
George Owen Rd 28306
Georgetown Cir 28314
Georgia Ave 28312
Geranium Dr 28314
Gerbing Cir 28306
Gerhart St 28312
German St 28301
Gertrude St 28303
Gettysburg Dr 28301
Geyser Peak Rd 28306
Gibson St 28301
Gigi St 28311
Gilabend Dr 28306
Gilbert Rd 28312
Gilbert Edge Rd 28312
Gilbert Mclaurin Rd 28312
Gillespie St
100-599 28301
600-4199 28306
Gillingham Cir 28304
Gillis St 28301
Gillis Hill Rd
100-599 28306
2200-2599 28304
2700-3099 28306
Gilmore St 28301
Ginger Cir 28314
Ginseng Dr 28312
Gip Rd 28312
Girard Ave 28311
Gist Pl 28306
Glacier Cir 28311
Glade Ct 28311
Gladiola Dr 28306
Gladstone Ct 28304
Gladys St 28303
Glamorgan Rd 28312
Glanis Dr & Pl 28304
Glasgow Dr 28303
Glen Pl 28305
Glen Canyon Dr 28303
Glen Iris Dr 28314
Glen Raven Dr 28306
Glen Reilly Dr 28314
Glenallen St 28314
Glenbarry Cir & Pl 28314
Glenbrook Rd 28314
Glenburney Dr 28303
Glencorra Dr 28314
Gleneagles Ct 28311
Glenlea Cir 28314
Glenola St 28311
Glenpine Dr 28306
Glenridge Rd 28304
Glenrock Ct & Dr 28303
Glensford Dr 28314
Glenville Ave 28303
Glenwick Dr
1800-2099 28304
3200-3299 28312
Glenwood Dr 28305
Glenwood Ln 28312
Glidden St 28301
Glynn Mill Farm Dr 28306
Goat Aly 28312
Gobbler Ln 28312
Godfrey Dr 28303
Godwin Cir 28312
Goins Dr 28306
Gola Dr 28301
Gold Hill Dr 28312
Golden Rd 28311
Goldeneye Ct 28303
Goldenrain Dr 28314
Goldfinch St 28306
Golf Dr 28314
Good Middling Dr 28304
Gooden Dr 28314
Goodview Ave 28305
Goodyear Ave 28303
Goose Creek Ln 28304
Gordon Way 28303
Gore Ave 28311
Gorham Aly 28301
Gorrenberry Dr 28311
Gosfield Pl 28304
Gotts Ln 28306
Gowan Ln 28311
Grace Ave 28301
Grace Black Cir 28301
Grace View Pl 28305
Grackle Dr 28306
Gradersi Rd 28312
Grady St 28306
Grafton Ave 28301
Graham Rd 28304
Grambling Ct 28311
Grampian Ct 28304
Granada Dr 28314
Granby Ct 28311
Grand Prix Dr 28303
Grande Oaks Dr 28314
Grandford Rd 28306
Grandview Dr 28314
Granger Pl 28303
Granite Sq 28311
Grant Ave 28312
Grantham Rd 28312
Granther Ct 28311
Grantsboro Rd 28312
Granville Dr 28303
Grape Arbor Dr 28312
Grassmere Pl 28304
Grassy Branch Dr 28304
Graves St 28311
Gravley Pl 28306
Gray St
200-299 28301
5700-5799 28311
Gray Goose Loop 28306
Graye Fryers Ln 28312
Grayhawk Pl 28311
Graylyn Pl 28314
Graystone Rd 28311
Graysville Ln 28306
Grayton Pl 28311
Grazing Ct 28312
Great Oaks 28303
Green Cir 28304
Green St 28301
Green Bush Ave 28312
Green Creek Rd 28314
Green Heron Dr 28306
Green Meadow Ct &
Rd 28304
Green Shore Cir 28311
Green Tree Ct 28314
Green Valley Rd
3100-3299 28301
3300-3599 28311
Green Way Dr 28314
Greenbay Rd 28303
Greenbriar Dr 28303
Greendale Dr 28304
Greengate Hill Rd 28303
Greenland Dr 28305
Greenleaf Dr 28314
Greenleigh Ct 28303
Greenock Ave 28304
Greenridge Dr 28306
Greensboro St 28301
Greenwood Dr 28311
Gregg Ct 28311
Gregory Ct & St 28311
Grenada Rd 28306
Grenedine Dr 28306
Gressitt Point Ln 28306
Grey Fox Ln 28303
Greycliff Dr 28314
Greyfield Rd 28303
Greyson Ct 28314
Greywalls Ct 28311
Griffin St 28312
Grimes Rd 28306
Grip Dr 28312
Gristmill Rd 28314
Grooms St 28303
Groton Ave 28305
Grouper Dr 28306
Grouse Run Ln 28314
Grove St 28301
Grove View Ter 28301
Growers Way 28314
Grundy Pl 28314
Guildhall Pl 28311
Guildsmen Ct 28306
Guilford Pl 28303
Guinevere Ct 28314
Gulf Dr 28311
Gumwood Dr 28306
Gunston Ct 28303
Gunter Ct 28306
Gurley St 28305
Gus Dr 28306
Guthrie St 28301
Guy Cir 28303
Gwen St 28312
Habersham Dr 28304
Hacienda Dr 28306
Hackamore St 28306
Hackney Loop 28304
Haddock St 28303
Hadley Ct 28301
Hagley Ct 28306
Hagram Dr 28304
Haigh St 28312

Hair Rd 28312
Halberton Ln 28314
Halcyon Cir 28306
Hale St 28301
Half Moon Cir 28311
Halfacre Ct 28312
Halifax Dr 28303
Hall St 28301
Hall Park Rd 28306
Hallberry Dr 28314
Hallmark Rd 28303
Hallstead Cir 28303
Hambeass Dr 28304
Hamburg Dr 28303
Hamilton St 28301
Hamlet St 28306
Hammerfest Cir 28306
Hammersley Rd 28306
Hammond St 28312
Hampshire Dr 28311
Hampton Rd 28311
Hampton Oaks Dr 28314
Hampton Ridge Rd 28311
Hanbury Ln 28304
Hangar Rd 28306
Hanley Ct 28314
Hanna St 28304
Haonani Dr 28303
Harbin Walk Ln 28306
Harbison Ct 28311
Harbor Rd 28311
Harbour Pointe Pl 28314
Harcourt Cir 28304
Hardwick Ln 28306
Hardy St 28306
Hargett Ct 28303
Hargrove Ct 28303
Harlee St 28303
Harlow Dr 28314
Harmon Pl 28314
Harmony Ln 28314
Harmony Hall Way 28303
Harper St 28312
Harrington Rd 28306
Harris St 28301
Harrisburg Dr 28306
Harrison St 28301
Harrogate Ct 28311
Harrow Pl 28304
Harry Truman Rd 28311
Hartfield Ct 28311
Hartford Pl 28303
Hartshorne Ct 28311
Hartwell Rd 28304
Harvard Dr 28306
Harvest Ct 28306
Harvey Dr 28301
Harvey Dale Dr 28301
Hasbrook Ct 28304
Hastings Dr 28311
Hatcher Ln 28312
Hatherleigh Dr & Pl 28304
Hatteras Ct 28311
Havelock St 28306
Haven Ct 28301
Haverford Ct 28314
Haverhill Dr 28314
Havilah Rd 28303
Hawfield Dr 28303
Hawick Dr 28312
Hawley Ln 28301
Hawthorne Rd 28301
Hay St
208-1A-208-1B 28301
100-799 28301
800-1299 28305
101-1-101-2 28301
Hayden Ln 28304
Haymarket Rd 28306
Haymount Ct 28305
Hayston Ct 28306
Haywood St 28312
Haywood Vann Dr 28312
Hazelcrest Dr 28304
Hazelhurst Dr 28314
Hazelwood Ave 28314
Hazleton Ct 28304
Headwind Dr 28306
Hearthstone Dr 28314
Heartland Dr 28314
Heartpine Dr 28306
Heathcliff Ct 28303
Heathcote Dr 28314
Heather Brooke Dr 28306
Heather Ridge Dr 28311
Heatherly Ct 28312
Heavens Trl 28312
Hedgelawn Way 28311
Hedgepeth St 28306
Hedrick Dr 28303
Helaman Ct 28303
N Helen St 28303
Helmsley Dr 28314
Helmsman Dr 28306
Hemlock Dr 28304
Hemphill Cir 28303
Henderson Ave 28301
Hennessy Pl 28303
Henriette Dr 28306
Henry St 28306
Hereford Dr 28314
Heriot Dr 28311
Heritage Ln 28312
Hermania Way 28306
Hermitage Ave 28304
Hermosa Ct 28314
S Herndon St 28303
Heron Lake Ct 28306
Herring Gull Dr 28306
Hersey Cir 28312
Hewitt Dr 28311
Hialeah Ct 28311
Hibernia Dr 28314
Hibiscus Rd 28311
Hickory St 28303
Hickory Hill Rd 28301
Hickory Knoll Rd 28314
Hickory Ridge Ct 28304
Hickory View Ct 28314
Hickorywood Dr 28314
Hicks Ave 28304
Hidden Creek Dr 28314
Hidden Forge Dr 28304
Hidden Lake Loop 28304
Hidden Oaks Dr 28306
Hidden Oasis Dr 28312
Hidden Pond Dr 28311
Hidden Valley Dr & Pl 28311
Higgins St 28303
High St 28312
High Kite Pl 28314
High Rock Ln 28314
Highfield St 28303
Highgrove St 28303
Highland Ave 28305
Highpoint Ct 28304
Highstan Ct 28304
Highview Dr 28306
Hilco Dr 28314
Hildreth Pl 28314
N Hill Rd 28303
Hillcrest Ave 28305
Hilliard Ct & Dr 28311
Hillsboro St 28301
Hillside Ave
100-299 28301
7500-7599 28311
Hilltop Ave 28305
Hillview Ave 28301
Hilton Dr 28311
Himalayan Rd 28312
Hinsdale Ave 28305
Hissop St 28311
Hiwassee Pl 28304
Hodge St 28303
Hodhat Dr 28314
Hoe Ct 28314
Hoffer Dr 28301
Hogan St 28311
Hoke Loop Rd 28314
Holbrook Ln 28314
Holder Ln 28311
Holland St 28311
Holland Park Ave 28314
Hollins Dr 28306
Hollister Dr 28306
Holloman Dr 28312
Hollow Springs Ct 28311
Holly Ln 28305
Holly Oak Dr 28314
Hollyberry Ln 28314
Hollydale Ln 28314
Hollyhock Ct 28303
Hollyridge Pl 28304
Hollywood Blvd 28312
Holman St 28306
Holmfield Rd 28306
Holstein Dr 28311
Holyrood Ct 28311
Homeplace Ct 28311
Homestead Ct & Dr 28303
Homewood St 28306
Hondo Dr 28306
Honeycutt Rd 28311
Honeydew Ln 28312
Honeysuckle Dr 28304
Hood Ave 28301
Hooks St 28306
Hope Mills Rd
2598A-2598B 28306
100-2499 28304
2500-2999 28306
Hopedale St 28306
Hopkins St 28314
Hopper Rd 28314
Horizon Dr 28312
Hornbeam Rd 28304
Hornbuckle Dr 28311
Horncastle Ct 28311
Horne St 28312
Horner Dr 28306
Horse Chestnut Pl 28304
Horse Tail Rd 28306
Horsepen Br 28304
Horseshoe Rd 28303
Horton Pl 28314
Hoss St 28306
Hoswick Ct 28306
Hot Dog St 28306
Hotspur Pl 28306
Hounds Chase Ct 28311
Houndsear Ct 28311
House Mover Dr 28304
Houston Rd 28311
Howard Clark Rd 28306
Howards Ln 28301
Howe Ct 28306
Howell St 28301
Hubbard St 28301
Huckleberry Dr 28311
Huckleberry Rd 28312
E Hudson St 28306
Huff St 28311
Hugh Shelton Loop 28301
Hughes Rd 28312
Hull Rd 28303
Hulon St 28311
Humboldt Pl 28314
Hummingbird Pl 28312
Humphrey Ln 28301
Huntcroft Dr 28312
Hunter Cir 28304
Hunters Run 28304
Hunters Point Dr 28311
Hunters View Dr 28312
Huntington Rd 28303
Huntleigh Ct 28303
Huntsfield Rd 28314
Huntsman Ct 28303
Huntsville Cir 28306
Hurley Dr 28304
Hurleys Landing Dr 28306
Huron St 28303
Hurrican Ln 28314
Hushpuppy Ct 28311
Huske St 28305
Hutchins Ct 28304
Hutton Pl 28303
Hyannis Dr 28304
Hybart St 28303
Hyde Pl 28306
Hyman Pl 28303
Icarus Cir 28304
Iceland Dr 28306
Ida St 28306
Ideal Trailer Park 28314
Idlewild Ct 28306
Idlewild Dr 28311
Idlewood Ct 28314
Idol Ct 28306
Idyllic Ln 28311
Ijams St 28301
Ike St 28303
Ile Ct 28314
Illinois Ct 28304
Immanuel Dr 28306
Impala Dr 28312
Imperial Dr 28303
Independence Place
Dr 28303
Indian Dr 28312
Indian Creek Rd 28312
Indian Wells Cir 28312
Indiana Ct 28312
Indigo Bush Pl 28304
Industrial Dr 28301
Ingate Dr 28314
Inglenook Cir 28314
Ingleside Dr 28303
S Ingleside Dr 28314
Inglewood Ln 28314
Ingram St 28301
Inman Cir 28306
Innisfree Pl 28306
Innovative Ct 28312
Interban Dr 28314
Interchange Dr 28311
Inverness Dr 28304
Inwood Ct 28303
Ira St 28306
Ireland Dr
1000-1999 28304
2000-2499 28306
Irene St 28301
Iron Hill Loop 28312
Iron Wheel Rd 28311
Irongate Dr 28306
Ironwood Dr 28304
Iroquois St 28303
Irrigation Dr 28312
Irving Dr 28301
Irvington Ct 28314
Irwin Cir 28303
Isabella Ln 28312
Isham St 28304
Isley St 28305
Isometric Ct 28306
Issac Dock Dr 28314
Italy St 28301
Ithaca Pl 28311
Ivan Dr 28306
Ivanhoe Ct 28314
Iverleigh Cir 28311
Ivey Commons Rd 28306
Iveystone Ct 28301
Ivory Ct 28311
Ivy Rd 28303
Ivyridge Ct 28314
J Herbert Rd 28312
J W Dawson Ct 28306
Jackie St 28312
Jackie Hood Ln 28312
Jacklyn Rd 28306
Jacks Ford Dr 28303
Jackson Ave 28312
Jacob St
1100-1199 28311
1200-1250 28312
1251-1300 28311
1301-1321 28312
1322-1398 28311
1323-1399 28312
1400-1499 28311
Jacobs Creek Cir 28306
Jade Ct 28311
Jakes Aly 28306
Jamaica Ct 28314
James Dail Rd 28312
James Hamner Way 28311
Jamestown Ave 28303
Janet St 28303
Janice St 28303
Janike Ln 28314
Japonica Dr 28304
Jarmarkis Ln 28312
Jarmon Ct 28306
Jarvis St 28314
Jasmine Dr 28306
Jason Ct 28314
Jason Keith Ct 28306
Jasper St 28301
Java Dr 28311
Jean St 28306
Jean Bullock Rd 28312
Jedridge Dr 28306
Jefferey Dr 28314
Jefferson Dr 28304
E & W Jenkins St 28306
Jenna Shane Dr 28306
Jennifer Ln 28314
Jennings Ln 28303
Jennings Farm Rd 28314
Jenny Rd 28314
Jenson Ct 28311
Jereens Creek Rd 28312
Jericho Dr 28314
Jernigan St 28306
Jerrico Dr 28314
Jerry Dr 28312
Jersey Dr 28314
Jesse Dr 28311
Jessus Christ Way 28312
Jet Cir 28314
Jewel Ave 28306
Jim Johnson Rd 28312
Jimmy Ct 28306
Jimree Ave 28312
Jody Cir 28306
Joefield Dr 28311
Joel St 28304
John St 28305
John B Carter Rd 28312
John Brady Rd 28306
John Deere Rd 28312
John Hall Rd 28312
John Marshall Rd 28304
John Smith Rd 28306
Johnson Rd 28312
Johnson St
100-999 28303
1001-1799 28303
6100-6499 28311
Johnson Farm Rd 28311
Jonas Reep Dr 28306
Jonathan Ct 28314
Joncee Dr 28312
Jones St 28301
Jordan St 28305
Joseph St
100-199 28303
2300-2499 28306
Jossie St 28311
Joy Dr 28312
Joyce St 28301
Jubilee Dr 28306
Judah Ct 28314
Judd St 28305
Judd Newton Dr 28304
Judson Church Rd 28312
Judy Dr 28314
Julia St 28301
Julian Dr 28304
Juliet Dr 28303
Julliard Dr 28311
July Ct 28314
Jumalon St 28306
Junco Pl 28304
June Dr & Pl 28314
Juneberry Ln 28304
Juni Dr 28303
Junior St 28306
Juniper Dr 28304
Jupiter Dr 28303
Jura Dr 28303
Justin Ct 28304
Kamenbury Dr 28311
Kansas Ct 28312
Kara Ct 28304
Karen St 28312
Karen Lake Dr 28303
Karl Rd 28306
Karr Dr 28314
Kathryn St 28306
Kathy St 28303
Katie St 28306
Katonah Dr 28314
Kaywood Dr 28311
Kearny Ave 28314
Keats Pl 28306
Keeler Ct & Dr 28303
Keg Ct 28314
Keithville Dr 28303
Kelburn Dr 28311
Kellam Cir 28311
Kellogg St 28301
Kelly St 28305
Kellys Landing Rd 28306
Kelmscot Ct 28303
Kelso Pl 28306
Kelton Cir 28303
Kemper Ct 28303
Kempton Pl 28304
Kenbrian St 28311
Kendall Dr 28301
Kendall Grove Ct 28306
Kendallwood Dr 28314
Kenleigh Dr N 28314
S Kenleigh Dr 28304
Kenmore Dr 28304
Kenmure Pl 28311
N Kennedy St 28301
Kennesaw Dr 28314
Kennicot Ct 28311
Kennybunk Dr 28304
Kensington Cir 28301
Kensington Park Rd 28311
Kent Rd 28306
Kent St 28311
Kentberry Ave 28301
Kentwell Ct 28303
Kentyre Dr 28303
Kenwood Dr 28311
Kerfield Ct 28306
Kerr Pl 28314
Kerrow Rd 28314
Kershaw Loop 28314
Keswick Dr 28304
Key Ct 28314
Keyboard Ln 28304
Keystone Ct 28304
Kids Cove Cir 28311
Kienast Dr 28314
Kilkeel Ct 28311
Kilkenny Rd 28312
Killcare Ct 28311
Killdeer Dr 28303
Killeen Rd 28303
Kilmory Dr 28304
Kilt Rock Way 28306
Kim St 28306
Kimberly Dr 28306
Kimberwicke Dr 28311
Kimbolton Dr 28306
Kimbrook Dr 28314
Kimridge Rd 28314
Kincross Ave 28304
Kindley Dr 28311
Kindness Ct 28314
King Rd 28306
N King St 28301
S King St 28301
King Arthur Dr 28314
King Charles Rd 28306
King George Dr 28303
King George Apts 28303
King James Ln 28306
Kingdom Way 28301
Kingdom Estate Dr 28301
Kingfisher Dr 28306
Kings Creek Dr 28311
Kings Lynn Loop 28304
Kingsberry Ln 28304
Kingsford Ct & Rd 28314
Kingsgate Dr 28314
Kingsland Dr 28306
Kingsley Rd 28314
Kingstree Dr 28304
Kingsway Ct 28304
Kingswood Rd 28303
Kinkead Ct 28314
Kinlaw Rd 28311
Kipling Cir 28303
Kipp Cir 28314
Kirbirnie Ln 28306
Kirby Ct 28304
Kirk Dr 28306
Kirkcaldy Ct 28314
Kirkland Dr 28301
Kirkwall Rd 28311
Kirkwood Dr & Pl 28303
Kisco Dr 28303
Kistler Ct 28304
Kitimat Ct 28311
Kittrell Dr 28311
Kittridge Dr 28314
Kizer Dr 28314
Klondyke Dr 28311
Knightbridge Pl 28311
Knob Ct 28303
Knollwood Dr 28304
Knotty Elm Loop 28304
Knotty Oak Ct 28314
Knox St 28306
Kodiak Dr 28304
Kooler Cir 28305
Korea Cir 28306
Kornbow St 28301
Kornbow Lake Rd 28303
Kort Cir 28306
Kozy Trailer Park 28304
Krista Dr 28303
Kubinski St 28312
Kumquat Dr 28306
Kyle St 28301
L R Bullard Cir 28312
La Dunham Rd 28312
Lacewood Ct 28306
Lacy St 28305
Lacy Crumpler Ln 28312
Ladley St 28306
Ladonia Dr 28314
Ladson Cir 28311
Lady Bird Dr 28306
Lady Cheryl Dr 28301
Lady Viola Dr 28301
Ladyslipper Dr 28306
Lagoon Dr 28314
Lagu Pl 28314
Laguna Dr 28314
Laguna Vista Dr 28311
Lainey Ln 28314
Laird Ct 28304
Lake Ave 28301
Lake Bend Dr 28311
Lake Clair Pl 28304
Lake Club Dr 28304
Lake Farm Rd 28306
Lake Francis Pl 28304
Lake Gordon Dr 28312
Lake Mont Ct 28311
Lake Pine Dr 28311
Lake Shannon Dr 28312
Lake Stone Pl 28311
Lake Terrace Ct 28304
Lake Trail Dr 28304
Lake Valley Dr 28303
Lake View St 28311
Lake Villa Dr 28304
Lakebarry Cir 28304
Lakebluff Pl 28304
Lakecrest Dr 28301
Lakedale Dr 28306

Street	ZIP
Lakehaven Dr	28304
Lakeheath Ct	28306
Lakehurst Dr	28304
Lakeland St	28301
Lakemeadow Dr	28304
Lakemoore Pl	28304
Lakeport Cir	28304
Lakeridge Dr	28304
Lakeshore Dr	28305
Lakeside Dr	28311
Lakeview Dr	
300-399	28311
1400-1499	28305
2400-2799	28306
Lakeway Dr	
5900-5999	28304
6000-6599	28306
Lakewell Cir	28306
Lakewood Ct	28303
Lakewood Dr	28306
Lamar Rd	28311
Lamb St	28305
Lambert St	28305
Lamboll Dr	28306
Lambrusco Pl	28306
Lamon St	28301
Lamplighter Dr	28306
Lamure Dr	28311
Lancaster Rd	28303
Lancers Dr	28306
Landau Rd	28311
Landmark Dr	28311
Landover Dr	28312
Landrum Ct	28304
Lands End Dr	28304
Lands End Rd	28314
Langdon St	28301
Lansdowne Rd	28314
Lansford Dr	28314
Lansing Ct	28303
Lantana Ln	28314
Lanyard Ct	28312
Laraine St	28303
Laramie Ct	28303
Larchmont Rd	28311
Laredo Ct	28303
Largo Pl	28314
Lariat Ct	28303
Lark Ct	
100-199	28306
900-999	28314
Lark Dr	28314
Lark St	28312
Larkfield Ct	28314
Larkhall Dr	28304
Larkhaven Ct	28303
Larkspur Dr	28311
Larry St	28306
Larue Ct	28303
Larwood Dr	28306
Lasalle Ave	28303
Lass St	28314
Latonea Dr	28306
Latrobe Ave	28304
Laughton Dr	28306
Laura Ann Ct	28314
Laurel St	28303
Laurel Lakes Rd	28301
Laurel Oak Dr	28314
Laurelwood Pl	28306
Lauren Mcneill Loop	28303
Laurent Dr	28312
Lava Trl	28311
Laverne Dr	28306
Law Rd	28311
Lawhorne Dr	28304
Lawndale St	28306
Lawnwood Dr	28304
Lawrence Ave	28301
Lawson St	28314
Layton Dr	28314
Lazy Acres St	28306
Lazybrook Ct	28314
Leabrook Dr	28306
Leacroft Ct	28311
Leanna Dr	28312
Lee Hill Cir	28306
Lee Wright Ct	28312
Leeds Ct	28304
Leesburg Ct	28311
Leffew Ave	28304
Legacy Ln	28314
Legend Ave	28303
Legion Rd	28306
Leisure Ln	28314
Leland Dr	28306
Lemont Dr	28303
Lemonwood Rd	28311
Lemuel Farm Rd	28312
Lena Spell Dr	28312
Lennox Dr	28303
Leona Ave	28314
Leroy Dr	28301
Leslie Dr	28314
Lester Dr	28311
Levenhall Dr	28314
Levi Rd	28314
Levy Dr	28305
Lewis Ln	28304
Lewis St	28303
Lewisburg Ct	28306
Lewiston Ct	28314
Lexi Ln	28314
Liberty Ln	28311
Libeth Pl	28314
Lido St	28301
Lieber St	28303
Lifestyle Rd	28312
Light Wood Ct	28314
Lillian Pl	28306
Lilly Dr	28305
Lime St	28314
Lime Kiln Ln	28312
Limestone St	28312
Limwert Ln	28306
Lincoln Dr	28301
Lincolnshire Pl	28306
Linda Ave	28306
Lindale Ct	28314
Lindbridge Dr	28306
Linden Rd	28312
Lindfield Ct	28314
Lindsay Cir & Rd	28304
Lindsey Dr	28306
Lineman Dr	28306
Link St	28301
Linkwood Dr	28311
Linton Ct	28306
Linton Hall Rd	28311
Linwood Rd	28306
Lioncoward Dr	28314
Lionel Ln	28311
E & W Lionfish Ct	28306
Lionshead Rd	28311
Lisa Ave	28314
Litchfield Pl	28305
Litho Pl	28304
Little Ave	28312
Little Dr	28314
Little Ln	28304
Little Beaver Dr	28306
Little Bridge Rd	28311
Little Gem Dr	28314
Little John Ct	28306
Little Rock Pl	28306
Littlestone Ct	28311
Live Oak Dr	28306
Lively Ct	28306
Livermore Dr	28314
Livestock Ln	28314
Livingston Dr	28311
Lizzie Ln	28312
Loader Ct	28306
Loblolly Ct	28314
Lochcarron Dr	28304
E Lochhaven Dr	28314
Lochland Ct	28311
Lochness Ct	28304
Lochstone Ct	28303
Lochview Dr	28311
Lock Trl	28312
Lockamy Dr	28306
Lockerbie Ct	28306
Lockheart Cir	28303
Locklear St	28306
Lockridge Rd	28311
Locks Creek Rd	28312
Locks Creek Church	
Rd	28312
Lockwood Ct & Rd	28303
Locust St	28301
Locust Grove Dr	28314
Lofton Dr	28311
Log Cabin Rd	28312
Logan Ct	28304
Loganberry Dr	28304
Lois Cir	28312
Lombardy Dr	28304
London Ct	28311
Londonderry Pl	28301
Lone Pine Dr	28306
Lonestar Rd	28303
Long St	28312
Long Creek Ct	28311
Long Iron Dr	28312
Longbranch Ct & Dr	28303
Longfield Rd	28306
Longhill Dr & Pt	28311
Longhorn Dr	28303
Longleaf Dr	28305
Longmoor Dr	28314
Longparrish Ct	28304
Longview Dr	
100-799	28311
5700-5799	28306
Longview Drive Ext	28311
Longwood Dr & Pl	28314
Look Ave	28311
Lookout Pl	28311
Loon Dr	28306
Loquat Dr	28306
Lorell Ct	28304
Lost Tree Ct	28314
Lothbury Dr	28304
Lotus Dr	28303
Lou Dr	28311
Loucada Ct	28301
Loufield Dr	28311
Louisburg Pl	28311
Louise Cir & St	28314
Lounging Ln	28314
Lovell St	28311
Lovington Dr	28303
Lowbranch Ct	28306
Lowell Harris Rd	28314
Lowery Ct	28303
Lox Ct	28314
Loxley Dr	28314
Loyalty Dr	28301
Loyola Ln	28311
Lucas St	28301
Lucerne St	28303
Ludgate Trl	28306
Ludin Ln	28312
Ludlow Pl	28314
Lufkin Cir	28311
Lugsail Ln	28306
Lull Water Dr	28306
Lumberly Ln	28303
Lumina Pl	28306
Lunar Dr	28304
Lune Cir	28314
Lupin Dr	28306
Lure Ct	28311
Luther Ave	28304
Luther Dr	28303
Lydia St	28304
Lynbrook Ct	28314
Lynette Cir	28314
Lynhurst Dr	28314
Lynn Ave	28301
Lynnhaven Dr	28312
Lyon Rd	28303
Lyric Ln	28314
Lytteton Dr	28311
Mabe Rd	28306
Mac Dr	28311
Maccumber Ct	28311
Macedonia Church Rd	28312
Macgregor Ct	28304
S Machami Pl	28301
Macie Ave	28312
Mack Simmons Rd	28312
Macks Ln	28312
Macon Dr	28306
Macqueen Ct	28314
Maddox Ct	28304
Madiera Ct	28311
Madison Ave	28304
Madonna Dr	28311
Madrid Dr	28303
Maffitt Ct	28303
Magellan Ct & Dr	28311
Maggie Cir	28314
Maggie St	28303
Magma Dr	28311
Magnolia Ave	28305
Mahogany Rd	28314
Maiden Ln	28301
Maitland Dr	28314
Majestic Ct	28306
Malina St	28311
Mallard Ct	28311
Mallard Way	28314
Malloy Cir	28312
Malloy St	28305
Maloney Ave	28301
Malvern Cir	28314
Mammoth Dr	28311
Manassas St	28304
Manchester St	28303
Mandalay St	28303
Mandolin Ct	28305
Mango Cir	28304
Mangrove Dr	28314
Mangum Ct	28314
Manley St	28306
Mann St	28301
Manning Cir	28306
Manor Haven Ct	28304
Manorbridge Ct	28306
Manos St	28303
Mansfield Ct	28306
Manteo St	28303
Maple St	28306
Maple Hill Ln	28306
Maple Leaf Ct	28306
Maplewood Ct	28314
Maracay Ct	28314
Marachino Ln	28311
Marble Ct	28311
March Dr	28314
Marchland Dr	28303
Marcia St	28303
Marcus James Dr	28306
Mariah Ct	28314
Marie Dr	28311
Marigold Dr	28306
Mariners Landing Dr	28306
Marion Ct	28301
Mariposa Dr	28311
Marita Dr	
3000-3399	28301
3400-3498	28311
Mark Ave	28306
Market Sq	28301
Market Hill Dr	28306
Marketview Ct	28301
Marklett Dr	28312
Marksbury Dr	28314
Marlborough Rd	28304
Marlin Ct	28306
Marlowe Dr	28314
Marquette St	28311
Marquis Pl	28303
Marracco Ct	28314
Mars Pl	28301
Marsh Rd	28306
Marsh St	28301
Marshall Rd	28303
Marshtree Ln	28314
Marshwood Lake Rd	28306
Marsville Ct	28306
Martha Ct	28314
Martin Ct	28304
Martin Rd	28312
Martindale Dr	28304
Martine Rd	28305
Martinique Ln	28314
Martinleer Ct	28311
Mary St	28301
Mary Jordan Ln	28311
Marykirk Dr	28304
Maryland Dr	28311
Mason St	28301
Matchwood Ct	28306
Mateo Cir	28312
Mathau Ct	28304
Matilda Ct	28304
Matlock Pl	28314
Matt Hair Rd	28312
Matthew Johnson Rd	28312
Matthews St	28301
Maude St	28306
Maverick Ct	28303
Mawood St	28314
Maxine St	28303
Maxtoke Rd	28312
Maxwell St	28301
May St	28306
Mayfair Dr & St	28306
Mayflower Ct	28314
Mayo Ct	28314
Mayodan Dr	28314
Mayview St	28306
Maywood St	28305
Mazarron Dr	28314
Mazie Loop	28305
Mcallister St	28305
Mcalphin Dr	28301
Mcarthur Rd	28311
Mcarthur Landing Cir	28311
Mcbain Dr	28305
Mccarthy St	28303
Mcchoen Dr	
3200-3399	28301
3400-3499	28311
Mccloskey Rd	28311
Mccoy Cross	28311
Mcdaniel St	28301
Mcdonald St	28312
Mcdougal Dr	28304
Mcdowell Ct	28306
Mcduffie St	28301
Mcduffies Mill Rd	28311
Mcfadyen Dr	28314
Mcfayden Rd	28306
Mcfrench Dr	28311
Mcgill Dr	28305
Mcgilvary St	28301
Mcgougan Rd	28303
Mcgrath Ct	28311
Mcinnis St	28306
Mciver St	28301
Mckeithan St	28301
Mckerre Dr	28303
Mckimmon Rd	28303
Mckinley Dr	28311
Mckinnon Rd	28312
Mckinnon Farm Rd	28304
Mcknight Dr	28306
Mclamb Dr	28301
Mclaurins Way	28312
Mclean Trl	28311
Mcmillan St	28301
Mcnatt St	28304
Mcneil Rd	28312
Mcneill Cir	28303
Mcphee Dr	28305
Mcpherson Ave	28303
N & S Mcpherson	
Church Rd	28303
Mcrae Dr	28305
Meadow Ln	28306
Meadow Creek Rd	28304
Meadow Wood Rd	28303
Meadowbrook Dr	28304
Meadowcroft Dr	28311
Meadowmont Ln	28306
Meadowsweet Dr	28301
Meadowview Ln	28312
Mechanic St	28301
Media Dr	28314
Medical Dr	28304
Medina Dr	28306
Medlo Rd	28303
Medway Ct	28306
Meed Ct	28303
Meeting St	28301
Megan Ct	28314
Meharry Dr	28311
Melba Dr	
3200-3399	28301
3400-3499	28311
Melba St	28301
Melbourne Dr	28314
Melissa Ct	28314
Mellwood Dr	28306
Melody Ln	28304
Melrose Rd	28304
Melstone Dr	28311
Melvin Pl	28301
Melvin Rd	28312
Melvinville Ct	28312
Memorial Dr	28311
Memory Rd	28306
Memory St	28304
Memphis Dr	28311
Mena Dr	28306
Mendel Ct	28304
Menola Ct	28301
Mercedes Dr	28312
Mercury Ct	28311
Merganser Ct	28306
Meridion St	28314
Meriweather Dr	28306
Merle Ct	28312
Merlin Ct	28306
Mernell Rd	28303
Merrick Ct	28311
Merriefield Ct	28301
Merrimac Dr	28304
Merritt Dr	28314
Merry Maple Ln	28304
Merry Oaks Dr	28304
Mesa Ct & Dr	28303
Mescal Ct	28303
Mesquite Dr	28306
Messenger St	28311
Metromedical Dr	28304
Metthame Dr	28306
Michelle Ct	28304
Michie Pl	28314
Michigan Dr	28311
Mid Iron Ct	28312
Mid Pine Rd	28306
Midan Ln	28306
Middle Rd	28312
Middle Creek Ct	28314
Middle River Loop	28312
Middlebury Pl	28303
Middlecoff Dr	28303
Middlefield Pl	28304
Middleham Ct	28311
Middlesbrough Dr	28306
Middlesex Rd	28306
Middleton Ct	28306
Midhurst Ct	28306
Midland Ct	28306
Mike St	28303
Milburn Dr	28314
Milden Rd	28314
Mildred St	28301
Miles Ct	28303
Milford Rd	28303
Mill Cove Ct	28314
Mill Creek Rd	
3600-3699	28306
3700-4699	28312
Mill Park Dr	28306
Mill Pond Ct	28314
Millan Dr	28305
Millbrook Rd	28303
Miller Ave	28304
Millmann Rd	28304
Millstone Ln	28306
Millstream Rd	28314
Milton Dr	28304
Mimosa Ln	28301
Mindenhall Ct	28311
Mingary Ave	28306
Mini Ranch Trl	28314
Ministry Rd	28312
Minnow Ct	28312
Minor St	28301
Mintz Ave	28303
Mintz Mill Rd	28303
Minurva Ct & Dr	28301
Miracle Ln	28311
Miracle Hill Dr	28312
Mirror Lake Dr & Pl	28303
Missenburg Ct	28314
Mission Dr	28304
Mistletoe Ct	28312
Misty Meadow Ln	28304
Mittie Ln	28314
Mittie Johnson Rd	28312
Mobile Ln	28311
Mobius Rd	28312
Mockernut Dr	28312
Mohawk Ave	28303
Molly Ct	28312
Monagan St	28301
Moncreiffe Rd	28311
Mondavi Pl	28314
Monica St	28311
Monks Walk Ct	28311
Montana Rd	28306
Montclair Rd	28314
Monterey Ct	28314
Montgomery St	28301
Monticello Ave	28301
Montoro Ct	28314
Montrose Dr	28314
Monza Ct	28314
Moody St	28306
Moonstone Ct	28311
Moore St	28301
Moorgate Cir	28304
Morehead Ave	28303
Morgan Ln & St	28305
Morganton Rd	
1300-2199	28305
2200-3799	28303
3800-6399	28314
6401-6499	28314
Morganton St	28305
Moriston Rd	28314
Morley Dr	28314
Morningside Dr	28311
Morris St	28314
Morrowick Ct	28304
Morrozoff Dr	28306
Morton Ct	28314
Moss Ct	28306
Mosswood Ln	28311
Mossy Cup Ln	28304
Mottram Ct	28306
Mount Gilead Dr	28314
Mount Haven Lake Dr	28306
E & W Mountain Dr	28306
Mountain Ash Ln	28311
Mountain Home Dr	28314
Mountroyal Ct	28306
Mourning Dove Pl	28314
Mudhole Dr	28312
Muirfield Ave	28306
Mulberry St	28303
Mullins Ave	28301
Mullis St	28303
Mulranny Dr	28311
Mum Creek Ln	28304
Munford Dr	28306
Munsey Rd	28306
Murchison Rd	
4029A-4029B	28311
400-3199	28301
3400-6299	28311
Muriel Dr	28306
Murphy Rd	28312
Murray Fork Dr	28314

Street	ZIP
Murray Hill Rd	
200-799	28303
800-899	28314
Musical Ct	28314
Muskegon Dr	28311
Myers Ct	28311
Myron Rd	28306
Myrover St	28305
Myrtle Dr	28301
Myrtle Ln	28312
Myrtle St	28305
Nag Dr	28311
Nakoma Way	28306
Nan St	28314
Nance St	28304
Nandina Ct	28311
Nantuckett Ct	28306
Naphtaly St	28312
Naple St	28311
Narwhal Ct	28314
Nash Rd	28306
Nashville Dr	28306
Nassau Dr	28314
Natal St	28306
Natchez Loop	28304
Nathan Dr	28303
Nathaniel Ave	28306
Nato Rd	28306
Nature Ln	28306
Navajo St	28303
Navarro St	28314
Navy Rd	28306
Naylor Ln	28312
Nc Highway 210 S	28312
Nc Highway 53 W	28312
Nc Highway 87 S & W	28306
Neal St	28312
Nebular Rd	28312
Ned Ashley Rd	28312
Needham Dr	28311
Needle Ln	28306
Nelson Ave	28314
Neptune Dr	28303
Nesbit Rd	28311
Nessee St	28314
Netherdale Dr	28314
Netherfield Pl	28314
E & W Netherland Dr	28303
Nettletree Ln	28301
Neville St	28301
New Ellenton Rd	28312
New Moon Dr	28306
Newark Ave	28301
Newburgh Dr	28311
Newcastle Rd	28303
Newgate St	28306
Newland Cir	28314
Newmarket Ct	28304
Newport Rd	28314
Nexus Ct	28304
Ney Ct	28312
Niarada Dr	28306
Nickey Ave	28301
Nickfield Rd	28303
Nicklaus Dr	28303
Nielsen Dr	28306
Nighthawk Pl	28314
Nimocks Ave	28301
Nix Rd	28314
Nobie St	28306
Nora Dr	28312
Norberry Ct	28304
Norcliff Dr	28304
Nordic Dr	28304
Norfolk Ct	28311
Norge St	28311
Normal Ave	28301
Norman Pl	28314
North St	28301
Northampton Rd	28303
Northbank St	28306
Northeast Blvd	28312
Northfield Ct	28303
Northgales Cir	28314
Northstone Pl	28303
Northumberland Ct	28314
Northview Dr	28303
Northwest Ave	28301
Norton Dr	28304
Norwick Dr	28314
Norwood St	28305
Nostalgia Ln	28311
Notland Ct	28304
Notlob Pines Dr	28306
Notlobpines Dr	28306
Notre Dame Pl	28304
Notting Hill Rd	28311
Nottingham Dr	28311
Nova Glen Dr	28311
Noxon St	28306
Nuffield Rd	28312
Nugget Ct	28311
Nutbush Pl	28314
Nuthatch Rd	28304
Nutley Dr	28303
Nutmeg Pl	28311
W Oak St	28306
Oak Hill Dr	28312
Oak Knolls Dr	28314
Oak Meadow Ct	28314
Oak Tree Ct	28304
Oakcrest Dr	28301
Oakdale Dr	28311
Oakdale Apts	28304
Oakfield Ct	28314
Oakgrove Dr	28314
Oakhill Ln	28314
Oakland Ave	28306
Oakland Dr	28301
Oakley Dr	28311
Oakmont Cir	28311
Oakridge Ave	28305
Oakstone Dr	28314
Oakview Dr	28304
Oakwood St	28303
Oates Dr	28311
Oberlin Ct	28303
Oblu Ct	28306
Ocala Dr	28311
Ocarina Cir	28311
October Pl	28314
Odd Ct	28303
Odom Dr	28304
Odom Farm Rd	28312
Offing Ct & Dr	28314
Offshore Dr	28305
Oglethorp Ct	28303
Ohmer Dr	28314
Ok Ct	28304
Oklahoma Ct	28304
Ola Burns Dr	28306
Old St	28301
Old Bunce Rd	28314
Old Castle Dr	28314
Old Colony Pl	28303
Old Elizabethtown Rd	28306
Old English Ct	28304
Old Farm Rd	28314
Old Fayetteville Rd	28312
Old Field Rd	28304
Old Gate Rd	28314
Old Hunt Pl	28314
Old Mcpherson Church Rd	28303
Old Raeford Rd	28304
Old Raleigh Rd	28312
Old Savannah Church Rd	28312
Old Shaw Rd	28303
Old Spears Rd	28304
Old Vander Rd	28312
Old Wilmington Rd	28301
Oldstead Dr	28306
Oldtown Dr	28314
Ole Bluff Mill Rd	28306
Olena Ln	28306
Olive Rd	28305
Oliver St	28304
Olivia Ct	28311
Olted Rd	28314
Olympia Ct	28301
Omni Ct	28314
Onie Ct	28314
Onslow St	28311
Ontra Dr	28311
Onyx Ct	28311
Opal Ct	28311
Openview Dr	28312
Orange St	28301
Orangeburg Dr	28312
Orbie Cir	28306
Orchard Dr	28303
Oregon Ct	28304
Oriole Ct	28306
Orlando St	28306
Ormond Ct	28314
Ormskirk Dr	28304
Orville St	28312
Osage Ct	28303
Osceola Dr	28301
Osprey Pl	28303
Ostendorf Ln	28311
Otis F Jones Pkwy	28301
Our St	28314
Outback Dr	28312
Outwood Pl	28306
Overbrook Dr	28303
Overland Ct & Rd	28306
Overlook Dr	28301
Overton Pl	28303
Overview Dr	28306
Owen Dr	
100-1899	28304
1900-4299	28306
Owen Park Ln	28304
Owls Head Rd	28306
Oxford St	28312
Oxnop Ct	28306
Ozie Dr	28312
Pacific Ave	28314
Packard Pl	28311
Paddington Ct	28304
Paddington Pl	28314
Paddlefish Ct & Dr	28306
Paddlewheel Rd	28314
Paddy Hollow Ct	28312
Painters Mill Dr	28304
Paisley Ave	28304
Pala Verde Dr	28304
Paladin St	28304
Palm Cir	28304
Palm Springs Dr & Rd	28311
Palma Pl	28314
Palmer Dr	28303
Palmetto Ln	28304
Palomar St	28314
Palomino Dr	28311
Pamalee Dr	
800-1599	28303
1600-1999	28301
Pamlico Rd	28304
Panelway Pl	28304
Pantego Dr	28314
Papa St	28306
Par Dr	28311
Parable St	28312
Paradise Ct	28314
Parcstone Ln	28314
Pardoner Pl	28306
E & W Park Ave, Dr & St	28305
Park Hill Dr	28311
Park Knoll Ln	28304
Park Lane Cir	28303
Parker Dr	28311
Parkhill Dr	28314
Parkridge Dr & St	28306
Parkview Ave	28305
Parkwood Cir	28303
Partners Way	28314
Partridge Ct	28304
Partridge Dr	28304
Partridge Rd	28306
Pasture Ln	28312
Pate Dr	28305
Patina Ct	28301
Patricia Dr	28311
Patrick Dr	28314
Patterson Cir	28301
Patton St	
5000-5299	28303
6300-6399	28311
Paul St	28312
Paulson Dr	28304
Pavilion Dr	28304
Pawling Ct	28304
Pawtucket Pl	28304
Paxton Dr	28303
Peabody Pl	28311
Peace St	28301
Peaceful Farm Dr	28312
Peachtree St	28305
Peacock Dr	28306
S Peak Dr	28306
Pear Ln	28301
N Pearl St	28303
Pearman Dr	28306
Peatmoss Dr	28311
Pebble St	28311
Pebble Ridge Ct	28311
Pebblebrook Dr	28314
Pecan Dr	28303
Pechman Ct	28303
Pecos Ct	28303
Pedro Dr	28303
Pee Jay Ln	28303
Peele St	28311
Pegasus Ln	28306
Pelican Ct	28306
Pella Pl	28314
Pelt Dr	28301
Pence Dr	28311
Pendleton Ct	28314
Penelope Dr	28314
Penfield Dr & Pl	28314
Penguin Dr	28312
Penhurst Ct	28311
Penick Ct	28314
Pennmark Pl	28301
Pennsylvania Ave	28301
Penny Dr	28306
Pennystone Dr	28306
Penrose Dr	28304
Penshore Dr	28314
Penwall Ct	28303
People St	28304
Pep Cush Dr	28312
Pepperbush Dr	28304
Pepperchase Dr	28312
Peppermint Ct	28314
Pepperridge Dr	28311
Pepperwood Dr	28311
Pepsi Ln	28301
Perch Dr	28306
Peregrine Pl	28306
Pericat Dr	28306
Peridot Ct	28311
Periwinkle Dr	28306
Perley St	28305
Pershing St	28301
Person St	
100-1099	28301
1100-1199	28312
Perth St	28314
Peteland Dr	28312
Peterson Pl	28301
Pettigrew Dr	28314
Petunia Ave	28306
Pheasant Ct	
100-199	28306
5400-5499	28311
Philadelphia St	28301
Phillies Cir	28306
Phillippine Dr	28306
Phillips St	28301
Phoenician Dr	28306
Picador Ct	28314
Pickerel St	28306
Pickettence Ln	28312
Pickford Rd	28311
Pickington Cir	28303
Pickney Ct	28314
Piedmont Ave	28306
Pierce St	28305
Pierron Dr	28303
Pigeon River Rd	28306
Pigeonhouse Ct	28311
Pike Pl	28306
Pikeville Ct	28306
Pilona Ct	28314
Pilot Ave	28303
Pin Oak Ln	28314
Pine St	28311
Pine Bark Ct	28306
Pine Cone Ln	28306
Pine Creek Ct	28314
Pine Haven Dr	28306
Pine Hill Rd	28305
Pine Lake Dr	28311
Pine Meadow Dr	28303
Pine Needle Ct	28314
Pine Springs Dr	28306
Pine St Ct	28311
Pine Valley Loop	28305
Pinebrook Dr	28314
Pinebuff Ct	28311
Pinecrest Dr	
100-399	28305
2500-2999	28306
Pinedale Ct	28314
Pinelawn Ct	28306
Pineview Dr	
1600-1699	28314
2400-2799	28306
Pineview Rd	28311
Pineview St	28311
Pinewood Ter	28304
Piney Rd	28306
Piney Creek Pl	28304
Ping Ct	28312
Pink Dr	28314
Pinnacle Dr	28306
Pinpoint Rd	28312
Pintail Dr	28311
Pinto Ct	28303
Piping Plover Ct	28306
Pirates Landing Dr	28312
Pisgah Dr	28306
Pitcairn Dr	28306
Pitt St	28306
Pittsfield Dr	28303
Placharn Dr	28314
Placido Pl	28306
Plainfield Ct	28304
Plainview Ct	28304
Plantation Rd	28301
Plantation Garden Blvd	28303
Plateau Ct & Rd	28303
Platinum St	28311
N Platte Rd	28303
Player Ave	28304
Plaza Dr	28304
Pleasant Loop	28311
Pleasant St	
6300-6499	28314
7000-7099	28306
Pleasant Oak Dr	28314
Pleasant View Dr	28312
Pleasantburg Dr	28312
Plowright Dr	28311
Plum St	28301
Plum Ridge Rd	28306
Plummers Ln	28301
N & S Plymouth St	28312
Poe St	28306
Poinciana Ln	28306
Poinsett Ct	28311
Point Pl	28301
Point East Dr	28306
Point Hill Dr	28306
Point Pleasant Ln	28303
Poland Ct	28314
Polo Dr	28306
Polygon Pl	28306
Pompton Dr	28314
Pond St	28301
Ponderosa Dr	28304
Ponsett Ct	28311
Ponton Dr	28314
Pony Run Dr	28304
Poole Dr	28303
Poplar Dr	28304
Poplar Hill Rd	28312
Poppy Ct	28303
Porpoise Cir	28306
Port Ellen Dr	28312
Porterfield Ct	28301
Portnall Pl	28311
Porto Pl	28314
Portsmouth Dr	28314
Possum Holler Rd	28306
Post Ave	28301
Post Oak Dr	28311
Potash Pl	28314
Potomac Rd	28304
Potters Ct	28314
Poultry Pl	28314
Powatan St	28301
Powell St	28306
Prairie Ct	28303
Prestige Blvd	28314
Preston Ave	28301
Preston Woods Ln	28304
Prestwick Dr	28303
Previs Rd	28306
Prices Cir	28306
Pridemore Ct	28303
Pridgeonfarm Rd	28306
Priego Pl	28314
Primrose Dr	28301
Prince St	28301
Prince Charles Dr	28311
Princess Ann Dr	28306
Princeton St	28306
Prioress Dr	28306
Pritchett Rd	28314
Private Road 100 Rd	28306
Privateer Way	28306
Privet Ct	28311
Proctor Ct	28311
Procurement Cir	28303
Produce Ln	28312
Production Dr	28306
Progress St	28306
Providence Rd	28301
Pryer St	28312
Public Works Dr	28301
Puddingstone Dr	28311
Pudy St	28314
Pueblo Ct	28303
Puffin Pl	28306
Pugh St	28305
Pummill Rd	28306
Pumpkin Rd	28304
Pungo Pl	28314
Purdue Dr	
1500-1599	28303
1600-1899	28304
Puritan St	28306
Purple Dr	28314
Purple Martin Pl	28306
Putte Williams Rd	28303
Pyramid Way Ct	28314
Quail Ct	28303
Quail Forest Dr	28306
Quail Hollow Ct	28304
Quailmeadow Dr	28314
Quailridge Dr	28304
Quailwood Dr	28314
Quality Rd	28306
Quarry Dr	28303
Quarry Hollow Dr	28306
Quartz Dr	28311
Quebec Ct	28304
Queen St	28303
Queen Anne Loop	28306
Queensberry Dr	28303
Queensdale Dr	28304
Quick St	28306
Quiet Cv	28304
Quiet Pine Rd	28314
Quietwood Pl	28304
Quill Ct	28312
Quillan St	28303
Quimby Ct	28303
Quincy St	28301
Rabakdu St	28314
Raccoon Path	28312
Racefan Dr	28306
N & S Racepath St	28301
Rachel Rd	28311
Radar Rd	28306
Radcliff Ct	28311
Radial Dr	28311
Radnor St	28314
Radstock Dr	28306
Radway Ct	28306
Raeburn Ct	28314
Raeford Rd	
1300-2599	28305
2600-2799	28303
2800-3498	28303
2800-2800	28304
2801-3499	28303
3600-8199	28304
S Raeford Rd	28304
Rafe Ave	28312
Rail Fence Ct	28314
Railroad St	28312
Rainbow Ct	28311
Raincloud Rd	28306
Rainfall Ct	28312
Rainham Ct	28314
Rainier Dr	28314
Rainsford Dr	28311
Raintree Dr	28304
Raintree Trailer Park	28306
Raleigh St	28301
Ralph St	28301
Ramblewood Dr	28304
Ramona Dr	28303
Rampart Dr	28311
Ramsey St	
400-2899	28301
2812-2812	28302
2900-3398	28301
2901-3399	28301
3400-7899	28311
Ramshorn Dr	28303
Ranaldi St	28314
Ranch House Rd	28314
Rancho Dr	28303
Randinita Dr	28311
Randleman St	28304
Randolph Ave	28311
Randy Reid Rd	28314
Ranger Dr	28311
Rangoon Ct	28314
Rankin St	28301
Rannock Ct & Dr	28304
Ransom St	28312
Rathburn Ct	28303
Raven Pl	28314
Ravencroft Ct	28314
Ravenhill Dr	28303
Ray Ave	28301
Ray Rd	28306
Ray Gillis Rd	28312
Rayconda Rd	28304
Raymede Ct	28311
Raymond St	28301
E Raynor Dr	28311
Rebecca Dr	28303
Reclining Ln	28314
Rectory Ct	28314
Red Cedar Ln	28306
Red Hawk Dr	28312
Red Oak Dr	28306
Red Tip Rd	28314
Redbud Dr	28311
Redcliff Dr	28311
Redding Ct	28314
Redfield Ct	28303
Redfin Dr	28306
Redfish Dr	28306
Redspire Ln	28306
Redstone Dr	28306
Redwood Ave	28314
Redwood Dr	28304
Reedy Branch Rd	28312
Reedy Creek Dr	28314

Reese Mclaurin Rd 28312
Reeves St 28306
Reflex St 28311
Regal Ct 28314
Regan Ave 28301
Regatta St 28301
Regency Dr 28314
Regent Ct 28314
Regiment Dr 28303
Regis Ct 28314
Rehder Dr 28306
Reid Ct 28314
N Reilly Rd 28303
S Reilly Rd 28314
S Reilly Road Trailer
Park 28314
Relaxing Ct 28314
Rembrandt Dr 28314
Remington Rd 28311
Renee Ct 28314
Renfrow Dr 28301
Reno Dr 28306
Renton Ct 28311
Renwick Dr 28304
Republican Rd 28311
Research Dr 28306
Restful Ct 28314
Retirement Cir 28306
Retriever Ct 28311
Revere St 28304
Revolution Rd 28311
Rexdale St 28301
Rexham Dr 28312
Rhemish Dr 28304
Rhew St 28303
Rhodhiss Ct 28311
Rhone St 28312
Richardson Ave 28314
Richardson Park Rd 28306
Richborough Ct 28314
Richmond Dr 28304
Richwood Ct 28314
Ridge Rd 28311
Ridge Line Ct 28301
Ridge Manor Dr 28306
Ridge Pointe Ln 28311
Ridgecrest Ave 28303
Ridgefield Rd 28312
Ridgemont Pl 28314
Ridgeway Ct & Dr 28311
Ridgewood St 28306
Ridley Ct 28303
Rieglewood St 28314
Rigsbee Ct 28306
Rim Rd 28314
Rimrock Ct 28303
Ringtail Dr 28306
Ringwood Rd 28312
Ripley Pl 28314
Ritchie Ct 28314
Ritter Dr 28314
Rivanna Dr 28312
Rivendale Dr 28314
Rivenhurst Dr 28301
Rivenoak Dr 28303
River Rd 28312
River Front Ln 28314
River Landing Dr 28312
River Ridge Rd 28311
Riverbasin Ct 28301
Riverbirch Dr 28311
Riverchase Pl 28306
Rivercliff Rd 28301
Rivercroft Rd 28304
Riverdell Dr 28311
Rivergate Rd 28304
Riverland Dr 28312
Rivermeade Dr 28306
Riverpoint Dr 28306
Riverwalk Pl 28311
Riyhad Rd 28314
Roanoke Rd 28304
Roberta Ct 28304
Robeson St
100-499 28301
600-2499 28305
Robin Pl 28306
Robin St
200-299 28312
4900-4999 28304
Robmont Dr 28306
Rochester Dr 28305
Rock Ave 28303
Rock Branch Rd 28312
Rock Canyon Dr 28303
Rock Creek Ln 28301
Rock Hill Rd 28312
Rock Spring Rd 28314
Rockabye Ln 28312
Rockcliff Rd 28314
Rockcrest Rd 28311
Rockfish Rd 28306
Rockford Dr 28304
Rockhurst Dr 28306
Rockingham Rd 28311
Rockledge Ave 28305
Rockport Dr 28311
Rockridge Ln 28306
Rockrose Dr 28312
Rockspur Ln 28306
Rocktree Ct 28306
Rockwood Dr 28311
Rocky River Rd 28312
Rocoso Pl 28306
Rod St 28306
Rodie Ave 28304
Rodriguez Ct 28303
Rodwell Rd 28311
Rogers Dr 28303
Rolling Hill Rd 28304
Rolling Meadows Ln 28306
Rollingwood Cir 28305
Rolls Ave 28311
Romain Ct 28303
Ron St 28301
Ronald Reagan Dr 28311
Roosevelt Dr 28301
Rosamond Dr 28311
Rosebank Dr 28311
Rosebud Dr 28312
Rosecroft Dr 28304
Rosehill Rd
1900-3299 28301
3300-4999 28311
Rosemary St 28301
Rosemeade Dr 28306
Rosewood Ave
700-899 28301
7700-7899 28314
Ross St 28301
Rosser Dr 28311
Rossmore Dr 28314
Rottingham Ct 28304
Rougemart Dr 28304
Roundtree Dr 28303
Rouse Dr 28306
Rowan St 28301
W Rowan St
400-999 28301
1000-1199 28305
Rowland Cir 28301
Roxie Ave 28304
Roy Dr 28314
Royal Ave 28312
Royal Gorge Rd 28304
Royal Springs St 28312
Royston Ct 28311
Rr55 Brm 28312
Ruby Rd 28311
Rudland Ct 28304
Rudolph St 28301
Rufus Johnson Rd 28306
Rugby Ct 28312
Ruggles Ct 28314
Rulnick St 28304
Rumford Pl 28303
Running Rivers 28312
Runnymede Ct & Dr 28314
Runway Rd 28306
Ruritan Dr 28314
Rush Rd 28305
E & W Russell St 28301
Russellville Ct 28306
Rustburg Dr 28303
Rustic Trl 28306
Rustic Haven Dr 28311
Rustland Dr 28301
Rustlewood Dr 28304
Rusty Rail Rd 28312
Rutgers Ave 28306
Ruth St 28305
Rutherglen Dr 28304
Rutledge Dr 28311
Ruton Ct 28303
Ryan St 28314
Ryder Ct & St 28311
Rye St 28312
Ryefield Dr 28314
Sabine Dr 28303
Sable Dr 28303
Sack St 28303
Saddle Ridge Rd 28311
Sage St 28312
Sage Creek Ln 28305
Sahara Pl 28312
Sailfish Ct 28306
Saint Augustine Ave 28304
Saint Clair Dr 28306
Saint George Rd 28306
Saint Georges Hl 28303
Saint Hardy Ln 28312
Saint Ives Ct 28306
Saint Johns Wood 28303
Saint Josephs Dr 28306
Saint Jude Rd 28312
Saint Julian Way 28314
Saint Lawrence Rd 28306
Saint Louis St 28314
Saint Margarets Pl 28312
Saint Marys Pkwy 28303
Saint Michaels Dr 28306
Saint Patricks Dr 28306
Saint Paul Ave 28304
Salinas Ct 28314
Salisbury Rd 28301
Sallie Ln 28306
Sally Hill Cir 28306
Salmon Dr 28306
Salter Way 28306
Saltwell Pl 28314
Saltwood Rd 28306
Sam Cameron Ave 28301
Samet Dr 28301
Samuel St 28312
San Carlos Ct 28314
San Juan Dr 28314
Sanchez Dr 28314
Sand Dollar Ct 28306
Sandalwood Dr 28304
Sanderosa Rd 28312
Sandfield Ct 28304
Sandhill Dr & Rd 28306
Sandhurst Dr 28304
Sandpiper Rd 28312
Sandra Dr 28304
Sandra Ln 28311
Sandra St 28314
Sandridge Dr 28314
Sandstone Dr 28311
Sandwedge Dr 28311
Sandy Ln 28303
Sandy Acres Loop 28312
Sandy Bay Cir 28312
Sandy Run Rd 28306
Sandy Valley Rd 28306
Sandystone Cir 28311
Sanford Dr 28301
Sangi Ln 28312
Sangria Pl 28306
Santa Fe Dr 28303
Santee Dr 28303
Santiato Dr 28314
Sapcote Rd 28312
Sapona Rd 28312
Sapphire Rd 28303
Sara Ln 28312
Sarah Ln 28306
Sarasota Dr 28311
Saraya Dr 28312
Sarazen Dr 28303
Sardonyx Rd 28303
Satinwood Ct 28312
Satterwhite Pl 28303
Saturn Dr 28303
Savannah Dr 28306
Saw Wood Ct 28314
Sawfish Ct 28306
Sawtooth Dr 28314
Saxony Pl 28304
Scales Ct 28306
Scallywag Rd 28306
Scampton Dr 28303
Scarborough St 28301
Scarecrow Ct 28314
Scarlett Pl 28306
Scary Creek Rd 28312
Scenic View Dr 28306
Schaffer Pl 28314
Schick Pl 28306
Schiller St 28314
Schley Dr 28314
Schmidt St 28303
Schonner Ct 28306
School Rd 28306
School St
200-699 28301
4000-4099 28312
Schram Rd 28306
Schrams Ave 28306
Schreiber Dr 28306
Schult Dr 28314
Scotch Hall Way 28303
Scotia Ln 28314
Scotland Dr 28304
Scott Ave 28301
Scottholm Dr 28306
Scottsdale Dr 28314
Scotty Hill Rd 28303
Scottywood Dr 28303
Scrub Oak Ct 28311
Scully Dr 28314
Scuppernong Dr 28312
Sea Water Ct 28306
Seabrook Rd 28301
Seabrook School Rd
1300-1899 28312
1900-1998 28301
1900-2098 28312
1901-1999 28301
1901-2099 28312
Seafarer Dr 28306
Seaford Dr 28314
Seahorse Dr 28306
Seaton Pl 28303
Seavista Ct 28306
Seawell St 28306
Second St 28306
Sedberry St 28305
Sedgefield Dr 28306
Sedgemoor Rd 28311
Selhurst Ct & Dr 28306
Selkirk Pl 28304
Selma Dr 28306
Selwyn Ct 28303
Selznick Pl 28311
Seminole Dr 28306
Senator Dr 28304
Seneca Dr 28301
Senoma Pl 28314
Sentinel Dr 28314
September Ct 28314
Sequoia Rd 28304
Serenity Pl 28312
Serro Dr 28314
Sessoms Dr & St 28301
Setter Dr 28311
Seven Mountain Dr 28306
Sevenoaks Ct 28303
Sevilla Cir 28303
Sewell St 28301
Sexton Ct 28314
Shaber St 28303
Shadbush Ln 28312
Shade Tree Dr 28306
Shadow Ln 28304
Shadow Oak Ln 28303
Shadow Wood Rd 28306
Shadowlawn Dr 28303
Shadowmoss Dr 28312
Shads Ford Blvd 28314
Shady Ln 28304
Shady Grove Ln 28314
Shady Knoll Ln & Rd 28314
Shadyside Ln 28306
Shagbark Rd 28304
Shaker Town Rd 28312
Shakerstone Dr 28311
Shallow Ridge Dr 28306
Shaloam Ct 28314
Shambrey St 28301
Shamrock Dr 28303
Shamus Ct 28311
Shannon Dr 28303
Sharon St 28306
Sharon Church Rd 28312
Sharpsburg Rd 28311
Shasta St 28314
Shaw Rd
1615A-1615B 28311
100-899 28303
900-2099 28311
2101-2109 28311
Shaw Mill Rd 28311
Shaw Rd Ext 28311
Shawcroft Rd 28311
Shawcross Ln 28314
Shawnee St 28303
Shea Ct 28311
Shearwater Dr 28304
Shedd Ave 28306
Sheely Rd 28303
Sheffield Ct 28314
Shelby Cir 28314
Shem Creek Dr 28306
Shenandoah Dr 28304
Shep Dr 28311
E Shepard St 28304
Sheraton Dr 28303
Sheraton Rd 28312
Sheringham Dr 28311
Sherman Dr
100-699 28301
6400-6499 28306
Sherrod Dr & Pl 28314
Sherwood Dr 28305
Shetland Dr 28303
S Shield Dr 28314
Shillinglaw Cir 28314
Shiloah Church Rd 28306
Shiloh Ct & Dr 28304
Shimmer Dr 28304
Shindine Dr 28311
Shirley Ct 28304
Shively Ct 28304
Shockley Dr 28303
Shopton Ct 28303
W Shore Ct 28306
Shoreline Dr 28311
Shoreway Dr 28304
Short St 28301
Shorthill Ln 28311
Shortridge Rd 28303
Shoshone Pl 28314
Shoveler Ct 28303
Shumont Dr 28314
Shuttle Rd 28311
Sickle Way 28306
Sids Mill Rd 28312
Sierra Ct 28303
Siesta Ct 28303
Sigman St 28303
Silk Ln 28301
Silver Bell Loop 28304
Silver Oaks Dr 28311
Silver Pine Ct & Dr 28303
Silver Ridge Ct 28304
Silverhill Rd 28311
Silverleaf Rd 28312
Silverstone Dr 28304
Sim Cotton 28306
Simmons St 28301
Simmons Carter Rd 28312
Simon St 28312
Simpson St 28305
Sinclair St 28301
Singletary Pl 28314
Singleton Cir 28304
Singletree Ln 28306
Siple Ave 28304
Sisal Dr 28311
Skateway Dr 28304
Skibo Rd
1918A-1918G 28314
200-1899 28303
1900-5199 28314
Skyburst Dr 28314
Skycliff Ct 28311
Skycrest Dr 28304
Skye Dr & Pl 28303
Skyhawk Dr 28314
Skyline Dr 28314
Skyview Dr 28304
Slater Ave 28301
Sleepy Hollow Dr 28311
Slim Cir 28306
Slippery Rock Ct 28311
Sloan Ave 28312
Slocomb Rd 28311
Smiling Faces 28306
Smith Dr 28306
Smith Rd 28306
Smith St
400-499 28301
6100-6199 28306
Smithfield St 28303
Snapper Ct 28306
Snapping Turtle Rd 28312
Snead Ave 28303
Snow Goose Ct 28304
Snow Hill Church Rd 28306
Snowbird Rd 28312
Snowhill Rd 28306
Snowvalley Dr 28311
Snowy Egret Dr 28306
Soacha Ct 28306
Society Ln 28311
Soffe Dr 28312
Somerset Ct 28314
Son Tay Ct 28311
Sonnet Ct & Dr 28303
Sonora Pl 28314
Sonya St 28312
Sophia Bill Rd 28312
Sorghum Way 28314
Sourwood Dr 28301
Southampton Ct 28305
Southbend Dr 28314
Southern Ave 28306
Southern Oaks Dr 28314
Southgate Rd 28314
Southland Dr 28311
Southpaw Dr 28312
Southport Rd 28311
Southridge Ct 28306
Southview Cir 28311
Southwick Dr 28303
Southwind Ct 28312
Southwood Dr 28304
Spain Cir 28306
Spanish Oak Dr 28306
Sparrow Dr
100-499 28306
7500-7599 28314
Spaulding St 28301
Spearfish Dr 28306
Spears Dr 28304
Spell Dr 28306
Spellman Dr 28311
Spellow Ln 28314
Spencer St 28306
Sperry Branch Way 28306
Spike Rail Dr 28312
Spindle Tree Dr 28304
Spinel Dr 28311
Spiralwood Dr 28304
Spivey Dr 28303
Spokane Rd 28304
Spotted Fawn Rd 28314
Spotted Horse Ln 28304
Spotted Owl Ct 28314
Spring Ct 28304
Spring St 28305
Spring Hill Dr 28311
Spring Moss Ln 28306
Spring Valley Rd 28303
Spring Water Ct 28314
Springbrook Pl 28305
Springdale Rd 28312
Springfield Rd 28301
Springrun Rd 28306
Springwood Pl 28304
Spruce Dr 28304
Spruce St 28303
Sprucewood Rd 28304
Spur Ave 28306
Spurge Dr 28311
Spy Glass Dr 28311
Squatting Bear Rd 28312
Squire Ln 28303
Squirrel St 28303
St Andrews Ct 28311
St Martins Pl 28311
St Thomas Rd 28311
Stackhouse Dr 28314
Stackpole Dr 28301
Stacy Weaver Dr 28311
S Staff Rd 28306
Stamper Rd 28303
Stanberry Ct & St 28301
Standard Dr 28306
Standingstone Dr 28311
Standish Ct 28303
Stanford Ct 28314
Stanhope St 28304
Stanley St 28306
Stansfield Dr 28303
Stanton St 28304
Stanworth Dr 28312
Star Ln 28306
Starbeam Dr 28306
Starboard Way 28314
Starbrook Dr 28304
Starburst Dr 28306
Starfish Ct 28306
Starhill Ave 28303
Starling St 28303
Starlit Cir 28312
Starmount Dr 28311
Starpoint Dr 28303
Starview Ln 28312
State Ave 28301
State St 28306
Steamboat Ct 28314
Stedman St 28305
Stedman Cedar Creek
Rd 28312
Steed Ct & Rd 28306
Steephill Ln 28311
Steeple Run Dr 28312
Stein St 28303
Stella St 28301
Stencil Smith Dr 28312
Sterling St 28306
Stetson Ln 28304
Stevens St 28301
Stewarts Creek Dr 28314
Stiles Pl 28314
Stillwater Dr 28304
Stirrup Ln 28312
Stitch St 28314
Stockbridge Ct 28311
Stockport Cir 28303
Stockton Dr 28304
Stokes Ct 28303
Stone Carriage Cir 28304
Stone Mason Ct 28304
Stone Mountain Farm
Rd 28311
Stonebrook Pl 28305
Stonecastle St 28306
Stoneclave Pl 28304
Stonecoal Dr 28311

Street	ZIP
Stonecrop Dr	28312
Stonecutter Cir	28306
Stonehaven Dr	28306
Stonehenge Ct	28306
Stonehouse Ct	28311
Stoneleigh Dr	28311
Stoneridge Rd	28311
Stoneway Ct	28301
Stonewood Dr	28306
Stoney Ct	28306
Stoney Point Loop	28306
Stoney Point Rd	
100-999	28304
7000-8799	28306
9000-9099	28304
9200-9299	28306
Stoneykirk Dr	28314
Stonington Dr	28311
Stornoway Ct	28306
Stout St	28301
Straight Oak Dr	28304
Stratford Rd	28304
Strathdon Ave	28304
Strathmore Ave	28304
Stratsfield Ct	28311
Stretton Ave	28306
Strickland Bridge Rd	
1098A-1098B	28304
700-2399	28304
2400-3199	28306
Stride Ln	28304
Stuart Ave	28301
Stubbs St	28301
Sudbury Dr	28304
Suffolk Ct	28311
Suga Cir	28314
Sugar Bush Ln	28311
Sugar Cane Cir	28303
Sugarbin Ln	28314
Sugaridge Ln	28311
Sugarloaf Pl	28311
Suggs Dr	28306
Sulky Cir	28312
Sullivan Rd	28312
Sullivan St	28301
N & S Sumac Cir	28304
Summer Cove Dr	28306
Summer Duck Rd	28314
Summer Hill Rd	28303
Summer Ridge Rd	28303
Summerberry Dr	28306
W Summerchase Dr	28311
Summerfield Ln	28306
Summerhill Ct	28303
Summerlea Ct & Dr	28311
Summerlin Dr	28306
Summertime Rd	28303
Summerwind Dr	28311
Summitt Ave	28305
Sumner Dr	28303
Sumter Pl	28314
Sun River Rd	28306
Sun Valley Dr	28314
Sunbeam Dr	28314
Sunburst Ct	28312
Sunbury Dr	28311
Sunchase Ct & Dr	28306
Sunday Dr	28306
Sundown Dr	28303
Sunfish Ct	28303
Sunny Acres	28312
Sunny Crest Dr	28314
Sunny Pines Pl	28312
Sunnydale Dr	28312
Sunnyside Cir	28305
Sunnyside School Rd	28312
Sunnyview Ln	28312
Sunrise Cir	28301
Sunset Ave	28301
Sunset Blvd	28312
Superb Dr	28312
Superior Pointe Pl	28301
Suregrow Ct	28314
Surf Pl	28314
Surf Scooter Dr	28311
Surrey Rd	28306
Sussex Dr	28311
Sutton St	28305
Suzanne St	28314
Swain St	28303
Swainey Ave	28303
Swallowtail Ct	28306
Swan Island Ct	28311
Swann St	28303
Sweetbay Cir	28311
Sweetbriar Loop	28306
Sweetgum Cir	28304
Sweetgum Rd	28306
Sweetie Rd	28312
Sweetwater Dr	28311
Swiftcreek Dr	28303
Swindon Dr	28312
Switzerland Dr	28306
Sycamore Ct	28301
Sycamore St	28306
Sycamore Dairy Rd	28303
Sydney Dr	28304
Sykes Loop	28314
Sykes Pond Rd	28304
Sylvan Rd	28305
Symphony Ct	28312
Syrene Dr	28306
Tablerock Dr	28303
Tabor Ct	28303
Tabor Church Rd	28312
Tacoma Ct	28303
Taft St	28306
Tahoe Ct	28303
Tailwinds Ct	28312
Tallpine Dr	28306
Tallstone Dr	28311
Tally Dr	28303
Tally Ho Dr	28303
Tallywood Dr	28303
Tallywood Shopping Ctr	28303
Talus Rd	28306
Tamarack Dr	28311
Tammy St	28311
Tampa Ave	28311
Tampico Ct	28303
Tamworth Ct	28314
Tanager Ct	28306
Tanbark Ct	28303
Tangerine Dr	28304
Tanglewood Dr	28311
Tango Dr	28312
Tangora Ln	28304
Tannen Ct	28314
Tapestry Trl	28306
Tar Kiln Dr	28304
Tarare Pl	28304
Taraway Dr	28304
Tarbert Ave	28304
Tareyton Rd	28314
Tarheel Dr	28314
Tarmore Ct	28311
Tarpon Ct	28306
Tarrytown Dr	28314
Tart St	28306
Tartan Ct	28311
Tarwick Ave	28304
Tashina Cir	28306
Tattersal Ct	28306
Tatum Dr	28314
Taurus Way	28311
Tavistock Ct	28304
Tayberry Ct	28306
Taylor Dr	28301
Teachers Dr	28301
Teague St	28306
Teal Ct	28311
Technology Dr	28306
Teeters Rd	28306
Tega Cay Dr	28312
Telegraph Cir	28301
Telfair Dr	28303
Telluride Ct	28304
Tempe Ct	28303
Temperance Dr	28314
Temple Ave	28301
Templeoak Ave	28312
Ten Ten Rd	28312
Tennessee Dr	28306
Tenter Dr	28306
Tern Pl	28311
Terrace Ct	28314
Terrals Creek Rd	28312
Terrapin Dr	28312
Terry Cir	28304
Terry Hill St	28311
Tettenbury Dr	28306
Tew St	28306
Texas Cir	28304
Thackeray Dr	28306
Thad St	28301
Thames Dr	28306
Thamesford Rd	28311
Thatcher Trl	28306
Thatford Ct	28304
Thelbert Dr	28301
Thicket Rd	28314
Thistle Ct	28303
Thomas Dr	28304
Thomas Trailer Park	28312
Thomasville Ct	28304
Thompson Ave	28306
Thorlieshope Dr	28311
Thorncliff Dr	28303
Thorndike Dr	28311
Thorngate Dr	28303
Thorngrove Ct	28303
Thornhill Rd	28306
Thornsby Ln	28306
Thornwald Ct	28304
Thornwood Pl	28304
Thorp Dr	28306
Three Points Rd	28311
Three Wood Dr	28312
Thresher Ct	28306
Thurman Dr	28312
Thursby Cross	28306
Thurston Ct	28314
Thymus Ct	28306
Tibs Run Dr	28314
Tiffany Ct	28301
Tillery Ln	28314
Tillinghast St	28301
Tillman Ct	28306
Tilton Ct	28314
Timbercroft Ln	28314
Timberlake Dr	28314
Timberland Dr	28314
Timberline Dr	28311
Timberrock Ct	28306
Timberwood Dr	28314
Tin Lizza Dr	28314
Tina Dr	28306
Tindall Ct	28311
Tine Rd	28314
Tinman Dr	28314
Tip Top Ave	28306
Tipperary Ct	28301
Tippit Trl	28306
Tiree Dr	28304
Tissington St	28311
Titleist Dr	28312
Titus Ct	28314
Tiverton St	28314
Tobacco Rd	28312
Tobago Pl	28306
Tobermory Rd	28306
Todd St	28306
Toggel Ave	28306
Tokay Dr	28301
Tolar St	28306
Toledo Ct	28306
Tolgate Rd	28304
Tollhouse Dr	28314
Tom Burns Rd	28312
Tom Geddie Rd	28312
Tom Starling Rd	28306
Tony Dr	28306
Top Hat St	28303
Topaz Ct	28311
Topcon St	28314
Topeka St	28301
Torbay Dr	28311
Torchie St	28304
Torcross Dr	28304
Toronto Ct	28303
Torrance Ln	28314
Torrey Dr	28301
Torrington Way	28314
Tortola Dr	28306
Totley Dr	28306
Touchstone Dr	28311
Towbridge Rd	28306
Towhee St	28304
Town Center Dr	28306
Townhouse Ln	28311
Townsend St	28303
Toxaway Ct	28314
Trace Ave	28306
Tractor Rd	28311
Tracy Hall Rd	28306
Trade St	28306
Tradewinds Dr	28314
Traemoor Villiage Dr	28306
Trailwood Dr	28306
Trainer Dr	28304
Trampas Ct	28303
Tranquility Rd	28306
Transylvania Dr	28314
Trappers Rd	28311
Traven Ct	28306
Travis Rd	28312
Treadway Ct	28311
Tree Pl	28314
Tree Farm Rd	28306
Tree Ring Ct	28306
Treeside Dr	28312
Treetop Dr	28311
Tregony Pl	28304
Trenton Rd	28304
Trentwood Ct	28304
Tres Ct	28314
Trespar Ln	28311
Trevino Dr	28303
Trevor Ln	28314
Triangle Pl	28312
Tribune Ct	28311
Tricia Dr	28306
Trimble Ln	28312
Trinity Dr	28301
Trogdan Dr	28306
Troll Ct	28303
Troon Ct	28306
Trophy Ct	28314
Trotwood Dr	28314
Trout Creek Rd	28304
Troy Dr	28312
Troy Fisher Rd	28312
Truewinds Dr	28306
Truly Blessed Dr	28312
Truman Dr	28311
Trumilla Dr	28312
Trust Dr	28301
Truth Ct	28301
Tryon Dr	28303
Tuckahoe Ct	28314
Tucker Rd	28312
Tucker St	28306
Tuckertown Ln	28314
Tucson Dr	28303
Tulip Dr	28304
Tulsa Ct	28311
Tunis Ct	28304
Tunnel Rd	28314
Tupelo Cir	28304
Turkey Run	28312
Turkey Ridge Dr	28314
Turnberry Cir	28303
Turnbull Rd	28312
Turner Rd & St	28306
Turners Ln	28301
Turnkey Dr	28312
Turnpike Rd	28305
Turquoise Rd	28311
Turtle Point Dr	28304
Tuscaloosa Dr	28306
Tuxford Pl	28303
Tweed Dr	28304
Twin Acres Dr	28303
Twin Creek Ct	28314
Twin Oaks Dr	28305
Twin Pond Dr	28312
Twinflowers Ct	28304
Twinleaf Ct	28306
Twisted Oaks Dr	28312
Two Bale Ln	28304
Two Rut Rd	28306
Tyburn Rd	28311
Tyler Dr	28314
Tyner Rd	28306
Tyrus Rd	28312
Tyson Plantation Rd	28306
Tysor Dr	28304
Umstead Rd	28304
Unaka Ct	28306
Underwood Rd	28312
Underwood St	28301
Uniform Dr	28312
Union St	28301
United Dr	28301
University Ave	
100-1099	28301
1700-1799	28306
1900-1999	28301
3200-3499	28306
Upchurch Dr	28306
Uphill Dr	28306
Uppingham Rd	28306
Upton St	28301
Upton Tyson Rd	28306
Uriah Dr	28314
Utile Rd	28304
Vagabond Dr	28314
Valdese Ct	28304
Vale Ln	28306
Valencia Ct & Dr	28303
Valerie Dr	28306
Valhalla Ct	28304
Valiant Dr	28314
Valley Rd	28305
Valley Pointe Ln	28311
Valley Ridge Dr	28303
Valleygate Dr	28304
Valmead Ct	28312
Valor Way	28301
Van Buren Ave	28303
Van Dyke Pl	28314
Van Grayson Loop	28314
Van Nobbing Ct	28306
Vance Melvin Rd	28312
Vancouver Dr	28303
Vandemere Ave	28304
Vandenburg Dr	28312
Vander St	28312
Vandora Dr	28311
Vann St	28311
Vanstory St	28301
Vara Dr	28304
Varga St	28314
Varrene St	28303
Varsity Dr	28301
Vassar Cir	28306
Vaughn Rd	28304
Veanna Dr	28301
Veda St	28306
Venice Ct	28306
Venture St	28314
Vernon Ct	28301
Vesper Ln	28311
Vestal Ave	28301
Vicksburg Ct	28304
Victor Hall Ln	28306
Victoria Ct	28311
Victorian Pl	28301
Victory Ln	28312
Vida Cir	28311
Viewsite Dr	28306
Vigilante Ct	28303
Viking Rd	28303
Villa Dr	28311
Village Dr	28304
Villagio Pl	28303
Vinchenn St	28305
Vineland Dr	28306
Vineyard Dr	28304
Vintage Ct	28304
N & S Virginia Ave	28305
Vision Pl	28312
Vista Dr	28305
Vivian Dr	28311
Vixen St	28303
Volunteer Dr	28301
Voyager Dr	28306
Waccamaw Ct	28314
Waco Dr	28306
Waddell Dr	28301
Waddell St	28314
Wading Creek Ln	28306
Wadsworth Pl	28314
Wagon Wheel Ct	28314
Wagon Wheel Rd	28306
Wagoner Dr	28303
Wake St	28306
Wake Forest Rd	28311
Wakefield Dr	28303
Walcott Pl	28304
Walden Rd	28303
Waldo Ave	28306
Waldos Beach Rd	28306
Waldwick Rd	28311
Walesby Dr	28306
Walker Ct & St	28311
Walking Ln	28311
Wall St	28301
Wallaby Ct	28314
Wallbrook Dr	28306
Wallingford Ct	28314
Walnut Dr	28304
Walsh Pkwy	28311
Walstone Rd	28301
Walta Ct	28306
Walter Dr	28306
Walter Reed Rd	28304
Walter West Rd	28312
Walworth Rd	28311
Wanda Cir	28314
Warbler Ln	28306
Ward Dr	28306
Wareham Ct	28311
Warhorse St	28306
Warmsprings Dr	28303
Warren St	28312
Warton Ln	28314
Washington Dr & St	28301
Watauga Rd	28304
N Water St	28301
Water Oaks Dr	28312
Water Trail Dr	28311
Waterbury Dr & Pl	28311
Watercrest Ct	28304
Waterdale Ct	28304
Waterdown Dr	28314
Waterford Dr	28303
Watergap Dr	28314
Waterless St	28306
Waterloo Ave	28314
Waters Edge Dr	28314
Watershed Dr	28311
Watersplash Ln	28311
Waterview Ct	28301
Waterwood Dr	28314
Watford Way	28306
Watling Ct	28311
Watson Lake Rd	28306
Wattle Bird Dr	28312
Wave Runner Ct	28306
Waverly Ct	28304
Wavetree Dr	28306
Waxhaw Dr	28314
Wayah Creek Dr	28314
Wayberry Dr	28303
Waycross Rd	28312
Wayde St	28301
Wayland Dr	28314
Wayne Ln	
1700-1999	28304
3100-3399	28306
Wayside Rd	28314
Weatherford Rd	28303
Weathergreen Dr	28306
Weatherstone Dr	28311
Weaverhall Dr	28314
Webb Ct	28312
Webb St	28301
Webster Ave	28303
Wedgeview Dr	28306
Wedgewood Dr	28301
Weeping Water Run	28314
Weeping Willow Way	28304
Weisiger St	28301
Weiskopf Ct	28303
Weiss Ave	28305
Welbeck Ct	28306
Welcome Ct	28314
Weldon Ave	28305
Welford Pl	28304
Wellington Dr	28314
Wellons Dr	28304
Welmont Dr	28304
Welsh Pl	28303
Welsh Lake Dr	28306
Wendell Pl	28303
Wendover Dr	28304
Wendy Ter	28306
Wenona Loop	28303
Wentworth Pl	28304
Wesleyan Ct	28311
Wessex Ct	28306
West Dr	28301
Westarea St	28301
Westbranch Dr	28306
Westbury Ct	28314
Westchester Dr	28303
Westcliff Rd	28304
Westdale Dr	28303
Westerly Dr	28314
Westfield Rd	28314
Westfork Dr	28304
Westgate Dr	28304
Westhaven Dr	28303
Westhill Dr	28304
Westlake Rd	28314
Westland Ridge Rd	28311
Westlawn Ave	28305
Westminster Dr	28311
Westmont Dr	28305
Weston Cir	28306
Westover Pl	28304
Westview Dr	28303
Westwater Way	28301
Westwick Ln	28314
Westwood Dr	28303
Westwood Shopping Ctr	28314
Wetherby Ct	28306
Wexford Oaks Ct	28303
Weymouth Ct	28304
Wheat Way	28314
Wheeler Rd	28306
Wheeling St	28303
Whelling St	28306
Whipple Tree Ln	28314
Whiskerlake Dr	28312
Whisper Ln	28303
Whisper Oaks Ct	28306
Whisper Wood Dr	28306
Whispering Meadow Dr	28306
Whispering Pines Rd	28311
Whitaker Dr	28312
Whitburn Ave	28304
Whitcomb Dr	28311
White St	28305
White Ash Dr	28306
White Oak Ct	28303
White Plains Dr	28312
Whitebridge Ln	28306
Whitehall Dr	28303
Whitehead Rd	28312
Whitehouse Ln	28306
Whitfield St	28306
Whithorn Ct	28311
Whitman Rd	28306
Whitmore Ct	28306
Whitney Dr	28314
Whitted Town Rd	28312
Whitwell Pl	28306

Wichita Dr 28303
Wicker Ct 28304
Wickersham Dr 28314
Wickford Ct 28314
Wicklow Pl 28304
Wieland St 28312
Wiggins Dr 28306
Wigwam Dr 28314
Wilberforce Ct 28311
Wilbon Dr 28305
Wilbur St 28312
Wild Pine Dr 28312
Wildcat Rd 28312
Wilder Ct & Dr 28314
Wildlife Way 28314
Wildwood Dr 28304
Wiley St 28301
Wilkersham Way 28306
Wilkes Rd 28306
Wilkins Dr 28311
Willa Ct 28306
Willard Dr 28312
Willborough Ave 28303
William Clark Rd 28303
Williams St 28301
Williamsburgh Dr 28304
Williamson Ln 28312
Willie Ln 28312
Williford St 28312
Willis Cir 28304
Williston St 28301
Williwood Rd 28311
Willougby Dr 28312
Willow Ct 28314
Willow St 28303
Willow Bend Ln 28303
Willow Gate Dr 28312
Willow Run Ln 28311
Willowbrae Dr 28312
Willowbrook Dr 28314
Wilma St 28301
Wilmington Hwy 28306
Wilson Ave 28314
Wilson St 28305
Wilton Dr 28312
Wiltshire Rd 28314
Wimbledon Cir 28314
Winchester Ct & St 28314
Wind Sock Ct 28312
Windcross Ct 28314
Windermere Dr 28314
Windfield Ct 28303
Windflower Dr 28314
Windham Ct 28303
Winding Creek Rd 28305
Windjammer Cir 28306
Windlock Dr 28304
Windmill Rd 28312
E Winds Ln 28311
Windsong Cir 28306
N Windsor Dr 28301
Windward Ct 28306
Windward Cv 28314
Windwood On Skye 28303
Windy Birch Cir 28304
Windy Creek Way 28306
Windy Fields Dr 28306
Windy Grove Ct 28314
Windy Hill Cir 28303
Windy Knoll Pl 28304
Wingate Rd
2100-2399 28304
2600-2699 28306
Winnabow Dr 28304
Winslow St
100-599 28301
600-1099 28306
Winston Ave 28303
Winter Hawk Ln 28312
Winter Park Dr 28304
Winterberry Dr 28314
Wintergreen Dr 28314
Winterlochen Rd 28305
Winterwood Dr 28306
Winthrop Ct & Dr 28311
Winton Dr 28306
Wipperwill Dr 28306
Wisconsin Dr 28311
Wishing Ln 28312
Wisteria Ln 28314
Withers Dr 28304
Wofford Ct 28311
Wolcott Ct 28314
Wolfberry Dr 28306
Wolfelee Dr 28311
Wolflair Dr 28311
Wolfpoint Dr & Ext 28311
Wolvey Rd 28312
Womble Dr 28306
Wood Creek Dr 28314
Wood Duck Dr 28304
Woodard Ct 28311
Woodberry Ln 28303
Woodbine Ave 28303
Woodbridge Way 28314
Woodburn Dr 28311
Woodclift Dr 28311
Woodcrest Rd 28305
Woodfield Rd 28303
Woodford Cir 28314
Woodglen Dr 28314
Woodhaven Cir 28311
Woodhill Ln 28314
Woodlake Ct 28311
Woodland Dr 28305
Woodleaf Ln 28303
Woodline Dr 28314
Woodlore Ln 28312
Woodmark Dr 28314
Woodrow St 28303
Woods Ct 28312
Woods End Dr 28312
Woodsage Cir 28303
Woodsdale St 28306
Woodside Ave 28301
Woodstone Ct 28311
Woodstream Trl 28314
Woodswallow Dr 28312
Woodview Dr 28314
Woodwind Dr 28304
Woody St 28306
Wordsworth Dr 28304
Workman St 28311
Worley St 28311
Worstead Dr 28314
Worth St 28301
Worthington Dr 28304
Wrangler Ave 28306
Wren Rd 28306
Wrenwood Ct 28303
Wright Ave 28314
Wright Ct 28314
Wright St 28301
Wrightsboro Rd 28304
Wriston Dr 28311
Wuycik Rd 28306
Wyatt Ct & St 28304
Wycliffe Ct 28306
Wynborne Ct 28306
Wynfare Dr 28306
Wynncrest Ln 28303
Wynnwood Dr 28314
Wyoming Ct 28304
Xavier Ct 28311
Yadkin Rd 28303
Yale St 28306
Yardley Ct 28303
Yarmouth Dr 28306
Yasmin Ave 28306
Yates Cir 28311
Yaupon Dr 28312
Yeager St 28312
Yellow Ribbon Dr 28314
Yellowbrick Rd 28314
Yellowstone Ct 28303
Yewelene Dr 28314
Yonkers Ct 28304
York Rd 28303
Yorkchester Dr 28314
Yorkshire Dr 28314
Young Dr 28311
Youngberry St 28314
Youngstown Dr 28303
Yovel Dr 28306
Yucca Ct 28303
Yuma Ct 28303
Zabell Dr 28312
Zadock Dr 28314
Zapata Ln 28314
Zareeba Dr 28306
Zenith Ct 28304
Zepher Rd 28311
Zinc Ct 28311
Zinnia Ct 28306
Zion Dr 28301
Zircon Ct 28311
Zollie Jones Rd 28303

NUMBERED STREETS

1st St 28306
71st School Rd 28314

FRANKLIN NC

General Delivery 28734

POST OFFICE BOXES MAIN OFFICE STATIONS AND BRANCHES

Box No.s
All PO Boxes 28744

NAMED STREETS

Acorn Dr 28734
Addington Pl 28734
Addington Bridge Rd 28734
Addington Meadows Dr 28734
Addington Villas Dr 28734
Admiral Dr 28734
Ag Camp Rd 28734
Aidan Ln 28734
Airport Rd 28734
Alamo Dr 28734
Alben Ln 28734
Alex Anderson Rd 28734
Allen Rd 28734
Allen Taylor Rd 28734
Allendale Hills Rd 28734
Allie Way 28734
Allison Creek Rd 28734
Allison Watts Rd 28734
Allman Dr 28734
Allman Farm Rd 28734
Alpine Dr 28734
Amber Dr 28734
Ammons Rd 28734
Amys Rdg 28734
Anderson St 28734
Anderson Creek Rd 28734
Andys Way 28734
Angel Rd 28734
Angel Cove Rd 28734
Angel Fields Rd 28734
Angel Knob Ln 28734
Annes Ln 28734
Antler Ridge Ln 28734
Apple Trl 28734
Apple Blossom Rd 28734
Apple Tree Ln 28734
Appleberry Ln 28734
Arbor Ln 28734
Archie Pt 28734
Archwood Ln 28734
Arland Mountain Rd 28734
Arnold Branch Rd 28734
Arrowhead Dr 28734
Arrowwood Ln 28734
Arthur Drake Rd 28734
Arvil Guyer Rd 28734
Ashewood Dr 28734
Ashleigh Ln 28734
Austin Welch Rd 28734
Autry Rd 28734
Autumn Trl 28734
Autumn Haze Ln 28734
Aylen Village Ln 28734
Azalea Ridge Rd 28734
Bailey Rd 28734
Bailey Hills Rd 28734
Baird Cove Rd 28734
Baldwin Ln 28734
Baldwin Cove Rd 28734
Balsam View Rd 28734
Baltimore Ave 28734
Bandarosa Dr 28734
Barbaras Pl 28734
Barn View Rd 28734
Barnard Rd 28734
Barnes Cove Rd 28734
Barrett Dr 28734
Bartram Trail Rd 28734
Basswood Dr 28734
Bateman Park Rd 28734
Bates Xing 28734
Bates Branch Rd 28734
Battle Branch Rd 28734
Battle Branch Ridge Rd 28734
Battle Branch Vista Dr 28734
Beacon Hill Rd 28734
Beale Dr 28734
Bear Trl 28734
Bear Back Ridge Rd 28734
Bear Mountain Rd 28734
Bear Paw Rdg 28734
Bear Paw Hill Rd 28734
Bear Ridge Rd 28734
Bear Wood Trl 28734
Bears Paw Trl 28734
Beasley Rd 28734
Beasley Mine Cir & Rd 28734
Beaver Ln 28734
Beaver Bend Rd 28734
Bee Branch Dr 28734
Bee Tree Ln 28734
Beechwood Ln 28734
Beeline Dr 28734
Bees Hive Dr 28734
Belden Cir 28734
Belden Terrace Ln 28734
Bella Ln 28734
Belle Dowdle Rd 28734
Belleview Rd 28734
Belleview Oak Cir 28734
Belleview Park Rd 28734
Belmont Dr 28734
Ben Lenoir Rd 28734
Bench Mountain Dr 28734
Benjamin Dr 28734
Bennett Rd 28734
Bennett Cove Rd 28734
Bennett Ridge Rd 28734
Bennington Rd 28734
Bent Oak Dr 28734
N Bentwood Dr & Ln 28734
Berry Cove Rd 28734
Berry Farm Rd 28734
Bert Waldroop Rd 28734
Bertha Rice Rd 28734
Betee Jay Ln 28734
Bethel Church Rd 28734
Betty Dolphy Rd 28734
Beulahland Way 28734
Beverly Dr 28734
Bidwell St 28734
Big Oak Dr 28734
Big Ridge Rd 28734
Bill Carver Rd 28734
Bill Dalrymple Rd 28734
Bingham Rd 28734
Birch Ln 28734
Birchwood Ln 28734
Bishop Cove Rd 28734
Black Bear Way 28734
Black Creek Dr 28734
Black Gap Rd 28734
Black Mountain Ln & Trl 28734
Black Mountain Creek Rd 28734
Black Oak Dr 28734
Black Walnut Dr 28734
Blackberry Ln & Rdg 28734
Blackburn Branch Rd 28734
Blaine Rd 28734
N Blaine Branch Rd 28734
Blaine Mountain Estate Rd 28734
Blanche Ln 28734
Blanton Rd 28734
Bloom Cottage Pl 28734
Blossom Ln 28734
Blossomtown Dr 28734
Blossomview Ln 28734
Blue Bird Cv 28734
Blue Jay Dr 28734
Blue Ridge Dr 28734
Blue Sky Ln 28734
Blueberry Ln 28734
Blueberry Hill Dr 28734
Board Tree Rd 28734
Bobbie Neal Dr 28734
Bobby Conley Rd 28734
Bobcat Trl 28734
Bobs Dr 28734
Bobwhite Ln 28734
Bonfire Dr 28734
Bow Tie Rd 28734
Bowers Mountain Rd 28734
Bowling Ln 28734
Bowman Rd 28734
Boyd Ln 28734
Bradley Rd 28734
Bradley Creek Rd 28734
Brandy Ln 28734
Brassy Creek Ln 28734
Breezy Knob Rd & Ter 28734
Breezy Oak Ln 28734
Brendle Ln & Rd 28734
Brendle Cove Rd 28734
Brentwood St 28734
Brewer Rd 28734
Brian Ln 28734
Brittany Ln 28734
Broadleaf Ln 28734
Brook Dr & Ln 28734
Brooklynn Trl 28734
Brooks Thomas Rd 28734
Brookshire Ct & Ln 28734
Brookside Dr 28734
Brookstone Forest Way 28734
Brookstone Mountain Trl 28734
Brookstone Vista Ln 28734
Brookwood Cv & Dr 28734
Brown Branch Rd 28734
Browning Rd 28734
Bruin Ln 28734
Bruin Ridge Trl 28734
Brushy Branch Rd 28734
Bryson Branch Rd 28734
Bryson City Rd 28734
Bryson Knob Rd 28734
Bryson Park Rd 28734
Buck Mountain Rd 28734
Buck Top Rd 28734
Buckeye Branch Rd 28734
Buckhead Trce 28734
Bud Perry Rd 28734
Buddy Hollow Ln 28734
Bulgin Dr 28734
Bullock Rd 28734
Bumgarner Ln 28734
Burgess Rd 28734
Burnette Ln & Rd 28734
Burnette Hill Rd 28734
Burningtown Rd 28734
Burningtown Church Rd 28734
Burningtown Falls Rd 28734
Business Park Dr 28734
Buster Cabe Rd 28734
Buttercup Rdg 28734
Butterfly Blvd 28734
Butterfly Park Dr 28734
Buttonwood Dr 28734
By Pass Ct 28734
Byrd Farm Rd 28734
Byrd Gap Rd & Trl 28734
Byron Waldroop Rd 28734
Ca Meadows Rd 28734
Cabe Cove Rd 28734
Cabin Rd 28734
Cactus Ln 28734
Cadon Gap Rd 28734
Calebs Way 28734
Calico Dr 28734
Callahan St 28734
Cals Cove Rd 28734
Camelot Est Rd 28734
Camp Rd 28734
Camp Ultima Blvd 28734
Campbell Ln 28734
Canary Ln 28734
Candy Dandy Ln 28734
Canine Way 28734
Cannon Trl 28734
Cardinal Dr & Ln 28734
Cardinal Ridge Farm Way 28734
Carl Dr 28734
Carl Ammons Rd 28734
Carl Henson Rd 28734
Carl Slagle Rd 28734
Carl Sorrells Rd 28734
Carnation Dr 28734
Carnes Rd 28734
Carolina Dr 28734
Carolina Crest Dr 28734
Carolina Mtn Dr 28734
Carolina Springs Ln 28734
Carolina Village Cir 28734
Carolyn Dr 28734
Carriage Ct 28734
Carson Branch Cir 28734
Carson Cove Rd 28734
Carter Ln & Rd 28734
Carvil Rd 28734
Cassada Dr 28734
Castle Cv 28734
Castleberry Ln & Vw 28734
Castleman Rd 28734
Cat Creek Ests & Rd 28734
Cat Creek Ridge Rd 28734
Cb Patton Pl 28734
Cd Moody Rd 28734
Cedar Ln 28734
Cedar Bluff Rd 28734
Cedar Estates Rd 28734
Cedar Field Rd 28734
Cedar Hill Rd 28734
Cedar Hills Dr 28734
Cedar Ridge Rd 28734
Cedar View Dr 28734
Cedar Wood Dr 28734
Center Ct & Trce 28734
Centre Farms Rd 28734
Chalet Dr 28734
Chalk Hill Rd 28734
Chapel Cove Cir 28734
Chapel Hill Dr 28734
Chapel View Dr 28734
Charles Nolan Rd 28734
Charles Sondheimer Rd 28734
Charlie Joe Rd 28734
Chateau Ln 28734
Chattahoochee Ln 28734
Chavis Rd 28734
Cheek Rd 28734
Cherokee Ln 28734
Cherokee Mine Rd 28734
Cherry St 28734
Ches Dr 28734
Chestnut Dr 28734
Chestnut Hill Dr 28734
Cheyanne Trl 28734
Chickadee Trl 28734
Childers Rd 28734
Chimney View Rdg 28734
China Springs Rd 28734
Chinquapin Hts 28734
Chinquapin Mountain Rd 28734
Chodl Ln 28734
Chris Ln 28734
Christa Ridge Rd 28734
Christy Dr 28734
Church St 28734
Church Hill Ln 28734
Cinnamon Hills Dr 28734
Circle Trce 28734
Circle D Farm Rd 28734
City View Dr 28734
Clampit Cove Rd 28734
Clara Ramsey Rd 28734
Clark Ct & Rd 28734
Clarks Chapel Rd 28734
Clarksville Ln 28734
Classic Dr 28734
Claude Arnold Rd 28734
Claude Sanders Rd 28734
Claude Scott Rd 28734
Clear Sky Dr 28734
Clear Stream Rd 28734
Cliff Dalrymple Rd 28734
Cliff View Dr 28734
Climbing Bear Dr 28734
Clint Cole Rd 28734
Clover Ln 28734
Clover Creek Rd 28734
Clyde St 28734
Clyde Downs Rd 28734
Clyde Lakey Dr 28734
Clyde Ruby Ln 28734
Co Op Rd 28734
Cochran Ln 28734
Cochran Ridge Rd 28734
Coddies Ter 28734
Cody Rd 28734
Cody Hill Rd 28734
Coffee Tree Ln 28734
Collette Ln 28734
Collins Ln 28734
Coman Rd 28734
Commerce St 28734
Commons Dr 28734
Compass Rose Ct 28734
Conley St 28734
Conners Park 28734
Cook Rd & St 28734
Cool Breeze Rd 28734
Coolbreeze Rd 28734
Coon Creek Rd 28734
Copperhead Rd 28734
Corbett Rd 28734
Corbin Rd 28734
Corbin Cove Dr 28734
Corbin Hill Rd 28734
Corey Ave 28734
Corkill Ln 28734
Cornerstone Dr 28734
Corpening Rd 28734
Corundum Hill Rd 28734
Corvette Dr 28734
Cottage View Dr 28734
Cotton Rd 28734
Cottontail Ln 28734
Cottonwood Rd 28734
Country Ln, Rd, Rdg & Walk 28734
Country Bend Rd 28734
Country Club Dr 28734
Country Woods Dr 28734
Countryside Dr 28734
Courson Rd 28734
Courson View Rd 28734
Courtney Ln 28734
Courtney Hill Rd 28734
Courtney Marie Dr 28734
W Cove Ct, Ln & Xing 28734

W Coventry Cir & Dr E 28734
Cowee Creek Rd 28734
Cowee School Dr & Rd 28734
Cowee View Ln 28734
Cowee Vista Rd 28734
Cowee Woods Ct & Dr 28734
Coweeta Church Rd 28734
Cozy Rocking Chair Ln 28734
Cr Cabe Rd 28734
Crabtree Ln 28734
Craig Rd 28734
Crane Cir 28734
Crawford Ln & Rd 28734
Crawford Hill Dr 28734
Creek Bottom Trl 28734
Creekside Dr, Ln & Ter 28734
Crepe Myrtle Ln 28734
Crescent Ridge Dr 28734
Crest Hill Ct 28734
Crestline Dr 28734
Crestview Hts 28734
Cricket Ln 28734
Crisp St 28734
Crisp Country Ln 28734
Crissy Ln 28734
Crooked Creek Ln 28734
Cross Rd 28734
Cross Creek Rd 28734
Crossroad Ln 28734
Crowes Branch Rd 28734
Crystal Cove Rd 28734
Crystal Ridge Trl 28734
Cszonka Rd 28734
Cullasaja Cir 28734
Cullasaja Hollow Rd 28734
Cullasaja Vista Ln 28734
Cunningham Rd 28734
Curtis St 28734
D Conley Rd 28734
D Long Rd 28734
D S Corbett Rd 28734
Daddys Trl 28734
Dairy View Rd 28734
Dale Dr 28734
Dalrymple Rd 28734
Dalton Creek Rd 28734
Dan St 28734
Dan Mar Rd 28734
Daves Creek Cir & Rd 28734
Davis Ln 28734
Davis Farm Dr 28734
Day Lily Ln 28734
Daybreak Ln 28734
Deal Rd 28734
Deal Farm Cir 28734
Dean Dr 28734
Dearmin Ter 28734
Dearmin Terrace Ln 28734
Deep Springs Dr 28734
Deer Run 28734
Deer Crossing Rd 28734
Deer Hollow Ln 28734
Deer Meadow Rd 28734
Deer Ridge Rd 28734
N Deer Run Trl 28734
Deerfield Ln & Rdg 28734
Deerwood Dr 28734
Deforest Ln 28734
Del Prado Ln 28734
Del Rio Ln 28734
Delia Dr 28734
Delightful Dr 28734
Dellwood Rd 28734
Delta Dr 28734
Dennis Ln 28734
Depot St
1-299 28734
250-250 28744
300-1198 28734
301-1199 28734
W Depot St 28734
Depot Industrial Park 28734
Derby St 28734
Dewey Ln 28734
Diamond Falls Blvd 28734
Dickerson Rd 28734
Dillon Dr 28734
N & W Dills Creek Rd 28734
Dills Knob Rd 28734
Dobson Rd 28734
Dobson Mountain Rd & Trl 28734
Dock Tallent Rd 28734
Doe Trl 28734
Dog Gone Cir 28734
E & W Dogwood Dr, Holw, Ln & Rd 28734
Donna Dr 28734
Doraul St 28734
Dorothy Mcconnell Rd 28734
Dorsey Dr 28734
Doster Dr 28734
Double Branch Cv 28734
Dove Haven Dr 28734
Dover D Blvd 28734
Dowdle Mountain Rd 28734
Dragonfly Cv 28734
Drake Trce 28734
Druid Hills Ln 28734
Dry Ridge Rd 28734
Dryman Rd 28734
Duck Cove Ln 28734
Dusty Rd 28734
Dutch Cove Rd 28734
Dutton Dr 28734
Duvall Trl 28734
Ea Watts Rd 28734
Eagle Crest Way 28734
Eagles Nest Rd 28734
Earnhardt Dr 28734
East Dr, Rdg & Trce 28734
Eastside Ct 28734
Echo Heights Rd 28734
Echo High Rd 28734
Echo Valley Rd 28734
Ed Crisp Ln 28734
Eddie Bateman Dr 28734
Edgewood Ave 28734
Edwards Rd 28734
Eight Belles Dr 28734
Eisenbach Cir 28734
Elders Rd 28734
Elizabeth Dr & Trl 28734
Elkhorn Ridge Dr 28734
Ellijay Rd 28734
Elliott Rd 28734
Elliott Cove Rd 28734
Ellis Ln 28734
Elmore Estates Rd 28734
Emerald Hl 28734
Emerald Hills Ln 28734
Emerson Crawford Rd 28734
Emmanuel Rd 28734
Enchanted Ln 28734
Enchanted Mountain Cv 28734
W End Dr 28734
Endoda Rd 28734
England Dr 28734
Enterprize Rd 28734
Eric Dr 28734
Erica Ln 28734
Ernest Cabe Rd 28734
Ervin Stockton Rd 28734
Estes Rd 28734
Eugene Ln 28734
Eulalie Ln 28734
Evans Rd 28734
Evans Creek Ln & Rd 28734
Everett Rd 28734
Evergreen Ln & Trl 28734
Fair Way Dr 28734
Fairlane Dr 28734
Fairmont Dr 28734
Fairway Knl 28734
Faith Dr 28734
Falcon Dr 28734
Falcon Crest Dr 28734
Falcon Point Trl 28734
Fallbrooke Ln 28734
Falling Rock Rd 28734
Falling Water Rd 28734
Family Cir 28734
Family Branch Rd 28734
Fantasy Dr 28734
Farm House Rd 28734
Farmstead Dr 28734
Fawn Hl & Rdg 28734
Featherstone Dr 28734
Fenno Hl 28734
Ferguson Rd 28734
Fern Hill Dr 28734
Fieldstone Dr 28734
Fireside Dr 28734
First St 28734
Fish Hawk Rd & Vw 28734
Five Oaks Dr 28734
Five Points Dr 28734
Flaming Azalea 28734
Flatrock Dr 28734
Flood St 28734
Florida Hills Rd 28734
Flowers Gap Rd 28734
Floyd Shuler Rd 28734
Forest Ave 28734
Forest Cove Rd 28734
Forest Hills Dr 28734
Forest Oak Rd 28734
Forest Ridge Dr 28734
N Forty Dr 28734
Fouts Ln 28734
Fox Hound Trl 28734
Fox Layre Rd 28734
Fox Ridge Cir 28734
Fox Run Dr & Rd 28734
Fox Valley Ln 28734
Foxden Ridge Rd 28734
Foxfire St 28734
Foxwith Rd 28734
Foxwood Dr 28734
Frank Cabe Rd 28734
Franklin Farm Rd 28734
Franklin Plaza Dr 28734
Frazier Rd 28734
Fred Crisp Rd 28734
Fred Dalton Rd 28734
Fred Slagle Rd 28734
Friendship Ln 28734
N & S Front St 28734
Frontier Ln 28734
Fuchs Dr 28734
Fulcher Rd 28734
Fulcher Creek Dr 28734
Fulcher Summit Dr 28734
Fulcher Vista Dr & Rd 28734
Fulton Rd 28734
Furman Welch Rd 28734
Gadd Rd 28734
Gaines Cove Rd 28734
Gale Trl 28734
Garden Ln 28734
Garden Branch Rd 28734
Garden Cove Rd 28734
Garden Flats Rd 28734
Garden Knoll Rd 28734
Garden Ridge Rd 28734
Garden Springs Way 28734
Garden View Dr 28734
Garnet Creek Rd 28734
Garnett Trace Rd 28734
Gaston St 28734
Gem Lake Estates Rd 28734
Gemstone Dr 28734
Gene Bateman Rd 28734
Genes Rd 28734
Geneva Cir 28734
George Dr 28734
George Doster Rd 28734
George Reid Rd 28734
George Taylor Rd 28734
Georgia Rd 28734
Gibson Rd 28734
Gibson Aquatic Farms Rd 28734
Gibson Cove Rd 28734
Gibson Cove Estates Dr 28734
Gibson Ridge Rd 28734
Gideon Cir 28734
Gilcrest Ln 28734
Giles Holler Rd 28734
Gillespie Dr 28734
Gilmer Russell Rd 28734
Ginger Tree Ln 28734
Gingers Way 28734
Gingerwood Dr 28734
Gladys B White Ln 28734
Glass Shanty Cir 28734
Glenn Campbell Rd 28734
Glennbrooke Ln 28734
Glennview Ln 28734
Glory Ln & Rd 28734
Goah Way 28734
Gold City Ln 28734
Gold Mountain Ln 28734
Golden Grv 28734
Golden Eagles Pt 28734
Golden Falls Dr 28734
Goldenseal Cv 28734
Golf Estates Rd 28734
Golf Vista Dr 28734
Golfview Dr 28734
Goodview Trl 28734
Gooseberry Ln 28734
Gorda Ln 28734
Gordon Trl 28734
Goshen Rd 28734
Grace Ln 28734
Grace Starr Rd 28734
Gracie Way 28734
Grand Horizon Way 28734
Grand Ridge Dr 28734
Grandview Ct & Dr 28734
Grandview Acres Rd 28734
Granny Kate Ln 28734
Grannys Rd 28734
Grannys Knob Rd 28734
Grassy Hill Dr 28734
Grateful Way 28734
Gravel Rd 28734
Gray Cove Rd 28734
Gray Fox Rd 28734
Grayson Higdon Rd 28734
Great Oak Dr 28734
Green Rd & St 28734
Green Acres Rd 28734
Green Holly Dr 28734
Green Knob Rd 28734
Green Vale Ln 28734
Green Valley Dr 28734
Greenbriar Ln 28734
Greenbrier St 28734
Greenleaf Ln 28734
Gregory Dr & Rd 28734
Grey Fox Ln 28734
Gribble Rd 28734
Gribble Hill Rd 28734
Griffin Rd 28734
Griffin Mountain Ln 28734
Groaning Hill Rd 28734
Grouse Rd 28734
Grouse Mountain Trl 28734
Guffey Ln 28734
Guffeys Gap Rd 28734
Guffie Ln & Rd 28734
Guy Knob Rd 28734
Guyer Homestead Rd 28734
Hailey Dr 28734
Hailey Brooke Ln 28734
Hailey Heights Ter 28734
Haley Ridge Rd 28734
Halfway Back Ln 28734
Hall Farm Rd 28734
Hall Mountain Rd 28734
Hallelujah Dr 28734
Haller Ln 28734
Hanak Way 28734
Hannah Dr 28734
Hannah Farms Rd 28734
Happy Ln 28734
Happy Hollow Rd 28734
Happy Jack Rd 28734
Hardwood Dr 28734
Harmony Ln 28734
Harmony Hill Rd 28734
Harold Ledford Rd 28734
Harper Ln 28734
Harrison Ave 28734
Harrison Gap Rd 28734
Hartman Ln 28734
Harvest Cove Rd 28734
Hatfield Rd 28734
Haughton Hills Rd 28734
Haughton Williams Rd 28734
Haven Dr 28734
Haven Meadow Ln 28734
Haven Of Rest Ln 28734
Haven Ridge Trl 28734
Hawk Hill Dr 28734
Hayes Cir & Ln 28734
Hayes Mill Rd 28734
Hazel Fouts Rd 28734
Hazels Creek Ln 28734
Heartland Ln 28734
Heathers Cove Rd 28734
Heatherstone Dr 28734
Heathwood Ln 28734
Hedden Ct 28734
Hedden Flats Rd 28734
Heflin Branch Rd 28734
Helen Ln 28734
Hemlock Trl 28734
Hemlock Creek Dr 28734
Hemlock Falls Rd 28734
Hemlock Gap Ln 28734
Hemlock Hills Dr 28734
Henderson Rd 28734
Henderson Farm Rd 28734
Henry Rd 28734
Henry Mashburn Ln 28734
Hensley Dr 28734
Henson Rd 28734
Heritage Ln 28734
Heritage Hollow Cir & Dr 28734
Heron Lake Rd 28734
Hi Lo Hills Dr 28734
Hibschman Holw 28734
Hickory Trl 28734
Hickory Barn Rd 28734
Hickory Gap Rd 28734
Hickory Hollow Ln & Rd 28734
Hickory Knob Rd 28734
E Hickory Knoll Rd 28734
Hickory Knoll Ridge Rd 28734
Hickory Ridge Trl 28734
Hidden Ln & Trl 28734
Hidden Acres Trl 28734
Hidden Hills Rd 28734
Hidden Meadow Ln 28734
Hidden Valley Dr & Rd 28734
Hideaway Ln 28734
Higdon Rd 28734
High Rd 28734
High Brace Rd 28734
High Country Dr 28734
High Point Dr 28734
High Ridge Rd 28734
Highaven Ln 28734
Highland Ave 28734
Highland Ridge Trl 28734
Highland Woods Dr 28734
Highlander Loop 28734
Highlands Rd 28734
Higlands Gorge Pt 28734
Hiland Ter 28734
Hiland Park Ln 28734
Hill St 28734
Hillcrest Ave & Cir 28734
Hillside Dr & St 28734
Hilltop Rd 28734
Hillview Dr 28734
Hodgins Rd 28734
Hoffman Ln 28734
Holbrook Branch Ln 28734
Holbrook Hill Dr 28734
Holbrooks Rd 28734
Holland Dr 28734
Holland Ayers Rd 28734
Holly Dr & Ln 28734
Holly Creek Rd 28734
Holly Hill Ln 28734
Holly Hills Vista Rd 28734
Holly Leaf Trl 28734
Holly Mountain Dr 28734
Holly Ridge Dr 28734
Holly Spring Vill Rd 28734
Holly Springs Plz 28734
Holly Springs Church Rd 28734
Holly Springs Estates Rd 28734
Holly Springs Park Dr 28734
Holly Terrace Rd 28734
Holly Tree Dr 28734
Hollyview Cir 28734
Homer Owens Rd 28734
Homestead Dr 28734
Homeward Dr 28734
Hominy Mill Rd 28734
Honey Maple Ln 28734
Honeysucle Ln 28734
Hook Ln 28734
Hooper Ln 28734
Hootin Holler 28734
Hootowl Hollow Rd 28734
Hope Dr 28734
Hopes Hill Rd 28734
Hopkins Rd 28734
E Horizon Dr 28734
Horizon Hill Dr 28734
Horseshoe Cir 28734
Horseshoe Ridge Rd 28734
Hougie Heaven Ln 28734
Houston Farm Rd 28734
Houston Gap Rd 28734
Howell Rd 28734
Hp Mccoy Rd 28734
Huckelberry Creek Rd 28734
Hudson Dr 28734
Hughes Ln 28734
Hummingbird Ln, Rd & Trl 28734
Hummingbird Hill Rd 28734
Hunnicut Ln & Rd 28734
Hunter Green Rd 28734
Hunters Ln & Trl 28734
Huntleigh Dr 28734
Hurst Cir & Rd 28734
Huscusson Dr 28734
Hyatt Rd 28734
Icenhower Rd 28734
Ida Ln 28734
Imperial Dr 28734
Independence Dr 28734
Indian Dr & Trl 28734
Indian Creek Rd 28734
Indian Springs Dr 28734
Indian Walk Rd 28734
Indigo Ln 28734
Industrial Park Loop & Rd 28734
Iotla St 28734
Iotla Church Rd 28734
Iotla Hill Dr 28734
Iotla Valley Park Rd 28734
Ivar St 28734
Ives Ln 28734
Ivy Rd 28734
Ivy Hills Ter 28734
Jack Cabe Rd 28734
Jack Stamey Rd 28734
Jackpine Dr 28734
Jackson Hts 28734
Jackson Hill Dr 28734
Jacobs St 28734
Jacobs Branch Rd 28734
Jacobs Mountain Rd 28734
Jake Dr 28734
Jakobs Way 28734
James Rd 28734
James Lyman Rd 28734
Jander Mountain Rd 28734
Janelle St 28734
Jasons Meadow Dr 28734
Jay Ln 28734
Jay Bird Trl 28734
Jegs Rdg 28734
Jennings Dr 28734
Jenny Ln 28734
Jenny Lee Ln 28734
Jess Sanders Rd 28734
Jewel Ln 28734
Jim Berry Rd 28734
Jim Cochran Rd 28734
Jim Corbin Rd 28734
Jim Deal Rd 28734
Jim Donald Rd 28734
Jim Mann Rd 28734
Jim Messer Rd 28734
Jin Ln 28734
Joe Harrison Rd 28734
Joe Plant Rd 28734
Johanna Dr 28734
John B Deal Rd 28734
John Justice Rd 28734
John Tallent Rd 28734
John Teague Rd 28734
Johnny Stanfield Rd 28734
Johnnys Mountain Rd 28734
Johnson Rd & Way 28734
N Jones Creek Rd 28734
Jones Creek Acres Dr 28734
Jones Ridge Rd 28734
Jordan Dr 28734
Joshua Ln 28734
Journey Ln 28734
Joy Ln 28734
Joyce Cir 28734
Judd Duvall Ln 28734
Judds Trl 28734
Julian Kiser Rd 28734
June Rd 28734
Junior Pruitt Rd 28734
Justice Rd 28734
K Ln 28734
Kangas Dr 28734
Katie Ln 28734
Katydid Ln 28734
Keener Mountain Rd 28734
Kelly Cove Rd 28734
Kelly Hi Rd 28734
Kempf Cir 28734
Keystone Dr 28734
Kimsey Ln 28734
Kincaid Rd 28734
Kings Rd 28734
Kings Cove Rd 28734
Kingwood Cir 28734
Kinsland Rd 28734
Kinsland Park Rd 28734
Kirkland Rd 28734
Kiser Rd 28734
Kivi Rd 28734
Knepp Rd 28734
Knob Hill Rd 28734
Knobby Ln 28734
Knoll Dr 28734
Knotting Ln 28734
Kooi Ln 28734
Kovacs Rd & Trl 28734
Krinklewood Dr 28734
Lady Slipper Ln 28734
Lake Rd 28734
W Lake Charles Rd 28734
Lake Emory Rd 28734
Lake Ledford Rd 28734
Lakes Estate Rd 28734
Lakeshore Dr 28734
Lakeside Cir, Ct & Dr 28734
Lakeview Cir & Dr 28734
Lakey Creek Rd 28734
Lamar Ln 28734

Lamplighter St 28734
Landon Ln 28734
Langston Howell Dr 28734
Laurel Dr, Rdg & Way 28734
Laurel Canyon Rd 28734
Laurel Falls Rd 28734
Laurel Hill Ln 28734
Laurel Lake Dr & Rd 28734
Laurel Mountain Rd 28734
Laurel Vista Trl 28734
Lauren Ln 28734
Lavona Joy Cir 28734
Law Ln 28734
Leaf Tree Ln 28734
Leaning Pine Rd 28734
Leaning Tree Ln 28734
Leatherman Rd 28734
Leatherman Gap Rd 28734
Leatherman Raby Rd 28734
Ledbetter Ln & Vw 28734
Ledbetter Hill Dr 28734
Ledford Dr & Rd 28734
Ledford Branch Rd 28734
Ledford Fields Rd 28734
Lee Bates Rd 28734
Lee Tallent Rd 28734
Leebrook Dr 28734
Leonard Ln 28734
Level Ln 28734
Lewis Rd 28734
Liberty Dr 28734
Lickskillet Rd 28734
Lightning Bug Ln 28734
Lilli Ln 28734
Lillian Hopkins Rd 28734
Limestone Dr 28734
Liner Dr 28734
Lion St 28734
Little Rd 28734
Little Brook Ln 28734
Little Cove Rd 28734
Little Ellijay Cir & Rd 28734
Little Nickajack Rd 28734
Little Ridge Rd 28734
Little Rocky Ln 28734
Lively Ln 28734
Liz Ln 28734
Lloyd Stewart Ln 28734
Lloyd Tallent Rd 28734
Lockwood Dr 28734
Locust Tree Rd 28734
Lodge Vw 28734
Lofty Ln 28734
Log Cabin Rd 28734
Log Haven Ln 28734
Log N Rd 28734
Logan Rd 28734
Lois Ln 28734
Lonesome Dove Ln 28734
Long Rd 28734
Long Bow Ln 28734
Longview Ct & Ln 28734
Longwood Dr 28734
Lopes Cir & Loop 28734
Lori Hill Rd 28734
Lorraine Rd 28734
Lost Gulls End 28734
Louisa Chapel Rd 28734
Louisa Ridge Rd 28734
Love St 28734
Love Cove Rd 28734
Loverly Way 28734
Loves Dr 28734
Low Brace Rd 28734
Lower Burningtown Rd 28734
W Lowery Ln 28734
Luke Still Rd 28734
Lullwater Rd 28734
Lullwater Ranch Acres 28734
Luther Raby Rd 28734
Lyle St 28734
Lyle Downs Rd 28734
Lyle Knob Rd 28734
Lyle Mill Rd 28734
Mac Cove Dr 28734
Mack Branch Rd 28734
Maclor Forest Cir, Ln & Rd 28734
Maclor Forest Heights Rd 28734
Macon Ave 28734
Macon Center Dr 28734
Macon Plaza Dr 28734
Macs Mountain Retreat Ln 28734
Magnolia Ln & Way 28734
Maidens Chapel Rd 28734
E, NE & W Main St & Trce 28734
Mallory Mtn 28734
Mann Rd 28734
Maple Dr & St 28734
Maple Breeze 28734
Maple Ridge Rd 28734
Maples Park Dr 28734
Margaret Dr 28734
Marion Thomas Rd 28734
Mariposa Way 28734
Mark Dowdle Rd 28734
Market St 28734
Marks Dr 28734
Marsh Ln 28734
Marshall Cove Rd 28734
Marshwood Way 28734
E Martha Ln 28734
Martin Peek Rd 28734
Marvic Hills Ln 28734
Mary B Ln 28734
Mashburn St 28734
Mashburn Branch Rd 28734
Mashburn Branch Cove Rd 28734
Mashburn Branch Estates Rd 28734
Mashburn Ridge Rd 28734
Mashburn Waters Dr 28734
Mashburn White Rd 28734
Mason Branch Rd 28734
Mason Hill Rd 28734
Mason Marion Dr 28734
Mason Mountain Dr 28734
Matlock Creek Rd 28734
Matlock Hills Rd 28734
Matlock Memories Rd 28734
Matthew Dr 28734
Matties Dr 28734
Maxies Corner Rd 28734
Maxwell Home Rd 28734
May Dr 28734
May Apple Ln 28734
Mc Dr 28734
Mccall Cir 28734
Mccall Mountain Rd 28734
Mcclure Rd 28734
Mcclure Mill Rd 28734
Mccollum Dr 28734
Mcconnell Rd 28734
Mccoy Rd & St 28734
Mccoy Hill Rd 28734
Mcdaniel Dr 28734
Mcdonald Rd 28734
Mcgaha Rd 28734
Mcintosh Trl 28734
Mckay St 28734
Mclaws Rd 28734
Meadow Ln 28734
Meadow Creek Rd 28734
Meadow Mtn Est Rd 28734
Meadow Rose Ln 28734
Meadow View Ln & Rd 28734
Meadow Wood Cir & Ct 28734
Meadowbrook Ct, Dr & Ln 28734
Meadowlark Ln 28734
Meadows Rd 28734
Meadowview Trl 28734
Medical Park Dr 28734
Medlin Rd 28734
Melody Ln 28734
Memorial Cir 28734
Memory Ln 28734
Mi Mountain Rd 28734
Mica Cir 28734
Mica City Rd 28734
Middle Dr 28734
Middle Burningtown Rd 28734
Middle Skeenah Rd 28734
Milk Run Ln 28734
Mill St 28734
Mill Creek Rd 28734
Millbrook Hts & Ln 28734
Millbrook Cove Rd 28734
W Mills Rd 28734
W Mimosa Dr & Ln 28734
Mincey Rd 28734
Mine Valley Trl 28734
Mint Lake Ct & Rd E & W 28734
Mirror Lake Dr 28734
Misty Dawn Cir 28734
Misty Hill Ln 28734
Misty Meadow Ln 28734
Misty Mountain Ln, Rd & Rdg 28734
Misty Ridge Dr 28734
Misty Valley Trl 28734
Mitten Ln 28734
Moffitt Cove Rd 28734
Monarch Ln 28734
Money Ln 28734
Moonstone Dr 28734
Moore Rd & St 28734
Moose Run Rd 28734
Morgan Rd 28734
Morning Glory Ln 28734
Morning Ridge Dr 28734
Morningside Dr 28734
Morrison Church Rd 28734
Moses Rd 28734
Mossy Oak Rd 28734
Mountain Cir 28734
Mountain Air Rd 28734
Mountain Breeze Rd 28734
Mountain Glory Way 28734
Mountain Grove Rd 28734
Mountain Laurel Dr 28734
Mountain Meadows Rd 28734
Mountain Paradise Dr 28734
Mountain Pride Rdg 28734
Mountain Springs Rd 28734
Mountain Terrace Rd 28734
Mountain View St 28734
Mountain View Villas 28734
Mountain Whispers Dr 28734
Mountainside Rd 28734
Mulligan Dr 28734
Murphy Rd 28734
Muskrat Rd 28734
Muskrat Valley Ln 28734
Mustang Ln 28734
My Place Ln 28734
Myers Cove Rd 28734
Mystic Mountain Rdg 28734
Nantoria Way 28734
Narrs Rd 28734
Nash Hill Dr 28734
Natural Dr 28734
Natures Way 28734
Natures Edge 28734
Natures Walk Rd 28734
Ned Hill Rd 28734
Neil Beasley Rd 28734
Nelson Hill Dr 28734
Nelson Waldroop Rd 28734
Nettie Hurst Rd 28734
New Hope Rd 28734
Newfound Ln 28734
Newman Rd 28734
Nichols Branch Rd 28734
Nickajack Rd 28734
Nikwasi Ln 28734
No Name Rd 28734
Noah Rd 28734
Noah Gibson Rd 28734
Nolen Cv 28734
Nonah Pl 28734
Norris Hl 28734
Norris Mcconnell Rd 28734
Northrup Dr 28734
Northside Dr 28734
Norton Tallent Rd 28734
Notta Rd 28734
Np And L Loop 28734
Nuthatch Ln 28734
Nuthouse Dr 28734
Oak Dr 28734
Oak Creek Rd 28734
Oak Forest Ln 28734
Oak Grove Church Rd 28734
Oak Hill Dr 28734
Oak Knob Dr 28734
Oak Leaf Trl 28734
Oak Ridge Dr 28734
Oak Tree Ct 28734
Oak Valley Dr 28734
Oakdale Dr 28734
Oaklawn Ave 28734
Oakleaf Dr 28734
Oakmont Way 28734
Oakridge School Rd 28734
Oakwood Dr 28734
Old Addington Bridge Rd 28734
Old Apple Tree Ln 28734
Old Barn Dr 28734
Old Buck Ln 28734
Old Cabin Rd 28734
Old Cat Creek Rd 28734
Old Chestnut Ln 28734
Old Clarks Chapel Rd 28734
Old Dairy Rd 28734
Old Frazier Rd 28734
Old Georgia Rd 28734
Old Highlands Rd 28734
Old Laurel Ln 28734
Old Mill Rd 28734
Old Mill Creek Rd 28734
W Old Murphy Rd 28734
Old Patton Rd 28734
Old Phillips Bridge Rd 28734
Old Poplar Rd 28734
Old Powerhouse Rd 28734
S Old Prentiss Rd 28734
Old Printers Way 28734
Old Siler Rd 28734
Old Smoky Gap Rd 28734
Old Sophie Rd 28734
Old Still Rd 28734
Old Thomas Rd 28734
Old Well Rd 28734
Olive Hill Holw & Rd 28734
Oliver Ln 28734
Olsen Dr 28734
Omega Hills Ln 28734
One Center Ct 28734
One Way Ter 28734
Onion Mountain Br & Rd 28734
Orchard Hill Rd 28734
Orchard View Dr 28734
Orenda Dr 28734
Oriole Dr 28734
Otto Heights Rd 28734
Outback Country Knl 28734
Over Dr 28734
Overlook Dr 28734
Owenby Ln 28734
Owl Knob Rd 28734
Paddock Rd 28734
Paige Ln 28734
E & W Palmer Dr, Rd & St 28734
Palmer Street Cir 28734
Pannell Ln 28734
Panorama Dr & Rdg 28734
Panther Dr 28734
Panther Ridge Ln 28734
Papas Mountain Rd 28734
Papaws Pl 28734
Paradise Rd 28734
Park Ave & Pl 28734
Park Ridge Dr 28734
Parker Farm Rd 28734
Parkview Ln 28734
Parrish Ln 28734
Parrish Cove Dr 28734
Parsons Way 28734
Passmore Rd 28734
Pastureview Dr 28734
Pat Rogers Rd 28734
Patterson Ln 28734
Pattis Pl 28734
S Patton Ave & Rd 28734
Patton Church Rd 28734
Patton Creekside Dr 28734
Patton Downs Rd 28734
Patton Farm Rd 28734
Patton Hill Rd 28734
Patton Valley Farms Rd 28734
Paul Hurst Rd 28734
Paul Rice Rd 28734
Paul Swafford Ln 28734
Pauline Ave & Cir 28734
Peace Haven Ln 28734
Peace Valley Ln 28734
Peaceful Rd 28734
Peaceful Cove Ln & Rd 28734
Peach Orchard Rd 28734
Pear Tree Ln 28734
Pearley Ln 28734
Pearly Gates Ct 28734
Peeks Creek Rd 28734
Peeks Pike Rd 28734
Pendergrass Rd 28734
Penhurst Ln 28734
Penland Ln, Rd & Trl 28734
Pennington Dr 28734
Penny Ln 28734
Peppermint St 28734
Perks Rd 28734
Perry Rd & St 28734
Pete Mccoy Rd 28734
Pheasant Dr 28734
Phillips Ln & St 28734
Pigeon Dr 28734
Pine Ave, Dr & Ln 28734
Pine Hill Rd 28734
Pine Ridge Dr 28734
Pinecone Dr 28734
Pinecrest Cir, Dr & Ln 28734
Piney Grove Rd 28734
Pinnacle Pt 28734
Pintail Rdg 28734
Pioneer Trl 28734
Pioneer Village Rd 28734
Piper Ln 28734
Pisgah Meadow Ct 28734
Pisgah Mountain Rd 28734
Pitts Rd 28734
Pitts Farm Rd 28734
Placid View Dr 28734
Plainview Ln 28734
Plantation Dr 28734
Pleasant Dr 28734
Pleasant Hill Dr & Rd 28734
Pleasant Valley Ln 28734
Plum Ln 28734
Plum Tree Ln 28734
Point Pleasant Dr 28734
Pond House Ln 28734
Ponderosa View Dr 28734
Pope Rd 28734
W Poplar Trl 28734
Poplar Cove Rd 28734
Poplar Grove Rd 28734
Poplar Ridge Ln 28734
Poplar Springs Rd 28734
Porter St 28734
Porter Creek Dr 28734
Possum Trl 28734
Possum Trot Trl 28734
Potts Branch Rd 28734
Poverty Branch Dr 28734
Prater Cove Rd 28734
Prentiss Bridge Rd 28734
Prentiss View Dr 28734
Preserve Dr 28734
Pressley Rd 28734
Pressley Circle Rd 28734
Prevost Ln 28734
Prison Camp Rd 28734
Promise Ln 28734
Prosperity Dr 28734
Prosperous Pt 28734
Punchbowl Dr 28734
Quail Walk N 28734
Quail Hollow Ln & Rd 28734
Quail Ridge Dr, Rd & Trl 28734
Queen Branch Rd 28734
Rabbit Ln 28734
Rabbit Creek Rd 28734
Rabbit Trac Rd 28734
Rabbit Track Trl 28734
Raby Dr 28734
Radio Hill Rd 28734
Rain Ridge Rd 28734
Rainbow Falls Rd 28734
Rainbow Springs Rd 28734
Rainbow Woods Dr 28734
Ralph Taylor Rd 28734
Ramblewood Rd 28734
Ramey Rd 28734
Randolph St 28734
Randy Dr 28734
Ransom Hill Cir 28734
Rass Justice Rd 28734
Rattlesnake Knob Rd 28734
Ray Cove Rd 28734
Ray Creek Rd 28734
Ray Downs Rd 28734
Rebecca Ln 28734
Red Cedar Ln 28734
Red Dog Rd 28734
Red Fox Ln & Run 28734
Red Leaf Ln 28734
Red Maple Ln 28734
Red Oak Rd 28734
Red Rock Rd 28734
Red Wolf Run 28734
Redbird Mountain Rd 28734
Redbud Ln 28734
Reserve Rd 28734
Restin Rd 28734
Reynolds Farm Rd 28734
Rich Rd 28734
Rickman Creek Rd 28734
E & W Ridge Rd & St 28734
Ridgecrest Baptist Ch Rd 28734
Ridgecrest Heights Rd 28734
Ridgecrest Villas Dr 28734
Ridgetop Rd 28734
Ridgewood Dr 28734
Rinehart Creek Rd 28734
River Dr & Rd 28734
River Bottom Ln 28734
River Ridge Rd 28734
River Roar Trl 28734
River Rock Ln 28734
W River Run Dr 28734
River Whispers Ln 28734
Riverbend Rd 28734
Riverbend Rv Cir 28734
Rivers Edge Trl 28734
Riverside Rd 28734
Riverview St 28734
Riverview Heights St 28734
Riverwood Dr 28734
Roane Rd 28734
Roanoke Rd 28734
Robbins Rd 28734
Roberts Rd 28734
Robin Crest Rd 28734
Robinet Ridge Rd 28734
Robinhood Ln 28734
Robins Nest Rd 28734
Robinson Ave 28734
Rock Quarry Rd 28734
Rockhaven Dr 28734
Rocking Chair Ln 28734
Rocky Branch Rd 28734
Rocky Cove Dr 28734
Rocky Creek Rd 28734
Rocky Hill Rd 28734
Rocky River Ln 28734
Rocky Top Ln 28734
Rodeo Dr 28734
E & W Rogers Rd & St 28734
Rogers Knob Rd 28734
Roland Rickman Rd 28734
Roller Mill Rd 28734
Rolling Acres Trl 28734
Rolling Hills Dr 28734
Rolling Meadows Dr 28734
Ronnie Vanhook Rd 28734
Roper Rd 28734
Roper Homestead Rd 28734
Roper Knob Rd 28734
Rose Ln 28734
Rose Creek Rd & Trl 28734
Rose Creek Cove Rd 28734
Rose Hill Dr 28734
Rosemary Ln 28734
Rosemont Dr 28734
Rosewood Dr 28734
Rough Hill Rd 28734
Roundstone Dr 28734
Rowland Rdg 28734
Roxie Ln 28734
Roy Cook Rd 28734
Roylston Rd 28734
Rozeta Gap Dr 28734
Ruby Cir & Ln 28734
Ruby Holland Rd 28734
Ruby Knoll Ln 28734
Ruby Mine Rd 28734
Ruby Ridge Rd 28734
Rufus Ridge Rd 28734
Runaway Hills Rd 28734
Runaway Ridge Rd 28734
Running Brook Dr 28734
Running Deer Rd 28734
Running Wolf Dr 28734
Russ Ln 28734
Russell Cove Rd 28734
Ruth Ledford Rd 28734
Rv Park Ln & Trl 28734
Ryan Rd 28734
Sab Rd 28734
Saddle Up Dr 28734
Sage Rd 28734
Saint Johns Church Rd 28734
Saldeer Mountain Rd 28734
Saldeer Summit Rd 28734
Sam Hill Rd 28734
Sam Mcclure Rd 28734
Sam Stockton Rd 28734
Sam Vanhook Ln 28734
Samantha Rd 28734
Sams Holw 28734
San Doria Rd 28734
Sanctuary Ln 28734
Sandefur Ln 28734
Sanders Rd 28734
Sanderstown Rd 28734
Sanderstown Ridge Rd 28734
Sandy Rd 28734
Santeetlah Rdg 28734
Sanwood Dr 28734
Sapphire Ln 28734
Sarawak Rd 28734
Sassy Trl 28734
Satinwood Dr 28734
Saunders Rd 28734
Sawdust Trl 28734
Sawmill Ln 28734
Sawmill Village Ln 28734
Scarlet Oak Dr 28734
Scenic View Dr 28734
Schley Farm Rd 28734
School House Rd 28734
Schurman Cove Rd 28734
Scofield Rd 28734

Street	ZIP
Scott Mickler Rd	28734
Scroggs Rd	28734
Scruffie Dr	28734
Scutter Ln	28734
Second St	28734
Selah Ln	28734
Seminole Dr	28734
September Embers Dr	28734
Sequoyah Ridge Dr	28734
Serenity Ridge Dr	28734
Setser Rd	28734
Setser Branch Rd	28734
Settlers Ln	28734
Shadow Ln	28734
Shadow Branch Rd	28734
Shady Ln	28734
Shady Brook Ln	28734
Shady Cove Ln	28734
Shady Knoll Rd	28734
Shady Oaks Dr	28734
Shady Ridge Rd	28734
Shallow Hollow Rd	28734
Shamrock Pl	28734
Sharons Blf	28734
Shawn Pack Cir	28734
Sheffield Farms Rd	28734
Sheldon Miller Rd	28734
Shepherd Dr	28734
Shepherd Creek Rd	28734
Sherrill Dr	28734
Sherry Ln	28734
Sherwood Dr	28734
Shiloh Springs Rd	28734
Shiver Phillips Dr	28734
Shope Cove Rd	28734
N Shore Dr	28734
Short Ridge Rd	28734
Shuler Rd	28734
Sierra Dr	28734
Siler Rd	28734
Siler Farm Rd	28734
Silo Branch Rd	28734
Silver Spruce Ln	28734
Silvercrest Rd	28734
Silverleaf Ln	28734
Sisk Branch Rd	28734
Skeenah Rd	28734
Skip Walters Rd	28734
Skyland Dr	28734
Skylark St	28734
Skyline Dr	28734
Skyline View Rd	28734
Skyview Ln	28734
Slagle Farm Rd	28734
Sleepy Hollow Ln	28734
Slep Orchard Rd	28734
Sloan Rd & St	28734
Sloan Industrial Park	28734
Slope Dr	28734
Smith Rd	28734
Smith Hill Rd	28734
Smoke Rdg	28734
Smokerise Rd	28734
Smoky Mountain Dr	28734
Snapfinger Hills Rd	28734
Snob Hill Rd	28734
Snookers Ln	28734
Snow Hill Falls Cir & Ln	28734
Snowhill Rd	28734
Snowy Knoll Ln	28734
Soaring Eagle Dr	28734
Soper Rd	28734
Sorrells Rd	28734
Sound Forest Ln	28734
Sourwood Dr	28734
Southard Valley Ln	28734
Southern Trce	28734
Southside Ln	28734
Sparrow Dr	28734
Spence Ledford Rd	28734
Spencer Ln	28734
Split Creek Rd	28734
Spradlin Rd	28734
Spring Rd & St	28734
Spring Blossom Dr	28734
Spring Branch Rd	28734
Spring Breeze Dr	28734
Spring Creek Rd	28734
Spring Hill Rd	28734
Spring Mountain Cir	28734
Springbrook Dr	28734
Springside Dr & Ln	28734
Sprinkle Rd	28734
St Johns Church Rd	28734
Stahelin Ln	28734
Stamey Cv	28734
Stamey Mountain Rd	28734
Stanfield Br & Rd	28734
Stanley Dr	28734
Starfire St	28734
Starlight Dr	28734
Stars Hollow Dr	28734
Starview Ln	28734
Steeplechase Rd	28734
Steves Pl	28734
Stewart St	28734
Stiles Dr	28734
Still House Branch Rd	28734
Stillhouse Rd	28734
Stiwinter Mountain Rd	28734
Stockman Dr	28734
Stockton Rd	28734
Stonebriar Xing	28734
Stonebrook Dr	28734
Stonebrook Hgts	28734
Stonecreek Dr	28734
Stonehouse Dr	28734
Stonewall Jackson Rd	28734
Stonewood Ln	28734
Stoneybrook Ln	28734
Stony Ln	28734
Stoudemire Dr	28734
Studebaker Ln	28734
Sugar Cove Rd	28734
N Sugar Creek Rd	28734
Sugar Maple Ln	28734
Sugar Ridge Rd	28734
Sugarcrest Ln	28734
Sugarfork Rd	28734
Sugarfork Church Rd	28734
Sugarfork Mountain Rd	28734
Summer Cir	28734
Summer Oaks Ln	28734
Summerfield Rd	28734
Summerhill Dr	28734
Summertime Hl	28734
Summit Dr	28734
Summit Hill Dr	28734
Summit Ridge Rd	28734
Sunburst Dr	28734
Suncrest Ln	28734
Sundance Dr	28734
Sunday Dr	28734
Sunny Ln	28734
Sunrise Ln	28734
Sunrise Ridge Rd	28734
E Sunset Dr & Rd	28734
Sunset Mountain Trl	28734
Sunset Ridge Rd	28734
Sunset Trace Trl	28734
Sunshine Dr	28734
Suttles Cir & Rd	28734
Sutton Ln & Pl	28734
Swallow Ln	28734
Sweet Grass Ln	28734
Sweet Nectar Ln	28734
Sweet Water Dr & Way	28734
W Swift Creek Rd	28734
Sycamore Dr	28734
Sylva Hwy & Rd	28734
T And E Ln	28734
T Bird Ln	28734
Tall Ridge Rd	28734
Tall Timber Dr	28734
Tallent Dr & St	28734
Tallent Cove Rd	28734
Talley Ln	28734
Talley Mountain Ln	28734
Tan Trough Trl	28734
Tanasi Ln	28734
Tanasi Landing Pl	28734
Tanglewood Ln	28734
Tarheel Trl	28734
Tate Cove Rd	28734
Tater Trl	28734
Tater Knob Rd & Rdg	28734
Tattnall Rd	28734
Taylor Rd & Trce	28734
Tcs Ln	28734
Teaberry Ln	28734
Teds Cir	28734
Teebear Trl	28734
Teem Hl & Trl	28734
Tellico Rd	28734
Templewood Dr	28734
Tennessee View St	28734
Tennis Court Dr	28734
Teran Cir	28734
Teris Way	28734
Terrace Ln	28734
Terrace Ridge Dr	28734
Terrell Rd	28734
Tessentee Ln & Rd	28734
Tessentee Woods Rd	28734
Thickety Trace Dr	28734
Third St	28734
Thomas Rd	28734
Thomas Heights Rd	28734
Thompkins Ln	28734
Thompson Rd	28734
Thorn Wood Rd	28734
Three Cabin Trl	28734
Thump Thunder Dr	28734
Thumpers Trl	28734
Thunder Rdg & Trl	28734
Thunder Creek Dr	28734
Thunderstruck Ln	28734
Tiger Lily Trl	28734
Timber Ln	28734
Timber Creek Dr	28734
Timber Ridge Rd	28734
Timbercrest Dr	28734
Timberland Trl	28734
Timberland Ridge Trl	28734
Tippett Ln	28734
Tippett Branch Rd	28734
Tippett Creek Rd	28734
Tisit Dr	28734
Todd Trl	28734
Tokumto St	28734
Town Mountain Dr	28734
Townhouse Pl	28734
Traces Pl	28734
Trae Rd	28734
Trampus Trl	28734
Tranquil Dr	28734
Travis Trl	28734
Treasure Ln	28734
Tree Top Ln	28734
Treeline Trl	28734
Trillium Trl	28734
Trimont Cir & Trl	28734
Trimont Branch Rd	28734
Trimont Lake Rd	28734
Trimont Lake Estates Rd	28734
Trimont Lake Overlook	28734
Trimont Mountain Rd & Trl	28734
Trimont View Dr	28734
Tulip Ln	28734
Tulip Tree Ln	28734
Tumblewood Dr	28734
Turkey Chase Ln	28734
Turkey Creek Dr	28734
Turkey Hollow Rd	28734
Turkey Pen Rd	28734
Turner Anderson Rd	28734
Turtle Cove Rd	28734
Turtle Dove Ln	28734
Twin Hills Rd	28734
Two Barn Ln	28734
Two Turtle Rd	28734
Two Waters Trl	28734
Tyding Rd	28734
Ulco Dr & Ln	28734
Ulco Bluffs Dr	28734
Ulco Ridge Rd	28734
Uncle Joes Blf	28734
Underburg Ln	28734
Union Otto Day Care Rd	28734
Union School Rd	28734
Up The Creek Rd	28734
Upper Burningtown Rd	28734
Upper Dalton Creek Rd	28734
Upper Peeks Creek Rd	28734
Valhalla Ln	28734
Valley Crst, Ln & Rd	28734
N Valley View Dr, Rd & Trl	28734
Van Carter Rd	28734
Van Raalte St	28734
Vandyke Dr	28734
Vanhook Rd	28734
Varner Rd	28734
Vaughn Rd	28734
Vester Ledford Rd	28734
Victory Ln	28734
Village Cir, Rd & Trce	28734
Vine Dr	28734
Vista Cir & Pt	28734
Vista Villa Hls	28734
Wadesboro Cir	28734
Wadhams Pl	28734
Wald Haus Way	28734
Waldroop Rd	28734
Walkerville Way	28734
Wallace St	28734
Wallace Branch Rd	28734
Walnut Dr, Hl & Ln	28734
Walnut Cove Rd	28734
Walnut Creek Rd	28734
Walters Dr	28734
Warren Ln	28734
Watauga Cv, Rd & St	28734
Watauga Church Rd	28734
Watauga Creek Trl	28734
Watauga Heights Rd	28734
Watchman Ln	28734
Water Gauge Rd	28734
Waterfall Dr & Ln	28734
Watkins Ln	28734
Watson Rd	28734
Watson Cove Rd	28734
Wayah Dr, Rd, St & Way	28734
Wayah Cove Rd	28734
Wayah View Dr	28734
Wayah Woods Ln	28734
Wayne Duvall Dr	28734
Wayside Dr	28734
Weaver Cabe Rd	28734
Wedgewood Rd	28734
Welch Rd	28734
Wells Grove Rd	28734
Welm Way	28734
Wendover Dr	28734
West Blvd & Rd	28734
Westfield Trce	28734
Westgate Plz	28734
Westside Ln	28734
Westwood Dr	28734
Wheat Field Rd	28734
Whipporwill Trl	28734
Whisper Mountain Rd	28734
Whispering Meadows Dr	28734
Whispering Pines Trl	28734
White Oak Cir & St	28734
White Pine Cir	28734
White Rock Ridge Rd	28734
White Tail Trl	28734
Whitfield Rd	28734
Whitlock Rd	28734
Whitney Ln	28734
Whits Trl	28734
Wide Horizon Dr	28734
Wide View Ln	28734
Wiggins Rd	28734
Wild Deer Trl	28734
Wild Flower Dr	28734
Wild Magnolia Way	28734
Wild Meadows Rd	28734
Wild Mint Rd	28734
Wild Pear Ln	28734
Wild Rose Ln	28734
Wild Strawberry Ln	28734
Wild Turkey Ln	28734
Wildcat Trl	28734
Wilderness Way	28734
Wildflower Dr	28734
Wilds Cove Rd	28734
Wildwood Acres Rd	28734
Wiley Brown Rd	28734
Wilkes Branch Ln	28734
Wilkes Knob Rd	28734
Wilkie St	28734
Williamson Dr	28734
Willis Cove Rd	28734
Willow Ct & Pl	28734
Willow Cove Rd	28734
Willow Grove Ln	28734
Willow Pond Rd	28734
Willow View Dr	28734
Willowbrook Est & Run	28734
Wilson Ave	28734
Wind Forest Dr	28734
Winding Way Dr	28734
Winding Woods Trce	28734
Windsong Ln	28734
Windsong Mountain Dr	28734
Windswept Ridge Rd	28734
Windwood Ln	28734
Windy Acres	28734
Windy Corner Rd	28734
Windy Gap Rd	28734
Windy Hill Dr	28734
Windy Hill Farm Rd	28734
Windy Poplar Rd	28734
Winners Cir	28734
Winston St	28734
Wispering Creek Ln	28734
Wisperwood Rd	28734
Wolf Rdg	28734
Wolf Run Rd	28734
Wolf View Rd	28734
N Womack St	28734
Wonder Ln	28734
Wood Ln	28734
Wood Pond Rd	28734
Wood Song Ln	28734
Woodbridge Rd	28734
Woodbrooke Hl	28734
Woodcastle Ln	28734
Woodchuck Ln	28734
Woodcove Dr	28734
Woodcrest Cir	28734
Woodhaven Dr	28734
Woodland Cir, Dr, Hts & Trl	28734
Woodland Cove Rd	28734
Woodland Hills Dr	28734
Woodpecker Way	28734
Woodrow Shope Rd	28734
Woodrows Ln	28734
Woods Ln	28734
Woods Edge Trl	28734
Woodside Villa Dr	28734
Woody Rd	28734
Wooten Cir & Rd	28734
Wooten Ridge Rd	28734
Wykle Rd	28734
Wyman Way	28734
Wymer Mason Rd	28734
Yearling Way	28734
York Ln	28734
Younce Ln	28734
Younce Creek Rd	28734
Young Cove Rd	28734
Youns Mtn	28734
Zurich Cir	28734

NUMBERED STREETS

Street	ZIP
All Street Addresses	28734

GASTONIA NC

General Delivery	28052

POST OFFICE BOXES MAIN OFFICE STATIONS AND BRANCHES

Box No.s	ZIP
1747A - 1747A	28053
1 - 2814	28053
3501 - 5299	28054
6001 - 6500	28056
8600 - 8600	28053
9998 - 9998	28052
9998 - 9998	28055
12151 - 13186	28052
550001 - 551434	28055

RURAL ROUTES

Route	ZIP
05	28056

NAMED STREETS

Street	ZIP
A C Widener Dr	28056
Abbotsford Ct	28056
Aberdeen Blvd	28054
Acapulco Dr	28054
Accent Ln	28052
Acorn Ct	28056
Acorn Dr	28052
Adams Ave, Ct, Dr & Rd	28052
Aden Ave	28054
Adirondak Dr	28052
E Airline Ave	28054
W Airline Ave	28052
Airport Rd	28056
Aj Wesley St	28056
Akinbac Rd	28056
Alexander Trl	28052
Alexandria Ct	28056
Allison Ave	28052
Allston Ct	28056
Almond Dr	28052
Alpine Ln	28054
Alton Dr	28054
Amanda Dr	28056
Amber Crest Dr	28052
Amberhill Ln	28052
Ambrose Dr	28056
American St	28052
Amhurst Dr	28056
Amity Ave	28054
Amy Ct	28052
Anderson St	28054
Andover Cir	28056
Andrea Ln	28056
Andrew Cir	28056
Andy Ln	28056
Angela Ct	28056
Angels Haven Ct	28056
Angler Way	28052
Angus Dr	28056
E Ann St	28054
Anna Elizabeth Dr	28052
Anne Neely Rd	28056
Annie Boyce Rd	28056
Anthony Dr	28052
Antlers Ct	28052
Appaloosa Way	28056
N Apple St	28054
Apple Blossom Cir	28052
Applegate Ct	28054
Applegate Rd	28056
Appling Dr	28052
April Dr	28056
April Valley Dr	28052
Araglin Dr	28056
Aragon Ln	28056
Arbors Dr	28054
Arbroath Trce	28054
Archie Rd	28052
Archie Whitesides Rd	28052
Archwood Dr	28052
Arkray St	28052
Armstrong Cir	28054
Armstrong Ln	28056
Armstrong St	28054
Armstrong Park Dr & Rd	28054
Arrowhead Cir	28054
Arrowood Dr	28056
Arthur Ave	28052
Ashbourne Dr	28056
Ashe Pl & St	28056
Ashley Ct	28054
Ashley Ln	28056
Ashton Ave	28052
Ashton Pl	28054
Ashwood Ct	28054
Ashworth Dr	28054
Aspen Dr	28052
Aspen Way Ct	28054
Aster Ln	28054
Atchley Ave	28054
Athenian Dr	28052
Atkins Pl	28056
Audrey Dr	28054
Audubon Dr	28054
Augusta Ct	28056
Austin St	28052
Auten Rd	28054
Autumn Dr	28056
Autumn Chase Ln	28056
Autumnwood Trl	28056
Avalon Rd	28056
Avery Pl	28056
N & S Avon St	28054
Avondale Rd	28054
Azalea Dr	28054
B St	28054
Babbling Brook Ln	28052
Backcreek Ln	28054
Badger Rd	28052
Bailey Ln	28056
Bainbridge St	28052
Baker Blvd & St	28052
Ballantyne Dr	28054
Ballard Dr	28054
Balsam Ct	28052
Balthis Dr	28054
Baltic St	28054
Banks Ave	28056
Barber Rd	28056
Barkley St	28052
Barn View Rd	28052
Barnstable Ct	28056
Baronwood Ct	28052
Barrett Ln	28054
Barrington Dr	28056
Bartlett St	28056
Barwick Rd	28052
Basswood Way	28052
Baugh St	28052
Baxter Ave	28054
Bayberry Ct	28056
Baytree Ct	28056
Bayview St	28054
Baywoods Ct	28056
Beacon St	28054
Beacon Hills Dr	28056
Beam Ave	28052
Beam Rd	28056
Bearbrook Ln	28052
Beartooth Ct	28054
Beatrice Costner Ave	28052
Beaty Rd	28056
Beaverbrook Dr	28052
Beckingham Ct	28056
Becky Ave	28052
Bedfordshire Dr	28056
Bedgood Dr	28056
Bee Dr	28056
Beech St	28052
Beechwood Cir	28054
Beechwood Dr	28052
Belfast Dr	28052
Belhaven Forest Dr	28056

Bell St 28052
Bellevue Ter 28056
Belmar Dr 28052
Belt Dr 28056
N & S Belvedere Ave 28054
Belvon Dr 28056
Benfield Rd 28056
Bent Branch St 28054
Benton Ave 28056
Berger St 28052
Berkshire Dr 28052
Bermuda Ave 28054
Bernice Dr 28052
Berry St 28054
Berryview Ln 28056
Berwick Ln 28054
Bessemer City Rd 28052
Bethany Rd 28052
Bethesda Oaks Dr 28056
Bethlehem St 28054
Bethlehem Church St 28056
Betty St 28054
Beverly Dr 28054
Bickett Ave 28052
Bicycle Ct 28054
Big Oak Rd 28052
Biggers Ave 28052
Billings St 28052
Binwhe Ln 28052
Birchfield Ln 28056
Birchwood Ct 28056
Birchwood Dr 28052
Black St 28052
Black Oak Dr 28054
Black Powder Ct 28056
Black Springs Dr 28054
Black Walnut Trl 28056
Blackburn Ct 28056
Blackwood St 28052
Blake Dr 28056
Bluedevil Dr 28056
Bob Nolen Rd 28056
Bob White Ln 28056
Bolding St 28052
Bolivia Dr 28054
Bond Ave 28052
Booker St 28054
Boone Dr 28056
Bordeaux Ave 28056
Borderline Dr 28056
Boulware Ave 28052
Bounty Ln 28056
Bowden Ln 28056
Boxwood Ln 28054
N Boyce St 28052
N & S Boyd Rd & St 28052
Bradbury Ct 28052
Braddy Ln 28052
Bradford St 28054
Bradford Heights Rd 28054
Bradley Ave 28052
E Bradley St 28052
W Bradley St 28052
Bradley Trl 28056
Braeburn Ct 28054
Brainard Ct 28056
Branch Ave & St 28054
Branding Iron Dr 28052
Brandon St 28052
Brandywine Ct 28054
Brandywine Dr 28052
Braswell Dr 28056
Brentwood Cir 28052
Brentwood Dr
300-399 28052
3500-3699 28056
Brian Cir 28056
Briar Creek Rd 28056
Briar Oak Dr 28052
Briarcliff Rd 28056
Briarwood Ave 28054
Briarwood Ln 28056
Brice Rd 28056
Bridgeport Ln 28056
Bridgestone Ct 28056
Bridgewood Ln 28054

Bridle Path Trl 28054
Bridlewood Ct 28054
Briggs Ct 28054
Brimwood Ct 28056
Brindle St 28052
Bristlecone Ct 28056
Bristol Cir 28052
Brittany Ct 28056
N Broad St 28054
S Broad St
100-598 28054
101-499 28052
501-599 28054
Broadcast St 28052
Broadview Ln 28056
Broadwater Ct 28056
Broadwing Ct 28056
Brookberry Ln 28056
Brookhaven Dr 28056
Brooklet Dr 28052
Brookneal Dr 28054
Brooks Rd & St 28052
Brookside Dr 28056
Brookside St 28054
Brookstone Ct 28052
Brown St
900-1099 28052
1900-1999 28054
Brownstone Ct 28054
Brunett St 28052
Bryant St 28052
Bryantcole Way 28056
Brymer Rd 28056
Bryson St 28054
Buckeye Ln 28056
Buckingham Ave 28054
Bucknell Ave 28054
Buckskin Dr 28052
Buckthorn Ct 28056
Bud Eye Pl 28056
Bud Wilson Rd 28056
Buena Vale Dr 28056
Buena Vista Way 28054
Bulb Ave 28052
Bur Oak Dr 28056
Burke Ave 28054
Burlington Ave 28054
Burmil Dr 28054
Burning Willow Ct 28054
Burrington Ct 28054
Burt Ave 28054
Burton Hills Cir 28054
Burtonwood Dr 28054
Bush St 28056
N Bush St 28054
Business Park Ct 28052
Butch Dr 28056
Butler Ct & St 28054
Butterfly Ct 28056
Butternut Dr 28054
Button Bush Ct 28052
Byrd Dr 28056
C V Ln 28056
Cabin St 28056
Cagle Ct 28056
Cain Ct 28052
Cairnsmore Pl 28054
Caldwell St 28052
N Calvary St 28054
S Calvary St 28052
Cama Dr 28056
Cambridge Ave 28054
Camelot Ct 28052
Cameo Trl 28056
Cameron Ave 28056
Camille St 28056
Camp St 28052
Camp Rotary Rd 28052
Can Do Ct 28056
Candleberry Dr 28056
Candleglow Dr 28056
Candlewick Trl & Way 28056
Candlewood Dr 28052
Canoby Ct 28054
Canterberry Dr 28056
Canterbury Ct 28052

Canvasback Ct 28052
Cape Breton Trl 28056
Capel Ct 28056
Capella Ct 28056
Capitol Dr 28056
Cardinal Dr 28052
Carl St 28054
Carla Ct 28056
Carlton Dr 28054
Carmel Dr 28056
Carmel Hills Dr 28056
Carmen Ln 28054
Carnoustie Ct 28056
Carol Dr 28054
Carolina Ave 28052
Carolina Cir 28054
Carolina Cherry Ct 28056
Carolyn Cir 28056
N Carpenter St 28054
Carriage House Ln 28054
Carrid Dr 28052
Carrie Elizabeth Ct 28056
Carrigan Dr 28056
Carson Dr & Rd 28052
Carson Spring Ct 28056
Carver Dr 28056
Cascade Dr 28056
Cassidy Dr 28054
Castle Ct 28052
Castlegate St 28054
Castlehill Rd 28052
Castlewood Dr 28056
Caswell Ct 28054
Catalina Dr 28052
Catawba Cove Dr 28056
Catawba Creek Dr 28056
Catawba Hills Dr 28056
Catawba Spring Pkwy 28054
Catfish Dr 28056
Catskill Ct 28052
Cauthen Way 28056
Cavney Ct 28052
Cecelia Dr 28054
E Cedar Ave 28054
Cedar Ct 28056
Cedar St 28056
Cedar Grove Dr 28056
Cedar Oak Cir 28052
Cedar Point Rd 28056
Cedarwood Dr 28052
Cemetary Rd 28056
Centennial St 28056
Center St 28054
Central Ave 28054
Chantilly Dr 28056
Chapel Grove Rd 28052
Chapel Grove School Rd 28052
Chapelwood Dr 28052
Charlwood Dr 28052
Chartres Dr 28056
Chastaine Ln 28052
Chateau Dr 28056
Chelsea Way 28056
Chelston Ct 28054
Cherbough Way 28056
Cherokee Ct 28056
Cherokee Dr 28052
N Cherry St 28052
Cherry Bark Oak Ct 28056
Cherry Park Dr 28052
Cherrywood Ln 28052
Cheshire Ln 28056
Chespark Dr 28052
Chesser Ave 28054
N & S Chester St 28052
Chesterfield Ct 28052
Chestnut Ln 28052
N Chestnut St 28054
S Chestnut St 28054
Cheviot Ln 28054
Chewacla Ln 28052
Chickasaw Rd 28056
Chinaberry Ct 28052
Chrisco Ln 28056
Christian Dr 28052

Chronicle Ave 28052
Church St 28054
Churchill Dr 28054
Cindy Ln 28056
Circle Dr 28054
Circle View Dr 28054
Citation Ln 28056
Clara St 28054
Clark Ave 28052
Clarke Ct 28056
Claudette Dr 28052
Clay Dr 28056
S Clay St 28052
Clay Court Dr 28056
Claybrook Cir 28054
Clear Creek Ct 28054
Clearview Ct 28054
Clearwood Ct 28052
Clell Dr 28052
Clenso Dr 28056
Cleveland Ave 28052
Clifton Fox Ct 28052
Cline Park Dr 28054
Clinton Dr 28054
Cloister Dr 28056
Cloninger Ave 28052
Clouse St 28052
Cloverdale Cir & Ln 28052
Cloverwood Ln
2200-2299 28054
4600-4699 28052
E Club Dr 28054
W Club Circle Dr 28054
E & W Club Colony Dr 28056
Clubhouse Dr 28054
Clubview Cir 28056
Clyde St 28052
Clyde May Dr 28056
Clydesdale Dr 28056
Coachwood Ln 28056
Cobb St 28054
Cobblestone Ct 28056
E Cole St 28054
Colebrook Dr 28052
Colfax Ct 28056
Collier St 28054
Collinston Dr 28052
Colony Ct 28056
Colony Ridge Dr 28056
Colony Woods Dr 28054
Colorado Ct 28056
S Columbia St 28054
Colvard Dr 28056
Confederate Dr 28056
Congaree Dr 28052
Congress Ct & St 28054
Connemara Ct 28054
Conner St 28054
Conrad Ave 28052
Cook Sears Rd 28056
Cooks Lake Rd 28056
Copper Ridge Ct 28056
Copperfield Rd 28056
Cora St 28054
Cordoba St 28054
Corl Dr 28052
Cornwallis Ave 28054
Cottage Ct 28054
Cotton Blossom Cir 28054
Cottonwood Ln 28052
Country Club Dr 28056
Country Club Rd 28054
Country Meadows Dr 28056
Country Pines Dr 28052
Country Village Dr 28056
Court Dr 28054
Courtland Dr 28056
Courtney Cove Ct 28052
Cove Rd 28052
Cove Creek Dr 28056
Covenant Dr 28054
Covington Ln 28056
Cox Rd 28054
Cp Groves Rd 28052
Cr Wood Rd 28056

Craig Ave 28054
Craigland Ln 28056
Cramer Woods Dr 28056
Cramerton Rd 28056
Craven St 28052
Crawford Ave 28052
Crawford Rd
200-299 28056
5000-5999 28052
Creek Bed Cir 28054
Creek Haven Dr 28056
Creek Meadow Dr 28054
Creek Ridge Dr 28056
Creekbriar Ave 28054
Creekview Dr 28052
Crescent Ave
1-199 28054
1200-1299 28052
Crescent Ln 28052
Crestview St 28054
Crestwood Ave 28054
Cricket Ln 28052
Crimson Ct 28056
Crisp Rd 28056
Cross Creek Dr 28056
Cross Ridge Dr 28056
Crossway Cir 28054
Crowders Trl 28052
Crowders Creek Rd 28052
Crowders Creek Church Rd 28052
Crowders Crest Dr 28052
Crowders Crossing Ln 28052
Crowders Ridge Ct 28052
Crowders View Dr 28052
Crowders Woods Dr 28052
Cuckleburr Ln 28056
Cumberland Ave 28054
Curtis St 28052
Cypress Ct 28056
Cypress Dr 28052
Cypress Oak Ln 28056
Cypress Pond Ln 28056
Daffodil Ct 28054
Daisy Ct 28052
Daisy Dr 28056
Dale Ave 28052
Dalewood Dr 28054
Dallas Bessemer City Hwy 28052
Dallas Spencer Mtn Rd 28056
N & S Dalton St 28052
Damascus Dr 28056
Dana Ln 28056
Danbury St 28052
Daniel Dr 28052
Daniel Ellis Dr 28056
Dare Ct 28054
Darrell Ave 28054
Darren Dr 28054
Dartmouth Dr 28054
Davenport St 28054
David Allen Ln 28056
E Davidson Ave 28054
W Davidson Ave 28052
Davie St 28052
E Davis Ave 28054
Davis Heights Dr 28052
Davis Park Rd 28052
Dawnshire Dr 28054
Dawnwood Dr 28056
Dean St 28052
Deep Forest Ct 28056
Deepwood Ct 28054
Deer Crossing Trl 28056
Deer Haven Ter 28056
Deer Hunter Trl 28052
Deerwood Dr 28054
Dellinger Ave 28054
Dellview Dr 28054
Delta Dr 28052
Denada Ct 28054
Denali Ct 28054
Denise Dr 28056
Derby Ct 28054

Derbydowns Dr 28056
Derrydowne Ln 28056
Devonshire Ct 28054
Devonwood Ct 28052
Dewey St 28054
Diamond T Rd 28052
Dicky Mill Rd 28052
Digh St 28052
Dix St 28052
S Dixie St 28052
Dixon Ave 28052
Dixon Cir 28054
Dixon Rd 28054
Dixon Howe Rd 28056
Dobbs Pond Rd 28056
Doe Creek Ct 28056
Doffin Ln 28052
Dogwood Dr
700-999 28054
1000-1099 28056
Dogwood Pl 28056
Dogwood St 28056
Dolphin St 28056
Donalds Dr 28054
Donegal Ct 28054
Donna Ave 28052
Donnabrook Ln 28052
Donnell Dr 28056
Donnington Way 28056
Donohoe Rd 28052
Dooley Rd 28054
Dorchester Rd 28056
Doris St 28056
Dornoch Rd 28054
Dorset Dr 28054
Double Oaks Rd 28056
Douglas Dr 28054
Dove Ln 28056
Dove Trl 28052
Dove Creek Ct 28054
Dove Meadows Dr 28052
Dove Tree Ln 28054
Dovewind Ct 28056
Dovewood Ln 28056
Dow Dr 28056
Dowd Dr 28054
Downey Pl 28054
Drake St 28052
Drayton Ct 28056
Drayton Hall Way 28056
Dresden Dr 28056
Driftwood Dr 28056
Dry Creek Ct 28054
Dublin Ct 28054
Duff St 28054
Dugar Ct 28056
Duhart Ave 28054
Duke St 28056
Dukes Cir 28052
Dumbarton Rd 28054
Dunbar Ln 28056
Duncan Ln & Rd 28056
Dundeen Dr 28052
Dunham Rd 28054
Eagle Ct 28054
Eagle Crest Ln 28056
Eagle Glen Ct 28056
Eaglebrook Dr 28056
Eagles Walk 28056
Eaglewood Dr 28052
Earl Ln 28052
East Dr 28052
Eastford Ct 28056
Easthampton Dr 28056
Eastover Dr 28054
Eastridge Dr 28056
Eastside St 28054
Eastwood Dr 28054
Eastwynn Cir 28052
Easy Ave 28054
Ebony Ave 28054
Echo Ln 28052
Eddie St 28054
Edenton Ct 28054
Edgefield Ave 28052
N & S Edgemont Ave 28054

Edgewater Rd 28056
Edgewood Cir 28052
Edinburg Dr 28054
Edison Dr 28052
Edna Dr 28056
Edward Graham Rd 28056
Edwards Ave 28054
Edwin St 28052
Efird St 28054
Elam St 28054
Elder Ct 28054
Elderwood Ct 28052
Elgin Ct 28056
Eli Cir 28056
Elizabeth Cir 28054
Elizabeth Dr 28052
Elizabeth Ln 28052
Elizabeth St 28054
Elkhart Cir 28054
Elkhorn Ln 28052
Ellabe St 28052
Eller Rd 28056
Ellis Rd
100-199 28056
300-399 28052
E Elm St 28054
S Elm St 28052
Elmwood Dr 28054
Elva Ira Ln 28054
Emerald Ln 28056
S Emerson St 28052
Emily Ct 28054
English Garden Dr 28056
Eppinette Ct 28056
Eric Ct 28052
Erika Ln 28056
Erskine Dr 28054
Ervin Dr 28056
Essen Ln 28054
Essex Ave 28052
Ethel Dr 28056
Etta Pl 28052
Evening Shade Ln 28052
Everest Dr 28054
Evergreen St 28054
Fair St 28056
Fair Meadows Ct 28056
Fair Oaks Dr 28054
Fairfax Dr
400-499 28056
2500-2599 28054
Fairfield Dr 28054
Fairgreen Dr 28056
Fairlane Dr
1700-1799 28054
1801-1899 28054
3700-3799 28056
Fairstone Dr 28056
Fairview Dr 28052
Fairway Ln 28054
Falcon Ct 28054
Falcons Nest Ct 28056
Falling Oak Ln 28052
Fallingwood Cir 28056
N Falls St 28052
S Falls St 28056
Falls Ferguson Rd 28052
Fallsdale Dr 28052
Fallswood Dr 28052
Farewell Dr 28054
Farm Pond Ct 28054
Farmbrook Rd 28056
Farmhouse Ln 28056
Farmview Dr 28056
E Farmview St 28054
W Farmview St 28054
Farmville Dr 28056
Farragut Ct 28056
Fawnbrook Ln 28052
Faye St 28054
Featherstone Ct 28056
Federal St 28052
Fenwick Hall Ct 28056
Ferguson Estates Rd 28052
Ferguson Ridge Rd 28052
Fern Forest Dr 28054

Ferncliff Dr & Rd 28056
Fernwood Dr 28052
Ferrell Ave 28056
Ferrell Grove Ave 28056
Ferris St 28054
Fewell Dr 28056
Fieldstone Dr 28056
Findlay St 28052
N & S Firestone St 28052
Firethorn Ct 28056
Firmin Ct 28056
Fl Maiers Rd 28056
Flag Pole Dr 28056
Flanagan Ln 28054
Fleetwood Cir 28052
Fleetwood Dr 28054
Flint Ln & St 28054
Flintshire Ln 28056
Florida St 28052
Flowe St 28052
Flowers Rd 28056
Floyd Ln 28052
Floyd Rd 28056
Flynn Dr 28054
Fonda St 28054
Forbes Rd
2400-3099 28056
4200-4299 28054
S Forbes St 28054
Forest Dr 28054
Forest Creek Ct 28052
Forest Heights Dr 28056
Forest Hill Ln 28052
Forest Pointe Ln 28056
Forestbrook Dr 28056
Forestwood Ct 28056
Forge Creek Ct 28054
Forington Ln 28056
Fostoria Dr 28054
Fox Ct 28052
Fox St 28054
Fox Fire Run 28052
Fox Hunt Dr 28054
Foxborough Ct 28056
Foxfield Ct 28054
Foxworth Ln 28052
Foy Rd 28052
Fraggle Rock Trl 28052
Fraley Rd 28052
Fraley Church Rd 28054
Frances Ct 28056
Francis St 28054
E Franklin Blvd
100-299 28052
300-2499 28054
2500-4499 28056
W Franklin Blvd 28052
N Franklin St 28054
Freedom Ct 28054
Freedom Mill Rd 28052
Freeport Dr 28052
Freida Ln 28054
Front St 28052
Frostwood Dr 28056
Frosty Bit Trl 28052
Fuller Dr 28052
Furman Cir 28056
Furr St 28056
Gail Ave 28052
Gaines Ave 28054
Gallagher Dr 28052
Galloway Dr 28052
Garden St 28052
Gardenside Dr 28056
Gardner St 28056
S Gardner St 28054
Gardner Park Dr 28054
Gardner Ridge Dr 28056
Garfield Dr 28052
Garland Ave 28052
E Garrison Blvd
100-127 28052
128-1999 28054
W Garrison Blvd 28052
Garrison St 28052
Gaston Ave 28052

Gaston Rd 28056
Gaston Way 28054
Gaston Day School Rd 28056
Gatehouse Ct 28056
Gateshead Ct 28054
Gatewood Dr 28056
Gayle Ave 28056
Gelinda Ct 28056
Gene Falls Cir 28056
Genes Rdg 28056
George Ln 28056
Georgemont Ct 28054
Georgetowne Dr 28054
Gibbons St 28052
Gilmer St 28052
Ginger Dr 28056
Gingles Farm Trl 28052
Glacier Ct 28056
Glasgow Ct 28056
Glenbriar Dr 28056
Gleneagles Dr 28056
Glenmore Ct 28056
Glenn St 28052
Glennallen Dr 28052
Glenraven Ave 28052
Glenridge Dr 28054
Glenview Ave 28054
Glenwood Dr 28054
Glover Rd 28056
Glyncastle Way 28056
Goble St 28056
Goddard Ln 28056
Goforth Ave 28054
Gold Mine Creek Rd 28056
Golden Bell Dr 28056
Golf Course Dr 28054
Golfview Dr 28056
Goodman Cir 28054
Gordon Dr 28056
Gothic Ct 28052
Governors Sq 28056
Grace St 28052
Graceland Ave 28054
Gracette Ln 28052
Graceway Dr 28052
Graham Rd 28056
Graham St 28052
Grampian Dr 28054
Grandover Dr 28054
W Granite Ave 28052
Granny Trl 28056
Grant St 28052
Grassy Ct 28052
Gray Ave 28054
N Gray St 28052
S Gray St 28052
Gray Bark Dr 28054
Grayson Ridge Ct 28056
Graystone Dr 28054
Graywood Dr 28052
Green Dr 28054
Green Chapman Rd 28056
Green Circle Dr 28054
Green Meadow Ct 28056
Green Meadow Dr 28052
Green Needle Trl 28056
Greenfield Ave 28052
Greenhaven Ln 28056
Greenhill Ave 28054
Greenleaf Dr
2100-2199 28054
2300-2399 28052
Greenpack Pkwy 28056
Greens Ave 28052
Greenview Dr 28054
Greenwich Ter 28052
Greenwood Dr 28052
Greg Dr 28052
Greylyn Ct 28054
Grice Ave 28054
Grier St 28056
Grimsby Ln 28056
Grissom Rd 28052
Grissom St 28056
Grove St 28054

Grover St 28054
Grovont Ct 28056
Gum St 28054
Hailey Ln 28056
Halifax Ct 28056
Hall Rd 28056
Hallmark Dr 28052
Hamilton Dr 28052
Hamme Ln 28054
Hampton St 28052
Hamptonbrook Dr 28056
Hamrick Rd 28056
Hancock St 28054
Hanks Cir 28052
Hanna St 28052
Hannaford Pl 28052
Hanover St 28054
Hantonte Rd 28052
Hardwood Cir 28056
Hardy Aly 28052
Hargrove Ave 28052
Harmon Ln 28056
Harmony Trl 28056
Harper Ln 28054
Harper Rd 28056
Harrington Dr 28056
E Harrison Ave 28054
W Harrison Ave 28052
Harrison Ln 28056
Hart Dr 28056
Hart St 28054
Hartford Dr 28052
Hartman St 28052
Harvell St 28052
Harvest Ln 28056
W Harvie Ave 28052
Hatley Rental Rd 28056
Havencrest Ct 28052
Hawk Ridge Dr 28056
Hawkins St 28052
Hawthorne Ln 28054
Hayden Ct 28056
Haynes Ave 28052
Haywood Ter 28056
Hazelnut Pl 28056
Hazelwood Ct 28056
Hearthstead Ln 28056
Hearthstone Dr 28056
Heather Ln & Trce 28056
Heatherloch Dr 28054
Heatherstone Dr 28056
Heathwood Dr 28052
Heddington Ct 28056
Hedgerow Rd 28056
Hedgestone Dr 28056
Hedgewood Cir 28052
Helen Ave 28056
Helen Dr 28054
Hemlock Ave 28054
Hemlock Ct 28056
Hemphill Rd 28056
Henderson St 28052
Henry Ave 28056
Heritage Ct 28056
Heritage Commons Ln 28054
Herman Dr 28052
Herron St 28052
Herschel Ct 28056
Hickory Ct 28056
Hickory Creek Dr 28052
Hickory Grove Rd 28056
Hickory Hill Ct 28054
Hickory Hollow Rd 28056
Hidden Glen Ct 28056
Hidden Meadow Ct 28056
High Cliff Ct 28056
High Ridge Ct 28056
N & S Highland St 28052
Hill Ln 28054
Hill St 28054
S Hill St 28052
Hillcrest Ave 28052
Hillgate Ave 28054
Hillmont St 28052
Hillside Dr 28052
Hilltop Cir 28054

W Hilltop Cir 28052
E Hilltop Dr 28054
Hillwood Dr 28052
Hodgin St 28056
Hoffman Blvd, Rd & St 28054
Holder Dr 28052
Holiday Rd 28054
Holland Ave 28052
Hollandale Dr 28054
Hollifield St 28056
Hollow Pine Ct 28056
Holly Dr 28054
Holly Pl 28056
Holly Hills Dr 28052
Holly Leaf Ave 28052
Holly Oak Ln 28056
Hollybrook Ave 28054
Hollycrest Ln 28056
Hollywood Dr 28052
Home Trl 28052
Homer Dr 28052
Homestead Dr 28056
Homewood Dr 28052
Honey Bee Ln 28056
Honeywood Ln 28056
Hoofbeat Dr 28056
Hooper Ave 28052
Hope Forbes Rd 28056
Hope Marian St 28052
Horseman Dr 28056
Horsley St 28056
Horton Rd 28052
Hospital Dr 28054
Houston St 28052
Hovis Ct 28056
Howard Ave 28054
Howe Dairy Rd 28056
Hoyle Cir & St 28052
Huckleberry Ln 28054
Hudson Ave 28054
E Hudson Blvd 28054
W Hudson Blvd 28052
Hudson Landings Dr 28054
Huffman Rd 28056
Huffstetler Rd 28056
Huffstetler St 28052
Hughes Ave 28052
Hughey Dr 28056
Hugo Dr 28056
Humphrey Blvd 28052
Hunsinger Ave 28052
Hunt Ave 28054
Hunter Ln 28056
Hunter Lee Ln 28052
Hunters Crossing Ln 28054
Hunters Glen Trl 28054
Hunting Wood Ct 28052
Huntington Dr 28056
Huntington Forest Ln 28056
Huntsman Ct 28054
Huntsmoor Dr 28054
Hyatt Dr 28056
Ida St 28054
Idlewood Cir 28054
Imperial Dr 28054
Independence Way 28056
Indigo Run Ln 28056
Industrial Ave 28054
Industrial Pike Rd 28052
Ingle Woods Dr 28056
Ingonish Dr 28056
Interstate View Ave 28052
Inwood Hill Dr 28056
Iredell Ct 28054
Iris Dr 28056
Irvin Ct 28054
Isley Rd 28052
Issac Ln 28056
Iva Ave 28054
Iverness Ct 28056
Ivey Dr 28052
Ivy St 28052
Ivy Creek Rd 28056
J And J Ln 28056
Jackson Rd & St 28052

Jacobs Rd 28054
Jake Long Rd 28052
Jakes Trl 28052
Jamaica Ln 28054
Jamee Dr 28056
James St 28052
James Adams Ave 28052
James Holland Dr 28052
Jamestown Dr
800-899 28056
3000-3099 28054
Jannee Ct 28052
Jasin Dr 28054
Jason Wolfe Ct 28052
Jaspers Trl 28052
Jay Ave 28052
Jaybird Ln 28056
Jefferson Ave 28056
W Jefferson Ave 28052
Jenkins Rd 28052
Jenkins Dairy Rd 28052
Jenny St 28054
Jeran Ln 28052
Jewitt St 28052
Jim Torrence Ln 28052
John Ave 28052
John D Rd 28056
John Freeman Ln 28056
John Kelly Ln 28056
John Logan Ln 28056
Johns Ln 28052
Johnston St 28054
Jondon Ln 28056
Jones St 28052
Jorache Ct 28052
Jordanview Ln 28056
Joselynn Dr 28054
Joy St 28052
Judith Ave 28054
Junius St 28052
Jupiter St 28052
K M Murphy Rd 28056
Kale St 28056
Kate St 28054
Katie Ln 28056
Katrina Dr 28052
Kay Dr 28056
Kaylin Ct 28052
Kaylor Ct 28052
Keith Dr 28054
Keith Ln 28056
Kelly Ln 28056
Kelly St 28054
Keltic Meadows Dr 28056
Kemswick Cir 28054
Kendall Ct 28056
Kendrick Rd 28056
Kendrick Estates Dr 28056
Kenilworth Dr 28052
Kennedy Rd 28056
Kennett Ave 28054
Kensington Ave 28054
Kent Ave 28052
Kentberry Ct 28056
Kentwood Dr 28056
Kerr Ct 28056
Kiawah Ct 28056
Kickapoo Ave 28054
Kilborne Dr 28052
Kimberly Dr 28052
N & S King St 28052
King Arthur Dr 28056
King Crowder Dr 28052
King David Ln 28056
King George Ln 28056
King Henry Ln 28056
King James Ln 28056
King John Cir 28056
Kings Ct 28054
Kings Dr 28054
Kings Mountain Ln 28054
Kingston Dr 28052
Kingstree Cir 28054
Kinmere Dr & Rd 28056
Kirby Ave 28054
Kirkcaldy Yard 28054

Kirkland Rd 28056
Kirkley St 28056
Kirkwood Cir 28054
Kitten Dr 28056
Knight Dr 28052
Knighton Ln 28056
Knightwood Dr 28056
Knollwood Dr 28052
Knotty Pine Trl 28056
Kodiak Dr 28052
Kuykendoll Ln 28052
Kyle Ct 28052
Lacey Ln 28056
Lagrande St 28056
Lake St
100-199 28056
1400-1699 28052
Lakefield Cir 28056
Lakencon Dr 28054
Lakeview St
200-299 28056
700-1099 28052
Lakewood Dr
300-599 28056
2600-2799 28052
Lakhany Rd 28056
Lamar Ave 28056
Lamar St 28052
Lamb Dr 28054
Lamp Glow Ct 28056
Lamppost Ct 28056
Lampwick Ct 28056
Lana Ln 28054
Lance Froneberger Rd 28056
Lancer Ct 28054
Lander Ave 28054
Landsdowne Dr 28054
Lane 3 St 28054
Lane Road Ext 28056
Lane Xang Rd 28056
Lanterntree Ct 28056
Larkhall Ct 28052
Larkspur Ct 28056
Larry Ln 28052
Laurel Ln 28054
Laurel Brook Ct 28056
Laurel Hill Ln 28056
Laurel Oak Ln 28056
Laurel Ridge Ct 28056
Laurel Woods Dr 28052
Lauren Ct 28056
Lauren Marie Ct 28052
Laurie Ct 28056
Laver Ct 28056
Lavington Ct 28056
Leafsmoke Dr 28054
Learning Pl 28052
Ledford Dr 28056
Ledia Dr 28056
Ledwell St 28056
Lee Rd 28056
Lee St 28054
S Lee St 28052
Legion Dr 28054
Lena Ln 28056
Lenden Hall Ct 28056
Lenox Ave 28052
Lenox St 28054
Leonard Dr 28056
Leroy Ave 28054
Leslie Dr 28056
Lewallen St 28052
Lewis Rd
300-399 28054
5000-6199 28052
Lewis St 28054
Lewiston Dr 28054
Leyland Dr 28056
N & S Liberty Ln & St 28052
Liberty Oak Ct 28056
Lighthouse Church Ln 28056
W Lincoln Ave 28052
Lincoln Ln 28056
Linda St 28054
Linden Cir 28054
Lindsey St 28056

Lineberger Ave 28052
Linford Ct 28056
Lingerfelt Dr 28052
Linn St 28056
Linsbury Ct 28056
Linwood Rd 28052
Lisa Dr 28056
Lisa Rayna Rd 28056
Lismore Ln 28056
Little Ave 28052
Little Creek Ct 28056
Little Mountain Rd 28056
Littlejohn St 28052
Live Oak Ct 28056
Ll Harwell Rd 28056
Lloyd White Rd 28052
Loblolly Pine Dr 28054
Loch Stone Dr 28054
Lochness Dr 28054
Lochshire Ln 28054
Locust Cir 28052
Log Cabin Dr 28054
N Logan St 28052
Logan Patrick Ct 28052
Lois Ln 28056
Londonderry Dr 28056
E Long Ave
100-299 28052
300-3099 28054
W Long Ave 28052
Long St 28052
Long Foot Rd 28056
Long Hungry Ln 28056
Longbriar Dr 28056
Lookout Ln 28054
Lorrie Ann Ln 28056
Lou Dr 28052
Louisbourg Ct 28056
Love Ct 28056
Love St 28054
Lowell Rd 28054
Lowell Bethesda Rd 28056
Lowell Spencer Mtn Rd 28056
Lunsford Dr 28056
Lynhaven Dr 28052
Lynhurst Dr 28054
Lynland Ln 28056
Lynn Ave 28052
Lynn Dr 28054
Lyon St 28052
Mackey Ct 28056
Madison Ln 28056
Madison St 28052
Madison Green Dr 28054
Maggie Elizabeth Way 28056
Maggie Lee Ln 28052
Magna Ct 28054
Magnolia St 28054
Main 28053
E Main Ave
100-299 28052
300-699 28054
W Main Ave
100-302 28052
301-301 28053
303-999 28052
304-998 28052
Main St 28056
Majestic Ct 28054
Malcolm St 28054
Mallard Ln 28052
Mallotte Ln 28054
Mamie St 28056
Manchester Ct 28056
Mandel Dr 28056
Mantooth Rd 28052
E Maple Ave 28054
Maplecrest Dr 28056
Mapleleaf Ln 28056
Maplewood Dr 28052
Mara Ave 28052
Marbel Ct 28054
Marblewood Ct 28056
Marcela Dr 28054
Maria Lynn Ct 28056

N Marietta St
  100-799 28052
  800-2399 28054
S Marietta St
  100-799 28052
  900-2199 28054
Marigold Ln 28052
Marilyn St 28054
Mark Ave 28054
Mark Whitesides Rd 28052
Marlborough Cir 28056
Marldale St 28052
Marlin St 28056
Mars St 28052
Marshall Ave 28052
Martha Ave 28052
Martin Ave 28052
Marve St 28052
Marvin St 28054
Mary Ave 28052
Mary Ln 28056
Mary Lee St 28052
Mathew St 28056
Matthews Dr 28052
E Mauney Ave 28054
W Mauney Ave 28052
Mauney Cir 28052
Mauney Ln 28052
Maw Dye Rd 28056
Maxton Ave 28052
W May Ave 28052
May Ct 28054
May St 28052
Mays Ct 28054
Mcarver St 28052
Mccall Ct 28054
Mccarver Rd 28056
Mcchesney Dr 28056
Mccormick Ave 28054
Mccoy Dr 28052
Mccully Rd 28052
Mcdade Ln 28056
W Mcfarland Ave 28052
N Mcfarland St 28054
Mcgarry Ln 28052
Mcgregor Rd 28056
Mcguire St 28052
Mclean St 28054
Mcneil St 28054
Mcpherson Ct 28052
Meade Ave 28052
Meadow Dr 28054
Meadow St 28056
Meadow Lark Ln 28056
Meadow View Dr 28054
Meadowbrook Ln 28052
Medallion Ct 28056
Meek Rd 28056
Meeting St 28054
Melody Ct 28054
Melody Dr 28056
Melvin Dr 28054
Memory Ln 28052
Merrywood Ln 28052
Mesa Ct 28054
Miami Dr 28052
Michael St 28054
Middle St 28052
Middlesbrough Rd 28056
Middleton Dr 28054
Midway Dr 28054
Midway St 28056
Midwood Dr 28052
Miguel Dr 28054
Mike Rd 28052
Mill Dr & St 28054
Miller Dr 28056
Miller St 28052
S Millon St 28052
Millstone Dr 28054
Milton Ave 28052
Mintwood Dr 28056
Miss Ellie Ln 28056
Mistletoe Ln 28056
Misty Ln 28052
Misty Hill Ln 28056
Misty Ridge Ct 28056
Mitchem Rd 28054
Mobile Ln 28054
Modena St 28054
N Modena Street Ext 28054
Monica Dr 28056
Monk Ave 28052
Monroe Dr 28054
Monroe Ter 28052
Montana Dr 28056
Montclair Ave 28054
Monte Vista Ln 28052
Monterey Park Dr 28054
Monticello Dr 28056
Montrose Dr 28054
Monument Ave 28052
Moonlite Ave 28052
Moore Dr
  100-299 28056
  1500-1599 28054
Moores St 28052
Moorsman Ct 28054
Moose St 28056
Mooseberry Ln 28052
N Moran St 28052
N Morehead St 28054
Morgan Dr 28056
Morgan St 28054
Morning Dove Ct 28052
Morningside Dr 28054
Morningside Park Dr 28054
N Morris St 28052
Morrocroft Trl 28054
Morton Ave 28052
Moss Ct 28054
Moss Bank Pl 28056
Mount Hebron Church Rd 28054
Mount Olive Church Rd 28052
Mount Vernon Dr 28056
Mountain Ave 28052
Mountain Oak Ln 28052
Mountain View St 28052
Mountain Village Cir 28052
Mountainbrook Dr 28052
Mountainview St 28056
Mutual Rd 28052
Myers St 28056
N Myrtle Ave & St 28052
N & S Myrtle School Rd 28052
Myrtlewoods Dr 28052
Nandina Ct 28056
Nash Ct 28054
Nassau Pl 28052
Nat Barber Ave 28052
Neal Hawkins Rd 28056
Neely St 28054
Neely Grove Rd 28056
Neely Smith Ln 28056
Neil St 28052
New Beginnings Ave 28052
New Haven Dr 28052
N New Hope Rd 28054
S New Hope Rd
  100-1899 28054
  1882-1882 28055
  1900-2498 28054
  1901-2499 28054
  2500-4699 28056
New Salem Acres Rd 28052
New Way Dr 28052
Newcastle Rd 28052
Newcombe Ct 28056
Newport Ct 28056
Newport Landing Way 28056
Niblick Dr 28054
Nichols Trl 28052
Nick N Shell Trl 28056
Nightingale Dr 28054
Nila Dawn Ave 28052
Nolen St 28056
Norfolk Pine Ct 28056
Norman St 28056
Normandy View St 28052
W Norment Ave 28052
Norseman Ct 28056
Northerly Island Ct 28056
Northgate Rd 28052
Northwest Blvd 28052
Northwestern Trl 28052
Northwynn Rd 28052
Norton Dr 28052
Norwick Ct 28052
Nottingham Dr 28054
Oak St 28056
S Oak St 28054
Oak Hollow Rd 28054
Oak Valley Dr 28054
Oakdale St 28054
Oakhill Ln 28056
Oakhurst Ave 28052
N Oakland St
  100-699 28052
  700-999 28054
S Oakland St
  100-601 28052
  602-899 28054
Oakleaf Ln 28056
Oakley Dr 28052
Oakmont Dr 28056
Oakstone Cir 28052
Oaktree Dr 28052
Oakview Trl 28052
Oakwood Ave 28052
Oakwood Cir
  300-399 28054
  4500-4999 28056
Oakwood Dr 28052
Oakwood Ln 28056
N Oakwood St 28052
Oates Rd 28052
Obarr Dr 28054
Ogden Dr 28056
Old Bridge Ct 28056
Old Church Rd 28052
Old Depot Rd 28052
Old English Dr 28054
Old Farm Rd 28056
Old Field Rd 28056
Old Forge Dr 28056
Old Granite Ct 28056
Old Knobbley Oak Dr 28056
Old Logging Trl 28056
Old Mill Rd 28056
Old Modena St 28054
Old Peach Orchard Rd 28052
Old Post Ln 28056
Old Providence Rd 28052
Old Redbud Dr 28056
Old South Ln 28056
Old Stage Rd 28052
Old Stone Ln 28056
Old Town Ln 28056
Old Well Ln 28054
Old West Ln 28052
Old York Rd 28056
Olde Oak Ln 28056
Ole Lamp Ln 28056
Oliver St 28052
Ollis Ln 28056
Olney Church Rd 28056
Omega Dr 28052
One Eagle Pl 28056
Only St 28052
Orange St 28054
Orange Hill Ct 28056
Orchard Trace Dr 28054
Oregon Way 28056
Osceola St 28054
Oshea Ave 28056
Osprey Ct 28056
Overhead Bridge Rd 28052
Overhill St 28052
Overman Ave 28052
Owens Dr 28054
Owens Ln 28056
Oxford St 28054
E Ozark Ave 28054
Pacemont Ln 28056
Packard St 28052
Pacolet Dr 28052
E Page Ave 28052
Paige Ct 28054
Palmer Dr 28052
Pam Dr 28056
Pamela St 28054
Panama Ave 28054
Paramount Cir 28052
Parham St 28054
E Park Ave 28054
Park Dr 28054
E Park Dr 28054
Park Ln 28052
Park St 28054
Park Ter 28054
Parkdale Ave 28052
Parker Dr 28056
Parkview Dr 28054
Pasco Pl 28054
Pasture Ln 28056
Path Way 28054
Patio Ln 28056
Patricia St 28052
Patrick Rd 28056
Patrick St 28054
Patriots Way 28056
Pattie Ann Dr 28052
Paul Revere Rd 28056
Paula Dr 28054
Pauline Ln 28056
Payton Dr 28056
Peabody Ct 28052
Peaceful Trl 28052
Peaceful Plains Ln 28056
Peachtree St 28054
Peacock Dr 28056
Peak View Ln 28052
N Pear St 28054
Pearl St 28054
Pearsons Tpke 28056
Pebble Stone Ct 28056
Pebblestone Ct & Way 28054
Pecan Grove Cir 28052
Pembroke Rd 28054
Penn Cir 28052
Penny Park Dr 28052
Pensbury Ct 28056
Pepper Ln 28056
Peppercorn Ct 28056
Pepperhill Dr 28054
Peregrine Ct 28056
Perkins St 28054
E Perry St 28054
S Perry St 28052
Petersburg Ct 28056
Petty Rd 28056
Petunia Ct 28056
Pharr Blvd 28056
Pheasant Run 28054
Phillips Ct 28052
Picadilly Cir 28054
Piedmont St 28054
Pikes Peak Dr 28052
Pinacle Ridge Ct 28056
S Pine Dr 28054
Pine St 28056
N Pine St 28054
Pine Trl 28056
Pine Bark Ct 28056
Pine Burr Ct 28056
Pine Circle Loop 28056
Pine Cove Dr 28056
Pine Creek Rd 28056
Pine Inn Dr 28056
Pine Knoll Ct 28054
Pine Needle Ct 28056
Pine Ridge Dr 28054
Pine Top Dr 28054
Pinebrook Ct 28056
Pinecrest Dr 28056
Pinefield Ct 28056
Pineforest Dr 28056
Pinehaven Dr 28054
Pinehurst St 28052
Pineola Ln 28054
Pineridge Ln 28056
Pineview Ln 28054
Pinewood Ln 28056
Pinewood Rd 28054
Piney Grove Rd 28056
Pinhook Loop Rd 28056
Pintail Way 28052
Pinto Ln 28052
Pioneer Ln 28052
Pisgah Rd 28052
Pit Row Ln 28056
Placid Ct 28054
Planer Ter 28054
Plantation Trl 28056
Planters Ridge Dr 28056
Plastics Dr 28054
Player Ct 28054
Plaza Rd 28056
Plum Tree Ln 28052
Plyler Lake Rd 28054
Plymouth St 28054
Poconos Dr 28052
Polly Jane Ln 28056
Polo Dr 28052
Pompano Pl 28056
Pondarosa Trl 28056
Pools Dr 28056
Pope Ave 28052
N Poplar St 28054
S Poplar St 28054
W Poplar St 28052
Poplar Down Rd 28056
Posey St 28052
Post Oak Ln 28056
Posterity Ct 28056
Poston Cir 28054
Power Dr 28052
Powerline Dr 28054
Prancer Ct 28056
Preslar Trl 28056
E Price Ave 28054
Princess St 28052
Princeton Ave 28054
Princeton Dr 28056
Proctor St 28052
Promise Creek Ln 28056
Propst St 28056
E Propst St 28054
Providence Dr 28052
Provincial Rd 28056
Pryor St 28052
Puritan St 28052
Quail Hollow Ct 28054
Quail Ridge Dr 28056
Quail Woods Rd 28054
Quailcrest Ln 28052
Quay Ct 28056
Queen Brogan Ct 28054
Queens Ct 28052
Queens Ln 28052
Queens Rd 28052
Queens St 28056
Queensberry Dr 28052
Queensberry Rd 28056
Queensgate St 28054
Quill Ct 28056
Quinn Ave 28054
Quinn St 28052
Rabbit Trl 28052
Raby Rd 28056
Radio St 28052
Raeford Ct 28052
Ragan Dr 28054
S Railroad St 28056
Rainbarrel Ln 28054
Raindrops Rd 28054
Rainforest Ct 28054
Rainier Ln 28052
Raintree Dr 28056
Raleigh Ct 28054
Ralphs Blvd 28052
Ramblewood Ln 28056
Ramsack Dr 28056
Ramsey Cir 28052
Ramsgate Dr 28056
Randolph Park Cir 28056
Randy Dr 28052
Ranier Ln 28052
Rankin Ave 28052
Rankin Rd 28056
Rankin St 28054
Rankin Lake Rd 28052
Ranlo Ave 28054
Ranlo Spencer Mtn Rd 28056
N & S Ransom St 28052
E Ratchford Ave
  200-299 28052
  300-699 28054
Ratchford Dr 28056
Ratchford Farm Rd 28056
Raven Hill Dr 28056
Ravenglass Turn 28054
Raxtetler Rd 28052
Ray St 28052
Rebecca Cir 28056
Red Bud Ct 28056
Red Cedar Rd 28054
Red Oak Ct & Ln 28052
Red Talon Ct 28056
Red Tip Ln 28052
Redbird Ln 28056
Redbud Dr 28056
Redding St 28054
Redford Ln 28054
Redlair Ln 28056
Redland Dr 28054
Redwood Ln 28052
Reese St 28056
Reford Ln 28054
Regal Dr 28056
Regal Oaks Rd 28056
Regent Ct 28054
Reid St 28054
Reimer Ct 28056
Remount Rd 28054
Reo Rd 28054
Reserve Ct 28056
Reverse Curv 28054
Rex Ave 28054
Reynolds Dr 28056
Rhoden Ct 28054
Rhonda Ct 28056
Rhonda Dr 28054
Rhyne Cir 28054
Rhyne Pl 28054
Rhyne St 28056
E Rhyne St 28054
N Rhyne St 28054
S Rhyne St 28054
Rhyne Carter Rd 28054
Rhyne Oakland Rd 28054
Rhyneland Cir & St 28054
Rice Hope Ct 28056
Richards Cir 28056
Richland Ave 28052
Rickard Dr 28056
Riddle Rd 28056
Ridge Ave
  1000-1099 28052
  2400-2599 28054
Ridge Cir 28052
Ridge Ln 28054
Ridge St 28052
Ridgecrest Rd 28052
Ridgecrest St 28056
Ridgefield Ln 28056
Ridgehaven Ct 28054
Ridgeway Dr 28054
Ridgewood Dr 28054
Riding Trail Rd 28054
Riley Ct 28052
Rillview Ct 28056
Rita Ln 28052
River Trce 28056
River Birch Dr 28056
River Creek Ln 28056
River Ridge Dr 28056
River Rock Dr 28054
Rivermont Dr 28054
Riverton Pl 28056
Riverwood Pkwy 28056
Roadrunner Dr 28052
Robbins St 28052
Robert Abram Dr 28056
Robert Schooler Ct 28052
Roberts Dr 28054
Robin Ln 28054
Robin Rd 28056
Robindale Rd 28056
Robins Nest Ct 28054
Robinson Cir 28056
Robinson Rd 28056
Robinson St 28052
Robinwood Rd 28054
Robinwood Village Dr 28054
Robusta Ct 28056
Rock Creek Ct 28056
Rockledge Dr 28052
Rocks Dr 28056
Rocky Rd 28056
Rocky Falls Ln 28054
Rocky Ridge Way 28052
Rogers Ave 28052
Rohm Rd 28056
Rolling Meadow Ln 28054
Rollingwood Dr 28052
Rosa C Ferguson Dr 28052
Roscoe Ln 28056
Rosebriar Ln 28052
Rosegarden Dr 28056
Rosegate Dr 28056
Rosemary Ln 28054
Rosemond Cir 28056
Rosewood Ln 28052
Ross St 28052
Rossmont Rd 28056
Rotan St 28052
Rousseau Ct 28054
Rowan Ct 28054
Rowe St 28056
Rowland Dr 28052
Roxburgh Ln 28056
Roy St 28052
Royal Oaks Ln 28056
Royalty Ct 28054
E Ruby Ave 28054
W Ruby Ave
  100-299 28054
  300-499 28052
Ruby Ln 28054
Rudd Rd 28054
Rufus Ratchford Rd 28056
Russ Ln 28056
Russell St 28052
Ryan Conley Ct 28056
Sabra St 28054
Saddlehorse Ln 28056
Saddlewood Dr 28056
Safeway Dr 28056
Saint Andrews Ln 28056
Saint Charles Ct 28056
Saint Marys Ct 28056
Saint Michaels Ln 28052
Saint Regis Dr 28056
Salem Dr 28052
Salemview Rd 28052
Saluda Dr 28054
Salvadore Ct 28056
Sam Brown Rd 28056
Sam Ferguson Rd 28052
San Paula Ln 28054
Sand Ln 28056
Sand Wedge Dr 28056
Sandhurst Ct 28054
Sandlewood Dr 28054
Sandswood Dr 28054
Sandy Ct 28056
Sandy Ln 28054
Sandy Creek Dr 28052
Sandy Oaks Trl 28052
Sanford Rd 28056
Sante Cir 28052
Sapphire Dr 28054
Sara Ct 28052
Saratoga Dr 28056
Sarn Ct 28054
Saturn St 28052

Sawbill Ln 28052
Sawgrass Ct 28056
Scalybark Rd 28054
Scarborough Ct 28054
Scarlet Oak Dr 28056
Schenley Ave 28056
School Ave 28052
Scotch Dr 28054
Scott Dr 28056
Scottwood Dr 28054
Scruggs St 28052
Seabrook Ct 28056
Sedgefield Dr 28052
Seejay Ct 28052
Seigle Ave 28054
Self Dr 28054
Selwyn Cir 28052
Seminole St 28054
Separk Cir 28054
Sequoia Dr 28052
Seth Ct 28054
Seward Dr 28052
Shade Tree Ct 28056
Shadow View Dr 28054
Shadwell Ct 28056
Shady Ave 28052
Shady Ct 28056
Shady Ln 28052
Shady Bark Dr 28054
Shady Bluff Dr 28052
Shady Nook Cir 28052
Shady Oak Trl 28052
Shady Pine Ct 28054
Shallowood Ln 28054
Shamrock Rd 28056
Shannon Dr 28054
Shannon Rdg 28056
Shannon Bradley Rd 28052
Sharon Ave 28054
Sharon Ln 28052
Shaw Ave 28054
Sheffield Dr 28054
Shenandoah Dr 28052
Shepherd St 28056
Sheridan Ct 28054
Sheringham Dr 28056
Sherman St 28052
Sherrill Rd 28056
Sherrill Farms Rd 28056
Sherry Ln 28054
Sherry Painter St 28056
Sherwood Ave 28052
Sherwood Cir 28056
S Shields Dr 28056
Shires Rd 28052
Shuda Ave 28054
Signal Ave 28052
Silver Creek Dr 28052
Silverberry St 28054
Silversmith Cir 28056
Silverstone Dr 28052
Simmons St 28052
Sims Cir 28052
Sinclair St 28054
Skating Rink Dr 28054
Skeet Rd 28056
Skyland Dr 28052
Slide Dr 28056
Sloan Ave 28052
Smethwick Ln 28056
Smith Ave 28052
Smitty Ln 28052
Smoke Tree Ct 28056
Smyre Dr 28054
Snoopy Dr 28056
Snowbird Ln 28056
Snowbrook Ln 28052
Snowshoe Ct 28052
Snyder Pl 28052
Somerset Dr 28052
N & S South St 28052
Southampton Cir 28056
Southern Farm Rd 28056
Southfork Meadows Rd 28052
Southgate Ct 28052
Southside Ave 28052
Southwood Dr 28056
Spaight Ct 28054
Spanish Oak Ln 28056
Spargo St 28056
Sparrow Dairy Rd 28056
Sparrow Springs Rd 28052
Sparta Ct 28052
Spencer Ave 28052
E Spencer Ave 28054
Spencer Mountain Rd
  1-99 28054
  100-199 28056
  1200-2299 28054
Spindle Ridge Ln 28056
Split Oak Trl 28052
Split Rail Ct 28056
Spooler Ct 28056
Spring Dr 28052
Spring St
  800-1199 28054
  5000-5099 28052
Spring Garden Dr 28052
Spring Lake Dr 28054
Spring Valley Dr 28052
Spring Wyatt Dr 28056
Springbrook Cir 28052
Springdale Ln 28052
Springfield Ct 28052
Springs St 28056
Springwater Dr 28056
Springway Dr 28052
Springwood Rd 28056
Spruce Ln 28052
Stablefarm Rd 28052
Stablegate Dr 28052
Stableview Dr 28056
Stacey Tucker Cir 28056
Stacy Ridge Rd 28052
Stagbuck Dr 28052
Stagecoach Rd 28052
Stallion Way 28056
Stanley Spencer Mtn Rd 28056
Stark Rd 28052
Starling Dr 28056
Starnes Ct 28052
Starr St 28056
Starrland Dr 28052
Starview Dr 28056
Staton Rd 28056
Stayman Ct 28054
Steele Dr 28052
Steeplechase Rd 28056
Stephanie Ct 28056
Sterling Ave 28054
Sterling Rd 28056
Stevens Cir & St 28054
Stewart Trl 28056
Stiles Dr 28052
Still Forest Ct 28056
Stockwood Dr 28056
Stone Creek Dr 28056
Stone Mountain Dr 28054
Stone Pine Dr 28056
Stone Ridge Dr 28056
Stonebrook Ln 28056
Stonegate Ct 28056
Stonehaven Ln 28052
Stonehedge Rd 28052
Stoneleigh Pl 28056
Stoneman Dr 28056
Stonemark Ct 28054
Stoney Oaks Dr 28052
Stoneybrook Ave 28054
Stoneycreek Ct 28056
Stony Dr 28056
Stowe Ave 28054
Stowe Ln 28056
Stowe Rd 28056
Stowe Dairy Rd 28052
Stradford Dr 28054
Strawberry Ln 28054
Strong Box Ln 28052
Stroupe Rd 28056
Su San Farms Rd 28056
Suburban Ter 28052
Sue Ellen Ct 28056
Suequay Ct 28056
Sugar Ln 28056
Sugar Spring Rd 28054
Sugarcane Ln 28056
W Sullivan St 28052
Summer Dr 28052
Summer Pl 28056
Summerell Ave 28056
Summerglen Dr 28056
Summit St 28052
Summit Crossing Pl 28054
Sumner Dr 28056
Sun Trl 28052
Sundance Dr 28054
Sunflower Ct 28052
Sunnydale Dr 28054
Sunrise Dr 28054
Sunriver Rd 28054
Sunset Ave 28052
Sunset Dr 28054
Sunshine Ave 28052
Superior Stainless Rd 28052
Surry Ln 28054
Susan Ln 28056
Susan Elaine Dr 28056
Sutton Carpenter Rd 28052
Swain Ct 28054
Swan Run Ct 28056
Sweet Birch Ct 28054
Sweetgum St 28054
Sweetwood Ln 28056
Sycamore Ave 28052
W Sycamore Ave 28054
Sydnor Ave 28052
Sykes St 28052
T And A Dr 28056
Table Rock Dr 28052
Tall Timber Ct 28056
Tamworth Ln 28052
Tanglewood Dr 28054
Tanner St 28052
Tanya Ct 28056
Tara Ct
  1500-1599 28052
  3000-3099 28056
Tareyton Dr 28056
Tarheel Dr 28056
Tate St 28052
Taylor Dr 28052
Taylor Ln 28056
Tea Olive Rd 28056
Teby Dr 28056
Tekoa Dr 28056
Telegraph Dr 28056
Temple Ct 28056
Terra Dr 28054
Teton Dr 28056
Thistlebrook Ct 28056
Thomas Trl 28054
Thornhill Dr 28052
Thoroughbred Ct 28056
Tillery Ln 28056
Timber Ln 28056
Timber Creek Trl 28056
Timberlane St 28054
Timberline Ln 28056
Timberwood Dr 28056
Timothy Ct 28056
Tiny Ave 28052
Tipperary Dr 28056
Titman Rd
  2900-3199 28054
  4000-4699 28056
Todd Ct 28054
Todd Reece Ln 28056
Tompkins Ct 28054
Tomshire Dr 28056
Tony Ave 28056
Tony Rd 28052
Torrence Ave 28054
Torrence Dr 28054
Torrence Rd 28052
Tottenham Ct 28056
Townsend Ave 28052
Townsend Dr 28056
Trabert Ct & Dr 28056
Trace Ave 28056
Tracy Ln 28056
Trad Ct 28056
Tradewind Ct 28054
Trafalger Dr 28056
Trail Ridge Ct 28056
Train Ln 28056
Trakas Blvd 28052
Tralee Dr 28056
Tranquil Ct 28056
Trapper Ct 28056
Travis Dr 28056
Treasure Ln 28054
Tree Haven Ct 28056
Trent Ct 28056
N & S Trenton St 28052
Trexlar Ave 28052
Trinity Ave 28052
Trotters Rd 28054
Tryon Pl 28054
Tukaway Ct 28056
Tulip Dr 28052
Turf Ct 28056
Turn Berry Dr 28056
Turner Dr 28052
Turner Rd 28056
Turtle Creek Ln 28052
Twin Ave 28052
Twin Tops Rd 28056
Twisted Oaks Ln 28052
Union Rd
  500-2999 28054
  3000-7099 28056
Union Ter 28056
Union New Hope Rd 28056
Unity Ave 28052
Upton Ave 28052
Uwharrie Dr 28052
Valley St 28056
Valleydale Dr 28056
Valleywood Dr 28054
Van Story Dr 28056
N & S Vance St 28052
Vancouver Ln 28052
Vanderlip Dr 28052
Vanwick Dr 28052
Venn Dr 28056
Venus Ave 28052
Verde View Dr 28056
Verisoun Rd 28056
Versailles Ln 28056
Victory Trl 28056
View Heights Ct 28052
Village Ct 28054
Village Ridge Dr 28056
Villagewood Ct 28054
Villard St 28054
N & S Vine St 28052
Virginia Ln 28056
Vista Mountain Ln 28052
Wagner Cir 28054
Wahoo Ct 28056
Walker Ln 28056
Walls St 28054
Walnut Ave 28054
E Walnut Ave
  100-199 28052
  300-499 28054
W Walnut Ave 28052
Walnut Hill Ct 28054
Walter Holland Dr 28052
Warburton Ave 28056
E Ward Ave 28054
N Ward St 28052
S Ward St 28054
Ware Ave 28052
Warren Ave 28054
Warren Cir 28052
Warren St
  100-199 28056
  901-997 28054
  999-1099 28054
Warton Ct 28056
N & S Washington St 28052
Water Oak Ln 28056
Waterfall Ct 28056
Waterford Ln 28056
Watergate Cir 28052
Watkins Rd 28054
Wayles Ct 28056
Wayne Ln 28056
Wayside Dr 28054
Weavers Row 28056
N & S Webb St 28052
Wedgewood Dr 28056
Wedowee Ln 28052
Weeping Willow Way 28052
Weir Ln 28052
Welch Ave 28054
Welch Ln 28056
N & S Weldon St 28052
Wellington Dr 28054
Wellman St 28054
Wellons Dr 28054
Wendy Ln 28052
Wesley Dr 28056
Wesleyan Dr 28056
West Cir 28054
Westbrook Cir 28052
Westerland Ct 28056
Westerly Hills Dr 28052
Westland Ct 28056
Weston Ave & St 28052
Westover St
  600-699 28054
  1600-1799 28056
Westview St
  1500-1599 28052
  2700-2899 28056
W Westview St 28052
Westway Dr 28054
Westwood Cir 28052
Westwynn Cir 28052
Wexford Ct 28054
Weymouth Dr 28056
White Ln & St 28052
White Cedar Dr 28056
White Dove Trl 28052
White Hall Pl 28056
White Oak Cir 28052
White Oak Ct 28056
White Pond Dr 28056
White Willow Ave Ave 28054
Whiteheath Ct 28056
Whitehorse Rd 28052
Whitener Ave 28052
Whitesides St 28052
Whitethorn Dr 28054
Whitson Rd 28054
Wicklow Dr 28054
Wicklow Ln 28056
Wilbur Rd 28056
Wild Country Way 28054
Wild Wing Dr 28052
Wildflower Dr 28052
Wildwood Rd 28054
Wiley Ave 28054
Wilkins Ave 28054
Wilkinson Blvd 28056
Willdon Ct 28056
William Forest Ln 28056
Williams St 28052
Williamsburg Dr 28054
Willimax Ave 28054
Willow St 28054
Willow Creek Dr 28054
Willow Oak Ln 28054
Willow Pond Rd 28056
Willow Run Dr 28056
Willow Wind Dr 28054
Willowbrook Cir 28056
Wilmington St 28054
Wilmont Dr 28054
Wilmot Dr 28054
Wilmot Trl 28054
Wilson Rd 28056
Wilson St 28052
Wilson Farm Rd 28056
Wimbledon Dr 28056
Windcrest Ave 28052
Winder Trl 28056
Windsong Ct & Dr 28056
Windsor Dr 28056
Windsor Woods Dr 28054
Windwood Dr 28056
Windy Hill Dr 28052
Windy Rush Ln 28054
Wingdale Ct 28056
Winget Cir 28054
Winget St 28052
Wingfield Dr 28056
Winnsboro Cir 28052
Winnsford Ln 28056
Winsor St 28052
Winston Dr 28052
Winterberry Ln 28056
Winterfield Dr 28056
Winterlake Dr 28054
Winterwood Dr 28056
Withers St 28054
Witten Ln 28052
Wix Way 28054
Wolfpack Rd 28056
Womble Ln 28054
Wonderwood Dr 28056
Wood St 28052
Wood Duck Ct 28056
Woodbeam Ln 28056
Woodbriar Trl 28056
Woodbridge Dr & St 28056
Woodbury Ln 28056
Woodcrest Dr 28052
Woodcut Rd 28052
Woodend Ln 28052
Woodfield Cir 28056
Woodfox Ct 28056
Woodgreen Dr 28052
Woodhaven Ln 28056
Woodhill Dr 28054
Woodhurst Ct 28056
Woodland Dr 28054
Woodlark Ct 28056
Woodlawn Ave 28052
Woodleaf Dr 28056
Woodleigh Dr 28056
Woods Trl 28052
Woodside Ave 28054
Woodside Dr 28056
Woodstream Dr 28056
Woodvale Ave 28054
Woodwynn Dr 28054
Woody Ct 28056
Wren Rd 28056
Wren Tpke 28052
Wrens Song Way 28052
Wrentree Ln 28056
Wright St 28056
Wynbourne Dr 28056
Wynewood Ct 28056
Wynnchester Rd 28056
Wynnhurst Ct 28054
Wyoming Ln 28056
X Ray Dr 28054
Yarmouth Ln 28056
N & S Yates St 28052
Yellow Jasmine Dr 28056
Yellowstone Ct 28054
N & S York Hwy, Rd & St 28052
York Union Rd 28056
Yorktown St 28054
Yorkwood Rd 28052
Yosemite Dr 28056
Zekes Pl 28056
Zeldazbelle Dr 28056

NUMBERED STREETS

1st St 28054
  5000-5099 28052
E 2nd Ave
  100-299 28052
  300-1099 28054
W 2nd Ave 28052
2nd St 28054
N 2nd St 28054
E 3rd Ave
  100-299 28052
  300-899 28054
W 3rd Ave 28052
E 4th Ave
  100-299 28052
  300-1099 28054
W 4th Ave 28052
E 5th Ave
  100-199 28052
  200-699 28054
W 5th Ave 28052
E 6th Ave
  100-199 28052
  200-1099 28054
W 6th Ave 28052
W 6th Avenue B 28052
7 1/2 Th Ave 28054
W 7th Ave 28052
E 8th Ave 28054
  100-119 28054
  120-599 28052
E 9th Ave 28054
W 9th Ave 28052
E 10th Ave 28054
W 10th Ave 28052
W 11th Ave 28052
E 12th Ave 28054
W 12th Ave 28052
W 19th Ave 28052
W 20th St 28052

GOLDSBORO NC

General Delivery 27530

POST OFFICE BOXES MAIN OFFICE STATIONS AND BRANCHES

Box No.s
A - P 27533
1 - 8012 27533
9998 - 10954 27532
9998 - 9998 27533
11001 - 11558 27532

NAMED STREETS

A St 27530
Aarons Pl 27530
Abbey Pl 27530
Abigail St 27534
Abington Pl 27534
Acacia Ave 27530
Ace St 27534
Acorn Rd 27534
Acreview Dr 27530
Adams St 27530
Addison Cir 27530
Adler Ln 27530
Agave Ln 27534
Agona Pl 27530
Airle Pl 27530
Airline Pl 27534
N & S Alabama Ave 27530
Albert Dr 27530
Alert Apron Rd 27531
Allen Dr & St 27534
Almond Ln 27534
Alpha Ct 27530
Alvin St 27530
Amandas Way 27534
Amaziah Pl 27534
Amblewood Ln 27534
Amelia Ct 27530
Amherst Pl & Rd 27534
Amhurst Dr & Pl 27534
Amy Ct 27534
Anderson Dr 27530
Andrea Dr 27530
N Andrews Ave 27530

S Andrews Ave 27530
Andrews St
1000-1599 27531
3600-3699 27534
S Andrews St 27531
Angel Pl 27530
Angela Dr 27530
Angie Dr 27530
Angus Dr 27530
Ann St 27534
Annabelle St 27530
Anthony Ln 27530
Antioch Rd 27534
Antler Creek Rd 27534
E & W April Ln 27530
Argo St 27530
Armstead Ave 27534
Armstrong Dr 27530
Arnold Ave 27531
W Arrington Bridge Rd 27530
Arrowpoint Dr 27530
Ash Lndg 27530
E Ash St
100-2299 27530
2300-3999 27534
W Ash St 27530
Ashby Ln 27530
Ashland Dr 27530
Ashley Ave 27530
Ashworth Dr 27530
Askew Pl 27530
Aspen Cir 27530
Astor Ct 27530
Atkinson Chapel Rd 27534
Atlantic Ave 27530
Atsur Pl 27534
N & S Audubon Ave 27530
Aulander Dr 27530
Aurora Ln 27530
Autumn Winds Dr & Pl 27530
Ava St 27530
Avalon Dr 27530
Avery Pl 27534
Avionics St 27531
Avon Dr 27534
Aycock Dr 27530
Aycock St 27534
E Azalea Dr 27530
N & S Baden Ct 27534
Bain St 27530
N & S Baines Pl 27534
Baler Dr 27534
Ball St 27530
Balsam Pl 27534
Banks Ave & Ct 27534
Barden Scott Ln 27530
Barkridge Pl 27534
Barnes Ct 27530
Barrow Ct 27534
Bartlett Ave 27530
Basil St 27530
Bay Dr 27530
Bayleaf Dr & Pl 27534
Bayview Pointe 27534
Beale St 27530
Bear Creek Rd 27534
Beatrice Dr 27530
Beaver Dam Rd 27530
Beck Rd & St 27534
Beckfield Dr 27530
Becton Cir 27530
S Becton Ln 27534
Beech St 27530
Beechwood Dr 27530
Beems St 27530
Belfast Ave & Rd 27530
Bell Ct 27530
Bell Court Dr 27534
Bellview Dr 27530
Ben Brewington Ct 27530
Benelli Cir 27530
Benjamin Ln 27534
Bennett Rd 27530
Bennett Farm Ln 27530
Benton St 27530
Bergstrom St 27531
N & S Berkeley Blvd 27534
E & W Berkshire Ct 27530
Berry St 27530
Best Ave 27534
N Best St 27530
S Best St 27530
Best Sand And Gravel
Rd 27534
Bethune Ave 27530
Bett Dr 27534
Betty Dr 27530
Beverly Dr 27534
Beyer St 27530
Biggs Ct 27534
Biggs St
100-299 27534
1000-1099 27531
Bill Cir 27530
Billy Francis Dr 27534
Biltmore Dr 27534
Birch Cir & Dr 27534
Bitterwood Pl 27530
Bizzell Ct 27530
Bj Dr 27530
Bk Cir 27534
Black Jack Church Rd 27530
Blackwater Dr 27530
Blaire Ln 27530
Blairridge Dr 27534
Blakeslee Ave 27531
Blessed Ln 27530
Bloomingfield Pl 27530
Blue Bird Ln 27534
Blue Bonnet Ln 27534
Blueberry Rd 27530
Bluecrest Ln & Pl 27534
Blythwood Ct 27530
Bob Braswell Ct 27530
Bobwhite Ln 27530
Bolingbrooke Dr 27534
Bolling Dr 27534
Bomb Loaders Ln 27531
Bonnie Pl 27534
Border Ln 27530
Boxwood Ln 27534
Boyette Dr 27534
Bradford Pl 27530
Brady Pl 27534
Branchwater Pl 27534
Brandywine Dr 27534
Brantwood Dr 27534
Braswell Cir & Rd 27530
Braxton Dr 27530
Brazil St 27530
Brebati Dr 27534
Breezewood Dr 27534
Brenn Loop 27530
Brentwood Dr 27530
Briarwood Pl 27530
Brick St 27530
Bridle Path Rd 27534
Bright St 27530
Brightleaf Rd 27530
Brighton Dr 27530
Broad Oak Pl 27534
Brock Rd & St 27530
Brockwood Ave 27530
Brogden St 27530
Brooks St 27531
Brookshire Dr 27534
Brookwood Dr & Ln 27534
Browning Pl 27530
Brownrigg St 27530
Bruce St 27530
Bryan Blvd 27530
Bryan Pond Ln 27530
Bryant Cir 27534
Bryant St 27530
Bryanwood Dr & Pl 27534
Buck Pl 27530
Buck Run Dr 27530
Buck Swamp Rd 27530
Buckhorn Rd 27530
Buckson Dr 27530
Bunche Dr 27530
Burge Rd 27531
Burnham Pl 27530
Burtus Dr 27534
Buttercup Ln 27530
Buttonwood Rd 27530
Byron Pl 27530
C R Lewis Dairy Rd 27534
Cadel Ln 27534
Callaway Ct 27530
Callie Dr 27530
Calvary St 27530
Calvin Ln 27530
Cambria Ln 27530
Cambridge Dr 27530
Camden Park Dr 27530
Camellia Dr 27530
Camelot Ct 27530
Cameron Rd 27534
Camp Fed Ln 27531
Canal St 27530
Candler Dr 27534
Cannon Ave
1000-1089 27531
1090-1090 27534
1091-1799 27531
1092-1348 27531
1350-1350 27534
1352-1798 27531
3600-3699 27534
Cardinal Dr 27534
Care Rd 27534
Carlyle Cir & Ct 27530
Carmel Ln 27530
Carol Ct & St 27534
N & S Carolina Cir &
St 27530
Carolina Commerce Dr 27530
Carolina Forest Dr 27534
Carolina Wren Cir 27530
Carriage Rd 27534
Carswell Ln 27534
Carver Blvd & Dr 27530
Cascade Dr 27530
Casey Dairy Rd 27534
Cashwell Dr
100-3099 27534
3100-3100 27532
3100-3398 27534
3101-3399 27534
Cashwell Pl 27534
Casino Dr 27530
Cassedale Dr & Pl 27534
Catalpa St 27530
Catherine St 27530
Caudill Ave 27534
Cedar Rd 27534
Cedar Creek Dr 27530
Cedar Lake Dr 27530
Cedarwood Dr 27534
Celia Ln 27534
Cella St 27534
N & S Center St 27530
Centina Ln 27530
Central Dr 27534
Central Heights Rd 27534
Centura Dr 27530
Century Ave 27531
Chafin Pl & Rd 27534
Challen Ct 27534
Challis Pl 27534
Chancery Dr 27530
Chandler Rd 27534
Chanute Rd 27534
Charles St 27530
Charlie Braswell Rd 27530
Chatwood Cir 27530
E & W Chestnut Cir &
St 27530
Chris Taylor Ln 27534
Christian Dr 27530
Christopher Dr 27534
Christopher Allen Dr 27534
Church St 27530
Church Of God Rd 27534
Cindy Cir 27530
N & S Claiborne St 27530
Clairmont Rd 27534
Clara Ct 27530
Clara Monte Dr 27534
Clarence Ct 27530
Claridge Nursery Rd 27530
Clay Rd 27534
Clay Brook Dr 27530
Clearwater Ct 27534
Cleatus Dr 27534
Cliffwell Dr 27530
Cline Dr 27534
Clingman St 27534
Clydes Ln 27530
Coach House Cir 27534
Coachmans Pl 27534
Cobb St 27534
Coburn Dr 27530
Cogdell Dr 27530
Cola Dr 27530
Colby Pl 27534
Coley Rd 27534
Collier Ave 27531
Collier St 27530
Colonial Ct & Dr 27534
Colonial Terrace Dr 27530
Combs Rd 27530
Comer Lumber Yard
Rd 27530
Comet Dr 27530
Commerce Ct 27534
Commercial Dr 27534
Commonsgate Dr 27530
Community Dr 27534
Cone St 27534
Connie Cir 27530
Cooke St 27530
Corbel Pl 27530
Corbett Rd & St 27534
Corbin Rd 27534
Corney St 27530
Corporate Dr 27534
Corral Dr 27530
Cotton Field Dr 27534
Cottontail Ln 27530
N & S Cottonwood Dr 27530
Country Ln 27534
Country Acres Rd 27534
Country Day Rd 27534
Country Run Ln 27530
Country View Dr 27534
Courtland Ave & Pl 27534
Courtney Rd 27534
Coventry Dr 27530
Cox Blvd 27534
Coy Pl 27534
Crabapple Ln 27530
Crawford St 27530
Creech St 27530
Creek Ct 27530
Creek Ridge Dr 27530
Creek Run Dr 27534
Creekside Dr 27534
Creekwood Rd 27530
Crepe Myrtle St 27530
Crestwood Dr & Pl 27530
Crisp St 27534
Crissy St 27531
Crooked Creek Ct 27530
Croom Dr 27530
Cross Pl 27530
Crosscut Pl 27534
Crossing Pl 27530
Crosswinds Cir & Dr 27530
Crump St 27530
Curlew St 27534
Cuyler Best Rd 27534
Cynthia Ct 27534
Cypress Dr 27530
D And W Cir 27534
Dail St 27530
Daisy St 27530
Dakota Ave 27534
Daleview Dr 27534
Dallas Rd 27534
Daniel Dr 27534
Danny Cir 27534
Darby Pl & Rd 27534
Dargue Ave 27531
Daryl Dr 27534
Davelin Pl 27530
David St 27530
Davis Rd 27530
Daw Pate Rd 27534
Dawn Cir 27534
Dawson Dr 27530
Day Cir 27530
De Priest St 27530
Deans Ln 27530
Debbie Dr 27530
Deborah Ln 27530
Dee Dee Pl 27530
Deer Acres Dr 27530
Deer Meadow Dr 27534
Deerborn Cir & Dr 27534
Delbert Dr 27534
Delia Trl 27534
Dellwood Pl 27534
Deluca Rd 27534
Deluxe Dr 27530
Denmark St 27530
Denton Pl 27534
Derek Dr 27530
Devereaux St 27530
Devonshire Dr 27530
E & W Dewey St 27530
Diana Ct & St 27534
Dillard St 27530
Ditchbank Rd 27534
Dixie Cir 27534
Dixie Trl 27530
Dobbers Creek Dr 27530
Dobbersville Rd 27530
Dobbs Pl 27534
E & W Doe Trl 27530
Dogwood Ct, St & Trl 27534
Dogwood Estates Ln 27534
Dollard Town Rd 27534
Don Allen Ct 27534
Donaldson Dr 27534
Doral Dr 27534
Doris Dr 27534
Dorsey St 27530
Dosia Dr 27534
Double D Ln 27534
S Douglas St 27534
Dove Pl 27534
Downing Pl 27530
Drake Village Dr 27530
Driftwood Dr 27534
Duffy Dr 27534
Dulcet Ct 27530
Dupont Cir 27530
Durwood Dr 27534
Dutch Pines Ct 27534
Duval Dr 27530
Dwight St 27534
Eagle Pl 27530
Eagle Scout Pl 27530
Eagles Pointe Dr & Pl 27530
Eagleston Ct 27534
Earl Dr 27530
Earl Rd 27534
Earnest Ave 27534
Eason St 27530
East St 27534
Easter Ln 27534
Eastern Pl 27534
Eastgate Dr 27534
Ebenezer Church Rd 27530
Eddington Dr 27534
Eden Pl 27530
Edgar St 27530
Edgerton St 27530
Edna Ln 27530
Edray Dr 27530
Edwards St
1000-1249 27531
1250-1252 27534
1251-1399 27531
1254-1308 27531
1310-1310 27534
1312-1338 27531
1340-1340 27534
1342-1398 27531
Egret Pl 27534
Elanor Ave 27530
Eleanor Pl 27534
Elizabeth St 27530
Ellis Dr 27534
Ellis St 27530
Elm Ave 27530
E Elm St
100-2299 27530
2401-2699 27534
W Elm St 27530
Elton Dr 27530
Emerald Pl 27534
Emily St 27530
Emmitte Dr 27534
E End Cir 27530
W End Ln 27534
W End Rd 27534
Englewood Dr 27534
Erin Pl 27530
Ervin Dr 27534
Essex Ct 27530
Etchberger Rd 27534
Etheridge Ln 27530
Eunice St 27530
Evans St 27534
Evergreen Ave 27530
Ew Ln 27534
Ewing Dr 27530
Exum Mill Ln 27534
Fairfield Dr 27530
Fairmax Rd 27534
Fairview Cir 27530
Fairway Dr 27534
Faith Pl 27530
Fall Leaf Dr 27530
Fallin Blvd 27534
Falling Creek Ln 27530
Falling Creek Church
Rd 27530
Farm Rd 27530
Farm Club Rd 27534
Farmview Ln 27530
Farnsworth Dr & Pl 27530
Farrington Pl 27534
Fawn Creek Dr 27530
Feather Ln 27534
Fedelon Trl 27530
N & S Fernwood Pl 27530
Ferrell Dr 27530
Ferry Bridge Rd 27530
Fetchet St 27534
Fickel St 27531
Fieldcrest Pl 27534
Fighter Plz 27531
Fighter Dock Rd 27531
Fisher Dr 27530
Fitch Ln 27530
Fleetwood St 27534
Fleming Ln 27534
Flight Line Rd 27531
Flint St 27534
Florence Dr 27530
Florida St 27530
Force Rd 27534
Forest Cir 27530
Forest Ct 27530
Forest Dr 27534
Forest Rd 27534
E Forest Hill Dr 27534
Forest Knolls Rd 27534
Forsyth St 27534
Fox Den Ln 27534
Foxcroft Dr 27530
Foxwood Dr & Pl 27530
Frank St 27530
Frankies Ln 27530
Franklin Ct & St 27530
Freeman St 27530
Friendly Dr & Rd 27530
Friendswood Dr 27530
Fussell St 27530
G And K Farm Rd 27534
Gainey Dr 27530
Garden Cir 27534
Gardner Manor Dr 27534
Garrald St 27530
Garrick Ln 27534
Gary Ln 27534
Gateway Dr 27534
Gator Dr 27530
Gayle Dr 27534
Geiger Ln 27534
Genoa Crossing Dr 27530
N & S George St 27530
N & S Georgia Ave 27530
Gerald Ln 27530
Gertrude Grady Rd 27534
Gilbert Ct 27534
Gin Ln 27530
Ginn Ln 27534
Glen Oak Dr 27534
Glendas Cir & Dr 27534
Glenhaven Ln 27530
Glenn Dr 27530
Glenwood Dr 27530
Glenwood Trl 27534
Gloucester Rd 27534
Gobble Dr 27534
Goldleaf Dr 27534
Goodson St 27531
Gordon Dr 27530
Gracie Pl 27534
Graham St 27530
Grand Oaks Dr 27530
Granny Dr 27530
Grant Dr 27534
W Grantham St 27530
Grantham Farm Ln 27530
Grantham School Rd 27530
Granville Dr & Pl 27530
Grasshopper Ln 27530
Graves Dr 27534
Gray St 27534
Green Dr 27534
Green St 27530
Green Valley Dr 27530
Greenbrier Dr 27534
Greene Dr 27534
Greenleaf St 27530
Greenwood St 27530
Greg Dr 27534
Grey Fox Ct 27534
Greystone Ct & Dr 27534
Grist Mill Dr 27534
Grove Dr 27534
Guardian Rd 27531
Guilford St 27530
Gulley St 27530
Gurley Ave 27534
Guyton St 27534
Hailey Dr 27534
Hamilton Dr 27530
Handley Pl 27534
Handley Acres Dr 27534
Handley Park Ct 27534
Hanger Row 27531
Hannah Way 27530
Harbor Ln 27530
Hard Oak Ln 27530
N & S Harding Dr &
Pl 27534
Hardingwood Dr 27534
Hare Rd 27534
Hargrove St 27530
Harley Trl 27534
Harmony Cir 27534
Harolds Pond Ln 27530
Harrell St 27530
Harris St 27530
Harrison Dr 27530
Hart Cir 27530
Harvest Ln 27530
Hawthorne St 27530
Haywood Dr 27530
Hazel St 27530
Head St 27530
Heather Ln 27534
Heather Glen Dr 27530
Helms Ct & Dr 27530
Hemlock St 27530

Street	ZIP
Henry St	27530
Henrys Hill Dr	27530
Herbert St	27530
N & S Herman Pl & St	27530
Heron Dr & Pl	27534
Herring Rd	27530
Herring St	27534
Hickam St	27531
Hickory Rd	27534
Hickory St	27530
Hicks Rd	27530
Higgins St	27534
High Meadow Cir	27530
Highland Ave	27530
Highland St	27534
Highwoods Dr	27530
Hilda Pl	27534
Hill Ct	27530
Hill St	27530
E Hill St	27534
W Hill St	27534
Hill Circle Dr	27534
Hill Loop Rd	27534
N & S Hillcrest Dr & Pl	27534
Hilldale Ln	27534
Hillside Dr	27534
Hilltop Cir & Ln	27530
Hillview Ln	27530
Hillwinds Pl	27534
Hilly Sands Rd	27534
Hines Dr	27530
Hinnant Rd	27530
Hinson St	27530
Hinton Ln	27534
Hitching Rack Pl	27534
Hofer Ct	27534
Holland Dr	27534
Holland Hill Dr	27530
Hollingsworth Rd	27530
Hollowell Rd & St	27530
Holly Rd	27534
E Holly St	27530
W Holly St	27530
Holly Berry Ln	27530
Holly Point Rd	27534
Hollybrook Ave	27530
Holmes Ln	27534
Homestead Dr	27530
Hood Dr	27530
Hood Swamp Rd	27534
E & W Hooks River Rd	27530
Hooping Crane Ln	27530
Hopkins St	27530
Horseshoe Dr	27534
Hospital Rd	27534
Hounds Run Dr	27530
House St	27530
Howell Rd	27530
Hubert Dr	27530
Hugh St	27530
Hummingbird Ln	27534
Humphrey St	
1000-1399	27531
1400-1899	27534
Hunters Pl	27530
Hunters Creek Dr & Pl	27534
Huntington Dr	27530
Huntington Pl	27534
Huntsman Pl	27534
Hyacinth Rd	27534
Hyde Park Dr	27530
Igloo Rd	27531
Imperial Dr	27534
Industry Ct	27530
Inez Ln	27534
Ingram Ln	27530
Inspection Ln	27531
Ironwood Rd	27530
Isaac Dr	27530
Isler St	27530
Ivey Ct	27534
Ivy St	27530
J And L Dr	27530
J R Pl	27530
Jabarrah Ave	27531
N & S Jackson St	27530
Jacksons Holw	27530
Jacobs Ridge Dr	27534
N & S James St	27530
James Hinson Rd	27530
James White Ct	27530
E & W Jamestown St	27534
Jay Ryan Rd	27534
Jeannine Dr	27534
N Jefferson Ave	
100-1099	27530
1100-1399	27534
S Jefferson Ave	27530
Jeffreys Ln	27530
E Jenkins Rd	27530
Jennifer Pl & Rd	27534
Jessica Pl	27534
Jj Ln	27530
N & S John Ct & St	27530
John Deere Dr	27530
Johnathans Pl	27534
Johnson Ln	27530
Johnson Branch Rd	27534
Jordan Blvd	27530
Joscara Dr	27534
Josh Ln	27534
Judy Pl	27530
Julie Ln	27534
Juniper St	27530
K And M Dr	27530
Kandis Dr	27530
Karen Cir	27530
Kasler Ln	27534
Kathy Ln	27534
Kay Dee St	27534
Kayla Ct	27534
Kayla Marie Ln	27530
Kearney Ln	27530
Keesler Ln	27534
Keith Ln & Pl	27534
Kelliwood Dr	27534
Kelly Ave	27531
Kelly Ct	27534
Kelly Dr	27530
Kelvin Ln	27530
Kelway Dr	27530
Kendall Ln	27534
Kenly Rd	27534
Kennedy Dr	27530
Kennon Ave & Ct	27530
Kenton Ln	27530
Kentucky Dr	27530
Kestrel Ct	27530
Kevin Dr	27530
Killdeer Dr	27530
Kimberly Ln	27534
King Dr & Rd	27530
Kingdom Ln	27534
Kings Way	27530
Kingston Cir	27530
Kirtland Dr	27534
Knollwood Dr	27530
Koonce St	27530
N & S Kornegay St	27530
Kosuda Ln	27534
Kristen Ct	27530
Krystal Cir	27534
L And D Ln	27530
La Rue Cir	27530
Lackland St	27534
Lake Dr	27530
E Lake Dr	27530
Lake Ridge Dr	27530
Lake Shore Ct & Dr	27534
Lake Wackena Rd	27534
Lakeview Dr	27530
Lamm Dr	27534
Lamp Lighter Cir	27534
Lancashire Dr	27534
Landmark Dr	27534
Lane Ridge Dr	27530
Lane Tree Dr	27530
Langley Ave	27531
Langston Dr	27534
Larchmont Cir	27530
Laredo Dr	27530
Lariat Rd	27534
Laura Ln	27530
Laurel St	27530
Laurel Patch Pl	27530
Lauren Pl	27534
Leafwood Dr	27534
Leatherwood Cir	27534
Lee Dr	27534
Lee St	27530
Leigh Pl	27534
Lemon St	27530
Lemuel Dr	27534
Leon Dr	27530
Leonard Dr	27534
N & S Leslie Rd & St	27530
Level St	27530
Lewis Dr	27534
Lexington Ave	27534
Lexington Dr	27530
Lillian St	27530
Lily Pl	27530
Lime St	27530
Lincoln Dr	27530
Lindsey St	27534
Linen Ln & Pl	27530
Linwood Ave	27530
Lionel St	27530
Lisa Cir & Ln	27534
Little River Dr	27530
Littleton Pl	27530
Live Oak Dr	27530
Livingston Dr	27530
Livius Ct	27534
Ljr Ln	27530
E & W Lockhaven Ct & Dr	27534
Log Oak Pl	27534
Logan St	27534
Lois Pl	27534
Londonderry Dr	27530
Long Leaf Ln	27534
Longleaf Ave	27534
Longs Plant Farm Rd	27534
Longview Dr	27534
Loop Rd	27530
Lou Dr	27530
Lou Alma Dr	27534
Louise Cir	27530
Louisville Rd	27534
Louvenia Ave	27534
Lowe St	27531
Lowry Dr	27534
Lucky Oak Rd	27530
Lufbery Ave	27534
Luke St	27531
Luther Dr	27534
Lynch Dr	27530
Lynn Ave & Pl	27534
Lyster St	27531
Mabe St	27534
Mack Rd	27530
N & S Madison Ave	27530
Magnolia St	27530
Malloy St	27534
Mann Ln	27530
Mansion Ln	27530
Maple St	27530
Maplewood Dr	27534
March Ln	27534
Marcia Dr	27530
Margaret Dr	27530
Marianna Dr	27534
Marie Ave	27530
N & S Marion Dr	27534
Mark Edwards Rd	27534
Marlette Dr	27534
Marshall St	27530
Marshburn Dr	27534
Marshview Pl	27534
Martha Vineyard Dr	27530
Martin Rd	27530
N Martin Rd	27530
Martin St	27531
Marvin St	27530
Mary Ln	27530
Marybeth Pl	27534
Marygold St	27530
Massey St	27534
Maxwell St	27534
Mcarthur St	27530
Mcdaniels St	27530
Mcduffie Pl	27530
Mckayla Ln	27530
Mclain St	27534
Mclamb Pl	27534
Mcneill Ln	27534
Mcwood Pl	27530
Meadow Ln	27530
Meadow Rd	27534
Meadow St	27534
Meadowcrest Dr	27534
Meadowlark Rd	27534
Meastowe Ave	27531
Medical Rd	27531
Medical Office Pl	27534
Megan Ln	27534
Melinda Ct	27534
Melodie Ln	27530
Memory Ln	27530
Mendenhall Cir	27530
Mercer St	27530
Meredith Dr	27530
Merritt Rd	27534
Merrywood Dr	27530
Mert Cir	27530
Michelle Dawn Dr	27534
Middle St	27530
Middleton Rd	27530
Mike Cir	27530
Mildred St	27530
Miles Ln	27534
Mill Pl & Rd	27534
Mill Creek Ct	27534
Mill Dam Ln	27530
Mill Run Pl	27534
Mill Stone Dr	27530
Millbrook Village Dr	27530
Miller Ave	27530
Miller St	27534
Millers Chapel Rd	27534
Mills Rd	27530
Milwood Dr & Pt	27534
Mimosa St	27530
Mimosa Park Dr	27534
Mint Ct & Dr	27530
Mira Dr	27534
Misty Ln	27530
Mitchell Ave	27531
Mollie Dr S	27534
Monticello Cir	27530
Mooring Ln	27534
Morgan Trace Ln	27530
Moss Pl	27534
Moss Hill Dr	27530
Mossburg Dr	27530
Mount Airy Rd	27534
Mourning Dove Ln	27534
Muirfield Pl	27534
E & W Mulberry St	27530
Mull Smith Ln	27534
Munitions Cir	27531
Munroe Ln	27534
Muriel St	27534
Muriel Hooks Dr	27530
Murphy St	27530
Murray St	27530
Myers Ave	27530
Myrna Dr	27534
Myrtle Ct	27530
Myrtle Rd	27534
Nahunta Rd	27530
National Dr	27534
Nc 111 Hwy N	
1300-1999	27530
2000-3699	27534
Nc 111 Hwy S	27534
Nc 581 Hwy	27530
Neal Dr	27530
Nealy Dr	27530
Neicees Dr	27534
Neil St	27530
Nellis Dr	27534
Nelson Ct & Dr	27534
Neuse Islands Ln	27530
New Hope Rd	27534
E New Hope Rd	27534
W New Hope Rd	
100-1699	27534
1700-1899	27530
New Hope Village Dr	27534
Newsome Rd	27534
Newsome St	27530
Newton Dr	27534
Nicholas Dr	27534
Nick Dr	27534
Nicole Cir	27530
Night Hawk Dr	27534
Nile St	27530
No Record St	27531
Noland Pl	27534
Norlee Dr	27534
Norman St	27530
North Dr	27534
North St	27530
Northgold Dr	27534
Northview Dr	27534
Northwood Dr	27534
Norwood Ave	27534
Nottingham Dr	27530
E & W Oak St	27530
Oak Circle Dr	27534
Oak Forest Rd	27531
N Oak Forest Rd	27534
S Oak Forest Rd	27534
Oak Heights Dr	27530
Oak Hill Dr	27534
Oak Hollow Ct	27534
Oak Knoll Dr	27530
Oak Tree Ln	27530
Oak Valley Farms Dr	27530
Oakland Church Rd	27530
Oakwood St	27530
Oberry Center Rd	27530
Odell St	27530
Old Farm Rd	27530
Old Grantham Rd	27530
Old Mill Pl	27530
Old Nc Highway 111	27534
Old Smithfield Rd	27530
Old State Road 1909	27534
Olde Mill Creek Dr	27530
Ole Vineyard Rd	27530
N & S Oleander Ave	27530
Olive St	27530
Olivia Ln	27530
Orange St	27530
Orbit Rd	27534
Orchard St	27530
Orchestra St	27530
Orchid Row	27534
Ormond Ave	27530
Oscar Ln	27534
Osprey Pl	27534
Overbrook Rd	27534
Overby Ln	27530
Overman Rd	27530
Oxford Dr	27530
Oxley Ave	27530
Page Dr	27530
Paine St	27534
Palm St	27530
Palmer Pl	27530
Panorama Ct	27534
Par Dr	27530
Park Ave	27530
N Park Dr	27530
Park Pl	27534
Park Avenue A	27530
Park Avenue B	27530
Park Ridge Rd	27530
Parks Rd	27534
Parkway Dr	27534
Parkwood Dr	27534
Parkwood Ln	27530
Partridge Cir	27534
Partridge Ln	27530
Pastoral Rd	27530
Pate Cir	27530
Pate Farm Ln	27534
Patetown Rd	27530
Patricia Ct	27534
Patrick Ct	27534
Patrick St	27530
Patsy Ln	27534
Paul Pl	27534
Paul St	27530
Paul Hare Rd	27530
Paxton Pl	27534
Peachtree Dr	27534
Peachtree St	
1300-2199	27530
2400-2599	27534
Peanut Ct N	27530
Pear St	27530
Pearson St	27530
Pebble Cir	27530
Peele Rd	27534
Peele St	27530
Peggy Ln	27530
Penn Cir	27530
Perkins Dr, Rd & St	27530
Perkins Mill Rd	27530
Perry Dr	27530
Perry Farm Ln	27530
Peru St	27530
Peters Branch Ct	27534
Peterson St	27531
Peyton St	27530
Phelps Aly	27530
Phillip Ct	27534
Phillips Ridge Ln	27530
Phyllis Dr	27530
Pickens Dr N	27530
Piedmont Pl	27530
Piedmont Airline Rd	27534
Pine Cir	27530
Pine Ct	27534
E Pine St	27530
W Pine St	27530
Pine Valley Rd	27530
Pinecrest Dr	27534
Pinehaven Ct	27534
Pineland Dr	27534
Pinemont Cir	27534
Pineneedles Ct & Rd	27534
Pineridge Ln	27530
Pinetops Ct	27530
N & S Pineview Ave	27530
Pinewood Cir & Dr	27534
Pittman St	27530
Pizza Inn Ln	27530
Plantation Dr	27534
Plantation Pl	27534
Plantation Rd	27530
Planters Pl	27530
Pleasant Pines Dr	27530
Pleasant Ridge Rd	27530
Poinsettia Dr	27534
Point Shore Dr	27534
N Pointe Dr	27530
Pope Ave	27531
Poplar St	27530
Poplar Ridge Dr	27534
Porter St	27530
Post Oak Dr	27534
Potley St	27530
Pou St	27530
Powell Rd	27534
Powers Ct	27534
Prince Ave	27530
Princess Dr & St	27530
Proctor St	27530
Propulsion Rd	27531
Providence Church Rd	27530
Psc 2000	27531
Quail Dr	27534
Quail Run	27530
N Quail Croft Dr	27534
Quaker Dr	27530
Rab Trl	27530
Rabbit Run Ln	27534
Rachel Dr	27534
Rackley Dr	27534
Racquet Ln	27534
Radford Dr	27530
Rae Ann Dr	27530
E & W Raintree Ln	27534
Rand Rd	27530
Randa Ln	27534
Randall Ln & Pl	27534
N & S Randolph St	27530
Rapcon Pl	27531
Raven Ridge Dr	27530
Rawlings St	27530
Raynor St	27530
Ream St	
100-399	27534
1000-1099	27531
Reavis Dr	27534
Red Cedar Ln	27530
Red Oak Dr	27530
Red Tip Ln	27530
Redfield Pl	27530
Redwood Trl	27534
Refueling Plz	27531
Regal Rd	27534
Remington Ct	27530
Remount Pl & Rd	27534
Renee Dr	27534
Research Farm Rd	27534
Retha St	27530
Rex Anna Dr	27530
Reynolda Pl	27530
Rhonda Dr & Pl	27530
Rhythm Pl	27530
Richard St	27530
Ridge Dr	27530
Ridge Runner Dr	27530
Ridgecrest Dr	27534
Ridgewood Dr	27534
Rifle Range Rd	27534
Rita Ln	27530
River Cir	27530
River Bluff Dr	27530
River Haven Dr	27530
River Run Pl	27530
Riverbend Pl & Rd N	27530
Riverview Cir	27534
Riverwoods Dr	27530
Riway St	27530
Roberts St	27530
Robin Pl & St	27534
Robinson Dr	27534
Robinson Pl	27530
Robson Cir	27530
Rock Rd	27534
Rockefeller Ct	27530
Rocky Ct	27530
Rodell Barrow Rd	27534
Rodney Ct	27530
Rollins Rd	27534
Rook Rd	27530
Rosa Howell Ln	27534
Rose Dr	27534
Rose St	27530
Rose Landing Dr & Pl	27530
Rosemary Cir	27530
Rosewood Ave	27530
Rosewood Gdns	27534
Rosewood Rd	27530
Roundtree Ln	27530
Rouse St	27534
Rowe St	27530
Royall Ave	27534
Ruby Rd	27534
Ruby Belle Way	27530
Rudolph St	27530
Runnel Pl	27530
Runningbranch Cir	27530
Rutledge Ln	27534
Ryan Blvd, Ct & Way	27534
Sable Dr	27530
Saddlewood Dr	27534
Sagewood Pl	27530
Saint Charles Dr	27530
Saint John Church Rd	27534
Sal Ct	27534
Salem Church Rd	27530

Salem Country Ln 27530
Salem Hill Ln 27530
Sallie Pl 27534
Sambo Lambert Rd 27530
Sami St 27530
Samuel Rd 27534
Sanborn Ln & Pl 27534
Sanderling Way 27530
Sanders Pl 27534
Sandhill Dr 27530
Sandstone Dr 27534
Sandy Cir & Dr 27534
Sandy Lane Rd 27534
Sandy Ridge Rd 27530
Sandy Spring Dr 27534
Sasser Dr 27530
Saulsberry Dr & Pl 27534
Saulston Rd 27534
Sawgrass Pl 27534
Sawwood Pl 27534
Saxon St 27534
Scale Dr 27530
Scallop Pl 27530
Schoodic Pt 27534
Scotland Dr 27530
Scott St 27534
Scott Hills Dr 27530
Scotty Dr 27534
Scriven Rd 27534
Seaboard St 27530
Sedgefield Dr 27534
Selah Church Rd 27530
Selfridge Rd 27534
Serenity Cir & Dr 27530
Sevendales Dr 27534
E & W Seymour Dr & St 27530
Shadowy Ln 27530
Shadywood Dr 27534
Shamrock Ave, Ct & Rd 27530
Sharon Dr 27534
Shaw Ct 27530
Sheba Ct 27534
Sheha Ter 27534
Shelley Dr & Pl 27534
Shelton St 27530
Sherard Ct 27530
Sheridan Rd 27534
Sheridan Forest Rd 27534
Sherman St 27530
Sherrell Pl 27534
Sherrington Dr 27534
Sherwood Ave 27534
Sherwood Cir 27530
Sheryl Ter 27534
Short St 27530
Silver Fox Cir 27530
Simmons St 27530
Simpson St 27530
Skeet Pl 27531
Skitt Dr 27534
Slaughter St 27530
Slick Rock Rd 27534
Slocumb St 27531
N Slocumb St 27530
S Slocumb St 27530
Small Arms Pl 27531
Smith Dr & Pl 27534
Smith Farm Rd 27534
Smith Logging Ln 27530
Smitty Ln 27530
Solara Dr 27534
Somerset Dr 27530
Somervale Ln 27530
Sourwood Rd 27534
South Dr 27534
South St 27530
Southeast Dr 27534
Southern Pine Rd 27534
Southfield Ln 27530
Southfork Pl 27530
Southwood Dr 27530
Spaulding Ave 27530
Spearwood Dr 27534
N & S Spence Ave 27534

Spoonbill Dr & Pl 27534
Spring Ct 27534
Spring St 27530
Spring Bank Rd 27534
Spring Branch Rd 27530
Spring Creek Rd 27534
Springwood Dr 27530
E & W Spruce St 27530
Squier Ave 27534
Stacy Dr 27530
Stadium Dr 27530
Stallings St 27530
E & W Stargrass Cir 27534
State 2121 Rd 27530
Steeplechase Cv 27534
Stephens Ct & St 27530
Steven Pl 27530
Stevens Church Rd 27530
Stevens Memorial Pl 27534
Stevens Mill Rd 27530
Stillwater Creek Cir & Dr 27534
Stonegate Ct 27530
Stonewood Dr & Pl 27534
N & S Stoney Creek Ln 27530
Stoney Creek Church Rd
1420A-1420Z 27534
100-733 27530
734-1599 27534
Stoney Hill Rd 27530
Stoney Manor Dr 27534
Stoney Run Dr 27530
Stratford Rd 27534
Striding Ridge Dr 27534
Strike Eagle Run 27530
Stronach Ave 27534
Stuart St 27530
Sue Ellen Cir 27534
Summer Wind Dr 27530
Summerlin Dr 27530
Summit Dr 27530
Summit Rd 27534
Sumpter Dr 27534
Sunburst Dr 27534
Sunflower Dr 27530
Sunny South St 27534
Sunnyhill Ct 27534
Sunset Dr & Pl 27534
Surry Ln
100-199 27534
3400-3499 27530
Susan Cir 27530
Sussex Pl 27530
Suttons Run 27534
Swan St 27530
Swine Rd 27530
Sycamore St 27530
Talbert Dr 27530
Tall Pines Pl 27534
Tammy Ln 27534
Tampa St 27534
Tanager Ct 27530
Tanglewood Ln 27534
Tarboro St 27530
Tarheel Pine Dr 27530
W Tarklin Dr 27530
N & S Taylor Pl & St 27530
Teakwood Dr 27534
Teal Cir 27534
Tenderfoot Cir 27530
Tenth Pl 27534
Teresas Way 27534
Terrace Ct 27530
Thad Ln 27534
The First Church Rd 27534
Thel Dr 27534
Theo Dr 27534
Thomas St & Trl 27534
Thomick Pl 27530
Thompson Ln 27530
Thoroughfare Rd 27534
Thrasher Cir 27534
S Tiffany Rd 27534
Tilghman Dr 27534
Till Dr 27530

Timber Lake Dr 27534
Timberline Oak Dr 27534
Tindale Pl 27534
Tinder Pl 27534
Tinderwood Dr 27534
S Tinker St 27531
Tipton Ln 27530
Titleist Dr 27530
Todd Dr 27534
Tolar St 27530
Tom Herring Rd 27534
Tommys Rd
100-599 27530
800-2199 27534
W Tommys Rd 27530
Tonya Dr 27534
Topaz Ct 27530
N Torhunta Dr 27534
Towbridge Ln 27534
Tower Ln 27530
Tower Rd 27531
Tracy Pl 27534
Trailwater Dr 27530
Tramway Dr & Pl 27534
Trappers Run Dr 27530
Trappers Wood Dr 27530
Treetop Rd 27530
Trey Dr 27530
Trollingwood Dr 27534
Trotwood Dr 27534
True Vine Rd 27534
Truman St 27530
Tryon Dr 27530
Turner Rd 27530
Tuskeegee St 27530
Twilight Dr 27534
Twin Dr 27534
Twin Creeks Dr 27530
Twin Oaks Pl 27530
Tyndall Ln 27534
Union St 27530
Us Highway 117 Byp N & S 27530
Us Highway 13 N 27534
Us Highway 13 S 27530
Us Highway 70 E 27534
Us Highway 70 W 27534
Us Highway 70 Byp E 27534
Us Highway 70 Byp W 27530
Uzzell Rd 27534
Valencia Ave 27534
Valerie St 27534
Valley Dr 27530
Valleyview Dr 27534
Valleywood Dr 27530
Vance Dr 27534
Vandenburg St 27534
Vanderbilt Cir 27530
Vann St 27530
Vera Ave 27534
Veranda Pl 27530
Veronica Ave 27534
Veterans Dr 27530
Victor Pl 27530
Village Cir & Dr 27534
Village Grove Dr 27530
E & W Vine St 27530
Vinson Rd 27534
Vinwood Ave 27534
Violeta Cir 27534
N & S Virginia St 27530
Wackena Point Rd 27534
Walker Ave 27531
Walker St 27530
E Walnut St 27530
W Walnut St 27530
Walnut Trl 27534
Walnut Creek Dr 27534
Walnut Ridge Dr 27534
Walters Dr 27534
Warners Ct & Dr 27530
Warren St 27530
Warrick Cir 27534
Wash Station Ln 27534
Washington Ct 27530
Washorie Rd 27534

Watergate Ct 27530
Waters Cir 27534
Waters St 27530
Wayne Ave 27530
E Wayne Rd 27534
Wayne Memorial Dr 27534
Waynewoods Dr & Pl 27534
Weapons Ln 27531
Weatherby Dr 27530
Weaver Dr, Pl & Rd 27530
Wedgewood Pl 27530
Welford Pl 27534
E & W Wendy Cir & Way 27530
Wescott Pl 27534
Wesley Dr 27534
Wessex Ct 27530
Westbrook Ave & Rd 27530
Westfield St 27534
Weston Cir 27530
Westover Dr 27530
Westover Rd 27534
Westview Ct 27530
Westview Meadows Dr 27530
E Westwood Dr 27530
Wharton Ln 27530
Wheel Coach Pl 27534
Wheeler Dr 27530
Whisner St 27534
White Dogwood Ln 27530
White Oak Rd 27534
Whitfield Dr 27530
Whitney Pl 27530
Whitted Ct 27530
Wildwood Ct & Dr 27530
Will Dr 27534
William Ct 27530
William Dr 27530
N William St
100-201 27530
200-200 27533
202-2998 27530
203-2999 27530
S William St 27530
Willow Pl 27534
Wilmington Ave 27530
Wilshire Way 27534
Wilson St 27530
Windham Ct 27530
Windsor Dr 27534
Windsor Creek Pkwy 27534
Windy Acres Ln 27534
Windyfield Dr 27530
Wingspread Dr 27530
Winslow Cir & Pl 27530
Winston Dr 27530
Wintergreen Pl 27534
Wisteria Rd 27530
Wolf Ln 27530
Wood Pl & St 27534
Wood Cock Dr 27530
Wood Peck Rd 27534
Woodberry Dr & Ln 27534
Woodbine St 27534
Woodcroft Dr 27534
Woodford Ct 27530
Woodhaven Dr 27530
Woodhille Dr 27530
Woodland Church Rd 27530
Woodmere Ln 27530
Woodrose Ave & Dr 27534
Woodrow St 27530
Woods Mill Rd 27534
Woodside Cir & Dr 27534
Woodview Cir & Dr 27530
Wooten Point Rd 27534
Workman St 27530
Worth Dr 27534
Wren Pl 27534
Wright Ave 27534
Wright Brothers Ave
1000-1814 27531
1815-1815 27534
1816-2098 27531
1817-2099 27531
3600-3699 27534

Wyatt Dr 27534
Yearling Dr 27534
Yelverton Pl 27530
York Dr 27534
Zekes Ln 27534
Zeno Ln 27530

NUMBERED STREETS

1st St 27534
2nd St 27534
3rd St 27534
4th St 27534
5 Points Rd 27530
5th St 27534
6th St 27534
7th St 27534
8th St 27534
9th St 27534
11th St
400-799 27530
800-1199 27534
12th St 27534

GREENSBORO NC

General Delivery 27420

POST OFFICE BOXES MAIN OFFICE STATIONS AND BRANCHES

Box No.s
1 - 2934 27402
745 - 745 27420
2971 - 3942 27402
4001 - 4996 27404
5001 - 5994 27435
7001 - 7999 27417
8001 - 8996 27419
9001 - 9992 27429
9998 - 9998 27402
10001 - 10994 27404
13001 - 14999 27415
16001 - 16992 27416
18001 - 19998 27419
20000 - 26099 27420
26100 - 26299 27402
26300 - 26306 27438
26401 - 26499 27404
26501 - 26599 27415
26600 - 26625 27416
26701 - 26725 27417
26800 - 26899 27429
26901 - 26975 27419
27000 - 27081 27425
27404 - 27404 27404
27415 - 27415 27415
27416 - 27416 27416
27417 - 27417 27417
27419 - 27419 27419
27420 - 27420 27420
27425 - 27425 27425
27427 - 27427 27427
27429 - 27429 27429
27435 - 27435 27435
27438 - 27438 27438
27494 - 27498 27495
29001 - 29714 27429
35002 - 35992 27425
36001 - 36619 27416
38001 - 39860 27438
41001 - 41320 27404
42001 - 42130 27425
46700 - 46799 27420
49001 - 49964 27419
77001 - 77959 27417
78001 - 78208 27427
79001 - 79119 27417

NAMED STREETS

Abbey Ct 27410

Abbots Glen Ct 27455
Abbott Dr 27455
Abelia Ct 27455
Aberdeen Ter 27403
Abington Dr 27401
Abner Pl 27407
Ackland Dr 27455
Acorn Ct & Rd 27406
Acorn Forest Rd 27410
Acorn Ridge Rd 27407
W Acres Dr 27405
Ada Rd 27406
Adair Rd 27409
Adams St 27401
Adams Farm Ln & Pkwy 27407
Adams Ridge Dr 27407
Adamson Rd 27407
Addison Pointe Dr 27409
Adonica Ln 27410
Aero Ct 27409
Afton Dr 27401
Aftonshire Dr 27410
Aggie Ct 27401
Ailanthus Pl 27407
Ainsworth Ct & Dr 27410
Air Harbor Rd 27455
Airline Rd 27409
Airport Center Dr 27409
Akin Dr 27409
Aladdin St 27407
Alamance Ct 27406
Alamance Rd 27407
Alamance Church Rd 27406
Albany St 27401
Albatross St 27403
Albemarle Dr 27410
Albert Pick Rd 27409
Albright Dr 27408
Alcorn Rd 27409
Alcott Rd 27405
Alder Way 27407
Alderman Ct & Dr 27408
Alderwood Dr 27409
Aldine Rd 27405
Alert Ct 27407
Alex Dr 27406
Alexander Rd 27406
Alexandria Rd 27405
Alice Ave 27401
Allen St 27406
Allenbrooke Dr 27407
Allendale Rd 27408
Allerton Cir 27409
Alliance Dr 27407
Alliance Church Rd 27406
Allisons Way 27409
Allred Farm Way 27406
Allwood Ct 27410
Allyson Ave 27405
Alma St 27407
Alma Pinnix Dr 27405
Aloe Rd 27409
Alonzo Ct 27405
Altamont Ct 27410
Alton St 27405
Amber Ln 27407
Amberhill Ct & Dr 27455
Ambleside Ct 27407
American Ave 27409
American Legion St 27405
Americhase Dr 27409
Amesbury Rd 27403
Amethyst Ct 27409
Amidon Dr 27410
Amity Ct & Dr 27406
Amos Dr 27405
Anchor Dr 27410
Anderson St 27405
Andorra Ct 27410
Andover Ave 27405
Andrew St 27406
Andrew Paul Way 27410
Andrews Dairy Rd 27406
Angelica Ln 27410
Angler Ln 27455

Anita Ln 27405
Anita Glen Dr 27405
Ann St 27405
Annadale Dr 27407
Annalisa Dr 27455
Annie Ave 27406
Annie Laurie Dr 27455
Annies Ct 27406
Anson Cir & Rd 27407
Anthony Ct 27406
Antilla Pl 27407
Antioch Dr 27406
Antiqua Ln 27406
Antler Ct 27406
Antoine Dr 27407
Anvil Pl 27407
Apache St 27401
Apple Ridge Ct & Rd 27406
Apple Tree Ln 27455
Applegate Rd 27455
Appleton Rd 27405
Applewood Ct 27410
April Ln 27405
Arbor Dr 27401
Arbor Crossing Ct 27405
Arbor Linda Dr 27405
Arby Ct 27401
Arcadia Dr 27410
Arcaro Dr 27455
Archer Ct 27407
Archer Glen Ct 27407
Archwood Dr 27406
Ardale Pl 27403
Arden Pl 27403
Ardmore Dr 27401
Ardoch Ct & Dr 27410
Ardsley Ct 27407
Argonne Blvd 27407
Argyle Ln 27406
S Ariel Farm Ct & Rd 27455
Arlee St 27401
Arlington St 27406
Armhurst Ct & Rd 27405
Armstead Dr 27407
Arnold Ln & St 27405
Arrow Rd 27409
Arrowhead Dr 27410
Arta Ln 27406
Artic Fox Cir 27405
Arundel Ct 27406
Arvid Dr 27405
Asa Ln 27406
Asbury Ter 27408
Ashcroft Rd 27406
Ashdale Rd 27405
Ashe St 27406
Ashebrook Dr 27409
Asheland Ridge Ct 27410
Asher Downs Dr 27405
Ashgrove Dr 27410
Ashland Dr
100-699 27403
4100-4198 27407
4200-4399 27407
Ashley Dr 27405
Ashley Hill Dr 27405
Ashmont Dr 27410
Ashmore Dr 27405
Ashton Ct 27410
Ashton Dr 27410
Ashton Sq 27408
Ashway Ct 27407
Ashwood Ct 27455
Ashworth Rd 27405
Aspen Ct 27408
Aspen Dr 27409
Assembly Rd 27405
Associate Dr 27405
Aster Dr 27401
Atchison Rd 27409
Athena Ct 27407
Atherton Ct 27405
Atlanta St 27406
Atlas Ct & St 27405
Attar Ct 27410
Atwater Rd 27407

Atwell Ave 27406
Auburn Hill Dr 27407
Auburn Hills Dr 27407
Auburndale Dr 27410
Auden Dr 27406
Audrey Rd 27406
Audubon Dr 27410
Augusta Ct 27455
Aunt Mary Ave 27405
Austin Ct 27406
Autumn Ct & Dr 27405
Autumn Ridge Ct 27455
Autumn Woods Dr 27407
Autumncrest Dr 27407
Ava Leigh Way 27405
Avalon Rd 27401
Avery Pl 27408
Avis Dr 27406
E & W Avondale Dr 27403
S Aycock St 27403
Azalea Dr 27407
Bach Ter 27405
Badenridge Ct 27407
Baggage Master Ct 27455
Bailey Rd 27406
Bailiff St 27403
Bain St 27406
Baity Bend Rd 27406
Baker Ave 27407
Baker Dr 27406
Balboa St 27405
Bald Eagle Dr 27410
Baliol Ct 27407
Ball St 27405
Ballinger Rd 27410
Bally Brook Dr 27410
Baltic Ave 27406
Bancolle Dr 27407
Bancroft Rd 27405
Banking St 27408
Banks St 27401
Banner Ave 27401
Banner Oak Ct 27406
Bannock Ln 27410
Barberry Dr 27406
Barbour Rd 27406
Barclay St 27405
Bardwell Pl & Rd 27410
Barham Rd 27455
Barksdale Dr 27401
Barkwood Dr 27406
Barmot Dr 27455
Barn Owl Ct 27406
Barnes Ct 27405
Barnfield Rd 27455
Barnhardt St 27406
Baron Walk 27406
Barrett Ct & Pl 27455
Barringer St 27403
Barrington Dr 27408
Barrymore Ct 27410
Bartholomews Ln 27407
Bartlett Dr 27406
Bartlett St 27409
Barto Pl 27405
E & W Barton St 27407
Base Leg Rd 27409
Bashford Ln 27405
Basington Rd 27406
Baskerville Ct 27410
Bass Chapel Rd 27455
Bass Landing Pl 27455
Basset Trl 27410
Batchelor Dr 27410
Batten Rd 27406
Battenburg Ct 27410
Battery Ct & Dr 27409
Battle Rd 27410
Battle Forest Ln 27455
Battleground Ave
300-799 27401
801-899 27401
900-3000 27408
2941-2941 27438
3001-3299 27408
3002-3298 27408
3300-5099 27410
Battleground Ct 27408
Bay Hill Ct 27410
Bay Meadows Ct 27406
Bay Willows Ct 27406
Bayberry Ct & Ln 27455
Bayer Ln 27409
Bayfield Ln & Rd 27455
Bayleaf Ct & Ln 27455
Baylor Ct 27405
Baylor St
3800-3999 27405
4000-4699 27455
Baynes Forest Ln 27406
Baytree Ct & Dr 27455
Bayview Rd 27405
Baywater Ln 27408
Beacon St 27405
Beaconwood Dr 27455
Beale Ave 27407
Beaman Pl 27408
Bear Cub Dr 27406
Bear Ridge Ct 27406
Bearberry Pt 27455
Bearhollow Rd 27410
Bearkling Pl 27407
Bears Creek Rd 27406
Bearwick Cir 27406
Beaumont Ave 27401
Beaver Creek Ct 27406
Beaverbrook Dr & Pl 27406
Beaverdale Dr 27406
Beck St 27405
Beckford Dr 27407
Beckwith Dr 27410
Bedstone Dr 27455
N Beech Ln 27455
Beech St 27401
Beech Cliff Ln 27455
Beech Grove Ct & Dr 27455
Beech Ridge Ct 27455
Beechcroft Ct & Dr 27407
Beechdale Rd 27409
Beechmont Ct & Dr 27410
Beechtree Rd 27408
Beechwood Dr 27410
Beechwood St 27403
Belcrest Dr 27406
Belden Dr 27405
Belfast Ct 27406
Belfield Ct & Dr 27405
Belfry Ct 27410
Belhaven Dr 27407
Bell House Cv 27455
Bell Orchard Dr 27455
Bell Tower Ct 27406
Bellaire St 27406
Bellemeade St 27401
Belles Ct 27401
Bellevue St 27406
Bellinghaus Ln 27455
Bellows Ct 27407
Bellwick Dr 27406
Belmar St 27407
Belmont St 27406
Belrose Ct 27406
Belvidere Ct & Pl 27410
Belvoir Dr 27406
N Benbow Rd 27401
S Benbow Rd
300-800 27401
802-898 27401
900-2299 27406
Benedict Rd 27406
Benfield Dr 27410
Benjamin Pkwy 27408
Benjamin Bensen St 27406
Bennett St 27406
Bennie Ct 27406
Bennington Ct & Dr 27410
Bent Creek Ct 27410
Bent Oak Ct 27455
Bentford Rd 27406
Bentley Rd 27409
Benton Ln 27455
Benway Pl 27410
Berea Ct 27406
Berkley Pl 27403
Berkshire St 27403
Bernard St 27405
Bernau Ave 27407
Berryhill Pl 27406
Berryman St 27405
Bertie St 27403
Berwick St 27403
Berwyn Ct 27407
E Bessemer Ave
100-499 27401
500-3399 27405
W Bessemer Ave
100-499 27401
800-1299 27408
Bessemer Ct 27401
Beta Pl 27407
Beth Rd 27406
Bethania St 27401
Bethany Trce 27406
Bethel Spring Dl 27410
Betula St 27407
Beverly Pl 27403
Bevill Pl 27406
Bewcastle Ct 27407
Bienvenue Dr 27409
Big Poplar Ln 27406
Big Tree Way 27409
Bilbro St 27406
Binford St 27407
Bingham St 27401
Birch Ln 27408
E & W Birch Bark Ln 27455
Birch Hammock Dr 27409
Birch Knoll Rd 27455
Birch Pond Rd 27410
Birch Ridge Rd 27405
Birch Tree Way 27410
Birchbrook Cir 27410
Birchcrest Dr 27406
Birchdale Dr 27455
Birchwood Ln 27410
Birkdale Ct & Dr 27410
Birnamwood Trl 27407
Bisbee Dr 27407
Biscayne Dr 27410
Bishop Rd 27406
Bismark Rd 27407
Bitter Creek Ln 27407
Bitternut Trl 27410
Bittersweet Ct 27405
Bitting St 27403
Black Gum Pl 27405
Black Locust Ter 27405
Black Stallion Ct 27407
Black Willow Dr 27405
Blackberry Rd 27406
Blackmoor Rd 27406
Blackwood Ct 27405
Bladen Rd 27405
Blainmore Dr 27405
Blair St 27408
Blair House Rd 27410
Blair Khazan Dr 27405
Blakeney Pl 27408
Blakeshire Rd 27406
Blakewood Ter 27407
Blandwood Ave 27401
Blanton Pl 27408
Blazer Rd 27407
Blazing Star Ln 27410
Blazingwood Ct & Dr 27406
Bledsoe Dr 27410
Blue Bell Rd 27406
Blue Gill Cv 27455
Blue Heron Dr 27455
Blue Ridge Dr 27455
Blue Robin Way 27409
Blue Rock Ct 27405
Blue Spruce Ct 27406
Blue Stone Ln 27407
Blue Violet Dr 27410
Blueberry Ln 27401
Bluebonnet Dr 27407
Bluefield Rd 27455
Bluejay Dr 27407
Bluemont Dr 27408
Blueslate St 27406
Bluestem Cir, Ct & Dr 27405
Bluff Ridge Ct 27455
Bluff Run Dr 27455
Bluford St 27401
Blumenthal Rd 27406
Blunt St 27407
Blythewood Ct 27455
Bodie Ln 27455
Boeing Dr 27409
Bogart St 27405
Bonaire Ln 27405
Bonaventure Rd 27408
Bond St 27405
Bonita Dr 27405
Bonnybrook Ct 27410
Bontura Dr 27455
N & S Booker St 27401
Boone St 27405
Borders Ter 27401
Boren Dr 27407
Boston Rd 27407
Bostonian Ct & Dr 27455
Bothwell Ct 27401
Bothwell St
1200-1399 27406
1800-2499 27401
Boughton Ct 27410
Boulder Ct & Rd 27409
Boulevard St 27407
Bowman Ave 27407
Boxborough Ct 27407
Boxelder Ct & Cv 27405
Boxer Ln 27406
Boxford Rd 27406
Boxwood Dr 27410
Boyd St
400-599 27401
600-699 27405
Boyden St 27403
Boyle Ave 27406
Brackenwood Ct 27407
Brackin Ln 27406
Bracyridge Rd 27407
Brad Ln 27406
Bradbury Dr 27410
Bradenton Ct & Dr 27406
Bradford St 27405
Bradley St 27406
Brady St 27401
Braeburn Ln 27409
E & W Bragg St 27406
Brahman Trl 27405
Bramblegate Rd 27409
Brambletye Ct & Dr 27407
Bramblewood Dr 27407
Brame Rd 27405
Bramlet Pl 27407
Branch Ct 27408
Branchwood Dr 27408
Brandermill Ct 27407
Branderwood Dr
2200-2299 27407
2900-3099 27406
Brandon St 27405
Brandonshire Ct 27409
Brandt St 27407
Brandt Vlg 27455
Brandt Forest Ct 27455
Brandt Lake Ct 27410
Brandt Ridge Dr 27410
Brandt Trace Farm Rd 27455
Brandy Ct 27409
Brandy Dr 27409
Brandy Rd 27407
Brandywine Cir 27409
Brandywine Dr 27410
Brannigan Cir 27407
Brannock Dr 27406
Bransford Ct 27407
Brass Cannon Ct 27410
Brass Eagle Loop 27410
Brassfield Rd 27410
Brassfield Oaks Ct & Dr 27410
Brassfield Park Pl 27410
Braswell Ct 27408
Braxton Ln 27408
Brecon Ln 27407
Breezeway Ln 27405
Breezewood Rd 27410
Brenock Ct 27410
Brentlen Way 27406
E & W Brentwood Rd 27403
Brevard St 27407
Brewington Sibert Pl 27406
Brewster Dr 27409
Briar Rose Ct 27410
Briar Run Dr 27405
Briarbend Dr 27410
Briarbranch Ct 27405
Briarcliff Rd 27408
Briargate Dr 27405
Briargrove Ct 27410
Briarlea Rd 27405
Briarmeade Rd 27405
Briaroak Ct 27410
Briarwood Dr 27403
Brice St 27403
Bricker St 27401
Brickhaven Dr 27407
Bridford Pkwy 27407
Bridford Downs Dr 27407
Bridford Lake Cir 27407
Bridgehill Ct 27406
Bridgepoint Rd 27405
Bridges Creek Dr 27406
Bridgestone Ct 27406
Bridgetown Ct 27407
Bridgette Blvd & Ct 27407
Bridgeview Dr 27406
Bridgewater Dr 27410
Bridgeway Dr 27406
Bridle Trl 27407
Bridle Creek Ct 27410
Bridle Path Ln 27410
Bridlington Dr 27455
Brigham Rd 27409
Brighton Pl 27410
Brighton St 27405
Brightwood Landing Ln 27405
Brightwood School Rd 27405
Brill Rd 27406
Brim Rd 27405
Brinton Dr 27410
Bristle Cone Rd 27406
Bristol Rd 27406
British Lake Dr 27410
Britley Ct 27406
Britton St 27406
Brixham Dr 27455
Broad Ave 27406
Broadacres Dr 27407
Broadmoor Pl 27410
Broadview St 27405
Broadway Dr 27406
Broken Tree Rd 27406
Bromley Rd 27406
Bromley Wood Ln 27410
Brompton Dr 27407
N Brook Dr 27410
Brook Rd 27407
Brook Pine Cir & Dr 27406
Brook Shadow Ct & Dr 27410
Brook Valley Cir 27406
Brookcliff Ct 27408
Brookcliff Dr
1600-1899 27408
1900-1999 27410
Brookfield Dr 27410
Brookforest Dr 27406
Brookglen Ct, Dr & Ln 27410
Brookgreen Dr 27406
Brookhaven Ct & Dr 27406
Brookhaven Mill Rd 27406
Brookmont Ct 27406
Brooks Ct 27406
Brooks Ln 27410
Brookshire Ct 27455
Brookside Dr 27408
Brookway Dr 27410
Broome Rd 27406
Broughton Dr 27410
Brown Blvd 27401
Brown Bark Dr 27410
Browning Rd 27410
Brownstone Ln 27410
Bruce St 27403
Bruin Ct & Rd 27405
Brunswick Rd 27407
Brush Rd 27409
Brush Arbor Ct 27455
Brushwood Ct & Rd 27410
Brushy Fork Dr 27406
Bruton Pl N & S 27410
Bryan Blvd 27409
Bryan Ct 27408
Brye Ct 27406
Brynhurst Dr 27407
Bryson St 27405
Buccaneer Ct 27455
Buchanan Rd 27405
Buchanan Church Rd 27405
Buchanan Heights Rd 27405
Buckboard Ln 27410
Buckhaven Ct 27409
Buckhorn Rd 27410
Buckingham Rd 27408
Buddingwood Dr 27409
Buena Vista Cir 27455
Buff St 27406
Buffalo St 27405
Buffalo Tom Dr 27455
Buffington Pl 27410
Bufflehead Ct 27455
Builtwell Rd 27405
Bull Run Ct 27407
Bulla St 27406
Bullard Loop 27405
Buncombe Dr 27407
Bundy Dr 27403
Bunkhouse Ct 27405
Bur Mill Club Rd 27410
Burbank St 27406
Burgenfield Dr 27407
Burgess Rd 27409
Burgundy Dr 27407
Burlingate Dr 27407
Burlington Rd 27405
Burlwood Dr 27410
Burnette Dr
2300-2499 27406
3100-3199 27405
Burnetts Chapel Rd
1200-1399 27406
1400-1599 27407
Burning Tree Dr 27406
Burns St 27406
Burnt Poplar Rd 27409
Burntleaf Pl 27410
Burtner St 27406
Burton Farm Rd 27455
Busic Ave 27401
Business Park Dr 27409
Butterfield Dr 27405
Buxton Ct & Rd 27406
Byers Rd 27405
Byers Ridge Dr 27405
Byrd St 27401
Byron Pl 27405
Bywood Ct & Rd 27405
Cabarrus Ct & Dr 27407
Cabin Ct 27406
Cabot Ct & Dr 27407
Cactus Ct 27410
Cahill Dr 27406
Caindale Dr 27409
Caldwell St 27406
Caleb Rd 27409
Calico Dr 27409
Callan Dr 27405
Calumet Pl 27405
Calvert St 27405
Calyx Ct 27410
Cam Pl 27406
Camann St 27407
Camber Rd 27407
Camborne St 27407
Cambridge St 27406
Cambridge Oak Cir 27410
Camden Rd 27403
Camden Falls Cir & Ct 27410
Camden Ridge Dr 27410
E & W Camel St 27401
Cameo Dr 27403
Cameron Ave 27401
Campbell St 27405
Campbell Farm Rd 27410
Campground Rd 27406
Camrose Rd 27406
Canaan Dr 27408
Canaan Forest Dr 27405
Canary Ct 27409
Candace Ridge Ct & Dr 27406
Candlenut Rd 27405
Candlewick Rd 27455
Candlewood Dr 27403
Cannes Way 27406
Cannon Rd 27410
Cannonball Ct & Rd 27455
Canoe Rd 27409
Canonero Dr 27410
Canterbury St 27408
Canterwick Ct 27410
Canterwood Dr 27410
Canton Ave 27405
Canvasback Pt 27455
Cape Pl 27405
Cape May Pt 27455
Capital Dr 27409
Captains Pt 27455
Caraway Ct 27406
Cardella Dr 27405
Cardigan Ct 27405
Cardinal Ct 27410
Cardinal Pl 27408
Cardinal Way 27410
Cardinal Cove Ln 27410
Cardinal Crest Rd 27406
Cardinal Downs Dr 27410
Cardinal Forest Ct 27410
Cardinal Health Ct 27407
Cardinal Lake Dr 27410
Cardinal Ridge Dr 27410
Cardinal Wood Dr 27410
Cardova Dr 27410
Cardwell Pt 27407
Cargo Rd 27409
Carilla Dr 27407
Carissa Ct 27407
Carla Ln 27405
Carlisle Rd 27408
Carlo Ct 27410
Carlson Dr 27455
Carlson Ter 27410
Carlson Dairy Rd 27410
Carlton Ave 27406
Carlynn Ct 27455
Carlys Way 27410
Carmel Rd 27408
Carnegie Pl 27409
Carnoustie Trl 27407
Carol Ave 27406
Carolina St
900-998 27401
1000-1399 27401
4800-5099 27406
Carolina Circle Mall 27405
Caroline Ct 27407
Carolwood Dr 27407
Carowill Dr 27455
Carpenter Ct & St 27403
Carr St 27403
Carrborough Rd 27406
Carriage Ln 27410
Carriage Crossing Ln 27410
Carriage Hill Ct 27410
Carrieland Dr 27405

Carrington St 27407
Carroll St 27408
E Carteret St 27406
Cartwright Dr 27406
Carver Dr 27401
Cascade Ct 27410
Cascade Dr 27410
Cascade Rd 27406
Caspian Ln 27455
Casting Way 27455
Castle Bridge Ct 27407
Castle Croft Rd 27407
Castleberry Ln 27406
Castlerock Rd 27406
Castleton Rd 27406
Castlewood Dr 27405
Caswell Dr 27408
Catalina Dr 27403
Catawba Dr 27407
Cates Dr 27409
Cathy Rd 27455
Cattail Ct 27455
Caulfield Dr 27410
Causeway Ct 27455
Causey St 27407
Causey Lake Rd 27406
Cavalier Ter 27408
Cavendish Cir 27455
Cecil St 27455
Cecilside Ln 27405
N & S Cedar St 27401
Cedar Bend Ct 27410
Cedar Bluff Ct 27407
Cedar Branch Dr 27407
Cedar Chase Dr 27455
Cedar Fork Dr 27407
Cedar Glen Rd 27410
Cedar Hollow Rd 27455
Cedar Knoll Ct & Dr 27407
Cedar Park Rd 27405
Cedar View Dr 27455
Cedar Waxwing Ct 27455
Cedarcroft Ct 27409
Cedardale Ct 27455
Cedarline Dr 27409
Celeste Ct & Dr 27407
Celtic Rd 27406
Centenary Rd 27407
Center St 27407
Center Grove Ct 27455
Centerview Dr 27407
Central Ave 27401
Central Park Ave 27407
Centre Camp Ct 27455
Centreport Dr 27409
Century Oaks Ct & Dr 27455
Cessna Dr 27409
Cezanne Dr 27407
Chadbury Ct & Dr 27407
Chadford Pl 27410
Chadmoor Ct 27406
Chaftain Pl 27410
Chamberlain Dr 27406
Chamblee Ct 27410
Champagne Dr 27410
Champion Ct 27410
Chance Rd 27410
Chancery Pl 27408
Channel Ct 27410
Channing Rd 27410
Chantilly Pl 27407
Chapel Bend Ct 27405
Chapel Brook Way 27405
Chapel Cross Ct 27405
Chapel Downs Ct 27405
Chapel Edge Dr 27405
Chapel Glen Ln 27405
Chapel Park Ln 27405
Chapel Ridge Dr 27405
N & S Chapman St 27403
Chapparal Dr & Ln 27406
Char Mar Ct & Dr 27406
Charing Cross Rd 27455
Chariot Dr 27406
Charity Ct 27401
Charles St 27405

Charles Harper Rd 27406
Charles Harshaw Ave 27401
Charleston Sq 27408
Charlotte St 27401
Charlottesville Ct & Rd 27410
Charolais Dr 27406
Charter Pl 27405
Chateau Ct & Dr 27407
Chatfield Dr & Sq 27410
Chatham Dr 27408
Chatterson Ct 27410
Chatwick Dr 27405
Chaucer Ct & Dr 27407
Chavis Dr 27401
Checkerberry Ln & Sq 27455
Cheek Dr & Rd 27406
Chelsea Ln 27406
Cheltenham Blvd & Ct 27407
Cherbonne Dr 27407
Cherine Way 27410
Cherokee Dr 27408
Cherry Ln 27405
Cherry St 27401
Cherry Hill Dr 27410
Cherry Tree Dr 27405
Cherrydale Dr 27406
Cherrywood Dr 27405
Chesapeake Ct & Dr 27410
Cheshire Way 27405
Chesterbrooke Dr 27455
Chesterfield Ct 27410
Chesterton Dr 27406
Chestfield Ln 27407
Chestnut St 27405
Chestnut Bend Dr 27406
Chestnut Bluffs Ct 27407
Chestnut Hill Ct 27455
Cheswick Ct & Dr 27410
Cheviot Rd 27455
Cheyenne Dr 27410
Chianti Way 27410
Chicory Ln 27405
Chiles Higgins Ct 27406
Chillon Ct 27407
Chimney Center Blvd 27409
Chimney Rock Ct 27409
Chimney Rock Rd 27409
N Chimney Rock Rd
100-399 27409
400-499 27410
S Chimney Rock Rd 27409
Chimney Springs Dr 27407
Chinaberry Ct & Pl 27405
Chipmunk Dr 27407
Chippendale Trl 27406
Chippers Ct 27407
Chiswell Ct 27410
Chorus Ln 27405
Chowan Rd 27407
Christmas Pl 27410
Christophers Dr 27455
Chuck Rd 27406
Chuckwood Dr 27407
Church Ct 27401
N Church St
100-1499 27401
1500-3899 27405
3900-6199 27455
S Church St 27401
Church View Dr 27455
Churchill Dr 27410
Cicero Rd 27455
Cimmaron Ct 27407
Cinnabar Ct 27409
Circle Dr 27405
Circle Pine Ct 27407
Circleview Dr 27406
Citation Ct 27409
Clair Pl 27407
Clapp St 27401
Clapp Farms Rd 27405
Clara Lawrence Dr 27406
Clarendon Dr 27410
Clarfield Dr 27407
Claridge Ct 27407
Clarinda Dr 27405

Clark Ave & Ct 27406
Clarkland Rd 27410
Clarkson Rd 27410
Clarkwood Cir 27410
Clay St 27405
Clayburn Rd 27406
Cleburne St 27408
Clegg St 27407
Clement Ct 27410
Clemmons St 27406
Clermont St 27407
Cleveland St 27401
Cliffside Ter 27403
Cliffwood Ct & Dr 27406
Clifton Rd 27407
Clopton Dr 27455
Clovelly Ct & Dr 27406
Clover Ln 27410
Clover Rd 27405
Cloverdale Dr 27408
Club Rd 27407
Clubview Ct 27410
Clustermill Dr 27407
Clydebank Rd 27455
Clymer St 27407
Coach Hill Rd 27410
Coachman Ct 27407
Coapman St 27407
Cobb St 27403
Cobble Ln 27407
Cobble Glen Ct 27407
Cobbler Ridge Ct 27455
Cobblestone Ct 27406
Cobblestone Walk 27455
Cobia Ln 27455
Cocklereece Dr 27405
Cocoa Dr 27406
Cody Ave 27405
Coefield Rd 27406
Colby St 27407
Cold Harbor Ct & Dr 27410
Cole St 27401
Coleridge Dr 27410
Coliseum Blvd 27403
Coliseum Dr 27406
College Rd 27410
College Lakes Dr 27410
N & S College Park
Dr 27403
Collier Dr 27403
Collins Grove Church
Rd 27410
Collinswood Ln 27405
Collwood Ct 27409
Colonial Ave 27408
Colson St 27401
Coltrain Rd 27455
Coltrane Mill Rd 27406
Coltsfoot Ct & Rd 27455
Coltsgate Dr 27410
Coltswood Dr 27406
Columbus Ct & St 27406
Colwyn Ct 27455
Comanche Trl 27406
Commerce Pl 27401
Commercial Rd 27407
Compton Ct 27407
Comstock Ln 27406
Concord St 27406
Concord Church Rd 27406
Condor Dr 27410
E Cone Blvd 27405
W Cone Blvd 27408
Conrad St 27405
Conway Ct 27455
Coon Hollow Ln 27406
Coopers Farm Ct &
Rd 27406
Coopers Oak Way 27410
Coopers Ridge Ct 27407
Copper Hill Ct 27407
Copthorne Dr 27410
Coquina Ln 27406
Coral Ave 27407
Corbin Rd 27405
Coriander Ct 27406

Corinth Dr 27406
Corinthian Way 27410
Cork St 27401
Corliss St 27406
Cornell Ave 27407
Cornerrock Dr 27406
Cornerstaff Dr 27407
E Cornwallis Dr
200-399 27408
400-1199 27405
W Cornwallis Dr
100-3099 27408
3200-3299 27410
Coronado Dr 27410
Coronet Ct 27410
Corporate Center Blvd &
Ct 27408
Corregidor St 27406
Cotswold Ave 27410
Cotswold Ter
3400-3699 27455
3700-3799 27410
Cottage Pl 27455
Cottingham Ct 27410
Country Ln 27410
Country Club Dr 27408
Country Club Rd 27406
Country Lake Dr 27406
Country Park Rd 27455
Country Pine Ln 27405
Country Ridge Rd 27405
Country View Ct & Dr 27406
Country Walk Ln 27407
Country Woods Ct &
Ln 27410
Countryside Dr 27405
County Clare Ct & Rd 27407
W Court St 27407
Courtfield Dr 27455
Courtland St 27401
Courtney Ln 27408
Cove Cay Ln 27410
Covenant Ln 27406
Covent Garden Ct 27455
Coventry Pl 27455
Coventry Woods Ct 27405
Covered Bridge Cir 27407
Coveview Ct 27407
Covey Ln 27406
Covington Pl 27407
Cox Pl 27409
Coxton Tower Ct 27407
Crab Tree Ct 27455
Crabapple Ct & Ln 27405
Crabtree Valley Ct 27455
Craig St 27406
Cramer Ct 27455
Cranberry Ct 27405
Cranbourn Ct 27455
Cranbrook St 27407
Crane Ave 27407
Cranebridge Pl 27407
Cranleigh Dr 27407
Cranwell Ct 27407
Cranwood Ct 27455
Craven St 27405
Crawford Ct 27406
Creek Mill Rd 27406
Creek Pointe Ct &
Way 27407
Creek Ridge Rd 27406
Creekdale Dr 27406
Creekmoor Ct 27455
Creekstone Ct 27407
Creekwood Dr 27407
Crest Dr 27406
Crestbrook Ct 27455
Crestland Ave 27401
Creston Dr 27406
Crestridge Rd 27406
Crestway Dr 27409
Crestwick Ct 27406
Crestwood Dr 27408
Creswell Ct 27407
Creswell Manor Dr 27407
Cricklewood Dr 27407

Cridland Rd 27408
Crimson Leaf Dr 27406
Crimson Wood Dr 27410
Crite Ct 27405
Crofton Springs Ct 27407
Cromwell Rd 27407
Cross Ridge Ln 27410
Cross Vine Cv & Ln 27455
Crossfield Ct & Dr 27408
Crossland Ct 27455
Crossroads Dr 27455
Crosstimbers Ct & Dr 27410
Crows Nest Ln 27455
Croydon Pl 27406
Crystal Ln 27403
Crystal Lake Dr 27410
Crystal Spring Ct 27410
Culpepper Cir 27410
Cumberland St 27401
Cunningham St 27401
Curfman Rd 27455
Currituck Pl 27407
Curry St 27406
Curtis St 27406
Cushing St 27405
Custer Dr 27407
Cynthia Rd 27406
Cypress St 27405
Cypress Grove Ln 27455
Cypress Park Rd 27407
Cypresswood Ct 27455
Cyril Ln 27401
Cyrus Rd 27406
Dairyfield Way 27410
Dakota Dr 27401
Dale St 27406
Daleview Ct & Pl 27406
Dalton Rd 27408
Damascus St 27403
Dan Hughes Ct 27405
Dana Pl 27406
Danbury Rd 27408
N & S Danby Castle
Rd 27407
Dane St 27405
Daniel St 27401
Daniel Pierce Dr 27410
Dans Rd 27401
Dante Ln 27410
Darden Rd
2500-2699 27406
2700-3599 27407
Dare Ct 27407
Darlington Pl 27405
Darrin Dr 27405
Dartford Dr 27407
Dartmouth St 27407
Daventry Ct 27410
David Caldwell Dr 27408
David Christian Pl 27410
David Richmond Ct 27405
N & S Davie St 27401
Davis Cup Dr 27406
Davis Mill Rd 27406
Davis Ridge Ct 27405
Dawn Rd 27405
Dawn Ridge Ct & Trl 27410
Dawson Ave 27401
Daybreak Sq N & S 27455
Daye Dr
2500-2799 27406
3800-4099 27407
Dayton St 27407
Dean Robert Ct 27409
Debbie Ln 27406
Decatur St 27406
Decca St 27406
Dedham Ct 27407
Deep Forest Dr 27406
Deep Green Dr 27410
Deer Pl 27407
Deer Forest Ct & Dr 27406
Deer Park Cir 27455
Deer Pointe Ct 27406
Deer Track Ln 27455
Deercroft Ct 27407

Deerglade Ct 27410
Deering Pl 27406
Deerview Ct 27410
Deerwood Ct 27410
Deidre Ct 27406
Deidre Tyler Ct 27406
Delancy St 27405
Delaware Ave 27408
Delchester Pl 27410
Dellwood Dr 27408
Delmar Dr 27406
Delmonte Dr 27406
Delta Pl 27406
Delwin Ct 27406
Denim Rd 27405
Denise Dr 27407
Denny Rd 27405
Densmore Ct 27455
Dent St 27408
Denver Dr 27406
Derby Pl 27405
Derbyshire Dr 27410
Derbywood Dr 27410
Derrick Dr 27405
Desmond Dr 27405
Desmond Woods Dr 27405
Desoto Pl 27408
Deverow Pl 27407
Devon Dr 27406
Devonmille Ct 27455
Devonna Ct 27455
Devonshire Dr 27410
Devonwood Ct 27405
Dewberry Dr 27407
Dewey St 27405
Dewitt St 27401
Dexter Ave 27407
Diamond Hill Ct 27406
Dick St 27403
Dickens Dr 27410
Dickerson Ln 27405
Dillard St 27403
Dillingham Pl 27455
Dillon Rd 27405
Dinsmore St 27401
Distribution Dr 27410
Divot Dr 27407
Dixon St 27455
Doak St 27406
Dobson Rd 27410
Dockery St 27405
Dodson St 27405
Dogwood Dr
3400-3899 27403
3900-4399 27410
Dollar Ct 27405
Dolley Madison Rd 27410
Dolphin Rd 27406
Donathan Pl 27405
Doncaster Dr 27406
Donegal Ct & Dr 27406
Donlora Ct & Dr 27407
Donnell St 27405
Donnington Ct 27407
Donvic Dr 27409
Dora Pl 27406
Doral Dr 27406
Dorchester Rd 27407
Dorgan St 27401
Dornoch Dr 27410
Dorothy Brown St 27406
Dorsey St 27407
Double Oaks Rd 27410
Dougherty St 27406
Douglas St
500-1799 27406
2200-2299 27401
Dove St 27405
Dover Rd 27408
Dover Park Rd 27407
Dovercrest Ct 27407
Doverstone Ln 27407
Downing St 27410
Downing Ridge Ct 27407
Downwind Rd 27409
Doyle St 27406

Drake Rd 27406
Drakestone Ct 27455
Drawbridge Pkwy 27410
Dreiser Pl 27405
Dressage Dr 27410
Drewsbury Dr 27455
Drexel Ct & Rd 27405
Drexmore Ave 27406
Driftwood Rd 27455
Drum Rd 27409
Dublin Dr 27408
Dublin Castle Rd 27407
Duck Club Ct & Rd 27410
N & S Dudley St 27401
Duffers Ln 27407
Duffield Dr 27410
Duffy Ave 27455
Duke St
800-899 27401
900-1299 27406
Dulaire Rd 27407
Duluth Loop 27406
Dumaine Ct 27407
Dumfries Rd 27407
Dumont Ct & Dr 27403
Dunaway Ct 27408
Dunbar St 27401
Dunbarton Dr 27406
Dunchurch Ct 27455
Dundas Cir & Dr 27407
Dunhagen Dr 27410
Dunkirk Pl 27410
Dunleith Ct & Way 27455
Dunlevy Way 27455
Dunlin Sq 27455
Dunnberry Ct 27455
Dunnhill Dr 27405
Dunrobin Dr 27409
Dunstan Rd 27405
Dunwoody Cir 27410
Duplin Ct & Dr 27407
Durant Pl 27408
N Durham St 27401
Durness Way 27455
Dutch Ct 27406
Dutchmans Pipe 27455
Duval Dr 27410
Eagle Rd 27407
Eagle Nesting Ln 27407
Eagle Perch Way 27407
Eagle Rock Rd 27410
Earl Dr 27406
Earnhardt Dr 27410
Eastcote Pt 27410
Eastern Shore Dr 27455
Eastern Star Ct 27407
Eastland Ave
3900-3999 27401
4000-4099 27405
4100-4198 27401
4200-4299 27401
Easton Rd 27405
Eastwood Ave & Ct 27401
Echo St 27407
Eckerson Rd 27405
Eddington Dr 27410
Eden Rock Rd 27406
Edenham Way 27410
Edenton Dr 27407
Edenwood Dr 27406
Edgar St 27403
Edgar Andrew Ln 27406
Edgedale Rd 27408
Edgefield Ct & Rd 27409
Edgemont Rd 27406
Edgemore Rd 27455
Edgerton Dr 27410
Edgewater Dr 27403
Edgewood Dr 27406
Edgewood Terrace Dr 27406
N & S Edgeworth St 27401
Edinborough Ct & Rd 27406
Edison Park Rd 27405
Edith Ln 27409
Edmond Dr 27401
Edney Ridge Rd 27408

Edwardia Dr 27409
Edwards Rd 27410
Efland Dr 27408
Eight Belles Ln 27410
Eisenhower Ave 27406
Elaine Wright Ct 27401
N Elam Ave
200-599 27403
600-1599 27408
S Elam Ave 27403
Elcebe Ln 27406
Elder Pl 27405
Elderbush Cir, Ct & Dr 27405
Elderwood Pl 27410
Eldorado Dr 27406
Electra Dr 27405
Elgin Pl 27410
Elium St 27405
Elizabethan Dr 27410
Elk Hound Trl 27409
Elkhart Dr 27408
Ella Pl 27409
Ellenwood Dr 27410
Ellery Ct 27407
Ellington St 27403
Ellis St 27406
Elliston St 27407
N Elm St
100-1299 27401
1301-1399 27401
1700-3299 27408
3300-3599 27405
3600-3999 27455
S Elm St
100-499 27401
500-1399 27406
S Elm Eugene St 27406
Elm Grove Ct & Way 27405
Elm Ridge Ct & Ln 27408
Elmcrest Dr 27406
Elmer St 27405
W Elmsley St 27406
Elmsley Meadows Ln 27406
Elmwood Dr & Ter 27408
Elmyra Dr 27407
Elsielee Rd 27405
Elton Way 27406
Elwell Ave 27405
Elwood Ave 27403
Emerald Dr 27403
Emerald Springs Ct 27407
Emerson Rd 27405
Emerywood Rd 27403
Emory Dr 27406
Emsley Rd 27407
Enchanted Ln 27406
W End Pl 27403
End O Trail Ln & Rd 27409
Endrick Ct 27409
Englewood St 27403
N English St 27405
S English St 27401
Enoch Ln 27405
Enterprise Rd 27408
Eric Rd 27409
Erin Ln 27406
Erskine Dr E & W 27410
Erwin St 27406
Esquire Ct 27405
Estate Dr 27405
Esterwood Rd 27405
Estes Cir & Ct 27410
Esteswood Ct 27406
Esther Rd 27406
Eton Dr 27406
Etta Ct 27406
Euclid St 27407
Eugene Ct 27401
N Eugene St 27401
S Eugene St
100-399 27401
600-1399 27406
Eula St 27403
Eva Ln 27455
Evans Dr 27401
Evans Town Rd 27406

Evelyn Dr 27406
Eventide Dr 27409
Evergreen Dr 27408
Everitt St 27401
Evlind Rd 27406
Ewing Dr 27405
Ewo Church Rd 27405
Exchange Pl 27401
Executive Dr 27406
Fairall Dr 27401
Fairbrother St 27405
Faircrest Ln 27405
Fairfax Rd 27407
Fairfield Ave 27408
Fairgreen Rd 27410
Fairhaven Dr 27455
Fairland Rd 27407
Fairmont St
600-1099 27401
1300-1499 27403
1501-1599 27403
Fairside Dr 27405
Fairview St 27405
Fairway Dr 27408
S Fairway Dr 27407
Fairwood Dr 27406
Fairystone Dr 27406
Falconridge Ct & Rd 27405
Falistr Dr 27408
Falkener Dr 27410
Falkirk Dr 27409
Fall Cliff Ln 27407
Fallen Oak Rd 27455
Falling Leaf Ln 27410
Fallingbrooks Ct & Dr 27407
Falmouth Dr 27410
Falworth Cir 27406
Fargis St 27403
Fargo Trl 27406
Farlin Ave 27407
Farlow Dr 27406
Farmbrooke Dr 27407
Farmington Dr 27407
Farmridge Ct 27410
Farragut St 27406
Farrar Dr 27410
Farrell St 27405
Farrington Ct 27407
Fast Ln 27406
Fatham Dr 27455
Fawcett St 27405
Fawn St 27403
Fawnbrook Dr 27455
Fawnwood Ct 27407
Faye Dr 27410
E & W February 1 Pl 27401
Federal Dr 27410
Federal Pl
300-499 27401
500-599 27406
Feldspar Ct 27409
Fellowship Dr 27410
Fence Dr 27409
Fenton Dr 27406
Fentress St 27407
Fern Pl 27408
Fern Bluff Ct 27410
Fern Hill Dr 27405
Fernbrook Rd 27405
Ferncrest Dr 27410
Fernhurst Way 27406
Fernwood Dr 27408
Fewell Rd 27405
Field Horney Rd 27406
Fieldale Ct & Rd 27406
Fieldbrook Dr 27455
Fieldcrest Rd 27406
Fieldgate Rd 27406
Fielding Pl 27405
Fields St 27405
Fieldstone Ct 27455
Fieldswood Dr 27406
Fiesta Dr 27406
Fig Leaf Ct 27406
Filmore Rd 27409
Filton Dr 27406

Finley St 27406
Fintry Ct & Dr 27409
Fir Pl 27407
Fireside St 27407
Firestone Dr 27406
Firewood Trl 27410
E & W Fisher Ave 27401
Fisher Hill Dr 27406
Fisher Park Cir 27401
Fitzgerald Pl 27405
Fitzsimmons Dr 27406
Flag St 27406
Flagship Cir & Cv 27455
Flagstaff Ct 27406
Flagstone St 27406
Flatiron Ct 27406
Fleetwood Ln 27407
Fleming Rd 27410
Fleming Terrace Cir &
Rd 27410
Flemingfield Rd 27405
Fletcher Dr 27406
Flint St 27405
Flint Ridge Ct 27407
Flintrock Ct 27455
Flora Vista Ct & Rd 27406
Florence St 27401
E Florida St
100-1299 27406
1600-2299 27401
2301-2599 27401
W Florida St
100-899 27406
900-2499 27403
2500-3399 27407
Flowering Path Ln 27405
Floyd St 27406
Foch St 27405
Folkestone Dr 27403
Folly Ct 27409
Fontaine Rd 27407
Fontana Dr 27406
Forbes Dr 27407
Forbis Farm Ln 27406
Ford Pl 27406
Fore Pl 27406
Fore St 27407
Forest Rd 27406
Forest St 27403
Forest Brook Dr 27406
Forest Crest Dr 27406
Forest Edge Ct & Dr 27406
Forest Glen Rd 27410
Forest Hill Ct & Dr 27410
Forest Lake Cir 27407
Forest Lawn Dr 27455
Forest Manor Dr 27410
Forest Oaks Dr & Ln 27406
Forest Ridge Ct 27406
Forest Vale Ct 27410
Forest Valley Ct & Rd 27410
Forest Village Ct & Dr 27406
Forest Walk Dr 27455
Forestdale Dr 27403
Forestglade Dr 27406
Forestside Dr 27406
Forestwood Dr 27405
Forsyth Dr 27407
Forsythia Ct & Dr 27410
Fortune Ln 27408
Fosseway Dr 27455
Founders Dr 27410
Founders Hall 27410
Fountain Head Ct &
Dr 27455
Fountain Manor Dr 27405
Fountain Meadow Ln 27409
Fountain View Cir 27405
Four Farms Cir & Rd 27410
Four Seasons Blvd
2100-2799 27407
2800-3399 27406
Four Seasons Town
Ctr 27407
Fourmile Loop 27405
Foushee St 27405

Foust Ct & Rd 27405
Fox Pl 27408
Fox Briar Ct & Dr 27455
Fox Chase Rd 27410
Fox Cove Ln 27407
Fox Glen Dr 27406
Fox Grove Trl 27406
Fox Hollow Rd 27410
Fox Hunt Dr 27407
Fox Tail Ct 27455
Fox Trot Rd 27406
Foxburrow Rd 27406
Foxcroft Rd 27410
Foxdale Dr 27455
Foxdown Ct 27410
Foxfire Ct & Dr 27410
Foxglove Ln 27455
Foxhall Ct & Ln 27410
Foxhaven Ct & Dr 27455
Foxridge Rd 27406
Foxwood Ct 27407
Foxwood Dr 27410
Foxworth Dr 27406
Framingham Ln 27410
Francis King St 27410
Francisco Dr 27410
Franklin Blvd 27401
Franklin Mccain Ct 27405
Franklinwood Ct & Dr 27401
Fraternity Dr 27407
Frazier Rd 27407
Frederick Rd 27455
Freedom Gate Dr 27410
Freeman Mill Rd 27406
Freemasons Dr 27407
Freida Ln 27406
N & S Fremont Dr 27407
Friar Tuck Ct & Rd 27408
Friars Ln 27455
E Friendly Ave 27401
W Friendly Ave
101-197 27401
199-1199 27401
1200-2399 27403
2401-2499 27403
3100-3299 27408
3300-7399 27410
7401-7499 27410
Friendly Acres Ct & Dr 27410
Friendly Center Rd 27408
Friendly Chapel Rd 27406
Friendly Farms Ln &
Rd 27406
Friendly Manor Dr 27410
Friendship Dr 27409
Friendsmeadow Dr 27410
Friendsview Dr 27410
Friendswood Dr 27409
Friendway Cir 27409
Friendway Rd
100-399 27409
400-699 27410
Frontier Ln 27406
Frost Pl 27405
Frostbrook Ct 27455
Fry St 27403
Fuller St 27403
Fulton Pl 27401
Fulton St
400-599 27401
600-698 27403
601-699 27401
Fuquay Pl 27410
Furman Pl 27409
Gadwall Ct & Dr 27455
Gaines Dr 27410
Gainsboro Dr 27410
Galax Trl 27410
Galaxie Dr 27406
Galearke Rd 27409
Gallenwol Ct 27405
Galleria Ct 27410
Gallimore Dairy Rd 27409
Galway Dr 27406
Gamble Pl 27410
Gant St 27401

Gar Pl 27406
Garden Lake Cir & Dr 27410
Garden Place Rd 27406
Garden Village Way 27410
Gardengate Rd 27406
Gardner Ct 27409
Garibaldi Pl 27407
Garland Dr 27408
Garrett St 27406
Garwin Rd 27406
Gaston Ct & Rd 27407
Gate Post Ct & Dr 27455
Gatehouse Ln 27407
Gatestone Dr 27406
Gatesville Rd 27405
Gatewood Ave 27405
Gatley Ct 27405
Gatwick Ct 27406
Gay Ter 27407
Gayle Oak Ln 27405
Genoa Ct 27455
Gentry St 27407
George Brook Ln 27406
George White Rd 27410
Georgette Dr 27405
Georgia St 27408
Gervais Ct 27455
Ggo Dr 27406
Gilbert St 27406
Gillespie St 27401
Gilmore Dr 27407
Giltspur Ct 27455
Giovanni Way 27410
Girard Rd 27406
Gladstone Ter 27406
Glass Rd 27406
Glen Burnie Dr 27406
Glen Cross St 27410
Glen Forest Ct 27410
Glen Hollow Rd 27407
Glen Laurel Dr 27406
Glen Meadow Dr 27455
Glen Raven Ct 27410
Glendale Ct & Dr 27406
Glendale Oaks Ct 27406
Gleneagle Ct 27408
Glengarry Cir 27410
Glenhaven Dr 27406
Glenoaks Dr 27407
Glenridge Ct & Rd 27405
Glenrock Dr 27406
Glenrose Ct 27407
Glenshire Way 27407
Glenside Dr 27405
Glentower Dr 27410
Glenview Dr 27406
Glenwood Ave
800-1799 27403
2000-2099 27406
Glouchester Ln 27410
Glover St 27406
Glynis Ln 27406
Godwin Ct 27405
Gold Dust Ct & Trl 27455
Gold Nugget Dr 27409
Golden Ct 27401
Golden Eagle Way 27410
Golden Fern Ct 27406
Golden Gate Dr 27405
Golden Valley Dr 27455
Goldeneye Ct 27455
Goldenrod Dr 27455
Goldfield Ct 27455
Goldfinch Ave 27409
Goldsboro St 27405
Good Hope Dr 27406
Goodall Dr 27407
Gordon St 27405
Gorrell St
300-1199 27406
1200-1799 27401
Grace Chapel Ct 27405
Grace Williams Rd 27410
Graceland Dr 27406
Gracewood Ct & Dr 27408
Grafton Rd 27405

Graham Rd 27410
Gramercy Rd 27410
Gramercy Park Ct &
Dr 27406
Granada Ct & Ln 27407
Granbury Dr 27405
Grandmont Ct 27405
Grandover Pkwy 27407
Grandview Ave 27408
Grandview Rd 27406
Grandway Cir 27409
Granite St 27403
Grantland Pl 27410
Granville Rd 27408
Granville Oaks Ct 27408
Grapevine Ct 27405
Grasmere Dr 27410
Grasswren Way 27409
Grassy Knoll Cir 27406
Grassy Meadow Ct &
Rd 27410
Grassy Moss Dr 27409
Gray Bluff Ct 27410
Gray Wolf Way 27406
Graybark Ct 27407
Graycliff Dr 27406
Grayland St 27408
Graymont Dr 27407
Graystone Ct 27406
Great Castle Ct 27455
Grecade St 27408
N Green Ct 27406
W Green Ct 27407
Green Acres Ln 27410
Green Apple Dr 27405
Green Crest Ct 27406
Green Forest Rd 27410
Green Lake Ct 27407
Green Market Ct 27406
Green Meadow Dr 27410
Green Needle Dr 27405
Green Oaks St 27401
Green Point Dr
3800-4399 27407
4500-4599 27410
Green Valley Rd
101-299 27403
500-899 27408
Greenbriar Rd 27405
Greenbrook Ct & Dr 27408
N & S Greene St 27401
Greenes Xing 27410
Greengate Dr 27406
Greenhaven Dr 27406
Greenhollow Dr 27410
Greenleaf Dr 27407
Greenlee Rd 27410
Greenmont Ct 27455
Greenough Way 27410
Greensboro St 27401
Greenside Dr 27406
Greentree Dr 27410
Greenview Dr 27409
E & W Greenway Dr N &
S 27403
Greenwich Dr 27410
Greenwood Dr & Ter 27410
Greghill Dr 27406
Gregory St 27403
Grenadier Guard 27410
Grendel Rd 27410
Grenham Rd 27455
Gresham Dr 27405
Gretchen Ct & Ln 27410
Grey Oaks Cir 27408
Greybark Dr 27406
Greycrest Dr 27406
Greystone Pt 27410
Greywood Dr 27406
Griggs Rd 27405
Grimsley St 27403
Grinsted Ct 27455
Grist Mill Ct 27455
Groometown Rd 27407
Grove St 27403
Groveland Trl 27407

Grover Dr 27405
Grumman Rd 27409
Guerrant St 27401
Guest St 27405
Guida Dr 27410
Guilding Dr 27455
Guilford Ave 27401
Guilford College Rd
100-1099 27409
4400-5899 27407
Guilford School Rd 27410
Gulf Ct 27401
Gwaltney Rd 27407
Gwyn Ln 27403
Hackamore Rd 27410
Hackett St 27401
Hacketts Lake Rd 27406
Hackney Rd 27409
Haddon Dr 27406
Hadham Pl 27405
Hadley Park Ct & Dr 27407
Hagan Ct 27406
Hagan Stone Park Rd 27406
Hahns Ln 27401
Haig Ct & St 27405
Hairston St 27409
Halcyon St 27407
Haldane Dr 27406
Halifax Rd 27407
Hall St 27406
Hallmark Ln 27406
Halsbrook Rd 27406
Hamden Ct & Dr 27405
Hamilton Rd 27408
Hamilton Hills Dr 27406
Hamlet Pl 27406
Hammel Rd 27408
Hammond Dr 27406
Hampshire Dr 27405
Hampton St 27401
Hanahan Ct 27409
Hanberry Dr 27410
Hancock Dr 27410
Hanging Leaf Pt 27409
Hannaford Rd 27401
Hannah Dawn Dr 27455
Hannah Mckenzie Ct &
Dr 27455
Hanner St 27403
Hanover Ter 27407
Harbor Gate Ct 27455
Harbor House Dr 27410
Harbor Ridge Dr 27406
Harbor View Ln 27410
Hardie Ct & St 27403
Hardie Farm Dr 27405
Hardindale Dr 27410
Hardwick Dr 27406
Hargett St 27406
Harleck Ct 27407
Harlequin Dr 27455
Harley Dr 27406
Harmont Dr 27406
Harmony Ln 27406
Harnett Dr 27407
Harold Dr 27406
Harrington St 27406
Harris Dr 27406
Harrison St 27407
Harrod Ct & Ln 27410
Harrow Pl 27455
Hart Ridge Ct 27407
Harte Pl 27405
Hartley Rd 27406
Hartridge Way 27407
Hartsfield Ct 27407
Hartsford Dr 27406
Harvard Ave 27407
Harvest Glen Dr 27406
Harvest Hill Rd 27405
Harvest Springs Ct &
Dr 27406
Harvest Time Way 27410
Harvester Dr 27406
Harvick Ct 27405
Harwood Rd 27406

Haskins Ct 27410
Hassall St 27401
Hastings Cir 27406
Hatcher Pl 27407
Hathaway Dr 27408
Hatteras Ct 27455
Haven Rd 27410
Havenwood Dr 27407
Haverford Pt 27455
Haverhill Dr 27405
Hawkins Dr 27410
Hawks Nest Rd 27406
Hawthorne St 27408
Hayden St 27407
Hayfield Ln 27410
Haynie Manor Ln 27410
Hayward Ct & Dr 27406
Haywood St 27403
Hazel Ln 27408
Hazelwood Dr 27401
Hci Blvd 27409
Headquarters Dr 27405
Healing Well Rd 27406
Hearthside Pl 27410
Hearthwood Ct 27407
Heath St 27401
Heather Ct 27403
Heather Hill Dr 27406
Heather Ridge Ct 27455
Heatherwood Ct 27407
Heathridge Ter 27410
Heathrow Ct & Dr 27410
Heddon Way 27455
Hedgeshire Ct 27407
Hedrick Dr 27410
Heilwood Dr 27407
Helen Rd 27405
Helmwood Ct & Dr 27410
Hemingway Dr 27405
Hempstead Dr 27410
Henderson Ct & Rd 27410
E Hendrix St
100-399 27401
400-599 27405
W Hendrix St 27401
Henry St 27405
Heraldry Ln 27455
Herbin St 27407
Herfshire Dr 27406
Heritage Pl 27405
Heritage Creek Way 27405
Heritage Woods Ct & Dr 27407
Herman Gist Rd 27401
Hermitage Rd 27403
Hern Ave 27405
Hertford St 27403
Hewitt St 27407
Hi Pocket Ln 27409
Hiatt St 27403
Hiatts Dr 27455
Hiawatha Dr 27408
Hibler Rd 27409
Hickory Ave 27405
Hickory Branch Dr 27409
Hickory Creek Rd
6000-6099 27407
6200-6299 27406
Hickory Grove Rd 27409
Hickory Hill Dr 27410
Hickory Knoll Ct 27407
Hickory Meadow Rd 27406
Hickory Ridge Dr 27409
Hickory Trace Dr 27407
Hickory Tree Ln 27405
Hickory Valley Rd 27406
Hickory Woods Ct & Dr 27410
Hicks Ct 27403
Hicone Rd 27405
Hidden Brook Ln 27405
Hidden Forest Dr 27405
Hidden Oak Ct & Dr 27407
Hidden Orchard Dr 27410
Hidden Timber Ln 27405
Hidden Valley Ct & Rd 27407

Hiddenwood Ct 27407
Hideaway Ct 27409
Higgins St 27406
High St 27406
High Meadows Ct & Rd 27455
High Point Rd
2100-2298 27403
2300-3099 27403
3100-4700 27407
4615-4615 27417
4701-6299 27407
4702-6298 27407
High Ridge Ct 27410
High View Cir & Rd 27410
Highberry Rd 27410
Highgate Ct 27407
Highgrove Ave 27405
Highland Ave 27403
Highland Bluff Ct 27410
Highland Oak Ct & Dr 27410
Highlawn Dr 27409
Highstone Dr 27406
Highstream Ct 27407
Highwoods Blvd 27410
Hill St 27408
Hill N Dale Dr 27408
Hill Valley Ct 27410
Hillcrest Dr 27403
Hillrise Ct & Dr 27405
Hillsboro St 27401
Hillside Dr 27401
Hilltop Rd 27407
Hilltop Forest Ct 27407
Hillway Dr 27407
Hillwind Ct 27408
Hillwood Ct 27410
Hiltin Pl 27409
Hiltons Landing Dr 27455
Hines Chapel Rd 27405
Hines Park Ln 27455
Hirank Ct 27405
Hobbs Pl 27403
Hobbs Rd
400-799 27403
800-4399 27410
Hobbs Landing Ct 27410
Hodge Ct 27407
Hogan Rd 27406
Hohn Ct 27407
Hohnway Ln 27406
Hoke Ln 27407
Holbrook St 27403
N Holden Rd
100-1399 27410
1600-2099 27408
S Holden Rd
100-3699 27407
3700-4799 27406
Holders Rd 27405
Holdsworth Ct 27455
Holgate Dr 27410
Holland Rd 27405
Hollandsworth Ct & Dr 27409
Holliday Dr 27403
Hollister Dr 27407
Holliston St 27406
Holly Dr 27408
Holly Crest Ct 27410
Holly Ridge Ct & Rd 27455
Holly Springs Ln 27455
Hollywood Dr 27405
Holmes Rd 27405
Holstein Ln 27405
Holt Ave 27405
Holts Chapel Rd 27401
Holyoke Rd 27406
Home St 27403
Homedale Dr 27406
Homeland Ave 27405
Homewood Ave 27403
Honan Dr 27401
Honey Locust Ct 27410
Honeycutt Ct 27407
Honeysuckle Dr 27408
Hood Pl 27408

Hooks St 27401
Hooting Hollow Rd 27406
Hope Ct 27407
Hope Valley Ln 27401
Hornaday Rd
5400-5499 27407
5500-5699 27409
Horse Pen Creek Rd 27410
Horseshoe Ct & Ln 27410
Hounslow Dr 27410
Houston St 27401
Howard St 27403
Howell Pl 27455
Hubbard St 27405
Hubert St 27403
Huckabee Dr 27401
Hudgins Dr 27406
Hudson Cir 27410
Huff St 27405
Huffine Mill Rd 27405
Huffman St
100-499 27401
800-1099 27405
Hugh Patrick Ct 27455
Hughes St 27401
Hulme Ct 27455
Humble Rd 27406
Hunsucker Rd 27405
Hunt Chase Ct & Dr 27407
Hunt Club Rd 27410
Hunter St 27401
Hunters Dr 27455
Hunters Path Ct 27409
Hunting Meadow Rd 27406
Huntington Rd 27408
Huntley Ct 27406
Huntmaster Trl 27407
Hurston Way 27405
Husbands St 27407
Hyalyn Ct 27406
Hyde Dr 27406
Hydrangea Ct 27455
Hywood Dr 27409
Ibis Cir 27455
Idlewild Ave 27410
Idlewood Ct & Dr 27408
Idol Ct 27407
Idolbrook Ct 27406
Ilchester Ct & Dr 27408
Immanuel Rd 27407
Imperial Dr 27406
Independence Ct & Rd 27408
Indian Wells Dr 27406
Indigo Cv 27455
Indigo Lake Ter 27455
Industrial Ave 27406
Industrial Village Rd 27409
Ingleside Ave 27405
Inman Rd 27410
Innisbrook Ct 27410
Integrity Oaks Dr 27401
International Dr 27409
Inverness Ct & Dr 27406
Iredell Rd 27407
Ireland St 27406
Iris Pl 27405
Iron Carriage Ct 27410
Ironwood Cir 27410
Irving Pl 27408
Irving Park Ct 27408
Irving Park Ln 27455
Irwin St 27405
Isaacs Pl 27408
Isabel St 27401
Isler Ct 27407
Isley St 27401
Ivy Hts 27401
Ivy Brook Ct 27407
Ivy Ridge Ct 27407
Ivyglen Ct 27406
Ivywood Rd 27455
J Ave 27403
J B Ln 27455
E & W J J Dr 27410
SE Jack Pine Ct 27406

Jackson St 27403
Jacobs Way 27455
James Pl 27405
James Doak Pkwy 27455
Jamison Pl 27407
Jane St 27407
Jane Edwards Rd 27406
Janell Dr 27406
Janet Ln 27405
Jans Ct 27405
Japonica Ln 27410
Jarvis Rd 27407
Jason Rd 27405
Jasper Rd 27409
Jay Lynn Dr 27406
Jaycee Park Dr 27455
Jefferson Rd 27410
Jefferson St 27403
Jefferson Wood Ct & Ln 27410
Jenna Dr 27405
Jennifer St 27401
Jerome Dr 27406
Jessup Ct 27455
Jessup Ln 27410
Jessup Grove Ct & Rd 27410
Jfh Dairy Rd 27405
Jidemi Rd 27406
Jm Hunt Jr Expy 27406
Joan Ave 27455
Jobe Ct 27407
Jock Dr 27405
Joe Brown Dr 27405
Joe Louis Ave 27401
John Dimrey Dr 27406
John Ross Dr 27405
John Tarpley Ln 27401
John Wesley Way 27401
Jolson Ct & St 27405
Jonah Ter 27406
Jonathan Ln 27406
Jones Rd 27406
Jonquil Dr 27407
Jordan Riley Ln 27407
Joseph Ter 27405
Joseph Mcneil Ave 27405
Josephine Cir 27410
Joy Ann Ter 27405
Joyce St 27405
Joyner St 27403
Judkins Ct 27407
Julian St 27406
Juliet Pl 27406
Julius Ct 27406
Juniper St 27407
Jupiter Dr 27406
Justamere Farm Rd 27455
Justin Ct 27410
Kacey Meadows Ct & Dr 27410
Kacia Ct 27407
Kallamdale Ct & Rd 27406
Kalloramo Dr 27407
Karlingdale Dr 27455
Kasarda Dr 27406
Kathleen Ave 27408
Katie Ct & Dr 27410
Kaufelt St 27407
Kay St 27405
Keats Pl 27408
Keeler St 27407
E & W Keeling Rd 27410
Kehoe Dr 27401
Keith St 27405
Kelford Dr 27406
Kellam Ridge Dr 27455
Kellenberger Dr 27406
Kelley Ct & Rd 27401
Kello Dr 27455
Kellom St 27409
Kelly Grove Rd 27409
Kelvington Ct 27410
Kemp Rd E & W 27410
Kempton Dr 27406
Kenbridge Ct & Dr 27410
Kenilworth St 27403

Kenion St 27405
Kenmont Rd 27409
Kenmore St 27408
Kenneth Rd 27455
Kenny Ln 27406
Kensington Rd 27403
Kentbury Cir 27406
Kentmere Rd 27406
Kentwood St 27405
Kenview St 27410
Kenwick Cir 27406
Kenwood Ct 27410
Keppen Trl 27410
Keren Dr 27405
Kersey Ct & St 27406
Kerwick Dr 27409
Kery Dr 27408
N Keswick Way 27410
Kettering Pl 27410
Key Blvd 27409
Keystone Rd 27406
Kilbourne Dr 27407
Kildare Dr 27405
Kildare Woods Ct & Dr 27407
Kilkenny Ave 27406
Killarney Dr 27406
Killington Pl 27407
Kilmarnock Ct 27410
Kilpatrick White Rd 27406
Kimberly Dr & Ter 27408
Kimmeridge Rd 27406
Kinbuck Pt 27410
Kincaid Dr 27406
Kindistr Rd 27406
Kindley Ct & St 27406
King St 27406
King Arthur Pl 27405
King Edward Ct 27455
King George Ct & Dr 27410
Kinglet Cir 27455
Kings Forest Ct 27405
Kings Mill Ct & Rd 27407
Kings Pond Ct & Rd 27407
Kingsland Dr 27455
Kingsport Rd 27406
Kingston Rd 27405
Kingswood Dr 27410
Kinlock Trl 27410
Kinnakeet Way 27455
Kinnley Ct 27455
Kinsman Rd 27406
Kipling Dr 27407
Kirby Dr 27403
Kirk Rd 27455
Kirkland St 27406
Kirkman St 27406
Kirkpatrick Pl 27408
Kirkwood Ct 27408
Kitly Ct 27455
Kitty Ln 27406
Kitty Hawk Rd 27407
Kivett Dr
2000-2429 27406
2430-2899 27407
Kizer Ct 27405
Kloster Ct 27455
Knight Pl 27410
Knightbridge Rd 27455
Knightway Ln 27455
Knightwood Dr 27410
Knoll Brook Ct 27407
Knollwood Dr 27403
Knox Place Dr 27407
Koger Blvd 27407
Korem Dr 27409
Koury Blvd 27407
Krebbs Ct 27405
Kruze St 27406
Kyla Dr 27455
Kylemore Dr 27406
La Grange Dr 27406
Labrador Ct 27406
Lacy Ave 27405
Lady Ln 27406
Lafayette Ave & Ct 27408

E Lake Dr
100-299 27403
300-400 27401
402-898 27401
W Lake Dr
1300-1599 27408
3300-3399 27407
Lake Bluff Ct 27410
Lake Brandt Pl & Rd 27455
Lake Breeze Ct 27455
Lake Forest Ct & Dr 27408
Lake Jeanette Rd 27455
Lake Laurel Ct 27455
Lake Spring Ct 27405
Lake Walk Dr 27410
Lakebend Ct & Way 27410
W Lakefield Dr 27406
Lakefront Dr 27406
Lakehaven Dr 27407
Lakeland Rd 27406
Lakemont Dr 27410
Lakepoint Ct 27406
Lakeshore Ct & Dr 27407
Lakeside Ct 27410
Lakeview St 27401
Lakewood Dr 27410
Lama St 27406
Lambert Ln 27406
Lamont Ct 27405
Lamp Post Ln 27410
Lamroc Ct & Rd 27407
Lanada Rd 27407
Lancaster Rd 27410
Lancer Ct 27405
Land Rd 27406
Landaff Dr 27406
Landerwood Ct & Dr 27405
Landmark Dr 27409
Landmark Center Blvd & Dr 27407
Landover Rd 27407
Landry Ct 27405
Lands End Dr 27408
Landsberg Ct N & S 27407
Landview Dr 27407
Lane Rd 27408
Langdon Dr 27410
Lange Trl 27407
Langley Ave 27406
Langside Rd 27405
Langston Dr 27405
Lankford St 27405
Lannigan Dr 27406
Lansbury Rd 27406
Lansdown Ave 27401
Laramie Dr 27406
Larch Ln 27406
Larchmont Dr 27405
Lardner Rd 27405
Largo Dr 27406
Lark Dr 27407
Larkin St 27406
Larkspur Dr 27405
Larkwood Dr 27410
Larson St 27407
Lasalle Way 27406
Lashley Ct & Rd 27455
Latham Rd 27408
Laughlin Ct 27406
Laurel Cv 27455
N Laurel St 27401
Laurel Brook Ct 27407
Laurel Creek Ct & Dr 27405
Laurel Lee Ter 27405
Laurel Oaks Dr 27406
Laurel Run Dr 27410
Laurel Springs Dr 27410
Laurelwood Ct 27410
Laurinda Dr 27410
Lausanne Dr 27410
Lava Rd 27406
Lavergne Dr 27405
Law St 27401
Lawndale Dr
2100-3699 27408
3700-5499 27455

Lawndale Pl 27455
Lawrence St 27406
Lea Ray Dr 27410
Leadership Pl 27410
Leaf Ln 27405
Leafmore Dr 27407
Leaning Tree Dr 27410
Leawood Ct & Dr 27410
Lebanon Rd 27409
Ledford Rd 27406
Ledger Stone Ln 27407
E Lee St
100-1499 27406
1601-1797 27401
1799-2999 27401
3200-5099 27406
W Lee St
100-599 27406
600-2399 27403
Lees Chapel Rd
1300-1399 27455
1400-2699 27405
Leesford Trl 27406
Leeward Ct 27455
Leftwich St
200-299 27401
300-399 27405
Lehigh St 27407
Leitzel Ave & Ct 27406
Leland Dr 27455
Lendew St 27408
Lennie Dr 27406
Lenoir Dr 27408
Lenox Ct 27408
Leo Dr 27405
Leona Dr 27406
Leonard Dr 27410
Leslie Rd 27408
Letha Ln 27406
Levelwind Ct 27455
Lewellyn Dr 27408
Lewey Dr 27405
Lewis St 27406
Lewiston Rd 27410
Lewiston Oaks Ct 27410
Lexington Ave 27403
Liberty Dr 27408
Liberty Rd 27406
Liberty Oaks Dr 27406
Liberty Square Cir & Dr 27455
Liberty Valley Rd 27406
Lilac Rd 27408
Lilly Ave 27403
Lilly Farm Rd 27406
Lillys Cir, Ct & Dr 27455
Limerick Ct 27406
Limerock Ct 27410
Lincoln St 27401
Lincoln Oaks Ct 27407
Linda Ln 27403
N & S Lindell Rd 27403
Linden Ln 27410
Lindenshire Dr 27406
Lindley Rd 27410
Lindley Woods Dr 27410
E Lindsay St
100-500 27401
502-798 27401
800-1399 27405
W Lindsay St 27401
Link Rd 27405
Linwood St 27403
Lion St 27406
Lionne Dr 27407
Lipscomb Rd 27410
Little Rd 27405
Little Oak Dr 27410
Live Oak Dr 27407
Livingston St 27406
Llano Ct & Pl 27401
Loch Pl 27405
Loch Ridge Ct & Dr 27408
Lochmere Ct 27406
Lochside Ct 27410
Lochwood Dr 27406

Street	ZIP
Lockhaven Cir	27407
Lockheed Ct	27409
Locksley Ln	27406
Logan St	
500-899	27401
900-1199	27406
Logandale Ct	27406
Lolly Ln	27405
Lombardy St	27405
London Rd	27405
Londonderry Dr	27410
Loney Cir	27406
Long St	27406
Long Cove Ct	27407
Long Run Dr	27405
Long Valley Rd	27410
Longacre Rd	27406
Longale Rd	27409
Longbrook Dr	27406
Longfellow St	27405
Longford Ave	27406
Longhorn Ct & Dr	27455
Longview St	27403
Longwood Dr	27455
Lonita St	27407
Lord Finwick Pl	27405
Lord Foxley Ct & Dr	27405
Lord Jeff Dr	27405
Loretta Ln	27405
Lormar Rd	27406
Lourance Blvd	27407
Love Dr	27406
Lovett St	27403
Low Meadow Ln	27405
Lowdermilk St	27401
Loxwood Ct	27405
Lucan Dr	27406
Lucas Ave	27405
Lucas Park Dr	27455
Lucca Promenade Way	27410
Lucerne St	27406
Lucille Way	27406
Lucye Ln	27410
Ludlow Ct	27407
Ludwick Ln	27405
Luewood Rd	27405
Luray Dr	27406
N Luther St	27401
Lutheran St	27401
Lydia Ct	27406
Lynbrook Dr	27405
S Lyndon St	27401
Lynette Dr	27403
Lynfield Ln	27406
Lynhaven Ct & Dr	27406
Lynn Rd	27405
Lynn Oak Dr	27406
Lynwood Dr & Loop	27406
Lytham Ct	27410
Macgregor Trl	27410
Mack St	27406
Mackinaw Dr	27455
Macklin Ct	27410
Macon St	27406
Macy St	27408
Madison Ave	
1700-3899	27403
3900-3999	27410
Madison Farm Rd	27406
Madison Oaks Ct	27407
Madre Pl	27406
Madrid Ct	27406
Magnolia Ct & St	27401
Mainsail Ct	27455
Malamute Ln	27407
Mallard Creek Dr	27405
Mallard Lake Dr	27406
Manard Ct & Ln	27407
Manchester Pl	27410
Mandela Ct	27401
Mandy Ct	27405
Maness Rd	27405
Manet Dr	27407
Manila Rd	27406
Manley Ave	27407
Manning Dr	27410
Manor Ct & Dr	27403
Manor House Ct	27407
Manor Ridge Ct & Trl	27407
Manorwood Rd	27406
Mansfield Cir	27455
Mantura Ln	27406
Manuel St	27455
Manufacturers Rd	27406
Map Ln	27455
Maple St	27405
Maple Hill Rd	27406
Maple Ridge Ct	27455
Mapleleaf Dr	27410
Mapleway Ln	27455
Maplewood Ln	27407
Marboro Dr	27406
Marchester Way	27407
Margaret Ct	27410
Marguerite Dr	27406
Maribeau Woods Ct & Dr	27407
Marietta Rd	27409
Marigold Way	27410
Mariner Rd	27406
Marion Rd	27455
Marion St	27403
Marion Elsie Dr	27407
Marisa Dr	27455
Marithe Ct	27407
Mark Pl	27406
E Market St	
100-2699	27401
2700-3199	27405
W Market St	
101-197	27401
199-1099	27401
1100-3799	27403
3800-5099	27407
5100-5703	27409
5704-8798	27409
5704-5704	27419
5704-5704	27425
5705-8799	27409
Markham Rd	27405
Markland Dr	27408
Marksbury Dr	27405
Marriott Dr	27409
Marsh St	27406
Marshall St	27401
Marston Rd	27408
Marthas Pl	27408
Martin Ave	27405
Martin St	27406
Martin Luther King Jr Dr	27406
Martinsville Rd	
2700-2999	27408
3000-3099	27455
Martlet St	27403
Mary St	27409
Mary Beth Cir	27407
Mary E Black Dr	27406
Mary Eula St	27401
Mary Scott Pl	27410
Mary Wil Ct	27455
Masonic Dr	27403
Massey St	27401
Matt Pl	27405
Matthew Oaks Ct	27405
Matthews Ln	27405
Matthews St	27408
Maudan Ct	27406
Maury Ln	27401
Maxfield Rd	27405
Maxmillan Dr	27406
Maybank Dr	27403
Maybrook Dr	27405
Mayfair Ave	27405
Mayflower Dr	27403
Mayo Ct	27406
Maywood St	27403
Mcadams Ct	27409
Mcadoo Ave	27406
Mcallen Dr	27409
Mcallister Pl	27455
Mcarthur Dr	27406
Mccallum St	27409
Mccarron Ct	27406
Mcclellan Pl	27409
Mccloud Rd	27409
Mcconnell Rd	
1400-2999	27401
3001-3099	27401
3100-3899	27405
3900-4399	27406
Mcconnell Center Dr	27405
Mccormick St	
800-1599	27403
1800-1899	27406
Mccoy St	27405
Mccuiston Ct & Rd	27407
E Mcculloch St	27406
Mcdowell Dr	27408
Mcelveen Ct	27401
E Mcgee St	27401
W Mcgee St	
100-899	27401
901-997	27403
999-1199	27403
Mcginty Dr	27406
Mcgirt St	27401
Mcintosh St	27407
Mciver St	27403
Mckee Huger Dr	27405
Mckelvey Dr	27406
Mcknight Mill Rd	27405
Mclaughlin Dr	27406
Mcleansville Rd	27405
Mcmanus St	27403
Mcmurray Cir	27410
Mcnairy Dr	27455
Mcpherson St	27405
Mcrae St	27401
Meade Dr	27410
Meadow St	27405
Meadow Crossing Ct	27410
Meadow Gate Dr	27455
Meadow Oak Dr	27406
Meadow Run Dr	27455
Meadowbriar Ct	27410
Meadowbrook Ter	27408
Meadowcroft Rd	27406
Meadowdale Dr	27406
Meadowland Ter	27406
Meadowood St	27409
Meadowood Glen Way	27409
Meadowshire Dr	27406
Meadowview Ct	27403
E Meadowview Rd	27406
W Meadowview Rd	
100-600	27406
602-1298	27406
1300-2199	27403
2200-2499	27407
Meadowville Ln	27406
Mecklenburg Rd	27407
Medford Ln	27408
Medhurst Dr	27410
Medley St	27406
Medlock Trce	27405
Medway Ct	27407
Meeting House Dr	27410
Melbourne Rd	27405
Melchior Cir	27406
Melissa Rd	27410
Melissa Carol Cir	27407
Melissa Laine Rd	27406
Melody Ln	27407
Meloine Ln	27407
Melrose Ct	27406
Melvin Pl	27407
Melvina Rd	27406
Memorial Ln	27407
Memory Way	27406
Memphis St	27406
N Mendenhall St	27401
S Mendenhall St	27403
Menfro Pl	27409
Menlo Park Rd	27405
Mepps Ln	27455
Mercury Dr	27410
Meredith Dr	27408
Merlin Dr	27407
Merlot Way	27410
Merrick Ct	27409
Merrill Dr	27410
Merritt Dr	27407
Merry Oaks Ct	27410
Merryweather Rd	27407
Mersey Rd	27406
Merton Rd	27455
Metals Dr	27407
Methodist Rd	27406
Miami St	27406
Mica Ct	27409
Michael Ct	27407
Michaux Rd	27410
Michelle Ln	27407
Middle Dr	27409
Middleburg Rd	27406
Middlebury Pl & Way	27410
Middlefield Ct	27455
Middlethorpe Ct	27407
Middleton Dr	27406
Midkiff Rd	27407
Midland Park Ln	27455
Midway St	27403
Mieh Mieh Dr	27407
Milan Rd	27410
Milburn St	27406
Milford Rd	27405
Mill St	27408
Mill Chase Ct	27455
Mill Creek Ct	27407
Mill Path Ln	27407
Mill Shire Ct	27455
Mill Spring Ct & Pl	27410
Millburn Dr	27407
Miller Dr	27405
Millhouse Ct	27407
Millikin St	27455
Millis Rd	27407
Millpoint Rd	27406
Millridge Ct & Dr	27407
Millwood School Rd	27409
Millwright Ct	27410
Milner Dr	27410
Milpond Ln	27455
Milton St	27403
Miltwood Dr	27455
Mimi Ln	27406
Mimosa Dr	27403
Mine Crest Ct	27407
Minnow Rd	27405
Minor St	27406
Minorwood Rd	27405
Miss Ellie Dr	27405
Mistletoe Dr	27403
Mistywood Ct	27407
Mitchell Ave	
2000-2299	27405
4700-4899	27410
Mizell Ct & Rd	27405
Mobile St	27406
Mockernut Ct	27455
Mockingbird Rd	27406
Monmouth Ct & Dr	27410
Monrovia Dr	27455
Montague Rd	27409
E & W Montcastle Dr	27406
Montclair Rd	27407
Monterey St	27406
Montevista Ct & Dr	27407
Montford Ct	27455
Monticello St	27410
Montlieu Ave	27409
Montmartre Rd	27409
Montpelier Dr	27410
Montreal Ave	27406
Montrose Ct	27410
Montrose Dr	
200-499	27407
500-999	27410
Moody St	27401
Moonlight Ln	27405
Mooresville Rd	27410
Moran Dr	27410
Morehead Ave	
600-799	27401
900-999	27403
Morgan Ashley Dr	27410
Morgan Smith Rd	27405
Morley Rd	27405
Morning Dew Rd	27407
Morning Joy Pl	27401
Morning View Dr	27401
Mornstar Pl	27406
Morris St	27406
Morris Farm Dr	27409
Morton St	27403
Mosby Dr	27407
Moser Rd	27406
Mosley Ct & Rd	27455
Moss Cove Ct	27407
Moss Creek Dr	27410
Mossborough Dr	27410
Mossdale Rd	27406
Mossy Wood Cir	27409
Mossyrock Rd	27406
Moton Dr	27401
Moultrie Ct	27409
Mount Hope Church Rd	27405
Mount Olive Dr	27406
Mount Zion St	27405
Mountain Rdg	27401
Mountain Ash Ct	27410
Mountain Brook Rd	27455
Mountain Laurel Dr	27406
Mountain View Rd	27410
Mourning Dove Ter	27409
Moutline Ct & Dr	27409
Mowbray Trl	27407
Muirfield Dr	27410
Muirs Chapel Rd	27410
Mulligan Cir	27406
Mullin Dr	27401
Mullis Ct	27405
Muncey Ln	27401
Munsford Hills Ln	27410
Munsford Woods Ln	27410
Munster Ave	27406
Murchie St	27405
Murray St	27406
Murrayhill Rd	
1800-1899	27406
1900-2300	27403
2302-2698	27403
Murraylane Rd	27405
N Murrow Blvd	
100-202	27401
201-201	27402
201-201	27420
201-201	27429
201-201	27435
204-498	27401
301-499	27401
S Murrow Blvd	27401
Musket Ln	27455
Myers Ln	27408
Myrawood Dr	27406
Myrtle St	27405
Mystic Ct & Dr	27406
Nabors Rd	27405
Naco Rd	27401
Nana Ln	27405
Nancy Jean Rd	27406
Nandina Dr	27455
Nantucket Rd	27455
Napper Dr	27455
Narrow Leaf Ct	27455
Nash St	27401
Natchez Ct & Trce	27455
Nathan Hunt Rd	27410
Nathanael Rd	27408
Nathanael Green Dr	27455
National Service Rd	27409
Natural Lake Ct	27410
Nc Highway 150 E & W	27455
Nc Highway 62 E & W	27406
Nc Highway 68 S	27409
Neal St	27403
Nealtown Rd & Way	27405
Needleleaf Ln	27410
Nelson St	27401
Nelson Creek Ln	27406
Nelson Farm Ct & Rd	27406
Nelson Meadow Ln	27406
Nesbitt Rd	27406
Nestleway Ct & Dr	27406
Netfield Rd	27455
Netherwood Dr	27408
Neuse Ct	27407
New St	27405
New Avedon Dr	27455
New Bailey Trl	27455
New Bedford Dr	27410
New Bern Sq	27408
New Castle Rd	27406
New Creek Ln	27405
New Garden Park	27410
New Garden Rd	27410
New Garden Rd E	27455
New Garden Commons	27410
New Garden Village Dr	27410
New Hanover Dr	27408
New Orleans St	27406
Newkirk Dr	27407
E & W Newlyn St	27408
Newman Davis Rd	27406
Newton St	27406
Niagara St	27405
Nicholas Rd	27409
Nichols Ave	27405
Nicholson Ct	27407
Nighthawk Pl	27409
Nightingale Ct	27405
Nile Pl	27409
No Record 27401	27401
No Record 27403	27403
No Record 27408	27408
No Record 27409	27409
No Record 27410	27410
No Record 27455	27455
No Record 27495	27495
Noble Pl	27408
N Nocho St	27401
Nolen Ct	27408
Nora Dr	27410
Norman Park Rd	27406
Normandy Rd	27408
Normandy Hills Cir	27410
Norsaw Ct	27410
Northampton Dr	27408
Northbrook Ct	27410
Northern Shores Ln & Pt	27455
Northfield St	27403
Northgate Dr	27405
Northlake Dr	27410
Northland Dr	27405
Northline Ave	
2900-3299	27408
3400-3499	27410
Northline Pl	27410
Northmoor Trce	27455
Northridge St	27403
Northside Dr	27405
Northumberland Dr	27406
E Northwood St	27401
W Northwood St	
100-398	27401
800-1599	27408
Norwalk St	27407
Norwich Dr	27410
Norwood Dr	27407
Notting Hill Ct	27410
Nottingham Rd	27408
Nut Bush Rd E & W	27410
Oak Ct	27401
W Oak Ct	27407
W Oak Dr	27407
Oak St	27403
Oak Arbor Rd	27455
Oak Bend Trl	27410
Oak Branch Dr	27407
Oak Gate Dr	27405
Oak Glen Ct	27408
Oak Grove Ave	27405
Oak Hill Dr	27408
Oak Leaf Dr	27406
Oak Tree Rd	27455
Oakbrook Ct	27410
Oakbury Ct	27455
Oakcliffe Ct & Rd	27406
Oakcrest Ave	27408
Oakland Ave	27403
Oakmont Ct	27407
Oakmoor Cir & Dr	27406
Oaks Ct & Dr	27455
Oaktop Cir	27410
Oakvale St	27407
Oakwood Dr	27407
Oberlin Dr	27405
N Obermeyer St	27401
Obriant Ct & Pl	27410
Obrien St	27407
Oconnor St	27406
October Ln	27405
Odell Pl	27403
Oferrell St	27405
Ogburn Rd	27405
Ogden St	27406
N Ohenry Blvd	
301-499	27401
1000-4199	27405
S Ohenry Blvd	27401
Ola St	27405
Old Acre Ct	27410
Old Barn Rd	27410
Old Battleground Rd	27410
Old Brandt Trce	27455
Old Brickstore Rd	27455
Old Burlington Rd	27405
Old Chapman St	27403
Old Farm Ct	27407
Old Fox Trl	27407
Old Friendly Rd	27410
Old Heritage Trl	27401
Old Hickory Dr	27405
Old Iron Ct	27455
Old Ironworks Rd	27455
Old Jones Rd	27406
Old Lake Jeanette Rd	27455
Old Liberty Pl	27406
Old Mcconnell Loop	27405
Old Oak Ridge Rd	27410
Old Onslow Rd	27407
Old Orchard Ln	27455
Old Park Rd	27407
Old Pegram Rd	27406
Old Randleman Rd	27406
Old Saybrook Dr	27455
Old School Rd	27405
Old Scotney Ct	27407
Old Stage Coach Trl	27410
Old Towne Dr	27455
Old Treybrooke Dr	27406
Old Well Pl	27406
Olde Forest Dr	27406
Olde Oaks Ln	27406
Olde Province Ct	27406
Olde Sedgefield Way	27407
Oldham Ct	27406
Oldsquaw Dr	27455
Oleander Pt	27407
Olive St	27401
Oliver Ct & Dr	27406
Oliver Hills Rd	27406
Olivet Ct	27406
Olympia Dr	27406
Olympic Ct	27410
Omaha St	27406
Oneida Rd	27410
Oneill Pl	27405
Onslow Dr	27408
Ontario St	27403
Opal Dr	27403
Orange St	27405
Orchard St	27406
Orchard Grass Ct	27410
Orchard Knoll Dr	27405

Orchard Ridge Ln 27455
Oriole Pl 27408
Orlando St 27406
Orleans Dr 27409
Orlon Pl 27407
Orourke Dr 27409
Orville Wright Dr 27409
Osborne Rd 27407
Osmond Pl 27455
Overbrook Dr 27408
Overland Hts 27407
Overland Park Dr 27410
Overlea Dr 27407
Overlook St 27403
Overman St 27410
Overshoot Ct 27455
Overton Dr 27408
Owens Ct & St 27405
Owls Roost Ct & Rd 27410
Oxford St 27406
P P G Rd 27409
Pacific Ave 27406
Paddington St 27406
Paddock Ct 27455
Pageland Dr 27410
Pai Park 27409
Paisley St 27401
Palazzi Way 27410
Pall Mall Pl 27455
Palladium Dr 27410
Palm St 27405
Palm Tree Ct 27406
Palmetto St 27405
Palmyra Dr 27410
Pamlico Dr 27408
Panarama Dr 27405
Pandora Dr 27409
Panners Trl 27455
Pardue Ct 27409
Parish St 27408
Park Ave 27405
N Park Dr 27401
S Park Dr 27401
Park Pl 27410
Park Ter 27403
Park Hill Dr 27410
Park Village Ct & Ln 27455
Parker St 27405
Parker Baldwin Ln 27406
Parkland Dr 27409
Parkmont Ct & Dr 27408
Parks St 27405
Parkway 27401
Parkway Vista Rd 27409
Parkwood Dr 27403
Parnell Dr 27405
Parsons Pl 27410
Partnership Ct 27405
Pasadena St 27406
Paschal St 27407
Pasquinelli Pl 27410
Pasquotank Rd 27407
Pasteur Dr 27403
Pastor Anderson Way 27401
Patillo Rd 27406
Patio Pl 27405
Patrick Henry Way 27410
Patriot Ct & Way 27408
Patterson Ct & St 27407
Patton Ave 27406
Paul St 27407
Pawnee Rd 27410
Pax Rd 27455
Paxton Ct 27405
Peach Orchard Dr 27455
Peachtree St 27401
Peale Ter 27407
Pear St 27401
Pear Tree Ct & Ln 27401
Pearl Rd 27406
Pearson St 27406
Pearview Dr 27405
Pebble Dr 27410
Pebble Garden Ct 27407
Pebble Ridge Ct 27455
Peebles Dr 27403

Pegg Rd 27409
Peggy Sue Ct 27407
Pelham Dr 27406
Pemberton Rd 27407
Pembroke Rd
600-699 27408
610-610 27404
700-2098 27408
701-2099 27408
Pence Ct 27455
Pender Ln 27408
Pendleton Dr 27409
Penn Pl 27405
Penn Wyne Dr 27410
Pennoak Ct, Ln, Rd & Way 27407
Pennsylvania St 27406
Pennydale Dr 27407
Penrose Ct 27410
Penry Rd 27405
Penton Pl 27455
Penton Ridge Ct 27455
Pepper Hill Ct & Rd 27407
Pepperbush Dr 27405
Peppercorn Ln 27406
Pepperdine Rd 27410
Pepperstone Dr & Pl 27406
Peppervine Trl 27455
Pepperwood Cir 27410
Perch Pl 27455
Percy St 27405
Perga Ct 27406
Periwinkle Ct & Dr 27407
Perkins St 27401
Perquimans Rd E & W 27407
Perrou Ct 27410
Perry St 27403
Pershing Ct 27408
Pershing St 27405
Persimmon Ct 27410
Perth Pl 27405
Pertland Trl 27405
Peterford Dr 27405
Peterson Ave 27405
Pewter Pl 27455
Pheasant Dr 27406
Pheasant Run Dr 27455
Phelps Ct 27409
Phifer Luther Ct 27406
Philadelphia Lake Ct 27408
Phillips Ave 27405
Phillips Park Dr 27401
Phillipsburg Ct 27410
Phipps Ave & St 27405
Phoebe Dr 27403
Phoenix Ct & Dr 27406
Picard St 27405
Piccadilly Cir 27410
Pichard St 27401
Pickerel Pl 27455
Pickering Rd 27407
Pickman Dr 27410
Pickwick Pl 27407
Piedmont Pkwy 27410
Piedmont Trace Dr 27409
Piedmont Triad Pkwy 27409
Piermont Dr 27410
Pigeon Cove Dr 27410
Pilgrims Church Rd 27409
Pilot Cir 27407
Pilot Ridge Ct 27407
Pindals Rd 27405
Pine St 27401
Pine Bark Ct 27406
Pine Bluff St 27403
Pine Branch Dr 27405
Pine Brook Ln 27406
Pine Cone Trl 27406
Pine Cove Ct & Rd 27410
Pine Glen Ct 27410
Pine Hollow Ln 27410
Pine Knoll Pl 27407
Pine Lake Dr 27407
Pine Meadows Ct 27406
Pine Ridge Ct & Dr 27406

Pine Vista Ln 27406
Pineburr Ct & Rd 27455
Pinecrest Rd 27403
Pinecroft Ct & Rd 27407
Pinedale Rd 27408
Pinehaven Dr 27410
Pineland St 27407
Pineneedle Dr 27405
Pinetop Rd 27410
Pinetuck Rd 27407
Pineview Dr 27407
Pineway Ct & Dr 27405
Pinewood Dr 27410
Pinewood Acres Dr 27405
Pinnix St 27405
Pinoak Ct & Rd 27455
Piper Pl 27408
Pipers Glen Ct 27406
Pisgah Ct & Pl 27455
Pisgah Church Rd 27455
Pitkin Ct 27406
Pitlockry Pl 27407
Pitman Rd 27406
Pitt Pl 27408
Placid Ln 27406
Plainfield Rd 27455
Plantation Dr 27410
Plantation Farms Rd 27409
Plantation Ridge Ln 27409
Planters Ct 27455
Planters Wood Trl 27407
Plateau Ct 27455
Platinum Dr 27409
Plaza Dr 27406
Pleasant Dr 27410
Pleasant Field Ct 27455
Pleasant Garden Rd 27406
Pleasant Oaks Rd 27410
Pleasant Ridge Rd
1100-1799 27409
1800-2414 27410
Pleasant Valley Rd 27406
Plott St 27406
Plummer Dr 27410
Plymouth St 27406
Plympton Pl 27410
Poe St 27403
Poinsettia Rd 27407
N Pointe Ct 27408
E Police Plz 27401
Pomona Dr 27407
Pompano Dr 27410
Pomroy St 27403
Ponderosa Ct & Dr 27406
Pondfield Ct & Dr 27410
Pondside Ct 27455
Pontesbury Pl 27408
Pontiac Dr 27405
Poplar Brook Ln 27406
Poplar Grove Trl 27410
Poplar Hill Ct 27407
E & W Poplar Ridge Ct 27455
Porte Pl 27405
Portico Ct 27410
Portland St 27403
Portrait Dr 27410
Portside Ct 27406
Post St 27405
Post Oak Ln 27406
Postbridge Ct & Dr 27407
Potomac Dr 27403
Potters Field Ct 27455
Power St 27405
Prairie Trl 27410
Preddy Blvd
500-599 27406
2500-2600 27407
2602-2698 27407
Prentiss Rd 27409
Presbyterian Rd 27406
Prescott St 27401
Presley Way 27405
Presnell Way 27405
Prestbury Ct & Dr 27455
Prestwood Ct 27406

Preyer Ct 27405
Preys St 27410
Price Park Dr 27410
Prima Ct & Dr 27455
Primrose Ave
3500-3699 27408
3700-4199 27455
Primrose Ct 27408
Prince Rd 27455
Prince Albert Dr 27405
Princess Rd 27455
Princess Ann St 27408
Princeton Ave 27407
Printers Ln 27407
Professional Vlg 27401
Promise Land Dr 27406
Provence Ct & Dr 27410
Province Spring Cir 27403
Provincetown Ct 27408
Pti Dr 27409
Puritan Dr 27410
Putters Cir 27406
Pyracantha Ct 27405
Pyramid Village Blvd 27405
Pyrus Ct 27401
Quad Oak Dr 27405
Quail Dr 27408
Quail Canyon Ct 27410
Quail Cove Ct 27406
Quail Hollow Rd 27410
Quail Oaks Dr 27405
Quail Ridge Ct & Dr 27455
Quaker Landing Ct & Rd 27455
Quaker Run Dr 27410
Quakeridge Dr 27410
Quate Dr 27406
Queen Alice Rd 27407
Queen Beth Dr 27405
Queen Victoria Pl 27455
Queenanne Ct 27406
Queens Ct 27408
Queensberry Ct 27405
Quick Silver Ct 27455
Quincemoor Ct 27407
Quincy St 27401
Quinlan Dr 27406
Rabb Pl 27410
Rachel Carson Ct 27410
Rachel Smothers Dr 27455
Radar Rd 27410
Radbrook Dr 27406
E & W Radiance Dr 27403
Radnor Dr 27410
Raelans Cir 27407
Rail St 27407
Railway Ave 27407
Rainbow Dr 27403
Raintree Ct & Dr 27407
N Raleigh St
101-197 27401
199-499 27401
800-1100 27405
1102-1198 27405
S Raleigh St 27401
Ralph St 27401
Ralph Johns St 27405
Ram Rd 27405
Ramblewood Dr 27406
Rambling Rd 27409
Ramsgate Ct 27403
Randall St 27401
Randleman Rd 27406
Randolph Ave 27406
Random Dr 27407
Rankin Pl 27403
Rankin Rd 27405
Rankin King Dr 27405
Rankin Mill Rd 27405
Ransom Rd 27455
Rappahannock Ct 27407
Rasheeda Ct 27406
Rath St 27406
Ravendale Dr 27406
Ravenstone Dr 27407
Ravenwood Dr 27409

Ray St 27406
Ray Alexander Dr 27410
Raybrook Rd 27406
Raylewood Ct & Dr 27406
Raymond Rd 27405
Rayston Dr 27405
Red Brook Ln 27406
Red Chief St 27406
Red Coat Ln 27410
Red Fern Ct 27455
Red Forest Ct & Rd 27410
Red Hill Ct 27407
Red Lure Way 27455
Red Sail Ln 27410
Redberry Rd 27407
Redbud Dr 27410
Redfield Dr 27410
Redford Dr 27408
Redhead Ct 27455
Redington Dr 27410
Redor St 27405
Redwine Dr 27410
Redwood Dr 27405
Reedy Fork Pkwy 27405
Reel Ct 27455
Regal Ct & Ln 27410
N Regan St 27401
Regency Dr
2300-2399 27407
4200-4299 27410
Regents Park Ln 27455
N & S Regional Rd 27409
Register Rd 27406
Rehobeth Ct 27406
Rehobeth Church Rd 27406
Rehobeth Oaks 27406
Reid St 27406
Remora Rd 27406
Remount Ct 27409
Renard Rd 27406
Renee Dr 27407
Renfrew Rd 27409
Rental Car Dr 27409
Renville Dr 27406
Renwick Ct 27410
Repon St 27407
Retriever Ct 27410
Retriever Ln 27455
Rev Williams Dr 27401
Revelle Ln 27407
Revere Dr 27407
Revolan Ct & Dr 27407
Revolution Mill Dr 27405
Rex Ct 27406
Rexdale Pl 27407
Reynolds Pl 27403
Rheims Dr 27407
Rhododendron Dr 27455
Rhynewood Dr 27410
Ribbon Grass Ter 27405
Richard St 27405
Richardson St 27403
Richardson Village Way 27405
Richfield Rd 27410
Richland St 27409
Richmond Rd 27407
Riderid St 27401
Ridge Grove Ct 27455
Ridge Haven Ct & Rd 27410
Ridgecrest Dr 27410
Ridgedale Dr 27455
Ridgefall Rd 27410
Ridgemore Ct 27407
Ridgeway Dr & St 27403
Ridgewood Ave 27405
Riding Ridge Dr 27410
Ridingate Ct 27455
Ring Rd 27405
Ringold Rd 27405
Ripley Rd 27406
Rising River Ln 27409
Ritters Lake Rd 27406
River Birch Loop 27409
River Bluff Ter 27409
River Brook Ct 27409

River Chase Ct 27407
River Crest Ln 27409
River Forest Ln 27409
River Glen Ct & Dr 27455
River Hills Ct & Dr 27410
River Knoll Ct 27409
River Lake Ct 27410
River Oaks Ct & Dr 27409
River Rock Pt 27409
River Springs Ct 27410
Riverdale Dr 27406
Riveria Dr 27406
Riverside Ct 27409
Riverside Dr 27406
Riverwood Ct 27410
Rivington Way 27455
Roanne Way 27409
Roanoke Dr 27408
Robalo Rd 27406
Robbins St 27406
Robbs Ct 27406
Roberson Comer Rd 27455
Robert St 27407
Robert Andrew Rd 27406
Robert Jessup Dr 27455
Robert Porcher Way 27410
Roberts Ct 27406
Robin Hood Ct & Dr 27408
Robinridge Rd 27410
Roblyn Rd 27410
Robyns Glen Cir 27409
Rock Haven Dr 27410
Rock Spring St 27405
Rock Springs Rd 27410
Rockbridge Rd 27407
Rockett St 27406
Rockford Rd 27408
Rockglen Ln 27410
Rocking Ct 27405
E Rockingham Rd 27407
Rockport Ct 27406
Rockwood Mnr 27405
Rockwood Rd 27408
Rocky Ann Ln 27406
Rocky Brook Ct 27409
Rocky Knoll Cir & Rd 27406
Rocky Ridge Pt 27405
Rocky Valley Rd 27407
Roediger Ct 27407
Rogers Ct 27455
Roland Rd 27407
Roldan Ln 27408
Rolling Rd 27403
Rolling Brook Rd 27406
Rolling Meadows Ct & Dr 27406
Rollingwood Dr 27410
Rollins Rd 27408
Rollins St 27405
Romaine St 27407
Ronald Rd 27406
Ropley Dr 27455
Rose Dr 27407
Rose Hill Ct 27407
Rose Lake Dr 27407
Rosebank Ct 27407
Rosebay Cir & Ln 27455
Rosebriar Ct 27407
Rosecliff Ct 27407
Rosecrest Dr 27408
Roseheim Ct 27405
Roseland St 27408
Rosemary Dr 27406
Rosetta Rd 27401
Rosevilla Ln 27455
Rosewood Cir 27410
Ross Ave
500-1399 27406
1600-1699 27401
Ross Ct 27401
Roswell Ct 27408
Rotherwood Rd 27406
Rothwood Acres Rd 27406
Rougon Dr 27405
Round Hill Ct & Rd 27408
Round Oak Ct 27455

Round Tree Ct 27410
Roundtable Rd 27407
Roundup Cir & Dr 27405
Routh Cir & Ct 27406
Rowe St 27407
Roxanna Rd 27410
Roxby Ct 27455
Royal Ave 27407
Royal Coach Rd 27410
Royal Palm Ct 27408
Royalshire Rd 27406
Royalton Dr 27406
Royce Cir 27405
Royster Rd 27455
Ruayne Rd 27406
Rucker St 27407
Rudd Rd 27405
Ruddy Duck Dr 27455
Ruffin Rd 27407
Rugby St 27406
Rugosa Dr 27410
Running Brook Dr 27408
Running Ridge Rd 27407
Runyon Dr 27405
Rustic Rd 27410
Rustic House Ln 27406
Rutgers Rd 27407
Rutherford Dr 27408
Rutherglen Ln 27455
Ruths Ln 27407
Rutledge Dr 27455
Ryan St 27405
Ryan Nicole Ln 27407
Ryderwood Dr 27407
Rye Mill Ct 27410
Sable Ln 27406
Sabre Ct 27406
Sacramento Dr 27406
Saddle Trl 27406
Saddleberry Way 27410
Saddlegate Ct 27407
Saferight Rd 27406
Saffron Close St 27410
Sagamore Dr 27410
Sage Dr 27410
Sage Brush Ct & Trl 27409
Sail View Cv 27455
Sails Way 27406
Sainsbury Ln 27409
Saint Andrews Rd 27408
Saint Augustine Sq 27408
Saint Charles Ln 27405
Saint Christopher Sq 27410
Saint Croix Pl 27410
Saint Francis Ct & Rd 27408
Saint James Ct 27401
Saint John Ct 27401
Saint Jude St 27405
Saint Katherines Cir 27455
Saint Lauren Dr 27410
Saint Leo St 27405
Saint Luke Ct 27401
Saint Mark Rd 27403
Saint Martin Pl 27455
Saint Matthew Ct 27401
Saint Patrick Dr 27406
Saint Pauls Ln 27410
Saint Regis Ct & Rd 27408
Saint Simons Sq 27408
Salem St 27401
Salisbury Pl 27405
Saltee Rd 27406
Sam Snead Dr 27410
Sampson St 27406
Sanctuary Dr 27405
Sandburg Dr 27405
Sanderling Pl 27407
Sandhurst Rd 27406
Sands Dr 27405
Sandy Springs Rd 27455
Santa Fe Trl 27406
Sapp Rd 27409
Saratoga Ln 27455
Sassafras Ct 27410
Satin Wood Dr 27410
Satterfield Pl 27410

Saturn Dr 27406
Sauls Dr 27401
Savannah Ct & St 27406
Savannas Run Dr 27405
Savoy Ln 27410
Sawgrass Rd 27410
Sawmill Ct 27407
Saxon Ct & Pl 27406
Scarlet Haw Ct & Dr 27410
Scaup Dr 27455
Schangto 27495
Schisler Dr 27401
NW School Rd 27409
SE School Rd 27406
Schoolway Dr 27406
Schuyler Ln 27410
Scotland Rd 27407
Scotland Oaks Ct 27407
Scotney Dr 27407
Scotridge Pt 27455
Scott Ave 27403
Scottish Rite Ct & Dr 27407
Scottsdale Rd 27455
Scottville Rd 27405
Seabrook Ct 27455
Seacliff Dr 27407
Seasons Way 27403
Seattle Dr 27406
Seawell Rd 27407
E & W Sedgefield Dr 27407
Sedgefield Gate Rd 27407
Sedgegrove Rd 27407
Sedgegrow Dr 27407
Sedgehill Ct 27407
Sedgelane Ct & Dr 27407
Sedgewood Ln 27407
Sedley Ct 27455
Selborne Dr 27410
Selkirk Dr 27410
Sellars Ave 27407
Selsey Ct 27405
Seminole Dr 27408
Seneca Rd 27406
Sequoia Ct 27455
Serene Ln 27406
Serenity Rd 27406
Service Center Rd 27410
Servomation Rd 27407
Settlers Ln 27410
Seven Gates Dr 27410
Seven Oaks Ct & Dr 27410
Sevier St 27406
Shadd Ln 27406
Shady Lawn Dr 27408
Shady Maple Dr 27406
Shady Oak Dr 27410
Shady Pine Dr 27455
Shadygrove Ln 27407
Shagbark Dr 27406
Shaker Dr 27410
Shallowford Dr 27406
Shamrock Dr 27408
Shanahan Ct 27406
Shandwick Way 27410
Shane Dr 27406
Shannon Dr 27405
Shannon Ridge Ct 27455
Sharing Ter 27405
Sharon Ave 27405
Sharon Donna Dr 27406
Sharonbrook Dr 27405
Sharp Ridge Rd 27406
Sharpe Rd 27406
Sharps Airpark Ct 27409
Shaw St 27401
Shaw Farm Cir 27406
Shawfield Ct 27409
Shawnee Rd 27403
Shelburne Ct 27455
Shelby Dr 27409
Sheldon Rd 27405
Shelia Dr 27406
Shell Dr 27407
Shelley Dr 27406
Shellford St 27406
Shelton St 27405
Shenandoah Rd 27405
Shenango Rd 27405
Shepherd Watch Ct 27403
Shepherds Way 27410
Shepway Loop 27405
Sheraton Ct 27410
E & W Sheraton Park Rd 27406
Sherbourne Ct & Ln 27405
Sheree Ct & Ln 27406
Sheridan Rd 27455
Sherman St 27410
Sherrill St 27403
Sherrilwood Dr 27406
Sherrod Watlington Cir 27406
Sherwin Rd 27409
Sherwood St 27403
Shiland Dr 27406
Shimer Dr 27407
Shipley Ct 27405
Shirley Ln 27401
Shoal Creek Dr 27410
Shoffner Ct 27406
E Shore Dr 27406
Shoreham Rd 27455
Shorelake Dr 27455
Shoreline Dr 27410
Short St 27406
Short Farm Rd 27406
Short Horn Ct & Way 27405
Shoveler Ct & Dr 27455
S & E Side Aly, Blvd & Dr 27406
Sidney Marie Ct 27407
Sidney Porter Dr 27405
Sidon Dr 27407
Siena Ter 27410
Sierra Dr 27410
Silent Spring Ct 27410
Siler Rd 27406
Siler St 27407
Silhouette Dr 27405
Silver Ave 27403
Silver Creek Dr 27410
Silver Oak Ct 27455
Silver Sky Way 27410
Silver Springs Rd 27455
Silverbriar Ct 27410
Silverwood Ct 27410
Simmons Ct 27407
Simpson St 27401
Simpson Calhoun Rd 27455
Sims St 27409
Sir Buxton Pl 27405
Sir Galahad Rd 27405
Sir Walter Rd 27405
Skylark Dr 27405
Skyway Dr 27409
Sloan St 27401
Slope Rd 27409
E & W Smith St 27401
Smithfield Dr 27406
Smokeridge Ln 27407
Smokerise Ct 27407
Smoketree Dr 27410
Smokey Quartz Ct 27409
Smothers Pl 27401
Smyres Pl 27403
Snow Rd 27409
Snowgoose Cv 27455
Snowy Owl Ct 27409
Snyder St 27407
Soabar St 27406
Solar Pl 27406
Solara Trce 27410
Soldiers Retreat Ct 27455
Somerset Pl 27410
Somersworth Dr 27407
Sommerton Ct & Dr 27408
Song Sparrow Ln 27409
Soto St 27406
Sourgum Ct 27410
Sourwood Rd 27408
South St 27406
Southall Dr 27406
Southbrook Dr 27406
Southern St 27401
Southern Gates Ct & Dr 27410
Southern Oxygen Rd 27407
Southern Webbing Mill Rd 27405
Southlake Dr 27410
Southport Rd 27410
Southside Sq 27406
Southstone Dr 27406
Southview Dr 27407
S Southwest Park Dr 27407
Southwick Dr 27455
Southwind Rd 27455
Spanish Oak Cir & Dr 27409
Sparger Pl 27455
Sparta Dr 27406
Spencer St 27401
Spencer Dixon Rd 27455
Spicebush Trl 27410
Spicewood Dr 27405
Spinnaker Ct 27410
Spirea Pl 27455
Splitrail Ct 27406
Sportime Pl 27410
Spray Rd 27406
Spring St 27405
N Spring St 27401
S Spring St
100-499 27401
600-699 27406
Spring Bridge Cir & Trl 27410
Spring Chapel Ct 27455
Spring Garden St
200-699 27401
700-3099 27403
3100-4199 27407
Spring House Pl 27410
Spring Leaf Ct 27455
Spring Mill Rd 27406
Spring Oak Ct & Dr 27410
Springberry Ct 27455
Springbrook Dr
2400-2699 27406
3800-4099 27407
Springdale Ct 27403
Springhill Rd 27403
Springmont Dr 27405
Springtime Dr 27409
Springwood Dr 27403
Spruce St 27405
Sprucewood Dr 27407
Spruill Ct 27409
Spry St 27405
Spur Rd 27406
Spyglass Ct & Dr 27410
Squire Ct 27405
Stable Ct 27410
Stadler Pl 27410
Stadleridge Dr 27410
Stafford St 27407
Stage Coach Ct 27409
Stage Coach Trl
100-400 27409
402-598 27409
700-800 27410
802-998 27410
Staghorn Ct 27410
Stamey St 27401
Standard Dr 27409
Standish Dr 27401
Stanfield Rd 27405
Stanford Rd 27407
Stanhope Rd 27406
Stanley Rd 27407
Starboard Dr 27410
Starhill Ct 27410
Starlight Dr 27407
Starling Ct & Dr 27405
Starmount Dr
3200-3300 27403
3302-3798 27403
3900-4999 27410
Starmount Farms Ct & Dr 27408
State St
100-399 27408
400-799 27405
Staunton Ct & Dr 27410
Stedman St 27401
Steeple Dr 27405
E & W Steeple Chase Ct, Ln & Rd 27406
Steepleshire Pl 27410
Steepleton Way 27410
Steepleton Colony Ct 27410
Stephen Oaks Way 27405
Stephens St 27406
Sterlingshire Dr 27409
Stevendale Ct & Rd 27410
Stewart St 27401
Still Run Dr 27455
Stinson Ln 27406
Stirrup Dr 27407
Stockbridge Ct & Dr 27410
Stockton Way 27406
Stokes St 27407
Stone Bluff Ct 27410
Stone Leigh Rd 27455
Stone Quarry Rd 27405
Stonebrook Farms Ct & Rd 27406
Stoneburg Ct 27409
Stonebury Ct 27410
Stonecreek Ct 27455
Stonecrest St 27405
Stonecutter Ter 27455
Stonedale Dr 27406
Stonegate Ct 27406
Stonehaven Dr 27406
Stonehenge Rd 27406
Stonehouse Ct 27455
Stonekirk Ct 27407
Stonewater Pl 27408
Stonewood Dr 27455
Stoney Creek Dr 27406
Stoney Glen Loop & Pl 27409
Stoney Hill Cir 27406
Stoneykirk Dr 27409
Stonypointe Dr 27406
Storms End Trl 27455
Strasburg Ct & Dr 27407
Stratford Dr 27408
Strathmore Dr 27410
Stratton Hills Ct & Dr 27410
Straw Hat Rd 27410
Strawridge Dr 27406
Studio Ln 27407
Sturbridge Ln 27408
Suburban Ct 27406
Success Rd 27409
Sudberry Ct 27405
Sue Ellen Ct 27405
Sues Blues Aly 27406
Suffolk Trl 27407
Sullivan St 27405
Sullivans Lake Dr 27410
Sumac Rd 27406
Summer Pl 27410
Summerglen Ct & Dr 27406
Summerlyn Ct 27409
Summertree Ln & Loop 27406
Summerwalk Ct & Rd 27455
Summerwood Dr 27455
Summit Ave
100-299 27401
301-397 27405
399-5599 27405
Summit Hill Dr 27405
Summit View Ct & Dr 27405
Summit Wood Ct 27405
Sumner Church Rd 27406
Sun Oak Ct 27410
Sun Shadow Ct 27410
Sunburst Ln 27406
Sunbury Dr 27405
Sundown Dr 27410
Sunfish Pt 27455
Sunnycrest Ave 27405
Sunnyside Dr 27405
Sunrise Dr 27406
Sunrise Valley Dr 27405
Sunset Cir & Dr 27408
Sunshine Way 27409
Surry Dr 27408
Susan Ter 27410
Sussex Ct 27410
Sussmans St 27406
Sutter Rd 27455
Sutton Ct & Rd 27406
Sutton Oaks Ln 27407
Suttonwood Dr 27407
Swan St 27407
Swan Haven Ln 27405
Swanley Dr 27405
Swannanoa Dr 27410
Swanson Rd 27406
Sweet Birch Dr 27406
Sweetbriar Rd 27455
Sweetwater Ct 27407
Swift St 27407
Swiftcreek Ct 27407
Swiggett Rd 27409
N & S Swing Ct & Rd 27409
E & W Sycamore St 27401
Sycamore Glen Rd 27405
Sydney Shores Ct 27410
Sykes Ave 27405
Sylvan Rd 27403
Tabor St 27406
Tagus Dr 27410
Taliaferro Rd 27408
Tall Cedar Rd 27406
Tall Oaks Dr 27455
Talley St 27407
Talleyrand Rd 27406
Tallowood Ct 27455
Tallwood Dr 27410
Tally Ho Ct 27455
Talmaga Ln 27410
Tam Oshanter Dr 27409
Tamannary Dr 27455
Tamarack Dr 27407
Tamaron Dr 27410
Tambeado St 27403
Tambenew Rd 27455
Tampa St 27406
Tanbark Ct 27407
Tanglewood Dr 27410
Tannenbaum Cir 27410
Tanner Woods Ln 27410
Tansley Ct 27407
Tapawingo Trl 27406
Tara Dr 27410
Tareyton Dr 27410
Tarkington Dr 27407
Tarr Dr 27407
Tarrant Rd 27409
Tarrywood Ct & Dr 27455
Tate St 27403
Tattershall Dr 27410
Tatum Pl 27455
Taunton Dr 27410
Taybrook Way 27407
Taylor St 27405
Taylorcrest Rd 27405
Teaberry Ct 27455
Teague St 27406
Teakwood Dr 27406
Teal Ct 27455
Tealbriar Way 27410
Tealwood Dr 27407
Ted Johnson Pkwy 27409
Temple St 27406
Tenby Ct & Dr 27455
Tennyson Ct & Dr 27410
Tenuss Ln 27410
Terminal Rd 27409
Terminal St 27407
N Terminal Service Rd 27409
Terrace Way 27403
Terrault Dr 27410
Terre Ct 27406
E & W Terrell Pl & St 27406
Terry Ln 27405
Terry Shell Rd 27406
Tesi Ct 27455
Tew St 27407
Textile Dr 27405
Thacker Dairy Rd 27406
Thames Ct 27455
Thatcher Rd 27409
Thayer Cir 27407
The Kings Rd 27455
Thicket Ln 27405
Thimbleberry Sq 27455
Thistle Trce 27410
Thornaby Dr 27410
Thornberry Dr 27455
Thornblade Ct 27410
Thornbrook Rd 27406
Thorncliff Dr 27410
Thorncrest Dr 27407
Thorncroft Rd 27406
Thorndike Rd 27409
Thornton Ct 27407
Thorny Rd 27406
Three Meadows Ct & Rd 27455
Throughbrook Ct 27405
Thurston Ave 27406
Tiffany Ct & Pl 27408
Tillbrook Pl 27408
Tillery Dr 27405
Tilley Ct 27405
Tillie Scott Ct 27455
Tillman Ave 27405
Timber Ln 27408
Timber Ridge Ct 27407
Timberbrooke Dr 27409
Timberidge Pl 27410
Timberline Dr 27409
Timberoak Ct & Dr 27410
Timberview Cir 27410
Timmons Ave 27406
Tin Pan Aly 27406
Tinderbox Ln 27455
Tinker Ct 27455
Tinkermill Ct 27406
Tipperary Ct & Dr 27406
Tippy Rd 27406
Tipton Ct & Pl 27406
Titanium Ct 27406
Tobacco Ln 27409
Todd Rd & St 27406
Tokay Ct 27406
Tolar Dr 27406
Tom Rd 27406
Tomahawk Dr 27410
Tonkins St 27407
Top Ridge Ct 27407
Topping Dr 27407
Topwater Ln 27455
Torrence Dr 27406
Torwood Ct & Dr 27409
Tory Hill Dr 27410
Tower Ln & Rd 27410
Town St 27407
Towne Ridge Ct & Dr 27455
Towneley Ct 27455
Tradd Ct & Dr 27455
Trade St 27401
Traders Way 27407
Trail Ridge Dr 27410
Trailbend Ct 27410
Trailshead Dr 27405
Trailwood Dr 27407
Treasure Trl 27455
Treeble Ct 27406
Treestead Cir 27410
Treford Ct 27406
Trellis Ct N 27410
N & S Tremont Dr 27403
Trent St 27405
Trenton Rd 27408
Trentwood Dr 27408
Tresant Ter 27410
Treva Dr 27409
Treycastle Ln 27406
Tri City Blvd 27407
Tri Port Ct 27409
Triad Dr 27409
Triad Center Dr 27409
Triangle Dr 27405
Trier Dr 27455
Trillium Ln 27410
Trinity Ave 27407
Triston Dr 27407
Triumphant Rd 27406
Trogdon St 27403
Trosper Rd 27455
Trotting Pl 27405
Trouble Ln 27406
Troublesome Creek Dr 27455
Trox St 27406
Troxler Rd 27405
Troxler Farm Ct 27406
Troy St 27406
Trull Ave 27455
Trulove Ln 27455
Tryon St 27403
Tucker St 27405
Tucson Dr 27406
Tudor Ln 27410
Tulip Ct 27406
Tuliptree Dr 27455
Tulsa Dr 27406
Tumbleweed Dr 27407
Turfwood Dr 27410
Turk Pl 27405
Turnage Dr 27407
Turnberry Ct & Ln 27410
Turner Grove Dr & Pl 27455
Turnstone Cir & Trl 27455
Turtle Cove Ct 27410
Tuscaloosa St
500-1699 27406
1700-1898 27401
1900-2299 27401
Tuscany Ln 27410
Tuskegee St 27405
Twain Rd 27405
Twin Brooks Ct & Dr 27407
Twin Lakes Dr 27407
Twin Oak Dr 27407
Twin Sail Dr 27410
Twining Rd 27406
Two Oaks Dr 27410
Twyckenham Dr 27408
Tyler Rd 27409
Tyndale Ct 27406
Tynecastle Ct 27455
Tyrol Ct 27410
Tyrone Loop 27406
Tysinger Dr 27406
Ulster Ave 27406
Underwood Dr 27409
Union St 27403
United St 27407
University Dr 27403
Upland Dr 27405
Urban Dr 27403
Us Highway 29 N 27405
Utah Pl 27405
Utility St 27405
V F Dr 27409
Vale Pl 27401
Valecian Way 27410
Valeen Dr 27405
Valentine Ct 27405
Valhalla Cir 27406
Valley Crest Dr 27407
Valley Crossing Dr 27410
Valley Falls Rd 27455
Valley Lake Dr 27410
Valley Oak Dr 27406
Valley Stream Ct 27407
Valley View St 27405
Valleydale Ln 27406
Valleymede Rd 27410
Van Allen Cir & Ct 27410
Van Noppen Rd 27406
Van Wert St 27403
Vance St 27406
E Vandalia Rd 27406
W Vandalia Rd
100-1999 27406

2000-2999 27407
Vanderbilt Rd 27407
Vanstory St
1900-2299 27403
2300-2899 27407
Vantage Point Pl 27407
Varner Rd 27406
Veasley St 27407
Ventura Ct & Dr 27406
Venus Dr 27406
Veranda Ct & Ln 27455
Veranda Lake Ct 27409
Verdant Way 27406
Verdun Dr 27409
Vermont St 27405
Vernon St 27408
Vernon Owen Ct 27405
Vernondale Rd 27406
Vershire Ave 27406
Vestal St 27406
Vetra Dr 27405
Vianiang St 27405
Viburnum Ln 27455
Vickrey Chapel Rd N 27407
Victor Pl 27406
Victoria St 27401
Victory St 27407
Viewmont Dr 27406
Villa Dr 27403
Village Ln 27409
Village Crest Dr 27405
Village Green Dr 27406
Village Square Ct 27409
Village View Dr 27406
Villastone Pl 27410
Vincent St 27405
Vine St 27405
Vinegar Hill Dr 27410
Virgilwood Dr 27409
Virginia St 27401
Vivian Ln 27406
Vodington Cir 27405
Voltz St 27406
Voss Ave 27405
Waccamaw Way 27410
Wachovia Dr 27403
Waco Dr 27406
Wadena Ct & Dr 27407
Wades Store Rd 27406
Wafco Ln 27401
Wagon Wheel Dr 27410
Wagoner Bend Rd 27405
Wakefield Dr & Pl 27410
Wakerobin Ct 27407
Wakewood Dr 27407
Waldenbrook Ct & Rd 27407
Waldorf Dr 27455
Waldridge Ct & Rd 27406
Waldron Ct & Dr 27408
Walker Ave
600-699 27401
700-4099 27403
4100-4199 27407
Walking Horse Ln 27410
Walkover Dr 27455
Wall Rd 27407
Wallace Dr 27407
Wallingford Rd 27409
N Walnut Cir 27409
S Walnut Cir 27409
Walnut St 27405
Walser Rd 27406
Walter Reed Dr 27403
Walters St 27408
Wanda Dr 27408
Warang Dr 27410
Ward Rd 27405
Ward St 27406
Warehouse St 27405
Warfield Ct & Dr 27406
Warm Springs Pt 27455
Warren St 27403
Warwickshire Dr 27455
E & W Washington St 27401
Watauga Dr
2800-2899 27408
3100-4099 27410
Water St 27405
Water Gap Ct 27455
Watercourse Ct 27407
Watercrest Dr 27407
Waterleaf Ct 27410
Waterline Dr 27455
Waterlyn Ct & Dr 27405
Waters Edge Ln 27410
Waterside Dr 27406
Waterstone Dr 27406
Waterthrush Ct 27455
Waterwheel Ct 27409
Watkins St 27407
Watkins Grove Pt 27406
Watlington Rd 27405
Watson St 27406
Watts St 27407
Waugh St 27405
Waverly Way 27403
Waxwing Cv 27455
Way St 27405
Waycross Ct & Dr 27410
Wayfarer Dr 27410
Wayne Rd 27407
Waynoka Dr 27410
Wayside Dr 27405
Wayward Dr 27407
Wealdstone Cv 27410
Weatherby Ln 27406
Weatherly Rd 27406
Weatherstone Dr 27406
Webster Rd 27406
Weddington Ct 27407
Wedgedale Ave & Pl 27403
Wedgewood Ct & Pl 27403
Weeping Willow Ln 27405
Well Spring Dr 27410
Wellington Dr 27405
Wells Rd 27406
Wellsley Dr E & W 27407
Wellstone Ct 27410
Wembley Ct 27410
Wenchelsa Ct & Rd 27410
Wending Ln 27405
E Wendover Ave
100-400 27401
402-498 27401
800-3699 27405
W Wendover Ave
101-197 27401
199-200 27401
202-298 27401
300-1499 27408
3400-3700 27407
3701-3701 27495
3702-4498 27407
3703-4499 27407
4500-4799 27409
Wendy Ct 27409
Wentworth Dr 27408
Wesley Harris Cir 27455
Weslo Willow Cir & Dr 27409
West Ave 27407
Westbourne Ct & Rd 27410
Westbrook St 27407
Westchester Dr 27408
Westcliff Rd 27409
Westdale Pl 27403
Westerborne Dr 27407
Western Trl 27410
Westfield Dr 27410
N & S Westgate Dr 27407
Westhampton Dr 27405
Westhaven Dr 27403
Westland Dr 27410
Westlock Ct 27407
Westminster Ct & Dr 27410
Westmoreland Dr 27408
Westmount Ct & Dr 27410
Weston Dr 27407
Westover Ter
101-397 27403
399-499 27403
600-1699 27408
Westport Triad Dr 27409
Westridge Ct & Rd 27410
Westridge Forest Ct 27410
Westside Ct & Dr 27405
Westwarren Rd 27407
Westwind Dr 27410
Westwood Rd 27410
Wetherburn Ct & Way 27410
Wexford Dr 27406
Weybridge Ln 27407
Weyland Dr 27405
Weymouth Pl 27408
Wharton St 27401
Whaton Oaks Ct 27408
Wheatfield Ct & Dr 27405
Wheaton Cir 27406
Wheel Wright Ct 27455
Whilden Pl 27408
Whipple Trl 27455
Whippoorwill Dr 27407
Whispering Ct 27407
Whispering Oaks Ln 27401
SE Whispering Willows Dr 27406
Whisperwood Ct 27407
Whistling Oak Trl 27407
Whistling Swan Dr 27455
Whitby Pl 27406
Whitdale Pt 27455
White St 27405
White Bass Pl 27455
White Blossom Dr 27410
White Chapel Ct 27405
White Chapel Way
4000-4098 27405
4001-5897 27455
5899-5999 27455
6000-6099 27405
White Elder Rd 27405
White Horse Dr 27410
White Oak Ct & Dr 27405
White Pine Dr 27407
Whitehurst Rd 27410
Whiteley Pl 27406
Whiterock Rd 27405
Whitestone Dr 27455
Whitfield Dr 27455
Whitley Ct & Way 27407
Whitman Rd 27405
Whittier Dr 27403
E Whittington St 27406
W Whittington St
100-599 27406
600-699 27403
Whitworth Dr 27405
Wichita Pl 27405
Wicker St 27403
Wigeon Ct & Dr 27455
Wilburn Rd 27406
Wilcox Dr 27405
Wild Cherry Ct 27410
Wild Duck Cir 27407
Wild Iris Way 27410
Wild Lark Ct 27455
Wild Oak Ln 27406
Wild Partridge Ct 27455
Wild Poplar Way 27405
Wild Wolf Dr 27406
Wildberry Ct & Dr 27409
Wilder Ct 27409
Wildflower Dr 27410
Wildmere Ct 27407
Wildrose Ct & Dr 27410
Wildwood Dr 27407
Wiley St 27406
Wiley Davis Rd 27407
Wiley Lewis Rd 27406
Wiley Park Dr 27407
Wilhoit Ct 27410
Will Doskey Ct & Dr 27410
Willard St 27405
Willett Way 27408
Williams St 27403
Williams Dairy Rd 27406
Williamsburg Rd 27410
Willie Ellis Ct 27406
Willimantic Dr 27455
Willomore St
1500-1699 27403
1800-1899 27406
Willora St 27406
Willoughby Blvd 27408
Willow Rd
900-1899 27401
1900-2399 27406
Willow Bend Rd 27406
Willow Glen Trl 27455
Willow Grove Ct 27410
Willow Hope St 27401
Willow Oak Ct & Dr 27408
Willow Rock Ln 27410
Willow Spring Ct 27410
Willow View Dr 27455
Willow Wick Dr 27408
Willow Wind Dr 27406
Willowbrook Dr 27403
Willowlake Rd 27405
Willowside Cir 27401
N Wilpar Dr & Ter 27406
Wilshire Dr 27408
Wilson St 27401
Wilsonwood Rd 27405
Wilton Dr 27408
Wimberly Dr 27410
Wimbledon Ln 27455
Wimbril Dr 27455
Winberry Dr 27407
Winborne Ln 27410
Winburn Dr 27410
Winchester Ct & Dr 27406
Wind Rd 27405
Wind Hill Ct 27405
Windale Ct 27406
Windcrush Ct 27455
Windermere Dr 27407
Windhurst Ct 27410
Winding Ridge Ct & Dr 27406
Windlestraw Ln 27410
Windrift Dr 27410
Windrock Way 27455
Windsong Rd 27406
Windsor St 27401
Windsor Castle Ct 27408
Windsor Creek Way 27455
Windy Hill Dr 27410
Windy Oaks Ct 27410
Winford Rd 27407
Winfree Boren Rd 27410
Wingate St 27408
Winged Foot Rd 27410
Wingrave Ter 27410
Winlock Ter 27407
Winnington Ct 27410
Winola Ct 27409
Winona Rd 27406
Winstead Pl 27408
Winston St
100-499 27401
700-1099 27405
Winter Pl 27407
Winterberry Ct 27455
Winterberry Ridge Ct 27407
Wintergarden Ln 27407
Winterlochen Dr 27410
Winters Way 27410
Winterset Dr 27406
Winterton Ct 27455
Winthrop Dr 27407
Winview Dr 27410
Wireless Dr 27455
Wolf Pack Way 27406
Wolf Run Dr 27406
Wolfe Rd 27405
Wolfetrail Rd 27406
Wolverine Ct 27406
Wonder Dr 27409
Wonderwood Cir 27407
Wood Ln 27410
Wood Leaf Dr 27407
Woodbark Ln 27406
Woodberry Dr 27403
Woodberry Forest Rd 27406
Woodberry Lake Dr 27455
Woodbine Ct 27403
Woodbluff Dr 27406
Woodbourne Rd 27410
Woodbriar Ave 27405
Woodbrook Dr 27410
Woodburn Dr 27406
Woodcliff Dr 27410
Woodclub Ct 27406
Woodcock Dr 27406
Woodcote Dr 27410
Woodcreek Ct & Dr 27406
Woodcrest St 27406
Woodcroft Cir 27407
Wooddale Ln 27405
Woodedge Dr 27406
Woodfield Rd 27409
Woodgreen Dr 27405
Woodhaven Rd 27406
Woodhill Ln 27406
Woodhue Dr 27406
Wooding Pl 27407
Woodlake Ct & Dr 27406
Woodland Dr 27408
Woodlark Ln 27406
Woodlawn Ave 27401
Woodlea Dr 27406
Woodlea Hollow Ln 27406
Woodlea Ridge Ct 27406
Woodlea Valley Cv 27406
Woodleaf Ct & Dr 27406
E & W Woodlyn Way 27407
Woodmark Dr 27407
Woodmeadow Rd 27455
Woodmere Dr 27405
Woodnell St 27405
Woodpine Dr 27455
Woodridge Ave 27405
Woods End Ln 27410
Woodsage Dr 27410
Woodsfield Dr 27406
Woodside Dr 27405
Woodsouth Ct 27406
Woodstock Ct 27408
Woodstone Ct 27410
Woodstream Ln 27410
Woodthorne Pl 27407
Woodvale Dr 27410
Woodview Dr 27408
Woodwind Dr 27406
Woody Ln 27406
Woody Mill Rd 27406
Worchester Ct 27406
Wordsworth Ct 27455
Worldwide Dr 27410
Worsham Pl 27408
Worthdale Ct 27408
Worthing Ct 27455
Worthing Chase Dr 27455
Worthington Pl 27410
Wrenn St 27408
Wrenwood Ct & Dr 27455
Wright Ave 27403
Wright Yow Ln 27406
Wroxton Rd 27406
Wyn Dan Ct & Ln 27406
Wyndmoor Ter 27407
Wynnewood Ct & Dr 27408
Wynterhall Way 27405
Wythe St 27401
Yalta Dr 27410
Yanceyville St
500-1586 27405
1585-1585 27415
1587-4099 27405
1588-4098 27405
Yarborough Dr 27405
Yardarm Ct 27455
Yarmouth Dr 27407
Yeardleys Ct 27455
Yellowbell Pl 27410
Yeoman Ln 27409
Yester Oaks Cir, Ct & Way E & W 27455
York St 27401
York House Dr 27407
York Rite Ct 27407
Yorkshire Dr 27406
Yorkwood Dr 27407
Youngs Mill Rd
1200-1399 27405
1400-1999 27406
Youngstown Dr 27405
Younts Ln 27406
Yow Rd 27407
Yunoka Ln 27405
Ywca Pl 27401
Zola Dr 27405
Zornbrook Dr 27406

NUMBERED STREETS

3rd St 27405
4th St 27405
5th Ave 27405
9th St 27405
10th St 27405
11th St 27405
12th St 27405
14th St 27405
16th Ct & St 27405
17th St 27405
18th St 27405
19th St 27405
20th St 27405
S 40 Dr 27407

GREENVILLE NC

General Delivery 27834

POST OFFICE BOXES MAIN OFFICE STATIONS AND BRANCHES

Box No.s
A - H 27835
1 - 1992 27835
2001 - 4550 27836
5001 - 8716 27835
9998 - 9998 27833
9998 - 9998 27835
9998 - 9998 27836
12001 - 12011 27835
20121 - 20774 27858
30001 - 31240 27833

RURAL ROUTES

01, 04, 05, 06, 08, 10, 11, 14, 15, 17, 21, 24 27834
02, 03, 07, 09, 12, 13, 16, 19, 20, 25 27858

NAMED STREETS

Aaron Cir 27834
Abbey Ln 27834
Abbotts Ln 27858
Abby Dr 27834
Abby Lynn Dr 27858
Abee Rd 27834
Abel St 27834
Abercroft Ct 27858
Abington Ct 27858
Academy Dr 27834
NW & W Acres Dr & Ln 27834
NW Acres Trailer Park 27834
Adams Blvd 27858
Airlee Dr 27858
Airport Rd 27834
Airport Village Park 27834
Albemarle Ave 27834
Alder Cir 27858
Aldersgate Ct 27858
Alexander Cir 27858
Alice Dr 27834
Allegheny Rd 27834
Allegro Ct 27858
Allen Rd 27834
Allen Ridge Dr 27834
Allendale Dr 27834
S Alley St 27834
Allison Rd 27834
Allpine Taylor Rd 27834
Alton Loop 27834
Alton Village Dr 27858
Altons Trl 27834
Alvah Dr 27858
Amanda Ct 27834
Amber Ln 27834
Amos Haddock Rd 27858
Amy Cir 27858
Anderson Rd 27834
Anderson St 27858
Anderson Creek Dr 27858
Angels End 27858
Ann Ln 27834
Antler Rd 27834
Applejack Dr 27858
April Ln 27834
Aqua Ln 27834
Arbor Dr 27858
Arbor St 27834
Archers Way 27858
E Arlington Blvd 27858
W Arlington Blvd 27834
Arlington Cir 27834
Arlington Park Dr 27858
Armstrong Ct 27858
Arrendal Cir 27858
Arrowhead Dr 27858
Arthur St 27834
Asbury Rd 27858
N & S Ash St 27858
Ashburton Dr 27858
Ashland Dr & Park 27834
Ashley Dr 27834
Ashley Pl 27858
Ashley Way 27858
Ashley Jones Ln 27834
Ashley Wilkes Ct 27834
Ashton Dr 27834
Aspen Ln 27834
Atkinson Dr & Ln 27834
Atlantic Ave 27834
Augusta Ln 27858
Aurora Dr 27858
Austin Ln 27834
Austin Pl 27858
Autumn Dr 27834
Autumn Blaze Ct 27858
Autumn Chase Ct 27858
Avalon Ln 27858
Avery St 27858
Avon Ln & Rd 27858
Aycock Hall 27858
Azalea Dr 27858
Azalea Gdns 27858
Azalea St 27858
Aztec Ln 27834
B B Ln 27834
B Stokes Rd 27858
Bach Cir 27858
Badger Cir & Ln 27834
Baker St 27858
Ballards Crossroads Rd 27834
Banbury Cir 27858
Bancroft Ave 27834
Baptist St 27834
Barn Ln 27834
Barnes St 27858
Barnhill Ln 27834
Barnies Ln 27834
Barr Ct 27834
Barrier Ln 27834
Barrington Dr 27834
Barrus Construction Rd 27834
Bass Ln 27834
Battle Dr & St 27834

Batts Ct 27834
Baugh Ct 27834
Bayhill Ct 27858
Bayley Ln 27858
Baytree Dr 27858
E & S Baywood Ln 27834
Beachwood Dr 27834
Bear Ln 27858
Beargrass Rd 27834
Beasley Dr 27834
Beatty St 27834
Beaumont Cir & Dr 27858
Beauvoir Ct 27834
Beaver Beach Ln 27834
Beaver Creek Rd 27834
Beaver Lodge Dr 27834
Beddard Rd 27858
Beech St 27858
Belaire Cir 27858
Belk Hall 27858
Bell Arthur Rd 27834
Bell Arthur Crossing Rd 27834
Bellamy Cir 27858
Belle Gray Pl 27834
Bells St 27858
Bells Chapel Rd 27858
Bells Fork Rd & Sq 27858
Belmont Dr 27858
Belvedere Dr 27834
W Belvoir Hwy & Rd 27834
Belvoir School Rd 27834
E Bend Est 27858
Bending Tree Ln 27858
Benin Ct 27858
Benjaman Dr 27834
Bent Creek Dr 27834
E & W Berkley Rd 27858
E & W Berkshire Rd 27858
Bernice Ln 27834
Bert Ct 27834
Bertha Ln 27834
Berwick Ct 27834
Bess Farm Rd 27858
Bessemer Dr 27858
Best Rd 27834
Beth St 27858
Bethesda Dr 27834
Betsy Ross Rd 27834
Betty Ln 27858
Beunavista Ct 27834
Bexhill Ct 27858
Big Ben Dr 27858
Billy Loop 27834
Biltmore St 27858
Birchwood Dr 27834
Birchwood Sands Mobile Est 27834
Birdneck Cir 27858
Birkdale Cir 27834
Bismarck St 27834
Black Jack Grimesland Rd 27858
Black Jack Simpson Rd 27858
Blacksmith Ln 27834
Blarney St 27834
Bloomsbury Rd 27858
Blount St 27834
Blue Banks Farm Rd 27834
Blue Beech Dr 27858
Blue Heron Dr 27834
Blue Jay Ln 27858
Bluebeech Ln 27834
Bluebill Dr 27858
Bluebird Ln 27858
Bluewillow Way 27834
Bluff View Ct & Dr 27834
Boardwalk Ln 27834
Bobbie Ln 27858
Bobwhite Ct 27858
Bonners Ln 27834
Boone Ct 27834
Boss Ln 27834
Bostic Dr 27834
Bowman Gray Dr 27834
Boxelder Way 27858
Boxwood Ln
1400-1499 27858
3800-3899 27834
Boyd Park Dr 27858
Bradbury Dr 27858
Bradford Dr 27858
Bradley St 27834
Bradshaw Ln 27858
Bragg Cir 27834
Bramblewood Dr 27858
Branch Ridge Dr 27834
Brandenburg St 27834
Brandy Ln 27858
Brandy Creek Dr 27858
Brandywine Cir 27858
Breezewood Dr 27858
Bremerton Dr 27858
Brenbrook Ln 27834
Briarcliff Dr 27834
Briarwood Dr 27834
Brick Kiln Rd 27858
Brickyard Ct 27858
Bridle Cir 27834
Brighton Park Dr 27834
Briley Rd 27834
Brimley Dr 27834
Brinkley Rd 27858
Bristol Ct 27834
Britannia Dr 27834
British Ct 27834
Britlyn Ln 27858
Britt Rd 27858
Brittany Rd 27858
Broad St 27834
Brompton Ct 27858
Brompton Ln 27858
Bronty Rd 27834
Brook Rd 27858
Brook Creek Ln 27858
Brook Hollow Dr 27834
Brookhaven Dr 27834
Brookline Ct 27834
Brookridge Cir 27834
Brooks Mills Ln 27858
Brookside Dr 27858
Brookview Pl 27858
Brookville Dr 27834
Brookwood Dr 27858
Brown Place Dr 27834
Brownlea Dr 27858
Brownstone Ct 27858
Bruce Strickland Rd 27834
Brunswick Ln 27858
Bruton Cir 27858
Bryan Cir 27858
Bryant Cir 27858
Bryson Dr 27858
Bs Barbecue Rd 27834
S Bubba Blvd 27834
Buck Ln 27834
Buck Trailer Park 27834
Bud Parker Rd 27834
Bullock Ln 27834
Bunch Ln 27834
Bundy Rd 27834
Burford St 27834
Burnette Rd 27858
Burrington Rd 27858
Burruss Pl 27858
Butts Ln 27858
Buxton Rd 27858
C And R Ln 27834
Caddie Ct 27858
Cadenza Ct & St 27858
Cadillac St 27834
Cady Dr 27834
Caldwell Ct 27834
Caleb St 27834
Calvary Dr 27834
Calvin Way 27834
Cambria Dr 27834
Cambridge Dr & Rd 27834
Camden Ct 27834
Camellia Ln 27858
Camilla Dr 27834
Campden Way 27858
Cancion St 27858
Candlewick Dr 27834
Candlewood Dr 27834
Cannon Ln 27834
Cantata Dr 27858
Canterbury Ct & Rd 27858
Cape Point Ln 27858
Cardinal Dr 27858
Caribou Cir 27834
Carlisle Ct 27858
Carlos Dr 27834
Carlson St 27834
Carlton Dr 27858
Carmon Cir 27834
Carnoustie Dr 27858
Carol Ct 27858
Carolina Ave 27834
Carolina East Ctr & Mall 27834
Carolina Leaf Rd 27834
Carolyn St 27858
Carrico Ln 27834
Casey Brooke Ct 27858
Cash Ln 27834
Castillo Ct 27834
Castle Dr 27834
Castlewood Dr 27834
Casual Cir 27858
Catalpa Rd 27858
E Catawba Rd 27834
Cattail Ct 27858
Cattail Ln 27858
Ce Senior Ln 27834
Cedar Ct 27858
Cedar Dr 27834
Cedar Ln 27858
Cedar St 27858
Cedar Creek Rd 27834
Cedarhurst Rd 27834
Celtic Ct 27858
Cemetery Rd 27858
Center St 27834
Century Dr 27834
Chadwick Ln 27834
Chance St 27834
Chandler Dr 27834
Chaney Dr 27858
Chaplain St 27834
Chappell Ct 27834
Charity Ln 27858
Charles Blvd & St 27858
Charles Buck Dr 27834
Charleston Ct 27834
Charlestowne Dr 27834
Charlies Ln 27834
Charlton Pl 27858
Charter Dr 27834
Chatham Way 27834
Chaucer Ln 27834
Chauncey Ln 27834
Chavis Ct & Dr 27858
Cheltenham Dr 27834
Cherokee Dr 27834
Cherry Ct 27858
Cherry St 27858
Cherry Run Rd 27834
Cherry Stone Ln 27834
Cherrywood Dr 27858
Cheryl Cir 27858
Chesapeake Pl 27858
Cheshire Dr 27858
Chesterfield Ct 27834
Chestnut St 27858
Chestnut Ridge Ct 27834
Cheyenne Ct 27858
Childs Way 27834
Chilwel Ct 27834
Chipaway Dr 27834
Chippendail Dr 27858
Chowan Rd 27858
Christenbury Dr 27858
Christie Cir 27858
Christina Dr 27858
Christopher Dr 27858
Church St 27834
Churchill Dr 27858
Churchside Dr 27858
Cindas Ln 27834
Circle Dr 27858
Circle M Ln 27834
Clairmont Cir 27834
Claredon Dr 27858
Claret Way 27858
Clark Dr & St 27834
Clark Farm Rd 27834
Clarks Farm Rd 27858
Clarks Mobile Home Park 27834
Claybourne Ct 27834
Clearview Ln 27834
Clearwater Dr 27834
Cleere Ct 27858
Clement Hall 27858
Clifton St 27858
Clover Ct 27858
Clover St 27834
Club Pines Dr 27834
Clubway Dr 27834
Cobblestone Dr 27834
Cody Ln 27834
Coghill Ln 27834
Coit Tower Ct 27834
Coleman Dr 27858
Colindale Ct 27858
College Court Dr 27858
College View Dr 27858
Collins St 27858
Colonial Ave 27834
Colonial Mobile Home Park 27834
Colony Ct 27834
Colony Woods Dr 27834
Columbia Ave 27834
Commerce St 27858
Compton Rd 27858
Concho Cir 27834
Concord Dr 27834
Conetoe Rd 27834
Conference Dr 27858
W Conley St 27834
Connie St 27834
Contentnea St 27834
Cool Acres Ln 27834
Cool Acres Trl Park 27834
Cooper Ln 27834
Cooper River Ct 27858
Copper Beech Way 27858
Copperfield Rd 27834
Coral Ln 27858
E & W Corbett Ave & St 27834
Cornelius Ln 27834
Cornwall Ct 27834
Corporate Dr 27858
Cortland Rd 27834
Cotanche St 27858
Cotten Rd 27858
Cotten Hall 27858
Cottondale Rd 27834
Coughlin Ct 27834
Council Ln 27834
Council Trailer Park 27834
Countess Rd 27834
Country Est 27858
Country Mnr 27834
Country Club Dr 27834
Country Paradise Est 27834
Countrydown Dr 27834
Countryside Dr 27834
Countrywood Ln 27858
County Home Rd 27858
Couples Ct 27834
Courtier Dr 27834
Courtney Pl 27834
Courtney Square Apts 27858
Covenant Ln 27858
Covengton Way 27858
Coventry Ct 27858
Covey Ln 27834
Coward Ln 27834
Cox St 27834
Coy Forbes Rd 27834
Cozy Ln 27834
Craftsman Ln 27834
Craig St 27834
Crawfords Pointe Dr 27834
Credle Ct 27858
N Creek Dr 27834
Creekside Dr 27858
Crepe Myrtle Ln 27858
Crest Cir 27858
Crestline Blvd & Pl 27834
Crestway Pl 27858
Crestwood Dr 27858
Cricket Dr 27834
Criswell Dr 27834
Crockett Dr 27858
Cromwell Dr 27858
Crooked Creek Rd 27858
Cross St 27834
Cross Creek Cir 27858
Cross Winds St 27834
Crown Point Rd 27858
Croyden Cir 27834
Crudie Ln 27834
Cumberland Pl 27858
Cutler Ct 27834
Cypress View Dr 27858
D And N Edwards Ests 27834
Dail Farm Ln 27834
Dails Ln 27834
Dalebrook Cir 27858
Dallas St 27834
Danielle Dr 27834
Dansey Rd 27834
Darcole Ln 27834
Darden Dr 27834
Darrell Dr 27834
Dartmouth Dr 27858
Darwin Ct 27858
Daughtridge Dr 27834
Davenport St 27834
Davenport Farm Rd 27834
Davenport Store Rd 27834
Daventry Dr 27858
Daves Ln 27858
David Dr 27858
Davids Dr 27858
Davidson Dr 27834
Davis St 27834
Dawson St 27834
Daystar Mobile Home Park 27858
Deal Pl 27858
Deans Mdws 27834
Deborah Ct 27834
Debra Ct 27834
Debsan Cir 27834
Deck St 27834
Decorah Ct 27834
Deejay Ln 27834
Deep Run Rd 27834
Deer Creek Ln 27834
Deer Run Est 27834
Deerfield Rd 27858
Deerwood Dr 27858
Delano Ct 27858
Deliverance Dr 27858
Della Ln 27858
Dellwood Dr 27858
Derbyshire Ln 27858
Derek St 27834
Derwent Ct 27858
Devereux Ln 27834
Deveron St 27834
Dexter St 27834
Diamond Dr & Ln 27834
Diamond Creek Ln 27834
Diane Way 27834
Dickinson Ave
500-599 27858
600-4599 27834
Director Ct 27858
Dixie Ct & Ln 27858
Dobbs Ct 27858
Doctors Park 27834
Dogwood Ct 27858
Dogwood Dr 27834
Donna Ct 27858
Donovan Ln 27834
Dorcus Ter 27858
Doreen Ct 27858
Doris Cir 27858
Dorothy Ln 27834
Dortches Ct 27834
Doublegate Ln 27834
Douglas Ave 27834
Dovedale Ct & Dr 27834
Dover Cir 27834
Downing Rd 27834
Draft Ct 27858
Drewry Ln 27858
Drexel Ln 27858
Driftwood Dr 27858
Drum Ave 27834
Duce Dr 27834
E & W Dudley St 27834
Dundee Ln 27858
Dunhagan Rd 27858
Dunhaven Dr 27834
Dunn St 27834
Dupont Cir 27858
Duran St 27858
Durant Rd 27834
Durwood Pollard Rd 27834
Dusk Ct 27834
Dusty Ln 27834
Dynamite Dr 27834
Eagle Ct 27858
Eagle Landing Ln 27834
Eagle Ridge Dr 27834
Eaglechase Ln 27858
Earl Cir 27858
Earl Rd 27834
Eastbend Dr 27858
Eastbrook Dr 27858
Eastbrook Apartments 27858
N & S Eastern St 27858
Eastern Pines Rd 27834
Eastgate Dr 27858
Eastman Rd 27858
Eastpoint Dr 27858
Eastridge Ct 27834
Eastview Dr 27858
Eastwood Country Est 27834
Easy St 27834
Eckerts Ln 27834
Eddie Ln 27834
Eden Pl 27858
Edgebrook Dr 27858
Edgewood Cir 27858
Edgewood Mobile Home Park 27834
Edna Ln 27834
Edward Ln 27834
Edwards Ct 27858
Edwards Ln 27834
Edwards Rd 27858
Edwards St 27858
Edwards Farm Rd 27858
Egan Ct 27834
Elaina Dr 27834
Eleanor St 27858
Elender Dr 27834
Elias Ln 27834
Elite Pl 27834
Elizabeth St 27834
Elk Horn Ct 27858
Elkin Ridge Dr 27834
Elks Rd 27858
Elks St 27834
Ellery Dr 27834
Ellison Ct 27858
Ellsworth Dr 27858
Ellwood Dr 27834
N & S Elm St 27858
Embarcadero Ave 27834
Emerald Pl 27834
Emergency Access Rd 27834
Emerson Rd 27858
Emmas Pl 27834
W End Trailer Park 27834
Englewood Dr 27858
English Ct 27834
English Gardens Dr 27858
English Oak Ct 27858
Eric Ct 27858
Erith Ct 27858
Ernul St 27858
Ervin Buck Rd 27858
Essex St 27834
Esther Cir 27834
Ethel Ln 27834
Evans St
100-559 27858
560-4099 27834
S Evans Apartments 27834
Evanswood Dr 27858
Everett Ln 27858
Evergreen Dr 27858
Excaliber Dr 27858
Exchange Dr 27858
Executive Cir 27834
Fair Oaks Ct 27834
Fairbanks Ct 27834
Fairfax Ave 27834
Fairlane Rd 27834
Fairmont Ave 27834
Fairview Est 27834
Fairview Way 27858
Fairway Dr 27858
Fairwood Ln 27834
Faith Dr 27858
Falcon Cir 27834
Falling Creek Dr 27834
Family Ln 27834
Fannie Rd 27834
Fantasia St 27858
Farm Dr 27834
Farmers St 27834
Farmhouse Pl 27834
Farmingwood Rd 27858
Farmville Blvd 27834
Fault Cir 27858
Fayes Ct & Ln 27858
Fenner Dr 27834
Fern Dr 27858
Fernleaf Dr 27858
Fernwood Ln 27834
Fescue Dr 27834
Ficklen St 27834
Field St 27834
Fieldside St 27858
Fieldstone Pl 27858
E Fillmore Ct 27834
E Fire Tower Rd 27858
Fireside Rd 27834
Fishermans Wharf Rd 27834
Fishpond Rd 27834
Flagstaff Ct 27858
Flagstone Ct 27834
Fleming St 27834
Fleming Hall 27858
Flemming School Rd 27834
Fletcher Pl 27858
Fletcher Hall 27858
Flint Ridge Rd 27834
Flow St 27834
Flower St 27834
Floyd Harris Rd 27834
Flutter Ln 27834
Flynn Ln 27834
Fontana Ct 27834
Forbes St 27858
Forbes Trailer Park 27834
Ford St 27834
Forest Acres Dr 27834
Forest Glen Dr 27858
Forest Hill Cir & Dr 27858
W Fork Ln 27834
Forrest Park 27858
Fort Fisher Rd 27858
Fort Sumter Dr 27858
Fosbury Way 27834
Foster Rd 27858
Fox Den Way 27858
Fox Haven Dr 27858
Fox Hunt Ln 27834

Fox Pen Rd 27858
Fox Run Cir 27858
Fox Trot Ln 27858
Foxberry Cir 27858
Foxwood Ln 27858
Francis Asbury Ln 27858
Frank House Tr Park 27834
Frankie Coburn Rd 27834
Franklin Dr 27858
Fred Dr 27834
Freestone Rd 27834
French Ct 27834
Friendly Ln 27834
Frog Level Rd 27834
Frontgate Dr 27834
Fur Ct 27834
Galahad Dr 27858
Galleria Dr 27834
Garden Cir 27858
Garden Ter 27834
Garden Grove Way 27858
Gardenia St 27834
Garland St 27834
Garner Rd 27834
Garrett Hall 27858
Garris Rd 27834
Gateway Blvd 27858
Gawain Rd 27858
Geneva Ct 27834
Genoa Ct 27858
Gentle Breeze Dr 27834
Gifford Pl 27858
Gilman Ct 27858
Glasgow Ln 27858
Glen Abbey Dr 27858
Glen Arthur Ave 27858
Glen Dale Dr 27834
Glenda St 27834
Glenn Ct 27858
Glenview Dr 27834
Glenwood Dr 27834
Gloria St 27858
Golden Rd 27858
Goldfinch Ln 27858
Golf Club Wynd 27834
Golf View Dr 27834
Gooden Pl 27834
Gordon Dr 27834
Gosford Gate 27858
Government Cir 27834
Governors Ln 27858
Grace Ave 27834
Grace St
 1300-1399 27858
 1700-1799 27834
Gracewood Dr 27834
Graham St 27858
Grande Ave 27834
Grandin Ln 27834
Granite Ct 27834
Granville Dr 27858
Graves St 27834
Gray Wood Ln 27858
Graystone Pl 27834
Great Laurel Ct 27834
Green Haven Ln 27834
Green Leaf St 27834
Green Springs Dr 27858
Greenbriar Dr 27834
N & S Greene St 27834
Greene Hall 27858
Greenfield Blvd 27834
Greenmeade Ct 27858
Greenridge Apartments 27834
Greenview Dr 27834
Greenville Blvd 27834
Greenville Blvd NE
 2200-2399 27858
 3500-3699 27834
Greenville Blvd SE
 100-2199 27858
Greenville Blvd SW
 800-2099 27834
SE Greenville Blvd
 800-1099 27858

SW Greenville Blvd
 100-699 27834
Greenville Mobile Ests 27858
Greenway St 27834
Greenway Apts 27834
Greenwood Dr 27834
Gretna Dr 27834
Grey Fox Trl 27858
Griffin St 27834
Grove Ave 27834
Groveland Dr 27858
Grovemont Dr 27834
Grover Hardee Rd 27858
Guilder Ln 27858
Guinevere Ln 27858
E & W Gum Rd 27834
Gum Swamp Church Rd 27834
Gunston Ct 27834
Haight Ct 27834
Halifax St 27834
S Hall Cir 27834
Hall Ln 27858
Ham Ln 27834
Hamilton St 27834
Hampton Cir 27858
Hams Woods Ln 27858
Hannah Cir 27834
Hanover Ct 27834
Hardaway Pl 27858
Hardee Cir, Rd & St 27858
Hardees Ln 27858
N & S Harding St 27858
Hardwick Ct 27834
Hardy Rd 27834
Harell St 27858
Harley Ln 27834
Harmony St 27834
Harness Ct 27858
Harrahs Dr 27858
Harrelson Dr 27834
Harris St 27834
Harrow Cir 27834
Hartford St 27834
Harvest Mnr 27858
Harvey Dr 27858
Harvey Ln 27858
Hastings Ct 27858
N Haven Dr & Ln 27834
Haw Dr 27834
Hawick Pl 27858
Hawkins Ln 27858
Hawthorne Rd 27858
Hayley Ct 27834
Health Dr 27834
Heart Dr 27858
Hearthside Dr 27834
Heath St 27858
Heather Ln 27834
Heber Hudson Rd 27858
Hemby Ln & Rd 27858
Hemlock Dr 27858
Hendrix St 27834
Henry St 27834
Herbert Ct 27834
Heritage St 27858
Herman Garris Rd 27858
Heron Ln 27858
Hickory St 27858
Hidcote Ct 27834
Hidden Hills Dr 27858
Hidden Laurel Ct 27834
Higgs St 27834
High Place Ct 27858
High Ridge Farm Ln 27858
Highland Ave 27858
Hillard Ln 27858
Hillcrest Dr 27834
Hillendale Cir 27858
W Hills Dr 27834
W Hills Apartments 27834
Hillsdale St 27834
Hillside Dr 27858
Hilltop Rd & St 27858
Hodges Ln 27858
Holbert St 27834

Holden Dr 27858
Holland Rd 27834
Holliday Ct 27834
Holloman St 27834
Hollow Dr 27858
N Holly St
 100-199 27858
 800-1299 27834
S Holly St 27858
Holly Branch Rd 27858
Holly Glen Dr 27834
Holly Hills Rd 27858
Hollybriar Ln & Pl 27858
Hollywood Dr 27858
Holman Dr 27858
Home St 27834
Homestead Dr 27834
Honeysuckle Ct 27834
Honor Cir 27858
Hooker Rd 27834
Hoots Rd 27858
Hoover St 27858
Hop Tyson Rd 27834
Hope Dr 27858
Hopkins Dr 27834
Horseshoe Dr 27834
Howard Cir 27834
Howell St 27834
Hubert Boyd Rd 27858
Hudson St 27834
Hudsons Crossroads Rd 27858
Hummingbird Ln 27858
Hungate Dr 27858
Hunt Club Ln 27834
Hunterchase Ln 27858
Hunters Ln 27834
Hunters Run 27858
Huntingridge Rd 27834
Huntington Rd 27858
Huntingwood Dr 27858
Huntley Dr 27858
Hyde Dr 27858
Ida And Mary Mclawhorn Rd 27858
Idle Fox Ln 27834
Idlewild Dr 27834
Imperial St 27834
Independence Blvd 27834
Indian Wells Pl 27858
Indus Trailer Park 27834
Industrial Blvd 27834
Inez Ln 27858
Ione St 27834
Iris Cir 27858
Iron Gate Ct 27834
Ironwood Dr 27834
Irvin Ln 27834
Ivan Harris Rd 27858
Ivy Cir 27834
Ivy Rd 27858
J C Galloway Rd 27858
Jackie Field Rd 27834
Jackrabbit Run 27834
Jacks Cir 27834
Jackson Ave 27834
Jackson Dr 27858
Jake Ln 27858
James St 27858
Jamestown Rd 27858
Jane Dr 27858
Jared Ct 27858
N & S Jarvis St 27858
Jarvis Hall 27858
Jasper Rd 27834
Jasper Lee Ct 27834
Jay Cir 27858
Jaybird St 27834
Jays Trailer Park 27834
Jean Ct 27834
Jeanette Ct 27858
Jefferson Dr 27858
Jenkins St 27858
Jennifer Pl 27834
Jesse Ln 27834
Jethro Mills Rd 27858

Joe Stocks Rd 27858
Joe Teel Rd 27834
Joel Dr 27834
Joes Ln 27834
Joes Walk Ln 27834
John Ave 27858
John Brown Ct 27834
John Cox Ln 27834
John Harris Ln 27858
John Wesley Rd 27858
Johnny Haddock Rd 27858
Johns Hopkins Dr 27834
Johnson Rd 27834
Johnsons Mill Dr 27834
Johnston St 27858
Jonathan Pl 27834
Jones St 27834
Jones Hall 27858
Jones Park Rd 27834
Jones Staton Rd 27834
Jordan Dr 27858
Joseph Pl & St 27858
Josh Ct 27834
Joshua Ct 27834
Josie Ln 27834
Joyce Dr 27858
Julia Ln 27834
Julie Cir 27858
Juniper Ln 27858
K And K Dr 27858
Kaley Ct 27858
Kanine Rd 27834
Kara Ct 27858
Kariblue Ln 27834
Karl Hardee Rd 27858
Katherines Pl 27858
Kathleen Dr 27858
Kathryn Ln 27834
Katie Ln 27834
Kay Rd 27858
Keith Dr 27834
Kelham Ct 27858
Kempton Dr 27834
Ken Ln 27858
Kendall Ct 27834
Kenilworth Rd 27834
Kennedy Cir 27834
Kensington Dr 27858
Kent Dr & Rd 27858
Kenwood Ln 27834
Keys Ct 27858
Kiesee Dr 27834
Kilby Dr 27858
Kimberly Dr 27858
Kineton Cir 27834
King Dr 27834
King Arthur Rd 27858
King George Rd 27858
King Lear Ct 27858
King Richard Ct 27858
Kings Rd
 201-299 27834
 600-699 27858
 1400-1499 27834
Kings Branch Dr 27834
Kings Crossroads Rd 27834
Kingsbrook Rd 27834
Kingston Cir 27858
Kinsaul Willoughby Rd 27834
Kipling Ct 27834
Kirkland Dr 27858
Kittrell Cir 27834
Kittrell Rd 27834
Kittrell Farms Dr 27858
Knights Ct 27858
Knoll Cir 27858
Knollwood Dr 27858
Knoreld Rd 27858
Kristin Dr 27834
L T Hardee Rd 27858
Ladybug Ln 27834
Lake Rd 27834
Lakeside Pl 27834
Lakeview Dr 27858
Lakeview Ter 27834
Lakewood Dr 27834

Lambeth Cir 27858
Lamont Rd 27858
Lancaster Dr 27834
Lance Dr 27858
Lancelot Dr 27858
Landfill Rd 27834
Landmark St 27834
Largo Rd 27858
Larkin Ln 27834
Larkspur Ln 27834
Larry Ln 27858
Latham St 27858
Laughinghouse Dr 27834
Laura Ln 27858
Lauray Dr 27834
Laurel St 27858
Laver Ln 27858
Lawrence St 27858
Leanne Dr 27858
Lee Ct 27834
Lee Dr 27858
Lee St 27858
Legion St 27834
Leighton Dr 27834
Lemon Rd 27834
Len Dr 27834
Lena Ln 27858
Lenair St 27834
Lennie Ln 27834
Lennon St 27858
Leon Dr 27858
Leon Hardee Rd 27858
Lester Mills Rd 27858
Lewis Rd 27834
Lewis St 27858
Lewis Dudley Rd 27834
Lexington Dr 27834
Lexington Downs Dr 27858
Lexington Farms Ct 27858
Liberty Dr 27858
N & S Library Dr & St 27858
Lighthouse Ln 27858
Lillian Ln 27834
Lillies Dream Ln 27834
Limber Pine Dr 27834
Lincoln Dr 27834
Linda Ln 27834
Lindbeth Dr 27834
Lindell Rd 27834
Lindenwood Dr 27834
Lindsay Dr 27858
Line Ave 27858
Lis Ln 27834
Lisa Ln 27858
Live Oak Ln 27858
Loblolly Cir 27858
Loblolly Pine Dr 27858
Lochview Dr 27858
Locksley Woods Dr 27858
Locust Dr 27858
Logan Ln 27834
Lois Ln 27858
Lombard Ave 27834
Lonesome Pine Ln 27858
Long Dr 27858
Long Branch Dr 27834
Longleaf Dr 27834
Longleaf Ln 27858
Longleaf Pine Dr 27834
E Longmeadow Rd 27858
Longview Dr 27858
Longwood Dr 27858
Loran Cir 27858
Lord Ashley Dr 27858
Lori Dr 27858
Los Alamitos Ln 27834
Loudon Ct 27834
Louis St 27858
Luci Dr 27858
Lum Buck Rd 27858
Lumber Rd 27834
Lyme Ct 27834
Lynn Ln 27858
Lynndale Ct 27858
Mabery Ln 27834
Macgregor Downs Rd 27858

Mackay Rd 27834
Macs Ln 27834
Madison Cir 27858
Madison Grove Rd 27858
Maggie Ln 27834
Magnolia Creek Dr 27834
Mahogany Dr 27834
Majenta Dr 27834
Major Ln 27858
Major Smith Rd 27858
Mall Dr 27834
Mallard Rd 27858
Malone Ct 27834
Manchester Dr & St 27834
Mandy Dr 27834
Manhattan Ave 27834
Mann Farm Ln 27858
Manning Rd 27858
Manning Forest Dr 27834
Mannsfield Cir 27834
Manor Ct 27858
Maple St 27858
Maple Leaf Ln 27834
Maple Ridge Rd 27858
Maplewood Ct 27858
Maraschino Dr 27858
Marble Ct 27858
Mares Way 27858
Margaret Ct 27858
Marin Way 27834
Marine Dr 27834
Marion Dr 27858
Maritime Pine Ln 27834
Marjorie Ln 27858
Marthas Ln 27834
Martin St 27834
Martin Luther King Jr Dr & Hwy 27834
Martinsborough Rd 27834
Mary Beth Dr 27858
Maryland Dr 27858
Marylebone Cir 27858
Massanutten Rd 27834
Masters Ln 27834
Mattox Rd 27834
Maxwell St 27834
May St 27834
Maye Ln 27834
Mayes Cir 27834
Mayes Apartments 27834
Mayo Ln 27834
Mcarthur Ln 27834
Mcclellan St 27834
Mccoy Rd 27858
Mcdonald Ct & St 27858
Mcdougald Way 27834
Mcdowell St 27834
Mcgregor Ln 27858
Mckinley Ave 27834
Mclawhorn Dr 27834
Mclawhorn Farm Rd 27858
Mcmillan Ln 27834
N & S Meade St 27858
Meadow Ln 27858
Meadowbrook Dr 27834
Meadowglenn Dr 27858
Meadowland Dr 27834
Medical Dr 27834
Medical Oaks Apartment 27834
Medical Pavilion 27834
Meeting Pl 27858
Megan Dr 27858
Melody Ln 27834
Melonie Ct 27834
N Memorial Dr 27858
S Memorial Dr
 100-2799 27834
 2728-2728 27833
 2800-3798 27834
 2801-3799 27834
Mercury Dr 27858
Meridian Dr 27834
Merriewood Ln 27834
Merry Ln 27858
Middlebury Dr 27834

Middleton Pl 27858
Midgette Ln 27858
Midland Ct 27834
Midway Trailer Park 27834
Mill St 27858
Mill Creek Dr 27834
Mill Run Rd 27834
Millbrook Dr 27858
Millbrook St 27834
Mills Rd 27858
Mills St 27834
Mimosa Ln 27834
Minuette Pl 27858
Misty Pines Rd 27858
Mitchell Dr 27834
Mizell St 27834
Monroe St 27858
Montclair Dr 27834
Monument Rd 27834
Moonlight Way 27834
E & W Moore Rd & St 27834
Mooring Ln 27858
Morgan St 27834
Morningside Cir 27858
Morris Cir 27834
Morton Ln 27834
Mosby Cir 27834
Moseley Dr 27858
Moses Dr 27858
Moss Point Ln 27834
Moye Blvd 27834
Moyewood Dr 27834
Mozingo Rd 27834
Ms Paul Ln 27834
Muir Ct 27834
Muirfield Dr 27858
Mulberry Ln 27858
Mumford Rd 27834
My Way 27858
Myrtie Ct 27834
Myrtle St 27834
Nantucket Ct 27834
Naples Dr 27858
Nash St 27834
Nathaniel Dr 27834
Nathans Ln 27834
National Ave 27834
Nc Highway 11 N 27834
Nc Highway 121 27834
Nc Highway 222 27834
Nc Highway 30 27834
Nc Highway 33 E 27858
Nc Highway 33 W 27834
Nc Highway 43 N 27834
Nc Highway 43 S 27858
Nc Highway 903 N 27834
New St 27834
New Hope Rd 27834
Nichols Dr 27858
Nicklaus Dr 27834
Nicole Ct 27834
No Record St 27858
Noah Ct 27834
Norcott Cir 27834
Norris St 27834
North Dr 27834
Northland Dr 27834
Northwoods Dr 27834
Nottingham Rd 27858
N & S Oak St 27858
Oak Bend Dr 27834
Oak Grove Ave 27834
Oak Hill Dr 27858
Oak Hills Dr 27834
Oak Ridge Ct 27834
Oak Square Trailer Park 27834
Oakdale Rd 27834
Oakenshaw St 27858
Oakhurst Cir 27834
Oaklawn Ave 27858
Oakmont Dr 27858
Oaksong Dr 27834
Oaktowne Dr 27858
Oakview Dr 27858
Ofarrell Ave 27834

- Ohagan Pl 27834
- Okie Acres Ln 27834
- Ola Ln 27834
- Old B Ln 27834
- Old Cafeteria Complex 27858
- Old Courthouse Dr 27858
- Old Creek Rd 27834
- Old Fire Tower Rd 27858
- Old Fort Rd 27834
- Old Heritage Pl 27858
- Old Mill Ct 27858
- Old Oak Walk 27858
- Old Pactolus Rd 27834
- Old River Rd 27834
- Old Stantonsburg Rd 27834
- Old Village Rd 27834
- Oldwell Dr 27834
- Ole London Rd 27834
- Olivia Dr 27834
- Ontario Dr 27858
- Opal Ln 27834
- Opera Ct 27858
- Orton Dr 27858
- Osborne Ln 27834
- Osceola Dr 27858
- N Overlook Dr 27858
- Owens St 27834
- Oxbow Ln 27834
- Oxford Ct 27834
- Oxford Rd 27858
- Pacific Cir 27834
- Pacolet Dr 27834
- Pactolus Hwy 27834
- Paddington Dr 27858
- Page Rd 27858
- Paige Dr 27834
- Palace Dr 27834
- Paladin Dr 27834
- Palmer Ct & Dr 27834
- Palmetto Dr 27834
- Palmetto Pl 27858
- Pam Dr 27834
- Pamlico Ave 27834
- Pams Ln 27858
- Papas Pl 27834
- Paramore Dr & Rd 27858
- Parcel St 27834
- Paris Ave 27834
- Park Ave 27834
- Park Dr 27858
- Park West Dr 27834
- Parkside Dr 27834
- Parkway Ct 27834
- Parkwood Ct 27834
- Parmer Pl 27858
- Patrick St 27834
- Patsy Dr 27858
- Patsy Mclawhorn Rd 27834
- Paul Cir 27834
- Paul Jones Ln 27834
- Peace Ridge Ct 27834
- Pearl Dr 27834
- Pecan Ridge Dr 27858
- Peed Dr 27834
- Pendleton St 27834
- Peninsula Pt 27834
- Pennant Dr 27834
- Penncross Dr 27834
- Pennsylvania Ave 27834
- Penny Hill Rd 27834
- Pepper Ln 27834
- Peppertree Townhouses 27834
- Periwinkle Pl 27834
- Perkins Ln, Rd & St 27834
- Petes Ln 27834
- Peyote Ct 27834
- Peyton Cir & Ln 27834
- Pheasant Run 27858
- Phillip Sutton Ln 27834
- Phillippi Dr 27834
- Phillips Cir & Rd 27834
- Pin Oak Ct 27858
- Pine Rd 27858
- Pine St 27834
- Pine Bark Ln 27858
- Pine Brook Ct 27858
- Pine Needle Pl 27858
- Pine Water Ln 27834
- Pinecrest Dr 27858
- Pinecrest Park 27834
- Pinehurst Dr 27834
- Pinelog Ln 27834
- Pinepoint Rd 27834
- Pineridge Dr
  - 100-200 27858
  - 202-204 27858
  - 1400-1499 27834
- Pines Crossing Way 27858
- Pinetree Ln 27858
- Pineview Dr 27834
- Pinewood Rd 27858
- Pinnacle Pl 27834
- Pinner Ln 27834
- Pintail Ct 27834
- N & S Pitt St 27834
- Pittman Dr 27834
- Placid Way 27834
- Plant St 27834
- Plantation Cir 27858
- Planters Walk 27858
- Plateau Dr 27834
- Plaza Dr 27858
- Pleasant Dr 27834
- Pleasant Acres Mob Hm Park 27834
- Pleasant Place Ln 27858
- Pleasure Mount Ln 27858
- Plymouth Dr 27858
- Poe Cir 27858
- Pointer Pl 27834
- Polk Ave 27858
- W Pollard St 27834
- Ponderosa Ln 27834
- Ponderosa Pine Ln 27834
- Poplar Dr 27834
- Poplar Grove Dr 27858
- Pops Ln 27834
- Port Royal Pl 27858
- Port Terminal Rd 27858
- Porter Pl 27858
- Porter Rd 27834
- Porters Ridge Dr 27858
- Portertown Rd 27858
- Possum Ln 27834
- Poundbury Ct 27858
- Powell St 27834
- Prairiefield Ct 27858
- Praise Way 27858
- Prescott Ln 27858
- Presidio Ln 27834
- Presley Dr 27834
- Preston Pl 27858
- Prestwick Pl 27834
- Price Dr 27834
- Prickle Pine Ln 27834
- Prickly Pear Dr 27834
- Prince Pl & Rd 27834
- Princess Dr 27834
- Professional Dr 27858
- Progress Rd 27834
- Prudoe Bay Dr 27858
- Pumpkin Ln 27834
- Quail Vlg 27834
- Quail Hollow Rd 27858
- Quail Pointe Dr 27858
- Quail Ridge Rd 27858
- Quail Ridge Trailer Park 27834
- Quality Ln 27834
- Quartz Dr 27834
- Queen Dr 27834
- Queen Annes Rd 27858
- Rackley Dr 27834
- Radford Dr 27858
- Radford Ln 27834
- Radio Station Rd 27834
- W Ragsdale Rd 27858
- S Railroad St 27834
- Rainbow St 27834
- Raintree Dr 27858
- Raleigh Ave 27834
- Rams Ct 27834
- Rams Horn Rd 27834
- Ramsey Ct & Dr 27834
- Randolph Ct 27858
- Randomwood Dr 27858
- Ravenwood Dr 27834
- Rawl Rd 27834
- Ray Hardee Cir 27858
- Rayfield Cir 27834
- Raynez Dr 27858
- Reade Cir
  - 100-199 27858
  - 600-699 27834
- Reade St 27858
- Reba Dr 27834
- Rebecca Rd 27858
- Rebecca Dare Ln 27834
- Recycling Ln 27834
- Red Banks Rd 27858
- Red Birch Ln 27858
- Red Bud Cir 27858
- Red Pine Cir 27834
- Redman Ave 27834
- E & W Redmond Ave & Ln 27834
- Redstone Ct 27858
- Regalwood Rd 27858
- Regency Blvd 27834
- Regents Cir 27858
- Reggie Ct 27834
- Reins Ct 27858
- Remington Ct 27834
- Remington Dr 27858
- Rhema St 27858
- Rhett Butler Rd 27858
- Richard Dr 27834
- Richard Lee Dr 27858
- Rick Cir 27834
- Ricky Ln 27834
- Ridge Pl 27834
- Ridge Rd 27858
- Ridgeway St 27834
- Ridgewood Dr 27858
- Riggs Ln 27834
- Ripley Dr 27834
- River Dr 27858
- River Bank Ln 27834
- River Birch Dr 27858
- River Bluff Rd 27858
- River Bluff Apts 27858
- River Branch Dr & Rd 27858
- River Chase Dr 27858
- River Hill Dr 27858
- River Oak Dr 27858
- River Road Estate Rd 27834
- Riverbend Rd 27834
- Rivercrest Dr 27858
- Riverdale Ct 27858
- Riverview Rd 27858
- Riverview Estates Trailer Park 27858
- Rivit St 27834
- Roanoke Pl 27834
- Roberson Dr 27858
- Robert Dr 27834
- Robin Rd 27858
- Robin Hood Rd 27858
- Rock Ln 27834
- Rock Spring Rd 27834
- E Rock Spring Rd 27834
- W Rock Spring Rd 27858
- Rocket Rd 27858
- Rockland Ct & Dr 27858
- Rockport Dr 27834
- Rockwood Ct 27834
- Rodney Rd 27834
- Roger Ln 27858
- Rolling Hills Ct 27858
- Rolling Meadows Dr 27858
- Rolling Rock Ln 27858
- Rollins Dr 27834
- Rolston Rd 27858
- Roman Ln 27834
- Rondo Dr 27858
- Roosevelt Ave 27834
- Roosevelt Spain Rd 27834
- Rosalind Ln 27858
- Rose Rd & St 27858
- Rosedown Ln 27834
- Rosemond Dr 27834
- Rosemont Dr 27858
- Rosewood Dr 27834
- Ross Ln 27834
- Rotary Ave 27858
- E & W Roundtree Dr 27834
- Rouse Rd 27858
- Running Bear Ln 27858
- Rupert Dr 27858
- Rustic Cir 27858
- Rustic Ln 27834
- Ruth Ct 27834
- Ruth Dr 27858
- Rutledge Rd 27858
- Saddle Way 27858
- Saddle Club Dr 27834
- Saddle Ridge Pl 27858
- Saddlewood Dr 27858
- Sage Ln 27834
- Saguaro Rd 27834
- Saint Andrews Dr 27834
- Saint Charles Cir 27834
- Saintsville Rd 27834
- Salem Cir 27858
- Sands Rd 27834
- Sandstone Ct 27834
- Sandy Field Ln 27834
- Sanibelle Ln 27834
- Santree St 27834
- Santree Mobile Home Park 27834
- Sapphire Ct 27834
- Sara Ln 27834
- Sassafras Ct 27858
- Satterfield Dr 27834
- Satterthwaite Rd 27834
- Savannah Ct 27858
- Saxon Ct 27834
- Scales Pl 27834
- Scarborough Rd 27858
- Scarlet Oak Dr 27858
- Scarlett Ohara Rd 27834
- Scotch Pine Ln 27834
- Scott Ln 27834
- Scott St 27858
- Scott Hall 27858
- Scottish Ct 27858
- Sean Dr 27834
- Sedgefield Dr 27834
- Seneca Dr 27858
- Sennie Dr 27834
- Setter Ct 27834
- Seven Pines Rd 27834
- Seville Rd 27834
- Seymour St 27834
- Shadowood Ct 27858
- Shady Ln 27858
- Shady Acres Trailer Park 27834
- Shady Knoll Trailer Park 27834
- Shale Ct 27858
- Shamrock Cir & Way 27834
- Shawnee Pl 27834
- Sheffield Ct 27834
- Sheffield Dr 27858
- Shenandoah Ct 27834
- Sheppard St 27834
- Sheppard Mill Rd 27834
- Sher Dan Ln 27858
- Sheraton Dr 27834
- Sherri St 27834
- N & S Sherrod Rd 27834
- Sherwin Dr 27834
- Sherwood Dr 27858
- Shiloh Dr 27834
- Short Ln 27834
- Short Bridge Rd 27834
- Short Leaf Pine Cir 27834
- N Side St 27858
- Sidney St 27834
- Silas Ln 27834
- Silver Creek Dr 27834
- Silver Maple Ln 27858
- Silver Wood Ln 27834
- Silverleaf Ct 27834
- Singletree Dr 27834
- Sir Eugene Ct 27858
- Sir Hugh Ct 27858
- Sir Hunter Dr 27858
- Sir Morris Ct 27858
- Sir Norman Ct 27858
- Sir Raleigh Ct 27858
- Sir Walter Dr 27834
- N & S Skinner St 27834
- Slate Ln 27834
- Slauter St 27834
- Slay Dr 27858
- Slay Hall 27858
- Sloan Dr 27858
- Slocum St 27834
- Smith St 27834
- Smiths Trailer Park 27834
- Smythewyck Dr 27858
- Soco Ct 27834
- Somerset Dr 27834
- Sonata Pl & St 27858
- Southampton Ct 27834
- Southberry Wynd 27834
- Southern Oaks Dr 27858
- Southgate Dr 27834
- Southland Dr 27858
- Southridge Dr 27834
- Southview Dr 27858
- Spain Farm Ln 27858
- Speight Dr 27834
- Spencer Loop Rd 27858
- Spinnaker Ct 27858
- Spiny Star Dr 27834
- Spirit Way 27834
- Splash Dr 27834
- Spring Creek Rd 27834
- Spring Forest Rd 27834
- Springbrook Dr 27834
- Springhill Rd 27834
- Sprinkle Rd 27858
- Spruce St 27834
- Square St 27834
- St Augustine Dr 27834
- Staccato Ct 27858
- Staffordshire Rd 27834
- Stancil Dr 27858
- Stancils Mobile Home Park 27834
- Stanley Rd 27858
- Stanton Dr 27834
- Stanton Squareshop Ctr 27834
- Stantonsburg Rd 27834
- Stanwood Dr 27858
- W Star St 27858
- Star Hill Farm Rd 27834
- Starnes Ct 27834
- Staton Ct & Rd 27834
- Staton House Rd 27834
- Staton Mill Rd 27834
- Steinbrook Dr 27858
- Steven St 27834
- Stevenson Ln 27834
- Steward Ln 27858
- Stirrup Ct 27858
- Stocks Ln 27834
- Stokes Rd 27834
- Stokestown Saint Johns Rd 27858
- Stone Creek Dr 27858
- Stone Gate Dr 27858
- Stonehenge Dr 27858
- Strange Ct 27834
- Stratford Rd 27858
- Stuart Cir 27834
- Stub Rd 27834
- Student St 27858
- Stueben Ct 27858
- Stutz St 27834
- Sugar Pine Ln 27834
- Sugg Pkwy 27834
- Sulgrave Rd 27858
- Sullivan Dr 27834
- Summer Pl 27834
- Summerhaven Dr 27858
- Summerwinds Dr 27834
- N & S Summit St 27858
- Sumrell St 27858
- Sunny Side Rd 27834
- Sunnybrook Rd 27834
- Sunnyfield Dr 27858
- Sunset Ave 27834
- Surrey Ln 27858
- Sussex St 27834
- Sweet Bay Dr 27834
- Sweet Gum Ct 27834
- Sweet Gum Meadow Dr 27834
- Sweetbriar Rd 27858
- Sycamore St 27858
- Sycamore Church Rd 27834
- N & S Sylvan Dr 27834
- Syme Cir 27858
- Taberna Dr 27834
- Tabitha Ln 27834
- Tall Pines Ln 27834
- Talton Dr 27834
- Tamarind Rd 27834
- Tammie Trl 27858
- Tanglewood Dr 27858
- Tar Heel Dr 27834
- Tara Ct 27858
- Tatten Ct 27834
- Tayloe St 27834
- Taylor St 27834
- Taylors Creek Dr 27834
- Teakwood Dr 27834
- Teels Estate Rd 27834
- Templeton Dr 27858
- Tempo Ct 27858
- Tenderleaf Ct 27834
- Terra Dell Dr 27858
- Terrace Ct 27834
- Terry St 27858
- Thackery Rd 27858
- N & S Thames Ct 27858
- Thigpen Rd 27834
- Thistle Down Ct 27858
- Thomas St 27834
- Thomas Mobile Home 1 Park 27834
- Thomas Mobile Home 2 Park 27834
- Thomas Mobile Home 3 Park 27834
- Thornbrook Dr 27834
- Three Sisters Ln 27834
- Tiburon Ct 27834
- Tice Cir 27834
- Tice Charles Rd 27834
- Tice Trailer Park 27834
- Tiffany Dr 27858
- Tifgreen Dr 27834
- Timber Dr 27858
- Tipton Dr 27834
- Toby Cir 27834
- Tollie Ct 27858
- Toms Trl 27834
- Tower Pl 27858
- Townes Dr 27858
- Trace Ct 27858
- Tracey Cir 27834
- Trade St 27834
- Trails End 27858
- Tram Ln 27834
- Tree St 27834
- Treemont Dr 27858
- Trent Cir 27834
- Trey Dr 27834
- Treybrooke Cir 27834
- Treyburn Cir 27858
- Triangle Trailer Park 27834
- Trinity Dr 27834
- E & W Tripp Ave & Ln 27834
- Trolling Wood Ct 27858
- Trotters Way 27858
- Trotters Ridge Ct 27858
- Troutman Dr 27858
- Troy Rd 27858
- Truman St 27834
- Tryon Dr 27858
- Tuckahoe Dr 27858
- Tucker Dr 27858
- Tucker Bullock Rd 27834
- Tull Rd 27858
- Tupelo Ln 27834
- Tupper Dr 27834
- Turkey Oak Ct 27858
- Turnage Ln 27834
- Turnberry Ln 27834
- Turnbury Dr 27858
- Turquoise Ln 27834
- Turtle Creek Dr 27858
- Tuscany Dr 27858
- Twin Creeks Rd 27858
- Twisting Creek Rd 27834
- Tyland Acres Trailer Park 27834
- Tyler Ln 27858
- Tyler Hall 27858
- Tyson St 27834
- Umstead Ave 27858
- Umstead Hall 27858
- Union St 27834
- United Dr 27834
- Unity Ln 27834
- University Square Shop Ctr 27858
- University Suites Dr 27834
- Upland Dr 27858
- Upton Ct 27858
- Us Highway 13 S 27834
- Us Highway 264 E 27834
- V O A Site C Rd 27834
- Vail Dr 27834
- Valley Ln, Pl & Rd 27858
- Valley Ridge Trailer Park 27834
- Valleyway Rd 27858
- Van Ness Ave 27834
- Van Nortwick St 27834
- Vance St 27834
- Vanderbilt Ln 27834
- Vandyke St 27834
- Vassar Rd 27858
- Vauxhall Ct 27858
- Venice Ln 27858
- Venture Tower Dr 27834
- Verdant Dr 27858
- Vernon St 27858
- Vicky Ln 27858
- Victor Dr 27834
- E Victoria Ct 27858
- W Victoria Ct 27834
- Victorious Pl 27858
- View St 27834
- N Village Dr 27834
- Vineyard Cir 27858
- Violet Ln 27834
- Vivian St 27858
- Voa Site B Rd 27858
- Wade St 27834
- Wainright Ln 27834
- Walden Dr 27858
- Wallace Ln 27858
- Wallingford Rd 27858
- Walnut Dr 27834
- Wanda Ln 27858
- Wandsworth Dr 27834
- Wapping Ct 27858
- Ward St 27834
- Wards Bridge Rd 27834
- N & S Warren St 27858
- Warrenwood Rd 27834
- Warwick Ct & Dr 27858
- N Washington St 27834
- S Washington St
  - 100-599 27858
  - 800-1499 27834
- Watauga Ave 27834
- Water Oak Ln 27834
- Water View Rd 27858
- Water Way Rd 27834

Waterford Commons Dr & Rd 27834
Watts St 27858
Wayne Dr 27834
Waynes Village Ln 27834
Wc Cobb Rd 27834
Webb St 27834
Webster Ct 27834
Wedgewood Dr 27858
Wedgewood Arms 27858
Weigum Ct 27834
Wellcome Dr 27858
Wellcome Ln 27834
Wellingham Ave 27834
Wellness Dr 27834
Wellons Dr 27858
Wellons Rd 27834
Wesley Ln & Rd 27858
West St 27834
Westchester Dr 27858
Westgate Dr 27834
Westhaven Rd 27834
Westminster Cir & Ct 27858
Westmont Dr 27834
Westover Dr 27834
Westpark Dr 27834
Westpointe Dr 27834
Westridge Ct 27834
Westview Dr 27834
Westwind Vlg 27834
Westwood Dr 27834
Wexford Ln 27858
Wh Mills Ln 27858
Wh Smith Blvd 27834
Wheaton Village Dr 27858
Wheatstone Dr 27858
Whichard Rd 27834
Whichard Building 27858
Whichard Cherry Lane Rd 27834
Whisper Rd 27858
Whitaker Dr 27834
White St 27834
White Bark Pine Ln 27834
White Hall 27858
White Hollow Dr 27858
White Horse Dr 27834
White Oak Dr 27858
White Pine Ln 27834
Whitehurst Rd 27834
Whitetail Ct 27834
Whitford Ln 27834
Whitten Ct 27858
Whittington Cir 27834
Widgeon Ct 27834
Wildflower Ln 27858
Wildwood Dr 27858
Wilkshire Dr 27858
Willette Dr 27834
William Henry Ln 27834
William Horice Cir 27834
Williams Rd 27834
Williams St 27858
Williamsbrook Ln 27858
Williamsburg Dr 27858
Willoughby Rd 27858
Willow St 27858
Willow Oak Ct 27858
Willow Run Dr 27858
Wilson St 27834
Wilson Farm Ln 27858
Wilton Ln 27858
Wimbledon Dr 27858
Winchester Dr 27858
Windchime Dr 27834
Windermere Ct 27858
Windham Rd 27834
Winding Ln 27858
W Winds Dr 27834
Windsong Dr 27858
Windsor Rd 27858
Windy Ln 27834
Winestone Ct 27858
Winslow Pointe Dr 27858
Winstead Rd 27834
Wistar Ct 27858
Wisteria Ln 27858
Wolf Pit Rd 27858
Woodbay Ct 27834
Woodberry Dr 27858
Woodfield Cir 27834
Woodhaven Ct & Rd 27834
N & S Woodlawn Ave 27858
Woodmen Rd 27858
Woodmoor Dr 27858
Woodridge Park Rd 27834
Woodsend Ln 27834
Woodside Rd 27834
Woodspring Ln 27834
Woodstock Dr 27834
Woodview Pl 27834
Woodwind Dr 27858
Worth Ct 27858
Worthington Ln & Rd 27858
Wrench Cir 27834
E Wright Rd 27858
Wyatt St 27834
Wyndham Cir 27858
Wyneston Rd 27858
Wyngate Dr 27834
Yadkin Ct 27858
Yankee Hall Rd 27834
Yarrell Pl 27834
Yaupon Ln 27834
Yorianso Rd 27834
York Rd 27858
Yorkshire Dr 27858
Yorktown Sq 27858
Zeb Ln 27834

NUMBERED STREETS

E 1st St 27858
101-299 27858
300-499 27834
2nd St 27834
E 2nd St 27858
W 2nd St
300-300 27834
300-300 27835
301-399 27834
E 3rd St 27858
W 3rd St
100-201 27858
400-1999 27834
E 4th St 27858
100-200 27858
300-1799 27834
E 5th St 27858
W 5th St
100-114 27858
116-201 27858
203-205 27858
300-2899 27834
E 6th St 27858
W 6th St 27834
E 7th St 27858
E 8th St 27858
W 8th St 27834
E 9th St 27858
W 9th St 27834
E 10th St 27858
806-806 27836
900-4698 27858
901-4699 27858
W 10th St 27834
E 11th St 27858
W 11th St 27834
E 12th St 27858
W 12th St 27834
E 13th St 27858
W 13th St 27834
W 14th Ave 27834
E 14th St 27858
W 14th St 27834

HENDERSON NC

General Delivery 27536

POST OFFICE BOXES MAIN OFFICE STATIONS AND BRANCHES

Box No.s
All PO Boxes 27536

RURAL ROUTES

02 27537

NAMED STREETS

A Garrett Rd 27537
Abbeys Ln 27537
Abbott Rd 27537
Abbott St 27536
Abbott Way 27537
Abbott Crossing Ln 27537
Abi Ln 27537
Ace Ln 27537
Acorn Ln 27537
Adams St 27536
Al Brown Ln 27537
Alexander Ave 27536
Alexander Ln 27537
Alice Faye Ln 27537
Allen Dr 27536
Allen Ln 27537
Allen Rd
1-100 27537
101-103 27536
102-598 27537
105-599 27537
Allen Kelly Rd 27537
Allison Cooper Rd 27537
Alpha Rd 27536
Americal Rd 27537
Amigo Ln 27537
Anchor Dr 27537
Anderson Creek Rd 27537
E & W Andrews Ave 27536
Angel Ln 27537
Anne St 27536
Annie Lee Rd 27537
Antioch Church Rd 27537
Antler Ct 27537
Apple St 27536
Arch St 27536
Arendell Pl 27536
Arrow St 27536
Arrowhead Ln 27537
Arvis Ln 27537
Ashley Ln 27537
Ashmont Ln 27537
Autumn Ln 27537
Autumn Winds 27537
Avery Ln 27537
Avis Ln 27536
Avista Ln 27537
Avon Ct 27537
Aycock Rd 27537
Ayscue Ln 27537
Azalea Dr 27536
N & S B Harrison Ln 27537
Bane Ave 27536
Baptist Church Rd 27537
N Barham Ln 27537
Barker Rd 27537
Barn Ln 27537
Baytree Ln 27537
Beach Ln 27537
Beacon Ave 27536
Beacon Hill Ln 27537
Beacon Light Apartments 27536
Bearpond Rd 27537
Beaver Creek Ln 27537
Beaver Dam Rd 27537
Beavertail Rd 27537
Beck Ave 27536
N & S Beckford Dr 27536
Beechwood Dr & Trl 27536
Begonia Ln 27537
E & W Belle St 27536
Bellwood Dr 27536
Belmont Dr 27536
Bent Creek Ln 27537
Ber Lake Dr 27537
Berry Ave & St 27536
Betty Ln 27537
Beverly Ln 27537
Beverly Hills Ln 27537
Bickett St 27536
Big Buck Rd 27537
Big Ruin Creek Ln 27537
Bill Bragg Morton Rd 27537
Bill Spain Rd 27537
Billy Burwell Rd 27537
Birch Cir & St 27536
Blackberry Ln 27537
Bliley Ln 27537
Bluebird Ln 27537
Bobbitt St 27536
Bobbitt Vlg 27537
Bobcat Ln 27537
Boddie St 27536
Bogey Ln 27537
Bolton Ln 27537
Booker St 27536
Booth Ave & St 27536
W Boulder Rd 27537
Bowman Ln 27537
E Boyd Ln & Rd 27537
Brame Rd 27537
Branch Ln 27537
Breckenridge Aly & St 27536
Breeze Hill Ln 27537
Breland Dr 27537
Brentwood Ln 27537
Briarcliff St 27536
Briarwood St 27536
Brick St 27536
Bridgers Aly & St 27536
Briggs Rd 27537
Broad St 27537
Brodie Rd 27536
Broken Fence Loop Ln 27537
Brookcove Way 27537
Brookhaven Ct & Pl 27537
Brookrun Rd 27536
Brookside Ln 27537
Brookston Rd 27537
Brookwood Ln 27537
Brown Hills Rd 27537
E Brunswick Ln 27537
Bryant Abbott Rd 27537
Buchan Best Ln 27537
Buckhorn St 27536
Buckskin Ln 27537
Bucktail Ct 27537
Bullock Ln 27537
N Bullock St 27536
S Bullock St 27536
Bumper Ln 27537
Bunn St 27536
Buoy Dr 27537
Burning Tree Dr 27537
Burnside Rd 27537
Burr St 27536
Burwell Ave 27536
Callie Ln 27537
Cambridge Way 27536
Cameron Dr 27536
Canary Ln 27537
Cannady St 27536
Canterbury Ct 27537
Cardinal Dr 27536
Cardinal Ln 27537
Carey Chapel Rd 27537
Carmel Ridge Rd 27537
S Carolina Ave 27536
Carolina Woods Dr & Ln 27537
Carolyn Ct 27536
Carroll Rd 27536
Carter St 27536
Carver Ln 27537
Carver School Rd 27537
Casei Ln 27537
Catherine Weldon Ln 27537
Caudle Ln 27537
Cedar St 27536
Cedar Cove Rd 27537
Cedar Grove Dr 27537
Cedar Hurst St 27536
Cedar Pine Ln 27537
Cedar Rock Ln 27537
Cedar Tree Ln 27537
Cedarwood Dr & Ter 27536
E & W Center Ln & St 27536
Champion St 27536
Charles St 27536
Charles Rollins Rd 27536
Charles Wade Ln 27537
Chavasse Ave 27536
Cheatham Ln 27537
Cheatham Mabry Rd 27537
Cheeks Quarter Rd 27537
Cherry St 27536
Cherryville Ln 27537
Chester Ln 27536
N & S Chestnut Aly & St 27536
Chicken Hollow Way 27537
Chloe Ln 27537
Chris Bowman Ln 27537
Christopher Tyler Ln 27537
N Church St 27536
N & S Cinnebar Ct 27537
Clare Dr 27537
Clark Ln 27537
N Clark St 27536
S Clark St 27536
N & S Clearview Dr 27536
Clements Rd 27537
Cleveland St 27536
Closs Ct 27536
Club Pond Rd 27537
E & W Coachway Dr 27537
Cobble Way 27537
N & S Cobble Creek Dr 27537
Coble Blvd 27536
Coghill Rd 27537
Coghill Dickerson Ln 27537
N & S Cokesbury Ct & Rd 27537
Cokesbury Village Dr 27537
Coleman Pl 27536
Colenda Ln 27537
Coley Rd 27537
N & S College St 27536
Colonial Ave 27536
Comfort Dr 27537
Commerce Dr 27537
Community College Rd 27537
Community House Rd 27537
Computer Ln 27537
Cone Ln 27537
N & S Cooper Dr 27536
Coopers Grove Rd 27537
Corbitt Rd 27536
Cotton Plz 27537
Cotton Pickin Pl 27537
Country Ln 27537
Country Acres Dr & Rd 27537
Country Club Dr 27536
Country Lake Dr 27537
Countrywood Ln 27537
County Home Rd 27536
Court St 27536
Cousins Ln 27537
Coventry Ln 27537
Coyote Ct 27537
Craig Ave 27536
Crawley Rd 27537
W Creek Rd 27537
Crescent Dr 27536
Crest Rd 27536
Crestwood Rd 27536
Crews Ln 27537
Croscill Dr 27537
Cross St 27536
Cross Creek Ct & Rd 27537
Crowder Ct & Ln 27537
Crozier St 27536
Currin Rd 27537
Cypress Dr 27536
D K Stainback Rd 27537
Dabney Dr 27536
E Dabney Dr 27536
Dabney Rd 27537
Dabney Depot Ln 27537
Dabney Drive Ext 27536
Dabney Heights Ln 27537
Dabney Woods Dr & Ln 27537
Daffodil Dr 27537
Daisy Ln 27537
Dalton Ln 27537
Daniel Ln 27537
Daniel St 27536
Daniel Boone Trl 27537
Daniel Harris Rd 27537
David Ave & St 27536
Davis Rd 27537
Davis St 27536
Debnam Ave 27536
Dee Ave 27537
Deepwood Dr 27536
Deer Chase Ln 27537
Deer Crossing Ct 27536
Deer Tick Ln 27537
Deer Track Ln 27537
Deer Wood Trl 27537
Deerfield Run 27537
Deerhound Ct 27537
Delta Pl 27536
Dement Ln 27537
Denver St 27536
Destiny Ln 27537
Diamond Point Ln 27537
Dick Faines Rd 27537
Dick Yancey Ln 27537
Dickie Dr 27537
Dillard St 27536
Dockside Ln 27537
Doctor Finch Rd 27537
Dodi Ln 27537
Doe Ct 27537
Dogwood Dr 27536
Dogwood Trl 27537
Dorsey Ave & Pl 27536
Dry Dock Ln 27537
Duke St 27536
Dutchess Ln 27537
Dy Hoyle Ln 27537
Eagle Ct 27536
Eagle Ln 27537
East Ave 27536
Eastern Blvd 27536
Eastern Minerals Rd 27537
Eastside Dr 27536
Eastway Dr 27536
Eaton St 27536
Eaves Rd 27537
Edgar Harris Rd 27537
Edgewater Ln 27537
Edgewood Dr 27536
Edward St 27536
Edward Wade Ln 27537
Edwards Rd 27537
Edwards St 27536
Eileen Ct 27537
N & S Elizabeth St 27536
Elk St 27536
Ellington Path & Rd 27537
Elm Ln 27537
Elm St 27536
Elsie St 27536
Elsie Smith Dr 27537
Embargo Ln 27537
Emerson Ln 27537
Emerson Grove Ln 27537
Ennis Murphy Rd 27537
Epsom Rocky Ford Rd 27537
Erica Ln 27537
Ernest Ln 27537
Estate Ln 27537
Evans Rd & St 27537
Evergreen Pl 27537
Ew Lester Ln 27537
Exchange St 27536
Facet Rd 27537
Fairview Dr 27537
Fairway Dr 27536
Faith Hope Ln 27537
Falkner Ln 27537
Falkner St 27536
Falkner Trail Park 27537
Farm St 27536
Farmington Ln 27537
Farmwood Ln 27537
Farrar Ave 27536
Faucette Ln 27537
Faulkner Dr 27536
Faulkner Town Rd 27537
Fawn Ct & Dr 27537
Fern Ln 27537
Fernbrook Pl 27536
Fernwood Ct, Dr & Way 27536
Fernwood Creek Ct 27536
Fields Ave 27536
Finch Rd 27537
Flanagan Rd 27537
Flat Rock Ln 27537
Flemingtown Ln & Rd 27537
Fletcher Fuller Rd 27537
Flint St 27536
Flour Ln 27537
Ford Ln 27537
Ford St 27536
Forest Rd 27536
Forest Hills Dr 27537
Forest Home Ln 27537
Foster Rd 27537
Foster Road Ext 27537
Four Oaks Ln 27537
Fowler Ln 27537
Fox Run 27536
Fox Trl 27537
Fox Pond Rd 27537
Foxborough Ln 27536
Foxfire Dr 27537
Foxy Ln 27537
Francis Ave 27536
Franklin Ln & Rd 27537
Frazier Dement Rd 27537
Fred Royster Rd 27537
Freedom Ln 27537
Friendly Ln 27537
Friendship Ln 27537
Fulcher Farm Ln 27537
Fuller St 27536
Furman Ln 27537
Garden Ln 27537
Garden Walk Dr 27536
Garland St 27536
N Garnett St
100-2199 27536
2200-2799 27537
S Garnett St 27536
S Garnett Street Ext 27536
Garrett Rd 27537
Garrett Farm Rd 27537
Gary St 27536
Gay St 27536
George Floyd Rd 27537
Geranium Ln 27537
Gholson Ave & Dr 27536
Gillburg Ln & Rd 27537
Gillburg Estates Ct 27537
Glass House Rd 27537
Glebe Rd 27537
Glendas Ln 27537
Glenn Ave & St 27536
Glover Rd 27537
Glover St 27536
Gold Finch Ln 27537
Gooch Rd 27537
Gordon St 27536
Gorman St 27536
Grace Ln 27537
Graham Ave 27536
Grain Ln 27537
Granite St 27536
Grant St 27536
Gray Owens Ln 27537
Green St 27536
Green Meadow Ln 27537
Greenbriar Rd 27536
Greta Ln 27537

Grey Fox Ln 27537
Greystone Rd 27537
Griffith Ln 27537
Grove Park Ln 27537
Gun Club Rd 27537
Gupton Ln 27537
Gupton St 27536
Gupton Lane Ext 27537
Gwynn Pond Ln 27537
N & S Hacienda Ln 27537
Hall St 27536
Hamilton Ln 27537
Hamilton St 27536
Hamlett Dr 27536
Hamp Falkner Rd 27537
Handyman Ln 27537
Hanford Ln 27537
Hargrove St 27536
Harpers Ln 27537
Harrell St 27536
Harriett St 27536
Harrington Rd 27537
Harris St 27536
Harrison Ave & St 27536
Hatch St 27536
Haw Pond Ln 27537
Hawkins Dr 27536
Hawkins Ln 27537
Hayes Way 27537
Hayes Farm Rd 27537
Hayesville Rd 27537
Haywood Wright Rd 27537
Hazel Rd 27537
Health Center Rd 27536
S Heartland Ln 27537
Heather Way 27537
Hedrick Dr 27537
N Henderson Mobile Ct 27536
Henry St 27536
Henry Ayscue Rd 27537
Heritage Hl 27537
Hester Dr 27537
Hibernia Rd 27537
Hibernia Cove Loop 27537
Hickory St 27536
Hicks St 27536
Hicksboro Rd 27537
High St 27536
Highland Ave 27536
Hight St 27536
Hightower Rd 27537
Highway 158 Business 27537
Hillandale Dr 27537
Hillcrest Dr 27536
Hilliard St 27536
Hillside Aly 27536
Hillside Ave 27536
Hillside Pl 27536
Hillside Way 27537
Holden Ln 27537
Holiday Ln 27537
Holly Cir 27537
Holly Ct 27536
E Holly Ln 27537
W Holly Ln 27537
Holly Rd 27537
Hood Loop Rd 27537
Hootin Owl Holw 27537
Horner St 27536
Horseshoe Bend Rd 27537
Horton Ln 27537
Howell Rd 27537
Hoyle Ln & Way 27537
Hoyletown Rd 27537
Huff Ln 27537
Hughes St 27536
Hughes Hollow Ln 27537
Hummingbird Ln 27537
Hunter Ln & Rd 27537
Hunters Rdg 27537
Hunting Trail Ln 27537
Huntstone Ct 27537
Indiana Ave 27536
Industry Dr 27537
Inlet Cove Ln 27537
Institute St 27536
Intake Ln 27537
Internet Ln 27537
Ipock Rd 27537
Irene Bullock Ln 27537
Island Creek Estates Rd 27537
Ivey St 27536
J And J Ln 27537
J P Taylor Rd 27537
Jack Court Ln 27537
S Jackson Ave 27537
Jackson Royster Rd 27537
Jacksontown Rd 27537
James Way 27537
James Matthews Rd 27537
Jane Ave 27536
Jefferson St 27536
Jeffress Dr 27537
E & W Jennette Ave 27536
Jewel Ln 27537
Jigs Way Ln 27537
Joe Ayscue Rd 27537
Joe Taylor Rd 27537
Joes Ln 27537
John St 27536
John Deere Rd 27537
John H Bullock Rd 27537
Johnson Ln 27537
Johnson St 27536
Jones Ln 27537
Jordan Ln 27537
Joshua Ln 27537
Julia Ave 27536
Julia St 27537
Julian Smith Rd 27537
Kaplan Ln 27537
Kate Bullock Rd 27537
Katie Ln 27537
Kearney St 27536
Keene St 27537
Kelly Rd 27537
Kemps Ln 27537
Kenny Ln 27537
Kerr Cir 27537
Kerr Lake Rd & Shrs 27537
Kerr Lake Club Dr 27537
Kimball Rd 27537
Kims Ln 27537
Kinderhook Ln 27537
King St 27536
Kings Ct & Rd 27537
Kirby Ln 27537
Kirklen Ln 27537
Kitchen Ave 27536
Kittrell St 27536
Kitts Landing Ln 27537
Kyle Ln 27537
L And S Ln 27537
Lake Rd 27537
Lake Haven Rd 27537
Lake Lodge Ext & Rd 27537
Lake Shore Ln 27537
Lake View Rd 27537
Lakeside Dr 27536
Lakeview Dr 27536
Lakewood Ct 27537
Lamb St 27536
Lanning Rd 27537
Lark Ln 27537
Larry St 27536
Lattimore Wright Rd 27537
Laurie Ball Rd 27537
Lawndale Cir 27536
Lawrence St 27536
Lee Ave & Ln 27537
Legacy Ln 27537
Lehman St 27536
Leland Cir 27536
Lemay Ln 27537
Lenora St 27536
Leon Frazier Rd 27537
Lewis Ln 27537
Lewis St 27536
Lewis Williams Rd 27537
Lightwood Ln & Way 27537
Lillie Harris Ln 27537
Lilly Ln 27537
Lincoln Ave & St 27536
Lindy Ln 27537
Links Ct 27536
Linwood Ln 27537
Little Mill Rd 27537
Little Rosewood Ln 27537
Loblolly Ln 27537
Log Cabin Dr 27537
Lone St 27536
Lone Wolf Dr 27537
Louisburg Rd 27536
Lowry St 27536
Lucie St 27536
Lucinda Ln 27537
Lucy St 27536
Lydia Ln 27537
Lynn Haven Ave 27536
N & S Lynnbank Rd 27537
Lynne Ave 27536
Mabry Mill Rd 27537
Macey Dr 27537
Maconville Ln 27537
Madison Grove Ln 27537
Main St 27536
Mallard Ln 27537
Manor Ln 27537
Mansfield Ln 27537
Maple St 27536
Margie Ln 27537
Marigold Ln 27537
Marilyn St 27536
Market St 27536
Marrow Dr 27536
Marsha Ave 27536
Marshall St 27536
Martin Creek Rd 27537
Mason St 27536
Massenburg Rd 27537
Matthews Dr & Rd 27537
Max Wilson Trail Park 27537
Maynard St 27536
Mayo St 27536
Mcarthur St 27536
Mcborn St 27537
Mccoin Ave 27536
Mcdaniel Ln 27537
Mcnair Cir & Dr 27537
Meadow Ct 27537
Meadow Dr 27537
Meadow Ln 27536
Meadow Way 27537
Meagan Ln 27537
Medical Ct 27536
Melinda Ln 27537
Melrose Ln 27537
Memory Ln 27537
Meredith Ln 27537
Meridian Way 27537
Merle Jones Ln 27537
Merriman St 27536
Mickey Ln 27537
Milford Way 27537
W Mill Creek Ln 27537
Milton Stainback Rd 27537
Mindy Ln 27537
Miriam St 27536
Mitchell St 27536
Monroe St 27536
Montgomery Ln 27537
E Montgomery St 27536
W Montgomery St 27536
Moody Rd 27537
Morgan Rd 27537
Morgans Pl 27537
Morning Glory Ln 27537
Morris Wilson Rd 27537
Morton Ln 27537
Moss Ln 27537
Mount Carmel Church Rd 27537
Mountain Ln 27537
Mulberry St 27536
Mum Ln 27537
Murphy Rd 27536
Nans Ln 27537
Nature Ln 27537
Nautical Way Ln 27537
Nc 39 Hwy N 27537
Nc 39 Hwy S
1700-1844 27536
1845-1897 27537
1846-1898 27536
1899-9099 27537
Nc 39 Loop Rd 27537
Nc Highway 39 N 27537
Neal Ln 27537
Neal Farm Rd 27537
Neathery St 27536
Nelson St 27536
Nethery Rd 27537
New Bethel Church Rd 27537
New Circle Ln 27537
Newton Dairy Rd 27537
Nicholas St 27536
Nightingale Ln 27537
No Record St 27537
Noel Ln 27537
North St 27536
Northern Oak St 27536
Norvell St 27536
Norwood Ln 27537
Norwood St 27536
Nottingham Ct 27537
Nutbush Rd 27537
Nutbush Farm Rd 27537
Oak St 27536
Oak Forest Dr 27537
Oak Hill Loop 27537
Oak Tree Ln 27537
Oakdale Cir 27536
Oakhill St 27536
Oakland Ave 27536
Oakridge Ave 27536
N & S Oakwood Ln 27537
Old County Home Rd 27537
Old Epsom Rd
100-1499 27536
1500-1999 27537
Old Hester Pl 27537
Old Norlina Rd 27536
Old Poplar Creek Rd 27537
Old Thomas Ln 27537
Old Warrenton Rd 27537
Old Watkins Rd 27537
N & S Oliver Dr 27537
Omega St 27536
Opie Ln 27537
Opie Frazier Rd 27537
Orange St 27536
Orchard Rd 27536
Orrs Ln 27537
Orville St 27536
Outrigger Ln 27537
Overhill Cir 27536
Owen St 27536
Oxford Rd 27536
Paige St 27536
Par Dr 27536
Parham Rd & St 27536
Parham Spring Ln 27536
Park Ave 27536
E & W Parker Ln & St 27536
W Parkview Dr E 27536
Parkway Dr 27536
Parrott Rd 27537
Partin St 27536
Patterson Ln 27537
Patton Cir 27536
Peace St 27536
Peach St 27536
Peachtree St 27536
Pearl St 27536
Pearson Ln 27537
Pebble Hill Ln 27537
Peebles Ln 27537
Pegram Ln 27537
Pendergrass Dr 27537
Pepper Ln 27537
Pernell Ln 27537
Perry Ave & St 27536
Pete Abbott Ln 27537
Peter Gill Rd 27537
Peter Harris Farm Ln 27537
Peters Ln 27537
Pettigrew St 27536
Phyllis Ln 27536
Pier Dr 27537
Pilgram Ln 27537
Pin Oak Cir 27537
Pincedal St 27536
Pine St
1-99 27537
1200-1399 27536
N Pine St 27536
Pine Trl 27537
Pine Forest Dr
1-99 27537
100-120 27536
121-123 27537
122-124 27536
125-199 27537
Pine Meadow Trl 27537
Pine Ridge Rd & Trl 27537
Pine View Rd 27537
Pine Way Dr 27537
Pinecone Ln 27537
Pinecrest Rd 27536
E & W Pinehill Dr 27537
Pineview Dr 27536
Pinewood Dr 27537
N & S Pinkston St 27536
Pinnacle Pl 27537
Pintail Ln 27537
Plum Ln 27537
Plum Nutty Rd 27537
Pollyanna Rd 27537
Pool Rock Rd 27537
Pool Rock Plantation Ln 27537
Pool Rock Shores Ln 27537
Poplar St 27536
Poplar Creek Rd 27537
Poppys Ln 27537
Porenner Rd 27537
Port Dr 27537
Pounder Branch Trail Park 27537
Powell St 27536
Poythress Ln 27537
Prosperity Dr 27536
Puckett Rd & Trl 27537
Puddle Stone Ln 27537
Pueblo Ln 27537
Quail Rdg & Run 27536
Quarry Ln 27537
Quarter Horse Ln 27537
Queens Ln 27537
Rabbitt Ln 27537
Raccoon Xing 27537
Radio Ln 27536
Ragland Ln 27537
Railroad St 27536
Raleigh Rd
100-2399 27536
2400-6499 27537
Raleigh St 27536
Ramblewood Ln 27537
Ramblewoods Dr 27537
Ramsey St 27536
Randy Yancey Ln 27537
Ranes Dr 27536
Ransom St 27536
Raydale Ln 27537
Red Bud Cir & Dr 27536
Red Clay Ln 27537
Red Fox Run 27537
Red Head Ln 27537
Red Maple Ln 27537
Red Oak Ln & Rd 27537
Redwing Ln 27537
Regina Ln 27537
Regional Water Ln 27537
Renn Ln 27537
Reservoir St 27536
Rev Henderson Rd 27537
Rice Rd 27537
W Ridge Dr 27537
Ridge Rd 27536
Ridge Circle Rd 27537
Ridgecrest Ln & Trl 27537
Ridgepath Ln 27537
Roanoke Ave 27536
Roberson St 27536
Roberson Hollow Ln 27537
Roberts Ave 27537
Robin Ln 27537
Rock Mill Rd 27537
E & W Rock Spring St 27536
Rock Spring Church Rd 27537
Rocky Ln 27537
Rollins Ave 27536
Romeo Ct 27537
Rook St 27536
Roosevelt St 27536
Rose Ave 27536
Rose Ln 27537
Rose St 27536
Rose Bud Ln 27537
Ross Ave 27537
Ross Mill Rd 27537
Rowland St 27536
Ruin Creek Rd
1-99 27537
100-1051 27536
1052-1098 27537
1053-1099 27536
1100-1699 27537
1700-1710 27536
1711-1800 27537
1801-1805 27536
1802-1898 27537
1807-1999 27537
1900-1924 27536
1930-2598 27537
2001-2099 27536
2101-2599 27537
Ryans Way Ln 27537
Sagefield Dr & Way 27537
Saint Andrews Church Rd 27537
Saint Matthews St 27536
Salt And Light Ln 27537
Sam Brummitt Rd 27537
Sandstone Rd 27537
Sandy Ln 27537
Sandy Pines Ln 27537
Sandy Plains Ln 27537
Sarah Ln 27537
Satterwhite Point Ln & Rd 27537
Saucy Ln 27537
Scott Rd 27537
Scott Bluff Dr 27537
Scuffletown Ln 27537
Settlement Ln 27537
Seven Springs Ln 27537
Shadowbrook Dr 27537
Shady Ln 27537
N & S Shank St 27536
Shearin Ct & Ln 27537
Sherwood Rd 27536
Shirley Dr 27536
Short Rd 27537
Shorts Ln 27537
Sidney Hl 27536
Simmons Dr 27536
Simon Harris Rd 27537
Sims Ave & St 27536
Skenes Ave 27536
N & S Skylark Ln 27537
Sleepy Eye Ln 27537
Small Pond Ln 27537
Smith Rd 27537
Smithwick Trail Park 27537
Sollie Ayscue Rd 27537
Sombrero Ln 27537
Somerset Ln 27537
Songbird Ln 27537
South St 27536
Southall St 27536
Southerland Pl 27537
Southerland St 27536
Southerland Mill Rd 27537
Southern Ave 27536
Southern Pine St 27536
Southland Dr 27537
Southpark Dr 27536
Southside Ln 27537
Southside Estates Ct 27537
Southwood Trailer Park 27537
E & W Spain Middleburg Rd 27537
Sparrow Ln 27537
Spring Ct
100-199 27537
400-599 27536
Spring Ln 27537
E Spring St 27536
W Spring St 27536
Spring Hill Ln 27537
Spring Trail Ln 27537
Spring Valley Dr 27536
Spring Valley Rd 27537
Spring Valley Lake Rd 27537
Springwood Dr 27537
Squirrel Holw 27537
Stagecoach Rd 27537
Standish St 27536
Stanley St 27536
Stantonville Ln 27537
Starling Ln 27537
State St 27536
Steed Dickerson Rd 27537
Stewart Ave 27536
Stewart Rd 27537
Stewart Farm Rd 27537
Stone St 27536
Stonebridge Ln 27537
Stonecrest Dr 27536
Stonehedge Dr 27537
Stoneridge Dr 27537
Stony Ridge Ln 27537
Stratford Dr 27537
Strawberry Ln 27537
Sultons Ln 27537
Summer Breeze Ln 27537
Summer Lake Ln 27537
Summer Shores Ln 27537
Summer Winds Ln 27537
Summerfield Ln 27537
Summit Rd 27537
Summitt Rd 27536
Sumter Ln 27537
Sunny Ln 27537
Sunnyview Rd 27536
Sunrise Ave 27536
Sunset Ave 27536
Sunset Cir 27536
Sunset Ln 27537
Swain Dr & St 27536
Sweet Gum Dr 27537
Sycamore Ln 27537
Sydnor Dr 27537
Tabor Ln 27537
Tall Pines Dr 27537
Tanner Pl 27537
Tanner St 27536
Tarheel Ln 27537
Taylor St 27536
Taylor Farm Ln 27537
Taylors Pointe Ln 27537
Technology Ln 27537
Terrace Ave 27536
E Terry Ln 27537
Tharrington Ln 27536
Thomas Ln
100-199 27537
1800-2299 27536
Thomas Rd 27537
Thomas St 27536
Thompson Ln 27537
Thorpe St 27536
Thurston St 27536
Tiffany Ln 27537
Timber Ln 27537

Tiny Ln 27537
Tobacco Rd 27537
Tollie Weldon Rd 27537
Tom Terry Ln 27537
Tony Ln 27537
Toots Way 27537
Topleman St 27536
Torri Dr 27537
Tower Ln & Rd 27537
Townsville Landing Rd 27537
Toyota Ln 27537
Trade St 27536
Travis Ln 27537
Trey Ln 27537
Tripp Ln 27537
Tripp St
300-999 27537
1600-1699 27536
Tristen Ln 27537
Truman Ave 27537
Tucker Lumber Rd 27537
Tulip Dr 27537
Turner Ave 27536
Turner Ln 27537
Turner Avenue Ext 27536
Twelve Oaks Ln 27537
Tyler Ct 27537
Us 1 Byp & Hwy 27537
Us 1/158 Hwy 27537
Us 158 Byp 27537
Us Grant Ct 27537
Us Highway 401 N & S 27537
Valley Way 27537
Valley View Dr 27536
Van Dyke Rd 27537
S Vance Dr 27537
Vance St 27536
Vance Academy Rd 27537
Vance Lake Trailer Park 27537
Vanco Mill Rd 27537
Vandora Ln 27537
Vann Ln 27537
Vaughan Rd 27537
Vaughan St 27536
Vicksboro Rd
1-399 27536
400-1699 27537
1700-1798 27536
1701-6999 27537
1800-6998 27537
Victory Ln 27537
Victory St 27536
Village Ct & Dr 27537
Vincent Hoyle Rd 27537
Vintage Ln 27537
Virginia Ave 27536
Virginia Dare Ln 27537
Vulcan Ln 27537
Waddill St & Way 27536
Wakefield Ave 27536
Walker Rd 27537
Wall St 27536
N Walnut Rd & St 27536
Walter Bowen Rd 27537
Walters St 27536
Warehouse Rd 27537
Warren Bullock Rd 27537
Warrenton Rd 27537
Washington Ave & St 27536
Washout Rd 27537
Water St 27536
Water Front Dr 27537
Waterfall Rd 27537
N & S Waters Edge Cv, Ext, Ln, Loop & Rd 27537
Waterstone Ln 27537
Waterway Ln 27537
Watkins Way 27537
Watson Dr 27536
E & W Waycliff Rd 27537
Wayview Rd 27537
Wedgewood Ln 27537
Welcome Ave
1-99 27537
100-599 27536
Welcome Ln 27537
Weldon Rd & Way 27537
Weldon Goodwin Rd 27537
Weldons Mill Rd 27537
Welshie Way Ln 27537
Wendover Rd 27536
Wendy Ct 27537
Wesley Dr 27536
Wester Ave 27536
Wester Rd 27537
Western Blvd & Ln 27537
Westhills Dr 27537
Westlake Dr 27536
Westover Dr 27536
Weybossett Rd 27537
Whaley Ln 27537
Wheat Ln 27537
White Deer Ln 27537
White Oak Dr 27536
White Tail Ct 27537
Whitten Ave 27536
Wilbur St 27536
Wildwood Ln 27537
Wilkens Ln 27536
Will Jefferson Rd 27537
Williams Ln 27537
N Williams St 27536
S Williams St 27536
Williams Acres Dr 27537
Williamsboro Ln 27537
Willie Currin Rd 27537
Willieville Ln 27537
Willow Ln 27536
Willow Creek Cir & Run 27537
Willow Oak Dr & Pl 27537
Willowood Dr 27536
Wilson St 27536
Wilson Trailer Park 27537
E & W Winder St 27536
Windsor Ct 27537
Winona Ln 27537
Wintergreen Rd 27537
Witherspoon St 27536
Wj Ln 27537
Wolf Pack Ln 27537
Wood St 27536
Wood Trail Way 27537
Wood Valley Ln 27537
Woodbridge Ct 27537
Woodhaven Rd 27537
N & S Woodland Rd 27536
Woodlawn Rd 27537
N Woods Rd 27536
Woodsworth Rd 27537
Wortham Ct 27537
Wright Ave 27536
Wyche St 27536
Yadkin St 27536
Yancey Ln 27536
Yarborough Ln 27537
E & W Young Ave & St 27536
Yowland Rd 27536
Zeb Robinson Rd
1-99 27536
100-799 27537
Zene St 27536
Zollicoffer Ave 27536

NUMBERED STREETS

All Street Addresses 27536

HENDERSONVILLE NC

General Delivery 28739

POST OFFICE BOXES MAIN OFFICE STATIONS AND BRANCHES

Box No.s
All PO Boxes 28793

RURAL ROUTES

03, 04, 10, 13, 15, 16, 20, 21 28739

NAMED STREETS

Aaron Pace Ln 28792
Aarons Way 28792
Abbey Ln 28739
Abbey Fields Ln 28792
Abigail Ln 28739
Academy Rd 28792
W Acorn Dr 28792
Acorn Creek Dr 28792
Acorn Hill Ln 28792
Acton Briar Pl 28739
Adams St 28739
Adams View Dr 28739
Adden Ln 28739
Adeles Way 28792
Adger Dr 28739
Aftermath Ln 28792
Aiken Place Rd 28792
Aileen Dr 28792
Airport Rd 28792
Alabama Ave 28739
Albea Dr 28792
Alex Cove Dr 28792
Alfs Cv 28792
Alfson Cir 28792
Algeria St 28792
Alice Nuckolls Way 28792
N Aliette Ln 28792
N Allen Rd 28792
E Allen St 28792
W Allen St
100-198 28792
200-1099 28739
Allen Claire St 28739
Allen Paul Dr 28791
Allenwood Cir 28792
Alley St 28792
Allgood Dr 28792
Allstar Ln 28739
Alma Way 28792
Almond Branch Dr 28791
Almond Joy Ln 28792
Almost Home Rd 28739
Alpine Dr 28791
Alta Cir 28739
Alta Vista Ln 28791
Alton Way 28791
Alverson Ln 28791
Amazing Grace Ln 28792
Amber Hill Ln 28792
Amber Jean Dr 28791
Amber Knoll Dr 28792
Amber Ridge Ln 28792
Amberjack Dr 28792
Amberly Ln 28739
Amberwood Ln 28791
Amblewood Trl 28739
Amelia Dr 28792
Amity Ct 28791
Ancestor Ln 28792
Anders Dr 28791
Andrew Johnstone Dr 28739
Angel Girl Ln 28792
Angel Mountain Ln 28739
Angel Whisper Ln 28792
Angels Cove Trl 28792
Angelwood Ln 28792
Ann Dr 28739
Anne Ave W 28739
Ansel Way 28792
Anthony Ryan Dr 28792
N & S Anvil Ave 28792
Apache Dr 28739
Appalachian Ave 28792
Apple Ln 28739
Apple Blossom Ln & Trl 28792
Apple Creek Ln 28792
Apple Jack Ln 28792
Apple Meadow Ct 28739
Apple Orchard Rd 28792
Apple Tree Ln 28792
Apple Valley Rd 28792
Apple Valley Park Dr 28792
S Apple View Ln 28792
Applecross Ln 28791
Appledore Ave 28739
Appleola Rd 28792
Applewood Dr 28792
April Ln 28792
April Dew Ln 28792
April Flowers Ln 28792
Arabian Ln 28792
Arbor Ln 28791
Arbutus Ln 28739
E Arbutus Ln 28792
Archangel Ln 28739
Archer Cir 28791
E Ardis Ln 28792
Ariel Loop 28792
Arlington Pl 28791
Armour Ct 28739
Armstrong Ave 28739
Arrowhead Trl 28739
Arrowood Ln 28791
Arrowroot Pl 28739
Arthur Ln 28791
Ash Path Ln 28739
Ashby Ln 28791
Ashe St 28792
Ashefield Ct 28791
Asheville Hwy 28791
Ashley Ln 28791
Ashley Pl 28739
Ashley Bend Trl 28792
Ashley Hill Ln 28791
Ashmore Ave 28791
Ashton Ln 28792
Ashton Forest Ct 28739
Ashwood Rd 28791
Askew Ln 28739
Aspen Ln 28791
Aspen View Ln 28739
Aspenbrook Ln 28791
Aster Ct 28792
Atwood Dr 28792
Audrey Trl 28791
Aunt Ettas Pl 28792
Auto Fixit Ln 28792
Autumn Chase Ln 28792
Autumn Hills Dr 28739
Autumn Sky Dr 28792
Autumn View Dr 28792
Autumn Wind Trce 28792
Autumnwood Ln 28792
Avalon Ln 28739
Avirea Dr 28739
Aycock Ave 28792
Azalea Way 28792
Azalea Bush Ln 28792
Azalea Park Dr 28792
Azalea Ridge Rd 28739
Azalea View Ln 28792
Azalea Woods Dr 28792
Babbling Brook Ln 28739
Baber Rd 28792
Baby Jane Ln 28792
Back Mountain Trl 28792
Badger Run 28739
Bag End Rd 28739
Bald Ridge Rd 28792
Bald Rock Rd 28792
Bald Rock View Dr 28792
Bald Top Dr 28792
Baldmar Rd 28791
Baldwin Hill Ave 28792
Balfour Rd 28792
Ballantyne Common Cir 28792
Ballard Ln 28792
Balsam Rd 28792
Bamboo Ln 28739
E Bane St 28792
Banks Ter 28791
Banks Mountain Dr 28792
Banks View Ln 28792
Bansha Dr 28791
Barbara Blvd 28739
Barker St 28792
Barksdale Ave 28792
Barn Owl Way 28792
Barnes Ct 28739
Barnsdale Ln 28791
E Barnwell St 28792
W Barnwell St
100-199 28792
200-299 28739
Barnwell Acres Dr 28792
Baskins Ln 28792
Basswood Ln 28739
Baton Ln 28792
Baxter Ln 28792
Bay Laurel Ln 28791
Bay Magnolia Ct 28791
Bay Willow Ct 28791
Bayberry Way 28739
Bayless Dr 28791
Baystone Dr 28791
Beach Dr 28792
Bear Butte Farm Ln 28739
Bear Landing Dr 28792
Bear Rock Rd 28739
Bear Rock Loop Rd 28739
Bearcat Blvd
1-138 28791
139-330 28792
Bearcat Loop 28791
Bearfoot Ln & Trl 28792
N Bearwallow Rd 28792
Bearwallow Mountain Rd 28792
Bearwallow View Ln 28792
Beaucrest Dr 28792
Beaumont Dr 28739
Beddingfield Hill Ln 28792
Bee Tree Way 28792
Beech St 28792
Beech Path Ln 28739
Beech Tree Pl 28792
Beechnut Dr 28739
Beechwood Cir 28739
Beechwood Lakes Dr 28792
Beehive Rd 28792
Beehive View Ln 28792
Belinda Dr 28792
Bellariva Dr 28739
Belle Meadow Ln 28792
Belmont Dr 28739
Belvidere Ct 28791
Ben Hogan Dr 28739
Ben Mar Ln 28791
Ben Ray Ln 28739
Benhurst Ct 28791
Benjamin Way 28792
Benning Ct 28792
Bent Arrow Ln 28792
Bent Laurel Ct 28792
Bent Oak Dr 28792
Bent Pine Trce 28739
Bent Tree Dr 28739
Bent Twig Ln 28739
Berea Church Rd 28739
Berkeley Rd 28792
Berna Knoll Ct 28792
Berry Cir 28739
Berry Hill Dr 28791
Berry View Ln 28792
Berrywood Ln 28792
Beth Dr 28791
Beth Ann Ln 28792
Bethea Dr 28791
Betty Joyce Cox Ln 28792
Beverly Ave 28792
Beverly Hanks Ctr 28792
Bicknell Dr 28791
Big Oak Rd 28792
Big Pine Rd 28792
Big Willow Rd 28739
Bigstone Rd 28792
Bill Moore Dr 28792
Birch Ln 28791
Birch Breeze Ln 28792
Birch Tree Ln 28792
Birchwood Dr 28739
Birchwood Views Dr 28739
Bird Haven Rd 28792
Bird Nest Ln 28792
Bird Song Ln 28792
Birdland Dr 28739
Bittersweet Dr 28792
Black Bear Ct & Trl 28739
Black Cherry Ln 28792
Black Creek Ln 28739
Black Hickory Ln 28739
Black Iron Ln 28792
Black Oak Ln 28791
Black Smith Run Dr 28792
Black Walnut Ct 28792
Blackberry Pl 28739
Blackgum Ct 28739
Blackjack Rd 28739
Blackwell Dr 28739
Blade Rd 28791
Blanche St 28792
Blanche Carlisle Ln 28792
Blazing Valley Ln 28739
Blessing Ct 28739
Bliss Dr 28739
Blooming Laurel Dr 28792
Blossom Branch Dr 28792
Blue Goose Ct 28792
Blue Haven Way 28739
Blue House Rd 28792
Blue Moon Ln 28739
Blue Ridge Ave & St 28792
Blue Rock Rd 28792
Blue Sky Ln 28792
Blue Spruce Ln 28739
Blue Star Way 28739
Blueberry Ln 28739
Bluebird Dr 28792
W Blythe Cir 28739
Blythe St
1-699 28739
700-1099 28791
Blythe Commons Ct 28791
Blythe Stepp Rd 28792
Blythe Street Ct 28739
Blythewood Dr 28792
Bob Cat Spur Ln 28792
Bobby Jones Dr 28739
W Bobcat Ct 28792
Bobcat Ln 28792
Bobcat Hill Ln 28739
Bobs Rd 28792
Bodges Ln 28792
Bogey Ln 28792
Bollers Knob Ln 28739
Bolt Action Trl 28792
Bolton Ct 28792
Bonaire Dr 28739
N & S Bonita Breeze Ln 28739
Bonner St 28739
Bostwick Rd 28791
Bothwell Rd 28792
Boulder Heights Ln 28792
Boulder Ridge Dr 28792
Bow Hunter Dr 28739
Bowden Ln 28792
Bowen Blvd 28739
Bowen Terra Dr 28791
Bower Ln 28792
Bowman Rd 28791
Bowman Ridge Rd 28739
Boxcar St 28792
Boxwood Branch Ln 28792
Boyd Hill Dr 28792
Bracton Rd 28791
Bradford Pl 28792
Bradford Terrace Ln 28792
Bradley Rd 28791
Bradley Ascent Ct 28792
Bradley Mountain Ln 28792
Bradshaw Ave 28792
Braemar Dr 28791
Bragg Ct 28792
Brandon Rd 28739
Breckenridge Ct 28739
Breezewood St 28792
Brentwood Dr 28739
Brevard Rd 28791
Brevard Knoll Dr 28792
Brewster Cir 28791
Brians View Dr 28792
Briarcliff Dr 28739
N & S Briarcreek Ct 28739
Briarwood Ln 28791
Bridgette Loop Rd 28791
Bridle Path Ct 28791
Brightwater Dr 28739
Brightwater Falls Rd 28739
Brightwater Farm Rd 28739
Brightwater Heights Dr 28791
Bristol Ln 28792
Brittany Place Dr 28792
Britton Ave 28791
Britton Creek Ct & Dr 28791
Broad Creek Rd 28739
Broadleaf Dr 28739
Broadway St 28739
Brogden Ln 28791
Brook Forest Ln 28791
Brookdale Ave 28792
Brookfield Ln 28739
Brookgreen Ln 28739
Brooklyn Ave 28792
Brooklyn Acres Rd 28792
Brookside Dr 28792
Brookside Camp Rd 28792
Brookstone Ct 28792
Brooktree Cir 28739
Brown Ct & Rd 28791
Brown Bear Trl 28792
Brown Farm Rd 28792
Brown Trout Ln 28791
W Browning Ave & Rd 28791
Broyles Rd 28791
Bruce Ln 28791
Bryan Ave 28739
Buck Trl 28792
Buckeye Dr 28792
Buckhorn Xing 28792
Buckingham Dr & Trl 28739
S Buena Vista Dr 28792
Buena Vista Ln 28791
Bugtussle Ln 28792
Bumble Bee Dr 28792
Bumont Dr 28739
Buncombe St
100-599 28739
600-799 28791
Bunny Trl 28791
Burge Mountain Rd 28792
Burke Ln 28791
Burnside Trl 28792
Butler Ridge Trl 28792
Buttercup Fields Ln 28792
Butternut Trl 28739
Buttons Dr 28739
Byers Dr 28792
Byers Cove Rd 28792
Bynums Pl 28792
E Byrd Ln & Ter 28792
C Ln 28791
C E Mabry Ln 28792
C M K Park Ln 28792
Cabin Cove Ln 28739
Cabinwood Dr 28792
Cagle Farm Rd 28792
Cairn Ct 28792
Calhoun St 28739
Calico Rock Ln 28792
Calloway Ln 28792
Cambria Ln 28791
Cambridge Dr 28792
Camellia Way 28739
Camelot Dr 28739
Camp Judaea Dr 28792
Camp Kanuga Cir 28739
Campground Rd 28791
Canal Dr 28739
Canary Ln 28792
Canarys Song Ln 28791

Candy Land Ln ... 28792
Cannalily Dr ... 28792
Cannon Dr ... 28792
Cannons Place Dr ... 28791
Canterbury Way ... 28792
Canterbury Hill Ln ... 28792
Cantrell Loop Rd ... 28739
Canvasback Way ... 28791
Cape Martin Cir ... 28791
Capps Rd ... 28792
Capri Ln ... 28791
Captains Cir ... 28792
Cardinal Ct ... 28792
Cardinal Ln
100-199 ... 28739
3100-3299 ... 28792
Cardinal Haven Ln ... 28739
Carleton Ter ... 28791
Carlisle Dr ... 28792
Carmack Dr ... 28792
Carolina Ave ... 28791
N Carolina Ave ... 28739
S Carolina Ave ... 28739
Carolina Cir ... 28792
Carolina Village Rd ... 28792
Carolyn Dr ... 28739
Carousel Ln ... 28792
Carousel Corner Dr ... 28739
Carpenters Son Ln ... 28792
Carriage Ct ... 28791
Carriage Commons Dr ... 28792
Carriage Crest Dr ... 28791
Carriage Falls Ct ... 28791
Carriage Forest Ct ... 28791
Carriage Highlands Ct ... 28791
Carriage Springs Way ... 28791
Carriage Square Ct & Dr ... 28791
Carriage Summitt Way ... 28791
N Carriage Walk Ln ... 28791
Carriage West Dr ... 28791
Carrie Dr ... 28792
Carrie Elizabeth Dr ... 28792
Carrie Hill Ln ... 28739
Carrington Ct ... 28739
Carson Dr ... 28791
Cart Wheel Ln ... 28792
Carverwood Ln ... 28791
Case St ... 28792
Case Estate Ln ... 28792
Casper Pointe Ln ... 28792
Cassie Ln ... 28792
Castleton Ln ... 28791
Casual Corner Ln ... 28792
E Caswell St ... 28792
Catalpa Trl ... 28792
Catawba Path ... 28739
Cathedral View Ln ... 28792
Cathy Ct ... 28792
Cathys Cove Rd ... 28792
Cattle Dr ... 28739
Caudle Way ... 28792
Causby Ln ... 28791
Cecil Rogers Rd ... 28792
Cecils Way ... 28792
Cedar Ter ... 28739
Cedar Bluffs Dr ... 28792
Cedar Creek Dr ... 28792
Cedar Rock Trl ... 28739
Cedarbrook Dr ... 28792
Cely Dr ... 28791
Center Park Ln ... 28792
Centerway Dr ... 28792
Centipede Ln ... 28792
Central Dr ... 28739
E Central St ... 28792
Chabb Wood Acres Ln ... 28792
Chadwick Ave ... 28792
Chadwick Square Ct ... 28739
Challenger Ln ... 28739
Chambers Ln & Rd ... 28739
Chandler Ln ... 28792
Chanteloup Dr ... 28739
Chanticleer Ln ... 28739
Chantilly Pl ... 28739
Chapman Dr ... 28792
Chapman Hills Dr ... 28792
Chariot Ct ... 28791
Chariton Ave ... 28739
Charles Ln & Trl ... 28792
S Charleston Ct & Ln ... 28792
Charleston View Ct ... 28792
Charlestown Dr ... 28792
Charlyne Dr ... 28792
Charming Ln ... 28792
Chatham Path ... 28791
Chattooga Run ... 28739
Cheerful Cir ... 28739
Chelsea St ... 28791
Chelsea Nix Ln ... 28792
Cherie Ln ... 28739
Cherokee Dr ... 28739
Cherry St ... 28792
Cherry Blossom Ln ... 28791
Cherry Hill Dr ... 28791
Cherrywood Ln ... 28792
Cheryl Dr ... 28792
Chestnut Cir ... 28739
W Chestnut Dr ... 28739
Chestnut Ln ... 28792
Chestnut Trl ... 28792
Chestnut Creek Trl ... 28792
E Chestnut Gap Rd ... 28792
Chestnut Hills Ct ... 28792
Chestnut Oak Ln ... 28791
Chestnut Path Ln ... 28739
Chestnut Stump Rd ... 28792
Chestnut Tree Rd ... 28792
Chestnut Way Trl ... 28792
Chickadee Cir & Trl ... 28792
Chickadee Hill Ln ... 28739
Chickadee Hollow Ln ... 28792
Chickasaw Trl ... 28792
E & W Chicory Xing ... 28739
Childs Dr ... 28791
E & W Chimney Xing ... 28739
Chimney Glen Dr ... 28739
Chimney Rock Rd ... 28792
Chinaberry Ln ... 28792
Chinquapin Oak Ln ... 28791
Chipmunk Dr ... 28739
Chippewa Ln ... 28791
Choctaw Cir ... 28739
Chris View Ln ... 28792
Christian Ln ... 28792
Christian Walk Ln ... 28792
Christy Ann Ln ... 28792
Chukkar Trl ... 28792
N & S Church St ... 28792
Ciccone Dr ... 28791
Cider Mill Dr ... 28792
Cimarron Blvd ... 28791
Circle Dr ... 28739
Circle L Farm Dr ... 28792
Circle Top Dr ... 28739
Circle View Dr ... 28792
Citadel Ln ... 28739
Citation Cir ... 28739
Clairmont Dr ... 28791
Claridge Way ... 28739
Clark Rd ... 28792
Clark St ... 28739
N & S Classic Ct ... 28791
Classic Breeze Ln ... 28792
Classic Oaks Cir ... 28792
Claude Justice Ln ... 28792
Clays Cv ... 28739
N Clear Creek Rd ... 28792
Clear Creek Park Dr ... 28792
Clear Creekside Dr ... 28792
Clear Oak Rd ... 28792
Clear Stone Rd ... 28792
Clear View Run Dr ... 28792
Clearview Dr ... 28792
Cleo Ct ... 28792
Cliff Dr ... 28739
Climbing View Ln ... 28792
Clingenpeel Ln ... 28792
Clipper Ln ... 28739
Cloverdale Dr ... 28791
Club Knoll Ct ... 28791
Club View Dr ... 28739
Cody Trl ... 28792
Cold Springs Rd ... 28792
Cold Stream Way ... 28791
Cold Wind Dr ... 28792
Coldwater Ln ... 28739
College St ... 28792
Colonial Way ... 28791
Colony Ln ... 28791
Colony Rd ... 28792
Columbia Cir ... 28792
Comet Dr ... 28791
Comfort View Ln ... 28791
Commerce Dr ... 28791
Commercial Hill Dr ... 28792
Commons Way ... 28792
Conde Pl ... 28739
Condor Ct ... 28792
Conger Dr ... 28739
Congress Ln ... 28739
Connell Dr ... 28739
Connemara Overlook Dr ... 28739
Connie Dale Ln ... 28792
Connor Ave ... 28791
Connor Hill Rd ... 28792
Conservative Ln ... 28739
Constance Ct & Way ... 28792
Coolridge St ... 28792
Coon Branch Trl ... 28791
Cooper Cv S ... 28739
Coopers Dr ... 28739
Copper Ct ... 28792
Copper Penny St ... 28792
Copperhead Rd ... 28739
Coral Dr ... 28791
Coral Bells Ln ... 28792
Corbly Dr ... 28739
Cori Dr ... 28792
Corlin Dr ... 28739
Corn Mountain Rd ... 28792
Cornerstone Way ... 28791
Cornflower Ln ... 28739
Cornsilk Ln ... 28739
Corntown Rd ... 28792
Cornwallis Ln ... 28792
Coronet Ln ... 28792
Cosmopolitan Ln ... 28739
Cosmos St ... 28791
Coston Cemetery Rd ... 28792
N Cottage Ct ... 28739
S Cottage Ct ... 28739
Cottage Ln ... 28792
E Cotton Ln ... 28792
Cotton St ... 28739
Cotton View Ln ... 28792
Cottontail Ln ... 28739
Country Rd ... 28791
Country Brook Trl ... 28739
Country Club Rd ... 28739
Country Meadows Ln ... 28792
Country Place Dr ... 28792
Country Ridge Rd ... 28739
Country View Dr & Ln ... 28792
Countryside Dr ... 28792
Courtland Blvd ... 28791
Courtney Dr ... 28792
Courtney View Dr ... 28792
Courtwood Ln ... 28739
Courtyard Square Ln ... 28739
Cove Creek Xing ... 28739
Cove Landing Ln ... 28792
Cove Loop Rd ... 28739
Cove Overlook Dr ... 28739
Cove Park Ln ... 28739
Cove Summitt Dr ... 28739
Cove View Ln ... 28792
Covington Cove Ln ... 28739
Cow House Rd ... 28739
Cox St ... 28739
Coy Evie Ln ... 28739
Coyote Ln ... 28791
Cozy Cv ... 28792
Cozy Cabin Trl ... 28792
Crab Creek Rd ... 28739
N & S Crab Meadow Dr ... 28739
Crabapple Cir ... 28792
Crabapple Hill Ln ... 28792
Craftsman Way ... 28739
Craig Dr ... 28739
Craigs Cove Ln ... 28792
Crail Farm Rd ... 28739
Cranbrook Cir ... 28792
Craven Ln ... 28792
Crawford Valley Ln ... 28792
Crecy Pl ... 28739
Creek Hollow Ln ... 28792
Creeks Edge Dr ... 28739
N & S Creekside Ct ... 28791
Creekside View Trl ... 28792
Creekstone Ln ... 28791
Creekwalk Ln ... 28792
Crepe Myrtle Gln ... 28739
Crescent Ave ... 28792
Crescent Point Dr ... 28739
Crest Blvd & Dr ... 28739
S Crest View Ct ... 28739
Crestmont Ln ... 28792
Crestview Dr ... 28791
Crestview Hills Dr & Ln ... 28792
Crestwood Dr & Rd ... 28739
Cricket Dr ... 28792
Crimson Ln ... 28792
Crisp Ln ... 28739
Crocus Dr ... 28792
Crooked Creek Ln & Rd ... 28739
Crooked Oak Ct ... 28791
Crooked Path Ln ... 28792
Cross Ln ... 28792
Cross Keys Ln ... 28792
Crossvine Trl ... 28739
Crosswick Ln ... 28739
Crow Ridge Ln ... 28739
Crown Ln ... 28791
Crows Nest Rd ... 28791
Croydon Dr ... 28791
Crystal Dr ... 28791
Crystal Creek Ln ... 28739
Crystal Heights Dr ... 28739
Crystal Mountain Dr ... 28739
Crystal Ridge Dr ... 28739
Crystal Spring Dr ... 28739
Crystalwood Ln ... 28739
Cub Run ... 28739
Cub Paw Ln ... 28792
Cumberland Dr ... 28792
S, E & W Cumming Woods Ct & Ln ... 28739
Cummings Rd ... 28739
Cummings Battle Trl ... 28739
Cummings Cove Pkwy ... 28739
Cummings Crest Dr ... 28739
Cummings Ridge Trl ... 28739
S Cureton Pl ... 28791
Curlew Ct ... 28792
Curry Ln ... 28791
Curtis Dr ... 28739
Cypress Pt ... 28739
Cypress Estates Ln ... 28792
Cyprus Creek Ln ... 28791
Daddys Girl Ln ... 28792
Daffodil Dr ... 28792
Dairy St ... 28739
Daisy Dr ... 28792
Daisy Dream Ln ... 28739
Dakota Ct ... 28791
S Dale Ave ... 28792
Dale St ... 28739
Dale Nix Cir ... 28792
Dallas Dr ... 28739
Dalmation Trl ... 28792
Dalton Clan Ln ... 28791
Dalton Farm Rd ... 28792
Dalton Pine Rdg ... 28792
Dalton Trail Dr ... 28792
Dana Rd ... 28792
Dania Dr ... 28792
Daniel Dr ... 28792
Daniel Ridge Dr ... 28792
Danner Ln ... 28739
Dantes Peak ... 28739
Darnell Dr ... 28791
Dartcrest Dr ... 28792
Dartmouth Rd ... 28791
Dausuel Trl ... 28791
Dave Edward Dr ... 28792
Davidson Ln ... 28792
Davies Way ... 28792
Davis Cir ... 28791
Davis St ... 28739
Davis Mountain Rd ... 28739
Dawley Dr ... 28791
Dawn Mist Ct ... 28791
Dawn Valley Dr ... 28792
Dawnview Dr ... 28791
Dawnwood Ln ... 28791
Daylilly Ct ... 28739
Daylily Dr ... 28739
De Witt Ln ... 28792
Debbie Dr ... 28791
Declaration Ln ... 28739
Dee Dee Ln ... 28791
Deep Valley Ln ... 28791
Deep Woods Dr ... 28739
Deer Run & Trl ... 28739
Deer Meadow Ln ... 28739
Deerfield Ct ... 28792
Deerfield Ridge Rd ... 28792
Deerhaven Ln ... 28791
Deermouse Way ... 28792
Deerpath Ln ... 28739
Deerwood Ln ... 28739
Del And Bettys Pl ... 28792
Delacy Dr ... 28739
Delaware Ln ... 28791
Delicious Ln ... 28792
Dellford Ct ... 28792
Dellwood Ter ... 28791
Dellwood View Ln ... 28791
Delozier Cir ... 28792
Delphi Ter ... 28791
Delta Dr ... 28792
Dena Nix Ln ... 28792
Denny Ln ... 28792
Derby Dr & Ln W ... 28739
Derbyshire Dr ... 28792
Dermid Ave ... 28792
Devon Wood Dr ... 28739
Dewberry Dr ... 28792
Diamond Mine Ln ... 28739
Dickens Ln ... 28792
Didrikson Way ... 28739
Diesel Dr ... 28739
Dillard Ave ... 28791
Dillon Ln ... 28792
Dismal Creek Rd ... 28739
Dixie Blvd ... 28792
Dixie Ln ... 28739
Dixie Trails Ln ... 28792
Dixon Dr ... 28792
Doanbury Ct ... 28792
Docks Rd ... 28792
Doctors Dr ... 28792
Doe Trl ... 28792
Doe Ridge Ln ... 28792
Doe Run Rd ... 28792
Doelger Dr ... 28792
Dogwood Dr ... 28791
E Dogwood Ln ... 28792
Dogwood Trl ... 28791
Dogwood Dell Ln ... 28739
Dogwood Path Ln ... 28739
Dollie Ln ... 28739
Dollie Case Ln ... 28792
Dolly Rogers Dr ... 28792
Don Wilkie Ln ... 28792
Donnatina Dr ... 28792
Dono Ln ... 28792
Dooley Dr ... 28792
Dorado Ln ... 28792
Doris Lisa View Dr ... 28792
Dorne Dr ... 28739
Dorothy St ... 28791
Dorothy Jane Ln ... 28792
Dorothy Nix Ln ... 28792
Dorset Ct & Ln ... 28792
Doties Ln ... 28792
Dotson Rd ... 28792
Dotson Half Loop ... 28792
Dotson Nelon Dr ... 28792
Double Creek Dr ... 28792
Douglas Dr ... 28792
Dove Trl ... 28792
Dove Haven Ln ... 28791
Dove Valley Ln ... 28792
Dover Ln ... 28739
Doverwood Ln ... 28792
Dovetree Ln ... 28739
Downing Ct ... 28739
E Downing St ... 28792
Drake St ... 28739
Drake Mountain Ln ... 28739
E Dream Rd & St ... 28792
Dreamworks Ct ... 28792
Drexel Rd ... 28739
S Drexel Farm Dr ... 28739
Dried Apple Ln ... 28792
Drifting Cloud Ln ... 28792
Driver Ct ... 28739
Druid Hills Ave ... 28791
Drummond Cir ... 28791
Dry Creek Ln ... 28792
Dry Creek Rdg ... 28739
Drystone Ln ... 28739
Dublin Ln ... 28792
Duchess Ln ... 28739
Ducks Walk Trl ... 28792
Due West Rd ... 28792
E Duncan Hill Rd ... 28792
Dundee St ... 28791
Dundeve Cir ... 28792
Dunean Ln ... 28739
Dunigan Dr ... 28791
Dunlap Rd ... 28792
Dunleer Ln ... 28791
Dunroy Dr ... 28739
Dupont Rd ... 28739
Dupont Estates Dr ... 28739
Dwight Dr ... 28792
Dynasty Dr ... 28792
Eagle Dr ... 28792
Eagle Claw Ln ... 28792
Eagle Rock Trl ... 28739
Eagle Valley Ln ... 28792
Eagles Ct ... 28739
Eagles Eye Dr ... 28792
Earl Baker Ln ... 28739
Earl Culbreth Dr ... 28792
Eastbrook Dr ... 28792
Eastbury Dr ... 28792
Eastwind Dr ... 28739
Easy St ... 28791
Ebb Ida Ln ... 28792
Echo Ave, Cir, Dr & Ln ... 28739
Echo Lakes Dr ... 28739
N Edenburg St ... 28791
Edgehill Rd ... 28739
Edgemont Ln ... 28792
N & S Edgerton Rd ... 28792
Edgewood Ave ... 28792
Edith Dr ... 28792
Edna Oaks Rd ... 28792
Edney St ... 28792
Edney Inn Rd ... 28792
Edney Lane Dr ... 28792
N Edwards St ... 28792
Edwards Mountain Dr ... 28792
Ehringhaus St ... 28739
Eisenhower Dr ... 28792
Elden St ... 28791
Elissa Ct & Way ... 28739
Elizabeth St ... 28792
Ellaberry Trl ... 28792
Ellerslie Acre ... 28739
Elliott Ln ... 28792
Elliott Ridge Ln ... 28792
Elm Ln ... 28739
Elm St ... 28792
Elson Ave ... 28739
Elzie Hill Dr ... 28792
Emerald Ln ... 28792
Emerald Cove Ct ... 28792
Emerald Pond Cv ... 28739
Emily Way ... 28792
Empress Ln ... 28792
Enchanted Acres Dr ... 28792
Enchanted Hills Way ... 28791
Englewood Dr ... 28739
Enigma Ln ... 28792
Eric M Ln ... 28792
Erkwood Dr & Hts ... 28739
Erwin Hill Dr ... 28739
Espresso Ln ... 28739
Essex Ct & Path ... 28791
Essie Orr Cir ... 28792
Essowah Dr ... 28739
Estate Dr & Ln ... 28739
Estelle Ln ... 28792
Esther King Dr ... 28792
Ethan Pond Way ... 28791
Ethel Ln ... 28791
Eton Dr ... 28792
Etowah Rd ... 28791
Etowah School Rd ... 28739
E Evans Ave ... 28792
Evans Rd ... 28739
Evanwood Pl ... 28792
Evening Shade Ln ... 28792
Evenstar Crst ... 28739
Everette Pl ... 28791
Evergreen Dr ... 28792
Ewart Dr ... 28739
Ewarts Hill Rd ... 28739
Ewarts Pond Rd ... 28739
Ewbank Dr ... 28791
Ewbank Gardens Dr ... 28791
Excalibur Ct ... 28739
Exeter Ct ... 28791
Expectation Ln ... 28792
F H Justus Rd ... 28792
Fair St ... 28792
Fair Hollow Ln ... 28792
Fair Oaks Dr ... 28791
Fairbanks Ln ... 28792
Fairfax Ln ... 28792
Fairfield Dr ... 28792
Fairgate Dr ... 28739
N Fairground Ave ... 28792
E Fairlane Dr ... 28792
Fairview Ave ... 28792
Fairview Heights Dr ... 28739
Fairway Dr ... 28739
Fairway Knoll Dr ... 28739
Fairway Seven Pl ... 28739
Fairwinds Dr ... 28791
Falcon Ct ... 28792
Falcon Wood Way ... 28739
Fallen Timber Rd ... 28791
Falling Oak Ln ... 28739
Falling Snow Ln ... 28739
Falling Star Ln ... 28792
Falling Waters Rd ... 28792
Falls Ln ... 28739
Falls Summit Rd ... 28739
Falls View Ct ... 28739
Fallswood Ct ... 28739
Fannie Collins Ln ... 28792
Farm View Dr ... 28791
Farmington Cir ... 28739
Farside Dr ... 28739
Fascination Dr ... 28792
Fassifern Ct ... 28791
Fawnview Ln ... 28791
Fax Jones Dr ... 28792
Fay Ln ... 28792
Feagan Rd ... 28792
Fenwick Ct ... 28739
Ferenvilla Dr ... 28791
Fern Ln ... 28739
Fernbrook Way ... 28791
Ferncliff Ln ... 28791
Fernhaven Pl ... 28792
Fernwood Dr
1-99 ... 28791
100-199 ... 28791
200-299 ... 28791
Fess Dr ... 28792

Street	ZIP
Ficker Cir	28739
Fickley Dr	28792
Fiddlers Green Ln	28791
Field Crest Ct	28791
Field Sparrow Ln	28792
Fiesta Ln	28792
Finlay Ridge Rd	28739
Finley St	28739
Finley Brook Way	28739
Finley Cove Rd	28739
Finley Creek Ct	28739
Fir St	28791
Fire Azalea Ln	28739
Fire Box Ln	28792
Fire Thorn Ln	28792
Firehouse Rd	28792
Firemender Valley Trl	28792
Fish Hawk Dr	28739
Fitzsimmons St	28792
Fiver Ln	28792
Flame Azalea Trl	28792
Flameleaf Ln	28739
Flanders Ave	28792
Flat Rock Fields Ln	28739
Fleetwood Ave	28791
Fleetwood Plz	28739
Fleming St	
100-599	28739
600-1099	28791
Flintlock Trl	28792
Flintstone Dr	28791
Flintwood Ln	28791
Floral Peak Ln	28792
Florence St	28792
Florida Ave	28739
Florida Dr	28792
Foggy Ridge Ln	28739
Folly Rd	28739
Folsmont Rd	28792
Foothills Dr	28792
Forest Dr	28791
Forest St	28739
Forest Edge Dr	28792
Forest Garden Dr	28739
Forest Hill Dr	28791
Forest Lawn Dr	28792
Forest Park Dr	28792
Forest Ridge Dr	28791
Fork Ridge Ln	28792
Forrestwood Ct	28792
Forsythia Ct	28739
Foster Cir	28739
Foster Hill Dr	28739
Fountain Dr	28739
Fountain Trace Dr	28739
Four Seasons Blvd & Mall	28792
Fox Chase	28739
Fox Chase Ct	28792
Fox Den Ct	28792
Fox Lair Ln	28791
E Fox Ridge Dr	28739
Fox Run Dr	28792
Fox Valley Ct	28791
Foxboro Rd	28739
Foxfire Ln	28739
Foxglove Rd	28739
Foxhorn Ct	28791
Foxhunt Ln	28791
Foxtail Ct	28792
Foxwood Dr	28791
Francis Rd	28792
Frank Hill Rd	28792
Franklin Farm Ln	28792
Fred Orr Dr	28792
N Frederick Ln	28792
Fredrick Ln	28792
Freeborn Ln	28792
Freedom Rd	28792
Freeman St	28792
Freeman Knolls Dr	28792
Freeman Place Trl	28792
Fresh Spring Dr	28791
Friendly Cir	28792
Fringetree Trl	28792
Frog And Fern Rd	28792
Frost Ln	28792
Fruitland Rd	28792
Fruitland Cemetery Rd	28792
Fuchsia Dr	28792
Fullam Farm Dr	28739
Fulton Dr	28792
Furman Dr	28739
Furniture Dr	28792
Fynch St	28791
Gage Ln	28792
Gaither Ln	28792
Galax Ln	28791
Galilee Ln	28792
Gander Way	28792
Garden Ln	28792
Garden Hill Dr	28739
Garden Hollow Ln	28739
Garren Rd	28792
Gateway Dr	28739
Gebe Ln	28792
Geneva Ln & St	28739
George St	28792
Georgetown Rd	28739
Georgia Ave	28739
Gerton Hwy	28792
Gibbs Rd	28792
Gibbs St	28739
E & W Gilbert St	28792
Gilbert Cove Dr	28739
Gilberts Way	28739
Gilliam Rd	28792
Gilliam Mountain Rd	28792
Gilliam Ridge Ln	28792
Ginseng Ln	28791
Gladewood Ln	28792
Gladiola Ln	28739
Glasgow Ln	28739
Glasgow Rd	28791
Glaspy Mountain Rd	28792
Glasson Ct	28792
Glassy Mountain Dr	28739
Glen Rd	28739
Glen Echo Ln	28739
Glen Park Dr	28791
Glenbrook Dr	28739
Glendale Ave	28739
Glenheath Dr	28791
Glenview Ave	28791
Glenwood Ln	28792
E Glenwood Ln	28792
Glenwood Rd	28791
Gloria Orchard Ln	28792
Glover St	28792
Goat Farm Trl	28792
Golden Eagle Way	28739
Golden Gate Dr	28739
Golden Pond Way	28791
Golden Valley Dr	28792
Goldfinch Dr	28792
Goldview Dr	28791
Golf Club Ct	28739
Golf View Condo Ln	28739
Golfside Ln	28739
Goodview Dr	28792
Goodwood Dr & Ln	28792
Gosling Cir & Dr E	28792
Gossamer Ct	28739
Gossett Dr	28739
Governors Dr	28791
Gowan Ln	28792
Grace Ct	28792
Gracewood Dr	28739
Graham Ln	28792
Grand Canyon Dr	28792
Grand Daughters Dr	28792
Grand Highland Dr	28792
Grand Oaks Dr	28792
Grand Teton Dr	28792
Grand Vista Ct	28739
Grandmas Gang Cir	28792
E Grandview Ln	28791
Granite Dr & St	28792
Granny Apple Rd	28792
Grant Mountain Rd	28792
Grassy Hills Dr	28792
Grassy Meadow Ct	28739
Gravel St	28739
Gray Wolf Ln	28792
Grayling Ln	28739
Great Oaks Ln	28792
Great Smoky Ln	28792
Greater Druid Hills Blvd	28791
Green Way	28739
Green Acres Hill Ln	28739
Green Berry Ln	28792
Green Haven Ln	28791
Green Mountain Rd	28792
Green Pine Ct	28739
Green Springs Rd	28739
Green Valley St	28739
Greenbriar Oval Way	28739
S Greenbriar Woods Rd	28739
Greenbrier Rd	28739
Greenfield Ln	28792
S Greenleaf Rd	28792
Greentree Ln	28739
Greenville Hwy	28792
Greenwood Dr	28791
Greg Ct	28792
Greg Albea Dr	28792
Gregory Way	28791
Grey Fox Trl	28739
Greyhawk Ln	28792
Greystone Dr & Way	28792
Gridley Rd	28739
Griffin Dr	28792
Grimes Golden Loop	28792
Grist Mill Dr	28739
Grizzly Bear Trl	28792
Grouse Ln	28739
N & S Grove St	28792
Grove Park Rd	28739
Gum St	28791
Gwens Dr	28739
Gypsy Ln	28792
Hackleburg Ln	28792
Hagen Dr	28739
Half Circle Ln	28791
Half Moon Trl	28792
Half Way Tree Ln	28739
Halford Ct & Dr	28792
Hall St	28739
Halliburton Rd	28791
Hals Way	28792
Halsbury Ave	28791
Halstead Blvd	28791
Hamilton Dr	28739
Hampton Ct & Dr	28791
Hannah Grace Way	28792
Hannah Knoll Ln	28792
Hannen Ln	28792
Happy Ln	28792
Harbor Rd	28792
Harden Cir	28739
Hardwood Summit Dr	28739
Harmony Ln	28791
Harmony Forest Trl	28739
N Harper Dr	28791
Harper Rd	28792
Harper Meadow Way	28792
Harris St	28792
Hart Ln	28792
Hartstone Hill Ln	28791
Harvey Dr	28792
Hawk Meadow Dr	28792
Hawke Ter	28792
Hawke Crest Rd	28792
Hawke Woods Rd	28792
Hawkins Creek Rd	28791
Hawks Ln	28792
Hawksnest Dr	28739
Hawkstepp Dr	28792
Hawthorn Dr	28791
Haydens Way	28792
Haynes Blvd	28792
Haynes St	28791
Haywood Rd & Ter	28791
Haywood Knolls Dr	28791
Haywood Manor Rd	28791
Haywood Park Dr	28791
Hazel St	28739
Hazelton Dr	28739
Headwater Dr	28739
Health Nut Ln	28792
Heath Bar Ln	28739
Heathcote Rd	28791
Heather Cir	28739
Heather Ln	28792
Heather Marie Dr	28792
Heatherwood Dr	28792
Heaton St	28739
Heavenly Valley Ln	28792
Heavenly View Ln	28792
Hebron Dr & Rd	28739
Helen Ln	28792
Hemingway Ln	28792
Hemlock Trl	28739
Henderson St	28739
Henderson Crossing Plz	28792
Henderson Ridge Ln	28792
Heritage Cir	28791
Heritage Ct	28791
Heritage Dr	28791
S Heritage Dr	28791
Heritage Ln	28739
Hibiscus Hill Dr	28792
Hickory Acres Rd	28792
Hickory Court Ln	28792
Hickory Cove Ln	28739
Hickory Hill Rd	28792
Hickory Hollow Estates Dr	28739
Hickory Mountain Ln	28739
Hickory Nut Trl	28739
Hickory Wood Trl	28739
Hicks Lake Dr	28739
Hicks Mountain Rd	28792
Hidaway Cv	28739
Hidden Brook Dr	28739
Hidden Cove Ln	28739
Hidden Creek Rdg	28739
Hidden Forest Dr	28792
E & W Hidden Hills Dr	28792
Hidden Lake Rd	28739
Hidden Meadow Dr	28792
Hidden Pines Ct	28792
Hidden Treasure Ln	28792
Hidden Valley Dr	28739
Hidden View Rd	28792
Hidden Woods Ct & Ln	28791
Hideaway Cabin Trl	28792
Hideaway Park Trl	28792
Higate Rd	28791
Higgins Dr	28791
High St	28791
High Canyon Ln	28791
High Cliffs Rd	28739
High Country Ln	28792
High Falls Rd	28792
High Fields Ct	28791
High Heaven Ln	28739
High Hills Rd	28791
High Meadow Ln	28739
High Mountain Trl	28791
High Park Ct	28791
High Peak Rd	28739
High Plains Dr	28739
E & W High Point Ln	28791
High Quarry Rd	28791
High Road Overlook	28739
High Rocks Trl	28739
Highland Ave	28792
Highland Point Dr	28739
Highlander Dr & Ln	28792
Highlands Square Dr	28792
Hilda Capps Ln	28792
Hilgirt Rd	28792
E Hill Dr	28792
Hillbilly Ln	28791
Hillcrest Cir	28792
Hillcrest St	28739
Hillpark Dr	28739
N & W Hills Dr & Rd	28791
Hills Ridge Rd	28792
Hillside Ln	28739
N Hillside Rd	28791
Hillside Commons Dr	28792
Hilltop Cir N	28791
Hilltop Ln	28739
Hillview Blvd	28792
Hilton Ln	28739
His Way	28792
Historic Courthouse Sq	28792
Hobby Horse Ln	28792
Hobe Crst	28792
Hobes Way	28792
Hog Hill Dr	28792
Hog Rock Rd	28792
Hogans View Cir	28739
Holbert Rd	28791
Holbrook Ln	28739
N Holiday Dr	28739
Holland Ln	28792
Hollingsworth Ln	28792
Holly Berry Ln	28739
Holly Hill Dr N	28791
Holly Hill Rd	28792
Holly Oak Dr	28792
Holly Springs Rd	28739
Holly Tree Cir	28792
Holly Tree Hl	28739
Hollywood St	28792
Holmes St	28739
Home Place Dr	28792
Homers Ln	28792
Homestead Cir	28792
Homestead Farm Cir	28792
Hominy Branch Rd	28792
Honey Ln	28792
Honey Sweet Path	28791
N Honeysuckle Dr	28791
Honor Ln	28792
Hood Hts	28739
Hoot Owl Ln	28792
Hoots Dr	28792
Hoover Dale Ln	28791
Hope Cir	28792
Hope Creek Ln	28792
Hope View Dr	28792
Horace Ln	28792
Horse Pasture Dr	28739
Horse Shoe Farm Dr	28791
Horse Shoe Gap Ln	28739
Horsefeather Ln	28792
Horseshoe Dr	28791
Horseshoe Loop Ln	28792
Horseshoe Ridge Trl	28739
Hospital Dr	28792
Hosta Ln	28739
Hot Rod Ln	28792
Hounds Trl	28791
Hounds Chase Dr	28791
Houston St	28792
N Howard Ln	28792
Howard Gap Rd	28792
Howard Gilbert Ln	28792
Howell Ln	28791
Hs Dalton Rd	28739
W Huckleberry Rd	28792
Huckleberry Mountain Rd	28792
Hudgins Rd	28792
Hudson Dr	28739
Huff St	28739
Huff N Puff Ln	28792
Hull Ln	28792
Hummingbird Ln	28792
Hunsinger Ln	28792
Hunters Ln	28791
Hunters Trl	28739
Hunters Glen Ln	28739
Hunting Trl	28792
Huntington Ct	28739
Huntley Stepp Ln	28792
Hurricane Dr	28792
Hyacinth Ln	28739
Hyde Well Dr	28792
Hyder St	28792
Hyder Allen Ln	28792
Hyder Farm Rd	28792
Hyder View Dr	28791
Hydrangea Dr	28739
Hyman Ave	28792
Hysong Ln	28791
Ida Rogers Dr	28792
Ideal Way	28739
Imperial Dr	28792
Indian Bend Dr	28739
Indian Bluff Trl	28739
Indian Cave Rd	28739
Indian Cave Park Rd	28739
Indian Hill Rd	28791
Indian Ridge Trl	28739
Indian River Rd	28791
Indian Springs Trl	28792
Indian Woods Trl	28739
Indigo Way	28739
Industrial Dr	28739
Industrial Park Rd	28792
Inglenook Rd	28792
Inkberry Rd	28739
Interlude Pl	28739
Investor Ln	28792
Iowa St	28739
Iris Dr	28792
Ironwood Dr	28739
Iroquois Dr	28791
Israel St	28739
Italy Ln	28792
Ives St	28739
Ives Farm Ln	28739
Ivy Ln	28792
Ivy Way	28739
Ivy Brook Ln	28792
Ivy Hill Rd	28792
Ivy Knoll Ln	28791
Ivywood Ln	28739
J And B Glaspy Dr	28792
J D Hogg Ln	28792
J H Hyder Rd	28792
J J Ln	28792
J P Garren Dr	28792
J R Matthews Dr	28792
Jacamar Way	28739
Jack St	28792
Jack Frost Ln	28739
Jack Rabbit Run Ln	28792
Jackal Ln	28792
Jacks Legacy Ln	28739
Jacks Mountain Ln	28792
W Jackson St	28792
Jackson Park Rd	28792
Jackson Parkview Ct	28792
Jacobs Apple Ln	28792
Jacobs Way Dr	28792
Jade Dr	28791
Jade Walker Dr	28792
James Way	28792
Jamestown Ln	28792
Jane Ln	28792
Jane Moore Dr	28792
Jane Way Dr	28792
Jannies Way	28792
Jarrod Dr	28739
N & S Jarvis Dr	28792
Jasmine Pl	28739
Jason Dr	28792
Jasper Ln	28792
Javelin Dr	28791
Jaymar Park Dr	28792
Jeans Way	28792
Jearl Ln	28739
Jeff St	28739
Jefferson St	28739
Jefferson Forest Dr	28739
Jenny Lind Dr	28791
Jeromy Ln	28739
Jerry Ln	28739
Jesse Ln	28792
Jesse Lamb Dr	28792
Jessica Ln	28792
Jet St	28792
Jeter Mountain Rd & Ter	28739
Jim Collins Dr	28792
Jims Pl	28739
Joanne Ln	28792
Jodhpur Ct	28791
Joel Wright Dr	28792
Joelle Ct	28792
John Delk Rd	28792
John Halford Ct	28792
John Laughter Dr	28792
John Lee Montgomery Dr	28792
John Maxwell Dr	28792
John Thomas Dr	28739
Johnnys Ln	28791
Johnson Dr	28792
Johnson Valley Dr	28792
Jolly Ln	28739
Jonas St	28792
S Jones St	28739
Jones Levy Ln	28792
Jonesborough St	28739
Jordan St	28739
Jordans Park Ln	28791
Joshua Springs Ln	28792
Josiah Ln	28792
Journey Ln	28792
Joy Ln	28739
Joyce Rd	28792
Joyful Dr	28791
Jp Huggins Dr	28791
Jr Matthews Dr	28792
Jubilation Dr	28791
Judsen Ln	28739
Julias Way	28792
Jumbo Ln	28792
Jump Creek Rd	28739
Junco Way	28792
N June Ln	28792
W June Ln	28791
Jungle Ln	28792
Juniper Ln	28739
Justamere Ln	28739
N Justice St	
100-599	28739
600-1199	28791
S Justice St	28739
Justice Hills Dr	28792
Justice Ridge Rd	28792
Justus Case Mountain Pl	28792
Justus Case Mtn Rd	28792
Justus View Dr	28739
Kalimar Hts	28739
Kalmia Ln	28791
Kalmia Terrace Ct	28739
Kanuga Rd	28739
Kanuga Chapel Dr	28739
Kanuga Conference Dr	28739
Kanuga Falls Ln	28739
Kanuga Forest Dr	28739
Kanuga Heights Ln	28739
Kanuga Lake Rd	28739
Kanuga Pines Dr	28739
Kanuga Ridge Rd	28739
Kanuga Valley Ln	28739
Kapfer Ln	28792
Karen Dr	28792
Karla Cir	28739
Karo Dr	28792
Kassandra Way	28739
Katherine Ave	28791
Kathryn Dr	28792
Kathy Lake Dr	28792
Katie Dr	28792
Katie Lee Ln	28792
Katie View Ln	28792
Katydid Ln	28739
Kay Anderson Ln	28792
Kay Thomas Dr	28792
Kayla Susan Rd	28792
Keela Ct	28792
Keeneland Dr	28792
Keith St	28792
Kelly Ln	28791
Kendall Diane Ln	28792
Kendra Rd	28792
Kennedy Hill Ln	28792

Kennerly Dr 28791
Kensington Rd 28791
Kent Ln 28739
Kentucky Ave 28739
Kenwood Dr 28739
Kerr Rd 28792
Kerr Ridge Dr 28792
Kestral Ct 28792
Ketchwood Ln 28792
Kevin Ln 28792
Kidder Ln 28792
Kids Way 28792
Killarney St 28792
Kilpatrick Rd 28739
Kim Ln 28792
Kimberly Ann Dr 28792
Kimbrell Farm Ln 28792
W Kindy Forest Dr 28739
N & S King St 28792
King Creek Blvd 28792
King Edward Ln 28792
King William Rd 28739
Kingsbury Rd 28791
Kingswood Dr 28792
Kira Ln 28739
Kirkwall Ln 28791
Kirkwood Hill Ln 28739
Kit Carson Ln 28791
Klondike Ln 28792
Knoll Ln 28791
Knollwood Dr 28791
Koala Bear Ln 28792
Kodiak Bear Trl 28792
Kristey Ln 28792
Kristilia Ln 28739
S Kuykendall 28739
Kyles Creek Ln & Rd 28792
L Lyda Continental Dr 28792
La Salle Ln 28791
La Terre Ln 28739
Lacey Ln 28739
Lacoste Dr 28739
Ladies Mantle Ct 28792
Ladys Fern Trl 28739
Ladyslipper Ln 28791
Lafolette St 28792
W Lake Ave 28739
Lake Dr 28739
N Lake Ln 28791
Lake Circle Dr 28792
Lake Club Cir 28792
Lake Edna Dr 28792
Lake Falls Rd 28739
Lake Forest Ln 28739
Lake Pointe Cir 28792
Lake Rugby Dr 28791
E & W Lake View Rd 28739
Lakeledge Ct 28739
Lakemoor Ln 28739
Lakeshore Dr 28739
Lakeside Dr 28739
Lakeview Estate Rd 28792
Lakewood Cir 28739
S Lakewood Cir 28739
Lakewood Rd 28792
Lamb Mountain Rd 28792
Lamonda Dr 28792
Lamy Dr 28792
Lancaster Rd 28792
Landia Dr 28739
Landrum Ln 28792
Lands End Dr W 28791
Lanier Ln 28792
Lanning Rd 28792
Lanning Mill Rd 28792
Larchmont Dr 28791
Largo Ln 28792
Lark Spur Dr 28792
Larry Mcdonald Memorial Dr 28739
Las Brisas Ln 28739
Laughter Rd 28792
Laughter Country Ln 28792
Laughter View Ln 28792
Laura Trce 28792
Laurel Ave & St 28792
Laurel Brook Dr 28792
Laurel Creek Dr 28792
Laurel Ivy Ln 28791
Laurel Oak Ln 28791
Laurel Park Hwy 28739
Laurel Park Pl 28791
Laurel Ridge Pl 28739
Laurel Woods Rd 28739
Laureldale Farm Dr 28792
Laurelhurst Dr 28739
Laurelwood Cir W 28791
Laurlea Ln 28792
Lavender Ln 28792
Lavern Rd 28792
Lawn Ave 28792
Laycock Rd 28792
Lazy Boy Ln 28792
Lazy Lake Ln 28792
Leatherwood Ln 28739
Ledbetter Rd 28792
Ledge Ter 28792
Ledgeview Dr 28792
Lee Dr 28739
Lee Smith St 28791
Legacy Layne Dr 28792
Legendary Rd 28739
Lennox Park Dr 28739
Lenox Pl 28739
W Leslie Way 28792
E Lester Ln 28739
Leucothae Way 28791
Level Plains Dr & Ln 28739
Leverette Dr 28791
Levi Ln 28791
Lewis Creek Dr 28792
Lexington Ln 28792
Libby Home Ln 28739
Lichen Ln 28791
Licklog Ln 28739
Lightwood Ct 28792
Lilac Breeze Ln 28792
Lillie Lee Ln 28792
Lillyfair Ln 28792
Lillys Ln 28791
Lily Pond Rd 28739
Limberlost Dr 28739
Limerick Ln 28791
Lincoln Cir 28792
Linda Vista Dr 28792
Lindas Orchard Ln 28792
Linden Turn 28739
Lindsley Ct 28792
Linkside Dr 28739
Linwood Pond Rd 28739
Little Ln 28739
Little Branch Ln 28739
Little Cherokee Rdg 28739
Little Creek Rd 28792
Little Dove Ct 28739
Little Hungry Rd 28792
Little Hungry Creek Ln 28792
Little Lake Dr 28739
Little Rise Trl 28792
Little River Ln & Rd 28739
Little Willow Cir & Rd 28739
Live Oak Ln 28791
Lloyd Dr 28739
Lloyd Barnwell Rd 28792
Lloyd Griffin Dr 28792
Lloyd Williams Rd 28792
Loblin Ln 28792
Locust St 28792
Locust Creek Ln 28792
Locust Grove Rd 28792
Locust Knoll Ln 28792
Lodge Dr 28791
Lodi Ln 28792
Logan Ln 28739
Loggers Run 28739
London Rd 28739
Lone Eagle Ln 28739
Lone Laurel Trl 28792
Lonesome Dove Trl 28792
Long John Dr 28791
E & W Long View Vista Ln 28792
Longview Dr 28791
Loop Rd 28792
Lora Cantrell Dr 28792
Lost Horse Ln 28739
Lotus Ln 28792
Louisiana Ave 28739
Lovdia Ln 28739
Love St 28791
Love Dove Ln 28792
Loveland Ln 28792
Low Gap Rd 28792
Lower Ln 28791
Lower Bat Cave Dr 28792
Lower Ridgewood Blvd 28791
Lower Sylvan Ter 28791
Lowery Ln 28792
Lr Smith Ave 28791
Lucas St 28791
Lugano Dr 28791
Luke Martin Ln 28739
Luna Trl 28792
Lure View Ln 28792
Luredon Hills Dr 28792
Luther Capell Ln 28792
E Lyda Rd 28792
Lydia Ln 28792
Lyndale Rd 28739
Lyndhurst Dr 28791
Lyndhurst Grove Ct 28791
Lyndon Ln 28792
Lynia Ln 28792
Lynn Estate Rd 28792
Lynnwood Ln 28792
Lynwood Cir 28791
Lytle Rd 28792
Lytle Park Rd 28792
Macintosh Ln 28792
Mack Hill Dr 28739
Macks Way 28739
Madewood Ln 28792
Madison Ln 28792
Madrid Ln 28792
Maewood Hill Ln 28792
Magnolia Dr 28792
Magnolia Spring Pl 28792
Mahshie Ln 28739
N & S Main St 28792
Majestic Trce 28739
Majestic View Ct 28791
Major Way 28792
Mallard Trl 28792
Mallee Ln 28792
Malvern Dr 28739
Manassa Dr 28791
Mandalay Dr 28792
Mansfield St 28791
Maple St 28792
Maple Crest Ln 28792
Maple Leaf Dr 28739
Maple Path Ln 28739
Maple Village Dr 28792
Maplewood Ct 28791
Maplewood Dr 28739
Marathon Ln 28792
Marble Ct 28792
March Ln 28791
Maren Ct 28739
Margate Ln 28792
Marigold Ln 28792
N Marjorie Ln 28792
Mark Freeman Rd 28792
Market St 28739
Marquette Ln 28739
Marshall Rd 28792
Marshall Ridge Rd 28792
Martin Cir & Dr 28792
Martin Luther King Jr Blvd 28792
Mary Elizabeth Dr 28792
N Mason Way 28792
S Mason Dixon Ln 28739
Mason View Ln 28792
Massac Ln 28739
Massey Rd 28792
Massey Road Ext 28792
Mastermind Ln 28792
Matthew Dr 28739
Maui Ln 28792
Max Ln 28792
Maximillian Ln 28792
Maxine Ln 28739
Maxwell Dr 28791
Maxwell Farm Ln 28792
May Dr 28791
May Apple Dr 28792
Mayapple Ct 28739
Maybank Dr 28739
Mayer Ln 28792
Maywood Rd 28792
Mazyck Ln 28792
Mccarson Dr 28739
Mccarson Ln 28791
Mccastle Ln 28792
Mccraws Hill Dr 28792
Mccredie Ct 28792
Mcfarlane Way 28739
Mckee Cir 28792
Mcmillan Dr 28792
Mcminn Rd 28792
Mcminn Woods Dr 28792
N Meadow Run 28792
Meadow Park Ln 28792
Meadow Ridge Ln 28739
Meadow View Ln 28739
Meadow Woods Dr 28792
Meadowbrook Ct 28792
Meadowbrook Ter 28791
Meadowlark Ln 28792
Meadowood Trl 28739
Melbourne Ln 28792
Melinda Dr 28791
Melinda G Ln 28739
S Melissa Way 28791
Melon Ridge Ln 28791
Mels Dr 28792
E Memminger Ct 28739
Memorial Day Ln 28792
Mercedes Ln 28791
Meredith Dr 28792
Mergans Ln 28791
Merlin Path 28792
Merrell Rd 28792
Merri Dr 28792
Merri Acres Ln 28739
Merribrook Ln 28791
Merriman Rd 28791
Merritt Ln 28791
Merriwood Ln 28791
Meyer Rd 28792
Miami Ter 28791
Michael Dr 28791
Mid Allen Rd 28792
Middle St 28792
Middle Fork Rd 28792
Middleton Cir 28791
Middleton Pl 28791
Middleton Rd 28739
Middleton Vis 28791
Middleton Way Ct 28791
Midland Ln 28791
Midnight Dr 28739
Midway St 28739
Milburn Ln 28792
Miley Ln 28792
Mill Creek Way 28739
Mill Pond Way 28791
Millard Xing 28792
Millard J Dr 28739
Millbrae Loop 28791
Miller Ln 28791
Millgate Ln 28791
Millionaire Ln 28792
S Mills Gap Rd 28792
Mimosa Way 28739
Minnow Creek Ln 28792
Minuet Ln 28791
Mistletoe Trl 28791
Misty Ln 28739
Misty Cove Ln 28739
Misty Dawn Cove Rd 28792
Misty Meadow Ln 28739
Misty View Dr 28791
Misty Woods Ln 28792
Mitchell View Dr 28792
Mitchelle Dr 28792
Mo Dr 28792
Mockingbird Dr 28792
Moll Dr 28792
Monarch Rd 28739
Mono Ln 28792
Monroe Dr 28792
Montchannin Hts 28792
Montevilla Dr 28739
Montiel Ln 28792
Moody St 28739
Moonrise Ln 28792
Moonstone Ln 28791
Moore St 28739
Moore Hill Ln 28791
Moores Creek Ln 28792
Morgan Rd 28739
Morgan Paige Dr 28792
Morincen Dr 28739
Morning Ln 28792
Morning Air Ln 28792
Morning Dew Ln 28791
Morning Glory Dr 28792
Morning Star Ln 28792
E Morningside Dr 28791
W Morningside Dr 28791
Morningside Ln 28792
Morrill Dr 28792
Morris Ln 28791
Morris Kaplan Dr 28739
Morton Ln 28739
Moss Ln & Rd 28792
Moss Valley Trl 28791
Mount Airy St 28792
Mount Hebron Rd 28739
Mount Pleasant Vw 28739
Mountain Pl & Rd 28791
Mountain Ash Cir 28739
Mountain Bluff Trl 28792
Mountain Cove Rd 28792
Mountain Crest Dr 28739
Mountain Elder Ln 28739
Mountain Home St 28791
Mountain Lake Dr 28739
Mountain Meadow Dr 28739
Mountain Mist Rd 28792
Mountain Shadow Ln 28792
Mountain Spring Dr 28739
Mountain Sunset Trl 28739
Mountain Top Way 28739
Mountain Trail Ln 28792
Mountain Valley Ct & Dr 28739
E Mountain View Dr & St 28739
Mountain View Estate Rd 28739
Mountain Vista Dr 28739
Mountainaire Ct 28792
Mountainside End Dr 28792
Mt Shady Oak Ct 28739
Muir Ln 28791
Muirfield Ct 28791
Mulberry Ct 28739
Mulberry Hill Dr 28792
Muley Hollow Ln 28792
Mull Dr 28792
Nagel Cir 28792
Nandina Way 28739
Naomi Dr 28792
Napier Dr 28792
Naples Rd 28792
Naples Glenn Trl 28792
Narrows Run Loop 28791
Narva Rd 28792
Nash Ln 28792
Nathaniel Ln 28792
Nature Dr 28792
Natures Rose Ln 28792
Navaho Dr 28739
Nc Hwy 9 28792
Needle Ln 28791
Neely Dr 28792
Nell Ave 28791
Nelson Ln 28739
Nelson Rd 28791
Nelson St 28792
Nelson Valley Ln 28739
Nestlewood Dr 28792
Nettie Way 28792
New Carlyle Way 28792
New Hope Rd 28792
New Smythe Dr 28792
New Village Dr 28791
New Vista Ln 28791
W Newman Dr 28792
Newman Knob Ln 28792
Newport Rd 28739
Newton Pl 28739
Nicole Rene Ln 28792
Nightcastle Ln 28792
Nighthawk Ln 28739
Nile Dr 28792
Nimbus Ln 28739
Nix Rd 28792
Nob Hill Rd 28791
Nobies Way 28792
Norleon Ave 28791
Norman St 28791
Northern Lights Ln 28739
Northfield Ct 28739
Northside Ln 28739
Northview Ln 28792
Northwoods Trl 28792
Norwood Pl 28791
Nuthatch Rd 28792
N Oak St
100-599 28739
600-899 28791
S Oak St 28739
Oak Apple Ln 28792
Oak Briar Dr 28739
Oak Creek Ln 28739
Oak Gate Dr 28739
W Oak Hill Ct & Ln 28739
Oak Hills Ln 28739
Oak Knoll Dr 28739
Oak Meadow Ln 28792
Oak Path Ln 28739
Oak Ridge Rd 28792
Oak Terrace Ln 28791
Oak Tree Ln 28791
Oakdale Dr 28791
Oakhurst St 28792
Oakland St
600-1099 28791
1100-1499 28792
Oakshire Ln 28739
Oakvale Dr & Pl 28791
Oakwilde Dr 28791
Oakwood Pl 28792
Oakwood Rd 28791
Ocain Ct 28792
Ocb Ln 28739
Ochlawaha Dr 28792
Odells Way 28739
Offense Ln 28792
Ogdon Dr 28792
Ohara Cir 28739
Oklahoma Ave 28739
Oklawaha Cir 28739
Old 5th Ave 28739
Old Applewood Ln 28739
N & S Old Asheville Rd 28791
Old Barn Rd 28791
Old Beddingfield Pl 28792
Old Cannon Dr 28792
Old Ccc Rd 28739
Old Chimney Rock Rd 28792
Old Clear Creek Rd 28792
Old Creek Ln 28739
Old Dana Rd 28792
Old Distillery Rd 28739
Old Farm Cir 28792
Old Gait Dr 28739
Old Hemlock Ct 28739
Old Hickory Trl 28739
Old Holbert Rd 28792
Old Homestead Rd 28739
Old Kanuga Pl & Rd 28739
Old King Rd 28792
Old Laurel Dr 28739
Old Logging Trl 28739
Old Maxwell Rd 28792
Old Mill Dr & Rd 28792
Old Mountain Pass 28792
Old Naples Rd 28792
Old Oak Dr 28791
Old Oklahoma Dr 28739
Old Orchard Dr 28739
Old Overlook Trl 28739
Old Pace Farm Ln 28739
Old Park Rd 28791
Old Pasture Way 28739
Old Piney Trl 28792
Old Place Rd 28792
Old Place Bluff Dr 28792
Old Possum Holler Rd 28739
Old Quarry Rd 28791
Old Roper Rd 28791
Old South Carolina Ave 28739
Old Spartanburg Hwy & Rd 28792
Old Springdale Dr 28791
Old Stoneledge Rd 28792
Old Sunset Hill Rd 28792
Old Tanglewood Trl 28739
Old Tom Morris Ln 28739
Old Town Way 28739
Old Twin Oak Rd 28792
Old Village Rd 28791
Old Wagon Trl 28791
Old White St 28791
Olde Chanteloup Ct 28739
Olds Ln & Trl 28739
Ole Blue Rd 28792
Oleta Rd 28792
Oleta Falls Path 28792
Oleta Knoll Ln 28792
Oleta Mill Trl 28792
Oliver Ln 28792
Oliver Orr Cir 28792
Ollace Ct 28792
One Penny Dr 28791
Onuska View Dr 28792
Openview Rd 28739
Orange Peel Ln 28792
Orchard Cir, Ct & St 28739
Orchard Ridge Rd 28792
Orchard Ridgetop Dr 28792
Ore Brae Ln 28739
Oriole Dr 28792
Orleans Ave 28791
Orr Ave 28791
Orrs Camp Rd 28792
Oscelake Way 28739
Osceola Rd 28739
Osceola Inn Rd 28739
Osprey Dr 28792
Osteen Dr 28792
Ottanola Rd 28792
Otter Tail Ln 28792
Our Boys Ln 28792
Outer Park Dr 28792
Overhill Dr 28792
Overlook Pt 28792
N Overlook Ter 28739
Overlook Park Dr 28792
Overlook Point Rd 28792
Overlook View Dr 28739
Overton Hills Dr 28739
Owensby Rd 28792
Oxford Dr 28792
Oxford Valley Dr 28791
P And J View Ln 28792
P E M Dr 28792
E Pace Rd & St 28792
Pace Creek Rd 28792
Pack Rd 28792
Paddock Ct 28791
Paisley Ct 28739
Pait Dr 28791
Palatka St 28739
Panorama Dr 28739

Panther Path Dr 28792
Panther Ridge Rd 28792
Papa Joes Way 28792
Paradise Falls Rd 28792
Parham Rd 28792
Park Dr 28739
Park Ln 28791
E Park Pl 28791
N Park Pl 28791
S Park Pl 28791
Park St 28739
Park Hill Ct 28739
Park Place Trl 28792
Parkview Dr 28792
Parkwood Rd 28739
Partner Dr 28792
Partridge Path 28739
Pastoral Way 28739
Pathfinder Ln 28791
Patriots Dr 28739
Pats Pl 28792
E Patterson Rd & St 28739
Patton St 28792
Peace Wood Ln 28792
Peaceful Orchard Dr 28792
Peaceful Pond Ln 28792
Peaceful View Trl 28792
Peachtree Ln 28791
Peacock View Dr 28792
Pearl Ln 28739
Pearson Dalton Ln 28792
Pebble Creek Ln 28739
Pebble Ridge Rd 28739
Pebble Stone Trl 28792
Pebblebrook Ct 28739
Pecks Trl 28792
Pegasus Ln 28792
Pennsylvania Ave 28739
Pennwood Ln 28739
Penny Ct 28739
Peregrine Dr 28739
Peregrine Perch Trl 28792
Periwinkle Ln 28791
Perry Pl 28739
Perseverance Pathway 28739
Persimmon Woods Ln 28739
Perspective View Ln 28792
Petal Drop Ln 28792
Petunia Dr 28792
Peyton Dr 28739
Pfirrmann Ln 28792
Pheasant Run 28739
Pheasant Branch Ct 28739
Pheasant Ridge Dr 28739
Phipps Ln 28791
Piedmont Dr 28739
Pilot Mountain Rd 28792
Pilot Point Ln 28739
Pilot View Ln 28792
Pin Oak Trl 28739
N Pine St 28792
S Pine St 28792
W Pine St 28739
Pine Bark Ln 28739
Pine Berry Cir 28739
Pine Bluff Rd 28792
Pine Cone Hl 28739
Pine Cove Ln 28739
Pine Forest Trce 28739
Pine Haven Dr 28791
E Pine Hill Ln 28792
Pine Knot Trl 28739
Pine Mount Ct 28739
Pine Path Ln 28739
Pine Ridge Rd 28792
Pine Shadow Dr 28739
Pine Spring Dr 28739
Pine Top Ct 28739
Pinebrook Cir 28739
N Pinecrest Dr & Ln 28739
Pinehurst Dr 28792
Pineland Rd 28792
Pinellas St 28791
E Pineview Dr 28739
Pinewood Cir 28739
Pinewood Knoll Dr 28739

Piney Knoll Ln 28739
Piney Mountain Rd 28792
Piney Oak Hills Cir 28792
Piney Plains Dr 28739
Piney Ridge Ct & Dr 28791
Piney View Rd 28792
Pinnacle Cir 28739
Pinnacle Mountain Rd 28739
Pinnacle View Way 28739
Pinner Pl 28792
Pintail Ct 28792
Pioneer Ln 28792
Pioneer Mountain Rd 28791
Pisgah Dr 28791
Pisgah Heights Ln 28791
Pisgah Shadows Rd 28739
Pittillo Pass 28792
Pjs Pl 28792
Plantation Dr 28792
Pleasant Grove Rd 28739
Pleasant Grove Church Rd 28739
Pleasant Hill Dr & Rd 28739
Pleasant Meadow Ln 28792
Pleasant Ridge Rd 28739
Plum Branch Cir 28792
Plum Tree Ln 28739
Poetry Ln 28791
Point Hope Ln 28792
Point Lookout Cir 28792
W Pointe Dr 28792
Pommel Rd 28791
Pond View Ln 28792
Pondside Ct 28739
Poor Boy Ln 28792
Pop Corn Dr 28792
Poplar Ct 28792
E Poplar Dr 28792
W Poplar Dr 28792
Poplar Ln 28739
Poplar Forest Trce 28739
Poplar Spring Trl 28739
Poplar Top Ln 28739
Poppy Ln 28791
Pops Perry Ln 28739
Posey Ln 28792
Post Oak Trl 28739
Powder River Ln 28739
Powell St 28792
Prairie Ln 28739
Preserve Ct 28791
Pressley Rd 28792
N & S Prestonwood Dr 28739
Prestwick Dr 28791
Prestwood Ln 28792
E Price Rd & St 28739
Prickley Brier Trl 28739
Prickly Briar Rd 28739
Pridmore Hollow Rd 28739
Primrose Dr 28792
N Primrose Dr 28792
Primrose Ln 28739
Prince Dr 28791
E Prince Rd 28792
W Prince Rd 28792
Princess Ann Dr 28739
Priscilla Ln 28739
Private Cove Ln 28739
Pro Court Dr 28739
Promised Ridge Dr 28791
Prophet Ln 28792
Prospect St 28792
Prosperity Ave 28792
Pryor Dr 28792
Ptarmigan Ln 28739
Puma Dr 28791
Pumphouse Rd 28739
Puncheon Camp Creek Rd 28792
Puncheon Creek Rd 28792
Puppet Pl 28792
Putter Ct 28739
Q P Ln 28792
Quacker Dr 28792
Quail Ln 28792

Quail Hollow Rd 28739
Queen St 28792
Quiet Breeze Trl 28739
Quiet Pine Ln 28792
Quiet Stream Ln 28791
Quiet Water Rd 28739
Quincey Ln 28792
R And R Hyder Ln 28792
S Rabbit Ln 28739
Rachel Fay Dr 28739
Racine Pl 28739
Racing Ln 28792
Rackley Pl 28739
Radcliff Ct 28739
Rainbow Ln 28791
Rainbow Lake Dr 28739
Raintree Dr 28791
Ralphs Ln 28739
Ramble Hill Ln 28739
S Ramblewood Trl 28739
Rambling Dr & Trl 28739
Rambling Creek Rd 28739
Rambling Oaks Trl 28739
Ramsay Ln 28792
Ranch Vista Dr 28792
Randall Cir 28791
Randall Farm Rd 28739
Randy Dr 28791
Ransier Dr 28739
Raven Cliff Dr 28739
Raven Creek Dr 28739
Ray Ave 28792
Raymond St 28791
Rd Morgan Ln 28739
Rebeccas Pond Dr 28739
Rebels Lair 28739
Red Apple Dr 28792
Red Birch Ct 28739
Red Bird Ln 28791
Red Bow Ln 28791
Red Cardinal Ln 28739
Red Cedar Dr 28792
Red Fox Ct 28792
Red Gates Ln 28792
Red Hawk Trl 28739
Red Huckleberry Ln 28792
Red Laurel Ct 28739
Red Oak Dr 28791
Red Oak Farm Rd 28739
Red Tail Dr 28792
Red Turn Dr 28792
Redden Rd 28739
Redtop Farm Dr 28739
Redwing Dr 28792
Reedy Creek Ct 28792
Reedy Ridge Rd 28792
Reeses Ridge Ct 28739
Refreshing Rdg 28792
Regal St 28792
Regal Oaks Dr 28792
Regency Loop Dr 28792
Reisha Ln 28739
Relyea Ave 28792
Reservoir Dr 28739
Resort St 28792
Reuben Dr 28792
Reward Dr 28792
Rhodes Rd 28739
Rhodes St 28739
Rhodes Park Dr 28791
Rhododendron Dr 28739
Riannon Ln 28791
Richards Dr 28792
Rick Barfield Dr 28792
Rick Lenas Dr 28792
Rickel Dr 28739
Rico Trl 28739
Rider Dr 28792
N Ridge Rd 28792
Ridge Field Dr 28792
Ridge Top Pl & Trce 28739
Ridgecrest Dr 28792
Ridgemont Rd 28739
Ridgemount Forest Trl 28739
Ridgestone Dr 28792
Ridgeview Dr 28792

N Ridgeview Hill Dr 28791
Ridgewood Ave & Blvd 28791
Ridgewood Acres Dr 28792
Riding Gate Rd 28791
Riford Rd 28792
Rising Star Ln 28739
Rising View Dr 28791
River Rd 28739
Riverside Dr 28792
Riverview Ct 28739
Riverwind Dr 28739
Rivoli Blvd 28739
Roaring Fork Ln 28739
Roasted Chestnut Trl 28792
Rob And Jims Ln 28739
Roberts Dr 28739
Robin Ln & St 28739
Robin Crest Dr 28791
Robinson Ln 28739
Robinson Ter 28792
Robinwood Trl 28791
Robleigh Dr 28739
Rock Broad River Rd 28792
Rock Hill Ave 28792
Rock House Rd 28792
Rock Ridge Trl 28792
Rock View Ct 28739
Rockaway Ln 28791
Rockmoor Way 28791
Rockwood Dr & Ln 28792
Rocky St 28792
Rocky Hill Dr 28792
Rocky Mountain Dr 28739
Rocky Ridge Rd 28739
Rocky Spur Ln 28739
Rocky Top Ct 28739
Rogat Rd 28792
Roland Jones Rd 28792
Rolfe St 28791
Rolling Oaks Dr 28791
Rollins St 28792
Romance Ln 28792
Rome Ln 28792
Rome Beauty Ln 28792
Ronald Lively Rd 28792
Rork Dr 28739
Rosa Ln 28739
Rose St 28739
Rose Evelyn Trl 28739
Rose Garden Ln 28792
Rose Park Ln 28739
Rosebud Ln 28739
Rosemont Ct 28791
Rosewood Ln 28791
Rosewood Trl 28739
E Rosewood Trl 28739
W Rosewood Trl 28739
Round Pond Dr 28739
N & S Rowe Ct & Rd 28792
Rowland Dr 28739
Royal Dr & Knl 28739
Royal Oaks Dr 28791
Ruby Dr 28792
Ruffed Grouse Run 28739
N & S Rugby Dr & Rd 28791
Rugby Cove Ln 28791
Rugby Forest Ln 28791
Rugby Hollow Dr 28791
Rugby Knoll Dr 28791
Rugby View Pl 28791
Rugged Top Rd 28792
Runaway Farm Ln 28792
Running Bear Trl 28792
Running Brook Trl 28739
Runway Dr 28792
Rural Retreat Dr 28792
Russell Rd 28792
Rustic Dr 28739
Rustling Pines Dr 28739
Rusty Ln 28791
Ruth Whitaker Rd 28791
Rutledge Anx & Dr 28739
Ryans Way 28792
Sabine Cir & Dr 28739
Sacanon Ln 28792

Saconon Orchard Ln 28792
Saddle Club Ln 28739
Saddlebred Ct 28739
Saddlebrook Dr 28739
Saddletree Ln 28739
Sadie Ln 28739
Sahalee Trl 28739
W Saint Johns Way 28791
Saint Marys Dr 28792
Saint Pauls Rd 28792
Salamander Ln 28739
Salisbury Rd 28792
Saluda St 28791
Sam King Rd 28739
Sam Mills St 28791
Samara Dr 28739
Sandburg Ter 28791
Sandpiper Palisades St 28792
Sandra Way 28739
Sandstone Ln 28739
Sandy Dr 28792
Sandy Creek Ct 28792
Sandy Hill Ln 28792
Sanguine Ct 28739
Sarasota Ln 28792
Sargeant Ln 28792
Sassafras Dr 28739
Satchwell Ln 28792
Savage Ln 28792
N Scarlet Oak Ln 28791
Scenic Ln 28739
Scenic Mountain Ln 28792
Scenic Ridge Dr 28792
Scenic View Dr 28792
Schafer Knoll Dr 28792
Scheppegrell Dr 28791
Schepper St 28792
Schmidt Ter 28739
School St 28739
Scomaill Dr 28791
Scottish Ln 28739
Sea Lark Ln 28791
Sean Way 28792
Searcy Ln 28792
Secret Ln 28792
Secretariat Dr 28792
Seminole Dr 28791
Seneca Blvd 28739
Sentell Creek Ct 28739
Sequoyah Trail Rd 28792
Serendipity Dr 28792
Serendipity Cove Rd 28792
Serenity Cir 28792
Serenity Hill Rd 28792
Serenity Mountain Dr 28792
Settlers Ridge Rd 28739
Sevier Dr 28791
Shacoba Ln 28792
Shadblow Ln 28791
Shadow Mountain Ln 28739
Shadow Run Rd 28792
Shadow Valley Dr 28739
Shadowleaf Dr 28739
Shady Dr 28792
Shady Branch Trl 28739
Shady Creek Ln 28739
Shady Laurel Ct 28739
Shady Oak Ln 28739
Shady Summit Rd 28792
Shadybrook Trl 28739
Shadywood Ln 28792
Shalom Ln 28739
Shannon Rd 28791
Shano Dr 28791
Sharon Hill Dr 28792
Shatto Estate Dr 28792
Shawn Rachel Pkwy 28792
Shaws Creek Ln 28739
Shaws Creek Church Rd 28791
Shaws Creek Farm Rd 28739
E & W Shay Cir 28791
Sheen Cir 28791
Sheila Ct 28792

Shelly Dr 28792
Shenandoah Dr 28792
Sheneman Dr 28792
Shepherd St 28792
Sherman Dr 28739
Sherwood Ln 28791
N & S Shiff Rd 28792
Shiloh Dr 28792
Shining Sun Ln 28792
Shipp St 28791
Shoals Falls Rd 28739
Shoeing Box Way 28792
N Shore Dr 28739
Short St 28739
Showy Orchis Dr 28792
Sidetrack Ln 28792
Sierra Dr 28739
Signal Hill Rd 28792
Silk Tree Rd 28739
Silver Loop 28792
Silver Birch Ln 28739
Silver Dapple Ln 28792
Silver Fox Run 28792
Silver Loop Dr 28792
Silver Pine Dr 28739
Silver Spring Dr 28739
Silverglen Way 28739
Silverleaf Dr 28739
Sims Aly 28792
Sinclair Ln 28739
Sioux Dr 28739
Sir Galahad Dr 28791
Skipper Ln 28792
Sky Trl 28739
Sky Lake Dr 28739
Sky Ridge Ln 28739
Sky Valley Rd 28739
Sky Valley Camp Rd 28739
Sky View Ln 28739
Sky Vista Ln 28792
Skybrook Farm Dr 28739
Skyline Dr 28791
Skyline Drive Ext 28791
Skytop Estates Ct 28791
Skytop Farm Ln 28791
Skyvillage Ln 28739
Skyway Dr 28739
Sleepy Creek Ln 28791
Sleepy Hollow Ln 28792
Slick Rock Rd 28792
Small Creek Ln 28792
Smith Dr 28739
Smith Rd 28792
Smokey Pines Way 28739
Smoky Ln 28739
Smoky Ridge Ln 28739
Smyth Aly 28739
Smyth Ave 28792
Snapdragon Ln 28739
Sneaky Hollow Ln 28739
Snow Dr 28791
Snowy Egret Way 28792
Solar Ln 28739
Solomon Cir 28739
Somersby Pkwy 28739
Somerset Dr 28791
Somerton Ct 28791
Song Sparrow Dr 28792
Songbird Ct 28792
Sonny Walker Trl 28792
Sophia Ln 28792
Sourwood Trl 28739
South Dr 28739
Southbrook Rd 28792
Southern Dr 28792
Southern Scenic Hts 28792
Southern Visions Dr 28792
Southridge Dr 28739
Southside Dr 28792
Southwind Dr 28792
Spanish Oak Ln 28791
Sparrow Rd 28792
Spartan Hts 28792
Spartanburg Hwy 28792
Speckled Trout Ln 28792
Spelter St 28792

Spicebush Ct 28792
Spicer Cove Rd 28792
Spicewood Ln 28791
Spring Path, Rd & St 28739
Spring Garden Ave 28739
Spring Heights Ct 28791
Spring Hill Dr 28792
Spring Place Dr 28791
Spring Rain Dr 28792
Spring Ridge Ln 28739
Spring Village Ln 28739
Springhead Trl 28739
N Springs Dr 28791
Springside Ct 28791
Springside Dr 28792
N Springside Dr 28792
Spruce St 28791
Spruce Hill Dr 28792
Spruce Path Ln 28739
Spruce Pine Ln 28739
Spurgeon Gilbert Rd 28792
Squirrel Trl 28791
Squirrel Hollow Dr 28791
Squirrel Trail Ct 28791
Stacy Ln 28792
Stanley Ln 28739
Stanley Haven Ln 28739
N Stanwood Ln 28739
Star Ln 28791
Star Gazer Way 28739
Star Point Dr 28792
Star Ridge Rd 28739
Starburst Dr 28739
Starcrest Trl 28739
Stardust Ln 28739
Starlight Ln 28792
Starling Way 28792
Starmount Ln 28791
Starview Ln 28739
State St 28792
Staton Ave 28792
Staton Rd 28739
Stayman Winesap Ln 28792
Steeplechase Ct 28791
Stephanie Ln 28792
Stepp Ave 28739
Stepp Rd 28792
Stepp Acres Ln 28792
Stepp Mill Rd 28792
Stepp Orchard Dr 28792
Stepp Ponderosa Trl 28792
Stepp Ridge Ct 28792
Stewart St 28792
Stillwater Ln 28791
Stone Gate Ln 28739
Stone House Rd 28739
Stone Valley Way 28792
Stonebridge Dr 28739
Stonebrook Dr 28791
Stoneledge Rd 28792
Stones Throw Dr 28739
Stoney Trce 28791
Stoney Brook Rd 28739
Stoney Creek Rd 28792
Stoney Creek Mountain Ln 28792
Stoney Gardens Ct 28791
Stoney Mountain Rd
1-99 28791
100-199 28792
101-199 28791
200-1999 28791
Stoney Nob Dr 28792
Stoney Ridge Ct 28792
N & S Stoney View Ct 28792
Storynook Ln 28739
Strawberry Dr 28792
Streamside Dr 28791
Substation St 28792
Sugar St 28792
Sugar Foot Rd 28739
Sugar Hill Dr 28792
Sugar Hollow Rd 28739
E & W Sugar Maple Dr & Hts 28739
Sugar Park Dr 28792

Sugarbear Ln 28792
Sugarberry Ln 28739
Sugarloaf Ln & Rd 28792
Sugarloaf Mountain Rd 28792
Sugarloaf Park Way 28792
Sugarloaf Ridge Rd 28792
Sujo Trl 28792
Sulo Dr 28792
Sultana Dr 28739
Summer Rd 28792
Summer Glen Rd 28739
Summer Path Ln 28739
Summer Place Ln 28791
Summer Rain Dr 28739
Summerset Dr 28792
Summerwind Dr 28739
Summey Farm Ln 28739
Summit Ave & Cir 28739
Summit Farm Ln 28739
Summit Hill Rd 28791
Sunlight Ridge Ct & Dr 28792
Sunny Ln 28792
Sunny Ridge Rd 28739
N & S Sunnydale Way 28792
Sunoake Ct 28739
Sunrise Dr 28791
Sunrise Hill Ln 28792
Sunrise Path Ct 28792
Sunrise Ridge Dr 28792
E Sunset Dr 28791
Sunset Acres Trl & Way 28792
Sunset Crest Ln 28739
Sunset Horizon Ln 28791
Sunset Vista Rd 28792
E & W Sunshine Ln 28792
Surrey Run 28791
Surrey Glen Cir 28739
Surry Ln 28791
Susan Ln 28739
Sutton Pl 28791
Suzannes Place Ln 28792
Sweet Ln 28792
Sweet Basil Ln 28791
Sweet Briar Path Way 28792
Sweet Clover Ln 28739
Sweet William Ln 28791
Sweetbriar Dr 28739
Sweetgrass Ln 28792
Sweetgum Trl 28739
Sweetpea Ln 28791
Sweetwater Hills Dr 28791
Sweetwater Valley Ct 28791
Sycamore Cir 28791
Sycamore Ridge Dr 28792
Sylvan Blvd 28791
Sylvania Dr 28792
T J Trl 28792
Talbot St 28791
Tall Pines Rd 28739
Tall Poplar Smt 28739
Tall Timbers Trl 28792
Talley Rd 28739
Tallwood Cir 28791
Tallyho Ln 28791
Tamarac Ter 28791
Tanager Ln & Trl 28792
Tanglewood Acres Dr 28791
Tara Pl 28739
Tarheel Blue Ln 28792
Tartana Cir 28791
Tatham Rd 28792
Taylor Rd 28792
Taylor St 28739
Teaberry Ln 28739
Teaneck Cir & Trl 28791
Tebeau Dr 28791
Tee Off Ln 28792
Temon St 28739
Tennis Ranch Rd 28791
Teresa Ln 28792
Termite Ln 28739
Terrace Ln 28792
Terrace Mountain Dr 28739
Terrys Gap Rd 28792
Texas St 28739
The Old Buggy Rd 28739
Theatre Rock Rd 28792
Theodore Ln 28792
Thistledown Ct 28739
Thistlewind Trl 28739
Thistlewood Ln 28791
Thomas Rd 28739
Thompson Rd & St 28792
Thornapple Dr 28739
Thornbird Ave 28792
Thorngate Dr 28739
Thornhill Ln 28739
Thornton Pl 28791
Thornwood Ln 28792
Thrashing Rock Dr 28739
Thrift Ln 28792
Thunder Aly 28792
Thunder Bay Ln 28792
Thunder Cloud Trl 28792
Thunder Mtn Rd 28792
Thunderbird Ln 28739
Tierra Trl 28792
Tifco Trl 28791
Tillman Dr 28792
Timber Trl 28792
Timber Cove Ct 28791
Timber Creek Rd 28739
Timber Run Rd 28739
Timberland Dr 28792
Timberline Trl 28792
Tioga Trl 28791
Tiptop Dr 28792
Tisha Ln 28739
Titleist Way 28739
Tobacco Rd 28792
Tom Fazio Trce 28739
Toms Dr 28739
Toms Falls Rd 28792
Toms Hill Dr 28739
Toms Park Cir 28739
W Ton A Wondah Rd 28792
Toney Dr 28739
Toone Town Ter 28792
Tootsie Ln 28792
Top Of The Mountain Rd 28739
Torrey Dr 28792
Tower Cir 28739
Tower View Dr 28792
Towhee Dr 28792
Town Mountain Rd 28792
Towne Place Dr 28792
Townsend Rd 28792
Toxaway Cir, Ct & Dr 28791
Tracy Grove Rd 28792
Tradition Way 28791
Trail Creek Rd 28792
Trail Ridge Rd 28739
Trailmaster Dr 28739
Trails Peak Ln 28739
Trailside Dr 28739
Tranquil Ct 28739
Tranquility Ln & Pl 28739
Transfer Station Dr 28791
Trappers Trl 28739
Tree Frog Ln 28739
Tree Haven Blvd 28791
Tree Top Dr 28791
Treeland Rd 28739
Treeline Dr 28739
Treemont Ln 28792
Trellis Ln 28739
Trenholm Rd 28739
Trenholm Woods Dr 28739
Trigger Ln 28792
Trillium Glen Ln 28792
Trio Ln 28792
Triple Creek Dr 28791
Triple Fairways Dr 28739
Triple Oaks Dr 28792
Triple Springs Rd 28792
Trudy Ln 28739
Try And Find It Dr 28792
Tuckaway Dr 28792
Tudor Ln 28739
Tudor Crescent Ct 28739
Tulip Trl 28792
Tulip Poplar Ln 28739
Tullahoma Farms Ln 28792
Tumble Bug Ln 28792
Turkey Creek Dr 28739
Turkey Foot Trl 28739
Turkey Knob Rd 28792
E & W Turkey Paw Trl 28739
Turkey Roost Ct 28739
Turley Falls Rd 28739
Turnabout Ln 28739
Turnberry Ct 28791
Turner Ln 28791
Turtle Ln 28791
Turtle Dove Ln 28792
Turtledog Ln 28739
Tuttle Rd 28792
Twin Brook Dr 28791
Twin Elm Knl 28792
Twin Ponds Ln 28739
Twin Springs Rd 28792
Twin Willow Dr 28792
Twisted Birch Dr 28792
Two Tree Dr 28791
Ty Mason Ln 28792
Tyler Pl 28739
Underhill Rd 28792
Underwood Dr 28739
Union Hill Rd 28792
Union Hill Church Rd 28792
Upland Way 28739
Upper Fairway Dr 28739
Upper Laurel Dr 28739
Upper Red Oak Trl 28792
Upper Ridgewood Blvd 28791
Valencia Dr 28791
Valle Way 28739
Vallevue Estates Ln 28739
Valley St
300-699 28739
700-799 28791
Valley Hill Dr 28791
Valley View Ct 28739
Valley Vista Dr 28792
Valmont Dr 28791
Valois Pl 28739
Vance St 28739
Venture Way 28792
Victoria Park Dr 28792
Victory Ln 28739
Victory Heir St 28792
View Rock Ln 28791
Viewcrest Dr 28739
Viking Trl 28739
Villa Cir 28739
Village Springs Ln 28739
Vincent Pl 28739
Vinewood Ln 28792
Vintage Barn 28791
Violet Dr 28792
Virginia Ave 28739
Virginia Loop Ln 28792
S & W Vista Dr 28739
Wa Glaspy Ln 28792
Waddell Dr 28792
Wade Lee Dr 28739
Wagram Pl 28739
Wake Robin Pl 28739
Wakefield Dr 28792
Walden Pond Dr 28791
Walking Horse Way 28792
N Wall St 28792
Walnut Ct 28792
Walnut Loop 28739
Walnut Cove Rd 28739
Walnut Grove Rd 28792
Walnut Heights Ln 28739
Walnut Loop Rd 28739
S Walnut Tree Cir & St 28792
Walnut Valley Ln 28739
Walter Edney Ln 28792
Walton Dr 28739
Wanteska Hls 28791
Ward Holler Rd 28792
Waridarr Rd 28792
Warren Ln 28739
Warrens Run Dr 28792
Wash Creek Dr 28739
Wash Freeman Rd 28792
N & S Washington St 28739
Water Oak Ln 28791
Waterbury Ct 28791
Waterfall Cv 28739
Waters Rd 28792
Waterside Dr 28791
Waterview Ln 28792
Waterwind Dr 28792
Waterwood Ln 28739
Watzel Ln 28792
Waxwing Way 28792
Wayne Lamb Dr 28792
Waynes Way 28792
Waynesville Ave 28792
Wayside Ln 28792
Weaver Mountain Ln 28792
Wedge Ct 28739
Weeping Willow Cir 28739
Wells Ave & St 28739
Wendy Ln 28792
Wesley Way 28792
Westbridge Dr 28739
Westbrook Rd 28739
Westbury Dr 28792
Western Blue Bird Dr 28792
Western Eagle Dr 28792
Westminster Ct 28739
Westridge Ct 28791
Westside Village Rd 28791
Westview Dr 28791
Westwind Dr 28791
Westwood Dr 28739
Wethero Ridge Rd 28792
Wetmur St 28739
Wexford Dr 28791
Whippoorwill Ln 28739
Whirlaway Ct 28792
Whiskey Creek Rd 28739
Whispering Hills Dr 28792
Whispering Pines Dr 28792
Whispering Stream Trl 28739
Whisperwood Cir & Dr 28791
Whistlewood Ln 28739
Whit Whiteside Ln 28792
White St 28739
White Ash Cir 28739
White Cedar Ln 28791
White Fence Ln 28792
White Hickory Rdg 28739
White Oak Dr 28791
E White Pine Dr 28739
White Quail Trl 28792
White Sparrow Dr 28792
White Squirrel Ln 28739
White Stone Ln 28791
White Water Dr 28792
Whitehall Ln 28739
Whitehead Rd 28792
Whiteside Trl 28792
Whitestone Farm Dr 28739
Whitfield Ln 28791
Whitmire Cir 28791
N Whitted St
100-599 28739
600-899 28791
S Whitted St 28739
Wickham Way 28791
Wickins Dr 28791
Widows Peak Ln 28791
Wild Flower Holw 28739
Wild Iris Ln 28739
Wild Ivy Run 28739
N Wild Oak Ln 28791
Wild Pheasant Run 28792
Wild Rose Dr 28792
Wild Rose Ln 28739
Wild Turkey Trl 28792
Wild Wind Ln 28792
Wildflower Ln 28792
Wildlife Trl 28739
Wildwood Rd 28739
Wilken St 28739
Will Rd 28792
Will Hill Rd 28792
Willard Ln 28792
Williams Ln 28739
N Williams Ln 28739
E Williams Rd 28792
Williams St 28792
Williams Acres Ln 28792
Williams Meadow Loop 28739
Willow Bnd 28792
Willow Ln 28739
Willow Rd 28739
Willow St 28739
Willow Way 28739
Willow Creek Rd 28739
Willow Falls Ln 28739
Willow Forest Dr 28739
Willow Lake Dr 28739
Willow Oak Ln 28791
Willow Park Ln 28739
Willow Peak Rd 28739
Willow Place Cir 28739
Willowide Dr 28739
Willow Run Farm Dr 28791
Willow Springs Cv & Dr 28739
Willow Valley Ln 28739
Willow Valley Farm Way 28739
N Willow Wood Trl 28739
Willowbrook Rd 28792
Willowood Trl 28739
Wills Way 28739
Wilmont Dr 28792
Wilson Hill Ln 28791
Wind Chime Ln 28792
Wind Song Way 28792
Windham Way 28739
Winding Creek Ln 28739
Winding Trail Dr 28791
Winding Way Ln 28792
Windjammer Way 28792
Windsock Ln 28792
Windsor Ct 28792
Windsor Dr 28791
Windswept Way 28792
Windwood Hill Rd 28739
Windy Acres Dr 28792
Windy Knoll Dr 28739
Windy Mountain Ln 28792
Winesap Dr 28792
Winslow Dr 28791
Winsome Trl 28739
Winter Holly Ln 28739
Winter Sun Trl 28792
Winter Wren Cir 28792
Winterberry Dr 28739
Winterview Trl 28739
Wintry Dr 28792
Wisdom Ln 28739
Wise Owl Dr 28739
Wisteria Ln 28791
Wistonia Pl 28792
Wolf Creek Dr 28792
Wolf Mountain Trl 28792
Wolf Shoals Dr 28739
Wolfe Lake Dr 28739
Wonderview Ln 28792
Wood Dale Dr 28791
Wood Duck Way 28792
Wood Owl Ct 28791
Wood Sorrel Ln 28792
Woodbridge Dr 28739
Woodbyne Ave & Ln 28739
Woodcock Dr 28792
Woodcrest Ln 28739
Wooden Bridge Ln 28739
Woodfield Ct & Ln 28791
Woodhaven Dr 28739
Woodland Dr 28792
Woodland Trl 28739
W Woodland Trl 28792
N & S Woodlawn Ave, Ln & Ter 28791
Woodlyn Etch Dr 28792
Woodmont Dr 28791
Woodpecker Walk 28792
Woodridge Dr 28739
N & S Woodridge View Ct 28791
Woods End Dr 28739
Woodside View Dr 28792
Woodsong Dr 28791
Woodys Dr 28792
Worlds Edge Rd 28792
Wormie Ln 28792
Wren Dr 28792
Wren Glen Ct 28792
Wyatt Ln 28792
Wyatt Hill Rd 28739
Wynnbrook Dr 28792
Yale Rd 28739
Yarborough St 28739
Yardley Ct 28739
Yellow Buckeye Ln 28739
Yellow Rock Rd 28739
N Yellow Rose Ln 28792
Yon Hill Rd 28792
Yosemite Dr 28792
Young St 28792
Zeb Corn Rd 28792
Zelda Ct 28792

NUMBERED STREETS

1st Ave E 28792
100-199 28792
200-999 28739
2nd E & W 28792
3rd Ave E 28792
100-199 28792
200-1599 28739
4th Ave E 28792
1-199 28792
200-1399 28739
5th Ave E 28792
1-199 28792
200-2399 28739
6th Ave E 28792
6th Ave W 28739
7th Ave E 28792
100-199 28792
200-1199 28791
8th Ave E 28792
8th Ave W 28791
9th Ave E 28792
9th Ave W 28791

HICKORY NC

General Delivery 28603

POST OFFICE BOXES MAIN OFFICE STATIONS AND BRANCHES

Box No.s
All PO Boxes 28603

NAMED STREETS

A Ave SE 28602
Abernethy Ln 28602
Abernethy Farm Rd 28602
Abernethy Park Dr 28602
Acres St 28601
Adarrint Rd 28602
Addison Ln 28601
Advent Rd 28602
Airport Rhodhiss Rd 28601
Alex Rd 28602
Alex Lee Blvd 28601
Alexander Pl NE 28601
Alexander Heritage Dr 28601
Alexander Pointe Dr 28601
Allison St 28601
Alpine Ct NE 28601
Anastasia Way 28602
S And K Rd 28601
S And W Farm Rd 28602
Andy Rd 28601
Anna Belle Ln 28601
Annette Dr NE 28601
Apache Dr 28601
Applehill Dr 28602
Arrow St 28601
Arrowhead Dr NE 28601
Arrowwood Dr 28601
Ashbury Ln 28602
Ashley Ct & Ln 28601
Ashton Glen Cir 28602
Atwood Dr 28601
Auction Ln 28601
Austin Ln 28602
Automotive Ln 28601
Autumn Ln 28602
E Avenue Ct SE 28602
B Ave SE 28602
B And J Hosiery Mill St 28602
B And S Ln 28601
Baker Barn Rd 28602
Bakers Pt 28602
Bakers Glade Ln 28602
Bakers Mountain Rd 28602
Barger Home Pl 28602
Barnhardt St 28602
Bartley Rd 28601
Bass Ln 28601
Bayberry Dr 28601
Beach St 28602
Bear Paw 28602
Beaver Ct 28602
Beechtree Ct 28601
Benson Ln 28601
Berkshire Dr 28602
Bernard St 28602
Berra Pl 28602
Berry Rd 28602
Berryhill Ct NE 28601
Beth Pl NE 28601
Bethel Church Rd 28602
Bethlehem Mfg Ln 28601
Bethlehem School Rd 28601
Betty Dr NE 28601
Beulah Dr & Rd 28601
Beverly Hills Dr 28602
Big Sky Ln 28602
Bill Keller Rd 28601
Billings Dr 28602
Biltmore Ave 28602
Birch Cir 28602
Bishop Dr 28602
Black Oak Rd 28602
Black Walnut Dr 28602
Blackberry Ln 28602
Blackburn Wike Rd 28601
Blendwood Ln NE 28601
Blue Grass Dr 28602
Blue Star Rd 28602
Bobcat Ln 28601
Bolick Farm Rd 28601
Boot Hill Rd 28602
Bowman Rd 28602
Bowman Lowman Ave 28601
Bowman Lowman Avenue Ext 28601
Boxwood Ct 28602
Boyd Bolick Rd 28601
Bradshaw Rd 28602
Brady Ln 28601
Branderr Dr 28602
Brandywine 28602
Brannock Rd 28602
Brannock Smith Dr 28602
Braxton Gate Ln 28602
Brent St 28601
Briarwood Dr 28602
Brickfield St 28602
Bridge Pointe Ln 28601
Brittain St 28602
Brittains Holw 28601

Street	ZIP
Brittian Rd	28602
Brookford Blvd	28602
Brookford Church Rd	28602
Brookridge Dr NE	28601
Brooksouth Dr	28602
Brookstone Dr	28602
Brookwood Ln	28602
Bruce Teague Ln	28601
Bryan Ln	28602
Bryant St	28602
Buckingham Dr	28602
Buckskin Dr	28601
Buena Vista Ct & Dr	28601
Buff St	28602
Buff And Allen Rd	28602
Buffett Cir	28602
Burke St	28601
Burke County Line Rd	28602
Butner Dr	28602
Byrd Farm Rd	28602
C Ave SE	28602
C And S Ln	28601
Caitlins Way	28602
Caldwell Ln	28602
Calhoun Dr	28601
Calvary Rd	28602
Cambrian Dr	28601
Camp Creek Rd	28602
Canino Hvn	28602
Canseco Ln	28602
Cape Hickory Rd	28601
Cape Hickory Cutoff Rd	28601
Capri Dr	28602
Carolina Ave	28601
Carolina Mill Rd	28602
Carriage Ln	28602
Carroll St	28601
Carson Ct	28602
Cascades Dr	28601
Castell Ln	28601
Castle Ave	28601
Castlewood Ct	28602
Catawba Ave	28601
Catawba Shores Ln	28601
Catawba Valley Blvd SE	28602
Cathedral Dr	28601
Cathrines Ln	28601
Cauble Dairy Rd	28602
Cedar Ln & Rd	28601
Cedar Bark Ln & St	28602
Cedar Forest Loop	28601
Cedar Road Ext	28601
Cedar Springs Dr	28602
Cemetery Loop	28601
N Center St	28601
S Center St	28602
Century Pl SE	28602
Charleston Ct	28601
Charlie Smith Rd	28602
Charlotte Ann Ln	28601
Charlynn Dr	28601
Chase Ln	28601
Cherokee Dr	28601
Cherry Grove Dr	28602
Chestnut Dr	28602
Childers Rd	28602
Christopher Ct	28601
Christopher Dr	28602
Church Dr	28602
Claralee Ln	28602
Clarence Pl	28601
Claridge Dr	28602
Claude Brittain Rd	28602
Clay Trl	28602
Clearlake Dr	28601
Clement Blvd NW	28601
Cliftwood Cir	28601
Cline Yoder Rd	28602
Cloninger Mill Rd NE	28601
Clontz Dr	28601
Clover St	28602
Cole Rd	28602
Coliny Rd	28602
Colonial Ln	28601
Commscope Pl SE	28602
Cone Ct	28601
Cook Ln	28601
Cook Hollow Dr	28601
Cookes Rolling Hill Dr	28601
Cool Water Dr	28601
Cooper Ln	28602
Corbin Ln	28601
Corral Dr	28602
Costner Rd	28602
Cottingham Dr	28602
Coulwood Ct NE	28601
Country Valley Rd	28602
Country View Ln	28602
Countryside Dr	28602
County Line Rd	28602
Courtney Dr	28602
Crafton Rd	28602
Crafton Farm Rd	28602
Creek Dr & St	28602
Creek Point Dr	28601
Creek View Dr	28601
Creekside Ln	28601
Creekside Rd	28602
Creekside Lane Ext	28601
Crookhorn Cir	28602
Crotts Tree Farm Rd	28602
Crown Ter	28601
Cruz Ln	28601
Cruz Hill Ln	28601
Crystal Cove Pl	28601
Crystal Falls Ave	28601
Csi Farm Rd	28602
D Ave SE	28602
D And H Farm Ln	28602
D And K Glass Rd	28602
D Avenue Dr SE	28602
Daisy Ln	28602
Dalton Pl	28601
Debras Ln	28602
Deerfield Ln	28602
Den Dr	28602
Derby St	28602
Dickinson Rd	28602
Dietz Ave & Rd	28602
Divot Ct	28601
Dixie Cir	28601
Doan Ogden Ct	28602
Doberman Ln	28601
Dockside Dr	28601
Doe Ln & Run	28602
Dogwood Dr	28601
Donalds Dr	28602
Dowell St	28602
Driftwood Ct	28601
Driftwood Dr	28602
Dunn Rd	28601
Dwayne Starnes Dr	28602
E Ave SE	28602
Earl Ct	28601
Earl St	28602
Eastwinds Dr	28601
Easy St	
1300-1399	28601
5200-5299	28602
Eckard Rd	28601
Eddies Dr	28602
Edgewater Rd	28601
Elizabeth Ave	28602
Elizabeth St	28601
Elk Trak	28602
Ellis Dr	28602
Elmhurst Dr NE	28601
Emory Dr & Ln	28601
Eps Rd	28602
Erdell Ln	28601
Eudy Ln	28602
Ewing Dr	28602
F Ave SE	28602
F And R Dr	28601
F Avenue Dr SE	28602
Fairgrove Church Rd	28602
Fairlane St	28602
Fairway Ct NE	28601
Faith Olive Church Rd	28602
Falling Creek Rd	28601
Fawn Trl	28602
Field Cir	28602
Fieldcrest Dr	28602
Finger Bridge Rd	28602
Fish Pond Rd	28602
Five Oaks Ln	28601
Flameview Ave	28602
Fleetwood Dr	28602
Flint Hill Dr	28602
Flintlock Ct	28601
Flowerfield Dr	28602
Floyd Darvin Rd	28601
Flynnwood Ct NE	28601
Foley Dr	28602
Forest Oaks Ln	28601
Forest Point Dr	28602
Forest Ridge Dr	28602
Fork Ave & St	28602
Fortenberry St	28602
Fox Trl	28601
Fox Ridge Ln	28601
Foxboro Ln NE	28601
Frances Ct	28602
Freedson Dr	28602
Frosty Ridge Dr	28602
Frye Ave	28602
Full Gospel Church Rd	28602
G W Carson Rd	28602
Gaines St	28602
Garren Dr	28601
Gary Ln	28602
Gatlin Pl	28602
Gazebo Rd	28601
Gene Cook Ln	28601
Gene Moretz Ln	28601
George Baker Dr	28601
George Henry Dr	28602
George Hildebran Rd	28602
George Hildebran Sch Rd	28602
George Pitts Rd	28602
Givens St	28602
Glen Hollow Ct & Ln	28601
Glenview Dr	28602
Glenwood Place Ct	28602
Goat Farm St	28601
Gold Creek Bay	28601
Gold Creek Estate Dr	28601
Gordon Rd	28602
Government Ave SW	
101-197	28602
199-299	28602
231-231	28603
Grace Dr	28601
Grace Chapel Rd	28601
Grady Ln	28602
Grand Oaks Ln	28602
Granfloral Dr	28602
Grant St	28602
Greedy Hwy	28602
Greenbriar Dr	28602
Greenfield Ct	28602
Gregory And Michaels Ln	28601
Griffin Rd	28602
Gross Rd	28602
Grove Park	28602
Grovewood Ln	28602
Gull Cove Ln	28601
Gunpowder Dr	28601
Gurney St	28602
Guy Rd	28602
Guy Cline Rd	28602
H And H Ln	28601
H M Hefner Rd	28602
Hahn Point Dr	28601
Halloway St	28602
Hamilton St	28602
Hanging Rock Ct	28601
Harley Dr	28602
Harmony Dr	28602
Harris Farm Rd	28602
Harrison Pl	28601
Harry James Ln	28601
Hart Ln	28601
Hart Hill Rd	28601
Harvest Dr	28601
Hathaway Dr NE	28601
Havenhurst Rd	28601
Hawks Rdg	28601
Hawthorne Ln	28602
Hayden Dr	28601
Heartwood Ln	28602
Heavenly Place Dr	28602
Hedgerow Cir	28601
Helmsley Dr	28602
Hemingway Dr	28601
Hemphill Rd	28602
Henry Falls Dr	28602
Henry River Rd	
300-399	28601
1000-4599	28602
Henry Smith St	28601
Hepler Dr	28602
Heritage Way	28601
Heritage Creek Dr	28601
Heritage Farm Rd	28601
Heritage View Rd	28601
Herman Pitts Icard Rd	28602
Heron Cove Loop	28601
Hickory Blvd & Hbr	28601
Hickory Airport Rd	28601
Hidden Creek Cir & Ct	28602
Hidden Point Dr	28601
Hideaway Ct NE	28601
Highland Ave NE	28601
Highland Ave SE	28602
Highland Pl	28601
Hildebran Shelby Rd	28602
Hilferty Rd	28601
Hillcrest Ln & St	28601
Hillsboro Ave	28602
Hillside Cir & Ct	28602
Hillstar Dr	28602
Hilltop Dr	28602
Hilltop Ln	28601
Hobbitsrow	28602
Holly Ridge Dr	28602
Home Place Ln	28601
Homer Burns Ave	28602
Homestead Dr	28602
Honda Dr	28602
Honey Ln	28601
Honeycutt Ln	28601
Honeysuckle Dr	28602
Hoot Owls Hollow Rd	28602
Hop Creek Dr	28602
Horse Rock Rd	28602
Horseshoe Bend Rd NE	28601
Hotel Dr SW	28602
Hounds Way	28601
Houston Ave	28602
Howell St	28601
Howell Farm Dr	28601
Hubbard Rd	28601
Hudson Rd	28602
Huffman Farm Rd	28602
N Hughes Blvd	28601
Hunsucker Rd	28601
Hunter Ave & Ct	28601
Hunters Chase Dr & Ln	28601
Hunterwood Dr	28601
I 40 Access Rd	28602
Icard Dam Rd	28601
Icard Ridge Rd	28601
Idlewood Acres Rd	28601
Indian Hills Ave, Cir & St	28601
Ingram St	28602
Ione Baker Rd	28602
Iron Pebble Dr	28602
Ironwood Dr	28602
Isaac Creek Dr	28601
Isaiah Ct	28601
J C Raulston Ct	28602
J Carswell St	28602
J J Hefner Rd	28602
J V Parker Dr	28602
Jack London St	28601
Jack Starnes Mhp Ln	28601
Jackie Ln	28601
Jacob Dr	28602
Jacobs Hartland Rd	28601
James Dr	28601
James Farm Rd	28602
Jeff Crafton Ln	28602
Jenjalo Dr	28601
Jennie Ln	28601
Jeremiah Ct	28601
Jess Monroe Dr	28602
Jetty Ln	28602
Jills Cir	28601
Jimmy Pl NE	28601
Jks Dr	28602
Joe Teague Rd	28601
John Bowman Rd	28602
John Martin Dr	28602
Johns Dr	28601
Johnson Bridge Rd	28602
Jonas Ct	28602
Joseph Ct	28602
Joy Rd	28602
Juniper Ln	28602
Kahill St	28602
Katherines Ln	28601
Kenlane Dr	28601
Kennedy St	28602
Kensington Park Ct	28602
Kilby Ln	28602
Kincaid Ct	28602
King Arthurs Ct	28601
Kings Ct & Rd	28602
Kingsway Blvd	28602
Kirby Farm Rd	28601
Kirkwood St	28602
Kiziah Ln	28601
N Knoll Pl	28601
Knoll Ridge Ct	28602
Kool Park Rd NE	28601
Kristy Dr	28602
Lackey Dr	28602
Lago Ct	28601
Lake Acres Dr	28601
Lake Breeze Ct	28601
Lake Hickory Pl	28601
Lake Park Dr	28601
Lake Pond Dr	28601
Lake Shore Dr	28601
Lake Valley Pl	28601
Lakemont Park Rd	28601
Lakeside Loop & Pl	28601
Lakeside Hill Ct	28601
Lakeside Loop Ext	28601
Lakeside Mhp Dr	28601
Lakeview Dr, Ln & Ter	28601
Lancer Dr	28602
Landing Ct	28602
Landon Ave	28601
Laurel Ridge Rd NW	28601
Lauren Ln	28602
Lee Dr	28602
Leigh Ln	28602
Leigh Ann Dr	28601
Leil Rd	28602
Lenoir Rhyne Blvd SE	28602
Leona Rd	28602
Leslie Ave	28602
Lewis Townsend Rd	28602
Liberty Church Rd & St	28601
Lillian Ln	28602
Limbaugh Ln	28601
Linda Ln	28601
Lindsay Mdws	28601
Linkside Ln	28601
Linville Dr	28602
Lisa Ln	28602
Little River Rd	28602
London Ct	28601
Lonesome Hollow Rd	28602
Longview Ln	28601
Looking Glass Ct	28601
Lost Creek Ct	28602
Loudonya Ln	28601
Lowmans Dr	28602
Lucky Hollow Rd	28601
Luna Pt	28601
Lynchburg Rd	28601
Lynwood Rd	28601
M C M Ln	28601
M J Berry Rd	28602
Machine Shop Rd	28602
Madison Ln	28602
Maggie Dr	28602
Magnolia Ln	28602
Magnum Rd	28602
Mahogany Ln	28602
Main Ave NE	28601
Main Ave NW	28601
Main Ave SE	28602
Main Ave SW	28602
Main Avenue Dr NW	28601
Main Avenue Pl NW	28601
Main Avenue Pl SE	28602
Mamas Garden Dr	28602
Marina Dr	28601
Mariners Point Ln	28601
Marion Ave	28601
Mark Dr NE	28601
Markland Dr	28602
Martin Fish Pond St	28602
Martin Mill Rd	28602
Mattingly Dr	28602
Maw Huffman Rd	28602
Maxwell Dr NE	28601
Maybrook Blvd	28601
Mayline Ct	28601
Maynard Dr	28602
Mcclough Rd	28602
Mccoy Rd	28602
Mccray Farms Dr	28601
Meadow Ln	28602
Meadow Crest Ln	28602
Meadow Lark Ln	28602
Meadowbrook Ln & Ter	28602
Medical Park Dr	28602
Melrose Dr	28602
Melton Road Loop	28601
Memory Ln	28602
Mennonite Church Rd	28602
Miami St	28602
Michaels Gap Ln	28601
Midarriv Ave NE	28601
Midnight Dr	28601
Midway Sand Rd	28601
Mikey Trl	28602
Miller Mill Rd	28602
Miller Ridge Ln	28601
Mini Acres Ln	28602
Mintwood Dr	28602
Missy St	28602
Misty Ln	28601
Misty Valley Rd	28602
Mitchell Dr	28602
Mockingbird Ln	28601
Monaco Ct	28601
Monroe Rd & St	28601
Montclair Cir	28601
Monte Carlo Ln	28601
Moretz Ct	28601
Moretz Dr	28602
Moretz Hall Ln	28601
Morning Glow Ln	28602
Morrison Dr	28602
Moss Farm Rd	28602
Mosteller Estate Ave SE	28602
Mounira Ave	28602
Mountain Grove Rd	28602
Mountain Oak Ln	28601
Mountain Terrace Dr	28602
Mountain View Rd	28602
Mountainside Ct & Dr	28601
Muangmoke Rd	28601
Mulberry Ln	28602
Munger Ln	28602
Murphy Weaver Rd	28602
Musket Dr	28601
My Pl	28602
Naguib Amin St	28602
Nathaneal Ct	28601
W Nc 10 Hwy	28602
S Nc 127 Hwy	28602
Nc Highway 127 Rd	28601
Nello Dr	28602
Nelson Gates St	28601
Newhall Dr NW	28601
Night Heron Pl	28601
No Record	28601
Norcross Ln	28601
Northlakes Dr	28601
Northview Dr	28601
Northwest Rd	28601
Northwood Dr	28601
Oak Ln & St	28602
Oak Leaf Dr	28601
Oakmont Ct, Dr, Ln & Pl	28602
Obie Ct	28602
Oglesby Ln	28602
Olas Dr	28602
Old Brittain Pl & Rd	28602
Old Buff St	28602
Old Dragstrip St	28601
Old Farm Dr	28602
Old Ferry Ln	28601
Old Laurel Rd	28602
Old Lenoir Rd	28601
Old Nc 10	28602
Old River Dr	28602
Old Shelby Rd	28602
Olde School Dr	28602
Olive Branch Rd	28601
Oliver Lowman Rd	28602
Ollen Dr	28602
Orchard Park Dr	28602
Orders St NW	28601
Oren Stephens Rd	28602
Paige St	28602
Paige Street Ext	28602
Park Rd	28602
Paul Rd	28602
Peaceful Pines Ln	28602
Peaceful Valley Dr	28602
Peggy St	28601
Pennwood Dr	28602
Penny Ln	28601
Performance Dr SE	28602
Perrywood Dr	28601
Pickering Dr	28602
Pine Ln	28601
Pine Lake Ct	28601
Pine Meadows Cir	28601
Pine Ridge Ct	28601
Pinecone Ln	28602
Pinecrest Ct & Dr	28601
Pineknoll Dr	28602
Pineview Ct	28601
Pinewinds Dr	28602
Piney Rd	28602
Piney Mountain St	28602
Pinoak Dr	28602
Pioneer Dr	28601
Pittstown Rd	28602
Players Ridge Rd	28601
Plaza Dr	28602
Pleasant Ct	28601
Pleasant Point Dr	28601
Poe Cir	28601
Pokey St	28602
Ponderosa Rd	28602
Pooveys Grove Church Rd	28601
Powder Point Dr	28601
Powell Dr S	28602
Price Dr	28602
Price Meat Cutting Rd	28602
Prince St	28602
Private View Dr	28602
Privette Dr	28601
Propst Dr	28602
Providence Church Rd	28602
Pyramid Rd	28602
Quail Rdg	28602
Quailwood Dr	28601
Queens Rd	28602

Queens Creek Rd 28602
Quiet Ln 28602
Quiet Cove Ln 28601
R And S Cir 28601
R H Rd 28602
R P Whitener Ln 28602
Rainbow Hills Dr 28602
Rainey Earp Dr 28601
Ralph L Rd 28602
Randall Dr 28602
Randolph Ct NE 28601
Raven Hill Dr 28602
Rayland Dr 28601
Recreation Club Rd 28602
Redwood Ave 28602
Redwood Ct 28601
Regents Park Dr 28602
Reitzel Dr 28601
Renwick Dr 28602
Renwick Ln 28601
Restful Ln 28601
Rhodhiss Rd 28601
Rhoney School Rd 28602
Richard Caldwell Ln 28602
Ridgeland Dr 28602
Rink Dam Rd 28601
Rio De Luna 28601
Ripken Dr 28602
River Rd 28602
River Birch Ln 28602
River Lookout St 28602
River Pointe Dr 28601
River Rock Dr 28602
River Run Cir 28602
Riverdell Rd 28601
Rivermont Dr 28602
Riverview Dr 28602
Riviera Run Estates Dr 28601
Rock Ln 28602
Rock Hill Rd 28601
Rockshire Ln 28602
Rocky Acres Rd 28601
Rodeway Ct NE 28601
Rogers Rd 28602
Rolling Ln 28602
Rolling Hills Ave 28602
Rolling Ranch Dr 28602
Rolling Ridge Dr 28602
Rosenbalm Ln 28601
Rosewood Dr 28602
Roten Rd 28601
Royal St 28602
Royal Heights Cir 28602
Royal Oak Ct 28602
Rucker Rd 28601
Rudisill St 28602
Rusty Lynn Rd 28602
Ruth Dr 28602
Saddle Ridge Dr 28602
Sage Meadow Cir 28601
Sagemeadow Cir 28601
Sain Rd 28602
Saint Charles Ct 28601
Salem Rd 28602
Salisbury St NE 28601
Saltwood Dr 28602
Sand Clay Rd 28602
Sand Pit Rd 28602
Sandgate Dr 28602
Sandhurst Rd 28602
Sandy Ford Rd 28602
Saratoga Dr 28602
Sardis Church Rd 28602
Scenic Ridge Dr 28601
Schumann Ln 28602
Scout Cabin Rd 28601
Seaver Ct 28602
Secrest Dr 28602
Section House Rd 28601
Selkirk Dr 28601
Serenity Dr 28602
Serenity Ln 28601
Settlemyre Lail St 28601
Shadowfax Wynd 28602
Shadowood Ln NE 28601
Shady Creek Dr 28602
Shady Falls Ln 28601
Shakespeare Dr 28601
Shamrock Dr 28602
Shamrock Village Ave 28602
Sharon St 28601
Sharon Valley Dr 28601
Shiloh Church Rd 28601
Shipwatch Dr 28601
Shirebourn 28602
N Shore Dr 28601
Short Rd 28602
Shoupes Grove Church Rd 28602
Siecor Park 28601
Sienna Dr 28601
Sigman St 28602
Sigmon Dr
100-1599 28601
2400-2499 28602
Sigmon Drum Rd 28601
Silver Fox Trl 28601
Simon Dr 28602
Singer Dr 28602
Skyline Rd 28601
Skyline Road Ext 28601
Skyview Dr 28602
Sleepy Hollow Dr & Rd 28601
Slick Rock Ct 28601
Sliding Rock 28602
Smith Dr 28601
Snider Cir 28602
Snipes Ct 28602
Snipes Williams Rd 28602
Snow Creek Rd NE 28601
Somerset Dr 28601
Song Bird Ln 28601
Sonnys Cove Dr 28601
Southgate Corporate Park SW 28602
Southlake Dr 28601
Southshore Ct 28601
Spencer Ln 28601
Spencer Woods Ln 28601
Spring St 28602
Spring Meadow Dr 28601
Springbrook Ave 28602
Springfield Rd 28602
Springs Rd NE 28601
Spur Tree Ln 28602
Spurgeons Rd 28602
Startown Rd 28602
Steel Bridge Loop 28601
Steele St 28602
Steeplechase Dr 28601
Stephanys Way 28602
Stephen Ln 28602
Stephensville Rd 28602
Sterling Dr 28602
Sterling Pl 28601
Steve Ikerd Dr NE 28601
Stillwater Ln 28601
Stillwell Hill Rd 28602
Stilwell St 28602
Stirewalt St 28602
Stonehenge Ct 28602
Stonewood Dr 28602
Strebor Ln 28602
Sulphur Springs Rd NE 28601
Sumpter Dr 28602
Sundance Cir 28602
Sunnyside Ln 28602
Sunrise Dr 28602
Sunshine Lake Ct 28601
Suttlemyre Ln 28601
Swayngims Ln 28601
Sweet Bay Ln 28602
Sweetbriar Ln 28602
Sycamore Dr 28601
T And D Ln 28601
Talbot Ln 28602
Tangle Dr 28602
Tanglewood Dr & Ln NE 28601
Tansie Ln 28602
Tate Blvd SE 28602
Taylor Ct 28602
Teague Town Rd 28601
Teakwood Rd 28602
Ted Bolick Ln 28601
Telephone Exchange Rd 28601
Terra Cotta Dr 28602
Theodore Trl 28602
Thistlebrook 28602
Tico Rd 28602
Timber Valley Ln 28602
Timberlane Ter 28601
Timberwood Ln 28602
Tipps Rd 28602
Touchberry Ln NE 28601
Townsend Rd 28601
Track Pl SW 28601
Tracy Bolick Ln 28601
Trade Ave NW 28601
Treasures Cv 28601
Triangle Cir 28602
Trinity Ln 28602
Trotters Ln 28601
Tuckborough 28602
Tucker St 28601
Turn Four Dr 28602
Tuscany Ct 28602
Twillingate 28602
Twin Ponds Dr 28602
Twinbrooke Rd 28602
Tyson Ln 28601
Union Sq NW 28601
Unity Church Rd 28602
Us Highway 321 NW 28601
Us Highway 321 SW 28602
Us Highway 321 Byp S 28602
Us Highway 70 28603
Us Highway 70 SE 28602
Us Highway 70 SW 28602
Us Highway 70a W 28601
Valley Ct 28602
Valley Rd 28601
Valley Arbors Dr 28602
Valley Field Rd 28602
Valley Haven Dr 28602
Valley Run Ct & St 28601
Valley View Ct 28602
Vandresser Pt 28601
Venice Ct 28601
Victoria Ln 28601
View Ave, Dr, St & Trl 28601
View Acres Ave & St 28601
W View Acres Avenue Ext 28601
View Court Park 28602
Village Cir 28602
Vine Arbor Dr 28602
Virginia Dr 28602
Wagner St 28601
Wagon Ln NE 28601
Wagon Wheel Rd 28602
Wallace Cir 28602
Wallace Dairy Rd 28602
Wallace Hollow Dr 28601
Walnut Acres Dr 28602
Walnut Grove Ln 28602
Wandering Ln NE 28601
Warlick Dr 28602
Waterbury Ct 28602
Waterford Dr 28602
Waterfront Dr & Ln 28601
Waterloo St 28602
Wellman Rd 28602
Wesley St 28601
Wessex Ln 28602
Westover Rd 28602
Westridge Dr 28601
Westwinds Dr 28601
Wexford Pt 28601
Wheelis St 28602
Whispering Pines Ct 28601
White Eagle Ln 28602
White Eagle Ranch Rd 28602
White Pine Dr 28602
White Tail Ln 28601
White Water Ct 28602
Whitener Dr & Rd 28602
Whitewater Dr 28601
Whitney Dr NE 28601
Wildlife Access Rd 28601
Wildwood Dr 28601
Wilkes Grove Rd 28602
Wilkies Grove Church Rd 28602
Willowbottom Rd 28602
Wiltshire Dr 28601
Windemere Ln 28602
Winding Oak Dr 28602
Windsor Ct 28602
Winston Dr 28602
Winstone Dr 28602
Winterfield Ct NE 28601
Wisteria Dr 28602
Wolfe Rd 28601
Woodfield Dr 28602
Woodhall 28602
Woodland Hills Dr & Rd 28602
Woodridge Cir & Dr 28602
Woodring Ln 28601
Woodwinds Ct & Dr 28601
Wortman Dr 28601
Wright Dr 28602
Wrong Rd 28601
Wynnshire Dr 28601
Yacht Pl 28601
Yoder Rd & St 28602
Yoder Farm Rd 28602
Yorkland Dr 28601
Young Rd 28602
Zion Church Rd 28602

NUMBERED STREETS

1st Ave NE 28601
1st Ave NW 28601
1st Ave SE 28602
1st Ave SW 28602
1st St NE 28601
1st St NW 28601
1st St SE 28602
1st St SW 28602
1st St W 28601
1st Avenue Cir NW 28601
1st Avenue Ct NW 28601
1st Avenue Ct SE 28602
1st Avenue Pl NW 28601
1st Avenue Pl SE 28602
1st Avenue Pl SW 28602
1st Street Cir NW 28601
1st Street Cir SE 28602
1st Street Ct NW 28601
1st Street Ct SE 28602
1st Street Dr NW 28601
1st Street Dr SW 28602
1st Street Ln NW 28601
1st Street Pl NE 28601
1st Street Pl NW 28601
1st Street Pl SE 28602
2nd Ave NE 28601
2nd Ave NW 28601
2nd Ave SE 28602
2nd Ave SW 28602
2nd St NE 28601
2nd St NW 28601
2nd St SE 28602
2nd St SW 28602
2nd Avenue Cir, Ct, Dr & Pl SW & SE 28602
2nd Street Ct NE 28601
2nd Street Ct NW 28601
2nd Street Ct SE 28602
2nd Street Ct SW 28602
2nd Street Dr NE 28601
2nd Street Dr NW 28601
2nd Street Dr SE 28602
2nd Street Dr SW 28602
2nd Street Ln NW 28601
2nd Street Pl NE 28601
2nd Street Pl NW 28601
2nd Street Pl SE 28602
2nd Street Pl SW 28602
3rd Ave NE 28601
3rd Ave NW 28601
3rd Ave SE 28602
3rd Ave SW 28602
3rd St NE 28601
3rd St NW 28601
3rd St SE 28602
3rd St SW 28602
3rd Avenue Ct SW 28602
3rd Avenue Dr NW 28601
3rd Avenue Dr SE 28602
3rd Avenue Ln SE 28602
3rd Avenue Pl NW 28601
3rd Avenue Pl SE 28602
3rd Street Ct NW 28601
3rd Street Ct SW 28602
3rd Street Dr NE 28601
3rd Street Dr NW 28601
3rd Street Dr SW 28602
3rd Street Ln NE 28601
3rd Street Ln NW 28601
3rd Street Pl NE 28601
3rd Street Pl NW 28601
3rd Street Pl SE 28602
3rd Street Pl SW 28602
4th Ave NE 28601
4th Ave NW 28601
4th Ave SE 28602
4th Ave SW 28602
4th St NE 28601
4th St NW 28601
4th St SE 28602
4th St SW 28602
4th Avenue Ct SW 28602
4th Avenue Dr NW 28601
4th Avenue Pl SE 28602
4th Avenue Pl SW 28602
4th Street Blvd NW 28601
4th Street Cir NE 28601
4th Street Cir NW 28601
4th Street Ct NE 28601
4th Street Ct NW 28601
4th Street Ct SW 28602
4th Street Dr NE 28601
4th Street Dr NW 28601
4th Street Dr SW 28602
4th Street Ln NE 28601
4th Street Ln NW 28601
4th Street Pl NE 28601
4th Street Pl NW 28601
4th Street Pl SE 28602
4th Street Pl SW 28602
4th Street Way NE 28601
5th Ave NE 28601
5th Ave NW 28601
5th Ave SE 28602
5th Ave SW 28602
5th St NE 28601
5th St NW 28601
5th St SE 28602
5th St SW 28602
5th Avenue Ct NE 28601
5th Avenue Ct NW 28601
5th Avenue Pl NE 28601
5th Avenue Pl SE 28602
5th Street Cir NW 28601
5th Street Ct NE 28601
5th Street Ct NW 28601
5th Street Ct SE 28602
5th Street Dr NE 28601
5th Street Dr NW 28601
5th Street Ext NE 28601
5th Street Ln NW 28601
5th Street Pl NE 28601
5th Street Pl NW 28601
6th Ave NE 28601
6th Ave NW 28601
6th Ave SE 28602
6th Ave SW 28602
6th St NE 28601
6th St NW 28601
6th St SE 28602
6th St SW 28602
6th Avenue Ct SW 28602
6th Avenue Dr NW 28601
6th Avenue Pl NW 28601
6th Avenue Pl SW 28602
6th Street Cir NW 28601
6th Street Ct NE 28601
6th Street Ct SE 28602
6th Street Dr NW 28601
6th Street Pl NE 28601
6th Street Pl NW 28601
6th Street Circle Ct NW 28601
7th Ave NE 28601
7th Ave NW 28601
7th Ave SE 28602
7th Ave SW 28602
7th St NE 28601
7th St NW 28601
7th St SE 28602
7th St SW 28602
7th Avenue Ct SE 28602
7th Avenue Dr SW 28602
7th Avenue Pl NW 28601
7th Avenue Pl SE 28602
7th Avenue Pl SW 28602
7th Street Blvd SE 28602
7th Street Ct SE 28602
7th Street Dr NE 28601
7th Street Dr SE 28602
7th Street Ln SE 28602
7th Street Pl NW 28601
7th Street Pl SE 28602
8th Ave NE 28601
8th Ave NW 28601
8th Ave SE 28602
8th Ave SW 28602
8th St NE 28601
8th St NW 28601
8th St SE 28602
8th St SW 28602
8th Avenue Cir SE 28602
8th Avenue Ct SE 28602
8th Avenue Dr NW 28601
8th Avenue Dr SE 28602
8th Avenue Dr SW 28602
8th Avenue Ln NW 28601
8th Avenue Loop NW 28601
8th Avenue Pl NE 28601
8th Street Cir NW 28601
8th Street Cir SE 28602
8th Street Ct NE 28601
8th Street Ct NW 28601
8th Street Ct SE 28602
8th Street Dr NE 28601
8th Street Dr NW 28601
8th Street Dr SE 28602
8th Street Dr SW 28602
8th Street Ln NE 28601
8th Street Ln NW 28601
8th Street Ln SE 28602
8th Street Pl NE 28601
8th Street Pl NW 28601
8th Street Pl SE 28602
9th Ave 28601
9th Ave NE 28601
9th Ave NW 28601
9th Ave SE 28602
9th St NE 28601
9th St NW 28601
9th St SE 28602
9th St SW 28602
9th Avenue Dr NE 28601
9th Avenue Dr NW 28601
9th Avenue Dr SE 28602
9th Avenue Pl NE 28601
9th Avenue Pl SW 28602
9th Street Cir NE 28601
9th Street Ct NE 28601
9th Street Ct NW 28601
9th Street Dr NE 28601
9th Street Dr NW 28601
9th Street Dr SE 28602
9th Street Ln NE 28601
9th Street Ln NW 28601
9th Street Ln SE 28602
9th Street Pl NE 28601
9th Street Pl NW 28601
9th Street Pl SE 28602
10th Ave NE 28601
10th Ave NW 28601
10th Ave SE 28602
10th Ave SW 28602
10th St NE 28601
10th St NW 28601
10th St SE 28602
10th St SW 28602
10th Avenue Ct NE 28601
10th Avenue Ct SE 28602
10th Avenue Dr NE 28601
10th Avenue Dr NW 28601
10th Avenue Dr SE 28602
10th Avenue Dr SW 28602
10th Avenue Ln SE 28602
10th Avenue Pl NE 28601
10th Street Blvd NW 28601
10th Street Cir NW 28601
10th Street Ct 28602
10th Street Ct NE 28601
10th Street Ct NW 28601
10th Street Dr NE 28601
10th Street Dr NW 28601
10th Street Ln NW 28601
10th Street Pl NE 28601
10th Street Pl NW 28601
10th Street Pl SW 28602
10th Street Place Cir NW 28601
11th Ave NE 28601
11th Ave NW 28601
11th Ave SE 28602
11th Ave SW 28602
11th St NE 28601
11th St NW 28601
11th St SW 28602
11th Avenue Blvd SE 28602
11th Avenue Cir NW 28601
11th Avenue Dr SE 28602
11th Avenue Pl NE 28601
11th Avenue Pl NW 28601
11th Street Cir NW 28601
11th Street Ct NE 28601
11th Street Ct NW 28601
11th Street Ct SE 28602
11th Street Dr NW 28601
11th Street Pl NE 28601
11th Street Pl NW 28601
11th Street Pl SW 28602
11th Street Circle Dr NW 28601
12th Ave NE 28601
12th Ave NW 28601
12th Ave SE 28602
12th Ave SW 28602
12th St NE 28601
12th St NW 28601
12th St SE 28602
12th St SW 28602
12th Avenue Ct NE 28601
12th Avenue Ct SE 28602
12th Avenue Dr NE 28601
12th Avenue Dr NW 28601
12th Avenue Ln NW 28601
12th Avenue Pl NE 28601
12th Street Cir NE 28601
12th Street Ct SE 28602
12th Street Dr NE 28601
12th Street Dr NW 28601
12th Street Dr SE 28602
12th Street Dr SW 28602
12th Street Ln NE 28601
12th Street Pl NE 28601
12th Street Pl NW 28601
13th Ave NE 28601
13th Ave NW 28601
13th Ave SE 28602
13th Ave SW 28602
13th St NE 28601
13th St NW 28601
13th St SE 28602
13th St SW 28602

13th Avenue Cir NE 28601
13th Avenue Dr NW 28601
13th Avenue Dr SE 28602
13th Avenue Pl NW 28601
13th Street Cir NE 28601
13th Street Ct NE 28601
13th Street Ct SW 28602
13th Street Dr NE 28601
13th Street Pl NE 28601
13th Street Pl SW 28602
14th Ave NE 28601
14th Ave NW 28601
14th Ave SE 28602
14th Ave SW 28602
14th St NE 28601
14th St NW 28601
14th St SE 28602
14th St SW 28602
14th Avenue Cir NW 28601
14th Avenue Cir SE 28602
14th Avenue Ct NW 28601
14th Avenue Ct SW 28602
14th Avenue Dr NE 28601
14th Avenue Dr NW 28601
14th Avenue Dr SE 28602
14th Avenue Dr SW 28602
14th Avenue Pl NW 28601
14th Avenue Pl SW 28602
14th Street Cir NE 28601
14th Street Ct NE 28601
14th Street Ct SW 28602
14th Street Dr NE 28601
14th Street Dr SW 28602
14th Street Ln NE 28601
14th Street Pl NE 28601
14th Street Pl NW 28601
15th Ave NE 28601
15th Ave NW 28601
15th Ave SE 28602
15th Ave SW 28602
15th St NE 28601
15th St NW 28601
15th St SE 28602
15th St SW 28602
15th Avenue Cir & Pl 28602
15th Street Ct NE 28601
15th Street Dr NE 28601
15th Street Dr SW 28602
15th Street Pl NE 28601
16th Ave NE 28601
16th Ave NW 28601
16th Ave SE 28602
16th Ave SW 28602
16th St NE
800-1300 28601
1269-1269 28603
1301-4399 28601
16th St NW 28601
16th St SE 28602
16th St SW 28602
16th Avenue Cir NW 28601
16th Avenue Cir SW 28602
16th Avenue Dr NE 28601
16th Avenue Dr SE 28602
16th Avenue Ln NW 28601
16th Avenue Pl NE 28601
16th Avenue Pl NW 28601
16th Avenue Pl SW 28602
16th Street Cir NE 28601
16th Street Dr NE 28601
16th Street Pl NE 28601
16th Street Pl SE 28602
17th Ave NE 28601
17th Ave NW 28601
17th Ave SE 28602
17th St NE 28601
17th St NW 28601
17th St SE 28602
17th St SW 28602
17th Avenue Cir SW 28602
17th Avenue Ct NE 28601
17th Avenue Ct NW 28601
17th Avenue Ct SW 28602
17th Avenue Dr NE 28601
17th Avenue Dr SE 28602
17th Avenue Ln NW 28601
17th Avenue Pl NW 28601
17th Street Ct, Dr, Ln &
Pl NE & NW 28601
18th Ave NE 28601
18th Ave NW 28601
18th Ave SE 28602
18th St NE 28601
18th St NW 28601
18th St SE 28602
18th St SW 28602
18th Avenue Cir, Ct,
Dr, Ln & Pl NE & NW 28601
18th Street Cir SE 28602
18th Street Ct NE 28601
18th Street Dr NE 28601
18th Street Ln NE 28601
18th Street Ln SE 28602
18th Street Pl NW 28601
18th Street Pl SW 28602
19th Ave NE 28601
19th Ave NW 28601
19th Ave SE 28602
19th Ave SW 28602
19th St NE 28601
19th St NW 28601
19th St SE 28602
19th St SW 28602
19th Avenue Cir NE 28601
19th Avenue Cir NW 28601
19th Avenue Ct NE 28601
19th Avenue Ct NW 28601
19th Avenue Dr NE 28601
19th Avenue Dr NW 28601
19th Avenue Dr SW 28602
19th Avenue Ln NW 28601
19th Avenue Pl NE 28601
19th Avenue Pl NW 28601
19th Street Ct NE 28601
19th Street Ct SE 28602
19th Street Dr SE 28602
19th Street Ln NE 28601
19th Street Ln NW 28601
19th Street Pl NE 28601
19th Street Pl SE 28602
20th Ave NE 28601
20th Ave NW
1-199 28601
200-499 28602
1000-1299 28601
20th Ave SE 28602
20th Ave SW 28602
20th St NE 28601
20th St NW 28601
20th St SE 28602
20th St SW 28602
20th Avenue Ct NE 28601
20th Avenue Ct NW 28601
20th Avenue Dr NE 28601
20th Avenue Dr NW 28601
20th Avenue Ln NE 28601
20th Avenue Ln NW 28601
20th Avenue Pl NE 28601
20th Avenue Pl NW 28601
20th Avenue Pl SE 28602
20th Street Cir NE 28601
20th Street Cir SW 28602
20th Street Ct NE 28601
20th Street Dr NE 28601
20th Street Ln NE 28601
20th Street Pl NE 28601
20th Street Pl SE 28602
20th Street Pl SW 28602
21st Ave NE 28601
21st Ave NW 28601
21st Ave SE 28602
21st St NE 28601
21st St NW 28601
21st St SE 28602
21st St SW 28602
21st Avenue Ct, Dr & Pl
NE & NW 28601
21st Street Ct NE 28601
21st Street Dr NE 28601
21st Street Dr SE 28602
21st Street Ln NE 28601
21st Street Ln SE 28602
21st Street Pl NE 28601
22nd Ave NE 28601
22nd Ave NW 28601
22nd Ave SE 28602
22nd St NE 28601
22nd St NW 28601
22nd St SE 28602
22nd St SW 28602
22nd Avenue Ct SE 28602
22nd Avenue Pl NE 28601
22nd Avenue Pl SE 28602
22nd Street Ct NE 28601
22nd Street Ct SE 28602
22nd Street Ext SW 28602
22nd Street Ln NE 28601
22nd Street Pl NE 28601
22nd Street Pl SE 28602
23rd Ave NE 28601
23rd St NE 28601
23rd St NW 28601
23rd St SE 28602
23rd St SW 28602
23rd Avenue Ct, Dr, Ln
& Pl NE 28601
23rd Street Cir NE 28601
23rd Street Ct NE 28601
23rd Street Ct SE 28602
23rd Street Dr NE 28601
23rd Street Dr SE 28602
23rd Street Ln NE 28601
23rd Street Pl NE 28601
23rd Street Pl NW 28601
24th Ave NE 28601
24th Ave SE 28602
24th St NE 28601
24th St NW 28601
24th St SE 28602
24th St SW 28602
24th Avenue Cir, Ct, Dr
& Pl NE & NW 28601
24th Street Cir NE 28601
24th Street Ct NE 28601
24th Street Ct SE 28602
24th Street Dr NE 28601
24th Street Dr SE 28602
24th Street Ln NE 28601
24th Street Pl NE 28601
24th Street Pl SE 28602
25th Ave NE 28601
25th Ave NW 28601
25th St NE 28601
25th St NW 28601
25th St SE 28602
25th St SW 28602
25th Avenue Ct & Dr 28601
25th Street Ct NE 28601
25th Street Dr NE 28601
25th Street Ln NE 28601
25th Street Pl NE 28601
25th Street Pl SE 28602
25th Street Pl SW 28602
26th Ave NE 28601
26th St NE 28601
26th St NW 28601
26th St SE 28602
26th St SW 28602
26th Avenue Ln & Pl 28601
26th Street Blvd SE 28602
26th Street Ct NE 28601
26th Street Dr NE 28601
26th Street Dr SE 28602
26th Street Ln NE 28601
26th Street Pl SW 28602
27th Ave NE 28601
27th St NE 28601
27th St NW 28601
27th St SW 28602
27th Avenue Cir & Dr NE
& NW 28601
27th Street Dr NE 28601
27th Street Dr SE 28602
27th Street Ln NE 28601
27th Street Pl NE 28601
27th Street Pl SW 28602
28th Ave NE 28601
28th Ave NW 28601
28th St NE 28601
28th St NW 28601
28th St SW 28602
28th Avenue Ct, Dr, Ln
& Pl NE & NW 28601
28th Street Cir NE 28601
29th Ave NE 28601
29th St NE 28601
29th St NW 28601
29th St SE 28602
29th St SW 28602
29th Avenue Ct, Dr, Ln
& Pl NE & NW 28601
29th Street Cir SW 28602
29th Street Ct NE 28601
29th Street Dr NE 28601
29th Street Pl SW 28602
29th Street Place Cir
SW 28602
30th Ave NE 28601
30th Ave NW 28601
30th St NE 28601
30th St NW 28601
30th St SW 28602
30th Avenue Cir, Ct,
Dr, Ln & Pl NE & NW 28601
30th Street Dr NE 28601
30th Street Ln NE 28601
30th Street Pl NE 28601
30th Street Pl NW 28601
30th Street Pl SW 28602
31st Ave NE 28601
31st Ave NW 28601
31st St NE 28601
31st St NW 28601
31st St SW 28602
31st Avenue Cir, Ct,
Dr, Ln & Pl NE 28601
31st Street Ct NE 28601
31st Street Dr NE 28601
31st Street Ln NE 28601
31st Street Pl SE 28602
32nd Ave NE 28601
32nd Ave NW 28601
32nd St NE 28601
32nd St SW 28602
32nd Avenue Ct, Dr &
Pl 28601
32nd Street Ln NE 28601
32nd Street Pl NE 28601
32nd Street Pl SW 28602
33rd Ave NE 28601
33rd Ave NW 28601
33rd St NE 28601
33rd St NW 28601
33rd St SW 28602
33rd Avenue Dr & Pl 28601
33rd Street Cir SW 28602
33rd Street Ct NE 28601
33rd Street Dr NE 28601
33rd Street Dr SE 28602
33rd Street Dr SW 28602
33rd Street Ln NE 28601
33rd Street Pl NE 28601
34th Ave NE 28601
34th Ave NW 28601
34th St NE 28601
34th St NW 28601
34th St SW 28602
34th Avenue Cir, Ct,
Dr, Ln & Pl NE & NW 28601
34th Street Cir, Ct, Dr
& Pl NE & NW 28601
35th Ave NE 28601
35th Ave NW 28601
35th St NE 28601
35th St NW 28601
35th St SW 28602
35th Avenue Ct, Dr, Ln
& Pl NE & NW 28601
35th Street Ct, Dr, Ln &
Pl NE & NW 28601
36th Ave NE 28601
36th Ave NW 28601
36th St NE 28601
36th St NW 28601
36th St SW 28602
36th Avenue Cir, Ct, Dr
& Pl NE & NW 28601
36th Street Dr & Pl 28601
37th Ave NE 28601
37th Ave NW 28601
37th St NE 28601
37th St NW 28601
37th St SW 28602
37th Avenue Ct, Dr & Pl
NE & NW 28601
37th Street Ct & Dr 28601
38th Ave & St 28601
38th Avenue Ct & Ln 28601
38th Street Dr NE 28601
39th Ave NE 28601
39th Ave NW 28601
39th St NW 28601
39th St SW 28602
39th Avenue Ct, Dr & Pl
NE & NW 28601
39th Street Cir & Pl 28602
40th St NW 28601
40th St SW 28602
40th Avenue Ct, Dr, Ln
& Pl NE & NW 28601
40th Street Dr SW 28602
41st Ave NW 28601
41st St NW 28601
41st St SW 28602
41st Avenue Ct, Dr, Ln
& Pl NE & NW 28601
42nd Avenue Cir, Ct,
Dr, Ln & Pl NE & NW 28601
43rd NE & NW 28601
43rd Avenue Ct, Dr, Ln
& Pl NE & NW 28601
44th NE & NW 28601
44th Avenue Cir, Ct,
Dr, Ln & Pl NE & NW 28601
45th Ave NE 28601
45th Avenue Ln & Pl 28601
46th Ave NE 28601
46th Avenue Dr & Ln 28601
47th Ave NE 28601
47th Avenue Ln & Pl 28601
48th Ave NE 28601
48th Avenue Ln NE 28601
49th Avenue NE &
NW 28601
50th Avenue Cir NE 28601
54th Ave NE 28601
55th Ave NE 28601

HIGH POINT NC

General Delivery 27260

POST OFFICE BOXES MAIN OFFICE STATIONS AND BRANCHES

Box No.s
HP2 - HP11 27261
B - H 27261
1 - 2838 27261
4000 - 4000 27263
5001 - 6770 27262
7001 - 9998 27264
9998 - 10044 27261
10300 - 10310 27263
16001 - 16400 27261
27260 - 27265 27260

NAMED STREETS

Abberton Way 27260
Abbie Ave 27263
Abbotts Xing 27265
Abbotts Creek Church Rd
& Xing 27265
Abbotts Ford Ct 27265
Abbotts Grove Ct 27265
Aberdare Dr 27265
Aberdeen Rd 27265
Academy St 27260
Adams St 27262
Addington Rd 27263
Addison Blvd 27262
Admiral Dr 27263
Afton Park Ln 27265
Agnes St 27265
Aileen Ct 27265
Akers Ct 27263
Alamosa Dr 27265
Albert Ave 27262
Albertson Rd
200-1899 27260
5500-5799 27263
Albertson Road Ext 27263
Alderbrook Dr 27265
Alderny Cir & Pl 27265
Aldridge Ln & Rd 27263
Alison Ln 27263
Alleghany St 27263
Allen Dr 27262
Allen Jay Rd 27263
Allendale Dr 27263
Allred Pl 27262
Almina Pl 27262
Alpha St 27263
Alpine Dr 27260
Alton Pl 27263
Ambassador Ct 27265
Amber Way 27263
Ambridge Ct 27265
Amhurst Ave 27260
Amos St 27260
Anaheim St 27260
Anchoridge Ave 27265
Anderson Pl 27260
Andover Ct 27265
Anji Ct 27265
Ann Arbor Ave & Ct 27265
Anna Ct 27263
Anne St 27263
Annmore Cir 27262
Ansley Way 27265
Apache Dr 27263
Apex Pl 27260
Apollo Cir 27263
Apple Orchard Cv 27265
Apple Tree Rd 27263
Appletree Ct & Rd 27263
Appling Rd 27263
Arbordale Ave 27262
Arbrook Ln 27265
Arch St 27260
Archdale Blvd & Rd 27263
Ardale Dr 27260
Arden Ct & Pl 27265
Ardmore Cir 27262
Arlington St 27260
Armory Dr 27260
Armstrong Ct 27263
Arnette Dr 27263
Arrowhead Ct 27265
Arthur Ave 27263
Artisan Ave 27263
Asbill Ave 27265
Ascot Ct 27262
Ashbrook Cir 27263
Ashburn St 27260
Ashe St 27262
Asheboro St 27260
Ashebrook Dr 27265
Ashfield Ct 27265
Ashford Cir 27262
Ashland St 27263
Ashley Ave 27262
Ashley Park Ct 27265
Ashton Oaks Ct 27265
Aston Ct 27265
Auction Rd 27263
Auction Road Ext 27263
Audubon St 27265
Augusta Pl 27265
Austin St 27260
Autumn Hill Ct 27263
Avalon Pl 27262
Avalon Acres Ln 27265
Avalon Springs Ct 27265
Avery Ave 27265
Avondale St 27260
Azalea Ct 27265
Aztec Dr 27263
Azure Ct & St 27265
Bacon Ct 27263
Bailey Cir 27262
Baileys Way 27263
Bainbridge St 27263
Baker Ct 27263
Baker Rd
100-1999 27263
200-699 27263
2000-2099 27260
Baldwins Mill Ct 27265
Balfour Dr 27263
Ballard Pond Dr 27265
Baltimore St 27263
Banbridge Dr 27260
Banoak Ct & St 27265
Barbee Ave 27260
Barbee St 27262
Barker Ave 27262
Barney Rd 27265
Barrett Dr 27263
Barrow Rd 27265
Barston Way 27260
Basalt Ct 27265
Basswood Ave 27265
Bay Ct 27265
Bayford Ct 27265
Baylesford Ln 27265
Bayswater Dr 27265
Baytree Ct 27265
Baywater Pt 27265
Beach St 27260
Beacon Ridge Dr 27265
Beane Rd 27263
Beard Ave 27263
Bearded Iris Ln 27265
Beaucrest Ave 27265
Beaumont Ave 27260
Beddington St 27260
Bedford St 27263
Beechnut Dr 27265
Belgian Dr 27263
Belle Ave 27265
Bellemeade St 27263
E & W Bellevue Dr 27265
Belmar St 27260
Belmont Dr 27263
Belo Rush Dr 27263
Belva Ct 27263
Bencini Pl 27260
Bennington Way 27262
Bent Trace Dr 27265
Bentbrook Dr 27265
Bergamot Loop 27260
Berkley St 27260
Berkshire Ct 27265
Bethel Dr 27260
Bethel Drive Ext 27260
Bethel Park Dr 27260
Betty Ct 27260
Beverly Hills Dr
1200-1299 27260
3800-4099 27265
Bexley Ct 27262
Big Creek Ct 27265
Big Oak Ct 27265
Big Tree Rd 27265
Billy Ave 27263
Billy Swaim Rd 27265
Biltmore Ave 27260
Bingham Ct 27265
Birch View Dr 27265
Birchgarden Dr 27265
Birchwood Dr 27262
Birdwood Way 27260
Birkdale Ct & Dr 27265
Blackberry Brook Trl 27265
Blackberry Ridge Rd 27265

Blain Ct & St 27262
Blair Ave 27260
Blair Ct 27263
Blair Dr 27263
Blair Farm Rd 27263
Blairwood St 27265
Blake Ave 27260
Blandwood Dr 27260
Blazing Star Dr 27263
Bluewood Ct 27263
Blythe Ct 27265
Boles Ave 27260
Bolingbroke Ct & Rd 27265
Bolivar Ave 27260
Bolton Pl 27260
Bonnie Pl 27263
Boulder Ct & Dr 27263
Boulding Ave 27265
Boulevard St 27262
Boundary Ave 27260
Bowen Dr 27263
Bowers Ave 27260
Bowman Loop Dr 27263
Boyer St 27262
Bracknell Dr 27265
Bradbury Way 27265
Braddock Rd 27265
Bradford Ln 27263
Bradley Pl 27260
Bradshaw St 27262
Braemar Ct 27265
Bragg Ave & Ct 27265
Branch St 27260
Brandemere Dr 27265
Brandon Dr 27265
Brandywine St 27265
Braniff Pl 27263
Branson Meadows Rd 27263
Brantley Cir 27262
Breckenridge Ct 27265
Brennen Ln 27262
Brentonshire Ln 27265
Brentwood St
100-1999 27260
2000-2599 27263
Brentwood Ter 27260
Brevard Rd 27263
Brian Hollars Ct 27265
Brian Jordan Pl 27265
Briarcliff Ct & Dr 27265
Briarcreek Rd 27265
Briarwood Ave 27265
Bridgend Dr 27260
Bridgeport Ter 27265
Bridges Dr 27262
Bridlewood Ave 27265
Briggs Pl 27262
Brightleaf Ct 27263
Brightleaf Ln 27265
Brighton Ave 27262
Brighton Village Ln 27263
Brightwood Dr 27262
Brinkley Pl 27265
Bristol Pl 27262
Brittany Way 27263
E Broad Ave 27260
W Broad Ave
100-299 27260
300-499 27262
Broadstone Village Dr 27260
Brockett Ave 27260
Bronzie Lawson Rd 27263
Brook Cir & St 27263
Brook Circle Ext 27263
Brookdale Ave 27265
Brookdale Dr 27263
Brookfield Ct 27262
Brookhollow Ln 27263
Brooks Ave 27260
Brookside Dr 27262
Brookwood Cir 27263
Brookwood Dr 27262
Brown Pl 27260
Brownsfield Ct 27262
Browntown Ln 27265
Brumley Ct 27262

Brummell Ln 27265
Brunswick Ct 27262
Buckleigh Ln 27265
Buena Vista Ave 27265
Bundy Dr 27263
Bunratty Ct 27260
Burch Pt 27265
Burge Pl 27260
Burgemere St 27263
Burguss Ct & Rd 27265
Burkston Ct 27262
Burning Tree Cir & Ct 27265
Burrwood Dr 27263
Burton Ave 27262
Burton Run Rd 27262
N Business Loop 85
Hwy 27263
Buttonwood Ct 27265
Buxenbury Dr 27263
Byerly Rd 27262
Byron Ln 27263
Cable St 27260
Caitlin Nicole Ct 27265
Calabria Ct 27265
Callahan St 27263
Calloway Farm Rd 27265
Calumet Ct 27265
Calvin St 27263
Cambridge Dr 27265
Cambridge Oaks Dr 27262
Camden Ave 27260
Camden Park Ct 27265
Cameron Ter 27263
Camillia Cv 27265
Campbell St 27262
Candelar Dr 27265
Candlewood Ct 27265
Canopy Oak Ct 27265
Canter Ln & Rd 27263
Canter Lane Ext 27263
Canterbury Rd 27262
Cantering Rd 27262
Cantus Ct 27265
Cantwell Ct 27265
Cardiff Ln 27265
Cardinal Pl 27263
Carey Ave 27262
Caribou Ct 27265
Carlisle Way 27265
Carneros Cir 27265
Carolina Ct
100-199 27263
1700-1799 27265
Carolina St
1200-1399 27262
1400-1899 27265
Carolyndon Dr 27262
Carr St 27262
Carrick St 27262
Carrington Ln 27263
Carroll St 27263
Carroll Brook Rd 27265
Carroll Ridge Ct 27265
Carson Ln 27265
Carsten Ave 27262
Carter St 27260
Carter Mill St 27260
Carthage Ln 27263
Carvette Ct 27265
Cascade Ct & Dr 27265
Cashatt Rd 27263
Cassell St 27260
Castle Oaks Ct 27265
Castlegate Ct 27265
Castleloch Ct 27265
Caudell Pl 27260
Cayley Ct 27260
Cecil Dr 27260
Cecil Farm Rd
100-499 27265
6800-6999 27263
Cedar Ln 27263
Cedar St 27260
Cedar Crest Ln 27265
Cedar Post St 27263
Cedar Ridge Ln 27265

Cedar Square Rd 27263
Cedar Trail Ct 27265
Cedarbrook Ct 27265
Cedarwood Trl 27265
Cedrow Dr 27260
Ceebee Dr 27263
Celtic Crossing Dr 27265
N Centennial St
100-299 27260
300-2199 27262
2200-3499 27265
S Centennial St 27260
Central Ave & Ct 27260
Chadwick Dr 27263
Challock Way 27260
Chambers St 27263
Chandler Ave 27262
Chanterelle Dr 27263
Charing Cross Ln 27260
Charity Church Ln 27263
Charles Ave 27260
Charlotte Ave 27262
Chas Ct 27265
Chase Ave 27260
Chatfield Dr 27260
Chatham Dr 27265
Checker Rd 27263
Chelsea Sq 27263
Cherokee Ct & Dr 27262
Chesapeake Ln 27263
Cheshire Ct 27262
Chester Dr 27265
Chester Ridge Dr 27262
Chester Woods Ct 27262
Chestnut Dr
100-1899 27262
2300-3799 27265
Chestnut Glen Way 27262
Chestnut Street Ext
1900-2299 27262
3800-4999 27265
Cheyenne Dr 27263
Chickadee Pt 27262
Chilton Rd 27263
Chilton Way 27265
Christene St 27265
Christopher Ct 27265
Church Ave 27262
Churchill Ct 27262
Cilgerran Ct 27265
Circle Dr
200-399 27263
800-999 27262
Circle Drive Ext 27263
Clara Cox Way 27260
Clark Pl 27265
Clay Ave 27260
Clay Huey Rd 27265
Claybrooke Ct 27265
Clayton St 27263
Cleveland St 27260
Cliffside Ave 27260
Cliffvale Ct & Dr 27262
Clifton Dr 27265
Clifton St 27260
Clinard Ave 27265
Clinard Farms Rd 27265
Cline 27265
Clinton Ave 27260
Clish Pl 27260
N Clodfelter Rd 27265
Clover Dr 27262
Cloverdale Ct 27263
Cloverdale Dr 27263
Cloverdale St 27260
NW Cloverleaf Pl 27260
SW Cloverleaf Pl 27263
Cloverwood Dr 27265
Cloverwood Meadow
Ln 27265
Clubhouse Ct 27265
Clyde Pl 27262
Clydesdale Dr 27263
Coachmans Ct 27262
Cobblestone Bend Dr 27265
Coe Ave 27263

Cole Ave 27265
E College Ave 27260
E College Dr
600-799 27260
1100-1399 27265
N College Dr
300-399 27260
700-1399 27262
S College Dr 27260
W College Dr
700-1099 27262
1100-1199 27260
Colonial Dr 27262
Colonial Pl 27262
Colonial St 27263
Coltrane Ave & Ct 27260
Coltrane Mill Rd 27263
Columbus Ave 27263
Comanche Rd 27263
E & W Commerce
Ave 27260
Connor Pl 27260
Cook St 27262
Copeland Ave 27263
Copperleaf Ct 27265
Copperstone Dr 27265
Core Ave 27265
Corina Cir 27263
Cork Tree Ln 27263
Cornell St 27260
Cornish Glen Ct 27265
Corporation Dr 27263
Corvair Dr 27265
Cory Rd 27265
Coryton Way 27260
Cos Cob Ct 27265
Cosway Ct 27265
Cottage Ct 27263
Cottesmore Dr 27265
Council St 27262
Country Ct & Ln 27263
Country Club Dr 27262
Country Dream Ln 27263
Countryside Dr 27265
Courtesy Rd 27260
Courtland Ln 27263
Courtland St 27265
Cove Ct 27265
Covedale St 27265
Covent Oak Ct 27265
Coventry Rd 27262
Covewood St 27265
Cox Ave & Ct 27263
Crafton St 27260
Craig Dr & Pt 27263
Cranberry Ridge Dr 27265
Cranbrook Pt 27265
Craven Rd 27262
Crawford Ave 27260
Cray Dr 27263
Cray Drive Ext 27263
Creek Bed Ln 27265
Creek Wood Dr 27263
Creekridge Dr 27265
Creekside Dr
100-399 27265
800-1099 27262
N Creekside Dr 27265
Creekside Ridge Dr 27265
Creekview Ct 27265
Crescent Dr 27263
Crest Ln 27265
Crestlin Dr 27262
Crestline Dr 27260
Crestview Dr
100-199 27265
3200-3399 27260
Crestwood Cir 27260
Crestwood Dr 27263
Crinan Ct 27265
Crocker Pl 27265
Croquet Cir 27262
Cross St 27260
Cross Creek Ct 27262
Crossing Way Ct 27262
Crosswinds Dr 27265

Crotts Dr 27263
Croyden St 27262
Cruthis Rd 27263
Culler Pl 27260
Cumberland Pl 27260
Cummins St 27262
Curry Rd 27265
Cypress Ct & Ln 27265
Dairy Point Dr 27265
Dale St 27263
Dalewood Ave 27265
Dallas Ave 27265
Danbury Ct 27262
Dancy Rd 27263
Dandelion Dr 27265
Dane St 27263
Daniel Paul Dr 27263
Danmar Ave 27260
Dantzler Ct & Rd 27265
Darden St
1400-1403 27262
1404-1599 27265
Dartmouth Ave 27260
Daveler Dr 27265
David St 27263
Davidson Ave 27260
Davidson Ct 27262
Davidson Rd 27262
Davidson St 27263
Davis Ave 27260
Dawn Dr 27263
Day Pl 27260
E Dayton Ave 27262
Deacon Ct 27265
Deborah Ave 27263
Deep River Rd 27265
Deerfield Dr 27262
Deerfield Pl 27263
Deerfield St 27265
Delaine Pt 27265
Delaware Pl 27260
Delk Dr
1100-1299 27262
1400-1599 27265
Dellwood St 27263
Delmar Ln 27265
Delmont St 27262
Deloach Ct 27265
Delray Ave 27265
Delta Ct 27263
Delwood Dr 27263
Denny St 27262
Densbury Dr 27260
Depot Pl 27260
Derby Cir 27265
Devane Ct 27265
Devlin Ct 27262
Devonshire Ave 27262
Dewitt Coltrane Dr 27263
Dill St 27263
Dillon Rd 27260
Dilworth Rd 27265
Dixie Pl 27260
Dogwood Cir 27260
Dogwood Ct 27260
Dogwood Ln 27263
Domino Pl 27265
Donna View Dr 27263
Donvic Dr 27262
Dora Wade Dr 27262
Dorado Cir, Ct & Dr 27265
Dorothy St 27262
Dorris Ave 27260
Dorsett St 27263
Double Pond Ln 27265
Dove Meadows Dr 27263
Dover Pl 27265
Dovershire Ct & Pl 27262
N & S Downing St 27260
Drake Rd 27263
Dresden Rd 27263
Dresher Ct 27265
Drew Ave 27260
Driftwood Dr 27263
Druid St 27265
Dry Creek Ct 27265

Dublin Ave 27260
Dukes Hollow Ct 27265
Dunloy Way 27262
Dunmore Ct 27263
Dunning Ct 27265
Dunwood Dr 27265
Durand Ave 27263
Dylan Scott Dr 27263
Eagle Glen Rd 27265
Eagle Hill Dr 27265
Eagle Point Dr 27265
Eagles View Ct 27265
Eagleston Ct 27265
Earle Pl 27265
Earlham Pl 27263
East Ave 27260
Eastchester Dr
100-1099 27262
1100-2799 27265
Eastover Pl 27265
Eastview Pl 27260
Eastward Ave 27260
Eastward Avenue Ext 27260
Eastway Ct 27260
Eastwind Dr 27263
Eaton Dr 27265
Eaton Pl 27262
Ebb Shore Dr 27263
Ebenezer Church Rd 27263
Eccles Pl 27260
Edbury Ct 27265
Eden Ter 27263
Edenridge Dr 27265
Edgar Rd 27263
Edgar View Dr 27263
Edgedale Dr 27262
Edgeview Rd 27260
Edgewater St 27265
Edgewood Ct 27263
Edgewood Dr 27262
Edgeworth St 27262
Edmonds Trl 27263
Edmondson Pl 27260
Edward Walker St 27263
Eight Oaks Dr 27263
Election Oak Dr 27265
Elgin Ave 27262
Eli Moore Ct 27265
Elk Pl 27262
Elkes Pl 27263
Elkhorn Ct 27263
Ellen Ave 27263
Elliott St 27263
Ellwood Dr 27260
N Elm St 27262
S Elm St 27260
Elmer Beeson Rd 27263
Elmhurst Ave 27262
Elmont St 27263
Elmwood Ave 27265
Elon Pl
1100-1199 27260
1200-1299 27263
Ember Oaks Ave 27265
Embers Ct 27265
Emerson St 27263
Emery Cir 27262
Emerywood Dr 27262
Emilia Ct 27262
N & S Emily Ct & St 27265
Enfield Dr 27263
Englewood Dr 27263
English Ct & Rd 27262
Ennis St 27260
Enterprise Dr 27260
Erica Dr 27263
Erica Marie Ct 27265
Ernest Ct & St 27263
Erwinwood Dr 27263
Esco Pl 27260
Eskdale Dr 27260
Essex Ct 27265
Essex Sq 27263
Ethan Dr 27265
Ethel Ave 27263
Eugene Ave 27260

Eva Trellis Ct 27265
Evans St 27260
Evans Mill Rd 27265
Evelyn View Dr 27263
Everett Ln 27262
Evergreen Ave 27262
Everton Ct 27265
Fair Oaks Ln 27265
Faircloth Way 27265
E & W Fairfield Rd 27263
Fairlane St 27265
Fairmeadow Ave 27265
Fairport Ct 27265
Fairstone Pl 27265
Fairview St 27260
Fairway Dr 27262
Fala St 27260
Farlow Ln 27262
Farlow St 27263
Farlow Farm Rd 27263
Farnsworth Ct 27262
E & W Farriss Ave 27262
Feld Ave 27263
Fern Ave 27260
Ferndale Blvd 27262
Fernwood Dr
1400-1499 27262
3600-3699 27263
Fieldale Pl 27265
Filbert Pl 27260
Finch Ave 27263
Finsbury Ln 27260
Firethorn Dr 27265
First Heights Dr 27263
First Tee Dr 27263
Fisher Ave 27262
Fishing Pond Ct 27265
Five Points Pl 27260
Flaherty St 27262
Flanders Ct 27265
Flannery Ln 27265
Flicker Ln 27262
Flint Ave 27260
Flintlock Ct 27265
Flintwood Ct 27265
Florence School Dr 27265
Florham Dr 27265
Florida St 27262
Flormont Dr 27265
Flynt Rd 27265
Foggy Ln 27265
Foliage Ln 27265
Folwell Dr 27263
Forage Dr 27265
Forest Hill Dr 27262
Forest Shade St 27263
Forester Dr 27265
Forestview Dr 27260
Forestwood Dr 27263
E Fork Rd 27265
Forrest St 27262
Fountain St 27263
Fountain Grove Cir &
Dr 27265
Fountain Village Cir &
Ln 27265
Foust Ave 27260
Fowler Pl 27260
Fox Creek Ct 27265
Fraley Rd 27263
Fraley Fields Rd 27262
Francis St 27263
Francis Mill Ct 27265
Frank White Dr 27263
Franklin Ave 27260
Frazier St 27263
Frazier Marsh Rd 27263
Fred Alexander Pl 27260
Freeman Pl 27263
Freestone St 27265
Friddle Dr 27260
Friendly Ave 27260
Friends Ave 27260
Friends Ln 27263
Frontier St 27263
Fulton Pl 27263

Furlough Ave ... 27260
Futrelle Dr ... 27262
Gable St ... 27260
Gable Way ... 27262
Gaines Ave ... 27263
Gaither Ct ... 27263
Gallimore Dairy Rd ... 27265
Gallop Way ... 27263
Garden Club St ... 27265
Garden Creek Dr ... 27265
Gardena Ct ... 27265
Garner Pl ... 27263
Garnett Dr ... 27263
Garrell St ... 27263
Garrison St ... 27260
Gate St ... 27263
Gatehouse Rd ... 27262
Gatewood Ave ... 27262
Gateworth Dr ... 27265
Gavin Dr ... 27260
Gaylord Ct ... 27260
Geddie Pl ... 27260
Gelding Ct ... 27265
Gene St ... 27263
Gentry Ct ... 27265
George Pl ... 27260
George Clyde Ln ... 27262
Georgetown Ct ... 27262
Georgia Pond Ln ... 27265
Gilbreth Ln ... 27263
Gilbrook Ct ... 27262
Giles St ... 27263
Glasgow Ct ... 27265
Glen Cove Way ... 27265
Glen Echo Ct ... 27265
Glendale Dr ... 27263
Glenmore Ave ... 27263
Glenn Meade Dr ... 27265
Glenola Industrial Dr ... 27263
Glenstone Trl ... 27265
Glenview Dr ... 27263
Glenwick Ln ... 27262
Glyn Water Ln ... 27265
Godnick Ln ... 27263
Goodman St ... 27263
Gordon Rd ... 27263
Gordon St ... 27260
Gordon Farm Rd ... 27265
Gower Ct ... 27265
Grace St ... 27260
Gracewood Ln ... 27262
Gracie Ct ... 27263
Granby Ave ... 27260
Grand St ... 27260
Grand Tri Ct ... 27260
Grant St ... 27262
Grantham Dr ... 27265
Granville St ... 27263
Graves Ave ... 27260
Gray Dawn Ct ... 27265
Gray Farm Rd ... 27263
Graylyn Dr ... 27263
Grayson St ... 27260
Green Dr ... 27265
E Green Dr
100-316 ... 27260
315-315 ... 27261
318-3098 ... 27260
401-3099 ... 27260
W Green Dr ... 27260
Green Acres Dr ... 27263
Green Farm Ln ... 27265
Greendale Rd ... 27263
Greendale Road Ext ... 27263
Greenhaven Dr ... 27263
Greenhill Dr ... 27265
Greenoak Dr ... 27263
Greenpoint Ct ... 27265
Greensboro Rd ... 27260
Greenstone Pl ... 27265
Greenvalley Dr ... 27262
Greenview Ter ... 27260
Greenway Dr ... 27262
Greenwood Dr ... 27262
Greer Ave ... 27260
Gregg St ... 27263

Grey Beard Ct ... 27265
Griclar St ... 27262
E & W Grimes Ave ... 27260
Grind Stone Ct ... 27265
Grindstaff Ave ... 27265
Groometown Rd ... 27263
Grove Forrest Dr ... 27263
Guarad Ct ... 27265
Guilford Ave ... 27262
Guilmont Ct ... 27265
Guyer St
1100-1299 ... 27262
1300-2699 ... 27265
Habersham Rd ... 27260
Haleys Way ... 27265
Halifax Ct ... 27265
N & S Hall St ... 27263
Halldale Rd ... 27265
N Hamilton St
100-399 ... 27260
400-1799 ... 27262
S Hamilton St ... 27260
Hammock Dr ... 27265
Hampstead Dr ... 27260
Hampton Dr ... 27265
Hampton Park Dr ... 27265
Hanes Brook Ct ... 27265
Haney Way ... 27263
Hanover Ct ... 27265
Hardaway Dr ... 27265
Hardin Ct ... 27265
Hardin St ... 27263
Harlow Dr & Rd ... 27263
Harrington Pt ... 27265
Harrison St ... 27260
Harrogate Ct ... 27262
E Hartley Dr ... 27262
W Hartley Dr ... 27265
Hartley Hill Ct ... 27265
Hattie St ... 27263
Havasu Way ... 27265
Havenridge Dr ... 27265
Havenwood Dr ... 27263
Haverly Dr ... 27265
Hawick Dr ... 27262
Hawthorne Ave ... 27262
Hay St ... 27260
Hayden Pl ... 27260
Haynes Rd ... 27262
Hayworth Cir ... 27262
Hayworth Rd ... 27265
Hayworth St ... 27263
Hazel Ave ... 27263
Hazelwood Ln ... 27263
Hearthstone Point Dr ... 27265
Heartland Dr ... 27263
Heathcliff Ct & Rd ... 27262
Heatherbrook Dr ... 27265
Heathgate Pt ... 27262
Hedgecock Cir & Rd ... 27265
Hedgepath Ter ... 27265
Hedgewood Ln ... 27265
Hedrick Ave ... 27262
Heidi Dr ... 27265
Hemlock Dr ... 27265
Hempshire Ct ... 27262
Henderson St ... 27263
Hendrix St ... 27260
Henley St ... 27260
Henry Pl ... 27260
Herbert Pl ... 27260
Heritage Glenn Ct ... 27265
Herman Ct ... 27265
Herrell Ter ... 27265
Herron Pt ... 27265
Hickory Ct & Ln ... 27265
Hickory Chapel Rd ... 27260
Hickory Creek Rd ... 27263
Hicks Pl ... 27262
Hickswood Rd ... 27265
Hickswood Creek Dr ... 27265
Hickswood Forest Ct & Dr ... 27265
Hidden Cove Pt ... 27265
Hidden Creek Ter ... 27260
Hidden Pond Cv ... 27265

Hidden Valley Farm Rd ... 27265
E & W High Ave ... 27260
High Point Rd ... 27265
Hilburn Dr ... 27260
Hill St ... 27260
Hill Farm Rd ... 27263
Hillcrest Dr & Pl ... 27262
Hillside Ct ... 27263
Hillside Dr ... 27265
Hilltop Dr ... 27263
Hilltop St ... 27260
Hilton Ct ... 27265
Hines St ... 27260
Hitchcock Way ... 27265
Hobart Pl ... 27262
Hobson St ... 27260
Hodgin St ... 27262
Hohn Rd ... 27263
Hohn Davis Rd ... 27263
Holland Park Ln ... 27265
Holleman St ... 27263
Holly St ... 27260
Holly Orchard Ct ... 27265
Hollyfield Pl ... 27265
Holt Ave ... 27260
Holton Pl ... 27262
Homestead Ave ... 27262
Homewood Ave ... 27262
Hood Pl ... 27260
Hoover Ave ... 27260
Hope Ct ... 27263
Hope Valley Dr ... 27263
Hopewell St ... 27263
Horidene St ... 27260
Horney Rd ... 27263
Horneytown Rd ... 27265
Hoskins St ... 27260
Howard Cir ... 27263
Howard Pl ... 27262
Howard Russell Rd ... 27263
Hudson St ... 27263
Huff Rd ... 27263
Hughes Ct ... 27263
Hummingbird Ct ... 27265
Hunter Oaks Ct & Dr ... 27265
Hunterwoods Dr ... 27265
Huntingridge Dr ... 27265
Huntington Cir & Dr ... 27262
Hunts Knoll Ln ... 27263
Hurdover St ... 27262
Hutton Ln ... 27262
Huttons Lake Ct ... 27265
Hyde Away Ln ... 27263
Hyde Park Dr ... 27263
Idol St ... 27262
Impala Ave ... 27265
Imperial Dr ... 27265
Indigo Pt ... 27265
Ingleside Dr ... 27265
Ingram Rd ... 27263
Inlet Ave ... 27263
Innwood St ... 27263
Interim Way ... 27265
Interstate Dr ... 27263
Irbywood Dr ... 27262
Ironwood Flat Dr ... 27265
Irwin Ave ... 27262
J Bar D Ln ... 27265
Jack Wall Ln ... 27263
Jackie Ave ... 27263
Jacklyn Ct ... 27265
Jackson Lake Rd ... 27263
Jacob Ct ... 27263
Jacobs Pl ... 27260
Jade Ct ... 27265
Jake White Ct ... 27265
Jamac Rd ... 27260
James Ct & Rd ... 27265
Jamestown Rd ... 27260
Janice Dr ... 27263
Jarrell St ... 27260
Jasper Dr ... 27263
Jay Pl & Rd ... 27263
Jeanette Ave ... 27265
Jefferson Ct ... 27263

Jefferson St ... 27260
Jeffrey Lane Pt ... 27265
Jennifer Ct ... 27263
Jennifer Ln ... 27265
Jeremey Way ... 27265
Jesse Green Rd ... 27265
Jessica Dr ... 27263
Jill Ct ... 27260
Joan Dr ... 27263
Joe Dr ... 27265
Joe Hoffman Dr ... 27263
Joe Lyda Dr ... 27265
John A Hall Rd ... 27265
John Gordon Ln ... 27265
John Green Rd ... 27263
Johnson Rd ... 27265
Johnson St
900-1899 ... 27262
3500-4499 ... 27265
5300-5399 ... 27263
Johnson Street Ext ... 27263
Joiner St ... 27263
Joines St ... 27263
Joplin Dr ... 27263
Jordan Pl ... 27260
Jordans Mill Ct ... 27265
Joseph Ct ... 27265
Joshua Cir ... 27260
Joyce Cir ... 27265
Juanita Hills St ... 27262
Julian Ave ... 27263
June Pl ... 27262
Junior St ... 27260
Juniper Dairy Ct ... 27265
Kacey Elaine Ct ... 27265
Kathert Ct ... 27265
Kaye St ... 27263
Kayla Ct ... 27265
E & W Kearns Aly & Ave ... 27260
Kello Rd ... 27263
Kelly Pl ... 27262
Kellywood Dr ... 27263
Kelso Dr ... 27265
Kelton Pl ... 27265
Kemper Ct ... 27265
Ken Dan Ct & St ... 27265
Kendale Rd ... 27263
Kendall Ave ... 27260
Kenilworth Dr ... 27260
Kenmare Ct ... 27260
Kennedy Ave ... 27262
Kennison Ct ... 27260
Kensington Ct & Dr ... 27262
Kent Ct & St ... 27260
Kentucky St ... 27262
Kentwood Ct ... 27265
Kersey Dr ... 27263
Kersey Valley Rd ... 27263
Kettering Rd ... 27263
Kim Dr ... 27265
Kimberly Pl ... 27265
Kimery Dr ... 27260
King St ... 27260
Kings Arms Ct ... 27262
Kingsfield Ct ... 27263
Kingsfield Forest Dr ... 27263
Kingston Dr ... 27262
Kingsway Dr ... 27260
Kingwood Ct ... 27265
Kinley Trl ... 27263
Kinview Dr ... 27263
Kippenshire Ln ... 27262
Kirkman Ct ... 27263
Kirkstone Dr ... 27265
Kirkwood St ... 27262
Kivett Dr ... 27263
E Kivett Dr ... 27260
W Kivett Dr
100-299 ... 27260
300-999 ... 27262
Kivlow Pl ... 27260
Knightdale Ave ... 27263
Knoll Ct ... 27265
Knollcrest Hill Ln ... 27265
Knollwood Dr ... 27263

Kreamer Dr ... 27263
Krista Kim Dr ... 27265
Kroll Ct & Ln ... 27260
La Dora Ct & Dr ... 27265
La Joy Ct ... 27265
La Port Ct ... 27265
La Salle Dr ... 27265
La Vera St ... 27265
La Vista Ct & Dr ... 27265
Ladford Ln ... 27265
Lafayette Pl ... 27263
Lake Ave ... 27260
Lake Dr ... 27263
Lake Forest Dr ... 27265
Lake Front Rd ... 27263
Lake Hill Ct ... 27265
Lake Oak ... 27265
Lake Ridge Dr ... 27265
Lake Run Dr ... 27265
Lake Village Dr ... 27263
Lakecrest Ave ... 27265
Lakeland Pt ... 27265
Lakes Edge Pt ... 27265
Lakeshore Dr ... 27265
Lakeside Dr ... 27263
Lakeview Ave ... 27263
Lakeview Heights Dr ... 27265
Lakewood Dr ... 27262
Lamb Ave ... 27260
Lambeth Ave ... 27262
Lamplight Cir & Way ... 27265
Lamuel Field Ln ... 27265
Lancaster Pl ... 27262
Lancer Dr ... 27263
Land Dale Dr ... 27263
Landover Dr ... 27265
Lane Ave ... 27260
Langdale Ct & Dr ... 27265
Langford Ave ... 27260
Lansdowne St ... 27262
Lansing St ... 27260
Laport Ct ... 27265
Lardner Ct & Pl ... 27260
Larkin St ... 27262
Lassiter Dr ... 27265
Laura Ave ... 27260
Laura Ln ... 27262
Laurel Ln ... 27262
Laurel Bluff Cir ... 27265
Lauren Pl ... 27265
Lawndale Ave ... 27260
Lawrence Dr ... 27263
Lazy Ln ... 27265
Ledford Cir ... 27265
Leeds Ave ... 27265
Leighton Dr ... 27263
Leonard Ave ... 27260
Lewis Jones Rd ... 27265
Lexham Ct ... 27265
E & W Lexington Ave ... 27262
W Lexington Avenue Ext ... 27265
Liberty Pl & Rd ... 27263
Lichen Ct ... 27265
Lifestyle Ct ... 27265
Lillie St ... 27265
Lilliefield Ln ... 27265
Lilly Flower Rd ... 27263
Limestone Ct ... 27265
Lincoln Dr ... 27260
Linda Dr ... 27263
Lindale Dr ... 27265
W Linden Ave ... 27260
Lindo Rd ... 27263
Lindsay Dr ... 27263
Lindsay St ... 27262
N Lindsay St ... 27262
S Lindsay St ... 27260
Linton Ct ... 27262
Little Ave ... 27260
Little Cricket Ln ... 27265
Loch Mere Rd ... 27265
Locke St ... 27262
Lockhart St ... 27263
Locust Pl ... 27265
Loflin Ave ... 27260

E & W Loftyview Ct & Dr ... 27260
Log Cabin Cv ... 27265
Logan St ... 27263
Logbridge Rd ... 27265
Lois Ln ... 27263
London Ct & Dr ... 27260
Londonderry Dr ... 27265
Long St ... 27262
Long Leaf Ct ... 27265
Longcreek Ct & Dr ... 27262
Longview Dr ... 27263
Longview Rd ... 27260
Lonita St ... 27263
Lori Dr ... 27263
Lorraine Ave ... 27263
Lost Tree Ln ... 27265
Louise Ave ... 27262
Lovington Ct ... 27260
Lowe Ave ... 27260
Lowell Rd ... 27263
Luck Dr ... 27263
Lumsden Ln ... 27265
Lunar Dr ... 27263
Lupton Ct ... 27262
Lynbrook Dr ... 27263
Lyndhurst Dr ... 27262
Lynn Dr
100-299 ... 27263
300-1599 ... 27265
Lynn Tree Ct ... 27265
Lynwood Ter ... 27265
Macedonia Ct & Way ... 27260
Macon Dr ... 27263
Maddy Ln ... 27263
Madison St ... 27262
Mae Matilda Ct ... 27263
Maggie Ct ... 27262
Magnolia Ct ... 27262
Magnolia Ln ... 27263
Mahala Dr ... 27265
N Main St
100-699 ... 27260
700-2599 ... 27262
2600-4199 ... 27265
10000-11199 ... 27263
11200-11699 ... 27263
S Main St
100-2099 ... 27260
2100-3099 ... 27263
10000-10699 ... 27263
Maize Dr ... 27265
Malachi Ct ... 27265
Maldon Way ... 27260
Malibu Dr ... 27265
Mall Loop Rd ... 27262
Malta Pl ... 27260
Malverne Dr ... 27265
Mandustry St ... 27262
Manley St ... 27260
Manning St ... 27260
N Manor Dr ... 27260
Manor Ridge Dr ... 27263
Manora Ct ... 27265
Maple Ct ... 27263
Maple Pl ... 27262
Maple Branch Dr ... 27265
Maple Grove Ct ... 27263
Maple Oak Dr ... 27263
Maple Ridge Ln ... 27262
Mapleview Ct ... 27265
Maplewood Ave ... 27265
Marble Dr ... 27265
Marie Ave ... 27263
Marion Ct ... 27263
Mariondale Dr ... 27265
Mark St ... 27260
E & W Market Center Dr ... 27260
Marlboro St ... 27260
Marshall St ... 27263
Martha Pl ... 27263
Martin St ... 27260
Mary Lee Way ... 27265
Maryfield Ct ... 27260
Maryland Pl ... 27263

Marywood Dr ... 27265
Mast Ave ... 27265
Mauldin Dr ... 27263
Maxine Dr ... 27265
Mayview Ave ... 27265
Mccain Pl ... 27262
Mcderr Rd ... 27265
Mcghee Ave ... 27265
Mcguinn Dr
1100-1599 ... 27262
1600-2099 ... 27265
Mckinley St ... 27265
Mclaurin Ct ... 27265
Mclong Dr ... 27265
Mcnair Ct ... 27265
Mcneill Rd ... 27263
Mcway Dr ... 27263
Meadow Pl ... 27262
Meadowbrook Blvd ... 27260
Meadowlark Rd ... 27265
Meadowlawn Ave ... 27262
Meadowside Ter ... 27265
Median Ct ... 27260
Meeting Way St ... 27265
Melco Ct ... 27265
Melissa Ct ... 27263
Melrose Ave ... 27262
Mendenhall Pl & Rd ... 27263
Mendenhall Oaks Pkwy ... 27265
Mendenhall Road Ext ... 27263
Meredith Dr ... 27263
Meredith St ... 27260
Meridian Ave ... 27262
Merrimon Pl ... 27265
Merry Hills Ct & Dr ... 27262
Meta Ct ... 27265
Meyers St ... 27263
Middle Point Rd ... 27263
Middlewood Ct ... 27265
Midland Ave ... 27260
Midview Dr ... 27265
Mill Ave ... 27260
Mill Ln ... 27265
Mill Pond St ... 27265
Mill Stone Ct ... 27265
Mill Wheel Ct ... 27265
Millbourne Pl ... 27265
Miller Dr ... 27265
Miller St ... 27262
Miller Hill Rd ... 27265
Millis St ... 27260
Millwood School Rd ... 27265
Mineral Springs Ct ... 27265
Mint Ave
400-699 ... 27262
700-1099 ... 27260
Mirabeau Ct ... 27265
Miriam Ave & Ct ... 27263
Mirus Ct ... 27265
Missionary Church Rd ... 27260
Misty Ln ... 27263
Misty Hill Cir ... 27265
Mitchell Pl ... 27262
Mitchell St ... 27263
Mobile Dr ... 27263
Mobile St ... 27260
Mock Rd ... 27265
Model Farm Rd ... 27263
Modlin Dr ... 27263
Modlin Grove Rd ... 27263
Moffitt Dr ... 27265
N & S Mohawk Ct & Dr ... 27262
Monnell Dr ... 27265
Monroe Pl ... 27262
Montclaire Ct ... 27265
Monteray Cir ... 27265
Montgomery St ... 27262
Montlieu Ave
100-719 ... 27262
720-730 ... 27260
721-731 ... 27262
732-799 ... 27260
800-899 ... 27262
900-998 ... 27260

901-1299 27262
1000-1298 27262
1400-1499 27265
Montree Ct 27265
Moon Pl 27260
E Moore Ave 27263
W Moore Ave 27263
Moore Rd 27265
Moreland Ave 27262
Morgan Pl 27260
Morgans Mill Way 27265
Mose Dr 27263
Mossbrook Cir 27260
Mossy Meadow Dr 27265
Motes Ct 27263
Motsinger St 27260
Mowery Dr 27265
Muddy Creek Rd 27263
Muirfield Ct 27265
Mulberry Ln 27265
Murphy Dr 27265
Murray Cir 27263
Murray St 27260
Myerwood Dr 27262
Nance Ave 27263
Naola Ct 27263
Nathan Hunt Dr 27260
National Highway Rd 27262
Navajo Dr 27263
Navy Pl 27265
N Nc Highway 109 27265
Nc Highway 62 W 27263
Nc Highway 68 S 27265
Neal Pl 27262
Nee Nee Ln 27263
Nesters Ct 27265
Netherstone Ln 27265
New St 27260
Newell St 27265
Newlin Pl 27260
Newport Ct 27265
Newton Pl 27262
Newview Rd 27260
Nicole Dr 27265
Nina Ct 27265
Nip St 27263
No Record
9998-9998 27262
No Record
9998-9998 27263
9998-9998 27265
Norman Pl 27265
Norse St 27265
North Ave 27262
North St 27265
Northbridge Dr 27265
Northeast Dr 27263
Northfield Ave & Pl 27265
Northfork Ter 27265
Northgate Ct 27265
Northland Dr 27263
Northpoint Ave 27262
Northshore Ct & Dr 27265
Northside Ct 27265
Northview Pl 27263
Northview St 27260
Norton St 27263
N & S Norwood Ave & Ct 27262
Nottingham Rd 27262
Nova Ave 27265
Nubbin Ridge Rd 27265
Nuggett Rd 27263
Nuthatch Ct 27262
O A Kirkman Way 27262
Oak St
100-399 27260
400-1799 27265
Oak Chase Dr 27265
Oak Field Ct 27265
Oak Forest Dr 27265
Oak Haven Rd 27265
Oak Hollow Ct & Dr 27265
Oak Spring Ln 27263
Oakcrest Ave 27260
Oakhurst Ave 27262
Oakland Pl 27262
Oakland Hills Ct 27265
Oaklawn St 27262
Oakley Ct 27263
Oakmont Cir & Rd 27263
Oakmont View Rd 27260
Oaks Ln 27265
Oakton Dr 27265
Oakview Rd 27265
Oakwood St 27262
Oberlin Dr 27260
Obsidian Ct 27265
Oconnell Ave 27265
Ogden Ct & St 27260
Old Cedar Square Rd 27263
Old Creek Crossing Ln 27265
Old Glenola Rd 27263
N Old Greensboro Rd 27265
Old Jackson Lake Rd 27263
Old Mendenhall Rd 27263
Old Mill Rd 27265
Old Park Ln 27265
Old Plank Rd 27265
Old Pond Ln 27265
Old Poole Rd 27263
Old South Ct 27262
Old Spencer Rd 27263
Old Thomasville Rd
200-1499 27260
1500-5899 27263
Old Turnpike Rd 27263
Old Winston Rd 27265
Olde Eden Dr 27265
Olivia Pl 27260
Oneil St 27260
Oneka Ave 27260
Orchard Knob Ln 27265
Orinoco Dr 27265
Orlando Pl 27262
Orville Dr 27260
Osborne Pl 27260
Ossi Ct 27265
Otteray Ave 27262
Overbrook Ct & Dr 27262
Overland Dr 27262
Overlook Pt 27265
Overview Ter 27265
Oxford Pl 27262
Packrite Ct 27260
Pallas Way 27265
Palmer St 27265
Pam St 27260
Paramount St 27260
Park Dr
100-299 27263
100-399 27265
Park St 27260
Park Ter 27260
Park Hill Crossing Dr 27265
Park Springs Dr 27265
Parker St 27263
Parkside Dr 27262
Parkview Ct 27263
E & W Parkway Ave 27262
Parkwood Cir & Dr 27262
Parliament St 27265
E Parris Ave 27262
W Parris Ave
100-499 27262
700-799 27265
Patrick Ave 27260
Patterson Pl 27260
Paul St 27263
Payne Ct & Rd 27265
Peace St 27262
Peaceford Glen Dr 27265
E Peachtree Dr 27265
W Peachtree Dr 27262
Pearson Pl 27260
Pecan Dr 27263
Pegram Ave 27263
Pemberton Way 27265
Pembroke Ter 27265
N Pendleton Ct & St 27260
Penman Rd 27263
Penn Pl 27260
Pennfield Way 27262
Penny Rd
100-199 27260
1100-2599 27265
Pennywood Dr 27265
Peregrine Ct 27265
Perrywood St 27262
Pershing St 27260
Peters Ct 27265
Petty St 27263
Phillips Ave 27263
Pickett Pl 27262
Piedmont Pkwy 27265
Piedmont Crossing Dr 27265
Pike St 27263
Pike Street Ext 27263
Pilgrim Ave 27262
Pine St 27262
Pine Circle Dr 27265
Pine Grove Dr 27263
Pine Needles Rd 27265
Pine Tree Ln 27265
Pine Valley Rd 27265
Pinebrook Dr 27263
Pinecrest Dr 27263
Pinecroft St 27260
Pinehurst Dr 27262
Pinelyn Dr 27265
Pineridge Dr 27262
Pinestone Ct 27265
Pineview Ave 27260
Pinewood Dr 27263
Pinewood Ln 27262
Pinnacle Ct & Dr 27265
Pioneer Ln 27262
Pipers Way 27265
Plainview Dr 27265
Planters Dr 27265
Plateau Ct 27265
Player Dr 27260
Playground Rd 27263
Plaza Ct & Ln 27263
Plentant Rd 27265
Plum River Cv 27265
Plummer Dr 27263
Plymouth St 27263
Pointer Ct 27265
Pomeroy Pl 27260
Ponce De Leon Dr 27265
Pond Meadow Dr 27265
Pondhaven Dr 27265
Poole Rd
500-899 27265
5300-6199 27263
Poole Road Ext 27263
Poplar Creek Ln 27265
Poplar Knoll Dr 27262
Porsha Ln 27265
Porter St 27263
Potts Ave 27260
Powell Way 27263
Precision Way 27265
Preferred Way 27260
Prelude Ct 27265
Premier Dr 27265
Prescott Pl 27262
President Ln 27265
Preston Ct 27263
Preston Pt 27265
Prestwick Dr 27265
Preswick Ct 27265
Price St 27260
Primrose Ln 27263
Princeton Ave 27262
Proctor Dr
100-299 27265
900-1199 27260
Progress Ave 27260
Promenade Dr 27265
Prospect Ct 27263
Prospect St
100-1699 27260
5000-6299 27263
Providence Ave 27262
Pump Station Rd 27260
Purdy Ave 27260
Purvis Ln 27263
Putnam St 27262
Quail Hollow Rd 27265
Quail Marsh Ct 27265
Quail Run Dr 27265
Quaker Ln 27262
Quaker Lake Dr 27263
Quakerwood Dr 27263
Quarry Ct & Dr 27265
Quarter Gate Dr 27265
Quarterstaff Ct 27265
Queens Grant Ct 27265
R C Baldwin Ave 27260
Radford St 27260
Ragan Ave 27260
Raleigh Ct 27262
Ralph Dr 27263
Ralston Ct 27265
Ramsay St 27265
Ranch Dr 27263
Rand Blvd 27263
Randall St 27260
Randolph St 27260
Random Acres Ln 27265
Range Crest Ct 27265
Rankin Pl 27265
Ravina Dr & Ln 27260
E & W Ray Ave 27262
Raymond Gray Ln 27263
Red Cedar Dr 27265
Red Oak Ct 27265
Red Robin Ln 27263
Red Run Ct 27265
Reddick St 27263
Redding Dr 27260
Reese Rd & St 27265
Regency Dr 27265
Reginald Ct 27260
Renaissance Ln 27262
Renola Dr 27263
Resthaven Rd 27265
Rice Ct 27265
Rich Fork Creek Dr 27265
Richard Byerly Rd 27262
Richardson Ave 27260
Richardson Rd 27263
Richland St 27260
Richmond Row Ct 27265
Richmont Ct 27262
Richview Cir 27265
Ridge Landing Rd 27263
Ridgebrooke Dr 27265
Ridgecrest Dr 27262
Ridgeland Dr 27262
Ridgerock Ct 27260
Ridgeview Rd 27263
Ridgeway Pl 27260
Ridgeworth Ave 27265
Rindle Dr 27262
Ring St 27260
E River Way 27265
River Cross Rd 27265
River Pointe Pl 27265
River Valley Rd 27265
Riverbrook St 27265
Riverdale Dr 27263
Rivermeade Dr
200-299 27263
2100-2199 27265
Rivershore Ct 27265
Rivertrace Pt 27265
Rob Cruthis Rd 27263
Rob Swaim Rd 27262
Robbins St 27263
Robert Ln 27263
Roberts Ct & Ln 27260
Roberts Star Ln 27265
Robin Cir, Ct & Ln 27265
Robin Hood Rd 27262
Robinwood Ct 27265
Roby Dr 27263
Rock Bridge Rd 27262
Rock Meadow Cir 27265
Rock Pond Cir 27265
Rockcreek Rd 27263
Rockford Rd 27262
Rockingham Rd 27265
Rockland Cir & Ct 27265
Rocklane Dr 27263
Rockledge Cir 27262
Rockspring Rd 27262
Rockwood Dr 27265
Rogar St 27263
Rolling Rd 27265
Rolling Green Dr 27260
Rose Haven Rd 27265
Rosecrest Dr 27260
Roseland St 27265
Rosemary Dr 27263
Rosewood Pl 27262
N & W Rotary Dr 27262
Rowan Ave 27260
Roy Ave 27260
Royal Pl 27260
Royal Oak Ave 27262
Runner Stone Dr 27265
Running Cedar Trl 27265
Runyon Dr 27260
Ruskin Dr 27265
E & W Russell Ave & Ter 27260
Ryley Ct 27265
Saddlewood Club Dr 27265
Sadler Ct 27260
Sage Dale Ct 27265
Sagewood Ln 27263
Saint Andrews Ct & Dr 27265
Saint Ann Dr 27265
Saint Giles Ct 27262
Saint Johns St 27265
Saint Michaels Ln 27265
Saint Stephens Ct 27265
Salem St 27262
Sales St 27260
Salisbury St 27263
Samet Dr 27265
San Fernando Dr 27265
Sandhurst Ct 27265
Sandlewood Rd 27265
Sandy Camp Rd 27265
Sandy Ridge Rd 27265
Sandy Woods Ct 27265
Sanford Ct 27263
Saunders Pl 27260
Scarborough Rd 27265
Scarlett Ct & Dr 27265
Schirra Pl 27263
SW School Rd 27265
School Park Rd 27265
N & S Scientific St 27260
Scott Ave 27262
Scouting Ct 27265
Seashire Ct 27260
Sechrest Cir 27263
Second Heights Dr 27263
Sedgebrook St 27265
Sedgewick Ln 27262
Seminole Ct 27265
Seminole Dr 27263
Seminole Ln 27265
Setliff Dr 27265
Seven Oaks Pl 27265
Seward Ave 27265
Shade Tree Ct 27265
Shadow Ridge Dr 27265
Shadow Valley Rd
100-499 27262
2200-2499 27265
Shady Ln 27262
Shady Lawn Ct 27263
Shady Oak Ln 27263
Shady View Dr 27265
Shadybrook Rd 27265
Shalimar Ct & Dr 27265
Shalotte Dr 27262
Shamrock Ct
100-699 27263
1000-1099 27265
Shamrock Rd 27265
Sharon Cir, St & Way 27260
Sharon Dale Dr 27263
Shaver St 27265
Shean Dr 27263
Sheffield St 27260
Sheldon Ct 27260
Shenandoah Dr 27262
Shepard Pl 27262
Sherbrook Dr 27262
Sherman Ct 27260
Sherrie Dr 27263
Sherrill Ave 27260
Sherwood Pl 27262
Shober Rd 27265
Shore St 27263
Shorewell Dr 27260
Silver Ct 27263
Silver Fox Ct 27265
Silver Ridge Dr 27265
Silverstone Ct 27265
Simmons Creek Ct 27263
Sinclair Ave 27260
Single Leaf Cir & Ct 27265
Single Tree Rd 27265
Sink Lake Rd 27265
Sisters Ln 27263
Skeet Club Rd 27265
Slatey Dr 27265
Sleepy Hollow Dr 27263
Smith Ln 27263
Smith St 27260
Smithwick Pt 27265
Snider St 27265
Somerset Ct 27260
Somma Ct 27265
Sonoma Ln 27265
Sorrell Ct 27265
South Rd 27262
Southern Pl 27260
Southern Oak Dr 27265
Southland Dr 27263
Southpark Dr 27263
Southtree Ln 27263
Southwest St 27260
Spanish Peak Dr 27265
Sparrowhawk Dr 27265
Spencer Rd 27263
Spencer St 27263
Spencer Lake Rd 27263
Spinning Wheel Pt 27265
Splitbrook Dr 27265
Spring St 27263
Spring Brook Cir 27263
Spring Garden Cir 27260
Spring Hill Church Rd 27262
Spring Hollow Rd 27262
Spring Oak Ct 27263
Spring Tree Ct 27265
W Springdale Ave 27260
E & W Springfield Rd & St 27263
Springview Dr 27265
Springwood Ln 27263
Spruce St 27262
Spruce Wood Ct 27263
Spurgeon Way 27265
Stafford Run Ct 27265
Staffordshire Dr 27263
Staley Rd 27265
Stanley Rd 27263
Stansbury Ln 27265
Stanton Pl 27260
Stapleton Way 27265
Starflower Dr 27263
Starr Dr 27260
E & W State Ave 27262
Station Ct 27260
Steele St
200-399 27260
400-599 27262
Steep Oak Ct 27265
Sterling Ave 27265
Sterling Ridge Dr 27263
Sternly Way 27260
Stillbrook Ln 27265
Stockwood Ct 27265
Stone Pl 27262
Stonebrier Ct 27265
Stonehurst Pl 27265
Stonemill Dr 27265
Stoney Creek Dr 27263
Stoneybrook Ct & Dr 27265
Stoneycreek Dr 27265
Stratford Ct 27265
Stratford Rd 27263
Stratton St 27260
Sturbridge Ave 27262
Suffolk Ave 27265
Suits Rd 27263
Summey Ave 27263
Summit Rd 27265
Sumter Dr 27265
Sunburst Dr 27265
Suncrest Dr 27265
Sunny Ln 27263
Sunnybrook St 27260
Sunnyvale Dr 27265
Sunset Dr 27262
Sunset Hollow Ct & Dr 27265
Sunset View Dr 27263
Sunset View Drive Ext 27263
Sunview Ave 27265
Sunwood Ct 27263
Surrett Ct 27263
Surrett Dr
1000-1699 27260
1900-6099 27263
2400-2699 27263
Sussex Dr 27260
Sutton Way 27265
Swan Lake Dr 27262
Swanner Ct 27262
Swansea Ct 27265
Swansgate Ln 27262
E Swathmore Ave 27263
Sweetbriar Ct & Rd 27262
Switchback Ct & Dr 27265
Sycamore Cir 27265
Sycamore Point Trl 27265
Sylvia St 27263
Tabor St 27262
Tahoe Ct 27265
Talavera Dr 27265
Tambeary Dr 27262
Tanager Rd 27260
Tangle Ln 27265
Tanglebrook Rd 27265
Tanglewood Ave 27265
Tanin Ct 27265
Tank Ave & Ct 27260
Tanyard Mill Ct 27265
Tara Dr 27265
Tarheel Dr 27263
Tarrant Trce 27265
Tarrant Trace Cir 27265
Tate St 27260
Taylor Ave 27260
Tealwood Vista Ct 27265
Tecumseh St 27265
Tellmont Ct 27265
Ternberry Rd 27262
Terrace Trace Ct 27263
Terrell Dr 27262
Tesa Ct 27265
Tesh Ct 27265
Textile Pl 27260
The Oaks Ln 27265
Thissell St 27260
Thistle Down Ct 27265
Thomas St 27263
Thompson Rd 27263
Thompson Road Ext 27263
Thornhill Dr 27262
Three Oaks Dr 27265
Timber St 27260
Timberlake Ave 27265
Timberlane Dr 27265
Timberwolf Ave 27265
Timberwood Dr 27260
Tinsley Dr 27265
Tipton St 27262
Tom Hill Rd 27263
Tomball Rd 27263

Tomlinson St 27260
Tonsley Ct & Pl 27265
Topaz Ln 27265
Tory Ct 27265
Totera Pl 27262
Tower Ave 27260
Townsend Ave 27263
Tracer Pl 27260
Traceway Rd 27265
Trafalgar Ct & Dr 27262
Trappers Run Ct 27265
Treebark Ln 27265
Trenton St 27262
Trey Ln 27263
Treyburn Ln 27265
Triangle Lake Rd 27260
Trindale Rd 27263
Trinity Ave 27260
Trinity Ct 27263
Trotter Country Rd 27263
Trowbridge Ct 27265
True Ln 27260
Truman Ave 27263
Tryon Ave 27260
Tulane Dr 27263
Turner Pl 27262
Turney Ct 27262
Turnpike Rd 27263
Turtle Creek Rd 27265
Turtle Rock Way 27265
Tuttle Rd 27263
Tuxedo Way 27260
Twain Ave 27260
Tweedmore Ct 27265
Twin Oak Ct 27260
Twisting Creek Dr 27265
Ty Cir 27260
Tyning St 27265
Tyson Ct & St 27263
Underhill St 27260
Union Hill Ct 27260
Us Highway 311 27263
Uwharrie Rd 27263
V V Willard Rd 27265
Vail Ave 27260
Valley Dr 27260
Valley Fields Farm 27265
Valley Ridge Dr 27260
Valleywood Pl 27265
Van Buren St 27260
Vandever St 27260
Vedra Ct 27265
Venable Ct 27262
Vera Ct 27262
Vernon Pl 27260
Verta Ave 27263
Viceroy Ct 27265
Vickers Ave 27262
Viking Dr 27265
Villa Ave 27260
Village Ln 27263
Village Springs Dr 27265
Vine St 27262
Vinebury Ln 27265
Virginia Pl 27262
Vista Cir 27263
Wade Pl 27260
Wadsworth Ct 27263
Wakefield Pl 27262
Walden Ln
3600-3699 27265
6100-6299 27263
Waldo St 27262
Waldon Ct 27265
Waldorf Ct 27265
Wales Ct & Dr 27262
Walker Pl 27260
Wall St 27263
Wallaby Ct 27265
Wallburg High Point Rd 27265
Walnut St 27260
Walnut Grove Rd 27263
Walnut Tree Ln 27263
Walpole Rd 27265
Walton St 27263
Warbler Ct 27260
N Ward Ave 27262
W Ward Ave 27260
Ward Ct 27260
E Ward St 27260
Warielin Rd 27263
E Washington Dr 27260
Water Run Ct 27265
Waterbury Dr 27263
Waterloo Dr 27260
Watermark Ct 27265
Waters Edge Dr 27263
Waterstone Ln & Loop 27265
Waterview Rd 27265
Waverly Ct 27262
Waverly St
1200-1399 27262
1500-1799 27265
Wayland Ct 27265
Wayne Ave 27260
Waynick St 27265
Wayside St 27260
Weant Rd 27263
Weaver Ave 27263
Weavil St 27265
Wedgewood St 27263
Welborn St 27262
Welch Dr 27265
Wellfleet Ct & Dr 27265
Wellingford Dr 27265
Wellingham Ln 27265
Wellington St 27262
Wendell Ave 27260
W Wendover Ave 27265
Wendover Dr 27262
Wesley Dr 27260
Wesseck Dr & Rd 27265
Wesson Ct 27265
West Ave 27260
West St 27265
N West Point Ave 27262
S West Point Ave 27260
Westbrook Ct 27263
Westchester Dr 27262
Westdale Dr 27265
Westfield St 27265
Westfork Ln 27265
Westgate Dr 27265
Westland Pl 27265
Westminster Ct & Dr 27262
Westover Dr 27265
Westridge Dr 27262
Westview Pl 27260
Westwood Ave 27262
Wexford Pl 27265
Wheatfield Creek Ct 27265
Wheeler Ave 27260
E & W White Dr & Ln 27260
White Beard Rd 27265
White Farm Ln 27265
White Fence Way 27265
White Oak St 27260
Whitehall St 27262
Whites Mill Rd 27265
Whitetail Ct 27265
Whitman Pl 27260
Whitney Ct 27265
Whittier Ave 27262
Wickham Ave & Ct 27265
Wickliff Ave 27262
Wildcat Trl 27265
Wildcrest Ct 27265
Wildwood Ave & Ct 27265
Wiley Pl 27262
Wiliton Way 27260
Wilkes St 27260
Willard Ave 27260
Willard Rd 27265
Willard Dairy Rd 27265
Williams Ave 27262
Williamsburg Ter 27262
Willie Bodenheimer Rd 27265
Williford Ct 27265
E & W Willis Ave 27260
Willoubar Ter
600-699 27260
700-1099 27262
Willoughby Pl 27265
Willoughby Park Dr 27265
Willow Pl 27260
Willow Oak Rd 27262
Willowood Dr 27260
Willows Ct 27265
Wilma Ave 27260
Wilson Pl 27260
Wilson View Dr 27263
Wiltshire St 27265
Wimbledon Pl 27262
Wincrest Dr 27263
Windchase Ct 27265
Windcreek Ct 27263
Windhaven Ct 27263
Windley St 27260
Windshore Ct 27265
Windsor Dr 27262
Wingate Pl 27260
Wingo St 27262
Winslow St 27260
Wintergreen Ct 27265
Wise Ave 27260
Wisteria Ct 27265
Wood Ave 27263
Wood Cove Dr 27265
Woodbend Ct 27265
Woodbine St 27260
Woodbrook Dr 27262
Woodbury St 27260
Woodduck Ln 27265
Woodhaven Ave 27260
Woodland Pl 27262
Woodlawn Rd 27265
Woodpark Dr 27265
Woodridge Ln 27262
Woodrow Ave 27262
Woodruff Ave 27265
Woods Ln 27265
Woodside Ave
1500-1599 27262
1600-1699 27265
Woodside Ct 27265
Woodsman Ct 27265
Woodvalley Ct 27265
Woodview Ct & Dr 27265
Woodymede Dr 27262
Worth St 27260
N Wrenn St
100-499 27260
500-599 27262
S Wrenn St 27260
Wright St 27262
Wrightenberry St 27260
Wyndham Ave & Ct 27265
Wynnewood Ave 27262
Wynnewood Dr 27263
Wynnfield Dr 27265
Yale Ct 27260
Yates Mill Ct 27265
York Ave 27265
Yorkshire Dr 27262
Young Pl 27260
Younger Pl 27265
Zachary Kent Dr 27263
Zelma Ave 27265
Zelma Blvd 27263

NUMBERED STREETS

4th St 27260
5th Ct 27262
5th St
600-699 27260
700-1299 27262
6th St 27262

HUNTERSVILLE NC

General Delivery 28078

POST OFFICE BOXES MAIN OFFICE STATIONS AND BRANCHES

Box No.s
1 - 3592 28070
9998 - 9998 28078

NAMED STREETS

Abberley Ct 28078
Abbey House Ln 28078
Aberdeen Park Dr 28078
Aberfeld Rd 28078
Abingdon Cir 28078
Abundance Cir 28078
Acorn Ridge Ln 28078
Addbury Ln 28078
Adderfield Ln 28078
Aegean Ct 28078
Agincourt Dr 28078
Agnes Park Ln 28078
Aiken Aly 28078
Alamosa Pl 28078
Alba Rose Ln 28078
Aldbury Ln 28078
Alden Ln 28078
Aldenbrook Dr 28078
Alexander Ln 28078
Alexander Place Dr 28078
Alexanderana Rd 28078
Alley Baster St 28078
Alley Cat St 28078
Alley Son St 28078
Allison Ferry Rd 28078
Allison Forest Trl 28078
Alluvial Dr 28078
Almondell Dr 28078
Alston Forest Dr 28078
Alton St 28078
Alwood Ln 28078
Amazona Dr 28078
Ambassador Park Dr 28078
Amber Field Dr 28078
Amsworth Ln 28078
Amwell Dr 28078
Amy Arnoux Dr 28078
Andover Cresent Ln 28078
Andres Duaney Pkwy 28078
Angel Oak Dr 28078
Angela Dawn Ln 28078
Angela Neal Rd 28078
Ansonborough Sq 28078
Anthea Ln 28078
Antigua Rd 28078
Appleseed Ct 28078
April Knoll Ct 28078
April Mist Trl 28078
Arahova Dr 28078
Arcadia View Ct 28078
Archer Notch Ln 28078
Ardry End Ln 28078
Arledge Ln 28078
Arlen Park Dr 28078
Arran Ct 28078
Arthur Auten Rd 28078
Arthur Davis Rd 28078
Artisan Hill Dr 28078
Asbury Dr 28078
Asbury Chapel Rd 28078
Ashby Glen Dr 28078
Ashford Knl 28078
Aurora Ln 28078
Auten St 28078
Autumn Cove Ln 28078
Autumn Trace Dr 28078
Autumncrest Rd 28078
Autumnview Ct 28078
Avensong Terrace Ct 28078
Babe Stillwell Farm Rd 28078
Bailes Ct 28078
Balcony Bridge Rd 28078
Bald Cypress Ct 28078
Balkan Way 28078
Ballara Pl 28078
Ballevue Ct 28078
Ballymore Ct 28078
Ballypat Ln 28078
Bankside Dr 28078
Banner Court Ln 28078
Barkley Farm Rd 28078
Barnburgh Ln 28078
Barnsbury Dr 28078
Barnstable Dr 28078
Baron Aly 28078
Barry Zito Pl 28078
Batemans Rd 28078
Bath Cir 28078
Baucom Ln 28078
Bayart Way 28078
Bayberry Glen Way 28078
Baylis Dr 28078
Bayshore Dr 28078
Baytown Ct 28078
Beatties Ford Rd 28078
Beech Hill Dr 28078
Bell Song Ln 28078
Bellingham Ct 28078
Bernick Way Ln 28078
Berryfield St 28078
Berrywood Cir 28078
Bertram Ct 28078
Bevin Ct 28078
Biddick Ln 28078
Bigham St 28078
Billings Pl 28078
Billingshurst Ct 28078
Billsdale Ct 28078
Binnaway Rd 28078
Birchwalk Dr 28078
S Birkdale Commons Pkwy 28078
Birkdale Crossing Dr 28078
Bishopstone Ct 28078
Black Farms Rd 28078
Blackgum Falls Ct 28078
Blackpool Ct 28078
Blackstock Rd 28078
Blackstone Dr 28078
Blakemore Ave 28078
Blooming Arbor St 28078
Blossom Hill Dr 28078
Blue Grass Dr 28078
Blue Moon Ct 28078
Bluff Meadow Trl 28078
Boatway Ct 28078
Bonnerby Ct 28078
Borealis Way 28078
Boren St 28078
Boulder Run 28078
Boulder Park Dr N 28078
Bradford Ln 28078
Bradford Hill Ln 28078
Braeloch Ct 28078
Bramborough Rd 28078
Bramfield Dr 28078
Branchside Ln 28078
Brandie Meadow Ln 28078
Bravington Rd 28078
Breckshire Dr 28078
S Brent Dr 28078
Brentfield Rd 28078
Brenthaven Park Dr 28078
Breton Brook St 28078
Brickingham Ln 28078
Brickle Ln 28078
Bridgeford Dr & Ln NW 28078
Bridgegate Dr 28078
Bridgestone Dr 28078
Bridgeton Ln 28078
Bridgewater Dr 28078
Brightpine Ln 28078
Britley Ridge Dr 28078
Broadway St 28078
Broadwell Ct 28078
Bronx Dr 28078
Brook Glen Ln 28078
Brook Line Ln 28078
Brookline Dr 28078
Brookway Dr 28078
Brown Gelly Dr 28078
Brown Mill Rd 28078
Bryton Town Center Dr 28078
Bud Henderson Rd 28078
Bur Ln 28078
Burlingame Dr 28078
Bushnell Ct 28078
Byrum Way St 28078
Bytham Castle Dr 28078
Cabarrus Crossing Dr 28078
Cadgwith Cove Dr 28078
Calaveras Ct 28078
Caldwell Creek Dr 28078
Caldwell Station Rd 28078
Caldwell Track Dr 28078
Callicut Spring Ct 28078
Calluga Aly 28078
Calvert Commons Dr 28078
Calverton Rd 28078
Camberly Rd 28078
Cambridge Rd 28078
Cambridge Grove Dr 28078
Camden Hollow Rd 28078
Canadice Rd 28078
Canal Dr 28078
Cane Branch Way 28078
Caneel Ct 28078
Canoe Cove Ln 28078
Canterbury Ln 28078
Cape Cedar Ct 28078
Capri Dr 28078
Capsdale Ct 28078
Carbert Ln 28078
Cardross Ln 28078
Carlos Dr 28078
Carlton Way Rd 28078
Carrigan Ct 28078
Carrington Pointe Dr 28078
Carrington Ridge Dr 28078
Carver Ave 28078
Cascade Loop 28078
Cascade Dream Ct 28078
Cashion Rd 28078
Cask Way 28078
Castledown Dr 28078
Castlehill Dr 28078
Catawba Ave & Ext 28078
Cattaloochee Ln 28078
Caverly Ct 28078
Cedar Ln 28078
Cedar Fall Dr 28078
Cedar Hollow Ln 28078
Cedar Pond Cir 28078
Cedar River Rd 28078
Cedarford Ct 28078
Cennetta Ct 28078
Centennial Commons Pkwy 28078
Centennial Forest Dr 28078
Center Ln 28078
Centerview Ln 28078
Central Ave 28078
Century View Dr 28078
Chaddsley Dr 28078
Chadhill Ln 28078
Chandlers Green Ct 28078
Chandos Pl 28078
Chapel Chase Ln 28078
Charterhouse Ln 28078
Chatham Glen Dr 28078
Checkerberry Ln 28078
Cheery Meadow Dr 28078
Chelsea Ridge Ln 28078
Chenault Dr 28078
Cheverly Dr 28078
Chewtonglen Ln 28078
Cheyenne Dr 28078
Chickasaw Dr 28078
Chilgrove Ln 28078
Chiltern Ln 28078
Chipping Dr 28078
N Church St 28078
Church Wood Ln 28078
Cimarron Close Ln 28078
Cimmaron Rd 28078
Cinder Ln 28078
Cinnabar Pl 28078
Citronelle Ln 28078
Citrus Ct 28078
Clarendon Point Ct 28078
Cletus Brawley Rd 28078
Cleveleys Trl 28078
Cliffcreek Dr 28078
Cliffhaven Ln 28078
Closest Pin Dr 28078
Clover Berry Dr 28078
Clover Pack Dr 28078
Coalcliff Dr 28078
Coastal Way 28078
Cobb Ct 28078
Cobbleview Ln 28078
Cobham Ct 28078
Cocheco Ct 28078
Cockerham Ln 28078
Cold Creek Pl 28078
Coleford Dr 28078
Coley Dr 28078
Colonial Garden Dr 28078
Colonial Park Dr 28078
Columbia Dr 28078
Comanche Rd 28078
Commerce Centre Dr 28078
Commerce Station Dr 28078
Common Oak Ln 28078
Compass St 28078
Compton Ln 28078
Conner Glenn Dr 28078
Cool Meadow Dr 28078
Cool Mist Ln 28078
Copans Glen Ln 28078
Copley Square Dr 28078
Coral Sunrise Dr 28078
Cordelia Oaks Ln 28078
Cordial Ln 28078
Coristar Pl 28078
Cotesworth Ct 28078
Cottsbrooke Dr 28078
Covington Point Ln 28078
Crabapple Ln 28078
Craig Mill Ln 28078
Cramur Dr 28078
Cranebridge Dr 28078
Cranleigh Dr 28078
Cranlyn Rd 28078
Cranwood Ave 28078
Creekhill Dr 28078
Cross Dale Dr 28078
Cross End Dr 28078
Cross Meadow Rd 28078
Cross Oak Pl 28078
Crusader Way 28078
Culcairn Rd 28078
Cumberland Crest Dr 28078
Cumbria Ct 28078
Cupworth Ct 28078
Curling Ct 28078
Cypress Springs Rd 28078
Cypress Woods Dr 28078
Dallas St 28078
Damson Dr 28078
Darblay St 28078
Dark Crystal Ct 28078
David St 28078
David Kenney Farm Rd 28078
Davidson Concord Hwy 28078
De Soto Aly 28078
Deer Meadows Ln 28078
Deerland Ct 28078
Delancey Ln 28078
Dellwood Dr 28078
Delstone Dr 28078
Denbolme St 28078
Dennehy Ct 28078
Desota Ln 28078
Detroiter Dr 28078
Devin Allen Dr 28078
Devonshire Dr 28078
Dinniston Dr 28078
Dixon Farm Rd 28078
Doe Path Ln 28078
Dogwood Ln & Ter 28078
Donahue Dr 28078
Dori Dr 28078
E & W Douglas Park Dr 28078

Dowling Dr NW 28078
Doyers Dr 28078
Drake Cove Rd 28078
Drake Hill Dr 28078
Drakeson Dr 28078
Drew Ct 28078
Dry Stone Dr 28078
Dryburgh Cir 28078
Duane Ct 28078
Dumphries Dr 28078
Dunbeth Dr 28078
Dunmore Dr 28078
Dunster Ln 28078
Dunton St 28078
Dutch Fork Dr 28078
Eastfield Rd 28078
Edenfield Dr 28078
Edgecliff Rd 28078
Edinburgh Ave 28078
Edna Dr 28078
Elham Ln 28078
Eliza Long Wilkie Dr 28078
Ellenwood Rd 28078
Elmcrest Ct 28078
Emerald Wood Dr 28078
Emily Magen Ct 28078
Emory Pl 28078
Epiphany Ct 28078
Epping Forest Dr 28078
Eric Kyle Dr 28078
Ervin Cook Rd 28078
Ethyln Cir 28078
Evanston Falls Rd 28078
Evanston View Rd 28078
Everett Keith Rd 28078
Ewart Rd 28078
Ewart Farm Ln 28078
Excalibur Way 28078
Fairsted Ln 28078
Fairwoods Dr 28078
Falgren Ct 28078
Fallcross Ct 28078
Fallonview Ct 28078
Farmall Dr 28078
Farnborough Rd 28078
Feather Oak Aly 28078
First Broad Dr 28078
First Laurel Dr 28078
Flanagan Ct 28078
Flatbush Dr 28078
Flatwoods Ct 28078
Folkston Dr 28078
Foreleigh Rd 28078
Forest Ct 28078
Forest Lake Ave 28078
Forest Ridge Ct 28078
Formby Rd 28078
Forrester Ave 28078
Fox Tail Ln 28078
Foxlyn Trail Ct 28078
Framfield Ct 28078
Framingham Ln 28078
Fred Brown Rd 28078
Freedom Valley Dr 28078
Fremington Rd 28078
Friarsgate Rd 28078
Front Park Cir 28078
Frontier Pl 28078
Galashiels Dr 28078
Gallant Ridge Pl 28078
Garden District Row 28078
Garden Hill Dr 28078
Garnkirk Dr 28078
Gathering Oaks Dr 28078
Gibralter Dr 28078
Gibson Dr 28078
Gibson Park Dr 28078
Gilderstern Glen Ct 28078
Gilead Rd
- 1-399 28078
- 400-400 28070
- 400-10398 28078
- 401-10399 28078

Gilead Grove Rd 28078
Gilead Hill Ct 28078
Gilpatrick Ln 28078
Ginny Louise Ln 28078
Glade Ct 28078
Gladwick Ct 28078
Glassfield Dr 28078
Glassonby Ct 28078
Gleen Oak Ln 28078
Glen Garden Ln 28078
Glen Miro Dr 28078
Glencastle St 28078
Glencreek Ln 28078
Glencrest Dr 28078
Glendale Dr & Rd 28078
Glenfurness Dr 28078
Glengarrie Ln 28078
Glenkinchie Dr 28078
Glenora Dr 28078
Glenside St 28078
Glenwyck Ln 28078
Glessner Pl 28078
Goodwood St 28078
Grace Park Ln 28078
Grafham Cir 28078
Grapperhall Dr 28078
Grassy Creek Dr 28078
Great Glen Ln 28078
Great Pine Ln 28078
Green Ashe Dr 28078
Green River Dr 28078
Green Spring Dr 28078
Greenfarm Rd 28078
Greenheather Dr 28078
Greenpoint Ln 28078
Greenpond Ln 28078
Greenway St 28078
Grimbsy Ct 28078
Grosson Ct 28078
Grove Tree Ln 28078
Groveland St 28078
Guthrie Dr 28078
Hagers Rd 28078
Hagers Ferry Rd 28078
Halcyon Dr 28078
Hallaton Dr 28078
Halston Cir 28078
Hambright Rd 28078
Hampton Crossing Dr 28078
Hampton Falls Dr 28078
Hampton Heritage Dr 28078
Hampton Trace Rd 28078
Handon Ln 28078
Harbert Rd 28078
Harkers Ct 28078
Harlow Creek Rd 28078
Harmon Ln 28078
Harold Ln 28078
Harris Rd 28078
Harrisons Sabbath Dr 28078
Harvest Moon Ct 28078
Harvest Point Dr 28078
Harvington Dr 28078
Hasley Woods Dr 28078
Hastings Farm Rd 28078
Hawk Grove Ct 28078
Hawks Perch Ln 28078
Hawksridge Rd 28078
Hayenridge Ct 28078
Hayes Ridge Ct 28078
Hearnerl Rd 28078
Hearthside Way 28078
Heath Grove Dr 28078
Heather Leanne Rd 28078
Heckscher Dr 28078
Hedrick Cir 28078
Hemlock Way 28078
Henderson Hill Rd 28078
Henderson Park Rd 28078
Henry Ln 28078
Henry Harrison Stillwell Dr 28078
Herbert Wayne Ct 28078
Heritage Orchard Way 28078
Heritage Vista Dr 28078
Herring St 28078
Hiawatha Ct 28078
Hickorywood Hill Ave 28078
Hidcote Ct 28078
Higgins Ln 28078
Highcrest Dr 28078
Hightower Oak Rd 28078
Highway 73 W 28078
Hill St 28078
Hill Tree Cir 28078
Hillcrest Dr & Ln 28078
Hillmoor Ln 28078
Hillspring Dr 28078
Hillston Ridge Rd 28078
Hinman Cir 28078
Hiwassee Rd 28078
Hodges Cir 28078
Holbrook St 28078
Holbrooks Rd 28078
Holkham Ln 28078
Hollingbourne Rd 28078
Hollis Hill Ln 28078
Hollow Wood Rd 28078
Holly Bend Ln 28078
Holly Crest Ln 28078
Holly Glade Cir 28078
Holly Point Dr 28078
Holly Springs Dr 28078
Holly Stream Dr 28078
Hollyhock Ln 28078
Holyhead Ln 28078
Hope Ct & St 28078
Hope Springs Ct 28078
Hopewell Ave 28078
Hord Dr 28078
Horseshoe Creek Dr 28078
Hortulan Ct 28078
Howell Ridge Rd 28078
Hubbard Rd 28078
Hudson Park Ln 28078
Hugh Mcauley Rd 28078
Hugh Torance Pkwy 28078
Hunt Valley Dr 28078
Hunters Rd 28078
Hunters Pointe Dr 28078
Huntersridge Rd 28078
Huntersville Cmns Dr 28078
Huntersville Concord Rd 28078
Huntersville Crossing Dr 28078
Huntersville Gateway Blvd 28078
Huntington Dr 28078
Huntingtowne Village Rd 28078
Hunton Ln 28078
Hus Mcginnis Rd 28078
Hutten Ct 28078
Ilse Helene Ln 28078
Ingleburn Ln 28078
Inglenook Ln 28078
Inglewood Ln 28078
Interlaken Pl 28078
Invermere Ave 28078
Iris Dr 28078
Island Dr 28078
Islay Ct 28078
Ithaca Ln 28078
Jamesburg Dr 28078
Janeiro Dr 28078
Jester Park Dr 28078
Jim Kidd Rd 28078
Joe Blanton Dr E 28078
Johnson Davis Rd 28078
Joleen Ct 28078
Journeys End Trl 28078
Joyce Ave 28078
Julian Clark Ave 28078
Kane Alexander Dr 28078
Karah Jane Ct 28078
Kaufinger St 28078
Kedleston Rd 28078
Keith Hill Rd 28078
Kelly Park Cir 28078
Kemerton Ln 28078
Kencot Ct 28078
Kennerly Dr 28078
Kennicott Way 28078
Kennon Ridge Ln 28078
Kent Ave 28078
Kenton Cir & Dr 28078
Kerns Rd 28078
Kerns Meadow Ln 28078
Kimberly Jane Ct 28078
Kimbolten Dr 28078
Kincardin Dr 28078
Kincey Ave 28078
Kingsway Dr 28078
Kinlocke Dr 28078
Kinross Ct 28078
Kirkin Way 28078
Klamath Pl 28078
Knockando Ln 28078
Knoll Oak Ct 28078
Knox Hill Rd 28078
Knox Ridge Rd 28078
Knox Run Rd 28078
Knoxwood Dr 28078
Krestridge View Dr 28078
Lacrosse Dr 28078
Lafoy Dr 28078
Lakehaven Dr 28078
Lakewood Dr 28078
Lamesa Pl 28078
Landings Dr 28078
Lariat Ct 28078
Lasaro Way 28078
Latta Gordon Rd 28078
Latta Plantation Cir 28078
Latta Springs Cir 28078
Laura Michelle Rd 28078
Laureate Rd 28078
Laurel Berry Ln 28078
Laurel Hill Ln 28078
Laurel Tree Ln 28078
Lavenham Rd 28078
Lawings Corner Dr 28078
Lawther Rd 28078
Lea Point Ct 28078
Leaning Oaks Ct 28078
Lear Ct 28078
Ledbury Ct 28078
Lee Dr 28078
Leeward Ln 28078
Lefferts House Pl 28078
Leisure Ln 28078
Leroy And Katies Way 28078
Leslie Brook Rd 28078
Levins Hall Rd 28078
Leyanne Ct 28078
Linderman Rd 28078
Lindholm Dr 28078
Linksland Dr 28078
Linksview Ln 28078
Linwood Dr 28078
Lithgow Pl 28078
Lizzie Ln 28078
Loch Raven Rd 28078
Lochrein Ridge Dr 28078
Locust Grove Ln 28078
Loftywood Ct 28078
Long Bow Ln 28078
Long Common Pkwy 28078
Long Cross Ct 28078
Long Iron Dr 28078
Long Pickett Ct 28078
Longstock Ct 28078
Lora Lynne Ct 28078
Lottingly Dr 28078
Louth Ct 28078
Lullwater Cv 28078
Lyman Oak Ct 28078
Lyon Hill Ln 28078
Mac Wood Rd 28078
Macbeth Ct 28078
Maclauren Ln 28078
Magnolia Bend Dr 28078
Mahafey Ln 28078
N & S Main St 28078
Malford Rd 28078
Mallory Baches Ln 28078
Maple Hill Ct 28078
Marguerite Ln 28078
Marion Lavern Rd 28078
Mariposa Ln 28078
Market Square Dr 28078
Marsh Field Ct 28078
Martello Ln 28078
Marthas View Dr NW 28078
Mascot Ln 28078
Maxwell Ave 28078
Maxwelton Dr 28078
Mayberry Place Ln 28078
Mayes Rd 28078
Mcauley Rd 28078
Mccahan Ln 28078
Mccord Rd 28078
Mccormick Pl 28078
Mccoy Rd 28078
Mccoy Ridge Dr 28078
Mcdiarmid Ln 28078
Mcdowell Run Dr 28078
Mcdunkeld Dr 28078
Mcginnis Ln 28078
Mcginnis Woods Dr 28078
Mcilwaine Rd 28078
Mcintosh Rd 28078
Mclothian Ln 28078
Meacham Farm Dr 28078
Meadow Crossing Dr 28078
Meadowmere Rd 28078
Melrose Meadow Ln 28078
Memory Ln 28078
Mendenhall View Dr 28078
Menifee Dr 28078
Mephan Aly 28078
Mercer Dr & Pl 28078
Mercia Ave 28078
Merlon Ct 28078
Merry Chase Ln 28078
Michael Andrew Rd 28078
Midas Springs Rd 28078
Middlethorpe Ln 28078
Milan Dr 28078
Millbank St 28078
Miriam Dr 28078
Misty Lilac Dr 28078
Moate Ct 28078
Monaco Dr 28078
Montecarlo Dr 28078
Monteith Grove Dr 28078
Moonbrook Ct 28078
Moonshadow Ln 28078
Moores Mill Rd 28078
Morehouse St 28078
Morgan Horse Trl 28078
Morlet Sq 28078
Mossy Rock Ct 28078
Mount Holly Hntrsvlle Rd 28078
Mountain Majesty Way 28078
Moxon Aly 28078
Muir Ct 28078
Mull Ct 28078
Mullen Rd & St 28078
Myston Ln 28078
Naworth Ln 28078
Nealy Rd 28078
Neck Rd 28078
Nethermead Ct 28078
New Birth Dr 28078
New Bond Dr 28078
New Haven Dr 28078
New Market Dr & Ln 28078
New Oak Ln 28078
New River Dr 28078
Newstead Rd 28078
Nicodemus Ln 28078
Nicole Campbell Rd 28078
Nitsa Ln 28078
Noble Pl 28078
Norman View Ln 28078
Norseman Ln 28078
Northbourne Rd 28078
Northcross Dr 28078
Northcross Center Ct 28078
Northdowns Ln 28078
Northgreen Dr 28078
Northstar Dr 28078
Northstone Dr 28078
Notchwood Ct 28078
Nottingham Dr 28078
O Hara St 28078
N Oak Dr 28078
Oak Hill Dr 28078
Oak Park Ln 28078
Oakham St 28078
Oakhill Park Ln 28078
Old Barnette Pl 28078
Old Bud Henderson Rd 28078
Old Dobbin Dr 28078
Old Grove Ln 28078
Old Statesville Rd 28078
Old Vermillion Dr 28078
Olive Park Dr 28078
Oliver Hager Rd 28078
Olmsford Dr 28078
Orange Sun Trl 28078
Overhill Rd 28078
Oxford Holw & Pl 28078
Oxford Glenn Dr 28078
Oxfordshire Ct 28078
Pacemaker Ln 28078
Palomar Dr 28078
Pamela St 28078
Paramount Dr 28078
Parcell St 28078
Park Ln 28078
Park Grove St 28078
Park Meadows Pl 28078
Parkcrest St 28078
Parkton Gate Dr 28078
Parr Dr 28078
Parsons Ridge Ln 28078
Patterson Rd 28078
Pavilion Estates Dr 28078
Pavilion Hill Cir 28078
Pavilion Hills Cir 28078
Pavilion Loop Dr 28078
Pavilion Valley Cir 28078
Pearl Moon Ct 28078
Pearwood Mews Dr 28078
Pecan Hill Ct 28078
Pembroke Rd 28078
Pendley Ln 28078
Pennington Dr 28078
Pennyhill Dr 28078
Pepperwood Ct 28078
Perthsire Ct 28078
Philip Michael Rd 28078
Pickford Ct 28078
Pine St 28078
Pine Springs Ct 28078
Pineknoll Ln 28078
Pineridge Dr 28078
Pinewood Dr 28078
Pinnacle Ln 28078
Pinnacle Cross Dr 28078
Platon Ave 28078
Plessis Pl 28078
N Point Rd 28078
N Pointe Executive Park Dr 28078
Polonius Ct 28078
Pontiac Pl 28078
Poplar Shadow Dr 28078
Poplar Tent Rd 28078
Prairie Rose Ln 28078
Prestwoods Ln 28078
Pristine Ct 28078
Professional Center Dr 28078
Promenade Dr 28078
Providence Ln 28078
Providence Hall Dr 28078
Province Valley Pl 28078
Provincial Ct 28078
Puckett Rd 28078
Quail Xing 28078
Queensway Pl 28078
Quilbray Dr 28078
Railway Dr 28078
Rainy Bend Dr 28078
Ramah Church Rd 28078
Ramah Creek Ct 28078
Ramah Oaks Ln 28078
Ranger Trl 28078
Rangeworth Ct 28078
Ranson Rd & St 28078
Rayneridge Dr 28078
Red Falcon Ct 28078
Red Sorrell Ln 28078
Redcliff Dr 28078
Reese Blvd E & W 28078
Regal Lily Ln 28078
Regency Park Dr 28078
Regent Grove Ln 28078
Remally Ln 28078
Remembrance Trl 28078
Repose Ln 28078
Rhiannon Ln 28078
Rich Hatchet Rd 28078
Richford Dr 28078
Richland Dr 28078
Rickstead Ct 28078
Rio St 28078
Riverside Oaks Dr 28078
Robert St 28078
Robins Way 28078
Rockhouse Ct 28078
Rocky Ford Club Rd 28078
Rocky Top Dr 28078
Rodanthe Pl 28078
Rolling Meadows Ln 28078
Rollingwood Dr 28078
Roosevelt Dr 28078
Rose Brook Ln 28078
Rose Commons Dr 28078
Rosedale Hill Ave 28078
Rosemary Way Dr 28078
Rosewood Meadow Ln 28078
Royal Park Ln 28078
Royalton Pl 28078
Rudyard Ln 28078
Rush Lake Ln 28078
Rustic Arch Way 28078
Rustic Barn Dr 28078
Rutledge Ridge Dr NW 28078
Ryddell Ct 28078
Sagefield Dr 28078
Salem Ridge Rd 28078
Salford Ct 28078
Salm Ridge Rd 28078
Sam Furr Rd 28078
Sample Rd 28078
Samuels Way Dr 28078
Sandowne Ln 28078
Santa Fe Trl 28078
Santa Rosa Ct 28078
Sao Paula Dr 28078
Sarah Ann Stephens Dr 28078
Sarsfield Ln 28078
Satinwood Ln 28078
Savannah Grace Ln 28078
Sawtimber Ct 28078
Saxon Trace Ct 28078
Schuyler Dr 28078
Scotsway Dr 28078
Scottsboro Dr 28078
Seafield Ln 28078
Seagle St 28078
Sedalia Pl 28078
Sedgebrook Ln 28078
Segars Ln 28078
Senate Court Way 28078
Sendler Way Dr 28078
Serenity St 28078
Shadetree St 28078
Shady Vale Ln 28078
Shamley Ct 28078
Sharrow Bay Ct 28078
Shaw Dr 28078
Shephards Rd 28078
Shepparton Dr 28078
Sherrill Estates Rd 28078
Sherrwynn Rd 28078
Sherwood Dr 28078
Shields Dr 28078
Shiella Caruth Dr 28078
Shinner Dr 28078
Shiro Ct 28078

Shoreway Dr ... 28078
Silbury Ln ... 28078
Silver Branch Ln ... 28078
Silver Chime Way ... 28078
Silver King Ct ... 28078
Silverton Way ... 28078
Sims Rd ... 28078
Singleton Ct ... 28078
Sky Vista Dr ... 28078
Skybluff Cir ... 28078
Skybrook Dr ... 28078
Skybrook Falls Dr ... 28078
Skypark Dr ... 28078
Skyscape Dr ... 28078
Skytop Dr ... 28078
Sloe Way ... 28078
Slumber Oaks Ct ... 28078
Snapdragon Ln ... 28078
Snapping Turtle Ln ... 28078
Sojourn Ct ... 28078
Soloman James Ln ... 28078
Southland Rd ... 28078
Sparkling Way ... 28078
Spotted Owl Ct ... 28078
Spring Tree Ln ... 28078
Springsure Ct ... 28078
Spruell St ... 28078
St Barts Ln ... 28078
St Brides Ct ... 28078
Standerwick Ln ... 28078
N Statesville Rd ... 28078
Stawell Dr ... 28078
Stayman Ct ... 28078
Steel St ... 28078
Stephens Rd ... 28078
Stephens Grove Ln ... 28078
Steuben Dr ... 28078
Steve Bondurant Dr ... 28078
Stillbrook Bend Ct ... 28078
Stilling St ... 28078
Stillwater Crossing Ln ... 28078
Stinson Ave ... 28078
Stinson Cove Rd ... 28078
Stockland Ct ... 28078
Stone Cross Dr ... 28078
Stone Garden Dr ... 28078
Stone Hollow Dr ... 28078
Stonegreen Ln ... 28078
Stonemason Dr ... 28078
Stonemont Rd ... 28078
Stonewall Rd ... 28078
Stourbridge Dr ... 28078
Strandhill Rd ... 28078
Strathburn Ct ... 28078
Stratton Farm Rd ... 28078
Strattonville Ct ... 28078
Streamview Dr ... 28078
Stumptown Rd ... 28078
Stumpview Ct ... 28078
Sulgrave Dr ... 28078
Sullivan Glen Way ... 28078
Sullivan Watch Dr ... 28078
Summer Serenade Dr ... 28078
Summerchase Trl ... 28078
Summerfield Ln ... 28078
Sunriver Rd ... 28078
Sunset Dr ... 28078
Sunset Grove Dr ... 28078
Sunset Walk Ln ... 28078
Surrey Crest Ln ... 28078
Surreykirt Ln ... 28078
Sutherland Dr ... 28078
Sutters Run Ln ... 28078
Swan Wings Pl ... 28078
Swansboro Ln ... 28078
Sweetfield Dr ... 28078
Swinton Rd ... 28078
Swiss Gate Ct ... 28078
Sycamore Terrace Ct ... 28078
Taft Ct ... 28078
Tallent Ln ... 28078
Tanners Creek Dr ... 28078
Tartan Ridge Dr ... 28078
Tatebrook Ln ... 28078
Taunton Dr ... 28078
Taviston St ... 28078
Taybrook Dr ... 28078
Tayside Ct ... 28078
Terry Ln ... 28078
Thach Ct ... 28078
Thames Way ... 28078
Thistlebrook Ln ... 28078
Thornbury Ln ... 28078
Thousand Oaks Dr ... 28078
Three Greens Dr ... 28078
Tidal Ct ... 28078
Tigers Paw Rd ... 28078
Timbergreen Dr ... 28078
Timberview Ln ... 28078
Tin Pan Aly ... 28078
Titan Ave ... 28078
Titus Ln ... 28078
Toka Ct ... 28078
Toledo Rd ... 28078
Tooley St ... 28078
Topsail Cove Dr ... 28078
Torrence Creek Ct ... 28078
Torrence Crossing Dr ... 28078
Torrence Trace Dr ... 28078
Tosomock Ln ... 28078
Townley Rd ... 28078
Tracy Beth Rd ... 28078
Trails End Ln ... 28078
Train Station Dr ... 28078
Treasure Cv ... 28078
Trenton Place Rd ... 28078
Trestlebrook Dr ... 28078
Tribute Place Dr ... 28078
Troubadour Ln ... 28078
Truitt Ct ... 28078
Tulip Poplar Pl ... 28078
Tulipfera Ln ... 28078
Tuscaloosa Rd ... 28078
Tuxford Dr ... 28078
Twelvetrees Ln ... 28078
Twin Cove Dr ... 28078
Twin Trail Dr ... 28078
Ulsten Ln ... 28078
Union Square Dr ... 28078
Uxbridge Ln ... 28078
Van Buren Pl ... 28078
Van Strattan Ct ... 28078
Vance Rd N ... 28078
Vanessa Ln ... 28078
Vanguard Pkwy ... 28078
Vanstory Dr ... 28078
Vantage Point Ln ... 28078
Verhoeff Dr ... 28078
Vesper Dr ... 28078
Vickers St ... 28078
Villanova Rd ... 28078
Vintage Hill Ln ... 28078
Virginia Ave ... 28078
Vixen Ln ... 28078
Walden Lea Dr ... 28078
Waldrop Hill Ct ... 28078
Walker St ... 28078
Wallace Pond Dr ... 28078
Warder Ct ... 28078
Warfield Ave ... 28078
Warton Way ... 28078
Water Iris Ct ... 28078
Waterfront Dr ... 28078
Waterperry Ct ... 28078
Waterton Ct ... 28078
Watkins St ... 28078
Waverton Ln ... 28078
Waycross Dr ... 28078
Weatherly Way ... 28078
Wedgewood Dr ... 28078
Wedgewood Drive Ext ... 28078
Wedmore Ln ... 28078
Welder Ct ... 28078
Wescott Hill Dr ... 28078
Wesson Hunt Rd NW ... 28078
Westgreen Dr ... 28078
Westminister Dr ... 28078
Westmoreland Rd ... 28078
Whispering Pines Ln ... 28078
White Point Dr ... 28078
Wickson Ct ... 28078
Wild Lilac Ct ... 28078
Wildlife Ln ... 28078
Williamsburg Cir ... 28078
Willingdon Rd ... 28078
Willingham Rd ... 28078
Willow Breeze Ln ... 28078
Willow Grove Way ... 28078
Willow Trace Ct ... 28078
Wilmington Rd ... 28078
Windblown Ct ... 28078
Winding Ridge Rd ... 28078
Windknob Ct ... 28078
Windward Oaks Dr ... 28078
Windy Falls Dr ... 28078
Windy Lea Ln ... 28078
Windy Mist Way ... 28078
Windyedge Rd ... 28078
Winmau Ln ... 28078
Woodcote Dr ... 28078
Woodhall Dr ... 28078
Woods Run Ln ... 28078
Worden Ct ... 28078
Wyncrest Dr ... 28078
Wynfield Creek Pkwy ... 28078
Wynford Hall St ... 28078
Wynstone Ridge Cir ... 28078
Yadkin River Dr ... 28078

NUMBERED STREETS

All Street Addresses ... 28078

JACKSONVILLE NC

General Delivery ... 28540

POST OFFICE BOXES MAIN OFFICE STATIONS AND BRANCHES

Box No.s
1 - 3003 ... 28541
4001 - 7624 ... 28540
12001 - 12957 ... 28546
28540 - 28540 ... 28540
28546 - 28546 ... 28546

NAMED STREETS

Aaron Ln ... 28540
Aberdeen Ln ... 28540
Acorn Ct ... 28540
Adam Ct ... 28546
Adobe Ln ... 28546
Aerie Ct ... 28546
Afton Villa ... 28540
Agerholm St ... 28540
Agler Ln ... 28540
Albany Dr
100-499 ... 28540
600-699 ... 28546
Alden Dr ... 28546
Aldersgate Rd ... 28546
Allen Pl ... 28546
Allison Ln ... 28540
Allison Hatchel Ave ... 28540
Altavista Loop ... 28546
Altman Ln ... 28546
Alum Spring Ct ... 28546
Aman Ln ... 28540
Amber Stone ... 28546
Ambray Ct ... 28546
Amelia Ln ... 28540
America Ct ... 28540
Amy Dr ... 28540
Andrea Ave ... 28540
Andrea Dawn Ln ... 28540
Anne St ... 28540
Annie Ave ... 28546
Annie Pearle Ln ... 28540
Anson Ct ... 28540
Apartment Dr ... 28546
Apex Ln ... 28540
Appaloosa Dr ... 28540
Applecross Pl ... 28546
Appling Ct ... 28546
Aquamarine Cir ... 28546
Arabella Dr ... 28546
Aragona Blvd ... 28540
Arbitrary Ln ... 28540
Archdale Dr ... 28546
Archer Ln ... 28540
Arlington Ct ... 28546
Arlington Meadows Dr ... 28546
Armistead Way ... 28540
Armstrong Dr ... 28540
Arnold Rd ... 28546
Arnold Road Ext ... 28546
Arthur Ct ... 28546
Ash Ct & Pl ... 28546
Ashbury Ct ... 28546
Ashcroft Dr ... 28546
Ashe St ... 28540
Ashley Pl ... 28540
Ashley Meadows Ln ... 28546
Ashwood Dr ... 28546
Aspen Ln ... 28540
E Aspen Ln ... 28540
Aspen Pl ... 28540
At Waller Rd ... 28540
Atlas Brown Dr ... 28540
Auburn Ct & Ln ... 28540
Audrey Ct ... 28540
Audubon Dr ... 28546
August Ln ... 28540
Autumn Cir & Dr ... 28546
Autumn Cove Ct ... 28546
Autumn Ridge Dr ... 28546
Avon Pl ... 28540
Azalea Garden Apts ... 28540
Aztec Rd ... 28540
Backer Cir ... 28540
Backfield Pl ... 28540
Bailey Dr ... 28540
Baker Ln ... 28546
Baldwin Ct ... 28546
Balsam Ct & Rd ... 28546
Bamboo Ln ... 28540
Bancroft St ... 28540
Banister Loop ... 28546
Banks St ... 28540
Barden St ... 28540
Barkley Ct ... 28546
Barksdale Dr ... 28540
Barn St ... 28540
Barnette Ln ... 28540
Barry Ln ... 28540
Basswood Ct ... 28546
Batchelor Trl ... 28546
Bates St ... 28540
Batting Cage Ln ... 28540
Baxter St ... 28540
Bayberry Ct ... 28546
Baymeade Ct ... 28546
Baysden Dr ... 28540
Baysden Dr Ext ... 28540
E Bayshore Blvd ... 28540
Baytree Dr ... 28546
Bayview Dr ... 28540
Beacham Ln ... 28540
Beacham Apts ... 28540
Beacon Hill Ct ... 28546
Beagle Ln ... 28540
Beasley Trailer Park ... 28546
Beaver Ct ... 28540
Beaver Creek Ct ... 28540
Becky Ln ... 28540
Bedford Grn ... 28546
Beech St ... 28540
Beech Tree Rd ... 28546
Beechtree Ln ... 28540
Bell Fork Rd ... 28540
Bellchase Dr ... 28540
Bellchasse Way ... 28540
Belmont Ct ... 28540
Belvedere Ct ... 28546
Belwood Ct ... 28540
Ben Williams Rd ... 28540
Benjamin Ct ... 28540
Bennie Ct ... 28540
Berks Ct ... 28546
Berkshire Dr ... 28546
Bernard Ln ... 28540
Berry Ln ... 28540
Bertie Ct ... 28540
Berwick Ct ... 28546
Bethesda Ct & St ... 28546
Bev Ln ... 28540
Beverly Dr ... 28540
Beverly Hills Ct ... 28540
Big Branch Ln ... 28540
Big Fish Run ... 28540
Big John Est ... 28546
Bills Ln ... 28546
Billy Hudson Rd ... 28540
Biltmore Ln E & W ... 28546
Birch Ct ... 28540
Birch Rd ... 28546
Birchleaf Ct ... 28546
Birchwood Ct & Ln ... 28546
Birdie Ct ... 28540
Biscayne Ct ... 28546
Bishop Dr ... 28540
Bishopsgate ... 28540
Blackbird Ln ... 28546
Blackthorn Ln ... 28546
Blake Ct ... 28546
Blue Angel Ct ... 28540
Blue Claw Bay Rd ... 28540
Blue Creek Rd ... 28540
Blue Creek Farms Dr ... 28540
Blue Creek School Rd ... 28540
Blue Diamond Ct ... 28540
Blue King Ln ... 28540
Blue Leaf Pl ... 28546
Blue Moon Ct ... 28540
Blue Swan Ct ... 28540
Blue Top Rd ... 28540
Bluegrass Cir ... 28546
Bluestone Ct ... 28546
Bluff Cir & St ... 28540
Bluff Ridge Ct ... 28540
Blur Angel Ct ... 28540
Bobcat Ln ... 28540
Bolder Ln ... 28540
Bonair Dr ... 28540
Bordeaux St ... 28540
Bordelon St ... 28540
Bosco Ct & Dr ... 28546
Bow Sprit Ct ... 28546
Bracken Pl ... 28540
Bradford Ct ... 28546
Branch Dr ... 28540
Branchwood Ct & Dr ... 28546
Branchwood Shopping Ctr ... 28546
Brandon Way ... 28540
Brandy Ct ... 28546
W Brandymill Ln ... 28546
Brass Ln ... 28540
Bratton Dr ... 28540
Brenda Dr ... 28546
Brentcreek Cir ... 28546
Brenton Pl ... 28540
Brentwood Ave & Dr ... 28546
Bret Ct ... 28540
Brevard Ct ... 28546
Briar Hollow Dr ... 28540
Briarcreek Ln ... 28540
Briarneck Rd ... 28540
Briarwood Ct ... 28546
Bribster Ct N & S ... 28540
NW Bridge Rd ... 28540
Bridge Side Dr ... 28540
N Bridgeside Ct ... 28540
Bridget Ln ... 28540
Bridgewater Ct ... 28546
Bridgeway Ct ... 28540
Bridgewood Dr ... 28546
Bridlewood Dr ... 28540
Brigham Ct ... 28540
Bright Leaf Ln ... 28540
Brighton St ... 28546
Brinkley Ln ... 28540
Broadhurst Rd ... 28540
Broadleaf Dr ... 28546
Broadwater Dr ... 28540
Brogdan Ln ... 28540
Broken Oak Ct ... 28540
Bronco Ln ... 28540
Brookdale Plz ... 28546
Brookshire Ct ... 28546
Brookside Ct ... 28546
N Brookside Ct ... 28540
S Brookside Ct ... 28540
Brookstone Ct & Way ... 28546
Brookview Ct & Dr ... 28540
Brothers Ln ... 28540
Brown Rd ... 28540
Bruce Dr ... 28540
Brunswick Dr ... 28546
Bryan Ct ... 28540
Bryan Pl ... 28540
Bryan Rd ... 28546
N Bryan Rd ... 28546
Bryan St ... 28540
Bryleigh Ln ... 28540
Brynn Marr Rd ... 28546
N Brynn Marr Trailer Park ... 28546
Bubbling Brook Ln ... 28546
Buff Ct ... 28540
Bunker Ct ... 28540
Burgaw Hwy ... 28540
Burlingame Pl ... 28540
Burnett St ... 28546
Burning Tree Ln ... 28546
Burton Pl ... 28540
Buster Ct ... 28540
Butternut Cir ... 28546
Butternut Ln ... 28540
Byron Ln ... 28546
C And B Trailer Park ... 28546
Cabernet Ct ... 28540
Cabin Cir ... 28540
Caldwell Ct ... 28540
Caldwell Loop ... 28546
Calico Ct ... 28546
California Cutoff ... 28546
Cambridge Ct ... 28546
E & W Cameron Ct ... 28546
Campbell Pl ... 28540
Canaan Ct ... 28546
Canady Rd ... 28546
Candlewood Dr ... 28540
Cando Pl ... 28540
Canterbury Ln ... 28546
Canterbury Rd ... 28540
Canterbury Hills Apts ... 28540
Cantle Ct ... 28540
Capri Ln ... 28546
Cardiff Ct ... 28546
Cardinal Dr & Rd ... 28546
Cardinal Village Apts ... 28546
Carl Williams Rd ... 28540
Carlisle Ct
100-199 ... 28546
300-399 ... 28540
S Carlisle Ct ... 28546
Carly Ln ... 28540
Carmen Ave ... 28540
Carole Ct ... 28540
Carole Dr
100-199 ... 28546
400-499 ... 28540
E Carole Dr ... 28546
N Carole Dr ... 28546
W Carole Dr ... 28546
Carolina Cir, Dr & Pl ... 28546
Carolina Forest Blvd ... 28546
Carolina Park Ave & Ln ... 28546
Carolina Pines Dr ... 28546
Carolina Plantations Blvd ... 28546
Carriage Ct ... 28540
Carriage Dr ... 28540
Carriage Ln ... 28540
E & W Carrington Way ... 28546
Carters Grove Cir ... 28540
Carver Dr ... 28546
Carver Rd ... 28540
Casey Ct ... 28540
Castelnau Ct ... 28540
Castle Ct & Dr ... 28546
Caswell Ct ... 28546
Cates Ct ... 28540
Catherine Ct ... 28546
Catherines Lake Rd ... 28540
Catino Farms Ln ... 28546
Catnapper Ln ... 28540
Cattail Ct ... 28540
Cavalier Dr ... 28546
Caviness Dr ... 28540
Cedar Ct ... 28546
Cedar Creek Dr ... 28540
Center St ... 28546
Chandler Ct ... 28546
Chaney Ave ... 28540
Chaparral Trl ... 28546
Chapman Ct ... 28540
Chaps Ct ... 28546
Charles Rd ... 28546
Charleston Ln ... 28546
Chastain Ct ... 28546
Chatham Ct ... 28540
Chauncery Ct ... 28546
Cheerful Ln ... 28540
Chentran Rd ... 28540
Cherokee Dr ... 28540
Cherokee Nation Ln ... 28540
Cherrybark Dr ... 28546
Cherrywood Ct ... 28546
Cheryll Ct ... 28546
Chestnut Ct ... 28546
Chestnut Rd ... 28540
Cheyenne Rd ... 28540
Chief Ct ... 28546
Chinkapin Ct ... 28546
Chisholm Trl ... 28546
Chris Ln ... 28540
Christian Ct ... 28546
Christine Ave & Ct ... 28540
Christine Thompson Ct ... 28540
Christopher Ct ... 28546
Church St ... 28540
Cider Hill Rd ... 28546
Circle Dr ... 28540
Circuit Ln ... 28546
Claudia Ct ... 28546
Claymore Ct & Dr ... 28546
Clayton Rd ... 28546
Clayton Humphrey Rd ... 28546
Clayton James Rd ... 28546
Clear Brook Ct ... 28546
Clemson Ct ... 28546
Cliff Ct ... 28546
Clifton Rd ... 28540
Clover Dr ... 28546
Club Ln ... 28546
Clyde Dr ... 28540
Clydesdale Ct ... 28546
Coachman Ct ... 28546
Coastal Ln ... 28546
Cobalt Stream Ct ... 28546
Cobble Creek Ln ... 28546
Cobblestone Ct & Trl ... 28546
Cobia Ct ... 28546
Coke Pl ... 28546
Cole Dr ... 28540
Cole Porter Ln ... 28546
Coleman Dr ... 28546
Coles Farm Dr ... 28546
College Plz ... 28546
College St ... 28540
Collins St ... 28546
Colonial Dr ... 28546
Colony Plz ... 28546
Columbia Dr ... 28546
Comet Ln ... 28540
Comfort Country Mobile Park ... 28540
Commerce Rd ... 28546
Commons Dr N & S ... 28546
Community Dr ... 28546
Compton St ... 28540

Conifer Cir 28540
Conover St 28540
Constitution Ave 28540
Converse Dr 28546
Coot Davis Rd 28540
Corbin St 28546
Cordell Cir & Dr 28540
Corey Cir & Ct 28546
Cornell Ct & Dr 28546
Cornerstone Pl 28546
Cornhusk Ct 28546
Cornsilk Ct 28546
Corolla Ct 28546
Corral Way 28546
NW Corridor Blvd 28540
Cottage Ln 28546
Cottonwood Ct 28546
Cougar Ln 28546
Country Rd 28546
Country Club Blvd 28540
Country Club Dr 28546
Country Club Rd 28546
Country Squire Ln 28540
Countrywood Blvd & Dr 28540
Courie Way 28540
Court St 28540
Courtland Dr 28546
Courtney Dr 28540
Coventry Ct 28540
Covered Wagon Trl 28546
Covington St 28540
Cowell Ln 28546
Cox Ave 28540
Cozy Crow Trl 28540
Cozy Haven Trailer Park 28546
Crawford St 28540
Creative Ln 28540
Creedmoor Rd 28546
N Creek Dr 28546
S Creek Dr 28540
Creekview Dr 28540
Creighton Dr 28546
Creon Ct 28540
Crest Pl 28540
Crickett Ln 28540
Crissy Dr 28540
Croatan Ct 28546
Crooked Creek Rd 28540
Croom Ln 28546
Croom Rentals 28546
Crooms Trailer Park 28546
Cross Creek Dr 28540
Crystal Falls Ct 28546
Crystal Stone Way 28546
Curtis Rd 28540
Cutlass St 28546
Cypress Ct 28540
Cypress Bay Dr 28546
Cypress Manor Ct 28540
Cyrus Pl 28546
Cyrus Thompson Dr 28546
D And J Farm Ln 28546
Dacard Ct 28540
Daffodil Ln 28540
Dahlia Ct 28546
Daisy Ct 28540
Daisy St 28546
Dale Ct & Dr 28540
Danbury Ct 28540
Daniel Ct, Dr & Pl 28546
Daplin Pl 28540
Darden St 28540
Dartmoor Trl 28540
David Pl 28540
E Davis Rd 28546
Davis St 28540
Dawn Ct 28540
Dawson Cabin Rd 28540
Dawson Place Rd 28540
Daylily Ln 28546
Deblea Ct 28546
Deborah Pl 28540
Debra Lee Ln 28540
Decatur Rd 28540

Deer Creek Dr 28540
Deer Crossing Rd 28546
Deerfield Rd 28540
Delaney Dr 28546
Delight Ct & Dr 28546
Dellview Ct 28540
Delmar Rd 28540
Deloss Ct 28546
Denise Ct & Dr 28540
Dennis Ct & Rd 28546
Derby Run Rd 28546
Devon Ct 28546
Dewitt St 28540
Diamond Ct 28546
Diane Ct & Dr 28540
Dickens St 28540
Diplomat Ln 28546
Dixie Trl 28546
Djs Ln 28540
Dockside Dr 28546
Doctors Dr 28546
Dogwood Dr & Ln 28540
Dolly Ln 28546
Dolphin Dr 28546
Domino Ln 28546
E & W Donna Ct 28546
Doris Ave & Ct 28540
Doris Place Dr 28540
Dorsett Ct 28546
Dover Ln 28540
Drake Ct 28540
Drayton Hall 28546
Dressler Ct & Dr 28540
Druid Ct 28546
Drummer Kellum Rd 28546
Dudley St 28540
Duff Ct 28546
Duffy Ln 28546
Duke Ct 28546
Dunbar Ln 28546
Dundee Ct 28546
Dunhill Ct 28546
Dunleith Pl 28546
Dunwoody Dr 28546
Duplin Ct 28540
Durban Ln 28546
Durbin Ln 28546
Dutchman Ln 28546
Dynamo Ln 28546
Dynasty Dr 28546
Eagle Ct 28540
Eagle River Ct 28546
Early Dr 28540
East Ct & Dr 28546
Eastgate Dr 28540
Eastview Ct 28546
Eastwood Dr 28546
Easy St 28546
Ed Coles Ct 28546
Edenton Ct 28540
Edgecombe Ct 28546
Edgefield Dr 28546
Edgewood Dr
200-299 28546
800-899 28540
Edinburgh Ct 28546
Edith Dr 28540
Edmunds Ln 28546
Edward Jarman Ln 28546
Edwards Rd 28540
Eider Loop 28540
El Dorado Ct 28546
Elaine Ct & Dr 28546
Elbert Way 28540
Elijah Ct 28540
Elizabeth St 28540
Elk Ct 28546
Ellen Ct 28540
Ellington Pl 28540
Ellis Blvd 28540
Elm St 28540
Elwood Rd 28546
Emerald Ridge Rd 28546
Emily Loop 28540
Emma Thompson Rd 28546
Emmerdale Way 28546

Empire Blvd 28546
Enouch Ln 28540
Enterprise Rd 28546
Epperson St 28540
Epworth Dr 28546
Erastus Ln 28540
Erica Ln 28540
Ernest Gurganus Rd 28540
Ernest King Rd 28540
Erskine Ct 28540
Ervin Ct 28546
Estate Dr 28540
Estates Ln 28540
Esther Ln 28546
Eton Ct & Dr 28546
Eucalyptus Ln 28546
Eva St 28540
Evergreen Dr 28546
Exmoor Dr 28540
Fairbanks Ct 28546
Faires Trailer Park 28540
Fairfax Ct 28540
Fairfield Ct 28540
Fairmont Ln 28540
Fairway Dr & Rd 28546
Fairwood Ct 28546
Falcon Crest Rd 28540
Fall Ct & Dr 28540
Fall Creek Dr 28540
Falling Leaf Ct 28546
Falls Cv 28546
Falls Creek Ct 28540
Farmers Ln 28540
Fawn Trl 28540
Fawns Creek Chase 28540
Fenton Pl 28540
Ferris Ln 28540
Festive Ln 28540
Field St 28540
Fieldcrest Dr 28546
Fieldgate Dr 28546
Fieldstone Pl & Way 28546
Filmore Ct 28540
Finley Ln 28540
Fire House Ln 28546
Fire Tower Rd 28540
Firethorn Ln 28546
First Post Rd 28546
Fisher Ln 28540
Flagstone Ln 28546
Fletcher St 28540
Flower Trl 28546
Foal Ct 28540
Foggy River Way 28546
Foliage Ct 28540
Forbes Ln 28540
Forbes Estates Dr 28546
Ford St 28540
Forest Cir & Ct 28540
Forest Bluff Dr 28540
Forest Grove Ave 28546
Forsythia Ct 28546
Foscue Dr 28540
Fosse Way 28546
Foster Rd 28540
Fountain Dr 28546
Fox Creek Trailer Park 28540
Fox Run Rd 28546
Foxberry Pl 28546
Foxfire Cir 28546
Foxhorn Rd 28540
Foxwood Ct 28540
Foy Lockamy Rd 28540
W Frances St 28546
Fred Garganus Rd 28540
Freedom Ct 28546
Freeman St 28546
Fremont Dr 28540
Friendly Ln 28540
Funny Farm Rd 28546
Furia Dr 28540
Futrell Trailer Park 28540
Gabriel Branch Apts 28546
Gadwell Loop 28540
Gainey Trailer Park 28546
Gaitway Ct 28546

Garden Pl 28546
S Gardenia Ln 28540
Gardenview Dr 28540
Garlands Way 28546
Garnet Ln 28546
Gary Ct 28546
Gaston Ct 28540
Gateway Dr S 28546
Gattis Rd 28546
Gency Ct 28546
Genora Pl 28540
George Ln 28540
George Howard Rd 28540
Georgetown Rd 28540
Gerald Dr 28540
Gilbert Thompson Ct 28540
Gilcrest Dr 28540
Ginko Cir 28546
Gladstone Dr 28546
Gladys Ln 28540
N & S Glen Ct 28540
Glen Cannon Dr 28546
Glenburney Dr 28546
Glendale Rd 28540
Glenhaven Ln 28546
Gloria Pl 28540
Gold Ln 28540
Gold Leaf Ct 28540
Golden Ct 28540
Goodson Trl 28546
Gospel Way Ct 28546
Gould Rd 28540
Grace St 28546
Grafton Ct 28540
Grainbin Ln 28546
Grandeur Ave 28546
Grandford Pl 28546
Granite Ct 28540
Grantham Ln 28546
Grants Creek Rd 28546
Gravely Creek Rd 28540
Grayborn Rd 28540
Graytown Rd 28540
Green Way 28546
Green Pines Trailer Park 28546
Greenbriar Ct & Dr 28546
Greencrest Cir 28540
Greenford Pl 28540
Greenleaf Ct 28540
Greenway Ct & Dr 28546
Greenwood Ct 28546
Greer Ln 28546
Gregory Dr 28540
Grey Barn Rd 28540
Grey Fox Ln 28546
Grey Squirrel Ct 28540
Greystone Ave 28540
Grier St 28540
Grimsby Pl 28540
Grismill Ct & Rd 28540
Grove Ct 28540
Guldin Rd 28540
Gum Branch Rd 28540
Guys Rd 28540
H Sanders Rd 28540
Hac St 28540
Hackney Ridge Ln 28540
Haddock Ct 28546
Hailey Ln 28540
Half Moon Church Rd 28546
Halltown Rd 28546
Halltown Apts 28546
Hammock Ln 28546
Hamp Ln 28546
Hampshire Pl 28546
S Hampton Ct & Dr 28546
Hampton Inn Way 28546
Hardin St 28540
Hardison Hills Ct 28546
Harenner Rd 28546
Hargett St 28540
Harness Rd 28546
Harpers Ln 28540
Harrells Loop Rd 28540
Harris Creek Rd 28540

Harris Creek Loop Rd 28540
Harris Creek Rentals 28540
Harrow Ct 28546
Hartford Ln 28540
Harther Dr 28540
Harvard Cir 28546
Harvest Dr 28540
Hawkins Blvd & Lndg 28540
Hawks Bill Dr 28540
Hawks Nest Rd 28540
Hawks Point Rd 28540
Hawkside Rd 28546
Haws Run Rd 28540
Hawthorne Rd 28540
Hayden Pl 28540
Hays Ln 28546
Haywood Ln 28540
Hearthstone Ct & Dr 28546
Heath Ln 28540
Heatherton Ln 28546
Heavens Gate Dr 28546
Hedgerow Ln 28546
Heiress Wynd Dr 28546
Helen St 28546
Hemby St 28540
Hemlock Dr 28546
Henderson Dr
100-1199 28540
2400-2498 28546
2500-5099 28546
Henderson Rd 28540
Hendricks Ave & Ct 28540
Heritage Ct 28540
Heritage Dr 28540
Heritage Ln 28546
Hershey Ln 28540
Hibiscus Ln 28540
Hickory Ct & Rd 28540
Hickory Grove Dr 28546
Hidden Oaks Dr 28546
High Hill Rd 28540
High Stepper Ct 28540
Highland Ct 28540
Highwood Ct 28546
Hilda Rd 28546
N & S Hill Ct 28540
Hills Lorough Loop 28546
Hills Trailer Park 28546
Hillside Ct 28546
E & W Hilltop Ct 28546
Hilltop Ridge Rd 28540
Hilton Sanders Rd 28540
Hines Farm Rd 28540
Hinestown Rd 28540
Hinson Arms Apts 28540
Hinson Lake Rd 28540
Hinsons Ct 28540
Hobbs Dr 28540
Hofmann Ct & Dr 28546
Hogg Ln 28540
Holly Ct & Dr 28540
Holly Grove Ct & Ln 28540
Holly Shelter Rd 28540
Hollyfield Ct 28546
Holmes Point Ct 28546
Honey Ct E & W 28540
Hoot Owl Ln 28546
Hope Ct 28540
Horizon Ln 28540
Horse Shoe Bnd 28546
Hosanna Ln 28546
Hourglass Ln 28540
Houston Rd 28540
E & W Howard Dr & Rd 28540
Howell Dr 28540
Hudson Ln 28540
Huerth St 28540
Huff Ct 28546
Huff Dr
100-198 28546
200-278 28546
279-279 28544
279-1199 28546
280-1298 28546
Hughes Ln 28546

Humphrey Rd 28540
N Humphrey Rd 28546
Humphrey Acres 28546
Hunter Ct & Dr 28546
Hunters Trl 28546
Hunters Ridge Dr 28540
Hunterswood Ct 28546
Hunting Green Dr 28546
Huntington Ct 28540
Hyannis Ct 28540
Hyatt Cir 28546
Hybrid Ct 28540
Idaho Dr 28540
Imperial Ln 28540
Independence Dr 28546
Indian Dr 28546
Inez Ct 28540
Investment Ln 28540
Ireland Ct 28546
Ironwood Ct 28546
Issac Ln 28540
Iverleigh Ln 28540
Ives Ln 28540
Ivey Ct 28540
Ivey Ridge Pl 28540
Ivy Glen Ln 28546
Jackson Ct 28540
Jacksons Trl 28540
Jacksonville Mall 28546
Jacob Ct 28540
Jade Ct 28546
Jade Tree Ct 28540
James St 28540
James Newbold Ct 28540
James Waters Pl 28540
Jamestown Ct 28546
Janie Ave 28540
Jarman St 28540
Jasmine Ln 28546
Javelan Ln 28546
Jay Cir 28540
Jaybyrd Ln 28540
Jean Cir 28540
Jeffrey St 28540
Jenkins Rd 28540
Jennie Dr 28546
Jennifer Dr 28546
Jim Blake Rd 28540
Jim Parker Rd 28540
Jld Dr 28540
Joe Powell Ln 28540
Joes Ct 28540
John Boy Ln 28540
Johnny Parker Rd 28540
Johnson Blvd 28540
Johnson Ct 28546
Jolly Dr 28540
Jonathan Dr & Rd 28540
Jones St 28540
Jordan Ln 28546
Joshua Ln 28546
Joy Ct 28540
Jubilance Ln 28540
Julia Ct 28540
Junction Ln 28540
Juniper Pl 28540
Jupiter Ct & Trl 28546
Justice Rd 28540
Kalli Dr 28546
Kane Ct 28540
Kant Pl 28540
Kanton Dr 28540
Kathryn Ave 28546
Kay St 28546
Kayla Ct 28540
Keating Ct 28546
Keller Ct 28540
Kellogg Ln 28540
Kellum Loop Rd 28546
Kelly St 28540
Kemberly Ct 28540
Kenan Loop 28546
Kenna Ct 28540
Kennel Ln 28540
Kensington Dr 28546
Kenwood Dr 28540

Kerr St 28540
Kerry Ct 28546
Kevin Ct 28546
Key Ln 28546
Kim Ln 28540
Kimberly Ln 28546
King Rd & St 28540
King Estates Rd 28540
King George Ct 28546
King Richard Ct 28546
Kings Pond Dr 28546
Kingsmill Ct 28546
Kingston Rd 28546
Kingswood Ct 28546
Kinsey Ln 28540
Kip Ct 28540
Kitt Dr 28540
Knight Pl 28546
Kodiak Ct 28540
Koonce Cir 28540
Kureb Ct 28546
Kyle Dr 28546
L P Willingham Pkwy 28540
Ladd St 28540
Laguna Ln 28540
Laguna Bay Dr 28540
Lake Ln 28540
E & W Lakeridge Lndg 28546
Lakeside Ct 28546
Lakewood Ct & Dr 28546
Lamm Ln 28540
Lancaster Ct 28540
Lance Ct 28546
Lancer Ln 28546
Lands End Ln 28540
Langtry St 28540
Lanier Dr 28546
Lansing Ct 28540
Lanza Pl 28546
Laran Rd 28540
Laredo Dr 28540
Lariat Ln 28546
Lasalle Ln 28546
Lasso Loop 28546
Lauradale Apts 28540
Laurel Ln 28546
Lava Ct 28540
Lee Ct 28546
Lee Dr 28540
Lees Ln 28546
Lejeune Blvd
900-1599 28540
1601-1897 28546
1899-2499 28546
Lela Ln 28540
Lemon Tree Ln 28540
Len South Dr 28546
Lennox Cir 28546
Lenox St 28546
Leonard St 28540
Lewis St 28546
Lib Ln 28540
Liberty Dr 28546
Liberty Crossing Apts 28540
Liberty Park Rd 28540
Limeston Dr 28546
Lincolnton Ct & Way 28546
Linda Dr & Loop 28546
Lindsey Dr 28540
Lindsey James Ln 28540
Lindsey Paige Ln 28546
Linton Trailer Park 28546
Linwood Dr 28546
Lionel Ave 28540
Lisa Ct 28540
Little Cardinal Ct 28540
Little Creek Ct 28546
Little Man Ln 28540
Little Rabbit Way 28540
Little Roxy Ct 28540
Littlejohn Ave 28546
Littleleaf Ct 28540
Live Oak Dr 28540
Loblolly Ct 28540
Locust Ct 28546

Logan Ct 28540
Logan Douglas Ln 28540
London Ct & Ln 28546
London Berry Ln 28540
Long Acre Dr 28546
Longstaff St 28540
Loop Road Rentals 28540
Lorraine Ct 28540
Louie Ln 28540
Louise Ave 28540
Louvre Ln 28546
Loxley Ct 28546
N & S Loy Ave 28540
Loyola Dr 28540
Luann Rd 28540
Lucinda Ln 28540
Lulu Jarman Ln 28540
Lynchburg Ct & Dr 28546
Lynn Ct 28540
Mabry Ct 28546
Madison Ct 28546
Magnolia Ln 28546
Magnolia Gardens Dr 28540
Mahogany Dr 28540
Maiden Ct & Ln 28546
Majestic Ln 28546
Mallard Dr 28540
Mandarin Trl 28540
Maple St 28540
Maplehurst Dr & Rd 28540
Maplewood Ct 28546
Marapese Ln 28540
Marble Ct 28546
Maready Rd 28546
Marian Pl 28546
Marie St 28546
Marina Ct 28540
Marine Blvd 28540
N Marine Blvd
2507A-2507C 28546
1-101 28540
103-1599 28540
1600-3499 28546
S Marine Blvd 28540
Marine Plz 28546
Marion Ct 28546
Mariposa Ct 28546
Marissa Ct 28540
Mark Ln 28546
Market St
1-99 28540
100-599 28546
Marlene Dr 28546
Marley Ct 28540
Marlo Cir 28540
Mars Dr 28546
Marseille Ct 28546
Marshall Chapel Rd 28546
Marshall Farm Rd 28546
Martha Ln 28540
Massey Ct & Rd 28546
Matthew Ct 28546
May Ct 28540
Mayfair Ct 28546
Mayfield Ct 28540
Maynard Blvd 28546
Maypatch Rd 28546
Mcarthur Dr 28546
Mcavoy St 28540
Mccall Dr 28540
Mccallister Rd 28540
Mccoy Ln 28546
Mcdaniel Dr 28546
Mcgowan Rd 28540
Mckinnon Pl 28540
Mcrae Ct 28546
Meadow Ln & Trl 28546
Meadow Oaks Ct 28546
Meadowbrook Ln 28546
Meadowbrook Apts 28546
Meadowview Ct 28546
Meadowview Rd 28540
Medlock Pl 28540
Melody Ln 28540
Memorial Ct & Dr 28546
Memory Ln 28546

Mendover Dr 28546
Mercer Rd 28546
Merin Height Rd 28546
Merlin Ct 28546
Mesa Ln 28546
Middle St 28546
Middleton Pl 28540
Mike Loop Rd 28546
Mildred Ave 28540
Mildred Thomas Ct 28540
Milestone Ct 28546
Milford St 28540
Mill Ave 28540
Mill Pond Rd 28546
Mill River Rd 28540
Millie Ln 28540
Mills Ct 28540
Mimosa Cir 28540
Miracle Dr 28546
Misty Ln 28546
Mitchell Rd 28540
Mitchell Trailer Park 28540
Mittams Point Dr 28546
Mohawk Trl 28546
Monarch Ln 28540
Monk Ln 28546
Monteith St 28540
Montford Ln 28546
Moonstone Ct 28546
Moosehart Ave 28540
Moosehaven Rd 28546
Morgan Cir 28546
Morgan View Ln 28540
Morning Dr 28546
Morningside Dr 28540
Morris Ct 28540
Morths Ln 28540
Morton Rd 28546
Morton St 28540
Morton Farm Rd 28546
Morton Trailer Park 28546
Moseley Dr 28540
Moss Creek Dr 28540
Mossy Oak Ln 28540
Muhammad Rd 28540
Mulberry Ln 28546
Mullholland Pl 28546
Murifield Dr 28540
Murphy Dr 28540
Murrill Hill Rd 28540
Murville Ct 28546
My Way 28546
Myna Dr 28540
Myrtle Pl 28546
Myrtlewood Cir 28546
Nace Jarman Ln 28540
Nancy Dr 28540
Nassau Ln 28546
Nature Dr 28546
Navarro Loop 28540
Navy Blue Dr 28540
Needmore Dr 28540
Nelson Ct & Dr 28540
Neptune Ln 28540
Nere Ln 28540
New St 28546
New Bern Hwy 28546
New Bridge St 28546
New Castle Dr 28546
New Fronteir St 28546
New Hanover Trl 28546
New Miracle Pl 28546
New River Dr 28546
Newberry St 28540
Newbold Rd 28546
Newbold Trailer Park 28540
Newell St 28540
Newhan Ct & Ln 28546
Newport Dr 28540
Nia Ct 28546
Nicolas Andrew Ct 28546
Nicole Ct 28540
Nikki Ln 28540
Nina Ct 28540
Noble Ct & Ln 28546
Nordell St 28540

North Dr 28540
Northridge Apts 28546
Northview Ct 28546
Northwest Cir 28546
Northwoods Dr 28540
Nottingham Rd 28546
Novel Ln 28546
Oak Dr 28546
Oak Ln 28540
Oak St 28540
Oak Dr Ext 28546
Oak Hill Ct 28546
Oak Hills Trailer Park 28540
Oaklawn Ct 28546
Oakley Trl 28540
Oakwood Ave, Ct & Dr 28546
Oci Dr 28540
Ocracoke Ct 28546
Odell Ln 28540
Office Park Dr 28546
Old 30 Rd 28540
Old Beechtree Ln 28540
Old Bridge St 28540
Old Bridge Street Ext 28540
Old Chadwick Ln 28540
Old Crist Ln 28540
Old Dam Rd 28540
Old Glory Ln 28540
Old Hickory Est 28540
Old Loy Ave 28540
Old Maplehurst Rd 28540
Old Northwest Bridge Rd 28540
Old Pond Ct 28540
Old Post Ct 28546
Old Stone 28546
Old Tar Landing Rd 28540
Old Timber Rd 28540
Old Wilmington Rd 28540
Oldtowne St 28546
Ole Henry Ln 28540
Ole Pine Trailer Park 28540
Oleander St 28540
Olive Ct 28540
Olivewood Ln 28546
Onslow Dr 28540
Onslow Pines Rd 28540
N Onsville Dr & Pl 28546
Onyx Ct 28546
Opal Ln 28546
Oriole Ct 28546
Orkney Dr 28540
Ormandy Ave 28546
Ornate Dr 28546
Osage Ln 28546
Otto Ln 28546
Overdale Cir 28546
Owens Aly 28546
Oxford Dr 28546
Pacer Ln 28540
Pactolous Dr 28546
Paddock Pl 28546
Paderick Ct 28546
Page Dr 28540
Palace Cir 28546
Palamino Ct & Trl 28546
Palm Pl 28546
Palmetto Ct 28546
Pantego Ct 28546
Papa John Ln 28540
Par Dr 28540
Park Ln & Pl 28546
W Park Shop Ctr 28546
Park Wood Dr 28546
N Parker Rd 28546
Parkway Ct & Dr 28540
Pasture Ln 28540
Patrick St 28540
Patrick Alan Ln 28540
Patriot Pl 28540
Paula Pl 28546
Pawn Ct 28546
Peach Ln 28540
Peachtree Dr 28540
Pearl Ct 28540

Pearl Valley Ct 28546
Pease Ct 28546
E & W Pebble Ct & Ln 28546
Pebble Creek Ct 28546
Pebble Island Ln 28546
Pebble Spruce 28546
Pecan Ct & Ln 28546
Peeds Trailer Park 28540
Peerce St 28546
Pekin St 28540
Pelletier Pl 28540
Penguin Ln 28546
Pennington St 28540
Penny Ln 28546
Penrose Ct 28540
Peppertree Ct 28540
Periwinkle Ct 28546
Perry Dr 28546
Persimmon Ct 28546
Pet Ln 28540
Peters Ln 28546
Petteway Dr & Ln 28546
Phillips Rd 28540
Phoenix Park Dr 28546
Pickett Rd 28540
Pine Ct & St 28540
N & S Pine Cone Ln 28546
Pine Crest Dr 28546
Pine Thicket Ln 28546
Pine Valley Ct & Rd 28546
Pine View Trailer Park 28540
Pinegrove Ct 28546
Pinetown Rd 28546
Pineview Rd 28546
Pinewood Ct & Dr 28546
Piney Ln 28540
Piney Green Rd 28546
Pink Ln 28540
Pintail Ct 28546
Pinto Pl 28546
Pinyon Ct 28546
Piper St 28540
Pisgah Ct 28546
N Plain St 28540
Plantation Blvd 28540
Planters Ln 28546
Player Ct 28540
Plaza Dr 28540
Plaza Manor Ct 28546
Pleasant Ct 28540
Plow Point Ln 28546
Plum Ln 28540
Plum Pointe Plz 28540
Pluto Ln 28540
Pocosin Ct 28540
Pollard Dr & Ln 28546
Pommel Ct 28540
Pompano Pl 28546
Ponderosa Dr 28540
Ponderosa Pl 28546
Pony Express Trl 28546
Pony Farm Rd 28540
Poplar St 28540
Poplar Ridge Rd 28546
Porters Ridge Rd 28540
Preston Dr & Rd 28540
Primrose Ct 28546
Princess Pl 28540
Princeton Dr 28546
Profit Ln 28540
Progress Way 28546
Providence Dr 28546
Provincial Ln 28546
W Pueblo Dr 28546
Puller Dr 28540
Puppy Ln 28540
Quail Hollow Dr 28540
Quail Ridge Rd 28546
Quaker Bridge Rd 28546
Quality Ln 28540
Quarterhorse Ln 28546
Quartz Dr 28540
Quartz Ln 28546
Queens Rd 28540
Rachel Pl 28540

Radcliffe Cir 28546
Radford St 28540
Radiant Dr 28546
Rae Ct 28540
Rag Ln 28540
Ragged Point Ct 28546
E & W Railroad St 28540
Rainbow Dr 28546
Rainmaker Dr 28540
Raintree Cir, Dr & Rd 28540
Ramona Ave & Ct 28540
Ramsey Ct 28546
Ramsey Dr 28540
Ramsey Rd 28546
Ramsey Loop Rd 28546
Randy Ct 28540
Raven Ln 28546
Ravenscroft Way 28540
Ravenwood Dr 28546
Rawls Ct 28540
Ray Rhodes Ln 28546
Raynor Ave 28540
Rea St 28546
Recreation Cir 28546
Red Leaf Ct 28540
Red Man Rd 28540
E Red Oak Ct 28546
W Red Oak Ct 28546
Red Oak St 28540
Redemption Ct 28546
Redhead Ct 28540
Redwood Ct & Pl 28546
Regalwood Dr 28546
E & W Regent Ct 28546
Reid Ct N & S 28540
Renee Ct 28546
Republic Ct 28540
Rex Ct 28546
Rhodes Ln 28540
Rhodestown Rd 28540
Rhodestwn Fire Dept Rd 28540
Rich Ln 28540
Richards Dr 28540
Richlands Ave & Hwy 28540
Richmond Dr 28540
E & W Ridge Ct, Dr & Rd 28540
Ridge View Dr 28540
Ridgecrest Ln 28546
Ridgeway Ct 28546
Ridgewood Ct 28546
Riggs St 28540
Rising Sun Ln 28540
Rita Pl 28540
Rivendale Ct 28546
River Ct, Dr & St 28540
River Bend Rd 28540
River Bluff Ct & Dr 28540
River View Ct 28540
River Winding Rd 28540
Riverbirch Pl 28546
Rivers Edge Ct 28540
Riverstone Ct 28546
Riverwalk Lndg 28540
Roan Ct 28546
Robert Ln 28540
Robin Rd 28540
Robinhood Dr 28546
Robinson Dr 28540
Roblee Dr 28540
Rock Creek Dr N & S 28540
Rockford Ct 28540
Rockledge Ct 28546
Rocky Run Rd 28546
Rodeo Ln 28540
Rogers Ave 28540
Ronny Ct 28546
Roosevelt Rd 28546
Rosewood Cir 28546
Roswell Ln 28546
Royal Ct & Dr 28546
Royal Bluff Rd 28540
Royce Ave 28540
Ruddy Ct 28546
Running Rd 28546

Runnymeade Dr 28540
Rustic Ln 28546
Rusty Ct 28540
Ruth St 28540
Rutherford Way 28540
Rye Mill Ct 28540
Saber St 28546
Sabrina Ct 28540
Saddle Ln 28546
Saddle Ridge Ct 28540
Sage Ct & Pl 28540
Sagefield Dr 28540
Saint Charles Ln 28546
Saint George Cv 28546
Salem Ln 28546
E & W Saltwood Pl 28540
Samuel Run Dr 28546
San Antonio Trl 28546
Sand Ct 28546
Sand Hill Rd 28540
Sanders St 28540
Sandhills Trailer Park 28540
Sandlin Dr 28540
Sands Ct 28546
Sandstone Ct 28546
Sandy Dr 28546
Santa Fe Trl 28546
Sara Kay Est & Ln 28546
Sarah Ct 28540
Saturn Ln 28540
Savannah Dr 28546
Savoy Ln 28546
Saw Briar Ct 28540
Saw Mill Ln 28546
Schall Pl 28540
School St 28540
Scientific Ln 28540
Scotsdale Ct & Dr 28546
Scott Ave 28546
Scott Jenkins Rd 28540
Sedgefield Ct 28540
Seminole Trl 28540
Serena Dr 28546
Settlers Cir 28546
Seville St 28546
Sewell Rd 28540
Shad Boat Ct 28546
Shadow Brook Dr 28546
Shadowood Dr 28540
Shadowridge Rd 28546
Shadwell Dr 28540
Shady Ct 28540
Shady Knoll Ln 28546
Shady Oak Ln 28546
Shadyside Ct 28540
Shamrock Dr 28540
Sharon Way 28546
Sharp Ln 28546
Sheffield Rd 28546
N & S Sheila Ct 28540
Shelby Dr 28540
Shell Ln 28546
Shelmore Ln 28546
Shelton Ln 28546
Shenandoah Rd 28546
Sherwood Rd 28540
Shetland Pl 28546
Shifting Winds 28546
Shipmans Pike 28546
Shirley Dr 28540
N & S Shore Dr 28546
Shoreham Dr 28546
Shoreline Dr 28540
Shroyer Cir 28546
Sidesaddle Ln 28546
Sidney Ln 28540
Sierra Pl 28546
Silance Rd 28540
Silver Hills Dr 28546
Silver Stream Way 28546
Silverleaf Dr 28546
Simpson St 28546
Singletree Ct & Dr 28540
Sioux Ct & Dr 28540
Siskin Ct 28546
Sitton Pl 28546

Skipping Stone Ln 28546
Sky Blue Ln 28540
Skye Ct 28546
Slate Ct 28546
Small Leaf Ct 28546
Smallwood Dr 28540
Sofia Ct 28540
Softwood Ct 28540
Solar Ln 28546
Solomon Dr 28546
Somerset Cv 28546
Sonoma Rd 28546
Sophia Dr 28540
Sourwood Ct 28540
South Dr 28540
Southbridge Dr 28546
Southwest Dr 28540
Southwoods Ln 28540
Spanish Trl 28546
Spargo St 28540
Sparkling Brook Way 28546
Spencer Ct 28546
Spinnaker Pl 28546
Spring Ct, Dr & St 28540
Spring Branch Trailer Park 28540
Spring Leaf Ln 28540
Spring Meadows Cir 28546
Spring Villa Ct & Dr 28540
Springdale Dr 28540
E & W Springhill Ter 28546
Springwood Dr 28546
Spruce Ct 28546
Stable Ln 28540
Stafford Ln 28546
N & S Stage Coach Trl 28546
Stagecoach Dr 28546
Stallion Dr 28540
Staples Mill Rd 28540
Starling St 28540
Starwood Cir 28540
Starwood Trailer Park 28540
Stateside Blvd 28546
Station St 28546
Steadfast Way 28540
Steeple Chase Ct 28546
Steller Rd 28540
N & S Stephanie Ct 28540
Stephens Ln 28546
Stepping Stone Trl 28546
Sterling Ct & Rd 28546
Sterling Farms Rd 28546
Steve Aman Dr 28546
Stewart Ct 28546
Still Forest Pl 28540
Stillbrook Ct 28546
Stillwater Cv 28546
Stillwood Cir, Ct, Dr & Rd 28540
Stone Ct 28540
Stone Gate 28546
Stone Point Ln 28540
Stonecroft Ln 28546
Stonemark Ct 28540
Stoneridge Dr 28546
Stonewall Ave 28546
Stonewater Ln 28546
Stoney Creek Dr 28540
Stony Brook Way 28546
Stratford Rd 28540
Strawberry Ln 28540
Streamwood Dr 28546
Stuart Ct 28540
Stump Grove Ct 28540
Stumpy Ln 28540
Suffolk Cir & Ct 28546
Sugar Ct 28540
Sugarberry Ct 28546
Sugarwood Ct 28546
Summer Ln 28546
Summerbrook Pl 28540
Summercreek Dr 28546
Summerfield Ct 28546
Summersill Dr 28540
Summersill School Rd 28540

Sumner St 28540
Sumter St 28540
Sunny Vale Ct 28540
Sunset Rd 28546
Sunset Strip 28540
Sunstone Ct 28546
Surrey Dr 28540
Surry Ct 28540
Sussex Ct 28540
Suzanne Ct 28540
Swains Loop Rd 28546
Swamp Junction Rd 28546
Sweet Melissa Ln 28546
Sweetwater Dr 28540
Sword St 28546
Sybil St 28540
Sycamore Dr 28546
Sycamore Pl 28540
Sycamore St 28546
Tall Oak Ct 28546
Tallman St 28540
Talon Cir & Dr 28546
Tamarack Ct 28546
Tanager Ct 28546
Tanbark Dr 28546
Tanglewood Dr 28540
Tara Pl 28540
Tarpon Trl 28546
Taylor St 28540
Tee Ln 28540
Terrace Ct 28546
Terry Ln 28546
Terry Lee Lanier Dr 28546
Texie Ln 28546
Thames Dr 28546
Thelma Ruth Ct 28540
Theresa Ln 28540
W Thomas Dr 28546
Thomas Humphrey Rd 28546
Thomas Loop Rd 28540
E Thompson St 28540
Thorn Ln 28540
Thorn Tree Ct 28540
Thornberry Pl 28540
Three Bridge Estates
Cir 28540
Threshing Ct 28540
Thrush Ct 28546
Thyme Ct 28540
Tiffany Ct & Pl 28546
Tiffin Ct 28546
Tiger Hill Dr 28546
Tillage Ct 28540
Timber Ln 28540
Timberlake Trl 28546
Timmerman St 28540
Timothy Rd 28546
Tina Ln 28540
Titus Ln 28540
Tobe Ln 28540
Toni Dr 28546
Topaz Dr 28546
Torrence Ave 28540
Tory Cir 28540
Totem Dr 28546
Toudle Ln 28540
Tower Dr 28546
Town Point Rd 28540
Townsend Pl 28546
Trailwood Trailer Park 28540
Treehaven Ln 28540
Treetop Ct 28540
Trenton Pl 28546
Triple C Ln 28540
Trotter St 28540
Trotters Run 28546
Troy Ave 28540
Trudie Ln 28540
Tryon Ct 28546
Tucker Ln 28540
Tucson Ct 28540
Tundra Pl 28540
Tupelo Ct 28546
Turner Ln 28540
Turquoise Dr 28546
Turtle Creek Ct 28540

Tweed Dr 28540
Twinlakes Trailer Park 28540
Twinwood Ct & Dr 28546
Tyler Ct 28540
Tyndall Trailer Park 28540
University Dr 28546
Uranus Ln 28540
Utica Rd 28540
Valencia Ct & Dr 28546
Valley Ct 28540
Valley Ridge Ln 28540
Vandergrift Dr 28540
Vandermere Pl 28540
Vauhan Ct 28540
Venus Ct & Rd 28546
Vera Dr 28540
Vera Elizabeth Ln 28540
Verdie Ave 28540
Vernon Dr 28540
Vernon Shepard Ln 28540
Verona Rd 28540
Victoria Rd 28546
Victory Way 28540
Vilas Way N & S 28546
Villa Dr 28546
Village Cir, Ct & Dr 28546
Vulcan Cir 28540
Walden Pl 28546
Walkens Woods Ln 28546
Wallace Creek Trailer
Park 28546
Waller Ln 28540
Wallis St 28546
Walnut Dr
1-1 28546
3-19 28546
21-21 28546
100-999 28540
Walnut Creek Ct & Dr 28546
Walter Lanier Rd 28540
Waltmore St 28540
Wantland St 28540
Ward St 28540
Ward Darst Plz 28540
Wardola Dr 28540
Warlick St 28540
Warn St 28540
Warren Ct 28546
Warren Dr 28540
Warrenton Way 28546
Warrenton Way Ct 28546
Washington Dr 28546
Waterfall Dr 28540
Waters Rd 28546
Waterstone Ln 28540
Waverly Way 28540
Weatherford Dr 28540
Weatherington Rd 28546
Webb Ct 28546
Webbs Apts 28546
Webster Ln 28546
Wedgewood Dr 28546
Weeping Hollow Ct 28546
Weeping Willow Ln 28540
Wellington Pl 28546
Wells Rd 28540
Welsh Ln 28546
Welton Cir 28546
Wesleyan Ct 28546
West Ct 28546
Weste Ave 28540
Western Blvd 28546
Westminister Dr 28540
Westmont Rd 28540
Westmoreland Dr 28546
Westridge Est 28540
Westwind Ct 28546
Wetherington Trailer
Park 28546
Whaley Field Rd 28546
Whispering Winds Ln 28546
Whitby Ct & Ln 28540
White St 28546
White Oak Blvd 28546
White Oak Ct 28546
White Oak St 28540

White Place Ln 28540
White Stone Ct 28546
Whitecap Lake Rd 28540
Whitehall Ln 28546
Whiteleaf Dr 28546
Wickersham Ct 28540
Wigeon Rd 28540
Wilbur Rd 28540
Wilda Dr 28546
Wildwood Dr 28546
Willbarry Rd 28540
William Sharp Way 28546
Williams Dr, Pl, Rd &
St 28540
Williamsburg Pkwy 28546
Willie Kellum Rd 28546
Willis Pkwy 28546
Willis Lake Dr 28546
Willoughby Ln 28546
N & S Willow Ln 28546
E & W Willowood Ln 28546
Wilmington Hwy 28540
Wilson Ct 28546
Wiltshire Ct 28546
Winchester Rd 28546
E & W Windgate Ct 28546
Windham Ct & Ln 28540
Windmill Ln 28540
Windsong Ct 28540
Windsor Cir, Ct & Pl 28546
Windy Bluff Ct 28540
Windy Branch Way 28540
Winestone Pl 28546
Winfall Ct 28546
Winn Ct 28540
Winners Cir N & S 28546
Winson Green Ln 28546
Winter Ct, Pl & Rd 28540
Winterberry Ct 28540
Winterlochen Dr 28540
Winthrope Way 28546
Wisteria Rd 28546
Wolf Glen Ct 28546
Wolf Laurel Ct 28546
Wolf Run Dr & Ln 28546
Wolf Swamp Rd 28546
Wolverine Pl 28546
Woodberry Pl 28540
Woodbridge Ct 28546
Woodbury Farm Dr 28540
Woodcrest Ct 28540
Woodhaven Dr 28540
Woodlake Ct 28546
Woodland Dr 28540
Woodlawn Dr 28546
Woodleaf Ln 28540
Woodleaf Pl 28546
Woodside Ct 28546
Woodview Ct 28540
Workshop Ln 28546
Worthington Pl 28546
Wren Ct 28546
Wt Whitehead Dr 28546
Wynbrookee Ln 28546
Wyndham Pl 28540
Wynstone Ln 28540
Wythe Grv 28546
Yale Cir 28546
Yankee Ln 28540
Yaupon Dr 28546
Yearling Loop 28540
Yellowwood Dr 28546
Yopp Rd 28540
York Ct & St 28540
Yorkshire Dr 28546
Yucca Ct 28546
Yukon Ct 28546
Zack Cir 28540
Zack Elwood Ct 28540
Zaner Dr 28540
Zircon Ct 28546

NUMBERED STREETS

2nd Ave 28546
2nd St 28540
3rd Ave 28546
3rd St 28540
4th Ave 28546
5th Ave 28546

KANNAPOLIS NC

General Delivery 28081

POST OFFICE BOXES MAIN OFFICE STATIONS AND BRANCHES

Box No.s
1 - 7020 28082
8091 - 9998 28081

NAMED STREETS

W A St 28081
A Bare St 28081
Abby Ln 28081
Academy St 28081
Acadia Ct 28083
Addison Cir 28083
Afton Rd 28081
Aggie Ave 28083
Aiken St 28081
Aileen Ave 28081
Airline Dr 28083
Airport Rd 28081
Akron Ave 28081
Alabama Ave 28083
Alder St 28081
Aldwick St 28081
Alexa Ave 28083
Alexander Ave 28083
Alexander Rd 28081
Allen St 28083
Allman Farm Rd 28081
Alma Ave 28081
Alpine St 28081
Alton Ln 28083
Amanda Dr 28081
Anchor Way NE 28083
Angela Ln 28083
Ann St 28081
Annex Ave 28083
Anson Ave 28081
Applewood Ave & St 28081
Aqua Ln 28081
N & S Arbor Ave 28081
Archie Ln 28083
Arden Ave 28081
Arizona Pl 28081
Arlene Ave 28081
Arlington Ave 28083
Arnette Dr 28081
Ashby St 28081
Ashe Ave 28083
Ashland Rd 28083
Ashmont Dr 28081
Ashwood St 28081
Athens Hls 28083
Athens St 28081
Atlanta St 28081
Atlantic Ct 28081
Auburn St 28081
Austin Ave 28083
Austin Run Ct 28083
Autumn Ln 28083
Avalon Dr 28081
N Avenue Ext 28083
Azalea Ave 28081
W B St 28081
Back Acres Ln 28081
Back Bay Ct NE 28083
Bahama Dr 28081
Bailey St 28081
Baker St 28081
Baldwin Ave 28083
Balsam Ave 28081
Baltimore Ln 28081
Bamboo Ln 28081
Barbara Ann Cir 28083
Barber St 28081
Barlow Ave 28081
Barncliff Ct 28081
Barnette St 28083
Barnhardt Ave 28083
Barons Ridge Rd 28081
Basin Ave 28083
Basinger Ln 28083
Baylor St 28083
Bealgray Rd 28081
Beaumont Ave 28083
Beaver Ln 28081
Beaver Rd 28081
Beaver St 28083
Beaver Lane Ext 28081
Beaver Leyvas Way 28081
Beaver Pond Rd 28083
Beechwood St 28081
Beendow St 28081
Bel Aire Ave 28083
Bell St 28081
Belva St 28081
Ben Ave 28081
Berkshire Dr 28081
Bernard Ave 28083
Bertha St 28083
Bertie Ave 28081
Bessie St 28081
Beth Dr 28083
Bethpage Rd 28081
Betty St 28083
Beuna St 28081
Billy St 28083
Biotechnology Ln 28081
Birch St 28081
Bismark Ave 28081
Black Maple Dr 28081
Blackhawk Dr 28083
Blackwelder Ave 28081
Blair St 28083
Blake Rd 28081
Blue Crown Ct 28081
Blue Jay Dr 28081
Blue Springs Dr 28081
Bo Dr 28083
Boone Ave 28081
Bost St 28081
Bostian Ave 28083
Bostian Oaks Ln 28081
Boston Grace Ln 28081
Boulevard Park Cir 28083
Boxwood Ct 28081
Boy Scout Camp Rd 28081
Boyd St 28081
Bradford Dr 28083
Brady Ave 28083
Branch Ave 28083
Brancy St 28081
Brantley Rd 28083
Brantley Creek Dr 28083
Brat Ln 28081
Brecken Ct 28081
Breckenridge Rd 28083
Breden St 28081
Brentwood Cir 28081
Briarcliff Dr 28081
Briarwood St 28081
Bridgeport Dr 28081
Brighton Cir & Dr 28081
Broad St 28081
Brodie Ct 28083
Brook Ave & St 28083
Brookcrest Dr 28081
Brookdale St 28083
Brookhaven Dr 28083
Brookshire Ave 28083
Brookside Ave 28081
Brookview Ave 28081
Browdis Ave 28083
Brumley Ct 28081
Brushwood Ave 28083
Bryan Ave 28083
Buddy Ln 28081
Buffalo St 28081
Buick Ave 28083
Bunker Ct 28081
Burgin St 28081
Burke St 28081
Burning Lantern Ln 28081
Butler Ct 28083
Buttercup Ln 28081
E C St 28083
W C St 28081
Cabarrus Arms Dr 28081
Cade Ln 28081
Cadillac St 28083
Calab Dr 28081
Caldwell St 28083
California St 28083
Callie St 28081
Cambridge St 28083
Cambrook Ct 28081
Camden Ave 28081
Camp Cabarrus Dr 28081
Camp Julia Rd 28083
Campbell Rd 28081
Candlewyck Ct 28081
Caneview Ct 28083
Cannon Ave 28081
N Cannon Blvd 28083
S Cannon Blvd 28083
Canterbury Dr 28081
Canyon Ln 28083
Captains Watch 28083
Cardinal Ct 28083
Caremoor Pl 28081
Caribean Ct 28081
Carlton Ave 28083
Carolina Ave 28083
Carolyn Ave 28083
Carriage House Dr 28081
Carriage Woods Ln 28081
Carsil Way 28083
Carson Ct 28083
Carter St 28083
Carver St 28083
Carwen Ct 28081
Caswell Ave 28081
Cavin Ln 28081
Cedar Ave 28081
Cedar Brook Dr 28081
Cedar Creek Rd 28083
Cedar Hill Dr 28083
Cedar Park Dr 28081
Celia St 28083
Center St 28083
Centergrove Rd 28083
Centerview St 28083
Central Ave 28081
Central Dr
700-2099 28083
6400-6499 28081
Century Dr 28081
Chamar Cir 28081
Chambers St 28083
Chantilly Ct 28081
S Chapel St 28083
Chapman Ave 28081
Chardonnay Cir 28081
Charles St 28083
Charles Towne Ct 28083
Charleston Ave 28081
Charlie Walker Rd 28081
Cherry Brook Ct 28083
Cherry Wood St 28081
Chesapeake Dr 28083
Cheshire Pl 28081
Chestnut Ave 28081
Chiccarello Dr 28081
Chics Pond Rd 28081
Chilton Pl 28081
China Grove Rd 28083
Chipola St 28083
Chisolm Trl 28081
Chris Dr 28081
Chris Ann Ln 28083
Christina Ct 28083
Christy Cir 28081
Chrysler St 28083
Church Ave & Ct 28081
Churchview St 28081
Cimmaron Cir 28081
Cinco Ave 28081
Circle Dr & St 28081
Circlewood Dr 28081
Citadel Ct 28083
Clanton Ct 28083
Clawson St 28081
Clay St 28083
Clear Brook Dr 28083
Clemson Ct 28083
Clermont Ave 28081
Cliffside Dr 28081
Clifton St 28081
Climbing Peace Ct 28081
Cloverfield Dr 28081
Cloverleaf Pkwy & Plz 28083
Clydesdale Ct 28081
Coach St 28083
Coach House Ln 28081
Cobb St 28081
Coggins St 28083
Cold Water Ext 28083
Coldwater Ridge Dr 28083
Cole St 28083
Coleraine Ave 28081
Coley St 28083
Coliseum Ave 28083
Collins St 28083
Colonial Dr 28081
Colony Dr 28081
Colorado Ln 28081
Commonwealth Dr 28083
Concord Lake Rd 28083
Congress Ct 28083
Cook St 28083
Cool Springs Ct 28083
Cooper Ave 28081
Coopers Ridge Dr 28083
Copel St 28083
Copper Creek Trl 28081
Copperhead Rd 28081
Cora St 28083
Corriher St 28081
Cosby St 28081
Cottage Ct 28081
Cottage Dr 28083
Cottage Rd 28081
Countryside Dr 28081
County Down Ave 28081
Coupe St 28083
Courtland Ct 28081
Cove Rd 28081
Coventry Rd 28081
Cowan St 28083
Cox Ave 28081
Craven Ave 28083
Crescent St 28081
Crest St 28081
Crestmont St 28081
Crestwood Ct 28083
Crestwood Dr 28081
Cricket Ct 28083
Cripple Creek Rd 28081
Crofton Ave 28081
Crooked Oak Ln 28081
Crosby St 28081
Cross St 28081
Crosswinds Ct 28083
Crystal Ln 28081
Cub St 28081
Curecanti Ct 28083
Cypress Ave 28081
E D St 28083
W D St
100-499 28083
500-699 28081
Dakota St 28083
Dale Ave & St 28081
Dale Earnhardt Blvd
100-999 28081
1000-3099 28083
Dalewood Ave 28083
Dallas St 28083
Dalrymple St 28083

Danfield Dr 28081
Daniels St 28081
Danlow Dr 28081
Danville Dr 28081
Dare Dr 28083
Dark Hollow Rd 28081
Darty St 28081
Davie Ave 28081
Davis St 28081
Dawn St 28081
Dawson St 28081
Daybreak Rdg 28081
Daybrook Dr 28081
Dean Dr 28081
Deaton St 28081
Debbie Cir & St 28083
Delane St 28083
Delco St 28081
Dellwood Dr 28081
Dennis Ave 28081
Denny Rumple Rd 28081
Denver St 28083
Denwood St 28083
Derbyshire Rd 28081
Desoto Ave 28083
Devonshire Dr 28081
Dexter St 28081
Dial St 28083
Diesel Leak Ln 28081
Dillery Ct 28083
Dixie Dr 28083
Dixon Ave 28081
Doby St 28081
Dodge St 28083
Dog Days Ln 28081
Dogwood Ave, Blvd, Dr & Ln 28081
Donegal Dr 28081
Doris St 28083
Dot Ave 28083
Douglas St 28083
Dovefield Ln 28081
Dover St 28081
Drakestone Rd 28081
Draper Ln 28081
Due West St 28081
Duke St 28081
Duke Adam St 28083
Dundee Dr 28083
Dunlap St 28081
Dunnmon Dr 28081
Dusty Oaks Trl 28081
Dyer St 28083
E E St 28083
Eagle St 28081
Earle St 28081
Earley Cir & St 28083
N & S East Ave 28083
Eastminister Dr 28083
Eastway Ave 28083
Eastwood Dr 28083
Ebenezer Rd 28083
Echerd St 28083
Echo Ave 28081
Eddie Ave 28081
Eddleman Rd 28083
Edgewood Ave 28081
Edinburg Dr 28083
Edsel Ct 28083
Edwards St 28083
El Paso St 28083
Elder Ln 28083
Elizabeth Ave 28083
Ellerbe Dr 28083
Elliot Jacob Ave 28083
Ellis St 28083
Elm St 28081
Elon St 28081
Elsinore Ln 28081
Elwood St 28081
Emanuel St 28081
Emily Ivy Ct 28083
Englewood St 28083
N & S Enochville Ave, Cir & Rd 28081
Enochville School Rd 28081
Entrance Rd 28083
Ervin Woods Dr 28081
Esther Cir 28083
Ethan Dr 28081
Evandale Rd 28081
Evelyn Ave 28083
Evergreen Ave 28081
Evermore Cir 28081
Evie Dr 28083
Excel Dr 28081
E F St 28083
W F St 28081
Fairfax St 28083
Fairmont Cir 28083
Fairview St 28083
Fairway Dr 28081
Fanning Springs Dr 28081
Farmbrook Dr 28081
Farmstone Dr 28081
Fellowship Dr 28081
Ferguson Park Dr 28081
Field Ave 28081
Fieldbrook Dr 28081
Fields Manor St 28081
Finch St 28081
Finger St 28083
Fir Ave 28081
Firehouse Dr 28083
Fisher Ridge Rd 28083
Florence Ave 28083
Florida Ave 28083
Flowe Ave 28083
Floyd St 28083
Ford St 28083
Forest Ave 28081
Forest Glen Ln 28081
Forest Park Dr 28083
Forest Pond Rd 28083
Forest Ridge Rd 28083
Forest View Ln 28081
Forestridge Ln 28081
Forrestbrook Dr 28083
Fort Worth St 28083
Fortress Ln 28083
Foster St 28083
Fowler St 28083
Fox Ave 28083
Frances St 28083
Frank St 28081
Franklin Ave 28083
Frederick Ave 28083
Freeze Rd 28081
Friar Tuck Trl 28081
Front St 28083
Furman Ct 28083
W G St 28083
Gaddy St 28081
Gaddy Mobile Home Dr 28081
Galena Ct 28081
Garnet St 28083
Gary St 28081
Gaston Dr 28083
Gateway Center Dr 28081
Gathering Pl 28081
Gault Ave 28081
Gay St 28083
Gee Dr 28081
Gem St 28083
N & S Gemini Springs Dr 28081
Geneva Dr 28081
Genoa St 28083
Georgia Ave 28081
Gessner Ct 28083
Gilling Ct 28081
Ginnie Springs Dr 28081
Glass Ct 28081
Glendale Ave 28081
Glenn Ave 28081
Glenwood St 28083
Goble Ave 28083
Goldfish Rd 28083
Goldston St 28081
Golfcrest Dr 28081
Goodnight Ln 28081
Grace Ave 28083
Graham Ave 28083
Grand Canyon Rd 28081
Grant Ave 28083
Grass St 28081
Gray Barn Ln 28081
Grayson Ln 28081
Graystone Dr 28083
Green St 28083
Greenridge Ln 28081
Greenview Dr 28083
Greystone Mobile Home Park 28083
Grove St 28083
Guinn Ave 28083
Gumtree Dr 28083
Gurley Ave 28083
W H St 28083
Haas Way 28081
Haley St 28083
Hall St 28081
Hallman Rd 28081
Halverson Ct 28083
Hamblin Ct & Rd 28083
Hambridge Ave 28081
Hammock Ln 28083
Hampshire Dr 28081
Hampton Ln 28081
Harbour View Cv NE 28083
N & S Harding Ave 28083
Harkey Ave 28081
Harmon Pl 28083
Harrington Dr & St 28081
Harris Ave 28081
Hartsoe St 28081
Harvard St 28081
Haven St 28083
Hawfield St 28083
Hawthorne St 28083
Haywood Ave 28083
Hazel Ave 28083
Heather Dr 28083
Heather Glen Rd 28081
Heintz St 28081
Helen St 28083
Hemlock Ave 28081
Heritage Ct 28083
Heritage Oaks Dr 28083
Hickory Wood Dr 28083
Hideaway St 28083
High Cliffs Rd 28083
Highland Woods Dr 28083
Hillcrest St 28083
Hillside St 28083
Hilltop Ave 28081
Hilton Ave 28081
Hilton Lake Rd 28083
Hinson St 28081
Hobbs Ave 28083
Hoke St 28081
Holland St 28083
Holly Ave 28081
Homestead Ave 28083
Hopedale St 28083
Horne St 28081
Horseshoe Cir 28083
Horton Ave 28083
Hoskins Dr 28081
Hospice Ln 28081
Houston Ave 28083
Howard Ave 28081
Hudson St 28083
Hunter Ave 28083
Hunter Oak Dr 28083
Hunteridge Ln 28081
Huntingdon Rd 28081
Huron St 28083
Hutton Ave 28081
Hyde St 28083
Ian Patrick Ave 28083
Ians Turn 28081
Idlewood Dr 28083
Independence Sq 28081
Independent Ave 28081
Indiana St 28083
Inez St 28083
Ingram Ave 28083
Innis Ave 28081
Inspired Way 28083
Integra Springs Dr 28081
Irene Ave 28083
Ireton Pl 28083
Iris Ave 28083
Iris Ln 28081
Irish Potato Rd 28083
Isabelle St 28083
Isenhour Ave 28081
Isenhour Rd 28081
Isenhour St 28083
J Ave 28081
J R Ln 28081
J Shreffler Ct 28081
J W Cline Rd 28083
Jack St 28081
Jackson St 28083
Jackson Park Rd 28083
Jacob St 28083
Jamaica Rd 28083
James St 28083
Janie St 28083
Jasper St 28083
Jay Ave 28081
Jaybird Ct 28081
Jayhawk Way 28081
Jean Ave 28083
Jefferson Ave 28081
Jenkins Dr
800-899 28081
6000-6099 28083
Jennie Linn St 28083
Jet St 28083
Jimmy St 28083
Joe St 28083
Johndy Ave 28083
Johnson St 28083
Jolly Dr 28081
Jonathon Ct 28083
Jordan Rd 28083
Joyce St 28083
N & S Juniper Ave & St 28081
Kannapolis Pkwy 28081
Kansas St 28083
Karriker Rd 28081
Kart Dr 28081
Katherine St 28083
Keady Mill Loop 28081
Keever Ave 28083
Keller Ave 28081
Kellswater Bridge Blvd 28081
Kelsey Plz 28081
Kendallwood Ct 28081
Kendra Dr 28081
Kenlough Dr 28081
Kennedy Ave 28083
Kent St 28083
Kentucky St 28083
Kentwood Dr 28081
Kenwood Dr 28081
Kevin Ave 28083
Key West Ave 28081
Kidd St 28083
Kimball St 28081
Kimberly Ln 28083
King Ave 28081
King Arthur Ct 28081
Kingston Dr 28083
Kirk Ave 28083
Kiser Ave 28083
Kizer Ct 28081
Klondale Ave 28081
Klutz St 28083
Knight Ave 28081
Knollwood Dr 28083
Knowles St 28083
Kristen Ln 28083
Lake Circle Dr 28083
Lake Fisher Rd 28083
Lake Hill Dr 28081
Lakeview St 28083
Lakewood Dr 28081
Lamp Post Ln 28081
Lamplighter Dr 28081
Landmark Dr 28083
Lane St 28083
Lantern Way 28081
Lark Dr 28081
Larry Dr 28083
Laugenour Pl 28081
Laundry St 28083
Laura Ave 28083
Laureate Way 28081
Laurel Crest Dr 28081
Lawn Side Pl 28083
Leader Ln 28081
Leazer St 28081
Lee Ave 28081
Legacy Maple Dr 28081
Leisure Park Cir 28083
Lenncass Dr 28081
Lenwood Ln 28083
Leonard Ave 28081
Leroy St 28083
Lighthouse Ln 28081
Lin Oaks Pl 28081
Lincoln St 28083
Linda Ave 28083
Lindsey St 28083
Linn Ave 28083
Little St 28083
Little John Trl 28081
N & S Little Texas Rd 28083
Live Oaks Ct 28081
Living Way 28083
Lock Erne Ave 28081
Lockhart Rd 28083
Locust St 28081
Lombardi St 28081
Long St 28083
Longbow Dr 28081
Longbriar Dr 28081
Longview Ave 28081
Lookout Point Rd 28083
Loop Rd N & S 28081
Louise Ave 28083
Lowe Ave 28083
Lower Pond Rd 28083
Lowrance Ave 28081
Lumber Ln & St 28083
Lydia St 28083
Lyndon St 28083
Lynn St 28083
Lynnview Ct 28081
Mable Ave 28083
Macon St 28081
Madison Ave 28081
Magnolia Ave 28081
Magpie Dr 28081
Maid Marion Ln 28081
N & S Main St 28081
Mallard Pointe Dr 28083
Mann Rd 28083
Manning Pl 28081
Maplanco St 28083
Maple Ave 28083
Maplewood Ave 28083
Margaret Ave 28081
Margate Ave 28083
Marie Ave 28083
Marigold Dr 28083
Marion Ave 28081
Marlin Dr 28081
Marlowe St 28081
Martha St 28083
Martin Cir 28083
Mary St 28083
Mary Wynn Ct 28083
Maryland Ave 28083
Mason St 28081
Matthew Allen Cir 28081
May St 28083
Mayfair Dr 28081
Maywood St 28083
Mcbeth Dr 28083
Mccombs Ave 28083
Mccray Ave 28081
Mccreary St 28081
Mcdaniel Park Dr 28081
Mcgee St 28081
Mcgill St 28081
Mcknight St 28081
Mclain Rd 28083
Mclain Heights Ct 28083
Mclain Road Ext 28083
Mcshag Dr 28081
Meadow Ave 28083
Meadowood Cir 28081
Measmer St 28081
Medlin Ct 28083
Melchor St 28083
Melinda Ave 28083
Memory Wood Dr 28081
Messina Ct 28083
Michelle Dr 28083
Michigan St 28083
Middale St 28083
Middlebury Ct 28081
Midlake Rd 28083
Milestone Ave 28081
Miller Rd & St 28081
Millie St 28081
Milton Ave 28081
Milton St 28083
Miss Daisey Ln 28083
Mission Oaks St 28083
Mission Tripp St 28083
Misty Cv 28083
Misty Ln 28081
Mitchell Glen St 28083
Mocking Bird Ln 28083
Montana Dr 28081
Moorecrest Pl 28083
Mooresville Rd 28081
Moose Rd 28083
Moreland Ave 28081
Morgan Dr 28083
Morningside Ct 28083
Moser St 28081
Moss Ave 28081
Moss Acres Ct 28081
Mount Olivet Rd 28083
Mount Vernon Ave 28083
Mountain St 28081
Mountain Vine Ave 28081
Mullis Rd 28083
Murabito Ln 28083
Murphy St 28081
Nance St 28083
Naomi Ct 28083
Nash Ave 28083
Nathan Ave 28083
Nathaniel Ln 28081
Needle Ct 28081
Nellie St 28083
Nellie Yale Pl 28083
Nevada Pl 28083
Nevada St 28083
New Dawn Ct 28081
New Potato Dr 28083
Newell Ave 28081
Newport Dr 28081
Ney St 28083
Nob Hill Dr 28081
Nola Ave 28083
Norfolk Dr 28081
Norland Ave 28083
Normandy Rd 28083
North Ave 28083
Northcrest Dr 28081
Northdale Ave 28081
Northside St 28081
Norwich Ct 28081
Nottingham Rd 28081
Oak Ave & Cir 28081
Oak Avenue Mall Dr 28081
Oak Grove St 28083
Oak Leaf Way 28081
Oakcrest Dr 28083
Oakdale Ave 28083
Oakhurst Ct 28081
Oakland Dr 28081
N & S Oakmont Dr 28081
Oakridge Dr 28081
Oakshade Ave 28083
Oakwood Ave 28081
Oakwood Villa Dr 28081
October Ln 28081
Odell Dr 28083
Odessa St 28083
Off Kimball Rd 28081
Ohio Ave 28083
Oklahoma St 28083
Old Centergrove Rd 28083
Old Creek Ct 28081
Old Earnhardt Rd 28083
Old Freeze Rd 28081
Old Heritage Rd 28081
Old Plank Rd 28083
Old Salisbury Concord Rd 28083
Old Sapp Rd 28083
Oliphant Ln 28081
Ontario Dr 28083
Onyx Ave 28083
Opal St 28083
Orangewood St 28081
Orchard Ave 28081
Oregon Ave 28083
Osborne Rd 28083
Oval St 28081
Overcash Ave 28081
Overcash Garden Rd 28083
Overcrest Dr 28081
Oxford Dr 28081
Pacific Ct 28081
Packard Ave 28083
Pagemont Rd 28081
Park St 28083
Park Edwards Rd 28081
Parks Field Dr 28083
Parksdale Dr 28083
Patricia Dr 28081
Patterson Ave & Rd 28083
Patton Ln 28081
Payne Rd 28083
Peace Haven Rd 28083
Peach St 28083
Peachtree Dr 28081
Pearl Ave 28083
Pembrook Ln 28081
Pendleton Dr 28081
Pennsylvania Ave 28083
Penny Ln 28083
Penny Earley Ln 28083
Perkins Dr 28083
Petes Pond Rd 28081
Pethel St 28081
Phillips Mobile Home Park 28081
Pickwick Ave 28083
Piedmont Dr 28081
Pine St 28081
Pine Bluff Cir 28081
Pine Cape Ct 28081
Pine Hill Ln 28083
Pinebrook Trl 28081
Pineview St 28083
Pinewood Ave 28081
Planters Ave 28083
Plaza Ave 28081
Pleasant Ave 28081
Pleasant Grove Church Rd 28081
Pleasant Hill Dr 28081
Plum Rd 28081
Plyler Rd 28081
Plymouth St 28083
Poindexter Dr 28081
Polo Ave 28081
Pom Orchid Ln 28081
Pond Ct 28081
Pond Ridge Ct 28083
Pond Side Ct 28083
Poplar Ave 28083
Poplar Glen Dr 28083
Poppy Ln 28083
Power St 28081
Power Line St 28081
Price Ave 28081
Prince St 28083

Princeton Ave 28081
Prism Pl 28083
Pritchard St 28081
Professional Park Dr 28081
Psalms St 28083
Pump Station Rd 28081
Quail Woods Ct 28081
Queens Gate Dr 28083
Quiet Cv 28083
Quill Ct 28083
Quinn Ave 28083
Raccoon Ridge Trl 28083
Rae Ln 28081
Rain Place Ct 28081
Rainbow Dr 28081
Randolph Rd 28081
Rankin St 28081
Raven Dr 28081
Ravendale St 28083
Red St 28081
Red Birch Pl 28081
Red Maple Dr 28081
Redfern Dr 28081
Redleaf Rd 28083
Redwood Ct 28081
Refuge Way 28081
Reid St 28083
Rena St 28081
Renee Ct 28081
Rental Dr 28081
N Research Campus Dr 28081
Rhode Island Ave 28083
Rice St 28081
Richard Ave 28081
Richard St 28083
Richmond Dr 28081
Richwood Cir 28081
N & S Ridge Ave & Rd 28083
Ridgecrest Dr 28081
Ridgeway Dr 28083
Rilan Pl 28081
Riverdale Rd 28081
Roanoke Dr 28081
Roberts Dr 28081
Robin Ave 28081
Robinhood Ln 28081
Robinhood Lane Ext 28081
Rochelle St 28081
Rod Dr 28081
Roger Dale Carter Dr 28081
Rogers Ave 28081
E Rogers Ln 28083
Rogers Lake Rd 28081
Rogers Lake Rd E 28083
Rogue Ct 28083
Rolling Rd 28081
Rolling Ridge Dr 28081
Rollingwood Dr 28081
Romsey Ct 28081
N & S Rose Ave 28083
Rosebud Pl 28083
Rosemary Ave 28083
Rosemont Ave 28081
Rosewood Ave 28081
Ross Ave 28083
Roth Ave 28083
Roxie St NE 28083
Royal Ave 28083
Royce St 28083
Ruby St 28081
Rumple Estates Rd 28081
Running Brook Dr 28081
Russell St 28083
Russell Farm Rd 28081
Ruth Ave 28083
Sabre Dr 28081
Safrit Ave 28083
Saguaro Ln 28083
Saint Joseph St 28083
Sam Broadway Loop 28081
Samantha Dr 28083
Samuel Richard St 28083
Sandy Ct 28083
Sapp Rd 28083
Sardis Ave 28081
Sassy Ln 28081
Scott St 28083
Scottish Square Ln 28083
Seaford Ave 28081
Sears St 28083
Security St 28083
Sedan Ave 28083
Self Rd 28081
Sellers St 28081
Settlers Ridge Dr 28081
Shadowbrook Dr 28081
Shady Cir 28081
Shady Dr 28083
Shady Ln 28083
Shady Brook Dr 28081
Shady Lane Ext Ave 28081
Shady Oaks Cir 28083
Shamrock Dr 28081
Sharon St 28083
Sharon Hills Ct 28083
Sharpe Ave 28083
Sheffield Dr 28083
Shepard St 28083
Sherrill Dr 28081
Sherry Ct 28081
Sherwood Dr & St 28081
Shirley Dr 28081
Short St 28081
Sibbie Ct 28081
Sides Ave & Rd 28083
Silas Ave 28081
Silver Maple Dr 28081
Silverleaf Cir 28083
Simmons St 28083
Skyland St 28083
Skyway Dr 28083
Sloop Ave 28083
Small St 28083
Smith Rd 28081
Smith St 28083
Snipe St 28081
Snow St 28081
Sorrel Dr 28081
Sorrow Farm Rd 28081
Southaven Ct 28083
Southern Ave 28081
Spider Dr 28083
Spring St 28083
Spring Acres Dr 28083
Spring Garden Ave 28081
Springdale Ave 28081
Springway Dr 28081
Sprucewood St 28081
Starnes Farm Rd 28081
State Ave 28081
Steepleton Dr 28083
Stephen Ct 28083
Stirewalt Rd 28081
Stone St 28083
Stone Ridge Ct 28081
Stonegate Ct 28081
Stonewood Vw 28081
Stonewyck Ave 28081
Stratton Ct 28081
Strickland Ct 28081
Strider Cir 28083
Suburban Ave 28083
Suffolk Dr 28083
Summerpine Pl 28081
Summit Ave 28081
Summit Park Ct 28083
Summit Ridge Ln 28083
Sumner St 28083
Sumter Ave 28081
Sundale St 28083
Sunny Ridge Ln 28081
Sunrise Dr 28083
Sunset Dr 28081
Sunset End 28083
Supercenter Dr NE 28083
Superior Ave 28083
Surrey Dr 28081
Swan St 28081
Sweet Gum St 28083
Sweet Home Ln 28081
Swiss Ln 28081
Sycamore Ave 28081
Sycamore Ridge Ct 28081
Talbert Farm Rd 28083
Tammy Ct 28083
Tanbark Ln 28083
Tanglewood Dr 28081
Tara Ave 28083
Tara Elizabeth Pl 28083
Taylor St 28083
Teakwood Dr 28083
Teate Dr 28081
Tee Pee Trl 28081
Temple St 28081
Tennessee St 28083
Terrace Dr 28083
Terrapin Station Rd 28081
Texas Pl 28081
Texas St 28083
Therrell Rd 28081
Thomas Ave 28081
Tiffany Dr 28081
Timberwood Dr 28083
Timway Dr 28081
Todd Ave 28081
Tony Ct 28083
Town House Dr 28083
Townsend Ct 28081
Townsgate Ct 28081
Townview Dr 28081
Trade Ave 28081
Trail Ave 28081
Trailwood Ct 28081
Tree Limb Ln 28083
Triece St 28081
Trinity Church Rd 28081
Trostan Turn 28081
Trotters Rdg 28081
Troutman Hill Rd 28083
Tuckaseegee Rd 28081
Tucker Ave 28081
Turfwood Dr 28083
Turkey Rd 28083
Turner Dr 28081
N Turner Dr 28081
Turner St 28083
Tuttlewood Dr 28083
Twining Vine Ct 28081
Tybeth Cir 28083
Tygress St 28081
Tyler St 28083
Unity Church Rd 28081
E Universal St 28083
W Universal St 28083
Upper Enochville Rd 28081
Utah St 28083
V 8 St 28083
Vale Ave 28081
Valley St 28081
Valwood Ct, St & Ter 28083
Vance Ave 28081
Vantage St 28083
Venice St 28083
Venus St 28083
Vermont Ave 28083
Verona St 28083
Victoria Ave 28081
Villa St 28083
Village Green Dr 28081
Village Park Rd 28081
Vincent St 28081
Vine Ave 28081
Virginia St 28083
Waco Ave 28083
Wagner Acres Trl 28083
Waldroup Ln 28081
Walker St 28081
N & S Walnut St 28081
Walter St 28083
Wankel Dr 28083
Washington Ln 28083
Water Ridge Ave 28083
Wayne Ave 28081
Weddington Ave 28081
Wedgewood Rd 28083
Wednesbury Ct 28083
Wensil Ln 28083
Wentworth Dr 28081
West Ave 28083
Westbrook Dr 28081
Westchester Dr 28081
Westen Acres Rd 28081
Westlake Dr 28081
Westover Ave 28081
Westview St 28081
Westwinds Ct 28081
Westwood Dr 28081
Wetherburn Dr 28081
White Ave 28081
White Oak Ln 28083
Whiting Ave 28083
Wig St 28081
Wildwood Dr 28081
Wilkerson St 28081
Wilkes Dr 28081
Wilkie Dr 28081
Willard Ave 28083
Williams St 28081
Willow Dr 28083
Willow Leaf Ct 28081
Willowood Rd 28081
Wilson St 28083
Wiltshire Dr 28081
Winbeck Turn 28081
Windermere Dr 28083
Windingbrook Dr 28083
N & S Windsor Dr 28081
Windy Rush Rd 28081
Winfield St 28083
Winona Ave 28081
Winter St 28081
Winter Jasmine Pl 28081
Winton St 28081
Wisteria Ln 28083
Wonder Dr 28083
Wood Ave 28083
Woodacres Cir 28081
Woodchuck Dr 28081
Woodcrest Dr 28081
Woodfield Dr 28081
Woodglen Rd 28081
Woodland Cir 28081
Woodlawn St 28083
Woodmoore Ln 28081
Woods Ln 28083
Woodsdale St 28081
Woodside St 28083
Woodwind Ct 28081
Wrenn Ave & St 28081
Wright Ave 28083
Wright Rd 28081
Wright Meadow Ln 28081
Wyoming Dr 28081
Wyrick Ln 28083
Y M C A Dr 28081
Yale Ave 28081
Yates Ave 28083
York Ave 28083
Youngsdale Dr 28083

NUMBERED STREETS

E 1st St 28083
W 1st St 28081
E 2nd St 28083
E 3rd St 28083
E 4th St 28083
E 5th St 28083
W 6th St 28081
W 7th St 28081
W 8th St 28081
W 9th St 28081
E 10th St 28083
W 10th St 28081
E 11th St 28083
E 12th St 28083
W 12th St 28081
E 13th St 28083
W 13th St 28081
E 14th St 28083
E 16th St 28083
W 16th St 28081
E 17th St 28083
W 17th St 28081
E 18th St 28083
W 18th St 28081
E 19th St 28083
W 19th St 28081
E 20th St 28083
W 20th St 28081
E 21st St 28083
W 21st St 28081
E 22nd St 28083
W 22nd St 28081
E 23rd St 28083
E 24th St 28083
E 25th St 28083
E 26th St 28083
E 27th St 28083
E 28th St 28083
E 29th St 28083
E 30th St 28083
E 31st St 28083

KERNERSVILLE NC

General Delivery 27284

POST OFFICE BOXES MAIN OFFICE STATIONS AND BRANCHES

Box No.s
All PO Boxes 27285

RURAL ROUTES

01, 02, 03, 04, 05, 06, 07, 08, 09, 10, 11, 12, 13, 14 27284

NAMED STREETS

Aaron Place Ln 27284
Abbey Park Ct & Rd 27284
Abbott Oaks Dr 27284
Abbotts Creek Cir & Ct 27284
Abbotts Creek Church Rd 27284
Abbotts Lake Ct 27284
Abbottsford Dr 27284
Abington Ct & Dr 27284
Adams St 27284
Afton Park Dr 27284
Allen St 27284
Allyson Kay Dr 27284
Alverstone Dr 27284
Ambridge Ln 27284
American Dr 27284
Amersham Ct 27284
Amos Farm Rd 27284
Amylee Trl 27284
Andrew Acres Dr 27284
Andrews Dr 27284
Angel St 27284
Angela Run Dr 27284
Angus Ridge Dr 27284
Anne Tyler Ct & St 27284
Anthony Rd 27284
Antler Ct & Trl 27284
Appaloosa Trl 27284
Apple Grove Rd 27284
Applecross Ct 27284
Applegate Ct & Rd 27284
Aquaview Ct & Dr 27284
Arbor Hill Rd 27284
Arborwood Dr 27284
Armfield St 27284
Armistead Dr 27284
Arpeace Ln 27284
Arrowhead Dr 27284
Artie Ln 27284
Asbury Dr 27284
Ash Forest St 27284
Asheby Ridge Ct 27284
Asheby Woods Ct & Rd 27284
Ashington Ct 27284
Ashley Park Dr 27284
Ashton Brook Dr 27284
Augusta Ct 27284
Autumn Harvest Ct & Dr 27284
Avenbury Cir & Ct 27284
Avery Way 27284
Avery Way Ct 27284
Aviary Ct 27284
Avondale Mobile Ct 27284
Avondale Woods Ct & Ln 27284
Bagley Rd 27284
Bainburgh Ct 27284
Ballard Ct 27284
Bambi Ln 27284
Banbridge Rd 27284
Bannon St 27284
Bantry Trl 27284
Barbera Dr 27284
Barden Dr 27284
Barn Swallow Ln & Rd 27284
Barnsdale Ridge Ct & Rd 27284
Barrington Park Cir & Ln 27284
Barrington Ridge Ct 27284
Barrister Ct & Rd 27284
Barrow Rd 27284
Barry Knolls Rd 27284
Barry Oak Ct 27284
Bass St 27284
Bastille Dr 27284
Baxter St 27284
Bay Brook Dr 27284
Bayhill Ct 27284
Bear Run Ln 27284
Beard St 27284
Beaucrest Rd 27284
Beaufort Ct 27284
Becky Ann Dr 27284
Beech Leaf Ct 27284
Beechview Ln 27284
Beeson Ct & Rd 27284
Beeson Park Ct & Ln 27284
Beesons Field Dr 27284
Bell West Dr 27284
Ben Joyce Rd 27284
Ben Nevis Dr 27284
Ben Smith Rd 27284
Benefit Church Rd 27284
Benjamin Ct 27284
Bent Creek Trl 27284
Bentridge Forest Dr 27284
Berkley Rd 27284
Berry Garden Rd 27284
Bessie St 27284
Bethel Dr 27284
Bethel Church Rd 27284
Bethel Forest Dr 27284
Beulah Ln 27284
Bexley Place Ln 27284
Bickford Rd 27284
Big Mill Farm Rd 27284
Biloxi Ave 27284
Birch Ln 27284
Birch Forest St 27284
Birch Hill Ct & Dr 27284
Birch Springs Ct 27284
Birchridge Dr 27284
Birgeheath Rd 27284
Blackmoor Ct & Rd 27284
Blanco Peak Dr 27284
Blue Stone Ln 27284
Bluff School Rd 27284
Blythe St 27284
Bobby Ln 27284
E & W Bodenhamer St 27284
Bolestein Dr 27284
Bona Ct 27284
Bonanza Dr 27284
Bonita Ct 27284
Bonvon Dr 27284
Bost St & Xing 27284
Bost Street Ext 27284
Bowen Lake Dr 27284
Bradford Village Ct 27284
Braemore Ct 27284
Bramblegate Ct 27284
Branch Dr & St 27284
Branchwood Dr 27284
Brett Ct & Dr 27284
Briar Hill Ct 27284
Brickyard Ln 27284
Bridgehead Rd 27284
Bridgeport Dr 27284
Bridlington Rd 27284
Brightington Ct & Dr 27284
Brimmer Place Ct & Dr 27284
Brittainywood Rd 27284
Brittany Ridge Dr 27284
Brittany View Ln 27284
Broad St 27284
Broadwater Dr 27284
Broken Saddle Ln 27284
Bromley Dr 27284
Brook Ct 27284
Brookdale Forest Dr 27284
Brookford Rd 27284
Brookford Industrial Dr 27284
Brookgreen Ct & Ln 27284
Brookgreen Mobile Ct 27284
Brookside Ct 27284
Brown Rd 27284
Brown Stone Ct 27284
Browns Run Dr 27284
Buck Forest Dr 27284
Buck Run Dr 27284
Buckhurst Dr 27284
Bunker Hl Sandy Ridge Rd 27284
Bunyan Ct 27284
Burger Ct 27284
Burke St 27284
Burke Hollow Rd 27284
Burnt Mill Rd 27284
Cabot Pl 27284
Caladium Ct 27284
Calla Lilly Ln 27284
Calmeria Ct 27284
Camberwell Ln 27284
Cambridge Farm Ct 27284
Cambridge Square Ln 27284
Cameronden Ct 27284
Camillabrook Ct 27284
Campbell Gardens Rd 27284
Camrose Ln 27284
Candlewood Dr 27284
Cane Mill Ln 27284
Canstaff Dr 27284
Carignan Ct 27284
Carlisle Dr 27284
Carlisle Park Dr 27284
Carmel Ct 27284
Carotec Dr 27284
Carriage Trail Ct 27284
Carries Pl 27284
Carrollton Crossing Dr 27284
Carter St 27284
Cartwright Dr 27284
Carvie Smith Rd 27284
Castaway Dr 27284
Caswell Kern Rd 27284
Cathi Ln 27284
Catrina Way 27284
Cavendish Ct 27284
Cawdor Ln 27284
Caxton Dr 27284
Cedar Ln 27284
Cedar Breeze Ct 27284
Cedar Canyon Rd 27284
Cedar Creek Dr 27284
Cedar Grove Ln 27284
Cedar Grove Trailer Ct 27284

Cedar Lake Ct 27284
Cedar Meadows Ln 27284
Center St 27284
Century Blvd & Ct 27284
Century Park Ave & Ct 27284
Century Place Blvd 27284
Century Wood Ct 27284
Chamelin Rd 27284
Chancery Park Ct 27284
Charles Conner Ct & Dr 27284
Charles Place Dr 27284
Charleston Dr 27284
Charlie Rd 27284
Charring Dr 27284
Chaucer Manor Cir & Ln 27284
Chaucer View Cir 27284
Chelsea Place Dr 27284
N & S Cherry St 27284
Cherry Blossom Dr 27284
Cherry Cove Dr 27284
Cherryvale Dr 27284
Cheryl Dr 27284
Ches Ln 27284
Chesham Dr 27284
Chestnut Chase Trl 27284
Chestnut Village Ln 27284
Chestnutwood Dr 27284
Cheviot Dr 27284
Chica Ct 27284
Chillingham Ct 27284
Chimney Rock Ct & Dr 27284
Chipchase Rd 27284
Christi Ln 27284
Church Ln & St 27284
Cinema Ct & Dr 27284
Cingma Dr 27284
Claxton Dr 27284
Claxton Ridge Dr 27284
Clay Flynt Rd 27284
Clayton Forest Dr 27284
Clear Springs Dr 27284
Clematis Way 27284
Cliffwood Dr 27284
Clifton St 27284
Clipstone Ln 27284
Cloud Peak Ct 27284
Clubb Rd 27284
Clyde Edgerton Dr 27284
Cokesbury Dr 27284
Colchester Dr 27284
Colston Ct 27284
Coltrane Dr 27284
Coltsgate Dr 27284
Combs Rd 27284
Conning Ct 27284
Constantine Ct 27284
Cope Ln 27284
Copperfield Ct 27284
Corjon St 27284
Corum St 27284
Cottingham Dr 27284
Country Ln 27284
Country Hill Ct 27284
Country Meadows Ct & Ln 27284
Countrymans Ct 27284
County Line Rd 27284
Covington Cv 27284
Cranfill Farm Rd 27284
Creek Bed Rd 27284
Creekridge Ct & Ln 27284
Creekview Ct & Dr 27284
Creekwood Forest Dr 27284
Crest Stone Ct 27284
Crestland Dr 27284
Crews St 27284
Crews Farm Rd 27284
Cricket Ct 27284
Critter Hollow Ln 27284
Croaisdale Ct 27284
Crooked Tree Dr 27284
Crosscreek Rd 27284
Crosspointe Ln 27284
Crossridge Ln 27284
Crouse Rd 27284
Croyden Ct & Dr 27284
Culloden Ct 27284
Curry Rd 27284
Cyrus Cir 27284
Daffodil Dr 27284
Dalton Ridge Rd 27284
Danay Dr 27284
Darvel Ct 27284
Dascomb Ct 27284
Davenport Ct 27284
Davis St 27284
Davis Meadows Ct 27284
Davis Ridge Rd 27284
Day Break Dr 27284
Daylilly Ct 27284
Dean Rd 27284
Debra Ln 27284
Deer Crossing Ln 27284
Deer Meadow Ln 27284
Deer Path Ln 27284
Deer Rack Cir 27284
Deere Hitachi Rd 27284
Dellas Aly 27284
Delmont Dr 27284
Denbigh Ct 27284
Derby St 27284
Dewberry Farm Ln 27284
Dewey St 27284
Dilworth Rd 27284
Dixie Dr 27284
Dobson Ct & St 27284
Doe Run Dr 27284
Doefield Dr 27284
Dogwood Trl 27284
Dolcetto Ct 27284
Donnell St 27284
Dora Dr 27284
Double D Rd 27284
Dowden St 27284
Drake Ct 27284
Drawbridge Ct 27284
Drayton Park Dr 27284
Drexdale Dr 27284
Driftwood Acres Dr 27284
Driftwood Trail Ct 27284
Drummond St 27284
Duffield Ct 27284
Duggins St 27284
Dunlap St 27284
Dunlap Springs Ct 27284
Durango Dr 27284
Eagle Point Ct & Dr 27284
Eagle Valley Ct 27284
Eagle Watch Ln 27284
Eastcrest Dr 27284
Eastgrove Ct 27284
Eastview St 27284
Echols Cir & Rd 27284
Eden Bridge Dr 27284
Eden Terrace Dr 27284
Edenfield Dr 27284
Edgebaston Dr 27284
Edgedale Ct 27284
Edgehill Ct 27284
Edgewood St 27284
Edwin Dr 27284
El Matador Dr 27284
El Toro Dr 27284
Elliott Rd 27284
Ellis Forest Rd 27284
Elsworth Ct 27284
Embark Ct & Dr 27284
Ember Ln 27284
Emerywood Ct 27284
Emily Dr 27284
Emmaus Ct & Rd 27284
Emperor Ln 27284
English St 27284
Essen Pl 27284
Fagg Farm Rd 27284
Fairaday Dr 27284
Fairbridge Dr 27284
Fairidge Ct & Dr 27284
Fairview St 27284
Fairweather Dr 27284
Fall St 27284
Fallfield Dr 27284
Farley Dr 27284
Farm Creek Rd 27284
Farmwood Dr 27284
Fawn Ridge Ln 27284
Fearington Dr 27284
Federal Hall Ln 27284
Fennell Dr 27284
Fenway Rd 27284
Fiddlers Knoll Ct & Dr 27284
Fiddlers Run Ct & Dr 27284
Fielding Dr 27284
Fieldmount Rd 27284
Finborough Ct 27284
Fireplace Ct 27284
Firestone Rd 27284
Floyd Berrier Dr 27284
Flynnwood Dr 27284
Flynt St 27284
Foothills Dr 27284
Fording Bridge Rd 27284
Fording Creek Ln 27284
Forest Dr 27284
Forest Creek Cir 27284
Forest Lake Cir 27284
Forestdale Ct 27284
Forrest Acres Dr 27284
Forsyth Rd 27284
Fosterdale West Ln 27284
Foxfire Rd 27284
Foxlair Dr 27284
Fred Chapel Ln 27284
Freeman Rd 27284
Friends Ln 27284
Frontier Dr 27284
Fulp Rd 27284
Fulp Farm Rd 27284
Fulps Pond Rd 27284
Fulton Ln 27284
Furlong Industrial Dr 27284
Gateway Center Dr 27284
Gateway Place Ln 27284
Gehring Dr 27284
Geoffrey Way 27284
George Place Dr 27284
George West Ct & Rd 27284
Georgetown Rd 27284
Gerry Dr 27284
Gibson Park Dr 27284
Glen Cross Dr 27284
Glen Gate Cir 27284
Glen Hollow Rd 27284
Glenacre Ct & Dr 27284
Glenn St 27284
Glennview Dr 27284
Glenridge Ct & Dr 27284
Glenwood Rd 27284
Glidewell Ln 27284
Goode Farm Rd 27284
Goodwill Church Rd 27284
Gordon St 27284
Gordon Terrace Rd 27284
Gortman Rd 27284
Grace Lndg 27284
Gracewood Ln 27284
Gralin St 27284
Grande Ln 27284
Gravelawn Dr 27284
Graves St 27284
Graves Mill Rd 27284
Grays Farm Rd 27284
Green St 27284
Green Holly Trl 27284
Greencastle Ct 27284
Greenlawn Dr 27284
Greenvalley Est & Rd 27284
Greenview Dr 27284
Greenway St 27284
Gregory Way Dr 27284
Gretas Way Ct 27284
Griffin Farm Rd 27284
Grindelwald Dr 27284
Grove Pines Ct & Ln 27284
Gunstock Dr 27284
Habersham Dr 27284
Halton Ridge Ct 27284
Hambersham 27284
Hamlin Park Dr 27284
Hammermill Ln 27284
Hammond St 27284
Hampton Plaza Dr 27284
Hancock Dr 27284
Hanes St 27284
Hanging Valley Ct 27284
Hap Ct 27284
Happy Hill Rd 27284
Harlan Dr 27284
Harmon Ct & Ln 27284
Harmon Creek Rd 27284
Harmon Mill Rd 27284
Harmon Ridge Ct & Ln 27284
Harris Ct 27284
Harvest Wind Ct 27284
Hastings Dr & Rd 27284
Hastings Hill Rd 27284
Havenstraat St 27284
Haw Meadows Dr 27284
Haw River Rd 27284
Hawick Ct 27284
Hearrai Rd 27284
Heartland Dr 27284
Heathbrook Ln 27284
Heathwood Ct 27284
Hedgecock Rd 27284
Hedgecock Farm Rd 27284
Hedgemore Dr 27284
Hedrick Dr 27284
Hendrix Dr 27284
Hendrix View Ln 27284
Hepler St 27284
Heston Farm Rd 27284
Hibiscus Ln 27284
Hickory Ln 27284
Hickory Bluff Ct 27284
Hickory Grove Ct 27284
Hickory Hill Ln 27284
Hicks Edwards Dr 27284
Hidden Branches Ct 27284
Hidden Hills Dr & Ln 27284
Hideaway Hills Ln 27284
High Creek Ct 27284
High Point Rd 27284
High Ridge Ct & Rd 27284
Highfield Aly 27284
Hill N Dale Dr 27284
Hillcrest St 27284
Hillside Dr 27284
Hillwood Dr 27284
Hollow Creek Ln 27284
Hollow Hill Rd 27284
Holly Tree St 27284
Hollyhock Rd 27284
Holt St 27284
Hooker Ln 27284
Hopkins Rd 27284
Horse Creek Ct & Run 27284
Horseman Cv 27284
Horsemens Cv 27284
Houndsbay Ct 27284
Howe Rd 27284
Howell Ct 27284
Hoyd Ln 27284
Huff Farm Rd 27284
Humberside Dr 27284
Hunter Path Rd 27284
Hunters Ln 27284
Huntington Run Ln 27284
Huntsman Rd 27284
Idlebrook Dr 27284
Idlewild Rd 27284
Idlewild Haven Ct 27284
Indeneer Dr 27284
Indian School Rd 27284
Industrial Park Dr 27284
Industrial Way Dr 27284
Inez Ct & Ln 27284
Inland Ct & Dr 27284
Interlaken Dr 27284
Irving Park Ct & Dr 27284
Ivorhing Ct 27284
Ja Mar Dr 27284
James St 27284
James East Dr 27284
Janeway Ct 27284
Jefferson St 27284
Jennings Park Trl 27284
Jewell St 27284
John Austin Ct 27284
John Ehle Ct 27284
Johnson Controls Dr 27284
Jones Brothers Rd 27284
Joyce Ln 27284
Joyceland Rd 27284
Joyner Cross Rd 27284
Jubilee Trl 27284
Julian Pond Ln 27284
Justice St 27284
Kakie Jennings Ct 27284
Kanoy Farm Rd 27284
Katherine Ridge Dr 27284
Kaye Gibbons Ct 27284
Kayla Cir 27284
Kelly Dwayne Rd 27284
Kelvdon Dr 27284
Kempsford Ct 27284
Kendallwood Dr 27284
Kenosha Dr 27284
Kensal Green Ct & Dr 27284
Kentland Ridge Dr 27284
Kenton Dr 27284
Kenville Green Cir & Ct 27284
Kerner Rd & St 27284
Kerner Farm Rd 27284
Kerner Knolls Dr 27284
Kerners Row Dr 27284
Kernersville Rd 27284
Kernersville Medical Pkwy 27284
Kerwin Cir 27284
Kilburn Cir 27284
Kilburn Way Ln 27284
King St 27284
King William Dr 27284
Kings Ct 27284
Kingsridge Rd 27284
Kingston Ave 27284
Kingsway Ln 27284
Kingswood Dr 27284
Kippen Dr 27284
Kirkman St 27284
Klompen Dr 27284
Knight Rd 27284
Knightsbridge Ct 27284
Knightwood Ct 27284
Korner Rock Ct & Rd 27284
Koury Dr 27284
Kristens Gate Dr 27284
Kristi Glen Ct 27284
Lagerfield Ct 27284
Lake Dr & Way 27284
Lake Garden Ct 27284
Lake Meadow Ct 27284
Lake Ridge Dr 27284
Lakecrest Dr 27284
Lakeside Ct & Dr 27284
Lakeview Dr 27284
Lambeth Farm Ln N 27284
Lambley Ln 27284
Lambs Ln 27284
Lamshire Ct & Rd 27284
Lance Ln 27284
Landreth Rd 27284
Laplata Ct & Dr 27284
Laquita Ct 27284
Larchwood Dr 27284
Larkhill Ct & Dr 27284
Latimer Dr 27284
Laverne Ln 27284
Lawson Acres Dr 27284
Lear Ct 27284
Lee St 27284
Lee Hy Dr 27284
Lee Smith Ln 27284
Lees Ridge Rd 27284
Leichester Square Ct 27284
Lenbrook Rd 27284
Leonard Farm Rd 27284
Leston Gilbert Dr 27284
Lilac Dr 27284
Lilly Dr 27284
Lindsay St 27284
Linview Dr 27284
Linville Ave, Ct, Rd & St 27284
Linville Springs Rd 27284
Lisa Run Ct & Dr 27284
Littlejohn Rd 27284
Littlewood Rd 27284
Loch Lorien Rd 27284
Londonderry Rd 27284
Long Branch Ct & Dr 27284
Long Mill Ct 27284
Long Walk Dr 27284
Longbridge 27284
Longburn Dr 27284
Longmont Ct & Dr 27284
Longreen Ct & Dr 27284
Longridge Dr 27284
Longview Dr 27284
Longworth Dr 27284
Lonnie Ct 27284
Loradale Dr 27284
Loughborough Ct 27284
Louis Sells Rd 27284
Lowell St 27284
Lower Creek Ln 27284
Lowergate Ln 27284
Lucinda Ln 27284
Lynnwood Park Dr 27284
Lyons Path Ct 27284
Lyons Walk Ct & Dr 27284
Mabe Hill Rd 27284
Macy Grove Rd 27284
Madison Place Cir 27284
Mae Stone Ct 27284
N & S Main St 27284
Majestic Way Ct 27284
Malbec Ct 27284
Malone Brook Ln 27284
Manorwood Dr 27284
Mantlewood Ln 27284
Manuel Farm Ln 27284
Mar Vista Ln 27284
Margate Cir & Ln 27284
Marietta Dr 27284
W Market St 27284
Martha Ct 27284
Martinlake Rd 27284
Marylebone Dr 27284
Mastel St 27284
Masten Dr 27284
Matt Rd 27284
Matthews Place Ln 27284
Maverick Rd 27284
Maxine St 27284
Mayford Dr 27284
Mayview Ct 27284
Mcbride Forest Ln 27284
Mcbryde Dr 27284
Mccollem Ln 27284
Mcconnell Dr & Ldg 27284
Mccoy St 27284
Mccracken Rd 27284
Mcidol Rd 27284
Mckaughan St 27284
Mcneil Rd 27284
Meadow Creek Ln 27284
Meadow Grove Trl 27284
Meadowbrook Park Dr 27284
Meadowbrook Trailer Park 27284
Meadowbrook Village Ln 27284
Meadowland Rd 27284
Meadows Field Ct 27284
Medford Cir 27284
Megan Cross Ln 27284
Mellon Dr 27284
Melva Ln 27284
Merrilu Ln 27284
Mic Mac Trl 27284
Michael St 27284
Micol Ln 27284
Middleham Dr 27284
Millbrook Trl 27284
Millers Creek Ct 27284
Millis St 27284
Milton St 27284
Misty Meadow Dr 27284
Monitor Ave 27284
Montcrest Dr 27284
Moore Acres Dr 27284
Moore Farm Dr 27284
Moravian Church Ln 27284
Morning Glory Dr 27284
Morris St 27284
Morro Dr 27284
Morton Dr 27284
Motsinger Farm Ln 27284
Moultrie Ct 27284
Mounce Rd 27284
E Mountain St 27284
W Mountain St
100-326 27284
325-325 27285
327-2799 27284
328-2798 27284
Mountain View Dr 27284
Musket Dr 27284
Myra Ct 27284
Nandina Ln 27284
Naomi Ave 27284
Nc Highway 66 S 27284
Nebbiolo Ct 27284
Needlewood Dr 27284
Nelson St 27284
Neptune Dr 27284
Nevada St 27284
New St 27284
Nickel Creek Ct 27284
Nicole Rd 27284
Nokomis Dr 27284
Norcross Rd 27284
Northpark Dr 27284
Notees Dr 27284
Novella Dr 27284
Oak St 27284
Oak Acres Dr 27284
Oak Forest Dr 27284
Oak Garden Dr 27284
Oak Meadows Dr 27284
Oak Ridge Rd 27284
Oakcliff Dr 27284
Oakdale Park Ct 27284
Oakhurst St 27284
Oakhurst Park Ct & Ln 27284
Oakland Ave 27284
Oakleaf Forest Dr 27284
Oakmont Cir, Ct & Dr 27284
Oakmont Park Ct 27284
Oakmont Place Ct 27284
Oakway Ct 27284
Oakway Ridge Ct 27284
Oakwood Forest Ln 27284
Odell Dr 27284
Ogden Avenue Ln 27284
Ogden School Ct & Rd 27284
Old 66 Cir 27284
Old Cabin Ln 27284
Old Coach Rd 27284
Old Flat Rock Rd 27284
Old Greensboro Rd 27284
Old High Point Rd 27284
E Old Hollow Rd 27284
Old Hunt Trl 27284
Old Jubilee Pl 27284
Old Linville Rd 27284
Old Orchard Rd 27284
Old Salem Rd 27284
Old Still Trl 27284
Old Stone Ln 27284
Old Us Highway 421 27284
Old Valley School Rd 27284

Old Winston Rd 27284
Old Wood Ct & Ln 27284
Ole Log Ln 27284
Opal Park Ln 27284
Open Hearth Dr 27284
Orr St 27284
Oscar Ln 27284
Osnek Ln 27284
Overbrook Meadow Ct 27284
Oxbow Ln 27284
Oxford Ridge Ln 27284
Paddison St 27284
Panther Pointe Dr 27284
S Park Dr 27284
Park Centre Dr 27284
Park Lawn Ct 27284
Park Place Dr 27284
Parkcrest Cir 27284
Parry View Ln 27284
Partridge Ln 27284
Patio Ct 27284
Patriot Ct 27284
Paul Joyce Rd 27284
Payne Rd 27284
Peace Rollins Ct 27284
Peach Grove Ct 27284
Peachtree Meadows Cir 27284
N Peak Dr 27284
Pearman Quarry Rd 27284
Pecan Ln 27284
Pecan Ridge Cir 27284
Peddycord Rd 27284
Peddycord Park Ct, Dr & Rd 27284
Pegg Ave 27284
Pegg Farm Ln 27284
Peppermint Ln 27284
Perlette Ct 27284
Perry Rd 27284
Perrywinkle Dr 27284
Phillips Farm Rd 27284
Phineas Dr 27284
Phippswood Ct 27284
Picardy Ct 27284
Pickney Ct 27284
Pike Place Ct 27284
Pine St 27284
Pine Burr Rd 27284
Pine Forest Dr 27284
Pine Knolls Rd 27284
Pine Meadow Ct, Dr & Rd 27284
Pine Shadows Ct 27284
Pine Tree Ln 27284
Pineland Dr 27284
Pinelawn Dr 27284
Pineview Dr 27284
Pinewood Ter 27284
Piney Grove Rd 27284
Pisgah Cir 27284
Pisgah Church Rd 27284
Pisgah View Dr 27284
Pitts St 27284
Plaza South Dr 27284
Pond Ct 27284
Pondarosa Dr 27284
Pope Ln 27284
Pope Creek Rd 27284
Pope Farm Dr 27284
Pope Hill Ct 27284
Popes Creek Rd 27284
Porter Ct & Ln 27284
Porter Trace Dr 27284
Portia Ln 27284
Portico Ln 27284
Post Oak Rd 27284
Pratt Rd 27284
Prescott St 27284
Prince Charles Ct & Dr 27284
Prince Edward Rd 27284
Prince Haven Ct & Ln 27284
Princeton Square Ct 27284
Pumpkin Ridge Rd 27284
Punkin Ct 27284
Quail Hollow Rd 27284
Quail Hunt Cir 27284
Quaker Ridge Dr 27284
Quaker Way Ave 27284
Quawatha Dr 27284
Rachel St 27284
Ragland St 27284
Ragland Place Ln 27284
E & W Railroad St 27284
Rains Davis Rd 27284
Rambling Dr 27284
Ramsey Rd 27284
Ranger Trl 27284
Raven Ridge Ct, Dr & Rd 27284
Ray St 27284
Ray West Dr 27284
Red Oak Ct 27284
Redcoat Dr 27284
Regents Park Rd 27284
Reidsville Rd 27284
Reigate Dr 27284
Renee Dr 27284
Renn Rd 27284
Retford Park Ln 27284
Reynard Dr 27284
Reynolds Price Dr 27284
Ribier Dr 27284
Richmond Ter 27284
Ridge Hill St 27284
Ridgeline Dr 27284
Ridgestone Ln 27284
Ridgewood 27284
Rierson Rd 27284
Riesling Dr 27284
Rivendell Rd 27284
Robbins Perch Trl 27284
Robbins Perch West Ct 27284
Robbinsperch West Ct 27284
Roberson Farm Ct & Rd 27284
Robert West Rd 27284
Robinette Ln 27284
Roburton Rd 27284
Rock Barn Rd 27284
Rockbridge Ct & Dr 27284
Rockford Ct & Rd 27284
Rockwood Ln 27284
Rocky Springs Ct & Ln 27284
Roddys Ct 27284
Rolling Ct & Rd 27284
Rosehaven Ct 27284
Rosehill Ct 27284
Roswell Ct & Dr 27284
Rougemount Ln 27284
Round Hill Cir & Ct 27284
Round Meadow Dr 27284
Round Oaks Ln 27284
Round Tree Ct 27284
Roxbury Ct & Ln 27284
Roxbury Forest Ct 27284
Royal Coach Trl 27284
Running Springs Ln 27284
Rustic Cut Dr 27284
Ryefield Ct 27284
Saddle Creek Dr 27284
Saddle Ridge Trl 27284
Sahabi Rd 27284
Saint Andrews Rd 27284
Saint Charles Ct 27284
Saint Mary Ct & Dr 27284
Saint Regis Ln 27284
Saints Delight Church Rd 27284
Salem Crossing Cir & Rd 27284
Salisbury Ct & St 27284
Salisbury Crossing Ct 27284
Sam St 27284
Sandy Ct 27284
Sangiovese Dr 27284
Sanwood Ln 27284
Sattlewood Dr 27284
Savannah Ct & Ln 27284
Sawtooth Ct 27284
Scarlet Oaks Ln 27284
School St 27284
Schoolview Dr 27284
Scott Dr 27284
Seacrest Dr 27284
Seaton Rd 27284
Sedge Brook Rd 27284
Sedge Garden Rd 27284
Sedge Haven Ln 27284
Sedge Hill Rd 27284
Sedge Lake Ct 27284
Sedgewood Dr 27284
Sells Farm Rd 27284
Selwyck Ln 27284
Serenity Pointe Dr 27284
Shaddowfax Dr 27284
Shagbark Ln 27284
Sheffield Place Dr 27284
Shepherd Grove Rd 27284
Sheppard Hill Ct & Rd 27284
Sheppards Run Dr 27284
Sherbow Rd 27284
Shields Rd 27284
Shields Park Dr 27284
Short St 27284
Silver Creek Trl 27284
Silver Dapple Ln 27284
Slate Rd 27284
Smith St 27284
Smith Branch Ct 27284
Smith Edward Rd 27284
Smith Haven Dr 27284
Smith Hollow Rd 27284
Smithwick Rd 27284
Smoke Crest Dr 27284
Smoke Glen Ct & Rd 27284
Smoke Hollow Ct & Rd 27284
Smoke View Dr 27284
Smokerise Ln 27284
Snow Garden Ln 27284
Solomon Dr 27284
Somerset Crossing Ln 27284
Southern St 27284
Southwood Dr 27284
Spring St 27284
Spring Hill Cir & Ct 27284
Spring Hill Mobile Ct 27284
Spring Ridge Dr 27284
Springbrook Dr 27284
Springhorn Dr 27284
Springhouse Ct 27284
Squire Davis Rd 27284
Squire Manor Ct & Pl 27284
Squires Ct & Ln 27284
Stable Hill Trl 27284
Stafford Anx & Dr 27284
Stafford Center Dr 27284
Stafford Country Ln 27284
Stafford Creek Ct 27284
Stafford Farm Rd 27284
Stafford Oaks Dr 27284
Stafford Park Ct & Dr 27284
Stanley Farm Ct & Rd 27284
Starkhill Dr 27284
Steen Rd 27284
Stella Blue Ct 27284
Stephenshire Ct 27284
Steve St 27284
Stigall Rd 27284
Stone Meadow Ct & Dr 27284
Stonehaven Rd 27284
Stonington Way Ct 27284
Stuart Run Rd 27284
Stunstall Rd 27284
Summercrest Ct 27284
Summerlyn Park Dr 27284
Summerlyn Place Dr 27284
Summit St 27284
Sun Meadows Dr 27284
Sun Valley Ln 27284
Sunbrook Dr 27284
Sunflower Ct 27284
Sunnyfield Dr 27284
Sunset Dr 27284
Susanna Ct & Dr 27284
Sutter Ln 27284
Sweetwood Ct 27284
Swindon Ln 27284
Swisher Center Rd 27284
Sydney Ct 27284
Sylvan Ln 27284
Tall Meadows Dr 27284
Tam O Shanter Rd 27284
Tammy Dr 27284
Tanbark Ct & Ln 27284
Tannelson Dr 27284
Tanner Ct 27284
Tanyard Ln 27284
Tar Heel Ln & Trl 27284
Tave Beeson Rd 27284
Teague Ln 27284
Teague Farm Ln 27284
Teakettle Ct 27284
Templeton Ln 27284
Tennyson Dr 27284
Thelbe Ln 27284
Thomas Drake Ct 27284
Thomas Ross Ln 27284
Thorndike Ct 27284
Thurston Ct 27284
Tilleys Grv 27284
Timber Creek Ln 27284
Timber Forrest Ct 27284
Timber Oaks Ln 27284
Timber Ridge Ct & Rd 27284
Timber Village Ct 27284
Timberview Dr 27284
Timberwood Trl 27284
Tipton Dr 27284
Todd Ct 27284
Tom Ct 27284
Toucan Ln 27284
Trail Inn Ln 27284
Trailwood Ln 27284
Trebbiano Ct & Dr 27284
Tredegar Rd 27284
Trent St 27284
Trenton Dr & St 27284
Trilliumplace Dr 27284
Trotters Ridge Ln 27284
Tryon Trl 27284
Tulane Dr 27284
Turner Manor Ct 27284
Tuxford Ln 27284
Twelve Oaks Dr 27284
Twin Creek Rd 27284
Twin Hill Ct 27284
Twin Lakes Dr 27284
Twin Pines Dr 27284
Tysonridge Ct 27284
Union Cross Rd 27284
Unity Ln 27284
Uppergate Ln 27284
Valley Forge Ln 27284
Valley Village Rd 27284
Valleydale Ln & Rd 27284
Valleymeade Ct & Dr 27284
Valleyspring Rd 27284
Van Hoy Rd 27284
Vance Rd & St 27284
Vancouver Ct 27284
Vandyke St 27284
Varner Dr 27284
Venable Dr 27284
Venus Rd 27284
Vernon Cir, Ct & St 27284
Vernon Farms Blvd 27284
Vernon Mill Rd 27284
Villa Dr 27284
Village Pines Ln 27284
Vista Way Dr 27284
Vivian St 27284
Vixen Ct 27284
Volta Rd 27284
Vossdale Dr 27284
Wagon Trace Ln 27284
Wakefield Farm Ln 27284
Wards Pond Ct 27284
Warner Rd 27284
Warren Rd 27284
Water Mill Ct & Rd 27284
Water Oak Rd 27284
Watercrest Ct 27284
Watermill Ct 27284
Watkins Ford Rd 27284
Watmead Rd 27284
Wear Ln 27284
Weather Ridge Ct & Rd 27284
Weatherfield Ln 27284
Weathergreen Ct 27284
Weatherstone Dr 27284
Weatherton Dr 27284
Weavil Rd 27284
Weavil Ridge Dr 27284
Welborn Rd 27284
Wembly Ct 27284
Wendy Ct 27284
Wenson Rd 27284
Wesley Park Dr 27284
Weslo Dr 27284
West Rd 27284
Westbourne Ct 27284
Westbury Dr 27284
Westhill Pl 27284
Weston Brooke Trl 27284
Westside Dr 27284
Westwood Dr 27284
Wheatsheaf Ct 27284
Whicker Rd 27284
Whicker Farm Ln 27284
Whispering Brook Dr 27284
Whispering Brook Trail Park 27284
Whispering Pines Dr 27284
White Oak Ct 27284
White Pine Trailer Ct 27284
White Tail Trl 27284
Whitehorn Rd 27284
Whitt Rd 27284
Whitworth Ct 27284
Wickham Rd 27284
Wilchester Ln 27284
Wiley Farm Rd 27284
Willa Place Ct & Dr 27284
Willamont St 27284
William Brown Ln 27284
Williams Way 27284
Williams Farm Rd 27284
Williamshire Ct 27284
Willoughby Dr 27284
Willow Bend Ct & Dr 27284
Willow Creek Rd 27284
Willow Oak Ct, Dr & Pl 27284
Wilson Dairy Rd 27284
Wilson Davis Dr 27284
Wilson Farm Ln 27284
Wilton Ct 27284
Wimberly Way Ct 27284
Windsor Manor Way 27284
Windsor Park Rd 27284
Windsor Way Ct 27284
Windwood Dr 27284
Winesapp Dr 27284
Winfree St 27284
Winsom Rd 27284
Winterberry Place Trl 27284
Wishbone Farm Rd 27284
Wood Dale Dr 27284
Woodbine St 27284
Woodbridge Dr 27284
Woodbrook Dr 27284
Woodfield Dr 27284
Woodlake Park Dr 27284
Woodland Trl 27284
Woodland Pointe Dr 27284
Woodlyn St 27284
Woodruff Rd 27284
Woods Edge Ln 27284
Woodstaff Rd 27284
Woodway Dr 27284
Worchester St 27284
Wright Rd 27284
Wyndfall Dr 27284
Yorktown Rd 27284
Zana Ct 27284
Zinfandel Dr 27284

KINSTON NC

General Delivery 28502

POST OFFICE BOXES MAIN OFFICE STATIONS AND BRANCHES

Box No.s
1 - 998 28502
1001 - 1980 28503
2001 - 4820 28502
5001 - 5999 28503
6001 - 6598 28501
7001 - 7660 28502
28501 - 28501 28501
28502 - 28502 28502
28503 - 28503 28503
99311 - 99997 28502

NAMED STREETS

A St 28504
A M Phillips Rd 28504
Aaron Dr 28504
Aaron Johnson Ln 28504
Abana St 28501
Abbott St 28504
Abby Ct 28504
Academy Heights Rd 28504
Acorn Cir 28504
Acrebrook Dr 28504
Acreridge Dr 28504
Adams Dr 28501
Addie Ln 28504
N & S Adkin St 28501
Aerosystems Blvd 28504
Airlee Dr 28504
Airport Rd
100-199 28501
200-2799 28504
Airy Grove Church Rd 28501
Albemarle Rd 28501
Albert Baker Rd 28504
Alberta St 28501
Albrittons Rd 28504
Alexander St 28501
Alexander Rouse Rd 28504
Alison Rd 28504
Allens Aly 28501
Alliance Dr 28504
Alma Dr 28501
Alpha Dr 28504
Alphin Rd 28504
Alton Phillips Rd 28504
Andrew Johnson Dr 28501
Andy Ln 28504
Ann Blvd 28504
Anne Dr 28501
Arnold Family Rd 28501
Arrendell Hodges Ln 28504
Arrow Dr 28501
Arrowhead Ln 28501
Arthur Ln 28504
Asa Ln 28504
Ashland Dr 28504
Ashlee Nicol Trl 28501
Ashton Ln 28504
Ashton Place Ln 28504
Atlantic Ave
300-699 28501
701-999 28501
1300-1999 28504
Autumn Dr 28501
Avalon Dr 28504
Back St 28504
Bagby Aly 28501
Bailey Dr 28501
Bailey St 28504
Baileys Park Ln 28504
Baker Bradley St 28504
Banks School Rd 28504
Barbara Ln 28501
Barnett Ln 28504
Barton Ave 28501
Barwick Rd 28504
Baxter Dr 28504
Beasley St 28501
Becton Farm Rd 28501
Beech Ave 28501
Beechnut Dr 28504
Bell Rd 28504
Bell St 28501
Belvidiere St 28504
Bennies Dr 28504
Berkley Ave 28504
Berneice Ilene Rd 28501
Bethlehem Rd 28504
Betty St 28504
Big Oak Rd 28504
Bill Herring St 28501
Bill Smith Rd 28501
Bill Stroud Rd 28504
Billy Becton Rd 28504
Birch Cir 28504
Bl Hamilton Ln 28504
Black Harper Rd 28504
Black Walnut Dr 28504
Blacksmith Cir 28504
Bland Howell Rd 28504
Blizzard Farm Rd 28504
E & W Blount St 28501
Bohannon Rd 28501
Bond St 28501
Bonnie Ln 28501
Booker St 28501
Boston St 28501
Bosworth Rd 28504
Bowden St 28504
Boy Scout Blvd 28501
Branchwood Dr 28504
Breckenridge Ln 28504
Brell Dr 28504
Brentwood Dr 28501
Brer Rabbit Pl 28504
Brian Ln 28501
Briarfield Rd 28501
Briarwood Dr 28501
Briary Run Rd 28501
E & W Bright St 28501
Brinson St 28504
Briss Dr 28504
British Rd 28501
Broadway St 28501
Brookhaven Dr 28504
Brooks Blvd 28504
Brookwood Rd 28504
Broomcorn Ln 28504
Brown St 28504
Buckingham Ct 28504
Buddy Dawson Dr 28504
Buddy Williams Rd 28504
Buena Vista Ct 28504
Burncoat Rd 28504
Burney Town Rd 28501
Butterfield Ln 28504
Buxton St 28504
Bynum Blvd 28501
C B Wade Ln 28504
Cabin St 28504
Cabin Branch Rd 28504
Cambridge Dr 28504
Camellia St 28504
Camelot Dr 28504
Cameron Dr 28501
Cameron Langston Rd 28501
Campbell St 28501
Candace Rd 28504
Candlewood Dr 28501
Canterbury Rd 28504
Cap Ln 28504
E & W Capitola Ave 28501
Caprice Dr 28504
Capstone Lodge Ln 28501

Street	ZIP
Carey Rd	
600-2099	28501
2100-3399	28504
3219-8-3219-8	28504
Cargo Dr	28504
Carl Ball Ln	28504
Carlton Dr	28504
Carolina Ave	28504
Caroline Nicole Dr	28504
Carolyn St	28504
Carr Lyles Dr	28501
Carraway Dr	28501
Carriage Dr	28504
Carriage Hill Dr	28504
Carrie Hill Dr	28504
Carver Cts & St	28501
Casey Rd	28501
Castle Rd	28501
E Caswell St	28501
W Caswell St	
100-199	28501
401-499	28504
Caswell Station Rd	28501
Catherine Ave	28504
Causey Rd	28501
Cavalier Cir	28501
Cayla Beths Ln	28501
Cecelia Ave	28501
Cecil Dr	28504
Cedar Ln	28501
Cedar Dell Ln	28504
Cedar Fresh Rd	28504
Centennial Trl	28501
Central Ave	28504
Charles Dr	28504
Charlie Cir	28504
Charlie Grant Rd	28504
Charlie Herring Rd	28504
Charlotte Ave	28501
Chase Dr	28504
Cherry Ln	28504
Cherry Oil	28504
Chestnut St	28501
Chevy Ln	28501
Chris St	28504
Christian Ln	28504
Christina Ln	28504
Churchill Dr	28504
Cindy Ln	28504
Cindy Lou Dr	28501
Clarence Potter Rd	28504
Clark Dr	28501
Clay St	28501
Clayton St	28504
Cleveland Dr	28504
Clifton Ter	28501
Clover Ln	28501
Cobb Rd	28501
Cobblestone Dr	28504
Cody Ln	28504
Cogdell Dr	28501
Coleman Dr	28504
Colemans Fast Ln	28501
Colgate Dr	28501
College St	28501
Collier Loftin Rd	28504
Colonial Cir	28504
Colonial Colony Blvd	28504
Colony Pl	28501
Commerce Dr	28504
Community Center Dr	28504
Conner Ln	28504
Cooks Aly	28501
Copeland Farm Rd	28501
Corey Ct	28504
Cornwallis Rd	28504
Cotton Ln	28501
Cotton Field Rd	28504
Cotton Patch Ln	28501
Country Trl	28504
Country Brook Dr	28504
Country Club Dr	28504
Country Squire Rd	28504
Country View Ln	28501
Covington Dr	28501
Cox Ave	28501
Craven Ln	28501
Crawford St	28504
Creekside Rd	28504
Crepe Myrtle Rd	28504
Crescent Dr	28504
Cresswell St	28504
Crestview St	28504
Crestwood Dr	28504
N & S Croom Bland Rd	28504
Crooms Dr	28504
Cummings Aly	28501
Cunningham Rd	28501
Curtis St	28504
Cypress Rd	28504
N Cypress St	28501
S Cypress St	28501
Dahlia St	28504
Dale Dr	28504
Dallas Dr	28504
Dallas Turner Rd	28504
Daly Waldrop Rd	28504
Danfield Dr	28504
Dani Ct	28501
Daniel Johnson Rd	28504
E & W Daniels St	28501
Daniels Farm Rd	28501
Darby Ave	28501
Darden Dr	28504
Dare Dr	28504
Daughety Rd	28501
Daughety White Rd	28501
David Ave	28501
N & S Davis St	28501
Davis Hardy Rd	28504
Daw Dr	28501
Dawson Station Rd	28504
Deabler Ln	28504
Dean Dr	28504
Deann Ln	28504
Deanswood Dr	28504
Debbie Ave	28504
Deerwood Ln	28504
Delilah Dr	28501
Demille Dr	28504
Dempsey Dr	28504
Derby Dr	28504
Derby Apts	28504
Desmond St	28501
Detroit St	28501
Dewey St	28501
Dexter Cir	28501
Diamond Ln	28504
Diane Blvd	28504
Diddy Bo Ln	28504
Dixon Rd	28504
Dixon St	28501
Dobbs Farm Rd	28504
Doctors Dr	28501
Dogwood Ln & Rd	28504
Donna Ave	28504
Donnelly Rd	28504
Dons Ln	28504
Dorcas Ter	28504
Doris Dr	28501
Doris Grady Rd	28504
Doug Dr	28504
Douglas St	28501
N & S Dover St	28501
Downing Ct	28504
Dr J E Reddick Cir	28501
Dr Martin Luther King Jr Blvd	28501
Driftwood Dr	28504
Dubose Dr	28504
Duck Pond Ct	28504
Dudley Park Rd	28504
Duffie St	28501
Duggins Dr	28501
Dunn Rd	28501
Dunn Family Rd	28504
Dupont Cir	28501
Dupree St	28504
Durwood Smith Ln	28504
Dylan Dr	28504
Eagle Rd	28501
N & S East St	28501
Eastover Ave	28501
Eastridge Cir	28501
Eastwood Dr	28504
Edgehill Ave	28501
Edgewood Dr	28504
Edmondson Ln	28504
Edwards Ave	28501
Eleanor Dr	28504
Elijah Loftin Rd	
1100-1949	28504
1950-2399	28501
2401-2691	28501
Elijah Sykes Rd	28501
Elise S Jones Rd	28504
Elizabeth Dr	28504
Elm St	28501
Elm Grove Rd	28504
Elma Dr	28501
N & S Elmore Davis Rd	28504
Elmore Farms Rd	28501
Elwoods Ln	28504
Emerald Rd	28504
Emerson Rd	28504
Emma Webb Dr	28501
Emmanuel St	28501
Emmitt Dr	28504
En Dickerson Rd	28501
Energy Dr	28504
Englewood Dr	28504
English Squire Dr	28504
English Walnut Ct	28504
Enterprise Blvd	28504
Eric Dr	28504
Essex St	28504
Eubanks Rd	28501
Evans Dr	28501
Evelyn Dr	28504
Everett Dr	28504
Executive Dr	28501
Fairfax Rd	28504
Fairfield Ave	28504
Fairgrounds Rd	28504
Faison St	28504
Fallacha Rd	28504
Falling Creek Rd	28504
Farmgate Rd	28504
Farmingwood Dr	28504
Faulkner Rd	28501
Faye Dr	28501
Ferguson Ln	28504
Ferndale Ln	28501
Ferrell Rd	28501
Fields St	28501
Fire Fighter Cir	28504
Firefighters Ln	28501
Fitzgerald Dr	28501
Fleming Ave	28501
Fletcher Rd	28504
Fordham Ln	28504
Fordham Rd	
200-499	28501
600-799	28504
Fordham Grady Cemetery Rd	28504
Forehand Ct	28501
Forest Hill Rd	28504
Forrest Dr	28504
Forrest St	28501
Fountain Park Dr	28504
Fourth St	28504
Fox Hunters Rd	28504
Fox Run Cir & Dr	28504
Frances Pl	28501
Fred Everett Rd	28504
Fred Sugg Rd	28504
Freedom Dr	28501
Futrell Ln	28504
Futrell Family Ln	28504
Gardenia St	28504
Garland Ave	28504
Garner Dr	28501
Garnett Pl	28504
Gary Dr	28501
George Ave	28501
George Dr	28504
George Earl Dr	28504
Georgetown Rd	28501
Ginger Rd	28504
Girl Scout Rd	28501
Glenwood Ave	28501
Glorias Way	28504
Gold Leaf Cir	28504
Goldstar Rd	28501
Gooding Dr	28501
Goodman Rd	28504
E & W Gordon St	28501
Grace Dr	28504
Grady St	28504
Graham Dr	28504
E & W Grainger Ave	28501
Grainger Station Rd	28501
Grant St	28501
Gray Grant Rd	28504
Gray Tilghman Rd	28501
Green Acres Dr	28504
Greenbriar Rd	28504
Greene Haynes Rd	28504
Greenleaf Rd	28501
Greenmeade Dr	28501
Greezzneck Trl	28501
Groff Dr	28504
Guinea Town Rd	28501
Gulick Dr	28504
H B Smith Rd	28504
Hadley St	28501
Ham St	28501
Hamilton Blvd	28504
Hamilton Rd	28501
Hampton Rd	28504
Hanover Dr	28501
Harbor St	28504
Hardee Rd	28504
Harding Ave	28501
Hardy Bridge Rd	28504
Hargett Dr	28501
Harlow St	28504
Harold Hall Rd	28501
Harper Dr	28501
Harriette Dr	28504
Harrison Rd	28504
Hartland Rd	28501
Hartley Dr	28504
Hartsfield Ln	28504
Harvey Cir & St	28501
Haskett Ct & Rd	28501
Hawthorne Ave	28501
Hayes Rd	28501
Hayloft Cir	28504
Hazel Dr	28504
Hazel Hill Rd	28504
Hazelwood Dr	28504
Heard St	28501
Heather Ln	28501
Heber Smith Ln	28504
Hedge St	28504
Helen Ct	28501
Hemlock Dr	28504
Henry Blvd	28504
Herbert Dr	28501
Herring Family Rd	28504
N & S Herritage St	28501
Hickory Rd	28504
Hickory Hills Rd	28504
Hicks Ave	28501
Hidden Valley Cir	28504
E & W Highland Ave	28501
Hill Dr	28504
Hill St	28501
Hill Allen Ln	28501
Hill Family Rd	28504
Hill Farm Rd	28504
Hill Trail Ln	28504
Hillandale Dr	28504
Hillcrest Rd	28504
Hillery Stewert Ln	28504
Hillman Rd	28504
Hines Ave	28504
Hitching Post Ln	28504
Hodges Rd	28504
Hoke Ln	28501
Holding Pl	28501
Holloway Dr	28501
Holly Ln	28501
Holly Ridge Rd	28504
Holman St	28501
Home Front Dr	28501
Hood Farm Ln	28501
Hooker St	28501
Hoosies Ln	28501
Hope Dr	28504
Howard Dr	28504
Howard St	28501
Hubert St	28504
Hugo Rd	28501
Hull Rd	28504
Hullwood Dr	28504
Hummingbird Ln	28504
Humphrey Rd	28501
Hunt Hill Pl	28504
Huntington Cir	28504
Hussey St	28501
Hwy 11 S	28504
Hwy 11 55	28504
Hwy 258 N & S	28504
Hwy 55 W	28504
Hwy 58 N & S	28504
Hyman Ave	28501
Idlewild Dr	28504
N & S Independence St	28501
Indian Ln	28504
Indigo Ln	28501
Industrial Dr	28504
Innovation Way	28504
Institute Rd	28504
Irene Ln	28504
Irvin Dr	28504
N & S Isler St	28501
Ives Ln	28501
Ivy Rd	28501
J P Harrison Blvd	28501
Jack Lillier Ln	28501
Jack Rountree Apts	28501
Jackson Ln	28501
Jackson Heights St	28504
Jade Rd	28504
James Albert Rd	28504
James E Baker Ln	28504
Jamestown Ct	28504
Jane K Farm Ln	28504
Jefferson Dr	28504
Jennifer Ln	28504
Jerald Dr	28504
Jericho Rd	28501
Jesse Grant Rd	28501
Jessica Ln	28501
Jessie T Bryan Rd	28504
Jetport Rd	28504
Joe Clay Cir	28504
Joe Nathan Rd	28504
Joe Nunn Rd	28504
Joe Temple St	28504
Joe Williams Rd	28501
John C Hood Homes	28501
John Davis Rd	28504
John Green Smith Rd	28504
John M Baker Rd	28501
John Mewborne Rd	28504
John N Baker Rd	28501
Johna Brooke Ln	28504
Johnson St	28504
Johnson Place Rd	28501
Jones Ave	28501
Jones Barnes Ln	28504
Jones Smith Rd	28501
Jordan Rd	28504
Joyner Dr	28501
Judy Ln	28504
K Cir	28504
Kaci Leighs Ln	28501
Kaitlyn Ct	28501
Karhu Ln	28504
Kathy Sue Dr	28504
Kayla Ln	28504
Kays Path Rd	28501
Kelly Rd	28504
Kember Dr	28504
Kendle Rayes Dr	28501
Kennedy Farm Cir	28504
Kennedy Home Rd	28504
Kenneth Cir	28504
Kent St	28504
Kevin Dr	28501
Kilpatrick Rd	28501
Kimberly Ln	28504
E & W King St	28501
King Heath Ln	28504
King Heights Blvd	28501
King William Ct	28504
Kingston Dr	28501
Kleber Croom Rd	28504
Knobb St	28501
Kornegay St	28504
Kristi Ln	28501
Kristin Leigh Dr	28501
Kyle Ln	28504
Lakeland Dr	28504
Lakeview Trl	28504
Lakewood Dr	28504
Lamp Lighter Cir	28504
Lanay Dr	28504
Lane St	28504
Larkspur Rd	28501
Laroque Ave	28501
Larry Loftin Ln	28504
Latham Dr	28504
Laura Ln	28504
Laurel Ridge Ln	28504
Lawrence Ln	28501
Lazy R Blvd	28501
Leach St	28501
Leah St	28501
Lee St	28501
Leeward Dr	28504
Leigh St	28504
Lemuel Dawson Rd	28501
E & W Lenoir Ave	28501
Leon Dr	28504
Leslie R Stroud Rd	28504
Levi Dr	28504
Levi Ln	28501
Levi Sutton Ln	28504
Lewis Ln	28501
Lewis E Sugg Rd	28504
Liberty Ln	28501
Liberty Heights Rd	28501
Liberty Hill Rd	28501
Lightwood Knot Rd	28504
Lincoln St	28501
Linden Ave	28501
Lisa Ln	28504
Live Oak Dr	28501
Lockwood Rd	28501
Loftin Ln	28501
Lonesome Pine Dr	28504
Longleaf Pine Dr	28504
Longview Dr	28504
Lotus Pl	28501
Louise St	28504
Lovers Ln	28501
Loveta Dee St	28501
Lovick Rd	28501
Lyle Rd	28504
Lynley Place Dr	28501
Lynn Dr	28504
Mable St	28504
Macon St	28501
Madison Ave	28501
Magnolia Dr	28504
Manchester Rd	28504
Manley Creek Rd	28504
Manning St	28501
Maple Leaf Rd	28504
Marble Bush Ln	28501
Marcella Dr	28504
Margaret Ln	28501
Margies Ln	28504
Marie Ln	28504
Marilyn Dr	28501
Marion Ln	28504
Marsha Ave	28501
Marshburn Cir	28504
Martha Dr	28504
Martha Ann Blvd	28504
Martin Dr	28501
Mary Ann Ln	28504
Mary Beth St	28504
Massey Dr	28504
Mattie Dr	28504
Maylon Ln	28504
Mcadoo St	28501
Mccaskill Dr	28501
Mcdaniel Gray Rd	28501
Mcdaniels St	28501
N & S Mclewean St	28501
Meadowbrook Dr	28504
Meadowood Dr	28501
Meadows Ln	28501
Measley Rd	28504
Medlin Rd	28504
Melissa Ln	28504
N & S Melvin St	28501
Memory Ln	28504
Meriwether Ln	28501
Mewborn Ave	28501
Michael Dr	28501
Michelle Dr	28504
Middle Rd & St	28501
Miller St	28501
Mina Dr	28504
Mindy Ln	28504
Miriam St	28504
Misty Dr	28501
Mitchell St	28501
Mitchell Wooten Ct	28501
Mitchiner Park Rd	28501
Monroe St	28504
Monticello Dr	28504
Morgan Dr	28504
Morningside Dr	28501
Moseley Ln	28501
Mount Vernon Park Dr	28504
Mt Vernon Estates Dr	28504
Mulberry Ln	28501
Murphy Ave	28504
Murray Cir	28501
Murray Hill Rd	28504
N & S Myrtle Ave & St	28501
Nancy Gooding Ln	28501
Nansemond Trl	28501
Nathan Rd	28504
Nautica Pl	28504
Nc Highway 11 N	28501
Nc Highway 55 E	28501
Nc Highway 58 N	28501
Nelson St	28501
Neuse Rd	28501
Neuse Haven Rd	28504
New St	28501
E New Bern Rd	
100-699	28504
700-1599	28501
W New Bern Rd	28504
New York St	28501
Newport St	28504
Newton Baker Rd	28501
Nobles Ln	28501
Noland St	28504
Norma Dr	28504
E & W North St	28501
Northridge Pl	28504
Northview Dr	28501
Northwest St	28504
Northwood Dr	28501
Nova Scotia Rd	28501
Nyra Ln	28501
Oak St	28501
Oak Bluff Rd	28504
Oak Bridge Park Cir	28501
Oak Leaf Dr	28504
Oak Tree Ln	28501
Oakdale Dr	28504
Oakland Dr	28504
Oakmont Dr	28501
Oakridge Pl	28504
Oaks Dr	28504
Oakview St	28504

Street	ZIP
Oakwood Dr	28504
Offutt Dr	28501
Ok St	28504
Old 2nd St	28504
Old Asphalt Rd	28504
Old Brooks Cir	28504
Old Colony Rd	28504
Old English Ln	28504
Old Homestead Rd	28504
Old Macon St	28504
Old Mission Ln	28504
Old Oak Rd	28504
Old Plantation Dr	28504
Old Poole Rd	28504
Old Ridgeway Dr	28501
Old Snow Hill Rd	28501
Old Vance Dr	28504
Old Well Rd	28504
Olde Dutch Ct	28504
Olde Jamestown Rd	28504
Olive St	28501
Olivia Rd	28504
Onyx Ln	28504
Opal Ln	28504
Oquinn Ln	28504
Orange St	28504
Oriental Ave	28504
N & S Orion St	28501
Owen Smith Dr	28501
Oxford Rd	28504
Paddock Dr	28504
Paige Anna Ln	28501
Pamela Dr	28504
Pamlico Rd	28504
Pantego St	28504
Par Dr	28504
Park Ave	28501
Parker St	28501
Parker Fork Rd	28504
Parkers St	28501
Parrott Ave	28501
Parrott Dickerson Rd	28504
Patterson Rd	28504
Paulowania Dr	28501
Pauls Path Rd	28504
Pawnee Dr	28504
Paylor Dr	28501
Peachtree St	28501
Pear St	28504
Pearson Rd	28504
Perry St	28501
Perry Park Dr & Ln	28501
Perry Woods Pl	28501
Pershing Ter	28504
Pete Dr	28501
E & W Peyton Ave	28501
Phillips Rd	28504
Phillips Farm Rd	28501
Picadilly Rd	28504
Pierce Rd	28501
Pin Oak Dr	28504
Pine St	28501
Pine Knoll Dr	28504
Pine Street Rd	28501
Pinehurst Dr	28504
Pineridge Dr	28504
Pinewood Dr	28504
Pink Hill Rd	28504
Plantation Cir	28504
Planters Dr	28501
Plaza Blvd	28501
Pleasant Hill Rd	28501
Poley Branch Ln	28501
Pollock St	28501
Pony Ln Dr	28501
Poole Rd	28504
Poplar St	28504
Postrider Dr	28504
Presbyterian Ln	28501
Preston Dr	28504
Primrose Ln	28504
Professional Dr	28501
Pruitt Rd	28504
Quail Haven Dr	28504
Quail Ridge Rd	28504
N Queen St	28501
S Queen St	
100-1299	28501
1300-1399	28504
Queens Rd	28501
Quinerly St	28501
Race Track Rd	28501
Rae Rd	28504
Railfence Dr	28504
Raleigh Rd	28504
Raleigh St	28501
Rambo Ln	28501
Randall Ct	28501
Randolph Farrow Rd	28501
Random Rd	28504
Randy Rd	28504
Ravenwood Dr	28504
Ray Smith Rd	28504
Rayner St	28501
Raynor Rd	28504
Reagan Dr	28504
Rebecca Ln	28504
Redfield Rd	28504
Reed St	28501
Register Dr	28504
Remus Iv Keaira Dr	28504
Renee Rd	28504
Reynolds Ln	28504
Rhem St	28501
Rhodes Ave	28501
Richard Green Ct	28501
Richlands Rd	28504
Ridge Rd	28504
Ridgeview Dr	28504
Ridgewood Dr	28504
Riley Rd	28504
River Watch Rd	28504
Riverview Ln	28501
Roanoke Ave	28504
Robert E Lee Dr	28501
Robinson Rd	28504
Robinwood Dr	28504
N & S Rochelle Blvd	28501
Rockwood Dr	28504
Rolling Hills Rd	28504
Rons Path Rd	28504
Roosevelt Ln	28501
Rosa Bell Dunn Ln	28501
Rosanne Dr	28504
Rose Vista Rd	28504
Rosedale Ave	28504
Roses Ln	28504
Rountree Ave	28501
Rouse Rd	28504
Rouse Adams Ln	28504
Rouse Road Ext	28504
Ruby Cir	28504
Ruffin Ter	28504
Rufus Dr	28504
Rustic Cir	28504
Rusty Lee Rd	28504
Ruth Rd	28504
Ruth Hill Dr	28501
Ryan Ln	28501
Sabra Dr	28504
Saddle Ridge Ct	28501
Saint Andrews Pl	28504
Saint Edmunds Cir	28504
Saint George Pl	28504
Saint James Cir & Pl	28504
Saint John Cir	28504
Salina Dr	28504
Sam Dr	28504
Sand Clay Rd	28504
Sandcastle Dr	28504
Sanderson Way	28504
Sandhill Dr	28501
Sandy Cir	28504
Sandy Foundation Rd	28504
Sandy Hope Ct	28501
Sandy Ridge Dr	28501
Sanview Dr	28504
Sapphire Pl	28504
Sarah Ln	28501
Sasser St	28501
Savannah Ln	28501
Savannah Heights Dr	28501
Savannah School Rd	28501
Savannahs Way	28501
Scott St	28504
Scott Daughety Cir	28501
Seashell Dr	28504
N & S Secrest St	28501
Sedgefield Dr	28504
Seth West Rd	28501
Shackle Ford Rd	28504
Shameka Dr	28504
Sharon Ct	28504
Sharon Church Rd	28501
Shaw Ln	28501
Shepard Dr	28501
Sherman St	28501
Sherry Dr	28504
Sherwood Ave	28501
Sheryl Dr	28504
Shindarr Rd	28501
E & W Shine St	28501
Shirley St	28504
Short St	28501
Silo Rd	28501
Silver Leaf Dr	28501
Silverdale St	28504
Silversmith Cir	28504
Simmons Aly	28501
Simon Bright Ct	28501
Sj Well Drilling Ln	28504
Sloan St	28504
Smith Colony Rd	28501
Smith Farm Rd	28504
Smithfield Way	28504
E & W South St	28501
Southpark Ln	28504
Southwood Rd	28501
Sparre Dr	28504
Speight Dr	28504
Spence Dr	28504
Spence Family Ln	28501
Spiritual Dr	28504
Spring Branch Rd	28501
Spring Court Rd	28504
Spring Creek Dr	28504
Springhill St	28501
Springwood Ln	28504
Squire Pl	28504
Stadiem Dr	28501
Stallings Dr	28504
Stanford Ave	28501
Stanley Mission Rd	28504
Stanton Rd	28504
Starburst Rd	28501
Starfish Ln	28504
State Dr	28501
Steeplechase Dr	28504
Stephanie Dr	28501
Stephen Mccoy Rd	28501
Stewart Pl	28501
Stockton Rd	28504
Stokes Cir	28504
Stony Dr	28501
Stonyton Ln	28501
Stough Aly	28501
Stratford Blvd	28504
Strawberry Branch Rd	28501
Strickland Ter	28504
Stroud Ave	28501
Strouds Corner Rd	28504
Stu Ln	28504
Sullivan Rd	28504
Summerhill Ter	28504
Summit Ave	28501
Sumrell Rd	28504
Sunset Ave	28504
Sunset Ln	28504
Sunshine St	28501
Surry St	28504
Susan Ave	28504
Susan Gray Ct	28504
Susie St	28504
Sussex St	28504
Sutton Dr	28501
Sutton Place Dr	28504
Suttontown Dr	28504
Sweetbriar Cir	28501
Sybil Dr	28504
Sycamore Ave	28504
Sycamore Rd	28501
Sykes Rd	28504
Sylvan Cir	28501
Sylvia Ln	28501
Tacoma Dr	28504
Tammy Dr	28504
Tanglewood Dr	28504
Tara Dr	28504
Taylor Ln	28501
Taylor Heath Rd	28501
Taylor Spence Rd	28504
Temple Ave	28504
Teresa Cir	28504
Terminal St	28504
Thatcher Dr	28504
Thomas Dr	28501
Thompson St	28501
N & S Tiffany St	28501
Tilghman Mill Rd	28501
Timberlake Ct	28504
Tobacco Ln	28501
Tom White Rd	28504
Tomlyn Dr	28504
Tonya Dr	28504
Topaz Dr	28504
Tower Hill Rd	28501
Towncrier Dr	28504
Trails End Dr	28504
Tremain Dr	28504
Trey St	28504
N & S Trianon St	28501
Trinity Ln	28504
Trinity Club Dr	28504
Troy Ct	28504
Truman Ave & Ct	28501
Tryon Dr	28501
Tulip Ln	28501
Tulls Aly	28501
Tully Hill Rd	28504
Turnage Dr	28501
Twin Oaks Dr	28501
Twinwood Rd	28501
Tyler Rd	28504
Tyndall Dr	28504
Tyree Rd	28504
Tyrell Dr	28504
Us Highway 70 E	28501
Us Highway 70 W	28504
Valerie Rd	28504
Valley Springs Rd	28504
Valleyview Ct	28504
Vance St	28501
E Vernon Ave	28501
W Vernon Ave	
100-1299	28501
1300-4899	28504
4901-4999	28504
Vernon Hall Msn	28501
Victoria Pl	28504
Victory Ln	28504
Viking Dr	28501
Villa Dr	28504
Village Sq	28504
Village Creek Dr	28504
Vine Swamp Rd	28504
Virginia Ave	28501
Wadeland Dr	28504
Wake Ave	28504
Walker Dr	28501
Wallace Ln	28501
Wallace Family Rd	28501
Waller Farm Rd	28504
Walnut Cir & Dr	28504
Walnut Place Dr	28504
Walnut Tree Dr	28504
Walston Ave	28504
Walter Ramsey Rd	28501
Wanda St	28504
Warren Ave	28501
E Washington Ave	28501
W Washington Ave	
100-1299	28501
1300-1999	28504
Water Chestnut Dr	28504
Waters St	28501
Waverly Ave	28504
Webbs Aly	28501
Welling Coples St	28504
Welsh Ct	28504
Wendy Ln	28504
West Rd	28501
Westbrooke Dr	28504
Westdowns Ter	28504
Westminster Cir & Ln	28501
Westover Ave	28504
Westridge Rd	28504
Westwood Dr	28504
Whaley Rd	28501
Wheat St	28504
Wheat Swamp Rd	28504
Whitaker Dr	28501
White Oak Dr	28504
Whitehall Dr	28504
Whitfield Dr	28504
Whitfield Ridge Dr	28504
Whitley Dr	28501
Wilcox Rd	28501
Will Baker Rd	28504
William Pearce Rd	28501
William Vause Ln & Rd	28504
Williams Aly & St	28501
Williams Loop Rd	28504
Willow St	28501
S Wilshire Ct	28504
Wilson Ave	28501
Winchester Rd	28504
Winding Oaks Rd	28504
Windsor Rd	28504
Windsor Farm Rd	28504
Wingate Dr	28501
Winter Forest Dr	28504
Wolf Ln	28501
Woodberry Rd	28501
Woodington Rd	28504
Woodlawn Dr	28501
Woodview Ln	28501
Woodview Rd	28504
Wootens Aly	28501
Worley Hill Rd	28501
Worthington Pl	28501
Yardly Ln	28504
Yogi St	28504
York St	28504
Young St	28501
Zebe Grady Rd	28504
Zurkle Ln	28504

NUMBERED STREETS

Street	ZIP
All Street Addresses	28504

LAURINBURG NC

Street	ZIP
General Delivery	28352

POST OFFICE BOXES MAIN OFFICE STATIONS AND BRANCHES

Box No.s	ZIP
1 - 3621	28353
5001 - 5951	28352
8000 - 8000	28353
28352 - 28352	28352

NAMED STREETS

Street	ZIP
Aberdeen Rd	28352
Acacia St	28352
Academy Rd	28352
Adams Ave & St	28352
Airbase Rd	28352
Alder Rd	28352
Alexander Ave	28352
W Allen Ln	28352
Allison Dr	28352
Alpha St	28352
Andrew Jackson Hwy	28352
Andrews Dr	28352
Angus Dr	28352
Anita Dr	28352
Anne St	28352
Anson Ave	28352
Antler Cir	28352
Appaloosa Ct	28352
Appin Rd	28352
Apple Ln	28352
Appomattox Cir	28352
Arch Mcloud Rd	28352
Argyleshire Rd	28352
Arthur Rd	28352
Asheville St	28352
Ashley Dr	28352
Ashton Dr	28352
Atkinson St	28352
Aurora St	28352
Avery St	28352
Azalea Dr	28352
Azure Ct	28352
Bag Pipe Ln	28352
Baker Cir	28352
Banawie Cir	28352
Barnes Dr	28352
Barnes Bridge Rd	28352
Barnhill Cir	28352
Barrett St	28352
Bay Ridge Dr	28352
Beech St	28352
Belhaven Cir	28352
Belk Cir	28352
Beman Ave	28352
Berry St	28352
Berwick Dr	28352
Beta St	28352
Biggs St	28352
Birchwood Cir	28352
E & W Bizzell St	28352
Blair Ave	28352
Blake Cir	28352
Blakely Rd	28352
Blue Dr	28352
Blue Heron Ct	28352
Blue Woods Rd	28352
Bluebell Ln	28352
Blues Farm Rd	28352
Bobwhite Trl	28352
Bonnie Ln	28352
Bostic Rd	28352
Bowyer Dr	28352
Boykin Ln	28352
Braemar Cir	28352
Brandon Cir, Dr & Rd	28352
Briarwood Dr	28352
Bridge Creek Dr & Rd	28352
Bridle Path Dr	28352
Britt St	28352
Bronco Dr	28352
Bryant St	28352
Buckingham Rd	28352
Bucknell Ln	28352
Buffkin Dr	28352
Bundy Ln	28352
Butler St	28352
C K Dr	28352
N & S Caledonia Rd	28352
Calhoun Rd	28352
Cameron Dr	28352
Candlewood Cir	28352
Captain St	28352
Carl Dr	28352
Carlson St	28352
Carnostie Dr	28352
Carolina Bay Rd	28352
Carriage Cir	28352
Carver St	28352
Cary St	28352
Cedar Dr & Ln	28352
Celebrity Dr	28352
Center St	28352
Champion St	28352
Charles Dr	28352
Charleston Cir	28352
Charlotte St	28352
Cherry St	28352
Chestnut St	28352
E & W Church St	28352
Circular Dr	28352
Cleveland St	28352
Cliffdale Dr	28352
Coble Dr	28352
Colinwood Cir	28352
College Dr, Plz & St	28352
Colonial Village Apts	28352
Colony Ln	28352
Common Wealth St	28352
Conegal Cir	28352
Cook St	28352
Cooper St	28352
Cornelia St	28352
Cornwall Dr	28352
Corona Ave	28352
Cotton Dr	28352
Cottonwood Rd	28352
Covenant Way	28352
E & W Covington St	28352
Craig Ln	28352
Crandall St	28352
Crawford St	28352
Creed Rd	28352
Creedle St	28352
Creekside Dr	28352
Crepe Myrtle Ave	28352
Crestline Rd	28352
Crestwood Dr	28352
E & W Cronly St	28352
Currie Dr	28352
Cypress Dr & St	28352
D Graham St	28352
Dana Dr & Pl	28352
Daves Rd	28352
Dawn Cir	28352
Debra Dr	28352
Deerfield Cir	28352
Delta St	28352
Deluca St	28352
Devon Dr	28352
Dickson St	28352
Dillon Dr	28352
Dixie Guano Rd	28352
Doe Cir	28352
Dogwood Dr & Ln	28352
Dogwood Mile St	28352
Donna Dr	28352
Dornoch Cir	28352
Dorset Dr	28352
Douglas Ave & St	28352
Dove St	28352
Dunbar Dr	28352
Duncan St	28352
Duncan Smith Apts	28352
Dundee Cir	28352
Durso St	28352
Eastover Ln	28352
Ed Mcnair Rd	28352
Edinburgh Dr	28352
El Moro Trailer Park	28352
Elizabeth Dr	28352
Elliott Dr	28352
Elm Ave	28352
Elmhurst Dr	28352
Elmore Rd	28352
Emily Dr	28352
Emory St	28352
Everett St	28352
Evergreen Ln	28352
Executive Park Rd	28352
Fair Ln	28352
Fairfield Dr	28352
Fairley St	28352
Fairmont St	28352
Fairway Dr	28352
Falkirk Ln	28352
Farmwood Dr	28352
Fawn Cir	28352
Fayetteville St	28352
Fernwood Dr	28352
Festival Cir	28352

Fieldcrest Rd 28352
First St 28352
Fleetwood Rd 28352
Flowers St 28352
Foraker St 28352
Forest Rd 28352
Formosa Dr 28352
Fox Crossing Rd 28352
Fox Run Cir 28352
Franklin Ave 28352
Frederick Ave 28352
Fulton Ave 28352
Gabriel Ave 28352
Galand Rd 28352
Gamble St 28352
Gameland Dr 28352
Gamma St 28352
Gardenia Ln 28352
Gaston Ave 28352
Geneva St 28352
Gettysburg Cir 28352
Gibson Rd & St 28352
Gilchrist St 28352
N Gill St 28352
S Gill St
100-199 28352
109-109 28353
Glasgow Dr & St 28352
Glen Eden Way 28352
Glencoe Cir 28352
Glenn St 28352
Gold St 28352
Graham Ct & Rd 28352
Granada Terrace Apts 28352
Grant St 28352
Green Acres Rd 28352
Greenbrier St 28352
Greensboro St 28352
Greenway Cir 28352
Gulf St 28352
Gulf Port Rd 28352
Guns Run 28352
Hackamore Ln 28352
Hall St 28352
Hammond Dr 28352
Hampton Cir 28352
Haney Dr 28352
Hardin St 28352
Harrison Rd & St 28352
Harry Malloy Rd 28352
Harvell Ln 28352
Hasty Rd 28352
Hasty Woods Farm Rd 28352
Havelock Dr 28352
Heather Ln 28352
Heather Glen Dr 28352
Heck Norton Rd 28352
Heritage Dr 28352
Hickory St 28352
N & S Highland Dr & Rd 28352
Highland Garden Apts 28352
Highland Vlg Trailer Park 28352
Hill St 28352
Hillcrest Ave 28352
Hillside Ave 28352
Holly Ln 28352
Homer St 28352
Honey St 28352
Hood St 28352
Hooper Dr 28352
Horace Cir 28352
Horne Rd 28352
Hospital Dr 28352
Howell Cir 28352
Hunt Dr 28352
Hunter Dr 28352
Hunters Ridge Dr 28352
Huntington Dr 28352
Hurley Dr 28352
Idlewood Dr 28352
Ingleside Dr 28352
Inverness Cir 28352
Isabelle St 28352

Jackson St 28352
James St 28352
Jamestown Dr & St 28352
Jamison Ct 28352
Japonica Dr 28352
Jean Cir 28352
Jefferson St 28352
Jerusalem Rd 28352
Jessica Rd 28352
Jim Calhoun Rd 28352
John St 28352
Johns Rd 28352
Jones Cir & Rd 28352
Joy St 28352
Kay Rd 28352
Kelly Dr 28352
Kennedy St 28352
Kenwyn Dr 28352
Kerrimur Dr 28352
Keystone Way 28352
N & S King St 28352
Kingsdale Dr 28352
Kinlaw Dr 28352
Kinston St 28352
Kintyre Ct 28352
Kiser Rd 28352
Knapp St 28352
Knox St 28352
Lake Dr 28352
Lakewood Dr 28352
Lamar Ave 28352
Lanoca Ave 28352
Last Stand Rd 28352
W & E Lauchwood Cir, Dr & Ln 28352
Laurel Ln & St 28352
Laurel Hill Church Rd 28352
Laurelcrest Rd 28352
Laurin Ln 28352
Lee Ln 28352
Lees Mill Rd 28352
Leisure Rd 28352
Lennox Ave 28352
Liberty Cir 28352
Lila Dr 28352
Lincoln St 28352
Liza Ln 28352
Loch Lomond Dr 28352
Lochstone Dr 28352
Locklear Rd 28352
Log Cabin Ln 28352
Longleaf Dr 28352
Lonnie Ln 28352
Lowery Dr 28352
Lumbee Heritage Ln 28352
Lynn Ln 28352
Lytch Dr, Rd & St 28352
Madera Ave 28352
N & S Main St 28352
Malcolm St 28352
Mallard Creek Dr 28352
Malloy St 28352
Maple St 28352
Maplewood Dr 28352
Marcellus St 28352
Marie Ct 28352
Martie Ln 28352
Mary Anne Ln 28352
Marys Rd 28352
Mcalpine Ln 28352
Mcarn Rd 28352
Mcbride Ave 28352
Mccallum St 28352
Mccarter Ave 28352
Mcclelland St 28352
Mccoll Rd 28352
Mcdougald Ave 28352
Mcduffie Village Apts 28352
Mcfarland Rd 28352
Mcgirts Bridge Rd 28352
Mcgregor Rd 28352
Mcintosh Rd 28352
Mckay St 28352
Mckenzie Ave, Rd & St 28352
Mckinnon Dr 28352

Mclaughlin Rd 28352
Mclaurin Ave 28352
Mclean St 28352
Mcleod Dr & Rd 28352
Mcmillian Rd 28352
Mcnair Aly & Ave 28352
Mcnair Mill Rd 28352
Mcneill Dr 28352
Mcqueen Rd 28352
Mcrae St 28352
Meadow Brook Dr 28352
Medical Dr 28352
Melanie Ln 28352
Melton St 28352
Memorial Park Rd 28352
Memory Ln 28352
Midland Way 28352
Mills St 28352
Millstone Rd 28352
Milton St 28352
Mistletoe Dr 28352
Mobile Home Est & Rd 28352
Moe Rd 28352
Monica Dr 28352
Monroe Rd 28352
Montclair Dr 28352
Monticello Dr 28352
Montrose Ln 28352
Morgan Cir 28352
Morrimac Ln 28352
Morris Dr & St 28352
Morrison Ln 28352
Mosley Dr 28352
Muirfield Dr 28352
Muse St 28352
Mustang Cir 28352
Nashville Church Rd 28352
Neal Ln 28352
New St 28352
Nichols St 28352
Nobles Dr 28352
Normas Rd 28352
Northgates Dr 28352
Norton Rd 28352
Oak St 28352
Oak Croft Trl 28352
Oakdale St 28352
Oakgrove School Rd 28352
Oakwood Dr 28352
Oat Dr 28352
Oban Dr 28352
Odom Rd 28352
Old Charleston Cir 28352
Old Johns Rd 28352
Old Lumberton Rd 28352
Old Maxton Rd 28352
Old Stage Rd 28352
Old Track Rd 28352
Old Wire Rd 28352
Olde Farm Cir 28352
Omega St 28352
Ormsby Dr 28352
Palomino Rd 28352
Pankey Town Rd 28352
Park Cir, Dr & Ln 28352
Parkdale Dr 28352
Parliament Ave 28352
Partridge Dr 28352
Patricia St 28352
Patsy Ln 28352
Patterson Cir & Rd 28352
Pea Bridge Rd 28352
Pecan Ln 28352
Peden St 28352
Peele St 28352
Peels St 28352
Pelham Dr 28352
Perks St 28352
Phillip Dr 28352
Phritz St 28352
Pie Ln 28352
N & S Pine St 28352
Pine Harbor Rd 28352
Pine Needle Cir 28352
Pine View Cir 28352

Pine Villa Dr 28352
Pinecroft St 28352
Pineview Dr 28352
Pinewood Trl 28352
Pintail Pt 28352
Pinto Pl 28352
Pitt St 28352
Plant Rd 28352
Plantation Rd 28352
Plaza Dr & Rd 28352
Pond Dr 28352
Ponderosa Cir 28352
Poplar Ln 28352
Port St 28352
Pranchea Rd 28352
Presbyterian Ave 28352
Pressley Ln 28352
Price St 28352
Prince St 28352
Produce Market Rd 28352
Progress Pl 28352
Providence Rd 28352
Purcell Rd & St 28352
Quail Ridge Dr 28352
Queen Rd 28352
Queensdale St 28352
R Graham St 28352
E & W Railroad St 28352
Raleigh St 28352
Randomwood Dr 28352
Randy Dr 28352
Ray Locklear Rd 28352
Raymond Cir 28352
Rea Magnet Rd 28352
Reed St 28352
Revel St 28352
Richardson Rd 28352
Richmond St 28352
Ridgecrest Cir 28352
Ridgewood Cir 28352
Riverton Rd 28352
Robin Run 28352
Rocky Ford Rd 28352
Roosevelt St 28352
Roper St 28352
Rose Ct 28352
Rosemary Ln 28352
Roseville St 28352
Rosewood St 28352
Ross St 28352
Saddle Path Cir 28352
Saint Andrews Dr 28352
Saint Luke Church Rd 28352
Salem St 28352
Salley Mcnair Rd 28352
Samantha Pl 28352
Samoa St 28352
Sanders Cir & Rd 28352
Sandhurst Dr 28352
Sanford Rd 28352
Sarah Ln 28352
Savannah Dr 28352
Sawdust Ln 28352
Saymon Cir 28352
Scarlet Ct 28352
Scotch Meadows Dr 28352
Scotia Ln 28352
Scotland St 28352
Scotland Crossing Dr 28352
Scotland Farm Rd 28352
Scotland High Rd 28352
Scotland Manor Apts 28352
E & W Scotsdale Rd 28352
Scottish Ave 28352
Seals Rd 28352
Shady Ln & St 28352
Sharla St 28352
Shaw Dr, Rd & St 28352
Shaw Currie Rd 28352
Shepherd Ave 28352
Sherbrooke Cir 28352
Short St 28352
Sidney Bean Rd 28352
Sierra Cir 28352
Sigma St 28352
Silver Ln 28352

Silver Hill Rd 28352
Simmons Ave 28352
Skye Ct & Dr 28352
Smart Dr 28352
Smith St 28352
Smyrna Church Rd 28352
Sneads Grove Rd 28352
Sneadtown Rd 28352
Sophies Ct 28352
Southgates Dr 28352
Southwood Dr 28352
Speller St 28352
Spring Branch Dr 28352
Spring Hill Dr 28352
Springs Mill Rd 28352
Spruce St 28352
St. Luke Church Rd 28352
Stanley St 28352
State Line Rd 28352
Sterling Ln 28352
Stevens Cir 28352
Stewartsville Rd 28352
Stewartsville Cemetery Rd 28352
Stonewall Rd 28352
Stratford Dr 28352
Strickland Dr 28352
Stubbs Rd 28352
Sugar Rd 28352
Summer Ln 28352
Sunset Dr 28352
Surrey Dr 28352
Sweetgum Cir 28352
Sy Dr 28352
Sycamore Ln 28352
Taft St 28352
Tara Dr 28352
Tarboro St 28352
Tartan Rd 28352
Taylor Cir & Rd 28352
Tens Dr 28352
Terrace Cir 28352
Todd Cir 28352
Tom Gibson Rd 28352
Trad St 28352
Troon Cir 28352
Tucker St 28352
S Turnpike Rd 28352
Tuskeegee Dr 28352
Us Highway 15 401 Byp S 28352
Us Highway 401 Byp 28352
Us Highway 501 S 28352
E Us Highway 74 28352
E & W Vance St 28352
Victoria Cir 28352
Village Dr 28352
Virginia Pl 28352
Wagram Rd & St 28352
Walker St 28352
Wall St 28352
Walnut St 28352
Ward St 28352
Warren Ave 28352
Washington Ave & St 28352
Washington Park Apts 28352
Webb Way 28352
Welch St 28352
Wells Cir 28352
Wesleyan Dr 28352
West Blvd 28352
Westwood Way 28352
Westwood Village Shopp Ctr 28352
Whiteville St 28352
Whitlock Rd 28352
Wiley Cir 28352
N Wilkinson Dr 28352
Will St 28352
Williams St 28352
Williamson Trailer Park 28352
Willow Dr 28352
Willow Wood Apts 28352
Wilmington St 28352
Wilson St 28352

Windmere Dr 28352
Woodbridge Dr 28352
Woodburn Rd 28352
Woodlawn Dr 28352
Woodpecker Ln 28352
Woodrun Dr 28352
Woodwinds Cir 28352
Wooster St 28352
X Way Rd 28352
Yadkin Ave 28352
York St 28352
Zion St 28352

NUMBERED STREETS

All Street Addresses 28352

LEXINGTON NC

General Delivery 27292

POST OFFICE BOXES MAIN OFFICE STATIONS AND BRANCHES

Box No.s
A - U 27293
949C - 949C 27293
1 - 5092 27293
9998 - 9998 27292
9998 - 9998 27293

RURAL ROUTES

01, 02, 06, 07, 09, 11, 16, 19, 20, 23 27292
03, 04, 05, 08, 10, 12, 13, 14, 15, 18, 21, 22, 24, 25 27295

NAMED STREETS

Abbid St 27292
Abbotts Ave & Ct 27292
Aberdeen Dr 27292
Abram Young Rd 27292
Acacia Cir 27292
Academy Dr 27295
Ada C Shaw Ln 27295
Adair Ln 27295
Adam Ln 27292
Adams Ct & St 27292
Adams Farm Dr 27295
Agner Ln 27292
Aimee Dr 27295
Alan Adale Ct 27292
Albemarle St 27292
Albert Dr 27292
Albert Varner Rd 27295
Aldean Dr 27295
Alicen Dr 27295
Allen Dr & Rd 27295
Allen Yountz Ln & Rd 27295
Allie Dr 27292
Allred Rd 27292
Alma Owens Dr 27292
Aloysius Dr 27292
Alpine Dr 27292
Amandale Ln 27295
Amber Ln 27292
Amberly Dr 27295
Amelia Ln 27295
American Way 27295
Anchor Ln 27292
Andrea Ln 27292
Andrew Sink Rd 27295
Angel Ln 27295
Angus Ct 27295
Angus Ln 27292
Ann Ave 27295
Anna Lewis Dr 27292

Anne Ct 27292
Anne St 27295
Annette Cir 27295
Annette Dr 27292
Antelope Dr 27292
Antha Ln 27295
Anthony Dr 27295
Antler Ct 27295
Apache Way 27295
Apex Dr 27295
Appaloosa Trl 27292
April Ln 27295
April Curry Ln 27292
E & W Arbor Ave & Dr 27292
Arcadia Dr & Ln 27295
Archdale Dr 27292
Archery Dr 27292
Archie Ln 27295
Arden Rd 27295
Arland Dr 27292
Arlene Dr 27295
Arnold Rd 27295
Arnold Farms Ln 27295
Arrington Dr 27295
Arrowhead Cir 27295
Arrowhead Dr 27295
Arrowhead Pt 27292
Arthur Dr 27292
Arthur Kepley Rd 27292
Arthur Murph Dr 27292
Arthur Tussey Rd 27295
Arvil Hunt Rd 27295
Arvin Hill Ln 27295
Ashbury Ct 27295
Ashby Ln 27292
Ashland Dr 27295
Ashley Ct 27295
Ashmoor Ct & Ln 27295
Ashwood Ln 27295
Aspen Ln 27295
Astoria Ct 27295
Audrey Ln 27292
Augusta Dr 27295
Austin Dr & St 27292
Autumn Ln 27295
Autumn Ridge Dr 27295
Avalon Dr 27295
Avenue A 27292
Avenue B 27292
Avenue C 27292
Avenue I 27292
Avenue J 27292
Avenue K 27292
Avenue L 27292
Avenue M 27292
Aviation Way 27292
Avondale Dr 27295
S Avondale Rd 27292
Azalea Ln 27295
B R Hunt Rd 27295
Baby Bear Ln 27295
Baker Ln 27295
Balsam Dr 27292
Baney Dr 27292
Barbry Ave 27295
Barrett Dr 27292
Baxter Ct 27292
Bay Meadow Ct 27292
Bayleaf Dr 27292
Beach Rd 27292
Bear Ln 27295
Beaver Creek Rd 27295
Beaver Dam Creek Rd 27295
Beaver Farm Rd 27295
Beaver Lodge Ln 27295
Beck Dr & Rd 27292
Beckford Dr 27295
Beckner Rd & St 27292
Beckner Cove Rd 27292
Becks Church Rd 27292
Becks Nursery Rd 27292
Becky Hill Rd 27295
Bedford Dr 27295
Beech Dr 27292

Beech Retreat Dr & Ln 27292
Beech Tree Ln 27295
Beechwood Dr 27292
Beethoven Ave 27292
Belair St 27292
Belgian Dr 27295
Bellwood St 27292
Ben Allyn Ln 27295
Bending Brook Ln 27292
Bennies Ln 27292
Bent Creek Dr 27295
Bentleys Dr 27295
Berger Dr 27292
Berkeley Dr 27295
Berrier Ave & Rd 27295
Berryfield Ln 27292
Berrywood Ln 27295
Bertessa Ln 27295
Berwick Ct 27295
Bethany Rd 27292
Bethesda Dr & Rd 27295
Biesecker Rd 27295
Big M Farm Rd 27292
Bill Lohr Rd 27292
Bill Medlin Rd 27292
Billy Smith Rd 27292
Birch Ln 27292
Birchwood Ct 27292
Birkdale Dr 27295
Black Angus Ct 27295
Black Dairy Rd 27295
Black Sawmill Rd 27295
Blackberry Ln 27292
Blossom Cir 27292
Blue Heron Ln 27292
Blue Jay Dr 27292
Blue Rose Ln 27295
Blue Water Pt 27292
Blueberry Ln 27295
Boardwalk Ln 27292
Boaze Rd 27295
Bob Allred Rd 27292
Bob Callicut Dr 27292
Bob Mountain Rd 27292
Bob Musgrave Rd 27292
Bob Smith Dr 27292
Bobcat Cv 27292
Bodine Pl 27295
Bonne Venture Rd 27292
Booker Ave 27292
Bookington Dr 27292
Boones Cave Rd 27295
Boss Hog Ave 27292
Bowers Rd 27292
Bowtie Rd 27292
Bradford Pl 27295
Bradley Tysinger Rd 27295
Branch Rd 27295
Branch Creek Dr 27295
Brandi Dr 27295
Brandon Ct 27295
Brandon Wayne Dr 27292
Breckenridge Ct 27292
Breezewood Ln 27292
Bremen Dr 27295
Bremen Garden Dr 27295
Brentwood Dr 27292
Brerose Ln 27292
Brewer Path & Rd 27295
Brian Center Dr 27292
Briar Patch Dr 27292
Briarcliff St 27292
Briarwood Dr 27295
Bridge St 27292
Bridgewood Ct 27292
Bridle Creek Trl 27295
Brierpatch Ln 27292
Briggs Rd 27292
Briggstone Rd 27292
Briggstown Rd 27292
Brinkley Dr 27295
Bristol St 27292
Brittany Ln 27295
Broad St 27295
Broadus Smith Rd 27292

Broadview Ave 27295
Broadway Rd 27295
Brody Ln 27295
Brookgreen Dr 27292
Brookhill Dr 27292
Brooks Cir & Rd 27295
Brookside Dr 27295
Brown St 27292
Bruce St 27292
Brushy Dr 27295
Bryan Woods Ln 27295
Bryant Rd 27292
Bryce Dr 27295
Buckstone Ct 27292
Bud Sink Rd 27295
Bud Yarborough Rd 27295
Buddle Dr 27292
Buddle Bay Ln 27292
Buddy Ln 27295
Buela Hairston Rd 27295
Buena Vista Dr 27295
Burbank Dr 27295
Burgess St 27292
Burgin Dr 27292
Burke Dr 27295
Burkeview Ct 27295
Burkewood Dr 27295
Burkhart Rd 27292
Burl Owens Rd 27295
Burler St 27292
Burrow Ct 27295
Business Blvd 27295
Butterfly Dr 27295
Byerly Rd 27295
Byerly St 27292
Caden Village Dr 27295
Caitlin Ln 27295
Caldcleugh Rd 27295
Callahan Hill Rd 27295
Calvin Sowers Ln & Rd 27295
Cambodian Cultural Center Rd 27292
Cambridge Rd 27292
Camden Cir 27292
Cameron Ct & Rd 27295
Camp Joel Trl 27295
Camper Ln 27292
Canary Dr 27292
Candlewood Dr 27295
Candy Ln 27295
Cane Creek Rd 27292
Canoe Ln 27295
Canterbury Ln & Pl 27292
Canvasback Dr 27292
Cap Ingram Rd 27292
Capistrano Shrs 27292
Capistrano Shores Blvd 27292
Captain Dr 27295
Carawood Ln 27295
Cardinal Dr & Ln 27292
Carl B Rd 27292
Carl Lee Dr 27292
Carl Pressley Rd 27295
Carl Snider Rd 27292
Carl Swing Dr 27295
Carley Ln 27295
Carlile Dr 27295
N Carolina Ave 27292
Carolina Acres Rd 27295
Carriage Trace Ln 27295
Carrick Rd 27292
Carrie Ln 27295
Carries Cove Ln 27295
Carrol Hills Ct 27295
Carroll St 27292
Carters Grove Rd 27292
Carver Dr 27292
Casper Ln 27295
Cecil Rd 27292
N Cecil St 27292
S Cecil St 27292
Cedar Dr & Ln 27292
Cedar Creek Ln 27292
Cedar Creek Rd 27295

Cedar Grove Dr 27295
Cedar Lane Dr 27295
Cedar Ridge Dr 27295
Cedar Rock Rd 27292
Cedar Springs Rd 27292
Cedarcrest Ln 27295
Cedarwood Dr 27292
E & W Center St 27292
Center Church Rd 27295
E Center Street Ext 27292
W Center Street Ext 27295
Central Ave 27292
Central Hts 27292
Century St 27292
Chandler Dr 27295
Chapel Dr 27295
Chapman Dr 27295
Charles Ave 27295
Charleswood Ln 27295
Charlie Hinkle Rd 27295
Charlie Owens Ln 27295
Charlotte Dr 27292
Charlotte Drive Ext 27292
Cher Lo Dr 27295
Cherokee Dr 27295
Cherry Dr, Ln & St 27292
Chester Tysinger Dr 27292
Chestnut St 27292
Chestnut Grove Ln 27295
Chestnut Grove Church Rd 27295
Chestnut Ridge Dr 27295
Chickadee Dr 27292
Chickasaw Rd 27295
Childers Ct 27292
Childrens Trl 27292
Childress Vinyard Rd 27295
Chimney Rock Dr 27292
Choctaw Dr 27295
Choyce St 27292
Chrisonya Ln 27295
Christie Ln 27295
Christmas Ln 27292
Chub Rd 27295
N & S Church St 27292
Cid Rd 27292
Circle Dr 27295
City Club Blvd & Cir 27292
City Lake Rd 27295
Cj Ln 27292
Cl Wagner Rd 27295
Clapp Farm Rd 27295
Clara Hill Ln 27292
Clarence Mock Ln 27295
Clark Snider Rd 27295
Claude Dr 27295
Clay Floyd Dr 27292
Clearfield Dr 27295
Clearview St 27295
Clell Dr 27295
Cleveland Dr 27292
Cliffview Dr 27292
Cliffwood Dr 27295
Clover Ct & Trl 27295
Cloverdale Rd 27295
Cloverfield Ln 27295
Clyde Dr 27292
Coble Cir 27295
Cody St 27292
Coe Rd 27292
Coleman Dr 27292
College Ln 27295
College Park Rd 27295
Colonial Dr 27295
Comanche Trl 27295
Comer Ln 27295
Commercial Blvd 27292
Commodore Dr 27295
Community Rd 27295
Conard Sowers Rd 27295
Confederate St 27295
Conner St 27292
Conrad Ln 27295
Conrad St 27295
Conrad Hill Mine Rd 27295
Converse Dr 27292

Copeland Dr 27295
Copley St 27292
Copper Ln 27292
Copperfield Ln 27292
Coree Dr 27295
Cornelia St 27292
Cornerstone Ln 27295
Cornerstone Rd 27292
Cornflower Ln 27292
Corvette Ln 27292
Cosie Ln 27292
Cotton Cross Dr 27292
Cotton Grove Rd 27292
E Country Ln 27292
Country Club Blvd, Cir & Dr 27292
Country View Dr 27292
Country Villa Dr 27295
Country Woods Dr 27292
County Home Rd 27292
County School Rd 27292
Court Sq 27292
Courtney Ln 27295
Cove Rd 27292
Covenant Ln 27292
Cow Palace Rd 27295
Coyote Trl 27292
Crabapple Way 27295
Crane Creek Way 27295
Cranford St 27295
Craver Dr 27292
Craver Rd 27295
Creek Meadow Dr 27295
Creek Ridge Dr 27295
Creekside Ln 27295
Creekview Ln 27292
Creekwood Ct & Dr 27292
Crepe Myrtle Ln 27295
Crescent Dr 27292
Cress Rd 27292
Crest Cir 27295
Crestwood Cir 27295
Crews Lake Rd 27295
Crimson Dr 27292
Critcher Dr 27295
E Cross Ln & Rd 27292
Crossbow Ln 27292
Crosscreek Rd 27292
Crossfield Ct 27295
Crotts Dr 27292
Crouse Mountain Ln 27292
Crousetown Rd 27295
Crow Creek Dr 27292
Crowfoot Ct 27295
Crutchfield Ave 27292
Crystal Ridge Dr 27295
Cul De Sac Ct 27295
Cullen Ct 27292
Cummings Ct 27295
Cunningham Brick Yard Rd 27292
Curry St 27292
Curtis Dr 27295
Curtis Leonard Rd 27295
Cuthrell Ln 27295
Cyndi Ln 27295
Cynthia Ln 27295
Cypress Ln 27295
D And O Dr 27292
Dacotah St 27292
Daisy Ln 27295
Daisy St 27292
Dale Ridge Ln 27292
Dalewood St 27292
Dallas St 27295
Dalton Dr 27295
Dalton Jackson Ln 27295
Daniel Ln 27295
Darr Pl 27295
Daryl Dr 27295
David Smith Rd 27295
Davidson Ave 27292
W Davidson Ave 27295
Davidson Dr 27295
N Davidson Dr 27295

Davidson County Landfill Rd 27292
Davis Dr 27295
Daybreak Ln 27292
Daydream Ln 27295
Dearr Dr 27292
Deaton Young Rd 27292
Deer Creek Ln 27292
Deer Crossing Ln 27292
Deer Haven Ln 27292
Deer Hunter Ln 27295
Deer Path Ln 27295
Deer Run Ln 27292
Deer Track Ln 27295
Deerfield Ct 27295
Deerwood Dr 27295
Del Vista Dr 27292
Delana Ave 27292
Delk Rd 27292
Della Wilson Rd 27295
Dellwood Dr 27292
Delta St 27295
Dennis Ln 27292
Der San Dr 27295
Derfmar Dr 27295
Dermont Dr 27292
Devonshire Dr 27295
Dew West Ct 27295
Dewey Ln 27295
Dillard Cir 27292
Dixie St 27292
Dixon St 27295
Doc Beck Rd 27292
Doc Mcculloch Rd 27292
Dock Post Ln 27292
Dockside Dr 27292
Dodge Dr 27295
Doe Xing 27295
Doe Run Ct 27292
Dogpatch Trl 27292
Dogwood Dr 27292
Dogwood Ln 27295
Dogwood Pt 27292
Dogwood Trl 27295
Domino Dr 27292
Donna Dr 27295
Donnell Ct 27295
Dora Ln 27292
Dorsett Rd 27292
Double Spring Ln 27295
Douglas Dr 27295
Dove Pt & St 27295
Dover Rd 27295
Doverstone Ct 27292
Dr Zimmerman Rd 27295
Dragon Dr 27295
Drake Ln 27295
Drew Ln 27295
Drexel Cir 27292
Druid Hills Dr 27292
Dry Branch Trl 27292
Duke Dr 27295
Dunbar St 27292
Dusty Dr 27295
Dutch Club Dr 27292
Dykers Creek Rd 27295
Eagle Ridge Ct 27295
Eanes St 27292
Earlie Hedrick Rd 27292
Early James Rd 27295
Early Miller Rd 27295
Earwood Ln 27295
Eastdale Dr 27292
Easter Cir & Rd 27295
Eastside Dr 27292
Eastview Dr 27295
Eastwood Dr 27295
Ebert Farm Rd 27295
Echoview Cir 27292
Ed Byerly Rd 27295
Ed Essick Rd 27295
Ed Lo Dr 27295
Ed Rickard Rd 27295
Ed Tiser Rd 27292
Edgar Ct 27295
Edgemont Ln 27292

Edgewood Dr 27292
Edgewood Ln 27295
Edna St 27292
Edwin Dr 27295
Egret Pl 27292
El Mcmahan Farm Rd 27295
El Myers Rd 27295
Elden Dr 27295
Eleanor Dr 27295
NW Elementary Rd 27295
Eliason Ln 27295
Elijah Beck Rd 27292
E Elizabeth St 27295
Elk St 27292
Ellenton Ct 27295
Eller Rd 27295
Eller St 27292
Ellington Ave 27292
Elm Dr 27295
Elvernia Ave 27292
Elwin Cir 27295
Embler Rd 27292
Emerald Isle Ct 27292
Emergency Dr 27292
Emile St 27292
Emily Ln 27295
Emlee St 27295
Enos Dr 27295
Enterprise Ct & Rd 27295
Ernest Cook Rd 27295
Ernest Snider Rd 27292
Ervin Dr 27292
Erwen Rd 27295
Essick Rd 27295
Estates Dr 27295
Esther Eigner Ln 27295
Eugene Ct 27292
Eulah Ct 27292
Eulala Leonard Rd 27295
Eva Ln 27295
Evans St 27295
Evergreen Ave & Cir 27292
Fair Cir & St 27292
Fairfax Rd & St 27295
Fairground Rd 27295
Fairview Dr 27292
Fairview Acres Rd 27295
Fairway Dr 27295
Fairystone Ln 27295
Faith Dr 27292
Fallie Ln 27295
Family Cir 27292
Family Ct 27295
Family Feud Dr 27295
Farabee Homestead Rd 27295
Farm Rd 27295
Farmer Ave 27292
Farmland Rd 27292
Fast Ln 27295
Fawn Trl 27292
Fawn Brook Dr 27292
Federal St 27292
Feezor Rd 27292
Fellowship Ln 27295
Fern Crk 27292
Fern Creek Dr 27292
Ferris Rd 27292
Field View Ct 27295
Fine Dr 27295
Fining Ct 27295
Fisher St 27292
Fisher Farm Rd 27292
Fleabo Rd 27295
Flicker Ln 27295
Flint Ridge Rd 27292
Florence St 27292
Flossie Ln 27295
Floyd Rd 27295
Floyd Church Rd 27292
Floyd Shoaf Rd 27292
Flying M Ln 27295
Flying M Airport Rd 27295
Flynt St 27295
Foothill Dr 27295
S Ford St 27292

S Forest Dr & Ln 27292
Forest Green Dr 27292
Forest Hill Rd 27295
Forest Ridge Ln 27292
Forest Service Rd 27295
Forestrose Dr 27295
Forrest Hedrick Rd 27295
Fowler Ave 27292
Fox Ln 27295
Fox Run 27292
Fox Chase Ct & Dr 27295
Fox Creek Dr 27292
Fox Den Dr 27295
Fox Haven Ct 27292
Fox Run Trl 27295
Foxcroft Dr 27292
Foxfire Cir 27295
Foxglove Ln 27292
Foxwood Dr 27295
Foy Ave 27292
Foyell St 27292
Frank Fleer Rd 27292
Frank Hinkle Rd 27295
Frank Hulin Rd 27295
Frank Stoner Rd 27292
Frankie St 27292
Franklin St 27292
Frankwood Dr 27292
Fred Miller Rd 27292
Freedom Ln 27295
Freewill Cir 27295
Freewood Rd 27295
Friar Tuck Ter 27292
Friendly Way 27292
Friendship Church Rd 27295
Fritts Rd 27295
Fritts St 27292
Fritts Farm Ct 27295
Frog Pond Dr 27295
Front St 27295
Frontier Dr 27292
Fuller St 27292
Ga Nan Dr 27292
Gabriel Pt 27295
Gainey Cir 27292
Gallimore Dr & Rd 27292
Gambrell Ln 27292
Game Farm Rd 27292
Gandy Ln 27295
Gap Dr 27295
Garden Dr 27292
Gardenia Ct 27295
Garland Dr 27295
Gate Cir 27292
Gate West Dr 27295
Gateway Ln 27295
Gene Hege Rd 27295
George Hege Rd 27295
George Surratt Rd 27295
Georgies Pl 27295
Gibson Pond Way 27295
Gil Mac Dr 27295
Giles Rd 27295
Glendale Ct & Rd 27292
Gleneagle Ln 27295
Glenn Link Rd 27295
Glenoaks Dr 27292
Glenwood Dr 27292
N Goat Pasture Rd 27295
Gobble Rd 27295
Gobble Creek Dr 27295
Godfrey Ct 27295
Goforth Lake Rd 27295
Golden Dr 27292
Golden Eagle Ln 27292
Golden Rod Ln 27295
Goodluck Dr 27292
Goose Dr 27292
Gordon Ln 27292
Gordontown Rd 27292
Graceway Dr 27295
Grady Dr 27295
Grady Michael Dr 27295
Granite Trl 27295
Grant St 27292
Gray Rd 27292

Gray Farm Ln ... 27292
Gray Mill Rd ... 27292
Grayland St ... 27295
Green Acres Ln ... 27292
Green Duck Ln ... 27292
Green Heron Dr ... 27292
Green Meadows Dr ... 27292
Green Meadows Drive Ext ... 27292
Green Needles Dr
- 100-299 ... 27292
- 300-399 ... 27295
- 700-999 ... 27292

Green Valley Dr ... 27292
Greenbriar Ln ... 27295
Greenfield Ct & Dr ... 27295
Greenhaven Dr ... 27292
Greenhills Dr ... 27292
N & S Greensboro St ... 27292
Greensboro Street Ext ... 27295
Greentree Dr ... 27295
Greenway Dr ... 27292
Greenwood St ... 27292
Grey Fox Ln ... 27295
Grey Fox Run ... 27292
Griffin Ln ... 27292
Grimes Blvd & Cir ... 27292
W Grove Rd ... 27295
Grove Park Ln ... 27295
Grubb Rd ... 27295
Guilford St ... 27292
Gurney Kerns Rd ... 27292
Guy Dr ... 27295
Guy Pressley Rd ... 27295
H H Farm Rd ... 27292
H L Palmer Rd ... 27292
Habersham Ct ... 27295
Hackney St ... 27292
Hadley Dr ... 27295
Hairston Rd ... 27295
Hal Parrish Rd ... 27292
Hallmark Dr ... 27292
Haltom Rd ... 27292
Hames St ... 27295
Hamil St ... 27292
Hamilton Ln ... 27292
Hamilton Rd ... 27295
Hammerhead Dr ... 27292
Hammond Rd ... 27295
Hampton Rd & St ... 27295
Hampton Estates Dr ... 27295
Hanes Ln ... 27295
Hanes Acres Dr ... 27295
Hanes Park Ln ... 27295
Hankins Dr ... 27292
Hannah Ln ... 27295
Hannersville Rd ... 27292
S Happy Hill Ct & Rd ... 27295
Happy Hollow Ct ... 27295
Happy Trails Rd ... 27295
Harb Dr ... 27295
Harbor Dr E & W ... 27292
Hardwood Ln ... 27292
S Hargrave Ln, Rd & St ... 27292
Harkey St ... 27292
Harmony Pl ... 27295
Harold Hinkle Dr ... 27295
Harrington Ave ... 27292
Harris Ln & Rd ... 27292
Hartley Ln ... 27295
Hartley Rd ... 27292
Hartman Rd ... 27295
Hartman St ... 27292
Harvey Tussey Dr ... 27295
Harvick Ln ... 27292
Hassie Ln ... 27295
Haven Hill Rd ... 27292
Havenwood Dr ... 27295
Hawk Nest Dr ... 27292
Hawthorne Ln ... 27295
Hayfield Ln ... 27292
Hays Harris Rd ... 27292
Haywood Ln ... 27292
Haywood Rd ... 27295
Hazelwood Ct ... 27295

Heath Ln ... 27292
Heath Church Rd ... 27292
Heather Cir ... 27295
Hedrick Ave ... 27292
Hedrick Cir ... 27295
Hedrick Ln ... 27292
Hedrick St ... 27292
Hedrick Heritage Dr ... 27295
Hedrick Lodge Rd ... 27292
Hedrick Mill Rd ... 27292
Heels Ct ... 27292
Hege Dr
- 1-99 ... 27292
- 100-1499 ... 27295

Hege Rd ... 27295
Heitman Rd ... 27295
Helmstetler Rd ... 27295
Hemlock Dr & Ln ... 27295
E & W Hemstead St ... 27292
Henderson Ln ... 27295
Henry Link Access Rd ... 27292
Henry Lomax Rd ... 27295
Heritage Dr ... 27295
Heritage Hill Ln ... 27295
Heritage Manor Cir ... 27295
Heron Rd ... 27292
Hershey Dr ... 27295
Hettie Dr ... 27295
Hhg Rd ... 27295
Hickory Pl ... 27295
Hickory Rd ... 27292
Hickory St ... 27292
Hickory Hills Ln ... 27295
Hickory Point Dr ... 27292
Hickory Wood Dr ... 27295
Hicks Ct & Rd ... 27295
Hidden Springs Dr ... 27292
Higgins Hill Dr ... 27295
High Bluff Dr ... 27295
High Meadows Dr ... 27292
High Ridge Ct ... 27295
High Rock Dr ... 27292
High Rock Shores Dr ... 27292
Highgate Ln ... 27295
Highland Dr ... 27292
Hilary St ... 27295
Hill Dr ... 27295
Hill Ln ... 27295
Hill Rd ... 27295
Hill St ... 27295
Hill Everhart Rd ... 27295
Hillbilly Trl ... 27292
Hillcrest Cir, Ct, Dr & Rd ... 27292
Hillie Byerly Ln ... 27292
Hillsdale Dr ... 27295
Hillside Dr ... 27295
Hilltop Dr ... 27292
Hillview Ct & Dr ... 27292
Hillwood Ct ... 27295
Hilton St ... 27292
Hinkle Ln & Rd ... 27295
Hl Frank Ln ... 27295
Hobbs Rd ... 27295
Hodge Dr ... 27295
Hoffman Ln ... 27295
Hoilman Ln ... 27295
Holiday Dr ... 27295
Hollis Dr ... 27295
Hollow Crk ... 27295
Hollow Ln ... 27295
Hollow Ridge Ln ... 27295
S Holloway Church Rd ... 27292
Holly Ct ... 27295
Holly Ln ... 27292
Holly Berry Ln ... 27292
E Holly Grove Rd ... 27292
Holly Grove Luthern Church Rd ... 27292
Hollyberry Ct ... 27292
Hollybrook Cir ... 27292
Hollyhill Rd ... 27292
Holston Rd ... 27292
Holt St ... 27292
Homer St ... 27292
Homer Leonard Rd ... 27295

E Homestead Dr ... 27292
Homewood Ln ... 27292
Hoover Dr ... 27292
Hoover Rd ... 27295
Hope Dr ... 27295
Hope Crossing Dr ... 27295
Hopedale St ... 27292
Horse Farm Rd ... 27295
Horse Haven Rd ... 27295
Horseshoe Neck Rd ... 27295
Hospice Way ... 27292
Hospital Dr ... 27292
Howard Ln ... 27295
Howard Black Rd ... 27292
Hoyle Grubb Ln ... 27295
Huckle Pl ... 27292
Hugh Miller Rd ... 27292
Hughes Rd ... 27292
Hummingbird Pass ... 27295
Hunt Rd ... 27292
Hunter Rd ... 27295
Hunter Creek Rd ... 27292
Hunters Pt ... 27295
Hunters Way ... 27292
Hunters Chase ... 27292
Hunters Path Ct ... 27292
Hunters Ridge Ct & Dr ... 27295
Huntingdon Rd ... 27292
Huntington Trl ... 27295
Huntington Woods Dr ... 27295
Hurd Ln ... 27292
Hw Phillips Rd ... 27295
Hyde St ... 27292
Hylian Ln ... 27295
Idlewild Dr ... 27295
Idlewood St ... 27295
Indian Grave Rd ... 27295
Indian Wells Cir ... 27295
Industrial Dr ... 27295
Inez Ln ... 27295
Ira Dr ... 27295
Ira Lewis Dr ... 27295
Irma Ave ... 27292
Iroquois Trl ... 27295
Isabel Dr ... 27292
Isaiah Ct ... 27292
Island View Dr ... 27292
Ivy Ln ... 27295
J Goins Dr ... 27292
J Nettie Dr ... 27292
J R Lambert Rd ... 27295
Jack Jowers Rd ... 27295
Jack Young Rd ... 27292
Jackie Dr ... 27292
Jackson Ave, Blvd & St ... 27295
Jackson Square Dr ... 27295
Jacob Dr ... 27295
Jada Dr ... 27295
Jake Ln ... 27292
Jake Shoaf Rd ... 27295
Jala Ln ... 27292
Jamaica Dr ... 27292
James St ... 27295
James Harper Trl ... 27295
James Owen Rd ... 27292
Jamie Dr ... 27295
Jane Blvd ... 27295
Jane Grubb Dr ... 27292
Jared Dr ... 27295
Jarrell Rd ... 27292
Jarvis Rd ... 27295
Jason Dr ... 27295
Jc Dr ... 27295
Jd Essick Rd ... 27295
Jeanette Dr ... 27295
Jeff Ave ... 27295
Jeff Nichols Ln ... 27292
E & W Jefferson Ct, Dr, Rd & St ... 27295
Jenkins Rd ... 27295
Jerome Simon Pl ... 27295
Jerry Dr ... 27292
Jersey Ln ... 27292
Jersey Church Rd ... 27292
Jerusalem Rd ... 27292

Jes Wes Ln ... 27295
Jess Cross Rd ... 27292
Jesse Ray Ln ... 27295
Jessie James Dr ... 27295
Jessup St ... 27292
Jessup Street Ext ... 27292
Jim Ln ... 27292
Jim Bell Rd ... 27292
Jl Temple Rd ... 27295
Jm Penninger Rd ... 27292
Jo Jo Ln ... 27292
Joan Dr ... 27292
Joe Dr ... 27292
Joe Cecil Rd ... 27292
Joes Beach Blvd ... 27292
John Beck Rd ... 27292
John Black Rd ... 27292
John Deere Ln ... 27295
John Hinkle Rd ... 27295
John Hoover Rd ... 27295
John Lookabill Rd ... 27292
John M Ward Rd ... 27295
John Snider Rd ... 27295
John T Farabee Ln ... 27295
John W Berrier Rd ... 27295
John Ward Rd ... 27295
John Wright Rd ... 27292
John Young Rd ... 27292
Johns Rd ... 27295
Johnson Farm Rd ... 27292
Jolly Rd ... 27292
Jordan Ln & Rd ... 27295
Joshua Ct ... 27295
N Joy Ct ... 27292
Joyce Dr ... 27295
Julia Ln ... 27295
Julie St ... 27295
Junior Order Home Rd ... 27292
Juniper Dr ... 27292
Junius Dr ... 27295
Justin Ct ... 27295
Kapstone Xing ... 27295
Kara Ln ... 27295
Kate St ... 27292
Kathryn Oak Ln ... 27295
Kathy Ln ... 27292
Kathys Park Dr ... 27295
Katlyn Dr ... 27295
Katy Ln ... 27295
Kaufman Blvd ... 27292
Kaye Dr ... 27292
Kayla Lyn Dr ... 27295
Kearns Dr ... 27295
Keely Ln ... 27292
Keiffer Dr ... 27295
Keith Cecil Rd ... 27292
Keith Sink Rd ... 27292
Kelly Ln ... 27295
Kellys Ct ... 27295
Kendlebrook Farm Rd ... 27295
Kenny Ln ... 27295
Kenton Ln ... 27295
Kentwood Ln ... 27295
Kenwood Ln ... 27295
Kepley Rd ... 27292
Kepley Craver Ave ... 27295
Kepley Sink Ln ... 27295
Kerney Kepley Dr ... 27292
Kert Dr ... 27292
Kesler Rd ... 27292
Kevin Dale Dr ... 27295
Kildee Dr ... 27292
Kimberly Dr & Ln ... 27292
Kimbrell St ... 27292
Kimrey St ... 27292
Kindley St ... 27292
King St ... 27292
King Richard Dr ... 27292
Kingfisher Ct ... 27292
Kinley Farm Rd ... 27292
Kinlucky Dr ... 27295
Kinney Dr & Ln ... 27292
Kirkman Rd ... 27292
Kirkwood Ave & St ... 27292
Kittery Ct ... 27295

Kiwanis Kiddie Kamp Rd ... 27295
Klap Dr ... 27292
Knob Dr ... 27295
Knollwood Ave ... 27292
Knopf Rd ... 27295
Knouse Dr ... 27295
Koo Leo Farm Rd ... 27295
N Koontz Ave & Rd ... 27295
Koontz Farm Dr ... 27295
Kyles Ct ... 27295
L And M Rd ... 27295
L F I Complex Ln ... 27292
Lady Bug Ln ... 27292
Lake Dr ... 27295
Lake St ... 27292
Lake Creek Dr ... 27292
Lake Drive 10 ... 27292
Lake Drive 2 ... 27292
Lake Drive 4 ... 27292
Lake Drive 6 ... 27292
Lake Drive 8 ... 27292
Lake Drive 9 ... 27292
Lake Leonard Rd ... 27295
Lake Pines Ln ... 27292
Lake Shore Ave & Ln ... 27292
Lakeshore Dr ... 27292
Lakeview Dr ... 27292
Lakewood Ct & Dr ... 27292
Lamb Rd ... 27295
Lambe Dr ... 27292
Landmark Pl ... 27292
Lanie Creek Dr ... 27295
Lanier Dr & Rd ... 27295
Lantanna Ave ... 27295
Lantern Dr & Ln ... 27295
Larkspur Ln ... 27292
Larry Dr ... 27295
Larry Ln ... 27292
Lashmit Ln ... 27295
Latham Dr ... 27295
Laura Ln ... 27295
Laurel Ave ... 27292
Laurel Bank Ln ... 27292
Laurel Brook Trl ... 27292
Laurel Ridge Ln ... 27292
Lawrence Dr ... 27295
Lawrence Beck Ln ... 27292
Lawrence Farm Rd ... 27292
Lazy H Ranch Rd ... 27292
Lazy River Dr ... 27295
Le Beau Ln ... 27292
Lea Meadow Rd ... 27295
Lee Ave ... 27295
Lee St ... 27292
Lee Ann Dr ... 27292
Lee Black Rd ... 27292
Lee Parks Rd ... 27292
Lee Smith Rd ... 27292
Legacy Ln ... 27292
Leggett And Platt Rd ... 27292
Legion Club Rd ... 27292
Lenalan Dr ... 27295
Lenox Ct ... 27295
N Leonard Ave & Rd ... 27295
Leonard Berrier Rd ... 27295
Leonard Creek Farm Rd ... 27295
Leonard Wade Ln ... 27295
Leonford St ... 27292
Leroy Dr ... 27295
Lester Dr ... 27292
Lester Powell Rd ... 27295
Letha Dr ... 27292
Lewie Berrier Farm Rd ... 27295
Lexington Ave ... 27292
S Lexington Dr ... 27292
Lexington Pkwy ... 27295
Lexington Thomasville Rd ... 27295
Liberty Ave ... 27292
Lillie Dr ... 27295
Lily Trl ... 27295
Limited Dr ... 27292
Lincoln Ave ... 27292
Lincoln St ... 27295

Linda Ave & Pl ... 27292
Linda Kay Ln ... 27295
Lindel Ct ... 27292
Linden Ln ... 27292
Lindy Rd ... 27292
Lineberger Dr ... 27295
Lingle Farm Rd ... 27295
Link Cir ... 27292
Link Rd ... 27295
Link Perry Trl ... 27295
Link Ridge Rd ... 27295
Linwood Rd ... 27292
Linwood Southmont Rd ... 27292
Little Beaver Rd ... 27295
Little John Ln ... 27292
Little Rock Ave ... 27295
Live Oak Ln ... 27295
Livestock Market Rd ... 27295
Lloyd Lookabill St ... 27292
Lockhart Dr ... 27292
Locust Dr ... 27292
Logan Ln ... 27292
Lohr St ... 27292
Lois Ln ... 27295
Lois Reich Ct ... 27295
Lona Daye Dr ... 27295
London Ct ... 27292
Lone Oak Dr ... 27295
Long St ... 27292
Long Bow Dr ... 27292
Longbranch Trl ... 27295
Longhorn Trail Rd ... 27295
Longview Rd ... 27292
Longview St ... 27295
Lookout Pt ... 27292
Lopp Dr & St ... 27292
Lori Belle Ln ... 27292
Lorven Dr ... 27292
Lothridge Ln ... 27292
Lou Ln ... 27292
Louya Rd ... 27292
Love Rd ... 27292
Low Creek Ln ... 27295
Lowe Dr ... 27295
Lowell St ... 27295
Lowes Blvd & Rd ... 27295
Lsb Plz ... 27292
Lumina Dr ... 27295
Lynda Ln ... 27295
Lynn Dr ... 27292
M Carrick Rd ... 27292
Mabrys Acres ... 27292
Madelyn Dr ... 27295
Madison Pl ... 27295
Mae Zimmerman Dr ... 27295
Maegeo Dr ... 27292
Magnolia Rd ... 27292
Maid Marian Ln ... 27292
N & S Main St ... 27292
Maley Ln ... 27292
Mallard Dr ... 27295
Manhattan Dr ... 27292
Manie Craver Dr ... 27295
Manor Dr ... 27295
Manor Ridge Way ... 27292
Manteo Rd ... 27295
Manus Ln ... 27292
Maple Ave ... 27292
Maple Ct ... 27295
Maple St ... 27295
Maple Tree Rd ... 27295
Marble Aly ... 27292
March Ln ... 27295
March Manor Dr ... 27295
Marco Blvd ... 27292
Margaret Lanier Dr ... 27295
Marhart Ln ... 27295
Marigold Ln ... 27292
Marion Cir, Dr & Ln ... 27292
Marion Drive Ext ... 27292
Market St ... 27292
Markwood Dr & Ln ... 27295
Marlin Dr ... 27292
Marquis Ln ... 27295
Marshall Byerly Rd ... 27295

Martha Dr ... 27292
Martin Ave & St ... 27292
Martin Luther King Jr Blvd ... 27292
Martindale Forrest Dr ... 27295
Marty Ln ... 27292
Marvin Hedrick Rd ... 27292
Mary Carter Dr ... 27292
Matt Dr ... 27292
Matthew Dr ... 27295
Maxine Dr ... 27292
Maxwell Dr ... 27295
Mayfair Rd ... 27292
Mayflower Ln ... 27295
Mayflower Rd ... 27292
Maymead St ... 27292
Mb Bailey Rd ... 27295
Mccann Ln ... 27292
Mccarn Rd ... 27292
Mccoy Rd ... 27292
Mcculloch Ln ... 27292
Mckinley Dr ... 27295
Mcpherson Ln ... 27292
Meadow Dr ... 27295
Meadow Ln
- 100-299 ... 27295
- 1000-1299 ... 27292

Meadow Trl ... 27295
Meadow Creek Dr ... 27295
Meadow Run Ln ... 27292
Meadow Way Dr ... 27295
Meadowbrook Farm Rd ... 27295
Meadowview Rd ... 27295
Meathouse Ln ... 27292
W Medical Park Dr ... 27292
Melrose Dr ... 27292
Melvin Myers Rd ... 27292
Memory Ln ... 27295
Mendota Ave ... 27292
Mercado Ln ... 27295
Mercy Ln ... 27295
Meredith Ave ... 27292
Merritt Way ... 27295
Michael Aly ... 27295
Michael Dr ... 27295
Michael Ln ... 27295
Michael Rd ... 27295
Michael St
- 100-199 ... 27295
- 400-499 ... 27292

Michael Ridge Ln ... 27295
Michelle Ln ... 27292
Midbrook Run ... 27295
Middle Creek Ct ... 27295
Midvalley Ct ... 27295
Midway Dr ... 27295
Midway School Rd ... 27295
Miles Dr ... 27295
Mill St ... 27295
Mill Stream Ln ... 27292
Miller Ln & St ... 27292
Millstone Dr ... 27295
N & S Miners Trl ... 27292
Miracle Dr ... 27295
Miss Emery Ln ... 27295
Mitchell Ave ... 27292
Mize Rd ... 27295
Mobile Ln ... 27295
Mock St ... 27295
Mock Myers Rd ... 27292
Mocksville Ave ... 27292
Mockwood Dr ... 27295
Mockwood Farms Ln ... 27295
Monroe Dr ... 27295
Monroe Rd ... 27295
Montclair Dr ... 27292
Monticello Dr ... 27292
Moore Dr ... 27292
Moose Lodge Rd ... 27295
Moretz Ln ... 27292
Morgan Dr ... 27292
Morgan Ln ... 27295
Morgans Way ... 27292
Morning Star Ln ... 27292
Morrison Dr ... 27295

Moss Brook Dr 27292
Motor Rd 27295
Mount Carmel Rd 27295
Mount Carmel Church Rd 27295
Mount Moriah Dr 27295
Mount Olivet Church Rd 27295
Mount View Ct 27292
Mountain Harbor Dr 27292
Mountain Ridge Dr 27292
Mountain View Ct 27292
Mountain View Church Rd 27292
Mountainbrook Dr 27295
Mud Run Dr 27292
Muirfield Dr 27295
Mulberry Ct 27292
Mundy House Rd 27295
Murphy Dr 27295
Murphy Ln 27292
Musgrave Rd 27295
Myers Dr & Rd 27295
Myers Hill Trl 27295
Myers Park Dr 27292
Myrtle St 27292
Nascar Fan Aly 27295
Nat Conrad Rd 27292
Natalie St 27295
Nathan Dr 27295
National Blvd 27292
Nautical Winds 27295
Navajo Rd 27295
S Nc Highway 109 27292
N & S Nc Highway 150 27295
Nc Highway 47 27292
Nc Highway 8 27292
Nealey Dr 27292
Needleworks Ln 27295
New Bowers Rd 27292
New Cut Rd 27292
New Jersey Church Rd 27292
Newhaven Dr 27292
No Record 27295
Norma Dr 27292
Norman Leonard Ln 27295
Norman Mckinley Dr 27292
Northeast St 27295
Northpoint Dr 27295
Northridge Dr 27295
Northside Dr 27295
Northview Dr 27295
Northwood Ct 27295
Nottingham Dr 27292
Numa Byerly Rd 27292
Oak Ave & Rd 27292
Oak Hill Dr 27295
Oak Hollow Rd 27295
Oakdale Ct 27295
Oakdale Ln 27295
Oakdale St 27292
Oakleaf Dr 27295
Oakmont Ter 27295
Oakridge Ct & Dr 27295
W Oaks Ln 27295
Oakwood Blvd 27292
Oakwood Cir 27295
Oakwood Dr
- 100-399 27292
- 1000-1299 27295

Oakwood Pl 27292
Oakwood Rd 27292
Octa St 27292
Octavia St 27292
Odell Owen Rd 27295
Ol Evans Farm Rd 27295
Old Brushy Dr 27292
Old Bud Sink Rd 27295
Old Buggy Trl 27295
Old Burkhart Rd 27292
Old Cabin Ln 27295
Old Doc Ct 27295
Old Garden Rd 27295
Old Golden Ln 27295
S Old Greensboro Rd 27292
Old Hargrave Rd 27295
Old Highway 29 27292
Old Indian Trl 27292
Old Lamp Ln 27292
Old Linwood Rd 27292
Old Mill Farm Rd 27295
Old Mountain Rd 27292
Old Nc Highway 109 27292
Old Nc Highway 75 27292
Old Oak Ct 27295
Old Rock Dr 27295
Old Salisbury Rd 27295
Old Silver Hill Rd 27292
Old Stone Xing 27292
Old Town Rd 27295
Old Us Highway 52 27295
E Old Us Highway 64 27292
W Old Us Highway 64 27295
W Old Us Hwy 64 27295
Old Wagon Rd 27295
Old Walnut Ln 27295
Old Willowmore Springs Rd 27292
Olde Fox Trl 27292
Olin Rd 27295
Olive St 27292
Olivia Dr 27295
Ollie Ln 27292
Olympia St 27295
Oriole Dr 27292
Osprey Trl 27295
Otter Run 27295
Outlook Ave 27292
Overbrook Dr 27292
Owen Rd 27292
Owens Rd 27292
Owens Farm Rd 27295
Oxford Rd 27292
Pack Dr 27295
Paddington Dr 27295
Palmer Rd 27295
Palomino Trl 27295
Pam Ave 27292
Parish Dr 27292
E Park Ave 27292
Park Cir 27295
Park Dr 27292
Park Ln 27292
Park St 27292
E Parker Ave, Ln & St 27292
Parks Rd 27292
Parks Meadows Dr 27292
Parks Pond Dr 27292
Parkview Dr 27295
Parnell Pl 27295
Parrot Cir 27295
Partridge Dr & Ln 27292
Patricia Ln 27295
Patterson St 27292
Paul Dr & St 27292
Paul Beck Rd 27292
Paul Hartley Ln 27295
Paul Musgrave Rd 27295
Paul Workman Rd 27292
Pauline Dr & Ln 27295
Payne Rd 27295
N Payne St 27292
S Payne St 27292
Peace Haven Dr 27292
Peachtree St 27292
Peacock Ave & Dr 27292
Pearce Rd 27295
Pearl Dr 27292
Pears Hart Ln 27295
Pebble Creek Rd 27295
Pebblestone Ct 27295
Pecan Ln 27295
Peeler St 27292
Peggy Ln 27295
Penninger Dr 27295
S Pennington Ave 27292
Penny Ln 27295
Penny Metcalf Dr 27295
Penry St 27292
Peppermill Dr 27295
Perfect Peace Rd 27292
Periwinkle Ln 27292
Periwinkle Lane Ext 27292
Perrell Ln 27295
Perry Cir 27292
Perryman Rd 27295
Pete Barnes Rd 27295
Pete Fritts Rd 27295
Peter Hedrick Dr 27292
Petrea Rd 27295
Pheasant Dr 27292
Phelps Dr 27292
Phillips Ln 27292
Phillips Rd 27295
Pickard Cir 27292
Pickett Dr & Rd 27295
Piedmont Dr 27295
Piedmont Plz 27292
Pilgrim Ct & Ln 27295
Pilgrim Church Rd 27295
N Pine Rd & St 27292
Pine Knot Rd 27295
Pine Lodge Rd 27292
Pine Meadow Dr 27292
Pine Park Dr 27292
Pine Ridge Rd 27295
Pine Top Park & Rd 27295
Pine Tree Dr 27295
Pinecrest Dr 27295
Pinecrest Ln 27292
Pinecrest Rd 27292
Pinecroft Blvd 27295
Pinehaven Dr 27292
Pineland Ave 27295
Pinewood Dr 27292
Piney Cross Dr 27292
Pinky St 27292
Pinnix Dr 27295
Pintail Dr 27295
Pitts Ln 27295
Placid Park 27295
Plantation Dr 27292
Plaza Pkwy 27292
Pleasant Hills Rd 27295
Point Harbor Rd 27295
Pond St 27292
Ponders Creek Dr 27292
Pope Rd & St 27292
Popeye Ln 27295
Poplar Dr & St 27292
Poplar Springs Rd 27295
Popper Jack Ln 27292
Poppy Ln 27295
Porter Dr 27292
Post Oak Trl 27295
Poverty Ln 27295
Prairie Dr & Ln 27292
Preston Ct 27295
Prestwick Ct 27295
Prevette Rd 27295
Price Rd 27295
Primrose Dr 27292
W Primrose Dr 27292
Primrose Ln 27292
Primrose Drive Ext 27292
Printers Aly 27292
Proctor Ln 27292
Promise Ln 27292
Prospect St 27292
Prospectors Trl & Way 27292
N & S Pugh St 27292
Quail Ln & Rd 27292
Quail Hill Dr 27295
Quail Ridge Ct & Dr 27292
Queens Dr, Ln & Rd 27292
Quentonya St 27295
Quiet Dr 27295
Rabbit Run 27292
Rabbit Ridge Dr 27292
Rachael Ln 27295
Radcliff Dr 27295
Radds St 27295
Radio Dr 27292
Raeford Ave 27292
N & S Railroad Ln & St 27292
Raleigh Rd 27292
Ralph Craver Rd 27295
Ralph Hege Farm Rd 27295
Ralph Miller Rd 27295
Ramkey Dr 27295
Random Dr 27292
Randy Hill Dr 27295
Raper Cir 27295
Raven Cir 27292
Ravenwood Cir & Ln 27292
Ray Lin Dr 27295
Raylenn Farm Dr 27295
Raymer Dr 27292
Raymond Clodfelter Rd 27292
Raymond Lanier Rd 27295
Rb Sink Rd 27295
Red Barn Rd 27292
Red Brick Rd 27295
Red Dog Ln 27292
Red Maple Ln 27292
Red Oak Dr 27292
Red Sparrow Ln 27295
Red Tip Ln 27295
Redbird Ln 27295
Redbud Rd 27292
Redwine St 27292
Redwood Ln 27295
Reeds Baptist Church Rd 27295
Reedy Creek Ct & Rd 27295
Reedy Creek Baptist Church Rd 27295
Reedy Creek School Dr 27295
Reedy Fork Dr 27295
W Regan Rd 27292
Regents Center Cir & Ln 27295
Reich St 27292
Reich Farm Ct 27295
Reid Dr 27292
Remer Regan Rd 27292
Rettie Ln 27292
Reynolds Rd 27292
Rhodes Rd 27292
Ricann Dr 27292
Rice St 27295
Richard Rd 27292
Richmond Dr 27295
S Ridge Dr, Ln, Rd & St 27295
Ridge Hill Ct 27295
Ridge Mill Cir 27295
Ridgecrest Dr 27292
Ridgeway Ln 27295
Ridgewood Dr 27292
River Pt 27292
River Oak Ln 27292
River Ridge Ln 27295
River Rock Dr 27292
Riverhouse Rd 27292
Riveroaks Ln 27292
Rivers Edge Pl 27292
Riverside Ct & Dr 27292
Riverview Blvd, Ct, Dr, Ln & Rd 27292
Riverview Road Ext 27292
Riverwood Dr & Rd 27292
Riviera Dr 27295
Ro Fritts Dr 27295
Rob Shoaf Rd 27295
Robbins Cir, Ln & St 27292
Robert St 27295
Robert Beck Rd 27292
Robert Everhart Rd 27292
Robert Floyd Dr 27295
Robert Hargrave Rd 27292
Robertson St 27295
Robinhood Rd 27292
Rochelle Dr 27292
Rock Harbor Dr 27292
Rockcrusher Rd 27292
Rockway Dr 27295
Rockwood Dr 27295
Rocky Ln 27292
Rocky Rd 27295
Rocky Knob Rd 27295
Rocky Trail Rd 27292
Rodeo Dr 27292
Rogers Rd 27292
Rolling Heights St 27295
Rolling Park Dr 27295
Ronald Ave 27295
Ronnie Mock Rd 27295
Roosevelt Ln 27292
Rosebriar Dr 27292
Rosemary Dr 27292
Rosemont Ln 27295
Rosewood Dr 27292
Ross Wood Rd 27292
Rotha Dr 27292
Rothrock Rd 27292
Rowe Rd 27295
Rowland Trl 27292
Roy Coppley Rd 27292
Roy Hartley Rd 27292
Roy Lopp Rd 27292
Royal Ave 27295
Royal Ashdown Ln 27295
Ruby Ln 27295
Ruff Leonard Rd 27295
Rumfelt Dr 27292
Rupert Bailey Dr 27295
Russell Dr & St 27292
Ruth Dr 27292
Ryan Rd 27292
Ryan St 27295
Saddlebrook Ct 27295
Sagebrush Trl 27292
Sailors Rest Rd 27292
Saint Albans Ct & Ln 27292
Saintsbury Pl 27292
Salem Ln 27292
Salem Rd 27292
Salem St 27292
E Salisbury Dr 27295
N Salisbury St 27292
S Salisbury St 27292
Salvage Rd 27295
Sandalwood Ct 27295
Sandy Creek Ln 27295
Sapona Rd 27292
Sapona Business Park 27292
Sara Beth Dr 27292
Sassafras Ln 27295
Sawgrass Ln N & S 27295
Sayber Ln 27295
Scarlet Ln 27295
School St 27292
Scott Dr 27295
Scout Rd 27292
Sea Mountain Ln 27295
Selbrook Ln 27292
Seminole Ln 27295
Sequoia Dr 27292
Sequoia Rd 27295
Serenity Ln 27295
Settlers Ln 27292
Shady Hanes Rd 27295
Shadybrook St 27292
Shamrock Dr 27295
Shando Dr 27295
Shannon Dr 27292
Shannon Brook Dr 27295
Shannon Park Dr 27295
Sharon Dr 27292
Shaw Ln 27292
Shawnee Cir, Dr & Rd 27295
Shelly Leonard St 27295
Shelton Ave 27295
Sheppard Pt 27292
Shepps Boat Dock Rd 27292
Sherman Dr 27295
Shermans Xing 27295
Sherwen Ln 27295
Sherwood Dr & Rd 27295
Shiloh Rd 27295
Shimmer Dr 27292
Shiptontown Rd 27292
Shirley Rd 27292
Shoaf Dr 27295
Shoaf Rd 27295
Shoaf St 27292
N & S Shore Dr & Ln 27292
Shoreline Dr & Ln 27292
Short St 27295
Short Pines Ln 27295
Shoshone Rd 27295
Shuford Everhart Ln 27292
Sides Rd 27295
Sidney St 27295
E & N Silver St 27292
Silver Hill Rd 27292
Silver Ridge Dr 27292
Silver Valley Rd 27292
Silverwood Ln 27292
Simeon Ct 27295
Simerson Rd 27295
Sink Cir 27292
Sink Rd 27295
Sink Farm Rd 27295
Sink Inn Rd
- 100-399 27292
- 400-499 27295

Siouan Dr 27295
Sir Abbott Ln 27292
Sk Dr 27295
Skylen Dr 27295
Skyline Dr 27292
Skyview Ln 27295
Sleepy Hollow Ln 27295
Smindela Rd 27292
Smith Ave & Rd 27292
Smith Farm Rd 27292
Smith Grove Church Rd 27292
Smithfield Ct 27295
Smokehouse Ln 27295
Snider Ave, Ln & Rd 27292
Soles Dr 27292
Sonlight Ln 27295
South Rd 27292
Southbound St 27292
Southern Ash 27295
Southlake Ct 27295
Southland Dr 27295
Southmont Pond Rd 27292
Southview Rd 27292
Southwind Dr 27292
Southwood Dr 27295
Sowers Pl 27295
Sp Lohr Dr 27292
Spainhour Ln 27295
Spains Mill Rd 27295
Spartan Dr 27292
Speedy Ln 27292
Spinnaker Ct 27292
Spring Dr
- 1-399 27295
- 1000-1499 27292

Spring St 27292
E Spring St 27292
Spring Lake Ct 27295
Spring Valley Dr 27295
Springfield Ct 27295
Spruce St 27292
Squaw Valley Dr 27295
Squirrel Ln 27295
Sr Fritts Dr 27295
St Dylan Dr 27295
Stamey Ave 27292
Stanford Rd 27292
Stanley Ln 27295
Staplewood Rd 27295
Star Dr 27295
Star Light Dr 27295
Starboard Reach 27292
Starfire Dr 27295
N State St
- 1-111 27292
- 110-110 27293
- 112-598 27292
- 113-599 27292

S State St 27292
Station Dr 27292
Stella Dr 27295
Stephanie Dr 27295
Stewart Rd 27292
Still Meadows Ln 27292
Stone Creek Dr 27292
Stoney Creek Ln 27292
Stoney Point Dr 27292
Stonybrook Dr 27295
Stover Ct & Way 27295
Stratford Rd 27292
Sugar Maple Ln 27295
Summit Dr 27295
Summit Crest Dr 27295
Sumner Ln 27292
Sundance Trl 27295
Sundial Dr 27295
Sunflower Dr 27295
Sunnyside Dr 27292
Sunrise Ave 27292
Sunrise Cir 27295
Sunrise Ln 27295
Sunset Blvd 27292
Sunset Dr 27295
Sunset Pl 27292
Sunset Ridge Ln 27295
Sunshine Ln 27295
Super Sport Ln 27292
Supply Dr 27292
Susan Dr 27295
Suzanne Ln 27295
Swans Way 27295
Swearing Creek Dr & Rd 27292
Sweetbriar Dr 27295
Swicegood Waitman Rd 27295
Swing Dr 27292
Swing Dairy Rd 27295
Sycamore Dr & St 27295
N & S Talbert Blvd 27292
Tall Oak Ct & Ln 27295
Tall Pines Rd 27295
Tamara Ln 27295
Tan Oak Dr 27292
Tancam Dr 27295
Tanglewood Dr 27295
Tannin Way 27295
Tanyard St 27292
Tar Heel Trl 27295
Tarawood 1 27292
Taylor Rd 27295
Taylors Park Rd 27292
Taylorstone Ln 27295
Ted R Daniels Rd 27295
Teebo Dr 27295
Temple St 27292
Terrace Dr 27295
Terrace Ln 27295
Tesh St 27295
Texas Dr 27295
Theodore Ave 27292
Thicket Dr 27295
Thomas Rd 27295
Thomason St 27292
Thompson Ln & St 27295
Thore Dr 27292
Three Hat Mountain Rd 27292
Thrugood Ave 27292
Thurman Beck Rd 27292
Tilden Dr 27295
Tilden Nursery Rd 27295
Timber Ridge Dr 27292
Timberbreak Dr 27295
Timberlane Dr 27295
Timberline Dr 27295
Timberview Dr 27292
Tip Top Ln 27295
Tj Hedrick Rd 27295
Tom Rd 27292
Tom Briggs Rd 27292
Tom Caudle Rd 27292
Tom Everhart Rd 27292
Tom Levitt Dr 27295
Tom Wood Rd 27295
Tomahawk Trl 27295
Tony Loflin Dr 27292
Tori Ln 27295

Towhee Dr 27292
Tp Sowers Rd 27295
Tr Koontz Ln 27295
Tracy Gail Ln 27295
Tracy Marshall Dr 27295
Trafalgar Dr 27292
Trailer Dr 27292
Trali Ln 27295
Transou Dr 27295
Trantham Dr 27292
Travis Ln 27295
Trencreek Farm Rd 27295
Trevor Dr 27295
Trey Ln 27295
Tricycle Hill Ln 27292
Trieglaff Dr 27292
Trina Ln 27295
Tripp Rd 27292
Trips Run 27292
Tristan Meadows Ln 27292
Troy Mcelrath Rd 27295
Ts Payne Rd 27295
Tucker Ln 27295
Tupelo Ln 27292
Turf Ln 27295
Turlington Dr 27295
Turnberry Ln 27295
Turner Rd 27292
Turtle Path Ct 27295
Tussey Ave 27295
Tussey Rd 27295
Tussey St 27292
Tuttle Rd 27295
Twin Acres Dr 27292
Twin Branch Dr 27295
Two Pond Ln 27295
Ty Koon Dr 27292
Tyler Dr 27295
Tyler Ln 27292
Tyro Rd 27295
Tyro Heights Rd 27295
Tyro School Rd 27295
Tysinger Family Rd 27292
Tysinger Hill Rd 27292
Ulysses St 27292
Union St 27292
S Union Grove Rd 27295
Union Pointe Ln 27295
United Furniture Dr 27292
United Furntiure Dr 27292
Uphill Dr 27295
Upton St 27292
Us Highway 29 70 S 27295
Us Highway 29 70
Service Rd 27292
E Us Highway 64 27292
W Us Highway 64 27295
Valentine Dr 27295
Valiant Dr 27292
Valley Ave & Dr 27292
Valley Hill Ln 27295
Valley Mine Rd 27292
Valley Oak Ct 27295
Valleyview Dr 27295
Vance Cir & St 27292
Vanmar Dr 27295
Varner Dr 27292
Verdeen Dr 27295
Veterans Ave 27292
Vi Mae Dr 27295
Vickie Lee Dr 27295
Victor St 27292
Victory Lane Dr 27295
Village Dr
1-299 27292
300-1399 27295
Village Ln 27292
Vine Dr 27292
Vineyard Ln 27295
Vineyards Xing 27295
Viola Dr 27292
Violet Rd 27295
Virgie Grubb Ln 27295
Virgil Wyatt Rd 27295
Virginia Dr & Rd 27295
Virginia Dare Dr 27295
Vlee Dr 27295
Von Dr 27295
Wa Grubb Rd 27295
Wafford Cir & Rd 27292
Wagner Dr 27295
Wagon Trail Ln 27295
Waitman Rd 27295
Walford St 27292
Wall Rd & St 27292
Waller Rd 27295
Walltown Rd & St 27292
Walnut Ct 27292
Walnut Dr 27295
Walnut Rd 27292
Walnut St 27292
Walnut Grove Rd 27292
Walser Ln & Rd 27295
Walter Ln 27295
Walton Farm Dr 27292
Waraleas Rd 27295
Ward Curry Rd 27292
Ward Farm Rd 27292
Warf Rd 27292
Warmoth Ln 27292
Warrior Way 27295
Washburn St 27292
Washington Ave 27292
Waterbury Pl 27292
Waterford Pointe Rd 27292
Waterway Dr 27292
Watkins Rd 27292
Watson Ln 27292
Wayne Love Dr 27295
Waywood Dr 27295
Weaver Dr 27292
Weaver Rd 27295
Weaver Wagner Ln 27295
Webb Rd 27295
Wedgewood Dr 27292
Weisner Dr & St 27295
Welcome Rd 27292
Welcome Arcadia Rd 27295
Welcome Bethesda Rd 27295
Welcome Center Blvd &
Ct 27295
Weldon Smith Rd 27295
Wenco Dr 27295
Wesley St 27295
West Ave 27295
Westdale Ave 27295
Western Blvd 27295
Westgate Ct 27295
Westmill Dr 27295
Westover Dr 27292
Westridge Dr 27295
Westside Dr 27292
Westside Drive Ext 27292
Westwood Dr & Ln 27295
Whippoorwill Ridge Dr 27292
Whispering Oaks Dr 27292
White St 27295
White Dove Dr 27292
White Oak Ct & Dr 27295
White Pine Ln 27292
White Street Ext 27295
White Tail Ct 27292
Whitman Dr 27295
Wild Cherry Ln 27292
Wildberry Ct 27295
Wildflower Trl 27295
Wildlife Cir & Rd 27292
Wildlife Rec Area Access
Rd 27292
Wiley Ln 27292
Wilfred Ave 27292
Wilkes Ln 27292
Will Hunt Rd 27295
Will Jose Dr 27295
Will Lanier Rd 27295
William Ln 27295
William Bell Rd 27292
Williams Cir & St 27292
Williamson St 27292
Willie Hoover Dr 27295
Willis St 27292
Willotesh Ln 27295
Willow Oak Cir, Dr &
Ln 27295
Willowbrook Cir 27295
Willowmore Springs
Rd 27292
Wilmar Cir 27295
Wilson Dr 27295
Wilson St
100-399 27295
900-1199 27292
Winchester Ct & Dr 27295
W Wind Ct 27295
Wind Terrace Ct 27295
Windchime Ct 27295
Winding Ridge Ln 27292
Windmill Ln 27292
Windsor Ave 27292
Windy Pointe Ct 27295
Winston Rd 27295
Winter Pl 27295
Wintergreen Ct 27295
Wm Craver Ln 27295
Wolf Creek Trl 27292
Wonderland Dr 27292
Wood Duck Run 27295
Wood Heirs Dr 27295
Wood Pointe Ct 27295
Wood View Ln 27295
Woodard Rd 27292
Woodberry Dr 27292
Woodbrier Dr 27292
Woodcrest Dr 27295
Woodfield Dr 27295
Woodhaven Dr 27295
Woodhaven Shores Dr 27292
Woodland Ave 27295
Woodlawn Dr & St 27292
Woodleen Ct 27295
Woodleon Ct 27295
Woods Island Rd 27292
Woodsedge Dr 27292
Woodside Dr 27292
Woodsway Dr 27292
Woodwind Dr 27295
Woosley Dr 27295
Workman Rd 27292
Wrenn Blvd, Dr & Rd 27292
Wright Rd 27295
Yachtsmans Point Dr 27292
Yadkin College Rd 27295
Yadkin College Church
Rd 27295
Yarborough Dr 27295
Yellow Poplar Ln 27295
Yokley Rd 27295
Young Dr & Rd 27292
Young Mill Rd 27292
Yountz Rd 27292
Zach Cir 27295
Zane Perkins Dr 27292
Zimmerman Rd 27295

NUMBERED STREETS

E 1st Ave 27292
W 1st Ave 27292
1st Cir 27292
E 1st St 27292
N 1st St 27295
W 1st St 27292
E 1st Avenue Ext 27292
1st Rainbow St 27295
E 1st Street Ext 27292
E 2nd Ave 27292
W 2nd Ave 27292
E 2nd St 27292
N 2nd St 27295
W 2nd St 27292
2nd Rainbow St 27295
E & W 3rd Ave & St 27292
E 3rd Ave Ext 27292
E & W 4th Ave & St 27292
E 5th Ave 27292
W 5th Ave
1-999 27292
1000-1399 27295
E 5th St 27292
W 5th St 27292
E 5th Avenue Ext 27292
E & W 6th Ave & St 27292
E 7th Ave 27292
W 7th Ave 27292
W 7th St
1-199 27295
200-299 27292
E 8th Ave 27292
W 8th Ave 27292
E 8th St 27295
W 8th St 27295
E 9th Ave 27292
W 9th Ave 27292
E 9th St 27295
W 9th St 27295
E 9th Street Ext 27295
E 10th Ave 27292
W 10th Ave 27292
E 10th St 27295
E 10th Avenue Ext 27292
E 11th Ave 27292
W 11th Ave 27292
E 11th St 27295
E & W 12th 27292
E 13th Ave 27292
W 13th St 27295
E 14th Ave 27292
E 15th Ave 27292
E 16th Ave 27292
E 17th Ave 27292

LINCOLNTON NC

General Delivery 28092

POST OFFICE BOXES MAIN OFFICE STATIONS AND BRANCHES

Box No.s
All PO Boxes 28093

NAMED STREETS

A St 28092
Abby Ave 28092
Abby Park Ln 28092
N & S Abernethy St 28092
N & S Academy St 28092
N Academy Street Ext 28092
Acre Hts 28092
Adams Ln 28092
Aderholdt Rd 28092
Alberry Ave 28092
Alcott Ln 28092
Alexander St 28092
Alf Hoover Rd 28092
Allen Ln 28092
Allendale St 28092
W Amber Dr 28092
Amy Dr 28092
Anastasia Ln 28092
Ancroft Ln 28092
Anderson Ln 28092
Andrea Ln 28092
Andrews Dr 28092
Andy Logan Rd 28092
Angela Ct 28092
Ann Gaither Ct 28092
Antique Rd 28092
Appalachian Ct 28092
Arbor Ln 28092
Arbor Hills Dr 28092
Arbor Run Dr 28092
Arcadia Heights Rd 28092
Arden Dr 28092
Armstrong Farm Way 28092
Arney St 28092
Arrow St 28092
Arrowood Ln 28092
Asbury Church Rd 28092
Ashlee Meadows Ln 28092
N & S Aspen St 28092
Atlantic Ln 28092
Auton St 28092
Autumn Rdg 28092
Autumn Wood Ct 28092
Avery Farm Rd 28092
Babs Ct 28092
Baby Bears Ln 28092
Bailey Springs Dr 28092
Baldwin Ln 28092
Balsam Dr 28092
Bancroft Ln 28092
Banks Rd 28092
Banyon Ln 28092
Barclay Trl 28092
Barkley Ave 28092
Barsdale Ln 28092
Battleground Rd 28092
Baxter Deaton Ln 28092
Bcs Trl 28092
Beagles Run Dr 28092
Beal Rd 28092
Beal Pond Trl 28092
Beard Rd 28092
Beason Dr 28092
Beaumont Ln 28092
Beaver Dam Ln 28092
Bedford Ln 28092
Beechnut St 28092
Bel Air Dr 28092
Ben Lee Ln 28092
Benbrook Ln 28092
Benfield St 28092
Bennington Ct 28092
Berryhill Reed Ln 28092
Bethel Church Rd 28092
Better Brook Ln 28092
Beverly Ln 28092
Bexley Ln 28092
Bill Lynch Rd 28092
Billess Ct 28092
Birch St 28092
Birkdale Ln 28092
Bishop Dr 28092
Bishs Way 28092
Bittersweet Ln & Trl 28092
Black Hawk Trl 28092
Black Oak Ln 28092
Blackburn Bridge Rd 28092
Blake Ct 28092
Blossom Hill Rd 28092
Boat Trl 28092
Bob Burgin Rd 28092
Bogey Ln 28092
Boggs St 28092
Bolton Ln 28092
Bonview Ave 28092
Bost St 28092
Bostic Ln 28092
Boulder Dr 28092
Boy Scout Rd 28092
Boyd Ave 28092
Brady Branch Trl 28092
Brady Hoffman Rd 28092
Branch Ridge Ct 28092
Branchview Trl 28092
Braswell Ln 28092
Breezy Trl 28092
Brent Trl 28092
Briarcliff Acres 28092
Briarwood Ln 28092
Bridgeport Ln 28092
Bridle Ct 28092
Broad River Ln 28092
Brocton Trl 28092
Brookfield Dr 28092
Brookhaven Dr 28092
W Brookside St 28092
Brookstone Ct 28092
Brookwood Rd 28092
Broome St 28092
Broomsage Ln 28092
Bryans Way 28092
Bryant Cooper Ln 28092
Buck Ct 28092
Buck Oak Rd 28092
Buff St 28092
Buffalo Run 28092
Buffalo Forest Rd 28092
Buffalo Shoals Rd 28092
Bulldog Ln 28092
Bumgarner James Ln 28092
Burris Blvd 28092
Burton Estates Ln 28092
Burtonwood Ln 28092
Butterfield Ln 28092
Bynum Rd 28092
C Alexander Rd 28092
Cabelos Ln 28092
Cadenhead 28092
Calloway Rd 28092
Calvary Church Rd 28092
Cameo St 28092
Cameron Rd 28092
Campbell Ln 28092
Caprice Cir 28092
Car Farm Rd 28092
Car Wash Dr 28092
Cardinal Ct 28092
Carla Ct 28092
Carlos Rd 28092
Carolina Cir 28092
Carolina Mill Cir 28092
Carpenter Dr & St 28092
Carriage Ln 28092
Carrie St 28092
E Carter St 28092
Cascade Rd 28092
Cat Square Rd 28092
Cataler Dr 28092
Catalina Ln 28092
Catawba Hts & St 28092
Catfish Dr 28092
N & S Cedar St 28092
Cedar Spring Ln 28092
Center Dr 28092
Central Ln 28092
Chapman St 28092
Chapman Wyant Ln 28092
Charles Ct 28092
Charles Heavner Ln 28092
Charlesvoix Ave 28092
Charlie Miller Rd 28092
Charlottes Ln 28092
Chavis Ln 28092
Cherry St 28092
Chestnut Rd & St 28092
Childs St 28092
Chinook Trl 28092
E & W Church St 28092
Circle Dr 28092
City View Ave 28092
Clark Dr 28092
Clark Creek Rd 28092
Clay St 28092
Clear Creek Cir 28092
Clear Lake Trl 28092
Clemmay Trl 28092
Clerthen Rd 28092
Cliffside Trl 28092
Cline St 28092
Cline Farm Rd 28092
Cloudburst Cir 28092
Cloverleaf Ln 28092
Clubhouse Rd 28092
Cobb St 28092
Cobblestone Ln 28092
Cochrane Rd 28092
Coffeytown Rd 28092
Colonial Village Dr 28092
Colorado Ct & Trl 28092
Colwick Ln 28092
Commonwealth Dr 28092
Confederate Rd 28092
E & W Congress St 28092
Coolwood Rd 28092
Coopertown Rd 28092
Coral Dr 28092
Corral Ln 28092
Correll Ln 28092
Corriher Farm Rd 28092
Cory Ln 28092
Country Club Rd 28092
Country Crossing Dr 28092
Country Way Dr 28092
County Line Trl 28092
Court Sq NE, NW &
SE 28092
Covey Ct 28092
Cowboy Way 28092
Creek Meadow Ln 28092
Creekside Dr 28092
Creekstone Ct 28092
Crescent Ct 28092
Crestview Dr 28092
Crossover Dr 28092
Crystal Ct 28092
Crystal Springs Dr 28092
Curveview Rd 28092
D St 28092
Dale Ave 28092
Danbrook Cir 28092
Daniel Ridge Dr 28092
Daniel Shrum Rd 28092
Daniels Rd 28092
Dave Warlick Dr 28092
Davis Rd & St 28092
Dawn Trl 28092
Dawnview Ln 28092
Deal St 28092
Dean Ln 28092
Deaton Ave 28092
Deer Crk 28092
Deerhorn Rd 28092
Del Mar Ln 28092
Dennis Reinhardt Ln 28092
Dental Aly 28092
Detter Rd 28092
Diesel Dr 28092
E Dixon St 28092
Doctors Park 28092
Dogwood Ave 28092
Dogwood Flower Ln 28092
Dolphin Ln 28092
Don Mcginnis Rd 28092
Donaldson Dr 28092
Dontia Dr 28092
Doris Ct 28092
Dorset Ln 28092
Dove Tree Ln 28092
Downing Ct 28092
Drew Dr 28092
Drexall Ln 28092
Driftwood Rd 28092
Drive Inn Rd 28092
Drum St 28092
Dunbrook Ln 28092
Duplin Ln 28092
Eagle Dr 28092
Eagle Nest Rd 28092
Early Bird Ln 28092
Eastview Dr 28092
Eastwood Dr 28092
Echo Ln 28092
Edgehill Ln 28092
S Edwards St 28092
Edwards Farm Ln &
Rd 28092
Elaine Ave 28092
Elizabeth Ave 28092
Ellen Finger Trl 28092
Ellys St 28092
Elm St 28092
Elm Grove Rd 28092
Embassy Trl 28092
Emerson Way 28092
Emorywood Ln 28092
English Oak Dr 28092
Erica Ln 28092
Ernest Houser Rd 28092
Ernest Huss Ln 28092
Estate Dr 28092
Eurey St 28092
Eva Ct 28092
Fair Oaks Dr 28092
Fairfield Ct 28092

Street	ZIP
Fairground Rd	28092
Fairland Ln	28092
Fairview Dr	28092
Fairview Church Rd	28092
Fairway Ln	28092
Falconview Rd	28092
Fallen Oak Trl	28092
Family Dr	28092
Ferguson Acres Dr	28092
Fernwood Rd	28092
Finger St	28092
Finger Merrick Trl	28092
Finger Mill Rd	28092
Fitzgerald Stowe Ln	28092
Flat Rock Dr	28092
Flay Rd	28092
N & S Flint St	28092
Flint Fire Ct	28092
Flower Ln	28092
Ford Ln	28092
Forest Rd	28092
Forney Ave	28092
Fox Creek Trl	28092
Foxberry Rd	28092
Fradell Dr	28092
Fran Ave	28092
Franks Rd	28092
Freeman Rd	28092
Friar Tuck St	28092
Fringewood Ln	28092
Frontier Ln	28092
Fuchia Ln	28092
Fulbright Way	28092
Fulton Trl	28092
Furnace Rd	28092
Furnace Road Ext	28092
Gainsville Church Rd	28092
Gallup Ln	28092
Galway Dr	28092
Gamble Dr	28092
Garland Ln	28092
Garrett Trl	28092
Garrison Ln	28092
E Gaston St	28092
Gaston Hillside Rd	28092
Gaston Webbs Chapel Rd	28092
Gastonia Hwy	28092
Gates Rd	28092
Gateway Ln	28092
Ge Hauss Ln	28092
General Hoke Dr	28092
N & S Generals Blvd	28092
Gentry Hill Ln	28092
Georgetown Rd	28092
Georgia Trl	28092
Gideon Dr	28092
Gilbert Rd	28092
Gladden Dr	28092
Glen Gar Dr	28092
Glen Manor Ct	28092
Glenn St	28092
Gloster Ln	28092
Gold Rush Dr	28092
Golden Pond Ct	28092
Goldrock Trl	28092
Goodson Forest Ln	28092
Gordon St	28092
N & S Government St	28092
Grandview Ln	28092
Grassy Meadow Ct	28092
Grazing Meadows Ct	28092
Green St	28092
Green Acres Rd	28092
Green Hill Ln	28092
Green Tree Ln	28092
Greenwood Rd	28092
Grier St	28092
Grigg Rd	28092
N & S Grove St	28092
S Grove Street Ext	28092
Grovedale Dr	28092
Gun Powder Trl	28092
Guy F Beal Ln	28092
Guy Heavner Rd	28092
Hamlet St	28092
Hampton Rd	28092
Hannah Trl	28092
Harbinson Ln	28092
Hares Way	28092
Harless Rd	28092
Harmon Rd	28092
Harolds Ln	28092
Harris Dr	28092
Harrison Sanders Ln	28092
Hartman St	28092
Hartsoe Rd	28092
Harvey Rd	28092
Hatchett Rd	28092
Hauss Rd	28092
Hawks Bill Dr	28092
Haynes Rd	28092
Haywood Ct	28092
Hayworth Ln	28092
Hd Trl	28092
Heartland Trl	28092
Heather Dr	28092
Heavner Rd	28092
Heavners Farm Ct	28092
Helms Ln	28092
Helms End Of Trl	28092
Henry Rhodes Rd	28092
Herb Valley Ln	28092
Herman Dr	28092
Herndon Chapel Church Ln	28092
Hershel Lackey Rd	28092
Herter Rd	28092
Hestertown Rd	28092
Hibiseus Trl	28092
Hickory Lincolnton Hwy	28092
Hickory Nut Ln	28092
Hickory Springs Ln	28092
Hidden Valley Ave	28092
N & S High St	28092
High Knoll Rd	28092
High Shoals Rd	28092
Highland Dr	28092
Highland Bluff Ct	28092
W Highview Ln	28092
E & W Highway 150 Byp	28092
Highway 182 W	28092
E & W Highway 27	28092
N Highway 321	28092
Highway 73	28092
Hill Dr & Rd	28092
Hillard Ln	28092
Hillcrest Dr	28092
Hillside Dr	28092
Hilltop Rd	28092
Hoffman Rd	28092
Hoffman Acres St	28092
Hoke St	28092
Holbrook Ln	28092
Holden Dr	28092
Hollow Rd	28092
Hollow Oak Ln	28092
Holloway Rd	28092
Hollybrook Ave	28092
Home Trl	28092
Homesley Trl	28092
Homestead Rd	28092
Honey Bee Ln	28092
Hoover Rd	28092
Hoover Elmore Rd	28092
Horseshoe Lake Rd	28092
Hovis Rd	28092
Howard Self Ln	28092
Howards Creek School Rd	28092
Howell Trl	28092
Hoyle St	28092
Hubbard St	28092
Huckleberry Dr	28092
Huddleston Sisk Trl	28092
Hudson White Trl	28092
Hull Mcginnis Rd	28092
Hunter Fields Ct	28092
Hunter Oaks Dr	28092
Hunter Rhyne Rd	28092
Hunters Hope Ln	28092
Hunting Ave	28092
Huntington Hills Dr	28092
Huss St	28092
Idlewood Dr	28092
Imperial Ln	28092
Indian Trl	28092
Indian Creek Rd	28092
S Industrial Park Rd	28092
Ingle Houser Rd	28092
Isenhour Farm Rd	28092
Ivan Ln	28092
Ivey Church Rd	28092
J E Carpenter Rd	28092
J Huffstetler Ln	28092
Jacks Trl	28092
Jackson Dr	28092
Jaclyn Ln	28092
Jacob Trl	28092
James St	28092
Janice Rd	28092
Jason Rd	28092
Jc Brooks Ln	28092
Jeb Seagle Dr	28092
Jeff Kaylor Ln	28092
Jenkins Rd	28092
Jennings St	28092
Jerrico Ln	28092
Jerry Crump Rd	28092
Jerry Poovey Ln	28092
Jessica Ann Rd	28092
Jim Carnes Ln	28092
Jim Wise Rd	28092
Joe Ross St	28092
Joe Scronce Ln	28092
John Beaver Ln	28092
John Chapman Rd	28092
John Cline Ct	28092
John Howel Memorial Dr	28092
John Lutz Cir	28092
John Williams Ln	28092
Johns Place Dr	28092
Johnson Blake Dr	28092
Jonas Dr	28092
Jordan Cir	28092
Jordans Chase Ct	28092
Joshua Ct	28092
Julia Dr	28092
Jw Huss Rd	28092
K N Victor Way	28092
Kanewood Trl	28092
Kawai Rd	28092
Kc Ln	28092
Keener Rd	28092
Keener Acres St	28092
Keever St	28092
Keever Dairy Farm Rd	28092
Kellom Ln	28092
Kendra Trl	28092
Kennedy Dr	28092
Kershaw Trl	28092
Kettle Creek Ct	28092
Kilborne Dr	28092
Killian Rd	28092
Kinfolk Ln	28092
King Wilkinson Rd	28092
Kings Grant Rd	28092
Kiser Rd	28092
Kistler St	28092
Knollwood Ln	28092
Kowaleski Ln	28092
Labans Ln	28092
Laboratory Rd	28092
Lady Marian St	28092
Lail Ln	28092
Lake St	28092
Lake Sylvia Rd	28092
Lakeland Ave	28092
Lakeside Ln	28092
Lakewood Ave	28092
Lama Ln	28092
Lancrest Ln	28092
Landers Chapel Rd	28092
Landers Church Rd	28092
Landon Ray Trl	28092
Lansdale Ave	28092
Lantern Ridge Dr	28092
Lariat Dr	28092
Larkview Dr	28092
Larkyn Dr	28092
Laudun Dr	28092
N & S Laurel St	28092
Laurel Hill Dr	28092
Laurel Ridge Dr	28092
Laurelwoods Acres Ln	28092
Lauren Ln	28092
Lawing St	28092
Lawndale Ln	28092
Lazy Meadow Ln	28092
Leaf Ln	28092
Leaning Pine Dr	28092
Leaping Brook Rd	28092
Ledford Dr	28092
Lee Ave	28092
Lee Huss Ln	28092
Lee Lawing Rd	28092
Lee Mccurry Rd	28092
Legionaire Dr	28092
Leisure Trl	28092
Lenhaven Trl	28092
Lenora Cir	28092
Leonard Rd	28092
Leonards Fork Church Rd	28092
Leroy Johnson Ln	28092
Levinfield Ct	28092
Levistock Ln	28092
Lewis Rd	28092
Liberty St	28092
Lightview Ln	28092
Lincoln St	28092
Lincoln County Pkwy	28092
Lincoln County Parkway Ext	28092
Lincoln Medical Park	28092
Lincoln Park St	28092
Lincolnview Rd	28092
Lincolnview One Rd	28092
Lincolnview Three Rd	28092
Lincolnview Two Rd	28092
Linden St	28092
Lineberger Rd	28092
Linwood Dr	28092
Lippards Creek Ln	28092
Lithia Ln	28092
Lithia Inn Rd	28092
Lithia Park Dr	28092
Lithia Springs Rd	28092
Little St	28092
Little Echo Ln	28092
Little John St	28092
Little River Ct	28092
Little Valley Ln	28092
Livingstone Trl	28092
Loafers Glory Trl	28092
Loblolly Trl	28092
Lockman Ln	28092
Lockridge Ln	28092
Logan Sain Trl	28092
Lonesome Dove Trl	28092
Lonetree Ln	28092
Long Meadow Ln	28092
Long Shoals Rd	28092
Loomis St	28092
Loop Rd	28092
Lore Rd	28092
Lotties Ln	28092
Loudlin Rd	28092
Louise Ave	28092
Love Memorial School Rd	28092
Loviee Rd	28092
Lucille Ln	28092
Lucy Dr	28092
Luther Shrum Ln	28092
Lutz Dairy Farm Rd	28092
Lydia Suzanne Pl	28092
Lyn Well Rd	28092
Lynch Rd & St	28092
Lyndsey Brook Ct	28092
Mace Ln	28092
Madison St	28092
Madison Furnace Trl	28092
Magan Dr	28092
Magna Vista Dr	28092
N & S Magnolia St	28092
Magnolia Grove Rd	28092
Maiden Hwy	28092
E Main St	
100-399	28092
326-326	28093
400-2798	28092
401-2799	28092
W Main St	28092
W Main Street Ext	28092
Majesty Ct	28092
Mallory Tai Dr	28092
Mansion Dr	28092
Maple Ln	28092
Marigold Ln	28092
Mariott Ln	28092
Marsh Trl	28092
Mason St	28092
Mason Spring Dr	28092
Massapoag Rd	28092
Mauney Dr	28092
Mcalister Rd	28092
Mcbee St	28092
Mcclain Trl	28092
Mccorkle Rd	28092
Mcdaniel Springs Rd	28092
Mcgee Rd	28092
Mcginnis Ave	28092
Mckellar St	28092
Mcree Rd	28092
Meadow Ln	28092
Meadow Hill Ct	28092
Meadowland Dr	28092
Meandering Ln	28092
Megan Ann Ln	28092
Mehling Dr	28092
Memory Ln	28092
Mesa Ln	28092
Mid Oak Ln	28092
Miller Woods Trl	28092
Millstead Trl	28092
Mineral Ln	28092
Miners Rd	28092
Miners Creek Dr	28092
Mintew Cir	28092
Miracle Ln	28092
Mirror Lake Rd	28092
Mission Dr	28092
Misty Dawn Ln	28092
Mize Ln	28092
Ml Goodson Ln	28092
Mockingbird Cir & Ln	28092
Modern Estates Rd	28092
Moline Dr	28092
Molly Acres Ln	28092
Monroe St	28092
Montgomery St	28092
Moore St	28092
Mooregate Ln	28092
Moorland Ln	28092
Moose Ln	28092
Morrison Houser Rd	28092
Moss Trl	28092
Mosteller Ln	28092
Motz Ave	28092
Mount Branch Rd	28092
Mountcrest Ln	28092
Mull Rd	28092
Myra Ln	28092
Myrtle Hill Ln	28092
Nandina Trl	28092
Narrow Ln	28092
Neighborhood St	28092
Nellwood Ln	28092
Nelson Dr	28092
Newbold St	28092
Newcastle Ave	28092
Newground Rd	28092
Newton Ln	28092
Nicholson Rd	28092
Nolen Farm Ln	28092
Noles Cir	28092
Norman Fair Ave	28092
North St	28092
Northcrest Dr	28092
Northpark Ln	28092
Norville Rd	28092
Nottingham Rd	28092
Null Rd	28092
Nutmeg Trl	28092
N & S Oak St	28092
Oak Canopy Rd	28092
Oak Grove Church Rd	28092
Oak Ridge Cir	28092
Oaklane Dr	28092
Oaklin Ln	28092
Oklahoma Ct	28092
Old Carpenter Ln	28092
Old Church Ln	28092
Old Farm Rd	28092
Old Home Place Way	28092
Old Lake Rd	28092
Old Lincolnton Crouse Rd	28092
Old Mill Rd	28092
Old Oak Ln	28092
Old Pond Dr	28092
Old Salem Ln	28092
Old Shady Brook Trl	28092
Old Silo Ln	28092
Old Tram St	28092
Oldwell Ln	28092
Olivia Ln	28092
Openview Dr	28092
Ore Bank Dr	28092
Oregon Trl	28092
Osprey Creek Rd	28092
Otis Dellinger Rd	28092
Our Pl	28092
Overbrook Trl	28092
Overhill Ln	28092
Owls Den Rd	28092
Paint Shop Rd	28092
Painter Ln	28092
E & W Park Cir & Dr	28092
Park Circle One	28092
Park Circle Two	28092
Pat Harrill Ln	28092
Paul Elmore Rd	28092
Paul Heavner Ln	28092
Paul Lyday Ln	28092
Paysour Trail Rd	28092
Peach Tree St	28092
Peak Rd	28092
Peakwood Ln	28092
Pebble Creek Ct	28092
Pecan Ln	28092
Pell Dr	28092
Performance Dr	28092
Periwinkle St	28092
Pervie Hovis Ln	28092
Petal Ct	28092
Petes Rd	28092
Pettus Ln	28092
Philadelphia Church Rd	28092
Pickwick Pl	28092
E & W Pine St	28092
Pine Tree St	28092
Pinewood Dr	28092
Pinewoods Circle Ln	28092
Plum Ln	28092
Poarch Rd	28092
Pointview Ln	28092
Policarp St	28092
Polo Trl	28092
Pond View Ln	28092
Ponderosa Rd	28092
Ponds Trl	28092
Poorboy Ln	28092
Poovey Hill Ln	28092
Poplar St	28092
Portwood Ln	28092
Poston Dr	28092
Potts Creek Rd	28092
Powell Dr	28092
Power Line Rd	28092
Pressley Dr	28092
Prince Dr	28092
Pristine Trl	28092
Proctor St	28092
Progress Dr	28092
Promise Ln	28092
Prue Sain Ln	28092
Pruitt Houser St	28092
Putnam St	28092
Quail Trl	28092
Quartz Trl	28092
Queens Dr	28092
Quinlan Ln	28092
Railroad St	28092
Raintree Ln	28092
Ralph B Keener Rd	28092
Ram Ln	28092
Ramble Trl	28092
Ramseur St	28092
Range Rd	28092
Rash Rd	28092
Red St	28092
Redbud Rd	28092
Redding Ln	28092
Redleaf Trl	28092
Redwood Ln	28092
Reep Brothers Rd	28092
Reep Hill Trl	28092
Reepsville Rd	28092
Reid St	28092
Reynards Cir	28092
E Rhodes St	28092
Rhodes Rhyne Rd	28092
Rhyne St	28092
Rhyneland Rd	28092
Ribbon Cir	28092
Ridge Ct & St	28092
Ridgewood Ln	28092
Rinck Hill Ln	28092
Rippy Ln	28092
Ritchfield Dr	28092
Ritchie Rd	28092
River Rd	28092
River Hill Trl	28092
River Meadows Ct	28092
River Village Ln	28092
Riverside Dr	28092
Riverstone Dr	28092
Riverview Rd	28092
Riverwood Ln	28092
Rob Heavner Farm Rd	28092
Robert Sherrill Ln	28092
Roberta Ave	28092
Robin Rd	28092
Robinhood Ln	28092
Rock Creek Dr	28092
Rock Dam Rd	28092
Rock Hill Ln	28092
Rock Ola Ln	28092
Rockdam Creek Ct	28092
Rocky Ln	28092
Rocky Hill Ln	28092
Rolling Rd	28092
Rolling Meadow Ln	28092
Ronald Broome Ln	28092
Roper Rd	28092
Rose St	28092
Rosebury Ln	28092
Rosedale Dr	28092
Rosehill Dr	28092
Roseland Dr	28092
Ross Rd & St	28092
Ross Farm Rd	28092
Roundtree Ln	28092
Royal Ct	28092
Royal Oaks Dr	28092
Royster Sain Ln	28092
Rucker Ln	28092
Rudisill Rd	28092
Rustic Trl	28092
Sabo Dr	28092
Saddletree Rd	28092
Sagefield Ct	28092
Sain Rd	28092
Saint Dorothys Ln	28092
Saint Matthews Church Rd	28092

Saint Patricks Way 28092
Salem Ave 28092
Salem Church Rd 28092
Sandhill Dr 28092
Sandra Ln 28092
Sandy Ln 28092
Sandy Farm Rd 28092
Sandy Lee Ct 28092
Sandy Park Rd 28092
Sapplings Ct 28092
Sarah Elizabeth Rd 28092
Sarver Ln 28092
Saunders St 28092
Sawmill Rd 28092
School House Rd 28092
Scottswood Ln 28092
Seaford Ln 28092
Sedgewood Ln 28092
Sentry Ln 28092
Serenity Ct 28092
Seterra Ln 28092
Shady Ln 28092
Shady Brook Ln 28092
Shady Pine Ln 28092
Shaw Estates Ln 28092
Shell St 28092
Sheppard Trl 28092
Sherrill Ave 28092
Sherrill Farm Rd 28092
Sherrod Ln 28092
Sherwood Forest Rd 28092
Shiloh Run Ln 28092
Shoal Rd 28092
Short Cut Rd 28092
Shrum St 28092
Shuford Rd 28092
Shuttle Ln 28092
Sierra Ln 28092
Sigmon Rd & St 28092
Silo Rd 28092
Silver Maple Trl 28092
Sipe Rd 28092
Sj Crawford Dr & Rd 28092
Skyview Ln 28092
Skyway Ln 28092
Smith St 28092
Smith Family Ln 28092
Smith Farm Rd 28092
Softwind Ln 28092
Sourwood Ct 28092
Southfork Rd 28092
Southland Trl 28092
Southside Rd 28092
Southside Church Rd 28092
Spake Rd 28092
Spartan Ln 28092
Spring Meadows Dr 28092
Spring Side Dr 28092
Spring Valley Ln 28092
Springdale Park Dr 28092
Springfield Dr 28092
Springhill Trl 28092
Springs Rd 28092
Springs East Rd 28092
Springside Ln 28092
Springview Dr 28092
Springwater Ln 28092
Sprouse St 28092
Stamey Ln 28092
Stanford Rd 28092
Stanley Dr 28092
Starlight Dr 28092
Startown Rd 28092
State St 28092
Staton Ln 28092
Stillview Ln 28092
Stockton Trl 28092
Stonecroft Dr 28092
Stonegate Ln 28092
Stonewall Ln 28092
Stoney Creek Dr 28092
Stony Ridge Rd 28092
Story St 28092
Story Woods Rd 28092
Strawberry Ct 28092
Sugar Maple St 28092
Sulpher Branch Dr 28092
Summerow Rd 28092
E Sumner St 28092
Sun Valley Trl 28092
Sunbeam Dr 28092
Sundale Ln 28092
Sundown Ln 28092
Sunny Hill Dr 28092
Sunray Dr 28092
Sunridge Dr 28092
Surrey Dr 28092
Sweet Gum Dr 28092
Sweet Pea Ln 28092
Sweetbriar Ln 28092
Sweetwater Trl 28092
Swift Crk 28092
Swing Trl 28092
E & W Sycamore St 28092
Tablerock Ln 28092
Tait St 28092
Tallpine Ln 28092
Taswell Ln 28092
Teague St 28092
Teakwood Ln 28092
Technolgy Dr 28092
Tennessee Ct & Trl 28092
Teresa Dr 28092
Terra Cotta Dr 28092
Terrace Pl 28092
Thel Ln 28092
Thomas Trl 28092
Thornhill Ln 28092
Threse Ln 28092
Thrift Dr 28092
Timberhill Trl 28092
Timberlake Ln 28092
Timberlane Dr 28092
Timmons Marie Ln 28092
Timothy Ln 28092
Timpken Dr 28092
Tin Ln 28092
Tin Lane Cir 28092
Tin Mine Rd 28092
Tinsel Trl 28092
Tiny Trl 28092
Tomes Rd 28092
Treehaven Trl 28092
Trey Trl 28092
Tripple H Ln 28092
Trivia Trl 28092
Turner St 28092
Underwood Ln 28092
Union Church Rd 28092
Union Ridge Dr 28092
Untold Way 28092
Upland Ln 28092
Valerie Dr 28092
Valley Ave 28092
Valley View Ln 28092
Vandiver Dr 28092
Vauxhall Ln 28092
Vellis Wright Rd 28092
Victor St 28092
Victor Woods Ln 28092
Victory Grove Church Rd 28092
Viewmont Rd 28092
Village Rd 28092
Vista Dr 28092
Wagon Trl & Way 28092
Walker Dr 28092
Walker Branch Rd 28092
Walker Mountain Rd 28092
Wallace Acres Ln 28092
Walnut St 28092
Walston Ln 28092
Walt Burgess Rd 28092
Walter Dr 28092
Wandering Trl 28092
Warwick Ct 28092
E & W Water St 28092
E & W Water Street Ext 28092
Waterfalls Dr 28092
Waterford Dr 28092
Waters Rd 28092
Waterview Trl 28092
Weatherfield Dr 28092
Weatherwood Dr 28092
Weaver St 28092
Wellington Dr 28092
Wellons St 28092
Wendover Dr 28092
Wesley Ln 28092
Wesleyan Church Rd 28092
West Ave 28092
Westdale Ln 28092
Western Sky Ct 28092
Westfork Trl 28092
Westover Dr 28092
Westridge Ln 28092
Westview Dr 28092
Westward Trl 28092
Westwinds Rd 28092
Wh Kiser Rd 28092
Wheat Field Ct 28092
Whim Shaft Dr 28092
Whipporwill Rdg 28092
Whispering Pnes 28092
Whispering Hill Trl 28092
Whistle Way 28092
White St 28092
White Hall Ln 28092
White Pine St 28092
Whiteners Farm Rd 28092
Whitesides Dr 28092
Wichitah Dr 28092
Wicket Ln 28092
Wildale Ln 28092
Wilfong Rd 28092
Will Schronce Rd 28092
Williams St 28092
Willow Dr & St 28092
Willow Ridge Rd 28092
Wilma Sigmon Rd 28092
Wiltshire Ln 28092
Windmill Trl 28092
Windsor Trl 28092
Windy Hill Rd 28092
Windy Knob Trl 28092
Wintercrest Ln 28092
Wise Rd 28092
Wisteria Ln 28092
Wood Hill Pt 28092
Woodcreek Ln 28092
Woodfield Ln 28092
Woodgate Rd 28092
Woodgreen Dr 28092
Woodland Hill Trl 28092
Woodmont Cir 28092
Woodridge Ln 28092
Woodsbury Ln 28092
Woodvale Cir 28092
Woolie Rd 28092
Worm Farm Ln 28092
Worthington Pl 28092
Wt Carpenter Dr 28092
Yarborough Rd 28092
Yorkdale Ln 28092
Zane Rd 28092
Zeb Hull Ln 28092
Zeb Johnson Rd 28092

NUMBERED STREETS

All Street Addresses 28092

LUMBERTON NC

General Delivery 28358

POST OFFICE BOXES MAIN OFFICE STATIONS AND BRANCHES

Box No.s
1 - 7640 28359
28358 - 28358 28358

NAMED STREETS

Abby Ln 28360
Abby Rd 28358
Aberdeen Dr 28358
Abernathy Dr 28360
Adrian Dr 28360
Airport Blvd 28358
Alamac Rd 28358
Albion St 28358
Aldwych St 28358
Alexander St 28358
Alexis Dr 28358
Alicia Dr 28358
Allen St 28358
Allenton Rd 28358
Alton B Rd 28358
Alyssa Ct 28360
Amanda St 28358
Amberdale West Cir 28358
Amberleaf Dr 28358
Amberleaf East Cir 28358
Ambrose Dr 28360
Amethyst Rd 28358
Ampack Dr 28358
Amy Ln 28360
Angel Dr 28360
Anna Dr 28360
Anne St 28358
Anthy Dr 28360
Antioch Ln 28358
Appaloosa Ct & St 28360
Apple St 28358
Arabian Dr 28360
Arbor Ln 28360
Arcadia Dr 28360
Archie Fairella Rd 28360
Ariella St 28358
Arlean Dr 28360
Arlington Dr 28358
Arnette St 28358
Arnold St 28358
Arrowhead Dr 28360
Arrowhead Trailer Park 28360
Arry Jane Rd 28360
Asbury Dr 28358
Ascot Ln 28358
Ash St 28358
Atlanta St 28358
Aundrea Ave 28358
Austaca Dr 28358
Austin Dr 28358
Autumn Chase Blvd 28358
Avon Ln 28360
Axiom Ln 28358
Ayers Ct 28358
Azalea Dr 28360
B And W Rd 28358
Back Bay Rd 28360
Back Swamp Rd 28360
Bailey Rd 28358
Bakersfield Dr 28358
Ball Park Rd 28358
Barber Shop Rd 28360
Barefoot Dr 28358
N Barker St 28358
Barker Church Rd 28358
Barker Ten Mile Rd
200-5499 28358
5500-5599 28360
5700-6999 28358
Barley Green Dr 28360
Barnes St 28358
Barnhill Rd 28358
Barry Rd 28360
Baucom Ave 28360
Baxter St 28358
Bay St 28358
Baymeadow Bnd 28358
Beach Dr 28358
Beal St 28358
Beam Rd 28360
Beam St 28358
Bear Ln 28360
Bear Bay Rd 28358
Beau Dr 28358
Beaver Dr 28360
Bee Gee Rd 28358
Beech Ct 28358
Bell Farm Rd 28360
Belle St 28358
Belmont St 28358
Benny Rd 28358
Bens Dr 28360
Benton Dr 28360
Berkley Ln 28360
Berkshire Pl 28358
Bernis St 28358
Berry St 28358
Bessie Dr 28358
Best Dr 28358
Beth Cir & Dr 28358
Beulah Church Rd 28358
Beverly Cir 28360
Bighorn Dr 28360
Birch St 28358
Birkdale Ct 28358
Birtie Rd 28358
Bishop Cir 28358
Bl Cox Dr 28358
Blair Dr 28360
Blake St 28358
Blessing Dr 28358
Blount St 28358
Blueberry Cir 28360
Bluejay Dr 28358
Bobbys Cir 28358
Bobs Lndg 28360
Bodiford Pl 28358
Bois Dr 28358
Boland Rd 28358
Bollinger Ave 28360
Bonnie Ln 28358
Booker Ave 28358
Boone Rd 28360
Bourbon St 28358
Bovine Dr 28360
Bowden Ln 28358
Bowman Rd 28358
Bracey Sampson Rd 28360
Bradford Dr & St 28358
Bragg St 28358
Branch Rd & St 28358
Branch Farm Acres Dr 28358
Brandons Rd 28360
Brewington Rd 28360
Briarcliff Rd 28358
Briarpath Cir 28358
Brightside Rd 28358
Brigman Rd 28358
Brisson St 28358
Brittany Dr 28358
Broadridge Rd 28358
Broadway Dr 28358
Broken Arrow Dr 28360
Bronco Ln 28360
Brooke Ln 28358
Brookfield St 28358
Brookgreen Dr 28358
Brookwood Dr 28360
Brown Stone Dr 28360
Browning Dr 28358
Bruce Ln 28360
Brunswick Rd 28358
Bryan St 28358
Bryant St 28358
Buchanan St 28358
Buck Trail Rd 28358
Bucket Rd 28360
Buckingham Cir 28360
Buckshot Rd 28358
Buie Philadelpus Rd 28360
Bullard St 28358
Bundy Dr 28358
Bunk Dr 28360
Bunny Rd 28358
Bunny Trail Rd 28358
Burch Rd 28360
Burgaw Rd 28360
Burke St 28358
Burnette Dr 28360
Burns Rd 28358
Burnt Island Rd 28358
Buttercup Ln 28358
Byrd Ave 28358
C Ave 28358
Cadaris Cir 28358
Caldonia Dr 28358
Caldwell St 28358
California Dr 28358
Cambridge Blvd 28358
Camellia Ln 28360
Camero Rd 28360
Campbell St 28358
Canaday Farm Rd 28360
Canal St 28358
Candor Dr 28360
Canecutter Rd 28358
Canterbury Cir 28358
Caple St 28358
Capuano Rd 28358
Cardinal Ave 28360
Cardwell Dr 28360
Carol Cir 28358
N & S Carolina Ave 28358
Carolyn St 28358
Carson Ave 28360
Carthage Rd 28358
W Carthage Rd 28360
Carver St 28358
Case St 28358
Castle Rd 28358
Caton Rd 28360
Cattle Rd 28360
Cavalier Dr 28358
N & S Cedar St 28358
Cedar Bay Dr 28358
Cedar Grove Rd 28358
Center St 28358
Centerville Church Rd 28358
Chambers St 28358
Charles Rd & St 28358
Charmant Rd 28358
Chavis St 28358
Cheater Ln 28358
Cheetah Dr 28358
Cherokee St 28358
Cherry Ln & St 28358
Cheryl Dr 28358
N & S Chestnut St 28358
Chicken Rd 28360
Chickenfoot Rd 28358
Chicos Dr 28360
Chimmey Rd 28358
N & S Chippewa St 28358
Christian Rd 28358
Christopher Rd 28360
Church St 28358
Circle Dr 28360
Civitan Rd 28360
Clark Ave 28358
Claude St 28358
Clay Dr 28358
Clewis Ln 28360
Clewis St 28358
Cliffridge Dr 28358
Cline St 28358
Clyborn Church Rd 28360
Clyde Cir 28358
Coe Rd 28358
Cold Storage Rd 28360
Coleman Dr 28360
Coleman St 28358
Collins Dr, Ln & St 28358
Colson Dr 28360
Columbia Ave 28358
Commerce Ave 28358
Community Way 28358
Concord Dr 28358
Confort Ln 28358
Contempora Dr 28358
Cooper St 28358
Corda Dr 28360
Coree St 28358
Corporate Dr 28358
Cottonwood St 28358
Country Ln 28360
Country Club Rd 28360
N Court Sq 28358
Covington Rd 28360
Cowboy Ln 28360
Cox Ln & Rd 28360
Cox Pond Rd 28360
Cozy Dr 28360
Crabtree Ln 28358
Crandlemire Rd 28358
Craven Rd 28358
Crawford Rd 28358
Creekwood Rd 28358
Crescent St 28358
Crestwood Dr 28360
Cricket Hollow Rd 28358
Cricklewood St 28358
Cromwell Pl 28358
Crystal Ln 28358
Crystaline Rd 28358
Cunningham Cir 28360
Cupcake Rd 28358
Curt Dr 28360
Cy Williams Blvd 28360
Cydney St 28358
Cynthia Dr 28360
Cypress Cv & St 28358
Dairy Ave 28358
Daisey Dr 28360
Daisy Cir 28358
Dallas Rd & St 28358
Damian Dr 28358
Dana Rd 28358
Dartmoor Ln 28360
Daughters Dr 28360
David St 28358
Davis Dr
1-99 28360
100-2499 28358
Davita Dr 28360
Dawn Dr 28360
Dayalpur Ave 28358
Deacon Rd 28360
Deacons Rd 28358
Deep Branch Rd 28360
Deer Stand Dr 28358
Deerfield Dr 28358
Delicate Dr 28358
Delmar St 28358
Deltons Rd 28358
Denium Rd 28360
Denmark Rd 28358
Denver Rd 28358
Derrick Rd 28358
Derwood Rd 28358
Desam Dr 28360
Deuce Dr 28358
Devin Dr 28358
Devon Rd 28360
Dewey Dr 28358
Diamond Cir 28358
Diane Rd 28358
Dickerson Rd 28358
Discovery Dr 28358
Doe Trail Rd 28358
Dogwood St 28358
Donnie Dr 28360
Doris E Ln 28358
Dorsey Rd 28360
Dot Rd 28360
Douglas Dr & St 28358
Drake Dr 28358
Dresden Ave 28358
Duart Rd 28358
Dundee Rd 28358
Dunn Rd 28358
E Ave 28358
Eagle Dr 28360
Eaglewood Loop 28358
Earl St 28358
Earnhardt Dr 28358
East St 28358
Eastwind Dr 28358
Eastwood Ter 28358
Ebermoor Rd 28358
Ed Rd 28358
Eddie Sampson Rd 28360

Street	ZIP
Edens Ave	28358
Edgewood Dr	28360
Edgewood St	28358
Edinborough Dr	28358
Edmund Dr	28360
Edwards Cir	28360
Edwards St	28358
Eisenhower St	28358
El Paso Dr	28360
Elba St	28358
Elijah Rd	28358
Elizabeth Ave	28358
E & W Elizabethtown Rd	28358
Elliotte Dr	28360
Ellis Dr	28360
N & S Elm St	28358
Elmhurst Dr	28358
Elmo Rd	28358
Eltons Dr	28358
Emerald Lake Dr	28358
Emory Cir	28358
Eternity Dr	28358
Ethan St	28358
Ethel Dr	28360
Ethridge Ln	28358
Eugina Ln	28360
Evelyns Dr	28360
Evergreen Ave	28358
Evergreen Church Rd	28360
Evers Rd & St	28358
Exand Rd	28360
Fairsite St	28358
N & S Falling Leaves Ln	28358
Farm Brook Dr	28358
Farringdom St	28358
Faulk Rd	28358
Fawn Trail Rd	28358
Faye Dr	28358
Fayetteville Rd	28358
N Fayetteville Rd	28360
Feather Ln	28360
Fernwood Cir	28360
Fieldcrest Dr	28358
Fields Rd	28358
Fieldstone Dr	28360
Fig St	28358
Flamingo Dr	28358
Florence Ct	28358
N Floyd Ave	28358
Fluffy Dr	28358
Flynn Dr	28360
Ford Dr	28358
Forest Rd	28358
Fork Pine Rd	28358
Fowler Rd	28358
Fralear Rd	28360
Frances Cir	28358
Franklin Ave	28358
Freedom Dr	28358
French Ave	28358
Friendly Ave	28360
Friendship Rd	28358
Front St	28358
Fuller Ave	28358
Furhan Rd	28358
Furman Dr	28358
G And M Dr	28360
Gainys Dr	28358
Gairlock Pl	28358
Garden Rd	28360
Gardenias Dr	28358
Gardner Dr	28358
Gateway Dr	28360
Gavintown Rd	28358
Gem Rd	28358
Gentry Rd	28360
George St	28358
Geronimo Dr	28358
Gertie Dr	28358
Giant Rd	28358
Glasgow Dr	28358
Glen Cove Dr	28360
Glen Cowan Rd	28360
Glendale Ave	28358
Glenn St	28358
Glisson St	28358
Gloucester St N	28358
Goats Dr	28360
Godwin Ave	28358
Gough St	28358
N & S Grace St	28358
Graham Cir	28360
Grande Oak Blvd	28358
Grandma Ln	28358
Grant Dr	28358
Grayton St	28358
Greenbiar Rd	28358
Greenock Pl	28358
Greenview Dr	28360
Greenville Rd	28358
Grey St	28358
Griffin St	28358
Grooms Dr	28358
Grumpy Dr	28358
Guinea Ln	28358
Hadassah Dr	28360
Halsey St	28358
Hammonds Rd	28360
Hammonds Apts	28360
Hamp Dr	28358
Hampstead Rd	28360
Hanks Dr	28360
Hanover St	28358
E Hardin Rd	28358
Hargrave St	28358
Harleesville Rd	28358
Harlie Rd	28360
Harrill Rd	28358
Harris Rd	28358
Harv Ln	28360
Hatfield Ct	28358
Havalih Dr	28358
Havelock Pl	28358
Hawthorne Ln	28360
Hay St	28358
Hayes Dr & St	28358
Hayswood Ave & St	28358
Hearty Rd	28358
Hedge Dr	28358
Hedgpeth Ct	28358
Helen Dr	28360
Helena Dr	28360
Hendrens Pond Dr	28358
Henry Hammond Rd	28360
Herndon Cir	28358
Herring St	28358
Hestertown Rd	28358
Hickory Leaf Ct	28358
High St	28358
Highland Ave	28358
Hillcrest Dr	28358
Hilly Branch Rd	28360
Hines St	28358
Holly Ln	28360
Holly St	28358
Holly Swamp Church Rd	28360
Hollywood Dr	28360
Homeland Dr	28360
Hood Rd	28358
Hooper St	28358
Horace Rd	28360
Horne St	28358
Hornets Rd	28358
Howard St	28358
Howell Rd	28358
Huetter Ln	28360
Huggins Rd	28360
Hull St	28358
Humphrey Ave	28358
Hundley Rd	28360
Hunt St	28358
Idlewood St	28358
Independence Dr	28358
Indian Heritage Rd	28358
Indigo Dr	28358
Iners Dr	28360
Inglewood Ave	28358
Inman St	28358
Ira Rd	28360
Iris Ln	28358
Isaac Dr	28360
Israel Dr	28358
Ivene Dr	28360
Ivey Rd	28358
Jackson Ct	28360
Jacobs St	28358
Jacobsville Rd	28358
James St	28358
Jamie Dr	28358
Jane St	28358
Jasmine Ln	28360
Jason Rd	28358
Jasper Dr	28358
Java Ln	28358
Jaybob Ln	28360
Jenkins St	28358
Jenny St	28358
Jeremy Dr	28358
Jerome St	28358
Jessup Dr	28360
Jewels Ln	28358
Jingle Dr	28360
Jlow Dr	28360
Joan St	28358
Jodis Dr	28358
John St	28358
John Henry Lee Rd	28358
Johnson St	28358
Jones St	28358
Jordan Dr	28358
Josephine Dr	28358
Journey Rd	28360
Judas Dr	28360
Judge Rd	28358
Judston Dr	28360
June Rd	28358
K B Rd	28358
Kahn Dr	28358
Kale Dr	28358
Kappa Ln	28358
Kayla Dr	28358
Kelsey Dr	28358
N Kenan Ave	28358
Kennedy Cir	28358
Kenny Biggs Rd	28358
Kenric Rd	28360
Kensington St	28358
Kentucky Cir	28358
Kiara Dr	28360
Kids Dr	28358
Kildeere Ln	28360
Kim Dr	28358
King St	28358
Kings Cross Rd	28360
Kingsdale Blvd	28358
Kinlaw Rd & St	28358
Kipling Dr	28360
Kite Rd	28358
Knight St	28358
Knot Dr	28358
Kristian Dr	28360
Krystin Ln	28358
Kyle St	28358
Kylon Dr	28358
La Hacienda Dr	28358
Lackey St	28360
Laclaire Rd	28360
Lafayette St	28358
Lafayette Park Rd	28358
Lake Dr	28358
Lakeside Dr	28360
Lamb Rd	28358
Lambeth St	28358
Lambshire Dr	28358
Landon Dr	28358
Langum Dr	28360
Lanye St	28358
Lark Ave	28358
Larry St	28358
Laurel Ct	28358
Laurel Oak Ln	28358
Ledoux Dr	28358
Lee Cir	28358
Lee Britt Rd	28358
Legend Rd	28358
Leggett St	28358
Leigh Ln	28358
Lenards Dr	28358
Lenors Dr	28360
Leola Dr	28360
Leon Dr	28360
Leonard Hunt Dr	28360
Lessane St	28358
Letties Dr	28358
Lewis West Dr	28358
Lexi Logan Rd	28358
Lexus Dr	28360
Liberty Hill Rd	28358
Limbo Dr & Rd	28360
Lincoln St	28358
Linden Ln	28358
Lindsey Ct	28358
Linkhaw Rd	28358
Linwood Ave	28358
Little St	28358
Little Rod Rd	28358
Littlefield Acres Loop Rd	28358
Live Oak Ln	28358
Lizzie Belle Dr	28360
Loch Raven Rd	28358
Lochern Rd	28358
Locklear St	28358
Locust St	28358
Lois Ln	28358
Loletas Ln	28358
Lollipop Dr	28360
Londonderry Dr	28358
Loneoak Dr	28358
Long Rd	28358
Long Branch Dr	28358
Longleaf Dr	28358
Lonnies Rd	28360
Loretta Dr	28358
Lorraine Dr	28358
Lottie Cir	28360
Lou Ave	28360
Louise Dr	28360
Lovette Rd	28358
Lowe Rd	28360
Lowery St	28358
Lucretia Dr	28358
Ludgate St	28358
Lumbee Ave	28360
Lumbee St	28358
Lummie Dr	28360
Lynn Rd	28358
Macarthur St	28358
Macon St	28358
Madison Ave	28358
Madonna Dr	28360
Magna Blvd	28360
Magnolia Way	28358
Main St	28358
Mallard Cir & Dr	28360
Manchester Ln	28360
Maple Dr & St	28358
Maple Leaf Way	28358
March Dr	28358
Marigold Ln	28358
Marine Dr	28360
Marion Rd	28358
Marley Dr	28358
Marracco Dr	28360
Marshall St	28358
Martin Rd	28358
N Martin Luther King Jr Dr	28358
Marvin Dr	28358
Maryland St	28358
Matilda Dr	28360
Matthews Bluff Rd	28358
Maverick Rd	28360
Maxwell Rd	28358
Mcarn Rd	28358
Mccollum St	28358
Mcdaniel Rd	28360
E Mcdonald Rd	28358
Mcdougald St	28358
W Mcduffie Crossing Rd	28360
Mckeller St	28358
Mckensie St	28360
Mckinnon Rollin Rd	28358
Mclamb St	28360
Mclean Rd	28358
Mcleod Rd	28358
Mclettan Rd	28360
N Mcmillan Ave	28358
Mcneely Dr	28358
Mcneill St	28358
Mcphail Rd	28358
Mcqueen St	28358
Meadow Ln	28360
Meadow Rd	28358
Meadow View Rd	28358
Medley Ln	28358
Meka Ln	28360
Melvin Ln	28360
Mercedes Ln	28358
Mercer Mill Rd	28358
Michelle Dr	28358
Michigan Cir	28358
Middle St	28358
Milan Ave	28358
Milestone Rd	28360
Mill St	28358
Millbrook Ln	28358
Mimosa St	28358
Minnesota Ct	28358
Miriam Ln	28360
Mockingbird Ln	28360
Monroe St	28358
Moore Cir	28358
Moores Ln	28358
Mopar Ln	28360
Morelia Dr	28360
Morgan St	28358
Moses Rd	28358
Moss Neck Rd	28360
Mount Moriah Church Rd	28360
Mount Olive Church Rd	28360
Mount Zion Rd	28360
Mud Alley Rd	28358
Mueller Dr	28358
Mule Rd	28360
Musselwhite Cir	28358
Mylow Dr	28358
Myrtle Ct	28358
Mystery Ln	28360
Naples Dr	28358
Narcissus Dr	28360
Narsons Cir	28360
Nathan Dr	28358
National Ave	28358
Native Rd	28360
Nc Highway 211 E	28358
Nc Highway 211 W	28360
Nc Highway 41 N & S	28358
Nc Highway 711	28360
Nc Highway 72 E	28358
Nc Highway 72 W 2000-6499	28360
Nc Highway 72 W 8300-8399	28358
Neal Dr	28358
Nealy Ave	28358
Nealy Cir	28358
Neighborhood Dr	28358
Nelson Way	28360
Nestle Ln	28360
Nevada Dr	28360
Nevada St	28358
New Kent St	28358
Newberry St	28358
Newgate St	28358
Newman Dr	28360
Nigel Dr	28360
Nimocks Dr	28360
Noir St	28358
Norman Dr	28360
Norment Rd	28360
Norris Dr & St	28358
North Blvd	28360
North St	28358
Northfield Rd	28360
Norton Rd	28358
Norwood Ave	28358
Nottingham Cir	28358
Nye Rd	28358
Nynelle Dr	28360
Oak Pt & St	28358
Oakgrove Rd	28360
Oakgrove Church Rd	28360
Oakridge Blvd	28358
Oakwood Ave	28358
Oakwood Heights Dr	28358
Oban Dr	28358
Oberry Ln	28358
Odum Rd	28360
Offie Jones Rd	28360
Olan Dr	28360
Old Allenton Rd	28358
Old Elizabethtown Rd	28358
Old Goat Rd	28358
Old Kingsdale Rd	28358
Old Oak Ct	28358
Old Saw Mill Rd	28360
Old Stage Rd	28358
Old Tower Rd	28360
Old Whiteville Rd	28358
Old Wilkins Dr	28358
Oleander St	28358
Olive Dr	28358
Oliver Ln	28358
Oliver St	28360
Olsen Dr	28358
Orange St	28358
Oras Dr	28360
Oregon St	28358
Oriole Rd	28360
Osborne Dr	28358
Osterneck Dr	28358
Owen Dr	28358
Oxendine Cir	28360
Oxford Rd	28358
Page St	28358
Paizley Dr	28358
Palm Ct	28358
Panther Dr	28358
Paris St	28358
Park St	28358
Parker Dr	28358
Parkview Dr	28358
Parmele Ave	28358
Parnell Cir	28358
Parnell Rd	28360
Parrot Dr	28360
Pate St	28358
Patsy Dr	28360
Patterson Rd	28358
Patton St	28358
Paul Rd	28360
Peachtree St	28358
Peacock Ln	28358
Pearl Rd & St	28358
Pebble Dr	28358
Pecan St	28358
Pecan Park Trailer Park	28360
Pentecostal Ave	28358
Pepper Dr	28358
Peril St	28358
Perry Rd	28360
Peterson Dr	28358
Phillips Dr	28358
Piccadilly Cir	28360
Pin Oak Dr	28358
N Pine St	28358
Pine Log Rd	28360
Pine Meadow Rd	28360
Pine Run Dr	28358
Pine Tree Rd	28360
Pinecrest Cir W	28360
Pinecrest Dr	28358
Pinedale Blvd	28358
Pinelog Rd	28360
Pineview Rd	28360
Pinewood Ct & Rd	28358
Piney Grove Rd	28360
Pinto Dr	28360
Pinwheel Cir	28358
Pirates Rd	28358
Pittman Rd	28358
Planetarium Rd	28360
Pleasant Hope Rd	28358
Pleasant Meadow Rd	28358
Polo Dr	28360
Pond Dr	28360
Ponk Cir	28360
Poochie Dr	28360
Pope Crossing Rd	28358
Poplar St	28358
Porky Dr	28358
Porter Dr	28360
Portsmouth Cir	28358
Possum Dr	28360
Post Oak Ct	28358
Pot Hole Rd	28360
Powell St	28358
Power Plant Rd	28358
Powers Rd	28358
E Powersville Rd	28358
W Powersville Rd	28360
Powhatan Dr	28360
Prather Dr	28360
Pratt Ln	28358
Pretty Ln	28358
Prevatte St	28358
Pridgen Rd	28358
Princeton St	28360
Promise Ln	28360
Prosperity Dr	28360
Pruitt St	28358
Pug St	28358
Quail Run Rd	28358
Quevero Dr	28358
Quincey Dr	28358
R And L Ln	28358
Rabbit Hill Dr	28358
Race Dr	28360
Rachel St	28358
Raft Swamp Dr	28360
Rambo Dr	28360
Randy St	28360
Ranger Ct	28358
Ransom Rd	28360
Raspberry Ln	28360
Raven Rd	28358
Raymond Rd	28358
Rdw Farm Rd	28360
Reaves St	28358
Red Bird Dr	28360
Red Fox Rd	28360
Red Oak Ct	28358
Red Tip Dr	28358
Redwood Ct & Way	28358
Reel Dr	28358
Regan Church Rd	28358
Regan Cutoff Rd	28358
Regents St	28360
Renee Cir	28358
Rennert Rd	28360
Resa Loop Dr	28358
Rgh Farm Rd	28360
Rhodies Dr	28360
Ricco Ln	28358
Rice Rd	28358
Ridge Dale Dr	28360
Ridgecrest Ct	28358
Ridgefield Dr	28358
Ridgeview Dr	28358
Riley Cir	28360
Rim Rd	28360
Ringo Dr	28358
River Rd	28360
River Ridge Rd	28360
River Run Dr	28360
Riverbrook Rd	28358
Rivermeade Dr	28360
Riverside Blvd & Dr	28358
Riverwood Ave	28358
Robbies Ln	28358
Robert Bessie Rd	28358
Roberts Ave	28358
N Roberts Ave 100-2899	28358

3000-3599 28360
S Roberts Ave 28358
Roberts Rd 28358
Robeson Dr & St 28358
Robin Rd 28358
Robotex Dr 28358
Rocket Rd 28360
Rodeo Dr 28358
Rogers St 28358
Rolling Ln 28358
Ron Dr 28358
Ronald Blvd 28360
Rose Ct 28358
Roseheart Dr 28358
Rosenwald St 28358
Rosewood Dr 28358
Roslyn Dr 28358
Rowan Rd 28358
N Rowland Ave 28358
N & S Rozier Ln, Rd & St 28358
Rozier Church Rd 28360
Rozier Siding Rd 28358
Rudolph Rd 28358
Rudys Dr 28358
Rufus St 28358
Russ Rd 28358
Ruth Rd 28358
Rutherglen Dr 28358
Ryan Dr 28358
Saddletree Rd 28360
Sadie Dr 28358
Saint James Cir 28358
Saint Johns Cir 28358
Salena Dr 28358
Sampson St 28358
Sanchez Dr 28358
Sandlin Dr 28358
Sandpit Rd 28358
Sanford St 28360
Saxon Ave 28358
Schaeman Cir 28358
School St 28358
Scott Rd 28360
Seals Dr 28360
Seals St 28358
Seaney Dr 28358
Sedgefield Dr 28360
Sellers Dr 28358
Selma Rd 28358
N & S Seneca St 28358
Sequoia Dr 28360
Serenity Ln 28360
Sessoms St 28358
Seth Rd 28358
Shamiya Dr 28358
Shamrock Dr 28360
Shane Dr 28360
Shannon Rd 28360
Shauna Dr 28360
N Shaw Ave 28358
Shawn Rd 28358
Sheeba Dr 28358
Shelton Cir 28360
Sherwood Rd 28358
Shiloh Rd 28360
Shirley St 28358
Short Dr 28360
Shot Dr 28358
Show Case Cir 28358
Sibley Rd 28358
Side St 28358
Silky Rd 28360
Silver Cir 28358
Silver Fox Rd 28360
Simmons Dr 28360
Sinclair St 28358
Singletary Rd 28358
Singletary Church Rd 28358
Sj Rd 28360
Skipper St 28358
Skitize Dr 28360
Skycrest Rd 28358
Smith Dr 28360
Smith Mill Rd 28358
Smyrna Church Rd 28358

Snake Rd 28358
Sonoma St 28360
South St 28358
Southfield Rd 28360
Spanish Oak Ln 28358
Spanky Rd 28360
Sparrow Ln 28360
Spearman St 28358
Speedway Dr 28360
Spiritwind Dr 28360
Spring Moon Ln 28358
Spruce St 28358
Sprunt Ave 28358
Spurgeon Dr 28360
Stable Dr 28358
Stacy Cir 28358
Stallings Dr 28358
Stanley Ln 28358
Star Dust Cir 28358
Starburst Rd 28360
Starlite Dr 28358
State St 28358
Steele St 28358
Stephens Ln, Rd & St 28358
Stewart Dr 28360
Stirling Dr 28358
Stone St 28358
Stratford Ln 28358
Styles Dr 28360
Suggs Rd 28360
Summer Ln 28358
Summit Ave 28358
Sun Rd 28360
Sunflower Dr 28360
Sunset Rd 28360
Surry Dr 28360
Sussex Ln 28360
Swann Dr 28360
Sweeping Cross Blvd 28360
Sweet Briar Ct 28358
N & S Sycamore Ln & St 28358
T P Rd 28358
Tammy Rd 28358
Tanglewood Ter 28358
Tanner Ln 28360
Tanya Ln 28358
Tar Heel Rd 28358
Tartan Rd 28358
Taylor Dr & St 28358
Tennessee Rd 28360
Terrance Dr 28358
Terry Dr 28360
Tessie Dr 28358
Theory Dr 28360
Thomas Dr 28358
Thomasville Dr 28360
Thompson Rd & St 28358
Thorps Rd 28358
Thunderbird Rd 28358
Tickle Rd 28358
Tiger Ln 28360
Tilman Cox Rd 28358
Tinas Rd 28360
Titus Rd 28360
Todd Farm Rd 28358
Tofah Ranch Rd 28358
Tolarsville Rd 28358
Toma Hawk Rd 28360
Tootsie Rd 28358
Toria Dr 28358
Tow Truck Dr 28360
Tower Rd 28358
Town Common St 28358
Townsend St 28358
Tracy Dr 28360
Tralliso Rd 28358
Traveler Rd 28358
Travis Dr 28360
Trevor Dr 28358
Tribe Rd 28360
Tricky Dr 28358
Trinity Dr 28358
Trinity Rd 28360
Trio Ln 28360
Troy Dr 28358

Truman Ln 28358
Turner Pl 28358
Turnpike Rd 28358
Turtle Dr 28360
Turtlecove Dr 28358
Tyner Rd 28360
Udell Rd 28360
Union Chapel Rd 28360
Us Highway 301 N
1100-11399 28360
Us Highway 301 N
11700-11999 28358
Us Highway 74 E 28358
Us Highway 74 W 28360
Utah St 28358
Valencia Cir 28358
Valtlee Dr 28360
Van Born Dr 28360
Vance Dr 28358
Vanlanot Dr 28358
Vann Dr 28358
Vate Rd 28360
Velcord Dr 28358
Velton Dr 28358
Venture Rd 28360
Vergie Dr 28360
Vester Rd 28358
Vfw Rd
1-199 28360
500-599 28358
Vicki Dr 28360
Victoria Est 28358
Vidalia Cir 28358
Village Walk E & W 28358
Virginia Dr 28358
Vollie Dr 28360
Von St 28360
Vonda Dr 28360
Wagon Loop Rd 28358
Walker St 28358
Wall St 28358
Wallace Rd 28360
N & S Walnut St 28358
Walnut Cove Dr 28358
Walter Cir 28360
War Path Rd 28360
Ward St 28358
Warren Rd 28360
Warrior Rd 28360
Warwick Mill Rd 28358
Washington St 28358
Watauga St 28358
N Water St 28358
Water View Ln 28358
Waterford Cir 28360
Watts Rd 28360
Waynes Rd 28358
Wd Locklear Rd 28360
Webb Rd 28358
Wellington Rd 28360
Wendell Rd 28360
Wesley Pines Rd 28358
West Dr & Rd 28358
Westchester Pl 28358
Westminster Rd 28360
Whale Dr 28360
White St 28358
White Oak Dr 28358
Whitney Rd 28358
Wildwing Rd 28358
Wilkerson Rd 28358
Wilkes Dr 28358
Wilkins Rd & St 28358
Willard Rd 28358
Williams St 28358
Willie Rd 28360
Willis Ave 28358
Willoughby Rd 28358
N & S Willow St 28358
Willow Oak Dr 28358
Willow Point Dr 28358
Wilson St 28358
Wilton Dr 28358
Windchester Dr 28358
Windsor Dr & Rd 28358
Windy Dr 28360

Winona Ave 28358
Winslow Dr 28360
Wintergreen Dr 28358
Wire Grass Rd 28358
Wiseman Rd 28360
Wisper Ln 28360
Wisteria Dr 28360
Wood St 28360
Woodcliff Dr 28358
Woodland Ave 28358
Woodlawn St 28358
Woodridge Dr 28358
Woody Farm Rd 28360
Worth Dr 28360
Wren St 28358
Wyatt St 28360
Wyndam Blvd & Ct 28358
Wyvin Ln 28360
Yedda Rd 28358
Yorkshire Pl 28358
Yvonne Dr 28360
Zach Dr 28358
Zippo Ln 28358
Zular Dr 28360

NUMBERED STREETS

E 1st St 28358
E & W 2nd 28358
E & W 3rd 28358
E & W 4th 28358
E & W 5th 28358
E & W 6th 28358
E 7th St
200-300 28358
301-2299 28358
301-301 28359
302-2298 28358
7th Street Rd 28358
E & W 8th 28358
E & W 9th 28358
E & W 10th 28358
E 11th St 28358
E 12th St 28358
E 13th St 28358
E 14th St 28358
E & W 15th 28358
E & W 16th 28358
E & W 17th 28358
E & W 18th 28358
E & W 19th 28358
E & W 20th 28358
E & W 21st 28358
E & W 22nd 28358
E & W 23rd 28358
E & W 24th 28358
W 25th St 28358
W 26th St 28358
W 27th St 28358
W 28th St 28358
W 29th St 28358
W 30th St 28358
W 31st St 28358
W 32nd St 28358
W 33rd St 28358
W 34th St 28358
W 35th St 28358
W 36th St 28358

MATTHEWS NC

General Delivery 28105

POST OFFICE BOXES MAIN OFFICE STATIONS AND BRANCHES

Box No.s
1 - 3958 28106
4001 - 9998 28105
10100 - 10200 28106

NAMED STREETS

Abbey Walk Ln 28105
Abergele Ln 28104
Ablow Dr 28105
Acacia St 28105
Acadia Ln 28105
Adagio Ct 28105
Adare Ct 28104
Afternoon Sun Rd 28104
Ainsdale Dr 28104
Alaqua Ct 28105
Albatross Ln 28104
Aldergrove Rd 28105
Alexander St 28105
Alexander Ridge Dr 28105
Allison Dr 28104
Altara Ln 28104
Amanda Dr 28104
Ambassador Ct 28104
Amen Ct 28104
N & S Ames St 28105
Amhurst Ct 28104
Amir Cir 28105
Ammanford Ct 28104
Ancestry Cir 28104
Andiron Dr 28105
Andulusian Dr 28105
Anglesey Ct 28104
Annabel Ct 28105
Anne St 28104
Annecy Dr 28105
Antioch Ct 28104
Antioch Church Rd 28104
Antioch Plantation Rd 28104
Antioch Woods Dr 28104
Apple Hill Rd 28105
Apple Tree Ct 28104
Arborfield Dr 28105
Arborlea Ct 28105
Aringill Ln 28104
Arlington Downs Blvd 28104
Armadale Ln 28105
Arrow Dr 28104
Arroyo Vista Ln 28104
Arundale Ln 28104
Ashby Woods Dr 28105
Ashford Glen Dr 28104
Ashie Ave 28104
Ashley Creek Dr 28105
Ashley Farm Dr 28105
Ashstead Ln 28105
Ashwell Oaks Ln 28105
Aston Ct 28105
Atrium Way 28105
Aubrey Bell Dr 28105
Auckland Ln 28104
Aurora Blvd 28105
Autumn Gold Ct 28104
Avery Ct 28104
Avington Pl 28105
Axford Ln 28105
Azteca Dr 28104
Bailey Ct 28104
Balintoy Ln 28104
Ballade Dr 28105
Ballards Pond Ln 28105
Ballymote Ct 28104
S Bank Ct 28105
Banteer Rd 28105
Bards Ct 28105
Bardsey Ct 28104
Barington Pl 28105
Barnard Castle Ln 28104
Barney Ct 28104
Barnyard Ct 28105
Basking Ridge Ct 28105
Bathgate Ln 28105
Bayleaf Ct 28105
Belfield Commons Ct 28105
Bellasera Way 28105
Belle Grove Manor Ln 28105
Beltway Blvd 28104
Bent Oak Dr 28104
Bent Tree Trl 28104
Bent Wood Ct 28105

Bentcreek Ln 28105
Benton Woods Dr 28105
Berkley Square Ln 28105
Bermuda Ct 28104
Bernadine Ct 28105
Bethesda Ct 28104
Bethune Pl 28105
Bethwyck Ct 28105
Beulah Church Rd 28104
Beulah Oaks Way 28104
Bideford Ct 28105
Big Creek Ct 28105
Big Pine Dr 28105
Biggers Brook Dr 28104
Biltmore Forest Dr 28105
Birchdale Ct 28104
Birchhaven Dr 28104
Birdie Ct 28104
Birkenhead Ln 28105
Bitter End Ct 28105
Black Oak Dr 28105
Blackberry Ln 28104
Blackfoot Ln 28104
Blacksmith Ct 28105
Blackvine Dr 28105
Blarney Ct 28104
Bloom Wood Ln 28105
Blossom Hill Dr 28104
Blossomwood Ln 28105
Blue Iris Dr 28104
Blueberry Ridge Rd 28105
Bluebird Hill Ln 28104
Bluebonnet Ln 28104
Bogey Ct 28104
Bonito Ct 28104
Botetourt Ct 28104
Bounty Ct 28104
Bow Club Trl 28104
Bow Hunter Trl 28104
Bow Wood Trl 28104
Bowbrook Trl 28104
Bowen Ct 28105
Bower Ct 28105
Boyd Dr 28105
Boyd Funderburk Dr 28104
Bracey Ct 28105
Brad Ct 28104
Bradwyck Ct 28105
Bramble Creek Dr 28105
Bramwell Pl 28105
Branch Lewis Cir 28105
Brandonwood Ln 28105
Brandywine Dr 28105
Brecon Ct 28104
Brenham Ln 28105
Brenner Ct 28104
Brenwyck Ct 28105
Briar Trail Ct 28104
Briarwood Ct 28105
Bridgemere Ter 28105
Brightmoor Dr 28105
Brightmoor Ridge Dr 28105
Brightwood Ln 28105
Brigmon Ln 28105
Brittle Creek Dr 28105
Bromley Dr 28104
Brook View Ct 28104
Brookfield Ct 28104
Brookgreen Ter 28104
Broomstraw Ct 28105
Brownstone Ct 28104
Brush Hollow Rd 28105
Bubbling Well Rd 28105
Buckton Ln 28105
Bumble Bee Dr 28105
Bungalow Dr 28104
Bunker Ct 28104
Burlwood Ct 28104
Burnt Mill Run 28104
Burnwood Ct 28105
Butter Churn Ln 28105
Butterburr Dr 28104
Butternut Ln 28105
Bydeford Ct 28105
Caddy Ct 28104
Caernarfon Ln 28104

Calabassas Ln 28105
Caliterra Dr 28104
Calpher Ct 28105
Cambria Ct 28104
Cambridge Oaks Dr 28104
Camden Dr 28104
Cameron Commons Way 28104
Cameron Creek Dr 28105
Cameron Matthews Dr 28105
Cameron Run Ln 28105
Cameron Village Dr 28105
Campus Ridge Rd 28105
Camrose Crossing Ln 28104
Candalon Way 28105
Candlelight Woods Dr 28105
Candlewood Ridge Ln 28105
Cannonade Ct 28105
Cantata Ct 28105
Canterbury Ln 28104
Canterfield Dr 28104
Canterfield Ln 28105
Cape Fear Ct 28105
Capriole Ln 28105
Cardiff Ln 28104
Cardigan Ct 28104
Carding Pl 28105
Cari Ln 28104
Carls Rd 28104
Carmarthen Ct 28104
Carmona Ct 28104
Carnegie Ln 28105
Carole Ct 28104
Caroline Dr 28104
Carolyn Ln 28104
Carpenter Grove Ln 28105
Carriage Crossing Dr 28105
Carrington Forest Ln 28105
Casetta Dr 28105
Cashel Ct 28104
Casswell Cir 28104
N Castle Ct 28105
Castle Cliff Dr 28105
Castlebridge Ln 28104
Castleford Blvd 28104
Castlemaine Dr 28104
Castlestone Ln 28104
Catawba Cir N & S 28104
Catskill Dr 28105
Cedar Bnd 28104
Cedar Chase Dr 28105
Cedar Point Ave 28104
Cedar Ridge Ln 28104
Cedarbark Dr 28105
Cedarwood Ln 28104
Cerretto Ct 28105
Chambers Dr 28105
Champion Rd 28105
Chanelstone Way 28104
Chaney Ct 28105
Chanson Pl 28105
Chaphyn Ln 28105
Charcoal Ridge Ct 28105
Chardmore Dr 28105
Charing Cross Dr 28105
E & W Charles St 28105
Chateau Ct 28105
Chaucer Ln 28104
Chaucery Ln 28104
Chelsea Pl 28105
Cherry Hollow Ln 28104
Cherrywood Ln 28104
Cheryl Cir 28105
Chesney Glen Dr 28105
Chesson Ct 28105
Chesswood Ln 28105
Chestnut Ln 28104
Chestnut Hill Dr 28105
Chickadee Ct 28104
Chimore Ln 28105
China Berry Ct 28104
Chip Shot Dr 28104
Chipwood Ln 28105
Chistow Rd 28105
Choctow Rd 28104

Christ Covenant Church Rd 28105
Churchill Glen Cir 28104
Cindy Carr Dr 28105
Cinnamon Dr 28104
Circa Dr 28105
E Circle Dr 28104
Citation Ct 28105
Cithara Dr 28105
Clairborne Ct 28104
Claire St 28105
Clairview Ln 28105
Clam Bed Ct 28105
Clarks Wynd 28105
Claybrooke Ct 28105
Clearbrook Rd 28105
Clearkirk Ct 28105
Clement Morris Rd 28105
Clifden Dr 28104
Clifton Dr 28104
Clifton Meadow Dr 28105
Climbing Rose Ln 28104
Clonmel Dr 28104
Cloudburst Dr 28105
Clover Crest Ln 28104
Club View Ln 28105
Clydesdale Ct 28104
Coach Ridge Trl 28105
Coatsdale Ln 28104
Cobblecreek Dr 28104
Cobblers Dr 28104
Cochrane Woods Ln 28105
Colchester Ln 28104
Colt Ct 28105
Colts Foot Dr 28105
Coltsview Ln 28105
Comanche Ln 28104
Commercial Dr 28104
Community Park Dr 28104
Cone Mill Ct 28104
Connemara Dr 28105
Connie Ct 28105
Copeland Ct 28104
Corduroy Ct 28105
Corner Stone Dr 28104
Cotton Gin Aly 28105
Cotton Mill Ct 28104
Council Pl 28105
Country Club Dr 28104
Country Place Dr 28105
Country Squire Ct 28105
County Haven Rd 28104
Couples Ct 28104
Courtney Ln 28105
Covenant Church Ln 28105
Covington Xing 28104
Cox Rd 28104
Cpcc Ln 28105
Craftsman Ridge Dr 28104
Creek Ct
2400-2499 28105
2800-2899 28104
Creek Pointe Dr 28105
Creekberry Dr 28104
Creekside Dr 28105
Creekwood Ct 28105
Crescendo Ct 28105
Crescent Ln 28105
Crescent Knoll Dr 28105
Crestdale Rd 28105
Crestdale Crossing Dr 28105
Crews Rd 28105
Cricket Ln 28105
Cricketwood Ct 28104
Cross Point Cir & Rd 28105
Cross Tie Ln 28105
Crusaders Ct 28105
Cupped Oak Dr 28104
Curry Way 28104
Cyprus Ct 28105
Dalwen Green Ct 28105
Dan Hood Rd 28105
Dancy Dr 28105
Dandridge Cir 28105
Danhill Pl 28105
Danny Ct 28105
Dark Wood Ct 28105
Darley Dale Ct 28105
Darlington Rd 28105
Dartmoor Ct 28105
David Dr 28105
Davidson Dr 28104
Davonport Rd 28104
Daylilly Rd 28104
Deal Rd 28104
Dean Hall Ln 28105
Deer Creek Dr 28105
Deerberry Ct 28105
Deerfield Creek Dr 28105
Delacourt Ln 28104
Delamere Dr 28104
Delaney Dr 28104
Demaree Ln 28105
Denhem Ct 28105
Derbyshire Ln 28104
Desborough Dr 28104
Devereaux Dr 28105
Devonport Rd 28104
Devore Ln 28105
Dilwyn Ct 28104
Dion Dr 28105
Divide Dr 28104
Divot Ct 28104
Dockside Ct 28104
Dogleg Ct 28105
Donegal Ct 28104
Donnelaith Ln 28105
Double Girth Ct 28105
Doverstone Ct 28104
Doves Nest Ct 28105
Doylestown Rd 28105
Draymore Ln 28105
Drew Ct 28104
Drexel Dr 28104
Driftway Point Rd 28105
Drumcliff Ct 28104
Drummond Ln 28104
Drye Ln 28104
Dubberly Ct 28105
Duffy Ct 28105
Dulins Knob Ct 28105
Dumont Ct 28105
Dundin Pl 28104
Dunfries Rd 28105
Dunham Dr 28105
Dunnwood Hills Dr 28105
Dunraven Ct 28104
Dylan Dr 28105
Eagle Pass Ct 28104
Eagle Point Ct 28104
Eaglecrest Dr 28104
East Cir 28104
Eastpoint Dr 28105
Eastville Ct 28105
Eberle Way 28105
Echo Ridge Rd 28105
Eden Wood Ct 28105
Edgebrook Cir 28105
Edgefield Ct 28104
Edgeland Dr 28105
Edmund Ct 28105
Eidy Dr 28105
Eirlys Ln 28104
Elderberry Ct 28104
Eliah Dr 28104
Elibren Ln 28105
Elizabeth Ln 28105
Elizabeth Manor Ct 28105
Elkins Park Dr 28105
Elmsford Ln 28105
Elsmore Dr 28104
Emerald Lake Dr 28104
Enchanted Dr 28104
English Knoll Dr 28105
Enid Ln 28105
Epperstone Ln 28105
Equestrian Dr 28105
Estate Ln 28104
Eva St 28105
Evans Manor Dr 28104
Evian Ln 28105
Ezra Ct 28105
Fair Forest Dr 28105
Fairchelsea Way Ln 28105
Fairfax Woods Dr 28105
Fairfield Dr 28104
Fairforest Dr
100-499 28105
3000-3299 28104
Falcon Rdg 28104
Falesco Ln 28105
Falkenburg Ct 28105
Falkirk Ln 28104
Falkland Dr 28104
Farmridge Ln 28105
Fawn Hill Rd 28105
Feather Oak Ln 28104
Fence Post Ln 28105
Fernridge Ln 28105
Fieldstone Dr 28104
Fieldstone Manor Dr 28105
Fincher Rd 28104
Fincher Farm Rd 28105
Fir Place Ct 28104
Firewood Dr 28105
Fitzhugh Ln 28104
Fitzpatrick Ln 28105
Five Gait Ct 28105
Flagstick Dr 28105
Fleming Ln 28104
Flint Ct 28104
Flourmill Ct 28104
Flowe Dr 28104
Foggy Glen Pl 28104
Forbishire Dr 28104
Forest Dr 28105
Forest Lawn Dr 28104
Forest Park Rd 28104
Forest Ridge Rd 28104
Forest Trail Dr 28105
Forest Wood Dr 28104
Forestmont Dr 28105
Fortis Ln 28105
Fortuna Ct 28105
Four Lakes Dr 28105
Four Oaks Ln 28105
Four Wood Dr 28104
Fox Hedge Rd 28105
Fox Run Rd 28104
Foxbridge Dr 28104
Foxfield Ln 28105
Foxlair Ct 28105
Foxmeade Dr 28105
Foxton Rd 28105
Franklin Meadows Dr 28105
Fraserburgh Dr 28105
Fredricksburg Rd 28105
N & S Freemont St 28105
Freesia Pl 28104
Friendship Dr 28105
Fullwood Rd 28105
Gable Way Ln 28104
Gainsborough Dr 28104
Galway Ct 28104
Gander Cove Ln 28105
Ganzert Ct 28105
Garden Rose Ct 28104
Garden View Ln 28104
Gatebrook Ct 28105
Gateshead Ln 28105
Gatewood Ln 28104
Gatwick Ln 28104
Gaye Pl 28104
Gelderland Dr 28104
George Clay Ln 28105
George Guin Rd 28105
Gifford Dr 28105
Gilchrest Cir 28105
Giles Ct 28105
Gladewater Dr 28105
Gladiateur Ct 28105
Gladstone Ct 28104
Gladwyn Ct 28105
Glamorgan Ln 28105
Glen Lyon Dr 28105
Glen Oaks Dr 28104
Glen Verde Ct 28105
Glendalough Ln 28105
Glenmeadow Dr 28105
Glenn Valley Dr 28105
Glenshannon Rd 28105
Gloucester St 28104
Gold Cup Ct 28105
Gold Spike Ct 28105
Golden Hill Rd 28105
Golden Rain Dr 28104
Goldfinch Ln 28104
Golf View Ct 28104
Grand Provincial Ave 28105
Grassy Knoll Cir 28104
Grayfox Ln 28105
Grayson Ct 28105
Green Ash Ln 28104
Greenbriar Dr 28104
Greenbrook Pkwy 28104
Greenhurst Dr 28104
Greenway Ct 28104
Gregan Ct 28104
Greylock Ridge Rd 28105
Greylyn Dr 28104
Greystone Dr 28104
Greystone Fair Ln 28105
Greywood Ln 28104
Gribble Rd 28104
Grier Pl 28105
Grindstone Ct 28104
Gulfstream Ct 28105
Gum Wood Ct 28105
Gupton Ct 28105
Habitat Manor Dr 28105
Hackamore Dr 28105
Hadco Ln 28105
Hadley Ct 28105
Hadley Park Ln 28104
Hallmark Dr 28105
Hamlet Ct 28105
Hammond Dr 28104
Hampden Ln 28105
Hampshire Hill Rd 28105
Hampton Glen Ct 28105
Hardwood Dr 28104
Hardwood Pl 28105
Harefield Ln 28105
Harewood Ct 28105
Hargett Rd 28105
Harmony Ct 28105
Harness Ln 28105
Harrogate Ln 28104
Harrogate Rd 28105
Hartford Way 28104
Hartis Ln 28105
Hashanli Pl 28105
Hathwyck Ct 28105
Haven Lodge Rd 28104
Havenchase 28104
Hawker Rd 28105
Hawksnest Ct 28104
Hayden Way 28105
Heather Glen Dr 28104
Heathershire Ln 28105
Heirloom Ct 28104
Heison Ct 28104
Helena Park Ln 28105
Hemby Rd 28104
Heritage Acres 28104
Hickory Hl 28105
Hickory Glen Dr 28105
Hickory Knoll Ct 28105
Hickory Lake Ln 28105
Hidden Manor Dr 28104
Hidden Trail Ct 28105
Hideaway Ridge Ct 28105
High Echelon Dr 28105
High Hill Ct 28105
High Meadow Dr 28105
High Oak Dr 28104
High Vista Ct 28104
Highbury Pl 28104
Highland Ridge Ct 28104
Highview Rd 28104
Hillcrest Ct 28104
Hillshire Meadow Dr 28105
Hillwood Ct 28104
Hinson Dr 28105
Holcroft Ct 28105
Holleybank Dr 28105
Hollice Pl 28104
Holly Ct 28104
Holly Grove Ct 28104
Holly Ridge Dr 28105
Home Pl 28105
Homestead Pl 28104
Homewood Way 28104
Honey Creek Ln 28105
Honeysuckle Dr 28104
Honeysuckle Ridge Dr 28105
Hooks Rd 28105
Horizon Ct 28104
Horseback Cir 28105
Horseman Cv 28104
Horseshoe Bnd 28104
Hounds Run Dr 28105
Hugh Crocker Rd 28104
Hunley Ridge Rd 28104
Hunleyhill Ct 28104
Hunter Ln 28104
Hunters Bluff Dr 28105
Hunters Moon Ln 28105
Hunters Run Ln 28105
Hunting Ct 28105
Hunting Creek Rd 28104
Huntington Dr 28104
Huntington Ridge Ct 28105
Idle Dr 28105
Idlefield Ln 28105
Idlewild Rd
9800-14699 28105
14700-15599 28104
Ilsemont Pl 28105
E Independence Blvd
8900-13599 28105
14000-14199 28104
Independence Commerce Dr 28105
Independence Pointe Pkwy 28105
Indian Brook Dr 28104
Indian Cross Trl 28104
Indian Wood Dr 28104
Industrial Dr
100-299 28104
900-11099 28105
Innishmoor Ct 28104
Irish Moss Ln 28105
Ironwood Dr 28104
Irwin Ln 28105
Ivey Wood Ln 28105
Ivy Bluff Way 28105
Ivy Brook Pl 28104
Jackson Pl 28105
James Madison Dr 28104
James Wall Ln 28105
Jameston Ct 28104
Jamesville Dr 28105
Jared Ct 28105
Jarrett Ct 28105
Jaywick Ln 28105
Jaywood Ln 28105
Jean Place Ct 28104
Jeffers Dr 28105
Jefferson St 28105
Jerry Ln 28105
Jessica Ln 28104
Jody Dr 28104
E John St
1-302 28105
301-13799 28105
301-301 28106
304-13798 28105
W John St 28105
Johnson Ln 28105
Joines Dr 28105
Jonesberry Rd 28105
Joseph Dr 28105
Juniper St 28105
K Line Dr 28104
Kalanchoe Dr 28105
Kale Ln 28105
Kale Wood Dr 28105
Karras Commons Way 28105
Katie Ct 28105
Keegan Ct 28104
Kelly Dr 28104
Kendall Knoll Ct 28105
Kensrowe Ln 28104
Kent Dr 28105
Kenwood Terrace Dr 28105
Kerry Greens Dr 28104
Keziah Rd 28105
Kidwelly Ln 28104
Kilarney Ct 28104
Kilkenney Hill Rd 28105
Kilkenny Ct 28104
Killian Ct 28104
Kilmarnock Ct 28105
Kimberfield Rd 28105
Kimbrell Ct 28105
Kimway Ct & Dr 28105
Kinard Ct 28104
King Henrys Way 28104
King Richards Ct 28104
Kings Grant Way 28104
Kings Manor Ct 28105
Kings Manor Dr 28104
Kingsford Ct 28104
Kintyre Ct 28105
Kirby Ln 28104
Kirkbridge Ct 28105
Kirkholm Dr 28105
Kite Ct 28104
Knox Ave 28105
Ladys Slipper Ln 28105
Lafayette Park Ln 28104
Lago Vista Dr 28104
Lake Dr 28104
Lake Bluff Dr 28105
Lake Forest Dr 28104
Lake Point Dr 28104
Lake Prairie Dr 28104
Lake Providence Dr 28104
Lakehurst Xing 28104
Lakeland Dr 28104
Lakenheath Ln 28105
Lakeview Cir 28105
Lakewood Dr 28104
Lamington Rd 28105
Lamplighter Close Dr 28105
Landry Dr 28105
Laurel Fork Dr 28105
Laurel Grove Ln 28104
Laurelwood Dr 28105
Lawing Ct 28104
Lawley Ln 28105
Lawrence Daniel Dr 28104
W Lawyers Rd 28104
Leahurst Ct 28105
Leahy Mill Ct 28104
Leeswood Ln 28105
Legends Ln 28105
Leicester Dr 28104
Leighton Ct 28105
Lemmond Dr
9100-9199 28104
13100-13199 28105
Lexington Pointe Pl 28104
Leyland Ct 28104
Liberty St 28105
Library Ln 28105
Liddington Rd 28105
Light Brigade Dr 28105
Lightwood Dr 28105
Limerick Dr 28104
Linden St 28105
Linden Glen Dr 28104
Lindenwood Dr 28104
Lindsay Ln 28105
Lineview Dr 28104
Links Ln 28104
Linville Dr 28105
Lion Heart Ln 28105
Lipizzan Ct 28105
Liriope Ct 28105
Little River Ct 28105
Little Stream Ct 28105
Lochmeade Ln 28105
Lois St 28105
Longbridge Dr 28105
Longleaf Ct 28104
Longspur Dr 28105
Longview Ct 28104
Longwood Ct 28104
Lost Cv 28104
Ludman Way 28105
Lugano Ct 28104
Lynderhill Ln 28105
Lyonshead Ct 28105
Lytton Ln 28104
Macie Glen Ct 28105
Macroom Ct 28104
Main St 28105
Majestic Ln 28104
Mangionne Dr 28105
Manicott Dr 28105
Mann Dr 28105
Manor Ridge Dr 28105
Mansard Ct 28105
Manus Ct 28105
Maple Grove Church Rd 28104
Maple Shore Dr 28104
Maple Valley Ct 28104
Mara Ct 28105
Marblebrook Dr 28105
Maremont Ct 28104
Mareshead Ln 28105
Margaret Wallace Rd 28105
Marglyn Dr 28105
Marion Dr 28105
Marjorie Dr 28105
Mark Pl 28105
Markay St 28105
Markwell Dr 28105
Marque Pl 28105
Marquis Ct 28104
Marshall Hooks Rd 28105
Marshbrooke Rd 28105
Marville Ct 28105
Matoka Trl 28104
Matt Wdng Rd 28104
E & W Matthews St & Xing 28105
Matthews Chapel Rd 28105
Matthews Commons Dr 28105
Matthews Estates Rd 28105
Matthews Indian Trail Rd
2200-2599 28105
2600-4299 28104
Matthews Mill Rd 28105
Matthews Mint Hill Rd 28105
Matthews Park Dr 28105
Matthews Plantation Dr 28105
Matthews School Rd 28105
Matthews Station St 28105
Matthews Street Ext 28105
Matthews Township Pkwy 28105
Matthews Weddington Rd
3200-3899 28105
3900-7199 28104
Mattridge Rd 28105
Mccamey Dr 28104
Mcclendon Ct 28105
W Mcdowell St 28105
Mckee Rd 28105
Mckirkland Ct 28105
Mclendon Rd 28104
Mcleod St 28105
Mcnabb Ct 28105
Meadow Ln 28105
Meadow Crest Ct 28104
Meadow Lake Dr 28105
Meadow Run Dr 28104
Meadowbrook Dr 28104
Mellon Rd 28104
Melrose Club Dr 28105
Melrose Cottage Dr 28105
Merancas Ct 28105
Merribrook Dr 28105
Mezzo Ct 28105
Michelle Ct & Dr 28104

Middlesborough Dr 28104
Middleton Ave 28104
Mikelynn Dr 28105
Mill House Dr 28105
Mill House Ln 28104
Mill Race Ln 28104
Mill Stream Ct 28104
Mill Valley Ct 28105
Millbank Dr 28104
Millbrook Ln 28104
Mills End Cir 28105
Millstone Ln 28104
Millwright Ln 28104
Minden Dr 28104
Minden Ln 28105
Minor Ln 28104
Mint Lake Dr 28105
Misty Glen Ct 28105
Mollie Irene Dr 28104
Monaghan Ct 28105
Mondavi Ct 28105
Monerria Rd 28104
Monroe Rd 28105
Monroe Weddington
Rd 28104
Moonstone Dr 28105
Moore Rd 28105
Moorefield Dr 28104
Morab Dr 28104
Morning Dale Rd 28105
Morning Star Dr 28105
Morningside Meadow
Ln 28104
Morningwood Dr 28105
Morris Rd 28105
Moss Creek Ct & Dr 28105
Mossy Branch Ct 28104
Mount Harmony Ch Rd
2000-2499 28104
2500-3199 28105
Mountain Ashe Ct 28105
Mountain Laurel Ct 28104
Mourning Dove Dr 28104
Mulberry Ct 28104
Mullis Ln 28105
Murandy Ln 28104
Muses Ct 28105
Myrtle Garden Ct 28105
Nashua Dr 28105
Natchez Ln 28105
Nathaniel Glen Ct 28105
Nedmore Ct 28105
Neill Ridge Rd 28105
Nelson Rd 28104
Nettleton Ct 28105
New Towne Dr 28105
Newburg Ln 28105
Newby Ln 28105
Newport Ln 28105
Nickalaus Dr 28104
Nightshade Pl 28105
Northeast Pkwy 28105
Northfield Ct 28105
Nottaway Dr 28105
Nottaway Place Dr 28105
Nutfield Ln 28105
O Malley Dr 28105
O Toole Dr 28105
Oak Forest Cir 28104
Oak Tree Trl 28105
Oak View Ct 28105
Oakberry Ct 28104
Oakcroft Dr 28105
Oakglade Ct 28105
Oakhaven Trailer Park 28105
Oakridge Ct 28104
Oakshade Ln 28105
Oakspring Rd
2400-2600 28104
2501-2599 28105
2601-2699 28104
2602-2698 28104
Oakton Ridge Ct 28105
Oakville Ct 28105
Oakwood Dr 28104
Ocaso Ct 28104

Odell Ct 28105
Old Acres Ct 28105
Old Depot Ln 28105
Old Farm Ct 28104
Old Gate Dr 28105
Old House Cir 28105
Old Monroe Rd
100-999 28104
1000-1299 28105
1300-3799 28104
3801-6599 28104
10001-12297 28105
12299-12399 28105
12401-12899 28105
13600-13799 28104
Old Pine Ln 28105
Old Pond Ln 28105
Olde Creek Trl 28105
Olde Roxbury Dr 28105
Olde Stone Ln 28104
Olive Mill Ln 28104
Optomist Ct 28104
Orchard Knob Dr 28105
Oscar Dr 28105
Oscar Privette Rd 28104
Over Stream Ln 28105
Overwood Dr 28105
Oxborough Dr 28105
Oxbow Ct 28105
Oxford Ter 28104
Paces Ave 28105
Painted Trillium Ct 28105
Palomino Rdg 28104
Panache Dr 28104
Panhandle Cir 28104
Park Center Dr 28105
Park Square Pl 28105
Parkgate Dr 28105
Parkhill Ct 28104
Parkstone Dr 28104
Parkview Way 28105
Partridge Ln 28104
Patrick Springs Ct 28105
Patten Hill Dr 28105
Paul Rose 28104
Pawnee Trl 28105
Peachtree Ct 28104
Pearlstone Ln 28104
Pearwood Ct 28105
Pebble Run Dr 28105
Pebble Stone Ln 28104
Peggy Ridge Ter 28105
Penderlea Ln 28105
Pennridge Pl 28105
Pepper Ann Ln 28104
Percheron Ct 28105
Pesca Ln 28104
Pheasantwood Ln 28105
Phillips Rd 28105
Phillips Woods Ln 28105
Piersland Dr 28104
Pine Chase Ln 28105
Pine Haven Ct 28105
Pine Laurel Dr 28104
Pine Needle Ct 28104
Pine Pointe St 28105
Pine Twig Way 28105
Pine Valley Ct 28105
Pineapple Ct 28105
Pinecliff Ct 28104
Pinehill Ln 28104
Pinetree Dr 28105
Pineville Matthews Rd 28105
Pinewood Ct 28104
Pinewood Hill Dr 28105
Plainview Dr 28104
Plantation Center Dr 28105
Plantation Estates Dr 28105
Pleasant Pine Ct 28105
Pleasant Plains Rd
1300-3399 28105
3400-4199 28104
Pleasantwood Dr & Ln 28104
Plentywood Dr 28105
Plum Ridge Ct 28105
Plum Royal Dr 28105

Plymouth Dr 28104
Polo Club Blvd 28105
Polo View Ln 28105
Polyantha Rose Cir 28104
Pommel Ln 28105
Pondmeade Ln 28104
Poplar Glen Dr 28104
Poplar Knoll Dr 28105
Porch Swing Ln 28104
Port Royal Dr 28105
Porters Pond Ln 28105
Portpatrick Ln 28105
Potter Cove Ln 28104
Potters Rd 28104
Prescott St 28104
Princessa Dr 28104
Privette Rd
1600-1799 28105
3300-3999 28104
Providence Rd 28105
Providence Forest Dr 28104
Providence Hills Dr 28105
Providence Oak Ln 28104
Purple Vale Dr 28104
Putney Ct 28104
Quail Ridge Ln 28104
Quarterhorse Ln 28104
Quill Ln 28105
Quilting Rd 28105
Quintessa Dr 28104
Raccoon Run Ct 28105
Rainbow Ridge Dr 28105
Raintree Dr 28104
Ranchview Ct 28104
Randwick Way 28104
Rapidan Ln 28104
Rappahannock Ct 28104
Ravens Ct 28104
Raywood Ct 28105
Red Barn Trl 28105
Red Fox Trl 28104
Red Porch Ln 28105
Red Willow Ln 28104
Redan Ct 28105
Redhaven St 28105
Reefton Rd 28104
Reid Hall Ln 28105
Reid Harkey Rd 28105
Restoration Dr 28105
Revelwood Dr 28104
Reverdy Ln 28105
Reverdy Oaks Dr 28105
Rexford Rd 28104
Rexford Chase Ct 28104
Rheinwood Ct 28105
Rhoderia Dr 28104
Rhyll Ct 28105
Rice Rd 28105
Rice Road Ext 28105
Riddick Pl 28105
Ridge Lake Dr 28104
Ridgebury Ter 28105
Ridgeview Rd 28105
Rising Sun Ln 28104
Ritz Ln 28105
River Banks Rd 28105
River Birch Cv 28104
Riverton Rd 28105
Robert Ln 28105
Robinet Pl 28105
Robinlynn Rd 28105
Robinson Ave 28105
Rock Hill Church Rd 28104
Rock Ridge Pass 28104
Rockfish Dr 28105
Rocking Chair Rd 28105
Rockwell View Rd 28105
Rondeau Ct 28105
Rose Arbor Ln 28105
Rosecrea Ct 28104
Rosedale Ln 28105
Rosedown Dr 28105
Royal Commons Ln 28105
Royal Troon Dr 28104
Rural Hill Ct 28105
Russet Glen Ln 28104

Sabot Ln 28105
Saddle Horn Trl 28104
Saddletree Ct 28105
Sadie Dr 28105
Sagemont Ave 28105
Saint Johns Ave 28104
Saint Peters Ln 28105
Salvo Dr 28105
Sam Boyd Ct 28105
Sam Newell Rd 28105
Sandy Ridge Ln 28105
Sandymead Rd 28105
Sangtong Dr 28105
Sapwood Ct 28104
Saranac Ln 28105
Sarandon Dr 28104
Sardis Rd 28105
Sardis Glen Dr 28105
Sardis Grove Ln 28105
Sardis Mill Dr 28105
Sardis Plantation Dr 28105
Sardis Pointe Rd 28105
Savannah Dr 28105
Savannah Hills Dr 28105
Scarborough Ln 28105
Scarlet Dr 28104
Scenic Dr 28105
Scenic Way 28104
Schuster Ct 28105
Scottsdale Ln 28104
Sea Mist Dr 28105
Seaboard St 28104
Secotan Ln 28105
Selma Burke Ln 28105
Senconee Rd 28104
Senna Dr 28105
Serel Dr 28104
Serenity Pl 28104
Seton Dr 28105
Shade Tree Ct 28104
Shadow Forest Dr 28105
Shadow Lake Ln 28104
Shadow Rock Ct 28104
Shadowmere Ln 28104
Shadowy Retreat Dr 28104
Shady Grove Ln 28104
Shady Knoll Cir 28104
Shady Knoll Ct 28105
Shagbark Ln 28104
Shalford Ln 28104
Shanelle Ln 28104
Shannamara Dr 28104
Shannon Bridge Ln 28105
Shannon Woods Ln 28104
Shasta View Way 28105
Shawnee Trl 28104
Sheckler Ln 28104
Shelby St 28105
Shirley Dr 28104
Shoreline Dr 28104
Short St 28104
Shrewsbury Ln 28105
Sills Creek Pl 28105
Silverleaf Ln 28105
Simfield Church Rd 28105
Siskey Pkwy 28105
Slate Ridge Rd 28104
Smith Cir 28104
Smith Farm Rd 28105
Snapdragon Ct 28104
Soleado Dr 28104
Solera Ln 28105
Somersby Ln 28105
Song Sparrow Dr 28104
Sonoma Ct 28105
Southern Cross Ln 28105
Spokeshave Ln 28105
Spring St 28105
Spring Hill Rd 28104
Spring Oaks Dr 28104
Spring Rose Ln 28105
Spring Stone Dr 28105
Springwater Dr 28105
Spruce St 28104
Squirrel Lake Ct 28105

Stallings Rd
100-4399 28104
4500-5099 28105
Stallings Road Ext 28104
Stallingswood Dr 28104
Stallion Ct 28105
Stanbury Dr 28104
Stanhope Ln 28105
Staunton Rd 28105
Stevens Rdg 28105
Stevens Mill Rd 28104
Stevens Schultz Ln 28104
Stillwell Rd 28105
Stillwood Pl 28105
Stilwell Rd 28104
Stirrup Ct 28104
Stonedown Ln 28104
Stoneham Ct 28105
Stonehedge Ct 28105
Stonehedge Dr 28104
Stonehill Ln 28104
Stonemede Ln 28105
Stoney Ridge Rd 28104
Stoneybrook Ct 28104
Strabane Dr 28104
Straffan Ct 28104
Stratford Woods Rd 28105
Stratfordshire Dr 28105
Strathaven Dr 28105
Straussburg Woods Ln 28105
Strawberry Rd 28104
Streatley Ln 28105
Stryker Dr 28104
Sudbury Ln 28104
Sugar Plum Ct 28104
Sultana Ln 28104
Summerfield Ridge Ln 28105
Summergrove Ct 28105
Summerland Dr 28105
Sunflower Field Pl 28104
Sunnyview Cir 28105
Sustare Ct 28105
Suttle Pl 28104
Swaim Dr 28105
Swancroft Ln 28105
Sweet Bay Ln 28105
Sweetbriar Dr 28104
Sweetgum Ln 28105
Swift Ct 28105
Sycamore Knoll Ct 28105
Tabard Ln 28104
Taconic Pl 28105
Tadlock Pl 28105
Talbot Ct 28105
Tall Oaks Ct 28104
Tall Pines Ln 28105
Tamarack Dr 28105
Tan Yard Rd 28104
Tanfield Dr 28105
Tanglebriar Ct 28104
Tank Town Rd 28105
Tarlton Dr 28105
Tatting Rd 28105
Tavistock Ct 28105
Team Rd 28105
Tenby Ln 28104
Tensing Ct 28105
Terra Glen Ct 28105
Terry Ter 28105
Thames Ct 28104
Thistledown Ct 28104
Thomas Payne Aly 28104
Thornblade Ridge Dr 28105
Thornsby Ln 28105
Three Wood Dr 28104
Tilbury Trl 28105
Tilley Morris Rd 28105
Tillingmere Cir 28104
Tillot Dr 28104
Timber Ln 28104
Timber Knoll Dr 28105
Timber Oak Ct 28104
Timber Top Ct 28104
Timber Wood Ct 28105
Toddington Ln 28105
Tommy Ln 28105

Toms Farm Rd 28105
Topsail Ct 28104
Torino Rd 28105
Tory Oak Pl 28105
Tournament Dr 28104
Tracelake Dr 28105
Tracy Cir 28104
N & S Trade St 28105
Trafalgar Pl 28105
Trail Ridge Rd 28105
Tralee Ct 28104
Tranquil Cove Ct 28105
Tranquil Falls Ln 28104
Trapper Cove Ln 28104
Trappers Run Dr 28105
Treasure Hill Ct 28105
Tree Hill Rd 28104
Treeside Ln 28105
Treverton Dr 28105
Triple Crown Ct 28105
Tulip Ln 28104
Tullamore Ct 28104
Twelve Mile Creek Rd 28104
Twin Falls Ln 28105
Twin Lakes Dr 28104
Twin Pines Dr 28104
Two Iron Dr 28104
Tynecastle Ln 28105
Umi Ct 28105
Underwood Rd 28104
Union Rd 28104
Union West Blvd 28104
Valley Ranch Ln 28104
Valleyview Ct 28104
Veery Ct 28104
Vermonte Dr 28105
Vicino Ct 28105
Vickie Ln 28104
Vine Arden Rd 28105
Vinecrest Dr 28105
Vinings Creek Dr 28105
Vinings Oak Ln 28105
Viscount Dr 28104
Wade Hampton Dr 28104
Wagon Hill Rd 28105
Wainsley Pl 28105
Walden Ln 28104
Walker Rd 28105
Wallbrook Dr 28105
Walnut Crest Ln 28105
Walnut Knoll Dr 28105
Walnut Point Dr 28105
Walsingham Ct 28105
Wanda Dr 28104
Wardlow Ct 28105
Warehouse Dr 28104
Water Oak Ln 28104
Water Wheel Ct 28104
Waterby Way 28104
Waterleaf Ln 28105
Waxhaw Indian Trail
Rd 28104
Waybridge Way 28104
Weatherly Way 28104
Weddington Rd
100-699 28104
1700-1919 28105
1920-1998 28104
1921-4499 28105
2000-4498 28105
4700-6999 28104
Weddington Brook Dr 28104
Weddington Downs Dr 28104
Weddington Hills Dr 28104
Weddington Lake Dr 28104
Weddington Manor Ct 28104
Weddington Matthews
Rd 28104
Weddington Monroe
Rd 28104
Weddington Oaks 28104
Weddington Ridge Ln 28105
Wedge Ct 28104
Wedgewood Dr 28104
Weeping Willow Ln 28105
Wellingshire Ct 28105

Wellington Dr 28104
Wesley Chapel Rd 28104
West Cir 28104
Westbury Dr 28104
Westchire Ct 28105
Wester Ross Ct 28105
Westfork Run Rd 28104
Westminster Ln 28104
Whetstone Dr 28104
Whirlaway Ct 28105
Whisper Ridge Ln 28105
Whisperfield Ln 28104
Whispering Oaks Cir 28104
Whispering Spring Dr 28105
Whisperwood Ct 28104
Whistler Way 28105
White Birch Trl 28104
White Locust Ct 28104
White Oak Ln 28104
Whitebeam Way 28105
Whitefriars Ln 28105
Whitfield Dr 28105
Wickerby Ct 28105
Wicklow Hall Dr 28104
Wilcrest Dr 28105
Wild Rose Ct 28104
Williams Rd 28105
Williams Station Rd 28105
Williamstown Rd 28105
Willow Brook Dr 28105
Willow Oaks Trl 28104
Willow Trace Ln 28104
Willow View Ct 28105
Willowbrook Dr 28104
Willowdale Ln 28105
Wilrose Pl 28105
Winding Trl 28105
Windrow Ln 28105
Windrow Wood Ct 28105
Windsor Chase Dr 28105
Windsor Glade Dr 28105
Windsor Hill Dr 28105
Windsor Meadow Ln 28105
Windsor Square Dr 28105
Windsorwood Ct 28105
Windward Cv 28104
Windy Hill Ln 28105
Wineberry Ct 28105
Winter Wood Dr 28105
Winterbrooke Dr 28105
Wonderland Dr 28104
Wood Sorrel Ct 28105
Wood Star Ct 28105
Woodbend Dr 28105
Woodburn Ter 28105
Woodcalm Dr 28105
Woodfern Dr 28105
Woodglen Ln 28104
Woodkirk Ln 28104
Woodland Ct 28104
Woodshorn Dr 28104
Woodstar Rd 28105
Woodview Ln 28104
Woodway Hills Dr 28105
Woodway Oak Cir 28105
Woody Creek Rd 28105
Worthington Dr 28104
Wyndmere Hills Ln 28105
Wyntree Ct 28104
Wythe Ct 28105
Yarrow Rd 28104
Yearling Ct 28105
Yellow Daisy Dr 28104
Zelda Ln 28105
Zinnia Dr 28104

MONROE NC

General Delivery 28110

POST OFFICE BOXES MAIN OFFICE STATIONS AND BRANCHES

Box No.s
1 - 5041 28111

9998 - 9998 28110

NAMED STREETS

A G R Nance Rd 28110
Abbey Way 28110
Abingdon Ave 28110
Acme Dr 28112
Acorn Ln 28112
Adams St 28110
Aegean Way 28110
Aero Pointe Pkwy 28110
Afton Ct 28112
Airport Rd 28110
Airport Extension Rd 28110
Alda Dr 28110
Aldersbrook Dr 28110
Alexander St 28110
Alexander Farm Rd 28110
Alisa Dr 28112
E & W Allen St 28110
Alloy Way 28110
Altan Ridge Dr 28112
Alton St 28110
Alton Woods Rd 28112
Ambrose Ln 28110
American Ln 28110
Andrew St 28112
Ann St 28112
Annaberg Ln 28110
Antler View Ct 28112
Appian Ln 28110
Apple Dr 28110
Applebrook Dr 28110
Apricot Ln 28110
Aprilia Ln 28112
Arant Rd 28112
Arbor Ln 28110
Arbor Creek Ct 28110
Arcadia Ln 28112
Archie Ln 28112
Archie Hargette Rd 28110
Arden Dr 28112
Armfield Mill Rd 28112
Arminius Ct 28110
Arnold Dr 28110
Arrowhead Ct 28110
Asbury Dr 28110
Ashcraft Ave 28110
Ashley Ln 28110
Ashley Woods Ct 28112
Ashmore Ln 28110
Aspengold Ct 28110
Astoria Dr 28110
Atkinson Way 28110
Augustus Rd 28112
Austin Rd & St 28112
Austin Chaney Rd 28110
Autumn Cv 28112
Autumn Dr
400-499 28112
1900-2199 28110
Autumn Wood Dr 28112
Ava Ct 28110
Avery Parker Rd 28112
Aviation Dr 28110
Avocet Ln 28110
Avon St 28110
Avondale Ln 28110
Aycoth Rd 28112
Back Rd 28110
Baker Rd 28112
Barbee Ct 28110
Barbee Farm Dr 28110
E Barden St 28112
Barkley Cir 28112
Basilwood Cir 28110
Bass Creek Ct 28110
Battle Ln 28110
Baucom Rd 28110
Baucom And Son Rd 28110
Baucom Deese Rd 28110
Baucom Manor Rd 28110
Baucom Tarlton Rd 28110
Bay St 28112
Beard St 28110
Bearskin Ln 28110
N Beasley St 28112
Beaver Dam Dr 28110
Becky Ln 28112
Beechwood Ln 28112
Belk Mill Rd 28112
Belleview Ct 28110
Belmont Church Rd 28112
Belton St 28110
Bendanna Ln 28110
Bentgrass Ct 28110
Benton St 28110
Benton Acres Dr 28110
Bentwood Ln 28110
Berea Ct 28110
Bernard Simpson Rd 28110
Berrywood Ln 28110
Bert Williams Rd 28110
Bethel Ln 28110
Bethphage Ln 28112
Bickett St 28112
Bickett Ridge Dr 28110
Biggers Cemetary Rd 28110
Billybrook Ct 28110
Birmingham Ln 28110
Bishop Bowens Dr 28110
Bishops Ridge Ct 28110
Bitter Root Ct 28110
N Bivens Rd 28110
S Bivens Rd 28112
Black Horse Run Ct 28110
Blackvine Dr 28110
Blair St 28112
Blakeney Rd 28112
Blazing Star Ln 28110
Blueberry Dr 28110
Bonanza Rd 28110
Bougainvillea Ct 28110
Bovender Rd 28110
Boxer St 28112
Boyce Rd 28112
Boyd Griffin Rd 28110
Boyte St 28110
Bradford Pl 28110
Bradley Dr 28112
N & S Bragg St 28112
N & S Branch St 28112
Brandon Ct 28110
Braswell Rushing Rd 28110
Bravo Pl 28110
Brawinal Ct 28110
Brekonridge Centre Dr 28110
Brett Dr 28110
Brewer Dr 28112
Briarberry Ln 28112
Briarcliff Dr 28110
Brice Love Rd 28112
Brick Landing Dr 28110
Brickyard Rd 28110
Bridgewater Dr 28112
E Brief Rd 28110
Brightland Run 28110
Broadview Dr 28110
Bronte Ln 28110
Brook Farm Ln 28112
Brook Valley Run 28110
Brooke Dr 28112
Brookgreen Dr 28112
Brookhaven Ave 28110
Brookline Ct 28112
Brooks St 28110
Brookside Dr 28110
Broome St 28110
Broome Acres 28110
Brown St 28110
Bruce Ct 28110
Bruce Thomas Rd 28112
Buck Hill Rd 28112
Bud Plyler Rd 28112
Buena Vista Rd 28112
Buford Shortcut Rd 28112
Bundy St 28110
Bunnybrook Ln 28110
Burgess Helms Rd 28112
Burke St
100-199 28112
400-1199 28110
Burning Ridge Dr 28110
Butler Ct 28110
Buttermilk Ln 28110
Cabin Creek Ct 28112
Calhoun St 28112
Camelia Dr 28110
Cameron Ct 28112
Cameron Woods Dr 28110
Camp Dubois Ct 28110
Campobello Dr 28110
Campus Park Dr 28112
Canal Rd 28112
Candlewood Dr 28110
Cannon Dr 28110
Canterbury Ln 28112
Capital Dr 28110
Capstone Dr 28110
Cardinal Landing Dr 28110
Carl Belk Rd 28112
Carl Funderburk Rd 28112
Carl Polk Rd 28110
Carlson Dr 28110
Carly Scott Dr 28110
Carmel Church Rd 28112
Carmel Oak Ln 28112
Carr St 28110
Carriker Rd 28110
Carriker Williams Rd 28110
Carroll St 28110
Carson Ave 28112
Carson St 28110
Carter Rd 28110
Castle Rd 28110
Castleberry Ct 28110
Castlebrook Dr 28112
Catawba Ave 28112
Catskill Ct 28110
Cattail Cv 28110
Cedar St 28110
Cedar Hill Ct & Dr 28110
Cedar Park Ct 28110
Cedarwood Dr 28112
Cemetary Dr 28112
Center St 28112
Ceria Dr 28112
Chadwyck Dr 28110
Chamber Dr 28110
Chambwood Rd 28110
Chancellor Ln 28110
Chaney Rd 28110
Chantress Ln 28110
Charles St 28112
Charles Franklin St 28110
Charleston St 28112
Charlie Williams Rd 28112
N Charlotte Ave
100-599 28112
600-1899 28110
S Charlotte Ave 28112
Chatterleigh Dr 28110
Chelle Ct 28112
Chelsey Ln 28110
Cherry St 28110
Cherry Tree Dr 28110
Cherrybrook Ln 28110
Cherryridge Rd 28112
Cheshire Glen Dr 28110
Chinkapin Ln 28110
Chippendale Rd 28110
Christian Ct 28110
Christopher Jacob Ct 28110
Christopher Run Dr 28112
N & S Church St 28112
Churn Ct 28110
Cindy Dr 28112
Circle Dr 28110
Circle S Ranch Rd 28112
Circle Trace Rd 28112
Citrus Dr 28110
E & W Cj Thomas Rd 28110
Clara St 28112
Clarence Secrest Rd 28110
Clark Rd 28110
Clarkdale St 28110
Clarksville Campground Rd 28112
Classic Dr 28112
Claude Austin Rd 28112
Clear Creek Dr 28110
Clear Hill Ct 28110
Clearview Dr 28110
Clontz Rd 28110
Clontz Long Rd 28110
Clover Bend Dr 28110
Club Dr 28112
Coakley St 28110
Cobblestone Pkwy 28110
N & S College St 28112
Colony Rd 28112
Colony Oaks Dr 28112
Columbus Ln 28110
Comfort Ln 28112
Commerce Dr 28110
Compostela Ct 28110
Concord Ave & Hwy 28110
Confederate St 28110
Constance Ct 28110
Continental Dr 28110
Coral Bell Ct 28110
Cori Jon Dr 28110
Corinth Church Rd 28112
Corporate Center Dr 28110
Cottage Dr 28112
Cotton St 28112
Cotton Ridge Dr 28110
Cottonwood Cir 28110
Counselors Dr 28110
Country Ln 28110
Country Land Ct 28110
Country Villa Dr 28110
Country Wood Rd 28110
Countryside Ln 28110
Courtney Store Rd 28110
Courtyard Ln 28112
Cox Rd 28112
Coy Way 28110
Craig St 28112
Cranberry St 28110
N & S Crawford St 28112
Creekridge Dr 28110
Creekside Dr 28112
Creekwood Dr 28110
Crescent St 28112
Cresthaven Dr 28110
Crestview Trl 28110
Crestwood Dr 28112
Cripple Creek Ct 28110
Crooked Creek Church Rd 28110
Crooked Stick Dr 28112
Crossbridge Dr 28112
Crow Rd & St 28112
Crowder Rd 28112
E & W Crowell St 28112
Crown Forest Ln 28112
Crown Vista Ct 28110
Cruz Bay Dr 28110
Crystal Ln 28112
Culpepper St 28112
Cureton St 28112
Curtis St 28112
Cuthbertson St 28112
Cyrus Edwards Rd 28110
Cyrus Lee Ln 28110
D A Simpson Rd 28112
Dahlonega Ct 28110
Dairy Farm Dr 28110
Dairy Meadow Ct 28110
Dairywood Ln 28110
Dale St 28112
Dale Jarrett Blvd 28110
Damascus Dr 28110
Dana Ct 28112
Darby Dr 28112
Davenport St 28112
Dawn Rdg 28110
Daybreak Dr 28110
Deans Ct 28110
Debbie Dr 28112
Deer Track Ln 28110
Deerfield Dr 28112
Deese Rd 28110
Deese St 28112
Dellwood Dr 28112
Delmar Griffin Rd 28112
Dennis St 28110
Depot St 28112
Devon Dr 28110
Dewberry Ln 28110
Dewdrop Ct 28110
Dewitt Helms Rd 28112
Dexter Pl 28110
Diana Lee Ln 28112
Dickens Ln 28110
Dickerson Blvd 28110
Dogwood Cir 28110
Dogwood Dr 28112
Donald St 28110
Donnom St 28112
Doster Rd 28110
Double Oaks Dr 28112
Dove St 28112
Dover Pl & St 28110
Downwind Dr 28110
Drake Ln 28110
Dresden Ct 28110
Dublin Pl 28112
Duck Point Dr 28110
Dudley Rd 28112
Duncan Rd 28110
Duncan Keziah Rd 28110
Durant St 28112
Dusty Hollow Rd 28110
Eagle View Ln 28110
Earl Griffin Rd 28112
Early Mist Ct 28110
E & W East Ave 28110
Eastridge Ct 28110
Eastview Cir 28110
Edd Rorie Rd 28112
Eddystone Ln 28110
Edgehill Dr 28110
Edwards Farm Ln 28112
Effie Whitley Rd 28112
Efird St 28112
Elizabeth Ave 28112
Ellen St 28112
Ellis Belk Rd 28112
Elm St 28110
Embassy Ct 28110
Emily Ln 28110
Emmanuel Dr 28110
Engleside St 28110
English St 28110
Eric Sustar Ln 28110
Erica Dr 28112
Erindale Ct 28110
Ervena Ct 28110
Ervin Thomas Rd 28112
Essex Pointe Dr 28110
Ethel Sustar Dr 28110
Eubanks Rd 28112
Euclid St 28110
Eudy Rd 28112
Eugene Hobbs Rd 28110
Eustace Richardson Rd 28112
Everette St 28112
Evergreen Pl 28112
Executive Point Dr 28110
Exodus Ct 28110
Fair Meadows Dr 28110
Faircroft Way 28110
Fairley Ave 28110
Fairmont St 28110
Fairview Ct 28110
Falcon Ln 28110
Falling Leaf Ct 28110
Fallingtree Ln 28112
Family Cir 28110
Faramount St 28110
Farm House Ln 28110
Farmview Dr 28110
Farmwood Dr 28110
Faulk St 28112
Faye Dr 28110
Fence Post Ln 28110
Ferguson Farms Ln 28110
Few St 28110
Field Master Dr 28110
Field Pond Ln 28112
Fieldridge Ln 28110
Fieldstone Gate Ct 28112
Fincher St 28112
Fisher Ridge Dr 28110
Fitzgerald St 28112
Fletcher Broome Rd
800-999 28110
1000-2599 28112
Florence Dr 28110
Floyd Moore Rd 28112
Foch St 28110
Fola Dr 28110
Folger Dr 28112
Forbis Ln 28112
Ford St 28110
Forest Ave & Ln 28112
Forest Hills Dr & Ln 28112
Forest Springs Dr 28112
Forest Valley Ln 28112
E Fork Ln 28110
Formosa Dr 28110
Fort Clapsop Ct 28110
Fort Manden Dr 28110
Fosteria Ln 28112
Fowler Rd 28110
Fowler Secrest Rd 28110
Fox Den Dr 28110
Fox Hunt Dr 28110
Foxmoor Dr 28110
Foxworth Dr 28110
Frances St 28110
Frank Broome Rd 28112
E & W Franklin St 28112
Fuller Dr 28112
G B Hill Rd 28110
Gables Dr 28112
Galesburg Dr 28110
Gambrel Way 28112
Garden Gate Dr 28112
Garden Glen Ct 28112
Garrison Ct 28110
Gate Rd 28112
Gay Rd 28112
Genesis Dr 28110
Georgia Ave 28112
Gilman Pl 28110
Gladedale Ln 28110
Gleneagles Dr 28110
Glenn Dr 28110
Goldmine Rd 28110
Gordon Ln 28110
Gordon St 28112
Granville Pl 28110
Grassy Ln 28110
Gray Fox Rd 28110
Grayson Pkwy 28110
Great Falls Dr 28110
E & W Green St 28112
Green Haven Ln 28110
Green Meadow Way 28110
Greene Rd 28110
Greenfield Dr 28112
Greenloch Ct 28110
Greenwood Ln 28110
Grey Cir 28110
Grey Pond Ln 28112
Greyfield Dr 28110
Grier St 28110
Griffin Cir 28110
Griffin Cemetery Rd 28110
Griffith Rd 28112
Griffith Hill Dr 28112
Grimes St 28110
Guild St 28110
Gulledge Parker Rd 28112
Gum Ln 28112
Gumtree Rd 28110
Gus Eubanks Rd 28112
Gusty Ln 28110
Gw Broome Rd 28112
Gwen Hartis Ct 28110
H C Baucom Rd 28110
Habitat Ln 28110
Haigler Rd 28110
Haigler Baucom Rd 28110
Haigler Gin Rd 28110
Halcyon Ln 28112
Hamilton St 28112
Hampton Downs Dr 28112
Hampton Meadows Rd 28110
Hannah Pl 28110
Hanover Dr 28110
Hargette Rd
2300-2399 28110
2400-3099 28112
Harley St 28112
Harrington Quick Rd 28110
Harris Ln 28112
Hart St 28110
Harvard St 28112
Harvest Way 28112
Harvey Ln 28110
Hasty St 28112
Hawk Valley Dr 28110
Hayes Rd 28110
N & S Hayne St 28112
Haywood Rd 28110
Heath St 28110
Heather Ln 28110
Heather Pl 28112
Heatherwood Dr 28112
Heathrow Ct 28110
Helen St 28112
Helms St 28110
Helms Belk Rd 28110
Helms Pond Rd 28110
Helms Short Cut Rd 28112
Helmsville Rd 28110
Henderson St 28112
Henry Baucom Rd 28110
Henry Smith Rd 28110
Hepburn Ct 28110
Herkimer Dr 28110
Heron Point Dr 28110
Hickory Ln 28112
Hickory Grove Dr 28110
Hickory Nut Cir 28112
Hickory Woods Dr 28112
High School Dr 28112
High Shoals Dr 28110
Highland Pointe Dr 28110
E & W Highway 218 28110
E Highway 74 28112
W Highway 74 28112
Hill St 28110
Hillcrest Dr 28110
Hillcrest Church Rd 28110
Hillsdale Dr 28110
Hillsdale Rd 28112
Hillside Dr 28112
Hilltop Ct 28110
Hilton Way 28110
Hilton Meadow Dr 28110
Hinson Rd 28110
Holly St 28110
Holly Tree Ln 28110
Hollybrook Ln 28110
Holton Dr 28110
Honey Bee Rd 28110
Honeybrook Ct 28110
Honeycutt Simpson Rd 28110
Honeysuckle Ln 28110
Honeywood Ln 28110
Hood St 28112
Hopeton Ct 28110
Hopewell Church Rd 28110
Hopewood Ln 28110
Horton Ln 28110
Hospital Dr 28112
Hough St 28112
Hounds Run Ct 28110
Houston Dr 28110
E Houston St 28112
W Houston St 28112
E & W Hudson St 28112
Hunley St 28112
Hunt Club Ave 28110

Street	ZIP
Hunter Davis Ct	28110
Hunter Oak Dr	28110
Hunters Blf & Way	28110
Hunters Knoll Dr	28110
Hunters Trace Dr	28110
Huntingdon Ln	28110
Huntley Acres Ct	28110
Huntsman Ln	28110
Ib Shives Rd	28110
Iceman St	28110
Iceman Street Ext	28110
Icemorlee St	28110
Indigo Run	28110
Industrial Dr	28110
Irby Rd	28112
Irma Wolfe Rd	28110
Irongate Dr	28110
Ivah Lee Way	28110
Iveywood Dr	28110
J D Helms Rd	28112
J Frank Moser Rd	28112
Jack Davis Rd	28112
Jackson St	28112
Jacobs Ct	28110
Jade Ct	28110
James Dr	28110
James Hamilton Rd	28110
Jamestowne Dr	28110
Janes Ln	28112
Jannock Ct	28110
Jason Ct	28112
E & W Jefferson St	28112
Jerome St	28110
Jerry St	28110
Jim Cir	28110
Jim Parker Rd	28110
Joe Collins Rd	28112
Joe Griffin Rd	28112
John St	28110
John Baker Rd	28112
John Moore Rd	28110
John Stevenson Rd	28110
Johnsie Thomas Ln	28110
N Johnson St	
100-699	28112
700-999	28110
S Johnson St	28112
Jonathan Cir	28112
Jones St	28110
Jug Broome Rd	28112
Julian St	28112
Justin Ct	28110
Justin Braswell Rd	28110
Kansas City Dr	28110
Karen Ln	28110
Karrington Pl	28110
Kate Rd	28110
Kathryn St	28112
Kathy St	28110
Katie Leigh Ln	28110
Keel Rd	28110
Keith Dr	28110
Kelly Grove Ln	28110
Kellystone Dr	28110
Kempsar Ln	28110
Ken Ryan Dr	28110
Kennedy St	28110
Kenneth St	28110
Kensington Pl	28112
Kent Ct	28110
Kerr St	28110
Keswick Pl	28112
Kevinshire Ct	28112
Keystone Ct	28110
Kiddle Ln	28110
Killdeer Ln	28110
Kimberly Dr	28110
King St	28110
King Arthur Dr	28110
Kings Pointe Dr	28112
Kingstree Dr	28112
Kingswood Dr	28112
Kintyre Dr	28112
Kirkland Ct	28110
Knights Ct	28110
Knollgate Dr	28112
Kristen Cir	28110
L J Whitley Rd	28112
Labon St	28110
Lacharette Ln	28110
N Lake Dr	28112
Lake James Ct	28110
Lake Lee Dr	28112
Lake Monroe Dr	28112
Lake Stone Dr	28112
Lake Twitty Dr	28110
Lakeshore Dr	28112
Lakeview Dr	28112
Lakewood Dr	28112
Lameshur Ln	28110
Lamplight Rd	28112
Lanaken Ln	28110
Lancaster Ave & Hwy	28112
Lancelot Dr	28110
Landen Chase Dr	28110
Lander Benton Rd	28110
Landsford Rd	28112
Lane St	28110
Laney Rogers Rd	28112
Lanier Ln	28110
Lark Trail Rd	28110
Lasalle St	28110
Latham Woods Dr	28110
Lathan Rd	28112
Latimer Way	28110
Laurel Creek Ln	28110
Laurel Oak Ln	28110
Lawrence Ct	28110
E & W Lawyers Rd	28110
Lee St	28112
Lee Cooke Rd	28112
Leeds Ct	28110
Leewood Dr	28112
Legacy Lake Dr	28110
Lenox Ln	28110
Lesa Lin Dr	28112
Leslie Dr	28112
Lewis St	28110
Lexington Ave	28112
Lileswood Dr	28112
Lindpoint Ln	28110
Lindsborg Trl	28110
Linville Falls Ln	28110
Little Rd	28110
Little Leaf Ln	28112
Little Rock Ct	28110
Little Tom Starnes Rd	28112
Lockhart St	28110
Locust Run Pl	28110
Logan Caroline Ln	28110
Lois Ln	28112
Lomax St	28110
Lone Eagle Dr	28110
Long Hope Rd	28112
Longmeadow Ln	28110
Longpond Ln	28110
Longs Trailer Park Rd	28110
Lonnie D Aldridge Rd	28112
Loretta St	28112
Lorna Dr	28110
Louise Dr	28110
Love Rd	28110
Love Mill Rd	28110
Loxdale Farms Dr	28110
Lucille Ave	28112
Lucy Dr	28110
Luke Ct	28112
Lundy Ln	28110
Luther Ln	28112
Lydia St	28110
Lynn St	28110
M L King Jr Blvd S	28112
N M L King Jr Blvd	28110
Macedonia Church Rd	28112
Mackenzie Ln	28110
Magnolia Ct & Dr	28112
Maho Ln	28110
N & S Main St	28112
Mallard Landing Dr	28110
Mallard Pond Ln	28112
Mammoth Oaks Dr	28110
Manchester Ave & Ln	28110
Manchineel Ln	28110
Mangum St	28110
Mangum Dairy Rd	28112
Maple Hill Rd	28110
Maple Knoll Dr	28112
Mara Ln	28110
Marble Clay Ct	28112
Marion St	28112
Marion Lee Rd	28112
Marshall Ct	28110
Marshall St	28112
Martha Dr	28112
Martin Luther King Jr Blvd	28110
Martin Tucker Rd	28110
Marvin Watkins Rd	28112
Mary Ct	28112
Mary Point Rd	28110
Mason St	28110
Massey St	28110
Matfield Ct	28110
Matthew Dr	28110
Maurice St	28112
Mayflower Trl	28110
Mcarthur Cir	28110
Mcateer Rd	28112
Mccarten St	28112
Mccauley St	28112
Mccray St	28112
Mcdonald St	28110
Mcgee Ln	28110
Mcintyre St	28110
Mclarty St	28112
Mcmanus Cir, Rd & St	28112
Mcrorie Rd	28112
Meadow St	28110
Meadow Creek Ln	28110
Meadow Wind Ct	28110
Meadowland Pkwy	28112
Meadowmere Dr	28110
Meadowood Ct, Dr & Ln	28110
Meadowview Dr	28110
Medlin Rd	28112
Medlin Farms Dr	28112
Megan Ct	28110
Meleto Dr	28110
Melody Dr	28110
Melrose Ln	28110
Melton Rd	28110
Memory Ln	28112
Mendelson Ct	28110
Meriwether Lewis Trl	28110
Michael St	28110
Michaels Ln	28112
Midwood Dr	28112
Milkfarm Ct	28110
Milkwood Ln	28110
Mill Creek Church Rd	28110
Miller St	28110
Millington Ct	28110
Millstone Ln	28112
Mine Shaft Dr	28110
Missouri River Ln	28110
Mistywood Dr	28110
Molly Pop Ln	28112
Monroe Way	28110
Monroe Ansonville Rd	28110
Montcalm Ct	28110
Montcalry Ct	28110
Monte Dr	28110
Monterrey Ln	28110
Monticello Dr	28110
Moores Trailer Park Rd	28110
Moravian Falls Ct	28110
W Morgan St	28112
Morgan Academy Rd	28110
Morgan Mill Rd	28110
Morgan Park Dr	28110
Morgans Cove Rd	28110
Morning Dew Ln	28110
Morrow Ave	28112
Moss Cove Ct	28110
Mossy Cup Ln	28110
Mount Pleasant Church Rd	28112
Mountain Dr	28112
Mountain Springs Church Rd	28112
Mullin St	28112
Mullis Rd	28112
Mullis Newsome Rd	28110
Murphy Ln	28112
Muscadine Ln	28110
E & W Myers Rd & St	28110
Nanny Point Dr	28110
Nash Rd	28112
Nash St	28110
Nature Way Pl	28110
Nazareth Ct	28110
Neal St	28112
Neal Boyce Rd	28110
Neely Evans Ct	28110
Nelda Dr	28110
Nesbit Rd	28112
New Castle Ln	28110
New Hope Church Rd	28110
New Salem Rd	28110
New Town Rd	28110
Newell Dr	28112
Nez Perce Ln	28110
Niagra Ct	28110
Normand St	
100-299	28110
300-499	28112
North St	28110
Northhills Dr & Ln	28110
Northwood Dr	28110
Nottingham Ln	28110
O Henry Dr	28110
Oak Dr	28112
Oak St	28110
Oak Forest Dr	28112
Oak Hill Dr	28112
Oak Meadow Ln	28110
Oakdale Dr	28110
Oakstone Dr	28110
Odessa Pl	28110
Oglethorpe Ln	28110
Old Camden Rd	28110
Old Charlotte Hwy	28110
Old Course Rd	28112
E Old Dutch Rd	28110
Old Ferry Rd	28110
Old Fish Rd	28110
Old Highway Rd	28112
E Old Highway 74	28112
Old Montgomery Place Rd	28112
Old Morgan Mill Rd	28110
Old Pageland Marshville Rd	28112
Old Pageland Monroe Rd	28112
Old Waxhaw Monroe Rd	28112
Olde Elizabeth Ln	28110
Olde Towne Dr	28110
Olive Branch Rd	28110
Omaha Dr	28110
Onset Pl	28110
Oriole Ct	28112
Orr Rd	28110
Out Of Bounds Dr	28112
Overhill Dr	28110
Overlook Dr	28110
Oxbow Ln	28110
P E Bazemore Dr	28110
Page Mar Dr	28112
Pageland Hwy	28112
Pamela Dr	28112
Paperbark Dr	28110
Paradise St	28112
E & W Park Dr	28112
Parker St	28112
Parks Mccorkle Rd	28112
Parks Medlin Rd	28112
Parkside Dr	28110
Parkwood Cir	28112
Parkwood School Rd	28112
Pasture View Ln	28110
Pate St	28112
Patricians Ln	28110
Patriot Dr	28110
Patterson St	28112
Patton Ave	28110
Paul J Helms Dr	28110
Peach Orchard Dr	28110
Peachtree St	28112
Pebble Dr	28110
Pedro St	28110
Peninsula Ct	28110
Penn St	28112
Pennigar Rd	28110
Pepperridge Ln	28110
Perrault Cir	28110
Persimmon Ct	28110
Persing Ct	28110
Perth Dr	28110
Phala Ct	28112
E & W Phifer St	28110
Phil Hargett Ct	28110
Pickford Ct	28110
Piedmont Dr	28110
Piedmont School Rd	28110
Piellord Rd	28112
Pigg Mattox Rd	28112
Pilgrim Forest Dr	28110
Pine St	28110
Pine Cone Ln	28110
Pine Lake Dr	28110
Pine Lane Dr	28112
Pine Oaks Dr	28112
Pine Tops Dr	28112
Pinedell Ave	28110
Pinewood Forest Dr	28110
Pinyan Ave	28110
Plain View Rd	28110
Plantation Dr	28112
Planters Knoll Dr	28110
Pleasant Knoll Ln	28112
Plum Creek Ct	28112
Plum Thicket Ct	28112
Plyler St	28110
Plyler Mill Rd	28112
Polk St	28110
Pond Bluff Dr	28112
Pope St	28112
Poplin Rd	28110
S Potter Rd	
100-1499	28110
3600-5299	28112
Potters Rd S	28112
Potters Bluff Rd	28110
Potters Trace Rd	28110
Poxon Ln	28110
Pressley Dr	28110
Presson Rd	28112
Presson Farm Ln	28110
Prestwick Ln	28110
Price Dairy Rd	28110
Price Pointe Dr	28110
Price Rushing Rd	28110
Price Short Cut Rd	28110
Price Tucker Rd	28110
Priceton Dr	28110
Princess Kelly Way	28110
Prospect Pt & Rd	28112
Prospect Pointe Dr	28112
Prospectors Ct	28110
Proverbs Ct	28110
Pulaski Dr	28110
Pumpernickel Ln	28110
Pumpkin Pl	28110
Purser Ave	28110
Purser Rushing Rd	28110
Quail Dr	28112
Quail Ridge Rd	28110
Quail Run Rd	28112
Quarry Rd	28112
Queensdale Dr	28110
Raccoon Run	28110
Rainbrook Dr	28112
Rainwater Ct	28110
Rams Ct	28110
Rape Rd	28112
Raymond St	28112
Red Cedar Ln	28110
Red Fox Run Rd	28110
Red Hook Rd	28110
Red Maple Dr	28110
Redwine St	28110
Reece Rd	28110
Reflections Dr	28112
Reid Cir	28112
Revelation Way	28110
Revere Rd	28110
Reynolds St	28112
Rhett Ct	28110
Richard St	28110
Richardson Rd	28112
Richardson St	28112
Richfield Rd	28112
Richland Ct	28110
Richmond Ln	28110
Ridge Rd	28110
Ridgewood Ave	28110
Ridgewood Dr	28112
Riggins St	28110
Rilla Hamilton Rd	28110
River Chase Dr	28110
Rivercrest Ct	28110
Riverside Ln	28110
Roanoke Church Rd	28110
Roberts St	28112
Robin Dr	28112
Rochester Ct	28110
N Rocky River Rd	28110
S Rocky River Rd	
100-1399	28110
1400-7799	28112
Rockycreek Ln	28112
Rogers Rd	28110
Roland Dr	28110
Roll Baker Rd	28112
Rolling Hills Dr	28110
Rollingwood Ln	28112
Rollins Pointe Dr	28110
Romany Dr	28110
E Roosevelt Blvd	28112
W Roosevelt Blvd	28110
Rosa Dr	28112
Rosemeade Dr	28110
Rosetta Dr	28110
Round Table Rd	28110
Roy Kindley Rd	28110
Ruben Rd	28112
Runaway Cir	28110
Rushing Rd & St	28112
Rushing Benton Rd	28110
Russell Courtney Rd	28112
Ryefield Way	28110
Saco St	28110
Saddlebred Way	28110
Saddlebrook Dr	28112
Sagebrush Bnd	28110
Saint Andrews Dr	28112
Saint James Way	28110
Saint Regis Ct	28110
Salem Dr	28110
Salem Church Rd	28110
Salem Pointe Dr	28110
Sallonge Rd	28110
Salmon River Dr	28110
Sand Dollar Ct	28112
Sand Trap Ct	28112
Sandstone Ln	28110
E & W Sandy Ridge Rd	28112
Sanford Ln	28110
Sanford St	28112
Sanlee Dr	28110
Sanlee Church Rd	28110
Santa Claus Rd	28110
Santiago Cir	28110
Sara Ln	28112
Sara Hinson Rd	28112
Sara Margaret Dr	28110
Sardis Church Rd	28110
Savannah Way	28110
Saye Brook Dr	28112
Schiller Dr	28110
Scott St	28110
Scotty Ln	28110
Seabrook Dr	28110
N Secrest Ave	28110
S Secrest Ave	28112
Secrest Hill Dr	28110
Secrest Price Rd	28110
Secrest Shortcut Rd	28110
Sells St	28110
Serenity Hills Dr	28110
Seven Lot Dr	28110
Seven Oaks Dr	28110
Seymour St	28110
Shadowood Dr	28112
Shady Ln	28110
Shady Ridge Ln	28112
Shaw Rd	28112
Shea Ct	28110
Shelby Dr	28110
Sherwood Forest Ln	28110
Shiloh Club Rd	28110
Shining Light Church Rd	28110
Shute St	28112
Sidney Ct	28110
Sierra Chase Dr	28112
Sikes St	28112
Sikes Mill Rd	28110
Silo Ct	28110
Silver Run Dr	28110
Silverthorne Dr	28110
Sim Williams Rd	28112
Simpson St	28112
Sincerity Rd	28110
Sinclair Dr	28112
Sioux St	28110
Sizemore Rd	28110
Skywatch Ln	28112
Skyway Dr	28110
Sl Polk Rd	28110
Sm Benton Ln	28110
Smith St	28112
Smithfield Dr	28110
Snake River Ct	28110
Snowcrest Ct	28112
Solitaire Ct	28112
Solomons Ct	28110
Sonny Ct	28112
Sonoma Way	28110
Southridge Dr	28112
Southwick Dr	28110
Southwood Pl	28112
Sowell St	28110
Sparrow Way Ct	28112
Sparta Dr	28110
Speer Dr	28112
Spence Ct	28110
Spring St	28110
Spring Breeze Way	28110
Spring Harvest Dr	28110
Spring Lake Dr	28110
Spring Meadow Ln	28110
Spring Morning Ln	28110
Springview Dr	28112
N Square Dr	28110
Stack Rd	28112
Stafford St	28110
Stafford Street Ext	28110
Standish Dr	28110
Starcrest Dr	28110
Starnes Cemetary Rd	28112
Station Dr	28110
Steele St	28110
Stepping Stone Ln	28110
Stevens Rd	28110
Stevens St	28112
N & S Stewart St	28112
Stitt St	28110
Stockbridge Dr	28110
Stone Mill Cir	28110
Stonegate Rd	28110
Stonewood Dr	28112
Stoney Creek Dr	28110
Stoney Point Cir	28112
Stonington Dr	28110
Story Ln	28112

Streamlet Way 28110
Stump Lake Dr 28110
Sturdivant Landing Dr 28112
Styx Dr 28112
Suburban Ln 28110
Sue St 28110
Sugar And Wine Rd 28110
Summerfield Dr 28110
Summit St 28112
Sumpter Ln 28110
Sun Catcher Ct 28110
Sunlight Path Dr 28110
Sunnybrook Dr 28110
Sunnywood Pl 28110
Sunrise Ln 28112
E & W Sunset Dr & Ln 28112
Sunshine Path 28110
Sunshower Ct 28110
Supreme Dr 28110
Sustar Dr 28110
N Sutherland Ave 28110
S Sutherland Ave 28112
Sutton Pl 28112
Sutton St 28110
Swan Sea Ct 28110
Swedish Ivy Ln 28110
Sweet Gum Ct 28110
Sweetgrass Ln 28112
Swilcan Burn Dr 28112
Sycamore St 28112
T J Dr 28112
Tabitha Ct 28110
E & W Talleyrand Ave 28112
Tammy Dr 28110
Tanglewood Dr 28110
Tara Dr 28112
Tara Plantation Blvd 28110
Tarheel Dr 28112
Tarlton Ridge Dr 28110
Teak Ct 28110
Teledyne Rd 28110
Telefair Ln 28110
Temple St 28110
Tesh Rd 28110
N & S Thompson St 28112
Thornburg Ct 28110
Thornhill Dr 28110
Three Knotts Rd 28112
Tiffany Dr 28110
Timber Lane Dr 28110
Timber Ridge Rd 28112
Timbercrest Cir 28110
Timnah Ln 28112
Tina Cir 28112
Tipton Rd 28112
Titus Ct 28110
Tom Boyd Rd 28110
Tom Greene Rd 28112
Tom Helms Rd 28110
Tom Laney Rd 28112
Tom Starnes Rd 28112
Tom Williams Rd 28112
Tomberlin Rd 28110
Tomberlin St 28112
Top Hill Rd 28110
Topeka Ct 28110
Toquima Trl 28110
Tower Ct 28112
Tower Industrial Dr 28110
Tradd Cir 28110
Tradewinds Dr 28112
Trafalgar Ct 28110
Treeway Dr 28110
Trellis Ln 28110
Trey Ct 28112
Tricia Ct 28110
Trinity Church Rd 28112
Trinity Trace Ln 28110
Triple Oaks Rd 28112
Troy Medlin Rd 28112
Trull Pl 28110
Trunk Bay Dr 28110
Tucker Rd & St 28110
Turner St 28110
Turtle Ridge Dr 28110
Twilight Ln 28110
Twin Cedars Dr 28110
Twin Peaks Ct 28110
Tyler Ridge Ct 28110
Tyson Rd 28110
Union St 28110
Union Power Way 28110
Unionville Rd 28110
Unionville Brief Rd 28110
Unionville Church Rd 28110
E & W Unionville Indian Trail Rd 28110
Unity Ct 28110
V F W Rd 28110
Vagabond Dr 28110
Valdosta Ct 28110
Valley Pkwy & St 28110
Valley Creek Dr 28112
Valleydale Rd 28110
Van Dyke Ct 28110
Vance Pl 28110
Vander Ln 28110
Vann St 28112
Varner Dr 28110
Vaugelas Ct 28110
Velma Dr 28110
Venture Oaks Ln 28110
Venus St 28112
Victoria Ave 28112
Victoria Pl 28110
Victorian Ln 28112
Vidalia Ct 28110
E Village Dr 28112
Village Ln 28110
Village Lake Dr 28110
Vineyard Dr 28110
Vintage Ln 28112
Viola Ln 28110
Virginia Ave 28112
Virginia St 28110
Voltaire Dr 28110
Volvo St 28112
Von Ct 28110
Wagon Wheel Ct 28110
Walkup Ave 28110
Wallace Rd 28110
Walnut Ln 28112
Walnut St 28110
Walt Gay Rd 28112
Walter Hasty Rd 28110
Walters Rd & St 28112
Walters Division Rd 28110
Walters Mill Rd 28112
Warren St 28110
Washburn Ct 28110
N & S Washington St 28112
Water Oak Ln 28110
Waterlemon Way 28110
Watersmark Dr 28112
Waterton Ct 28110
Waterview Ln 28110
Watkins Rd 28110
Watson Church Rd 28110
Waverly Dr 28112
Waxhaw Hwy 28112
Waxwood Dr 28110
Waycross Dr 28110
Weddington Rd
1900-1999 28112
2000-6299 28110
Wellness Blvd 28110
Welsh St 28112
Wesley Chapel Stouts Rd 28110
Wesley Downs Rd 28110
Wesley Hills Trl 28112
Wesley Woods Rd 28110
Wessex Ct 28110
N & S West St 28112
Westend Dr 28112
N & S Westover Dr 28112
Westwood St 28110
Westwood Industrial Dr 28110
Wexford Pl 28110
Wg Medlin Rd 28112
Wh Smith Dr 28110
Wheaton Way 28112
Whisper Ridge Ln 28110
White Cliffs Dr 28110
White Marsh Ct 28110
White Oaks Cir 28112
White Pines Ct 28112
White Store Rd 28112
Wiatt St 28110
Wild Dogwood Ln 28110
Wildwood Rd 28110
Wilkes Dr 28110
Will Helms Rd 28110
William Clark Trl 28110
Williams Rd 28110
Williams Road Ext 28110
Williamsburg Ln 28110
Willis Long Rd 28110
Willoughby Rd 28110
Willoughby Woods Dr 28110
Willow St 28110
Willow Run Dr 28110
Willoway Ln 28110
Wilson Ave 28110
Wilson St 28112
Winburn St 28112
Winchester Ave & Rd 28110
Wind Carved Ln 28110
Wind Chime Ct 28110
Windcrest Way 28110
Winding Brook Rd 28112
Winding Way Dr 28110
Windjammer Dr 28110
Windmere Dr 28110
E & W Windsor St 28112
Windsor Greene Dr 28110
Windswept Ln 28110
Windy Dr 28110
Windy Hill Ln 28110
Winfield Dr 28110
Winston Ave 28110
Winterberry Ln 28110
Winthrop Ln 28110
Wishbone Rd 28112
Wisteria Ln 28112
Wm Griffin Rd 28112
Wolf Pond Rd 28112
Wolfe Rd 28110
Wolfe Mill St 28110
Wood Duck Point Rd 28112
Wood Lake Dr 28110
Wood Side Pl 28110
Woodbrook Ln 28110
Woodhill Cir 28110
Woodhurst Dr 28110
Woodland Ave & Ln 28112
Woodlands Creek Dr 28110
Woodlark Pl 28112
Woodridge Dr 28110
Woody Knoll Ct 28110
Worley St 28112
Worthwood Cir 28112
Wren Way Ct 28110
Wynbrook Way 28112
Yellow Bell Way 28112
Zack Rd 28110
Zeb Helms Rd 28112
Zebulon Williams Rd 28110
Zee Ct 28110
Zephyr Cir 28110

NUMBERED STREETS

All Street Addresses 28110

MOORESVILLE NC

General Delivery 28115

POST OFFICE BOXES MAIN OFFICE STATIONS AND BRANCHES

Box No.s
1 - 1858 28115
3001 - 5672 28117
9998 - 9998 28115

RURAL ROUTES

01, 03, 15 28115

NAMED STREETS

Abberly Green Blvd 28117
Abbotswood Pl 28117
Abj Way 28117
N & S Academy St 28115
Accent Loop 28117
Acorn Ln 28117
Adrian Ln 28117
Adventure Ln 28117
Agape Dr 28115
Agnew Rd 28117
Airpark Dr 28115
Airplane Ct 28117
Airstream Ct 28115
Akerman Pl 28115
Alameda Cir 28117
Albany Dr 28115
Alborn Dr 28115
Alcove Rd 28117
Alder Springs Ln 28117
Alexander St 28115
Alexander Acres Rd 28115
Alexander Place Ln 28115
Alexandria Dr 28115
Alisha Ln 28117
Aljen Ct 28115
Alley Lake Rd 28117
Allman Rd 28115
Almond Rd 28115
Almora Loop 28115
Alo Dr 28115
Alton Ct 28117
Alyah Ln 28117
Ameena Chase Trl 28117
Amelia Ln 28117
Anderson Farm Ln 28117
Andover Pl 28117
Angel Ln 28115
Anglers Pl 28117
Apple Blossom Dr 28117
Aqua Dr 28117
Aquarius Ln 28117
Arabian Dr 28115
Aragon Ct 28115
N & S Arcadian Way 28117
Archbell Point Ln 28117
Archer Club Ln 28115
Ardmore Pl 28117
Argus Ln 28117
Ariel Dr 28117
Armour Ln 28115
Arrington Way Ln 28117
Artisan Ct 28117
Asbury Cir 28117
Ash Aly 28115
Ashcraft Dr 28115
Ashe St 28115
Ashford Hollow Ln 28117
Ashley Woods Dr 28115
Ashlyn Creek Dr 28115
Ashton Dr 28115
Ashwood Ln 28117
Assembly Dr 28117
Astor Rd 28115
Atlantic Way 28115
Attleboro Pl 28117
Atwell Farm Ln 28115
Audrey Ln 28117
N & S Audubon Ave 28117
Autry Ave 28117
Autumn Grove Ln 28115
Autumn View Ln 28115
Avocet Ct 28117
Avon Place Ln 28115
Azalea Rd 28115
Aztec Cir 28115
Babbling Brook Rd 28117
Backlog Ln 28115
Backstretch Ln 28117
Badin Ln 28117
Bailey Ct 28115
Bailey Rd 28117
Bain Ln 28117
Bald Cypress Ln 28115
Ballston Dr 28117
Ballycastle Rd 28117
Balmoral Dr 28117
Balmy Ln 28117
Balsam Ct 28115
Bandit Ln 28117
Bantam Pl 28117
Banterling Ct 28115
Banty Rd 28117
Barber Loop 28117
Barclay Ln 28115
Barefoot Ln 28117
Barfield Rd 28115
Barington Dr 28117
Barkland Ln 28117
Barksdale Ln 28117
Barley Park Ln 28115
Barnette Point Ln 28117
Barnhardt Loop 28117
Barnstable Ct 28117
Barnswallow Ln 28115
Barrister Bay Ln 28117
Barton Pl 28117
Bassett Cove Ln 28117
Basswood Ln 28117
Bath Creek Dr 28117
Bay Crossing Dr 28117
Bay Harbour Rd 28117
Bay Laurel Dr 28115
Bay Port Ln 28115
Bay Shore Loop 28117
Bayberry Creek Cir 28117
Baybreeze Ct 28117
Bayview Dr 28117
Baywatch Dr 28117
Beach Ln 28117
Beach Fern Ct 28117
Beachview Dr 28117
Beam Dr 28115
Bear Ln 28117
Bear Run Cir 28117
Bearcreek Rd 28117
Beaten Path Rd 28117
Beatty Ave 28115
Bechtler Loop 28117
Bedford Ln 28115
Beech Pointe Ln 28117
Beech Tree Rd 28117
Beechfield Ct 28117
Belfry Loop 28117
Belk Pt 28117
Belk Rd 28115
Bell St 28115
Bellelaine Dr 28115
Bellflower Ln 28115
Bellhaven Ln 28117
Bellingham Dr 28115
Bells Run 28117
Bells Crossing Dr 28117
Beracah Pl 28115
Besford Rd 28117
Bevan Dr 28115
Beverly Chase Ln 28117
Bevington Way 28117
Bexley Rd 28117
Bibry Way 28117
Big Dukes Ln 28117
Big Indian Loop 28117
Billingsgate Ct 28117
Billy Jo Rd 28117
Biltmore St 28115
Binns Rd 28117
Birch River Pl 28117
Birdie Ct 28117
Birdsong Ln 28117
Biscayne Ct 28117
Biscuit Ct 28115
Bite Size Ln 28115
Black Alder Ct 28115
Black Angus Ln 28115
Blackbeard Ln 28117
Blackberry Ln 28117
Blackberry Creek Ln 28115
Blacksmith Ln 28115
Blackwelder Farm Dr 28115
Blair St 28115
Blake Ln 28117
Blarney Rd 28117
Blessing Ln 28117
Blossom Ridge Dr 28117
Blue Bonnett Cir 28117
Blue Devil Blvd 28115
Blue Eyes Ln 28117
Blue Ridge Trl 28115
Blue Sky Ct 28117
Bluebell Dr 28115
Bluefield Rd 28117
Bluegrass Cir 28117
Bluewing Ln 28117
Bluff Meadow Ln 28115
Bluffton Rd 28115
Blume Rd 28117
Bobby Lee Ln 28115
Bobwhite Ln 28117
Boger St 28115
Bogey Ln 28117
Bolivia Ln 28115
Bonner Ln 28117
Boone Ln 28117
Bosburg Dr 28115
Bost Rd 28115
Bow Ln 28115
Bowfin Cir 28117
Bradberry St 28115
Bradford Glyn Dr 28115
Bradshaw Rd 28115
Branchview Dr 28115
Brantley St 28115
Brantley Acres Dr 28115
Brantley Place Dr 28117
Bratton Ct 28117
Brawley Ave 28115
Brawley Harbor Pl 28117
Brawley School Rd 28117
Brazington Ln 28115
Breakwater Ct 28117
Breezeview Pl 28117
Brentwood Ct 28115
Breton Ct 28117
Brewer Ln 28115
Brewster Ct 28115
Briarcliff Rd 28115
Briarfield Dr & Ln 28115
Briarhill Rd 28115
Briarwood Dr 28115
Brick Kiln Way 28117
Bridgeport Dr 28115
Bridges Farm Rd 28115
Bridgewater Ln 28117
Bridlepath Ln 28117
Bridlewood Dr 28117
Brigadoon Dr 28115
Bright Star Cir 28115
N & S Broad St 28115
Broad Sound Pl 28117
Broadbill Dr 28117
Broadleaf Loop 28115
Broadview Cir 28117
Brockton Ln 28115
Brockway Dr 28117
Broken Pine Ln 28117
Broken Pines Ln 28115
Brook Dr 28115
Brook Glen Dr 28115
Brookfield Cir 28115
Brookleaf Ln 28115
Brookridge Ln 28115
Brookstone Ln 28117
Brooktree Dr 28117
Brookwood Dr 28115
Broome Farm Ln 28115
Brown Ridge Ln 28117
Browns Hill Ln 28115
Browns Rink Rd 28115
Brownstone Dr 28117
Bruce Ave 28115
Brumley Rd 28115
Brunswick St 28115
Brushwood Ln 28115
Buckingham Place Rd 28115
Buckthorn Ct 28115
Bufflehead Dr 28117
Bullfinch Rd 28117
Bunker Way 28117
Burke Cir 28115
Burley Dr 28115
Burtons Barn Rd 28115
Bushnell Pl 28115
Bushney Loop 28115
Buttercup Dr 28117
Byers Commons Dr 28117
Byers Creek Rd 28117
C And C Ln 28115
Cabana Dr 28117
Cabarrus Ave 28115
Cabin Creek Rd 28115
Caboose Ln 28115
Cades Cove Ln 28117
Caladium Dr 28115
Caldwell Ave 28115
E & W Callicutt Trl 28117
Cambria Pl 28117
Camforth Dr 28117
Camino Real Rd 28117
Camp Ln 28117
Camphill Rd 28117
Candy Park Ln 28115
Canopy Ct 28115
Canter Ct 28115
Canterbury Place Rd 28115
Canvasback Rd & Trl 28117
Cape Cod Way 28117
Capital Ave 28117
Caraway Ln 28117
N & S Cardigan Way 28117
Cardinal Ln 28117
Cardinal Berry Ct 28115
Cardinal Ridge Ln 28115
Carlson Dr 28117
Carlton Dr 28117
Carolina Ridge Ct 28115
Carolina Wren Dr 28115
Carolwoods Dr 28115
Carpenter Ave 28115
Carriage Club Dr 28117
Carrie Ln 28117
Carsons Pl 28117
Cascade Rd 28115
Cassidy Ln 28115
Castaway Trl 28117
Castle Dr 28117
Castle Bay Ct 28117
Castle Tower Dr 28117
Castles Gate Dr 28117
Castleton Dr 28117
Catalina Dr 28117
Catalina Place Dr 28117
E & W Catawba Ave 28115
Catawba Air Rd 28117
Catesby Ln 28117
E & W Cavendish Dr 28115
Cayuga Dr 28117
Cbs Ln 28115
Cedar St 28115
Cedar Bluff Ln 28117
Cedar Branch Ct 28117
Cedar Pointe Dr 28117
Cedar Woods Dr 28117
Cedarcrest Dr 28115
Cedarcroft Dr 28115
Cedarview Ln 28115
E & W Center Ave 28115
Center Point Dr 28115
Center Square Dr 28117
Central Ave 28115
Centre Church Rd 28115
Chaco Ln 28117
Chaffee Pl 28115
Chandeleur Dr 28117
Channel Point Ln 28117
Channelview Dr 28117

Charing Pl 28117
Charity Ln 28115
Charleston Dr 28117
Charlotte Hwy
  1200-1999 28115
  2000-3299 28117
Charlotte St 28115
Charter Pl 28117
Charter Oak Ct 28115
Chasestone Ln 28117
Chatfield Cove Dr 28117
Chatham Rd 28117
Chatworth Ln 28117
Chaucer Ln 28117
Chawton Ln 28117
Chere Helen Dr 28115
Cherokee Dr 28117
Cherry Bark Dr 28117
Cherry Grove li 28115
Cherry Tree Dr 28117
Cherrycrest Ln 28115
Chertsey Dr 28115
Cheshire Ln 28117
Chesterwood Ct 28117
Chestnut Bay Ln 28117
Chestnut Tree Rd 28117
Chimney Crest Ave 28115
Chinook Ct 28117
Chollywood Dr 28115
Christy Ln 28117
Chuckwood Rd 28117
N & S Church St 28115
Churchill Ln 28117
Cicero Ln 28117
Cider Mill Pl 28117
Cinebar Rd 28115
Circle Dr 28115
Circle Lynn Dr 28115
Circleview Dr 28117
Citation Dr 28117
Clacton Ct 28117
Claiborne Dr 28117
Claire Ln 28117
Claremont Way 28117
Clark Branch Ln 28115
Clarktown Dr 28115
Clay St 28115
Clear Creek Ln 28115
Clear Springs Rd 28115
Clearfield Dr 28115
Clearwater Dr & Ln 28117
Clematis Pl 28117
Cleveland Ave 28115
Cliff Loop 28117
Cliffview Ln 28117
Cliffwood Cir 28115
Clipper Ln 28117
Clodfelter Rd 28115
Cloister Ln 28117
Cloud Top Ln 28115
Clover St 28115
Clover Bank Rd 28115
Cloverhill Rd 28117
Club Dr 28115
Clusters Cir 28117
Cobbler Cove Rd 28117
Cobblestone Ln 28117
Coddle Creek Hwy &
Rd 28115
Cohen Ln 28115
Colborne Dr 28115
Cold Harbor Ln 28117
E & W Cold Hollow
Farms Dr 28117
Cole Dr 28115
College St 28115
Collenton Ln 28115
Collingswood Rd 28117
Collins Dr 28117
Colonial Ridge Cir 28117
Colony Dr 28115
Colony Hills Ln 28115
Colvard Farms Ln 28117
Colville Rd 28117
Comata Rd 28117
Commerce Park Rd 28117
N Commercial Dr 28115
Commodore Loop 28117
Common Way 28117
Commons Dr 28117
Community Park Ln 28117
Consumers Sq 28117
Continental Dr 28117
Conway Ct 28117
Cook St 28115
Cool Branch Ln 28117
Cool Breeze Dr 28117
Cooley Rd 28117
Copperhead Dr 28115
Coral Ln 28117
Coral Bells Ct 28117
Corinth Church Rd 28115
Cornelian Ct 28115
Cornelius Rd 28117
Corona Cir 28117
Coronilla Rd 28117
Corporate Park Dr 28117
Corriher Grange Rd 28115
Corriher Springs Rd 28115
Cottage Grove Ln 28117
Cottage Place Ln 28117
Country Ln 28115
Country Brook Ln 28115
Country Stroll Ln 28115
Court Ln 28115
Courtland Ln 28117
Courtney Ln 28117
S Cove Dr 28117
Cove Creek Loop 28117
N & S Cove Key Ln 28117
Cove View Dr 28117
Craftsman Loop 28115
Cranbrook Ln 28117
Creek Branch Dr 28115
Creek View Rd 28117
Creekridge Cir 28115
Creekwood Dr 28117
Creeky Hollow Dr 28117
Crescent Place Ln 28117
Creston Ct 28115
Crianson Ct 28115
Cricklewood Ln 28115
Crimson Orchard Dr 28115
Crois Ct 28115
N & S Cromwell Dr 28115
Cross Meadow Ln 28115
Crossbow Ln 28115
Crosslake Park Dr 28115
Crosspoint Ln 28115
Crossrail Rd 28115
Croton Ct 28117
Crusoe Dr 28115
Crystal Cir 28117
Crystal Bay Dr 28115
Culbreth Ln 28115
Cullen Place Ln 28117
Culp St 28115
Culpeze Rd 28117
Currituck Ct 28117
Curtis Dr 28115
Cypress Cove Ln 28117
Cypress Landing Dr 28117
Dabbling Duck Cir 28117
Dairy Farm Rd 28115
Dale Earnhardt Hwy 28115
Dale View Ct 28117
Dalton Dr 28115
Dandy Ln 28115
Danica Pl 28117
Dannyn Grove Ct 28117
Daventry Pl 28117
Davidson Ridge Ln 28117
Davis St 28115
Dawson Downs Ln 28115
Days Inn Dr 28117
Deacons Pond Ct 28117
Deal Rd 28115
Dearborn Ln 28117
E Decatur Ave 28117
Dedham Loop 28117
Dee Dee Ln 28115
Deer Path Pl 28115
Deerfield Dr 28115
Deerwood Ln 28117
Delany Ln 28115
Delargy Cir 28117
Denham Pl 28115
Denver Business Park
Dr 28115
Devon Forest Dr 28115
Devonshire Ct 28115
Deward Loop 28115
Diamond Dr 28117
Diamond Head Dr 28117
Diamondhead Dr 28117
Dickens Ct 28115
Didio Cir 28115
Digh Cir 28117
Dime Ln 28117
Dingler Ave 28115
Dixie Dr 28115
Dobbin Ln 28117
Dodge Dr 28115
Dogwood Ln 28115
Dolphin Cir 28117
Donaldson Ct 28117
Donnive Dr 28117
Doolie Rd 28117
Doolittle Ln 28115
Dorothy Ln 28117
Doster Ave 28115
Double Eagle Dr 28117
Double Rose Ln 28115
Dovetail Dr 28115
Downey Ln 28117
Downey Thistle Ln 28115
Doyle Farm Ln 28115
Drawbridge Ct 28115
Driftwood Dr 28117
Dry Dock Loop 28117
Drye Dr 28117
Due East Rd 28117
Due West Rd 28117
Duffy Dr 28115
Dun Rovin Ln 28115
Dunbar St 28115
Dunn Ross Ct 28117
Dunnell Rd 28115
Dunsmere Ln 28117
Dupree Ln 28115
Dusty Farm Rd 28117
Duval Ct 28117
Duxbury Dr 28115
Eagle Ct 28117
Early Frost Ln 28115
Eastbend Ct 28117
Eastham Ct 28117
Easton Dr 28117
Eastport Ln & Trl 28115
Eastridge Ln 28115
Easy St 28117
Echo Hill Ln 28115
Eclipse Way 28117
Eddie Wayne Dr 28115
Edenton Ln 28117
Edenwood Cir 28115
Edgartown Ct 28117
Edgemoor Dr 28115
Edgeway Rd 28115
Edgington St 28115
Edwards Rd 28115
Egrets Walk Pl 28117
El Cardenal Farm Ln 28115
Elba Dr 28115
Elderbury Dr 28115
Elgin Ln 28115
Elizabeth Hearth Rd 28115
Ellington Dr 28117
Elm St 28115
Elmhurst Ln 28115
Elrosa Rd 28115
Elysian Dr 28117
Emerald Dr 28115
Emerald Point Ln 28117
Emerson Dr
  100-199 28117
  500-1099 28115
Emily Cir 28115
Endicott Ct 28115
English Hills Dr 28115
English Ivy Ln 28117
Enochville Ave 28115
Ensign Pl 28115
Equestrian Dr 28115
Eric Dr 28117
Erie Rd 28117
Ervin Rd 28117
Ervin Farm Rd 28115
Ervin Ranch Ln 28115
Esquire Ln 28117
Essex Ct 28117
Estate View Ct 28117
Estelle Rd 28115
Estes Park Dr 28117
Ethan Ln 28117
Evelyn Ln 28117
Evening Shade Ln 28115
Everett Park Dr 28115
Evergreen St 28115
Ewart Pl 28117
Excellance Ln 28115
Executive Dr 28117
Exmore Rd 28117
Fairburn Dr 28117
Fairview Rd 28117
Fairway Dr 28117
Faith Rd 28115
Fallon Ln 28115
Falmouth Rd 28117
Fandy Croft Dr 28117
Fantasy Ln 28117
Farm Knoll Rd & Way 28117
Farmcrest Ln 28115
Farmers Folly Dr 28115
Farmington Ln 28117
Farmplace Dr 28115
Farmstead Ln 28117
Farnham Way 28115
Farthing Ln 28115
Fast Ln 28117
Fawn Ln 28117
Felicity Ln 28117
Fellspoint Rd 28115
E Fenway Ave 28117
Fern Haven Ln 28117
Fern Hill Rd 28117
Fernbrook Dr 28117
Ferncliff Dr 28115
Fernwood Ln 28115
Field Trce 28115
Fieldmaster Ln 28115
Fieldstone Rd 28115
Firethorn Ct 28115
Fitchburg Ct 28115
Flagstone Ln 28115
Flanders Dr 28117
Fleishhacker Pl 28117
Flowering Cherry Ln 28115
Flowering Grove Ln 28115
Folkstone Rd 28117
Fontanelle Dr 28115
Forest Ln 28115
Forest Cove Ln 28115
Forest Glen Rd 28115
Forest Lake Blvd 28117
Forest Ridge Rd 28115
Forest Walk Way 28115
Forestdale Loop 28117
Forester St 28115
Forgotten Ln 28115
Forrest Edge Rd 28115
Forum Dr 28117
Foundation Ct 28117
Four Seasons Way 28115
Foursquare Rd 28115
Fourtrax Dr 28115
Fox Glove Dr 28115
Fox Hollow Rd 28117
Fox Hunt Dr 28117
Foxfield Park Dr 28115
Foxgate Ln 28115
Foxtail Dr 28117
Franklin Dr 28115
Franklin Grove Dr 28115
Fransher Ln 28117
Fred Ln 28115
Fredericks Ct 28117
Freeman St 28115
Freeze Crossing Dr 28115
Fremont Loop 28115
Freshwater Ln 28117
Freunds Ln 28117
Frost Ln 28115
Frost Cliff Ln 28117
Fugitt Rd 28115
Fuller Dr 28115
Fulton Farms Ln 28117
Gable Rd 28115
Gabriel Dr 28115
Gage Dr 28115
Gainswood Dr 28117
Gallery Center Dr 28117
Galway Dr 28117
Gambrill Trl 28115
Gammon Point Ct 28117
Gannett Rd 28117
Gantt St 28115
Garden Gate Ln 28115
Gasoline Aly 28117
Gatehouse Ln 28117
Gateway Blvd 28117
Gateway Dr 28115
Gibbs Rd 28117
Gilden Way 28115
Ginger Ln 28115
Gladbrook Dr 28115
Glade Valley Ave 28117
Glastonbury Dr 28115
Glen Oaks Ct 28117
Glencoe Ln 28117
Glenholden Ln 28115
Gleniris Trl 28115
Glenmere Ln 28115
Glenmont Ct 28117
Glenn Allen Rd 28115
Glenwood Dr 28115
Glory Rd 28117
Glynwater Dr 28117
Goathill Rd 28117
Godspeed Ln 28117
Gold St 28115
Gold Finch Ln 28117
Golden Bell Ct 28117
Golden Pond Ln 28115
Golden Valley Dr 28115
Golf Course Dr 28115
Gondola Rd 28117
Good Luck Ln 28115
Goodnight St 28115
Goodspring Ln 28115
Goodwin Cir 28115
Gossett Ct 28115
Grace Meadow Dr 28115
Gracie Ln 28115
Gradys Farm Dr 28115
Gramados Ln 28115
Gran Ct 28117
Grand Bay Dr 28117
Grasshopper Cir 28115
Gravenstein Dr 28117
E & W Gray Ave & Ln 28115
Grayfox Dr 28117
Grayland Rd 28115
Grayson Dr 28115
Great Lakes Rd 28115
Great Point Dr 28117
Green Acres Rd 28115
Green Dragon Ct 28115
Green Morris Ln 28115
Greenbay Rd 28117
Greenhill Ln 28117
Greentree Dr 28117
Greggs Woods Dr 28115
Gresham Ln 28117
Grey Lady Ct 28117
Grey Oaks Ln 28115
Greycliff Dr 28117
Greyfriars Rd 28117
Grove Creek Ln 28115
Gudger Rd 28117
Gum St 28115
Haddington Pl 28115
Hadley Harbor Ct 28117
Hager Farm Ln 28115
Hager Lake Rd 28115
Hager Point Ln 28117
Hagerty Ln 28117
Haley Ct 28115
Hammersmith Farm Ln 28117
Hampshire Dr 28115
Hampton Pl 28115
Hanes Bee Ln 28117
Haney Way 28115
Hanson Pl 28115
Happy Oaks Rd 28117
Harbor Cove Ln 28117
Harbor Landing Dr 28117
Harbor Pine Rd 28117
Harbor Shore Ct 28117
Harborcrest Ln 28117
Harborview Pl 28117
Hardwick Rd 28115
Harris St 28115
Harris Farm Rd 28115
Harrison Point Ct 28117
Hartine Ct 28115
Harvest Ln 28117
Harwell Rd 28117
Harwick Ct 28117
Hawks Nest Ln 28117
Hawks Prey Dr 28115
Hawleyville Ln 28115
Hayden Ct 28117
Hayes Erwin Ln 28115
Hazelton Dr & Loop 28117
Heath Ln 28117
Heatherly Rd 28115
Heathland Ln 28117
Heathstead Ln 28115
Hedges Ln 28115
Hedgewood Dr 28115
Heglar Rd 28115
Henfield Way 28117
Henry Ln 28117
Heritage Pl 28115
Hermance Ln 28117
Herons Gate Dr 28117
Heywatchis Dr 28115
Hickory Dr 28115
Hickory Hill Rd 28117
Hidden Ln 28117
Hidden Harbor Rd 28117
Hideaway Ln 28117
High Bluff Cir 28115
High Hills Dr 28117
High Ridge Rd 28117
High Sail Ct 28117
Highland Dr 28117
Highland Ridge Rd 28115
Hightower Ct 28117
Highway 150 W 28117
Highway 152 W 28115
Hileath Dr 28117
Hillbilly Hollar Ln 28115
Hillcrest Dr 28115
Hillside Dr 28115
Hilltop Ln 28115
Hiram Rd 28117
Hobbs Ln 28115
Hogan Ln 28117
Hollen Ln 28117
Holly Oak Way 28115
Holly Pond Ln 28117
Hollycock Ln 28115
Holt Ln 28117
Holton Ln 28117
Home Dr 28117
Homer Ln 28117
Homers Woods Dr 28115
Honeyboy Ln 28115
Honeycutt Knoll Dr 28117
Honeysuckle Ln 28117
Honeysuckle Creek
Loop 28117
Hopedale Ct 28117
Hopkinton Dr 28117
Horsestable Ct 28115
Hoskins House Ct 28117
Hotrod Hill Ln 28117
Hughes Ln 28117
Humbold Pl 28115
Hunter Dr 28115
Hunter Green Ln 28115
Hunter Spring Ln 28117
Hunters Creek Dr 28115
Hunters Pointe Ln 28117
Huntfield Way 28117
Huntington Ln 28117
Huntington Ridge Pl 28115
Huntly Ln 28115
Hyannis Ct 28117
Ideal Dr 28115
Indian Trl 28117
Indian Paint Brush Dr 28115
Indian Springs Dr 28117
Indigo Ln 28117
Infield Ct 28117
Institute St 28115
Inverness Loop 28117
E & W Iredell Ave 28115
S Iredell Industrial Park
Rd 28115
Iris Meadow Dr 28115
Irish Rd 28117
Iron Gate Cir 28117
Ironstone Ln 28115
Ironwood Ct 28117
Irving Ave 28117
Island Ln 28117
Island Cove Ln 28117
Island Forest Ln 28117
Isle Of Pines Rd 28117
Isle Run Dr 28117
Ivy Creek Ln 28115
Ivy Hollow Ln 28117
Ivygate Ln 28115
Ivyridge Ct 28117
J And M Ln 28117
J C Cir 28115
Jack Pine Ct 28117
Jackson Rd 28115
Jade Ct 28117
Jade Spring Ct 28117
Jakes Rdg 28115
James Robert Ln 28115
Jamitat Rd 28115
Jamiwind Ct 28115
Jase Ct 28117
Jason Ln 28115
Jenkins Farm Ln 28115
Jennifer Way 28115
Jennymarie Rd 28115
Jeremy Point Pl 28117
Jess Ct 28117
Jib Ln 28117
Jillians Ln 28115
Joann Ln 28117
Jocelyn Ln 28117
Jodie Ct 28115
Joe Knox Ave 28117
Joels Hill Ln 28117
Johns Pond Ln 28115
Johnson Dairy Rd 28115
Jonquil Ct 28117
Joseph Ln 28115
Joshua Ln 28117
Jousters Ct 28117
Judas Rd 28117
Juliette Dr 28115
Julius Ln 28117
Juniper Rd 28115
Kalista Ln 28115
Kallie Loop 28117
Kam Dr 28115
Kapp Place Rd 28117
Karlstad Ln 28115
Karlyn Ct 28115
Karriker Farms Rd 28115
Karrimont Rd 28115
Kase Ct 28117
Keats Rd 28117
Keel Ct 28117

Keenan Dr 28117
Keller Ridge Ln 28115
Kelly Ave 28115
Kelly Cove Ct 28117
Kelly Point Ln 28117
Kelsey Ln 28117
Kemp Rd 28117
Kendra Dr 28117
Kenley Pl 28117
Kennerly Ave 28115
Kennette St 28115
Kensington St 28117
Kent Ct 28117
Kenway Loop 28117
Kenyon Loop 28115
Kerr St 28115
Keswick Ln 28117
Ketch Ct 28117
Ketchie Dr 28115
Key St 28115
Key West Ln 28115
Keyside Ln 28115
Kilborne Rd 28117
Kilkee Ln 28117
Killarney Dr 28117
Kilmer Ln 28115
Kilson Dr 28117
Kingfisher Dr 28117
Kings Crest Dr 28117
Kings Cross Ln 28117
Kingsbury Ct 28117
Kipka Ln 28115
Kipling Ln 28115
Kirkwall Pl 28117
Kirsche Ct 28115
Kisa Ct 28117
Kiskadee Dr 28117
Kistler St 28115
Kistler Farm Rd 28115
Kitty Hawk Rd 28117
Klutz Rd 28115
Knight Ln 28115
Knight N Gail Dr 28115
Knight Woods Ln 28117
Knob Hill Rd 28117
Knops Nob Rd 28115
Knotty Pine Ln 28117
Knox Haven Ln 28117
Knoxview Ln 28117
Koinonia Ln 28117
Kristens Court Dr 28115
Krosper Ln 28117
Krystal Nicole Ln 28115
Kyle Ln 28117
Lacona Trce 28115
Lady Slipper Dr 28115
Lake Campus Dr 28117
Lake Hills Dr 28117
Lake Mist Dr 28117
Lake Pine Rd 28117
Lake Spring Loop 28117
Lakefront Dr & Rd 28117
Lakehaven Ln 28115
Lakeland Rd 28117
Lakeshore Dr 28117
Lakeshore Hills Dr 28117
Lakeshore School Dr 28117
Lakeview Shores Loop 28117
Lakewind Dr 28115
Lakewood Circle Dr 28117
Lamplighter Ln 28115
Landings Dr 28117
Landis Hwy 28115
Landover Ln 28117
Langdon Rd 28117
Langtree Rd E 28117
Langtree Village Dr 28117
Lansdowne Pl 28115
Lansing Cir 28115
Laporte Ln 28115
Lark Glen Dr 28115
Larkhaven Ln 28117
Larkspur Dr 28115
Laura Rd 28117
Laurel Glen Dr 28115
Laurel Hedge Ln 28117
Lavender Bloom Loop 28115
Lawnhaven Dr 28115
Lawrence Tee Ln 28117
Lazy Ln 28117
Leaning Oak Dr 28117
Leaning Tower Dr 28117
Leazer Rd 28115
Ledgewood Ln 28115
Lee St 28115
Leeward Ln 28117
Legacy Village Blvd 28117
Leisurewood Dr 28117
Leonard St 28115
Leslie Loop 28115
Leyton Loop 28117
Liberty St 28115
Lightship Dr 28117
Lilac Mist Loop 28115
Limerick Rd 28115
Lindbergh Ln 28117
Linden Falls Ct 28117
Lineberger Dr 28117
Linker Farm Loop 28115
Linwood Rd 28115
Lisa Carol Dr 28115
Lismark Dr 28117
Litewood Ln 28117
Little Acorn Ln 28117
Little Chapman Ln 28117
Little Creek Rd 28115
Little Daisy Dr 28115
Little Indian Ln 28117
Little Ranch Rd 28115
Liva Ln 28117
Live Oak Ln 28117
Livingston Ln 28117
Loc Doc Pl 28115
Lochfoot Ln 28117
Lockerbie Ln 28115
Locomotive Ln 28115
Locust St 28115
Logan St 28115
Loghouse Ln 28115
Loma Hill Dr 28117
London Rd 28117
Lone Oak Ln 28115
Long Cove Ln 28117
Longboat Rd 28117
N & S Longfellow Ln 28117
Longfield Dr 28115
Longford Way 28117
Lookout Point Pl 28115
Lorenzo Ln 28115
Lost Tree Ln 28115
Louden Dr 28117
Louise Dr 28115
Lowes Blvd 28117
E & W Lowrance Ave & Rd 28115
Lucent Ln 28117
Lugnut Ln 28117
Lutz Ave 28115
Lynch Cir 28117
Lynn Cove Ln 28117
Lynnbrook Ln 28117
Lynnfield Ct 28117
M And M Farms Dr 28115
Mackey Ave 28115
Mackwood Rd 28115
Macleod Rd 28117
Maddaket Loop 28117
Madelia Pl 28117
Madison Place Cir 28115
N & S Magnolia St 28115
Magnolia Farms Ln 28117
Magnolia Park Dr 28117
Magnolia Ridge Dr 28115
N & S Main St 28115
Main Channel Dr 28117
Mainview Dr 28117
Malibu Rd 28117
Mallard Ln & Way 28117
Mallard Head Ln 28117
Mallbrook Dr 28117
Manall Ct 28115
Mandarin Dr 28117
Mangum Cir 28117
Manitoba Ln 28117
Manor Cir 28115
N & S Maple St 28115
Maple Falls Way 28115
Maple Grove Ln 28117
Marakery Rd 28115
E & W Maranta Rd 28117
Marbury Ct 28117
Marietta Rd 28117
Marina Ln 28117
Mariner Pointe Ln 28117
Marisol Ln 28115
Market Pl 28117
Market Rd 28115
Market Place Ave 28117
Markham Dr 28115
Marlin Dr 28117
Marlowe Cove Ln 28117
Marston Ct 28115
Marstons Mill Dr 28117
Mary Ida Ln 28117
Mast Ct 28117
Masthead Ct 28117
Matlen Dr 28117
Maxamy Ln 28117
Mayberry Ln 28115
Mayfair Rd 28117
Mayflower Ave 28115
Mayhen Park Ln 28117
Mayhew St 28115
Mayhew Park Ln 28117
Mazeppa Rd 28115
Mcadam Ln 28117
Mccarns St 28115
Mccauley Ct 28117
Mccleod Rd 28117
Mccrary Rd 28117
Mcinnis Rd 28117
Mckendree Rd 28117
Mckenzie Rd 28115
Mcknight Ln 28115
Mclaughlin Rd 28117
Mclaughlin Farm Rd 28115
Mclean Cir 28117
E & W Mclelland Ave 28115
Mcnaron Ln 28117
E & W Mcneely Ave 28115
Meadow Ln 28115
Meadow Creek Ln 28117
Meadow Crest Ln 28115
Meadow Hill Cir 28117
Meadow Lilly Ct 28115
Meadow Pond Ln 28117
Meadow Run Ln 28117
Meandering Way Ln 28117
Mebane St 28115
Mecklenburg Hwy 28115
Mecklynn Rd 28115
Medical Park Rd 28117
Meeting House Sq 28117
Megis Ln 28117
Melody Ln 28115
Melrose Ln 28117
Melville Ct 28117
Meredith Ln 28115
Merrin Ct 28117
Merrywood Ct 28115
Messick Ave 28115
Michigan Dr 28117
Middle Grove Dr 28115
Middleton Pl 28117
Midfield St 28115
Midglen Ct 28117
Midnight Ln 28117
Midway Lake Rd 28115
Mikron Ln 28117
Milan St 28115
Milbros Ln 28117
Mile Long Rd 28115
Milford Cir 28117
Mill Chase Cir 28115
Milledge Dr 28117
Millen Dr 28115
Millers Hollow Ln 28115
Millhouse Rd 28117
E & W Mills Ave 28115
Mills Forest Ln 28117
Mills Pond Ln 28115
Mills Valley Dr 28117
Millswood Dr 28115
Milo Ln 28115
Milroy Ln 28115
Mimi Ln 28117
Misty Ct 28117
Misty Arbor Ln 28117
Misty Cove Ln 28117
Misty Harbor Ln 28115
Misty Meadows Ct 28117
Misty Pond Ct 28115
Misty Tunnel Ln 28115
Moffet Ln 28115
Moffett Ln 28115
Molly Rex Ln 28117
Monarch Ln 28115
Montclair Dr 28115
Monterey Dr 28117
Montibello Dr 28117
Montrose Dr 28115
Monument Ct 28115
Moonflower Ct 28115
Moonridge Ln 28115
E & W Moore Ave 28115
Moore Farm Ln 28115
Mooreland Rd 28117
Mooresville Blvd & Rd 28115
Mooresville Commons Way 28117
Moors End 28117
E & W Morehouse Ave 28115
Morgan Bluff Rd 28117
Morlake Dr 28117
Morning Mist Ln 28117
Morning Sun Dr 28115
Morrison Cove Rd 28117
Morrison Plantation Pkwy 28117
Morrison Plantation Park Dr 28117
Morrocroft Ln 28115
Morrow St 28115
Morrows Ridge Ln 28117
Moser Ln 28115
Motorplex Dr 28115
Motorsports Rd 28115
Mott Rd 28115
Mount Joy Ln 28115
Mount Mourne Loop 28117
Mount Ulla Hwy 28115
Muirfield Dr 28115
Muskedine Loop 28117
Mussell Ln 28117
Myrtlewood Ln 28117
Mystic Lake Loop 28117
Nahcotta Dr 28115
Nance Farm Rd 28115
Nantucket Ct 28117
Naomi Rd 28115
Nash Ct 28115
Nathaniel Ct 28115
Nautical Point Ct 28117
Navigator Ct 28117
W Nc 152 Hwy 28115
Neds Cove Ct 28117
Neel Ave 28115
Neel Ranch Rd 28115
Nesbit Ave 28115
Nesting Quail Ln 28117
Nevis Ln 28117
New Haven Dr 28117
Newark Ln 28117
Newbury Dr 28115
Newcastle Ct 28115
Nichols Ln 28115
Nile Cir 28117
Norcross Ln 28117
Norman Dr 28115
Norman Station Blvd 28117
Normandy Rd 28117
Northbridge Dr 28115
Northhampton Dr 28117
Northington Woods Dr 28117
Northland Ave 28115
Oak St 28115
Oak Breeze Cir & Dr 28115
Oak Brook Dr 28115
Oak Fork Dr 28117
Oak Meadow Rd 28115
Oak Ridge Ln 28117
Oak Ridge Farm Hwy 28115
Oak Tree Rd 28117
Oak Village Pkwy 28117
Oakhurst Dr 28115
Oakpark Dr 28115
Oakridge Dr 28115
Oakwood Ave 28115
Oakwood Meadow Dr 28115
Oasis Ln 28117
Oates Rd 28117
Oberkirch Ln 28115
Ogburn St 28115
Ogden Ln 28117
Old Arborway Rd 28117
Old Meadowbrook Rd 28115
Old Post Rd 28115
Old Squaw Rd 28117
Old Stage Ln 28117
Old Timber Ln 28117
Old Willow Rd 28115
Oliphant Rd 28115
Olympia Dr 28115
Onslow Ct 28117
Onsrud Ln 28117
Ontario Rd 28117
Orange Ln 28115
Orbison Rd 28115
Orchard Farm Ln 28115
Orchid Ln 28115
Osprey Ln 28117
Outside Loop Ln 28117
Overcash Farm Ln 28115
Overcreek Rd 28117
Overhead Bridge Rd 28115
Overhill Dr 28117
Overlook Cove Loop 28117
Owens Farm Rd 28115
Oxford Dr 28117
P And C Path Ln 28115
Pallisades Ct 28117
Palmer Marsh Pl 28117
Palmetto Dr 28117
Palos Verde Dr 28115
Pamlico Ln 28117
Pampas Ln 28117
Panasonic Way 28115
Pandora Rd 28115
Panther Hill Ln 28115
Par Pl 28115
Paradise Penn Rd 28117
E Park Ave 28115
W Park Ave 28115
Park Rd 28117
Park Creek Dr 28115
Parker Ave 28115
Parkertown Rd 28115
Parkside Ln 28117
Paseo Dr 28117
Passage Ct 28117
Patience Place Ln 28115
Patrice Rd 28115
Patrose Ln 28115
Patternote Rd 28117
Patternote Cove Ln 28117
Patterson Ave 28115
Patterson Farm Rd 28115
Patterson Hill Ln 28115
Patton Ct 28115
Paulas Parkway Ln 28117
Pauls Ln 28117
Pavillion Ln 28117
Peace Ln 28115
Peaceful Valley Ln 28115
Pebble Ct 28117
Pebble Brook Ln 28117
Pecan Hills Dr 28115
Pelham Ln 28115
Pelican Ct 28117
Peninsula Dr 28117
Peninsula Place Ln 28117
Penske Way 28115
Pentland Ct 28117
Pepaw Dr 28115
Pepper Cir 28117
Peralta Cir 28117
Peregrin Ct 28117
Perennial Dr 28117
Performance Dr & Rd 28115
Periwinkle Ln 28117
Perrin Dr 28117
Perrin Park Ln & Loop 28117
Perth Rd 28117
Peterborough Dr 28115
Phillips Hollow Dr 28115
Phonesavanh Rd 28115
Phyllis Ln 28115
Picardy Place Ln 28117
Pickens Ln 28115
Picwyck Dr 28115
Piedmont Pointe Dr 28115
Pier 33 Dr 28117
Pin Oak Ln 28117
Pine St 28115
Pine Bluff Dr 28117
Pine Cliff Ln 28117
Pine Meadow Ln 28117
Pine Mist Dr 28117
Pine Needle Ln 28115
Pinebridge Dr 28115
Pineridge Dr 28115
Pinewood Cir 28115
Pink Jasmine Ct 28115
Pink Orchard Dr 28115
Pinnacle Ln 28117
Pinnacle Shores Dr 28115
Pintail Run Ln 28117
Pinto Rd 28117
Pipeline Dr 28117
Pitt Rd & St 28115
Plainview Ct 28115
Plantation Dr 28117
Plantation Creek Dr 28117
Plantation Pointe Loop 28117
Plantation Ridge Dr 28117
Planters Ln 28115
E Plaza Dr 28115
W Plaza Dr 28117
Plaza Ln 28115
Pleasant Grove Ln 28115
Pleasant Way Ln 28115
Plyler St 28115
Plymouth Rd 28115
Poinsettia Ln 28117
Point Of View Dr 28117
Pointe Harbor Ln 28117
Points End Dr 28117
Polpis Rd 28117
Pomeroy Ln 28117
Pompano Pl 28117
Pond St 28115
Pond View Rd 28115
Ponderosa Cir 28117
Pondhaven Cir 28117
Pondridge Ln 28117
Poplar Grove Rd 28117
Poplar Pointe Dr 28117
Poplar Springs Rd 28115
Poppy Field Ln 28115
Portestown Way 28115
Possum Knob Dr 28117
Powder Horn Rd 28115
Powers Farm Rd 28115
Powers Hill Dr 28115
Prelude Dr 28117
Presbyterian Rd 28115
Preserve Way 28117
E & W Pressley Ave 28115
Preston Rd 28117
Prestwood Ln 28117
Professional Park Dr 28117
Promenade Dr 28117
Purple Finch Ln 28117
Putter Pl 28115
Pyler St 28115
Quail Ln 28117
Quail Hill Dr 28115
Quail Hollow Dr 28117
Quail Ridge Dr & Rd 28117
Quaker Rd 28117
Quarter Ln 28117
Queens Rd 28117
Queens Cove Rd 28117
Queensbury Ln 28117
Quiet Cove Rd 28117
Quiet View Rd 28115
Quiet Waters Dr 28117
Quincy Ct 28117
Quinn Ln 28115
Raceway Dr 28117
Ragsdale Trl 28117
Rain Shadow Ln 28115
Rainberry Dr 28117
Rainbow Ln 28117
Rainford Ct 28117
Raintree Ln 28117
Rankin St 28115
N & S Ranney Way 28117
Raspberry Ln 28117
Rathbone Dr 28115
Ray Dawn Ln 28117
Raykecki Dr 28117
Raymond Rd 28117
Rebecca Jane Dr 28115
Rebel Hill Dr 28115
Red Arrow Pl 28117
Red Brook Ln 28117
Red Dog Dr 28115
Red Rose Ln 28115
Red Tip Ln 28117
Reed Creek Rd 28117
Regal Cir 28117
Regatta Ln 28115
Regency Rd 28117
Regency Center Dr 28117
Rehoboth Ln 28117
Renville Pl 28115
Renwick Ln 28117
Rescue Ln 28117
Revere Dr 28117
Rhinehill Dr 28117
Richards Ln 28115
Richland Ln 28115
Ricks Ln 28115
Ridge Ave 28115
Ridge Bluff Rd 28115
Ridge Top Rd 28117
Ridgebrook Dr 28117
Ridgecrest Dr 28115
Riding Trl 28117
Rinehardt Rd 28115
Ringneck Trl 28117
Rio Vista Dr 28117
Ripplewater Ln 28117
River Hwy 28117
River Birch Cir 28115
River Park Rd 28117
Riverbend Dr 28117
Riverchase Ln 28115
Riveria Dr & Rd 28117
Riverwood Rd 28117
Roanoke Ln 28117
Rob Ln 28117
Robin Aubrey Ln 28117
Robinson Rd 28117
Rockabill Ln 28117
Rockridge Point Dr 28117
Rockspring Rd 28117
Rockwell Loop 28115
Rocky Point Ct 28115
Rocky Ridge Ln 28117
Rocky River Rd 28115
Rolling Hill Rd 28117
Rolling Stone Ct 28117
Rollingwood Ln 28117
Romany Ln 28117
Rose St 28117
Rosehaven Ln 28117
Roseland Ct 28115
Rosewood Ln 28117
Ross Rd 28117

Rougemont Ln ... 28115
Round Keep Ln ... 28117
Royal Coach Ln ... 28115
Royal Pointe Way ... 28117
Royalton Rd ... 28115
Ruby Rd ... 28117
Runningdeer Dr ... 28117
Rush St ... 28115
Rustic Rd ... 28115
Rustic Way Ln ... 28117
Rustwood Ln ... 28117
Rusty Nail Dr ... 28115
Rutan Ct ... 28117
Ryan Ln ... 28115
Saddle Rd ... 28115
Saddle Back Ln ... 28115
Sadie Ln ... 28115
Sagemore Rd ... 28117
Sagewood Dr ... 28115
Sago Ln ... 28117
Sail High Ct ... 28117
Sailors Bay Ct ... 28117
Sailview Rd ... 28117
Sailwinds Rd ... 28115
Saint Charles Ln ... 28117
Saint Thomas Ln ... 28115
Salisbury Hwy ... 28115
Samdusky Ln ... 28117
Sample Rd ... 28115
San Agustin Dr ... 28117
Sand Spur Dr ... 28117
Sandhills Ct ... 28115
Sandpiper Dr ... 28117
Sandreed Dr ... 28117
Sandstone Loop ... 28115
Sandy Cove Ct ... 28117
Sandy Shore Dr ... 28117
Sanibel Ln ... 28117
Sansome Rd ... 28115
Sapphire Dr ... 28117
Sardis Rd ... 28115
Sasserbrook Ln ... 28117
Satellite Dr ... 28115
Saturday Ln ... 28117
Savannah Crossing Dr ... 28115
Sawhorse Dr ... 28115
Sawyer Ln ... 28117
Saye Pl ... 28115
Scanlon Rd ... 28115
Scarlet Oaks Dr ... 28117
Scenic Dr ... 28115
School St ... 28115
Schoolhouse Ln ... 28117
Schooner Rd ... 28117
Scotland Dr ... 28115
Scottish Dr ... 28115
Scottsdale Ln ... 28117
Sea Hide Ct ... 28117
Sea Trail Dr ... 28117
Seabreeze Ln ... 28117
Seabury Dr ... 28117
Seagrove Ln ... 28117
Secretariat Ln ... 28117
Selma Dr ... 28115
Seneca Pl ... 28117
Serenity Hill Rd ... 28115
Shadow Ln ... 28117
Shadowbrooke Ln ... 28117
Shadyview Ln ... 28117
Shagbark Ln ... 28115
Shaleigh Ln ... 28117
Shall Mar Ln ... 28117
Sharpe St ... 28115
Shavender Dr ... 28117
Shearers Rd ... 28115
Shearers Chapel Rd ... 28115
Sheep Path Dr ... 28115
Sheets Dr ... 28117
Sheets Ln ... 28115
Shelbourne Pl ... 28117
Shelter Cove Ln ... 28117
Shephard Hill Dr ... 28115
Shepherd Rd ... 28115
Shepherd Valley Rd ... 28115
Shepherds Bluff Dr ... 28115
Sherbrook Ln ... 28117
Sheridan Ct ... 28115
Sherman Ct ... 28115
Sherman Oaks ... 28115
N & S Sherrill St ... 28115
Sherwood Pl ... 28115
Sherwood Pines Dr ... 28115
Shetland Pl ... 28117
Shining Armor Ct ... 28117
Shinn Farm Rd ... 28115
Shinnville Rd ... 28115
Shipyard Pointe Rd ... 28117
N Shore Dr ... 28117
Shoreline Loop ... 28117
Shoreview Dr ... 28117
Short Ave ... 28115
Short Ridge Ln ... 28117
Sienna Ln ... 28117
Sienna Pace Ct ... 28117
Silver Eagle Ln ... 28117
Silver Hook Dr ... 28117
Silver Lake Trl ... 28117
Silverleaf Ln ... 28115
Silverlining Rd ... 28117
Silverspring Pl ... 28117
Sinclair Ln ... 28115
Singleton Rd ... 28117
Sink Farm Rd ... 28115
Sister Farm Rd ... 28115
Ski Haven Pl ... 28117
Skip Jack Point Ct ... 28117
Skylark Way ... 28115
Sleepy Cove Trl ... 28117
Smith St ... 28115
Smith Deaton Dr ... 28115
Smyrna Ln ... 28115
Snooter Trl ... 28115
Snow Fountain Ln ... 28115
Sonora Ln ... 28115
Soule Ln ... 28115
Southfork Rd ... 28115
Southhaven Dr ... 28117
Southpark Dr ... 28117
Southpoint Dr ... 28117
Southside Ave ... 28115
Southwood Park Rd ... 28117
Sparta Dr ... 28117
Spartina Ct ... 28117
Spears Creek Dr ... 28117
Speedway Dr ... 28117
Spencer St ... 28115
Sport Court Way ... 28117
Spring Grove Dr ... 28117
Spring Run Dr ... 28117
Springdale Acres Dr ... 28115
Springtime Ln ... 28115
Springwood Ln ... 28117
Spruce St ... 28115
Squam Ct ... 28117
St. Sophia Ct ... 28117
Stacy Rd ... 28115
Staff Ln ... 28115
Stafford Ln ... 28115
Stallings Ln ... 28115
Stallings Mill Dr ... 28115
Stamford Ct ... 28117
Standish Ln ... 28117
Stanton Ln ... 28117
Stanwood Pl ... 28115
Starwood Dr ... 28115
Stat Cir ... 28117
E & W Statesville Ave & Hwy ... 28115
Steam Engine Dr ... 28115
Steeple Gate Dr ... 28117
Steeplechase Ave ... 28117
Steinbeck Way ... 28117
Stepaside Ln ... 28117
Sterling Ter ... 28115
Sterling Oak Ln ... 28117
Stevenson St ... 28115
E & W Stewart Ave ... 28115
Stingray Ct ... 28117
Stone Point Ct ... 28117
Stone Ridge Ln ... 28117
Stonecrest Dr ... 28117
Stonehaven Dr ... 28115
Stonemarker Pt & Rd ... 28117
Stonemason Ct ... 28115
Stonewall Beach Ln ... 28117
Stonewood Dr ... 28115
Stoney Crest Ct ... 28115
Stormy Pointe Ln ... 28117
Stover Rd ... 28117
Stowe Away Ln ... 28115
Stratus Ln ... 28117
Strawpocket Ln ... 28117
Streamside Pl ... 28115
Stucomb Ln ... 28117
Studio Ln ... 28115
Stump Hill Trl ... 28115
Stumpy Creek Rd ... 28117
Stutts Rd ... 28117
Sugar Magnolia Dr ... 28115
Sugar Thyme Ln ... 28115
Summer St ... 28115
Summer Pines Ln ... 28115
Summerbrook Ln ... 28117
Summerchase Ln ... 28117
Summersong Ln ... 28117
Summerville Dr ... 28115
Summerwind Dr ... 28117
Summerwood Dr ... 28117
Sumter Dr ... 28117
Sun Ln ... 28115
Sundown Rd ... 28117
Sundown Cove Dr ... 28117
Sunfish Dr ... 28117
Sunhaven Ln ... 28117
Sunridge Dr ... 28117
Sunrise Cir ... 28117
Sunset Ln ... 28115
Sunset Cove Ln ... 28117
Sunshine Dr ... 28115
Sunstede Dr ... 28117
Superior Dr ... 28117
Surfside Ln ... 28117
Swan Lake Rd ... 28115
Swayne Dr ... 28117
Sweet Magnolia Ct ... 28115
Sweet Martha Dr ... 28115
Sweetbriar Ln ... 28115
Swift Arrow Dr ... 28117
Swift Creek Ln ... 28115
N & S Sycamore Ln & St ... 28115
Sycamore Slope Ln ... 28117
Syllabub Ln ... 28115
Talbert Rd ... 28115
Talbert Pointe Dr ... 28117
Talbert Town Loop ... 28117
Talbert Woods Dr ... 28117
Tall Fern Ln ... 28115
Tall Oak Dr ... 28117
Tamer Rd ... 28115
Tammy Dr ... 28115
Tanager Ln ... 28115
Tannenbaum Ct ... 28117
Tara Rd ... 28117
Tara Lynn Ct ... 28115
Tartan Pl ... 28115
Tawny Bark Dr ... 28117
Taylor Ct ... 28115
Tea Olive Ln ... 28117
Teaberry Ct ... 28117
Teague Dr ... 28115
Teakwood Ln ... 28115
Teeter Dr & Rd ... 28115
Teeter Farms Dr ... 28115
Templeton Ave ... 28115
Templeton Rd ... 28117
Templeton Bay Dr ... 28117
Tennant Ln ... 28115
Tennessee Cir ... 28117
Tennyson Ct ... 28117
Terrace Rd ... 28117
Tessies Ln ... 28115
Tgpl Dr ... 28117
Thayer Ct ... 28115
The Point Dr ... 28117
Thompson Farm Rd ... 28115
Thornbrook Ln ... 28115
Thorsen Dr ... 28117
Thrasher Ln ... 28117
Thunder Hill Rd ... 28117
Thurstons Way ... 28117
Tiger Ln ... 28117
Tigris Ct ... 28117
Tillman Dr ... 28115
Tilton Dr ... 28115
Timber Rd ... 28115
Timberbrook Ln ... 28117
Timberland Loop ... 28115
Timberlane Ter ... 28115
Timberview Ln ... 28115
Tisbury Ct ... 28117
Tomahawk Ln ... 28117
Tommys Ln ... 28117
Topaz Pl ... 28117
Topsail Pl ... 28117
Torrence Chapel Rd ... 28117
Toucan Rd ... 28117
Towell St ... 28115
S Tower Dr ... 28115
Town Loop ... 28117
Town Center Dr ... 28117
Town Square Cir ... 28117
Town Squire ... 28117
Trade Ct ... 28117
Tradewinds Ct ... 28115
Tradition Ln ... 28115
Tranquil Cove Rd ... 28117
Transco Rd ... 28117
Travis Point Dr ... 28117
Treasure Ln ... 28117
Trent Pines Dr ... 28117
Triplett Rd ... 28115
Trollingwood Ln ... 28117
Trotter Ridge Dr ... 28117
Troutman Ave ... 28115
Trump Sq ... 28117
Tuckernook Ln ... 28117
Tuckernuck Dr ... 28117
Tulip Dr ... 28117
Turbyfill Rd ... 28115
Turnberry Ln ... 28117
Turner St ... 28115
Turnerlair Ct ... 28117
Tuscany Trl ... 28117
Tuskarora Trl ... 28117
Tuskarora Point Ln ... 28117
Tweed Pl ... 28117
Twiggs Ln ... 28115
Umberly Ct ... 28115
Underhill Ln ... 28115
Union Chapel Dr ... 28117
Unity Church Rd ... 28115
Uppercrest Dr ... 28115
Valleydale Dr ... 28115
Valleyview Rd ... 28115
Vance Crescent Dr ... 28115
Vandalia Rd ... 28117
Vandenbrook Ln ... 28115
Ventana Ct ... 28117
Venus Ln ... 28117
Verde Rd ... 28115
Vestal Dr ... 28117
Vetana Ct ... 28117
Vick Rd ... 28115
Viewpoint Ln ... 28115
Village Green Blvd ... 28117
Village View Dr ... 28117
Vineyard Dr ... 28117
Vintage Dr ... 28117
Vista Bluff Ln ... 28117
E & W Vista View Pl ... 28117
Voyager Way ... 28117
Waddell Rd ... 28117
Waderich Ln ... 28115
Wades Way ... 28117
Waitsfield Ct ... 28117
Wal Hollow Ln ... 28115
Walden Dr ... 28117
Walden Ridge Ln ... 28115
Wallaces Grant Dr ... 28115
Walmsley Pl ... 28117
Walnut St ... 28115
Walnut Cove Dr ... 28117
Walnut Hill Dr ... 28115
Walnut Hollow Ln ... 28115
E & W Warfield Dr ... 28115
Warlick Dr ... 28117
Washam Rd ... 28117
Washburn Range Dr ... 28115
Water St ... 28115
Water Ash Ct ... 28115
Water Oak Dr ... 28117
Waterbury Dr ... 28117
Waterford Dr ... 28117
Waterfowl Ln ... 28117
Waterhouse Ct ... 28117
E Waterlynn Rd
100-268 ... 28117
269-499 ... 28115
W Waterlynn Rd ... 28117
Waterlynn Club Dr ... 28117
Waterlynn Ridge Rd ... 28117
Waters Edge Ct ... 28117
Waterview Dr ... 28117
Watson Ct ... 28115
Watts Farm Ln ... 28115
Wayman Rd ... 28115
Weathers Creek Rd ... 28115
Webbed Foot Rd ... 28117
Wedgewood Dr ... 28115
Weeping Spring Dr ... 28115
Wellcraft Ct ... 28117
Wellesley Ln ... 28115
Wellfleet Ln ... 28117
Wellshire St ... 28115
Welton Way ... 28117
N & S Wendover Trce ... 28117
Wescoe Dr ... 28117
Wesley Woods Ln ... 28115
Westbury Dr ... 28117
Westmoreland Rd ... 28115
Westpaces Rd ... 28117
Whaling Ln ... 28117
Wheaton Ln ... 28115
Whimbrel Ln ... 28117
Whippoorwill Rd ... 28117
Whispering Cove Ct ... 28117
Whispering Oaks Ct ... 28115
Whistle Stop Ln ... 28115
Whitby Ln ... 28117
White St ... 28115
White Crest Ct ... 28117
White Horse Dr ... 28117
White Oaks Rd ... 28115
White Pine Dr ... 28115
Whitefield Trce ... 28115
Whitehall Dr ... 28117
Whitewater Ln ... 28115
Whitman Cir ... 28115
Wickford Ln ... 28117
Wiggins Rd ... 28115
Wild Harbor Rd ... 28117
Wild Rose Loop ... 28115
Wildcat Ln ... 28117
Wildiris Dr ... 28117
Wildwood Acres ... 28115
Wildwood Cove Dr ... 28117
Wilk Rob Rd ... 28115
Wilkinson Rd ... 28115
Willhaven Dr ... 28115
Williams St ... 28115
Williamson Rd ... 28117
Williford Rd ... 28115
Willow St ... 28115
Willow Bend Ct ... 28117
Willow Oak Ln ... 28115
Willup Trl ... 28115
E Wilson Ave ... 28115
W Wilson Ave
200-699 ... 28115
900-1099 ... 28117
Wilson Lake Rd ... 28117
Wilton Pl ... 28117
Winborne Dr ... 28115
Windchime Ln ... 28115
Windrift Ln ... 28117
Windy Run ... 28117
Windy Knoll Ln ... 28117
Winedale Ln ... 28115
Winged Elm Ln ... 28115
Winghaven Ct ... 28117
Wingmaster Dr ... 28115
Winter Oaks Ln ... 28115
Winter Wien Ln ... 28117
Winter Wren Ln ... 28117
Winterbell Dr ... 28115
Winterfield Dr ... 28115
Winthrow Creek Rd ... 28115
Wisteria Ln ... 28117
Wits End Ln ... 28115
Wolf Hill Dr ... 28117
Wood Acre Dr ... 28115
Wood Duck Loop ... 28117
Wood Ridge Dr ... 28115
Wood Thrush Ln ... 28117
Woodberry Dr ... 28115
Woodchase Ln ... 28115
Woodcrest Dr & Rd ... 28115
Woodfern Pl ... 28115
Woodlawn School Loop ... 28115
Woodlea Ct & Rd ... 28115
Woodridge Dr & Ln ... 28115
Woods Hole Ct ... 28117
Woodsmans Ln ... 28115
Woodsong Ln ... 28117
Woodstork Cove Rd ... 28117
Woodstream Cir ... 28117
Woodwinds Dr ... 28115
Wordsworth Way ... 28115
Worley Dr ... 28117
Wren Ln ... 28117
Wren Hill Dr ... 28115
Wrights View Ln ... 28115
Wynswept Dr ... 28117
Wynward Ln ... 28117
Yacht Rd ... 28117
Yacht Cove Ln ... 28117
Yacht Harbor Rd ... 28117
Yacht Harbour Dr ... 28117
Yale Loop ... 28117
Yardley Ct ... 28115
Yeager Rd ... 28117
Yellow Brick Rd ... 28115
Yellow Jacket Cir ... 28117
Yellow Wood Cir ... 28115
Yeoman Rd ... 28117
Yorke Ln ... 28117
Yorkshire Ln ... 28115
Young St ... 28115
Zephyr Ln ... 28117
Zolder Ln ... 28117

MORGANTON NC

General Delivery ... 28655

POST OFFICE BOXES MAIN OFFICE STATIONS AND BRANCHES

Box No.s
1 - 8478 ... 28680
9998 - 9998 ... 28655
9998 - 9998 ... 28680

NAMED STREETS

All Street Addresses ... 28655

NUMBERED STREETS

All Street Addresses ... 28655

NEW BERN NC

General Delivery ... 28562

POST OFFICE BOXES MAIN OFFICE STATIONS AND BRANCHES

Box No.s
A - X ... 28563
1 - 1776 ... 28563
3001 - 3778 ... 28564
12001 - 15590 ... 28561
28562 - 28562 ... 28562
28563 - 28563 ... 28563
28564 - 28564 ... 28564

NAMED STREETS

A St ... 28560
Abner Nash Rd ... 28562
Academic Dr ... 28562
Acorn Dr ... 28562
Acorn Ln ... 28560
Adell Ln ... 28562
E & W Ag Dr ... 28562
Airport Rd ... 28560
Alabama Ave ... 28560
Alanwood Dr ... 28560
Albacore Ln ... 28560
Albatross Dr ... 28560
Albemarle Ct ... 28562
Albury Ct ... 28562
Alex Dr ... 28562
Alexander Ln ... 28562
Alexandria Cir ... 28560
Alexis Ct & Dr ... 28562
Allante Dr ... 28562
Allen Dr ... 28562
Allison Dr ... 28562
Amanda Ct ... 28562
Amber Dr ... 28560
Amberwood Ln ... 28562
Amelia Ln ... 28560
Amhurst Blvd ... 28562
Amy Dr ... 28562
Anchor Way ... 28562
Andre Ln ... 28560
Ann Ct ... 28560
Antioch Rd ... 28560
Antioch Lakes Rd ... 28560
Antler Ln ... 28562
Appenzell Ln ... 28562
Applewood Ln ... 28560
Arbon Ct & Ln ... 28562
Arbor Green Way ... 28562
Arcane Cir ... 28562
Argosy Dr ... 28560
Arlington Cir ... 28560
Armstrong Ave ... 28560
Arrowhead Trl ... 28562
Asheville St ... 28560
Ashland Ave ... 28560
Ashley Pl ... 28562
Atlas Ct ... 28560
Attmore Dr ... 28560
Auburn Ct ... 28562
Audrey Ln ... 28560
Augusta Ct ... 28562
Austin Ave ... 28562
Austin Bradley Ln ... 28562
Autumn Pl ... 28562
Avenue A ... 28560
Avenue B ... 28560
Avenue C ... 28560
Avenue D ... 28560
Avery Rd ... 28560
Aviation Dr ... 28562
Aycock Ave ... 28562
B St ... 28560
Baden Ct & Ln ... 28562
Balboa Ct ... 28560
Ballard Dr ... 28562
Bandon Dr ... 28562
Banks Dr ... 28560
Barbara Dr ... 28562
Barbary Coast Dr ... 28560
Bargate Dr ... 28562
Barkentine Dr ... 28560
Barkside Ln ... 28562
Baron Point Rd ... 28562
Barons Way ... 28562
Barrington Way ... 28562
Basil Dr ... 28562
Batchelder Rd ... 28560
Batchelor Creek Ln ... 28560

Battleground Ave 28560
Batts Hill Rd 28562
Bay St 28560
Bay Hill Ct 28562
Bayberry Park Dr 28562
Bayleaf Rd 28560
Bayside Dr 28560
Bayswater Ct 28562
Baytree Way 28560
Baywood Ct 28562
Beach St 28560
Beacon Hill Rd 28562
Beaman Rd 28562
Beamans Frk 28562
Bear Trl 28562
Beaufort St 28560
Beaver Dam Trl 28560
Bee Tree Ct 28560
Beech St 28560
Belle Oaks Dr 28562
Belles Way 28562
Bellwood Dr 28560
Belmont Blvd & Ct 28562
Benfield Ave 28562
Bennett Farm Rd 28560
Bennett Tingle Rd 28560
Bentley Ln 28560
Berkley Dr 28562
Bermuda Vw 28560
Bern St
200-399 28562
400-1099 28560
N Bern St 28560
Berne Sq 28562
Bernhurst Rd 28560
Berry Hill Rd 28562
Bettye Gresham Ln 28562
Bicentennial Park 28560
Biddle St 28560
Biel Ln 28562
Big Cypress Rd 28562
Billy Dr 28562
Birch Ct 28562
Birchwood Ln 28562
Black Bear Ln 28562
Black Horse Run 28560
Black Swan Rd 28560
Blackbeard Ln 28560
Blackheath Dr 28560
Blackledge Cir 28562
Blades Ave 28560
Bloomfield St 28560
Blount Brimage Dr 28562
Blue Grass Ct 28562
Blue Heron Dr 28560
Blue Jay Ct 28562
Blue Top Rd 28560
Bluebeard Dr 28560
Bluebell Trce 28562
Blueberry Ln 28562
Bluebird Dr 28560
Bluff Ct 28562
Boatswain Dr 28562
Boleyn Loop 28562
Booms Aly 28560
Booth Ln 28560
Booty Ln 28560
Boros Lndg & Rd 28560
Bosch Blvd 28562
Bouy St 28560
Bowline Rd 28562
Boxwood Ct 28562
Bracken Fern Dr 28560
Bradford Dr 28560
Brame St 28560
Branch Canal Rd 28560
Brandywine Dr 28562
Bray Ave 28562
Breckenridge Ln 28560
Breighmere Dr 28560
Brems Battery 28562
Brentwood Ct 28562
Briarhill Ct & Rd 28562
Briarwood Ln 28560
Brices Ct 28562
Brices Creek Rd 28562
Bricewood Ln 28562
Bridge Pointe Dr 28562
Bridge Town Blvd 28560
Bridle Path 28562
Brig Ct 28560
Brigadoon Ct 28562
Broad St 28560
Broad Creek Rd 28560
Brody Ln 28562
Brooks Dr 28560
Brookshire Dr 28562
Brown Dr & St 28560
Brugg Ct 28562
Brunswick Ave 28562
Bryan St 28562
Bryant Ln 28562
Bucco Reef Rd 28560
Buckingham Rd 28562
Buckskin Dr 28562
Buffalo Rd 28562
Bullens Creek Dr 28562
Bungalow Dr 28562
Bur Ben Ln 28560
S Business Plz 28562
Butler Rd 28560
Buttercup Ct 28562
Butterfly Cir 28560
Buxton Way 28562
N C St 28560
Cabot Cir 28560
Calico Dr 28560
Cambridge Ct 28562
Camden Square Dr 28562
Camelia Rd 28562
Camelot Dr 28560
Cameron Shores Dr 28562
E Camp Kiro Rd 28560
W Camp Kiro Rd 28562
Canaan Rd 28562
Canal St 28560
Candlewood Ln 28562
Canebrake Dr 28562
Canovan Rd 28560
Canterbury Rd 28562
Canterwood Ln 28562
Cape Fear Ln 28560
Capeson Ln 28562
Capstan Ct 28560
Captain Haitien Rd 28560
Captains Cv 28562
Caracara Dr 28560
Cardinal Dr 28560
Cardinal Rd 28562
Carmel Ln 28562
Carmer St 28560
Carolina Ave 28562
S Carolina Ave 28562
N Carolina Dr 28562
Carolina St 28562
Carolina Pines Blvd 28560
Caroline Ct 28560
Carragood Trl 28560
Carraway Ln 28560
Carriage House Ct 28562
Carroll St 28560
Carteret Dr 28562
Carver St 28560
Casey Rd 28562
Cashmere Ln 28562
Cassowary Ln 28562
N & S Castle Dr 28562
Castle Ridge Rd 28562
Castlegate Rd 28560
Castleton Ct 28560
Caswell St 28560
Catarina Ln 28562
Catfish Lake Rd 28562
Catherine St 28560
Cavanaugh Ln 28560
Cavendish Ct 28560
Cayenne Ct 28562
Cedar Rd & St 28560
Celadon Ln 28562
Cemetery Rd 28562
Center Ave
2000-2299 28560
2300-2399 28562
Cerise Cir 28560
Chair Rd 28560
Change St 28560
Channel Run Dr 28562
Chapman St 28560
Charles St 28562
Charmer Ct 28560
Chateau Dr 28560
Chatham Pass 28562
Chattawka Ln 28560
Chelsea Rd 28562
N & S Cherie Ct 28562
Cherry Ln 28562
Cherry Point Rd 28564
Cherry Tree Dr 28562
Chestnut Ave 28562
Chevy Ln 28560
Chinquapin Ln & Rd 28562
Christian Ct 28560
Christopher Ave 28560
Church Rd 28560
Church St 28562
Church Hill Ct 28562
Cinnamon Run 28562
Circle Dr 28562
Circle L Dr 28562
Cl Scott Ave 28560
Clark Ave & St 28560
Clarks Rd 28562
Clearbrook Way 28562
Clearview Dr 28562
Clermont Rd 28560
Cleveland St 28560
Cliffridge Rd 28560
Clipper Ct
100-199 28562
800-899 28560
Clubhouse Dr 28562
Cobb St 28560
Cobblestone Aly 28562
Cobia Ln 28560
Coley Ln 28562
College Ct, St & Way 28562
Colleton Way 28562
Colonel Burgwyn Dr 28562
Colonial Pl & Way 28560
Colonial Mobile Home Park 28562
Colony Dr 28562
Columbus Ct 28560
Commander Cir 28562
Commerce Dr & Way 28562
Commons Ct 28560
Compass Ct 28562
Cona Ct 28560
Concord St 28560
Conner Grant Rd 28562
Connie Lee Dr 28562
Connors Way 28560
Contentnea Ave 28560
N Cool Ave 28560
Coopers Ct 28562
Copperfield Dr 28562
Coral Ct 28560
Coral Reef Ct & Dr 28562
Coree Way 28562
Corena Dr 28562
Coriander Dr 28562
Corinth Dr 28562
Corporate Ln 28562
Corral Cir 28562
Cottonwood Ln 28562
Country Club Cir, Dr & Rd 28562
Country Springs Rd 28562
Counts Ct 28562
County Line Rd 28562
Couples Ln 28560
Courtney Ln 28562
Cove Hbr 28562
Covey Ct 28560
Covington Ct 28560
Cowan Ln 28560
Crabtree Cir 28562
Craftsman Dr 28562
Cranberry Ln 28562
Crane Dr 28560
N Craven St & Ter 28560
Craven County Rd 28560
NW & SW Craven Middle School Rd 28562
Crawford St 28560
Creek Bank Dr 28560
Creek Bend Rd 28560
Creek Pointe Rd 28560
Creek Spring Dr 28560
Creekscape Xing 28562
Creekside Dr 28562
Creekview Rd 28562
Creekwood Dr 28562
Creeping Phlox Dr 28562
Crepe Myrtle Ct 28562
Crescent St 28560
Crestview Ct & Dr 28562
Crimson Walk 28562
Croatan Ln 28562
Croatan Woods Dr 28562
Crockett Ave 28560
Crooked Creek Dr 28560
Crooked Run Dr 28560
Crows Nest Ct 28560
Crump Farm Rd 28562
Crump Woods Dr 28562
Crystal Ct 28560
Crystle Pt 28560
Culpeper Rd 28562
Currituck Ct 28562
Cutlass Ct 28560
Cutler St 28560
Cypress Pt & St 28560
Cypress Shores Dr 28562
D St 28560
Dail St 28560
Daniels St 28560
Darby Rd 28560
Dare Ct 28560
Dare Dr 28560
Darst Ave 28560
Dartmouth Ln 28560
Daughety Ct 28562
David Alvania Ct 28562
Davis St 28562
Davit Ln 28560
Davy Jones Ct 28560
Day Star Ln 28560
Dean Dr 28560
Decatur Ln 28562
Deep Creek Dr 28560
Deep Gully Ln 28562
Deep Run Dr 28560
Deer Haven Trl 28560
Deer Path Cir 28560
Deer Run Rd 28562
Deerfield Dr 28562
Deerfoot Cir 28562
Degrafenreid Ave 28560
Delanie Way 28562
Delesa Ct 28560
Delft Dr 28562
Delta Ct 28560
Delwood Ln 28562
Den Tree Ct 28562
Denim Ct 28562
Derby Ct 28562
Derby Park Ave 28562
Devers Ave & Cir 28560
Devonshire Dr 28562
Diamond Ct 28560
Dianne Dr 28562
Dickinson Ct 28562
Didrikson Dr 28560
Dillahunt St 28560
Discovery Bay 28562
Distant Creek Ct 28560
Dixie Ln 28560
Dixon Rd 28560
Dobbs Spaight Rd 28562
Docks Way 28560
Doe Ln 28562
Dogwood Dr & Ln 28562
Doral Ct 28562
Dorchester Ln 28562
Dorset Way 28562
Douglas Dr 28562
Dovefield Ct 28560
Downing Cir 28562
Dr M L King Jr Blvd
1800-2299 28560
2300-4799 28562
Dragstrip Rd 28560
Drake Lndg 28560
Drew Ave 28562
Driftwood Dr 28560
Drummond Pl 28562
Drury Ln 28560
Dry Monia Rd 28560
Duchess Ct 28562
Duck Pond Rd 28560
Ducks Way 28562
Dudley St 28560
Duds Dr 28562
Duffy St 28560
Dukes Ct 28562
Dunn St 28560
Dupree Ave 28560
Durham St 28560
Durwood Ct 28562
Duval Ln 28560
Duzan Dr 28560
Dylan Ln 28562
E St 28560
Eagle Trl 28560
Earls Ct 28562
Eastchurch Rd 28560
Easterly Dr 28560
Easy St 28560
Eden St 28562
Edenton St 28560
Edgecomb St 28562
Edgehill Rd 28562
Edgerton St 28560
Edgewood Dr & St 28562
Educational Dr 28562
Edwards Ave 28560
Edwards Way 28562
Ef Thompkins Ln 28562
Efird Blvd 28562
Egret Cir 28562
Elder St 28560
Elizabeth Ave 28562
Ella Sophia Ln 28562
Ellen Ave 28560
Ellington St 28560
Elm Dr 28562
Elm St 28560
Elmwood St 28560
Els Ln 28560
Elsmore Dr 28562
Elveden Rd 28562
Elza Ct 28562
Emerson St 28562
Emily St 28560
Emmen Rd 28562
Englewood Ln 28562
English Ivy Ln 28562
Erna Ln 28560
Esquire Ct 28562
Eubanks St 28560
Evans St 28562
Evans Mill Rd 28562
Evergreen Ln 28562
Executive Pkwy 28562
F St 28560
Fairfax Ln 28560
Fairmount Way 28562
W Fairway Dr 28562
Fairways 7 Ct 28562
Fairways West Ct & Dr 28562
Fairwoods Ln 28562
Falcon Dr 28560
Falcon Bridge Dr 28560
Falcon Landing Ct 28560
Faldo Ln 28560
Fall Walk 28562
Farrior Cir 28562
Farrow Rd 28562
Fawn Ln 28562
Fayetteville St 28560
Felicity Ln 28562
Felucca Ct 28560
Fern Ct 28562
Fernie Ln 28560
Fernwood Ln 28562
Ferret Run Ln 28562
Fieldgreen Ct 28562
Fields Rd 28560
Finch Ln 28560
Firefly Ct 28560
Firestone Ct 28562
Fish Cay Ct 28560
Fish Farm Rd 28560
E Fisher Ave 28560
W Fisher Ave 28562
Fishing Creek Dr 28562
Flanners Beach Rd 28560
Fleet St 28562
Florence St 28560
Florida Ave 28560
Florist Dr 28562
Foggy Landing Rd 28560
Forbes Ave 28560
Ford St 28560
Foreman St 28560
Forerunner Ct 28562
Forest Dr 28562
Forest Oaks Dr 28562
Forest Park Dr 28562
Forsythe Ln 28560
Fort Rd 28560
Fort Place Ct 28562
Fort Totten Dr 28560
Fowlers Ln 28560
Fox Chase Rd & Vlg 28562
Foxhorn Rd 28562
Foxwood Trl 28560
Frances Ave 28562
Franklin Ave 28560
Franks Ave 28560
Freeport Ct 28560
Friburg Rd 28562
Friendly Ave 28562
E Front St 28560
S Front St
1-499 28560
500-899 28562
Frontier Ln 28562
Frost Ct 28560
Fulcher Ln 28562
G St 28560
Gables Rd 28562
Galeashe Rd 28562
Galloway Rd & St 28560
Gangplank Rd 28562
Garden St 28560
Gardner Aly 28560
Garfield St 28560
Garner Rd 28560
Gary Thomas Rd 28560
Garys Ln 28562
Gaskins Rd 28560
Gaston Blvd 28560
Gaston Ct 28562
Gatewood Dr 28562
Geer Ct 28562
General Branch Dr 28562
Geneva Ct & Rd 28562
Gentry Cv 28562
George St
300-399 28562
400-1199 28560
Georgia Ave 28560
Gethsemane Church Rd 28562
Gibbs Rd 28560
Gladewood Cir 28560
Gladiola Dr 28562
Glenbrook Ln 28562
Glenburnie Dr 28560
N Glenburnie Rd 28560
S Glenburnie Rd
100-198 28560
200-1199 28560
1200-1900 28562
1851-1851 28561
1901-2199 28562
1902-2198 28562
Glenn Dr 28562
Glenwood Ave 28562
Gloucester Dr 28562
Gold Ct 28560
Golden Rd 28560
Golden Acres Rd 28560
Goldfinch Ln 28560
Goldsboro St 28560
Gondolier Dr 28560
Goose Creek Rd 28562
Gordon Ave 28560
Grace Ave
2000-2299 28560
2300-2500 28562
2502-2698 28562
N Grace Ave 28562
Grace St 28560
Gracie Farms Rd 28560
Grant Ct 28562
Grantham Pl 28560
E Grantham Rd 28560
W Grantham Rd 28562
Granville Ct 28562
Graves St 28562
Great Inagua Ct 28560
Green Ave 28562
Green St 28560
Green Park Ct & Ter 28560
Green Springs Rd 28560
Green Trees Dr 28560
Greenbrier Ct & Pkwy 28562
Greensboro St 28560
Greenside Ct 28562
Greenview Rd 28562
Greenwood Dr 28562
Grenada Ct 28560
Grenville Ave 28560
Grenville Ct 28562
Greywood Ln 28562
Griffin Ave
2100-2299 28560
2300-2499 28562
Grooms Dr 28560
Grouse Ct 28562
Grove Ln 28562
Guilford Ct 28562
Guion St 28560
Gulf Stream Ct 28560
Gull Ln 28560
Gull Pt 28562
Gum St 28560
Gurten St 28562
Gus Ln 28562
H St 28560
Hale Rd 28560
Half Moon Rd 28560
Halifax Cir 28562
Hall Rd 28560
Halls Bluff Ln 28560
Halls Creek Rd 28560
Hamilton Dr 28562
Hampton Way 28562
Hancock St
200-399 28562
400-699 28560
Hanes Farm Rd 28562
Harbor Ctr 28562
Harbor Dr 28560
Harbor Walk 28562
Harbor Hut 28562
Harbor Island Rd 28562
Harbortown Villas 28562
Harbour Master Villas 28560
Harbour Pointe Dr 28560
Harbourside Dr 28560
Hardee Farms Dr 28562
Hardison Rd 28560
Hardy Ave & St 28560
Hare Holw 28560
Harkers Way 28562
Harrison St 28560
Hart Dr 28560

Hartford Ave 28562
Harvard Way 28562
Hatcher Rd 28562
Hatties Ln 28560
Havenwood Ln 28562
Hawkes Pt 28560
Hawks Bluff Dr 28560
Hawks Pond Rd 28562
Hawksbill Ct 28560
Hawthorne Rd 28562
Haywood Pl 28560
Haywood Creek Dr 28562
Haywood Farms Rd 28562
Hazel Ave 28560
Hazeldale Ln 28560
Health Dr 28560
Hearthside Ct 28560
Heather Ct 28562
Heckathorne Dr 28560
Hedgerow Cir 28562
Helen Ave, Dr & Ln 28560
Helm Dr 28560
Hemlock Dr & Rd 28560
Henderson Ave
2000-2299 28560
2300-2499 28562
Henna Pl 28562
Heritage Dr 28562
Hermitage Rd 28562
Hickory St 28562
Hickory Hills Ct 28560
Hidden Dr 28562
Hidden Harbor Dr 28562
Hidden Pond Dr 28562
High St 28560
W High St 28562
High School Dr 28560
Highland Ave 28562
Highland Rd 28560
E & W Hightree Ln 28562
Hilda Dr 28562
Hill St 28560
Hill Randolf Ln 28562
Hillandale Rd 28562
Hillard Rd 28562
Hillcrest Rd 28562
Hillmont Rd 28562
Hills Ct & Dr 28562
Hillsboro Dr 28562
Hines Dr 28562
Hinson Ln 28560
Hogan Rd 28560
Hoke St 28560
Holland Dr 28560
Holly St 28560
Holly Berry Rd 28560
E Holly Ridge Rd 28562
Holstein Dr 28562
Homestead Dr 28562
Honeysuckle Ct 28560
Hoods Creek Dr 28562
Hopewell Ct 28562
Horgen Ct 28562
Horse Shoe Bnd 28562
Horseshoe Rd 28562
Hospital Dr 28560
Hotel Dr 28562
Hound Cir 28562
Hounds Trl 28562
Howard St 28560
Howell Rd 28562
Hoyle Farm Rd 28560
Hudson Ln 28560
Hudson Park Rd 28560
Hughes Ln 28560
Hunt Club Ln 28562
Hunt Master Rd 28562
Huntcliff Rd 28560
Hunterfield Ln 28560
Hunters Rd 28562
Hunters Landing Dr 28562
Hunting Wood Ln 28560
Hurricane Ct 28560
Hyacinth Ln 28562
Hyde Ct 28562
Hydes Cor 28562

Hyman Ct & Rd 28562
I St 28560
Ibis Ln 28560
Indigo Ln 28562
Industrial Dr 28562
Inge Ct 28562
Innisbrook Ct & Ln 28562
Inverness Ct 28562
Ipock Ln 28562
Ironwood Ln 28562
Iverson Ln 28562
Ives Ave 28562
Ivy Ct 28562
Jack Dail Rd 28560
Jack Rabbit Ln 28562
Jackson St 28560
Jade Ct 28562
Jamaicanwood Ln 28562
James St 28560
James Arthur Ave 28560
Jamestown Ct 28562
Jarvis St 28560
Jasper Dr 28562
Jefferson Ave 28560
Jenny Lisa Ln 28560
Jeri Dr 28560
Jessie Ln 28560
Jewell Ct 28560
S Jimmies Creek Dr 28562
Jimmys Rd 28560
John St 28560
John Patt Rd 28562
John Willis Rd 28562
Johnson St 28560
Johnson Point Rd 28560
Johnston Ln 28562
Jolly Roger Ct 28560
Jones St 28562
Jones Farm Rd 28562
Jordan Dr 28562
Joshua Norman Dr 28562
Joshwood Dr 28560
Jr Rd 28560
Juanita Ln 28560
Jubilee Pl 28560
Judge Manly Dr 28562
Julia Clay St 28560
Jura Ct 28562
Justin Dr 28562
K St 28560
Kaitlyn Ln 28562
Kale Rd 28560
Karen Dr 28562
Karen St 28560
Karissa Ct 28560
Kea Ct 28562
Keener Ave 28560
Keith Cir 28562
Kelly Ln & Rd 28560
Kelso Rd 28562
Kenmore Ct 28560
Kennedy Ave & Dr 28560
Kensington Park Dr 28560
Kestrel Ct 28560
Ketch Ct 28562
Kilmarnock St 28560
Kilroy St 28560
Kimberly Rd 28562
King St 28560
King Neck Rd 28560
Kingdom Way 28560
Kings Way 28562
Kingsmill Ct 28562
Kinnakeet Ln 28562
Kinnett Blvd 28560
Kinston St 28560
Kirolina Pl 28560
Kit Ct 28562
Knights Ct 28562
Knollwood Ct 28562
Knotline Rd 28562
Kriens Ct 28562
Lafitte Way 28560
Lagoon Rd 28562
Lagrange St 28560
Lake Pointe Rd 28562

Lake Tyler Dr 28560
Lake View Dr 28560
Lakemere Dr 28562
Lakeshore Dr 28562
Lakeside Green Dr 28560
Lancewood Ct 28562
Lancy Ln 28562
Landmark Cir 28560
Landscape Dr 28562
Lantern Ln 28562
Lanyard Ln 28560
Lapis Ct 28562
Lariat Cir 28562
Lark St 28560
Larkspar Ct 28562
Laroque Ln 28560
Lathams Battery Dr 28562
Laura Dr 28562
Laurel St
100-199 28560
1400-1599 28562
Laurel Valley Dr 28562
Lauren Ct 28562
Lavenham Rd 28562
Lawson St 28560
Leaf Ct 28562
Leaf Ln 28560
S Lee Rd 28560
Lee Landing Rd 28560
Lees Ave 28560
Lees Lake Dr 28562
Leeward Dr
900-999 28562
1000-1099 28560
Lefringhouse Ln 28562
Leonard Dr 28560
Lewis Dr 28560
Lewis Farm Rd 28560
Lexington Cir 28562
Liberty St 28562
Lichen Ln 28562
Liestal Ln 28562
Lighthouse Ln 28560
Lilliana Ct 28562
Lilliput Dr 28562
Lima Rd 28562
Lincoln St 28560
Linden St 28560
Linksiders Rd 28562
Linson Rd 28560
Linwood Ln 28560
Lisa Ln 28560
Little Lake Cir 28560
Little Rossie Rd 28560
Llewellyn Dr 28562
Loblolly Ln 28562
Lochbridge Dr 28562
Locklear Dr 28560
Lodge Dr 28562
Lofland Way 28562
Lombardi Cir 28562
Longleaf Dr 28560
Longleaf Ln 28560
Longview Dr 28562
Longwood Dr 28562
Lookout Ln 28562
Lopez Ct 28560
Louisia Mae Way 28560
Louisiana Ave 28560
Lowell St 28562
Lowes Blvd 28562
Lucerne Way 28560
Luferry Rd 28560
Lugano Rd 28562
Luke Ct 28560
Lupton Ln 28560
Lynchfield Dr 28562
Lynden Ln 28560
Lynn St 28562
Lynwood Dr 28560
Mack Scott Ave 28560
Macon Ct 28562
Macy Ct 28562
Madam Moores Ln 28562
Madera Ct 28562
Madison Ave 28562

Magellan Dr 28560
Maggie Ln 28560
Magnolia Dr 28562
Magnolia Ln 28560
Mahaffey Ct & Ln 28562
Main St 28560
Mallard Ln 28560
Mallard Cove Lndg & Rd 28562
Mandy Ln 28562
Manila Ln 28560
Manning Rd 28562
Manteo Ct 28562
Maple St 28560
Mapleleaf St 28560
Margo Ct 28562
Margret Ct 28560
Marina Dr 28560
Marina Rd 28562
Marina Townes Dr 28560
Mariners Ct 28562
Marion Dr 28562
Market St 28560
Marsh Dr 28560
Martin Dr 28562
Mary Jane Ln 28560
Mason Cir 28562
Massachusetts Rd 28562
Masters Court Dr 28562
Matthews Ln 28562
Matties Ln 28562
May St 28562
Mcarthur Ave 28560
Mcbride Pl 28560
Mccarthy Blvd 28562
Mcdaniel Ln 28562
Mcilwean Farm Rd 28560
Mckinley Ave 28562
Meadow Court Dr 28562
Meadow View Dr 28562
Meadowbrook Ave & Dr 28562
Meadowinds Dr 28560
Meadows St 28560
Mechanic St 28560
Medical Park Ave 28562
Mellen Ct & Rd 28562
Melody Ln 28562
Mercer Ave 28562
Meridian Ct 28562
Merriwood Ct 28562
Metcalf St
200-399 28562
400-699 28560
Michael Dr 28560
Michele Dr 28560
Mickelson Dr 28560
Mickey Ct 28562
Middle St
100-300 28560
233-233 28563
301-699 28560
302-698 28560
Midway Dr 28560
Midyette Ave 28560
Mill Brooke Dr 28562
Mill Dam Rd 28560
Mill Pond Rd 28560
Mill Run Dr 28562
Millcreek Ln 28560
Miller St 28560
Millinder Ln 28560
Miramar Ct 28560
Mistique Ct 28560
Mitchell Cir 28562
Mocha Ct 28560
Mockingbird Ln 28562
Mom Ln 28562
Mona Passage Ct 28560
Moncks Ct 28562
Monroe Dr 28562
Monterey Cir 28562
Montgomery Ct 28562
Montreux Ln 28562
Moonlight Lake Dr 28560
Moore Ave 28562

Moore Swamp Rd 28560
Morgan Ln 28562
Morgan Swamp Rd 28560
Morning Star Dr 28562
Morton Rd 28562
Moses Griffin Ln 28562
Moss Bnd 28562
Mount Pleasant Rd 28560
Mourning Dove Trl 28560
Moye Rd 28562
Muirfield Ct & Pl 28560
Mulberry Ln 28562
Mullen Rd 28560
Mulligan Ct 28562
Murdock Way 28560
Murphy Rd 28562
Murray St 28560
Myrtle Ave 28560
Myrtle Grove Rd 28562
Nassau Ct 28560
Nathan Tisdale Ln 28562
National Ave 28560
National Court Dr 28560
Nature Ct 28560
Nautical Dr 28560
Nautillus Ct 28560
Navidad Bank Ct 28560
W Nc 55 Hwy 28562
Nc Highway 55 E 28560
Nc Highway 55 W 28562
Neeley Ln 28560
Neely Ln 28560
Neely St 28562
Nelson St 28562
Neuchatel Ct & Rd 28562
Neuse Ave 28560
Neuse Blvd
1300-2399 28560
2400-2899 28562
2900-3699 28560
Neuse Dr 28560
Neuse Rd 28560
Neuse Cliffs Cir, Dr & Rd 28560
Neuse Forrest Ave 28560
Neuse Harbour Blvd 28560
Neuse Landing Dr 28560
Neuse River Dr 28560
New St 28560
New Bern Ave 28562
New Hampshire Ln 28562
New Liberty Rd 28562
Newman Rd 28562
Newood Dr 28562
Newsome Dr 28562
Newton Dr 28560
Nicklaus Dr 28562
Nina Ln 28562
Nj Scott Ave 28560
Noah Ln 28560
Norbury Dr 28562
Nordhoff St 28560
Norman Ct 28560
Norman Rd 28562
North Ave 28560
Norwich Rd 28562
Norwood St 28562
Nova Ct 28560
Nunn St 28560
Nursery Rd 28560
Nydegg Ct & Rd 28562
Nyon Ct & Rd 28562
O Hara Dr 28562
Oak Dr 28562
Oak St 28560
Oak Hill Ln 28562
Oak Leaf Bnd 28560
Oak Meadow Dr 28560
Oakdale Ave 28562
Oakgrove Ct 28562
Oakland Ave 28560
Oakleaf Ct 28560
Oakley Dr 28560
Oakmont Cir 28562
Oaks Rd 28560
Oakview Dr 28562

Oakwood Ave & Dr 28560
Old Airport Rd 28562
Old Cherry Point Rd
100-199 28562
200-1699 28560
1620-1620 28564
1700-4798 28560
1701-4799 28560
Old Cross Rd 28560
Old Pollocksville Rd 28562
Old Us 70 Hwy W 28562
Old Us Highway 70 W 28562
Old Vanceboro Rd 28560
Olde Towne Pl 28562
Olony Cir 28560
Olympia Rd N 28560
Onslow Ct 28562
Onyx Ln 28562
Opal St 28560
Oscar Dr 28562
Osprey Ct 28560
Otter Creek Rd 28560
Outrigger Rd 28562
Owls Nest Ct 28562
Oxford Ln 28562
Palisades Way 28560
E & W Palmer Dr 28560
Parisher Dr 28560
Park Ave 28560
Park Dr 28562
Parker Ct & Rd 28562
Parkwood Ct 28562
Parsons Ave 28560
Partridge Dr 28562
N Pasteur St 28560
Pate Rd 28562
Patten Rd 28560
Pattswood Dr & Rd 28560
Paula Ln 28562
Pavie Ave 28560
Peace Rd 28562
Peace And Plenty Ct 28560
Peach Tree Ln 28562
Pearson Cir & St 28562
Pebblebrook Dr 28562
Pecan Ct 28562
Pecan Grove Ct 28562
Pecan Ridge Dr 28562
Pelican Dr 28560
Pella Ln 28562
Pembroke Ave 28562
Pender St 28560
Penn St 28562
Pennyroyal Ct & Rd 28562
Peppercorn Ct & Rd 28562
Percy Dr 28560
Peregrine Ridge Dr 28560
Periwinkle Pl 28562
Perry Meadow Dr 28562
Perrytown Rd 28562
Perrytown Loop Rd 28562
Petite Terre Ct 28560
Pettiford Ln 28560
Phillips Ave 28562
N Phillips Rd 28560
Pickett Ln 28562
Pier Pt 28562
Pillory Cir 28562
Pilot Pl 28562
W Pine Cir, Rd & St 28560
Pine Cove Rd 28562
Pine Crest Rd 28562
Pine Needle Pl 28562
Pine Ridge Ave 28560
Pine Valley Dr 28562
Pinecrest Ave 28560
Pinehurst Dr 28562
Pinetree Dr & Ln 28562
Pinewood Dr & Ln 28562
Pioneer Trl 28560
Pirates Rd 28562
Plantation Dr 28562
Plantation Oaks Dr 28560
E & W Pleasant Hill Dr 28562
Plum St 28560

Plymouth Ct 28560
Plymouth Dr 28562
Point Ct 28560
Pollock St
100-499 28560
500-1099 28562
1101-1199 28562
1200-1299 28560
Pompano Dr 28560
Pond Pine Trl 28562
Poplar St 28560
Port Dr 28560
Port Royal Ct 28560
Portia Ct 28560
Portside Ln 28562
Portsmouth Ct 28562
Possum Trot Rd 28562
Powell St 28560
Preakness Pl 28562
Premier Dr 28562
Prescott Rd 28560
Primrose Ct 28560
Princeton Ln 28562
Professional Dr 28560
Purifoy Rd & St 28560
Quail Holw 28560
Quailwoods Dr 28560
Quarterdeck 28562
Quartre Cir 28560
Queen St 28560
Queen Anne Ln 28560
Queens Ct 28562
Quincy Ct 28560
Race Track Rd 28562
Raft Rd 28562
Rail Ct 28560
Railroad St 28560
Rainmaker Dr 28562
Raleigh St 28560
Ramonas Lake Ct 28560
Ramsey Ln 28560
Randomwood Ln 28562
Rankin Ct 28560
Rawley Rd 28560
Red Fox Rd 28562
Red Oak Dr 28562
Red Robin Ln 28562
Red Sail Rd 28560
Red Shoulder Ln 28560
Redwood Ln 28560
Redwood Ter 28562
Reedy Rd 28562
Reinach Ln 28562
Reisenstein St 28560
Remona Ct 28560
Rennys Creek Dr 28560
Reunion Pointe Ln 28562
Rhem Ave 28560
Rhem St 28560
Richard Ct 28560
Richardson Rd 28562
Richmond Ct 28562
N Ridge Rd 28560
Ridgewood Trl 28560
River Cv 28560
River Dr 28560
River Ln 28562
River Rd 28562
River Bluffs Dr 28560
River Island Rd 28562
River Reach Ct 28560
River Ridge Rd 28560
Riverbank Ln 28562
Riverdale Rd 28562
N Rivershore Dr 28560
Riverside Dr 28560
Rivertides Ln 28562
Riverview Dr 28560
Riverwalk Ln 28562
Riverwood Ln 28560
Riviera Ct 28562
Roanoke Ave 28562
Robbie Ln 28562
Robertson Ln 28560
E & W Rock Creek Dr, Ln & Rd 28562

Rockledge Rd 28562
Rocky Run Rd 28562
Rogers Ct 28562
Rolling Ln 28560
Rollingwood Dr 28562
Rollover Creek Rd 28562
E Rose St 28560
Rosemary Rd 28562
Rossie Rd 28562
Roundtree St 28560
Roxboro Ct 28562
Royal Pines Dr 28560
Runaway Bay 28562
Ruth Ave 28560
Sage Close 28562
Sailors Ct 28562
Saint Andrews Cir 28562
Saint John St 28562
Saint Paul St 28562
Saints Delight Church Rd 28560
Salt Cay Ct 28560
Salvo Dr 28562
Sampson St 28560
San Juan Rd 28560
Sand Hill Rd 28560
Sand Ridge Rd 28560
Sanderling Ln 28562
Sanders Ln 28562
Sandhurst Rd 28562
Sandpiper Ct 28562
Sandy Chase Rd 28560
Sandy Curve Dr 28560
Sandy Point Rd 28560
Sandy Trail Rd 28560
Santa Lucia Rd 28560
Santo Domingo Ct 28560
Sarahs Cir 28562
Saratoga Ln 28562
Sardis Ln 28562
Satterfield Dr 28560
Savannah Rd 28560
Savoy Dr 28562
Sawgrass Ct 28560
Scamozzi Dr 28562
Schooner Ct 28560
Scott St 28560
Scott Farm Ln 28562
Scott Town Rd 28560
Scotts Creek Dr 28562
Sea Holly Ct 28560
Seabiscuit Ln 28562
Seafarers Ct 28562
Seafoam Ct 28562
Seifert Rd 28560
Sellhorn Blvd 28562
Selover Ave 28560
Serenity Ct 28560
Sermons Blvd 28560
Sextant Ct 28562
Shadetree Dr 28560
Shadow Brook Ln 28562
Shady Ln 28562
Shady Oaks Ct 28562
Shady Side Ln 28562
Sheri Ct 28560
Sherman Point Ln 28562
Sherwood Ave 28562
Shingle Brook Rd 28560
Shinnecock Ct & Dr 28562
Ship Trl 28560
Shippoint Ave 28560
Shipyard Pt 28562
Shoo Fly Rd 28560
Shore Hills Rd 28560
Shoreline Dr 28562
Shoreview Dr 28562
Side Saddle Ln 28562
Sienna Pl & Trl 28562
Sierra Dr 28560
Sim Dawson Rd 28562
Simmons St 28560
Simmons Loop Rd 28562
Sir James Ln 28562
Skinner Ct 28560
Skippers Ln 28562
Sky Sail Blvd 28560
Slaughterhouse Rd 28562
Sloop Ct 28560
Smith St 28560
Smokey Dr 28560
Snead Rd 28560
Solomito Ct 28560
Somerset Ct 28562
Sothel Ct 28562
South St 28560
Southern Hills Dr 28562
Spar Ct 28560
Sparta Way 28562
Spencer Ave
2305EXT-2305EXT 28562
1300-2299 28560
2300-2499 28562
Spiegel St 28562
Spivey St 28560
Split Oak Way 28562
Spring Garden Rd 28562
Spring Green Pass 28562
Spring Hope Church Rd 28560
Spring Ridge Ct 28562
Springwater Ct 28560
Springwood Dr 28562
Spruce Ct 28562
Squirrel Ln 28560
St Gallen Ct 28562
Stacy Ln 28560
Stadiem Dr 28560
Stadler Dr 28560
Stafford Ct 28562
Staffordshire Dr 28562
Stallings Pkwy 28562
Stanberry Hick Rd 28562
Stanley St 28560
Stapleford Rd 28560
Starboard Dr 28562
Stately Pines Rd 28560
Staten Rd 28562
Station House Rd 28562
Steeple Chase Dr 28562
Sterling Dr 28562
Stern Ct 28560
Stevenson Rd 28562
Stewart Blvd 28560
Stillwater Ct 28562
Stillwood Ct 28560
Stimpson St 28562
Stone Hawk Ln 28560
Stonewall Cir 28562
Stoneyhill Trl 28560
Stony Branch Rd 28562
Stony Brook Dr 28562
Strange Ln 28560
Stratford Rd 28562
Stratton Dr 28562
Street Field Rd 28562
Sumatra Ct 28560
Sunrise Way 28560
Sunset Rd 28562
Surrey Ln 28562
Sursee Ct 28562
Susan Dr 28562
Sutton St 28560
Suttons Ave 28560
Swallow Ct 28560
Swashbuckle Ct 28560
Sweet Gum Way 28562
Sweetbay Dr 28560
Sweetbriar Ct 28562
Swiss Rd 28560
Sycamore St 28562
Taberna Cir & Way 28562
Tack House Rd 28562
Taliaferro Ln 28560
Tammy Ct 28560
Tanglewood Ct 28562
Tar Lndg 28562
Tara Hills Dr 28562
Tarragon Ct 28562
Tartan Ct 28560
Tatum Dr 28560
Taylor St 28560
Teachey Ct 28562
Teakwood Dr 28562
Tebo Rd 28562
Ten Tall Trl 28560
Tenella Rd 28562
Terminal Dr 28562
Terrapin Ct 28560
Territorial Rd 28560
Terthol Rd 28560
Tesie Trl 28562
Teufen Rd 28562
Thatcher Ct 28562
Theodore Ln 28560
Thomas Ave 28562
Thomas Sugg Dr 28560
Thorpe Abbotts Ln 28562
E Thurman Rd 28560
W Thurman Rd 28562
Thyme Ct 28562
Ticino Ct & Rd 28562
Tiger Woods Pl 28560
Timberwolf Ct 28560
Timothy Ct 28562
Tina Ct 28562
Tobacco Rd 28562
Tobiano Dr 28562
Token Ct 28560
Toler Rd 28560
Tomlinson Blvd 28562
Towne Woods Dr 28562
Trade Winds Rd 28560
Tram Rd 28562
Trappers Trl 28560
Traveller Ln 28562
Travers Ln 28562
Tree Ln 28562
Tremayne Dr 28560
Trent Ave 28560
Trent Blvd 28560
Trent Ct
A1-A10 28562
A2-195-A2-200 28562
B2-201-B2-206 28562
B11-B18 28562
C2-207-C2-212 28562
C19-C28 28562
D2-213-D2-218 28562
D29-D36 28562
E37-E46 28562
F47-F56 28562
G57-G66 28562
H67-H76 28562
I77-I86 28562
J87-J96 28562
K97-K106 28562
L107-L116 28562
M117-M122 28562
N123-N128 28562
O129-O134 28562
P135-P140 28562
Q140-Q146 28562
R147-R152 28562
S153-S158 28562
T159-T164 28562
U165-U170 28562
V171-V176 28562
W177-W182 28562
X183-X188 28562
Y189-Y194 28562
1-211 28562
Trent Rd 28562
Trent St 28562
Trent Farm Rd 28562
Trent Pines Dr 28562
Trent River Dr 28562
Trent Shores Dr 28562
Trent Villa Landing Dr 28562
Trent Woods Dr & Rd 28562
Trevino Ln 28560
Trilliums Hideaway 28562
Trinidad Ct 28560
Trinity Dr 28560
Trolley Ct 28560
Truitt Rd 28560
Tryon Rd 28560
Tryon Palace Dr 28560
Tucker St 28560
Tupelo Trl 28562
Turnberry Ct 28562
Turtle Bay Dr 28562
Tuscan Ln 28560
Tuscarora Rhems Rd 28562
Two Lakes Trl 28560
Two Putt Ct 28560
Tyler Ryan Trl 28562
Tyndall Ln 28562
Union Ct 28562
E Us 70 Hwy 28562
Us Highway 17 N 28560
Us Highway 17 S 28562
Us Highway 70 E
100-4000 28560
Us Highway 70 E
4001-7999 28562
4002-8098 28560
Uster Ct 28562
Vail St 28560
Valais Ct 28562
Van Moreadith Rd 28562
Vaud Ct 28562
Venturi Dr 28560
Vernon Dr 28562
Victoria Way 28562
Victory Cir 28560
Vida Ln 28560
Village Rd 28560
Village Way 28562
Village Green Ct & Dr 28562
Vineyard Dr 28562
Virginia Ave, Ct & Ln 28562
Viridian Trce 28562
Wadkins Blvd 28560
Wadsworth Ln 28562
Wahoo Dr 28560
Wake St 28562
Wakefield Dr 28562
Walden Ct & Rd 28562
Walker Rd 28560
Wallace Meadows Ln 28560
Walnut Rd 28562
Walnut Way 28560
Walt Bellamy Dr 28562
Walter Dr 28562
Walter Ln 28560
Walton Dr 28562
Wanchese Way 28560
Wanda Ave 28562
Washington Cir, Ct & St 28560
Washington Post Rd
100-200 28560
201-457 28562
202-450 28560
459-461 28562
463-2199 28562
500-2198 28560
Water St 28560
Water View Rd 28560
Waterleaf Pt 28562
Waters St 28560
Waterscape Way 28562
Watson Ave 28560
Weathersby Dr 28562
Weatherstone Park Rd 28562
Wedgewood Dr 28562
Wehoe Rd 28560
Wellons Blvd 28560
Wentworth Ct 28562
Wesley Dr 28562
West St 28560
Westchester Dr 28562
Westerly Rd 28560
Westminster Dr 28562
Westover Ln 28562
Westward Ct 28562
Westwood Ct 28562
Wetherington Rd 28562
Wexford Pl 28562
White St 28560
White Ash Ln 28562
White Oak Dr 28562
Whitehurst Rd 28560
Whitford Ln 28562
Whooping Crane Ln 28562
Widgeon Cir 28562
Wilcox Rd 28562
Wild Turkey Rd 28562
Wildlife Rd 28560
Wildwood Dr 28562
Wildwood Pointe Dr 28560
Williams Ln 28560
Williams Rd 28562
Williams St 28560
Williamson Dr 28562
Willis Rd 28560
Willow Tree St 28560
Willowbrook Ct 28562
Wilmington St 28560
Wilson St 28560
W Wilson Creek Dr 28562
Wilson Point Rd 28562
Winchester Ct 28562
Wind Ct & Way 28560
Wind Hill Ct 28560
Windjammer Villas 28560
Windley St 28560
Windsor Dr 28562
Windward Dr 28560
Windy Trl 28560
Wingate Dr 28562
Winged Foot Ct 28562
Winter Pl 28562
Woodbrook Dr 28562
Woodcrest Cir 28560
Woodcroft Ct 28562
Woodland Ave
2000-2299 28560
2300-2599 28562
2601-3199 28562
Woods Cir & Run 28562
Woodvine Ct 28562
Woolard Trl 28560
Wyndsor Park Dr 28562
Yacht Ct 28560
Yacht Club Dr 28562
Yadkin Ct 28562
Yarmouth Rd 28562
Ymca Ln 28560
York Ct & St 28562
Yucca Ln 28562
Zeb Rd 28560
Zurich Pl 28562

NUMBERED STREETS

1st Ave 28560
N 1st Ave 28560
1st St
100-299 28562
300-499 28560
2nd Ave 28560
3rd Ave 28560
5th St 28560
7th St 28560
8th St 28560
9th St 28560

PINEHURST NC

General Delivery 28374

POST OFFICE BOXES MAIN OFFICE STATIONS AND BRANCHES

Box No.s
1 - 2020 28370
205 - 2000 28374
2101 - 2158 28370
2200 - 2200 28374
2201 - 2458 28370
3000 - 28374 28374

NAMED STREETS

Abbottsford Dr 28374
Abington Dr 28374
Adams Cir 28374
Airdrie Ct 28374
Airport Rd 28374
Alexander Ln 28374
Alpine Pl 28374
Amboy Pl 28374
American Legion Ln 28374
Apaloosa Pl 28374
Apawamis Cir, Pl & Rd 28374
Appin Ct 28374
Applecross Rd 28374
Aronimink Ln 28374
Ash Ct 28374
Asheville Way 28374
Ashkirk Dr 28374
Augusta Way 28374
Augusta National Dr 28374
Aviemore Ct & Dr 28374
Azalea Rd 28374
Ballybunion Ln 28374
Baltusrol Ln 28374
Bangor Ln 28374
Bankfoot Dr 28374
Barkley Ln 28374
Barons Dr 28374
Barrett Rd E 28374
Barton Hills Ct 28374
Batten Ct 28374
Bay Ct 28374
Beasley Dr 28374
Beaver Ln 28374
Beckett Rdg 28374
Bedford Cir 28374
Bel Air Dr 28374
Belair Ct & Pl 28374
Belmont Ct 28374
Bent Tree Ct 28374
Berwick Ct 28374
Berwyn Ct 28374
Beryl Cir, Ct & Ln 28374
Beula Hill Rd N 28374
Biltmore Pl 28374
Birkdale Dr & Way 28374
Blair Ct & Pl 28374
Blake Blvd
1-99 28374
80-80 28370
100-498 28374
101-499 28374
Blue Rd 28374
Board Branch Rd 28374
Bob O Link Rd 28374
Boswell Pl 28374
Bradley Ln 28374
Braemar Rd 28374
Brandon Trl 28374
Brechin Ct 28374
Briarwood Cir & Pl 28374
Bridle Path Cir 28374
Brinyan Ct 28374
Broadmoor Pl 28374
Brook Hollow Dr 28374
Brookfield Dr 28374
Brookhaven Rd 28374
Brookline Dr 28374
Browns Ct 28374
Brunswick Ln 28374
Buckingham Pl 28374
Bur Ct & Pl 28374
Burning Tree Pl & Rd 28374
Butte Ct 28374
Cabot Cir 28374
Caddell Rd 28374
Calhoun Ln 28374
Camden Pl 28374
Camelia Pl 28374
Cameron Ln 28374
Campbell Rd 28374
Canter Ln & Pl 28374
Canterbury Cir 28374
Cardinal Run 28374
Carolina Vista Dr 28374
Carrick Ct 28374
Carroll Ct 28374
Carson Way 28374
Carter Ln 28374
Castlecombe Ct 28374
Castlewood Ln 28374
Catalpa Ln N & S 28374
Cedar Ct & Ln 28374
Cedar Wood Ct 28374
Central Park Ave 28374
Chalford Pl 28374
Chatham Ln 28374
Cherokee Rd 28374
Cherry Ln 28374
Cherry Hill Dr & Pl 28374
Chester Way 28374
Chesterfield Dr 28374
Chestertown Dr 28374
Chestnut Ct & Ln 28374
Chinquapin Rd 28374
Chipping Campden Way 28374
Choke Cherry Ln 28374
Clarendon Ln 28374
Clubhouse Dr 28374
Cochrane Castle Cir 28374
Cohassett Ln 28374
Coldstream Ln 28374
Collett Ln 28374
Colonial Ln 28374
Colonial Pines Cir 28374
Colt Ct 28374
Comanced Rd 28374
Community Rd 28374
Cone Ct 28374
Cosgrove Rd 28374
Craig Rd 28374
Creekside Ct 28374
Cruden Bay Cir 28374
Crystal Ct 28374
Culdee Rd 28374
Culross Ct 28374
Cumberland Dr 28374
Cumnock Ct 28374
Curtis Ln 28374
Cypress Ln 28374
Cypress Point Dr 28374
Dalcross Ct 28374
Dalrymple Rd 28374
Danville Ln 28374
Dawn Rd 28374
Deepdale Ln 28374
Deerwood Ct & Ln 28374
Derby Dr 28374
Deuce Dr 28374
Devon Dr 28374
Diamond Head Dr S 28374
Dogwood Rd & Ter 28374
Donald Ross Dr 28374
Doral Ct & Dr 28374
Dove Run 28374
Dowd Cir 28374
Driving Range Rd 28374
Duncan Ln 28374
Dundee Rd 28374
Dunedin Cir 28374
Dungarvan Ln 28374
Dunvegan Ct 28374
Eastman Pl 28374
Edgewater Pl 28374
Edinburgh Dr & Ln 28374
El Dorado St 28374
Eldorado Ln 28374
Elkington Way 28374
Elkton Dr 28374
Ellen Ct 28374
Ellington Dr 28374
Elmhurst Pl 28374
Emerald Ln 28374
Emerald Necklace Ln 28374
Evans Ln 28374
Everett Rd 28374
Evergreen Ct 28374
Fairway Cir, Ct & Dr 28374
Farmington Ln 28374
Ferguson Rd 28374
Fields Rd 28374
Filly Ct, Dr & Pl 28374

Firestone Dr & Ln 28374
First Village Dr 28374
Flint Ct 28374
Florence Dr 28374
Forest Dr & Ln 28374
Forest Hills Dr & Ln 28374
Fortrose Cir 28374
Fox Hollow Ct & Rd 28374
Fox Hound Run 28374
Fox Run Rd 28374
Frye Rd 28374
Fur Ct E & W 28374
Furlong Pl 28374
Gadsten Ct 28374
Gaeta Dr 28374
Gallop Ct 28374
Galston Ct 28374
Gambel Ct 28374
Garden Villa Dr 28374
Garner Ln 28374
Georgia Ct 28374
Gerry Ct 28374
Gilbert Ct 28374
Gilmore Rd 28374
Gingham Ln & Pl 28374
Ginkgo Ct 28374
Glasgow Dr 28374
Glen Abbey Trl 28374
Glen Eagles Ln 28374
Glen Meadow Ct 28374
Glen Ross Dr 28374
Glenbarr Ct 28374
Golfers Way 28374
Grafton Ct 28374
Graham Rd & St 28374
Granger Dr 28374
Granville Dr 28374
Gray Fox Run 28374
Grayson Ln 28374
Greenbrier Ln 28374
Greencastle Dr 28374
Greenville Ln 28374
Grey Abbey Dr 28374
Greystones Ct 28374
Gull Ln 28374
Gun Club Rd 28374
Haddington Dr & Way 28374
Halkirk Dr 28374
Hall Ct 28374
Halter Pl 28374
Hampshire Ln 28374
Hampton Dr & Pl 28374
Harding Ct 28374
Harlow Rd 28374
Harness Pl 28374
Hawick Ct & Pl 28374
Hearthstone Pl & Rd 28374
Heather Ln 28374
Heatherhurst Pl 28374
Hempstead Way 28374
Hialeah Pl 28374
High Point Rd 28374
Hillard Rd 28374
Hillcrest Rd 28374
N Hills Rd 28374
Hobkirk Ct 28374
Holly Knl & Ln 28374
Holly Pines Dr & Ln 28374
Hollycrest Ln 28374
Horse Creek Run 28374
Hot Springs Ln 28374
Hunt St 28374
Huntington Valley Dr 28374
Ice Ct 28374
Idlewild Rd 28374
Innisbrook Pl 28374
Interlachon Ln 28374
Inverness Pl & Rd 28374
Inverness Lake Pl 28374
Inverrary Ct & Rd 28374
Invershin Ct 28374
Ivy Way 28374
Jade Ct 28374
James River Pl 28374
Juniper Ln 28374
Juniper Creek Blvd 28374

Kahkwa Trl 28374
Kelly Rd 28374
Kemper Woods Ct 28374
Kenilwood Ct 28374
Kenwood Ct 28374
Keswick Ln 28374
Kilberry Dr 28374
Kilbride Dr 28374
Killarney Ct 28374
Killearn Ct 28374
Killiney Ct 28374
Kilrea Ct 28374
Kinbuck Ct 28374
Kincaid Pl 28374
Kincraig Ct 28374
Kings Xing 28374
Kingswood Cir 28374
Kippen Ct 28374
Kirkhill Ct 28374
Kirkton Ct 28374
Knickerbocker Ln 28374
Knollwood Pl & Rd 28374
La Quinta Loop 28374
Lacosta Ln 28374
Laggan Ct 28374
Lagorce Pl 28374
Lake Ct 28374
Lake Dornoch Dr 28374
Lake Forest Dr, Ln & Pl SE & SW 28374
Lake Hills Rd 28374
Lake Pinehurst Villa 28374
Lake Point Dr 28374
Lake Shore Ct & Dr 28374
Lake View Dr E 28374
Lake Vista Ln 28374
Lakeside Ct & Ln 28374
Lakewood Dr 28374
Lamplighter Village Cir, Ct & Dr 28374
Lassiter Ln 28374
Lasswade Dr 28374
Laurel Ln & Rd 28374
Lee Ct 28374
Lenoir Ct 28374
Leven Links Ln 28374
Lima Ct 28374
Linden Ln & Rd 28374
Linton Ct 28374
Linville Dr 28374
Live Oak Ln 28374
Loblolly Ct 28374
Loch Lomond Ct 28374
Lochdon Ct 28374
Lochmere Dr 28374
Lochmoor Ct 28374
Lockerbie Ct 28374
Lockwinnock Ln 28374
Locust Ct 28374
Lodge Pole Ln 28374
Long Cove Dr 28374
Longleaf Dr E 28374
Lookaway Ln 28374
Lost Tree Rd 28374
Love Ln 28374
Love Fifteen Dr 28374
Love Forty Dr E & W 28374
Love Thirty Dr 28374
Macon Ln 28374
Magnolia Ave & Rd 28374
Maidstone Ct 28374
Mallard Ln 28374
Manakiki Ln 28374
Maples Ln & Rd 28374
Market Sq 28374
Marshall Pl 28374
Match Point Ave 28374
Maverick Pl 28374
Mccaskill Rd E & W 28374
Mcdairmid Rd 28374
Mcdonald Pl & Rd 28374
Mcfarland Rd 28374
Mcgrath Ln 28374
Mcintrye Rd 28374
Mckenzie Rd E 28374
Mckinnon Rd 28374

Mclean Rd 28374
Mcleod Rd 28374
Mcmichael Dr 28374
Mcnair Rd 28374
Mcqueen Pl & Rd 28374
Meadowlark Ln 28374
Medlin Rd 28374
Melfort Dr 28374
Melrose Dr 28374
Memorial Dr 28374
Merion Cir & Pl 28374
Merrywood Pl 28374
Meyer Ct 28374
Meyer Farm Dr 28374
Middlebury Ct & Rd 28374
Midland Dr, Ln, Rd & Trl 28374
Miles Ct 28374
Minikahada Trl 28374
Mitchell Ct 28374
Mockingbird Ct & Way 28374
Monmouth Ct & Pl 28374
Monroe Ln 28374
Montclair Ct & Ln 28374
Monteith Pl 28374
Monticello Dr 28374
Montrose Ct 28374
Moore Dr 28374
Morganton Rd 28374
Morris Ln 28374
Mount Washington Cir 28374
Muirfield Pl & Rd 28374
Mulbren Ct 28374
Muster Branch Rd 28374
Nashua Ct 28374
National Dr 28374
Nc Highway 5 S 28374
New Bedford Cir 28374
New Castle Pl 28374
Newberry Ln 28374
Norfolk Ct 28374
Northam Ct 28374
Nottingham Dr 28374
Oak Ct, Ln & Mdws 28374
Oak Hills Rd 28374
Oak Meadow Rd 28374
Oak Tree Ln 28374
Oakmont Cir & Rd 28374
Old Hunt Pl & Rd 28374
Olmsted Blvd 28374
Onyx Ln N & S 28374
Opal Ln 28374
Orange Rd 28374
Orrin Ct 28374
Osage Ln 28374
Ouimet Ln 28374
Overcup Ln 28374
Overpeck Ln 28374
Oxton Cir 28374
Pace Ct 28374
Page Dr, Rd & St 28374
Palm Ln 28374
Palmetto Rd 28374
Park Ct 28374
Parker Ln 28374
Parson Rd 28374
Passion Dr 28374
Peachtree Ln 28374
Pearl Ct 28374
Pebble Beach Pl 28374
Peebles Pl 28374
Perth Pl 28374
Petitt Ct 28374
Piedmont Ln 28374
Pierce Ct & Pl 28374
Pin Cherry Ln 28374
Pin Oak Ct 28374
Pine Ct 28374
Pine Linn 28374
Pine Meadows Pl & Rd 28374
Pine Orchard Ln & Pl 28374
Pine Valley Cir & Rd 28374
Pine Vista Dr 28374
Pinebrook Dr 28374
Pinehurst Mnr S 28374

Pinehurst Race Trak 28374
Pinehurst Trace Dr 28374
Pinewild Dr 28374
Pinto Ct 28374
Pinyon Cir, Ln & Rd 28374
Pitch Pine Ln 28374
Pitt Ct 28374
Polk Ct 28374
Pomeroy Dr 28374
Ponte Vedra Dr 28374
Post Ct 28374
Power Plant Rd 28374
Presbrey Ln 28374
Prestonfield Dr 28374
Prestwick Ct & Ln 28374
Prichard Ln 28374
Princeville Ln 28374
Quail Run 28374
Quail Hollow Dr 28374
Quail Lake Rd E & W 28374
Quaker Ridge Rd 28374
Queens Ct 28374
Quincy Pl 28374
Racquet Ln 28374
Raintree Ct 28374
Raleigh Dr 28374
Randolph Ct 28374
Rathlin Ct 28374
Rattlesnake Trl 28374
Red Cedar Ln 28374
Red Fox Run 28374
Regal Way 28374
Regional Cir & Dr 28374
Rein Pl 28374
Remington Ln 28374
Revere Ct 28374
Ridgeland St 28374
Ridgewood Pl & Rd 28374
Ritter Rd W 28374
Riverside Ct 28374
Riviera Dr 28374
Robin Ln 28374
Rockland Ln 28374
Roslin Ct 28374
Rossmore Ct 28374
Rothes Ct 28374
Royal County Down 28374
Royal Dornoch Ln 28374
Royal Dublin Downs 28374
Royal Troon Dr 28374
Ruby Ln 28374
Rutledge Ln 28374
Saddle Pl 28374
Safford Dr 28374
Saint Andrews Dr & Pl 28374
Saint Georges Dr 28374
Saint Mellions 28374
Sakonnet Trl 28374
Salem Dr & Ln 28374
Sandhills Cir & Pl 28374
Sarclet Ct 28374
Sassafras Ln 28374
Saunders Ln 28374
Sawgrass Pl 28374
Sawmill Ct & Rd 28374
Scarborough Pl 28374
Scioto Ln & Rd 28374
Scotscraig Ct 28374
Scott Ct, Ln & Rd 28374
Sedgefield Ln 28374
Sedgwyck Dr 28374
Seminole Pl 28374
Shadow Creek Ct 28374
Shamrock Way 28374
Shaw Rd 28374
Shenecossett Ln 28374
Sherwood Ct 28374
Short Rd 28374
Short Hills Ln 28374
Sodbury Ct 28374
Southern Hills Pl 28374
Spring Lake Dr & Rd 28374
Spring Valley Ct 28374
Spruce Ct & Ln 28374
Spur Pl & Rd 28374
Spyglass Ct 28374

Squires Ln 28374
Stallion Pl 28374
Stanton Cir 28374
Starlit Ct & Ln 28374
Statler Ln 28374
Sterling Ct 28374
Stickney Cir 28374
Stirrup Pl 28374
Stone Ct 28374
Stoneykirk Dr 28374
Stratford Pl 28374
Strathaven Ct & Dr 28374
Sugar Gum Ln 28374
Sugar Pine Dr 28374
Sulky Ln 28374
Sunny Ct 28374
Surry Cir & Ln 28374
Sweet Birch Ln 28374
Tall Timbers Dr 28374
Tall Trees Dr 28374
Talladale Ct 28374
Tamarisk Ln 28374
Tandem Dr 28374
Taylor Pl 28374
Tayport Ct 28374
Tewkesbury Ct 28374
Thompson Ln 28374
Thorne Rd 28374
Thunderbird Cir & Ln 28374
Timuquana Trl 28374
Toome Ct 28374
Topaz Ln 28374
Torrey Pines Ln & Pl 28374
Towhee Run 28374
Travis Ln 28374
Troon Dr 28374
Trotter Dr 28374
Troy Ct 28374
Tull Ln 28374
Turnberry Way 28374
Turnberry Wood 28374
Turner Rd 28374
Turtle Point Rd 28374
Tyler Way 28374
Us Highway 15 501 28374
Vail Pl 28374
Valley Rd 28374
Van Buren Ln 28374
Vardon Pl & Rd 28374
Vernon Ln 28374
Victoria Way 28374
Village Grn & Ln 28374
Village Green Rd 28374
Village Club Ct 28374
Vinson Ln 28374
Vixen Ln 28374
Wake Ct 28374
Wakefield Way 28374
Walnut Creek Rd 28374
Wampanoag Ln 28374
Wanamoisett Ln 28374
Watson Ct 28374
Wee Burn Ln 28374
Weeburn Pl 28374
Weldon Ct 28374
Wellington Dr 28374
Wentworth Cir 28374
Westchester Cir & Pl 28374
Westlake Rd 28374
Westlake Point Dr 28374
Wheeling Dr 28374
Whinhill Ct 28374
Whippoorwill Run 28374
Whirla Way 28374
Whistling Straight Rd 28374
White Ct 28374
White Birch Ln 28374
Whitecraigs Ct 28374
Whitehaven Dr 28374
Whithorn Ct 28374
Wicker Ln & Pl 28374
Wicker Sham Ct E & W 28374
Wicklow Ct 28374
Wild Turkey Run 28374
Wilkes Ct 28374

Wilshire Ln 28374
Wilson Rd 28374
Wimbleton Dr 28374
Winchester Rd 28374
Windmere Rd 28374
Windsor Ter 28374
Wingate Ct 28374
Winged Foot Rd 28374
Wood Dr 28374
Woodburn Rd 28374
Woodenbridge Ln 28374
Woodland Dr 28374
Woods Rd 28374
Woodward Pl 28374
Woodway Ln 28374
Wye Ct 28374
York Pl 28374

RALEIGH NC

General Delivery 27611

POST OFFICE BOXES MAIN OFFICE STATIONS AND BRANCHES

Box No.s
R - R 27626
MV - MV 27626
1 - 2779 27602
1 - 2 27676
2801 - 3069 27602
5010 - 5988 27650
6001 - 6774 27628
9200 - 9998 27676
9998 - 9998 27602
9998 - 9998 27611
9998 - 9998 27619
9998 - 9998 27620
9998 - 9998 27622
9998 - 9998 27623
9998 - 9998 27624
9998 - 9998 27626
9998 - 9998 27627
9998 - 9998 27628
9998 - 9998 27629
9998 - 9998 27636
9998 - 9998 27650
9998 - 9998 27658
9998 - 9998 27661
9998 - 9998 27675
10001 - 13018 27605
14001 - 15000 27620
17002 - 21118 27619
24081 - 28978 27611
25000 - 29650 27626
30000 - 32298 27622
33001 - 33812 27636
37000 - 38038 27627
40001 - 41998 27629
46001 - 46898 27620
50102 - 50406 27650
52001 - 52320 27612
58000 - 59900 27658
61000 - 61476 27661
80001 - 81059 27623
90001 - 91774 27675
97001 - 99838 27624
130000 - 130013 27605
140000 - 140001 27620
150000 - 150099 27624
176001 - 177800 27619
300001 - 322490 27622
500000 - 900075 27675

RURAL ROUTES

10, 28, 32, 34, 52, 71 27603
25 27604
09, 27 27606
02, 12, 40 27610
08, 43 27612
11, 13, 15, 17, 18, 19, 26, 29, 30, 31, 36, 49, 50, 51 27613
07, 14, 20, 22, 23, 46, 47 27614
21, 37 27615
05, 24 27616
44 27617

NAMED STREETS

Aaron Dr 27610
Abbey Ln 27613
Abbey Grove Trl 27614
Abbey Park Way 27612
Abbey Woods Dr 27614
Abbington Way 27610
Abbotsbury Ct 27615
Abbotts Pointe Ct 27616
Aberdeen Dr 27610
Aberloch Ct 27606
Abington Ln 27604
Abney Pl 27607
Academy St 27603
Acc Blvd 27617
Accabee St 27616
Accabonac Pt 27612
Acentala Ct 27603
Acer Ct 27615
Ackley Ct 27607
Acorn Cir 27616
Acorn St 27604
Acres Way 27614
Adaba Dr 27606
Adallont Rd 27613
Adams Dr 27603
Adams Rd 27603
Adams St 27605
Adams Mountain Rd 27614
Adcox Pl 27610
Addison Pl 27610
Adler Pass 27612
Admaston Dr 27613
Adrian Ct 27604
Advantis Dr 27610
Agawam Ct 27610
Agecroft Rd 27608
Agent Ct 27603
Aggravation Ln 27610
Agnes St 27606
Agriculture St 27603
Aileen Dr 27606
Airline Dr 27607
Airmax Dr 27616
Ajinomoto Dr 27610
Akron St 27616
Al Boat Dr 27603
Alabaster Ct 27610
Alafia Ct 27616
Alamance Dr 27609
Alamo Ct 27616
Alanda Ct 27612
Albacore Ln 27612
Albany Ct 27615
Albatross Ct 27613
Albemarle Ave 27610
Alberon Pl 27603
Alborz Dr 27612
Albright Rd 27612
Alcazar Walk 27617
Alco Dr 27615
Alcott Ct 27609
Alder Grove Ln 27610
Alder Ridge Ln 27603
Alderman Cir 27603
Alders Gate Way 27615
Aldie Ct 27610
Alenja Ln 27616
Alercia Ct 27606
Alero Rd 27610
Alexander Rd 27608
Alexander Hall 27607
Alexander Promenade Pl 27617
Alfred Ct 27603
Alison Ct 27615

Alistar Ct 27612
All Points View Way 27614
All Saints Pl 27607
Allansford Ln 27613
Alleghany Dr 27609
Allen Ct 27617
Allen Dr 27610
E Allen St 27603
W Allen St 27603
Allen Grove Ct 27610
Allenby Dr 27604
Allendale Dr 27604
Allison Dr
1500-1599 27608
14100-14299 27615
Allister Dr 27609
Alloway Ct 27606
Allsbrooke Dr 27613
Allscott Way 27612
Allsdale Dr 27617
Allwood Dr 27606
Allyns Landing Way 27615
Allyson Dr 27603
Alm St 27617
Almond Ct 27615
Alpern Ct 27614
Alpha Dr 27603
Alpine Dr 27609
Alpine Creek Dr 27614
Alpine Meadow Ln 27614
Alpinis Dr 27616
Alslee Oaks Dr 27606
Alston St 27601
Alta Vista Ct 27610
Altama Cir 27610
Altha St 27606
Althorp Dr 27616
Altice Dr 27603
Altman Rd 27614
Alton Pl 27610
Alumni Dr 27606
Alva Dr 27606
Alwin Ct 27604
Alwoodley Pl 27613
Amador Way 27616
Amanda Lynn Ln 27613
Amandcroft Way 27616
Amaris Ln 27612
Amber Bluffs Cres 27616
Amber Clay Ln 27612
Amber Dawn Ln 27603
Amber Lantern St 27613
Amber Leaf Ct 27612
Amber Ridge Ln 27607
Amberfield Way 27604
Amberlock Ct 27606
Amberton Ct 27615
Ambleside Dr 27605
Amelia Ave 27615
Amelia Park Dr 27606
Amerjack Ct 27603
Ameron Ct 27617
Amery Ln 27616
Amethyst Ridge Dr 27604
Amherst Ln 27609
Amistad Ln 27610
Amity Hill Ct 27612
Ammons Dr 27615
Amoretto Way 27613
Amos Cir 27610
Amstel Way 27613
Amsterdam Pl 27606
Anchor Ct 27615
Anchorage Way 27610
Anclote Pl 27607
Andalusia Walk 27617
Anderson Dr
2200-2999 27608
3000-3299 27609
Anderson Point Dr 27610
Andiron Ln 27614
Andor Pl 27604
Andover Glen Rd 27604
Andrea Ln 27613
Andrews Ln 27607
Andron Dr 27616
Andsley Dr 27609
Andy Dr 27610
Anfield Rd 27606
Angel Ct 27606
Angel Falls Rd 27614
Angel Fire Ct 27610
Angel Hare Ln 27606
Angel Oaks Ct 27610
Angela Dr 27603
Angelfish Ct 27610
Angelus Dr 27610
Angelwing Ct 27613
Angie Rd 27603
Angier Ave 27610
Angle Park Dr 27617
Anglewood Ct 27614
Angus Dr 27617
Anihinga Ct 27616
Ann Ave 27610
Ann St 27608
Ann Arbor Ct 27604
Anna Brook Ln 27614
E & W Annaley Dr 27604
Annapolis Dr 27608
Annaron Ct 27603
Anne Carol Ct 27603
Annsbury Ct 27616
Ansleigh Hills Dr 27616
Ansley Ln 27612
Anson Way 27615
Anson Grove Ln 27615
Antebellum Rd 27606
Antel Ct 27615
Antelope Ln 27610
Anthony Dr 27603
Antionette Ln 27616
Antique Ln 27610
Antiquity Ave 27613
Antler Ridge Ct 27616
Antside Ct 27610
Anvil Pl 27603
Anwood Pl 27603
Apache Dr 27609
Apalachicula Dr 27616
Apollo Ct 27604
Appalachian Dr 27603
Appaloosa Run E & W 27613
Apperson Dr 27610
Apple Blossom Ct 27606
Apple Orchard Way 27615
Apple Valley Dr 27606
Applebrook Ter 27617
Applecreek Ct 27610
Applegarth Ln 27614
Applegate Ct 27609
Appleton Dr 27606
Applewood Ln 27609
Appliance Ct 27604
April Dr 27603
April Pl 27612
April Moon Ln 27614
Aptos Ct 27613
Aqua Ln 27603
Aquila Way 27614
Aquinas Ave 27617
Aralia Ct 27614
Arbaugh Ct 27610
Arboles Ct 27613
Arbor Dr 27612
Arbor Chase Dr 27616
Arbor Grande Way 27615
Arbor Lodge Dr 27616
Arbor Oak Ln 27616
Arbutus Dr 27612
Arcade Dr 27601
Arcadian Ct 27616
Archdale Dr 27614
Archean Way 27616
Archer Cir 27615
Archibald Way 27616
Arckelton Dr 27612
Arco Corporate Dr 27617
Ardara Ln 27607
Arden Cir 27612
Arden Branch Ln 27616
Ardleigh Ct 27616
Arete Way 27607
Argent Valley Dr 27616
Argonne Way 27610
Argyle Dr 27609
Arinto Dr 27612
Aris Ct 27615
Aristides Cir 27617
Aristotle Ct 27616
N & S Arizona Dr 27616
Arlington St 27608
Armada Dr 27610
Armadale Ln 27616
Armitage Ct 27615
Armorton Ln 27615
Armsleigh Ct 27603
Armstrong Cir 27610
Arneson St 27614
Arnold Rd 27607
Arnold Palmer Dr 27617
Arnold Park Dr 27603
Arrington Rd 27607
Arrow Dr 27612
Arrow Creek Dr 27617
Arrowood Ln 27606
Arrowspring Ln 27610
Arrowwood Dr 27604
Arsenal Ave 27610
Arthur Ct 27607
Arties Aly 27613
Artillery Ln 27615
Asbury Cir 27606
Asbury Cove Cir 27612
Ascot Ct & Ln 27615
Asgar Ct 27610
Ash Hollow Dr 27617
Ashburn Ct 27610
Ashburton Rd 27606
Ashbury Ct 27615
Ashby Pl 27604
Ashdown Ct 27613
Ashe Ave
1-299 27605
300-599 27606
Ashe Ter 27601
Ashebrook Dr 27609
Ashel St 27612
Asher View Ct 27606
Ashford St 27610
Ashford Park Dr 27613
Ashire Xing 27616
Ashland St 27608
Ashland Gate Dr 27617
Ashland Mill Ct 27617
Ashley Ct 27607
Ashley Dr 27616
Ashley Ridge Dr 27612
Ashmead Ln 27614
Ashmont Ct 27616
Ashton Dr 27612
Ashton Sq 27604
Ashton Hall Ln 27609
Ashton Hollow Dr 27603
Ashton Woods Ln 27614
Ashtonshire Ct 27613
Ashwell Ct 27603
Ashwood Dr 27603
Ashworth Ct 27615
Askew Ln 27608
Aspen Ct 27615
Aspen Mountain Ct 27616
Aspenshire Ct 27613
Aspenwald Dr 27614
Associate Dr 27603
Asterwood Dr 27606
Astor Hill Dr 27613
Astoria Pl 27612
Astro Ct 27604
Astwell Ct 27615
Atamasco Cir 27616
Athena Woods Ln 27606
Athens Dr 27606
Athens Clark Way 27610
Atherton Bridge Rd 27613
Athlone Pl 27606
Atkins Dr 27610
Atkins Farm Ct 27606
Atlantic Ave
2001-2097 27604
2099-4799 27604
4800-5299 27616
5300-5599 27609
5600-5699 27615
Atlantic Springs Rd 27616
Atrium Dr 27607
Atterbury Ct 27604
Atticus Rd 27614
Attingham Dr 27615
Atwater St 27607
Auburn Rd
1200-2399 27610
4900-5099 27609
Auburn Estates Rd 27610
Auburn Hills Dr 27616
Auburn Knightdale Rd 27610
Audley Cir 27615
Audubon Dr 27615
August Way 27610
Augusta Ct 27607
Aukland St 27606
Auldbury Way 27617
Auman Rd 27603
Aurora Dr 27615
Austin St 27603
Auston Grove Dr 27610
Australia Dr 27610
Authority Ln 27601
Automotive Way 27604
Autrey Ct 27613
Autumn Ct 27609
Autumn Breeze Ln 27615
Autumn Chase Dr 27613
Autumn Field Dr 27603
Autumn Hill Ter 27617
Autumn Oaks Ln 27614
Autumn Pine Ct 27603
Autumn Sage Lndg 27616
Autumn Sunset Ct 27616
Autumn Winds Dr 27615
Avalon Ct 27612
Avebury Ct 27609
Avenida Del Sol Dr 27616
Avensburg Ct 27614
Avenshire Cir 27606
Avent Ct & Hl 27606
Avent Ferry Rd 27606
Avent Ridge Rd 27606
Averell Ct 27615
Averette Field Dr 27616
Averette Hill Dr 27616
Avery Dr 27608
Avery St 27610
Aviara Dr 27606
Aviemore Cres 27604
Avocado Cir 27615
Avocet Ln 27617
Avon Dr 27608
Avondale Ct 27613
Awls Haven Dr 27614
Axle Ln 27616
E & W Aycock St 27608
Ayr Ct 27609
Azalea Dr
1300-1499 27607
4200-4399 27612
Azalea Pl 27613
Azari Ct 27614
Aztec Dr 27612
Aztec Dawn Ct 27613
Azure Ln 27613
Babble Ln 27615
Babbling Brook Dr 27610
Babock Ct 27609
Back Sail Ct 27613
Baden Pl 27613
Badger Springs Rd 27603
Badham Pl 27609
Baez St 27608
Baggett Ave 27604
Bagwell Ave 27607
Bagwell Farm Rd 27610
Bagwell Hall 27607
Bagwell Pond Rd 27610
Bailey Dr 27610
Bailey Grove Ct 27613
Baileycroft Dr 27615
Baileyfield Dr 27612
Baileys Landing Dr 27606
Baileywick Rd
9001-9097 27615
9099-9799 27615
9800-10499 27613
Bainbridge Ter 27614
Baird Dr 27606
Baker Rd 27607
Bakers Grove Way 27610
Bakersfield Dr 27606
Balance Fox Dr 27616
Balboa Rd 27603
Baldpate Ct 27616
Ball Complex 27610
Ballou Ct 27609
Ballybrook Ct 27614
Ballybunion Way 27613
Ballyclare Ct 27614
Ballyhask Pl 27607
Balm Ct 27610
Balmy Dawn Ct 27613
Balsam Dr 27612
Balsam Pl 27603
Banana Key Pl 27603
Banbury Rd
1200-1298 27607
1300-1500 27607
1502-1698 27607
1700-2199 27608
Banbury Woods Pl 27607
Bancroft St 27612
Banded Iron Ln 27616
Bandford Way 27615
Baney Ct 27610
Banks Rd 27603
Banks St 27604
Banks Haven Ct 27603
Banks Stone Dr 27603
Bankscrest Dr 27603
Bankshill Row 27614
Bankshire Ln 27603
Bankswood Dr 27603
Bannf Ct 27604
Bannister Ct 27615
Bannock Ct 27603
Bantry Ct 27615
Banwell Pl 27613
Barbara Dr 27606
Barber Bridge Rd 27603
Barberry Ct 27615
Barbour Dr 27603
Barclay Dr 27606
Barclay Manor Way 27614
Barclay Woods Ct 27614
Barcroft Pl 27615
Barday Downs Ln 27606
Barden Dr 27605
Bardwell Rd 27604
Bare Back Ct 27606
Bare Creek Ln 27603
Barefoot Industrial Rd 27617
Barfield Ct 27612
Barham Ct 27613
Barker Pl 27604
Barksdale Dr 27604
Barley Pl 27615
Barleymoor Dr 27615
Barlon Ct 27616
Barlows Knoll St 27610
Barmettler St 27607
Barmouth Ct 27614
Barngate Way 27614
Barnhart Way 27617
Barnhill Dr 27603
Barnsley Ln & Trl 27604
Barnstable Ct 27612
Baron Cooper Pass 27612
Baron Monck Pass 27612
Baronsmede Dr 27615
Barony Lake Way 27614
Barrett Dr 27609
Barringer Dr 27606
Barrington Dr 27610
Barrington Pl 27615
Barrington Manor Dr 27612
Barrington Village Ln 27610
Barron Berkeley Way 27612
Barrow Dr 27616
Barrowood Dr 27612
Barryknoll Ct 27613
Barrymore St 27603
Barsanlaw Dr 27613
Barset Pl 27607
Barstow Dr 27606
Bart St 27610
Bartholomew Cir 27604
Bartlett Dr 27609
Barton Oaks Dr 27614
Barton Park Pl 27613
Barton Pines Rd 27614
Barton Place Dr 27608
Barton Ridge Ct 27613
Bartons Rd 27613
Bartons Creek Rd 27615
Bartons Enclave Ln 27613
Bartons Grove Pl 27614
Bartons Landing Rd 27613
Bartram Pl 27617
Bartwood Dr 27613
Barwell Rd 27610
Barwell Park Dr 27610
Bascomb Dr 27614
Baseline Rd 27610
Basewood Dr 27609
Bashford Rd 27606
Bashford Bluffs Ln 27603
Bashford Crest Ln 27606
Basil Dr 27612
Basinger Ct 27612
Basketweave Dr 27614
Baslow Brook Ct 27614
Bason Ct 27609
Bassett Hall Ct 27616
Basswood Dr 27610
Bastion Ln 27604
Batavia Ct 27604
Bates St 27610
Batesville Dr 27617
Bath Cir 27610
Batholith Ct 27616
Batiste Rd 27613
Baton Rd 27610
Batteau Ct & Ln 27613
Batterhayes Rd 27615
Battery Dr 27610
Battle Bridge Rd 27610
Battleford Dr
6000-6399 27612
6400-6699 27613
Battleview Dr 27613
Battom Ct 27613
Batts Rd 27604
Batts St 27603
Baucom Rd 27610
Bauer Ct 27604
Baugh St 27604
Bavin Pl 27613
Baxley Dr 27610
Bay Ct 27615
Bay Creek Ct 27614
Bay Harbor Dr 27604
Bay Hill Ct 27615
Bay Horse Ln 27614
Bay Meadow Ct 27615
Bay Rum Ln 27610
Bayberry Ln 27612
Bayberry Hills Dr 27617
Baybriar Dr 27613
Baybridge Wynd 27613
Baybush Dr 27615
Bayfield Dr 27606
Bayleaf Dr 27615
Bayleaf Trl 27614
Bayleaf Church Rd 27614
Bayliner Dr 27604
Baylor Ct 27609
Baymar Dr 27612
Bayridge Xing 27604
Bayshore Ct 27613
Bayside Ct 27613
Bayspring Ln 27613
Baystone Ct 27615
Bayswater Trl 27612
Baytree Ln 27615
Baywood Dr 27613
Beach Plum Ct 27616
Beach Pointe Ave 27604
Beach Water Dr 27604
Beacon Bluff St 27604
Beacon Crest Way 27604
Beacon Heights Dr 27604
Beacon Hill Ct 27616
Beacon Lake Dr 27610
Beacon Valley Dr 27604
Beacon Village Dr 27604
Beaded Stone St 27613
Beagle Retreat Dr 27616
Beagle Run Dr 27616
Beane Dr 27604
Beardsley Ct 27609
Bearglades Ln 27615
Beargrass Ln 27616
Bearmont Pl 27610
Bearskin Ct 27606
Beastrad Dr 27612
Beaufain St 27604
Beaufort St 27609
Beaufort Inlet Ct 27610
Beaumont Ct 27604
Beauty Ave 27610
Beauvoir St 27614
Beaux Ct 27616
N & S Beaver Ln 27604
Beaver Creek Dr 27604
Beaver Dam Rd 27607
Beaver Lake Ct 27613
Beaver Lodge Ct 27604
Beaver Oaks Ct 27606
Beaver Pond Ln 27614
Beaverbrook Rd 27612
Beaverwood Dr 27616
Beckley Ct 27615
Beckridge Ln 27615
Becky Cir 27615
Becton Hall 27607
Bedell St 27616
Bedford Ave 27607
Bedford Green Dr 27604
Bedford Hills Ct 27613
Bedford Pines Ct 27613
Bedford Woods Dr 27614
Bedfordshire Ct 27604
Bedfordshire Dr 27606
Bedfordtown Dr 27614
Bedrock Dr 27603
Bee Hive Dr 27614
Beech Bluff Ln 27616
Beech Gap Ct 27603
Beech Glen Dr 27617
Beech Valley Ct 27617
Beech Wood Ct 27614
Beecham Cir 27607
Beechcrest Ln 27614
Beechgrove Dr 27612
Beechleaf Ct 27604
Beechnut Trl 27613
Beechridge Rd 27608
Beechtree Camp Dr 27613
Beechtree Ridge Trl 27612
Beechview Ct 27615
Beechwood Dr
1-499 27603
1500-1699 27609
Beechwood Hills Dr 27603
Beehnon Way 27603
Beeler Rd 27607
Beestone Ln 27614
Bekonscot Ave 27604
Belafonte Dr 27610
Belden Pl 27614
Belfast Dr 27610
Belford Valley Ln 27615
Belgium Dr 27606
Belgreen Ct 27612

Belin Ct 27616
Belington Ct 27604
Bell Ave 27603
Bell Dr 27610
Bell Forest Trl 27615
Bell Grove Way 27615
Bella Park Trl 27613
Bellaire Ave 27608
Bellard Ct 27617
Bellcamp Ct 27610
Belle Crest Dr 27612
Belle Patch Cir 27604
Belleau Woods Dr 27610
Bellechasse Dr 27615
Bellemeade St 27607
Bellenden Pl 27604
Bellevue Rd 27609
Bellewood Farms Rd 27603
Bellford Ct 27614
Bellingham Cir 27615
Bellow St 27609
Bells Valley Dr 27617
Bellstone Ln 27614
Bellview Ct 27613
Bellweather Ct N & S 27615
Bellwood Dr 27605
Belmont Dr 27610
Belmont Forest Way 27606
Belmont Valley Ct 27612
Belneath Ct 27613
Belsay Dr 27612
Belspring Ln 27612
Belvedere Ct 27604
Belvin Dr 27609
Bembridge Dr 27613
Ben Bur Rd 27612
Ben Hill Cir 27610
Ben Lloyd Dr 27604
Benar Dr 27603
Benchmark Dr 27615
N Bend Dr 27609
Bend Of The Barton Ln 27614
Bender Dr 27603
Bending Birch Dr 27613
Bending Tree Ct 27613
Benedict Ln 27614
Benehan St 27605
Beneventum Ct 27606
Benevolence Dr 27610
Benhart Dr 27613
Benjamin St 27604
Benjamin Hill Cir 27610
Bennett St 27604
Bennettwood Ct 27612
Bennington Dr 27615
Bensley Ct 27615
Benson Dr 27609
Bent Branch Dr 27603
Bent Fork Cir 27606
Bent Green St 27614
Bent Leaf Dr 27606
Bent Oak Ct 27603
Bent Pine Pl 27615
Bent Ridge Pl 27615
Bent Twig Dr 27613
Bentgrass Dr 27610
Bentham Dr 27614
Bentley Cir 27616
Bentley Ln 27610
Bentley Bridge Rd 27612
Bentley Brook Dr 27612
Bentley Forest Trl 27612
Bentley Hill Rd 27612
Bentley Meadow Ln 27612
Bentley Wood Ln 27616
Benton Cir 27615
Bentonville Ct 27610
Bentpine Dr 27603
Bentwood Pl 27615
Benzinger Dr 27613
Berdan Ct 27616
Beret Ct 27615
Bergamot Ct 27614
Bergot St 27616
Bergstrom Dr 27616

Berkeley St 27612
Berkeley Springs Pl 27616
Berkely Club Dr 27617
Berks Way 27614
Berkshire Rd 27608
Berkshire Downs Dr 27616
Berkshire Village Ct 27616
Berley Ct 27609
Bermouth Sq 27615
Bermwood Ct 27610
Bernadette Ln 27615
Bernard St 27608
Bernie Pl 27616
Berry Ct 27610
Berry Creek Cir 27613
Berry Crest Ave 27617
Berry D Sims Wynd 27612
Berry Hall 27607
Berry Hill Dr 27615
Berryville Ct 27617
Bertie Dr 27610
Bertini Rd 27616
Bertram Dr 27604
Berwickshire Cir 27615
Berwyn Way 27615
Beryl Rd
3800-3899 27607
3901-3919 27607
3919-3919 27636
3921-3999 27607
4000-5299 27606
Bessborough Dr 27617
Bethany Dr 27603
Bethel Cir & Rd 27610
Bethlehem Rd 27610
Bethune Dr 27603
Bethwicke Ct 27604
Betimca Dr 27603
Betry Pl 27603
Betterton Dr 27613
Betts Ln 27614
Beverly Dr 27610
Bianco Dr 27607
Bickett Blvd 27608
Bickley Pl 27613
Biddestone Ct 27612
Big Bass Dr 27610
Big Creek Rd 27613
Big Cypress Ct 27603
Big Hoof Run 27610
Big Lake Ct 27607
Big Nance Dr 27616
Big Oak St 27610
Big Sandy Dr 27616
Big Sky Ln 27615
Big Stone 27610
Bilbury Ct 27614
Billingham Ct 27604
Billingsgate Ln 27614
Billingsworth Way 27613
Biloxis Ct 27603
Biltmore Ct 27610
Bilyeu St 27606
Bimini Ct 27603
Bingham Dr 27614
Binghampton Ln 27604
Binley Pl 27615
Birch Ct 27616
Birch Pl 27609
Birch Brook Ct 27613
Birch Ridge Dr 27610
Birchbark Ct 27615
Birchfalls Dr 27614
Birchfield Ct 27616
Birchford Ct 27604
Birchleaf Dr 27606
Birchmoor Way 27616
Birchwood Ct 27612
Birkwood Ct 27616
Birmingham Way 27604
Birnamwood Rd 27607
Biroc Ct 27614
Bishopgate Dr 27613
Bishops Park Dr 27605
Bisland Dr 27610
Bismith Dr 27610

Bison Hill Ln 27604
Bittersweet Ct 27609
Bivens Dr 27616
Black Diamond Ct 27604
Black Horse Run 27613
Black Lion Way 27610
Black Maple Dr 27616
Black Marble Ct 27612
Black Mountain Path 27612
Black Rock Dr 27610
Black Walnut Ct 27606
Black Willow Ct 27606
Blackard Pond Rd 27604
Blackbeard Ln 27604
Blackberry Ln 27609
Blackbrook Ct 27614
Blacket Ct 27604
Blackham Ct 27610
Blacklan Cir 27610
Blacksmith Dr 27606
Blackwell Dr 27617
Blackwing Ct 27615
Blackwolf Run Ln 27604
Blackwood Dr 27612
Bladen St 27601
Blaine Ct 27609
Blair Dr 27603
Blair Cee Ln 27613
Blaire Woods Dr 27610
Blairmore Ct 27612
Blairstone Ct 27612
Blake St 27601
Blakehurst Dr 27617
Blakeley Ln 27613
Blakeman Ln 27617
Blakenham Rd 27610
Blakewood Dr 27609
Blanchard St 27603
Blanche Dr 27607
Bland Rd 27609
Blaney Bluffs Ln 27606
Blaney Franks Rd 27606
Blarney Ct 27610
Blaydon Dr 27606
Blazing Star Ln 27610
Bledsoe Ave 27601
Bleeker Ct 27606
Blenheim Dr 27612
Blessing House St 27614
N Bloodworth St
1-399 27601
400-899 27604
S Bloodworth St
1-1399 27601
1400-1599 27610
Bloomfield Way 27616
Blooming St 27612
Blooming Acres 27603
Bloomsbury Park Dr 27609
Blossom Hill Ct 27613
N Blount St
1-499 27601
500-1299 27604
S Blount St
1-1399 27601
1400-1599 27603
Blue Blossom Dr 27616
Blue Coral Dr 27610
Blue Cypress Ln 27606
Blue Dun Way 27614
Blue Heron Way 27615
Blue Lagoon Ln 27610
Blue Moon Ct 27603
Blue Oak Ter 27608
Blue Ribbon Ln 27610
Blue Ridge Rd
500-999 27606
1001-1097 27607
1099-2999 27607
3000-4299 27612
Blue River Rd 27603
Blue River Farm Dr 27603
Blue Rock Ct 27610
Blue Run Ln 27604
Blue Sage Dr 27606
Blue Slate Ct 27603

Blue Stem Ct 27606
Blue Water Ct 27606
Bluebeard Way 27604
Blueberry Dr 27612
Bluebill Ct 27615
Bluebird Ct 27606
Bluemont Ct 27617
Bluestone Dr 27612
Bluetick Rd 27616
Bluewing Rd 27616
Bluff St 27603
Bluff Pointe Ct 27615
Bluff Top Ct 27615
Bluffridge Dr 27615
Bluffside Ct 27615
Bluffwind Dr 27603
Boars Head Ct 27613
Boathouse Ct 27615
Boaz Rd 27610
Bobwhite Ct 27609
Boca Pt 27616
Boddie Dr 27609
Bodie Island Ln 27604
Bodkin Ct 27613
Bog Sage Ln 27603
Bogey Way 27603
Bogle Branch Ct 27606
Bolder Vw 27610
Bolero Cir & Way 27615
Bolin Ct 27603
Boling Dr 27603
Bolingbrook Ln 27613
Bolitar Dr 27610
Bolo Trl 27615
Bolton Pl 27610
Bon Marche Ln 27615
Bona Ct 27604
Bonbright Ct 27614
Bond St 27604
Bonneau Dr 27616
Bonneville Ct 27604
Bonnibee Ct 27612
Bonnie Ridge Ct 27615
Booker Dr 27610
Booker Oak Cir 27612
Boone Trl 27610
Boone Hall Ct 27614
Boot Ct 27615
Boothbay Ct 27613
Borders Ct 27613
Bordesley Ct 27609
Boren Ct 27616
Boros Pl 27615
Boscobel Way 27615
Boswell Rd 27610
Botany Bay Dr 27616
Bothwell St 27617
Boulder Ct 27607
Boulder Creek Ln 27613
Boulder Ridge Dr 27610
Boulders View Dr 27610
Bouncy Day Ct 27614
N Boundary St 27604
S Boundary St 27601
Bouree Cir 27606
Bournemouth Dr 27615
Bowdoin Dr 27615
Bowen Hall 27607
Bowling Dr 27606
Bowling Farm Ct 27603
Bowling Green Trl 27613
Bowman Ln 27610
Boxelder Ct 27610
Boxelder Dr 27613
Boxwood Rd 27612
Boyce Mill Rd 27613
Boyer St 27610
N Boylan Ave
1-699 27603
700-800 27605
802-998 27605
S Boylan Ave 27603
Boysenberry Ln 27616
Braceridge Rd 27613
Bracey Pl 27610
Brack Pl 27603

Brack Penny Rd 27603
Bracken Ct 27615
Bracknell Ct 27603
Bradbury Ct 27613
Braddock Dr 27612
Bradford Pl 27610
Bradford Grove Pl 27606
Bradford Pear Ct 27606
Bradkin Ct 27610
Bradley Pl 27607
Bradwell Ct 27613
Brady Hollow Way 27613
Braefield Dr 27616
Braes Mdw 27612
Brafferton Ct 27604
Bragaw Hall 27607
Bragg St
1-514 27601
516-518 27601
519-1099 27610
Braid Ct 27603
Braidwood Ct 27612
Bramble Ct 27615
Brambleberry Way 27616
Brambleton Ave 27610
Bramblewood Dr 27612
Bramer Dr 27604
Branch Rd 27610
Branch St 27601
Branchview Ct 27610
Branchwood Rd 27609
Brandermill Ln 27614
Brandon Ct 27609
Brandon Allen Ave 27613
Brandon Hall Dr 27614
Brandon Station Rd 27613
Brandy Bay Rd 27613
Brandyapple Dr 27615
Brandycrest Dr 27610
Brandytrace Cir 27610
Brandywine Cir 27614
Brandywine Dr 27607
Brandywine Rd 27607
Brandywood Ct 27615
Brantford Pl 27607
Brass Kettle Rd 27614
Brass Lantern Ct 27606
Brass Mill Ln 27617
Brassfield Rd 27614
Braxton Ct 27606
Braxwood Pl 27617
Breadfruit Ct 27616
Break Dance Ct 27610
Breakspear Ct 27603
Breamore Cir 27615
Brecken Ridge Ave 27615
Breckon Way 27615
Breda Ct 27606
Bredon Ct 27613
Breeland Way 27613
Breeze Rd 27608
Breezeway Dr 27614
Breezewood Rd 27607
Breezy Point Ln 27617
Bremer Hall Ct 27615
Bremerton Ct 27613
Brenda Dr 27610
Brenfield Dr 27606
Brennan Dr 27613
Brent Rd 27606
Brentmoor Dr 27604
Brentwood Rd
2000-2778 27604
2777-2777 27629
2779-3899 27604
2780-3898 27604
Brereton Dr 27615
Breton Ln 27613
Brett Cir 27603
Bretton Mill Dr 27616
Brevard Pl 27609
Brewer St 27608
E Brewer St 27610
Brewington Ct 27615
Brewster Dr 27606
Brewton Pl 27604

Briana Dr 27603
Briar Mill Trl 27612
Briar Oak Ln 27612
Briar Patch Ln 27615
Briar Stream Run 27612
Briarcliff Rd 27610
Briarforest Pl 27615
Briarmont Ct 27610
Briarstone Ct 27610
Briarthorne Pl 27613
Briarwood Dr 27603
Briarwood Pl 27614
Brickell Ave 27617
Brickhaven Dr 27606
Brideveil Ct 27610
Bridford Pl 27613
Bridge Way 27615
Bridgehampton Ct 27615
Bridgeport Dr 27615
Bridget Dr 27603
Bridgetender Dr 27615
Bridgeton Park Dr 27612
Bridgetowne Way 27609
Bridgeville Rd 27610
N & S Bridgewater Ct 27615
Bridle Ln 27614
Bridle Path Dr 27606
Bridle Ridge Ln 27609
Bridlespur Ln 27604
Bridlington Ln 27612
Brielson Pl 27616
Brier Creek Pkwy & Pl 27617
Brier Leaf Ln 27617
Brier Oak Pl 27617
Brierley Hill Ct 27610
Briertownes Pkwy 27617
Brigadoon Dr 27606
Brigham Rd 27610
Bright Loop 27613
Bright Creek Way 27601
Bright Future Way 27614
Bright Hedge Ct 27613
Bright Horizons Way 27614
Bright Oak Trl 27616
Bright Passage Dr 27616
Bright Pebble Ct 27604
Brighthaven Dr 27614
Brighthurst Dr 27605
Brighton Rd 27610
Brighton Hill Ln 27616
Brighton Village Dr 27616
Brightwater Ct 27614
Brightwell Ln 27610
Brightwood Ct 27612
Brigmore Ct 27617
Brilliant Dr 27616
Brimfield Ct 27614
Brimming Lake Ct 27614
Brimstone Ln 27613
Brimwater Dr 27604
Brinell Pl 27610
Bringle Ct 27610
Brinkley Dr 27604
Brinkman Ct 27614
Brinleys Cove Ct 27614
Brintons Cottage St 27616
Brisbayne Cir 27615
Bristoe Station Ln 27610
Bristol Pl 27610
Bristol Meadow Dr 27603
Britmass Dr 27616
Britt Dr 27610
Britt Farm Ct 27603
Britt Ridge Ct 27603
Britt Valley Rd 27603
Britt Vintage Rd 27603
Brittabby Ct 27606
Brittany Bay E & W 27614
Brittdale Ln 27617
Brittlebank Dr 27610
Brittonwood Ct 27616
Brixham Ct 27615
Broad St 27613
Broad Head Ln 27616
Broad Leaf Cir 27613
Broad Oaks Pl 27603

Broadfield Ct 27617
Broadhaven Dr 27603
Broadingham Ct 27615
Broadlands Dr 27604
Broadmore Ct 27613
Broadrun Dr 27617
Broadview Dr 27617
Broadwell Ct 27613
Broadwell Dr 27606
Brockfield Ct 27614
Brockton Dr 27604
Brockwell Ct 27614
Broken Arrow Ct 27610
Broken Branch Ct 27610
Broken Sound Way 27615
Brokers Tip Ln 27617
Bromley St 27610
Bromley Way 27615
Brompton Ct 27615
Bromwich Ln 27607
Brook Dr 27609
Brook Crossing Cir 27606
Brook Edge Dr 27613
Brook Fern Way 27609
Brook Garden Ct 27615
Brook Knoll Pl 27609
Brook Mill Dr 27612
Brook Ridge Ct 27615
Brook Run Dr 27614
Brook Top Ct 27606
Brook View Ct 27613
Brookbank Ln 27615
Brookchase Dr 27617
Brookdale Dr
7500-7999 27616
8600-8699 27613
Brooke Lauren Ln 27616
Brookfield Rd 27615
Brookgate Ter 27617
Brookhaven Dr 27612
Brookhollow Dr 27615
Brookhurst Pl 27609
Brooklane Dr 27610
Brooklyn St 27605
Brookmeade Pl 27612
Brookmont Dr 27613
Brooks Ave & Ct 27607
Brookshadow Dr 27610
Brookside Dr 27604
Brookstone Ct 27615
Brookton Ct 27615
Brookvalley Dr 27616
Brookway Ct 27613
Brookwood Ct 27613
Brookwood Dr
900-999 27607
2500-2899 27603
Broome Bay Ct 27616
Broomfield Way 27615
Broomsedge Ct 27610
Brost Ct 27616
Brothers Way 27603
Brothwell Ct 27606
Browder St 27614
Brown Pl 27604
Brown Bark Pl 27615
Brown Field Rd 27610
Brown Owl Dr 27610
Brown Straw Dr 27610
Brownairs Ln 27610
Browning Pl 27609
Brownleigh Dr 27617
Brownlow Ct 27610
Brownsburg Pl 27613
Brownstone Ct 27609
Broyhill Cir 27604
Bruce Cir 27603
Bruckhaus St 27617
Brumbley Pl 27612
Brumlow Ln 27610
Brunetti Ct 27614
Brunswick St 27609
Brunswick Ter 27601
Brushwood Ct 27612
Bryan St 27605
Bryanstone Pl 27610

Bryant St 27603
Bryant Falls Ct 27613
Bryarton Village Way 27606
Bryarton Woods Dr 27606
Bryn Athyn Way 27615
Bryn Brooke Dr 27614
Bryn Mawr Ct 27606
Bryna Ct 27615
Bubbling Brook Ct 27610
Buck Jones Rd 27606
Buck Spring Ct 27603
Buckboard Ln 27603
Buckeye Ct 27612
Buckhead Dr 27615
Buckingham Rd 27607
Buckle Ct 27609
Buckridge Ct 27616
Bucksport Ln 27613
Bucktail Pl 27610
Buckthorne Ct 27610
Buckwater Ct 27615
Buddha Ave 27610
Budwood Dr 27609
Buffaloe Rd
3200-4100 27604
4101-4199 27616
4102-4398 27604
4201-4399 27604
4400-8099 27616
Buffaloe Farm Ln 27603
Bufflehead Rd 27616
Bugle Ct 27616
Bullard Ct 27615
Bulmer Ter 27615
Bunchberry Ct 27616
Bunche Dr 27610
Bunchgrass Ln 27614
Buncombe St 27609
Bunker Hill Dr 27610
Bunnalley Ct 27610
Bunnwood Ln 27617
Bunting Dr 27616
Bur Trl 27616
Bur Oak Cir 27612
Burberry Dr 27614
Burchard Dr 27616
Burchfield Ct 27616
Burgundy St 27610
Burke St 27609
Burkwood Ln 27609
Burleigh Manor Dr 27616
Burnaby St 27616
Burnette Pl 27603
Burning Oak Ct 27606
Burningbush Ln 27614
Burnlee Pl 27609
Burns Pl 27609
Burntwood Cir 27610
Burrell Pl 27607
Burt Dr 27606
Burton Ave 27606
Burton St 27608
Burtons Barn St 27610
Burwell St 27615
Burwell Rollins Cir 27612
Buscot Ct 27615
Bush St 27609
Bushmills St 27613
Bushveld Ln 27613
Business Park Dr 27610
Busted Rock Trl 27610
Butler Blvd 27604
Butler Cabin Dr 27610
Buttar Ln 27614
Byers Dr 27607
Byrd St 27608
Byrnwick Pl 27615
Byron Pl 27609
Byrum Woods Dr 27613
Bywood Ct 27615
E Cabarrus St 27601
W Cabarrus St
1-499 27601
500-1199 27603
Caber Rd 27613
Cabin Pl 27609

Cabin Creek Ln 27614
Cablewood Dr 27603
Cabochon Diamond Ct 27610
Cadbury Ct 27615
Caddy Rd 27603
Cadences Dr 27615
Cadenza Ln 27614
Cadler Ct 27616
Cadmore Ct & Dr 27613
Cadwell Ct 27606
Cagle Dr 27617
Cahaba Way 27616
Cahill Rd 27614
Caines Way 27614
Caistor Ln 27614
Calabria Dr 27617
Calais Ct 27613
Calculus Ln 27603
Caldbeck Dr 27615
Caldera Ln 27616
Calderwood St 27614
Caldwell Dr 27607
Caledonia St 27609
Caliber Woods Dr 27616
Calibre Chase Dr 27609
Calico Jack Ct 27604
N & S California Dr 27616
Callaway Gap Rd 27614
Calliope Way 27616
Calloway Dr 27610
Calorie Ct 27612
Calton Dr 27612
Calumet Dr 27610
Calvary Dr 27604
Calvert Dr 27610
Calverton Dr 27613
Calvin Rd 27605
Calypso Ct 27610
Camargo Ln 27604
Camaro Ct 27604
Camberwell Ct 27614
Cambium Ct 27613
Cambridge Rd 27608
Cambridge Woods
Way 27608
Camden St 27601
Camden Creek Dr 27610
Camden Park Dr 27613
Camden Woods Ct 27612
Camellia Dr 27613
Camellia St 27603
Camelot Dr 27609
Cameo Glass Way 27612
Cameron Dr 27603
Cameron St 27605
Cameron Crest Cir 27613
Cameron View Ct 27607
Camfirth Way 27613
Camille Ct 27615
Caminetto Ct 27603
Caminos Dr 27607
Camley Ave 27612
Camp Durant Rd 27614
Camp Mangum Wynd 27612
Campanella Ln 27610
Campbell Rd 27606
Campbell Woods Dr 27606
Campfire Trl 27615
Campton Mill Ct 27616
Campus Dr 27613
Campus Shore Dr 27606
Camrose St 27608
Canaan Ln 27615
Canadero Dr 27612
Canadian Ct 27616
Canal Dr 27606
Canary St 27614
Candelaria Dr 27616
Candle Ct 27616
Candlehurst Ln 27616
Candlelight Oaks Ln 27603
Candler Falls Ct 27614
Candlewood Dr 27612
Candor Ln 27601
Candor Oaks Dr 27615
Candyflower Pl 27610

Cane Garden Dr 27610
Canemount St 27614
Canenaugh Dr 27604
Canes Way 27614
Canewood Pl 27612
Canfield Ct 27608
Cannold Ct 27610
Canoe Ct 27615
Canoe Brook Pkwy 27614
Canoga Pl 27615
Canolder St 27614
Canonero Pl 27613
Canter Ln 27604
Canterbury Rd
900-1199 27607
1200-1799 27608
Cantilever Way 27613
Cantwell Ct 27610
Canvas Art Ter 27617
Canvasback Ct 27616
Canyon Rock Ct 27610
Cap Collins Ln 27604
Capability Dr 27606
Cape Ave 27601
Cape Breton Dr 27616
Cape Charles Dr 27617
Cape Henry Dr 27615
Cape Scott Ct 27614
Capehart Ct 27616
Capers Ct 27612
Capital Blvd
300-1599 27603
1600-4749 27604
4750-4798 27616
4751-4799 27604
4800-6399 27616
6320-6320 27661
6400-9498 27616
6401-9499 27616
Capital Center Dr 27606
Capital Club Ct 27616
Capital Hills Dr 27616
Cappozzi St 27606
Caprice Ct 27606
Capstone Dr 27615
Caraleigh Mills Ct 27603
Caramoor Ln 27614
Cardamon Ct 27610
Cardhu Way 27603
Cardiff Ct 27615
Cardigan Pl 27609
Cardinal Dr 27604
Cardinal Grove Blvd 27616
Cardinal Landing Dr 27603
Cardinal View Dr 27610
Cardington Ln 27614
Careway Pl 27607
Carileph Ct 27615
Carisbrook Ct 27615
Carl Sandburg Ct 27610
Carl Williamson Rd 27610
Carlisle St 27610
Carlos Dr 27609
Carlow Ct
1100-1199 27615
3600-3699 27612
Carlswood Ct 27613
Carlton Ave 27606
Carlton Dr 27616
Carlton Square Pl 27612
Carlyle Dr 27614
Carlyle Hills Way 27617
Carmel Ln 27609
Carmen Ct 27610
Carnage Dr 27610
Carnegie Ln 27612
Carnelian Dr 27610
Carnoustie Way 27613
Carolina Ave 27606
Carolina Cherry Dr 27610
Carolina Hills Ln 27603
Carolina Marlin Ct 27603
Carolina Pines Ave 27603
Carolingian Ct 27615
Carolton Dr 27606
Carolyn Dr 27604

Carovel Ct 27612
Carp Rd 27610
Carpathian Way 27615
Carpenter Pond Rd 27613
Carr St 27608
Carr Pur Dr 27603
Carrack Ct 27613
Carrbridge Way 27615
Carretta Ct 27610
Carriage Dr 27612
Carriage Trl 27614
Carriage Farm Rd 27603
Carriage Hills Ct 27614
Carriage Lantern Ln 27615
Carriage Light Ct 27604
Carriage Oaks Dr 27614
Carriage Pine Dr 27616
Carriage Tour Ln 27615
Carriage Woods Cir 27607
Carrier Way 27603
Carries Reach Way 27614
Carrington Dr 27615
Carrington Ridge Dr 27615
Carroll Dr 27608
Carroll Hall 27607
Carruthers Ct 27615
Carson St 27608
Cart Track Trl 27615
Carter St 27612
Carter Finley Pl 27606
Carteret Dr 27612
Cartersville Ct 27617
Carthage Cir 27604
Cartier Dr 27608
Cartier Ruby Ln 27610
Cartway Ln 27616
Cartwright Dr 27612
Carvel Ct 27613
N & S Carver St 27610
Cary Lee Dr 27603
Carya Dr 27610
Casa Del Rey Dr 27616
Cascade Ct 27604
Cascades Blvd 27617
Cascadia Dr 27610
Casco Cir 27610
Case Ter 27606
Casey Leigh Ln 27612
Cashew Dr 27616
Cashlin Dr 27616
Casland Dr 27604
Casona Way 27616
Caspan St 27610
Casper Ln 27606
Casper Creek Ln 27616
Caspian Tern Dr 27616
Cass Ct 27613
Cassimir Ct 27603
Cassino Ln 27610
Cassock Ct 27613
Castain Dr 27617
Castine Ct 27613
Castle Ct 27613
Castle Crest Ct 27616
Castle Hill Rd 27616
Castle Pines Dr 27604
Castle Ridge Rd 27614
Castlebar Dr 27604
Castlebrook Dr 27604
Castlegate Dr 27616
Castlelake Ct 27615
Castlemoor Ct 27606
Castlereagh Ln 27614
Castleton Ln 27615
Caswell Ct 27613
Caswell Pl 27613
Caswell St 27608
Catalano Dr 27607
Catalina Ct & Dr 27607
Catalpa Ct 27609
Catamaran Dr 27615
Catamount Ct N & S 27615
Catandpolly Ln 27603
Catara Dr 27614
Catawba St 27609
Catfish Creek Ct 27604

Cathedral Bell Rd 27614
Cathedral Rock Ct 27610
Catkins Ct 27616
Catsby Cir 27603
Cattail Cir 27610
Cattail Creek Pl 27616
Cattle Farm Dr 27603
Cavalier St 27603
Cavanaugh Dr 27614
Cave Creek Ct 27613
Caversham Way 27617
Cayuga Pl 27612
Cayuse Ln 27603
Cazavini Ct 27613
Cedar Cir 27616
Cedar Ln 27614
Cedar St 27604
Cedar Bend Ct 27612
Cedar Downs Dr 27607
Cedar Forest Way 27609
Cedar Hill Ln 27609
Cedar Oak Wynd 27612
Cedar Park Pl 27609
Cedar Rail Rd 27610
Cedar Springs Dr 27603
Cedar Waters Dr 27607
Cedarbluff Ct 27615
Cedarbrook Ct 27603
Cedarcrest Ct 27609
Cedarfield Dr 27606
Cedarhurst Dr 27609
Cedarview Ct 27609
Cedarwood Dr 27609
Cedric Dr 27603
Celbridge Pl 27613
Celtic Ct 27612
Centennial Pkwy 27606
Centennial Ridge Way 27603
Centennial View Ln 27606
Centennial Woods Dr 27603
Center Rd 27608
Center Creek Cir 27612
Center Cross Ct 27617
Center Spring Ct 27603
Centerview Dr 27606
Centerwood Dr 27617
Centipede Trl 27610
Central Dr 27613
Centrebrook Cir 27616
Century Dr 27612
Centway Park Dr 27617
Ceremonial Ct 27615
Cerny St 27617
Cha Cha Ln 27610
Chadbourne Ct 27613
Chadford Dr 27612
Chadstone Ct 27615
Chadwick Dr 27609
Chagford Way 27614
Chalcedony St 27603
Chalcombe Ct 27615
Chalfant Ct 27607
Challenge Rd 27603
Chamber Ct 27607
Chamberlain St 27607
Chambers Rd 27603
Chambersbury Rd 27613
Chamisal Pl 27613
Chamonix Pl 27613
Champaign Pl 27615
Champion Ct 27606
Chancellor Pl 27603
Chancellorsville Ct 27610
Chancery Pl 27607
Chander Dr 27615
Chandler Way 27614
Chandler Grove Ct 27612
Chandler Ridge Cir 27603
Chandlewood Knl 27615
Chandon Ln 27615
Chaney Rd 27606
Channel Park Ct 27616
Channery Way 27616
Chapanoke Rd 27603
Chapel Cove Ln 27617
Chapel Hill Rd 27607

Chapman Ct 27612
Chappell Dr 27606
Chappells Way 27614
Chardon Ct 27609
Charenson Pl 27614
Charland Ct 27603
Charles Dr 27612
Charles St 27610
Charles B Root Wynd 27612
Charles G Dr 27606
Charlesgate Ct 27614
Charleston Rd 27606
Charleston Oaks Dr 27614
Charleston Park Dr 27604
Charleycote Dr 27614
E & W Charlotte Ct 27607
Charlton Ct 27613
Charment Ct 27616
Charmford Way 27615
Charny Dr 27604
Charterhouse Dr 27613
Charwood Pl 27612
Chase Ct 27607
Chasemill Ct 27617
Chasewick Cir 27615
Chasscot Ct 27606
Chastain Dr 27614
Chasteal Trl 27610
Chatahoochie Ln 27616
Chatelaine Pl 27614
Chatford Dr 27612
Chatham Ln 27610
Chatham Ter 27601
Chatmoss Dr 27610
Chatsworth Ln 27614
Chatt Ct 27616
Chatterleigh Cir 27615
Chatterson Dr 27615
Chattouga Ct 27612
Chaucer Pl 27609
Chauncey Dr 27615
Chavis Way 27601
Cheerful Ct 27615
Cheery Knl 27614
Chehaw Dr 27610
Chello Ct 27612
Chelmshire Ct 27610
Chelray Ct 27616
Chelsea Dr 27603
Chelsea Pl 27612
Chelsford Pl 27604
Chelton Oaks Pl 27614
Cheltonham Ct 27614
Chemistry Rd 27603
Chenault Ct 27604
Cherimoya Ln 27616
Cherokee Dr 27608
Cherry Cir 27603
Cherry Dr 27603
Cherry Ln 27607
Cherry Creek Blvd 27617
Cherry Field Dr 27603
Cherry Laurel Dr 27603
Cherrybark Ln 27616
Cherrycrest Ct 27609
Cherryrain Ct 27610
Cherrywood Ct 27609
Chesborough Rd 27612
Cheshire Ct 27615
Cheshire Downs Ct 27603
Chesley Ct 27613
Chesnee Ct 27604
Chesson Dr 27614
Chester Rd 27608
Chesterbrook Ct 27615
Chesterfield Rd 27608
Chesters Hollow Dr 27603
Chesthill Dr 27606
Chestnut Cv 27616
Chestnut St
200-399 27604
5000-5099 27606
Chestnut Branch Ct 27612
Cheswich Dr 27614
Cheswick Dr 27609
Cheswick House Ln 27614

Chevelle St 27607
Cheviot Ct 27615
Cheviot Hills Dr 27616
Cheyenne Rd 27609
Chi Rd 27603
Chichester Ct 27615
Chickapay Dr 27610
Chicora Ct 27615
Chicora Wood Dr 27606
Childers St 27612
Chilham Pl 27612
Chilton Pl 27616
Chimneycap Dr 27613
Chinese Fir Trl 27610
Chinkapin Pl 27613
Chinook Ct 27610
Chinquoteague Ct 27613
Chipaway Ct 27614
Chipmunk Ln 27607
Chippendale Rd 27604
Chippenham Ct 27613
Chipstone Dr 27610
Chittim Ct 27616
Chivalry Ct 27612
Chokecherry Ln 27616
Cholderton Ct 27604
Cholla Ct 27616
Chow Ln 27616
Chowan St 27609
Chowning Ct 27612
Chowning Pl 27614
Chris Dr 27603
Chris St 27610
Chrisdale Ct 27607
Christabelle Cir 27603
Christine Ct 27604
Christman Ct 27609
Christmas Ct 27604
Chrysanthemum Way 27614
Chubkey Ln 27603
Church St 27601
Church At North Hills
St 27609
Churchdown Ct 27613
Churchill Rd
2200-2799 27608
2800-3599 27607
Cicero Dr 27617
Cilantro Dr 27610
Cilcain Ct 27614
Cinabar Rd 27610
Cinch Trl 27610
Cinder Bluff Dr 27603
Cindy Dr 27603
Cinnamon Cir 27610
Circle Ln 27603
Circlebank Dr 27615
Circlewood Ct 27615
Citizen Ct 27615
Citris Glen Dr 27610
City Loft Ct 27613
City Of Oaks Wynd 27612
Civic Blvd 27610
Claflin Ct 27614
Claiborne Ct 27606
Clairbourne Pl 27615
Clairebrook Ct 27615
Clandon Park Dr 27613
Clanton St 27606
Clare Ct 27609
Claremont Rd 27608
Clarendon Cres 27610
Clareys Forrest Ln 27616
Claribel Ct 27612
Clarion Heights Ln 27606
Clark Ave
1900-2199 27605
2200-3500 27607
3502-3698 27607
Clark Ridge Ct 27613
Clarks Branch Dr 27613
Clarks Fork Dr 27616
Clarksburg Pl 27616
Clarkson Hall 27612
Clasara Cir 27613
Clava Dr 27616

Claverack Way 27613
Claxton Cir 27615
Clay St 27605
Clay Hall Ct 27606
Claybank Pl 27613
Claybourne Dr 27616
Clayette Ct 27612
Clean Ct 27603
Clear Brook Dr 27615
Clear Creek Farm Dr 27615
Clear Falls Ct 27615
Clear Meadow Ct 27615
Clear Sailing Ln 27615
Clear Skyview Cir 27603
Clear Springs Ct 27615
Clearbay Ln 27612
Clearfield Dr 27616
Clearview St 27603
Clearwater Ct 27603
Clearwater Springs Rd 27610
Cleaver Ct 27617
Clee Cir 27603
Clemson Ct 27609
Clerestory Pl 27615
Clerkenwell Way 27603
Clerriso Rd 27606
Cleveland St 27605
Cliff Haven Dr 27615
Cliff Top Ct 27613
Cliffside Cir
1200-1299 27615
12000-12199 27614
Cliffwood Ct 27609
Clifton Ct & St 27604
Climbing Vine Dr 27617
Cline Dr 27616
Clingmans Pl 27614
Clinton Pl 27607
Clivedon Dr 27615
Clonnel Ct 27604
Cloud Cover Ln 27614
Cloud Mist Cir 27614
Cloudview Ln 27613
Clove Meadow Ct 27604
Clovehitch Ct 27615
Clovelly Ct 27614
Clover Ln 27604
Clover Creek Ct 27613
Clover Crest Ct 27617
Clover Ridge Ct 27610
Clovermill Cir 27617
Cloves Ct 27614
Club Dr 27613
Club Hill Dr 27617
Club Manor Dr 27616
Club Plaza Rd 27603
Clubhaven Pl 27617
Clubmont Ln 27617
Clubvalley Way 27617
Cluette Dr 27615
Cluskey Way 27615
Clyborn Ct 27617
Clyden Cv 27612
Clymer Ct 27614
Coach Ct 27604
Coach And Four Ct 27614
Coach House Ln 27615
Coach Light Cir 27613
Coachmans Way 27614
Coalinga Ln 27610
Cobble Ct 27616
Cobble Creek Ln 27616
Cobbler Pl 27613
Cobblestone Ct 27607
Coben Dr 27610
Cobia Ct 27604
Cobridge Sq 27609
Coburn Pl 27616
Cobworth Ct 27613
Coconut Ln 27603
Codes Ridge Rd 27612
Coffeetree Dr 27613
Coffey St 27604
Cog Hill Ct 27604
Cohosh Ct 27616
Coit Ln 27614

Cokesbury Ln 27614
Colbert Creek Loop 27614
Colby Dr 27609
Cold Harbour Dr 27610
Cold Springs Rd 27615
Coldstream Ct 27615
Coldwater Ct 27612
Coldwater Springs Dr 27616
Cole St 27605
Cole Brook Dr 27610
Coleman St 27610
Coleraine Ct 27615
Coleridge Dr 27609
Colesbury Dr 27615
Colewood Dr 27604
Coley Forest Pl
2100-2299 27607
2300-2499 27612
Colgate Pl 27609
Colinwood Ln 27606
Collection River Dr 27617
College Pl 27605
College Crest Aly 27607
Collegeview Ave 27606
Collegiate Cir 27606
Colleton Rd 27610
Collingdale Way 27617
Collingswood Dr 27609
Collins Dr 27609
Collins Farm Rd 27603
Collinsworth Ct 27614
Colonial Dr 27603
Colonial Rd 27608
Colonnade Center Dr 27615
Colony Ct 27612
Colony Dr 27603
Colony Village Ln 27617
S Colorado Dr 27616
Colorcott St 27614
Colossae Ct 27610
Colton Pl 27609
Coltrane Ct 27610
Columbia Dr 27604
Columbine Dr 27613
Columbus Club Dr 27604
Colville Ct 27617
Colworth Way 27614
Combe Hill Trl 27613
Comelia Dr 27603
Comet Dr 27604
Comfort Ct 27604
Commerce Pl 27601
Commerce Park Dr 27610
Commercial Ave 27612
Commodity Pkwy 27610
Common Oaks Dr 27614
Community Dr 27610
Community Garden Rd 27603
Como Dr 27610
Compass Ln 27615
Compassionate Dr 27610
Compatible Way 27603
Competition Rd 27603
Compton Rd 27609
Computer Dr 27609
Comstock Rd 27603
Concord Hill Ct 27613
Condor Ct 27615
Condorwood Way 27610
Cone Manor Ln 27613
Conference Dr 27607
Congeniality Way 27613
Conifer Dr 27606
Conley Cove Ct 27613
Conly Dr 27603
Connally Ln 27614
Connell Dr 27612
Connestee Ct 27612
Conover Ct 27612
Consett Ct 27613
Consortium Dr 27603
Constance Cir 27603
Constellation Dr 27604
Constitution Dr 27615
Contender Dr 27603
Continental Way 27610

Contour Dr 27612
Converse Dr 27609
Cook Ridge Ct 27615
Cooke St
1-399 27601
1200-1299 27610
Cookefield Ct 27606
Cooksbury Ct 27604
Cookshire Dr 27604
Cookwood Ct 27610
Cool Pond Rd 27613
Cool Spring Rd 27614
Cool Vista Ln 27613
Cooleemee Dr 27608
Coolmore Dr 27614
Coolridge Ct 27616
Cooper Dr 27607
Cooper Rd 27610
Cooper Falls Ln 27614
Coopers Ridge Ln 27613
Coopershill Dr 27604
Coosa Ct 27616
Copernicus Ct 27617
Copley Dr 27604
Coppedge Ln 27616
Copper Trl 27606
Copper Mine Ln 27615
Copperdale Dr 27614
Coppergate Dr 27614
Coppersmith Ct 27615
Coral Ridge Ct 27616
Coral Seas Way 27610
Corbarron Ct 27606
Corberrie Ln 27613
Corbett Grove Dr
2800-2999 27616
8500-8599 27617
Corbin St 27612
Corbon Crest Ln 27612
Cordiss Ct 27603
Corin Ct 27612
Corinthian Way 27607
Corley Wood Dr 27606
Cornell Pl 27607
Cornerstone Park Dr 27613
Cornwall Pl 27612
Coronado Dr 27609
Corporate Center Dr 27607
Corporate Ridge Rd 27607
Corporation Pkwy
800-1399 27610
1400-1799 27604
Corvette Ct 27613
Corvus Rd 27614
Corydon Ct 27610
Cosmos Ct 27613
Cotkin Ln 27603
Cotswold Ct 27609
Cottage Cir 27613
Cottage Oaks Ln 27616
Cottage Rose Ln 27612
Cottage Stone Dr 27616
Cotten Rd 27603
Cottingham Way 27615
Cotton Pl 27601
Cotton Exchange Ct 27608
Cotton Grove Run 27610
Cotton Mill Dr 27612
Cotton Press St 27614
Cottonrose Ln 27606
Cottonwood Cir 27609
Cottrell Pl 27614
Cotydon Ct 27610
Coulwood Ct 27610
Council Ct 27615
Count Fleet Dr 27617
Country Ct 27609
Country Trl 27613
Country Brooke Dr 27603
Country Charm Rd 27614
Country Club Ct 27608
Country Cove Ln 27606
Country Forest Dr 27606
Country Pines Ct 27616
Country Ridge Dr 27609
Country Village Dr 27606

Countryview Ln 27606
Countrywood Rd 27615
Countrywood North Rd 27615
Courage Ct 27615
Courier Ct 27603
Courtland Dr 27604
Courtney Ln 27616
Courtney Estates Dr 27617
Courtside Pl 27604
Cove Dr 27604
Cove Bridge Rd 27604
Cove Point Dr 27613
Covenant Creek Dr 27607
Coventry Ct 27609
Coventry Ridge Rd 27616
Covered Bridge Ct 27614
Covered Wagon Ln 27610
Covey Ct 27609
Covina Dr 27613
Covington Bend Dr 27613
Cowan Ln 27610
Cowden Ct 27612
Cowper Dr 27608
Cox Ave 27605
Coxindale Dr 27615
Crab Creek Dr 27612
Crab Orchard Dr 27606
Crabapple Ln 27607
Crabberry Ln 27609
Crabtree Blvd
1100-1599 27610
2300-2499 27604
Crabtree Park Ct 27612
Crabtree Pines Ln 27612
Craddock Rd 27613
Crafton Way 27607
Craftsman Dr 27609
Crag Burn Ln 27604
Craig St 27608
Crampton Pl 27604
Cranberry Dr 27609
Cranbrook Rd 27609
Crandon Ln 27604
Crane Ct 27616
Cranes View Pl W 27615
Cranesbill Dr 27613
Cranmer Dr 27603
Cranmoore Ct 27604
Crassen Trl 27612
Craven Dr 27609
Crawford Rd 27610
Crawley Pl 27615
Crayford Dr 27604
Creech Rd 27610
Creedmoor Rd
4400-6399 27612
6400-8399 27613
8400-10999 27615
11000-12499 27614
N Creek Run 27613
Creek Mill Dr 27612
Creek Ridge Ln 27607
Creek Rock Ln 27615
Creekdale Cir 27612
Creekside Dr
500-699 27609
3600-3799 27616
Creekstone Ct 27615
Creekwood Ct 27603
Creel Ct 27610
Cremshaw Ct 27614
Crepe Myrtle Ct 27609
Crescent Ct 27609
Crescent Creek Dr 27606
Crescent Forest Dr 27610
Crescent Knoll Dr 27614
Crescent Moon Ct 27606
Crescentview Pkwy 27606
Cressage Ct 27613
Cresskill Pl 27615
Crest Rd 27606
Crest Mist Cir 27613
Cresta Dr 27603
Crestdale Cir 27612
Crestgate Ter 27617
Cresthill Ct 27615

Crestland Woods Dr 27615
Crestline Ave 27603
Crestmont Dr 27613
Crestmore Rd 27612
Creston Rd 27608
Crestscene Trl 27603
Crestview Rd 27609
Crestview Bluff Ct 27606
Crestwood Dr 27603
N & S Crestwyck Ct 27615
Crete Dr 27606
Crichton St 27617
Cricket Ridge Dr 27610
Crickett Rd 27610
Cricklewood Ct 27603
Crimson Cross Ct 27606
Crimson Tree Ct 27613
Crisfield Ct 27613
Crisp Dr 27614
Crispin Ct 27610
Criswell Cres 27615
Crocker Dr 27615
Crockett Ct 27606
Crofton Ct 27604
Crofton Springs Dr 27615
Croftwood Dr 27616
Croix Pl 27614
Cromwell Ct 27614
Cromwell Rd 27608
Crook Shank Cir 27605
Crooked Chute Ct 27612
Crooked Stick Trl 27612
Crooked Tree Ln 27617
Crookpine Trl 27610
Cross St 27610
Cross Brook Ln 27610
Cross Clay Ct 27614
Cross Creek Ct 27607
Cross Creek Dr 27615
Cross Current Ln 27610
Cross Link Rd 27610
Crosschurch Ln 27614
Crossfield Dr 27613
Crossgar Ct 27614
Crosspine Dr 27603
Crossroads Arbor Way 27606
Crossroads Crest Way 27606
Crossroads Forest Pl 27606
Crossroads Heights Dr 27606
Crossroads Valley Ct 27606
Crossroads Vista Dr 27606
Crowder Rd 27603
Crowfield Dr 27610
Crown Ct 27608
Crown Crest Ct 27615
Crown Crossing Ln 27610
Crown Glenn Pl 27613
Crown Oaks Dr 27615
Crown Vetch Rd 27614
Crowntree Ct 27614
Croydon St 27610
Croydon Mill Way 27616
Crump Rd 27606
Crupper Ct 27613
Crusader Dr 27606
Crutchfield Rd 27606
Crystal Bluff Ln 27601
Crystal Breeze St 27614
Crystal Clay Ct 27613
Crystal Downs Ln 27604
Crystal Hill Ct 27604
Crystal Lake Dr 27603
Crystal Oaks Ln 27614
Crystal Ridge Ln 27610
Crystal Springs Cir 27617
Cub Trl 27615
Cuchalain Rd 27616
Culater Ct 27616
Culpepper Ln 27610
Culps Hill Ct 27610
Cum Laude Ct 27606
Cumberland St 27610
Cumberland Creek Rd 27613
Cumberland Plain Dr 27616
Cumberland Pond Rd 27606
Cumming Cir 27613

Cupine Ct 27604
Cupola Dr 27603
Cupp Ct 27603
Curfman St 27603
Currie Ct 27613
Currin Fox Ct 27616
Currituck Dr 27609
Curthay Ct 27610
Curtis Dr 27610
Curvature Ln 27616
Cushing St 27613
Customs House Ct 27615
Cutler St 27603
Cutright Dr 27617
Cutstone Ct 27610
Cy Ln 27603
Cyanne Cir 27606
Cynthia Pl 27610
Cynthiana Ct 27610
Cypress Ln 27609
Cypress Club Dr 27615
Cypress Grove Run 27612
Cypress Knee Ct 27607
Cypress Lakes Dr 27615
Cypress Plantation Dr 27616
Cypress Ridge Ct 27616
Cypress Wood Ct 27606
Cyprine Ct 27603
Cyrus St 27610
Dacian Rd 27610
Daddy Rd 27603
Dade St 27612
Daffodil Dr 27603
Dahlberg Dr 27603
Dahlgreen Rd 27615
Dail Dr 27603
Daimler Way 27607
Daingerfield Dr 27616
Daisy St 27607
Dakar St 27601
Dakins Ct 27615
Daladams St 27603
Dalcross Rd 27610
Dale Rd 27613
Dale St 27605
Daleland Dr 27612
Daleview Dr 27610
Dalewood Dr 27610
Dalford Ct 27604
Dality Dr 27604
Dallas St 27610
Dalmore Pl 27614
Dalton Ct 27613
Dalton Dr 27615
Daltrey Ct 27613
Daly Rd 27604
Damon Ct 27610
Dan David Dr 27606
Dana Dr 27606
Dana Ln 27604
Danang Ct 27610
Danbury Cir 27613
Dancer Ct 27610
Dandelion Ct 27610
Dandridge Dr 27610
Danesfield Ct 27603
Danforth Ct 27615
Daniels St 27605
Daniels Landing Dr 27610
Dansey Dr 27616
Dansington Ct 27615
Dantree Pl 27609
Danube St 27615
Danville Dr 27612
Dapping Dr 27614
Darby St 27610
Darcy Ln 27606
Dare St 27608
Dare Ter 27601
Darfield Dr 27615
Darien Dr 27607
Darling St 27613
Darlington Pl 27612
Darnell Ct 27615
Darrow Dr 27612
Dartford Ct 27615

Dartmoor Ln 27614
Dartmouth Rd 27609
Darwin Ct 27612
Daufuskie Dr 27604
Daventry Ln 27613
Davidson St 27609
E Davie St
1-1099 27601
1300-1699 27610
W Davie St 27601
Davis Cir 27613
Davis St 27608
Davis Creek Dr 27610
Davis Meadow St 27616
Davishire Dr 27615
Daviton Ct 27615
Davy Ln 27601
Dawn Pl 27603
Dawn Piper Dr 27613
Dawn Smoke Ct 27615
Dawnalia Ct 27617
Dawnbrook Dr 27604
Dawnshire Rd 27615
Dawnwood Ct 27609
N Dawson St 27603
S Dawson St 27601
Dawson Mill Run 27606
Daybrook Cir 27606
Daycroft Ct 27615
Daystar Ln 27613
Dayton Ct 27617
Daytona Dr 27610
Daywood Ct 27609
Dean Ave 27616
Deana Ln 27604
Deanwood Dr 27615
Deblyn Ave 27612
Debmoor Pl 27614
Deboy St 27606
Debra Dr 27607
Dechart Ln 27616
Deckbar Pl 27617
Declaration Dr 27615
Dedmon Pl 27616
Deeda Ct 27610
Deep Forest Trl 27603
Deep Glen Ct 27603
Deep Hollow Dr 27612
Deep Pine Run 27603
Deep River Ct 27610
Deep Valley Run 27606
Deer Run 27614
Deer Cove Ln 27610
Deer Creek Trl 27616
Deer Crossing Dr 27616
Deer Fern Dr 27606
Deer Forest Trl 27614
Deer Garden Ct 27606
Deer Haven Dr 27606
Deer Hill Ct 27613
Deer Knoll Ct 27603
Deer Manor Dr 27616
Deer Oaks Ct 27603
Deer Pointe Dr 27616
Deer Stream Ln 27603
Deer Track Dr 27613
Deerfield Rd 27609
Deergrass Ct 27613
Deerhurst Dr 27614
Deering Dr 27616
Deerland Grove Dr 27615
Deershire Ct 27615
Deerview Dr 27606
Deerwood Dr 27612
Deerwood Pl 27607
Dehijuston Ct 27614
Dekoven Pl 27608
Del Monte Dr 27613
Delany Dr 27610
Delaval Ln 27614
Delavan Cir 27613
Delbarton Ct 27606
Delco Ct 27610
Dell Dr 27609
Dellbrook Ct 27617
Dellcain Ct 27617

Dellwood Dr 27607
Delmont Dr 27606
Delshire Ct 27614
Delta Bluff Ln 27606
Delta Lake Dr 27612
Delta Ridge Ct 27612
Delta Vision Ct 27612
Deltona Dr 27615
Delventon Ct 27614
Delway St 27604
Dembridge Dr 27606
Demille Pl 27610
Democracy St 27603
Den Ct 27615
Den Heider Way 27606
Denbel Cir 27604
Denberg Ln 27606
Denbigh Ct 27604
Deneb Ct 27614
Denfield Ct 27615
Denham Ct 27613
Denise Dr 27606
Denlee Rd 27603
Denmark St 27612
Denmead Way 27613
Dennis Ave 27604
Densmore Pl 27612
Denton Ct 27609
Departure Dr
 4900-5898 27616
 4901-5899 27616
 4901-4901 27658
Deponie Dr 27614
Deptford Ct 27609
Derbton Ct 27617
Derby Dr 27610
Derby Ln 27613
Derbyshire Pl 27604
Derek Dr 27613
Dermotte Ln 27604
Derry Ct 27616
Destiny Dr 27604
Detail Dr 27614
Detrick Dr 27609
Devan Oaks Way 27606
Devere Ct 27613
Devereux St 27605
Devlin Ct 27614
Devon Cir 27604
Devonport Dr 27610
Devonshire Dr 27607
Devonwood Ct 27609
Dew Drop Ct 27613
Dewees Ct 27612
Dewing Dr 27616
Dexter Pl 27605
Diamond Dr 27610
Diamond City Ct 27612
Diamond Creek Rd 27614
Diamond Shoal Cv 27604
Diamond Springs Dr 27610
Diamondhitch Trl 27615
Diane Dr 27603
Dianne Ct 27604
Dice Dr 27616
Dickens Dr 27610
Dickinson Cir 27614
Diehl St 27608
Digby Ct 27613
Diggs Dr 27603
Dilford Dr 27604
Dillard Dr 27606
Dillingham Ct 27604
Dillmark Ct 27610
Dillon Cir 27610
Dillswood Ln 27606
Dillwyn Dr 27603
Dime Dr 27606
Dinwiddie Ct 27604
Diploma Ct 27606
Diquedo Dr 27604
Dirt Peeler Dr 27603
Disco Ln 27610
Discovery Dr 27616
District Dr 27607
Division Dr 27603
Dix St 27609
S Dixie Trl 27607
Dixie Forest Rd 27615
Dixon Dr 27609
Dobbin Pl 27604
Dobson Ct 27612
Doby Cir 27610
Doc Arnold Dr 27614
Dockery Ln 27606
Dockside Cir 27613
Dodsworth Dr 27612
Doe Hill Ct 27612
Doe Valley St 27617
Does Run Ct 27613
Dogtrott Ct 27616
Dogwood Dr
 3000-3699 27604
 5800-5899 27616
Dogwood Ln 27607
Dogwood Acres Dr 27603
Dogwood Branch Ct 27612
Dogwood Valley Ct 27616
Dogwood View Ln 27614
Doie Cope Rd 27613
Dolans Way 27614
Dolle Ct 27610
Dolphin Pl 27603
Dolphin Key Ct 27603
Dolphin Waters Ln 27603
Dominion Blvd 27617
Donald Ross Dr 27610
Doncaster Ct 27612
Donegal Ct 27615
Donerail Way 27617
Donna Rd 27604
Donnelly Rd 27610
Donnington Dr 27615
Donny Brook Rd 27603
Donnybrook Rd 27606
Donovan Pl 27610
Dora Pine Ln 27603
Doral St 27608
Doran Pl 27604
Dorcas St 27606
Dorety Pl 27604
Dorleath Ct 27614
Dormitory Rd 27603
Dorner Cir 27606
Dorothea Dr
 400-599 27601
 600-1099 27603
Dorothy Sanders Way 27601
Dorrington Trl 27615
Dorsett Dr 27603
Dorsie Dr 27603
Dorton Rd 27607
Dothan Ct 27614
Double E Ct 27613
Doublebit Dr 27615
Doughton St 27608
Douglas St 27607
Dove Ln 27604
Dove Field Pl 27613
Dove Tree Ln 27610
Dover Rd 27608
Dover Farm Rd 27606
Doverton Ct 27615
Dowling Rd 27610
Dowling Haven Pl 27610
Downey Ct 27612
Downeymeade Ln 27603
Downhill Slide Trl 27614
Downholme Ct 27603
Downing Rd 27610
Downing Way Ct 27614
Downpatrick Ln 27615
Downs Ct 27612
S Downs Dr 27603
Dowse Cir 27610
Doyle Rd 27607
Dr Bill Gilbert Way 27603
Dracena Dr 27610
Draco Rd 27614
Dragby Ln 27603
Drake Cir 27607
Draper Rd 27616
Dray Ct 27613
Drayton Ct 27615
Dream Farm Ln 27616
Dreamy Way 27613
Dresden Ln 27612
Dresden Village Dr 27604
Dressage Ct 27613
Dresser Ct 27609
Drew St 27604
Drewbridge Way 27604
E & W Drewry Ln 27609
Drexel Dr 27609
Driewood Ct 27609
Driftwood Dr 27606
Drolmond Dr 27615
Drommore Ln 27614
Druids Ln 27613
Drum Inlet Pl 27610
Drummond Dr 27609
Drumquin Dr 27614
Dry Bed Ln 27610
Dry Fork Ln 27617
Dryden Ct 27609
Drystone Dr 27613
Dublin Rd 27609
Duck Creek Dr 27616
Duck Pointe Dr 27603
Duckdown Ct 27604
Duckling Way 27610
Duckwing Dr 27604
Duckworth Ct 27616
Dudley Cir 27610
Duffy Pl 27603
Duke Dr 27609
Dukes Dynasty Dr 27615
Dumfries Dr 27609
Dunard St 27614
Dunbar Rd 27606
Dunbarton Way 27613
Dunbrook Ct 27604
Duncan St 27608
Duncanshire Ct 27613
Dundee Pl 27612
Dunes Ct 27615
Dunforest Ct 27614
Dunham Ln 27613
Dunhill Dr 27608
Dunhill Ter 27615
Dunkirk Dr 27613
Dunlee Falls Rd 27613
Dunleith Dr 27614
Dunlin Ln 27614
Dunn Dr 27616
Dunn Rd 27614
Dunnington Cir 27613
Dunraven Dr 27612
Dunrobin Ct 27610
Dunsinane Ct 27604
Dunstable Ct 27614
Dunstan Ct 27613
Duntrune Ct 27606
Dunwood Ct 27613
Dunwoody Dr 27615
Dunwoody Trl 27606
Dunzo Dr 27617
Duplin Rd 27607
Dupont Cir 27603
Duraleigh Rd 27612
Durant Rd
 8600-8699 27614
 8700-9299 27616
 9300-14099 27614
Durham Dr 27603
Durham Rd
 3300-4499 27614
 4501-4699 27614
 5000-5399 27613
Durlain Dr 27614
Durweston Ct 27615
Durwood Dr 27603
Durwood Ln 27604
Duskywing Dr 27613
Dusty Ln 27604
Dusty Rd 27610
Dusty Fox Ln 27606
Dutch Creek Dr 27606
Dutch Garden Ct 27613
Dutch Grove Cir 27610
Dutch Harbor Ct 27606
Dutchman Dr 27606
Dutchman Rd 27610
Duval St 27614
Duval Hill St 27603
Duveneck Dr 27616
Duxbury Dr 27607
Duxford Dr 27614
Dwellinghouse Ct 27615
Dwight Pl 27610
Dyer Ct 27604
Dylan Ct 27606
Dylan Heath Ct 27608
Eagle Trl 27615
Eagle Beach Ct 27610
Eagle Bluff Cir 27613
Eagle Cliff Ct 27613
Eagle Cloud Trl 27606
Eagle Creek Ct 27606
Eagle Stone Ln 27610
Eagle Trace Dr 27604
Eaglebrook Ct 27617
Eaglerock Dr 27613
Eagles Landing Dr 27616
Eaglesfield Dr 27613
Eagleshire Pl 27610
Eagleton Cir 27609
Eaglewood Dr 27610
Eakley Ct 27606
Earl Grey Ct 27612
Earle Rd 27606
Earle Ridge Ln 27606
Earlham Ct 27613
Early St 27610
Early Rise St 27610
Earthstone Ct 27615
Eason Cir 27613
N East St
 1-399 27601
 400-799 27604
S East St 27601
Eastbrook Dr 27615
Eastern Branch Rd 27610
Easthampton Dr 27604
Easthorpe Dr 27613
Eastover Dr 27603
Easy St 27603
Eatmon Mill Ct 27610
Ebb Ct 27615
Ebenezer Church Rd
 3400-8199 27612
 8200-8799 27617
Ebon Ct 27615
Ebony Ct 27610
Eby Dr 27610
Echo Ridge Rd 27612
Eck Dr 27604
Ed Dr 27612
Eddystone Rd 27612
Eden Ln 27608
Eden Close Ct 27613
Eden Croft Dr 27612
Eden Park Dr 27613
Edenburgh Rd 27608
E Edenton St
 1-1099 27601
 1100-1199 27610
 1201-1299 27610
W Edenton St
 1-5 27601
 7-99 27601
 100-499 27603
Edenwood Ln 27615
Edgebury Rd 27613
Edgecombe Ter 27601
Edgedale Dr 27612
Edgehill Ct 27612
Edgemont Dr 27612
Edgerton Ct & Dr 27612
Edgeside Ct 27609
Edgetone Dr 27604
Edgeview Ct 27613
Edgewater Ct 27614
Edgewood Rd 27609
Edington Ln 27604
Edison Rd 27610
Edmund St 27604
Edmundson Ave 27614
Edridge Ct 27612
Edsel Dr 27613
Edward Pride Wynd 27612
Edwards Ln 27606
Edwards Mill Rd
 1000-1499 27607
 3000-5899 27612
Edwell Ct 27617
Edwin Dr 27610
Eel Ct 27616
Effingham Cir 27615
Eglantyne Ct 27613
Egrets Nest Ln 27603
Eider Ct 27616
Eilla Bluffs Ct 27606
Elaine Ave 27616
Elberon Pl 27609
Elbridge Dr 27603
Elders Grove Way 27610
Elderson Ln 27612
Eleanor Rigby Ct 27603
Electra Dr 27607
Electronics Dr 27604
Elegance Dr 27614
Elham Ct 27615
Eliot Pl 27609
Elizabeth Dr 27604
Elizabeth Bennet Pl 27616
Elkhart Dr 27610
Elkpark Dr 27610
Elkton Dr 27610
Elkwood Ct 27613
Ellerbe Ln 27610
Ellesmere Ct 27614
Ellington St 27601
Ellington Oaks Ct 27603
Elliott Dr 27613
Ellis Ct 27603
Ellis Dr 27612
Ellsmere Ln 27604
Ellstree Ln 27617
Ellwood Dr 27609
Elm Cir 27616
Elm St
 200-399 27601
 400-999 27604
Elm Heights Ln 27616
Elm Tree Ln 27614
Elmbrook Ct 27614
Elmfield St 27614
Elmgate Way 27614
Elmhurst Cir 27610
Elmhurst Ridge Ct 27616
Elmleaf Ct 27614
Elmsford Way 27608
Elmwood Dr 27603
Elmwood View Rd 27614
Elon Dr 27613
Elsie Lorraine Dr 27603
Elsmore Ct 27607
Elvin Ct 27607
Embleton Dr 27612
Emcutta Ct 27604
Emerald Club Ct 27617
Emerald Creek Dr 27617
Emerald Hill Ct 27613
Emerson Dr 27609
Emerywood Dr 27615
Emmit Dr 27604
Emmitt Pond Rd 27616
Emory Ln 27609
Empire Lakes Dr 27617
Enchanted Rd 27606
Enchanted Hollow
Way 27614
Enchanted Oaks Dr 27606
Enchanting Way 27616
Enderbury Dr 27614
Endsley Ct 27610
Enduring Freedom Dr 27610
Endwell Dr 27616
Enfield Ct 27615
Englefield Dr 27615
Englehardt Dr 27617
English Garden Way 27612
English Ivy Ln 27615
English Laurel Ln 27612
English Oaks Dr 27615
English Rose Ln 27614
Enka Dr 27610
Ennis Ct 27613
Ennismore Cir 27613
Enoree Ln 27616
Enson Pl 27603
Enterprise St 27607
Entheos Ln 27610
Entrepreneur Dr 27606
Eolian Ct 27607
Epperly Ct 27616
Epping Forest Dr 27613
Erie Rd 27610
Erin Ct 27615
Erinridge Rd 27610
Erins Way Ln 27614
Erinsbrook Dr 27617
Ervin Ct 27614
Es Kings Vlg 27607
Escambia Ln 27616
Esher Ct 27609
Esmond Pond Rd 27616
Essex Garden Ln 27612
Essie St 27610
Essington Pl 27603
Estate Hill St 27617
Estate Ridge Rd 27617
Ethan Ln 27613
Ethans Overlook Dr 27614
Ethridge Ct 27615
Eton Rd 27608
Etta Burke Ct 27606
Euclid St 27604
Euston St 27610
Eva Mae Dr 27610
Evander Way 27613
Evans Dr 27610
Evans Mill Pl 27613
Evening Song Cir 27610
Everett Ave 27607
Evergreen Ave 27603
Evergreen Ct 27613
Evergreen Chase Way 27613
Evergreen Forest Way 27616
Evergreen Spring Pl 27614
Evers Dr 27610
Eversfield Dr 27615
Everspring Ln 27616
Everview Ct 27613
Ewing Pl 27616
Exacta Ln 27613
Exchange Plz 27601
Executive Dr 27609
Exeter Cir 27608
N Exeter Way 27613
Exeter Field Cir 27614
Exeton Ct 27615
Exhibit Ct 27617
Exposition Pl 27615
Express Dr 27603
Extine Ln 27610
Exton Woods Dr 27614
Eyrie Ct 27606
Faber Dr 27606
Fabric Ridge Ln 27603
Fair Chase Ct 27617
Fair Meadows Ln 27607
Fair Rain Dr 27616
Fair Valley Ct 27617
Fairall Dr 27607
Fairbanks Dr 27613
Fairbridge Rd 27613
Fairbrook Ter 27617
Fairburn Ct 27615
Faircloth St 27607
Fairfax Dr 27609
Fairfield Dr 27608
Fairforest Pl 27604
Fairhaven Ct 27612
Fairhill Dr 27612
Fairlawn Dr 27615
Fairley Dr 27607
Fairlie Pl 27613
Fairmead Cir 27613
Fairmont Ct 27615
Fairpoint Ct 27613
Fairview Rd
 1300-2008 27608
 2009-2009 27628
 2010-3098 27608
 2011-3099 27608
Fairway Dr 27603
Fairway Ridge Dr 27606
Faison Pl 27608
Falcon Knoll Cir 27616
Falcon Rest Cir 27615
Faldo Cv 27603
Falkirk Pl 27604
Falkland Ave 27617
Falkwood Rd 27617
Fall Ln 27604
Fall Mall Dr 27614
Fallbrook Cir 27604
Fallen Leaf Ct 27606
Fallen Log Ct 27610
Falling Leaf Ct 27615
Falling Water Ct 27603
Falling Wind Ct 27610
Fallon Oaks Ct 27608
N Falls Ct & Dr 27615
Falls Bridge Dr 27614
Falls Church Rd 27609
Falls Common Dr 27609
Falls Farm Xing 27614
Falls Forest Dr 27615
Falls Glen Ct 27614
Falls Lake Cir 27614
Falls Landing Dr 27614
Falls Meadow Ct 27617
Falls Mill Dr 27614
Falls Of Neuse Rd
 4301-4397 27609
 4399-6299 27609
 6300-7801 27615
 7800-7800 27624
 7803-9799 27615
 7900-9798 27615
 9800-14599 27614
Falls Preserve Dr 27615
Falls River Ave 27614
Falls Tower Dr 27614
Falls Valley Dr 27615
Fallston Ct 27613
Fallswood Pl 27613
Falmouth Dr 27604
Falstaff Rd 27610
Fan Palm Ct 27616
Fanleaf Trl 27612
Fanny Brown Rd 27603
Fares Wall Ct 27616
Fargo Ct 27612
Faringdon Pl 27609
Farless Rd 27613
Farley Dr 27609
Farlow Rd 27603
Farlow Gap Ln 27603
Farm Rd 27603
Farm Gate Rd 27606
Farm Meadow Rd 27603
Farmdale Rd 27610
Farmer Ln 27606
Farmers Market Dr 27603
Farmington Ct 27615
Farmington Grove Dr 27614
Farmingwood Ln 27615
Farmlea Cir 27616
Farmridge Rd 27617
Farmstone Dr 27603
Farmville Rd 27614
Farmwell Rd 27610
Farmwood Dr 27613
Farnborough Rd 27613
Farnham Ct 27615
Farrier Ct 27603
Farrington Dr 27615
Farrior Rd 27607

Farris Ct 27610
Farside Pl 27616
Farthingale Ct 27603
Fast Park Dr 27617
Father And Sons Dr 27613
Fathom Ct 27606
Fatima Ct 27610
Faucette Dr 27607
Faulkner Pl 27609
Faversham Pl 27604
Favorwood Ct 27615
Fawn Creek Ct 27616
Fawn Glen Dr 27616
Fawn Hill Ct 27617
Fawn Lake Dr 27617
Fawnbrook Cir 27612
Fawncrest Dr 27603
Fawndale Dr 27612
Fayetteville Rd 27603
Fayetteville St
100-299 27601
300-1298 27601
300-300 27602
301-1299 27601
1300-1899 27603
Feather Grass Ln 27613
Feathers Ln 27606
Featherstone Dr 27615
Felbrigg Dr 27615
Feldmen Dr 27603
Fellers Pond Dr 27610
Fellowship Dr 27617
Felton Pl 27612
Felucca Pl 27617
Fenham Ct 27604
Fenn Brook Ln 27613
Fenner Ln 27603
Fenton St 27604
Fenwick Dr 27603
Fenwood Dr 27609
Feralenc Rd 27614
Ferdilah Ln 27610
Fereday Ct 27616
Ferguson Rd 27612
Fern Dr 27603
Fern Creek Ct 27613
Fern Forest Dr 27603
Fern Grass Ln 27604
Fern Stone Ct 27604
Fernbrook Rd 27610
Ferncliff Cir 27609
Ferndell Ln 27607
Ferndown Ct 27603
Fernham Pl 27612
Fernhill Ln 27612
Fernhurst Ct & Ln 27604
Fernwood Dr 27612
Ferrell Woods Ln 27603
Ferret Ct 27610
Ferriday Ct 27616
Ferry Launch Way 27617
Fetlock Dr 27613
Fiddler Ct 27616
Fiddlewood Ct 27613
Fidelis Ln 27613
Fidelity Blvd 27617
Field St 27604
Field And Stream Rd 27613
Field Hill Rd 27603
Field Towne Ln 27614
Fieldale Dr 27610
Fieldcross Ct 27610
Fieldgrass Pl 27603
Fieldhouse Ave 27603
Fielding Dr 27606
Fieldland Ct 27614
Fieldmist Dr 27614
Fieldmont Ct 27614
Fields Dr 27603
Fields Of Broadlands
Dr 27604
Fieldspring Ln 27606
Fieldstone Ct & Dr 27609
Fieldstream Farm Rd 27603
Fieldview Ct 27607
Fieldwood Ct 27616
Fiesta Way 27615
Fifebrew Ln 27614
Fig Leaf Ct 27610
Fig Vine Dr 27609
Filbert St 27610
Filbin Creek Dr 27616
Filgate Ct 27615
Filigree Ct 27614
Filmore St 27605
Final Trail Ct 27603
Finale Pt 27604
Fincastle Dr 27607
Finestra Way 27610
Finland Dr 27612
Finley Ridge Ln 27615
Finsbury Ct 27609
Finsbury Park Way 27614
Fire Pink Way 27613
Firecracker St 27610
Firelight Rd 27610
Firerun Ct 27610
Fireside Dr 27609
Firestone Ln 27604
Firewood Cir 27607
Firth Of Tay Way 27603
Firwood Ln 27614
N & S Fisher St 27610
Fishers Island Ct 27604
Fisk Ct 27604
Fitzgerald Dr 27610
Fitzwilliam St 27614
Five Heart Cir 27603
Five Leaf Ln 27613
Flagstone Pl 27612
Flamingo Ln 27610
Flanagan Pl 27612
Flanking Ln 27610
Flat Fern Dr 27610
Flat Keystone Dr 27613
Flat Sedge Ln 27604
Flavion Dr 27608
Fleet Service Dr 27617
Fleetwood Dr 27612
Fletcher Dr 27603
Flint Pl 27605
Flint Ridge Pl 27609
Flint Rock Cir 27613
Flintshire Rd 27604
Flintwood Ct 27609
Floral Ridge Ct 27613
Florence St 27603
Floretta Pl 27676
Florida Ct 27615
Flower Bed Ct 27614
Flower Blossom Cir 27610
Flower Garden Dr 27610
Flower Round Ct 27610
Flowerfield Ln 27606
Flowering Peach Trl 27610
Flowery Branch Rd 27610
Flowing Dr 27610
Flowing River Ct 27610
Floyd Dr 27610
Flutterby Way 27610
Fly Fish Ln 27610
Fly Way Dr 27604
Flying Buttress Dr 27613
Focal Pt 27617
Foggy Bottom Dr 27613
Foggy River Ct 27610
Folger St 27604
Folinsbee Ct 27616
Folk Ln 27610
E & W Folkestone Pl 27604
Follow Me Way 27610
Fontana Pl 27615
Fontana Ridge Ln 27613
Footman Way 27615
Fordham Ln 27604
Fordland Dr 27606
Forest Dr 27616
E Forest Dr 27605
Forest Rd
100-399 27605
3400-3499 27604
Forest Creek Rd 27606
Forest Garden Ln 27606
Forest Glade Ct 27615
Forest Glen Dr 27603
Forest Highland Dr 27604
Forest Lawn Ct 27612
Forest Mill Cir 27616
Forest Oaks Dr 27609
Forest Pines Dr 27614
Forest Point Rd 27610
Forest Ridge Rd 27609
Forest Shadows Ln 27614
Forestchase Ct 27603
Forestdale Rd 27603
Forestford Ct 27610
Forestview Rd
3700-3899 27612
3900-4199 27607
Forestville Rd
2900-5099 27616
5100-5198 27604
5200-6899 27604
Formal Garden Way 27603
Forsyth St 27609
Fort Aly 27601
Fort Hill Ct 27615
Fort Macon Ct 27615
Fort Sumter Rd 27606
Fortingale Cir 27613
Fortress Gate Dr 27614
Fortune Way 27617
Forum Dr 27615
Forward Way 27614
Fossil Creek Ct 27617
Fostoria Ct 27606
Foundry Pl 27616
Fountain Dr 27610
Fountain Park Dr 27613
Fountainhead Dr 27609
Four Sons Ct 27610
Four Townes Ln 27616
Four Winds Dr 27615
Fourfoot Ct 27616
Fowler Ave 27607
Fowler Ridge Dr 27616
Fowlkes Pl 27612
Fownes Ct 27613
Fox Rd 27616
Fox Bluff Ct 27616
Fox Branch Ct 27614
Fox Chase Ct 27606
Fox Crossing Dr 27603
Fox Fern Ln 27604
Fox Haven Pl 27616
Fox Hollow Dr 27610
Fox Hunt Ln 27615
Fox Pen Dr 27603
Fox Ridge Manor Rd 27610
Fox Run Dr 27610
Fox Sterling Dr 27606
Fox Stone Dr 27603
Fox Valley St 27614
Foxbrook Dr 27603
Foxburrow Ct 27613
Foxcroft Rd 27614
Foxfire Pl 27615
Foxford Ct 27614
Foxgate Dr 27610
Foxgrove Ct 27617
Foxhall St 27609
Foxhall Village Rd 27616
Foxhill Cir 27610
Foxhound Rd 27616
Foxlair Ct 27609
Foxmoor Ct N & S 27616
Foxtail Ct 27610
Foxtrot Rd 27610
Foxvale Ct 27610
Foxwood Dr 27615
Framingham Ct 27615
Frank St 27604
E Franklin St 27604
W Franklin St 27604
Franklin Ter 27601
Franklin Ridge Ct 27616
Franks Dr 27610
Franz Liszt Ct 27615
S Fraternity Ct 27606
S Fraternity Court Dr 27606
Frazier Dr 27610
Freedom Dr 27610
Freeman St 27601
Freemont Ln 27613
Freestone Ln 27603
Freewood Ct 27606
French Dr 27612
French Lake Dr 27604
Frenchill Cir 27610
Frenchwood Dr 27612
Freys Hill Ct 27612
Friar Tuck Rd 27610
Friars Walk Pl 27609
Friedel Pl 27613
Friedland Pl 27617
Friendly Dr 27607
Friendly Trl 27610
Friendly Way 27614
Friendly Neighbor Ln 27614
Frinks St 27610
Frogstool Ln 27610
Front St 27609
Frost Ct 27609
Fugate Ct 27617
Fulham Pl 27615
Full Cir 27613
Full Meadow Pl 27603
Fuller St 27603
Fullerton Pl 27607
Fullwood Pl 27614
Fulton Ct 27610
Fun Park Dr 27617
Funster Ln 27615
Furches St 27607
Furman Hall 27612
Futura Ln 27610
Gabe Ct 27613
Gable Top Ln 27607
Gabriel Trl 27606
Gabriels Bend Dr 27612
Gaddy Dr 27609
Gadland Ct 27609
Gadsen Ct 27613
Gadwell Ct 27606
Gaelic Trl 27604
Gaheris Ct 27614
Gaillard Dr 27614
Gainsborough Dr 27612
Gainswood Ct 27615
Gala Ct 27615
Gala Farm Ln 27603
Galand Ct 27614
Galax Dr 27612
Gallatree Ln 27616
Galleria Ave 27614
Gallop Ct 27614
Galloway Ct 27615
Galon Glen Rd 27613
Galway Dr 27613
Gamble Dr 27610
Gamelyn Walk 27612
Gann Trl 27612
Gannett St 27606
Gansett Ln 27612
Garden Pl 27607
Garden City Ct 27604
Garden Crest Cir 27609
Garden Grove Ln 27610
Garden Hill Dr 27614
Garden Knoll Ln 27614
Garden Oaks Ct 27606
Garden Springs Ln 27610
Garden Tree Ln 27614
Garden View Ln 27614
Garden Wall Ct 27614
Garden Warbler Ln 27613
Gardenbrook Dr 27606
Gardenia Ct 27603
Gardenlake Dr 27612
Gardner St 27607
Garfield St 27603
Garland Dr 27606
Garner Rd
1000-1199 27601
1200-3699 27610
E Garner Rd 27610
Garner Glen Dr 27603
Garner Station Blvd 27603
Garnet Ridge Way 27607
W Garrali Blvd 27623
Garrett Ct 27616
Garrett Rd 27606
Garrison Ct 27612
Garvey Dr 27616
Gary St 27606
Gaspari Ct 27615
Gaston St
600-699 27603
700-799 27605
Gaston Wood Ct 27605
Gatcombe Pl 27604
Gateridge Dr 27613
Gates St 27609
Gateway Pl 27617
Gateway Access Pt 27607
Gateway Park Dr 27601
Gathering Pl 27604
Gatling St 27610
Gatwick Ct 27613
Gavin St 27608
Gaylord Dr 27612
Geary Trl 27610
Gelder Dr 27603
Gemini Dr 27604
General Jos Martin Cir 27606
Generation Dr 27612
Geneva St 27606
Genford Ct 27609
Gentle Breezes Ln 27614
Gentle Slope Way 27603
Gentle Springs Ct 27603
Gentle Valley Ln 27603
George V Strong
Wynd 27612
Georgetown Rd 27608
Georgian Ter 27607
Gerber Ct 27614
Germantown Rd 27607
Gibbs Hill Ct 27613
Gibney Dr 27610
Gideon Creek Way 27603
Gidleigh Xing 27616
Gilbert Ave 27603
Gilliam Ln 27610
Gilman Ln 27610
Gin St 27610
Ginger Trl 27614
Giralda Walk 27617
Girard Ln 27613
Girth Ln 27603
Glackens Ct 27616
Glade Cv 27617
Glade Aster Ct 27604
Glade Spring Ct 27612
Gladstone Dr 27610
Glamorgan Ct 27612
Glascock St
100-198 27604
200-799 27604
801-999 27604
1001-2097 27610
2099-2799 27610
Glasgow St 27610
Glass Ridge Rd 27616
Glass Tower Way 27612
Glassman Ln 27606
Glassville Ct 27604
N Glen Dr 27609
Glen Abbott Ln 27613
Glen Autumn Rd 27617
Glen Brack Ct 27603
Glen Branch Ct 27603
Glen Burnie Dr 27607
Glen Canyon Rd 27616
Glen Currin Dr 27612
Glen Dean Ct 27603
Glen Eden Cir & Dr 27612
Glen Erin Way 27613
Glen Forest Dr 27612
Glen Garnock Cir 27613
Glen Henry Dr 27612
Glen Iris Ln 27612
Glen Kirk Dr 27612
Glen Lake Ct 27606
Glen Laurel Dr 27612
Glen Mill Ct 27606
Glen Oak Ct 27606
Glen Royal Rd 27617
Glen Valley Dr 27609
Glen Verde Trl 27613
Glenanneve Pl 27608
Glenbrittle Way 27615
Glenbrook Dr 27610
Glencastle Way 27606
Glencree Ct 27612
Glencross Ct 27604
Glendale Dr 27612
Glenden Falls Way 27614
Glendower Rd 27613
Gleneagles Dr 27613
Glenferrie Ct 27616
Glenfiddich Way 27613
Glenfield Ln 27613
Glengrove Rd 27616
Glenharden Dr 27613
Glenhaven Rd 27606
Glenhurst North Dr 27603
Glenlake Ct 27606
Glenlake Garden Dr 27612
Glenlivet Way 27613
Glenmartin Dr 27615
Glenmist Ct 27612
Glenmorgan Ln 27616
Glenn Ave 27608
Glenraven Dr 27604
Glenridge Dr 27604
Glenriver Ct 27616
Glenrock Cir 27613
Glenroy Ct 27616
Glenthorne Dr 27613
Glenwood Ave
1-699 27603
700-1499 27605
1500-2999 27608
3000-8599 27612
8600-10799 27617
S Glenwood Ave 27603
Glenwood Gardens Ln 27608
Glenwood Springs Ct 27616
Global St 27610
Globe Rd 27617
Gloria Pl 27614
Glorietta Cir 27613
Glosson Rd 27606
Gloucester Rd 27612
Glover Ln 27605
Godfrey Dr 27612
Godley Ln 27617
Godwin Ct 27606
Gold Hall 27607
Gold Mine Ct 27615
Gold Star Dr 27607
Goldcrest Ln 27616
Golden Ave 27603
Golden St 27610
Golden Amber Ct 27610
Golden Arrow Ln 27613
Golden Bell Dr 27610
Golden Branch Ln 27603
Golden Heights Dr 27606
Golden Lantern Ct 27613
Golden Moss Trl 27613
Golden Oak Ct 27603
Golden Sun Dr 27614
Goldeneye Ct 27606
Goldengate Ct 27613
Goldenglow Way 27606
Goldenrain Way 27612
Goldfinch Way 27606
Goldsmith Ct 27613
Golf Course Dr 27610
Golf Link Dr 27617
Goode St 27603
Goodrich Dr 27614
Goodrum Ct 27617
Goodstone Dr 27616
Goodview Ct 27613
Goose Pond Rd 27615
Goosedown Ct 27604
Gordon St 27608
Gordon Glen Ct 27617
Goren Pl 27603
Gorman St
400-700 27607
702-798 27607
800-3199 27606
Goshawk Ln 27603
Gotherstone Ct 27615
Goudy Dr 27615
Governor Manly Way 27614
Governors Ct 27604
Governors Hill Ln 27603
Grace St 27604
Grace Brook Rd 27609
Graceland Ct 27606
Graduate Ln 27606
Grady Cir 27615
Graedon Dr 27603
Grafton Rd 27615
Graham St 27605
Graham Newton Rd 27606
Grahamstone Rd 27610
Gralyn Rd 27613
Gramercy Ct 27609
Granada Dr 27612
Granada Hills Dr 27613
Grand Ave 27606
Grand Carolina Way 27603
Grand Cypress Ct 27604
Grand Estate Dr 27617
Grand Gate Dr 27613
Grand Journey Ave 27614
Grand Look Ct 27610
Grand Manor Ct 27612
Grand Prince Ln 27603
Grand Traverse Dr 27604
Grande Meadow Way 27603
Grandiflora Ln 27604
Grandmas Ln 27603
Grandover Dr 27610
Grandview Ct 27615
Grandview Heights Ln 27614
Granite St 27603
Granite Ridge Trl 27616
Grant Ave
1200-2298 27608
2300-2699 27608
2700-3099 27607
Grantland Dr 27610
Granville Dr 27609
Granville Ter 27601
Grasmere Ct 27609
Grasshopper Rd 27610
Grassington Way 27615
Grassy Banks Dr 27610
Grassy Creek Pl 27614
Grassy Field Dr 27610
Grassy Knoll Ln 27616
Graves Ct 27608
Graylyn Dr 27612
Graymar Ct 27616
Graymont Pl 27615
Grayson Ridge Ct 27613
Great Bear Ln 27614
Great Laurel Dr 27616
Great Meadows Ct 27609
Great Oaks Dr 27608
Great Pine Way 27614
Greater Hills St 27614
Grecian Woods Pl 27606
Greek Way 27606
Greek Village Dr 27606
Green Rd
3900-4799 27604
4800-4999 27616
Green St 27603
Green Acres Ln 27616
Green Cliff Ct 27615
Green Downs Dr 27613
Green Feather Ln 27604
Green Jacket Trl 27610
Green Knight Ct 27612

Green Lantern St 27613
Green Meadow Dr 27603
Green Mill Dr 27616
Green Needles Blvd 27610
Green Pine Ct 27614
Green Pine Dr 27603
Green Ridge Dr 27609
Green Tap Ct 27603
Green Tunnel Ln 27613
Green Valley Dr 27606
Green Vista Way 27604
Greenbranch Ln 27603
Greenbrier Rd 27603
Greencastle Ct 27604
Greencove Ct 27609
Greenevers Dr 27613
Greenfield Dr 27615
Greenhead Ct 27615
Greenlawn Dr 27609
Greenleaf St 27606
Greenock Dr 27604
Greens Dairy Rd 27616
Greenside Dr 27609
Greentree Ct 27615
Greenvale Rd 27603
Greenway Ave 27608
Greenway St 27615
Greenwich St 27610
Greenwood St 27608
Gregg St 27601
Gregmoor Ct 27614
Gregory Ln 27610
Grenadine Ct 27612
Grenelle St 27603
Gresham Grove Ln 27615
Gresham Hills Dr 27615
Gresham Lake Rd
2000-3499 27615
3700-3799 27616
Gresham Trace Ln 27615
Gretna Green Ln 27603
Grettle Ct 27617
Gretton Pl 27615
Grey Abbey Pl 27615
Grey Coat Ct 27616
Grey Harbor Dr 27616
Grey Oak Dr 27615
Grey Paw Ct 27603
Greylock Ct 27603
Greys Landing Way 27615
Greyson St 27610
Greystone Dr 27615
Greystone Overlook Ct 27615
Greystone Park Dr 27615
Greywalls Ln 27614
Greywinds Dr 27615
Greywood Dr 27604
Griffice Mill Rd 27610
Griffin Cir 27610
Griffis Glen Dr 27610
Griffith Park Rd 27613
Grilse Way 27613
Grimaldi Ct 27612
Grimstead Ln 27613
Grinding Stone Dr 27604
Grinnell Dr 27612
Grissom St 27603
Grist Mill Rd 27615
Groomsbridge Ct 27612
Grosbeak Way 27616
Grosvenor Dr 27615
Groundnut Ct 27613
Groundwater Pl 27610
Grove Ave 27606
Grove St 27601
Grove Barton Rd 27613
Grove Church Rd 27612
Grove Crabtree Cres 27613
Grove Creek Ln 27610
Grove Crest Ct 27613
Grove Estates Ter 27606
Grove Hill Ct 27610
Grove Hollow St 27601
Grove Lake Ct 27613
Grove Point Ct 27609
Grove Ridge Rd 27614
Grovechase Ln 27617
Grovehurst Dr 27613
Groveland Ave 27605
Grovemont Rd 27603
Groveshire Dr 27616
Groveside Ct 27613
Grovewood Pl 27606
Guard Hill Dr 27610
Guerro Ct 27613
Guffy Dr 27603
Guiding Light Rd 27610
Guilford Cir 27608
Gulf Ct 27617
Gulley Ln 27603
Gumtree Ct 27610
Gumwood Ln 27615
Gun Powder Pl 27616
Gunnette Dr 27610
Gunnison Pl 27609
Gunston Pl 27612
Gushing Dr 27610
Guy Cir 27613
Guy Johnson Ln 27603
Guyandotte Ln 27616
Gw Ct 27603
Gwynn Oaks Dr 27614
Gwynnebrook Cir 27613
H And R Dr 27610
Habbot Dr 27603
Habersham Pl 27610
Habitat Ct 27610
Hackney Ct 27613
Haddon Ct 27606
Hadley Rd 27610
Hadley Meadows Dr 27603
Hagney St 27614
Haig Point Way 27604
Hailey Dr 27606
Haines Creek Ln 27616
Haithcock Rd 27604
Halberd Ct 27613
Halburton Rd 27613
Halcott Ct 27613
Hales Rd 27608
Halethorpe Dr 27613
Haleytree Ct 27606
Halfhitch Trl 27615
Halfmoon Ct 27613
Halford Dr 27604
Halifax St 27604
S Hall Dr 27610
Hall Pl 27607
N & S Hall Dormitory 27607
Hallam Way 27616
Hallberg Ln 27614
Hallingdale Ct 27614
Halliwell Dr 27606
Halstead Ln 27613
Halton Ct 27615
Hambledon Ct 27615
Hamilton Rd 27604
Hamilton Club Dr 27617
Hamilton Mill Dr 27616
Hamlet Dr 27604
Hamlet Green Dr 27614
Hamletville St 27614
Hamlin Ct 27616
Hammell Dr 27603
Hammersmith Dr 27613
Hammock Pl 27606
Hammond Rd 27603
Hammond Business Pl 27603
Hampshire Ct 27612
Hampstead Ct 27613
Hampstead Pl 27610
Hampton Rd 27607
Hampton Ridge Rd 27603
Hampton Woods Ln 27607
Hamptonshire Ct & Dr 27613
Hamrick Dr 27615
Hampstead Xing 27612
Hanarry Ct 27614
Handsworth Ln 27607
Handy Ln 27603
Hanford Ct 27614
Hanging Fern Ln 27604
Hanging Rock Rd 27613
Hank Aaron Ln 27604
Hannover Sq 27601
Hanover St 27608
Hanska Way 27610
Happiness Hill Ln 27614
Happy Ln 27614
Harbins Ct 27613
Harbison Way 27615
Harbor Dr 27615
Harbor Crest Rd 27614
Harborough Ct 27613
Harbour Towne Dr 27604
Harbourgate Dr 27612
Harcourt Dr 27613
Hardee Rd 27614
Harden Rd 27607
Hardeth Way 27616
Hardimont Rd 27609
Harding St 27604
Hardwick Ct 27614
Hardwick Dr 27615
Haresnipe Ct 27613
E Hargett St
1-1099 27601
1100-1399 27610
W Hargett St
1-399 27601
400-899 27603
Hargrove Rd
4400-4699 27604
4700-4899 27616
Haringey Dr 27615
Harkers Ct 27615
Harkers Island Ct 27604
Harline Ct 27614
Harmont Dr 27603
Harmony Ct 27610
Harness Cir 27614
Harnett Dr 27616
Harp St & Ter 27604
Harper Rd 27603
Harps Mill Rd 27615
Harps Mill Woods Run 27615
Harptree Ct 27613
N Harrington St 27603
S Harrington St
1-399 27603
400-599 27601
Harrington Grove Dr 27613
Harris St 27607
Harrod St 27604
Harrogate Ct 27613
Harter Ct 27610
Hartford Rd 27610
Hartham Park Ave 27616
Hartland Ct 27614
Hartwick Ct 27613
Harvard St 27609
Harvest Ct 27616
Harvest Ln 27606
Harvest Acres Ct 27617
Harvest Brook Ln 27617
Harvest Mill Ct 27610
Harvest Oaks Dr 27615
Harvey St 27608
Harvey Johnson Rd 27603
Harvey Meadows Rd 27603
Harward Ln 27606
Harwich Ct 27609
Hasty St 27603
Hatchies Dr 27610
Hatfield Ln 27603
Hathaway Rd 27608
Hatherleigh Ct 27612
Hatteras Ct 27607
Hatton Way 27604
Haven Rd 27610
Haven Hill Ct 27603
Havenhurst Ct 27603
Havenwood Ct 27615
Havenwood Dr 27616
Haverford Ct 27614
Haverhill Ct 27609
Havering Pl 27604
Havershire Dr 27613
Haverty Dr 27610
Hawes Ct 27608
Hawick Rd 27615
Hawkhurst St 27604
Hawkins St 27610
Hawksbury Ln 27606
Hawkshead Rd 27613
Hawksmoor Dr 27615
Hawley Ct 27609
Haworth Dr 27609
Hawser Ct 27606
Hawthorne Park 27613
Hawthorne Rd 27605
N Hawthorne Way 27613
Hawtree Dr 27613
Hay Ln 27601
Hay Meadow Ct 27603
Hayden Ct 27612
Hayfield Dr 27610
Hayling Dr 27610
Hayloft Cir 27606
Haymarket Ln 27615
Haynes St 27604
Haywood St 27601
Hazelnut Dr 27610
Hazelwood Dr 27608
Heacham Ct 27614
Header Stone Dr 27613
Headwater Ct 27606
Health Park 27615
Hearth Dr 27609
Hearth Fire Ln 27604
Hearthridge Ct 27609
Hearthstone Dr 27615
Heartley Dr 27615
Heath St 27610
Heather Dr 27606
Heather Garden Way 27613
Heather Meadow Ln 27614
Heather Ridge Ln 27610
Heatherbrook Cir 27612
Heatherfield Way 27604
Heathermill Ln 27617
Heathersmith Ct 27604
Heatherstone Dr 27606
Heatherview Dr 27614
Heathfield Dr 27615
Heathgate Ln 27613
Heathill Ct 27603
Heathrowe Pl 27609
Heathshire Dr 27616
Heathwood Ct 27615
Heck St 27601
Hedge Maple Dr 27603
Hedgelawn Way 27615
Hedgemoor Dr 27612
Hedgerow Dr 27616
Hedgestone Run 27603
Hedgewood Village Pl 27612
Hedingham Blvd 27604
Heel Stone Ct 27613
Heelands Ct 27610
Hegarty Ter 27606
Helena Ct 27613
Helix Ct 27606
Helmond Way 27617
Helms Pl 27610
Helmsley Ave 27616
Hemingway Dr 27609
Hemingway Forest Pl 27607
Hemingwood Ct 27613
Hemlock Ct 27615
Hemlock Forest Cir 27612
Hempbridge Dr 27614
Hemphill Dr 27609
Hempshire Pl 27613
Hemsbury Way 27612
Henderson St 27607
Hendren Cir 27610
Henley Park Ct 27612
Henline Dr 27604
Henning Dr 27615
Henny Pl 27614
Henry Dr 27613
Henry J Menninger Wynd 27612
Henrys Garden Ln 27612
Hensley Dr 27615
Henslowe Dr 27603
Hepworth Ct 27615
Herdsman Way 27614
Heritage Ln 27606
Heritage Pl 27604
Heritage Falls Dr 27614
Heritage Grove Rd 27603
Heritage Manor Dr 27610
Herman Pl 27616
Hermitage Dr 27612
Herndon Oaks Way 27604
Herndon Village Way 27610
Herringbone Dr 27614
Hershey Ct 27613
Herston Rd 27610
Hertford St 27609
Hester Cir 27604
Hester Dr 27606
Hewberry Ln 27610
Heydon Ct 27614
Heygill Ln 27604
Hi Bridge Ct 27615
Hichalde Rd 27616
Hickman Dr 27614
Hickory Dr 27603
Hickory Ln 27603
Hickory Rd 27616
Hickory Grove Church Rd 27613
Hickory Hollow Ln 27610
Hickory Leaf Dr 27606
Hickory Mill Xing 27617
Hickory Nut Dr 27613
Hickory Pond Ct 27612
Hickory Ridge Dr 27609
Hickory Tree Pl 27610
Hidden Branches Dr 27613
Hidden Cove Ct 27604
Hidden Creek Dr 27616
Hidden Dove Ln 27606
Hidden Glen Ln 27606
Hidden Harbor Ln 27615
Hidden Knoll Pl 27606
Hidden Pond Dr 27613
Hidden Ridge Dr 27613
Hidden River Ct 27614
Hidden Tree Ct 27606
Hidden Vale Dr 27614
Hidden View Ct 27613
Hidden Waters Cir 27614
Hiddenbrook Dr 27609
Hideaway Ct 27613
High Dr 27610
High Bluff Ct 27612
High Glen Pt 27614
High Grove Dr 27610
High Holly Ln 27614
High Knoll Ct 27603
High Lake Ct 27606
High Mountain Dr 27603
High Oaks Ln 27606
High Ridge Dr 27606
High Rock Ct 27604
High Summit Dr 27603
Highbrook Trl 27616
Highcastle Ct 27613
Highcourt Dr 27610
Highcross Ct 27613
Highgate Pl 27610
Highgate Rd 27603
Highhill Rd 27615
Highland Pl 27607
Highland Glen Ct 27612
Highland Park Ct 27613
Highlander Dr 27603
Highlandview Cir 27613
Highline St 27616
Highmore Trl 27603
Highpark Ln 27608
Highstream Dr 27614
Hightower St 27610
Highview Ct
1400-1499 27606
4700-4799 27613
Highview Pl 27606
Highway 64 E 27610
Highway 98 27614
Highwoods Blvd 27604
Hihenge Ct 27615
Hiking Trl 27615
Hilburn Dr 27613
Hill Pl 27613
Hill St
1-599 27610
2200-2499 27604
Hill Haven Dr 27610
Hillandale Dr 27609
Hillbrow Ln 27615
Hillcreek Ct & Dr 27603
Hillcrest Dr 27610
Hillcrest Rd 27605
Hillcross Ct 27615
Hillewood Ln 27603
Hillingdon Way 27614
Hillmer Dr 27609
Hillock Dr 27612
N Hills Dr
1800-5799 27612
5800-6299 27609
Hillsborough St
100-1299 27603
1300-1899 27605
1900-3999 27607
4001-4099 27607
4100-6999 27606
Hillside Ct 27607
Hillside Dr 27612
Hillston Ridge Rd 27617
Hillstone Dr 27615
Hilltop Dr 27610
Hilltop Rd
1900-1999 27610
5500-5999 27603
Hillwood Ct 27615
Hillyridge Ct 27603
Hilton St 27608
Hines Dr 27609
Hinnants Creek St 27610
Hinsdale St 27605
Hinton St 27612
Hinton Grove Pl 27604
Hip Hop Ln 27610
Historian St 27603
History Trl 27612
Hobby Ct
1-99 27603
3300-3399 27604
Hobhouse Cir 27615
Hobson Ct 27607
Hoch Cv 27603
Hocutts Ln 27610
Hodfield Ct 27604
Hodges St 27604
W Hodges St 27608
Hodges Creek Dr 27609
Hogan Ln 27607
Hoke St 27601
Holbrook Ct 27604
Holburn Pl 27610
Holden Rd 27616
Holden St 27604
Holdenby Trl 27616
Holiday Dr 27610
Holiday Rd 27613
Holkham Ct 27614
Holland Church Rd 27603
Holland Farms Way 27603
Holland Ridge Dr 27603
Hollander Pl 27606
Hollenden Dr 27616
Hollirose Pl 27616
Hollister Hills Dr 27616
Hollow Tree Ct 27616
Holloway Rd 27610
Holloway Ter 27608
Hollowell Ln 27604
Hollowgate Rd 27614
Holly Cir 27603
Holly Dr
5900-5999 27616
6800-7099 27615
Holly Ln 27612
Holly Pl 27606
Holly Berry Ct 27615
Holly Forest Dr 27616
Holly Lake Trl 27604
Holly Mill Ct 27613
Holly Ridge Farm Rd 27616
Holly Rock Rd 27616
Holly Springs Rd 27606
Holly View Dr 27610
Hollybrook Farm Rd 27610
Hollycrest Ct 27612
Hollyheight Ln 27615
Hollyridge Dr 27612
Holm Oak Ln 27613
Holman St 27601
Holmes St 27601
Holston Ln 27610
Holt Dr 27608
Holt Pl 27607
Holyoke Ct 27603
Home Ct 27603
Homeland Dr 27603
S Homestead Dr 27616
Hometown Dr 27615
Homewood Ct 27609
Homewood Banks Dr 27612
Honey Berry Ct 27615
Honey Locust Ct 27606
Honeychurch St 27614
Honeycutt Rd
8300-9699 27615
9700-12099 27614
Honeysuckle Rd 27609
Hooker Dr 27607
Hoot Owl Ct 27603
Hope St 27607
Hope Diamond Ct 27610
Hopeton Ave 27614
Hopper St 27616
Hopson Dr 27604
Horaderi Rd 27607
Horizon Dr 27615
Horizon Hike Ct 27603
Horizon Line Dr 27617
Horizons Hope Way 27607
Hornbeck Ct 27614
Hornblower Trl 27610
Horne St 27607
Horse Buggy Dr 27603
Horse Creek Rd 27603
Horse Farm Rd & Trl 27603
Horse Track Aly 27607
Horseback Ln 27610
Horsemans Trl 27613
Horsepen Pl 27615
Horseshoe Bnd 27615
Horseshoe Dr 27603
Horseshoe Farm St 27610
Horton St 27607
Hospice Cir 27607
Hostetler St 27609
Hounds Ear Pl 27606
Houndsman Ct 27616
Hourglass Ct 27612
Housewren Pl 27613
Hovingham Way 27616
Hovis Ct 27615
Howard Cir 27604
Howard Dr 27603
Howard Rd 27613
Howie Rd 27613
Howson Rd 27603
Hoyle Dr 27604
Hubert St 27603
Hubo Ct 27603
Huckabay Cir 27612
Huckleberry Dr 27612
Huddlestone Dr 27612
Hudson Ln 27603
Hudson St 27608
Hudson Hill Ln 27612
Huey Ct 27615
Huff Dr 27606
Hula Ct 27610

Hummer Way 27614
Hunnicutt Dr 27610
Hunt Club Ln 27606
Hunt Farms Ln 27603
Hunt Manor Ct 27616
Hunter Rd 27615
Hunter St 27612
Hunter Chase Ct 27610
Hunter Hill Rd 27604
Hunter Hollow Dr 27606
Hunterfield Ln 27609
Hunterfox Ct 27603
Hunters Way 27615
Hunters Bluff Dr 27606
Hunters Club Dr 27606
Hunters Creek Ln 27606
Hunters Farm Dr 27603
Hunters Meadow Ln 27606
Hunters Oak Trl 27616
Huntford Ln 27606
Hunting Trl 27613
Hunting Ridge Rd 27615
Huntingdon Dr 27606
Huntington Ct 27609
Huntingwood Dr 27606
Huntleigh Dr 27604
Huntride Ct 27616
Huntscroft Ln 27617
Huntwyck Dr 27603
Hurley St 27606
Hurmax Ln 27610
Huron Rd 27610
Hurricane Alley Way 27607
Hurst St 27603
Hushpuppy Ct 27616
Hutton St 27606
Hyde Pl 27614
Hyde St 27609
Hyde Ter 27601
Hydra Rd 27614
Hylton Dr 27616
Hymettus Ct 27607
Hyson Pl 27604
Ice Dr 27617
Idlewild Ave 27601
Idlewood Village Dr 27610
Idolbrook Ln 27615
Ikes Pond Ln 27610
Ileagnes Rd 27603
Image Pt 27614
Iman Dr 27615
Imperial Oaks Dr 27614
Independence Pl 27603
Indian Lake Gln 27603
Indian Trail Dr 27609
Indian Valley Ln 27603
Indianwood Ct 27604
Indica Dr 27613
Indigo Moon Way 27613
Industrial Dr 27609
Industry Dr 27603
Inez Ct 27604
Infinity Ln 27610
Ingate Way 27613
Inglehurst Dr 27613
Ingleside Pl 27614
Inglewood Ln 27609
Ingomar Pl 27609
Ingram Dr 27604
Inkster Cv 27603
Inland Ct 27606
Inland Trl 27613
Inlet Pl 27615
Inman Park Dr 27612
Innisbrook Ct 27612
Inona Pl 27606
Interlachen Pl 27612
Interlock Dr 27610
Intrepid Ct 27610
Inverbrass Ct 27616
Inverness Ct 27615
Inverrary Ct 27615
Inverstone Ln 27606
Involute Pl 27617
Inwood Rd 27603
Inwood Forest Dr 27603

Ione Ln 27603
Iredell Dr 27608
Iredell Ter 27601
Irelan Dr 27606
Irene Ln & Way 27603
Iris Dr 27612
Iris Lake Ct 27604
Iron Bark Ct 27606
Iron Horse Rd 27616
Iron Meadow Run 27601
Iron Rock Dr 27604
Iron Sight Ct 27616
Ironstone Ct 27615
Ironwood Ln 27613
Irving Ct 27609
Isabella Dr 27603
Isabella Cannon Dr 27612
Islamorada Ln 27603
Island Ford Dr 27610
Isle Worth Ct 27617
Islehurst Ct 27613
Ithaca Ln 27606
Ivanhoe Dr 27615
Iver Johnson Dr 27606
Iverson St 27604
Iverstone Ln 27606
Ives Ct 27616
Ivin Dr 27610
Ivory Rose Ln 27612
Ivory Run Way 27603
Ivy Ln 27609
Ivy Blossom Ln 27604
Ivy Commons Dr 27606
Ivy Crest Ct 27604
Ivy Hill Rd 27616
Ivy League Ln 27616
Ivy Ridge Rd 27612
Ivybridge Ln 27610
Ivydale Dr 27606
Ivymount Way 27613
J J Ct 27603
J Richard Dr 27617
Jackknife Trl 27615
Jacklin Ct 27603
Jackson St
2900-3000 27607
3002-3998 27607
3801-3999 27606
Jackson Dane Dr 27613
Jackson King Rd 27603
Jacqueline Ln 27616
Jade Forest Trl 27616
Jade Tree Ln 27615
Jagalene Ln 27616
Jamaica Dr 27601
Jamboree Rd 27613
James Pl 27605
James Rd
4100-4199 27604
4200-4499 27616
James D Newsome
Wynd 27612
E & W Jameson Rd 27604
Jamestown Cir 27609
Jamie Ct 27613
Jamison Dr 27610
Jamison Valley Dr 27617
Jane Ln 27604
Janet Ct 27615
Janice Rd 27614
Jansmith Ln 27615
Janston Dr 27613
Jarden Ct 27613
Jarman Dr 27604
Jarratt Cv 27617
Jarvis St 27608
Jasmine Cove Way 27614
Jasper Ln 27613
Jaybee Ct 27604
Jayman Dr 27617
Jean Dr 27612
Jeanette Marie Ln 27613
Jeanew Ct 27613
Jeff Dr 27603
Jefferson Ln 27616
Jefferson St 27605

Jefferson Town Rd 27606
Jeffrey Dr 27603
Jeffrey St 27610
Jeffrey Alan Ct 27613
Jeffreys Creek Ln 27616
Jeffreys Grove School
Rd 27612
Jeffries St 27606
Jehossee St 27616
Jekyl Cir 27615
Jellison Ct 27615
Jelynn St 27616
Jenkins Ridge Ct 27613
Jennifer Dr 27603
Jerome Ct 27617
Jersey Ct 27617
Jesella Dr 27610
Jesmond Pl 27613
Jessamine Way 27612
Jessica Dr 27610
Jessup Dr 27603
Jetton Ct 27610
Jimmy Carter Way 27610
Jimmy Ridge Pl 27610
Jitterbug Ln 27610
Jo Dell St 27616
Joanne Dr 27603
Jobs Journey Ct 27610
Joe And Ruth Lee Dr 27610
Joe Leach Rd 27603
Joe Louis Ave 27610
Jogging Ct 27603
John Allen Rd 27614
John H Rencher Wynd 27612
John Haywood Way 27604
John Hopkins Ct 27616
John Humphries Wynd 27612
John Rex Blvd 27614
John S Raboteau
Wynd 27612
John White Dr 27610
Johnsdale Pl & Rd 27615
W Johnson St
100-799 27603
800-999 27605
Johnston Rd 27603
Johnston Ter 27601
Johnston Busbee
Wynd 27612
Jonas Ridge Ln 27613
E Jones St
1-1299 27601
1300-1599 27610
W Jones St
1-99 27601
100-799 27603
Jones Franklin Rd 27606
Jonesbay Ln 27616
Jonesboro Ct 27603
Jonesbury Way 27604
Jordan Rd 27603
Jordan Oaks Way 27604
Jordan Ridge Ln 27603
Jordan View Dr 27603
Jordan Woods Dr 27603
Jordanmill Ct 27616
Jordanus Dr 27617
Jordy Dr 27617
Joseph Dr 27614
Joseph Michael Ct 27606
Joyce Glow Ct 27613
Joydon Ct 27616
Joyner Pl 27612
Juaquin Ln 27603
Julia Ln 27609
Julian Dr 27604
Julie Ct 27613
Junction Blvd 27603
Juneberry Pl 27613
Juniper Ave 27603
Juniper Ct 27612
Juniper St 27612
Juno Ct 27610
Jupiter St 27604
Jupiter Hills Ct 27604
Justice Dr 27615

Justification Ln 27603
K-Wesley Way 27610
Kabanek Dr 27603
Kanaskis Rd 27603
Kanawa Ln 27614
Kanawha Ct 27616
Kanga Cir 27603
Kangaroo Ct 27615
S Kansas Dr 27616
Kapalua Way 27610
Kaplan Dr 27606
Karcia Ct 27617
Karen Ct 27615
Karlbrook Ln 27616
Karns Pl 27614
Kary Dr 27603
Kaseys Cir 27603
Kassia Ln 27616
Kate Denson Way 27612
Katesbridge Ln 27614
Katharina Ct 27613
Kavkaz St 27610
Kaycee Ct 27616
Kayla Ct 27606
Kaysmount Ct 27614
Kaytree Ln 27613
Kaywoody Ct 27615
Keats Pl 27609
Kedvale Ave 27617
Kedzie Ct 27617
Keegan Ct 27613
Keenland Dr 27613
Keeter Center Dr 27601
Keighley Pl 27612
Keith Dr 27610
Kelford St 27606
Kellett Ln 27616
Kelley Ct 27615
Kellwood Ct 27609
Kelly St 27610
Kelly Austin Dr 27606
Kelmscot Way 27615
Kelterson Pl 27616
Kelton Dr 27615
Kelway St 27614
Kemp Rd 27613
Kempsford Pl 27604
Kempton Rd 27615
Kencot Ct 27615
Kendricks Ct 27613
Kenilworth Dr 27613
Kenly Ct 27607
Kenmore Dr 27608
Kennebuck Ct 27613
Kennedy St 27610
Kennett Village Ct 27615
Kenning Park Dr 27616
Kennington Rd 27610
Kennington Park Dr 27614
Kensett Way 27616
Kent Cv 27617
Kent Rd 27606
Kentfield Dr 27615
Kentford Ct 27603
Kentish Town Ln 27612
Kentmere Way 27615
Kentwell Pl 27604
Kenwick Ct 27613
Kenwood Ct 27609
Kenwood Meadows Dr 27603
Kenwyck Manor Way 27612
Keowee Way 27616
Kernstown Dr 27610
Kerrigan Ln 27603
Kershaw Dr 27609
Kesslers Cross Dr 27610
Kestrel Dr 27615
Keswick Dr 27609
Keswick Woods Ct 27615
Ketley Ct 27613
Kettner Ct 27615
Kevin Cir 27609
Key Ct 27614
Key Biscayne Ct 27603
Keynes Ct 27615
Keystone Dr 27612

Kidd Rd 27610
Kilburn Rd 27604
Kilcullen Dr 27604
Kilgore Ave 27607
Kilkenny Pl 27612
Killarney Hope Dr 27613
Killington Dr 27609
Kilnstone Ln 27613
Kilpeck Ln 27610
Kimbal St 27606
Kimberly Dr 27609
Kimbrook Dr 27612
Kimbrough St 27608
Kimsey Ct 27606
Kincaid Dr 27604
Kincross Ct 27610
Kindle Wood St 27616
King Cir 27610
King Arthur Rd 27610
N & S King Charles
Rd 27610
King Crest Ln 27614
King Cross Ct 27614
King Croydon Ct 27603
King Lawrence Rd 27607
King Richard Rd 27610
King William Ct 27613
King William Rd 27610
Kingdom Way 27607
Kings Ct 27606
Kings Pkwy 27610
Kings Arms Way 27615
Kings Branch Way 27614
Kings Cross Way 27615
Kings Garden Rd &
Way 27612
Kings Grant Dr 27614
Kings Hollow Dr 27603
Kings Lassiter Way 27614
Kings Mill Pl 27615
Kingsberry Ct 27615
Kingsboro Rd 27610
Kingscote Ct 27617
Kingsland Dr 27613
Kingsley Pl 27609
Kingsley Rd 27612
Kingston Heath Way 27604
Kingstree Ct 27610
Kingswood Ct 27613
Kingwood Dr 27609
Kinlawton Pl 27614
Kinleys Way 27613
Kinleywood Ct 27603
Kinross Ct & Dr 27613
Kinsdale Dr 27615
Kinsey St 27603
Kinsfolk Cir 27610
Kinsley Pl 27616
Kinsman Ct 27603
Kintail Dr 27613
Kintyre Cir 27612
Kipawa St 27607
Kipling Pl 27609
Kira Ln 27614
Kirby St 27606
Kirk Ave 27603
Kirkby Ln 27614
Kirkhill Dr 27615
Kirkland Rd 27603
Kirkman St 27601
Kirks Grove Ln 27603
Kirks Penny Rd 27606
Kirks Ridge Dr 27606
Kirkstall Ct 27615
Kirkwood Ct 27609
Kirkwood Park Dr 27612
Kirkwood Ridge Dr 27612
Kirner Ct 27613
Kissimmee Ln 27616
Kissing Ct 27613
Kitchen Dr 27603
Kitledge Dr 27610
Kitt Pl 27610
Kittansett Ct 27604
Kittrell Dr 27608
Kitty Ln 27615

Kitzel Way 27615
Kivet Cir 27604
Klondike Ct 27615
Knaresborough Rd 27612
Knebworth Ct 27613
Knickerbocker Pkwy 27612
Knights Way 27615
Knightsbridge Way 27604
S Knoll Ct 27603
Knollbrook Ct 27616
Knollrock Dr 27612
Knollwood Rd 27609
Knotty Pine Ln 27617
Knowles St 27603
Knox Rd 27608
Kohler Ln 27616
Kon Tiki Ct 27603
Koomen Ln 27606
Kornegay Dr 27603
Koupela Dr
9300-9699 27615
9700-9999 27614
Krandon Dr 27603
Kresson Pl 27616
Kristy Cir 27613
Kroll Ct 27616
Krume Ct 27613
Kukui Ct 27613
Kumar Ct 27606
Kundinger Ct 27606
Kure Ct 27603
Kushima Ct 27604
Kyle Dr 27616
Kyle Abbey Ln 27613
La Costa Way 27610
La Manga Dr 27610
La Matisse Rd 27615
La Sombre Dr 27616
Labrador Dr 27616
Lacebark Ln 27613
Lacy Ave 27609
Ladbrooke St 27617
Ladden Ct 27615
Ladish Ln 27610
Lady Myrtle Ln 27610
Lady Of The Lake Dr 27612
Ladys Slipper Ct 27606
Ladywood Ct 27616
Lafayette Rd 27604
Lafferty Ct 27616
Lagrange Dr 27613
Lail Ct 27606
E Lake Clb 27617
E Lake Ct 27613
W Lake Ct 27613
Lake Dr
2300-2499 27609
2600-2799 27607
7900-7999 27613
E Lake Dr 27609
W Lake Dr 27609
Lake Allyn Dr 27615
Lake Anne Dr 27612
Lake Boone Pl 27608
Lake Boone Trl
100-599 27608
600-4699 27607
Lake Brandon Trl 27610
Lake Cove Ct 27606
Lake Dam Rd
1000-2099 27606
2100-2298 27606
2100-2100 27627
2101-2299 27606
Lake Eva Marie Dr 27603
Lake Ferry Dr 27606
Lake Forest Dr 27615
Lake Front Dr 27613
Lake Garden Ct 27610
Lake Hill Dr 27609
Lake Lynn Dr 27613
Lake Moraine Pl 27607
Lake Mountain Pl 27607
Lake Nona Ct 27604
Lake Point Cir 27606
Lake Raleigh Rd 27606

Lake Ridge Dr 27604
Lake Springs Ct 27613
Lake Trout Ln 27610
Lake Villa Way 27614
Lake Vista Dr 27613
Lake Wheeler Rd 27603
Lake Woodard Dr 27604
Lakefield Dr 27603
Lakegreen Ct 27612
Lakehaven Dr 27612
Lakehill Dr 27613
Lakeland Dr 27612
Lakemont Dr 27609
Lakenheath Ct 27614
Lakepark Dr 27612
Lakerest Ct 27612
Lakerun Ct 27612
Lakeshore Dr
1901-1997 27604
1999-2599 27604
11100-11199 27613
S Lakeside Dr 27606
Lakeside Trl 27603
Lakestone Dr 27609
Laketree Dr 27615
Lakeview Dr
400-699 27603
2400-2899 27609
3000-3099 27603
Lakeway Dr 27612
Lakewind Ct 27603
Lakewood Dr 27613
Lakinsville Ln 27610
Lamarsh Ct 27617
Lambeth Dr 27609
Lambroll Ln 27613
Lambshire Dr 27612
Lamesa Dr 27603
Lamont St 27610
Lancashire Ct 27606
Lancashire Dr 27613
Lancaster Dr 27612
Lancelot Ct 27604
Landale Ct 27610
Landfall Ct 27613
Landguard Dr 27613
Landing Brook Ln 27616
Landing Falls Ln 27616
Landings Way 27615
Landis St 27603
Landmark Dr 27607
Landor Rd 27609
Landover Ct 27612
Landover Ln 27616
Landover Arbor Pl 27616
Landover Bluff Way 27616
Landover Charge Ln 27616
Landover Crest Dr 27616
Landover Dale Dr 27616
Landover Glenn Ct 27616
Landover Keep Pl 27616
Landover Pine Pl 27616
Landover Ridge Dr 27616
Landover Vale Way 27616
Landover Woods Ln 27616
Landreaux Dr 27610
Landrum Ln 27616
Lands End Ct 27606
Landsburg Dr 27603
Landscape Ln 27614
Landshire View Ln 27616
Lane Ave 27610
E Lane St
1-1299 27601
1300-1599 27610
W Lane St 27603
Laneridge Ct 27603
Langdon Rd 27604
Langford Pl 27609
Langham Ln 27615
Langley Cir 27609
Langston Rd 27610
Langtree Ln 27613
Langwood Dr
8900-8999 27613
9000-9399 27617

Lanham Pl 27615
Laniel Ct 27612
Lanier Club Dr 27617
Lansdale Dr 27617
Lansdowne Pl 27609
Lansing St 27610
Lantern Pl 27612
Laodicea Dr 27610
Larchmont Dr 27612
Larchwood Dr 27609
Largo Springs Ct 27613
Lark Cir 27604
Larka Ct 27613
Larkdale Ct 27609
Larrantr Dr 27615
Larson Dr 27610
Lasalle Ln 27612
Lash Ave 27607
Lasilla Way 27616
Laskin Ct 27617
Lassiter Pl 27609
Lassiter At North Hills Ave 27609
Lassiter Falls Cir 27609
Lassiter Farm Rd 27603
Lassiter Mill Rd 27609
Lassiter Summit Ct 27609
Last Oak Ct 27613
Latham Ct 27606
Latham Way 27604
Latimer Rd 27609
Latitude Way 27610
Latrobe Ct 27604
Latta St 27607
Lattice Grove Pl 27610
Lattimore Dr 27614
Lattyes Ln 27613
Laurdane Rd 27613
Laurel Cir 27612
Laurel Coach Ln 27617
Laurel Falls Ln 27603
Laurel Glen Dr 27610
Laurel Grove Ln 27616
Laurel Hills Rd 27612
Laurel Manor Ct 27612
Laurel Mountain Rd 27613
Laurel Ridge Dr 27612
Laurel Rock Ln 27613
Laurel Valley Way 27604
Laurelbrook St 27604
Laurelcherry St 27612
Laureldale Dr 27609
Lauren Oaks Dr 27616
Laurie Dr 27606
Lauriston Rd 27616
Laurnet Pl 27614
Lavista Ct 27616
Law Enforcement Dr 27610
Lawhorn St 27606
Lawn Ct 27613
Lawrence Dr 27603
Layden St 27603
Layla Ave 27617
Layton Ray Cir 27613
Lazy River Dr 27610
Leach St 27603
Lead Crystal Ct 27610
Lead Mine Rd
4300-6999 27612
7000-8499 27615
8501-8899 27615
Leadenhall Way 27603
Leader Ln 27615
Leaf Ct 27612
Leafcrest Ct 27604
Leafwood Pl 27613
Leagan Dr 27603
Leaning Tree Rd 27612
Leanne Ct 27606
Lear Pl 27609
Leas Mill Ct 27606
Lease Ln 27617
Leatherwood Ct 27613
Ledbetter Ct 27608
Lee Rd 27604
E Lee St 27601
W Lee St 27601
Lee Hall 27607
Leebrook Rd 27616
Leeds Ct 27615
Leeds Pl 27613
Leeds Forest Ln 27615
Leesburg Ln 27617
Leeshire Ln 27615
Leesville Rd
6500-6799 27612
6800-12399 27613
Leesville Church Rd 27617
Leesville Towns Ct 27613
Legacy Ct 27615
Legare Ct 27613
Legend Rd 27603
Legging Ln 27615
Lehigh Ct 27609
Leiden Ln 27606
Leigh Dr
1700-1899 27603
4800-4999 27616
Lela Ct 27606
Leland Dr 27616
Lemay Ct 27604
Lemon Springs Ct 27612
Lemuel Dr 27615
Lendermans Cir 27603
Lennox Pl 27612
Lennox Laurel Cir 27617
E Lenoir St
1-899 27601
900-1799 27610
W Lenoir St
1-599 27601
600-1299 27603
Lenoraway Dr 27613
Lenox Hill Ter 27615
Lenoxplace Cir 27603
Leonard St 27607
Leonard Mill Rd 27616
Leone Landing Ct 27603
Leonidas Ct 27604
Leota Dr 27603
Leslie Dr
10400-10799 27615
10800-10899 27614
Leslieshire Dr 27615
Lethbridge Ct 27606
Leven Ln 27616
Leveret Cir 27615
Leverton Ln 27615
Lewis Cir 27608
Lewis Farm Rd
2500-2799 27608
2801-2997 27607
2999-3599 27607
Lewis Grove Ln 27608
Lewis P Olds Wynd 27612
Lewisand Cir 27615
Lewisham Ct 27612
Lewiswood Ln 27608
Lexington Dr 27606
Liana Ln 27613
Liatris Ln 27613
Liberty Pl 27610
Liberty Woods Way 27613
Life Ln 27615
Light Brigade Ln 27612
Lighthall Ln 27604
Lightner Ln 27610
Lightwood Ct 27616
Ligon St 27607
Lila Ln 27614
Lila Blue Ln 27612
Lilac Ln 27612
Liles Rd 27606
Lilley Ct 27606
Lillington Dr 27607
Lillyhurst Dr 27612
Lilymount Dr 27610
Limber Ln 27616
Limebay Ln 27613
Limehouse Ct 27613
Limerick Dr 27604
Limestone Ct 27615
Limousine Dr 27617
Lincoln Ct 27610
Lincoln Ter 27601
Lincolnville Rd 27607
Linden Ave 27601
Linden Crest Rd 27603
Lindenshire Rd 27615
Lindley Dr 27614
Lindoby Ln 27616
Lindsay Dr 27612
Line Dr 27603
Lineberry Dr 27603
Links Club Dr 27603
Linville Dr 27606
Linville Rdg 27604
Lion Ridge Ct 27612
Lionel Ln 27607
Lions Way 27604
Lipkin Holw 27613
Lipscomb Ct 27609
Lissa Jon Ct 27614
Liston Dr 27616
Litchfield Downs Ln 27612
Litchford Rd 27615
Litchford Creek Ct 27615
Litchford Pines Cir 27615
Little Brier Creek Ln 27617
Little Bud Ln 27610
Little Creek Dr 27603
Little Falls Dr 27609
Little John Rd 27610
Little Lake Hill Dr 27607
Little Sandy Dr 27616
Littlefield Ct 27606
Littlerock Rd 27616
Littleton Dr 27616
Littrell Cir 27613
Live Oak Rd 27604
Live Oak Trl 27613
Liverpool Ln 27604
Livery Way 27603
Livia Cir 27604
Lizei St 27616
Llewellyn Ct 27613
Lloyd Allyns Way 27615
Lobelia St 27603
Lobley Hill Ln 27613
Loblolly Ct 27615
Loblolly Pine Dr 27614
Lobo Dr 27604
Loch Harbour Ln 27606
Loch Highlands Dr 27606
Loch Laural Ln 27613
Lochbroom Rd 27612
Lochgarton Ln 27614
Lochmore Dr 27608
Locke Ln 27610
Locke Woods Rd 27603
Lockhart Ln 27614
Lockwood Folly Ln 27610
Locust Ln 27603
Lodestar Dr 27615
Lodge Allen Ct 27616
Lodgepole Ln 27616
Loft Ln 27609
Lofton Pl 27610
Lofty Heights Pl 27614
Log Cabin Dr 27616
Logan Ct 27607
Loganshire Ln 27616
Logger Ct 27609
Logos Ct 27610
Logsdon Ln 27615
Lomas Ct 27615
Lombar St 27610
London Dr 27608
London Bell Dr 27614
London Bridge Ct 27613
London Park Ct 27615
Londonderry Cir 27610
Londonville Ln 27604
Lone Holly Way 27610
Lone Oak Pl 27615
Lone Valley Ct 27603
Long And Winding Rd 27603
Long Barrow Ct 27614
Long Bow Dr 27604
Long Branch Trl 27604
Long Cove Ct 27604
Long Meadow Ct 27613
Long Neck Ct 27604
Long Pine Ln 27603
Long Point Ct 27604
Longacre Dr 27613
Longdale Dr 27616
Longeria Ct 27612
Longfield Dr 27616
Longford Dr 27615
Longhill Ln 27612
Longholme Way 27614
Longistic Way 27617
Longitude Way 27610
Longleaf Branch Ct 27612
Longneedle Ct 27603
Longridge Dr 27603
Longstone Way 27614
Longstreet Dr 27615
Longview Lake Dr 27610
Longwood Dr 27612
Loniker Dr 27615
Lontress Dr 27604
Looking Glass Ct 27612
Lookout Loop 27612
Lookout Mountain Rd 27613
Lookout Point Ct 27612
Loon Ln 27616
Lora Ln 27604
Lord Anson Dr 27610
Lord Ashley Rd 27610
Lord Berkley Rd 27610
Lord Britton Pl 27603
Lord Nelson Dr 27610
Lorimer Rd 27606
Loring Ct 27613
Lorraine Rd 27607
Lost Ln 27603
Lost Cove Ln 27603
Lost Feather Ct 27610
Lost Forest Way 27616
Lost Key Ct 27617
Lost Valley Rd 27612
Lostwood Ln 27614
Lothian Way 27612
Lottery Ln 27610
Louisburg Rd
1500-4399 27604
4400-8200 27616
8202-8498 27616
Louise St 27610
Louson Pl 27614
Lovdal Dr 27613
Lovell Ct 27613
Loves Ln 27601
Lovko Ln 27613
Lowden St 27608
Lowell Ridge Rd 27616
Lower Dry Falls Ct 27603
Lowery Dr 27615
Lowery Farm Ln 27614
Lowery Ridge Dr 27614
Lowndes Grove Dr 27616
Lownwood Way 27616
Loxley Pl 27610
Loyal Ln 27615
Loylane Ct 27610
Lubbock Dr 27612
Lucerne Pl 27604
Ludwell Branch Ct 27612
Lullwater Dr 27606
Lumley Rd 27617
Lumpkin St 27610
Lunar Dr 27610
Lunar Stone Pl 27613
Lunceston Way 27613
Lundy Dr 27606
Lunenburg Dr 27603
Lungren Ct 27610
Lupine Ct 27606
Lupton Cir 27606
Luray Ct 27609
Luther Rd 27610
Lutz Ave 27607
Luverly Ln 27604
Lyle Rd 27603
Lyman Ave 27616
Lyme Ct 27609
Lymington Dr 27616
Lynchester Ct 27615
Lyndhurst Dr 27610
Lynn Dr 27603
Lynn Rd
1-699 27609
1000-2799 27612
3500-3799 27613
Lynn Brook Dr 27609
Lynn Cove Ln 27613
Lynn Crest Ln 27609
Lynn Garden Ct 27610
Lynn Meadow Dr 27609
Lynn Point Ln 27613
Lynn Ridge Dr 27613
Lynn Townes Ct 27613
Lynnberry Pl 27617
Lynndale Dr 27612
Lynne Carol Way 27616
Lynnoak Dr 27613
Lynnridge Ln 27609
Lynwood Ln 27609
Lyon St 27608
Lytham Pl 27604
M And T Farm Rd 27610
M E Valentine Dr 27607
Mabledon Ct 27613
Mabry Mill St 27614
Maccheever Ct 27606
Macintyre Commons 27606
Mackinac Island Ln 27610
Macon Pl 27609
Macon Rd 27613
Macon Forest Pl 27613
Macon Pond Rd 27607
Macon Ridge Rd 27613
Mactavish Way 27613
Maddry Oaks Ct 27616
Madeline Way 27610
Madelyn Watson Ln 27610
Madiera Ct 27615
Madison Park Ln 27615
Madison Ridge Way 27613
Maeve Ct 27616
Mafolie Ct 27613
Magellan Way 27612
Magenta Ct 27617
Maggie Ct 27603
Magic Hollow Ct 27614
Magical Pl 27614
Magnolia Ct 27612
Magnolia Green Ln 27604
Magnolia Grove Ct 27614
Magnolia Pond Rd 27610
Maham Pl 27616
Mahonia Ct 27615
Maiden Ln 27607
Maidenhair Dr 27610
Maidstone Ct 27613
Main At North Hills St 27609
Main Campus Dr 27606
Maitland Dr 27610
Majestic Prince Ct 27606
Major Loring Way 27616
Makena Dr 27615
Mal Weathers Rd 27603
Malachite Ct 27603
Malbay Ln 27615
Malbec Cres 27612
Malersid Dr 27617
Malibu Dr
3300-3499 27607
6100-6699 27603
Mallard Ln 27609
Mallard Grove Dr 27616
Mallory Ct 27616
Mallory Glen Cir 27616
Malone Ct 27616
Malone Pl 27610
Malta Ave 27610
Malvern Ct 27615
Mambo Ln 27610
Man O War Trl 27613
Manassa Pope Ln 27612
Manassas Ct 27609
Manatee Ct 27616
Manchester Dr 27609
Mandarin Ct 27614
Mandrake Ct 27613
Mandrel Way 27616
Mango Dr 27610
Mango Key Ct 27603
Mangrove Dr 27616
Mangrove Sky Ln 27603
Mangum St 27601
Manhasset Ln 27604
Mankoma Ter 27612
Manndell Ln 27606
Manning Pl 27608
Manor Park 27612
Manor Bluff Way 27613
Manor Club Dr 27612
Manor Field Way 27612
Manor Glen Way 27615
Manor Oaks Dr 27615
Manor Plantation Dr 27603
Manor Ridge Dr 27603
Manor Valley Ct 27613
Manor Village Way 27612
Manorbrook Rd 27607
Manovill Pl 27609
Mansfield Dr 27613
Mansura Dr 27610
Mantachie Ct 27610
Manteo Ct 27615
Manthorp Ter 27610
Mantle Ct 27607
Mantua Way 27604
Manuel St 27612
Maple Ln 27603
Maple St 27610
Maplecroft Ct 27617
Maplefield Dr 27613
Mapleridge Rd 27609
Mapleshire Dr 27616
Mapleside Ct 27609
Maplestead Dr 27615
Mapleton Ln 27613
Maplewood Ln 27610
Marabou Ct 27614
Maraketch Ct 27603
Maram Ct 27609
Marathon Ln 27616
Marble St 27603
Marblehead Ln 27612
Marbletree Ct 27604
Marblewood Ct 27604
Marcom St 27606
Marcony Way 27610
Mardela Spring Dr 27616
Mardella Dr 27613
Margarets Ln 27614
Margate Ct 27612
Margie Helen Rd 27603
Maria Luisa Pl 27617
Marie Dr 27604
Marietta Ct 27612
Marigold St 27603
Marilyn Dr 27607
Mariner Cir 27603
Mariner Dr 27615
Marion Rd 27610
Marion Stone Way 27614
Mark Ln 27603
Mark St 27601
Mark Massengill Dr 27610
Mark Oak Ct 27610
Markay Cir 27603
N Market Dr 27609
Market Plz 27601
Market At North Hills St 27609
Market Bridge Ln 27608
Markridge Rd 27607
Markwood Ct 27613
Marlborough Rd 27610
Marleybone Dr 27617
Marlin Ct 27604
Marlowe Rd 27609
Marni Ct 27617
Marriott Dr 27612
Mars St 27604
Marsh Ave 27606
Marsh Creek Rd 27604
Marsh Field Dr 27614
Marsh Grass Dr 27610
Marsh Hollow Dr 27616
Marshall St 27604
Marshall Brae Dr 27616
Marshlane Way 27610
Marshville Ct 27616
Martello Ln 27613
Martha St 27610
Marthalyn Dr 27610
Marthas Way
10700-10799 27615
10800-10899 27614
Marthonna Way 27616
E Martin St
1-1099 27601
1100-1699 27610
W Martin St
1-399 27601
400-699 27603
Martin Farm Rd 27613
Martin Luther King Jr Blvd
100-799 27601
1600-2099 27610
Martindale Dr 27614
Martinsburg St 27616
Martinwood Ct 27604
Marvin Pl 27609
Marvino Ln
8100-8299 27613
8600-8699 27617
Marwood Dr 27604
Mary Frances Pl 27606
Mary Hobby Rd 27603
Mary Lou Ln 27603
Maryel Way 27615
Maryton Pkwy 27616
Mason Pl 27604
Mason Ridge Dr 27614
Masonboro Ct 27604
Masota Rd 27612
Mass Rock Dr 27610
Massachusetts Ct 27615
Massey Run 27616
Massey Pond Trl 27616
Massey Preserve Trl 27616
Massey Wood Trl 27616
Master Ct 27615
Master Craft Rd 27603
Matharlyn Dr 27610
Mathias Ct 27615
Maton Pl 27603
Matson Pl 27614
Matt Dr 27604
Matterly St 27612
Mattlyn Ct 27613
Maury Ct 27615
Max Ln 27603
Maxwell Dr 27603
May Ct 27609
Mayapple Pl 27613
Mayberry Pl 27609
Maybrook Dr 27610
Maybrook Crossing Dr 27610
Mayfair Rd 27608
Mayfair Mill Dr 27616
Mayfaire Crest Ln 27615
Mayflower Dr 27604
Mayhurst Pl 27614
Maylands Ave 27615
Maymont Dr 27615
Mayo St 27603
Mayridge Ln 27610
N Mayview Rd 27607
Maywood Ave 27603
Mazurka Ct 27610
Mc Alister Pl 27612
Mcadams Dr 27604
Mcaden St 27610

Mcandrew Dr 27610
Mcbride Dr 27613
Mcburnie Dr 27603
Mccarthy St 27608
Mcchesney Ct 27612
Mccleary Ct 27607
Mcclure Dr 27603
Mcconnell Oliver Dr 27604
Mccoy Rd 27603
Mcculloch St 27603
Mcdade Farm Rd 27616
Mcdaniel Rd 27603
Mcdevon Dr 27617
Mcdonald Ln 27608
N Mcdowell St 27603
S Mcdowell St 27601
Mcelveen Ct 27603
Mcgee Ct 27604
Mcgrath Way 27616
Mcguire Dr 27616
Mchines Pl 27616
Mckee Dr 27616
Mckimmon View Ct 27606
Mcknight Ave 27607
Mclean Dr 27609
Mcmakin St 27610
Mcmullan Cir 27608
Mcneely Dr 27612
Mcneill St 27608
Mcpherson St 27610
Mead Ln 27613
S Meadow Rd 27603
Meadow Chase Dr 27617
Meadow Cove Ln 27612
Meadow Creek Ln 27616
Meadow Field Ln 27606
Meadow Hill Pl 27609
Meadow Mist Ct 27617
Meadow Moss Ct 27613
Meadow Ridge Ct 27615
Meadow Ridge Dr 27604
Meadow Rue Pl 27603
Meadow Star Ct 27615
Meadow Sweet Ct 27603
Meadow View Dr 27609
Meadow Wood Blvd 27604
Meadowbrook Rd 27603
Meadowgreen Dr 27603
Meadowland Ln 27603
Meadowlark Ln 27610
Meadowmont Ln 27615
Meadowvista Ct 27606
Meakin Dr 27614
Mearralt Dr 27609
Mechanicsville Run Ln .. 27610
Mecklenberg Ter 27601
Medfield Rd 27607
Mediate Dr 27603
Medinah Ct 27604
Medlar Ln 27616
Medlin Dr 27607
Medoc Ln 27615
Medway Dr 27608
Meerbrook Ct 27603
Meeting House Cir 27615
Megan Hill Ct 27614
Megson Ct 27614
Melanie Dr 27603
Melbourne Rd
5000-5299 27606
5900-6399 27603
Mellow Field Dr 27604
Melrose Dr 27604
Melrose Club Blvd 27603
Melrose Forest Ln 27603
Melrose Ridge Ct 27603
Melrose Valley Cir 27603
Melton Ct 27615
Melvid Ct 27610
Melvin Arnold Rd 27613
Memo Ct 27610
Memorial Dr 27612
Memory Ln 27604
Memory Rd 27609
Memory Ridge Dr 27606
Mendi Ct 27606

Mentone Way 27612
Mercury Cir 27604
Mercury St 27603
N & S Mere Ct 27615
Mere View Ct 27606
Meredith St 27606
Meredith Anne Ct 27606
Merendino St 27606
Merganzer Rd 27616
Meridian Dr 27616
Merion Pl 27615
Merrell Dr 27610
Merrianne Dr 27607
Merrie Rd 27606
Merrill Ct 27604
Merriman Ave 27607
Merrington Cir 27615
Merritt St 27606
Merriweather Cir 27616
Merrywood Dr 27610
Mersey Ln 27615
Merton Dr 27609
Merwin Rd 27606
Meryton Park Way 27616
Mesa Ct 27607
Messer Rd 27603
Metacomet Way 27604
Metcalf Dr 27612
Metcalf Hall 27607
Metedeconk Ln 27604
Method Rd
500-800 27607
802-898 27607
900-1099 27606
Method Townes Ct 27607
Metronome Ln 27613
Metts Dr 27610
Mevan Ct 27613
Mezzanine Dr 27614
Mial St 27608
Mial Plantation Rd 27610
Michael Dr 27603
Michael J Smith Ln 27610
Michelle Dr 27614
Mickleson Ridge Dr 27603
Micollet Ct 27613
Mid Lakes Dr 27612
Mid Pines Rd 27606
Middle Branch Rd 27610
Middle Oaks Dr 27616
Middleberry Ln 27603
Middleboro Dr 27612
Middlebrook Dr 27615
Middlefield Ct 27615
Midhurst Ct 27614
Midland St 27603
Midlavian Dr 27614
Midstone Ln 27610
Midtown Pl 27609
Midway Island Ct 27610
Midway Park Ct 27610
Midway West Rd 27617
Midwood Dr 27604
Mifflin St 27612
Mike Levi Ct 27610
Milan Ct 27613
Milburnie Rd 27610
Milden Hall Ct 27615
Miles Dr 27615
Milestone Ct 27615
Milky Way 27604
Mill Cv 27617
Mill Run 27612
Mill Bend Dr 27616
Mill Bluff Ct 27616
Mill Creek Ct 27603
W Mill Forest Ct 27606
Mill Glen Cir 27614
Mill Greens Ct 27609
Mill Ridge Rd 27613
Mill Rock Ln 27616
Mill Tree Rd 27612
Mill Village Rd 27612
Millbank St 27610
Millborough Ct 27604
Millbridge Ct 27615

E Millbrook Rd
100-1899 27609
1900-1998 27604
2000-2999 27604
W Millbrook Rd
1-499 27609
900-2399 27612
2401-2599 27612
2900-3599 27613
Millbrook Green Dr 27604
Millbrook Manor Cir 27604
Millbrook Village Pl 27604
Millbrook Woods Dr 27604
Millchest Pl 27606
Millenium Dr 27614
Miller St 27610
Millhaven Dr 27610
Millpine Dr 27614
Millrace Trl 27606
Mills St 27608
Millstaff Ct 27613
Millstone Dr 27604
Millstone Harbour Dr 27603
Millstone Landing Dr 27603
Millstone Ridge Ct 27614
Millstream Ct 27615
Millstream Pl 27609
Milltrace Run 27615
Millwright Ct 27614
Milner Dr 27606
Milroy Ln 27610
Milton Rd 27609
Milvaney Ct 27615
Mimetree Ct 27616
Mimosa St 27604
Mimosa Grove Dr 27610
Mimosa Tree Ln 27612
Mims Ct 27603
Mindees Ct 27609
Minden Ln 27607
Mindspring Dr 27610
Mine Creek Ln 27615
Mine Lake Ct 27615
Mine Shaft Rd 27615
Mine Valley Rd 27615
Mineral Springs Ln 27616
Minerva St 27601
Minnie Dr 27603
Minuet Pl 27610
Miranda Dr 27617
Mirkirk Xing 27616
Mirror Dr 27610
Mishicot Ct 27604
Mission Hills Ct 27617
Missionary Ridge Dr 27610
Missions Ln 27603
Misskelly Dr 27612
Mistiflower Dr 27606
Misty Creek Ln 27617
Misty Dawn Pl 27615
Misty Fog Ct 27603
Misty Glen Trl 27606
Misty Isle Pl 27615
Misty Morning Way 27603
Misty Oak Dr 27613
Misty River Dr 27610
Mitchell St 27607
Mitchell Mill Rd 27616
Mitford Woods Ct 27614
Mizelle Ln 27614
Mizner Ln 27617
Mocha Ln 27616
Mockingbird Dr 27615
Modern Ct 27610
Mogollon Ct 27610
Mollington Ct 27614
Monarda Ct 27616
Moncacy Dr 27610
Moncreiffe Rd 27617
Monie Ln 27601
Monk Dr 27603
Monkwood Pl 27603
Monnell Dr 27617
Monroe Dr 27604
Monrreiffe Rd 27617
Monsieur Ct 27610

Montague Ln 27601
N & S Montana Dr 27616
Montauk Dr 27615
Montcastle Ct 27612
Montclair Dr 27609
Montclair St 27603
Monte Alto Dr 27613
Montego Ct 27603
Monterey St 27604
Montesino Dr 27603
Montgomery St 27607
Monticello Dr 27612
Montreat Ct 27609
Montrose St 27603
Monument Ln 27615
Moon Bay Ct 27613
Moon Beam Dr 27603
Moonglow Dr 27610
Moonsprite Way 27614
Moonview Ct 27606
Moore Dr 27607
Mooreland Ct 27603
Moorfoote Ct 27614
Moorgate Ct 27615
Moorhaven Dr 27603
Moorsfield Ct 27604
Moosecreek Dr 27614
Moratuck Dr 27604
Moray Dr 27613
Mordecai Dr 27604
Mordecai Towne Pl 27604
Morden Ct 27615
Morehead Dr 27612
E Morgan St 27601
W Morgan St
1-399 27601
400-999 27603
Morgan Valley Dr 27603
Morgans Way
8000-8199 27615
8200-8699 27613
Morgans Mill Ct 27610
Morgantown St 27616
Morgause Dr 27614
Moriah Way 27614
Moring St 27603
Morman Springs Ln 27610
Morning Blossum Pl 27616
Morning Creek Way 27610
Morning Edge Dr 27613
Morning Forest Dr 27609
Morning Mountain Rd ... 27614
Morning Ridge Ct 27616
Morningsdale Dr 27609
Morningside Dr 27607
Morocroft Dr 27615
Morrison Ave 27608
Morrocroft Dr 27615
Morson St 27601
Morton Rd 27604
Morvan Way 27612
Mosely Ln 27601
Moses Ct 27604
Moss Run 27614
Moss Bluff Ct 27613
Moss Garden Path 27616
Moss Hill Dr 27616
Moss Oak Cir 27606
Moss Pointe Ln 27606
Moss Spring Dr 27616
Moss Valley Ct 27603
Mossbank Rd 27604
Mossgreen St 27614
Mossy Glen Ct 27614
Mossy Ridge Ct 27613
Moton Pl 27610
Motor Pool 27607
Motorsport Ln 27603
Moultrie Ct 27615
Mount Herman Rd 27617
Mount Prospect Cir 27614
Mount Valley Ln 27613
Mount Vernon Rd 27607
Mount Vernon Church Rd
100-2699 27614
2700-3199 27613

S Mountain Dr 27603
Mountain Ash Ct 27614
Mountain Brook Ln 27615
Mountain Falls Ct 27617
Mountain Lake Dr 27610
Mountain Laurel Dr 27603
Mountain Mill Dr 27614
Mountain Mist Ct 27603
Mountain Ridge Rd 27612
Mountain View Cir 27614
Mountbatten Way 27613
Mountford St 27603
Mourning Dove Rd 27615
Mowbray Dr 27604
Mt Vernon Church Rd .. 27614
Muddy Creek Ct 27610
Muirfield Club Dr 27615
Muirfield Village Way ... 27604
Mulberry St 27604
Mullens Dr 27607
Mumm Ln 27615
Munford Rd 27612
Murad Ct 27606
Murray Hill Dr 27615
Murrillo Walk 27617
Murry Rd 27603
Musket Ball Ct 27616
Myakka Ct 27616
Myers Ave 27604
Myra Rd 27606
Myron Dr 27607
Myrtle Ave 27608
Myrtle Ct 27604
Myrtlewood Ct 27609
Mystery Ln 27604
Mystic Ct 27603
Nagami Ct 27610
Najma St 27613
Nakoma Pl 27607
Namozine Ct 27610
Nancy Ln 27604
Nancy St 27610
Nancy Ann Dr 27607
Nantahala Dr 27612
Napa Valley Dr 27612
Naples Ct 27617
Narrawood St 27614
Narron Ct & St 27617
Narrow Valley Way 27615
Narrow Water Ln 27614
Nash Dr 27608
Nash Ter 27601
Nashford Pl 27604
Natalie Dr 27603
Natalie Brook Way 27609
Nathans Landing Dr 27603
National Ave 27610
National Dr 27612
Native Dancer Dr 27606
Nature Ct 27609
Nautia St 27606
Nautical Ln 27610
Navaho Dr 27609
Nazareth St 27606
Nc 42 Hwy 27603
Nc Highway 42 27603
Neals Creek Dr 27610
Nealstone Way 27614
Neath Hill Ct 27610
S Nebraska Dr 27616
Neches Ln 27616
Nectarine Dr 27616
Needham Rd 27604
Neeley St 27606
Neil St 27607
Neils Branch Rd 27603
Neiman Cv 27612
Neland St 27614
Nellman Ln 27617
Nelson St 27610
Nelson Ridge Ct 27617
Neptune Dr 27604
Nesbit Ct 27616
Nesfield Pl 27606
Nesting Ct 27610
Netherby Ct 27613

Netherfield Ln 27610
Netherlands Dr 27606
Neuse St 27610
Neuse Bend Dr 27616
Neuse Bluff Ct 27603
Neuse Club Ln 27616
Neuse Commons Ln 27616
Neuse Creek Pl 27616
Neuse Crossing Dr 27616
Neuse Farm Dr 27616
Neuse Forest Rd 27616
Neuse Garden Dr 27616
Neuse Grove Ln 27616
Neuse Hunter Dr 27616
Neuse Landing Ln 27616
Neuse Lawn Rd 27616
Neuse Meadow Cir 27610
Neuse Planters Ct 27616
Neuse Rapids Rd 27616
Neuse Ridge Rd 27610
Neuse Run Ct 27616
Neuse Stone Dr 27616
Neuse Tavern Ct 27616
Neuse Timbers Ct 27616
Neuse Town Dr 27616
Neuse View Dr 27610
Neuse Village Ct 27616
Neuse Vista Way 27616
Neuse Wood Dr 27616
Neusehill Ln 27610
N & S Nevada Dr 27616
New Rd 27608
New Arden Way 27613
New Bern Ave
100-298 27601
300-400 27601
311-311 27611
401-1199 27601
402-1198 27601
1200-5799 27610
New Bern Pl 27601
New Bern Ridge Dr 27610
New Birch Dr 27610
New Briarwood Cir 27616
New Brunswick Ln 27615
New Castle Ct 27603
New Cypress Cv 27616
New Dogwood Dr 27616
New Hall Ct 27615
New Hampshire Ct 27615
New Hanover Pl 27603
New Hickory Dr 27616
New Hill Park Rd 27606
N New Hope Rd
900-1299 27610
1300-5199 27604
S New Hope Rd 27610
New Hope Church Rd
1701-1797 27609
1799-1899 27609
1901-1999 27609
2000-3699 27604
New Leesville Blvd 27613
New Light Rd 27614
New London Ln 27613
New Maple Ct 27616
New Market Way
6100-6299 27609
6300-6599 27615
N & S New Mexico Dr ... 27616
New River Cir 27603
New Strickland Ln 27603
New Walnut Pl 27616
New Willow Cv 27616
New Windsor Pl 27603
New World Cir 27615
Newark Dr 27610
Newberry Dr 27609
Newbold St 27603
Newburgh Cir 27603
Newby Ct 27603
Newcastle Rd 27606
Newcombe Rd 27610
Newell Ln 27616
Newfield Ln 27603
Newham Ct 27612

Newport Ave 27613
Newsome St 27603
Newstead Manor Ln 27606
Newton Rd 27615
Niayah Way 27612
Nichols Dr 27605
Nichols Rd 27615
Nicholwood Dr 27605
Nickleby Way 27614
Nicolas Pl 27606
Nicolson Ct 27616
Nicolyn Dr 27616
Nightfall Ct 27607
Nightshade Way 27610
Nikole Ct 27612
Nimich Pond Way 27613
Nina Ct 27603
Nine Iron Way 27603
Nipper Rd 27614
No Record 27606
No Record 27601 St ... 27601
No Record 27603 St ... 27603
No Record 27605 St ... 27605
No Record 27607 St ... 27607
No Record 27608 St ... 27608
No Record 27612 St ... 27612
No Record 27614 St ... 27614
No Record 27616 St ... 27616
No Record 27617 St ... 27617
Noble Rd 27608
Noble Creek Ln 27610
Noble Oak Way 27601
Noblin Rd 27604
Nodding Oak Ct 27610
Noel Ct 27607
Nolichucky Ct 27612
Nolstead Ct 27614
Nomar Rd 27610
Norbury Pl 27614
Noremac Dr 27612
Norfleet Cir 27604
Noridara Rd 27608
Norman Pl 27606
Norman Estates Way ... 27613
Norman Ridge Ln 27613
Normanshire Dr 27606
Norris St 27604
E North St 27601
W North St 27603
Northampton St 27609
Northbrook Dr 27609
Northchester Way 27614
Northclift Dr 27609
Northern Telecom Pl ... 27607
Northfield Ct 27603
Northfield Dr 27609
Northop Ct 27614
Northpines Dr 27610
Northside Dr 27615
Northstone Dr 27604
Northview Ct 27603
Northway Ct 27615
Northwood Dr 27609
Northwyck Pl 27609
Norton Ln 27616
Nortonbridge Rd 27603
Norway Ct 27616
Norwegian Woods Ct ... 27603
Norwich Dr 27613
Norwood Rd
5100-13099 27613
13100-14699 27614
Norwood St 27610
Norwood Crest Ct 27614
Norwood Knolls Way ... 27614
Norwood Oaks Dr 27614
Notchmill Dr 27616
Nottingham Rd 27607
Nottoway Ct 27609
Nouveau Ave 27615
Nowell Rd 27607
Nowell Pointe Dr 27607
Nowell Ridge Rd 27607
Nugget Ln 27615
Nunamaker Ct 27616
Nur Ln 27606

Nutmeg Ct 27614
Nuttree Pl 27606
Nydale Dr 27606
Oak Rd 27603
Oak Way 27613
Oak Bridge Dr 27610
Oak Brook Cir 27609
Oak Chase Ln 27604
Oak Creek Rd 27615
Oak Estate St 27617
Oak Forest Dr 27616
Oak Grove Cir 27607
Oak Hill Dr 27616
Oak Hollow Ct 27613
Oak Lake Ct 27606
Oak Leaf Ct 27615
Oak Marsh Dr 27616
Oak Meadow Ln 27612
Oak Orchard Ct 27613
Oak Park Rd 27612
Oak Point Ct 27610
Oak Ridge Ct 27603
Oak Ridge Dr 27612
Oak Run Dr 27606
Oak Springs Way 27614
Oak Stand Cir 27606
Oak Stone Ct 27614
Oak Stump Ln 27606
Oak Top Ct 27603
Oak Tree Way 27604
Oak Twig Dr 27603
Oakboro Dr 27614
Oakcrest Ct 27612
Oakcroft Dr 27614
Oakdale Dr 27606
Oakes Plantation Dr 27610
Oakgreen Ct 27612
Oakhill Ct 27610
Oakland Dr 27609
Oakland Hills Way 27604
Oaklyn Springs Dr 27606
Oakmont Pl 27615
Oakmoor Ct 27614
Oakshyre Way 27616
Oakside Ct 27609
Oakthorne Way 27613
Oakton Dr 27606
Oakvale St 27603
Oakview Ct 27604
Oakwood Ave
300-1299 27601
1300-2199 27610
Oakwood View Dr 27614
Oates Dr 27604
Oatgrass Ln 27604
Oatstone Pl 27606
Obedient Ln 27603
Oberlin Rd
100-1199 27605
1200-2999 27608
Oberry St 27607
Obion Ct 27616
Ocean Crest Cir 27603
Ocean Key Pl 27603
Ocean Reef Pl 27603
Ocoee Ct 27612
Oconner St 27617
Ocotea St 27607
Ocracoke Ct 27610
Octavia St 27606
Octawa Trl 27610
October Rd 27614
Offshore Dr 27610
Ogden Ct 27613
Ogilvy Ct 27610
Oglebay Ct 27617
Ohmann Ct 27615
Okamato St 27603
Okelly St 27607
N & S Oklahoma Dr 27616
Old Avent Ferry Rd 27606
Old Barbee Ln 27604
Old Baucom Rd 27610
Old Bellows Ct 27607
Old Bern Ct 27612
Old Brick Ct 27616

Old Buffaloe Rd 27604
Old Coach Rd 27616
Old Colony Rd 27613
Old Country Ln 27616
Old Creedmoor Rd 27613
Old Creek Ct 27604
Old Crews Rd 27616
Old Deer Trl 27615
Old Elizabeth Rd 27616
Old English Ct 27615
Old Farm Rd 27606
Old Forge Cir 27609
Old Fox Trl 27613
Old Greenfield Rd 27604
Old Hickory Ln 27610
Old Holiday Rd 27613
Old Horseman Trl 27613
Old Hundred Rd 27613
Old Lane St 27610
Old Lantern Ct 27614
Old Lassiter Mill Rd 27609
Old Lead Mine Rd 27615
Old Leesville Rd 27613
Old Lewis Farm Rd 27604
Old Louisburg Rd 27604
Old Lowery Ct 27614
Old Maple Dr 27610
Old Mccullers Rd 27603
Old Meetinghouse
Way 27615
Old Milburnie Rd
1000-3099 27604
3100-4799 27616
Old Mill Pl 27612
Old Mill Creek Ct 27614
Old Mill Ridge Ct 27616
Old Mill Stream Ct 27610
Old Millcrest Ct 27609
Old Oliver Farm Rd 27606
Old Orchard Rd 27607
Old Pine Ct 27613
Old Plank Rd 27604
Old Ponderosa Cir 27603
Old Poole Rd 27610
Old Post Rd 27612
Old Preserve Ct 27615
Old Raven Ridge Ln 27613
Old Ridge Rd 27610
Old Saybrook Ct 27612
Old Spring Dr 27606
Old Stage Rd 27603
Old Stagecoach Ln 27603
Old Stones Mill St 27610
Old Timber Rd 27613
Old Tom Way 27613
Old Trafford Way 27606
Old Trinity Cir 27607
Old Us Highway 64 E 27610
Old Valley St 27603
Old Vanteen Ln 27614
Old Village Rd 27612
Old Wake Forest Rd
4400-6000 27609
6002-6098 27609
6100-6299 27615
6300-8099 27616
Old Warden Rd 27615
Old Warson Ct 27612
Old Watkins Rd 27616
Old Well Ln 27615
Old Westgate Rd 27617
Old Willard Dr 27613
Old Williams Rd 27610
Old Woodard St 27610
Old World Pl 27612
Oldbrook Ct 27614
Olde Birch Dr 27610
Olde Chimney Ct 27614
Olde Hill Ct 27615
Olde Mill Forrest Dr 27606
Olde Province Ct 27609
Olde South Rd 27606
Olde Station Dr 27615
Olde Stream Ct 27612
Olde Tannton Ct 27614
Oldgate Dr 27604

Oldham Ct 27604
Oldtowne Rd 27612
Ole Ct 27603
Oleander Rd 27603
Olive Rd 27606
Oliver Rd 27614
Olivias Ln 27606
Olivula Ter 27613
Ollie St 27609
Olustee Dr 27610
Olympia Dr 27603
Omni Pl 27613
On Track Rd 27603
Oneal Rd 27613
Oneida Ct 27610
Oneonta Ave 27604
Onslow Rd 27606
Onyx Mill Ct 27616
Opal Ct 27615
Opal Falls Cir 27616
Open Sight Ct 27616
Opequon Dr 27610
Oporto Ct 27610
Opportunity Ln 27603
Opus St 27616
Orabelle Ct 27606
Orallari Rd 27603
Orange St 27609
Orangebrook Rd 27610
Orchard St 27606
Orchard Beach Ln 27616
Orchard Farm Ln 27610
Orchard Gate Way 27616
Orchard Grove Way 27612
Orchard Hollow Ln 27603
Orchard Knob Dr 27610
Orchard Pond Dr 27616
Orchard Trace Way 27616
Orchardgrass Ln 27614
Orchid Ln 27603
Orchid Hill Dr 27613
Orchid Valley Rd 27613
Oregano Ct 27614
Oregon Inlet Ct 27603
Oregon Landing Pl 27610
Orford Ct 27615
Oris Dr 27603
Orkney Pl 27604
Orleans Pl 27609
Ortega Rd 27609
Ortin Ln 27612
Orton Pl 27607
Orwin Manor Dr 27617
Osbourne Ct 27604
Oshanter Pl 27604
Osprey Cir 27615
Osprey Cove Dr 27604
Osterley St 27614
Otterburn Pl 27616
Otters Run Ct 27609
Otura Way 27612
Outback Creek Trl 27603
Over Hadden Ct 27614
Overbrook Dr 27608
Overdale Ln 27603
Overflow Cir 27610
Overhill St 27603
Overland Trl 27615
Overleaf Ct 27615
Overlook Dr 27609
Overlook Rd 27616
Overlook Creek Way 27612
Overlook Village Cir 27612
Overtop Ln 27603
Ovid Ln 27613
Oviedo Dr 27603
Owen Hall 27607
Owens Ln 27610
Owensboro Ct 27603
Owenston Ct 27612
Owl Roost Pl 27617
Owl Tree Ct 27610
Owls House Ln 27603
Owls Nest Dr 27613
Oxalis Dr 27613
Oxbow Ct 27613

Oxbridge Ct 27613
Oxen Cir 27603
Oxford Rd 27608
Oxford Hills Dr 27608
Oxfordshire Ct 27606
Oxgate Cir 27615
Oxley Pl 27616
Oxleymare Dr 27610
Pace St 27604
Pacer Ct 27614
Paces Arbor Cir 27609
W Paces Ferry Rd 27613
Paces Forest Ct 27612
Pacesferry Dr 27614
Pacific Dr 27609
Pack Pl 27615
Paddington Ct 27613
Paddle Pl 27615
Paddle Wheel Dr 27615
Paddock Cir 27613
Paddock Dr
1000-1399 27609
7200-7399 27613
Paddy Hollow Ln 27614
Paducah Dr 27610
Pagan Rd 27603
Page Dr 27603
Page Rd 27603
Page St 27610
Paine Ct 27609
Paint Rock Ln 27610
Painted Sunset Rd 27616
Paisley Pl 27604
Palace Garden Way 27603
Palafox Ct 27604
Pale Moss Dr 27606
Palm Ct 27607
Palm Bay Cir 27617
Palm Island Ct 27603
Palmer Dr 27603
Palmer Spring Ln 27616
Palomino Dr 27606
Pamela Dr 27603
Pamlico Dr 27609
Pampers Ln 27616
Pangea Ln 27616
Panhill Way 27604
Pannonia St 27615
Panther Dr 27603
Panther Branch Dr 27612
Panther Creek Dr 27603
Panther Hill Ln 27603
Panther Springs Ct 27603
Pantops St 27603
Papaya Dr 27613
Paper Birch Ct 27606
Paprika Ct 27614
Par Dr 27603
Paradise Key Way 27603
Paradise Valley Ct 27610
Paragon Park Rd 27616
Parakeet Dr & Ln 27614
Parapet Ln 27610
Pardue Woods Pl 27603
Parham St 27601
Park Ave
100-399 27605
400-499 27606
Park Dr 27605
E Park Dr 27605
W Park Dr 27605
Park Pl 27616
Park At North Hills St 27609
Park Falls Dr 27614
Park Glen Dr 27613
Park Hill Dr 27616
Park Ridge Way 27614
Park Side Dr 27612
Parkander Ct 27603
Parkchester Rd 27616
Parker St 27607
Parker Croft Ct 27609
Parker Falls Dr 27613
Parkersburg St 27616
Parkham Ln 27603
Parklake Ave 27612

Parkland Rd 27603
Parkridge Ln 27605
Parkstone Dr 27613
Parkville Dr 27604
Parkway Dr 27603
Parkwood Dr
4300-4499 27603
5300-5699 27612
Parlor St 27614
Parnell Dr 27610
Parott Dr 27616
Parr Vista Ct 27612
Parrish St 27610
Parrott Dr 27603
Parsley Ct 27614
Partners Way 27606
Partridge Ln 27609
Partridge Berry Dr 27606
Pasquotank Dr 27609
Passage Way 27617
Passage Marseille Ct 27615
Passenger Pl 27603
Passmore Ct 27614
Pastille Ln 27612
Pasture Ln 27614
Pasture View Ln 27603
Pat Reed Rd 27616
Patbrook Ln 27610
Patch Pl 27616
Pathview Ct 27613
Patrick Rd 27604
Patrie Pl 27613
Patriot Pl 27615
Patriot Ridge Ct 27610
Pats Branch Dr 27612
Patton Rd 27608
Patton Ridge Ct 27612
Patuxent Dr 27616
Paul Rd 27616
Paula St 27608
Paula Ann Ct 27612
Paulawood Ln 27603
Pauley Ct 27610
Pauls Penny Ln 27603
Paumier Ct 27615
Paverstone Dr 27615
Pavilion Pl 27615
Pawleys Mill Cir 27614
Paxton Pl 27613
Payton Ct 27614
Pea Ridge Ln 27610
E Peace St 27604
W Peace St
1-599 27603
600-1099 27605
Peace Ter 27604
Peacenest Dr 27610
Peach Rd 27603
Peach Creek Ct 27603
Peach Haven Ct 27607
Peachford Ln 27616
Peachleaf St 27614
Peachtree St 27608
Peachwood Pl 27609
Peacock Pl 27616
Peacock Moss St 27613
Peakton Dr 27614
Peakwood Dr 27603
Pear Orchard Cir & Ln 27616
Pearl Rd 27610
Pearl Crescent Ct 27613
N Peartree Ln 27610
Pebble Ct 27613
Pebble Beach Dr 27616
Pebble Gate Dr 27612
Pebble Hill Ct 27604
Pebble Meadow Ln 27610
Pebble Ridge Dr 27610
Pebblebrook Dr 27609
Pebblestone Ct 27613
Pecan Rd 27603
Peckover Ct 27615
Pecks Pl 27608
Pecore Pl 27615
Peddler Pl 27615
Peebles Rd 27616

Peebles St 27608
Peed Rd 27614
Peed Dead End Rd 27614
Peele Pl 27610
Pegasi Way 27614
Peggy Ct 27603
Pelham Rd 27610
Pelican Pl 27610
Pelican Post Ct 27604
Pell St 27604
Pemberton Dr 27609
Pembridge Ln 27613
Pembrook Pl 27612
Pence Ct 27616
Pendelton Dr 27614
Pender St 27610
Penderwood Ct 27617
Pendleton Lake Rd 27614
Pendragon Pl 27614
Penhurst Pl 27613
Penley Cir 27609
Penmarc Dr 27603
Penn Rd 27604
Penn Oak Cir 27615
Penncross Dr 27610
Pennfine Dr 27610
Pennsylvania Ct 27615
Penny Rd 27606
Penny Hill Ln 27615
Pennyshire Ln 27606
Pennythorne Ct 27615
Penrose Trl 27614
Penselwood Dr 27604
Pentland Ct 27614
Pentridge Ct 27614
Penwood Dr 27606
Pepper Ridge Ct 27615
Peppercorn Ct 27613
Pepperfield Dr 27604
Peppermill Dr 27614
Peppersauce St 27610
Pepperton Dr 27606
Peppertree Pl 27604
Perception Ln 27613
Percheron Pl 27613
Percy Ct 27613
Perennial St 27603
Peridot Ln 27615
Periwinkle Ct 27609
Periwinkle Blue Ln 27612
Perkins Dr 27612
Perkins Ridge Rd 27610
Pernod Way 27613
Perquimans Dr 27609
Perricrest Ct 27603
Perrimor Ct 27603
Perrin Pl 27613
Perry Cir 27616
Perry St 27608
Perry Creek Rd 27616
Perryclear Ct 27614
Perserverance Ct 27606
Pershing Rd 27608
Persimmon Ct 27615
Persimmon Ridge Dr 27604
N Person St
1-499 27601
500-899 27604
S Person St 27601
Pesta Ct 27612
Peter Ct 27610
Peterson St 27610
Petfinder Ln 27603
Petrucelli Ln 27614
N & S Pettigrew St 27610
Pettis Pl 27610
Petworth Ct & Pl 27615
Pewter Pl 27612
Peyton St 27610
Peyton Hall Way 27604
Peyton Oaks Ct 27612
Phaeton Cir 27606
Pheasant Ct 27604
Pheasant Run Cir 27610
Phebe Pl 27612
Pheiffer Dr 27603

Phellos Ct 27615
Phelps Ave 27607
Philcrest Rd 27612
Phillips Ct 27607
Phillipsburg Dr 27613
Philmont Dr 27615
Phlox Rd 27616
Phyllis Dr 27607
Picadilly Ln 27608
Picardy Dr & Pl 27612
Picket Fence Ln 27606
Pickwick Dr 27613
Picnic Pl 27603
Picnic Rock Ln 27613
Picot Dr 27603
Pictou Rd 27606
Pidgeon Hill Rd 27613
Piedmont Dr 27604
Piedmont River Way 27606
Pierce St 27605
Pierce Farm Rd 27610
Pike Rd 27613
Pile Rd 27610
Pilgrim Rd 27616
Pillar Gate Ln 27613
Pillory Pl 27616
Pilots View Dr 27617
Pilton Pl 27604
Pin Oak Rd 27604
Pinckney Pl 27604
Pine Ave 27603
N Pine Ct 27616
S Pine Ct 27616
Pine Dr
1900-2199 27608
4800-5099 27604
5100-5799 27606
Pine Banks Dr 27603
Pine Barren Ln 27610
Pine Birch Dr 27606
Pine Bluff Ct 27614
Pine Cluster Ct 27603
Pine Cove Ct 27614
Pine Creek Ct 27613
Pine Forest Dr 27610
Pine Grove Rd 27610
Pine Knoll Dr 27604
Pine Lakes Ct 27617
Pine Leaf Ct 27606
Pine Limb Ln 27606
Pine Meadow Ln 27615
Pine Needle Ct 27614
Pine Ridge Pl 27609
Pine Springs Ct 27613
Pine Stump Ln 27606
Pine Swell Way 27610
Pine Thicket Ct 27603
Pine Timber Dr 27613
Pine Top Cir 27612
Pine Trace Dr 27613
Pine Tree Ct 27609
Pine Village Rd 27615
Pinebark Ct 27615
Pinecrest Dr 27609
Pinecrest Rd 27613
Pinecrest Townes Dr 27613
Pinecroft Dr 27609
Pinedale Dr 27603
Pinehall Wynd 27604
Pinehurst Dr 27604
Pineland Cir 27606
Pinemist Pl 27614
Pineton Ct 27610
Pineview Dr 27606
Pineview St 27608
Pineville Rd 27617
Pinewild Ct 27615
Pinewinds Dr 27603
Pinewood Ln 27616
Piney Ct 27603
Piney Brook Rd 27614
Pinkham Way 27616
Pinna Ct 27606
Pinnacle Ridge Rd 27603
Pinot Noir Ln 27615
Pintail Ct 27616

Piping Plover Dr 27616
Pirate Ct 27612
Pirouette Ct 27606
Pitch Pine Ct 27617
Pitching Wedge Dr 27603
Pitchkettle Rd 27606
Pitkin Ct 27606
Pitt St 27609
Pittsford Rd 27604
Pj Farms Ln 27603
Plainsfield Cir 27610
Plainview Ave 27604
Plainview Dr 27610
Planet Dr 27604
Plano Ct 27616
W Plantation Cir 27603
Plantation Rd 27609
Plantation Center Dr 27616
Plateau Ln 27615
Platinum Ave 27610
Platinum Creek Ct 27616
Platte Xing 27617
Player Ct 27615
Plaza Pl 27612
Pleasant Creek Ct 27613
Pleasant Garden Ln 27610
Pleasant Grove Church Rd 27613
Pleasant Meadow Dr 27615
Pleasant Pines Dr 27613
Pleasant Quail Ct 27603
Pleasant Ridge Rd 27615
Pleasant Union Church Rd 27614
Pleasant Valley Rd 27612
Pleasantville Dr 27616
Plentywood Ct 27615
Plum Frost Dr 27603
Plum Nearly Ct 27610
Plumbridge Ct 27613
Plumleaf Rd 27613
Plymouth Ct 27610
Poe Dr 27610
Pogue St 27607
Point Owoods Ct 27604
Pointe Vista Cir 27615
Pointe Water Ct 27603
Pointer Dr 27609
Poison Ivy Pl 27614
Poland Pl 27609
Polaris Ct 27604
Polesdon Ct 27615
Polite Ln 27610
Polk St 27604
Polka Ln 27610
Pollock Pl 27607
Polly St 27610
Polo Dr 27603
Polonaise Pl 27610
Pomegranate Dr 27616
Pomfret Pt 27612
Pommell Dr 27613
Ponder Ln 27617
Ponderosa Dr 27603
Ponderosa Rd 27612
Pondsedge Trl 27603
Pony Chase Ln 27610
Pony Pasture Ct 27612
Pony Run Rd 27615
Pooh Corner Dr 27616
Poole Rd 27610
Poole Farm Ln 27610
Pooler Rd 27617
Poolside Dr 27612
Poplar Dr
500-699 27603
4400-4499 27610
Poplar St 27604
Poplar Creek Trl 27610
Poplar Grove Ct 27613
Poplar Springs Church Rd 27603
Poplarwood Ct 27604
Poppy Hills Ct 27603
Pops View Ln 27613
Porchlamp Ct 27615
Porchlight Ct 27603
Porellar Rd 27610
Port Chester Ct 27614
Port Royal Rd 27609
Porterdale Dr 27610
Portico Pl 27603
Portree Pl 27606
Portside Ln 27610
Portsmouth Ln 27615
Portview Dr 27613
Possum Track Rd 27614
Post Mill Pl 27615
Post Oak Rd 27615
Postell St 27601
Potecasi Dr 27610
Potomac Ave 27604
Potomac Ct 27613
Pottery Ln 27616
Potthast Ct 27616
Poulnot Ct 27604
Powder Horn Ct 27616
Powell Dr 27606
Powell Townes Way 27606
Powis Cir 27615
Poyner Dr 27612
Poyner Anchor Ln 27616
Poyner Pond Cir 27616
Poyner Village Pkwy 27616
Pradera Way 27615
Prairie Pond Cir 27614
Prancer Pl 27613
Prat Ct 27606
Precision Dr 27617
Prelude St 27616
Prescott Pl 27615
Preserve Rd 27610
Presidio Dr 27617
Presley Ct 27604
Preslyn Dr 27616
Presnell Ct 27615
Prestige Rd 27616
Preston Pl 27604
Price St 27606
Priceview Dr 27603
Pride Way 27613
Pride Rock Ct 27614
Pridwen Cir 27610
Primanti Blvd 27612
Primavera Ct 27616
Primland Ln 27610
Primrose Valley Ct 27613
Prince Dr 27606
Prince George Ln 27615
Princess Anne Rd 27607
Princeton St 27609
Princeton Mill Pkwy 27612
Princewood St 27612
Printer Ln 27613
Printice Pl 27604
Prisma Ct 27612
Pritchard Ct 27616
Proctor Rd 27610
Proctor Hill Dr 27613
Professional Ct 27609
Professor St 27616
Progress Ct 27608
Pronghorn Ln 27610
Proprietor Way 27612
Prospect Ave 27603
Prospector Pl 27615
Prosser Ct 27614
Providence Rd 27610
Providence Square Dr 27613
Provincial St 27603
Provost St 27603
Prynnwood Ct 27607
Puffin Pl 27616
Pullen Rd 27607
Pullman Ln 27616
Pumpkin Ln 27614
Pumpkin Ridge Way 27604
Punjab St 27604
Purchase Xing 27617
Purdue St 27609
Purland Dr 27603
Purple Garnet Way 27610
Purple Martin Ln 27606
Purplehorse Way 27606
Purser Dr 27603
Pursuit Ct 27616
Putters Way 27614
Pylon Dr 27606
Pyxis Ct 27614
Quadrilla Pl 27610
Quail Cir 27603
Quail Dr 27604
Quail Creek Ct 27609
Quail Forest Dr 27609
Quail Hollow Dr 27609
Quail Landing Ct 27606
Quail Meadow Dr 27609
Quail Oaks Cir 27603
Quail Point Dr 27603
Quail Ridge Rd 27609
Quail Side Ct 27603
Quail View Trl 27604
Quaker Lndg 27603
Quaker Ridge Pt 27615
Quarry St 27601
Quarry Ridge Ln 27610
Quarry Springs Rd 27610
Quarryman Rd 27610
Quarter Pt 27615
Quarton Dr 27616
Quartz Ct 27610
Queen Annes Dr 27613
Queen Charlotte Pl 27610
Queens Rd 27612
Queensbridge Ct 27613
Queensland Rd 27614
Queenstown Ct 27612
Quiet Cove Ct 27612
Quiet Mill Rd 27612
Quiet Ridge Cir 27614
Quillin Ct 27616
Quillstone Ct 27613
Quinby Ct 27613
Quince Dr 27610
Quinley Pl 27604
Quitman Trl 27610
R B Dr 27616
Rabbit Run 27603
Rabbit Box Cir 27610
Rabbit Hollow Trl 27614
Race Track Rd 27603
Raceview Ter 27615
Racine Way 27615
Radburn Pl 27615
Radcliff Rd 27609
Raddington St 27613
N Radner Way 27613
Rail Fence Rd 27606
Railroad St 27603
Rain Forrest Way 27614
Rainbow Ct 27612
Rainbow Hill Way 27614
Rainbow Ridge Ct 27603
Raindipper Dr 27614
Raindrop Ct 27615
Rainford Ct 27603
Raintree Ct 27609
Rainwater Rd 27615
Rainwood Ln 27615
Raleigh Blvd 27604
N Raleigh Blvd
701-997 27610
999-1999 27610
2400-2699 27604
S Raleigh Blvd 27610
Raleigh Beach Rd 27610
Raleigh Durham Hwy 27612
Raleigh Pines Dr 27610
Raleigh School Dr 27607
Raleigh View Rd 27610
Ralph Dr 27610
Rambeau Cir 27613
Ramble Way 27616
Ramblewood Dr 27609
Ramona Rd 27606
Rampart St 27609
Ramseur St 27610
Ramsey Rd 27604
Ramsgate St 27603
Ramson Ct 27603
Ranada Ct 27616
Ranburne Dr 27610
Ranch Farm Rd 27603
Ranch Mill Cir 27610
Rand Dr 27608
Rand Rd 27603
Randolph Ct 27606
Randolph Dr 27609
Random Pl 27616
Raney Ct 27604
Rangecrest Rd 27612
Rangeley Dr 27609
Rankin St 27604
Ranleigh Ct 27613
Ranlo Dr 27612
Rannette St 27603
Rannock Ct 27604
Ransdell Rd & Way 27603
Ranwick Ln 27603
Ranworth Way 27615
Rappahanock Rd 27614
Raspberry Ln 27614
Ratchford Dr 27604
Rattan Bay Dr 27610
Ravel St 27606
Ravelstone Ct 27610
Raven Rd 27614
Raven Ridge Rd 27614
Raven Rock Dr 27614
Raven Tree Dr 27617
Ravenglass Pl 27612
Ravenhill Dr 27615
Ravenhurst Dr 27615
Ravens Creek Ct 27603
Ravens Crest Ln 27616
Ravens Point Cir 27614
Ravenscar Dr 27615
Ravenscroft Dr 27615
Ravenwood Dr 27606
Ravi Rd 27604
Rawls Dr 27610
Ray Rd 27613
Raya Ct 27617
Raymond St 27607
Raymond Smith Rd 27603
Raytown Rd 27613
Razorbill Way 27616
Reading Cir 27615
Reanne Ct 27617
Reaves Dr 27608
Reavis Rd 27606
Reba Dr 27616
Rebecca Lynn Ln 27613
Rebel Cir 27604
Reconciliation Dr 27603
Red Ln 27606
Red Alder Ct 27610
Red Banks Ct 27616
Red Bay Dr 27616
Red Beech Ct 27614
Red Bud St 27603
Red Cap Ln 27616
Red Cedar Rd 27613
Red Clay Dr 27604
Red Coat Ct 27616
Red Eagle Ct 27617
Red Forest Trl 27615
Red Fox Run 27614
Red Grape Dr 27607
Red Inn Ct 27603
Red Jasmine Ln 27604
Red Lodge Pl 27603
Red Oak Ct 27613
Red Quartz Dr 27610
Red Robin Rd 27613
Red Ruby Ln 27610
Redbud Ln 27607
Redcrest Pl 27617
Reddick Smith Rd 27603
Reddington Trl 27616
Redford Dr 27603
Redhook Ct 27617
Redington Dr 27609
Redleaf Ct 27609
Redman Ct 27610
Redmond Ct 27612
Redtail Ct 27616
Redwood Cir 27609
Redwood Dr 27606
Redwood Ln
5800-5899 27606
6800-6999 27616
Reedham Way 27615
Reedham Oaks Ct 27615
Reedy Creek Rd 27607
Reedy Ridge Ln 27613
Reflection Ct 27610
Regal Run Dr 27603
Regalwood Dr 27613
Regatta Way 27613
Regent Pl 27608
Regina Dr 27603
Regulator St 27603
Reid St 27608
Reigate Ln
1800-1899 27610
8800-8899 27603
Rein St 27613
Relay Way 27603
Release Cir 27615
Rembert Dr 27612
Rembrandt Cir 27607
Remedios Walk 27617
Remington Rd 27610
Remington Lake Dr 27616
Renaissance Ln 27614
Rendezvous Dr 27610
Rendition St 27610
Renewal Pl 27603
Renfield Dr 27617
Renfrow Rd 27603
Rennit Ct 27603
Renwick Ct 27615
Renyard Ct 27616
Resco Ct 27617
Reservoir Rd 27610
Resolution Ln 27603
Resplendent Pl 27603
Rest Haven Dr 27612
Reston Ct 27614
Retriever Ln 27603
Reunion Pt 27609
Revelation St 27610
Revere Dr 27609
Revine Dr 27610
Revolution Cir 27603
Revolutionary Dr 27603
Rexview Ct 27607
Rexwoods Dr 27607
Reynolda Ct 27603
Reynolds Rd 27609
Rhett Dr 27606
Rhiannon Rd 27613
Rhinebeck Ct 27617
Rhododendron Dr 27612
Rhudy Pl 27612
Rhyne Ct 27610
Rhynes Gate Way 27606
Ribbon Trough Ct 27603
Ribbongrass Ct 27614
Ribcowski Ct 27616
Richardson Dr 27603
Richland Dr 27612
Richland Pointe Dr 27616
Richmond St 27609
Richmond Run Dr 27614
Richward Pl 27607
Richwood Ct 27612
Ricker Rd 27610
Ricky Cir 27612
Ricochet Dr 27610
Riddick Dr 27609
Riddle Pl 27615
N Ridge Dr 27615
Ridge Rd
1200-2199 27607
2200-3099 27612
Ridge Brook Ln 27610
Ridge Grove Ct 27615
Ridge Mill Run 27612
Ridge Pointe Ln 27615
Ridge Side Pl 27613
Ridge Trace Dr 27606
Ridgebluffs Ct 27603
Ridgebrook Bluffs Dr 27603
Ridgebury Rd 27603
Ridgecrest Ct 27607
Ridgecroft Ln 27615
Ridgefield Dr 27609
Ridgegate Dr 27617
Ridgeland Dr 27607
Ridgeline Dr 27613
Ridgeloch Pl 27612
Ridgeway Ct 27604
Ridgewell Ct 27613
Ridgewood Dr 27609
Ridley St 27608
Riese Dr 27613
Rigel Ct 27604
Riley Ridge Ln 27603
Rim Ct 27616
Rimwood Ct 27613
Ringland Rd 27613
Rink Rd 27617
Rio Bluff Dr 27614
Rio Falls Dr 27614
Rio Grande Dr 27616
Rio Springs Dr 27614
Rio Valley Dr 27614
Rio Vista Dr 27614
Rio Wild Dr 27614
Ripley Station Way 27610
Ripple Rd 27610
Ripplestir Ct 27615
Rippling Stone Ln 27612
Risdon Ct 27616
River Run 27613
River Bank Dr 27614
River Basin Ln 27610
River Birch Dr 27613
River Bluff Ct 27604
River Boat Landing Ct 27604
River Branch Dr 27610
River Breeze Ct 27604
River Chase Dr 27610
River Creek Run 27604
River Dance Dr 27613
River Down Dr 27603
River Dreams Dr 27610
River Edge Dr 27604
River Field Dr 27616
River Forest Dr 27614
River Glen Ct 27614
River Gold Ln 27616
River Haven Pl 27616
River Jasmine Ln 27604
River Keeper Way 27616
River Lake Cir 27604
River Landings Dr 27604
River Laurel Ct 27604
River Meadow Ct 27604
River Oak Turn 27613
River Pearl St 27603
River Rock Ct 27604
River Shadow Ct 27610
River Stream Way 27616
River Walk Dr 27616
River Watch Ln 27616
River Water Ct 27616
Riverbed Dr 27610
Riverbrooke Dr 27610
Rivercliff Ct 27610
Riverdale St 27610
Riverford Dr 27616
Rivergate Rd 27614
Rivergrass Ct 27610
Riverknoll Dr 27610
Rivermist Dr 27610
Riverport Rd 27616
Rivershyre Way 27616
Riverstone Pl 27614
Riverview Rd 27610
Riverview Park Dr 27613
Riverwind Ln 27617
Riverwood Ln 27617
Riviera Ct 27604
Roads Hill Dr 27610
Roadstead Way E & W 27613
Roan Mountain Pl 27613
Roanoke St 27606
Roaring Rapids Rd 27610
Robb Ct 27615
Robbie Dr 27607
Robbins Dr 27610
Roberts St 27607
Robin Hood Dr 27604
Robinfield Dr 27603
Robinson Ave
1200-1399 27610
2400-10699 27603
Rocca Cir 27603
Rock Ave & Dr 27610
Rock Barn Rd 27613
Rock Canyon Rd 27613
Rock Creek Dr 27609
Rock Creek Rd 27613
Rock Dam Ct 27615
Rock Field Dr 27610
Rock Hollow Rd 27617
Rock Hurst Ct 27603
Rock Oak Ct 27613
Rock Quarry Rd 27610
Rock Rose Ln 27612
Rock Service Station Rd 27603
Rock View Dr 27612
Rockbridge Ct 27604
Rockcliff Rd 27603
Rockdale Dr 27609
Rocket Ct 27610
Rockfall Ct 27614
Rockglen Way 27615
Rockingham Dr 27609
Rockledge Dr 27617
Rockrest Ct 27612
Rockridge Ct 27612
Rockside Hills Dr 27603
Rockwell Ct 27603
Rockwood Dr
2500-2799 27610
4400-4799 27612
Rocky Ct 27616
Rocky Bluff Ct 27614
Rocky Branch Dr
1-99 27603
700-799 27601
Rocky Brook Xing 27604
Rocky Falls Ct 27610
Rocky Ford Ct 27614
Rocky Gap Cir 27603
Rocky Point Ct 27613
Rocky Stream Ln 27610
Rocky Toad Rd 27614
Rocky Top Dr 27616
Rodessa Run 27607
N & S Rogers Ln 27610
Rogers View Ct 27610
Rogerson St 27614
Roller Ct 27604
Roller Mill Ct 27607
Rolling Ct 27616
Rolling Dale Ct 27615
Rolling Farm Dr 27603
Rolling Glenn Dr 27616
Rolling Green Ct 27604
Rolling Hills Dr 27603
Rolling Meadows Dr 27603
Rolling Oaks Ln 27606
Rollingwood Dr 27613
Rolston Dr 27609
Romealia Ln 27613
Ronal Cir 27603
Ronald Dr 27609
Rondan Cir 27612
Rondeau Woods Ct 27614
Rooksley Ct 27615
Rooster Way 27614
Rosalie St 27614
Rosalynn Ct 27610
Rosaria Way 27601
Roscoe Trl 27607

Rose Ln 27610
Rose Water Pl 27616
Rosebank Ln 27614
Rosecliff Ct 27617
Rosedale Ave 27607
Rosedale Dr 27603
Rosegate Ct 27617
Rosehaven Dr 27609
Roseland Ct 27613
Roselle Ct 27610
Rosemary St 27607
Rosemont Ave 27607
Rosengarten Aly 27603
Ross Ct 27613
Roswell Rd 27615
Roteny Ct 27610
Rothfield Ln 27616
Rothgeb Dr 27609
Rothschild Dr 27615
Rothshire Ct 27615
Rotterdam Ct 27606
Round Brook Cir 27617
Round Hill Ln 27616
Round Oak Rd 27616
Roundleaf Ct 27604
Roundstone Dr 27613
Roundtree Ct 27607
E Rowan St 27609
Rowland Rd 27615
Rowlock Way 27613
Roxanne Dr 27603
Roxton Ct 27613
Roxy St 27610
Roy Averette Dr 27603
Royal St 27607
Royal Acres Rd 27610
Royal Adelaide Way 27604
Royal Amber Way 27614
Royal Anne Ln 27615
Royal Coach Ct 27612
Royal Crest Dr 27617
Royal Dornoch Dr 27604
Royal Forrest Dr 27614
Royal Foxhound Ln 27610
Royal Kings Ln 27615
Royal Melbourne Dr 27604
Royal Oaks Dr 27615
Royal Pines Dr 27610
Royal Troon Dr 27604
Royalwood Ct 27613
Royster St 27608
Royton Cir 27613
Ruark Ct 27608
Rubblestone Path 27613
Rubra Cir 27616
Ruby Dr 27610
Ruddy Rd 27616
Rudolph Ct 27610
Rue Cassini Ct 27615
Rue Sans Famille 27607
Ruffin St 27607
Rugby Ct 27604
Ruggles Dr 27603
Rumba Ct 27610
Rumford Ct 27614
Rumshill Rd 27614
Rumson Rd 27610
Running Brook Trl 27609
Running Cedar Trl 27615
Running Oak Dr
1800-1899 27613
8800-8899 27617
Runnymede Rd 27607
Runon Cir 27603
Rupert Rd 27603
Ruritania St 27616
Rush St
100-199 27603
300-699 27610
Rush Springs Ct 27617
Rushing Creek Pkwy 27610
Rushingbrook Dr 27612
Russ St 27610
Russell Ct 27610
Russell Dr 27612
Russling Leaf Ln 27613

Rustic Brick Rd 27603
Rustic Country Dr 27603
Rutgers Ct 27609
Rutherford Dr 27609
Rutland Ct 27613
Rutledge Ct 27613
Rutledge Bay 27614
Ryan Ct 27606
Rydal Ct 27613
Ryder Cup Cir 27603
Ryegate Dr 27604
Ryegrass Ct 27610
Ryton Ct 27613
Sablewood Dr 27617
Sacred Woods Way 27607
Saddle Ct 27609
Saddle Seat Dr 27606
Saddle Springs Ct 27615
Saddlepath Cir 27606
Saddleridge Dr 27615
Saddleview Ct 27613
Saddlewood Ct 27614
Sadie Hopkins St 27603
Sadler Ct 27615
Sadora Ct 27610
Safran Ct 27606
Sagacity Dr 27601
Sagamore Ct 27604
Sage Green Ct 27610
Sagehurst Pl 27614
Sageland Ct 27604
Sageleaf Ct 27603
Sagewood Ct 27615
Saguaro Ct 27616
Sahalee Way 27604
Sailfish Ln 27610
Saint Agnes Way 27612
Saint Albans Dr 27609
Saint Andrews Ct 27615
Saint Augustine Ave 27610
Saint Chapelle Ct 27615
Saint Francis Dr 27613
Saint George Rd 27610
Saint Giles St 27612
Saint Ives Ct 27610
Saint James Rd 27607
Saint James Church Rd 27604
Saint Jens Ln 27603
Saint Johns Ct 27616
Saint Ledger Dr 27613
Saint Marys St
1-1399 27605
1500-2299 27608
2500-2799 27609
S Saint Marys St 27603
Saint Mellion St 27603
Saint Patrick Dr 27603
Saint Pauls Sq 27614
Saint Regis Cir 27606
Saint Stephan Ct 27615
Saint Thomas Pl 27612
Salamander Ct 27610
Salcomb Ln 27614
Salem Cir 27609
Salem Glen Ln 27617
Salem Woods Dr 27615
Salisbury Pln 27613
N Salisbury St
1-499 27603
500-600 27604
602-898 27604
S Salisbury St 27601
Sallies Pl 27603
Salsa Ct 27610
Salt Bush Ct 27603
Salterton Ct 27608
Saltree Pl 27614
Saltsby Ct 27615
Saltville Ct 27610
Saltwood Pl 27617
Saluda Ct 27608
Salute St 27615
Samantha Dr 27613
Sampson St 27609
San Gabriel St 27613

San Juan Hill Ct 27610
San Marcos Way 27616
San Pablo Dr 27616
Sanctuary Ct 27617
Sanctus Ln 27613
Sand Cove Ct 27616
Sand Pebble Ct & Pl 27613
Sandberry Ln 27613
Sandbridge Ct 27612
Sandel Ln 27603
Sanderford Rd 27610
Sanderson Dr 27608
Sandfiddler Dr 27604
Sandhurst Rd 27615
Sandia Dr 27607
Sandlewood Dr 27609
Sandlin Pl 27606
Sandown Pl 27615
Sandpiper Ct 27615
Sandra Dr 27603
Sandra Ln 27615
Sandringham Ct & Dr 27613
Sandusky Ln 27614
Sandwell Ln 27607
Sandwood Ct 27613
Sandy Banks Rd 27616
Sandy Bay Cir 27603
Sandy Bluff Rd 27616
Sandy Bottom Way 27613
Sandy Creek Dr 27615
Sandy Forks Rd
5900-6199 27609
6200-7299 27615
Sandy Grove Ct 27615
Sandy Lake Ct 27613
Sandy Oak Ln 27614
Sandy Ridge Ct 27615
Sandy Springs Dr 27610
Sandyfield Run 27603
Sandygrass Ct 27610
Sansome Trl 27610
Sap Ln 27603
Sapling Pl 27615
Sappello Ct 27604
Sapphire Valley Dr 27604
Sapwood Ct 27615
Sara Ln 27606
Sarah Lawrence Ct 27609
Sarahcreek Ct 27607
Sarant Oaks Ct 27614
Saratoga Dr 27604
Saratoga Falls Ln 27614
Saratoga Springs Ln 27613
Sarazen Pl 27615
Sardis Dr 27603
Sargas St 27614
Sarver Ct 27603
Sassafras Ln 27614
Sasser St 27604
Satellite Ct 27604
Satillo Ln 27616
Satinleaf Dr 27616
Satinwing Ln 27617
Saturn St 27603
Saubranch Hill St 27616
Sauls Rd 27603
Saulsridge Rd 27603
S Saunders St 27603
Savan Ct 27613
Savannah Dr 27610
Savannah Oaks Way 27614
Savior St 27610
Sawbuck Ct 27613
Sawgrass Ct 27615
Sawmill Rd
100-1699 27615
2400-2699 27613
Sawpit Dr 27610
Sawyer Dr 27613
Sawyer Rd 27610
Saxby Ct 27613
Saxon Way 27613
Saxony Pl 27604
Saybrooke Dr 27604
Sayornis Ct 27615
Scales St 27608

Scales Towne Ct 27608
Scarlet Maple Dr 27606
Scarlet Oak Pl 27610
Scarlet Sage Ct 27613
Scattered Oak Ct 27603
Scaup Ct 27616
Scenic Dr & Way 27614
Scenic Brook Ln 27616
Scenic View Ln 27612
Schaller Ct 27617
Schaub Dr 27606
Schenley Dr 27610
Scholar Cir 27606
School Chapel Dr 27605
School Creek Pl 27606
Schoolhouse St 27614
Schubba Ct 27614
Scofield Dr 27610
Scollay Ct 27609
Scotch Dr 27616
Scotch Castle Dr 27612
Scotland St 27609
Scotney Ct 27615
Scotridge Ct 27615
Scott Dr 27604
Scott Glen Ln 27614
Scottsdale Ln 27613
Scouting Trl 27615
Scribe Ct 27615
Scripps Ln 27610
Sea Daisy Dr 27606
Sea Fox Ct 27616
Seaboard Ave 27604
Seabrook Rd 27610
Seafarer Ct 27613
Seaforth Ct 27606
Seagate Dr 27615
Seagrams Ct 27610
Seasons Dr 27614
Seaspray Ln 27610
Seastone St 27603
Seaton Ct 27615
Seawell Ave 27601
Seawright Pl 27610
Seclusion Ct 27612
Seclusion Park Dr 27610
Second Star Ct 27613
Secret Dr 27612
Secretariat Way 27614
Sedalia Ct 27610
Sedgefield Dr
5200-5299 27609
11200-11299 27613
Sedgefield Pines Ave & Ln 27604
Sedgewick Dr 27616
Sedgewood Dr 27612
Sego Ct 27616
Selfridge Ct 27615
Selkirk Pl 27604
Sellona St 27617
Selwyn Aly 27601
Semana Walk 27617
Semart Dr 27604
Seminole Trl 27609
Sendero Dr 27612
Seneca Dr 27604
Sentinel Dr 27609
September Ct 27614
Serenade Cir 27610
Serendipity Dr 27616
Serenity Creek Dr 27610
Setter Cir 27609
Settle In Ln 27614
Settlers Ridge Ln 27614
Seven Springs Trl 27616
Sevillanos Walk 27617
Sextons Creek Dr 27614
Sgt Pepper Ct 27603
Shadbush St 27616
Shaded Villa Ct 27613
Shades Pl 27601
Shadetree Ct & Ln 27613
Shadow Ct 27613
Shadow Creek Dr 27604
Shadow Elms Ln 27614

Shadow Glen Dr 27604
Shadow Hills Ct 27612
Shadow Moss Cir 27603
Shadow Oak Way 27615
Shadow Stone Ct 27613
Shadow Wood Pl 27613
Shadowbark Ct 27603
Shadowbrook Dr 27612
Shadowland Xing 27616
Shadowlawn Dr 27614
Shadowood Ln 27612
Shadowview Ct 27614
Shadwell Ct 27613
Shady Ln 27604
Shady Crest Dr 27613
Shady Grove Cir 27609
Shady Grove Rd 27617
Shady Maple Ct 27607
Shady Rise Gln 27603
Shady River Ct 27610
Shadybrook Dr 27609
Shadyside Dr 27612
Shadywood Ln 27603
Shaftsberry Ct 27609
Shag Dr 27610
Shaker Heights Ln 27613
Shallcross Way 27617
Shallowbrook Trl 27616
Shallowford Dr 27614
Shamrock Dr 27612
Shanda Dr 27609
Shandwick Ct 27609
Shannon Ct 27603
Shannon St 27610
Shannonbrook Ln 27603
Shannondale Dr 27603
Shannonhouse Dr 27612
Sharnbrook Ct 27614
N & S Sharon Dr 27603
Sharon View Ln 27614
Sharpe Dr 27612
Sharpstone Ln 27615
Shasta Ct 27609
Shavenrock Pl 27613
Shavlik Trl 27606
Shaw Ct 27606
Shawood Dr 27609
Shedd Dr 27603
Sheetbend Ln 27606
Sheffield Rd 27610
Shelane Ct 27610
Shelden Dr 27610
Shellbrook Ct 27609
Shellburne Dr 27612
Shelley Rd
400-1399 27609
1400-2099 27612
Shellnut Rd 27615
Shellum St 27610
Shellwood Ct 27617
Shelly Ridge Ln 27609
Shelly River Dr 27609
Shelter Cv 27617
Shelton Ct 27609
Shelton Ham Way 27612
Shem Creek Ct 27613
Shenandoah Rd 27603
Shepherd St 27607
Shepherd Valley St 27610
Sherborne Pl 27612
Sherbrooke Ct 27612
Sherburg Ct 27606
Sherlock Ct 27613
Sherman Ave 27606
Sherrif Pl E & W 27610
Sherrill Dr 27604
Sherry Dr 27604
Sherrybrook Dr 27610
Sherwee Dr 27603
Sherwood Ave 27610
Sheryl Dr 27604
Shetland Ct 27609
Shield Cir 27603
Shilling Ct 27606
Shillingstone Pl 27615
Shiloh Ct 27609

Shiloh Creek Ct 27616
Shimer Farm Ln 27614
Shining Water Ln 27614
Shinleaf Ct 27613
Shinnwyck Ct 27604
Shipton Ct 27614
Shire Ln 27606
Shirley St 27610
Shoalcreek Pl 27612
Shofield Ct 27615
Sholliso St 27605
Shonnie Dr 27604
Shooting Club Rd 27613
Shore View Rd 27613
Short Pine St 27609
Shotwell Rd 27610
Shoveller Ct 27616
Shy Baby Ln 27610
S Side Dr 27612
Sidney Rd 27603
Sierra Dr 27603
Sierra Vista Way 27615
Signature Ln 27606
Signett Dr 27616
Silas Ridge Ct 27609
Silent Stream Ct 27607
Silhouette Pl 27613
Silkwater Ct 27610
Silkwood Way 27612
Silver Ct 27614
Silver Ash Dr 27616
Silver Beach Way 27606
Silver Birch Ct 27614
Silver Dollar Ln 27603
Silver Farm Rd 27603
Silver Forrest Ln 27614
Silver Lake Trl 27606
Silver Leaf Pl 27609
Silver Maple Pl 27603
Silver Mist Ct 27613
Silver Moon Ln 27606
Silver Oaks Ct 27614
Silver Quill Ct 27604
Silver Sage Dr 27606
Silver Star Dr 27610
Silver View Ln 27613
Silverdene St 27616
Silverling Way 27613
Silverpalm St 27612
Silvers Rd 27606
Silverthorne Dr 27612
Silverthread Ln 27617
Silverwood Creek Dr 27614
Simmons Branch Trl 27606
Simms Creek Rd 27616
Simpkins Rd 27603
Simpkins St 27606
Simpkins Farm Ln 27603
Simtree Ct 27615
Sinclair Dr 27616
Sinesis Ct 27609
Singing Wind Dr 27612
Singleleaf Ln 27616
Singleton St 27606
Singleton Industrial Dr 27604
Sioux Dr 27609
Sir Colleton Ct 27612
Sir Duncan Way 27612
Sissinghurst Ct 27615
Sisters Ln 27603
Sitterson Dr 27603
Situs Ct 27606
Sitwell Ct 27613
Sitzman Ct 27616
Six Forks Rd
3200-6199 27609
6200-10499 27615
10500-13299 27614
E Six Forks Rd
100-399 27609
350-350 27619
350-350 27622
400-898 27609
401-899 27609
900-999 27604
Six Oaks Ln 27601

Six Pence Ct 27613
Six Point Trl 27616
Six Siblings Cir 27610
Skeenes Ct 27614
Skibo Ln 27603
Skidmore St 27609
Skinner Dr 27610
Skinners Ridge Rd 27614
Skipjack Ct 27613
Skipton Ct 27606
Sky Point Ct 27603
Sky Ridge Dr 27603
Skycrest Dr 27604
Skycrest Park Ln 27604
Skyland Ridge Pkwy 27617
Skylark Way 27615
Skylock Dr 27610
Skyview Dr 27603
Slabstone Ct 27613
Slade Hill Rd 27615
Slate Dr 27610
Slatestone Ct
1300-1399 27615
12300-12499 27614
Sleepy Creek Dr 27613
Sleepy Hollow Dr 27612
Slide Rock Ln 27613
Slider Dr 27614
Slippery Creek Ct 27616
Slippery Elm Dr 27610
Sloan Ct 27606
Slopeside Ct 27610
Sly Ct 27616
Small Ct 27612
Small Oak Ln 27617
Small Pine Dr 27603
Small Pond Rd 27603
Small Ridge Cir 27614
Smallwood Ct 27613
Smallwood Dr 27605
Smart Dr 27603
Smedes Pl 27605
Smith Ct 27604
Smith Dr 27606
Smith Plz 27601
Smith Basin Ln 27614
Smith Creek Pkwy 27612
Smith Reno Rd 27603
Smithdale Dr 27606
Smithfield Rd 27604
Smoke Pl 27610
Smokeridge Ln 27615
Smokerise Ct 27615
Smoketree Ct 27604
Smokey Ridge Rd 27613
Smoky Chestnut Ln 27615
Smoky Topaz Ln 27610
Smooth Stone Trl 27610
Snapswell St 27614
Sneedhall Ln 27615
Snelling Rd 27609
Snipe Creek Ln 27613
Snodgrass Hill Ct 27610
Snow Ave 27603
Snow Goose Ct 27616
Snow Heights Ln 27613
Snow Peak Ct 27603
Snow Wind Dr 27615
Snowberry Dr 27610
Snowcrest Ln 27616
Snowden Pl 27615
Snowy Meadow Ct 27614
Soapstone Cir 27614
Soaring Talon Ct 27614
Society Pl 27615
Soco Ct 27614
Soco Gap Ct 27613
Sojourn Dr 27610
Sojournertruth Way 27610
Solar Dr 27610
Solheim Ln 27603
Solumbra Ct 27616
Soma Ct 27613
Somerford Ln 27614
Somerset Rd 27610
Somerset Hills Ct 27604

Somerset Mill Ln 27616
Somerset Springs Dr ... 27616
Somerset Valley Ln 27616
Somerton Pl 27604
Sommerville Park Rd ... 27603
Sommerwell St 27613
Sonesta Ct 27613
Sonora St 27607
Soquel Ln 27603
Sorrell Ln 27603
Sorrell Brook Way 27609
Sorrell Brothers Ct ... 27603
Sorrell Crossing Dr ... 27617
Sorrento Ct 27613
Sorrills Creek Ln 27614
Sosa Rd 27610
Sourwood St 27610
E South St 27601
W South St
2-98 27601
100-200 27601
202-598 27601
600-1099 27603
Southall Rd 27604
Southall Road Ext 27604
Southampton Ct 27604
Southampton Dr 27615
Southbriar Dr 27606
Southbridge Rd 27610
Southern Charm Ln 27603
Southern Cross Ave 27606
Southern Escape Way ... 27603
Southern Grace Ln 27603
Southern Hills Ct 27604
Southern Living Dr 27610
Southern Meadows Dr ... 27603
Southern Moss Ct 27603
Southern Oaks Dr 27603
Southern Times Dr 27603
Southfield Pl 27615
Southgate Dr 27610
Southview Ct 27603
Southwalk Ln 27614
Southwell Ct 27614
Southwind Dr 27613
Spacer Dr 27603
Spacious Skies St 27614
Spaldwick Ct 27613
Spanglers Spring Way .. 27610
Spanish Ct 27607
Spanish Bay Ct 27604
Sparkling Brook Dr 27616
Sparrow Pond Ln 27606
Spartina Ct 27606
Spaulding St 27610
Speight Cir 27616
Spencer Ct 27615
Spennymore Rd 27603
Spice Ridge Ln 27606
Spin Cast Pl 27610
Spiny Ridge Ct 27612
Spiralwood Ct 27613
Spirit Ct 27610
Split Branch Ct 27604
Split Oak Way 27609
Split Stone Ln 27613
Spoolin Ct 27604
Sporting Club Dr 27617
Spottswood St 27615
Sprague Rd 27613
Spring Ct 27616
Spring Dr
2600-2699 27610
6900-7099 27613
E Spring Dr 27607
W Spring Dr 27607
Spring Rd 27603
Spring St 27605
Spring Bluffs Ln 27606
Spring Farm Rd 27603
Spring Forest Rd
100-999 27609
1000-2499 27615
2500-5099 27616
N & S Spring Garden
Cir 27603

Spring Glen Ln 27616
Spring Lake Blvd 27617
Spring Meadows Ln 27606
Spring Oaks Way 27614
Spring Pines Way 27616
Spring Ridge Rd 27606
Spring Run Cir 27615
Spring Valley Dr
500-599 27609
5900-6099 27616
Spring Willow Pl 27615
Springcreek Cv 27613
Springdale Dr 27613
Springerly Ln 27612
Springfield Dr 27609
Springfield Commons
Dr 27609
Springfield Creek Dr .. 27616
Springfield Park Dr ... 27614
Springhill Ave 27603
Springhouse Ln 27617
Springlawn Ct 27609
Springmoor Cir, Ct &
Dr 27615
Springshire Ct 27610
Springsweet Ln 27612
Springwood Dr 27613
Spruce Dr 27612
Spruce Ln 27616
Spruce Grove Ct 27614
Spruce Hill Ln 27603
Spruce Shadows Ln 27614
Spruce Tree Way 27614
Spruce View Ln 27614
Sprucedale Dr 27613
Spungold St 27617
Spyglass Way 27615
St Clair Ct 27616
Stable Ct 27612
Stable End Rd 27613
Stacy St 27607
Stadler Dr 27616
Stafford Ave 27607
Staffordshire Ct 27609
Stage Dr 27603
Stage Ford Rd 27615
Stagecrest Dr 27603
Stageline Dr 27603
Staghorn Ln 27615
Stags Leap Cir 27612
Stagwood Dr 27613
Staley Ct 27609
Stallings Glen Rd 27603
Stallion Ct 27613
Stancil Dr 27603
Stancil Farm Rd 27603
Standing Oak Ln 27603
Standing Rock Way 27604
Standing Stone Ct 27613
Standonshire Way 27615
Stanford St 27609
Stanhope Ave 27607
Stannard Trl 27612
Stannary Pl 27613
Stanridge Dr 27613
Stanton Pl 27615
Stanton Hall Ct 27614
Star St 27610
Star Sapphire Dr 27610
Star Trek Ct 27604
Starboard Ct 27613
Starburst Ln 27603
Stargrass Ct 27613
Starkey St 27603
Starling Ct 27615
Starmount Dr 27604
Starrett Ct 27603
Startwood Pl 27609
N State St
1-399 27601
601-1097 27604
1099-1299 27604
S State St
100-1199 27601
1200-2099 27610
Stately Oaks Dr 27614

Station Dr 27615
Staunton Ct 27613
Staysail Ct 27613
Steams Ct 27616
Stedman Dr 27607
Steeds Run Dr 27616
Steel St 27603
Steeplechase Ct 27613
Steinbeck Dr 27609
Steiner Trl 27610
Stemmons Ct 27613
Stephanie Ln 27615
Stephen Boyd Ct 27616
Stepping Stone Ct 27603
Sterling Ct 27613
Sterling Pl 27612
Sterling Park Dr 27603
Sterlingworth Dr 27606
Stevens Rd 27610
Stewart Dr & Rd 27603
Stewart Ellison Wynd .. 27612
Stewart Pines Dr 27615
Stewartby Dr 27613
Stewarts Glen Cir 27615
Still Creek Ct 27614
Still Forest Pl 27607
Still Monument Way 27603
Still Pines Dr 27613
Still Pond Ct 27613
Stiller St 27609
Stillmeadow Rd 27604
Stillwater Dr 27607
Stillwater Pt 27613
Stillwell Ct 27604
Stinson Dr 27607
Stockbridge Cir 27615
Stockton Dr 27606
Stoddard Ct 27603
Stokesbury Ct 27606
Stone St 27608
Stone Branch Dr 27610
Stone Canyon Ct 27613
Stone Castle Ct 27613
Stone Cellar Dr 27613
Stone Creek Way 27615
Stone Eagle Ln 27610
Stone Falls Trl 27614
Stone Flower Ln 27603
Stone Gap Ct 27612
Stone Home Ln 27603
Stone Horse Cir 27612
Stone Kirk Dr 27614
Stone Manor Dr 27610
Stone Mason Dr 27613
Stone Mountain Rd 27613
Stone Pine Dr 27603
Stone Spring Rd 27613
Stone Station Dr 27616
Stone Summit Ln 27603
Stonebrook Ter 27617
Stonechase Dr 27613
Stonecliff Dr 27615
Stonecrest Ct 27612
Stonecroft Ln 27616
Stonecutter Ct 27614
Stoneferry Ln 27606
Stoneford Trace Dr 27616
Stonegate Dr 27615
Stoneglen Ln 27603
Stonehaven Dr 27609
Stonehenge Dr
1300-2399 27615
7100-7599 27613
Stonehenge Park Dr 27613
Stonehill Dr 27609
Stonehurst Rd 27607
Stonelake Ct 27610
Stonemill Way 27614
Stonemont Dr 27603
Stonemoor Ct 27606
Stonepond Ln 27603
Stoneridge Dr 27612
Stonerose Cir 27606
Stones End Pl 27610
Stonesthrow Ct 27610
Stonetown Ave 27612

Stonewall Dr 27604
Stonewater Dr 27603
Stonework Dr 27613
Stoney Moss Dr 27610
Stoney Run Dr 27615
Stoney Spring Dr 27610
Stoney Woods Dr 27614
Stoneyard Pl 27613
Stoneyford Ct 27603
Stoneyoak Ln 27610
Stoneyridge Dr 27614
Stoneytrace Ct 27614
Stonton Way 27615
Stony Bottom Dr 27610
Stony Brook Dr 27604
Stormy Ln 27610
Stormy Gale Rd 27614
Storrington Way 27615
Storybook Ln 27614
Stoutt Dr 27604
Stovall Dr 27606
Stowecroft Ln 27616
Stradshire Dr 27614
Straight A Way Ln 27613
Straley Pl 27614
Stranaver Pl 27612
Stratford Ct 27609
Stratford Hall Dr 27614
Strathmore Dr 27613
Stratlen Ct 27615
Stratton Pl 27609
Strawberry Meadows
St 27613
Strawbridge Ct 27615
Stream Side Rd 27613
Streamer Ct 27614
Streams Of Fields Dr .. 27604
Streeter Ln 27614
Strickland Rd
7900-11099 27615
11100-13399 27613
Strickland Farm Rd 27604
Strolling Ct 27614
Strome Ave 27617
Stropshire Ln 27614
Strother Rd 27606
Strothmore Ct 27615
Stryker Ct 27615
Stuart Dr 27615
Stubble Field Dr 27613
Sturbridge Ct 27612
Sturbridge Rd 27615
Sturdivant St 27610
Sturnebrook Rd 27612
Su John Rd 27607
Suburban Dr 27615
Sudbury Ct 27609
Sue Ct 27614
Sue Ln 27604
Sue Ellen Dr 27604
Suffolk Blvd 27603
Sugar Bush Rd 27612
Sugar House St 27614
Sugar Maple Ct 27615
Sugarbend Way 27606
Sugarberry Ct 27614
Sugarloaf Way 27603
Sugarwood Ct 27616
Sugg Farm Ln 27603
Sulkirk Dr 27617
Sullivan Hall 27607
Summer Pl 27604
Summer Azure Way 27613
Summer Elms Ct 27614
Summer Grove St 27610
Summer Leaf Ct 27615
Summer Music Ln 27603
Summer Shire Way 27604
Summer Stream Dr 27610
Summerdale Dr 27604
Summerford Dr 27607
Summerglen Dr 27615
Summerkings Ct 27610
Summerland Dr 27612
Summerlyn Ct 27609
Summerpointe Pl 27606

Summersprings Ln 27615
Summersweet Ln 27612
Summerton Dr 27614
Summerville Cir 27610
Summerwood Ct 27613
Summit Ave 27603
Summit Cv 27613
Summit Arbor Dr 27612
Summit Hills Way 27607
Summit Manor Ln 27613
Summit Overlook Dr 27612
Summit Park Ln 27612
Summit Waters Ln 27613
Sumner Blvd 27616
Sumter Crest Dr 27617
Sumter Heights Ct 27617
Sumter Ridge Ln 27617
Sun Dr 27614
Sun Hill Ln 27610
Sun Hollow Ln 27610
Sun Star Dr 27610
Sun Valley Dr 27606
Sunapee Ct 27616
Sunbelt Pl 27613
Sunbow Falls Ln 27609
Sunbriar Ln 27613
Sunbright Ln 27610
Sunburst Ct 27613
Suncreek Ct 27606
Suncrest Village Ln ... 27616
Sunday Dr 27607
Sunderland Ct 27603
Sundial Pl 27610
Sunfield Cir 27617
Sungate Blvd 27610
Sunhaven Pl 27615
Sunlit Ln 27604
Sunningdale Pl 27612
Sunny Ln 27603
Sunny Corners Ct 27614
Sunny Cove Dr 27610
Sunny Madison Ln 27604
Sunny Meadow Ln 27606
Sunnybrook Rd
1-237 27610
236-236 27620
238-2698 27610
239-2699 27610
Sunnyfield Dr 27610
Sunnystone Way 27613
Sunpointe Dr 27606
Sunridge Rd 27613
Sunrise Ave 27608
Sunrise Valley Pl 27610
Sunriver Pt 27610
Sunscape Ln 27613
Sunset Dr 27608
Sunset Branch Ct 27612
Sunset Glen Pt 27614
Sunset Maple Ct 27612
Sunset Ridge Rd 27607
Sunshadow Ln 27613
Sunswept Cir 27603
Suntan Lake Dr 27610
Suntree Ct 27617
Sunview St 27610
Super Sport Ln 27603
Supreme Dr 27606
Sure And Steadfast Ct . 27606
Surfbird Ct 27615
Susan Dr 27603
Sussex Rd 27607
Sutcliffe Dr 27613
Sutherland Ct 27615
Sutter Way 27613
Sutterton Ct 27615
Sutton Dr 27605
N & S Swain St 27601
Swales Way 27603
Swallow Ct & Dr 27606
Swallow Cove Ln 27614
Swallow Falls Ln 27614
Swallowtail Ln 27613
Swan Neck Ln 27615
Swanhaven Ct 27617
Swanley Ct 27612

Swann St 27612
Swans Mill Xing 27614
Swans Rest Way 27606
Swarthmore Dr 27615
Swatner Dr 27612
Sweden Dr 27612
Sweeny Dr 27609
Sweet Bay Ln 27615
Sweet Birch Ct 27613
Sweet Cherry Ct 27614
Sweet Chestnut Ln 27610
Sweet Oak Dr 27617
Sweet Shade Trl 27616
Sweetbriar Dr 27609
Sweetbrook Ln 27615
Sweetgum Cir 27610
Swepstone Ln 27615
Swerling Way 27614
Swift Dr 27606
Swift Creek Ln 27603
Swift Ridge Rd 27606
Swift Willow Cir 27606
Swiftbrook Cir 27606
Swimming Hole Cir 27610
Swinburne Rd 27610
Swindon Ct 27615
Swinford Ct 27604
Swing Ct 27610
Swingline Way 27610
Swinton St 27616
Swisswood Dr 27613
Swithland Ct 27614
Swordfish Dr 27603
Swordgate Pl 27613
Sycamore Rd 27613
Sycamore St 27604
Sycamore Grove Ln 27614
Sycamore Hill Ln 27612
Sycamore Knoll Rd 27614
Sylvan Ln 27613
Sylvania Dr 27607
Sylvester St 27610
Sylvia Dean St 27615
Syme Hall 27607
T W Alexander Dr 27617
Tabor Ct 27604
Tabriz Pt 27614
Tacketts Pond Dr 27614
Taconia St 27612
Tadley Ct 27603
Tadlock Dr 27614
Taft Ct 27610
Tafton Ct 27609
Tahoma Ct 27606
Talamore Ct 27604
Talbot Ct E & W 27610
Taliaferd Ct 27616
Talisman Way 27615
Talison Ct 27610
Tall Oak Trl 27612
Tall Oaks Ct 27613
Tall Pines Ct 27609
Tall Rock Ct 27610
Tall Timber Dr 27612
Tall Tree Pl 27607
Tallgrass Rd 27603
Tallis Ct 27610
Tallon Hall Ct 27607
Tallowtree Dr 27613
Tallwood Dr 27613
Tallyhoe Dr 27616
Talmage St 27603
Talman Ct 27615
Talon Ridge Way 27610
Talserwood Dr 27610
Talton Cir 27612
Tamarack Ct 27612
Tamerson Ct 27612
Tamor Way 27614
Tanager St 27606
Tanawha Ct 27603
Tanbark Way 27615
Tanby Ct 27613
Tandem Ct 27615
Tanglebrook Way 27615
Tanglewild Dr 27613

Tanglewood Dr
4700-5099 27612
5800-5899 27616
Tanglewood Creek Ct ... 27610
Tanglewood Oaks St 27610
Tanglewood Pine Ln 27610
Tango Ln 27613
Tanjier Bay 27613
Tannat Ct 27612
Tanner Dr 27610
Tanners Mill Pl 27614
Tantara Sq 27615
Tanworth Dr 27615
Tanzanite Ct 27615
Taos Trl 27603
Tapers Dr 27616
Tappersfield Ct 27613
Tara Ridge Rd 27616
Tarbell Ct 27616
N & S Tarboro St 27610
Target Cir 27616
Tarheel Dr 27609
Tarheel Club Rd 27604
Tarheel Clubhouse Rd .. 27604
Tarkdale St 27609
Tarleton Ct 27616
Tarnhour Ct 27612
Tarrywood Ct 27609
Tartan Cir 27606
Tarton Fields Cir 27617
Tassel Ct 27612
Tate Dr 27603
Tatten Hoe Ct 27610
Tattershale Ct 27613
Tatton Dr 27608
Taurus Ct 27613
Tavernier Knoll Ln 27603
Tawny Chase Dr 27617
Tawny View Ln 27603
Taybran Ln 27610
Tayloe Ct 27615
Taylor St 27607
Taylor Farm Rd 27603
Taylor Mill Ct 27617
Taylor Oaks Dr 27616
Taylors Creek Ct 27610
Taymouth Ct 27613
Tazwell Pl 27612
Teabrook Ct 27610
Teakwood Pl 27606
Teal Pl 27604
Teal Chappell Ct 27617
Teal Crest Ct 27604
Tealbriar Dr 27615
Tealbrook Dr 27610
Tealby Pl 27615
Tealeaf Dr 27610
Tealford Ct 27612
Tealwood Pl 27615
Technology Woods Dr ... 27603
Tecumseh Ct 27607
Ted Ave 27614
Tee Dee St 27610
Tee Time Way 27614
Tempest Rdg 27613
Tempia Ct 27610
Temple St 27609
Ten Oaks Ln 27606
Ten Ten Rd 27603
Tenbury Ct 27606
Tenderfoot Trl 27615
Tennessee Ct 27615
Tennyson Pl 27609
Tensity Dr 27604
Tenter Banks Sq 27609
Tera Springs Dr 27610
Terminal Dr 27604
Terra Cotta Dr 27613
Terra Verde Dr 27609
Terrace Ct 27615
Terrace Park Ct 27616
Terregles Dr 27617
Terrel Mill Rd 27616
Terrington Ln 27606
Terry St 27609
Tetbury Pl 27613

Teton Pines Way 27617
Tewkesbury Ct 27615
N & S Texas Dr 27616
Thacker Ct 27603
Thames Ct 27610
Thanet Pl 27612
Tharps Ln 27614
Thatcher Way 27615
Thaxton Pl 27612
Thayer Dr 27612
The Cir 27608
The Arts Dr 27603
The Circle At North Hills St 27609
The Dyke 27606
The Gates Dr 27614
The Greens Cir 27606
The Hague 27606
The Lakes Dr 27609
The Oaks Dr 27606
The Olde Pl 27614
The Pointe 27615
The Village Cir 27615
Thea Ln 27606
Thebes Dr 27616
Thelma St 27610
Thelonious Dr 27610
Thendara Way 27612
Theresa Ct 27615
Therfield Dr 27614
Thesis Cir 27603
Thetford Ct 27615
Theys Rd 27606
Thicket Hill Ln 27607
Thicket Run Ct 27616
Thistlebrook Ct 27610
Thistledown Dr 27606
Thistlegate Trl 27610
Thistlehill Ct 27616
Thistleton Ln 27606
Thomas Rd 27607
Thomasville Ct 27612
Thompson St 27603
Thoreau Dr 27609
Thorn Leaf Ct 27604
Thorn Ridge Rd 27613
Thornblade Dr 27604
Thornbury Crest Ct 27614
N & S Thorncliff Pl 27616
Thornrose Hill Dr 27616
Thornton Rd 27616
Thornton Garden Ln 27616
Thornton Knoll Way 27616
Thornton Town Pl 27616
Thornwell Ln 27610
Thornwood Ct 27613
Thorny Bush Rd 27616
Thoroughbred Ln 27610
Thorpshire Dr 27615
Thoughtful Spot Way 27614
Threave Rd 27617
Three Bridges Cir 27613
Three Frenchmen Ct 27610
Three Notch Rd 27615
Three Oaks Dr 27612
Thrush Ridge Ln 27615
Thunderidge Dr 27610
Thunderwood Dr 27617
Thurmount Pl 27604
Thyme Pl 27609
Tibury Ct 27615
Tibwin Dr 27606
Tide Ct 27615
Tie Stone Way 27613
Tierney Cir 27610
Tierra Del Sol Way 27616
Tiffany Bay Ct 27609
Tifton Dr 27610
Tilbrook Ct 27610
Tilden St 27605
Tilden Park Dr 27612
Tilford Ln 27613
Tillery Pl 27604
Tillinghast Trl 27613
Tilton Dr 27616
Tilton Woods Trl 27610
Timber Dr 27604
Timber Ln 27606
Timber Creek Ln 27612
Timber Crest Dr 27617
Timber Oaks Dr 27606
Timber Ridge Dr 27609
Timberbrook Dr 27616
Timbercroft Ct 27613
Timbergrove Ln 27614
Timberhurst Dr 27612
Timberknoll Dr 27617
Timberlake Dr & Rd 27604
Timberlane Ct 27613
Timberline Ct 27604
Timbermill Ct 27612
Timberwind Dr 27615
Timberwood Ct 27606
Timberwood Dr 27612
Timken Ct 27604
Tinderbox Ln 27603
Tinsley Ct 27614
Tipped Ct 27603
Tipperary Dr 27604
Tipping Cir 27609
Tipton St
800-999 27601
1000-1199 27610
Tischer Rd 27603
Tiverton Ct 27615
Tivoli Ct 27604
Tobermory Ln 27606
Tobiano Ln 27614
Tobin Pl 27612
Toccopola St 27604
Tolchester Pl 27613
Toll Mill Ct 27606
Tolley Ct 27616
Tollington Dr 27604
Tom Gipson Dr 27610
Tomahawk Trl 27610
Tomasita Ct 27616
Tommans Trl 27616
Tomotley Ct 27606
Tonsler Dr 27604
Tony Tank Ln 27613
Tonylee Ct 27603
Top Greene Ln 27601
Top Of The Pines Ct 27604
Topiary Ct 27614
Toppe Ridge Ct 27615
Topsfield Ct 27615
Topstone Rd 27603
Torbay Ct 27613
Torchlight Way 27603
Tori Trce 27613
Torness Ct 27604
Torquay Xing 27616
Torre Del Oro Pl 27617
Torrey Pines Pl 27615
Torrington St 27615
Torry Ridge Rd 27613
Tory Sound Ct 27613
Touchstone Forest Rd 27612
Touchwood Pl 27613
Tournament Dr 27612
Tower St 27607
Town Dr 27616
Town And Country Rd 27612
Town Center Dr 27616
Townedge Ct 27612
Towneley Pl 27615
Townesbury Ln 27612
Townfield Dr 27614
Towngate Dr 27614
Townhouse 27615
Townmeade Ct 27612
Township Cir 27609
Toxey Dr 27609
Toy Ct 27603
Toyon Dr 27616
Toyota Dr 27617
Trackside Dr 27603
Tractor Dr 27603
Tradd Ct 27607
Trade St 27603
Trademark Dr 27610
Traders Dock Ct 27616
Tradescant Ct 27613
Tradewind Ct 27610
Traherne Dr 27612
N Trail Dr 27615
Trail Ridge Dr 27613
Trailing Cedar Ct & Dr 27613
Trailridge Ct 27603
Trails End Ct 27614
Trailside Dr 27610
Trailwood Dr
900-2199 27606
2200-2299 27603
Trailwood Heights Ln 27603
Trailwood Hills Dr 27603
Trailwood Pines Ln 27603
Trailwood Valley Cir 27603
Tralee Pl 27609
Transom Ct 27603
Transport Dr 27603
Transylvania Ave 27609
Trappers Creek Dr 27614
Trassacks Dr 27610
Travel Lite Dr 27603
Travel Ridge Rd 27614
Travianna Ct 27609
Trawick Cir & Rd 27604
Treadstone Ct 27616
Treasure Chest Cv 27604
Treasure Key Pl 27603
Treasures Ln 27614
Tredwood Dr
10500-10599 27615
10600-10699 27614
Tree Bark Ct 27613
Tree Meadow Ln 27603
Tree Side Ct 27607
Tree Swallow Run 27616
Tree Top Ct 27612
Tree Vista Ln 27604
Treen St 27614
Treerose Way 27606
Treesdale Ln 27617
Trego Trl 27614
Trellis Ct
2300-2399 27604
2400-2499 27616
Tremont Dr 27609
Trent Rd 27603
Trently Ct 27609
Trenton Rd 27607
Trenton Park Ln 27607
Trenton Ridge Ct 27613
Trenton Woods Way 27607
Tresco Xing 27616
Trescott Ct 27614
Trestlewood Ln 27610
Treverton Pl 27609
Trevor Ct 27613
Trexler Ct 27606
Treymore Dr 27617
Triana Ct 27610
Triana Market Walk 27617
Triangle Dr 27617
Triangle Plantation Dr 27616
Triangle Promenade Dr 27616
Triangle Town Blvd 27616
Triassic Dr 27616
Tributary Dr 27609
Tribute Center Dr 27612
Trickle Ct 27615
Trillium Cir 27606
Trillium Whorl Ct 27607
Trimblestone Ln 27616
Trinity Cir & Rd 27607
Trinity Chase Ln 27607
Trinity Commons Ln 27607
Trinity Crest Rd 27607
Trinity Farms Rd 27607
Trinity Gate Ln 27607
Trinity Grove Dr 27607
Trinity Knoll Rd 27607
Trinity Oaks Ln 27607
Trinity Pine Ln 27607
Trinity Ridge Rd 27607
Trinity Village Ln 27607
Trinity Woods Dr 27607
Triple Creek Dr 27616
Tripp Ct 27616
Trollingwood Ln 27615
Troone Ct 27612
Tropical Dr 27607
Tropical Key Pl 27603
Tropical Paradise Way 27603
Tropical Sky Ln 27603
Trottenham St 27614
Trotter Dr 27603
Trotters Ridge Dr 27614
Trout Lilly Pl 27610
Trout Stream Dr 27604
Troutman Ln 27613
Trowbridge Ct 27613
Troy Pl 27609
Trueway Ln 27603
Trumpetor Way 27613
Trunecek Cir 27603
Trust Dr 27616
Trusty Trl 27615
Truth Ln 27606
Tryon Rd
1-3599 27603
3600-5799 27606
E Tryon Rd
100-199 27603
400-499 27610
Tryon St 27603
Tryon Grove Dr 27603
Tryon Hill Dr 27603
Tryon Park Dr 27610
Tryon Pines Dr 27603
Tryon Ridge Dr 27610
Tucca Way 27604
Tucker St 27603
Tucker Hall 27607
Tuckland Dr 27610
Tudor Pl 27610
Tufts Ct 27609
Tulane Dr 27604
Tulare Ct 27612
Tulip Cir 27606
Tuliptree Ln 27612
Tullamore Dr 27613
Tully Ct 27609
Tunas St 27616
Tupelo Ct 27610
Tupenny Ln 27606
Turf Grass Ct 27610
Turkey Creek Dr 27613
Turlington Hall 27607
Turnabout Ct 27604
Turnbridge Dr 27609
Turnbull Ct 27616
Turner St 27607
Turner Glen Dr 27603
Turner Meadow Dr 27603
Turner Store Ln 27603
Turner Woods Dr 27603
Turning Branch Ln 27603
Turning Brook Ln 27616
Turnstone Dr 27612
Turtle Cv 27609
Turtle Creek Ln 27606
Turtle Dove Ct 27614
Turtle Point Dr 27604
Turtle Ridge Way 27614
Turtleneck Ct 27616
Tuscan Lake Rd 27613
Tuscany Woods Ct 27612
Tusket Ct 27613
Tutman Ct 27614
Tuxford Dr 27612
Twatchman Dr 27616
Tweeds Mill Rd 27617
Twelvepole Dr 27616
Twickenham Ct 27613
Twin Branches Way 27606
Twin Leaf Dr 27613
Twin Oak Ct 27615
Twin Rock Rd 27616
Twin Springs Rd 27603
Twin Tree Ct 27613
Twinbrook Ct 27610
Twinfield Ct 27610
Twinwood Ct 27613
Twist Ln 27610
Twisted Branch Ct 27616
Twisted Oaks Dr 27612
Twisted Willow Way 27610
Two Brothers Run 27603
Two Courts Dr 27613
Two Robins Ct 27613
Twyford Pl 27612
Tybrook Ct 27612
Tyler Rd 27604
Tyler Bluff Ln 27616
Tyler Farms Dr 27603
Tylerton Dr 27613
Tyndall Ct 27615
Tyne Cir 27607
Tyrrell Rd 27609
Tyson St 27612
Ujamaa Dr 27610
Ulster Aly 27606
Umstead Dr 27603
Umstead Forest Dr 27612
Umstead View Dr 27607
Union St 27609
United Dr 27603
University Ct 27606
University Woods Rd 27603
Up Above Ln 27614
Upchurch St 27610
Upchurch Woods Dr 27603
Upland Cir 27607
Upland Ct 27615
Upper Creek Way 27614
Upper Dry Falls Ct 27603
Upper Lake Dr 27615
Upper Oaks Way 27615
Upper School Ln 27615
Uppercross Ct 27613
Urania Dr 27603
Urban Legend Dr 27603
Us 70 Hwy E 27610
S Utah Dr 27616
Utica Dr 27609
Uwharrie Ct 27606
Vailwood Ct 27613
Vale St 27604
Valencia Ct 27614
Valentine Ct 27615
Valerie Dr 27606
Valerie Anne Dr 27613
Valiant St 27610
Vallejo Trl 27610
Vallery Pl 27604
Valley Ct 27612
E Valley Ct 27606
S Valley Ct 27606
Valley Dr
1400-1499 27603
6700-7199 27612
Valley Brook Dr 27613
Valley Cove Ct 27616
Valley Edge Dr 27614
Valley Estates Dr 27612
Valley Forge Dr 27615
Valley Haven Dr 27603
Valley Lake Dr 27612
Valley Mist Ct 27613
Valley Ridge Ct
2000-2099 27603
6800-6999 27615
Valley Run Dr 27615
Valley Springs Pl 27615
Valley Star Ct 27614
Valley Stream Dr
3800-3999 27604
4600-4998 27616
5000-5099 27616
Valley View Dr 27605
Valley Woods Ct 27613
Valleycross Cir 27615
Valleyfield Cir 27612
Valton Dr 27604
Valview St 27613
Van Buren Rd 27604
Van Dyke Ave 27607
Van Haven Dr 27615
Van Hessen Dr 27614
Van Huron Dr 27615
Van Page Blvd 27607
Van Thomas Dr 27615
Vanburgh Ct 27615
Vancastle Way 27617
Vance St 27608
Vancouver Ln 27615
Vandemere Ct 27615
Vanderbilt Ave 27607
Vanessa Dr 27603
Vann St 27606
Vannstone Dr 27603
Vardaman St 27610
Varnell Ave 27612
Varnish Pl 27610
Varsity Dr 27606
Varve Ln 27616
Vaughn Ct 27603
Vauxhill Dr 27615
Veasey Mill Rd 27615
Vega Ct 27614
Vela Ct 27614
Velvet Ct 27614
Vendue Range Dr 27604
Ventana Ln 27604
Ventry Ct 27613
Venture Ct 27615
Venus Dr 27604
Vera Rd 27607
Veranda Ct 27615
Verde Dr 27603
Verde Farm Rd 27603
Verdugo Dr 27610
Vernie Dr 27603
Vernon Ter 27609
Verona Pl 27613
Versatile Rd 27603
Vesta Dr 27603
Vestavia Woods Dr 27615
Vestry Way 27613
Via Galardo Ln 27614
Via Las Cruces Cir 27615
Viceroy Dr 27613
Vick Ave 27612
Vick Charles Dr 27606
Vicky Dr 27603
Vico Ter 27610
Victor Pl 27604
Victoria Rd 27608
Victoria Park Ln 27614
Victoria Townes Ln 27612
Victoria Woods Dr 27613
Victory Church Rd 27613
Vienna Crest Dr 27613
Vienna Woods Dr 27606
N View Ct 27613
View Water Dr 27606
Viewcrest Way 27606
Viewmont Dr 27610
Viewpointe Cir 27617
Viking Dr 27612
Vilana Rdg 27612
Villa Green Ct 27612
Village Ct 27607
Village Bluff Pl 27603
Village Gate Way 27614
Village Glenn Dr 27612
Village Grass Ln 27614
Village Grove Rd 27613
Village Lawn Dr 27613
Village Manor Way 27614
Village Meadows Ct 27614
Village Mill Pl 27608
Village Oaks Ln 27614
Village Pines Ln 27614
Village Springs Rd 27614
Village Stone Ct 27614
Village Tavern Way 27606
Villawood Cir 27603
Villawood Ct 27615
Vineland Dr 27616
Vinnings Pl 27608
Vino Dr 27607
Vinson Ct 27604
Vintage Rd 27610
Vintners Ct 27610
Violet Bluff Ct 27610
Violet Hill Ln 27610
Vira Dr 27617
Vireo Ct 27616
Virgil Dr 27614
Virgilia Ct 27616
Virginia Ave 27604
Virginia St 27610
Virginia Dare Pl 27610
Vista Del Rey Ln 27613
Vista View Ct 27612
Vivian Ct 27610
Vixen Ct 27616
Vogel St 27617
Volant Dr 27609
Volkswalk Pl 27610
Von Hoyt Dr 27613
Vosburgh Dr 27617
Votive Ln 27604
Voyager Cir 27603
Wade Ave
300-1099 27605
2300-2398 27607
2400-3599 27607
Wade Park Blvd 27607
Wadford Dr 27616
Wagon Ridge Rd 27614
Wagon Wheel Ct 27610
Wagram Ct 27615
Wainwright Ct 27604
Wakashan Cir 27603
Wake Dr 27608
Wake Academy Dr 27603
Wake Bluff Dr 27614
Wake Forest Hwy 27613
Wake Forest Rd
800-1700 27604
1702-1798 27604
1800-2499 27608
2500-4399 27609
Wake Towne Dr 27609
Wakebrook Dr 27616
Wakefield Ave 27603
Wakefield Commons Dr 27614
Wakefield Crossing Dr 27614
Wakefield Pines Dr 27614
Wakefield Plantation Dr 27614
Wakefield Woods Dr 27614
Wakespring Ct 27614
Wakestone Ct
900-999 27609
2900-2999 27614
Wakewood Cir 27615
Walden Ct 27604
Walden Pl 27609
Walden Pond Dr 27604
Waldrop St 27610
Walenda Dr 27604
Walkelin Ct 27615
Walker St 27603
Walkertown Dr 27614
Walking Stick Trl
5900-6099 27603
8800-9199 27615
Wall Hill Rd 27604
Waller Pl 27610
Wallingford Dr 27616
Walnut St 27601
Walnut Bluffs Ln 27610
Walnut Cove Dr 27603
Walnut Creek Pkwy 27606
Walnut Ridge Ct 27610
Walser Pl 27601
Waltham Way 27614
Walton St 27610
Walton Heath Ct 27612
Waltz Ln 27610
Wapello Ln 27613
Ward Rd 27604
Ward St 27603
Warehouse Dr 27610

Warfield Pl 27604
Warm Springs Ln 27610
Warren Ave 27610
Warren Pond Ct 27614
Warwick Dr 27606
Warwickshire Park & Way 27613
Warwood Ct 27612
Washington St 27605
Wasser Ct 27617
Watauga St 27604
Watauga Hall 27607
Watch Tower Ct 27614
Water Oak Dr 27616
Water Spray Dr 27610
Water Willow Dr 27617
Waterbrook Ct 27603
Waterbury Rd 27604
Waterchase Ct 27613
Waterflower Ct 27616
Waterford Ct 27613
Waterford Bank Ln 27612
Waterford Bluff Ln 27612
Waterford Club Xing 27612
Waterford Cove Dr 27616
Waterford Crystal Ct 27610
Waterford Landing Ct 27610
Waterford Park Ln 27615
Waterford Point Dr 27612
Waterford Valley Cres 27612
Waterford Village Pl 27612
Watergate Ct 27615
Waterloo Ct 27613
Waterlow Park Ln 27614
Waterman Dr 27614
Watermark Ct 27609
Waters Dr 27610
Waters Edge Dr 27606
Waters Way Dr 27606
Waterside Ln 27613
Watersmeet Ln 27614
Watertown Cir 27613
Waterview Rd 27615
Waterville St 27603
Watervista Trl 27616
Waterwalk Ln 27616
Waterwheel Dr 27606
Waterwood Ct 27614
Watkins Rd 27616
Watkins St 27604
Watkins Glen Ct 27613
Watkins Ridge Ct 27616
Watkins Town Rd 27616
Watkinsdale Ave 27613
Watson St 27601
Wavendon Ct 27615
Waverly Pl 27613
Waxhaw Ct 27616
Waybridge Ct 27606
Waycross St 27606
Wayland Dr 27608
Wayne Dr 27608
Wayne St 27606
Waynesboro Ct 27615
Waynick Dr 27617
Weather Rock Ct 27613
Weatherford Cir 27604
Weathergreen Dr 27615
Weathersfield Ct 27613
Weaver Dr 27612
Webb St 27609
Webster Ct 27609
Weddington Rd 27610
Wedgedale Dr 27609
Wedgegate Dr 27616
Wedgeland Dr 27615
Wedgestone Ct 27615
Wedgewood Dr 27604
Wedgewood St 27612
Wee Burn Trl 27612
Weeks Dr 27603
Weeping Glen Ct 27614
Weeping Pine Ln 27603
Weidmann Dr 27614
Weimer Dr 27617
Weir Way 27616

Welborn St 27615
Welbury Ct 27617
Welch Ln 27614
Welch Hall 27607
Weldon Pl 27608
Welford Rd 27610
Welland Ct 27614
Wellesley Park N & S 27615
Wellhouse Dr 27603
Wellington Ct 27615
Wellington Downs 27613
Wells Ave 27608
Wellsley Way 27613
Wellwater Ct 27614
Wembley Ct 27607
Wenchelsea Pl 27612
Wendy Ln 27606
Wenesly Ct 27616
Wensford Ct 27615
Wentworth St 27612
Weobley Ln 27614
Werribee Dr 27616
Wertherson Ln 27613
Wescott Dr 27614
Weshel Dr 27610
Wesley Dr 27603
Wesley Farm Dr 27616
Wessel Way 27610
Wessex Ct 27613
N West St 27603
S West St
1-399 27603
400-999 27601
Westavia Dr 27613
Westborough Dr 27612
Westbridge Ct 27606
Westbrook Dr 27615
Westbury Dr 27607
Westbury Lake Dr 27603
Westchase Blvd 27607
Westchester Rd 27610
Westcliff Ct 27606
Westcreek Pl 27606
Wester Rd 27604
Western Blvd 27606
Westerwood Ct 27609
Westfall Ln 27612
Westfield Ave 27607
Westgate Rd 27617
Westgate Club Dr 27617
Westgate Park Dr 27617
Westglen Dr 27612
Westgreen Ct 27612
Westgrove St 27606
Westhall Ct 27612
Westham Pl 27604
Westhampton Pl 27604
Westhaven Dr 27607
Westinghouse Blvd 27604
Westmill Ct 27613
Westminister Dr 27616
Westminster Dr 27604
Westmoreland Dr 27612
Westmouth Bay 27615
Weston St 27610
Westpine Ct 27606
Westpoint Ct 27610
Westra Dr 27604
Westridge Dr 27609
Westview Ln 27605
Westwick Ct 27615
Westwood Dr 27607
Westwood Pl 27613
Wesvill Ct 27607
Wetherburn Ln 27615
Wetlands Dr 27610
Wettaw Ln 27616
Wexford Dr 27603
Wexford Woods Trl 27613
Weybridge Dr 27615
Weymouth Ct 27612
Whartons Park & Way 27613
Whatley Ln 27604
Whatsit Ln 27603
Wheat Mill Pl 27613
Wheatcross Pl 27610

Wheatland Dr 27603
Wheaton Pl 27609
Wheatstone Ln 27613
Wheeler Rd
2200-2299 27607
2300-2399 27612
Wheeler Bluff Dr 27606
Wheeler Ridge Ln 27606
Wheelerbrook Ct 27603
Wheeling Dr 27615
Whetstone Ct 27615
Whippletree Dr 27603
Whippoorwill Ln 27609
Whirlabout Way 27613
Whisper Ct 27616
Whisper Ridge Pl 27613
Whispering Branch Rd 27613
Whispering Falls Run 27613
Whispering Glen Ln 27614
Whisperwood Dr 27616
Whistle Ct 27603
Whistler Ct 27606
Whistling Way 27616
Whistling Straits Way 27604
Whitaker Ln 27603
E Whitaker Mill Rd
100-1024 27608
1025-1099 27604
W Whitaker Mill Rd 27608
Whitby Ct 27615
White Ash Ct 27615
White Bark Rd 27616
White Chapel Way 27615
White Crane Way 27615
White Daisies Ct 27610
White Dove Ct 27606
White Eagle Ct 27617
White Kestrel Dr 27616
White Leaf Ct 27610
White Oak Rd
1800-2399 27608
2400-3499 27609
White Pine Dr 27612
White Post Dr 27603
White Sock Ln 27610
White Springs Cir 27615
Whitebud Dr 27609
Whiteclay Ct 27617
Whitecroft Dr 27603
Whitehall Ave 27604
Whitehall Pl 27612
Whitehart Ln 27606
Whitehurst Way 27606
Whitestone Rd 27615
Whitfield Rd 27610
Whitford Ct 27606
Whitley Dr 27613
Whitley St 27603
Whitley Falls Dr 27610
Whitman Rd 27607
Whitmire Pl 27612
Whitmore Dr 27606
Whittier Dr 27609
Whittington Dr 27614
Whittlesea Pl 27616
Wicker Dr 27604
Wickersham Way 27604
Wickershire Ct 27614
Wickham Rd 27606
Wicklow Pl 27604
Wide River Dr 27614
Widgeon Way 27603
Wiggs St 27608
Wigmore Ct 27615
Wilcox Pl & St 27607
Wild Dunes Dr 27604
Wild Magnolia Dr 27617
Wild Mint Ct 27610
Wild Orchid Trl 27613
Wild Rose Ct 27615
Wild Waters Dr 27614
Wild Wood Forest Dr 27616
Wilder St 27607
Wilder Cliff St 27615
Wilderness Rd 27613
Wilders Ln 27603

Wilders Grove Ln 27604
Wildlife Trl 27613
Wildmarsh Dr 27613
Wildcat Pl 27610
Wildorlyn Cir 27603
Wildrock Cir 27610
Wildwood St 27612
Wildwood Links 27613
Wiles Ct 27610
Wilger Ct 27603
Wilhagan Ct 27616
Wilkes St 27609
Wilkins Pl 27610
Wilkinsburg Rd 27612
Will O Dean Rd 27616
Willano Way 27610
Willard Pl 27603
Willey St 27617
William And Mary Dr 27616
William J Cowan Wynd 27612
William Moore Dr 27607
William Pope Wynd 27612
Williams Rd 27610
Williamsborough Ct 27609
Williamson Dr 27608
Willmark Ct 27613
Willow Bnd 27616
Willow Ct 27610
Willow St 27604
Willow Bend Ln 27613
Willow Bluff Dr 27604
Willow Creek Dr 27604
Willow Cry Ln 27613
Willow Fox Ct 27616
Willow Haven Ct 27616
Willow Lake Rd 27616
Willow Oak Rd 27604
Willow Pines Pl 27614
Willow Run South Dr 27615
Willow Valley Ct 27617
Willow Winds Dr 27603
Willow Wood Ct 27613
Willowblue Ln 27604
Willowbrook Dr 27609
Willowglen Dr 27616
Wills Ave 27608
Wills Forest St 27605
Wills Grove Ln 27615
Wilmeth Dr 27614
N Wilmington St
1-499 27601
500-599 27604
S Wilmington St
1-1199 27601
1200-3899 27603
3901-3999 27603
Wilmington Ter 27604
Wilmore Dr 27614
Wilmot Dr 27606
Wilshire Ave 27608
Wilson Ln 27609
Wilson St 27610
Wilton Cir 27615
Wiltshire Ct 27614
Wimbish Ln 27612
Wimbleton Dr 27609
Winchester Dr 27612
Wind Chime Ct 27615
Wind Grove Way 27610
Wind Mountain Ln 27613
Windberry St 27612
Windblown Ct 27616
Windbreak Ln 27616
Windbur Pl 27609
Windchase Dr 27610
Windcove Pl 27612
Windcross Dr 27614
Windel Dr 27609
Windemere Pl 27604
Windfield Ct 27615
Windflower Ln 27612
Windgate Ct 27603
Windham Dr 27609
Winding Trl 27612
Winding Arbor Trl 27606

Winding Bluff Dr 27613
Winding Bluffs Dr 27613
Winding River Way 27616
Winding Stream Dr 27610
Winding Waters Way 27614
Winding Wood Trl 27613
Windjammer Dr 27615
Windlake Ct 27606
Windlass Ct 27616
Windmere Chase Dr 27616
Windmill Ln 27606
Windmill Harbor Way 27617
Windmont Ct 27610
Windproof Way 27616
Windrow Ln 27603
Windsock Ln 27616
Windsor Pl 27609
Windsor Trl 27615
Windsor Club Ct 27617
Windsor Ridge Dr 27615
Windsprint Way 27616
Windstorm Way 27616
Windtree Cir 27612
Windwitty Ct 27614
Windwood Ct 27609
Windy Gap Ct 27617
Windy Hill Dr 27609
Windy Hollow Ct 27609
Windy Knoll Rd 27616
Windy Meadow Ct 27614
Windy Ridge Ct 27606
Windy Woods Dr 27607
Windycrest Ct 27610
Wine Ct 27610
Winfield Ct 27610
Winfred Dr 27603
Wingate Dr 27609
Wingate Hill Ct 27606
Winged Elm Dr 27610
Winged Thistle Ct 27617
Wingfoot Dr 27615
Wingspread Way 27614
Winifred Ln 27609
Wininger Dr 27603
Winners Edge St 27617
Winnie Pl 27603
Winona Rd 27609
Winslow Ct 27604
Winsome Ct 27603
Winston Diamond Ct 27610
Winstone Ct 27615
Winter Pl 27616
Winter Breeze Ct 27607
Winter Holly Ct 27606
Winter Oak Way 27617
Winter Song Rd 27614
Winterbury Ct 27607
Wintergreen Dr 27609
Winterlochen Rd 27603
Winterpointe Ln 27606
Winterton Dr 27603
Winterwind Pl 27615
Winterwood Dr 27613
Winthrop Dr 27612
Wintu Ct 27603
Winway Dr 27610
Wireglass Ct 27603
Wirewood Dr 27605
Wisconsin Ct 27615
Wishing Willow Dr 27603
Wispy Green Ln 27614
Wispy Willow Ln 27609
Witherbee Ln 27603
Withers Rd 27603
Witterton Pl 27614
Woburn Dr 27615
Wofford Ln 27609
Wolf Way 27606
Wolf Creek Cir 27606
Wolf Dale Ct 27606
Wolf Den Ln 27606
Wolf Glade Ct 27606
Wolf Glen Ct 27606
Wolf Green Dr 27606
Wolf Park Dr 27606
Wolf View Dr 27606

Wolf Village Way 27607
Wolf Walk Way 27606
Wolfe St 27601
Wolfmill Dr 27603
Wolfpack Ln 27609
Wolftech Ln 27603
Wolftrap Rd 27616
Wolverhampton Dr 27603
Womans Club Dr 27612
Wood Cove Ct 27615
Wood Cutter Ct 27606
Wood Glen Ct 27609
Wood Hall 27607
Wood Henge Dr 27613
Wood Lawn Dr 27613
Wood Pond Ct 27610
Wood Spring Ct 27614
Wood Valley Dr 27613
Wood Way Ct 27606
Woodard Ln 27606
Woodard St 27610
Woodbend Dr 27615
Woodbine Ct 27610
Woodbine Rd 27612
Woodbridge Ct 27612
Woodburn Rd 27605
Woodbury Dr 27612
Woodchester Ct 27613
Woodchuck Pl 27610
Woodchurch Ct 27604
Woodcliff Dr 27609
Woodcock Cir 27615
E Woodcrest Dr 27603
Woodcroft Dr 27609
Wooded Ridge Rd 27606
Wooden Rd 27617
Wooden Shoe Ln 27613
Woodfern Ct 27613
Woodfox Ct 27610
Woodgate Manor Ct 27614
Woodgreen Dr 27607
Woodhall Spa Ct 27604
Woodhaven Ct 27615
Woodhill Ct 27615
Woodknoll Ct 27606
Woodlake Pl 27607
Woodland Ave 27608
Woodland Rd 27603
Woodlands View Ln 27614
Woodlaurel Ct 27613
Woodlawn Dr 27616
Woodlea Dr 27604
Woodline Dr 27603
Woodlinks Dr 27606
Woodmanor Dr 27614
Woodmark Trl 27606
Woodmeadow Pkwy 27610
Woodmere Dr 27612
Woodmont Dr 27613
Woodnell Dr 27603
Woodowl Dr 27613
Woodpecker Ct 27610
Woodridge Dr 27612
Woodrow Dr 27609
Woods Pl 27607
Woods Edge Ct 27615
Woods Of North Bend Dr 27609
Woods Ream Dr 27615
Woodsborough Pl 27601
Woodsdale Rd 27606
Woodshire Pl 27612
Woodside Ct 27606
Woodslope Dr 27610
Woodsmith Pl 27609
Woodsnipe Dr 27604
Woodsong Ct 27613
Woodstock Dr 27609
Woodstone Dr 27615
Woodthrush Ct 27603
Woodview Dr 27604
Woodvine Ct 27613
Woodward Pl 27607
Woodwind Ct 27614
Woodwyck Way 27604
Woodyglenn Dr 27614

Woodyhill Rd 27613
Worchester Pl 27604
Wordsworth Pl 27609
World Trade Blvd 27617
Worley Dr 27613
Worsham Dr 27616
Worth St 27601
Wortham Dr 27614
Worthington Ln 27604
Wrentree Cir 27610
Wrenwood Ave 27607
Wrexham Ct 27615
Wrightwood Dr 27616
Wyatt Ln 27614
Wyatt Brook Way 27609
Wyckford Forest Dr 27604
Wyckhurst Ct 27609
Wycliff Rd 27607
Wycombe Ln 27615
Wynalda Way 27613
Wynbrook Way 27612
Wyncote Dr 27603
Wyndcliff Ct 27616
Wyndfield Cir 27615
Wynewood Ct & Dr 27616
Wyngate Mill Ln 27617
Wyngate Ridge Dr 27617
Wynhurst Ct 27613
Wynmore Rd 27610
Wynncrest Ct 27603
Wynne St 27601
Wynne Trace Ct 27603
Wynneford Way 27614
Wynslow Park Dr 27616
Wyntree Pond Ln 27606
Wyntree Ridge Way 27606
S Wyoming Dr 27616
Wyrick Ct 27604
Wysong Ct 27612
Wythe Cir 27615
Xebec Way 27606
Yachtsman Ct 27615
Yadkin Dr 27609
Yakimas Rd 27603
Yale St 27609
Yancey St 27608
Yarborough Park Dr 27604
Yarmouth Rd
400-599 27608
600-999 27607
Yates Branch Ln 27603
Yates Forest Ln 27603
Yates Garden Ln 27606
Yates Mill Trl 27606
Yates Mill Pond Rd 27606
Yateswood Ct 27603
Yaxley Hall Dr 27616
Yeamans Way 27616
Yellow Wood Ln 27617
Yelverton Cir 27612
Yester Ct 27615
Yew Cir 27612
Yonkers Rd 27604
Yopon Ct 27603
E Yoreenti St 27601
York Rd 27608
Yorkchester Way 27615
Yorkgate Dr 27612
Yorkshire Ct 27604
Yorktown Pl 27609
Yorkwood Dr 27616
Young St 27608
Young Farm Dr 27610
Youngsbury Ct 27604
Youth Center Dr 27606
Yucca Trl 27615
Zachary Brook Ln 27609
Zaharis Cv 27603
Zaldivar Way 27612
Zara Ct 27616
Zelton Way 27610
Zephyr Pl 27603
Zermatt Ct 27617
Zinfandel Pl 27615
Zoa Ct 27607
Zuma Way 27613

Zuzu Dr 27614

NUMBERED STREETS

1st Pl 27613
2nd Ave 27609

REIDSVILLE NC

General Delivery 27320

POST OFFICE BOXES MAIN OFFICE STATIONS AND BRANCHES

Box No.s
All PO Boxes 27323

NAMED STREETS

All Street Addresses 27320

NUMBERED STREETS

All Street Addresses 27320

ROCKINGHAM NC

General Delivery 28379

POST OFFICE BOXES MAIN OFFICE STATIONS AND BRANCHES

Box No.s
1 - 2800 28380
28379 - 28379 28379

NAMED STREETS

A St 28379
Aab Ln 28379
Abrams Dr 28379
Adam St 28379
Adetha Ln 28379
Aginora Ln 28379
Airline St 28379
Airport Rd 28379
Alcan Rd 28379
Aleo Eighth Ave 28379
Aleo Fifth Ave 28379
Aleo First Ave & St 28379
Aleo Fourth Ave 28379
Aleo Ninth Ave 28379
Aleo Second Ave 28379
Aleo Seventh Ave 28379
Aleo Sixth Ave 28379
Aleo Third Ave 28379
Allen Rd & St 28379
Allen Hancock Rd 28379
Alma Green Rd 28379
Alsace St 28379
Amanda Ln 28379
Amber Way 28379
American Legion Rd 28379
Angee Dr 28379
Ann St 28379
Ann Mckinney Rd 28379
Ann Street Ext 28379
Anson Ave 28379
Anthony Ave & Ln 28379
Apple Dr 28379
April Ln 28379
Arbor Rd 28379
Ardsley Rd 28379
Arlos Ln 28379
Armstead St 28379
Arrowhead Trl 28379
Arthur Cir 28379
Arville Dr 28379
Ashe St 28379
Ashley St 28379
Ashworth Ln 28379
Aslington St 28379
Aspen Ln 28379
Avalon Dr 28379
Azie Dr 28379
Back St 28379
Bailey St 28379
Baker St 28379
Baldwin Rd 28379
Barbara Ct 28379
Barnes Dr 28379
Barrett St 28379
Bass Hollow Ln 28379
Bateman St 28379
Battley Dairy Rd 28379
Baucom Dr 28379
Baucoms Cor 28379
Bay St 28379
Beane Run 28379
Bear Branch Rd 28379
N Beaunit Ave 28379
Beaverbrook Rd 28379
Beaverdam Church Rd 28379
Beaverwood Ct 28379
Bedrock Rd 28379
Belle Dr 28379
Bellevue Dr 28379
Ben Hudson Rd 28379
Benji Rd 28379
Benny Watkins Rd 28379
Bernice Rd 28379
Bible Way Church Rd 28379
Bickett St 28379
Biggs Blvd 28379
Bills Pl 28379
Billy Covington Rd 28379
Biltmore Dr 28379
Birch St 28379
Bk Jones St 28379
Blackjack Dr 28379
Blewitt Ave 28379
Blewitt Falls Rd 28379
Blue Sky Dr 28379
Bluebird Ct 28379
Bolton Blvd 28379
Boon Dock Rd 28379
Boone St 28379
Bostic Rd 28379
Bowman St 28379
Boxhill Pl 28379
Brady St 28379
Branch Trl 28379
Brandywine Rd 28379
Breanner Ln 28379
Breleighs Ct 28379
Brewington Ave 28379
Bristow Ln 28379
Broad Ave 28379
Broad Street Sq 28379
Broadway St 28379
Brock St 28379
Brookbank Rd 28379
Brookfield Rd 28379
Brooks Ave 28379
Brookstone Ln 28379
N & S Brookwood Ave 28379
Brower Rd 28379
Brown St 28379
Bryan Cir & St 28379
Buck Wall Rd 28379
Bullard St 28379
Bunker St 28379
Bunkies Rd 28379
Bush St 28379
Butler Cir 28379
Bynum Rd 28379
Byrd Dr 28379
Cabel Blvd 28379
Cabin Cv 28379
Cagle Rd 28379
Caleb Dr 28379
Caley Ln 28379
Calvert St 28379
Camelot Dr 28379
Cameron Dr 28379
Cameron Hill Rd 28379
Campbell Dr 28379
Canopa Pt 28379
Cardinal Dr 28379
Carla Ct 28379
Carmen Cv 28379
Carolina Cv & Dr 28379
S Caroline St 28379
Carolyns Mill Pl 28379
Carpenter Dr 28379
Carroll Farm Rd 28379
Carrye St 28379
Cartledge Creek Rd 28379
Cascades Way 28379
Castlewood Dr 28379
Cauthen Dr 28379
Cecil Ln 28379
Cedar St 28379
Cedarwood Dr 28379
Central Ave 28379
Chalk Rd 28379
Chalk Fork Rd 28379
Chance Dr 28379
Charann Ln 28379
Charles Mcdonald Dr 28379
Charles Mcrae Dr 28379
Charlie Dr 28379
Chatham Rd 28379
Chelsea Dr 28379
Cherokee St 28379
Chestnut Ln 28379
Chickasaw Rd 28379
S Church St 28379
Church Street Ext 28379
Cicero Dr 28379
Circle Dr N 28379
Circlewood Dr 28379
City Lake Dr 28379
Clara Ln 28379
Clark St 28379
Clayton Steen Rd 28379
Clearfield Dr 28379
Clemmer Rd 28379
Cliff St 28379
Coble Rd 28379
Cole Train Rd 28379
Collins Church Rd 28379
Colonial Dr 28379
Commerce Pl 28379
Confederate Ave 28379
Connell Rd 28379
Connie Dr 28379
Copeland St 28379
Country Canyon Dr 28379
Country Club Dr 28379
Country Hideout Rd 28379
County Home Rd 28379
Court St 28379
Covington St 28379
Cox St 28379
Coy Rd 28379
Craddock Cir 28379
Craig St 28379
Crawford Creek Dr 28379
Creek Run Ln 28379
Crescent Dr 28379
Crestmont Dr 28379
Crestview Dr 28379
Crestway Dr 28379
Cricket Ln 28379
Crisco Rd 28379
Critter Xing 28379
Croft Ln 28379
Crow Run 28379
Crown Ct 28379
Crystal Ct 28379
Cumberland Cir 28379
Curtis Dr 28379
Cypress St 28379
Dale St 28379
Dan Mcdonald Rd 28379
Daniels Ln 28379
Dave Kings Rd 28379
Davidson Dr 28379
Davis St 28379
Dawkins St 28379
Dawn Dr 28379
Day Lilly Ln 28379
Deanna Ln 28379
Deer Creek Ln 28379
Deerfield Rd 28379
Denson Run 28379
Derek St 28379
Destiny Dr 28379
Devos Dr 28379
Deweese Ave 28379
Dewey Ave 28379
Dicks Rd 28379
Dixie Rd 28379
Dixieland Rd 28379
Dobbins Ln 28379
Dockery Rd 28379
Dodson Rd 28379
Dogwood Ln 28379
Doral Dr 28379
Double L Rd 28379
Dozier Ln 28379
Dublin Ct 28379
Dust Cir 28379
Dustin Vw 28379
Dyan St 28379
E & W Eason Dr 28379
Eastern Ave 28379
Eastside Dr 28379
Ebony Ln 28379
Edwards Cir 28379
Edwin St 28379
Edwin Park Rd 28379
Effie Jane Ln 28379
Elaine Ave 28379
Elder St 28379
Elf Ln 28379
Eli Dr 28379
Elizabeth Ave & St 28379
Ellen Rd 28379
Ellerbe Rd 28379
Ellerbe Grove Church Rd 28379
Ember Ln 28379
Emory Dr 28379
Enterprise Dr 28379
Entwistle Rd 28379
Entwistle Third St 28379
Erica Dr 28379
Essie Mae Ln 28379
Ev Hogan Dr 28379
Evans St 28379
Evelyn Ct 28379
Everett St 28379
Everetts Mill Rd 28379
Evergreen Ct 28379
Fairfield Dr 28379
Fairlane Dr 28379
Fairley Dr 28379
Fairley Hayes Rd 28379
Fairway Dr 28379
Fairwood Rd 28379
Falling Creek Rd 28379
Farmstead Ct 28379
Fayetteville Rd 28379
Fenton St 28379
Fh Hare Rd 28379
Firefly Woods Rd 28379
First Ave 28379
Flowers St 28379
Ford Hill Rd 28379
Fordtown Rd 28379
Forest Dr 28379
Forest Way Rd 28379
Forrest St 28379
Fourth St 28379
Fourth Avenue Pee Dee 28379
Foushee St 28379
Fox Rd 28379
Fox Run Ln 28379
Foxfield Dr 28379
Fran Rd 28379
Frank Davis Rd 28379
Frank Parker Rd 28379
E & W Franklin St 28379
Franklin Haigler Rd 28379
Freedom Dr 28379
Friends St 28379
Frosty Dr 28379
Galestown Rd 28379
Gardenia St 28379
Garrett St 28379
Gaston Mclean Rd 28379
Gene Smith Dr 28379
George Maddry Rd 28379
Gerrys Dr 28379
Gibson Dr 28379
Glen Haven Cir 28379
Glen Rose Dr 28379
Glendale Dr 28379
Glenmore Dr 28379
Glenwood Ave 28379
Golden Dr 28379
Golfcart Ln 28379
Goodman St 28379
Goose Creek Cv 28379
Gore Dr 28379
Gould St 28379
Graham Bridge Rd 28379
Grant St 28379
Graystone Ln 28379
Great Falls Cir 28379
E & W Green St 28379
Green Acres St 28379
Green Cedar Ln 28379
Green Lake Rd 28379
Green Lake Church Rd 28379
Green Ridge Dr 28379
Greenbriar Ln 28379
Greenland Dr 28379
Greenlawn Dr 28379
Greensboro St 28379
Grenaco Ln 28379
Grenaco Village Rd 28379
Grey Fox Run 28379
Greylyn Rd 28379
Griffin Rd 28379
N & S Grove Ave 28379
Gus Wall Rd 28379
Hall Rd 28379
Hamer Rd 28379
W Hamer Mill Rd 28379
Hammond St 28379
Hampton Ln 28379
N & S Hancock St 28379
Hanford Dr 28379
Hannah Pickett Ave 28379
Hannah Pickett Church St 28379
Hannah Pickett First Ave & St 28379
Hannah Pickett Fourth Ave 28379
Hannah Pickett Second Ave 28379
Hannah Pickett Seventh Ave 28379
Hannah Pickett Sixth Ave 28379
Hannah Pickett Third Ave 28379
Happy Valley Rd 28379
Harrington Rd 28379
Harris Dr 28379
Harvest Church Rd 28379
Hastings St 28379
Hatcher Rd 28379
Hattie Ruth Rd 28379
Hawkins Ln 28379
Hawthorne Ave 28379
Haywood Ave & St 28379
Haywood Cemetery Rd 28379
Hazelwood Ave 28379
Heather Ave 28379
Helton Ln 28379
Hemlock St 28379
Henry Dr 28379
Henry Snead Rd 28379
Hickory St 28379
Hidden Knoll Cir 28379
Hill St 28379
Hillary Ln 28379
Hillcrest Dr 28379
Hillside Dr 28379
Hilltop Dr 28379
Hillview Cir 28379
Hinson Ave & Ct 28379
Hinson Lake Rd 28379
Holiday Village Apts 28379
Hollow Trl 28379
Holly Rd 28379
Holly Berry Rdg 28379
Holly Grove Church Rd 28379
Hollywood Ln 28379
Home Ave 28379
Homeplace Rd 28379
Homeward Dr 28379
Honey Rd 28379
Hood St 28379
Hooper St 28379
Hopkins Rd 28379
Horne Dr 28379
Horseshoe Rd 28379
Hudson St 28379
Hudson Reese Rd 28379
Hummingbird Dr 28379
Hunt St 28379
Hunter Cir 28379
Hutchinson Dr 28379
Ida Run 28379
Ida Ellerbe Dr 28379
Industrial Park Dr 28379
Ingram St 28379
Irish St 28379
Isom Nichols Rd 28379
Ivy Trl 28379
J Elsie Webb 28379
Jabba Rd 28379
Jackson Dr & Rd 28379
Jacobs Ln 28379
James Hall Rd 28379
James Hand Rd 28379
Jasper Forrest Dr 28379
Jay Bird Dr 28379
Jayson St 28379
Jeanette Ln 28379
Jenkins Ave 28379
Jenkins Covington Rd 28379
Jennifer Dr 28379
Jerry Lynn Dr 28379
Jess Dr 28379
Jessica Ave 28379
Jewell Ln 28379
Jim Mcdonald Rd 28379
Joann Dr 28379
Joe Kanaris Rd 28379
Joes Ct 28379
John St 28379
John Chavis Rd 28379
John Elliott Rd 28379
John F Kennedy Dr 28379
John O Mcdonald Rd 28379
John Thomas Rd 28379
Johns Rd 28379
Jones Ave 28379
Joseph Rd 28379
Joyce St 28379
Judith Ann Dr 28379
Juniper St 28379
Karen Dr 28379
Katie Ln 28379
Keeler Ave 28379
Keith Ave 28379
Kellam Williams Rd 28379
Kellyville Dr 28379
Kenric Pt 28379
Kevin Roller Rd 28379
Kimberly St 28379
Kimmer Rd 28379
King St 28379
Kingstree Dr 28379
Kinney St 28379
Kitty Kat Dr 28379
Knight Cir 28379
Knoresta Rd 28379
Koala Dr 28379
Kristy Ln 28379
La Ron Dr 28379
Lady Mary Ln 28379
Lake Rd & Run 28379
Lake View Pass 28379
Lakeland Dr 28379
Lakepoint Rd 28379
Lakeshore Dr 28379
Lakeside Dr 28379
Lakeview Trl 28379
Lakewood Dr 28379
Lancaster Ln 28379
Lands End Rd 28379
Lasona Dr 28379
Lassiter Rd 28379
Laurel Ave & St 28379
Laurel Ledge 28379
Lauren Ln 28379
N & S Lawrence St 28379
Lawson Ln 28379
Leak St 28379
Leatha Ln 28379
N & S Ledbetter Rd & St 28379
Ledbetter Bay Cv 28379
Ledbetter Hailey Rd 28379
N & S Lee St 28379
Lee Thee Church Rd 28379
Legrand St 28379
Leonard St 28379
Lewarae St 28379
Lewis Cir 28379
Lewis Terry Rd 28379
Liberty Cir & Dr 28379
Lila Ln 28379
Lillians Ln 28379
Lincoln Ave & St 28379
Linden Dr 28379
Lindsey Dr 28379
Linwood Ln 28379
Little St 28379
Little Bo Ln 28379
Little Ingram St 28379
Loblolly Ct 28379
Loch Haven Rd 28379
Loch Laurin Ln 28379
Locklear Dr 28379
Logan Park 28379
N & S Long Dr 28379
Long Leaf Ln 28379
Lonnie Ln 28379
Loren Cir 28379
Lorraine St 28379
Louise Ave 28379
Love Ln 28379
Lovin Rd 28379
Lowery Ln 28379
Lucille Ln 28379
Lumyer Rd 28379
Luther St 28379
Lyerly St 28379
Lynch Ln 28379
Macs Ln 28379
Madison Ave 28379
Main Trl 28379
Mallard Ln 28379
Mandella Ln 28379
Maner Rd 28379
Maness Ave 28379
Maola Ln 28379
Maple St 28379
Marigold St 28379
Marilyn Ave 28379
Marshall Ave 28379
Martin St 28379
Martin Mcgee Rd 28379
Mary Evans Rd 28379
Mary Wall Rd 28379
Mattie Dr 28379
Matts Castle Rd 28379
Mcarthur Dr 28379

Mcbrothers Dr 28379
Mccroskey St 28379
Mcdonald Dr 28379
Mcdonald Church Rd 28379
Mcdowell Ln 28379
Mcgee Rd 28379
Mcinnis Rd 28379
Mckinnon Dr 28379
Mcleod St 28379
Mcnair Rd 28379
Mcneill Rd & St 28379
Mcqueen St 28379
Medical Cir 28379
Melton Dr 28379
Memory Ln 28379
Mid Pines Trailer Park 28379
Middle St 28379
Midland St 28379
Midway Rd 28379
Military Ln 28379
Mill Rd & St 28379
Minnie Pl 28379
Miranda Ln 28379
Mitchell Ave 28379
Mizpah Rd 28379
Montclair Ave 28379
Moore Ave 28379
Morman St 28379
Morningside Dr 28379
Morris Dr 28379
Morrow St 28379
Motlow Ln 28379
Mount Olive Church Rd 28379
Munns Farm Rd 28379
Murray Manor Ln 28379
Musket Ct 28379
Myrtle Dr 28379
Nannie Ln 28379
Napier Ln 28379
Nash Dr 28379
Nc Highway 177 S 28379
Needle Ln 28379
Nelson Rd 28379
Nelson Farm Rd 28379
New St 28379
Newborn Rd 28379
Nicholson Rd & St 28379
Nicole Ln 28379
Nika St 28379
Nonnie Dr 28379
Northam Rd 28379
Northshore Trl 28379
Northside Dr 28379
Northside Park Dr 28379
Northview St 28379
Oak Ave 28379
Oakdale St 28379
Old Aberdeen Rd 28379
Old Charlotte Hwy 28379
Old Cheraw Hwy 28379
Old Highway 1 S 28379
Old River Rd 28379
Old Salem Rd 28379
Old Time Way 28379
Old Us Highway 74 28379
Old Wix Rd 28379
Oliver St 28379
Olympic Dr 28379
Oral Bessie Ln 28379
Osborne Rd 28379
Ossie Flowers Cir 28379
Outside Ln 28379
Pa Gale Rd 28379
Page St 28379
Painted Acres Dr 28379
Palisade Cir 28379
Palmer St 28379
Panky Rd 28379
N Park Ave, Dr & St 28379
Parker Ln & St 28379
Parkwood Ct 28379
Parrot Ln 28379
Patterson Rd & St 28379
Patton Cir 28379
Pauline Dr 28379
Payton Ct 28379
Peace Dr 28379
Pearls Dr 28379
Pecan Rd & St 28379
Pee Dee St 28379
Pema Dr 28379
Pemberton Ln 28379
Pence St 28379
Perkins Cir 28379
Pernell Dr 28379
Perry Leviner Rd 28379
Petunia Ln 28379
Philadelphia Dr 28379
Phillips Cir 28379
Physicians Park Dr 28379
Pickett St 28379
Pine Cir, Ln & St 28379
Pine Bark Trl 28379
Pine Circle Dr 28379
Pine Forest Rd 28379
Pine Haven Park 28379
Pine Ledge Rd 28379
Pine Straw Rd 28379
Pine Tree Trl 28379
Pinecrest Trl 28379
Pinecroft St 28379
Pinedale Dr & Rd 28379
Pineleigh Ave 28379
Pineridge Dr 28379
Pinetop St 28379
Pineview Ct 28379
Pinewild Ln 28379
Pinewood Cir 28379
Pinion Dr 28379
Pirate Ln 28379
Pistol Ridge Rd 28379
Plantation Rd 28379
Plum Nelly Rd 28379
Poe Rd 28379
Polly Pt 28379
Ponds Ln 28379
Poole Rd 28379
Poplar St 28379
Poplar Springs Rd 28379
Poppy Seed Dr 28379
Potter Rd 28379
Power Line Dr 28379
Prudence Dr 28379
Purvis Rd 28379
Quail Creek Ct 28379
Quarter Horse Ln 28379
Rabbit Hare Rd 28379
Rachel Rd 28379
Raider Rd 28379
Railroad St 28379
Rainwater Ln 28379
Ralph Cecil Dr 28379
N & S Randolph St 28379
Ratliff Rd 28379
Ravenhill Dr 28379
Ravenwood Rd 28379
Rebecca Dr 28379
Rebel Rd 28379
Reddick Dr 28379
Rich Dr 28379
Richmond Rd 28379
Richmond Memorial Dr 28379
Richmond Pines Dr 28379
Richmond Road Ext 28379
W Ridge Ct 28379
River Park & Rd 28379
Road Runner Dr 28379
Roberdell Rd 28379
Roberdell School Rd 28379
Roberta Rd 28379
Robin Covington Rd 28379
Robinson St 28379
Rockingham Rd 28379
Rockingham Roofing Rd 28379
Rocky Ln 28379
Rocky Hill Rd 28379
Rogosin St 28379
Rohanen Ave 28379
Rolling Ave & Hls 28379
Ron Dr 28379
Rosa St 28379
Rosalyn Rd 28379
Rosemont Ln 28379
Roses Dr 28379
Rowan Ter 28379
Roy Moss Ln 28379
Rudy Ln 28379
Rush St 28379
Russell Dr 28379
Ruth Covington Rd 28379
Sadie Ln 28379
Safie Fifth Ave & St 28379
Safie First Ave & St 28379
Safie Fourth St 28379
Safie Second Ave & St 28379
Safie Sixth St 28379
Safie Third St 28379
Sagebrush Dr 28379
Saint Johns Ln 28379
Saint Stevens Church Rd 28379
Salem Dr 28379
Sam Richardson Rd 28379
Samaritan Dr 28379
Sandcrest Dr 28379
Sandhill Rd 28379
Sandhill Game Mgnt Rd 28379
Sandhurst Dr 28379
Sandspur Ln 28379
Sandy Ln 28379
Sandy Grove Church Rd 28379
Sandy Oaks Rd 28379
Sandy Ridge Church Rd 28379
Sanford St 28379
Sara Rose Ln 28379
Sarah Dr 28379
Sargent Dr 28379
Scales St 28379
Scaleybark Rd 28379
School St 28379
Scotch Ln 28379
Scotland Ave 28379
Scott Ln 28379
Scott Mcdonald Rd 28379
Seaboard St 28379
Seago Ln 28379
Second Avenue Pee Dee 28379
Sedgefield Rd 28379
Selah Dr 28379
Seven Oaks Dr 28379
Shady Ln 28379
Shady Wood Dr 28379
Shaffer Rd 28379
Shallow Ford Dr 28379
Shankle Ln 28379
Shannon Dr 28379
Sharon Rd 28379
Shaw Ln & St 28379
Shawns Ln 28379
Shelby Ln 28379
Shell Dr 28379
Short St 28379
Shultz Ln 28379
Silver Grove Church Rd 28379
Silver Leaf Dr 28379
N & S Skipper St 28379
Sky Run 28379
Skylar Ln 28379
Skyline Dr 28379
Slate Rd 28379
Sleepy Hollow Dr 28379
Smith St 28379
Smith Jones Rd 28379
Smokey Hollow Rd 28379
Snake Hill Rd 28379
Snead Ave 28379
Sneads Mill Rd 28379
Sonoco Paper Mill Rd 28379
South St 28379
Southwood Dr 28379
Sparks Dr 28379
Spencer Rd 28379
Spivey St 28379
Spring Dr & St 28379
Spring Drive Ext 28379
Spring Garden St 28379
Spring Lake Rd 28379
Springdale Dr 28379
Springer Mountain Rd 28379
Spruce St 28379
Stan Ave 28379
Stanback Ln 28379
Stanley Ave 28379
Starlight Dr 28379
N State Ln 28379
Steele St 28379
Steen Park Rd 28379
Stelleys Tabernacle Chu Rd 28379
Sterling Dr 28379
N & S Stewart St 28379
Stewart F Webb Ln 28379
Stillwell St 28379
Stokes Rd 28379
Strawberry Ln 28379
Sturdivant Dr 28379
Substation Rd 28379
Summit Dr 28379
Sun Glory Dr 28379
Sunday School Rd 28379
Sunflower Dr 28379
Sunrise Cir & Ln 28379
Sunset Belt 28379
Surginor Rd 28379
Sweet Haven Rd 28379
Sweetbriar Ln 28379
Sycamore Ln 28379
Tadlock Dr 28379
Tanner St 28379
Taylor Dr 28379
E & W Temple Ave 28379
Terry Bridge Rd 28379
The Pines Apts 28379
Third Avenue Pee Dee 28379
Thomas St 28379
Thomas Hill Rd 28379
Thompson Farm Rd 28379
Thrower Rd 28379
Tiffany Ln 28379
Tillman Rd 28379
Tiny Ln 28379
Tip Toe Cir 28379
Tisha Ln 28379
Torch Lounge Rd 28379
Tracey Ln 28379
Trail Hollow Ln 28379
Trailcrest Dr 28379
Trailwood Ln 28379
Travis Trl 28379
Tree Farm Rd 28379
Tree Top Dr 28379
Trent St 28379
Tri City Shopping Ctr 28379
Trinity Way 28379
Tulip Cir 28379
Twin Oaks Rd 28379
Two Branch Rd 28379
Two Sisters Ln 28379
N Us 220 Hwy 28379
N Us Highway 1 S 28379
N Us Highway 220 28379
E & W Us Highway 74 28379
Valley Rd 28379
Valley Hill Dr 28379
Vance St 28379
Vertis Covington Rd 28379
Village Terrace Dr 28379
Virginia Ave 28379
Vista Ln 28379
Waddell Rd 28379
Wadsworth Ln 28379
Wal Mart Shopping Ctr 28379
Walker Ln 28379
Wall St 28379
Wall Ferry Rd 28379
Wallace Ave 28379
Walnut Ln 28379
Walters Ct 28379
Warburton Ave 28379
Ware St 28379
E Washington St 28379
W Washington St
100-118 28379
119-699 28379
119-119 28380
120-698 28379
E Washington Street Ext 28379
Waters Ave 28379
Waters Edge Way 28379
Watkins Ave 28379
Watkins Loop Rd 28379
Watson Ave 28379
Waymon Ave 28379
Wayne Rd 28379
Webster Ave 28379
West Ave 28379
Westfield Dr 28379
Westside St 28379
Westside Shopping Ctr 28379
Westwood Dr 28379
Wheat St 28379
Wheel Slip Ln 28379
White St 28379
Whitekloud Trl 28379
Whitney Ln 28379
Wiggins Rd 28379
Wild Cherry Ave 28379
Wilderness Dr 28379
Wildlife Holw 28379
Wildwood Rd 28379
N & S Williams Ave & St 28379
Williamsburg Dr 28379
Willie Mae Ln 28379
Willie Williams Rd 28379
Willow Rd 28379
Wilson Ave & St 28379
Windy Knoll Knl 28379
Winsor Dr 28379
Wiregrass Rd 28379
Woodfield Dr 28379
Woodland Rd 28379
Woodside Dr 28379
Wright Ln 28379
Yates St 28379
Yates Hill Rd 28379
Zannie Dr 28379
Zeb Bailey Dr 28379
Zion St 28379
Zion Church Rd 28379

NUMBERED STREETS

All Street Addresses 28379

ROCKY MOUNT NC

General Delivery 27801

POST OFFICE BOXES MAIN OFFICE STATIONS AND BRANCHES

Box No.s
A - P 27802
1 - 2979 27802
4001 - 4940 27803
6001 - 6999 27802
7001 - 9120 27804
9995 - 9995 27801
9998 - 9998 27802

RURAL ROUTES

04 27801
07, 12, 16 27803
17 27804

NAMED STREETS

A St 27804
Abbey Rd 27804
Abbington Ct 27803
Aberdeen 27804
Abner Dr 27803
Academy Way 27804
Acie Ln 27801
Acorn Trl 27804
Acorn Ridge Rd 27804
Adams St 27804
Adams Ridge Rd 27804
Adamsville Ct 27803
Airport Rd 27804
Alabaster Way 27804
Albemarle Ave 27801
Alby Ct & St 27803
Alex Ln 27801
Alexander Dr 27804
Allen St 27803
Allison Ln 27803
Alta Vista Ln 27803
Alwood Ln 27804
Amanda Ln 27801
Ambler Ave 27801
Amherst Rd 27804
Amos St 27803
Anabella Dr 27803
Anchor Farm Ln 27801
Anderson St 27803
Anglers Cove Ct 27804
Anne St 27801
Annie Lee Way 27804
Ansley St 27803
Antioch Rd 27801
N & S Applewood Ct 27803
April Ln 27801
Aqua Ct 27801
Arbor Ln 27803
Arcenia Hines Dr 27803
Archer Dr 27801
Argus Pl 27801
Arlington Cir, St & Ter 27801
Arrington Ave 27803
Arrow Rd 27804
Arrowhead Ln 27801
Arthur Cir 27804
Ascot 27804
Ashcroft Ct 27804
Ashland Ave 27801
Ashley Way 27804
Ashmore Ln 27804
Ashton Rd 27803
Aspen Rd 27804
Atlantic Ave 27801
Audubon Ln 27804
Augustine Ln 27801
Augustus Dr 27801
Aunt Hattie Ln 27801
Authority Dr 27801
Autry Rd 27803
Autumn Ct 27804
Avalon Rd 27801
Avent Cir & St 27804
Avenue A 27801
Avenue B 27801
Avenue C 27801
Avondale Ave
400-899 27804
1000-1399 27803
Avondale Ct 27803
Aycock St 27803
Azalea St 27803
Azimuth Ct 27804
Aztec Ave 27801
B P Ln 27804
Baber Ct 27803
Badin Dr 27803
Baie Rd 27801
Bailey St 27803
Baker 27801
Baker Ln 27803
Bakers Trailer Park 27801
Banner Way 27804
Barfield 27801
Barn Yard Ln 27801
Barnes St 27801
Barnum Rd 27804
Barrington Ct 27803
E Bassett St 27801
W Bassett St 27803
Batchelor Rd 27801
Battle St 27801
Batts Dr 27803
Bay Dr 27803
Bayleaf Ln 27801
Bayridge Ct 27803
Baywood Ct 27803
Baywood Ln 27801
Baywood Rd 27803
Beal St 27804
Beamon St 27803
Bear Wallow Rd 27804
Beaver Pond Dr 27804
Beckman St 27801
Bedford Rd 27801
Beechwood Ct & Dr 27803
Beeston Flds 27804
Belgreen Dr 27804
Bell Dr 27803
Belleview Ave 27804
Belmont Club Way 27804
Belmont Farms Pkwy 27804
Belmont Lake Dr 27804
Belvedere St 27803
Ben Layton Cir 27804
Bend Of The River Rd 27803
Benjamin Ct 27803
Bennett St 27803
Benson Way 27803
Bent Creek Ct & Dr 27803
Benvenue Rd 27804
Benvenue Forest Rd 27804
Berkley Dr 27803
Berkshire Rd 27801
Bermuda Rd 27801
Berryhill Rd 27804
Berwick 27804
Bessemer Ln 27801
Bessie Ct & Ln 27804
Beth Eden Ct 27803
Bethlehem Rd 27803
Betty Ln 27801
Betty Lou Ln 27804
Betz St 27803
Beverly Rd 27801
Big Ed Ln 27801
Big Jim Rd 27804
Bills Ln 27801
Billy Buck Ln 27803
Biltmore Pl 27804
Bing Crosby Dr 27801
Binker Dr 27804
Birch Ct & St 27804
Birdie Ct 27804
Bishop Rd 27804
Bitterroot Rd 27803
Black Pearl Cv 27804
Blackthorne Rd 27803
Blaire St 27804
Blanch Ln 27803
Blandwood Dr 27801
Blanton St 27803
Blue Rug Rd 27801
Blue Water Lndg 27804
Blue Willow Ct & Ln 27804
Bobbys Ln 27804
Bobwhite Ln 27804
Boddie Ct 27804
Bonnie Ln 27801
Boone St 27803
Boseman Pl 27801
Boseman Rd 27804
Bowie Pl 27803
Boyd Ct 27803
Bradford Ln 27801
Bradley Farm Ln 27801

Brake Rd
1-3699 27801
5400-6299 27804
Brake Farm Ln 27801
Brake Loop Rd 27801
Bramblebush Ct 27804
Branch St 27801
Brandon Ln 27804
Brandymill Dr 27804
Brandywine Ct & Ln 27804
Brassfield Ct & Dr 27803
Brassie Club Dr 27804
Braswell Ln 27803
Braswell Rd 27803
Braswell St 27804
Braswell Memory Ln 27801
Braswell Woods Cir 27801
Braxton Pl 27804
Braylock Dr 27804
Breckenridge Ct 27804
Brentwood Dr 27804
Brewer Ct 27801
Briar Creek Rd 27803
Briar Glenn Rd 27804
Briarcliff Rd 27804
Briarfield Rd 27804
Briarwood Dr 27803
Bridge Tender Cir 27803
Bridgedale Dr 27803
Bridgeport Ct 27804
Bridgeton Rd 27804
Bridgeview Rd 27803
Bridgewood Rd 27804
Bridle Dr 27804
Brigadier Way 27804
Bristol Ct 27803
Brittany Ct & Rd 27803
Brook Dr 27804
Brook Valley Mobile
Park 27804
Brookdale Dr 27804
Brookfield Dr 27803
Brookmeade Ct 27804
Brooks Dr & St 27801
Brookview Dr 27804
Broom Straw Ct 27803
Brown Dr 27804
Brown Tower Ln 27801
Browning Ln 27804
Browns Cv 27801
Browns Trailer Park 27801
S Browntown Rd 27804
Brownview Dr 27801
Bryant St 27804
Buck Xing 27801
Buck Run Ct 27803
Buckboard Trl 27804
Buckingham Ct 27803
Buena Vista Ave 27801
Buff Rd 27803
Buffaloe Ridge Ct 27804
Buick St 27803
Bull Run Ln 27801
Bullock Trailer Park 27803
Bulluck Ave 27804
Bulluck School Rd 27801
Bunch Cir 27804
Bunn Ave 27804
Bunn Ln 27801
Burnette St 27803
Burnham 27804
Burnt Mill Rd 27804
Burt St 27801
Burton St 27803
N & S Business Ct &
Ln 27804
Business Park Dr 27804
Butternut Ct 27804
Calbrad Rd 27801
Caleb Ct 27804
Calhoun Ave & Rd 27801
Calloway Ct & Rd 27804
Calvary St 27803
Calvert St 27804
N Cambridge Cir 27801
S Cambridge Cir 27801
Cambridge Dr 27804
Camellia Ct 27801
Cameron St 27803
Camland Cir 27803
Canal St 27801
Canary Dr 27803
Candle Ct 27804
Candlewood Rd 27804
Cane Dr 27801
Canterbury Rd 27801
Canvasback Pt 27804
Capital Dr 27804
Capstone Ct 27804
Cardinal St 27804
Cardinals Knob 27804
Carnation Ct 27804
Carolina Ave 27801
Carr St 27804
Carriage Trl 27804
Carriage Farm Rd 27804
Carrington Rd 27804
Carroll Ave 27804
Carson Ct & Dr 27803
Carter St 27804
Carver Pl 27801
Carybrook Ct & Rd 27803
Cascade Ave 27803
Cash Ln 27803
Cassie Ct 27804
Castaways Trl 27804
Castlebury Ct 27804
Cathy Ln 27801
Cathy Way 27804
Cecils Ln 27803
Cedar St 27803
Cedarbrook Dr 27803
Cedarhurst Ln 27801
Center St 27803
Centipede Dr 27801
Centura Hwy 27804
Chad St 27803
Chaise Dr 27804
Challenge Ct 27801
Chamberlain Ct & Rd ... 27803
Champion Way 27804
Chandler Ln 27804
Chapman St 27803
Charity Ct 27801
Charlene Ln 27801
Charles Ln 27801
Charleston Ct 27803
Charlie Rd 27803
Charlotte St 27804
Charmin Ln 27804
Chartavia Ln 27801
Charter Dr 27801
Chartwell Rd 27804
Chase Ct & St 27801
Chason Ln 27801
Chateau Ln 27803
Chelsea Ct & Dr 27803
Cherokee Rd 27804
Cherry St 27801
Chesapeake Ct 27804
Cheshire Ln 27803
Chester St 27804
Chestnut St 27804
Chickasaw Ct 27804
Chicopee Ct 27804
Chicora Ct 27804
Chimney Hill Ct, Trl &
Way 27804
Chippenham Rd 27804
Christina Ln 27804
Christopher Ln 27801
Chrystal Way 27801
N Church St 27801
S Church St
100-499 27804
500-4499 27803
Churchview Dr 27804
E, N, S & W Circle Dr .. 27804
Claiborne Ln 27801
Clancy Ct 27803
Claremont Ct 27804
Clarence Ct 27803
Clark St 27801
Clayton St 27803
Clematis Ct 27804
Cleo St 27803
Cleveland St 27803
Cliff Ln 27801
Clifton Rd 27804
Clinton Ct 27804
Clints Ln 27803
Clover Rd 27801
Clubview Ct & Dr 27804
Clyde St 27803
Clyde Smith Ln 27803
Co Ah Bar St 27803
Coastline St 27804
Cobb Rd 27804
Cobb Corners Dr 27804
Cobb Farm Village Ln .. 27804
Cobblestone Ct 27804
Coeco Cir 27804
Coggins Ct 27804
Cokey Rd 27801
Colby Ct & Rd 27803
Coleberry Trl 27804
Coleman Ave 27801
Coleridge Ct 27803
Coley Rd 27804
Colleen Dr 27803
Collingbourne Ct 27804
Collington Ct 27804
Colon Dr 27804
Colonial Ln 27804
Colony Sq 27804
Columbia Ave 27804
Commerce Ct 27803
Commodore Dr 27801
Community Dr 27804
Como Way 27803
Compass Creek Dr 27804
Compton Ln 27804
Construction Dr 27804
Cool Spring Rd 27801
Cool Valley Ln 27801
Cooley Rd 27803
Cooper St 27803
Coppedge Rd 27804
Coral Dr 27801
Corbett St 27801
Cordiality Church Rd ... 27803
Cornell Dr 27803
Cornerstone Ct 27804
Cornwallis Dr 27804
Cottage Way 27803
Cottonwood Ct 27804
Country Ln & Rd 27803
Country Club Dr & Rd .. 27804
Country Ridge Dr 27803
Countryside Ln 27801
County Line Rd 27803
Courtland Ave 27801
Cove Ct & Dr 27804
Covenant Ct 27804
Coventry Ct 27801
Coventry Dr 27804
Covenwood Ln 27801
Covington Ln 27801
Cox Ave 27801
Crabapple Ln 27804
Craig St 27803
Creek Ln 27804
Creekridge Dr 27803
Creekside Dr 27804
Creekstone Rd 27803
Crescent Dr 27804
Crestview Rd 27801
Crosswinds Dr 27803
Crowell Rd 27803
Crumpler Dr 27803
Crusenberry Rd 27804
Crystal Ln 27804
Culpepper Dr 27803
Cummings Rd 27804
Cunningham Ct & Dr ... 27804
Curtis St 27803
Curtis Ellis Dr 27804
Cutchin Dr 27803
Cypress St 27801
Cypress Cove Ln 27803
Daffodil Way 27804
Dahlgren Ave 27804
Daisy Ln & St 27803
Dalewood Dr 27801
Dalton Rd 27803
Dana Ln 27803
Darden Ct 27804
Dare Ct 27804
Darrah Ln 27804
Dartmoor Ct 27803
Darwin Ln 27803
Daughtridge Rd 27803
Daughtridge St 27801
Daughtridge Farm Rd .. 27801
N Daughtry St 27801
Davenport Rd 27804
Davenport St 27803
David Way 27803
Davis Rd & St 27803
Davis Store Rd 27803
Davis Trailer Park 27801
Dawn Ln 27804
Dawsie Ln 27803
Dawson Pl 27804
Daybreak Ln 27804
Dayspring Dr 27804
De Leon Ln 27803
Debbie Ln 27801
Deer Run 27801
Deer Hunter Ln 27801
Deer Ridge Ct 27804
Deerchase Dr 27804
Deerwalk Dr 27804
Delane Dr 27804
Delaride Rd 27801
Delphia Dr 27801
Derby Dr 27804
Devon Ln 27804
Dexter St 27803
Dillon Ct 27803
N & S Discovery St 27801
Doe Ln 27801
Doe Run Ct 27803
Dogwood Ave & Ct 27804
Dominick Dr 27804
Donovan Ct 27801
Dorchester Ct 27803
Dorman Rd 27804
Dorothy Ln 27803
Dorothy St 27804
Dortches Blvd 27804
Douglas St 27804
Dove Ct 27804
Dover Rd 27804
Doves Mount Cir 27801
Dowdy St 27803
Dozier Rd 27804
Dreaver St 27801
Drew St 27801
Drexel Ct & Rd 27803
Drivers Cir 27804
Duck Pond Rd 27804
E & W Duke Cir 27804
Dunbarton Rd 27803
Duncan Dr 27801
Dunn Dr 27801
Dunn St 27801
Durham St 27801
S Eagle Ridge Dr 27804
Eaglecrest Cir 27801
Eagles Ter 27804
Eagles Mere Trl 27804
Earl St 27804
East St 27801
Eastern Ave
300-1699 27801
2000-3999 27804
7600-7699 27801
Eastfield Dr 27801
Eastwood Ln 27804
Echo Lake Ln 27803
Eden Ct 27801
Edgecombe St 27801
Edgecombe Meadows
Dr 27801
Edgewater Dr 27804
Edinborough Ct & Rd ... 27803
Eds Dr 27804
Edwards St 27803
Effie Smith Ln 27803
Elaine Ct & Dr 27801
Elizabeth Ln 27804
Elkhorn Ct 27803
Ella Dr 27803
Ellison Dr 27801
E & W Elm Ct & St 27804
Elmwood Rd 27804
Eltham 27804
Ely Dr 27804
Emerald Ln 27801
Emerson Dr 27803
Emily Way 27804
Emma Clint Ln 27801
W End St 27803
N & S Englewood Dr ... 27804
English Rd 27804
Enterprise Dr 27804
Epps Church Rd 27801
Eric Way 27803
Essex Ct 27803
Estell St 27803
Evans Ln 27801
Evergreen Rd 27803
Fabrication Way 27804
Fairfax Ct 27801
Fairfield Ct & Dr 27804
Fairhaven Dr 27803
N & S Fairview Rd 27801
Fairway Ter 27804
Faith Ct 27801
Faith Christian Dr 27803
Falcon Rd 27801
Falling River Walk 27804
Falls Rd 27804
Farley Ct 27801
Farmer St 27801
Farmington Rd 27801
Fenner Rd 27804
Ferndale Dr 27801
Ferro Rd 27803
Fidelia Rd 27804
Field Crest Rd 27803
Fieldcrest Dr & Rd 27804
Fieldstream Dr 27803
Finneman Ln 27803
Fleming Ct & St 27803
Fletcher Dr 27801
Flintshire Ln 27801
Floods Store Rd 27803
Flora Ln 27803
Floras Ln 27803
Flowers Ln 27803
Focus Ct 27801
Fords Colony Ct & Dr .. 27804
Foresome Ln 27804
Forest Dr 27804
Forest Hill Ave 27804
Forest Wood Rd 27804
Formby 27804
Fort St 27801
Fosteri Dr 27801
Fountain Rd & St 27801
Fountain Branch Ct &
Rd 27803
Fountain School Rd 27801
Foxden Ct 27804
Foxhall Ct & Dr 27804
Foxridge Ct 27804
Foy Dr 27804
Frank Wilkerson Dr 27801
N Franklin St 27804
S Franklin St
100-599 27804
600-2299 27803
Franks Rd 27803
Frazier Ct 27803
Freedom Ln 27801
Freer Dr 27804
Freight Rd 27804
Friendly Oak Ln 27801
Friendly Oaks Mobile
Park 27801
Gail Dr 27804
Garden Gate Dr 27803
Gardenia Cir 27804
Garvis St 27803
Gary Ct & Rd 27803
Gateway Blvd 27804
Gay Rd 27801
Gay St 27804
Gelo Rd 27804
N & S George St 27801
George Bulluck Ln 27801
Glasgow 27804
N & S Glendale Ave ... 27801
Glenn Ave 27803
Gloucester Ct & Rd 27803
Godwin Ln 27803
Gold St
300-399 27803
800-1199 27804
Golden Eye Cv 27804
E Goldleaf St 27801
Goldrock Rd 27804
Goose Branch Dr 27804
N Grace St 27804
S Grace St
100-599 27804
600-1699 27803
Graham St 27803
E Grand Ave 27801
W Grand Ave 27804
Grange St 27804
Granite Falls Ct 27804
Granville Ct 27804
Gravely Dr 27804
Great Gln 27804
Great Branch Dr 27803
Great State Ln 27803
Green Ave 27801
Green Bank Ct 27804
Green Cove Ln 27804
Green Forest Ct 27804
Green Hills Rd 27804
Green Hills Mobile
Park 27801
Green Meadow Ln 27804
Green Pasture Rd 27801
Green Ridge Ln 27804
Green Tee Ln 27804
Green Valley Ln 27804
Greenbriar Dr 27804
Greenfield Dr 27804
Greenleaf St 27803
Greenwood Ave 27804
Gregg Ct 27803
Greys Mill Ct & Rd 27804
Greyson Grv & Rd 27804
Greystone Dr 27804
Griffin St 27803
Grove Dr & Ln 27804
Guardian Ct 27804
Gulftide Ct 27801
Gwen St 27803
E & W Gypsy Trl 27803
Habersham Ct 27804
Hackberry Dr 27804
Hackney Rd 27804
Haggerty Trl 27803
N Halifax Rd 27804
S Halifax Rd
200-699 27804
700-8499 27803
Halifax St 27801
Hammond St
100-999 27804
1000-1899 27803
Hampton Ct 27803
Hampton Dr 27803
W Hampton Dr 27804
Hannah Ln 27803
Hansford Dr 27803
Happy Valley Ln 27804
Harbour West Dr 27803
Hargrove St 27801
Harlon Dr 27804
Harmingdale Ln 27804
Harper St 27801
Harper Farm Ln 27801
Harraler Rd 27803
N & S Harris St 27804
Harrison Dr 27804
Harrisontown Rd 27804
Harvey Dr 27803
W Haven Blvd 27803
Hawthorne Rd 27804
Hayfield Ct 27804
Haywood Dr 27803
Hazelwood Dr 27803
Health Dr 27804
Hearthstone Ct 27803
Heather Ln 27803
Heffner Rd 27803
Helms St 27804
Hemlock Ct 27804
Hendricks St 27801
Henna St 27801
Henry St 27803
Hermitage Rd 27804
Herraler Rd 27803
Herron St 27803
Hickory Ct & St 27804
High St 27803
E Highland Ave 27801
W Highland Ave 27804
Hill St 27801
Hillandale Way 27804
Hillandale Trailer Park .. 27803
Hillcrest St 27804
Hillsdale Dr 27801
Hillside Ct 27804
Hinton Rd 27803
Hinton Crest Ln 27801
Hodge Haven Trl 27801
Holleyfield 27801
Holly Dr 27803
E Holly St 27801
Home St 27803
Home Depot Plz 27804
Homestead Ct & Rd 27804
Honeysuckle Ln 27804
N & S Hornbeam Dr ... 27804
Horne St 27804
Horsepen Rd 27804
Horseshoe Dr 27804
Howard St 27804
Howard Avenue Ext 27801
N Howell St 27804
S Howell St
100-599 27804
600-899 27803
Hoylake 27804
Hubbard Ln 27801
Hudson St 27803
E Hudson St 27801
Huffines Ave 27804
Hummingbird Ln 27804
Humphrey Dr 27801
Hunter Ln 27803
Hunter St 27801
Hunter Hill Rd 27804
Hunter Ridge Ct & Rd .. 27803
Hunterbrook Ln 27804
Hunting Lodge Dr 27801
Huntington Ct 27803
Huntington Trailer
Park 27803
Hurt Dr 27804
Hyatt Way 27804
Hycliff Rd 27803
Independence Dr 27804
Indian Branch Rd 27804
Instrument Dr 27804
Irene Ct & Ln 27804
Iron Horse Rd 27803
Irwin Isle 27803
Irwin Isle Rd 27803
Isabella Ln 27804
Island Ct 27804
Ivy Ln & St 27801
Jackson St 27803

Street	ZIP
Jackson Walk	27801
Jacobs Ave & St	27804
Jake Ln	27801
James St	27803
Jarrett Dr	27803
Jasmine Dr	27804
Jason Ct & Dr	27803
Jasper St	27803
Jefferson St	27804
Jeffreys Ct	27804
Jeffreys Ln	27801
Jeffreys Rd	27804
Jeffries Cv	27804
Jenkins Farm Rd	27801
Jennifer Ct	27803
Jennifer Ln	27801
Jennings Ct	27803
Jeremy Ln	27803
Jesse Ln	27801
Jessica Ln	27801
Jessica Way	27803
Jimmie Ln	27801
Joelene Ct & Dr	27803
John Arthur Ln	27803
Johnson St	27801
Jones Rd	27804
Jordan Rd	27803
Jordan St	27801
Joseph Ln	27801
Joshua Clay Dr	27803
Joyner Rd	27803
Jubilee	27804
Judge St	27803
Julian Ct	27803
Juniper Ct	27804
Justin Ct	27804
Kaitlin Rd	27803
Kaitlyn Ln	27801
Kamlar Rd	27804
Kandemor Ln	27804
Karen Pl	27801
Kasey Ln	27801
Kasey Way	27803
Katherine Trl	27804
Katie Dr	27803
Keen St	27804
Kelly Ln	27801
Kennedy Cir & Ln	27801
Kent Ct & Dr	27804
Kentucky Ave	27803
Kenwood St	27801
Ketch Point Ct & Dr	27803
Killebrew Ln	27801
Killian Ct	27804
Kimberly Dr	27803
Kimberly Jo Dr	27804
Kinchen Dr	27803
King Cir	27801
N & S King Charles Ct	27803
N & S King Edward Ct	27803
N & S King Henry Ct	27803
N King James Ct	27803
N & S King Richard Ct	27803
Kingsboro Rd	27801
Kingston Ave	27803
Kingswood Mobile Home Park	27803
Kinlaw Ct	27803
Kirby Dr	27804
N & S Kirkwood Ave & Pl	27801
Kitty Ln	27801
Knight Ct	27801
Krista Ln	27803
Lacy Ln	27804
Ladybank	27804
Lafayette Ave & Cir	27803
E Lake Rd	27804
Lake Pointe Trl	27804
Lake Shore Dr	27801
Lake View Farm Ln	27804
Lake Vista Ct	27803
Lakeshore Mobile Park	27801
Lambert Ln	27804
Lancaster St	27801
Lancastershire Ct	27803
Lance Dozier Ln	27801
Landaus Ln	27804
Lane Ct	27804
Langley Rd	27803
Langwood Way	27803
Lansdowne Rd	27804
Lanwood Ln	27801
Lark Ln	27803
Larry Ln	27801
Larson Ln	27803
Laurel Ave	27803
Laurel Ct	27801
Laurel Trail Rd	27804
Lauren Dr	27804
Laurie Dr	27803
Lawrence Cir	27804
Layola Ave	27804
Lazy Oaks Ct	27804
Leaston Rd	27803
N & S Lee St	27804
Lee Roy Ln	27801
Legacy Dr	27804
Leggett Rd	27801
Leigh Ct & Rd	27803
Leighton Dr	27803
Lenoir Dr	27801
Leona Ln	27803
Leonard St	27803
Leslie Ln	27801
Lessie Trl	27804
Lewis St	27804
Lewy Ln	27801
Lexington St	27801
Lib And Johnnie Ln	27801
Liberty Ln	
100-199	27801
1000-1099	27804
Liberty St	27803
Ligustrum Ct	27801
Lily Walk	27804
Limestone Ln	27801
Lincoln Dr	27801
Linda Ln	27801
Linda Way	27804
Linden Ave & Pl	27801
Lindsey St	27803
Liriope Dr	27801
Lisa Ct	27803
Litchfield Ct & Dr	27803
Little Aston	27804
Little Falls Dr	27801
Live Oaks Trl	27804
Liverpool	27804
Living Stone Dr	27804
Loblolly Dr	27804
Loch Ct	27804
Lochinvar Ln	27804
Lochmere Bay Dr	27803
Lockewood Ct	27804
Loftin Dr	27804
Logan Ln	27801
Logan Trl	27803
Lois Ln	27803
Lone Oak Ln	27801
Long Ave	27801
Longleaf Rd	27804
Loop Ct	27801
Loretta Ln	27801
Lothian	27804
Lottie Ln	27801
Loveless Ln	27804
Lucas Cir	27801
Lucy Rose Ln	27801
Luper St	27803
Luther Ln	27803
Lynne Ave & Ct	27801
Lynnhaden Dr	27803
Macon Rd	27804
Madison St	27801
Magnolia Dr	27801
E Main St	27803
NE Main St	27801
NW Main St	27804
S Main St	27803
SE Main St	27801
SW Main St	
100-399	27804
1100-2300	27803
2302-2498	27803
2500-2599	27801
W Main St	27803
Maize Ct	27801
Malcolm Ln	27801
Malibu Ct	27804
Mallard Ct	27804
Mallory St	27801
Mamas Run Ln	27804
Manchester Ct	27803
Manning Ct	27803
Mansfield Dr	
3400-3699	27803
3800-3899	27804
Mansil Dr	27804
E Maple Ct	27804
W Maple Ct	27804
Maple St	27803
Maple Creek Dr	27803
Maplefield Ln	27801
Mapleton Dr	27803
Maranatha Dr	27804
Marble Ct	27803
Marcus Way	27803
Mare Ct	27804
Marigold St	27801
Market St	27804
Marlboro Pl	27803
Marlee Dr	27801
Marshall Ln	27801
Marshland Rd	27803
Martin Dr	27804
Martin Luther King Dr	27801
Martin Sasser Dr	27801
Marvelle Ave	27803
Mary Ln	27803
Marys Ln	27803
Mashie Ct & Ln	27804
Matie Rd	27803
Matthews St	27801
Maude Rd	27801
May Dr	27804
May Belle Ln	27801
Maybell Ln	27801
Mayfair Dr	
100-599	27804
600-899	27803
N & S Mayo St	27801
Mcdearman St	27804
Mcdonald St	27804
Mcduffers Rd	27804
Mcintyre Ln	27804
Mckendree Church Rd	27801
Mckinzie Ln	27801
Meadowbrook Rd	27801
Meadowview Ln	27804
Medlin Way	27803
Medpark Dr	27804
Melissa Dr	27801
Melrose Pl	27803
Melton Dr	27804
Melton Rd	27801
Melvin Ln	27803
Memory Ln	27804
N & S Mercer St	27801
Meredith Ct	27804
Merganser Cv	27804
Merrifield Ct & Rd	27804
Michael Scott Dr	27803
Middle St	27804
Middleton Rd	27804
Midway St	27801
Milby Ct	27804
Milestone Ct	27801
Mill St	27804
Mill Branch Rd	27803
Millbrook Way	27804
Miller Pl	27803
Milliefield Ln	27803
Millinium Ct	27801
Mills Ln	27801
Minges St	27804
Minnie Knight Ln	27801
Mitchell St	27801
Mno Ln	27801
Mobile Dr	27804
Mobile City Trailer Park	27801
Mockingbird Ln	27804
Modern Mobile Park	27803
Modlin Ave	27804
Montrose	27804
Moore St	27801
Morgan St	27804
N & S Moring Ave	27801
Morning Glory Way	27804
Morning Star Ct	27804
Morningside Ln	27804
Morris Ct & Rd	27803
Morris Trailer Park	27803
Moses Way	27801
Mosley Ct & Dr	27804
Moss Creek Way	27804
Mount Dr & Rd	27803
Moye Ct	27803
Mullins St	27803
Munn St	27803
Muscadine Rd	27804
Myers Rd	27801
Myrtle Ave	27801
Nairn	27804
Nance St	27803
Nancy Taylor Ln	27801
Nancys Cir	27804
Nancys Way	27803
Nandina Ct	27801
Nash St	27804
Nash Central High Rd	27804
Nash Medical Arts Mall	27804
Nashville Rd	27803
Nc Highway 43 N	27801
Nc Highway 97 W	27801
E Nc Highway 97	27803
Neal St	27803
Nelms Ln	27801
Nelson St	27803
Netherwood Rd	27803
Neville Ln	27801
New St	27803
New Castle Ct	27803
New Haven Ln	27804
Newby Ct & Rd	27804
Niblick Dr	27804
Nichole Ln	27803
Nichols Dr	27804
Nicodemus Mile	27804
No Record St	27803
Nobles Mill Pond Rd	27801
Noell Ln	27804
Noell Rd	27803
Nokes Mill Rd	27801
Nora Ln	27801
Norcrest Ct	27804
Norfolk St	27801
Norris Ave	27803
North St	27804
Northern Blvd	27804
Northern Estates Cir	27804
Northern Hills Dr	27804
Northern Nash Rd	27804
Northgreen Ln	27804
Northridge Dr	27804
Northstar Ct	27804
Northwood Dr	27804
Norwood Ln	27801
Nottingham Ct & Rd	27803
Nucar	27804
Nugent St	27801
Nutrition St	27801
O Berry St	27803
Oak St	27801
Oak Bend Rd	27804
Oak Forest Dr	27803
Oak Grove Rd	27804
Oak Leaf Dr	27804
Oak Leaf Ln	27803
Oak Level Rd	
1700-3699	27804
3800-5899	27803
Oakdale Rd	27804
Oakey St	27803
Oakland Ave	27804
Oakton Ln	27801
N & S Oakwood Dr	27801
Octavia Dr	27804
Old Barn Ct	27801
Old Barn Ln	27804
Old Barn Rd	27804
Old Battleboro Rd	27801
Old Carriage Rd	27804
N Old Carriage Rd	27804
S Old Carriage Rd	
100-1799	27804
2200-8599	27803
Old Coach Rd	27804
Old Colony Way	27804
Old Farm Rd	27801
Old Forge Rd	27804
Old Joyner Ln	27803
Old Mill Rd	
1-499	27803
500-599	27804
600-2999	27803
Old Sparta Rd	27804
E Old Spring Hope Rd	27804
Old Wilson Rd	27801
Olde Bass Farm Rd	27804
Olde Bay Ct	27803
Olive St	27801
Ollie Way	27804
Opossum Trot Ct & Ln	27804
Orange St	27801
Orchard Ct	27804
Otis Ln	27801
Ottermount Ct	27804
Outback Ln	27801
Overbrook Dr	27801
Overlook Dr	27803
Overton Ct & Dr	27804
Pamela Ln	27803
Panmure	27804
Parham St	27803
Park Ave	27801
Park Pl	27804
N Parker St	27801
Parkridge Ct & Rd	27804
Parrish Ct & St	27801
Parsons Park Dr	27801
Patrick Ct	27804
Patriotic Ln	27801
Patterson Dr	27804
Paul Ct & St	27803
Payne Ct	27801
Peace Ln	27801
Peachtree St	27804
Pear Tree Rd	27804
N Pearl St	27804
S Pearl St	
100-599	27804
600-899	27803
Pearlie Ln	27801
Peastrai Rd	27804
Pebble Brook Ct & Way	27804
Peebles Dr	27801
Peele Rd	27804
Peggy Ct	27803
Pelham Rd	27804
Pender St	27801
Penelo Farm Ln	27801
Pennsylvania Ave	27801
Pepper Ln	27801
Peppermill Ct & Way	27804
Periwinkle Pl	27804
Peter St	27803
Petty Ct	27803
Pheasant Ct	27804
Phillips Rd	27801
Photinia Ct	27801
Pickwick Ct	27801
Picturesque Trl	27803
Piedmont Ave	
100-199	27804
200-799	27803
N Pine St	27804
S Pine St	
100-299	27804
500-899	27803
Pine Knoll Dr	27804
Pine Needle Mobile Park	27803
Pine Terrace Dr	27804
Pine Tree Ln	27804
Pinecrest Rd	27803
Pinefield Dr	27804
Pinehaven Dr	27803
Pinehurst Dr	27801
N Pineview St	27801
Pinewood Ave	27804
Pinewood Trl	27803
Pintail Ln	27804
Pitt Rd & St	27801
Pittman St	27804
Planters St	27801
Pleasant Hill Rd	27801
Pleasonton Ln	27801
Plum Pl	27804
Plymouth Rd	27804
Pointe Ln	27803
Pole Cat Ln	27803
Polly Jones Ct	27804
Pond View Ct	27801
Pondview Ct	27804
Pope St	27804
Poplar Ct & St	27804
Poplar Ridge Ct	27803
Porter Rd	27803
Portland	27804
Positive Way	27801
Postal Dr	27804
Potter Clay Ct	27804
Powell Dr	27803
Powell Rd	27801
Preacher Joyner Rd	27803
Prescott Ln	27803
Preston Ct	27804
Price Ln	27804
Pridgen Rd	27803
Primrose Pl	27804
Privettes Hedge Rd	27801
Proctor St	27801
Professional Dr	27804
Progress Dr	27804
Providence Rd	27803
Province Cir	27804
Pumpkin St	27801
Quail Ct	27803
Quail Haven Rd	27804
Quarry Ln	27803
Queens Ct	27801
Rabbit Run Rd	27801
Rabbits Trce	27804
Raccoon Branch Rd	27804
Rainbow Ct	27801
Rainbow Ln	27804
Rainbow Trl	27801
E Raleigh Blvd	
200-400	27801
327-327	27802
327-327	27803
401-1899	27801
402-1898	27801
W Raleigh Blvd	27803
Raleigh Rd	27803
N Raleigh St	27801
S Raleigh St	27801
Ramsey Ln	27804
Randy Ln	27803
Raper Dr	27804
Ravenwood Dr	27803
Raymond St	27804
Reas Ln	27803
Red Barn Ln	27801
Red Iron Rd	27804
Red Maple Ct	27804
Red Oak Blvd	27804
Red Oak Ln	27801
Red Rose Ln	27801
Redgate Ave	27801
Redman Rd	27803
Reece Rd	27804
Reedy Branch Rd	27803
Regis Store Rd	27804
Remington Dr	27804
Renfrow St	27803
Rex St	27801
Rick St	27803
Ricks St	27804
E & W Ridge St	27804
Ridgecrest Dr	27803
Ridgemeadow Ln	27803
Ridgewood Dr	27803
River Dr	27804
River Farm Rd	27803
River Glenn Ct & Rd	27803
River Run Rd	27801
River Walk Dr	27803
Rivera Dr	27803
Riverbirch Rd	27803
Ro Bren Do Trailer Park	27803
Robbiewood Ln	27803
Robbins Ave & Rd	27803
Roberson Ln	27804
Robert Ave	27801
Robert Ryan Ct & Rd	27803
Robert Thompson Dr	27801
Robindale Ln	27801
Rock Creek Ct & Dr	27804
Rock Quarry Rd	27803
Rockaway Ct	27804
Rocking Horse Ln	27803
Rockwater Ct	27803
Rocky St	27803
Rolling Rock Rd	27803
Rollinwood Dr & Mnr	27801
Romie Ln	27801
Rons Country Ln	27804
Rooks Ln	27803
Rosa St	27803
Rosalie Ln	27804
Roscoe Ln	27803
Rose St	27801
Rosebud Dr	27804
Rosedale Ave	27804
Rosemont	27804
Rosewood Ave	27801
Roundabout Ct	27804
Roundtree Dr	27804
Rouse Rd	27801
Rowe Dr	27804
Royal St	27804
Royal Ridge Ct & Dr	27804
Ru Bob Ln	27801
Rum Barrell Cv	27804
Russell St	27803
Rustys Ln	27801
Ryals St	27801
Saddle Run Ct	27804
Saddlehorn Dr	27803
Saint Catherines Walk	27804
Saint Christophers Walk	27804
Saint Francis Ct	27801
Saint James Pointe Rd	27804
Saint John St	27803
Saint Marys Walk	27804
Saint Paul St	27803
Salem Ct	27804
Salisbury Dr	27801
Sand Stone Dr	27803
Sand Trap Dr	27804
Sandberg Ln	27803
Sanders Dr	27801
Sandona Cir	27801
Sandstone Ct	27803
Sandy Ln	27803
Sandy Hill Ct	27803
Sandy Knob Ct & Ln	27803
Sapphire Rd	27804
Sarah Ln	27801
Sarah Way	27803

Saw Mill Rd 27801
Sawgrass Rd 27804
Sawmill Ln 27803
Scarborough Ln 27804
School St
700-899 27801
8600-9099 27803
Scott Ct 27803
Scott St 27801
Sebastian Way 27804
Sector Pl 27804
Sedgefield Dr 27804
Seminole Dr 27804
Sexton Rd 27804
Shadwell Ct 27803
Shady Circle Dr 27803
Shamrock Ct & Ln 27804
Shannon Ct 27804
Sharpe Rd 27803
Shawn Ct 27804
Shearin St 27801
Shearin Andrew Rd 27804
Sheenas Ln 27803
Sheffield Dr 27803
Shellcastle Rd 27804
Shelly Dr 27804
Shenandoah Ct & Rd 27803
Shepard Dr 27801
Sherwood Dr 27804
Sheryl Ln 27801
Shire Ln 27804
Shirley Leak Ave 27801
Shore Dr 27801
Shorewood Ln 27801
Short St 27801
Short Spoon Cir 27804
Shreve Rd 27801
Sides Ln 27801
Silverleaf Rd 27804
Simmons St 27804
Singer Rd 27804
Singletree Ln 27804
Sion Ct 27803
Sipe Rd 27801
Sled Ct 27803
Smallwood Dr 27804
Smith St 27803
Smokey Rd 27804
Somerset Way 27804
Sonnys Ln 27803
Sophia Ln 27803
Sorsbys Aly 27804
South St 27804
Southall Ct 27804
Southbriar Dr 27804
Southbrook Rd 27804
Southern Blvd 27804
Southgate Rd 27803
Southlake Dr 27803
Southpark Village Ct & Dr 27803
Southwick Ct 27804
Sparrow Hawk Ln 27804
Spaulding Dr 27801
Speight Dr 27803
Speights Pond Ln 27801
Spencer Cockrell Rd 27803
Spinnaker Cv 27804
Sportsmans Trl 27804
E & W Spring St 27804
Spring Field Rd 27804
Spring Forest Ct & Dr 27803
Spring Glenn Ct 27803
Spring Haven Rd 27804
Spring Mill Trail Rd 27804
Springbrook Dr 27801
S Springfield Rd 27801
Spruce Ct 27804
Spruce St 27801
Stallion Rd 27804
Stancil Dr 27801
Stanley Park Dr 27804
Star Pl & St 27804
Starling Way 27803
Steeple Chase Rd 27804
Stephen Ln 27803
Steven Dr 27801
Stewart Ct & Ln 27803
Still Pond Ln 27803
Stillbrook Ct 27804
Stillmeadow Ln 27801
Stillwater Dr 27804
Stockbridge Cir 27804
Stokes St 27801
Stone Dr 27804
Stone Rose Dr 27804
Stoneridge Ln 27804
Stony Creek Dr 27804
Stonybrook Rd 27804
Storage Rd 27804
Stratford Dr & Rd 27801
Strawbush Rd 27804
Suburb St 27801
Success Ct 27804
Sugar Creek Rd 27804
Sullivan Ln 27804
Summer Ln 27801
Summerfield Ln 27801
Summerlea Pl 27804
Summerwalk Rd 27804
Summerwinds Ln 27803
Sunflower Rd 27804
Sunrise Ln 27803
Sunset Ave & Dr 27804
Sunset Harbour Ln 27803
Sunshine Dr 27804
Sunshine Ln 27801
Surrey Ct 27804
Susan Ln 27801
Sutters Creek Blvd 27804
Sutton Rd 27801
Swanson Ct 27801
Sweet Bay Rd 27804
Swift Rd 27801
Sycamore St 27801
Tabernacle Church Rd 27803
Tadlock Ave 27801
Talbott Dr 27803
Tam O Shanter Dr 27804
Tanglewood Rd 27804
Tanner Rd 27801
Tar Island Dr 27803
Tar River Cove Dr 27803
Tarboro Hwy 27801
E Tarboro Rd 27801
W Tarboro Rd 27803
Tarboro St 27801
Tarrytown Ctr 27804
Tartan Ln 27803
Taswell Dr 27804
Tavern Lndg 27804
Tay Riv 27804
Taylor Dr 27803
N Taylor St 27804
S Taylor St
100-299 27804
300-799 27803
Taylor Woods Cir 27803
Teal Ct 27804
Temperance Hall Rd 27801
Temple Pl 27803
Terri Wood Dr 27803
Terriwood Dr 27803
Tessie St 27801
Tharrington Rd 27804
The Oaks 27804
Thomas Rd
1-1299 27801
8800-9299 27803
E Thomas St 27801
W Thomas St 27804
Thomas A Betts Pkwy 27804
Thorne Rd 27801
Thorne Ridge Cir 27801
Thorne Town Rd 27801
Thorpe Rd 27804
Thru St 27801
Thunder Rd 27804
Tiffany Blvd 27804
N Tillery St 27804
S Tillery St
100-499 27804
500-899 27803
Timber Creek Dr 27804
Timberlane Dr 27804
Tims Rd 27803
Tobacco Rd 27801
Toddsberry Rd 27804
Toisnot Rd 27803
Toms Trl 27804
Tony Cir 27801
Topaz Ave 27801
Tower Ln 27801
E Tower Ln 27804
W Tower Ln 27804
Town Creek Rd 27803
Town Hall Rd 27804
Tracy Way 27803
Trailside Ln 27801
Trailwood Dr 27804
Tralee 27804
Trap Range Rd 27801
Travis Run 27804
Treefield Ct 27804
Treetop Ln 27804
Trevathan St 27804
Triple Ct 27801
Trudy Ln 27801
Tucker Trl 27804
Turkey Foot Rd 27804
Turnberry 27804
Turnip St 27803
Turnstone Dr 27803
Turtle Rock Ct 27803
Tyan St 27801
Tyler Dr 27804
Tyler Ln 27803
Tyson Ave 27804
Union St 27803
S Us Highway 301 27803
Us Highway 64 Alt W 27801
N & S Valley Ct 27804
Vance St 27801
Vans Dr 27801
Varnell Ln 27801
Ventura Dr 27804
Vernon Rd 27801
Vestal Rd 27801
Veterans Cir 27801
Vick Ln 27803
Vickers Rd 27803
Vicks Joyner Ln 27803
Victory Ave & Ct 27801
Villa St
200-699 27804
700-799 27803
Village Rd 27804
Vineyard Ct 27803
E Virginia St 27801
W Virginia St 27804
Virginia Way 27804
N Vyne St 27804
S Vyne St
100-299 27804
500-699 27803
Wagon Wheel Rd 27804
Wake St 27801
Walbrook Ct 27804
Walley St 27803
Wallhaven Ln 27803
Walnut St 27801
Walton Cir 27801
Waltrip St 27803
Ward Dr 27803
Warren St 27801
Warrington Ct 27803
N & S Washington Pl & St 27801
Water Front Dr 27803
Waterford Ln 27804
Waterloo Ct & Dr 27804
Waters Edge Dr 27803
Watsons Cove Rd 27803
Waverly Dr 27803
Wayfarer Ct 27801
Wayne St 27804
Weatherstone Dr 27804
Weathervane Way 27803
Weathervane Hill Dr 27803
Weaver Dr 27803
Weax Parker Ln 27803
Weldon Ave 27804
Welford Ln 27801
Wellington Ct & Dr 27803
Wells Ln 27801
N Wesleyan Blvd 27804
S Wesleyan Blvd
100-399 27804
400-3599 27803
Westburg Ln 27803
Westbury Ln 27803
Western Ave 27804
Westfield Ct 27803
Westminster Dr & Ln 27803
Westmoreland Dr 27804
Westover Ct 27803
Westridge Circle Dr 27804
Westry Rd 27804
Westview Park Dr 27804
Westwood Dr 27803
Whatley Dr 27801
Whetstone Ct 27804
Whispering Pine Dr 27804
Whitaker Rd 27801
Whitby Ct 27804
White Oak Rd 27803
White Owl Ln 27803
Whitehall Dr 27804
Whitehead Dr 27801
Whitfield Ave 27801
Whitley Circle Way 27803
Wiggins Lake Dr 27801
Wiggins Lake Mobile Park 27801
Wildberry Ct & Dr 27804
Wildlife Dr 27803
Wildwood Ave 27803
Wiley Acre Ln 27801
Wilkeshire Rd 27804
Wilkins St 27803
Wilkinson St 27804
Willard Ln & St 27803
William Ct 27803
Williams Mobile Home Est 27803
Williford Rd & St 27803
Willow St 27804
Willow Glynn Rd 27804
Willow Oaks Ct 27804
Willowby St 27803
Wimberly Ave 27804
Winchester Rd 27804
Wind Chime Ct 27803
Windchase Dr 27803
Windchase Pointe Ct 27803
Windchime Ct 27804
Windcrest Ln 27801
Winders Crk 27804
Windmere Ct 27803
Windsong Way 27803
Windsor Dr 27801
N Winstead Ave 27804
S Winstead Ave
100-499 27804
800-1799 27803
Winstead Rd 27804
Winstead Mobile Park 27801
Winston Walk 27803
Winterberry Dr 27804
Wintergreen Ct 27801
Winterhaven Dr 27803
Wisteria Dr 27804
Wits End Ln 27801
Wood Duck Dr 27804
Wood Duck Ln 27803
Woodbrook Dr 27804
Woodbury Dr 27801
Woodcrest Rd 27804
Woodland Ave 27801
Woodlawn Rd 27804
Woodleaf Cir 27803
Woodridge Ct 27804
Woodruff Rd 27804
Woods Walk Ln & Way 27804
Woodstock Rd 27803
Wooten Cir 27801
Worksop 27804
Worsley Rd 27801
Wren Ave 27804
Wye St 27801
Wynn Dr 27801
Wythe Way 27804
Yellow Rose Ln 27801
York St 27803
Yorkshire Ln 27803
Z St 27803
Zebulon Ct & Rd 27804
Zinnia Ct 27801

NUMBERED STREETS

All Street Addresses 27804

ROXBORO NC

General Delivery 27573

POST OFFICE BOXES MAIN OFFICE STATIONS AND BRANCHES

Box No.s
All PO Boxes 27573

RURAL ROUTES

01, 02, 03, 04, 05, 06, 07 27574

NAMED STREETS

Abbitt St 27573
Academy St 27573
Acey Reaves Rd 27573
Adams Farm Rd 27574
Admirals Dr 27574
Aintree Ln 27574
Alfred Palmer Ln 27574
Alleghany Dr 27573
Allens Chapel Church Rd 27574
Allensville Rd 27574
Allgood St 27573
Allie Clay Rd 27573
Allie Sidney Rd 27574
Allyson Ln 27574
Alva Oakley Rd 27574
Amethia Dr 27574
Amy Ln 27574
Anderbrock Dr 27573
Anderson Rd 27573
Anderson Jones Rd 27574
Anglers Way 27574
Anglers Cove Ct 27574
Annie Bell Ln 27574
Appaloosa Trl 27574
Apple Tree Ln 27574
Archie Clayton Rd 27574
Arrowood Dr 27573
Austyn Ave 27573
Autumn Dr 27573
Azalea Ave 27573
Badger Cir 27573
Baird Ct 27574
Banbury Ct & Dr 27573
Bannies Rd 27574
Barden Pl & St 27573
Barkwood Dr 27574
Barnette Ave 27573
Barnette Tingen Rd 27574
Batha Dr 27573
Bb Newell Dr 27573
Beacon St 27573
Beagle Rd 27574
Bear Run Ln 27574
Bearcreek Trl 27574
Beaver Creek Pkwy 27574
Beaver Crossing Rd 27574
Bedford Gentry Ln 27574
Benjamin Ct 27573
Berryhill Rd 27574
Bessie Daniel Rd 27574
Bethel Hill School Rd 27574
Billy Hicks Rd 27574
Blackard Rd 27574
Blalock Dairy Rd 27574
Blue Heron Ln 27574
Blue Wing Rd 27574
Bonnie Blue Ln 27574
Booth St 27573
Border Rdg 27574
Boston Rd
1900-4699 27573
4700-12099 27574
Boulder Ct 27574
Bowes Shotwell Rd 27574
Bowling Rd 27574
Bowmantown Rd 27574
Boyd Rogers Rd 27574
Bradsher Rd 27574
Brann Ln 27573
Brann Farm Rd 27574
Brater St 27573
Bravett Cir 27574
Breckenridge St 27573
Breeze Trl 27574
Brentwood Ct 27573
Bretts Trl 27573
Brian Ct 27574
S Bridalet Trl 27573
Brightleaf Ct 27574
Brittany Ln 27573
Broad Rd & St 27573
Brocks Ct 27573
Brook St 27573
Brookland Church Rd 27573
Brooks Car Dr 27573
Brooks Dairy Rd 27574
Brookstone Ln 27573
Brookwood Ter 27573
Brothers Dr 27574
Brunswick Ln 27573
Bry Chris Rd 27574
Bryce St 27573
Bryee St 27573
Buck Cash Rd 27574
Buck Street Rd 27574
Bucks Point Rd 27574
Bumpass Ln 27573
Burch Ave 27573
Burlington Rd
1-2199 27573
2200-6299 27574
Burlington Hall Rd 27573
Burton St 27573
Butcher Hollow Ln 27574
Butcher Place Rd 27574
Buttonwood Ln 27574
Bywood Dr 27573
Cadale St 27573
Caleb Epps Rd 27574
Calip Long Ln 27574
Cambridge Dr 27573
Canterbury Rd 27573
Captains Dr 27574
Cardinal Rd 27573
Carl Adcock Rd 27574
Carlyle Dr 27573
Carmichael Dr 27574
Carnaby Dr 27574
Carol Cropper Ln 27574
Carolina Ave 27574
Carr Farms Rd 27574
Carrington Ln 27573
Carter Ln 27574
Carver Dr
100-799 27573
900-1999 27574
Carver Farm Rd 27573
Carver Holt Rd 27574
Cates St 27573
Cates Mill Rd 27574
Cattle Dr 27574
Cavel Chub Lake Rd 27574
Cedar Grove Church Rd 27574
N & S Charles Cir & St 27573
Charlie Carr Rd 27574
Charlie Gentry Rd 27574
Charlie Jay Rd 27574
Charlie Stovall Rd 27574
Charlie Tapp Rd 27574
Charlie Winstead Rd 27574
Cherokee Ln 27574
Cheryl Cir 27574
Cheslies Ct 27574
Chestnut St 27573
Chris Tingen Rd 27574
Christopher Way 27574
Christys Way 27574
Chub Lake Rd
700-1099 27573
1100-4799 27574
Chub Lake St 27573
Chub Lake Loop Rd 27574
Church St 27573
City Lake Rd 27574
Claude Hall Rd 27574
Clay Rd 27573
Clay Thomas Rd 27573
Clayton Ave & St 27573
Clayton Glenn Rd 27574
Clayton Hollow Rd 27574
Clearwater Dr 27574
Cleotes Lawson Ln 27574
Cleveland Ln 27573
Club House Rd 27574
Cobblestone Ln 27573
Cody St 27573
Coleman Rd 27574
College Dr 27574
Collin Dr 27574
Colonial Estate Rd 27574
Commerce Dr 27573
Community House Rd 27574
Community Vale Rd 27573
Concord Rd 27573
Concord Ceffo Rd 27574
Concord Church Rd 27574
Coney Pine Ave 27574
Copper Rd 27574
Copper Ridge Ln 27574
Country Hls 27574
Country Brooke Ln 27574
Country Club Rd 27574
Country Side Dr 27574
Court St 27573
Coy Monk Rd 27574
Creek View Ln 27574
Crestwood Dr 27573
Critcher Wilkerson Rd 27573
Croper Rd 27574
Crowder Farm Rd 27574
Culpepper Ln 27574
D Hay Burrell Stewart Rd 27574
Dairyland Rd 27574
Daisy Thompson Rd 27574
Dale St 27573
Dan Winstead Rd 27574
Dancy Day Rd 27574
Daniel Ridge Ln 27574
Danwin Ln 27573
David Ln 27573
Davis Dr 27573
Dean Ln 27574
Decoy Dr 27574
Dee Long Rd 27574
Dee Yancey Rd 27574
Deep Woods Trl 27574
Delta Dr 27573
Denada Path 27574
Dennis Torain Rd 27574
Denny Cates Ln 27574

Dennys Store Rd 27574
Depot St 27573
Dickens St 27573
Dickey Dr 27574
Dirgie Mine Rd 27574
Divine View Ln 27573
Dixon Ln 27574
Doctors Ct 27573
Dogwood Ln 27573
Dolly St 27573
Dorothy Brooks Ln 27574
Dorrance Ct 27574
Dorsey Day Rd 27574
Doug St 27573
Dove Ln 27574
Dover St 27573
Duck Pointe Dr 27574
Duke Ln 27574
Duncan Dr 27573
Duncan Rd 27574
Durham Rd
700-3799 27573
3800-5699 27574
Dustin Ln 27574
Dylan St 27574
Eagle Place Dr 27573
Eastwood Long Ln 27574
Ec Cousin Rd 27574
Ed Lester Rd 27574
Eddie Hicks Rd 27574
Edgar St 27573
Edgemont Ave 27573
Edgewood Dr 27573
Edwards Dr 27573
Edwin Ct 27573
Edwin Robertson Rd 27574
Elizabeth Ct & St 27573
Ellen St 27573
Elliott Farms Rd 27574
Elm St 27573
Elmore St 27573
Elmwood Dr 27573
Emma Ct 27573
Enos Slaughter Rd 27574
Epps Martin Rd 27574
Esther Rd 27573
Eugene Faison Memorial Rd 27574
Evans Reagan Rd 27574
Evelyn Day Rd 27574
Everett Ave 27574
Evergreen Dr 27574
Executive Ln 27573
Fair Oaks Dr 27574
Fairway Dr 27574
Falcons Rest Dr 27574
Fannie Jones Rd 27574
Farm House Rd 27574
Faulkner Long Rd 27574
Fiddlers Rd 27574
Fiddlers Run Rd 27574
Fieldstone Rd 27574
Fifth Ave 27574
Fishermans Point Rd 27574
Flat River Church Rd 27574
Flem Clayton Rd 27574
Fontaine Rd 27574
Forest St 27573
Forest Creek Trl 27574
Forrestwood Dr 27573
Four Trailer Ct 27574
Fourth Ave 27573
N & S Foushee St 27573
Fox Ln 27574
Fox Crest Rd 27574
Fox Crossing Dr 27574
Frank St 27573
Frank Fox Rd 27573
Frank Oakley Rd 27573
Franklin St 27573
Friendly Dr 27573
Friendship Xing 27574
Front St 27573
Gabriel Jones Rd 27574
Garden Grove Rd 27574
Gardner Rd 27574
Garnet Dr 27573
Garrett St 27573
Garrison Rd 27574
Gates St 27573
Gates Worth Rd 27574
Geneva Cir 27574
Gentry St 27573
Gentry Dunkley Rd 27574
Gentry Massey Rd 27574
Gentry Ridge Rd 27574
George St 27573
Gillis Rd 27574
Gla Rd 27574
Glen Allen Ct 27574
Glendale Ln 27574
Glenview Dr 27574
Gm Robertson Rd 27574
Golden Leaf Ln 27574
Goldfinch Rd 27574
S & W Gordon St 27573
Gospel Ln 27574
Graham Dr 27573
Graham Day Rd 27574
Grandfather Oak Rd 27574
Granite Dr 27574
Grapevine Dr 27574
Graves Rd 27574
Gravitte Rd 27573
Green St
400-499 27573
2500-2599 27573
Green Meadow Ln 27574
Greentree Rd 27573
Gregory St 27573
Griesch Rd 27573
Griles St 27573
Gwinn Rd 27573
Hagers Ridge Rd 27574
Hal Melton Rd 27574
Halifax Rd
1-99 27574
100-2599 27573
2700-4599 27573
Hamlin Dr 27574
Hannah Ln 27574
Hard Rock Rd 27574
Hardwood Rd 27573
Hargrove Rd 27574
Harold Gill Rd 27574
Harrington Ln 27573
Harris St 27573
Harris Clayton Rd 27574
Harris Morris Rd 27574
Harry Turner Rd 27574
Hassel Clayton Rd 27574
Hawthorne Dr 27574
Haywood Bailey Rd 27574
Hazel Lawson Rd 27574
Heath Ln 27574
Henderson Rd 27573
Henderson Farm Rd 27574
Henry St 27573
Henry Long Rd 27574
Hensley Ave & Ln 27574
Heritage Rd 27574
Herman Oakley Rd 27574
Hess Perry Rd 27574
Hester St 27573
Hesters Store Rd 27574
Hickory Ct & St 27574
Hickory Leaf Ct 27573
Hicks Cir 27573
Hicks Yarboro Rd 27574
Hickson Rd 27574
Hidden Ln 27574
Hidden Hills Rd 27574
High St 27573
High Plains Rd 27574
High Plains School Rd 27574
High View Church Rd 27574
Hill St 27573
Hillcrest Ave 27573
Hillhaven Ter 27573
Hillsborough St 27573
Historic Village Rd 27574
Holloway Rd 27573
Holly St 27573
Holly Berry Ln 27574
Home Place Rd 27574
Homestead Rd 27573
Honeysuckle Ln 27573
Horseshoe Ct 27574
Houston Blalock Rd 27574
Huff Rd 27574
Huff Garrett Rd 27574
Hugh Blalock Rd 27574
Hugh Woods Rd 27574
Humphries Estate Rd 27574
Hurdle Mills Rd
1000-1399 27573
1400-6399 27573
Hutch Ln 27574
Industrial Dr
200-399 27573
700-899 27574
Ira Watson Ln 27574
Iris Ln 27573
Isaac Trl 27574
Ivey St 27573
Ivey Day Rd 27574
J B Ln 27574
J C Lunsford Rd 27574
J L Long Rd 27574
Jack Ln 27573
Jack Brann Rd 27574
Jack Crumpton Rd 27574
Jack Ford Rd 27574
Jack Hambrick Rd 27574
Jackson St 27573
Jackson Farm Rd 27574
James St 27573
James Clayton Rd 27574
James Long Rd 27573
James Mcghee Dr 27573
Jasper Clayton Rd 27574
Jaxson Ln 27574
Jean St 27573
Jeff Poole Rd 27574
Jefferson Dr 27573
Jesse Barrett 27573
Jessica Ln 27574
Jessie Banks Rd 27574
Jessie Hicks Rd 27574
Jeter Pritchett Woody Rd 27574
Jewel Wrenn Rd 27573
Jim Poole Rd 27574
Joe Mcghee Ln 27574
John St 27573
John Allen Rd 27574
John Brewer Rd 27574
John D Winstead Rd 27574
John Obie Rd 27574
John Wade Rd 27573
Johnny Palmer Rd 27574
Johnson St 27573
Jones St 27573
Jones Lester Rd 27574
Jones Paylor Rd 27574
Jones Store Rd 27574
Joy Ln 27574
Judith Lee Ln 27573
Jw Pulliam Rd 27574
Kappa Dr 27573
Katmandu Dr 27574
Kaylahs Path 27574
Kelly Carver Rd 27574
Kendrick Dr 27574
Kerr Dr 27573
Keyser Ln 27574
W King Rd 27574
Kinsman Trce 27574
Kirby St 27573
Kiser Hicks Rd 27574
Kitten Hill Rd 27574
Knolls Of Hyco 27574
Knolls Of Mayo Rd 27574
Kylasu Ln 27574
L And J Wrenn Rd 27574
Lack Dr 27573
Lacy Wilkerson Rd 27574
Lady Layne Dr 27574
Lake Dr 27573
Lake Shore Dr 27573
Lake Wood Dr 27573
S Lakewood Trl 27574
Lakewood Pointe Dr 27574
N & S Lamar St 27573
Lamberth St 27573
Landmark N 27574
Landmark South Dr 27573
Lankford St 27573
Larry Wrenn Rd 27574
Lasale Ave 27573
Latoma Dr 27574
Laura Ln 27573
Lawrence St 27573
Lawson Adcock Rd 27574
Lawson Chapel Church Rd 27574
Lawson Farm Rd 27574
Layne St 27573
Leasburg Rd
100-1199 27573
1200-7699 27574
Leb Oakley Rd 27574
Lee Ln & St 27573
Lee Chambers Rd 27574
Lester Rd 27574
Lester Burch Rd 27574
Lewis Winstead Loop Rd 27574
Lillian Ln 27573
Lily Lane Rd 27574
Lima Ln 27573
Lindsey Carver Rd 27574
Lions Dr 27573
Lisa Cheryl Ln 27573
Little Duck Ln 27573
Lochridge Dr 27573
Loftis Loop Rd 27574
Lonach Ln 27574
Lonerenn Rd 27574
Lonesome Oak Dr 27574
Long Ave 27573
Longhurst St 27573
Longs Store Rd 27574
Longwood Ter 27573
Lonnie Gentry Rd 27574
Lucy Garrett Rd 27574
Lunsford Knott Rd 27574
Lyle St 27573
Lyman Ln 27574
Lynn Dr 27574
Macbeth Ln 27574
Mackfieldson Rd 27574
N & S Madison Blvd 27573
Maggie Ln 27573
Magnolia Dr 27573
N & S Main Cir & St 27573
Manchester Dr 27573
Maple St 27573
Maple Ridge Rd 27574
Marandas Vw 27574
Marco Rd 27574
Margies Way 27573
Mariners Point Dr 27574
Marshalls Cv 27574
Martin St 27573
Martin Estates Rd 27574
Martin Hills Ln 27574
Marvin Gill Rd 27574
Maurice Daniels Rd 27574
Mayo Harbor Ln 27574
Mayo Lake Rd 27574
Mayoak Farm Rd 27574
Mccains Dr 27574
Mccoy Jeffers Dr 27574
Mcghees Mill Rd 27574
Mcmahon Faulkner Rd 27573
Meadowlands Pkwy 27574
Meadowwood Ct 27573
Megan Run 27574
Mellie Clayton Rd 27574
Melton Rd 27574
Melvin St 27573
Memorial Dr 27573
Merrill Hall Rd 27574
Merritt Pl 27573
Mica Ct 27573
Michael Jones Rd 27574
Mill Creek Rd 27574
Mill Hill Rd 27574
Mimosa Dr 27573
Miranda Ln 27574
Mollie Mooney Rd 27574
Mollys Place Rd 27574
Monroe St 27573
Montague Ave 27573
Montford Dr 27573
Montpelier Ave 27573
Moonshine Rdg 27574
S Moore Dr 27574
E & W Morehead St 27573
N & S Morgan St 27573
Morton Pulliam Rd 27574
Moss Creek Dr 27574
Mount Bethel Church Rd 27573
Mountain Rd 27574
Mountain View Rd 27573
Mullins Ln 27574
Munday Rd 27574
Murray Hazel Rd 27574
My Country Rd 27574
Nandina Dr 27573
Nannette Ln 27574
Natures Trail Ln 27574
Nc Highway 49 27574
Neals Store Rd 27574
Nelson Loop Rd 27574
New Country Rd 27574
New Mayo Dr 27574
Newell Dr & St 27573
Nichols Ave 27573
Nicole Dr 27574
Nirvana Rd 27574
No Record St 27574
Noah Davis Rd 27574
Nora Poole Rd 27574
Northpointe Dr 27574
Northside Vw 27574
Northwood Ct 27574
Novella Rd 27574
Oak St 27573
Oak Grove Rd 27574
Oak Grove Mount Zion Rd 27574
Oak Park Dr 27574
Oakdale Dr 27574
Oakwood Ln 27574
Obriant Miller Rd 27574
Obrien Dr 27574
Old Allensville Rd 27574
Old City Lake Rd 27574
Old Durham Rd 27573
Old Hickory Dr 27573
Old Mill Creek Rd 27574
Old Salem Rd 27574
Old Surl Rd 27574
Old Us 501 27574
Old Wagon Ln 27574
Ole Cabin Rd 27574
Olive Branch Rd 27574
Olive Crest Dr 27574
Oliver Loop Rd 27574
Omega Foushee Rd 27574
Outlaw Rd 27574
Overby Riley Rd 27574
Owens St 27573
Oxford Rd
1-1699 27573
1800-5099 27574
Painter Ln 27574
Painter-Hill Ln 27574
Palmer Ln 27574
Palmetto Dr 27574
Pappys Dr 27574
Paradise Rd 27574
Parham Rd 27574
Park Dr & St 27573
Parkview Cir 27573
Patterson Dr
1-599 27573
600-999 27574
Paul Tuck Farm Rd 27574
Paynes Tavern Rd 27574
Peace Rd 27573
Peaceful Rd 27573
Peachtree St 27573
Pearce St 27573
Peck Perry Rd 27573
Pepper Pot Pl 27574
Person Ct 27573
Personality Ln 27573
Peter Byrd Rd 27574
Pheasant Way 27574
Pin Oak Dr 27573
Pine St 27573
Pine Ridge Ct & Dr 27573
Piney Creek Dr 27574
Piney Forest Rd 27574
Piney Ridge Trl 27574
Plantation Dr 27574
Plum Tree Ln 27574
Poindexter Rd 27574
Point Sunset Trl 27574
Pointe Mayo Dr 27574
Pointer St 27573
Polk Huff Rd 27574
Ponderosa Trl 27574
Poplar Pl 27574
Poplar Lane Rd 27574
Portia Ln 27574
Prestige Ave 27573
Preston Pleasant Rd 27573
Primrose Ln 27573
Professional Dr 27573
Providence Rd 27573
Pulliam St 27573
Pulliam Boyd Rd 27573
Pulliam Tingen Mine Rd 27574
Puryear St 27573
Quail Creek Dr 27574
Quail Hollow Dr 27574
Quartergate Rd 27574
R T Hester Rd 27574
Rachael Ln 27573
Ralapen St 27573
Raney Crumpton Rd 27574
Ransome Slaughter Rd 27574
Raymond Lowery Dr 27574
Raymond Royster Rd 27574
Reade Dr 27573
Reams Ave 27573
Red Bud Ln 27574
Red Clay Rd 27573
Red Fox Ln 27574
Red Oak Ct & Dr 27573
Renee Dr 27573
Reuben Allen Rd 27574
Richland Rd 27574
Richmond Rd 27574
N Ridge Cir 27574
Ridge Rd 27573
Roach Dr 27573
Robert Norris Rd 27574
Robert Ramsey Rd 27574
Robert Reed Ln 27574
Robertson Rd 27574
Rock Farm Rd 27574
Rocky Way 27574
Rocky Mountain Rd 27574
Rocky Ridge Rd 27574
Rolling Creek Dr 27574
Rolling Hills Rd 27574
Romans Rd 27574
Rosemary Way 27574
Rosemary Creek Dr 27574
Roseville Loop Rd 27574
Rosewood Dr 27573
Roxboro St 27573
Roxdale Pl 27574
Roy Rogers Rd 27574
Royster Clay Rd 27574
Ruff Davis Rd 27574
Saddlebrook Rd 27574
Saint James Estates Dr 27573
Saint Paul Church Rd 27574
Saints Rd 27574
Sam Muldrow Rd 27573
Sand Trap Ln 27574
Sandstone Rd 27574
Sandstone Way 27573
Sandy Hill Rd 27574
Sappony Trl 27574
School St 27573
Schullers Point Dr 27574
Scotland Pl 27573
Scott Outlaw Rd 27574
Seamster Rd 27574
Semora Rd
1-699 27573
700-5999 27574
Service Rd 27574
Shady Hill Cir 27573
Shady Oak Rd 27574
Shale Cir 27573
Shelton Rd 27573
Shiloh Church Rd 27574
Shotwell Rd 27574
Shotwell St 27573
Sievers Cir 27573
Six Oaks Rd 27574
Sloan Rd 27574
Smith Hill Ln 27574
Snug Harbor Ct 27574
Solomon Ct 27573
Somerset Dr 27573
Somerset Church Rd 27573
South St 27573
Southern Middle School Rd 27573
Southern Village Dr 27573
Spencer Rd 27574
Sportsman Club Rd 27574
Spring Hill Rd 27574
Squirrel Hill Dr 27574
Squirrel Pathway 27574
Stagecoach Trl 27574
Stephens Dr 27573
Steve Long Rd 27574
Stewart St 27573
Stillwater Ln 27574
Stokes Dr 27573
Stonbraker Rd 27574
Stone Dr 27573
Stonegate Dr 27574
Stoneridge Ln 27574
Stories Creek Rd 27574
Stories Creek School Rd 27574
Streets Store Rd 27574
Sugar Bear Dr 27574
Sugartree Lndg 27574
Summer Ridge Rd 27573
Summitt St 27573
Sunnyvale Ln 27574
Sunset St 27573
Sweet Bay Ct 27574
Sycamore Rd 27574
Tall Oaks Dr 27573
Talley Loop Rd 27574
Tanglewood Cir 27573
Tatum Rd 27574
Tee Ct 27574
Thaxton Rd 27573
Thee Hester Rd 27574
Thomas Rd 27574
Thomas Green Rd 27574
Thomas Humphries Rd 27574
Thompson Rd 27573
Thorpe Subdivision Ln 27574
Three Star Ln 27574
Tingen St 27573
Tingen Mine Rd 27574
Tink Rd 27574
Todd Ct 27573
Todd Ln 27574
Todd Rd 27574
Tom Webb Rd 27574

Tombstone Dr 27573
Tonker Dr 27573
Trickling Branch Rd 27573
Trotter St
  1-199 27573
  200-299 27574
Trotter Clay Rd 27574
Tuck Rd 27574
Tulip Ln 27574
Turkey Feather Dr 27574
Turner St 27573
Turtle Creek Ln 27574
Turtle Hill Ct 27574
Tyler Ln 27574
Vance Wrenn Rd 27573
Vanhook Rd 27574
Vickamar Pl 27573
Victor Williford Rd 27574
Victoria Ln 27574
Virgilina Rd
  1-1772 27573
  1773-1797 27574
  1774-1798 27573
  1799-13599 27574
Virginia Ave 27573
Wade Powell Rd 27574
Wade Smith Rd 27574
Wagstaff St 27573
Wagstaff Carver Rd 27574
Walker St 27573
Walker Nelson Dr 27573
Walkers Path Rd 27574
Wall St 27573
Walnut Tree Ln 27574
Walters Place Rd 27574
Washboard Ave 27574
Wavy Twig Trl 27574
Webb St 27573
Webster Dr 27573
Weeks Dr 27573
Weldon Wrenn Rd 27574
Wesley Gravitte Rd 27573
Wesleyan Rd 27573
Wesleyan Heights Rd 27573
Westfield Dr 27574
Westover Dr 27573
Westwood Ln 27573
White Oak Dr 27573
Whitfield Rogers Rd 27574
Whitt Town Rd 27574
Wilbourne Run 27574
Wild Oak Ln 27574
Wildflower Ln 27574
Wiley Rd 27574
Wilkerson Ave 27573
Wilkins Ln 27573
Willifords Point Dr 27574
Willow St 27573
Willow Lake Rd 27574
Willow Oak Dr 27573
Wilsons Creek Rd 27574
Wimbledon Ct & Dr 27573
Wind Dancer Ln 27574
Winding Trail Dr 27574
Windsor Dr 27573
Winhaven St 27573
Winstead Farm Rd 27574
Winstead Hicks Rd 27574
Wisteria Dr 27573
Wood Lake Ct & Dr 27574
Woodberry Dr 27574
Woodchip Ln 27574
Woodhurst Ln 27573
Woodlawn Ave 27573
Woodsdale Rd
  1-508 27573
  509-6699 27574
Woodsy Vw 27573
Woody St 27573
Woody Fox Rd 27574
Woodys Store Rd 27574
Wrenn Rd 27573
Wrenn Crumpton Rd 27574
Wrenon Ave & St 27573
Ww Clayton Rd 27574
Yarborough St 27573
Yarbrough Rd 27574
Yearby Long Rd 27574
Yellington Ln 27574
Younger Rd 27573
Youngs Chapel Church Rd 27574
Zadock Slaughter Rd 27574

NUMBERED STREETS

S 2nd St 27573
S 3rd St 27573
S 4th Ave 27573
S 5th St 27573
12th Green Rd 27574

SALISBURY NC

General Delivery 28144

POST OFFICE BOXES MAIN OFFICE STATIONS AND BRANCHES

Box No.s
1 - 4639 28145
9998 - 9998 28144

NAMED STREETS

W A Ave 28144
A Trl 28147
Aaron Way 28144
Abbey Cir 28147
Aceland Cir 28146
Ackert Ave 28144
Acorn Ln 28144
Acorn Oaks Dr 28146
Acres Ln 28146
Adam St 28144
Adderly Dr 28146
Admiral Dr 28147
Adolphus Rd 28146
Adrian Rd 28146
Aggrey Ave 28146
Agner Dr & Rd 28146
Agner Creek Dr 28146
Airport Loop & Rd 28147
Alan Cir 28147
Alexander Ln 28144
Alleghany Dr 28147
Allen Ln 28146
Allen Farm Ln 28147
Allison Ct 28146
Alpha Dr 28146
Amber Dr 28147
Amberlight Cir 28144
American Dr 28147
American Quarry Rd 28146
Anderson Ave 28144
Andover Ct 28147
Andrews St 28144
Andrews Ford Rd 28146
Animal Dr 28147
Ann St 28146
Annadale Ave 28144
Antler Way 28147
Appalachian Dr 28146
Apple Ln & Rd 28147
Apple Down Ct 28147
Arabian Ln 28147
Arbor Dr 28144
Archer Rd 28147
Archer Acres Dr 28147
Archer Farm Dr 28144
Arden Dr 28144
N & S Arlington St 28144
Armour Ct 28144
Arrowhead Cir 28146
Arrowood Rd 28144
Artz Rd 28146
Asa Ln 28146
Asbury Rd 28147
Ashbrook Rd 28147
Ashford Cir 28146
Ashland Ct 28147
Ashley Dr 28147
Ashton Ln 28147
Ashwood Pl 28146
Aspen Gq Ave 28146
Athens Dr 28147
Auborn Pl 28147
Auction Dr 28147
Audrey Ln 28147
Audubon Ln 28147
Autumn Chapel Dr 28147
Autumn Wood Ln 28146
Autumnlight Dr 28147
N Avalon Dr 28146
Azalea Lake Dr 28146
E B Ave 28144
W B Ave 28144
B Trl 28147
B Leazer Rd 28147
Baden Ct 28147
Badger Rd 28147
Baker Ct 28146
Balfour Dr 28147
Balfour Quarry Rd 28146
Ball Park Rd 28144
E & W Bank St 28144
Bankett Ave 28146
Barber Lyerly Rd 28147
Barbour St 28144
Barger Dr
  1-99 28147
  100-399 28146
Barger Rd 28146
Barger Estates Dr 28147
Barker St 28144
Barley Run 28147
Barlow Ln 28147
Barn Dance Dr 28147
Barn Lao Dr 28146
Barrier Ln 28146
Barringer Rd 28147
Barringer St
  100-1099 28146
  1500-1599 28144
E Barrington Ct 28146
Barrow Ln 28146
Basinger Kluttz Rd 28146
Bass Ct & Run 28146
Basset Cir 28146
Baxter Rd 28146
Baxx Dr 28147
Bayberry Dr 28147
Bayleaf Dr 28146
Baymount Dr 28144
Bayridge Dr 28146
Bayview St 28147
Baywood Dr 28146
Beachnut Ln 28146
Beagle Run 28146
Beagle Club Rd 28146
Bean Rd 28146
Beard St 28144
Beck Rd 28144
Becton Rd 28147
Bee Lake Dr 28146
Bee Line Ln 28147
Bee Tree Ln 28144
Bee Tree Rd 28144
Beechcliff Ln 28146
Beechwood Dr 28147
Belfry Ct 28144
Bell St 28144
Belle Ct 28147
Bellemeade Dr 28144
Bellevue Rd 28144
N & S Bellwood Rd 28146
S Bend Dr 28147
Bendix Dr 28147
Benjamin Dr 28146
Benjamin Trott Ln 28147
Benson St 28144
Bent Oak Dr 28146
Benton Rd 28146
Berkshire Dr 28146
Bermuda Cir 28146
Bernhardt Rd 28147
Bertie Ave 28147
Best St 28144
Bethaven Dr 28144
Bethel Dr 28144
Beulah Ln 28146
Bhs Dr 28147
Big Rock Rd 28146
Billie Hope Dr 28146
Birch St 28146
Birchwood Dr 28146
Birdie Dr 28147
Birdshot Ln 28146
Birkdale Dr 28144
Birmingham Pl 28146
Black Rd 28146
Black Dog Ln 28146
Black Grubb Rd 28146
Blackberry Ln 28147
Blackwelder Rd 28146
Blackwell Woods Dr 28147
Blair St 28144
Blevens Ln 28146
Blue Heron Rd 28146
Blue Waters Dr 28146
Blueberry Rd 28147
Bluebird Ln 28146
Blues Dr 28146
Bluff Ln 28146
Boat Club Ln 28146
Boating Ter 28146
Bob White Run 28147
Bonanza Dr 28144
Bonaventure Dr 28147
Booth Rd 28146
Bost St 28144
Bostian Height St 28146
Boulder Run 28146
N & S Boundary St 28144
Boundary East Apts 28144
N & S Boundary Es St 28144
Boyden Rd 28144
Bradford Ct & Dr 28146
Bradley Dr 28147
Bradshaw Rd 28147
Bramblewood Dr 28147
Brandon Dr 28144
Brandon Cole Dr 28147
Bren Ln 28147
Brenner Ave 28144
Brians Way Dr 28146
Briar Creek Dr 28146
Briarwood Ter 28147
Briarwood Lake Dr 28147
Bridge Ct 28147
Briggs Rd 28147
Brighton Ln 28147
Brindles Hillside Ln 28147
Bringle Custom Butcher Rd 28147
Bringle Ferry Rd
  400-1399 28144
  1400-13099 28146
Brittany Way 28146
E & W Broad St 28144
Brook Cir 28147
Brook St 28146
Brook Valley Dr 28147
Brookfield Cir 28146
Brookmont Ave 28146
Brookshire Dr 28146
Brookstone Way 28146
Brookwood Dr 28146
Brown St 28146
Brown Acres Rd 28146
Brown Yadkin St 28144
Brownrigg Rd 28144
Browns Farm Rd 28147
Bryce Ave 28146
Buccaneer Cir 28146
Buck Dr 28146
Buckboard Ln 28147
Buckingham Pl 28144
Buckshot Trl 28146
Bull Hill Dr 28144
Burke St 28146
Burkesway Dr 28146
Burl Castor Rd 28146
Burmac Cir 28147
Burns Dr 28144
Burr Ln 28146
Burris Dr 28146
Burton St 28144
Butler St 28144
Butter Oveda Ln 28146
Byrd Rd 28146
Byron Dr 28144
E & W C Ave 28144
Cabagnot Ln 28144
N & S Caldwell St 28144
Calhoun St 28144
Callaway Dr 28146
Calvert Rd 28146
Calvin St 28147
Cambenew Rd 28146
Cambridge Rd 28147
Camelot Dr 28144
Camelot Rd 28147
Cameron Dr 28147
Camp Rd 28147
Campbell Ave E & W 28146
Candlewick Dr 28147
Cannon Rd 28147
Canteberry Dr 28144
Cantiberry Dr 28146
Carabelle Cir 28146
Carmi Ln 28144
Carola Ct 28146
Carolina Blvd 28146
Carolina St 28144
Carolyn Rd 28146
Carowood Dr 28147
Carpenters Cir 28144
Carriage Ln 28146
Carrie Dr 28147
Carrington Ln 28146
Carroll Ct 28146
Castle Dr 28146
Castle Keep Rd 28146
Castlebrook Dr 28146
N & S Castleview Rd 28146
Castlewood Dr 28147
Castor Rd 28146
Cat Fish Ter 28146
Catawba Dr 28147
Catawba Rd 28144
Cauble Rd 28144
Cauble Farm Rd 28147
Cauble Stout Cir 28146
Cedar Cir 28147
Cedar Dr 28147
Cedar St 28144
Cedar Drive Ext 28147
Cedar Farm Rd 28147
Cedar Pond Ln 28146
Cedar Springs Rd 28147
Cedar Valley Dr 28147
Cedar Village Trl 28147
Cedarfield Dr 28146
Cedarwood Cir & Dr 28147
Celebration Dr 28144
Celestial Dr 28146
Celtic Cir 28146
Cemetary Cir 28146
Cemetary Dr 28146
E Cemetary St 28144
W Cemetary St 28144
Century Pl 28147
Chalfont Ct 28146
Chalice Ct 28147
E Chamblee Dr 28147
Chandler Rd 28147
Chantilly Ln 28146
Chapel Ct 28147
Chapparal Dr 28146
Charleston Ln 28146
Charolais Dr 28146
Charter Way 28146
Chase Dr 28147
Chasestone Ct 28146
Chatham Ln 28146
Chelton Ct 28147
Cherokee Ln 28147
E Cherry St 28144
Cherry Tree Ln 28146
Chesapeake Dr 28147
Chesterfield Dr 28146
Chestnut St 28144
Chevy Ave 28146
Chez Charlois 28146
Chez Charolais Rd 28146
Choate Rd 28146
Christie Farm Rd 28147
N & S Church St 28144
Church Faith St 28146
E & W Church Gq St 28146
Churchill Dr 28144
Cindy Rd 28147
Circle Dr 28144
Circle M Dr 28147
Civic Park Apartments 28144
S Claiborne Rd 28146
Clairmont Rd 28146
Clancy St 28147
Clark Rd 28146
Claude Ave 28147
N & S Clay St 28144
Claymont Dr 28147
Claymoor Dr 28146
Clayton Trl 28146
Clearbrook Dr 28146
Clement St 28146
N & S Cleo Ave 28146
Cliff Eagle Rd 28146
Cliffdale Rd 28146
Cline Dr 28146
Cloudview Ln 28147
Cloudy Ln 28147
Clover St 28146
Cloverdale Dr 28146
Club House Dr 28144
Clyde St 28144
Clyde Poole Rd 28146
Colby Cir 28147
Coley Rd 28146
Colleton Pl 28146
E & W Colonial Dr 28144
Colony Rd 28144
Colton Ln 28144
Commodore Rd 28146
Community Ln 28146
Competition Dr 28146
Conestoga Trl 28147
Confederate Ave 28144
Cookout Ter 28146
Cool Side Dr 28146
Cool Wind Dr 28146
Cooper Rd 28147
Cooper St 28144
Copeland Trl 28146
Copper Leaf Ln 28146
Corbett Dr 28147
Cordova Ct 28147
Corliss Ave 28147
Cornerstone Ln 28146
Cornwall Dr 28147
Corporate Cir 28147
Corporate Center Dr 28146
Correll Park 28146
Correll St 28144
Correll Farm Rd 28146
Correll Loop Rd 28146
E & W Corriher Ave 28144
Corriher Farm Rd 28147
Cottage St 28147
Cotton St 28147
Cottontail Dr 28146
E Council St
  100-899 28144
  1200-1599 28146
W Council St 28144
Country Ln 28144
Country Club Ln 28146
Country Garden Ln 28146
Country Hill Dr 28147
Country Village Dr 28147
County View Dr 28147
Court Side Dr 28147
Courtland Dr 28144
Courtney Ln 28146
Cove Dr 28146
Covenant Woods Dr 28144
Coventry Ln 28147
Covington Ln 28147
Cox Ln & Rd 28146
Coyote Trl 28144
N & S Craige St 28144
Crane Dr 28146
Crane Creek Rd 28146
Crane Point Rd 28146
Crane View Rd 28146
Cranfield Ln 28147
Cranford Rd 28146
Craver Ave 28146
Crawford Dr 28147
Crawford Rd 28146
Crawford St 28144
Creekside Dr 28146
Creekwood Dr 28147
Crenerad St 28144
Crenshaw Ct 28144
Crescent Hts & Rd 28146
Crescent Heights Dr 28146
Cress Rd 28147
Cress Loop Rd 28147
Cress School Rd 28147
Crestview Ave 28144
Crestview Dr 28146
Cromer Rd 28146
Crook St 28146
Crosby St 28144
Cross Dr 28146
Cross St 28147
Crossridge Ave 28147
Crowder Dixon Rd
  100-299 28144
  1000-1399 28146
Crowell Ln 28146
Crown Point Dr 28146
Cruse Cir, Ln & Rd 28146
Cubby Ln 28146
Cypress Ln 28147
D Ave 28144
Daisy Ln 28146
Dalton Dr 28146
Dan St 28147
Dana Dr 28147
Dandridge Pl 28144
Daniels Rd 28144
Danley Dr 28146
Dappler Ln 28147
Darby Pl 28146
Darrell Whitley Ln 28147
Daves Dr 28146
Davis St 28146
Davis Farm Dr 28147
Dawn St 28147
De Lara Cir 28146
Deal Creek Dr 28147
Deck Ln 28146
Deer Rd 28146
Deer Brook Dr 28147
Deer Creek Dr 28146
Deer Lake Run 28146
Deer Springs Trl 28146
Deer Track Ln 28146
N Deerfield Cir 28147
S Deerfield Cir 28147
Deerfield Dr 28146
Delmar Dr 28146
Delray Dr 28147
Delta St 28146
Delta Downs Ln 28144
Demco Dr 28147
Denmark Dr 28147
Densmore Ln 28147
Depot St 28144
Derek Dr 28146
Devon Dr 28147
N & S Devon Park Pl 28147
Devonmere Pl 28144
Devonshire Ln 28146

Devynne Ct 28146
Dewberry Pl 28146
Dino Dr 28146
Dirt Rd 28146
Division Ave 28144
Dixie Ln 28144
Dixon Dr 28146
Dockside Dr 28146
Dogwood Ct 28144
Dogwood Ln 28146
Dogwood Rd 28144
Dollie Cir 28147
Dolly Madison Rd 28144
Dominion Dr 28146
Donner Dr 28147
Doral Ct 28144
Dorsett Dr 28144
Double J Ln 28147
Douglas St 28144
Dove Ln 28147
Dove Meadow Dr 28147
Down Yonder Dr 28144
Doyle Ave 28147
Dream Ln 28146
Drew Cir 28147
Driftwood Trl 28146
Duck Haven Ln 28146
Duke Cir 28144
Duke Dr 28146
Dukemont St 28146
Dukeville Rd 28146
Dulin Ave 28146
Dunham Ave 28146
Dunnbrook Dr 28146
Dunns Mountain Rd 28146
Dunns Mountain Church Rd 28146
Dunnsview Dr 28146
Dusty Ln 28146
Dutchmans Pt 28146
Eagle Dr 28144
Eaman Ave 28144
Earnhardt Ave 28144
Earnhardt Rd 28146
E Earnhardt St 28144
W Earnhardt St 28144
East Ave 28146
East St 28144
Eastbend Ln 28146
Eastbrook Cir 28146
Eastfork Dr 28146
Eastland Dr & Ln 28146
Eastover Dr 28147
Eastview Rd 28146
Eastville Dr 28146
Eastway Ln 28147
Eastwind Apartments 28144
Eastwood Dr 28146
Easy Dr 28146
Easy St 28144
Echo Hill Dr 28146
Ed Church Rd 28146
Ed Weavers Rd 28146
Eden Dr 28147
Edgedale Dr 28144
Edgefield Dr 28146
Edgewater Ct 28146
Edgewood Ct 28147
Edgewood Dr 28144
Edgewood Farm Rd 28147
Edie Ln 28144
Edzell Dr 28146
El Camino Dr 28146
Elderberry Ln 28147
Eldon Ln 28144
Elizabeth Ave 28144
Elk Trl 28147
Ellen St 28146
Eller Dr 28146
Ellerwood Dr 28146
Elliot Dr 28147
N & S Ellis St 28144
Ellis Loop Rd 28144
Elljoy Ln 28146
Elm St 28144
Elmwood Dr 28147
Elwood Ln 28144
Elyse Ave 28147
Emerald Ave 28144
Emerald Bay Dr 28146
Emerald Ridge Rd 28146
English St 28146
Enon Church Rd 28147
Ephraim Dr 28144
Epperson Rd 28147
Equestrian Dr 28144
Ermine Rd 28146
Ernest Miller Rd 28147
Estate Ln 28146
Eva Ln 28146
Evening Dr 28147
Evergreen Dr 28144
Everwood Ln 28147
Executive Dr 28147
Fair Share Rd 28147
Fairbluff Ave 28146
Fairfax Dr 28146
Fairfield Ln 28146
Fairhaven Dr 28146
Fairmont Ave 28144
Fairson Ave 28144
Fairview Hts 28144
Fairview St 28146
Fairway Ridge Rd 28146
Faith Rd 28146
Faith Farm Rd 28146
Faith Mountain Trl 28146
Falcon Ln 28146
Falcon Crest Ln 28147
Falcon Ridge Rd 28146
Fallsworth Ct 28147
Farley Ct 28146
Farm Creek Rd 28146
Farm House Rd 28147
Farmview Ct 28147
Fawn Creek Rd 28147
Faye Ln 28146
Ferncliff Dr 28147
Ferndale Dr 28147
Ferrell Ln 28147
Fieldbrook Dr 28146
Fieldcrest Dr 28146
Fieldstone Dr 28146
Filbert St 28144
File Rd 28146
File Farm Rd 28146
Fish Pond Rd 28146
E & W Fisher St 28144
Fisher Faith St 28146
N & S Fisherman Ln 28146
Five R Rd 28146
Five Row Rd 28144
Fleetwood Dr 28146
Flint School Rd 28146
Floral Ave 28144
Florence Ct 28147
Flowe Dr 28146
Flowers Ln 28146
Fly Fisher Dr 28147
Foggy Hollow Rd 28146
Foil St 28146
Follette Ln 28147
Forbes Ave 28147
Ford Rd 28146
Foresail Rd 28146
Forest Dr 28147
Forest St 28144
Forest Glen Dr 28147
Forest Meadow Ln 28144
Forest Oaks Dr 28146
Forest Pine Ln 28146
Forest Winds Dr 28144
Forestdale Dr 28144
Forney St 28146
Fortune Ln 28146
Foster Ln 28146
Foursons Dr 28146
Fox Trce 28147
Fox Chase Ct 28146
Fox Fire Dr 28147
Fox Grove Ln 28146
Fox Haven Dr 28146
Fox Hollow Ln 28146
Fox Hollow Farm Rd 28146
Fox Run Rd 28146
Foxbrook Pl 28147
Foxcress Dr 28147
Foxmeade Ct 28144
Foxwood Ln 28147
Fraley St 28146
Frances St 28147
E & W Franklin St 28144
Franklin Church Dr 28147
Franklin Comm Center Rd 28144
Franks Dr 28147
Franks Farm Ln 28146
Freedle Ln 28144
Freedom Dr 28147
Freeland Dr 28144
Freeman Ln 28147
French Ln 28146
Fries St 28144
Fuller Cir 28147
N & S Fulton St 28144
Furniture Dr 28147
G Goodnight Rd 28147
Gaither Dr 28146
Gallarie Pl 28144
Gallimore Rd 28147
Ganell Ave 28147
Ganton Rd 28147
Gantt St 28146
Garden Ln 28146
Gardner St 28146
Garland Dr 28146
Garner Dr 28146
Garrick Rd 28144
Gaskey Rd 28147
Gates St 28144
Geiger Ln 28147
Gentry Pl 28146
W Geroid St 28144
Gheen Rd 28147
Gibson Rd 28147
Gillan Dr 28146
Gillespie St 28144
Glendower Dr 28144
Glenfield Dr 28147
W & E Glenview Cir & Dr 28147
Glenwood Ave 28146
Glock Ct 28144
Glover Rd 28146
Godair Dr 28146
Godbey Rd 28147
Goff Acres Ln 28146
Gold Branch Rd 28146
Gold Hill Cir & Dr 28146
Gold Knob Rd 28146
Golden Ln 28147
Golfers Dr 28146
Good Fellow Dr 28146
Goodfellow Dr 28146
Goodman Dr
1-99 28147
100-499 28146
Goodman Lake Rd 28146
Goodnight Rd 28147
Goodnight Farm Rd 28147
Goodson Rd 28147
Goodson Acres Dr 28147
Goodwin Rd 28146
Government Rd 28144
Grace St 28144
Grace Church Rd 28147
Gracebrook Dr 28146
Graceland Pl 28146
Grady St 28144
Graham Pl 28147
Graham Acres Rd 28147
Grandeur Dr 28146
Granite Ln 28146
Grant Rd 28146
Grant St 28144
Grants Creek Rd 28147
Granville Ln 28146
Grayson Dr 28147
Green St 28144
Green Acres Mh Park 28146
Green Gable Ln 28147
Green Meadows Dr 28147
Greenbrier Creek Pl 28146
Greenheather Dr 28147
Greenside Cir 28146
Greentree Cir 28147
Greenway Dr 28144
Gregory Rd 28147
Grim St 28144
Grist Mill Run 28146
Grove St 28144
Grubb Ferry Rd 28144
Guffy St 28147
Gupton Dr 28147
Gwynn St 28147
Hackett St 28144
Hader St 28147
Hagen Ct 28144
Hailey Rd 28146
Halifax Cir 28144
Hall St 28144
Hall Es St 28144
Hallmark Cir 28147
Hallmark Estates Dr 28147
Hamby Way 28147
Hamilton Dr 28147
Hampshire Ct 28144
Hampshire Dr 28146
Hampton Cir & Rd 28144
Hannah Ave 28147
Hannah Ferry Rd 28144
Hanover Ct 28144
Happy Estates Mh Park 28146
Happy Lake Rd 28146
Happy Trails Rd 28147
Harbor Ct 28147
Harley Dr 28146
Harrel Ct & St 28144
Harrelson Dr 28146
Harris Rd 28147
Harris Granite Rd 28146
Harris Point Rd 28146
Harris Quarry Rd 28146
Harrison Rd 28147
E Harrison St 28144
W Harrison St 28144
Hartley Rd 28146
Hartman Ave 28144
Hartman Rd 28146
Hat Creek Rd 28146
Hawk Rd 28147
Hawkins Ave & Loop 28144
Hawkinstown Rd 28144
Hawkridge Ln 28146
Hawksnest Rd 28146
Hawthorne Ln 28147
Hayden St 28144
Haynes Dr 28146
Hazeltine Ct 28144
Heatherdale Rd 28146
Heatherwood Ln 28144
Heavens Trl 28146
Hedge St 28147
Hedrick St 28144
Hedrick Lambe Dr 28146
Heilig Ave 28144
Heilig Rd 28146
Heilig Es St 28144
Heiligtown Rd 28144
Helenas Way 28146
Hemlock Dr 28147
Henderlite St 28144
E & W Henderson St 28144
E Henderson Es St 28144
Henderson Grove Church Rd 28147
Hendricks Rd 28147
Henkle Craig Farm Rd 28147
Henry Ln 28146
Henry Laurens Cir 28147
Hereford Ln 28146
Heritage Ln 28147
Heritage Valley Dr 28144
Hickory Dr 28144
Hickory Ln 28147
Hickory Pl 28144
Hickory Gq St 28146
Hickory Hill Rd 28144
Hickory Springs Ln 28146
Hidden Cir 28147
Hidden Cove Dr 28146
Hidden Creek Cir & Dr 28147
Hidden Hill Ln 28144
Hidden Hut Rd 28147
Hidden Springs Dr 28147
Hidden Valley Rd 28147
Higgins Way 28147
High Meadow Dr 28144
High Meadows Ln 28144
High Ridge Trl 28146
High Rock Est 28146
Highland Ave 28144
Highland Creek Dr 28147
Highland Hills Trl 28144
Highland Lake Rd 28147
Highway 52 28146
Hildebrand Rd 28147
Hill St 28144
Hill Top Dr 28147
Hillcrest Pl 28144
Hillcrest Ridge Dr 28146
Hillsboro St 28144
Hillside Dr 28147
Hillview 28146
Hinkle Ln 28146
Hobson Rd 28144
Hodge St 28147
Hodge Place Rd 28146
Hoffman Ln 28147
Hogans Valley Way 28146
Holiday Dr 28146
Holland Dr 28147
Hollar Way 28147
Hollins Dr 28144
Holly Ave 28147
Holly Lake Dr 28146
Hollyberry Ln 28147
Hollybrook Ct 28147
Hollywood Dr 28144
Holmes Ave & St 28144
Holobough Ln 28146
Home Rd 28147
Honey Moss Ln 28146
Honeycutt Rd 28144
Honeysuckle Ln 28146
Hoot Cir 28147
Hope Ln 28147
Hope Hill Rd 28147
Hopkins Ln 28147
Hopkins St 28144
Hopper Rd 28146
E & W Horah St 28144
Horseshoe Dr 28146
Hounds Run Dr 28147
Howell Rd 28147
Hubert Ln 28147
Hudson St 28144
Hugo Dr 28146
Hummingbird Cir 28146
Hunt Ln 28144
Hunter St 28144
Hunters Ridge Rd 28146
Huntington Dr 28147
Hurley School Dr & Rd 28147
Hurst Dr 28146
Hutchins Way 28146
Hyde Ln 28146
Idlewheel Dr 28147
Idlewood Dr 28144
Imperial Dr 28147
Independence Dr 28147
Indian Trl 28144
Indigo Cir 28147
Industrial Ave 28144
Inglewood Ln 28146
Inlet Point Dr 28146
E Innes St
100-700 28144
605-605 28145
701-1299 28144
702-1298 28144
1300-2599 28146
W Innes St 28144
S Institute St 28144
Inverness Ln 28146
Irby Ln 28146
Isaiah Dr 28144
Ivy St 28146
J Bost Rd 28147
J Brown Rd 28146
Jack Brown Rd 28147
N & S Jack Gq St 28146
Jackson Rd 28146
N Jackson St 28144
S Jackson St 28144
Jackson Es St 28144
Jackson Farm Ln 28146
Jacob Bost Rd 28147
Jacobs Dr 28144
Jacobs Lambe Ln 28146
Jake Alexander Blvd N 28147
Jake Alexander Blvd S
100-1099 28147
1100-2899 28146
Jake Alexander Blvd W 28147
Jakes Dr 28146
James St 28146
Jane Rd 28146
Janis Ln 28146
Jarrett Dr 28144
Jasmine Cir 28147
Jaycee St 28146
Jenny Dr 28146
Jesse Safrit Rd 28147
Jibsail Rd 28146
Jim Neely Dr 28144
Joe Hess Rd 28146
Joe Lentz Rd 28146
Joe Lewis St 28144
John Michael Ln 28146
John Penn Cir 28147
John Rainey Rd 28147
Johnson St 28144
Jon Drake Dr 28147
Jonathan St 28147
Jones Rd 28147
Jordan St 28144
Journey Ln 28146
Joy Cir 28146
Joy St 28147
Joyner Ln 28144
Julia Dr 28147
Julian Rd
100-999 28147
1000-1599 28146
Julian St 28146
Julian Park Cir 28146
Julius Dr 28147
June Dr 28147
Juniper St 28146
Justin Ct 28146
Karri Ln 28147
Kay St 28146
N & S Kayla Dr 28146
Keck St 28146
Keener Pl 28146
Kelly Dr 28147
Kenly St 28144
Kensington Ln 28146
Kent Rd 28147
Kenton Pl 28147
Kentucky St 28144
Kentwood Ave 28146
Kepley Rd 28147
Kern Dr 28147
Kern Carlton Rd 28146
E Kerns St 28146
E & W Kerr St 28144
Kershaw Ct 28144
Kesler St 28144
Kesler Farm Dr 28146
Kesler Pastures Rd 28146
Kestrel Ct 28147
Keystone Dr 28147
Kincaid Rd 28146
King Rd 28146
Kings Dr 28144
Kings Ter 28146
Kingsbridge Rd 28144
Kingsway Dr 28146
Kingtree Rd 28146
Kirk St 28144
Kizer St 28147
Klumac Rd
100-899 28144
900-1599 28147
Kluttz Rd
100-699 28147
1200-2299 28146
Kluttz Gq St 28146
Kluttz Lake Dr 28146
Knights Pl 28146
Knoll View Dr 28147
Knollwood Ave 28144
Knollwood Dr 28146
Knollwood Park 28147
Knollwood Acres 28147
Knotty Pine Cir 28146
Knox St 28144
Krider Dr 28144
Kristy Ln 28147
Ladino Ln 28147
E & W Lafayette Cir & St 28144
Lake Dr 28144
Lake Rd 28146
Lake Forest Cove Rd 28146
Lake Fork Rd 28146
Lake High Rock Est 28146
Lake Landing Dr 28146
Lake Pointe Ln 28146
Lake Shore Dr 28146
Lakefront Dr 28146
Lakeside Dr 28146
Lakeview Dr & Rd 28147
Lakewood Dr 28147
Lamb Dr 28146
Lancaster Ct 28144
Lancelot Cir & Rd 28147
Landmark Dr 28146
Landover Dr 28147
Landsdown Dr 28147
Lane Pkwy 28146
Lane St 28147
Langley Dr 28147
Lanning Dr 28146
Lantz Ave 28144
Larch Rd 28147
Larchmont Pl 28144
Lariat Cir 28144
Larin Way 28146
Larkscraft Dr 28146
Larkspur Rd 28146
Larson Dr 28147
Lash Dr 28147
Laura Kate Ave 28147
Laura Springs Dr 28146
Laurel Ln 28147
Laurel St 28146
Laurel Pointe Cir 28147
Laurel Valley Way 28144
Lauren Ln 28146
Lawndale Dr 28147
Lawton Ln 28144
Lazy Lane Dr 28146
Leach Rd 28146
N & S Lee St 28144
Lee Es St 28144
Lee Trexler Rd 28146
Leewood Ln 28146
Legion Club Rd 28146
Legion Gq St 28146
Leigh Dr 28147
Leisure Ln 28146
Leisure Point Rd 28146
Lemly Ln 28146
Leonard Rd 28146
Lewis St 28146

Lexington Ave 28144
E Liberty St
100-899 28144
1500-1699 28146
W Liberty St 28144
Lighthouse Way 28146
N & S Lilac Ln 28147
Lillian Cir 28147
Lilly Ave 28144
Lilly Pad Dr 28146
Lincoln Ave 28144
Lincolnton Rd
400-1199 28144
1200-2599 28147
Linda St 28146
Lingle Ln 28146
N & S Link Ave 28144
Linn Cir & Ln 28144
Lippard Rd 28146
Lisk St 28144
Litaker Rd 28147
Litaker Farm Rd 28147
Little St 28144
Little Crane Cove Rd 28146
Little Creek Dr 28147
Litton Dr 28147
Livengood Dr 28147
Livingstone Ave 28144
Lizzie Ln 28147
Lloyd St 28144
Lm Overcash Rd 28146
Locke Cir 28147
Locke St 28144
Log Barn Rd 28146
Loganberry Ln 28146
Lois Ln 28147
Lone Star St 28146
N & S Long St 28144
Long Bow Rd 28144
Long Branch Dr 28146
Long Branch Rd 28147
Long Creek Ln 28146
N & S Long Es St 28144
Long Es Street Ext 28144
Long Ferry Rd
100-1099 28144
1100-6499 28146
Long Meadow Dr 28147
Longleaf Dr 28147
Longview Ave 28146
Lonzo Ave 28144
Loop St 28147
Lowder Rd 28147
Lower Palmer Rd 28146
Lu Dot Ln 28146
Lucerne Ln 28144
Lucky Ln 28146
Ludwick Ave 28146
Ludwick Heights Ln 28147
Lumber St 28144
Lumen Christie Ln 28147
Luther Ln 28144
Luther Barger Rd 28146
Lutheran Synod Dr 28144
Lyerly Dr 28146
E & W Lyerly Gq St 28146
Lyerly Pond Rd 28146
Lyn Rd 28147
Lynchburg Trl 28147
Lynn Rd 28147
Mack St 28146
Mae Rd 28146
Maggie Ave 28147
Magnolia Ave 28146
Magnolia Cir 28147
Magnolia Dr
100-199 28147
3400-3699 28144
Mahaffey Dr 28146
Mahaley Ave 28144
Mahaley Rd 28146
Maidstone Dr 28147
N Main St 28144
S Main St
100-2099 28144
2100-6899 28147

N & S Main Faith St 28146
N & S Main Gq St 28146
Mainsail Rd 28146
Majestic Dr 28146
Majestic Heights Dr 28144
Majolica Rd 28147
Malcolm Rd 28144
Manor Dr 28144
Maple Ave 28146
Maple Cir 28146
Maple St 28146
N Maple Es St 28144
Maple Gq St 28146
Maple Ridge Cir 28147
Maplewood Dr N 28147
Marina Pointe Rd 28146
Marion Brown Trl 28146
Marriot Cir 28144
Marsh Rd & St 28144
Martin Gq St 28146
N & S Martin Luther King
Jr Ave 28144
Mathis Ave 28146
Matika Dr 28147
Matthew Dr 28147
Maupin Ave 28144
Max Ave 28147
Maxwell St 28144
Mccanless Rd 28146
Mccombs Farm Dr 28146
N & S Mccoy Rd 28144
Mccoy Farm Rd 28146
W Mccubbins St 28144
Mcfarland Dr 28146
Mcintosh Ln 28147
Mckinley Ln 28147
Mcnair Cir 28144
Meadow Ln 28147
Meadow Green Dr 28147
Meadow Lake Dr 28146
Meadow Wood Ct &
Dr 28146
Meadowbrook Cir &
Rd 28144
Meadowview Ln 28147
Meah Ln 28147
Mellon Dr 28144
Melrose St 28144
Melton Gq Dr 28146
Memory Ln 28144
Mendenhall Dr 28146
Menius Rd 28146
N & S Merritt Ave 28144
Messick Rd 28147
Messner St 28144
Middle Rd 28146
Middle Oaks Dr 28146
Midsail Rd 28146
Midway Dr 28147
E Midway St 28144
W Midway St 28144
Midway Park Dr 28147
Mike Dr 28147
Milburn Dr 28147
Mildred Ave 28144
Miles Dr 28147
N & S Milford Dr 28144
Milford Hills Rd 28144
Military Ave & St 28144
Mill Haven Dr 28146
Mill Run Rd 28144
Mill Wheel Dr 28146
Millbridge Rd 28147
Millennium Dr 28146
Miller Ave 28144
Miller Dr 28146
Miller Rd 28147
E Miller St 28144
W Miller St 28144
Miller Chapel Rd 28147
Milton St 28144
Mining Ave 28147
Mink Dr 28146
Miracle Dr 28146
Mirror Lake Rd 28146
Mirror Park Dr 28146

Mist Valley Dr 28146
Mitchell Ave 28144
Mitchell Es St 28144
Mockingbird Ln 28146
Mocksville Ave 28144
Molasses Mill Rd 28147
Monarch Dr 28144
E & W Monroe St 28144
Montclair Dr 28144
Montego Ln 28147
Montgomery Ave 28146
Montieth Dr 28146
Montrose Rd 28146
Moon Cir 28147
Moon River Rd 28146
Moonlight Dr 28146
Moore St 28144
Moore Haven Dr 28147
Mooresville Rd
100-999 28144
1000-8999 28147
Mop Bucket Dr 28147
Morgan Pond Rd 28146
Morlan Park Rd 28146
Morningside Ln 28146
Morris Ln 28146
Morris Farm Rd 28146
Morrison Ave 28146
Mossy Oak Ln 28146
Mount Hope Church Rd
100-499 28147
500-5899 28146
Mount Vernon Park
Rd 28146
Mountain View Rd 28147
Moyle Ave 28146
Muirfield Way 28144
Mulberry Cir 28144
Mulberry Ln 28146
Murray Dr 28146
Muskedine Ln 28146
Mustrat Run 28146
Myers Pl 28147
Myron Pl 28147
Nanas Way 28146
National Guard Rd 28147
E Nc 152 Hwy 28146
Nc Highway 801 28146
Ned Marsh Rd 28146
Neel Rd 28147
Neita Dr 28147
Nesbitt Dr 28147
Nestlewood Ln 28144
New St 28144
New Jersey Dr 28146
Newcastle Cir 28144
Newport Dr 28144
Newsome Rd 28147
Nicholas Run 28147
Nine Hole Ter 28146
Noble Acres Dr 28147
Noodle Way 28146
Norris Dr 28147
North Cir 28144
North Rd 28147
North St 28147
Northwest St 28144
Norwood Dr 28146
Nottingham Rd 28147
Nuggett Ln 28146
O C Pine Dr 28146
Oak Dr 28144
Oak Rd 28147
Oak St 28147
Oak Brook Dr 28146
Oak Farm Rd 28146
Oak Forest Ln 28146
N & S Oak Gq St 28146
Oak Grove Ln 28146
Oak Hollow Dr 28146
Oak Leaf Ln 28146
Oak Mountain Rd 28147
Oakbluff Dr 28147
N & S Oakhurst Dr 28147
Oakmont Ct 28146
Oakridge Dr & Run 28146

Oakview Dr 28146
Oakwood Ave 28146
Oddie Rd 28146
Odell Dr 28146
Odom Dr 28146
Ohara Dr 28147
Old Barnyard Ln 28146
Old Bradshaw Rd 28147
Old Camp Rd 28147
Old Cherokee Cir 28146
Old Concord Rd
100-999 28144
1000-9999 28146
Old Cress Rd 28147
Old Farm Rd 28147
E Old Farm Rd 28146
Old Garden Rd 28146
Old Mocksville Rd 28144
Old Plank Rd 28144
Old South Main St 28144
Old Stone House Rd 28146
Old Tulip Farm Rd 28147
Old Union Church Rd 28146
Old Us Highway 70 28147
Old Volkswagon Pl 28146
Old West Innes St 28144
Old Wilkesboro Rd 28144
Old Wood Ln 28144
Olde Fields Dr 28146
Ole Point Ln 28146
Oleary Ct 28147
Olivia Ln 28147
Oradwar Rd 28147
Orchard Ln 28147
Ore Dr 28147
Organ Trl 28146
Organ Church Rd 28146
Oscar Ln 28147
Oslo Ln 28146
Overbrook Dr & Rd 28144
Overcash Rd 28147
Overhill Dr & Rd 28144
Overlook Dr 28146
Overman Ave 28144
Overview Rd 28147
Owens Dr 28146
Owl Dr 28147
Oxford Rd 28146
P And F Farm Rd 28146
Paige Dr 28147
Palasade Cir 28146
Palema St 28147
Palomino Dr 28146
Pamela St 28144
Panfish Ln 28146
Panther Creek Rd 28146
Par Dr 28147
Paradise Dr 28146
Park Ave
1-1099 28144
1200-1599 28146
Park Cir 28146
Park Dr 28147
N Park Dr 28144
E Park Rd 28144
W Park Rd 28144
Park Gq Ave 28146
Park Villa Rd 28146
Parkland Dr 28146
Parks Rd
100-1099 28146
2000-3099 28147
Parkside Dr 28147
Parkview Cir 28144
Parrish St 28144
Partee St 28144
Partridge Cir 28147
Partridge Run 28147
Partridge Trl 28146
Pathway Ln 28146
Patriot Cir 28147
Patterson Rd 28147
Paul St 28144
Peace St 28144
Peace Wood Rd 28146
Peach Orchard Ave 28147

Peach Orchard Ln 28147
Peach Orchard Rd
100-999 28147
1000-1999 28146
Peach Tree Ln
100-299 28146
3900-4099 28147
Pearl St 28146
Pebble Dr 28147
Pebble Pt 28146
Pecan Ln 28146
Peeler Rd
100-1099 28147
1100-2299 28146
W Peeler St 28146
Peeler Mobile Home
Park 28146
Penny Ln 28146
Pentecost Ln 28147
Perry Dr 28146
Perryman Dr 28147
Persimmon Ln 28146
Persimmon Cove Rd 28146
Peters Dr 28146
Peyton Ln 28147
Phillip Dr 28146
Phillip St 28147
Pickler Rd 28144
Piedmont Ave 28144
Pietryk Dr 28146
Pin Oak Cir 28146
Pine Dr 28144
Pine St
800-999 28144
4000-4199 28147
Pine Church Ln 28146
Pine Cone Ln 28147
Pine Grove Rd 28147
Pine Hill Dr 28146
Pine Hill Rd 28144
Pine Lake Dr 28146
Pine Needle Trl 28146
Pine Tree Pl & Rd 28144
W Pine Tree Es Dr 28144
Pine Valley Rd 28147
Pinecrest St 28147
Pinehaven Dr 28146
Pinehill Apartments 28144
Pinehurst St 28144
Pinevale Dr 28144
Pineview Cir 28144
Pinewood Ave 28144
Pinewood Dr 28147
Pinkney Dr 28144
Pinnacle Dr 28146
Pioneer Trl 28146
Piper Ln 28147
Plantation Ridge Dr 28147
Player Ct 28144
Playground Ln 28146
Pleasant Cove Rd 28146
Pleasant Place Rd 28147
Pleasant View Dr 28146
Plum Tree Dr 28147
Plymouth Ave 28144
Poe Dr 28146
Polliana Dr 28146
Polo Dr 28144
Pond View Dr 28147
Ponderosa Dr 28146
Poole Rd 28146
Pop Basinger Rd 28146
Pop Stirewalt Rd 28146
Poplar St 28144
Porter Rd 28146
Portsail Rd 28146
Post Oak Pl 28147
Poteat Ln 28147
Potneck Rd 28147
Prescott Dr 28144
Prestigue Ln 28144
Preston Ln 28147
Prestwick Ct 28146
Price Rd 28146
Price St 28144
Primrose Dr 28147

Princeton Dr 28144
Proctor Dr 28147
Propst Rd 28146
Prospect Trl 28147
Providence Church Rd 28146
Providence Country 28147
Putney Ct 28147
Quail Cir & Dr 28147
Quail Meadow Ln 28146
Quail Pointe Dr 28147
Quail Ridge Run 28146
Quarry Way 28146
Queen Anne Rd 28144
Queeners Ct 28146
Queens Rd 28144
Rachel Ln 28147
N & S Railroad Ave &
St 28144
N Railroad Es St 28144
Railroad Gq St 28146
Rainbow Dr 28146
Rainey Rd 28146
Rainwood Dr 28146
Ranchwood Dr 28146
Randall Ct 28147
Randolph Rd 28144
Random Dr 28147
Raney Faith St 28146
Rattlesnake St 28146
Raven Brook Way 28146
Ravenwood Ct 28147
Raymond Ave 28146
Raymond Meadows
Rd 28146
Reading Rd 28147
Reamer Cir 28144
Rebecca Ln 28146
Rebel Rd 28144
Recreation Dr 28146
Red Acres Rd 28147
Red Fox Run 28147
Red Oak Ln 28146
Redfield Dr 28146
Redhaven Dr 28147
Redman Dr 28147
Reeds Ln 28144
Reeves St 28144
Regency Dr & Rd 28147
Reid Farm Rd 28147
Remington Dr 28144
Rendleman Rd 28146
Rex Rd 28147
Reynolds St 28146
Rhema Ln 28146
Rhodes Dr 28147
Rhododendron Dr 28146
Ribelin Rd 28146
Rice Farm Rd 28147
Richard Rd 28147
Richard St 28144
Richmond Rd 28144
Riddle Forest Ln 28146
Ridenhour Rd 28144
Ridge Ave 28144
E Ridge Rd 28144
W Ridge Rd 28147
Ridge St 28147
Ridge Creek Ct 28144
Ridgecrest Rd 28146
Ridgeline Dr 28146
Ridgewood Ct 28146
Rimer Rd 28146
Rink St 28147
E Ritchie Rd 28146
W Ritchie Rd 28147
Ritchie St 28146
Rithmetic Rd 28147
Riting Rd 28147
River Birch Dr 28146
River Country Rd 28146
River Ranch Rd 28146
River Trace Ln 28144
Riverside Dr 28146
Riverview Cir 28146
Riverwalk Dr 28146
Riverwood Dr 28146

Riviera Dr 28144
Robert Dr 28147
Roberta St 28146
Roberts St 28144
Robertson Rd 28146
Robin Cir & Rd 28144
Robinson Rd 28144
Robinwood Dr 28146
Rock Cut Rd 28147
Rock Grove Church
Rd 28146
Rock Hump Rd 28147
Rock Pond Ln 28146
Rock Spring Rd 28147
Rocklyn Ln 28146
Rockwood Dr 28146
Rocky Crest Cir 28146
Rocky Hill Rd 28146
Rocky Ridge Trl 28146
Roger Dr 28147
Romana Dr 28146
Rose Ave 28146
Rose Ln 28144
Rose Brier Ln 28146
Roseman Rd 28147
Rosemont Rd 28146
Rosemont St 28144
Roundknob Ave 28144
Rouzer Rd 28146
Rowan Ave & Cir 28146
Rowan Gq St 28146
Rowan Mills Rd 28147
Rowland Ln 28146
Roy St 28144
Roy Miller Park Rd 28146
Rudder Cir 28146
Rudolph Rd 28146
Ruff Rd 28147
Ruffin Graham Rd 28146
Rufty Cir 28144
Rugby Rd 28144
Ruger St 28146
Rutherford St 28144
Ryan St 28144
Ryan Patrick Dr 28147
Ryans Crossing Dr 28147
Sable Rd 28146
Saddle Dr 28147
Sadie Ln 28146
Safety St 28144
Safrit Rd 28146
Sage Way 28147
Sagewood Ln 28146
Sailboat Dr 28146
Saint Cyril Ln 28147
Saint James Way 28147
Saint Johns Dr 28144
Saint Luke Church Rd 28146
Saint Matthews Church
Rd 28146
Saint Paul Church Rd 28146
Saint Peters Church
Rd 28146
N Salisbury Ave 28144
N & S Salisbury Gq
Ave 28146
Sandhill Ct 28144
Sandra Ave 28147
Sandvika Ln 28146
Sandy Creek Ln 28146
Sapona Dr 28146
Sarah Dr 28146
Sarah Ellen Ln 28147
Sarazen Way 28144
Sassafras Ln 28147
Saw Dust Trl 28144
Saxton Cir 28147
Scales St 28144
Scaley Bark Dr 28147
Schofield Pl 28144
Scotland Ln 28146
Scott Rd 28146
Scott Trce 28147
Scottsdale Dr & Est 28146
Scout Rd 28146
Scrub Pine Dr 28146

Sea Breeze Rd ... 28144
Secret Garden Ct ... 28146
Secretariat Ln ... 28144
Sells Rd ... 28144
Settlers Grove Ln ... 28146
Setzer Rd ... 28146
Shadow Spring Ln ... 28144
Shady Ln ... 28144
Shady Rest Ln ... 28146
Shag Bark Ln ... 28146
Shamrock Dr ... 28144
Shane Dr ... 28147
Shane Candy Ln ... 28146
Shannon Dr ... 28144
Shannon Bear Ln ... 28146
Shanrock Meadows
Rd ... 28146
Sharon Ct ... 28146
Sharon Ln ... 28146
Sharon Rd ... 28147
N & S Shaver St ... 28144
N Shaver Es St ... 28144
Sheila Ln ... 28146
Shenandoh Ln ... 28147
Sheridan Dr ... 28144
Sherrill Dr ... 28146
Sherrills Ford Rd ... 28147
Sherwood St ... 28144
Shirley St ... 28147
Shive Rd ... 28146
Shives St ... 28144
Shoaf Ridge Rd ... 28147
Shore Acres Rd ... 28146
Short St ... 28144
Shortsail Rd ... 28146
Shue Rd ... 28147
Shumac Ln ... 28146
Shuping Mill Rd ... 28146
Sides Ln ... 28144
Sides Rd ... 28146
Sidney Dr ... 28147
Sifford Ln ... 28146
Sills Dr ... 28146
Silver Point Ct ... 28147
Silvertrace Dr ... 28144
Simmerson Farm Rd ... 28147
Simmons Cir ... 28147
Sir Lance Cir ... 28146
Skylar Ln ... 28147
Skyline Cir & Dr ... 28146
Skysail Rd ... 28146
Skyview Cir ... 28147
Sleepy Hollow Rd ... 28146
Snead Ct ... 28144
Snider St ... 28144
Snooky Dr ... 28147
Sonny Acres Dr ... 28146
Sonoma Ln ... 28146
Southern Ln ... 28147
Southern Breeze Ln ... 28146
Southern Es St ... 28144
Southern Oaks Apts ... 28147
Southmark Dr ... 28147
Southwest St ... 28144
Southwood Rd ... 28147
Sowers Rd ... 28144
Sowers Ferry Rd ... 28144
Speedway Blvd ... 28146
Spence Dr ... 28144
Spicewood Ln ... 28147
Sportsman Dr ... 28146
Spring Dr ... 28144
Spring Estates Cir ... 28146
Spring Oak Dr ... 28147
Spring Rock Dr ... 28146
Spring Valley Ln ... 28147
Spruce Dr ... 28147
Spruce St ... 28146
N Spruce Es St ... 28144
Spyglass Hill Pl ... 28146
Squirrel Run ... 28146
Stafford Dr ... 28144
Stafford Estates Dr ... 28146
Stamper Dr ... 28146
Standish St ... 28144
Stanley St ... 28144

Stanwyck Cir & Rd ... 28147
Starhaven Ln ... 28147
Starnes Rd ... 28146
Statesman Dr ... 28147
Statesville Blvd
100-1940 ... 28144
1942-1998 ... 28144
1949-1997 ... 28147
1999-8899 ... 28147
Staysail Rd ... 28146
E & W Steele St ... 28144
Steele Trace Dr ... 28147
Steeple Chase Trl ... 28144
Sterling Ct ... 28144
Steven Dr ... 28147
Stevens Rd ... 28147
Stockade Ct ... 28147
Stokes Ferry Rd ... 28146
Stone Rd ... 28146
Stone Mill Cir ... 28146
Stone Pointe Dr ... 28146
Stone Ridge Dr ... 28146
Stonefield Ln ... 28146
Stonehaven Ct ... 28146
Stoner Morgan Rd ... 28146
Stones Throw Ln ... 28146
Stonewall Rd ... 28144
Stonewood Dr ... 28146
Stonewyck Dr ... 28146
Stoney Cove Pl ... 28147
Stoney Creek Dr ... 28146
Stoney Heights Dr ... 28146
Stoney Knob Ln ... 28146
Stoneybrook Rd ... 28147
Stratford Pl ... 28144
Stratford Rd ... 28146
Strawberry Ln ... 28147
Stuart St ... 28144
Stuckey Rd ... 28146
Sudley Cir ... 28144
Suggs Ave ... 28146
Summer Ln & Pl ... 28146
Summer Leigh St ... 28146
Summersett St ... 28147
Summit Ave ... 28144
Summit Park Dr ... 28146
Sumter Ct ... 28144
Sun Fish Ter ... 28146
Sun Valley Dr ... 28146
Suncreek Ln ... 28146
Sunday Dr ... 28146
Sunny Ln ... 28147
Sunrise Ridge Dr ... 28146
Sunset Dr ... 28147
Sunset Pointe Dr ... 28146
Sunshine Ln ... 28146
Surratt Dr ... 28144
Surveyors Dr ... 28146
Susan Ln ... 28144
Sussex Ln ... 28144
Suzannes Rd ... 28147
Swaim Ct ... 28147
Swanner Park Rd ... 28146
Sweet Gum Ln ... 28146
Sweet Pea Ln ... 28146
Sweetbriar Cir ... 28146
Swimmers Ln ... 28146
Swink Ave ... 28147
Sycamore Rd ... 28147
Sycamore St ... 28146
T Brown Rd ... 28146
Tabernacle St ... 28144
Tabor Dr & Rd ... 28144
Tall Cedar Dr ... 28146
Tall Oaks Cir ... 28147
Tall Pine Cir ... 28147
Talley Ln ... 28146
Talon Dr ... 28147
Tamarac Shores Dr ... 28146
Tammy Rd ... 28147
Tammys Park Rd ... 28146
Tanglewood Dr ... 28144
Tarbox Ln ... 28146
Tarheel Trl ... 28146
Tarheel Farm Rd ... 28147
Teague Rd ... 28146

Ted Ln ... 28146
Tennis Court Dr ... 28146
Terra Ct ... 28146
Terrace Dr ... 28146
Theodore Ln ... 28147
Thermoid Way ... 28144
Thetford Dr ... 28146
W Thomas St ... 28144
Thomason Rd ... 28147
Thompson Rd ... 28147
Thriftwood Ct ... 28146
Tidewater Rd ... 28146
Tigger Ln ... 28147
Tilman St ... 28144
Timber Creek Ln ... 28146
Timber Ridge Dr ... 28144
Timber Run Dr ... 28146
Timber Spring Ln ... 28147
Timberlake Ct ... 28146
Timberlake Dr ... 28147
Timberlane Cir & Trl ... 28147
Timberwolf Ln ... 28147
N Titan Dr ... 28147
Todd Cir ... 28147
Todd St ... 28144
Toms Trl ... 28146
Tonys Ln ... 28146
Tootsie Rd ... 28146
Topsail Rd ... 28146
Torrence St ... 28144
Tower Dr ... 28146
Town Ct ... 28147
Trading Path ... 28147
Trails End Ln ... 28146
Trantham Ln ... 28146
Traveller Ln ... 28146
Travis Ln ... 28146
Tree Top Ct ... 28147
Tremont Dr ... 28147
Trexler Loop ... 28144
Trexler Rd ... 28146
Trexler St
1-1099 ... 28144
3800-5899 ... 28147
Trinity Oaks Dr ... 28144
Troon Dr ... 28144
Troutman St ... 28144
Truck Ave ... 28146
Tumbleweed Dr ... 28146
Tupelo Cir ... 28146
Turnberry Cir ... 28147
Twin Chapel Dr ... 28147
Twin Creeks Dr ... 28146
Twin Lake Dr ... 28146
Twin Oaks Rd ... 28146
Tyler Ct ... 28146
Tyre Dr ... 28146
Union Church Rd ... 28146
Union Heights Blvd ... 28146
Uphill Dr ... 28146
Upper Palmer Rd ... 28146
N Us Highway 29 ... 28144
Us Highway 52 ... 28146
Us Highway 601 S ... 28147
Vacation Ct ... 28146
Valentine Ct ... 28147
Valley Dr ... 28147
Valleyview Pl ... 28144
Van Nuys St ... 28144
Vance Ave ... 28144
Vanderbuilt Dr ... 28147
Vanderford St ... 28144
Varnadore Rd ... 28146
Venture Ct & Dr ... 28147
Verlen Dr ... 28146
Veronia Ln ... 28146
Veronica Ln ... 28146
Victor St ... 28147
Victoria St ... 28147
Victory St ... 28144
E Villa Woods Dr ... 28146
Village Ln ... 28146
Village Creek Way ... 28147
Vincent Ct ... 28146
Vine St ... 28146
Vine Arden Dr ... 28146

Vineyard Cir & Dr ... 28146
Viola Ln ... 28146
Vista Dr ... 28146
Waccamaw Dr ... 28146
Waddell Dr ... 28147
Waggoner Rd ... 28144
Wagner Country Dr ... 28146
Wagon Ln ... 28146
Wagon Wheel Way ... 28147
Wake Dr ... 28144
Wakefield Dr ... 28146
Walden Ln ... 28146
Walen Dr ... 28147
Walker St ... 28144
Walker Valley Ln ... 28146
Walkers Park Cir ... 28146
Wall St ... 28146
Walnut St ... 28144
N Walnut St ... 28146
Walnut Cove Dr ... 28147
N & S Walnut Gq St ... 28146
Walnut Gq Street Ext ... 28146
Walton Pl & Rd ... 28146
Warehouse Dr ... 28144
Water St ... 28144
Waterford Dr ... 28147
Waters Rd ... 28146
Waverly Cir ... 28144
Weant St ... 28144
Weatherby Dr ... 28146
Webb Rd
100-899 ... 28147
900-2699 ... 28146
Webb Farm Rd ... 28147
Wedgefield Dr ... 28147
Wedgewood Dr ... 28146
Welch Rd ... 28144
Welder St ... 28144
Weldon Ln ... 28146
Wellington Dr ... 28144
Wellington Hills Cir ... 28147
Wendermere Dr ... 28144
Wendover Dr ... 28147
Wentwood Ln ... 28147
Wesley Dr ... 28146
Wesminster Ct ... 28146
Westerman Loop ... 28146
Westfork Dr ... 28146
Westway Ln ... 28147
Wheatfield Ln ... 28147
Wheaton Ct ... 28147
Whipporwill Ln ... 28146
Whisnant Dr ... 28144
Whisperwood Dr ... 28147
White Rd ... 28147
White Crane Rd ... 28146
White Farm Rd ... 28147
White Oak Cir ... 28146
White Oaks Dr ... 28147
White Rock Ave ... 28146
Whitetail Ln ... 28147
Whitney Ct ... 28146
Whitney Dr ... 28147
Whitney Ln ... 28146
Wild Turkey Way ... 28146
Wildflower Ln ... 28147
Wildwood Dr ... 28146
Wiley Ave ... 28144
Wiley Ln ... 28146
Wilhelm Ridge Ln ... 28146
Wilkins Ln ... 28144
Will Black Rd ... 28147
William Dr ... 28146
Williams St ... 28144
Willow Dr
100-299 ... 28146
1500-1599 ... 28144
Willow Ln ... 28146
Willow Rd ... 28147
Willow Run ... 28146
Willow St ... 28144
Willow Creek Dr ... 28146
Wilson Rd ... 28144
Wilton Ln ... 28147
Wiltshire Pl & Rd ... 28144
Winchester Cir ... 28144

Wind Dr ... 28144
Winding Way ... 28147
Winding Brook Ln ... 28146
Windmill Rd ... 28147
Windsor Dr ... 28144
Windwood Apartments ... 28146
Windy Hill Dr ... 28147
Windy Knob Way ... 28146
Windy Ridge Ln ... 28144
Winged Foot Dr ... 28144
Winning Way ... 28147
Winterlocken Rd ... 28144
Wisconsin Dr ... 28147
Wise Ln ... 28146
Withers Rd ... 28147
Wood Ave ... 28144
Wood Duck Run ... 28146
Woodberry Dr ... 28146
Woodbine Dr ... 28146
Woodbury Dr ... 28146
Woodlake Dr ... 28147
Woodland Dr ... 28146
Woodland Hls ... 28146
Woodland Rd ... 28144
Woodland Creek Dr ... 28147
Woodleaf Rd ... 28147
Woodmill Rd ... 28147
Woodrun Cir ... 28146
Woodside Dr ... 28146
Woodson St ... 28144
Woodvale Cir ... 28146
Woodwedge Cir ... 28144
Woody Ave ... 28146
Wrenwood Ct ... 28146
Wright Ave ... 28147
Wyndham Way ... 28147
Yachtman Dr ... 28146
Yadkin Baptist Church
Rd ... 28144
Yadkin Gq St ... 28146
Yadkin River Dr ... 28147
Yale Rd ... 28146
Yates Rd ... 28146
York Rd
100-199 ... 28144
300-599 ... 28147
Yorkshire Dr ... 28144
Yost Rd ... 28146
Yost St ... 28144
Yost Farm Rd ... 28146
Young Rd ... 28146
Young Farm Rd ... 28144
Yount Dr ... 28147
Zeb St ... 28144
Zebulon Ln ... 28146

NUMBERED STREETS

1st St ... 28144
2nd St ... 28144
2nd Es St ... 28144
3rd St ... 28144
E 3rd St ... 28146
3rd Es St ... 28144
3rd Street Ext ... 28144
4th St ... 28144
7th St ... 28144
W 10th St ... 28144
E & W 11th ... 28144
E & W 12th ... 28144
E & W 13th ... 28144
E & W 14th ... 28144
E & W 15th ... 28144
E 16th St ... 28144
E & W 17th ... 28144

SANFORD NC

POST OFFICE BOXES MAIN OFFICE STATIONS AND BRANCHES

Box No.s
All PO Boxes ... 27237

NAMED STREETS

A And B Rd ... 27332
A D Hall Rd ... 27332
Abbott Dr ... 27330
Abercorn Ln ... 27330
Academy St ... 27332
Acorn Dr ... 27330
Acorn Ln ... 27332
Advancement Center
Rd ... 27330
Adventure Ln ... 27330
Agnes Almary Ln ... 27330
Airport Rd ... 27332
Alabama Ave ... 27332
Albert Ct ... 27332
Alcott St ... 27330
Alder Ln ... 27332
Alfred Alston Rd ... 27330
Alisha Ln ... 27330
Allen Rd ... 27332
Allen Farms Rd ... 27330
Allendale Ln ... 27330
Alma Brown Rd ... 27330
Alpine Ave ... 27332
Alston House Rd ... 27330
Altons Ln ... 27332
Amanda Dr ... 27330
Amarillo Ln ... 27332
Amber Ln ... 27332
Amber Wood ... 27332
Amberwood Dr ... 27332
Amherst Rd ... 27330
Ammons Farm Rd ... 27330
Amos Bridges Rd ... 27330
Andrea Ct ... 27332
Andrews Dr ... 27332
Angel Rd ... 27330
Angus Ct ... 27332
Animal Ave ... 27330
Apache Trl ... 27332
Apple Dr ... 27332
Apple Ln ... 27330
Applecross Ct ... 27332
Applegate Way ... 27332
Appleton Way ... 27332
Appletree Rd ... 27330
Arbor Ln ... 27330
Argyll Dr ... 27332
Arlington Cir ... 27330
Arrowood Cir ... 27332
Arthur Maddox Rd ... 27332
Asbury Church Rd ... 27330
Ashby Rd ... 27332
Ashford Cir ... 27330
Ashley Island Rd ... 27330
Aspen Dr ... 27332
Asset Pkwy ... 27332
Atkins Ln ... 27330
Attie Lee Ln ... 27330
Auguston Ct ... 27330
Austin St ... 27330
Austin Farm Ln ... 27332
Autumn Ct ... 27330
Autumn Valley Dr ... 27330
Avents Ferry Rd ... 27330
Ayers Ln ... 27332
Azalea Ln ... 27332
Back Bay ... 27332
Badders Rd ... 27330
Bailes Dr ... 27330
Bailey Thomas Rd ... 27332
Baker Dr ... 27332
Ballentyne Ct ... 27332
Balsam Ln ... 27330
Bamboo Ln ... 27330
Bank St ... 27332
Barbecue Church Rd ... 27332
Bargin Ln ... 27332
Barnes St ... 27330
Barney Ct ... 27332
Barrett Bush Ln ... 27332
Barretts Landing Ln ... 27330
Barringer Rd ... 27330
Barrington Ct ... 27332

Bassett Hall Ln ... 27330
Battle St ... 27330
Bay Dr & Pt ... 27332
Bay Tree Ln ... 27332
Bayberry Ln ... 27332
Bayleaf Ln ... 27332
Baystone Dr ... 27332
Beach End ... 27332
Beachwood Dr ... 27330
Beacon Cir ... 27332
Beal Dr ... 27330
Beautiful Ln ... 27332
Beaver Br ... 27332
Beaver Farm Ln ... 27330
Beaver Lake Rd ... 27332
Bee Ln ... 27332
Beechtree Dr ... 27330
Beechtree Vlg ... 27332
Belfast Ln ... 27332
Belford Dr ... 27330
Belgium Horse Ln ... 27330
Bell Dr ... 27330
Bellaire Dr ... 27330
Belmont Cir ... 27332
Benhaven School Rd ... 27332
Bennett St ... 27330
Bent Pine Cir ... 27330
Bentcreek Ct ... 27330
Berke Thomas Rd ... 27330
Bermuda Trl ... 27332
Bethany Cir ... 27330
Bethany Springs Rd ... 27330
Beulah Brown Rd ... 27332
Bickett Rd ... 27330
Big Branch Rd ... 27332
Big Man Dr ... 27330
Big Oaks Ln ... 27330
Big Rock Ln ... 27330
Big Sky Rd ... 27330
Big Springs Rd ... 27330
Big Springs Road Ext ... 27330
Bighorn Ln ... 27332
Birch St ... 27330
Birchard Rd ... 27332
Birdie Ln ... 27330
Birdies Roost ... 27332
Birkdale Dr ... 27332
Blackberry Ln ... 27330
Blackjack Dr ... 27332
Blacks Chapel Rd ... 27332
Blackstone Rd ... 27330
Blackwelder Dr ... 27330
Blair St ... 27332
Blakely Rd ... 27332
Blanchard Rd ... 27332
Bland Cir ... 27330
Blue Heron Ct ... 27332
Blue Sky ... 27330
Blue Stone Dr ... 27330
Bluebird Ct & Dr ... 27332
Bluejay Dr ... 27332
Blumont Dr ... 27332
Bobbitt St ... 27330
Bobolink Rd ... 27330
Bobwhite Ln ... 27332
Bogan St ... 27330
Bond Ct ... 27332
Bone Oak ... 27332
Bonnie Path ... 27330
Booker St ... 27330
Boone Trail Rd ... 27330
Botany Woods Dr ... 27330
Boulder Dr ... 27332
Bouldin Ln ... 27332
Bounty Ln ... 27330
Bourbon St ... 27332
Bowles Ln ... 27332
Boyd Brafford Dr ... 27332
Boykin Ave ... 27330
Bracken St ... 27330
Bradford Pear Ln ... 27330
Bradley Rd ... 27330
Brady Rd ... 27330
Brafferton Ct ... 27330
Bragg St ... 27330
Branch Rd ... 27330

Brandons Cir 27330
Brandy Ln 27332
Brantley Rd 27330
Breezewood Rd 27330
Brent Wood 27332
Brentwood Pl 27330
Briar Oak Ct 27332
Briarcliffe Dr 27330
Briarwood Dr & Pl 27332
Brick Capital Ct 27332
Brickyard Rd 27330
Bridgeport Cir 27330
Bridges Rd 27330
Bridgewater Dr 27330
Bridle Path 27332
Bridle Wood Ln 27330
Brighton Pt 27330
Brights Mhp 27330
Brinn Dr 27330
Bristol St 27332
Bristol Way 27330
Brittany Woods Dr & Rd 27332
Britton Ct 27330
Broadmoor Ct 27332
Broadway Rd 27332
Brody Parker Rd 27330
Brookcliff Rd 27330
Brookfield Cir 27330
Brookhaven Dr 27330
Brookhollow Dr 27330
Brooks Dr 27332
Brookwood Trl 27330
Brothers Dr & Rd 27330
Brown Rd 27330
Brownstone Rd 27330
Bruce Coggins Rd 27332
Bryan Dr 27332
Bryant Dr 27330
Bryte Ter 27332
Bubbas Way 27332
Buchanan St 27330
Buchanan Farm Rd 27330
Buckhorn Rd 27330
Buckingham Dr 27330
Buckroe Dr 27330
Bucks Ct 27332
E & W Buffalo St 27330
Buffalo Church Rd 27330
Buffalo Lake Rd 27332
Buffalo Turn 27332
Bugfield Ln 27332
Bullard Rd 27330
Bumgarner Ln 27330
Bumpy Ln 27332
Burning Tree Cir 27332
Burns Dr 27330
Butler St 27330
Byrd Ave 27332
C And W Ct 27332
Cade Ln 27332
Calcutta Ln 27330
Calico Ct 27330
California Pl 27332
Calumet Dr 27332
Calvary Ct 27332
Calvary Church Rd 27332
Cambridge Dr 27330
Camden Ct E 27332
Camden Ct W 27332
Camden Sq 27330
Camelot Ln 27330
Cameron Dr 27332
Cameron Pines Dr 27332
Campbell Dr 27330
Campbell Ln 27332
Candace St 27332
Cannon Cir 27330
Canterbury Cir 27332
Canterbury Rd
1-199 27332
600-899 27330
Canyon Ct & Vw 27332
Canyon Creek Dr 27330
Cape Jasmine Dr 27330
Captain Hbr 27332
Captains Pt 27332
S Carbonton Rd 27330
Cardinal Cir
1400-1499 27330
5000-5199 27332
Cardinal Bay 27332
Carol St 27332
Carolina Ct, Dr, Trce & Way 27332
Carolina Lakes Rd 27332
Caroline Dr 27330
Carpenter Ln 27330
Carr St 27330
Carr Creek Rd 27332
Carr Creek Mhp 27332
Carrington Ln 27330
Carson Dr 27332
Carter Dr 27332
Carthage St 27330
Carver Dr 27332
Cary Ct 27330
Casablanca Ct 27332
Cascade Ct 27330
Cashmere Ct 27332
W Castle Ct 27330
Castle Bay Dr 27332
Castle Rock Dr 27332
Castle Wood 27332
Castleberry Rd 27332
Castleton Dr 27330
Cattle Dr 27332
Cave Rd 27332
Caviness Dr 27330
Cedar Cir, Ln & Rd 27332
Cedar Lake Rd 27330
Cedar Lane Rd 27332
Cedarhurst Dr 27330
Cellas Ln 27332
Cemetery Rd 27332
Center Church Rd 27330
Central Dr 27330
Chadwick Cir 27330
Chaffin St 27330
Chalmers Dr & Rd 27330
Chancellors Ridge Way 27330
Chapman Dr 27332
Char Lin Dr 27332
Chariot Dr 27330
Charles Riddle Rd 27330
Charleston Dr 27330
Charlotte Ave 27330
Charwood Pl 27332
Chason Ter 27332
Chateau Cir 27332
Chatham St 27330
Chatham Church Rd 27330
Chelsea Dr 27330
Cherokee Trl 27332
Cherry St 27330
Cherry Berry Ln 27332
Cheshire Dr 27332
Chestnut Ln 27330
Chicago Loop 27332
Chickadee Ct 27332
Chicken Farm Ln 27330
Chicks Ln 27330
Chilton Dr 27332
Chimney Rock Ln 27330
Chipmunk Cir 27332
Chippendale Trl 27330
Chipping Wedge 27332
E & W Chisholm St 27330
Chownings Dr 27330
Chris Cole Rd 27332
Christmas Ln 27332
Christopher Dr 27332
Christopher Ln 27330
Church St 27330
Circle Ave 27330
Cks Ln 27330
Clarence Mckeithen Rd 27330
Clark Cir 27330
Claude White Rd 27332
Clearview Ct 27332
Clearwater Dr 27330
Clearwater Hbr 27332
Clearwater Pt 27332
Cletus Hall Rd 27330
Cleveland Cir 27332
Cliffside Ct 27332
Cliffside Dr 27330
Clifton Ln 27330
Cloud Ct 27332
Club Ln 27330
Club House Dr 27332
Clyde Rhyne Dr 27330
Coachman Way 27332
Coastal Ct 27332
Cobb Ct 27330
Cobblestone Dr 27330
Cold Duck 27332
Cole St 27330
Colon Rd 27330
Colonial Dr 27330
Colorado Trl 27332
Columbine Rd 27330
Comfort Ln 27330
Commerce Dr 27332
Commercial Ct 27330
Compass Way 27330
Condor St 27330
Cone St 27330
Connecticut Pl 27332
Cool Springs Rd 27330
Cooper Store Rd 27332
Coopers Corner Ln 27332
Copeland Rd 27330
Copper Loop 27332
Copper Mine Dr 27332
Copper Ridge Dr 27330
Coradins Rd 27330
Coral Stone Ct 27330
Coralberry Cir 27332
Cornell Dr 27332
Cornsilk Dr 27332
Costa Maya Ct 27332
Cotten Rd 27330
Cottontail Ln 27330
Country Pl & Way 27332
Country Club Ct & Dr 27332
Country Estates Dr 27332
Country Squire Dr 27332
Country Walk Ln 27332
Court Sq 27330
W Courtland Dr & Vlg 27330
Courtney Ln 27330
Courtside Ln 27330
Cove Lndg 27332
Coventry Ct 27332
Covered Bridge Ln 27330
Covert Rd 27330
Cowboy Ln 27330
Cox Rd 27330
Cox Maddox Rd 27332
Cox Mill Rd 27332
Cozy Hollow Dr 27332
Craft Ln 27330
Craig Dr 27330
Cranberry Ln 27330
Cranes Dr 27332
Creek Run 27332
Creek Trl 27330
Creekside Dr 27330
Creekside Trl 27332
Creekview Ln 27330
Creekwood Rd 27330
Crepe Myrtle Dr 27330
Crest St 27330
Cresthaven Dr 27332
Crestview St 27330
Cricket Hearth Rd 27330
Cripple Creek Ln 27332
Cromarty Ave 27330
Cross St 27330
Crosswinds Cir 27332
Crown Pt 27332
Crusaders Dr 27330
Crystal Pt 27332
Crystal Spring Dr 27332
Cumberland Rd 27330
Cumnock Rd 27330
N & S Currie Dr 27330
Currituck Dr 27332
Curt Dowdy Rd 27330
Curtis Ln 27330
Cutter Cir 27332
Cypress Pt 27332
Cypress Creek Farm Rd 27332
D Seagroves Rd 27330
Daffodil Ln 27330
Daiquiri Turn 27332
Daisy St 27330
Dakota Loop 27332
Dale O Ln 27330
Dalrymple Rd 27330
Dalrymple St
2000-2499 27330
2500-2899 27332
Dalrymple Farm Rd 27330
Dana Ln 27332
Dandy Ln 27330
Daniels Creek Rd 27330
Darryls Dr 27330
Darwin Ct 27332
Days Ct 27332
Debra Ln 27330
Deep River Rd & Trl 27330
Deer Vw 27332
Deer Creek Rd 27330
Deer Track Trl 27332
Deerfield Dr 27332
Deerfoot Trl 27332
Delaware Cir 27332
Delwood St 27330
Denada Path 27332
Dennis Dr 27330
Detroit Blvd 27332
Dewayne St 27332
Dewitt St 27330
Dillon Ln 27332
Dinghy Dr 27332
Dinkins Dr 27332
Dino Ct 27332
Divot Dr 27332
Dixie Farm Rd 27332
Doctors Dr 27330
Dodson Rd 27332
Doe Run Dr 27332
Dogwood Ln & St 27330
Dogwood Acres Dr 27332
Doll House Rd 27332
Dorsett Rd 27330
Double D Ln 27330
Douglas Dr 27330
Douglas Farm Rd 27332
Dove Path & Trl 27332
Dover Ct E 27332
Dover Ct W 27332
Dover St 27330
Down Home Ln 27332
Doyle Cox Rd 27332
Dragon Fly Ln 27332
Dragonfly Ln 27332
Dry Branch Trl 27332
Dryfork Rd 27330
Dublin Dr & Rd 27330
Duck Ln 27330
Duck Crossing Ln 27332
Dudley Ave 27330
Duffers Ln 27332
Duke Dr 27330
Dumbarton Dr 27330
Dunbar Dr 27330
Dunes Cir & Dr 27332
Durgin Springs Rd 27330
Dycus Rd 27330
Eagles Nest Dr 27332
Eagles Roost 27332
Eakes Rd 27330
Eames Dr 27330
East Pt 27332
Ebony Ln 27330
Echo Ln
1-99 27332
100-199 27330
Edenberry Ln 27332
Edgedale Ln 27332
Edgemont Ter 27332
Edgewood Dr 27330
Edinburgh Dr 27332
Eds Ln 27332
Edwards Rd 27332
Electric Ln 27332
Elizabeth Ave 27330
Elkins Ln 27330
Elliott Rd 27332
Elm St 27330
Elsie Lamm Rd 27332
Elwin Buchanan Dr 27330
Emily Ln 27330
Emory Pointe 27332
Englewood Cir 27332
English Cir 27332
Erwin Rd 27330
Essex Ct 27332
Euphronia Church Rd 27330
Evans Dr 27330
Everett Dowdy Rd 27330
Evergreen Ln 27330
Evers Ave 27332
Eveton Ln 27330
Ewestbrook Dr 27332
F L Dowdy Ln 27330
F O R Ln 27332
Fair Vw 27332
Fair Barn Rd 27332
Fairfax Dr 27332
Fairview Ln 27330
Fairway Dr 27330
Fairway Ln 27332
Fairway Woods 27332
Falling Strm 27332
Falls Creek Rd 27330
Falls Park Dr 27332
Family Farm Ln 27332
Farm Rd 27330
Farm Wood 27332
Farmhouse Ct 27332
Farmington Ln 27330
Farmstead Dr 27332
Farmville Coal Mine Rd 27330
Farmwood Ct 27332
Farrell Rd 27330
Fawn Ln 27330
Fayetteville St 27332
Fern Creek Dr 27332
Ferndell Path 27330
Fernridge Dr 27332
Fields Dr 27330
Fieldstone Dr 27330
Fire Tower Rd 27330
Firestone Ln 27330
Firethorn Ln 27330
First Pt 27332
Fisher Ln 27332
Fitts St 27330
Fitzpatrick Dr 27330
Five Ponds Dr 27332
Flint Crk 27332
Flo Tom Ln 27332
Florence Harris Ln 27330
Florida Dr 27332
Flowers Dr & Ln 27332
Foggy Btm 27330
Foggy Mountain Loop 27330
Fore View Ln 27332
Forest Glen Dr 27330
Forest Hills Ct 27332
Forest Manor Dr 27332
Forest Mountain Ct 27332
E & W Forest Oaks Dr 27330
Forest Ridge Dr 27330
Forestwood Park Rd 27330
Forrest Dr 27330
Foster Dr 27330
Fountain Wood Dr 27332
Foushee Dr 27330
Fox Rdg 27332
Fox Run Rd 27330
Fox Trail Ln 27332
Fox Wood Dr 27332
Fraley Rd 27330
Fralick Rd 27330
Frances Louise Ln 27332
Francis Ct 27332
Frank Thompson Rd 27330
Frank Wicker Rd 27332
N & S Franklin Dr 27330
W Frazier Dr 27332
Fred Stone Rd 27332
Freeman Dr 27330
Friars Dr 27330
Friendship Dr 27330
Frog Pond Ln 27330
Fry St 27330
Gabby Ln 27332
Gabrielle Ter 27332
Gaines Rd 27330
Galaxy Ln 27330
E & W Garden St 27330
Garner Rd 27330
Gary St 27330
Gates St 27330
Georgia Bay 27332
Gettysburg Ct 27332
Gibson Dr 27330
Gilliam Rd 27330
Gilmore Dr 27330
Gilmore Farm Rd 27332
Gin Way 27332
Gladden Ln 27330
Glade Run Dr 27330
Glass Dr 27330
Glenaire Cir 27330
Glendale Cir 27330
Glenn Ct 27332
Glenn Oak Dr 27332
Glenwood Dr 27330
E & W Globe St 27330
Gloucester Dr 27330
Goat Hill Ln 27330
Godfrey Dr 27330
Gods Way 27330
Goins Dr 27330
Golden Hills Ln 27332
Golden Horseshoe Ln 27332
Goldfinch Turn 27332
Goldsboro Ave 27330
Goldston Blvd 27330
Golf Dr 27332
Golf Course Ln 27330
Gordon St 27330
Gordon Wicker Dr 27332
Gormly Cir 27330
Governors Creek Ln 27330
Graceland Ln 27330
Graham Rd 27332
Grant St 27330
Grassmere Ct 27330
Gravel Ln 27332
Gray St 27330
Gray Fox Ln 27332
Grayson Pl 27332
Great Dane Rd 27330
Green St 27330
Green Acres Dr 27330
Green Meadow Dr 27332
Green Spring Dr 27332
Green Valley Dr 27330
Greenbriar Dr 27330
Greenland Dr 27330
Greensboro Ave 27330
Greenside Ln 27332
Greenway Ct 27330
Greenwich Dr 27330
Greenwood Rd 27332
Grey Fox Ct 27332
Greystone Cir 27330
Grimm St 27332
Grogan St 27330
Grove St 27330
N & S Gulf Rd & St 27330
Gunter St 27330
Gunter Lake Rd 27332
Gunter Trailer Park 27332
H Atkins Rd 27330
H M Godfrey Ln 27330
Hal Siler Dr 27332
Halifax St 27330
Hall St 27330
Hamilton Dr 27330
Hampton Pl 27330
Hancock Rd 27332
Happy Ct & Ln 27332
Harbor Trce 27332
Harbor Side 27332
Harborview Dr 27332
Hard Oak Ct 27330
Hardwood Ln 27330
Harkey Rd 27330
Harley Ln 27332
Harriet J Ln 27332
Harrington Ln 27330
Harrington Pl 27332
Harrington St 27330
Hart Dr 27330
Hartshorne Ct 27330
Harvey Faulk Rd 27332
Harward Dr 27332
Hatteras Ln 27332
Haw Branch Rd 27330
Hawk Rd 27330
Hawkinberry Ln 27330
Hawkins Ave 27330
Hawthorne Dr 27330
Hayden Ave 27330
Hayes Rd 27332
Hearn Ln 27330
Hearthstone Dr 27330
Heather Dr 27330
Heavens Gate Ct 27332
Hel Mar Ln 27332
Hemi Ln 27330
Hemlock Dr 27332
Henley Rd 27330
Henry Cir 27330
Hermitage Rd 27330
Hiawatha Trl 27332
Hibiscus Ct 27332
Hickman Ln 27332
Hickory Ave 27330
Hickory Hill Dr 27332
Hickory House Rd 27332
Hickory Nut Ct 27332
Hickorydale Ln 27332
Hidden Pond Ln 27332
High Harbor Rd 27332
High Ridge Dr 27330
Highland Cir 27332
Highland St 27330
Highland Forest Dr 27332
Highland School Rd 27332
Highwoods Dr 27330
Hill Ave 27330
Hill Side Ln 27332
Hill Top Cir 27332
Hillandale Dr 27332
Hillcrest Dr 27332
Hillcrest Farm Rd 27330
Hilltop Ln 27332
Hilltop Rd 27330
Hillwood St 27332
Hiram Ter 27332
Holder Rd 27332
Holiday Rd 27330
Holly Ln 27332
Holly Berry Ln 27330
Holly Brook Rd 27330
Holly Pond Dr 27332
Holly Tree Ln 27330
Hollywood Rd 27330
Holman Ln 27332
Holt Rd 27330
Homestead Cv 27332
Honeybee Cir 27332
Honeysuckle Trl 27332
Hooker St 27330
Hoover Rd 27332
Hoover St
100-199 27330
300-799 27332

Hope St 27332
Hopemore St 27330
N Horner Blvd 27330
S Horner Blvd
100-1199 27330
1200-2498 27330
1200-1200 27331
1201-2499 27330
2500-3499 27332
Horsemans Ridge Ln 27330
Horseshoe Falls Rd 27330
Horton Cir 27330
Hospital Dr 27330
Howard Farm Ln 27330
Hubbard Rd 27330
Hudson Ave 27330
Hughes St 27330
Hughes Mhp Ln 27330
E & W Humber St 27330
Hummingbird Cir 27332
Hunt Springs Dr 27332
Hunter Fld, Rd & Rdg 27332
Hunter Farm Rd 27330
Hunters Glen Dr 27330
Hunters Ridge Rd 27332
Huntington Ln 27330
Hwy 87 S 27332
Idlewilde Ln 27332
Illinois Ave 27332
Imperial Dr 27330
Independent Dr 27330
Indian Trl 27332
Indian Wells Ct 27332
Indiana Cir 27332
Industrial Dr 27332
Inlet Vw 27332
Inverness Cir 27332
Irish Blvd 27332
Iron Furnace Rd 27330
Ivey Dr 27332
J And S Ln 27330
J Campbell Ln 27332
J D Murchison Ln 27332
J Mccrimmon Ln 27332
J R Industrial Dr 27332
J Stewart Ln 27330
Jackson St 27330
Jacobs Ln 27332
Jake Ln 27330
James St 27330
James River Ct 27330
James W Davis Ln 27332
Jamestown Dr 27330
Jasany Dr 27330
Jasper Ln 27330
Jefferson St 27330
Jefferson Davis Hwy
1800-2299 27330
2300-4199 27332
Jeffrey St 27332
Jeffries Dr 27330
Jenkins St 27330
Jenni Ln 27330
Jessica Ct 27332
Jewel Ln 27332
Jim Ln 27332
Jim Gordon Dr 27330
Jj Ln 27332
Joe Carson Rd 27332
Joe Matthews Rd 27332
Joels Ln 27330
Joey Ct 27330
John Garner Rd 27332
John Godfrey Rd 27332
John Rosser Rd 27332
John Waddell Ln 27332
Johnson Dr 27330
Johnson Cemetary Rd 27332
Johnsonville School
Rd 27332
Jonathon Ln 27332
Jones Cir & St 27332
Jones Chapel Rd 27330
Jonesboro Jct 27332
Joni Dr 27332
Jordan Ln & Rd 27330

Josie Ln 27332
Jp Ln 27332
Judd St 27332
Judson Rd 27330
Judy Ann Ln 27330
June Rd 27332
Junior Ln 27332
Juniper Dr 27330
Juniper Creek Rd 27332
Juno Dr 27332
K Bar Ln 27332
K M Wicker Memorial
Dr 27330
Kansas Loop 27332
Kate Ln 27332
Katherine Dr 27332
Kathleen Ter 27332
Keats Rd 27330
Keith Dr 27332
Keller Andrews Rd 27330
Kelly Dr 27330
Kelly Rd 27332
Kenan Dr 27330
Kendale Dr 27332
Kentucky Ave 27332
Kentyrewood Farm Rd 27332
Kenwood Ter 27332
Key Rd 27332
Khalif Ct 27332
Kids Ln 27330
Kildare Cir 27330
Kimberly Cir 27330
King St 27330
King Farm Ln & Rd 27330
Kingfisher Rd 27332
Kingwood Cir 27332
Kir Cir 27332
S Kirby Ln 27330
Kirk Ct 27332
Kirkmaiden Ave 27330
Kitten Cv 27332
Kittery Pt 27332
Knight Rd 27332
Knollwood Dr 27330
Knot Cir 27332
Knottwood Dr 27332
Knottwood Trailer Park 27330
Knotty Pine Trl 27332
Kristin Ln 27330
L And S Dr 27332
Labrador Ln 27330
Lafayette Dr 27330
Lake Frst & Pt 27332
Lake Willet Rd 27330
Lakebrook Cir 27330
Lakeforest Trl 27332
Lakehill Dr 27330
Lakeland Dr 27332
Lakeland Prt 27332
N Lakes Dr 27330
Lakeside Dr 27330
Lakeside Ln 27332
Lakeview Cir & Dr 27332
Lakewind Cir 27332
Lakewood Vw 27332
Lamm Ln 27332
E Landing 27332
S Landing 27332
W Landing 27332
W Landing Dr 27330
Landis St 27330
Landmark Ln 27330
Landor Cir 27330
Lanier Farm Rd 27330
Lanlier Dr 27330
Lansing Ct E 27332
Lansing Ct W 27332
Lansing St 27330
Lantana Cir 27332
Lantern Run 27330
Lark Ln 27332
Larkspur Dr 27330
Laurel Dr 27330
Laurel Ridge Dr 27332
Lawrence St 27330
Lazy Waters Ln 27330

Lee Ave
900-2499 27330
2500-4499 27332
Leeds Ct 27332
Lees Chapel Rd 27330
Lees Well Rd 27330
Legion Dr 27330
Leicester Cir 27332
Lemmond Dr 27330
Lemon Heights Dr 27332
Lemon Springs Rd 27332
Lenity Ln 27332
Leola Ln 27332
Leons Way 27332
Leslie Rd 27332
Lick Creek Rd 27330
Lightwood Ln 27330
Lillie Ln 27330
Lilly Loop 27332
Linden Ave 27330
Lindsey Ln 27330
Lineberger Ln 27332
Little Creek Rd 27330
Little John Ln 27330
Little River Ln 27330
Live Oak Dr 27330
Liverpool Dr 27332
Lizzie Hl 27332
Loblolly Ct & Trl 27332
Lochmere Dr 27332
Log Cabin Ln 27330
Logan Farm Ln 27330
Logging Trl 27332
Lone Pine Trl 27332
Long Dr 27332
Long Branch Rd 27330
Long Point Trl 27332
Longleaf Ct 27332
Longleaf Ln 27330
Longleaf Pine Way 27332
Longstreet Rd 27330
Longview Dr 27330
Longwood Ave 27330
Lookout Pt 27332
Lora Ann Ln 27332
Lord Ashley Dr 27330
Lori Ln 27332
Lorraine Ln 27330
Lotus Ln 27332
Louise St 27330
Louisiana Ln 27332
Love Grove Church
Rd 27332
Lower Moncure Rd 27330
Lower River Rd 27330
Loxley Ln 27330
Luanne St 27330
Lucas And Tucker Ln 27332
Luck Ln 27330
Lula Ln 27330
Lydia Perry Rd 27330
Lyman Kittrell Ln 27330
Lynn Ave 27330
Lynnbrook Dr 27332
Lynwood Cir 27330
Lyons St 27330
Macon Ct E & W 27332
Maddox Dr 27332
Mag Ln 27330
Maggie Ln 27332
Magnolia Ct 27332
Magnolia St 27330
Mahogony Ct 27332
Maideline Ave 27332
E Main St
100-899 27332
900-1299 27330
W Main St 27332
Maine Cir 27332
E & W Makepeace St 27330
Mallard Dr, Rd & Trl 27332
Mallard Cove Rd 27330
Manassas Dr 27332
Manhattan Row 27332
Maple Ave 27330
Maple Cir 27332

Maplewood Dr
1-399 27332
500-599 27330
Margarita Ln 27332
Marina Rd 27332
Market St 27330
Marketplace Dr 27332
Markham Dr 27332
Marks St 27330
Marsh St 27330
Martin Cir 27332
Martin St 27330
Mary Emma Ln 27330
Maryland Ct 27332
Marzy Ct 27332
Massachusetts Sq 27332
Masters Cir 27332
Matthews St 27330
Mattie Rd 27332
Maybee Hill Dr 27330
Mayflower Cir 27330
Mays Chapel Rd 27330
Mcauley St 27330
Mcauley Greaux Ln 27332
Mccleney Cir 27332
Mccormick Rd 27332
Mcdaniel Dr 27332
Mcdonald Dr & Rd 27332
Mcdougald Rd 27332
Mcgilberry Ln 27332
Mcgill St 27330
E & W Mcintosh St 27330
Mciver St 27330
Mckenzie Park Dr 27330
Mckinley Ln 27330
Mcleod Dr 27332
Mcmillian Ln 27332
Mcneill Rd
100-1499 27330
2800-4399 27332
Mcpherson Rd 27330
Mcqueen Chapel Rd 27332
Meade St 27330
Meadow Dr 27332
Meadow Reach Trl 27332
Meadow Spring Ln 27332
Meadow View Ln 27332
Meadowbrook St 27330
Meadowlark Trl 27332
Meerkat Ln 27330
Melvin Ln 27330
Melwood Ln 27332
Memory Ln 27330
Merchants Ct 27330
Mercury Ln 27330
Meridian Xing 27330
Merion Cir 27332
Merriwood Ct 27330
Meyers Ln 27330
Michigan Blvd 27332
Micro 27330
Midget Ln 27330
Midland Ave 27330
Mill Run 27332
Mill Creek Ct 27330
Mill Pond Rd 27330
Mill Ridge Rd 27330
Mill Run Rd 27332
Millbrook Dr 27330
Millstone Ct 27330
Milton Welch Rd 27332
Mini Mobile Ln 27330
Minow Johnson Rd 27330
Minter Ave 27332
Minter School Rd 27332
Misha Ln 27330
Mobile Home Park Ln 27330
Moblie Ln 27332
Mock Brothers Rd 27332
Mockingbird Ln 27330
Monarch Ln 27330
Monger Ln 27330
Monroe Ave 27330
Montague Ct 27330
Montana Sq 27332
Montclair Cir 27332

Moon Run 27332
Moonshine Ln 27332
N & S Moore St 27330
Moorehill Cir 27330
W Mooring 27332
Morning Star Dr 27330
Morning View Dr 27330
Morris Meadows Ct 27332
Mossy Oak Ln 27332
Mount Pisgah Church
Rd 27332
Mount Sands Ln 27332
Mountain View Dr 27332
Mountainside Ln 27332
Mourning Dove Dr 27332
Mugs Ln 27332
Mulberry Ln 27332
Murchison Rd 27332
Murchisontown Rd 27332
Myrtle Ln 27332
Mystic Wolf Ln 27332
Nance Rd 27330
Nancy Dr 27332
Nash St 27330
Nassau Ln 27332
Navaho Trl 27332
Nc 27 W 27332
Nc 87 N & S 27332
Nc Highway 27 27332
Nc Highway 42 27330
Nc Highway 87 S 27330
Neil Blue Ln 27332
Nevada Loop 27332
New Jersey Cir 27332
New York Ave 27332
Nicholson Rd 27332
Nicholwood Dr 27332
Nicole Dr 27332
Night Heron Ct 27332
Nixon Dr 27330
No Record 27332
Nob Hill Dr 27330
North Ave 27330
North Pt 27332
Northern Ranches Rd 27330
Northgate Cir 27332
Northridge Cir 27332
Northridge Dr 27330
Northridge Trl 27332
Northview Dr
1-1000 27332
1001-1099 27330
1001-8699 27332
1002-1198 27330
1002-1098 27330
8600-8698 27332
Nottingham Ln 27330
November Ln 27332
Nowhere Ln 27332
Nutbush Rd 27330
Oak Lndg 27332
Oak Rd 27332
W Oak Way 27330
Oak Branch Ln 27332
Oak Forest Dr 27332
Oak Hollow Ln 27332
Oak Park Rd 27330
Oak Point Ln 27332
Oak Shadows Ln 27330
Oakcrest Dr 27332
Oakdale St 27330
Oakhill Dr 27330
Oakland Dr 27330
Oaklawn Dr E 27332
Oakleaf Rd 27332
Oaktrail Ln 27332
Oakwood Ave 27330
Obed Olive Rd 27332
Oddfellow St 27330
Oelrich Cir 27332
Offset Farm Rd 27332
Ohio Ln 27332
Old Barn Ct 27332
Old Carbonton Rd 27332
Old Carriage Way 27330
Old Colon Rd 27330

Old Corral Ave 27332
Old E C Womack Rd 27330
Old Farm Rd 27332
Old Field Loop 27332
Old Jefferson Davis
Hwy 27332
Old Nc 87 27332
Old Place Ln 27332
Old Wagon Ln 27332
Olde Mill Dr 27330
Olde Towne Dr 27330
Oldham Lake Rd 27330
Olive Farm Rd 27332
Oliver Rd 27330
Olivia Rd 27332
Ontario Dr 27330
Openview Dr 27330
Oquinn Rd 27330
Orchard Ct 27330
Orchard Rd 27332
Orchard Crest Cir 27332
Oriole Cir 27330
Osgood Rd 27330
Osprey Pt 27332
Overbrook Ln 27330
Overlook Ct 27332
Owls Nest Rd 27330
Oxford Ln 27330
Oxon Ct 27332
Pacific Ln 27330
Pack House Ln 27332
Paige Cir 27330
Paint Horse Ln 27330
Palace Dr 27330
Palace Green Ln 27330
Palmer Dr 27330
Palmer Sloan Rd 27332
Palmetto Path 27332
Palomino Dr 27330
Pamela Dr 27330
Panners Pl 27330
Par Cir 27332
Par Dr 27330
Paradise Way 27332
Park Ave 27330
Parkton Ct E & W 27332
Parkwood Dr 27332
Parrish Ln 27332
Partridge Cir 27332
Pasture Ln 27330
Patchetts Creek Ln 27332
Pate Davis Ln 27332
Pathway Dr 27330
Patterson Ridge Ln 27332
Patton St 27332
Paul St 27330
Pauline Cir 27332
Peaceful Ln 27330
Peacehaven Ln 27332
Peach Blossom Cir 27332
Peach Orchard Rd 27332
Peach Tree Dr 27330
Peachtree Ln 27332
Peacock Dr & Rd 27332
E & W Pearl St 27330
Pearson Cir & St 27330
Pebble Bch 27332
Pebble Beach Pt 27332
Pebble Creek Mhp 27332
Pebblebrook Dr 27332
Pebbles Ct 27332
Pecan Ln 27332
Peele Ln 27332
Pegg St 27332
Pelican Ct 27332
Pendergrass Rd 27330
Pennsylvania Ave 27332
Penny Ln 27332
Peppermill Rd 27332
Periwinkle Rd 27330
Perkinson Rd 27330
Perry Rd 27332
Perry Pond Rd 27330
Pershing St 27330
Persimmon Path 27332
Perth Dr 27332

Peters Ln 27330
Petty Rd 27330
Petty Creek Rd 27330
Pheasant Cir, Ln & Rd 27332
Phil Johnson Rd 27330
Philadelphia St 27332
Phillips Dr 27330
Piccadilly Ct 27332
Pickard Rd 27330
Pickett Rd 27332
Piedmont Dr 27330
Pierce St 27330
Pilson Rd 27332
Pine Rd 27332
Pine St 27330
Pine Acres Dr 27330
Pine Branch Cir 27332
Pine Haven Dr 27332
Pine Haven Ln 27330
Pine Lake Dr 27330
Pine Line Dr 27332
Pine Ridge St 27330
Pine Wood Rd 27332
Pineburr Ln 27330
Pinecrest Ave 27330
Pinecrest Dr 27332
Pinecrest Ln
600-699 27330
9000-9099 27332
Pinehurst St 27330
Pineknoll Dr 27330
Pineland St 27330
Pineridge Cv 27332
Pineside Trl 27332
Pinevalley Ln 27332
Pinewinds Dr 27332
Pinewood Trl 27332
Piney Hollow Ln 27330
Pioneer Dr 27332
Pittsburgh Pl 27332
Placid Ln 27332
N & S Plank Rd 27330
Plant Bed Ln 27332
Plantation Dr 27330
Planters Rdg 27330
Plateau Ct 27330
Plaza Blvd 27330
Pleasant View Ln 27332
Pleasure Ln 27332
Pocket Church Rd 27332
Polly Ln 27330
Pond View Ln 27332
Ponderosa Rd 27332
Poplar St 27330
Poplar Springs Church
Rd 27330
Popular Turn 27332
Porches Way 27330
Port Bay 27332
Port Tack 27332
Port Turn 27332
Porter Ln 27330
Portico Cir 27330
Post Oak Ln 27330
Post Office Rd 27330
Pot Hole Ln 27332
Pottery Ln 27330
Pressly Foushee Rd 27330
Price St 27330
Primrose Ln 27330
Prospectors Ln 27330
Prosperity Dr 27332
Providence Hall Dr 27330
Pumping Station Rd 27330
Putters Cir & Path 27332
Pyrant Rd 27330
Quail Holw 27332
Quail Hollow Rd 27332
Quail Ridge Dr 27332
Quail Valley Ct 27332
Quality Ln 27332
Quartermaster 27330
Queens Rd 27330
Quiet Cv 27332
Quiet Country Ln 27332
Quince Loop 27332

R H Ln 27330
R Jordan Rd 27330
Rabbit Ridge Rd 27330
Raccoon Ct 27330
Racquet Ct 27332
Radcliff Dr 27330
Radford Rd 27332
Radius Cir 27330
Rafter Creek Ln 27332
Ragan Rd 27330
Railroad St 27330
Rainy Day Farm Dr 27330
E Raleigh St
100-200 27332
201-299 27330
202-398 27332
301-399 27330
W Raleigh St 27332
Ramseur St 27330
Rand St 27332
Randolph St 27330
Rascob Rd 27330
Raven Way 27332
Ravens Wood Cir 27332
Ray Ave 27330
Red Dr 27332
Red Cedar Ln 27332
Red Holly Dr 27330
Red Oak Dr 27332
Red Tip Ln 27332
Reece Dr 27332
Reedy Ln 27332
Reeves Dr 27332
Register St 27330
Rena Ln 27330
Renee Dr 27332
Rental Ln 27332
Revenel Dr 27330
Rex Mcleod Dr 27330
Reynwood Vista Ln 27330
Rhynewood Dr 27330
Ribbon Oak Ct 27332
Rice Rd 27330
Richmond Dr 27330
Riddle Rd 27330
Ridge Hvn 27332
Ridgecrest Dr 27330
Ridgefield Ct 27332
Ridgeway Ct 27332
Ridgewood Dr 27330
Ritter Ln 27332
River Bend Ln 27330
River Falls Rd 27332
River Forks Rd 27330
River Run Dr 27332
Riverbirch Ct 27330
Riviera Ln 27332
Roanoke Ln 27330
Robbins St 27330
Robert E Lee Rd 27332
Roberts Rd 27332
Robin Hill Rd 27332
Robin Hood Ln 27330
Robin Roost 27332
Rock Hill Dr 27332
Rock Springs Dr 27330
Rockwood Dr 27330
Rocky Fls 27330
Rocky Fork Church Rd 27332
N & S Rocky River Rd 27330
Rod Sullivan Rd 27330
Rolling Hill Rd 27330
Rolling Stone Ct 27332
Rollins Store Rd 27332
Rooster Ln 27332
Rorer Way 27332
E & W Rose St 27330
Rosebriar Dr 27330
Rosemary St 27330
Ross St 27330
Rosser Rd
2300-2999 27332
3300-4399 27330
Rosser Pittman Rd 27332
Rosy Ln 27332
Round Fish Dr 27330
Roxbury Ct 27332
Roy Wood Ln 27330
Royal Dr 27332
Royal Pines Dr 27330
Rubble Ct 27332
Ruby Ln 27330
Running Cedar 27332
Russell St 27330
Ryan Ave 27330
Rye Rd 27332
Sabre Dr 27332
Saddle Ridge Rd 27330
Saddlewood Ln 27330
Saffron Ct 27330
Sahara Cir 27332
Saint Andrews Dr & Loop 27332
Saint Andrews Chu Rd 27332
Saint Clair Ct 27330
Saint Joseph St 27332
Saintsbury Pl 27332
Salamander Creek Ln 27330
Salem Church Rd 27330
San Lee Dr 27330
Sand Doodle Ln 27332
Sandalwood Dr 27330
Sanders Rd 27332
Sandhill Crane Ct 27332
Sandollar Ct 27332
Sandpiper Dr 27332
Sandstone Ct 27330
Sandstone Ln 27332
Sandwedge 27332
Sandy Ln & Pt 27332
Sandy Bluff Ct 27332
Sandy Creek Church Rd 27330
Sandy Forge Ln 27330
Sapona Cir 27332
Sapphire Pl 27332
Saunders St 27330
Savage Ln 27332
Savannah Dr 27330
Saw Mill Ln 27332
Saw Timber 27332
Scarlet Ln 27330
Scarlett Oak Ln 27330
School St 27330
Scotch Row 27332
Scott Ave 27330
Scuppernong Ct 27332
Sea Mist Dr 27330
Sean Ln 27332
E & W Seawell St 27330
Seawell Rosser Rd 27332
Secretariate Cir 27330
Sedgefield Dr 27330
Serenity Ln 27330
Seth Dr 27330
Shade Wood 27332
Shadewood Ct 27332
Shady Lane Dr 27330
Shallow Creek Ln 27330
Shannon Dr 27330
Sharp Rd 27330
Sharpe Rd 27332
Shaw Pond Rd 27332
Shawnee Dr 27332
Shelly Fore Ln 27332
Shenandoah Ln 27330
Sheree Ln 27330
Sheriff Watson Rd 27332
Sherry Hl 27330
Sherwood Dr 27330
Sherwood Ln 27332
Shirleys Ln 27330
N & S Shoreline Dr 27330
Short St 27330
Shue Rd 27330
Sidney Ln 27330
Sierra Ln & Rd 27330
Silver Lake Pt 27332
Silverthorne Dr 27332
Simmons St 27330
Simpson Dr 27330
Skycroft Rd 27332
Skyline Ln 27330
Skyview Dr 27330
Sloan Ln & Rd 27330
Sloops Ct 27332
Sm Ln 27330
Smindard Rd 27332
Smith Rd 27330
Smoketree Ct 27330
Snow Cir 27330
Soco Ln 27330
Sommers St 27330
Sonya Ct 27330
Sophia Ln 27332
Sourwood Cir 27330
South Pt 27332
Southall Pl 27330
Southbrook Ln 27330
Southern Rd 27330
Southwind 27332
Sparrow Cir
1-4299 27332
4500-4599 27330
Spears Ln 27330
Spivey Ln 27332
Spottswood Dr 27330
Spring Ln 27330
Spring Branch Dr 27330
Spring Farm Ln 27330
Springfield Rd 27330
Springmoore Ct 27330
E & W Spruce St 27330
Spyglass Ln 27332
St James Way 27332
Stanley Rd 27332
Star Ln 27332
Starboard Bay 27332
Starboard Tack 27332
Steel Bridge Rd 27330
N & S Steele St 27330
Stihl Saw Ln 27332
Still Turn 27332
Stillwater Turn 27332
Stone St 27330
Stone Hill Ln 27330
Stone Mack Ln 27330
Stone Quarry Rd 27330
Stone Wood Ln 27330
Stonecliff Ln 27332
Stonegate N & S 27332
Stoneoak Ct 27330
Stoneridge Rd 27332
Stonewall Ct 27332
Stonewheel Dr 27332
Stoney Brook Dr 27330
Stoney Creek Dr 27332
Stoney Hill Ln 27332
Stroud St 27330
Stuart Dr 27330
Sue Mintz Ln 27330
Sugar Creek Dr 27332
Sugar Maple Rd 27332
Sugar Mill Rd 27330
Sugarneck Ln 27330
Sumac St 27330
Summer Creek Ln 27332
Summer Storm Pl 27332
Summerfield Dr 27332
Summerlin Dr 27332
Summerset Pl 27332
Summitt Dr 27330
Sunflower Cir 27330
Sunny Ln 27330
Sunnybrook Dr 27330
Sunrise Dr 27330
Sunset Dr 27330
Sure Fire Ln 27330
Sussex Ave 27330
Sutphin Rd 27330
Swan St 27330
Swanns Station Rd 27332
Swaringen Ln 27330
Sweet Bayberry Ct 27332
Sweet Gum Cir 27332
Sweet Patty Ln 27332
Swift Ln 27332
Sycamore St & Trl 27330
Sylvan Ct 27330
Sylvia Sue Ln 27330
T Tarpey Ln 27330
Tabitha Ln 27330
Tahoe Cir 27332
Talley Ave 27330
Tamben Ln 27330
Tanbarkway Rd 27330
Tanglewood Dr 27330
Tarheel Ln 27330
Taton Ct 27330
Taylors Chapel Rd 27330
Teakwood Ct 27330
Tee Trl 27332
Temple Ave 27330
Tempting Church Rd 27330
Tennessee Cir 27332
Tew St 27330
Texas Sq 27332
Thames Ct 27332
The Pointe 27332
Thistlecone Ln 27330
Thomas Rd 27330
Thomas Kelly Rd 27330
Thomas Mcgehee Rd 27332
Thomas Scott Rd 27332
Thomas Williams Rd 27330
Thornwood Ct, Dr, Loop & Pt 27330
Thoroughfare Branch Rd 27332
Thorpe Ct 27332
Thrush Cir 27332
Thunder Ln 27332
Thurn Dr 27330
Tidewater Dr 27332
Tiffany Dr 27330
Tillman Rd 27330
Tim Ln 27332
Timber Ridge Dr 27332
Timber Wolf Cir 27332
Timberlake Trl 27332
Timberline Dr 27332
Timberwood Ln 27332
Timberwood Pl 27332
Tobacco Rd 27332
Tomberlin Rd 27332
Toomer Ln 27330
Topside 27332
Tower Ridge Ln 27332
Traceway S 27332
E Trade St
100-200 27332
201-399 27330
202-398 27332
W Trade St 27330
Trail Rider Ln 27332
Tramway Rd 27332
Tramway West Rd 27330
Tranquility Ln 27330
Traveller Ln 27332
Travis Dr 27332
Tree Cutters 27332
Tree Master Rd 27332
Tree Top Cir 27332
Triple Farm Ln 27330
Triple Lakes Rd 27332
Troon Cir 27332
Truelove Dr & St 27332
Truman Dr 27330
Trundle Rdg 27330
Trundle Ridge Rd 27330
Tryon St 27330
Tucker House Ln 27330
Tucks Ct 27330
Tulip Tree 27332
Turnberry Cir 27332
Turnbury Ct 27332
Turtle Creek Ln 27330
Tuscany Pl 27330
Twin Bridge Cir 27332
Twin Oaks Farm Rd 27330
Twin Ponds Rd 27330
Tyndall Dr 27330
Tyrone Dr 27332
Ueberall Rd 27332
Ultra Lite Dr 27332
Ulysses Grant Ln 27330
Uncle Willie Ln 27332
Underwood Dr 27332
Underwood Rd 27330
Upchurch Farm Rd 27332
Upland Reach 27332
Upper Deck 27332
Uppergate Ln 27332
Us Highway 421 S 27330
Vail Ct 27332
Valley Rd 27332
Valley Pine Ln 27330
Valley View Ct 27332
Valley View Dr 27330
N & S Vance St 27330
Vantage Pt 27332
Variety Ln 27330
Veggie Ln 27330
Veranda Ct 27330
Vermont Ct 27332
Vermouth Loop 27332
Vic Keith Rd 27332
Vick Keith Rd 27332
Victory Dr 27330
View Ct 27330
Villa Cir 27330
Village Dr 27330
Villanow Dr 27332
Vine Ct 27332
Virginia Cir 27330
Vista Ridge Trl 27332
Vodka Cir 27332
Von Cannon Cir 27330
Waddell St 27330
Wade Dr 27330
Wade Bright Rd 27330
Wagon Trail Rd 27332
Wagon Wheel Ln 27332
Wakefield Rd 27330
Walden St 27330
Walkabout Ln 27330
Walker Rd 27332
Wall St 27330
Wallace Creek Ln 27330
Walnut Dr 27330
Walter Ln 27332
Walter Bright Rd 27330
Walter Waddell Ln 27332
Warbler Rd 27332
Washington Ave 27330
Washington St 27332
Watchacow Ln 27330
Water Oak Cir 27332
Wateredge Ln 27332
Waterford Ct 27332
Waters Edge Dr 27332
Waterside Dr 27332
Waterview Ln 27330
Watson Aly & Ave 27332
Watsons Nursery Ln 27330
Watts St 27332
Wayne St 27330
Waynes Landing Ln 27330
Wayview Ln 27330
Wd Graham Ln 27332
E & W Weatherspoon St 27330
Weatherwood Ct 27332
Weaver Ln 27332
Webb St 27330
Wedgewood Ct & Dr 27332
Weldon Ln 27330
Weller St 27330
Wellington Dr 27330
Wellington Ln 27332
Wellston Pl 27330
Wellstone Dr 27332
Welshire Dr 27332
Wendover Ct 27330
Wendy Ln 27330
Wentworth Ct 27330
West Pt 27332
Westbrooke Dr 27330
Westchase Run 27330
Westchester Dr 27332
Westcott Cir 27330
Western Hills Dr 27330
Westfall Cir 27330
Westgate Dr 27330
Westminster Ct 27330
Westover Ct 27332
Westover Dr 27330
Westport Pl 27330
Westwood Dr 27330
Wheel Hollow Trl 27330
Whippoorwill Ln 27330
Whistling Wind 27332
Whitaker Ln 27330
White St 27332
White Heron Ct 27332
White Hill Rd 27332
White Oak Cir 27332
White Oak Dr 27330
White Tail Ln 27332
Whitford St 27330
Whitney Ln 27332
Wicker St 27330
Wickfield Dr 27330
Wiggins Dr 27330
Wilburs Ln 27332
Wild Forest Ln 27332
Wild Forest Rd 27332
Wild Plum Ln 27332
Wilder Ln 27330
Wildflower Dr 27330
Wildlife Rd 27332
Wildwood Dr 27330
Wiley St 27330
Wilkins Dr 27330
Willett Rd 27332
William Ammon Dr 27332
E & W Williams St 27332
Williams Farm Rd 27332
Williamsburg Ct 27330
Willow Cir & Run 27332
Willow Creek Rd 27330
Willow Oak Ln 27330
Willow Ridge Dr 27332
Willowfield Ln 27332
Wills Ln 27330
Wills Way 27332
Wilma Ct & Way 27332
Wilmer Rd 27332
Wilmont Dr 27330
Wilmouth Rd 27330
Wilshire Ct 27330
Wilson Rd 27332
Wilson St 27330
Wimberly Wood Dr 27330
Wimberly Woods Dr 27330
Wimbledon Dr 27330
Winchester Dr 27332
Wind Tree Dr 27332
Windfall Rd 27330
Winding Rdg 27332
Windjammer Ct 27330
Windmere Dr 27330
Windmill Dr 27330
Windrace Trl 27332
Windsock Dr 27332
Windsong Dr 27330
Windsor Pl 27330
Windy Bch 27332
Wine Tree 27332
Winfield St 27330
Wingate Dr & St 27330
Winslow Dr 27330
Winstead Rd 27332
Wintergreen Rd 27330
Winterlocken Dr 27330
Winterwind Cir 27330
Winthrop Pl 27330
Wispy Willow Dr 27332
Wisteria Ln 27330
Wolf Trapp Pl 27330
Womack Rd 27332
Womack Lake Cir 27330
Womble Rd 27330
Womble Creek Rd 27330
Wood Hbr, Ln & Run 27332
Wood Croft 27332
Wood Duck Trl 27332
Wood Ridge Dr 27332
Wood Stream Trl 27332
Woodburn Cir 27330
Woodbury Ln 27332
Woodcreek Rd 27330
Woodcrest Dr 27330
Woodcroft Dr 27332
N Woodfield Dr 27332
Woodland Ave 27330
Woodland Heights Dr 27330
Woodland Trails Rd 27330
Woodridge Trl 27332
Woodrow Mcduffie Ln 27332
Woodside Dr 27332
Woodsleaf Ln 27332
Woodstone Ct 27332
Woodwedge Way 27332
Woody Dam Rd 27330
Woodyhill Ln 27330
Woolard Rd 27330
Worthy Rd 27330
Wren Way 27332
Wren Tree Cir 27330
Wycliff Ct 27330
Wynns Rd 27330
Yarmouth Tern 27332
Yellow Bird 27332
York Pl & St 27330
Yorkshire Cir 27332
Zimmerman Rd 27330
Zion Church Rd 27330

NUMBERED STREETS

All Street Addresses 27330

SHALLOTTE NC

General Delivery 28459

POST OFFICE BOXES MAIN OFFICE STATIONS AND BRANCHES

Box No.s
All PO Boxes 28459

NAMED STREETS

A I Clemmons Rd SW 28470
Ada Ln NW 28470
Al St 28470
Alice St SW 28470
Alton Loop NW 28470
Amos Way SW 28470
Arabian Way 28470
Arbor Branch Dr 28470
Arcadia Dr SW 28470
Argill Ln 28470
Arnold St 28470
Arnold Palmer Dr 28470
Ash Dr 28470
Ashley Trl SW 28470
Atlantic Ave SW 28470
Audell St SW 28470
Avocet Ct SW 28470
Back Bay Dr SW 28470
Bassett St 28470
Bay Rd & Vlg NW & SW 28470
Bay Hill Ct 28470
Bayberry Ct 28470
Beach Dr SW 28470
Beachway Trl 28470
Bear St NW 28470
Beaver Cir SW 28470
Beaver Pond Ln NW 28470
Bellamy Ave 28470
Betty Ln 28470

Big Oak Ct 28470
Bill Holden Rd SW 28470
Birch Pond Dr 28470
Bird Dr 28470
Blake St 28470
Blue Dogwood Trl SW 28470
Blue Heron Ln SW 28470
Bluebird Trl 28470
Bluejay Ct 28470
Bluff Dr 28470
Bobby Ln SW 28470
Boone St SW 28470
Bostic Pl 28470
Boverie St 28470
Bowen Dr 28470
Boyd Dr SW 28470
Bozeman Loop NW 28470
Brantley Cir SW 28470
Brick Landing Rd SW 28470
Bridge Ct 28470
Bridger Rd 28470
Bridgers Rd NW 28470
Brierwood Rd 28470
Brightleaf St 28470
Brookhollow Dr 28470
Brooks Ct 28470
Burke Ln NW 28470
Buttercup Ln NW 28470
Callender Rd 28470
Callis Ln 28470
Canna Pl 28470
Card St 28470
Cardinal Dr 28470
Carmel Ln SW 28470
Carolyn Ave SW 28470
Carter St SW 28470
Cedar Oak Ln 28470
Cedar Ridge Rd 28470
Cemetary Ln SW 28470
Central Ave SW 28470
Chadwick Lndg & Way SW 28470
Charlie St 28470
Charter Oak Dr 28470
Chavis Rd 28470
Cheers St 28470
Cheshire Way SW 28470
Chickadee Pl SW 28470
Chiquita Ln 28470
Church St SW 28470
Claremont Dr 28470
Coastal Horizons Dr 28470
Cockatoo Dr & St 28470
Columbus Rd 28470
Connie Pl SW 28470
Coot St 28470
Copas Rd SW 28470
Cotton Patch Rd SW 28470
Country Club Dr 28470
Country Club Villa Dr 28470
Cove Ct SW 28470
Coward Trl SW 28470
Creek Dr 28470
Crest St SW 28470
Cross St 28470
Crystal Ct SW 28470
Cumbee Loop SW 28470
Cypress Cir SW 28470
D E Robinson Trl 28470
Daddy Ct SW 28470
Daffodil Rd 28470
Darden Dr SW 28470
Dark Oak St SW 28470
Daught Rd SW 28470
Deep Branch Rd 28470
Deer St NW 28470
Deer Park Dr SW 28470
Dennis St SW 28470
Devane Rd SW 28470
Dillon Dr 28470
Dixie Ln SW 28470
Doogle Ln 28470
Doral Dr 28470
Drumar Ct 28470
Dusty Rd NW 28470
Eagle Dr 28470
Earl Della Dr SW 28470
East Dr 28470
Eastcoast Ln 28470
Edgewater Dr SW 28470
Edinburgh Dr 28470
Edna Way SW 28470
Egret St SW 28470
Ellis Way NW 28470
Elmers Dr 28470
Elmhurst Ave 28470
Emerald Valley Dr 28470
Estate Dr SW 28470
Evans Cir SW 28470
Evanwood Ln SW 28470
Express Dr 28470
Fairway Dr 28470
Fairway Crest Dr SW 28470
Farmer Ct 28470
Fieldview Way SW 28470
Fifth St SW 28470
Finch Dr SW 28470
First St SW 28470
Flamingo Dr 28470
Fletcher Hewett Rd 28470
Flicker Pl 28470
Floyd Rd 28470
Forest Dr 28470
Forest Drive Ext 28470
Forest Lake Dr SW 28470
Fourth St SW 28470
Fox St 28470
Frontage Rd NW 28470
Gallinule Dr SW 28470
Galt Ln E 28470
Gander Ct SW 28470
Garner St SW 28470
Gate 1 SW 28470
Gate 2 SW 28470
Gate 3 SW 28470
Gate 4 SW 28470
Gate V SW 28470
Golden Eagle Dr SW 28470
Goldfinch Pl 28470
Goose Ln SW 28470
Goose Creek Rd SW 28470
Grabee Way NW 28470
Gray Dr 28470
Gray Bridge Rd 28470
Grebe Ct SW 28470
Green Heron Dr SW 28470
Greenock Ct 28470
Grosbeak Pl SW 28470
Gum Tree Hole Rd SW 28470
Gurganus Rd SW 28470
Hale Swamp Rd 28470
Hannah Dr SW 28470
Happy Valley Ln 28470
Hardsmith St 28470
Hardwick Ct NW 28470
Hardy St SW 28470
Harrison Rd SW 28470
Harry Bell Rd 28470
Havelock Pl 28470
Haven Trl SW 28470
Hawick Dr 28470
Hazel St SW 28470
Hen Cove Ave SW 28470
Heron Ct 28470
Hewett Farms Rd 28470
Heyward St 28470
Hickory St 28470
Hickory Point Ct 28470
Hidden Way SW 28470
Hidden Shores Dr 28470
High St 28470
High Hill Dr SW 28470
High Meadows Dr 28470
Highfield Ct NW 28470
Highland Forest Cir 28470
Highlands St SW 28470
Highlands Glen Dr 28470
Hill Way 28470
Hilton Ct 28470
Hinson St 28470
Hogan Ct 28470
Holden Rd SW 28470
Holden Beach Rd SW 28470
Hollywood Dr SW 28470
Holmes St 28470
Hope Crest Loop 28470
Hughes Trl SW 28470
Hummingbird Dr SW 28470
Ibis Cir SW 28470
Industrial Dr 28470
Invishield Ct 28470
Isla Cabritos Rd 28470
Ivey Stone Ct SW 28470
J And E Ln 28470
Jack N Johnny Rd 28470
Jay St 28470
Jd Cox Ln SW 28470
Jennies Branch Way 28470
Jennys Ln SW 28470
Jim St SW 28470
Joey Ln SW 28470
John St 28470
Johnny Price Dr NW 28470
Johnsontown Way 28470
Jones St 28470
Joseph Lewis Rd 28470
Judith Ann Ct NW 28470
Jura Ct 28470
Kara Dr SW 28470
Kay St SW 28470
Kelsey Ln SW 28470
Kensington Pl & Sq NW 28470
Kerry Gail Ln 28470
Kestrel Dr SW 28470
Killdeer Dr SW 28470
Kimberly Ann Ln 28470
King Mackeral Dr SW 28470
Kingfisher Dr SW 28470
Kinglet Dr SW 28470
Kings Grant Ct 28470
Kinlaw Dr SW 28470
Lads Rd NW 28470
Lake St SW 28470
Lakeshore Dr SW 28470
Lakewood Dr SW 28470
Landing St 28470
Lansing Ct SW 28470
Latrobe Ln 28470
Laughing Gull Ct SW 28470
Laurel Valley Dr 28470
Lawndale Dr SW 28470
Lh Stanley Ln NW 28470
Lightwood Ln 28470
Lina Trl SW 28470
Linden Ln SW 28470
Little Ct 28470
Little Shallotte River Dr 28470
Live Oak St SW 28470
Lloyd Ct 28470
Loblolly Rd SW 28470
Log Landing Rd SW 28470
London St 28470
Long Cir SW 28470
Long Bay Ct SW 28470
Long Shore Dr SW 28470
Lyndhurst Ter 28470
Ma Stell Ln 28470
Macgregor Dr 28470
Madison St SW 28470
Magnolia St SW 28470
Main St 28470
Mallard Dr 28470
Mancy C Stanley Trl 28470
Maple St SW 28470
Maple Hill Rd SW 28470
Marie King Way NW 28470
Market St NW 28470
Marlin St 28470
Mars Dr 28470
Marsh Ave 28470
Marsh Hawk Ln 28470
Marsh Hen Dr SW 28470
Marsh Line Ct SW 28470
Marshall St 28470
Martin St 28470
Marvins Trl SW 28470
Mary St SW 28470
Mary Isiah Ln 28470
Mary Sheldon Dr SW 28470
Mattie Ln 28470
Mcmilly Rd NW 28470
Meadow Dr 28470
Meadowlark Ln 28470
Meander Ln 28470
Meredith Ln NW 28470
Merganser St SW 28470
Merlin Ct SW 28470
Mh Rourk Dr 28470
Middle Dr 28470
Middle Dam Rd SW 28470
Mill Pond Rd SW 28470
Milligan Ln SW 28470
Milliken St 28470
Minta Ln NW 28470
Mintz St 28470
Mirror Lite Ct NW 28470
Mithwick St SW 28470
Mockingbird Ln 28470
Mulberry Rd & St NW 28470
Murdock Ct 28470
Myra Way NW 28470
Naber Dr 28470
Nesting Ln SW 28470
Nicklaus Ct 28470
Nighthawk Ct SW 28470
Noble Ct NW 28470
Norlina Dr SW 28470
Northside Dr 28470
Oak Dr SW 28470
Oak Tree Ln 28470
Oakwest St NW 28470
Oban Ct 28470
Ocean Hwy W 28470
Ocean Breeze Ave SW 28470
Ocean Isle Beach Rd SW 28470
Ocean Pine St SW 28470
Old Berwick St 28470
Old New Britton Rd NW 28470
Old Shallotte Rd NW 28470
Olde Cypress Ln 28470
Oriole Ln 28470
Otter Ln SW 28470
Owendon Dr 28470
Pacific Dr SW 28470
Paisley Dr SW 28470
Palmer Dr 28470
Paradise Ln SW 28470
Parkview Pl NW 28470
Partridge Pl 28470
Pauls Trl 28470
Pelican Pl 28470
Pender Rd 28470
Peoples Way SW 28470
Peregrine Dr SW 28470
Phelps St SW 28470
Phoebe Ct SW 28470
Pigott Rd SW 28470
Pine St 28470
Pine Hill Dr SW 28470
Pine Lake Dr SW 28470
Pintail Ave SW 28470
E & W Pipers Gln 28470
Pittsboro Trl SW 28470
Plover Ct SW 28470
Plymouth Ln SW 28470
Pocono Trl 28470
Point Ln 28470
Point Vista Pl SW 28470
Point Windward Pl SW 28470
Pompano St 28470
Pond Way 28470
Pondview Pl SW 28470
Preacher Ln SW 28470
Price Farm Ct 28470
Pro Shop Dr SW 28470
Quail Cir & Cv 28470
Queens Grant Cir 28470
Rabbit Ct NW 28470
Radford Way SW 28470
Rail Ct SW 28470
Rainbow Ct 28470
Randall St 28470
Rebel Trl NW 28470
Red Breast Way NW 28470
Red Bug Rd SW 28470
Red Fox St NW 28470
Red Oak Dr SW 28470
Redgray Way SW 28470
Redwine Ave 28470
Redwood St SW 28470
Rest Pl SW 28470
Retha Dr SW 28470
Rhett Ct 28470
Ridge Rd & Way NW & SW 28470
Rising Meadows Ct SW 28470
Ritz Cir 28470
River Bluff Dr 28470
River Crest Dr 28470
River Hills Dr SW 28470
River Ridge Dr 28470
River Village Sq 28470
River Wynd 28470
Riverbend Dr SW 28470
Rivers Edge Dr 28470
Riverview Dr SW 28470
Roadrunner Way 28470
Robin Dr 28470
Rock Crab Way SW 28470
Rose Ln SW 28470
Rounding Run Rd SW 28470
Royal Oak Rd NW 28470
Ruby Way NW 28470
Ruddock Way 28470
Russell Rd SW 28470
Rusty Cir SW 28470
Rutledge Cross 28470
Saint Marys Dr 28470
Salem Ln SW 28470
Salt Works Ln SW 28470
Sanders Forest Dr NW 28470
Sandtrap Dr 28470
Sanguine Ln 28470
Sasspan Dr SW 28470
Sassy Trl 28470
Scarlet Sage Way 28470
Scotts Ln SW 28470
Scottsdale Dr SW 28470
Seamac St SW 28470
Sellers Rd 28470
Shady Rest Pl SW 28470
Shalamar Ln SW 28470
Shallotte Ave 28470
Shallotte Crossing Pkwy 28470
Shallotte Inlet Dr SW 28470
Shallotte Point Loop Rd SW 28470
Shannon St 28470
Sharon Dean Ln 28470
Shell Dr 28470
Shell Point Rd 28470
Shellys Ln SW 28470
Sherrow River Dr 28470
Silver Grove Way 28470
Skylee Pl 28470
Smintont Rd 28470
Smith Ave
100-299 28470
209-209 28459
Smokerise Dr SW 28470
Snapper St 28470
Snead Ct 28470
Songline St 28470
Southland Way SW 28470
Sparrow Pl 28470
Squirrel Ave NW 28470
Stanley Cove Way SW 28470
Star Cross Dr SW 28470
Starboard Rd NW 28470
Stone Haven Ct 28470
Stratford Pl 28470
Sturgis Dr 28470
Suburban St SW 28470
Sugarberry Dr 28470
Sun And Surf Ln NW 28470
Sundown Ln SW 28470
Sunnyside St SW 28470
Sunrise Ave 28470
Susan Dr 28470
Sussex Dr 28470
Swain Ln SW 28470
Swallow Pl SW 28470
Sylvan St 28470
Tallow Trce 28470
Tanner Dr SW 28470
Tar Landing Rd 28470
Tarkln Ct NW 28470
Tarpon St 28470
Tatum Rd SW 28470
Tavia Ln SW 28470
Tern Ct 28470
Third St SW 28470
Thomas Dr 28470
Tidewater Landing Dr SW 28470
Todd Rd 28470
Toms Trl 28470
Tony St SW 28470
Tripp St SW 28470
Trogon Pl 28470
Tryon Rd NW 28470
Tuna Dr 28470
Turkey St SW 28470
Twins Ct SW 28470
Union Ln NW 28470
Union School Rd NW 28470
Upper Mill Slough Rd SW 28470
Usher Ave 28470
Vanderhorst Ave 28470
Verdant St 28470
Village Pnes & Rd SW 28470
Village Green Trl SW 28470
Village Point Rd SW 28470
Walker St SW 28470
Walkinghorse Pt SW 28470
Wall St 28470
Walton St 28470
Waltz Cir 28470
Washington Rd SW 28470
Wendy Ln 28470
White St 28470
Whiteville Rd NW 28470
Widgen Ct SW 28470
Wild Hawk Ln 28470
Wild Raven St 28470
Wildwood St NW 28470
Willard Ln 28470
S Willis Dr 28470
Willow Run St SW 28470
Wilson Way SW 28470
Windward Pl SW 28470
Winfree Way SW 28470
Wm And Odell Gurganus Ln SW 28470
Wood St SW 28470
Woodpecker Ln 28470
Woodsong Ln 28470
Woodthrush Ln 28470
Wren Pl SW 28470
Wyndcrest Ln 28470
Yellowood Dr 28470
Young St SW 28470

SHELBY NC

General Delivery 28150

POST OFFICE BOXES MAIN OFFICE STATIONS AND BRANCHES

Box No.s
1 - 9089 28151
9998 - 9998 28150

NAMED STREETS

A A Barrett Rd 28150
Aaron Dr 28152
Abbington Ln 28150
Abernathy St 28150
Adair Dr 28150
Adams St 28150
Addie Ln 28152
Airline Ext 28150
Airport Rd 28150
Aken Dr 28150
Aladdin St 28152
Albert Blanton Rd 28152
Albertville Ln 28152
Alder Dr 28152
Alex Dr 28152
Alexander Ln 28150
Alexandra Dr 28150
Alfalfa Ln 28152
Allen St 28152
Allendale Dr 28150
Allison Dr 28150
Alma Ln 28152
Alpha Dr 28150
Amber Ln 28150
Amberwood Dr 28152
Amesbury Dr 28152
Andicot Ln 28152
Annie Carpenter Dr 28152
Annieline Dr 28152
Annies Cir 28152
Anthony Lake Dr 28152
Anthonys Mobile Home Park 28152
Antler Ct 28150
Antrum St 28150
Appaloosa Trl 28150
Appian Way 28150
Apple Hill Dr 28152
Applegate Dr 28152
April Dr 28152
Arbor Way Dr 28150
Arboretum Way 28150
Archdale Dr 28150
Arden Dr 28150
E & W Arey St 28150
Arlee Dr 28150
Arlon Dr 28150
Arnold Dr 28152
Arrowhead Dr 28150
Arrowood Dr 28150
Artee Rd 28150
Ashburne Dr 28152
Ashland Ct 28150
Ashley St 28150
Atlantic Ave 28150
Augusta Ln 28150
Austell Graham Rd 28152
Austin Dr 28152
Autumn Ln 28152
Avalon Ct 28152
Baker Dr 28152
Bankhead Rd 28152
Banyon Dr 28150
Barbee Rd 28150
Barclay Rd 28152
Barker Blvd 28152
Barrier Dr 28150
Barth Cir 28152
Barto Pl 28150
Bay Ct 28152
Baylor Dr 28150
Bayridge Dr 28150
Beacon Dr 28152
Beam Ct 28150
Beam Dr 28152
Beam St 28152
Beaman St 28152
Bear Creek Rd 28152
Beason St 28152
Beau Rd 28152
Beaumonde Ave 28150
Beaver Dam Dr 28150

- Beaver Dam Church Rd 28152
- Belaire Cir 28152
- Belinda Dr 28152
- Bellview Dr 28150
- Belmont Pl 28150
- Belvedere Ave 28150
- Ben Jones Rd 28152
- Benjamin Ct 28152
- Bentley Rd 28152
- Berry Dr 28150
- Berwick Rd 28152
- Best St 28150
- Betty Ct 28152
- Beverly Ave 28152
- Big Oak Rd 28150
- Biggers Lake Rd 28152
- Billet Dr 28152
- Billy Bob Dr 28150
- Billy Williams Dr 28150
- Billys Dr 28152
- Bingham Rd 28150
- Birchbrook Ln 28150
- Birdie Ln 28150
- Black St 28150
- Blackhawk Dr 28150
- Blackley Cir 28152
- Blackwood Pl 28150
- Blakemore Dr 28152
- Blanton St 28150
- Blazer St 28152
- Blevins Dr 28150
- Blue Jay Rd 28150
- Blue Ridge Dr 28150
- Blue Sky Cir 28152
- Blue Spruce Dr 28152
- Bluebird Ln 28152
- Blythe St 28152
- Bob Falls Dr 28150
- Bolt Dr 28150
- Bonny St 28150
- Booker St 28150
- Borders Rd
  - 1-599 28152
  - 600-1299 28150
- Botts Rd 28150
- Boulevard Interchange 28152
- Bowen Dr 28152
- Bowman St 28150
- Boyce Rd 28150
- Boyd Ct 28150
- Bradley Rd 28152
- Bramblewood Dr 28152
- E Branch Ave 28152
- Branchville Rd 28150
- Brandy Ln 28152
- Branton Dr 28152
- Brenard Dr 28152
- Brett Dr 28152
- Briar Ln 28150
- Briar Creek Dr 28152
- Briarcliff Rd 28152
- Bridges St 28152
- Bridges Dairy Rd 28150
- Brierwood Farms Rd 28152
- Bristol Ln 28150
- Brittain Dr 28150
- Broad St 28152
- Broadway Rd 28152
- Brookdale Dr 28150
- Brookfield Rd 28152
- Brookhaven Dr 28152
- Brookhill Rd 28150
- Brooks Ave 28152
- Brookside Dr 28150
- Brookside Pl 28152
- Brookview Dr 28152
- Brookwood Rd 28150
- Brushy Creek Rd 28150
- Bryson Rd 28150
- Buchanan Rd 28152
- Buck Creek Rd 28152
- Buck Landing Ct 28150
- Buckford Dr 28152
- Buckles Ave 28152
- Bucks Dr 28152
- Buffalo St 28150
- Buffalo Church Rd 28150
- Buford St 28152
- Burke Rd 28152
- Burl Turner Rd 28150
- Byrd Dr 28152
- Bytha Way 28152
- W Cabaniss Dr & Rd 28150
- Cabaniss Farm Rd 28150
- Cabin Creek Dr 28152
- Caddies Ct 28150
- Caldwell Cir 28150
- Caleb Rd 28152
- Calla Ln 28150
- Callahan Ct 28152
- Calvary St 28150
- Cambridge Dr 28152
- Camden Ct 28152
- Cameo Dr 28152
- Cameron St 28152
- Camille Dr 28150
- Camp Ct 28152
- Camp School Rd 28152
- Campbell St 28150
- Canterbury Cir & Rd 28152
- Caring Way 28150
- Carl Ln 28150
- Carla Dr 28150
- Carlos St 28152
- Carmel Dr 28152
- Carol St 28152
- Carolina Ave 28150
- Carolina Pl 28152
- Carolyn Dr 28152
- Carpenter St 28150
- Carriage Ct & Run 28150
- Carson Rd 28150
- Carter Rd 28150
- Carters Grove Rd 28152
- Carver St 28152
- Castlewood Dr 28150
- Catalina Ct 28152
- Cedar St 28152
- Cedar Circle Dr 28152
- Cedar Creek Rd 28152
- Cedar Hill Dr 28152
- Cedar Point Dr 28150
- Cedarline Dr 28150
- Cedarwood Dr 28152
- Centerfield Dr 28150
- Central Pl 28152
- Chagrin Farm Rd 28150
- Chambwood Ln 28152
- Champion St 28150
- Chapel Dr 28152
- Charger Ct 28152
- Charles Rd 28152
- Charlie Elliott Rd 28150
- Chatfield Rd 28150
- Cherry Ln & St 28152
- Cherry Mountain Rd 28150
- Cherryville Rd 28150
- Chesalon Farm Rd 28152
- Chesapeake Cir 28152
- Chesterfield Dr 28152
- Chestnut St 28150
- Chickasaw Dr 28152
- China Ave 28150
- Chiquitta St 28152
- Christopher Rd 28152
- Church Dr 28150
- Church St
  - 100-199 28150
  - 900-999 28152
- Churchill Dr 28150
- Cider Dr 28152
- Cinnbar St 28152
- Circle Dr 28152
- Circle Dr E 28150
- Circle Dr W 28150
- N Circle Dr 28150
- Circleview Dr 28150
- Claremont Dr 28150
- Clark Cir 28150
- Clary Dr 28152
- Claxton Dr 28150
- Clay Rd 28152
- Claytenna Rd 28152
- Clearbrook Dr 28150
- Clearview Dr 28150
- Clearwater Rd 28152
- Clegg St 28150
- Cleveland Ave & St 28150
- Cliffside Rd 28152
- Clifton Dr
  - 1-99 28152
  - 400-499 28150
- Clifton Oates Rd 28150
- Cline St 28150
- Clinton St
  - 100-199 28152
  - 200-399 28150
- Clive Harrill Rd 28152
- Clyde St 28150
- Clyde Wallace Rd 28152
- Cole Dr 28150
- College Ave 28150
- College Farm Rd 28152
- E, N & W College Manor Dr 28152
- Columns Cir 28150
- Comanche Dr 28152
- Combs St 28152
- Commerce Center Dr 28150
- Community Rd 28152
- Concord St 28150
- Condor Dr 28152
- Congress St 28152
- Conifer Way 28150
- Connie Ln 28150
- Cool Spring Ln 28150
- Cora St 28150
- Corine Ct 28150
- Cornwell Rd 28150
- Cornwell St 28152
- Corvair Ln 28150
- Costner Rd 28150
- Cotton Rd 28150
- Cottonwood Dr 28152
- Country Dr 28152
- Country Club Cir, Ct, Ln & Rd 28150
- Country Club Acres 28150
- Country Garden Dr 28150
- County Home Rd 28152
- Courtland Dr 28152
- Cove St 28152
- Covenant Ct 28152
- Cow Boy Rd 28150
- Cowboy Up Trl 28152
- Cox Rd 28152
- Craig Pl 28150
- Crane Ct 28152
- Crawford St 28152
- Crawley Rd 28150
- Crawley Gin Rd 28150
- Creek Rd 28150
- Creek Ridge Rd 28152
- Creekside Dr 28152
- N Crescent Ave & Cir 28150
- Crest Rd 28152
- Crestbrook Cir 28152
- Crestfield Ct 28152
- Crestland Dr 28150
- Crestview Dr 28150
- Crestwood Rd 28152
- Crosby Dr 28150
- Crow Rd 28152
- Crowder Rd 28150
- Crowder Ridge Rd 28150
- Crystal Ln 28150
- Crystal Springs Ln 28150
- Cumberland Dr 28150
- Cyclone St 28150
- Dakar Dr 28150
- E & S Dale St 28150
- Dalton Dr 28150
- Damon Rd 28150
- Dana Pl 28152
- Dart Dr 28150
- Daves Dr 28150
- David Dr 28150
- Davis Rd 28152
- Davis Ridge Dr 28152
- Dawn Dr 28150
- Deal Rd 28150
- E Debbie Dr 28150
- Debby Dr & Rd 28152
- Deborah Cir 28150
- Deep Green Dr 28152
- Deer Chase Rd 28150
- Deer Run Cir 28152
- Deer Track Pl 28152
- Deerbrook Dr 28150
- Deere Dr 28150
- Deerfield Dr & Rd 28150
- Degraw Dr 28150
- Dehart Dr 28152
- N Dekalb St 28150
- S Dekalb St
  - 100-500 28150
  - 405-405 28151
  - 501-999 28150
  - 502-998 28150
  - 1000-1799 28152
- Delano Pl 28152
- Delaware Dr 28150
- Dellinger Rd 28152
- Dellwood Dr 28152
- Delmar Rd 28152
- Delong Dr 28150
- Delta Dr 28152
- Delta Park Dr 28150
- Dennis Ct 28152
- Dennis Dr 28150
- Derby Dr 28150
- Destiny Ln 28150
- Devenny Rd 28150
- Devin Rd 28152
- Dewey Horn Rd 28150
- Dick Spangler Rd 28150
- Dillard Cir 28150
- Diploma Dr 28152
- Dixie Dr 28152
- E & W Dixon Blvd & St 28152
- Dockery Dr 28152
- Dodd St 28152
- Dogwood Ln & Trl 28150
- Donlynn Dr 28150
- Donna Dr 28152
- Dons Ct 28150
- Doris Dr 28152
- Doty Rd 28150
- Double Shoals Rd 28150
- Double Springs Ch Rd 28150
- Douglas St 28150
- Dover Dr & St 28150
- Downing St 28152
- Drake Cir 28152
- Dravo Rd 28152
- Drewery Ln 28152
- Drum Rd 28152
- Duck Pond Rd 28152
- Duffy Dr 28152
- Duke St 28150
- Duncan Dr 28152
- Dundee Ct 28150
- Durham St 28152
- E Durham St 28152
- Durham Johnson Rd 28150
- Dyer Ct & Dr 28152
- Eagle Spur Trl 28152
- Eagles Ter 28150
- Eagles Nest Way 28152
- Earl Rd
  - 100-499 28150
  - 500-1499 28152
- Earl St 28150
- East Ave 28152
- Easton Dr 28152
- Eastview Ext 28152
- Eastview St
  - 700-799 28150
  - 800-999 28152
- Eastway Dr 28150
- Eastwood Dr 28150
- Eaves Rd 28152
- Ed Hamrick Rd 28150
- Edgefield Ave 28150
- Edgemont Ave 28150
- Edgewater Rd 28150
- Edgewood Rd 28150
- Edgewood St 28152
- Edna St 28152
- Edwards St 28152
- Eleanor Dr 28150
- Elgin Dr 28150
- Elizabeth Ave & Rd 28150
- Elizabeth Church Rd 28150
- Elkwood Dr 28152
- Ella St 28152
- Elliott Dr 28150
- Elliott Cemetery Rd 28150
- Elliott Farm Rd 28150
- Ellis Rd 28152
- Ellis Ferry Rd 28152
- E Elm St 28150
- W Elm St
  - 500-999 28150
  - 1000-1199 28152
- Elmwood Dr 28152
- Elru Ct 28152
- Embert Ln 28152
- Emerald Ln 28152
- Emerald Mine Rd 28152
- Emerald Valley Dr 28152
- Emily Ln 28152
- Englewood Dr 28150
- Enola Dr 28150
- Eric Rd 28150
- Eva Ln 28152
- Evergreen Dr 28152
- Exeter Dr 28150
- Fabian Dr 28150
- Fairfax Cir 28150
- Fairmont Dr 28150
- Fairview Rd 28150
- Fairview St 28152
- Fairview Farms 28150
- Fairway Dr 28150
- Faith Dr 28150
- Falcon Cir 28150
- Fallston Rd 28150
- Fallston Waco Rd 28150
- Fanning Dr 28150
- Farm Rd & St 28152
- Farmhurst Pl 28152
- Farmington Rd 28150
- Farmville Rd 28150
- Farmway Ln 28150
- Featherway Ln 28152
- Felter St 28150
- Fenway Dr 28152
- Fermair Rd 28150
- Fern Pl 28150
- Ferndale St 28150
- Fernwood Dr 28152
- Fielding Rd 28150
- Fields Dr 28150
- Fieldstone Ln 28152
- Firefly Path 28150
- Fite Rd 28150
- Five Points Rd 28150
- Flagstone Ct 28152
- Fletcher Rd 28150
- Flint St 28152
- Flint Hill Church Rd 28152
- Floyd St 28150
- Fontana Ln 28150
- Ford St 28150
- Forest Dr 28152
- Forest Hill Dr 28150
- Forest Park Dr 28150
- Forest Ridge Dr 28152
- Forney St 28152
- Forrest St 28152
- Foust Rd 28152
- Fox Ridge Dr 28152
- Foxboro St 28152
- Foxcroft Cir 28152
- Foxhill Dr 28150
- Foxrun Rd 28152
- Francine Dr 28152
- Francis Ct 28152
- Frank Grigg Dr 28150
- Franklin Ave 28150
- Frederick St 28150
- Friendship Rd 28150
- Frost Pl 28152
- Fullerton St 28150
- G B Blanton Rd 28152
- Gaffney Rd 28152
- Gantt St 28152
- Gardner St 28150
- Garland St 28152
- Garrett Dr 28152
- Geneva Ln 28150
- Geno Dr 28150
- George Beam Rd 28150
- Gibson Rd 28152
- Gidney St 28150
- Gilbert St 28152
- Gilliatt St 28150
- Gin Rd 28150
- Glenbrook Dr 28152
- Glendale St 28150
- Glenwood Ave 28150
- Goddard Rd 28150
- Gold St 28150
- Gold Farm Rd 28152
- Goldfinch Ct 28150
- Goldwater St 28152
- Goodwin Dr 28152
- Gordon Ave 28152
- Gordon Rd 28150
- Gorman St 28152
- Gorrell St 28152
- Grace St 28150
- Gragg Dr 28152
- E & W Graham St 28150
- Granite Dr 28152
- Grassy Mdws 28152
- Gray Crest Ct 28150
- Green Ave 28152
- Green Ct 28152
- Green Dr 28150
- Green St 28150
- Green Oak Dr 28152
- Green Valley Dr 28152
- Greenbrook Dr 28150
- E Greene St 28150
- Greene Farm Rd 28150
- Greene Lake Dr 28150
- Greenway Dr 28150
- Greer St 28152
- Grice St 28150
- Grigg Rd & St 28150
- Grove St 28152
- E & W Grover St 28150
- Guffey Dr 28152
- Gum St 28150
- Hallelujah Blvd 28150
- Hals Pl 28150
- Hamilton Rd 28152
- Hammock Ave 28152
- S Hampton Ext 28152
- Hampton St
  - 700-799 28150
  - 800-1099 28152
- S Hampton St 28152
- Hamrick Ave 28152
- Hamrick Rd 28152
- Hamrick St
  - 600-799 28150
  - 800-899 28152
- Hanford Dr 28150
- Hanover Dr 28150
- Hardin Dr 28150
- Hardwick Dr 28152
- Hardy St 28152
- Harlans Rd 28152
- Harley Ct 28150
- Harmon Homestead Rd 28150
- Harold Ct 28152
- Harris St 28150
- Harvest Moon Way 28150
- Hastings Dr 28150
- Hatcher Rd 28150
- Hatcher Spangler Rd 28150
- Hause St 28150
- Haven Ln 28152
- Hawk Hollow Ln 28150
- Hawk Ridge Ct 28152
- Hawkins St 28150
- Hawthorne Ln 28152
- Hawthorne Rd 28150
- Hazel Dr 28152
- Heafner Dr 28150
- Hearthside Dr 28150
- Helen Mcbrayer Dr 28152
- Hemlock Dr 28150
- Hendrick St 28150
- Hendrick Lake Rd 28150
- Heritage Ln 28150
- Hermitage Ct 28150
- Hickory St 28150
- Hickory Nut Rd 28150
- Hidden Acre Dr 28150
- Hidden Cove Dr 28150
- Hidden Creek Dr 28152
- Hidden Valley Rd 28152
- Hideaway Hls 28152
- High Wedge Rd 28152
- Highfield Ct 28150
- Highland Ave & Cir 28150
- Highland Pines Dr 28152
- Hill St 28152
- Hillcrest Dr 28150
- Hillcrest St 28152
- Hillside Dr 28150
- Hillside St 28152
- Hilltop Dr 28150
- Hillview Cir & Dr 28152
- Hillwood St 28152
- Hinson Ln 28150
- Hinton Creek Rd 28150
- Hobbs Ave 28150
- Hoey Church Rd 28152
- Hogan Dr 28150
- Holder Dr 28152
- Holland Dr 28152
- Hollis Rd 28150
- Holly Ln 28150
- Holly Hill Rd 28152
- Holly Oak Rd 28152
- Holman Dr 28150
- Holmes St 28152
- Homeplace Dr 28152
- E & W Homestead Ave 28152
- Honey Haven Farm Rd 28152
- Honeysuckle Dr 28150
- Hope Ct 28152
- Hopewell Rd 28150
- Hopewell Church Rd 28150
- Hoppes Pl 28150
- Horace Grigg Cir 28152
- Horse Trail Dr 28152
- Horseshoe Dr 28150
- Hosch Dr 28152
- Hot Springs Ter 28150
- Houston St 28152
- Howard St 28152
- Howell St 28150
- Howie Dr 28150
- Howington St 28152
- Hubbard Ter 28152
- Huckleberry Dr 28150
- Hudson St 28150
- Hugh Harrill Rd 28150
- Humphries Rd 28150
- Hunt St 28152
- Hunter Valley Rd 28150
- Hunting Ridge Ln 28150
- Hurricane Dr 28150
- Ida Cir & St 28152
- Idlewild Dr 28152
- Immanuel Church Rd 28152
- Indian Creek Dr 28152
- Industry Dr 28152
- Irvin St 28150
- Isaac Pl 28152
- Island View Dr 28150

Ivywood Dr 28150
J B Dr 28150
J T Dr 28150
Jabez Ln 28150
Jack Francis Rd 28152
Jack Moore Mountain Ext & Rd 28150
Jack Wilson Rd 28150
Jackson St 28152
Jacob St 28150
Jake Anthony Rd 28152
James Love School Rd 28152
James Lovelace Rd 28152
Janeal Pl 28152
Jason Dr 28150
Jeanne Dr 28150
Jefferson St 28150
Jenkins Rd 28150
Jennings St 28150
Jenny Dr 28152
Jesse James Ln 28150
Jesslyn Ct 28150
Jim Elliott Rd 28150
Joe Rd 28150
Joes Lake Rd 28152
E & W John Crawford Rd 28152
John E Randall Rd 28152
Johnnie Bridges Rd 28150
Johnsfield Rd 28150
Johnson Rd 28152
Jonathon Trl 28150
Jones Rd 28150
Jordan Dr 28150
Jose St 28150
Joseph Ct 28152
Joyful Dr 28150
Juan St 28150
Julius St 28150
June Rd 28150
Juniper Ter 28152
Justice Pl 28150
Jw Borders Dr 28150
Kearney Dr 28152
Kee Ln 28150
Keen Dr 28152
Keeter St 28152
Kellom Dr 28152
Kelly Cir 28150
W Kelly Ln 28152
Kelly Jo Ln 28150
Kelso Dr 28152
Kemp Cir 28152
Kemper Rd 28152
Ken Daves Rd 28152
Kendall St 28150
Kendallwood Dr 28152
Kendrick Cir 28152
Kendricks Rd 28152
Kenmore St 28150
Kennedy St 28150
Kenwall Village Dr 28152
Kenwood Dr 28150
Keystone Dr 28152
Kilby Ln 28152
Kildare St 28152
Kimberlee Dr 28152
Kimbrell Dr 28152
King Arthur Ct 28152
Kings Cir 28150
Kings Rd
500-2299 28150
2300-2499 28152
Kingsbury St 28150
Kingston Rd 28150
Kingsview Ave 28152
Kirby St 28152
Knott St 28150
Knox St 28152
Lackey St 28152
Ladell Ln 28152
N Lafayette St 28150
S Lafayette St
1-899 28150
900-3099 28152

Lail Ter 28150
Lake Dr 28152
Lake St 28150
Lake George Rd 28152
Lakehurst St 28150
Lakemont Dr 28150
Lakeview Dr & St 28152
Lakeway Dr 28150
N Lakewood Dr 28150
Lamar Ave 28150
Lamar St 28152
Landor Dr 28152
Laney Dr 28152
Langston Dr 28152
Lapides Dr 28152
Laren Rd 28152
Lark Dr 28150
Lattimore Rd
3200-3399 28150
3400-3499 28152
Lattimore St 28150
Laura Rd 28150
Lavista Dr 28152
Lawhon St 28152
Lawndale Dr 28150
Lawrence St 28152
Leander St 28152
Leanna Ct 28152
Lear St 28152
Ledbetter Rd 28152
Ledgefield Dr 28150
Lee Dr 28152
N Lee Rd 28150
Lee St 28150
N Lee St 28150
Lee Cornwell Rd 28150
Leesburg Ct 28152
Legrand St 28150
Len Dr 28152
Lena Dr 28150
Lenick Dr 28152
Lenoir Dr 28152
Lenox Dr 28150
Leo Dr 28152
Leona Dr 28150
Leslie Dr 28152
Lester Ln 28150
Levi St 28152
Lexus Dr 28152
Life Enrichment Blvd 28150
Light Oak Cir 28152
Ligon St 28150
Lila Ln 28152
Lillco Dr 28150
Lily St 28152
Lincoln Dr 28152
Lincoln St 28150
Lindsey Dr 28152
Lindsey Lee Ln 28152
Lineberger St 28150
Linney Ln 28152
Linton Barnette Dr 28152
Lion St 28150
Lithia Springs Rd 28150
Lithia Springs Road Ext 28150
Little Ct 28150
Little Dr 28152
Little Pond Dr 28150
Littlejohn Cir 28152
Liveoak St 28150
Lloyd Dr 28152
Loblolly Ln 28150
Locust St 28150
Lodi Dr 28152
Logan St 28150
Lon St 28152
Longwood Dr 28152
Lori Ct 28150
Louise Dr 28150
Lowery St 28152
Lowman Rd 28150
Lyman St 28152
Lynn Cir 28152
Lynnhurst Ln 28150
Macedonia Church Rd 28150

Madison St 28150
Magel Rd 28152
Magness Rd 28150
S Main Rd 28150
E Main St 28150
N Main St 28152
S Main St 28150
Manchester Dr 28152
Manley Bridges Rd 28152
Maple St 28150
Maple Springs Ch Rd 28152
Maple Valley Dr 28152
Marable Pl 28150
Marcus Dr 28152
Marietta St 28150
Mario Dr 28152
E Marion St
1-1699 28150
1700-2099 28152
W Marion St 28150
Mark Dr 28152
Markanda Pl 28152
Market St 28150
Markway St 28152
Marlowe Ave 28150
Marlwood Dr 28150
Marshall Wolfe Rd 28150
Martin St 28150
Mason Sq & St 28150
Masonic Dr 28152
Maudie Ln 28152
Mauney Ln 28150
Max Rd 28152
Maxwell Ave 28152
Maynard St 28152
Mayo St 28152
Maysville Rd 28150
Mcbrayer St 28150
Mcbrayer Homestead Rd 28152
Mcbrayer Springs Rd 28150
Mcbrayer Street Ext 28150
Mcclurd St 28150
Mccoy Ln 28150
Mccracken Dr 28150
Mccurry Rd 28152
Mcdowell St 28150
Mcfarland Dr 28152
Mcgowan Rd 28150
Mckee Rd 28150
Mckinney Rd 28152
Mcswain Rd 28152
Meadowbrook Ln 28150
Meadowood Ln 28150
Meadowood St 28152
Mellon Rd 28150
Melody Ln 28152
Melrose Dr 28152
Melton Dr 28152
Memorial Dr 28152
Mercury Dr 28152
Merit Dr 28150
Metcalf Rd 28150
Metrolina Plz 28150
Michael Ct 28152
Mid St 28150
Midway Ave 28150
Miles Rd 28150
Mill St 28150
Miller Ct 28152
Millsap Rd 28150
Mimosa Dr 28150
Mint St 28150
Misenheimer Pl 28150
Mitchell St 28152
Mitchum Rd 28150
Mode Ct 28152
Monica Dr 28150
Monroe St 28150
Monteith Dr 28150
Montevista Dr 28152
Montrose Cir & Dr 28150
Moonshadow Ln 28150
Moor Dr 28150
Mooresboro Rd 28150
Moose Dr 28150

N Morgan St 28150
S Morgan St
1-899 28150
900-2099 28152
Morrison St 28152
Morton St 28152
Moses Ct 28152
Moss Rd 28150
Motion Picture Blvd 28152
Mount Sinai Church Rd 28152
Mountain Ln 28150
Mountain View Cir & Dr 28150
Mull St 28152
Mulligan Dr 28150
Murdock Cir 28150
Mustang Dr 28150
Nalley Dr 28150
Nancy Dr 28152
Navy Dr 28150
Neil Brown Rd 28150
Neisler St 28152
Nelson Cv 28150
Neva Rd 28150
New Crest Ln 28150
New House Rd 28150
New Prospect Church Rd 28150
Newton St 28150
Nickey Sharts Rd 28152
Nicole Dr 28152
Nixon Dr 28152
Normandy Ln 28152
Norris Acres Dr 28150
Northeastern Dr 28152
Northern St 28150
Northgate Dr 28150
Northside Dr 28150
Norwood St 28150
O G Lail Rd 28152
Oak Ave 28152
Oak Dr 28150
N Oak Dr 28150
S Oak Dr 28150
Oak St 28150
W Oak St 28150
Oak Grove Rd 28150
Oak Haven Ln 28150
Oakberry St 28150
Oakcrest Dr 28150
S Oakhurst Dr 28152
Oakland Dr 28150
Oakley St 28150
Oakridge Dr 28150
Oakvale Dr 28150
Oakwood Dr 28150
Oates Ct & Dr 28152
Ocean Dr 28152
Ohana Ln 28150
Ola Ct 28150
Olan Dr 28152
Old Boiling Springs Rd 28152
Old Buffalo Church Rd 28152
Old Charles Rd 28152
Old Cliffside Rd 28152
Old Friends Ln 28150
Old Gaffney Rd 28152
Old Lincolnton Rd 28150
Old Mill Rd 28150
Old Rutherford Rd 28150
Old School Rd 28150
Oliver Ave 28152
Olsen Dr 28152
Orange St 28150
Orchard Dr 28150
Osborne St 28150
Otho Ln 28152
Overlook Dr 28152
Owl Ln 28152
Oxford St 28152
Packard Rd 28152
Padgett Rd 28150
Palm St 28150
Palmer St 28150
Pamela Dr 28150

Pamlico Dr 28152
Parham Beam Rd 28150
N Park Ave, Cir & St 28150
Parkview St 28150
Parkwild Cir 28152
Parkwood Rd 28150
Parnell St 28150
Parrish Dr 28152
Patricia Ct 28152
Patrick Ave 28152
S Patterson Rd & St 28152
Patton Dr 28150
Peach St 28150
Peachtree Rd 28150
Pebble Crk 28152
Pebble Dr 28150
Pecan Dr 28152
Peck Pl 28152
Peeler St 28152
Peninsula Ave 28150
Penn Pl 28150
Penndale Dr 28152
Peppermint Dr 28152
Perry St 28150
Peterson Dr 28152
Petty Rd 28150
Peyton Pl 28150
Pheasant Dr 28150
Philbeck St 28150
Phillips St 28150
Phillips Vlg 28152
Pico Dr 28150
Piedmont Ave 28150
Pike Ct 28150
Pilbury Dr 28152
Pine St 28152
Pine Cone Ln 28152
Pine Forest Dr 28150
Pine Grove Church Rd 28152
Pine Ridge Dr 28152
Pineburr Dr 28152
Pinecrest Dr & St 28152
Pineland Ave 28152
Pinetop Dr 28150
Pineview Dr 28150
Pinkney St 28150
Pinoak Ln 28150
Plainfield Dr 28150
Plantation Ct 28150
Plaster Ave 28152
Plato Lee Rd 28150
Pleasant Dr 28152
Pleasant Grove Church Rd 28150
Pleasant Hill Church Rd 28152
Pleasant Ridge Church Rd 28152
Pleasantdale Dr 28150
Point Crossing Ct 28152
Polkville Rd 28150
Pontiac Dr 28152
Poplar Cir 28152
Poplar Dr 28152
Poplar St 28150
Poplar Springs Church Rd 28152
Porter St 28150
N Post Rd
100-399 28152
400-1799 28150
S Post Rd 28152
Posting Pl 28152
Poston Cir 28152
N Poston St 28150
S Poston St 28150
Power Dr 28152
Powerline Dr 28152
Prentice Dr 28152
Prestwick Ct 28152
Preyer St 28152
Price St 28150
Princess Ln 28150
Prospect Church Rd 28152
Providence Rd 28152
Putnam St 28152

Quail Ln 28152
Quail Meadow Rd 28150
Quail Run Dr 28150
Queens Cir 28150
Quinn Dr 28152
Rachel Ct 28152
Raft Pl 28152
Railroad Ave 28152
Rainbow Dr 28152
Ralph Green Rd 28152
Ramblewood Dr 28152
Ramseur Church Rd 28150
Ramsey Farm Ln 28152
Ramsgate Dr 28152
Ranchfield Dr 28152
Randall Rd 28152
E & W Randolph Rd 28150
Rayton Dr 28152
Red Rd 28152
Red Sun Dr 28150
Red Tail Ln 28152
Redman Rd 28150
Reece Rd 28152
Rehobeth Church Rd 28150
Rena Dr 28150
Rhapsody Ln 28152
Rhodann Dr 28152
Rhyne St 28152
Ria Ct 28152
Richard Dr 28150
Richards Dr 28150
S Ridge St 28152
Ridgedale Dr 28150
Ridgefield Rd 28150
Ridgemont Ave 28150
Ridgeview Dr 28150
Ridgewood St 28152
Ridings Rd 28150
Riley St 28152
Ritchie Dr 28152
River Rd 28152
River Chase Dr 28152
River Hill Dr 28152
Riveria Dr 28150
Riverside Rd 28152
Riverwood Dr 28152
Robert Riding Rd 28150
Roberts Ct 28152
Roberts St 28150
Robin Dr 28150
Robin Pl 28152
Robinwood Dr 28150
Robyn Ave 28152
Rockey Brook Rd 28150
Rockford Rd 28152
Rocky Creek Rd 28152
Rogers St 28150
Rollingwood Dr 28150
Ronald Dr 28152
Roper Rd 28152
Rosebank Dr 28150
Rosecrest Dr 28152
Ross Rd 28150
Ross Grove Rd E & W 28150
Royster Ave & Rd 28150
Rucker Rd 28152
Runnin R Trl 28150
Rural Ln 28152
Rustling Wind Dr 28150
Ruth St 28150
Ryburn St 28152
Sailers Dr 28150
Sam Lattimore Rd 28152
Sam Mitchell Ct 28152
Sanders Rd 28150
Sandie Dr 28150
Sandranette St 28152
Sandy Point Dr 28150
Santa Clara Dr 28152
Santa Fe Trl 28152
Santrest Rd 28150
Sarratt Dr 28152
Scenic Cir & Dr 28150
Schenck St 28150
Schweppe Ln 28152

Scottsdale Dr 28150
Seaboard Ave 28150
Seattle St 28152
Sedgefield Dr 28152
Seminole Ct 28152
Serenity Dr 28152
Serro Ct 28152
Seven Hawks Trl 28152
Shadowgate Dr 28152
Shadowood Dr 28150
Shady Ridge Ln 28150
Shamrock Rd 28152
E & W Shannonhouse St 28152
Sharon Cir 28152
N Sharon Dr 28150
Shawnee Dr 28152
Sheila Ln 28150
Sheree Ln 28150
Sheriff Allen Rd 28152
Sherrill Pl 28150
Sherwood Dr 28150
Shiloh Ct 28150
Shoal Creek Church Rd 28152
Shuford Dr 28152
Shull St 28152
Shytle Dr 28150
Silver St 28152
Silver Creek Ln 28152
Silverina Ct 28152
Simpson Park Rd 28150
Sioux Ct 28152
Sir Gregory Dr 28152
Skinner Rd 28152
Skycrest Ave 28152
Sleepy Ln 28152
Smarr Pl 28152
Smith St 28150
Sneed Rd 28150
Sonnet Dr 28152
Sounder Ln 28150
South Ave 28152
Southern Dr 28150
Southern Pines Dr 28152
Southern Springs Rd 28152
Southfork Dr 28152
E & W Southgate Dr 28152
Southglenn Dr 28152
Southmeadow Ln 28152
Spake Cir 28150
Spangler Dr 28150
Spann St 28150
Sparks Dr 28150
Sperling Dr 28150
Spiral Ln 28152
Spring Dr 28150
Spring Ln 28152
Spring St 28152
Spring Forest Dr 28152
Spring Garden Dr 28150
Spring Lake Dr 28150
Spring Valley Ter 28152
Springbrook Rd 28150
Springdale St 28150
Springmont St 28152
Spruce Dr 28152
Spurlin St 28150
W Stage Coach Trl 28150
Stamey Ave 28150
Stanton Dr 28150
Starlight Dr 28152
E & W Steeple St 28150
Stella Ct 28150
Stice Shoal Rd 28152
Stillwater Rd 28152
Stingray Dr 28152
Stockton St 28150
Stone St 28152
Stone Crest Rd 28152
Stone Gate Dr 28150
Stoneview Ct 28150
Stoney Ranch Rd 28150
Stony Point Rd 28150
Stroud Rd 28152
Sue Ln 28152

Suffolk Dr 28152
Sulphur Springs Rd 28152
Summit St 28150
E & W Sumter St 28150
Sunderland Dr 28150
Sunny St 28150
Sunrise Cir 28150
Surry Dr 28152
Suttle St 28150
Sweezy Rd 28152
Sycamore Ln 28152
Sylva Dr 28152
T R Harris Dr 28150
Tall Pine Dr 28152
Tallwood Dr 28152
Tan Yard Rd 28150
Tanglewood Ln 28152
Tanya Ln 28152
Tarheel Dr 28150
Tarlton Dr 28150
Taylor Rd 28152
Tenda Pl 28150
Textile St 28152
Thamon Rd 28150
Thea Dr 28150
Thisa Way 28150
Thistle Dr 28152
N & S Thompson St 28150
Thore Rd 28152
Thornhill Ln 28152
Three Brothers Ave 28152
Three Lakes Rd 28150
Thrift Rd 28152
Tiffany Rd 28152
Tilly Rd 28150
Timber Ridge Dr 28152
Timberlake Dr 28150
Timberland Dr 28150
Tina Dr 28152
Tobe Bridge Rd 28150
Tom Dedmon Rd 28150
Toms St 28150
S Toney St 28152
Tonga Dr 28152
Topic Ct & St 28152
Tower Dr 28152
Towery Rd 28150
Tracy St 28150
N & S Trade St 28150
Trail Run 28150
Tremont Pl 28150
Trent Mcswain Rd 28152
Troon Pl 28150
Troutman Ln 28152
Troy Rd 28150
Truman St 28150
Tryon St 28150
Turner Dr & Rd 28152
Turtle Xing 28150
Twelve Oaks Dr 28150
Twin Chimney Rd 28152
Twin Lake Dr 28152
Twin Oaks Ct 28150
Tyler Dr 28152
Union Church Rd 28150
Vale St 28150
Valentine Dr 28152
Valerie Dr 28152
Valley Stream Dr 28152
Van Aken Cir 28150
Vantage Dr 28150
Vassey Rd 28152
Vauxhall Dr 28150
Vermont St 28150
Vernell Ln 28150
Vernon Rd 28150
Veticusi Dr 28152
Vick St 28152
Vick Wilson Rd 28152
Victor Dr 28152
Victoria Park Dr 28150
Victory Ln 28152
Vintage Woods Ct & Ln 28150
Vista Dr 28150
Wal Mart Dr 28150
Walker Dr 28152
Walkers Ridge Rd 28152
Walksing Dr 28150
Wall Ave 28152
Wall St 28150
Wallace Grove Dr 28150
Walnut St 28150
Wanda St 28152
Wardell St 28150
Ware Rd 28152
Ware St 28150
E & W Warren Pl & St 28150
Warrenton Ct 28150
Washburn Rd 28150
Washburn Switch Rd 28150
N Washington St 28150
S Washington St
1-899 28150
900-1199 28152
Waters St 28152
Waterside Dr 28150
Waterwood Dr 28150
Watson St 28150
Waylen St 28150
Waynes Ct 28152
Wease Dr 28152
Weatherford Dr 28150
Weatherly Ln 28150
Weathers St 28150
Weaver Rd 28150
Webb Dr 28150
Webb Rd 28152
Webb Farm Rd 28152
Webber St 28152
Wedgewood St 28150
Wellington St 28152
Wellmon Rd 28150
Wells St 28150
Wendover Height Dr 28150
Wesley St 28150
Wesson Rd 28152
Western Ln 28152
Westfield Rd 28150
Westgate Dr 28152
Westlee St 28150
Westover Ter 28150
Westside Dr 28152
Westview St 28150
Westwind Dr 28152
Westwood Dr 28152
Whaley St 28150
Whisnant St 28150
Whitaker Rd 28152
White Ave 28150
White Haven Ct 28152
N & S White Oak Dr 28150
White Tail Dr 28152
Whitener St 28152
Whitmar Lake Rd 28150
Wichita Dr 28152
Wild Cherry Dr & Rd 28150
Wildwood Dr 28150
Wildwood Ranch Rd 28152
Wilkshire Dr 28150
Williamsfield Dr 28150
Williamson Rd 28150
Willis Dr 28152
Willow Ln 28150
Willow Brook Dr 28152
Willow Creek Ln 28152
Wilmouth St 28152
Wilson Rd 28152
Wilson St 28150
Wilson Cornwell Rd 28150
Wilson Farm Rd 28150
Winchester Dr 28152
Windcrest Dr 28150
Windermere Ln 28150
Winding Rd 28150
Windover Rd 28150
Windsor Dr 28150
Windy Ln 28152
Wingate Ct 28152
Winners Cir 28152
Winston Rd 28152
Winter Park Dr 28152
Withers St 28152
N & S Withrow Dr 28150
Wolfe Rd 28152
Woodbine Rd 28150
Woodbluff Dr 28150
Woodcove Ln 28150
Wooded Ln 28152
Wooden St 28152
N Woodhill Dr 28152
Woodland Ave 28152
Woodland Dr 28150
Woodlawn Ave 28150
Woodman Hall St 28152
Woodside Dr 28150
Worthington St 28150
Wright St 28150
Wyanoke Ave 28152
Wyke Rd 28150
Yancey St 28150
Yancy Branch Ln 28152
Yarn Mill Rd 28150
Yates Rd 28150
Yates Mcbrayer Dr 28152
Yorkfield 28150
Young St 28150
Zeb Cline Rd 28150
Zelda Dr 28150
E & W Zion Church Rd 28150

NUMBERED STREETS

1st St 28150
1st Broad Rd 28152
2nd St 28150
3rd St 28150

SOUTHERN PINES NC

General Delivery 28387

POST OFFICE BOXES MAIN OFFICE STATIONS AND BRANCHES

Box No.s
1 - 2750 28388
28387 - 28387 28387

NAMED STREETS

Aiken Rd 28387
Air Tool Dr 28387
Arbutus Rd 28387
Artillery Rd 28387
N & S Ashe St 28387
Aster Ct 28387
Augusta Dr 28387
Austins Ridge Cir 28387
Azalea Rd 28387
Barber Rd 28387
Barcroft Ct 28387
Barvis Ct 28387
Bayhill Ct 28387
Baystone Ct 28387
Becky Branch Rd 28387
Belfair Ct 28387
Bell Ave 28387
Belmont Ct 28387
Ben Nevis Cir 28387
N & S Bennett St 28387
Bentwood Ln 28387
Bethesda Rd 28387
Beverly Ln 28387
Bishops Rdg 28387
Blue Ln 28387
Boiling Springs Cir 28387
Boyd Ln 28387
N & S Brackenfern Ln 28387
Braden Rd 28387
Bradford Village Ct 28387
Branch Rd 28387
Brandt Ln 28387
Brewster Hussey Ln 28387
Bridgewater Dr 28387
Bristow Ln 28387
NE Broad St 28387
NW Broad St 28387
SE Broad St 28387
SW Broad St
100-199 28387
190-190 28388
200-1598 28387
201-1599 28387
Broadmeade Dr 28387
Bronwyn St 28387
Brooks Ln 28387
Brothers Rd 28387
Brucewood Rd 28387
Bumbalong Ln 28387
Burlwood Dr 28387
Burns Rd 28387
Byrd St 28387
Caitlin Ct 28387
Camelia Way 28387
Camp Easter Rd 28387
Canterbury Rd 28387
Capital Rd 28387
Cardinal Rd 28387
Caritas Ct 28387
N & S Carlisle St 28387
Carolina Trailer Park 28387
Cathleen Way 28387
Central Ct & Dr 28387
Champions Rdg 28387
Change Way 28387
E & W Chelsea Ct 28387
Cheviot Way 28387
Christine Cir 28387
Clark St 28387
Clearfield Ln 28387
Clematis Rd 28387
Cliff Ct & Rd 28387
Cliff Court Ext 28387
Club Pl 28387
Coats St 28387
Colorado Cir 28387
Columbine Rd 28387
Commerce Ave 28387
E, N, S & W Connecticut Ave 28387
Corran Cir 28387
Cottage Ln 28387
Cotton Patch Pl 28387
Country Club Cir & Dr 28387
Cox St 28387
Crest Rd 28387
Crestview Rd 28387
Creswell Dr 28387
Cross Country Rd 28387
Crosscut Ln 28387
Cypress Cir 28387
Daffodil Rd 28387
Davis Ct & Rd 28387
Deacon Palmer Pl 28387
Dean Ave 28387
E & W Delaware Ave 28387
Den Rd 28387
Doctor Neal Rd 28387
Dog Leg Rd 28387
E Dogwood Ln 28387
Dover St 28387
Downing Pl 28387
Dragonfly Ct 28387
Driftwood Cir 28387
Drumar Ct 28387
Duffers Ln 28387
Duncan Ct & Rd 28387
Dundee Trl 28387
Eagle Point Ln 28387
Eastbourne Dr 28387
Eastman Rd 28387
Edinboro Dr 28387
Elk Rd 28387
Elk Ridge Ln 28387
Essex Pl 28387
Fairway Ave, Ct, Dr & Ln 28387
Falcon Crest Ln 28387
Felton Capel Ln 28387
Fieldcrest Rd 28387
Firelane Ave 28387
Firleigh Rd 28387
Forest Glen Rd 28387
Fort Bragg Rd 28387
Fox Hunt Ln 28387
Foxfire Pl 28387
Fraser Ln 28387
Furth Ln 28387
N & S Gaines St 28387
Gatewood Ave 28387
Glasgow Cir 28387
Glen Devon Dr 28387
Glenmoor Dr 28387
N & S Glenwood Trl 28387
N & S Glover St 28387
Golfcrest Ln 28387
Goodwill Rd 28387
Gossman Rd 28387
Grampian Way 28387
Grannys Ln 28387
Greenhouse Ln 28387
Grove Rd 28387
Hadley Ct 28387
Haines Ct 28387
Halcyon Dr 28387
Haldane Dr & Pl 28387
N & S Hale St 28387
Haley St 28387
Hall St 28387
N & S Hardin St 28387
Harmony Ln 28387
Heather Ln 28387
E & W Hedgelawn Way 28387
S Henley Pl & St 28387
Henson St 28387
Highland Rd 28387
Highland Hills Ctry Clb 28387
Highland View Dr 28387
Hill Rd 28387
Hillside Rd 28387
Hillwood Ct 28387
Hodgins St 28387
Holiday St 28387
Holly Cir & Ln 28387
Horseshoe Dr & Rd 28387
Huntcliff Apts 28387
Hunter Ct & Trl 28387
Hutchinson Rd 28387
Hyland Ct 28387
Hyland Hills Rd 28387
E & W Illinois Ave 28387
Indian Trail Dr 28387
E & W Indiana Ave 28387
Inverness Rd 28387
W Iowa Ave 28387
James Creek Rd 28387
Jordan Chapel Ln 28387
Katavolos Dr 28387
Katherine Pl 28387
Kensington Rd 28387
Kings Ridge Ct 28387
S Knoll Rd 28387
Knollwood Dr 28387
Kyloe Rd 28387
Lake Dr 28387
Lakeview Dr 28387
Lanark Trl 28387
Landis Ct 28387
Lanson Trl 28387
Larkenda Rd 28387
Latrobe Ct 28387
Laurel Rd 28387
Laurel Valley Ct 28387
Laurelton 28387
Lauren Ln 28387
Lazar Ln 28387
N & S Leak St 28387
Lily Pl 28387
Lindley Rd 28387
Little Rd 28387
Llp Farm Rd 28387
Lone Pine Pl 28387
Long St 28387
Long Pine Hills Rd 28387
Longleaf Rd 28387
Lost Tree Pl 28387
W Lowe Ave 28387
Lupin Pl 28387
Luther Way 28387
E Magnolia Cir & Ct 28387
E & W Maine Ave 28387
E Manley Ave 28387
Maples Rd 28387
Marston Ave 28387
Martin Trl 28387
E Massachusetts Ave 28387
Masters Rdg 28387
N & S May St 28387
Mcdeeds Creek Rd 28387
Mclendon Ct 28387
Mcmillan Cir 28387
Mcneil Rd 28387
Mcnish Rd 28387
Mcsweeney Cir 28387
N & S Mechanic St 28387
Meeting House Rd 28387
Memaire Pl 28387
Memorial Park Ct 28387
Merced Ct 28387
Merry Way 28387
Merry Mock Hill Rd 28387
W Michigan Ave 28387
Middleton Pl 28387
Midland Rd 28387
Midlothian Dr 28387
Mile Away Ln 28387
Mill Rd 28387
Mitchell Rd 28387
Morganton Rd 28387
Murray Hill Rd 28387
Myrtlewood Ct 28387
New England Rd 28387
E & W New Hampshire Ave 28387
New Haven Pl 28387
E & W New Jersey Ave 28387
E & W New York Ave 28387
Newton Dr 28387
Niagara Rd 28387
Niagara Carthage Rd 28387
Northsouth Ct 28387
Northwood Dr 28387
Oak Dr 28387
Oconner Ct 28387
E Ohio Ave 28387
Old Clubhouse Ln 28387
Old Dewberry Rd 28387
Old Field Rd 28387
Old Mail Rd 28387
Old Morganton Rd 28387
Old Us Highway 1 S 28387
One Down St 28387
Orchard Rd 28387
Owens Ln 28387
Paddock Ln 28387
N & S Page St 28387
Palmer Dr 28387
Park Hill Rd 28387
Partner Cir 28387
Pebble Beach Pl 28387
Pee Dee Rd 28387
Penick Woods Ln 28387
Penn Carol Ln 28387
E & W Pennsylvania Ave 28387
Perry Dr 28387
Pettingill Pl 28387
Petty St 28387
N & S Pine Ln & St 28387
Pine Branch Ct 28387
Pine Cone Pl & Way 28387
Pine Grove Rd 28387
Pine Needles Ln 28387
Pinecrest Plz 28387
Pinecrest High School Rd 28387
Pinecrest School Rd 28387
Pinefield Ct 28387
Pinehurst Ave 28387
Piney Ln 28387
Plantation Dr 28387
Pleasant Dr 28387
N Poplar St 28387
Preakness Ct 28387
Preston Ln 28387
Prospect St 28387
Quail Glen Rd 28387
Quail Hollow Pl 28387
Railroad Ave 28387
Redwood Dr 28387
E & W Rhode Island Ave 28387
Rhyan Ct 28387
Richards St 28387
N & S Ridge St 28387
Ridgeview Rd 28387
Ridgewood Dr 28387
Riding Ln 28387
Rob Roy Rd 28387
Rothney Ave & Ct 28387
Round About Ct & Rd 28387
Roundabout Rd 28387
Roundtree Ln 28387
Saint Andrews Pl 28387
Saint James Cir 28387
Saint Joseph Rd 28387
Sandalwood Dr 28387
Sandavis Rd 28387
Sandhurst Pl 28387
Sandmoore Dr 28387
Sandy Ave 28387
Satinwood Ct 28387
Saunders Blvd 28387
N Saylor St 28387
Scots Glen Dr 28387
Selkirk Trl 28387
Serpentine Dr 28387
Service Rd 28387
Shady Ln 28387
Shaw Ave 28387
Sheldon Rd 28387
Shibui Gdns 28387
Shields Rd 28387
Short Rd 28387
Skye Dr 28387
Skyline Manor Rd 28387
Southern Rd 28387
Southwick Apts 28387
Spring Rd 28387
Stafford Ct 28387
Starland Ln 28387
Station Ave 28387
Steelman Rd 28387
Steeplechase Ct & Way 28387
Stephanie St 28387
N & S Stephens Cir & St 28387
Stoneyfield Dr 28387
Stornoway Dr 28387
Strathmore St 28387
Sundew Ct 28387
Swoope Dr 28387
Tabernacle Rd 28387
Talamore Dr 28387
Talmadge Way 28387
Tanglewood Ct & Dr 28387
Tannen Dr 28387
Tar Kiln Pl 28387
Tartan Trl 28387
Teakwood Ln 28387
Tella Dr 28387
The Commons Plz 28387
Tilgman Ave 28387
Timber Ln Rd 28387
Timothy St 28387
Tingley Ct 28387
Tower St 28387
Tray St 28387
Tremont Pl 28387

Trimble Plant Rd 28387
Triple Crown Cir 28387
Turner St 28387
Turnwell Pl 28387
Us Highway 1 N & S 28387
Us Highway 1 Bus 28387
Us Highway 1 Service Rd E 28387
S Us Highway 15 501 28387
Valentine Dr 28387
Valhalla Rd 28387
N & S Valley Park & Rd 28387
Valley View Rd 28387
Valleyfield Ln 28387
Van Dusen Way 28387
Vardon Ct 28387
E, N, S & W Vermont Ave 28387
Village By The Lk 28387
Village Green Cir 28387
Village In The Woods 28387
Virginia Rd 28387
Voit Gilmore Rd 28387
Wake Forest Ct 28387
Walsh Ln 28387
Wanamaker Ct 28387
Waters Dr 28387
Wayland St 28387
Westover Rd 28387
Weymouth Rd 28387
Wildwood Ct 28387
Williams Rd 28387
Willowood Ct 28387
Windsor Ln 28387
Windstar Pl 28387
Wiregrass Ln 28387
W Wisconsin Ave 28387
Woodbrooke Dr 28387
Woodcrest Rd 28387
Woodhaven Ct 28387
Woodland St 28387
Wooster Rd 28387
Yadkin Rd 28387
Youngs Rd 28387

NUMBERED STREETS

All Street Addresses 28387

STATESVILLE NC

General Delivery 28677

POST OFFICE BOXES MAIN OFFICE STATIONS AND BRANCHES

Box No.s
All PO Boxes 28687

RURAL ROUTES

01, 02, 04, 05, 06, 08, 09, 11, 12, 13, 15, 17, 18, 20, 21, 24, 25, 27, 28 28625
07, 10, 14, 16, 19, 22, 23 28677

NAMED STREETS

A St 28677
Abernathy Ave 28625
Abruzzo Ln 28625
Absher Park, Rd & St 28625
Absher Farm Loop & Rd 28625
Adams St 28677
Addie Rd 28625
Adeline Ln 28625
Adkins Ln 28677
Advantage Pl 28677
Aileen Ln 28677
Airborne Ln 28625
Airport Rd 28677
Alexander St 28677
Alexander Knoll Dr 28625
Allen Creek Rd 28625
Allis Dr 28625
E & W Allison St 28677
Alma Dr 28625
Almosta Cir 28625
Alpine Cir 28625
Altondale Dr 28625
Amanda Ln 28625
Amber Ln 28677
Amity Hill Rd 28677
Amos Lake Dr 28625
Anderson St 28677
Andes Dr 28625
Angdale Ln 28677
Angel Oaks Dr 28625
Angela Ln 28677
Anglers Cove Ln 28625
Angus Trl 28677
Anna Dr 28625
Annie Valley Ln 28625
Antietam Rd 28625
Antler Dr 28625
Appalachian Trail Ln 28677
Appaloosa Ln 28625
Apple Tree Ln 28677
Apple Valley Ln 28677
Apricot Ln 28677
April Showers Ln 28677
Arbor Dr 28677
Arborgate Loop 28625
Arey Rd 28677
Argyle Ct & Pl 28677
Arizona Dr 28625
Arlie Loop 28677
Arlington Ave 28677
Armfield St 28677
Armstrong St 28677
Arrington Rd 28625
Arrington Farm Ln 28625
Arrow Ln 28625
Artist Ln 28677
Ascending Ln 28625
Ashbrook Rd 28677
Asheville Ave 28677
Ashland Ave 28677
Ashley Acres Rd 28677
Ashley Brooke Ln 28677
Atwell Dr 28677
Aubry Dr 28677
Auburn Ln 28625
Auction Ln 28625
Augusta Dr 28625
Austin Rd 28625
Autumn Frost Ave 28677
Autumn Mist Rd 28677
Avalon St 28677
Aviation Dr 28677
Avondale Dr 28625
Aycock Rd 28625
B St 28677
Babson Ln 28625
Back End Ln 28625
Backcreek Ln 28677
Bacon Rd 28625
Badger Ln 28625
Bailey Farm Rd 28625
Baker St 28677
Bakery Ln 28677
Balerelm Rd 28625
Ball Dr 28677
Ballingarry Dr 28625
Bambi Ln 28625
Banberry Ct & Dr 28625
Bancroft Ln 28625
Baner Dr 28625
Barbary Dr 28677
Bard Ln 28625
Bargate Dr 28625
Barium Ln 28677
Barium Springs Dr 28677
Barker Ln 28625
E & N Barkley Rd 28677
Barn Owl Dr 28625
Barnes Airship Dr 28625
Barnyard Ln 28625
Barracuda Loop 28677
Barriere Cir 28677
Barringer Dr & Ln 28625
Barry Oak Rd 28625
Bass Ln 28625
Battle Rd 28625
Bauer Dr 28625
Bauyer Dr 28677
Baxter Dr 28677
Bayberry Ct 28677
Baymount Dr 28625
Baymount Acres Dr 28625
Bc Dr 28677
Beagle Ln 28625
Beam Farm Rd 28625
Beatty Farm Ln 28625
Beauty St 28625
Beaver Farm Rd 28625
Beaverbrook Rd 28677
Beaverwood Ln 28625
Beck Ln 28625
Beckham Rd 28625
Beech Brook Ln 28625
Beechnut Ln 28625
Beechwood Rd 28677
Beechwood Farm Rd 28625
Belfast Rd 28677
Belinda Loop 28677
Bell Rd 28625
E Bell St 28677
W Bell St 28677
Bell Chase Ln 28677
Bell Farm Rd 28625
Bell Meade Rd 28625
Belle Ave 28677
Belle Heritage Trl 28625
Belle Meade Ave 28677
Belle Terre Rd 28625
Bellfast Rd 28677
Bellwood Dr & Loop 28625
Benfield Rd 28677
Benfield Farm Dr 28625
Benjamia Hill Dr 28625
Benjamin Ln 28625
Bent Twig Dr 28677
Bentbrook Rd 28677
Berea Ln 28625
Berkshire Dr 28677
Berry St 28677
Bess Rd 28625
Bethany Rd 28625
Bethany Woods Ln 28625
Bethesda Rd 28677
Bethlehem Rd 28677
Beulah Rd
100-299 28677
300-499 28625
Beverly Dr & Pl 28625
Beverly Anne Dr 28677
Bevis Ln 28677
Big Bertha Dr 28677
Big Cedar Dr 28625
Big Forest Dr 28677
Big Oak Ln 28625
Big Tree Dr 28625
Bigham Ln 28677
E & W Bingham St 28677
Biondo Ct 28625
Birchcrest Dr 28677
Birchwood Rd 28625
Bird Haven Dr 28625
Birdsey St 28625
Black Rd 28677
Black Pine Rd 28625
Blackhawk Dr 28625
Blackwelder Rd 28625
Blanchwood Rd 28677
Blaythorne Ln 28625
Blimp Works Rd 28625
Bloomingdale Rd 28677
Blue Jay Way 28625
Blueberry Ln 28677
Blueberry Hill Dr 28625
Bluebird Ln 28677
Bluegill Ln 28625
Bluff Ct 28625
Boatlaunch Dr 28677
Bobbys Loop 28625
Bobcat Trl 28625
Boiling Brook Dr 28625
Bond St 28677
Bone Dr 28625
Bonnie Ln 28625
Book Ct 28677
N Bost St 28677
Bostian Hts 28677
Bostian Bridge Rd 28677
Bostian Lake Rd 28677
Boulder Pl 28625
Bowen Dr 28677
Bowles Farm Rd 28625
Bowman Rd 28625
Boyd St 28677
Boyuer Ln 28677
Brad Dr & St 28625
Bradford Ln 28625
Bradley Farm Rd 28625
Brady Ln 28625
Brady Circle Rd 28625
Brady Woods Ln 28625
Braeburn Ln 28677
Bramblewood Dr 28625
Branchside Ln 28625
Branchwood Rd 28677
Brandenburg Dr 28677
Brandon St 28677
Brandy Ln 28677
Brandywine Loop 28625
Brawley Park Dr 28625
Braxton Dr 28677
Breckenridge Ln 28625
Breeze Hill Pl 28625
Breezeway Ln 28677
Breezy Farm Ln 28625
Brenda Ln 28677
Brevard St 28677
Brick Bat Ln 28677
Brick Yard Rd 28677
Bridge Bottom Dr 28625
Bridge Mill Ct 28625
Bridges Creek Dr 28625
Bridle Ln
100-199 28625
2500-2599 28677
Brierwood Rd 28677
Bristol Dr, Rd & Ter 28677
Brittany Ln & Rd 28625
Britton Hill Rd 28677
E Broad St
100-1499 28677
1500-3599 28625
W Broad St 28677
Broad Meadow Dr 28625
Broadmoor Dr 28625
Broadway Ct & St 28625
Brock Ct 28625
Brody Dr 28625
Broken Arrow Dr 28677
Brook Run Ln 28625
Brookdale Dr 28677
Brookfield Dr 28625
Brookgreen Ave & Pl 28677
Brookhaven Rd 28625
Brookhollow Ct & Dr 28625
Brookmeade Dr 28625
Brookview Rd 28625
Brookwood Ct & Dr 28677
Broom St 28677
Broomsage Ln 28625
Brothers Ln 28625
Brotherton Rd 28625
Brown Summit Ave 28677
Bruce Farm Rd 28625
Bryant St 28677
Buck Ln 28625
Buck And Doe Ln 28625
Buck Deer Ln 28625
Buck Hollow Rd 28677
Buckbee Rd 28625
Buckingham Pl 28625
Bucks Industrial Rd 28625
Buckwheat Dr 28625
Buddy Ln 28625
Buena Vista Ave 28677
Buffalo St 28677
Buffalo Creek Dr & Rd 28677
Buffalo Shoals Rd 28677
Buffaloway Rd 28677
Bunch Dr 28677
Bunton Ln 28625
Burl Ln 28625
Burton Pl 28625
Business Park Dr 28677
Bussell Rd 28625
Bustle Farm Ln 28625
Butch Hollow Ln 28677
Butterfield Cir & Rd 28625
Buttke Dr 28625
C St 28677
Cabe Dr 28625
Cactus Ln 28625
Cadigan Ranch Rd 28625
Cady Ct 28677
Caldwell St 28677
Caldwell Farm Ln 28625
Calico Ln 28625
Cambridge Pl 28625
Cambridge Hill Dr 28625
Camden Dr 28677
Camden Rd 28625
Camelot Dr 28625
Cameron Dr 28625
Camp Oak Rd 28677
Campbell St 28625
Campground Rd 28625
Canal Dr 28625
Candlestick Dr 28625
Candy Dr 28677
Cannon Rd 28625
Canopy Oak Ln 28625
Caper St 28677
Capstone Ct 28625
Cara Ln 28677
Carderwoody Rd 28625
Caribou Dr 28625
Carigan Ranch Rd 28625
Carington Ln 28625
Carl Austin Rd 28625
Carney Ln 28677
Carodell Ln 28625
Caroldon Ln 28625
N & S Carolina Ave & Cir 28677
Caroline St 28625
Carolinian Dr 28625
Carolyn St 28677
Carpet Rd 28625
Carriage Rd 28677
Carroll St 28677
Carter Ln 28625
Carters Farm Dr 28625
Cartner Rd 28625
Cartway Ln 28625
Cash Ln 28677
Cashion Farm Dr 28677
Caskaddon Ln 28625
Cass St 28677
Castle Creek Rd 28625
Castle Pines Ln 28625
Castlefin Ct 28625
Caterpillar Ln 28677
Catfish Dr 28677
Catfish Pond Ln 28625
Catspaw Rd 28677
Cattlemans Rd 28625
Caudill Dr 28677
Cecil Dr, Ln & Park 28625
Cedar Hill Trl 28677
Cedar House Dr 28625
Cedar Lake Dr 28625
Cedar Ridge Loop 28625
Cedar Tree Ct 28677
Cedarbrook Dr 28625
Celeste Estates Rd 28677
Celeste Eufola Rd 28677
Celestial Ln 28677
N & S Center St 28677
Central Dr 28677
Centre Church Rd 28625
Chal Dr 28677
Chalet Heights Dr 28677
Chalice Ct 28625
Chambers St 28677
Chantilly Ln 28625
Chapel Hill Ln 28677
Chapman Place Ln 28677
Charis Ln 28677
Charles St 28677
Charlotte Ave 28677
Chase Dr 28677
Chatfield Loop 28677
Checkers Ln 28625
Chel Thom Ln 28677
Cheng Dr 28625
Cherry Ln & St 28677
Cheryls Pass Cir 28625
Chestnut Ln 28625
Chestnut Grove Rd 28625
Chevelle Dr 28677
Chevy Ln 28625
Cheyenne Ln 28677
Chico Dr 28625
Chimney Ln 28625
Chimney Ridge Ln 28625
N & S Chipley Ford Rd 28625
Chisam Dr 28625
Chisum Dr 28625
Christine Dr 28625
Christopher Ln 28625
Chrysanthemum Ln 28677
Church St 28677
Church Estate Ln 28625
Church Farm Dr 28677
Church Lake Rd 28625
Churchland Dr 28625
Cinema Dr 28625
Circle L Dr 28625
Clanton Rd 28625
Clara Dr 28677
Clarence Ln 28625
Clarice Ct 28625
Clark St 28677
Clark Cove Rd 28677
Classic Ln 28625
Clay St 28677
Claycamp Dr 28677
Clayton St 28677
Clear Meadow Ln 28625
Clearcrest Dr 28625
Clearcut Ln 28625
Clearview Rd 28625
Clegg St 28677
Clements Rd 28677
Cliffside Dr 28625
Cliffwood Dr 28677
Cline St 28677
Clinker Brick Rd 28677
Clint Dr 28625
Clio Ln 28625
E & W Cloaninger Ave 28625
Cloer St 28677
Clove Ln 28677
Cloverdale Ct 28677
Club Dr 28677
Club House Dr 28677
Clyburn Rd 28677
Clyde St 28677
Coachman Loop 28625
Cobalt Ln 28625
Cochran St 28677
Coco Ln 28625
Coddington Ln 28625
Coite Ln 28625
Colfax Rd 28625
Collier Ln 28625
Colonial Dr 28625
Colonial Heights Ln 28625
Colony Ct & Rd 28677
Columbia St 28677
Columbine Dr 28625
Comet Trl 28677
Commanche Ct 28677
Commerce Blvd 28625
Commonwealth Ave 28677
Commscope Way 28625
Community Ln 28677
Compton Park Rd 28677
Concord Ave 28677
Cone Ln 28625
Congo Rd 28625
Conifer Dr 28625
Connor St 28677
Constance Ln 28625
Cook Farm Ln 28625
Cool Spring Rd 28625
Coolidge Ave & Ct 28677
Coolwood Dr 28625
Cooper St 28677
Cooper Farm Rd 28625
Copper Creek Dr 28677
Cordova Ln 28677
Coretta Ave 28625
Corey Dan Farm Ln 28625
Corinthian Dr 28677
Cornflower Rd 28677
Corral Cir 28625
Corry Dr & St 28625
Cottontail Ln 28677
Council Ave 28625
Country Dr 28625
Country Hill Ln 28625
Country Life Dr 28625
Country Park Rd 28625
Country Side Est 28625
Country View Rd 28625
Country Woods Ln 28625
Court St 28677
Cove Gap Rd 28625
Coventry Ln 28677
Cowan Ln 28625
Cowart Dr 28625
Cowboy Trl 28625
Cowgirl Run Trl 28625
Crabapple Ln 28625
Craft Ln 28677
Craig St 28677
Crawford Rd 28625
Creedmore Dr 28625
Creek Bottom Ln 28625
Creek Cove Ln 28677
Creekside Dr 28625
Creekstone Dr 28625
Crescent Ln 28677
Crest Dr 28625
Crestridge Rd 28677
Crestview Acres Rd 28677
Crestwater Ln 28677
Crews Ln 28677
Cricket Ln 28677
Crider Rd 28625
Cripple Creek Ln 28677
Critter Ln 28625
Crofton Ct 28677
Crooked Ln 28625
Crosby Rd 28625
N Cross Ln 28625
Cross Country Rd 28625
Cross Creek Dr 28625
Crossroads Dr 28625
Crosswhite Ln 28625
Crouch St 28625
Crouse Ct 28625
Crowell Ave 28677
Crown Vue Ct 28625
Crystal St 28677
Cub Farm Dr 28677
Cubs Paw Ln 28625
Cuddles Dr 28625
Cullen Ln 28625
Culpepper Rd 28625
Cumberland Rd 28677
Cunningham Dr 28625
Cyclone Ln 28677

Cynthia St 28677
Cyprus Ln 28677
D St 28677
D And K Ln 28625
Dagenhart Farm Rd 28677
Daisey Bare Ln 28625
Dallas Ln 28677
Damascus Church Rd 28625
Dan Ln 28677
Danbury Ln 28625
Dancourt Ln 28677
Daniel Ct 28677
Daniels Dairy Dr 28625
Darty Ln 28625
David Dr 28677
Davidson Rd 28677
Davie Ave
200-1899 28677
2000-2899 28625
Davis St 28677
Davis Place Ln 28625
Dawnwood Ln 28677
Deal Ln 28677
Dealwood Dr 28625
Deans Ranch Dr 28625
Deaton St 28677
Deauville Pl & Rd 28625
E & W Debbie Ln 28625
Deep Water Rd 28625
Deer Haven Dr 28625
Deer Ridge Dr 28625
Deer Trail Rd 28677
Deerchase Cir 28625
Deercreek Trl 28677
Deercroft Dr 28625
Deerfield Ln 28677
Deertracks Dr 28677
Deerview Cir 28625
Deitz Rd 28625
Delaware Rd 28625
Delight Loop 28677
Della Dr 28625
Dellinger Dr 28625
Dellwood Dr 28677
Delmar Ln 28677
Delray St 28677
Delta Pl 28677
Denny Rd 28625
Depot Pl 28677
Derby Dr 28677
Desiree Dr 28677
Destiny Dr 28625
Devon Ln 28625
Dewberry Ln 28625
Dewey Dr 28625
Diamond St 28677
Diane Ln 28677
Dillon Dr 28625
Diner Ln 28625
Dishman Ln 28625
Dishman Estate Ln 28625
Dishmon Family Dr 28625
Dixie Dr 28677
Dj Dr 28625
Dobbs Dr 28625
Dobson Rd 28677
Dobson Farm Rd 28625
Dockery St 28677
Dodge Dr 28625
Doe Ridge Ln 28625
Doe Run Ln 28625
Doe Trail Ln 28625
Dogwood Ln 28625
Dogwood Rd 28677
Dogwood Est Cir 28625
Donna Ln 28625
Donsdale Dr 28625
Doodle Dr 28677
Doubletree Dr 28677
Douglas St 28677
Douglas Pine Dr 28625
Douglas Trail Ln 28625
Dove Cir 28625
Dove Haven Dr 28677
Dove Meadow Ln 28625
Dover Rd 28677
Dover Park Dr 28677
Drake St 28677
Draper Dr 28625
Draughn Dr 28677
Drew Trl 28625
Dry Pond Ln 28625
Dublin Ct 28677
Duchamp Ln 28677
Duck Creek Rd 28677
Duggits Den Ln 28625
Duke Ln 28625
Duke Farm Ln 28625
Dunavant Ln 28677
E & W Dundee Ct 28625
Dunlap Loop 28625
Dunlap Gate Cir & Rd 28625
Duplex Ln 28677
Duramo Rd 28625
Durand Ln 28625
Durham Ave 28677
Dustin Ln 28625
Dusty Loop 28677
Eagle Dr 28677
Eagles Nest Ln 28625
Eagles Refuge Dr 28625
Eaglewood Dr & Rd 28625
Earlwood Rd 28677
Eastbrook Ln 28625
Eastfield Cir 28625
Eastgate Dr 28625
Easthaven Dr 28625
Eastover Dr 28625
Eastside Dr 28625
Eastway Dr 28625
Eastwood Dr 28625
Easy Livin Ln 28625
Eaves Ln 28625
Ebenezer Rd 28625
Ebony Cir 28625
Echo Glen Dr 28625
Edenderry Dr 28625
Edgewood Dr 28625
Edgewood School Ln 28625
E & W Edinburgh Ct 28625
E & W Edison Dr 28625
Edna Ln 28625
Edra Dr 28625
Eds Ln 28677
Edsel Way 28625
Edwards Ln 28677
Edwina Ln 28677
Eeb Ln 28625
Effie Ln 28625
Eight Point Dr 28625
Elam Ave 28677
Elam Farm Ln 28625
Eldorado Dr 28677
E Elementary Rd 28625
Elizabeth Ave 28677
Elk Dr 28625
Ella Kay Ln 28625
Ellenburg Dr 28625
Ellis Rd 28625
N & S Elm St 28677
Elmridge Dr 28625
Elmwood Rd 28625
Elpine St 28677
Elsie Dr 28677
Emma Ln 28625
Emma Mae Dr 28677
End Ave SE 28677
Engine Dr 28677
English Ln 28625
English Oaks Ln 28677
Enwood Ct 28677
Erastus Ln 28625
Ericson St 28677
Ernest Rd 28625
Estate Dr 28625
Estes Rd 28625
Ethel Ln 28625
Euclid Ave 28625
Eufola Rd 28677
Eupeptic Springs Rd 28625
Evans Valley Ln 28625
Evening Star Dr 28625
Evergreen Woods Rd 28625
Excell Dr 28625
Eye View Ln 28625
Fair Wind Ln 28677
Fairdale Rd 28625
Fairgate Dr 28625
Fairmount Rd 28625
Fairpoint Ct 28625
Faith And Hope Ln 28677
Falcon Ln 28625
Falling Creek Dr 28625
Falling Leaf Ln 28677
Falls St 28677
Family Cir 28625
Family Tree Ln 28625
Fanjoy Rd 28625
Farm House Rd 28625
Farmbrook Dr 28625
Farmview Ln 28625
Farmwood Dr 28625
Fawn Trail Ln 28625
Fawnwood Dr 28625
Faye St 28677
Fayetteville Ave 28677
Feimster St 28677
Feimster Place Ln 28625
Fern Creek Dr 28625
Fern Gully Ln 28625
Ferndale Dr 28677
Field And Stream Ln 28625
Fieldcrest Dr 28677
Fieldpine Rd 28625
Fieldstone Cir 28677
Fieldstone Farm Dr 28625
Filbert St 28625
Filly Trl 28625
Finch Ln 28625
Findley Rd 28625
Fines Creek Dr 28625
Fink Rd 28625
Firefly Ln 28677
Fish Hill Dr 28677
Flatbed Dr 28625
Flatrock Ln 28625
Fleetwood Rd 28677
Fleming Dr 28677
Flint Cir & Dr 28677
Flintlock Ln 28677
Flintstone Dr 28677
Florence Cir & Rd 28625
Floyd Ln 28625
Foggy Bottom Ln 28677
Folger Dr 28625
Fonda Rd 28677
Foothills Dr 28625
Ford Farm Rd 28625
Fores Rd 28625
Forest Dr 28677
Forest Rd 28625
Forest Brook Dr 28677
Forest Creek Dr 28625
Forest Grove Dr 28625
Forest Hollow Dr 28677
Forest Park Dr & Ter 28677
Fort Dobbs Rd 28625
Fort Valley Ct 28625
Fortunes Trl 28625
Foster Ln 28625
Four Winds Dr 28625
Fourwheel Dr 28625
Fox Ave 28677
Fox Bottoms Rd 28625
Fox Creek Rd 28625
Fox Den Cir 28677
Fox Mountain Rd 28625
Fox Park Ln 28625
Fox Run Dr 28625
Fox Tail Ct 28677
Foxcroft Ln & Ter 28677
Foxfire Ct 28625
Foxglove Dr 28677
Foy Ln 28625
Fraley Rd 28625
Franke Ln 28625
Frazier Loop 28677
Fred-Lee Dr 28677
Freda Ln 28677
Freddie Dr 28625
Free Nancy Ave 28677
Freedom Dr 28625
Freedom Park Ln 28625
Freeland Cir 28677
Freeland Farm Rd 28625
Freeze Farm Dr 28677
Friar Tuck Rd 28625
Friendly Cir 28625
Friendship Rd 28625
E Front St 28677
W Front St
100-300 28677
205-205 28687
301-2799 28677
302-2798 28677
3100-3399 28625
Frye Ln 28625
Fulton Dr 28677
G St 28677
G And R Dr 28625
Gagner St 28677
Gains Ln 28677
Gaither Rd 28625
Galax Dr 28677
Gantt Horn Rd 28625
Gantts Landing Ln 28625
Garden Valley Rd 28625
Garfield St 28677
Garner Dr 28677
E Garner Bagnal Blvd 28677
Garrison Dr 28677
Gaston Ct 28625
Gator Hollow Ln 28625
Gatwick Ct 28677
Gay St 28625
Gaymont Cir 28625
Gays Chapel Rd 28625
Gemstone Dr 28625
Geneva Ln 28625
Gennusa Ln 28625
Georgia Ave 28677
Getgood Ln 28625
Gethsemane Rd 28625
Gibson Farm Ln 28625
Gilbert Rd 28677
Gilead Ln 28625
Ginko Woods Ct 28625
Ginny Ln 28625
Glade St 28677
Glaspy Rd 28677
Glen Cross Dr 28625
Glendale Dr 28677
Gleneagles Rd E & W 28625
Glenhaven Rd 28677
Glenview Dr 28677
Glenview Ext Dr 28677
Glenway Dr 28625
Gloria Brook Dr & Ln 28677
Glory Bound Ln 28625
Glover St 28625
Goble Rd 28625
Godfrey Pass Ln 28625
Gods Farm Dr 28625
Gold Leaf Ln 28677
Golden Oak Dr 28625
Goldenrod Ln 28677
Goldsboro Ave 28677
Goldwing Dr 28625
Gonzales Ln 28677
Goodin Farm Ln 28625
Goodwrench Dr 28625
Gordon Ave 28677
Grace Lynn Dr 28625
Grady Rd 28625
Gragg Ave 28625
Graham St 28625
Grainger Ln 28625
Grandview Dr 28677
Grannis Ln 28677
Granny Trail Ln 28625
Grant Rd 28625
Grassy Meadow Ln 28625
Gray St 28677
Grayrock Dr 28677
Grayson Park Rd 28625
Greater Living Pl 28677
N & S Green St 28677
Green Leaf Ct 28677
Green Meadow Ln 28625
Green Valley Rd 28677
Greenberry Ln 28625
E Greenbriar Rd 28625
Greencrest Ln 28677
Greenfield Dr W 28625
Greenland Dr 28677
Greenway Dr 28677
Greenwich Dr 28677
Greenwood Dr 28625
Greer Pass Ln 28625
Gregory Ln & Rd 28677
Grey Manor Dr 28677
Greylin Loop 28625
Greythorn Dr 28625
Grier St 28677
Grier Farm Rd 28625
Grouse Ct 28625
Grove Dr 28677
Gumbo Dr 28625
Guy St 28677
Guy Farm Ln 28625
Gypsy Dr 28677
H St 28677
Habersham Loop 28677
Hackett St 28677
Hager View Ln 28625
Hall Dr 28625
Hallmark Rd 28625
Hallmark Estates Dr 28625
Hamby Ln 28625
Hampton Glen Dr 28625
Hams Grove Rd 28625
Hanbury Ln 28625
Hangar Dr 28677
Hanging Tree Ln 28625
Hannah Rd 28625
Hannah Brooke Ln 28625
Happy Ln 28677
Happy Acres Dr 28625
Harbin Ln 28625
Harbor Ridge Dr 28677
N & S Harbor Watch
Dr 28677
Harborcliff Dr 28677
Harborgate Dr 28677
Hardwood Ct 28677
Harmony Dr 28677
Harold Ln 28677
Harper Dr 28625
Harrelson Ln 28677
Harriet Ln 28625
Harrill St 28677
Harris St 28677
Harrison St 28677
Harrys Dr 28677
Hartness Rd 28677
Harvest Moon Ct 28625
Hatchery Ln 28677
Hatfield Rd 28625
Hatford Ct 28677
E & W Haven Dr 28625
Hawks Rd 28625
Hawthorne Dr 28677
Hayes Farm Rd 28625
Haymeadow Ln 28625
Haywood Ln 28625
Hayworth Ln 28625
Hazeline Dr 28677
Hazelwood Cir & Dr 28625
Heart Pine Ln 28677
Hearthstone Dr 28677
Heartland Dr 28677
Heartwood Ln 28625
Heathcote Dr 28677
Heather Ln 28677
Heathro Cir 28677
Heathrow Ln 28677
Heaven Bound Ln 28625
Heavenly Dr 28625
Hebron Rd 28625
Hedrick Cir & Dr 28677
Helen Dr 28625
Hellman Ranch Rd 28625
Hemingway Ln 28625
Hempstead Pl 28677
Henderson Dr 28677
Henkel Rd 28677
Henry Martin Trl 28625
Herbert Ln 28625
Heritage Cir & Rd 28625
Hermit Ln 28625
Heron Pt 28677
Heronwood Rd 28677
Hezekiah Rd 28625
Hickory Ave, Hwy &
St 28677
Hickory Hollar Dr 28677
Hickory Nut Dr 28677
Hickory Point Ct 28677
Hicks Rd 28625
Hidden Brook Dr 28677
Hidden Oak Dr 28677
Hidden River Ln 28625
Hidden Valley Dr 28677
High Lake Dr 28677
High Point Ave 28677
High Shoals Ln 28677
High Springs Ct 28677
Highland Ave 28677
Highland View Dr 28677
Highview Cir 28625
Hill St & Ter 28677
Hill Dairy Rd 28625
Hill Haven Rd 28677
Hillard St 28625
Hillbilly Ln 28677
Hillcrest Dr 28677
Hillndale Rd 28677
Hillside Ln 28625
Hilltop Dr 28625
Hilton Dr 28677
History Ln 28677
Hodge Ln 28677
Hog Jaw Dr 28625
Hoke Ln 28677
Holland Cir & Dr 28677
Hollie Ln 28625
Hollie Lee Dr 28625
Hollingswood Dr 28625
Hollowbrook Ct 28625
Holly St 28677
Holly Brook Ln 28625
Holman Rd 28677
Homeplace Ln 28625
Homestead Estates Dr 28677
Homewood Ln 28625
Honeypath Ln 28625
Hoots Ln 28625
Hope St 28677
Hopewell Rd 28677
Hopewell Hill Dr 28625
Horizon Dr 28625
Horsemans Dr 28625
Horseshoe Loop 28625
Horton Dr 28677
Horvath Dr 28677
Hound Ln 28677
Houpe Ln & Rd 28625
Houpe Ridge Ln 28625
Houpes Farm Ln 28625
Howard Pond Loop 28625
Hudson Ln 28625
Hudspeth Rd 28677
Huff Rd 28625
Huggins St 28677
Hugh Ln 28625
Hugo Ln 28677
Hull St 28677
Hummingbird Ln 28625
Hunt St 28677
Huntcliff Dr 28677
Hunter St 28677
Hunterpond Ln 28677
Hunters Hill Dr 28677
Hunters Ridge Ln 28625
Huntwood Rd 28625
Hurst Dr 28677
Huskins St 28625
Husky Ln 28677
Hyde Ln 28625
Hydie Ln 28677
I St 28677
Idaho Rd 28625
Idalee Ln 28677
Idlebrook Rd 28677
Idlewild Dr 28677
Idlewile Dr 28677
Idlewood Ln 28625
Imes Ct 28625
Impala Dr 28677
W Imperial Heights Rd 28625
Inch Along Dr 28625
Independence Loop 28625
Indian Rdg 28625
Industrial Dr 28625
Inglewood Rd 28677
Ingram Rd 28625
Innisbrook Dr & Rd 28625
Intercraft Dr 28625
International Dr 28625
Intrepid Dr 28625
Investment Ln 28625
W & E Iredell Cir & Dr 28625
Irene Ln 28625
Isaac Rd 28625
Island Vw 28677
Island Farm Rd 28625
Island Ford Rd 28625
Island Park Ln 28625
Island Ridge Dr 28677
Island Sycamore Dr 28677
Island Terrace Rd 28677
Island View Rd 28677
Its My Dr 28677
Ivanhoe Ln 28625
Ivey Ln 28677
Ivey Ostwalt Rd 28677
Ivy Oak Rd 28625
Ivybrook Dr 28625
Ivyrun Ct 28625
Jack Dr 28677
Jack Terrace Ln 28677
Jackfabb Dr 28625
Jackson St 28677
Jacobs Dr 28625
Jacobs Farm Ln 28625
Jacobus Jib Ct 28625
Jafar Ln 28625
Jaley Ln 28677
James Way 28625
James Farm Rd 28625
Jamie Dr 28677
Jane Sowers Rd 28625
Japul Rd 28625
Jarab Hill Ln 28625
Jarrett Ln 28677
Jaybird Ln 28625
Jefferson St 28677
Jefferson Farm Rd 28625
Jehovahs Good Rd 28625
Jehue Rd 28625
Jen Ra Pen Ln 28625
Jenkins Rd 28625
Jennings Rd 28625
Jeremy Ln 28677
Jerry Dr 28677
Jessi Ln 28625
Jessica Ln 28625
Jet Stream Way 28625
Jim Ln 28625
Jim Bob Ln 28625
Jimmy Dr 28677
Jj Ln 28625
Jo Monni Loop 28625
Jobe Dr 28677
Joe Rd 28625
John Adams Ln 28625
John Long Rd 28625
Johns Ln 28677
Johnson Dr 28677
Johobe Dr 28625
Jonathan Ln 28677
Jones St 28625

Jones Brook Ln 28625
Jordan Ln 28677
Josey Rd 28625
Jost St 28677
Journeys End Rd 28625
Joy Dr 28625
Jubilee Ln 28625
Judea Ln 28625
Julia Ln 28625
Julie Dr 28625
June Rd 28625
Jurney Ave 28677
Kalen Dr 28625
Kammerer Dr 28625
Kansas Ln 28625
Karmen Rd 28677
Katie Ln 28625
Kay Ln 28625
Kaylas Ln 28625
Kaywood Ln 28625
Kellana Dr 28625
N Kelly St 28677
Ken Ln 28625
Kenhill Rd 28625
Kenilworth Rd 28677
Kenmore Dr 28625
Kennedy Ct & Dr 28677
Kennington Ln 28625
Kenny Bob Ln 28625
Kentwood Cir & Dr 28677
Kerley Ct 28677
Kerr St 28677
Kidd Ct 28677
Kimball St 28677
Kimball Estate Dr 28625
King St 28625
King Home Ln 28625
Kings Grant Ct 28625
Kingsdale Dr 28625
Kingsgate Ct 28625
Kingswood Rd 28625
Kirkland Dr 28625
Kiser Ln 28677
Kit Carson Rd 28625
Kitchings Dr 28677
Kite Ln 28625
Knollcrest Ln 28625
Knollern St 28677
Knox Ave & St 28677
Knox Farm Rd 28677
Koa Ln 28677
Kodak Dr 28625
Koi Ln 28677
Krumroy Dr 28625
Kyles Oak Dr 28677
N & S Lackey St 28677
Ladybug Ct 28625
Ladyslipper Dr 28677
Lago Ln 28625
Lake James Ln 28677
Lake Run Dr 28625
Lake Top Ln 28677
Lakeridge Dr 28625
Lakeside Dr 28677
Lakeview Dr 28677
Lakewood Dr 28677
Lamb Rd 28677
Lambert Ln 28677
Lamberth Ridge Dr 28677
Lancaster Dr 28625
Lancelot Ct 28625
Landerwood Ln 28625
Landlock Dr 28625
Landmark Aly 28677
Lands End Dr 28677
Landson Dr 28677
Lankford Dr 28625
Laredo Ln 28677
Lark Ln 28677
Larkin Ln 28625
Larue Cir 28625
Lasalle Ln 28677
Launceston Dr 28677
Laura Jeanne Ln 28625
Laura Knoll Ln 28625
Laurel Cove Rd 28677
Laurel Creek Rd 28625
Laurel Ridge Dr 28677
Lauren Dr 28677
Laws Ln 28625
Lazy D Ln 28625
Leatherwood Dr 28625
Leaway Ln 28625
Ledgehill Rd 28625
Lee St 28677
Legend Ln 28677
Leigh Ann Ln 28677
Leitz Pl 28677
Lena Dr 28677
Lentz Rd 28625
Lerain Ct 28677
Levi Ln 28677
Lewis Ferry Rd 28677
Lewis Ridge Ln 28677
Lexanna Dr 28625
Leyland Dr 28625
Liberty St 28625
Liberty Hill Rd 28625
Light St 28677
Lighthouse Ct 28625
Liles Ln 28625
Lillian Dr 28625
Limbo Rock Ln 28677
Limestone Ln 28677
Lincoln St 28677
Lincoln Village Dr 28625
Lindsey St 28625
Linkin Ln 28625
Links Dr 28677
Linville Falls Hwy 28625
Lippard St 28677
Lippard Farm Rd 28625
Lippard Springs Cir 28677
Lippards Hill Ln 28625
Lipton Ln 28625
Lisha Ln 28625
Little Adam Ln 28625
Little Farm Rd 28625
Little Forest Ln 28625
Little John Rd 28625
Little Valley Ln 28625
Liz Dr 28625
Loblolly Dr 28677
Locke Moore Ln 28625
Lockhart Farm Ln 28677
Lockly Dr 28625
Loftin Ln 28677
Log Dr 28677
Log Cabin Rd 28677
Logan St 28677
Logan New Amity Rd 28625
Logan Ridge Dr 28677
Loggerhead Rd 28625
Lois Ct 28625
Lone Pine Rd 28625
Lone Poplar Dr 28625
Lonely Dr 28625
Lonesome Dove Ln 28625
Lonesome Hollar Rd 28625
Long St 28677
Long Island Rd 28677
Long Meadow Dr 28625
Long Pond Dr 28625
Longbranch Rd 28677
Longdale Dr 28677
Longview Rd 28625
Lookout Dr 28625
Lookout Dam Rd 28625
Loraindale Dr 28677
Loray Ln 28625
Love Valley Rd 28625
Low Ln 28677
Lowes Aviation Dr 28677
Loyd Rd 28625
Luangthep Ln 28625
Lucas Ln 28677
Lucille St 28625
Lucky Ln 28625
Lucy Ln 28625
Lundy Rd 28625
Lydia Ln 28677
Lyndon Dr 28677
N & S Lynn Hollow Dr 28677
Lynns Ln 28677
Lynnwood Dr 28677
M And M Ln 28625
Mables Ct 28677
Macon Dr 28625
Macy Ln 28625
Madrid Ln 28677
Maggie Ln 28625
Magnolia St 28677
Magnolia Hill Ln 28625
Mahaffey Dr 28625
Mahogany Rd 28625
Malis End Ln 28625
Mallory Ln 28625
Mandy Beth Ln 28625
Manitou Trl 28677
Manley Ln 28625
Maple St 28677
Maple Care Ln 28625
Maple Creek Dr 28625
Maplehill Ct 28625
Mapleleaf Rd 28625
Maplewood Ln 28625
Marble Rd 28625
Marcel Rd 28625
Marcia Ln 28677
Mardon Ln 28677
Margaret Dr 28677
Margaret Rogers Cir 28625
Marian Ln 28625
Marie Duke Ln 28677
Marilyn Dr 28677
Maristone Dr 28625
Marjorie Rd 28625
Marlou St 28625
Marlowe St 28677
Marsh Dr 28625
Marshall St 28677
Marshall Forest Ln 28625
Martendale Ln 28625
Martha Ln 28625
Marthas Ridge Dr 28625
Martin Ln 28625
Mason Ln 28625
Mason Dixon Ln 28625
Mason Farm Rd 28625
Massey Deal Rd 28625
Masters Hollow Ln 28625
Matthew Dr 28625
Mattie Ln 28625
Maxfli Dr 28677
Maxwell Ln 28677
May Dr 28677
May Jean Dr 28677
Mayapple Ln 28625
Mayo St 28677
Mcallister Rd 28625
Mccarran Trl 28625
Mccollough St 28677
Mccoy Ln 28677
Mcelwee St 28677
Mcgregor Ln 28625
Mckinley Ave 28625
Mclaughlin St 28677
Mcness Rd 28677
Meacham Rd 28677
Meadow Ave 28625
Meadow Rd 28677
Meadow Oaks Dr 28625
Meadow Rue Ln 28625
Meadowbrook Rd 28677
Meadowlane Dr 28677
Meadowlark Ln 28625
Meadows Ct 28677
E & W Meadowview Dr 28625
Medlin St 28677
Meeting St 28677
Melviney St 28677
E Memorial Hwy 28625
Memory Ln 28625
Meredith Ln 28677
Merriman Rd 28625
Messick Farm Dr 28677
Messina Ln 28625
Mibbs Pl 28625
Michael Cir 28625
Middle Ridge Dr 28677
Midway Dr & Rd 28625
Mill Pond Dr 28625
Millbranch Ln 28625
Millbrook Ln 28625
N & S Miller Ave 28677
Miller Cove Ln 28625
Miller Farm Rd 28625
Millerwood Ln 28625
Mills St 28625
Mills Garden Rd 28625
Mills Hill Ln 28677
Millsaps Rd 28625
Millstone Dr 28625
Mimosa Rd 28625
Mindon Pl 28677
Mineral Rock Pl 28625
Minyard Ln 28677
Mitchell Ave 28677
Mitchell Farm Rd 28625
Mitchell Trail Rd 28625
Mobeal Ln 28625
Mocaro Dr 28677
Mock Mill Rd 28677
Mockingbird Dr 28625
Mocksville Hwy 28625
Modular Dr 28625
Mohler Ln 28625
Mojo Ln 28677
Molly Ln 28625
Molly B Rd 28625
E Monbo Rd 28677
Monroe St 28677
Monsanto Rd 28625
Montaigne Ln 28677
Monte Vista Rd 28625
Montgomery Dr 28625
Monticello Rd 28625
Moonglow Ln 28677
Moore Ridge Dr 28625
Moose Club Rd 28677
Moose Farm Dr 28625
Morehead Rd 28677
Morgan Ford Rd 28625
Morland Dr 28677
Morning Dew Dr 28677
Morning Dove Ln 28625
Morningstar Ct 28677
Morris Dr 28677
Morrison Ct 28677
Morrison Dr 28625
W Morrison Creek Rd 28625
Morrison Flats Rd 28625
Morrow Farm Rd 28677
N & S Morvue Loop & Rd 28625
Mosark Ln 28677
Moshier Hill Ln 28625
Moss Rd 28677
Mott Park Dr 28625
Mount Hermon Rd 28625
Mount Olive Rd 28625
Mount Vernon Ave 28677
Mount Zion Dr 28625
Mountain Crest Dr 28625
Mountain Oak Dr 28625
Mountain View Rd 28625
Mountaineer Dr 28677
Mouzon Ln 28625
Muddy Ln 28625
Muellers Cir 28625
N & S Mulberry St 28677
Munday Rd 28677
Museum Rd 28625
Musket Ln 28677
Mustang Dr 28677
My Dr 28677
Myers Dr 28625
Myers Mill Rd 28625
Myrtle Rd 28625
Nabors Rd 28677
Nanas Ln 28677
Nanny Pats Ln 28677
Natawest Dr 28625
Nathan Grove Ln 28677
Nathaniel Gracie Dr 28625
National Dr 28625
Natures Trl 28625
Neal Sherrill Ln 28677
Nelly Green Cir 28625
Nevermore Ln 28677
New Center Dr 28677
New Hope Rd 28625
New Mexico Dr 28625
New Salem Rd 28625
Newbern Ave 28677
Newland Ln 28625
Newton Ave & Dr 28677
Nicholson Way Rd 28625
Nikki Ln 28625
Nixon Rd 28625
No Record 28625
Nola Ln 28677
Nomad Ln 28677
Nook Ln 28625
Northfield Rd 28625
Northlake Dr 28677
Northmont Dr 28625
Northridge Ct 28625
Northside Dr 28625
Northstone Dr 28677
Norwood Rd 28677
Nottingham Cir 28625
Nursery Ln 28677
O Hara Ln 28625
N & S Oak St 28677
Oak Creek Rd 28625
Oak Forest Dr 28625
Oak Grove Rd 28677
Oak Haven Dr 28625
Oak Hill Ln 28625
Oak Knoll Dr 28677
Oak Post Ln 28625
Oakdale Dr 28677
Oakhurst Rd 28677
N Oakland Ave 28677
S Oakland Ave
100-300 28677
301-399 28677
301-301 28687
302-398 28677
Oaklawn Rd 28625
Oakmont Rd 28625
Oakstone Dr 28677
Oakview St 28677
N & S Oakwood Dr 28677
Odell Rd 28625
Odom Ln 28625
Olano Ln 28677
Old Airport Rd 28677
Old Charlotte Rd 28677
Old Cotton Dr 28625
Old Farm Rd 28625
Old Georgia Rd 28625
Old Hoover Farm Ln 28677
Old Lion Rd 28625
Old Loray Ln & Rd 28625
Old Mill Ln 28677
Old Miller Rd 28625
Old Mocksville Rd 28625
Old Mountain Rd
100-1967 28677
1968-2799 28625
Old Pond Ln 28625
Old Rocky Ford Ln 28625
Old Salisbury Rd
500-799 28677
1300-1599 28625
Old Stagecoach Ln 28625
Old Timer Dr 28625
Old Warren Dr 28677
W Old Well House Rd 28677
Old Wilkesboro Rd 28625
Oley Ln 28677
Olive Ct 28625
Oliver Farm Ln 28677
Omega Ln 28625
One Montgolfier Ln 28625
Opal St 28677
Ora Dr 28625
Orbit Rd 28677
Orchard Ln 28677
Original Dr 28625
Oriole Ct 28625
Orr Pl 28677
Orville Rd 28677
Osborne Ln 28625
Osborne Valley Dr 28625
Ostwalt Amity Rd 28677
Ostwalt Farm Ln 28677
Ottare Farm Ln 28625
Owl Hollow Ln 28625
Oxford Scenic Ct 28625
Pacer Ln 28677
Pacific Dr 28677
Padgett Ln 28677
W Page Hager Rd 28625
Palmer Ln 28677
Paola St 28677
Parcel Dr 28625
Park Dr, St & Ter 28677
Park Oak Cir 28625
Parker Lake Loop 28677
Parkers Grove Ln 28677
Parkway Dr 28677
Parkwood Ln 28677
Parlier St 28625
Partner Ln 28625
Partnership Way 28677
Partridge Dr 28677
Partridge Ln 28625
Partridge Hill Ln 28625
Pasture Dr 28625
Patchwork Dr 28677
Patricia Ln 28677
N & S Patterson St 28677
Pawnee Ct 28677
Payton Ct 28677
Pea Patch Ln 28625
Peaceful Ln 28625
Peachtree Rd 28625
Peacock Hollar Rd 28625
Pearce Farm Ln 28625
Pearl St 28677
Pebblestone Ct 28625
Pecan St 28677
Pecan Tree Ln 28625
Pecos Ln 28677
Pendergrass Dr 28677
Penguin Ln 28625
Pennell Farm Ln 28625
Penny Dr 28625
Penquin Ln 28625
Peppercorn Ln 28625
Pepperidge Ln 28625
Peridot Dr 28625
Persimmon Cir 28625
Pervie Ln 28625
Pheasant Ln 28625
Phifer Ln 28677
Phillips Ln 28625
Phipps Ln 28677
Phoenix St 28677
Picnic Ln 28677
Piedmont St 28677
Pierce Bluff Dr 28625
Pierce Woods Dr 28677
Pilch Rd 28677
Pilgrim Cir 28677
W Pine Cir 28677
Pine Bark Ct 28625
Pine Haven Rd 28677
Pine Hollow Dr 28625
Pine Tree Rd 28677
Pinedell Acres Dr 28677
Pinehurst Rd 28625
Pinehurst Forest Pl 28677
Pineview Ct 28625
Pineville Rd 28677
Pinewood Cir 28625
Pinewood Ln 28625
Ping Ct 28677
Pink Ln 28625
Pinkney Ln 28677
Pisgah Church Rd 28625
Planters Dr 28677
Players Park Cir 28677
Pleasant Dr 28677
Pless Ln 28625
Plum St 28677
Plumtree Ln 28677
Plyler Farm Ln 28677
Pneu Mech Dr 28625
N Pointe Blvd 28625
Polly Dr 28625
Pom Ln 28677
Pondasuzie Dr 28677
Ponder Ln 28625
Ponokah Ln 28677
Pony Run Ln 28625
Pooh Dr 28677
Pope Huss Dr 28677
Poplar St 28677
Poplar Leaf Ln 28625
Poplar Springs Rd 28625
Poppy Ln 28677
Pops Lake Rd 28625
Porter Rd 28625
Porter Farm Dr 28625
Post Ln 28625
Postell Dr 28625
Pottery Dr 28625
Potts Grant Ln 28625
Pounders Ridge Ln 28625
Poverty Hill Ln 28625
Powder Creek Dr 28677
Power St 28677
Powerball Cir 28677
Pratt Rd 28625
Primrose Ln 28625
Prince Albert Ct 28677
Prison Camp Rd 28625
Privette St 28677
Progress Pl 28677
Prospect Rd 28625
Prosperity Pl 28677
Proust Rd 28625
Pulpwood Ln 28625
Pump Station Rd 28625
Purebred Dr 28677
Purple Ln 28625
Purple Marten Ln 28625
Quality Works Ln 28625
Quarter Horse Ln 28625
Queens Ct 28677
Raccoon Hollow Dr 28625
N & S Race St 28677
Rachel Ln 28625
Rachels Creek Trl 28625
Racquet Ln 28625
Radio Rd
800-1221 28677
1236-1236 28625
1238-1599 28625
Raefield Dr 28677
Railroad Ave 28677
E & W Raleigh Ave 28677
Ralph Rd 28625
Ramblewood Ln 28677
Rambling Ln 28625
Ramsey Ct 28677
Ranchero St 28677
Randa Dr 28625
Randall Ln 28625
Randolph Rd
100-199 28677
2800-2899 28625
Randolph St 28677
Randolph Farm Rd 28625
Randys Loop 28625
Raspanti Ct 28625
Ravencrest Dr 28625
Ravenwood Dr 28677
Ray Ln 28625
Rayon St 28677
Rays Dr 28625
Rc Farm Dr 28677
Red Barn Ln 28677
Red Brick Dr 28677
Red Buck Ln 28625
Red Chimney Rd 28625
Red Fox Trl 28677

Red Maple Ln 28625
Red Oak Dr 28677
Red Rose Ln 28677
Red Walnut Dr 28677
Redbird Ln 28677
Redemption Rd 28625
Redmond Dairy Dr 28677
Redstone Ln 28625
Redtail Ln 28625
Redwood Ln 28625
Reeves Rd 28625
Reid St 28677
Rejoice Ln 28625
Remus Farm Dr 28625
Renaissance Pl 28625
Renegar Farm Ln 28625
Restmore Ln 28677
Retro Ln 28625
Reuben Dr 28677
Revel Ln 28625
Rex Ln 28625
Reynolda Dr 28677
Reynolds Rd 28677
Richard Ln 28625
Richie Ln 28625
Rickert St 28677
Ridge Ct 28625
Ridge Dr 28677
Ridge Run Dr 28625
Ridge Valley Dr 28677
Ridgecliff Dr 28677
Ridgegate Ln 28625
Ridgeview Rd 28625
Ridgeway Ave 28677
Ridgewood Ln 28677
Rimmer Rd 28625
Rimrock Rd 28625
Rita Ave 28677
Rita Gale Rd 28625
River Bank Rd 28625
River Haven Dr 28677
River Hill Rd 28625
River Ridge Ln 28677
River Run Rd 28625
Riverfield Dr 28625
Rivergreen Dr 28625
Riverside Rd 28625
Riverton Dr 28625
Riverview Dr 28625
Roadrunner Ln 28625
Robert Dr 28625
Roberts Farm Ln 28625
Robertson Rd 28677
Robin Ln 28677
Robinette Ln 28625
Robinhood Loop 28625
Robins Hill Ln 28677
Robys Pl 28625
Rock Island Dr 28625
Rockcrest Ln 28677
Rocker Ln 28677
Rockhaven Dr 28625
Rockhouse Dr 28677
Rockin N Ln 28625
Rockwood Ln 28677
Rocky Ln 28625
Roger Dr 28625
Rogers Ave 28677
Rogers Cir 28625
Rolling Ln 28677
Romans Ln 28625
Ropers Cir 28625
Rosa Jane Ct 28677
Rosalind Ln 28677
Rose St 28677
Rosebud Ln 28677
Roseman Ln 28625
Rosemary Ln 28677
Rosevine Rd 28625
Ross Catfish Dr 28625
Rosy Apple Ln 28625
Roten Ln 28625
Round House Dr 28625
Roundabout Ln 28677
Royalty Cir 28625
Roys Dr 28625
Rubbermaid Way 28625
Rumley Ln 28625
Rumple Farm Ln 28625
Rumple Hill Dr 28677
Rupard Rd 28625
Russell Dr 28625
Russell St 28677
Rydel Ln 28625
Saddlewood Ln 28625
Safriet Loop 28625
Sage Ln 28677
Sagebrush Rd 28677
Sagefield Dr 28625
Sain Rd 28625
Saint Andrews Rd 28625
Saint Cloud Dr 28625
Saint James Pl 28625
Saint Jill Cir 28625
Saint Johns Rd 28677
Saint Joseph Ct 28677
Saint Martins Ln 28677
Saint Paul Ln 28677
Salem Loop 28625
Salem Creek Dr 28625
Salem Meadow Dr 28625
Salisbury Ave 28677
Salisbury Hwy 28677
Salisbury Rd
100-1099 28677
1100-1499 28625
1500-1899 28677
Sallie Dr 28625
Sampson Dr 28625
Sams Way 28625
Sams Trail Ln 28625
Sandalwood Ln 28625
Sandra Dr 28625
Sandtrap Dr 28677
Sandy Ave 28625
Sara Ln 28625
Sarah Laura Ln 28625
Scalybark Rd 28625
Scenery Dr 28677
Schafer Hollow Dr 28677
School St 28677
Scott Rd 28625
Scott St 28677
Scotts Creek Rd 28625
Scroggs Cemetery Rd 28677
Scuggs Cemetry Rd 28677
Sebastian Ln 28677
Secor St 28677
Security Dr 28677
Sedgefield Rd 28625
Seed House Rd 28625
Sena Ln 28625
Serene Meadow Trl 28677
Serenity Ln 28625
Setter Ct 28625
Setzer Pt 28677
Seven Cedars Dr 28677
Seven Oaks Ln 28677
Seven Springs Loop 28625
Shadow Ridge Ct 28677
N & S Shady Rest Rd 28677
Shady Stream Dr 28625
Shadywood Ln 28677
Shalom Pl 28625
Shamrock Ln 28625
Shane Ln 28625
Shanna Ln 28625
Shannon Ct 28625
Sharon Dr 28625
Sharon Crest Dr 28625
Sharon Ridge Ln 28677
Sharon School Rd
100-499 28677
500-1099 28625
1100-1199 28677
E & W Sharpe St 28625
Sharpe Farm Dr 28625
Sharpes Landing Ln 28677
Shasta Dr 28625
Shaver Ln 28625
Shawver Ln 28625
Shearer Dr 28625
Sheep Hill Ln 28625
Shelia Ln 28625
Shelton Ave 28677
Sherlock Dr 28625
Sherrill Dr 28625
Sherwood Ln 28677
Shillington Ln 28625
Shiloh Rd 28677
Shoemaker Farm Rd 28625
Short St 28677
Short Dog Dr 28625
Shot Gun Ln 28677
Shotgun Ln 28677
Shovelhead Ln 28625
Shrub Ln 28625
Shuford Dr 28625
Shumaker Dr 28625
Side Track Dr 28625
Sides Ln 28625
Sierra Chase Dr 28677
Sigmon Rd 28677
Sigmon Ridge Dr 28677
Signal Hill Dr 28625
Signal Hill Drive Ext 28625
Silas Mill Dr 28625
Silhouette Ln 28625
Silver Pine Rd 28625
Silvermere Dr 28625
Simones Ct 28625
Simonton Rd 28625
Sir George Cir 28677
Skeeter Ln 28625
Sky Ln 28677
Skyland Dr 28625
Skyuka Rd 28677
Slate Ln 28625
Sleepy Creek Ln 28625
Slingerland Dr 28625
Slingshot Rd 28677
Sloan Rd 28625
Smith Farm Dr 28625
Smokestack Ln 28625
Smyre Ln 28625
Snow Creek Rd 28625
Snowbird Ln & Loop 28625
Society Rd 28625
Solano Dr 28625
Somerset Pl 28625
Songbird Ln 28625
Sonja Dr 28677
Southern Pines Ave 28625
Southview Dr 28677
Southway Ln 28625
Southwood Dr 28677
Sowers St 28677
Span Ln 28677
Sparkle Ln 28625
Sparrow Ln 28625
Spearpoint Ln 28625
Speedball Rd 28677
Speigle Ln 28677
Spirit Ln 28625
Spitfire Ln 28625
Sportsman Dr 28625
Spring St 28677
Spring Forest Dr 28625
Spring Garden Ct 28677
Spring Meadows Ln 28677
Spring Shore Rd 28625
Spring Valley Ln 28677
Springbranch Ln 28625
Springbrook Ln 28677
Springdale Rd 28625
Springfield Rd
100-299 28625
300-499 28677
7100-7199 28625
Springs Mountain Ln 28625
Sprinkle Rd 28625
Spud Ln 28625
Squeaky Tree Ln 28625
Squire Ct 28625
Stable Ln 28625
Staffordshire Dr 28625
Stallion Ln 28625
Stamey Farm Rd
100-350 28677
351-399 28625
Stampede Dr 28625
Stan Ln 28625
Stanley Dr 28625
Starbuck Dr 28625
Starlight Rd 28677
Starmount Dr 28677
Starr Ln 28677
State Park Rd 28677
N Statesville Dr 28625
Steele St 28677
Steep Ln 28625
Steeple Ln 28677
Stem Ln 28625
Stephanie Ln 28625
Stephens Ln 28625
Sterling St 28625
Sterling Moss Way 28625
Stevenson Farm Rd 28625
Stevenson Park Loop 28625
Steves Farm Ln 28677
Stewart Ct 28677
Stewart Acres Dr 28677
Stinson Ct 28677
Stockbridge Ln 28625
Stockton St 28677
Stokes Ave 28625
Stone Bridge Ln 28625
Stone Creek Dr 28625
Stone Harbor Ct 28677
Stone House Dr 28625
Stonecrest Dr & Loop 28625
Stonefield Dr 28677
Stonegate Ln 28677
Stonehenge Ln 28625
Stonewall Trl 28625
Stoney Ln 28625
Stoneybrook Rd 28677
Storm Ln 28625
Strawberry Ln 28625
Street Rod Loop 28625
Stroud Rd 28625
Stroud Mill Rd 28625
N Stu Dr 28625
Stump Ct 28625
Styers Ln 28677
Sugar Spring Dr 28625
Sullivan Rd 28677
Sullivan Farm Rd 28625
Summer Breeze Ct 28677
Summerhut Ln 28625
Summers Farm Rd 28625
Summit Ave 28677
Suncrest Ave 28677
Suncret Dr 28625
Sundance Cir 28625
Sunflower Rd 28625
Sunningdale Ln 28625
Sunny Path Ln 28677
Sunset Hill Rd 28625
Sunset View Ln 28677
Sunswept Loop 28625
Sunwood Ct 28625
Supreme Ct 28677
Susce Ct 28677
Sutton Ct 28677
Sutton Farm Ln 28625
Suzanne Ln 28677
Swann Rd 28625
Swann Crossing Ln 28625
Sweet Gum Ln 28625
Sweet Oaks Ln 28677
Sweet Ruby Ln 28625
Sweetwater Dr 28625
Sydney Ln 28625
Sylvan Dr 28677
Sylvia St 28677
T Bird Dr 28625
Tall Pine Ln 28625
Talons Trl 28677
Tanbridge Dr 28625
Tangent Dr 28625
Tangle Ln 28677
Taras Trace Dr 28625
Tarheel Ln 28677
Tarlton Rd 28625
Tarrington Dr 28625
E & W Tattersall Dr 28677
Taurus Rd 28625
Taxidermy Rd 28625
Taylor Made Dr 28677
Taylor Ridge Ln 28677
Taylors Pass Trl 28625
Taylorsville Hwy 28625
Taylorsville Rd 28677
Teak Dr 28625
Temperature Ln 28677
Tenth Green Ct 28677
Teresa Dr 28677
Teri Sha Rd 28677
Terry Mountain Rd 28625
Terry Springs Ln 28677
Tetley Ln 28625
Texas Ln 28625
The Glen St 28677
Thistle Ln 28625
Thomas St 28677
Thomas Meadow Dr 28625
Thompson Dr & Ln 28625
Three Lindas Ln 28625
Three Oaks Ln 28677
Thyme Ln 28677
Tiffany Ln 28625
Tilley Ln 28625
Tilley Farm Ln 28625
Timber Creek Stables
Rd 28625
Timber Ridge Ln 28625
Timberbrook Ln 28625
Timberlane Dr 28625
Tinsley Dr 28625
Titanium Dr 28625
Titleist Dr 28677
Tobacco Rd 28625
Tobacco Farm Ln 28625
Tobitha Rd 28625
Tokie Ln 28625
Tom Rd 28625
Tom Pass Ln 28625
Tomlin Mill Rd 28625
Tommy Dr 28625
Toms Cut Rd 28625
Top Flite Dr 28677
Tori Pass Ln 28625
N & S Toria Dr 28625
Tower Dr 28677
Tracey Ln 28625
N & S Tradd St 28677
Trailblazer Ln 28625
Trails End Ln 28625
Trailway Dr 28625
Train Ln 28677
Trappers Trail Ln 28625
Travis Loop 28625
Tree Ln 28677
Treebark Rd 28625
Treeline Dr 28677
Trent Rd 28677
Trillium Dr 28625
Trinity Rd 28625
Triple Oaks Ln 28625
Triton Dr 28625
Trophy Dr 28625
Troutman Dr 28625
Troutman Farm Rd 28677
Troutman Shoal Ct 28677
Troutman Shoals Rd 28677
Trumpet Branch Rd 28625
Tucker Rd 28677
Tuckers Grove Rd 28625
Tulip Tree Ct 28677
Turn Out Dr 28677
E & W Turner St 28677
Turnersburg Hwy &
Rd 28625
Turning Leaf Ln 28677
Turnipseed Ln 28625
Turtledove Ln 28677
Tweety Bird Ln 28625
Twilight Ln 28677
Twin Lakes Dr 28625
Twin Oaks Dr & Rd 28625
Twisted Oak Ln 28677
Twitty Ln 28625
Two Marys Ln 28625
Two Pond Dr 28677
Under The Oaks Ln 28625
Unity Dr 28625
Upland Dr 28625
Upper Lake Dr 28677
Upper Oak Dr 28625
Upright Dr 28677
Valahalla Ln 28625
Valencia Ln 28625
Valhalla Ln 28625
Valiant Dr 28677
Valley St 28677
Valley Stream Rd 28677
Van Buren St 28677
Van Haven Dr 28625
Vance St 28625
Vance Farm Dr 28625
Vance Po Rd 28625
Vanner Way 28625
Vaughn Mill Rd 28625
Vectra Dr 28625
Venture Ln 28625
Vermillion Loop 28625
Verna Dr 28625
Vernon Ln 28677
Victoria Dr 28625
Victory Ln 28625
Victory Farm Ln 28625
Viewmont Ct 28625
Village Dr 28677
Village Point Dr 28625
Vine St 28677
Vinson Rd 28677
Viola Ln 28625
Virgils Place Dr 28677
Virginia Ave 28677
Virginia Ridge Ln 28625
Visible Dr 28677
Vista Ter 28677
Viv Ln 28677
Volt Cir 28677
Wagner St 28677
Wagon Trail Ln 28625
Wagon Wheel Dr 28677
Wake Ct 28677
Walker Rd 28625
Walker St 28677
Walking Ln 28625
Wall St 28677
Wallace St 28677
Wallace Pass Ln 28625
Wallace Springs Rd 28677
Walnut St 28677
Walnut Creek Dr 28625
Walnut Tree Rd 28625
Walton Dr 28625
Warren Rd 28625
Warrior Dr 28625
Washboard Ln 28625
Washington Ave & St 28677
Washington Ridge Rd 28677
E & W Water St 28677
Water Ski Dr 28677
Water Tank Rd 28625
Watercrest Dr 28625
Watering Trough Rd 28677
Watermelon Rd 28625
Watermelon Hill Ln 28625
Waterside Ln 28677
Watts Ct 28625
Watts Meadow Dr 28677
Waugh Farm Rd 28625
Waverly Pl 28677
Wayne Dr 28677
Wayside Rd 28677
Weaver St 28625
Weaver Hill Dr 28625
Webb St 28677
Weco Ln 28625
Wedge View Way 28677
Wedgedale Ave 28677
Wedgeway Dr 28677
Wedgewood Dr 28677
Weeping Cherry Ln 28625
Weinig St 28677
Welcome Ln 28677
Wellwood Ave & Rd 28677
Wendover Rd 28677
Wentworth Pl & St 28625
Wesley Dr 28677
Westbrook Ln 28625
Westchester Rd 28625
Western Ave 28677
Westglow Rd 28625
Westhaven Dr 28625
Westminster Dr 28677
Westmore Dr & St 28677
Weston Rd 28625
Weston Dairy Rd 28625
Westover Rd 28677
Westridge Dr 28625
Westscott Dr 28625
Westview Ln 28625
Westwinds Loop 28625
Westwood Dr 28677
Wexford Way 28625
Wheatfield Dr 28677
Wheatland Ln 28625
Wheatridge Dr 28625
Whirlwind Ln 28677
Whisper Pine Rd 28625
Whistling Pines Dr 28677
White Dogwood Ln 28625
White Fox Trl 28625
White House Ln 28625
White Oak Branch Rd 28625
White Oak Farm Dr 28625
White Rock Farm Ln 28625
Whites Farm Rd 28625
Whites Mill Rd 28677
Whitetail Rd 28625
Whitney Ln 28625
Whittington Pl 28677
Wickersham Dr 28625
Wike Ln 28677
Wilcox Karriker Ln 28625
Wild Cherry Dr 28625
Wildeman Trl 28625
Wildflower Ln 28625
Wildhurst Ln 28625
Wildlife Haven Dr 28625
Wildmere Ln 28677
Wildwood Loop 28625
Wildwood Ter 28677
Wildwood Forest Ct 28625
Wildwood Ranch Rd 28625
Wildwood Trail Dr 28677
Wilhelm Ln 28625
Wilkesboro Hwy 28625
Willard Ln 28625
William Land Ln 28677
Williams Rd 28677
Willie Beatty Ct 28677
Willow St 28625
Willow Branch Ln 28625
Willowest Ln 28625
Wilmington Ave 28677
Wils Way 28625
Wilson Pass 28625
Wilson St 28677
Wilson Farm Rd 28625
Wilson Park Rd 28625
Wilson Pass Ln 28625
Wilson W Lee Blvd 28677
Wilworth Cir 28625
Winberry Ln 28677
Winchester Ln 28625
Windbluff Dr 28677
Windemere Isle Rd 28677
Windforest Dr 28677
Winding Brook Way 28625
Winding Cedar Dr 28677
Windingwood Dr 28677
Windmill Ridge Dr 28625
Windrow Ln 28625
Windrush Ct 28625
Windsor Ln 28677

Windsor Pl 28625
Windy Hill Rd 28625
Winfield Pl 28625
Wing Dr 28625
Winona St 28677
Winston Ave 28677
Winter Dr 28677
Winter Flake Dr 28677
Winterfield Rd 28677
Wintergreen Cir 28677
Winters Farm Ln 28625
Wise St 28677
Wishbone Rd 28677
Witherspoon Ln 28677
Wolf Creek Ln 28625
Wolf Ranch Dr 28625
Wood St 28677
Wood Bridge Rd 28625
Woodbrook Ln 28677
Woodfield Dr 28677
Woodhaven Dr 28677
Woodland Rd 28677
Woodland Cove Dr 28677
Woodlawn Dr 28677
Woodpecker Rd 28625
Woodruff St 28677
Woods Dr 28677
Woodsdale Dr 28625
Woodside Rd 28677
Woodtop Ln 28677
Woodview Dr 28625
Wooten St 28677
Wooten Farm Rd 28625
Wootie Dr 28677
Wright Ln 28677
Yadkin St 28677
Yadkin River Rd 28625
Yadkin Valley Rd 28625
Yang Dr 28625
Yellowstone Ln 28677
York Ave 28677
Younger Ave 28677
Zachary Rd 28625
Zircon Dr 28625
Zorse Ln 28625
Zurich Ln 28625

NUMBERED STREETS

1st Ave & St 28677
2nd Ave & St 28677
3rd St 28677
3rd Creek Rd 28677
4th St 28677
4th Creek Landing Dr 28625
4th Crescent Pl 28625
5th St 28677
5th Creek Rd 28625
7th St 28677
8th St 28677
9th St 28677
10th St 28677
11th St 28677
12th St 28677
17th Tee Ln 28677

THOMASVILLE NC

General Delivery 27360

POST OFFICE BOXES MAIN OFFICE STATIONS AND BRANCHES

Box No.s
All PO Boxes 27361

RURAL ROUTES

01, 02, 03, 04, 05, 06, 07, 08, 09, 10 27360

NAMED STREETS

All Street Addresses 27360

NUMBERED STREETS

All Street Addresses 27360

WAKE FOREST NC

General Delivery 27587

POST OFFICE BOXES MAIN OFFICE STATIONS AND BRANCHES

Box No.s
All PO Boxes 27588

RURAL ROUTES

01, 02, 04, 05, 06, 07, 08, 09 27587

NAMED STREETS

Abercrombie Rd 27587
Acanthus Dr 27587
Adlie Dr 27587
Adona Ln 27587
Agnew Ct 27587
Agora Dr 27587
Aiken Rd 27587
Alba Rose Ln 27587
Alberbury Commons Ct 27587
Albino Deer Way 27587
Aldershot Dr 27587
Aldoncaster Dr 27587
Alexander Springs Ln 27587
Alexis Anne Dr 27587
Alfalfa Ln 27587
N & S Allen Rd 27587
Allenwoods Rd 27587
Alpine Clover Dr 27587
Alstonburg Ave 27587
Alveston Cir 27587
Alydar Dr 27587
Amaryllis Way 27587
Amazon Trl 27587
Amber Ln 27587
Amberwine Ln 27587
Ambrose Dr 27587
Amersham Ln 27587
Amherst Creek Dr 27587
Anderbrook Ct 27587
Anderson Dr 27587
Andover Ln 27587
Andoversford Ct 27587
Andrew Ct 27587
Angel Star Ln 27587
Angelview Ct 27587
Anglesey Ct 27587
Annonhill St 27587
Anterra Dr 27587
Appaloosa Way 27587
Appleberry Ct 27587
Applenook Ct 27587
Aquaduct Dr 27587
Aquarius Ln 27587
Arbor Pl 27587
Arbor Mist Ln 27587
Armadale Ln 27587
Armida Dr 27587
Astrol Ln 27587
Austin Creek Dr 27587
Austin View Blvd 27587
Autumn Forest Trl 27587
Autumn Meadow Ln 27587
Avborough Ct 27587
Aventon Glen Dr 27587
Averette Rd 27587
Avinshire Pl 27587
B And B Ln 27587
Bacardi Ct 27587
Bagshot Ct 27587
Bakers Acres Ln 27587
Bakewell Ct 27587
Balbirnie Ct 27587
Bambi Ct 27587
Band Box Dr 27587
Bankwell St 27587
Barbaras Ct 27587
Bardeen Ct 27587
Barham Crossing Dr 27587
Barham Hollow Dr 27587
Barham Siding Rd 27587
Barkston Gardens Ln 27587
Barley Pl 27587
Barley Green St 27587
Barn Hill Ln 27587
Barnes House Ct 27587
Barnford Mill Rd 27587
Barrasett Ct 27587
Barrett Hall Ln 27587
Barrett Ridge Rd 27587
Basley St 27587
Battery Crest Ln 27587
Bay Laurel Ct 27587
Baya Vista Way 27587
Baynam Pond Dr 27587
Bayview Dr 27587
Bear Branch Way 27587
Bear Hollow Rd 27587
Beaver Falls Dr 27587
Bella Terra Ct 27587
Bellreng Dr 27587
Belmellen Ct 27587
Belmont Cir 27587
Bennett Ridge Ct 27587
Bent Rd 27587
Benthill Ct 27587
Beringer Forest Ct 27587
Bermondsey Market Way 27587
Berteau Dr 27587
Berwick Ct 27587
Best Ave 27587
Big Bend Ct 27587
Billiard Ct 27587
Binkley Chapel Ct 27587
Birch Tree Ln 27587
Bird Dog Ln 27587
Birkstone Ct 27587
Biscay Ln 27587
Bishop Falls Rd 27587
Bisque Ct 27587
Black Swan Way 27587
Blackley Lake Rd 27587
Blazing Sunset Trl 27587
Blue Bell Ln 27587
Blue Bird Ln 27587
Blue Bonnet Dr 27587
Blue Larkspur Ave 27587
Blue Lilac Ln 27587
Blue Ravine Rd 27587
Blueberry Hill Ln 27587
Blykeford Ln 27587
Bocage Pl 27587
Bold Run Hill Rd 27587
Bolus Ct 27587
Borage Dr 27587
Bostwick Dorm St 27587
Boulder Ct 27587
Boulder Springs Dr 27587
Bowlin Ct 27587
Bowling Forest Dr 27587
Bowtie Ct 27587
Boxer Pl 27587
Boxer Farm Dr 27587
Boyce Bridge Rd 27587
Bracken Ct 27587
Bradstone Ct 27587
Bragg Valley Ln 27587
Bramden Ct 27587
Branch Ferry Ct 27587
Branch River Way 27587
Brason Ln 27587
Bratt Ave 27587
Brayer Hill Path 27587
Breeders Hill Dr 27587
Brewer Ave & Cir 27587
Brewer Jackson Ct 27587
Brewers Glynn Ct 27587
Brianside Ct 27587
Briarwood Pl 27587
Brick St 27587
Bridges Pond Way 27587
Bridle Glen Ct 27587
Brierroot Ct 27587
Brighton Way 27587
Brimfield Springs Ln 27587
Brogden Woods Dr 27587
Brooks St 27587
Brookvale Dr 27587
Broyhill Hall Ct 27587
Bruce Dr 27587
Bruce Garner Rd 27587
Brumber Cir 27587
Bruna Ln 27587
Buccaneer Ct 27587
Buck Run Trl 27587
Buck Wallow Rd 27587
Buckeye Ct 27587
Buckhorn Ln 27587
Bud Dr 27587
Bud Morris Rd 27587
Bud Smith Rd 27587
Buggy Run Cir 27587
Buggy Whip Cir & Ct 27587
Burchblind Dr 27587
Burge Ct 27587
Burlington Mills Rd 27587
Burning Pine Ln 27587
Buttercup Ln 27587
C And L Ave 27587
Caddel St 27587
Cala Lilly Ln 27587
Caladium Dr 27587
Calico Ct 27587
Calliness Way 27587
Calvados Dr 27587
Cameron Dr 27587
Camp Kanata Rd 27587
Canning Pl 27587
Canonbie Ln 27587
Canopy Ct 27587
Cantlemere St 27587
Canvas Dr 27587
Capcom Ave 27587
Capefield Dr 27587
Capellan St 27587
Capital Blvd 27587
Capitol Heights Rd 27587
Capricorn Dr & Ln 27587
Cardinal Dr 27587
Cardinal Crest Ln 27587
Careme Ct 27587
Carlton Oaks Dr 27587
Carmel Woods Ct 27587
Carper Ct 27587
Carradale Ct 27587
Carriage Way 27587
Carriage Meadows Dr 27587
Carrie May Ln 27587
Carroll St 27587
Carter St 27587
Carthan Ct 27587
Cascade Creek Ct 27587
Casey Dr 27587
Casine Ct 27587
Cataska Ln 27587
Catlett Farm Rd 27587
Catrush Way 27587
Cats Paw Ct 27587
Caudle Woods Dr 27587
Caveness Farms Ave 27587
Caviness Farms Ave 27587
E & W Cedar Ave 27587
Cedar Branch Ct 27587
Cedar Falls Dr 27587
Cedar Knoll Dr 27587
Centaur Rd 27587
Chadwell St 27587
Chalk Rd 27587
Chamberwell Ave 27587
Charles Ct 27587
Charles Forest Rd 27587
Charmco Ct 27587
Checkmate Cir 27587
Chelridge Dr 27587
Cherry Pond Ct 27587
Chester St 27587
Chestley Farm Rd 27587
E & W Chestnut Ave 27587
Chestnut Hill Rd 27587
Chilmark Ave 27587
Chilton Pl 27587
Chimney Swift Dr 27587
Chipper Ln 27587
Choplin Rd 27587
Chouder Ln 27587
Churchill Dr 27587
Cimarron Pkwy 27587
Circle Dr 27587
Clamshell Dr 27587
Clapton Dr 27587
Clarincarde Ct 27587
Clatter Ave 27587
Clayshant Ct 27587
Clear Cut Ct 27587
Clearsprings Dr 27587
Cleason Ct 27587
Cliff Ln 27587
Clifton Blue St 27587
Cloey Dr 27587
Cloud Nine Ct 27587
Cloudy Day Ct 27587
Cloven Ct 27587
Clover Bank St 27587
Cloverleaf Park 27587
Clovis Ridge Dr 27587
Club Villas Dr 27587
Coach Lantern Ave 27587
Cobble Glen Ct 27587
Cobble Ridge Ct 27587
Cocharie Way 27587
Cochran Ct 27587
N & S College St 27587
Colombard Ct 27587
Colonial Club Rd 27587
Colt Dr 27587
Comphrey Ct 27587
Conaway Ct 27587
Connector Dr 27587
Coolbreeze Ct 27587
Coolwater Ct 27587
Copper Beech Ln 27587
Copper Creek Ct 27587
Coral Bell Dr 27587
Coram Fields Rd 27587
Corbeling Pt 27587
Corbet Grove Dr 27587
Corktree Ct 27587
Corner Rock Dr 27587
Cornwell Dr 27587
Corporate Chaplain Dr 27587
Corrina Rd 27587
Costa Verde Ct 27587
Cotesworth Dr 27587
Cottage View Path 27587
Cottesbrook Dr 27587
Cotton Field Ct 27587
Cottontail Ct 27587
Cottonwood Dr 27587
Country Club Dr 27587
Country Heritage Ln 27587
Country Tracts Dr 27587
Countryman Ct 27587
Cousins Ln 27587
Coveshore Dr 27587
Covington Ridge Rd 27587
Crappie Ln 27587
Creedmoor Rd 27587
Creeds Hill Ct 27587
Creek Moss Ave 27587
Creek Pine Dr 27587
Creekbend Dr 27587
Creekstone Way 27587
Crendall Way 27587
Crenshaw Dr & Pt 27587
Crescent Ridge Dr 27587
Crimson Clover Ave 27587
Critter Pond Rd 27587
Crooked Creek Rd 27587
Crookham Ct 27587
Crowder Ave 27587
Crozier Ct 27587
Crusher Run 27587
Crystal Rock Rd 27587
Cullingtree Ln 27587
Cureton Dr 27587
Curly Hill Ct 27587
Curly Willow Ln 27587
Dacus Pl 27587
Dagmar Ln 27587
Dairy House Ct 27587
Damson Ct 27587
Dandridge Oak Ln 27587
Daniel Ct & Rd 27587
Dannon Ct 27587
Dansforeshire Way 27587
Dargan Hills Dr 27587
Darmstadt Ct 27587
Dasher Ct 27587
Davis House Ln 27587
Daybreak Dr 27587
Deacon Ridge St 27587
Deacons Bend Ct 27587
Debenham Dr 27587
Deep Spring Cir 27587
Deep Woods Trl 27587
Deer Path 27587
Deer Hollow Ct 27587
Deer Lake Trl 27587
Deerberry Ln 27587
Deerchase Trl 27587
Deerfield Dr 27587
Deerfield Crossing Dr 27587
Degrace Dr 27587
Denby Pt 27587
Denwitty Dr 27587
Derby Ln 27587
Desert Marigold Ct 27587
Diazit Dr 27587
Dickel Dr 27587
Dillon Ln 27587
Dimock Way 27587
Docks Lndg 27587
Doctor Calvin Jones Hwy 27587
Dodford Ct 27587
Dogwood Ln 27587
Dogwood Hill Ln 27587
Domaine Dr 27587
Donlin Dr 27587
Donneeford Rd 27587
Donner Trl 27587
Doonan St 27587
Doris Ln 27587
Doss Ct 27587
Dotted Mint Ave 27587
Dougher Ct 27587
Drogheda Pl 27587
Drumantrae Ln 27587
Dry Gully Ct 27587
Dry Rock Ln 27587
Duckhorn Ct 27587
Dugway Ct 27587
Dumas Ct 27587
Dun Loring Dr 27587
Dunman Ct 27587
Dunmore Ct 27587
Dunn Ave 27587
Dunn Creek Xing 27587
Dunn Maple Dr 27587
E & W Dunpatrick Pl 27587
Dunsany Ct 27587
Durham Rd 27587
Durkyn Pl 27587
E & W Durness Ct 27587
Eagleroost Ct 27587
Eagleson Ln 27587
Easy Horse Trl 27587
Eaton Square Ct 27587
Ecola Valley Ct 27587
Eden Falls Dr 27587
Edgar Ln 27587
Edgefield Dr 27587
Edgeford Park Ln 27587
Edgeview Ct 27587
Edgeware Way 27587
Edinshire St 27587
Elf Ct 27587
Elizabeth Ave 27587
Elm Ave 27587
Elmo Dr 27587
Elmwood Ct 27587
Elsbeth Ct 27587
Emeron Rd 27587
Emily Ln 27587
Endgame Ct 27587
Endurance Dr 27587
Enville Ct 27587
Eppes Ln 27587
Epping Forest Way 27587
Ernest Ct 27587
Estes Crossing Ln 27587
Evans Ridge Rd 27587
Evening Shadows Ln 27587
Evening Snow St 27587
Everett Ridge Ct 27587
Everstone Rd 27587
Everton Way 27587
Evesham Ct 27587
Fairburn Ct 27587
Fairlake Dr 27587
Fairlong Rd 27587
Fairview Club Dr 27587
Fairway Villas Dr 27587
Faithful Pl 27587
Falcate Dr 27587
Falconhurst Dr 27587
Falkirk Ridge Ct 27587
Fall Branch Ct 27587
Falls Cove Ln 27587
Falls Farm Xing 27587
Falls Of Neuse Rd 27587
N Fallsview Ln 27587
Family Meadows Ln 27587
Fanning Dr 27587
Farm Rd 27587
Farm Hill Ct 27587
Farm Ridge Rd 27587
Farnsworth Rd 27587
Fauntlee Ct 27587
Fawn Ct & Dr 27587
Fawn Lily Dr 27587
Federal House Ave 27587
Fenmar Ln 27587
Fern Hollow Trl 27587
Ferry Ct 27587
Field Oak Dr 27587
Fieldstone Dr 27587
Finchurch Cir 27587
Findhorn Ln 27587
Fineberg Ct 27587
Fixit Shop Rd 27587
Flaherty Ave 27587
Flemming House St 27587
Flex Way 27587
Flicker Ct 27587
Fonville Rd 27587
Foothills Trl 27587
Forbes Rd 27587
Forest Rd 27587
Forest Lake Ct 27587
Forest Lynks Dr 27587
Forestville Rd 27587
Forgotten Pond Ave 27587
Fortune Head Ln 27587
Fountainside Ct 27587
Four Wheel Dr 27587
Foxbridge Ct 27587
Foxwild Ln 27587
Frank Bailey Rd 27587
N & S Franklin St 27587
Freeman Farm Way 27587
Freeman House Ln 27587
Freshwater Ct 27587
Friendship Chapel Rd 27587

Frog Hop Ct 27587
S Front St 27587
Front Gate Ln 27587
Frosty Hollow Rd 27587
Fruit Hill Ln 27587
Frye St 27587
Fullard Dr 27587
Fulworth Ave 27587
Galashiels Pl 27587
Galaxy Dr & Rd 27587
Gambit Cir 27587
Garffe Sherron Rd 27587
Garner Terrace Way 27587
Garnet Ln 27587
Gateway Commons Cir 27587
Gear Box Dr 27587
Genesis Ln 27587
German Shepherd Trl 27587
Ghoston Rd 27587
Gideon Dr 27587
Gilcrest Farm Rd 27587
Gillcrest Ln & Way 27587
Gilmore Dr 27587
Gironde Ct 27587
Glamis Cir 27587
Glencoe Dr 27587
Glennis Ct 27587
Golden Poppy Ct 27587
Golden Star Way 27587
Goldston Trl 27587
Gooch Ct 27587
Grace Cove Ln 27587
Gracechurch St 27587
Gracie Girl Way 27587
Graham Sherron Rd 27587
Grandmark St 27587
Granite Hill Trl 27587
Granville Ridge Rd 27587
Granville Woods 27587
Grapeland Dr 27587
Grason Crockett Dr 27587
Grateful Trl 27587
Grayson Creek Dr 27587
Great Woods Rd 27587
Green Apple Ct 27587
Green Drake Dr 27587
Green Edge Trl 27587
Green Farm Ln 27587
Green Hollow Ct 27587
Green Mountain Dr 27587
Greenhow Ln 27587
Greenville Loop Rd 27587
Gro Peg Ln 27587
Gross Ave & Rd 27587
Grove Crossing Way 27587
Groves Field Ln 27587
Groveton Trl 27587
Guernsey Ct 27587
Guinness Pl 27587
Gwen Dr 27587
Haldane Ct 27587
Hall Farm Ln 27587
Hallburg Ct 27587
Haltwhistle St 27587
Hamilton Yates Dr 27587
Hammond Oak Ln 27587
Hampton Chase Ct 27587
Hampton Way Dr 27587
Hanes Farm Rd 27587
Hares Ear Ct 27587
Harpers Ferry Ct 27587
Harpers Ridge Ct 27587
Harps Ln 27587
Harris Rd 27587
Harris Point Way 27587
Harrisdale Dr 27587
Harrison Ridge Rd 27587
Hartsfield Dr 27587
Hartsfield Forest Dr 27587
Harvest Ridge Ln 27587
Hasentree Way 27587
Hasentree Club Dr 27587
Hasentree Lake Dr 27587
Hasentree Villa Ln 27587
Havisham Ct 27587
Hawk Hill Ct 27587
Hawk Hollow Ln 27587
Hawkshead Rd 27587
Hayebury Dr 27587
Hayrick Ct 27587
Haywicke Pl 27587
Hazel Ln 27587
Hazeltown Rd 27587
Heartland Dr 27587
Heather Ln 27587
Heaven Bound St 27587
Heflin Ct 27587
Height Ln 27587
Hempton Cross Dr 27587
Hemsworth Ct 27587
Heritage Arbor Dr 27587
Heritage Branch Rd 27587
Heritage Center Dr 27587
Heritage Club Ave 27587
Heritage Commerce Ct 27587
Heritage Garden St 27587
Heritage Gates Dr 27587
Heritage Glenn Ln 27587
Heritage Greens Dr 27587
Heritage Heights Ln 27587
Heritage Hills Way 27587
Heritage Knoll Dr 27587
Heritage Lake Rd 27587
Heritage Lake Rd Dr 27587
Heritage Links Dr 27587
Heritage Reserve Ct 27587
Heritage Spring Cir 27587
Heritage Trade Dr 27587
Heritage View Trl 27587
Herring Gull Pl 27587
Heuristic Way 27587
Hialeah Ct 27587
Hidden Hills Dr 27587
Hidden Home Ln 27587
Hidden Jewel Ln 27587
Hidden Nook Ln 27587
Hidden Trail Ct 27587
High Spring Cir 27587
High Trail Ct 27587
Highgate Cir 27587
Highland Dr 27587
Hill St 27587
Hillsgrove Rd 27587
Hillsgrove Stone Rd 27587
Hillswick Pl 27587
Hinshaw Rd 27587
Hinton Rd 27587
Hipps Dr 27587
Hobblebush Way 27587
Hogan Dr 27587
E Holding Ave
100-225 27587
224-224 27588
226-798 27587
227-799 27587
W Holding Ave 27587
Holding Oaks Ct 27587
Holding Ridge Ct 27587
Holly Cir 27587
Holly Bend Ln 27587
Holly Forest Rd 27587
Holly Mist St 27587
Holmes Hollow Rd 27587
Home Garden Ct 27587
Homecamp Ct 27587
Homestead Lake Dr 27587
Hope St 27587
Hope Farm Ln 27587
Hopkinton St 27587
Hornbuckle Ct 27587
Horse Fly Trl 27587
Horse Shoe Farm Rd 27587
Horsetrail Way 27587
Hosmer Ct 27587
Hosta Valley Ct 27587
Houndsditch Cir 27587
Hugh Davis Rd 27587
Hunsford Pl 27587
Huntingcreek Dr 27587
Huntmaster Trl 27587
Hysop Ln 27587
Incline Dr 27587
Index Dr 27587
Ingalls Cir 27587
Iris Ct 27587
Irish Dr 27587
Ivy Creek Trl 27587
Ivy Stone Ct 27587
Iyar Way 27587
Jabbo Ct 27587
Jack Jones Rd 27587
Jackson Rd 27587
Jaffiley Ct 27587
Jasmine Ct 27587
Jeanne St 27587
Jeffreys Ln 27587
Jenkins Rd 27587
Jersey Ln 27587
Jewel Dr 27587
Jilandre Ct 27587
E Jones Ave 27587
Jones Dairy Rd 27587
Jones Farm Rd 27587
Jones Ridge Trl 27587
Jones Wynd 27587
Jonesville Rd 27587
Jordan Ln 27587
Joseph Dr 27587
Joshua Woods Dr 27587
Joyner Ct 27587
Jubilee Ct 27587
Judson Dr 27587
Julian Cir 27587
Julie Ann Ct 27587
Jumper Dr 27587
E & W Juniper Ave 27587
Kalworth Rd 27587
Kaplan Woods Way 27587
Karbas Rd 27587
Kayenta Ct 27587
Kearney Rd 27587
Keeter Cir 27587
Keighley Forest Dr 27587
Keith Rd 27587
Keith Store Rd 27587
Kelly Pine Ct 27587
Kemble Ridge Dr 27587
Kensington Manor Ln 27587
Kilmarnock Ct 27587
Kimi Rd 27587
Kimmon Way 27587
Kings Way Ct 27587
Kingsbridge Ct 27587
Kingsbrook Ct 27587
Kintail Ct 27587
Kinvara Ct 27587
Kirkham Ct 27587
Kirkwood Hill Way 27587
Kittinger Ct 27587
Knebford Cir 27587
Knoll Ridge Ln 27587
Knotty Pine Ct 27587
Knox Overlook Ct 27587
Kullana Ln 27587
Ladowick Ln 27587
Lagerfeld Way 27587
Lake Forest Dr 27587
Lake Hart Ln 27587
Lake Heart Trl 27587
Lake Valley Dr 27587
Lakefall Dr 27587
Lakeview Ave 27587
Lalla Ct 27587
Lamberley Ct 27587
Lambton Ave 27587
Landen Dr 27587
Lantern Walk Ln 27587
Lantus Ct 27587
Lapwing Trl 27587
Lariat Ridge Dr 27587
Las Brisas Ct 27587
Lasheral Rd 27587
Lassiter Rd 27587
Laura Lake Dr 27587
Laurel Field Cir 27587
Laurelford Ln 27587
Lavender Ln 27587
Lawn Artist Dr 27587
Lawrence Rd 27587
Lebatton Dr 27587
Ledbury Way 27587
Ledford Grove Ln 27587
Ledgerock Rd 27587
Ledyard Ct 27587
Lee St 27587
Legacy Greene Ave 27587
Leighton Ridge Dr 27587
Lemongrass Ln 27587
Lenmar Ln 27587
Lennox Pl 27587
Leroy Dr 27587
Liberty St 27587
Light Falls Dr 27587
Light Horse Trl 27587
Lightfoot Ct 27587
Lightning Bug Ln 27587
Ligon Creek Loop 27587
Ligon Mill Rd 27587
Lillie Liles Rd 27587
Lilliput Ln 27587
Lindenberg Sq 27587
Linenhall Way 27587
Linslade Way 27587
Litchborough Way 27587
Literary Ln 27587
Little Pine Way 27587
Little Tall Way 27587
Little Turtle Way 27587
Littlehampton Ct 27587
Loblolly Ln 27587
Lochmaben St 27587
Lockhurst St 27587
Locust Tree Ln 27587
Lodestar Ln 27587
Loftwood Ln 27587
Loghouse St 27587
Lois Ln 27587
Lola Ln 27587
Lolley Ct 27587
Lonesome Spur Cir 27587
Long Green Dr 27587
Longbourn Dr 27587
Longleaf Ct 27587
Longmire Pt 27587
Longmont Dr 27587
Lonnie Dr 27587
Lopez 27587
Loring Lake Dr 27587
Lotus Ln 27587
Lotus Tree Ct 27587
Louisburg Rd 27587
Louisbury Rd 27587
Lowenstein St 27587
Lower Lake Rd 27587
Lowery Farm Rd 27587
Lowery Ridge Dr 27587
Lumbermill Pt 27587
Lunsford Ct 27587
M And M Ln 27587
Magnolia Forest Ct 27587
N & S Main St 27587
Main Divide Dr 27587
Malindo Ct 27587
Mallard Crossing Way 27587
Malor Dr 27587
Mangum Ave 27587
Mangum Dairy Rd 27587
Mangum Hollow Dr 27587
Manly Farm Rd 27587
Marbank St 27587
Marcy Ct 27587
Margie Cir 27587
Margots Ave 27587
Marigold Ln 27587
Marjoram Ct 27587
Marshall Farm St 27587
Martin Bench Ct 27587
Massenburg Rd 27587
Massey Apartments 27587
Massimo Dr 27587
Matherly Dr 27587
Matrix Farm Dr 27587
Mauldin Cir 27587
May Apple Ct 27587
May Bell Ln 27587
Mayeville Ln 27587
Mcdowell Dr 27587
Mcgowan Ct 27587
Mcneil St 27587
Meadow Flowers Ave 27587
Meadow Glen Dr 27587
N Meadows Ct 27587
Medlin Ave 27587
Medlin Woods Rd 27587
Melcombe Way 27587
Melksham Rd 27587
Memphis Dr 27587
Merrilow Ct 27587
Mica Mine Ln 27587
Micklewaithe Ct 27587
Mid Ridge Ct 27587
Middle Bridge Rd 27587
Middlegame Way 27587
Middlestone Ct 27587
Middleton Dr 27587
Middletown Dr 27587
Midnight Ln 27587
Mill St 27587
Mill Dam Rd 27587
Millkirk Cir 27587
Millpoint Dr 27587
Minna Rd 27587
Mira Mar Pl 27587
Miracle Dr 27587
Miramir Woods Ct 27587
Missy Ln 27587
Mistletoe Dr 27587
Mitchell Mill Rd 27587
Mitchell Ridge Rd 27587
Mithrasdowne Ct 27587
Mockingbird Ln 27587
Moffat Ter 27587
Mollynick Ln 27587
Mondavi Woods Ct 27587
Montavista Ln 27587
Monthaven Dr 27587
Montonia St 27587
Montville Ct 27587
Montys Ln 27587
Moody Dr 27587
Moondance Ct 27587
Moores Pond Rd 27587
Moresham Way 27587
Moretz Creek Dr 27587
Morgan Cir 27587
Moultonboro Ave 27587
Mountain Branch Dr 27587
Mountain Grove Ln 27587
Mountain High Rd 27587
Mountain Oaks Way 27587
Murdock Cir 27587
Naxos Dr 27587
Nc 98 Byp 27587
Nc Highway 98 W 27587
Neasden Dr 27587
Neighbors Dr 27587
Nello Cir 27587
E Nelson Ave 27587
Neuse Banks Ct 27587
Neuse Rock Trl 27587
New Century Rd 27587
New Forest Ln 27587
New Grissom Way 27587
New Light Rd 27587
Newlyn Woods Dr 27587
Newquay Ln 27587
Night Heron Dr 27587
Nillkirk Cir 27587
Nolabee Ln 27587
North Ave 27587
Northlake Ct 27587
Northpark Dr 27587
Northshore Dr 27587
Nucassee St 27587
Nuthatch Ct 27587
E & W Oak Ave 27587
Oak Falls Dr 27587
Oak Grove Ct 27587
Oak Grove Church Rd 27587
Oak Lawn Way 27587
Oakcrest Dr 27587
Oakman Ridge Ct 27587
Oakview Dr 27587
Oakwood Dr 27587
Oatlands Ct 27587
Obrien Cir 27587
Old Ash Ct 27587
Old Bailey Ct 27587
Old Bayleaf Rd 27587
Old College Cir 27587
Old Crawford Rd 27587
Old Creedmoor Rd 27587
Old Jones Rd 27587
Old Kearney Rd 27587
Old Keith Rd 27587
Old Larkin Ct 27587
Old Magnolia Ln 27587
Old Murray Dr 27587
Old Nc 98 Hwy 27587
Old Neusiok Trl 27587
Old Pearce Rd 27587
Old Pond Ct 27587
Old Still Rd & Way 27587
Old Stone Way 27587
Old Weaver Trl 27587
Ole Mill Stream Rd 27587
Ole Neuse Trl 27587
One World Way 27587
Oneal Rd 27587
Opeushaw Ct 27587
Opposition Way 27587
Orange Cosmos Ave 27587
Orchard Oriole Trl 27587
Orchard Tree Ln 27587
Oriole Dr 27587
Ormand Way 27587
Oscar Barham Rd 27587
Ostrich Path 27587
Otway Rd 27587
Out Back Ln 27587
Overglen Ave 27587
Overlook Ct 27587
Overlook Ridge Rd 27587
E & W Owen Ave 27587
Oxford Rdg 27587
Oxford Ridge Dr 27587
Oxwich Ct 27587
Paddstowe Main Way 27587
Pageland Ct 27587
Palmer Ct 27587
Pamplona Dr 27587
Pantonbury Pl 27587
Paper Trl 27587
Park Falls Dr 27587
Parkside Townes Ct 27587
Parlange Woods Ln 27587
Partington St 27587
Pastor Ln 27587
Pasture Walk Dr 27587
Peaceful Rd 27587
Pearce Ave 27587
Pebblebrook Dr 27587
Peeler Ct 27587
Penfold Ln 27587
Pericchis Pond Dr 27587
Perini Ct 27587
E Perry Ave 27587
Petite Ct 27587
Pheasant Tail Ct 27587
Philbeck Ln 27587
Phillips Landing Dr 27587
Philly Ct 27587
E & W Pine Ave 27587
Pine Fork Ct 27587
Pine Needles Dr 27587
Pine Ridge Ct 27587
Pine Rock Ct 27587
Pine Valley Dr 27587
Pine View Dr 27587
Pine Warbler Ct 27587
Pineview Dr 27587
Piney Hill Run 27587
Pleasant Forest Way 27587
Pleasants Ridge Dr 27587
Plimoth Hill Dr 27587
Plott Hound Ln 27587
Plum Creek Ln 27587
Plummer Ct 27587
Plunket Dr 27587
Polanski Dr 27587
Polbida Dr 27587
Pompeii Pl 27587
Ponderosa Park Dr 27587
Ponderosa Service Rd 27587
Ponsonby Dr 27587
Poole Ln 27587
Porter Creek Ct 27587
Portmarnock Ct 27587
Porto Fino Ave 27587
Portpatrick Ct 27587
Possum Trot Rd 27587
Poteat Dr 27587
Powell Rd 27587
Prairie Aster Ct 27587
Prairie Smoke St 27587
Prancer Ct 27587
Prather Pl 27587
Precious Stone Dr 27587
Pressler St 27587
Primrose Meadow Ln 27587
Prindown Rd 27587
Pulley Town Rd 27587
Purisima Ct 27587
Purnell Rd 27587
Purnell Ridge Rd 27587
Quail Ave 27587
Quail Bluff Ct 27587
Quail Crossing Dr 27587
Quarry Rd 27587
Quatrefoil St 27587
Quercus Ct 27587
Rabbit Run 27587
Rachel Dr 27587
Railroad St 27587
Rainsong Dr 27587
Rainy Lake St 27587
Ralph Dr 27587
Rankin Ct 27587
Rayburn Ave 27587
Reagan Ln 27587
Recapture Ct 27587
Red Horse Way 27587
Red Pine Ct 27587
Red Quill Way 27587
Red Trillium Ct 27587
Redstart Ct 27587
Reezy Ln 27587
Registry Ct 27587
Reindeer Moss Dr 27587
Remington Woods Dr 27587
Rescue Estates Dr 27587
Retail Dr 27587
Reynolds Mill Rd 27587
Rhone Ct 27587
Rice Cir & Dr 27587
Richland Dr 27587
Richland Bluff Ct 27587
Richland Creek Ln 27587
Richland Hills Ave 27587
Richland Ridge Dr 27587
Ridgemount St 27587
Ridgetop Way 27587
Ridgeway Bluff Ct 27587
Ridley Field Dr 27587
Ripley Woods St 27587
Rising Sun Ct 27587
River Downs Ct 27587
River Hill Dr 27587
River Mill Dr 27587
River Park Dr 27587
River Ridge Rd 27587
Rivermead Ln 27587
Riverside Dr 27587
Robin Ave 27587
Robins Nest Ln 27587
Robinson Dr 27587
Rochelle Dr 27587
Rock Farm Rd 27587
Rock Pine Dr 27587
N Rock Springs Rd 27587
Rockhind Way 27587

Rockville Rd 27587
E Rockwood Ct 27587
Rocky Creek Way 27587
Rocky Knoll Ln 27587
Rocky Ridge Rd 27587
Rodinson Ln 27587
Rodney Bay Xing 27587
Rogers Cir & Rd 27587
Rogers Branch Rd 27587
Rolesville Rd 27587
Rolling Brooks Dr 27587
Rolling Rock Rd 27587
Rolling View Dr 27587
Rookfield Dr 27587
Rookwood Ct 27587
E Roosevelt Ave 27587
Rose Angel Cir 27587
Rose Petal Run 27587
Roseanna Dr 27587
Rowsby Ct 27587
Roxbury Dr 27587
Royal Coachmen Dr 27587
Rubicon Ln 27587
Ruby Lee Dr 27587
Running Deer Dr 27587
Rusted Oak Rd 27587
Rutherford Hill Ct 27587
Saint Catherines Dr 27587
Samuel Wait Ln 27587
San Remo Pl 27587
Sand Hollow Cir 27587
Sandaway Ln 27587
Sandy Plains Rd 27587
Sandy Woods Dr 27587
Sandybrook Ln 27587
Sanford Creek Ave 27587
Santorini Way 27587
Sarratt Ridge Ct 27587
Sawnwork Ct 27587
Scarborough Oak Trl 27587
Scotch Pine Trl 27587
Scotts Pine Cir 27587
Seattle Ct 27587
Seawell Dr 27587
Sebts 27587
Secluded Oaks Ct 27587
Secret Pond Rd 27587
Sedge Wren Dr 27587
Selsey Dr 27587
Sephora Ct 27587
Serena Pl 27587
Serenity Lake Dr 27587
Settlers Landing Ct 27587
Shady Bottom Ln 27587
Shady Glen Ln 27587
Shady Hill Ln 27587
Shannonford Ct 27587
Shapinsay Ave 27587
Shasta Daisy Dr 27587
Shearon Farms Ave 27587
Shellrock Dr 27587
Shenandoah Farm Rd 27587
Shephards Landing Dr 27587
Shepstone Pl 27587
Sherron Dr 27587
Shingleback Dr 27587
Shining Water Ln 27587
Shirehall Park Ln 27587
Shiretown Ln 27587
Shorrey Pl 27587
Shortleaf Ct 27587
Shropshire 27587
Shuford Rd 27587
Sid Jones Ln 27587
Siena Dr 27587
Silent Brook Rd 27587
Silo Glen Ln 27587
Silver Linden Ln 27587
Silver Water Ln 27587
Sinewell Dr 27587
Sky Hill Pl 27587
Skylar Ct 27587
Slater Dr 27587
Sleepy Hollow Rd 27587
Slow Gait Trl 27587
Smith Creek Way 27587
Snap Dragon Dr 27587
Snooks Trl 27587
Softbreeze Ln 27587
Soho Sq 27587
Solunar Ct 27587
Song Sparrow Dr 27587
Sonoma Creek Ln 27587
E & W South Ave 27587
Southern Pines Dr 27587
Southwick Ct 27587
Sovereign Way 27587
Sparhawk Rd 27587
Sparrow Dr 27587
Sparrowwood Dr 27587
E Spring Ln & St 27587
Spring Park Rd 27587
Spring Valley Rd 27587
Springflow Cir 27587
Springtime Fields Ln 27587
Springwood Dr 27587
Stable Point Cir 27587
Stacked Stone Trl 27587
Stackhurst Way 27587
Stadium Dr 27587
Star Rd 27587
Starboard Ct 27587
Stearns Way 27587
Steel Canyon Way 27587
Steeple Run Dr 27587
Stells Rd 27587
Sterling Lake Dr 27587
Steven Taylor Rd 27587
Stickman St 27587
Stillwood Dr 27587
Stirrup Ct 27587
W Stone Dr 27587
Stone Bridge Ct 27587
Stone Fly Dr 27587
Stone Forest Way 27587
Stone Monument Dr 27587
Stoneway Ct 27587
Stonewyck Ln 27587
Stoney Bluff Ct 27587
Stoningham Pl 27587
Stony Grove Ln 27587
Stony Hill Rd 27587
Strategy Way 27587
Stringbean Rd 27587
Stroud Cir 27587
Stuarts Ridge Rd 27587
Studbury Hall Ct 27587
Sugar Gap Rd 27587
Sugar Hollow Ln 27587
Sugar Maple Ave 27587
Summer Pines Way 27587
Sun Catcher Ln 27587
Sundance St 27587
Sunflower Meadows Ln 27587
Sunset Manor Dr 27587
Superior Dr 27587
Sweet Olive Ct 27587
Sweetclover Dr 27587
E & W Sycamore Ave 27587
Tackwood Ct 27587
Tacy Pl 27587
Talbot Ridge St 27587
Tamaras Cir 27587
Tannerwell Ave 27587
Tansley St 27587
Tarkiln Pl 27587
Taviston Ct 27587
Taviswood Way 27587
N & S Taylor St 27587
Taylors Ridge Rd 27587
Teacup Spring Ct 27587
Teletec Plaza Rd 27587
Templeridge Rd 27587
Ten Point Trl 27587
Tenbridge Ct 27587
Tenbury Woods Ct 27587
Territory Trl 27587
Tessier Ct 27587
Thamelink Ct 27587
Thaney Ct 27587
Tharrington Rd 27587
Theberton Way 27587
Thompson Glenn Pl 27587
Thompson Mill Rd 27587
Thornburg Dr 27587
Thorndike Dr 27587
Thornrose Way 27587
Thorny Vine Ct 27587
Tiffield Way 27587
Tilgate Ct 27587
Tillamook Dr 27587
Timberknoll Ln 27587
Timberland Dr 27587
Tipsy Sq 27587
Titanic Ct 27587
Tonawanda Trl 27587
Topaz St 27587
Torry Hill Ct 27587
Townsend Warbler Ct 27587
Trackertrace Ct 27587
Traders Trl 27587
Traditions Meadow Dr 27587
Trail Blazer Trl 27587
Trailing Rose Ct 27587
Trammel Ct 27587
Trap Ct 27587
Trappers Forest Dr 27587
Trappers Run Rd 27587
Trawden Dr 27587
Trayer Ln 27587
Traylee Dr 27587
Tree Top Dr 27587
Trentini Ave 27587
Trevi Fountain Pl 27587
Trifle Ln 27587
Trommel Ct 27587
Trophy Trl 27587
Trout Valley Rd 27587
Trouville Ct 27587
Tryst Ln 27587
Tuckahoe Trce 27587
Tucker Hollow Ln 27587
Tulip Grove Ln 27587
Tully Ridge Ct 27587
Turning Point Dr 27587
Twig Ct 27587
Twin Meadows Ln 27587
Two Pines Trl 27587
Tyler Run Dr 27587
Tynewind Dr 27587
Tyson Farm Rd 27587
Unicon Dr 27587
Universal Dr 27587
Upchurch Ln 27587
Us Highway 401 27587
Vail Springs Ct 27587
Vanagrif Ct 27587
Vann Dowda Pl 27587
Venflor Ct 27587
Ventura Cir 27587
Ventura Springs Ct 27587
Ventura Woods Ct 27587
Verdant Ct 27587
Vermilion Ct 27587
E & W Vernon Ave 27587
Vidal Ct 27587
Village Club Dr 27587
Vineyard Pine Ln 27587
Vinson View Ct 27587
Virginia Pine Ct 27587
Vista Del Lago Ln 27587
Vodin St 27587
Vonkramer Ct 27587
Wahlbrink Dr 27587
Wait Ave 27587
Wake Dr 27587
Wake Bluff Dr 27587
Wake Forest Business Park 27587
Wake Union Church Rd 27587
Wakecenter Dr 27587
Wakefalls Dr 27587
Wall Ave & Rd 27587
Wallberman Dr 27587
Wallridge Dr 27587
E & W Walnut Ave & St 27587
Walter Ridge Dr 27587
Walters Dr 27587
Warmoven St 27587
Washhouse Ln 27587
Watch Hill Ln 27587
Watchet Pl 27587
Water Ave 27587
Waterford Ridge Ln 27587
Waterline Dr 27587
Watershed Way 27587
Waterwinds Ct 27587
Waterwood Ct 27587
Watson Woods Ln 27587
Waverly Woods Pl 27587
Waxwing Ct 27587
Wayne Dr 27587
Welcome Dr 27587
Welding Rd 27587
Welsh Tavern Way 27587
Wendler Ct 27587
Wendy Ct 27587
West Ave 27587
Westerfield Rd 27587
Westerham Dr 27587
Wheddon Cross Way 27587
Whispering Pines Mh Park 27587
Whistable Ave 27587
Whistling Swan Dr 27587
N & S White St 27587
White Carriage Dr 27587
White Fir Dr 27587
White Flag Way 27587
White Pine Ct 27587
Whiteclover Ct 27587
E Whitier St 27587
Wide River Dr 27587
Wigton Ln 27587
Wild Duck Ct 27587
Wild Meadow Ln 27587
Wild Orchid Ct 27587
Wildhurst Ln 27587
Will Let Ln 27587
Willeva Dr 27587
Willington Pl 27587
Willow Creek Dr 27587
Willow Stone Ln 27587
Willow Wisp Ct 27587
Willowdell Dr 27587
Willowgrass Ln 27587
Willowhurst Dr 27587
Willowlawn Dr 27587
Willowshire Ln 27587
Wilts Dairy Pt 27587
Winburne Ct 27587
Windemere Ln 27587
Winding Way 27587
Winding Forest Trl 27587
Windmeade Rd 27587
Windsong Valley Dr 27587
Windsor Dr 27587
Winfree Ln 27587
N & S Wingate St 27587
Winkworth Way 27587
Winslet Dr 27587
Winter Bloom Ct 27587
Winter Spring Dr 27587
Wisley Way 27587
Wisteria Ct 27587
Wolverton Fields Dr 27587
Wood Duck Ln 27587
Wood Poppy St 27587
Woodbridge Ct 27587
Woodchase Ct 27587
Woodcross Way 27587
Woodfield Creek Dr 27587
Woodland Dr N 27587
Woodland Church Rd 27587
Woodlief Rd 27587
Woodrose Ln 27587
Woods Way 27587
Woods Mill Cir 27587
Wooten Ct 27587
Worthing Ct 27587
Wycombe Ridge Way 27587
Wylie Way 27587
Yam Dr 27587
Yellow Dunn Way 27587
Yellow Poplar Ave 27587
Yew Pine Ct 27587
Yonna Dr 27587
Young Forest Dr 27587
Youngsville Blvd 27587
Zebulon Rd 27587
Zennie Dr 27587

NUMBERED STREETS

All Street Addresses 27587

WAYNESVILLE NC

General Delivery 28786

POST OFFICE BOXES MAIN OFFICE STATIONS AND BRANCHES

Box No.s
All PO Boxes 28786

RURAL ROUTES

02 28785
10 28786

NAMED STREETS

Aaron Way 28786
Abbeys Cove Rd 28785
Abby Ln 28785
Abel Ln 28786
Abigail Dr 28786
Academy St 28786
Acadia Pl 28786
Access Rd 28785
Acorn Ln 28785
Acres View Dr 28786
Adams St 28786
Adarrad Rd 28786
Adcock Mountain Rd 28785
Addie Ln 28786
Adell Dr 28786
Admiration Ct 28785
Adrianne Ln 28785
Adventure Park 28785
Aerial Rdg 28785
Afton Pl 28786
Airdale 28786
Airish Ln 28785
Alavista Way 28786
Aldersgate Rd 28786
Alex Trl 28786
Allen Dr & St 28786
Allens Creek Ext, Park & Rd 28786
Alley Cat Dr 28786
Allison Acres 28786
Allison View Ln & Rd 28786
Alma Dr 28785
Almond Pl 28786
Aloha Ln 28785
Alpaugh Dr 28785
Alpine Ln 28786
Altima Ln 28786
Amanda Rd 28786
Amanda Jane Dr 28785
Ambria Dr 28785
Ambrosia Dr 28785
American Way 28785
Amethyst Trl 28786
Amhurst Ct 28786
Amity Pl 28785
Ammons Trl 28786
Amos Mountain Rd 28785
Anderson Dr 28786
Andrew Ln 28786
Anessa Kay Ln 28786
Angel Rdg 28785
Angel Puppy Ln 28786
Angelica Way 28786
Anglers Rdg 28786
Anglers Trl 28785
Angus Ln 28786
Animal Trl 28785
Annies Rd 28786
Anthony St 28786
Antler Pt 28785
Apache Dr 28785
Appaloosa Trl 28785
Apple Blossom Ln 28786
Apple Creek Rd 28786
Apple House Rd 28786
Apple Tree Ct 28786
Applehill Dr 28786
April Park 28786
Aqua Vista Loop 28785
Aquifer Brae Ln 28786
Arabian Pt 28786
Arbor Dr 28786
Ardella Trl 28786
Arden St 28786
Arlen Dr 28786
Arms Ave 28786
Arnold Hts 28786
Arrington Rd 28786
Arrington Acres Dr 28786
Arrowhead Ln 28786
Asa Trl 28785
Asbury Rd 28785
Ash Rdg & St 28786
Asheville Rd 28786
Ashley Ln 28786
Ashwood Ln 28786
Aspen Pl 28785
E Assembly St 28786
Aster Ln 28786
Atari Rd 28786
Atkin St 28786
Atwater Dr 28785
Aubrey Trl 28785
Auburn Rd 28786
Auburn Park Dr 28786
Augusta Cir 28786
Auld Rock Rd 28786
Aunt Belles Cv 28786
Aurora Way 28785
Austin Hts 28786
Autumn Ridge Ln 28785
Avalon Ct 28786
Avery St 28786
Avery Patrick Ln 28786
Awesome Rdg 28785
Awohali Cv 28785
Azalea Dr 28786
Babb St 28786
Babbling Brook Ln 28785
Baconton Cv 28786
Bage St 28786
Baguette Blvd 28785
Bait Shop Dr 28786
Baldwin Dr 28786
Ball Dr 28785
N & S Balsam Dr, Rd & St 28786
Balsam Meadows Rd 28786
Balsam Ridge Rd 28786
Balsam View Dr 28786
Bamboo Ln 28786
Banbury Ct 28786
Banjo Ln 28785
Banjo Hollow Ln 28786
Banker Dr 28786
Barber Blvd & Dr 28786
Barber Hill Dr 28786
Barber Orchard Dr 28786
Bark Trl 28786
Barlow Dr 28785
Barn Loop Ln 28786
Barn Owl Ln 28786
Barrel Ln 28786
Basil Ct 28786
Bass Ln 28785
Beacon Rock Ln 28786
Beanie Rd 28786
Beantown Ln & Rd 28785
Bear Hollow Rd 28785
Bear Vista Trl 28785
Bearfoot Ln 28786
Beatrice Way 28785
Beatty Springs Trce 28786
Becker Dr 28786
Beech St 28786
Begonia Dr 28786
Belair Dr 28785
Belle Meade Dr 28786
Belleview Rd 28786
Beltz Way 28785
Ben Dr 28785
Ben Mattrose Dr 28786
Ben Medford Rd 28785
Benjamin Trl 28786
Bennett St 28786
Bent Nail Blvd 28785
Bent Oak Dr 28786
Bent Pine Dr 28785
Berea Ct 28786
Bernard Ln 28785
Bernies Trl 28785
Berry Ln 28785
Berryknoll Dr 28786
Berthas Dr 28786
Beth Ln 28785
Bethel View Hts 28786
Bethesda Ln 28786
Bethharan Dr 28786
Betsy Acres Ln 28786
Bettys Dr 28786
Beverly Ln 28785
Bible Baptist Dr 28786
Big Bear Rd 28786
Big Cove Cir, Dr & Rd 28786
Big Holly Way 28786
Big Laurel Rd 28785
Big Oak Dr 28785
Big Spruce Ln 28786
Big Stomp Rd 28786
Bill Parks Rd 28785
Billy Bob Trl 28785
Biodome Dr 28785
Birch Springs Rd 28786
Bird Creek Dr 28786
Birdsong Trl 28786
Black Gum Dr 28786
Black Hawk Trl 28785
Black Pine Dr 28786
Blackberry Rdg 28786
Blair Athel Pt 28786
Blanton Dr 28786
Blayco Dr 28786
Blazing Trl 28786
Blessings Ln 28786
Blind Sams Cv 28785
Blink Bonny Dr 28786
Blooms Way 28786
Blossom Dr 28786
Blueberry Ln 28786
Bluebird Ln 28785
Bluegrass Ln 28786
Bluff Hollow Rd 28785
Boardwalk Ln 28786
Bob Ln 28785
Bob Boyd Rd 28785
Bob Cat Rd 28785
Bob White Loop 28786
Bobtail Dr 28785
Bodacious Dr 28786
Bogie Ln 28785
Bonita Ct 28785
Bonner Rd 28785
Bonnie View Dr 28786
Bonnies Ln 28786
Boomer Run Dr 28785
Boone Orchard Dr 28786
Boot Rdg 28785
Borges Ln 28785
Bosenberry Ln 28786

Street	ZIP
Bottom Ridge Rd	28785
Bottoms Way	28786
Boulder Dr	28786
Boundary St	28786
Bountiful Ln	28785
Bounty Ln	28785
Bow And Arrow Cv	28785
Bowden Ln	28786
Bowman Dr	28785
Boxwood Ln	28785
Boyd Ave	28786
Boyd Farm Rd	28785
Boyd Mountain Rd	28785
Brad St	28786
Bradford Cir	28786
Bradley Ct, Hts & St	28786
Bradshaw Rd	28785
Braeburn Way	28785
Bragg Ln	28786
Bramlett Dr	28785
Branch Ln	28786
Brandon Pl	28785
Brandywine Rd	28786
Brankris Dr	28786
Branner Ave	28786
Brannon Forest Dr	28785
Branscombe Rd	28785
Brantley Branch Ln	28786
Braxton Way	28786
Breckenridge Rd	28785
Breezemont Dr	28786
Breezy Rdg	28785
Brendle St	28786
Brian Hts	28786
Briarberry Ln	28786
Briarwood Dr	28786
Bridges St	28786
Bridget Dr & St	28786
Brigham Dr	28785
Bright St	28786
Bristle Cone Ln	28786
Britts Way	28786
Broad St	28786
Broadview Rd	28786
Brody Dr	28786
Broken Bow Rdg	28785
Bronzewing Ln	28786
Brook St	28786
Brookside Ct	28786
Brown Ave	28786
Brown Bear Way	28786
Brown Ridge Rd	28785
Browning Rd	28786
Browning Branch Rd	28786
Bruin Ln	28786
Bruna Dr	28785
Brunswick Rd	28786
Brushy Creek Ln	28785
Bryson St	28786
Bryson Heights Rd	28786
Buccaneer Dr	28785
Buchanan Dr	28786
Buchanan Cemetery Rd	28786
Buck Ridge Rd	28785
Buckeye Dr	28786
Buckeye Rd	28785
Buckskin Ln	28785
Budding Dr	28786
Buddleia Ln	28786
Buffalo Ln	28786
Buffy Ln	28785
Bug Hollow Rd	28786
Buglers Trl	28786
Bull Moose Ln	28786
Bumblebee Ln	28786
Bungalow Dr	28786
Bunk House Trl	28785
Bunny Run Ln	28785
Buntin St	28786
Burgess Loop	28785
Burgin Springs Rd	28785
Burke St	28786
Burley Dr	28786
Burma Rd	28786
Burnette Cir	28786
Burnt Fork Trl	28786
Burris Ln	28786
Bust O Dawn	28785
Buster Dr	28786
Butler Hills Dr	28786
Buttercup Ln	28786
Buxton St	28786
Cabin Breeze Ln	28786
Cactus Dr	28785
Cagle Dr	28785
Cajun Ln	28786
Caldwell Dr & Rd	28786
Caldwell Cove Dr	28786
Calhoun Rd & Rdg	28786
Calhoun Ridge Dr	28786
Caline Dr	28786
Callie Ln	28785
Calm Creek Rd	28785
Calusa Rd	28786
Calvary St	28786
Cambridge Way	28786
Camden Downs Rd	28785
Camellia Ct	28786
Camelot Dr	28786
Cameron Ln	28785
Camp St	28786
Camp Branch Rd	28786
Camp Schaub Rd	28786
Campbell Mountain Dr	28785
Campfire Loop	28785
Camry Pl	28786
Canary Rdg	28786
Candlelight Ln	28785
Candler St	28786
Candlewood Cir	28785
Cansadie Top Rd	28785
Canterbury Ln	28786
Cap St	28786
Caravan Ct	28786
Cardinal Dr & Ln	28786
Carillon Ct	28786
Carl Arrington Rd	28786
Carly Rd	28785
Carmal Dr	28785
Carolina Ave	28786
Carolina Mountain Dr	28785
Carousel Ln	28786
Carpathian Ln	28785
Carpenter Way	28786
Carriage Ln	28786
Carsen Loop	28785
Carswell Dr	28786
Cartwright Dr & Rd	28786
Carving Tree Ln	28786
Cassken Rd	28785
Castle Creek Dr	28786
Casual Ln	28786
Cataloochee Ln	28785
Catawba Ln	28786
Catbird St	28786
Caterpillar Dr	28786
Cathey Cove Rd	28786
Catholic Camp Rd	28786
Cattail Ln	28786
Cattle Dr	28786
Cavalier Dr	28786
Ce Smathers Dr	28786
Cecils Rd	28786
Cedar St	28786
Cedar Rock Rd	28786
Cedarwood Dr	28785
Celtic Ct	28786
Cemetary Rd	28785
Centennial Dr	28786
Central St	28786
Chambers Ln & Rd	28786
Champion Ct	28786
Chancery Ln	28786
Chanticleer Ln	28786
Charles St	28786
Charles Wesley Way	28786
Charlie Medford Rd	28785
Charlie Mull Rd	28786
Chase Cove Rd	28785
Chateau Pl	28785
Chatham St	28786
Cheerful Dr	28786
Chelsea Rd	28786
Chenoa Ridge Rd	28785
Cherokee St	28786
Cherry St	28786
Cherry Berry Dr	28785
Cherry Hill Dr	28785
Cherry Tree Ln	28785
Cherrywood Ln	28786
Chestnut Flats Ln & Rd	28786
Chestnut Hill Cv	28786
Chestnut Park Dr	28786
Chestnut Walk Cir, Dr & Pl	28786
Chestnut Wood Dr	28786
Cheyenne Pl	28786
Chickadee Rd	28785
Chickering Ln	28786
Children St	28786
Chilly Trce	28785
Chimney Ridge Trl	28786
Chinquapin Ln	28785
Chipmunk Cir	28785
Chipping Sparrow Ln	28786
Chipwood Ln	28785
Chloe Ln	28786
Choctaw Trl	28785
Christine Ct	28786
Christopher Farms Rd	28786
Church St	28786
Cicero Ln	28785
Cider Ln	28785
Cider Mill Rd	28786
Cimarron Trl	28786
Cindy Ln	28785
Cinnamon Rdg	28786
Cisco Cv	28785
City View Dr	28786
Cj Justice Dr	28785
Clancy Cv	28786
Clarity Ct	28785
Clark Dr	28786
Claudia Dr	28785
Claw Foot Trl	28785
Clay St	28786
Clay Hollow Rd	28786
Clayton Lake Rd	28785
Clearview Dr	28785
Clearwater Dr	28785
Clellie View Dr	28786
Clement Dr	28786
Clemson Rd	28786
Clif Dr	28786
Cliff Ln	28786
Clifton St	28786
Cline St	28786
Cloud Rdg	28785
Cloudland Dr	28786
Clover Pl	28785
Club Knoll Ave	28786
Club View Dr	28786
Clydesdale Rd	28785
Cobblestone Dr	28786
Cochran St	28786
Coco Way	28786
Cody Dr	28785
Coffee Cup Dr	28785
Cogdaview Dr	28786
Cohasset Dr	28785
Coldwater Creek Dr	28785
Coleman Mountain Rd	28785
Coljo Rd	28785
Collier Ln	28786
Colonial Ct	28786
Colony Ln	28786
Colten Dr	28786
Columbus Cv	28785
Columbine Dr	28786
Combo Ct	28786
Comet Ln	28785
Commerce St	28786
Commons Way	28786
Communications Dr	28786
Compromise Dr	28785
Conard Rd	28785
Conley St	28786
Conner Ridge Rd	28786
Constitution Ave	28785
Contentment Ln	28786
Continental Dr	28785
Conway Ln	28785
Cool August Hts	28785
Coon Hollow Rd	28786
Cope Rd	28786
Copper Way	28786
Copperhead Cv	28785
Corbin Ln	28786
Corbin Shady Ln	28785
Corn Patch Rd	28786
Corner Dr	28785
Cornerstone Rdg	28786
Cornwell Dr	28786
Coronado Ln	28786
Corsair Ct	28786
Cortland Ct	28786
Cory Ln	28786
Cosmic Ln	28786
Costalota Loop	28786
Cottage Loop	28785
Cottonwood Ln	28785
Cougar Ct	28786
Counsel Pl	28786
Country Ln	28785
Country Club Dr	28786
Country Haven Dr	28785
Country Meadows Ln	28786
Countryside Dr	28785
County Rd	28785
Courtney Ln	28785
Couzins Ln	28786
Cove Creek Rd	28785
Coventry Ln	28786
Covered Bridge Trl	28785
Covered Wagon Trl	28786
Covey Trl	28786
Cowan St	28786
Coy Dr	28786
Coyote Trl	28785
Coyote Hollow Rd	28785
Cozy Cv	28786
Crabapple Cv	28785
Crabtree Rd	28785
Cradling Cv	28785
Cranberry Ln	28785
Craven Rd	28786
Crawford Rd	28785
Creeds Cove Ln	28785
Creek Bend Ln	28785
Creekside Loop Rd	28786
Crestmont Dr	28786
Crestridge Dr	28785
Crestview Dr	28785
Crestview Pt	28786
Cricket Ln	28786
Crickhollow Ln	28786
Crimson Down Trl	28785
Cripple Creek Dr	28785
Crisp Dr	28786
Crocus Dr	28785
Crooked Branch Rd	28785
Crooked Fork Ln	28785
Cross View Dr	28786
Crosscreek Rd	28786
Crowbar Hill Dr	28786
Crown Pl	28786
Crows Nest Dr	28785
Crymes Pl	28786
Crymes Cove Rd	28786
Crystal Ln	28785
Crystal Tree Dr	28785
Cugees Ln	28786
Culpepper Dr	28786
Cumberland Pl	28785
Cunningham Dr	28785
Cupp Ln	28786
Cur Dog Trl	28785
Curtis Dr	28786
Cypress Villa Ln	28786
Daddo Dr	28785
Daffodil Dr	28785
Dahlia Ln	28785
Dairy Rdg	28785
Daisy Ave	28786
Dakota Ln	28786
Dale Dr	28786
Dalmahula Dr	28786
Dana Rd	28786
Dancing Deer Ln	28785
Dandelion Trl	28785
Daniel Ln	28785
Dapple Beauty Ln	28785
David Edwards Rd	28786
Davis Ln	28786
Davis Cemetary Rd	28785
Davis Cove Rd	28786
Dawen Cir	28786
Dawn Dr	28786
Dawn Valley Rd	28785
Dawnview Dr	28786
Day Lily Dr	28786
Dayco Dr	28786
Dayton Dr	28786
Dazzling Brook Ln	28786
Dean Riddle Dr	28785
Debbie Loop Ln	28786
Dee Ann Dr	28786
Deepwoods Ct	28785
Deer Glade Ln	28786
Deer Path Rd	28786
Deer Run Dr	28786
Deerglade Ln	28786
Deerwood Dr	28786
Delanne Dr	28786
Delia Wells Dr	28786
Delicious Rdg	28786
Dellwood Rd	28786
Denali Ln	28786
Denise Dr	28786
Dennis Farm Rd	28785
Depot St	28786
Derby Ln	28785
Destination Dr	28786
Destiny Rd	28785
Deva Trl	28786
Devine Way	28785
Devlin Dr	28785
Devoe Dr	28786
Dewberry Ln	28785
Dewdrop Ln	28785
Dewey Ross Rd	28786
Dicks Trl	28785
Divit Rd	28785
Dixie Way	28785
Dobbins St	28786
Dock Ratcliffe Rd	28786
Doe Trl	28785
Dogwood Dr, Hts, Ln & Trl	28786
Dogwood Acres	28785
Dogwood Rise Ter	28785
Dolan Dr & Rd	28786
Dolata Ln	28786
Dolly Dr	28786
Dolphin Dr	28786
Donaldson Pl	28786
Doodle Lou Dr	28786
Dorchester Rd	28785
Double Top Dr	28786
Douglas Dr	28786
Dove Crest Ln	28786
Dovetail Ln	28786
Downey Dr	28786
Downs Cove Rd	28786
Dragonfire Ln	28785
Dream Catcher Rdg	28785
Dream Forest Ln	28785
Drum Dr	28786
Dry Spring Cv	28785
Duckett Cove Rd	28786
Duff Ln	28786
Dulcimer Ln	28786
Duncan Rd	28786
Duncan Hill Dr	28786
Dungannon Dr	28786
Dusk Dr	28786
Dusty Rd	28786
Dutch Apple Ln	28786
Eagle Fork Dr & Rd	28786
Eagle Gap Rd	28786
Eagle Ridge Dr	28786
Eagle View Cir	28786
Eaglecrest Ln	28785
Eagles Nest Rd	28786
Earl Ln	28785
Earnhart Way	28785
East St	28786
Easy St	28786
Echo Dr	28786
Eclipse Est	28786
Eddies Trl	28785
Eden Ln	28785
Edgewood Dr	28786
Edward Allen Dr	28785
Edwards St	28786
Edwards Cove Rd	28786
Edwin Caldwell Rd	28786
Egret Ct	28786
Eindon Cir	28786
Elderberry Ln	28785
Eldorado Trl	28786
Eliza Cv	28785
Elizabeth Ln	28786
Elizabeth Chapel Rd	28786
Elkhound Rd	28785
Ellis Dr	28786
Elmer Price Ln	28785
Elmwood Way	28786
Elysinia Ave	28786
Emerald Trce	28786
Emerson Ln	28785
Emily Dr	28786
Emma Dr	28786
Empire Ln	28785
Empty Cabin Rd	28785
Enchanted Ln	28786
Enclave Dr	28786
Endeavor Ln	28786
English Sorrell Rd	28785
Entrata Dr	28786
Epsom St	28786
Equestrian Dr	28786
Erikas Way	28786
Erwin Ln	28785
Escalante Rd	28785
Essex Rd	28786
Estate Dr	28786
Estero Rd	28786
Estes Dr	28786
Estes Loner Ln	28786
Et Turner Rd	28786
Ethel Ln	28786
Etta Roy Pl	28786
Ettereve Ln	28785
Eva Creek Ln	28786
Evening Song Dr	28785
Evergreen Cir	28786
Evergreen Farm Cir	28786
Everview Ln	28785
Ewart Rd	28785
Explorer Dr	28786
Fairlane Dr	28786
Fairview Hts & Rd	28786
Fairway Dr	28786
Fairway Hills Dr	28786
Faith Ln	28785
Falcon Rdg	28786
Fall Creek Rd	28785
Fallen Timber Dr	28785
Falling Glen Dr	28785
Falling Waters Dr	28786
Falls Cv	28785
Family Rdg	28786
Fancy Ln	28785
Fannie Mae Ln	28786
Far Side Way	28786
Faren Ln	28786
Fargo Ln	28786
W Farley St	28786
Farm Boss Rd	28786
Farmland Rd	28785
Farmview Dr	28786
Fawn Dr	28785
Feather Ln	28786
Fellowship Ln	28785
Felmet St	28786
Fern Trl	28786
Fern Brook Dr	28786
Fernwood Pl	28786
Fiddlers Cv	28785
Fields Dr	28785
Finch Ct	28786
Fincher Mountain Rd	28785
Fir Ln	28785
Fireweed Park	28786
Fisher Ln	28786
Fishermans Trl	28785
Fitzgerald Ln	28786
Flag St	28786
Flat Creek Dr	28785
Flat Rock Rd	28786
Flat Rock Gap Rd	28785
Flat Top Rd	28785
Flint St	28786
Floppy Ear Trl	28785
Flora Ln	28785
Flossie Bell Ln	28785
Flowering Dr	28786
Flowing Brook Ln	28786
Floyd Rd	28786
Flying Hawk Trl	28786
Foggy Cv	28785
Foggy Bottom Rd	28786
Foliage Trl	28786
Fontana Dr	28786
Foothill Ln	28786
Forbidden Cv	28785
Ford Rd	28786
Forest Hill Rd	28785
Forest Park Dr	28785
Forest View Dr	28786
Forestway Ln	28786
Forever Joels Pl	28785
Forga Plaza Loop	28786
Forget Me Not Ln	28786
Forked Horn Trl	28785
Forsythe Ln	28785
Fortner Dr	28786
Fortune View Dr	28786
Fountain Springs Rd	28786
Fowler Trce	28786
Fox Trl	28786
Fox Chase Rd	28785
Fox Fire Estates Cir	28785
Fox Hill Ln	28785
Fox Run Rd	28786
Foxwood Dr	28785
Frady Ln	28786
Fragrant Pine Dr	28785
Francis Dr & St	28786
Francis Asbury Rd	28785
Francis Farm Rd	28786
Francis Orchard Rd	28786
Frank Davis Rd	28785
Frank Tucker Rd	28785
Franklin St	28786
N Frazier St	28786
Freedom Dr	28786
Freeman Dr & Rd	28786
French Cv	28785
Friendly Acres Dr	28786
Friendship Cir	28786
Frog Holler Rd	28785
Frog Pond	28786
Frontage Park Ave	28786
Frost Pl	28786
Fulbright Rd	28785
Full Moon Cv	28786
Fuller Dr & St	28786
Furry Ln	28786
Gables Pl	28786
Gaddy Hts	28786
Gala Ln	28786
Galax Trl	28785
Gale Wind Dr	28785
Gallant Moose Trl	28785
Galloway St	28786
Garci Dr	28786
Gardner St	28786
Garland St	28786

Street	ZIP
Gateway St	28785
Gatewind Dr	28785
Gator Dr	28785
Gazebo Ln	28786
Gem Dr	28785
Genesis Way	28785
Geneva Ln	28785
Genoa Ln	28786
Gentian Way	28785
Gentman Dr	28785
Gentry Dr	28786
George Sutton Rd	28785
Georges Branch Rd	28785
Georgia Ave	28786
Gerald Dr	28785
Germany Cove Rd	28785
Gibson Dr	28786
Giles Pl	28786
Ginger Ln	28785
Gingerbread Ln	28786
Gingham Dr	28785
Gingko Ln	28786
Ginseng Hollow Ln	28786
Glade Way	28785
Gladioli Pl	28786
Glen Eagle Dr	28786
Glendale Dr	28786
Glenwood Dr	28786
Gliding Hawk Way	28785
Gloria Way	28785
Go Way Rd	28785
Gobbler Ln	28785
Gods Country Rd	28785
Goldenrod Ln	28786
Goldfinch Way	28785
Golf Course Rd	28786
Goodin Ln	28786
Goodson Springs Rd	28786
Goodyear St	28786
Gooseberry Rdg	28785
Gordon Dr	28786
Government St	28786
Grace Ridge Rd	28786
Gracious Ln	28785
Grady Gibson Dr	28786
Graham St	28786
Grahl St	28786
Grahl Roost Rdg	28785
Grand Oak Trl	28785
Grandview Cir, Hts & Ln	28786
Granite Ln	28786
Granite Cliffs Ct	28785
Granny Smith Dr	28786
Grant Dr	28785
Grapeleaf Dr	28786
Grapevine Cove Rd	28785
Grassmere Ln	28786
Grassy Bald Rd	28786
Gray Squirrel Dr	28785
Graybark Ct	28786
Grayden St	28786
Grazing Deer Dr	28785
Great Smoky Mountain Expy	28786
Green Dr	28786
Green Pastures Dr	28786
Green Valley Cir & Rd	28786
Greenbriar Dr	28786
Greenleaf Dr	28785
Greenview Dr	28786
Greenwood Ln	28786
Greg Cir	28786
Grey Fox Ln	28785
Greystone Ln	28786
Griffin Rd	28786
Grimball Ct & Dr	28786
Grindstone Rd	28786
Gristmill Dr	28786
Groundhog Hill Dr	28786
Grouse Ln	28786
Grouse Ridge Rd	28786
Grove Park	28786
Grovers Mtn Trl	28786
Gudger St	28786
Gulley Rd	28786
Gunter Dr	28785
Gusty Knoll Trl	28785
Guy Chambers Rd	28785
Guyer Ln	28786
Gwen St	28786
Hackberry Ln	28785
Hailey Dr	28785
Halcyon Hills Dr	28785
Hale Farm Rd	28786
Halfback Trl	28786
Hall Dr	28785
Hall Top Rd	28786
Hallelujah Dr	28786
Hamer Ave	28786
Hammock Ln	28786
Hampshire Dr	28786
Hampton Ct	28786
Handsome Dr	28785
Hanks Rd	28785
Happy Ln	28786
Happy Acres Rd	28785
Happy Hill Rd	28786
Happy Hills Dr	28786
Happy Hollow Access Rd	28786
Hard Rdg	28785
Harleys Cv	28785
Harmony Ln	28785
Harmony Hill Ln	28786
Harrietts Trl	28786
Harris St	28786
Harris Street Ext	28786
Harvest Dr	28786
Harvey Ln	28785
Hassletime Ln	28785
Hathaway Ln	28785
Haven Park	28786
Hawk Haven Cv	28786
Hawk Mountain Rd	28785
Hawkeye Ln	28786
Hawks Crest Cir, Ct, Dr & Hts	28786
Hawks Lift Dr	28786
Hawktree Ln	28786
Hawthorne Rd	28785
Hayes St	28785
Hayfield Ln	28786
Haynes Holler Dr	28785
Haystack Rd	28785
N & S Haywood St	28786
Haywood Office Park	28786
Hazel St	28786
Hazelview Dr	28786
Hazelwood Ave	28786
Hazen Dr	28785
Head Rd	28786
Heartland Rd	28785
Heath Dr	28786
Heath Peak Rd	28785
Heath Retreat Rd	28786
Heavens Vw	28786
Heavens View Rd	28786
Hedge Way	28786
Heggie Ln	28785
Heidi Ln	28785
Helen Dr	28786
Heliport Dr	28786
Hemlock St	28786
Hemphill Rd	28785
Hendrix St	28786
Hengestone Cv	28786
Henry St	28786
Henry Hollow Ln	28785
Henson Dr	28786
Herbert Trl	28785
Heritage Ct	28785
Hermits Ln	28785
Hickory Dr	28786
Hickory Nut Ln	28786
Hidden Rdg	28786
Hidden Hill Ln	28786
Hidden Hollow Trl	28785
Hidden Oak Ln	28786
Hideaway Ln	28785
High St	28786
High Acres	28786
High Meadow Ln	28786
High Ridge Rd	28786
High Spring Trl	28786
Higher Ground Rdg	28785
Highland Rd	28786
Highland Ridge Dr	28785
N & S Hill St	28786
Hill Farm Ln	28786
Hillbrook Dr	28785
Hillside Rd	28786
Hillside Terrace Dr	28786
Hilltop Dr	28786
Hillview Cir	28786
Hilton Rdg	28785
Historic Oak Trl	28785
Hitching Post Dr	28786
Hodges Dr	28786
Hoglen Rdg	28785
Hollie Hill Dr	28785
Hollon Cv	28785
Hollow Trl	28786
Hollow Tree Ct	28786
Holly Berry Ln	28785
Holly Grove Dr	28786
Holly Ridge Rd	28786
Holstein Farm Rd	28785
Holston Village Rd	28786
Homestead Cove Rd	28786
Homeward Way	28785
Homlish Gdns	28785
Honeybee Way	28786
Honeycomb Dr	28786
Honeysuckle Dr	28786
Hooper Haven Dr	28786
Hoot Hill Rd	28785
Hoot N Holler Way	28785
Hoot Owl Rdg	28786
Hopalong Trce	28785
Hope Cir	28786
Hopper Cv	28786
Horizon Ln	28785
Hornbuckle Dr	28785
Horse Ridge Dr	28785
Horsecart Path Dr	28786
Horseshoe Trce	28785
Hosanna Way	28785
Hospital St	28786
Hound Rdg	28785
Howard Hts	28786
Howell St	28786
Howell Mill Rd	28786
Howling Meadows Ln	28786
Hub Patch Rd	28786
Huckleberry Ln	28785
Hugh Massic Rd	28786
Hugh Massie Rd	28786
Hughes Rd	28786
Humble Rdg	28786
Humingbird Ln	28786
Hummingbird Ln	28785
Hunt Estates Dr	28786
Hunters Crossing Dr	28786
Hy Tech Hts	28786
Hy Vue Dr	28786
Hyacinth Ln	28786
Hyatt St	28786
Hyatt Creek Rd	28786
Hyde St	28786
Hydrangea Dr	28785
Hydro Ln	28786
Idlewild Dr	28786
Idlewood Dr	28786
Impala Dr	28785
Imperial Ct	28785
Independence Dr	28786
Indian Rdg	28786
Indian Hills Loop	28786
Indian Springs Dr	28786
Indian Trail Loop	28786
Indigo Dr	28786
Industrial Park Dr	28786
Inglewood Cove Rd	28786
Inheritance Mountain Rd	28785
Inman Dr	28786
Inman Branch Rd	28786
Intrepid Dr	28786
Inverness Dr	28786
Irene Vernon Dr	28786
Iris Ln	28786
Iron Duff Rd	28785
Iron Will Cv	28785
Ironwood Rdg	28785
Isler Branch Rd	28785
Ithilien Dr	28786
Ivanhoe Ct	28785
Ivy Hills Dr	28785
J And J Farm Rd	28786
J C Rd	28785
Jack Pine Dr	28785
Jacks Way	28785
Jackson Dr	28786
Jacobs Dr	28786
Jade St	28786
Jamaica Way	28785
James Franklin Pl	28785
James Loop Rd	28786
Jan Dr	28785
January Hts	28785
Jarvis St	28786
Jasmine Way	28785
Jaybird Ln	28785
Jaynes Cove Rd	28785
Jefferson Ln	28786
Jeffrey Ln	28785
Jenkins Rd	28785
Jennings Ln	28786
Jenny Rae Ln	28786
Jericho Rdg	28786
Jerry Mcelroy Dr	28785
Jess Man Rd	28786
Jesse James Dr	28786
Jewel Ln	28786
Jf Morris Dr	28786
Jim Moody Dr	28785
Jims Cove Rd	28786
Joe Carver Rd	28785
Joe Davis Rd	28785
Joe Medford Rd	28785
Joe Walker Rd	28786
Joel Cv	28786
John Morrow Rd	28786
John Paul Dr	28785
John Rock Rd	28786
John Vance Rd	28786
Johnson Hill Dr	28785
Johnson Hollow Dr	28785
Jonathan Creek Rd	28785
Jonathan James Cv	28785
Jones Dr	28786
Jordan Dr	28786
Jordan Farm Dr	28786
Josh Hill Dr	28786
Joshua Ln	28786
Josiah Dr	28785
Journeys Way	28785
Joy Ln	28786
Joyce St	28786
Jubilee Way	28785
Judy Ln	28786
Jule Noland Dr	28786
Julia Dr	28785
Jumping Branch Trl	28785
Junaluska Oaks Dr	28785
Junco Trl	28785
Junebug Trl	28785
Juniper Ln	28785
Justice Trl	28785
Kammerer Dr	28785
Kanuga Pl	28785
Kasey Dr	28785
Kathy Dr	28786
Katrina Way	28786
Keaton Rd	28786
Keatons Rd	28785
Keeping Ct	28785
Keeter Rd	28786
Keever Cir	28786
Kel Mil Rd	28785
Keller Hts & St	28786
Kelly Ln & St	28786
Kelly Park Ln	28786
Kelly Springs Rd	28786
Kelso Rd	28785
Kenai Trl	28786
Kendor Ln	28786
Kennel Way	28786
Kent Ln	28786
Kentucky Ave	28786
Kerley St	28786
Kerovac Dr	28786
Kestrel Ct	28785
Key Cir	28785
Keystone Ln	28786
Kilgore Rd	28785
Killian St	28786
Kimberly Ln	28786
King Rd	28786
King Arthur Ct	28786
King Horn Rdg	28785
Kinross Ln	28785
Kirton Ln	28786
Kitty Ln	28785
Kitty Hawk Dr	28785
Knoll Rdg	28785
Knoll Ridge Ln	28785
Knollwood Dr	28786
Knothead Dr	28786
Kudzu Loop	28785
Kylie Ln	28785
L And E Meadows Dr	28786
La Vista Dream Ln	28785
Lab Ln	28786
Ladderback Rdg	28785
Lady Bird Dr	28786
Lady Bug Dr	28786
Ladyslipper Ln	28786
Lagrange Rd	28786
Laguna Ln	28785
Lake Logan Rd	28786
Lakeview Dr	28786
Lamp Post Ln	28786
Lamplighter Dr	28786
Lanes End Dr	28786
Langdale Way	28785
Langford Rd	28786
Lanier Ln	28786
Lanning Dr	28786
Lansing Rd	28786
Lantern Ln	28786
Laramie Ln	28786
Laras St	28786
Larchwood Pt	28786
Lariat Loop	28786
Lark Ct	28786
Larkspur Trl	28786
Lasso Ln	28786
Last Stop Ln	28785
Late September Way	28785
Laughter Ln	28786
Laurel Cir	28786
Laurel Branch Rd	28786
Laurel Ridge Dr	28786
Laurelwood Ln	28786
Lauren Dr	28786
Lavender Spring Ln	28786
Lawson Ln	28786
Layfield Dr	28786
Lazy Cir	28786
Lea Plant Rd	28786
Leaf Ln	28786
Leaping Cat Ln	28786
Leatherwood St	28786
Leatherwood Cove Rd	28785
Ledford Dr	28786
Lee Cir, Rd & St	28786
Legacy Dr	28785
Legion Dr	28786
Leisure Ln	28786
Leming Ln	28786
Lenoir Cir	28785
Lentini Dr	28785
Lenwood Dr	28785
Leo St	28786
Leopard Cir & Dr	28786
Lesco Dr	28785
Lester Ln	28785
Levis Ln	28786
Lewis Dr	28786
Lewis Buchanan Dr	28786
Lexington St	28786
Leyland Path Dr	28785
Libbies Ln	28786
Liberty Rd	28785
Liberty Church Rd	28785
Lickstone Rd	28786
Lighthouse Rd	28786
Lightning Bug Ln	28786
Lilac Ln	28785
Lily Ln	28786
Lima Ln	28785
Limb Ln	28786
Lincoln Way	28785
Lindera Ln	28785
Lindsey Way	28785
Liner Ct & St	28786
Liner Cove Rd	28786
Lingering Shade Ln	28786
Lingermore Dr	28786
Links Ln	28786
Linsonwood Rdg	28786
Lions Den Rd	28785
Lisa Rd	28785
Little Ln	28786
Little Acres Rd	28786
Little Chestnut Dr	28786
Little Cove Rd	28786
Little Horse Rd	28786
Little Mountain Rd	28786
Little Tree Ln	28785
Live Oak Loop	28785
Living Good Ln	28786
Lloyd Mountain Rd	28786
Loafer Ln	28786
Lobelia Ln	28786
Lochmoor Ln	28785
Locust Dr	28786
Locust Grove Dr	28785
Lode Star Ln	28785
Lodge Ln	28786
Lofty Ridge Dr	28786
Lofty View Dr	28785
Log Cabin Rd	28786
Logan Dr	28785
Lois Ln	28786
Lolly Joe Rdg	28785
Lombard St	28786
Lone Rock Ln	28785
Lonely October Rd	28786
Lonesome Dove Rd	28785
Long St	28786
Longridge Ln	28785
Longview Dr	28785
Lono Ln	28786
Lookout Ln	28785
Lorraine Dr	28785
Lost Cv	28785
Lost In The Woods Ln	28786
Lothlorian Rd	28786
Louise Ln	28786
Love Ln	28786
Love Carriage Loop	28785
Lovely Dr	28785
Lovett Ln	28785
Lowe Dr	28786
Lowe Branch Cv	28785
Lowell St	28786
Lucas Dr	28786
Lucky Cv	28785
Lucky Clover Ln	28786
Lum Boone Cir	28786
Lumbard St	28786
Lumber Ln	28785
Lumberton Ridge Rd	28785
Lunar Trace Rd	28786
Lundy Ln	28786
Luska Rdg	28785
Lynn St	28785
Lynne Birch Dr	28786
M And M Dr	28786
Mabelton Pl	28786
Mable Rose Rd	28785
Macallan Dr	28785
Macon St	28786
Macs Ln	28786
Madison Ln	28786
Maelarkin Trl	28785
Magellan Dr	28786
Maggie Dr	28786
Magnola Way	28786
Magnolia Way	28786
Mahan Ln	28786
Mahogany Dr	28786
Maid Knl	28785
E, N, S & W Main St	28786
Maintenance Way	28786
Majestic Ln	28785
Malibu Ln	28786
Mallard Loop	28785
Maloney Ct	28786
Mandolin Ln	28786
Mandy Ln	28785
Mann Dr	28786
Maple St	28786
Maple Grove Dr	28786
Maple Grove Church Rd	28786
Maple Knoll Ln	28786
Maple Lane Loop	28786
Maple Springs Dr	28785
Maranatha Way	28785
Marantha Way	28785
Marblegate Ct	28785
March Hillside Ct	28785
Margaret Ln	28785
Marigold Ct	28786
Marina Cv	28785
Mariville Ln	28786
Marjorie Ln	28786
Market St	28786
Marlin Trl	28785
Marneys Vista Rd	28786
Marquis Ln	28785
Marretta Ln	28786
E & W Marshall St	28786
Martha Way	28785
Martindale Rd	28785
Mary John Dr	28786
Maryland Ln	28786
Mason Hill Dr	28785
Massie Hill Dr	28785
Masterview Ln	28786
Mastiff Hollow Dr	28785
Matheny Acres Dr	28786
Mathis Cir	28786
Mattie Marion Rd	28785
Matties Ln	28786
Mauney Ln	28786
Mauney Cove Rd	28786
Maxima Ln	28786
Maxwell St	28786
Mayali Trl	28785
Mayapple Ln	28786
Mayflower Ct	28785
Mayo Mountain Rd	28786
Maywood Ter	28786
Mccracken St	28786
Mcelroy St	28786
Mcelroy Cove Rd	28785
Mcguires Rdg	28786
Mckay Farm Rd	28786
Mckenzie Pl	28785
Mclean Ln	28786
Mcnabb St	28786
Mead St	28786
Meadow St	28786
Meadow View Cir	28786
Meadowbrook Cir	28786
Meadowind Ct	28786
Meadowlark Ln	28786
Meadowood Cir & Ln	28786
Medcliff Dr	28786
Medford Ave	28786
Medford Farm Rd	28785
Medford Hannah Rd	28785
Medley Dr	28785
Meg Pie Ln	28785
Meghan Ln	28786
Melinda Dr	28786
Mellow Springs Rd	28786

Street	ZIP
Melody Dr	28786
Melrose St	28786
Memory Dr	28786
Mendenhall Dr	28785
Mercy Dr	28785
Merrie Way	28786
Merrimac Cir	28786
Merry Hill Ln	28786
Messer Rd	28786
Meteor Ct	28786
Mexico Dr	28785
Miami Dr	28785
Mica Mine Rd	28786
Micadale Ln	28786
Michael Dr	28785
Michaels Hwy	28786
Michigan Ln	28786
Middle Rdg	28785
Middleton Dr	28786
Midland Dr	28785
Midnight Ln	28786
Mill St	28786
Miller St	28786
Millwood Dr	28785
Milner Ln	28786
Mimi Mills Ln	28785
Mimosa Ln	28786
Miner Rd	28785
Minerva Dr	28785
Minnetonka Rd	28785
Minpin Dr	28786
Mint Dr	28786
Minuet Dr	28785
Mirah Ln	28786
Mississippi Ave	28786
Misti Leigh Ln	28786
Mistletoe Rdg	28786
Misty Mountain Way	28785
Mitchell Ln	28786
Mockingbird Dr	28785
Molasses Way	28785
Monalah Dr	28785
Monarch Sq	28786
Montalto Dr	28785
Montana Stone Trl	28785
Monte Vista Dr	28786
Monteagle Dr	28786
Monterey Pl	28786
Montgomery St	28786
Monticello Dr	28785
Montrose Ln	28785
Moody Dr	28786
Moondust Dr	28786
Moonlight Ln	28786
Moore St	28786
Moore Hill Dr	28786
Moorehill Dr	28786
Moose Dr	28786
Mopey Maple Rd	28785
Morgan St	28786
Morning Dr	28786
Morning Mist Ln	28785
Morning View Rd	28785
Morrow Dr	28785
Morrow Mountain Rd	28785
Mosa Dr	28786
Moss Ct	28786
Mount Olive Rd & St	28786
Mount Valley Rd	28786
Mountain Call Dr	28786
Mountain Cove Est & Rd	28786
Mountain Haven Rd	28786
Mountain Lake Dr	28785
Mountain Laurel Ln	28785
Mountain Mist Ln	28785
Mountain Spring Rd	28786
Mountain View Dr SW	28786
Mountaineer Dr	28786
Mountainside Dr	28786
Mounthaven Ln	28786
Mouzon Rd	28785
Muckle Cove Rd	28785
Mull St	28786
Multiflora Way	28785
Murdock Dr	28785
Murphys Way	28785
Muscadine Ln	28786
Muse St	28786
Muse Business Park	28786
Music Way	28786
Muskogee	28786
Mussie Hill Dr	28786
Mustang Ln	28786
Myers Ln	28786
Myrdice Dr	28786
Mystic Cv	28785
Nags Trl	28786
Nancy Ln	28785
Narcissus Ct	28786
Nathan Dr	28785
Nathaniel Dr	28786
Natural Springs Loop	28786
Nature Ln	28786
Nautilus Dr	28786
Navajo Trl	28786
Nazarene Way	28785
Ned Cove Rd	28785
Neighbors Loop	28785
Nelson Park Dr	28786
Neon Pl	28786
Nesbitt St	28786
Nesting Rdg	28785
Nettie Dr	28786
New Allens Creek Rd	28786
New Ground Trl	28785
New Liberty Dr	28786
Newkirk Rd	28785
Neyland Pl	28786
Nichols Rdg	28786
Nightingale Pl	28786
Ninevah Rd	28786
Ninevah View Dr	28786
Nitro Ln	28786
Noble Ct	28786
Noland Dr	28786
Noland Downs Rd	28786
Noland Gap Rd	28785
Nome Dr	28785
Nora Harrell Dr	28785
Norman St	28786
Norman Heights Dr	28786
Norris St	28786
North Ln	28786
Norway Manor Loop	28786
Nottingham Ln	28785
Nunnehi Trl	28786
Nursery Ln	28785
Nutcracker Ln	28786
Nutmeg Ct	28785
N Oak Ln & St	28786
Oakcrest Ln	28786
Oakdale Dr & Rd	28786
Oakstone Dr	28785
Oakview Dr	28786
Obscure Cv	28785
October Scenic Rd	28786
Ogden Dr	28786
Ola Bea Dr	28785
Old Balsam Rd	28786
Old Clyde Rd	28785
Old Country Rd	28786
Old Fiddle Rd	28785
Old Golf Course Rd	28786
Old Hickory St	28786
Old Orchard Rd	28786
Old River Rd	28786
Old School Rd	28786
Old Time Ln	28786
Oleander Dr	28786
Oliver Dr	28785
Olympia Ln	28786
Opal Ct	28786
Ora Cir	28786
Orchard Dr	28786
Orchard Cove Rd	28785
Orchard View Dr	28786
Orchid Ln	28786
Orion Davis Rd	28786
Oscar Banks Way	28786
Osceola Cir	28786
Oshea Ln	28786
Osprey Loop	28786
Oswego Way	28785
Ottinger Hts	28786
Our Loop	28786
Outpost Ln	28785
Overbrook St	28786
Overlook Ct & Dr	28786
Overlook Farm Ln	28786
Owens Rd	28785
Owl Ridge Rd	28786
Oxner Cove Rd	28786
P J Dr	28786
Pacific Dr	28785
Page Rd	28786
Palmer Rd	28786
Palmer Hill Rd	28786
Palmetto Dr	28785
Palomino Rd	28785
Panda Trl	28785
Panorama Dr	28786
Pansy Pl	28785
Panther Pt	28786
Panther Springs Gap Rd	28785
Paradise Ln	28785
Paragon Pt	28785
Paralee Ln	28786
Park Dr	28786
Parker Pt	28786
Parkview Dr	28786
Parkway View Dr	28786
Parkwood Pl	28786
Parliament Pl	28785
Parrish Farm Rd	28786
Parsley Pl	28786
Parsonage Ct	28786
Parton Dr	28786
Partridge Cir	28786
Pasco Loop	28786
Pastures Dr	28786
Patchen Rd	28786
Patchen Estate Rd	28786
Patered Rd	28785
Pates Ln	28785
Patrick Dr	28786
Patterson Ln	28785
Patton Park Dr	28785
Pavilion Ln	28786
Payne Ln	28786
Peace Mountain Rd	28786
Peaceful Falls Dr	28786
Peachy Keene Pl	28785
Peak Ave	28786
Pearson Rdg	28786
Pebble Brook Dr	28785
Pecan Pl	28785
Peddlers Sq	28786
Peele Rd	28786
Peggy Sue Ln	28785
Pelican Pl	28786
Pennant Ave & Dr	28786
Penny Ln	28785
Peregrine Pl	28786
Periwinkle Park	28786
Persimmon Ct	28786
Peters Cove Rd	28786
Petunia Cir	28786
Pewee Ln	28786
Pheasant Run Cir	28786
Phillips Rd	28786
Phlox Dr	28786
Phoenix Way	28786
Pica Ln	28785
Piccadilly Dr	28786
Piedmont Pl	28786
Piedmont View Dr	28786
Pigeon Rd & St	28786
Pigeon Gap Rd	28786
Pigpen Cove Rd	28786
Pika Ln	28785
Pike Pt	28785
Pilgrim Ln	28785
Pilipinas Dr	28786
N & S Pine Dr & St	28786
Pine Top Ln	28785
Pinecrest Ln	28785
Pinedale Ln	28786
Pinellas Ln	28785
Pineview Dr	28786
Pinewood Dr & Hts	28786
Piney Grove Rd	28786
Piney Mountain Rd	28786
Pink Dogwood Ln	28786
Pinnacle Dr	28786
Pinto Pl	28785
Pioneer Dr	28786
Pippin Ln	28786
Pisgah Dr	28786
Pisgah View Dr	28786
Pitch Fork Cv	28785
Pitts St	28786
Pj Dr	28786
Placid Knoll Dr	28785
Plantation Dr	28786
Plateau Pl	28786
Playground Ct & St	28786
Plaza Pl	28786
Pleasant Hill Cir	28786
Plemmons Park Ln	28786
Plott Hts	28786
Plott Creek Cir & Rd	28786
Plott Mountain Rd	28786
Plott Valley Rd	28786
Plow Pt	28786
Plum Tree Ln	28785
Poindexter Rd	28786
Point Of View Dr	28785
Pointer Trl	28786
Poison Ivy Trl	28785
Polaris Pl	28786
Polk St	28786
Polka Ln	28786
Polly Pl	28786
Pond View Dr	28786
Ponderosa Pl	28785
Pony Dr	28785
Poplar Dr, Loop & St	28786
Poplar Holler Rd	28786
Possum Trot Trl	28786
Pot Leg Rd	28785
Potts Dr	28785
Powderhorn Dr	28786
Precious Metal Dr	28785
Precipice Dr	28785
Preservation Way	28786
Presidential Dr	28786
Pressley Ln	28785
Pretty View Ln	28785
Prevost St	28786
Price Ln	28786
Pride Mountain Rd	28786
Primrose Ln	28786
Princess Pl	28786
Private Cv	28786
Promise Pl	28785
Prosperity Rdg	28785
Proud Merry Trl	28786
Providence Pl	28786
Pruett Ln	28786
Pumpkin Patch Pl	28786
Puppy Dog Rd	28785
Purchase Rd	28786
Pure Point Ct	28786
Putnam St	28786
Quail Rdg	28786
Qualla Rd	28785
Quartz Park	28785
Queen St	28786
Queen Cove Rd	28786
Queens Farm Ln	28786
Quest Ln	28786
Quincy St	28786
Quinlan Dr	28786
R And K Dr	28786
Rabb Dr	28786
Rabbit Skin Rd	28785
Raccoon Rd	28786
Rachael Dr	28785
Racking Horse Ln	28786
Racks Rd	28785
Radio Tower Rd	28785
Ragan Ln	28785
Ragwood Ln	28785
Railroad St	28786
Rainbow St	28786
Rainbow Park Cir	28786
Rainbow Ridge Dr	28786
Raindrop Way	28786
Raintree Rd	28786
Rambling Ridge Rd	28786
Ramp Patch Ln	28786
Ramsey Dr	28785
Ranch Boundary Dr	28785
Randall Rd	28786
Ranger Dr	28786
Ranger Station Rd	28785
Rangeview Ln	28786
Rapid Waters Way	28785
Raspberry Ln	28786
Ratcliff Cove Rd	28786
Rathbone Rd	28785
Raven Rock Dr	28786
Ray St	28786
Ray Wood Dr	28786
Raymond Dr	28786
Raytown Hts	28786
Razorback Rd	28786
Rebe St	28786
Red Bank Rd	28786
Red Barn Ter	28786
Red Maple Dr	28785
Red Oak Ln	28786
Red Snanger Rd	28786
Red Swanger Rd	28786
Redbud Ln	28786
Redsleeve Dr	28786
Reece Rd	28786
Reed Rd	28786
Reed Cove Rd	28786
Reflection Dr	28786
Regents Pl	28785
Regina Ln	28786
Reinertson Dr	28786
Remington Fork Dr	28786
Renegade Rdg	28785
Reservoir Dr	28786
Restoration Way	28786
Retrievers Ln	28786
Return Rd	28785
Rhinehart St	28786
Rhinehart Farm Rd	28786
Rhododendron Dr	28786
Rhonda Rd	28785
Rice Dr	28785
Rich Putnam Dr	28785
Richardson Ct	28786
Richland St	28786
Richland Creek Rd	28785
Riddle Dr	28786
Riddle Branch Dr	28785
N Ridge Dr	28786
Ridge Rd	28786
Ridgecrest Ln	28786
Ridgefield Rd	28786
Ridgetop Rd	28786
Ridgeview Cir	28786
Ridgewood Dr	28786
Ridgewood Estates Dr	28786
Riding High Rd	28785
Riding Horse Trl	28786
Rigdon Ln	28786
Riggins Park	28786
Riley Rdg	28786
Rimesdale Way	28786
Ringer Ln	28785
Rising Sun Rd	28786
River Wind Dr	28785
Riverbend St	28786
Riverview Dr	28785
Roadman Dr	28785
Roaring Creek Ln	28785
Roberta Dr	28785
Roberts Shop Rd	28786
Robin Ln	28786
Robinette Dr	28786
Robinson St	28786
Rock St	28786
Rockin Chair Ln	28785
Rockmont Rd	28785
Rockwood Rd	28786
Rocky Rd	28786
Rocky Branch Rd	28786
Rocky Ford Dr	28786
Rocky Knob Rd	28786
Rodeo Dr	28785
Rogers Dr & St	28786
Rogers Cove Rd	28785
Rolling Dr	28786
Rolling Green Dr	28786
Rome Beauty Rd	28785
Rons Rdg	28785
Rooney Rdg	28785
Rosalee Rd	28785
Rose Ln	28786
Rose Garden Ln	28786
Rose Path Ln	28786
Ross Rd & St	28786
Ross Farm Rd	28786
Roth Stream Dr	28786
Rough Creek Rd	28785
Roundtop Rd	28785
Rountoit Rd	28786
Rovingwood Dr	28786
Roxies Way	28786
Roy Dr	28785
Royal Crest Hts	28786
Rubes Dr	28786
Ruby Park	28785
Ruffed Grouse Ln	28786
Rugged Trl	28786
Rugged Top Rd	28785
Rugrats Ln	28786
Rumble Rd	28786
Rumbling Gap Trl	28786
Runaway Hill Dr	28786
Running Brook Dr	28785
Running Deer Trl	28785
Russ Ave	28786
Russell Dr	28786
Russell Cove Rd	28785
Russell Mountain Rd	28786
Rustic Rd	28786
Rustic Heights Rd	28785
Ruth Ln	28786
Sable Ln	28785
Saddle Ridge Dr	28785
Salamander Cv	28785
Salem Loop	28786
Sams Trl	28786
Sanborn Rd	28786
Sanctuary Dr	28786
Sandow Ln	28785
Sandsridge Way	28785
Sandtrapp Rd	28786
Sanford Dr	28786
Sang Way	28786
Santolina Ln	28785
Sapling Ln	28786
Sara Ridge Rd	28786
Saranac Ln	28785
Sarvice Berry Ln	28785
Sassy Ln	28785
Satinwood Dr	28785
Saunooke Dr & Rd	28786
Savannah Ln	28785
Sawbriar Ln	28786
Sawyer St	28786
Saxony Pl	28786
Scarlet Oak Dr	28785
Scates St	28786
Scenic Cir	28786
School Daze Dr	28786
Scotchmans Rd	28786
Scott St	28786
Screech Owl Cv	28786
Seagraves Ln	28786
Sears Ln	28786
Seasons Vista Ln	28785
Seay Mountain Rd	28785
Secluded Cv	28785
Secret Hollow Ln	28786
Seekhaven Way	28786
Seibert Rd	28786
Semeion Rdg	28786
Seminole Dr	28786
September Ln	28785
Sequoyah Dr	28785
Serendipity Ln	28785
Serenity Dr	28785
Serenity Mountain Rd	28786
Sesame St	28785
Set A Spell Rd	28785
Setting Sun Trl	28786
Settlers Ln	28785
Seymour St	28786
Shackford St	28786
Shadow Ln	28786
Shadowood Ln	28786
Shadrach Ln	28786
Shady Ln	28786
Shady Rest Dr	28785
Shady Ridge Rd	28785
Shadyside Dr	28785
Shadyview Way	28786
Shagbark Ln	28785
Shallow Dr	28786
Shamrock Ln	28786
Shannon Pl	28786
Sheep Ln	28786
Sheep Pasture Rd	28785
Sheila Dr	28785
Shelby Ln	28786
Shelton St	28786
Shelton Cove Rd	28786
Shena Dr	28785
Shenandoah Dr	28786
Shepherd Hill Ln	28786
Sherman Way	28786
Sherriff Dr	28786
Sherrill Dr	28786
Sherwood Trl	28786
Shetley Rd	28785
Shiloh Trl	28786
Shiners Trl	28786
Shingle Cove Rd	28786
Shining Rock Trl	28786
Shogun Pl	28785
Shondra Dr	28785
Shooting Star Rd	28786
Short St	28786
Shovel Creek Rd	28786
Shulers Ct	28786
Sierra Pt	28786
Signature Blvd	28785
Sigogglin Trl	28785
Silent Acres Rd	28785
Silo Acres Dr	28785
Silo Ridge Rd	28786
Silver Maple Ln	28786
Silverbell Ln	28786
Silverleaf Cir	28786
Silverweed Pt	28786
Silverwood Dr	28785
Simplicity Way	28785
Simpson Trl	28786
Sims Cir	28786
Singingwater Ln	28785
Singlefoot Ln	28786
Singleton Dr	28785
Sisk Ln	28786
Skipping Stone Way	28786
Skyland Rd	28786
Skylark Hts & Ln	28786
Skyline Dr	28786
Skyview Dr	28786
Sleepy Hollow Dr	28785
Slick Holler Dr	28786
Slippery Rock Rd	28785
Sloan Dr	28786
Slow Pace Ln	28785
Smathers St	28786
Smathers Branch Dr	28786
Smith Dr	28786
Smith Meadows Dr	28786
Smokemont Dr	28786
Smokey Hill Dr	28786
Smokey Hollow Dr	28785
Smokey Mountain Sanctuary	28786
Smokey Pines Dr	28786

Smokey Ridge Loop 28786
Smokies Rdg 28786
Smoky Ln 28786
Snakes Loop 28785
Snapdragon Ln 28785
Sneaking Creek Rd 28786
Snowden Field Rd 28786
Snowy Hill Rd 28785
Snyder Cir 28786
Snyder Farm Rd 28786
Soaring Mtn 28786
Soft Creek Ln 28786
Soft Winds Dr 28785
Solid Rock Ln 28785
Solitary Meadow Cir 28786
Solomon St 28786
Solstice Way 28786
Son Country Ln 28785
Sonata Ln 28785
Songbird Trl 28785
Sonoma Cir & Rd 28786
Sonora Ln 28786
Sorghum Dr 28785
Sorrells Cove Rd 28786
Sour Apple Ln 28786
Sourwood St 28786
Southern Way 28785
Southfork Rd 28785
Sparkleberry Rdg 28785
Sparks Dr 28786
Sparrow Dr 28786
Spellbound Rd 28785
Spice Ridge Rd 28786
Spirea Dr 28785
Spirit Mountain Rd 28786
Splendor Rdg 28785
Split Rail Ln 28786
Spring Cove Rd 28786
Spring Creek Dr 28786
Spring Valley Dr 28786
Springbrook Farm Rd 28786
Springview Dr 28786
Spruce St 28786
Spy Rock Rd 28785
Squaw Ridge Rd 28786
Ss Ln 28786
St Andrews Rd 28786
Stack Rock Trl 28785
Staghorn Dr 28785
Stamey Cove Rd 28786
Standing Rock Trl 28786
Star Crest Dr 28785
Starlight Dr 28786
Starnes Ridge Dr 28786
Staymon Rd 28786
Stealth Dr 28786
Steely Dan Dr 28785
Steep Trl 28786
Steep Hill Rd 28785
Steeple View Rdg 28786
Steinwald Trl 28786
Stephens Rd 28786
Stepping Stone Ln 28786
Sterling Way 28785
Stetson Trl 28785
Stevens Creek Rd 28785
Stevenson Cove Rd 28785
Stewart Rd 28786
Stick Weed Trl 28785
Stiles Rd 28786
Stillhouse Cove Rd 28785
Stillwater Dr 28786
Stone Haven Dr 28786
Stonecrest Hts & Ln 28786
Stoneridge Rd 28785
Stonewall Way 28786
Stoney Brook Ln 28786
Stovall St 28786
Stratford Dr 28786
Strauss Ln 28785
Strawberry Pl 28786
Streamside Dr 28785
Streamwood Cir 28786
Strickland Dr 28785
Strollers Ln 28785
Stroup Ridge Rd 28785
Stucco Rd 28786
Studio Ln 28785
Styles Rd 28786
Suburban Loop 28786
Sugar Maple Way 28785
Sugar Mountain Rd 28785
Sulphur Springs Rd 28786
Summer Way 28786
Summer Place Dr 28786
Summit Rdg & St 28786
Sun Country Ln 28785
Sunburst Dr 28786
Sundown Way 28785
Sunflower Ln 28785
Sunny Dr 28786
Sunny Acres Pl 28786
Sunnyside Rd 28786
Sunray Ct 28786
Sunrise Ln 28786
Sunset Dr 28786
Sunshine Cove Rd 28785
Surrey Rd 28786
Surveyors Pt 28785
Susie Ln 28786
Suttles Dr 28786
Sutton Loop 28786
Sutton Town Rd 28786
Suyeta Park Dr 28786
Swag Rd 28785
Swanger Ln 28786
Sweetbay Cv 28786
Sweethart Pl 28786
Sweetwater Ln 28786
Sycamore Ln 28786
Sylvan Dr & St 28786
Sylvan Acres Rd 28785
Symphony Ln 28786
Tacoma Trl 28786
Tadpole Ln 28785
Tahoe Dr 28786
Tall Pines Dr 28785
Tall Timbers Ln 28785
Talon Ct 28786
Tam Dr 28786
Tanglewood Rd 28786
Tango Ln 28785
Tannehill Ln 28786
Tanner Trl 28785
Tap Root Dr 28786
Tara Nova Dr 28786
Tarheel Dr 28786
Tarragon Pl 28786
Tate St 28786
Tater Patch Rd 28785
Taylor Ave 28786
Taylor Hill Dr 28786
Teaberry Ridge Rd 28785
Teague Loop 28786
Tedder Ln 28785
Tee Box Way 28786
Tempest Dr 28786
Teresa Trl 28786
Terrell Ln & St 28786
Tessa Ln 28786
Test Farm Rd 28786
Thankful Rdg 28785
The High Rd 28786
Thistle Ln 28786
Thomas Coke Dr 28785
Thomas Park Dr 28786
Thomasine Dr 28786
Thornapple Ln 28786
Thornton Dr 28785
Thoroughbred Trl 28785
Thrush Ct 28786
Thump Keg Cv 28785
Thunder Rd 28785
Thurman Evans Trl 28785
Tibi Ln 28786
Tierza Ln 28785
Tiffany Ln 28786
Tiger Lily Ln 28786
Tiger Mountain Rd 28786
Tightrun Gap Rd 28786
Tillarock Ln 28785
Timber Creek Dr 28786
Timberbarn Trl 28785
Timbergrove Ln 28786
Timberlane Rd 28786
Timothy Ln 28786
Timucua Trl 28786
Tipperary Trl 28786
Tipstill Cv 28786
Titleist Dr 28786
Tobacco Rd 28785
Tomahawk Rdg 28785
Tommy Boyd Rd 28785
Tommys Dr 28786
Tony Ln 28786
Top View Dr 28786
Topaz Dr 28786
Torda Trce 28786
Tortoise Trl 28785
Tosco Dr 28786
Touchstone Dr 28786
Tower Ln 28786
Towhee Ln 28786
Town Center Loop 28786
Town N Country Dr 28786
Tracking Elk Trl 28785
Tractor Trl 28786
Tracy Ln 28786
Traders Pl 28786
Trails End Dr & Ln 28785
Trambley Dr 28786
Tranquil Ln & Loop 28786
Trantham Dr 28786
Trantham Cove Rd 28786
Trapper Ln 28785
Travelers Pt 28785
Treasure Trce 28786
Treble Clef Ln 28786
Tree Line Trl 28786
Tree Top Ln 28785
Tri Lakes Dr 28786
Trials Gap Dr 28786
Trickle Creek Rd 28785
Trigger Rdg 28786
Trillium End Ln 28786
Trinity Pl 28786
Triple B Cir 28786
Triple Springs Ln 28786
Triston Dr 28785
Triton Ln 28785
Trois Lesbouche Loop 28786
Trotters Trl 28785
Trout Cove Rd 28785
Trout Stream Cir 28785
Troy Ct 28786
Truckers Cove Rd 28786
Trudy Ln 28786
Trull Ln 28786
Tsali Dr 28786
Tuckaway Rd 28786
Tug Fork Trl 28786
Tuka Loop 28785
Tulip Tree Ln 28786
Tumbleweed Trl 28785
Tumbling Fork Rd 28785
Turkey Trl 28786
Turkey Hollow Ct 28786
Turn About Ct 28785
Turner Ln & Rd 28785
Turning Leaf Ln 28786
Turnpike Rdg 28785
Turquoise Way 28786
Tuscola Ave & Rd 28786
Tuscola School Rd 28786
Twig Ln 28785
Twilight Dr 28785
Twin Brook Dr 28785
Twin Maple Ln 28786
Twin Spring Dr 28786
Twinkle Star Dr 28786
Twisted Trl 28786
Ty Lea Dr 28786
Tyler Rd 28786
Unagusta St 28786
Underwood Dr 28786
Underwood Cove Rd 28786
Unique Way 28785
Unity Dr 28786
Upchurch Rd 28786
Upper Scenic Cir 28786
Upward Way 28785
Utah Mountain Rd 28785
Utopia Ct 28785
Vacation Pt 28785
Valley Cove Pl 28785
Valley Fork Dr 28785
Valley Overlook 28786
Valley View Cir & Ter 28786
Valleybrook Ln 28785
Van Tassel Dr 28786
Vance St 28786
Varrieur Branch Rd 28785
Vaughn Cove Rd 28786
Veery Rd 28785
Venezia Way 28786
Ventura Dr 28785
Vera Lee Rd 28785
Veranda Dr 28786
Verlynne Ln 28785
Vermont Dr 28786
Vernon Ln 28786
Vero Ln 28786
Vesie Etta Way 28785
Victoria Way 28786
Victoria Rose Ln 28785
Victory St 28786
Viewpoint Dr 28785
Vigoro St 28786
Viking Dr 28786
Villa Ct 28786
Village Ln 28786
Vinewood Dr 28785
Vintage Dr 28785
Violet Rdg 28785
Vireo Ln 28785
Virginia Ave 28786
Vista Rd 28786
Vizsla Way 28786
Volley Ct 28786
Voyager St 28786
Wagon Wheel Cir 28785
Wahoo Dr 28785
Wahwah Way 28785
Wake St 28786
Wake Robin Rd 28785
Waldonpond Pl 28786
Walenty Trl 28785
Walkabout Ct 28785
Walker Rd 28786
Walking Horse Ln 28785
Wall St 28786
Wallace Ln 28786
Walnut St 28786
Walnut Cove Rd 28785
Walnut Creek Rd 28786
Walnut Ford Rd 28786
Walnut Holler Dr 28785
Walnut Trail Rd 28785
Walnut Valley Ln 28785
Walter Rd 28786
Walter C Rd 28785
Walts Path Way 28786
Wandering Rose Rdg 28785
Wapiti Dr 28785
Waring Way 28785
Warm Cv 28786
Warren St 28786
Warren Messer Dr 28785
Warwick Loop 28785
Water St 28786
Water Rock Cir 28785
Waterbrook Dr 28785
Watkins Harpe Dr 28786
Waverly Dr 28786
Way Up Yonder Rd 28786
Wayne St 28786
Waynesville Plz 28786
Wayneview Dr 28786
Waynewood Dr 28786
Wayview Pl 28785
We Too Ln 28786
Weathering Hts 28785
Weatherwatch Ln 28785
Weatherwood Ln 28786
Wedgewood Rd 28785
Wee Too Ln 28786
Weeping Willow Ln 28785
S Welch St 28786
Welch Farm Rd 28786
Welch Street Ext 28786
Welcome Ln 28786
Weldith Hts 28785
Wells Rd 28785
Welsh Rd 28786
Wenlock Way 28785
Wertz Dr 28786
Wesley Way 28785
Wessill Way 28785
West St 28786
Westbrook Dr 28786
Westend Cir 28785
Westream Dr 28786
Westview St 28786
Westwood Cir 28786
Wet Stone Trl 28786
Wet Weather Dr 28786
Wheatgrass Loop 28785
Whigham Ln 28786
Whipoorwill Way 28786
Whispering Hill Dr 28786
Whispering Pines Dr 28786
Whispering Winds Rd 28785
Whistle Ridge Rd 28785
White Rdg 28785
White Mountain Rd 28785
White Oak Dr 28786
White Oak Rd 28785
White Pine Dr 28786
Whitner Dr 28786
Wick Way 28785
Wiggins Dr 28786
Wild Turkey Run Rd 28785
Wildcat Mountain Rd 28786
Wilderness Trl 28786
Wildflower Ln 28786
Wildrose Dr & Rd 28786
Wildwood Way 28785
Wiley Franklin Rd 28786
Wilfred Way 28785
Wilkhaven Trl 28785
Wilkinson Pass Ln 28786
Will Hyatt Rd 28786
Williams St 28786
Willie Bills Ln 28786
Willow Rd 28786
Willow Brook Garden Dr 28786
Wills Way 28786
Wilson Dr 28786
Winchester Dr 28785
Winchester Creek Rd 28786
Windalier Ln 28786
Windfall Ln 28785
Winding Creek Dr 28786
Windingwood Trl 28786
Windmeadow Dr 28786
Windmere Trce 28785
Windsong Dr 28785
Windsor Ln 28786
Windswept Way 28785
Windy Rdg 28785
Windy Hill Dr 28786
Winesap Ln 28786
Winghaven Hts 28786
Winngray Ln 28785
Winslow Rd 28786
Winston Way 28785
Winter John Cv 28786
Winterberry Dr 28786
Winthrop Rd 28785
Wishbone Ln 28785
Wispy Willow Dr 28786
Wisteria Way 28786
Witch Way 28785
Wits End Way 28785
Wj Rd 28785
Wolfpen Rd 28786
Wolverine Ct 28785
Woodbine Rd 28785
Woodchuck Way 28786
Woodfield Dr 28786
Woodland Dr 28786
Woodlaurel Ln 28785
Woodmore Dr 28785
Woods Rd 28785
Woods Edge Rd 28786
Woodsedge St 28786
Woodside Cir 28786
Woodstream Rd 28786
Woodview Dr 28786
Woody Ln 28786
Woolsey Hts 28786
Worsham Dr 28786
Woven Cloud Ln 28785
Wren Way 28786
Wrestling Dr 28785
Wrights Rdg 28786
Wyatt Ln 28786
Yarborough St 28786
Yarrow Rd 28785
Yates Cove Rd 28785
Yellow Locust Dr 28786
Yellow Patch Rd 28785
Yellowood Rd 28785
Yonah Trl 28785
York Dr 28786
Yorkshire Rd 28786
Young Way 28786
Zemery Ln 28786
Zemery Caldwell Rd 28786
Zenith Dr 28785
Zurich Ln 28785

NUMBERED STREETS

1st St 28786
2nd St 28786
4th St 28786
5th St 28786
6th St 28786
7th St 28786
96 Trl 28785

WILMINGTON NC

General Delivery 28402

POST OFFICE BOXES MAIN OFFICE STATIONS AND BRANCHES

Box No.s
1 - 2896 28402
3001 - 7980 28406
9000 - 9025 28402
9998 - 9998 28412
10001 - 11438 28404
12001 - 12998 28405
15001 - 16718 28408
18000 - 18000 28406
20001 - 28399 28407
28401 - 28401 28401
28402 - 28402 28402
28403 - 28403 28403
28405 - 28405 28405
28411 - 28411 28411
28412 - 28412 28412
28500 - 29740 28407
99721 - 99997 28402

RURAL ROUTES

36 28405

NAMED STREETS

Abalone Dr 28411
Abbey Ln 28411
Abbey Glen Way 28411
Abbington Ter 28403
Abc Aly 28401
Abernethy Ct 28405
Acacia Dr 28403
Academy Cv 28403
Acer Ct 28411
Acorn Branch Rd 28405
Acres Dr 28411
Adams St 28401
Addenbury Ct 28409
Adelaide Dr 28412
Adele Ct 28412
Adonis Ct 28405
Aftonshire Dr 28412
Ainsdale Ct 28405
W Airlie Pl & Rd 28403
Airlie Brook Dr 28403
Airlie Forest Ct 28403
Airlie Oaks Ln 28403
Airport Blvd 28405
Alabama Ave 28401
Alamance Ct & Way 28411
Alameda Dr 28412
Alamosa Dr 28411
Alandale Dr 28405
Albemarle Rd 28405
Albert Cir 28403
Alcoa Way 28411
Alden Ct 28412
Alder Ridge Rd 28412
Aldrich Ln 28411
Alestone Dr 28411
Alexander Pl & Rd 28411
Alexandria Ct 28412
Alexis Ct 28409
Alida Pl 28409
Allens Ln 28403
Aloft Way 28411
Aloha Ln 28403
Alpine Dr 28403
Althea Way 28405
Amaryllis Dr 28411
Amber Dr 28409
Amberjack Ln 28405
Amberleigh Dr 28411
Ambleside Dr 28409
Amelia Ct 28405
Amesbury Ct 28411
Amhearst Ct 28412
Amity Way 28411
Ammons Dr 28405
Amphitheater Dr 28401
Amsden Ct 28412
Amsterdam Way 28405
Amy Dr 28403
Anaca Point Rd 28411
Anchors Bend Way 28411
Anderson St 28401
Andover Cir & Rd 28403
Andrews Reach Loop 28409
Andros Ln 28412
Angel Island Rd 28412
Angelfish Ln 28405
Anglewood Pl 28405
Ann St
1-1699 28401
1700-1999 28403
Anna Pennington Dr 28405
Anne Dr 28403
Anson Dr 28405
Answorth Ct 28405
Antares Rd 28405
Antelope Trl 28409
Antietam Dr 28409
Antilles Ct 28405
Antler Dr 28409
Antoinette Dr 28412
Apache Trl 28409
Apollo Dr 28405
Appaloosa Trl 28411
Appleton Way 28412
Appomattox Dr 28409
Aqua Dr 28409
Aqua Vista Dr 28409
Aqua Vista Farms 28409
Aquarius Dr 28411
Arbor Way 28409
Arboretum Dr 28405

Archdale Rd 28411
Archer Dr 28409
Arden Rd 28403
Ardley Ct 28409
Argonne Ct 28412
Arizona Ave 28401
Arjean Dr 28411
Arlington Dr 28401
Armada Ln & Pl 28405
Armstrong Rd 28401
N & S Arnlea Ct 28409
Arnold Rd 28412
Arrow Ct 28412
Artifact Ct 28411
Ascott Pl 28403
Ashborne Ct 28405
Ashbrook Dr 28403
Ashby Dr 28411
Ashe St 28401
Ashes Dr 28405
Asheton Rd 28411
Ashford Ave 28405
Ashland Ct 28405
Ashley Cir 28403
Ashley Park Dr 28412
Ashton Ct & Dr 28412
Ashworth Manor Ct 28412
Aster Ct 28409
Athena Ct 28411
Athens Ln 28405
Atlantic Dr 28411
Atlantis Ct 28403
Aubreys Aly 28401
Auburn Ln 28405
Audubon Blvd 28403
Aurora Pl 28405
Austin Ct 28411
Autumn Dr 28409
Autumn Crest Pl 28405
Autumn Hall Dr 28403
Autumn Leaves Ct 28411
Avalon Ave 28409
Avant Dr 28411
Avenel Dr 28411
Avenshire Cir 28412
Aventuras Dr 28409
Aviation Rd 28405
Avine Ct 28409
Avocet Ct 28411
Avon Ct 28405
Avondale Ave 28403
Azalea Dr
300-399 28409
1600-1899 28403
Backfin Pt 28411
Bagley Ave
100-199 28403
200-399 28409
Bahia Honda Dr 28412
Bailey Ave 28411
Bailey Buck Rd 28409
Bailey Harbor Ln 28411
Bailiwyck Way 28409
Bainridge Ct 28412
Bala Ln 28409
Bald Eagle Ln 28411
Balfoure Dr 28412
Balmoral Pl 28405
Balsam Dr 28409
Bancroft Dr 28412
Banded Tulip Dr 28412
E Bank Rd 28412
Banks Rd 28411
Banyan Trl 28411
Bar Harbor Dr 28403
Barclay Dr 28403
Barclay Hills Dr 28405
Bardmoor Cir 28411
Barefoot Dr 28403
Barkley Ave 28403
Barksdale Rd 28409
Barkwood Ct 28411
Barlow Ct 28409
Barnard Dr 28405
Barnards Landing Rd 28412
Barnett Ave 28403
Barnette Ln 28405
Barnsley Ct 28411
Barouche Ct 28412
Barren Inlet Rd 28411
Barton Oaks Dr 28409
Basset Ct 28411
Batsonwood Ct 28405
Battery Pl 28403
Battleship Rd 28401
Bavarian Ln 28405
Bay Blossom Dr 28411
Bay Branch Cir 28405
Bay Colony Ln 28405
Bay Cove Ln 28411
Bay Gull Ct 28405
Bay Head Cir 28405
Bayberry Pl 28411
Baycreek Dr 28405
Bayfield Dr 28411
Baylor Dr 28412
Baypointe Cv 28411
Bayshore Dr 28411
Bayside Cir E & W 28405
Baytree Rd 28409
Baywood Dr 28403
Beach Rd N & S 28411
Beach Bay Ln E & W 28411
Beach Mountain Ct 28405
Beachcomber Ct 28411
Beagle Trl 28409
Beamon Ln 28412
Bear Ct 28403
Bear Hunt Ct 28411
Beasley Rd 28409
Beattrice Rd 28412
Beau Rivage Dr 28412
Beaufort Ct 28411
Beaumont Ct 28412
Beauregard Dr 28412
Beaver Creek Ct 28409
Beawood Rd 28411
Beddoes Dr 28411
E & W Bedford Rd 28411
Bedford Forest Dr 28412
Bedminister Ln 28405
Bedrock Ct 28411
Beech St 28405
Beechcliff Dr 28409
Beeston Ct 28411
Bel Arbor 28403
Belgrave Cir 28403
Belhaven Dr 28411
Bell St 28401
Bella Sera Way 28411
Bellamy Aly 28401
Bellamy Parke Way 28412
Belle Ct 28411
Bellevue Ct 28405
Bellflower Ct 28412
Bellwood Ct 28412
Belmont Cir & Ct 28405
Belvedere Dr 28405
Benchmark Ct 28409
Benefield Dr 28409
Benfield Ct 28409
Benjamin Ave 28403
Bennington Pl 28412
Bent Creek Dr 28405
Bent Tree Ct 28405
Bent Twig Ct 28411
Bentley Dr 28409
Bentley Gardens Ln 28409
Berberis Way 28412
Beresford Ct 28409
Beretta Way 28409
Berkley Dr 28405
Bermuda Dr 28401
Bernhardt Ct 28409
Berridge Dr 28412
Berry Ct 28412
Bertha Rd 28411
Berwyn Rd 28409
Bess St 28401
Bethea Ln 28403
Bethel Rd 28409
Betten Court Aly 28401
Beval Rd 28401
Bexley Dr 28412
Bickett Ct 28411
Big Bay Dr 28409
Big Cypress Dr 28409
Big Gum Rd 28411
Big Horn Ct 28411
Billmark Dr 28409
Binford Ct 28405
Birch Ct 28409
Birch Creek Dr 28403
Birchbark Ct 28411
Birchwood Dr 28405
Bird Dog Ct 28411
Birdie Ln 28405
Birds Nest Ct 28405
Biscayne Dr 28411
E & W Bishop Ct 28412
Bittern Ct 28403
Black Chestnut Dr 28405
Black Diamond Dr 28411
Black Horse Trl 28412
Black Wing Ln 28403
E & W Blackbeard Rd 28409
Blackberry Rd 28405
Blackbrook Ln 28409
Blackburn Ct 28411
Bladen St 28401
Blake Trl 28409
Bland St 28401
Blenheim Pl 28409
Blockade Ct 28411
Bloom Aly 28401
Bloomfield Ln 28412
Bloomington Ln 28411
Bloomsbury Ct 28411
Blount Dr 28411
Blue Clay Rd 28405
Blue Grass Ct 28409
Blue Heron Dr E & W 28411
Blue Jay Ct 28409
Blue Point Dr 28411
Blue Tick Ct 28411
Blue Wing Ct 28409
Bluebell Ct 28409
Blueberry Rd 28405
Bluebird Ln 28409
Bluff Ct 28411
Bluffton Ct 28411
Blythe Rd 28403
Boardwalk Ave 28403
Boathouse Rd 28403
Boatswain Pl 28405
Bobby Jones Dr 28412
Bodega Bay Rd 28412
Bogey Dr 28405
Bohicket Way 28409
Bon Aire Rd 28412
Bonaventure Dr 28411
Bonfire Dr 28409
Bonham Ave 28403
Boone Ln 28411
Booth Bay Ct 28411
Bordeaux Ave 28401
Borden Ave 28403
Bors Run 28403
Botsford Ct 28412
Bougainville Way 28409
Boundary St 28405
Bouquet Ct 28409
Bow Hunter Dr 28411
Bowens Ln 28401
Bozeman Rd 28412
Bracken Fern Dr 28405
Bradbury Ct 28412
Braddock St 28409
Bradfield Ct 28411
Bradford Rd 28409
Bradley Dr 28409
Bradley Creek Point Rd 28403
N & S Bradley Overlook 28403
Bradley Pines Dr 28403
Braemar Ln 28409
Bragg Dr
701-799 28412
800-3499 28409
Bramton Rd 28405
S Branch Rd 28411
Brandon Rd 28405
Brandy Ct 28405
E & W Brandywine Cir 28411
Branford Rd 28412
Brantley Ct 28412
Brantwood Ct 28411
Brascote Ln 28412
Brass Eagle Ct 28409
Braxlo Ln 28409
Brays Dr 28411
Breadon Ct 28411
Breckenridge Dr 28412
Brecknock Ct 28412
Breedon Ct 28405
Breeland Ct 28412
Breeze Way 28409
Breezewood Dr 28412
Brenda Dr 28409
Brenton Ct 28412
Brentwood Dr 28401
Brenwood Ct 28409
Bretonshire Rd 28405
Brevard Dr 28405
Brewster Ln 28412
Brewton Ct 28403
Briarcliff Cir 28411
Briarcliff Dr 28409
Briarcreek Way 28411
Brickle Ave 28403
Bridge Rd 28411
Bridgeport Dr 28405
Bridgeton Ct 28411
Bridgewater Cv 28411
Bridle Ct 28411
Brief Rd 28411
Briercrest Dr 28405
Brierwood Rd 28405
Brigantine Dr 28405
Bright Leaf Rd 28411
Brighton Rd 28409
Brightwood Ct & Rd 28409
Brinkman Dr 28405
Brisbane Ct 28405
Bristol Rd 28409
Britford Ct 28409
Brittain Dr 28409
Brittany Lakes Dr 28411
Broad St 28403
Brockway Rd 28411
Brodick Ct 28411
Broken Limb Ct 28405
Brookbend Dr 28411
Brookfield Dr 28405
Brookforest Rd 28409
Brookhaven Rd 28403
Brooklyn Ln 28401
Brookmere Ct 28411
Brooks Aly 28401
Brooks Rd 28405
Brookshire Ln 28409
Brookside Gardens Dr 28411
Brookview Rd 28409
Brookwood Ave 28403
Brougham Dr 28412
Brown Pelican Ln 28409
Browning Dr 28405
Brownlow Cir 28409
Browns Aly 28401
Brucemont Dr 28405
Brunswick St 28401
Bryan Ave 28403
Bryan Rd 28412
Bryce Ct 28405
Buccaneer Rd 28409
Buckeye Dr 28411
Buckhorn Ct 28411
Buckhurst Ct & Dr 28411
Buckingham Ave 28401
Buckner Dr 28412
Buddy Rd 28405
Buena Vista Cir 28411
Buff Cir 28411
Buffington Pl 28409
Bull St 28403
Bullitt Ln 28409
Bump Along Rd 28411
Bunche St 28405
Bunting Dr 28403
Burbank Rd 28412
Burke Ave 28403
Burnett Blvd 28401
Burnett Rd 28409
Burney St 28412
Burning Tree Rd 28409
Burnt Mill Dr 28403
Burroughs Dr 28412
Burton Ln 28409
Business Dr 28405
Butler Ct 28412
Butler National Ln 28411
Butterclam Ct 28405
Butterfly Ct 28405
Butternut Ct 28409
Buxton Rd 28409
Cabbage Inlet Ln 28409
Cable Car Ln 28403
Cabot Dr 28405
Cactus Dr & Ln 28405
Caddy Cir 28405
Cadfel Ct 28412
Caesar Ct 28405
Caicos Ct 28405
Cain Ct 28409
Cainslash Ct 28405
Calabash Ct 28405
Calais Cir 28409
Calder Ct 28405
Cale Ct 28411
Calhoun Dr 28412
Caliber Ct 28405
Calico Xing 28411
Callawasse Island Dr 28411
Callie Ct 28409
Calvert Pl 28403
Cambridge Dr 28403
Camden Cir 28403
Camellia Dr 28403
Camellia Ln 28409
Camelot Ct 28409
Cameo Ct 28409
Cameron Ct 28401
Camp Wright Rd 28409
Campbell St 28401
Campus Cv 28403
Campus View Cir 28403
Camway Dr 28403
Canady Rd 28411
Canal St 28405
Candlewood Dr 28411
Cando St 28405
Canetuck Rd 28411
Cannon Rd 28411
S Canterbury Rd 28403
Canterwood Dr 28401
Cantwell Rd 28411
Cape Blvd 28412
Cape Fear Blvd 28401
Cape Harbor Dr 28411
Capeside Dr 28412
Capital Dr 28405
Capps Ct 28409
Capps Rd 28411
Capri Dr 28403
Captain Dexter Wynd 28411
Captains Ln 28409
Captiva Ct 28412
Carabas Ct 28412
N Cardinal Dr 28405
S Cardinal Dr 28403
Cardinal Drive Ext 28405
Caribe Ct 28409
Carl St 28403
Carl Seitter Dr 28401
Carleton Dr 28403
Carlton Ave 28403
Carlyle Ln 28405
Carmalia Ct 28411
Carmel Trl 28411
Carnation Ct 28401
Carol St 28412
Carolina Ave 28403
N Carolina Ave 28401
S Carolina Ave 28401
Carolina Beach Rd
1700-2599 28401
2600-5700 28412
5675-5675 28408
5701-8199 28412
5702-8198 28412
Carolina Inlet Acres Rd 28412
Carolyn Dr 28409
Carretta Ct 28412
Carrington Ct 28409
Carter Ave
1-99 28405
6500-6699 28411
Carthage Dr 28405
Carya Dr 28412
Cascade Rd 28409
W Cascade Rd 28412
Cashew Ct 28411
Caspian Ct 28411
Cassidy Dr 28409
Cassimir Pl 28412
Castine Way 28412
Castle St
1-1699 28401
1700-2199 28403
Castle Creek Ln 28401
Castle Hayne Rd 28401
Castleberry Ct 28412
Castleboro Ct 28411
Castlewood Dr 28409
Caswell St 28403
Catamaran Dr 28412
Cathay Rd 28412
Cauthen Way 28411
Cavalier Dr
1-99 28405
100-399 28403
Cayman Ct 28405
Cazaux Ct 28409
Cedar Ave 28403
Cedar Blf 28409
Cedar Is 28409
Cedar Branch Ln 28403
Cedar Find Cv 28411
Cedar Hope Cv 28411
Cedar Landing Rd 28409
Cedar Ramble Ln 28411
Cedar Ridge Dr 28405
Cedarwood Ln 28403
Celline Ct 28409
Centallion Ct 28411
Central Ave 28405
Central Blvd 28401
Chablis Way 28411
Chadsford Ct 28412
Chadwick Ave 28401
Chalfont Cir 28405
Chalice Ln 28409
Chalmers Dr 28409
Chamberlain Ln 28409
Champ Davis Rd 28411
Champion Hills Dr 28411
Champlain Rd 28412
Chancellorsville Dr 28409
Chancery Pl 28409
Chandler Dr 28405
N & S Channel Haven Dr 28409
Chanticleer Ct 28409
Chapel Way 28405
Chappell Ave 28412
Chapra Dr 28412
Chariot Ct 28412
Charles Langdon Rd 28411
Charles Paine Dr 28412
Charred Pine Dr 28411
Chart House Dr 28405
Charter Dr 28403
Chase Ln 28411
N Chase Pkwy W 28405
Chatham Pl 28412
Chattooga Pl 28412
Chaucer Dr 28405
Chelon Ave 28409
Chelsea Ln 28409
Chelwood Ct 28412
Cheney Pl 28412
Cheraw Ct 28411
Cherokee Trl 28409
Cherry Ave 28403
Cherry Hill Ct 28409
Cherry Laurel Ct 28405
Cheryl Ln 28405
Chesapeake Ct 28411
Cheshire Pl 28412
Chester Ave & St 28405
Chestnut St
1-1699 28401
1700-2999 28405
Chewning St 28411
Cheyenne Trl 28409
Chilcot Ln 28409
Childers Ct 28412
Chilmark Ct 28412
Chimney Ln 28409
Chipley Dr 28411
Chippenham Dr 28412
Chipshot Way 28412
Chisholm Dr 28405
Chissom Rd 28409
W Chop Way 28412
Chorley Rd 28412
Chowning Pl 28409
Christa Dr 28409
Christian Dr 28403
Christy Cir 28411
Chukka Way 28409
Chula Vista Dr 28412
Church Aly 28401
Church St
1-1699 28401
1700-1999 28403
S Churchill Dr 28403
Cicada Ct 28405
Cinema Dr 28403
Circle St 28403
Clairidge Dr 28412
Clairidge Rd 28403
Clairwood Ct 28411
Clamdigger Point Rd 28411
Clark Aly 28401
Clark Hill Rd 28412
Clay St 28405
Claymore Dr 28405
Clayton Pl 28405
Clear Run Dr 28403
Clearbrook Dr 28409
Clearwater Ct 28405
Clemmons Way 28411
Clemson Dr 28403
Clewis Ave 28411
Cliff Rd 28403
Cliffmore Pl 28405
Cliffside Dr 28409
Clinton St 28401
Clipper Ln 28405
Clover Rd 28405
Cloverfield Ct 28411
Cloverland Way 28412
Club Ct & Way 28412
Clydesdale Ct 28411
Coastal Ave 28409
Cobblestone Dr 28405
Cobia Ln 28409
Cocker Ct 28411
Coddington Loop 28405
Cohan Cir 28405
Coker Ct 28405
Colchester Pl 28409
Coleman Dr 28412
Coleridge Dr 28405
N College Rd 28405
S College Rd
1-2299 28403
2301-2697 28412

Street	ZIP
2699-6499	28412
College Acres Dr	28403
Collegiate Dr	28403
Colleton Ct	28403
Collier Aly	28401
Collinwood Ct	28403
Colonel Lamb Dr	28405
Colonial Dr	28403
Colony Cir N	
500-699	28409
200-499	28409
S Colony Cir	28409
Colony Way	28412
Colony Club Ct	28405
Colony Green Ct	28412
Colquitt Dr	28412
Columbia Ave	28403
Columbus Cir	28403
Colwell Ave	28403
Comber Rd	28411
Commerce Rd	28405
Commons Way	28409
Commonwealth Dr	28403
Compass Pt	28409
Compton St	28401
Conch Ln	28411
Condo Club Dr	28412
Confederate Dr	28403
Congressional Ln	28411
Conifer Ct	28411
Conner Ct	28412
Conservation Way	28405
Constable Way	28405
Constitution Blvd	28412
Contender Ln	28409
Control Tower Dr	28405
Convention Center Dr	28401
Converse Dr	28403
Cooper Ct	28405
Copley Rd	28403
Copper Mare Ct	28411
Copperfield Ct	28411
Coppers Trl	28411
Coquina Dr	28411
Corbett St	28401
Cores Ct	28411
Cornelius Harnett Dr	28401
Cornelius Moore Ave	28405
Cornus Dr	28412
Cornwall Ct	28409
Coronado Dr	28409
Corporate Dr	28405
Corum Ln	28411
Costins Ct	28409
Costmary Ln	28412
Cotesworth Dr	28405
Cotswald Ct	28411
Cottage Ln	28401
Coulter Pl	28409
Council St	28403
Country Club Rd	28403
Country Haven Dr	28411
Country Lakes Rd	28411
Country Place Rd	28409
Countywood Way	28411
Courtland Pl	28409
Courtney Pines Rd	28411
Cove Rd	28405
Cove Point Dr	28409
Covenant Ln	28403
Coventry Rd	28405
Covey Ln	28411
Covil Ave	28403
Covil Farm Rd	28405
Covington Rd	28409
Cowan St	28401
Cowpen Landing Rd	28401
Cowrie Ln	28411
Coxe Ln	28412
Crab Apple Ln	28412
Crab Catcher Ct	28409
Crabwalk Ct	28405
Craftsman Way	28411
Cranbrook Dr	28405
Cravens Pt	28409
Cravens Point Rd	28409
Crawdad Ct	28405
Crawford Ct	28409
Creecy Ave	28403
Creek Ridge Rd	28411
E & W Creeks Edge Dr	28409
Creekside Ln	28411
Creekside East Dr	28411
Creekwood Rd	28411
Crescent Ct	28411
Crestland Cir	28405
N & S Crestwood Dr	28405
Crete Dr	28403
Cricket Ct	
1-99	28411
1800-1899	28405
Crimson Ct	28405
Crockette Rd	28409
Crocus Ct	28401
Crofton Pl	28412
Crojack Ln	28409
Cromwell Cir	28409
Crooked Creek Ln	28409
Crooked Pine Rd	28411
Croquet Dr	28412
Cross St	28401
Cross Creek Rd	28403
Cross Staff Pl & Rd	28405
Crosscurrent Pl	28409
Crossover Rd	
2400-2499	28401
3600-3699	28405
Crosswinds Dr	28409
Crowley Aly	28401
Crown Point Ln	28409
Crows Landing Cir	28403
Crows Nest Ct	28409
Crystal Ct	28409
Culbreth Dr	28405
Culler Ct	28409
Culloden Ct	28409
Cumberland Pl	28411
Cupola Dr	28409
Curlew Dr	28409
Cypress Dr	28401
Cypress Grove Dr	28401
Cypress Island Dr	28412
Cypress Pond Way	28411
Dachshund Ct	28411
Dahlia Ct	28401
Daisy Lee Dr	28411
Dalkeith Rd	28409
Dallas Dr	28405
Dalton Ct	28405
Damon Ct	28405
Dandelion Dr	28405
Danie St	28401
Daniel Boone Trl	28411
Danton St	28412
Daphine Dr	28409
Daphne Ct	28401
Dapple Ct	28403
Darby St	28409
Darden Rd	28411
Dare St	28412
Darley Ln	28409
Darlington Ave	28403
Dartridge Dr	28412
Darwin Dr	28405
Davie Dr	28412
Davis St	28401
Davis Sound Ln	28409
Dawning Creek Way	28409
Dawson St	
1-1699	28401
1700-2099	28403
Day Lilly Dr	28405
Daybreak Ln	28411
Deacon Ln	28411
Dean Dr	28405
Deauville Pl	28405
Deborah Ct	28405
Decatur Dr	28403
Decoy Ln	28411
Deep Creek Run	28411
Deepwood Dr & Pl	28405
Deer Creek Ln	28405
Deer Glade Ct	28409
Deer Haven Ct	28409
Deer Hill Dr	28409
Deer Island Ln	28405
Deer Spring Ln	28409
Deerwood Dr	28405
Del Rio Ave	28409
Delaney Ave	28403
Delgado Ave	28403
Delham Ct	28412
Dellwood Dr	28405
Denise Dr	28411
Denly Ct	28411
Densiflorum Ct	28412
Departure Ct	28403
Derby Down Way	28409
Derry Ct	28411
Dever Ct	28411
Devon Ct	28403
S Devonshire Ln & Way	28409
Dewars Cir	28409
Dewberry Rd	28405
Dewitt Rd	28405
Dexter St	28403
Diamond Shoals Rd	28403
Diane Dr	28411
Dickens Dr	28405
Dieppe Ct	28405
Dijon Dr	28405
Dilworth Rd	28411
Disney Dr	28409
Division Dr	28401
Division Park Ln	28401
Dixie Ave	28403
Dj Morgan Trl	28401
Dobbs St	28412
Dock St	28401
Doctors Cir	28401
Doe Clearing Ct	28409
Dog Whistle Ln	28411
Dogwood Dr	28403
Dogwood Ln	28409
Dolphin Ct	28403
Dominion Dr	28403
Donald E Gore Dr	28412
Donegal Pl	28409
Donna Ave	28403
Donnelly Ln	28409
Dorchester Pl	28412
Dorothy Ave	28403
Dorrington Dr	28412
Dorsett Pl	28403
Dotson Ct	28405
Doughton Dr	28409
Dove Ct	28403
Dove Field Dr	28411
Dover Rd	28409
Down Rigger Ct	28409
Downey Branch Ln	28403
Dragons Eye Ct	28412
Drake Ct	28403
Drewman Ct	28405
Dron Pl	28409
Druid Ln	28403
Drummond Dr & Rd	28409
Drysdale Dr	28405
Duck Downe Ct	28409
Duck Hawk Ct	28409
Ducks Bill Ct	28411
Dullage Dr	28405
Dunbar Ct	28405
Dunbar Rd	28411
Dundee Dr	28405
Dunes Point Rd	28411
Dungannon Blvd	28403
Dunhill Ln	28412
Dunlea Ct	28405
Dunmore Rd	28409
Dunn Place Dr	28411
Dupree Dr	28403
Durands Lndg	28412
Durango Pl	28403
E & W Durant Ct	28412
Durbin Ct	28409
Duval Ct	28411
Duxbury Ct	28411
Dye Pl	28405
Eagles Nest Dr	28409
Earl Dr	28405
Early Dr	28412
Eastwind Rd	28403
Eastwood Rd	28403
Eastwood Service Rd	28405
Ebb Dr	
100-299	28411
1500-1799	28409
Ebb Tide Ln	28409
Echo Ln	28403
Echo Farms Blvd	28412
Edgehill Rd	28403
Edgemont Ln	28405
Edgewater Ln	28403
Edgewater Club Rd	28411
Edgewood Rd	28403
Edinboro Ln	28409
Edisto Dr	28403
Edith Ct	28411
Edward Hyde Pl	28405
Edwards St	28405
Efird Rd	28409
Egret Point Rd	28409
Ehler Ct	28409
Eider Ln	28409
N & S El Carol Ct	28409
El Ogden Dr	28411
Elance Moore Ln	28401
Eland Ct	28411
Elder Dr	28405
Elease Ln	28403
Elgin St	28409
Elisha Dr	28405
Elizabethan Ct	28409
Elk Trail Dr	28409
Elkmont Ct	28411
Elliot Dr	28405
Ellis Ct	28405
Elm St	28401
Elmhurst Rd	28411
Embassy Cir	28412
Emberwood Rd	28405
Emerald Cove Ct	28409
Emerald Dunes Rd	28411
Emerson Pt	28411
Emerson St	28403
Emily St	28401
Emmarts Ct	28409
Emory St	28405
Encarrow Ln	28411
Endeavour Ln	28403
Endicott Ct	28411
Englehard Pl	28403
Englewood Dr	28409
English Ct	28411
English Lndg	28409
Enterprise Dr	28405
Epling Dr	28411
Erie Ct	28412
Erin Ct	28403
Erinshire Ct	28412
Ern Way	28411
Eschol Ct	28409
Essary Ct	28411
Essex Dr	28403
Estate Rd	28405
Estelle Lee Pl	28401
Eucalyptus Ln	28412
Evans St	28405
Evans Way	28411
Evanston Ct	28412
Eventide Blvd	28411
Everbreeze Ln	28411
Everette Ct	28412
Everetts Creek Dr	28411
Evergreen Dr	28403
Ewell Dr	28409
Excalibur Way	28403
Exchange Dr	28405
Exeter Pl	28403
Exeter Rd	28405
Export Dr	28405
Exuma Ln	28412
Fair Lakes Dr	28405
Faircloth Rd	28405
Fairfield Dr	28401
Fairlawn Dr	28405
Fairlie Ct	28412
Fairview Dr	28412
Fairway Dr	28403
Fairway Lakes Pl	28405
Faith Ct	28411
Falcon Pointe Rd	28411
Falcon Ridge Way	28403
Fall Dr	28401
Fallen Leaf Ln	28403
Fallen Tree Rd	28405
Fanning St	28401
Farley Dr	28405
Farm Rd	28411
Farmers St	28403
Farrington Farms Dr	28411
Farrows Aly	28401
Faulkenberry Rd	28409
Fawn Creek Dr	28409
Fawn Settle Dr	28409
Fayemarsh Rd	28412
Fayemont Ct	28412
Fazio Dr	28411
Featherstone Ct	28411
Federal Park Dr	28412
Fenway Ln	28403
Fenwick Pl	28403
Ferlerri Rd	28409
Fern Ct	28405
Fern Dr	28401
Fern Bluff Ln	28409
Fern Valley Dr	28412
Ferndale Dr	28411
Ferry Dr	28401
Fiddler Cir	28405
Fiddlestick Way	28412
Field View Rd	28411
Fielding Dr	28405
Filmore Dr	28403
Fin Castle Pl	28409
Final Landing Ln	28411
Finian Dr	28409
Fireside Ct	28412
Fish Hawk Ct E & W	28403
Fisher Ln	28412
Fisherman Creek Dr	28405
Fitzgerald Dr	28405
Five Acres Rd	28411
Flagler Dr	28411
Fleet Rd	28409
Fleming St	28401
Flemington Dr	28401
Flight Path Dr	28405
Flightline Rd	28405
Flint Dr	28401
Flintrock Ct	28411
Flip Flop Ln	28409
Floral Pkwy	28403
Florida Ave	28401
Flounder Ln	28409
Floyd Dr	28412
Flushing Dr	28411
Foliage Ct	28411
Folly Island Ct	28411
Fontana Rd	28412
Fontenay Pl	28405
Forbes Ct	28405
Fordham Rd	28403
Forest Ave	28403
Forest Ln	28401
Forest Rd	28403
Forest Bend Ln	28411
Forest Creek Cir	28403
Forest Hills Dr	28403
Forest Island Pl	28405
Forest Lagoon Pl	28405
Forest Park Rd	28409
Formosa Dr	28403
Forwalt Pl	28409
Fountain Dr	28403
Fountain Grove Ct	28412
Fourth Quarter Apts	28412
Fowler St	28403
Fox Ct	28405
Fox Hunt Ln	28405
Fox Ridge Ln & Pl	28405
Fox Run Rd	28409
Foxfield Ct	28411
Foxglove Ct	28401
Foxhall Ct	28412
Foxhaven Ct	28412
Foxwerth Dr	28411
Foxwood Ln	28409
Foys Trl	28411
E Foys Creek Ln	28411
Fralders St	28401
Francis Marion Dr	
100-199	28411
600-1199	28412
Franklin Ave	28403
Fraternity Ct	28403
Frederica Ct	28412
Fredrickson Rd	28401
Freeboard Ct	28409
Freedom Rd	28409
French Rd	28403
Fresco Dr	28405
Friar St	28411
Friday Dr	28411
Friendly Ln	28409
Friendly Shores Rd	28409
Frog Pond Rd	28403
N & S Front St	28401
Fulbright St	28401
Fullford Ln	28412
Fullwood St	28401
Furtado Dr	28411
Futch Creek Rd	28411
Gabriel St	28412
Gaddy Dr	28403
Gadwall Ct	28403
Gainesford Ct	28412
Galahad Ct	28403
Galaxy Ct	28405
Gale Rd	28405
Galloway National Dr	28411
Gammon Ct	28409
Gander Dr	28411
Gantts Trl	28409
Garden Ave	28403
Garden Lake Est	28401
Garden Terrace Dr	28405
Gardenia Ct & Ln	28409
Gardner Dr	28405
Garnercrest Rd	28411
Garrett Lea Parke	28412
Garrison Ct	28411
Gaskins Ln	28411
W Gate Rd	28405
Gate Post Ln	28412
Gatefield Dr	28412
Gateway Dr	28403
Gatewood Ct	28405
Gaya Pl	28411
Gazebo Ct	28409
George Anderson Dr	28412
George Trask Dr	28405
Georgetown Rd	28409
Gerbe Ct	28409
Gerdes Aly	28401
Gerome Pl	28412
Gettysburg Dr	28409
Gibson Ave	28403
Giles Ave	
1-199	28403
200-299	28409
Gillette Dr	28403
Gillmoss Ln	28409
Gilmore Dr	28411
Gimme Ct	28412
Ginger Rd	28405
Gingerwood Dr	28405
Gladbrook Dr	28405
Glasgow Ave	28403
Glastonbury Ct	28409
Gleason Rd	28405
Glen Arbor Dr	28411
Glen Eagles Ln	28405
Glen Meade Rd	
1200-1299	28401
1800-2299	28403
Glenarthur Dr	28412
Glendale Dr	28401
Glenlea Dr	28405
Glenn St	28401
Glennburn Ct	28409
Glenora Pl	28405
Gloucester Pl	28403
Glynnwood Dr	28405
Godfrey Ct	28412
Godfrey Way	28409
Gold Ave	28409
Golden Rd	28409
Golden Astor Ct	28405
Golden Eagle Ct	28409
Golden Rod Dr	28405
Goldeneye Ct	28411
Goodwood Way	28412
Goose Creek Ct	28411
Goose Landing Cir	28403
Gordon Rd	
100-199	28401
4200-4499	28405
4500-6899	28411
Gordon Acres Dr	28411
Gordon Woods Rd	28411
Gores Row	28401
Gorham Ave	28409
Government Center Dr	28403
Governors Rd	28411
Grace St	
1-1699	28401
1800-1999	28405
Grackle Ct	28403
Grady Ave	28403
Graham St	28412
Grainger Point Rd	28409
Granada Ave	28409
Granby St	28409
Grand Banks Dr	28412
Grand Champion Rd	28412
Grande Manor Ct	28405
Grandiflora Ct	28405
Grange St	28411
Grantham Ct	28409
Grape Arbor Ct	28409
Grass Ln	28405
Grathwol Dr	28405
Gray Gables Ln	28403
Grayhawk Cir	28411
Graylyn Ter	28405
Graymont Dr	28403
Grayson Park Dr	28411
Graystone Rd	28411
Grayswood Ct	28411
Graywalsh Dr	28405
Great Oaks Dr	28405
Great Pine Ct	28411
Green Arbor Ln	28409
Green Bay Cir	28405
Green Berry Ct	28409
Green Forest Dr	28409
N Green Meadows Dr	28405
Green Tip Cv	28409
Green Turtle Ln	28409
Green Valley Dr	28412
Greenbriar Rd	28409
Greendale Dr	28405
Greenfield St	28401
Greenhowe Dr	28409
Greenleaf Dr	28403
Greens Ferry Ct	28409
Greentree Rd	28405
Greenview Dr	28411
Greenville Ave	28403
Greenville Loop Rd	28409
Greenville Sound Rd	28409
Greenway Ave	28403
Greenwell Ct	28409
Greenwich Ln	28409
Greenwood Ave	28403
Greenwood Rd	28409
Greg Dr	28405
Gregory Rd	28405

Grenezay Rd 28411
Grenoble 28409
Gresham Ct 28405
Grey Leaf Dr 28409
Grey Oaks Ct 28412
Grey Squirrel Dr 28409
Greythorne Ct 28411
Grinnellis Ct 28409
Grissom Rd 28409
Grizzly Bear Ct 28411
Groppo Cv 28412
Groundwater Way 28411
Grouper Ct 28409
Grouse Ct 28403
Grouse Woods Dr 28411
W Grove Dr 28409
Grove Point Rd 28409
Gruffy Ct 28411
Gufford Dr 28403
Guilford Ave 28403
Guinea Ln 28409
Guinevere Ln 28403
Gulf Stream Ln 28409
Gull Point Rd 28405
Gun Raven Ln 28411
Gunston Ln 28405
Guy Ct 28403
Habberline St 28412
Haberdeen Dr 28411
Hadley Ct 28405
Haig Dr 28412
Hailsham Dr 28412
Halcyon Ln 28411
Hales Ln 28401
Haley Ct 28412
Halifax Rd 28403
Hall Dr 28405
Hall St 28401
Hall Waters Dr 28405
Hallbrook Farms Cir 28411
Hallmark Ln 28405
Hallstead Ct 28411
Halyard Ct 28405
Halyburton Memorial Pkwy 28412
Hammock Pl 28409
Hammock Dunes Dr 28411
Hampshire Dr 28409
Hampstead Ct 28405
N Hampton Rd 28409
Hanging Moss Ct 28412
Hanna Dr 28412
Hanover St 28401
SE Harbor Dr 28409
Harbor Ln 28411
SE Harbor Ln 28409
Harborway Dr & Pl 28405
Harbour Dr 28401
Hardscrabble Ct 28409
Hardy Pl 28405
Hargate Ct 28405
Hargrove Dr 28411
Harlandale Dr 28411
Harley Dr 28405
Harmony Ct 28409
Harnett Ave & St 28401
Harrells Ln 28401
Harris Aly 28401
Harris Rd 28411
Harrison St 28401
Hart St 28401
Hartefield National Ln 28411
Harvard Dr 28403
Harvest Grove Ln 28409
Haskell Ct 28411
Hastings Ct & Dr 28411
Haven Pt & Way 28411
Hawes Ct 28411
Hawk Rd 28411
Hawks Bill Dr 28409
Hawthorne Dr
  1-299 28403
  400-499 28405
Hawthorne Rd 28403
Hayden Dr 28411
Hayfield Ct 28411
Haymarket Ln 28412
Haywood Dr 28405
Hazel Smith Dr 28412
Hazelton Ct 28411
Head Rd 28409
Headsail Ct 28409
Headwater Cove Ln 28403
Healy Cir 28412
Hearn Dr 28411
Hearthside Dr 28412
Heartwood Pl 28411
Heathcliff Rd 28409
Heather Ridge Dr 28405
Heatherstone Ln 28405
Heaton Pl 28411
Hedgerow Ln 28409
Hedingham Ct & Ln 28412
Heide Dr 28403
Hellene Dr 28411
Helmsdale Dr 28405
Henry St 28405
Henry H Watters Dr 28412
Henson Dr 28405
Hepworth Way 28412
Herford Ct 28411
Heritage Park Dr 28401
Heron Run 28403
Herring Ln 28403
Hervey Ln 28411
Hess Rd 28411
Hewlett Dr 28405
Hewletts Run 28409
Hiawatha Dr 28412
Hibiscus Way 28412
Hickory Knoll Rd 28409
Hidden Cv 28411
Hidden Lake Ln 28409
Hidden Lake Trailer Park 28405
Hidden Pointe Dr 28411
Hidden Valley Rd 28409
High Bush Ct 28405
High Rock Dr 28412
High Tide Dr 28411
Highgreen Dr 28411
Highgrove Pl 28409
Highland Dr 28403
Hill Rd 28401
Hill St 28403
Hill Valley Walk 28412
Hillandale Dr 28412
Hillcrest Anx 28401
Hilliard Ct 28411
Hillman Dr 28405
Hillsboro Rd 28403
Hillsdale Dr 28403
Hillside Dr 28412
Hillview Dr 28405
Hillwood St 28409
Hilton Rd 28401
Hinton Ave 28403
Hitch Ct 28411
Hixon Pl 28411
Hl Smith Rd 28411
Hobart Dr 28405
Hogan Ct 28412
Hoggard Dr 28403
Holbrook Ave 28412
Holiday Hills Dr 28409
Holland Dr 28401
Hollingsworth Dr 28412
Hollins Rd 28412
Hollis Ln 28409
Hollister Dr 28411
Holly Dr 28401
Holly Tree Rd
  4300-4599 28412
  4600-5399 28409
Hollybriar Dr 28412
Hollyholm Trce 28409
Holmlock Ter 28403
Holt Rd 28409
Homestead Ct 28411
Honey Bee Ln 28412
Honeydew Ln 28412
Honeysuckle St 28401
Honeywood Dr 28405
Hons Trl 28409
Hood Dr 28409
Hooker Rd 28403
Hooper St 28401
Hope Springs Ct 28405
Hopscotch Ct 28411
Horizon Ct 28411
Horn Rd 28412
Horndale Dr 28409
Horne Place Dr 28401
Horsham Ct 28405
Hospital Plaza Dr 28401
Hounds Chase Dr 28409
Howard St 28401
Howes Point Pl 28405
Huckleberry Rd 28405
Hudson Dr 28403
Hughes Cir 28411
Hugo Ct 28412
Hummingbird Ln 28411
Humphrey Dr 28411
Hunt Cliff Ct 28409
Hunt Club Rd 28403
Hunters Trl 28405
Hunters Mill Ln 28409
Hunting Ridge Rd 28412
Huntington Rd 28403
Huron Dr 28412
Hutaff Aly 28401
Hyannis Way 28409
Hyatt Ln 28411
Hydon Ct 28411
Hydrangea Pl 28403
Ibis Ct 28409
Ike Dr 28409
Ikner Ln 28403
Ilex Dr 28412
Independence Blvd
  1300-2099 28403
  2500-4199 28412
  4201-4299 28412
Indian Trl 28412
Indian Cove Ave 28409
Indian Wells Way 28411
Indica Ct 28405
Infantry Rd 28405
Inglehart Ct 28409
Ingleside Dr 28409
Inkberry Ct 28411
Inland Grn 28405
Inland Greens Cir & Dr 28405
Inlet Dr 28411
Inlet Acres Dr 28412
Inlet Hook Rd 28411
Inlet Point Dr 28409
Inlet View Dr 28409
Inman Park Ln 28403
Innovation Dr 28405
Inspiration Dr 28405
Interlachen Cir 28411
International Dr 28405
Inverary Way 28405
Invergordan Ct 28411
Inverness Ln 28405
Ireland Ct 28411
Iris St 28409
Irish Ct 28411
Iron Gate Dr 28412
Irwin Dr 28405
Islamerta Pl 28405
Island Cv 28412
Island Bridge Way 28412
Island Creek Dr 28411
Isle Of Palms Way 28412
Ivanhoe St 28411
Iverstone Ct 28409
Ivey Cir 28401
Ivocet Dr 28409
Ivory Ct 28411
Ivydale Ln 28405
J R Kennedy Dr 28405
E & W Jackson Dr & St 28401
Jacksonville St 28403
Jacobs Creek Ln 28409
Jacqueline Dr 28411
Jadewood Dr 28411
Jaeckle Dr 28403
Jamaica Dr 28401
James Aly 28401
James Pl 28405
Jamey Ct 28405
Janice Ln 28411
Jared Ct 28409
Jarvis Cir 28412
Jasmine Cv 28412
Jasmine St 28401
Jasmine Cove Way 28412
Jason Ct 28405
Jasper Pl 28409
Jay Bird Cir 28412
Jeanelle Moore Blvd 28411
Jeb Stuart Dr 28412
Jefferson Rd 28411
Jefferson St 28401
Jel Wade Dr 28401
Jennings Dr 28403
Jettys Reach 28409
Jewell Pt 28411
Jib Rd 28411
Joe Wheeler Dr 28409
Joey Ct 28409
John D Barry Dr 28412
John Henry Dr 28412
John S Mosby Dr 28412
John Yeamen Rd 28405
Johns Creek Rd 28409
Johns Orchard Ln 28411
Johnston Dr 28412
Jolly Boat Ct 28411
Jonathan Ct 28412
Jonquil Ct 28409
Jordan Ln 28403
Joshuas Lndg 28409
Joy Pl 28409
Judges Rd 28405
Julia Dr 28412
Jumpin Run 28403
Junction Cir 28412
Junction Creek Dr 28412
Junction Park Cir & Dr 28412
Juneberry Ct 28403
Jupiter Hills Cir 28411
Justus Ct 28405
Kannapolis Dr 28411
Karen Ln 28405
Karsten Creek Way 28411
Kathleen Dr 28412
Kauri St 28411
Keaton Ave 28403
Keats Pl 28405
Kellum Ct 28412
Kelly Rd 28409
Kenan Ct 28403
Kendall Ave 28401
Kenilworth Ln 28405
Kennedy Plz 28401
Kennedy Rd 28409
Kennesaw Ct 28412
Kenneth Ct 28405
Kennington St 28405
Kent St 28403
Kentucky Ave 28401
Kenwood Ave 28405
N Kerr Ave 28405
S Kerr Ave 28403
Kestral Dr 28409
Keswick Ct 28409
Kettering Pl 28412
Key Pointe Dr 28405
Kiawah Ln 28412
Kidder St 28401
W Kilarny Rd 28409
Kildare Pl 28409
Kilkenny Pl 28409
Kimberly Way 28403
King St 28401
King Arthur Dr 28403
Kingfisher Ct 28403
Kings Ct 28411
Kings Dr 28405
Kings Arm Ct 28409
Kings Grant Rd 28405
Kingsley Rd 28403
Kingston Rd 28409
Kinsella Ct 28409
Kipling Ct 28405
Kirby Smith Dr 28409
Kirkley Ct 28409
Kirkwood Dr 28412
Kitty Hawk Rd 28405
Kiwi Ln 28412
Klein Rd 28405
Knightsbridge Rd 28403
Knollwood Rd 28403
Knotty Ct 28405
Kolbe Ct 28403
Konlack Ct 28411
Koonce Ct 28411
Kornegay Ave 28405
Krause Ln 28401
Krystal Pond Dr 28411
Kubeck Ct 28403
Kyle Ct 28409
La Salle St 28411
Lacewood Ct 28409
Lady Bug Ln 28411
Lady Fern Ct 28409
Lafayette St 28411
Laffitte St 28411
Lagar Ln 28405
Lake Ave 28403
Lake Branch Dr 28401
E Lake Emerald Dr 28411
Lake Forest Pkwy 28401
Lake Nona Dr 28411
Lake Renaissance Cir 28409
E & W Lake Shore Dr 28401
Lakemoor Dr 28405
Lakes Edge Pl 28405
Lakeview Dr 28412
Lakewood Pl 28409
Lambeth Ct 28409
Lambrook Dr 28411
Lambs Ct 28412
Lame St 28403
Lampost Cir 28403
Lancaster Rd
  200-399 28409
  600-698 28411
Lance Dr 28405
Lancome Ct 28409
Land Line Dr 28411
Landalee Dr 28405
Landfall Dr 28405
Landis Farm Rd 28403
Landmark Dr 28412
Landon Ln 28412
Lands End Ct 28409
Langley Ln 28411
Lanham Dr 28409
Lansdowne Rd 28409
Lantana Ln 28411
Lantern Way 28409
Lapaloma Ct 28409
Larchmont Dr 28403
Largo Ct 28409
Lark Ct 28409
Lark Ln 28411
Larkspur Ct 28409
Larne Ct 28411
Larson Pl 28403
Latimer Dr 28403
Laughing Oak Ln 28401
Lauralis Bluff Ct 28409
Laurel Dr 28401
Lauren Place Dr 28405
Laveen Way 28412
Lawrence Dr 28405
Lawshe Ct 28412
Lawson Ln 28405
Lawther Ct 28412
Lawton Cir 28412
Le Gare Ct 28403
Leaf Point Ct 28411
Leaning Tree Ct 28405
Leatherwood Dr 28412
Lee Dr 28401
Lee Parker Dr 28409
Lee Shore Pl 28405
Leeward Ln 28409
Legacy Ln 28411
Legend Dr 28405
Lehigh Rd 28412
Leith Ct 28405
Lemming Ct 28411
Lennon Dr 28405
Lennox Pl 28412
Lenoir Dr 28412
Leslie Ln 28411
Lettered Olive Pl 28412
Levis Ln 28412
Lex Rd 28405
Lexington Dr 28403
Libby Ln 28409
N & S Liberty Ct 28401
Liberty Bell Ct 28411
Lido Dr 28411
Lightning Whelk Way 28412
Lilac Ct 28401
Lillington Dr 28412
Lilly Pond Ln 28411
Limpkin Ct 28403
N Lincoln Ct 28401
S Lincoln Ct 28401
Lincoln Rd 28403
Lincolnshire Ln 28411
Linden Ln 28409
Linden Rdg 28412
Line Dr 28412
Lineberry Ln 28403
Lingo St 28403
Linksider Dr 28412
Linkway Ln 28409
Lipkin Ct 28403
Lipscomb Dr 28412
Lisa Ct 28411
Liston Ct 28411
Litchfield Way 28405
Little John Cir 28401
Little Neck Rd 28411
Little Pony Trl 28412
Live Oak Ln 28411
S Live Oak Pkwy 28403
Liverpool St 28401
Lloyd Ct 28405
Loblolly Ct 28411
Locke St 28403
Lockerby Ln 28411
Locksley Ct 28405
Lockwood Dr 28405
Loder Ave 28409
Lodi Ct 28412
Loganberry Rd 28405
Logwood Ct 28412
Loman Ln 28412
London Ln 28405
Londonderry Dr 28411
Lone Eagle Ct 28409
Long Boat Cir 28405
Long Branch Dr 28412
Long Cove Ct 28405
Long John Silver Dr 28411
Long Leaf Acres Dr 28405
Long Leaf Hills Dr 28409
Long Pointe Rd 28409
Long Putt Ct 28412
Long Ridge Dr 28405
Longleaf Dr 28401
Longleaf Trailer Park 28412
Longmeadow Dr 28412
Longstreet Dr 28412
Lonicera Ct 28411
Loosestrife Ct 28411
Loqust Dr 28405
Lord Dr 28411
W Lord Byron Rd 28405
Lord Elkins Rd 28405
Lord Nance Ct 28405
Lord Tennyson Dr 28405
Lord Thomas Rd 28405
Loring Aly 28405
Lorraine Cir & Dr 28412
Lost Tree Rd 28411
Loubelle St 28405
Louisa Ln 28403
Louisiana St 28401
Lounsberry Ct 28405
Love Aly 28401
Love Grass Ct 28405
Lovingston Ln 28409
Low Bush Ct 28405
Lowes Island Dr 28411
Lowry Ct 28412
Lt Congleton Rd 28409
Lucky Fish Ln 28411
Ludlow Dr 28411
Lullwater Dr 28403
Lunar Ln 28405
Lupine Ct 28405
Lure Ln 28412
Lydden Rd 28409
Lydford Ct 28409
Lynbrook Dr 28405
Lynchfield Ct 28412
Lyndon Ave 28405
Lynette Dr 28409
Lynnwood Dr
  1700-1799 28401
  2000-2399 28403
Lyonia Ct 28411
Lytham Ct 28405
Mabee Way 28411
Mabry Ct 28405
Maccumber Ln 28403
Macdonald Dr 28403
Mackay Ct 28412
Mackenzie Dr 28409
S Macmillan Ave N 28403
Macon Ct 28412
Macumber Aly 28401
Madeline Dr 28405
Madison St 28401
Magazine St 28403
Magnolia Dr 28409
Magnolia Pl 28403
Magnolia St 28401
Mahogany Run 28411
Maid Stone Dr 28405
Maides Ave 28405
Main St 28405
Mainsail Ln 28412
Mako Dr 28409
Mallard Dr 28403
Mallard Xing 28409
Mallow Rd 28411
Malpass Ave 28403
Malvern Rd 28403
Mamie Ct 28409
Manassas Dr 28409
Manchester Dr 28405
Mandevilla Ct 28409
Manet Rd 28412
Mango Ct 28409
Mangum Dr 28409
Manhattan Dr 28403
Manly Ave 28405
Manor Ct 28405
Manteo Ct 28412
Maple Ave 28403
Maple Ridge Rd 28411
Marblehead Ct 28412
March Ct 28405
Marguerite Dr 28403
Maria Ct 28412
Marigold Ct 28401
Marina Club Dr 28409
Mariner Ct 28405
Mariner Ln 28403
Marion Dr 28412
Mark Twain Dr 28411
Market St
  6820B-3-6820B-3 28405
  1-1699 28401
  1700-4499 28403
  4500-6899 28405
  6900-8300 28411
  8207-8207 28404

8301-10099 28411
8302-10098 28411
Marlboro St 28403
Marlin Ct 28403
Marlin Ln 28409
Marlowe Dr 28405
Marlwood Dr 28403
Marne Dr 28405
Marquette Dr 28412
Marsdon Ave 28401
Marsh Ct 28412
Marsh Bay Dr 28409
Marsh Cove Ln 28409
Marsh Harbor Pl 28405
Marsh Hawk Ct 28409
Marsh Hen Dr 28409
Marsh Oaks Dr 28411
Marsh Reach Dr 28411
Marshall Ct 28411
Marshfield Dr 28411
Marshland Dr & Pl 28405
Marshview Dr 28403
Marshview Trl 28412
Marshwood Dr 28409
Marstellar St 28401
Martin St 28401
Martingale Ln 28409
Martinique Way 28411
Marvin K Moss Ln 28409
Maryland Ave 28401
Marymount Dr 28411
Marywood Dr 28409
Mascot Ct 28411
Mashenso Rd 28411
Masks Aly 28401
Mason Knoll Ct & Dr 28409
Mason Landing Rd 28411
Mason Reed Dr 28403
Mason Ridge Ln 28409
Masonboro Harbor Dr 28409
Masonboro Loop Rd 28409
Masonboro Sound Rd 28409
Masons Bluff Ct 28411
Masons Point Pl 28405
Masters Ln 28409
Max Flite Way 28412
Maxwell Pl 28409
Mayberry Ct 28409
Mayfair Dr 28403
Mayfaire Club Dr 28405
Mayfield Ct
800-899 28411
3700-3999 28412
Mayflower Dr 28412
Maypop Ct & Ln 28412
Mccalley Ct 28411
Mcclammy St 28405
Mcclelland Dr 28405
Mccormick Ln 28411
Mcculloch Ave 28403
Mceachern Ct 28412
Mcginnis Ln 28412
Mcgirt Pl 28412
Mcintyre Trl 28411
Mcivers Ln 28401
Mckinnon Dr 28409
Mcquillan Dr 28412
Mcrae St 28401
Meadow St 28401
Meadow Brook Ct 28409
Meadowlark Ln 28411
Meadowood Dr 28411
Meadowview Ave 28411
Meaninde Ave 28403
Mears St 28401
Medallion Pl 28411
Medeira Ct 28405
Medical Center Dr 28401
Meeting Ct 28401
Megans Place Dr 28409
Meherrin Ln 28403
Melba Ct 28405
Melbourne Ct 28411
Melinda Ct 28409
Melissa Ct 28409
Melody Ln 28405

Melton Rd 28412
Mendenhall Dr 28411
Mentone Ln 28403
Mercer Ave 28403
Merchant Ct 28405
Meredith Way 28405
Merestone Dr 28412
Meridian Ter 28411
Merklebay Ct 28411
Merlot Ct 28409
Merrimac Dr 28412
Metro Cir 28401
Metting Rd 28403
Metts Ave 28403
Mews Dr 28405
Michelas Bay Ln 28409
Michelle Dr 28403
Michigan Ave 28401
Middle Ln 28411
Middle Oaks Dr 28409
Middle Sound Rd 28411
Middle Sound Loop Rd 28411
Middleborough Dr 28409
Middlesex Rd 28405
Middleton Pl 28412
Midland Dr 28412
Midnight Channel Rd 28403
Milan Ct 28411
Milford Rd 28405
Military Cutoff Rd
100-1399 28405
1400-1699 28403
Mill Creek Ct 28403
Millhaven Ct 28409
Millheim Ct 28411
Milton Pl 28405
Mimosa Pl 28403
Minnow Way 28405
Mintwood Ct 28405
Miranda Ct 28405
Mission Hills Dr 28405
Misty Morning Ln 28409
Misty Oak Ln 28411
Mitchell Ct 28412
Mockingbird Ln 28409
Mohawk Trl 28409
Mohican Trl 28409
Mollys Ct 28411
Monarch Dr 28411
Monck Ct 28409
Monitor Dr 28412
Monlandil Dr 28403
Monroe St 28401
Montclair Dr 28403
Montego Ct 28411
Monterey Dr 28409
Montfaye Ct 28411
Montford Dr 28409
Montgomery Ave 28405
Monticello Dr 28405
Montrose Ln 28405
Monty Dr 28405
Monument Dr 28405
Moon Snail Dr 28412
Moonlight Ln 28409
Moore Plz 28401
Moores Creek Ln 28403
S Moorings Dr 28405
Moraga Ct 28412
Moreland Dr 28405
Morgan St 28412
Morley Ct 28411
E & W Morning Dove Ct 28403
Morning Glory Ct 28405
Morningside Dr 28401
Morris Ct & Rd 28405
Morrow Rd 28412
Morton Ct 28403
Mosley St 28405
Moss St 28403
Moss Tree Dr 28405
Moss Vine Pl 28405
Mossberg Rd 28405
Mosswood Ct 28411

Motts Creek Rd 28412
Motts Forest Rd 28412
Motts Village Rd 28412
Mount Pleasant Dr 28411
Mount Vernon Dr 28403
Mountaineer Ln 28412
Muirfield Ct 28403
Mulberry Ave 28403
Mullet Ct 28409
Mullington Ln 28409
Murphy Aly 28401
Murray Farms Rd 28411
Murrayville Rd
100-6099 28405
6100-7499 28411
Musevale Dr 28412
Muters Aly 28401
Mutual Rd 28405
Myna Cir 28403
Myric Ct 28411
Myrtle Ave 28403
Myrtle Gardens Dr 28409
Myrtle Grove Rd 28409
Nantucket Ct 28412
Naples Dr 28412
Narrow Way 28411
Narrows Hunt Ln 28403
Nash Dr 28403
Nassau Rd 28401
Nature Trail Dr 28405
Naudin Ct 28411
Nautica Yacht Club Dr 28411
Nautilus Dr 28412
Navaho Trl 28409
Navigator Ln 28409
Needle Grass Way 28412
Needle Sound Way 28409
Needlefish Ct 28411
Neelys Ct 28409
Neil Ct 28411
Nesbitt Ct 28401
Net Ln 28412
Netherlands Dr 28405
Nettle Cir 28405
Nevan Ln 28405
New Bern Ave & St 28403
New Centre Dr
4700-4799 28405
4800-5390 28403
New Colony Dr 28412
New Forest Dr 28411
New Hanover Medical
Park Dr 28403
New Haven Dr 28411
New Holland Dr 28412
New Hope Pl 28409
New Jack Rd 28409
New Kent Dr 28405
New Orleans Pl 28403
New Town Dr 28405
New Village Way 28405
New Wales Parke 28412
Newbury Way 28411
Newcastleton Dr 28412
Newington Ct 28405
Newkirk Ave 28412
Newkirk Rd 28409
Newry Ln 28411
Nicholas Creek Cir 28409
Niffer Ln 28405
Night Hawk Dr 28412
Nina Pl 28412
Nixon St 28401
Noble Ave 28405
Noland Dr 28405
Nordic Dr 28411
Norfleet Aly 28401
Norman St 28401
Normandy Dr 28412
Northbend Rd 28411
Northbrook Dr 28405
Northchase Pkwy NE 28405
Northcreek Rd 28409
Northeaster Dr 28409
Northern Blvd 28401
Northern Light Pl 28405

Northhills Dr 28411
Northshore Dr 28411
Northstar Pl 28405
Northwood Dr 28405
Norton Ct 28411
Norwich Rd 28405
Norwood Ave 28403
Nottingham Ln & Rd 28409
Nun St
1-1699 28401
1700-1999 28403
Nut Bush Ct 28411
Nutt St 28401
Nymue Pt 28403
Oak Ave 28411
Oak St 28401
Oak Bluff Ln 28409
Oak Creek Pl 28405
Oak Landing Rd 28409
Oak Ridge Ln 28411
Oakcliff Dr 28409
Oakcrest Dr 28403
Oakhurst Rd 28409
Oakland Dr 28405
Oakleaf Dr 28403
Oakvale Dr 28411
Oasis Dr 28409
Oban Ct 28411
Oberbeck Way 28409
Ocean Point Dr & Pl 28405
Ocean Ridge Dr & Pl 28405
Ocracoke Dr 28412
Odyssey Dr 28405
Offshore Ct 28409
Ogden Business Ln 28411
Ogden Park Rd 28411
Okeechobee Rd 28412
Old Baymeade Rd 28411
Old Branch Rd 28409
Old Brick Rd 28412
Old Camp Rd 28409
Old Dairy Rd 28405
Old Eastwood Rd 28403
Old Field Rd 28411
Old Foards Ln 28409
Old Fort Rd 28411
Old Garden Rd 28403
Old Lamplighter Way 28403
Old Maccumber Station Rd 28405
Old Mears Rd 28403
Old Military Rd 28409
Old Myrtle Grove Rd 28409
Old Oak Rd 28411
Old Orchard Dr 28403
Old Overton Way 28411
Old Winter Park Rd 28405
Old Wrightsboro Rd 28405
Olde Pond Rd 28411
Olde Well Loop Rd 28411
Oleander Dr
6314A-6314C 28403
1700-3999 28403
3916-3916 28406
4000-6798 28403
4001-6799 28403
Olive St 28401
Oliver Ct 28412
Olmstead Ln 28405
Olsen Ln 28405
Olympic Ln 28411
Omie Ln 28411
Oneal Pl 28405
Ontario Rd 28412
Onyx Ct 28412
Operation Center Dr 28412
Orange St
1-1699 28401
1700-1899 28403
Orchard Ave 28403
Orchard Trce 28409
Oriole Dr 28403
Orion Pl 28405
Orpin Ct 28411
Orton Point Rd 28409
Orville Wright Way 28405

Osprey Ln 28409
Osprey Pl 28411
Ottawa Ct 28411
Otter Hole Ln 28405
Out Island Dr 28409
Outrigger Ct 28412
Ovalberry Ct 28411
Overbrook Rd 28403
Overland Ct 28409
Owencroft Ct 28409
Owens Ct 28412
Owl Roost Ct 28411
Owls Ln 28405
Owteway Pl 28409
Oxford Rd 28403
Oxmoor Pl 28403
Oyster Dr 28411
Oyster Ln 28411
Oyster Lndg 28405
Oyster Bay Ln 28409
Oyster Catcher Rd 28411
Oyster Point Ln 28411
Pacific Rd 28409
Padrick Ln 28411
Page Ave 28403
Pages Creek Dr 28411
Painted Spindle 28405
Paisley Ct 28409
Palm St 28412
Palm Grove Dr 28411
Palmer Way 28412
Palmetto Rd 28401
Pampass Ct 28411
Pandy Ann Ln 28411
Panel Ct 28411
Paoli Ct 28409
Paramount Way 28405
Parham Dr 28403
Park Ave 28403
Parker Farm Dr 28405
Parkshore Dr 28409
Parkview Cir 28405
Parkway Blvd 28412
Parkway Dr 28409
Parkwood Dr 28409
Parliament Dr 28411
Parmele Dr 28401
Parsley St 28401
Partha Ln 28409
Partridge Rd 28412
Pasha Dr 28409
Passage Gate Way 28412
Patalanda Rd 28409
Patricia Dr 28409
Patrick Ave 28403
Patrick Ln 28411
Patriot Way 28412
Patsy Ln 28405
Pauline Ln 28405
Pavillion Pl 28403
Pawleys Ln 28411
Peabody Aly 28401
Peachtree Ave 28403
Pearwood Ct 28405
Pecan Ave 28403
Peden Point Rd 28409
Peeble Dr 28412
Peiffer Ave 28409
Pelican Point Rd 28409
Pelican Reach Pl 28405
Pemberton Dr 28412
Pembroke Jones Dr 28405
Pencade Rd 28411
Pender Ave 28403
Pendula Way 28411
Penn St 28412
Pennhurst Ct 28405
Pennington Dr 28405
Penny Ln 28405
Pennypacker Ct 28412
Pepper Hill Ln 28409
Peppercorn Ct 28411
Pepys Ln 28403
Perennial Ln 28403
Peristat Dr 28405
Perry Ave 28403

Pershing Ct 28412
Persimmon Pl 28409
Perth Dr 28412
Peters Ln 28411
Peterson Pl 28411
Petite Ct 28412
Petral Ct 28409
Pettigrew Dr 28412
Peyton Ct 28409
Pheasant Ct 28403
Physicians Dr 28401
Picadilly Ct 28403
Pickett Dr 28412
Pickway Ct 28411
Piedmont Pl 28411
Pierpoint Dr 28405
Pigfish Ln 28409
Pilgrim Cir 28401
Pilots Ridge Rd 28412
Pin Oak Dr 28411
Pin Tail Ct 28403
Pine Ave 28411
Pine St
1800-2199 28401
4900-5199 28403
Pine Bark Ct 28409
Pine Clay Rd 28403
Pine Cone Rd 28409
Pine Forest Rd 28409
Pine Grove Dr
100-299 28403
300-6699 28409
Pine Hills Dr 28403
Pine Hollow Rd 28412
Pine Knoll Rd 28411
Pine Marsh Ct 28409
Pine Needles Dr 28403
Pine Valley Dr
1-799 28412
800-1299 28409
Pinecliff Dr 28409
Pinecrest Pkwy 28401
Pinehurst Pl 28405
Piner Rd 28409
Pineview Dr 28412
Pinewood Cir 28409
Pinkerton Dr 28411
Pinnacle Pl 28411
Pioneer Ct 28411
Pipers Neck Rd 28411
Pitch Pine Ct 28412
Placid Dr 28411
Plainfield Ct 28411
Plantation Dr, Rd & Vlg 28411
Plantation Landing Dr 28411
Planters Row 28405
Player Way 28412
Plaza E
1900-1999 28403
E Plaza
1500-1699 28401
Plaza Dr 28405
Pleasant Dale Dr 28412
Pleasant Grove Dr 28412
Pleasant Oaks Dr 28412
Pleasant Pine Ct 28403
Plover Ct 28409
Plum Nearly Ln 28403
Plymouth Dr 28405
Point Dr 28411
Point Harbor Rd 28401
Point Reyes Dr 28412
Point Summerset Dr 28403
Point View Ct 28411
Pointer Ln 28411
Polk St 28401
Pollocks Way 28412
Polvogt Aly 28401
Pompano Ct 28403
Pompano Ln 28409
Pond Dr 28409
Ponderosa Ln 28409
Pontchartrain Rd 28412
Pope Ct 28405
Poplar St 28401

Poplar Grove Rd 28411
Poplar Knoll Ct 28409
Porches Dr 28409
Port O Pines Est 28405
Porters Crossing Way 28411
Porters Neck Rd 28411
Portofino Ct 28412
Portside Ln 28405
Portsmouth Pl 28411
Portwatch Way 28412
Poseidon Pt 28411
Possum Pl 28409
Post St 28401
Potomac Ct & Dr 28411
Powder Keg Ct 28411
Premier Ct 28405
Prescott Ct 28412
Preservation Way 28405
Presidio Dr 28412
Prestwick Ln 28405
Prestwick Close 28405
Prices Aly 28401
Prices Ln 28405
Primivera Ct 28409
Prince Albert Ct 28405
Princess St
1-1699 28401
1700-1999 28405
Princess Place Dr 28405
Princeton Dr 28403
Prior Dr 28412
Privateer Ct 28405
Privet Ct 28411
Promenade Ct 28405
Promontory Ct 28412
Prospect Ave 28403
Providence Ct 28412
Providence Rd 28411
Providence Point Rd 28411
Province Dr 28405
Purdue Dr 28403
Purl B Ingraham Rd 28412
Purple Martin Ct 28411
Purviance Ave & Ct 28409
Putnam Dr 28411
Quadrant Cir 28405
Quail Ct 28412
Quail Ridge Rd 28409
Quail Ridge Road Ext 28409
Quail Roost Cir 28403
Quail Run Rd 28409
Quail Woods Rd 28411
Quality Way 28401
Queen St
1-1699 28401
1700-1899 28403
Queens Ct 28411
Queensbury Ct 28405
Quiet Ln 28409
Quilon Cir 28412
Quince Aly 28401
Quinn Dr 28411
Rabbit Run 28409
Rabbit Hollow Dr 28411
Rachel Pl 28409
Racine Dr 28403
Radian Rd 28405
Radnor Rd 28409
Ragland Ct 28411
Railroad St 28401
E & W Rainbow Cir 28403
Raintree Ct & Rd 28411
Raleigh St 28412
Ramblewood Ln 28411
Ramon Rd 28405
Ramsbury Way 28411
Ranchwood Ct 28409
Randall Pkwy 28403
Randolph Rd 28403
Randy Pl 28411
Rankin St 28401
Raspberry Rd 28405
Ravens Glass Ct 28411
Rawles Ct 28412
Ray Dr 28405
Raye Dr 28412

Raynor Ct 28409
Rectory Ct 28411
Red Bay Ct 28405
Red Berry Dr 28409
Red Bird Rd 28412
Red Bud Cir 28403
Red Cedar Rd 28411
Red Cockaded Ct 28411
Red Fox Rd 28409
Red Hawk Rd 28405
Red Heart Dr 28412
Red Lighthouse Ln 28412
Red Wing Ln 28403
Redcross St 28401
Redwood Ct & Rd 28412
Reed Ct 28405
Reegan Ct 28409
Regatta Dr 28405
Regency Dr 28412
Regent Dr 28412
Register Ln 28411
Rehder Aly 28401
Reigate Way 28409
Reilly Dr 28409
Reisling Ave 28411
Remington Dr 28405
Renee Ct 28403
E & W Renovah Cir 28403
Rensler Ct 28409
Reserve Dr 28409
Reston Ct 28403
Retriever Dr 28411
Reunion Rd 28411
Revere Ct 28411
Rheims Way 28412
Rhine Ct 28412
Rhodes Ave 28405
Rice Rd 28409
Rice Gate 28411
Richard Bradley Dr 28409
Richardson Dr 28405
Richelieu Rd 28412
Richfield Ct 28411
Richmond Cir 28409
Ridge Rd 28412
Ridgeview Pl 28411
Ridgeway Dr 28409
Ridgewood Heights Dr 28403
Ridley Dr 28412
Riggs Trl 28412
Rill Rd 28403
Ringo Dr 28405
Rio Road East E 28401
Rio Vista Rd 28412
Riplee Dr 28405
Riptide Dr 28403
Ripwood Rd 28405
Rising Tide Ct 28405
Riva Ridge Rd 28411
Rivage Promenade 28412
Rivendell Pl 28411
River Ct & Rd 28412
River Bark 28405
River Front Pl 28412
River Gate Ln 28412
River Oaks Dr 28412
River Rock Rd & Way 28401
River Vista Dr 28412
Riverbirch Dr 28411
Riverwoods Dr 28412
Riviera Dr 28411
Rl Honeycutt Dr 28412
Roane Rd 28405
Robert E Lee Dr 28412
Robert Hoke Rd 28412
Robert S Garnett Dr 28412
Robert Stevenson Dr 28411
Robeson St 28405
Robin Dale Ct 28405
Robinette Rd 28412
Robinhood Rd 28401
Robmar Ct 28411
Rochelle Rd 28411
Rock Creek Cir 28405
Rock Spring Rd 28405
Rockledge Rd 28412
Rockwell Rd 28411
Roderick Ave 28401
Rogers Ave 28403
Rogers Dr 28411
Rogersville Rd 28403
Rollin Rd 28409
Rolling Rd 28405
Rolling Hills Cv 28409
Rondo Pl 28412
Rosa Parks Ln 28409
Roscoe Freeman Ave 28409
Rose Ave 28403
Rose Crest Ct 28412
Rose Trellis Ct 28412
Roseland Dr 28409
Roseman Ln 28409
Rosemary Ln 28411
Rosemont Ave 28403
Rosin Ct 28405
Rossmore Rd 28405
Roswell Gln 28411
Rothbury Way 28411
Rouen Ct 28412
Rounding Bend Ln 28412
Rowsgate Ln 28411
Rowsley St 28409
Royal Bonnet Ct & Dr 28405
Royal Fern Dr 28412
Royal Oak Dr 28409
Royal Palm Ln 28409
Roymac Dr 28401
Ruffin St 28412
Runningbrook Ter 28411
Rushing Dr 28409
Rushton Cir 28412
Rushwood Ct 28405
Russell Aly 28401
Russellborough Dr 28405
Ruth Ave 28411
Rutledge Dr 28412
Ruxton Way 28409
Ryans Ct 28412
W Rye Ln 28405
Sabal Ct 28409
Sabra Dr 28405
Saddle Pt 28411
Saddleworth Trl 28405
Sage Valley Dr 28411
Sagedale Dr 28405
Sagewood Dr 28411
Saginaw Ct 28411
Sago Bay Dr 28412
Sago Palm Dr 28412
Sailmaker Walk 28409
Saint Andrews Dr 28412
Saint Annes Moor 28412
Saint Barts Ct 28412
Saint Clair Dr 28412
Saint Francis Dr 28409
Saint Ives Pl 28411
Saint James Ct 28409
Saint James Dr 28403
Saint Johns Ct 28403
Saint Luke Ct 28409
Saint Mark Ct 28409
Saint Marys Pl 28403
Saint Nicholas Rd 28405
Saint Rosea Rd 28405
Saint Stephens Pl 28412
Saint Vincent Dr 28412
Salem Ct 28411
Salient Pt 28412
Salix Dr 28412
Salo St 28411
Salt Brick Ct 28411
Salt Wind Pl 28405
Saltaire Village Ct 28412
Saltcedar Dr 28411
Saltee Way 28409
Salters Rd 28411
Saltmeadow Rd 28411
Saltram Ct 28411
Saltwood Ln 28411
Salty Bay Lndg 28409
Sampson St 28401
San Jose Ct & Rd 28412
San Mateo Dr 28412
San Palo Ave 28409
Sand Bar Ln 28409
Sand Trap Ct 28412
Sandcastle Ct 28405
Sanderling Pl 28411
Sanders Rd 28412
Sandfiddler Pointe Rd 28409
Sands Hill Dr 28409
Sandwedge Pl 28405
Sandy Ct 28412
Sandy Pt 28411
Sandybrook Rd 28411
Sansberry Ct 28411
Santa Ana Dr 28412
Santa Maria Ave 28411
Sapling Cir & Ct 28411
Sapphire Ridge Rd 28409
Sardou Rd 28412
Sarensen Ct 28412
Satara Dr 28412
Saucier Way 28405
Saulnier St 28403
Sausalito Dr 28412
Savanna Run Loop 28411
Savannah Ct 28403
Saville Ct 28411
Savoy Cir 28412
Sawmill Creek Ln 28411
Saybrook Dr 28405
Scallop Ln 28409
Scarborough Dr 28409
Scenic Cir 28411
Schooner Pl 28412
Scientific Park Dr 28405
Scorpion Dr 28411
Scotland Ln 28409
Scots Pl E & W 28412
Scotts Glen Dr 28411
Scotts Hill Loop Rd 28411
Scotts Hill Medical Dr 28411
Scottsdale Dr 28411
Scout Camp Hatila Rd 28409
Scratch Ct 28412
Scrimshaw Pl 28405
Sea Bass Ln 28409
Sea Castle Ct 28412
Sea Eagle Ct 28409
Sea Gull Ln 28409
Sea Lilly Ln 28409
Sea Mist Ct 28409
Sea Robin Ct 28409
Sea Shell Ln 28411
N & S Seabreeze Blvd &
Rd 28409
Seabrook Ct 28403
Seabuoy Cir 28409
Seabury Ct 28403
Seacrest Rd 28405
Seahawk Sq 28403
Seascape Dr 28409
Seaview Rd 28409
Seawind Ln 28405
Sebastian Ln 28412
Sebrell Ave 28403
Sedgewick Ct 28412
Sedgewood Rd 28403
Sedgley Dr 28412
Selkirk Ct 28411
Seminole Trl 28409
Semmes Dr 28412
Senova Trce 28405
Sentinel Ct 28409
Sentry Oaks Dr 28409
Sequoia Ct 28403
Serena Ct 28411
Serenity Point Rd 28409
Sericea Ct 28412
Setter Ct & Ln 28411
Settlers Dream Pl 28409
Shackleford Dr 28411
Shadebranch Ct 28411
Shadow Ct 28409
Shadow Branch Ln 28409
Shadow Moss Ct 28412
Shady Brook Ln 28411
Shady Grove Dr 28401
Shady Oaks Ln 28412
Shaftesbury Pl 28409
Shakespeare Dr 28405
Shallowford Dr 28412
Shamrock Dr 28409
Shandy Ln 28409
Shannon Dr 28409
Sharaz Way 28411
Sharease Cir 28405
Sharon Dr 28409
Shaw Ct 28405
Shaw Dr 28411
Shawnee Trl 28412
Shaws Aly 28401
Sheffield Ct & Dr 28411
Shelby Ct 28409
Shell Midden Ct 28411
Shell Point Pl 28405
Shell Road Village Dr 28403
Shelley Dr
200-299 28409
4800-5099 28405
Shelter Cove Pl 28405
Shelton Ct 28412
Shenandoah St 28411
Sheppard Rd 28411
Sherbon Way 28411
Sheridan Dr 28401
Sherman Oaks Dr 28411
Sherwood Dr 28401
Shetland Dr 28409
Shiloh Dr 28409
Shinn Creek Ln 28409
Shinn Point Rd 28409
Shinnwood Rd 28409
Shipwatch Dr 28412
Shipyard Blvd
1-1699 28412
1700-4599 28403
Shipyard Walk 28401
Shire Ln 28411
Shirley Rd 28405
Shoalcreek Pl 28405
Shoals Dr 28411
Shoemakers Ln 28409
Shoreline Pl 28403
Shorepoint Dr 28411
Shorewood Hills Dr 28409
Short Putt Ct 28412
Shortfin Dr 28405
Shortwater Dr 28411
Shuney St 28409
Sidbury Rd 28411
Sidney Dr 28405
Sierra Dr 28409
Sigmon Rd 28403
Signature Pl 28405
Silkweed Ct 28405
Silva Terra Dr 28412
Silver Rd 28409
Silver Grass Ct 28405
Silver Lake Rd 28412
Silver Ring Ct 28411
Silver Stream Ln 28401
Silverbell Ct 28409
Simmons Dr 28411
Simon St 28401
Single Tree Ct 28411
Sir Galahad Ct & Dr 28403
Sir Tyler Dr 28405
Sirius Dr 28405
Six Run Creek Ln 28403
Skeet Rd 28409
Skimmer Rd 28411
Skipper Ln 28403
Skycrest Ct 28411
Skystasail Dr 28403
Sleepy Hollow Ln 28409
Slice Ct 28412
Slipper Shell St 28412
Sloop Lndg 28409
Small Dove Ct 28412
Smalley Ct 28409
Smallwood Ct 28411
Smilax Ln 28412
Smith Aly & St 28401
Smith Bay Cir E & W 28405
Smugglers Ct 28405
Snowberry Ct 28409
Snug Harbour Dr 28405
Soaring Spirit Dr 28409
Softwind Way 28403
Solera Dr 28403
Solid Hollow Rd 28412
Solomon Aly 28401
Somerset Ln 28409
Somersett Ln 28409
Song Sparrow Ct 28412
Songbird Ct 28411
Sophia Ct 28412
Sound View Dr 28409
Sound Watch Dr 28409
Sounds Point Rd 28411
Soundside Dr 28412
South Walk 28401
Southerland Farm Dr 28411
Southern Blvd 28401
Southern Charm Dr 28412
Southern Exposure 28412
Southfield Dr 28405
Southgate Dr 28405
Southgate Rd 28412
Southwind Dr 28409
Southwold Dr 28409
Spaniel Ct 28411
Spanish Moss Way 28412
Spanish Wells Dr 28405
Spargo Pl 28409
Sparrow Hawk Ct 28409
Spartan Rd 28405
Spaulding Dr 28405
Spearow Ln 28411
Spencer Ct 28412
Spicetree Dr 28412
Spicewood St 28405
Spike Rush Ct 28405
Spinnaker Pl 28405
Spirea Dr 28403
Split Rail Dr 28412
Splitbrook Ct 28411
Spofford Cir 28403
Spotswood Ct 28409
Spring Ave 28403
Spring Rd 28401
Spring Branch Rd 28405
Spring Creek Ln 28411
Spring Garden Dr 28403
Spring Peeper Ln 28411
Spring Valley Rd 28405
Spring View Dr 28405
Springdale Dr 28405
Springer Rd 28411
Springfield Dr 28405
Springhill Rd 28411
Springtime Rd 28405
Spruce Cir & Dr 28403
Spy Glass Ct 28411
Squire Ln 28411
St James St 28401
Staffordshire Dr 28412
Standsberry Ln 28412
Stanley St 28401
Stapleton Rd 28412
Star Harbor Rd 28409
Starfix Ter 28405
Starkey Aly 28401
Station Rd 28405
Staunton Ct 28405
Stearman Ct 28409
Stedwick Ct 28412
Steeplechase Rd 28412
Stembridge Ct 28409
Stephens Church Rd 28411
Sterling Pl 28403
Stetten Ct 28412
Stevenson Dr 28405
E Stewart Cir 28405
Still Meadow Dr 28412
Still Pine Dr 28412
Stillpond Rd 28409
Stillwater Pl 28405
Stillwell Rd 28412
Stockbridge Pl 28412
Stoddard Rd 28412
Stokley Dr 28403
Stone Ct 28412
Stone Wood Ct 28411
Stonebridge Rd 28409
Stonehaven Ct 28411
Stonehead Ct 28411
Stonemoor Ct 28405
Stones Edge Loop 28405
Stonewall Jackson Dr 28412
Stoneybrook Rd 28411
Stonington Dr 28412
Strada St 28409
Stradleigh Rd 28403
Stratford Blvd 28403
Stratton Village Ln 28409
Strawfield Dr 28405
Strickland Pl 28403
Striking Island Dr 28403
Stroud Aly 28401
Stumpy Ct 28405
Sturbridge Rd 28405
Sturdivant Dr 28403
Suffolk Ln 28409
Sugar Creek Ct 28412
Sugar Pine Dr 28412
Suisan Bay Ct 28412
Summer Haven Ave 28405
Summer Hideaway Rd 28409
Summer Rest Rd 28405
Summer Sands Pl 28405
Summer Woods Dr 28412
Summerlin Falls Ct 28412
Summertime Ln 28405
Summertree Ln 28412
Summit Walk 28401
Sumter Dr 28412
Sun Coast Dr 28411
Sunburst Ct 28411
Suncourt Villa Dr 28409
Sundance Way 28409
Sundial Ct 28405
Sunglow Dr 28405
Sunn Aire Ct 28405
Sunny Ct 28412
Sunnybranch Dr 28411
Sunnyside Dr 28411
Sunnyvale Dr 28412
Sunrise Ln 28409
Sunrunner Pl 28405
Sunseeker Dr 28411
Sunset Ave 28401
Sunset Woods Dr 28412
Sunwood Cir 28405
Superior Rd 28412
Surf Ct 28411
Surrey St 28401
Surrey Downs Ct 28403
Susquehanna Ln 28403
Sussex Ct 28411
Sutton Dr 28409
Sutton Lake Rd 28401
Sutton Steam Plant
Rd 28401
Swan Mill Rd 28405
Swann St 28401
Sweet Gum Holw 28409
Sweetbay Ct 28405
Sweetbriar Rd 28403
Sweetgrass Ct 28412
Sweetwater Dr 28411
Swift Wind Pl 28405
Swiss Stone Ct 28412
Sycamore St
100-799 28405
5500-5599 28403
Sycamore Hollow Dr 28409
Sylvan Dr 28403
Sylvan Ln
400-499 28409
6600-6799 28411
Tabor Ln 28405
Taft Aly 28401
Tahoe Rd 28412
Talamore Ct 28412
Talbury Ct 28411
Taliga Ln 28412
Tall Mast Ct 28409
Tall Pine Ct 28409
Tall Ships Ln 28409
Tall Tree Ln 28409
Talon Ct 28409
Tanager Ct 28403
Tanbark Dr 28412
Tanbridge Rd 28405
Tandem Ct 28405
Tangelo Dr 28412
Tangier Dr 28403
Tanglewood Dr 28409
Tanlaw Ct 28412
Tansey Close Dr 28409
Tara Dr 28409
Tara Ln 28411
Tarbert Ct 28411
Tarheel Ct 28403
Tarin Rd 28409
Tarpon Dr 28409
Tarrants Ct 28411
Tassle Ct 28411
Tate Aly 28401
Tattersalls Dr 28403
Taylor St 28401
Taylor Homes 28401
Teal St 28403
Teaticket Ln 28409
Technology Dr 28405
Telephone Rd 28403
E & W Telfair Cir 28412
Tenby Ct 28411
Tennessee Ave 28401
Tennwood Dr 28411
Terminal Rd N & S 28401
Terrace Walk 28401
Terrapin Ct 28409
Terrington Dr 28412
Terry Ln 28405
Tesla Park Dr 28412
Teviot Dr 28412
Tewkesbury Ct 28411
Thais Trl 28411
Thaxton Ct 28403
The Isle 28412
The Cape Blvd 28412
The Kings Hwy 28409
Thetford Ct 28411
Thickett Pl 28409
Thistle Ct 28411
Thomas Ave 28405
Thomas C Jervay
Loop 28401
Thornblade Cir 28411
Thornin Ct 28405
Thrasher Ct 28403
Thrush Dr 28403
Thurgood Rd 28411
Thursley Rd 28412
Thurston Ct 28411
Tiara Dr 28412
Tibbys Dr 28411
Tiburon Dr 28403
Tidal Oaks 28409
Tidal Reach Ct 28403
Tidalwalk Dr 28409
Tidefall Ct 28403
Tidewater Ln 28403
Tiffany Dr 28405
Tilbury Dr 28411
Tillson Ct 28411
Tillson Rd 28412
Timber Ln 28405
Timber Circle Ln 28411
Timber Creek Ln 28411
Timber Lake Ln 28411
Timme Rd 28401
Tipton Ct 28409
Tisbury Ln 28412
Titleist Ln 28412
Tiverton Way 28405
Toddlo Ct 28409
Tollington Dr 28412

Tonbo Trl 28409
Toomers Aly 28401
Top Flite Ln 28412
Topsail Ln 28411
Torchwood Blvd 28411
Tortoise Ln 28409
Tottenham Ct 28409
Touch Me Not Dr 28405
Toulon Dr 28405
Tower Ct 28412
Towles Rd 28409
Town Center Dr 28405
Trace Dr & Rd 28411
Tradd Ct 28401
Trademark Dr 28405
Trafalgar Rd 28405
Trail In The Pines St 28409
Trailing Vine Ln 28409
Trailmark Dr & Rd 28405
Trails End Rd 28409
Transcom Ct 28401
Trap Way 28412
Trask Rd 28405
Travelers Ct 28412
Treadwell St 28403
Treasure Ln 28411
Treasure Island Way 28411
Tree Frog Ct 28411
Tree Lake Ct 28411
Tree Swallow Ct 28411
Tree Toad Ct 28411
Tree Top Way 28409
Treeswallow Rd 28411
Trelawney Ct 28411
Trellis Ct 28409
Tremont Ct 28411
Trevis Ln 28412
Trey Ct 28403
Treybrooke Dr 28409
Treyburn Dr 28411
Trimaran Pl 28405
Trinity Ave 28411
Triplett Way 28409
Tristram Pl 28403
Trolley Ln 28403
Trombay Dr 28412
Troon Ct 28403
Tropic Ct 28409
Trowbridge St 28403
Troy Dr 28401
Truesdale Rd 28405
Trumpet Vine Way 28412
Tudor Ct 28409
Tulane Dr 28403
Tulip Dr 28409
Tullamore Pl 28409
Tumbril Ln 28412
Tupelo Dr 28411
Turgotine Ln 28412
Turnberry Ln & Pl 28405
Turnstone Ct 28409
Turtle Cay 28412
Turtle Dove Ct 28412
Turtle Hall Dr 28409
Tuscan Way 28411
Twin Leaf Rd 28405
Twin Magnolias Ln 28409
Twisted Oak Pl 28405
Two Mile Cir E & W 28405
Tyler Pl 28409
Ulloa Pl 28412
Ullswater Ln 28405
University Dr 28403
Upland Dr 28411
Upper Reach Dr 28409
Upton Ct 28409
Us Highway 17 28411
Us Highway 421 N 28401
Uss Battleship Rd 28401
Vale Dr 28411
Valencia Ct 28412
Valley Brook Rd 28412
Valley Forge Ct 28411
Vallie Ln 28412
Valor Dr 28411
Van Ambridge Aly 28401
Van Buren St 28401
Van Campen Blvd 28403
Van Dorn Ct 28412
Van Dyke Dr 28405
Vance St 28412
Vancouver Ct 28412
Vanderhorst Pl 28405
Vann Ave 28403
Varsity Dr 28403
Vella Ln 28411
Ventana Dr 28411
Ventura Dr 28412
Venus Ct 28405
Vera Ct 28403
Verandah Way 28411
Verbenia Dr 28409
Verdura Dr 28409
Verona Dr 28411
Verrazzano Dr & Pl 28405
Vespar Ct 28411
Vicar Ct 28405
Victoria Dr 28401
Victory Gardens Dr 28409
Viking Ct 28405
Villa Ct & Pl 28409
Village Dr 28401
Village At Greenfield 28401
Village Park Dr 28405
Vincennes Pl 28405
Vinewood Ct 28405
Vineyard Ln 28403
Vintage Club Cir & Dr 28411
Vintner Ct 28409
Violet Ct 28409
Virgie Rhodes Ln 28401
Virgil Ln 28412
Virginia Ave 28401
Vision Dr 28403
Vista Green Ct 28412
Vistamar Dr 28405
Vitamin Dr 28401
Voltaire Pl 28412
Vowel Ave 28411
Voyagers Way 28412
Waccamaw Ct 28412
Waddell St 28401
Wade Hampton Ct 28411
Wagon Ct 28412
Wagon Wheel Way 28411
Wakefield Rd 28403
Walden Dr 28401
Walker Ridge Ct 28412
Walking Horse Ct 28411
N Wallace Ave 28403
S Wallace Ave
100-199 28403
200-399 28409
N Wallace Cir 28403
Wallington Rd 28409
Walnut St 28401
Walston Dr 28412
Walter Ave 28409
Waltmoor Rd 28409
Waltonwood Ln 28409
Ward St 28412
Warlick Dr 28409
N & S Warrendale Ct 28409
Washington St 28401
Watauga Rd 28412
N & S Water St 28401
Watermill Way 28409
Waters Point Ct 28412
Watson Dr 28405
Waverly Dr 28403
Waxmyrtle Ct 28409
Waylon Rd 28411
Wayne Dr 28403
Wayneridge Ct 28411
Weatherby Ct 28405
Web Trce 28409
Wedderburn Dr 28412
Wedgefield Dr 28409
Weeping Willow Rd 28409
Weimarner Ct 28411
Welborn Rd 28409
Welch Way 28411
Welcome Ln 28409
Wellesley Dr 28409
Wellfleet Ct 28412
Wellington Ave
500-1699 28401
1700-1799 28403
Wellington Dr 28411
Wellspring Way 28403
Welmont Dr 28412
Wendover Ct & Ln 28411
Wentworth Ct 28403
Wescot Ct 28409
Wesley Dr 28403
West Dr 28401
Westbrook Ave 28403
Westbrook Dr 28405
Westbury Ct 28412
Westchester Rd 28409
Westminister Way 28405
Weston Ct 28409
Westover Rd 28403
Westport Dr 28409
Westprong Way 28403
Westridge Ct 28411
E & W Westwood Dr 28405
Wetherill Ln 28412
Wetland Dr 28412
Wetsig Dr 28403
Weybridge Ln 28409
Whaler Way 28409
Whaley Cir 28412
Wheatfields Ct 28411
Wheel Estate Trailer Park 28405
Whimberley Ct 28409
Whimbrel Ct 28409
Whimsy Way 28411
Whintert Dr 28412
Whipporwill Ln 28409
E Whisper Creek Ln 28409
Whisper Park Ct & Dr 28411
Whispering Doe Dr 28409
Whispering Pines Ct 28409
Whispering Woods Ct 28411
Whistler Ave 28401
White Rd
1500-1799 28405
2000-3099 28411
White Columns Way 28411
White Heron Rd 28412
White Ibis Ct 28412
White Oak Dr 28409
White Swan Ct 28412
Whitehorse Ct 28412
Whitehurst Dr 28409
Whites Ave 28403
Whiteweld Ter 28412
Whiting Cv 28412
Whitner Dr 28409
Whitney Dr 28411
Whittle Ct 28411
Wickford Dr 28409
Wickslow Rd 28412
Widgeon Dr 28403
Wild Cherry Ln 28411
Wild Dunes Cir 28411
Wild Iris Rd 28412
Wild Magnolia Rd 28411
Wild Rice Way 28412
Wild Turkey Pl 28405
Wildberry Ct 28411
Wilderness Rd 28412
Wildwood Cir 28409
Wilkinson Aly 28401
Willanda Dr 28403
Willard St 28401
William And Mary Pl 28409
William Louis Dr 28405
Williams Rd 28409
Williamsburg Ct 28411
Williamson Dr 28412
Willoughby Park Ct 28412
Willow St 28405
Willow Way 28412
Willow Glen Dr 28412
Willow Woods Dr 28409
Willowick Park Dr 28409
Wilmington Ave 28403
Wilshire Blvd 28403
Wilson St 28401
Wilton Ct 28409
Wimbledon Ct 28412
Winchester Ter 28405
Wind Bluff Cir 28409
Windchase Ln 28409
Windchime Dr 28412
Windemere Rd 28405
Windgate Dr 28412
Winding Branches Dr 28412
Windingwood Ln 28411
Windjammer Ln 28409
Windlass Dr 28409
Windlea Run 28409
Windmill Way 28405
Winds Ridge Dr 28409
Windsail Dr 28401
Windsong Rd 28411
Windsor Dr 28403
Windstar Ln 28411
Windswept Pl 28405
Windtree Rd 28412
Windward Dr 28409
Windy Hills Dr 28409
Wine Cellar Cir 28411
Winecoff Ct 28409
Winery Way 28411
Winforde Dr & Rd 28412
Winged Foot Ln 28411
Wingfoot Way 28412
Wingpointe Pl 28409
Winslow Ave 28412
Winston Blvd 28403
Winter Moss Ln 28411
Winterberry Ct 28403
Wintergreen Rd 28409
Wiregrass Rd 28405
Wishing Well Ln 28409
Wisteria Dr 28401
Wisteria Ln 28409
Wolcott Ave 28403
Wolfhead Ct 28411
Wolfhound Ct 28411
Wonder Way 28401
Wood Cove Rd 28409
Wood Ridge Rd 28409
Wood Sorrell Rd 28405
Woodberry Ct 28411
Woodbine St 28401
Woodburn Ct 28411
Woodcreek Cir 28411
Woodcroft Dr 28405
Wooddale Dr 28403
Woodduck Cir 28409
Woodfield Ct 28409
Woodhall Dr 28411
Woodland Dr 28403
Woodland Trce 28409
Woodland Forest Ct 28403
Woodlawn Ave 28401
Woods Ave 28401
Woods Edge Rd 28409
Woodscape Dr 28409
Woodstock Dr 28412
Wooler Ct 28411
Wooster St
1-1699 28401
1800-1899 28403
Wordsworth Dr 28405
Worth Dr 28412
Worthington Ct & Way 28411
Wrenwood Cir 28405
Wrexham Ct 28411
Wright St 28401
Wrights Aly 28401
Wrightsboro Rd 28405
Wrightsville Ave & Pl 28403
Wrightsville Green Ave 28403
Wyck Farm Way 28405
Wycliffe Ct 28405
Wyndham Way 28411
Wynfield Dr 28405
Wynnwood St 28401
Wynstone Ct 28405
Wythe Pl 28409
Yale Dr 28403
Yardley Ln 28412
Yarmouth Way 28409
Yaupon Dr 28401
Yearling Ln 28411
Yellow Bell Rd 28411
Yellow Daisy Dr 28412
Yester Oak Dr 28405
Yolanda Dr 28409
York Ct 28411
Yorkshire Ln 28409
Yorktown Dr 28401
Yucca Dr 28405
Yulan Dr 28412
Yvonne Rd 28411
Zekes Run 28411
Zephyr Dr 28412
Zest Ct 28411
Zinnia Ct 28401

NUMBERED STREETS

2 Chopt Rd 28405
N & S 2nd 28401
N & S 3rd 28401
N & S 4th 28401
N & S 5th 28401
N & S 6th 28401
7 Oaks Dr 28411
N & S 7th 28401
N & S 8th 28401
N & S 9th 28401
N & S 10th 28401
N & S 11th 28401
N & S 12th 28401
N & S 13th 28401
N & S 14th 28401
N & S 15th 28401
N & S 16th 28401
N 17th St 28401
1-2699 28401
2700-4499 28412
N 18th St 28405
S 18th St 28403
N 19th St 28405
S 19th St 28403
N 20th St 28405
S 20th St 28403
N 21st St 28405
S 21st St 28403
N 22nd St 28405
N 23rd St 28405
1800-2899 28401
S 23rd St 28403
N 25th St 28405
N 26th St 28405
N 27th St 28405
N 29th St 28405
S 29th St 28403
N 30th St 28405
N 31st St 28405
S 39th St 28403
S 41st St 28403
S 42nd St 28403
S 43rd St 28403
S 44th St 28403
S 47th St 28403
S 48th St 28403
51st St 28403
52nd St 28403
S 52nd St 28409
54th St 28403
S 58th St
100-199 28403
200-299 28409

WILSON NC

General Delivery 27893

POST OFFICE BOXES MAIN OFFICE STATIONS AND BRANCHES

Box No.s
1 - 2999 27894
3001 - 3999 27895
4001 - 5632 27893
6001 - 6356 27894
7001 - 7916 27895
8001 - 8358 27893
9001 - 9154 27895
9998 - 9998 27894
9998 - 9998 27895

RURAL ROUTES

07, 09 27896

NAMED STREETS

Academy St E 27893
Adams St N 27893
Adrian Rd 27896
Adventura Ln E 27893
Agnes Ct 27893
Airport Blvd NW 27896
Airport Blvd W 27893
Airport Cir NW 27896
Airport Dr NW 27896
Akron Rd 27893
Albany Ln SW 27893
Albert Ave NW 27893
Althorp Dr W 27893
Alton Rd 27893
Alyson Dr N 27896
American Eagle Ln NW 27896
Ammons Dr N 27896
Anderson Rd N 27896
Anderson St NW 27893
Andrea Ct N 27896
Anson St NE 27893
Anthony Rd & St W 27893
Anthony Trailer Park 27893
Apache Rd 27893
Appleberry Ct NW 27896
Arapahoe Rd 27893
Arbor Rd N 27893
Arch Ct NW 27896
Arch Finch Rd 27893
Archers Rd NW 27896
Ardsley Rd N 27896
Arrington Ave SW 27893
Arrowwood Dr N 27896
Ash St E 27893
Ashbrook Dr NW 27896
Ashford Dr 27896
Ashland Dr N 27893
Ashpark Ct NW 27896
Astor Dr NW 27896
Atlantic St E 27893
Atlantic Christian Col Dr N 27893
Audubon Pl NW 27896
Augusta Cir SE 27893
Aviation Pl NW 27896
Aycock St S & SW 27893
W Baker Dr & Rd 27896
Bakers Ct 27896
Baldree Rd S 27893
Banks Ln & St 27893
Bar Harbor Dr NW 27896
Barefoot Park Ln SW 27893
Barkley Dr NW 27896
Barnes St S 27893
Barnhill St S 27893
Barrington Dr N 27896
Barron St SW 27893
Bayberry Ln NW 27896
Baybrook Pl N 27896
Baybrooke Dr W 27893
Bayleaf Cir SW 27893
Bayview Dr 27896
Baywood Ct 27896
Beacon St W 27893
Bear Trap Rd NW 27896
Beaver Dam Rd S 27893
Bedgood Dr SW 27893
Beekman Pl NW 27896
Beeler Rd S 27893
Bel Air Ave SE 27893
Beland Ave NW 27896
Bell St NW 27896
Belle Meade Dr NW 27896
Belmont Ave SW 27893
Bennington Pl N 27896
Benton St E 27893
Berkley Rd N 27893
Berkshire Dr NW 27896
Best St E 27893
Biltmore Ct W 27893
Birch St S 27893
Birchwood Dr SE 27893
Black Creek Rd S & SE 27893
Blakewood St E 27893
Blalock Rd 27893
Blazing Star Ln 27896
Blenheim Pl NW 27896
Bloomery Rd 27896
Blount St S 27893
Bluebill Rd 27893
Bluebird Ln 27893
Bluff Pl 27896
Bobolink Ct NW 27896
Bobwhite Trl N 27896
Borden Rd 27893
Boswell St SW 27893
Boswellville Rd 27893
Boyette Dr SW 27893
Boykin Rd 27893
Bradford Dr N 27896
Bragg St NE 27893
Branch St NW 27893
Brandie Ln SW 27893
Brandon Cir NW 27896
Brentwood Cir N 27893
Brentwood Dr N
100-1799 27893
1800-3299 27896
Brentwood Center Ln N 27896
Brewer Ct 27896
Brians Dr E 27893
Briarwood Dr NW 27896
Brickstone Ct N 27896
Bridgers St NW 27896
Briggs St S 27893
Bristol Ct 27896
Britthill Ln 27893
Broad St W 27893
Brook Ln NW 27896
Brookfield Dr NW 27893
Brookhaven Dr NW 27896
Brookside Dr NW
900-1099 27893
1100-1399 27896
Broughton St N 27893
Browning Ct 27896
Bruton Cir & St 27893
Buck Branch Rd 27893
Buckingham Cir & Rd 27896
Bullard Ct 27893
Bunday Cir N 27896
Burkam Ct N 27896
Burning Tree Ln N 27896
Burnside Dr NW 27896
Butterfield Ln SE 27893
Buxton Cir & Rd 27896
Byerly Dr N 27896
Bynum St N 27893
Bynwood Cir & Dr 27893
Caldwell Ave NE 27893
Caleb Ct 27896
Callie Ct 27896
Cam Strader Dr 27896
Cambridge Rd NW 27896
Camden St SW 27893
Camellia Dr 27896
Cameron Rd SW 27893
Canal Dr NW
1300-1400 27893
1402-1798 27893
1900-3099 27896
Canal St E 27893
Canal St NE 27893

Candlewood Dr SW 27893
Cannon St NE 27893
Canterbury Rd NW 27896
Cardinal Dr NW 27896
Cargill Ave S & SE 27893
Carmel Ln N 27896
Carole Dr 27893
Carolee St S 27893
Carolina Ave & St NW & E 27893
Carr Rd 27893
Carrie Rd E 27896
Carroll St E & SE 27893
Carter Rd 27893
Cartwheel Ct 27893
Carver Pl 27893
Carver Trailer Park 27893
Castlewood Dr 27893
Caswell Pl W 27893
Cavalier Cir NW 27893
Cedar St S 27893
Cedar Run Pl NW 27896
Cemetery St S 27893
Center St 27893
Central Rd 27893
Centre St W 27893
Chalk Dr NE 27893
Chamberlain Dr NW 27896
Chandler Dr N 27896
Charles St NE 27893
Charleston St SE 27893
Chase Rd NW 27896
Chateau Ct W 27893
Chelsea Dr NW 27896
Cherokee Rd 27893
Cherry Ln NW 27896
Chesnee Dr NW 27896
Chickasaw Ct 27893
Chicken Dr SW 27893
Chinook Ct & Rd 27893
Chippendale Pl SW 27893
Chippenham Ct N 27896
Christian Rd 27896
Christman St SW 27893
Christopher Dr NW 27896
Church Loop & St 27893
Churchill Ave SW 27893
Citation Ct NW 27896
Claremont Cir E 27893
Clark Ave NE 27893
Claudie Rd 27893
Clearbrook Ln N 27896
Clifford Pl N 27896
Cliftonville Rd 27896
Cloverdale Dr NW 27896
Cloverleaf Dr E 27893
Clyde Ave N & NW 27893
Cockran St SW 27893
Coghill Dr N 27896
Coleman St SE 27893
College Cir & St N & NE 27893
Collinswood Ct 27893
Colonial Ave NW 27896
Columbia Ave NW 27896
Comanche Rd 27893
Commerce Rd S 27893
Community Grocery Rd 27893
Concord Dr N 27896
Cone St N & NW 27893
Conifer Ct N 27896
Connor St N & NW 27893
Contentnea Rd S 27893
Corbett Ave N & NE 27893
Cornish Ct NW 27896
Corporate Pkwy 27893
Cotton Cir SE 27893
Country Club Dr N & NW 27896
Countryside Rd 27896
Courtland Dr NW 27896
Covington Dr N 27896
Cozart Rd NW 27893
Crabtree Rd & St S 27893
Craft Ln 27893
Cranberry Ridge Dr SW 27893
Crane Dr SW 27893
Crawford St S 27893
Creekside Cir & Dr 27896
Crepe Myrtle Ct & Rd 27896
Crescent Dr W 27893
Crest Rd 27893
Crestview Ave SW 27893
Crisp Rd 27893
Crossmoor Dr 27896
Crowell St E 27893
Crystal Dr SW 27893
Cypress Dr NW 27896
Daffodil Dr N 27896
Daisy Ln N 27896
Dale St SW 27893
Daniel St W 27893
Darden Ln E 27893
Darien Pl NW 27896
Dartmore Dr N 27896
Davie St SE 27893
Davis St S 27893
Davis Farms Dr N 27896
Dayton Dr S 27893
Deans St W 27893
Deer Creek Dr N 27896
Deer Path Dr NW 27896
Deer Trail Ln 27893
Deerfield Ln N 27896
Dees Ct NW 27893
Delano Ave SW 27893
Delwood Dr W 27893
Denby St SW 27893
Devonshire Dr 27896
Dew St S 27893
Dewey St SW 27893
Dewfield Dr N 27896
Dianne Dr NW 27896
Dixie Inn Rd 27893
Dixon Ct NW 27896
Dogwood Ln NW 27896
Doral Ln N 27896
Dorothy Ln 27893
Douglas St E & S 27893
Dove Rd 27896
Dover St W 27893
Downing Rd & St SW 27893
Drakemoor Rd 27896
Drexel St N 27893
Drummond Dr 27896
Dryden Pl NW 27896
Dunbar St SE 27893
Dunn St S 27893
Durban Dr 27896
Eagle Rd NW 27893
Eagle Farm Dr N 27896
Eagle Point Ln 27896
Eaglechase Dr NW 27896
Early Bird Ln 27893
East St E & SE 27893
Eclipse Way 27896
Edgewood St S 27893
Edinburgh Dr NW 27896
Edwards St S 27893
El Ramey Cir SE 27893
Elba St E 27893
Eliza Pl N 27896
Elizabeth Rd W 27893
Ellington Dr NW 27896
Ellis St S & SW 27893
Elmwood Ln S 27893
Elvie St S & SE 27893
Elvie School Dr S 27893
Emma Dr N 27896
Emory St SW & W 27893
W End Ave NW 27893
Ensworth Rd NW 27896
Eon Dr 27893
Ernest Rd 27893
Essex Cir NW 27896
Etheridge Rd 27893
Evansdale Rd 27893
Evergreen Dr NW 27896
Expressway Dr 27893
Fair Pl S 27893
Fairfax Ave NE 27893
Fairfield Dairy Rd 27893
Fairview Ave SW 27893
Faison St E 27893
Falconcrest Ct 27896
Falling Maple Dr NW 27896
Fangra Ct 27893
Farmington Pl NW 27896
Farmwood Loop 27896
Farrior Ave SE 27893
Fawn Ct N 27893
Feldspar Ct SW 27893
Ferndale Ct NW 27893
Fieldcrest Rd E 27893
Fieldstream Dr N 27896
Fikewood St E 27893
Filmore Rd 27893
Finch St SE 27893
Firestone Ln N 27896
Firestone Pkwy NE 27893
Fisher Ct N 27896
Fitch Dr E 27893
Fleming St NE 27893
Flint Ln SW 27893
Flowers Dr N 27896
Flowers Rd 27893
Forest Hills Loop SW 27893
Forest Hills Rd NW
100-199 27893
200-1599 27896
Forest Hills Rd SW 27893
Forest Hills Rd W 27893
Forrest Rd W 27893
Fountain Dr NE 27893
Foxcroft Rd NW 27896
Foxfire Ln N 27896
Frank Price Church Rd 27893
Franklin Ave W 27893
Fred Ct 27893
Freeman St SE 27893
Friendship Dr N 27893
Fulton Pl NW 27896
Gardners School Rd 27893
Garner St SW & W 27893
Garrett Dr NW 27896
Garwin Dr W 27893
Gate House Ct 27896
Gay St S 27893
Gee Ln SE 27893
Geneva Ln & Pl 27896
Georgetown Dr N 27896
Gina Ct NW 27896
Glen Eagles Ln N 27896
Glen Laurel Rd 27893
Glendale Dr SW & W 27893
Glenview Cir E 27893
Glory Rd 27893
Gloucester Dr W 27893
Gold St E 27893
Goldfinch Ln NW 27896
Goldsboro St E 27893
Gooseneck Ln 27893
Grace Dr NW 27896
Grace St S 27893
Graham St SE 27893
Granger St S 27893
Granite Ct SW 27893
Grapevine Ct 27896
Gray St NE 27893
Green St E & NE 27893
Green Wing Rd 27893
Greenbriar Ct & Rd 27896
Greenbriar Mhp 27893
Greenbrier Ln N 27896
Greenwich Ln NW 27896
Gregory Ln SW 27893
Greystone Cir & Dr 27893
Grimsley Store Rd 27893
Grove St N & NE 27893
Gulfstream Dr 27893
Hackney St E 27893
Hadley St SE 27893
Hampton Ct & Rd 27896
Hanover Ave SW 27893
Harper St E & NE 27893
Harrison Dr N 27893
Hart Ave NW 27896
Harvest Ln SW 27893
Hatcher Ln N 27896
Hathaway Rd 27896
Hawker Cir 27896
Hawthorne Ln W 27893
Hayes Pl 27893
Hayes Pl W 27896
Heard Rd N 27896
Heather Ct 27893
Heaths Glen Rd 27893
Henry St W 27893
Heritage Dr & Vlg W 27893
Herman Dr NW 27896
Hermitage Rd NW 27896
Herring Ave E & NE 27893
Hicks St S 27893
Highfield Dr 27893
Highland Dr NW 27893
Highmeadow Ln N 27896
Hill St NE 27893
Hillcrest Dr W 27893
Hillman Dr SE 27893
Hines St S 27893
Hinson Acres S 27893
Holdens Cross Rd 27893
Holly St & Trl S 27893
Holman Dr 27893
Hood St SW 27893
Hooks St S 27893
Hope Dr NW 27896
Horace St NE 27893
Horace Watson Rd S 27893
Hornes Church Rd 27893
Horseshoe Ln 27896
Horton Blvd SW 27893
Howard Jones Ct E 27893
Hudson Rd NW 27896
Hunter St SW 27893
Hunting Ridge Rd NW 27896
Huntington St SW 27893
Huntsmoor Ln 27896
Hutchens Rd 27893
Hyannis Dr NW 27896
Hyatt Dr W 27893
Ida St 27896
Imperial Ave E 27893
Independence Dr 27896
Industrial Ave NE 27893
Industrial Park Dr SE 27893
Inkberry Cir N 27896
International Blvd 27893
Irene Dr NW 27896
Irma St SE 27893
Ironwood Dr N 27896
Iroquois Rd 27893
Ivy Ct 27893
Jackson St NE & W 27893
James St NE 27893
James Town Dr 27896
Janice Ct 27893
Jayne Ln NW 27896
Jefferson St W 27893
Jennette Cir N 27896
Jennings Farm Dr NW 27896
Jetstream Dr NW 27896
Joel Ln N 27896
Johns Ln 27896
Jonathan Ct 27896
Jones Rd & St 27893
Jonesey Rd 27893
Jordan St S & SW 27893
Joweaver Rd 27893
Juniper Ln NW 27896
Katharine Ct W 27893
Kauffman Ct E 27893
Kavanaugh Rd NW 27896
Kelly Pl N 27896
Kenan St NW 27893
Kenmore St N 27893
Kennedy Rd 27893
Kenroy Rd 27893
Kensington Ave NW 27896
Kent Dr & Rd N 27896
Kevin Ln 27896
Keystone Pl 27893
Killdeer Ln N 27896
Killette St SW 27893
Kimberly Ln SW 27893
Kincaid Ave N & NW 27893
King Charles Blvd SE 27893
Kings Mill Walk N 27896
Kingswood Rd NW 27896
Knightdale Dr S 27893
Knollwood Dr NW 27896
Koval Ct SW 27893
Kristin Ln 27893
Lady Marian Rd N 27896
Lafayette Dr NW 27893
Lake Forest Dr 27896
Lake Hills Dr 27896
Lake Wilson Rd N 27896
Lakehaven Ct 27896
Lakeside Dr NW 27896
Lamm Rd
4700-5599 27893
5600-6499 27896
Lamm Rd SW 27893
Lancaster Rd NW 27896
Landfill Rd 27893
Landover Ln 27893
Landrum Dr NW 27896
Lane St SE 27893
Larkspur Rd 27893
Lattice Rd 27893
Laurel Ln NW 27896
Laurents Rd 27893
Lawndale Dr NE 27893
Layton Ave S 27893
Leanne Cir 27893
Lear Ct NW 27896
Lee Ln 27896
Lee St E 27893
Lee St N 27893
Lee St NE 27893
Lely Rd 27893
Lennox Dr NW 27896
Lenoir Dr E 27893
Lewis St SE 27893
Lexington Dr NW 27896
Libby St W 27893
Lillian Rd W 27893
Lincoln St S & SE 27893
Linden Ln NW 27896
Linton Mobile Park 27893
Lipscomb Rd E 27893
Litchfield Rd N & S 27893
Litchford Ln NW 27896
Little John Dr N 27896
Live Oak Ln N 27896
Livedo Dr 27893
Lochmere Rd 27893
Lodge St E & S 27893
London Dr NE 27893
London Church Rd NE 27893
Long Branch Rd 27893
Longview Cir & Dr 27893
Lucas Ave N 27893
Luther Rd 27893
Lynch Cir NW 27893
Lynn Dr W 27893
Lynwood Ave NE 27893
Maclaga Rd S 27893
Macon St S 27893
Madison Dr W 27893
Mallard Ln 27893
Mallory Ave 27896
Malpass Dr S 27893
Mamie Rd 27893
Manchester St SE 27893
Maple Leaf Ln 27893
Maplewood Ave NE 27893
Marguerite Ln NW 27896
Marie St SE 27893
Marion Ct N 27896
Mark Pl 27893
Marlboro Dr E 27893
Marlow St E 27893
Marlowe Rd N 27893
Martha Ln N 27896
Martin Luther King Jr Pkwy E & SE 27893
Mary Ella Mobile Home Park 27893
Marybeth Ct N 27896
Masters Ln N 27896
Matthews Rd 27893
Maury St S 27893
Mayflower Dr NW 27893
Mayo St E 27893
Mclamb Cir N 27893
Mcnair St SW 27893
Mcrae Rd NW 27896
S Meade Pl NW 27896
Meadow St S & SW 27893
Meadowbrook Ln W 27893
Medical Park Dr W 27893
Mercer St SW
300-502 27893
501-501 27894
503-1499 27893
504-1498 27893
Merck Rd W 27893
Merrick St SE 27893
Merrills Park Dr NW 27896
Meteor Dr 27893
Micheal Dr 27896
Midway Trailer Park 27893
Mill Br 27893
Millbrook Dr SW 27893
Miller Rd S 27893
Millhaven Ct W 27893
Milliken Close N 27896
Millridge Cir W 27893
Minchew St SE 27893
Mink Rd 27896
Mitchell Pl SW 27893
Montgomery Dr SW & W 27893
Monticello Dr NW 27896
Montreat Ct NW 27896
Moore St S 27893
Morningside Rd 27893
Mosby St SW 27893
Moss St W 27893
Mount Vernon Dr NW 27893
Moye Ave NW 27893
Mulberry Ln NW 27896
Nantucket Dr NW 27896
Naomi Dr N 27896
Narrow Way E 27893
Nash Pl N 27896
Nash St E 27893
Nash St N
900-2014 27893
2016-4898 27896
Nash St NE 27893
Nash St NW
901-2015 27893
2017-4899 27896
Nash St S 27893
Nash St SE 27893
Nash St SW 27893
Nash St W 27893
Navaho Ln 27893
Nc Highway 42 E & W 27893
Nc Highway 58 N 27896
Nc Highway 58 S 27893
E Nc Highway 97 27896
Nealshire Dr NW 27896
New St S 27893
New Bern St SE 27893
Newton Ave NW 27896
Niki Dr 27896
No Record St 27896
Noland Rd E 27893
Nora St S 27893
Norfolk St S 27893
Norris Blvd W 27893
North Ave N 27893
Northmeade Pl NW 27896
Norwood Dr N 27896
Nottingham Rd NW 27896
Oak Ave E 27893
Oak Forest Dr NW 27896
Oakdale Cir, Dr & Rd E & W 27893
Oakview Ct E 27893
Old Bailey Hwy 27896
Old Dam Dr SW 27893
Old Farm Pl NW 27896
Old Manor Pl 27896
Old Merck Rd W 27893
Old Raleigh Rd 27893
Old Sharpsburg Loop 27893
Old Silver Lake Rd 27896
Old Stantonsburg Rd 27893
Olympic Ln N 27896
Opal Ct SW 27893
Orange St SE 27893
Ortho Dr W 27893
Otter Rd NW 27896
Oxford Cir NW 27893
Packhouse Rd 27896
Panther Branch Rd 27896
Par Three Dr S 27893
Park Ave, Ct & Dr W & SW 27893
Parker Ln S 27893
Parkside Dr NW 27896
Parkview St W 27893
Parkway St W 27893
Parkwood Blvd & Plz W 27893
Parrieli Dr NW 27896
Patrick Ln 27893
Patterson Way S 27893
Paxton Cir W 27893
Peachtree Pl NW 27896
Peachtree Rd NW
1000-1099 27893
1100-1699 27896
Pear Tree Ct NW 27896
Pearson Ct 27896
Pearson Ln 27896
Pearson St N 27893
Pebble Beach Cir N 27896
Pebble Creek Cir 27893
Pecan Ct N 27893
Pender St E 27893
Penny Ln SE 27893
Peppermill Dr N 27896
Petalcrest Cir SE 27893
Pettigrew St E & S 27893
Pheasant Rd NW 27896
Phillip St S 27893
Phillips Rd N 27896
Pickett St SW 27893
Pike St SW 27893
Pima Ct 27893
Pine St NE & W 27893
Pine Needles Ln N 27896
Pine Tree Ct 27896
Pinecrest Dr W 27893
Pinehurst Dr N 27896
Pineview Ave NW 27896
Pinewood Dr NW 27893
Pinnacle Dr N 27896
Pittman Dr NW 27896
Piute Rd 27893
Plaza Dr W 27893
Plum Dr N 27893
Poe St SW 27893
Point Dr NW 27896
Pond Dr N 27896
Ponte Vedra Ln N 27896
Poplar St S 27893
Portsmouth Dr NW 27896
Potato House Ct 27893
Powell St E & SE 27893
Poythress Rd 27893
Prairie Ct 27893
Prestwick Ln N 27896
Princess Anne Cir & Dr 27896
Privette St NE 27893
Providence Ln NW 27896
Purdie St SE 27893
Purdue Dr W 27893
Purina Cir S 27893
Quail Pt W 27893

Quail Rd NW 27896
Quaker Rd 27893
Quality Dr NE 27893
Queen St E 27893
Queen Anne Rd NW 27896
Queensferry Dr NW 27896
Quinn Dr NW 27896
Rabbit Trace Rd 27896
Raccoon Ct NW 27896
Radford Rd 27893
Radio Tower Rd 27893
Railroad St E & S 27893
Raleigh Road Pkwy N 27893
Raleigh Road Pkwy W
100-899 27893
900-5999 27896
Ralston St S 27893
Ramblewood Hill Dr 27893
Ranch Farm Ct 27893
Rand Rd W 27893
Randolph St S 27893
Raper Dr & Rd 27893
Rasberry Dr N 27896
Raven Ridge Dr NW 27896
Red Haven Ct SW 27893
Redbay Ln N 27896
Redwood Dr SW 27893
Reid St E & SE 27893
Retreat Ct 27893
Richards St W 27893
Richardson Acres Mh Park E 27893
Ricks Ct E 27893
Ricks Rd 27896
Ridge Rd NW 27893
Ridgecrest Rd 27893
Ridgeway St W 27893
Ripley Rd NW 27893
River Rd 27893
Riverbirch Rd N 27896
Riviera Dr NW 27896
Robert Rd W 27893
Robeson St S & SE 27893
Robin Hill Rd NW 27896
Rochester Ct NW 27896
Rock Ridge School Rd 27893
Rock Ridge Sims Rd 27893
Rockport Dr NW 27896
Rogers Ave N 27893
Rolling Brook Ct 27893
Rollingwood Dr NW 27896
Rosebud Church Rd 27893
Rountree Ave & St 27893
Rowe Ave NW 27893
Roxbury Dr N 27893
Ruann Dr SW 27893
Ruffleleaf Cir SE 27893
Runnymeade Rd NW 27896
Sabre Ln 27896
Saddle Run Rd N 27896
Saint Andrews Cir & Dr 27896
Saint Christopher Cir SW 27893
Saint Georges Dr N 27896
Saint John Dr SW 27893
Saint Marys Church Rd 27893
Saint Rose Church Rd 27893
Salem St NW & W 27893
Samuel St NE 27893
Sandford Rd 27893
Sandoz Dr 27893
Sandy Creek Dr SE 27893
Sandy Fork Pl & Rd 27896
Sandy Ridge Dr S 27896
Sauls St SW 27893
Sawdust Rd 27893
Saxby Ln NW 27896
Scotch Highlands Ln N 27896
Scotsfield Rd 27893
Scuppernong Rd 27893
Scythia St SW 27893
Sedgefield Ln N 27896
Selma St SW 27893

Seminole Rd 27893
Senior Village Ln NW 27896
Shadow Ridge Rd N 27896
Shady Rest Trailer Park 27893
Shamrock Dr E 27893
Sharpe Newton Way S 27893
Shawnee Rd 27893
Shepherd Rd 27893
Sherwood Dr N 27896
Shiloh Church Rd 27896
Shirley Rd 27893
Shreve St SW 27893
Sierra Dr NW 27896
Silver Lake Ct 27896
Silver Leaf Rd SW 27893
Silver Pines Trailer Park 27896
Sims St S 27893
Singletary St SE 27893
Skyland Loop 27893
Slabtown Rd 27893
Slate Ct 27893
Smallwood St SW 27893
Smith St E 27893
Snowden Dr SE 27893
Solaris Dr 27896
Somerset Dr N 27896
South St S 27893
Southern Village Dr 27893
Southmeade Pl NW 27896
Spaulding St SE 27893
Speight School Rd 27893
Spicebush Cir 27896
Springflower Dr N 27896
Springlake Pl N 27896
Spruce St S 27893
Squire Ct SW 27893
Stadium St SW 27893
Staff Sergeant Lucas Jr Rd 27896
Stafford Dr W 27893
Stantonsburg Cir & Rd 27893
Stark Cir N 27896
Starmount Cir W 27893
Starship Ln NW 27896
Stedman Dr NW 27896
Steeple Chase Rd N 27896
Steinbeck Dr W 27893
Stemmery St S 27893
Stephenson St S 27893
Stewart Rd N 27896
Stillwater Ct 27893
Stoddard Rd S 27893
Stone Henge Ln W 27893
Stonegate Ct N 27896
Stonemark Ct N 27896
Stoneybrook Dr NW 27896
Stratford Dr N 27893
Stronwood Dr N 27893
Stubb Ln 27893
Sturbridge Dr NW 27896
Sugar Hill Rd 27896
Suggs St S & SE 27893
Sulgrave Dr NW 27896
Summerfield Dr NW 27896
Summit Place Dr NW 27896
Sunflower Ct 27896
Sunnybrook Rd S 27893
Sunnyside Ln W 27893
Sunrise Ave S 27893
Sunset Cres & Rd 27893
Surry Rd NW 27896
Sussex Ln N 27893
Sutton Pl NW 27896
Sweet Williams Ln 27896
Sweetbriar Pl NW 27896
Sycamore St W 27893
Sylvia Ct SE 27893
Tacoma St E & SE 27893
Talon Ct NW 27896
Tamerisk Ln N 27896
Tammy Ln 27893
Tanglewood Dr NW 27896
Tar River Church Rd 27896

Tarboro St E 27893
Tarboro St NE 27893
Tarboro St SW 27893
Tarboro St W
100-1398 27893
1400-1485 27893
1470-1470 27895
1486-2198 27893
1487-1499 27893
Tarboro Street Anx SW 27893
Tarheel Rd S 27893
Tartts Mill Rd 27893
Teal Dr SW 27893
Technology Dr NW 27896
Thistle Dr NW 27896
Thompson Rd 27896
Thompson Chapel Rd 27896
Thompson Chapel Church Rd 27896
Thorne Ave S 27893
Thurston Dr W 27893
Tiffany Dr NW 27896
Tilghman Rd N
1100-2299 27893
2300-3299 27896
Timberlake Dr NW 27896
Tobacco Rd S 27893
Toisnot Ave NE 27893
Toisnot Trailer Park 27893
Tolly Ho Trailer Ct 27893
Tolson Rd S 27893
Toms Ct 27896
Top Ridge Ct 27893
Townes Ct 27896
Trace Dr W 27893
Trafalgar Pl W 27893
E Trail Dr SE 27893
Tranquil Dr SE 27893
Trappers Rd NW 27896
Treemont Rd NW 27896
Trey Rd 27893
Trinity Dr W 27893
Trotters Dr W 27893
Truesdale Dr S 27893
Trull St SW 27893
Tucker Ct 27893
Tumberry Dr 27896
Tunstall Pl SW 27893
Turnage Rd 27893
Turner Ave N 27893
Tuskeegee St E & SE 27893
Tyler Ln 27893
Upland Game Rd NW 27896
Us Highway 117 27893
Us Highway 264 E 27893
Us Highway 264 Alt E 27893
Us Highway 301 E 27893
Valley Cir E 27893
Valley Dale Rd & St W 27893
Vance St E 27893
Vancomer Rd 27893
Varnell Rd 27893
Vick St E & SE 27893
Village Dr W 27893
Villas Ct 27896
Vineyard Dr N 27893
Vintage Ct 27896
Viola St E 27893
Virginia Ave & Rd S 27893
Vogue St NE 27893
Wainwright Ave E & SE 27893
Walbrook Pl N 27896
Wales Pl N 27896
Walker Dr W 27893
Wallace Dr W 27893
Walnut Ln & St S, SW & W 27893
Walnut Creek Dr SW 27893
Walton St SW 27893
Ward Blvd E, NE, S, SE, SW & W 27893
Warehouse Ct 27893
Warren St W 27893

Warwick Pl 27893
Washington St E 27893
Waterford Dr NW 27896
Waterloo Ct 27896
Watson Dr NW 27893
Waverly Rd NW 27896
Wayne St S 27893
Wayside Ct 27893
Weaver Rd 27893
Webb Lake Rd 27893
Webster Dr N 27893
Wedgewood Mnr 27893
Welford Pl N 27896
Wellington Dr SW 27893
Wellons Ct 27893
Wells Ct 27893
Wembly Pl N 27896
Wentworth Ave NW 27896
Wescott Dr & Ln 27896
West Ct W 27893
Westbrook Dr NW 27896
Westchester Ct NW 27896
Westminster Dr NW 27896
Westover Ave W 27893
Westshire Dr N 27896
Westwood Ave W 27893
Wetherly Dr N 27896
Wexford Dr NW 27896
Whetstone Pl N 27896
Whipporwill Ln NW 27896
Whispering Pines Ln N 27896
White Oak Loop 27893
Whitehead Ave NE 27893
Whitley Rd E 27893
Whitlock Dr N 27896
Whitney Ln 27893
Widgeon St SW 27893
Wiggins St S 27893
Wiggins Mill Rd 27893
Wilco Blvd S 27893
Wild Turkey Ct NW 27896
Wildwood Ct NW 27896
Williams St NE 27893
Williamsburg Dr NW 27896
Williamson Rd 27893
Williamson Mobile Home Park N 27893
Willis Ct N 27896
Willow Creek Dr N 27896
Willow Springs Rd S 27893
Willowbrook Ln SW 27893
Wills St SE 27893
Wilshire Blvd & Cir 27893
Wilson St SW 27893
Wilson Christian Rd 27893
Wiltons Ct 27896
Wimbledon Ct N 27896
Winchester St NE 27893
Windemere Dr & Pl 27896
Winding Creek Dr SW 27893
Winding Ridge Dr W 27893
Windsor St W 27893
Wingate Dr N 27896
Winged Foot Ln N 27896
Winoca Rd SW 27893
Winstead St N 27893
Winthorp Ct NW 27896
Wolf Trap Dr NW & W 27896
Womble St SW 27893
Womble Brooks Rd E 27893
Wood Duck Rd 27893
Woodard Ave & St 27893
Woodbridge Rd 27893
Woodcroft Dr W 27893
Woodford Pl W 27893
Woodgreen Dr N 27896
Woodland Dr NW 27893
Woodrow St S & SW 27893
Woods Myrtle Ct N 27896
Woodside Dr & Rd W 27893
Woodstream Dr N 27896
Wooten Blvd SW 27893
Worth Dr E 27893
Wyattwood Dr N 27896
Wyck Pl N 27896

Wyncliff Dr N 27896
Wynfall Ln SW 27893
Wysteria Ln S 27893
Yank Rd 27893
York St SW 27893
Yorkshire Dr NW 27896
Yukon Rd S 27893
Yuma Rd 27893
Zulas Pl 27893

NUMBERED STREETS

All Street Addresses 27893

WINSTON SALEM NC

General Delivery 27102

POST OFFICE BOXES MAIN OFFICE STATIONS AND BRANCHES

Box No.s
1 - 3600 27102
4001 - 4996 27115
5001 - 5994 27113
6001 - 9999 27109
9998 - 9998 27120
10418 - 10418 27108
11001 - 11972 27116
12001 - 12956 27117
15000 - 15804 27113
16001 - 16774 27115
17001 - 18554 27116
20001 - 21694 27120
24001 - 26980 27114
27001 - 27117 27117
27102 - 27120 27102
27108 - 27108 27109
27113 - 27113 27113
27114 - 27114 27114
27115 - 27115 27115
27116 - 27116 27116
27120 - 27120 27120
27130 - 27130 27130
27201 - 27840 27117
28001 - 29999 27109
30001 - 30834 27130
77704001 - 77704030 27104

RURAL ROUTES

02 27103
03, 07, 17 27105
01, 08, 14 27106
09, 11, 12, 16, 19 27107
04, 10, 13 27127

NAMED STREETS

Aaron Ln 27106
Abattoir St 27101
Abbey Ct 27103
Aberdeen Ter 27103
Abingdon Way 27106
Academic Dr 27106
E Academy St 27101
W Academy St
400-1199 27101
1200-2099 27103
E & W Acadia Ave 27127
Acoma Ct 27103
Acorn Ct 27106
Acorn Ln 27107
Acorn Knoll Ln 27101
Act Dr 27107
Ada Ave 27105
Adams Ct 27127
Adams Gate Rd 27107
Adams Morgan Ct 27103

Addison Ave
1000-1299 27101
1300-1499 27105
Ader Dr 27105
Advantage Way 27103
Advent St 27127
Aftonshire Ct 27104
Airport Rd 27105
Airview Dr 27107
Airy Ct 27107
Ajane Ln 27105
Akre Dr & Ln 27107
Akron Dr 27105
Alacherm Dr 27103
Alameda Dr 27105
Alamo Dr 27104
Alani Ct 27103
Albert St 27101
Alcoa Ct 27106
Alcott St 27127
Alden Ln 27103
Alder St 27127
Alderney Ln 27103
Alex Dr 27127
Alexander Rd 27106
Alexander St 27127
Alexander Preston Ln 27127
Alice Ct 27127
Alice St 27105
Allen St 27107
Allen Easley Dr 27106
Allerton Lake Dr 27106
Allgood Rd 27106
Allington Ct 27104
Allison Ave 27105
Allistair Rd 27104
Alma Dr 27105
Almond St 27127
Alonzo Dr 27104
Alpine Ct & Rd 27104
Alspaugh Cir & Dr 27105
Altay Dr 27106
Althea St 27107
Alton St 27105
Alvarado St 27101
Alvis Ln 27107
Alyssum Pl 27127
Amanda Pl 27101
Amber Ln 27105
Ambercrest Dr 27106
Amesbury Rd 27103
Amhurst St 27105
Ampthill Ln 27103
Amy Ct 27106
Anderson Dr 27127
Anderson Rd 27107
Andover St 27107
Andrea Ln 27105
Andrews Dr 27106
Andys Dr 27107
Angel Dr 27101
Angel Oaks Ct & Dr 27105
Angelia Dr 27106
Angelo St 27104
Anglesey Ct 27103
Anita Dr 27104
Ann Ln 27106
Annapolis St 27103
Anne Ave 27127
Another Way 27107
Ansley Ct & Dr 27107
Anson St 27103
Ansonia St 27105
Antietam Ct & Dr 27106
Apache Dr 27107
Apollo Dr 27101
Apostles Ct 27107
Appalachian Rd 27105
Apple St 27101
Appledore Ct 27103
Appomattox Dr 27106
Aquadale Ln 27104
Araminta Dr 27104
Arbor Knl 27107
Arbor Rd 27104
Arbor Oaks Dr 27104

Arbor Place Ct & Dr 27104
Arbor View Ln 27105
Archer Rd 27106
Archie Yokeley Rd 27107
Arcola Dr 27107
Ardenton Dr 27127
Ardmore Ct 27127
Ardmore Mnr 27103
Ardmore Rd 27127
Ardmore Ter 27103
Ardmore Village Ct & Ln 27127
Ardsley St 27103
Argonne Blvd 27107
Arita Cir 27105
Arlington Dr 27103
Armstrong Dr 27103
Arnold Ave 27127
Arrowcrest Pl 27107
Arrowood Ct 27104
Art St 27107
Arthur Ct & St 27107
Asbury Ln 27103
Ashbry Run 27106
Ashburton Ln 27106
Asher Ct 27105
Asherton Ct & Dr 27127
Asheton Grove Ct 27127
Ashford Ct & Dr 27103
Ashlawn Ct 27106
Ashley Sq 27103
Ashley Ter 27127
Ashley Xing 27127
Ashley Glen Dr 27104
NE Ashley School Cir 27105
Ashleybrook Ln & Sq 27103
Ashlyn Dr 27106
Ashton Dr 27101
Ashton Place Cir 27106
Ashview Dr 27103
Ashwood Dr 27103
Asia Chanel Dr 27105
Aspen Ct, Pl, Trl & Way 27106
Aspen Ridge Ct 27103
Asphalt Dr 27105
Astoria Ct 27127
Athens Dr 27105
Atkins St 27101
Atlantic St 27127
Atlee St 27105
Attanook Dr 27106
Attucks St 27105
Atwood Ct & Rd 27103
Auburndale St 27104
Audrey Dr & St 27127
Audubon Dr 27106
Aurelia Ct 27107
Aureole St 27107
Austin Ln 27106
Austin Place Ct & Ln 27127
Autoserve St 27105
Autum Frst 27127
Autumn Chase Dr 27101
Autumn Crest St 27107
Autumn Leaf Ln 27106
Autumn Mist Dr 27103
Autumn Oak Cir 27103
Autumn Valley Dr 27103
Autumn View Dr 27103
N & S Avalon Rd 27104
Avera Ave 27106
Averlan Ct & Dr 27105
Aveson Ct 27107
Aviation Dr 27105
Avon Rd 27104
Avondale St 27127
Axle Dr 27107
Ayman Ln 27103
Azalea Dr 27105
Azalea Pl 27103
Azalea Terrace Ct 27105
Aztec Ct 27103
Aztec Dr 27107
Azure Ln 27127
B And B Trl 27107

Back Forty Dr 27127
Backwoods Ln 27107
Bacon St 27105
Baden Ln & Rd 27107
Bailey Ct 27127
Bailey Rd 27107
Bailey St 27106
Bailey Forest Cir 27106
Bainbridge Ct & Dr 27105
Baity St 27105
Bald Cypress Dr 27127
Baldwin Ln 27103
Baldwin Pl 27127
Balfour Rd 27104
Ballincourt Ln 27104
Ballpark Way 27101
Baltimore St 27127
Banbury Rd 27104
Bancroft St 27127
Bangor Dr 27107
E & W Bank St 27101
E & W Banner Ave 27127
Barbara Dr 27107
Barbara Ann Cir 27103
Barbara Jane Ave 27101
Barbaras Ln 27107
Barber St 27127
Barclay Ter 27106
Barclays Dr 27107
Barjean Ln 27106
Barkas Dr 27106
Barker Ct & Rd 27107
Barkerville Ln 27127
Barkwood Ct & Dr 27105
Barlow Cir 27105
Barndale Glen Ct 27106
Barnes Rd 27107
Barney Ave 27107
Barnsdale Rd 27106
Barnsley Ct 27106
Barnwell Dr 27105
Baron Rd 27106
Barrett Rd 27104
Barrington Ct & Pl 27104
Barrington Way Ct 27106
Barrow Ct 27103
Barry St 27101
Bartram Pl & Rd 27106
Bassford Ct 27104
Basswood Ct 27106
Bates Dr 27105
Battery Dr 27107
Baux Mountain Rd 27105
Baxter Rd 27107
Bay Creek Dr 27106
Bay Meadow Ct 27106
Bay Meadows Ct 27103
Bayeux Ct 27103
Baytree Ct 27127
Beach St 27103
Beacher Gardner Rd 27107
Beacon Dr 27106
Beacon Hill Dr 27106
Beagle Run Ln 27106
Bear Creek Rd 27106
Beatrice St 27127
Beau View Ct 27127
Beauchamp Rd 27106
Beaumont St 27101
Beaverton Trl 27103
Bechler Ln 27106
Beckel Ct & Rd 27127
Beckerdite Stewart Rd 27107
Beckner St 27103
Becks Church Rd 27106
Becks Park Ln 27106
Beckwood Dr 27103
Bedford St 27107
Bedford Knoll Dr 27107
Bedford Park Ct & Dr 27107
Beech Acres Ln 27106
Beechcliff Ct 27104
Beecher Rd 27104
Beechmont St 27101
Beechridge Rd 27106
Beechwood Cir 27105

Beeson Ln 27107
Beeson Acres Rd 27105
Beeson Dairy Rd 27105
Beeson Farm Rd 27107
Belews Creek Rd 27101
Belfast Pl 27106
Belle Ave 27105
Belle Vista Ct 27106
Belleauwood St 27107
Bellingham Rd 27127
Bellview St 27103
Belo St 27105
Belvedere Ct 27127
Belwick Dr 27106
Belwick Village Dr 27106
Benathon Ct 27104
Benbow St 27106
Benchley Rd 27106
S Bend Dr 27107
Benjamins Way 27103
Bennett Dr 27104
Bennington Ct 27106
Bent Grass Ln 27127
Bent Oak Dr 27107
Bent Tree Farm Rd 27106
Bent Twig Ct 27103
Bentley Ct 27104
Benton Pl 27127
Benton Rd 27104
Benton Creek Dr 27106
Berchfield Dr 27127
Berkeley Place Ct 27106
Berl St 27105
Bermen Dr 27107
Berryhill Ln 27106
Berrywood St 27105
Bertha St 27107
Berwick Rd 27103
Berwyn Ct 27107
Beth Ave 27127
Bethabara Rd 27106
Bethabara Haven Dr 27106
Bethabara Hills Ct &
Dr 27106
Bethabara Park Blvd 27106
Bethabara Pointe Cir &
Dr 27106
Bethabara Ridge Ct 27106
Bethania Rd 27106
Bethania Lot Dr 27106
Bethania Rural Hall
Rd 27106
Bethania Station Ct 27106
Bethania Station Rd
3600-4200 27106
4202-4398 27106
4400-4999 27105
Bethany Ct 27103
Bethany Church Rd 27107
Bethany Trace Ln 27127
Bethel Ct 27127
Bethel Church Rd 27103
Bethel Methodist Church
Ln 27103
Bethesda Ct, Pl & Rd 27103
Bethlehem Ln 27105
Betsy Dr 27105
Betty Dr 27107
Bevlon Ct 27106
Bexley Dr 27104
Big Fish Rd 27107
Big House Gaines
Blvd 27101
Big Oaks Dr 27107
Big Woods Rd 27105
Bigelow St 27106
Billie Sue Dr 27104
Billy Dr 27107
Birch St 27127
Birch Creek Trl 27106
Birchdale Dr 27106
Birchway Ln 27103
Birchwood Ct 27107
Birchwood Dr 27103
Birkner Ave 27103
Birmingham Ct 27106

Biscayne St 27104
Bishop St 27104
Bishop Gate Rd 27127
Bismark St 27105
Bittersweet Rd 27106
Bitting Rd 27104
Black Jack Hill Ln 27106
Blackburn Rd 27105
Blackwood Ave 27103
Blaine St 27101
Blair Ct 27104
Blair Path Ct 27107
Blake St 27104
Blakeford Ct 27106
Blaze St 27105
Blazingwood Rd 27107
Blecker Dr 27107
Bleeker Sq 27106
Blenheim Pl 27106
Bloomfield Dr 27107
Blue Bonnet Ln 27103
Blue Rock Ct 27103
Blue Stone Ln 27107
Bluebird Ln 27106
Bluegrass Ln 27107
Bluffridge Trl 27103
Bluffview Dr 27127
Blum St 27101
Blysworth Ct 27106
Bo-Cline Dr 27107
Bobby Willard Rd 27107
Bodford St 27103
Bodford Lake Rd 27127
Bogart Cir 27104
Bogue Dr 27127
Bohannon Dr 27104
Bohannon Park Cir 27105
Bolick Ave 27127
Bolton St 27103
NE Bon Air Ave 27105
Bonanza Dr 27104
Bonbrook Cir & Dr 27106
Bond St 27127
Boneyard St 27105
Bonhurst Dr 27106
Booker St 27105
Boone Ave 27103
Borg Rd 27127
Borum Dr 27107
Boulder Ct 27107
Boulder Park Ct & Rd 27101
Bowen Blvd 27105
Bower Ln 27104
Boxthorne Ct & Ln 27106
Brachel 27106
Bradberry Ln 27104
Bradbury Pl 27107
Bradenton Ct & Dr 27103
Bradford Ct 27106
Bradford Glen Cir 27107
Bradley Ave & Rd 27107
Bradstone Dr 27107
Bradwyck Cir 27104
Braeburn Ct & Dr 27127
Braehill Blvd & Ct 27104
Braehill Terrace Dr 27104
Braer Ct 27127
Braewyck Ln 27104
Bramblebrook Ln 27105
Brambleton Ct 27106
Brambleton Rd 27127
Brampton Ct 27106
Bramton Ct 27127
Branch Rd 27105
Branch St 27101
Brandemere Ct & Ln 27106
Brandiles Ln 27104
Brandon Pl 27104
Brandywine Rd 27103
Brannigan Village Cir &
Dr 27127
Brannon Ln 27105
Brantley St 27103
Brassfield Dr 27105
Braxton Ridge Ct 27104
Breck Ave 27105

Breckindale Cir & Ct 27104
Brecknock Dr 27103
Breeze Way 27106
Breeze Hill Rd 27106
Brencomb Dr 27107
Brenda Dr 27107
Brenner St 27101
Brennington Place Rd 27104
Brent St 27103
Brent View Ct 27103
Brentwood Ct 27104
Brentwood Rd 27107
Breslau Cir 27106
Bretton St 27107
Brevard St 27101
Brewer Rd 27127
Brian Center Ct & Ln 27106
Briar Glen Ct & Rd 27127
Briar Lake Cir & Rd 27103
Briar Ridge Cir 27104
Briarcliff Ct 27106
Briarcliffe Rd 27106
Briarcreek Dr 27107
Briaridge Ct 27107
Briarlea Rd 27104
Briarwood St 27127
Brickell Dr 27127
Brickwood Ct 27127
Bridal Crossing Ct &
Dr 27106
Bridalcreek W 27106
W Bridge Rd 27107
Bridge St 27101
Bridgegate Dr 27106
Bridgeport Dr 27103
Bridgton Rd 27127
Bridgton Cape Ct 27127
Bridgton Place Ct &
Dr 27127
Bridgton Run Ln 27127
Bridle Path 27103
Bridlespur Ct 27106
Brierhurst Rd 27104
Briers Circle Ct 27107
Brigham St 27103
Brighton Ct 27103
Brighton Park Dr 27103
Brighton View Ln 27104
Brightwood Ct 27127
Brindle St 27107
Brintonial Way 27104
Bristol St 27105
Bristol View Cir 27103
British Square Dr 27105
Britt Rd 27105
Brittany Ct 27103
Brittany Joy Dr 27107
N Broad St 27101
S Broad St
100-1299 27101
1400-2399 27127
Broadbay Dr 27107
Broadmoor Ln 27104
Broadsword Rd 27104
Brockton Ln 27106
Bromley Ter 27103
Bromley Park Ct & Dr 27103
Bromwich Dr 27127
Brondesbury Dr 27107
Brook Bend Dr 27107
Brookberry Dr 27104
Brookberry Farm Cir &
Rd 27106
Brookcrest Dr 27106
Brookdale Ct & Dr 27107
Brookdale Ridge Ct &
Dr 27106
Brooke Dr 27107
Brookfield Dr 27106
Brookfield Ridge Ct &
Dr 27105
Brookford Place Ct 27104
Brookforest Dr 27107
Brookhaven Dr 27107
Brookhill Dr 27127
Brookhurst St 27106

Brookland Dr 27103
Brookleigh Ct 27104
E Brookline St
1-399 27127
700-1099 27107
W Brookline St 27127
Brookmeade Ct & Dr 27106
Brookmere Ln 27106
Brookmont Dr 27107
Brookridge Dr 27103
Brooks Edge Dr 27107
Brooks Landing Dr 27106
Brookshire Ln 27107
Brookstone Ridge Dr 27107
Brookstown Ave 27101
Brookview Dr & Rd 27107
Brookview Hills Blvd 27103
Brookway Dr 27105
Brookwood Dr
100-399 27127
1200-1799 27106
Brown St 27105
Browndale St 27103
Browning Pl 27103
Brownsboro Rd 27106
Brownstone Ln 27106
Brownwood Dr 27105
Bruce St 27107
Bruce Nifong Rd 27107
Brunswick Ct 27104
Brushy Creek Rd 27107
Bryansplace Rd 27104
Bryant St 27107
Bryn Mawr Ln 27103
Brynfield Ct 27127
Bryson St 27107
Brysons Meadow Ct 27103
Buchanan Ct & St 27127
Buck Chase Ct 27101
Buckhead Rd 27127
Buckhorn Ct & Rd 27104
Buckingham Rd 27104
Bucklebury Ct 27103
Budd Blvd 27103
Buddingbrook Ln 27106
Buddy St 27103
Buena Vista Rd
1700-2699 27104
2700-3599 27106
Buffington Ct 27104
Buick St 27101
Bull Run Ln 27107
Bull Run Rd 27106
Bumgardner St 27104
Bunker Hill Ct 27107
Bunny Trl 27105
Burbank Ln 27106
Burdette Dr 27105
Burgandy St 27107
Burgess Rd 27106
Burgoyne Ct 27107
Burke St 27101
Burke Meadows Rd 27103
Burke Mill Ct & Rd 27103
Burke Park Ln 27103
Burke Place Ct 27103
Burke Village Ln 27105
Burkeridge Ct 27104
Burkes Crossing Dr 27104
Burkeshore Rd 27106
Burkewood Dr 27104
Burlwood Dr 27103
Burnette Dr 27105
Burnette Acres 27107
Burnham Cir, Ct & Dr 27105
Burning Tree Ln 27106
Burroak Ct 27106
Burtis St 27105
Burton Ct & St 27105
Burwell Rd 27107
Burwood Dr 27127
Bushberry Ct 27105
Bushfield Dr 27127
Business Park Cir &
Dr 27107
Butchwood Dr 27105

Butler Ave 27103
Butler St 27107
Butterfield Cir & Dr 27105
Buttonwood Ct & Dr 27104
Buxton St 27101
Byerly Rd 27101
Byron St 27105
C And C Rd 27107
C E Gray Dr 27101
Cabot Dr 27103
Cadallic Ln 27107
Cadillac St 27101
Cahill Ct & Dr 27127
Calderwood Dr 27107
Cale Bradley Ct 27127
Caledonia Dr 27105
Calumet St 27106
Calvert Dr 27107
Calvin Rd 27107
Cambridge Rd 27104
Cambridge St 27127
Cambridge Links Ct 27107
Cambridge Plaza Dr 27104
Camburn Ct 27127
Camden Ct & Rd 27103
Camden Forest Dr 27127
Camden Place Ct &
Dr 27103
Camden Ridge Dr 27105
Camel Ave 27101
Camel Heights Dr 27101
Camelot Ct 27106
Camerille Farm Rd 27106
N Cameron Ave
100-1300 27101
1302-1398 27101
1400-1499 27105
S Cameron Ave 27101
Cameron Village Ct &
Dr 27103
Cameron Way Cir 27103
Camp Cir 27106
Campbell Glen Ln 27103
Campus Ct 27127
Canaan Place Ct & Dr 27105
Canal Dr 27101
Canary Trl 27107
Candlelight Ct 27127
Candlelight Dr
500-599 27127
4800-4899 27107
Candlewood Dr 27127
Candlewyck Dr 27104
Candlewyck Manor Dr 27104
Cannon Ave 27105
Cannoy St 27105
Canter Ln 27127
Canterbury Dr 27107
Canterbury Trl 27104
Canterbury Park Ct &
Dr 27127
Capistrano Ct & Dr 27103
Capitol Lodging Ct 27103
Capri Rd 27103
Caradco Rd 27106
Caraway Ln 27103
Carbine Ct 27101
Cardiff Ct 27103
Cardinal St 27105
Carl Livengood Ln 27107
Carl Russell Ave 27101
Carlton Cir & Dr 27105
Carlyle St 27107
Carlyle Place Dr 27103
Carnation Dr 27105
Carnes Rd 27127
Carnlough Ln 27104
Carol Rd 27106
Carolina Ave 27101
Carolina Cir 27104
Carolyn Dr 27103
Carpenter Ave 27107
Carr Ct 27105
Carriage Ct 27105
Carriage Dr 27106
Carriage Cove Ln 27127

Carriage House Pl 27106
Carriage Manor Cv 27106
Carrie Ave 27105
Carrington Ln 27127
Carrisbrooke Ln 27104
Carrollwood Dr 27103
Carrowmore Ln 27106
Carson Trl 27107
Carter Cir 27106
Carver Glen Ct & Ln 27105
Carver School Rd 27105
Carversham Ct 27106
Casa Vista Ln 27107
Cascade Ave 27127
Casedy Dr 27107
Casey Trace Ct 27127
Cash Dr 27107
Caspian Way Ct & Ln 27127
Cassel Cir 27106
Cassell St
1-299 27127
300-999 27107
Castellum Sq 27127
Castillo Rd 27106
Castleford Ct 27106
Castlegate Ct & Dr 27103
Castlewind Ln 27105
Cat Tail Ln 27127
Catawba St 27127
Catesby Ct 27106
Catherines Way 27103
Caudle Place Ln 27103
N Causeway Rd 27106
Cavalier Dr 27104
Cayuga St 27105
Cebon Ave 27104
Cecil Dr 27105
Cedar Dr 27107
N Cedar Dr 27107
Cedar Trl 27104
Cedar Cove Ln 27104
Cedar Crest Ln 27103
Cedar Haven Ct 27127
Cedar Hills Ct 27104
Cedar Lake Trl 27104
Cedar Place Ct 27107
Cedar Post Ct & Rd 27127
Cedar Ridge Cir & Ln 27127
Cedar Springs Dr 27107
Cedar Trails Ct & Pl 27104
Cedarberry Ct 27127
Cedarbranch Trl 27105
Cedarfield Place Ct 27106
Cedarlimb Ct 27127
Cedarline Ln 27103
Cedarmere Dr 27106
Cedartree Ter 27127
Cedarview Trl 27105
Cedarwood Dr 27103
Cedarwood Creek Ct &
Dr 27104
Cemetery St 27101
SE Center St 27127
Center Rock Ct 27127
Center Stage Ct 27127
Central Dr 27107
Centre Park Blvd & Ct 27107
Century Sq 27106
Century Oaks Ct & Ln 27106
Chadbourne Ct & Dr 27104
Chadwyck Ct & Dr 27106
Chaftain Dr 27107
Chalet Dr 27101
Chamberlain Pl 27103
Champion Blvd 27105
Champlain St 27127
Chancellorsville Dr 27106
Chancy Ln 27104
Chandler St 27101
Chantilly Ln 27106
Chanute Rd 27106
Chanute Trl 27107
Chapel St 27127
Charity Ln 27105
N Charles Ct, Dr & St 27107
Charles Michael Ct 27103

Charleston Ct 27103
Charleston Dr
1000-1299 27107
4300-4499 27127
Charlestowne Cir 27103
Charlois Blvd 27103
Charlotte Ct 27103
Charlwood Dr 27103
Charmin Ln 27104
Charnel Rd 27127
Charton Pl 27106
Chartwell Cir 27106
Charwin Dr 27101
Chase Ln 27107
Chase St 27101
Chateau Rdg 27103
Chatfield Dr 27103
Chatham Rd 27101
Chatham Farm Rd 27106
Chatham Hill Dr 27104
Chaucer Ln 27107
Chelmsford Dr 27105
Chelsea St 27103
Chelsea Village Cir, Ct & Ln 27103
Cheltenham Dr 27103
Cherbourg Ave 27103
Cherokee Ln 27103
Cherokee Valley St 27107
Cherry St 27105
N Cherry St 27101
S Cherry St 27101
Cherry Blossom Ln 27127
Cherryhill Ln 27106
Cherrylaurel Ct & Ln 27106
Cherryrock Trl 27107
Cherryview Ln 27105
Cherthes 27109
Chesborough Rd 27127
Cheshire Ct 27106
Cheshire Place Ct & Dr 27106
Cheshire Woods Dr 27106
Chester Rd 27104
Chesterton Way 27104
Chestnut Ln 27107
N Chestnut St
100-1199 27101
1300-1699 27105
S Chestnut St 27101
Chestnut Trl 27101
Chestnut Way 27103
Chestnut Bend Dr 27103
Chestnut Heights Ct & Rd 27107
Chestnut Hill Ct & Ln 27106
Chestnut Plains Ct 27105
Chestnut Ridge Ct & Dr 27103
Chestnut View Ln 27105
Cheswyck Ln 27104
Chevelle Ln & Rd 27105
Chevy Chase St 27107
Cheyenne Ct 27106
Chickamauga Dr 27106
Childress St 27105
Chilton Dr 27106
Chinaberry Ln
100-299 27107
4500-4599 27106
Chippendale Way 27103
Chippenham Ct 27104
Chippewa Dr 27106
Chipping Ct 27104
Chipwood Ln 27106
Chloe Ct 27127
Choyce Ct 27106
Chrisfield Cir, Ct & Ln 27104
Christine Ct 27127
Chuppway Ct 27106
N & S Church St 27101
Church Hill Rd 27105
Churchland Dr 27101
Churchview Dr 27107
Churton St 27103
Circle Dr 27105

City Yard Dr & Ln 27101
Claim Jumper Trl 27127
Clamoor Dr 27127
Clara Ln 27105
Claratom Dr 27107
Claremont Ave 27101
N Claremont Ave 27105
NE Claremont Ave 27105
S Claremont Ave 27101
Clarendon Ave 27106
Clarendon Creek Ct 27106
Claridge Cir 27106
Clark Ave 27105
Claudias Ln 27103
Claverton Ct 27104
Clawson St 27106
Claxton Dr 27127
Clay Dr 27107
Clay Vann Ln 27107
Clayburne Ct & Dr 27103
Clayton Rd & St 27105
Clear Meadow Dr 27107
Clearview Dr
100-699 27107
5100-5299 27104
Clearwater Ct 27106
Cleburne Meadows Dr 27101
Clement St 27127
Clemmonsville Cir 27107
E Clemmonsville Rd
1-99 27127
100-1399 27107
W Clemmonsville Rd 27127
W Clemmonsville Road Ext 27127
Clemson Cir 27107
Cleta Ln 27107
N Cleveland Ave
100-1399 27101
1400-3199 27105
NE Cleveland Ave 27105
S Cleveland Ave 27101
Cleveland Ct 27101
Cliff Rdg 27107
Cliff St 27127
Cliff Pointe Ct 27106
N & S Cliffdale Dr 27104
Cliffspring Ct 27104
Clinard Ave 27127
Cline St 27107
Clodfelter Rd 27107
Cloister Dr 27127
Cloister Oaks Cir 27127
Clovelly Rd 27106
Clover St 27101
Cloverdale Ave
1500-1599 27104
2000-2098 27103
2100-2399 27103
Cloverdale Dr 27103
Cloverfield Ct
100-299 27127
3500-3598 27103
Cloverhurst Ct & Rd 27103
Cloverleaf Dr 27103
Club Ct 27103
Club Knoll Rd 27105
Club Oaks Ct 27104
Club Park Rd 27104
Club Pointe Ct & Dr 27104
Clyde Dr 27104
Clyde Hayes Dr 27106
Coachford Ln 27104
Coalson Place Ln 27104
Cobalt Ct 27127
Cobble Creek Cir 27105
Cobble Oak Ct 27105
Cobblestone Rd 27106
Cockerham St 27127
Cody Cir & Dr 27105
Cody Lee Ln 27107
Coghill Dr 27103
Colchester Ct 27127
Cold Springs Rd 27106
Coldsprings Ct 27127
Cole Rd 27107

Cole Ridge Cir & Ct 27107
Colerain Creek Dr 27106
Coletta Ln 27106
Colgate Dr 27105
Colin Village Way 27106
Coliseum Dr 27106
Coliseum Plaza Ct 27106
College Ln 27127
Collegian Ter 27106
Collier St 27103
Collingswood Dr 27127
Collingwood St 27103
NW Collins St 27105
Colonial Pl 27104
Colonial Arms Dr 27103
Colonial Village Ct 27103
Colony St 27107
Colony Lodge Ln 27106
Colton St 27107
Columbine Dr 27106
Comanche Trl 27107
Comenius Ct 27106
Commerce Ct 27105
Commercial Plaza St 27104
Commonwealth Dr 27104
Community Rd 27107
Compton Dr 27107
Concrete Works Rd 27107
Cone Rd 27127
Conestoga Trl 27101
Conley St 27105
Connor Rd 27105
Conrad Oaks Ln 27106
Contour Ln 27105
Conway Ct 27106
Cook St 27105
Cool Springs Ct & Rd 27107
Cool Water Ct 27107
Cooper Rd 27127
Cooper Cove Rd 27127
Cooper Lake Dr 27127
Copeland Rd 27103
Copperfield Place Ct 27106
Copperfield Ridge Ct & Ln 27106
Cora Dr 27127
Coral Dr 27105
Coral Garden Ln 27106
Coravan Ct & Ln 27106
Corbin Ct & St 27107
Corbridge Ln 27106
Cordova Dr 27103
Cornelius Ct 27101
Cornell Blvd
3600-3678 27107
3679-3699 27127
Corner Stone Ct 27104
Cornwallis St 27105
Corona St 27103
Corporate Square Dr 27105
Corry Cir 27107
Cortland Ct & Dr 27105
Cottage St 27107
Cottage View St 27104
Cottington Dr 27105
Cotton St 27101
Cottontail Ln 27127
Cottonwood Ct 27127
Cottonwood Ln 27103
Couningt St 27127
Countess Pl 27106
Country Ln 27107
Country Acres Ln 27107
Country Club Rd 27104
Country Meadow Ln 27107
Country View Dr 27107
Countryside Ct & Dr 27105
County Line Rd 27107
Court Rd 27106
Covenant Ln 27106
Coventry Park Ln 27104
Coventry Way Ln 27104
Covington Ridge Rd 27107
Cox Blvd 27105
Coyote Crossing Ct 27107
Crabtree Dr 27127

Craft Dr 27105
Crafton St
100-199 27101
200-499 27103
Cragmore Ct & Rd 27107
Craig St 27103
Crampton St 27107
Cranberry Hill Ln 27127
Cranford St 27107
Craven St 27127
Craven Way 27107
Craver Dr 27107
Craver Ln 27107
Craver St 27105
Craver Meadows Ct & Dr 27127
Craver Woods Ct 27127
Crawford Pl 27105
NW Crawford Pl 27105
Crawford St
500-799 27105
800-899 27101
Cread Ct 27127
Creek Bend Dr 27103
Creekfield Way 27106
Creekmoore Dr 27101
Creeksedge Ct 27105
Creekshire Ct & Way 27103
Creekside Ct 27127
Creekside Dr 27127
Creekside Ln 27107
Creekstone Ct 27104
Creekway Ct & Dr 27104
Creekwood Dr 27103
Creighton Ln 27127
Crepe Myrtle Cir 27106
Crescent Ct 27127
Crescent Rd 27105
Crescent Oaks Ct 27106
Crest Hill Dr 27107
Crest Hollow Dr 27127
Crestridge Ln 27105
Crestview Dr & Way 27103
Crestwood Cir 27107
Crestwood Dr 27101
Crews St 27101
Crews Village Trl 27105
Crickett Ln 27105
Crittenden Ct 27106
Croft St 27127
Cromartie St 27101
Cromford Ct 27106
Crooked Oak Ln 27106
Crosland Rd 27106
Crosland Hills Dr 27106
Cross Gate Ct & Rd 27106
Cross Tree Rd 27106
Cross Vine Ln 27103
Crossfield Dr 27107
Crossfield Ridge Ct & Ln 27127
Crossfield River Ln 27127
Crossglenn Dr 27103
Crosswinds Dr 27127
Croston Dr 27104
Crotts Ln 27107
Crow Hill Dr 27106
Crowder Ln & St 27107
Crowne Ct 27106
Crowne Chase Dr 27104
Crowne Club Dr 27104
Crowne Crest Dr 27106
Crowne Forest Ct 27106
Crowne Oaks Cir 27106
Crowne Park Dr 27106
Crowne View Dr 27106
Croydon Ln 27107
Crusade Dr 27101
Crystal Dr 27106
Cullen St 27105
Culpepper Ct 27104
Cumberland Ct 27103
Cumberland Rd 27105
Cumbie Rd 27107
Cunningham Ave 27107
Currier Ct 27104

Curtis Dr 27105
Cutty Sark Rd 27103
Cypress Cir 27106
Cypress Point Ct 27107
Dacian St 27107
Daddem Way 27107
Dahlia Dr 27107
Daisy St 27107
Daisy Station Ln 27105
Dalarna Pl 27107
Dalby Ln 27127
Dalewood Dr 27104
Dallas Ct & Dr 27107
Dalton St 27105
Dalton Manor Ct 27104
Dana Ct 27103
Danby Ct & Dr 27103
Dandoon Ct 27103
SW Daniel St 27127
Danny Motsinger Dr 27107
Dans Ln 27107
Danube Ct & Dr 27105
Darby Ln 27107
Dare Ave 27101
Darien Blvd 27105
Dartmoor St 27106
Dartmouth Rd 27104
Darwick Rd 27127
Darwood Estate Ln 27106
Daryl Ln 27105
Dave St 27127
David Smith Rd 27127
E Davidson Ave 27127
W Davidson Ave 27127
Davidson Dr 27107
N Davidson Dr 27107
Davidson Heights Cir & Dr 27107
Davie Ave 27127
Davis Rd 27105
Davis St 27107
Davis Acres Ln 27106
Dawn Ct 27106
Dawnview Dr 27107
Dawson St 27105
Day Rd 27105
Daylily Ln 27107
Daysbrook Rd 27105
Dayton St 27105
Deacon Blvd 27105
Deamon Ct 27101
Dean St 27101
Deborah Ln 27103
Decatur St 27101
Deckerleaf Ct 27106
Deep Ravine Ct 27103
Deepwood Ct 27104
Deer Trak 27127
Deer Ridge Rd 27107
Deerbrook Ct 27103
Deercreek Dr 27106
Deerfield Ct 27103
Deerglade Rd 27104
Deerwood Dr 27103
Deerwood Forest Rd 27105
Deighton Ct 27106
Del Rio Ct 27105
Deland St 27106
Delane Dr 27101
Delaware Ave 27105
Delburg Dr 27106
Dell Blvd & Ln 27107
Della Dr 27105
Della Crescent Rd 27106
Dellabrook Rd 27105
Dellwood Dr 27105
Delmonte Dr 27106
Delta Dr 27104
Demetrias Dr 27103
Dempsey Ave 27107
Denby Dr 27107
Denise Ln 27127
Denny Dr 27107
Densmore St 27103
Denver St 27101
Derbyshire Rd 27104

Derende St 27107
Derry St 27105
Deshler St 27106
Desoto Ct 27107
Devin Kathleen Ln 27127
Devoe Rd 27107
Devon Ct 27104
E Devonshire St
1-499 27127
600-1099 27107
W Devonshire St 27127
Dew Ave 27107
Dewitt Dr 27105
Dewsbury Rd 27104
Diamond Hill Rd 27105
Dianne Ave 27106
Diaz Ln 27103
Dier Ln 27107
Diercrest Ln 27107
Diggs Blvd 27107
Dillingham Rd 27105
Dillon Ave & St 27107
Dillon Farm Rd 27105
Dilworth St 27101
Dimholt Ct 27104
Dinmont St 27127
Dippen Rd 27105
Disher Rd 27107
Disher St 27105
Dixie Broadway 27127
Dixie Club Rd 27107
Dixieanna Dr 27107
Dize Dr 27107
Dober Ct 27127
Dogleg Dr 27103
Dogwood Dr
100-299 27107
5400-5799 27105
Dogwood Falls St 27103
Dolly Ln 27107
Dolphin Dr 27105
Dominion St 27105
Don Ave 27105
Donald St 27107
Doncaster Rd 27106
Donna Ave 27101
Donny Brook Ct 27103
Donovan Pl 27103
Dorgan Dr 27105
Doris Dr 27107
Doris St 27105
Dornoch Dr 27107
Dorset Rd 27127
Doss Dr 27107
Dottie Mae Dr 27107
Double Jack Ln 27127
Douglas St 27105
Douglas Hill Dr 27105
Doune St 27127
Doutholi Rd 27106
Dove Ave 27105
Dove Dr 27107
Doveland Cir 27127
Dover Dr 27104
Dover Rd 27107
Downing Rd 27106
Downing Creek Ct 27106
Downway Ln 27107
Doyle St 27107
Draper Ct & St 27105
Dresden Dr 27104
Drewry Ln 27105
Drexel St 27105
Drexmore Ct 27103
Driftwood Ln 27104
NW Druid Hills Dr 27105
Drumcliffe Rd 27103
Dryden Rd 27107
Dublin Ct 27101
Dublin Dr
100-399 27107
1200-1399 27101
Duchess Ct 27107
Duck Pond Ct 27107
Duckview Ct 27106
Duckworth Ct 27106

Dudley St 27107
Duke St 27103
Dumont Dr 27107
Dunbar St 27105
Dunbarton Ct & Dr 27107
Duncan Ln 27127
Dundee St 27107
N Dunleith Ave
100-1399 27101
1500-2499 27105
Dunn St 27103
Dunwoody Rd
100-199 27127
200-299 27107
300-399 27127
400-699 27107
700-799 27127
Dupont Rd 27103
Durant Dr 27107
Dust Devil Dr 27106
Dustin St 27127
Duvall Cir 27107
Eagle Path 27127
Eagle Creek Ct 27103
Eagles Nest Ct & Dr 27127
Eaglewood Ln 27127
East Dr 27105
Easton Dr 27107
Eastside Ct 27127
Eastview Dr 27107
Eastwell Pl 27106
Eastwin Dr 27104
Eastwood Dr & Rd 27107
Ebert Ct 27127
Ebert Rd 27127
Ebert St 27103
Ebert Farms Rd 27127
Ebert Village Ct 27127
Eby Dr 27104
Echo Pt 27106
Echo Bluff Dr 27127
Echo Glen Dr 27106
Ed Everhart Rd 27107
Eddystone Ln 27103
Edelweiss Dr 27127
Eden Ter 27103
Eden Park Dr 27107
Edenwood Dr 27103
Edgar St 27107
Edgebrook Dr 27106
Edgefield Dr 27127
Edgeware Rd 27106
Edgeway Dr 27104
Edgewood Cir 27127
Edgewood View Ln 27127
Edinburg Dr 27103
Edison Ct 27101
Edith Ave 27106
Edmon Ct 27105
Edna St 27101
Edrem Ave 27101
Edwards St 27127
Efird St 27105
Eisenhower Rd 27107
El Santos Ct 27105
Elaines Way 27127
Eland Ct & Dr 27127
Elbon Dr 27105
Elderwood Ave 27103
Eldora St 27105
Eldorada Rd 27103
Electric Dr 27107
Elgin Rd 27103
Elisha Ln 27105
Elizabeth Ave 27103
Elk Valley Ct 27103
Elkton Trl 27107
E Eller Dr 27107
Eller Way 27127
Ellerbe Ave 27127
Ellington Dr 27104
Elliott Rd 27104
Elm Dr 27105
Elm Ln 27107
Elmhurst St 27127
Elmwood Dr 27127

Street	ZIP
Elon St	27107
Eltha Dr	27105
Emerald St	27105
Emerald Creek Ct	27127
Emerson Ct & St	27127
Emily Ann Dr	27107
Emma Ave	27127
Emory Dr	27103
Empire Dr	27103
Emsley Dr	27103
W End Blvd	27101
Endsley Ave	27106
Englewood Ct	27127
Englewood Dr	27106
Enterprise Dr	27106
Enterprise Park Blvd	27107
Erie Dr	27106
Erin St	27105
Ernest St	27107
Ernest Lambeth Rd	27107
Ernsford Dr	27103
Esquire Place Dr	27106
Essex Rd	27105
Essex Country Ln	27103
Essick Ln	27127
Ethel Dr	27127
Euclid St	27106
Evans Ct & Rd	27127
Evanston Way	27107
Evelyn Rd	27106
Evergreen Dr	
1-299	27106
1100-1399	27107
Everidge Rd	27103
Evie Ct	27127
Ewing St	27106
Excelsior St	27101
Executive Dr	27105
Executive Park Blvd	27103
Exeter Ct	27103
Factory Row	27101
Faculty Dr	27106
Fair Oaks Ln	27127
Fairburn Dr	27106
Fairchild Rd	27105
Faircloth St	27106
Faircrest Dr	27106
Fairfax Dr	27104
Fairfield Dr	27127
Fairhope Ct	27104
Fairlawn Dr	27106
Fairmont Rd	27106
Fairstone Ct	27106
Fairview Blvd	27127
Fairway Dr	27103
Fairway Cove Ct	27105
Fairway Forest Dr	27105
Fairwind Dr	27106
Falcon Rd	27106
Falcon Crest Dr	27107
Falcon Pointe Dr	27127
Falcon Tree Ct	27127
Falcon Wood Ct	27127
Falling Leaf Ln	27107
Fanning Rd	27107
Fanning Oaks Dr	27107
Fanning Pointe Ln	27107
Fannwood Cir	27127
Fargo Dr	27106
Fariss Rd	27127
Farm Acres Ct	27103
Farm Bell Ct & Ln	27127
Farm House Trl	27103
Farmall St	27105
Farmbrook Rd	27103
Farmbrooke Ln	27127
Farmingdale Ave	27107
Farmoor Cir	27105
Farmstead Rd	27107
Farrington Point Dr	27107
Fath Dr	27104
Faw Rd	27103
Fayette St	27101
Fayetteville St	27127
Felicity Cir & Ln	27101
Fenimore St	27103
Fentriss Dr	27103
Fern Pl	27105
Fern Cliff Dr	27106
Fern Leaf Ln	27106
Fern Ridge Dr	27104
Fernbrook Dr	27127
Ferndale Ave	27107
Fernhaven Cir	27104
Fernhill Rd	27106
Fernwood Ln	27107
Ferrell Ave & Ct	27101
Ferrell Heights Ct	27101
Fiddlers Ct	27107
Fiddlers Glenn Ct & Dr	27127
Fiddlers Way Ct	27107
Field Ln	27105
Field Crossing Ct & Dr	27107
Field Sedge Dr	27107
Fieldale Ave	27104
Fieldcreek Ct	27105
Fieldcrest Rd	27127
Fieldgate Forest Dr	27103
Fieldstone Dr	
100-599	27127
3000-3599	27105
Fieldtop Dr	27107
Fieldwood Ct & Ln	27106
File St	27101
Fillgate Dr	27104
Finley Cir	27127
Finsbury Rd	27104
Fir Dr	27107
Fireside Ln	27127
Fishel Rd	
100-199	27107
200-499	27127
Fisherville Ln	27127
Fitch St	27107
Five Royales Dr	27105
Flag St	27101
Flagstone Ct	27103
Flaming Tree Ct	27103
Flanders Dr	27105
Flatrock Ct, St & Ter	27107
Fleet St	27127
Fleetwood Cir	27106
Flintfield Dr	27103
Flintshire Rd	27104
Flintwood Ct	27106
Flora Ln	
3600-3699	27106
5300-5399	27105
Floral Ln	27106
Florence St	27127
Flyntdale Rd	27106
Flyntvalley Ct & Dr	27104
Fogle St	27101
Foilage Dr	27105
Foliage Dr	27101
Folkstone Ridge Ln	27127
Follansbee Rd	
100-699	27107
4500-5199	27127
Foltz Dr	27127
Fondly Rd	27105
Fontana Ct	27103
Ford St	27103
Forest Dr	27104
Forest Brook Dr	27106
Forest Creek Dr	27107
Forest Glade Rd	27107
Forest Grove Dr	27104
Forest Hill Ave	27105
Forest Knolls Cir	27101
Forest Manor Dr	27103
Forest Park Cir	
100-199	27107
200-299	27127
300-599	27107
Forest Ridge Ct	27106
Forest Trails Dr	27107
Forest Valley Dr	27105
Forest View Ct & Dr	27104
Forestglen Dr	27103
Forrestgate Dr	27103
Forsyth Ct	27103
Forsyth St	27101
Fort Place Ct	27127
Fortune St	27103
Forty Foot St	27105
Fosterdale Ln	27107
Four Brooks Ct & Rd	27107
Four Winds Trl	27106
Fox Chase Dr	27105
Fox Hill Ln	27107
Fox Hollow Ln	27105
Fox Lake Ct	27106
Fox Meadow Ln	27107
Fox Point Cir	27104
Fox Ridge Ln	27104
Fox Trot Ct	27103
Foxbury Ct	27104
Foxcroft Dr	27103
Foxdale Dr	27103
Foxfield Ct	27106
Foxgate Cir	27106
Foxglove Dr	27106
Foxhall Dr	27106
Foxhunter Ct	27106
Foxton Dr	27105
Foxwood Ln	27103
Foxwood Pl	27127
Fraiser View Ln	27105
Fraizer Creek Rd	27105
Frampton St	27105
Frances Ct	27105
Frances Ln	27127
Francis St	27107
Franciscan Ter	27127
Frandale Dr	27104
Frandell Place Ct	27104
Frank St	27107
Frankie St	27105
Franklin Dr	27107
Franklin St	27101
Fraternity Church Rd	27127
Frazier St & Way	27127
Fred Sink Rd	27107
Freddy St	27105
Frederick Dr	27103
Fredonia Ave	27105
Freds Rd	27106
Free St	27127
Freedom Ct & St	27101
Freedom Ridge Ct	27101
Freeman St	27127
Fremont St	27107
Fresh Field Ln	27106
Friar Ln	27106
Friar Tuck Rd	27104
Friedberg Ct	27127
Friedberg Church Rd	27127
Friedberg Village Dr	27127
Friedland Church Rd	27107
Friendly Acres Dr	27107
Friendship Cir	27106
Friendship Church Rd	27107
Friendship Ledford Rd	27107
Fries Dr	27101
Fritz St	27104
Front St	27101
Frontis St	27103
Frontis Plaza Blvd	27103
Fulp St	27105
Fulton Farm Rd	27105
Funk Farm Ln	27106
Funtime Blvd	27103
Furman Dr	27107
Gail Ln	27107
Gaither Rd	27101
Gaither Forest Dr	27127
Galaxy Ct	27101
Gales Ave & Ct	27103
Gallant Ct & Ln	27101
Gallery Pl	27106
Galsworthy Dr	27106
Gamble Dr	27103
Garden Path	27104
Garden St	27105
Garden Park Ln	27106
Garden Valley Dr	27107
Garden View Dr	27107
Gardenia Rd	27107
Gardner Ct	27107
Gardner St	27101
Garfield Ave & Ct	27105
Garland St	27127
Garner Rd	27105
Gary Trl	27107
Gaston St	27103
Gateridge Ct	27106
Gateshaven Ln	27103
Gateshead Dr	27106
Gateway Ln	27107
Gatewood Dr	27104
Gauntlet Dr	27101
Gaynor St	27105
Gayron Dr	27105
Gemini Ct	27101
Gene Clodfelter Dr	27107
Geneva Rd	27103
Genia Dr	27103
Gentle Pond Ct	27107
George Big Redd Ct	27101
George Black Ln NE	27101
George Murphy Rd	27107
Georgetown Dr	27106
Georgetown Rd	27107
Georgia Ave	27104
Georgia Ln	27107
Gerald St	27101
Germanton Rd	27105
Gessner Pl	27104
Gholson Ave	27107
Gibb St	27106
Gibbons St	27107
Gideon St	27105
Gilbert St	27107
Gillcrest Dr	27127
Gillette St	27105
NE Gilmer Ave	27105
Ginger Dr	27103
Ginger Creek Ln	27107
Glade St	27101
Gladstonbury Rd	27104
Gladstone St	27104
Gladwyn Dr	27104
Glascoe St	27107
Glasmere Ct	27101
Glen Eagles Dr	27104
Glen Echo Trl	27106
Glen Forest Dr	27103
Glen Hill Dr	27127
Glen Laurel Ln	27107
Glen Lyon Dr	27107
Glen Meadow Dr	27107
Glen Oak Dr	27105
Glen Way Dr	27107
Glen Way West Dr	27107
Glenbrook Dr	27101
Glenburn Dr	27127
Glencairn Rd	27107
Glencoe St	27107
Glencove Ct	27106
Glendale St	27127
Glendare Ct & Dr	27104
Glenford Dr	27107
Glenhaven Ln	27106
Glenmont Rd	27107
Glenmore Creek Dr	27107
E Glenn Ave	27105
Glenn Hi Rd	27107
Glenn Knoll Ct & Ln	27107
Glenn Lake Trl	27107
Glenn Landing Dr	27107
Glenshire Ct & Dr	27127
Glenwood Dr	27107
Glenwood St	27106
Gloria Ave	27127
Gloria Rdg	27107
Gloucestershire Rd	27104
Glouchester Rd	27127
Glousman Rd	27104
Glovenia Dr	27127
Gobble Ct	27127
Gobble Ln	27107
Gobble Acres Dr	27103
Golden Acorn Ct	27107
Golden Lamb Ct	27105
Golden Oaks Cir & Dr	27107
Goldenberry Ct	27106
Goldfloss St	
300-499	27127
600-1099	27107
Golding Center Dr	27103
Goldwind Ct	27106
Goler Ct & St	27101
Gomar Ln	27106
Good Hope Rd	27106
Goodwood Rd	27106
Gordon Ct	27104
Gordon Dr	27107
N Gordon Dr	27104
S Gordon Dr	27104
Gordy Trl	27105
Gospel Light Church Rd	27101
Gossett St	27105
Gould St	27103
Grace Ln	27107
Grace St	27103
Gracefield Ct	27127
Gracemont Dr	27106
Grady St	27104
N & S Graham Ave & Ct	27101
Graham Farm Rd	27105
Grainwood Ct	27105
Gramercy St	27104
Gramercy Park Ln	27105
Granada Ct	27105
Granby St	27101
Grand Ct	27104
Grand St	27107
Grand Silo Way	27127
Grand Springs Dr	27127
Grandview Dr	27104
Granite St	27107
Granite Ridge Ln	27107
Grant Ave	27105
Grant Hill Ln	27104
Granville Dr	27101
Grassy Creek Blvd	27105
Grassy Knoll Cir	27107
Gray Ave	27101
N Gray Ave	27105
Graylyn Ct	27106
Graylyn Place Ct	27106
Grayson Dr	27107
Graystone Dr	27105
Graytuck Dr	27107
Graywood Ct	27127
Greeley St	27107
N & S Green St	27101
Green Acres St	27105
Green Cove Ct	27107
Green Oaks Ct & Dr	27107
Green Point Rd	27107
Greenbrier Rd	27104
Greenbrier Farm Rd	27106
Greencedar Ct & Ln	27127
Greencrest Dr	27106
Greendale Way	27103
Greene Cross Ct & Dr	27107
Greene Haven Dr	27107
Greenfield St	27127
Greenfield Way Dr	27103
Greenhaven Dr	
100-199	27107
5900-6099	27103
Greenhouse Ln	27107
Greenhouse Rd	27127
Greenhurst Rd	27104
Greenmanor Dr	27106
Greenmead Rd	27106
Greenmeadow Lakes Cir & Rd	27106
Greenturf Dr	27107
Greenvale Ct	27104
Greenvalley Rd	27106
Greenvine Cir	27103
Greenway Ave	27105
Greenwich Rd	27104
Gregor Ct	27106
Gregory St	27101
Gretel Ln	27127
Grey Fox Ct	27104
Grey Fox Ln	27106
Greyhound Ct	27101
Greystone Dr	27107
Greystone Place Ct	27106
Griffith Rd	27103
Griffith Commons Dr & Pl	27103
Griffith Meadows Dr	27103
Griffith Park Ct	27103
Griffith Plaza Dr	27103
Griffyn Way	27127
Grossman Ct	27104
Grosvenor Pl	27106
Grouse Hollow Ct & Rd	27106
Grove Ave	27105
Grove Garden Dr	27106
Grover St	27101
Grubbs St	27105
Grubbs Park Rd	27106
Guilford Dr	27127
Guinevere Ct & Ln	27104
Gumtree Rd	27107
Gun Club Rd	27103
Gunston Ct	27106
Guthrie Ct	27101
Gyddie Dr	27105
Gyro Dr	27127
Hacker Bend Ct	27103
Hadley Ct	27106
Hagen Ct	27106
Hailey Rd	27107
Halcyon Ave	27104
Haled St	27127
Haley Ct	27106
Half Wright Rd	27107
Hall Ln	27127
Halle Ann Cir	27103
Hambrick Ct	27106
Hamillak Dr	27105
Hamilton Ave	27107
Hamlin Ave	27107
Hammock Farm Rd	27105
Hampton Rd	27103
Hampton Club Ct	27104
Hampton Hall Ln	27127
Hampton Inn Ct	27103
Hampton Way Dr	27107
Handy Woods Dr	27104
Hanes Ave	27105
Hanes Mall Blvd & Cir	27103
E & W Hanes Mill Ct & Rd	27105
Hanes Square Cir	27103
Hanestown Ln	27103
Hanna Trce	27127
Hannaford Rd	27103
Hannon Dr	27101
Hanover Rd	27127
Hanover Arms Ct	27104
Hanover Park Dr	27103
Hardiman Place Ct	27127
Harding St	27107
Hardwick Ct	27101
Hardwood Dr	27106
Harmon Ave	27106
Harmon Ct	27106
Harmon Rd	27107
Harmony St	27105
Harper St	27104
Harpers Ferry Rd	27106
Harpwell Dr	27106
Harriet Tubman Dr	27105
Harrington Cir	27105
Harrington Village Dr	27105
Harrison Ave	27105
Harrow Cir	27103
E & W Harson St	27127
Hart St	27107
Hartfield Cir	27103
Hartfield Commons Ln	27103
Hartford St	27106
Hartle St	27127
Hartley St	27107
Hartman Rd & St	27127
Hartman Branch Ln	27127
Hartman Plaza Dr	27127
Hartsoe Rd	27107
Harvard Rd	27107
Harvest Dr	27101
Harvest Stone Ln	27106
Harvey St	27103
Harvey Teague Rd	27107
Harwick Place Ct	27103
Harwood St	27105
Harwyn Rd	27107
Hastings Ave	27127
Hathaway Dr	27103
Hattie Ave	
1100-1299	27101
1301-1329	27101
1400-1799	27105
Hattie Cir	27105
Hausman Dr	27103
Haven Crest Rd	27106
Haven Ridge Dr	27104
Haven Way Ct	27103
Havenwood Dr	
100-299	27127
4000-4299	27106
Haverhill St	27127
Haversham Park Cir & Dr	27127
Haweswater Rd	27105
Hawk Ridge Cir & Dr	27103
Hawk View Dr	27103
Hawkcrest Ct & Ln	27127
Hawkedale Dr	27106
Hawks Nest	27103
Hawksmoore Rd	27106
Hawkwood Trl	27103
N Hawthorne Rd	27104
S Hawthorne Rd	27103
Hay Rd	27127
Hayes Dr & Rd	27107
Hayes Forest Ct & Dr	27106
Hayfield Dr	27107
Haymore Dr	27107
Haymount St	27127
Haystack Hill Rd	27106
Haywood St	27105
Hazelwood Dr	27103
Healy Dr	
1800-3332	27103
3331-3331	27114
3334-3498	27103
3401-3499	27103
Hearthside Dr	27104
Hearthstone Dr	27107
Hearthwood Ct	27105
Heathcliff Pl	27104
Heathcote Dr	27104
Heather Ln	27127
Heather Ridge Dr	27127
Heather Trace Ln	27127
Heather View Ct & Ln	27127
Heatherstone Ct & Dr	27104
Heatherton Way	27104
Heatherwood Dr	27107
Heathrow Dr	27127
Hebron Ln	27107
Hebron Church Rd	27107
Hedgecock Ave	27104
Hedgewood Pl	27104
Hege St	27127
Heidelbury Ct & Dr	27106
Heitman Ct & Dr	27107
Helen Ave	27105
Helms Rd	27107
Hemingway St	27127
Hemlock Dr	27105
Hemphill Dr	27105
Hempstead St	27105
Henning Dr	27106
Henry St	27105
Herchel Ln	27106
Herinhut Rd	27127
Heritage Dr	27107

Heritage Acres Ln 27107
Heritage Oaks Ln 27106
Heritage Path Ct & Ln 27103
Heritage Pointe Dr 27127
Hermitage Dr 27103
Herndon Dr 27104
Heron Ridge Rd 27106
Herry St 27105
Hertford Rd 27104
Hester St 27105
Hewes Ln & St 27103
Hialeah Ct 27103
Hickman Ln 27103
Hickory Creek Ct & Rd 27107
Hickory Glen Rd 27106
Hickory Knoll Dr 27106
Hickory Ridge Dr 27127
Hickory Trails Rd 27105
Hickory Tree Rd
100-199 27107
700-3499 27127
Hicks St 27101
Hidden Creek Ln 27107
Hidden Creek Rd 27127
High St 27101
High Meadows Dr 27106
High Point Rd 27107
High Sedge Dr 27107
Higher Ground Dr 27127
Highfield Park Dr 27127
Highland Ave 27101
N Highland Ave 27101
Highland Ct
100-199 27127
800-999 27101
Highland Glen Rd 27103
Highland Oaks Dr 27103
Highland Park Ct, Dr & St 27106
Highland Trace Ct 27105
Highwood Ln 27104
Hilda St 27101
Hildebrand Dr 27106
S Hill Ave 27127
Hill Ct 27107
Hill Ln 27107
Hill St 27107
Hillcrest Center Cir 27103
Hillendale Dr 27107
Hillhaven Dr 27107
Hills Dr 27107
Hillsboro Dr 27104
Hillside Ct 27107
Hillstone Ct 27106
Hilltop Ct & Dr 27106
Hilltop Forest Ln 27106
Hilton Dr 27127
Hines Dr 27107
Hinshaw Ave 27104
Hogan Ln 27127
Hogan Point Ct & Dr 27127
Holbrook St 27107
Holiday St 27104
Holland St 27101
Hollin Way 27104
Hollinswood Ave & Ct 27103
Hollow Bridge Ct 27106
Hollow Forest Rd 27105
Hollow Stump Ln 27106
Hollow Tree Ct 27127
Hollow Wood Ct 27104
Hollowoak Ct 27104
Hollowridge Dr 27103
Holly Ave 27101
Holly Ct 27105
Holly Crescent Ln 27127
Holly Hill Ct & Ln 27106
Holly Place Ct 27101
Holly Ridge Dr 27105
Hollyrood St 27127
Holmes Dr 27127
Holmes Creek Pl 27127
Holton Dr 27127
Holyoke Pl 27106
Home Rd 27106
Homestead Ln 27106
Homestead Club Dr 27103
Homestead Hills Cir & Dr 27103
Hondo Dr 27103
Honeysuckle Ln
100-199 27105
300-399 27107
Hood Dr 27104
Hoots Dr 27107
Hootsdale Dr 27106
Hoover Ln & St 27107
Hope Ln 27105
Hope St 27107
Hope Church Rd
2500-2699 27103
2700-2899 27127
Hope Valley Rd 27106
Hopewell Church Rd 27127
Hopewood Ln 27103
Horace Mann Ave 27104
Horizon Ln 27105
Horn Of Plenty Ln 27107
Horncastle Rd 27104
Horne Dr 27105
Hornsway Dr 27104
Horseshoe Bnd 27101
Hoskins Dr 27105
Hospice Ln 27103
Houston St 27107
Howell St 27106
SE Howie St 27127
Hoy Long Rd 27127
Hoyle Trl 27107
Hoyt St 27103
Hsa Cir & Ln 27101
Hubbard Rd 27101
Hubert Ct 27107
Huckabee Cir 27105
Huckleberry Ct 27105
Huddington Ct 27106
Hudgins Hill Ct 27103
Hudler Rd 27107
Hudson Rd 27107
Hudson St 27105
Huff Cir 27105
Huff St 27107
Hughe Cir 27107
Humming Bird Ct & Dr 27107
Humphrey Ct & St 27127
Hundley Rd 27106
Hunsford Dr 27105
Hunt Club Rd 27104
Hunt Park Ct 27106
Huntcliff Trl 27104
Hunter Ave & St 27101
Hunters Forest Dr 27103
Hunters Grove Ct 27104
Hunters Horn Ct & Ln 27107
Hunters Knoll Rd 27106
Hunters Ridge Rd 27103
Hunterswood Dr 27104
Hunterview Ct 27107
Hunterwood Ln 27107
Huntfield Ct & Dr 27107
Huntingdon Rd 27104
Huntingreen Ln 27106
Huntington Ct 27106
Huntington Ridge Ln 27105
Huntington Woods Ct & Dr 27103
Huntmaster Trl 27107
Huntscroft Ct & Ln 27106
Huron Ct 27103
Hursh Ln 27105
Hutchins St 27106
Hutton St
600-999 27101
1000-1599 27103
1600-1699 27127
Hyatt Dr 27101
Hyde Ave 27104
Hyde Park St 27106
Hyde Place Cir 27103
Idlewild Industrial Dr 27105
Idlewilde Ct & Dr 27106
Idlewilde Heath Ct & Dr 27106
Idlewood Ct 27103
Idol Farm Rd 27101
Idolbrook Ln 27105
Inca Ct & Ln 27103
Independence Rd 27106
Indera Mills Ct 27101
Indian Trl 27106
Indian Peaks Dr 27107
Indiana Ave
2801-2897 27105
2899-4499 27105
4500-5799 27106
Indigo Ct 27107
Industrial Dr 27105
Ingle St 27106
Inlet St 27127
Inlet Place Dr 27127
Inverness Dr 27107
Inverness St 27105
NE Inverness St 27105
Inwood Dr 27106
Ionia St 27106
Irene Ln 27105
Ireton Ln 27103
Iris St 27107
Ironstone Ct 27127
Irving St 27103
Irving Grubbs Rd 27105
Ivanhoe St 27107
Ivors Ln 27106
Ivy Ave
900-1299 27101
1300-3099 27105
Ivy Bluff Trl 27106
Ivy Glen Ct & Dr 27127
Ivy Park Ln 27104
Ivy Ridge Ln 27104
Ivy Yokeley Rd 27107
Ivystone Ct & Ln 27104
J R Ln 27107
Jack Hoyle Ln 27106
N Jackson Ave
100-1399 27101
1400-2000 27105
2002-2298 27105
NE Jackson Ave 27105
S Jackson Ave 27101
Jackson View Rd 27105
Jacob Autumns Ln 27105
Jacobs Way 27106
Jadin Ct 27107
Jag Dr 27105
James St 27106
Jameson Ln 27106
Jamestown Rd 27106
Jammie Ct 27106
Janet Ave 27104
Janita Dr 27127
Jansu Ln 27106
Jarvis St 27101
N & S Jasmin Ct 27105
Jasper Ln 27127
Javan Dr 27107
Jay Ave 27127
Jay Dee Dr 27107
Jayson Ln 27107
Jazer Ln 27105
Jean Dr 27107
Jefferson Ave
100-299 27107
2300-2599 27103
Jefferson Forest Ct 27106
Jefferson School Ln 27106
Jeffrey Ln 27106
Jeketer Ct & Dr 27105
Jenkins Rd 27105
Jericho St 27105
Jerry St 27105
Jersey Ave 27101
Joe Shawn Rd 27107
Joel Ave 27105
John St 27105
John Ernest Rd 27107
John Green Rd 27107
Johnny Knl 27107
Johnny Knoll Ln 27107
Johnsborough Ct 27104
Johnson Cir 27101
Johnson Hardin Ct 27105
Jones Ct, Dr & Rd 27107
Jones Meadow Dr 27107
Jonestown Rd
100-499 27104
500-2699 27103
Jonestown Trl 27103
Joplin Dr 27107
Jordan Dr 27105
Joseph Samuels Dr 27105
Joshie Dr 27103
Joshua Ct & Ln 27127
Joshua Way Ln 27105
Joy Way 27101
Joyce Ave 27106
Joyce Dr 27107
Ju Lenor Dr 27107
Jude Ct 27103
Judy Ln 27127
Julie Ct 27106
Julius St 27106
June Ave 27106
June Ln 27127
Junia Ave
200-499 27127
600-1199 27107
Junior Dr 27105
Jutland Dr 27105
K Court Ave 27105
Kailey Ln 27107
Kaismore Ct 27106
Kanah Ct & Dr 27107
Kapalua Ct 27107
Kapp St 27105
Karen Cir 27105
Karenda Dr 27127
Karley Ct 27106
Karmel Dr 27127
Katherine Ct 27106
Katie Foltz Ln 27107
Katies Trl 27101
Katies Crossing Dr 27103
Katrina Dr 27127
Kaybrook Dr 27105
Kaymoore Dr 27127
Kaysboro Dr 27105
Kaywood Ln 27103
Kearns Ave 27106
Keating Dr 27104
Kedron Ct 27106
Keehlyn Ave 27105
Keighly Ct 27104
Keith Dr 27107
Kelley Moore Dr 27105
Kellum Pl 27105
Kelly Dr 27106
Kellys Trl 27101
Kellys Trail Ct 27101
Kelway Pl 27104
Kem Dr 27105
Kendale Dr 27104
Kendall Dr 27107
Kendall Farms Ct & Way 27107
Kenilworth Ave 27107
Kenleigh Cir 27106
Kennerly St 27105
Kennington Terrace Ct 27103
Kennison Village Dr 27127
Kensington Pl 27103
Kensington Rd 27106
E & W Kent Rd 27104
Kent Mews Ct 27104
Kent Park Cir 27106
Kent Place Ln 27104
Kentucky Ave 27101
Kenwick Dr 27106
Kenwood St 27103
Kepler St 27106
Keprechian Ln 27104
Kerensky St 27103
Kerfing Pl 27106
Kernersville Rd 27107
Kerry Rd 27127
Kerrybrook Ln 27104
Kershaw Ct 27107
Kester Mill Ct & Rd 27103
Kesteven Rd 27127
Keswick Ct 27103
Ketner St 27107
Kettle Ct 27104
Kevin Dr 27105
Kiawah Island Dr 27107
Kiger Farm Rd 27105
Kiger Way Ln 27107
NW Kilkare Ave & Ct 27105
Killarney Ct 27103
Kilpatrick St 27104
Kim St 27107
Kimball Ln 27105
Kimberly Rd 27105
Kimbrough St 27106
Kimel Forest Dr 27103
Kimel Park Dr 27103
E Kimwell Dr 27103
Kinard Dr 27101
Kinder Rd 27107
King Arthur Ct 27104
King George Ct 27103
King Rusty Ln 27106
Kingfish St 27107
Kinghill Dr 27105
Kings Ln 27107
Kings Row 27106
Kings Gate Dr 27101
Kings Meadow Ct & Dr 27127
Kingsberry Park Ct & Dr 27107
Kingsbridge Rd 27103
Kingsbury Cir 27106
Kingsdale Ct 27103
Kingsgate Dr 27101
Kingsland Cir 27106
Kingston Rd 27106
Kingstree Ridge Dr 27127
Kingswell Dr 27106
Kingswyck Cir 27104
Kinloch Ct 27104
Kinloch Dr 27107
Kinlough Ln 27106
Kinnamon Ct 27103
Kinnamon Pl 27103
Kinnamon Rd
2300-2399 27103
2900-3499 27104
4300-4999 27103
Kinnamon Village Loop 27103
Kirby St 27107
Kirk Rd 27103
Kirklees Rd 27104
Kirkridge Ln 27107
Kirkstone Dr 27107
Kirkwood St 27105
Kiser Rd 27106
Kittering Ln 27105
Kittery Ct 27104
Kivett Ct 27105
Knights Haven Ct 27106
Knightsbridge Ct 27127
Knob View Ct, Dr & Trl 27104
Knoll Rd 27107
Knollwood St
1-369 27104
370-378 27103
380-1099 27103
Knoristr Rd 27104
Knott St 27105
Knox St 27105
Knoxwood Rd 27107
Koger Dr 27106
Kona Dr 27127
Konnoak Dr 27127
Konnoak View Dr 27127
Konnoak Village Cir 27127
Kramer Ave & Ct 27106
Krause Ln 27127
Kreeger Rd 27106
Kress Dr 27106
Kress St 27127
Kristy Park Ct 27107
Krites St 27127
Kyle Rd 27104
Kyle Smith Ct 27127
L St 27105
La Casa Blvd 27105
La Deara Crest Ln 27105
Lackey Hill Rd 27104
Lafayette St 27105
Laguna Ave 27103
Lake Dr
100-699 27107
1800-2099 27127
N Lake Dr 27127
Lake Rd 27127
Lake St 27107
Lake Forest Dr 27106
Lake Point Dr 27103
Lake Valley Dr 27107
Lakeland Ave 27101
Lakeshore Dr 27106
Lakeside Valley Dr 27107
Lakespring Ct 27106
Lakeview Blvd 27105
Lakeway Dr 27127
Lakewood Dr 27106
Lakewood Glen Ct & Dr 27107
Lambeth Ln & St 27107
Lamond Ct & Dr 27101
Lamont Dr 27103
Lamore Ct 27107
Lampan Ln 27105
Lamplighter Cir 27104
Lancaster St 27106
Lancaster Park Ct & Dr 27103
Lance Dr 27103
Lance Ridge Ct & Ln 27127
Lancelot Ln 27103
Landis St 27107
Landmark Dr 27103
Landscape Ln 27107
Lane St 27105
Langden Dr 27107
Langhorne Dr 27106
Lankashire Rd 27106
Lansdale Ln 27103
Lansdowne Dr 27103
Lansdowne Pl 27107
Lansing Dr 27105
Lantana Dr 27127
Lantern Dr 27106
Lantern Ridge Dr 27104
Larch Ct 27104
Larck Crest Ln 27107
Laree Dr 27105
Largo Dr 27101
Lark Crest Ln 27127
Larkspur Dr & Pl 27105
Lash Rd 27106
Lashmit Dr 27103
Lasley Ct & Dr 27105
Latonia Rd 27127
Laura Ave 27105
Laura Dr 27107
Laura St 27107
N & S Laura Wall Blvd 27101
Laurel Ct 27127
Laurel Ln 27101
Laurel Run 27106
Laurel St 27101
Laurel Grove Rd 27127
Laurel Hill Ct 27127
Laurel Ridge Cir 27107
Laurel View Ct & Dr 27104
Lauren Acres Ct 27103
Lauren Hill Ct 27127
Lauren Woods Ct & Dr 27127
Laurenfields Way 27127
Lavada Dr 27103
Lavada South Dr 27103
Lavender Ln 27107
Lawndale Dr 27104
Lawrence St 27101
Lawrence Way 27105
Layla Ct 27105
Layston St 27106
Lazy Ln 27106
Lazyboy Ln 27103
Leafland St 27106
Leak Creek Ct 27127
Learwood Cir 27107
Ledford Rdg 27107
Ledford Farm Ln 27107
Lee St
100-199 27107
3400-3499 27106
N Lee St 27107
Leeds Ln 27103
Leeshire Way 27106
Legacy Park 27103
Legare Dr 27105
Leheigh Ct 27103
Leighswood Dr 27106
Leight St 27107
Leighton Ct 27104
Leinbach Dr 27106
Leisure Ln 27103
Leisure Time Ln 27107
Leland Dr 27106
E & SW Lemly St 27127
Lenetta Dr 27127
Lennox Rd 27105
Lenora Dr 27107
Leo St 27105
Leona St 27107
Leonard Ln 27107
Leonard St 27127
Leprechaun Ln 27127
Leslie Dr 27105
Lester Ln 27103
Letchworth Pl 27104
Lewey Ln 27105
Lewis St 27107
Lexwin Ave 27107
Liberia St 27127
N Liberty St
300-1299 27101
1300-4399 27105
S Liberty St 27101
Liberty Walk 27101
Liberty Hall Cir 27106
Liberty View Ct 27101
Lichfield Rd 27104
Lighthouse Ct & Ln 27127
Lillian Ct 27103
Lime Ave 27105
Limerick Ln 27104
Limner Ln 27106
Linbrook Dr 27106
Lincoln Ave 27105
Linda Cir 27106
Lindale St 27127
Lindbergh St 27104
Linden St 27101
Lindenleaf Ct 27106
Lindsay Ln 27107
Lindsey Ln 27106
Linecrest Dr 27106
Linger Rd 27127
Link Rd 27103
Linn Station Rd 27106
Linton Ct 27107
Linville Ln 27107
Linville Ridge Ct 27101
Lisa Dr 27103
Lissa Anne Ln 27104
Listonbrook Ct 27105
Little Brook Ln 27104
Little Creek Cir 27103
Little Pond Rd 27127
Little Stream Ln 27101
Livengood Dr 27107
Livengood Rd 27106
Loblolly Ln 27107

Loch Dr 27106
Loch Lomond Ct 27106
Lochmoore Ct 27127
Lochraven Dr 27104
Lockland Ave & Ter 27103
Locksley Ln 27104
Lockwood Dr 27103
Locust Ave
1300-1399 27101
1500-1999 27105
NE Locust Ave 27105
Lodge St 27105
Lodgecrest Dr 27107
Loeschs Ln & Trl 27106
Log Cabin Rd 27127
Log House Rd 27127
Logan Ln 27105
Logan Rae Ct 27107
Lois Ct & St 27127
Lombardy Ln 27103
Lomond Ct & St 27127
London Ln 27103
Long Dr 27106
Long St 27107
Long Leaf Dr 27101
Long Meadow Ln 27106
Long Perryman Rd 27107
Long Win Dr 27101
Longbow Rd 27104
Longbrook Cir 27105
Longfellow St 27127
Longview Dr 27107
Longwood Dr 27104
Lookout Ct 27106
Lorelei Ct 27103
Lori Ln 27127
Lorraine Dr 27107
Louella Dr 27107
Louise Rd 27107
Louise Wilson Ln 27101
Lovedale Ave 27127
Lovill Dr 27107
Lower Mall Dr 27103
Lowery Ct, St & Xing 27101
Lowery Mill Ln 27101
Loyelisa Ct 27106
Lu Wan Ln 27107
Lubet Ln 27107
Lucerne Ln 27104
Lucille St 27127
Ludlow Ln 27103
Ludwig St 27107
Luke St 27107
Lukon Ln 27104
Lula St 27101
Lullington Dr 27103
Lumber Ln 27127
Luna Ln 27107
Lunar Ct 27101
Lura Rd 27104
Luther St 27127
Luther Green Rd 27106
Luxbury Ct & Rd 27104
Luzelle Dr 27103
Luzenia Ln 27107
Lyman Rd 27105
Lynch Ct 27106
Lyndale Dr 27106
Lyndhurst Ave & Ct 27103
Lynhaven Ct & Dr 27104
Lynhaven Place Ct 27104
Lynn Ave 27104
Lynn Dee Dr 27106
Lynnhaven Park Dr 27107
Lynwood Ave 27104
Lyons St 27107
Lytchfield Ct & Pl 27104
Macarthur Rd & St 27107
Mace Cir 27103
Machine St 27105
Mackenzie Ln 27107
Macon Dr 27106
Madelyn Dr 27104
Madi Ct 27107
Madison Ave 27103
Mae Len Dr 27107

Mae Trappe Rd 27107
Magazine Dr 27106
Magnolia Ct 27107
Magnolia Ln 27107
Magnolia St 27103
Magnolia Branch Dr 27104
Magnolia Place Ln 27107
Magnolia View Ct 27107
Magnum Dr 27101
Maid Marion Ln 27106
Maiden Ln 27104
N Main St
100-899 27101
1300-1499 27105
S Main St
100-1299 27101
1300-4799 27127
4800-4898 27107
4900-5599 27107
Malbeth Ct 27104
Mallard Glen Cir 27106
Mallard Lakes Dr 27106
Mallard View Ct & Ln 27127
Mallory Cir 27106
Maloy Dr 27107
Malvern Ct 27106
Manchester Ave 27103
Manchester St 27105
Maner Place Ct 27103
Mangum St 27127
Manly St
700-899 27101
900-998 27105
1000-1199 27105
Manna Dr 27101
Manning St 27105
Manning Wood Dr 27105
Mansfield St 27107
Manteo Ln 27127
Maple Dr 27107
Maple Glen Ln 27106
Maple Hill Ct 27106
Maple Leaf Trl 27107
Maple Ridge Ln 27103
Maple Shade Ct 27106
Maplewood Ave & Ct 27103
Mar Don Dr 27104
Mar Don Hills Cir & Ct 27104
Mar Joe Dr 27127
Marajo Ct 27127
Maranda Rd 27107
Maranville Trl 27107
Marble St 27107
Marble Arch Rd 27104
Mardele Ln 27105
Margaret St 27103
Margie Ave 27127
Marguerite Dr 27106
Marguerite Park Dr 27106
Marian Ln 27104
Marie Dr 27127
Markwood Ln 27107
Marla Ct 27107
Marlborough Ln 27105
Marlowe Ave 27106
Marmion St 27127
Marne St 27107
Marriot Crossing Way 27103
N & S Marshall St 27101
Marshall View Ct 27101
Marshallberg Rd 27105
Marshallgate Dr 27105
Marta Rd 27107
Martin St 27103
N Martin Luther King Jr
Dr 27101
S Martin Luther King Jr
Dr
100-108 27101
110-399 27101
1200-2199 27107
Martin View Ln 27104
Martindale Rd 27107
Martins Dairy Rd 27107
Marty Dr 27105
Marvin Blvd 27105

Mary Belle Ln 27107
Mary Dee Ct & Ln 27127
Mary Young Ln 27106
Maryland Ave 27101
Mason St 27101
Mason Knoll Dr 27127
Mathews View Ln 27105
Maurine Way N 27127
Maverick St 27106
Max Dr 27106
Maxton Trl 27107
Maxwell Rd 27105
May St 27105
Mayan Ct 27103
Mayberry Ln 27106
Mayberry St 27107
Mayfair Dr 27105
Mayfield Ct & Rd 27104
Maynard Dr 27107
Maynard South Dr 27107
Maysol Dr 27105
Maywood St 27105
Mccanless St 27105
Mccreary St 27105
Mccuiston St 27105
Mcdaniel St 27105
Mcdowell Rd 27107
Mcgee Rd 27107
Mcgee St 27105
Mcgill Dr 27105
Mcgregor Rd 27103
Mcgregor Downs Rd 27103
Mcgregor Park Dr 27103
Mcguire Ave 27104
Mciver Ln 27127
Mckinley Dr 27107
Mclean Ave 27127
Mctavish Ln 27103
Meade Ln 27106
Meado Lee Ln 27127
W Meadow Dr 27103
Meadow Ln 27107
Meadow Trl 27107
Meadow Club Ct 27105
Meadow Glen Dr & Ln 27127
Meadow Hill Ct & Rd 27106
Meadow Ridge Ct 27107
Meadowbrook Dr 27104
Meadowdale Ct & Dr 27105
Meadowlands Dr 27107
Meadowlark Dr 27106
Meadowlark Glen Ln 27106
Meadowood Dr 27107
Meadowpark Ln 27107
Meadows Cir 27104
Meadowstone Dr 27104
Meadowsweet Ct 27107
Meadowview Dr 27107
Medical Park Dr 27103
Medinah Dr 27107
Megahertz Dr 27107
Meghan Elizabeth Ln 27127
Melba Ln 27107
Melinda Dr 27103
Mellon Dr 27107
Melody Ln 27105
Melrose St 27103
Melrose Village Ct 27105
Mendenhall Dr 27127
Menfreya Ct 27106
Mentor St 27105
Mercantile Dr 27105
Mercia Ct 27106
Merck Dr 27106
Meredith Dr, Ln &
Way 27107
Meredith Woods Ct, Dr &
Ln 27107
Merehunt Dr 27106
Mereledge Ct 27106
Mereworth Ct 27104
Meridian Way 27104
Merion Ct 27104
Merlendale Ln 27105
Merrell Dr 27127
Merrie Mill Ln 27103

Merrifield Way 27127
Merrimac St 27105
Merrimont Dr 27106
Merriweather Ct & Rd 27107
Merry Acres Ct & Ln 27106
Merry Dale Dr 27105
Merry Oaks Trl 27103
Merrymac Dr 27107
Merrywood Dr 27105
Mesa Ct 27106
Meta Dr 27106
Metairie Ln 27104
Methodist Dr 27105
Metropolitan Dr 27101
Mialina Forest Ct 27106
Miami Ave 27101
Mica Ct 27103
Michaels Trl 27101
Michigan St 27127
Mickey Rd 27107
Mid Salem Ct & Dr 27103
Middleton St 27107
Midian Ct 27105
Midkiff Rd 27106
Midpines Dr 27127
Midway Rd 27105
Midway School Rd 27107
Mikala Dr 27107
Mildred St 27105
Milford St 27107
Milhaven Rd 27106
Milhaven Lake Ct &
Dr 27106
Milhaven Park Ln 27106
Mill Dr 27127
Mill St 27103
Mill Creek Rd 27106
Mill Pond Ct & Dr 27106
Mill Works St 27101
Millbrook Dr 27105
Miller Rd 27106
Miller St
1-99 27104
100-1699 27103
Miller Crossing Ct 27103
Miller Park Cir 27103
Miller Pointe Cir, Dr &
Way 27106
Millers Creek Dr 27127
Millers Ridge Ln 27107
Millerwood Dr 27106
Millgate Dr 27103
Millhaven Cir 27103
Milnor Pl 27104
Milton Dr 27105
Minart Dr 27106
Mindona Dr 27106
Mineola St 27107
Mineral Ave 27105
Minorcas Dr 27106
Mint St 27127
Miracle Xing 27107
Miramar Rd 27105
Miriam Dr 27127
Mischief Ct 27127
Mission Rd 27103
Mistic Ln 27105
Misty Ridge Dr 27107
Mitch Dr 27104
Mitchell Dr 27106
Moat Dr
4100-4199 27101
4200-4399 27105
Mock St 27127
Mockingbird Ct 27107
Mockingbird Ln
300-399 27107
5900-5999 27105
Mohawk Dr 27107
Mollie Ln 27107
Monica Ct 27107
E Monmouth St
1-499 27127
600-699 27107
Monroe St 27104
Montague St 27107

Montclair Rd 27106
Monte Vista St 27105
Montgomery St 27101
Monticello Dr 27106
Montpelier Dr 27103
Montrose Ave 27105
Mooney St 27103
Moravia Rd 27127
Moravia St 27107
Moravian Way Dr 27106
Morgan Cir 27127
Morgan Rd 27105
Morgan Way 27127
Morgan Trace Dr 27127
Morgans Ct 27101
Morning Mist Rd 27107
Morning Ridge Ln 27101
Morning Side Dr 27107
Morning Star Ln 27107
Morningside Dr 27106
Morrell Rd 27105
Morris Rd 27101
Morsinie St 27107
Moses Lucas Ct 27101
Moss Dr 27106
Moss Brook Ct & Dr 27127
Mossbank Ln 27106
Mossy Oak Dr 27127
Motor Rd 27105
Motsinger Dr & Rd 27107
Mount Hope Dr 27107
Mount Olivet Dr 27107
Mount Olivet Church
Rd 27127
Mount Pleasant Dr 27105
Mount Tabor Ct 27106
Mount Vernon Ave 27101
Mount Vernon Church
Rd 27107
Mount Zion Pl 27101
Mountain Brook Trl 27105
Mountain View Rd 27104
Moyers Rd 27104
Mozart Ave 27104
Muddy Creek Dr 27107
Mueller Dr 27106
Muirfield Dr 27104
Mulberry St 27101
Mullins Dr 27107
Mumford St 27127
Murphy Ln 27104
Murray Rd 27106
Museum Dr 27105
Myer Lee Dr 27101
Myers Ct 27103
Myers St 27127
Myers Way Ln 27107
Myra St 27105
Myrick Dr 27101
Myrtle Ave 27106
Myrtle St 27107
Mystic Ln 27107
Nancy Ln 27107
Nantucket Ct & Dr 27103
Naomi Dr 27107
Narrow Way Ln 27105
Nash Ave 27101
Natalie Dr 27104
Natalie Temple Ln 27105
Nathan Ave 27107
Nathaniel Place Ct 27106
National Dr 27103
Nationwide Dr 27106
Navajo Ave 27103
N Nc Highway 109 27107
N Nc Highway 150 27127
E Ne St 27105
Nelson St 27105
Nesting Ln 27107
Neston Dr 27105
Netterillo Dr 27103
Nettlebrook Ct & Dr 27106
Neushore Ct & Dr 27127
Neva Ln 27107
Nevil Dr 27107
Neville Gardens Ln 27103

New Dr 27103
New Berry Ct 27103
New Castle Dr 27103
New Delhi Dr 27101
New Garden Rd 27107
New Greensboro Rd 27101
New Hampton Ct 27103
New Home St 27104
New Hope Ln & St 27105
New Plantation Rd 27104
New Providence Ln 27107
New Walkertown Rd
700-2699 27101
2700-4499 27105
Newark St 27105
Newland Dr 27107
Newport St 27105
Newton St 27105
Nicholas Dr 27107
Nicholson Rd 27107
Nieman Industrial Dr 27103
Nina Ct 27106
Ninfield Dr 27103
Nisbet Ct 27106
Nissen Ave 27107
Nita Dr 27105
No Record 27104 27104
No Record 27105 27105
No Record 27106 27106
No Record 27109 27109
No Record 27127 27127
Noble St 27105
Noel Dr 27105
Nokomis Ct 27106
Noralin Dr 27107
Nordwin Dr 27104
Norfleet Dr 27105
Norman Rd 27106
Norman Shoaf Rd 27107
Normandy Ln 27103
Normans Ln 27107
Northampton Dr 27105
Northbridge Rd 27103
Northchester Ln 27105
Northcliffe Dr 27106
Northeast Dr 27106
Northern Quarters Dr 27105
Northgate Dr 27104
Northgate Park Dr 27106
Northgate Plaza Dr 27105
Northoaks Ct & Dr 27105
Northpond Ln 27106
Northridge Dr 27105
Northriding Rd 27104
Northview St 27105
Northwest Blvd 27105
E Northwest Blvd 27105
W Northwest Blvd
100-599 27105
600-1099 27101
1400-1498 27104
1500-1699 27104
Northwest Dr 27105
Northwick Dr 27103
Northwind Dr 27127
Northwood Dr 27106
Northwoods Cir 27105
Norton St 27107
Norvista Cv 27107
Norwich Rd 27127
Norwood Hills Dr 27107
Nottingham Rd 27104
Nottingham Place Ln 27106
Nottinghill Dr 27107
Novack St 27105
Nowlin St 27127
Nylon Dr 27105
O Farrell St 27107
Oak St
700-1199 27101
1300-1599 27105
Oak Arbor Ln 27104
Oak Croft Ct 27107
Oak Forest Dr 27127
Oak Glen Dr 27107
Oak Grove Cir 27106

Oak Grove Rd 27103
Oak Grove Church Rd 27107
Oak Haven Dr 27105
Oak Hollow Ct 27106
Oak Plaza Blvd 27105
Oak Pointe Dr 27105
Oak Ridge Ct, Dr & Pl 27105
Oak Shadows Ct 27104
Oak Spring Ct 27104
Oak Summit Ct & Rd 27105
Oak Tree Dr 27107
Oakbury Ct 27107
Oakcrest Ct 27106
Oakdale Dr 27105
Oakdale St 27107
Oakhaven Forest Dr 27105
Oakland Dr 27106
Oaklawn Ave 27104
Oaklawn Rd 27107
Oakmont Rdg 27105
Oakridge Place Dr 27107
Oaks Ct 27107
Oaksburg Ct & Dr 27107
Oakshire Ct & Rd 27107
Oakside Rd 27104
Oakwood Cir 27106
Oakwood Ct 27103
Oakwood Dr 27103
Ocala Dr 27127
Oconnor Dr 27106
Ocono St 27105
Ogburn Ave 27105
Ohio Ave 27105
Okalina Ave 27105
Ola Dr 27107
Old Baux Mountain Rd 27105
Old Belews Creek Ct &
Rd 27101
Old Country Club Rd 27104
Old Cypress Dr 27127
Old Gaston Pl 27103
Old Greensboro Rd 27101
Old Grist Ct 27103
Old Hollow Rd 27105
Old Jonestown Rd 27103
Old Lexington Rd 27107
Old Mill Cir 27103
Old Milwaukee Ln 27107
Old Northwest Blvd 27105
Old Oak Cir & Dr 27106
Old Pfafftown Rd 27106
Old Plank Rd 27106
Old Plantation Cir &
Ct 27104
Old Rural Hall Rd 27105
Old Sage Ct 27127
Old Salem Rd 27101
Old Salisbury Ct & Rd 27127
Old Sides Mill Rd 27103
Old Thomasville Rd 27107
Old Timber Rd 27101
Old Town Dr & Rd 27106
Old Town Club Rd 27106
Old Us Highway 52
6000-6099 27105
Old Us Highway 52
10000-13199 27107
Old Vineyard Rd
3201-3297 27103
3299-3599 27103
3600-4199 27104
Old Wagon Rd 27106
Old Walkertown Rd 27105
Old Wayside Dr 27107
Olde Lantern Ct 27106
Olde Village Ln 27106
Olde Vineyard Ct 27104
Olive St 27103
Olivers Crossing Cir &
Dr 27127
Olivet Ln 27107
Olivet Church Rd 27106
Olympia Dr 27104
Omega Ct 27101
Ommache Trl 27107
One Triad Park 27101

Oneida St 27105
Ontario St 27105
Opportunity Rd 27105
Orchard Creek Ln & Way 27127
Orchard Park Ln 27127
Orchard View Dr 27127
Orchestra Dr 27127
Orchid Dr & Pl 27105
Oregon St 27107
Orlando St 27105
Ormond Dr 27106
Orosebriar Sq 27106
Orvil Ln 27107
Osborne Rd 27103
Osprey Ridge Rd 27106
Otis Dr 27105
Ottawa St 27106
Overbrook Ave 27104
Overbrook Dr 27107
Overcreek Ln 27127
Overdale Rd
100-199 27127
3300-5099 27107
Overlook Cir & Dr 27105
Owen Dr 27106
Owen Ln 27127
Owen Park St 27103
Oxford Dr 27104
Oxford St 27103
Ozark St 27105
Pacific Dr 27105
Paddington Ln 27106
Page St 27105
Paigebrook Cir & Dr 27106
Paint Horse Trl 27107
Palace Ave 27101
Palace Dr 27107
Palm Dr 27106
Palmer Ln 27107
Palmerston Ln 27104
Palmetto Dr 27107
Palmira Trl 27127
Palo Verde Ct & Dr 27106
Pam Dr 27107
Panola Rd 27106
Panther Crk Ct 27107
Papas Trl 27107
Par Pl 27107
Paradise Ln 27101
Paragon Dr 27127
Park Blvd 27127
Park Cir 27101
Park Ln 27104
Park Creek Ct 27104
Park Knoll Ct 27106
Park Plaza Dr 27105
Park Pointe Cir 27104
Park Ridge Cir, Ct & Ln 27104
Park Terrace Ct & Ln 27127
Park Vista Ln 27101
Parker Ct 27103
Parkgate Ct 27106
Parkhurst Dr 27103
Parkland Ct 27127
Parkside Cir 27107
Parkside Meadow Ct 27127
Parkside Place Dr 27127
Parkview Ct 27127
Parkway Dr 27103
Parkway Village Cir 27127
Parkwood Ave & Ct 27105
Parnell Rd 27107
Parrish Rd 27105
Parthelia Ct 27107
Partridge Ln 27106
Pasadena Dr 27127
Paschal Dr 27106
Pasture Ct 27101
Patria St 27127
Patricia Ln 27103
Patricia Ann Ct 27127
Patrick Ave 27105
Patsy Dr 27107
N Patterson Ave
101-197 27101
199-1299 27101
1300-1499 27105
1500-1500 27102
1500-1500 27105
1500-1500 27115
1501-4699 27105
1502-4698 27105
Patterson Center Ct 27105
Patton Ave 27107
Paul Howell Dr 27101
Paula Dr 27127
Pawley Ave 27103
Pawnee St 27105
N Payne Rd 27127
Peace Ct 27105
Peace Haven Ct 27106
Peace Haven Rd 27106
N Peace Haven Rd 27104
S Peace Haven Rd
100-399 27104
400-1099 27103
Peach Ave 27127
Peachtree St 27107
Pearl Valley Ln 27107
Pebble Ln 27107
Pebble Creek Rd 27107
Pebble Ridge Ln 27104
Pebblebrook Rd 27105
Peden St 27105
Pee Wee Ct 27101
Pelham Pl 27106
Pemberton Ct 27106
Pembroke Ave 27103
Pembrooke Rd 27106
Pembrooke Forest Ct & Dr 27106
Pendoric Cir 27106
Pendry St 27105
Penn Ave 27105
Penner St 27105
Pennington Ln 27106
Pennsylvania Ave 27104
Penny Ln 27127
Pensby Rd 27106
Pepper Ct 27107
Pepperidge Ct 27107
Peregrine Ct 27104
Perimeter Point Blvd 27105
Perks Dr 27127
Perry Ave 27107
Perry St 27105
Perry Maxwell Ln 27106
Perryco Ln 27127
Pershing Ave 27103
Pete Allen Cir 27103
Peters Creek Pkwy
100-599 27101
600-1599 27103
2000-12399 27127
Petree Rd 27106
Pewter Ct 27104
Peyton Ct 27103
Pfafftown Forest Dr 27106
Pheasant Ln 27106
Phelps Cir & Dr 27105
Philip St 27103
Phillips Bridge Rd 27104
Philpark Dr 27106
Phoenix Dr 27106
Phyllis Ridge Ln 27107
Piccadilly Dr & Ln 27104
Pickford Ct 27101
Piedmont Ave 27101
Piedmont Cir 27105
Piedmont Farms Way 27107
Piedmont Industrial Dr 27107
Piedmont Memorial Dr 27107
Piermont Ct 27103
Pilgrim Ct 27106
Pilot View St 27101
Pima Ct 27103
Pimlico Dr 27107
Pin Oak Dr 27127
Pine St 27107
Pine Bark Ln 27101
Pine Cove Ct & Dr 27127
Pine Lake Dr 27105
Pine Needles Dr 27104
Pine Top Dr 27104
Pine Tree Rd 27105
N Pine Valley Rd
100-499 27104
500-899 27106
S Pine Valley Rd 27104
Pinebluff Rd 27103
Pinebrook Ln 27105
Pinebrook Knolls Dr 27105
Pinecrest Dr 27127
Pinecroft Dr 27104
Pinedale Dr 27105
Pineridge Dr 27104
Pinetuck Ln 27104
Pineview Dr 27105
Pinewood Ct & Dr 27106
Pinewood Knolls Dr 27105
Piney Brook Ln 27107
Pinoak Dr 27104
Pinta Dr 27106
Pioneer Trl 27106
Pitcher Ct 27103
Pitts St 27127
Pittsburg Ave, Ct & St 27105
Pitzer Ln 27106
Placid St 27104
Plantation Dr & Rd 27105
Plata Dr 27101
Plaza Dr 27103
Plaza Hollow Dr 27107
Plaza Ridge Cir 27107
Plaza West Dr 27103
Pleasant St
1100-1996 27107
1995-1995 27117
1997-2399 27107
1998-2398 27107
Pleasant Fork Church Rd 27127
Pleasant View Dr 27105
Plesney Way 27103
Ploughboy Ct, Ln & Trl 27103
Plymouth Ave 27104
Poe St 27101
Poindexter Ave 27106
Poinsetta Dr 27107
N Point Blvd
7600-7841 27106
7840-7840 27116
7842-8098 27106
7843-8099 27106
8100-8199 27105
N Point Ct 27106
N Point Dr 27106
Pointe Ct 27103
Polk Ave 27106
Pollard Dr 27103
Pollyanna Dr 27105
Polo Rd
100-499 27105
500-3599 27106
Polo Oaks Ct & Dr 27106
Polo Ridge Ct 27106
Pomeroy Dr 27105
Pontiac St 27101
Poole Ct 27106
Pope Rd 27127
N & S Poplar St 27101
Poplar Grove Rd 27106
Poplar Valley Ln 27127
Poppy Ln 27105
Poteat Ct 27106
Potomac St 27127
Potter St 27107
Powell St 27127
Power Plant Cir 27101
Powers Rd 27106
Powers Point Ct 27106
Prague Cir 27106
Pratt Rd 27106
Premier Park Ln 27105
Prescott Dr 27107
Presley Dr 27107
Pressman Dr 27105
Preston Downs Way 27103
Preston Woods Dr 27127
Prestwick Pl & Xing 27106
Prestwick Manor Ct 27104
Primrose Path 27127
Princess Dr 27127
Princeton St 27103
Proctor Farm Rd 27107
Professional Park Dr 27103
Progress Ct & Ln 27106
Progressive Ln 27101
Promise Land Ct 27105
Prospect Dr 27105
Providence Ln 27106
Providence Church Rd 27105
Providence Pt Ln 27106
Prytania Rd 27106
Pugh Dr 27105
Pulliam Dr 27107
Punkin Ridge Ln 27107
Puritan Ln 27103
Quail Dr
200-299 27105
1100-1299 27107
Quail Haven Ln 27107
Quail Lakes Dr 27104
Quail Place Dr 27127
Quail Wood Ct & Dr 27104
Quantum Ct & Ln 27106
Quarterstaff Pl & Rd 27104
Queen St 27103
Queen Ann Cir 27106
Queen Catherine Ln 27106
Queens Grant Rd 27106
Queensbury Dr 27127
Queensbury Rd 27104
Queensway Rd 27127
Queenswood Ct & Dr 27106
Quick Silver Dr 27127
Quietwood Dr 27103
Quilling Rd 27104
Quillmark Ct & Rd 27127
Quincy Dr 27106
Quincy Caldwell Cir 27101
Quinn Forest Way 27127
R G B Dr 27107
Rachael Dr 27107
Racine Dr 27105
Radcliff St 27107
Radford St 27106
Radley Ct 27104
Railroad Ave 27105
Railway Ln 27107
Rainridge Dr 27104
Raintree Ct 27106
Rainwood Ct & Dr 27107
Rainy Day Dr 27107
Ralee Dr 27127
Raleigh Ave 27105
Ramillie Run 27106
Rams Dr 27101
Rams Horn Rd 27105
Ramseur Dr 27101
Ramsgate Ct 27106
Ranch Dr 27106
Randall St 27104
Rankin St 27101
Rannoch Ct 27107
Ransom Rd 27106
Ransom Trace Ct 27106
Ras Dr 27107
Raven Rd 27105
Raven Forest Ct & Dr 27105
Ravenscar Ct 27104
Rawson St 27127
Ray Lanning Rd 27107
Raye Dr 27107
Rayfield Dr 27107
Reaford Rd 27104
Reba Dr 27105
Red Copper Cir 27106
Red Cypress Ct 27127
Red Fox Trl 27103
Red Hawk Ln 27107
Red Oak Ln 27106
Red Sage Rd 27127
Red Willow Ln 27127
Redberry Ln 27107
Redbud Ln 27106
Redcoat Ln 27107
Redfern Pl 27107
Redigo Ave 27107
Redwing Cir & Ct 27106
Redwood Ct 27103
Reece Rd 27107
Reed St 27107
Reflection Ct 27105
Regal Ct & Dr 27127
Regalwood Dr 27107
Regency Dr 27106
Regent Dr 27103
Regent Village Dr 27103
Reich St 27105
Reid Rd & St 27107
Reidsville Rd 27101
Remington Dr 27104
Renigar St 27105
Renon Rd 27127
Renwood Dr 27106
Retford Cir 27104
Retnuh Dr 27105
Retreat Ln 27106
Reubens Ridge Dr 27105
Reuter Way 27127
Revere Rd 27103
Rex Ct & Rd 27107
Reynolda Rd
800-1799 27104
1800-6399 27106
Reynolda Vlg 27106
Reynolds Blvd
500-1199 27105
1200-1299 27106
Reynolds Dr 27104
Reynolds Sq 27106
Reynolds Creek Cir, Dr & Rd 27106
Reynolds Forest Ct & Dr 27107
Reynolds Manor Dr 27107
Reynolds Park Rd 27107
Rhue Rd 27107
Rhyne Ave
1-199 27127
200-399 27107
Ribbon Ln 27107
Rich Ave 27101
Richard Dr 27107
Richard Allen Dr 27105
Richmond Park Dr 27103
Rickard Dr 27101
Ricks Dr 27103
Rideout Way 27105
Ridge Aly 27101
S Ridge Ct 27107
Ridge Brook Ct 27127
Ridge Cove Ct 27104
Ridge Forest Ct 27104
Ridge Hollow Dr 27107
Ridgeback Dr 27107
Ridgecrest Rd 27103
Ridgecrest Place Ct 27103
Ridgehaven Cir & Dr 27104
Ridgelea Ct 27104
Ridgemeadow Dr 27127
Ridgemere Ct & Ln 27106
Ridgeview Ave 27127
Ridgeview Dr 27107
Ridgeview Ln 27103
Ridgewood Ct & Rd 27107
Ridgewood Park Dr 27107
Ridgewood Place Dr 27107
Riggins Ln 27107
Riley Forest Ct & Dr 27127
Rink Rd 27107
Rittenhouse Ct & Rd 27104
River Chase Rdg 27104
Rivertree Ln 27103
Robbins Ct, Ln & Rd 27107
Robbins Brook Dr 27107
Robbins Farm Rd & Way 27105
Robertson Dr 27101
Robie St 27107
Robin Ave 27106
Robin Wood Ln 27105
Robindale Dr 27107
Robinhood Cir 27106
Robinhood Rd
1700-2499 27104
2500-5899 27106
Robinhood Medical Plz 27106
Robinhood Valley Ct 27106
Robinhood Village Dr 27106
Robinson Ct 27105
Rock Cliff Ct 27104
Rock Crest Dr 27127
Rock Garden Cir 27104
Rock House Rd 27127
Rock Knoll Ct 27107
Rock Spring Dr 27105
Rockaway Dr 27107
Rockaway Ln 27106
Rockdale Dr 27104
Rockford St 27107
Rockingham Dr 27103
Rockmont Ct & Dr 27104
Rockridge Ct 27104
Rocky Ford Ln 27101
Rocky Gravel Dr 27107
Rogers Ln 27106
Rolling Green Dr 27107
Rolling Knoll Cv & Ln 27106
Rolling Meadow Ct 27107
Rollingreen Dr 27103
E & W Rollingwood Cir 27105
Romany Ct 27106
Romara Ct & Dr 27103
Rominger Rd 27127
Rookwood Ln 27106
Roosevelt St 27105
Rosa St 27105
Rosalie St 27104
Rosann Dr 27107
Roscoe Vaughn Dr 27105
Roscrea Ln 27104
Roseberry Ln 27107
Rosebriar Cir & Ln 27106
Rosebriar Square Dr 27106
Rosedale Cir 27106
Rosedown Ct 27106
Rosemary Dr
100-299 27107
2500-2899 27105
Rosemont Ave 27127
Rosencarrie Ln 27106
Rosetta Ln 27105
Rosewood Ave & Ct 27103
Rosie St 27107
Roslyn Rd 27104
Ross St 27101
Rothrock St 27107
Roundtree Ln 27103
Row St 27105
Rowell St 27101
Royal Dale Ln 27107
Royal Forest Ct 27104
Royal Gate Rd 27101
Royal Grey Ct 27107
Royal Highland Dr 27107
Royal Kings Ct 27127
Royal Oaks Dr 27107
Royall Dr 27106
Royalton St 27104
Rozianna Dr 27106
Ruby Rd 27106
Rugby Rd & Row 27106
Rumley Cir 27105
Rundell St 27105
Runnymede Rd 27104
Rural Retreat Rd 27107
Rushland Dr 27104
Ruskin Ct 27105
Russell Dr 27127
Russell Way Ln 27127
Rustic Ln 27107
Rustic Rd 27106
Ruth Ave 27105
Ruth Ct
100-3799 27127
5700-5799 27105
Rutledge Dr 27103
Ryan Way 27106
Ryandale Rd 27104
Rymco Dr 27103
Sabrina Lake Ct & Rd 27127
Saddlechase Ln 27107
Saddlegate Ct 27106
Saddler Dr 27105
Saddlewood Forest Ct & Dr 27106
Saffron Pl 27127
Sagamore Ln 27106
Sage Crossing Rd 27127
Sage Hill Dr 27127
Sage Meadows Dr 27127
Sagebrush Trl 27101
Sagewood Ln 27127
Sailway Rd 27127
Saint Alban Ct 27104
Saint Claire Rd 27106
Saint George Rd 27106
Saint George Square Ct 27103
Saint Johns Ct & Pl 27106
Saint Marks Rd 27103
E Salem Ave 27101
W Salem Ave 27101
Salem Ct 27103
Salem Xing 27103
Salem Bluff Dr 27127
Salem Creek Rd 27103
Salem Crest Cir & Ln 27103
Salem Garden Dr 27107
Salem Industrial Dr 27127
Salem Lake Rd 27107
Salem Landing Ct & Dr 27101
Salem Point Ct 27103
Salem Pointe Ln 27101
Salem Springs Ct & Dr 27107
Salem Trail Ct 27105
Salem Valley Rd 27103
Salem Vista Ct 27101
Salemtowne Dr 27106
Salisbury Sq 27127
Salisbury Ridge Rd 27127
Sallies Ln 27106
Sally Kirk Rd 27106
Salt St 27101
Sam Hollow Dr 27107
San Carlos Rd 27105
Sandalwood Ct & Ln 27106
Sandersted Rd 27103
Sandersted Village Cir 27103
Sandhill Dr 27105
Sandon Pl 27104
Sandrail Ln 27107
Sandusky St 27105
Sandy Lane Dr 27107
Sanford Dr 27105
Santa Maria Dr 27106
Saponi Village Ct & Trl 27127
Sapphire Valley Dr 27107
Sara Ln 27103
Sara Jean Ct 27127
Saratoga Ct & St 27103
Sassafras Ln 27106
Saura Ln 27107
Savannah Meadows Dr 27104
Saw Buck Dr 27127
Saw Tooth Trl 27127
Sawgrass Ct 27103
Sawmill Rd 27107
Sawyer Ct, Dr & St 27105
Saxon Ln 27104
Scarsborough Dr 27104

Scenic Dr 27105
Schaub Rd 27127
Schlitz Ave 27107
Scholastic Ct & Dr 27106
School St 27105
Scioto St 27103
Scotland Ridge Ct & Dr 27107
Scotney Ct 27127
Scott Hines Park Dr 27105
Scott Hollow Dr 27103
Scotthurst 27107
Scottie Lane Cir 27107
Scottsdale Ln 27127
Sea Pines Dr 27107
Seaman St 27103
Seasons Chase 27103
Seaton Rd 27104
Secret Garden Ln 27104
Sedge Meadow Dr 27107
E & W Sedgefield Dr 27107
Sedgemont Dr 27103
Sedgeview Ln 27107
Sedgewick St 27127
Selda Dr 27107
Selena St 27106
Selkirk Dr 27105
Sells Rd 27105
Sellwood Rd 27105
Selma St 27107
Selwyn Dr 27104
Seminole Ct 27127
Seminole Dr 27107
Seneca St 27103
Sennett Dr 27127
Sentry Ct 27127
Sentry Pointe Ct & Ln 27127
Serene St 27101
Serenity Way 27127
Settlers Run Dr 27101
Seville St 27106
Sewanee Dr 27106
Seymore Ln 27105
Shadetree Cir & Dr 27107
Shadow Ln 27107
Shadow Glen Ct 27106
Shadowbrook Ln 27103
Shadowmere Ct 27104
Shady Blvd 27101
Shady Ct 27107
Shady Ln 27107
Shady Rd 27107
Shady Acres Ln 27127
Shady Grove Ct 27103
Shady Grove Ln 27107
Shady Grove Church Rd 27107
Shady Hollow Ln 27127
Shady Maple Ln 27106
Shady Mount Ave 27105
Shady Oaks Ln 27106
Shady Stone Dr 27127
Shady Woods Dr & Trl 27107
Shadylawn Ct & Dr 27104
Shaffer Ct 27127
Shaftesbury Ln 27105
Shaker Ct 27104
Shalimar Ct & Dr 27107
Shallotte Ave 27127
Shallowcreek Ct 27127
Shallowford Rd 27104
Shallowford St 27101
Shamel Ct & St 27105
Shamrock Trl 27107
Shannon Dr 27106
Shannon Ln N 27107
Sharon Rd 27103
Shattalon Cir 27106
Shattalon Dr
3800-5599 27106
5600-5799 27105
Shattalon Enterprise Way 27105
Shattalon Grove Ln 27106
Shauna Dr 27107
Shaw Rd 27105
Shaw Hills Ct 27107
Shaw Ridge St 27105
Shawnee St 27127
Shea Ct 27107
Sheets St 27103
Sheffield Dr & Pl 27104
Shelburne Ln 27104
Shelby Ln 27107
Shell Ln 27107
Shelter Cv 27106
Shelton Cir 27106
Shelwin Ct 27106
Shenandoah Ct & Dr 27103
Shepherd St 27103
Shepley Ct 27104
Sheraton St 27105
Sherbrooke Dr 27105
Sherlie Weavil Rd 27107
Sherman Dr 27127
Sherwood Dr 27103
Sherwood Forest Rd 27104
Sherwood Hills Dr 27104
Shetland Dr 27127
Shieldale Dr 27107
Shillington Dr 27127
Shiloh Dr 27106
Shiloh Church Rd 27105
Shirley Jean Ct 27105
Shoaf Rd 27127
Shober Ct 27127
Shober St 27101
Shorefair Dr 27105
Shoreland Rd 27106
Short St 27105
Shouse Blvd 27105
Shrub St 27105
Shulbrook Dr 27105
Shuman St 27101
Sides Rd 27127
Sides St 27103
Sides Branch Rd 27127
Sides Meadow Ct & Dr 27107
Sides Village Dr 27127
Sidney St 27101
Signet Dr 27101
Silas Creek Pkwy
300-372 27127
374-1699 27127
1700-3329 27103
3320-3320 27130
3330-3398 27103
3331-3399 27103
4000-4298 27104
4300-4499 27104
5100-6699 27106
Silas Creek Rd 27103
Silas Ridge Ct & Rd 27106
Silver Chalice Dr 27101
Silver Chase Ct 27127
Silver Leaf Dr 27103
Silver Run Ct 27127
Silver Stone Ln 27106
Silverbrook Ct 27106
Silverthorne Ct 27103
Simmon Hill Dr 27107
Sina Ave 27127
Single Leaf Ct 27105
Sink St 27107
Sinkland Dr 27127
Sir Isaac Dr 27101
Skycrest Dr 27127
Skyline Vlg 27107
Skyview Dr 27127
Slater Ave 27101
Sledd Ct 27106
Sleepy Hollow Dr 27107
Slick Rock Trl 27107
Sloan Dr 27103
Sm Caesar Dr 27105
Smith Lndg 27107
Smith Farm Ln 27107
Smith Lake Rd 27103
Smith Meadow Ln 27107
Smithdale St 27107
Smokey Hollow Rd 27105
Smoky Ridge Ln 27127
Snead Rd 27103
Snyder Dr 27127
Snyder Ridge Ln 27107
Solon St 27105
Somerset Dr 27103
Somerset Center Dr 27103
Somerset Cove Dr 27103
Somerset Place Dr 27103
South St 27127
Southdale Ave 27107
Southern View Ct 27105
Southern Woods Dr 27107
Southfork Ave 27104
Southland Ave 27107
Southmont Dr 27103
Southoak Ct & Dr 27107
Southpark Blvd 27127
Southview Dr 27127
Southwin Dr 27104
Spach Dr 27127
Spangenberg Rd 27127
Sparkling Pl 27103
Sparks Ct 27103
Spaugh Ct 27107
Spaugh St 27101
Spaugh Industrial Dr 27103
Spaulding Dr 27105
Speas Rd 27106
Specialty Park Dr 27105
Spencer Dr
100-199 27107
1700-1799 27127
Spenway Pl 27106
Spice Meadow Ln 27106
Spicewood Ct & Dr 27106
Spicewood Trails Ln 27106
Spilsby Ln 27104
Spindletop Ct 27106
Split Creek Trl 27107
Split Rail Cir 27106
Sportsmans Dr 27101
Spotswood Dr 27107
Spradlin St 27106
Sprague Ct 27107
E Sprague St
1-499 27127
500-598 27107
600-2947 27107
2949-2999 27107
W Sprague St 27127
Spring Dr 27107
N Spring St 27101
S Spring St 27101
Spring Branch Dr 27107
Spring Creek Ct 27106
Spring Drive Ext 27107
Spring Garden Rd
2500-2599 27104
2700-2799 27106
Spring Green Ct 27107
Spring Grove Dr 27103
Spring Lake Farm Cir & Ct 27101
Spring Rock Ct 27104
Spring Run Dr 27106
Spring Tree Ct 27104
Spring Willow Way 27107
Springdale Ave 27104
Springhaven Dr 27103
Springhouse Ct 27107
Springhouse Farm Ct & Rd 27107
Springmeadow Knoll Ct 27103
Springview Dr 27105
Springwater Ct 27106
Springwood Cir 27107
Sprinkle Farm Ln 27106
N & S Spruce St 27101
Sprucepine Dr 27105
Spry Rd 27107
Squire Rd 27106
Stacy Ct 27107
Stadium Dr 27101
Stadler Ridge Rd 27106
Stafford Place Cir 27127
Staffordshire Ct & Rd 27104
Stagecoach Rd 27105
Staghorn Rd 27104
Stanaford Rd 27104
Standish Ct 27106
Stanley Ave & Ct 27101
Stanley Park Rd 27101
Stanleyville Dr 27105
Stanton Ct & Dr 27106
Stark St 27103
Starlight Dr 27107
Starmount Dr 27105
State St 27105
Staton Dr 27107
Stavanger Ct 27127
Stedman St 27101
Steed Ct 27104
Steelman Ln 27127
Steelwood Ct 27106
Steeple View Ct 27101
Stephen Blvd 27107
Sterling Brooke Ct & Ln 27103
Sterling Park Ct 27105
Sterling Point Ct 27104
Sterling Trail Ct 27127
Stewart Rd 27107
Stickney Rd 27107
Still Meadow Ln 27106
Still Point Ct & Dr 27103
Stilletto Rd 27107
Stillmere Ct & Dr 27101
Stillwater Ct & Dr 27106
Stillwell Dr 27106
Stixfield Ct 27103
Stockdale Pl 27104
Stockton St 27127
Stokes Ave 27105
Stokesdale Ave 27101
Stone Ln 27103
Stone Crossing Dr 27104
Stone Forest Ct & Dr 27105
Stone Mill Dr 27105
Stone Moss Ln 27127
Stone Ridge Dr 27106
Stone Ridge Pl 27107
Stonebridge Dr 27104
Stonebrook Ct & Ln 27104
Stonecroft Ct & Dr 27103
Stonecutter Ct & Dr 27103
Stonegate Ct 27104
Stonegate Dr 27107
Stonegate Ln 27104
Stonehenge Ct & Ln 27106
Stonekirk 27103
Stoneleigh Ct 27106
Stonemoor Dr 27104
Stones Throw Ct 27106
Stoneshire Ct 27127
Stonewall St 27105
Stoneway Ct 27105
Stonewood Dr 27103
Stoney Brook Blvd 27103
Stoney Glen Cir & Dr 27107
Stoney Ridge Rd 27107
Stoneybrook Cir 27105
Stonington Rd 27103
Stony Creek Ln 27127
Storm Canyon Rd 27106
Stovall Dr 27101
Stowe St 27105
Stratfield Ct 27104
Stratford Ct 27103
Stratford Rd 27103
N Stratford Rd 27104
S Stratford Rd
100-161 27104
162-3399 27103
Stratford Common Ct 27103
Stratford Crossing Dr 27103
Stratford Green Ct & Ln 27103
Stratford Lake Ct & Rd 27103
Strathmore Cir 27104
Stratton Ave 27101
Strawberry Ln 27106
Strickland Ave 27127
Student Dr 27106
Stump Tree Ln 27106
Sturbridge Rd 27104
Sturmer Park Cir 27105
Styers Rd 27105
Styers Ferry Rd 27104
Sudlicht Cir 27106
Sugar Maple Ct 27106
Sugarberry Ct 27107
Sugarcane Ln 27104
Sugarcreek Dr 27106
Sulgrave Ct 27104
Sullivan Way 27104
Summer Hill Ln 27106
Summer Trace Ln 27105
Summerfield Ln 27106
Summergate Dr 27103
Summerlin Rdg & St 27103
Summerour Ct 27106
Summers St 27106
Summerside Ct 27107
Summertime Pl 27107
Summertree Ct 27127
Summit St 27101
Summit Heights Dr 27104
Summit Point Ln 27105
Summit Square Blvd & Ct 27105
Sumner Pl 27101
Sun Creek Dr 27104
Sun View Rd 27105
Sunbridge Ct 27103
Sunburst Cir 27105
Sunderland Rd 27103
Sundown St 27127
Sunflower Cir & Pl 27105
Sunny Dr 27106
Sunny Park Cir 27103
Sunnydell Dr 27106
Sunnynoll Ct & Dr 27106
Sunnyside Ave 27127
Sunpath Cir 27103
Sunrise Ter 27105
Sunscape Dr 27103
Sunset Ct 27107
Sunset Dr 27107
N Sunset Dr 27101
S Sunset Dr
100-199 27101
200-1599 27103
Sunshine Ave 27107
Superior Dr 27106
Surrey Path Ct & Trl 27104
Surrey Way Ct 27106
Surtees Rd 27104
Susan Ln 27107
Susanna Wesley Dr 27104
Sussex Ln 27104
Sutherland Dr 27106
Sutters Place Ct 27104
Sutton Pl 27103
Swaim Ct 27127
Swaim Rd
1800-2199 27127
3100-3299 27107
3300-4299 27127
Swaim Woods Ln 27107
Swan Ct & Dr 27106
Swanson Ct 27105
Sweetwater Dr 27107
Swing Ct & Dr 27127
Sycamore Cir & Rdg 27105
Sycamore Trail Ln 27103
Sylvan Rd 27104
Sylvia St 27104
Tabor St 27106
Tabor View Ln 27106
Tadmore St 27127
Taft St 27105
Talcott Ave 27106
Tall Pines Ct 27107
Tall Tree Ct & Dr 27105
Talladega Ct 27107
Tallison Dr 27106
Talwood Ct 27106
Tam O Shanter Trl 27103
Tambente St 27101
Tamra Ln 27101
Tanders St 27101
Taney Ct 27106
Tangle Ln 27106
Tanner Ln 27107
Tanners Mill Ct 27101
Tanners Park Ct 27101
Tanners Run Dr 27101
Tannery Trl 27106
Tantelon Pl 27127
Tar Branch Ct 27101
Tara Ct 27107
Tara Gail Ln 27127
Tart-Murphy Ln 27107
Tartan Ct 27106
Tatton Park Cir & Dr 27103
Taylor St 27101
Taylor Ridge Rd 27106
Tea Berry Ct & Ln 27127
Tea Berry Ridge Rd 27127
Teague Ct & Rd 27107
Teague Meadow Ln 27107
Teague Mill Ln 27107
Teagues Xing 27103
Teakwood Ct 27106
Teakwood Dr 27127
Teal Ct & Dr 27127
Teapot Ct 27106
Tech Ave 27107
Technology Way 27101
Tekoa Ln 27105
Temple St 27101
Temple School Rd 27107
Tenney Ln 27106
Teresa Ave 27105
Tern Ct 27105
Terra Stone Ct 27103
Terrace Ave 27101
Terrence Dr 27103
Terrie Dr 27107
Terry Rd 27107
Terrybrook Ct 27104
Terrys Lndg 27104
Tesh Rd 27127
Thacker Hill Dr 27106
Thales Rd 27104
Thamer Ln 27107
Thomas St 27101
Thomas Mock Rd 27107
Thomas Park Dr 27107
Thomas School Rd 27107
Thomasville Rd 27107
Thompson Dr 27127
Thoresby Ct 27104
Thorn Ridge Rd 27106
Thornaby Cir & Dr 27107
Thornbrook Ln 27105
Thornbury Ridge Ct & Rd 27106
Thorncliffe St 27104
Thorndale Dr 27106
Thornfield Rd 27106
Thornhill Ln 27106
Thorntons Way 27105
Thrace Ct 27104
Three Hills Dr 27105
Thresher Ln 27127
Thurmond St 27105
Thurston St 27103
Tiffany Ave 27104
Tiger Eye Ct 27127
Tilmark Dr 27103
Tim Rd 27106
Timber Ln 27127
Timber Cove Ct & Ln 27127
Timber Wolfe Trl 27107
Timberlake Ln 27106
Timberline Dr 27101
Timberline Ridge Ct & Ln 27106
Timbrook Ln 27103
Timlic Ave 27107
Timothy Ln 27106
Tinley Park Dr 27107
Tipperary Ln & Pl 27104
Tise Ave 27105
Tiseland Dr 27104
Tiverton Dr 27105
Tobacco St 27106
Tochi Ct 27105
Todays Woman Ave 27105
Toddle Ct & Dr 27104
Toddler Place Dr 27105
Tohari Rd 27105
Tollesbury Ct 27127
Tolley Creek Dr 27106
Tolley Ridge Ln 27106
Tom Everhart Rd 27107
Tom Livengood Rd 27107
Tomahawk Rd 27106
Tombee Farm Rd 27106
Tommys Lake Rd 27105
Tonbridge Ln 27106
Tonifae Dr 27106
Tony Dr 27105
Tonya Dr 27105
Top Ct 27104
Topaz Dr 27127
Topsail Ln 27107
Torey Pines Ct 27105
Tori Ln 27127
Torrance Dr 27106
Torrington Ln 27104
Tortoise Ln 27127
Tower St 27107
Tower Circle Dr 27107
Towergate Ct & Dr 27106
Town Run Ln
200-200 27101
200-200 27120
200-200 27113
201-299 27101
Town Square Dr 27127
Townley St 27103
Townsend Dr 27107
Townsend Glen Cir 27106
Townsend Ridge Dr 27107
Trace View Dr 27106
Traci Ln 27107
Tracy St 27105
N Trade St
400-1299 27101
1300-2299 27105
Trademart Blvd 27127
Traden Ct 27107
Trafalgar Sq 27106
Trammel Ter 27106
Tranquil Ave 27101
Tranquil Meadow Ln 27107
Travis St 27101
Treadway Ct 27107
Treble Ct 27127
Tredwell Dr 27103
Tree Line Dr 27107
Treebrook Ct & Dr 27106
Treetop Ct 27127
Treetop Ln 27101
Trellis Ln 27105
Trenchard Ln 27127
Trendy Dr 27107
Trent Ct & St 27127
Trent Hill Dr 27105
Trenwest Dr 27103
Triad Ct 27107
Triangle Dr 27106
Trillium Ln 27127
Trinidad Ln 27106
Tro Tod Dr 27107
Troonsway Rd 27127
Trotter Farm Rd 27107
Trotters Way Ct 27106
Troy Dr & Lndg 27107
Truelove Ln 27127
Truliant Way 27103
Truman St 27106
Tryon St 27107
Tucker Ave 27104
Tudor Rd 27106

Tudor Downs Rd 27103
Tulip Dr 27105
Tully Sq 27106
Tumbleweed Dr 27127
Tumbleweed Trl 27103
Turkey Hill Ct & Rd 27106
Turnberry Ct 27104
Turnberry Forest Ct 27106
Turner St 27104
Turnwood Ln 27104
Turret Dr 27101
Turtle Bay Ct 27107
Turtle Creek Ct 27106
Turtle Rock Ln 27104
Tuscan Row 27105
Tutelo Trl 27127
Twain Dr 27107
Twickenham Ln 27127
Twin Branch St 27107
Twin Knolls Ct & Dr 27127
Twin Oak Dr 27105
Twisted Cypress Ln 27127
Tyler Ct & St 27107
Tyler Way Ct 27104
Tyndall St 27105
Underwood Ave 27105
Union St 27127
Union Cross Rd 27107
Union Grove Rd 27127
Union Knoll Dr 27107
University Ct 27101
University Pkwy
2700-3199 27105
3201-3697 27106
3699-5399 27106
5400-6399 27105
6401-6401 27105
University Rd 27104
University Center Dr 27105
Upton Rd 27107
Upton St 27103
Urban St 27107
Utah Dr 27107
Utica St 27107
Utopia Rd 27105
Valencia Cir & Ln 27106
Valjean Ln 27107
Valley Ct 27106
Valley Dr 27107
Valley Rd 27106
Valley Brook Ln 27104
Valley Cliff Dr 27106
Valley Hill Ct & Ln 27106
Valleydale Ln 27107
Valleyridge Ln 27103
Valleyside Ln 27107
Valleystream Rd 27104
Van Buren St 27103
Van Hoy Ave 27104
Vance Ct 27105
Vanclair Dr 27105
Vandalia Dr 27104
Vandar Dr 27106
Vanhorn St 27105
Vargrave St
1600-1699 27127
1700-1799 27107
1900-2599 27127
Velinda Dr 27106
Velma Ave 27127
Velyn Ct & Dr 27127
Verdun St 27107
Verita Ct 27104
Vernon Ave 27106
W Vernon Church Rd 27107
Vest Mill Cir & Rd 27103
Vicar Ln 27107
Viceroy Dr 27103
Vickie Dr 27106
Victoria Ct 27127
Victoria St 27105
Victoria Park Ln 27103
Victoria Village Ln 27107
Vienna Ln 27106
Viking Dr 27105
S Villa Dr 27104
Villa Club Dr 27106
S Village Dr 27127
Village Pl 27127
Village Trl 27106
Village Creek Cir & Ct 27104
Village Crossing Ln 27104
Village Green Sq 27104
Village Link Rd 27106
Village Oak Dr 27106
Village Park Ct 27127
Village Ridge Dr 27107
Villas Ct & Dr 27103
Vincent Rd 27106
Vine St 27101
Vinegar Hill Rd 27104
Vineland Ln 27103
Vineyard Brook Ct 27104
Vineyard Park Ct & Rd 27104
Vintage Ave 27127
Viola Ct 27127
Violet St 27127
Virginia Rd 27104
Virginia Branch Rd 27127
Virginia Dare Ln 27106
Virginia Lake Rd 27105
Virginia Newell Ln 27101
Visser Ln 27107
Vista Cir 27106
Vista Lindo Ct 27101
Vixen Ln 27104
Vogler Dr & St 27107
Voss St 27105
Wabash Blvd 27106
Waccamaw Path 27127
Wachovia Ct 27127
Wachovia St 27101
Waddill St 27105
Wade Frye Rd 27103
Wainwright St 27107
Wait Rd 27106
Wake Dr 27106
Wake Forest Dr 27106
Wake Forest Rd 27109
Wake Place Ct 27106
Wakefield Dr 27106
Wakeman Dr 27105
Wakewood Hill Ct 27106
Walcott St 27106
Walden Dr 27106
Walden Ridge Ct & Dr 27127
Waldenshire Rd 27127
Waldorf Cir 27106
Wales St 27101
Walkabout Ln 27107
Walker Ave 27103
Walker Rd 27106
Walkertown Ave 27105
Walkertown Guthrie Rd 27101
Walking Trail Rd 27107
Wallburg Rd 27107
Wallburg High Point Rd 27107
Wallburg Landing Dr & St 27107
Wallingford Rd 27101
Wallridge Dr 27106
Walnut Ave 27106
Walnut St 27101
Walnut Forest Ct & Rd 27103
Walnut Hill Dr 27106
Walnut Hollow Ct & Dr 27127
Walnut Park Ln 27106
Walnut View Ct 27103
Walsh St 27107
Walter Ct 27103
Waltrude Ln 27107
Wanda Way 27105
Wandering Way 27106
Wanger Dr 27127
Ward Rd 27107
Ward St 27101
Wareham Ln 27106
Warner Ave 27105
Warren Ave 27127
Warrington Ct 27127
Warwick Rd 27104
Warwick Green Rd 27104
Washington Ave 27101
Water St 27101
Water Lily Cir 27107
Waterbury St 27107
Wateree Trl 27127
Waterford Rd 27106
Waterwheel Cir & Dr 27103
Waterworks Rd 27101
Watkins Rd 27107
Watkins St 27101
Watson Ave 27103
Waughtown St
1-579 27127
580-3099 27107
Wavebrook Ct 27105
Waverly St 27127
Waverly Crossing Rd 27127
Waverly Dell Dr 27127
Waybridge Ln 27103
Waycross Dr 27106
Wayne Ave 27104
Wayside Dr 27107
We Flynt Rd 27105
Weamont St 27107
Weatherbee Dr 27103
Weatherwood Ct 27103
Weavil Rd 27107
Webster Fulton Ct 27105
Weddington Ln 27105
Wedgefield Ave 27106
Wedgewood Dr 27103
Weisner Ct & St 27127
Welch Cir 27127
Welco St 27107
Weldon St 27107
Welfare Rd 27127
Wellesborough Rd 27104
Wellington Rd 27106
Wells St 27127
Welter Dr 27107
Welwyn Rd 27104
Wendell St 27107
Wendover Cir 27104
Wentworth Dr 27107
Wentworth Rd 27105
Wesley Ct 27107
Wesley Dr 27106
Wesley Ln 27107
Wesleyan Ln 27106
Wessex Rd 27106
Wessyngton Rd 27104
West Dr 27107
West Ln 27107
West St 27101
Westbridge Rd 27107
Westbrook Dr 27103
Westbrook Plaza Dr 27103
Westchester Rd 27103
Westcliff Ct 27103
Westcott Dr 27105
Westdale Ave 27101
Westerly Dr 27106
Westfield Ave 27103
Westgate Cir 27106
Westgate Center Cir & Dr 27103
Westgreen Ct 27104
Westhaven Cir 27104
Westminister Ln 27106
Westmont Ct & Dr 27104
Westmore Ct 27105
Westmoreland Dr & St 27105
Westoak Trl 27104
Westover Ave 27104
Westover Dr 27103
Westpark Cir & Ct 27103
Westpoint Blvd 27103
Westridge Rd 27103
Westside Ct 27127
N Westview Dr 27104
S Westview Dr
100-499 27104
500-899 27103
Westwin Dr 27104
Wetherburn Ct 27104
Wexford Rd 27103
Wexham Rd 27103
Weymoth Rd 27103
Wharton Ave 27127
Wheatland Ct 27107
Wheatland Ln 27106
Wheaton Crest Ct 27107
Wheel Crest Dr 27127
Wheeler Ct 27106
Wheeler St 27101
Wheeling Village Mhp 27101
Whicker Dr 27107
Whirl Win Dr 27101
Whispering Oaks Dr 27106
Whispering Pines Dr 27107
Whitaker Ct & Rd 27106
Whitaker Ridge Dr 27106
White St 27105
White Hawk Ln 27106
White Meadow Ln 27107
White Oak Dr 27105
White Petals Ct 27107
White Rock Rd 27105
Whitehall Ct 27127
Whitehaven Rd 27106
Whitewood Ln 27104
Whitfield Ct & Rd 27105
Whitford Place Ct 27107
Whitlock Ct 27106
Whitman Dr 27104
Whitney Rd 27106
Whittier Rd 27105
Wickersham Ln 27106
Wicklow Rd 27106
Widaustin Dr 27127
Widgeon Ct 27106
Wilbur St 27107
Wilcox St 27105
Wild Dogwood Ln 27106
Wild Spruce Ct 27106
Wildlife Dr 27101
Wildwood Ct 27103
Wildwood Ln 27107
Wiley Ave 27104
Wilkes Dr 27106
Will Oliver Rd 27103
Will Scarlet Rd 27104
Will Taylor Ln 27107
Willard Rd 27107
William Dr 27107
Williams Meadow Ln 27127
Williams Place Ct 27106
Williamsburg Ct 27103
Williamsburg Rd
100-399 27107
5000-5199 27106
Williamsburg Manor Ct 27103
Williamsgate Ct 27107
Williamson St 27107
Williamston Park Ct 27107
Willie Davis Dr 27105
Willmeade Dr 27127
Willmor Dr 27127
Willomere Cir 27107
Willow Ct 27103
Willow St 27127
Willow Cove Dr 27107
Willow Knoll Ln 27106
Willow Oak Dr 27105
Willow Ridge Ln
300-599 27127
3600-3699 27105
Willow Ridge Way 27105
Willow Woods Way 27104
Willowbrook Ln 27104
Willowcrest Dr 27107
Willowee Ln 27127
Willowlake Ct & Rd 27106
Wilma Ave 27127
Wilmar Place Ct 27104
Wilmington Ct 27127
Wilshire Rd 27106
Wilson Hill Ct 27104
Wilsway Ln 27104
Wimberly Ln 27106
Wimbledon Dr 27104
Winberry Ct 27104
Winburn Ln 27106
Winchelsea Rd 27104
Winchester Rd 27106
Wind Haven Ln 27104
Wind Spring Dr 27105
Windalier Ln 27106
Windcastle Ln 27105
Winddrift St 27107
Windemere Ct 27127
Windermere Cir 27106
Windflower Rd 27106
Winding Creek Way 27106
Winding Forest Dr 27104
Winding Ridge Ct & Rd 27127
Windjammer Pl 27106
Windmere Ct & Dr 27103
Windmill Cir 27106
Windover Ln 27107
Windridge Ct 27106
Windrush Rd 27106
N Winds Dr 27127
Windsong Ct 27127
Windsor Rd 27104
Windsor Gate Ct 27104
Windsor Oaks Ct 27104
Windsor Place Ct & Dr 27106
Windworth Ct & Dr 27106
Windy Xing 27127
Windy Hill Dr 27105
Windy Point Ct 27127
Windy Ridge Dr 27127
Winfield Dr 27105
Winfield Bluff Ct 27104
Winfield Ridge Dr 27103
Wing Haven Cir & Ct 27106
Wingate Vlg 27103
Winghaven Forest Ct 27107
Winkfield Ct 27106
Winnabow Rd 27105
Winnipeg St 27105
Winona St 27106
Winslow Ln 27103
Winsted St 27127
Winster Cir & Dr 27106
Winston Ct 27103
Winston Lake Rd 27105
Winter Garden Rd 27107
Winterberry Dr 27106
Winterberry Ridge Ct 27103
Winterbrook Ct 27105
Wintergreen Rd 27107
Winterhaven Ln 27103
Winterhue St 27107
Winterlin Falls Dr 27103
Winterside Ct & Ln 27107
Winterwoods Ln 27103
Wise Ct 27127
Witherow Rd 27106
Witt St 27103
Witwould Ln 27107
Woccon Path 27127
Wonderwood Dr 27103
Wood Ct 27107
Wood St 27127
Wood Glen Ct 27107
Wood Valley Rd 27106
Woodard Rd 27127
Woodberry Ct 27107
Woodberry Dr 27106
Woodbine Rd 27104
Woodbriar Ct & Rd 27106
Woodbury Knolls Dr 27104
Woodcliff Dr 27106
Woodcote Dr 27107
Woodcove Dr 27104
Woodcreek Rd 27106
Woodcrest Dr 27104
Wooded Ave 27105
Woodfin Pl 27105
Woodgate Cir 27107
Woodgreen Rd 27106
Woodgrove Ln 27104
Woodhaven Forest Dr 27105
Woodhill Dr 27104
Woodhurst Dr 27105
Woodington Dr 27103
Woodlake Cir & Rd 27127
Woodland Ave
200-499 27101
1400-2499 27105
2501-3099 27105
NE Woodland Ave 27105
Woodland Hills Dr 27103
Woodland Trace Ct & Dr 27104
Woodleaf Ct 27107
Woodleigh St 27127
Woodlore Trl 27103
Woodmark Ct 27104
Woodmere Pl 27106
Woodmont Ct 27105
Woodrow Ave 27106
Woodruff Glen Dr 27105
Woodrun Ct 27103
Woods Ln 27107
Woods Rd 27106
Woodsboro Ln 27105
Woodside Dr 27106
Woodsman Way 27103
Woodsong Ct & Ln 27106
Woodspring Dr 27106
Woodstone Dr 27127
Woodtree Ln 27107
Woodvale Dr 27127
Woodview Dr 27106
Woodville St 27107
Woodwind Dr 27103
Woodworth Dr 27103
Worthdale Ct & Dr 27103
Worthland Ct & Dr 27103
Wrangler Dr 27101
Wright St 27127
Wrights Farm Rd 27103
Wyandotte Ave 27127
Wycliff Dr 27106
Wyman Ct & Rd 27106
Wynbrook Ct & Dr 27103
Wynbrook Square Ct & Ln 27103
Wyndham Ln 27107
Wyndhurst Ct 27106
Wynfield Crossing Ln 27103
Wyngate Village Dr 27103
Wyngrove Cir 27103
Wynnwood Dr 27127
Yadkinville Rd 27106
Yale Ave 27107
Yarbrough Ave 27106
Yardley Ter 27105
Yates Rd 27106
Yeaton Glen Cir & Dr 27107
Yellowstone Ln 27106
Yelton Ln 27127
Yokley St 27107
Yoreenco Rd 27107
York Ln 27107
York Rd
3300-3399 27106
3400-3599 27104
Yorkshire Rd 27106
Young Acres Farm Rd 27106
Yuma Ct
2800-2899 27103
4600-4699 27107
Yuma Dr 27107
Yvonne Ct 27107
Ywca Way 27127
Zachary St 27107
Zacharys Keep Ct 27103
Zane Dr 27127
Zeverly St 27127
Ziglar Ct & Rd 27105
Zinzendorf Rd 27127
Zuider Zee Ct & Dr 27127

NUMBERED STREETS

E 1st St 27101
100-1499 27101
1500-2099 27104
E & W 2nd 27101
E & W 3rd 27101
W 4 1/2 St 27101
E & W 4th 27101
E & W 5th 27101
E & W 6th 27101
E 7 1/2 St 27101
E & W 7th 27101
E & W 8th 27101
E & W 9th 27101
E 10th St 27101
E 11th St 27101
W 11th St 27105
E 12th St 27101
W 12th St
200-399 27101
800-999 27105
E 13th St 27105
1200-1799 27101
W 13th St 27105
E & W 14th 27105
E 15th St 27105
E 16th St 27105
E & W 17th 27105
E 18th St 27105
E 19th St 27105
E 20th St 27105
E & NE 21st 27105
E & NE 22nd 27105
E 23rd St 27105
E 24th St 27105
E 25th St 27105
NE 25th St 27105
NW 25th St 27105
W 25th St
1-999 27105
1000-1099 27104
NE & W 26th 27105
E, NE, NW & W 27th 27105
E 28th St 27105
E 29th St 27105
E 30th St 27105
E 32nd St 27105
E & NE 33rd 27105
E 12 1/2 St 27101
E 13 1/2 St 27101
E 16 1/2 St 27105
W 24 1/2 St 27105
W 25 1/2 St 27105

North Dakota

People QuickFacts	North Dakota	USA
Population, 2013 estimate	723,393	316,128,839
Population, 2010 (April 1) estimates base	672,591	308,747,716
Population, percent change, April 1, 2010 to July 1, 2013	7.6%	2.4%
Population, 2010	672,591	308,745,538
Persons under 5 years, percent, 2013	6.7%	6.3%
Persons under 18 years, percent, 2013	22.5%	23.3%
Persons 65 years and over, percent, 2013	14.2%	14.1%
Female persons, percent, 2013	48.9%	50.8%
White alone, percent, 2013 (a)	89.6%	77.7%
Black or African American alone, percent, 2013 (a)	1.8%	13.2%
American Indian and Alaska Native alone, percent, 2013 (a)	5.4%	1.2%
Asian alone, percent, 2013 (a)	1.2%	5.3%
Native Hawaiian and Other Pacific Islander alone, percent, 2013 (a)	0.1%	0.2%
Two or More Races, percent, 2013	1.9%	2.4%
Hispanic or Latino, percent, 2013 (b)	2.9%	17.1%
White alone, not Hispanic or Latino, percent, 2013	87.3%	62.6%
Living in same house 1 year & over, percent, 2008-2012	82.9%	84.8%
Foreign born persons, percent, 2008-2012	2.5%	12.9%
Language other than English spoken at home, pct age 5+, 2008-2012	5.2%	20.5%
High school graduate or higher, percent of persons age 25+, 2008-2012	90.5%	85.7%
Bachelor's degree or higher, percent of persons age 25+, 2008-2012	27.1%	28.5%
Veterans, 2008-2012	54,782	21,853,912
Mean travel time to work (minutes), workers age 16+, 2008-2012	16.5	25.4
Housing units, 2013	339,313	132,802,859
Homeownership rate, 2008-2012	66.4%	65.5%
Housing units in multi-unit structures, percent, 2008-2012	25.6%	25.9%
Median value of owner-occupied housing units, 2008-2012	$123,900	$181,400
Households, 2008-2012	282,667	115,226,802
Persons per household, 2008-2012	2.3	2.61
Per capita money income in past 12 months (2012 dollars), 2008-2012	$28,700	$28,051
Median household income, 2008-2012	$51,641	$53,046
Persons below poverty level, percent, 2008-2012	12.1%	14.9%

Business QuickFacts	North Dakota	USA
Private nonfarm establishments, 2012	23,551	7,431,808
Private nonfarm employment, 2012	331,278	115,938,468
Private nonfarm employment, percent change, 2011-2012	8.2%	2.2%
Nonemployer establishments, 2012	50,952	22,735,915
Total number of firms, 2007	61,546	27,092,908
Black-owned firms, percent, 2007	0.3%	7.1%
American Indian- and Alaska Native-owned firms, percent, 2007	1.6%	0.9%
Asian-owned firms, percent, 2007	0.7%	5.7%
Native Hawaiian and Other Pacific Islander-owned firms, percent, 2007	0.0%	0.1%
Hispanic-owned firms, percent, 2007	0.5%	8.3%
Women-owned firms, percent, 2007	24.8%	28.8%
Manufacturers shipments, 2007 ($1000)	11,349,799	5,319,456,312
Merchant wholesaler sales, 2007 ($1000)	13,099,348	4,174,286,516
Retail sales, 2007 ($1000)	10,527,300	3,917,663,456
Retail sales per capita, 2007	$16,495	$12,990
Accommodation and food services sales, 2007 ($1000)	1,214,201	613,795,732
Building permits, 2012	10,340	829,658

Geography QuickFacts	North Dakota	USA
Land area in square miles, 2010	69,000.80	3,531,905.43
Persons per square mile, 2010	9.7	87.4
FIPS Code	38	

(a) Includes persons reporting only one race.

(b) Hispanics may be of any race, so also are included in applicable race categories.

FN: Footnote on this item for this area in place of data

NA: Not available

D: Suppressed to avoid disclosure of confidential information

X: Not applicable

S: Suppressed; does not meet publication standards

Z: Value greater than zero but less than half unit of measure shown

F: Fewer than 100 firms

Source: US Census Bureau State & County QuickFacts

North Dakota

3 DIGIT ZIP CODE MAP

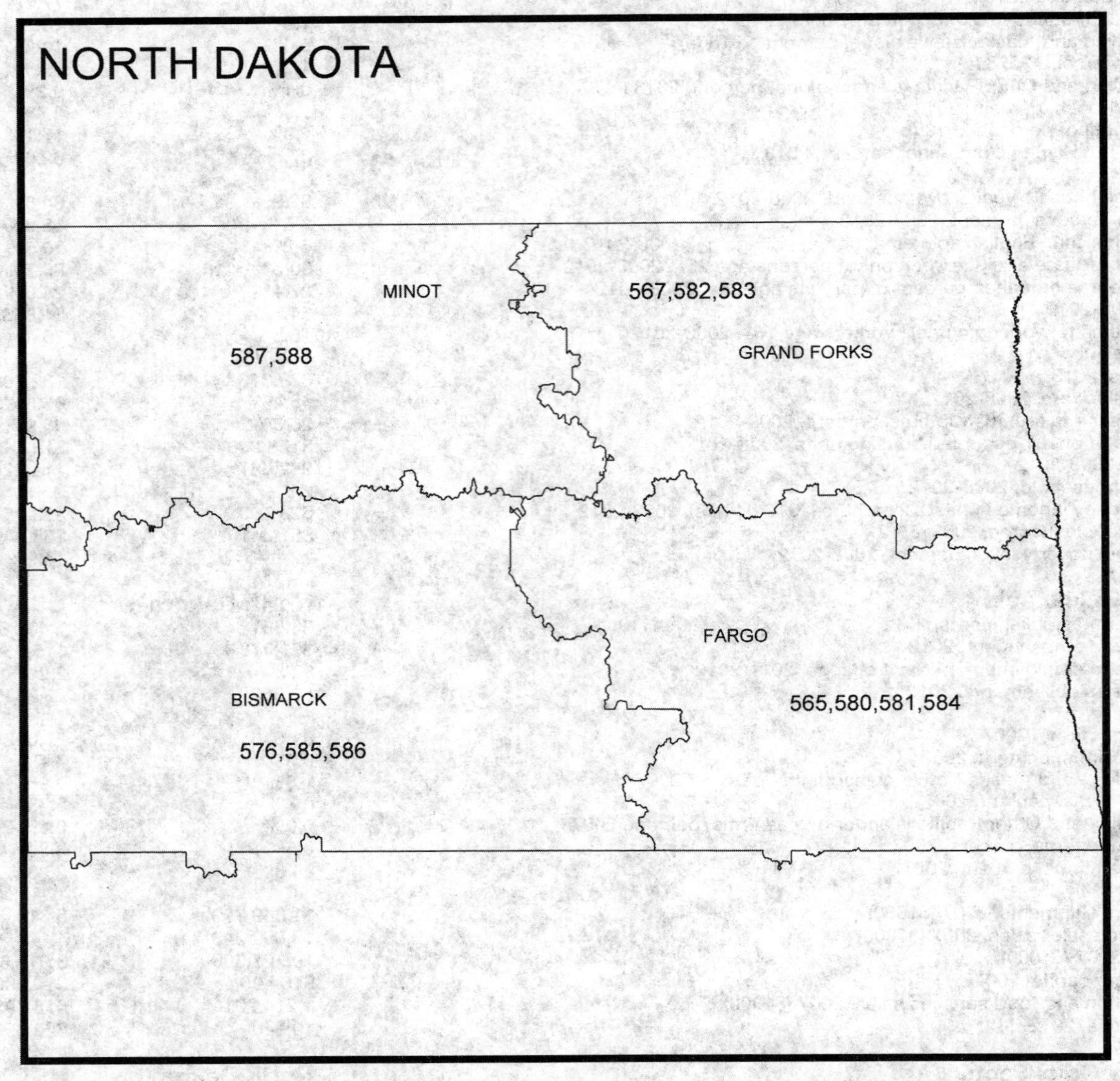

North Dakota

(Abbreviation: ND)

Places with more than one ZIP code are listed in capital letters, See pages indicated.

Post Office, County	ZIP Code
Abercrombie, Richland	58001
Absaraka, Cass	58002
Adams, Walsh	58210
Adrian, Stutsman	58472
Agate, Rolette	58310
Alamo, Williams	58830
Alexander, Mckenzie	58831
Alfred, Lamoure	58454
Alice, Barnes	58031
Alkabo, Williams	58845
Almont, Morton	58520
Alsen, Cavalier	58311
Ambrose, Divide	58833
Amenia, Cass	58004
Amidon, Slope	58620
Anamoose, Mchenry	58710
Aneta, Nelson	58212
Antler, Bottineau	58711
Appam, Williams	58830
Ardoch, Walsh	58261
Arena, Burleigh	58494
Argusville, Cass	58005
Arnegard, Mckenzie	58835
Arthur, Cass	58006
Arvilla, Grand Forks	58214
Ashley, Mcintosh	58413
Ayr, Cass	58007
Backoo, Pembina	58220
Baker, Benson	58386
Baldwin, Burleigh	58521
Balfour, Mchenry	58712
Balta, Pierce	58313
Bantry, Mchenry	58713
Barney, Richland	58008
Barton, Bottineau	58384
Bathgate, Pembina	58216
Battleview, Burke	58773
Beach, Golden Valley	58621
Belcourt, Rolette	58316
Belden, Mountrail	58784
Belfield, Stark	58622
Benedict, Mclean	58716
Bentley, Grant	58562
Bergen, Mchenry	58792
Berlin, Lamoure	58415
Berthold, Ward	58718
Berwick, Mchenry	58788
Beulah, Mercer	58523
Binford, Griggs	58416
Bisbee, Towner	58317
BISMARCK, Burleigh (See Page 2941)	
Blaisdell, Ward	58718
Blanchard, Traill	58009
Bonetraill, Williams	58801
Bordulac, Foster	58421
Bottineau, Bottineau	58318
Bowbells, Burke	58721
Bowdon, Wells	58418
Bowesmont, Pembina	58225
Bowman, Bowman	58623
Braddock, Emmons	58524
Brampton, Sargent	58017
Brantford, Eddy	58356
Breien, Sioux	58570
Bremen, Eddy	58356
Briarwood, Cass	58104
Brinsmade, Benson	58351
Brocket, Ramsey	58321
Buchanan, Stutsman	58420
Bucyrus, Adams	58639
Buffalo, Cass	58011
Buffalo Springs, Bowman	58623
Buford, Williams	58801
Burlington, Ward	58722
Burnstad, Mcintosh	58495
Burt, Hettinger	58646
Butte, Mclean	58723
Buxton, Traill	58218
Caledonia, Traill	58219
Calio, Cavalier	58352
Calvin, Cavalier	58323
Cando, Towner	58324
Cannon Ball, Sioux	58528
Carbury, Bottineau	58783
Carpio, Ward	58725
Carrington, Foster	58421
Carson, Grant	58529
Cartwright, Mckenzie	58838
Casselton, Cass	58012
Cathay, Wells	58422
Cavalier, Pembina	58220
Cavalier Afs, Pembina	58220
Cayuga, Sargent	58013
Center, Oliver	58530
Chaffee, Cass	58079
Charlson, Mountrail	58763
Chaseley, Wells	58423
Christine, Richland	58015
Churchs Ferry, Ramsey	58325
Cleveland, Stutsman	58424
Clifford, Traill	58016
Clyde, Cavalier	58352
Cogswell, Sargent	58017
Coleharbor, Mclean	58531
Colfax, Richland	58018
Colgan, Divide	58844
Colgate, Steele	58046
Columbus, Burke	58727
Concrete, Pembina	58220
Cooperstown, Griggs	58425
Corinth, Williams	58830
Coteau, Burke	58721
Coulee, Ward	58734
Courtenay, Stutsman	58426
Crary, Ramsey	58327
Crete, Sargent	58040
Crosby, Divide	58730
Crystal, Pembina	58222
Crystal Springs, Stutsman	58467
Cummings, Traill	58223
Dahlen, Nelson	58224
Davenport, Cass	58021
Dawson, Kidder	58428
Dazey, Barnes	58429
Deering, Mchenry	58731
Delamere, Sargent	58060
Denbigh, Mchenry	58788
Denhoff, Sheridan	58430
Des Lacs, Ward	58733
Devils Lake, Ramsey	58301
Dickey, Lamoure	58431
DICKINSON, Stark (See Page 2943)	
Dodge, Dunn	58625
Donnybrook, Ward	58734
Douglas, Ward	58735
Doyon, Ramsey	58327
Drake, Mchenry	58736
Drayton, Pembina	58225
Driscoll, Burleigh	58532
Dunn Center, Dunn	58626
Dunseith, Rolette	58329
Durbin, Cass	58059
Dwight, Richland	58075
Eckelson, Barnes	58481
Edgeley, Lamoure	58433
Edinburg, Walsh	58227
Edmore, Ramsey	58330
Edmunds, Stutsman	58476
Egeland, Towner	58331
Eldridge, Stutsman	58401
Elgin, Grant	58533
Ellendale, Dickey	58436
Elliott, Ransom	58054
Embden, Cass	58079
Emerado, Grand Forks	58228
Emmet, Mclean	58540
Emrick, Wells	58422
Enderlin, Ransom	58027
Englevale, Ransom	58033
Epping, Williams	58843
Erie, Cass	58029
Esmond, Benson	58332
Fairdale, Walsh	58229
Fairfield, Billings	58627
Fairmount, Richland	58030
FARGO, Cass (See Page 2943)	
Fessenden, Wells	58438
Fillmore, Benson	58332
Fingal, Barnes	58031
Finley, Steele	58230
Flasher, Morton	58535
Flaxton, Burke	58737
Flora, Benson	58348
Forbes, Dickey	58439
Fordville, Walsh	58231
Forest River, Walsh	58233
Forman, Sargent	58032
Fort Clark, Oliver	58530
Fort Ransom, Ransom	58033
Fort Rice, Morton	58554
Fort Totten, Benson	58335
Fort Yates, Sioux	58538
Fortuna, Divide	58844
Foxholm, Ward	58718
Fredonia, Logan	58440
Frontier, Cass	58104
Fryburg, Stark	58622
Fullerton, Dickey	58441
Gackle, Logan	58442
Galchutt, Richland	58075
Galesburg, Traill	58035
Gardar, Walsh	58227
Gardner, Cass	58036
Gardner, Cass	58042
Garrison, Mclean	58540
Gascoyne, Bowman	58653
Geneseo, Richland	58053
Gilby, Grand Forks	58235
Gladstone, Stark	58630
Glasston, Pembina	58236
Glen Ullin, Morton	58631
Glenburn, Renville	58740
Glenfield, Foster	58443
Golden Valley, Mercer	58541
Golva, Golden Valley	58632
Goodrich, Sheridan	58444
Gorham, Billings	58627
Grace City, Foster	58445
Grafton, Walsh	58237
GRAND FORKS, Grand Forks (See Page 2944)	
GRAND FORKS AFB, Grand Forks (See Page 2945)	
Grand Rapids, Lamoure	58458
Grandin, Cass	58038
Granville, Mchenry	58741
Grassy Butte, Mckenzie	58634
Great Bend, Richland	58075
Grenora, Williams	58845
Guelph, Dickey	58474
Gwinner, Sargent	58040
Hague, Emmons	58542
Halliday, Dunn	58636
Hamar, Nelson	58380
Hamberg, Wells	58341
Hamilton, Pembina	58238
Hamlet, Williams	58795
Hampden, Ramsey	58338
Hankinson, Richland	58041
Hannaford, Griggs	58448
Hannah, Cavalier	58239
Hannover, Morton	58563
Hansboro, Towner	58339
Harlow, Benson	58346
Harvey, Wells	58341
Harwood, Cass	58036
Harwood, Cass	58042
Hastings, Barnes	58049
Hatton, Traill	58240
Havana, Sargent	58043
Haynes, Adams	58639
Hazelton, Emmons	58544
Hazen, Mercer	58545
Heaton, Wells	58418
Hebron, Morton	58638
Heil, Grant	58533
Heimdal, Wells	58341
Hensel, Pembina	58241
Hensler, Oliver	58530
Hettinger, Adams	58639
Hickson, Cass	58047
Hillsboro, Traill	58045
Honeyford, Grand Forks	58235
Hoople, Walsh	58243
Hope, Steele	58046
Horace, Cass	58047
Huff, Morton	58554
Hunter, Cass	58048
Hurdsfield, Wells	58451
Inkster, Walsh	58233
Inkster, Grand Forks	58244
JAMESTOWN, Stutsman (See Page 2945)	
Jessie, Griggs	58452
Johnstown, Grand Forks	58235
Joliette, Pembina	58271
Juanita, Foster	58443
Jud, Lamoure	58454
Judson, Morton	58563
Karlsruhe, Mchenry	58744
Kathryn, Barnes	58049
Keene, Mckenzie	58847
Kelso, Traill	58045
Kempton, Grand Forks	58267
Kenmare, Ward	58746
Kensal, Stutsman	58455
Kief, Mclean	58723
Killdeer, Dunn	58640
Kindred, Cass	58051
Kintyre, Emmons	58549
Kloten, Nelson	58254
Knox, Benson	58343
Kramer, Bottineau	58748
Kulm, Lamoure	58456
Lake Williams, Kidder	58478
Lakota, Nelson	58344
Lamoure, Lamoure	58415
Lamoure, Lamoure	58458
Landa, Bottineau	58783
Langdon, Cavalier	58249
Lankin, Walsh	58250
Lansford, Bottineau	58750
Larimore, Grand Forks	58251
Lark, Morton	58535
Larson, Burke	58727
Lawton, Ramsey	58345
Leal, Barnes	58479
Leeds, Benson	58346
Lefor, Stark	58641
Lehr, Mcintosh	58460
Leith, Grant	58529
Leonard, Cass	58052
Leroy, Pembina	58282
Lidgerwood, Richland	58053
Lignite, Burke	58752
Lincoln, Burleigh	58504
Linton, Emmons	58552
Lisbon, Ransom	58054
Litchville, Barnes	58461
Loma, Cavalier	58311
Loraine, Renville	58761
Lostwood, Mountrail	58784
Ludden, Dickey	58474
Luverne, Steele	58056
Maddock, Benson	58348
Maida, Cavalier	58255
Makoti, Ward	58756
Mandan, Morton	58554
Mandaree, Mckenzie	58757
Manfred, Wells	58341
Manning, Dunn	58642
Mantador, Richland	58058
Manvel, Grand Forks	58256
Mapes, Nelson	58344
Mapleton, Cass	58059
Marion, Lamoure	58466
Marmarth, Slope	58643
Marshall, Dunn	58644
Martin, Sheridan	58758
Max, Mclean	58759
Maxbass, Bottineau	58760
Mayville, Traill	58257
Maza, Towner	58324
Mccanna, Grand Forks	58251
Mcclusky, Sheridan	58463
Mcgregor, Williams	58755
Mchenry, Foster	58464
Mckenzie, Burleigh	58572
Mcleod, Richland	58057
Mcville, Nelson	58254
Medina, Stutsman	58467
Medora, Billings	58645
Mekinock, Grand Forks	58258
Melville, Foster	58421
Menoken, Burleigh	58558
Mercer, Mclean	58559
Merricourt, Lamoure	58433
Michigan, Nelson	58259
Millarton, Stutsman	58472
Milnor, Sargent	58060
Milton, Cavalier	58260
Minnewaukan, Benson	58351
MINOT, Ward (See Page 2946)	
MINOT AFB, Ward (See Page 2947)	
Minto, Walsh	58261
Moffit, Burleigh	58560
Mohall, Renville	58761
Monango, Dickey	58436
Montpelier, Stutsman	58472
Mooreton, Richland	58061
Mott, Hettinger	58646
Mountain, Pembina	58262
Munich, Cavalier	58352
Mylo, Rolette	58353
Nanson, Rolette	58366
Napoleon, Logan	58561
Nash, Walsh	58237
Neche, Pembina	58265
Nekoma, Cavalier	58355
New England, Hettinger	58647
New Hradec, Stark	58601
New Leipzig, Grant	58562
New Rockford, Eddy	58356
New Salem, Morton	58563
New Town, Mountrail	58763
Newburg, Bottineau	58762
Niagara, Grand Forks	58266
Nome, Barnes	58062
Noonan, Divide	58765
Norma, Ward	58746
North River, Cass	58102
Northgate, Burke	58737
Northwood, Grand Forks	58267
Nortonville, Lamoure	58454
Norwich, Mchenry	58768
Oakes, Dickey	58474
Oberon, Benson	58357
Oriska, Barnes	58063
Orr, Grand Forks	58244
Orrin, Pierce	58368
Osnabrock, Cavalier	58269
Overly, Bottineau	58384
Oxbow, Cass	58047
Page, Cass	58064
Palermo, Mountrail	58769
Park River, Walsh	58270
Parshall, Mountrail	58770
Pekin, Nelson	58361
Pembina, Pembina	58271
Penn, Ramsey	58362
Perth, Towner	58363
Petersburg, Nelson	58272
Pettibone, Kidder	58475
Pick City, Mercer	58545
Pillsbury, Barnes	58065
Pingree, Stutsman	58476
Pisek, Walsh	58273
Plaza, Mountrail	58771
Pleasant Lake, Pierce	58368
Portal, Burke	58772
Portland, Traill	58274
Powers Lake, Burke	58773
Prairie Rose, Cass	58104
Prosper, Cass	58042
Raleigh, Grant	58564
Raub, Ward	58779
Rawson, Mckenzie	58831
Ray, Williams	58849
Reeder, Adams	58649
Regan, Burleigh	58477
Regent, Hettinger	58650
Reiles Acres, Cass	58102
Reynolds, Grand Forks	58275
Rhame, Bowman	58651
Richardton, Stark	58652
Riverdale, Mclean	58565
Riverside, Cass	58078
Robinson, Kidder	58478
Rocklake, Towner	58365
Rogers, Barnes	58479
Rolette, Rolette	58366
Rolla, Rolette	58367
Roseglen, Mclean	58775
Ross, Mountrail	58776
Roth, Bottineau	58783
Rugby, Pierce	58368
Ruso, Mclean	58778
Rutland, Sargent	58067
Ryder, Ward	58779
Saint Anthony, Morton	58554
Saint Anthony, Morton	58566
Saint John, Rolette	58369
Saint Michael, Benson	58370
Saint Thomas, Pembina	58276
San Haven, Rolette	58329
Sanborn, Barnes	58480
Sanish, Mountrail	58763
Sarles, Cavalier	58372
Sawyer, Ward	58781
Scranton, Bowman	58653
Selfridge, Sioux	58568
Selz, Wells	58341
Sentinel Butte, Golden Valley	58654
Sharon, Steele	58277
Sheldon, Ransom	58068
Sherwood, Renville	58782
Sheyenne, Eddy	58374
Shields, Grant	58569
Sibley, Barnes	58429
Silva, Pierce	58368
Solen, Sioux	58570
Souris, Bottineau	58783
South Heart, Stark	58655
Southam, Ramsey	58327
Spiritwood, Barnes	58481
Spring Brook, Williams	58843
Stanley, Mountrail	58784
Stanton, Mercer	58571
Starkweather, Ramsey	58377
Steele, Kidder	58482
Sterling, Burleigh	58572
Stirum, Sargent	58069
Strasburg, Emmons	58573
Straubville, Sargent	58017
Streeter, Stutsman	58483
Surrey, Ward	58785
Sutton, Griggs	58484
Sydney, Stutsman	58401
Sykeston, Wells	58486
Tagus, Ward	58718
Tappen, Kidder	58487
Taylor, Stark	58656
Temple, Williams	58852
Temvik, Emmons	58552
Thompson, Grand Forks	58278
Tioga, Williams	58852
Tokio, Benson	58379
Tolley, Renville	58787
Tolna, Nelson	58380
Tower City, Cass	58071
Towner, Mchenry	58788
Trenton, Williams	58853
Trotters, Golden Valley	58621
Turtle Lake, Mclean	58575
Tuttle, Kidder	58488
Underwood, Mclean	58576
Union, Cavalier	58260
Upham, Mchenry	58789

Valley City, Barnes 58072
Velva, Mchenry 58790
Venturia, Mcintosh 58413
Verona, Lamoure 58490
Voltaire, Mchenry 58792
Voss, Walsh 58261
WAHPETON, Richland
(See Page 2947)
Walcott, Richland 58077
Wales, Cavalier 58281
Walhalla, Pembina 58282
Walum, Griggs 58448
Warwick, Benson 58381
Washburn, Mclean 58577
Watford City, Mckenzie 58854
Webster, Ramsey 58382
Werner, Dunn 58636
West Fargo, Cass 58078
Westfield, Emmons 58542
Westhope, Bottineau 58793
Wheatland, Cass 58079
Wheelock, Williams 58849
White Earth, Mountrail 58794
White Shield, Mclean 58540
Whitman, Nelson 58259
Wild Rice, Cass 58047
Wildrose, Williams 58795
WILLISTON, Williams
(See Page 2947)
Willow City, Bottineau 58384
Wilton, Mclean 58579
Wimbledon, Barnes 58492
Windsor, Stutsman 58424
Wing, Burleigh 58494
Wishek, Mcintosh 58495
Wolford, Pierce 58385
Wolseth, Renville 58740
Woodworth, Stutsman 58496
Wyndmere, Richland 58081
York, Benson 58386
Ypsilanti, Stutsman 58497
Zahl, Williams 58856
Zap, Mercer 58580
Zeeland, Mcintosh 58581

BISMARCK ND

General Delivery 58501

POST OFFICE BOXES MAIN OFFICE STATIONS AND BRANCHES

Box No.s
1 - 5020 58502
5500 - 6276 58506
7001 - 7478 58507

NAMED STREETS

Adams Ln 58501
Adobe Dr 58503
Airport Rd 58504
Airway Ave 58504
Alamo Dr 58504
Albany Dr 58504
Albatross Dr 58504
Alberta Ave 58503
Aleutian Dr 58503
Allen Dr 58504
Allison Dr 58501
Almond Dr 58503
Alpine Ln 58503
Alta Dr 58503
Amberglow Dr & Pl 58503
American Ave 58504
N Anderson St 58501
S Anderson St 58504
Angus Dr 58504
Apache St 58501
W Apollo Ave 58503
Apostolic Way 58501
Apple Way 58504
Apple Creek Dr & Rd 58504
Apple Valley Dr 58501
Arabian Ave & Pl 58503
E & W Arbor Ave 58504
Arcata Dr 58503
E & W Arikara Ave 58501
Arizona Dr 58503
N Arlington Dr 58503
Arrow Ave 58504
Arthur Dr 58501
Ash Ln 58503
Ash Coulee Dr & Pl 58503
Ashlee Ave 58504
Ashton Cir 58504
Ashwood Ave 58504
Aspen Ave, Ln & Pl 58503
Assiniboin Dr 58503
Assumption Dr 58501
Aster Ln 58501
Astronaut Dr 58503
Atlanta Dr 58504
Atlas Dr 58503
Augsburg Ave 58504
Augusta Pl & Way 58503
Aurora Loop & St 58503
Autumblaze Way 58503
E & W Avenue 58501
E Avenue A 58501
W Avenue A
100-899 58501
1200-1300 58504
1302-1398 58504
E & W Avenue B 58501
E & W Avenue C 58501
E & W Avenue D 58501
E & W Avenue F 58501
Avondale Dr 58503
Baffin Loop 58503
Baine Dr 58503
Baker Pl 58504
Baltus Dr & Ln 58501
Bar D Rd 58504
Baracuda Dr 58503
N Barincor St 58501
SE Barston Ln 58501
Basin Ave 58504
Bayhill Loop 58503
Bayview Ct 58504
Beacon Loop 58501
Bear Path Dr 58504
Beaver Creek Pl & Rd 58504
Bedford Blvd 58504
Beech St 58504
Begonia Ave 58501
Belaire Dr 58501
Belk Dr 58504
N Bell St 58501
S Bell St 58504
Belmont Ln 58501
Benteen Dr 58504
Berkshire Dr 58503
Bernell Dr 58503
Berry Dr 58501
Bethany Loop 58503
Big Sky Cir 58503
Billings Dr 58504
Birch Pl 58504
Birchcrest Dr 58501
Birchwood Dr 58504
E Bismarck Expy
100-2200 58504
2202-2898 58504
3500-3598 58501
3701-3799 58501
N Bismarck Expy 58501
W Bismarck Expy 58504
Bitteroot Ave 58501
Bliss Ave 58503
Blue Spruce Rd 58503
Bluejay Ave 58504
Bluffview Dr 58504
Boehm Dr 58504
Boeing Ave 58504
Bogey Dr 58503
Bohe Dr 58503
Boise Ave 58504
Bonn Blvd 58504
Boston Dr 58504
Bottom Rd 58504
Boulder Dr 58504
Boulder Ridge Rd 58503
E Boulevard Ave
100-399 58501
401-2599 58501
600-998 58505
1100-2598 58501
W Boulevard Ave 58501
Boundary Rd 58503
Bouyer Pl 58504
E & W Bowen Ave 58504
Bozeman Dr 58504
Brads Way 58504
Braman Ave 58501
Brandenburg Loop 58504
E, W, N & S Brandon Cir, Dr, Loop & Pl 58503
Breen Dr 58501
Bremner Ave 58503
Brenda Berneta Ln 58503
Breton Dr 58503
Brevet Pl 58504
Briardale Dr & Loop 58504
Bridgeport Dr 58504
Bridger Dr 58503
E & W Bristol Dr 58501
Britanic Ln 58504
British Dr 58503
Broadview Ln 58503
E & W Broadway Ave 58501
Brome Ave & Loop 58503
Brook Loop & Pl 58503
Brookside Ln 58503
Brookwood Pl 58503
Browning Ave 58503
Brunswick Cir & Dr 58503
Buccaneer Pl 58504
Buckingham Pl 58501
Buckskin Ave 58503
Buckskin Rd 58504
Bunker Dr 58503
Burgundy Cir 58503
Burke Dr 58504
E & W Burleigh Ave 58504
Burlington Dr 58504
Burnside Dr 58503
Burnt Boat Dr 58503
Burnt Creek Loop 58503
Burnt Creek Island Rd 58503
Burntwood Pl 58503
Burr Oak Loop 58501
Butte Dr 58503
Butterfield Dr 58503
Cactus Cir 58503
Calahan Pl 58504
Calgary Ave, Cir & Loop 58503
Calvert Dr & Pl 58503
Calypso Dr 58504
Cambridge Dr 58504
Camden Loop 58503
Camellia Ln 58501
Canada Ave 58503
Canary Ave 58501
Cane Dr 58503
Canterbury Ln 58504
Canyon Cir & Dr 58503
E & W Capitol Ave & Way 58501
Caraway Dr 58503
Carbine Dr 58504
Carefree Cir 58503
Carlin Dr 58504
Carriage Cir 58503
Carrington Dr 58503
Cartridge Loop 58504
Catherine Dr 58501
W Cavalry Dr 58504
Cedar Ln & Pl 58503
Centennial Rd 58503
Center St 58504
Centerville Ln 58503
E & W Central Ave 58501
Centurion Dr 58504
E & W Century Ave 58503
Chamberlain Dr & Pl 58503
Chambly Ave 58503
Chandler Ln 58503
Channel Dr 58501
Cherokee Ave 58501
Cherry Ln 58503
Cherrybrook Dr 58503
Cherrywood Dr 58501
Chestnut Dr & Ln 58504
Chevelle Cir 58503
Cheyenne Ave 58501
Chisholm Pl & Trl 58503
Chivas Pl 58501
Chokecherry Dr 58503
Cimarron Dr 58503
Clairmont Rd 58503
Claridge Loop 58503
Clarke Rd 58504
Clearview Pl 58504
Clipper Pl 58504
Clover Ln & Pl 58503
Club House Dr 58503
Clydesdale Dr 58503
Cody Dr 58503
Coleman Ct & St 58503
College Dr 58501
Cologne Dr 58504
Colonial Dr 58503
E & N Colorado Dr & Ln 58503
Colt Ave 58503
Columbia Dr 58504
Columbine Ln 58501
Comet Ln 58503
Commerce Dr 58501
Commons Ave 58503
Compass Ln & Loop 58504
Concord Dr 58504
Connar Dr 58503
Connecticut St 58504
Constitution Dr 58501
Contessa Dr & Pl 58503
Continental Ave 58504
Coolidge Ave 58501
Copper Pt 58504
Copper Mountain Cir 58503
Copper Ridge Ln 58504
Cordgrass Dr 58503
Coriander Dr 58503
Cornice Dr 58503
Corona St 58503
Coronado Dr 58504
Cortland Pl & Xing 58501
Corvette Cir 58503
Cottage Dr 58501
Cottonwood Ln 58503
Cottonwood Loop 58504
Couch St 58501
E & W Coulee Rd 58501
Country Ln 58503
Country Brook Rd 58503
Country Club Dr 58501
Country Creek Dr 58503
Country Hills Dr 58503
Country West Rd 58503
Countryside Dr 58501
Crane Dr 58501
Creekside Dr 58504
Crescent Ln 58501
Crescent Ridge Cir & Rd 58503
Crest Cir 58503
Crested Butte Pl & Rd 58503
Crestfield Ave 58503
Cresthill Rd 58504
Crestland Pl 58503
Crestridge Ln & Pl 58503
Crestview Ln 58501
Crestwood Dr 58503
Crocus Ave 58501
Cross Rd 58503
Cumberland Loop 58503
Curtis St 58501
Custer Dr 58504
E Custer Park 58501
W Custer Park 58501
Daisy Ln 58503
Dakota Dr 58501
Dakota Country Dr 58503
Daniel St 58504
Darin Dr 58504
Day Hill Loop 58504
Daytona Dr 58503
Deadwood Dr 58503
Deer Lodge Dr 58504
Deer Valley Ln 58503
Deerewood Ln 58503
Del Rio Dr 58503
Delaware St 58504
Delta Ave 58504
Denali Pl 58503
E & W Denver Ave 58503
Derek Dr 58504
Desert Rd 58504
Desperado Pl 58503
Devon Dr & Pl 58504
Dietrich Pl 58503
Discovery Dr 58503
E & W Divide Ave 58501
Dodge Cir 58503
Dogwood Dr 58504
Dohn Ave 58503
Dolan Dr 58504
Dominion St 58503
Domino Dr 58503
Dondiant Dr 58504
Dortmund Dr 58504
Doubleday Dr 58503
Dove St 58504
Dover Dr 58504
Downing St 58504
Drake Dr 58503
Dream Cir 58503
Driftwood Ln 58503
Dublin Dr 58503
Duchess Dr 58501
Duncan Dr 58503
Durango Dr 58503
Eagle Crest Loop 58503
Eagles View Ln & Pl 58503
Earhart Ln 58504
Eastdale Dr 58501
Eastside Pl 58501
Eastview Dr 58501
Eastwood St 58504
Easy St 58504
Eckleson Rd 58504
Edgerly Ln 58504
Edgewood Cir, Dr, Pl & Pt 58503
Edgewood Village Ct & Loop 58503
E & W Edmonton Dr 58503
Edwards Ave 58501
El Paso Dr 58503
Elm St 58504
Emerald Pl 58503
Endeavor Pl 58504
Endicott Dr 58503
England St 58504
English Oak Dr 58501
Enterprise St 58501
Eric Ave 58504
Essex Loop 58504
Estate Ave 58504
Estevan Dr 58503
Evergreen Ave 58504
Fairfax Loop & Pl 58503
Fairhill Rd 58503
Fairview Pl 58501
Fairway Ct & Ln 58501
Falconer Dr 58504
Far West Dr 58504
Feldspar Dr 58503
Fennel Pl 58503
Fernwood Dr 58503
Fido Dr 58504
Finley St 58504
Flatrock Dr & Loop 58503
Flickertail Dr 58503
Florida Dr 58503
Fontenelle Dr 58504
Forest Dr 58503
Forestlawn Dr 58504
S Fork Jct 58504
Fountainblue Dr 58503
Fox Meadow Dr & Pl 58503
Foxden Loop 58503
Foxhaven Loop 58503
Foxtail Cir 58503
Fraine Barracks Ln, Loop & Rd 58504
Francis Pl 58504
Franklin Ave 58503
Freiburg Ln 58504
Fresno Dr 58504
Friendship Trl 58503
E & W Front Ave 58504
Frontage Pl 58501
Frontier Dr 58504
Frost Ln 58503
Fuller Ave 58504
Gallatin Dr 58504
Galleon Pl 58504
Garden Dr 58504
Garnet Dr & Pl 58503
Gary Ave 58501
Gates Dr 58503
Gateway Ave 58503
Gatlin Ave 58503
Gentry Cir 58503
Georgia St 58504
Gettysburg Dr 58504
Gibbons Dr 58504
Glendale Dr 58504
Glenwood Dr 58504
Golden Crest Rd 58503
Golden Eagle Ln 58503
Golden Wave Dr 58503
Golf Dr 58503
NE & SE Goodland Dr 58501
Governor Ln 58501
N & S Grandview Ln 58503
Granger Ave 58503
Granite Dr 58503
Grant Dr 58501
Grassy Ln 58503
Gray Fox Ln 58503
Greeley Dr 58504
Green Spruce Ln 58503
Green Tree Loop 58503
Greenfield Ln 58503
Greensboro Dr 58503
Greenwood Dr 58503
N Griffin St 58501
S Griffin St 58504
Grimsrud Dr 58501
Hackberry St 58503
Hale Ln 58503
Hamburg Dr 58504
Hamilton St 58503
Hampton St 58504
Hanaford Ave 58501
Hancock Dr 58501
N Hannifin St 58501
S Hannifin St 58504
W Harbor Dr 58504
Harding Ave & Pl 58501
Harmon Ave 58501
Harvest Ln 58503
Harvest Hills Dr 58503
Hawken St 58503
Hawktree Dr 58503
Haycreek Ct & Dr 58503
Haywood Dr 58504
Heart Pl & Rd 58504
Heartland Dr & Loop 58503
Heatherwood Ln 58501
Hemlock St 58504
Henry St 58503
Heritage Ave 58501
Hester Dr 58504
High Creek Rd 58503
High Meadows Cir & Pl 58503
High Plains Rd 58504
Highland Pl 58501
E Highland Acres Rd 58501
Highridge Dr 58503
Hightop Ln 58503
Highway 10 58501
Highway 1804 58504
Highway 1804 N 58503
Highway 1804 NE 58503
Highway 1804 NW 58503
Highway 1804 S 58504
Highway 83 58503
Hill St 58504
Hillsboro Dr 58503
Hillside Ter 58501
Hillview Ave 58501
Hitchcock Dr 58503
Hogue Rd 58503
Holden Ave 58504
Homestead Dr 58503
Hoover Ave 58501
Horizon Pl 58503
Horseman Loop & Pl 58501
Horseshoe Bnd 58503
Houston Dr 58504
Huber Dr 58504
Hudson St 58503
Humbert Dr 58504
Hunter Cir 58503
Huron Dr 58503
Illinois Dr 58503
Impala Ln 58503
Imperial Dr 58504
Independence Ave 58503
E & W Indiana Ave 58504
Industrial Dr 58501
E & W Ingals Ave 58504
Ingelwood Ln 58503
Interchange Ave 58501
E & W Interstate Ave & Loop 58503
Intrepid Cir 58504
Iowa Ln 58501
Irish Ln 58504
Island Dr 58504
Island Rd 58503
Ithica Dr 58503
Ivy Ave 58504
Jackson Ave 58501
Jeaner Pl 58504
Jefferson Ave 58504
Jericho Rd 58503
Joppa St 58503
Jordan St 58503
Junction Rd 58503
Juniper Dr & Pl 58503
Kambri Cir 58504
E Kavaney Dr 58501
Kayley Ct & Dr 58504
Keating Dr 58501
Keepsake Ln 58501
Keith Dr 58503
Kelly Dr 58503
Kendal Ct 58504
Kennedy Ave 58501
Kent Dr 58503
Kerry Ln 58503
Keystone Dr 58503
Kimball Ln 58504
Kimberly Ave 58501
Kings Ln 58503
Kingsford Rd 58504
Kingston Dr 58503
Kingswood Ln & Rd 58503
Kirkwood Mall 58504
Kittie Ln 58504
Knollwood Dr 58501
Koch Dr 58503
Kodiak Pl 58503
Kost Dr & Pl 58503
Kristen Ln 58503
Lacorte Loop & Pl 58503
Lafayette Dr 58503
Laforest Ave 58501
Lake Ave 58504
Lakota Ln 58504
Lambeau Ln 58503
Lambton Ave 58503
Langer Ln & Way 58504
Lansing Ln 58504
Laramie Dr 58504
Laredo Dr 58504
Lariat Ln, Loop & Pl 58503
Lark Ln 58504
Larson Rd 58504
E & W Lasalle Dr 58503
Lee Ave 58504
Leisure Ln 58503
Lewis Rd 58504
Lexington Dr 58503
Libby Rd 58504
Lilac Ct & Ln 58501
Lilly Dr 58503
Limestone Ln 58503
Lincoln Ave & Rd 58504
Linden Ln 58503
Link Dr 58503
Little Rock Ct 58503
Live Oak Ln 58504
Lockport St 58501
London Ave & Pl 58504
Longhorn Dr & Pl 58503
Longley Ave 58501
Lookout Trl 58504
Lora St 58501
Lorrain Dr & Pl 58503
E & W Loveland Rd 58503
Lovett Ave 58504
Lucas St 58504
Lunar Ln 58503
Macon Dr 58504
Madison Ln 58503
Magnolia Dr 58503
Mahone Ave 58503
E & W Main Ave 58501
Majestic St 58504
Maltby St 58503
Manchester Pl & St 58504
N Mandan St 58501
S Mandan St 58504
Manitoba Ln 58503
Maple Ln 58504
Mapleton Ave 58503

Maplewood Dr 58504
Marian Dr 58501
Marietta Dr & Pl 58504
Mariposa Pl 58503
Marston Dr 58503
Maryland St 58504
Mason Ave 58501
Masterson Ave 58501
Mayflower Cir & Dr 58504
Mayville Rd 58503
Mccomb Ave 58503
Mccurry Way 58504
Mcdonald Rd 58504
Mcdougall Dr 58504
Mcginnis Way 58504
Meade Cir 58503
Meadow Ln 58504
Meadow Ridge Pl 58503
Meadow Run Dr 58504
Meadowcrest Rd 58503
Meadowlark Ln 58501
Meadowview Dr 58504
Medora Ave 58503
Meledee Pl 58504
Mellowsun Dr 58503
Memorial Hwy 58504
Mercedes Dr & Pt 58504
Mercury Ln 58503
Meredith Dr 58501
Mesquite Loop 58503
Michigan Ave 58504
Middlefield Rd 58503
Midway Dr 58501
Milky Way Rd 58503
Mills Ave 58504
Mirage Pl 58503
Miriam Ave & Cir 58501
Missouri Ave 58504
Misty Waters Dr 58503
Modesto Cir 58504
Mohawk St 58501
Monreo Dr 58503
Montana Dr 58503
Montego Dr 58503
Montgomery Pl 58504
Montreal St 58503
Moonlite Rd 58503
Moonstone Ln 58503
Morgan Cir 58503
Morning View Ct 58501
Morningside St 58501
Morris Rd 58503
Morrison Ave 58504
Mouton Ave 58503
Mulberry Ln 58501
Mulligan Way 58503
Munich Dr 58504
Mustang Dr 58503
Mutineer Pl 58504
Nagel Dr 58501
Napa Loop 58504
Nautilus Dr 58504
Nebraska Dr 58503
Nelson Dr & Pl 58503
Neptune Cir 58504
Nevada St 58503
New Jersey St 58504
New Orleans Pl 58504
New York St 58504
Niagara Dr 58503
Nickerson Ave 58503
Nina Ln 58504
Nordic Ln & Pl 58503
Normandy St 58503
North Ave 58501
Northern Plains Dr 58504
Northgate Dr 58504
Northridge Dr 58501
Northrop Dr 58503
Northstar Dr 58503
Northview Ln 58501
Northwest Dr 58504
Northwood Dr & Pl 58503
Nottingham Dr 58504
Nova Dr 58503
Oahe Bnd 58504
Oak Dr 58503
Oakfield Dr 58503
Oakland Dr 58504
Oberhausen Dr 58504
Ogden Ln 58504
Ohio St 58503
Olive Ln 58503
Olive Tree Dr & Pl 58503
E Omaha Dr 58504
Omar St 58504
Ontario Ln 58503
Onyx Dr 58503
Opal Dr 58503
Oregon Dr 58503
Osage Ave 58501
Ottawa St 58503
Overland Rd 58503
Overlook Dr 58503
E & W Owens Ave 58501
Oxford Dr 58504
Pacific Ave, Ln & Pl 58501
Paige Dr 58503
Palmer Pl 58503
Palomino Dr 58504
Park Ave 58504
Parkerplum Dr 58503
Parkridge Ln 58503
N Parkview Dr 58501
Patriot Dr 58503
Peach Tree Dr 58504
Pearson Cir 58504
Pebbleview Cir, Loop & Pl 58503
Penenah Dr 58504
Penn Pl 58503
Pennsylvania Ave 58504
Pheasant St 58504
Piccadilly Cir 58504
Pin Oak Loop 58501
Pine Ave 58503
Pinewood Loop & Pl 58504
Pinto Pl 58503
Pioneer Dr 58501
Plainsman Rd 58503
Plainview Dr 58503
Pleasant St 58504
Pleasantview Rd 58503
Pocatello Dr 58504
Pointe Loop & Pl 58503
Pond Pl 58504
Ponderosa Ave 58503
Poplar Ln 58504
Portage Dr 58503
Porter Ave 58501
Portland Dr 58504
Poseidon Loop 58504
Powder Ridge Cir & Dr 58503
Prairie Dr 58501
Prairie Clover Pl 58503
Prairie Hills Dr 58503
Prairie Pines Loop 58503
Prairie Rose Loop 58501
Prairie Sage Pl 58503
Prairie View Dr 58501
Prairiewood Dr 58504
Preston Loop 58504
Primrose Pl 58501
E & W Princeton Ave 58504
Promontory Dr & Pl 58503
Prospect Pl & Pt 58501
Pumice Loop 58503
Quarts Ln 58503
Quebec Ln 58503
Railroad Ave 58501
Ranch Loop 58503
E Rancount Ave 58505
Raven Dr 58501
Rawhide Dr 58503
Raymar Pl 58504
Raymond St 58501
Rebel Dr 58503
Red Fox Ln 58503
Red Oak Dr 58501
Redcoat Dr & Loop 58503
Redstone Dr 58503
E & W Regent Dr 58504
Regina Ln & Pl 58503
Reily Rd 58504
Remington Ave 58503
Remuda Dr 58503
Renee Dr 58503
E, W & S Reno Ave & Dr 58504
Republic St 58504
Restful Dr 58503
Revere Dr 58501
Richmond Dr 58504
Ridge Pl & Way 58503
Ridgecrest Dr 58503
Ridgedale St 58503
Ridgeland Dr & Loop 58503
Ridgemont Ln 58504
Ridgeview Ln 58501
Ridgewood Dr 58501
Rifle Range Dr 58504
Ringneck Rd 58503
River Rd
400-598 58504
601-699 58504
1700-6399 58503
Riverbend Ln 58504
Riverside Park Rd 58504
Riverview Ave 58504
Riverwood Dr 58504
Roadrunner Ave 58504
Rock Creek Rd 58503
Rock Island Pl 58504
Rocky Rd 58503
Rocky Point Ln 58503
Rolling Dr 58501
Rolling Hills Rd 58503
Rolling Ridge Rd 58503
Roosevelt Dr 58503
Rooster Rd 58503
Rose Dr 58503
E Rosser Ave
100-299 58501
220-220 58502
220-220 58506
220-220 58507
300-3898 58501
301-3899 58501
W Rosser Ave 58501
E & W Roundup Rd 58503
Runnel Rd 58503
Rushmore Rd 58503
Russell Rd 58503
Rutland Dr 58504
Ryan Dr 58501
Saber Dr 58504
Saddle Ridge Rd 58503
Sage Dr 58503
Sagebrush Dr 58504
W Saint Benedict Dr 58501
Saint Joseph Dr 58501
Saint Louis Pl 58504
Salmon St 58503
San Angelo Dr 58504
San Diego Dr 58504
Sand Dune Ln 58503
Sand Hill Rd 58503
Sandpiper Ave 58504
Sandstone Dr 58503
Sandy River Dr 58503
Santa Barbara Dr 58504
Santa Fe Ave 58504
Santa Gertrudis Dr & Loop 58503
Santa Maria Ln 58504
Santee Rd 58503
Sapphire Ln 58503
Sarah Pt 58504
Saratoga Ave 58503
Saturn Dr 58503
Scenic Dr 58503
Scenic Hills Rd 58503
Schaan Dr 58504
Schafer St 58501
Schick Dr 58501
Schooner Pl 58504
Scotsman Dr 58504
Scout St 58504
Selkirk Rd 58503
Seminole Ave 58501
Senate Dr 58501
Seneca Cir & Dr 58503
Sentinel St 58504
Serene Cir 58503
Shady Ln 58501
Shady View Pl 58504
Shamrock Dr & Pl 58503
Shannon Dr 58501
Sharloh Loop & Pl 58501
Sharps Loop & Pl 58503
Sheehan Rd 58504
Shelburne St 58503
Sheridan Cir 58503
Sherman Dr 58504
Sherwood Ln 58504
Sheyenne Cir 58503
Shiloh Dr 58503
Shirley St 58504
Shoal Dr 58503
Showdown Ln 58503
Sibley Dr 58504
Sierra Cir 58503
Signal St 58504
Silica Pl 58503
Siltstone Dr 58503
Silver City Ln 58503
Silver Fox Cir & Ln 58503
Simle Dr 58501
Sioux Ave 58501
Sky Ln 58503
Skylark Ave 58504
Skyline Blvd 58503
Skyline Crossings 58503
Skyway St 58504
Slate Dr 58503
Sleepy Hollow Loop 58501
Smokey Ln 58504
Snappy Ln 58504
Socorro Pl 58501
Sonora Way 58503
Soo Line Dr 58501
Sorrento Cir & Pl 58501
Souris St 58503
Southport Loop 58504
Southridge Ln 58504
Southview Ln 58501
Southwood Ave 58504
Spaulding Ave 58501
Springfield St 58503
Spruce Pl 58504
Spruce Creek Rd 58503
Stagecoach Cir 58503
N Stanley Dr 58504
Star Ln 58503
N Star Acres Rd 58503
State St
1701-1799 58501
2401-2597 58503
2599-3699 58503
3701-4299 58503
Sterling Dr 58504
Stetson Dr 58503
Stevens St 58503
Stewart Dr 58503
Stone Loop 58503
Stoneridge Pl 58503
Stonewall Dr 58503
Stonewood Way 58504
Stoney Ln 58501
Stratford Dr 58504
Stream Pl 58503
Sturgis Loop 58504
Stuttgart Dr 58504
Sudbury Ave 58503
Sully Dr 58504
Summit Blvd 58504
Sumter Cir & Dr 58503
Sundance Loop 58503
Sundown Dr 58503
Sunflower Dr 58503
Sunlight Dr 58503
Sunny Pl 58503
Sunnyview Pl 58503
Sunnyview Rd 58504
Sunrise Ave 58504
Sunset Pl 58504
Sunshine Ln 58503
Superior Dr 58503
Susan Dr 58503
Sussex St 58504
E & W Sweet Ave 58504
Sycamore Ln 58504
Sykes Dr 58504
Tacoma Ave 58504
Tahoe Dr 58504
Talon Rd 58503
Tarry Town Pl 58501
Tatley Park Rd 58504
Tavis Rd 58504
Telluride Ln 58503
Telstar Dr 58503
Terrace Dr 58503
Territory Dr 58503
Teton Ave 58501
E & W Thayer Ave 58501
Thompson Ln 58503
Thompson St 58501
Thornburg Dr 58504
Thunderbird Ln 58503
Tiffany Dr 58504
Timber Bottom Ln 58504
Timberlane Pl 58504
Tj Ln 58503
Tolly Dr 58504
Toronto Dr & Loop 58503
Torrence Pt 58504
Toulon Dr 58503
Tower Ave 58501
Trademark Dr 58504
Trappers Cir 58503
Traynor Ln 58504
Trenton Dr 58503
Tucker Ln 58503
Tucson Ave 58504
Tulsa Ave 58504
Tumbleweed Cir 58504
Turnbow Ln 58503
E & W Turnpike Ave 58501
Twilight Rd 58503
Tyler Pkwy 58503
Tyndale Cir 58503
University Dr 58504
Utah Dr 58503
Valcartier St 58503
Valle Moor Dr & Pl 58501
N Valley Dr & Loop 58503
Valley Forge Dr 58503
Valley Vista Ln 58503
Valleyview Ave 58501
Vancouver Ln 58503
Vantassel Dr 58501
Vermont Ave 58504
Versailles Ave 58503
Victoria Cir 58504
Victory Pl 58501
Viewpoint Dr 58503
Viking Dr 58501
Village Cir & Dr 58503
Violet Ln 58503
Virginia Ave 58504
Vista Ln 58501
Volk Dr 58501
Voyager Dr & Pl 58504
E & W Wachter Ave 58504
Walker Dr 58504
Walter Way 58503
Ward Rd 58501
Warwick Loop & Pl 58504
N Washington St
200-2199 58501
2400-7699 58503
S Washington St 58504
Waterford Dr 58503
Weatherby Way 58503
Weir Dr 58504
Weiss Ave 58503
Welle Loop 58503
Wentworth Dr 58503
Westwood St 58504
Weyburn Dr 58503
Whisper Dr 58504
White Oak Loop 58501
White Spruce Rd 58503
Whitefox Cir 58503
Whitetail Dr 58503
Whitetail Ln 58504
Whitlow St 58504
Whitney Ct 58504
Wichita Dr 58504
Wild Rye Pl 58503
Wilderness Cove Rd 58503
Wildrose Cres 58503
Wildwood St 58503
Williams St 58501
Willow Ln 58504
Willow Oaks Cir & Rd 58504
Winchester Dr 58503
Windmill Rd 58504
Windsor Pl & St 58503
Winnipeg Dr 58503
Wisconsin Dr 58503
Wood Ln 58503
Wood Moor Pl 58501
Woodland Dr & Pl 58504
Woodlawn Dr 58504
Woodrow Ct & Dr 58504
Woodsman Pl 58504
Woodvale Dr 58504
Xavier St 58501
Yegen Pl & Rd 58504
York Ln 58503
Yorkshire Ln 58504
Yorktown Dr 58503
Yukon Dr 58503

NUMBERED STREETS

N 1st St 58501
S 1st St 58504
N 2nd St 58501
S 2nd St 58504
N 3rd St 58501
S 3rd St
100-2398 58504
101-199 58501
201-2399 58504
4th Ave SE 58501
N 4th St
100-2199 58501
2301-2397 58503
2399-2800 58503
2802-3098 58503
5th Ave NE 58501
N 5th St 58501
S 5th St
101-119 58501
121-197 58504
199-399 58504
401-599 58504
6th Ave SW 58504
N 6th St
100-198 58501
2400-2599 58503
7th St NE 58503
N 7th St
200-2199 58501
2400-2599 58503
S 7th St 58504
N 8th St
101-197 58501
2400-2599 58503
S 8th St 58504
N 9th St
200-298 58501
300-2199 58501
2400-2498 58503
2500-2599 58503
S 9th St 58504
10th Ave SE 58504
N 10th St
300-1099 58501
3100-3298 58503
S 10th St 58504
11th St NE 58503
N 11th St
201-397 58501
399-1999 58501
2901-3097 58503
3099-3102 58503
3104-3298 58503
S 11th St 58504
12th St SE 58504
N 12th St 58501
S 12th St 58504
N 13th St 58501
S 13th St 58504
N 14th St
200-1999 58501
2900-3499 58503
S 14th St 58504
15th St NW 58503
N 15th St
200-1999 58501
3001-3099 58503
S 15th St 58504
N 16th St 58501
S 16th St 58504
17th Ave NE 58501
N 17th St 58501
S 17th St 58504
N 18th St 58501
S 18th St 58504
19th St NE 58503
N 19th St
200-2099 58501
2501-2897 58503
20th Ave NE 58501
N 20th St 58501
S 20th St 58504
N 21st St 58501
22nd Ave SE 58504
N 22nd St 58501
S 22nd St 58504
N 23rd St 58501
S 23rd St 58504
N & S 24th 58501
N 25th St 58501
26th St NE 58503
N 26th St 58501
S 26th St
200-298 58501
201-497 58504
499-1000 58504
1002-1498 58504
27th St NE 58503
N 27th St 58501
28th Ave SE 58504
28th St NW 58503
N 28th St 58501
N 29th St 58501
30th Ave NE 58501
N 31st St 58501
N 32nd St 58501
33rd St SE 58504
N 33rd St 58501
34th St NW 58503
N 34th St 58501
N 35th St 58501
41st St NE 58503
41st St NW 58503
41st St SE 58504
42nd St NE 58503
43rd Ave NE 58503
44th St NE 58503
46th Ave SE 58504
46th St NE 58503
47th St NE 58503
48th SE & SW 58504
52nd Ave NE 58503
52nd Ave SE 58504
52nd St NE
100-1899 58501
3300-3898 58503
52nd St SE
100-799 58501
3601-3997 58504
N 52nd St 58501
53rd St SE 58504
54th St NW 58503
54th St SW 58503

55th Ave & St 58504
56th St NE 58501
57th Ave NE 58503
57th Ave NW 58503
57th St SE 58504
59th St NE 58501
62nd Ave SE 58504
62nd St NE 58503
64th Ave NW 58503
66th St NE
100-2099 58501
3200-9599 58503
66th St SE
500-999 58501
1500-9899 58504
67th St NW 58503
71st NE & NW 58503
73rd Ave NE 58503
76th Ave NE 58503
76th Ave SE 58504
78th Ave NE 58503
79th Ave NE 58503
80th St NE
800-2299 58501
3500-13799 58503
80th St NW 58503
80th St SE
300-799 58501
1100-11099 58504
81st St NE 58503
82nd Ave NE 58503
84th NE & NW 58503
87th St NE 58501
89th Ave SE 58504
90th Ave NE 58503
93rd St NE
800-1999 58501
10400-14499 58503
93rd St SE 58504
97th NE & NW 58503
100th St SE 58504
101st St SE 58504
102nd Ave SE 58504
104th Ave NW 58503
106th St NE
1500-1699 58501
3700-13299 58503
106th St SE 58504
110th NE & NW 58503
112th St NE 58501
115th Ave SE 58504
119th St NE 58503
119th St SE 58504
123rd NE & NW 58503
132nd St SE 58504
136th NE & NW 58503
145th St SE 58504
149th Ave NW 58503
154th Ave SE 58504
156th Ave NW 58503
162nd Ave NW 58503
171st St SE 58504
175th Ave NW 58503

DICKINSON ND

General Delivery 58601

POST OFFICE BOXES MAIN OFFICE STATIONS AND BRANCHES

Box No.s
All PO Boxes 58602

NAMED STREETS

All Street Addresses 58601

NUMBERED STREETS

1st Ave E 58601
1st Ave SE 58601
1st Ave SW 58601
1st Ave W 58601
1st St E
2-998 58601
15-15 58602
17-999 58601
1st St S 58601
1st St SE 58601
1st St SW 58601
1st St W 58601
2nd Ave & St E, SE, SW & W 58601
S 3rd Ave & St E, SE, SW & W 58601
4th Ave & St E, SE, SW & W 58601
5th Ave & St E, SE, SW & W 58601
6th Ave & St E, SE, SW & W 58601
S 7th Ave & St E, SE, SW & W 58601
S 8th Ave & St E, SE, SW & W 58601
S 9th Ave & St E, SE, SW & W 58601
S 10th Ave & St E, SE & W 58601
S 11th Ave & St E, SW, W & SE 58601
12th Ave & St E, W & SE 58601
13th Ave & St E, SW & W 58601
14th Ave & St E, W & SW 58601
15th Ave & St E, W & SE 58601
16th Ave & St 58601
17th Ave & St E & W 58601
18th Ave & St E, W & SW 58601
19th Ave & St W, E & SW 58601
20th Ave & St E, SW, SE & W 58601
21st Ave & St 58601
22nd Ave & St E, SW & W 58601
23rd Ave & St E, W & SW 58601
24th Ave & St E, SW & W 58601
25th Ave & St 58601
26th Ave & St E, SW & W 58601
27d St SW 58601
27j St SW 58601
27th Ave & St E, SW & W 58601
28m St SW 58601
28th Ave & St E, SW & W 58601
29d St SW 58601
29p St SW 58601
29t St SW 58601
29th Ave & St E, SW & W 58601
30g St SW 58601
30j St SW 58601
30th Ave & St 58601
31p St SW 58601
31st St SW 58601
31t St SW 58601
31u St SW 58601
32c St SW 58601
32k St SW 58601
32nd St E 58601
32t St SW 58601
32v St SW 58601
33m St SW 58601
33r St SW 58601
33rd St SW 58601
34j St SW 58601
34p St SW 58601
34th SW & W 58601
34y St SW 58601
35p St SW 58601
35r St SW 58601
35th Ave & St E & SW 58601
35u St SW 58601
35w St SW 58601
36th St SW 58601
36v St SW 58601
36x St SW 58601
37th Ave & St 58601
38th Ave & St E & SW 58601
39c St SW 58601
39l St SW 58601
39m St SW 58601
39th St SW 58601
40t St SW 58601
40th Ave & St SW, E & W 58601
41st St SW 58601
42nd St SW 58601
43rd SW & W 58601
44m St SW 58601
44th St SW 58601
45m St SW 58601
45th St SW 58601
46th St SW 58601
47t St SW 58601
47th St SW 58601
48th Ave & St 58601
49th Ave & St 58601
50th St SW 58601
50x St SW 58601
51st NW & SW 58601
52nd NW & SW 58601
62nd NE & SW 58601
63rd Ave NE 58601
64th NE & NW 58601
65th Ave NE 58601
71st NW & SW 58601
73rd St NW 58601
85th Ave NE 58601
86th Ave NE 58601
89th St SW 58601
92nd St NE 58601
93rd St NE 58601
96th St NE 58601
97th Ave NW 58601
98th Ave NW 58601
99th NW & SW 58601
101st Ave NW 58601
102nd Ave SW 58601
103rd Ave & St NW & SW 58601
104 1/2 Ave SW 58601
104 1/4 Ave SW 58601
104 3/4 Ave SW 58601
104m Ave SW 58601
104t Ave SW 58601
104w Ave SW 58601
104f Ave SW 58601
104th Ave & St NW & SW 58601
105th NW & SW 58601
106th Ave SW 58601
106t Ave SW 58601
107th Ave & St NW & SW 58601
108th Ave SW 58601
108h Ave SW 58601
108s Ave SW 58601
108w Ave SW 58601
108f Ave SW 58601
108x Ave SW 58601
108y Ave SW 58601
109 1/4 Ave SW 58601
109f Ave SW 58601
109th Ave SW 58601
109e Ave SW 58601
110th Ave SW 58601
110z Ave SW 58601
110p Ave SW 58601
110s Ave SW 58601
110v Ave SW 58601
110x Ave SW 58601
110k Ave SW 58601
111b Ave SW 58601
111f Ave SW 58601
111e Ave SW 58601
111th Ave SW 58601
111j Ave SW 58601
111h Ave SW 58601
111c Ave SW 58601
112th Ave SW 58601
112s Ave SW 58601
112t Ave SW 58601
113th Ave SW 58601
114u Ave SW 58601
114w Ave SW 58601
114y Ave SW 58601
114th Ave SW 58601
114v Ave SW 58601
115g Ave SW 58601
115c Ave SW 58601
115th Ave SW 58601
115l Ave SW 58601
116th Ave SW 58601
117th Ave SW 58601
118th Ave SW 58601
119th Ave SW 58601
121st Ave SW 58601
122nd Ave SW 58601
151g Ave SW 58601
189th St SW 58601
28 1/2 St SW 58601
44 1/2 St SW 58601
45 1/2 St SW 58601
47 3/4 St SW 58601

FARGO ND

General Delivery 58102

POST OFFICE BOXES MAIN OFFICE STATIONS AND BRANCHES

Box No.s
1 - 2172 58107
2181 - 3280 58108
4001 - 4030 58107
5036 - 5903 58105
6000 - 6161 58108
6201 - 6204 58106
6401 - 6583 58109
6700 - 6799 58108
7001 - 11459 58106

NAMED STREETS

Adams Dr 58102
Adams St S 58104
Administration Ave N 58105
Agassiz Xing S 58104
Aggregate Industries Dr N 58102
Albrecht Blvd N
1301-1317 58105
1319-1420 58105
1422-1698 58105
1601-1699 58102
Amber Valley Ct & Pkwy 58104
American Way S 58103
April Ln N 58102
Aquarius Dr 58104
Arbor Ct S 58104
Arrowhead Rd S 58103
Arthur Dr 58104
Ashton Ct S 58104
Atlantic Dr S 58103
Auburn Ave 58104
Autumn Dr S 58104
Avery Ln S 58104
Baja Ln S 58103
Bakers Ln 58102
N Bantania Dr 58105
Barrett St N 58102
S Bay Dr S 58103
Beach Ln S 58104
Bennett Ct S 58104
Birch Ln S 58103
Birchwood Ct S 58104
Birdie St N 58102
Bishops Blvd S 58104
E & W Bison Ct 58102
Blue Stem Ct S 58104
Bohnet Blvd N 58102
Bolley Dr 58105
Brandt Dr S 58104
Briarwood Pl 58104
Bristlecone Loop S 58104
Broadway N 58102
Broadway S 58103
Buchanan St S 58104
Burritt St S 58104
Calico Dr S 58104
Carrie Rose Ln S 58104
Casino St N 58102
Cedar Ave N 58102
Centennial Blvd 58105
Centennial Blvd N 58102
Centennial Rose Dr S 58104
Chelsea Ln S 58104
Cherry Ln N 58102
Chrisan Blvd & Way 58104
Christianson Pkwy S 58104
Circle Dr N 58102
Claire Dr S 58104
Clock Tower Ln S 58104
Clubhouse Dr S 58104
Cobblestone Ct S 58103
College St N
700-798 58102
800-1199 58102
1200-1299 58105
Columbus Cir S 58103
Comerive St N 58102
Copperfield Ct S 58104
Cossette Dr S 58104
E & W Country Club Dr 58103
Countryside Trailer Ct S 58103
County Road 31 58102
County Road 81 N 58102
Coventry Dr S 58104
Crofton Ln S 58104
Cypress Ln S 58104
Dakota Dr N 58102
Dakota Park Cir S 58104
Deer Creek Pkwy 58104
Demores Cir & Dr 58103
Domingo Rd S 58103
Dorothea Ct S 58104
Douglas Dr S 58104
Eagle St N 58102
Eagle Park Dr S 58104
Eagle Pointe Dr S 58104
Eastgate Dr S 58103
Eddy Ct S 58103
Edgemont St N 58102
Edgewood Dr N 58102
El Cano Dr S 58104
El Tora Blvd & Cv 58103
Elm Cir & St 58102
Elmwood Ave S 58103
Estate Dr S 58104
Evergreen Cir & Rd 58102
Fairway Rd N 58102
Farantra Ave S 58103
Farmstead Ct S 58104
Fayland Dr 58102
Fiechtner Dr S 58103
Fillmore St S 58104
N & S Flickertail Cir & Dr S 58103
Forest Ave N 58102
Forest River Dr & Rd 58104
Fremont Dr S 58103
Froemke Ln 58102
Frontier Way S 58104
Furnberg Pl S 58104
E & W Gateway Cir & Dr S 58103
Gemini Cir 58104
Gibraltor Ave N 58102
Gold Dr S 58103
Goldelin Ave S 58104
Golden Ln S 58104
Golden Valley Pkwy S 58104
Golf Course Ave N 58102
Great Northern Dr N 58102
Great Plains Dr S 58104
Hackberry Dr S 58104
Harrison St S 58104
Harvest Dr S 58104
Harwood Dr S 58104
Hawthorne St S 58104
Heritage Cir 58104
Hickory St N 58102
Highland Dr 58102
Highpointe Dr N 58102
Hillside Dr 58104
Houkum Ct S 58104
Interstate Blvd S 58103
Ironwood Ct S 58104
Jackson St S 58104
Jefferson St S 58104
Juniper Ct S 58104
Kelly St N 58102
Kennedy Ct N 58102
Kennedy St S 58104
Keno St N 58102
Kirsten Ln S 58104
La Casa Way S 58103
Landview Rd 58102
Laredo Dr S 58103
Lavonne Ct S 58104
Leahy Ave S 58103
Lee Ln S 58104
Libra Ln 58104
Lilac Ln N 58102
Lincoln St S 58104
Linden Ave S 58103
Lindenwood Dr S 58103
Loden Ct S 58104
Lone Tree Rd S 58104
Longfellow Rd N 58102
E & W Lynmar 58102
Machinery Row Ave N 58102
Madison Ave N 58102
Madison Square Dr S 58104
Main Ave 58103
Maple St N 58102
Maple Valley Dr S 58104
Maplewood Ct S 58104
Marion St S 58104
Martens Way S 58104
May Ln N 58102
Meadow Creek Cir & Dr 58104
Meadow Park Trailer Ct N 58102
Meadowlark Ln N 58102
Monroe St S 58104
Monte Carlo Dr N 58102
Montego Ave S 58103
Mountain Maple Ct S 58104
Nd State University 58108
Ndsu Research Cir N 58102
Ndsu Research Park Dr N 58102
Niskanen 58102
Nodak Dr S 58103
Norman Ct S 58104
Northwood Dr 58102
Np Ave N 58102
Oak St N 58102
Oak Manor Ave S 58103
Oakcreek Dr S 58104
Oakland Ave S 58103
Oakwood Ct S 58104
Orchard Park Dr 58104
Osgood Pkwy S 58104
Pacific Dr S 58103
Page Dr S 58103
Par St N 58102
Park Ave, Blvd & Dr 58103
Parkview Cir, Dr & Ln 58103
Peterson Pkwy N 58102
Pierce St S 58104
Pine Pkwy S 58104
Plumtree Rd N 58102
Polk St S 58104
Ponderosa Pl S 58104
Prairie Ln S 58103
W Prairiewood Cir, Dr & Xing S 58103
Rainier Rue St N 58102
Redwood Ln S 58104
Reed Dr 58102
River Dr 58102
River Dr S 58104
N River Rd N 58102
S River Rd S 58103
River View Rd 58104
Riverwood Dr N 58102
Roberts St N 58102
Rocking Horse Cir S 58104
Roger Maris Dr S 58103
E Rose Creek Blvd, Dr & Pkwy S 58104
Round Hill Dr S 58104
Royal Oaks Dr N 58102
Russet Ave S 58104
Sagittarius Cir S 58104
Samuel Dr S 58104
San Juan Dr S 58103
Santa Cruz Dr S 58103
Santiago Blvd S 58103
Scorpio Cir S 58104
Seter Pkwy S 58104
Shawnas Pl 58104
Short St N 58102
Sienna Dr S 58104
Silverleaf Dr S 58104
Smylie Ln S 58104
South Dr S 58103
Southgate Dr S 58103
Southwood Dr S 58103
Spencer Ln S 58104
Sterling Rose Ln S 58104
Sundance Cir S 58103
Sundance Dr S 58104
Sundance Sq S 58104
Sunflower Ln S 58104
Sungate Dr S 58103
Tanner Ave S 58104
Taylor St S 58104
N & S Terrace 58102
Thunder Rd S 58104
Timberline Cir & Dr 58104
Tom Williams Dr S 58104
Townsite Pl S 58104
Troy St S 58104
Tuscan Ct S 58104
Tyler Ave S 58104
Umber Ct S 58104
University Dr N
8-16 58102
18-1230 58102
1231-1231 58105
1232-1298 58102
1233-1299 58102
1300-1399 58105
1303-1529 58102
1531-1533 58102
1535-1799 58102
1600-1618 58105
1620-1626 58102
1700-1716 58105
1718-1746 58105
1748-1798 58105
1800-1900 58102
1835-1899 58105
1901-2615 58102
1902-2998 58102
University Dr S
21-97 58103
99-3199 58103
3201-3497 58104
3499-8599 58104
8601-9099 58104
University Vlg 58102

Us Highway 81 N 58102
Van Buren St S 58104
Veterans Blvd S 58104
Victoria Rose Dr & Ln .. 58104
Viking Cir S 58103
Villa Dr S 58103
Village Ln S 58104
Voodoo Dr 58102
Waco Ln S 58103
Walsh Ave S 58104
Washington St S 58104
Waterford Dr S 58104
Westgate Dr S 58103
Westrac Dr S 58103
Wheatland Dr S 58103
Wheatland Pines Dr S .. 58103
Whispering Creek Cir S 58104
Whitestone Cir S 58103
Willow Rd N 58102
Windwood St S 58104
Woodbury Ct S 58103
Woodbury Park Dr S ... 58103
N & S Woodcrest Dr ... 58102
Woodhaven Dr & St 58104
Woodland Dr N 58102

NUMBERED STREETS

1st Ave N 58102
1st Ave S 58103
1st St N 58102
2nd Ave N
  400-498 58102
  657-657 58105
  657-657 58107
  657-657 58108
  701-1423 58102
2nd Ave S 58103
2nd St N 58102
2nd St S 58103
3rd Ave N 58102
3rd Ave S 58103
3rd St N 58102
3rd St S 58103
4th Ave N 58102
4th Ave S 58103
4th St N 58102
4th St S 58103
5th Ave N 58102
5th Ave S 58103
5th St N 58102
5th St S 58103
6th Ave N 58102
6th Ave S 58103
6th St S
  801-811 58103
  813-2399 58103
  10000-10298 58104
  10300-10499 58104
7 1/2 Ave N 58102
7th Ave N 58102
7th Ave S 58103
7th Ln S 58103
7th St N 58102
7th St S 58103
8th Ave N 58102
8th Ave S 58103
8th St N 58102
8th St S 58103
9 1/2 St N 58102
9th Ave N 58102
9th Ave NE 58102
9th Ave S 58103
9th St N 58102
9th St S 58103
9th Avenue Cir S 58103
10th Ave N 58102
10th Ave S 58103
10th St N
  1-1799 58102
  1700-1798 58105
  1800-1898 58102
  1800-1898 58105
  1801-4799 58102
10th St S
  1-497 58103
  3500-3700 58104
11th Ave N 58102
11th Ave S 58103
11th St N 58102
11th St S
  2-98 58103
  100-3099 58103
  3200-5499 58104
12th Ave N
  301-697 58102
  1500-1616 58105
  1501-4399 58102
12th Ave NE 58102
12th Ave S 58103
12th St N 58102
12th St S
  2-98 58103
  3700-7299 58104
13th Ave N 58102
13th Ave S 58103
13th Cir S 58104
13th St N 58102
13th St S 58104
14th Ave N
  24-198 58102
  200-1299 58102
  1300-1498 58105
  1301-4399 58102
  4100-4298 58102
14th Ave S 58103
14th St N 58102
14th St S
  1-2699 58103
  5500-7299 58104
15th Ave N
  1-197 58102
  1500-1600 58105
  1801-1899 58102
  1801-1899 58105
  3800-4699 58102
15th Ave S 58103
15th St N 58102
15th St S
  1-97 58103
  3200-8099 58104
16th Ave N 58102
16th Ave S 58103
16th St N 58102
16th St S
  2-98 58103
  100-2499 58103
  5500-7499 58104
17th Ave N 58102
17th Ave S 58103
17th St N
  701-997 58102
  1400-1498 58105
  4700-6398 58102
17th St S
  1-897 58103
  3301-3397 58104
18th Ave N 58102
18th Ave S 58103
18th St N
  701-997 58102
  999-1199 58102
  1400-1499 58105
18th St S
  1-3199 58103
  3200-6199 58104
19th Ave N 58102
19th Ave S 58103
19th St N 58102
19th St S
  800-3099 58103
  3300-5700 58104
  5702-6498 58104
20th Ave N 58102
20th Ave S 58103
20th St N 58102
20th St S
  100-698 58103
  700-3099 58103
  3200-5599 58104
  5601-5799 58104
20th Street Cir S 58104
21st Ave N 58102
21st Ave S
  500-1100 58103
  1102-2198 58103
  4200-4298 58104
  4800-5298 58103
21st St N 58102
21st St S
  1-97 58103
  99-3099 58103
  3300-6999 58104
22nd Ave N 58102
22nd Ave S 58103
22nd St S
  100-3099 58103
  3101-3199 58103
  3200-3398 58104
  3400-6299 58104
23rd Ave N 58102
23rd Ave S
  500-3399 58103
  4201-4397 58104
  4399-5500 58104
  5502-5698 58104
23rd St N 58102
23rd St S
  100-3102 58103
  3104-3198 58103
  6000-6999 58104
24th Ave N 58102
24th Ave S 58103
24th St N 58102
24th St S
  100-198 58103
  200-499 58103
  5801-5897 58104
  5899-6999 58104
25th Ave N 58102
25th Ave S 58103
25th St N 58102
25th St S
  200-298 58103
  2400-2498 58104
  2501-3199 58103
  3200-8700 58104
26th Ave N 58102
26th Ave S
  501-1801 58103
  4100-4498 58104
26th St N 58102
26th St S
  2300-2498 58103
  5600-5798 58104
27th Ave N 58102
27th Ave S 58103
27th Cir S 58103
27th St N 58102
27th St S
  1-3099 58103
  3101-3199 58103
  5301-5697 58104
  5699-6199 58104
28th Ave N 58102
28th Ave NE 58102
28th Ave S
  1101-1497 58103
  4100-5499 58104
28th St N 58102
28th St S
  1-1299 58103
  3200-3398 58104
29th Ave N 58102
29th Ave NE 58102
29th Ave S 58103
29th St N 58102
29th St S 58104
30th Ave N 58102
30th Ave S
  1100-3599 58103
  4100-5400 58104
  5402-5498 58104
30th St N 58102
30th St S 58104
31st Ave N 58102
31st Ave S
  1500-3399 58103
  4100-5299 58104
31st St N 58102
31st St S
  101-2997 58103
  2999-3199 58103
  3500-5799 58104
32nd Ave N 58102
32nd Ave NE 58102
32nd Ave S
  1000-1098 58103
  4100-4200 58104
32nd St N 58102
32nd St S
  1300-1398 58103
  1455-1455 58106
  1455-1455 58109
  3201-3397 58104
33rd Ave N 58102
33rd Ave S 58104
33rd St N 58102
33rd St S
  1400-3100 58103
  3102-3198 58103
  3200-5799 58104
  4001-4097 58104
  4099-4100 58104
  4102-4198 58104
34th Ave S 58104
34th St N 58102
34th St S
  300-398 58103
  400-3099 58103
  3900-5799 58104
35th Ave N 58102
35th Ave NE 58102
35th Ave S 58104
35th St N 58102
35th St S
  1400-1899 58103
  5300-6299 58104
36th Ave N 58102
36th Ave NE 58102
36th Ave S 58104
36th St N 58102
36th St S
  300-3098 58103
  3200-3298 58104
  3300-3400 58104
  3402-5798 58104
37th Ave N 58102
37th Ave S 58104
37th St N 58102
38th Ave S 58104
38th St N 58102
38th St S
  201-1899 58103
  3401-4797 58104
  4799-7099 58104
  7101-7999 58104
39th Ave S 58104
39th St N 58102
39th St S
  1700-1899 58103
  2901-2997 58104
  2999-4899 58104
40th Ave N 58102
40th Ave S 58104
40th St N 58102
40th St S
  100-1800 58103
  1802-1898 58103
  3900-4698 58104
  4700-4899 58104
41st Ave N 58102
41st Ave S 58104
41st St N 58102
41st St S
  200-300 58103
  302-398 58103
  2601-3097 58104
  3099-3199 58104
  4700-4899 58104
42nd Ave N 58102
42nd Ave S 58104
42nd St N 58102
42nd St S
  101-197 58103
  199-1999 58103
  3100-3198 58104
  3200-5199 58104
  5201-5399 58104
43rd Ave N 58102
43rd Ave S 58104
43rd St N 58102
43rd St S
  901-997 58103
  999-1499 58103
  1501-1699 58103
  2101-3097 58104
  3099-5699 58104
44th Ave N 58102
44th Ave S 58104
44th St N 58102
44th St S
  401-997 58103
  999-2099 58103
  3100-4298 58104
  4300-5699 58104
45th Ave N 58102
45th Ave S 58104
45th St N 58102
45th St S
  200-698 58103
  700-1900 58103
  1902-1998 58103
  2200-5099 58104
  5101-8299 58104
46th Ave N 58102
46th Ave S 58104
46th St N 58102
46th St S 58104
47th Ave N 58102
47th Ave S 58104
47th St N 58102
47th St S
  1600-1698 58103
  2600-2698 58104
  2700-5000 58104
  5002-5298 58104
48th Ave N 58102
48th Ave S 58104
48th St S
  700-799 58103
  801-1599 58103
  3800-4398 58104
  4400-4499 58104
49th Ave N 58102
49th Ave S 58104
49th St N 58102
49th St S
  700-2099 58103
  3000-4499 58104
50th Ave S 58104
50th St N 58102
50th St S
  700-2099 58103
  3401-3497 58104
51st Ave S 58104
51st St S
  700-898 58103
  1601-1699 58103
  2701-3197 58104
  3199-4999 58104
51st Way S 58104
52nd Ave N 58102
52nd Ave S 58104
52nd St S
  1700-2099 58103
  2101-2199 58103
  4100-4799 58104
53rd Ave & St 58104
54th Ave & St 58104
55th Ave & St 58104
56th Ave & St 58104
57th Ave S 58104
57th St N 58102
58th Ave, Ct & St 58104
59th Ave & St 58104
60th Ave & St 58104
61st Ave & St 58104
62nd Ave N 58102
62nd Ave S 58104
62nd St S 58104
63rd Ave S 58104
64th Ave N 58102
64th Ave S 58104
65th Ave & St 58104
66th St S 58104
67th Ave & St 58104
68th Ave & St 58104
69th Ave S 58104
70th Ave S 58104
71st Ave S 58104
72nd Ave S 58104
73rd Ave S 58104
75th Ave S 58104
76th Ave N 58102
76th Ave S 58104
81st Ave S 58104
81st St N 58102
88th Ave S 58104
100th Ave S 58104
11 1/2 St N 58102
13 1/2 Ave S 58103
13 1/2 St N 58102
13 1/2 St S 58103
14 1/2 Ave S 58103
14 1/2 St N 58102
14 1/2 St S 58103
15 1/2 Ave S 58103
15 1/2 St N 58102
16 1/2 Ave N 58102
16 1/2 St S 58103
17 1/2 Ave N 58102
17 1/2 St S 58104
20 1/2 Ave S 58103
25 1/2 Ave S 58103
26 1/2 Ave & Ct 58103
27 1/2 St S 58103
28 1/2 Ave S 58103
30 1/2 Ave S 58103
33 1/2 Ave S 58104
34 1/2 Ave S 58104
35 1/2 Court Ave S 58104
35 1/2 Ave S 58104
36 1/2 Ave & Ct 58104
37 1/2 Ave S 58104
38 1/2 Ave S 58104
39 1/2 Ave N 58102
39 1/2 Ave S 58104
43 1/2 St N 58102
43 1/2 St S 58103
47 1/2 St S 58103

GRAND FORKS ND

General Delivery 58201

POST OFFICE BOXES MAIN OFFICE STATIONS AND BRANCHES

Box No.s
5001 - 6376 58206
12001 - 14972 58208

NAMED STREETS

Acorn Ct 58201
Adams Ave & Dr 58201
Air Cargo Dr 58203
Airport Ave NE 58203
Airport Dr
  2301-2399 58203
  2770-2810 58202
Airport Rd 58203
Allwood Ct 58201
Almonte Ave 58201
Alpha Ave 58203
Angela Dr 58201
Augusta Dr 58201
Austin Cir 58201
Autumn Ct 58201
Bacon Rd 58203
Balsam Cir 58201
Barley Ct 58201
Baron Blvd 58201
Beacon Cir 58201
Bek Hall 58202
Belmont Ct & Rd 58201
Berkley Dr 58203
Bethesda Cir 58201
Big Sky Cir 58203
Blackwood Ave 58201
Boyd Dr 58203
Brannon Hall 58202
Breezy Hills Cv 58201
Brenna Ave NE 58203
Broadway Blvd 58201
Brookshire Dr 58201
Bruce Ave 58201
Buffalo Ave 58203
Burbank 58201
Burdick Ct 58203
Burke Dr 58201
Burntwood Ct 58201
Cambridge St
  300-314 58202
  301-315 58203
  317-599 58203
Campbell Dr 58201
Campus Rd
  2800-3399 58202
  3401-4199 58202
  3600-3698 58203
  3612-4198 58202
Carleton Ct 58203
Cedar Cir 58201
Centennial Dr 58202
Center Ave 58203
Central Ct 58201
Central Plains Ct 58201
Charlie Ray Dr 58201
Charwood Ct 58201
Cherry St 58201
Cherry Lynn Dr 58201
Chestnut Pl & St 58201
Christian Ct & Dr 58201
Circle Dr E 58203
Circle Hills Dr 58201
Clearview Cir 58201
Clemetson St NE 58203
Cleo Ct 58201
Cleveland Ave 58201
Clover Dr 58201
Cole Creek Dr 58201
Columbia Ave NE 58201
Columbia Cir NE 58201
Columbia Ct 58203
N Columbia Rd 58203
S Columbia Rd 58201
Columbine Ct 58201
Conference Ctr 58202
Conklin Ave 58203
Continental Dr 58201
Copper Gate Dr 58203
Cornell St 58202
Cottonwood St 58201
Count Cir 58201
Countryside Ln 58201
Courtyard Dr 58201
Crescent Dr 58201
Crown Cv 58201
Cumberland Rd 58201
Curran Ct 58201
Cypress Point Dr 58201
Dacotah View Ct 58201
Daisy Cir 58201
Dakota Dr 58201
Dakota Hall 58202
Darwin Dr 58203
Davis Dr 58202
Dawn Cir 58203
Dellwood Ct 58201
Demers Ave
  200-298 58201
  300-3199 58201
  3201-3399 58201
  3500-3599 58202
  4301-4697 58201
  4699-8999 58201
  9001-9599 58201

Desert Star Ln 58201
Desiree Dr 58201
Division Ave 58201
Drees Dr 58201
Drews Dr 58201
Driftwood Dr 58201
Duke Dr 58201
Dyke Ave 58203
Earl Cir 58201
Edgewood Ct 58201
Elks Dr 58201
Ella Cir 58203
W Elm Ct 58203
E & W Elmwood Dr 58201
Emernera Ave N 58203
Estabrook Dr 58201
Evergreen Dr 58201
Fairview Dr 58201
W Fallcreek Ct 58201
Farmstead Dr 58201
Fenton Ave 58203
Filmore Ave 58203
Fountain Vista Dr 58201
Fox Farm Rd 58203
Franklin Ave 58201
Fulton Hall 58202
Gardenview Dr 58201
Garfield Ave 58201
Gateway Dr 58203
Gentle Hills Cir 58201
Gertrude Ave 58201
Glen Cir 58201
Glenwood Dr 58201
Golden Gate Dr 58203
Grassy Hills Ln 58201
Great Plains Ct 58201
Haleigh Dr 58201
W Hall 58202
Hamline St
300-599 58203
601-799 58203
750-800 58202
802-1198 58202
Hammerling Ave 58201
Hancock Hall 58202
Harrison Ave 58201
Harvard St
300-399 58202
500-599 58203
Harvest Cir 58201
High Plains Ct 58201
Highland Ct 58201
Hillcrest Ave 58201
Homestead Cir 58201
Hoover Ave 58201
Horizon Cir 58203
Hughes Ct 58201
Huntington Park Dr 58201
Inland Hills Ct 58201
Iron Gate Ct 58203
Ivy Dr 58201
Jackson St 58201
James Ray Dr
2500-4399 58202
4301-4399 58203
Jennie Ave 58203
Johnstone Hall 58202
Keystone Ct 58201
Kiana Ln 58203
Kimberly Ct 58201
King Cv & Pl 58201
Kings View Dr 58201
Kirkwood Dr 58201
Kittson Ave 58201
Knight Dr 58201
Knightsbridge Ct 58201
Kuster Cir & Ct 58201
E Lake Dr 58201
W Lanark Dr 58203
Landeco Ln 58201
Laraleas Ave S 58201
Lark Cir 58201
Lawndale Rd 58201
Leeward Hills Ln 58201
Legend Ln 58201
Letnes Dr 58201
Level Plains Cir 58201
Lewis Blvd 58203
Library Cir & Ln 58201
Lincoln Dr 58201
Linden Ct 58201
Lindsey Ln 58201
Loamy Hills Pl 58201
Lonesome Dove Dr 58203
Longbow Ct 58203
Lord Cir 58201
Lucke Ln E & W 58201
Lydia Cir 58201
Lynnbrook Ln 58201
Lynnwood Cir 58201
Mac Dr 58201
Mahlum Ct 58201
Manitoba Ave 58203
W Maple Ave 58203
Mckinley Ave 58201
Mcvey Hall 58202
Meadow Dr 58201
Meadow Brook Ct 58201
Mighty Acres Dr 58201
Mill Rd 58203
Minnesota Ave 58201
Mistwood Ct 58201
Monarch Ln 58201
Monroe Ave 58201
Morgan St 58201
Morning Dove Dr NE 58201
Mulberry Dr 58201
Mulholland Dr 58201
Mulligan St 58203
Noble Cv 58201
Norchip Cir 58201
Nordonna Cir 58201
Noren Hall 58202
Norkota Ct 58201
Norland Cir 58201
Northridge Hills Ct 58201
Northwestern Dr 58203
Oak St 58201
Oakfield Dr 58201
Oakwood Ave 58201
Odyssey Cir 58201
Olive St 58201
Olson Dr 58201
Omega Cir 58203
Orchard Cir 58201
Orchid Cir 58201
Oxbow Ct 58203
Oxford St
300-499 58202
500-599 58203
800-899 58202
Park Ave 58203
Park Dr 58201
Parkview Cir 58201
Patterson Ln 58201
Pembina Ct 58201
Pembrooke Dr 58201
Pendleton Dr 58201
Peyton Place Cir 58201
Phoenix Ct 58203
Pinehurst Ct & Dr 58201
S Pines Cir & Ct 58201
Pioneer Dr 58201
Plain Hills Dr 58201
W Plum Dr 58203
Poplar Cir 58201
Prairie Dr & Rd 58201
Prairie Rose Ct 58201
Prairieview Ct NE 58203
E & W Prairiewood Dr 58201
Primrose Ct 58201
Princeton St
301-319 58202
321-497 58203
499-599 58201
601-699 58203
800-899 58202
Promenade Ct 58203
Queens Ct 58201
Raboin Cir 58201
Raindale Ct 58201
Ralph Engelstad Arena Dr 58203
Red Dot Pl 58203
Reeves Ct & Dr 58201
Rider Rd 58201
Ridgewood Ln 58201
River St 58201
River Crest Cir & Rd 58201
River Oaks Cir 58201
Rivers Edge Dr 58201
N Riverside Dr 58203
Robert Cir 58201
Robertson Ct 58201
Robin Rd NE 58201
Rolling Hills Cir 58201
Royal Cir & Dr 58201
Ruemmele Rd 58201
Russet 58201
Rusty Ln NE 58201
Rylan Rd 58201
Sand Hills Ave 58201
Sandalwood Dr 58201
Sandy Hills Ln 58201
Sara Lyn Dr 58201
Schroeder Dr 58201
Seantans 58202
Selke Hall 58202
Selkirk Cir 58203
Seward Ave 58203
Shadow Rd 58201
Shady Ln 58201
Shadyridge Ct 58201
Shakespeare Rd 58203
Sheena Ct 58201
Sherwood Ln 58201
Silver Gate Dr 58203
Simonview Ct 58201
Skyview Cir 58201
Sleepy Hollow St 58201
Sloping Hills Cv 58201
Smith Hall 58202
W Springbrook Ct 58201
Spruce Ct 58201
Squires Hall 58202
Stadstad Ln 58203
Stanford Rd
301-497 58203
499-500 58203
502-1198 58203
525-599 58202
601-1399 58203
Star Ave S 58201
State St 58203
Summerset Ct 58201
Sun Cir 58201
Sunset Dr 58201
Swanson Hall 58202
Taft Ave 58201
Technology Cir 58203
Terrace Dr 58201
Times Square Ct 58201
Tulane Ct & Dr 58203
University Ave
400-498 58203
500-2500 58203
2502-2898 58203
2900-2909 58202
2911-3699 58202
2912-3698 58203
3700-3800 58203
3802-4398 58203
4101-4299 58202
5501-5599 58203
Us 2 58203
Vail Cir 58201
Valley Cir 58203
Victoria Ct 58201
Vineyard Cir & Dr 58201
Walnut Pl & St 58201
Walsh Hall 58202
N Washington St 58203
S Washington St 58201
Westminster Ct 58201
Westward Dr 58201
Wheatland Cir 58201
Whipperwill Ln 58203
Wilkerson Hall 58202
Willow Dr 58201
Windward Hills Ave 58201
Wintergreen Ct 58201
Wolf Cir 58201
Woodcrest Rd 58201
Woodland Ave NE 58203
Woodland Cir 58201
Yale Dr 58203

NUMBERED STREETS

1st Ave N 58203
1st Ave S 58201
N 1st St 58203
2nd Ave N 58203
2nd Ave N 58203
2500-2999 58202
2nd Ave S 58201
N 2nd St 58203
3rd Ave S 58201
N 3rd St 58203
S 3rd St 58201
4th Ave N 58203
4th Ave S 58201
N 4th St 58203
S 4th St 58201
5th Ave N 58203
5th Ave S 58201
N 5th St 58203
S 5th St 58201
6th Ave N 58203
6th Ave S 58201
N 6th St 58203
S 6th St 58201
7th Ave N 58203
7th Ave S 58201
N 7th St 58203
8th Ave N 58203
8th Ave S 58201
N 8th St 58203
9th Ave N 58203
9th Ave S 58201
N 9th St 58203
S 9th St 58201
10th Ave N 58203
10th Ave NE 58201
10th Ave S 58201
N 10th St 58203
S 10th St 58201
11th Ave N 58203
11th Ave NE 58201
11th Ave S 58201
11th St NE 58201
N 11th St 58203
S 11th St 58201
12th Ave N 58203
12th Ave NE 58201
12th Ave S 58201
12th St NE
1100-1198 58201
2300-2599 58203
N 12th St 58203
S 12th St 58201
13th Ave N 58203
13th Ave NE 58201
13th Ave S 58201
13th St NE 58201
14th Ave NE 58201
14th Ave S 58201
14th St NE 58201
N 14th St 58203
S 14th St 58201
15th Ave NE 58201
15th Ave S 58201
15th St NE 58201
N 15th St 58203
S 15th St 58201
16th Ave N 58203
16th Ave NE 58201
16th St NE
1000-1699 58201
1700-1799 58203
16th St SE 58201
N 16th St 58203
S 16th St 58201
16th Avenue Cir N 58203
17th Ave NE 58201
17th Ave S 58201
17th St NE
1000-1699 58201
1700-2399 58203
N 17th St 58203
S 17th St 58201
18th Ave S 58201
18th St NE
1100-1599 58201
1700-2399 58203
N 18th St 58203
S 18th St 58201
19th Ave S 58201
19th St NE
1100-1299 58201
1800-2399 58203
N 19th St 58203
S 19th St 58201
20th Ave NE 58203
20th Ave S 58201
20th St NE
1100-1199 58201
1900-2099 58203
N 20th St 58203
S 20th St 58201
21st Ave N 58203
21st Ave NE 58203
21st Ave S 58201
N 21st St 58203
S 21st St 58201
22nd Ave NE 58203
22nd Ave S 58201
N 22nd St 58203
S 22nd St 58201
23rd Ave NE 58203
23rd Ave S 58201
N 23rd St
1-99 58202
100-998 58203
1000-1100 58203
1102-1198 58203
S 23rd St 58201
24th Ave N 58203
24th Ave NE 58203
24th Ave S 58201
N 24th St 58203
S 24th St 58201
25th Ave NE 58203
25th Ave S 58201
N 25th St 58203
S 25th St 58201
26th Ave S 58201
N 26th St 58203
S 26th St 58201
27th Ave N 58203
27th Ave S 58201
28th Ave S
400-498 58201
500-2000 58201
2002-3498 58201
2501-2501 58206
2501-2501 58208
3401-3599 58201
S 29th Ave & St S 58201
30th Ave S 58201
N 30th St 58203
S 30th St 58201
S 31st St 58201
32nd Ave S 58201
S 34th Ave & St S 58201
S 35th St 58201
36th Ave S 58201
N 36th St 58203
S 36th St 58201
S 38th Ave & St S 58201
39th Ave S 58201
N 39th St 58203
40th Ave N 58203
40th Ave S 58201
N 40th St 58203
S 40th St 58201
41st Ave S 58201
42nd Ave S 58201
N 42nd St 58203
S 42nd St 58201
43rd Ave S 58201
43rd St 58202
N 43rd St 58203
S 43rd St 58201
44th Ave S 58201
N 44th St 58203
45th Ave S 58201
N 45th St 58203
46th Ave N 58203
46th Ave S 58201
S 46th St 58201
47th Ave S 58201
N 47th St 58203
S 47th St 58201
48th Ave S 58201
N 48th St 58203
S 48th St 58201
49th Ave S 58201
N 49th St 58203
N 50th St 58203
N 51st St 58203
52nd Ave S 58201
N 52nd St 58203
S 52nd St 58201
N 53rd St 58203
54th Ave N 58203
55th Ave S 58201
N 55th St 58203
S 55th St 58201
62nd Ave S 58201
62nd Ave SE 58201
N 62nd St 58203
65th Ave N 58203
69th Ave S 58201
N 69th St 58203
S 69th St 58201
70th Ave N 58203
72nd Ave N 58203
73rd Ave S 58201
N 73rd St 58203
74th Ave N 58203
74th Ave S 58201
78th Ave N 58203
79th Ave N 58203
N 83rd St 58203
S 83rd St 58201
84th Ave N 58203
N 84th St 58203
S 84th St 58201
N 86th St 58203
S 93rd St 58201

GRAND FORKS AFB ND

POST OFFICE BOXES MAIN OFFICE STATIONS AND BRANCHES

Box No.s
All PO Boxes 58204

NAMED STREETS

Alert Ave 58205
Ash Ave 58204
B St 58205
Beech Dr 58204
Birch Ave 58204
Cedar Ave 58204
Chenerai Dr 58204
Dogwood Dr 58204
Eielson St 58205
F St 58205
Fir Ave 58204
G St 58205
Gumwood Ave 58204
H St 58205
Hawaii St 58204
Hemlock Rd 58204
Hickam Dr 58204
Holly Dr 58204
Holzapple St
500-598 58204
501-575 58205
589-599 58204
600-699 58205
I St
1801-1849 58205
1808-1848 58204
1850-1999 58204
Indiana St 58204
Iowa St 58204
J St
1501-1707 58205
1711-1899 58204
Juniper Ave 58204
Kentucky St 58204
Korina Ave 58204
Langley Ave 58204
Lilac Ct 58204
Louisana St 58205
Louisiana St 58204
Lox Ave 58205
Malmstrom St 58205
Maxwell Ave 58204
Missouri St 58204
Montana St 58204
Nevada Dr 58204
New Jersey St 58204
Oregon St 58204
Poplar Ave 58204
Psc Box 58205
Randolph Ave 58204
Range Rd 58205
Red Oak Ave 58204
Redwood Ave 58205
Redwood Dr 58204
Spruce Dr 58204
Steen Ave
1-100 58205
101-199 58204
102-698 58205
201-699 58205
Sycamore Dr 58204
Teak Ave 58204
Tower Ave 58205
Winchean Ave 58205

NUMBERED STREETS

All Street Addresses 58205

JAMESTOWN ND

General Delivery 58401

POST OFFICE BOXES MAIN OFFICE STATIONS AND BRANCHES

Box No.s
All PO Boxes 58402

NAMED STREETS

All Street Addresses 58401

NUMBERED STREETS

1st Ave N 58401
1st St N 58401
2nd Ave N 58401
2nd Ave NE 58401
2nd Ave NW 58401
2nd Ave S 58401
2nd Ave SE 58401
2nd Ave SW 58401
2nd Pl NE 58401
2nd St NE 58401
2nd St NW 58401
2nd St SE 58401

2nd St SW
100-199 58401
212-212 58402
300-1698 58401
N 2nd St N 58401
S 2nd St S 58401
2nd Street A SW 58401
3rd Ave & St NE, NW, SE & SW 58401
3rd Ave & St NE, NW, SE & SW 58401
4th Ave & St NE, NW, SE & SW 58401
5 1/2 Ave NE 58401
5th Ave & St NE, NW, SE & SW 58401
6th Ave & St NE, NW, SE & SW 58401
7th Ave, Pl & St NE, NW, SE & SW 58401
8th Ave & St NE, NW, SE & SW 58401
9th Ave & St NE, NW, SE & SW 58401
10th Ave & St NE, NW, SE & SW 58401
11th Ave & St NE, SE, SW & NW 58401
12th Ave & St NE, SE, SW & NW 58401
13th Ave & St NE, SE, SW & NW 58401
14th Ave & St NE, NW, SE & SW 58401
15th Ave & St NE, SE, SW & NW 58401
16th Ave & St NE, SE, SW & NW 58401
17th Ave & St NE, SW, NW & SE 58401
18th Ave & St NE, SE, NW & SW 58401
19th Ave & St NE, NW & SW 58401
20th Ave & St 58401
21st Ave & St NE & SW 58401
22nd Ave NE 58401
23rd Ave & St NE & SW 58401
24th Ave & St 58401
25th Ave & St 58401
26th Ave & St 58401
27th Ave & St 58401
28th St SE 58401
29th St SE 58401
30th St SE 58401
31st St SE 58401
32nd St SE 58401
33rd St SE 58401
34th NW & SE 58401
35th St SE 58401
36th St SE 58401
37th St SE 58401
38th NW & SE 58401
39th St SE 58401
40th St SE 58401
41st NW & SE 58401
42nd St SE 58401
43rd St SE 58401
44th St SE 58401
45th NW & SE 58401
46th St SE 58401
47th NW & SE 58401
48th St NW 58401
68th Ave SE 58401
69th Ave SE 58401
70th Ave SE 58401
71st Ave SE 58401
72nd Ave SE 58401
73rd Ave SE 58401
74th Ave SE 58401
75th Ave SE 58401
76th Ave SE 58401
77th Ave SE 58401
78th Ave SE 58401
79th Ave SE 58401
80th Ave SE 58401
81st Ave SE 58401
82nd Ave SE 58401
84th Ave SE 58401
85th Ave SE 58401
86th Ave SE 58401
87th Ave SE 58401
88th Ave SE 58401
89th Ave SE 58401
90th Ave SE 58401
91st Ave SE 58401
92nd Ave SE 58401
94th Ave SE 58401
95th Ave SE 58401
15 1/2 Ave SW 58401
16 1/2 St NE 58401
31 1/2 St SE 58401
34 1/2 St SE 58401
76 1/2 Ave SE 58401
83 1/2 Ave SE 58401
86 1/2 Ave SE 58401

MINOT ND

General Delivery 58701

POST OFFICE BOXES MAIN OFFICE STATIONS AND BRANCHES

Box No.s
All PO Boxes 58702

NAMED STREETS

A Ave SW 58701
Academy Rd 58703
Adams Ave 58701
Airport Rd 58703
Airview Dr 58701
Anderson Dr 58703
Appaloosa Way NE 58703
Apple Way 58701
Arbor Ave 58701
Arthur Ln 58701
Ashland Ct 58701
Aspen Cir SW 58701
Aster Loop 58701
Bavaria Dr 58703
Beacon St 58701
Beaver Creek Rd 58701
Bel Air Ct, Dr & Pl 58703
Belview Dr 58701
Birch Pl SW 58701
Blake Rd 58703
Blue Bell Dr 58701
N Broadway 58703
S Broadway 58701
Brookside Dr 58701
Buchanan Blvd 58701
Buckskin Dr NE 58703
Burdick Expy E & W ... 58701
Buttercup Ln 58701
California Dr 58703
Cedon Dr 58703
Centennial St 58701
E & W Central Ave 58701
Cherry Dr 58701
Chestnut Cir NE 58703
Clarke Dr 58701
Colton St 58701
Coneflower Dr 58701
Cook Dr 58701
Coolidge Ave 58701
Cortland Dr 58703
Cottonwood Ave 58701
County Road 12 W 58701
County Road 15 W 58703
County Road 17 W 58701
County Road 19 S 58701
Crescent Dr 58703
Crocus Pt 58701
Dakota Dr SW 58701
Dakota Ridge Rd S 58701
Debbie Dr 58701
Debra Ct 58703
Dell Way 58701
Delmar Ct 58703
Dogwood Dr 58701
Donna Dr 58701
Eisenhower Dr 58701
El Rio Dr 58701
Elk Dr 58701
Elmwood Dr 58701
Evergreen Ave SW 58701
Fair Way 58701
Fillmore St 58701
Foothills Rd SW 58701
Forest Rd 58701
Foxtail Dr SE 58701
Galmac Dr 58701
Glacial Ct, Dr & Pt 58703
Gold Ct 58703
Golden Valley Ln 58703
Green Way 58701
Grey Eagle Pass 58703
Harmony Ct & St NW .. 58703
Harrison Dr 58703
Heritage Ct & Dr 58703
Hiawatha St 58701
Highland Dr 58703
Highview Ave NW 58703
Highway 2 Byp 58701
Highway 2 And 52 W
1800-2698 58701
2700-5400 58701
5402-5698 58701
6200-6899 58703
6901-7199 58703
Highway 52 S 58701
Highway 83 N 58703
Highway 83 S 58701
Hillcrest Dr 58703
Hilltop St NW 58703
Holbach Way 58701
Homestead Rd NW 58703
Ida Mae Ct 58703
Irma Ct 58703
Jefferson Dr 58701
Juniper Ct 58701
Kintrin St NW 58703
Lake St 58703
Lakeside St 58703
Landmark Cir & Dr 58703
Larson Ln 58701
Laurel Ln 58703
Lincoln Ave 58703
Main St N 58703
Main St S
2-4099 58701
2800-2898 58701
Maple St 58701
Meadowlark Dr 58701
Misty Glen Ln 58703
Moraine Pt 58703
Mount Curve Ave 58701
Mulberry Loop 58703
Mustang Trl NE 58703
Normal St 58703
Northwest Ave 58703
Oak Dr 58701
Olive Tree Cir 58703
Palomino Rd NE 58703
Park St & Way 58701
Parkside Dr 58703
Partridge Dr NE 58703
Pasadena 58701
Quail St NE 58703
Railway Ave 58703
Ramstad Ave 58701
Rebba Dr 58701
Rivers Edge Dr SE 58701
Riverside Dr 58701
Roberts St 58703
Rolling Hills Dr 58703
Ruyak Pt 58703
Sadie Ln 58701
Sage Dr 58701
Saint Peter Ave 58701
Sedona Ct SE 58701
Shirley Ct 58703
Skyline Dr 58703
Soo St 58701
Souris Ct & Dr 58701
Southwood Ln SE 58701
Springfield Ave 58703
Spruce Ln 58701
Summit Dr 58701
Sundown Dr 58701
Sunrise Ct SE 58701
Sunset Blvd 58703
Sunset Ridge Rd SE ... 58701
Sycamore Ave SE 58701
Tammy Dr 58701
Terrace Ct & Dr 58703
Timber Trl SE 58701
Timberwood Ave SE 58701
Timmothy Dr 58703
Tumbleweed Rd NW ... 58703
Tuttle Ave SE 58701
Tuxedo Rd 58703
Unity Dr SE 58701
University Ave E & W .. 58703
Valley St 58701
Valley View Dr 58703
Vie St 58701
Village Ave SE 58701
Vista Dr 58703
Walders St 58703
Wendy Way SE 58701
Western Ave 58701
Westfield Ave & Cir 58701
Wildwood Ave 58703
Willow Ln SE 58701
Woodside Cir & Dr 58701
Zaharia Dr SE 58701
Zander St 58701

NUMBERED STREETS

1st Ave NE 58703
1st Ave NW 58703
1st Ave SE 58701
1st Ave SW 58701
1st St NE 58703
1st St NW 58703
1st St SE 58701
1st St SW 58701
2nd Ave NE 58703
2nd Ave NW 58703
2nd Ave SE 58701
2nd Ave SW 58701
2nd St NE 58703
2nd St NW 58703
2nd St SE 58701
2nd St SW 58701
3rd Ave NE 58703
3rd Ave NW 58703
3rd Ave SE 58701
3rd Ave SW 58701
3rd St NE 58703
3rd St NW 58703
3rd St SE 58701
3rd St SW 58701
4th Ave NE 58703
4th Ave NW 58703
4th Ave SE 58701
4th Ave SW 58701
4th St NE 58703
4th St NW 58703
4th St SE 58701
4th St SW 58701
5th Ave NE 58703
5th Ave NW 58703
5th Ave SE 58701
5th Ave SW
101-117 58701
117-117 58702
421-427 58701
5th St NE 58703
5th St NW 58703
5th St SE 58701
5th St SW 58701
6th Ave NE 58703
6th Ave NW 58703
6th Ave SE 58701
6th Ave SW 58701
6th St NE 58703
6th St NW 58703
6th St SE 58701
6th St SW 58701
7th Ave NE 58703
7th Ave NW 58703
7th Ave SE 58701
7th Ave SW 58701
7th St NE 58703
7th St NW 58703
7th St SE 58701
7th St SW 58701
8th Ave NE 58703
8th Ave NW 58703
8th Ave SE 58701
8th Ave SW 58701
8th St NE 58703
8th St NW 58703
8th St SE 58701
8th St SW 58701
9th Ave NE 58703
9th Ave NW 58703
9th Ave SE 58701
9th Ave SW 58701
9th St NE 58703
9th St NW 58703
9th St SE 58701
9th St SW 58701
10th Ave NE 58703
10th Ave NW 58703
10th Ave SE 58701
10th Ave SW 58701
10th St NE 58703
10th St NW 58703
10th St SE 58701
10th St SW 58701
11th Ave NE 58703
11th Ave NW 58703
11th Ave SE 58701
11th Ave SW 58701
11th St NE 58703
11th St NW 58703
11th St SE 58701
11th St SW 58701
12th Ave NE 58703
12th Ave NW 58703
12th Ave SE 58701
12th Ave SW 58701
12th St NE 58703
12th St NW 58703
12th St SE 58701
12th St SW 58701
13th Ave NE 58703
13th Ave NW 58703
13th Ave SE 58701
13th Ave SW 58701
13th St NE 58703
13th St NW 58703
13th St SE 58701
13th St SW 58701
14th Ave NW 58703
14th Ave SE 58701
14th Ave SW 58701
14th St NE 58703
14th St NW 58703
14th St SE 58701
14th St SW 58701
15th Ave NE 58703
15th Ave NW 58703
15th Ave SE 58701
15th Ave SW 58701
15th Ct 58701
15th St NW 58703
15th St SE 58701
15th St SW 58701
16th Ave NE 58703
16th Ave NW 58703
16th Ave SE 58701
16th Ave SW 58701
16th St NW 58703
16th St SE 58701
16th St SW 58701
17th Ave NE 58703
17th Ave NW 58703
17th Ave SE 58701
17th Ave SW 58701
17th St NW 58703
17th St SE 58701
17th St SW 58701
18th Ave NE 58703
18th Ave NW 58703
18th Ave SE 58701
18th Ave SW 58701
18th St NW 58703
18th St SE 58701
18th St SW 58701
19th Ave NE 58703
19th Ave NW 58703
19th Ave SE 58701
19th Ave SW 58701
19th St NW 58703
19th St SE 58701
19th St SW 58701
20th Ave NW 58703
20th Ave SE 58701
20th Ave SW 58701
20th St NW 58703
20th St SE 58701
20th St SW 58701
21st Ave NW 58703
21st Ave SE 58701
21st Ave SW 58701
21st St NW 58703
21st St SE 58701
21st St SW 58701
22nd Ave NW 58703
22nd Ave SE 58701
22nd Ave SW 58701
22nd St NW 58703
22nd St SE 58701
22nd St SW 58701
23rd Ave NW 58703
23rd Ave SE 58701
23rd Ave SW 58701
23rd St NW 58703
23rd St SW 58701
24th Ave NW 58703
24th Ave SE 58701
24th Ave SW 58701
24th St NW 58703
24th St SE 58701
24th St SW 58701
25th Ave NW 58703
25th Pl NW 58703
25th St NW 58703
25th St SE 58701
25th St SW 58701
26th Ave NW 58703
26th Ave SW 58701
26th St NW 58703
26th St SW 58701
27th Ave NW 58703
27th Ave SE 58701
27th Ct NW 58703
27th St NE 58703
27th St NW 58703
27th St SE 58701
27th St SW 58701
28th Ave SE 58701
28th Ave SW 58701
28th St NW 58703
28th St SW 58701
29th SE & SW 58701
30th Ave NE 58703
30th Ave NW 58703
30th Ave SE 58701
30th St NW 58703
30th St SW 58701
31st Ave NW 58703
31st Ave SE 58701
31st Ave SW 58701
31st St SE 58701
31st St SW 58701
32nd SE & SW 58701
33rd Ave SE 58701
33rd Ave SW 58701
33rd Ct SE 58701
33rd St NW 58703
33rd St SW 58701
34th Ave NE 58703
34th Ave SE 58701
34th Ave SW 58701
34th St SW 58701
35th Ave NE 58703
35th Ave NW 58703
35th Ave SE 58701
35th Ave SW 58701
35th St NW 58703
35th St SE 58701
35th St SW 58701
36th Ave NE 58703
36th Ave NW 58703
36th Ave SE 58701
36th St SE 58701
36th St SW 58701
37th Ave & St SE & SW 58701
38th Ave NW 58703
38th St SE 58701
38th St SW 58701
39th Ave NE 58703
39th Ave SE 58701
39th Ave SW 58701
39th St SE 58701
40th Ave NE 58703
40th Ave NW 58703
40th Ave SW 58701
40th St SE 58701
41st Ave SE 58701
41st Ave SW 58701
41st St NW 58703
41st St SE 58701
42nd St NE 58703
42nd St SE 58701
43rd Ave & St 58701
44th Ave SW 58701
44th St NE 58703
44th St SE 58701
45th Ave & St 58701
46th Ave NE 58703
46th Ave NW 58703
46th St NW 58703
46th St SE 58701
46th St SW 58701
47th Ave, Loop & St ... 58701
48th St NW 58703
48th St SE 58701
49th St SE 58701
50th Ave SE 58701
50th St NW 58703
50th St SE 58701
50th St SW 58701
51st Ave & St 58701
52nd Ave & St SW & SE 58701
53rd Ave NE 58703
53rd Ave SW 58701
53rd St SE 58701
54th Ave NE 58703
54th Ave NW 58703
54th Ave SE 58701
54th Ave SW 58701
54th St NW 58703
54th St SE 58701
54th St SW 58701
55th Ave SE 58701
55th Ave SW 58701
55th St NE 58703
55th St SE 58701
56th St NW 58703
57th St NW 58703
58th Ave NW 58703
58th St SE 58701
58th St SW 58701
59th Ave & St SW & SE 58701
60th Ave NW 58703
60th Ave SE 58701
61st Ave & St SE & SW 58701
62nd Ave NE 58703
62nd Ave NW 58703
62nd St NW 58703
62nd St SE 58701

62nd St SW 58701
63rd Ave NE 58703
63rd St NW 58703
63rd St SE 58701
64th Ave NE 58703
64th St NW 58703
64th St SE 58701
65th St NW 58703
66th Ave SE 58701
66th Ave SW 58701
66th St NW 58703
67th St NW 58703
68th St NW 58703
69th St NW 58703
70th St SE 58701
72nd Ave NE 58703
72nd St NE 58703
72nd St NW 58703
72nd St SE 58701
72nd St SW 58701
73rd St NW 58703
73rd St SE 58701
74th St NW 58703
74th St SE 58701
75th St NW 58703
78th St SE 58701
79th SE & SW 58701
80th St SE 58701
82nd Ave SE 58701
83rd Ave SE 58701
84th Ave SE 58701
86th Ave NE 58703
86th St NE 58703
86th St NW 58703
86th St SE 58701
86th St SW 58701
89th St SE 58701
91st St SE 58701
93rd Ave & St 58701
94th St SE 58701
97th St NE 58703
97th St SE 58701
100th Ave NE 58703
100th Ave NW 58703
100th St SW 58701
104th St SE 58701
107th SE & SW 58701
11 1/2 Ave SW 58701
111th Ave & St 58701
114th NE & NW 58703
12 1/2 St SW 58701
121st SE & SW 58701
125th St SE 58701
128th Ave NW 58703
13 1/2 St SW 58701
135th SE & SW 58701
14 1/2 Ave SW 58701
142nd Ave NW 58703
142nd St SW 58701
149th Ave SW 58701
15 1/2 Ave & St 58701
156th Ave NW 58703
163rd SE & SW 58701
17 1/2 Ave SW 58701
170th Ave NW 58703
177th SE & SW 58701
18 1/2 Ave SW 58701
191st Ave SW 58701
25 1/2 Ave NW 58703
26 1/2 Ave NW 58703
N 83 Byp 58703

MINOT AFB ND

NAMED STREETS

Arrowhead Dr 58704
Avion Way 58704
B St 58704
Bomber Blvd 58705
Carlton Ct 58704
Chevy Chase 58704
Coral Ct 58704
Dakota Ct 58704
Dauphin Dr 58704
Delmar Ct 58704
Delta Dr 58704
Dorm 58705
Dundee Dr 58704
E St 58704
Eagle Way 58704
Firing Ln 58704
Garistan 58705
Glacier Dr 58704
Glencoe Ln 58704
Gramercy Ct 58704
H St 58704
Hampton Loop 58704
Huey Ln 58704
Indian Rock Cir 58704
Lamearal Dr 58704
Landing Ct 58704
Largo Ln 58704
Lariat Ln 58704
Lilac Ln 58704
Linden Ct & Loop 58704
Locke Ln 58704
Mallard Trl 58704
Missile Ave 58705
Peacekeeper Pl 58704
Pembrook Ln 58704
Polar Pl 58704
Prairie Pl 58704
Psc Box 58705
Raintree Cir 58704
Roaming Rd 58704
Rocket Rd 58704
Rockridge Cir 58704
Shawnee Rd 58704
Sherwood Cir 58704
Siesta Dr 58704
Singletree Cir 58704
Sirocco Dr 58704
Spruce St 58704
Sumerset Ln 58704
Summit Dr
100-199 58704
200-599 58705
Sunset Loop 58704
Tangley Ct & Rd 58704
Waverly Way 58704
Wedgewood Cir 58704
Winding Way 58704

WAHPETON ND

General Delivery 58075

POST OFFICE BOXES MAIN OFFICE STATIONS AND BRANCHES

Box No.s
All PO Boxes 58074

NAMED STREETS

All Street Addresses 58075

NUMBERED STREETS

All Street Addresses 58075

WILLISTON ND

General Delivery 58801

POST OFFICE BOXES MAIN OFFICE STATIONS AND BRANCHES

Box No.s
D - K 58802
1 - 6715 58802
7001 - 8498 58803
9000 - 9001 58802
10001 - 12241 58803

NAMED STREETS

Airport Rd 58801
Andong Ave W 58801
Angelica Ave 58801
Anna Ave 58801
Antelope Dr 58801
Aspen Loop 58801
Ave R 58801
Baldwin Ln 58801
Bennett Loop 58801
Bennett Industrial Dr 58801
Bergstrom Dr 58801
Bison Dr 58801
Blacktail Dr 58801
Border Ave 58801
Box Elder St 58801
Bradford Ct 58801
Brigham Dr 58801
E Broadway
1-99 58801
101-1399 58801
120-2198 58801
120-120 58802
W Broadway 58801
Buffalo Ridge Dr 58801
Carolville Loop 58801
Cartright Loop NW 58801
Chokecherry St 58801
Clearwater Ln 58801
Cochise St 58801
Commercial Dr 58801
Coteau St 58801
Cottonwood St 58801
Country Ln 58801
Creekside Dr W 58801
Crest St 58801
E & W Dakota Pkwy 58801
Darby Ln 58801
Davidson Dr 58801
Depot Ln 58801
Derrick Ave 58801
Dublin Ln 58801
Emily St 58801
Energy St 58801
Everson Dr 58801
Fairview Dr 58801
Ferndale Blvd 58801
Freedom Ln 58801
Freshwater Ln 58801
W Front St 58801
Gate Ave 58801
Golden Vista Ave 58801
Grandview Dr 58801
Hamilton Ln 58801
Harvest Hills Ave & Dr 58801
E & W Highland Dr 58801
Highway 1804 58801
Highway 2 58801
Highway 327 58801
Highway 85 58801
E Hillcourt 58801
Hillside Ct 58801
Independence St 58801
Izabella Ave 58801
Jackson Pl & St 58801
James Dr 58801
Janella St 58801
Janica St 58801
Jefferson Ln 58801
Julia Ave 58801
Karen St 58801
Kings View Ln 58801
Knoll St 58801
Kristina St 58801
Lake View Dr & Loop 58801
Laurice Ave 58801
Leah Ave 58801
Liberty Ln 58801
Linda Ln 58801
Long Branch Ave 58801
Loves Way 58801
Lukenbill Ave 58801
Madison Ln & Rdg 58801
Madison Industrial Dr 58801
N & S Main Ct & St 58801
Martinez Loop 58801
Mathew Ave 58801
Mila St 58801
Mortenson St 58801
Mountain Meadow Ln 58801
Muddy Valley Dr & Loop 58801
Natasha Ave 58801
Nicholas Ave 58801
Niehenke St 58801
Oil Ave 58801
Orange Willow St 58801
Owan Industrial Park Dr 58801
Painted Woods Dr 58801
Park Pl 58801
Parkway Dr 58801
Patriot Ln 58801
Petroleum Park Dr 58801
Pheasant Run Pkwy 58801
Pierce St 58801
Prairie Ln 58801
Prairie Commons St 58801
Prairie Meadow St 58801
Reclamation Dr 58801
Reiger Dr 58801
Ridge Ct & Dr 58801
Riverside Dr 58801
Rocky Wagon St 58801
Rose Ln 58801
Round Prairie Ave 58801
Sand Creek Dr 58801
Sarah Jane St NW 58801
Sherman Ln 58801
Sioux St 58801
Skyway Ct 58801
Sleepy Ridge Ave 58801
Snowy Water Ln NW 58801
Sophia St 58801
Southview Dr, Ln & St 58801
Spring Creek Dr 58801
Stoneview Ave 58801
Sunrise Dr 58801
Sunset Blvd St 58801
Sweet Clover Ln 58801
Tanya St 58801
Timbers St W 58801
Town And Country North Ct 58801
Town And Country South Ct 58801
Tyler St 58801
University Ave N 58801
Valley View Dr 58801
Vanessa Ave 58801
Victoria Ave 58801
Washington Ave 58801
Well St 58801
Western Way 58801
Wheat Ridge St 58801
Whitetail Cir 58801
Wyat St 58801
Yellowstone Meadow Ln 58801

NUMBERED STREETS

1st Ave & St E & W 58801
2nd Ave & St E & W 58801
2nd Avenue Cir E 58801
3rd E & W 58801
4th Ave & St E & W 58801
5th Ave & St 58801
6th Ave & St E, NW & W 58801
7th Ave & St E & W 58801
8th Ave & St E & W 58801
9th Ave E 58801
9th Ave NW 58801
9th Ave W
201-297 58801
299-2099 58801
2101-4315 58801
4315-4315 58803
9th St E 58801
9th St W 58801
10th Ave & St 58801
11th Ave & St E & W 58801
12th Ave & St 58801
13th Ave & St E & W 58801
14th Ave & St E & W 58801
15th Ave & St 58801
16th Ave, Ct & St E & W 58801
17th Ave, Cir, Ct & St E & W 58801
18th Ave, Cir, Ct & St E & W 58801
19th Ave & St 58801
20th Ave & St E & W 58801
21st Ave & St 58801
22nd Ave & St NE, W & E 58801
23rd Ct, St & Ter E & W 58801
24th Ave, Ct & St NE, W & E 58801
25th Ave, Cir, Ct & St E & W 58801
26th Ave & St NE, W & E 58801
27th Ave & St 58801
28th St W 58801
29th Ave & St 58801
30th E & W 58801
31st St W 58801
32nd Ave & St 58801
33rd St & Ter 58801
34th Pl & St 58801
35th Ave, Pl, St & Ter E & W 58801
36th Pl, St & Ter E & W 58801
37th Pl, St & Ter 58801
38th E & W 58801
39th Cir & Ln 58801
40th E & NW 58801
42nd St E 58801
43rd St NW 58801
44th Ln & St NW & W 58801
45th NW & W 58801
46th NW & W 58801
47th Ln & St 58801
48t Way NW 58801
48th NW & W 58801
49t Way NW 58801
49th Ln, Rd & St NW, E & W 58801
50t Way 58801
50th Dr, Ln, St & Way NW & W 58801
51st St NW 58801
52nd St NW 58801
53rd Ln & St NW, E & W 58801
54th St NW 58801
55th St NW 58801
56th St NW 58801
57j Loop NW 58801
57th St NW 58801
58th Ave & St NW, E & W 58801
59th St NW 58801
60th St NW 58801
61st St NW 58801
62nd St NW 58801
63rd St NW 58801
64th St NW 58801
65th E & NW 58801
66th E & NW 58801
67th St NW 58801
68th E & NW 58801
69th E & NW 58801
70th St E 58801
72nd St E 58801
73rd St E 58801
74th St E 58801
75th St E 58801
124th Ave NW 58801
125th Ave NW 58801
127th Ave NW 58801
128th Ave NW 58801
129th Ave NW 58801
130th Ave & Rd 58801
131st Ave NW 58801
132nd Ave, Dr, Ln, Rd & Trl NW 58801
133rd Ave, Dr & Ln 58801
134th Ave & Dr 58801
135th Ave NW 58801
137th Ave & Ln 58801
138th Ave NW 58801
139th Ave & Ln 58801
140th Ave NW 58801
141st Ave NW 58801
141t Ln 58801
142nd Ave & Dr 58801
143rd Ave NW 58801
144th Ave NW 58801
145th Ave & Dr 58801
146th Ave & Dr 58801
146m Ln NW 58801
147th Ave & Rd 58801
148th Ave NW 58801
149th Ave NW 58801
150th Ave NW 58801
151st Ave NW 58801
152nd Ave NW 58801
153rd Ave NW 58801
154th Ave NW 58801
155th Ave NW 58801
53 S Way NW 58801

Ohio

People QuickFacts	Ohio	USA
Population, 2013 estimate	11,570,808	316,128,839
Population, 2010 (April 1) estimates base	11,536,503	308,747,716
Population, percent change, April 1, 2010 to July 1, 2013	0.3%	2.4%
Population, 2010	11,536,504	308,745,538
Persons under 5 years, percent, 2013	6.0%	6.3%
Persons under 18 years, percent, 2013	22.9%	23.3%
Persons 65 years and over, percent, 2013	15.1%	14.1%
Female persons, percent, 2013	51.1%	50.8%
White alone, percent, 2013 (a)	83.2%	77.7%
Black or African American alone, percent, 2013 (a)	12.5%	13.2%
American Indian and Alaska Native alone, percent, 2013 (a)	0.3%	1.2%
Asian alone, percent, 2013 (a)	1.9%	5.3%
Native Hawaiian and Other Pacific Islander alone, percent, 2013 (a)	Z	0.2%
Two or More Races, percent, 2013	2.0%	2.4%
Hispanic or Latino, percent, 2013 (b)	3.4%	17.1%
White alone, not Hispanic or Latino, percent, 2013	80.5%	62.6%
Living in same house 1 year & over, percent, 2008-2012	85.4%	84.8%
Foreign born persons, percent, 2008-2012	3.9%	12.9%
Language other than English spoken at home, pct age 5+, 2008-2012	6.6%	20.5%
High school graduate or higher, percent of persons age 25+, 2008-2012	88.2%	85.7%
Bachelor's degree or higher, percent of persons age 25+, 2008-2012	24.7%	28.5%
Veterans, 2008-2012	893,168	21,853,912
Mean travel time to work (minutes), workers age 16+, 2008-2012	23	25.4
Housing units, 2013	5,123,997	132,802,859
Homeownership rate, 2008-2012	68.0%	65.5%
Housing units in multi-unit structures, percent, 2008-2012	22.9%	25.9%
Median value of owner-occupied housing units, 2008-2012	$133,700	$181,400
Households, 2008-2012	4,555,709	115,226,802
Persons per household, 2008-2012	2.46	2.61
Per capita money income in past 12 months (2012 dollars), 2008-2012	$25,857	$28,051
Median household income, 2008-2012	$48,246	$53,046
Persons below poverty level, percent, 2008-2012	15.4%	14.9%

Business QuickFacts	Ohio	USA
Private nonfarm establishments, 2012	250,842	7,431,808
Private nonfarm employment, 2012	4,548,143	115,938,468
Private nonfarm employment, percent change, 2011-2012	2.6%	2.2%
Nonemployer establishments, 2012	743,915	22,735,915
Total number of firms, 2007	897,939	27,092,908
Black-owned firms, percent, 2007	5.8%	7.1%
American Indian- and Alaska Native-owned firms, percent, 2007	0.3%	0.9%
Asian-owned firms, percent, 2007	2.0%	5.7%
Native Hawaiian and Other Pacific Islander-owned firms, percent, 2007	S	0.1%
Hispanic-owned firms, percent, 2007	1.1%	8.3%
Women-owned firms, percent, 2007	27.7%	28.8%
Manufacturers shipments, 2007 ($1000)	295,890,890	5,319,456,312
Merchant wholesaler sales, 2007 ($1000)	135,575,279	4,174,286,516
Retail sales, 2007 ($1000)	138,816,008	3,917,663,456
Retail sales per capita, 2007	$12,049	$12,990
Accommodation and food services sales, 2007 ($1000)	17,779,905	613,795,732
Building permits, 2012	16,905	829,658

Geography QuickFacts	Ohio	USA
Land area in square miles, 2010	40,860.69	3,531,905.43
Persons per square mile, 2010	282.3	87.4
FIPS Code	39	

(a) Includes persons reporting only one race.
(b) Hispanics may be of any race, so also are included in applicable race categories.
FN: Footnote on this item for this area in place of data
NA: Not available
D: Suppressed to avoid disclosure of confidential information
X: Not applicable
S: Suppressed; does not meet publication standards
Z: Value greater than zero but less than half unit of measure shown
F: Fewer than 100 firms
Source: US Census Bureau State & County QuickFacts

3 DIGIT ZIP CODE MAP

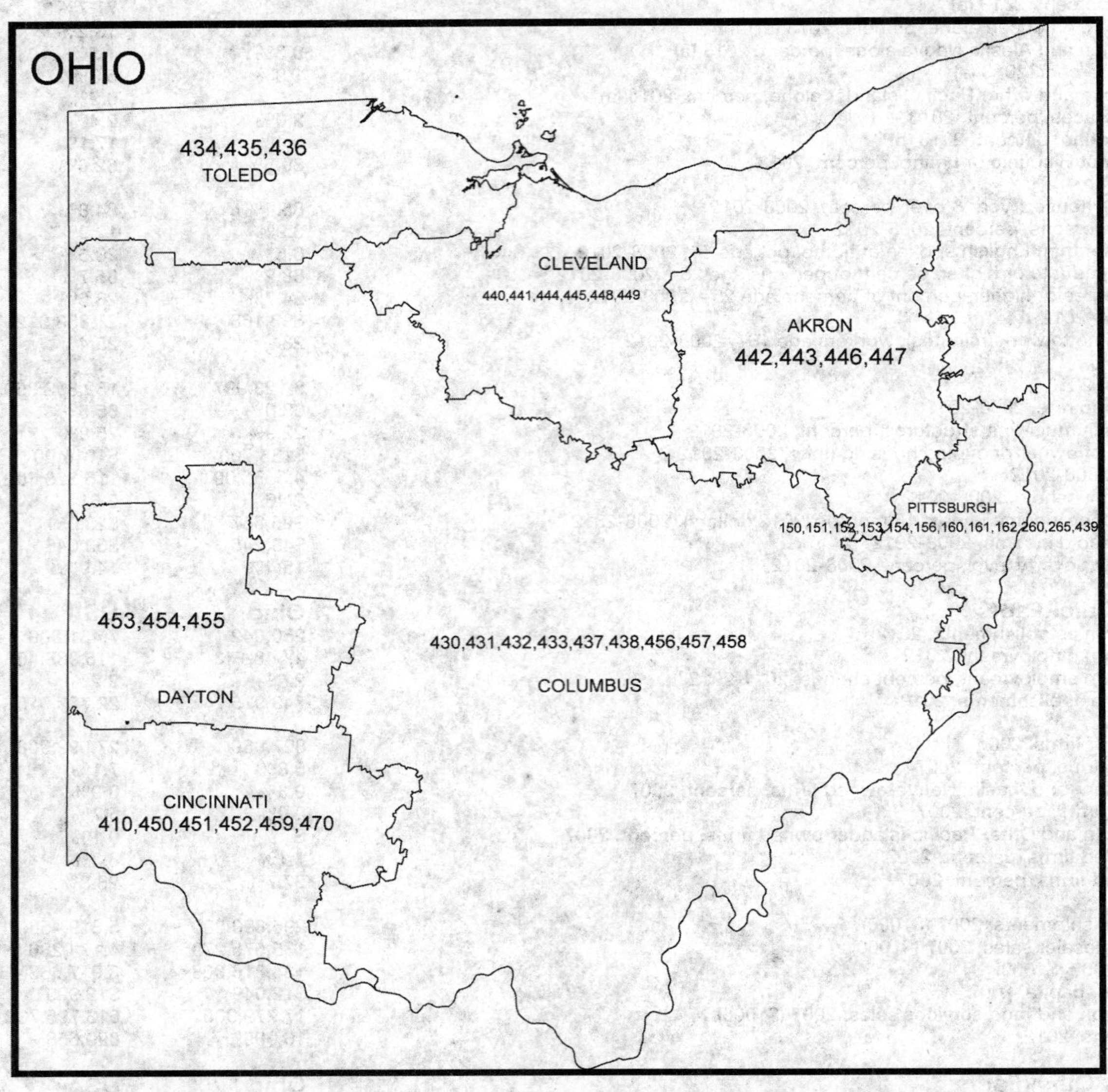
OHIO
434,435,436
TOLEDO
CLEVELAND
440,441,444,445,448,449
AKRON
442,443,446,447
PITTSBURGH
150,151,152,153,154,156,160,161,162,260,265,439
453,454,455
DAYTON
430,431,432,433,437,438,456,457,458
COLUMBUS
CINCINNATI
410,450,451,452,459,470

Ohio

(Abbreviation: OH)

Post Office, County — ZIP Code

Places with more than one ZIP code are listed in capital letters, See pages indicated.

Aberdeen, Brown 45101
Ada, Hardin 45810
Adams County, Adams 45144
Adams Mills, Muskingum 43821
Adamsville, Muskingum 43802
Addyston, Hamilton 45001
Adelphi, Ross 43101
Adena, Jefferson 43901
Adrian, Wyandot 43316
AKRON, Summit (See Page 2954)
Albany, Athens 45710
Alexandria, Licking 43001
Alger, Hardin 45812
Alledonia, Belmont 43902
Allensville, Vinton 45651
Alliance, Stark 44601
Alpha, Greene 45301
Alvada, Seneca 44802
Alvordton, Williams 43501
Amanda, Fairfield 43102
Amberley, Hamilton 45237
Amelia, Clermont 45102
Amesville, Athens 45711
Amherst, Lorain 44001
Amlin, Franklin 43002
Amsden, Seneca 44830
Amsterdam, Jefferson 43903
Anderson (See Cincinnati)
Anderson Township, Hamilton 45230
Andover, Ashtabula 44003
Anna, Shelby 45302
Ansonia, Darke 45303
Antioch, Monroe 43793
Antwerp, Paulding 45813
Apple Creek, Wayne 44606
Arcadia, Hancock 44804
Arcanum, Darke 45304
Archbold, Fulton 43502
Archbold, Williams 43570
Arlington, Hancock 45814
Arlington Heights, Hamilton 45215
Armstrong Mills, Belmont 43933
Ashland, Ashland 44805
Ashley, Delaware 43003
ASHTABULA, Ashtabula (See Page 2960)
Ashville, Pickaway 43103
Athalia, Lawrence 45669
Athens, Athens 45701
Attica, Seneca 44807
Atwater, Portage 44201
Auburn Township, Geauga 44023
Augusta, Carroll 44607
Aurora, Portage 44202
Austinburg, Ashtabula 44010
Austintown, Mahoning 44515
Ava, Noble 43711
Avon, Lorain 44011
Avon Lake, Lorain 44012
Avondale, Hamilton 45229
Bainbridge, Ross 45612
Bairdstown, Wood 45872
Bakersville, Coshocton 43803
Baltic, Tuscarawas 43804
Baltimore, Fairfield 43105
Bannock, Belmont 43972
Barberton, Summit 44203
Barlow, Washington 45712
Barnesville, Belmont 43713
Bartlett, Washington 45713
Barton, Belmont 43905
Bascom, Seneca 44809
Batavia, Clermont 45103
Bath, Summit 44210
Bay Village, Cuyahoga 44140
Beach City, Stark 44608
Beachwood, Cuyahoga 44122
Beallsville, Monroe 43716
Beaver, Pike 45613
Beavercreek, Greene 45305
Beavercreek Township, Greene 45305
Beavercreek Township, Greene 45305
Beaverdam, Allen 45808
Bedford, Cuyahoga 44146
Bedford Heights, Cuyahoga 44128
Bedford Heights, Cuyahoga 44146
Bellaire, Belmont 43906
Bellbrook, Greene 45305
Belle Center, Logan 43310
Belle Valley, Noble 43717
Bellefontaine, Logan 43311
Bellevue, Huron 44811
Bellville, Richland 44813
Belmont, Belmont 43718
Belmore, Putnam 45815
Beloit, Mahoning 44609
Belpre, Washington 45714
Bentleyville, Cuyahoga 44022
Benton Ridge, Hancock 45816
Bentonville, Adams 45105
Berea, Cuyahoga 44017
Bergholz, Jefferson 43908
Berkey, Lucas 43504
Berlin, Holmes 44610
Berlin Center, Mahoning 44401
Berlin Heights, Erie 44814
Bethel, Clermont 45106
Bethesda, Belmont 43719
Bettsville, Seneca 44815
Beverly, Washington 45715
Bexley, Franklin 43209
Bidwell, Gallia 45614
Big Prairie, Holmes 44611
Birmingham, Erie 44816
Blacklick, Franklin 43004
Bladensburg, Knox 43005
Blaine, Belmont 43909
Blakeslee, Williams 43505
Blanchester, Clinton 45107
Blissfield, Coshocton 43805
Bloomdale, Wood 44817
Bloomingburg, Fayette 43106
Bloomingdale, Jefferson 43910
Bloomville, Seneca 44818
Blue Ash (See Cincinnati)
Blue Creek, Adams 45616
Blue Rock, Muskingum 43720
Bluffton, Allen 45817
Boardman (See Youngstown)
Bolivar, Tuscarawas 44612
Bono, Ottawa 43445
Botkins, Shelby 45306
Bourneville, Ross 45617
Bowerston, Harrison 44695
Bowersville, Greene 45307
Bowling Green, Wood 43402
Bradford, Miami 45308
Bradner, Wood 43406
Brady Lake, Portage 44211
Bratenahl, Cuyahoga 44108
Brecksville, Cuyahoga 44141
Bremen, Fairfield 43107
Brewster, Stark 44613
Brice, Franklin 43109
Bridgeport, Belmont 43912
Brilliant, Jefferson 43913
Brinkhaven, Knox 43006
Bristolville, Trumbull 44402
Broadview Heights, Cuyahoga 44147
Broadway, Union 43007
Brook Park, Cuyahoga 44142
Brookfield, Trumbull 44403
Brooklyn, Cuyahoga 44144
Brooklyn Heights, Cuyahoga 44131
Brookpark, Cuyahoga 44142
Brookville, Montgomery 45309
Broughton, Paulding 45879
Brown County, Brown 45121
Brownsville, Licking 43721
Brunswick, Medina 44212
Bryan, Williams 43506
Buchtel, Athens 45716
Buckeye Lake, Licking 43008
Buckland, Auglaize 45819
Bucks, Tuscarawas 43804
Bucyrus, Crawford 44820
Buffalo, Guernsey 43722
Buford, Brown 45171
Burbank, Wayne 44214
Burghill, Trumbull 44404
Burgoon, Sandusky 43407
Burkettsville, Mercer 45310
Burton, Geauga 44021
Butler, Richland 44822
Byesville, Guernsey 43723
Cable, Champaign 43009
Cadiz, Harrison 43907
Cairo, Allen 45820
Calcutta, Columbiana 43920
Caldwell, Noble 43724
Caledonia, Marion 43314
Cambridge, Guernsey 43725
Cambridge, Guernsey 43750
Camden, Preble 45311
Cameron, Monroe 43914
Camp Dennison, Hamilton 45111
Campbell, Mahoning 44405
Canal Fulton, Stark 44614
Canal Whchstr, Franklin 43110
Canal Winchester, Franklin 43110
Canfield, Mahoning 44406
CANTON, Stark (See Page 2960)
Carbon Hill, Hocking 43111
Carbondale, Athens 45717
Cardington, Morrow 43315
Carey, Wyandot 43316
Carlisle, Warren 45005
Carroll, Fairfield 43112
Carrollton, Carroll 44615
Carrothers, Seneca 44807
Carthagena, Mercer 45822
Casstown, Miami 45312
Castalia, Erie 44824
Castine, Darke 45304
Catawba, Clark 43010
Cecil, Paulding 45821
Cedarville, Greene 45314
Celina, Mercer 45822
Celina, Mercer 45826
Centerburg, Knox 43011
Centerville (See Dayton)
CHAGRIN FALLS, Cuyahoga (See Page 2966)
Chandlersville, Muskingum 43727
Chardon, Geauga 44024
Charm, Holmes 44617
Chatfield, Crawford 44825
Chauncey, Athens 45719
Cherry Fork, Adams 45618
Chesapeake, Lawrence 45619
Cheshire, Gallia 45620
Chester, Meigs 45720
Chesterhill, Morgan 43728
Chesterland, Geauga 44026
Chesterville, Morrow 43317
Cheviot, Hamilton 45211
Chickasaw, Mercer 45826
Chillicothe, Ross 45601
Chilo, Clermont 45112
Chippewa Lake, Medina 44215
Christiansburg, Champaign 45389
CINCINNATI, Hamilton (See Page 2967)
Circleville, Pickaway 43113
Clarington, Monroe 43915
Clarksburg, Ross 43115
Clarksville, Clinton 45113
Clay Center, Ottawa 43408
Claysville, Guernsey 43725
Clayton, Montgomery 45315
Clermont County, Brown 45121
CLEVELAND, Cuyahoga (See Page 2984)
Cleveland Heights (See Cleveland)
Cleves, Hamilton 45002
Clifton, Greene 45316
Clinton, Summit 44216
Clinton County, Clinton 45169
Cloverdale, Putnam 45827
Clyde, Sandusky 43410
Coal Grove, Lawrence 45638
Coal Run, Washington 45721
Coalton, Jackson 45621
Coldwater, Mercer 45828
Colerain, Belmont 43916
Colerain Township (See Cincinnati)
College Corner, Butler 45003
College Hl, Hamilton 45224
Collins, Huron 44826
Collinsville, Butler 45004
Colton, Henry 43510
Columbia Station, Lorain 44028
Columbia Township, Hamilton 45243
Columbiana, Columbiana 44408
COLUMBUS, Franklin (See Page 2996)
Columbus Grove, Putnam 45830
Commercial Point, Pickaway 43116
Concord Township, Geauga 44024
Concord Township, Lake 44077
Conesville, Coshocton 43811
Congress, Wayne 44287
Conneaut, Ashtabula 44030
Conover, Miami 45317
Continental, Putnam 45831
Continental, Putnam 45837
Convoy, Van Wert 45832
Coolville, Athens 45723
Copley, Summit 44321
Corning, Perry 43730
Cortland, Trumbull 44410
Coshocton, Coshocton 43812
Covington, Miami 45318
Creola, Vinton 45622
Crestline, Crawford 44827
Creston, Wayne 44217
Cridersville, Allen 45806
Crooksville, Perry 43731
Croton, Licking 43013
Crown City, Gallia 45623
Cuba, Clinton 45114
Cumberland, Guernsey 43732
Curtice, Ottawa 43412
Custar, Wood 43511
Cutler, Washington 45724
CUYAHOGA FALLS, Summit (See Page 3012)
Cuyahoga Heights, Cuyahoga 44127
Cygnet, Wood 43413
Cynthiana, Pike 45624
Dalton, Wayne 44618
Damascus, Mahoning 44619
Danville, Knox 43014
Darbydale, Franklin 43123
Darbyville, Pickaway 43146
Day Heights, Clermont 45150
DAYTON, Darke (See Page 3013)
De Graff, Logan 43318
Decatur, Brown 45115
Deer Park, Hamilton 45236
Deerfield, Portage 44411
Deersville, Harrison 44693
Defiance, Defiance 43512
Delaware, Delaware 43015
Dellroy, Carroll 44620
Delphos, Allen 45833
Delta, Fulton 43515
Dennison, Tuscarawas 44621
Derby, Pickaway 43117
Derwent, Guernsey 43733
Deshler, Henry 43516
Dexter, Meigs 45741
Dexter City, Noble 45727
Diamond, Portage 44412
Dillonvale, Jefferson 43917
Dola, Hardin 45835
Donnelsville, Clark 45319
Dorset, Ashtabula 44032
Dover, Tuscarawas 44622
Doylestown, Wayne 44230
Dresden, Muskingum 43821
DUBLIN, Franklin (See Page 3025)
Dunbridge, Wood 43414
Duncan Falls, Muskingum 43734
Dundee, Tuscarawas 44624
Dunkirk, Hardin 45836
Dupont, Putnam 45837
East Canton, Stark 44730
East Claridon, Geauga 44033
East Cleveland (See Cleveland)
East Fultonham, Muskingum 43735
East Liberty, Logan 43319
East Liverpool, Columbiana 43920
East Orwell, Ashtabula 44076
East Palestine, Columbiana 44413
East Rochester, Columbiana 44625
East Sparta, Stark 44626
East Springfield, Jefferson 43925
EASTLAKE, Lake (See Page 3027)
Eaton, Preble 45320
Edgerton, Williams 43517
Edgewater, Cuyahoga 44107
Edison, Morrow 43320
Edon, Williams 43518
Elba, Washington 45746
Eldorado, Preble 45321
Elgin, Van Wert 45838
Elida, Allen 45807
Elkton, Columbiana 44415
Elliston, Ottawa 43432
Ellsworth, Mahoning 44416
Elmore, Ottawa 43416
Elmwood Pl, Hamilton 45216
Elmwood Place, Hamilton 45216
ELYRIA, Lorain (See Page 3027)
Empire, Jefferson 43926
Englewood, Montgomery 45322
Enon, Clark 45323
Etna, Licking 43018
EUCLID, Cuyahoga (See Page 3030)
Evansport, Defiance 43519
Evansport, Williams 43557
Fairborn, Greene 45324
FAIRFIELD, Butler (See Page 3030)
Fairlawn (See Akron)
Fairpoint, Belmont 43927
Fairport Harbor, Lake 44077
Fairview, Guernsey 43736
Fairview Park, Cuyahoga 44126
Farmdale, Trumbull 44417
Farmer, Defiance 43520
Farmerstown, Tuscarawas 43804
Farmersville, Montgomery 45325
Fayette, Fulton 43521
Fayette County, Highland 45135
Fayetteville, Brown 45118
Feesburg, Brown 45119
Felicity, Clermont 45120
FINDLAY, Hancock (See Page 3031)
Flat Rock, Seneca 44828
Fleming, Washington 45729
Fletcher, Miami 45326
Florida, Henry 43545
Flushing, Belmont 43977
Fly, Washington 45767
Forest, Hardin 45843
Fort Jennings, Putnam 45844
Fort Loramie, Shelby 45845
Fort Recovery, Mercer 45846
Fort Seneca, Seneca 44883
Fort Shawnee, Allen 45806
Fostoria, Seneca 44830
Fowler, Trumbull 44418
Frankfort, Ross 45628
Franklin, Warren 45005
Franklin Furnace, Scioto 45629
Frazeysburg, Muskingum 43822
Fredericksburg, Wayne 44627
Fredericktown, Knox 43019
Freeport, Harrison 43973
Fremont, Sandusky 43420
Fresno, Coshocton 43824
Friendship, Scioto 45630
Fulton, Morrow 43321
Fultonham, Muskingum 43738
Gahanna, Franklin 43230
Galena, Delaware 43021
Galion, Crawford 44833
Gallipolis, Gallia 45631
Galloway, Franklin 43119
Gambier, Knox 43022
Garfield Heights (See Cleveland)
Garrettsville, Portage 44231
Gates Mills, Cuyahoga 44040
Geneva, Ashtabula 44041
Genoa, Ottawa 43430
Georgetown, Brown 45121
Germantown, Montgomery 45325
Germantown, Montgomery 45327
Gettysburg, Darke 45328
Gibsonburg, Sandusky 43431
Gilboa, Putnam 45875
Girard, Trumbull 44420
Glandorf, Putnam 45848
Glencoe, Belmont 43928
Glendale, Hamilton 45246
Glenford, Perry 43739
Glenmont, Holmes 44628
Glouster, Athens 45732
Gnadenhutten, Tuscarawas 44629
Gomer, Allen 45809
Gordon, Darke 45304
Goshen, Clermont 45122
Grafton, Lorain 44044
Grand Rapids, Wood 43522
Grand River, Lake 44045
Grandview Heights, Franklin 43212
Granville, Licking 43023
Gratiot, Licking 43740
Gratis, Preble 45330
Graysville, Monroe 45734
Graytown, Ottawa 43432
Green, Summit 44232
Green Camp, Marion 43322
Green Springs, Seneca 44836
Greenfield, Highland 45123
Greenford, Mahoning 44422
Greentown, Stark 44630
Greenville, Darke 45331
Greenwich, Huron 44837
Grelton, Henry 43523
Grelton, Henry 43534
Groesbeck (See Cincinnati)
Grove City, Franklin 43123
Groveport, Franklin 43125
Grover Hill, Paulding 45849
Guernsey, Guernsey 43749
Guysville, Athens 45735
Gypsum, Ottawa 43433
Hallsville, Ross 45633
Hamden, Vinton 45634
Hamersville, Brown 45130
HAMILTON, Butler (See Page 3033)
Hamilton Township, Warren 45039
Hamler, Henry 43524
Hammondsville, Jefferson 43930
Hanging Rock, Lawrence 45638
Hannibal, Monroe 43931

Hanover, Licking 43055
Hanoverton, Columbiana 44423
Harbor View, Lucas 43434
Harlem Springs, Carroll 44615
Harpster, Wyandot 43323
Harrisburg, Franklin 43126
Harrison, Hamilton 45030
Harrisville, Harrison 43974
Harrod, Allen 45850
Hartford, Trumbull 44424
Hartville, Stark 44632
Harveysburg, Warren 45032
Haskins, Wood 43525
Haverhill, Scioto 45636
Haviland, Paulding 45851
Haydenville, Hocking 43127
Hayesville, Ashland 44838
Heath, Licking 43056
Hebron, Licking 43025
Helena, Sandusky 43435
Hemlock, Perry 43730
Hicksville, Defiance 43526
Hideaway Hls, Fairfield 43107
Higginsport, Brown 45131
Highland, Highland 45132
Highland County, Highland 45135
Highland Heights, Cuyahoga 44143
Highland Hills, Cuyahoga 44122
Highland Hts, Cuyahoga 44143
Hilliard, Franklin 43026
Hillsboro, Highland 45133
Hinckley, Medina 44233
Hiram, Portage 44234
Hockingport, Athens 45739
Holgate, Henry 43527
Holiday City, Williams 43543
Holland, Lucas 43528
Hollansburg, Darke 45332
Holloway, Belmont 43985
Holmesville, Holmes 44633
Homer, Licking 43027
Homerville, Medina 44235
Homeworth, Columbiana 44634
Hooven, Hamilton 45033
Hopedale, Harrison 43976
Hopewell, Muskingum 43746
Houston, Shelby 45333
Howard, Knox 43028
Hoytville, Wood 43529
Hubbard, Trumbull 44425
Huber Heights, Montgomery 45424
Hudson, Summit 44224
Hudson, Summit 44236
Huntsburg, Geauga 44046
Huntsville, Logan 43324
Huron, Erie 44839
Iberia, Morrow 43325
Idaho, Pike 45661
Independence, Cuyahoga 44131
Irondale, Jefferson 43932
Ironton, Lawrence 45638
Irwin, Union 43029
Isle Saint George, Ottawa 43436
Ithaca, Darke 45304
Jackson, Jackson 45640
Jackson Belden, Stark 44718
Jackson Center, Shelby 45334
Jacksontown, Licking 43030
Jacksonville, Athens 45740
Jacobsburg, Belmont 43933
Jamestown, Greene 45335
Jasper, Pike 45642
Jefferson, Ashtabula 44047
Jeffersonville, Fayette 43128
Jenera, Hancock 45841
Jeromesville, Ashland 44840
Jerry City, Wood 43437
Jerusalem, Monroe 43747
Jewell, Defiance 43530
Jewett, Harrison 43986
Johnstown, Licking 43031
Junction City, Perry 43748
Kalida, Putnam 45853
Kansas, Seneca 44841
Keene, Coshocton 43828
Kelleys Island, Erie 43438
Kensington, Columbiana 44427
KENT, Portage
(See Page 3035)
Kenton, Hardin 43326
Kerr, Gallia 45643
Kettering
(See Dayton)
Kettlersville, Shelby 45336
Kidron, Wayne 44636
Kilbourne, Delaware 43032
Killbuck, Holmes 44637
Kimbolton, Guernsey 43749
Kings Island, Warren 45034
Kings Mills, Warren 45034
Kingston, Ross 45644
Kingsville, Ashtabula 44048
Kinsman, Trumbull 44428
Kipling, Guernsey 43750
Kipton, Lorain 44049
Kirby, Wyandot 43330
Kirkersville, Licking 43033
Kirtland, Lake 44094
Kitts Hill, Lawrence 45645
Kunkle, Williams 43531
La Rue, Marion 43332
Lacarne, Ottawa 43439
Lafayette, Allen 45854
Lafferty, Belmont 43951
Lagrange, Lorain 44050
Laings, Monroe 43752
Lake Milton, Mahoning 44429
Lake Waynoka, Brown 45171
Lakeline, Lake 44095
Lakemore, Summit 44250
Lakeside, Ottawa 43440
Lakeside Marblehead, Ottawa 43440
Lakeview, Logan 43331
Lakeville, Holmes 44638
Lakewood, Cuyahoga 44107
Lancaster, Fairfield 43130
Langsville, Meigs 45741
Lansing, Belmont 43934
Latham, Pike 45646
Latty, Paulding 45855
Laura, Miami 45337
Laurelville, Hocking 43135
Laurelville, Hocking 43152
Leavittsburg, Trumbull 44430
Lebanon, Warren 45036
Lees Creek, Clinton 45169
Leesburg, Highland 45135
Leesville, Carroll 44639
Leetonia, Columbiana 44431
Leipsic, Putnam 45815
Leipsic, Putnam 45856
Lemoyne, Wood 43441
Lewis Center, Delaware 43035
Lewisburg, Preble 45338
Lewistown, Logan 43333
Lewisville, Monroe 43754
Lexington, Richland 44904
Liberty Center, Henry 43532
Liberty Tnsp, Butler 45050
Liberty Township, Butler 45011
Liberty Township, Butler 45044
Liberty Townshp, Butler 45069
Liberty Twnship, Butler 45050
LIMA, Allen
(See Page 3036)
Limaville, Stark 44640
Lindenwald, Butler 45015
Lindsey, Sandusky 43442
Lisbon, Columbiana 44432
Litchfield, Medina 44253
Lithopolis, Fairfield 43136
Little Hocking, Washington 45742
Lockbourne, Franklin 43137
Lockland, Hamilton 45215
Lodi, Medina 44254
Logan, Hocking 43138
London, Madison 43140
Londonderry, Ross 45647
Long Bottom, Meigs 45743
LORAIN, Lorain
(See Page 3039)
Lore City, Guernsey 43755
Loudonville, Ashland 44842
Louisville, Stark 44641
Loveland, Hamilton 45111
Loveland, Clermont 45140
Lowell, Washington 45744
Lowellville, Mahoning 44436
Lower Salem, Washington 45745
Lucas, Richland 44843
Lucasville, Scioto 45648
Luckey, Wood 43443
Ludlow Falls, Miami 45339
Lynchburg, Highland 45142
Lyndhurst, Cuyahoga 44124
Lynx, Adams 45650
Lyons, Fulton 43533
Macedonia, Summit 44056
Macedonia, Summit 44067
Macksburg, Washington 45746
Madeira, Hamilton 45243
Madison, Lake 44057
Magnetic Springs, Union 43036
Magnolia, Stark 44643
Maineville, Warren 45039
Malaga, Monroe 43757
Malinta, Henry 43535
Malta, Morgan 43758
Malvern, Carroll 44644
Manchester, Adams 45144
MANSFIELD, Richland
(See Page 3040)
Mantua, Portage 44255
Maple Heights, Cuyahoga 44137
Maplewood, Shelby 45340
Marathon, Brown 45118
Marble Cliff, Franklin 43212
Marblehead, Ottawa 43440
Marengo, Morrow 43334
Maria Stein, Mercer 45860
Marietta, Washington 45750
MARION, Marion
(See Page 3042)
Mark Center, Defiance 43536
Marshallville, Wayne 44645
Martel, Marion 43335
Martin, Ottawa 43445
Martins Ferry, Belmont 43935
Martinsburg, Knox 43037
Martinsville, Clinton 45146
Marysville, Union 43040
Mason, Warren 45040
MASSILLON, Stark
(See Page 3042)
Masury, Trumbull 44438
Matamoras, Washington 45767
Maumee, Lucas 43537
Maximo, Stark 44650
Mayfield, Cuyahoga 44143
Mayfield Village, Cuyahoga 44143
Maynard, Belmont 43937
Mc Arthur, Vinton 45651
Mc Clure, Henry 43523
Mc Clure, Henry 43534
Mc Comb, Hancock 45858
Mc Cutchenville, Wyandot 44844
Mc Dermott, Scioto 45652
Mc Donald, Trumbull 44437
Mc Guffey, Hardin 45859
Mcconnelsville, Morgan 43756
Mechanic, Tuscarawas 43804
Mechanicsburg, Champaign 43044
Mechanicstown, Carroll 44651
MEDINA, Medina
(See Page 3044)
Medway, Clark 45341
Melmore, Seneca 44845
Melrose, Paulding 45861
Melrose, Paulding 45873
Mendon, Mercer 45862
MENTOR, Lake
(See Page 3046)
Mentor On The Lake, Lake 44060
Mesopotamia, Trumbull 44439
Metamora, Fulton 43540
MIAMISBURG, Montgomery
(See Page 3047)
Miamitown, Hamilton 45041
Miamiville, Clermont 45147
Middle Bass, Ottawa 43446
Middle Point, Van Wert 45863
Middlebranch, Stark 44652
Middleburg, Logan 43336
Middleburg Heights, Cuyahoga 44130
Middlefield, Geauga 44062
Middleport, Meigs 45760
MIDDLETOWN, Butler
(See Page 3048)
Midland, Clinton 45148
Midvale, Tuscarawas 44653
Milan, Erie 44846
Milford, Clermont 45150
Milford Center, Union 43045
Millbury, Wood 43447
Milledgeville, Fayette 43142
Miller City, Putnam 45864
Millersburg, Holmes 44654
Millersport, Fairfield 43046
Millersville, Sandusky 43435
Millfield, Athens 45761
Milton Center, Wood 43541
Mineral City, Tuscarawas 44656
Mineral Ridge, Trumbull 44440
Minerva, Stark 44657
Minford, Scioto 45653
Mingo, Champaign 43047
Mingo Junction, Jefferson 43938
Minster, Auglaize 45865
Mogadore, Portage 44260
Monclova, Lucas 43542
Monroe, Butler 45044
Monroe, Butler 45050
Monroeville, Huron 44847
Montezuma, Mercer 45866
Montgomery, Clermont 45140
Montpelier, Williams 43543
Montville, Geauga 44064
Moraine
(See Dayton)
Moreland Hills, Cuyahoga 44022
Morral, Marion 43337
Morristown, Belmont 43759
Morrow, Warren 45152
Moscow, Clermont 45153
Mount Blanchard, Hancock 45867
Mount Cory, Hancock 45868
Mount Eaton, Wayne 44659
Mount Gilead, Morrow 43338
Mount Healthy, Hamilton 45231
Mount Hope, Holmes 44660
Mount Liberty, Knox 43048
Mount Orab, Brown 45154
Mount Perry, Perry 43760
Mount Pleasant, Jefferson 43939
Mount Saint Joseph, Hamilton 45051
Mount Sterling, Madison 43143
Mount Vernon, Knox 43050
Mount Victory, Hardin 43340
Mount Washington, Hamilton 45230
Mowrystown, Highland 45155
Moxahala, Perry 43761
Munroe Falls, Summit 44262
Murray City, Hocking 43144
N Canton, Stark 44721
Nankin, Ashland 44848
Napoleon, Henry 43545
Napoleon, Henry 43550
Nashport, Muskingum 43830
Nashville, Holmes 44661
Navarre, Stark 44662
Neapolis, Lucas 43547
Neffs, Belmont 43940
Negley, Columbiana 44441
Nelsonville, Athens 45764
Nevada, Wyandot 44849
Neville, Clermont 45156
New Albany, Franklin 43054
New Athens, Harrison 43981
New Bavaria, Henry 43548
New Bedford, Coshocton 43824
New Bloomington, Marion 43341
New Boston, Scioto 45662
New Bremen, Auglaize 45869
New Carlisle, Clark 45344
New Concord, Muskingum 43762
New Franklin, Summit 44203
New Franklin, Summit 44216
New Hampshire, Auglaize 45870
New Haven, Huron 44850
New Holland, Pickaway 43145
New Knoxville, Auglaize 45871
New Lebanon, Montgomery 45345
New Lexington, Perry 43764
New London, Huron 44851
New Lyme, Ashtabula 44047
New Madison, Darke 45346
New Marshfield, Athens 45766
New Matamoras, Washington 45767
New Middletown, Mahoning 44442
New Paris, Preble 45347
New Philadelphia, Tuscarawas 44663
New Plymouth, Vinton 45654
New Richmond, Clermont 45157
New Riegel, Seneca 44853
New Rome, Franklin 43228
New Rumley, Harrison 43984
New Springfield, Mahoning 44443
New Straitsville, Perry 43766
New Vienna, Clinton 45159
New Washington, Crawford 44854
New Waterford, Columbiana 44445
New Weston, Darke 45348
NEWARK, Licking
(See Page 3050)
Newburgh Heights
(See Cleveland)
Newbury, Geauga 44065
Newcomerstown, Tuscarawas 43832
Newport, Washington 45768
Newton Falls, Trumbull 44444
Newtonsville, Clermont 45158
Newtown, Hamilton 45244
Ney, Defiance 43549
Niles, Trumbull 44446
North Baltimore, Wood 45872
North Bend, Hamilton 45052
North Benton, Portage 44449
North Bloomfield, Trumbull 44450
North Canton
(See Canton)
North College Hill, Hamilton 45224
North Fairfield, Huron 44855
North Georgetown, Columbiana 44665
North Hampton, Clark 45349
North Industry, Stark 44707
North Jackson, Mahoning 44451
North Kingsville, Ashtabula 44068
North Lawrence, Stark 44666
North Lewisburg, Champaign 43060
North Lima, Mahoning 44452
North Olmsted, Cuyahoga 44070
North Randall, Cuyahoga 44128
North Ridgeville, Lorain 44035
North Robinson, Crawford 44856
North Royalton, Cuyahoga 44133
North Star, Darke 45350
Northfield, Summit 44056
Northfield, Summit 44067
Northwood, Lucas 43605
Northwood, Wood 43619
Norton, Summit 44203
Norwalk, Huron 44857
Norwich, Muskingum 43767
Norwood, Hamilton 45212
Nova, Ashland 44859
Novelty, Geauga 44073
Oak Harbor, Ottawa 43449
Oak Hill, Jackson 45656
Oakwood, Montgomery 45409
Oakwood, Montgomery 45419
Oakwood Village, Cuyahoga 44146
Oberlin, Lorain 44074
Obetz, Franklin 43207
Oceola, Crawford 44860
Ohio City, Van Wert 45874
Okeana, Butler 45053
Okolona, Henry 43545
Okolona, Henry 43550
Old Fort, Seneca 44861
Old Washington, Guernsey 43768
Olmsted Falls, Cuyahoga 44138
Olmsted Twp, Cuyahoga 44138
Ontario, Richland 44862
Ontario, Richland 44903
Orangeville, Trumbull 44453
OREGON, Lucas
(See Page 3051)
Oregonia, Warren 45054
Orient, Pickaway 43146
Orrville, Wayne 44667
Orwell, Ashtabula 44076
Osgood, Darke 45351
Ostrander, Delaware 43061
Ottawa, Putnam 45875
Ottawa Hills
(See Toledo)
Ottoville, Putnam 45876
Otway, Scioto 45657
Overpeck, Butler 45055
Owensville, Clermont 45160
Oxford, Butler 45056
Painesville, Lake 44077
Palestine, Darke 45352
Pandora, Putnam 45877
Paris, Stark 44669
Parkdale
(See Cincinnati)
Parkman, Geauga 44080
Parma, Cuyahoga 44129
Parma Heights, Cuyahoga 44130
Pataskala, Licking 43062
Pataskala, Franklin 43068
Patriot, Gallia 45658
Paulding, Paulding 45879
Payne, Paulding 45880
Pedro, Lawrence 45659
Peebles, Adams 45660
Pemberton, Shelby 45353
Pemberville, Wood 43450
Peninsula, Summit 44264
Pennsville, Morgan 43787
Pepper Pike, Cuyahoga 44124
Perry, Lake 44081
PERRYSBURG, Wood
(See Page 3051)
Perrysville, Ashland 44864
Petersburg, Mahoning 44454
Pettisville, Fulton 43553
Phillipsburg, Montgomery 45354
Philo, Muskingum 43771
Phoneton, Miami 45371
Pickerington, Fairfield 43147
Piedmont, Belmont 43983
Pierpont, Ashtabula 44082
Piketon, Pike 45661
Piney Fork, Jefferson 43941
Pioneer, Williams 43554
Piqua, Miami 45356
Pitsburg, Darke 45358
Plain City, Madison 43064
Plainfield, Coshocton 43836
Pleasant City, Guernsey 43772
Pleasant Corners, Pickaway 43146
Pleasant Hill, Miami 45359
Pleasant Plain, Warren 45162
Pleasantville, Fairfield 43148
Plymouth, Huron 44865
Poetown, Brown 45130
Point Pleasant, Clermont 45153
Poland, Mahoning 44514
Polk, Ashland 44866
Pomeroy, Meigs 45769
Port Clinton, Ottawa 43452
Port Jefferson, Shelby 45360
Port Washington, Tuscarawas 43837
Port William, Clinton 45164

Portage, Wood 43451
Portland, Meigs 45770
Portsmouth, Scioto 45662
Portsmouth, Scioto 45663
Potsdam, Miami 45361
Potsdm, Miami 45337
Powell, Delaware 43065
Powhatan Point, Belmont 43942
Proctorville, Lawrence 45669
Prospect, Marion 43342
Put In Bay, Ottawa 43456
Quaker City, Guernsey 43736
Quaker City, Guernsey 43773
Queen City (See Cincinnati)
Quincy, Logan 43343
Racine, Meigs 45771
Radcliff, Vinton 45695
Radnor, Delaware 43066
Randolph, Portage 44265
Rarden, Scioto 45671
Ravenna, Portage 44266
Rawson, Hancock 45881
Ray, Vinton 45672
Rayland, Jefferson 43943
Raymond, Union 43067
Reading (See Cincinnati)
Reedsville, Meigs 45772
Reesville, Clinton 45166
Reminderville, Portage 44202
Rendville, Perry 43730
Reno, Washington 45773
Republic, Seneca 44867
Reynoldsburg, Franklin 43068
Richfield, Summit 44286
Richmond, Jefferson 43944
Richmond Dale, Ross 45673
Richmond Heights, Cuyahoga 44143
Richwood, Union 43344
Ridgeville Corners, Henry 43555
Ridgeway, Hardin 43345
Rinard Mills, Monroe 45734
Rio Grande, Gallia 45674
Ripley, Brown 45167
Risingsun, Wood 43457
Rittman, Wayne 44270
Riverside, Greene 45431
Roaming Shores, Ashtabula 44084
Robertsville, Stark 44670
Rochester, Lorain 44090
Rock Camp, Lawrence 45675
Rock Creek, Ashtabula 44084
Rockbridge, Hocking 43149
Rockford, Mercer 45882
Rocky Ridge, Ottawa 43458
Rocky River, Cuyahoga 44116
Rogers, Columbiana 44455
Rome, Ashtabula 44085
Rootstown, Portage 44272
Roselawn, Hamilton 45222
Roseville, Muskingum 43777
Rosewood, Champaign 43070
Ross, Butler 45061
Ross County, Highland 45123
Rossburg, Darke 45348
Rossburg, Darke 45362
Rossford, Wood 43460
Rossville, Butler 45013
Roundhead, Hardin 43346
Rudolph, Wood 43462
Rushsylvania, Logan 43347
Rushville, Fairfield 43150
Russell, Geauga 44072
Russells Point, Logan 43348
Russellville, Brown 45168
Russia, Shelby 45363
Rutland, Meigs 45775
S Bloomingville, Hocking 43152
Sabina, Clinton 45169
Sagamore Hills, Summit 44067
Saint Bernard (See Cincinnati)
Saint Clairsville, Belmont 43950
Saint Henry, Mercer 45883
Saint Johns, Auglaize 45884
Saint Louisville, Licking 43071
Saint Marys, Auglaize 45885
Saint Paris, Champaign 43072
Salem, Columbiana 44460
Salesville, Guernsey 43778
Salineville, Columbiana 43945
SANDUSKY, Erie (See Page 3052)
Sandyville, Tuscarawas 44671
Sarahsville, Noble 43779
Sardinia, Brown 45171
Sardis, Monroe 43946
Savannah, Ashland 44874
Sayler Park, Hamilton 45233
Scio, Harrison 43988
Scioto Furnace, Scioto 45677
Sciotoville, Scioto 45662
Scott, Van Wert 45886
Scottown, Lawrence 45678
Seaman, Adams 45679
Sebring, Mahoning 44672
Sedalia, Madison 43151
Senecaville, Guernsey 43780
Seven Hills, Cuyahoga 44131
Seven Mile, Butler 45062
Seville, Medina 44273
Shade, Athens 45776
Shadyside, Belmont 43947
Shaker Heights, Cuyahoga 44118
Shandon, Butler 45063
Sharon Center, Medina 44274
Sharonville, Hamilton 45241
Sharpsburg, Athens 45777
Shauck, Morrow 43349
Shawnee, Perry 43782
Shawnee Hills, Delaware 43065
Sheffield Lake, Lorain 44054
Sheffield Village, Lorain 44035
Sheffield Village, Lorain 44054
Shelby, Richland 44875
Sherrodsville, Carroll 44675
Sherwood, Defiance 43556
Shiloh, Richland 44878
Shinrock, Erie 44839
Shreve, Wayne 44676
Sidney, Shelby 45365
Silver Lake, Summit 44224
Silverton, Hamilton 45236
Sinking Spring, Highland 45172
Smithfield, Jefferson 43948
Smithville, Wayne 44677
Solon, Cuyahoga 44139
Somerdale, Tuscarawas 44678
Somerset, Perry 43783
Somerton, Belmont 43713
Somerville, Butler 45064
Sonora, Muskingum 43701
South Amherst, Lorain 44001
South Bloomfield, Pickaway 43103
South Bloomingville, Hocking 43152
South Charleston, Clark 45368
South Euclid (See Cleveland)
South Lebanon, Warren 45065
South Point, Lawrence 45680
South Salem, Ross 45681
South Solon, Madison 43153
South Vienna, Clark 45369
South Webster, Scioto 45682
South Zanesville (See Zanesville)
Southington, Trumbull 44470
Sparta, Morrow 43350
Spencer, Medina 44275
Spencerville, Allen 45887
Spring Valley, Greene 45370
Springboro, Warren 45066
Springdale, Hamilton 45246
SPRINGFIELD, Clark (See Page 3053)
St Louisville, Licking 43071
Stafford, Monroe 43786
Sterling, Wayne 44276
STEUBENVILLE, Jefferson (See Page 3055)
Stewart, Athens 45778
Stewartsville, Belmont 43933
Stillwater, Tuscarawas 44679
Stockdale, Pike 45683
Stockport, Morgan 43787
Stone Creek, Tuscarawas 43840
Stony Ridge, Wood 43463
Stout, Adams 45684
Stoutsville, Fairfield 43154
Stow, Summit 44224
Strasburg, Tuscarawas 44680
Stratton, Jefferson 43961
Streetsboro, Portage 44241
STRONGSVILLE, Cuyahoga (See Page 3056)
Struthers, Mahoning 44471
Stryker, Defiance 43519
Stryker, Williams 43557
Sugar Grove, Fairfield 43155
Sugarcreek, Tuscarawas 44681
Sugarcreek Township, Greene 45305
Sugarcreek Township, Greene 45305
Sullivan, Ashland 44880
Sulphur Springs, Crawford 44881
Summerfield, Noble 43788
Summerford, Madison 43140
Summit Station, Licking 43073
Summitville, Columbiana 43962
Sunbury, Delaware 43074
Swanton, Fulton 43558
Sycamore, Wyandot 44882
Sycamore Valley, Monroe 43754
Sylvania, Lucas 43560
Sylvania Township (See Toledo)
Symmes, Hamilton 45249
Symmes Twp, Clermont 45140
Syracuse, Meigs 45779
Taft (See Cincinnati)
Tallmadge, Summit 44278
Tarlton, Pickaway 43156
Terrace Park, Hamilton 45174
The Plains, Athens 45780
Thompson, Geauga 44086
Thornville, Perry 43076
Thurman, Gallia 45685
Thurston, Fairfield 43157
Tiffin, Seneca 44883
Tiltonsville, Jefferson 43963
Timberlake, Lake 44095
Tipp City, Miami 45371
Tippecanoe, Harrison 44699
Tiro, Crawford 44887
TOLEDO, Lucas (See Page 3058)
Tontogany, Wood 43565
Toronto, Jefferson 43964
Tremont City, Clark 45372
Trenton, Butler 45067
Trimble, Athens 45782
Trinway, Muskingum 43842
Trotwood (See Dayton)
Troy, Miami 45373
Tuppers Plains, Meigs 45783
Tuscarawas, Tuscarawas 44682
Twinsburg, Summit 44087
Uhrichsville, Tuscarawas 44683
Union, Montgomery 45322
Union City, Darke 45390
Union Furnace, Hocking 43158
Unionport, Jefferson 43910
Uniontown, Stark 44685
Unionville, Ashtabula 44088
Unionville Center, Union 43077
Uniopolis, Auglaize 45888
University Heights, Cuyahoga 44118
University Hts, Cuyahoga 44118
Upper Arlington (See Columbus)
Upper Sandusky, Wyandot 43351
Urbana, Champaign 43078
Urbancrest, Franklin 43123
Utica, Licking 43080
Valley City, Medina 44280
Valley View, Cuyahoga 44125
Van Buren, Hancock 45889
Van Wert, Van Wert 45891
Vandalia, Montgomery 45377
Vanlue, Hancock 45890
Vaughnsville, Putnam 45893
Venedocia, Van Wert 45894
Vermilion, Lorain 44001
Vermilion, Erie 44089
Verona, Preble 45378
Versailles, Darke 45380
Vickery, Sandusky 43464
Vienna, Trumbull 44473
Village Of Indian Springs, Butler 45011
Village Of Indian Springs, Butler 45011
Vincent, Washington 45784
Vinton, Gallia 45686
WADSWORTH, Medina (See Page 3064)
Waite Hill, Lake 44094
Wakefield, Pike 45687
Wakeman, Huron 44889
Walbridge, Wood 43465
Waldo, Marion 43356
Walhonding, Coshocton 43843
Walnut Creek, Holmes 44687
Walnut Hills, Hamilton 45206
Walton Hills, Cuyahoga 44146
Wapakoneta, Auglaize 45895
Warner, Washington 45745
Warnock, Belmont 43967
WARREN, Trumbull (See Page 3064)
Warrensville Heights, Cuyahoga 44122
Warsaw, Coshocton 43844
Washington Court House, Fayette 43160
Washington Township (See Dayton)
Washingtonville, Columbiana 44490
Waterford, Washington 45786
Waterloo, Lawrence 45688
Watertown, Washington 45787
Waterville, Lucas 43566
Wauseon, Fulton 43567
Waverly, Pike 45690
Wayland, Portage 44285
Wayne, Wood 43466
Waynesburg, Stark 44688
Waynesfield, Auglaize 45896
Waynesville, Warren 45068
Wellington, Lorain 44090
Wellston, Jackson 45692
Wellsville, Columbiana 43968
West Alexandria, Preble 45381
West Carrollton (See Dayton)
West Carrollton City (See Dayton)
WEST CHESTER, Butler (See Page 3066)
West Elkton, Preble 45070
West Farmington, Trumbull 44491
West Jefferson, Madison 43162
West Lafayette, Coshocton 43845
West Liberty, Logan 43357
West Manchester, Preble 45382
West Mansfield, Logan 43358
West Millgrove, Wood 43467
West Milton, Miami 45383
West Point, Columbiana 44492
West Portsmouth, Scioto 45663
West Rushville, Fairfield 43150
West Salem, Wayne 44287
West Union, Adams 45693
West Unity, Williams 43570
WESTERVILLE, Franklin (See Page 3067)
Westfield Center, Medina 44251
Westlake, Cuyahoga 44145
Weston, Wood 43569
Westville, Champaign 43083
Westwood, Hamilton 45248
Wharton, Wyandot 43359
Wheelersburg, Scioto 45694
Whipple, Washington 45788
White Cottage, Muskingum 43791
Whitehall, Franklin 43213
Whitehouse, Lucas 43571
Wickliffe, Lake 44092
Wilberforce, Greene 45384
Wilkesville, Vinton 45695
Willard, Huron 44888
Williamsburg, Clermont 45176
Williamsfield, Ashtabula 44093
Williamsport, Pickaway 43164
Williamstown, Hancock 45897
Williston, Ottawa 43468
WILLOUGHBY, Lake (See Page 3070)
Willoughby Hills, Lake 44092
Willoughby Hills, Lake 44094
Willow Wood, Lawrence 45696
Willowick, Lake 44095
Willshire, Van Wert 45898
Wilmington, Clinton 45177
Wilmot, Stark 44689
Winchester, Adams 45697
Windham, Portage 44288
Windsor, Ashtabula 44099
Winesburg, Holmes 44690
Wingett Run, Washington 45789
Winona, Columbiana 44493
Wintersville (See Steubenville)
Wolf Run, Jefferson 43970
Woodmere, Cuyahoga 44122
Woodsfield, Monroe 43793
Woodstock, Champaign 43084
Woodville, Sandusky 43469
Wooster, Wayne 44691
Worthington, Franklin 43085
Wp Air Base, Greene 45433
Wpafb, Greene 45433
Wren, Van Wert 45899
Wright Patter, Greene 45433
Wright Patterson Afb, Greene 45433
Wyoming (See Cincinnati)
Xenia, Greene 45385
Yellow Springs, Greene 45387
Yorkshire, Darke 45388
Yorkville, Jefferson 43971
YOUNGSTOWN, Mahoning (See Page 3071)
Zaleski, Vinton 45698
Zanesfield, Logan 43360
ZANESVILLE, Muskingum (See Page 3075)
Zoar, Tuscarawas 44697
Zoarville, Tuscarawas 44656

AKRON OH

General Delivery 44309

POST OFFICE BOXES MAIN OFFICE STATIONS AND BRANCHES

Box No.s
9130C - 9130C 44305
9240C - 9240C 44305
1 - 3699 44309
3701 - 3996 44314
4501 - 4980 44310
5701 - 5938 44372
6001 - 6676 44312
7001 - 7999 44306
8000 - 8004 44305
8001 - 8414 44320
9001 - 9454 44305
10001 - 10380 44310
15001 - 15294 44314
19001 - 19240 44319
22001 - 22699 44302
26001 - 27734 44319
30900 - 30947 44309
72001 - 72118 44372
80001 - 80598 44308

NAMED STREETS

A St 44312
Abbey Ln 44319
Abbey Rd 44312
Abbott Ave 44307
Abbyshire Rd 44319
Aberdeen St 44310
Aberth Dr 44320
Abington Rd
500-1299 44312
2400-2799 44333
Acacia Dr 44333
Ace Dr 44319
Ackley St 44306
Acme Dr 44319
Acoma Dr 44306
Acre Rd 44320
Ada St 44306
N & S Adams Ct & St 44304
Adawood Dr 44321
Addyston Rd 44313
Adelaide Blvd 44305
Adelford Ave 44310
Adella Ave 44312
Adena Cir & Trce 44321
Adkins Ave 44301
N & S Adolph St 44304
Aegean Dr 44333
Aetna St 44304
Afton Ave 44313
Agate Pl 44305
Airenso Pkwy 44309
Akers Ave 44312
Akers Ct 44306
Akins Ave 44301
Akins Ct 44314
Akron General Ave 44307
Akron Peninsula Rd 44313
Alaho St 44305
Albert Aly 44307
Albert Pl 44303
Alberta Ave 44303
Alberti Ct 44310
Albion Ave 44320
Albrecht Ave 44312
Aldawood Hills Dr 44319
Alden Ave 44313
Alder Run Way 44333
Aldis Dr 44312
Alexander Ct 44321
Alexander St 44306
Alfaretta Ave 44310
Alfred Rd 44306
Alhambra Way 44302
Alice Ave 44310
Alice Ct 44301
Alice Dr 44319
Alicia Walk 44306
Allard Dr 44333
Allendale Ave 44306
Allenford St 44314
Allies St 44305
Allyn St
300-499 44304
500-899 44311
Alma Ave 44319
Almeter Rd 44306
Alonby Dr 44306
Alpha Ave 44312
Alpha Ct 44311
Alphada Ave 44310
Alta St 44314
Alta Vista Ave 44312
Althea Ave 44319
Alton Dr 44313
Ambassador Ct & Dr 44312
Amber Hills Dr 44313
Amberwood Dr 44312
Ambre Dr 44312
Ambrose Ct 44303
Amelia Ave 44302
Ames Ct 44305
Amesbury Rd 44313
Amherst St 44311
Amy Dr 44321
Anaconda Rd 44310
Anchor Dr 44319
Anderson Ave 44306
Andover Ct 44319
Andrew St 44307
Andrus St 44301
Angle Ln 44312
Angleterre Blvd 44312
Anna Ave 44314
Annabelle Dr 44320
Annadale Ave 44304
Annapolis Ave 44310
Anne Marie Pkwy 44305
Annetta Ave 44313
Ansel Ave 44312
Ansley Ct 44321
Anstock Dr 44319
Anthony Dr 44333
Anton Dr 44306
Anton St 44320
Apache Pl 44321
Appian Way 44333
Apple Ct 44306
Apple Dr 44319
Appletree Rd 44321
April Ct 44307
Aqua Blvd 44319
Aqueduct St 44303
Arbawr Ct 44304
Arborway Dr 44333
Arbour Green Dr 44333
Arbutus St 44307
Arcadia Rd 44312
Arch St 44304
Archmere Dr 44319
E Archwood Ave
1-599 44301
600-1600 44306
1602-1698 44306
W Archwood Ave 44301
Ardella Ave 44306
Arden Pl 44306
Ardendale Ave 44312
Ardleigh Dr 44303
Ardmore Ave 44302
Ardwell Ave 44312
Arenac Rd 44333
Argonne Ave 44310
Argonne Ct 44311
Ariels Way 44312
Arlington Cir 44306
Arlington Pl 44306
S Arlington Rd
1950-2199 44306
2200-2699 44319
2700-3649 44312
Arlington Rdg 44312
Arlington Rdg E 44312
N Arlington St 44305
S Arlington St 44306
Armante Ct 44313
Armil Dr 44312
Armory Rd 44306
Arnold Ave & Ct 44305
Arrow Ave 44319
Arrowhead Trl 44321
Artman Ave 44313
Asbury Rd 44333
Ashbourne Ct 44321
Ashford Dr 44321
Ashford Ln 44313
Ashland Ave 44311
Ashland St 44320
Ashwood Dr 44313
Ashwood Rd 44312
Aspen St 44307
Aspenwood Rd 44333
Aster Ave 44301
Atwood Ave 44301
Auberry Dr 44312
Auburn Pl 44312
Auburndale Ave 44313
Audubon Rd & Spur 44320
Augusta Ave 44302
Augusta Dr 44333
Auldfarm Rd 44320
Auman Dr 44312
Austin Ave 44306
Auten Dr 44320
Autumn Ln 44333
Autumn Leaves Dr 44333
Avalon Ave 44320
Averill Dr 44333
Avis Rd 44312
Avon St 44310
Avondale Dr 44313
Axline Ave 44319
Ayers Ave 44313
B St 44312
Bacher Pl 44303
Bachtel Ave 44311
Bacon Ave 44320
Bailey Ave 44302
Bailey Ct 44304
Baird St
200-649 44311
650-1099 44306
Baker Ave 44312
Baker Blvd 44333
N Balch St 44303
S Balch St 44302
Baldwin Ave & Rd 44312
Bali Dr 44319
Balmoral Dr 44333
Baltimore Ave 44306
Balton Dr 44319
Banbury Rd 44333
Bancroft Rd 44333
Bank Ct & St 44305
Banning Rd 44333
Bannock St 44310
Barbara Ave 44306
Barbara Ct 44319
Barcelona Dr 44313
Barder Ave 44305
Barn Hill Dr 44333
Barnsleigh Dr 44333
Barnstable Rd 44313
Barrett Rd 44333
Barrington Rd 44333
W Bartges St
2-98 44311
100-139 44311
140-499 44307
Barton Dr 44321
Barwell St 44303
Basin Ter 44311
Basswood Ave 44301
Bastogne Dr 44303
N & S Bates St 44303
W Bath Rd
4055A-4055B 44333
2000-2199 44313
2200-5299 44333
Bath Country Dr 44333
Bath Hills Blvd 44333
Battery B St 44305
Battles Ave 44314
Bauer Blvd 44305
Baughman St 44320
Bay Hill Dr 44333
Bay Path Dr 44319
Bayview Dr & Ter 44319
Beach Dr 44312
Beach Drive Ext 44312
Beachview Blvd 44319
Beacon St 44311
Beardsley St
700-949 44311
1000-1550 44301
1552-1598 44301
Beatrice Dr 44310
Beaumont Dr 44333
Beauparc Dr 44313
Beaver St
100-274 44304
276-354 44306
356-399 44306
Beaverbrook Dr 44333
Beck Ave 44302
Becker Ln 44306
Bee Bee Cir 44305
Beech St 44308
Beechnut Dr 44312
Beechnut Hl 44333
Beechview Dr 44305
Beechwood Dr
300-499 44320
500-699 44312
Belair Dr 44319
Belcher Ave 44314
Belden Ave 44310
Belhar Dr 44313
Bell St 44307
Bell Ridge Rd 44303
Bellaire Dr 44333
Bellbrook Dr 44321
Bellcrest Dr 44313
Belle Meade Dr 44321
Belleau Wood Dr 44303
Belleflower Rd 44307
Bellevue Ave
600-899 44307
900-1399 44320
1401-1499 44320
Bellewood Ave 44311
Bellfield Ave 44312
E & W Bellisle Ct & Dr 44319
Bellows St
800-864 44311
866-1046 44311
1048-1048 44311
1050-1499 44301
Belmont St
100-199 44304
1700-1799 44320
Beltz Ct 44311
Belvidere Way 44302
Bender Ave 44312
N Bender Ave 44319
S Bender Ave 44319
Bender Ln 44321
Beni Ct 44305
Benn Ct 44310
Bennett Ave 44320
Bennington Ct 44312
Bennington Rd 44313
Benson Rd 44333
Bent Bow Dr 44313
Bent Branch Ct 44333
Bentley Dr 44321
Benton Ave 44312
Berendo Ave 44313
Berger Rd 44312
Berghoff St 44311
Berkley St 44305
Berkshire Cir 44333
Berkshire Ct 44313
Berman Ave 44305
Berna Rd 44312
Berne St 44312
Bernice St 44307
Berry Ave 44307
Berry Rd 44320
Berrywood Dr 44333
Bertha Ave 44306
Bertsch Ter 44311
Berwick Ct 44321
Berwin St 44310
Berwyck Dr 44312
Beryl Rd 44312
Bessie St 44311
Betana Ave 44310
Beth St 44301
Bethany Ave 44305
Bethwayne Ct 44311
Bettes Ave 44310
Bettie St 44306
Betula Ave 44320
Betz Dr 44306
Beulah Ave 44314
Bevan St 44319
Beverly Ave 44312
Beverly Dr 44306
Bexley Cir 44312
Bey Rd 44312
Bicentennial Blvd 44333
Bickleigh Cir 44312
Big Falls Ave 44310
Big Spruce Dr 44333
Big Valley Dr 44319
Bigelow St 44314
Bilburston Rd 44312
Bina Ave 44314
Bingham Path 44305
Birch St 44301
Birchwood Ave 44310
Birdland Ave 44319
Birdwood Rd 44313
Biruta St 44307
Biscayne Dr 44319
Bishop St 44307
Bisson Ave 44307
Bittaker St 44306
Bittersweet Rd 44333
Bittman St 44303
Bittner Pl 44301
Black St 44306
Black Pond Dr 44320
Blackstone Ave 44310
Blaine Ave 44310
Blair Dr
300-399 44321
1400-1499 44312
Blake Pl 44307
Blanche Ct 44311
Blanche St 44307
Blanding Ave 44310
Blarlens Ave 44305
Blinn St 44310
Bloomfield Ave 44302
Blue Hill Ln 44333
Bluestone Ave 44310
Bluff St 44304
Boardwalk Dr 44319
Boat Dr 44319
Bobwhite Trl 44319
Boder St 44304
Bodine Ct 44320
Boltz Rd 44333
Bonar Ln 44320
Bond St 44313
Bonita Dr 44333
Bonnebrook Dr 44333
Bonnie Brae Ave 44307
Bonshire Rd 44319
Boone St 44306
Booth Ave 44305
Bordeaux Dr 44312
Borton Ave 44302
Boston Ave 44319
Bosworth Dr 44321
Botnick Plz 44301
Botzum Ct 44303
Boughton Dr 44320
Boulevard St 44311
Bowdoin Ln 44311
Bower Ave 44319
E Bowery St 44308
W Bowery St
1-245 44308
247-265 44308
266-999 44307
Bowmanville St 44305
E & W Boxwood Ave 44301
Boyd Ave 44305
Boyer Pkwy 44312
Boyle St 44310
Boylston Rd 44306
Bradford Pt 44313
Brady Ave 44314
Braewick Cir & Dr 44313
E & W Bramble Cir & Dr 44321
Branchwood Cv 44319
Brandon Ave 44305
Brandon Blvd 44312
Brandon Ct 44312
Brant Dr 44319
Brecht Ct 44311
Breckenridge St 44314
Breezewood Dr 44313
Breiding Rd 44310
Brenneman Blvd 44314
Brent Dr 44312
Brentwood Blvd 44321
Brentwood Dr 44333
Bretton Pl 44313
Brewer Ave 44305
Brewster Creek Dr 44306
S Briancol St 44308
Briar Club Trl 44313
Briar Ridge Ln 44313
Briarcliff Ct 44313
Briarcliff Trl 44321
Briarhill Dr & Spur 44333
Briarwood Cir 44321
Briarwood Dr
300-499 44320
4300-4499 44321
Brice Rd 44313
Bridge Rd 44312
Bridger Rd 44312
Bridget St 44306
Bridgewater Dr 44320
Bridle Trl 44333
Bridlewood Dr 44321
Briggle Rd 44320
Brighton Dr 44301
Briner Ave 44305
Bristol Dr 44312
Bristol Ter 44307
Brittain Cir 44310
Brittain Rd
2-8 44305
10-1224 44305
1225-2099 44310
Brittain Woods Rd 44310
Brittany Blvd 44312
Broad St 44305
Broadview Ave 44321
N Broadway St
1-74 44308
75-97 44304
99-199 44304
S Broadway St
1-499 44308
501-597 44311
599-1099 44311
Bronson Rd 44305
Brook Bend Dr 44333
Brookfield Dr 44313
Brookledge Ln 44321
Brookmont Rd 44333
Brookrun Dr 44321
Brookshire Rd 44313
E Brookside Ave 44301
Brookstone Ct 44321
Brookview Rd 44333
Brookwall Dr 44333
Brookwood Dr 44313
Brown St
375-999 44311
1000-1949 44301
1950-2099 44319
Brownstone Ave 44310
Bruce Rd 44306
Bruner St 44306
Brunk Rd 44312
Brunsdorph Rd 44333
Brutus Pl 44301
Bryden Dr 44313
Buchholzer Blvd 44310
E Buchtel Ave
1-40 44308
42-98 44308
100-699 44304
701-999 44305
W Buchtel Ave
1-51 44308
53-129 44308
131-165 44302
167-199 44302
Buchtel Mall 44304
Buckingham St 44306
Buddy Ln 44310
Buena Vista Dr 44319
Buffington Rd 44333
Bulger St 44306
Bungalow Way 44310
Bunker Dr 44333
Burbank Ave 44305
Burkhardt Ave 44301
Burlington Rd 44313
Burnham Rd 44333
Burning Tree Dr 44303
E & W Burns Ave 44310
Burnside St 44312
Burnwyke Ct 44321
Burr Pl 44306
Burr Oak Dr 44333
Burt Ct 44302
Burton Ave 44302
Butler Ave & Ct 44310
Buttercup Ave 44319
Butterfield Dr 44319
Bye St 44320
Byers Ave 44302
Bywood Ave 44333
C St 44312
Cabot Dr 44333
Caddo Ave 44305
Cadillac Blvd 44320
Caine Rd 44312
Cairo Pl 44306
Caladonia Ave 44333
Calderwood Dr 44333
Caldwell Dr 44319
Caleb Dr 44321
Calicoe Dr 44307
California Ave 44314
Callis Dr & Oval 44311
Calvin St 44312
Camborne Blvd 44312
Cambridge Ave 44305
Cambridge Ct 44319
Camden Ridge Blvd 44312
Camellia Dr 44320
Camelot Ct 44321
Cameroon Ct 44305
Campbell St 44307
Canadian Ave 44306
N Canal St 44308
Canal Square Plz 44308
Candlewood Ln 44333
Canfield Ave 44301
Canfield Rd 44312
Canova Dr 44319
Canterbury Cir 44319
Canterbury Rd 44333
Canton Rd 44312
N Canton Rd 44305
Canvasback Cir 44319

Canyon Pkwy 44313
Canyon Trl 44303
Cardigan Dr 44333
Cardinal Rd 44333
Carey Ave 44314
Cargo Ave 44319
Carle Rd 44333
Carlton Dr 44312
Carlysle St 44310
Carnegie Ave 44314
Caroline Ct 44301
Carpenter St 44310
Carper Ave 44312
Carriage Way 44313
Carroll St
  450-498 44304
  500-799 44304
  800-899 44305
Carson Rd 44333
Carter Ave 44301
Carter Dr 44312
Carter Ter 44310
Cartwright Dr 44333
Carver St 44305
Cascade Ct 44304
Cascade Plz 44308
Cascade Mills Dr 44307
N & S Case Ave 44305
Cassidy Ct 44310
Casterton Ave 44303
Castle Blvd 44313
Castle Rdg 44321
Castle Pines Dr 44333
Castlemaine Ct 44333
Castleton Ct 44312
E Caston Rd 44319
E Catawba Ave
  1-499 44301
  600-799 44306
W Catawba Ave 44301
Catawba Cir 44301
Cates Rd 44312
Cato Ave 44310
Catskill Dr 44306
Caxton Cir 44312
Cayuga Ave 44312
Cayugas Dr 44319
Cazenovia Ave 44303
Cedar Ct 44307
E Cedar St 44311
W Cedar St 44307
Cedar Chase Dr 44312
Cedar Creek Ln 44312
Celia Ave 44312
Celia Pl 44301
Celina Ave 44307
Celtic St 44314
W Center St
  2-8 44308
  10-134 44308
  200-299 44302
Centerview Cir & Dr 44321
Chaffin Ct & Rd 44306
Chalker St 44310
Chamberlain Rd 44333
Champlain St 44306
Chandler Ave 44314
Channelwood Cir 44307
Chapman Dr 44305
Charlada Way 44313
Charles Ln 44333
Charles St 44304
Charleston Dr 44319
Charlotte St 44303
Chatham Rd 44313
Chattford Ct 44312
Chaucer Cir 44312
Chelsea Dr 44312
Cheney Ave 44312
Chenoweth Ct 44319
Chenoweth Dr 44319
Chenoweth Ext 44319
Chenoweth Rd 44312
Cherimoya Ave 44319
N Cherry St 44303
Cherrywood Ln 44312

Cheshire Rd 44319
Chester Ave 44314
Chesterfield Dr 44319
W Chestnut St 44307
Chestnut Chase 44321
Chestnut Ridge Blvd 44314
Cheswyck Ct 44321
Chevelle Dr 44319
Childs Ave 44314
Chinook Ave 44305
Chippewa Ave
  900-999 44312
  1200-1499 44305
Chittenden St 44306
Chitty Ave 44303
Christensen Ave 44314
Christie St 44303
Christman Rd 44319
Christopher Dr 44312
Chuckery Ln 44333
Cicero Plz 44301
Cincinnati Ave 44320
Circle Dr 44310
City View Ave & Ter 44307
Clackenn Ave 44306
Clairmont Ave 44301
Clara Ave 44306
Clark St 44306
Claudia Ave 44307
Clay Dr 44311
Clay St
  800-999 44311
  1000-1099 44301
Clayben Dr 44312
Clayton Dr 44319
Clearbrook Dr 44313
Clearfield Ave 44314
Clearview Ave 44314
Clearwood Rd 44321
Clement St 44306
Clemmer Ave 44313
Cleveland St 44306
N Cleveland Massillon Rd 44333
S Cleveland Massillon Rd
  1-1029 44333
  1031-1031 44321
  1033-2499 44321
Cliff Spur Dr 44333
Clifford Ave
  401-473 44301
  475-599 44301
  600-638 44306
  640-999 44306
Clifford Dr 44321
Cliffside Cir 44313
Cliffside Dr
  500-999 44313
  2800-2850 44321
  2852-3199 44321
Clifton Ave 44310
Climax Ave 44310
Clinton Ave 44301
Clondens Ave 44302
Clouse Dr 44312
Clouse St 44333
Clover Hill Rd 44333
Cloverdale Ave 44302
Cloverfield Dr 44321
Cluster Ave 44305
Clyde St 44310
Coach Ln 44312
Cobble Creek Ln 44333
Cobblestone Dr 44321
Coburn St 44311
Cody Cir 44312
Colby Dr 44321
Colchester Ct 44319
Cole Ave
  34-98 44301
  100-649 44301
  650-764 44306
  766-1099 44306
Cole Pl 44308
Coleman Ave 44312
Coleridge Ln 44313

Colette Dr 44306
Coley Path 44306
Colfax Pl 44302
N College St 44304
S College St
  1-89 44308
  90-199 44304
Collier Rd 44320
Collinwood Ave 44310
Colon Dr 44321
Colonial Hills Dr 44310
Colonnade Dr 44333
Colony Cres 44305
Colony Hills Dr 44333
Colony Park Dr 44305
Colopy St 44319
Columbia Ave 44310
Columbine Ave 44312
Columbus Ave
  600-799 44306
  1900-2099 44320
Commerce Dr 44321
Commerce Park Dr 44310
Commercial Dr 44333
Commonwealth Dr 44313
Comstock Ct 44305
Concord Ave 44306
Conestoga Trl 44321
Conger Ave 44303
Congo St 44305
Congress Dr 44305
Conlin Dr 44319
Conmore Ct 44311
Conrad Ave 44314
Continental Pt 44321
Conway St 44314
Cook St 44305
Cookhill Cir 44312
Cooledge Ave 44305
Coon Rd 44321
Cooper Ave 44306
Cope Ave 44319
Copen Dr 44321
Copley Rd
  500-548 44320
  550-2369 44320
  2370-4899 44321
Copley Meadows Dr 44321
Cora Ave 44312
Coral Dr 44313
Corbett Ave 44305
Cordova Ave 44320
Corice St
  500-649 44311
  650-799 44306
Corley St 44306
Cormany Rd 44319
Cornell St 44310
Coronado Ave 44333
Corsham Cir 44312
Corson Ave 44302
Corunna Ave 44333
Corwin Ave 44310
Cory Ave 44314
Cosmos Ave 44319
Cotswold Dr 44321
Cottage Grove Rd 44319
Cotter Ave 44305
Cottonwood Cir 44312
Country Club Dr 44313
Court Dr 44333
Courtland Ave 44320
Courtland Dr 44314
Courtleigh Dr 44313
Courtney Pl 44311
Cove Blvd 44319
Coventry St
  877-1399 44306
  1550-1898 44301
Covington Rd 44313
Cox Rd 44319
Coy Dr 44333
Cramer Ave 44312
Cranberry Ln 44313
Crane Walk 44306
Cranz Pl 44310

Crawfis Blvd 44333
Crawford Rd 44313
Cree Ave 44305
Creekledge Ln 44321
Creekrun Dr 44321
Creighton Ave 44310
Crescent Dr 44301
Crestline Dr 44312
Crestmont Ct 44321
Creston Ave 44310
Crestview Ave 44320
Crestwood Ave 44302
Cricket Cir 44333
Croghan Way 44321
Cromwell Dr & Ter 44313
Crosby St
  100-449 44303
  451-497 44302
  499-799 44302
E Crosier St
  1-73 44311
  75-649 44311
  651-697 44306
  699-1099 44306
W Crosier St 44311
Cross Ct 44311
Cross St 44311
Cross Way 44312
Crouse St
  300-549 44311
  550-598 44306
  600-899 44306
  901-999 44306
Crown St 44302
Crusade Dr 44321
Crystal Dr 44312
Crystal Pt 44333
Crystal St 44305
Crystal Lake Rd 44333
Culpepper Dr 44313
Cumberland Dr 44306
Curtis St 44301
Cutler Pkwy 44305
Cuyahoga St
  2-18 44304
  20-299 44304
  300-677 44310
  678-1699 44313
E & W Cuyahoga Falls Ave 44310
Cynthia Cir 44333
Cypress Ave 44301
Cypress Ct 44321
Dahlgren Dr 44306
Daisy Ave 44319
Dale St 44313
Dales Dr 44312
Dallas Ave 44301
Dalton Rd 44333
E Dalton St 44310
W Dalton St 44310
Damar Dr 44305
Damon St 44310
Dan St 44310
Danbury Ln 44321
Danchite Ave 44320
Danforth Rd 44312
Dangel Ave 44312
Daniels Ave 44312
Danmead Ave 44305
Danville Ct 44311
Darkow St 44306
Darnell Dr 44319
Darrah Dr 44312
Darrell Ln 44312
Darrow Rd 44305
E & W Dartmore Ave 44301
Dartmouth Ave 44313
Darwin Ave 44306
Davenport Ave & Cir 44312
Davies Ave 44306
Davis St 44310
Dawes Ave 44302
Dawn Dr 44312
Dawson Rd 44320
Day St 44305

Daylesford Dr 44333
Dayton Pl & St 44310
Dean St 44304
Dearborn Dr 44313
Deepridge Cir 44313
Deepwood Dr 44313
Deerfield Dr 44333
Deering Dr 44313
Delaware Ave
  300-899 44303
  2000-2599 44312
Delaware Pl 44303
Delaware Trl 44321
Delba St 44307
Delcon Cir 44313
Delia Ave 44320
Dellenberger Ave 44312
Dellwood Rd 44312
Delmar Ave 44310
Delno Dr 44320
Delora Dr 44319
Delos St 44306
Delray Dr 44321
Delta 77 Dr 44312
Denaple Ave 44312
Denby Ave 44313
Denise Dr 44321
Denman Dr 44319
Dennis Dr 44312
Dennison Ave 44312
Denver St 44305
Derby St 44314
Derby Downs Dr 44306
Derbydale Rd 44306
Derbyshire Rd 44319
Derling Rd 44319
Derrwood Dr 44333
Detroit St 44305
Devalera St 44310
Devereux Dr 44321
Devon Ct 44312
Devon Ln 44313
Devonshire Ct 44321
Devonshire Dr 44312
Dewalt Dr 44312
Dewitt Dr 44313
Dewport Dr 44312
Dexter Rd 44320
Diagonal Rd
  500-1149 44320
  1150-1349 44307
  1350-1899 44320
Diana Ave 44307
Diandrea Dr 44333
Dick Ave 44302
Dickemery Dr 44303
Die Gem Way 44312
Dietz Ave 44301
Dillon Rd 44313
Division St 44303
Divot Spur 44319
Dodge Ave 44302
Dogwood Ln 44333
Dogwood Ter 44321
Dollar Dr 44319
Dolphin Dr 44313
Dolton Rd 44312
Dominion Dr 44313
Don Dr 44319
Donald Ave 44306
Donova Ln 44310
Dopler St 44303
Dorcas Ave 44305
Dorchester Ct 44312
Dorchester Rd
  100-299 44313
  300-799 44320
Doris Ave 44303
Dorothy Ave 44307
Dorset St 44305
Dorwil Ct & Dr 44319
Dot Ct 44319
Doty Dr 44306
Doubler Dr 44319
Douglas St 44307
Dover Ave 44320

Dover Dr 44312
Doves Xing 44319
Dow Dr 44313
Dowling Dr 44333
Downing Pl 44306
Doxey Dr 44312
Doyle Ct & St 44303
Dreisbach Dr 44320
Dremina Rock Dr 44333
E & W Dresden Ave 44301
Drexel Ave 44310
Driftwood Ct 44321
Druid Dr 44321
Druid Walk 44306
Drury Ave 44305
Duane Ave 44306
Duane Dr 44320
Dublin Ct 44321
Dublin St 44305
Dudley St 44305
Duer Ct 44311
Dunbar Dr 44311
Duncan Spur 44333
Dundee Ave 44305
Dunstone Ave 44312
Durand Rd 44333
Durst Blvd 44319
Durward Rd 44313
Eagle Dr 44312
Eaglenest Ave 44303
Eagles Ln 44306
Eagles Chase Dr 44313
Earhart Ave 44320
Earl Ct 44304
East Ave
  500-799 44320
  800-1499 44307
  1520-2599 44314
Easter Ave 44307
Eastgate Ave 44312
Eastgate Commons Dr 44312
Eastgay Dr 44313
Eastholm Ave 44312
Eastland Ave 44305
Eastlawn Ave 44305
Easton Dr 44310
Eastport Dr 44312
Eastview Dr 44312
Eastview Ter 44307
Eastwood Ave 44305
Eaton Ave 44303
Eaton Dr 44312
Eaton Park Ln 44303
Eber Ave 44305
Echo Hills Rd 44333
Eckard Ave 44314
Ecton Rd 44303
Eddishire Rd 44319
Edgar Ln 44312
Edge St 44306
Edgebrook Ave 44312
Edgehill Dr 44312
Edgemere Ct 44321
Edgemoor Ave 44313
Edgepark Dr 44319
Edgerton Ct & Rd 44303
Edgewood Ave 44307
Edinburg Ct 44319
Edington Rd 44333
Edison Ave 44301
Edith Ave 44312
Edmeyer Ct 44306
Edmore Rd 44333
Edmund Ave 44312
Edward Ave 44310
Edwards Dr 44306
Edwin Ave 44314
Egret Dr 44319
Eileen Dr 44319
El Dorado Dr 44319
Elbon Ave 44306
Elbur Ave 44306
Elder Ave 44301
Elderberry Ave 44319
Eldridge Ave 44301
Eleanor Ter 44303

Elgin Dr 44333
Elia Cir 44333
Elinor Ave 44305
Elizabeth Ave 44321
Elizabeth Pkwy 44304
Elko Ave 44305
Ella Ct 44314
Ellen Ave 44305
Ellen Dr 44312
Eller Ave 44306
Ellet Ave 44312
Ellet Grove Ave 44312
Ellsworth Dr 44313
Elm Dr 44305
Elm Grove Ave 44312
Elma St 44310
Elmdale Ave
  1-249 44313
  250-399 44320
Elmo St 44319
Elmore Ave 44302
Elmwood Ct 44302
Elora Ave 44319
Elwell Ct 44306
Ely Rd 44313
Embassy Pkwy 44333
Emerald Dr 44312
E & W Emerling Ave 44301
Emerson St 44305
Emma Ave 44302
Emmet Ct 44311
Emmett Dr 44312
Emmitt Rd 44306
Emmons Ave 44312
Emorey Cir 44312
Emory Ave 44310
Encell Dr 44321
Endicott Dr 44313
Englewood Ave
  1400-1698 44305
  1800-1898 44312
  1900-1954 44312
  1956-2298 44312
English Tern Dr 44333
Enright Ave 44312
Eric Dr 44305
Ericsson Ave 44306
Erie Ave 44312
Erie Dr 44333
Erskine Ave 44306
Essex St 44306
Essig Rd 44312
Esther Ave 44312
Euclid Ave 44307
Eugene St 44306
Eva Ave
  442-458 44301
  460-649 44301
  650-804 44306
  806-1099 44306
Eva Walk 44306
Evans Ave
  500-734 44310
  736-748 44310
  750-1390 44305
  1392-1398 44305
Evelyn Ct 44302
Evelyn Ln 44306
Everest Cir 44333
Everett Ave 44302
Everett Rd 44333
Evergreen Ave 44301
Evergreen Cir 44301
Evergreen Dr 44303
Evers St 44310
Everton Dr 44307
Ewart Dr 44306
Ewart Rd 44312
Ewing Ct 44304
Excelsior Ave 44306
E Exchange St
  1-99 44308
  100-549 44304
  550-910 44306
  912-998 44306
W Exchange St
  1-27 44308

29-99 44308
100-144 44302
146-1074 44302
1075-1799 44313
Exeter Rd 44306
Fair Ct & Ln 44312
Fairbanks Pl 44306
Fairdale Dr 44312
Fairfax Rd 44313
Fairfield Ave 44303
Fairhill Dr 44313
Fairington Ave 44321
E & W Fairlawn Blvd 44313
Fairlawn Knolls Cir & Dr 44313
Fairview Ave 44314
Fairview Dr 44319
Fairway Dr 44333
Fairway Park Dr 44321
Falcon Ave & Ct 44319
Fallen Log Ln 44333
Falmouth Rd 44333
Fan Dr 44319
Far View Rd 44312
Farmdale Rd 44312
Farr Rd 44319
Fawler Ave 44314
Fawn Meadows Dr 44321
Faye Rd 44306
Faylor Dr 44312
Fenton Ave 44312
Fern Rd 44312
Fern St 44307
Ferndale St 44304
Fernette Ave 44312
Fernway Dr 44321
Fernwood Dr 44320
Fess Ave 44307
Fettro Rd 44312
Field Circle Ave 44312
Fieldcrest Dr 44333
Fig Dr 44319
Fillmore Ave 44314
Finland Ave 44319
Finley Dr 44312
N Fir Hl & St 44304
Fireside Dr 44319
E Firestone Blvd 44301
N Firestone Blvd
173-237 44301
239-599 44301
600-999 44306
S Firestone Blvd 44301
W Firestone Blvd 44301
Firestone Pkwy 44301
Firestone Trce 44333
Firstmerit Cir 44307
Flanders Ave 44314
Fleming Dr 44311
Flickinger Rd 44312
Flight Memorial Pkwy 44333
Flint Ave & Dr 44305
Flora Ave 44314
Florida Ave 44314
Florida Pl 44303
Flower Ct 44304
Flowerdale Dr 44319
Floyd St 44310
Flynn Ave 44319
Forbes Ave 44306
Ford Ave 44305
Fordham Ct 44313
Forest Dr 44312
Forest Brook Dr 44321
Forest Cove Dr 44319
Forest Mill Ln 44319
Forest Oak Dr 44312
Forest Oaks Dr 44333
Forest Park Blvd 44312
Forest Pool Rd 44333
Forest Ridge Ct 44333
Forest View Dr 44333
N Forge St 44304
S Forge St
1-51 44304
53-99 44304
101-149 44308
151-299 44308
Forget Me Not St 44319
N Fork Dr 44333
Forrest Ct, Dr & St 44306
Fort Island Dr 44333
Fortuna Dr 44312
Fountain St
101-259 44304
261-399 44306
Four Seasons Dr 44333
Foursome Ave 44313
Fouse Ave 44310
Fowler Ave 44319
Fox Rd 44320
Fox Hollow Dr 44321
Fox Hollow Ln 44333
Fox Run Rd 44321
Foxboro Ave 44305
Foxchase Dr 44333
Foxford Ct 44312
Foxhollow Ct 44313
Foxtail Trl 44321
Foxwood Dr 44333
Frallea Rd 44312
Frances Ave 44310
Frank Blvd 44320
N Frank Blvd 44313
S Frank Blvd 44313
Franklin St 44304
Franz Dr 44333
Franzen Ln 44310
Frase Ave 44305
Frashure Dr 44321
Frazier Ave 44305
Frederick Ave 44310
Frederick Blvd 44320
Freedom Ave 44310
Fremont Ave 44312
Fried St 44320
Fritch Ave 44314
Fritsch Ave 44312
Fruit Dr 44319
Frye Dr 44312
Fryman Dr 44333
Fuller St 44306
Fulmer Ave 44312
Fulton Dr 44333
Fulton St 44305
Fultz St 44307
Furnace St
1-39 44308
41-74 44308
75-299 44304
Furnace Run Dr 44307
Gable Ave 44319
Gage St
400-574 44311
576-662 44306
664-700 44306
702-798 44306
Galat Way 44307
Gale Dr 44312
Gale Pl 44302
Gale St 44302
Galena Ave 44301
Galewood Dr 44312
Galsworthy Dr 44313
Ganyard Rd 44313
N & S Garden Ct & Pl 44312
Gardendale Ave 44310
Gardiner Run 44321
Garfield St 44310
Garland Ave 44313
Garman Rd 44313
Garner Ave 44310
Garnette Rd 44313
Garry Rd 44305
Garson Dr 44319
Garth Ave 44320
Gault St 44311
Gavington Pl 44313
Gaycroft Ct 44321
Gaylan Dr 44310
Gaylord Dr 44320
Gem Ave 44307
General St 44305
Genesee Rd 44303
Geneva Ave 44314
Genoa Ave 44305
George Washington Blvd
700-1299 44312
1345-1345 44306
Georgia Ave 44306
Geraldine Ave 44310
Gesten Dr 44321
Getz St 44301
Ghent Ct 44312
Ghent Rd 44333
Ghent Hills Rd 44333
Ghent Ridge Rd 44333
Ghentwood Dr 44333
Gibbs Pl 44306
Gibbs Rd 44312
Gilbert St 44314
Gilchrist Rd 44305
Gilpin Rd 44313
Girard St 44301
Glaser Pkwy 44306
Gleason Ave 44312
N & S Glencoe Dr 44319
Glendale Ave 44302
Glendora Ave 44320
Glengary Rd 44333
Glenhaven Ave 44321
Glenmoor Dr 44321
Glenmount Ave
1500-1900 44301
1902-1948 44301
2000-2299 44319
Glenn St 44320
N & W Glenridge Rd 44319
Glenway Dr 44305
E Glenwood Ave
1-159 44304
160-198 44310
200-799 44310
W Glenwood Ave 44304
Gless Ave 44301
Gloucester Ct 44313
Gojo Plz 44311
Gold St 44303
Golda Pl 44311
Goldleaf Dr 44333
Good St 44304
Good Park Blvd 44320
Goodenough Ave 44320
Goodhue Dr 44313
Goodview Ave 44305
Goodwin Ave 44303
Goodyear Blvd 44305
Gordon Dr 44302
Gorge Blvd 44310
Gotham Ct 44304
Gougler Rd 44319
Gowanda Ave 44312
Grace Ave 44320
Grace Rd 44312
Grafton Rd 44333
N & S Graham Ave & Cir 44312
Grand Ave
1-99 44303
100-102 44302
104-499 44302
Grand Blvd 44320
Grand Park Ave 44310
Grandin Rd 44313
Grandview Ave 44305
Grandview Dr 44333
Granger Rd 44333
Grant St
300-350 44304
351-1074 44311
1075-1499 44301
Grapevine Swing 44321
Gray Ct 44311
W Grayling Dr 44333
Graystone Ave 44310
Graystone Cir 44320
Great Run Ln 44333
Green Dr 44333
Green St 44303
Greencrest Ter 44313
Greenhaven Cir & Dr 44333
Greenhill Dr 44319
Greening Dr 44321
Greenlawn Ave 44301
Greenleaf Rd 44312
Greensfield Cir & Ln 44321
Greenspire Ln 44333
Greenvale Ave 44313
Greenville Ln 44333
Greenwing Ct 44319
Greenwood Ave
200-299 44313
309-329 44320
331-1499 44320
Greer Rd 44319
N Gregg Rd 44306
S Gregg Rd 44319
Gregory Ave 44301
Gregory Dr 44312
Greissing Ter 44311
Gresham Dr 44333
Grey Village Dr 44319
Gridley St 44306
Griffin Ct 44306
Griffith Rd 44312
Grifton Ave 44305
Grove St 44302
Grupe Ave 44319
Gunarh Dr 44319
Gurley Ave & Cir 44310
Guss Ave 44312
Guys Run Rd 44319
Hackberry St 44301
Hadden Cir 44313
Halcyon Dr 44319
Halifax Rd 44313
Hall St 44303
Hallandale Dr 44333
Hallie Ave 44305
N Hametown Rd 44333
S Hametown Rd 44321
Hamlin St 44320
Hammel St 44306
Hammond Blvd 44321
Hampshire Rd
1-559 44313
560-697 44333
699-699 44333
Hampton Rd 44305
Hampton Knoll Dr 44313
Hampton Ridge Dr 44313
Hancock Ave & Cir 44314
Hanley Ct 44303
Hanna Pkwy 44319
Hanover Ct 44313
Hanover Dr 44312
Hansen Ct 44305
Harbour View Dr 44319
Harcourt Dr 44313
Harden Ave 44310
Hardesty Blvd 44320
Harding Ave 44312
Hardy Rd 44313
Harlem Rd 44320
Harmon Ave 44307
Harmony Rd 44333
Harmony Hills Dr 44321
Harold St 44310
Harpster Ave 44314
Harrington Rd 44319
Harris Ct 44310
Harris St 44304
Harrison Ave 44314
Hart St 44306
Harter Ave 44305
Hartford Ave 44320
Hartford Ln 44312
Harts Landing Dr 44312
Harvard St 44311
Harvest Dr 44333
Harvey Ave 44314
Harvey Ct 44304
Haskell Dr 44333
Hastings Ct 44319
Haverhill Rd 44333
Hawk Ave 44312
N Hawkins Ave 44313
S Hawkins Ave
1-399 44313
400-418 44320
420-1799 44320
1800-2299 44314
Hawksfield Cir 44321
Hawthorne Ave 44303
Hayden Ave 44320
Hayne Rd 44312
Haynes St 44307
Hazel Pl 44304
Hazel St
600-1399 44305
1800-1899 44312
Hazelwood Ave 44305
Hearthstone Cir 44320
Heath Dr 44319
Heather Ct & Ln 44313
Heather Hills Rd 44333
Heatherleigh Dr 44333
Hedden Ave 44311
Hedgewood Dr 44319
Heights View Dr 44305
Heimbaugh Ave 44306
Helen Ave 44310
Helmsdale Dr 44312
Helston Ave 44312
Hemlock St 44301
Hemlock Hills Dr 44313
Hemsley Ave 44319
Henconto Dr 44321
Hennetta Ave 44320
Henry St 44305
Hentrado Rd 44333
Herberich Ave 44301
Herbert Rd 44312
Hereford Dr 44303
Heritage Ct 44320
Heritage Ln 44333
Heritage Woods Dr 44321
Herkender Ave 44310
Herman Ave 44307
Heron Watch Dr 44319
Herons Way 44319
Hessel Dr 44313
Hi Vue Dr 44312
Hiawatha Pl 44313
Hicircle Dr 44319
Hickory Rd 44333
Hickory St 44303
Hickory Farm Ln 44333
Hidden Hollow Ln 44313
Hidden Lake Blvd 44312
Hidden Valley Rd 44333
Hideway Cv 44319
High Ave 44305
N High St 44308
S High St
1-359 44308
360-398 44311
400-600 44311
602-698 44311
High Grove Blvd 44312
High Point Dr 44321
High Ridge Trl 44333
Highbrook St 44301
N & S Highland Ave 44303
Highlands Dr 44333
Highpoint Ave 44312
Highview Ave 44301
Hilbish Ave 44312
Hilen Rd 44333
Hillandale Dr 44333
Hillcrest St
1300-1449 44307
1450-1699 44314
Hillier Ave 44310
Hillman Rd 44312
Hillsdale Ave 44303
Hillside Dr 44321
Hillside Ter 44305
Hillstock Ave 44312
Hilltop Dr 44310
Hillview Dr 44319
Hillwood Dr 44320
Hilton Dr 44313
Himelright Blvd 44320
Hinman Ct 44301
Hite St
1200-1399 44307
1422-1599 44314
Hobart Ave 44306
Hogue Ave 44310
Hohman Ave 44319
Holgate Rd 44313
Holland Dr 44313
Hollibaugh Ave 44310
Hollinger Ave 44302
Hollis St 44305
Holliston Rd 44333
Holly Ave 44301
Holly Cir 44321
Hollythorn Dr 44321
Hollywood Ave 44313
Holy Cross Blvd 44306
Home Ave
500-649 44305
650-1699 44310
Home Care Pl 44320
Homer Ave 44320
Homestead St 44306
Homewood Ave 44312
Honeywell Dr 44313
Honodle Ave 44305
Honor Ln 44312
Hoover Ave 44312
Horizon Dr 44313
Horton Ave 44312
Hottle St 44319
House Dr 44319
Howard Ave 44312
Howard Ct 44303
Howard Ln 44312
N Howard St
1-159 44308
160-439 44304
440-472 44310
474-1300 44310
1302-1498 44310
Howe St 44307
Hoye Ave 44320
Hubbard St 44303
Huber St 44306
Hudson Ave 44306
Hue Dr 44319
Hughstowne Dr 44333
Hugill Ct 44304
Huguelet St 44305
Hull Dr 44321
Hummel Dr 44319
Hunsicker Dr 44319
Hunt St 44306
Hunt Club Dr 44321
Hunter Ridge Cir 44333
Hunters Trl 44313
Huntington Ave 44306
Hurlburt Ave 44303
Huron Ave 44312
Hyacinth Ave & Ct 44319
Hyde Ave 44302
Hyde Park Ave 44310
Hyfield Ave 44319
Hyland Dr 44312
Ibis Dr 44319
Idaho Ave 44314
Idalia Ave 44319
Idlebrook Dr 44333
Idlewild St 44313
Idlewood Ave 44313
Ido Ave 44301
Igleheart Rd 44312
Impala Dr 44319
Imrek Dr 44312
Ina Ave & Ct 44306
Inas Dr 44321
Income Dr 44305
Independence Ave 44310
Indian Trl 44314
Indian Hills Trl 44313
Indianola Ave 44305
Industrial Pkwy 44310
Ingalls Rd 44312
Ingersoll Dr 44320
E & W Ingleside Dr 44319
Inman St 44306
Inner Circle Dr 44333
Innovation Way 44305
Interstate Pkwy 44312
Inverness Rd 44313
Iona Ave 44314
Ira Ave 44301
Ira Rd 44333
Iredell St 44310
Ireland Ave 44301
Irene Ave 44305
E & W Iris Ave 44319
Irisdale Pl 44311
Ironwood Cir 44312
Ironwood Dr 44312
Ironwood Rd 44306
Iroquois Ave
352-398 44305
400-499 44305
1300-1399 44312
Irvin St 44306
Isaac Trl 44306
Isle View Dr 44319
Ithaca Ave 44312
Iuka Ave 44310
Ivan Pl 44304
Ivor Ave 44314
Ivy Ct 44307
Ivy Pl 44301
Jack Ave 44312
Jacoby Rd 44321
James Ave 44312
Janis Ave 44314
Janwood Dr 44321
Jarvis Rd 44319
N & S Jasmine Ave 44319
Jason Ave 44314
Java Ave 44305
Jean Ave 44310
Jeanette Ct 44308
Jeanie J Ave 44310
Jefferson Ave
900-1049 44302
1050-1541 44313
1543-1699 44313
Jenkins Blvd 44306
Jennifer Ln 44310
Jennifer St 44313
Jerome Ave 44320
Jesse Ave 44310
Jewell Dr 44311
Jewett St 44305
Johnland Ave 44305
N & S Johns Ave 44305
Johnston Ct 44311
Johnston St
500-649 44311
650-1099 44306
1100-1199 44305
Jolson Ave 44319
Jonah Dr 44321
Jonathan Ave
700-900 44306
902-998 44306
1000-1099 44333
Jonathan Ln 44333
Joplin Dr 44319
Jordan Ln 44306
Joseph Ave 44306
Joy Ave 44306
Joyce Ave 44319
Judith Ave 44313
Judy Ave 44319
Juliana Dr 44312
Julien Ave, Cir & Ct 44310
Jumpers Dr 44333
Juneau Ave 44320
Juniata Rd 44305
Junior Ave 44312
Juniper Ave 44310
Juno Pl 44333

Kalman Ln 44301
Kansas Ave 44314
Karen Dr 44313
Karg Dr 44313
Karl Dr 44321
Katherine Ave 44310
Katherines Ln 44321
Kathleen St 44303
Kathryn Pl 44304
Kays Dr 44306
Keck St 44305
Keeney St 44310
Keifer Ct 44307
Keith Ave 44313
Kellar Ave 44312
Keller St 44310
Kellogg Ave 44314
Kelly Ave 44306
Kelly Ct
100-199 44306
3000-3099 44312
Kelsey Dr 44321
Keltner Rd 44319
Kelty Ct 44312
Kemble Ave 44319
Kemery Rd 44333
Ken Dr 44312
Kendale Dr 44314
Kendall Rd 44321
Kenilworth Dr 44313
Kenmore Blvd
101-253 44301
255-499 44301
500-1599 44314
Kennebec Ave 44305
Kennedy Rd 44305
Kenneth Pl 44305
Kenridge Rd 44333
Kensington Pl 44314
Kensington Rd 44333
Kensington Way 44321
Kent Ct, Pl & St 44305
Kenton Ct 44313
Kentucky Ave 44314
Kenwick Dr 44313
Kenwood Ave 44313
Kenyon St 44311
Kermit Ave 44305
Kerns Dr 44305
Kessel Ave 44310
Kevin Dr 44313
Kew Dr 44319
Keys Pl 44306
Keyser Dr 44319
Keystone Blvd 44320
Kibler Rd
2500-2590 44320
2591-2799 44321
Kickapoo Ave 44305
Kildare Dr 44313
Kilgore St 44314
Killian Rd
1-874 44319
875-2399 44312
2401-2429 44312
Killingly St 44305
Kim Dr 44312
Kimball Ct 44314
Kimberly Rd 44313
Kimlyn Cir 44310
Kimwood Dr 44312
Kincoun Ave 44314
Kindig Spur 44321
King Ct 44303
King Dr 44302
Kings Ct 44321
Kingsbridge Ct 44313
Kingsbury Blvd 44321
Kingsley Ave 44313
Kingsley Dr 44319
Kingsport Way 44314
Kingston Pl 44320
Kingswood Dr 44313
Kinzie St 44305
Kipling St
500-649 44311
650-718 44306
720-799 44306
Kirby Dr 44319
Kirkwall Dr 44321
Kirkwood Ct 44304
Kirn Ave 44304
Kirn St 44311
Kline Ave 44305
Kling St
300-999 44311
1000-1099 44301
Klinger St 44319
Knapp Dr 44319
Knecht Ct 44311
Knight Rd 44306
Knightsbridge Dr 44313
Knofl Dr 44319
Knollcrest Ct 44313
Knollwood Dr 44312
Knollwood Ln 44333
Knox Ave 44314
Knox Blvd 44320
Koerber Ave 44314
Kohler Ave 44314
Koons Ct 44311
Kraus Ct 44307
Krebs Dr 44319
Kreiner Ave 44312
Kromer Ave 44306
Krumroy Rd
900-1699 44306
1700-2599 44312
Kryder Ave 44305
Kubic Dr 44313
Kubler Trl 44312
Kuder Ave 44303
Kumho Dr 44333
Kyle Ln 44310
La Belle Ave 44320
La Croix Ave 44307
Laburnum Dr 44319
Ladd St 44312
Lafayette Cir & Dr 44303
Laffer Ave 44305
Lafollette St
500-649 44311
651-697 44306
699-799 44306
Laforce Dr 44319
Lagoon St 44314
Laird St 44305
Lajoy Dr 44319
Lake Rd 44312
Lake St 44301
Lake Beach Blvd 44319
Lake Front Dr 44319
Lake James Dr & Ter 44312
Lake Of The Woods
Blvd 44333
Lake Pointe Dr 44333
Lake Vista Rd 44319
Lakeland Ave 44320
Lakemont Ave 44314
Lakeshore Blvd 44301
Lakeside Ct 44301
Lakeview Ave 44314
Lakeview Dr
801-817 44312
819-899 44312
1900-2199 44333
Lakeway St 44319
Lakewood Blvd 44314
Lakota Ave 44319
Lamb Dr 44319
Lamesa Dr 44333
Lamont St 44305
Lamparter St 44311
Lamprey Cir 44319
Lancaster Rd 44313
Landon St 44306
Landsbury Ct 44321
Lane St 44307
Lang Rd 44319
Lansing Rd 44312
Larch St 44301
Larchmont Rd 44313
Larkin Ave 44305
Larkspur Ln 44333
Lauby Ave 44306
Laura Ln 44312
Laurel Ave 44307
Laurel Valley Dr 44313
Lavada Dr 44312
Laverne Ln 44312
Lawn Dr 44312
Lawnshire Dr 44321
Lawton St 44320
Layden Ave 44310
League St 44305
Lease St 44306
Lecona Dr 44319
Leda Pl 44311
Ledgestone Ct 44321
Ledgewater Dr 44319
Ledgewick Cir 44333
Ledgewood Dr 44333
Lee Dr
100-798 44305
800-899 44305
2000-2299 44306
Leedom Ln 44312
Leeds St 44305
Leeser Ave 44314
Legan Ct 44319
Leicester Dr 44319
Leighton Ave 44314
Leighton Ln 44319
Leighurst Dr 44319
Leila St 44310
Leland Ave 44312
Lemar Ave 44319
Lenox Village Dr 44333
Leo St 44305
Leonard St 44307
Leonora Ave 44305
Leora St 44301
Leroy Ave 44307
Leslie Ave 44314
Lessig Ave 44312
Letchworth Dr 44303
Lethbridge Cir & Ln 44321
Lewis St 44301
Lexington Ave 44310
Ley Dr 44319
Liberty Dr 44313
Lido Ct 44319
Lillian St 44307
Lily St 44301
Linda Dr 44319
Linda Ln 44321
Linda St 44319
Lindakay Dr 44312
Lindale Cir, Dr & St 44312
Lindbergh Ave 44320
Lindell St 44305
Linden Ave 44310
Lindenwood Ave 44301
Lindsay Ave 44306
Linnway Dr 44312
E Linwood Ave 44301
W Linwood Ave 44301
Linwood Rd 44312
Lisa Ann Dr 44313
Litchfield Dr 44321
Litchfield Rd 44305
Little St 44320
Littledale Rd 44319
Lloyd St 44301
Loamshire Rd 44319
Loch Raven Blvd 44321
Lockert Ct 44311
Lockwood St 44314
Locust St
101-149 44302
151-300 44302
302-348 44302
351-397 44307
399-499 44307
Lodi St 44305
E & W Lods Ct & St 44304
Logan Cir 44319
Logan Dr 44320
Logan Pkwy 44319
Lois Dr 44333
Lola St 44305
Loma Dr 44319
Lomae Rd 44312
Lombard St 44310
Londonderry Dr 44333
Long Rd 44312
E Long St 44311
W Long St 44301
E & W Long Lake
Blvd 44319
Longacre Dr 44319
Longstone Ave 44310
Longview Ave 44307
Longwood Ln 44333
Longworth Ln 44319
Looker Ave 44319
Lookout Ave 44310
Lorain St 44305
Lorena Ave 44313
Lorenz Ave 44310
Lorielar St 44304
Louisiana Ave 44314
Lovers Ln
400-499 44301
500-649 44311
650-1099 44306
Lovisa St 44311
Lowe Dr 44319
E & W Lowell Ave 44310
Lownsdale Ave 44313
Lucille Ave 44310
Lucy St 44306
Luedella Ct 44310
Lumiere St 44306
Lurie Ave
500-599 44301
600-699 44306
Luzon Cir 44319
Lyman Ln 44313
Lynn Dr 44312
Lynndale Dr 44313
Lynne Rd 44312
Lynnhaven Ln 44313
Mack St 44305
Mackinaw Ave & Cir 44333
Madison Ave 44320
Madora Ave 44319
Madrid Dr 44313
Mafia Cir 44321
Magdalyn Dr 44320
Magennis Ave 44307
E & W Magnet St 44319
Magnolia Ave 44310
Magnolia Dr 44321
Magua Dr 44319
Maiden Ln 44308
N Main St
1-1 44308
3-149 44308
400-438 44310
440-1299 44310
S Main St
1-329 44308
331-339 44308
340-1079 44311
1080-2139 44301
2140-5000 44319
5002-5010 44319
Majesty Ct 44333
Malacca St 44305
Malasia Rd 44305
Malden St 44313
Mallard Dr 44319
Mallard Point Dr 44319
Mallard Pond Dr 44333
Malley Ave 44319
Mallison Ave & Ct 44307
Malta Dr 44319
Malvern Rd 44303
Manchester Rd
1100-1399 44307
1400-2524 44314
2525-4199 44319
Manderly Dr 44313
Mangold St 44311
Manila Pl 44311
Manister Ct 44314
Manitou Ave 44305
Manning Ave 44307
Manning Tree Dr 44321
Manor Rd 44313
Mansard Ln 44312
Mansfield Ave 44319
Manton Ct 44306
Maple Dr 44312
Maple Ln 44321
N Maple St
2-12 44303
14-124 44303
125-299 44304
S Maple St
1-33 44303
35-60 44303
61-426 44302
428-498 44302
Maple Hill Ln 44312
E & W Mapledale Ave 44301
Mapleleaf Hl 44333
Maplewood Ave 44313
Maralroy Way 44321
Marben Rd 44312
Marcy St 44301
Mardon Ave 44303
Marfa Cir 44321
Margaret Rd 44312
Margaret St 44306
Margate Dr 44313
Marie Ave 44314
Marie Ter 44306
Marietta Ave 44320
Marigold Ave 44301
Marilyn Dr 44320
Maringo Ave 44314
Marion Ave
191-399 44312
1400-1599 44313
Marion Pl 44311
Mark Dr 44313
Mark Trl 44321
E Market St
1-25 44308
27-299 44308
300-699 44304
700-1962 44305
1964-1998 44305
2000-2502 44312
2504-2598 44312
W Market St
23-97 44308
99-102 44308
103-899 44303
900-2625 44313
2626-2712 44333
2711-2711 44334
2714-3824 44333
2715-3825 44333
Markey St 44319
Markle St 44306
Marks Ave 44305
Marlowe Ave 44313
Marmont Dr 44313
Marne St 44310
Marquette Rd 44333
Marrow St 44320
Marsh Fern Ln 44312
Marsh View Dr 44319
Marshall Ave 44303
N & S Martadale Dr 44333
N Martha Ave 44305
S Martha Ave
1-200 44305
202-298 44305
300-399 44306
Martin Ave 44306
Martin Pl 44307
Martin Rd 44333
Martin Crest Dr 44312
Martin Luther King Jr
Blvd 44304
Marviel Dr 44333
Marview Ave 44310
Marvin Ave 44302
Marvo Dr 44306
Mary Peavey Eagle Ct 44307
Maryguard Dr 44312
Maryland Ave
1100-1399 44319
2200-2299 44314
Maryville Ave 44305
Mason Ave 44306
Massillon Rd
1-399 44312
400-1549 44306
1550-3449 44312
Matthews St 44306
Maxen Dr 44307
Maxfli Dr 44312
Maxine Pl 44305
Maxwell Rd 44312
May Ct & St 44311
Mayes Pl 44321
Mayfair Cir 44312
Mayfair Rd
800-999 44303
2400-3550 44312
Mayfield Ave 44313
Maylo Path 44312
Mayview Dr 44313
Maywood Ave 44306
Mcallister Rd 44312
Mcchesney Rd 44306
Mccoy Rd 44320
Mccoy St 44311
Mcdowell Ave 44313
Mcelwain Rd 44312
Mcfarland Ct 44304
Mcgowan Ct & St 44306
Mcintosh Ave 44314
Mckenna Ave 44305
Mckinley Ave
500-649 44311
650-1299 44306
Mcknight Way 44312
Mcmillan Cir 44306
Mcnaughton St 44305
Mcpherson Ave 44313
Mctaggart Dr 44320
Mcvey Rd 44333
Meade Ave 44305
N Meadow Cir 44333
S Meadow Cir 44333
Meadow Dr 44312
Meadow Run 44321
Meadow Spur 44333
Meadow Gate 44313
Meadow Park Dr 44333
Meadow Spring Cir 44312
Meadow Wood Ln 44321
Meadowcreek Ln 44321
N & S Meadowcroft Dr 44313
Meadowridge Rd 44312
Meadowvale Ct & Dr 44333
Meander Cir 44312
Medford Ave 44310
Medina Rd
3826-4299 44333
4300-5199 44321
N Medina Line Rd 44333
S Medina Line Rd 44321
Megglen Ave 44303
Melbourne Ave 44313
Melody Dr 44321
Melody Ln 44319
Melrose St 44305
Melville Ave 44312
Memorial Pkwy
200-599 44310
600-999 44303
Menlo Park Dr 44313
Mentor Rd 44303
Mercer Ave
700-1149 44320
1150-1299 44307
Meridian St 44310
Merridge Rd 44313
Merrill Ave 44306
Merriman Rd
1-1100 44303
1101-1899 44313
Merton Ave 44306
Merz Blvd 44333
Metlin Ave 44302
Metz Ave 44303
Miami St 44311
Michaels Dr 44312
Middle Way 44312
Middlebury Ave 44305
Middlebush Cir 44321
Middlecoff Dr 44313
Middlefield Dr 44312
Midway St 44310
Mila Ct 44314
Milan Ave 44320
E & W Mildred Ave 44310
Miles Ave 44306
E & W Mill St 44308
Mill Race Run 44312
Mill Run Dr 44312
Millbrook St 44314
Millcreek Dr 44307
E Miller Ave
31-259 44301
260-299 44311
W Miller Ave 44301
N Miller Rd 44333
S Miller Rd 44333
Miller Park Rd 44312
Millhaven Dr 44321
Millstone Cir 44312
Millstream Ct 44321
Millway St 44314
Milnar Ave 44319
Milo White Dr 44312
Milton St 44306
Mina Ave 44321
Mindora Dr 44319
Mineola Ave
200-204 44313
206-374 44313
375-799 44320
Minerva Pl 44320
Mingo Trl 44312
Minnie Ct 44311
E Minor Ave 44319
W Minor Ave 44319
Minor Rd 44321
Minordy Pl 44306
Minota Ave 44306
Minson Way 44306
Miriam St 44305
Mishler Ave 44312
Mission Dr 44301
Mistletoe Rd 44307
Misty Ln 44321
Mobile Ln 44312
Modena Dr 44306
Moe Dr 44310
Moeller Ave 44307
Mogadore Rd 44312
Mohawk Ave
450-899 44305
2800-2899 44312
Mohawk Dr
1500-1799 44306
4100-4199 44321
Mohawk Trl 44312
Mohican Ave 44305
Mohican Blvd 44312
Molane Ave 44313
Moler Dr 44312
Molly Dr 44312
Mona Ct 44319
Mong Ave 44319
Monmouth Dr 44313
Monroe St 44307
Montana Ave 44314
Monte Vista Dr 44319
Monteray Dr 44305
Montgomery St 44305
Montrose Ave
200-298 44310
300-399 44310

401-499 44310
3300-3599 44333
Montrose West Ave 44321
Moody St 44305
Moon Dr 44304
Moon St 44307
Moonlight Dr 44312
Moonlit Trl 44313
Moore Rd 44319
Moore St 44301
Moorfield Rd 44333
Moraine Ave 44310
Moray Dr 44319
Moreley Ave 44320
Moreview Dr 44321
Morewood Rd 44333
Morgan Ave
300-649 44311
650-799 44306
Morningside Dr 44303
Morningstar Dr 44307
Morningview Ave 44305
Morrison St 44312
Morse St
800-949 44314
950-1499 44320
Mosser Pl 44310
Motz Dr 44333
Mound Dr 44319
Mount Vernon Ave 44310
Mount View Ave 44303
Mountain Ash Dr 44312
Mountain Aven Rd 44321
Mowbray Rd 44333
Muchney Cir 44312
Mulberry St 44301
Mull Ave
1-475 44313
476-500 44320
477-1099 44313
502-1098 44313
2601-2697 44321
2699-2836 44321
2838-2898 44321
Multnoma Ave 44305
Munson St 44305
Mura Dr 44312
Murray Ave 44310
Muskoka Dr 44319
Mustill Ct & St 44304
Myers Ave 44305
Myersville Rd 44312
Myra St 44305
Myrtle Pl 44303
Nadia Ct 44306
Nanaula Cir & Dr 44305
Nancy Ave 44314
Nancy Dr 44319
Nancy Lee Dr 44312
Naomi St 44319
Naples St 44310
Narragansett Dr 44305
Narrows Way 44312
Nash St
300-549 44304
550-599 44306
Nathan St 44307
National Ave 44314
Neal Ct 44303
Neal Rd 44312
Nebraska St 44304
Nedra Ave 44305
Needle St 44319
Neil Evan Dr 44313
Nemes Dr 44301
Neptune Ave 44301
Neptune Dr 44319
Nesbitt Ave
2400-2452 44314
2454-2675 44314
2677-2697 44319
2699-2799 44319
Nesmith Lake Blvd 44314
Nestor Ave 44314
Nestor Ln 44312
Nevada St 44319

Neville Ave 44306
Nevin St 44310
New York St 44314
Newcastle Cir & Dr 44313
Newdale Ave 44320
Newell Ave 44305
Newport Rd 44303
Newton Cir 44305
Newton Pl 44310
Newton St 44305
Niagara Ave 44305
Nicholas Ave 44305
Nicholas Ct 44311
Nicholas Dr 44319
Nichols Rd 44312
Nickel St 44303
Nidover Dr 44312
Nieman St 44305
E Nimisila Rd 44319
Nina Ln 44333
Nine Iron Dr 44312
Noah Ave 44320
Nob Hill Dr 44303
Noble Ave
112-122 44302
200-758 44320
760-798 44320
Nokomis Dr
200-399 44319
900-1099 44313
Nola Ct & Ln 44319
Nolt Dr 44312
Nome Ave 44320
Nordica Ave 44314
Norka St 44307
Norledge Rd 44305
Norma Ave & Ct 44320
Norman St 44310
E North St
1-574 44304
575-799 44305
W North St
1-149 44304
150-361 44303
363-399 44303
North Way 44312
Northampton Rd 44313
Northgate Cir 44320
Northledge Ct 44321
Northwold Dr 44321
Northwood Dr 44313
Norton St 44305
Nottoway Ct 44313
Nutwood Rd 44305
Nye Dr 44333
Nye St 44320
Oak Crst 44321
Oak St 44310
Oak Ter 44304
Oak Glen Ct 44333
Oak Grove Dr 44319
Oak Knoll Dr 44333
Oak Park Dr 44302
Oak Point Dr 44321
Oak Tree Rd 44320
Oakdale Ave 44302
Oakdale Ct 44303
Oakes Dr 44312
Oakes Drive Ext 44312
Oakhurst Trl 44321
Oakland Ave 44310
Oakmont Dr 44321
Oakridge Dr 44313
Oakwood Ave 44301
N Oakwood Dr 44312
S Oakwood Dr 44312
Oberlin Ct & St 44311
Ocean Ave 44310
Ogden Ave 44312
Ogle Ter 44311
Oh Ave 44321
Ohio St 44304
Olalla Ave 44305
Old Home Rd 44312
Old Main St 44301
Old Spring Rd 44321

W Olden Ave 44319
Olentangy Cir & Dr 44333
Olive St 44310
Olivet Ave 44319
Onaway St 44319
Oneida Ave
500-599 44303
2701-2709 44312
2711-2899 44312
Oneida Pl 44313
Oneida Trl 44312
Onondago Ave 44305
Onondago Trl 44312
Ontario St 44310
Opportunity Pkwy 44307
Orchard Dr 44333
Orchard Ln 44312
Orchard Rd 44313
Orchard St 44304
Orchard Grove Ct 44333
Orchard View Dr 44321
Orcutt Dr 44321
Oregon Ave 44314
Organ Ave 44319
Oriole Ave 44312
Orlando Ave 44320
Ormsby Rd 44333
Orrin St 44320
Orton Dr 44319
Osage Ave
1400-1418 44305
1420-1699 44305
2700-2899 44312
Ostend Ave 44319
Oswego Ave 44312
Ottawa Ave
1200-1718 44305
1720-1798 44305
2700-2799 44312
Otter Dr 44319
Otto St 44304
Overland Dr 44319
Overlook Dr
1400-1699 44314
3200-3599 44312
Overlook Pl 44303
Overwood Rd 44313
Oviatt Pl 44302
Owego Dr 44312
Owen Ave 44311
Owosso Ave 44333
Oxford Ave 44310
Oxford Cir 44312
Oxford Ct 44319
Oxford Ln 44312
Ozark Dr 44312
E & W Pace Ave 44319
Packard Dr 44320
Paddock Dr 44333
Paige Ave 44302
Palace Way 44321
Palisades Dr 44303
Palm Ave 44301
Palmetto Ave
1-524 44301
526-598 44301
600-1299 44306
Palmyra Ave 44311
Pamer Dr 44319
Pamona Pl 44312
Panay Dr 44319
Par Dr 44312
Para Ave 44305
Pardee Ave 44306
Paris Ave 44301
Parisette Ln 44319
Park Ave 44312
Park Blvd 44312
E Park Blvd 44305
Park Dr 44312
Park Pl 44321
Park St
100-199 44308
200-399 44304
E Park Way 44312
W Park Way 44312

Park Lane Dr 44320
Park West Blvd 44320
Parkdale Dr 44307
Parker Rd 44313
Parkgate Ave
1400-1599 44313
1900-1999 44320
Parkhill Dr 44333
Parkside Dr 44313
Parkview Ave 44310
Parkwood Ave 44304
Parma Ln 44312
Parnell Dr 44319
Parsons Ct 44307
Partridge Ln 44333
Pasadena Ave 44303
Patapsco Pl 44306
Path Dr 44319
Patterson Ave 44310
Paul Williams St 44311
Pauline Ave 44312
Pawnee Blvd 44312
Paxton Ave 44312
Paxton Rd 44321
Payne Ave 44302
Peach Dr 44319
Pear Dr 44319
Pebble Beach Dr 44333
Pebblecreek Dr
700-799 44320
1500-1799 44333
Peckham St 44320
Peerless Ave 44320
Pelee Dr 44333
Pelton Ave 44314
Pembroke Rd 44333
Penelope Dr 44320
Penfield Ave 44310
Penguin Ave 44319
Peninsula Dr 44319
Penn Ave 44311
Penny Ln 44311
Penthley Ave 44312
Pepper Hill Cir 44312
Pepperhill Rd 44312
Perdue Ave 44310
Perkins Sq 44308
Perkins St 44304
Perkins Park Dr 44320
Perry Dr 44313
N & S Pershing Ave 44313
Petersburg Rd 44312
Pfeiffer Ave 44312
Pheasant Hill Dr 44333
Pheasant Run Rd 44305
Philip Ave 44305
Philomena Pl 44304
Phoenix Ave 44310
Phyllis Ave 44319
Picadilly Cir 44319
Pickford Ave 44320
Pickle Rd 44312
Picton Pkwy 44312
Piedmont Ave 44310
Pier Dr 44307
Piercy Dr 44312
Pikes Ave 44314
Pilgrim St 44305
Pilgrim Way 44313
Pilmore St 44305
Pin Oak Dr 44312
Pin Oak Rd 44333
Pine St 44307
Pine Grove Dr 44320
Pine Knolls Dr 44310
Pine Point Dr 44333
Pine Top Ct 44319
Pinecrest Dr 44321
Pinehurst Dr 44333
Pinehurst Ln 44313
Pineland Dr 44321
Pineview Dr 44321
Pinewood Path & Spur 44321
Pinnacle Dr 44312
Pintail Ct 44319
Pioneer St 44305

Pitkin Ave 44310
Pitt Rd 44312
Place De Bordeaux 44333
Plainfield Rd 44312
N & S Plainview Dr 44321
Plateau St 44319
Plato Ln 44301
Plaza Ct 44312
S Plaza Dr 44319
Pleasant Valley Dr 44319
Plum St 44305
Plymouth Ave 44310
Pocantico Ave 44312
Poe Ave 44306
Point Dr 44319
N Point Dr 44313
W Point Dr 44333
Polk Ave 44314
Polonia Ave 44319
Pomatan Ave 44312
Pomona Dr 44319
Ponciana Ave 44319
Pondview Ave 44305
Pontiac Ave 44307
Popham St 44314
Port Dr 44319
Portage Dr 44303
N Portage Path
1-949 44303
950-1599 44313
S Portage Path
1-149 44303
150-299 44302
300-499 44320
Portage Pl 44307
Portage Lakes Dr 44319
Portage Line Rd 44312
Portage Point Blvd 44319
Portage Trail Ext 44313
Portside Cir 44319
Poulsen Dr & Spur 44313
Powell Ave 44319
Power St
200-299 44304
300-499 44311
Prairie Dr 44312
Premae Dr 44312
Prentiss Ave
500-599 44301
600-699 44306
Pressler Rd 44312
Preston Ave 44305
Price Pl 44308
Primewood Rd 44305
Primrose Pl 44303
Princeton Cir 44312
Princeton St
700-774 44311
776-1049 44311
1050-1299 44301
N & S Prior Rd 44319
Priscilla Ave 44312
Proctor Rd 44306
N Prospect St 44304
S Prospect St 44308
N & S Prosser Ave 44319
Provence Pt 44333
Provens Dr 44319
Pruitt Blvd 44310
Putnam Rd 44313
Putnam St 44303
Quail Rdg 44319
Quaker Ridge Dr 44313
Quarry Dr 44307
Quarry Rd 44312
Quayle Dr 44312
Queens Ct 44321
Quincy Dr 44321
Raasch Ave 44307
Raceside Dr 44319
Raceway Ct 44312
Rachel Ct 44321
Radnor Ave & Ct 44319
Rainbow Dr 44320
Raintree Rd 44333
Raleigh Blvd 44321

Ralph St 44310
E & W Ralston Ave 44301
Rambling Way 44333
Ramp Ave 44319
Rampart Ave 44313
Ranchwood Rd & Spur 44333
Randel Ave 44313
Random Dr 44319
Randys Rd 44319
Rankin St 44311
Ranney St 44310
Rapids Way 44312
Ravenswood St 44306
Ravine St 44303
Ravine View Dr 44303
Ray St 44306
Raymond St 44307
Rea Ave 44312
Redbush Rd 44320
Redcrest Ln 44319
Redfern Ave 44314
Redfield Ln 44321
Redstone Ave 44310
Redwood Ave 44301
Redwood Cir 44312
Redwood Dr 44312
Reed Ave
300-551 44301
553-599 44301
600-1299 44306
Reeves Ct 44312
Regal Dr 44321
Regalstone Ln 44321
Regent Dr 44319
Regina Rd 44320
Reid Ter 44310
Remmington Ave 44321
Rentar Ln 44307
Rentham Rd 44313
Rentschler St 44304
Reserve Ave 44321
Reserve Dr 44333
Reston Dr 44312
Retreat Dr 44333
Revere Dr 44333
N Revere Rd 44333
S Revere Rd 44313
Rexford St 44314
Reynolds Ave 44313
Rhine Ave & Ct 44319
Rhoadesdale Ave & Ct 44312
Rhoda Ct 44307
Rhodes Ave
1-349 44302
350-670 44307
672-1098 44307
1101-1125 44311
1127-1199 44311
Richards Ct 44306
Richland St 44320
Richmond Pl 44303
Richmond St 44306
Rickel Cir & Dr 44333
N Ridge Dr 44333
S Ridge Rd 44333
Ridge St 44308
Ridge Crest Dr 44321
Ridge Park Dr 44333
Ridgecrest Rd 44303
Ridgedale Dr 44319
Ridgeway Dr 44311
Ridgewood Rd
1918-1998 44313
2000-2621 44313
2623-2699 44313
2700-3639 44333
3640-4899 44321
Ridgewood Xing 44333
Ridpath Ave 44313
Riley Ave 44306
Ripley Ave 44312
Rising Meadow Dr 44333
Rita Dove Ln 44307
Ritchie Ave 44320

Ritzman Ct 44314
River St 44305
Riverbed Ln 44312
Riverside Dr & Pl 44310
Riverview Rd 44313
Riverwoods Dr 44313
Riviera Dr 44333
Roanoke Ave 44312
Robbin St 44314
Robert St 44306
Roberts Rdg 44333
Robindale Ave 44312
Robinette Ct 44310
Robins Trce 44319
Robins Gate 44319
Robinson Ave 44319
Robinson Spur 44333
Robinwood Blvd 44312
Robinwood Ln 44321
Robinwood Hills Dr 44333
Rock Crk 44333
Rock Hill Ln 44313
Rock Ridge Ln 44333
Rockaway St 44314
Rockcliff Dr 44320
Rockford St 44301
Rockridge Way 44321
Rockwell Ct 44303
Rockwood Dr 44313
Rocky Brook Dr 44313
Rocky Hollow Dr 44313
Rocky Ridge Dr 44313
Rockys Run Rd 44319
Roe Dr 44319
Roger Ave 44305
Rohner Ave 44319
Roland Dr 44319
Roller Ave 44319
Rolling Meadows Ln 44312
Rolling Meadows Rd 44333
Rolling View Dr 44333
Romayne Dr 44313
Rome Dr 44319
Romig Rd 44320
Romney Rd 44333
Romona Rd 44305
Ronald Ave 44319
Ronald Rd 44312
Rood Dr 44319
Rook Dr 44319
Roosevelt Dr 44305
Rosa Ct 44313
Rosalind Ct 44304
Rosamond Ave 44307
Roscoe Ave 44306
N Rose Blvd 44302
S Rose Blvd
1-114 44302
116-188 44302
190-399 44313
400-499 44320
Rosedale Ave 44314
Roselawn Ave 44306
Roselle Ave 44307
Rosemary Blvd 44306
Rosemont Blvd 44333
E & W Rosewood Ave 44301
Roslyn Ave 44320
Ross Dr 44313
Roswell St 44305
Rothrock Ave 44314
Rothrock Cir 44321
Rothrock Loop 44321
Rothrock Pl 44321
Rothrock Rd 44321
Rotili Ln 44321
Rotunda Ave 44333
Roulhac Cir 44307
Round Rock Dr 44333
Roundhill Rd & Spur 44333
Rowe St 44306
Rowles Dr 44313
Royal Ave 44303
Royal Crst 44321
Royal Pl 44310
Royal Fern Dr 44312

Royal Rock Rd 44321
Ruckel Rd 44305
Rudd St 44307
Rugby Pl 44303
Russell Ave
 1-237 44311
 239-299 44311
 401-597 44307
 599-1099 44307
Russell St 44312
Russett Ln 44312
Ruth Ave
 700-899 44307
 1200-1399 44321
Rutland Ave 44305
Rutledge Dr 44319
Ryewood Ave 44321
Sabetha Pl 44313
Sackett Ave 44313
Sackett Hills Dr 44313
Saddlewood Ave 44313
Sadler St 44312
Safer Plz 44306
Sagamore Ave 44305
Sagamore Rd 44313
Sage Ave 44301
Sail Dr 44319
Saint Ambrose Dr 44307
Saint Andrews Ct 44312
Saint Andrews Dr 44303
Saint Ann Dr 44319
Saint Clair Dr
 100-298 44307
 2800-2999 44321
Saint Francis St 44333
Saint Leger Ave 44305
Saint Michaels Ave 44320
Saint Vincent Dr 44333
Salem Ave 44306
Salida St 44305
Salisbury Way 44321
Salmon Dr 44312
E & W Salome Ave 44310
Salton Dr 44333
Samoa Dr 44319
Samuel Ave 44314
Samuel Rd 44312
San Moritz Cir & Dr 44333
San Pier Dr 44333
San Raphael Dr 44333
Sanborn Dr 44333
Sanctuary Dr 44333
Sand Ct 44333
Sand Run Pkwy 44333
Sand Run Rd 44313
Sand Run Knolls Dr 44313
Sanders Rd 44320
Sandhill Dr 44313
Sandhurst Rd 44333
Sandin Rd 44333
Sandy Ln 44321
Sandy Beach Dr 44319
Sanford Ave 44305
Sanitarium Rd 44312
Santee Ave 44306
Sara Ave 44305
Sara Ln 44321
Sarah Dr 44312
Saralee Ave 44314
Sarcee Ave 44305
Sarlson Ave 44314
Sauer Dr 44319
Saunders Ave 44319
Savage Dr 44312
Savoy Ave 44305
Sawgrass Dr 44333
Sawmill Rd 44321
Sawyer Ave 44310
Saxon Ave 44314
Saxony Dr 44313
Scarlet Oak Dr 44321
Scenic Way
 1400-1600 44310
 1602-1698 44310
 1901-1979 44312
 1981-2099 44312
Scenic View Dr 44321
Scheck St 44307
Schiller Ave 44310
Schneider Park Dr 44313
Schneiderman Ln 44319
Schocalog Rd
 1-263 44313
 265-299 44313
 300-1299 44320
School St 44307
Schoolcraft Ave 44321
Schrop Ave 44312
Schumacher Ave 44307
Scorenco Ave 44303
Scotland Dr 44305
Scudder Dr 44320
Seaman Ave 44305
Seaton Ct 44319
Sedgewick Ave 44321
Seiberling St 44306
N Seiberling St 44305
S Seiberling St 44305
Selden Ave 44301
Selle St 44311
Sellman Dr 44333
Selzer St 44310
Seminola Ave 44305
Seneca Ave 44312
Seneca Pl 44305
Seneca Trl 44312
Senn Dr 44319
Serenity Ln 44321
Seth Ct 44307
Seth Roberts Dr 44306
Settlement St 44306
Sevilla Ave 44314
Seward Ave 44320
Sewell Ave 44319
Shade Rd 44333
Shade Park Dr 44333
Shadeside Ave 44320
Shadow Ridge Ln 44333
Shadowfax Cir 44305
Shady Way 44312
Shady Acres Dr 44312
Shady Hollow Ln 44313
Shady Ledge Dr 44313
Shadybrook Dr 44312
Shaefer St 44311
Shaker Dr 44305
Shakespeare Ave 44306
Shamokin Dr 44319
Shanabrook Dr 44313
Shanafelt Ave 44312
Shannon Ct 44312
Sharon St 44314
Shatto Ave 44313
Shaw Ave 44305
Shaw Rd 44333
Shaw Road Ext 44333
Shawnee Path 44305
Shawnee Trl 44321
Sheffield Dr 44320
Shelburn Ave 44312
Shelby Ave 44310
Shelby St 44320
Sheldon Dr 44313
Shelley Lynn Dr 44333
Shelton Ct 44312
Shelva Ln 44321
N & S Sheraton Cir &
Dr 44319
Sheraton Point Dr 44319
Sheridan St 44307
Sherman Ct 44311
Sherman St
 300-999 44311
 1100-1312 44301
Sherwood Ave 44314
Sherwood Dr 44303
Shiawassee Ave 44333
Shikellamy Dr 44319
Shillings Way 44321
Shirley Ave 44310
Shook Rd 44319
N Shore Dr 44333
Shoreline Dr 44314
Short St 44314
Short Way 44312
N & S Short Hills Dr 44333
Shoshone Ave 44305
Shrakes Hotel Dr 44319
Shreve Rd 44305
Shullo Dr 44313
Shultz St 44310
Sieber Ave 44312
Sierra Dr 44321
Sillars Ave 44303
Silver St 44303
Silver Maple Dr 44333
Silver Ridge Dr 44321
Silvercrest Ave 44314
Simcoe Ave 44305
Simmons Ct 44306
Simon Dr 44305
Singleton Dr 44321
Singley Ave 44310
Skelton Rd 44312
Skylark Dr 44313
Skyview Dr 44319
Slagle Dr 44312
Slosson St 44320
Slusser Rd 44305
Smith Rd
 1400-2199 44313
 2200-2599 44333
 2601-2631 44313
 2633-3199 44333
S Smith Rd 44333
Smith St 44303
Smithfarm Ave 44305
Smokerise Dr 44313
Snoderly Dr 44312
Snow Ave 44319
Snowfall Spur 44313
Snowgoose Ln 44319
Snyder St 44307
Sobul Ave 44305
Socrates Pl 44301
Sojourner Dr 44307
Solar Cir 44333
Sollman Ave 44321
Somerset Dr 44312
Somerset Rd 44313
Sommers Ct 44304
Sooy Rd 44333
Sorin Ave 44310
Sourek Rd 44333
Sourek Trl 44313
Sourek Road Ext 44333
E & W South St 44311
Southampton Ct 44321
Southampton St 44304
Southwold Rd 44321
Southwood Rd 44313
Sovereign Rd 44303
Spade Ave 44312
Spafford Dr 44321
Spangler Ln 44320
Sparhawk Ave 44305
Sparrow Pond Cir &
Ln 44333
Sparrows Crst 44319
Spaulding St 44310
Spellman Ct 44305
Spencer Ave 44306
Sperry Dr 44305
Spicer St
 100-369 44304
 370-570 44311
 572-698 44311
Sprague St 44305
Spring St 44304
Spring Valley Rd 44333
Spring Water Dr 44333
Springcrest Dr 44333
Springdale Dr 44310
Springfield Ave 44320
Springfield Center Rd 44312
Springfield Lake Blvd &
Dr 44312
Springhill Ter 44307
Springside Dr 44333
Spruce Run 44321
Spruce St 44304
Spyglass Dr 44333
Squires Ct 44333
Stabler Rd 44313
Stadelman Ave & Ct 44320
Staeger St 44306
Stage Coach Trl 44321
Stahl Rd 44319
Stanford St 44314
Stanley Rd
 300-699 44312
 2900-3499 44333
Stansberry Cir 44313
Stanton Ave 44301
Stanwood Ave 44314
Star St 44311
Starboard Cir & Dr 44319
Starlight Dr 44306
State Rd 44319
E State St 44308
W State St
 1-99 44308
 100-149 44302
State Mill Rd 44319
Steelwood Cir 44312
Stein Rd 44312
Steiner Ave
 2-38 44301
 40-199 44301
 201-249 44301
 251-273 44311
 275-299 44311
Stephanie Ln 44306
Stephens Rd 44312
Sterling Ct 44304
Stetler Ave 44312
Steve Dr 44319
Stevens Rd 44319
Stevenson Ave 44312
Stevenson Pt 44307
Stewart Way 44303
Stillwood Ln 44313
Stillwood Spur 44333
Stimson St 44320
Stinard Ave 44312
Stockbridge Rd 44313
Stockton St 44314
Stoddard Ave 44313
Stone St 44305
Stone Arch Dr 44307
Stone Circle Dr 44320
Stone Gate Blvd 44333
Stone Ridge Dr 44320
Stonebridge Blvd 44321
Stonecliff Dr 44313
Stonecreek Dr 44320
Stonegate Dr 44313
Stonehedge Rd 44333
Stonehenge Cir 44319
Stonehurst Dr 44321
Stoner St 44320
Stonewood Dr 44313
Storer Ave
 100-374 44302
 375-999 44320
Stouffer Rd 44333
Strader Rd 44305
Strand Ave 44312
Stratford Ave 44303
Stratford Cir 44312
Stratford Ln 44313
Stratford Rd 44333
Straw St 44304
Stroman Ave 44306
Stuber St 44304
Stull Ave 44312
Sturbridge Dr 44313
Success Rd 44310
Sucrose Dr 44312
Sue Ln 44321
Sues Ct 44311
Suffolk Ct 44319
Sugar Rd 44321
Sugar Knoll Dr 44333
Sullivan Ave 44305
Sullivan Pl 44310
Sumatra Ave 44305
Summerhill Dr 44333
Summit Rd 44321
N Summit St
 1-99 44308
 100-199 44304
S Summit St 44308
Summit Lake Blvd 44314
Summit View Ave 44314
Sumner Ct 44311
Sumner Pkwy 44321
Sumner St
 200-549 44304
 550-560 44311
 562-899 44311
Sun Dr 44312
Sun Valley Cir & Dr 44333
Sundale Rd 44313
Sunnyacres Rd 44321
N & S Sunnyfield Dr 44321
Sunnyside Ave 44303
Sunridge Rd 44333
Sunrise Dr 44307
Sunset Ave 44301
Sunset Dr 44321
Sunset View Dr
 400-799 44320
 1100-1299 44313
 1301-1423 44313
 1426-1472 44320
 1474-1699 44320
Sunside Dr 44321
Super Genius Cir 44306
Superior Ave 44307
Surfside Dr 44319
Susan Ct 44307
Sutherland Ave 44314
Sutton Pl 44313
Swan Ct 44319
Swan Lake Dr 44321
Swartz Rd
 1-1049 44319
 1050-1299 44306
Sweetbriar Dr 44321
Sweitzer Ave
 800-1049 44311
 1051-1097 44301
 1099-1500 44301
Swinehart Ave 44314
Swinehart Rd 44312
Sycamore Ln 44313
Sycamore St 44301
Sylvan Ave 44306
Sypher Rd 44306
Taft Ave 44314
Tahgajute Dr 44319
Tahiti Dr 44319
Talbot Ave 44306
Talent Dr 44319
Tallkron Dr 44305
E & W Tallmadge Ave 44310
Tallmadge View Ave 44305
N & S Tamarack Rd 44319
Tamarisk Dr 44333
Tamiami Trl 44303
Tampa Ave 44314
Tanager Rd 44333
Tandy Ln 44311
Tanglewood Dr 44313
Tarbell St 44303
Tarson Ter 44306
Tate Ter 44311
Tavondale Ave 44313
Taylor Ave 44312
Taylor St 44307
Teal Cir 44319
Tech Way Dr 44306
Tecumseh Ln 44321
Tecumseh Pl 44306
Teddy Ave 44305
Tee Dr 44333
Teeple Dr 44313
Tennyson Dr 44333
Terrace Ave 44312
Terrace Ct 44306
Terrell Dr 44313
Terrier Dr 44321
Thane Ave 44301
Thayer St 44310
The Brooklands 44305
Theiss Rd 44313
Thelma Ave 44314
Theodore St 44301
Theresa Dr 44321
Thierry Ave 44306
Thompson Ct 44304
Thompson Dr 44313
Thoreau Ave 44306
Thorlone Ave 44312
Thornapple Ave 44301
Thornbury Ln 44319
Thorndale Dr 44320
Thornhill Dr 44313
E Thornton St 44311
W Thornton St
 1-78 44311
 80-274 44311
 300-899 44307
Thorpe St 44304
Three Acres Dr 44312
Thrush Dr 44312
Thurmont Rd 44313
Thurston St 44320
Tiffany Cir 44313
Timber Trl 44313
Timber Creek Dr 44333
Timberline Dr 44333
Timothy Dr 44319
Tinkham Rd 44313
Tioga Ave 44305
Tippecanoe Dr 44319
Tisdale Dr 44312
Tisen Rd 44312
Titan Dr 44321
Titleist Dr 44312
Toby Ter 44306
Toepfer Rd 44312
Tomahawk St 44305
Tomahawk Trce 44321
Tompkins Ave 44305
Tonawanda Ave 44305
Toombs Dr 44306
Top Of The Hill Rd 44333
Topflite Dr 44312
Torrey St 44304
Torrey Pines Dr 44333
Totham Dr 44319
Tower Dr 44305
Tower Hill Dr 44319
Towpath Blvd 44313
Traci Ln 44321
Traian Cir 44312
Tralesto Dr 44319
Trapas Ave 44319
Travertine Way 44333
Traymore Dr 44319
Treaty Line Rd 44313
Treecrest Dr 44333
Treeside Dr 44313
Treetop Dr 44321
Treetop Spur 44321
Treetop Trl 44313
Trellis Green Dr 44333
Tremont Rd 44313
Trent Dr 44312
Trenton Rd 44312
Trentwood Dr 44313
Tresham Ct 44321
Tressel Ave 44307
Tributary Ln 44312
Trigonia Dr 44302
Trimble Dr 44307
Triplett Blvd
 600-1801 44306
 1803-2097 44312
 2099-2599 44312
Tritt Ave & Dr 44312
Tritts Mill Dr 44312
Trumbull Ave 44321
Trunko Rd 44333
Tryon Ave 44310
Tudor Ave 44312
Tulip Dr 44333
Tulip St 44301
Tupelo Ave 44320
N & S Turkeyfoot Rd 44319
E Turkeyfoot Lake Rd
 1-849 44319
 850-2499 44312
W Turkeyfoot Lake Rd 44319
Turner Dr 44321
Turner Ext 44304
Turner St 44304
Twain Ave 44306
Twin Creeks Dr 44321
Twin Oaks Rd 44313
Two Max Dr 44311
Tyler St 44307
Tyner St 44311
Tyredale Ave 44305
Tyro Ave 44305
Tyrone St 44312
Tyson Ave 44319
Uhl Dr 44319
Uhler Ave 44310
Ultra Cir 44312
Uncas Dr 44319
Unclmorse Ave 44314
Underwood Ave 44306
N & S Union Pl & St 44304
University Ave
 1-37 44308
 39-80 44308
 100-156 44304
 158-299 44304
Upham Dr 44319
Upland Ave 44301
Upper Merriman Dr 44303
Upson St 44305
Upton Ave 44310
Upton Ct 44319
Urban Dr 44306
Ute Ave 44305
Utica Ave 44312
Valdes Ave 44320
Vale Dr 44321
Valentine Farms Dr 44333
Valinda Pl 44304
Valisout Ave 44307
Valley Dr 44312
N Valley St 44303
S Valley St 44303
Valley Wood Rd 44333
Van Everett Ave 44306
Van Lynn Rd 44306
Vane Ave 44310
Vaniman St 44305
Vantine Dr 44319
Vaughn Rd & Trl 44319
Verde Ave 44314
Verdun Dr 44312
Vermont Pl 44312
Verndale Dr 44306
Vernon Odom Blvd
 101-149 44307
 151-1299 44307
 1300-1999 44320
Vesper Dr
 151-299 44310
 2800-2999 44333
Vesper St 44310
Vicgross Ave 44310
Vicheann Dr 44313
Vichendi Ave 44310
Victor Dr 44321
Victoria Ave 44310
Victory St
 900-1039 44311
 1040-1225 44301
 1227-1299 44301
Viers Ct 44310
Viewland Ter 44314
Villa Ave 44310
Village Dr 44313
Village Pkwy 44333
Village Pointe Dr 44313

Vincent St 44301
Vinderth Ave 44301
Vine St 44304
Vinita Ave 44320
Violet Ave 44319
N & S Viona Dr 44319
Virginia Ave 44306
E & W Vista Ave 44319
Vivian Pl 44302
Volga Way 44302
E Voris St 44311
Vosello Ave 44313
Wabash Ave 44307
Wade Park Ave 44310
Wadsworth Rd 44320
Wagon Wheel Trl 44321
Wagoner St 44319
Wakefield Dr 44320
Walbridge Dr 44319
Waldorf Dr 44313
Wall St 44310
Wallhaven Cir & Dr 44313
Wallwood Dr 44321
N Walnut St 44304
S Walnut St 44303
Walnut Ter 44303
Walnut Ridge Rd 44333
Walsh Ave 44310
Walt Ct 44319
Walter Pl 44311
Waltham Rd 44313
Walton Dr 44313
Wareham Cir 44312
Warner Ct 44307
E Warner Rd 44319
W Warner Rd 44319
Warren Ave 44320
Warrington Rd 44320
Warwick St 44305
Washburn St 44307
Washington St 44311
Water St
201-219 44308
221-399 44308
400-498 44307
E Waterford Ct 44313
W Waterford Ct 44313
Waterford St 44314
E Waterloo Rd
1-97 44319
99-649 44319
650-1899 44306
1900-3899 44312
W Waterloo Rd
1-349 44319
350-1425 44314
Waters Edge Dr 44313
Waterside Dr 44319
Watkins Ave 44305
Watson St 44305
Waverly Cir 44321
Way St 44310
Waycross Ave 44320
Wayne Ave
1-499 44301
1700-1799 44320
Wayside Dr 44320
Wealthy Dr 44321
Weatherstone Ct 44321
Weathervane Ln 44313
Weber Ave 44303
Wedgemere Ave 44313
Wedgewood Cir 44312
Wedgewood Dr
2000-2599 44312
4200-4499 44321
Wednesbury Cir 44313
Weehawken Pl 44306
Weeks St 44306
Weil Ave 44319
Weiler St 44312
Weiser Ave 44314
Weller Ave 44310
Wellesley Ave 44303
Wellington Ave 44305
Wellman Ct 44301
E & W Wellock Dr 44319
Wells Creek Run 44312
Wellsley Ln 44313
Welsh Ave 44314
Welton Ave 44306
Welton Pl 44301
Wembley Dr 44313
Wendling Dr 44333
Wesley Pl 44311
West St 44303
Westbourne Blvd 44321
Westchester Dr 44333
Westerly Rd 44307
Western Ave 44313
Westgate Cir 44313
Westgay Dr 44313
Westgrove Rd 44303
Westminster Cir 44319
Westmont Blvd 44321
Westmoreland St 44314
Westmoreland Ter 44302
Weston Ct 44321
Westover Dr 44313
Westpoint Ave 44310
Westport Dr 44312
Westridge Rd 44333
Westvale Ave 44313
Westview Dr
700-899 44312
4300-4499 44321
Westwick Way 44321
Westwood Ave & Pl 44302
Wexford Ct 44312
N & S Wheaton Rd 44313
Wheeler St
2-98 44311
100-101 44311
103-169 44311
170-399 44304
Wheeling Dr 44319
White Ave 44307
White Pond Dr
1-67 44313
69-249 44313
250-1299 44320
1900-2099 44313
White Tail Cir 44333
White Tail Ridge Dr 44333
Whitefriars Dr 44319
Whitepine Dr 44313
Whitestone Ave 44310
Whitney Ave 44306
Whittier Ave 44320
Whychwood Dr 44312
Wichita Pl 44313
Wicket Dr 44307
Wigeon Way 44319
Wigley Ave 44305
E Wilbeth Rd
2-98 44301
100-599 44301
600-999 44306
W Wilbeth Rd
2-98 44301
100-399 44301
400-1399 44314
Wilbur Ave 44301
Wild Brook Dr 44313
Wildon Ave 44306
Wildwood Ave 44320
Wilkinson Dr 44333
Willard St 44305
Williams Ct 44306
Williams St 44305
Williamston Ct 44313
Willow Ln 44333
Willow St 44307
Willow Creek Dr 44333
Willow Green Trl 44321
Willowedge Dr 44319
E & W Willowview Dr 44319
Wills Ave 44302
Wilmich Dr 44319
Wilmot St 44306
Wilpark Dr 44312
Wilshire Dr 44321
Wilson Dr 44312
Wilson Ln 44321
Wilson Rd 44312
Wilson St 44311
Wiltshire Rd 44313
Winans Ave 44306
Winchester Rd 44333
Windemere Ave 44312
Winding Way 44313
Windsor St 44306
Winfield Way 44303
Wing St 44305
Wingate Ave 44314
Wingerter St 44314
Wingfoot Way 44305
Winhurst Dr 44313
Winimac Ave 44319
Winnefeld Way 44320
Winnipeg St 44310
Winslow Ave 44313
Winston Rd 44313
Winston St 44314
Winter Fern Ave 44312
Winterberry Dr 44333
Winthrop Dr 44319
Winton Ave 44320
Wirth Ave 44312
Wise St 44304
Witner Ave 44314
Woburn Dr 44319
Wolcott Rd 44313
Wolf Ledges Pkwy
400-408 44311
410-624 44311
625-625 44309
626-744 44311
627-673 44311
675-675 44309
677-899 44311
Wonder Lake Dr 44319
Wood St 44303
Wood Duck Ln 44319
Wood Fern Dr 44312
Woodbine Ave 44313
Woodbirch Ave 44314
Woodbury Dr 44333
Woodcrest Ave 44319
Woodcrest Dr 44333
Woodhaven Blvd 44333
Woodhaven Dr 44321
Woodland Ave 44302
Woodland Pl 44312
Woodland Rd 44312
Woodlawn Reserve Rd 44305
Woodledge Dr 44313
Woodley Blvd 44319
Woodling Ct 44312
Woodmere Ave 44312
Woodpark Rd 44333
Woodridge St 44314
Woodrow Ct 44310
Woodrow St 44303
Woods Rd 44306
E & W Woodsdale Ave 44301
Woodsfield Dr 44319
Woodside Dr 44303
Woodstock Rd 44312
Woodsview Dr 44313
Woodthrush Cir & Rd 44333
Woodview Dr 44319
Woodward Ave 44310
Woodward Ct 44310
Woodward Rd 44312
Woolf Ave 44312
Work Dr 44320
Worron Ct 44304
Worthington Rd 44313
Wren Walk 44306
Wrens Path 44319
Wrico St 44319
Wright Blvd 44312
Wright Rd 44320
Wyandot Ave 44305
Wyant Rd 44313
Wybell Ct 44302
Wycliff Ln 44313
Wye Dr 44303
Wye Rd 44333
Wykeham Ct 44319
Wyley Ave 44306
Wymore Ave 44319
Wyndham Rd 44313
Wyndham Way 44321
Wynne Dr 44319
Wyoming Ave 44314
Yale St
700-774 44311
776-999 44311
1000-1099 44301
Yardley Ln 44313
Yarmouth Rd 44313
Yarrowdale Dr 44319
Yellow Creek Ln & Rd 44333
Yellowstone Ave 44310
Yerrick Cir & Rd 44312
Yorindia St 44311
E & W York St 44310
Yorkshire Ct 44321
Yorkshire Dr 44310
Young St 44305
Youtz Ave 44301
Yukon Ave 44320
Yuma Ave 44305
Zahn Ct & Dr 44313
Zeller Ave 44310
Zemil Ave 44320
Zents Ct 44310
Zesiger Ave 44312

NUMBERED STREETS

1st Ave 44306
1st St SW 44314
2nd Ave 44306
2nd St SW 44314
4th Ave 44306
4th St SW 44314
5th Ave
800-1350 44306
1400-1599 44312
5th St SW 44314
6th Ave 44306
6th St SW 44314
7th Ave 44306
7th St SW 44314
8th Ave 44306
8th St SW 44314
9th Ave 44306
9th St SW 44314
10th St SW 44314
11th St SW 44314
12th St SW 44314
13th St SW 44314
14th St SW 44314
15th St SW 44314
16th St SW 44314
17th St SW 44314
18th St SW 44314
19th St SW 44314
20th St SW 44314
21st St SW 44314
22nd St SW 44314
23rd St SW 44314
24th St SW 44314
25th St SW 44314
26th St SW 44314
27th St SW 44314
28th St SW 44314
29th St SW 44314
30th St SW 44314
31st St SW 44314
32nd St SW 44314

ASHTABULA OH

General Delivery 44004

POST OFFICE BOXES MAIN OFFICE STATIONS AND BRANCHES

Box No.s
All PO Boxes 44005

NAMED STREETS

All Street Addresses 44004

NUMBERED STREETS

All Street Addresses 44004

CANTON OH

General Delivery 44711

POST OFFICE BOXES MAIN OFFICE STATIONS AND BRANCHES

Box No.s
1 - 236 44707
6001 - 6935 44706
7001 - 7906 44705
8001 - 9975 44711
20001 - 24929 44701
35001 - 36970 44735
80001 - 80876 44708

NAMED STREETS

Abbey Church Ave NW 44718
Abbeyshire Ave SE 44720
Abbots Pond Cir NE 44721
Abbotsford Blvd NW 44718
Abbott Pl NW 44708
Abigail Cir NW 44720
Acacia Ave NW 44718
Ada Pl NW 44708
Adele Ave NW 44708
Adena St NE 44720
Afton Cir SW 44709
W Airport Dr 44720
Akcan Cir NW 44720
Akin Ct SW 44706
Alan Page Dr SE 44707
Albany Dr NW 44708
Albert Ct SE 44707
Alden Ave SW 44706
Alderglen St NW 44720
Alderidge St NE 44714
Alex Neal Cir SW 44706
Alexander Ave SW 44706
Alexander Pl NE 44704
Alexandria Pkwy SE 44709
Algona Dr 44720
Allen Ave SE 44707
Allenford Dr SE 44707
Allenwood St SW 44706
Allison Pl NW 44720
Allma Dr 44720
Alpine St NE 44721
Alta Pl NW 44703
Alton Pl NE 44705
Amarillo St NW 44720
Amberidge Ave NW 44708
Amberly Cir NW 44720
Ambler Ave SW 44709
Amblewood St NW 44718
Ambrose Ave NW 44708
American St NW 44720
Americana Dr NW 44720
Amerman Pl NE 44704
Ames Ct NW 44703
Amford St SE 44707
Amsel Ave NE 44721
Anchorport Cir NW 44718
Andalor St NW 44708
Anderson Pl SW
2200-2299 44706
2301-2399 44706
2400-2699 44710
Andiron Cir NW 44718
Andover Ave NW 44709
Andrew Pl SW 44706
Angel Dr NW 44720
Anglo Cir NW 44708
Angora Cir NW 44720
Anna Ave NW 44708
Annaruth Ave SW 44706
Apollo St NW 44720
Apple Ct NE 44720
Applegrove St NE
100-399 44720
1000-2699 44721
Applegrove St NW 44720
Aquarius St SW 44706
Aran Cir NW 44720
Arbor Rd SW 44710
Arbor Creek Ave NW 44718
Arboretum Cir NW 44718
Arbury Ave SE 44720
Arch Ct NE 44704
Arden Ln NW 44708
Ardmore Ave SW 44710
Argyle Rd SE 44707
Arlington Ave NW
100-1199 44708
7700-8799 44720
Arlington Ave SW 44706
Arlington Rd 44720
Armandale Ave NW 44718
Armistice Ave NW 44718
Arnesby Cir NW 44720
Arnold Ave NW
1200-1799 44703
1800-4099 44709
Arrowbrook St NW 44708
Arter Ave NW 44720
Arthur Ct NW 44703
Asbury Cir NE 44721
Ashburn St NW 44718
Ashburton Cir NW 44720
Ashby St NW 44708
Ashdale St NW 44720
Ashford Cir NE 44720
Ashford St NW 44718
Ashford Glen Cir NW 44718
Ashland Ave SW 44709
Ashley Ave NE 44720
Ashmont Ave SW 44706
Ashmoore Ave NW 44720
Ashway Ave SE 44707
Ashwood Cir & St 44708
Aspen St NE 44721
Aspen Valley Ave NE 44721
Aspenwood Cir NW 44720
Asshan St NW 44720
Aster Ave NE 44705
Astrojet St NW 44720
Atlantic Blvd NE 44705
Atwood Ave SE 44707
Auburn Ave SE 44709
Auburn Pl NW 44703
Audrey St SW 44706
Augusta Ave NW 44718
Aultman Ave NW
100-599 44708
1500-4498 44720
4501-4599 44720
Aultman Rd 44720
Aurora St NW 44708
Autumncrest St SW 44706
Autumnwood St NW 44720
Avalon Ave NE 44705
Avalon St NW 44708
Avon Pl NE 44705
Avondale Blvd & Ln 44708
Aylesbury St NW 44720
Ayrshire Ave NE 44721
Azalea Ave NE 44705
Bachert Ct SW 44707
Bachtel St SE & SW 44720
Baier Cir NE 44721
Bainbridge St NW 44720
Baker Ct SE 44720
Baker St SE 44707
Baldridge Ave SE 44707
Baldwin Ave NE 44705
Ballyshannon Cir NW 44718
Balmore St NW 44720
Balsam St NW 44720
Bambi St NW 44709
Banbury Cir NW 44720
Bank Pl SW 44706
Banner Ct NW 44703
Bantry Cir NW 44718
Barchester Ave NW 44720
Barclay Cir NW 44720
Barn Dr SW 44706
Barnstable Cir NW 44718
Barnstone Ave SW 44706
Baron St NW 44720
Barr Ave NW 44708
Barrett Ct NW 44703
Barrie St NW 44708
Barrington Pl NW 44708
Barrister Ave SE 44720
Barton Pl NE 44705
Bass Cir NW 44708
Batton St NW 44720
Bauer Ct NE 44704
Baum St SE 44707
Baumford Ave SE 44707
Baunach St NW 44708
Bausher Ct NW 44708
Baycliff Ave NW 44718
Baycrest Dr NW 44708
Baycrest St SW 44706
Baylor Cir NW 44720
Baymore St SE 44707
Bayshore Cir NW 44718
Bayside St NW 44718
Bayview Dr NW 44718
Beachland Cir NW 44718
Beachview Cir NW 44708
Beau Ct NW 44708
Beaver Place Ave SW 44706
Bebington St NW 44720
Bechel Pl NW 44708
Beckleigh Cir NW 44708
Becky Cir NW 44709
Becky Jo Ln SW 44706
Bedford Ave NW 44708
Bedford Ave SW
100-1299 44710
1400-2099 44706
Bedivere St NW 44708
Beech Hill Rd NW 44720
Beechgrove Ave NE 44705
Beechmoor Dr NW 44720
Beechtree Cir NW 44709
Beechwood Ave NE 44720
Begonia Ave NE 44705
Bel Air Ave NW 44718
Bel Air Dr NW 44720
Belden Ave NE
100-750 44704
752-798 44704
1000-1198 44705
1200-1299 44705
Belden Ave SE 44707
Belden Park Dr NW 44720
Belden Village Mall & St NW 44718
Bellarbor Ave NW 44708
Bellflower Ave NW 44708
Bellflower Ave SW
100-1499 44710
1600-2199 44706
Bellview St NE 44721
Bellwood Dr NW 44708
Belmont Pl SW 44710
Belpar St NW 44718
Benham Ct SE 44707
Benjamin St SW 44706
Bennington Cir SW 44709
Benskin Ave SW 44710
Benson Ct NW 44703
Benson Ct SW 44707
E & W Bent Oak Cir 44720
Bentham Cir NW 44720
Bentler Ave NE 44721
N Bentley Dr SE 44709
S Bentley Dr SE 44709
Bentley Pl NE 44704
Bentrina St NE 44704

Bentwood Cir NW 44720
Berdel Pl SE 44707
Berger Pl NE 44705
Bergess Rd NW 44718
Bergold Ave SW 44710
Berkshire Dr SW 44706
Bernard Ave NW 44709
Bernewood Cir NW 44709
Bernice Ct NE 44705
Berrywood Ave SW 44706
Bertram Ave NW 44718
Berwick Ave NE 44721
Beth Ave SW 44706
Beth Park Ave NE 44721
Bethany Cir NW 44720
Bethel Ave NW 44718
Beverly Ave NE
2600-5399 44714
5401-5499 44714
5500-7899 44721
Bevington St NW 44709
Bexley Cir NW 44718
Bexwell St NE 44714
Biery St SW 44706
Big Spring Ave NE 44721
Billendon Cir NW 44720
N & S Billingsgate Cir 44708
Birch Ave NE 44721
Birchbark Ave NE 44721
Birchdale Rd NW 44708
Birchdale St SW 44706
Birchdell Ave NE 44705
Birchmont Ave SW 44706
Birk Cir NE 44705
Birkdale St NW 44708
Birmingham Rd NE 44721
Bishops Gate Rd NW 44708
Blackberry Ave NW 44709
Blackburn Rd NW 44718
Blackfriars Dr NW 44708
Blackthorne St NW 44718
Blair Pl SW 44710
Blake Ave NW
1800-2550 44708
2551-2697 44718
2699-2999 44718
Blakemore Trl NW 44718
Blarney Cir NW 44720
Blecker Pl NE 44705
Blendon Ave NW 44718
Blendwood Ave NE 44721
Bletchley Ave NW 44720
Blitzen Rd NW 44720
N & S Bloomsbury Cir 44708
Blossomwood Cir NE 44721
Blue Ave SE 44707
Blue Ash Ave NW 44708
Blueberry Ave NW 44709
Blueridge St NW 44720
Bly Pl NW 44709
Bob O Link St NW 44720
Bobby Ave SW 44706
Bobwhite St NW 44720
Boettler St NE 44721
Bolivar Rd SW 44706
Bollinger Ave NE 44705
Bonnett St SW 44720
Bonnot Pl NE 44705
Bordner Ave SW
100-1499 44710
2400-2699 44706
Bornique Pl SW 44707
Boston Ave & Pl 44720
Bosworth Ave NE 44705
Boulder Creek Ave NE 44721
Bowdale Ave NW 44708
Bowen Cir NW 44708
Boylan Ave SE 44707
Bracken Rd SW 44706
Brad Ave NE 44704
Brad Ave SE 44707
Braden Pl NE 44705
Bradley Cir NW 44718
Braemar Cir 44720
Bramshaw Rd NW 44718
Brancoli St NW 44703

Brandy Cir NW 44720
Brant Ave NW 44708
Braucher St NW 44720
Bravado Rd SW 44706
Breea Cir NE 44720
Breezewood Dr NE 44705
Bremen Cir NW 44708
Brentwood Ave NW 44720
Brentwood Rd NW 44708
Brentwood Close St NW 44708
Bretton St NW 44720
Briar Ave NE 44720
Briarview Ave NW 44720
Briarwood Ave NW 44720
Bridgecreek Ave NW 44718
Bridgestone Cir NE 44721
Bridlewood Cir NE 44714
Bridlewood St NW 44720
Briton Cir NW 44708
Brittanny Dr NE 44720
Broad Ave NW 44708
Broadmoor Cir NW 44709
Brodie Cir NW 44720
Bromo Ct NE 44704
Bromo Ct SE 44707
Brookdale St NW 44709
Brookdell Dr NW 44720
Brookhaven Cir NE 44705
Brookledge Ave NW 44720
Brookline Rd 44720
Brooklyn Ave SW
100-1499 44710
2200-2699 44706
Brookpark St NW 44718
Brookpoint St NW 44720
Brooks Ave SW 44706
Brookstone St NW
5100-5299 44720
5400-5699 44718
Brookview Dr SW 44709
Brookway Rd NW 44718
Brookwood Dr NW 44708
Broughton Cir NW 44720
Brown Ave NW 44703
Browning Ave NW 44720
Brownlee Ave NE 44705
Brownstone Cir NW 44718
Bruening Ave SW 44706
Brumbaugh St NW 44720
Brunnerdale Ave NW
2900-3599 44708
3600-5299 44718
Brush Pl NE 44705
Brushmont Cir NW 44720
Brushmore Ave NW 44720
Brut Cir NW 44708
Bryan Ave SW 44706
Brycewood Cir NW 44720
Buchanan Blvd NW 44720
Buckhorn Dr NW 44708
Bucknell Cir NW 44720
Buddy Ave SW 44706
Buena Vista St NE 44714
Bundoran St NW 44720
Bur Oak St NE 44705
Burberry St NW 44720
Burger Ave NW 44709
Burgundy Ave NW 44720
Burkey Rd NW 44720
Burkhardt Ave NE 44704
Burkshire Dr SW 44709
Burlawn St NW 44708
Burrshire Dr NW 44709
Butler Cir & St 44720
Butternut St NW 44720
Buttonshoe Ave NW 44720
Byron Ave NE 44721
Byron Dr 44720
Bywood St SE 44707
Cable Point Cir NW 44718
Cadney St NE 44714
Cain St NW 44720
Calvin Ave SW 44706
Camaro St NE 44721
Cambridge Ave SW 44709

Camden Ave SW 44706
Campton Cir NW 44720
Campus Ave SE 44720
Campus Hill Cir NW 44720
Candlestick Ave NE 44721
Candlewood Ave NW 44720
Canter Hill Cir NE 44721
Canterbury St NW 44708
Canton Ave NW 44708
Caprice Ave NW 44709
Capricio St NE 44721
Captens St NE 44721
Car Mar Cir SW 44720
Cardiff Ave NW 44708
Cardinal Ave & Hl 44720
Cardington Green Cir NW 44718
Carl Pl NW 44708
Carlew St NW 44720
Carlisle Ave NE 44714
Carlton Ave NW 44709
Carlton Ave SE 44709
Carlton St NW 44720
Carmen Ct NW 44703
Carmen Dr NW 44720
Carnahan Ave NE 44704
Carnelian St NE 44721
Carnoustie Cir NW 44708
Carnwise St SE 44707
Carnwise St SW 44706
Carol St NE 44720
Carosel Cir NW 44720
Carr Ave SW 44706
Carriage Lane Ave NE 44721
Carrington St NW 44720
Carrolldale Ave NE 44704
Carrolldale Ave SE 44707
Cascade Cir E & W 44708
Case Pl NW 44703
Casern Ave NW 44720
Cashmere Cir 44720
Casper Dr NW 44718
N & S Casswell Cir 44720
Castlebar St NW 44708
Castleton Rd NE 44720
Castlewood Ave SW 44720
Catherine Pl SE 44707
Cathy Dr NE 44705
Cato Ct NW 44703
Cauley Ave NW 44720
Cayuga Ave & Cir 44708
Cedar Ln NW 44708
Cedar St NW 44720
Cedar Glen Cir NE 44714
Cedar Grove Ave NW 44720
Center Ct NW 44709
E Center Dr NE 44721
Center St SW 44706
Center Hill Sq NE 44714
Central Ave SE 44707
Central Plz N 44702
Central Plz S 44702
Century St NW 44718
Chaderton Cir NW 44720
Chadford Gate SE 44709
Chadwell Cir NW 44720
Chagrin Ave SW 44706
Chalford Cir NW 44720
Chandler Ave NW & SW 44720
Channel Dr NW 44718
Channelside Dr SE 44707
Channonbrook St SW 44710
Chanticleer Cir NW 44720
Chantilly Cir NE 44721
Chapel Rdg NE 44714
Chapple Hill Dr NE 44720
Charing Cross Rd NW 44708
Charlane Cir NW 44718
Charlene Ave SW 44706
Charles Ede Blvd SE 44707
Charlotte Ave SE 44707
Charlotte St NW 44720
Charm St SW 44706
Charring Court Cir NW 44718
Chatfield Ave NE 44721

Chatham Ave NE & NW 44720
Chatsworth St NW 44718
Chaucer Dr NE 44721
Chelmsford St NW 44720
Chelsea Dr SW 44706
Chermont St NW 44718
Cherokee Ave NW 44720
Cherry Ave NE
100-899 44702
900-1199 44704
1200-1749 44714
Cherry Ave SE
100-699 44702
700-1999 44707
Cherry Dr NW 44720
Cherry Blossom Cir NW 44720
Cheryl Ave SW 44706
Chesham Ave NE 44721
Cheshire Cir SW 44706
Chestnut Hill St NW 44720
Cheswold Cir NE 44720
Cheyenne St SE 44707
Chianti St NW 44720
Chicago Pl NW 44703
Chidwell St NE 44714
Chillingsworth Cir NW 44718
Chilmark St NW 44708
Chippewa Ave NW 44720
Choctaw St NW 44720
Christian Pl NW 44708
Christmas Seal Dr NW 44709
Church St SW 44720
Churchmont St SE 44707
Cinderford St NW 44718
Circle Dr SW 44706
N Circle Dr 44709
Circle Hill Rd SE 44720
Clardell Ave SW 44706
Claremont Ave NW 44708
Clarendon Ave NW 44708
Clarendon Ave SW
100-1399 44710
1500-2299 44706
Clark Ave SW 44706
Clearmount Ave SE 44720
Clearview Ave NW
1800-2540 44708
2541-3299 44718
Clearwater Dr 44720
Cleveland Ave NW
100-1199 44702
1200-1799 44703
1800-2649 44709
2650-2698 44711
2651-4999 44709
2700-4998 44709
7700-9701 44720
Cleveland Ave SW
100-899 44702
900-5399 44707
Cliffwood Ave NW 44708
Cliftmont Ave NE 44705
Cline Dr 44720
Clinton Ave SE 44720
Clinton Ave SW 44706
Cloister Ave NW 44709
Clover Ct NW 44703
Cloverhill St SW 44706
Cloverhurst St NE 44721
Clyde Pl SW
2200-2399 44706
2400-3499 44710
Clydesdale St NE 44720
Cobbledale Ave NW 44720
Cobblefield St NE 44721
Cobra Blvd NW 44720
Cockleburr St NW 44720
Cody Ct NW 44703
Cody Dr SW 44706
Cold Stream Ave NE 44721
Coldwater Ave NW 44708
Cole Ave SE 44707
Cole Ave SW 44720
Colebrook Cir NW 44720

College St SE 44720
Collins Ct NW 44703
Colonial Blvd NE 44714
Colony Wood Cir SW 44706
Columbus Ave NW 44708
Columbus Rd NE 44705
Comanche St NW 44720
Comet Cir NW 44720
Commerce St SW 44706
S & W Commons Cir & St 44721
Concord Ave SW 44710
Congress Dr SW 44706
Constance Cir NW 44718
Convenience Cir NW 44718
Cook Ave SW 44707
Coppercove Cir NW 44720
Coral Blvd NW 44720
Cord Pl SE 44709
Cordelia St SW 44720
Cornelia Ave NE 44704
Cornell Ave SW 44706
Cornwall Dr NW 44708
Corporate St SW 44706
Correll Ave NE 44704
Corrib Ave NW 44708
Corrine Dr NW 44718
Cottage Pl NW 44703
Cottington Cir & St 44720
Cottonwood Dr 44720
Coty Dr SW 44706
Cougar St NE 44721
Court Ave NW 44702
Court Ave SW
100-899 44702
1000-1299 44707
Cove Cir NW 44708
Coventry Blvd NE 44705
Coventry Ln NW 44708
Crabapple Ave NE 44721
Crafton Cir NW 44720
Cranberry Ave NW 44709
Cranwood St NW 44720
Creekside Cir NE 44720
Creekview Cir 44720
Crescent Ave SW 44709
Crescent Rd SW 44710
Crestdale St NE 44714
Crestdale St NW 44709
Crestfield St SW 44706
Crestland Ave NW & SE 44720
Crestmont Ave NE 44704
Crestmont Ave SE 44707
Creston Dr SW 44706
Crestpark St SW 44706
Crestwood St NW 44708
Cromdale Cir 44720
Cromer Ave NW 44709
Crompton St NE 44721
Cropf St NW 44708
Crosshaven Rd NW 44708
Crowl Pl SW 44706
Crown Pl NW 44708
Croydon Dr NW 44718
Crystal Pl NE 44705
Culpepper St NW 44718
Culver Cir NW 44709
Cupid Cir NW 44720
Cynthia Dr 44720
Cypress Ct NE 44705
Daffodil St NE 44705
Dahlia St NE 44705
Daisybrook St NW 44720
Daisywood Ave NW 44720
Dalbury Ave NE 44714
Dale Pl NW 44703
Daleford Ave NE 44705
Dalemont Ave SE 44707
Dallas Pl SE 44707
Dalton Pl SW 44710
Danbury Rd NW 44720
Dancer Ave NW 44720
Dane Ave NE 44704
Danforth Cir NW 44718
Danna Ave NE 44721

Danube Way SW 44706
Dapplegray St NW 44709
Darien Ave NW 44718
Darlington Ave NW
2900-2999 44718
3400-3999 44708
4700-4999 44718
Dartmouth Ave SW 44710
Dasher Ave NW 44720
Dauphin Dr NE 44721
Dave Ave SW 44706
Daventry St NW 44720
David Ave NW 44709
Davide Cir NW 44709
Davis Pl SW 44707
Davis St SW 44706
Dawn Cir NW 44703
Dawnridge Cir NW 44709
Dawnwood Ave NE 44721
Dayspring Cir NW 44720
Deacon Ave & Dr 44720
Deanna Ln 44720
Deberg Ct NW 44703
Deborah St NW 44720
Deer Pass Dr SW 44706
Deer Trace Ave NW 44708
Deer Trail Ave NE 44721
Deerfield Dr SW 44720
Del Corso Ave NE 44721
Delaware Ave SW
100-1399 44710
2200-2699 44706
Dell Cir NW 44720
Dellwood Ave NW 44708
Delverne Ave SW 44710
Demington Ave NW
1800-2699 44708
2700-3099 44718
Democracy Dr NW 44720
Denham Cir NE 44721
Denise Cir SW 44706
Denne St NW 44709
Dennis Ct NE 44705
Dennison Pl NW 44709
Dent Pl SW 44707
Depot St NE 44721
Derby Cir SE 44707
Derby Ct SW 44706
Derbyshire Ave NW 44720
Desert Inn Ct NW 44703
Deville Ave NW 44708
Devon Dr NE 44720
Devonshire Dr NW 44708
Dewalt Ave NW
100-599 44702
700-799 44703
801-1199 44703
Dewalt Ave SW 44707
Dewey Pl SW 44710
Diamond St NE 44721
Diamond Park Ave NE 44721
Diana Pl NW 44703
Diane Ave SW 44706
Dill Ct NE 44704
Dillon Cir NE 44720
Dillon Pl NE 44705
Discovery Rd 44720
Division St NE 44705
Dodge Rd SW 44706
Doeskin St NE 44704
Dogwood Ave NE 44720
Dolores St SW 44706
Donald Pl SW 44706
Doncaster Ave NW 44720
Donegal Dr NE 44721
Donelson Cir 44708
Donner Ave & St 44720
Doral Dr NW 44718
Doris Cir NW 44718
Dornestr St SW 44706
Dorothy Ave NE 44705
Dorrington Ave NE 44721
Dotwood St NW 44720
Dougherty Pl NW 44703
Douglas Cir NW 44718
Dover Ave NE 44714

Downing Ct NE 44714
Downingsgate Cir NW 44718
Drake St NW 44718
Dreamwood Ave SW 44706
Dresden Dr NW 44708
Dressler Rd NW
3600-4421 44718
4420-4420 44735
4422-5298 44718
4423-5299 44718
5300-6499 44720
Driftwood Cir NW 44720
Drossel Ave NE 44721
Drumcliff Dr NW 44708
Dryden Ct SW 44706
Dublin Cir NW 44720
Duck Hollow Cir 44720
Dueber Ave SW 44706
Dunbarton Ave NW 44708
Dunberry St NW 44720
Duncannon Ave NW 44708
Dunfred Cir SE 44707
Dungannon Cir NW 44720
Dunkeith Dr NW 44708
Dunkeith Woods Dr NW 44708
Dunmore Ave NW 44708
Dunoon Cir NW 44718
Dunwoody Cir NW 44718
Duo Ave NW 44708
Duplain St NW 44720
Durkin Way SW 44720
Dutch Cir NE 44721
Eagle St NW 44720
Eagle Watch St NE 44721
Earlington Cir NW 44708
Earlscourt Cir NW 44718
East Blvd NW 44718
Eastbranch Cir NE 44705
Eastbury Ave NE 44720
Eastern St NE 44721
Eastgate St NW 44718
Eastgreen St NE 44721
Eastham Cir NW 44708
Easthill Sq NE 44714
Easthill St SE 44720
Eastlake St NW
5100-5399 44720
5400-5699 44718
Easton St NE 44721
Eastpointe Blvd NE 44714
Eastview Ave NE 44705
Eastwind Cir NW 44720
Eastwood Cir SE 44720
Eastwood St NE 44714
Eastwood St NW 44709
Easy Pace Cir NW 44718
Eaton Rd NW 44708
Eby Dr NE 44705
Echo St NE 44721
Echodell Ave NW 44720
Echoglenn St NW 44720
Echohill Ave NW 44720
Echolake Dr NW 44720
Echosprings St NW 44720
Echovale St NW 44720
Echovalley St NW 44720
Economy Ct NE 44704
Eddie Ave SW 44706
Edelweiss St NE 44721
Edgedale Ave NE 44721
Edgefield Ave NW 44709
Edgehill Cir NW 44709
Edgemont St NW 44718
Edgewood St SE 44720
Edinburg Ave NW 44708
Edinderry Dr NW 44708
Edith Ct NE 44705
Edmeyer Ave NW 44708
Edwards Ave NE 44705
Edwin Dr NW 44718
El Mar Dr NW 44720
Elaine Ave NW 44720
Elberta Ave NW & SW 44709
Elcar Ave NW 44708
Elderwood Ct SW 44707

Eldon Cir SE 44707
Elgin Ave NW 44708
Elizabeth Pl NW 44709
Ellen Cir NW 44718
Ellenhurst St NE 44714
Ellesmere Ave NW 44720
Ellinda Cir NW 44709
Elliott Pl NW 44703
Ellis Ave NE 44705
Ellwood Ave SW 44710
Elmcreek St NW 44720
Elmdale St NW 44718
Elmhurst Ave NW 44720
Elmport Ave NE 44704
Elmwood Ave SW 44720
Elrod Pl NE 44705
Elva Ct SW 44710
Emerald Ave NE 44721
Emerson Ave NW 44720
Emerson Pl NE 44704
Emma Pl NW 44708
Emmett Boyd Cir NW 44720
Empire Rd NE 44705
E End Ave SE 44707
Endrow Ave NE 44705
Enfield Ave NW 44708
Engle Pl SW 44710
Englewood Dr NE 44721
Ennis Cir NE 44705
Essex Ave NW 44720
Essig Ct NW 44703
Estep Pl SW 44707
Esther Ave NE 44714
Esther Ave SW 44706
Ethel St NW 44718
Etna Pl SW 44706
Euclid St NE 44704
Evergreen Dr NW 44720
Everhard Rd NW
3400-3999 44709
4200-5899 44718
Everhard Rd SW 44709
Everhart Dr 44720
Eversholt Cir NW 44708
Eversole Ave SW 44706
Evesham Cir NE 44721
Excalibur Cir NW 44708
Executive Cir NW 44718
Exeter Ave SW 44710
Fair Oaks Ave NW & SW 44720
Fairacres St SW 44706
Faircrest St SE 44707
Faircrest St SW 44706
Fairfax Ct NW 44708
Fairfax St NW 44720
Fairhart Ave SE 44720
Fairhaven Ave NW 44709
Fairknoll Ave SE 44707
Fairlane Ave SW 44710
Fairmount Blvd & St 44705
Fairview St SE 44720
Fairwood Ave NW 44720
Falcons Ridge Cir NW 44708
Fall Ave SW 44706
Fallen Timber St NE 44721
Falmouth Way SE 44709
Far View Dr SW 44720
Faridark St SE 44707
Farmcrest Cir NW 44720
Farmdale Ave NW 44720
Farmington Cir SW 44706
Farmview St NW 44720
Farnham St NW 44720
Farrell St SE 44720
Farringdon Rd NW 44708
Fawcett Ct NW 44708
Fawn Dr NW 44720
Fay Pl SW 44710
Fencegate St NE 44705
Fenchurch Cir NE 44720
Fenton Ave NE 44704
Fenwick Ave NE 44721
Ferndale Rd NW 44709
Fernwood St NW 44718
Fiddler Court Cir NE 44721
Fiddlers Creek Cir NW 44720
Field St NW 44709
Fieldmont St NW 44720
Fields Ave SW 44706
Fieldstone Dr NW 44718
Fife Cir NW 44720
Figueroa Pl SE 44707
Finn Cir NW 44720
Firestone Ave NE 44721
Firethorn Ave NW 44720
Firwood Dr 44720
Fitzjames Dr NW 44708
Flagstone Cir NW 44718
Flamos Cir NE 44704
Fleetwood Ave NW 44718
Fletcher Ave NE 44705
Floral Ave NW 44708
Florian Dr NW 44709
Flory Ct NE 44704
Flory Ct SE 44707
Fohl St SW 44706
Fohldale St SW 44706
Folmer Pl NE 44704
Ford Ave SW 44720
Ford Ct NW 44708
Fordham Cir NW 44720
Forest Ave SW 44710
Forestdale Ave SW 44706
Forestview Cir & St 44721
Forestwood St NW 44718
Forsythia Dr 44720
Foster Ave SE 44720
Fox Hill Dr NW 44708
Fox Hollow Dr NW 44720
Fox Ridge Dr 44720
Fox Run Ave NW 44720
Fox Tail Cir NW 44718
Foxboro Ave NW 44718
Foxchase Ave NW 44718
Foxford St SW 44706
Foxhaven Ave NW 44718
Foxhill Cir NE 44705
Foxview Ave NW 44718
Foxway Cir NW 44720
Francie Ave NW 44718
Francis Ct NE 44705
Franciscan St NE 44705
Frank Ave NW 44720
Franklin Pl NW 44709
Frazer Ave NW
1500-1799 44703
1800-4899 44709
5500-6099 44720
Frazer Dr NW 44720
Frederick Ave SW 44706
Fredricksburg Ct NE 44720
Freed Ct SE 44707
Freedom Ave NE 44704
Freedom Ave NW 44720
Freitag St NW 44718
Fremont Pl SW
1800-2199 44706
2600-2699 44710
Frey Ave SW 44706
Friarsgate Dr NW 44718
Friarwood Cir NW 44718
Friendly Ln NW 44720
Fromes Ave NE 44721
Fromm Ave NW 44708
Fuller Ct NW 44718
Fulton Dr NW 44718
Fulton Rd NW
201-297 44703
299-1799 44703
1800-2501 44709
Furbee Ave SW 44720
Gage Ave NE 44705
Galway Cir NW 44720
Gambrinus Ave SW 44706
Gans Ave NE 44721
Garaux St NE 44704
Gardendale Ave NE 44714
Gardenia Dr 44720
Gardenstone Cir NE 44721
Garfield Ave SW 44706
Garity Ct SW 44706
Garnet Ave NE 44721
Garth Cir NW 44718
Gaslight Cir SE 44720
Gatekeepers St NE 44721
Gateway Blvd SE 44707
Gatewood Cir NW 44720
Gayle Pl SW 44706
Geltz Ct NW 44709
Gem Cir NE 44721
Gem Ct NW 44708
Genoa Ave SW 44706
Gensen Lake Rd NE 44721
George Pl SW 44707
George St SW 44706
George Halas Dr NW 44708
Georgene Cir SW 44706
Georgetown Rd & St 44704
Geranium Ave NE 44705
Gertrude Ct SW 44706
Giacomo Ct NW 44709
Gibbs Ave NE
100-799 44704
800-1899 44705
1900-1902 44714
1904-2999 44714
Gilbert Ave & Cir 44705
Gill Pl NW 44709
Gillariv Ave NW 44708
Gilmore Ave NW 44703
Girard Ave NE 44704
Girard Ave SE 44707
Gladiola St NE 44705
Glastonbury Cir NW 44708
Glavera Ave NE 44704
Gleenwillow Dr 44720
Glen Abbey Ave NE 44720
Glenburn St NW 44720
Glendale Pl NE 44705
Glendale St SW 44720
Glenennis Cir NW 44708
Glengarry Ave NW 44718
Glenhill Ave NE
5200-5499 44705
5500-5699 44721
Glenhurst St SW 44706
Glenmar Oval SE 44709
Glenmere Ave NE 44721
Glenmont Dr & Rd 44708
Glenmoor Rd NW 44718
Glenn Pl NW 44708
Glennview St NE 44721
Glenport Cir NW 44709
Glenridge Cir NE 44714
Glenwood St SE & SW 44720
Glessner Ave NE 44721
Global Gtwy 44720
Glorine St NW 44720
Glouchester Dr NE 44721
Glyn Dr NW 44720
Glynhaven Ave NE 44704
Glynhaven Ave SE 44707
Gobel Ave NE 44704
Gobel Ave SE 44707
Gonder Ave SE 44707
Gooding St SW 44706
Governors Ave NW 44718
Grace Ave NE 44705
Gracie Dr NW 44718
Graham Ct SW 44710
Grail Cir NW 44708
Grand Dr NW 44708
Grand Blanc Dr SW 44706
Grandjean Ln 44720
Grandview Ave NE 44705
Grandview Ave NW 44708
Grandview Ave SW 44710
Granite Ct NW 44703
Granite St NW 44718
Grant Ct NE 44704
Grassmere St SE 44709
Gray Fox Dr 44720
Gray Fox Dr NW 44718
Graydon Ave SW 44706
Grayson Cir NW 44718
Graystone Cir NW 44718
Great Oak Cir NW 44708
Green Ct NE 44704
Greenbriar Sq NE 44714
Greenbrook Rd 44720
Greencrest St NW 44720
Greenfield Ave SW 44706
Greenfield Cir NW 44720
Greenmeadow Ave NW 44709
Greenock Dr NW 44720
Greenport Ave SE 44707
Greensburg Rd 44720
Greentree Ave SW 44706
Greenview Cir NW 44708
Greenway Rd SE 44709
Greenwood Pl SW 44710
Greg Cir NW 44708
Grenada Dr NE 44714
Gressel Ave NW 44720
Greyhawk St NW 44708
Greystone Dr 44720
Gridley Ave NE 44705
Griffith Ave NW 44720
Grigsby Pl SW
2300-2399 44706
2400-3099 44710
Grimes Ave NW 44720
Grimsby St NW 44720
Gross Ave NE
1201-1297 44705
1299-1899 44705
1900-1998 44714
2000-3599 44714
5500-5699 44721
Grossi Cir NE 44714
Groton St NW 44708
Grove Pl SW
2100-2399 44706
2400-3199 44710
Grove St NE 44721
Grovewood Cir SW 44706
Grubb Ct NE 44721
Grunder Ave NW 44709
Guilford Ave NW
3400-3899 44718
4001-4699 44709
Hadrian Cir NW 44708
Hafer Ct SW 44706
Hahn St NE 44721
Hale Ave SW 44706
Halifax Way SE 44709
Hall St NW 44720
Hallersi Ave SW 44710
Hallum St SW 44720
Halter Ave & Ct 44708
Halwyck Cir NW 44720
Hamilton Ave NE 44704
Hammerly Ct SE 44707
Hammerstone Cir NW 44720
Hammond Ave SW 44706
Hancock St SW 44706
Hannah Cir 44709
Hanover Ct SE 44709
Harbor Dr NW
1401-1499 44708
6200-6999 44718
Harborview Ave NW 44718
Harbour Cir NW 44708
Harmon St NE 44705
Harmon St SW 44720
Harmont Ave NE 44705
Harmony Ct NE 44705
Harmony Ln SW 44709
Harness Cir NE 44721
Harriet Ave NW 44703
Harris Ave NW 44708
Harrisburg Rd NE 44705
Harrison Ave NW
100-1799 44708
1801-2199 44708
2500-4699 44709
4701-4799 44709
Harrison Ave SW 44706
Harter Ave NW 44708
Hartford Ave NE 44704
Hartford Ave SE 44707
Hartman St SE 44720
Hartung Pl NE 44704
Harvard Ave NW
1500-1799 44703
1800-3999 44709
E Harvard Blvd 44709
W Harvard Blvd 44709
Harvest Cir SE 44707
Harvest Ridge Ave NE 44721
Harvey Ave NW 44720
Harvey Pl SE 44707
Hauer Ct NW 44709
Havana Pl NE 44714
Hawick St NW 44708
Hawk Ave & Pl 44707
Hawthorne Ave SW 44710
Hazeldell Dr 44720
Hazlett Ave NW 44708
Heang Ave NE 44702
Hearthstone Ave NW 44720
Heather Cir NE 44720
Heather St NW 44708
Heatherwood Cir & St NW & SW 44720
Heggy Ct NE 44704
Heisers Way SW 44720
Heising Ct SW 44706
Helen Pl NW 44708
Helmsworth Dr NE 44714
Heminger Ct NE 44721
Hemlock St NW 44720
Henrietta Ave NE 44704
Henry Ave SW 44706
Henrys Mill Cir NW 44718
Hensley St 44708
Henton Cir NE 44705
Herbert Pl NW 44703
Herbruck Ct NE 44704
Heritage Ave NW 44718
Hickory St NE 44721
Hidden Glen Ave NE 44721
Hidden View St NW 44720
Hiddenbrook St NE 44721
Higbee Ave NW 44718
High Ave NW 44703
High Ave SW 44707
High Line Ave NW 44720
High Vista Cir NE 44714
Highgate Cir NW 44720
Highland Park NW 44720
Highland Rd NE 44704
Highland Creek Ave 44720
Highpoint Cir NW 44718
Highspire St NE 44721
Highview Ave SW 44706
Highwood Ave SW 44706
Hillbrook Ave SE 44709
Hillcrest Ave NW 44720
Hillcrest Ave SW 44720
Hillcrest Rd NW 44709
Hilldale Rd NW 44718
Hillfield St NW 44720
Hillford Ave NE 44721
Hillmont Ave SW 44706
Hillport Dr SW 44706
Hillridge Ave NE 44721
Hills And Dales Rd NW 44708
Hillsboro Ave SE 44707
Hilltop Dr NW 44708
Hillview Cir NW
300-399 44709
5300-5399 44718
Hillway Ave NW 44720
Hilscher Ave NE 44705
Hiner Pl NE 44705
Hines St SW 44720
Hiram Rd NW 44718
Hoffman Ct NE 44705
Hogan Way NW 44718
Holiday St NW 44718
Holl Rd NE 44720
Holland Ct SW 44706
Hollydale Ave NE 44721
Hollyhock Ave NW 44718
Hollyridge St NW 44720
Hollythorne Rd NE 44721
Hollyview Ave NE 44721
Hollywood Ave NE 44704
Holmes Dr NW 44718
Holt St SE 44707
Homedale Ave NW 44708
Homer Ave NW 44703
Homes Pl NW 44703
Homewood Ave SW 44710
Honeymoon Dr 44720
Honeysuckle Dr 44720
Hoover Pl NW 44703
Hope Ct SE 44707
Hopple Ave SW 44706
Horallia Ave NE 44705
Horeener St NW 44720
Horseshoe Ave NE 44721
Hossler Dr NW 44720
Houghton Pl NE 44705
Housel Ave SE 44707
Hower St NE 44720
Howington Cir SE 44707
Huck Cir NW 44720
Huckleberry St NW 44720
Hudson Pl SW 44706
Hughes St NW 44709
Humberside Ave NW 44720
Humbert Rd NW 44720
Hume St NE & NW 44720
Huntcliffe Rd NE 44721
Hunters Ridge Blvd NE 44721
Hunting Vly NW 44720
Huntington Pl SW 44707
Huntshire Ave NW 44720
Huntsman St NW 44718
Hurless Dr SW 44706
Hursh Pl NW 44708
Hyacinth Dr NE & NW 44720
Hyke Ct SE 44707
Hythe St NW 44708
Ida Pl SE 44707
Immel St NE 44721
Independence Cir & Dr 44720
Indian Creek Cir NW 44718
Indiana Way NE 44705
Industrial Pl SE 44707
Inglewood Ave NW 44718
Ingram Ave SW 44710
Inn Cir NW 44720
Inner Dr SW 44706
International Pkwy 44720
Inverness Pkwy NW 44708
Inverrary Dr NW 44718
Iowa Pl NE 44705
Ira Cir SW 44706
Ira Turpin Way NE 44705
Iris Ct NW 44709
Irondale Cir NE 44720
Ironstone St NE 44705
Ironwood St SE 44707
Ironwood St SW 44706
Irvine Cir NW 44718
Irwin Pl NE 44705
Island Dr NW 44718
Isler Cir NW 44708
Isley Rd NW 44718
Ivanhoe Ave NW 44709
Ivy Ct NE 44704
Ivy St NW 44720
Ivy Way NE 44705
Ivydale Ave NW 44720
Ivydale Ave SW
1300-1599 44710
1700-1899 44706
Jacque Dr NW 44718
Jaguar St NE 44721
James St SW 44720
Janet Ave NW 44720
Janet Ct NE 44704
Janet Ct SE 44707
Jaquelyn Dr 44720
Jasmine Cir NW 44720
Jasper St NE 44721
Jefferson Cir NW 44718
Jennifer Dr NW 44720
Joan Dr 44720
Jobe Ct NE 44704
Jobe Ct SE 44707
John Ct SE 44707
Johnnycake Rdg NE 44705
Johnson Pl SE 44707
Joleda Dr SW 44706
Jonathan Ave SW 44720
Jones Ct NW 44703
Jordan Cir NW 44720
Joseph Pl NW 44708
Josephine St NW 44720
Junction Ct NW 44708
Kaiser Ave NE 44705
Kalahari St NE 44705
Kalurah St NE 44721
Kandel Cir SE 44720
Kasper St NE 44705
Katrina Ct NW 44709
Keats St NE 44721
Keiffer Ave SW 44706
Keller Dr SW 44706
Ken Pl NW 44709
Kendal St SW 44706
Kennebuck Cir & St 44718
Kennedy St NW 44720
Kennemer Cir NW 44720
Kennesaw Cir NW 44708
Kennet Ct NW 44708
Kensington Ct NW 44708
Kent Ave NE 44721
Kentview Ave NW 44720
Kenwood Cir NE 44714
Kerry Cir NW 44718
Ketterer Cir & St 44720
Kevin St NW 44720
Kildare Cir NW 44718
Killington Ave NW 44720
Kimball Rd SE 44707
Kimberly Cir NE 44705
King Ct NW 44703
King St SW 44706
Kingman Ave NW 44709
Kings Cross Cir NE 44721
Kings Gate Cir NE 44721
Kingsboro Cir NW 44720
Kingsbury Dr SW 44706
Kingscote Cir NE 44720
Kingsrow Ave NW 44709
Kingston Dr NW 44708
Kingston Dr SE 44707
Kingswood St NE 44721
Kinlinwood Ct NW 44708
Kinross Cir 44720
Kirby Ave NE
2500-4999 44705
6600-7199 44721
Kirk Ct NW 44709
Kistler Pl NE 44705
Knight Ave NW 44708
Knightsbridge Ave NW 44718
Knob Hill Dr NW 44718
Knoll St SE 44709
Knollridge Ave & Cir 44721
Knollwood Rd NW 44708
Kolp Pl NW 44709
Kolp Pl SW 44720
Konen Ave NW 44718
Koons Rd 44720
Koran Ave NW 44708
Krisher Ave SW 44706
Krisko Cir SW 44706
Kropf Ave SW 44706
Kuemerle Ct NE 44705
Kurtz Ct NE 44705
La Salle Ct SE 44709
Lacave Pl NW 44703
Ladonna Cir NW 44720
Laiblin Pl NE 44705
Lake Breeze Dr 44720
Lake Cable Ave NW
5700-6499 44718
6700-6899 44720
Lake Heights Rd NW 44708

Lake O Springs Ave NW
5500-6699 ... 44718
6700-8300 ... 44720
8302-8652 ... 44720
Lake Road Blvd NW ... 44708
Lakecrest St NW ... 44709
Lakemere Cir NW ... 44718
Lakemoor Cir NW ... 44718
Lakeridge Dr NE ... 44714
Lakeside Ave NW ... 44708
Lakeview Ave NW ... 44708
Lakewood Ct NW ... 44708
Lakewood St NW ... 44718
Lamb Cir NW ... 44720
Lambert Cir NW ... 44718
Lamennais Ave SE ... 44720
Lancaster Gate SE ... 44709
Lancer St NW ... 44720
Landmark Blvd ... 44720
Landscape Ave & Cir ... 44709
Lang Pl NW ... 44708
Langley St NW ... 44718
Lanner St NW ... 44720
Lansdale Ave NW ... 44720
Lantern Hill Cir NW ... 44718
Larch Ave NE ... 44721
Larchmoor Pkwy NW ... 44708
Larchwood Cir NW ... 44718
Larkspur Ave NW ... 44720
Las Olas Blvd NW ... 44720
Lasater Dr NW ... 44718
Lattavo St NE ... 44714
Lauby Rd ... 44720
Laurel Dr NW ... 44718
Laurel Green Dr NE ... 44720
Laurel Lane St NW ... 44708
Laurelview Cir NE ... 44721
Laverton Ave NE ... 44705
Lavonne Ave NE ... 44721
Lawn Ave NW ... 44708
Lawn Ave SW ... 44706
Lawndale St NW ... 44708
Lawnview St NW ... 44718
Lawrence Rd NE
501-597 ... 44704
599-1099 ... 44704
1100-1399 ... 44705
1401-1499 ... 44705
Leander Pl NE ... 44704
Leawood Dr NE ... 44714
Ledbury Cir NE ... 44721
Lee Ct SW ... 44706
Lee St NW ... 44720
Leemont Ave NW ... 44709
Lehigh Ave SW ... 44720
Leigh Ave NW
4700-4999 ... 44709
6800-6999 ... 44720
Len Pl NW ... 44703
Leo Ave SW ... 44706
Leonard Ave SW ... 44706
Leonard Pl SE ... 44707
Lesh St NE ... 44705
Leslie St NW ... 44720
Leyland Ave NW ... 44720
Leyton Ave NE ... 44721
Libbie St NW ... 44718
Liberty Ln NW ... 44720
Libra Cir SW ... 44706
Lillian St SW ... 44706
Lillys Ln NW ... 44718
Limerick Ave NW ... 44720
Limington St NW ... 44720
Lincoln Ave NW ... 44708
Lincoln St E ... 44707
Linda Pl NE ... 44704
Linda St NW ... 44720
Linda St SW ... 44720
Lindbergh Ave NW ... 44718
Lindell Ct NW ... 44718
Lindenwood Ave NE ... 44714
Linder Cir NE ... 44721
Lindford Ave NE
4500-5499 ... 44705
5501-5551 ... 44721
5553-5699 ... 44721

Lindy Lane Ave NW &
SW ... 44720
Linmar Dr ... 44720
Linwood Ave NW ... 44708
Linwood Ave SW
300-1299 ... 44720
600-1599 ... 44710
1600-2199 ... 44706
Lippert Rd NE
700-798 ... 44704
800-1099 ... 44704
1101-1197 ... 44705
1199-1599 ... 44705
Lipton Ave SW ... 44720
Lisburn Cir NW ... 44720
Lismore Ave NW ... 44718
List St NW ... 44708
Lloyd Ct NE ... 44704
Lochness Cir NW ... 44718
Loddy Ave NE ... 44714
Loehrmoore Ave NE ... 44705
Logan Ave NW
1200-1699 ... 44703
2100-4999 ... 44709
Lois Ave NW ... 44720
Loma Linda Ln NE
5200-5399 ... 44714
5500-5899 ... 44721
Lombardi Ave SW ... 44706
Long Ave NE ... 44705
Longbranch Dr NE ... 44714
Longfellow St NE ... 44721
Longshadow Ave ... 44720
Longview Pl NW ... 44720
Lorena St SW ... 44720
Lorenz Ln SE ... 44720
Lorindow St NE ... 44721
Lorraine Ave NW ... 44720
Lorrell Ave SW ... 44720
Los Angeles Blvd NW ... 44720
Lost Trail Ave NE ... 44721
Lost Tree Dr NW ... 44708
Lotus Pl SW ... 44710
Louise Dr NW ... 44718
Louisiana Ave NW ... 44703
Louisville St NE ... 44705
Lourelton Ave NW ... 44720
Lovers Ln NE ... 44721
Loyal St SW ... 44706
Loyola Cir NW ... 44720
Lucille Ave SW ... 44720
Lucinda Ave SE ... 44707
Luna Ct SE ... 44707
Lupe Ave NW ... 44720
Luther Pl NE ... 44704
Lutz Pl NE ... 44704
Lydford St NW ... 44720
Lyman Ct NE ... 44704
Lynbrook St SE ... 44720
Lynch Ave SW ... 44707
Lynhurst Cir SW ... 44720
Lynleigh Cir NW ... 44708
Lynn Cir NW ... 44708
Lynncrest St SW ... 44706
Lynx Ave NE ... 44721
Mabry Mill Dr SW ... 44709
Macduff Dr NW ... 44720
Macintosh St SW ... 44709
Mackay Cir NW ... 44720
Mackenzie Ave NW ... 44720
Macnaughten St NW ... 44720
Macthomas Ave NW ... 44720
Maddrell Ct NE ... 44705
Madison Ct SE ... 44707
Magnolia Ave NE ... 44705
Magnolia Cir SE ... 44709
Magnolia Rd NE ... 44705
Mahogany Run Cir
NW ... 44720
Mahoning Rd NE ... 44705
N Main St ... 44720
S Main St
100-1477 ... 44720
1478-1799 ... 44709
Malhaven St SW ... 44706
Malory Cir NW ... 44708

Malvern Ct NW ... 44709
Manor Ave NW ... 44708
Manor Ave SW ... 44710
Maple Ave NE
1217-1297 ... 44705
1299-1899 ... 44705
1900-2999 ... 44714
3001-3599 ... 44714
E Maple St ... 44720
E Maple St NW ... 44720
W Maple St ... 44720
Maple Glen Ave NW ... 44720
Maplecrest St SW ... 44720
Mapledell St NW ... 44718
Maplelynn St SW ... 44706
Mapleridge Cir NW ... 44718
Mapleton St SE ... 44707
Maplewood Ave SW ... 44706
Marbury Ave NE ... 44705
Marcellus St NW ... 44708
Marelis Ave NE ... 44721
Maret St NE ... 44705
Margaret Ave SW ... 44706
Margate Cir NW ... 44718
Marguerite Ct NW ... 44708
Marietta Ave NE ... 44704
Marietta Ave SE ... 44707
Marilyn Ave NW ... 44708
Mariners Island Dr
NW ... 44708
Mariol Ct SW ... 44706
Marion Ave SW ... 44707
Marion Motley Ave NE ... 44705
Mark Twain Cir NW ... 44720
Market Ave N
200-1199 ... 44702
1200-5499 ... 44714
5500-8999 ... 44721
Market Ave S
201-203 ... 44702
205-899 ... 44702
901-997 ... 44707
999-1799 ... 44707
Markley St NE ... 44721
Markley St NW ... 44720
Marlin Ave NW ... 44708
Marquardt Ave NE &
NW ... 44720
Mars St NW ... 44720
Marsden Ave SW ... 44710
Marsh Ave NW ... 44708
Marshall St NW ... 44718
Martha Ave NE ... 44705
Martindale Rd NE
3000-3098 ... 44714
3100-4030 ... 44714
4031-4199 ... 44705
Marvella Dr NE ... 44714
Marvin Pl NE ... 44705
Maryland Ave SW
100-1599 ... 44710
1600-2199 ... 44706
Marzilli Cir & St ... 44718
Mason Pl NW ... 44703
Massillon Rd ... 44720
Mattie St SE ... 44707
Maureen Dr NW ... 44718
Max Rd ... 44720
Maxim Cir NE ... 44721
Maxine Ave NE ... 44705
Maxwell Cir NW ... 44720
May Ave NW ... 44709
May Pl NE ... 44705
Mayapple Cir NE ... 44705
Mayfair Rd ... 44720
Maywood Pl SW ... 44710
Mcalmont Rd NE ... 44720
Mcdowell St NE ... 44721
Mcginty Rd NW ... 44720
Mcgregor Ave NW ... 44703
Mckinley Ave NW
100-599 ... 44702
600-1299 ... 44703
Mckinley Ave SE ... 44720
Mckinley Ave SW
300-499 ... 44702
500-598 ... 44707
600-1399 ... 44707
1401-1599 ... 44707
Mckinley Monument Dr
NW ... 44708
Meadowbluff Dr ... 44720
Meadowlands Ave NW ... 44720
Meadowlane Dr NW &
SE ... 44709
Meadowlark St NW ... 44720
Meadowridge Ave NW ... 44708
Meadowsweet Ave
NW ... 44718
Meadowview Dr NW ... 44718
Mears Gate Dr NW ... 44720
Medley Dr ... 44720
Meek Pl SW ... 44707
Mega St NW ... 44720
Mehaffie Dr NE ... 44721
Melchoir Pl SW ... 44707
Melody Rd NE ... 44721
Melrose Pl NE ... 44714
Mendell Dr NW ... 44720
Menlough Ave NW ... 44708
Menlough Wood Dr
NW ... 44708
Mercy Dr NW ... 44708
Meridian Cir NW ... 44720
Merriman Pl SE ... 44707
Metric Ave SW ... 44706
Metro Cir NW ... 44720
Meyerson Ave SE ... 44707
Miami Ct NE ... 44714
Michael Dr NW ... 44718
Michael Pl SW ... 44707
Middlebranch Ave NE
3101-3197 ... 44705
3199-5100 ... 44705
5102-5498 ... 44705
5500-10099 ... 44721
Middlebury Cir SW ... 44706
Middlesworth Ave SW ... 44720
Midvale Rd NW
2400-2949 ... 44708
2950-3299 ... 44718
Midway Ave NE ... 44705
Miles Ave NW
100-1899 ... 44708
3000-4099 ... 44718
Miles Ave SW ... 44710
Milford St NE ... 44714
Militia Hill St NW ... 44718
Mill St SE ... 44707
Mill St SW ... 44706
Mill Ridge Cir NW ... 44708
Millerton St SE ... 44707
Millheim Cir NW ... 44718
Millport Ave SW ... 44706
Millvale Ave NE ... 44705
Millview Pl SW ... 44706
Millwood Ave SW ... 44706
Millwood St NW ... 44720
Milton Ct NW ... 44708
Milton St NW ... 44720
Minerva Ct NW
1000-1799 ... 44703
1800-1899 ... 44709
Missenden St NW ... 44720
Mississippi St SE ... 44720
Modred Cir NW ... 44708
Mohawk Ave NW ... 44708
Mohler Ct & Dr ... 44720
Mohr St NW ... 44708
Monica Ave SW ... 44706
Monnot Pl NW ... 44703
Monroe Ave NE ... 44704
Monroe Ave SE ... 44707
Montabella Pl NW ... 44709
Monterey Blvd NW ... 44720
Montgomery St NW ... 44718
Monticello Ave NW ... 44708
Montrose Ave NW ... 44708
Monument Rd NW
700-1798 ... 44703
1800-2298 ... 44709
Moock Ave SW ... 44706

Moon Ave NW ... 44708
Moonbeam Cir NW ... 44708
Moonlight Bay Dr NW ... 44708
Moore Ave SE ... 44707
Moore Ct NW ... 44703
Morello St SW ... 44709
Morgate Cir NW ... 44708
Morrilton Cir NW ... 44720
Morris Ave NE ... 44705
Mosley Ct SW ... 44710
Moss Wood Cir NE ... 44705
Mount Marie Ave NW ... 44708
Mount Pleasant Ln
NW ... 44720
Mount Pleasant St NE ... 44721
Mount Pleasant St
NW ... 44720
Mount Vernon Blvd
NW ... 44709
Mozart Cir SW ... 44706
Muirfield Ave NW ... 44708
Mulberry Rd SE ... 44707
Munson St NW ... 44718
Murray St NW ... 44718
Myrtle Ave NW
1600-1799 ... 44703
1800-2799 ... 44709
Nan Bet Cir NW ... 44709
Nancy Cir NW ... 44720
Nancy Jo St NW ... 44720
Nathan Cir NE ... 44720
Nathan Ct SW ... 44702
Navarre Rd SW
100-899 ... 44707
1100-6299 ... 44706
Nave St SW ... 44706
Neal Ct NW ... 44709
Negley Ave SW ... 44706
Neil Cir NE ... 44705
Nella Ave NW ... 44720
Nelson Pl NE ... 44705
Nemo Pl SW ... 44707
Neptune Ave NW ... 44720
Netherwood Ave NW ... 44708
New England Dr SE ... 44720
Newburg St NW ... 44709
Newgate Ave NW ... 44720
Newton Ave NW ... 44703
Newton Ave SW ... 44707
Ney Pl NW ... 44703
Nicholas Pl NW ... 44708
Nicklaus Ave NW ... 44718
Niles Pl NW ... 44703
Nimishillen Church Rd
NE ... 44721
E Nimisila Rd ... 44720
Nobles Pond Dr NW ... 44718
Norman Ave NW ... 44709
Norris Pl NE
800-1099 ... 44704
1100-1199 ... 44705
Norriton Cir NW ... 44720
Northam Cir NW ... 44720
Northbury Cir NE ... 44720
Northern St NE ... 44721
Northfield Ave SE
1300-1399 ... 44720
1400-1599 ... 44709
Northgate St NW ... 44720
Northland Ave NW ... 44720
Northridge St NW ... 44720
Northview Ave NE ... 44721
Northview Ave NW ... 44709
Northwind Cir NW ... 44720
Norwood Pl NW ... 44709
Notre Dame St NE ... 44721
Nottaway Cir SE ... 44709
Nottinghill Cir NW ... 44720
Numan Pl NE ... 44702
Oak Ave NW ... 44708
Oak Dr NW
100-299 ... 44720
5600-5799 ... 44718
Oak Glen Cir NW ... 44720
Oakbriar Cir NE ... 44705
Oakbridge Ave NW ... 44720

Oakcliff St SW ... 44706
Oakcrest Ave NW
6100-6699 ... 44718
6700-7099 ... 44720
Oakmont St NW ... 44709
Oakpark St NW ... 44720
Oakridge St SW ... 44720
Oakside St NE ... 44721
Oakvale St SW ... 44706
Oakway St NW ... 44720
Oakwood St SE ... 44720
Oberlin Ct NW ... 44703
Oby Pl NW ... 44703
Ocelot St NE ... 44721
Ohio Ave NE ... 44705
Ojays Pkwy NE
400-799 ... 44704
800-1099 ... 44705
1101-1199 ... 44705
Old Colony Dr NW ... 44718
Old Elm St NE ... 44721
Old Hickory Ave NW ... 44718
Old Mill Cir NW ... 44720
Old Spring St NW ... 44720
Old Trail Ln SE ... 44707
Olde Stone Cir NE ... 44721
Olive Pl NE ... 44705
Olive St NW ... 44708
Oliver Pl NE ... 44704
Olivette Pl NW ... 44703
Olympia Dr NW ... 44708
Onahom Cir NE ... 44705
Oneida Ave NW ... 44708
Orchard Ave NE
101-197 ... 44704
199-599 ... 44704
300-1099 ... 44720
Orchard Dale Dr NW ... 44709
Orchard Hill Dr SW ... 44720
Orchard Park St NW ... 44718
Orchard Trail Rd NE ... 44721
Orchardway St NW ... 44720
Orchid St NW ... 44720
Ord Pl NW ... 44709
Oren Pl NE ... 44714
Oriole Ave NW ... 44720
Orion St NE & NW ... 44720
Orlando Pl NE ... 44714
Otto Pl NE ... 44704
Outer Dr SW ... 44706
Overbrook Ct NW ... 44709
Overdale Ave NW ... 44708
Overhill Dr NW ... 44718
Overland Ave NE ... 44720
Overlook Cir NW ... 44718
Overlook Dr SW ... 44706
Overridge Ave SE ... 44720
Overwood Ave NW ... 44720
Oxford Ave NW ... 44703
Oyer St SE ... 44707
Oyler Ave NW ... 44720
Paar Pl NE ... 44714
Pacific Ave SE ... 44709
Packard Ave NW ... 44709
Paddington Down Rd
NW ... 44718
Paige Ave NW ... 44709
Palmer Dr NW ... 44718
Panther Ave NE ... 44721
Paolo Cir NW ... 44709
Paradise St SW ... 44706
Park Ave NE ... 44720
Park Ave NW ... 44708
Park Ave SW ... 44706
N Park Ave NW ... 44708
S Park Ave NW ... 44708
W Park Ave NW ... 44708
W Park Rd NW ... 44720
Parkdale Ave NW ... 44718
Parker Ave NE ... 44704
Parkhaven Ave NE ... 44705
Parkhill Cir NW ... 44718
Parkhill Pl NE ... 44705
Parklane St NW ... 44709
Parkridge Cir NW ... 44718
Parkview Ave NW ... 44720

Parkview St NW ... 44708
Parkway St NW ... 44708
Parwich Cir NE ... 44705
Pasadena Blvd NW ... 44720
Patricia Ave NW ... 44720
Patrick St SW ... 44706
Patriots Pt SE ... 44709
Patterson Ave SW ... 44707
Patton Pl NW ... 44708
Paul Pl NE ... 44705
Pawnee St NW ... 44720
Paxton St NE ... 44721
Payne Ct NE ... 44705
Peach St NE ... 44720
Peachmont Ave NW ... 44720
Peachtree Ave SW ... 44709
Pear Ave NW ... 44718
Pear Ct NE ... 44720
Pearl Pl SE ... 44720
Pearl Pl SW
200-299 ... 44720
1400-1699 ... 44706
Pearmont St SW ... 44706
Pebble Beach Dr NW ... 44718
Pebble Creek Ave NW ... 44718
Pebblebrook Dr SW ... 44709
Pebblestone Ave NW ... 44720
Peerless Cir SW ... 44706
Pelham St NE ... 44714
Penhurst Cir NE ... 44720
Peninsula Dr NW ... 44718
Penn Pl NE ... 44704
Pennington St NW ... 44709
Penny St SE ... 44720
Penrose Ct NE ... 44714
Peppergrass Dr NE ... 44720
Perkins Ave NW ... 44703
Perry Dr NW ... 44708
Perry Dr SW
100-1550 ... 44710
1551-2999 ... 44706
Perry Hills Dr SW ... 44706
Pershing Ave NE &
SE ... 44720
Perue Pl NW ... 44708
Peterson Ave NE ... 44721
Pheasant Ave NW ... 44720
Pheasant Run Cir NW ... 44709
Pheasant Valley Ave
NW ... 44720
Phillips Dr SW ... 44706
Philzer St NW ... 44720
Piccadilly St SW ... 44706
Pickett St NW ... 44720
Pickforde Dr ... 44720
Pickwick Cir NW ... 44720
Piedmont Ave NE
200-499 ... 44702
900-1098 ... 44704
1100-1199 ... 44704
1201-1297 ... 44714
1299-1399 ... 44714
Piedmont Ave SE ... 44702
Pierce Ave NW ... 44720
Pilgrims Knob SE ... 44709
Pin Oak St NE ... 44704
Pine St NW ... 44720
Pine Bluff Ave NE ... 44721
Pine Ridge St NW ... 44720
Pinecone St NW ... 44720
Pinecreek St NW ... 44720
Pinecrest St NE ... 44721
Pinedrive Cir NW ... 44718
Pinetree Ave NE ... 44721
Pineview Ave SE ... 44720
Piper Ct NW ... 44703
Pisces St SW ... 44706
Pittsburg Ave & Pl ... 44720
Plain Ave NE
1000-1199 ... 44704
1200-1699 ... 44714
Plain Center Ave NE ... 44714
Plainfield Ave SW ... 44706
Plainview St SE ... 44709
Pleasant Pl & St ... 44720
Pleasant Hill Rd NW ... 44708

Pleasantview Ave SE ... 44720
Pleasantwood Ave NW . 44720
Plymouth Ct NW ... 44703
N Pointe Dr NW ... 44708
Pond Dr NW ... 44720
Pondsford St NW ... 44720
Ponteberry St NW ... 44718
Pontiac Cir NW ... 44720
Pontius Pl NE ... 44705
Poplar Ave NW ... 44708
Poplar Ave SW ... 44710
Poplarwood Rd NW ... 44720
Port Jackson Ave NW .. 44720
Portage St NW ... 44720
Portage Glen Ave NW .. 44720
Portview Ave NW ... 44720
Postiy St NW ... 44720
Prairie College St SW .. 44706
Prancer Ave NW ... 44720
Preserve Dr NW ... 44708
Prince Cir NE ... 44720
Progress St NE ... 44705
Promler St NW ... 44720
Promway Ave NW ... 44720
Prospect Ave SW ... 44706
Psolla St NE ... 44721
Pulley St SE ... 44707
Puma St NE ... 44721
Purdue Cir NW ... 44720
Purney Ct SE ... 44707
Puskas Ct NE ... 44721
Quail Hill St NW ... 44720
Quail Hollow Ave NE ... 44704
Queen Ct NW ... 44703
Queensgate St NW ... 44718
Queensway St NW ... 44718
Quimby Ave SW ... 44706
Quincy St NW ... 44708
Race Ct SW ... 44706
Rachel St NW ... 44709
Radford St NE & NW ... 44720
Raebel Pl SW ... 44706
Raff Rd NW ... 44708
Raff Rd SW ... 44710
Railway Ave NE ... 44721
Raintree St NE ... 44705
Ralph Ct NW ... 44708
Ramsgate St NW ... 44720
Randal Cir NE ... 44720
Ravenwood Ave NW
6500-6699 ... 44718
6700-6999 ... 44720
Ravine Dr NW ... 44720
Ray Pl NW ... 44703
Raymar St NW ... 44718
Raymont Ct NW ... 44708
Raymont Ct SW ... 44706
Raynolds Pl SW
100-198 ... 44702
200-299 ... 44702
300-1000 ... 44707
1002-1098 ... 44707
Ready Ave NE ... 44721
Ream Ave NW ... 44720
Rebar Ave NE ... 44705
Rebecca Ave NW ... 44709
Rebel St SW ... 44706
Red Coach Rd & St NW
& SE ... 44720
Red Deer Cir NW ... 44708
Redford Rd NW ... 44720
Reed Ave NW ... 44720
Regal Ave NE ... 44705
Regent Ave NE ... 44705
Regentview St NE ... 44705
Regina Cir NW ... 44708
Reicosky Ln NW ... 44718
Rem Cir NE ... 44705
Rennick Ct SE ... 44707
Reno Ct NW ... 44708
Renwick Cir SW ... 44709
Renworth Ave NE ... 44714
Ressler Ct SW ... 44710
Rex Ave NE
100-899 ... 44702
900-1199 ... 44704
1300-1499 ... 44714
Rex Ave SE ... 44702
Rex Dr NW ... 44718
Rexdale St SW ... 44706
Ricciardi St NW ... 44720
Rice Ave NE ... 44704
Rich Ave NW ... 44720
Richard Pl NW ... 44703
Richmond Ave NE ... 44705
Richville Dr SW ... 44706
Ridge Ave SE ... 44707
Ridge Rd NW ... 44703
Ridgecliff Cir NE ... 44721
Ridgecourt St NW ... 44720
Ridgedale Ave NW ... 44708
Ridgeglen Cir NW ... 44708
Ridgeside Cir SE ... 44707
Ridgeway Pl NW ... 44709
Ridgewood Ave ... 44720
Ridgewood St SW ... 44706
Ridgley Cir SE ... 44720
Riley Cir SE ... 44707
Rip Ave SW ... 44706
River Run Cir NW ... 44720
Riverside Dr NE ... 44704
Roberts Ave NW ... 44709
Robin Ct SE ... 44707
Robin Hill Ct NW ... 44720
Rochelle St NW ... 44720
Rockbridge Ct SE ... 44709
Rockside Cir NW ... 44718
Rockwood Ave SW ... 44710
Rocky Rill Ave NE ... 44705
Roden Ct SE ... 44707
Roe Ct SE ... 44707
Rogwin Cir NW & SW .. 44720
Rohn Ave NE ... 44705
Rohrer St NW ... 44720
Rolena Cir NW ... 44708
Rolling Hill Ave NW ... 44720
Rolling Ridge Rd NE ... 44721
Romy Pl SE ... 44707
Ronald St NW ... 44718
Ronelle Cir NW ... 44720
Roosevelt Ave NE ... 44705
Root Ave NE ... 44705
Rose Ct NW ... 44703
Rose Ct SW ... 44720
Rose Lane St SE &
SW ... 44720
Rose Marie Ave NW ... 44720
Rosecreek Dr NE ... 44721
Rosemont Ct NW ... 44708
Rosewood Ave NW ... 44720
Rosewood Cir SE ... 44720
Rosewood Pl NW ... 44708
Roslyn Ave NW ... 44708
Roslyn Ave SW
600-1499 ... 44710
1600-2199 ... 44706
Ross Ave NE
600-799 ... 44704
1032-1098 ... 44705
Rowland Ave NE
100-799 ... 44704
800-1851 ... 44705
1900-3699 ... 44714
Rowland Ave SE ... 44707
Royal Ave NE ... 44705
Royal Hill Cir NE ... 44721
Royer Ave NW & SW .. 44720
Rucker Pl NE ... 44705
Ruggles Ave SE ... 44707
Run Rabbit Run Ave
NE ... 44705
Rusty Ave SW ... 44706
Rutgers St NW ... 44720
Ruth Ave SW ... 44720
Ruth Pl NW ... 44709
Ryan Ct NE ... 44704
Saddle Creek St NE ... 44721
Saginaw Cir NW ... 44720
Sahara Ave NE ... 44705
Sailboat St NW ... 44718
Saindiso St NE ... 44714
Saint Albans Cir NW ... 44720
Saint Andrews St NW .. 44708
Saint Augustine Dr
NW ... 44718
Saint Edmund Ave
NW ... 44718
Saint Elmo Ave NE
1200-1216 ... 44705
1218-1899 ... 44705
1900-3699 ... 44714
Saint Georges St NW .. 44720
Saint James Cir NW ... 44708
Saint Leger Ave NE ... 44721
Saint Michaels Blvd
NW ... 44718
Saint Patrick Ave NW .. 44720
Salerno St NW ... 44718
Sally Ann Ave NW ... 44708
Salway Ave NW
1401-1499 ... 44720
3800-4599 ... 44718
Salway Ave SW
1100-1400 ... 44720
1402-1498 ... 44720
1500-1699 ... 44709
Sanborn Ave NW ... 44709
Sandal Pl NE ... 44704
Sandalwood Ave NE ... 44721
Sandava Ave NW ... 44718
Sandgate St NW ... 44720
Sandhurst Ave NW ... 44718
Sandleford Ave NW ... 44720
Sandpiper Ave NW ... 44720
Sandrock Cir NW ... 44718
Sandwith Ave SW ... 44706
Sandy Ave SE ... 44707
Sandy Cir NW ... 44718
Sandy Ridge Cir NW ... 44720
Santa Clara St NW ... 44709
Santry Cir NW ... 44720
Sapphire Ave NE ... 44721
Saratoga Ave NW ... 44708
Saratoga Ave SW
100-1499 ... 44710
2200-3099 ... 44706
Saratoga Hills Dr NE ... 44721
Satellite Cir NW ... 44720
Satinwood Cir NW ... 44718
Saturn Ave NW ... 44720
Savannah Ave NE ... 44704
Savannah Ave SE ... 44702
Sawyer St NW ... 44720
Saxon St NE ... 44721
Saxony Cir NW ... 44708
Saybrook Ave NW ... 44720
Sayler Pl SW ... 44707
Scales St SW ... 44706
Scarborough Rd NW ... 44718
Scenic View St NE ... 44721
Schario Rd NW ... 44718
Schauer Pl SW ... 44707
Scheiring Ave SW ... 44706
Schneider St NE ... 44721
Schneider St NW ... 44720
Schneider St SE ... 44720
Schoen Ave NE ... 44704
School Ave NE ... 44720
Schory Ave SE ... 44707
Schroyer Ave SW
101-197 ... 44702
199-599 ... 44702
600-898 ... 44707
Schuller Dr NE ... 44705
Schwalm Ave NE ... 44704
Schwalm Ave SE ... 44707
Scofield St NE ... 44714
Scotland St NW ... 44709
Scotney Ave NW ... 44720
Scoville Ave SW ... 44706
Sea Pines Cir NW ... 44718
Seabjscuit Dr NE ... 44721
Searielm St NW ... 44709
Searls Dr NW ... 44720
Seaview Cir NW ... 44708
Secretariat St NE ... 44721
Seel Ave NW ... 44720
Seeley Ct NW ... 44703
Selkirk Cir NW ... 44718
Seneca Pl NE ... 44704
Severn Cir NW ... 44708
Shady Hollow Rd NW ... 44718
Shadygrove Cir NE ... 44721
Shadyside Ave SW ... 44710
Shaftesbury Dr NW ... 44708
Shaheen Ave SW ... 44706
Shaker Ave NW ... 44720
Shaker Valley Cir SE ... 44707
Shakertown Dr NW ... 44718
Shalimar Cir NW ... 44720
Shallowford Rd NE ... 44721
Shamrock Ave NW ... 44720
Shanabruck Ave NW ... 44709
Sharon Ave NW ... 44720
Sharonwood Ave NW
2800-2999 ... 44708
4700-4999 ... 44718
Sharp Ave NW ... 44718
Shawn Cir NW ... 44720
Sheaters Dr ... 44720
Sheffield St NE & NW .. 44720
Shellburne Ave NW ... 44708
Shelley St NE ... 44721
Shenandoah Ave NW .. 44718
Shepherd St NW ... 44720
Shepler Church Ave
SW ... 44706
Sheraton Cir & Dr ... 44720
Sherbourne Dr SW ... 44706
Sherbrook Cir NE ... 44720
Sherer Ave SW ... 44706
Sheridan Rd NW ... 44708
Sherlock Pl NE
700-1099 ... 44714
1200-1299 ... 44705
Sherman Church Ave
SW ... 44706
Shermont Ave SW ... 44706
Sherr Ave SE ... 44707
Sherrick Rd SE ... 44707
Shetland Cir NE ... 44721
Shillingford Cir NW ... 44720
Shiloh Run ... 44709
Shiloh St NW ... 44708
Shipslanding Ave NW .. 44718
Shipton Cir NW ... 44720
Shirley Ann Ave SW ... 44706
Shisler St NE ... 44721
Shorb Ave NW
100-198 ... 44703
200-1799 ... 44703
2000-2098 ... 44709
2100-2799 ... 44709
Shorb Ave SW ... 44707
E & W Shore Dr ... 44718
Shore Line Ave NW ... 44708
Shoreview Cir NW ... 44708
Shortridge Ave NE ... 44705
Shrine Pl NW ... 44709
Shriver Ave NE ... 44705
Shriver Rd ... 44720
Shuffel St NW ... 44720
Sibila Rd NW ... 44718
Sierra Ave SW ... 44706
Silent Ct NW ... 44709
Sill Pl SE ... 44707
Simone Dr ... 44720
Sinclair Dr NW ... 44708
Sippo Ave SW
100-1399 ... 44710
1700-2299 ... 44706
Sir Thomas Blvd NW ... 44708
Sites Pl NE ... 44702
Skycrest Dr NW ... 44718
Skylane St NW ... 44720
Skylark St SW ... 44706
Skyline Cir SE ... 44709
Skyview St NW ... 44718
Skyway St NE ... 44721
Slate Run Cir NE ... 44721
Smetts Pl NW ... 44703
Smith Ave ... 44720
Smith Ave NW ... 44708
Smith Ave SW ... 44706
Snowshoe Cir NW ... 44718
Snyder Ave NE ... 44714
Soehnlen Ave SW ... 44706
Softwind Ave NW ... 44720
Sol Beck Ct NE ... 44705
Somerset Ave SW ... 44706
Songbird Cir NE ... 44721
Sorrento Ave NW ... 44718
South Blvd NW ... 44718
Southberry Cir SW ... 44706
Southmoor Cir NE ... 44721
Southpointe Cir NE ... 44714
Southway St SW ... 44706
Southwood Dr NW ... 44720
Southwoods Ln SE ... 44720
Southwyck Ave NW ... 44720
Spangler Rd NE
100-1899 ... 44714
1900-1999 ... 44705
Spencer Ave NW ... 44720
Sperry Ln SE ... 44709
Spring Ave NE
300-1199 ... 44704
1200-2199 ... 44714
Spring Blossom Cir
NW ... 44720
Spring Valley Ave NW .. 44708
Spring Walk Dr NE ... 44721
Springfield Ave SW ... 44706
Springlake Rd NW ... 44718
Springline St ... 44720
Springvale Ave SW ... 44706
Spruce Ave & Dr ... 44720
Spruce Hill Dr NW ... 44718
Sprucewood Ave & St
NW & SE ... 44720
Squirrel Hollow St NE .. 44704
Stadium Overlook Dr
NW ... 44708
Stadium Park Dr NW ... 44718
Staffordshire Court Cir
NW ... 44718
Stalnaker Dr ... 44720
Stambaugh St NW ... 44720
Standish Ave SW ... 44706
Stanley Ct NE ... 44705
Stanwood Pl SW ... 44706
Star St NW ... 44708
Starcliff Ave NW ... 44720
Stardust Ave NW ... 44708
Stark Ave SW ... 44706
Starlight Cir NW ... 44708
State St NE ... 44721
State St NW ... 44720
Staten Cir NW ... 44720
Stayman Ave SW ... 44709
Stedman Ave NW ... 44708
Steepleview Dr NW ... 44708
Steese Ave NW ... 44709
Steiner Pl SE ... 44707
Steiner St NW ... 44720
Steinway Blvd SE ... 44707
Stella Cir SE ... 44707
Stephens Cir NW ... 44718
Sterling Ave SE ... 44707
Sterling St NW ... 44718
Stillmeadow Ave SW ... 44706
Stillwater Ave NW ... 44708
Stockbridge St NE ... 44720
Stockbridge St NW ... 44718
Stone Ln & Way ... 44720
Stone Crossing St NE .. 44721
Stone Ledge Ct ... 44720
Stonebridge Ave NW ... 44720
Stonecreek Ave NE ... 44721
Stoneham Rd ... 44720
Stonehill St SW ... 44709
Stoneridge St NE ... 44714
Stonewall St NE ... 44721
Stonewood Dr NW ... 44720
Stoney Creek Dr & Ln .. 44720
Stoney Pointe Dr ... 44720
Stoney Ridge Rd NW ... 44718
Stoneybrook St SW ... 44706
Stoneywood Cir NW ... 44718
Stonington Rd NW ... 44720
Stover Ave NW ... 44720
Stowell Ave NW ... 44709
Strasser Pl SW
2200-2399 ... 44706
2400-2799 ... 44710
Stratavon Dr NW ... 44720
Stratham Cir NW ... 44708
Strathmore Dr NW ... 44708
Strauss Ave NW ... 44720
Strauss Ln SW ... 44706
Strausser St NW ... 44720
Strawberry Ct NW ... 44709
Strawberry St NW ... 44720
Strawberry Fields Cir
NE ... 44721
Stream Ave NE ... 44721
Strip Ave NW ... 44720
Strouble Dr NW ... 44718
Struble Ave NE ... 44705
Stuber Dr NW ... 44718
Sudbury Cir NW ... 44720
Suffield Cir NW ... 44708
Sugargrove Cir NE ... 44721
Sugarwood Rd NE ... 44721
Summerchase Rd NE .. 44721
Summit Cir & St ... 44720
Summitview Cir NW ... 44708
Sumser St NW ... 44720
Sun Valley Ave NE ... 44721
Sunford Ave SE ... 44720
Sunlight Ct NW ... 44709
Sunnydale Ave NE ... 44721
Sunnyfield Dr NE ... 44720
Sunquest Cir NW ... 44718
Sunrise St NW ... 44720
Sunset Blvd SW ... 44720
Sunset Strip Ave NW ... 44720
Sunshine Ct NW ... 44708
Superior Ave NE ... 44705
Supreme St NW ... 44720
Surbey Ave NW ... 44720
Surmay Ave SW ... 44706
Susetta Ave NW ... 44709
Sussex St NW ... 44718
Sutherland Cir NW ... 44720
Sutton Ave NE ... 44720
Swan Ave NE ... 44721
Swanhurst Cir NE ... 44720
Swathmore Cir NW ... 44720
Sweeney Ave NW ... 44720
Sweet William Cir NW .. 44718
Sweetwater Rd NE ... 44721
Swepstone St NW ... 44708
Swiss Ave SW ... 44706
Sycamore Ave SE ... 44707
Sycamore Dr NW ... 44720
Sylvan Ave NW ... 44720
Sylvan Ct NE
700-799 ... 44704
900-1099 ... 44705
Sylvian St NW ... 44720
Taft Ave NE
100-299 ... 44720
1600-3999 ... 44705
Tallwood Cir NW ... 44718
Tamara Ave SE ... 44707
Tamarack Ave ... 44720
Tamarack Cir NE ... 44721
Tamworthy Cir NW ... 44720
Tanager Ave NE ... 44705
Tanglewood Cir NE ... 44714
Tanglewood Dr SW ... 44720
Tanner Ave SW ... 44706
Tannybrooke Ln NW ... 44718
Teakwood St NE ... 44721
Techwood St NW ... 44720
Telford Dr NW ... 44718
Terrace Ave NW ... 44708
Terrace Rd NW ... 44720
Terri Bate Cir NE ... 44705
Tewksbury Court Cir
NW ... 44718
Thatcher Ave NW ... 44720
Thicket St NW ... 44708
Thistlehill Cir NW ... 44708
Thompson St NE ... 44721
Thornbriar St NW ... 44718
N & S Thornham Cir ... 44720
Thornton St NW ... 44720
Thornwood St NW ... 44718
Thunderbird Cir NW ... 44720
Thursby Rd ... 44720
Tidewater St NW ... 44708
Tim Ave NW ... 44720
Timber Run St NW ... 44708
Timbercreek Ave NE ... 44721
Timbercreek Cir ... 44720
Timberlane St NE ... 44721
Timberview St NW ... 44720
Times Ave SW ... 44706
Timken Pl SW ... 44706
Tioga St NW ... 44708
Tipperary Cir NW ... 44720
Tobin Cir NW ... 44720
Tommy St NW ... 44720
Torrey Pines Cir NW .. 44708
Tradewinds Cv NW ... 44708
Trafalgar St SW ... 44706
Tralee Cir NW ... 44720
Travelo St NW ... 44708
Tree Line Cir NW ... 44720
Treecrest Cir ... 44720
Treeside St NW ... 44709
Treetop Cir NE ... 44705
Treeview Dr ... 44720
Tremont Cir NW ... 44708
Trent Rd NW ... 44708
Tricaso Dr ... 44720
Trillium Ave NW ... 44708
Trinity Ave NE ... 44721
Trinity Pl NW ... 44709
Troy Pl NW ... 44703
Trump Ave SE ... 44707
Tudore St NE ... 44721
Tulip St NE ... 44705
Tully Ave NW ... 44720
Turnberry Cir NW ... 44708
Turnberry Cir SW ... 44709
Turquoise Ave NE ... 44721
Tuscany Cir NW ... 44718
Tuscarawas St E
101-197 ... 44702
199-699 ... 44702
700-2614 ... 44707
Tuscarawas St W
100-1599 ... 44702
1600-5299 ... 44708
Twickenham St NW ... 44708
Twin Pl NE ... 44705
Tyler Ave SE ... 44707
Tyner Ave NW ... 44708
Tyro St NE ... 44721
Unger Ln SW ... 44706
Union Ave SW ... 44707
University Ave NW ... 44709
University Heights Cir
NW ... 44720
Utah Ct NW ... 44709
Val Ct SW ... 44702
E & W Valentine Cir ... 44708
N Valley Blvd NW ... 44720
S Valley Blvd NW ... 44720
Valley Dr NW
800-1399 ... 44720
4100-4299 ... 44708
Valley View Dr NW ... 44720
Valleydell Cir & St ... 44720
Valleyview Ave NW ... 44708
Valleyview Ave SW ... 44710
Van Pl SW ... 44706
Van Horn Pl SE ... 44707
Van Kirk Ct NE ... 44705
Vanderbilt Dr NW ... 44720
Varley Ave SW ... 44706
Vassar Ave NW ... 44703
Veldon Cir NE ... 44721
Velvet Pl NW ... 44709
Venus St NW ... 44720
Vera Pl NW ... 44708
Vereldel Ave NW ... 44718
Vermont Pl NE ... 44714
Vermont St NW ... 44720

Vermouth St NW 44720
Vernon Ave NW 44709
Vicary Sq NE 44714
Vicary Hill Ln NE 44714
Vicksburg Ave NW 44708
Victor St NW 44718
Victoria Ave NW 44708
Victoria Court St NW ... 44718
Vienna Rd SW 44706
Vienna Mill Ct SW 44706
Vienna View Ct SW 44706
Vienna Woods Ave SW 44706
View Ct NW 44709
Viking St NW 44720
Villa Glen Cir NW 44708
Villa Padova Dr NW 44718
Village St SE 44707
Vinal Ave NW 44709
Vince Ave NW 44708
Vincent Rd NW & SE .. 44720
Vincine Cir NW 44718
Vine Ave SW 44706
Vineyard Ave NW 44708
Viola Pkwy NW 44708
Violet Ave SE 44707
Violet Knoll Ave NE 44705
Virginia Pl NE 44705
Vixen St NW 44720
Vliet St SW 44710
Wabash Ct NE 44705
Wackerly Dr NW 44718
E & W Wadora Cir 44720
Walbrook St NW 44718
Walcott St NW 44720
Walden Ave NW
1700-1799 44703
1800-2000 44709
2002-2298 44709
Wales Ave NW 44720
Walker Ct NE 44704
Walker Ct SE 44707
Wallace Ave NE 44705
Wallace Ave SE 44707
Wallbridge St NW 44720
Wallingford Cir SW 44706
Wallington Court Cir NW 44718
Walnut Ave NE
100-899 44702
900-1199 44704
1200-1499 44714
Walnut Ave SE 44702
Walnut St 44720
Walnut Ridge Cir NW .. 44720
Walsh Ave SE 44720
Waltham Pl SW 44706
Waltham St NW 44708
Waltham Crossing Ave NW 44718
Wareham Cir NW 44720
Warner Rd NE
100-399 44704
801-899 44705
Warner Rd SE 44707
Warrick Pl NE 44714
Washington Blvd NW ... 44709
Water Ct SE 44707
Water Line Cir NW 44708
Waterbury St NW 44720
Waterford Ave NW 44708
Watson Pl SE 44707
Wayland Cir SW 44706
Wayne Ave NE 44705
Waynesburg Dr SE 44707
Wayview St NW 44720
Weaver St SW 44706
Weber Ave NE 44720
Webster Ave NE 44704
Wedgefield Ct 44720
Wedgewood Ave NW ... 44720
Weiler Ct NE 44704
Weiss Ave SW 44706
Wellingshire St NE 44721
Wells Ave NW 44703
Wells Ave SW 44707

Wellspring Ave NW 44720
Wendover Cir NE 44720
Wendy Cir NE 44720
Wentworth Ln SW 44706
Werner Church Rd NE . 44721
Werstler Ave NW 44720
Wertz Ave NW 44708
Wertz Ave SW
200-1399 44710
1400-1498 44706
1500-2299 44706
West Blvd NW 44718
West Dr SW 44706
Westdale Rd NW 44708
Western Ave SW 44710
Westfield Ave SW
1200-1499 44720
1500-1699 44709
Westgate Cir NW 44718
Westmoreland Ave NW 44718
Weston Ave NW 44718
Weston Place Ave NW 44720
Westridge Cir NW 44720
Westview Ave NW 44709
Westview Cir SE 44720
Westwind Cir NW 44720
Westwood Ave NW 44709
Wexford Cir NW 44708
Wheeling Pl NE
900-999 44704
1400-1498 44705
Wherry Pl SW 44707
Whipple Ave NW
100-2999 44708
3000-5199 44718
5400-8099 44720
Whipple Ave SW
125-697 44710
699-1699 44710
2200-2298 44706
2300-5099 44706
Whippoorwill St NW 44720
White Oaks Cir SW 44710
White Stone Cir NE 44721
White Tail Ave NW 44708
Whitehouse Ave NW ... 44709
Whiteridge Cir NW 44720
Whitetail Trl NE 44704
Whitewood St NW 44720
Whitingham St SE 44720
Whitmer Ave NE 44721
Whittier Ave NW 44720
Whittier St NE 44721
Wickford Ave NW 44708
Wicklow Way NW 44708
Wiclif St NE 44721
Widmer Ct NE 44714
Wilben Pl NW 44703
Wilbur Dr NE 44720
Wilbur Allen Jr Ave SE 44707
Wildflower Dr 44720
Wildwood Ave NE 44714
Wilkshire Cir SW 44720
Willaman Ave NW 44720
Willet Ave SE 44707
William St NE 44721
William Tell Ave NW ... 44720
Williamsburg Ln NW ... 44708
Willow Creek St NE 44720
Willow Run Cir NW 44718
Willoway Ave SE 44720
Willowcrest Dr NW 44718
Willowdale Lake Ave NW 44720
Willowdell Dr NE 44714
Willowhurst Cir NW 44720
Willowrow Ave NE 44705
Wilson Pl NW 44703
Windbur Cir NW 44720
Windcrest St NW 44720
Windem Cir NW 44720
Windgate Ave NE 44721
Windham St NE 44721

Windmill Cir NE 44721
Windsor Cir NE 44714
Windsor Pl SW 44710
Windsor St NE 44721
Winesap Ave SW 44709
Winfield Way NE 44705
Wingate Way NW 44708
Winning Way 44720
Winston Ave NE 44720
Winterdale St SW 44706
Winterwood Ave NW ... 44720
Winton Pl NW 44709
Wise Ave NE 44720
Wise Ave NW
2400-2999 44708
3000-3199 44718
6300-6899 44720
Wise Ave SE 44720
Wise Rd 44720
Wiseland Ave SE 44707
Wisner St NE 44721
Withersfield St NE 44721
Witney Ave NW 44720
Witwer St NE 44720
Wolverine St NE 44705
Wood Owl St NE 44704
Wood Trail Ave NE 44705
Woodacres Ave 44720
Woodchuck St NE 44705
Woodcliff Dr NW 44718
Woodcrest Ave NE 44721
Woodell Ave NE 44721
Woodfern Ave NE 44705
Woodford Ave NW 44709
Woodhaven Dr NW 44718
Woodhill Dr NW 44718
Woodington Ave SW ... 44706
Woodland Ave NW
1200-1799 44703
1800-4799 44709
Woodland Ave SW 44720
Woodlawn Ave NW 44708
Woodlawn Ave SW 44710
Woodlawn Cir NW 44708
Woodleigh Ave NW 44718
Woodlore Cir NW 44720
Woodmoor Ave NW ... 44718
Woodridge Ave NW 44718
Woodrow St NW 44720
Woodrush Dr NW 44720
Woodside Ave NE 44720
Woodside Ave NW 44709
Woodside Ave SE 44720
Woodthrush St NE 44721
Woodview St SW 44706
Woodward Pl NW
800-1399 44709
2300-2599 44708
Woodway Ave & St 44721
Wooster Ave NE 44705
Worley Ave NW 44703
Worthington Cir NW 44708
Wren Ave NW 44720
Wuske Pl SE 44707
Wyndgate Court Ave NW 44720
Wynnbrook Rd SW 44706
Wynnridge Ave NE 44720
Wynstone Cir NE 44720
Wynterhall Ave NE 44714
Yale Ave NW
1300-1799 44703
1800-4999 44709
Yoder Ave SW 44706
York Ave NE 44721
Yorkshire Trce SE 44709
Yost St NW 44718
Young Ave NE
100-799 44704
800-1099 44705
1101-1199 44705
Young Ave SE 44707
Youngdale Ave NW 44718
Yukon St NW 44708
Zellars Pl NW 44720
Zimmer Pl NW 44703

Zink Dr NW 44718
Zinnia Ave NE 44705
Zircon St NE 44721

NUMBERED STREETS

2nd St NE
100-699 44702
700-2399 44704
2nd St NW
100-499 44702
600-698 44703
2600-5099 44708
2nd St SE
200-699 44702
700-3799 44707
2nd St SW
100-399 44702
900-1323 44707
1324-1398 44702
1901-1919 44706
3rd St NE
100-198 44702
700-4099 44704
3rd St NW
100-499 44702
500-1199 44703
2200-5099 44708
3rd St SE
100-198 44702
700-3299 44707
3rd St SW
100-399 44702
500-1299 44707
1300-1499 44702
4th St NE
100-699 44702
600-699 44720
700-4099 44704
4th St NW
100-499 44702
500-1399 44703
1700-5299 44708
4th St SE
100-400 44702
1000-3299 44707
4th St SW
101-217 44702
500-1299 44707
5th St NE
100-699 44702
100-1199 44720
700-3099 44704
5th St NW
100-499 44702
100-699 44720
500-1399 44703
2600-4799 44708
5th St SE
101-197 44702
1700-3216 44707
5th St SW
300-400 44702
500-1399 44707
1400-1499 44702
6th St NE
100-899 44720
101-197 44702
700-2299 44704
6th St NW
100-499 44702
400-699 44720
500-1399 44703
2200-2999 44708
6th St SE
100-198 44702
2600-3299 44707
6th St SW
100-198 44702
300-1499 44707
1600-2399 44706
2400-3399 44710
7th St NE
100-1399 44720
500-3099 44704
7th St NW
100-999 44720
601-697 44703
1600-1898 44708
7th St SE 44702
7th St SW
100-299 44702
300-1299 44707
1500-2399 44706
2400-4799 44710
8th St NE 44704
8th St NW
300-498 44703
500-1499 44703
2200-2202 44708
2204-4699 44708
8th St SE 44707
8th St SW 44707
9th St NE
100-999 44720
201-397 44704
1100-1899 44705
9th St NW
100-299 44702
100-799 44720
500-1499 44703
2200-4999 44708
9th St SW
100-299 44702
300-1399 44707
1400-1598 44706
2400-3499 44710
10th St NE
100-599 44720
800-1099 44704
1400-2099 44705
10th St NW
500-1599 44703
2200-4699 44708
10th St SW
1500-2399 44706
2400-3899 44710
11th St NE 44704
11th St NW
400-1599 44703
2300-4699 44708
11th St SE 44707
11th St SW
1500-2399 44706
2400-4699 44710
12th St NE
100-1099 44704
1100-1499 44705
1501-1699 44705
12th St NW
100-1599 44703
2400-6099 44708
12th St SE 44707
12th St SW
1500-2399 44706
2400-5299 44710
13th St NE
100-1099 44714
1100-2499 44705
2501-2599 44705
13th St NW
100-1499 44703
2200-4799 44708
13th St SE 44707
13th St SW 44710
14th St NE
100-1099 44714
1100-2599 44705
14th St NW
100-1599 44703
2800-4899 44708
14th St SE 44707
14th St SW
1419-1999 44706
3000-5299 44710
15th St NE
100-198 44714
200-1099 44714
1100-2400 44705
15th St NW
100-1499 44703
2600-4899 44708
15th St SE 44707
15th St SW
100-499 44707
1200-2599 44706
4500-5099 44710
16th St NE
101-297 44714
1100-2599 44705
16th St NW
100-1699 44703
2600-5099 44708
16th St SE 44707
16th St SW
1400-3099 44706
4000-4299 44710
17th St NE
100-999 44714
1001-1005 44714
1100-2699 44705
17th St NW
100-1699 44703
2301-2597 44708
2599-4899 44708
17th St SE 44707
17th St SW 44706
18th St NE
700-798 44714
800-1005 44714
1007-1099 44714
1100-2699 44705
18th St NW
100-1799 44703
2900-4999 44708
18th St SE 44707
18th St SW 44706
19th St NE
100-198 44714
200-1900 44714
1902-1998 44714
2000-2010 44705
19th St NW
100-1621 44709
2400-4599 44708
19th St SE 44707
19th St SW 44706
20th St NE
100-1899 44714
2001-2111 44705
2113-2499 44705
20th St NW
1400-1611 44709
1613-1699 44709
2901-2905 44708
2907-4799 44708
20th St SW 44706
21st St NE
100-1499 44714
2000-2499 44705
21st St NW
100-1799 44709
2100-4499 44708
21st St SW 44706
22nd St NE
100-1899 44714
2000-3299 44705
22nd St NW
100-1400 44709
1402-1598 44709
2600-4599 44708
22nd St SW 44706
23rd St NE
1300-1627 44714
1629-1699 44714
1900-2499 44705
23rd St NW
100-1899 44709
2900-3599 44708
23rd St SW 44706
24th St NE
700-1699 44714
2000-2499 44705
24th St NW
501-1215 44709
1217-1799 44709
3200-3499 44708
24th St SE 44707
25th St NE
100-1699 44714
1800-3400 44705
3402-3698 44705
25th St NW
100-1699 44709
2600-3799 44708
25th St SE 44707
25th St SW 44706
26th St NE
100-1300 44714
1302-1398 44714
1800-3299 44705
26th St NW
1300-1699 44709
2600-2699 44718
3000-3699 44708
26th St SE 44707
26th St SW 44706
27th St NE
100-1699 44714
3800-4098 44705
4100-4199 44705
27th St NW
1400-1799 44709
2600-2699 44718
3000-3599 44708
27th Ter NE 44705
28th St NE
101-697 44714
699-1699 44714
2001-4097 44705
4099-4499 44705
28th St NW 44709
28th St SW 44706
29th St NE
100-1499 44714
2000-3916 44705
3918-4198 44705
29th St NW 44709
29th St SW 44706
30th St NE
100-1799 44714
1901-2097 44705
2099-4399 44705
30th St NW 44709
30th St SW 44706
31st St NE
1000-1799 44714
2200-2322 44705
2324-3699 44705
3701-3899 44705
31st St NW 44709
32nd St NE 44714
32nd St NW 44709
32nd St SE 44707
32nd St SW 44706
33rd St NE
100-1699 44714
2700-3999 44705
33rd St NW 44709
33rd St SE 44707
33rd St SW 44706
34th St NE
100-1699 44714
2100-4299 44705
34th St NW 44709
34th St SE 44707
34th St SW 44706
35th St NE
100-1699 44714
2100-3899 44705
35th St NW 44709
35th St SE 44707
36th St NE
100-1699 44714
1900-2099 44705
36th St NW
100-2199 44709
3800-3999 44718
37th St NE 44714
37th St NW
100-2199 44709
3800-3999 44718
37th St SE 44707
37th St SW 44706
38th St NE 44705
38th St NW
100-2799 44709

2900-4599 44718
38th St SE 44707
38th St SW 44706
39th St NE
800-898 44714
900-1199 44714
1201-1299 44714
1900-2099 44705
39th St NW 44709
39th St SE 44707
39th St SW 44706
40th St NE
1000-1099 44714
1900-2499 44705
40th St NW 44709
40th St SE 44707
40th St SW 44706
41st St NE 44705
41st St NW 44709
42nd St NW
600-2699 44709
4200-4399 44718
43rd St NW 44709
43rd St SW 44706
44th St NE 44714
44th St NW 44709
45th St NE 44705
45th St NW 44709
45th St SW 44706
46th St NE 44705
46th St NW 44709
46th St SW 44706
47th St NE
800-1099 44714
2000-2699 44705
47th St NW
100-1399 44709
1401-2099 44709
4000-4399 44718
48th St NE
100-1099 44714
1800-2499 44705
2501-2599 44705
48th St NW 44709
48th St SE 44707
48th St SW 44706
49th St NE
100-1099 44714
1801-1897 44705
1899-2499 44705
49th St NW 44709
49th St SE 44707
49th St SW 44706
50th St NW
1700-1720 44709
1722-2098 44709
4000-4399 44718
50th St SE
100-299 44707
1721-2099 44709
51st St NE 44705
51st St SE 44707
51st St SW 44706
52nd St NE
900-1199 44714
2200-2499 44705
52nd St NW 44709
52nd St SE 44707
52nd St SW 44706
53rd St SE 44707
53rd St SW 44706
54th St NE 44705
55th St NE 44721
55th St NW 44720
56th St NE 44721
57th St NE 44721
58th St NE 44721

CHAGRIN FALLS OH

General Delivery 44022

POST OFFICE BOXES MAIN OFFICE STATIONS AND BRANCHES

Box No.s
1 - 8099 44022
23001 - 238099 44023

NAMED STREETS

Abbey Rd 44023
Acorn Trl 44022
Akron St 44023
Alden St 44023
Alderwood Dr 44022
Alex Way 44023
Amber Trl 44023
American St 44022
Anderson Ct 44023
Anglers Dr 44022
Annandale Dr 44022
Anne Ln 44023
Apple Hill Rd 44023
Applebrook Dr 44022
Arch St 44022
Arrow Wood Cir 44022
Ascot Ln 44023
Ashleigh Dr 44022
Aspenwood Dr 44022
Auburn Rd 44023
Auburn Glen Dr 44023
Auburn Lakes Dr 44023
Auburn Springs Dr 44023
Auburndale Rd 44023
Azalea Cir 44023
Bainbridge Rd 44023
Bainbrook Dr 44023
Baker Ln 44023
Bartholomew Rd 44023
Basswood Ln 44022
Bayberry Dr 44023
Baybrook Ln 44023
Beacon Hill Dr
400-598 44022
600-699 44022
701-799 44022
8500-8899 44023
Bedford St 44022
Beech Grove Trl 44023
Beech Tree Ln 44023
E & W Bel Meadow Ln 44022
Bell Rd & St 44022
Bell Tower Ct 44022
Bellflower Cir 44022
Bellview St 44022
Belmont Ln 44023
Bent Tree Ln 44023
Bentleyville Rd 44022
Berkeley Ave 44022
Berkshire Park Dr 44022
Bernwood Ln 44022
Bingham Ln 44023
Birch Hill Dr 44023
Birchbark Grv 44023
Birchmont Dr 44022
Bishop Dr 44022
Bittersweet Trl 44023
Blackford Dr 44023
Blossom Ln 44022
Blue Spruce Trl 44023
Bradley St 44022
Brainard Rd 44022
Bramley Ct 44022
Bramshill Cir 44023
Brandon Ct 44022
Brayton Trl 44023
Brewster Rd 44023
Bridge Creek Trl 44023
Bridgeway Dr 44023
Brigadoon Dr 44023
Brighton Park Ct 44023
Brittany Woods Dr 44023
Broadway Dr & St 44022
Brookfield Rd 44023
Bryce Ct 44023
Buckthorn Dr 44023
Burton Trl 44022
Button Bush Cir 44022
Cableknoll Ln 44023
Cabot Ln 44022
Candlenut Ct 44022
Cannon Rd 44022
Canterbury Ct 44023
Canton St 44023
Canyon Rd 44022
Capital Hill Cir 44022
Cardinal Ln 44022
Carnes Rd 44023
Carriage Dr 44022
Carriage Hill Dr 44023
Carriage Stone Dr 44022
Carrington Pl 44023
Cascade Dr 44022
Catsden Rd 44023
Cedar St 44022
Center St 44022
Chadwick Ct 44023
Chagrin Blvd 44022
Chagrin Rd 44023
Chagrin Mills Rd 44022
Chagrin River Rd
2401-2497 44022
2499-6899 44022
17300-17899 44023
Champion Ln 44022
Champlain Trl 44023
Chanticleer Ct 44023
Charles Rd 44023
Chase Dr 44023
Chateau Trl 44023
Chelsea Ct 44022
Chestnut Ct & Ln 44022
Chickashay Ln 44023
Chillicothe Rd
5000-15799 44022
16300-19199 44023
Chipping Ln 44023
Church St 44022
Cinnabar Trl 44023
Cinnamon Trl 44023
Circle Dr 44022
Clarion Dr 44023
Cleveland Dr 44023
Cleveland St 44022
N Cleveland St 44022
Clover Ln 44022
Cloveridge Rd 44022
Club Ln 44023
Clubside Dr 44022
Cobblestone Ln 44023
Colchester Ln 44023
Coldwater Trl 44023
Colonial Ct 44023
Columbus St 44022
Commons Ct 44022
Community Dr 44022
Concord Ct 44023
Cooper Ct 44023
Cope Dr 44023
Corban Dr 44023
Cothelstone Ln 44022
Cotswold Ln 44022
E & W Cottage St 44022
Cottonwood Trl 44023
Country Ln 44023
Countryside Dr 44022
County Line Rd 44023
Courtney Trl 44022
Cove Ct 44023
Coventry Ct 44023
Covington Ln 44023
Coy Ln 44022
Crabtree Ln 44023
Crackel Rd 44023
E & W Craig Dr 44023
Cranberry Ridge Ln 44023
Creekside Dr 44023
Creekview Cir 44022
Creekview Trl 44023
Creighton Dr 44023
Crown Pointe 44023
Crystal Trl 44023
Cumberland Trl 44022
Curry Ln 44023
Daisy Ln 44023
Dale Rd 44022
Darbys Run 44023
Dawson Dr 44023
Dayton St 44023
Deep Creek Ln 44022
Deepview Dr 44023
N & S Deepwood Dr & Ln 44022
Deer Ct 44022
Deer Run Dr 44022
Deerfield Dr 44022
Derbyshire Ln 44023
Devon Ct 44023
Devonshire Ln 44023
Division St 44022
Doe Ct 44022
Dogwood Ln 44023
Dorset Dr 44022
Downey Glen Trl 44023
Eaglenest Dr 44022
Eagles Pointe 44023
Eaglewood Trl 44023
Eastbrook Cir & Trl 44023
Easton Ln 44022
Eastview Dr 44023
Eastwood Dr 44023
Eaton Dr 44023
Edgewood Ct 44022
Edinboro Ln 44023
Edwards Ln & Lndg 44023
Ellendale Rd 44023
Elliott Dr 44023
Elm Ct 44022
Elmwood Ln 44023
Elyria St 44023
Emery Rd 44022
English Dr 44023
Fairfax Dr 44022
Fairlawn Dr 44023
Fairmount Blvd 44022
Fairview Rd 44022
Fairway Trl 44023
Fairway Vw 44023
Falling Water Dr 44023
Falls Rd 44022
Falls Creek Cir & Trl 44022
Falls Walk Way 44022
Falsgraf Ln 44022
Faraway Trl 44023
Farmcote Dr 44022
Farwood Dr 44022
Fawn Ct 44022
Fernwood Rd 44022
Fields Rd 44023
Findlay St 44023
Fircrest Ln 44023
Fireside Dr 44023
Firwood Ln 44022
Fish Creek Trl 44023
Flintlock Rdg 44023
Forest Dr 44022
N Fork Dr 44022
Fossil Dr 44023
Fox Ln 44022
Fox Rd 44023
Fox Run 44022
Fox Trl 44022
Fox Way 44022
Fox Glen Rd 44022
Fox Ledges Ln 44023
Foxhall Dr 44022
Franklin Rd 44023
N Franklin St 44022
S Franklin St
1-300 44022
302-498 44022
401-497 44023
499-1200 44022
1202-6698 44023
16301-16335 44022
16400-17298 44022
16433-17499 44023
Franks Rd 44023
Frostwood Dr 44023
Garden Park Dr 44023
Gardiner Ln 44023
Geauga Lake Rd 44023
Geneva St 44023
Giles Rd 44022
Glen Rd 44022
Glenridge Ct 44022
Golden Pond Dr 44023
Gottschalk Pkwy 44023
Granite Rdg 44023
Greatwood Ln 44023
Green Valley Dr 44022
Greenbrier Dr 44022
Greenhaven Dr 44022
Greentree Rd 44022
Greenway Trl 44023
Grey Fox Run 44022
Hackney Rd 44022
Hall St 44022
Hamlet Hills Dr 44022
Harris Farm Dr 44023
Harvard Rd 44022
Harvest Dr 44023
Haskins Rd 44023
Hastings Ln 44022
Hawksmoor Way 44023
Hawksview Ln 44023
Hawthorne Dr & Ln 44022
Hazelwood Dr 44023
Hearthstone Ln 44023
Heather Ct 44022
Heather Hl 44023
Heatherwood Ln 44023
Hemlock Ln & Rd 44022
Hemlock Point Rd 44022
Heritage Ln 44022
Hickory Ln 44022
Hickory Hill Rd 44022
Hickory Nut Trl 44023
Hidden Point Dr 44023
Hidden Valley Dr 44022
High Ct & St 44022
High Point Ln 44022
High Point Rd 44022
Highland Ln 44022
Hillbrook Dr & Ln N 44022
Hillside Ln
200-300 44022
302-398 44022
18900-19099 44023
N & S Hilltop Rd 44022
Hilltop Park Pl 44023
Hiram Trl 44022
Holbrook Rd 44023
Holly Ln 44022
Holly Springs Trl 44023
Honey Bell Oval 44022
Honeysuckle Ln 44023
Hopewell Trl 44023
Horseshoe Dr 44023
Hunting Ln & Trl 44022
Hunting Hill Farm Dr 44022
Huron St 44023
Indian Hills Dr 44023
Industrial Pkwy 44022
Island View Cir 44023
Ivy Ln 44023
Jackson Dr
100-299 44022
18600-18700 44023
18702-18798 44023
Jackson Rd
7000-7799 44023
28200-38799 44023
Jacobs Dr 44023
Jasmine Ln 44023
Jennifer Ln 44023
Jensen Ct 44023
Jordan Gardner Oval 44023
E & W Juniper Ln 44022
Kensington Ct 44023
Kensington Dr 44022
Kenston Lake Dr 44023
Kent St 44022
Kenton Rd 44022
Kimberwick Ct 44022
Kings Orchard Trl 44023
Kingsley Dr 44023
Kingswood Dr 44022
Knight Ln 44023
Knolls Way 44023
Knorentr Rd 44023
Kurzemes Dr 44023
Ladue Trl 44023
Lake Dr 44023
Lake Forest Ct & Trl 44023
Lake House Ln 44022
Lake In The Woods Trl 44023
Lake Shore Dr 44023
Lakedge Ln 44022
Lakesedge Trl 44023
Lakeview Ln 44022
Lancaster Ct 44022
Lancaster Dr 44023
Lander Rd 44022
Lansmark Ct 44023
Larkspur Rd 44022
Laurel Ct, Ln & Rd 44022
Laurelbrook Dr 44022
Le Land Trl 44023
Leaview Ln 44022
Ledgebrook Ln 44022
Lewis Dr 44023
Liberty Rd 44022
Lindsay Ln 44023
Lochspur Ln 44022
Locust Ln 44022
Long Dr 44023
Long Meadow Trl 44023
Longview Trl 44023
Longwood Dr 44022
Lookout Dr 44022
Lorain St 44023
Lost Trl 44023
Lost Lakes Trl 44023
Louise Dr 44022
Low St 44022
Lucerne Dr 44023
Lucky Bell Ln 44023
Lyndale Dr 44022
Magnolia Ln 44023
N & S Main St 44022
Majestic Oaks 44023
Mallard Pt 44023
Manderly Ln 44022
Manor Brook Dr 44022
Maple Dr 44023
Maple Ln 44022
Maple St 44022
Maple Hill Dr 44022
Maple Springs Dr 44022
Mapleridge Rd 44022
Maplewood Ln 44022
Martingale Ct 44022
Marydale Dr 44023
Mather Ln 44022
May Ct
1-199 44022
18400-18599 44023
Meadow Ln
300-399 44022
10800-11000 44023
11002-17320 44023
33900-33999 44022
Meadowhill Ln 44022
Meadowood Ln 44022
Medina St 44023
Merrill Ct 44023
Merry Oaks Trl 44023
Messenger Rd 44023
Miles Rd 44022
Mill St 44022
Mill Hollow Dr 44022
Millbrook Dr 44023
Millcreek Ln 44022
Millstone Dr 44023
Misty Lake Gln 44023
Mitchell Ln 44022
Moccasin Run 44023
Mock Orange Cir & Ln 44023
Mogul St 44022
Mohican Trl 44023
Monticello Dr 44022
Moreland Ln 44023
Morning View Ct 44023
Morningside Dr 44022
Moss Pt 44023
Mount Pleasant Dr 44022
Mountain View Dr 44022
Muirwood Ct 44023
Munn Rd 44023
Murcott Cir 44022
Murwood Dr 44022
Music St 44022
Mystic Ridge Rd 44023
Nighthawk Dr 44023
Nob Hill Dr & Oval 44022
Noll Ct 44023
Normandy Ln 44023
North Blvd 44023
North St 44022
Northampton Ct 44023
Northbrook Trl 44023
Northview Dr 44023
Northwood Lakes Dr 44023
Nottingham Ln 44022
Oak St 44022
Ober Ln 44023
Old Farm Rd 44022
Old Kinsman Rd 44022
Old Meadow Dr 44023
Old Plank Ln 44022
Old Som Ln 44022
Old Tannery Trl 44023
Olive St 44022
Orange Ln 44023
E Orange St 44022
W Orange St 44022
E & W Orange Hill Cir 44022
Orange Meadow Ln 44022
Orange Tree Dr 44022
Orangedale Rd 44022
Orchard Cir & St 44022
Overlook Dr 44023
Overlook Rd 44022
Overlook Brook Ct & Dr 44023
Owls Hollow Ln 44023
Oxgate Ln 44022
Park Dr 44022
Park Ln 44022
Park Pl 44022
W Park Circle Dr 44023
Park Wood Cir 44022
Parkland Dr 44022
Partridge Ln 44022
Paw Paw Lake Dr 44022
Pear Tree Cir 44022
Pebble Creek Ct 44023
Pebblebrook Ln 44022
Pecan Ct 44022
Penny Ln 44023
Peppermill Run 44023
Pettibone Rd 44023
Pheasant Ln 44022
Pheasant Run Dr 44022
Philomethian St 44022
Pike Dr 44022
E Pilgrim Ave & Dr 44023
Pine St 44022
Pine Creek Ct 44022
Pine River Dr 44022
Pinecrest Dr 44022
N & S Pintail Dr 44023
Plarrins Rd 44022
Plaza Dr 44022
Pleasant Aly & Dr 44022
Plum Creek Trl 44023
Potomac Dr 44022
Primrose Ct 44023
Quail Ln & Rdg 44022
Quail Hollow Dr 44022
Queens Way 44023
Quinn Rd 44023
Raea Ln 44022
Rail King Ct 44023
Railroad Pl 44023
Rambling Creek Trl 44023
Ravenna Rd 44023
Red Fox Trl 44023
Regal Pl 44023

Renaissance Ct 44023
Reserve Trl 44022
Riddle Rd 44022
Ridgecrest Trl 44022
Ridgecrest Dr 44022
Ridgeview Trl 44023
Ridgewood Rd 44022
River St 44022
River Mountain Dr 44022
River Stone Dr 44022
Rivers Edge Dr E & W 44023
Riverside Ln 44023
Riverview Ct 44022
Riverview Dr 44023
Riverwood Ln 44023
Robens Ct 44022
Robert Ln 44023
Robin Wood Ln 44023
Rocker Ave 44023
Rockspring Dr 44023
Rolling Brook Dr 44023
Root Rd 44023
Roundwood Rd 44022
Royal Oak Dr 44022
Runny Meade Trl 44022
Russell Rd 44022
Rydalwood Ln 44022
Sablewood Dr 44023
Sagewood Dr 44023
Saint James Pl 44023
Samuel Lord Dr 44023
Sanctuary Dr 44023
Sandlewood Dr 44023
Savage Rd 44023
Saybrook Ln 44023
Scarsdale Ln 44022
Scotland Dr 44023
Sedge Ct 44023
Senlac Hills Dr 44022
Settlers Trl 44023
Shadow Wood Cir 44023
Shaker Blvd 44022
Sharon Dr 44023
Shaw Rd 44023
Sheerbrook Dr 44022
Shopping Plz 44022
Signal Hl 44023
Silica Rdg 44023
Silver Springs Trl 44022
Skyline Dr & Ln 44022
Smithfield Rd 44022
Snow Rd 44023
Snow Shoe Trl 44023
Snyder Rd
16100-16299 44022
16300-16306 44023
16301-16307 44022
16308-19199 44023
Solether Ln 44022
Solon Rd 44022
Som Center Rd 44022
Somerset Dr 44022
Sorrelwood Ln 44022
South Blvd 44023
South Ln 44023
South St 44022
Southbrook Trl 44023
Southwyck Dr 44022
Spice Bush Ln 44023
Spiceberry Cir 44023
Spring Dr 44022
N & S Spring Valley Park Dr 44023
Springdale Ln 44022
Stafford Rd 44023
Staffordshire Ct 44022
Stanridge Rd 44022
Starbush Ct 44023
Stella Ln 44023
Sterling Glen Ln 44023
Sterncrest Dr 44022
Stockton Ln 44023
Stone Ridge Rd 44023
E & W Stonebrooke Ct, Dr & Oval 44022
Stonecreek Dr 44022
Stonehill Ln 44022
Stonewood Dr 44022
Stoney Brook Ct & Dr 44023
N & S Strawberry Ln 44022
Stump Hollow Ln 44022
Suffolk Ln 44022
Sugar Bush Ln 44022
Sugar Hill Trl 44023
Summit Dr 44023
E Summit St 44022
W Summit St 44022
Sun Ridge Ln 44022
Sundew Ln 44022
Sunset Dr 44022
Sylvan Dr 44022
Tall Tree Trl 44023
Tamarack Trl 44023
Tanglewood Ct, Sq & Trl 44023
Tartan Ct 44022
Taylor May Rd 44023
Teaberry Cir 44022
Thorpe Rd 44023
Timber Ln & Trl 44023
Timber Ridge Dr 44022
Topping Ln 44022
Townsend Ct 44023
Trails End 44023
Traymore Dr 44023
Treetower Dr 44023
Trillium Dr 44023
Trolley Trl 44022
Tulip Ln 44023
Twin Acre Ct 44022
Twin Creeks Dr 44023
Twin Lakes Trl 44022
Valencia Cir 44022
Valley Dr, Ln & Rd 44023
Valley Ridge Farm 44022
Victoria Dr 44022
Village Circle Dr 44022
Vincent St 44022
Walden Trl 44022
Walnut Ct 44022
Walnut St 44022
Walnut Trl 44023
Walters Rd 44022
Warren Ct 44023
Washington St
500-599 44022
7600-11999 44023
E Washington St
2-161 44022
160-160 44023
162-498 44022
163-499 44022
W Washington St 44022
Water St 44022
Water Fall Trl 44022
Waterford Dr 44022
Waterford Trl 44023
Waverly Ln 44022
Weathertop Ln 44023
Weathervane Dr 44022
Wembley Ct 44023
Wenhaven Dr 44022
West St 44022
Westhill Dr 44023
Westover Dr 44022
Westview Dr 44022
Whisper Wood Cir 44023
Whisperwood Ln 44022
White Oak Dr 44023
Whitetail Dr & Ln 44022
Wick Ln 44023
Widgeon Dr 44023
Wilderness Psge 44023
Wilding Chase 44022
Wildoak Pl 44023
Williams St 44022
Williamsburg Ct 44023
Willow Ln 44022
Willow Wood Ln 44022
Willson Dr 44023
Wiltshire Rd 44022
Winding River Trl 44022
Windrush Dr 44022
Windswept Cir 44023
Windward Ln & Way 44023
Windy Lakes Cir 44023
Wing Rd 44023
Wingate Dr 44023
Winterberry Ln 44022
Wisteria Dr 44023
Wolfpen Dr 44022
Wood Acre Trl 44023
Woodberry Blvd 44023
Woodburn Dr 44022
Woodcrest Rd 44022
Woodland Ave 44023
Woodland Ct 44022
S Woodland Rd 44022
Woodmere Dr 44023
Woodrush Cir 44022
Woodside Rd 44022
Woodsong Way 44023
Wren Rd 44023
Wychwood Dr 44022
Yorkshire Dr 44023

CINCINNATI OH

General Delivery 45202

POST OFFICE BOXES MAIN OFFICE STATIONS AND BRANCHES

Box No.s
1 - 2239 45201
1 - 378 45242
1 - 465 45222
249 - 250 45205
946 - 946 45215
2301 - 3766 45201
2900 - 2913 45209
3900 - 5000 45201
5001 - 5488 45205
5046 - 5900 45201
5901 - 5999 45249
6000 - 6636 45206
6464 - 6600 45201
6701 - 6999 45206
7001 - 7116 45205
8001 - 8898 45208
8010 - 8110 45280
8172 - 8292 45249
8778 - 8820 45212
8902 - 8986 45249
9001 - 9994 45209
9998 - 9998 45204
11001 - 11720 45211
12001 - 12970 45212
14001 - 14999 45250
15001 - 15995 45215
16001 - 16239 45216
17001 - 17259 45217
18001 - 18355 45218
19001 - 19976 45219
20001 - 20244 45220
23003 - 23360 45223
24001 - 24506 45224
25022 - 25495 45225
27005 - 27477 45227
29001 - 29864 45229
30001 - 30586 45230
31001 - 31486 45231
32001 - 32379 45232
33011 - 33186 45233
36001 - 36700 45236
37001 - 37999 45222
40101 - 40955 45240
42001 - 42894 45242
43001 - 43594 45243
44001 - 44349 45244
46101 - 46969 45246
53001 - 53956 45253
54001 - 54992 45254
58001 - 58740 45258
62001 - 62999 45262
63701 - 68124 45206
80001 - 80111 45280
92900 - 92913 45209
111010 - 112300 45211
128701 - 128820 45212
141011 - 145900 45250
156301 - 157296 45215
162801 - 162811 45216
172701 - 172705 45217
193700 - 198074 45219
317611 - 317844 45231
322901 - 323456 45232
367701 - 369942 45236
371000 - 371805 45222
389001 - 389256 45238
405001 - 405020 45240
422405 - 429598 45242
465600 - 465662 45246
488011 - 488068 45248
495901 - 499050 45249
508100 - 508100 45250
531001 - 538710 45253
541001 - 548506 45254
587101 - 587101 45258
621000 - 628360 45262
802501 - 804527 45280

NAMED STREETS

Abbie Pl 45237
Abbington Rdg 45242
Abbott Ln 45249
Abbottsford St 45212
Abby Ct 45248
Abelia Ct 45213
Aberdeen Aly 45230
Aberdeen Rdg 45245
Abilene Trl 45215
Abington Ave 45229
Able Ct 45215
Academy Ave 45205
Access Pl 45241
Ackley Rd 45255
Acomb Ave 45213
Acorn Dr 45231
Acre Dr 45239
Acreview Dr 45240
Acton Ct 45241
Ada St 45219
Adair Ct 45251
Adams Ave
2200-2326 45212
2328-2398 45212
6500-6599 45243
Adams Rd 45231
Adams St 45215
Adams Xing 45202
Adams Creek Dr 45231
Adams Ridge Dr 45231
Addice Way 45224
Addingham Pl 45223
Addison St 45214
Adelle Walk 45218
Adelphi St 45227
Adena Trl 45230
Adler St 45214
Admiral Ct 45238
Adnored Ct 45219
Advance Ave 45217
Adwood Dr 45240
Affinity Dr 45231
Afton Ave 45213
Agnes St 45223
Ahrens St 45219
Ahwenasa Ln 45243
Aicholtz Ln & Rd 45245
Aikenside Ave 45213
Ainsworth Dr 45251
Airport Rd 45226
Airy Ct 45239
Airycrest Ln 45211
Airymeadows Dr 45252
Airymont Ct 45211
Akochia Ave 45205
Akron Ave 45204
Alabama Ave 45225
Alameda Pl 45229
Alamo Ave 45209
Alamosa Dr 45251
Alaska Ave & Ct 45229
Alba Ct 45241
Albano St 45246
Albany Ter 45224
Alberly Ln 45243
Albert Pl 45227
Albert St 45217
Albert Sabin Way 45229
Alberts Ct 45209
Albion Ave 45246
Albion Ln 45246
Albion Pl 45219
Alcliff Ln 45238
Alcor Ter 45230
Alcott Ln 45218
Aldbough Ct 45251
Alder Ln 45233
Aldermont Ct 45239
Aldine Dr 45242
Aldon Ln 45236
Aldor Ln 45255
Aldrich Ave 45231
Alex Ave 45211
Alexandras Oak Ct 45248
Alexis Rd 45239
Alfred St 45214
Algiers Dr 45246
Algona Pl 45207
Algonquin Dr 45243
Algus Ln 45248
Alhambra Ct 45236
Alicante Ln 45255
Alicemont Ave 45209
Aljoy Ct 45215
Allaire Ave 45239
Allarank Rd 45249
Allegheny Dr 45251
Allen Ave
1-99 45215
600-799 45246
Allencrest Ct 45231
Allendale Dr 45209
Allendorf Dr 45209
Allenford Ct 45238
Allenham St 45204
Allenhurst Blvd E & W 45241
Allenhurst Close 45241
Allenwood Ct 45238
Allet Ave 45239
Alliance Rd 45242
Allison St 45212
Allston St 45209
Allview Cir & Ct 45238
Alma Ave 45242
Almahurst Ct 45249
Almester Dr 45211
Alms Pl 45206
Almsgate Ln 45226
Alnetta Dr 45230
Alomar Dr 45238
Alpha St 45227
Alphonse Ln 45238
Alpine Ave
4500-4799 45242
6700-6899 45236
Alpine Pl
2100-2199 45206
3200-3399 45211
Alpine Ter 45208
Alsace Way 45245
Alta Ave 45236
Alta Crest Ln 45219
Alta Vista Ave 45211
Altadena Ave 45230
Altaview Ct 45231
Alter Pl 45229
Althaus Rd 45247
Althea Dr 45248
Altoona St 45206
Altura Dr 45239
Alvera Dr 45238
Alvernoridge Dr 45238
Alvernovalley Ct 45238
Alvin St 45219
Alvina Ave 45212
Alvina Ln 45255
Alwil Dr 45215
Alydar Ct 45242
Amanda Pl 45205
Amandas Oak Ct 45248
Amarillo Ct 45231
Amazon Ave 45220
Ambar Ave 45230
Ambassador Dr 45231
Amber Trl 45244
Amberacres Dr 45237
Ambercreek Dr
9000-9071 45236
9073-9073 45236
9088-9199 45237
Amberlawn Ave 45237
Amberson Ave 45208
Amberway Ct 45251
Amberwood Ct 45224
Ambler Dr 45241
Ambleside Pl 45208
Ambrose Ave 45224
Amelia Dr 45241
Ameliamont Ave 45209
Amesbury Dr 45231
Amethest Ln 45238
Amigo Ct 45251
Ammon Ave 45223
Amor Pl 45214
Amy Ave 45227
Amylynn Dr 45211
Anaconda Dr 45211
Anaheim Ct 45251
Anchor Dr 45255
Anchor Rd 45244
Anchorage Rd 45226
Andalus Ct 45217
Andalusia Close 45241
Andamo Dr 45238
Andarant Ave 45215
Anders Ct 45238
Anderson Ave 45255
Anderson Pl 45227
Anderson Way 45242
Anderson Cove Ln 45244
Anderson Ferry Rd 45238
Anderson Glen Dr 45255
Anderson Hills Dr 45230
Anderson Manor Ct 45244
Anderson Oaks Dr 45255
Anderson Woods Dr 45244
Andina Ave 45237
Andover Rd 45218
Andreas Ave 45211
Andres Ln
500-599 45244
3100-3199 45248
Andrew Ave 45209
Andrew Pl 45209
Andrew St 45217
Andrews Ave 45205
Andy Ct 45238
Angel Nook St 45238
Angela Ave 45231
Angels Way 45217
Angie Ct 45248
Anioton Ct 45227
Anita Pl 45237
Anna St 45215
Anna Mae Dr 45244
Anna Marie Ln 45247
Annadale Ln 45246
Annajoe Ct 45233
Annapolis Dr 45244
Annesdale Dr 45243
Anniston Dr 45248
Annuity Dr 45241
Annwood Ln & St 45206
E & W Anson Dr 45245
Antares Ct 45231
Anthony St 45223
Anthony Wayne Ave 45216
Antioch Ct 45241
Antique St 45202
Antoinette Ave 45230
Antoninus Dr 45238
Antrim Ct 45236
Apache Cir 45243
Apache Run Dr 45245
Apalachee Dr 45249
Apawana Ct 45255
Apjones St 45223
Appaloosa Ct 45231
Apple Ln 45255
Apple St 45223
E Apple St 45232
Apple Blossom Ln 45244
Apple Farm Ln 45230
E Apple Gate 45245
Apple Hill Rd 45230
Apple Orchard Ln 45248
Apple Ridge Ln 45236
Applebud Dr 45247
Applecreek Ct 45238
Applecrest Ct 45242
Applegate Ave 45211
Applejack Ct 45249
Appleknoll Ln 45236
Appleridge Ct 45247
Appleseed Dr 45249
Appleton St 45209
Appletree Ct 45247
Applevalley Ct 45247
Applewood Dr 45236
April Dr 45239
Aquadale Ln 45211
Aquarius Dr 45231
Arabian Ct 45242
E & W Aracoma Dr 45237
Aracoma Forest Dr 45237
Arapaho Ln
1200-1299 45244
8300-8399 45243
Arbor Ave 45209
Arbor Cir 45255
Arbor Ct 45246
Arbor Ln 45255
Arbor Pl
500-599 45255
2600-2699 45209
Arbor Green Dr 45255
Arbor Montgomery Ln 45249
Arbor Trail Ct 45231
N Arbor Woods Ct 45248
Arborcreek Dr 45242
Arborcrest Ct & Dr 45236
Arborhill Ln 45241
Arborrun Dr 45233
Arborview Ct 45239
Arborwood Dr 45251
Arcadia Pl 45208
Arch St 45202
Archer Ave 45208
Archland Dr 45224
Arcola St 45215
Ardmore Ave
2400-2699 45237
3900-3999 45229
Ardon Ln 45215
Ardwick Ln 45246
Argentine Ct 45244
Argus Rd 45224
N & S Argyle Pl 45223
Aries Ct 45251
Arklow Ct 45212
Arlington Ave
300-799 45215
7600-7799 45255
Arlington Dr 45244
Arlington St 45225
Armada Pl 45227
Arnett St 45243
Arnold St 45208
Arnsby Pl 45227
Arroka Dr 45231
Arrow Ave
3300-3399 45213
5200-5299 45247

Street	ZIP
Arrow Point Way	45227
Arrowhead Ct	45231
Arrowood Pl	45231
Arthur Pl	45225
Artwood Dr	45230
Arundel Ct	45231
Arvin Ave	45231
Asbury Ln	45243
Asbury Rd	45255
Asbury Hills Dr	45255
Asbury Lake Dr	45247
Ascot Ct	45251
Ash Ave	45215
Ash Ct	45242
Ash St	45212
Ashbourne Pl	45233
Ashbrook Dr	45238
Ashburn Rd	45240
Ashby St	45218
Ashcroft Ct	45240
Ashfield Dr	45242
Ashford Ct	45231
Ashgrove Dr	45244
Ashhill Ct	45247
Ashhollow Dr	45247
Ashinewo St	45203
Ashland Ave	
2300-2999	45206
4200-4599	45212
Ashleigh Ct	45246
Ashley Ct	
200-299	45215
6000-6099	45242
Ashley Ln	45215
Ashley Meadow Ct	45227
Ashley Oaks Dr	45227
Ashley View Dr	45227
Ashmont Ave	45208
Ashmore Ct	
1200-1299	45231
11800-11899	45246
Ashsteade Ln	45255
Ashtabula St	45233
Ashton Ct	45244
Ashtree Dr	45223
Ashview Pl	45242
Ashwood Ct	45245
Ashwood Dr	
3200-3399	45213
4700-4799	45241
Ashworth Ct	45255
Ashworth Dr	45208
Asmann Ave	45229
Aspasia St	45226
Aspen Ave	45224
Aspen Ct	45246
Aspen Way	45224
Aspen Glen Dr	45244
Aspen Point Ct	45247
Aspen View Ct	45247
Aspenhill Dr	45240
Aspenknoll Ct	45230
Assisi Ln	45238
Assisiknoll Ct	45238
Assisiview Ct	45238
Aster Pl	45224
Aston Ct	45209
Aston Dr	45244
Aston Pl	45241
Astoria Ave	45208
Athenia Dr	45244
Athens Ave	45226
Atkinson St	45219
Atlantic Ave	45209
Atson Ln	45205
Attica Ave	45212
Atwater Dr	45251
Atwood Ave	45224
Aubrey Ln	45245
Auburn Ave	45219
Auburncrest Ave	45219
Auburnview Dr	45206
Audie Ct	45246
Audrey Ter	45219
Audro Dr	45247
Audubon St	45226
Augcliffe Dr	45245
August Pl	45238
Augusta Ave	45211
Augusta Ln	45243
Ault Ln	45246
Ault Park Ave	45208
Ault View Ave	45208
Aultwoods Ln	45208
Aurora Ave	45248
Austin Dr	45255
Austin Ter	45220
Austin Ridge Dr	45247
Austin Woods Ln	45247
Auten Ave	45213
Autumn Ln	45239
Autumn Hill Ct	45230
Autumnleaf Ln	45230
Autumnridge Dr	45251
Autumnwind Dr	45249
Autumnwood Dr	45242
Auxier Dr	45244
Avalon St	45216
Avarit Ln	45249
Avenell Ln	45218
Avery Ln	45208
Avilla Pl	45212
Avon Dr	45229
Avon Pl	45225
Avon Fields Ln & Pl	45229
Avondale Ave	45229
Avonlea Ave	45237
Axminster Dr	45251
Ayerdayl Ln	45255
Ayers Rd	45255
Ayershire Ave	45230
Aylesboro Ave	45208
Azalea Ave	45227
Azimuth Dr	45251
Aztec Ct	45241
Azure Ct	45230
Babb Aly	45226
Babson Pl	45227
Babygold Ct	45247
Baccarat Dr	45245
Bach Ave	45209
Bachman St	45218
Back St	45202
Bacon St	45215
Bader Ct	45236
Bader St	45225
Badgeley St	45223
Baen Rd	45242
Bagdad Dr	45230
Bahama Ter	45223
Bailey Ave	45248
Bainbridge Dr	45241
Bainsbrook Ct	45249
Bainwoods Dr	45249
Bake Ave	45239
Baker Ave	
1-199	45217
2700-2899	45211
Baker Cir	45212
Baker Pl	
2700-2799	45206
4700-4799	45217
Baker St	45212
Balboa Dr	45231
Balbriggan Ct	45255
Balfour Dr	45245
Balfour Ln	45231
Balincot Ave	45208
Ballantrae Ct	45238
Ballard Ave	45209
Ballyclare Ter	45240
Ballymore Ct	45245
Ballymore Ln	45233
Balmoral Dr	45233
Balsam Ct	45246
Balsamridge Dr	45239
Baltic Ct	
500-599	45245
7200-7299	45244
Baltimore Ave	
1600-2599	45225
2600-2699	45211
Banbury Ln	45255
Banbury St	45216
Bancroft Cir	45246
Bancroft St	45227
Bandanna Dr	45238
Bank Ave	45217
Bank Ct	45211
Bank Rd	
10900-11099	45252
11100-11799	45251
Bank St	45214
Banks Rd	45245
Bankwood Ln	45224
Banning Rd	45239
Bantam Ln	45245
Bantry Ave	45213
Baps Dr	45246
Bar Harbor Dr	45255
Barbara Ln	45244
Barbara Pl	45229
Barberry Ave	45207
Barg Ln	45230
Barg Salt Run Rd	45244
Baribill Pl	45230
Barjo Ln	45239
Barker Rd	45229
Barkley St	45204
Barnesburg Rd	45247
Barneswood Ct	45249
Barney Ave	45215
Barnsby Ln	45244
Barnsdale Ct	45230
Barnstable Ct	45244
Baronwood Ct	45240
Barony Pl	45241
Barridar Ave	45223
Barrington Ct	45242
Barron Dr	45215
Barrow Ave	45209
Barry Ln	45229
Bartels Rd	45244
Barthas Pl	45239
Bartlett St	45214
Barvac Ave	45223
Basil Ln	45238
Bassett Rd	45205
Basswood Ln	45239
Batavia Rd	45244
Bates Aly	45225
Bates Ave	
1100-1399	45225
1200-1299	45246
Bath Ct	45241
Bathgate St	45206
Bauer Ave	
400-499	45214
6400-6499	45239
Bauerwood Dr	45251
Baum St	45202
Baumer St	45204
Baurichter St	45204
Baxter Ave	45220
N Bay Ct	45238
Bayard Dr	45208
Bayberry Dr	45242
Baybro Ct	45224
Bayham Dr	45218
Bayhill Ct	45233
Bayley Place Dr	45233
Baymiller St	
300-399	45203
1700-2299	45214
Baymiller Walk	
1000-1099	45203
1300-1699	45214
Bayou Ct	45248
Bayswater Dr	45255
Baytowne Dr	45247
Baytree Ct	45230
Baywood Ln	45224
Beacon St	45230
Beacon Hill Rd	45243
Beacon Hills Dr	45241
Beaconwood Dr	45230
Beacraft Ave	45213
Beamer Ct	45245
Bear Valley Ct	45241
Bearcat Dr	45248
Bearcat Way	45219
Bearcreek Dr	45249
Beatrice Dr	45229
Beau Ln	45231
Beaufort Ct	45240
Beaufort Hunt Ln	45242
Beaumont Pl	45205
Beaver Ave	45213
Beaver Creek Cir	45244
Beavercreek Cir	45241
Beaverton Ave	45237
Beckford Dr	45218
Beckham Ln & Way	45246
Beckridge Ct	45247
Becky Ct	45215
Beckys Ridge Dr	45251
Bedford Ave	45208
Bedford St	45227
Bedford Ter	45208
Bedford Glen Ln	45246
Bedivere Ct	45241
Beech Ave	
300-398	45215
319-399	45215
836-1599	45205
7800-8499	45236
Beech Ct	45245
Beech Dr	45231
Beech Ln	
1-99	45208
2500-2599	45237
10100-10199	45215
Beech St	
300-499	45216
3800-4299	45227
4200-4299	45212
4300-5099	45212
5200-5299	45217
Beech Trl	45243
Beech Crest Ln	45206
Beech Dell Dr	45233
Beech Grove Dr & Ln	45233
Beech Hill Ave	45223
Beech Hollow Dr	45236
Beech Knoll Dr	45224
Beech Tree Ln	45244
Beech View Cir	45213
Beecham Ln	45208
Beechcreek Ln	45233
Beechcrest Dr	45255
Beechcrest Pl	45230
Beechcroft Ct	45233
Beecher St	45206
Beecherfalls Ct	45233
Beechglen Ct	45233
Beechhollow Ct	45233
Beechlands Dr	45237
Beechmar Dr	45230
Beechmeadow Ln	45238
Beechmont Ave	
2000-2599	45230
3742-4999	45226
5000-7399	45230
7400-8899	45255
Beechmont Cir	45226
Beechmont Ct	45226
Beechmont Dr	45244
Beechnut Dr	45230
Beechpoint Dr	45231
Beechridge Dr	45216
Beechshire Dr	45255
Beechtop Dr	45233
Beechtop Ln	45226
Beechtree Dr	45224
Beechurst Woods Ln	45233
Beechwood Ave	
700-799	45232
3900-4099	45229
Beechwood Dr	45215
Beechwood Rd	45244
Beechwood Ter	45230
Beechwood Farms Dr	45244
Beekley Woods Dr	45241
Beekman St	
2200-2499	45214
2500-3099	45225
3100-3354	45223
3101-3355	45225
3356-3999	45223
Behles Ave	45215
Behymer Rd	45245
Belclare Rd	45247
Belcross Ct	45238
Beldare Ave	45220
Belden Cir	45211
Belfast Ave	45236
Belgreen Ln	45240
Belhaven Dr	45239
Belkay Dr & Ln	45237
Belkenton Ave	45236
Belknap Pl	45218
Bell Ave	45242
Bell Pl	45206
Bell St	45212
Bella Vista Pl	45206
Bella Vista St	45237
Bellacre Ct	45248
Bellaire Ct	45244
Bellbranch Ct	45231
Belle Meade Ct	45230
Belleair Pl	45224
Bellecrest Ave	45208
Bellehaven Ct	45248
Belleview Ave	45242
Bellevue Ave	45219
Bellewood Ave	45213
Bellfield Ln	45238
Bellglade Ter	45238
Bellmeadows Dr	45224
Bello Ct	45231
Bells Ln	45244
Bells Lake Dr	45244
Belltone Ave	45211
Bellune Dr	45231
W Belmar Pl	45224
Belmont Ave	
3701-3797	45227
3799-3899	45227
5500-6099	45224
Belmont Blvd	45245
Belsage Ct	45231
Belsaw Pl	45220
Belvedere St	45202
Belvoir Ln	45238
Benadir Rd	45246
Benchmark Ln	45242
N Bend Rd	
2900-3599	45239
3800-5199	45211
5205-5219	45247
5221-5599	45247
Bend St	45244
Bender Rd	45233
Benedict Ct	45246
Benham Ct	45255
Benhill Dr	45247
Benjamin St	45245
Benken Ln	45248
Benkert Dr	45241
Bennett Ave	45212
Bennett Ln	45245
Bennett Rd	
3700-3899	45245
6700-7199	45230
Bennett Spur	45245
Bennettwoods Ct	45230
Benneville St	45230
Bennington Dr	45241
Bennington Way	45246
E & W Benson St	45215
Bent Creek Dr	45244
Bent Tree Ct	45244
Bentbrook Dr	45251
Bentley Ct	45244
Benton Ridge Ln	45255
Bentwood Ct	45241
Benvue St	45233
Benz Ave	45238
Beranger Ct	45255
Berauer Rd	45248
Bercliff Ave	45223
Berdale Ln	45244
Beredith Pl	45213
Beresford Ave	45206
Bergen Ct	45244
Berkinshaw Dr	45230
Berkley Ave	45237
N Berkley Cir	45236
S Berkley Cir	45236
Berkshire Ln	45220
Berkshire Rd	45230
Berkshire Club Dr	45230
Bermuda Pl	45231
Bern Ln	45246
Bernard Ave	
200-299	45215
7200-7499	45231
Bernhart Ct	45246
Berry Ave	45208
Berry Ct	45244
Berryhill Ln	45242
Berrypatch Dr	45244
Berrywood Dr	45244
Berte St	45230
Berthbrook Dr	45231
Bertus St	45217
Berwick St	45227
Berwood Dr	45243
Berwyn Pl	45209
Beryl Ave	45242
Bess Ct	45249
Bessinger Dr	45240
Best Pl	45241
Bestview Ter	45230
Besuden Ct	45208
Beta Ave	45231
Beth Ln	45230
Bethany Ln	45255
Bethesda Ave	45229
Betlin Ct	45238
Bettman Dr	45232
Betton St	45214
Betts Ave	
6200-6432	45224
6434-6478	45224
6435-6477	45239
6479-6899	45239
Betty Ln	45238
Bettyhill Ln	45245
Betula Ave	45229
Beverly Dr	45245
Beverly Hill Dr	45208
Bevis Ave	45207
Bevis Ln	45251
Bickel Ave	45214
Biddle St	45220
Biegler St	45214
Biehl Ave	45248
Big Ben Ct	45241
Big Ben Ln	45226
Big Chief Dr	45227
Big Moe Dr	45244
Big Sky Dr	45255
Bigelow St	45219
Bighorn Ct	45211
Bilamy Ct	45224
Bilby Ln	45244
Biloxi Dr	45231
Birchbark Dr	45249
Birchdale Ct	45230
Birchgrove Ct	45251
Birchhill Dr	45251
Birchknoll Ct	45230
Birchridge Dr	45240
Birchway Dr	45251
Birchwood Ave	45224
Birchwood Dr	45255
Birkdale Way	45245
Birney Ln	45230
Biscayne Ave	45248
Biscoe Dr	45215
Bishop St	45220
Bishopsbridge Dr	45255
Bishopsgate Dr	45246
Bising Ave	45239
Bitteroot Ln	45224
Bittersea Ct	45255
Black Watch Way	45245
Blackberry Trl	45233
Blackbird Holw	45244
Blackcomb Dr	45244
Blackhawk Cir	45240
Blackstone Pl	45237
Blackthorn Dr	45255
Blackwolf Run	45247
Blackwood Ct	45236
Blade Ave	45216
Blaesi St	45227
Blaine Rd & St	45214
Blair Ave	
500-920	45229
922-998	45229
1400-1699	45207
Blair Ct	45229
Blairhouse Dr	45244
Blanchard Ave	45205
Blanche Ave	45215
Blanchetta Dr	45239
Blaney Ave	45227
Bleecker Ln	45225
Blenheim Ct	45238
Blome Rd	45243
Blong Rd	45249
Bloom St	45214
Bloomingdale Ave	45230
Bloor Ave	45226
Blossom Dr	45236
Blossom Ln	45244
Blossomhill Ln	45224
Blue Ash Rd	
7000-8599	45236
8600-8900	45242
8901-8997	45242
8902-10328	45242
8999-9453	45242
9455-9499	45242
Blue Bell Dr	45224
Blue Boar Dr	45230
Blue Grass Ln	45237
Blue Haven Ter	45238
Blue Heron Ln	45251
Blue Lake Dr	45247
Blue Meadow Ln	45251
Blue Ridge Ave	45213
Blue Rock Rd	
2700-3555	45239
3556-7099	45247
Blue Rock St	45223
Blue Rock Hill Rd	45247
Blue Spruce Ln	45224
Blue Spruce Rd	45223
Blue Teal Dr	45246
Blueacres Dr	45239
Blueberry Hill Ct	45248
Bluebird Dr	45248
Bluebird Ln	
600-699	45244
5400-5499	45239
Bluecrest Dr	45230
Bluecrystal Ct	45224
Bluecut Ln	45243
Bluefield Pl	45237
Bluegate Dr	45241
Bluehill Dr	45240
Bluejacket Rd	45244
Bluejay Ct	45244
Bluejay Dr	45231
Bluelark Dr	45231
Blueorchard Dr	45230
Bluepine Dr	45247
Bluesky Dr	45247
Bluestone Ct	45241
Bluewing Ter	
9200-9399	45236
9400-9599	45236
Bluffcrest Ln	45238
Boake Aly	45216
Boal St	45202
Boardwalk Ct	45242
Bob Dr	45238
Bobby Ln	45243
Bobolink Ave	45231
Bobolink Ct	45244

Street	ZIP
Bobolink Dr	45224
Bobwood Ave	45231
Boca Ln	45239
Bodley Ave	45205
Bodmann Ave	45219
Bodwell Ct	45241
Bogart Ave	45229
Bogarts Pointe Dr	45230
Boggs Ln	45246
Boleyn Dr	45239
Bolser Dr	45215
Boltwood Ct	45225
Bomark Ct	45242
Bona Vista Pl	45213
Bonair Ct	45230
Bonanza Ln	45255
Bonaparte Ave	45207
Bonaventure Ct	45238
Bond Pl	45206
Bondick Ct	45230
Bonfield Dr	45220
Bonham Rd	45215
Bonita Dr	45238
Bonnell St	45215
Bonneville Ln	45231
Bonnie Dr	45230
Bonnieview Ln	45220
Boomer Rd	45247
Boone St	45206
Borden St	45223
Bornholm Pl	45244
Borrman Ave	45229
Bosley St	45219
Bossi Ln	45218
Boston Way	45244
Bostwick Ct	45244
Bosworth Pl	45212
Bouchaine Way	45208
Boudinot Ave	
2300-3099	45238
3100-4399	45211
Boulder Path Dr	45247
Boutique Ct	45238
Bouton St	45208
Bowden Ln	45246
Bowdle Pl	45220
Bowen Ave	45255
Bowling Green Ct	45225
Bowman Ave	45204
Bowman Ter	45229
Boxwood Cir	45241
Boxwood Ct	45246
Boyd St	45223
Boyne Ct	45238
Boynton Pl	45208
Bracebridge Dr	45231
Brachman Ave & Ln	45230
Bracken Ridge Ave	45213
Bracken Woods Ln	45211
Bradbury Dr	45240
Bradbury Rd	45245
Braddock St	45204
Bradford Ct	45233
Bradford Place Dr	45243
Bradhurst Dr	45244
Bradley Ave	45215
Bradnor Pl	45218
Braemore Ln	45233
Braewing Ct	45245
Braewood Dr	45241
Braintree Dr	45255
Bramble Ave	45227
Bramble Hill Dr	45227
Brampton Dr	45251
Branch St	45214
Brandon Ave & Ln	45230
Brandonburg Ln	45213
Brandonhill Ct	45244
Brandonmore Dr	45255
Brandsteade Ct	45255
Brandtmanor Dr	45248
Brandy Way	45244
Brandychase Way	45245
Brandywine Dr	45246
Branford Ct	45236
Brannon Dr	45255
Brant Ln	45244
Brantner Ln	45244
Brashears St	45223
Brasher Ave	45242
Brater Ave	45238
Braxton Campbell Ct	45206
Brayton Ave	45215
Brazee St	45209
Breckenridge Ct	45244
Breckenridge Dr	45247
Breedshill Dr	45231
Breen St	45208
Breezewood Dr	45248
Breezy Ln	
400-499	45244
10100-10199	45241
Breezy Vis	45215
Breezy Way	45239
Breezy Acres Dr	45251
Brehm Rd	45252
Bremont Ave	45237
Brent Dr	45231
Brentwood Ave	45208
Brestel Rd	45225
Brettmer Dr	45239
Bretton Dr	45244
Brevier Ave	45205
Brewster Ave	45207
Briarcliffe Ave	45212
Briarcove Ln	45242
Briarfield Ct	45240
Briargreen Ln	45248
Briarhill Dr	45238
Briarpatch Ln	45236
Briarrose Ct	45231
Briarwood Ln	
1-99	45218
4900-4999	45244
Bridge Point Pass	45248
Bridgecreek Dr	45231
Bridgeknoll Ct	45248
Bridgepoint Dr	45248
Bridgeport Ln	45240
Bridges Rd	45230
Bridgestone Ct	45248
Bridgetown Rd	
4100-4599	45211
5500-7753	45248
7755-7769	45248
Bridgeview Ct	45248
Bridgewater Ln	45243
Bridgewood Ct	45249
Bridle Path	45231
Bridle Rd	45244
Bridlemaker Ln	45249
Bridlepath Ln	45241
Brierly Creek Rd	45247
Brierly Ridge Dr	45247
Briertho Rd	45248
Brigade Ct	45239
Brigadoon Dr	45255
Briggs Pl	45209
Brighton	45249
Brighton Manor Ln	45208
Brightview Dr	45231
Brill Rd	45243
Brillwood Ln	45243
Brinkmeier Ave	45225
Brinton Trl	45241
Brisben Pl	45249
Brisco Ct	45244
Bristol Ln	45229
Bristol Hill Ct	45239
Britesilks Ln	45249
Brittany Dr	45242
Brittany Ridge Ln	45233
Brittany Woods Ln	45249
Britton Ave	45227
Britton Blvd	45245
Brixton Ln	45255
Broadhurst Ave	45240
N & S Broadlawn Cir	45236
Broadmore Dr	45247
Broadview Dr & Pl	45208
Broadway St	45202
Broadwell Ave	45211
Broadwell Rd	45244
Brocdorf Dr	45215
Brockton Dr	45251
Brodbeck Pl	45211
Broerman Ave	45217
Brokaw Ave	45225
Brokensound Ln	45242
Brompton Ln	45218
Brook Ave	45241
Brookbridge Dr	45249
Brookcrest Dr	45237
Brookdale Dr	45211
Brooke Ave	45230
Brookfield Ave	45208
Brookfield Ct	45244
Brookfield Dr	45245
Brookforest Dr	45238
Brookgreen Ct	45242
Brookhaven Ave	45215
Brookline Ave	
3400-3499	45220
7200-7299	45236
Brookline Dr	45220
Brooks Ave	
700-799	45215
3600-3699	45207
Brooks Creek Dr	45249
Brookside Ave	45223
Brookside Dr	45251
Brookston Dr	45240
Brookstone Dr	
3500-3699	45209
5600-5799	45230
Brookview Dr	45238
Brookway Dr	45240
Brookwood Ln	45237
Brookwood Mdws	45208
Bross Ct & Ln	45238
Brotherton Rd	
3200-5199	45209
5200-5399	45227
Brown Ave	45242
Brown St	
100-199	45215
200-299	45226
700-1499	45215
9700-9799	45242
Browning Ave	45209
Brownsboro Pl	45255
Brownsway Ln	45239
Brownway Ave	45209
Bruce Ave	
1000-1199	45230
1500-1899	45223
Brucehills Dr	45224
Bruestle Ave	45211
Brunner Dr	45240
Brunnerwood Dr	45238
Bruns Ln	45244
Brunswick Dr	45240
Brushwood Ave	45224
Bryant Ave	45220
Bryn Mawr Dr	45224
Bryson St	45230
Buck St	45214
Buckeye Cres	45243
Buckeye Rdg	45247
Buckingham Pl	45227
Buckingham Rd	45243
Buckland Dr	45249
Buckskin Trl	45245
Budd St	45203
Buddleia Ct	45239
Budmar Ave	45224
Budwood Ct	45230
Buell Rd	45251
Buell St	45211
Buena Vista Pl	45206
Buff Ct	45231
Bufler Ln	45227
Bunker Hill Ct	45215
Bunny Ct	45215
Burbank St	45206
Burch Ave	45208
Burdett Ave & Ct	45206
Burgenland Ave	45255
Burgess Ct	45245
Burgess Dr	45251
Burgoyne Dr	45245
Burgoyne St	45223
Burgundy Ln	45224
Burhaven Ln	45230
Burhen Dr	45238
Burke Ave	45241
Burkhart Ave	
100-299	45215
2800-2899	45213
Burkhart St	45237
Burklin Dr	45244
Burley Cir	45218
Burley Hills Dr	45243
Burlinehills Ct	45244
Burlington Pl	45225
Burlington Rd	45231
Burman Meadow Dr	45243
Burnet Ave	
2000-3099	45219
3100-3599	45229
4301-4799	45217
Burnet Woods Dr	45220
Burney Ln	45230
Burnham St	45218
Burning Tree Ln	45237
Burns Ave	
1-911	45215
913-935	45215
1003-1003	45230
1005-1042	45230
1024-1038	45215
1040-1199	45215
1044-1060	45230
8100-8499	45216
Burns Ct	45216
Burns Ln	45216
Burns St	45204
Burr Oak Dr	45255
Burr Oak St	45232
Bursal Ave & Ct	45230
Burton Ave	45229
Burton Woods Ln	45229
Burwood Ave	45212
Burwood Ct	45218
Bush St	45227
Bushnell St	45204
E Business Way	45241
Business Center Dr	45246
Butlersbridge Ct	45244
Buttercup Ln	45239
Butterfield Pl	45227
Butterfly Ct	45231
Butterwick Dr	45251
Buttonwood Ct	45230
Buxton Ave	45212
Byerstone Ln	45242
Byrd Ave	45215
Byrnes Ln	45229
Byrneside Dr	45239
Byrneslake Ct	45216
Byron St	45214
Cabinet Cir	45244
Cablecar Ct	45244
Cabot Dr	45231
Cachepit Way	45227
Cadillac Ave	45209
Caerleon Ct	45241
Caesar Dr	45231
Calderwood Ln	45243
Caldwell Dr	45216
Caledon Ln	45244
Caledonia Ct	45245
Calgary Ct	45244
Calgery Dr	45255
Calhoun St	45219
Calico Ct	45215
California Ave	45237
Calmhaven Dr	45248
Calumet Dr	45245
Calumet St	45219
Calumet Way	45249
Calvert St	45209
Calverton Ln	45238
Calvin Cliff St	45206
Camargo Cyn	45243
Camargo Pike	45227
Camargo Pnes	45243
Camargo Rd	45243
Camargo Club Dr	45243
Camargo Greene Ct	45243
Camargowoods Ct & Dr	45243
Camaridge Ln & Pl	45243
Camberly Dr	45215
Camberwell Rd	45209
Cambridge Ave	
5800-6499	45230
6600-7099	45227
Cambridge Dr	45241
Camden Ave	
500-599	45229
3700-3899	45227
Camellia Ct	45211
Cameo Ln	45239
Cameron Ave	45212
Cameron Gln	45245
Cameron Pl	45205
Cameron Rd	45246
Camner Ave	45236
Camp Superior Dr	45241
Campbell St	45202
Campus Ln	45230
Camvic Ter	45211
Canal Rd	45241
Canal Rdg	45223
Canary Ct	45242
Candice Ln	45248
Candle Ct	45244
Candlelite Ter	45238
Candlemaker Dr	45244
Candleridge Dr	45233
Candlestick Dr	45233
Candlewick Dr	45231
Candy Ln	45231
Canfield Ct	45240
Cannas Dr	45238
Cannon Gate Dr	45245
Canterbury Ave	45237
Cantrell Dr	45246
Canvas Back Cir	45246
Canyon Dr	45217
Capitol Dr	45244
Cappel Dr	45205
Capri Dr	45224
Capstan Dr	45251
Caralee Dr	45242
Caraway Dr	45244
Cardiff Ave	45209
Cardinal Ct	45242
Cardinal Dr	45244
Cardinal Hill Ct	45230
Carefree Ct	45238
Carefree Dr	45244
Carey Walk	45215
Caribou Cir	45245
Caribou Ct	45243
Carillion Blvd	45240
Carini Ln	45218
Carley Ln	45248
Carlin St	45223
Carll St	45225
Carlos Dr	45251
Carlsbad Rd	45240
Carlsbory Dr	45231
Carlton St	45227
Carlynn Dr	45241
Carmalt St	45219
Carmania Ave	45238
Carmel Ter	45211
Carnaby Ln	45249
Carnation Ave	
4400-4599	45238
7100-7199	45236
Carnation Cir	45238
Carnegie Dr	45240
Carnes St	45214
Carney St	45202
Carol Dr	
800-899	45245
2400-2499	45215
Carolann Ln	45215
Carolina Ave	45237
Carolines Trl	45242
Carothers St	45227
Carpathia Ave	45213
Carpenter Dr	45239
Carpenters Rdg & Run	45241
Carpenters Creek Dr	45241
Carpenters Green Ln	45241
Carpenters Run Ct	45241
Carpenterview Dr	45241
Carplin Pl	45229
Carpol St	45241
Carr St	45203
Carrahen Ave & Ct	45237
Carrel St	45226
Carriage Hl	45248
Carriage Ln	45242
Carriage Trl	45242
Carriage Circle Dr	45246
Carriage Hill Ln	45243
Carriage Station Dr	45245
Carriagelite Dr	45241
Carriageview Ln	45248
Carrie Ave	45211
Carrington Ct	45249
Carrol Ave	45231
Carroll Ave	
2600-3099	45248
6900-6999	45236
Carrousel Park Cir	45251
Carruthers Pond Dr	45246
Carson Ave	
300-399	45215
1000-1399	45205
3600-3799	45211
Carter Ave	
4000-4699	45212
6100-6299	45242
Carthage Ave	
1-299	45215
301-699	45215
4900-5899	45212
Carthage Ct	45212
Cartwheel Ter	45251
Carver Rd	45242
Carver Woods Dr	45242
Cary Ave	45224
Casa Loma Blvd	45238
Cascade Rd	45240
Case Ln	45215
Casey Dr	45223
Cashold Rd	45242
Casper St	45225
Cass Ave	45223
Cassandra Ct	45238
Cassatt Ave	45219
Cassidy Ct	45233
Castle Pl	45227
Castle Pines Ln	45244
Castle Stone Ln	45247
Castlebay	45245
Castleberry Ct	45255
Castlebridge Ct & Ln	45233
Castlebrook Ct	45247
Castlegate Ln	45231
Castleton Pl	45237
Castlewood Ln	45248
Castro Ln	45246
Casual Ct	45238
Catalina Ave	45237
Catalpa Ave	45239
Catalpa Rd	45233
Catalpa Creek Dr	45242
Catalpa Woods Ct	45242
Catawba Valley Dr	45226
Cathedral Ave	45212
Cathedral Hills Dr	45244
Catherine Ave	
100-199	45215
400-499	45229
3900-4099	45212
Causeway Ln	45255
Cavalier Dr	45231
Cavanaugh Ave	45211
Cave Hill Ln	45230
Cavett Dr & Ln	45215
Cavour St	45209
Cayuga Dr	45243
Cecil St	45223
Cecilia Ct	45247
Cedar Ave	
1100-1699	45224
1703-1768	45224
1716-1740	45231
5700-6199	45216
Cedar Crest Ln	45230
Cedar Crossing Ln	45230
Cedar Knolls Ct	45230
Cedar Point Dr	45230
Cedar Ridge Dr	45245
Cedarbluff Ct	45233
Cedarbreaks Ln	45249
Cedarbrook Dr	45237
Cedarcreek Dr	45240
Cedarhill Dr	
600-749	45246
750-999	45240
Cedarhurst Dr	45251
Cedaridge Dr	45247
Cedarpark Dr	45233
Cedarville Ct	45255
Cedarwood Ct	45213
Cedarwood Ln	45245
Cedarwood Pl	45213
Cei Dr	45242
Celedon Ct	45251
Celeron Ave	45209
Celestial St	45202
Cella Dr	45239
Centennial Ave	45242
Centennial Dr	45227
Center Ave	45236
Center St	
3600-3720	45227
6800-6899	45244
7000-7099	45243
E Center St	45227
W Center St	45227
Center Hill Ave	
5500-5622	45216
5623-5899	45232
5900-6399	45224
Centerbrook Ct	45240
Centerbury Ct	45246
Centerdale Rd	45246
Centerridge Ave	45231
Centerview Dr	45238
Central Ave	
22-98	45202
100-399	45215
100-1099	45202
1200-2199	45214
Central Pkwy	
1100-1200	45202
1201-1703	45214
1202-1704	45202
1705-2699	45214
2700-3399	45225
3400-3699	45223
E Central Pkwy	45202
W Central Pkwy	45202
Central Ter	45215
Central Trust Tower	45202
Centron Pl	45246
Centurion Dr	45211
Century Blvd	45246
Century Cir E	45246
Century Cir N	45246
Century Cir W	45246
Century Ct	45244
Century Ln	45205
Chadwick Ln	45255
Chagrin Way	45251
Chalet Dr	45217
Chalfonte Pl	45229
Challen St	45211
Chalmers Ct & Ln	45218
Chamberlain Ave	45215
Chambers St	45223
Champdale Ln	45238

Champion Way 45241
Champlain St 45214
Chancery Ln 45249
Chandler St 45227
Channing St 45202
Chanticleer Way 45245
Chantilly Dr 45238
Chaparal Ct 45233
Chapel St 45206
Chapel Heights Ln 45247
Chapel Ridge Dr 45223
Chapelacres Ct 45233
Chapelhill Dr 45233
Chapelsquare Ln 45249
Chapelview Ct 45233
Chapman St 45227
Charann Ln 45224
Chardale Ct 45248
Chardon Ln 45246
Chardonnay Rdg 45226
Charing Way 45246
Charingcross Ct 45238
Charity Dr 45248
Charlemar Dr 45227
Charles St
210-212 45202
211-232 45215
Charlesfield Ln 45243
Charloe Ct & St 45227
E Charlotte Ave 45215
W Charlotte Ave 45215
Charlotte St 45214
E & W Charlton St 45219
Charteroak Dr 45236
Charwood Ct 45211
Charwood Dr 45244
Chase Ave 45223
Chase Plz 45240
Chaswil Dr 45255
Chateau Ave 45204
Chateau Dr 45244
Chatelaine Ct 45247
Chatham Ct 45215
Chatham St 45206
Chatsworth Ave 45215
Chatterton Dr 45231
Chatwood Ct 45248
Chaucer Dr 45237
Chelmsford Rd 45240
Chelsea Pl 45233
Cheltenham Dr 45231
Chelton Ln 45249
Chenora Ct 45215
Cherevilla Ln 45238
Cherokee Ave 45233
Cherokee Dr 45243
Cherry Ln
6700-6799 45227
8300-8399 45255
Cherry St
300-399 45246
3800-4299 45223
8800-9099 45242
Cherry Blossom Ln 45231
Cherrybend Dr 45247
Cherrywood Ct 45224
Cherwin Dr 45243
Chesapeake Run 45248
Cheshire Dr 45240
Chesney Ln 45249
Chesswick Dr 45242
Chesswood Dr 45239
Chester Ave 45232
Chester Rd
9900-10699 45215
10700-11699 45246
Chesterdale Cir, Ct, Dr & Rd 45246
Chesterfield Ct 45239
Chesterhill Dr 45231
Chesterton Way 45230
Chesterwood Ct 45246
Chestnut Ave 45215
Chestnut Ct 45245
Chestnut Ln 45230
Chestnut St
400-799 45203
5600-6199 45216
6600-6799 45227
Chestnut Commons 45244
Chestnut Creek Dr 45244
Chestnut Ridge Dr 45230
Chetbert Dr 45236
Cheviot Ave 45211
Cheviot Rd
5767A-5767C 45247
5500-8549 45247
8550-8999 45251
Cheyenne Dr 45216
Chicago Ave 45215
Chickadee Ct 45227
Chickasaw St 45219
Chickering Ave 45232
Chicory Ln 45244
Chidester Ln 45241
Childress Ct 45240
Childs Ave 45248
Chili Hill Dr 45238
Chimney Hill Dr 45241
Chimneysweep Ln 45241
Chinquapin Ln 45243
Chipley Ct 45240
Chippenham Ct 45231
Chippewa St 45227
Chisholm Trl 45215
Chopin Dr 45231
Christmas Ln 45224
Christopal Dr 45231
Christopher Ln 45233
Chuck Harmon Way 45237
Chuckfield Dr 45239
Chukker Point Ln 45244
Chumani Ln 45243
Church Ave 45246
Church Ln 45211
Church Pl
4700-4799 45226
4800-4899 45208
Church St
1-299 45217
300-399 45246
300-399 45217
400-599 45217
600-699 45204
900-1199 45215
3201-3930 45244
3932-3998 45244
Churchill Ave 45206
Churchview Ln 45211
Churchwood Dr 45238
Cider Mill Dr 45245
Cimarron Trl 45238
Cincinnati Ave 45249
Cincinnati Batavia Pike 45245
Cincinnati Dayton Pike 45241
Cincinnati Mills Dr 45240
Cindy Ln 45239
Cinergy Fld 45202
Cinnamon Cir 45244
Cinnamon Ct 45244
Cinnamon Dr 45244
Cinnamon St 45208
Circle Ave 45232
Circlefield Dr 45246
Circlewood Ln 45215
Citadel Pl 45255
Citrus Ln 45239
City View Cir 45225
City View Pl 45219
Citycentre Dr 45216
Cityscape West Dr 45205
Civic Center Dr 45231
Clairmont Woods Dr 45244
Clanora Dr 45205
Clara Ave 45239
Clara St 45214
Claramont Ave 45209
Clare Rd 45227
Clarebluff Ct 45238
Clareknoll Ct 45238
Clareridge Ct 45238
Claretta Dr 45231
Clarevalley Dr 45238
Clarewood Ave 45207
Clarion Ave 45207
Clark Ave 45215
Clark Rd 45215
Clark St 45203
Clarke Ct 45246
Clarkwood Pl 45208
Classic Dr 45241
Claudia Ct 45230
Claxton Trl 45241
Clay St
1-99 45217
1100-1116 45202
1118-1499 45202
Clayburn Cir 45240
Claymore Ter 45238
Claypole Ave 45204
Clayton Ave 45206
Clayton Dr 45244
Cleander Dr 45238
Clearbrook Dr 45229
Clearfield Ln 45240
Clearidge Ln 45247
Clearlake Dr 45247
Clearmeadow Ln 45251
Clearpoint Dr 45247
Clearview Ave
4500-4599 45205
5500-5599 45248
Clearwater Pl 45248
Clearwood Ct 45236
Cleinview Ave 45206
Clemmer Ave 45219
Clemray Dr 45231
Clemson Cir 45255
Cleneay Ave 45212
Clephane Ave 45227
Clepper Ln 45245
Clermont Ave 45212
N & S Clerose Cir 45205
Cleveland Ave
200-208 45217
210-499 45217
301-321 45217
304-364 45246
323-323 45217
800-999 45229
1700-1899 45212
Cleveland Ct 45229
Cleves Warsaw Pike
4800-5699 45238
5700-7299 45233
Clevesdale Dr 45238
N Cliff Ln 45220
W Cliff Ln 45220
Cliff St 45219
N Cliff Ter 45220
Cliff Laine Dr 45208
Cliff Ridge Ln 45213
Clifford Rd 45236
Cliffside Dr 45251
Clifftop Dr 45220
Clifton Ave
2501-2513 45219
2515-2599 45219
2600-4099 45220
4100-4299 45232
E Clifton Ave 45202
W Clifton Ave
1-199 45202
2000-2519 45219
2521-2599 45219
Clifton Colony Dr 45220
Clifton Crest Ter 45220
Clifton Hills Ave & Ter 45220
Clifton Ridge Dr 45220
Clinton St 45215
Clinton Springs Ave
1-599 45217
600-999 45229
Clinton Springs Ln 45217
Clio Ave 45230
Clippard Park 45251
N & S Clippinger Dr 45243
Cloister Ct 45208
Cloister Dr 45220
Close Ct 45208
Clough Hts 45245
Clough Ln 45245
Clough Pike
400-551 45244
552-1080 45245
1082-1098 45245
5200-8699 45244
Clough Ridge Dr 45230
Clover Dr 45245
Clover Ln 45224
Clover St 45230
Clover Crest Dr 45239
Clover Leaf Ln 45239
Cloverdale Ave 45246
Cloverfield Ln 45224
Cloverhill Ter 45238
Cloveridge Ct 45244
Clovernoll Dr 45231
Clovernook Ave 45231
Cloverton Ct 45240
Cloverview Ave 45231
Cloverwood Ct 45231
N & S Club Crest Ave 45209
Club View Dr 45209
Clybourn Pl 45219
Clydes Xing 45244
Clydesdale Dr 45231
Coachlite Way 45243
Coachman Ct 45238
Coachtrail Ln 45242
Coad Dr 45237
Cobblechase Ct 45251
Cobblestone Ct 45244
Cochise Ct 45215
Cody Pass 45215
Coffey St 45230
Coghill Ln 45239
Cohasset Dr 45255
Cohoon St 45208
Colbert Cir 45240
Coldbrook Ln 45255
Coldstream Dr 45255
Coldstream Woods Dr 45255
Cole Ave 45246
Coleen Dr 45251
Colerain Ave
1900-2699 45214
2700-3499 45225
3700-5499 45223
5501-5513 45239
5515-8499 45239
8500-8800 45251
8721-8721 45253
8801-10399 45251
8802-10398 45251
10400-12099 45252
Coleridge Ave 45213
Colette Ln 45224
Collegevue Pl 45224
Collegewood Ln 45231
Collins Ave
300-308 45202
310-499 45202
500-599 45206
Collinsdale Ave 45230
Collinspark Ct 45230
Collinwood Pl 45227
Colmar Ln 45237
Colonial Dr 45238
Colonial Ridge Ct 45212
Colony Dr 45205
Colorama Dr 45224
Colter Ave 45230
Colton Ln 45236
Columbard Ct 45255
Columbia Ave 45249
E Columbia Ave 45215
W Columbia Ave 45215
Columbia Pkwy
1800-2198 45202
2800-4699 45226
Columbine Ct 45231
Columbus Ave
1200-1399 45255
3600-3699 45208
Comet Ct 45231
Comet Dr 45244
Comfort St 45225
Commerce Blvd 45241
N Commerce Way 45246
N Commerce Park Dr 45215
Commercial Blvd 45245
Commodity Cir 45241
Commodore Ln 45251
Common Wealth Dr 45244
Commons Cir 45251
Commons Dr 45246
Commonwealth Dr 45224
Compton Rd
1-31 45216
32-98 45215
33-99 45216
100-522 45215
523-2799 45231
2800-3399 45251
Compton Hills Dr 45215
Compton Lake Dr 45231
Compton Ridge Dr 45215
Comstock Dr 45231
Conant St 45227
Conca St 45218
Concerto Dr 45241
Concord Ln 45241
Concord St 45206
Concord Glen Dr 45244
Concord Hills Cir, Ln & Pl 45243
Concordgreen Dr 45244
Concordia St 45206
Concordridge Dr 45244
Condor Dr 45251
Conestoga Ct 45241
Congress Ave
1-299 45226
700-841 45246
843-885 45246
866-866 45215
889-903 45215
905-927 45246
929-931 45246
932-956 45215
933-945 45246
958-960 45215
962-966 45215
965-967 45246
969-971 45246
973-985 45246
976-1008 45215
1010-1016 45215
1018-1098 45215
1065-1097 45246
1099-1101 45246
1103-1105 45246
1108-1110 45215
1112-1126 45215
1115-1125 45246
1130-1140 45246
1133-1147 45246
1135-1149 45215
1149-1167 45246
1151-1339 45215
1169-1215 45246
1341-1399 45215
Congress Run Rd 45215
Congresswood Ln 45224
Congreve Ave 45213
Conifer Ln 45247
Conina Dr 45233
Conklin Ave 45242
Conklin Rd 45242
Conklin St 45219
Conlan Ct 45230
Conley Rd 45245
Connecticut Ave & Ct 45224
Connie Ln
700-799 45245
6100-6199 45233
Conover St 45227
Conrad Dr 45231
Conrey Rd 45249
Conroy St 45214
Considine Ave
400-1199 45205
1200-1399 45204
Considine Ln 45205
Constance Ln 45231
Constitution Ct 45248
Constitution Dr 45215
Constitution Sq 45255
Container Pl 45246
Continental Dr 45246
Convent Ln 45208
W Convention Way 45202
Converse Dr 45240
Conway St 45227
Coogan Dr 45231
Cook Ave 45242
Cook St 45214
Cookie Ln 45238
Coolidge Ave
100-199 45246
1200-1399 45230
Coolwood Ct 45236
N Cooper Ave 45215
S Cooper Ave 45215
Cooper Ln 45242
Cooper Rd
2800-3399 45241
3400-4099 45241
4100-7999 45242
Cooper Spgs 45241
Cooper St
300-300 45215
302-399 45215
401-499 45215
1600-1699 45223
Cooper Woods Ct 45241
Cooperhill Dr 45241
Copelen St 45206
Copperfield Ct 45241
Copperfield Dr 45241
Copperfield Ln 45238
Copperglow Ct 45244
Copperleaf Ln 45230
Coppice Ln 45223
Cora Ave 45211
Coral Ave 45246
Coral Gables Rd 45248
Coral Park Dr 45211
Coralberry Ct 45230
Coralsea Dr 45230
Coran Dr 45255
Corbett Ave 45208
Corbett Dr 45219
Corbett Rd 45231
Corbin Dr 45208
Corbin St 45226
Corbin Park Ct 45226
Corbly Rd 45230
Corcoran Pl 45224
Cordova Ave 45239
Corine Ave 45242
Corinth Ave 45237
Corinthian Ct 45244
Cornavin Ct 45246
Cornelia Ave 45216
Cornell Pl 45220
Cornell Rd
3400-4817 45241
4201-4249 45241
4251-4799 45241
4818-7899 45242
4900-7099 45242
7900-8399 45249
Cornell Park Dr 45242
Cornell Woods Dr 45241
Cornish St 45227
Cornstalk Ln 45244
Cornwall Dr 45231
Corona Rd 45240
Coronado Ave 45238
Corporate Dr 45242
Corporate Park Dr 45242
Corporation Aly 45202
Corrine Ave 45238
Corry St 45219
Corsica Pl 45227
Cortelyou Ave & Pl 45213
Corvallis Ave 45237
Corwine St 45202
Cosby St 45223
Coshocton Ct 45233
Costello Ave 45211
Cotillion Dr 45231
Cottage Ct 45230
Cottage Pointe Ct, Dr & Pl 45247
Cottingham Dr 45241
Cottontail Ct 45239
Cottonwood Dr 45231
Councilrock Ln 45243
Country Club Dr 45245
Country Club Pl 45208
Country Mills Ln 45240
Country Park Dr 45251
Country Walk Dr 45248
Country Woods Ln 45248
Countryhills Dr 45233
Countrylake Dr 45233
Countrymeadow Ln 45233
Countryridge Ln 45233
Countryside Ct 45233
Countrytrace Ct 45233
Countryview Ter 45233
Courageous Cir 45252
Courier Ct 45238
E Court St 45202
W Court St
1-399 45202
400-899 45203
Courtland Ave 45212
Courtland Pl 45255
Courtropes Ln 45244
Cove Ct 45238
S Cove Dr 45233
Covedale Ave 45238
Coventry Ln 45240
Coventry Pl 45247
Coventry Woods Dr 45230
Covered Bridge Rd 45231
Covey Trce 45244
Coveyrun Ct S 45230
Covington Ave 45227
Cox Ln 45209
Coxbury Cir 45246
Coy St 45219
Coyote Ct 45241
Crabapple Ln 45208
Crabtree Ln 45243
Craft St 45232
Cragview Ct 45241
Craig Ave 45211
Craig Ct 45211
Craig Rd 45244
Craigland Ct & Ln 45230
Cranbrook Dr
2300-2699 45231
2700-3099 45251
Crane Ave 45207
Cranfield Dr 45251
Cranford Dr 45240
Cranwood Ct 45240
Crawford Ave 45223
Crawford St 45244
Creek Rd
3300-4166 45241
4167-4197 45241
4168-4198 45241
4199-4399 45241
4400-6899 45242
Creekhill Dr 45231
Creekscape Ln 45249
Creekside Dr 45242
Creekview Dr
3600-3799 45241
7200-7299 45247
Creekwood Ln 45237
Creekwood Sq 45246
Creighton Pl 45226
Crenshaw Ln 45240
Cresap Ave 45223
Crescent Ave 45215
Crescent Dr 45245

Crescentville Rd
  2501-2699 45241
  3055-3055 45235
E Crescentville Rd 45246
W Crescentville Rd 45246
Cresentview Ln 45248
Crest Cir 45208
E Crest Dr 45215
W Crest Dr 45215
Crest Rd
  1800-2199 45240
  2300-2699 45231
  2700-3599 45251
Crest Hill Ave 45237
Crest Hill Dr 45246
Crestbrook Dr 45231
Crestdale Ct 45236
Crestfield Ct 45249
Cresthaven Ct 45236
Crestland Ct
  10000-10199 45246
  10200-10399 45251
Crestline Ave 45205
Crestmont Dr 45215
Crestmont Ln 45220
Crestmoor Ln 45238
Crestnoll Ln 45211
Crestpoint Dr 45211
Crestridge Cir 45213
Crestview Ave 45213
Crestview Pl 45230
Crestview Ter 45230
Crestwind Cir 45242
Crestwood Ave 45208
Creswell Dr 45240
Crevelings Ln 45226
Crimson Ln 45239
Crinstead Ct 45243
Crisfield Dr 45245
Cristway Ct 45230
Crittenden Dr 45244
Crittwoods Ct 45244
Crocus Ln 45208
Cromwell Rd 45218
Crooked Stick Ct 45244
Crooked Stone Rd 45220
Crookshank Rd 45238
Crosier Ln 45242
Crosley Ave
  900-1099 45215
  4000-4099 45212
Crosley Farm Dr 45251
Crosley Field Ln 45214
Croslin St 45230
Cross Ln 45206
Cross St
  100-199 45215
  3700-3799 45211
  8800-8899 45242
Cross Ridge Trl 45251
Crossgate Ln 45236
Crossing Dr 45241
Crossing Pointe 45231
Crossings Dr 45246
Crosspointe Dr 45255
Croton Dr 45242
Crotty Ct 45255
Crowden Dr 45224
Crown Ave 45212
Crown Ct 45241
Crown St 45206
Crowne Point Ct, Dr &
Pl 45241
Crull St 45244
Crusader Dr 45251
Cryer Ave 45208
Crystal Ave 45242
Crystal Creek Dr 45245
Crystal Springs Rd 45227
Crystal View Ct 45241
Crystalhill Ct 45240
Culpepper Ct 45231
Culvert St 45202
Cumber St 45202
Cummings Farm Ln 45242
Cummins St 45225

Cunningham Rd
  2500-2999 45241
  9000-9899 45243
Curly Maple Sq 45246
Current Ln 45251
Currier Ln 45249
Curt Ln 45242
Curtis St 45206
Curzon Ave 45216
Custer Ave 45208
Cutter St 45203
Cyclorama Dr 45211
Cynthia Ct 45242
Cypress St 45206
Cypress Way 45212
Cypress Garden St 45220
Cypresspoint Ct 45245
Cypresspoint Ln 45249
Cypresswood Dr 45249
Dacey Ave 45209
Daffodil Ave 45242
Dahlgren St 45227
Dahlia Ave 45233
Dakota Ave 45229
Dalbren Ln 45231
Dale Ave 45238
Dale Rd
  1700-1999 45237
  2000-2199 45212
Dalehurst Dr 45211
Daleview Rd 45247
Dalewood Pl 45237
Dallas Ave 45239
Dallas Blvd 45231
Dalmellington Ct 45251
Dalton Ave
  500-1299 45203
  1300-1588 45214
  1589-1591 45234
  1590-2098 45214
  1593-1619 45214
  1621-1623 45234
  1623-1623 45250
  1625-2099 45214
  7700-8199 45236
Daly Rd
  6200-8199 45224
  8200-10099 45231
Dalzell St 45227
Dameron Ln 45244
Damon Rd 45218
Dana Ave
  900-1017 45229
  1019-1099 45229
  1401-1457 45207
  1459-2199 45207
  2200-2398 45208
  2201-2221 45207
Danbury Rd 45240
Dance Ct 45203
Dandridge St 45202
Dane Ave 45223
Daniel Ct 45244
E & W Daniels St 45219
Danielson Ave 45248
Danny Dr 45245
Danroth Ct 45239
Dante Ave 45213
Dantzler Dr 45215
Danvers Dr 45240
Danville Dr 45233
Daphne Ct 45240
Darbi Dew Ln 45251
Darby Ln 45233
Dargate Ln 45231
Darke Ct 45233
Darling Rd 45227
Darnell Ave 45236
Darrow Ave 45232
Dartmoor Ct 45236
Dartmouth Cir 45244
Dartmouth Dr
  3100-3399 45211
  4200-4299 45217
Darwin Ave 45211
Dauner Ave 45207

Dautel Ave 45211
Davenant Ave 45213
Davenport Ave 45204
Davey Ave 45224
David Ct 45215
David St 45214
Davids Way 45233
Davies Pl 45227
Davis Ave 45211
Davis Ct 45247
Davis Ln 45237
Davis Rd 45255
Davis St 45215
Davlin Ave 45230
Davoran Ave 45205
Dawes Ln 45230
Dawn Rd 45237
Dawson Ave 45223
Dawson Rd 45243
Day Ct 45238
Day Rd 45252
Daylight Ct 45251
Dayspring Ter 45218
Dayton St 45214
Daytona Ave 45211
De Armand Ave 45239
De Camp Ave 45216
De Forest Dr 45209
De Sales Ln 45206
De Votie Ave
  300-399 45220
  500-699 45225
Deaconsbench Ct 45244
Dean Ct 45230
Dean Dr 45246
Deanview Dr 45224
Dearborn Ave 45236
Dearborn Ct 45244
Dearwester Dr 45236
Deauville Rd 45240
Debbe Ln 45229
Debby Carol Dr 45245
Deblin Dr 45239
Debolt Rd 45244
Debonair Ct 45237
Debonhill Ct 45238
Deborah Ln 45239
Debreck Ave 45211
Decatur Ct 45240
December Ct 45251
Decima St 45242
Deckebach Ave 45220
Dee St 45243
Deephaven Dr 45238
Deeprun Ln 45243
Deepwood Ln 45245
Deepwoods Ln 45208
Deer Path 45243
Deer Chase Dr 45240
Deer Crossing Ln 45243
Deer Meadow Dr 45240
Deer Park Ave 45236
Deer Run Ln 45233
Deercove Ct 45211
Deercreek Ln 45249
Deercross Pkwy 45236
Deerfield Blvd 45245
Deerfield Rd 45242
Deerfield St 45206
Deerhaven Dr 45244
Deerhill Ln 45218
Deerhollow Ln 45252
Deerhorn Dr 45240
Deeridge Ln 45247
Deerlake Ct 45247
Deerpath Ln 45248
Deershadow Ln 45242
Deervalley Ct 45247
Deervalley Dr 45245
Deerview Ct 45230
Deerway Dr 45236
Defender Dr 45252
Dehaviland Dr 45231
Del Monte Pl 45205
Delaney St 45223
Delas Cv 45244

Delaware Ave
  1900-2099 45212
  7100-7299 45236
Delaware Ridge Ln 45226
Delehanty Ct 45238
Delhi Ave
  600-4199 45204
  4200-5699 45238
Delhi Rd 45233
Delhill Dr 45238
Delight Dr 45238
Deliquia Dr & Pl 45230
Dell Ter 45230
Dellbrook Ct 45241
Dellers Glen Dr 45238
Dellway St 45229
Delmar Ave
  100-599 45217
  3000-3099 45213
  3800-3999 45211
Delmar Ct 45217
Delmont Dr 45245
Delphos Ave 45213
Delridge Dr 45205
S Delridge Dr 45238
Delryan Dr 45238
Delta Ave
  200-899 45226
  1000-3499 45208
Delta Ter 45226
Demar Rd 45243
Demarc Ct 45248
Dempsey St 45225
Dena Ln 45237
Denallen Dr 45255
Denfield Ct 45255
Dengail Dr 45238
Denham St 45225
Denier Pl 45224
Denmark Dr 45244
Dennis St 45219
Dennler Ln 45247
Denny Pl 45227
Dent Rd 45248
Dent Xing 45247
Depalma Dr 45251
Depot Ln 45246
Depot St 45204
Derby Ave 45232
Derby Dr 45245
Derbyday Ct 45249
Deronda St 45219
Derrick Turnbow Ave 45214
Desertgold Dr 45247
Deshler Dr 45251
Desmond St 45227
Desoto Dr 45231
Destiny Ct 45237
Detzel Pl 45219
Devils Backbone Rd 45233
Devon Ct 45248
Devonshire Dr 45226
Devonwood Dr 45224
Dewdrop Cir 45240
Dewey Ave 45205
Dewhill Ln 45251
Dewitt Ct & St 45218
Dexter Ave
  400-499 45215
  1600-1999 45206
Dexter Pl 45206
Dexter Park Blvd 45241
Dhonau St 45223
Diamondview Dr 45241
Diane Dr 45245
Dianna Dr 45239
Dick St 45220
Dickens Ave 45213
Dickens Dr 45241
Dickinson Ave 45211
Dicks Aly 45223
Dickson Ave 45229
Dieckman Ln 45245
Diehl Ave 45236
Diehl Rd 45211
Digby Ave 45220

Dillon Ave 45208
Dillward Ave 45216
Dimmick Ave 45246
Dina Ave & Ter 45211
Dinsmore Dr 45240
Diplomat Dr 45215
Dirheim Ave 45211
Dirr St 45223
Disney St 45209
Diston Ln 45246
Dix St 45206
Dixie Ave 45216
Dixie Ct 45215
Dixie Dr 45245
Dixmont Ave 45207
Dixmyth Ave 45220
N & S Dixon Cir 45224
Doberrer Ave 45232
Dobson Ct 45215
Dodgeon Ct 45231
Doe Run Ct 45240
Doe Run Dr 45245
Doepke Ln 45231
Doerger Ln 45212
Doeview Ct 45230
Dog Leg Ct 45245
Dog Trot Rd 45248
Dogwood Ln 45213
Dolomar Dr 45239
Dolphin Dr 45239
Dominion Cir 45249
Don Ln 45238
Don Rich Ct 45237
Donahue St 45219
Donald St 45213
Donaldson Pl 45223
Donata Dr 45251
Donegal Dr 45236
Dones Ave 45243
Donham Ave 45226
Donjoy Dr 45242
Donlar Ave 45238
Donna Ln 45236
Donnington Ln 45244
Donnybrook Ln 45251
Donora Ln 45240
Donovan Ct 45249
Doolittle Ln 45230
Doon Ave 45213
Dora St 45227
Dorchester Ave 45219
Dordine Ln 45231
Doresa Pl 45238
Dorgene Ln 45244
Dorian Dr 45215
Dorideld Ave 45227
Dorino Pl 45215
Dorothy Ct 45215
Dorothy Ln 45205
Dorsey St 45202
Dot Dr 45213
Dottie Ct 45215
Dougherty Hill Rd 45230
Doughman Ct 45242
Douglas St 45215
Douglas Ter 45212
Douglas Walk 45215
Douglas Fir Ct 45247
Dove St 45245
Dovehill Ln 45248
Dover St 45206
Dovetail Ln 45223
Dowlin Dr 45241
Downing Dr 45208
Dragon Way 45227
Drake Ave 45209
Drake Rd 45243
Drake St 45244
Drakewood Dr 45209
Draper St 45214
Dreier Ln 45224
Dreman Ave 45223
Dresden Ct 45238
Drew Ave 45248
Drewry Farm Ln 45243
Drex Ave 45212

Drexel Ln 45246
Drexel Pl 45229
Driftwood Cir 45239
Driftwood Ln 45241
Drott Ave 45205
Droxford Ct 45246
Drummond St 45218
Drummore Ln 45245
Druwood Ln 45243
Dry Ridge Rd 45252
Dry Run View Ln 45244
Dryden Ave 45213
Dryhorse Ct 45233
Dublin Ct 45236
Duchess Ln 45255
Duck Creek Ct 45227
Duck Creek Rd
  1700-2399 45207
  2400-2799 45212
  2801-2999 45212
  3400-3499 45213
  3500-5299 45227
Dudley Walk 45214
Duebber Dr 45238
Duet Ln 45239
Duke St 45220
Duluth Ave 45220
Dumont St 45226
Dunaway Ave 45211
Dunaway Ct 45238
Duncan Ave 45208
Dundalk Ct 45236
Dundas Dr 45238
Dundee Ct 45231
Duneden Ave 45236
Dunes Ct 45245
Dunham Ln & Way 45238
Dunkirk St 45220
Dunlap Rd 45252
Dunlap St 45214
Dunleith Ct 45243
Dunloe Ave 45213
Dunn Ct 45238
Dunn Rd 45230
Dunn St 45215
Dunning Pl 45227
Dunore Rd 45220
Dunraven Dr 45251
Dunview Ct 45255
Dunwoodie Dr 45230
Duramed Rd 45213
Durban Dr 45220
Durham St 45232
Durhams Xing 45245
Durrell Ave
  300-399 45215
  3000-3199 45207
Dury Ave 45229
Dutch Colony Dr 45232
Dutchess Ln 45240
Duvall Pl 45231
Duxbury Ct 45255
Dyer Ave 45230
Eagle Ct 45237
Eagle Creek Rd 45247
Eagle Ridge Dr 45243
Eaglepoint Ct 45238
Eagles Lndg 45245
Eagles Vw 45244
Eagles Lake Ct & Dr 45248
Eagles Walk Ln 45255
Eaglescout Ct 45249
Eaglesknoll Ct 45255
Eaglesnest Dr S 45248
Eaglesridge Ln 45230
Eaglesview Ct 45230
Eagleswatch Ct 45230
Eagleview Way 45215
Earl Rd 45239
Earls Court Vw 45226
Earlwood Ct 45238
Earnshaw Ave 45219
Eashalia Rd 45233
Eashante Ave 45230
East Ave 45236

East St
  1400-1499 45215
  3700-3999 45227
East Way 45224
Eastborne Rd 45255
Eastdale Dr 45255
Eastern Ave
  3500-4795 45226
  4796-5099 45208
Eastern Hills Ln 45209
Eastgate Blvd 45245
Eastgate Dr 45231
Eastgate North Dr 45245
Eastgate South Dr 45245
Eastgate Square Dr 45245
Easthill Ave 45208
Eastknoll Ct 45239
Eastland Ter 45230
Eastlawn Dr 45237
Eastridge Ln 45247
Eastside Ave 45208
Eastwick Ct & Dr 45246
Eastwind Ct 45230
E & W Eastwood Cir &
Dr 45227
Eaton Ln 45229
Eatondale Dr 45204
Ebenezer Rd
  1000-3099 45233
  3100-4999 45248
Ebersole Ave 45227
Ebony Ln 45224
Ebro Ct 45231
Echo Ln 45230
Eclipse Dr 45231
Edalbert Dr 45239
Eddy Dr 45244
Eddystone Dr 45251
Eden Ave
  2500-2556 45219
  2558-3199 45219
  3500-3599 45229
Eden Park Dr 45202
Eden Place Dr 45247
Eden Ridge Dr 45247
Edenton Ln 45242
Edfel Way 45238
Edgar St 45204
Edge Hill Pl 45229
Edgebrook Dr 45248
Edgecliff Pl, Pt & Rd 45206
Edgemere Ct 45244
Edgemont Rd 45237
Edger Dr 45239
Edgetree Ln 45238
Edgeview Dr 45213
Edgewater Dr 45240
N Edgewood Ave 45232
Edgewood Dr 45211
Edgewood Ln 45241
Edgeworth Ct 45240
Edinburgh Dr 45245
Edinburgh Ln 45246
Edington Ct & Dr 45249
Edison Dr 45216
Edith Ave 45227
Edith St 45244
Edmar Ct 45239
Edmondson Rd 45209
Edmunds St 45219
Edna Ave 45223
Edroy Ct 45209
Edvera Ln 45239
Edwards Ave 45242
Edwards Rd
  900-3713 45208
  3714-4199 45209
  3800-4000 45244
  4002-4098 45244
Edwilla Dr 45245
Edwin Ave 45204
Edwood Ave 45224
Egan Ct 45229
Egan Ln 45215
Egan Hills Dr 45229
Egbert Ave 45220

Eggerding Dr 45215
Eggers Pl 45211
Eggleston Ave 45202
Eglington Ct 45255
Ehrling Rd 45227
Ehrman Ave 45220
Eider Dr 45246
Eileen Dr 45209
Eiler Ln 45239
Elaine Cir 45239
Elam St 45225
Elberon Ave
300-1699 45205
2300-2499 45204
Elbow Dr 45252
Elbrook Ave 45237
Elco St 45233
Elda Ln 45224
Elder St 45227
W Elder St 45202
Elderberry Ct 45239
Elderwood Dr 45255
Eldora Dr 45236
Eldorado Ave 45230
Eleanor Pl 45219
Eleanor St 45227
Eleck Pl 45243
Eliza St 45214
Elizabeth Pl
1500-1699 45237
4600-4799 45242
Elizabeth St
1-199 45215
400-799 45203
4500-4599 45242
7200-8099 45231
Elizabeths Oak Ct 45248
Elk Ave 45246
Elkgrove Ct 45251
Elkhorn Dr 45251
Elkridge Dr 45240
Elkton Pl 45224
Elkwater Ct 45248
Elkwood Dr 45240
Ella St 45223
Elland Ave 45229
Ellen Ave 45239
Ellen Dr 45255
Ellenwoods Dr 45249
Ellery Dr 45245
Ellington Ct 45249
Elliott Ave 45215
Ellis Ave 45245
Ellis St 45223
Ellison Ave 45226
Elljay Dr 45241
Ellman Ave 45242
Ellmarie Dr 45227
Ellson Rd 45245
Elm Ave
1-299 45215
1800-2199 45212
3900-3999 45236
Elm Ct 45215
Elm Dr 45255
Elm Ln 45215
Elm St
100-324 45215
300-312 45202
314-322 45202
325-399 45215
326-398 45215
405-410 45238
411-411 45202
412-414 45238
413-419 45238
435-597 45202
599-2099 45202
6600-7499 45227
Elm Park Dr 45216
Elm Ridge Ct 45244
Elm Tree Ct 45244
Elm View Pl 45216
Elm Wood Dr 45245
Elmcrest Ln 45242
Elmdale Dr 45230
Elmgrove Cir 45240
Elmhill Ct 45248
Elmhurst Ave & Pl 45208
Elmont Dr 45245
Elmore Ct & St 45223
Elmtree Ave 45231
Elmwood Ave 45216
Elsie Ave 45224
Elsinboro Dr 45226
Elsinore Ave & Pl 45202
Elsmere Ave
3700-4299 45212
4400-4599 45242
Elstun Rd 45230
Elwynne Dr 45236
Elysian Pl 45219
Embassy Dr 45240
Embrett Ct 45238
Emeantat Ave 45237
Emerald Ave 45242
Emerald Rdg 45211
Emerald Walk 45211
Emerald Glade Ln 45255
Emerald Lakes Dr 45211
Emerson Ave 45239
Emery Ln 45227
Emilys Oak Ct 45248
Emma Pl 45223
Emma Belle Pl 45244
Emming St 45219
Empire Ct 45231
Empress Ave 45226
Endeavor Dr 45252
Endicott St 45218
Endor Ct 45240
Endovalley Dr 45244
Enfield St 45218
Englewood Ave 45237
English Dr 45244
English Creek Dr 45245
English Garden Ln 45230
Enright Ave 45205
Enslin St 45225
Enterprise Cir 45252
Enterprise Dr 45241
Enterprise Park Dr 45241
Enyart Ave 45209
Epley Ln 45247
Eppert Walk 45230
Epworth Ave 45211
E Epworth Ave 45232
Epworth Ct 45238
Equine Ln 45244
Erickson Ct 45244
Erie Ave
1-99 45246
2400-3999 45208
4000-6499 45227
Erie Ct 45227
Erie Station Ln 45227
Erin Dr 45251
Erindale Dr 45238
Erkenbrecher Ave
1-99 45220
100-209 45215
203-213 45229
211-211 45215
215-499 45229
Erlene Dr 45238
Ernst St 45204
Errun Ln 45217
Erskine Rd 45242
Escalon St 45216
Esmonde St 45214
Essex Pl 45206
Estate Ct 45224
Estate Ridge Dr 45244
Este Ave 45232
Estecreek Rd 45232
Estelle St 45219
Estermarie Dr 45236
Estes Pl 45229
Esther Dr 45213
Esther Ln 45243
Eswin St 45218
Ethan Ave 45225
Etoncross Ct 45244
Euclid Ave
1-99 45215
2500-3099 45219
3300-3399 45220
6400-8099 45243
Euclid Rd 45236
Eugenie Ln 45211
Eula Ave 45248
Eureka Ter 45219
Eustis Ct 45236
Eustis Farm Ln 45243
Evangeline Rd 45240
Evanor Ln 45244
Evans St
600-1099 45204
7800-12199 45249
Evanston Ave 45207
Evanswood Pl 45220
Evelyn Dr 45230
Evelyn Rd 45247
Evencrest Dr 45231
Evendale Dr 45241
Evendale Commons
Dr 45241
Evening Whisper Way 45244
Eveningstar Ln 45220
Everett Ave 45211
Everglade Pl 45214
Evergreen Ave 45211
Evergreen Cir 45215
Evergreen Ct 45215
Evergreen Ridge Dr 45215
Evers St 45205
Eversole Rd 45230
Everson Ave 45209
Ewald Pl 45211
Executive Ct 45244
Executive Park Dr 45241
Exmoor Dr 45240
Exon Ave 45241
Eyrich Rd 45248
Ezzard Charles Dr
300-1298 45214
401-899 45203
F V Geier Dr 45209
Faber Ave 45211
Faehr Ave 45214
Fair Ln 45227
Fair Acres Dr & Ln 45213
Fair Oaks Ave, Dr &
Ln 45237
Fairbanks Ave
1-499 45204
500-1299 45205
Fairborn Rd 45240
Faircrest Ct & Dr 45224
Fairdale Ct 45238
Fairfax Ave 45207
Fairfield Ave
2900-3099 45206
3100-3399 45207
Fairglen Dr 45251
Fairgreen Dr 45238
Fairgrove Ct 45244
Fairhaven Ln 45237
Fairhill Dr 45239
Fairhope Ct 45224
Fairhurst Ave 45213
Fairmount Ave 45214
Fairpark Ave 45216
Fairsprings Ct 45246
Fairview Ave
2300-2599 45219
4800-4999 45242
Fairview Pl 45219
Fairway Dr
700-899 45245
6100-6199 45212
Fairway Ln 45230
Fairway View Ln 45233
Fairwayglen Dr 45248
Fairways Blvd 45245
Fairwood Rd 45239
Faith Dr 45237
Faith Way 45240
Falcon Ln 45218
Falconbridge Dr 45238
Fallbrook Ln 45240
Fallen Br 45241
Fallentree Ln 45236
Falling Brk 45241
Falling Waters Ln 45241
Fallshill Cir 45231
Fallsington Ct 45242
Fallson Ct 45242
Fallsridge Ct 45231
Fallstone Dr 45246
Falmouth Dr 45231
Fancycab Ct 45231
Far Hills Dr 45208
Faraday Rd 45223
Farcrest Ct 45247
Fardale Dr 45247
Farhaven Dr 45247
Farlenta St 45214
Farlook Dr 45247
Farm Acres Dr 45237
Farm Hill Ct 45231
Farm House Ln 45238
Farmbrook Dr 45230
N & S Farmcrest Dr 45213
Farmdale Rd 45237
Farmedge Ln 45231
Farmington Rd 45240
Farmsworth Ct 45255
Farnham Ct 45240
Farragut Rd 45218
Farrell Ct 45233
Farrell Dr 45211
Farrow Dr 45245
Farview Ln 45247
Farwick Ct 45249
Fashion Ave 45238
Faske Dr 45231
Fath Ct 45239
Fawn Cir 45245
Fawn Knoll Ct 45247
Fawn Lake Ct 45247
Fawn Wood Ln 45247
Fawncreek Dr 45249
Fawnhill Ln 45205
Fawnmeadow Ln
7500-7699 45241
8600-8900 45242
8902-8998 45242
Fawnridge Ct 45239
Fawnrun Ct & Dr 45241
Fawnvista Ln 45246
Faxon Ct 45215
Fay Ln 45251
Faycrest Dr 45238
Fayebanks Ln 45245
Fayhill Dr 45238
Faymeadow Ct 45238
Fayridge Ct 45238
Faysel Dr 45233
Fayvista Dr 45238
Faywood Dr 45238
Fdr Walk 45218
Fearman Ave 45211
February Dr 45239
Federal Dr 45248
Feemster St 45226
Fehl Ln 45230
Fehr Rd 45238
Feist Dr 45238
Feist Manor Dr 45238
Feldkamp Ave 45211
Feldman Ave 45212
Felecia Dr 45238
Felicity Dr & Pl 45211
Fellsmere Ln 45240
Feltz Ave 45211
Fenchurch Ct 45230
Fenmore Dr 45237
Fenton Ave
1300-1399 45215
2500-2699 45211
Fenwick Ave 45212
Ferdinand Pl 45209
Fergus St 45223
Ferguson Dr 45245
Ferguson Pl 45238
Ferguson Rd
2000-3099 45238
3100-3199 45211
Fern Ct 45244
Fernbank Ave 45233
Fernbrook Ct 45231
Ferncrest Ct 45211
Ferncroft Dr 45211
Ferndale Ave 45216
Fernhaven Ct 45251
Fernhill Dr 45241
Fernland Ave 45204
Fernside Pl 45207
Fernview Ave & Ct 45212
Fernwell Dr 45231
Fernwood Dr
4100-4199 45245
7500-7599 45237
Fernwood St 45206
Ferrars Ct 45217
Festive Ct
4400-4499 45245
7900-7999 45236
Fiddlers Green Rd 45248
Fiddlers Ridge Dr 45248
Fiddlers Trail Dr 45248
Fidelis Dr 45242
Field Ln
1-99 45208
3800-3899 45255
Fieldcrest Ct 45231
Fieldcrest Dr 45211
Fieldglen Ct 45231
Fieldhouse Way 45227
Fielding St 45209
Fields Ertel Rd
4237-4267 45241
4269-4699 45241
4522-4716 45241
4700-5354 45249
4701-7699 45241
4718-4876 45241
4878-6586 45241
5400-5404 45241
5406-5520 45249
5560-5712 45241
5714-5714 45249
5726-5732 45241
5770-5776 45249
5780-5798 45241
5836-5872 45249
5890-5890 45241
5892-6076 45249
6080-6298 45241
6336-6606 45249
6620-7298 45241
7700-9499 45249
Fieldside Dr 45244
Fieldsted Dr 45249
Fieldstone Ct 45241
Fiesta Ct 45240
Filson Pl 45202
Filview Cir 45248
Findlater Ct 45230
Findlay St
1-299 45202
300-1299 45214
Finley Ln 45242
Finnegan Ln 45244
Finney Trl
700-999 45224
4400-4599 45244
Finsbury Ct 45230
Fireside Dr 45255
Firestone Ave 45215
Firethorn Ct 45242
Firewood Dr 45215
Firshade Ter 45239
Firtree Ct 45223
Fischer Ave 45217
Fischer Ln
900-999 45231
4300-4399 45244
Fischer Pl
900-999 45217
2800-2999 45211
Fisher St 45255
Fishwick Dr 45216
Fisk Ave 45205
Fitchburg Ln 45240
Fithian St 45204
Fitzpatrick St 45204
Fitzwalter Ct 45230
Flagler Ln 45240
Flagstaff Dr 45215
Flagstone Ct 45239
Flamingo Ln 45239
Flanders Ln 45218
Flanigan Ct 45239
Flat Top Dr 45251
Flatt Ter 45232
Flaxen Ct 45244
Fleet St 45226
Fleetwood Ave 45211
Flembrook Ct 45231
Fleming Rd
1-399 45215
400-448 45231
401-449 45231
450-799 45231
Fleming St 45206
Flemington Dr 45231
Flemridge Ct 45231
Flick Rd 45247
Flint St 45214
Flintlock Dr
1000-1099 45231
4700-4899 45244
Flintpoint Way 45227
Flintshire Ct 45230
Flomar Ct 45233
Flora Ave 45231
Flora St
300-499 45215
2200-2399 45219
Floral Ave
3700-4799 45212
9200-9499 45242
Floral Run Ct 45239
Florence Ave
2000-2012 45202
2013-2019 45206
2014-2020 45202
2021-2399 45206
3500-3599 45211
3800-3999 45248
5000-6299 45242
5100-5999 45242
Florida Ave 45223
Floridale Ln 45239
Flower Ave 45205
Flowerwood Ct 45230
Flyer Dr 45248
Fogle Ave 45224
Folchi Dr 45224
Foley Rd 45238
Folkstone Dr 45240
Follett Ave 45223
Fondulac Dr 45231
Fontaine Ct 45236
Fontainebleau Ter 45231
Foraker Ave
900-1299 45206
2000-2099 45212
Foran Dr 45238
Forbes Rd 45233
Forbus St 45214
Ford Cir 45227
Ford St 45223
Fordham Ct 45255
N Fordham Pl 45213
S Fordham Pl 45213
W Fordham Pl 45213
Fordon Ct 45244
Foremark Dr 45241
Forest Ave
8-12 45220
14-126 45220
15-17 45215
19-340 45215
128-166 45220
201-201 45229
203-699 45229
800-999 45246
3800-5099 45212
7300-7599 45231
10100-10199 45215
Forest Ct
1200-1299 45215
3700-3799 45211
Forest Pl 45246
Forest Rd 45255
Forest Trl 45244
Forest Acres Dr 45255
Forest Hill Dr 45208
Forest Hill Ln 45227
Forest Meadows Ct 45244
Forest Park Dr 45229
Forest Ridge Ct 45244
Forest Valley Dr 45247
Forest View Ct & Ln 45233
Forestcrest Way 45244
Forestdale Dr 45240
Forester Dr 45240
Forestlake Dr 45244
Forestoak Ct 45208
Forestpine Dr 45255
Forestway Ln 45230
Forestwood Ct 45244
Forestwood Dr 45216
Forfeit Run Rd 45247
E Fork Ave 45227
W Fork Rd
1500-1999 45223
2000-3599 45211
3600-6599 45247
Forrer St 45209
E Forrer St 45215
W Forrer St 45215
Forsythia Dr 45245
Fort Lee Pkwy 45244
Fort View Pl 45202
Forthmann Pl 45211
Fortney Ln 45241
Fortune Ave 45219
Fosdick St 45219
Fossway Ct 45230
Foster Ave 45230
Foster St 45202
Foulke St 45220
E Fountain Ave 45246
W Fountain Ave 45246
Fountain Ct 45245
Fountain Square Plz 45202
Four Worlds Dr 45231
Fourson Dr 45233
Fourtowers Dr 45238
Fowler Ave 45243
Fowler St 45206
Fox Ln 45223
Fox Rd 45239
Fox Rdg 45248
Fox St 45219
Fox Creek Ln 45245
Fox Cub Ln 45243
Fox Den Ln 45244
Fox Hill Ln 45236
Fox Hollow Dr 45241
Fox Hollow Ln 45243
Fox Ridge Ct 45247
Fox Run Dr 45236
Fox Run Trl 45255
Fox Trail Cir 45245
Fox Trail Ln 45255
Fox Trails Way 45233
Foxboro Ct 45236
Foxchase Ln 45243
Foxcove Ct 45211
Foxcreek Ln 45233
Foxcroft Dr 45231
Foxdale Ct 45243
Foxgate Ln 45243
Foxglove Ct 45245
Foxglove Ln 45239
Foxhall Ct 45219
Foxhollow Dr 45255
Foxhunter Ln 45242
Foxknoll Ct 45230

Foxrun Ct 45239
Foxtail Ln 45248
Foxvalley Ct 45230
Foxview Dr 45230
Foxwood Dr 45231
Foxworth Ln 45218
Fralisto Rd 45243
Framingham Dr 45240
Frances Ave 45211
Francis Ave
4100-4199 45205
4600-4799 45242
Francis Ln 45206
Francis Xavier Way 45207
Francisco St 45206
Francisridge Dr 45238
Francisvalley Ct 45238
Francisview Dr 45238
Frane Ln 45236
Franklin Ave
1100-1599 45237
4200-4999 45212
N & S Fred Shuttlesworth Cir 45229
Freddie Dr 45205
Frederick Ave 45223
Fredericksburg Ct 45227
Fredonia Ave 45229
E Freedom Way 45202
Freeland Ave 45208
Freeman Ave
500-999 45203
1600-2162 45214
2164-2198 45214
Freestone Ct 45240
Freightliner Dr 45241
Fremantle Dr 45240
French Park Pl 45237
Fresno Rd 45240
Friartuck Ln 45230
Frick Ct 45246
Fricke Rd 45225
Frintz St 45202
Frogdan Ct 45248
Frolic Dr 45236
Frondorf Ave 45211
Front St 45241
Frontenac Ave 45236
Frontier Ct 45240
Froome Ave 45232
Frost Ct 45231
Fruit Hill Ln 45230
Fuhrman Rd 45215
Fulbourne Dr 45231
Fuller St 45202
Fullerton Dr 45240
Fulsher Ln 45243
Fulton Ave 45206
Fulton Grove Rd 45245
Funston Ln 45218
Fyffe Ave 45211
Gable Glen Ln 45249
Gablefield Ct 45255
Gables Ct 45238
Gabriel Ave 45204
Gadwell Dr 45246
Gaff Ave 45206
Gaffney Pl 45240
Gage St 45219
Gahl Ter 45215
Gail Dr 45236
Gailynn Dr 45211
Gaines Rd 45247
Gainsborough Ln 45230
Galaxy Ct 45224
Galaxy Ln 45244
E Galbraith Rd
1-253 45216
255-299 45216
300-2099 45215
2100-3020 45237
3021-6899 45236
6900-7699 45243
W Galbraith Rd
1-199 45216
200-699 45215
700-1599 45231
1600-3599 45239
3600-4199 45247
W Galbraith Pointe Ln 45231
Galecrest Dr 45231
Galion Ln 45246
Gallahad Ct 45240
Gallatin Ct 45240
Gallia Dr 45233
Galloway Ct 45240
Galsworthy Ct 45240
Galvin Ave 45204
Gambier Cir 45218
Gamble Ave 45211
Gamma Ct 45231
Gammwell Dr 45230
Gander Dr 45238
Gano Aly 45202
Gano Ave 45220
Gantzfield Ct 45241
Gapstow Brg 45231
Garden Cir 45215
Garden Ln 45237
Garden Pl
1-99 45208
1400-1499 45246
Garden Rd 45236
Garden St 45214
Garden View Ct 45247
Gardenhill Ln 45232
Gardenia Ln 45239
Gardenlake Ct 45233
Gardenview Ln 45232
Gardenwood Ct 45231
Gardner Ave 45236
Gardner Ln 45245
Gareth Ln 45241
Garfield Ave
100-199 45246
2100-2199 45224
Garfield Pl 45202
Garland Ave 45209
Garmar Ln 45248
Garnoa Dr 45231
Garrard Ave 45225
Garrison Dr 45231
Gary Ct 45248
Gaskins Rd 45245
Gassaway Rd 45226
Gate St 45211
Gateclub Dr 45241
W Gatehouse Dr E 45215
Gateway Dr 45242
Gatewood Dr 45245
Gatewood Ln 45236
E Gatewood Ln 45236
Gayheart Ct 45239
Gaylord Dr 45240
Gayway Ct 45239
Gazelle Ct 45239
Gebert St 45215
Gehrum Ln 45238
Geiger St 45225
Gellenbeck St 45205
Genenbill Dr 45238
Genessee St 45214
Geneva Rd 45240
Genevaview St 45214
Gennie Ln 45244
Genoma Dr 45215
N & S Gensen Loop 45245
Georgeann Ln 45245
Georges Way 45233
Georgetown Ct 45224
Georgetown Rd 45236
Georgia Ave 45223
Georgia Ct 45223
Georgia Ln 45215
Georgianna Dr 45239
Gerald Ct 45245
Geraldine Dr 45239
Gerard St 45219
Gerdsen Dr 45236
Geringer St 45223
Gerity Ct 45240
Germania St 45227
Gerold Dr 45238
Gertrude Ln 45231
Gertrude Rose Ln 45238
Gest St
1-1530 45203
1531-2399 45204
Gholson Ave 45229
Gibralter Dr 45251
Gideon Ln 45249
Giffindale Dr 45239
Gila Dr 45251
Gilbert Ave
400-1899 45202
1901-2055 45202
2000-2054 45206
2056-3115 45206
3116-3299 45207
6900-6999 45239
Gilchrest Ct 45244
Gilcrest Ln 45238
Giles Ct 45238
Gilligan Ave 45233
Gilman Ave 45219
Gilmore Ave 45209
Gilna Ct 45211
Gilpin Ave 45206
Gilsey Ave 45205
Ginger Ln & Way 45244
Ginnala Ct 45243
Girard Ave 45213
Given Rd 45243
Giverny Blvd 45241
Glade Ave 45230
Gladstone Ave 45202
Gladys Ave 45224
Glasgow Dr 45240
Glastonbury Ct 45248
Glen Aly 45246
Glen Ave 45213
N Glen Rd 45248
Glen Acres Dr 45237
Glen Armand Ave 45223
Glen Cove Ct 45238
Glen Creek Dr 45238
Glen Eagle Ct 45238
Glen Eden Ln 45244
Glen Edge Ln 45213
Glen Este Pl 45217
Glen Este Withamsville Rd 45245
Glen Lyon Ave 45229
Glen Meadow Ct 45246
Glen Oaks Dr 45238
Glen Parker Ave 45223
Glenaire Dr 45251
Glenbar Ct 45236
Glenbrook Ct 45224
Glenburney Ct 45236
Glencary Ct 45248
Glencoe Pl 45219
Glencrest Ct 45251
Glencross Ave 45217
Glencrossing Way 45238
Glendale Ave 45246
Glendale Rd 45215
Glendale St 45216
Glendale Milford Rd
1-1999 45215
2400-4099 45241
4100-4799 45242
Glendon Pl 45237
Glendora Ave
2600-3099 45219
3200-3299 45220
Gleneagles Cir 45245
Gleneagles Ct 45233
Glenellyn Dr 45236
Glenfalls Ct 45246
Glenfarm Ct 45236
Glenfield Ct 45238
Glengariff Dr 45230
Glengary Ln 45236
Glengate Ln 45212
Glengyle Ave 45208
Glenhaven Rd 45238
Glenhills Way 45238
Glenhurst Pl 45209
Glenknoll Ct 45251
Glenmary Ave 45220
Glenmeadow Ln 45237
Glenmill Ct 45249
Glenmont Ln 45248
Glenmore Ave
3000-3099 45238
3100-3999 45211
Glenna Dr 45238
Glenorchard Dr 45237
Glenover Dr 45236
Glenridge Dr 45245
Glenridge Pl 45217
Glenrock Dr 45231
Glenrose Ave 45215
Glenrose Ln 45244
Glenroy Ave 45238
Glensford Ct 45246
Glenshade Ave & Ct 45227
Glensharon Rd 45246
Glenshire Ave 45226
Glenside Ave 45212
Glensprings Dr 45246
Glenview Ave 45224
Glenview Pl 45205
Glenway Ave
600-699 45215
2300-3299 45204
3300-4599 45205
4163-4169 45236
4171-4351 45236
4353-4353 45236
4600-5999 45238
6000-6614 45211
6616-6698 45211
Glenwood Ave
1-399 45217
400-1099 45229
Glenwood Pl 45229
Globe Ave 45212
Glohaven Ct 45247
Gloria Ave 45231
Gloria Dr 45239
Gloss Ave 45213
Glow Ct 45238
Glynn Ct 45233
Goal Post Ln 45244
Gobel Ave & Ct 45211
Goda Ave 45211
Goethe St 45202
Goetz Aly 45202
Goff Ter 45243
Gold Dust Dr 45247
Goldcoast Dr 45249
Goldcrest Dr 45238
Golden Ave & Holw 45226
Golden Hill Dr 45241
Goldengate Dr 45244
Goldenrod Dr 45239
Goldrush Ct 45211
Golf Dr 45239
Golf Club Ln 45245
Golfway Dr 45239
Gondola St 45241
Good News Ln 45252
Good Samaritan Dr 45247
Goodfield Ct 45240
Goodhue Cir 45240
Goodman Ave
1500-1599 45224
1600-1999 45239
Goodman St 45219
Goodrich Ln 45233
Gordon St 45223
Gorham Dr 45245
Gorman Ln 45215
Gorman Heritage Farm Ln 45241
Gosling Rd 45252
Goss Rd 45229
Gotham Pl 45202
Governor Ter 45215
Governors Way 45249
Governors Hill Dr 45249
Grace Ave
1200-3499 45208
3900-3999 45211
5700-6820 45227
6700-6720 45236
6722-6840 45236
6822-7098 45227
6825-6843 45239
6828-6898 45239
6900-6999 45239
6901-7099 45227
Graceland Ave 45237
Gracely Dr 45233
Gracewind Ct 45231
Gracewood Ave 45239
Graebe Ave 45214
Graf Dr 45230
Grafton Ave 45237
Graham St 45219
Granada St 45227
Grand Ave
300-999 45205
1000-1699 45204
1700-2399 45214
3900-4099 45236
11000-11199 45242
Grand Ct 45245
Grand Cypress Ct 45245
Grand Haven Ct 45248
Grand Oaks Dr 45255
Grand Vista Ave 45213
Grandin Ave
400-599 45246
600-699 45240
Grandin Ln 45208
Grandin Pl 45208
Grandin Rd
2100-2961 45208
2963-2999 45208
3500-3799 45226
Grandin Ter 45208
Grandin Farm Ln 45208
Grandin Gate Ln 45208
Grandin Hollow Ln 45208
Grandin Ridge Dr 45208
Grandin Riverview St 45208
Grandle Ct 45230
Grandmere Ln 45206
Grandview Ave
2300-2499 45206
3400-3699 45241
4400-4499 45244
9200-9299 45242
10000-10299 45215
Grandview Pl 45212
Grange Ct 45239
Granite Ave 45215
Grant Ave
2200-2799 45231
6600-6699 45230
Grant St 45202
Grantham Way 45230
Grantwood Ave 45207
Granville Ln 45224
Grasscreek Ct 45231
Grasselli Ave 45211
Gravenhurst Dr 45231
Graves Rd 45243
Graves Lake Dr 45243
Gray Rd 45232
Graydon Ave 45207
Graydonmeadow Ln 45243
Graymont Ct 45240
Grayrick Dr 45231
Grayview Ct 45224
Great Oak Dr 45255
Green Rd 45255
Green St 45202
Green Acres Ct 45248
Green Arbors Ln 45249
Green Glen Ln 45238
Green Hill Ave 45220
Green Hills Rd 45208
Green Meadow Ln 45242
Greenarbor Dr 45255
Greenbriar Ln 45243
Greenbriar Pl 45237
Greenbrook Ln 45251
Greenbush Ave 45251
Greencastle Dr 45246
Greencrest Ct 45248
Greendale Ave 45220
Greenery Ln 45233
Greenfarms Dr 45224
Greenfield Cir 45245
Greenfield Dr 45224
Greenfield Ln 45245
Greenfield Woods Dr N & S 45224
Greenfringe Ln 45224
Greenhaven Ct 45251
Greenhills Pl 45238
Greenhouse Ln 45209
Greenland Pl 45237
Greenlawn Ave
3400-3499 45207
11600-11699 45246
Greenleaf Dr 45255
Greenlee Ave 45217
Greenmount Dr 45248
Greenoak Dr 45248
Greenpine Dr 45231
Greenridge Dr 45251
Greenriver Dr 45231
Greensfelder Ln 45241
Greensprings Ct 45231
Greentree Dr 45224
Greenvalley Ter 45239
Greenview Pl 45237
Greenview Way 45245
Greenville Ave 45246
Greenwald Ct 45248
Greenway Ave 45248
Greenwell Ave 45238
Greenwich Ave 45238
Greenwood Ave
400-599 45246
600-799 45229
1600-1899 45246
1901-1925 45246
Greenwood Ln 45245
Greenwood Ter 45226
Gregory Ct 45251
Gregory Ln 45206
Gregson Pl 45208
Greismer Ave 45239
Grenada Dr 45231
Grenoble Ct 45255
Gresham Pl 45240
Gretna Ln 45240
Greylock Dr 45243
Greystone Ct 45240
Griest Ave 45208
Griffin Dr 45237
Griffin Gate Dr 45255
Griffiths Ave 45208
Grigg Ave 45207
Grimsby Ln 45241
Grinnell Dr 45236
Grischy Ln 45208
Groesbeck Rd 45224
Grooms Rd 45242
Grosse Pointe Ln 45238
Grosvenor Dr
2400-2699 45231
2700-2899 45251
Groton Ct 45233
Grotto Ct 45211
Grove Ave
1-99 45246
200-699 45215
3800-3999 45212
4000-4000 45212
4001-4015 45227
4002-4036 45212
4017-4053 45227
4038-4038 45212
4040-4098 45212
4100-4105 45212
4106-4110 45227
4107-4231 45212
4112-4112 45212
4200-4210 45227
4212-4212 45212
4300-4400 45227
4400-4482 45211
4402-4416 45227
4484-4490 45211
10600-10699 45242
S Grove Ave 45215
Grove Ct 45215
Grove Rd 45215
Grove St 45225
Grovedale Pl 45208
Grover Hill Ave 45212
Grovesnor Sq 45245
Grovewood Dr 45251
Guam Ct 45236
Guards Ln 45244
Guenther St 45225
Guerley Rd 45238
Guido St 45202
Guild Ct 45240
Guise Ct 45215
Gulfport Dr 45246
Gulow St 45223
Gungadin Dr 45230
Gwendolyn Dr 45230
Gwendolyn Rdg 45238
Gwenwyn Dr 45236
Gwilada Dr 45236
Gwinnet Dr 45232
Habits Glen Ct 45244
Hackamore Ct 45215
Hackberry St
2500-3099 45206
3100-3399 45207
Hackett Dr 45240
Haddington Ct 45251
Hader Ave 45211
Hadley Rd 45218
Haft Rd 45247
Hageman Ave 45241
Hagewa Dr 45242
Haight Ave 45223
Haines Ave 45227
Halcor Ln 45255
Hale Ave 45229
Halesworth Dr 45240
Haley Ave 45227
Half Circle Ct 45230
Halidonhill Ln 45238
Halifax Cir 45244
Halker Ave 45215
Hall Rd 45240
Hall St 45244
Hallfield Ln 45245
Hallmar Ave 45225
Hallridge Ct 45231
Hallwood Pl 45229
Halpin Ave 45208
Halsey Ave 45204
Halstead St 45214
Hamblen Dr 45255
Hambletonian Dr 45249
Hamblin Dr 45255
Hamden Dr 45240
Hamer St 45202
Hamilton Ave
4000-5099 45223
5100-6899 45224
6900-12199 45231
Hamilton Blvd 45215
Hamilton Hills Dr 45244
Hamlet Rd 45240
Hamlin Dr 45218
Hammel Ave 45237
Hammersmith Ln 45248
Hammerstone Way 45227
Hampshire Ave 45208
Hampton Dr 45236
Hampton Ln 45208
Hampton Place Ln 45244
Hampton Pointe Dr 45248
Hand Ave 45232
Handasyde Ave, Ct & Ln 45208
Handel Ln 45218
Handman Ave 45226

Haney St 45230
Hanfield St 45223
Hankwood Ln 45255
Hanley Rd 45247
Hanna Ave 45211
Hannaford Ave 45212
Hanois Ct 45251
Hanover Cir 45230
Hanover Rd 45240
Hansford Pl 45214
Hanson Dr 45240
Hantradi Ave 45224
Happiness Ln 45245
Happiness Way 45236
Happy Dr 45238
Harbeson Ave 45224
Harbor St 45230
Harborpoint Dr 45248
Harborside Dr 45248
Harbortown Dr 45249
Harborway Dr 45241
Harbury Dr 45224
Harcourt Dr 45246
Harcourt Estates Dr 45244
Harden Ct 45240
Harding Ave
3700-4499 45211
7300-7399 45231
Harding Rd 45248
Hardisty Ave 45208
Hardwick Dr 45238
Hargrove Way 45240
Harington Ct 45240
Harkin Dr 45240
Harkness St 45225
Harmar Ct 45211
Harmes Ave 45215
Harmon Ct & Dr 45215
Harmony Ave 45246
Harmony Ln 45248
Harper Ave 45212
Harper Point Dr 45249
Harriet Ln 45244
Harriet St
100-299 45215
400-599 45203
Harris Ave
800-999 45205
2200-3099 45212
Harris Pl 45212
Harrison Ave
1100-2127 45214
2128-2140 45211
2129-2141 45214
2142-4468 45211
4470-4498 45211
4485-4493 45236
4497-4497 45211
4500-4599 45236
5500-6049 45248
6050-7584 45247
7327-7339 45231
7341-8099 45231
7586-7880 45247
Harrison Ln 45244
Harrison Woods Ct 45244
Harrogate Ct 45240
Harrow Ave 45209
Harry Aly 45220
Harry Lee Ln 45239
Harrywood Ct 45239
Hart Ave 45223
Harter Ave 45246
Hartford St 45229
Hartshorn St 45219
Hartwell Ave & Ct 45216
Hartwood Dr 45240
Harvard Ave 45207
Harvard Acres 45227
Harvest Ave 45213
Harvest Ln 45237
Harvest Rdg 45211
Harvestridge Dr 45211
Harvey Ave 45229
Harvey Cir 45233
Harvey Ct 45217
Harwick Dr 45240
Harwinton Ln 45248
Haskell Dr 45239
Hasler Ln 45216
Hassman Ct 45223
Hastings Ave 45231
Hastings St 45219
Hatch St 45202
Hatmaker St 45204
Haubner Rd 45247
Hauck Rd 45241
Haus Ln 45211
Haven St 45220
Haven Crest Ln 45248
Havensport Dr 45240
Havenwood Ct 45237
Havenwood Dr 45245
Haverhill Ln 45236
Haverknoll Dr 45231
Haverkos Ct & Ln 45251
Haverstraw Dr 45241
Havilland Ct 45240
Hawaiian Ter 45223
Hawk St 45241
Hawk Ridge Ln 45243
Hawkhurst Dr 45231
Hawkins Ave 45225
Hawkins Ln 45255
Hawkins Rdg 45230
Hawkslanding Dr 45244
Hawkstone Dr 45230
Hawthorne Ave
300-999 45205
5800-6499 45227
Hawthorne Dr 45245
Hayden Dr 45218
Hayes Rd 45248
Hays Ave 45223
Hayward Ave & Ct 45208
Hazel Ave 45212
Hazelcrest Ln 45231
Hazelgrove Dr 45240
Hazelhurst Dr 45240
Hazelton Ct 45251
Hazelwood Ave 45211
Healy Ct 45208
Hearne Ave 45229
Hearne Rd 45248
Heart Ct 45255
Hearthside Ln 45244
Hearthstead Ln 45239
Hearthstone Ct 45245
Hearthstone Dr 45231
Heather Ct
5400-5499 45248
9400-9699 45242
Heather Hill Blvd N 45244
Heather Hill Blvd S 45244
Heather Hill Ct 45245
Heathercrest Cir 45241
Heatherdale Dr 45231
Heatherglen Dr 45255
Heatherhill Ln 45206
Heatherstone Dr 45240
Heathertree Ct 45249
Heatherwood Ln 45244
Heathgate Rd 45255
Heavenly Ln 45238
Hebron Ct 45232
Hector Ave 45227
Hedge Ave 45213
Hedgerow Ln
1-99 45220
700-899 45246
3600-3699 45220
Heekin Ave 45208
Heger Dr 45217
Hegner Ave 45236
N & S Hegry Cir 45238
Heights Ct 45247
Heile Dr 45215
Heimert Ave 45215
Heis Ter 45230
Heitzler Ave 45224
Helen St
200-399 45219
5600-5699 45216
Helen M Glassmeyer
Ln 45229
Helena Dr 45244
Helmsburg Ct 45240
Helmsley Way 45231
Helston Ct 45244
Hemesath Dr 45242
Hemlock St 45206
Hemphill Ave & Way 45236
Hempstead Dr 45231
Hempwood Ave 45224
Hendent Ave 45211
Henderson Ct 45246
Hengehold Dr 45211
Henkel Dr 45205
Hennge Dr 45239
Henrianne Ct 45225
Henrietta Ave 45204
Henshaw Ave 45225
Herald Ave 45207
Herbert Ave
300-599 45215
3200-3799 45211
Hereford Ct & St 45216
Heritage Ct 45241
Heritage Dr 45249
Heritage Rd 45241
Heritage Glen Dr 45245
Heritage Square Dr 45251
Heritageoak Ct 45238
Herlerel Ave 45229
Herlin Pl 45208
Herman St 45219
Hermes Dr 45247
Hermitage Ln 45236
Hermosa Ave 45238
Herrick Ave 45208
Herron Ave 45223
Herschel Ave 45208
Herschel View St 45208
Herschel Woods Ln 45208
Herzog Pl 45238
Hess Ave 45211
Hetherington Ct & Ln 45246
Hetz Dr 45242
Hetzell St 45227
Heuwerth Ave 45238
Hewitt Ave 45207
Hewitt Crescent St 45207
Heyward St 45205
Heywood St 45225
Hialea Ct 45230
Hiawatha Ave 45227
Hibernia Dr 45238
Hickman Ave 45229
Hickman St 45231
Hickok Ln 45238
Hickory Holw 45241
E Hickory Rd 45245
Hickory St
400-599 45229
11400-11599 45246
Hickory Bark Ct 45247
Hickory Hill Ln 45215
Hickory Nut Ct 45241
Hickory Place Dr 45247
Hickory Point Dr 45242
Hickory Ridge Ln 45239
Hickory Trail Ln 45242
Hickorycreek Dr 45244
Hickoryknoll Dr 45233
Hickorylake Dr 45233
Hickorytree Ct 45233
Hickoryview Dr 45233
Hickorywood Ct 45233
Hidden Creek Dr 45251
Hidden Glen Dr 45230
Hidden Hills Dr 45230
Hidden Valley Ln 45215
Hidden Wood Pl 45208
Hiddenlake Ln 45233
Hiddenmeadows Dr 45231
Hiddenpoint Dr 45230
Higbee St 45211
High Pt 45244
High St
2100-2199 45214
5800-6199 45227
6700-6799 45244
W High St 45238
High Forest Ln 45223
High Hollow Ln 45223
High Meadows Dr 45230
High Point Ave 45211
High Pointe Ln 45248
High Tree Dr 45247
Highcedar Ct 45233
Highcliff Ct 45224
Highcrest Ct 45251
Highfield Ct 45242
Highgate Pl 45236
Highgrove Ct 45239
Highland Ave
100-199 45215
1600-1899 45202
1900-2332 45219
2000-2099 45224
2232-2306 45212
2308-2847 45212
2333-2361 45212
2334-2508 45219
2403-2405 45219
2407-2411 45212
2421-2449 45219
2501-2507 45212
2509-2511 45212
2512-2608 45219
2610-2651 45219
2653-2669 45219
2700-2780 45212
2801-2801 45212
2803-2823 45219
2825-2825 45212
2828-2917 45219
2849-2909 45212
2919-3041 45219
2920-2940 45212
3130-3130 45219
3200-3499 45213
5700-6399 45216
6500-6799 45236
9400-9799 45242
Highland Grn 45245
Highland Oaks Dr 45248
Highland Ridge Dr 45232
Highlander Ct 45245
Highorchard Dr 45239
Highridge Ave 45238
Highton Ct 45236
Highview Dr 45238
Highway Dr 45241
Highwood Ln 45239
Hilda Ave 45211
Hildreth Ave 45211
Hill Ave 45231
N Hill Ln 45224
W Hill Ln 45215
Hill St
700-899 45215
900-1099 45202
3200-3399 45241
Hill And Dale Dr 45213
Hill And Hollow Ln 45208
Hill Crest Rd 45224
Hill Smith Dr 45215
Hill Top Ln 45243
Hillary Dr 45239
Hillbrook Dr 45238
Hillcrest Dr 45215
Hillfred Ln 45238
Hillgrove Ct 45246
Hilliard Dr 45238
Hillridge Ct 45244
Hillrose Ct 45240
Hillsdale St 45216
Hillside Ave
300-499 45215
3300-4299 45204
4300-7338 45233
Hilltop Dr 45244
Hilltop Ln
1-99 45208
200-699 45215
Hilltree Dr 45255
Hillview Dr 45245
Hillvista Ln 45239
Hilsun Pl 45238
Hilton Pl 45219
Hines Aly 45207
Hinkley Dr 45240
Hinton Pl 45240
Hires Ln 45212
Hirsch Dr 45237
Hitchcock Dr 45240
Hitchens Ave 45211
Hitching Post Ln 45230
Hoadly Ct 45211
Hobart Ave 45223
Hobbit Rd 45243
Hobbs Ln 45240
Hocking Dr 45233
Hoff Ave
2590-2798 45202
2800-2899 45226
Hoffman Ave 45236
Hoffman Farm Ln 45242
Hoffner St
1400-1499 45231
1600-2099 45223
Hoge St 45226
Hohum Dr 45245
Hokel Ln 45230
Holbrook Ave 45226
Holden St 45214
Holderness Ln 45240
Holgate Dr 45240
Holiday Dr 45245
Holiday Hills Dr 45255
Holland Dr 45232
Hollenshade Ave 45211
Hollingsworth Way 45240
Hollis Dr 45251
E & W Hollister St 45219
Holliston Pl 45255
Hollow Oak 45241
Holloway Ave & Ct 45207
Hollowview Ct 45233
Holly Ave 45208
Holly Hl 45243
Holly Ln 45208
Holly Ridge Dr 45245
Hollybrook Ct 45239
Hollyglen Ct 45251
Hollyhock Dr 45231
Hollyridge Ct 45251
Hollytree Dr 45231
Hollywood Ave 45224
Holman Cir 45236
Holman View Dr 45215
Holyoke Dr 45240
Holz Ave 45230
Home Ave 45215
Home St 45236
Home City Ave 45233
Homelawn Ave 45211
Homer Ave
4000-4599 45227
5500-5699 45212
Homeside Ave 45224
Homestead Pl 45211
Homewood Rd 45227
Honesdale Ct 45251
Honeyhill Ct 45236
Honeysuckle Ct 45241
Honeysuckle Dr 45230
Honeysuckle Ln 45230
Honeywell Dr 45241
Honeywood Ct 45230
Honnert Dr 45247
Hoock Ct 45239
Hood Ct 45231
Hope Ave 45232
Hope Ln 45211
Hopedale Ct 45240
Hopewell Rd
8300-9299 45242
9300-9599 45249
Hopewellhills Dr 45249
Hopewoods Ct 45249
Hopkins Ave 45212
Hopkins St 45203
Hopper Rd 45255
Hopper Hill Rd 45255
Hopper Hill Farms Rd 45255
S Hopper Ridge Cir &
Rd 45255
Hopper View Blf 45255
Hopple Ct & St 45225
Horace St 45214
Horatio Ct 45240
Horizonvue Dr 45239
Horncastle Dr 45241
Horton St 45214
Hosbrook Rd
7100-7999 45243
8000-8099 45236
Hosea Ave
100-266 45220
115-213 45215
216-226 45215
268-298 45220
Houston Rd
2400-2699 45231
2700-2899 45251
Howard Ave 45223
Howdy Ct 45239
Howell Ave 45220
Howland Pl 45223
Hoy Ct 45231
Hubble Rd 45247
Huddleston Dr 45236
Hudepohl Ln 45231
Hudepohl St 45203
Hudson Ave
1900-2599 45212
3400-3599 45207
Hudson Pkwy 45213
Huey Ave 45233
Huffman Ct 45231
Hughes Rd 45251
Hughes St 45202
Hulbert Ave 45214
Hull Ave 45211
Humbert St 45226
Hummingbird Ct 45239
Humphrey Rd & St 45242
Humphrey Manor Ct 45242
Hunincou Dr 45231
Hunley Rd 45244
Hunnicutt Ln 45238
Hunsford St 45216
Hunt Rd
1500-2499 45215
2500-3900 45236
3901-3907 45236
3902-3908 45236
3909-4199 45236
4200-4999 45242
Huntcrest Dr 45255
Hunter Ave 45212
Hunter Ct 45215
Huntergreen Dr 45251
Hunters Lk 45249
Hunters Pl 45249
Hunters Rdg 45249
Hunters Trl 45243
Hunters Vw 45249
Hunters Creek Dr 45242
Hunters Creek Ln 45247
Hunters Ridge Ln
7100-7399 45247
7281-7283 45249
Huntersknoll Ln 45230
Hunterspoint Ln 45244
Huntersrun Ln 45242
Hunterton Ct 45249
Hunting Horn Ct 45255
Huntington Pl 45219
Huntridge Ave 45231
Huntsman Ct 45230
Huntwicke Pl 45241
Hurd Ave 45227
Hurley Ave 45237
Hurlingham Way 45244
Huron Ave 45207
Hust Aly 45202
Huston Ave 45212
Hutchins Ave 45229
Hutchinson Rd 45248
Hutchinson Glen Dr 45248
Hutton St 45226
Hyacinth Rd 45245
Hyacinth Ter 45248
Hyannis Dr 45251
Hyde Park Ave
2700-2899 45209
3600-3699 45208
3700-3899 45209
Hyde Park Pl 45208
Iberis Ave 45213
Ibsen Ave 45209
Icicle Ct 45251
Ida Ave 45212
Ida St 45202
Idaho St 45204
Idalia Ave 45242
Ideal Ter 45238
Idlewild Ave 45207
Ihle Dr 45238
Iliff Ave 45205
Illinois Ave
2-199 45215
3100-3199 45204
Illona Dr 45218
Imbler Dr 45218
Imboden Ct 45218
Imhoff Ct 45240
Immaculate Ln 45255
Impala Dr 45231
Imprint Ln 45240
Imwalle Ave 45217
Indeco Ct & Dr 45241
Independence Dr 45255
Indian Ln 45233
Indian Run 45243
Indian Bluff Dr 45242
Indian Bluff Ln 45241
Indian Creek Dr 45241
Indian Heights Dr 45243
Indian Hill Pl 45227
Indian Hill Rd
6801-6853 45227
7000-9299 45243
Indian Hill Trl 45243
Indian Mound Ave 45212
Indian Ridge Ln 45243
Indian Springs Dr 45241
Indian Trace Ct 45255
Indian Trail Dr 45243
Indian Walk Dr 45241
Indian Woods Dr 45215
Indiancreek Rd 45255
Indianview Ave 45227
Indianwoods Dr 45251
Indra Ct 45240
Ingalls St 45204
Inglenook Pl 45208
Ingleside Ave 45206
Ingram Rd 45218
Ingrams Ridge Dr 45244
Inman Ln 45218
Inner Circle Dr 45240
Innes Ave
1900-2099 45224
4300-4599 45223
Innisfree Ln 45255
Innsbrook Pl 45244
Intern Ct 45239
Intersection St 45204
Interstate Cir 45242
Intervine Pl 45220
E Interwood Ave & Pl 45220
Intrepid Dr 45252
Inverness Pl 45209
Invicta Ct 45231
Inwood Dr 45241
Inwood Pl 45219
Iona Ave 45213
Iowa Ave 45206
Ipswich Dr 45224

Ireland Ave 45218
Iris Ave 45213
Iris Ln 45255
Iroll Ave 45225
Iron Bridge Way 45248
Iron Woods Dr 45239
Ironliege Ln 45249
Ironstone Dr 45240
Ironwood Ct 45249
Iroquois St 45214
Irvella Pl 45238
Irving Pl 45212
Irving St 45220
Irwin Ave 45236
Irwin Pl 45229
Isabella Ave 45209
Isis Ave 45208
Island View Dr 45252
Islandale Dr 45240
Islington Ave 45227
Iuka Ave 45243
Ivanhoe Ave
1-299 45233
3800-4499 45212
Ivory Ct 45238
Ivy Ave
700-899 45246
2200-2499 45208
Ivy Way 45244
Ivy Hills Blvd, Dr, Ln & Pl 45244
Ivy Pointe Blvd 45245
Ivy Trails Dr 45244
Ivybrook Ct 45236
Ivyfarm Rd 45243
Ivyhill Dr 45238
Ivyrock Ct 45240
Jachanso Dr 45230
Jack Malloy Ln 45218
Jackfrost Way 45251
Jackie Ct 45244
Jackie Dr 45245
Jackie Ln 45244
Jackies Dr 45239
Jackpine Ct 45231
Jacks Way 45233
Jackson Ave 45217
Jackson Ln 45245
Jackson St
100-1113 45215
1115-1187 45215
1120-1150 45202
1160-1160 45215
1201-1209 45202
1211-1217 45202
1219-1227 45202
1300-1399 45215
Jackway Ct 45239
Jacob Ave 45238
Jacobs Way 45247
Jadaro Ct 45248
Jadwin St 45216
Jager Ct 45230
Jail Aly 45202
Jakaro Dr 45255
Jamar Dr 45224
Jamerine Ct 45239
James Dr 45245
James Pl 45246
James St 45216
James Hill Dr 45230
Jameson St 45227
Jamestown Dr 45241
Jamestown St 45205
Jamies Oak Ct 45248
Jandaracres Dr 45248
Jane Ave 45211
Jane Ct 45241
Janet St 45223
Janett Ave 45211
Janlin Ct 45211
January Ct 45218
Janward Dr 45211
Japonica Dr 45218
Jardin Pl 45241
Jarole Dr 45245
Jasmine Ct 45215
Jason Dr 45240
Jasper Ct 45231
Jay St 45229
Jeanette Ln 45249
Jeannie Ave 45230
Jeff Ln 45241
Jefferson Ave
200-300 45217
302-320 45217
303-401 45217
311-401 45215
403-1010 45215
403-422 45217
1012-1020 45215
1025-1027 45246
1029-1089 45246
1091-1099 45246
1101-1103 45215
1105-1107 45246
1109-1121 45246
1123-1125 45246
1200-1499 45215
2200-2499 45212
2600-3099 45219
3100-3399 45220
9600-9799 45242
S Jefferson Ave 45212
Jefferson St
6700-6999 45244
11300-11399 45241
Jeffrey Ct 45236
Jenkins Pl 45241
Jennie Ln 45238
Jennifer Ct 45211
Jennifer Lynn Dr 45248
Jennings Rd 45218
Jeremy Ct 45240
Jericho Dr 45231
Jerome Ave 45223
Jerome Park 45244
Jerome St 45202
Jerry Ln 45208
Jersey Ave 45233
Jessamine St 45225
Jesse Ln 45224
Jessicas Oak Ct 45248
Jessup Rd
2600-3599 45239
3600-6199 45247
Jester St 45223
Jethve Ln 45243
Jewel Ln 45218
Jewett Dr 45215
Jillmarie Dr 45251
Jimbet Ct 45239
Jimjon Ct 45248
Jimmar Ct 45239
Jimray Ct 45233
Jo Williams St 45223
Joan Pl 45227
Joana Pl 45238
Jody Lynn Ct 45231
Joe Nuxhall Way 45202
Joetta Dr 45230
Joey Ter 45248
John St
100-400 45202
415-497 45215
499-599 45215
1000-1319 45203
1320-1899 45214
John Gray Rd
1601-2299 45240
2301-2749 45231
2751-3199 45251
Johnny Appleseed Ct 45255
Johnson Rd 45247
Johnson St 45243
Johnston Ln 45242
Johnstone Pl 45206
Joliet Ave 45215
Jonas Dr 45238
Jonathan Ave 45207
Jonathan Ct 45255
Jones Aly 45215
Jones Pl 45244
Jones St 45214
Jonfred Ct 45231
Jonkard Rd 45247
Jonlen Dr 45227
Jonquil Ln 45231
Jonquilmeadow Dr 45240
Jonrose Ave 45239
Jonte Ave 45215
Jonte St 45214
Jora Ln 45209
Jordan Ln 45227
Joselin Ave 45220
Joseph Ct 45231
Joseph Rd 45251
Joseph St
1300-1699 45237
7300-7899 45231
Joseph E Sanker Blvd 45212
Josephine St 45219
Joslyn Rd 45242
Joyce Ln 45237
Joywood Dr 45218
Jud Dr 45236
Judge St 45212
Judiann Ct 45215
Judson St 45225
Judy Ln
500-599 45238
900-999 45245
Judy Con Dr 45255
Juergens Ave 45220
Julep Ln 45218
Juler Ave 45243
Julian Dr 45215
Julianne Dr 45241
Julie Ter 45215
Juliemarie Ct 45239
Julmar Dr 45238
July Ct 45239
June St
100-199 45217
400-599 45244
600-699 45206
3600-3699 45211
5200-5499 45217
Juneberry Dr 45240
Junedale Dr 45218
Junefield Ave 45218
Junietta Ave 45211
Juniper Ave 45238
Juniper Ct 45241
Juniperview Ln 45243
Jupiter Dr 45238
Justicia Ln 45218
Justis St 45219
Juvene Way 45233
K Of C Dr 45245
Kaitlyn Ct 45248
Kalama Ct 45236
Kaldy St 45244
Kalmar Dr 45240
Kanauga Ct & St 45227
Kanawah Ave 45236
Karahill Dr 45240
Kardon Ct 45247
Karen Ave 45248
Karenlaw Ln 45231
Karla Ave 45211
Karnak Ct 45233
Kary Ln 45240
Kasota St 45229
Kathleen Ct 45239
N & S Kathwood Cir 45236
Kathy Ln 45238
Katiebud Dr 45238
Katies Ct 45244
Katies Green Ct 45211
Kaywood Dr 45243
Kearney St 45216
Keats Ln 45224
Keen Ave 45237
Keenan Ave 45232
Keith Dr 45215
Keller Ct 45245
Keller Rd 45243
Kellerman Ave 45237
Kellogg Ave
3500-4899 45226
4900-6299 45230
Kellogg Rd
6300-6999 45230
7000-7799 45255
Kellway Ct 45239
Kellywood Ave 45238
Kelsch Ln 45227
Kelseys Oak Ct 45248
Kelso Ct 45231
Kelvin Ct 45240
Kemper Ave
1600-1799 45231
4400-5099 45217
11000-11199 45242
Kemper Ln
1600-1999 45202
2000-2699 45206
E Kemper Rd
1-1899 45246
2000-6499 45241
6500-8900 45249
8902-9198 45249
W Kemper Rd
1-749 45246
750-2299 45240
2300-2799 45231
2800-4999 45251
5000-5499 45252
Kemper Commons Cir 45246
Kemper Meadow Dr 45240
Kemper Springs Dr 45240
Kemper Woods Dr 45249
Kemperknoll Ln 45249
Kemperridge Ct 45249
Ken Arbre Dr 45236
Kenard Ave 45232
Kenbyrne Ct 45239
Kencrest Cir 45243
Kendale Ct 45236
Kendall Ave 45208
Kendara Ct 45230
Kenilworth Ave 45212
Kenilworth Ct 45246
Kenilworth Pl 45226
Kenkel Ave 45211
Kenker Pl 45211
Kenlee Dr 45230
Kenmore Ave 45227
Kenn Rd 45240
Kennebel Ln 45244
Kennecot Dr 45244
Kennedy Ave 45213
Kennedy Ln 45242
Kennedy Trl 45255
Kennedys Lndg 45245
Kenner St 45214
Kenneth Ave 45224
Kenoak Ln 45213
Kenova Ave 45237
Kenray Ct 45215
Kenridge Dr 45242
Kenross Ct 45240
Kenshire Dr 45240
Kensington Ln 45245
Kensington Pl 45205
Kensington Ridge Dr 45230
Kentbrook Ct 45240
Kentford Ct 45233
Kentland Ct 45236
Kenton Ave 45236
Kenton Ct 45245
Kenton St 45206
Kentucky Ave 45223
Kentuckyview Dr 45230
Kenview Dr 45243
Kenwood Ave 45230
Kenwood Rd
5000-5699 45227
5700-6999 45243
7000-8599 45236
8600-8700 45242
8701-8757 45242
8702-8758 45242
8759-11299 45242
Kenwood Crossing Way 45236
Kenwood Hills Dr 45227
Kern Dr 45247
Kerper Ave 45206
Kerr Ave 45245
Kerrianna Dr 45242
Kessen Ave 45211
Kessler Ave & Pl 45217
Kesta Pl 45240
Keswick Pl 45230
Kettering Dr 45251
Kewanee Ln 45230
Keyridge Dr 45240
Keys Crescent Ln 45206
Keysport Ln 45231
Keystone Dr
600-699 45244
2700-2999 45230
Keywest Dr 45239
Kibby Ln 45233
Kiefer Ct 45224
Kieley Pl 45217
Kilbourne Ave 45209
Kilbride Dr 45251
Kildare Dr 45233
Kilgour St 45202
Kilkenny Dr 45244
Killarney Ct 45236
Killington Ln 45244
Kimbee Dr 45244
Kimberly Ave & Ct 45213
Kimmey Ct 45244
Kimpel Aly 45214
Kims Arbor Ln 45249
Kincaid Rd 45213
Kincardine Dr 45238
Kincora Ct 45233
Kindel Ave 45214
King Pl 45223
King James Ct 45247
King Louis Ct 45255
Kingfisher Ln 45246
Kingman Dr 45251
Kingoak Dr 45248
Kings Auto Mall Rd 45249
Kings Run Ct & Dr 45232
Kings Water Dr 45249
Kingsbury Dr 45240
Kingscove Way 45230
Kingsford Dr 45224
Kingslake Dr 45242
Kingsley Dr 45227
Kingsmere Ct 45231
Kingspath Dr 45231
Kingsport Dr 45241
Kingston Dr 45244
Kingston Pl 45204
Kingstonhill Ct 45255
Kingstonview Ct 45255
Kingsway Ct 45230
Kingsway Ct W 45215
Kingswood Ct 45255
Kinmont St 45208
Kinney Ave
1400-1699 45231
1700-1999 45207
1715-1739 45231
1741-1799 45231
Kinoll Ave 45213
Kinsey Ave 45219
Kinsman Ct 45238
Kipling Ave 45239
Kiplington Dr 45239
Kiplingwood Dr 45239
Kipp Dr 45255
Kirbert Ave 45205
Kirby Ave
4100-5499 45223
5500-5799 45239
Kirkland Dr 45224
Kirkridge Dr 45233
Kirkup Ave 45213
Kirkwood Ln 45233
Kirtley Dr 45236
Kismet Ct 45231
Kistner St 45204
Kittery Ln 45255
Kittrun Ct 45231
Kitty Ln 45238
Kittywood Dr 45252
Klatte Rd 45244
Klausridge Ct 45247
Kleeman Ct & Rd 45211
Kleeman Green Dr 45211
Kleeman Lake Ct 45211
Kleindale Ave 45231
Klemme Dr 45238
Kleybolte Ave 45226
Kline Ave 45211
Kling Ave 45211
Klondike Ct 45251
Klotter Ave
200-339 45219
340-699 45214
Knight Ave 45212
Knightsbridge Dr 45244
Knob Ct 45225
Knoll Rd 45237
Knollcrest Dr 45237
Knollridge Ln 45231
Knollsprings Ct 45246
Knollview Dr 45241
Knollwood Ln 45224
Knorr Ave 45214
Knott St 45229
Knottypine Dr 45230
Knowlton St 45223
Knox St 45214
Kodiak Dr 45240
Koehler Ave 45215
Koenig Ave 45211
Koenig St 45215
Komura Ct 45240
Kosta Dr 45231
Koszo Dr 45255
Kottmann St 45214
Kovach Dr 45215
Kreis Ln 45205
Kremer Ave 45225
Kress Aly 45214
Krierview Dr 45248
Kristen Pl 45240
Kristiridge Dr 45252
Kroegermount Dr 45239
Kroger Ave & Ln 45226
Kroger Farm Rd 45243
Kroger Valley Dr 45226
Krug Ave 45216
Krug Cir 45212
Krylon Dr 45215
Krystal Ct 45252
Kuertzmill Dr 45249
Kugler Meadow Ct 45236
Kugler Mill Rd
4100-6899 45236
7700-9399 45243
Kuhlman Ave 45205
Kuliga Park Dr 45248
Kumler Ave 45239
La Boiteaux Ave
6900-7099 45239
7100-7199 45231
La Crosse Ave 45227
Labelle Ave 45242
Laclede Ave 45205
Laconia Ave 45237
Lady Ellen Dr 45230
Lafayette Ave
300-999 45220
500-591 45246
593-595 45246
4200-4599 45212
7200-7299 45236
Lafayette Cir 45220
Lafayette Ln 45220
Lafeuille Ave & Cir 45211
Lagrange Ln 45239
Laidlaw Ave 45237
Lake Ave
2-99 45246
7800-8499 45236
N Lake Ave 45246
S Lake Ave 45246
E Lake Ln 45244
Lake St 45244
Lake Chetac Dr 45241
Lake Circle Dr 45246
Lake Forest Dr 45242
Lake Forest Ln 45244
E Lake Shore Dr 45237
Lake Thames Dr 45242
E Lake View Dr 45237
Lakefront Dr 45247
Lakehaven Ct 45246
Lakehill Dr 45230
Lakehurst Ct 45242
Lakeland Ave 45237
Lakeman St 45223
Lakemeadow Ct 45239
Lakenoll Dr 45231
Lakepark Dr 45231
Lakepointe Ct 45248
Lakeridge Dr 45231
Lakeshore Dr 45231
Lakeside Dr 45231
Laketrail Dr 45233
Lakevalley Dr 45247
Lakeview Dr 45231
Lakeview St 45211
Lakeville Dr 45233
Lakewood Ave 45220
Lakewood Dr
3500-3799 45248
7100-7199 45241
Lakewood Ln 45242
Lakewood Pt 45244
Lakota Dr 45243
Lamarc Trl 45241
Lamarque Dr 45236
Lambert Pl 45208
Lambston St 45223
Lamont Ave 45242
Lamplighter Way 45245
Lamplite Ct 45244
Lancaster Ave 45242
Lancelot Dr 45244
Lancer Ln 45239
Lancewood Ct 45243
Landan Ln 45246
Landis Ln 45231
Landon Ct 45229
Landy Ln 45215
Lane Ave 45214
Lanette Dr 45230
Lang Rd 45244
Lang St 45202
Langdon Ave 45212
Langdon Farm Rd
1700-2499 45237
2500-2899 45212
Langhorst Ct 45236
Langland St 45223
Langley Ave 45217
Lanius Ln 45224
Lanny Ln 45231
Lansdowne Ave 45236
Lansford Dr 45242
Lantana Ave 45224
Lanter Ln 45230
Lapland Dr 45239
Laramie Trl 45215
Larann Ln 45231
Larch Ave 45224
Larchmont Dr 45215
Larchview Dr 45236
Larchwood Pl 45237
Laredo Ave 45206
Largo Dr 45236
Lariat Dr 45238
Lark Ct 45242
Larkfield Dr 45237
Larkhall St 45245
Larking Dr 45242
Larkspur Ave 45208
Larma Ln 45245
Larmon Ct 45224
Larona Ave 45229

Larrieli Rd 45247
Larry Ave 45224
Larry Joe Dr 45230
Larrywood Ln 45224
Larue Ct 45211
Lasalle Ave 45205
Lassiter Dr 45240
Latham Ave 45205
Lathrop Pl 45224
Latiff Ln 45230
Latina Ct 45218
Lauderdale Dr 45239
Lauk St 45220
Laura Ln
  1-199 45233
  2500-5499 45212
Laured Pl 45238
Laurel Ave
  900-1099 45246
  4816-4820 45242
  4822-4999 45242
  7000-7899 45243
Laurel St 45216
Laurel Grove Ct 45244
Laurel Oak Ln 45237
Laurel Park Dr 45214
Laurel Ridge Ct 45244
Laurel View Dr 45244
Laurelridge Ln 45247
Laurelwood Cir 45224
Lauren Close 45244
Laurence Rd 45215
Laval Dr 45255
Laverne Dr 45251
Laverty Ln 45230
Laveta Ct 45215
Lavinia Ave 45208
Lawn Ave
  1700-1999 45237
  2000-2299 45212
Lawndale Ave & Pl 45212
Lawnview Ave 45246
Lawrence Ave 45212
Lawrence Rd 45248
Lawrence St 45217
Lawyer Rd 45244
Lawyers Point Dr 45244
Le Beau Dr 45244
Le Blond Ave 45208
Le Conte Ave 45230
Le Mar Dr 45238
Le Roy Ct 45219
Le Roy Pl 45230
Le Roy Rd 45230
Leacrest Rd 45215
Leadwell Ln 45242
Leaftree Ct 45208
Leafwood Dr 45224
Leander Ct 45240
Leath Ave 45238
Lebanon Ave 45242
Lebanon Rd 45241
Lebanon St 45216
Leda Ct 45211
Leders Ln 45238
E Ledge St 45227
Ledgewood Dr
  3700-3899 45207
  3900-4099 45229
Ledlie St 45225
Ledro St 45246
Lee Ct 45248
Lee Ann Dr 45255
Leebrook Dr 45231
Leeds Ln E & W 45215
Leelanau Ave 45215
Leeper St 45223
Lees Crossing Dr 45239
Leesburg Ln 45209
Leeside Trl 45248
Leeward Way 45248
Leffingwell Ave 45224
Legacy Ct 45241
Legacy Ln 45249
Legacy Trce 45237
Legacy Ridge Ln 45248

Legend Ct 45244
Legend Hls 45255
Legendary Ln 45255
Legendary Pass 45249
E Legendary Run 45245
W Legendary Run 45245
Legendary Trails Dr 45245
Legends Ln 45244
Legendwood Ln 45245
N & S Leggett Ct & St 45215
Legrove Cir 45239
Lehigh Ave 45230
Lehman Rd
  2300-3299 45204
  3300-3499 45205
Leibel Rd 45248
Leland Ave 45204
Lemarie Dr 45241
Lemaster Dr 45255
Lemontree Dr 45240
Lengel Rd 45244
Lengwood Dr 45244
Lenkenann Dr 45255
Lenore Dr 45215
Lenox Dr 45245
Lenox Ln 45229
Lenox Pl 45229
Leo St 45217
Leon Ct 45238
Leona Dr 45238
Leonard Ave 45217
Leonard St
  100-399 45215
  3500-3599 45244
  4900-5099 45208
Leota Ln 45251
Leslie Ave
  2500-2699 45212
  4400-4599 45242
E Leslie Ave 45215
W Leslie Ave 45215
Leslies Woods Ct 45211
Lester Rd 45213
Leumas Rd 45239
Lever Ct 45238
E & W Levitt Pl 45245
Lewis Ave 45242
Lewis Clark Trl 45241
Lewiston Ct 45240
Lexa Ct 45231
W Lexington 45212
Lexington Ave
  800-999 45229
  1800-2200 45212
  2202-2298 45212
Lexington Dr 45241
Lexington Green Dr 45245
Ley Ave 45214
Leyman Dr 45229
Libbejo Dr 45233
Liberty Hl 45202
E Liberty Hl 45202
E Liberty St 45202
W Liberty St
  1-299 45202
  300-1099 45214
  3000-3209 45204
  3210-4299 45205
Liberty Hill Ct 45242
Libra Ln 45251
Lick Rd 45251
Liddell St 45225
Liddle Ln 45215
Ligorio Ave 45218
Lilac Ave 45208
Lilbur Ln 45230
Lilibet Ct 45238
Lilienthal St 45204
Lillian Ave 45213
Lillian Dr 45237
Lillie Pl 45223
Lillilee Ln 45233
Lillwood Ln 45251
Lilly Ln 45245
Limberlost Ln 45238
Limerick Ave 45236

Limestone Cir 45239
Lina Pl 45239
Lincoln Ave
  600-1117 45206
  1119-1119 45206
  1160-1162 45246
  1164-1191 45246
  1193-1199 45246
  1200-1212 45206
  1214-1599 45206
  1700-1899 45212
  2100-2228 45224
  2230-2236 45224
  2231-2235 45231
  2237-2799 45231
  4500-4599 45212
  7800-7899 45231
Lincoln Pl 45206
Lincoln Rd 45247
Lincoln Ter 45206
Lincolnshire Dr 45240
Lincrest Dr 45240
Lind St 45215
Linda Dr 45238
Linda Sue Dr 45245
Lindale Ct 45215
Linde Ln 45244
Lindell Ln 45226
Linden Ave
  1-6 45246
  7-899 45215
  4100-4421 45236
  4250-4498 45212
  4500-5099 45212
Linden Dr
  1-299 45215
  1600-1699 45224
Linden Ln 45215
Linden Pl 45227
Linden Rdg 45215
Linden St
  1-599 45216
  2500-2899 45225
Linder Ln 45244
Linderwood Ln 45255
Lindley Ave 45212
Lindsay Ln 45251
Lindsey Ln 45230
Lindy Ave & Walk 45215
Linfield Dr 45242
Lingo St 45223
Link Side Dr 45245
Linn St
  400-1319 45203
  1320-2099 45214
Linnehill Ln 45238
Linneman Rd 45238
Linneman St 45230
Linsan Dr 45239
Linshaw Ct 45208
Linton St 45219
Linview Ave 45208
Linwood Ave
  2800-3199 45208
  3200-3699 45226
Lionel Ave 45214
Lippelman Rd 45246
Lisa Ln 45243
Lisbon Ave 45213
Lisbon Ln 45246
Lischer Ave 45211
Little Creek Ln 45246
Little Dry Run Rd 45244
Little Flower Ave 45239
Little Harbor Dr 45244
Little John Ct 45230
Little Turtle Ln 45244
Littlefield Ln 45247
Liveoak Ct 45224
Livingston Rd
  7600-8499 45247
  8500-8999 45251
Livingston St 45214
Llanfair Ave 45224
Llewellyn Ave 45223
Lloyd Ave 45212
Lloyd Pl 45219

Loannes Ct & Dr 45243
Lobelia Dr 45241
Lobob Ct 45205
Locharbour Ln 45251
Lochcrest Dr 45231
Lock St 45215
Lockard Ave 45230
Lockbourne Dr 45240
Locker Ct 45224
Lockhurst Ln 45214
Lockland Rd 45215
Lockman Ave 45238
Lockport Ct 45240
Locksley Ct 45241
Locksley St 45230
Lockwood Pl 45204
Lockwood Hill Rd 45247
Locust Ave 45238
Locust Ln
  800-999 45245
  3400-3599 45238
  4100-4199 45242
  7700-7999 45243
Locust St
  100-209 45215
  211-299 45215
  300-302 45216
  304-315 45216
  316-316 45215
  317-599 45216
  318-598 45216
  400-499 45255
  400-415 45215
  1400-1499 45206
  4100-4299 45227
  5200-5299 45238
  8400-8499 45216
Locust Corner Rd 45245
Locust Hill Rd 45245
Locust Log Ln 45239
Locust Run Rd 45245
Locust View Ln 45239
Loda Dr 45245
Lodgeview Ct 45240
Lofty View Ln 45247
Logan Lndg 45245
Logan St 45202
Loganfield Ct 45249
Logans Oak Ct 45248
Logenberry Cir 45240
Loire Dr 45245
Lois Dr
  1100-1199 45237
  6900-6999 45239
Loisdale Ct 45255
Loiska Ln 45224
Loisview Ln 45255
Loiswood Dr 45224
Lombardy St 45216
London Ct 45245
Londonderry Ct 45242
Londonderry Dr 45241
Londonridge Ct 45242
Loneoak Ct 45243
Lonerent Ave 45236
Long Ln 45231
Long Acres Dr 45245
Longacre Dr 45240
Longbourn St 45230
Longbow Ct 45230
Longfield Dr 45243
Longford Dr 45236
Longlake Ct 45247
Longmeadow Ln 45236
Longren Ct 45242
Longview St 45216
Longwood Ct 45239
Longwood Ln 45232
Longworth St 45215
Lonsdale St 45227
Lookout Cir & Dr 45208
Lookover Dr 45251
Lora Ave 45211
Loraine Ave 45220
Loralinda Dr 45251
Lord Alfred Ct 45241

Lorelei Dr 45231
Loretta Ave 45238
Loretta Dr 45239
Lory Ln 45215
Losantiridge Ave 45213
Losantiville Ave
  1700-2699 45237
  2700-3199 45213
Losantiville Ter 45213
Lossing St 45220
Lost Xing 45231
Loth St
  2100-2199 45202
  2200-2299 45219
Lotushill Dr 45240
Loubell Ln 45205
Louden St 45202
Louese Ln 45248
Louis Ave 45220
Lourdes Ln 45238
Love Ct 45215
Loveland Madeira Rd
  7600-9099 45243
  9100-9499 45242
Lovell Ave 45211
Lowell Ave 45220
Lowland Rd 45233
Lowry Ave
  3900-3999 45229
  4100-4399 45212
Lu Clare Dr 45233
Lucenna Dr 45238
Lucerne Ave 45227
Lucille Dr 45213
Luckey Ave 45214
Ludlow Ave
  200-999 45220
  1000-3999 45223
Ludlow Ln 45245
Ludlow Pl
  1-99 45217
  1400-1499 45223
Luhn Ave 45227
Lullaby Ct 45238
Lumardo Ave 45238
Lumberjack Dr 45240
Lumberwill Ct 45239
Lumford Pl 45213
Lumsden St 45226
Luna Ave 45219
Lunken Park Dr 45226
Lupine Dr 45241
Luray Ave 45206
Lurline Pl 45233
Lusanne Ter 45230
Luschek Dr 45241
Lusitania Ave 45205
Luwista Ln 45230
Lux St 45216
Lyceum Ct 45230
Lydia St 45214
Lyleburn Pl 45220
Lyncris Dr 45242
Lyncross Dr 45240
Lyndhurst Ct 45249
Lyndon Center Ct 45236
Lyness Dr 45239
N & S Lynndale Ave 45231
Lynne Ter 45215
N & S Lynnebrook Dr 45224
Lynnehaven Ct & Dr 45236
Lynnfield Ct 45243
Lynnfork Ave 45231
Lyon St 45219
Lyonia Ct 45239
Lysle Ln 45212
Lytham Ct 45233
Lytle St 45202
Lytle Woods Pl 45227
Mac Nicholas Ave 45236
Macar Dr 45241
Macarthur Ct 45211
Mace Ave 45216
Macey Ave 45227
Machende St 45216
Mack Ave 45248

Mackenzie Ave 45233
Mackenzie Xing 45245
Macon St 45225
Macpherson Pl 45245
Mad Anthony St 45223
Maddux Dr & Ln 45230
Madeira Ct 45255
Madeira Hills Dr 45243
Madeira Pines Dr 45243
Madeleine Cir 45231
Madison Ave
  1500-1999 45231
  2200-2499 45212
  11400-11599 45246
S Madison Ave 45212
Madison Ln 45208
Madison Rd
  1500-1598 45206
  1501-1599 45206
  1600-1960 45206
  1962-2696 45208
  2698-2698 45208
  2700-3799 45209
  3800-6799 45227
Madison St
  1200-1299 45215
  3400-3499 45244
Madison Park Ave 45209
Madisonville Rd 45227
Madonna Dr 45238
Magdalena Dr 45231
Magee Ct 45215
Magic Ln 45215
Magill Ave 45229
Magly Ct 45230
Magnolia Ave 45246
Magnolia Dr 45215
Magnolia St 45202
Mahoning Ct 45233
Maid Marian Dr 45230
Maidstone Ct 45230
Main Ave 45242
Main St
  300-312 45202
  314-1799 45202
  6501-6597 45244
  6599-7999 45244
  9301-9341 45242
  9343-9529 45242
  9531-9555 45242
  10800-11199 45241
  11600-11699 45246
Maisel Dr 45220
Majestic Ct 45244
Majestic Ln 45251
Makro Dr 45241
Malabar Ter 45236
Malaer Dr 45241
Malcolm Ave 45212
Malden Walk 45214
Malibu Ct 45251
Malin St 45219
Mall Dr 45251
Mallard Dr
  4000-4099 45245
  5400-5499 45247
Mallard Cove Dr 45246
Mallard Crossing Ln 45247
Mallet Dr 45246
Mallet Hill Dr 45244
Mallory Ln 45231
Malory Ct 45207
Malsbary Rd 45242
Malvern Pl 45219
Mancelona Ct 45251
Mandarin Dr 45240
Mandery Ave 45214
Mandrake Dr 45251
Manford Ct 45240
Mangham Dr 45215
Mangrove Ln 45246
Manhattan Dr 45251
Manistee Way 45251
Manitoba Dr 45255
Manitou St 45206
Mann Pl 45229

Manning Ave 45211
Mannington Ave 45226
Manor Hill Dr 45220
Manor Hill Ln 45243
Manortree Ct 45238
Manover Ln 45252
Mansfield St 45202
Mansion Ave 45205
Manss Ave 45205
Mantell Ave 45236
Manuel St 45227
Maphet St 45227
Maple Ave
  421-421 45215
  431-507 45229
  509-617 45229
  520-618 45215
  619-631 45229
  1200-1299 45246
  1400-1599 45215
  1800-2199 45212
  3500-3599 45241
  7000-7146 45243
  7148-7156 45243
  7300-7599 45231
Maple Dr
  500-899 45215
  4100-4199 45209
Maple St
  8-12 45215
  9-13 45216
  14-799 45215
  15-599 45216
  200-216 45215
  218-218 45215
  801-899 45215
  900-999 45238
  6700-6799 45227
  11100-11199 45241
Maple Trce 45246
Maple Circle Dr 45246
Maple Dale Ln 45255
Maple Knoll Cir 45246
Maple Knoll Dr 45251
Maple Knoll Ter 45246
Maple Leaf Ct 45246
Maple Leaf Dr 45243
Maple Park Ave 45209
Maple Ridge Ct 45244
Maple Tree Ct 45236
Maple View Pl 45246
Maplecove Ln 45255
Maplecrest Pl 45209
Maplecroft Ct 45255
Maplefield Ct 45255
Maplehill Dr 45240
Mapleleaf Ave
  2900-2999 45212
  3000-3199 45213
Mapleleaf Dr 45255
Mapleport Way 45255
Mapleridge Dr 45227
Maplespur Ln 45227
Mapleton Ave 45233
Maplevalley Ct 45244
Mapleview Ct 45236
Maplewood Ave 45219
Mar Bev Dr 45239
Mar Del Dr 45243
Mar Ric Ln 45215
Marbill Ln 45238
Marble St 45223
Marblehead Dr 45243
Marburg Ave
  3600-3699 45208
  3700-5099 45209
Marburg Square Ln 45209
Marcarol Ln 45230
Marcella Dr 45248
March Ter 45239
Marchwind Ct 45239
Marcrest Dr 45211
Mardon Pl 45205
Marette Dr 45245
Margaret St 45214
Margaretta Ave 45242
Margate Ter 45241

Marge Pl 45238
Margo Ln 45227
Maria Ave
3600-3699 45205
10200-10499 45231
Marias Oak Ct 45248
Marie Ave
5500-5599 45248
6200-6399 45224
Marieda Dr 45245
Mariemont Ave & Cres . 45227
Marietta St 45227
Marieview Ct 45236
Marilyn Ln
500-599 45255
1600-1799 45231
Mariners Cv 45249
Marino Dr 45251
Marion Ave
200-299 45215
900-1099 45229
4900-5199 45212
Marion Rd 45215
Marions Way 45255
Mariposa Dr 45231
Mariwood Ln 45230
Marjorie Ln 45244
Mark Ct 45255
Markay Ct 45248
Markbreit Ave 45209
Markdale Ct 45248
Marker Dr 45251
Market Pl 45216
Market St 45215
S Market St 45219
Markley Rd 45230
Markley Woods Way ... 45230
Marksberry Ln 45249
Marlborough Dr 45230
Marlette Dr 45249
Marley St 45216
Marlin Ave 45211
Marlington Ave 45208
Marlou Ln 45230
Marlowe Ave 45224
Marmet Ave 45220
Marmion Ln 45212
Marquette Ave 45230
Mars Ct 45231
Marsh Ave 45212
Marshall Ave
1000-2895 45225
2896-3099 45220
Marsue Ln 45211
Martha Ave 45223
Martha Rd 45230
Martin Dr 45202
Martin Pl 45202
Martin St
1-199 45217
7300-7899 45231
Martin Luther King Dr E
1-47 45219
49-229 45219
231-299 45219
400-599 45229
800-1399 45206
Martin Luther King Dr W 45220
Martini Rd 45233
Marview Ave 45236
Marview Ter 45231
Marvin Ave
6700-6804 45243
6700-6842 45224
6806-6812 45243
6814-6822 45243
Marwood Ln 45246
Mary Ln
100-199 45217
1000-1099 45215
Mary St
1-99 45216
6000-6199 45227
Mary Ann Ln 45213
Mary Crest Ave & Dr ... 45237
Mary Jane Dr 45211
Mary Lee Ln 45244
Marydell Pl 45211
Maryland Ave
2300-2899 45204
7100-7299 45236
Mason Montgomery Rd 45249
Mason Way Ct 45249
Massachusetts Ave 45225
Massachusetts Dr 45245
Massey Ct 45255
Massies Grant 45244
Mathers St 45206
Mathis St 45227
Matlock Ave 45237
Matson Ave 45236
Matson Ct 45236
Matson Pl 45204
Matthews Ct 45246
Matthews Dr 45215
Mattingly Blvd 45233
Maureen Ln 45238
Maverick Dr 45231
Maxfield Ln 45243
Maxim Way 45249
Maxwell Ave 45219
May St
2100-2899 45206
3900-3999 45245
6300-6699 45243
7400-7499 45236
8000-8199 45216
Mayapple St 45226
Mayberry Ln 45239
Maycliffe Pl 45230
Mayfair Ave 45211
Mayfair St 45216
Mayfield Ave
3600-3799 45205
6900-7199 45243
Mayflower Ave 45237
Mayhew Ave 45238
Mayjo Ct 45224
Mayland Dr 45230
Maylee Pl 45238
Maynard Dr 45242
Mayridge Ct 45211
Mayrow Dr 45249
Mayview Forest Dr & Pl 45215
Maywood Ct 45211
Maywood Dr 45241
Mc Cane Dr 45243
Mcalpin Ave 45220
Mcauley Pl 45242
Mcbrayer St 45214
Mcbreen Ave 45211
Mccabe Ln 45255
Mccaulay St 45219
Mccauly Ct & Rd 45241
Mccauly Woods Dr 45241
Mcclelland Ave 45217
Mcclellans Ln 45246
Mcclure Ave 45237
Mccormick Ln 45245
Mccormick Pl 45219
Mccray Ct 45224
Mccreary Ct 45231
Mccullough St 45226
Mcdowell St 45226
Mcfadden Ave 45211
Mcfarlan Rd 45211
Mcfarlan Park Dr 45211
Mcfarlan Woods Dr 45211
Mcfarland St 45202
Mcfarran Ave 45211
Mcgary Dr 45245
Mcgill Rd 45251
Mcgillard St 45246
Mcgregor Ave
200-399 45219
400-799 45206
5700-6100 45216
6102-6298 45216
Mcgregor Pl 45219
Mcgrew St 45241
Mcguffey Ave 45226
Mcguire Ln 45215
Mchenry Ave
3000-3339 45211
3340-3699 45225
Mchugh Pl 45213
Mcintosh Dr 45255
Mcintyre Ave 45215
Mckelvey Rd
800-10099 45231
10500-10699 45240
Mckeone Ave 45205
Mckerai Dr 45255
Mckinley Ave
2100-2199 45224
2600-2999 45211
Mckinley Rd 45242
Mclaren Ave 45215
Mclaughlin Pl 45226
Mclean Ave 45203
Mclean Dr
300-399 45237
4000-4299 45255
Mclean St 45215
Mclelland Ave 45211
Mcmakin Ave
700-799 45232
1500-1699 45231
Mcmann Rd & Spur 45245
E Mcmicken Ave 45202
W Mcmicken Ave
1-199 45202
200-2728 45214
2729-3099 45225
E Mcmillan St
1-399 45219
400-1799 45206
W Mcmillan St 45219
Mcneil Ave 45212
Mcpherson Ave 45205
Mcswain Dr 45241
Mcwhorter St 45215
Mcwilliams St 45204
Mead Ave 45226
Meadow Ave
100-199 45217
3400-3699 45211
Meadow Ln
400-499 45215
3600-3699 45220
Meadow Bluff Ct 45249
Meadow Bluff Ln 45241
Meadow Brook Dr 45237
Meadow Estate Dr 45247
Meadow Gold Ln 45203
Meadow Grove Ln 45243
Meadow Ridge Dr 45245
Meadow Ridge Ln 45237
Meadow Walk Ln 45247
Meadowbright Ln 45230
Meadowcreek Dr 45244
Meadowcrest Cir & Rd . 45231
Meadowdale Cir 45243
Meadowglen Dr 45231
Meadowind Ct 45231
Meadowland Dr 45255
Meadowland Pl 45244
Meadowlark Ln 45227
Meadowmar Ln 45230
Meadowood Ct 45238
Meadowtrail Ct 45231
Meadowview Dr 45211
Meadowvista Ct 45224
Meagans Ln 45255
Mearl Ave 45239
Mears Ave 45230
E & W Mechanic St 45215
S Medallion Dr 45241
Medosh St 45215
Medpace Way 45227
Meeker St 45225
Mefford Ln 45241
Megans Oak Ct 45248
Mehmert Ave 45223
Mehring Way 45203
E Mehring Way 45202
W Mehring Way 45202
Meier Ave 45208
Meigs Ln 45233
Meis Ave 45224
Mel Carl Dr 45251
Melbourne St 45229
Melbourne Ter 45206
Melcrest Dr 45245
Melish Ave & Pl 45206
Melissa Ct 45251
Melissaview Ct 45248
Mellowbrook Ct 45239
Mellwood Ave 45232
Melody Ln
4600-4699 45245
8600-8699 45231
Melodymanor Dr 45239
Melrose Ave
2502-2578 45212
2503-2597 45212
2525-2539 45206
2585-2587 45212
2599-2636 45212
2600-3099 45206
2638-2642 45212
Melville Ln 45208
Memory Ln 45239
Mendon Hill Ln 45244
Mendova Ln 45230
Menlo Ave 45208
Menominee Dr 45251
Mentola Ave 45205
Mentor Ave 45212
Mentor St 45206
Menz Ln 45233
Mercer St 45202
Mercers Pointe Dr 45244
Merchant St 45246
Mercury Ave 45231
Mercury Dr 45244
Mercy Health Blvd 45211
Meredith Dr 45231
Merganser Dr 45246
Meridian St 45233
Meriweather Ave 45208
Merlin Ct 45244
Mernic Dr 45248
Merrell Ln 45215
Merrick Ln 45242
Merrifield Ct 45239
Merrimac St 45207
Merritt Grove Ln 45255
Merrittview Ln 45231
Merriway Ln 45231
Merrymaid Ln 45240
Merrymaker Ln 45236
Merton St 45214
Merwin Ave 45227
Merwin 10 Mile Rd 45245
Meryton Pl 45224
Merzen Ct 45217
Meta Dr 45237
Meyer Pl 45211
Meyerfeld Ave 45211
Meyerhill Dr 45211
Meyers Dr 45215
Meyers Ln 45242
Miami Ave
3700-5499 45226
6500-8199 45243
Miami Ct 45211
Miami Rd
3800-4012 45227
4300-8699 45243
Miami Run 45227
Miami Bluff Dr 45227
Miami Hills Dr 45243
E Miami River Rd
7100-10134 45247
10135-12199 45252
Miamitrail Ct & Ln 45252
Michael Dr
3800-3999 45255
6500-7099 45243
Michael Anthony Ln 45247
Michaels Run 45251
Michelles Oak Ct 45248
Michelles Whisper 45245
Michigan Ave
1200-3699 45208
3700-3799 45209
Mickey Ave 45204
Microwave Plz 45249
Midarene Ave 45212
Midden Cir 45238
Middlebrook Ave 45208
Middleton Ave 45220
Midfield Rd 45244
Midforest Ln 45233
Midland Ave 45205
Midpines Dr 45241
Midway Ave 45238
Mignon Ave 45211
Milaine Dr 45245
Milan Ave 45212
Mildmay Ct 45239
Miles Ct 45245
Miles Ln 45245
Miles Rd 45231
Miles Woods Ct & Dr ... 45231
Milgin Dr 45238
Miljoie Dr 45244
Mill Rd
9900-10399 45231
10400-12199 45240
Mill St 45215
Mill Farm Ct 45231
Mill Spring Ct 45231
Millbank Ln 45249
Millbrook Dr 45231
Millcliff Dr 45231
Millcreek Rd 45223
Millennium Pl 45211
Miller Rd 45242
Miller St 45223
Millies Ct 45247
Millington Ct 45242
Millrich Ave 45211
Mills Ave 45212
E Mills Ave 45215
W Mills Ave 45215
Millsbrae Ave 45209
Millsdale St
101-199 45215
200-899 45216
E & W Millvale Cir & Ct 45225
Millview Dr 45249
Millwood Ln 45224
Milton Ct 45229
Milton St 45202
Milverton Ct 45248
Mimosa Ln 45238
Minaret Dr 45230
N & S Mingo Ln 45243
Minion Ave 45205
Minmor Dr 45217
Minnesota St 45206
Minnewaukan Dr 45243
Minot Ave 45209
Minto Ave 45208
Minute Man Dr 45245
Miralake Ln 45243
Miramar Ct 45237
Mirror Ln 45248
Mission Ln 45223
Missouri Ave 45226
Mistyhill Dr 45240
Mistymeadow Ln 45230
Mistymorn Ln 45242
E Mitchell Ave
1-400 45217
401-697 45229
402-698 45217
699-899 45229
W Mitchell Ave
1-199 45217
200-4699 45232
Mitchell Way Ct 45238
Mockingbird Ln
600-699 45244
8200-8999 45231
Moeller Ave
600-699 45217
5300-5499 45212
Moellering Ave 45214
Moerlein Ave 45219
Moffat Ct 45211
Mohawk Pl & St 45214
Mohican Ln 45243
Mohler Rd 45241
Moline Ct 45223
Molly Green Ct 45211
Monalisa Ct 45239
Monardi Cir 45213
Monastery St 45202
Monerier Ave 45220
Monets Ln 45241
Monette Ct 45231
Monfort St 45206
Monfort Heights Dr 45247
Monfort Hills Ave 45239
Monica Ct 45238
Monitor Ave 45233
Monmouth St 45225
Monning Pl 45227
Monon Ave 45216
Monongahela Dr 45244
Monroe Ave
2100-2399 45212
8200-8599 45236
8600-9799 45242
Monroe St 45206
Monsanto Dr 45231
Montana Ave 45211
Montchateau Dr 45244
Montclair Ave 45211
Monte Vista Dr 45247
Montegor Dr 45230
Monteith Ave 45208
Monterey Ave 45236
Monterey Ct 45223
Montevista Dr 45224
Montezuma Dr 45251
Montgomery Rd
3300-3717 45207
3718-5899 45212
5900-6699 45213
6700-7199 45236
9000-10899 45242
10900-10980 45249
10982-12179 45249
Monticello Ave
5900-6099 45224
7700-7799 45236
Montoro Dr 45231
Montreal St 45204
Montridge Dr 45244
Montrose St 45214
Montvale Dr 45231
Montview Ct 45238
Moock Ave 45215
Moon Ln 45219
Moon Valley Ln 45230
Mooney Ave 45208
Moonflower Ct 45251
Moonkist Ct 45230
Moonlight Dr 45231
Moonridge Dr 45248
Moore Rd 45244
Moore St 45202
Moorehead St 45212
Moorfield Dr 45230
Moorhill Dr 45241
Moorman Ave 45206
Moosewood Ave & Ct .. 45225
Morado Dr 45238
Moran Rd 45244
Morgan St 45206
Morganraiders Ln 45236
Morning Dew Ct 45237
Morning Glory Ln 45240
Morning Watch 45244
Morningcalm Dr 45255
Morningdale Ct 45211
Morningridge Dr 45211
Morningstar Ln 45231
Morningview Ln 45211
Morris Pl 45226
Morris St 45206
Morrison Ave 45220
Morrison Pl
3400-3499 45220
6900-6999 45243
Morrocco Ct 45240
Morrow Pl 45204
Morrow St
100-299 45215
6100-6199 45230
Morrvue Dr 45238
Morse Ave 45246
Morse St 45226
Morten St 45208
Morton Ave 45212
Morts Pass 45215
Mosaic Ln 45237
Moss Ct 45236
Mosswood Ct 45224
Mosteller Rd 45241
Moubray Dr 45241
Moulton Ave 45205
Mound St
300-399 45215
900-1099 45203
Mound Way 45227
Moundcrest Dr 45212
Moundview Dr 45212
Mount Adams Cir 45202
Mount Airy Ave 45239
Mount Alverno Rd 45238
Mount Carmel Rd 45244
Mount Carmel Tobasco Rd
4000-4242 45255
4243-4599 45244
Mount Echo Rd 45204
Mount Echo Park Dr 45205
Mount Holly Ct 45240
Mount Hope Ave 45204
Mount Moriah Dr & Vlg 45245
Mount Pleasant Ave 45215
Mount Vernon Ave
3700-3899 45209
6800-7199 45227
Mount Vernon Dr 45241
Mountfort Ct 45244
Mountville Dr 45238
Mowbray Ln 45226
Moyer Pl 45208
Mozart Ave 45211
Muchmore Ave 45227
Muchmore Pt 45243
Muchmore Rd
4100-4199 45227
4200-4899 45243
Muchmore Close 45243
Muddy Creek Rd
3300-5699 45238
5700-6699 45233
Muirfield Dr 45245
Muirfield Ln 45241
Muirwood Dr 45233
Muirwoods Ct 45242
Mulberry Ct 45215
Mulberry St
1-399 45202
600-799 45215
6900-7099 45239
Mullen Rd 45247
Mulligan St 45241
Mullins Way 45245
Murat Ct 45231
Murdock Ave 45205
Muriel Ct 45219
Murkett Ct 45231
Murray Ave 45227
Murray Rd 45217
Muscogee St 45216
Muskegon Dr 45255
Musket Dr 45244
Musketeer Dr
1600-1676 45207
1678-1698 45207

6000-6099 45248
Mustafa Dr 45241
Mustang Dr 45211
Myerdale Dr 45242
Myrtle Ave
1-99 45246
1100-1499 45206
4100-4399 45236
4801-4823 45212
4814-4816 45212
4816-4826 45242
4828-4999 45242
Myrtlewood Ave 45236
Mystic Ave 45216
Mystical Rose Ln 45238
Nabida Dr 45247
Naeher St 45214
Nagel Rd
1200-1319 45255
1320-1320 45254
1320-1998 45255
1321-1999 45255
Nagelwoods Dr 45255
Nahant Ave 45224
Nancy Ln 45226
Nancy Lee Ln 45238
Nandale Dr 45239
Nansen St 45216
Naomi Ave 45243
Napa Ct 45255
Napoleon Ln 45240
Narcissus Ct 45238
Narrowsburg Dr 45231
Nash Ave 45226
Nassau St 45206
Natamac Cir 45230
Nathanial Dr 45240
Nathaniel Glen Dr 45248
Nathanshill Ln 45249
Nature Trl 45244
Nature Trail Way 45231
Navaho Trl 45243
Navarre Pl 45227
Navona Ct 45246
Naylor Ct 45246
Neave St 45204
Nebraska Ave 45238
Neeb Rd 45233
Needlewood Ct 45236
Neff Ave 45204
Neiheisel Ave 45248
Neil Dr 45231
Neilson Pl 45206
Neisel Ave 45248
Nelson Ln 45246
Neptune Dr 45231
Neptune Way 45244
Netherland Ct 45240
Neumann Way 45215
Neuss Ave 45246
Nevada St 45204
New St
100-199 45233
300-499 45202
New England Ct 45236
New Hope Dr 45240
New John Gray Rd 45251
New Year Dr 45251
Newbedford Ave 45237
Newberry Acres Dr 45251
Newbridge Dr 45239
Newbrook Dr 45231
Newbury St 45216
Newcastle Dr 45231
Newell Pl 45226
Newfield Ave 45237
Newgate Ln
9500-9599 45231
11400-11599 45240
Newlun Ct 45244
Newmarket Dr 45251
Newport Dr 45231
Newton Ave 45207
Newtown Rd 45244
Neyer Ave 45225
Niagara St
2500-2699 45231
2700-3599 45251
Nicholson Ave 45211
Nicklaus Ct 45245
Nickview Dr 45247
Nieman Dr 45224
Nightfall Ct 45251
Nighthawk Dr 45247
Nightingale Ct & Dr 45227
Niles St 45208
Nimitz Ln 45230
Nimitzview Dr 45230
Nina Dr 45244
Ninann Ct 45211
Nita Ln 45208
Nitram Ct 45230
E Nixon St 45219
W Nixon St 45220
Noble Ave & Ct 45239
Nodding Way 45243
Noel Ln 45243
Nohunta Ct 45231
Nolan Ave 45211
Nolen Cir 45227
Noralma Dr 45239
Norbourne Dr 45240
Norcol Ln 45231
Norcrest Dr 45231
Nordica Ln 45255
Nordyke Rd 45255
Norfolk Dr 45231
Norham Ave 45213
Norman Ave 45231
Normandy Ave 45227
Normandy Pl 45241
Normandy Close 45241
North Aly 45246
North Ave
1-199 45215
4100-4299 45236
North St 45202
E North St 45215
W North St 45215
North Way 45224
E North Bend Rd 45216
W North Bend Rd
1-23 45216
25-469 45216
470-498 45224
471-499 45216
500-2195 45224
2196-2899 45239
Northampton Dr 45237
Northbend Xing 45247
Northbrook Ct 45231
Northcreek Dr 45236
Northcrest Ln 45247
Northcut Ave 45237
Northdale Pl 45213
Northern Ave
200-399 45229
1900-2099 45224
Northern Pkwy 45224
Northfield Ln 45231
Northfield Rd 45242
Northgate Dr 45248
Northlake Dr 45249
Northland Blvd
2-380 45246
382-398 45246
385-397 45240
399-699 45240
670-670 45218
670-670 45246
700-898 45240
701-899 45240
Northpoint Dr 45247
Northport Dr 45255
Northridge Dr 45231
Northside Ave 45214
Northview Ave 45223
Northwest Blvd 45246
Northwest Dr 45231
Northwest St 45252
Northwich Dr 45230
Northwood Dr 45237
Northwoods Ln 45212
Norton St 45225
Norway Ave 45229
Norway Ct 45244
Norwell Ct 45240
Norwich Ave & Ln 45220
W Norwood Ave 45212
Nottingham Dr 45255
Nottingham Rd 45225
Nottinghill Ln 45255
Nottingwood Dr 45255
Nova Ave 45238
November Ct 45251
Novner Dr 45215
Nuby Ln 45217
Nuevelle Ln 45243
Nutmeg Knls 45244
O Brien Pl 45212
O Bryon St 45208
O Leary Ave 45236
O Meara Pl 45213
Oak Ave
500-1099 45215
800-898 45215
11001-11051 45242
11053-11199 45242
Oak Dr 45246
Oak Ln 45209
Oak Rd
500-699 45246
2100-2199 45241
Oak St
20-34 45246
20-50 45217
36-199 45246
200-524 45219
300-531 45216
526-538 45219
533-535 45216
600-899 45206
800-832 45206
3800-3941 45227
3901-3909 45236
3911-4399 45236
3943-3949 45227
4800-4899 45212
6800-6899 45236
7000-7099 45244
11100-11199 45241
Oak Brook Dr 45244
Oak Crest Ave 45236
Oak Hollow Ct 45255
S Oak Knoll Dr 45224
Oak Post Ln 45241
Oak View Pl 45209
Oakapple Dr 45248
Oakbrook Ct 45243
Oakcreek Dr 45247
Oakdale Ave 45237
Oakerli Ave 45209
Oakfield Ave 45224
Oakhaven Dr 45233
Oakhill Ln 45247
Oakhurst Ct 45241
Oakland Ave 45205
Oakland Farm Dr 45245
Oaklawn Dr 45227
Oakleaf Ave 45212
Oakleaf Ct 45241
Oakley Station Blvd 45209
Oakmeadow Ln
3300-3599 45239
3600-3699 45247
Oakmont St 45216
Oakpark Pl 45209
Oakridge Dr 45237
Oaks Dr 45245
Oakside Ct 45236
Oakstand Dr 45240
Oaktree Ln & Pl 45238
Oakville Dr 45211
Oakvista Dr 45227
Oakwood Ave
4100-4399 45236
5900-6099 45224
Oakwood Ct 45246
Oakwoodpark Dr 45238
Oasis Ct 45247
Oberlin Ave 45237
Oberlin Blvd 45237
Oberlin Ct 45246
Observatory Ave
1300-1399 45215
2300-3699 45208
Observatory Dr
500-699 45246
1300-1399 45208
Observatory Hl 45208
Observatory Pl 45208
Ocala Ct 45239
Ocenceda Dr 45251
Ocentria Dr 45241
Ocosta Ave 45211
October Dr 45251
Odeon St 45202
Odessa Ct 45240
Odin Ave 45213
Odin Dr 45244
Ogden Pl 45202
Ogle Ln 45245
Ohio Ave
200-300 45215
302-398 45215
1900-2131 45202
2132-2198 45219
2200-2500 45219
2502-2598 45219
6800-7299 45236
10900-10999 45241
Ohio Cir 45215
Ohio Pike
400-599 45255
600-1092 45245
1094-1104 45245
Old 5 Mile Rd 45255
Old Beechwood Rd 45244
Old Blue Rock Rd 45247
Old Carriage Trl 45242
Old Chapel Dr 45244
Old Chimney Ct 45241
Old Coach Rd 45249
Old Course Ln 45245
Old Court St 45203
Old Hickory Dr & Ln 45243
Old Indian Hill Rd 45243
Old Kellogg Rd 45255
Old Kincaid Ln 45213
Old Locust Hill Rd 45245
Old Ludlow Ave 45220
Old Mcmillan St 45219
Old Merwin Ln 45245
Old Oak Trl 45238
Old Orchard Ct
1-99 45255
6800-6899 45230
Old Orchard Dr 45255
Old Orchard Rd 45230
Old Pfeiffer Ln 45242
Old Red Bank Rd 45227
Old Savannah Dr 45245
Old Stable Rd 45243
Old State Route 74 45244
Old Stone Mill Rd 45251
Oldbarn Ct 45243
Oldbridge Rd 45230
Olde Commons Dr 45246
Olde Dominion Dr 45249
Olde Gate Dr 45246
Olde Savannah Dr 45247
Olden Ave 45215
Oldforge Ln 45244
Oldtimber Pl 45230
Oldwick Dr 45215
Olentangy Ln 45244
Olinchit Ave 45207
Olive Ave 45205
Oliver Ct
500-599 45215
5300-5599 45241
Oliver Rd 45215
Oliver St 45214
Olivette Ave 45211
Olivia Ln 45238
Olympia Way 45240
Omar Pl 45208
Omena Pl 45238
Omni Dr 45245
Omnicare Ctr 45202
Omniplex Ct & Dr 45240
Onondago Ave 45213
Ononta Ave 45226
Ontario St 45231
Onyx Ct 45240
Opal Ct 45242
Opengate Ct 45247
Orange St 45246
Orangeblossom Ln 45251
Orangeburg Ct 45251
Orangelawn Dr 45238
Orangewood Dr 45231
Orchard Ave
1-99 45215
3900-3999 45236
Orchard Ct 45211
Orchard Dr 45230
Orchard Ln
4100-4799 45236
6200-6499 45213
Orchard St
1-99 45217
200-299 45202
5000-5099 45212
7400-7499 45227
11200-11399 45241
Orchard Hill Ct 45251
Orchard Hills Ln 45252
Orchard Knoll Dr 45215
Orchard View Pl 45238
Orchardcreek Ct 45239
Orchardgate Ct 45239
Orchardknoll Ct 45239
Orchardpark Dr 45239
Orchardridge Ct 45239
Orchardtree Ct 45239
Orchardvalley Dr 45239
Orchardwood Ct 45251
Oregano Dr 45244
Oregon St 45202
Oregon Trl 45215
Orient Ave 45232
Orillia Dr 45239
Oriole Ct 45227
Orion Ave 45213
Orkney Ave 45209
Orland Ave 45211
Orland Rd 45244
Orlando Pl 45227
Orleans Ct 45224
Ormond Ave 45220
Ortiz Pl 45219
Osage Ave 45205
Osborne Ave 45242
Osceola Dr 45243
Osgood St 45227
Oslo Ct 45244
Osprey Ln 45246
Ostenhill Ct 45238
Osterfeld St 45214
Ottawa St 45233
Otte Ave 45223
Otterbein Rd 45241
Ottercreek Dr 45240
Outlook Ave 45208
Outlookridge Ln 45244
Overbrook Pl 45227
Overcliff Rd 45233
Overdale Dr 45251
Overhill Ln 45238
Overland Ave 45226
N Overlook Ave 45238
Overlook Hills Ln 45244
Overton Ln 45248
Overview Ln 45231
Ovid Ave 45231
Owasco St 45227
Owenton Ct 45240
Owl Creek Rd 45252
Owlcrest Dr 45231
Owlwoods Ln 45243
Oxbow Trl 45241
Oxford Ave 45230
Oxford Pl 45230
Oxford Ter 45220
Oxfordshire Ln 45240
Oxley St 45216
Oyster Bay Ct & Ln 45244
Oysterbay Dr 45255
P G Graves Ln 45241
Pace Ave 45213
Pacora Dr 45231
Paddington Ln 45249
Paddison Rd 45230
Paddison Trails Dr 45230
Paddock Ln 45229
Paddock Rd
4000-4799 45229
4800-5199 45237
6200-7499 45216
Paddock Hills Ave & Ln 45229
Page St 45226
Paisley Dr 45236
Palace Dr 45249
Palermo Rd 45244
Palisades Dr & Pt 45238
Palm Ave 45223
Palmer Ct 45245
Palmer St 45215
Palmerston Dr 45238
Palmetto St 45227
Palmhill Ln 45239
Palmore Ln 45215
Palmwood Ct 45224
Palmyra Dr 45251
Palomar Rd 45251
Palomino Dr 45238
Palos St 45205
Pamela Rd 45255
Pameleen Ct 45239
Pamlico Ln 45243
Panama St 45230
Pancoast Ave 45211
Pandora Ave 45213
Panola Dr 45215
Panorama Ct 45238
Panther Ct
1100-1199 45205
5300-5399 45238
Pape Ave 45208
Paprika Ct 45251
Para Dr 45237
Paradrome St 45202
Paragon Ct 45240
Paramount Ridge Ln 45247
Parchman Pl 45217
Parfore Ct 45245
Parfour Ct 45241
Paris St 45219
Park Ave
300-599 45215
600-799 45246
2201-2211 45206
2205-2597 45212
2213-2245 45206
2247-2399 45206
2250-2250 45212
2260-2384 45206
2403-2427 45212
2429-2431 45212
2433-2433 45212
2500-3099 45206
2599-2627 45212
2629-2641 45212
6800-6899 45236
7200-7499 45231
N Park Ave 45215
W Park Dr 45238
Park Ln 45227
Park Mnr 45242
Park Pl
1-99 45219
400-599 45244
4500-4599 45217
6700-6799 45239
Park Rd 45243
Park St 45249
Park 42 Dr 45241
Park Ridge Pl 45208
Parkcrest Ln 45211
Parkdale Ave 45237
Parker Ln 45230
Parker Pl 45217
Parker St 45219
Parkfield Dr 45240
Parkhill Dr 45248
Parkhurst Ct 45224
Parkland Ave 45233
Parkland Dr 45244
Parkline Ave 45208
Parkman Pl 45213
Parkmont Dr 45238
Parkridge Ct 45240
Parkside Ct 45238
Parkside Pl 45202
Parkson Pl 45204
Parktrace Ct 45238
Parktrail Ln 45238
Parkvalley Ct 45239
Parkview Ave
3000-3199 45213
5200-5299 45238
Parkview Dr 45224
Parkview Ln 45236
Parkwalk Dr 45239
Parkway Ave 45216
Parkwood Pl 45217
Parmalee Pl 45212
Parnell Ave 45230
Parrakeet Dr 45247
Parrish Ave 45239
Parrot Ln 45236
Parry Ln 45213
Partnership Way 45241
Partridge Pl 45214
Partridgelake Ct 45248
Pasadena Ave
1500-1637 45238
1617-1618 45224
1620-1636 45224
1639-1641 45238
Pasco Dr 45247
Pashori Rd 45218
Passage Way 45240
Pastoral Ln 45244
Pat Ct 45233
Patricia Ln 45230
Patrick Dr 45204
Patrick Way 45245
Patricks Glen Ln 45242
Patrilla Ln 45249
Patrisal Ct 45236
Patron Ct 45238
Patterson St
100-599 45215
2100-2199 45214
Patterson Farms Ln 45244
Pattie Ct 45247
Pattison St 45204
Patton Ave 45255
Paul Rd 45238
Paul St 45208
Paul Brown Stadium 45202
Paul Farm Ln 45231
Paul Margaritis Way 45249
Paulmeadows Dr 45249
Pavilion St 45202
Pavlova Dr 45251
Paw Paw Ln 45236
Pawnee Dr 45224
Pawtucket Dr 45255
Paxton Ave
1000-3679 45208
3680-3899 45209
3874-3874 45227
3900-4298 45209
3901-4299 45209
Paxton Knoll Ln 45208
Paxton Woods Dr & Ln 45209
Peabody Ave 45227

Street	ZIP
Peach St	
300-399	45246
7400-7499	45227
Peachblossom Ct	45231
Peachey Ct	45241
Peachtree Ct	45231
Peachview Dr	45247
Peacock Dr	45239
Peak Dr	45246
Peaks Edge Dr	45247
Peancene Dr	45244
Pear St	
300-399	45246
7400-7499	45227
Pearl St	45215
Pearton Ct	45224
Peasenhall Ln	45208
Peaslee Ave	45224
Pebble Ct	45255
Pebble Ridge Ln	45252
Pebble View Dr	45252
Pebblebrook Ln	45251
Pebblecreek Ln	45252
Pebbleknoll Dr	45252
Pebblevalley Dr	45252
Pecos Dr	45244
Pedretti Ave	45238
Pee Wee Dr	45244
Peete St	45202
Pegroy Ct	45239
Pelham Pl	45237
Pelican Dr	45231
Pell St	45223
Pellston Ct	45240
Pemberton Ave	45212
Pembina Dr	45238
Pembridge Dr	45255
Pembroke Ave	45208
Pemmicanrun Dr	45249
Penarth Dr	45251
Pendery Ave	45215
Pendinda Ave	45206
Pendleton St	45202
Penelope Ln	45236
Penfield Ln	45238
Penn Ave	45230
Pennington Ct	45240
Pennsbury Dr	45238
Pennsylvania Ave	45226
Penrose Pl	45211
Pensacola Dr	45251
Penway Ct	45239
Pepper Cir	45231
Pepper Ln	45230
Pepper Ridge Rd	45244
Pepperell Ln	45236
Peppermill Ln	45242
Peppermint Ln	45238
Percivale Ct	45241
Percy Ave	45211
Peregrine Ln	45243
Perignon Pl	45226
Perin Rd	45242
Perinwood Dr	45248
Perkins Ave	45229
Perkins Ln	45208
Perry St	
4500-4699	45242
7300-7999	45231
Pershing Ave	45215
Pershing Ct	45211
Persimmon Ct	45231
Perth Ln	45229
Perthview Dr	45244
Perthwood Dr	45244
E Pete Rose Way	45202
W Pete Rose Way	
1-599	45202
601-699	45202
700-899	45203
Petobego Ct	45251
Petoskey Ave	45227
Petri Dr	45230
Petworth Ct	45236
Pewter Rd	45244
Pfeiffer Rd	45242
Pharo Dr	45245
Pharoway Dr	45245
Pheasantwalk Ct	45241
Phillips Ave	
1-99	45217
3000-3399	45205
Phillips Rd	45230
Philloret Dr	45239
Philnoll Dr	45247
Philomena Ave	45223
Phoenix Ave	
3100-3399	45211
7400-7499	45231
Pica St	45205
Picardy Ln	45248
Picasso Ct	45244
Piccadilly Cir & Sq	45255
Pickbury Dr	45211
Picket Way	45245
Pickmeier Ln	45211
Pickway Dr	45233
Pickwick Dr	45255
Pickwick Pl	45241
Pictoria Dr	45246
Pictureview Ln	45247
Picuda Ct	45238
Picwood Dr	45248
Piedmont Ave	45219
Pieper Way	45237
Pike St	
1-599	45215
300-308	45202
310-314	45202
316-408	45202
Pilgrim Pl	45246
Pillars Dr	45209
Pin Ct	45239
Pin Oak Dr	45239
Pina St	45248
Pinallas Ct	45238
Pinckney St	45214
S Pine Dr	45241
Pine Rd	
8200-8599	45236
8600-8899	45242
Pine St	
1-99	45216
3300-3399	45244
4800-4999	45212
Pine Brook Cir	45247
Pine Grove Ave	45208
Pine Isle Ct	45244
Pine Knoll Dr	45224
Pine Needle Ct	45244
Pine Run Dr	45244
Pine Valley Ln	45245
Pinebluff Ln	45255
Pinebrook Ct	45224
Pinecliff Ln	45247
Pinecove Ct	45249
Pinecrest Dr	45238
Pinecroft Dr	45211
Pinedale Dr	45231
Pineglen Dr	45224
Pinehill Dr	45238
Pinehollow Ln	45231
Pinehurst Ave	45208
Pinehurst Dr	45244
Pinehurst Ln	45208
Pineknot Dr	45238
Pinemeadow Ln	45224
Pineneedle Ln	45243
Pineridge Ave	45208
Pineterrace Dr	45255
Pinetree Ln	45245
Pinetree St	45214
Pineview Ln	45247
Pinewell Dr	45255
Piney Meadow Ln	45244
Pinnacle Dr	45247
Pinney Ln	45231
Pinto Ct	45242
Pinwood Ln	45239
Pioneer Dr	45247
Pipewell Ln	45243
Pippin Ct	45231
Pippin Ln	45231
Pippin Rd	
7100-8399	45239
8400-9199	45251
9200-12199	45231
Pippin Meadows Dr	45231
Piqua Ave	45224
Pitt St	45219
Pitts Ave	45223
Pittsburg St	45226
Placid Pl	45236
Plainfield Ln	45236
Plainfield Rd	
6000-6599	45213
6600-8999	45236
9000-9799	45236
10201-10297	45241
10299-10799	45241
10400-10599	45241
Plainville Rd	45227
Planet Dr	45231
Plantation Way	45224
Plateau Pl	45241
Playfield Ln	45226
Playtime Ln	45231
Plaza Ave	45230
Plazaview Ct	45255
Pleasant St	
1400-1899	45202
3600-3799	45227
4000-4099	45245
6600-6799	45227
E Pleasant St	45215
W Pleasant St	45215
Pleasant Hill Dr	45215
Pleasant Run Dr	45240
Pleasant View Ave	45207
Pleasanthill Dr	45240
Pleasantwood Ct	45236
Pleasure Dr	45205
Plerrall Ave	45226
Plersida Dr	45246
Plover Ln	45238
Plum Rd	45238
Plum St	
1-315	45202
317-333	45202
346-364	45246
366-367	45246
369-369	45246
401-597	45202
599-1099	45202
E Plum St	45244
W Plum St	45244
Plumhill Dr	45249
Plumridge Dr	45238
Plymouth Ave	45230
Poage Farm Rd	45215
Pocahontas Ave	45227
Pogue Ave	45208
Poinsettia Dr	45238
Pointe Pl	45244
Pointer Ln	45213
Pointwood Way	45241
Polaris Ave	45231
Polk St	45219
Pollux Ct	45231
Polmeyer Aly	45227
Polo Woods Dr	45244
Pomeroy St	45230
Pomo Ct	45249
Pomona Ct	45206
Pompano Ave	45215
Ponce Ln	45238
Pond Run Ave	45244
Pond View Ct	45247
Pond Woods Ln	45241
Ponder Dr	45245
Ponderosa Dr	45239
Ponds Ln	45242
Pondside Ct	45241
Pondview Pl	45244
Pontius Rd	45233
Poole Rd	45251
Pope Dr	45215
Poplar Ave	45215
Poplar Crk	45245
Poplar Ln	45216
Poplar St	
1-99	45216
400-999	45214
4700-5099	45212
Poppy Ln	45249
Portage St	45233
Porthaven Way	45248
Portman Ave	45237
Portsmouth Ave	45208
Portway Dr	45255
Post And Rail Ln	45243
Postage Due St	45219
Potomac Ave	45208
Potter Pl	45207
Potter Farm Ln	45255
Pottinger Rd	45251
Powderhorn Dr	45244
Powell Dr	45211
Power St	45226
Powers St	45223
Powfoot Rdg	45245
Powner Rd	45248
Powner Farm Dr	45248
Prairie Ave	45215
Prang St	45223
Preakness Ln	45249
Preakness Pike	45245
Preble Ct	45233
Prechtel Rd	45252
Prelariv Dr	45239
Prentice St	45227
Prentiss Ave	45212
Prescott St	45233
Preserve Ln	45239
President Dr	45225
Presidio Ct	45244
Preston St	45206
Prestwick Ct	45233
Price Ave	
2600-2999	45204
3000-3699	45205
Pridenew Rd	45252
Prilla Ln	45255
Prince Ln	45241
Princess Ct	45215
Princeton Pike	45246
Princeton St	45204
Princeton Glendale Rd	45246
Princewood Ct	45246
Principio Ave	45208
Pringle Dr	45231
Prior St	45202
Priscilla Ln	45208
Probasco Ct & St	45220
Procter And Gamble Plz	45202
Produce Dr	45202
Production Dr	45237
Production Plz	45219
Progress Pl	45246
Promenade Dr	45240
Prospect Ave	45242
Prospect Pl	
500-699	45229
1200-1299	45231
Prosperity Pl	45238
Prosser Ave	45216
Proudhon Way	45239
Providence St	45214
Providence Way	45241
Province Ln	45239
Provincial Ct	45214
Pueblo St	45202
Puhlman Ave	45211
Pullan Ave	45223
Pulte St	45225
Pulver Dr	45251
Purcell Ave	45205
Purdue St	45220
Putnam Rd	45230
Putz Pl	45211
Quail Ct	45240
Quail Run	45244
Quail Run Farm Ln	45233
Quailhill Dr	45233
Quailhollow Pl	45240
Quailhollow Rd	45243
Quaillake Dr	45248
Quailridge Ct	45240
Quailwood Ct	45238
Quailwood Dr	45240
Quaker Ct	45251
Quaker Hill Dr	45211
Quante Ave	45211
Quarter Maine Ave	45236
Quarterhorse Ct	45249
Quatman Ave	45212
Quebec Rd	
1200-1923	45205
1924-2399	45214
Queen City Ave	
1200-2299	45214
2300-3399	45238
Queen Crest Ave	45236
Queens Ave	45236
Queensgate Ln	45203
Queensway Ln	45230
Queenswood Dr	45211
Race Rd	
3800-5099	45211
5100-5599	45247
Race St	45202
Raceview Ave	
3900-4499	45211
5500-5599	45248
Rachel St	45225
Rachel Anne Ct	45241
Rack Ct	45239
Rackacres Dr	45211
Rackview Rd	45248
Radcliff Dr	45204
Radcliff Ln	45241
Raeann Dr	45252
N & S Raeburn Dr, Ln & Ter	45223
Raglan St	45230
Ragland Rd	45244
Raiders Run Rd	45236
Railroad Ave	
1-399	45217
7700-7899	45243
9400-9599	45242
Rainbow Ct	45230
Rainbow Ln	45230
Rainbow Rdg	45215
Raleigh Ln	45215
Ralph Ave	45238
Ralston Ave	45223
Ramble Vw	45231
Rambler Pl	45231
Rambling Hills Dr	45230
Ramblingridge Dr	45247
Rammelsberg St	45206
Ramona Ave & Cir	45211
Ramondi Pl	45240
Ramsdale Ct	45246
Ramundo Ct	45230
Ranchill Dr	45231
Rancho Ln	45244
Ranchvale Dr	45230
Randall Ave	45225
Randolph Ln	45245
Randolph St	45220
Randomhill Rd	45231
Randy Ct	45247
Rangoon Ct	45240
Rankin St	45214
Ranlyn Ave & Ct	45239
Raphael Pl	45240
Rapid Ave	45205
Rapid Run Rd	
4500-5699	45238
5700-6999	45233
Rathman Pl	45255
Ratterman Ave	45211
Raven Ln	45242
Ravenal Ct	45213
Ravencrest Ct	45255
Ravenna St	45227
Ravens Run	45244
Ravens Ridge Ln	45247
Ravensburg Ct	45240
Ravenswalk Ln	45243
Ravenwood Ave	45213
Ravenwood Ct	45244
Ravine St	
2000-2199	45214
2200-2599	45219
Ravogli Ave	45211
Rawhide Ct	45238
Rawson Pl	45209
Rawson Farm Ln	45220
Rawson Woods Cir & Ln	45220
Ray Norrish Dr	45246
Raymar Blvd & Dr	45208
Raytee Ter	45230
Raywill Ct	45227
Reading Ln	45229
Reading Rd	
300-2499	45202
2500-3099	45206
3100-4699	45229
4700-8399	45237
8400-9799	45215
9800-11100	45241
11069-11069	45262
11101-12199	45241
11102-12198	45241
Rebold St	45230
Rebor Ct	45239
Red Bank Rd	
3300-5799	45227
5800-6699	45213
Red Bud Ave & Pl	45229
Red Cedar Dr	45224
Red Coat Dr	45245
Red Deer Ct	45245
Red Fox Dr	45245
Red Fox Ln	45243
Red Hawk Ct	45251
Red Maple Way	45246
Red Stag Pl	45245
Red Villa Ct	45209
Redbird Dr	45231
Redbird Hollow Ln	45243
Redcloud Ct & Dr	45249
Redeagle Way	45216
Redfern Ct	45251
Redfield Pl	45230
Redhaven Ct	45247
Redhill Dr	45242
Redmaple Dr	45244
Redmill Dr	45231
Redmont Ave	45236
Redna Ter	45215
Redoak Dr	45238
Redondo Ct	45243
Redskin Dr	45251
Redsky Dr	45249
Redstar Ct	45238
Redway Ave	45229
Redwing Ct	45239
Redwood Ct	45244
Redwood Ter	45217
Reed Hartman Hwy	
9500-10899	45242
10900-11199	45242
11200-11500	45241
11501-11597	45241
11502-11598	45241
11599-12200	45241
12202-12598	45241
Reedy St	45202
Reemelin Ave	45223
Reemelin Rd	
3400-5519	45211
5520-5850	45248
Regal Ln	45251
Regatta Dr	45252
Regency Ct	45251
Regency Ridge Ct	45248
Regency Run Ct	45240
Regency Square Ct	45231
Regent Ave	
1100-1499	45237
3700-3999	45212
Regent Rd	45245
Regiment Dr	45244
Regimental Pl	45239
Regina Ave	45205
Regina Graeter Way	45216
Regis Ct	45244
Reid Ave	45224
Reily Rd	45215
Reinhold Dr	45237
Reisling Knls	45226
Reliance Dr	45240
Relleum Ave	45238
Relluk Dr	45238
Reltas Ct	45249
Rembold Ave	45227
Remington Rd	45242
Renee Ct	45239
Renetta Ct	45251
Renfro Ave	45211
Rennel Dr	45226
Renner Pl & St	45214
Renoir Pl	45241
Renshaw St	45219
Renslar Ave	45230
Rentz Pl	45238
Republic St	45202
Reserve Cir	45230
Resolute Cir	45252
Resor Ave & Pl	45220
Retford Dr	45231
Rettig Ln	45243
Rev Dr	45232
Revel Ct	45217
Revere Ave	45233
N Revere Rd	45255
S Revere Rd	45255
Revmal Ln	45238
Rex Ave	45227
Rexford Dr	45241
Reynard Ave	45231
Rhode Island Ave	
5101-5737	45212
5738-5999	45237
Rice St	
2100-2199	45202
2200-2299	45219
Richard Ave	45224
Richard Ln	45244
Richardson Dr	45246
Richardson Pl	45233
Richford Dr	45231
Richland Dr	45255
Richmond Ave	45236
Richmond St	45203
Richwill Ct	45239
Richwood Ave	45208
Rickshire Dr	45248
Riddle Rd	
1-399	45215
400-799	45220
404-410	45231
412-539	45231
541-549	45231
Riddle Crest Ln	45220
Riddle View Ln	45220
Ridge Ave	
4100-5099	45209
5200-6899	45213
Ridge Cir	45213
S Ridge Ct	45224
S Ridge Dr	45224
Ridge Rd	
7100-8199	45237
8200-8599	45236
8601-8699	45236
Ridge Pointe Ct	45237
Ridgeacres Dr	45237
Ridgebrook Ln	45231
Ridgecliff Ave	45212
Ridgecliff Dr	45215
Ridgecombe Dr	45248
Ridgecrest Dr	45242
Ridgedale Dr	45247
Ridgefield Dr	45224
Ridgeland Pl	45212

Ridgeley St 45226
Ridgemoor Ave 45231
Ridgepoint Dr 45230
Ridgestone Dr 45255
Ridgetop Way 45238
Ridgevale Dr 45240
Ridgevalley Ct 45247
Ridgeview Ave 45238
Ridgeview Dr 45215
Ridgeway Ave
500-899 45229
1800-1899 45212
3400-3499 45229
4700-4799 45212
9700-9799 45242
Ridgeway Rd
4-299 45216
300-399 45215
Ridgeway Close 45236
Ridgewood Ave
2700-2999 45213
3400-3799 45211
Ridlen Ave 45205
Riehle Rd 45247
Riesenberg Ave 45215
Riesling Dr 45245
Riga Ct 45240
Riley Ln 45227
Rinda Ln 45239
Ring Pl 45204
Ringgold St 45202
Ringwood St 45239
Rio Grande Ln 45244
Rion Ln 45217
Riovista Dr 45255
Ripplebrook Dr 45231
Ripplegrove Dr 45251
Ripplewood Ln 45230
Risingwind Ct 45249
Rita Ln 45243
Ritchie Ave
1-399 45215
2500-2599 45208
Ritter Ave 45242
River Rd
1800-4699 45204
4700-7599 45233
River Dee Ct 45230
River Hills Dr 45244
River Oaks Ct 45238
Riverama Dr 45238
Riverby Dr 45255
Riverpoint Ln 45255
Riverside Dr
900-2799 45202
2800-3499 45226
Riverview Pl 45202
Riverwatch Dr 45238
Riviera Pl 45231
Roan Ln 45242
Roanoke St 45227
Rob Vern Dr 45239
Robb Ave 45211
Robb St 45226
Robben Ln 45238
Robbins Ln 45241
Robers Ave 45239
Robert Ave
2700-2899 45211
5300-5499 45248
8200-8299 45239
Robert Ct 45239
Robert A Taft Dr 45244
Roberta Dr 45215
Roberts St 45227
Robertson Ave
2300-2759 45212
2760-3199 45209
Robindale Dr 45241
Robinet Dr 45238
Robinhill Dr 45211
Robinson Cir 45223
Robinway Dr 45230
Robinwood Ave 45237
Robison Rd 45213
Robley Ave 45223
Robroy Dr 45247
E & W Rochelle St 45219
Rock Hill Ln 45243
Rockacres Ct 45239
Rockaway Ave 45233
Rockcrest Dr 45246
Rockdale Ave 45229
Rocker Dr 45239
Rockfield Ct 45241
Rockford Pl 45223
Rockhurst Ln 45255
Rockingham St 45237
Rockland Ave 45230
Rocknoll Ln 45247
Rockport Dr 45231
Rockwell Rd 45238
Rocky Ridge Rd 45251
Rodeo Ct 45211
Rodoan Ct 45240
Roe St 45227
Roebling Rd
400-499 45204
500-699 45238
Roettele Pl 45231
Rogan Dr 45246
Rogers Pl 45206
Rogers Park Pl 45213
Rohde Ave 45230
Rohling Oaks Dr 45245
Rohs St 45219
Rokeby Ct 45241
Roland Ave 45216
Roland Creek Dr 45245
Rolef Ave 45215
Roll Ave 45223
Rollaway Rd 45236
Rolling Ln 45236
Rolling Hills Ct 45215
Rolling Hills Dr
1-399 45215
1100-1199 45255
1600-1699 45215
Rolling Oaks Ct 45239
Rolling Ridge Ct 45236
Rollingknolls Dr 45237
Rollingridge Ln 45238
Rollingrock Ln 45255
Rollman Estates Dr 45236
Rollymeade Ave 45243
Rolston Ave 45212
Romaine Dr 45209
Romana Pl 45209
Romance Ln 45238
Romilda Dr 45238
Romohr Rd 45244
Romohr Acres 45244
Ronald Reagan Dr 45236
Ronaldson Ave 45230
Ronda Ave 45212
Roney Ln 45244
Ronnie Rd 45215
S, W & E Rookwood Ct, Dr, Ln & Pl 45208
Roosevelt Ave
1800-2199 45240
2200-2799 45231
3100-3199 45211
Ropes Dr 45244
Roppelt Rd 45252
Rosa Parks St 45202
Rosalee Ln 45236
Rose Ave 45212
Rose Ln 45246
Rose Pl 45237
Rose St 45215
Rose Crest Ave 45243
Rose Hill Ave
500-699 45217
3900-4299 45229
Rose Hill Ln 45217
Rose Meadow Ln 45230
Rose Petal Dr 45247
Roseann Ln 45239
Rosebud Dr 45238
Rosecliff Ave 45237
Rosecliff Dr 45205
Rosedale Ave 45237
Roseland Mound 45212
Roselawn Pl 45207
Rosella Ave 45208
Rosemary Ln 45236
Rosemont Ave
300-399 45204
400-1699 45205
Rosetree Ln 45230
Rosetta Ct 45246
Rosewood St 45216
Roslyn Ave 45238
Ross Ave
1000-1699 45205
1800-2199 45212
7400-7599 45237
E Ross Ave 45217
W Ross Ave 45217
Ross Ln 45244
Rossash Rd 45236
Rosslyn Dr 45209
Rossmore Ave 45237
Rossplain Dr 45236
Roswell Ave 45211
Roth Ave
1-99 45215
4500-4599 45238
Rothesay Ct 45251
Round Bottom Rd 45244
Round Top Rd 45251
Roundhill Rd 45236
Roundhouse Dr 45245
Roundtree Ct 45230
Rowan Hill Dr 45227
Rowanta Ave 45230
Rowley Ct 45246
Roxanna Dr 45231
Roxbury St 45230
Roxie Ln 45224
Royal Pl 45208
Royal Glen Dr 45239
Royal Heights Dr 45239
Royal Oak Ct 45237
Royal Point Dr 45249
Royal Stewart Ct 45245
Royalgreen Dr 45244
Royalview Ct 45244
Royalwoods Ct 45244
Ruberg Ave 45211
Rubicon Pl 45240
Ruckle Ave 45211
Ruddy Ct 45239
Rudgate Ct 45244
Rudyard Ln 45230
Rudyard Pl 45239
Rue Center Ct 45245
Rue De La Paix 45220
Ruebel Pl 45211
Ruehlmann Pl 45211
Rugby Rd 45224
Rugg St 45231
Rulison Ave 45238
Rumford Ct 45251
Rumpke Rd 45245
Runningfawn Dr 45247
Runyan Dr 45241
Rural Ln 45220
Rush St 45214
Rushton Rd 45226
Ruskin Dr 45246
Russell Ave 45208
Russell Heights Dr 45248
Russett Dr 45251
Rust Ln 45244
Rustic Ln 45215
Rustic Way 45245
Rusticwood Ln 45255
Ruth Ave
1500-1699 45207
3100-3199 45211
10700-10899 45231
Ruth Ln 45211
Ruth Lyons Ln 45202
Ruther Ave 45220
Rutherford Ct 45239
Rutland Ave 45207
Rutledge Ave 45205
Ruwes Oak Dr 45248
Ryan Ave 45219
Ryans Way
4400-4499 45245
10200-10399 45241
Rybolt Rd 45248
Rydel Dr 45238
Ryland Ave 45237
Sabino Ct 45231
Sable Dr 45238
Sachem Ave 45226
Sacramento St 45231
Sacred Heart Ln 45255
Saddleback Dr 45244
Saddleridge Rd 45247
Safari Dr 45231
Safe Ln 45215
Saffer St 45211
Saffin Ave 45214
Sagamore Dr 45236
Sage Ave 45225
Sagebrush Ln 45251
Sagecrest Dr 45239
Sagemeadow Dr 45251
Sagola Pl 45209
Saguin St 45227
Saint Albans Ave 45237
Saint Andrews Dr 45245
Saint Andrews Pl 45236
Saint Ann Pl 45211
Saint Anns Turn 45245
Saint Catherine Pl 45211
E Saint Charles Pl 45208
Saint Clair Ave
1400-1599 45231
8200-8499 45236
Saint Claire Ave 45215
Saint Dominic Dr 45238
Saint Edmunds Dr 45230
Saint Edmunds Place Dr 45246
Saint Elmo Ave 45224
Saint Georges Ct 45233
Saint Gregory St 45202
Saint Ives Pl 45255
Saint James Ave
2100-2399 45206
3900-4199 45236
Saint James Pl 45239
Saint Joe St 45219
Saint Johns Pl 45208
Saint Johns Ter 45236
Saint Jonathan Ct 45230
Saint Lawrence Ave 45205
Saint Leger Pl 45207
Saint Leo Pl
2100-2199 45211
2500-2599 45225
Saint Martins Pl 45211
Saint Michael St 45204
Saint Paul Dr 45206
Saint Paul Pl 45202
Saint Peters St 45226
Saint Regis Dr 45236
Saint Rita Ln 45215
Saint Thomas Ct 45230
Saint Williams Ave 45205
Saleasho Ave 45204
Salem Rd 45230
Salem St 45208
Salem Hills Ln 45230
Salem Ridge Ln 45230
Salem Woods Ln 45230
Salisbury Dr 45226
Sally Ct 45233
Salmar Ct 45231
Salty Ln 45244
Salutaris Ave 45206
Salvador St 45230
Salvia Ave 45224
Salway St 45232
Salzberg Ln 45246
Samoht Ridge Rd 45238
Sampson Ln 45236
Samstone Ct 45242
Samver Rd 45239
San Marco Ct 45243
Sanborn Ct & Dr 45215
Sanctuary Cir 45230
Sandal Ct & Ln 45248
Sandalwood Ln 45224
Sandcliff Dr 45255
Sanderson Pl 45243
Sandgate Ct 45241
Sandheger Pl 45220
Sandhurst Dr 45239
Sandover Dr 45233
Sandra Pl 45238
Sandra Lee Ln 45244
Sandralin Dr 45247
Sandstone Ct 45245
Sandy Ln 45239
Sandymar Dr 45242
Sanfan Ave 45231
Sanoma Ave 45243
Sanoma Ct 45255
Sanoma Dr 45243
Sanrio Ct 45247
Sanro Dr 45244
Sapphire Ln 45238
Sarah Bend Dr 45251
Sarah Joy Ct 45238
Sarahs Oak Dr 45248
Saranac Ave 45224
Saratoga Ct 45255
Sarazen Ct 45241
Sarbrook Dr 45231
Sargasso Ct 45251
Sargent St 45203
Sarita Pl 45208
Sarnia Ct 45244
Sarvis Ct 45214
Sassafras St 45225
Saturn St 45214
Sauer Ave 45219
Savannah Ave
6200-6411 45224
6412-6899 45239
Savannah Ct 45247
Savannah Way 45224
Saville Row 45246
Savoy Pl 45229
Sawgrass Ct
2600-2699 45233
3100-3199 45244
Sawgrass Ln 45209
Saxon Ave 45223
Saybrook Ave 45208
Sayler Ave 45233
Scamper Ln 45242
Scarborough Dr 45238
Scarborough Way 45215
Scarlet Dr 45224
Scarletoak Dr 45239
Scarsdale Cv 45248
Scenic Ave 45217
Scenic Dr 45219
Schappelle Ln 45240
Schenck Ave 45236
Schiff Ave 45205
Schiller St 45202
Schinkal Rd 45248
Schirmer Ave 45230
Schneider Ave 45223
Schneiders Farm Ct 45251
Schoedinger Ave 45214
Scholten Ln 45244
Schon Dr 45231
School Rd 45249
School St 45244
School Section Rd 45211
Schroeder Ln 45217
Schroer Ave 45238
Schubert Ave 45213
Schulte Dr 45205
Schumard Ave 45215
Schunk Ct 45239
Schuster Ct 45239
Schwartze Ave 45211
Schweitzerhoff Rd 45247
Scioto Dr 45244
Scioto St 45219
Scotland Dr 45238
Scottwood Ave 45237
Scoutmaster Dr 45241
Scripps Ctr 45202
Scull Rd 45252
Scully St 45214
Seabrook Ln 45244
Seabrook Way 45245
Seaford Dr 45231
Season Dr 45251
Sebastian Ct 45238
Sebright Ln 45230
Sebring Dr 45240
Secretariat Dr 45230
Section Ave 45212
Section Rd
1200-1699 45237
1701-3699 45237
1730-1730 45222
1732-3698 45237
3700-6999 45236
Sedam St 45204
Sedgewick Dr 45236
Sedler St 45205
Seegar Ave
2400-2499 45214
2500-2799 45225
Seibel Ln 45238
Seiler Dr 45239
Seitz St 45202
Selby Ct 45211
Selim Ave 45214
Seminary Ln 45206
Seminole St 45219
Semloh Ave 45247
Senate Ct 45244
Senator Pl 45220
Seneca St 45226
Sentinel Ridge Ln 45243
September Dr 45251
Sequoia Ct 45239
Serben Dr 45233
Serenade Dr 45238
Sesame St 45244
Setchell St 45226
Seton Ave 45205
Settle Rd & St 45227
Sevenhills Dr 45240
Seville Ct 45247
Seward Ave 45231
Seymour Ave
1200-2199 45237
2200-2399 45212
E Seymour Ave 45216
W Seymour Ave 45216
Shade Rd 45255
Shademore Park 45244
Shadetree Dr 45242
Shadowleaf Ln 45247
Shadowood Ct 45244
Shadowridge Ln 45240
Shadowslope Ln 45244
Shady Ln
3400-3499 45208
10100-10199 45215
Shady Hollow Ln 45230
Shady Lane Dr 45245
Shady Lawn Ter 45238
Shady Pine Dr 45255
Shadybrook Dr 45216
Shadycrest Dr 45239
Shadyglen Rd 45243
Shadymist Ln 45239
Shadyoak Ct 45231
Shadyside Ln 45249
Shadyslope Ct 45224
Shadywoods Ct 45244
Shaffer Ave 45211
Shagbark Dr 45242
Shaker Ct 45238
Shallowford Ln 45231
Shamrock Ave 45231
Shangrila Dr 45230
Shanmoor Ave 45212
Shannon Ln 45255
Shannon St 45204
Sharjoy Ct 45230
Sharkey Ln 45206
Sharlene Dr 45248
E Sharon Rd
1-699 45246
2000-3399 45241
W Sharon Rd
1-499 45246
500-1599 45240
Sharon Knoll Ct 45241
Sharon Meadows Dr 45241
Sharon Park Ln 45241
Sharondale Rd 45241
Sharonview Dr 45241
Sharonwoods Ct 45241
Shasta Pl 45211
Shattuc Ave 45208
Shaw Ave 45208
Shawnee Ln 45243
Shawnee Hills Dr 45243
Shawnee Pines Dr 45243
Shawnee Ridge Ln 45243
Shawnee Run Rd 45243
Shawnee Trace Ct 45255
Shayler Rd & Xing 45245
Shea Pl 45219
Sheakley Way 45246
Sheed Rd 45247
Sheehan Ave 45216
Sheffield Ave 45208
Sheffield Rd 45240
Sheits Rd
5100-5199 45251
5200-6499 45252
Shelby St 45204
Sheldon Ave 45239
Sheldon Close 45227
Shell Rd 45236
Shellbark Ln 45231
Shelley Ln 45224
Shelrich Ct 45247
Shenandoah Ave 45237
Shenstone Dr 45255
Shepard Rd 45212
Shepherd Ave 45215
Shepherd Dr 45215
Shepherd Ln 45215
Shepherd Rd 45223
Shepherd Creek Rd
4300-4499 45211
4700-5199 45223
Sheralee Dr 45231
Sheraton Ln 45246
Sherborn Dr 45231
Sherbrooke Dr 45241
Sherel Cir & Ln 45209
Sheridan Dr 45212
Sheridan St 45211
Sherlock Ave 45220
Sherman Ave
200-299 45215
1500-2199 45212
6400-6699 45230
Sherman Ter 45231
Sherry Ln 45255
Sherry Rd 45215
Sherrybrook Dr 45248
Sherwood Ave 45227
Sherwood Dr 45231
Sherwood Ln 45212
Shewango Way 45243
E Shields St 45220
Shillito Pl 45202
Shiloh St 45220
Shimmering Bay Ln 45244
Shipley Ct 45231
Shireton Ct 45245
Shirley Dr 45217
Shirley Pl 45238
Shirljune Dr 45215
Shivers Ct 45215
Shollenberger Ave 45239
Shona Dr 45237
Shore View Run 45248
Shoreham Ct 45255

Shorewood Ln 45241
Shorthill Way 45240
Shortridge Cir 45247
Shorts Dr 45230
Shoshone Ct 45215
Showcase Dr 45237
Shuman Ln 45231
Sibley Ave 45236
Sidney Ave 45225
Sidney Rd
5000-5699 45238
5700-5799 45233
Sidona Ln 45238
Siebenthaler Ave 45215
Siebern Ave 45236
Sienna Dr 45251
Sierra Park & St 45227
Siesta Dr 45247
Sigbee Ave 45208
Sigma Cir 45255
Signal Hill Ln 45244
Signal Pointe Dr 45247
Silkyrider Ct 45249
Silofarm Ln 45248
Silva Dr 45251
Silver St
5100-5199 45212
5600-5699 45216
Silver Crest Dr 45236
Silver Maple Way 45246
Silver Streak Dr 45245
Silverbrook Dr 45240
Silverfox Dr 45230
Silvergate Ln 45231
Silverglade Ct 45240
Silverhedge Dr 45231
Silverleaf Ave 45212
Silverpoint Dr 45247
Silverspring Dr 45238
Silverton Ave 45236
Silverwood Cir 45246
Simbury Ct 45224
Simca Ln 45211
Simmons Ave 45215
Simon Dr 45233
Simpson Ave
100-199 45215
3700-4899 45227
6200-6469 45224
6470-6899 45239
Simpson Ct 45215
Sinton Ave 45206
Sirius Dr 45231
Sitka Dr 45239
Skies Edge Ct 45247
Skillman Dr 45215
Sky Bridge Ct 45248
Skylark Dr 45238
Skyline Dr 45213
Skyridge Dr 45252
Skytop Ln 45244
Skyview Cir 45248
Skyview Ln 45213
Slack St 45202
Slane Ave 45212
Slaven Rd 45245
Sleepy Hollow Dr 45243
Sleepy Hollow Ln 45244
Sliker Ave 45205
Smalley Rd 45215
Smallwood Ln 45236
Smiley Ave
400-749 45246
750-1199 45240
Smith Ln 45215
Smith Rd
3800-3999 45211
4000-4008 45209
4004-4008 45211
4010-4023 45211
4010-4034 45209
4025-4039 45211
4036-4098 45209
4100-4899 45212
Smithfield Ln 45239
Smokey Woods Ln 45230

Snider Rd 45249
Snowflake Ln 45251
Snowvalley Ct 45251
Snyder Rd 45247
Soaring Eagle Ct 45244
Softspring Dr 45241
Sohn St 45219
Solar Vista Pl 45213
Solarama Ct 45238
Solon Dr 45242
Solzman Rd 45249
Somerset Dr 45224
Somerset Chase 45249
Songbird Dr 45239
Sonny Dr 45230
Sonny Ln 45244
Sonoma Ct 45227
Sonora Ct 45215
Sorrel Ln 45243
Sorrento Dr 45236
South Ave 45236
South Rd
2000-3099 45233
3100-3499 45248
South St 45204
Southacres Dr 45233
Southampton Ct 45231
Southern Ave
1-199 45215
200-299 45219
300-399 45215
3700-3999 45227
Southern Trce 45255
Southerness Dr 45245
Southfield Ct 45231
Southfork Dr 45248
Southgate Dr 45241
Southknoll Dr 45248
Southland Rd 45240
Southmeadow Cir 45231
Southpointe Dr 45233
Southridge Ln 45231
Southside Ave
3000-3599 45204
7300-7499 45243
Southstead Ct 45240
Southview Ave 45219
Southwick Ln 45241
Southwind Ter 45247
Southwoods Ln 45213
Sovereign Dr
2700-3399 45251
5600-6099 45241
Spalding Dr 45231
Sparkle Dr 45237
Spartan Dr 45215
Spechtview Dr 45248
Spencer Ave
3700-3999 45212
4400-4599 45236
Spencer Hill Dr 45226
Sperber Ave 45214
Spicewood Ln 45255
Spindlehill Dr 45230
Spindletop Hl 45245
Spindlewick Ln 45230
Spinner Ave 45241
Spinningwheel Ln 45244
Spiral Pass 45249
Spire Ridge Ct 45247
Spirea Dr 45236
Spiritknoll Ln 45252
Spiritoak Ln 45252
Spiritridge Ln 45252
Spiritwood Ct 45243
Spokane Ave 45207
Spooky Hollow Rd 45242
Spooky Ridge Ln 45242
Spring Ct 45227
Spring St
1100-1399 45202
3600-4099 45227
Spring Grove Ave
2100-2699 45214
2700-3466 45225
3467-3467 45223
3468-3468 45225
3469-4399 45223
4400-5107 45232
5108-5399 45217
Spring Hill Dr 45227
Spring Hill Ln 45226
Spring House Ln 45217
Spring Knoll Dr 45227
Spring Lawn Ave 45223
Spring Leaf Dr 45247
Spring Leaf Lake Dr 45247
Spring Park Walk 45215
Spring Rose Dr 45232
Spring View Dr 45208
Springbeauty Ln 45231
Springbrook Dr 45224
Springcrest Cir 45243
Springdale Rd
1200-1399 45218
1400-2699 45231
2700-5699 45251
5700-7199 45247
Springdale Lake Dr 45246
Springdew Dr 45231
Springer Ave
600-799 45215
2900-3099 45208
Springfield Pike
1-10699 45215
10700-12199 45246
Springfield Rd 45246
Springgarden Ct 45238
Springknob Ct 45251
Springlake Ct 45247
Springlen Ct 45251
Springmeadow Dr 45229
Springmyer Dr 45248
Springoak Dr 45248
Springrock Dr 45251
Springrun Dr 45231
Springs Ln 45255
Springside Ct 45240
Springvalley Dr 45236
Springwater Ct
1001-1041 45215
1043-1218 45215
1220-1798 45215
8400-8499 45247
Springwood Ct 45248
Spruce St 45216
Spruceglen Dr 45224
Sprucehill Dr 45240
Spruceway Dr 45251
Sprucewood Dr 45239
Spurrier Ln 45241
Spyglass Ct
1-99 45241
100-199 45238
7400-7499 45244
Spyglassridge Dr 45230
Squirehill Ct
5700-5899 45241
6000-6099 45230
Squirrel Run 45247
Squirrel Creek Dr 45247
Squirrel Run Ln 45247
Squirrelridge Dr 45243
Squirrelsnest Ln 45252
Squirrelwood Ct 45247
Squirrelwoods Ln 45247
Stable Watch Ct 45249
Stablehand Dr 45242
Staburn Ave 45216
Stacey Ave 45207
Stadia Dr 45251
Staebler St 45204
Stafford St 45227
Staghorn Dr 45245
Stahley Dr 45239
Standish Ave 45213
Stanford Dr 45223
Stanhill Ct 45230
Stanhope Ave 45211
Stanley Ave 45226
Stanley Ln 45226
Stanley Rd 45230

Stanlyn Dr 45245
Stanton Ave 45206
Stanwin Pl 45241
Stapleton Ct 45240
Starcrest Dr 45238
Stargate Ln 45240
Starhaven Trl 45248
Stark St 45214
Starling Ct 45238
Starlite Ct 45248
Starridge Ct 45248
Startinggate Ln 45249
Starvue Dr 45248
State Ave
600-1999 45204
2000-2199 45214
State Rd
7200-7463 45230
7495-7497 45255
7499-8099 45255
Stateland Ct 45251
Statewood Dr 45251
Stathem Ave 45211
Station Ave
100-199 45217
300-599 45215
4300-4499 45232
4600-4899 45212
Steamboat Dr 45244
Stearns Ave 45215
Steel Pl 45209
Steeplechase Dr 45242
Steffen Ave 45215
Steger Dr 45237
Steiner St 45204
Stella Ave 45224
Sterling Ave 45239
N Sterling Way 45209
S Sterling Way 45209
Sterlingridge Ct 45247
Sternblock Ln 45237
Sterrett Ave 45204
Stetson St 45219
Stettinius Ave 45208
Stevens Ave 45231
Stevens Pl 45226
Stevenson Ln 45206
Stevie Ln 45239
Stewart Ave
600-799 45215
4700-6499 45227
Stewart Park 45212
Stewart Pl 45229
Stewart Rd 45236
Stiegler Ln 45243
Stille Dr 45233
Stillmeadow Dr 45245
Stillmeadow Ln 45236
Stillwater Dr 45238
Stillwell Rd 45237
Stillwind Dr 45249
Stirrup Rd 45244
Stites Ave 45226
Stites Cv 45245
Stites Pl 45226
Stock Ave 45225
Stockholm Ln 45244
Stockport Ct 45231
Stokeswood Ct 45238
Stoll Ln 45236
Stone Arbor Ln 45226
Stone Barn Rd 45243
Stone Creek Dr 45209
Stone Crest Ln 45247
Stone Mill Rd 45251
Stone Snail Ln 45242
Stonebridge Dr
700-899 45233
3600-3699 45209
Stonechapel Ln 45223
Stonecreek Blvd 45251
Stonecreek Way 45241
Stonecrest Ct 45249
Stonegate Dr 45255
Stoneham Pl 45236
Stonehaven Dr 45245

Stonehearst Ln 45231
Stonehenge Dr 45242
Stonehill Dr 45255
Stonehill Run 45245
Stonehouse Ln 45255
Stoneleigh Ln 45255
Stonemill Ct 45215
Stonequarry Ct 45251
Stonetrace Dr 45251
Stonewall St 45214
Stonewood Ct 45240
Stoney Bridge Dr 45244
Stoney Culvert Ln 45215
Stoney Ridge Dr 45247
Stoneybrook Rd 45244
Stoneybrooke 45231
Stonington Rd 45230
Stonybrook Dr 45237
Stonypoint Dr 45231
Storm Dr 45251
Stormy Way 45230
Storrs St 45204
Stout Ave 45215
Stout Rd 45251
Stover Ave 45237
Strader Ave 45226
Strafer St 45226
Strahli Rd 45251
Straight St
300-699 45219
700-1299 45214
Strand Ln 45232
Stratford Ave
2100-2626 45219
2627-2899 45220
Stratford Pl 45229
Stratford Hill Dr 45230
Strathburn Ct 45230
Strathcoma Dr 45255
Strathmore Dr 45227
Stratton 45230
Strawberry Ln 45231
Stream Ridge Ln 45255
Stream View Ct 45255
Streambrook Dr 45231
Streamside Ct 45230
Streng St 45223
Strifler Pl 45243
Stroschen Dr 45248
Struble Rd
1900-2750 45231
2751-3999 45251
Stuart Ln 45245
Sturbridge Dr 45236
Sturdy Ave 45230
Sturgeon Ln 45251
Sturgis Ave 45217
Sturm St 45205
Stutly Ct 45230
Style Ln 45238
Styrax Ln 45236
Sudbury Dr 45231
Sue Ln 45238
Suehaven Ct 45248
Suffolk St 45230
Sugar Maple Ct 45255
Sugar Maple Ln 45246
Sugarball Ln 45215
Sugarberry Ct 45224
Sugarmaple Ct 45236
Sugartree Ct 45231
Sugarun Ln 45243
Suire Ave 45205
Sullivan Ave 45217
Sulsar Ave 45207
Sultana Dr 45238
Sumac Ter 45239
Summe Dr 45231
Summer St 45204
Summer Crest Dr 45251
Summer View Dr 45255
Summerdale Ln 45248
Summerfield Ln 45240
Summerhouse Rd 45243
Summerside Rd 45244
Summerville Dr 45246

Summerwind Ct 45252
Summit Ave
700-936 45204
938-950 45204
940-942 45246
944-974 45246
7000-7199 45243
7300-7599 45236
8900-9099 45242
Summit Rd 45237
Summit East Ct 45237
Summit Hills Dr 45255
Summit Lake Dr 45247
Summit Oak Ln 45248
Summit View Ct 45247
Summitridge Dr 45255
Sumter Ave
3900-3940 45244
5000-5199 45238
Sun Ave 45232
Sun Ridge Ln 45247
Sunaire Ter 45238
Sunappe Ct 45247
Sunbright Dr 45247
Sunburst Ln 45238
Sunburst Rdg 45248
Sunbury Ln 45251
Suncreek Ct 45238
Suncrest Dr 45208
Sundale Ave 45239
Sundance Dr 45233
Sunderland Dr 45255
Sunfield Dr 45237
Sungrove Ct 45241
Sunland Dr 45238
Sunlight Dr 45231
Sunliner Ct 45231
Sunmont Dr 45255
Sunny Acres Dr 45255
Sunnybrook Dr 45237
Sunnyhill Dr 45225
Sunnyhollow Ln 45239
Sunnyside Dr 45251
Sunnyslope Dr & Ter 45229
Sunnywoods Ln 45239
Sunray St 45230
Sunridge Dr 45224
Sunrise Ave 45231
Sunset Ave
800-1399 45205
1400-2099 45238
Sunset Ln 45238
Sunshine Ave 45211
Sunvalley Ln 45230
Sunwalk Dr 45237
Sunwood Ct 45231
Superior Ave 45236
Surfwood Ln 45241
Surrey Ave 45248
Surrey Rdg 45245
Surrey Trl 45245
Surrey Way 45245
Surreyhill Ln 45243
Susann Ln 45215
Susanna Dr 45251
Susanview Ln 45244
Susanwoods Ct 45249
Sussex Ave 45230
Susshine Ln 45243
Sutter Ave 45225
Sutters Mill Dr 45247
Sutton Ave, Pl & Rd 45230
Suwanee Ct 45244
Swallow Ct 45242
Swanbrook Ln 45233
Swanson Ct 45249
Sweetbriar Ln 45239
Sweetgum Ct 45241
Sweetwater Dr 45215
Sweetwood Ct 45251
Swift Ave 45212
Swindon Ct 45241
Swing Rd 45241
Swirlwood Ln 45239
Swiss Chalet Ct 45220
Swissvale Ct 45251

Sycamore Blvd 45245
Sycamore Rd 45236
Sycamore St
300-1899 45202
5700-6199 45216
Sycamore Grove Ln 45241
Sycamore Terrace Dr 45249
Sycamore Trace Ct 45242
Sycamorehill Ln 45243
Sylmar Ct 45233
Sylvan Ave 45223
Sylvan Ln 45215
Sylved Ln 45238
Sylvia Ln 45215
Symmes St 45206
Symmes Gate Ln 45249
Symphony Ln 45242
Syracuse St 45206
Tacoma Ave 45220
Taconic Ter 45215
Tafel St 45225
Taft Ave 45211
Taft Pl 45243
Taft Road Ln 45206
Tag Dr 45231
Tahiti Dr 45224
Tahoe Ter 45238
Talbert St 45205
Talbott Ave 45211
Tall Trl 45242
Tall Pines Ln 45244
Tall Trees Dr 45245
Tallahassee Dr 45239
Tallant Ave 45220
Tallberry Dr 45230
Talloak Ct 45247
Tam O Shanter Ct 45255
Tamarack Ave 45207
Tamarco Dr 45242
Tammy Ct 45238
Tampico Dr 45231
Tamworth Cir 45213
Tanager Ln 45215
Tanagerhills Dr 45249
Tanagerwoods Dr 45249
Tanbark Ct 45231
Tances Dr 45243
Tangent Dr 45211
Tangleberry Ct 45240
Tangleridge Dr 45243
Tanglewood Ln 45224
Tannehill Ln 45208
Tanner Ave 45213
Tansing Dr 45231
Tappan Ave 45223
Tarawa Dr 45224
Tarpis Ave 45208
Tarryton Dr 45241
Tartan Hl 45245
Tassie Ln 45231
Taulman Aly 45242
Tavel Ct 45246
Taylor Ave
3000-3099 45220
3900-4199 45209
4400-4599 45236
Taylor Ct 45215
Taylor Rd 45248
Teaberry Ct 45238
Teakwood Ave & Ct 45224
Teal Dr 45241
E Tech Dr 45245
Techview Dr & Pl 45215
Techwood Cir 45242
Tecumseh Dr 45244
Tecumseh Trl 45243
Ted Gregory Ln 45242
Telegraph Ct 45244
Telford Ave 45224
Telford St 45220
Telluride Dr 45244
Telluride Way 45247
Temple Ave 45211
Templeton Dr 45251
Tenderfoot Ln 45249

Tennessee Ave
900-1899 45229
1900-1999 45212
Tennis Ln 45217
Tennyson Dr 45241
Tennyson St 45226
Tepe Ct 45241
E Teralta Cir 45211
Terlerie St 45202
Terleriv Dr 45240
Terra Ct 45248
Terrace Ave 45220
Terrace Dr
1-9 45215
11-123 45215
4200-4399 45245
S Terrace Dr 45215
Terrace Ridge Dr 45244
Terrace View Dr 45255
Terry Ct 45215
Terry Ln 45241
Terry St 45205
Terrydel Ln 45245
Terrylynn Ln 45239
Terrytown Ct 45246
Terway Ln 45231
Terwilligers Hill Ct 45249
Terwilligers Run Dr 45249
Terwilligers Valley Ln 45249
Terwilligers View Ct 45249
Terwilligers Wood Ct 45249
Terwilligerscreek Dr 45249
Terwilligersknoll Ct 45249
Terwilligersridge Dr & Ln 45249
Teuton Ct 45244
Tewkesbury Ct 45255
Texas Ave 45205
Thames Pl 45241
Thayer Ln 45249
Thelma Ave 45233
Theodore Ave 45236
Theresa St 45204
Thicket Ln 45255
Thill St 45219
Thimbleglen Dr 45251
Thinnes St 45214
Thisbe Ave 45233
Thistle Ct 45231
Thoburne Ln & St 45227
Thole Rd 45230
Thomaridge Ct 45248
Thomas Ct
1-9 45246
1100-1299 45215
Thomas Dr 45243
Thomas Ln 45244
Thomasview Ct 45231
Thomasville Ct 45238
Thompson Ave 45214
Thompson Rd 45247
Thompson Heights Ave 45223
Thomwood Dr 45224
Thornberry Dr 45231
Thornbird Dr 45230
Thorndale Ct 45239
Thorndale Ln 45244
Thorndike Rd 45227
Thornfield Ln 45224
Thornhill Ave 45224
Thornton Ave 45233
Thornton Dr 45236
Thornview Dr 45241
Thornwood Cir 45230
Thornwood Ln 45240
Thoroughbred Ln 45231
Thrall St 45220
Thrasher Dr 45247
Thrush Ct 45242
Thrushfield Ter 45238
Thunderbird Ave 45231
Thunderhill Ln 45233
Thurnridge Dr 45215
Tice Ct 45227
Ticonderoga Ct 45230

Tidewater Ct 45255
Tiffany Ln 45230
Tiffany Hill Ct 45241
Tiffany Ridge Ln 45241
Tiki Dr 45243
Tilbury Ct 45238
Tilden Ave 45212
Tillie Ave 45214
Tillotson St 45219
Tillsam Ct 45242
Timber Cir 45240
Timber Trl 45224
Timber Creek Dr 45245
Timber Ridge Ln 45241
Timber Top Ct 45238
Timber Trail Pl 45238
Timber Way Dr 45238
Timberbreak Dr 45249
Timberchase Ct 45247
Timbercreek Dr 45244
Timbercrest Dr 45238
Timbercroft Ct 45239
Timberdale Ct 45238
Timberhill Ct 45233
Timberhollow Ln 45247
Timberknoll Rd 45244
Timberlake Dr 45249
Timberland Dr 45215
N & S Timberlane Dr 45243
Timbermill Ct 45231
Timberpoint Dr 45247
Timbers Dr 45242
Timbershadows Ct 45238
Timbervalley Ct 45233
Timberview Ct 45215
Timberview Dr 45211
Timberwood Ln
700-899 45245
10900-10999 45241
Timely Ter 45233
Timrick Ct 45238
Tina Dr 45244
Tinaview Ct 45211
Tipton Ct 45231
Titian Dr 45244
Tiverton Ln 45231
Tivoli Ln 45246
Tobermory Ct 45231
Todd Ave 45223
Todd Rose Ave & Ct 45244
Tohatchi Dr 45215
Tokay Ct 45255
Tolland Ct 45248
Toluca Ct 45224
Tompkins Ave 45227
Tonopah Dr 45255
Tony Ct 45238
Topaz Dr 45230
Topeka St 45231
Topfield Dr 45255
Topichills Dr 45248
Topinabee Rd 45233
Topridge Pl 45232
Topview Pl 45251
Toronto Ct 45255
Torrence Ct 45202
Torrence Ln 45208
Torrence Pkwy 45208
Torrey Dr 45246
Torrington Ct 45248
Totempole Dr 45249
Totten Ave & Way 45226
Tottenham Dr 45231
Toulon Dr 45240
Toulouse Ln 45246
Tournament Dr 45244
Towanda Ter 45216
Tower Ave 45217
W Tower Ave 45238
E Tower Dr 45238
W Tower Ln 45238
Tower Rd 45248
Tower St 45220
Towering Ridge Way 45247
Towerview Ln 45255
Towerwoods Dr 45224

Towhee Ln 45243
Towne St 45216
Towne Commons Way 45215
Towne Square Ave 45242
Townhill Dr 45238
Townsend Rd 45238
Townsend St 45223
Township Ave 45216
Township St 45225
Townterrace Dr 45251
Townvista Dr 45224
Track Ln 45245
Tracy Ct 45245
Trade St 45227
Trafalgar Ct 45251
Trafford Ct 45231
Trail Ridge Ln 45223
Trailbridge Dr 45241
Trailridge Dr 45215
Trailview Ct 45244
Trailwood Ct 45240
Trailwood Dr 45230
Tralee Ct 45236
Tramore Dr 45236
Tramway Dr 45241
Tramwood Ct 45242
Tranquility Ln 45223
Transpark Dr 45229
Trapp Ct & Ln 45231
Traskwood Cir 45208
Treasure Ct & Ln 45211
Trebor Dr 45236
Tree Top Ln 45247
Treeknoll Dr 45244
Treeridge Dr 45244
Treetop Ln 45240
Treevalley Ct 45244
Treeview Dr 45238
Trelawney Ct 45251
Tremont Ln 45224
Tremont St 45214
Trenton Ave
500-588 45238
589-799 45205
Tressel Dr 45248
Tressel Wood Dr 45248
Trevino Ct 45245
Trevor Ave 45211
Trevor Pl 45225
Tri County Pkwy 45246
Triangle Park Dr 45246
Trianins Ave 45205
Tricon Rd 45246
Tridale Ct 45230
Trierlia St 45219
Triert Ave 45213
Triesta Ct 45230
Trillium Ct 45215
Trillium Ridge Ln 45255
Trimble Ave 45207
Trinidad Dr 45231
Trinity Ln 45237
Trio Ct 45238
Tripoli Dr 45251
Trockene Ave 45232
Troon Ct 45241
Trotters Chase 45249
Trotters Trail Ct 45249
Troubador Ct 45238
Trowbridge Dr 45241
Troy Ave 45213
N Troy Ave 45246
S Troy Ave 45246
Truitt Ave 45212
Trumbull Ct 45233
Tucson Ct 45239
Tudor Ct 45242
Tulane Rd 45212
Tulipwood Ct 45242
Tulsa Ct 45238
Tupelo Ln 45243
Turf Ln 45211
Turf Wood Cir 45240
Turfridge Ct 45248
Turfwood Ct 45241
Turgot Cir 45241

Turnberry Dr 45244
Turnkey Ct 45244
Turpin Ln 45244
Turpin Hills Dr 45244
Turpin Knoll Ct 45244
Turpin Lake Pl 45244
Turpin Oaks Ct 45244
Turpin Valley Ln 45244
Turpin View Dr 45244
Turpin Woods Ct 45244
Turquoise Dr 45255
Turrill St 45223
Turtledove Ct 45233
Turtleview Ln 45244
Tuscany Pl 45226
Tusculum Ave 45226
Tuskeegee Ln 45216
Tuxedo Pl 45206
Tuxworth Ave 45238
Twain Ave 45233
Tweed Ave 45226
Twelve Oaks Ct 45255
Twig Ln 45230
Twigwood Ln 45237
Twilight Dr 45241
Twilight Tear Ln 45249
Twin Hills Ridge Dr 45230
Twin Lakes Ct 45247
Twin Oak Dr 45224
Twinbrook Ct 45242
Twincrest Ct 45231
Twinridge Ln 45224
Twinview Dr 45247
Twinwillow Ln 45247
Tyndall Ave 45233
Tyne Ave 45213
Tyson Ct 45248
Underwood Pl 45204
Union St 45229
Union Cemetery Rd 45249
E & W University Ave & Ct 45219
Upland Pl 45206
Upper Rd 45233
Uranus Ct 45231
Urbancrest Dr 45226
Uright Pl 45208
Urwiler Ave 45211
Us Highway 52 45255
Utah Ave 45214
Utopia Pl 45208
Vacationland Dr 45231
Vail Ct 45247
Valdosta Dr 45246
Vale Ave 45215
Valence Dr 45238
Valencia St 45219
Valerie Ct 45236
Valiant Dr 45231
Vallangs Dr 45245
Valley Ln
1000-1099 45229
6900-7099 45244
Valley Brook Dr 45211
Valley Crossing Dr 45247
Valley Ford Ln 45230
Valley Ridge Rd 45247
Valley View Ave
5700-5899 45213
11700-11799 45246
Valley View Ct 45219
Valley View Pl 45244
Valley Vista Way 45247
Valleyway Ct 45247
Valwood Dr 45248
Van St 45219
Van Antwerp Ct & Pl 45229
Van Blaricum Rd 45233
Van Buren Ave
400-1199 45215
3100-3199 45229
Van Camp Ln 45246
Van Cleve Ave 45246
Van Dyke Ave 45226
Van Dyke Dr 45208
Van Fleet Ave 45231

Van Hart St 45214
Van Kirk Ave 45216
Van Lahr Dr 45244
Van Lear Aly 45202
Van Lear St 45219
Van Leunen Dr 45239
Van Meter St 45202
Van Nes Dr 45246
Van Roberts Pl 45215
Van Vey St 45205
Van Vista Dr 45244
Van Zandt Dr 45211
Vancover Ct 45244
Vancross Ct 45230
Vandalia Ave 45223
Vangeres Dr 45238
Vaquera Pl 45255
Varelman Ave & Ct 45212
Varner Rd 45243
Vassar Ct 45232
Vaughn St 45219
Vaukvalley Ln 45249
Veazey Ave 45238
Vegas Dr 45239
Velma Ct 45255
Velvet Ct 45255
Vendome Pl 45227
Venetian Ter 45224
Ventura Ct 45246
Venus Ln 45231
Vera Ave 45237
Veraview Ct 45244
Verbena Dr 45241
Verdale Dr 45230
Verde Ct 45255
Verde Ridge Dr 45247
Verdin Ave 45211
Verger Ln 45237
Vermona Dr 45245
Vermont Ave 45215
Verne Ave 45209
Vernier Dr 45251
Vernon Pl 45219
Verona Ave 45227
Verona Ln 45246
Versailles 45240
Verton Ln 45238
Verulam Ave 45213
Vestry Ave 45219
Vicbarb Ln 45244
Vicksburg Dr 45249
Victor Ave
1200-1399 45255
4300-4599 45242
Victor St 45219
Victoria Ave 45208
Victoria Ct 45215
Victoria Ln 45208
Victoria Pl 45208
Victorian Way 45241
Victorian Green Dr 45211
Victory Dr 45233
Victory Pkwy
2100-3199 45206
3200-3898 45207
3301-4097 45229
4099-4299 45229
Victoryview Ln 45233
Vienna Woods Dr 45211
View Ct 45219
View Dr 45245
View St 45244
View Place Dr 45224
Viewcrest Ct 45231
Viewland Pl 45238
Viewpointe Dr 45213
Viki Ter 45211
Viking Ct 45244
Viking Way 45246
Villa Dr 45242
Villa Ln 45208
Village Dr
5000-5099 45244
7800-8199 45242
Village Sq 45246
Village Brook Dr 45249

Village Woods Dr 45241
Villageview Ct 45241
Villas Cir 45215
Villaview Ct 45238
Vinca Dr 45237
Vincennes Ct 45231
Vincent Ave 45205
Vine St
200-514 45202
516-2198 45202
525-525 45201
525-2199 45202
2200-3000 45219
2917-2917 45223
2917-2917 45225
3001-3199 45219
3002-3198 45219
3200-3699 45220
3700-3798 45217
3701-3799 45220
3800-5200 45217
5115-5115 45216
5115-5115 45232
5201-5553 45217
5202-5558 45217
5555-5557 45216
5559-8499 45216
E Vine St 45215
W Vine St 45215
Vine Vista Pl 45217
Vinecrest Pl 45220
Vinedale Ave 45205
Vinegarten Dr 45255
Vinemont Dr 45231
Vinewood Ave 45227
Vineyard Pl 45226
Vineyard Rdg 45241
Vineyard Bluff Ln 45226
Vineyard Green Dr 45255
Vineyard Hills Dr 45255
Vineyard Woods Dr 45255
Vinings Dr 45245
Vinnedge Ct 45243
Vinton St
1500-1699 45225
1700-1719 45214
1720-1835 45225
1836-1899 45214
Violeta Ln 45237
Virbet Dr 45230
Virescent Ct 45224
Virgil Rd 45238
Virginia Ave
3700-4099 45227
4100-4499 45223
7100-7299 45236
Virginia Crk 45244
Virginia Ct 45248
Virginia Ln 45244
Viscount Dr 45238
Visitation Dr 45248
Vista Ave, Pl & Ter 45208
Vista Glen Dr 45246
Vista Point Dr 45247
Vista View Ct 45247
Vistaridge Ln 45227
Vittmer Ave 45238
Vivian Pl 45232
Vixen Dr 45245
Vockell Ln 45219
Vogel Rd 45239
Volkert Ave & Pl 45219
Voll Rd 45230
Vollmer Pl 45248
Volterra Ln 45206
Von Seggern St 45202
Von Seggren St 45202
E & W Voorhees St 45215
Vorhees Ln 45236
Voss St 45205
Voyager Way 45252
Vyvette St 45236
Wabash Ave
900-1500 45215
1502-1700 45215
3300-3699 45207
Wachendorf St 45215

Wade St
200-299 45202
300-799 45214
Wade Walk 45214
Wadell Dr 45230
Wadsbury Dr 45230
Wagner Rd 45245
Wagner St 45225
Wagners Ct 45227
Wahl Ter 45211
Wainwright Dr 45246
Waits Ave 45230
Wakefield Dr 45226
Wakefield Pl 45212
Walcot Ln 45249
Walden Glen Cir 45231
Waldon Dr 45231
Waldons Pond Dr 45247
Waldorf Pl 45230
Waldway Ln 45224
Wales Dr 45249
Walker Ave 45213
Walker St 45202
Walkerton Dr 45238
Wall St 45212
Wallace Ave
500-3499 45226
7000-7199 45243
Wallingford Dr 45244
Walls St 45217
Walnut Ave
1-13 45215
2-14 45215
15-99 45215
11100-11199 45246
Walnut St
1-12 45216
6-598 45215
13-13 45215
14-20 45216
15-17 45216
100-198 45202
100-100 45216
102-530 45216
109-401 45215
110-134 45215
200-242 45215
312-324 45202
326-345 45202
347-1699 45202
404-404 45215
406-1698 45202
600-729 45215
731-801 45215
3300-3599 45241
11400-11699 45246
Walnut Woods Ln 45243
Walnutridge Ct 45242
Walnutview Ct 45230
Walsh Ln & Rd 45208
Waltella Pl 45212
Walter Ave
3000-3099 45206
4000-4099 45211
4500-4599 45212
Waltham Ave 45239
Walton Creek Rd
3700-4210 45227
4211-4799 45243
Walts Way 45247
Walworth Ave 45226
Wanda Ave 45212
Wanderling Ln 45237
Wanninger Ln 45255
Ward Ln 45246
Ward St 45227
Wardall Ave 45211
Warder Dr 45224
Wardwood Dr 45251
Wareham Dr 45202
Warfield Ave 45239
Waring Dr 45243
Warner St 45219
Warren Ave
1-100 45215
102-198 45215
300-499 45220

3900-3999 45227
5100-5799 45212
Warrick St 45227
Warsaw Ave
2300-3099 45204
3100-3799 45205
Warwick Ave 45229
Warwick Pl 45246
Washalew Ave 45217
Washburn St 45223
Washington Ave
1-100 45246
102-102 45246
103-167 45246
105-105 45217
108-110 45215
110-218 45217
112-127 45215
145-199 45246
169-211 45246
207-221 45217
213-217 45246
225-235 45215
237-248 45215
300-320 45217
303-319 45217
310-336 45215
321-337 45215
400-499 45217
2203-2209 45212
2211-2230 45212
2250-2274 45212
2255-2261 45231
2263-2281 45231
2276-2424 45212
2283-2289 45231
2309-2309 45212
2311-2321 45212
2323-2415 45212
2324-2450 45231
2325-2397 45231
2452-2799 45231
3500-3864 45229
3820-3836 45211
3838-3844 45211
3866-3874 45229
3900-4299 45211
Washington Cir
1300-1399 45255
1700-2599 45215
Washington Ter 45206
Wasigo Dr 45230
Wasson Rd 45209
Watch Creek Dr 45230
Watch Hill Ln 45230
Watch Point Dr 45230
Watchcove Ct 45230
Watchview Ct 45230
W Water St 45202
Waterbury Cir 45231
Waterford Way 45245
Waterpoint Ln 45255
Watersedge Dr 45241
Waterstone Blvd 45249
Watertower Ct 45227
Waterview Way 45241
Watson St 45226
Watterson Rd & St 45227
Waveland Pl 45214
Waverly Ave
1-399 45215
1500-1899 45214
1900-1999 45212
Waxwing Dr
1-199 45236
9400-9699 45241
Waycross Rd 45240
Wayland Ave 45212
Waymont Ln 45224
Wayne Ave
2000-2199 45212
9000-9698 45215
9700-10361 45215
10363-10399 45215
N Wayne Ave 45215
S Wayne Ave 45215
Wayne Ct 45215
Wayne St 45206
Wayne Park Dr 45215
Wayside Ave 45230
Wayside Ct 45230
Wayside Dr 45241
Wayside Pl 45230
Wayward Winds Dr 45230
Weatherly Ct 45252
Webbland Pl 45213
Weber Ln 45205
Weber Pl 45223
Weber St 45223
Webman Ct 45223
Webster Ave
3900-3979 45236
3980-3998 45212
3981-4399 45236
4000-4398 45236
4000-4144 45212
4146-4168 45212
Wedgewood Ave 45217
Weebetook Ln 45208
Weekly Ln 45249
Wegman Ave 45205
Wehrman Ave
700-899 45229
900-999 45206
Weigold Ave 45223
Weik Rd 45252
Weil Dr 45244
Weil Rd
10400-10500 45242
10501-10599 45249
Weiner Ln 45244
Weirman Ave 45211
Weiss Rd 45247
Weitz Dr 45248
Welge Ln 45248
Welland Dr 45238
Weller Rd 45242
Wellesley Ave 45224
Wellington Dr 45245
Wellington Pl 45219
Wellington Chase Ct 45248
Wellingwood Ct 45240
Wells St 45205
Wellspring Dr 45231
Wellston Pl 45208
Weltner Ave 45227
Welton St 45213
Wemblywood Ct 45240
Wemyss Dr 45251
Wenatchee Ln 45230
Wenbrook Dr 45241
Wenchris Dr 45215
Wendee Dr 45238
Wendover Ct 45238
Wengate Ln 45241
Weninger Cir 45203
Wenner St 45226
Wenning Rd 45231
Wentworth Ave
1-124 45215
133-133 45220
135-144 45220
146-160 45220
200-599 45215
Werk Rd
2800-3499 45211
3500-3643 45248
3644-3644 45258
3645-6699 45248
3646-6698 45248
Werkastle Ln 45211
Werkmeadows Dr 45248
Werkridge Dr 45248
Werkshire Estates Dr 45248
Werner Ave 45231
Weron Ln 45225
Wescott Rd 45231
Wesken Ln 45241
Wesley Ave
1000-1099 45203
4600-5099 45212
Wesley Dr 45244
Wess Park Dr 45217
Wesselman Rd 45248
Wessels Ave 45205
West Ave
1400-1499 45215
1501-1505 45215
9400-9699 45242
West Ct 45211
West St
2-6 45220
8-22 45220
24-26 45220
1500-1600 45215
1686-1696 45212
1699-1713 45212
1700-1708 45212
1700-1700 45215
2000-2099 45215
3500-3599 45244
3701-3721 45227
3723-3999 45227
West Way 45224
Westbourne Dr 45248
Westbrook Dr
2600-2899 45211
2900-3299 45238
Westbury Dr 45231
Westchase Park Dr 45248
Westchester Way 45244
Westerly Dr 45231
Western Ave
1100-1318 45203
1319-2199 45214
Western Hills Ave &
Ln 45238
Westfield Ave 45209
Westgate Ave 45208
Westgrove Dr 45248
Westhaven Ave 45205
Westknolls Ln 45211
Westlake Ctr 45242
Westminster Dr 45229
Westmont Cir 45239
Westmont Dr 45205
Westmont Ln 45205
Westmoreland Ave 45223
Weston Ct 45248
Westonridge Dr 45239
Westover Cir 45236
Westpoint Dr 45231
Westport Ct 45248
Westridge Ave 45238
Westside Ave 45208
Westview Ave
300-699 45215
4500-4599 45223
Westview Ct 45215
Westwood Ave 45214
Westwood Northern Blvd
1700-2399 45225
2400-4499 45211
5500-5699 45248
Wetherfield Ln 45236
Wetheridge Dr 45230
Wexford Ave 45236
Wexford Ln 45233
Wexler Ct 45251
Wexwood Ln 45255
Weyer Ave 45212
Weymouth Ct 45240
Whallon Ct 45246
Whatley St 45204
Wheatcroft Dr 45239
Wheatfield Dr 45251
Wheeler St 45219
Wheelright Ave 45225
Whetsel Ave 45227
Whetstone Aly 45202
S Whetzel St 45227
Whipple St 45233
Whippoorwill Dr 45244
Whipporwill Dr 45230
Whisper Ln 45230
Whisper Way 45241
Whispering Way
5400-5599 45247
7300-7499 45241
Whispering Oak Trl 45247
Whispering Pines Dr 45230
Whispering Valley Dr 45247
Whisperinghill Dr 45242
Whisperwoods Ln 45249
Whistling Elk Run 45247
White St
2300-2599 45214
4000-4099 45255
White Oak Rd 45245
White Pine Ct 45255
Whiteacres Dr 45239
Whitebirch Dr 45231
Whitechapel Dr 45236
Whitegate Ln 45243
Whitehall Ave 45230
Whitehead Dr 45251
Whitehouse Ln 45244
Whitekirk Way 45245
Whiteman St 45214
Whiteoak Dr 45247
Whitestone Ct 45231
Whitetail Ct 45241
Whitetail Meadow Dr 45240
N & S Whitetree Cir 45236
Whitewood Ct 45244
Whitewood Ln 45239
Whitfield Ave 45220
Whitley Ct 45251
Whitman Ct 45202
Whitmore Dr 45238
Whitney Ave & Pl 45227
Whitthorne Dr 45215
Whittier St 45229
Whittington Ln 45249
Wiborg Dr 45244
Wichman Ct 45215
Wickham Pl 45214
Wicklow Ave 45236
Widhoff Ln 45236
Widman Pl 45226
Wiehe Rd 45237
Wielert Ave 45239
Wieman Ave 45205
Wigeon Dr 45246
Wilaray Ter 45230
Wilbud Dr 45205
Wilcox Dr 45251
Wildbrook Ln 45231
Wildcherry Ct 45248
Wilder Ave 45204
Wilderness Trl 45238
Wildflower Trl 45230
Wildhaven Way 45230
Wildoak Ct 45238
Wildwood St 45216
Wiley Ln 45208
Wilfert Dr 45245
Wilk Ln 45233
Wilke Dr 45238
Wilkens Short Rd 45233
Wilkinson St 45206
Willard Ave
2700-2799 45209
3300-3399 45241
Willet Ter 45238
Willfleet Dr 45241
William Henry Harrison
Ln 45243
William Howard Taft Rd
2-599 45219
600-1999 45206
William P Dooley Byp 45223
Williams Ave
1700-2599 45212
2600-2799 45209
4200-4399 45236
Williams Ct 45214
Williams Dr 45255
Williams St 45215
Williams Creek Dr 45244
Williamsburg Ct
300-499 45215
500-599 45244
Williamsburg Dr 45225
Williamsburg Ln 45241
Williamsburg Rd 45215
Williamsburg Rd N 45215
Williamsburg Rd NW 45215
Williamson Ct 45240
Williamson Dr 45240
Williamson Pl 45223
Williamson Rd 45241
Willis Ave 45208
Willnet Dr 45238
Willow Ave 45246
E Willow Ave 45246
Willow St 45215
Willow Hills Ln 45243
Willow Hollow Ln 45243
Willow Oak Ln 45239
Willow Ridge Dr 45251
Willow Run Ct 45243
Willowbrook Dr 45237
Willowbrook Ln
300-399 45215
7000-7799 45237
Willowcove Dr 45239
Willowcrest Ct 45251
Willowdale Dr 45248
Willowgate Dr 45251
Willowlake Ct 45233
Willowlea Ct 45208
Willowood Ave 45238
Willowridge Ln 45237
Willowspring Ct 45231
Willowview Ct 45251
Wilma Cir 45245
Wilma Ct 45245
Wilma Dr 45241
Wilmar Dr 45211
Wilmer Ave 45226
Wilmer Ct 45226
Wilmer Rd 45247
Wilmont Ct 45224
Wilmuth Ave 45215
Wilshire Ave
1100-1199 45230
3600-3699 45208
Wilson Ave
2200-2749 45231
2750-2899 45251
3400-3699 45229
Wilson St 45215
Wilsonia Dr 45205
Wilton Ave 45236
Wincanton Dr 45231
Winchell Ave 45214
Winchester Ave 45230
Wind St 45227
Windcrest Dr 45231
Windemere Way 45224
Windfern Forest Ln 45244
Windfield Ln 45249
Windham Ave 45229
Windhill Ter 45255
Winding Way
600-799 45245
3801-3897 45229
3899-4099 45229
6900-7399 45236
E Winding Way 45236
Windings Ct & Ln 45220
Windisch Ave 45208
Windknoll Ct 45243
Windmere Dr 45248
Windmill Way 45240
Windon Dr 45251
Windridge Ct 45243
Windridge Dr
5505-5513 45248
5515-5655 45248
5560-5698 45243
5657-5695 45248
5700-5799 45243
Windridge Vw 45243
Windrose Ct 45238
Windsong Ct 45243
Windsong Dr 45251
Windsong Ln 45241
Windsor Ct 45245
Windsor St 45206
Windsorhill Dr 45238
Windswept Ln 45251
Windview Dr 45248
Windward St 45227
Windword Way 45241
Windy Holw 45249
Windy Hills Rd 45230
Windy Knoll Ln 45239
Windy Way Dr 45251
Winesap Ct 45236
Winfield Ave 45205
Winford Ct & Ln 45240
Wing St 45204
Wingate Dr 45245
Wingate Ln 45249
Winged Foot Way 45245
Wingham Dr 45238
Winkler St 45219
Winlake Dr 45231
Winnebago Trl 45241
Winners Cir 45233
Winneste Ave & Ct 45232
Winnetka Dr 45236
Winona Ter 45227
Winslow Ave 45206
Winsray Ct 45224
Winstead Ln 45231
Winston Cir & Ln 45240
Winstone Ct 45255
Winter St 45226
Wintergreen Ct 45241
Winton Rd
4300-6099 45232
6400-8199 45224
8200-10299 45231
10400-11199 45218
11200-12199 45240
Winton Hills Ln 45215
Winton Ridge Ln 45232
Wintonview Pl 45232
Wintrop Ave 45224
Wionna Ave 45224
Wirham Pl 45220
Wirtz Way 45215
Wiscasset Way 45251
Wisconsin Ave 45204
Wismar Dr 45255
Wisnew Dr 45245
Wiswell St 45216
Witham Ln 45245
Witham Woods Dr 45245
Withany Ave 45213
Witherbone Ct 45242
Witherby Ave 45224
Withers Ln 45242
Witler St 45223
Witt Rd 45255
Wittekind Ter 45224
Wittlou Ave 45224
Wittmeyer Dr 45230
Witts Meadow Ln 45255
Witts Mill Ln 45255
Wittshire Cir & Ln 45255
Wocher Ave 45233
Wold Ave
2900-3099 45206
3100-3299 45207
Wolf Run Ct 45244
Wolfangel Rd 45255
Wolfangle Rd 45244
Wolff St 45211
Wolseley Ln 45229
Wood Ave
1-99 45246
300-499 45220
11040-11040 45242
11042-11199 45242
Wood St 45212
Wood Duck Dr 45246
Wood Meadow Dr 45243
Woodacre Dr 45231
Woodbine Ave
700-899 45246
3400-3999 45211
8000-8002 45216
8004-8499 45216
Woodbine St 45246
Woodbluff Ct 45231
Woodbriar Ln 45238
Woodbridge Ct 45240
Woodbridge Pl 45226
Woodbrook Ln 45215
Woodburn Ave
2500-3099 45206
3100-3699 45207
Woodchuck Dr 45251
Woodcreek Ct 45238
Woodcreek Dr 45241
Woodcrest Dr
1-99 45246
6600-6699 45233
Woodcroft Dr
7100-7375 45230
7367-7391 45241
7374-7398 45241
7377-7399 45230
7400-7499 45241
Wooden Shoe Hollow
Dr 45232
Woodfield Dr
700-799 45231
4600-4799 45244
Woodford Ct & Rd 45213
Woodgate Rd 45244
Woodglen Dr 45255
Woodhall Dr 45247
Woodhaven Dr 45248
Woodhill Dr 45251
Woodhurst Ct 45238
Woodknoll Ter 45215
Woodlake Dr 45238
Woodland Ave
1200-1499 45237
3700-3799 45209
Woodland Holw 45249
Woodland Ln 45227
Woodland Rd 45227
Woodland Trl 45255
Woodland Reserve Ct 45243
Woodland View Dr 45244
Woodlands Pl & Way 45241
Woodlands Path Ln 45238
Woodlands Ridge Dr 45238
Woodlark Dr 45230
Woodlawn Ave
500-1199 45205
4200-4399 45236
4700-4799 45212
Woodlawn Blvd 45215
Woodleigh Ct & Ln 45241
Woodlyn Dr N & S 45230
Woodmere Ct 45238
Woodmill Ln 45231
Woodmont Ave 45213
Woodpine Ln 45255
Woodridge Dr 45230
Woodrow Ave 45211
Woodrow St 45204
Woodruff Ln 45215
Woodruff Rd 45255
Woods Pt 45249
Woodscene Ct 45230
Woodsdale Ave 45216
Woodsedge Dr 45230
Woodsfield St 45213
Woodshire Dr 45233
Woodside Ct 45246
Woodside Hts 45217
Woodsong Dr 45251
Woodstate Dr 45251
Woodstock Dr 45215
Woodstone Dr 45244
Woodsview Ln 45241
Woodsway Dr 45236
Woodthrush Dr
600-699 45244
3800-4099 45251
Woodtrail Ln 45251
Woodvale Ct 45246
Woodvalley Ln 45238
Woodview Ct 45246
Woodview Dr 45231
Woodward Ln 45241

Woodward St 45202
Woodwick Ct 45255
Woody Ln 45238
Woodyhill Dr 45238
Wool St 45226
Woolper Ave 45220
Wooster Pike
  5100-5500 45226
  5501-8699 45227
Wooster Pl 45211
Wooster Rd 45226
Worth Ave 45212
Worth St 45226
Worthington Ave
  1-799 45215
  3000-3199 45211
Wortman St 45226
Wren St 45233
Wrenwood Ln 45231
Wuebold Ln 45245
Wuest Rd
  8200-8499 45247
  8500-8999 45251
Wuest St 45217
Wulff Run Rd 45233
Wunder Ave 45211
Wyandotte Dr 45233
Wyatt Ave 45213
Wycliffe Dr 45244
Wyler Park Dr 45245
Wyman Ln 45243
Wymart Ave 45231
Wyndwatch Dr 45230
Wynnburne Ave & Dr 45238
Wynne Pl 45233
Wynnecrest Dr 45242
Wynnewood Ln 45237
Wyoming Ave
  1-518 45215
  1600-2199 45205
  2200-2399 45214
E Wyoming Ave 45215
W Wyoming Ave 45215
Wyoming Club Dr 45215
Wyoming Point Pl 45231
Wyoming Woods Ln 45215
Wyscarver Rd 45241
Yakima Ct 45236
Yale Ave 45206
Yarabee Trce 45255
Yarger Dr 45230
Yarmouth Ave & Pl 45237
Yates Ln 45244
Yearling Ct 45211
Yeatman Rd 45252
Yellowglen Dr 45255
Yellowstone Dr 45251
Yellowwood Dr 45251
Ymca Dr 45242
Ymca Rd 45244
Yoast Ave 45225
Yonkers Ave 45225
York Ln 45215
York St
  400-1299 45214
  8200-8399 45236
Yorkhaven Rd
  300-749 45246
  750-999 45240
Yorkridge Dr 45231
Yorkshire Pl 45237
N Yorkshire Sq 45245
S Yorkshire Sq 45245
Yorktown Dr 45245
Yorktown Rd 45237
Yorktowne Dr 45241
Yorkway Ln 45249
Yorkwood Ln 45238
Yosemite Dr 45237
Young St
  1602-1602 45202
  1604-1899 45202
  1900-2199 45219
Youngman Dr 45245
Youngs Ln 45245
Yuba Ct 45231
Yukon St 45202
Zagar Dr 45245
Zan Ct 45226
Zaring Ct 45241
Zeller Dr 45244
Zenith Ct 45231
Zephyr Ln 45242
Zetta Ave 45217
Ziegle Ave 45208
Zier Pl 45219
Zig Zag Ln & Rd 45242
Zind Ln 45241
Zinn Pl 45233
Zinsle Ave 45213
Zocalo Dr 45251
Zodiac Dr 45231
Zoellner Dr 45251
Zula Ave 45238
Zumstein Ave 45208

NUMBERED STREETS

1st Ave
  1200-1899 45205
  2000-2099 45224
  11900-12199 45249
2 Mile Rd 45230
2nd Ave
  2000-2099 45224
  11900-12199 45249
2nd St 45215
E 2nd St 45202
3rd Ave
  2000-2099 45224
  11600-11898 45249
  11900-12199 45249
3rd St 45215
E 3rd St 45202
W 3rd St
  1-699 45202
  700-899 45203
4 Mile Rd 45230
4th Ave
  2000-2099 45224
  11900-12199 45249
4th St 45215
E 4th St 45202
W 4th St 45202
5 Mile Rd 45230
5th Ave
  2000-2099 45224
  11900-12199 45249
5th St 45215
E 5th St 45202
W 5th St
  1-399 45202
  741-797 45203
  799-999 45203
6th Ave
  2000-2099 45224
  11900-12199 45249
E 6th St 45202
W 6th St
  1-399 45202
  700-1299 45203
7 Gables Rd 45249
7th Ave 45249
E 7th St 45202
W 7th St
  1-300 45202
  302-398 45202
  400-1399 45203
8 Mile Rd
  100-1999 45255
  2000-3299 45244
E 8th St 45202
W 8th St
  200-399 45202
  800-1499 45203
  1900-2999 45204
  3000-4399 45205
  4400-4599 45238
9 Mile Tobasco Rd 45255
E 9th St 45202
  1-399 45202
  400-1299 45203
E & W 12th 45202
E & W 13th 45202
E 14th St 45202
  1-299 45202
  300-399 45214
E 15th St 45202
  1-299 45202
  300-399 45214
28th St 45209
31st Ave 45209
32nd Ave 45209
33rd Ave 45209
34th Ave 45209
W 64th St 45216
W 65th St 45216
E & W 66th 45216
E 67th St 45216
W 68th St 45216
E & W 69th 45216
E & W 70th 45216
E & W 72nd 45216
E & W 73rd 45216
E 75th St 45216
E 76th St 45216
E 77th St 45216

CLEVELAND OH

General Delivery 44101

POST OFFICE BOXES MAIN OFFICE STATIONS AND BRANCHES

Box No.s
1801 - 1998 44106
5000 - 6978 44101
10001 - 10999 44110
12001 - 12780 44112
14001 - 14999 44114
15002 - 15583 44115
18001 - 18999 44118
19001 - 19540 44119
20001 - 20956 44120
21001 - 21892 44121
24001 - 24956 44124
25004 - 25998 44125
26011 - 26446 44126
27101 - 27580 44127
28001 - 28956 44128
29001 - 29660 44129
30001 - 30999 44130
34001 - 34360 44134
35101 - 35950 44135
43001 - 43838 44143
44001 - 44660 44144
50700 - 76999 44101
78026 - 78051 44103
78200 - 78299 44102
78300 - 78399 44103
78400 - 78499 44104
78503 - 78512 44105
78600 - 78695 44106
78800 - 78899 44108
78900 - 78910 44109
81001 - 81999 44181
89400 - 96724 44101
99001 - 99958 44199
101000 - 108099 44110
110001 - 118099 44111
128000 - 128099 44112
141000 - 148099 44114
181000 - 188099 44118
198000 - 198099 44119
200361 - 208099 44120
210011 - 218099 44121
241001 - 248199 44124
251000 - 258099 44125
268000 - 268099 44126
278000 - 278099 44127
281001 - 288099 44128
298000 - 298099 44129
301000 - 309870 44130
347001 - 348099 44134
358000 - 358007 44135
438000 - 438099 44143
448000 - 448099 44144
602001 - 602780 44102
603001 - 603996 44103
604001 - 604420 44104
605001 - 605969 44105
606011 - 606306 44106
608001 - 608999 44108
609001 - 609720 44109
811000 - 818100 44181
894300 - 933180 44101
991201 - 998099 44199
6031001 - 6031298 44103

NAMED STREETS

Aaron Dr 44130
Abbey Ave 44113
Abbey Ct
  3600-3698 44105
  6600-6699 44125
Abbot Dr 44134
Abby Ave 44119
Abell Ave 44120
Aberdeen Ave 44103
Aberdeen Blvd 44143
Aberdeen Dr 44143
Aberdeen Rd 44120
Abigail Dr 44124
Ablewhite Ave 44108
Abraham Ave 44130
Acacia Cir 44124
Acacia Dr 44121
Acacia Park Dr 44124
W Access Rd 44135
Ackley Rd
  5400-5800 44129
  5802-5898 44129
  5900-5999 44105
  5900-5998 44129
  6000-8499 44129
  8500-10399 44130
Ada Ave 44108
Adams Ave 44108
Addington Blvd & Ct 44126
Addison Rd 44103
Adelaide Ave 44111
Adelbert Rd 44106
Adeline Ave 44111
Adena Ln 44124
Admiral Dr 44109
Adolpha Ave 44127
Adrian Ave 44111
Adrian Rd 44121
Aec Pkwy 44143
Aetna Rd 44105
Agnes Ct 44113
Ainsworth Dr 44124
N Aintree Park 44143
Aintree Park Dr 44143
Alachana Rd 44120
Alameda Pkwy 44128
Alan Pkwy 44130
Alber Ave 44129
Albers Ave 44111
Albert Ct 44143
Alberta Dr 44124
Albertly Ave 44134
Albion Rd 44120
Albrus Ave 44135
Alcester Rd 44124
Alcoy Rd 44112
Alden Ave 44111
Alden Dr 44134
Alden Ln 44143
Aldene Ave 44135
Aldenham Dr 44143
Alder Ave 44112
Aldersgate Dr 44124
Aldersyde Dr
  7600-7799 44130
  12100-12499 44125
  15500-15898 44120
  15900-17499 44120
Alderwood Rd 44130
Alexander Rd
  5401-5599 44130
  9300-13799 44125
  22000-22398 44126
  22001-22399 44126
Alexandria Dr 44130
Alfred Lerner Way 44114
Alger Rd 44111
Algiers Dr 44124
Algonac Rd 44112
Alhambra Rd 44110
Ali Ave 44130
Allbey Ave 44115
Alice Ave 44105
Allandale Ave 44112
Allanwood Dr 44129
Allegheny Cir 44112
Allen Dr 44125
Allen Bradley Dr 44124
Allendale Dr 44143
Allien Ave 44111
Allison Dr 44143
Allison Rd 44118
Allman Ct 44113
Allston Rd 44121
Almar Dr 44122
Almira Ave
  8000-8098 44102
  8100-9800 44102
  9802-9898 44102
  10000-10098 44111
  10100-10999 44111
Alonzo Ave 44128
Alpha Ave 44105
Alpha Dr 44143
Alpha Park 44143
Alpine Ave 44104
Alpine Rd 44121
Altamont Ave 44118
Althen Ave 44109
Alton Rd 44112
Altoona Rd 44109
Alvason Rd 44112
Alvey Rd 44124
Alvin Ave
  1700-2099 44109
  13100-13899 44105
Alvord Pl 44124
Amber Dr 44111
N Amber Dr 44144
S Amber Dr 44144
Amber Ln 44130
Amberley Ave 44109
Ambler Ave 44104
Ambleside Dr 44106
American Rd 44144
Ames Rd 44129
Amesbury Ave 44106
Amherst Dr 44129
Ammon Rd 44143
Amor Ave 44108
Amos Ave 44104
Amrap Dr 44130
Amsterdam Rd 44110
Anderson Ave 44105
Anderson Rd
  4401-4497 44121
  4499-4709 44121
  4710-5099 44124
W Anderson Rd 44121
Andover Blvd 44125
Andover Dr 44134
Andrea Ln 44109
Andrews Rd 44118
Angela Dr
  4300-4399 44121
  4400-4499 44121
  4400-4499 44126
  4500-4699 44126
  23000-23699 44128
  23701-23799 44128
Angelus Ave 44105
Anita Dr 44130
Anita Kennedy Rd SE 44104
Ann Ct 44108
Ann Arbor Dr 44130
Annandale Rd 44124
Annette Pl 44128
Ansel Rd
  800-1099 44103
  1100-1299 44108
  1301-1309 44106
  1311-1900 44106
  1902-1998 44106
Anson Ave 44127
Ansonia Ave 44144
Anthony Ln 44130
Anthony St 44143
Antietam Rd 44130
E Antisdale Ave & Rd 44118
Antoinette Dr 44129
Apache Dr 44130
Apelt Dr 44135
Apollo Dr 44130
Apple Ave 44113
Apple Dr 44143
Apple Creek Dr 44144
N & S Applecross Rd 44143
Appleton Dr 44130
Applied Plz 44115
Arabella Rd 44112
Arbor Ct 44134
Arbor Dr 44130
Arbor Rd 44108
Arbor Way 44134
Arbor Park Dr 44134
Arcade Ave 44110
Arcadia Dr 44129
Archer Rd 44105
Archmere Ave
  3200-4799 44109
  4801-4899 44109
  4900-4998 44144
  5000-6999 44144
Archwood Ave 44109
Arden Ave
  7400-7699 44129
  11001-11097 44111
  11099-11899 44111
Ardenall Ave 44112
Ardendale Rd 44121
Ardleigh Dr 44106
Ardmore Ave
  3900-4499 44109
  4500-4699 44144
  4701-4899 44144
Ardmore Dr 44144
Ardmore Rd
  3200-3399 44120
  3900-4499 44121
Ardoon Ave 44120
Ardoon St 44121
Ardoyne Ave 44109
Arey Rd 44106
Argonne Rd 44121
Argus Ave 44110
Arkansas Ave 44102
Arlington Ave
  3800-4199 44105
  12300-13099 44108
Arlington Dr 44124
Arlington Ln 44134
Arlington Rd 44118
Arlis Ave 44111
Armitage Ct 44105
Arnold Ct 44109
Arrow Ln 44134
Arrow Wood Oval 44129
Arrowhead Ave 44119
Arrowhead Trl 44130
Arsenio Way 44128
Arthur Ave 44106
Ascot Rd 44124
Ashburton Ave 44110
Ashbury Ave 44106
Ashby Rd 44120
Ashcroft Dr 44124
Ashdale Rd 44124
Ashford Rd 44120
Ashland Rd 44103
Ashley Cir 44143
Ashley Rd 44122
Ashton Rd 44118
Ashurst Rd 44118
Ashwood Dr 44124
Ashwood Rd 44120
Aspen Cir 44129
Aspen Ct 44102
Aspinwall Ave 44110
Associate Ave 44144
Asterhurst Trce 44130
Astor Ave 44135
Atherstone Rd 44121
Attica Rd 44111
Attleboro Rd 44120
Atwood Dr 44108
Auburn Ave 44113
Auburndale Ave 44112
Audrey Dr 44143
Audubon Blvd 44104
Augustine Dr 44134
Augustus Dr 44143
Austen Ln 44143
Austin Ave 44108
Austrian Ct 44104
Autumn Ln 44144
Avalon Dr 44134
Avalon Rd
  1600-1799 44112
  3200-3799 44120
Avennewo Ave 44115
Avenue Of Peace 44135
Avery Ave 44127
Avion Park Dr 44143
Avon Ave 44105
Avondale Ave
  2701-2797 44118
  2799-2900 44118
  2902-2998 44118
  7600-7799 44125
  7801-7899 44125
Avondale Rd 44121
Aylesworth Dr 44130
Azalea Dr 44143
Bader Ave 44109
Bagley Rd 44130
Bailey Ave & Ct 44113
Bain Park Dr 44126
Bainbridge Rd 44118
Baintree Rd 44118
Baker Ave 44102
Baldwin Ave 44112
Baldwin Ct 44130
Baldwin Rd 44104
Baldwin Creek Dr 44130
W Baldwin Reserve Dr 44130
Balmoral Dr 44143
Baltic Rd 44102
Banbury Cir & Ct 44128
Bancroft Ave 44105
Band Dr 44125
Bangor Ave
  5400-5698 44144
  5700-5999 44144
  12100-12198 44125
  12200-13904 44125
  13906-13998 44125
Bank St 44125
Banner Ln 44129
Baraleas Ave 44112
Barbara Ave 44135
Barber Ave & Ct 44113
Barberton Ave 44102
Bard Ave 44126
Bardbury Ave 44130
Bardwell Ave 44112
Barkston Dr 44143
Barkwill Ave 44127
Baron Dr 44130
Barrett Ave 44108
Barriemore Ave 44130
Barrington Ave 44108
Barrington Blvd 44130
Barrington Rd 44118
Bartfield Ave 44108
Bartholomew Dr 44130
Bartlam Ave 44125

Bartlett Ave 44120
Barton Cir 44129
N Barton Rd 44124
S Barton Rd 44124
Barton Hill Dr 44129
Bartow Ln 44143
Bartter Ave 44111
Batavia Ave 44105
Battery Park Blvd 44102
Bauerdale Ave 44129
Bavaria Ave 44129
Baxter Ave 44105
Bayard Rd 44121
Bayliss Ave 44103
Bayreuth Rd 44112
Beach Ct 44134
Beachdell Dr 44130
Beachwood Ave 44105
Beacon Ave 44105
Beacon Pl 44103
Beacon Rd 44124
Beaconfield Rd 44124
Beaconsfield Dr 44130
Beaconwood Ave 44121
Beau Ct 44129
Beaumont Ave 44112
Beaumont Ct 44103
Beaver Ave 44104
Becker Ct 44103
Becket Rd 44120
Beckman Ave 44104
Beech Ave
8500-9499 44144
14000-14299 44111
Beech Hill Rd 44143
Beechers Brook Rd 44143
Beechgrove Ave 44125
Beechwood Ave 44118
Beersford Rd 44112
Beham Dr 44124
Behrwald Ave
3500-4499 44109
4500-9500 44144
9502-9598 44144
Belcourt Rd 44124
Belden Ave 44111
Belfair Dr 44130
Belfiore Rd 44128
Belgrave Rd 44124
Belistri Ave 44119
Bell Ave 44104
Bella Dr 44119
Bellaire Rd
10600-11699 44111
11700-13700 44135
13702-13898 44135
Bellaston Rd 44143
Belleshire Ave 44135
Bellevue Ave 44103
Bellfield Ave 44106
Bellflower Ct & Rd 44106
Bellford Ave 44127
Bellingham Rd 44124
Belmar Rd 44118
Belmeadow Dr 44130
Belmere Dr 44129
Belmont Ave 44111
Belmore Rd 44112
Belrose Rd 44124
Belt Line Ave 44109
Belvidere Ave
6000-6799 44103
20500-20999 44126
Belvoir Blvd
1800-1900 44112
1902-1998 44112
2000-2098 44121
2001-2127 44121
2129-2599 44121
2665-3199 44122
S Belvoir Blvd
100-180 44121
182-2149 44121
2150-2399 44118
2400-2664 44118
Belvoir Mews 44121

E Belvoir Oval 44122
Belwood Dr 44143
Belwood Rd 44121
Beman Ave 44105
Bendemeer Rd 44118
Bender Ave 44112
Benedict Dr 44130
Benham Ave 44105
Bennington Ave 44135
Bennington Blvd 44130
Bennington Dr 44130
Bentwood Dr 44144
Benwood Ave
12300-13999 44105
14000-14599 44128
14601-15099 44128
Berdelle Ave 44105
Berea Rd
3000-3098 44111
3100-3499 44111
10200-11699 44102
11700-12999 44111
Beresford Ave 44130
Berg Ave 44115
Berkeley Rd 44118
N & S Berkley Sq 44143
Berkshire Ave 44108
Berkshire Rd
2500-2548 44106
2550-2799 44106
2800-3399 44118
9100-9499 44130
Berlerle Ln 44113
Bern Ave 44109
Bernard Ave 44111
Berrimore Ln 44128
Berry Ave 44102
Berry Blvd 44128
Bert Ave 44105
Bertha Ave 44129
E Berwald Rd 44121
Berwick Ln 44121
Berwick Rd 44104
Berwyn Ave 44111
Berwyn Rd 44120
Bessemer Ave
6500-8799 44127
8800-9999 44104
Beta Ave 44105
Beta Dr 44143
Bethany Ave 44111
Bethany Rd 44118
Beulah Ave 44106
Beverly Ct 44102
Beverly Dr 44130
Beverly Rd 44121
Beverly Hills Dr 44143
Bexley Blvd 44121
Beyerle Pl & Rd 44105
Beyerle Hill Rd 44125
Bicentennial Pl 44106
Biddulph Ave
3500-4399 44109
4501-5097 44144
5099-5929 44144
Biddulph Rd 44144
Bidwell Ave 44111
Big Creek Pkwy
5201-5451 44129
5453-5508 44129
5510-5598 44129
6000-6398 44130
6400-7899 44130
Big Met Pl 44135
Biltamy Blvd 44121
Biltmore Ave 44128
Biltmore Rd 44124
Bingham Ln 44108
Birch Ln 44109
Birch Tree Path 44121
Birchdale Ave 44106
Birchwold Rd 44121
Birchwood Ave 44111
Birchwood Rd 44125
Biscayne Blvd 44134
Bishop Rd 44143

Bittern Ave 44103
Bivens Dr 44115
Blackmore Rd 44118
Blaine Ave 44106
Blair Dr 44143
Blakley Dr 44143
Blanche Ave
3300-3799 44118
3450-3679 44118
5200-5298 44127
5300-5399 44127
5401-5607 44127
Blanchester Rd 44124
Blandford Rd 44121
Blarkenc Ave 44104
Blatt Ct 44109
Blenheim Rd 44110
Bletch Ct 44125
Bliss Ave 44103
Blossom Ave 44130
Blue Bell Dr 44124
Blue Spruce Oval 44130
Blueberry Cir 44143
Bluestone Rd 44121
Blythin Rd 44125
Bobko Blvd 44130
Bohn Rd 44104
Bohning Dr 44125
Bolingbrook Rd 44124
Bolivar Rd 44115
Bolton Rd 44118
Bonna Ave 44103
Bonnie Ln & Pl 44124
Bonnie Bank Ln 44126
Bonnieview Rd 44143
Bonniewood Dr 44110
Bonny Blvd 44134
Booth Ave 44105
Born Ave 44108
Boston Ave 44127
Bosworth Rd 44111
Botanica Ln 44124
Botany Ave 44109
Boundary Ln 44130
Bower Ave 44127
Bowmen Ln 44134
Boxwood Ave 44105
Boxwood Cir 44144
Boyce Rd 44122
Boynton Rd 44121
Brackland Ave 44108
Braddock Ave 44110
Bradenton Blvd 44134
Bradford Ave 44113
Bradford Rd
3201-3237 44118
3239-3499 44118
3501-3799 44118
4600-4699 44121
Bradgate Ave 44111
Bradley Ave 44129
Bradley Rd 44109
Bradwell Ave 44109
Bradwell Rd 44125
Braemar Rd 44120
Bragdon Ave 44102
Bragg Rd 44127
Brainard Ave 44109
Brainard Dr 44130
Brainard Rd
800-1099 44143
1100-3099 44124
3101-3499 44124
Brainard Hills Dr 44124
Bramblewood Ln 44143
Branch Ave 44113
Brandon Rd 44112
Brandywine Dr
2100-2199 44143
20700-20799 44126
Brandywine Ln 44126
Brandywine Rd 44130
Brandywine Sq 44143
Brandywood Dr 44124
Branford Ave 44125
Branford Dr 44143

Brantley Rd 44122
Bratenahl Pl & Rd 44108
Brayton Ave 44113
Brazil Rd 44119
Breakwater Ave 44102
Bremen Ave 44129
Bremerton Rd 44124
Brentwood Ct 44143
Brentwood Rd 44121
Breton Dr 44109
Brevier Ave 44113
Brewster Rd
2800-2899 44124
15300-16399 44112
Brian Ave 44119
Brian Dr 44134
Briar Rd 44135
Briarbanks Dr 44126
Briarcliff Dr 44125
Briarcliff Pkwy 44130
Briarwood Dr 44126
Briarwood Rd 44118
Bridge Ave
2300-2398 44113
2400-4499 44113
4500-6499 44102
6501-6899 44102
Bridge Ct 44102
Bridgeport Trl 44143
Bridgeview Ave 44105
Bridgeview Dr 44121
Bridgewater Rd 44124
Briggs Rd 44111
Brighton Ave 44111
Brighton Rd
2800-3099 44120
10300-10499 44108
Brightwood Ave 44112
Brinbourne Ave 44130
Brinkmore Rd 44121
Brinsmade Ave 44102
Bristol Ave 44104
Bristol Ct 44124
Bristol Rd 44110
British St 44113
Britt Oval 44104
Britton Dr 44120
Broadale Rd 44109
Broadrock Ct 44134
Broadview Ct 44109
Broadview Rd
2000-4999 44109
5100-5198 44134
5200-6400 44134
6402-7898 44134
Broadway Ave
800-1502 44115
1504-1600 44115
1602-3998 44115
1801-2299 44101
2653-3299 44115
4000-4398 44127
4400-6299 44127
6300-9099 44105
9101-9199 44105
9800-9898 44125
9900-14599 44125
Brockway Dr 44125
Brockway Rd 44118
Bromley Rd 44118
Bromton Dr 44124
Brook Ln 44144
Brook Hill Cir 44144
Brookdale Ave 44134
Brookdale Rd 44143
Brookfield Ave
1-99 44110
11700-12999 44135
Brookhigh Dr 44144
Brookhill Dr 44125
Brooklawn Ave 44111
Brookline Ave 44103
Brookline Rd 44121
Brooklyn Ave 44109
Brookmere Dr 44130
Brookpark Rd
700-2099 44109

2100-5399 44134
5400-9800 44129
9802-9998 44129
10000-10198 44130
10200-12999 44130
13000-21098 44135
21600-22999 44126
Brooks Rd 44105
Brookside Blvd
3800-4099 44111
4100-4299 44135
Brookside Dr 44144
Brookside Pkwy 44130
Brookstone Trl 44130
Brookton Rd 44128
Brookview Blvd 44134
Brookway Dr 44126
Brookway Ln 44144
Brookwood Dr
4600-4734 44144
4736-4775 44144
4776-30999 44124
31001-31099 44124
Brow Ave 44105
Brown St 44110
Brownell Ct 44115
Brownfield Dr 44129
Browning Ave 44120
Broxton Ave 44111
Broxton Rd 44120
Bruening Dr 44134
Brunner Ave 44105
Brunswick Ave 44125
Brunswick Rd 44112
Brush Rd 44143
Brushview Dr 44143
Brussels Rd 44110
Bryan Dr 44121
Bryant Ave 44108
Bryce Ave 44128
Bryce Rd 44124
Bryden Ct 44125
Bryden Rd 44122
Bryn Mawr Rd 44112
Brysdale Ave 44135
Buck Ave 44103
Buckeye Ct 44109
Buckeye Rd
8401-11599 44104
11600-13199 44120
Buckingham Ave 44120
Buckingham Ct 44130
Buckingham Dr 44129
Buckstone Ct 44134
Bucyrus Ave 44109
Bucyrus Dr 44144
Buechner Ave 44109
Buffalo Ct 44119
Buhrer Ave 44109
Bundy Dr 44104
Bunker Hill Dr 44126
Bunker Hill Rd 44130
Bunnell Ct 44113
Burbridge Rd 44121
Burden Dr 44134
Burger Ave 44109
Burger Rd 44121
Burgess Rd 44112
Burke Ave 44105
Burleigh Rd 44125
Burlington Rd 44118
Burnette Ave 44112
Burnham Pl 44103
Burnside Ave 44110
Burten Ct 44115
Burton Ave 44108
Burton Ct 44113
Burwell Ave 44115
Burwick Rd 44143
Busa Oval 44128
Bush Ave 44109
Bushnell Ct 44104
Bushnell Rd 44118
Butler Ave 44127
Butternut Ln
2580-2699 44124

20001-20197 44128
20199-20399 44128
Butterwing Rd 44124
Buxton Rd 44121
Byron Ave 44120
Byron Blvd 44130
Byron Dr 44124
Byron Rd 44122
Cable Ave 44127
Cadwell Ave 44118
Caine Ave
13100-13999 44105
14000-14599 44128
Calamie Dr 44130
Calcutta Ave 44110
Caldwell Ave 44111
Caleb Ct 44127
Caledonia Ave 44112
Camberly Dr 44124
Cambridge Ave 44105
Cambridge Dr 44129
Cambridge Ln
26001-26399 44128
27900-28499 44124
Cambridge Rd 44121
Camden Ave 44102
Camelot Dr 44134
Campbell Rd 44105
Campus Dr 44126
Campus Rd 44121
Canal Rd
301-597 44113
599-2599 44113
4900-5098 44125
5100-7699 44125
7701-7899 44125
W Canal Rd 44125
Candlewood Ct 44134
Cannon Ave 44105
Canova Ave 44109
Canterbury Dr 44130
Canterbury Ln 44143
Canterbury Rd
2200-2699 44118
17800-18399 44119
N Canterbury Rd 44129
S Canterbury Rd 44129
Canton Ave 44105
Cantwell Dr 44124
Canyon Cir 44130
Canyon Rd 44126
Capers Ave 44115
Capitol Ave 44104
Cardinal Ave 44110
Cardwell Ave 44105
Care Dr 44125
Carey Dr 44125
Cargo Rd 44135
Carl Ave 44103
Carlone Pl 44121
Carlos Ave 44102
Carlton Ct 44124
Carlton Rd
1600-1999 44134
2001-2105 44134
2801-2897 44122
2899-3099 44122
11800-11999 44106
Carlyle Ave 44109
Carlyon Rd 44112
Carnation Ct 44108
Carnegie Ave
300-498 44115
500-3999 44115
4000-8499 44103
8500-10999 44106
Carol Dr 44119
Carol Jean Blvd 44125
Carolina Rd 44108
Caroline Dr 44128
Carolyn Ave 44126
Caronia Dr 44124
Carpenter Ave 44127
Carpenter Rd 44125
Carr Ave 44108
Carrbridge Dr 44143

Carrington Ave 44135
Carrmunn Ave 44111
Carroll Ave 44113
Carroll Blvd 44118
E Carroll Blvd 44118
Carry Ave 44103
Carrydale Ave 44111
Carson Ave 44104
Carter Rd 44113
Carton Ave 44104
Carver Rd 44112
Cary Jay Blvd 44143
Cascade Xing 44144
Case Ave 44124
Case Ct 44104
Casper Rd 44110
Cass Ave 44102
Cassius Ave 44105
Castalia Ave 44110
Castle Ave 44113
Castlehill Dr 44143
Castleton Rd 44121
Castlewood Ave 44108
Catalano Dr 44124
Catalpa Rd 44112
Catharina Ave 44109
Catlin Dr 44143
Caton Ct 44115
Cavaliers Way 44115
Cayuga Ct 44111
Cecelia Dr 44134
Cecilia Ave 44109
Cedar Ave
2200-2498 44115
2500-3999 44115
4000-8499 44103
8500-11300 44106
11302-11498 44106
Cedar Rd
12350-12350 44106
12352-12799 44106
12800-14071 44118
13200-13460 44118
13461-13700 44118
13702-13748 44118
14073-14079 44118
14100-14499 44121
24201-24597 44124
24599-33799 44124
Cedar Glen Pkwy 44106
Cedarbrook Rd 44118
Cedarwood Rd 44124
Cedarwood Trce 44130
Celestia Dr 44143
Center Ave 44125
Center Ct 44115
Center Dr 44134
Center St
1-99 44110
1100-2599 44113
Center Ice 44115
Central Ave
1800-2206 44115
2208-3900 44115
3902-3998 44115
4000-8499 44104
Central Via 44115
Central Furnace Ct 44115
Century Cir 44144
Century Dr 44109
Cesko Ave 44109
Chadbourne Dr 44125
Chadbourne Rd 44120
Chagrin Blvd
15600-17699 44120
17700-18799 44122
18801-20499 44122
29801-29997 44124
29999-32099 44124
32101-32299 44124
Chaincraft Rd 44125
Chalfant Rd 44120
Chamberlain Ave 44104
Chambers Ave 44105
Champion Ave 44111
Channing Rd 44118
Chanticleer Dr 44126

Chapek Pkwy ... 44125
Chapelside Ave ... 44120
Chapman Ave ... 44112
Chard Ave ... 44105
Chardon Rd ... 44143
Chardonview Dr ... 44143
Charles Ave ... 44129
Charles Dr ... 44125
Charles Pl ... 44143
Charles Rd ... 44112
Charles Carr Pl ... 44104
Charleston Sq ... 44143
Charlton Rd ... 44121
Charney Rd ... 44118
Charter Ave ... 44127
Chase Dr ... 44143
Chateau Ave ... 44128
Chateau Dr ... 44130
Chatfield Ave ... 44111
Chatfield Dr ... 44106
Chatham Ave ... 44113
Chatham Rd ... 44124
Chatham Way ... 44124
Chelford Rd ... 44143
Chelmsford Dr & Rd ... 44124
Chelsea Dr ... 44118
Chelston Rd ... 44121
Cheltenham Blvd ... 44124
Chelton Rd ... 44120
Cherie Dr ... 44125
Cheriton Dr ... 44143
Cherokee Ave ... 44119
Cherokee Dr ... 44124
Cherokee Trl ... 44130
Cherrywood Ln ... 44128
Cheshire Rd ... 44120
Chester Ave
901-3999 ... 44114
1030-1100 ... 44115
1102-3998 ... 44114
4000-5499 ... 44103
9300-10498 ... 44106
10500-10699 ... 44106
Chester Pkwy
8100-8398 ... 44103
8400-8698 ... 44106
Chester Rd ... 44125
Chesterfield Ave
7500-8399 ... 44129
11601-11697 ... 44108
11699-12499 ... 44108
Chesterfield Dr ... 44130
Chesterton Rd ... 44122
Chestnut Dr ... 44129
Chestnut Ln
129-199 ... 44143
31800-32599 ... 44124
Chestnut Pl ... 44104
Chestnut Hills Dr
1800-2259 ... 44106
2261-2299 ... 44106
5800-6347 ... 44129
6349-7699 ... 44129
Chestnutdale Ave ... 44109
Chevrolet Blvd ... 44130
Cheyenne Trl ... 44130
Chickadee Ln ... 44124
Chickasaw Ave ... 44119
Chintriv Ave ... 44144
Chippewa Trl ... 44130
Christine Ave ... 44105
Church Ave ... 44113
N Church Dr ... 44130
Churchill Ave ... 44106
Churchill Blvd ... 44118
Churchill Rd ... 44124
Circle Ct ... 44113
Circle Dr
2100-2299 ... 44106
5800-5899 ... 44124
Circlewood Ct & Dr ... 44126
City View Dr ... 44113
Claasen Ave ... 44105
Claiborne Rd ... 44112
Clairdoan Ave ... 44108
Claire Ave ... 44111

Claire Freeman Ln ... 44104
Clairview Ave ... 44111
Clakeney Rd ... 44125
Clarebird Ave ... 44105
Claremont Ave ... 44130
Claremont Blvd ... 44125
Claremont Rd ... 44122
Clarence Rd ... 44121
Clarendon Rd ... 44118
Claridge Oval ... 44118
Clark Ave
301-697 ... 44113
699-999 ... 44113
1000-4499 ... 44109
4500-7699 ... 44102
7701-8999 ... 44102
Clarkson Rd ... 44118
Clarkstone Rd ... 44112
Clarkwood Pkwy ... 44128
Clarkwood Rd ... 44103
Claver Rd ... 44118
Claymore Blvd ... 44143
Claythorne Rd ... 44122
Clayton Ave ... 44109
Clayton Blvd ... 44120
Clayton Ct ... 44105
Clearaire Rd ... 44110
Clearview Ave
900-1399 ... 44134
4900-4999 ... 44125
15900-16499 ... 44128
Clearview Dr ... 44130
Clearview Rd ... 44124
Clearwater Dr ... 44134
Clement Ave ... 44105
Cleminshaw Rd ... 44135
Clermont Rd ... 44110
Cleveland Rd ... 44108
Cleveland Heights Blvd ... 44121
Cleveland Memorial Sh
200-298 ... 44114
Cleveland Memorial Sh
5800-6898 ... 44102
7301-7399 ... 44102
Cleveland Pkwy Dr ... 44135
Cleviden Rd ... 44112
Cliff Cir ... 44126
Cliff Dr ... 44102
Clifford Ave
13200-13298 ... 44111
13300-13399 ... 44111
13500-14299 ... 44135
Clifford Dr ... 44126
Clifford Rd ... 44121
Cliffview Rd
1600-1799 ... 44112
1801-1863 ... 44112
1965-1997 ... 44121
1999-2099 ... 44121
Clifton Blvd ... 44102
Clinton Ave
900-1000 ... 44121
1002-1098 ... 44121
2800-4499 ... 44113
4500-4799 ... 44102
W Clinton Ave ... 44102
Clinton Ln ... 44143
Clinton Rd
7301-7497 ... 44144
7499-9999 ... 44144
10000-10098 ... 44111
Cloud Ave ... 44113
Clover Ave ... 44109
Cloverdale Ave ... 44111
Cloverleaf Pkwy ... 44125
Cloverside Ave ... 44128
Club Dr ... 44143
Clubside Rd ... 44124
Clybourne Ave ... 44109
Coath Ave ... 44120
Cobb Ct ... 44108
Cobblestone Dr ... 44143
Cobleigh Ct ... 44104
Cochran Ave ... 44110
Cocoa Dr ... 44134

Coffinberry Blvd ... 44126
Coit Ave ... 44112
Coit Rd
12101-12197 ... 44108
12199-12899 ... 44108
13300-14799 ... 44110
Colburn Ave ... 44109
Colby Rd ... 44122
Colchester Rd ... 44106
Coldstream Dr ... 44143
Colebrook Rd ... 44130
Coleridge Rd ... 44118
Colfax Rd ... 44104
Colgate Ave & Ct ... 44102
Collamer Ave
1600-1699 ... 44110
1700-1799 ... 44112
College Ave ... 44113
College Rd ... 44121
Colletta Ln ... 44111
Collier Ave ... 44105
Colonel Dr ... 44109
Colonial Ave ... 44108
Colonial Ct ... 44106
Colonial Dr ... 44118
Colonial St ... 44110
Colonial Heights Blvd ... 44112
Colonnade Rd ... 44112
Colony Dr ... 44143
Colony Ln ... 44108
Colony Rd
3700-3999 ... 44118
4000-4299 ... 44121
Coltman Rd ... 44106
Colton Rd ... 44122
Columbia Ave ... 44108
Columbine Ave ... 44111
Columbine Ct ... 44130
Columbus Rd ... 44113
Colwyn Rd ... 44120
Commanche Ct ... 44130
Commerce Ave ... 44103
Commerce Ct ... 44130
Commerce Pkwy
4600-5099 ... 44128
19601-19999 ... 44130
Commerce Pkwy W ... 44130
Commerce Park Dr ... 44103
Commercial Rd ... 44113
Commodore Rd ... 44124
N Commons Blvd ... 44143
Commonwealth Ave ... 44124
Commonwealth Blvd ... 44130
Commonwealth Dr ... 44134
Community College Ave ... 44115
S Compton Rd ... 44118
Comstock Cir ... 44130
Concept Dr ... 44128
Concord Ct ... 44130
Concord Dr ... 44126
Concord Rd ... 44124
Concord Trl ... 44130
Congress Ct ... 44104
Connecticut Ave ... 44105
Conover Rd ... 44118
Consul Ave ... 44127
Continental Ave
11100-11599 ... 44104
11600-12099 ... 44120
Cook Ave ... 44109
Cooley Ave ... 44111
Cooper Ave ... 44103
Cooper Ct ... 44125
Copper Trce ... 44118
Coral Pl ... 44118
Coral Gables Dr ... 44134
Corbin Dr ... 44128
Corbus Rd ... 44108
Corby Rd ... 44120
Cordova Rd ... 44124
Corlett Ave ... 44105
Corliss Rd ... 44124
Cormere Ave ... 44120
Cornado Ave ... 44108
Cornelia Ave ... 44103

Cornell Rd ... 44106
Corning Ave ... 44109
Corning Dr ... 44108
Cornwall Rd ... 44119
Corona Ct ... 44102
Corporate Cir ... 44125
Corporate Dr ... 44130
Corsica Ave ... 44110
Corwin Rd ... 44121
Cory Ave ... 44103
Corydon Rd ... 44118
Cotes Ave ... 44105
Cottage Grove Dr ... 44118
Cottingham Dr ... 44124
Cottonwood Ln ... 44129
Cottonwood Oval ... 44130
Country Ln
1-99 ... 44124
300-399 ... 44143
4600-4800 ... 44128
4802-4898 ... 44128
Countryside Rd ... 44124
Courtland Ave ... 44111
Courtland Blvd
2600-2630 ... 44118
2632-2698 ... 44118
2751-2797 ... 44122
2799-3399 ... 44122
Courtland Ct ... 44102
Courtland Oval ... 44118
Coventry Dr ... 44134
Coventry Rd
1500-2499 ... 44118
1749-2149 ... 44118
2500-2899 ... 44120
Covert Ave ... 44105
Covington Ave
8100-8399 ... 44129
9401-9497 ... 44105
9499-9699 ... 44105
9701-9799 ... 44105
Covington Rd ... 44121
Cowan Ave ... 44127
Craigleigh Dr ... 44129
Craigmere Dr ... 44130
Cranbrook Cir ... 44130
Cranbrook Dr ... 44143
Crane Ave ... 44105
Cranleigh Ct ... 44143
Cranlyn Rd ... 44122
Cranover Rd ... 44124
Cranston Rd ... 44118
Cranwood Dr ... 44105
Cranwood Pkwy ... 44128
Cranwood Park Blvd ... 44125
Craven Ave ... 44105
Crawford Ct
700-799 ... 44113
8900-8999 ... 44106
Crawford Rd ... 44106
Crayton Ave ... 44104
Creek View Dr ... 44119
Creekhaven Dr ... 44130
Creekside Dr
400-499 ... 44143
6000-6100 ... 44130
6102-6104 ... 44130
31400-33099 ... 44124
Creekwood Ln ... 44143
Crennell Ave ... 44105
Crenshaw Dr ... 44130
Crescent Ave ... 44102
Crescent Rd ... 44111
Cress Rd ... 44111
Crest Ave ... 44125
Crest Dr ... 44109
Crest Rd ... 44121
Crestland Rd ... 44119
Crestline Ave ... 44109
Creston Ave ... 44109
Crestview Ct ... 44143
Crestwood Ave ... 44104
Crestwood Dr ... 44130
Crestwood Rd ... 44124
Crete Ave ... 44105
Cricket Ln ... 44128

Crofoot Ave ... 44105
Crofton Rd ... 44125
Cromwell Ave
11600-12099 ... 44120
21000-21999 ... 44126
Crossburn Ave ... 44135
Crossline Dr ... 44134
Croton Ave ... 44115
Crowell Ave ... 44104
Croyden Rd
1-99 ... 44110
1001-1097 ... 44124
1099-1499 ... 44124
Crudele Dr ... 44125
Crumb Ave ... 44103
Cudell Ave ... 44102
Cullen Dr ... 44105
Cumberland Ave
1-99 ... 44110
8900-10199 ... 44104
Cumberland Dr ... 44125
Cumberland Rd ... 44118
Cummings Rd ... 44118
Curran Ave ... 44111
Curry Dr ... 44124
Curtis Ct ... 44103
Curtiss Wright Pkwy ... 44143
Cushing Ln ... 44143
Cutters Creek Dr ... 44121
Cyclone Dr ... 44135
Cynthia Ct ... 44143
Cypress Ave ... 44109
Cyrano Ct ... 44113
Cyril Ave ... 44109
Czar Ave ... 44127
Dade Ln ... 44143
Daisy Ave ... 44109
Daisy Ln ... 44124
Dakota Ave ... 44127
Dale Ave ... 44111
Daleford Rd ... 44120
Daleside Ave ... 44134
Dalewood Rd ... 44124
Dallas Rd ... 44108
Dalton Ave ... 44127
Dalwood Dr ... 44110
Damon Ave ... 44110
Dana Ave ... 44111
Danbury Ave ... 44125
Danbury Ct ... 44103
Danbury Ln ... 44143
Dandridge Cir ... 44104
Dandridge Dr ... 44128
Daniel Ave ... 44110
Danville Ct ... 44104
Darley Ave ... 44110
Darlington Ave ... 44125
Dartford Rd ... 44121
Dartmoor Ave ... 44134
Dartmoor Rd ... 44118
Dartmouth Ave ... 44111
Dartmouth Dr ... 44129
Dartworth Dr ... 44129
Darwin Ave ... 44110
Darwin Pl ... 44130
Daryl Dr ... 44124
Davenport Ave ... 44114
David Ave ... 44134
David Dr ... 44121
David Rd ... 44125
Davidson Dr ... 44143
Davinwood Dr ... 44135
Dawn Ave ... 44104
Dawn Haven Dr ... 44130
Dawn Vista Oval ... 44129
Dawncliff Dr ... 44144
Dawning Ave ... 44109
Dawning Dr ... 44144
Dawnshire Dr ... 44134
Dawnwood Dr ... 44134
Day Dr ... 44129
Daytona Dr ... 44134
Dean Dr ... 44121
Deanwood St ... 44112
Dearborn Ave ... 44102
Debby Dr ... 44130

Deborah Dr ... 44130
Deborah Lynn Dr ... 44144
Debra Ann Ln ... 44112
Decker Ave ... 44103
Decker Dr ... 44134
Deepwood Ln ... 44143
Deer Ln ... 44126
N Deer Creek Ln ... 44124
Deer Run Dr & Trl ... 44130
Deerfield Dr ... 44129
Deering Ave ... 44130
Deforest Ave ... 44128
Deise Ave ... 44110
Delamere Dr ... 44106
Delavan Ave ... 44119
Delaware Dr
2100-2399 ... 44106
7600-13900 ... 44130
13902-13998 ... 44130
Delevan Dr ... 44124
Dell Ave ... 44104
Dell Haven Dr ... 44130
Dellbank Dr ... 44144
Delleang ... 44101
Dellenbaugh Ave ... 44103
Dellrose Dr ... 44130
Dellwood Dr ... 44134
Dellwood Rd ... 44118
Delmar Ave ... 44109
Delmont Ave ... 44112
Delmore Rd ... 44121
Delora Ave ... 44144
Delrey Ave ... 44128
Delroy Rd ... 44121
Demington Dr ... 44106
Denison Ave
800-1198 ... 44109
1200-4450 ... 44109
4452-4498 ... 44109
4700-10099 ... 44102
Denison Blvd ... 44130
Denley Ave ... 44109
Denmark Ave ... 44102
Dennis Cir ... 44121
Denton Dr ... 44106
Dentzler Rd ... 44134
Denver Dr ... 44130
Derby Ave ... 44125
Derby Dr ... 44143
Derbyshire Ct ... 44106
Derbyshire Dr ... 44128
Derbyshire Rd ... 44106
E Derbyshire Rd ... 44118
Dercum Rd ... 44105
Desmond Ave ... 44102
Desota Ave ... 44118
Detour Ave ... 44103
Detroit Ave
1500-2198 ... 44113
2200-4499 ... 44113
4501-4597 ... 44102
4599-11699 ... 44102
Deveny Ave ... 44105
Devon Rd ... 44119
Devonshire Dr ... 44106
Devonshire Rd ... 44109
Dewitt Dr ... 44143
Dexter Dr ... 44130
Dexter Pl ... 44113
Diamond Ave ... 44104
Diana Ave ... 44110
Diana Ct ... 44143
Diane Dr ... 44126
Dibble Ave ... 44103
Dickens Ave ... 44104
Dickens Dr ... 44143
Diemer Ct ... 44103
Dill Rd ... 44121
Dillard St ... 44115
Dille Ave ... 44127
Dillewood Rd ... 44119
Division Ave
2500-2900 ... 44113
2902-3498 ... 44113
4000-4599 ... 44102
Dix Ct ... 44103

Dixon Rd ... 44111
Doan Ave ... 44112
Dobson Ct ... 44109
Dodge Ct ... 44114
Doering Ct ... 44109
Dogwood Cir ... 44130
Dogwood Ln ... 44130
Dogwood Trl ... 44124
Doll Dr ... 44125
Dollar Ct ... 44113
Dolloff Rd ... 44127
Donald Ave
4700-4999 ... 44143
6601-6697 ... 44125
6699-6799 ... 44125
7100-7899 ... 44103
Doncaster Ave ... 44129
Dondinso Ave ... 44135
Donna Dr ... 44143
Donovan Dr ... 44125
Donover Rd ... 44128
Donwell Dr ... 44121
Dorchester Dr ... 44119
Dorchester Rd ... 44120
Doris Ave ... 44126
Doris Rd ... 44111
Dornoch Ln ... 44143
Dornur Dr ... 44109
Dorothy Ave
7300-8300 ... 44129
8302-8398 ... 44129
9400-9699 ... 44125
Dorothy Ct ... 44103
Dorset Rd ... 44124
Dorsh Rd ... 44121
Dorshwood Rd ... 44121
Dorver Ave ... 44105
Douglas Blvd ... 44143
Douse Ave ... 44127
Dove Ave ... 44105
Dover Ave ... 44112
Dover Ln ... 44130
Doxmere Dr ... 44130
Drake Ave ... 44127
Drayton Dr ... 44124
Dresden Ave ... 44129
Dresden Rd ... 44112
Dressler Ave & Ct ... 44125
Drexel Ave ... 44108
Drexmore Rd ... 44120
Drummond Rd ... 44120
Drury Ct & Ln ... 44124
Dryden Rd ... 44122
Drydock Ave ... 44113
Du Sable Ct ... 44128
Dudley Ave ... 44102
Duffield Rd ... 44122
Duke Ave ... 44102
Duluth Ave ... 44103
Dumbarton Blvd ... 44143
Dunbar Ln ... 44143
Dundee Dr
301-397 ... 44108
399-499 ... 44108
24700-24799 ... 44143
Dunellon Dr ... 44124
Dunfield Dr ... 44143
Dunham Ave ... 44103
Dunlap Ave ... 44105
Dupont Ave ... 44108
Durant Ave ... 44108
Durkee Ave ... 44105
Duval Rd ... 44124
Dynes Ave & Ct ... 44128
Dysart Rd ... 44118
Eagle Trce ... 44124
Eagle Point Dr ... 44124
Eaglesmere Ave ... 44110
Eardley Rd ... 44118
Earle Ave ... 44108
Earlwood Rd ... 44110
East Blvd
701-1299 ... 44108
1301-1397 ... 44106
1399-11150 ... 44106
11152-11198 ... 44106

Eastgate Dr
6601-6729 44124
6730-6899 44143
Eastham Ave 44112
Eastland Rd 44130
Eastlane Dr 44144
Eastlawn Dr 44143
Eastlawn Rd 44128
Easton Ave 44104
Eastondale Rd 44124
Eastover Rd 44124
Eastway Rd
3700-3999 44118
4000-4299 44121
Eastwick Dr 44118
Eastwood Ave
1100-1499 44124
20400-21499 44126
Eastwood Blvd 44125
Eaton Ct 44130
Eaton Rd
2400-2661 44118
2663-2699 44118
2670-2749 44118
2750-3099 44122
20800-21999 44126
Eddington Rd 44118
Eddy Rd
100-298 44108
300-1399 44108
1401-1499 44108
1600-1799 44112
Eden Ln 44130
Edendale St 44121
Edenhall Dr 44124
Edenhurst Rd 44124
Edenwood Rd 44121
Edgebrook Blvd 44130
Edgecliff Ave 44111
Edgecliff Dr
6900-7099 44134
19600-19698 44119
19700-19999 44119
Edgecliff Ter 44111
Edgedale Rd 44124
Edgefield Rd 44124
Edgehill Dr
3700-3799 44121
5600-5688 44130
5690-6099 44130
Edgehill Rd
2200-2799 44106
2800-3199 44118
Edgemont Rd 44143
Edgepark Dr 44125
Edgerly Rd 44121
Edgerton Rd
2100-2699 44118
2282-2352 44118
2354-2419 44118
18300-18499 44119
Edgewater Dr 44102
Edgewood Ave
13100-13999 44105
14000-15199 44128
Edgewood Rd
600-799 44143
2100-2299 44118
2900-31600 44124
31602-31698 44124
E & W Edinburgh Dr 44143
Edison Rd 44121
Edmond Dr 44121
Edmonton Ave 44108
Edmunds Ave 44106
Edna Ave 44103
Edolyn Ave 44111
Edsal Dr 44124
Edward Ct 44130
Edwin Ct 44112
Effie Rd 44105
Eggers Ave 44105
Eglindale Ave 44109
Eichorn Ave 44102
Elandon Dr 44106
Elberon Ave 44112
Elberta Ave 44128
Elbon Rd 44121
Eldamere Ave 44128
Elderdale Dr 44130
Elderwood Ave 44112
Eldon Dr 44130
Eleanore Dr 44135
Elgin Ave 44108
Eliot Ave 44104
Elise Dr 44130
Eliza Ave 44105
Elizabeth Ave
5401-5599 44130
9300-10199 44105
21700-21999 44126
Elizabeth Ln 44144
Elk Ave 44108
Ella Ave 44105
Ellacott Pkwy 44128
Ellen Ave 44102
Ellen Dr 44126
Ellianch Ave 44103
Elliffe St 44115
Ellison Rd 44121
Ellwood Ave 44135
Elm Ave 44112
Elm Ct 44102
Elm St 44113
Elmarge Ave 44105
Elmdale Rd
2400-2499 44118
6460-6700 44130
6702-6798 44130
Elmore Dr 44130
Elmore Rd 44126
Elmwood Ave
10600-11099 44125
11800-12799 44111
12801-12999 44111
Elmwood Rd
1100-1399 44124
3900-4499 44121
Eloise Dr 44112
Elsa Ct 44102
Elsetta Ave
10000-10042 44130
10044-10100 44130
10102-10198 44130
13600-14399 44135
Elsienna Ave 44135
Elsinore Ave 44112
Elsmere Ave 44135
Elsmere Dr 44130
Elsmere Rd 44120
Elston Ave 44109
Elton Ave 44102
Elwell Ave 44104
Elwood Rd 44112
Ely Ave 44120
Ely Vista Dr 44129
Emerald Ct 44135
Emerald Pkwy 44135
Emerald Pt 44130
Emerald Vw 44126
Emerson Dr 44124
Emerson Rd 44121
Emery Ave 44135
Emery Rd 44128
Emily St 44112
Emma Ln 44130
Emmet Rd 44124
Empire Ave 44108
Enderby Dr 44130
Enderby Rd 44120
Endicott Rd 44120
Endora Rd 44112
Enfield Dr 44124
Engel Ave 44127
Engle Rd 44130
Engle Lake Dr 44130
Englewood Ave 44108
Englewood Dr
900-1599 44134
17700-17999 44130
18001-18099 44130
Englewood Rd 44121
Ensign Ave 44104
Enterprise Ave 44135
Eric Ln 44109
Erieside Ave 44114
Erieview Plz 44114
Erieview Rd 44121
Erin Ave 44113
Ernadale Ave 44111
Ernest Ave 44111
Erwin Ave 44135
Erwin Ct 44130
Esmeralda Ave 44110
Essen Ave 44129
Essex Rd 44118
Esterbrook Ave 44108
Esther Ave 44126
Esther Rd 44143
Euclid Ave
140-198 44114
200-529 44114
530-532 44115
531-699 44114
600-898 44114
900-3999 44115
4000-8299 44103
8401-8497 44106
8499-12499 44106
12500-18599 44112
Euclid Beach Blvd 44110
Euclid Chagrin Pkwy 44143
Euclid Heights Blvd
2330-2358 44106
2360-2799 44106
2800-3099 44118
3101-3183 44118
3185-3499 44118
Eureka Pkwy 44130
Euston Dr 44130
Evangeline Rd 44110
Evans Dr 44130
Evanston Rd 44124
Evarts Rd 44104
Eve Ave
6700-6798 44125
7601-7797 44102
7799-7999 44102
Evelyn Dr 44125
Eventide Dr 44129
Everett Ct 44103
Evergreen Dr 44129
Evergreen Pl 44110
Everton Ave 44108
Evins Ave 44104
Exchange St 44125
Exeter Rd
2500-2699 44118
11100-11300 44125
11302-11398 44125
Fairchild Ave 44106
Fairdale Ave 44109
Fairfax Ave 44128
Fairfax Rd 44118
E Fairfax Rd 44118
Fairfield Ave 44113
Fairhaven Rd 44124
Fairhill Rd 44120
Fairlane Cir 44126
Fairlawn Ave 44111
Fairlawn Cir 44126
Fairlawn Dr
300-399 44143
10400-11399 44130
Fairlawn Rd 44124
Fairmount Blvd
2400-2754 44106
2755-3000 44118
3000-22899 44118
3002-3298 44118
18701-18797 44118
18799-19199 44118
19201-19699 44118
22901-22999 44118
23001-23197 44122
23199-24199 44122
27501-27597 44124
27599-33699 44124
Fairoaks Rd 44121
Fairpark Dr 44126
Fairport Ave 44108
Fairview Ave 44106
Fairview Pkwy 44126
Fairview Center Dr 44126
Fairville Ave 44135
Fairway Dr
4301-4499 44135
4700-4799 44144
17700-18399 44135
Fairweather Dr 44130
Fairwood Dr 44124
Fairwood Rd 44111
Falkirk Rd 44124
Fall St 44113
Falmouth Oval 44130
Falmouth Rd 44122
Faraday Rd 44124
Farinacci Ct 44106
Farland Rd 44118
Farmington Dr 44125
Farmington Rd 44112
Farnhurst Rd 44124
E Farnhurst Rd 44124
W Farnhurst Rd 44121
Farnsleigh Rd 44122
Farnsworth Dr 44129
Farnum Ave 44130
Farringdon Ave 44105
Father Caruso Dr 44102
Father Frascati Dr 44102
Fatima Dr 44134
Faversham Rd 44118
Fay Dr
1800-2199 44134
4700-4799 44121
Fayette Rd 44122
Federal Dr 44128
Felch St 44128
Felton Rd 44121
Fenemore Rd 44112
Fenley Rd 44121
Fenway Dr 44129
Fenwick Ave
4201-4297 44113
4299-4499 44113
4500-4799 44102
4801-4899 44102
Fenwick Rd 44118
Fenwood Rd 44118
Fergus Ave 44109
Ferman Ave 44109
Fern Ct 44109
Ferncliffe Ave 44135
Ferndale Ave 44111
Fernhill Ave 44129
Fernhurst Ave 44130
Fernshaw Ave 44111
Fernway Ave 44111
Fernway Rd
15601-15697 44120
15699-17699 44120
17701-17997 44122
17999-18299 44122
Fernwood Ave 44112
Ferrell Ave 44102
Ferris Ave 44105
Fidelity Ave 44111
Filo Ave 44105
Finn Ave 44127
Finney Ave 44105
Fir Ave 44102
Firsby Ave 44135
Firwood Rd 44110
Fischer Rd 44111
Five Points Rd 44135
Flamingo Ave 44135
Fleet Ave 44105
Fleger Dr 44134
Fleming Ave 44115
Flora Ave 44108
Florian Ave 44111
Florida Ave 44128
Flower Ave 44111
Flower Dr 44130
Flowerdale Ave 44144
Folk Ave 44108
Follett Ct 44113
Folsom Ave 44104
Fontenay Rd 44120
Force Ave 44105
Ford Dr 44106
Ford Rd
800-1089 44143
1090-1098 44124
1100-1432 44124
1434-1498 44124
Fordham Dr 44129
Fordham Rd 44125
Fordwick Rd 44130
Forest Ave
5400-7200 44129
7202-7298 44129
11000-11599 44104
11600-12999 44120
Forest Dr 44124
Forest Oval 44130
Forest Edge Dr 44144
Forest Grove Ave 44108
Forest Hill Ave 44112
Forest Hills Blvd
1200-1298 44118
1300-1499 44118
1800-1899 44112
4200-6799 44134
15500-16299 44112
Forestdale Ave 44109
Forestdale Dr 44125
Forestview Dr 44118
Forestwood Ave 44135
Forestwood Dr 44134
Forman Ave 44105
Forsythia Ln 44143
Fort Ave 44104
Fort Myers Ct 44134
Fortune Ave
2400-3499 44134
10400-11699 44111
Fosdick Rd 44125
Foster Ave 44108
Fowler Ave 44127
Fowles Rd 44130
Fox Hollow Ct
101-199 44124
6600-6699 44130
Fox Hollow Dr
100-198 44124
200-3299 44124
10000-10198 44130
10200-10400 44130
10402-10498 44130
30800-31200 44124
31202-31298 44124
Foxboro Dr 44143
Foxcroft Dr 44125
Foxglove Ln 44130
Foxhall Ln 44130
Foxlair Trl 44143
Foxwood Ln 44124
Foxwynde Trl 44143
Frances Dr 44125
Francis Ave 44127
Francis Ct 44121
Frank Ave 44106
Franke Rd 44130
Frankfort Ave
200-700 44113
702-798 44113
5701-5799 44129
Franklin Blvd
600-799 44143
2500-2512 44113
2514-4499 44113
4500-11699 44102
Frazee Ave 44127
Frederick Ave 44104
Freehold Ave 44134
Freeman Ave 44113
Freemont Rd 44121
Freeway Cir 44130
French St 44113
Friar Cir 44126
Friar Dr 44134
Frick Ct 44111
Friendly Ct 44104
Front Ave 44113
E & S Frontenac Dr 44128
Frontier Ave 44102
Fruit Ave 44113
Fruitland Ave 44124
Fruitland Ct 44102
Fruitland Dr 44134
Fruitside Rd 44125
Fry Rd 44130
Fulham Dr 44124
Fuller Ave 44104
Fullerton Ave 44105
Fulton Ct 44113
Fulton Pkwy 44144
Fulton Pl 44113
Fulton Rd
1600-3099 44113
3100-3799 44109
4000-4098 44144
4100-4700 44144
4702-4998 44144
Gable Ln 44121
Gabriella Dr 44130
Gainsboro Ave 44112
Galaxy Dr 44109
Galaxy Pkwy 44128
Galemore Dr 44130
Galewood Dr 44110
Galion Ave 44109
Gallup Ave 44127
Gambier Ave 44102
Gamma Ave 44105
Garden Ave 44109
Garden Blvd 44128
Garden Ct 44104
Garden Dr 44121
Garden Rd 44112
Garden Valley Ave 44104
Garfield Ave 44108
Garfield Blvd 44125
Garfield Dr 44125
Garfield Ln 44108
Garfield Rd 44112
Garland Ave 44125
Garrett A Morgan Pl 44105
Garwood Rd 44109
Gaslight Ln 44124
Gates Ave 44105
Gates Mills Blvd 44124
Gateway 44119
Gateway Plz 44115
Gay Ave 44105
Gaylord Ave 44105
Gedeon Ave 44102
Gehring Ave 44113
Genesee Ave 44124
Genesee Rd 44121
Gentry Cir E & W 44143
George Ave
2500-3499 44134
3501-3599 44134
9100-9299 44105
Georgetown Rd & Sq 44143
Georgette Ln 44109
Gerald Ave 44129
Gerald Dr 44130
Geraldine Ave 44111
Geraldine Rd 44143
Germaine Ave 44109
Germantown Dr 44126
Gerome Ct 44105
Gertrude Ave 44105
Gettysburg Dr 44134
Gibson Ave 44105
Giddings Rd 44103
Giesse Dr 44124
Gifford Ave
4000-4499 44109
4500-5399 44144
5401-5799 44144
Gifford Dr 44144
Gilbert Ave 44129
Gilbert Ct 44102
Gilbert Dr 44124
Giles Rd 44135
Gilford Ln 44130
Gill Ave 44104
Gilmer Ln 44143
Gilmore Ave 44135
Ginger Wren Rd 44124
Gino Ln 44109
Glade Ave 44104
Gladwin Dr 44124
Glamer Dr 44130
Glasgow Dr 44143
Glastonbury Cir 44143
Glazier Ave 44127
Gleeson Dr 44125
Gleeten Rd 44143
Glen Ave 44110
Glen Oval
1800-1899 44143
11200-11499 44130
Glen Allen Dr 44121
Glen Daniel Cir 44144
E & W Glen Eagle Dr 44143
Glenbar Ct & Dr 44126
Glenboro Dr 44105
Glenbrooke Chase 44124
Glenburn Ave 44128
Glencairn Dr 44134
Glencairn Rd 44122
Glencliffe Rd 44111
Glencoe Ave
6201-6497 44144
6499-7699 44144
15300-15599 44110
Glencoe Ln 44143
Glendale Ave
13100-13999 44105
14000-17599 44128
17601-17699 44128
Glendon Rd 44118
Glendora Ln 44130
Glenfield Rd 44119
E Glengary Cir 44143
W Glengary Cir 44143
Glengary Ln 44124
Glengary Rd 44120
Glenlyn Rd 44124
Glenmere Cir 44128
Glenmont Rd 44118
Glenmore Rd 44122
Glenn Dr 44134
Glenn Oval Dr 44130
Glenpark Ave 44128
Glenridge Ave 44130
Glenridge Rd 44121
Glenshire Ave 44135
Glenside Rd
900-1099 44121
13400-14299 44110
Glenview Ave 44108
Glenview Rd
4300-4599 44128
6600-6899 44143
Glenville Ave 44108
Glenwood Ave 44106
Glenwood Rd 44121
Gloucester Dr 44143
Glouchester Dr 44124
Glynn Rd 44112
Goans Pl 44134
Goebel Dr 44134
Golden Ave 44103
Golden Gate Blvd & Plz 44124
Golf View Dr 44135
Golfview Ln 44143
Golfway Ln 44124
Golfway Rd 44121
Gollangs Dr 44134
Goller Ave 44119
Gooding Ave 44108
Goodman Ave 44105
Goodnor Rd 44118
Goodwalt Ave 44102
Gordon Dr 44130
Gordon Rd 44124
Gorman Ave 44105
Governor Ave 44111

Street	ZIP
Grace Ave	
7500-7898	44102
9900-10899	44125
Graham Dr	44124
Graham Rd	44112
Gramatan Ave	44111
Granada Blvd	44128
Granby Ave	44109
Grand Ave	44104
Grand Division Ave	44125
Grandview Ave	
2100-2399	44106
10300-10999	44104
Grandview Ter	44112
Granger Rd	44125
Grannis Rd	
4200-4399	44126
12100-13499	44125
20100-20199	44126
Grant Ave	
4900-5499	44125
5700-7100	44105
7102-7898	44105
Grant Blvd	44130
Grant Dr	
1200-1699	44134
1983-1989	44143
1991-2035	44143
2037-2069	44143
Grantham Rd	44112
Grantleigh Rd	44121
Granton Ave	44111
Grantwood Ave	44108
Grantwood Dr	44134
Grapeland Ave	44111
Grasmere Ave	44112
Gray Ave	44108
Grayton Rd	44135
Green Ct	44104
Green Dr	44125
Green Rd	
1851-1905	44112
1907-1947	44121
1949-2387	44121
2389-2399	44121
2800-2900	44122
2902-2998	44122
4201-4297	44128
4299-4999	44128
E Green Rd	44121
N Green Rd	44121
S Green Rd	44121
Green Acres Dr	44134
Green Valley Dr	44134
Greenbriar Ct	44143
Greenbriar Dr	44130
Greenheath Dr	44130
Greenhill Rd	44111
Greenlawn Ave	
8200-8500	44129
8502-8598	44129
10500-10900	44108
10902-10998	44108
Greenleaf Ave	44130
Greenvale Rd	44121
Greenview Ave	
9717-9897	44125
9899-10299	44125
10301-10399	44125
11100-11299	44108
N Greenway Ct	44143
S Greenway Ct	44143
Greenway Rd	
4300-4499	44121
15400-15799	44111
Greenwich Ave	44105
Greenwold Rd	44121
Greenwood Ave	44111
Greenwood Dr	44124
Greenwood View Dr	44129
Grenleigh Rd	44124
Grenville Rd	44118
Grenway Rd	44122
Gretna Green Dr	44143
Greyton Rd	44112
Gridley Rd	44122
Griffing Ave	44120
Grimsby Ave	44135
Griswold Ave	44104
Gross Dr	44130
Grosvenor Rd	44118
Groton Rd	44121
Grove Ct	44113
Grove Dr	44125
Grove Ln	44134
Grove Park Dr	44134
Groveland Ave	44111
Groveland Rd	44118
Groveland Club Dr	44110
Grovewood Ave	
1600-3499	44134
15200-17199	44110
17200-17799	44119
17801-17899	44119
Gruss Ave	44108
Guadalupe Dr	44134
Guardian Blvd	44135
Guilford Rd	44118
Guthrie Ave	44102
Guy Ave	44127
Haber Dr	44126
Habersham Ln N & S	44143
Hacienda Dr	44130
Haddam Rd	44120
Hadleigh Rd	44118
Hague Ave	44102
Halcyon Dr	44130
Haldane Rd	44112
Hale Ave	44110
Halle Ave	44102
Halle Dr	44125
Hallford Cir	44124
Halliday Ave	44110
Halsey Rd	44118
Haltnorth Ct & Walk	44104
Halton Trl	44143
Halworth Rd	44122
Hamden Rd	44130
Hamilton Ave	44114
Hamlen Ave	44120
Hamlet Ave	44127
Hamlet Ct	44108
Hamm Ave	44127
Hammond Ave	44144
Hampden Ave	44108
Hampshire Ln	44106
Hampshire Rd	
2501-2597	44106
2599-2799	44106
2800-2999	44118
3001-3099	44118
Hampstead Ave	
5400-7299	44129
14700-14799	44120
Hampstead Rd	44118
Hampton Ct	
119-127	44108
4500-4599	44128
4601-22699	44128
Hampton Rd	
1301-1317	44112
1319-1399	44112
2801-2897	44120
2899-2999	44120
Hancock Ave	44113
Hand Ave	44127
Hanford Dr	44143
W Hanger Rd	44135
Hanks Ave	44108
Hanley Rd	44124
E & W Hanna Ct & Ln	44108
Hanover Dr	44112
Hansford Rd	44124
Harbor View Dr	44102
Harcourt Dr	44106
Harkness Rd	44106
Harland Ave	44119
Harlem Ave & Ct	44103
Harleston Dr	44124
Harley Ave	44111
Harmony Ln	44144
Harms Rd	44143
Harold Ave	44135
Harold Dr	44130
Harris Ave	44104
Harris Ct	44104
Harris Rd	44143
Harrison Dr	44143
Harrison St	44113
Harrow Dr	44129
Harsax Ave	44135
Hartford Rd	44112
Hartley Dr	44124
Hartley Rd	44110
Hartshorn Rd	44112
Hartwood Rd	
3300-3499	44112
3500-3599	44121
Harvard Ave	
500-598	44105
600-698	44105
600-5299	44105
1000-1099	44109
2100-2198	44105
2200-13999	44105
14100-18299	44128
Harvey Ave	44104
Harvey Rd	44118
Harwich Rd	44124
Harwood Ave	44105
Harwood Rd	44121
Haselton Rd	44121
Haskell Dr	44108
Hastings Ave	
1800-1899	44112
7300-7399	44105
Hastings Rd	44125
Hathaway Ave	44108
Hathaway Rd	44125
Hauserman Rd	44130
Havana Rd	44125
Havel Ave	44120
Haverford Dr	44124
Haverhill Ave	44129
Haverhill Rd	44112
Haverston Rd	44124
Hawthorne Ave	44103
Hawthorne Cir	44134
Hawthorne Dr	
1500-1799	44124
5501-5597	44143
5599-5700	44143
5702-5798	44143
6500-6599	44134
Hayden Ave	
1100-1219	44110
1220-2000	44112
2002-2098	44112
Hayes Ct	44143
Haywood Dr	44121
Hazel Dr	44106
Hazel Rd	44112
Hazeldell Dr	44108
Hazelmere Ave	44111
Hazelmere Rd	44122
Headley Ave	44111
Hearthstone Rd	44134
Heath Ave	44104
Heather Ct	44124
Heather Ln	
4700-4799	44144
16201-16297	44130
16299-16500	44130
16502-16598	44130
25000-25099	44143
Heather Field Cir	44134
Hecker Ave	44103
Hector Ave	44127
Hege Ave	44105
Heidtman Pkwy	44105
Heinton Dr	44125
Heisley Ave	44105
Helen Rd	44122
Helena Ave	44108
Helmsdale Dr	44143
Helmsdale Rd	44112
Hemingway Rd	44143
Hemlock Ave	44113
Hemlock Ln	44130
Hempstead Rd	44125
Hencenco Ave	44106
Henderson Rd	44112
Henia Cir	44125
Henley Rd	44112
Henning Dr	44124
Henninger Rd	44109
Henritze Ave	44109
Henry Rd	44126
Henry St	44125
Hepburn Rd	44130
Hereford Rd	
1000-1199	44112
1201-1399	44118
Heresford Dr	44134
Heritage Ln	44124
Herman Ave	44102
Hermit Ave	44105
Hermitage Rd	44122
Herold Rd	44121
Herrick Mews	44106
Herrick Rd	44108
Herschel Ct	44113
Hessler Ct & Rd	44106
Hetzel Dr	44134
Hialeah Dr	44134
Hickory Dr	44124
Hickory Ln	
2500-2699	44124
4200-4299	44128
Hickory Hill Dr	44143
Hickory Hill Ln	44130
Hickox Blvd	44130
Hidden Valley Cir & Ln	44129
Hidden Woods Trl	44143
High St	44115
High Point Ct	44134
S Highland Ave	44125
Highland Rd	
3601-3629	44111
3631-3899	44111
5300-27699	44143
Highland Hills Ct	44129
Highland Place Ct	44143
Highland Ridge Dr	44143
Highland View Dr	44134
Highlandview Ave	44135
Highview Ave	44109
Highview Dr	
7200-7335	44129
7337-7399	44129
16200-16499	44128
Hildana Rd	44120
Hilgert Dr	44104
Hilland Dr	44109
N Hillary Ln & Oval	44143
Hillbrook Rd	44118
Hillburn Rd	44128
Hillcrest Ave	44109
Hillcrest Dr	
400-499	44143
6000-6599	44125
Hillcrest Ln	44134
Hillcrest Rd	44118
Hillcroft Dr	44128
Hiller Ave	44119
Hillgrove Ave	44119
Hillman Ave	44127
Hillock Ave	44108
Hillrock Dr	44121
S Hills Dr	44109
Hillsboro Rd	44112
Hillsdale Ave	44126
Hillsdale Rd	44134
Hillside Ave	
1800-1899	44112
1901-1999	44112
4600-4799	44125
Hillside Rd	
7500-7899	44104
20300-20999	44135
Hillstone Rd	44121
Hilltop Dr	44134
Hilltop Oval	44134
Hilltop Rd	44143
Hillview Rd	44112
Hilton Rd	44112
Hinckley Ave	44109
Hinckley Industrial Pkwy	44109
Hinde Ave	44127
Hinsdale Ct	44130
Hinsdale Rd	44121
Hipple Ave	44135
Hirst Ave	44135
Hlavin Ave	44105
Hodgman Dr	44130
Hodgson Ave	44109
Hoertz Rd	44134
Holborn Ave	44105
Holbrook Rd	44120
Holburn Rd	44129
Holden Ln	44108
Holiday Cir	44109
Hollenbeck Cir	44129
Hollister Rd	44118
Holliston Ln	44130
Holly Cir	44134
Holly Hill Dr	44128
Hollyhock Ct	44124
Hollywood Ave	44111
Hollywood Dr	44129
Holmden Ave	44109
Holmden Ct	44109
Holmden Rd	44121
Holmes Ave	44110
Holmwood Rd	44122
Holton Ave & Ct	44104
Holyoke Ave	
1500-1799	44112
4700-5099	44104
Holyrood Rd	44106
Home Ct	44103
Homer Ave	44103
Homestead Ave	44105
Homestead Rd	44121
Homeway Rd	44135
Homewood Ave	44130
Homewood Way	44143
Homeworth Ave	44125
Honeydale Ave	44120
Hood Ave	44109
Hoover Ave	44119
Hope Ave	44102
Hope Haven Dr	44134
Hopkins Ave	44108
Hoppensack Ave	44127
Horace Ct	44113
Horizon Dr	44143
Horner Ave	44120
Horton Rd	44125
Hosmer Ave	44105
Hough Ave	
5500-8499	44103
8500-9699	44106
House Ave	44127
Houston Ave	44113
Houston Dr	44130
Howard Ave	44113
Howard St	44134
Hower Ave	44112
Howlett Ave	44113
Hoy Ave	44105
Hub Pkwy	44125
Hubbard Ave	44127
Huckleberry Dr	44143
Hudson Ave	44106
E Huffman Rd	44130
Hulda Ave	44104
Hull Ave	44106
Humphrey Ct	44110
Humphrey Rd	44130
Hunt Cir	44143
Hunter Dr	44125
Hunting Hollow Dr	44124
Huntington Ln	44118
Huntington Rd	44120
Huntington Reserve Dr	44134
Huntmere Ave	44110
Hurley Ave	44109
Huron Rd	44124
Huron Rd E	44115
Huron Rd NW	44115
W Huron Rd	44113
Hurston Ct	44121
Huss Ave	44105
Hy Ct	44125
Hyde Ave	44109
Hyde Park Ave	44118
Hyde Park Dr	44130
Ida Ave	44103
Idarose Ave	44110
Idlehurst Dr	44143
Idlewood Ave	44112
Idlewood Dr	44144
Idlewood Rd	44118
Ignatius Ave	44111
Imperial Ave	44120
Independence Blvd	44130
Independence Rd	
2900-2999	44115
3100-3749	44105
3751-3899	44105
Indian Creek Dr	44130
Indian Mound Rd	44125
Indiana Ave	
6500-6699	44124
6800-7599	44105
Industrial Pkwy	44135
Infinity Corporate Centre Dr	44125
Ingalton Ave	44110
Ingleside Dr	44134
Ingleside Rd	
3200-3799	44122
4300-4499	44128
17600-17999	44119
Inglewood Dr	44121
Ingomar Ave	44108
Inman Ave	44105
Interchange Corporate Center Rd	44128
Invermere Ave	
15401-15497	44128
15499-18299	44128
18300-18999	44122
E Inverness Dr	44143
W Inverness Dr	44143
Inverness Rd	44122
Iowa Ave	44108
Ira Ave	44144
Irene Rd	44124
Irma Ave	44105
Iron Ct	44115
Ironwood Ave	44110
Ironwood Cir	44129
Iroquois Ave	
1100-1499	44124
12600-12799	44108
12801-13099	44108
Irving Ave	
1000-1499	44109
9701-9799	44125
Irvington Ave	44108
Irvington Ter	44103
Isaac Dr	44130
Issler Ct	44105
Itasca Ave	44106
Ithaca Ct	44102
Ivandale Dr	44129
Ivanhoe Rd	
900-974	44110
976-1199	44110
1700-1799	44112
Ivy Ave	44127
Ivy Ln	44130
N Ivy Ln	44130
Ivydale Rd	44118
Ivywood Dr	44144
Jackie Ln	44124
Jackson Blvd	44118
Jackson Rd	44135
Jacqueline Dr	44134
Jaeger Dr	44124
James Dr	44130
Jameson Rd	44129
Jamestown Dr	44134
Jamestowne Dr	44130
Janette Ave	44118
Japan Ct	44113
Jasmine Cir	44124
Jasper Rd	44111
Jay Ave	44113
Jean Ave	44110
Jeanne Dr	44134
Jeannette Dr	44143
Jefferson Ave	44113
Jefferson Dr	44143
Jefferson Ln	44143
Jefferson Park Rd	44130
Jeffries Ave	44105
Jelliffe St	44115
Jenne Ave	44110
Jennifer Dr	44134
Jennings Rd	44109
Jennings St	44128
Jennings Ridge Dr	44109
Jenny Ln	44125
Jesse Ave	44105
Jesse L Jackson Pl	44108
Jewett Ave	44127
Jill Dr	44134
Jo Ann Dr	
1401-1497	44134
1499-2099	44134
3700-3999	44122
Joan Ave	44111
John Ave & Ct	44113
John Carroll Blvd	44118
John Nagy Blvd	44144
John P Green Pl	44105
Johnson Ct	44113
Johnson Dr	44130
Johnston Pkwy	44128
Joliet Rd	44105
Jones Rd	44105
Joslyn Rd	44111
Joy Ct	44113
Joyce Ave	44128
Joyce Dr	44130
Joyce Rd	44143
Judie Dr	44109
Judson Dr	44128
Judy Ct	44111
Judy Dr	44134
Julia Ave	44104
Junction Rd	44102
Juniata Ave	44103
Juniper Rd	44106
Kadel Ave	44135
Kader Dr	44130
Karen Isle Dr	44143
Kares Ave	44122
Karl Dr	44143
Katey Rose Ln	44143
Kazimier Ave	44105
Keemar Ct	44106
Keene Ct	44113
Kelley Ave	44114
Kelley Ln	44134
Kelsey Rd	44129
Kelso Ave	44110
Kelton Ave	44106
Keltonshire Rd	44129
Kemper Rd	44120
Kempton Ave	44108
Kenarden Dr	44143
Kenbridge Dr	44143
Kenbridge Rd	44130
Kendall Rd	44120
Kenilworth Ave	
1000-1599	44113
7301-7397	44129
7399-8399	44129
Kenilworth Mews	44106
Kenilworth Rd	44106
Kenmore Ave	
3700-5299	44134
8600-9399	44106
Kenmore Rd	44122
Kennard Ct & Rd	44104
Kennedy Ave	44104
Kennedy Dr	44144

Kennelwood Dr 44143
Kenneth Ave
1801-2097 44109
2099-2100 44109
2102-2298 44109
5400-7199 44129
7201-7299 44129
Kensington Ave 44111
Kensington Rd 44118
Kent Rd 44106
Kenton Ave 44129
Kenton Cir 44124
Kenyon Ave 44105
Kenyon Dr 44129
Kenyon Rd 44120
Keppler Ct 44105
Kerneywood Rd 44129
Kerns Ave 44102
Kerrwood Rd 44118
Kersdale Rd 44124
Kerwick Rd 44118
Kerwin Rd 44118
Keswick Dr 44130
Keswick Rd 44120
Kew Rd 44118
Kewanee Ave 44119
Key Plz 44114
Key West Dr 44134
Keyes Ave 44104
Keystone Dr 44121
Keystone Pkwy 44135
Keystone Rd 44134
Kidder Ave 44102
Kilbourne Dr 44124
Kilbridge Dr 44143
Kildare Rd 44118
Kildeer Ave 44119
Kilson Ave 44135
Kimberley Ave 44108
Kimberly Dr 44125
Kimmel Rd 44105
King Ave 44114
King George Blvd 44121
King Richard Dr 44134
Kingman Dr 44130
Kings Hwy
5200-5399 44126
5800-5999 44130
21400-21499 44126
Kingsbury Blvd 44104
Kingsdale Blvd 44130
Kingsford Ave 44128
Kingsley Rd 44122
Kingston Rd 44118
Kingswood Dr 44124
Kinkel Ave 44109
Kinsman Rd
5500-11599 44104
11600-15599 44120
Kipling Ave 44110
Kipling Ct 44143
Kirby Ave 44108
Kirkham Ave 44105
Kirkshire Ct 44143
Kirkwood Ave 44102
Kirkwood Rd 44121
Kirton Ave 44135
Kiwanis Dr 44130
Klein Dr 44130
Klonowski Ave 44105
Klusner Ave 44134
Kneale Dr 44124
Knollwood Dr 44129
Knollwood Trl 44143
Knowles Dr 44134
Knowles St 44112
Knowlton Ave 44106
Koch Dr 44134
Kolar Ave 44104
Kollin Ave 44128
Korman Ave 44103
Kosciuszko Ave 44103
Krakow Ave 44105
Krather Rd 44109
Krueger Ave 44134
Kuhlman Ave 44110

La Grange Ave 44103
La Rose Ave 44105
La Salle Ave 44119
Laclede Rd 44121
Lafayette Dr
2500-2599 44118
10600-11999 44130
Laird Ave 44102
Laisy Ave 44104
Lake Ave 44102
S Lake Blvd 44130
Lake Ct 44114
Lake Abrams Dr 44130
Lake Cove Ct 44108
Lake Front Walk 44110
Lake Harbor Ct 44108
Lake Shore Blvd
8701-9397 44108
9399-13399 44108
13400-17199 44110
17300-19999 44119
S Lake Shore Blvd 44119
Lake Shore Dr 44110
Lakefront Ave
1200-1499 44108
1500-1799 44112
Lakehurst Dr 44108
Lakeland Blvd 44119
Lakeport Ave 44119
Lakeside Ave E 44114
W Lakeside Ave 44113
Lakeside St 44110
Lakeview Cir 44129
Lakeview Dr 44129
Lakeview Rd
600-1299 44108
1301-1313 44106
1315-1399 44106
1400-1899 44112
Lakeview Ter 44130
Lakota Ave 44111
Lalemant Dr 44129
Lalemant Rd 44118
Lamar Ct 44143
Lambert Ave 44120
Lambert Rd 44121
Lambert St 44112
Lamberton Rd 44118
Lamoille Ct 44113
Lamont Ave 44106
Lamontier Ave 44104
Lampson Rd 44112
Lanark Ln 44124
Lancashire Rd 44106
Lancaster Rd 44121
Lancelot Ave 44108
Lancelot Dr 44134
Landchester Rd 44109
Lander Dr 44143
Lander Rd
701-721 44143
723-1099 44143
1100-3699 44124
3701-3739 44124
Landerbrook Dr 44124
Landerhaven Ct & Dr 44124
Landerwood Rd 44124
Landon Ave 44102
Landon Rd 44122
Landover Ct 44134
Landseer Rd 44119
Langerdale Rd 44121
Langerford Dr 44129
Langly Ave 44128
Langston Ave 44115
Langton Ave 44125
Langton Rd 44121
Lanier Dr 44130
Lanken Ave 44119
Lansbury Ln 44124
Lansdale Rd 44118
Lansing Ave 44105
Lansmere Rd 44122
Lantern Ln 44130
Lanyard Dr 44129
Larchmere Blvd & Sq 44120

Larchmont Dr 44124
Larchmont Rd 44110
Larchwood Ave 44135
Lardet Ave 44104
Lares Ln 44130
Larkspur Dr 44124
Larkspur Ln 44128
Larnder Ave 44102
Lassiter Dr
400-599 44143
7000-7299 44129
Lassiter Oval 44129
Latimore Rd 44122
Laumer Ave 44105
Laurel Ln 44125
Laurel Rd
3000-3098 44120
3100-3199 44120
4400-4498 44121
4500-4599 44121
Laurel Trce 44130
Laurel Hill Dr 44121
Laurel Hill Ln 44124
Laureldale Rd 44122
Laurelhurst Rd 44118
Laurent Dr 44129
Lausche Ave 44103
Laverne Ave
5400-7199 44129
16200-17599 44135
Lawn Ave 44102
Lawndale Ave 44128
Lawndale Dr 44130
Lawnview Ave 44103
Lawnway Rd 44121
Lawnwood Ave 44130
Lawrence Ave 44125
Lawrence Rd 44128
Lawton Ln 44124
Layor Dr 44130
Leading Ave 44109
Learidge Rd 44124
Leavitt Ct 44104
Lecona Rd 44121
Lederer Ave 44127
Ledgewood Ave 44111
Ledgewood Trl 44124
Lee Ave 44106
Lee Blvd
1801-2249 44112
2251-2397 44118
2399-2499 44118
Lee Dr 44134
Lee Rd
1600-2699 44118
2501-2535 44118
2537-2599 44118
2800-3749 44120
3750-4999 44128
Lee Heights Blvd 44128
Leedston Dr 44124
Leedy Ct 44113
Leeila Ave 44135
Legacy Dr 44143
E & W Legend Ct & Ln 44143
Legends Way 44124
Leigh Ellen Ave 44135
Leighton Rd 44120
Lena Ave 44135
Lenacrave Ave 44105
Lennox Ave 44134
Lennox Rd 44106
Lenox Dr 44126
Leonard St 44113
Leopold Ave 44109
Leroy Ave
9300-9399 44104
13500-14299 44135
Lester Ave 44127
Leuer Ave 44108
Leverett Ln 44143
Lexington Ave 44103
Lexington Sq 44143
Lexington Green St 44130
Liberty Ave
7300-7398 44129

7400-8299 44129
13000-14299 44135
Liberty Rd 44121
Library Ave 44109
Lido Ct 44129
Liggett Dr 44134
Lilac Rd 44121
Lima Ave 44108
Lime Ln 44129
Lime Rd 44113
Lincoln Ave
2000-5099 44134
11001-11097 44125
11099-11299 44125
14800-15299 44128
Lincoln Blvd 44118
Lincoln Dr 44110
Lincolnshire Ln 44134
Linda Ln 44125
Lindazzo Ave 44114
Lindbergh Ave 44119
Linden Ln 44124
E Linden Ln 44130
N Linden Ln 44130
S Linden Ln 44130
W Linden Ln 44130
Lindholm Rd 44120
Lindsey Ln & Oval 44143
Linn Ave 44125
Linn Dr 44108
Linnell Rd 44121
Linnet Ave 44111
Linton Ave 44105
Linwood Ave 44103
Lipton Ave 44128
Lisbon Rd 44104
List Ct 44113
List Ln 44130
W List Ln 44130
Litchfield Dr 44143
Litchfield Rd 44120
Literary Rd 44113
Little Met Pl 44135
Littleton Rd 44125
Livingston Rd 44120
Ljubljana Dr 44119
Lloyd Rd 44111
Locherie Ave 44119
Locke Ave 44108
Locklie Dr 44143
N Lockwood Ave 44112
Lockyear Ave 44103
Logan Ct 44106
Logan Dr 44130
Loganberry Dr 44143
Lombardy Ln 44124
Lomond Blvd
16600-17699 44120
17700-20199 44122
London Ave 44135
London Rd
700-1099 44110
1700-1800 44112
1802-1898 44112
Longbrook Rd 44128
Longfellow Ave 44103
Longleaf Rd 44128
Longman Ln 44128
Longmead Ave 44135
Longridge Rd 44124
Longspur Ct 44125
Longspur Rd 44143
Longton Rd 44124
Longwood Ave
3500-3900 44115
3700-3702 44134
3704-3910 44134
3901-3915 44134
3902-3998 44115
3917-3999 44115
4000-5399 44134
Longwood Ct 44118
Longwood Dr 44124
Lonna Ct 44111
Lookout Cir 44126
Loop Dr 44113

Lorain Ave
1600-2098 44113
2100-4499 44113
4500-9999 44102
10000-18299 44111
Lorain Ct 44113
Lorain Rd 44126
Loren Ave 44105
Lorenzo Ave 44120
Loretta Ave
9700-9899 44102
9901-9999 44102
10001-10097 44111
10099-10399 44111
10401-10499 44111
Lorient Dr 44128
Lorimer Dr 44134
S Lotus Dr 44128
Lotusdale Dr 44130
Louis Ave 44135
Louis Dr 44124
Louisa Ct 44127
Louise Harris Dr 44104
Louisiana Ave 44109
Lourdes Dr 44134
Lowden Rd 44121
Lowell Ave 44108
Lowell Dr 44143
Lowell Rd 44121
Lownesdale Rd 44112
Loxley Dr 44143
Loyola Dr 44129
Loyola Rd 44118
Lucerne Ave
2700-3599 44134
6600-6899 44103
Lucerne Dr 44130
Lucia Ave 44104
Lucille Ave
4200-4499 44121
15900-16999 44111
Lucknow Ave 44110
Lucy Dr 44130
Ludgate Rd 44120
Ludlow Rd 44120
Luelda Ave 44129
Lufkin Ave 44127
Luke Ave 44120
Luther Ave 44103
Luxor Rd 44118
Lydian Ave 44111
Lyle Ave 44134
Lyman Blvd 44122
S Lyn Cir 44121
Lynd Ave 44124
Lynden Dr 44143
Lynden Oval 44130
Lyndhurst Rd 44124
Lyndway Dr 44125
Lyndway Rd 44121
Lynett Dr 44129
Lynford Cir 44143
Lynn Ct 44111
Lynn Park Dr 44121
Lynnfield Rd 44122
Lynnhaven Rd 44130
Lynton Rd 44122
Lyric Ave 44111
Mabel Ct 44113
Macauley Ave 44110
Macbeth Ave 44126
Machinery Ave 44103
Mack Ct 44109
Mackall Rd 44121
Macomb Ave 44105
Macon Ave 44102
Madison Ave 44102
Madison Ct 44103
Magdala Dr 44130
Magnet Ave 44127
Magnolia Dr
1-51 44110
53-199 44110
10701-10797 44106
10799-11199 44106
Magnolia Oval 44124

Mahoning Ave 44113
Main Ave 44113
Main St 44130
Makayla Ct 44143
Malden Rd 44121
Malibu Dr 44130
W Mall Dr 44114
Mallard Cv 44130
Mallard Dr 44124
Mallo Pl 44130
Malvern Dr 44129
Malvern Rd 44122
Manassas Oval 44134
Mancende Ave 44105
Mancenwo Ave 44111
Manchester Ct 44143
Manchester Rd
2800-3099 44122
6000-6499 44129
Mandalay Ave 44110
Mandalay Dr 44130
Manhattan Ave
1600-1699 44112
7300-7398 44129
7400-8199 44129
Manila Ave 44144
Mann Ave 44112
Mannering Rd 44112
Manoa Ave 44144
Manor Ave 44104
Manorford Dr
7801-7897 44129
7899-8399 44129
8700-8744 44130
8746-10499 44130
Mansfield Ave 44105
Manufacturing Ave 44135
Maple Ave 44108
Maple Dr
1000-1098 44134
1100-1399 44134
22500-22899 44126
Maple Rd 44121
Maple St 44110
Maple Leaf Dr 44125
Maplecliff Dr 44130
Maplecliff Rd 44119
Maplecrest Ave
2800-5399 44134
6400-6599 44130
Mapledale Ave 44109
Maplegrove Rd 44121
Maplerow Ave 44105
Mapleside Rd 44104
Maplewood Ave 44135
Maplewood Rd
2100-2299 44118
5900-6699 44124
6701-6797 44130
6799-7399 44130
Marah Ave 44104
Marble Ave 44105
Marcella Rd 44119
Marcelline Ct 44125
Marchmont Rd 44122
Marcie Dr 44109
Marda Dr 44134
Margate Ave 44135
N Marginal Rd 44114
S Marginal Rd
2301-3897 44114
3899-5499 44114
5500-6898 44103
Marguerite Ave 44125
Marian Cir 44126
Marian Dr 44124
Mariana Dr 44130
Marietta Ave
1600-1999 44134
9800-9999 44102
Marina Ct 44102
Marioncliff Dr 44134
Mark Ter 44128
Markal Dr 44130
Market Ave 44113
Market Square Park 44113

Marko Ln 44134
Marlboro Rd 44118
Marlborough Ave 44129
Marleen Dr 44126
Marlene Ave 44135
Marlindale Rd 44118
Marloes Ave 44112
Marlowe Ave 44108
Marmore Ave 44134
Marne Ave 44111
Marnell Ave 44124
Marquardt Ave 44113
Marquette St
1000-1349 44114
1350-1398 44103
Marquis Ave 44111
Marrus Cir & Ln 44143
Marshall Ave 44104
Marshfield Rd 44124
Marsol Rd 44124
Marston Ave 44105
Martha Rd 44135
Martin Ave 44127
Martin Dr
12900-12999 44130
13600-13800 44125
13802-13898 44125
Martin Luther King Jr Blvd 44105
Martin Luther King Jr Dr
1801-1899 44106
2401-2499 44120
2500-2598 44104
2600-3499 44104
3500-12099 44105
Marvin Ave 44109
Marvin Rd 44128
Marwood Ave 44135
Mary Ann Dr 44125
Maryland Ave 44105
Marymount Village Dr 44125
Massie Ave 44108
Mastick Rd 44126
W Mather Ln 44108
Matherson Ave 44135
Matilda Ave 44105
Maud Ave 44103
Maureen Dr 44130
Maurice Ave 44127
Maxwell Ave 44110
May Ave 44105
Mayberry Ave 44124
Mayberry Dr 44130
Maydor Ln 44121
Mayfair Ave 44112
Mayfair Blvd 44124
Mayfair Ln 44128
Mayfield Rd
2500-2712 44106
2714-2799 44106
2800-3649 44118
3663-3713 44121
3715-4749 44121
4750-6805 44124
6807-6849 44124
11400-12699 44106
Mayfield Ridge Rd 44124
Mayflower Ave 44124
Mayland Ave 44124
Maynard Ave 44109
Maynard Rd 44122
Maypine Farm Blvd 44143
Maysday Ave 44129
Mayview Ave 44109
Mayview Rd 44124
Maywood Ave 44102
Maywood Rd 44121
Mazepa Trl 44134
Mcbride Ave 44127
Mccann St 44128
Mccauley Rd 44122
Mccracken Blvd 44125
Mccracken Rd
10800-13999 44125
15101-15397 44128
15399-16399 44128

Street	ZIP
Mccurdy Ave	44104
Mcelhattan Ave	44110
Mcfarland Rd	44121
Mcgowan Ave	44135
Mcgregor Ave	44105
Mead Ave	44127
Meadow Ln	
6700-6811	44130
7100-7499	44134
S Meadow Ln	44109
Meadow Lark Way	44124
Meadow Wood Blvd	44124
Meadowbrook Ave	44144
Meadowbrook Blvd	44118
Meadowbrook Dr	44130
Meadowbrook Rd	44125
Meadowlane Dr	44143
Meadowlark Ln	44128
Meadowlawn Blvd	44134
Meadowood Dr	44143
Meadowvale Ave	44128
Medfield Rd	44124
Medford Rd	44121
Medina Ave	44103
Medway Rd	44143
Meech Ave	44105
Mehling Ct	44102
Melba Ave	44104
Melber Ave	44144
Melbourne Ave	44111
Melbourne Rd	44112
Melgrave Ave	44135
Melgrove Ave	44105
Melody Ln	
3100-3200	44134
3202-3298	44134
9500-9699	44144
Melrose Ave	44103
Melville Rd	44110
Melzer Ave	44120
Memphis Ave	
3400-4499	44109
4500-11299	44144
Memphis Villas Blvd S	44144
Menlo Rd	44120
Mentor Ave	44113
Meredith Ave	44119
Meridian Ave	44106
Merit Dr	44143
Merkle Ave	44129
Merl Ave	44109
Merrill Ave	44102
Merrimeade Dr	44111
Merrygold Blvd	44128
Merrymound Rd	44121
Merwin Ave	44113
Messenger Ct	44121
Metcalf Ave	44120
Methyl Ave	44120
Metro Park Dr	44143
Metrohealth Dr	44109
Metropolitan Dr	44135
Metropolitan Park Blvd	44121
Metta Ave	44103
Meyer Ave	44109
E & N Miami Dr	44134
Micka Dr	44144
Middlebrook Blvd	44130
Middledale Rd	44124
Middlefield Rd	44106
Middlehurst Rd	44118
Middleton Rd	44121
Midland Ave	44110
Midvale Ave	44135
Midwest Ave	44125
Milan Ave	
11700-12400	44111
12402-12498	44111
13300-13799	44112
Milan Cres	44128
Milan Dr	44119
Milburn Ave	44135
Mildred Ave	44126
Miles Ave	
9001-9097	44105
9099-13999	44105
14000-17699	44128
Miles Pkwy	44128
Miles Rd	44128
S Miles Rd	44128
Miles Park Ave	44105
Milford Ave	44134
Milford Rd	44118
W Mill Dr	44143
Millcreek Blvd	44105
Miller Ave	44119
Miller Ct	44113
Millerwood Ln	44130
Milligan Ave	44135
Millikin Ct	44118
Millridge Rd	44143
Milo Rd	44125
Milton Rd	44118
Milverton Rd	44120
Mina Ave	44135
Miner Rd	44143
E Miner Rd	44124
W Miner Rd	44124
Minkon Ave	44113
Minnie Ave	44104
Minor Ave	44105
Minster Ct	44105
Mira Ct	44109
Mirabeau Dr	44129
Miramar Blvd	
1701-1997	44121
1999-2149	44121
2151-2289	44118
2291-2400	44118
2402-2598	44118
Mission Rd	44135
Mistletoe Dr	44106
Mitchell Ave	44111
Mobile Ct	44109
Mohawk Ave	44119
Mohawk Trl	44130
Mohican Ave	44119
Moltke Ct	44113
Monarch Rd	44121
Monica Ln	44125
Monmouth Rd	
2900-2998	44118
3000-3199	44118
6300-6499	44129
E Monmouth Rd	44118
Monroe Ave	44113
Mont Ave	44118
Montagano Blvd	44121
Montana Ave	44102
Montauk Ave	44134
Montclair Ave	44109
Monterey Ave	44119
Monterey Dr	44124
Montevista Rd	44121
Montford Rd	44121
Montgomery Ave	44104
Montgomery Pl	44144
Montgomery Rd	
2800-3200	44122
3202-3298	44122
7801-7821	44130
7823-7899	44130
Monticello Blvd	
1-2897	44118
2899-3399	44118
3400-4350	44121
4352-4398	44121
4400-4999	44143
Monticello Place Ln	44143
Montrose Ave	44111
Montville Ct	44128
Mooncrest Dr	44129
Moonglow Ln	44109
Moore Ct	44113
Moore Dr	44130
N Moreland Blvd	44120
S Moreland Blvd	44120
W Moreland Rd	44129
Morgan Ave	44127
Morison Ave	44108
Morley Rd	44122
Morningside Ave	44130
Morningside Dr	
4500-4598	44109
4600-4799	44109
5400-6600	44129
6602-6610	44129
6701-6799	44125
Mornington Ln	44106
Morris Ct	44106
Morris Black Pl	44104
Mortimer Ave	44111
Morton Ave	
6100-6199	44127
8501-8597	44144
8599-9499	44144
22000-22699	44126
Moulton Ave	44106
Mound Ave	44105
Mount Auburn Ave	44104
Mount Carmel Rd	44104
Mount Laurel Rd	44121
Mount Overlook Ave	
10800-10898	44104
10900-11599	44104
11701-11897	44120
11899-12699	44120
Mount Sinai Dr	44106
Mount Union Ave	44112
Mount Vernon Blvd	44112
Mountview Ave	
5401-5499	44125
10500-10699	44104
10500-10699	44125
10700-11399	44125
Mozina Dr	44119
Mt Hermon Ave	44115
Muirfield Dr	
380-394	44143
396-499	44143
5100-5460	44124
Mulberry Ave	44113
Mulberry Cir	44143
Mumford Ave	44127
Munich Dr	44130
Munn Oval & Rd	44111
Muriel Ave	44109
Murray Rd	
900-999	44121
8400-9699	44125
Murray Hill Rd	44106
Muskoka Ave	44119
Myron Ave	44103
Myrtle Ave	44128
Nan Linn Dr	44143
Nancy Ct	44128
Nancy Dr	44121
Nanford Rd	44102
Nantucket Ct	44108
Nantucket Ln	44130
Naomi Ave	44111
Naomi Dr	44130
Naples Ave	44128
Narraganset Oval	44130
Nassau Dr	44130
Natchez Ave	44109
Nathan Dr	44130
Nathaniel Rd	44110
Naumann Ave	44119
Navahoe Rd	44121
Navajo Ln	44130
Navarre Ct	44108
W Neff Rd	44119
Neil Dr	44130
Nela Ave	44112
Nela View Rd	44112
Nelacrest Rd	44112
Neladale Rd	44112
Nelamere Rd	44112
Nelawood Rd	44112
Nell Ave	44110
Nelson Ave	44105
Nelson Blvd	44134
Nelwood Rd	44130
Neo Pkwy	44128
Nethersole Dr	44130
Nevada Ave	44104
Neville Ave	44102
Neville Rd	44121
New York Ave	44105
Newark Ave	44109
Newberry Ave	44121
Newberry Dr	44144
Newbury Dr	
2000-2299	44112
2301-2397	44118
2399-2599	44118
Newbury Ln	44130
Newcomb Dr	44129
Newcome St	44143
Newkirk Dr	44130
Newland Rd	44130
Newman Ave	44127
Newport Ave	44129
Newport Ln	
4500-4599	44128
16700-16899	44130
22501-22597	44128
22599-22899	44128
22901-22999	44128
Newton Ave	
9700-10099	44106
18700-19998	44119
Newton Rd	44130
Nicholas Ave	
9800-9999	44102
16301-16599	44120
Nichols Rd	44103
Nickel Pl	44104
Nickel Plate Dr	44115
Nicky Blvd	44125
Niessen Ct	44109
Night Vista Dr	44129
Nightjar Ct	44125
Nobb Hill Dr	44130
Noble Rd	
1700-2235	44112
2236-2999	44121
S Noble Rd	44121
Nobleshire Rd	44121
Nordica Ct	44102
Nordway Rd	44118
Norfolk Dr	44134
Norfolk Rd	44106
Norma Dr	44121
Norman Ave	44106
Norman Ln	44143
Normandie Blvd	44130
Normandy Ave	44111
Normandy Dr	44134
Normandy Rd	44120
Norris Ave	44134
North Ave	44134
North Blvd	44108
North Ct	44111
North Dr	44105
North Rd	44111
Northampton Rd	44121
Northboro Dr	44143
Northcliff Ave	44144
Northcliffe Rd	44118
Northfield Ave	44112
Northfield Rd	44128
Northland Rd	44128
Northlane Dr	44144
Northline Cir	44119
Northridge Oval	44144
Northvale Blvd	44112
Northwood Ave	
12800-12898	44120
20700-21499	44126
Northwood Dr	44124
Northwood Rd	44118
Norton Rd	44111
Norway Ave	44111
Norwell Ave	44135
Norwood Rd	
1001-1119	44103
1121-1299	44103
3200-3699	44122
Notabene Dr	44130
Notre Dame Ave	44104
Nottingham Dr	
2400-3499	44134
21100-21599	44126
21601-21699	44126
Nottingham Rd	
17400-18599	44119
18600-19699	44110
Novicky Ct	44121
Nursery Ave	44127
Nyack Ct	44110
Nye Rd	44110
Oak Ave	44105
Oak Rd	44118
Oak St	44125
Oak Knoll Dr	44124
Oak Park Ave	44109
Oak Park Blvd	44125
Oakbrook Oval	44129
Oakdale Ave	44128
Oakdale Rd	
2100-2299	44118
9100-9699	44129
Oakfield Ave	44105
Oakhill Dr	44143
Oakhill Rd	44112
Oakland Ave	44106
Oakland Dr	44124
Oaklawn Dr	44134
Oakley Ave	44102
Oakmont Dr	44124
Oakmount Rd	44121
Oakridge Dr	44121
Oakshire Ct	44130
Oakshore Dr	44108
Oakton Cir	44143
Oakview Ave	44108
Oakview Blvd	44125
Oakview Dr	44143
Oakville Rd	44124
Oakwood Dr	44121
Oakwood Rd	44130
Ocala Dr	44134
Octavia Rd	44112
Ohio Ave	44128
Ohlman Ave	44108
Okalona Rd	44121
Old Brainard Rd	44124
Old Brookpark Rd	44109
Old Granger Rd	44125
Old Grayton Rd	44135
Old Oak Blvd	44130
Old Pleasant Valley Rd	44130
Old River Rd	44113
Old Rockside Rd	
821-897	44134
899-1599	44134
8000-11499	44125
Old Salem Trl	44143
Old Virginia Ln	44130
Olde York Rd	44130
Olistinc Ave	44110
Olive Ct	44103
Oliver Rd	44111
Olivet Ave	44108
Olney Ct	44105
Olympia Rd	44112
Omalley Dr	44134
Onaway Oval	44130
Onaway Rd	44120
Oneal Pt	44128
Onoko Dr	44126
Ontario St	
1200-1350	44113
1351-1399	44114
1352-1398	44113
2000-2299	44115
2301-2499	44115
Orange Ave	
2200-2400	44101
3500-3698	44115
3700-4000	44115
4002-4002	44115
Orchard Ave	
4200-4399	44113
5400-7199	44129
8501-8597	44144
8599-9499	44144
Orchard Blvd	44130
Orchard Rd	
3900-3999	44121
4500-4699	44126
4700-4999	44128
Orchard Grove Ave	44144
Orchard Grove Dr	44130
Orchard Heights Dr	44124
Orchard Park Ave	44111
Orchard Park Dr	44134
Orchardview Rd	44134
Orey Ave	44105
Orinoco Ave	44112
Orlando Dr	44134
Orleans Ave	44105
Orme Rd	44125
Ormiston Ave	44119
Ormond Rd	44118
Orton Ct	44103
Orville Ave	44106
Osage Ave	44105
Osborn Rd	44128
Osceola Ave	44108
Osmond Ct	44105
Ostend Ave	44108
Othello Ave	44110
Otis Ct	44104
Otokar Ave	44127
Ottawa Rd	44105
Otter Ave	44104
Otto Ct	44102
Outhwaite Ave	44104
Outlook Ave & Dr	44144
Overbrook Rd	44124
Overdrive Way	44125
Overlook Dr	44126
Overlook Ln	44106
Overlook Rd	
2101-2197	44106
2199-2599	44106
4901-4999	44125
5500-5699	44129
E Overlook Rd	
2600-2799	44106
2800-2969	44118
2970-3399	44118
S Overlook Rd	44106
Overlook Park Dr	44110
Overlook Ridge Dr	44109
Ovington Ave	44127
Owosso Ave	44105
Ox Ridge Trl	44143
Oxford Ave	44111
Oxford Dr	44129
Oxford Rd	
900-1299	44121
18801-18897	44122
18899-19099	44122
19101-19199	44122
Ozark Ave	44119
Pacific Ave	44102
Packard Ave & Cir	44130
Page Ave	44112
Palda Dr	44128
Pallarra Rd	44143
Pallister Dr	44105
Palm Cir	44126
Palmerston Rd	44122
Pamela Dr	44125
Panama Dr	44134
Panna Ln	44109
Paris Ave	44109
Park Ave	44105
N Park Blvd	
1601-2699	44106
2701-18299	44118
2901-20197	44118
18301-18497	44118
18499-18599	44118
18700-19699	44122
19701-19999	44122
20001-20099	44118
20199-20700	44118
20702-20798	44118
S Park Blvd	
2600-2698	44120
2701-2999	44120
5600-6499	44134
13900-18498	44120
18501-18597	44122
18599-20099	44122
W Park Blvd	44120
Park Dr	
2400-2700	44134
2700-2799	44134
2701-2799	44120
2702-3898	44134
2801-3899	44134
4701-5599	44144
E Park Dr	44119
N Park Dr	44126
S Park Dr	44126
W Park Dr	44126
Park Ln	
3801-3899	44105
10500-10598	44106
Park Pl	44109
Park Rd	44135
W Park Rd	44111
Park Fulton Oval	44144
Park Heights Ave	44125
Park Heights Rd	44104
Park Knoll Dr	44125
Park Lane Dr	44124
Park Midway St	44104
Park Pointe Ct	44124
Park West Oval	44135
Parkcliff Ct & Dr	44126
Parkdale Ave	
14000-14299	44111
21700-21999	44126
Parkdale Rd	44121
Parkedge Cir	44126
Parkedge Dr	
4500-4699	44126
10900-11199	44104
Parker Dr	44124
Parkgate Ave	44108
Parkgrove Ave	44110
Parkhaven Dr	44134
Parkhill Ave	44120
Parkhill Dr	44130
Parkhill Rd	44121
Parkhurst Dr	44111
Parkland Blvd	44124
Parkland Dr	
5700-9799	44130
15600-17699	44120
17700-18398	44122
18400-18699	44122
Parklane Dr	
2800-3499	44134
20900-20999	44126
Parklawn Ave	44130
Parklawn Dr	44108
Parkleigh Dr	44134
Parkmount Ave	44135
Parkridge Ave	44144
Parkside Blvd	44143
Parkside Cir	44124
Parkside Dr	
4000-4198	44144
7500-7799	44130
S Parkside Dr	44144
Parkside Rd	44108
Parkton Dr	44128
Parkview Ave	
6800-6899	44134
9400-11599	44104
9701-9801	44125
9803-10300	44125
10302-10302	44125
11600-12199	44120
Parkview Dr	44124
E Parkview Dr	44134
W Parkview Dr	44134
Parkview Ln	44126
Parkway Dr	
1801-1897	44118
1899-1999	44118
4801-4999	44125
N Parkway Dr	
6901-6999	44130

12500-12598 44105
12600-13099 44105
S Parkway Dr
6900-6998 44130
12700-13899 44105
Parkway Rd 44108
W Parkway Rd 44135
Parkwood Ave 44126
Parkwood Dr 44108
Parma Heights Blvd 44130
Parma Park Blvd 44130
Parmaview Ln 44134
Parmelee Ave 44108
Parmenter Dr 44129
Parnell Rd 44122
N & S Partridge Dr 44125
Pasadena Ave 44108
Pasnow Ave 44119
Patton Rd 44109
Paul Ave 44106
Paula Dr 44130
Pawnee Ave 44119
Pawnee Trl 44130
Paxton Rd
800-999 44108
2800-2999 44120
Payne Ave
1300-3899 44114
3901-3999 44114
4000-4999 44103
Peachtree Ln N & S 44134
Pear Ave 44102
Pearl Rd
3600-5069 44109
5071-5097 44129
5099-5799 44129
5800-7899 44130
Pearldale Ave 44135
Pearse Ave 44105
Pecan Oval 44130
Peck Ave 44103
Peeper Hollow Ln 44124
Pelham Dr
4601-4699 44144
5400-8500 44129
8502-8598 44129
Pelley Dr 44109
Pelton Ct 44113
Pembrook Rd 44121
Pendind Dr 44129
Penfield Ave 44125
Penhurst Rd 44110
Penn Ct 44113
Pennfield Rd 44121
Pennington Rd 44120
Pennsylvania Ave 44103
Penrose Ave 44112
Pensacola Ave 44109
Peony Ave 44111
Pepper Ave 44110
Pepper Creek Dr 44124
Pepper Ridge Dr 44144
Pepper Ridge Rd 44124
Pepperwood Ln 44124
Percy Ave 44127
Peridert Ave 44108
Periwinkle Ln 44143
Perkins Ave
3001-3097 44114
3099-3999 44114
4000-5299 44103
Perkins Ct 44103
Pershing Ave
3700-4199 44134
4200-5099 44134
4201-4297 44127
4299-4599 44127
4600-4700 44134
4701-4797 44127
4702-4798 44134
4799-5099 44127
5100-5399 44134
Perth Dr 44143
Petrarca Rd 44106
Pheasant Run 44124
Philena Ave 44109
Philetus Ave 44127

Phillips Ave
11700-12499 44108
12501-12697 44112
12699-12950 44112
12952-12998 44112
Piercefield Dr 44143
Piermont Rd 44121
Pierpont Ave 44108
Pierson Dr 44143
Pilgrim Ave 44111
Pilsen Ave 44102
Pin Oak Dr 44130
Pine Oval 44134
Pine Cone Dr 44134
Pine Forest Dr 44134
Pine Hill Trl 44130
Pine Ridge Ct 44130
Pine River Ct 44130
Pine Tree Ct 44130
Pine Valley Trl 44130
Pinebrook Ln 44124
Pinegrove Ave 44129
Pinehurst Ct
5700-5899 44143
7300-7498 44130
Pinehurst Dr 44129
Pinehurst Rd 44143
Pinetree Rd 44124
Pineview Ct 44130
Pinewood Cir 44124
Pinewood Dr 44130
Pipers Ct 44134
Pittsburgh Ave 44115
Pixley Ct 44109
Plainfield Ave 44144
Plainfield Rd 44121
Plato Ave 44110
Platt Ave & Ct 44104
Platten Ave 44102
Plaza Dr 44130
Pleasant St 44130
Pleasant Trl 44143
Pleasant Hill Dr 44130
Pleasant Lake Blvd 44130
W Pleasant Valley Rd
900-4699 44134
4700-7199 44129
7201-7299 44130
7300-12999 44130
Pleasant View Dr 44134
Pleasantdale Rd 44109
Plymouth Ave 44125
Plymouth Dr 44121
Plymouth Pl 44112
Plymouth Rd
1300-1599 44109
1601-1699 44109
2800-2900 44124
2902-2998 44124
4100-4250 44109
4252-4298 44109
Poe Ave 44109
W Point Dr 44126
N Pointe Dr 44124
Pointe Pkwy 44128
Poland Ct 44105
Polonia Ave 44105
Pomeroy Ave 44110
Pomona Dr 44130
Pomona Rd 44121
Pompano Ct 44134
Ponciana Ave 44135
Pontiac St 44112
Pontonto Dr 44130
Poplar Ave 44110
Porieriv Ave 44109
Port Ave 44104
Portage Ave 44127
Portage Rd 44124
Portman Ave 44109
Postal Rd
5701-5799 44135
5801-5801 44181
5805-5999 44135
Potomac Ave 44112
Potter Ct 44113

Powell Ave 44118
Powers Blvd 44129
Praha Ave 44127
Prame Ave 44109
Prasse Rd 44121
Pratt Ave 44105
Preble Ave 44104
Prentice Ct 44110
Preston Ave 44102
Preston Rd 44128
Prestwick Ln 44143
Preyer Ave 44118
Priebe Ave 44128
Primary Rd 44135
Primrose Ave 44108
Primrose Cir 44130
Prince Ave 44105
Princeton Ave 44105
Princeton Blvd 44121
Princeton Ct 44130
Princeton Pl 44130
Princeton Rd 44118
Prior Ct 44106
Priscilla Ave 44134
Private Dr
5900-6099 44130
14700-14998 44112
Proctor Ct 44105
Professor Ave 44113
Professor Rd 44124
Project Ave 44115
Prospect Ave 44103
Prospect Ave E 44115
W Prospect Ave
3-107 44115
109-113 44115
115-199 44115
200-298 44113
301-399 44113
Prospect Rd 44103
Prosser Ave 44103
Providence Ct 44108
Providence Rd 44124
Public Sq
1-3 44114
2-2 44113
4-124 44113
125-200 44114
202-228 44114
Pulaski Ave 44103
Puritan Ave 44105
Puritas Ave 44135
Puritas Park Dr 44135
Putnam Ave 44105
Pythias Ave 44110
Quail Roost 44124
Quarry Dr 44121
Quarry Ln 44143
Quarrystone Ln 44130
Quebec Ave 44106
Queen Ave 44113
Queen Ann Ct 44121
Queen Anns Way 44126
Queen Mary Dr 44121
Queens Hwy 44130
Queens Park Ave 44124
Queensboro Dr 44143
Queenston Rd 44118
Quentin Rd 44112
Quigley Rd 44113
Quilliams Rd 44121
Quimby Ave 44103
Quincy Ave
4101-4297 44104
4299-8499 44104
8500-10699 44106
Quinebaug Ct 44130
Quinn Ct 44103
Rabbit Run Dr 44144
Rabun Ln 44143
Rachel Ln 44143
Radcliff Rd 44121
Radford Dr 44143
Radio Ln 44114
Radnor Rd 44118
Rae Rd 44124

Ragall Pkwy 44130
Rainbow Ave 44111
Rainbow Rd 44121
Rainier Ct 44134
Raleigh Sq 44143
Ralph Ave 44109
Ralston Dr 44129
Ramblewood Trl 44121
Ramona Blvd 44104
Ramona Dr 44130
Ranchland Dr 44124
N Randall Dr 44128
Randall Rd 44113
Randolph Rd 44121
Random Rd 44106
Ransome Rd 44143
Rathbun Ave 44105
Ravenswood Dr 44129
Ravine Blvd 44134
Ravine Dr 44112
Rawlings Ave 44104
Rawnsdale Rd 44122
Raymond Ave
9300-9999 44104
10600-10799 44125
Raymont Blvd 44118
Recher Ave 44119
Red Raven Rd 44124
Redding Rd 44109
Redell Ave 44103
Redfern Rd 44134
Redwood Rd
3100-3300 44118
3302-3398 44118
19200-19319 44110
19321-19499 44110
Reed Ave 44125
Reese Rd 44119
Regal Dr 44129
Regalia Ave 44104
Regency Dr 44129
Regent Rd 44127
Reichert Rd 44130
Reid Ave 44127
Reid Dr 44130
Reindeer Ave 44125
Remington Ave 44108
Renaissance Pkwy 44128
Renee Dr 44143
Renfield Rd 44121
Reno Ave 44105
Reno Dr 44130
Renrock Rd 44118
W Rental Rd 44135
Renwood Ave 44119
Renwood Dr 44129
Renwood Rd 44121
Reserve Ct 44126
Reserve Ln 44130
Reservoir Place Dr 44104
Revere Ave 44105
Revere Cir 44130
Revere Ct 44109
Revere Rd
1800-2099 44118
6800-6999 44130
Rexford Ave 44105
Rexwood Ave 44105
Rexwood Rd 44118
Reyburn Rd 44112
Rhodes Ct 44109
Richard Dr
9801-9897 44144
9899-9999 44144
10400-11500 44130
11502-11598 44130
Richland Ave 44125
Richmond Ave 44105
Richmond Park E 44143
Richmond Park W 44143
Richmond Rd
100-106 44143
108-825 44143
826-2099 44124
4400-4498 44128
4500-4999 44128

Richmond Sq 44143
Richmond Bluffs Dr 44143
Richmond Park Dr 44143
Richner Ave 44113
S Ridge Dr 44109
Ridge Rd
3400-3609 44102
3700-4936 44144
4938-4998 44144
4951-5097 44129
5099-7899 44129
Ridgebury Blvd 44124
Ridgefield Ave 44129
Ridgefield Rd 44118
Ridgehill Rd 44121
Ridgeland Ave & Cir 44135
Ridgeline Ave 44129
Ridgemore Ave 44144
Ridgeton Dr 44128
Ridgeview Rd
4000-4299 44144
6590-6699 44124
Ridgewood Ave 44129
E Ridgewood Dr 44131
W Ridgewood Dr
1200-5399 44134
5500-8499 44129
8500-8898 44130
8900-11199 44130
Ridgewood Lakes Dr 44129
Ridpath Ave 44110
Riedham Rd 44120
Riester St 44134
Rinard Rd 44118
Ripley Rd 44120
River Rd 44113
River Trl 44124
River Creek Rd 44124
River Ridge Dr 44109
Riverbed St 44113
Rivercliff Dr 44126
Riveredge Dr 44130
Riveredge Rd 44111
Riverside Ave
2600-4199 44109
4300-4499 44102
Riverside Dr 44135
Riverview Ct 44130
Riviera Dr 44126
Roadoan Rd 44144
Roanoke Ave 44109
Roanoke Cir 44134
Roanoke Dr 44134
Roanoke Rd 44121
Robert Ave 44109
Robert Dr 44130
Robert Rd 44121
Robert St 44134
Robertson Ave 44105
Robin Cir 44143
Robinhood Ave 44126
Robinhood Dr
2400-2899 44134
13501-13599 44125
Robinson Ave 44125
Rochelle Ave 44135
Rochelle Blvd 44130
Rochester Rd 44122
Rock Ct 44118
Rockefeller Ave 44115
Rockfern Ave 44111
Rockland Ave 44135
Rockland Dr 44144
Rockledge Ln 44143
Rocklyn Rd 44122
Rockport Ave 44111
Rockport Ln 44126
Rockridge Ct 44130
Rockside Rd
1013-1397 44134
1399-1490 44134
1492-1498 44134
8003-8197 44125
8199-13999 44125
Rockwell Ave 44114
Rockwood Rd 44125

Rocky River Dr
3101-3249 44111
3251-3999 44111
4000-4999 44135
Roedean Dr 44129
Roehl Ave 44109
Roeper Rd 44134
Rogers Ave 44127
Roland Ave 44127
Roland Dr 44125
Roland Rd 44124
Rolling Hills Dr 44124
Rolling Meadow Dr 44134
Rolliston Rd 44120
Romilly Oval 44129
Ronald Dr 44130
Rondel Rd 44110
Rook Cir 44112
Rookhill Cir 44112
Rookwood Cir & Rd 44112
Rosa Parks Dr 44106
Rosalie Dr 44125
Rosalind Ave
1800-1899 44112
9200-9219 44106
9221-9299 44106
Rosbough Blvd 44130
Rose Blvd 44143
Rosebury Ct 44124
Rosecliff Rd 44119
Rosedale Ave 44112
Rosedale Ct 44106
Rosedale Rd 44112
Rosehill Ave 44104
Roseland Rd 44112
Roselawn Rd 44124
Rosemary Ave 44111
Rosemond Rd 44121
Rosemont Rd 44112
Roseside Ave 44134
Roseville Ct 44127
Rosewood Ave 44105
Rosewood Ct 44130
Ross Ave 44105
Rossmoor Rd 44118
Rouse Ave 44104
Rousseau Dr 44129
Rowley Ave 44109
Roxboro Ave 44111
Roxboro Dr 44130
Roxboro Rd 44106
Roxbury Rd
1800-1999 44112
9100-9499 44130
Roxford Rd 44112
Roy Ave 44104
Roy Rd 44143
Royal Blvd 44125
Royal Rd 44110
Royal Oak Blvd 44143
Royal Parkway Dr 44130
Royal Ridge Dr 44129
Royalview Dr 44129
Roycroft Dr 44129
Rozelle Ave 44112
Ruble Ct 44104
Ruby Ave 44109
Ruby Ln 44128
Rubyvale Rd 44118
Rudolph Ave 44125
Rudwick Rd 44112
Rudyard Rd 44110
Rue Saint Anne Ct 44128
Rue Saint Gabriel Ct 44128
Rugby Rd 44110
Ruggiero Cir 44130
Rumson Rd 44118
Running Brook Dr 44130
Runnymede Ave 44125
Runnymede Blvd 44121
Ruple Rd
800-900 44110
902-998 44110
4100-4199 44121
Rushleigh Rd 44121
Rushmore Ct & Dr 44143

Rushton Rd 44121
Russell Ave
2000-5099 44134
10001-10097 44125
10099-10499 44125
Russell Ct 44103
Russell Ln 44144
Russell Rd 44103
Rustic Rd 44135
Rustic Trl 44134
Ruth Ellen Dr 44143
Rutherford Rd 44112
Rutland Ave 44108
Rutland Dr 44143
Rutledge Ave 44102
Rybak Ave 44125
Rydalmount Rd 44118
Rye Rd 44122
Sable Rd 44119
Sackett Ave 44109
Sacramento Ave 44111
Safeguard Cir 44125
Sagamore Ave 44103
Sagamore Rd 44134
N Sagamore Rd 44126
S Sagamore Rd 44126
W Saillake St 44126
Saint Albans Rd 44121
Saint Andrews Ct 44130
Saint Andrews Dr
392-400 44143
3200-3499 44134
E Saint Andrews Dr 44143
W Saint Andrews Dr 44143
Saint Anthony Ln 44111
Saint Catherine Ave 44104
Saint Clair Ave
4000-8499 44103
8700-8798 44108
8800-13099 44108
13101-13199 44108
13300-13398 44110
13400-18999 44110
Saint Clair Ave NE 44114
W Saint Clair Ave 44113
Saint Germain Blvd 44128
Saint James Ave 44135
N Saint James Pkwy 44106
W Saint James Pkwy 44106
Saint John Ave 44111
Saint Mark Ave 44111
Saint Olga Ave 44113
Saint Petersburg Dr 44134
Saint Roccos Ct 44109
Saint Stephens Ct 44102
Saint Tikhon Ave 44113
Salem Ave 44127
Salisbury Dr 44129
Salisbury Rd 44121
Samuel Dr 44143
San Diego Ave 44111
Sand Ct 44134
Sandalhaven Dr 44130
Sandhurst Dr 44143
Sandpiper Dr 44134
Sandusky Ave 44105
Sandy Ln 44126
Sandy Hill Dr 44143
Sandy Hook Dr 44134
Sanford Ave 44110
Sanford Dr 44134
Sapphire Ct 44130
Sarah Ln 44128
Saranac Dr 44126
Saranac Rd 44110
N Sarasota Dr 44134
Saratoga Ave 44109
Saratoga Dr 44126
Saratoga Rd 44130
Sassafras Dr 44129
Sauer Ave 44102
Savannah Ave 44112
Savoy Dr 44126
Sawtell Rd 44127
Saxe Ave 44105
Saxon Dr 44125

Saybrook Ave 44105
Saybrook Dr 44144
Saybrook Rd 44118
Saywell Ave 44108
Scarborough Rd
2600-2749 44106
2750-3199 44118
2836-2889 44118
E Scarborough Rd 44118
Scarlet Oak Ln 44130
Scenic Park Oval 44130
W Schaaf Rd 44109
Schade Ave 44103
Schaefer Ave 44103
Schell Ave 44109
Schenely Ave 44119
Schiller Ave 44109
Schneider Ct 44102
Scholl Rd 44118
School Ave 44110
Schreiber Rd 44125
Schuyler Ave 44111
Schwab Dr 44130
Scioto Ave 44112
Scotham Ave 44113
Scott Ct 44102
Scottsdale Blvd
15500-15598 44120
15600-17699 44120
17700-20399 44122
Scottwood Ave 44108
Scovill Ave 44104
Scranton Ct 44109
Scranton Rd
1800-3099 44113
3100-3599 44109
Scullin Dr 44111
Seabury Ave 44126
Searsdale Ave 44109
Seaton Rd 44118
Sebastian Ct 44143
Sebert Ave 44105
Sebor Rd 44120
Secondary Dr 44135
Sector Ave 44111
Sedalia Ave 44135
Sedgewick Rd 44120
N Sedgewick Rd 44124
S Sedgewick Rd 44124
Sedley Rd 44143
Sellers Ave 44108
Selma Ave 44127
Selwick Dr 44129
Selwyn Rd 44112
Selzer Ave 44109
Semra Cir 44130
Seneca Ct 44111
Seneca Rd 44143
Seneca Trl 44130
Seneca Trl N 44143
Seneca Trl S 44143
Sequoia Dr 44134
Service Ct 44105
Service Rd 44111
Settlers Ln 44124
Seven Oaks Dr 44124
Severance Cir 44118
Severance Place Ln 44118
Severn Rd 44118
Seville Rd 44128
Sexton Rd 44105
Seymour Ave 44113
Shadeland Ave 44108
Shady Ln 44144
Shady Oak Blvd 44125
Shadyway Rd 44125
Shaker Blvd
10000-10198 44104
10200-10999 44104
11001-11599 44104
11600-18499 44120
18501-18597 44122
18599-24200 44122
24202-24398 44122
27500-32300 44124
32302-33598 44124

Shaker Rd 44118
Shaker Sq 44120
Shaker Glen Ln 44122
Shakespeare Pkwy 44108
Shale Ave 44104
Shaleside Ct 44130
Shamrock Ave 44111
Shannon Rd 44118
Sharon Dr 44130
Sharon Ln 44126
Shaw Ave
1700-1700 44112
1702-1799 44112
12500-13099 44108
13200-14899 44112
Shawnee Ave 44119
Shawnee Dr 44124
Shawnee Trl 44130
Shawview Ave 44112
Sheffield Rd 44121
Shelburne Dr 44130
Shelburne Rd
17400-18199 44118
18200-19899 44118
19901-20399 44118
20400-23999 44122
24001-24199 44122
Sheldon Ave 44112
Sheldon Rd
5500-5598 44124
5600-5699 44124
13351-20099 44130
Shelley Rd 44122
Shelton Dr 44110
Shenandoah Oval 44134
Sheraton Dr 44134
Sherborn Rd 44130
Sherbrook Rd 44121
Sherbrooke Rd 44122
Sheridan Dr 44134
Sheridan Pl 44127
Sheridan Rd 44121
Sherman Ave 44104
Sherman Ct 44104
Sherman Dr 44134
Sherrington Rd 44122
Sherry Ave 44135
Sherwood Cir 44125
Sherwood Dr
2400-2899 44134
5200-21999 44126
Sherwood Rd
3700-3899 44121
9300-9399 44104
Sheryl Dr 44109
Shetland Ct 44143
Shiloh Cir 44134
Shiloh Rd 44110
Shipherd Ct 44106
Ships Channel 44113
Shirley Dr 44121
Shore Acres Dr 44110
Shoreby Dr 44108
Shurmer Dr 44128
Siam Ave 44113
Sidaway Ave 44104
Side Ave 44102
Sierra Oval 44130
Signet Ave 44120
Silk Ave 44102
Silmor Ave 44108
Silsby Rd
3200-3438 44118
3439-3659 44118
3660-4095 44118
3800-3999 44111
4096-4098 44118
4097-4099 44118
4100-4499 44118
4501-4599 44118
Silver Rd 44125
Silverdale Ave 44109
Silverton Ave 44102
Simon Ave 44103
Sinton Pl 44124
Sky Lane Dr 44109

Skye Rd 44143
Skylark Dr 44130
Skyline Dr 44143
Skyview Rd 44109
Sladden Ave 44125
Slate Ct 44118
Sleepy Hollow Dr 44130
Smith Ave 44109
Smith Ct 44113
Smith Rd 44130
Snavely Rd 44143
Snow Rd
1500-5399 44134
5400-8399 44129
8401-8499 44129
8701-8797 44130
8799-12986 44130
12988-12990 44130
Snowberry Ln 44124
Snyder Ave 44109
Sobieski Ave 44135
Soika Ave 44120
Som Ct 44143
Som Center Rd
200-1099 44143
1100-3599 44124
3601-3699 44124
Somerset Ave 44108
Somerset Dr 44122
Somerton Rd 44118
Somia Dr 44134
Sonora Ave 44114
Sophia Ave 44104
South Blvd 44108
Southern Ave 44125
Southfield Ave 44144
Southington Dr 44129
Southington Rd 44120
Southland Ave 44111
Southland Dr 44130
Southlane Dr 44144
Southpoint Dr 44109
Southview Ave 44120
Southwood Ave 44111
Southwood Dr
4600-4999 44144
21100-21199 44126
Sowinski Ave 44103
Spafford Pl & Rd 44105
Spangler Ct 44103
Spangler Rd 44112
Speedway Overlook 44112
Speidel Ave 44126
Spencer Ave 44103
Spencer Ln 44126
Spencer Rd 44124
Spilker Ave 44103
Spokane Ave
3500-4699 44109
4701-4799 44144
Spotswood Dr 44124
Sprague Ave 44108
W Sprague Rd
1100-8998 44134
9600-16998 44130
10400-14098 44130
Sprecher Ave 44135
Sprengel Ave 44135
Spring Rd 44109
Spring Crest Dr 44144
Spring Garden Rd 44129
Springdale Ave
7900-7998 44129
8000-8199 44129
18500-19199 44135
Springdale Dr 44130
Springfield Rd 44128
Springvale Dr 44128
Springwood Dr 44144
Springwood Rd 44130
Spruce Ave & Ct 44113
Squirrel Run Dr 44130
Stacy Ct 44143
Stafford Dr 44124
Stanard Ave 44103
Stanbury Rd 44129

Standish Ave 44134
Stanfield Dr 44134
Stanford Ave
3500-3699 44109
20400-20999 44126
Stanford Rd 44122
Stanley Tolliver Ave 44115
Stanton Ave 44104
Stanwell Dr 44143
Stanwood Rd 44112
Star Ave 44103
Starkweather Ave 44113
Starlight Dr 44109
Stary Dr 44134
State Rd
4200-4870 44109
4872-4898 44109
4900-7899 44134
State Road Parkway Blvd 44134
Staunton Dr 44134
Staunton Rd 44118
Stearns Rd 44106
Steelyard Dr 44109
Steinway Ave 44104
Steven Blvd 44143
Stevenson Rd 44110
Stevenson St 44143
Stewart Ave 44108
Stickney Ave
3500-4499 44109
4500-4598 44144
4600-5799 44144
Stillman Rd 44118
Stillson Ave 44105
Stillwood Ave 44111
Stilmore Rd 44121
Stimson Ct 44109
Stirling Ct 44115
Stirling Dr 44143
Stock Ave 44102
Stockbridge Ave 44128
Stockholm Rd 44120
Stoer Rd 44122
Stokes Blvd
1952-1998 44106
2000-2299 44106
11201-11213 44104
11215-11299 44104
Stone Ave 44102
Stone Rd 44125
Stonebridge Ct 44143
Stonecreek Dr 44143
Stonecutters Ln 44121
Stoneham Rd 44130
N Stonehaven Dr 44143
S Stonehaven Dr 44143
Stonehaven Rd 44121
Stoneledge Dr 44143
Stoneleigh Rd 44121
Stoneloch Ct 44130
Stones Levee 44113
Stoney Rdg 44143
Stoney Creek Ln 44130
Stonington Rd 44130
Stonybrook Dr 44130
Storer Ave
3300-4499 44109
4500-6699 44102
Stormes Dr 44130
Storrington Oval 44134
Story Rd 44126
Stoughton Ave 44104
Strandhill Rd
3501-3639 44122
3641-3779 44122
3780-3999 44128
4001-4099 44128
Stratford Dr
6100-6499 44130
7900-7999 44129
8000-8399 44129
8401-8499 44129
Stratford Rd 44118
Strathaven Dr 44143
Strathavon Rd 44120

Strathmore Ave 44112
Strathmore Dr 44125
Stroud Rd 44130
Strumbly Dr 44143
Stuart Dr 44121
Stuber Ct 44114
Stumph Rd 44130
Sturbridge Dr 44143
Sudbury Rd 44120
Suffield Rd 44124
Suffolk Ln 44124
Suffolk Rd 44121
Sulgrave Oval & Rd 44122
Summer Ln 44144
Summerdale Ave 44125
Summerfield Rd 44118
Summerland Ave 44111
Summit Dr 44124
Summit Ln 44124
Summit Oval 44134
Summit Rd 44124
Summit Park Rd 44121
Sumner Ave 44115
Sumpter Ct 44115
Sumpter Rd 44128
Sun Ray Dr 44134
Sun Vista Dr 44129
Suncrest Ct 44134
Sunderland Dr 44129
Sunhaven Oval 44134
Sunningdale Rd 44124
Sunny Dr 44128
Sunny Ln 44144
Sunny Glenn Ave 44128
Sunny Hill Cir 44109
Sunnyside Dr 44130
Sunrise Oval
7400-7499 44130
7501-7575 44134
7577-7699 44134
Sunset Ct 44103
Sunset Dr
1700-1999 44143
6300-6399 44125
12100-12699 44125
Sunset Ln 44134
Sunset Oval 44144
Sunset Rd 44124
Sunset Trl 44144
Sunview Ave 44128
Sunview Rd 44124
Superior Ave
4000-8499 44103
8500-12499 44106
12500-13299 44112
13301-13399 44112
Superior Ave E 44114
W Superior Ave 44113
Superior Rd
13500-13848 44112
13851-13897 44118
13899-14781 44118
14654-14718 44118
14783-14899 44118
Superior Via 44113
Superior Park Dr 44118
Surrey Ln 44110
Surrey Rd 44106
Susan Ave 44111
Sutherland Ave 44130
Sutherland Dr 44143
Sutherland Rd 44122
Sutton Pl
1-99 44120
6800-6899 44130
Sutton Rd 44120
Svec Ave 44120
Swaffield Rd 44121
Sweeney Ave 44127
Sweet Valley Dr 44125
Swetland Blvd & Ct 44143
Swingos Ct 44115
Sycamore Dr 44126
Sycamore Rd 44118
Sycamore St
1-99 44110

2000-2098 44113
Sydenham Rd 44122
Sykora Rd 44105
Sylvanhurst Rd 44112
Sylvania Rd 44121
Sylvia Ave 44110
Symphony Ln 44124
Syracuse Ave 44110
Tacoma Ave 44108
Taft Ave 44108
Talbot Ave 44106
Talbot Dr 44129
Talford Ave 44128
Tally Ho Ln 44143
Tamalga Dr 44121
S Tamarack Dr 44134
Tamearis Rd 44124
Tamiami Dr 44134
Tampa Ave 44109
Tanglewood Ln 44129
Tanner Ave 44108
Tarkington Ave 44128
Tarlton Ave 44109
Tarrymore Rd 44119
Tate Ave 44109
Taunton Ave 44144
Taylor Dr 44128
Taylor Ln 44128
Taylor Rd 44112
N Taylor Rd
2100-2399 44112
2400-2549 44118
2551-2599 44118
S Taylor Rd 44118
Teal Trce 44124
Telfair Ave 44128
Telhurst Rd 44121
Templethurst Rd 44121
Temblett Ave 44108
Temblett Ter 44121
Temple Ave
1500-1799 44124
6801-6999 44127
Tennyson Rd 44104
Terminal Ave & Dr 44135
Terrace Ct 44130
Terrace Ln 44144
Terrace Rd 44112
Terrace View Ln 44134
Terrell Ct 44143
Terrett Ave 44113
Terry Ct 44119
Thackeray Ave 44103
Thackeray Trl 44143
Thames Ave 44110
Thayer Ct 44104
Theota Ave
3700-4899 44134
4901-5399 44134
5400-8399 44129
Thistle Trl 44124
Thoreau Dr 44129
Thorn Ave 44108
Thornapple Dr 44143
Thornapple Ln 44124
Thornbury Rd 44124
Thorncliffe Blvd 44134
Thorne Rd 44112
Thornhill Dr 44108
Thornhope Rd 44135
Thornhurst Ave 44105
Thornridge Ave & Cir 44135
Thornton Ave 44125
Thornton Dr 44129
Thornwood Ave 44108
Thraves Ave 44125
Three Village Dr 44124
Throckley Ave 44128
Thrush Ave 44111
Thurgood Ave 44115
Thurman Ave 44113
Tiedeman Rd 44144
Tiffany Ct 44124
Tiffany Ln 44130
Tillman Ave 44102

Timber Ln
14700-14999 44130
18800-18899 44126
Timberlane Rd 44128
Timberline Trl 44143
Timothy Ln 44109
Tinkers Creek Rd 44125
Tioga Ave 44105
Tiverton Rd 44110
Tobik Trl 44130
Tolland Rd 44122
Tom Ln 44109
Tompkins Ave 44102
Tonsing Dr 44125
Torbenson Dr 44112
Torrance Ave 44144
Torrington Ave 44134
Torrington Rd 44122
Torwood Ct 44109
Tourelle Dr 44143
Towl Ct 44127
Townley Rd 44122
Towns Ln 44143
Townsend Ave 44104
Towpath Dr 44125
Track Ave 44127
Tracy Trl 44130
Tradewinds Cir 44124
Tradex Pkwy 44102
Trafalgar Ave 44110
Trail Run 44144
Train Ave
1700-2599 44113
2601-4499 44113
4500-4598 44102
4600-5899 44102
5901-5999 44102
Transport Rd 44115
Transportation Blvd 44125
Travis Dr 44143
Traymore Ave 44144
Traymore Rd 44118
Treadway Ave 44109
Trebec Blvd 44119
Trebisky Rd 44143
Treetop Ct 44134
Tremont Ave 44113
Tremont Rd 44121
Trent Ave 44109
Trenton Ave 44104
Trenton Sq 44143
Trenton Trl 44130
Trevitt Cir 44143
Trevor Ln 44129
Triedstone St 44115
Trillium Trl 44124
E Trinceda St 44114
Triskett Rd 44111
Trowbridge Ave 44109
Troy Oval 44129
Truax Ave 44111
Trumbull Ave 44115
Truscon Ave 44127
Tuckahoe Ave 44111
Tucks Trak 44102
Tucson Dr 44130
Tudor Ave 44111
Tudor Dr 44106
Tullamore Rd 44118
Turnberry Ln 44143
Turney Rd
4200-4298 44105
4300-4599 44105
4600-6399 44125
Tuscora Ave 44108
Tuttle Ave 44111
Tuxedo Ave 44134
Twin Lakes Dr 44129
Twinkie Ln 44113
Two Village Dr 44124
Tyler Ave 44111
Tyndall Rd 44118
Tyronne Ave 44119
Uhlin Dr 44130
Underwood Ave 44119
Uninsou Ave 44128

Union Ave
6400-13099 44105
13100-13999 44120
Unity Ave 44111
University Blvd
2500-2699 44118
20500-20598 44122
20600-20799 44122
University Ct 44113
University Pkwy 44118
University Rd 44113
University St 44130
University Hospital Dr .. 44106
Unwin Rd 44104
Upton Ave 44110
Uptown Ave 44106
Urban Dr 44121
Urbana Rd 44112
Utica Ave 44103
Utopia Ave 44110
Valentine Ave 44109
Valewood Dr 44134
Vallevista Dr 44124
N Valley Dr 44126
S Valley Dr 44126
W Valley Dr 44126
Valley Ln 44130
W Valley Ln 44126
Valley Pkwy 44126
Valley Rd 44109
Valley Forge Dr
4300-4599 44126
9800-10399 44130
20700-20999 44126
Valley Lane Dr 44125
Valley Villas Dr 44130
Valleyside Rd 44135
Valleyview Ave 44135
Van Pl 44103
Van Aken Blvd
2700-2798 44120
2800-17699 44120
17700-20399 44122
Van Buren Rd 44112
Vandalia Ave 44144
Vandemar St 44121
Varian Ave 44103
Vashti Ave 44108
Vassar St 44112
Vega Ave 44113
Velma Ave 44129
Velour Ave 44110
Venning Ct 44104
Ventnor Ave 44135
Venture Dr 44130
Vera St 44128
Vermont Ave 44113
Vernon Ave 44125
Vernon Rd 44118
Vernondale Dr 44130
Verona Rd 44121
Vestry Ave 44113
Vicksburg Dr
1000-1599 44134
10600-10999 44130
Victor Ave 44127
Victoria Rd 44112
Victory Blvd
3900-3999 44111
4000-4100 44135
4102-4298 44135
Victory Dr 44121
Vienna Dr 44130
View Dr 44143
View Rd 44109
Villa Bch 44110
Villa Dr 44121
Villa Carabelli Dr 44106
Villaview Rd 44119
Ville Ct 44129
Vincent Ave 44114
Vincolde Ave 44102
N Vine Ave 44119
Vine Ct
3001-3097 44113
3099-3199 44113
3201-4499 44113
4501-4599 44102
4700-4798 44102
Vineshire Rd 44121
Vinewood Dr 44134
Vineyard Ave 44105
Viola Ave
2-99 44110
14000-14298 44111
14300-14599 44111
Violet Ave 44135
Virginia Ave
1-99 44110
3300-3599 44109
5400-7599 44129
7601-7699 44129
Virginia Dr 44126
Vista Ave 44125
Vista Dr 44134
Vista Ln 44130
Vista Way 44125
Vivian Ave 44127
Wade Ave 44113
Wade Oval Dr 44106
Wade Park Ave
5800-8499 44103
8500-12299 44106
12301-12399 44106
Wadena St 44112
Wadsworth Ave 44125
Wagner Ave 44104
Wainfleet Ave 44135
Wainstead Ave 44111
Wainstead Dr 44129
Wake Robin Dr 44130
Wakefield Ave 44102
Walbrook Ave 44109
Walden Ave 44128
Walden Rd 44112
Wales Ave 44134
Walford Ave 44102
Walford Rd 44128
Walker Ave 44105
Wall St 44125
Wallingford Ave 44125
Wallingford Gln 44143
Wallingford Rd 44121
Walnut Ave 44114
Walt Ct 44111
Walter Ave 44134
Walton Ave 44113
Walworth Ave 44102
Wamelink Ave 44104
Wanda Ave 44135
Wandsworth Rd 44121
War Ave 44105
Ward Rd 44134
Wareham Dr 44129
Warner Rd
4200-4599 44105
4600-5499 44125
Warren Ave 44127
Warren Rd 44111
Warrendale Rd 44118
Warrensville Center Rd
1300-1398 44121
1400-2149 44121
2150-2664 44118
2300-2499 44118
2665-2673 44122
2675-3349 44122
3351-3399 44122
3675-3677 44120
4211-4245 44128
4247-4999 44128
Warridar Rd 44121
Warrington Rd 44120
Warsaw Ave 44105
Wartholi Ave 44127
Warwick Dr 44129
Warwick Rd 44120
Washington Ave 44113
Washington Blvd
1-99 44110
1070-1098 44143
1100-1499 44124
2800-3599 44118
3600-14599 44118
Washington Ct 44105
Washington Dr 44143
Washington Sq 44143
Washington Park Blvd .. 44105
Waterloo Rd 44110
S Waterloo Rd
15250-17298 44110
17600-19998 44119
Waterman Ave 44127
Watterson Ave 44105
Waverly Ct 44102
Waverly Pl 44121
Way Ave 44105
Wayland Ave 44111
Wayne Dr 44128
Wayside Rd
700-1000 44110
1002-1098 44110
1600-1799 44112
Webb Ter 44105
Webster Ave 44115
Webster Rd 44130
Wefel Ave 44144
Wellesley Ave 44112
Wellington Ave 44134
Wellington Rd
2400-2674 44118
5600-5799 44124
Welton Dr 44112
Wemple Rd 44110
Wendell Ave 44127
Wenden Ct 44108
Wendy Dr
3700-3999 44122
12100-12299 44130
Wengatz Dr 44130
Wentworth Ave 44102
Werdell Ct 44113
Wesley Ave 44111
Wesley Dr 44129
West Ave
901-999 44113
13001-13097 44111
13099-13999 44111
West Blvd
1200-2299 44102
3000-3799 44111
4001-4199 44144
Westborough Rd 44130
Westbourne Rd 44124
Westbrook Dr 44144
Westburn Ave 44112
Westbury Rd 44120
Westchester Ave 44108
Westchester Rd 44122
Westdale Ave 44135
Westdale Rd 44121
Westerham Rd 44124
Western Ave 44111
Westfield Ave 44110
Westgate Mall 44126
Westlake Ave 44129
Westland Ave 44111
Westlawn Rd 44128
Westminster Dr 44129
Westminster Rd 44118
Weston Rd 44121
Westover Rd 44118
Westport Ave 44135
Westropp Ave 44110
Westview Ave 44128
Westview Dr 44129
Westwood Rd
3700-3899 44118
20800-22959 44126
Wethersfield Ct 44143
Wetzel Ave
3600-5499 44109
5600-5798 44144
5800-6104 44144
6106-7298 44144
Wexford Ave 44134
Wexford Ln 44130
Weybridge Rd 44120
Weyburne Ave 44135
Weymouth Rd 44120
Wheeler Ave 44112
Wheelock Rd 44103
Whippoorwill Ln 44130
Whiskey Is 44102
Whispering Oaks Blvd .. 44134
Whitaker Dr 44130
Whitby Rd 44112
Whitcomb Rd 44110
White Ave 44103
White Rd
2400-2499 44118
6400-26298 44143
26300-26599 44143
White Oak Cir 44130
E Whitedove Ln 44130
Whiteford Dr 44143
Whitehall Dr 44121
Whitehaven Dr 44129
Whitethorn Ave 44103
Whitethorn Rd 44118
Whiteway Dr 44143
Whitfield Ln 44143
Whitman Ave 44113
Whitmore Ave 44108
Whitney Ave 44103
Whiton Rd 44118
Whittier Ave 44103
Whittington Dr 44129
Wichita Ave
4000-4499 44109
4500-6099 44144
Wickfield Dr 44130
Wickford Rd 44112
Wicklow Rd 44120
Wilber Ave 44129
Wilburn Dr 44121
Wilderness Ln 44130
Wildlife Way 44109
Wildwood Dr 44119
Wildwood Ln 44119
Wildwood Trl 44143
Wilhelm Ct 44104
Wilkes Ln 44143
Willard Ave
8500-9799 44102
11600-13199 44125
Willey Ave 44113
William Cir 44134
Williams Ave 44120
Williamsburg Ct 44130
Williamsburg Dr
500-700 44143
702-6098 44143
2001-2199 44134
5601-6099 44143
Williamston Ave 44144
Williston Dr 44129
Willman Ave 44135
Willow Pkwy 44125
Willow Brook Dr
3200-3499 44124
4900-5099 44125
Willowdale Ave 44109
Willowhurst Rd 44112
Willowmere Ave 44108
Willshire Rd 44124
Wilmar Rd 44121
Wilmington Rd 44121
Wilsmere Rd 44124
Wilson Mills Rd 44143
Wilton Ave 44135
Wilton Rd 44118
Wimbledon Rd 44122
Winchell Rd 44122
Winchester Ave 44110
Winchester Dr 44134
Winchester Rd 44124
Windermere St 44112
Windham Rd 44130
Winding Creek Ln 44124
Winding Oak Dr 44130
Windrush Ct 44134
Windsor Cir 44124
Windsor Dr 44124
Windsor Rd 44121
Windward Rd 44119
Windy Hill Dr 44124
Winfield Ave 44105
Winona Cir 44130
Winsford Rd 44112
Winslow Ave 44113
Winslow Rd
17300-17699 44120
17700-20099 44122
Winston Rd 44121
Winter Ln 44144
Winterpark Dr 44134
Winthrop Dr 44134
Winthrop Rd 44120
Wire Ave 44105
Woburn Ave
3700-4699 44109
5100-6599 44144
6601-7299 44144
Wolf Ave
7000-7200 44129
7202-7298 44129
13300-13999 44125
Wolverton Dr 44128
Wood Ave 44134
Wood Rd 44121
Wood Creek Dr 44130
Wood Thrush Dr 44134
Woodbine Ave 44113
Woodbine Cir 44143
Woodbridge Ave 44109
Woodbridge Gln 44143
Woodbury Ave 44135
Woodbury Rd 44120
Woodbury Hills Dr 44134
Woodhaven Ave 44144
Woodhawk Dr 44124
Woodhill Ct 44104
Woodhill Rd
2300-2399 44106
2401-2497 44104
2499-3099 44104
Woodhurst Ave 44124
Woodland Ave
2201-3297 44115
3299-3999 44115
4000-11599 44104
N Woodland Rd
2901-2999 44118
27300-28499 44124
S Woodland Rd
13200-13298 44120
13300-18399 44120
18401-18499 44120
18500-18698 44122
18700-21999 44122
27500-27598 44124
27600-33400 44124
33402-33498 44124
Woodland Park Way 44115
Woodlane Dr 44143
Woodlawn Ave 44112
Woodlawn Dr 44134
Woodleigh Rd 44124
Woodmere Dr 44106
Woodridge Rd 44121
Woodrow Ave
1500-1699 44124
3700-5399 44134
Woodruff Ct 44130
Woodside Ave 44108
Woodside Rd 44143
Woodstock Ave
10800-10900 44104
10902-11698 44104
20400-20999 44126
Woodview Blvd 44130
Woodview Rd 44121
Woodward Ave
1800-1898 44118
1900-1960 44118
9700-10099 44106
Woodward Blvd 44125
Woodway Ave 44134
Woodworth Rd
13200-13298 44112
13300-14699 44112
14701-14849 44112
14901-14997 44110
14999-15199 44110
Woolman Ct 44130
Wooster Pkwy 44129
Wooster Rd 44126
Wordsworth Ct 44143
Worley Ave 44105
Worthington Ave 44111
Worton Blvd 44124
Worton Park Dr 44143
Wrenford Rd
1500-1699 44121
1701-2149 44121
2200-2326 44118
2328-2398 44118
Wright Ct 44108
Wyatt Rd
4300-4499 44128
15501-15597 44112
15599-15799 44112
Wymore Ave 44112
Wyncote Rd 44121
Wynn Rd 44118
Yale Ave 44108
Yarmouth Oval 44130
Yeakel Ave 44104
Yellowstone Rd 44121
Yorancol Rd 44118
Yorick Ave 44110
York Ave 44113
York Blvd 44125
York Dr 44124
York Rd 44130
Yorkshire Ave 44134
Yorkshire Rd 44118
Yorktown Dr 44134
Yorktown Ln 44130
Zelis Rd 44135
Zimmer Ave 44102
Zoeter Ave 44103
Zona Ln 44130
Zorn Ln 44143

NUMBERED STREETS

1st Ave
13300-13499 44112
20200-20599 44130
2nd Ave 44112
E 2nd St 44115
W 2nd St 44113
3rd Ave 44112
W 3rd St
1000-1099 44114
1100-2700 44113
4th Ave 44112
E 4th St 44115
W 4th St
1200-2398 44113
2400-2499 44113
4400-4499 44109
5th Ave 44112
W 5th St 44113
6th Ave 44112
E 6th St 44114
W 6th St
1100-1198 44113
1200-2599 44113
4500-4599 44109
W 7th St 44113
E 8th St 44115
W 8th St 44113
E 9th St
823-1099 44114
1101-1999 44114
1240-1240 44199
1300-1998 44114
2000-2499 44115
2501-2699 44115
W 9th St 44113
W 10th St
1000-2599 44113
4300-4499 44109
5200-5299 44134
W 11th Pl
2000-2099 44113
3100-3199 44109
W 11th St
2000-3099 44113
3100-4799 44109
W 12th Pl 44109
E 12th St
1200-1899 44114
2400-2498 44115
W 12th St
2800-3099 44113
3100-4999 44109
W 13th Pl 44113
E 13th St 44114
W 13th St 44109
E 14th St
1401-1431 44114
2000-2299 44115
W 14th St
2000-3099 44113
3100-4999 44109
W 15th Pl 44113
E 15th St 44114
W 15th St
2100-2599 44113
2601-2699 44113
3600-3798 44109
3800-3899 44109
3901-4299 44109
W 16th Pl 44113
W 16th St
2900-2998 44113
3000-3099 44113
3100-3899 44109
3901-4187 44109
5200-5299 44134
5301-5499 44134
W 17th Pl 44109
E 17th St
1282-1800 44114
1802-1898 44114
1900-1998 44115
W 17th St
2000-2999 44113
3100-4299 44109
4301-4399 44109
W 18th Pl
2400-2498 44113
2500-2699 44113
3100-3199 44109
E 18th St
1282-1799 44114
1900-2098 44115
W 18th St
2000-2699 44113
3800-3999 44109
W 19th Pl 44113
E 19th St
1500-1698 44114
2000-2167 44115
2169-2199 44115
W 19th St
1901-1961 44113
1963-2699 44113
3800-4899 44109
W 20th Pl 44113
W 20th St
1900-2599 44113
3800-4299 44109
E 21st St
1300-1883 44114
1885-1899 44114
2001-2097 44115
2099-2199 44115
W 21st St
1801-1997 44113
1999-2199 44113
3800-4399 44109
W 22nd Pl 44113
3700-3899 44109
E 22nd St
1500-1859 44114
1861-1895 44114
2000-2599 44115
W 22nd St
1800-1999 44113

3900-4299 ... 44109
W 23rd Pl ... 44109
E 23rd St
1301-1497 ... 44114
1499-1899 ... 44114
2501-2599 ... 44115
W 23rd St ... 44109
E 24th St
1300-1700 ... 44114
1702-1898 ... 44114
2300-2398 ... 44115
W 24th St
1800-1899 ... 44113
4200-4299 ... 44109
5200-5498 ... 44134
5500-6060 ... 44134
6062-6098 ... 44134
E 25th St ... 44114
W 25th St
1200-3099 ... 44113
3100-3599 ... 44109
3601-4799 ... 44109
5200-5299 ... 44134
E 26th St
1100-1198 ... 44114
1200-1400 ... 44114
1402-1498 ... 44114
3900-4099 ... 44105
W 26th St
1400-2200 ... 44113
2202-2298 ... 44113
3100-4698 ... 44109
5200-5299 ... 44134
W 27th Pl ... 44113
E 27th St
1500-1799 ... 44114
4000-4099 ... 44105
W 27th St ... 44113
W 28th Pl ... 44113
E 28th St ... 44115
W 28th St
1300-2399 ... 44113
4200-4499 ... 44109
4501-4599 ... 44109
5200-5230 ... 44134
W 29th Pl ... 44113
E 29th St ... 44105
W 29th St
1200-2200 ... 44113
5800-6499 ... 44134
E 30th St
1300-1900 ... 44114
2049-2049 ... 44115
W 30th St
1700-1764 ... 44113
3100-4399 ... 44109
W 31st Pl
1600-1899 ... 44113
3700-3799 ... 44109
E 31st St
1300-1899 ... 44114
2101-2199 ... 44115
W 31st St
2000-2199 ... 44113
3100-3899 ... 44109
W 32nd Pl
2600-2699 ... 44113
3700-3799 ... 44109
E 32nd St
1300-1899 ... 44114
2101-2199 ... 44115
W 32nd St
1400-3099 ... 44113
3100-4799 ... 44109
W 33rd Pl ... 44113
E 33rd St
1200-1867 ... 44114
2100-2999 ... 44115
W 33rd St
1400-1998 ... 44113
2000-2299 ... 44113
3100-3999 ... 44109
5200-5249 ... 44134
W 34th Pl
2000-2199 ... 44113
3100-3199 ... 44109

E 34th St
1300-1699 ... 44114
2300-2700 ... 44115
2702-2798 ... 44115
W 34th St ... 44109
E 35th St ... 44115
W 35th St ... 44109
E 36th St
1300-1849 ... 44114
2001-2139 ... 44115
2141-2599 ... 44115
W 36th St
2100-2299 ... 44113
3700-4299 ... 44109
E 37th St
1700-1899 ... 44114
2100-2999 ... 44115
W 37th St
2100-2399 ... 44113
3700-4299 ... 44109
E 38th St
1100-1899 ... 44114
2100-2599 ... 44115
3800-3899 ... 44105
W 38th St
1400-3099 ... 44113
3100-4299 ... 44109
W 39th Pl ... 44109
E 39th St
1300-1799 ... 44114
2100-2599 ... 44115
W 39th St ... 44109
W 40th Pl ... 44113
E 40th St
1100-1349 ... 44114
1350-2299 ... 44103
2300-2559 ... 44104
2560-2598 ... 44115
2561-2599 ... 44104
2600-2799 ... 44115
3800-3898 ... 44105
W 40th St
2100-2198 ... 44113
3100-3899 ... 44109
W 41st Pl ... 44113
E 41st St
1350-1699 ... 44103
3900-4099 ... 44105
W 41st St
2000-2700 ... 44113
2702-2798 ... 44113
3100-4599 ... 44109
4601-4651 ... 44109
E 42nd St
2300-2399 ... 44104
3800-4099 ... 44105
W 42nd St
2000-2199 ... 44113
3700-4599 ... 44109
E 43rd St
1350-2299 ... 44103
2400-2599 ... 44104
3800-3999 ... 44105
W 43rd St
3000-3099 ... 44113
3101-3115 ... 44109
3117-3899 ... 44109
E 44th Pl ... 44127
E 44th St ... 44105
W 44th St
1300-3099 ... 44113
3100-3899 ... 44109
5200-5799 ... 44134
E 45th Pl ... 44104
E 45th St
1200-1300 ... 44114
1350-1899 ... 44103
3100-3199 ... 44127
W 45th St
1201-1397 ... 44102
4352-4398 ... 44109
5200-5799 ... 44134
W 46th Pl ... 44102
E 46th St
2000-2098 ... 44103
2100-2299 ... 44103
2400-2599 ... 44104

3400-3498 ... 44105
3500-3699 ... 44105
W 46th St
3000-3699 ... 44102
5200-5799 ... 44134
W 47th Pl ... 44102
E 47th St
1350-1899 ... 44103
2400-2799 ... 44104
3500-3598 ... 44105
3600-3699 ... 44105
3701-3799 ... 44105
W 47th St
1700-3799 ... 44102
4300-4400 ... 44144
4402-4498 ... 44144
E 48th St
2400-2799 ... 44104
3200-3399 ... 44127
3600-3698 ... 44105
W 48th St
1400-3699 ... 44102
4000-4499 ... 44144
5200-5299 ... 44134
5301-5599 ... 44134
E 49th Pl ... 44127
E 49th St
1100-1198 ... 44114
1350-2299 ... 44103
2500-2599 ... 44104
2900-3198 ... 44127
3501-3799 ... 44105
4200-5000 ... 44125
W 49th St
1300-3699 ... 44102
4000-4500 ... 44144
5200-5299 ... 44134
E 50th Pl ... 44103
E 50th St
2500-2542 ... 44104
2900-2998 ... 44127
3000-3499 ... 44127
3600-3899 ... 44105
W 50th St
1400-3699 ... 44102
4000-4499 ... 44144
5200-5299 ... 44134
E 51st Pl ... 44127
E 51st St
1350-1499 ... 44103
2534-2717 ... 44104
2719-2799 ... 44104
3400-3499 ... 44127
W 51st St
3000-3099 ... 44102
4400-4499 ... 44144
E 52nd Pl ... 44127
E 52nd St
1350-1499 ... 44103
3300-3499 ... 44127
3600-3899 ... 44105
W 52nd St
1400-3599 ... 44102
4300-4499 ... 44144
5200-5299 ... 44134
E 53rd St
1201-1349 ... 44114
1350-1499 ... 44103
2700-2799 ... 44104
3300-3499 ... 44127
3501-3597 ... 44105
3599-3899 ... 44105
3900-4099 ... 44105
W 53rd St
2000-2299 ... 44102
4400-4499 ... 44144
E 54th St
2900-2999 ... 44127
3500-3596 ... 44105
3598-3924 ... 44105
3925-4099 ... 44105
W 54th St
1201-1297 ... 44102
1299-3599 ... 44102
4592-4698 ... 44144
5200-6499 ... 44129
W 55th Pl ... 44102

E 55th St
1100-2299 ... 44103
2300-2766 ... 44104
2768-2838 ... 44104
2841-2897 ... 44127
2899-3460 ... 44127
3500-3594 ... 44105
3596-4099 ... 44105
W 55th St ... 44102
E 56th Pl ... 44127
E 56th St ... 44105
W 56th St
3000-3098 ... 44102
3100-3569 ... 44102
3571-3699 ... 44102
4000-4699 ... 44144
E 57th St
1400-1999 ... 44103
2300-2599 ... 44104
2900-3299 ... 44127
3500-4119 ... 44105
4121-4199 ... 44105
W 57th St
1400-1999 ... 44102
4000-4699 ... 44144
E 58th St
1100-1299 ... 44103
3900-4099 ... 44105
W 58th St
1200-1258 ... 44102
1260-3566 ... 44102
3568-3798 ... 44102
4000-4700 ... 44144
4702-4898 ... 44144
W 59th Pl ... 44102
E 59th St
1200-1999 ... 44103
2300-2599 ... 44104
2900-2999 ... 44127
3500-4131 ... 44105
4133-4157 ... 44105
W 59th St
1300-3599 ... 44102
4100-4299 ... 44144
E 60th St ... 44103
3300-3699 ... 44102
4300-4499 ... 44144
E 61st Pl ... 44103
E 61st St
1000-1999 ... 44103
2300-2799 ... 44104
2801-2897 ... 44127
2899-2999 ... 44127
3001-3099 ... 44127
3500-3799 ... 44105
W 61st St
1300-3599 ... 44102
4300-4499 ... 44144
E 62nd St
1000-1099 ... 44103
2600-2799 ... 44104
W 62nd St
3301-3397 ... 44102
3399-3599 ... 44102
4100-4599 ... 44144
E 63rd St
800-2299 ... 44103
2300-2699 ... 44104
2900-3199 ... 44127
3600-3799 ... 44105
W 63rd St
2200-2212 ... 44102
2214-3599 ... 44102
3900-4399 ... 44144
W 64th Pl ... 44102
E 64th St
900-1199 ... 44103
2400-2799 ... 44104
2840-2999 ... 44127
3900-4199 ... 44105
W 64th St ... 44102
E 65th St
1300-2199 ... 44103
2300-2799 ... 44104
2900-3499 ... 44127
3501-3597 ... 44105
3599-3899 ... 44105

W 65th St ... 44102
E 66th Pl ... 44103
E 66th St
1049-1999 ... 44103
2400-2498 ... 44104
2900-3450 ... 44127
3801-3897 ... 44105
W 66th St
3500-3599 ... 44102
4300-4499 ... 44144
W 67th Pl
3200-3399 ... 44102
4400-4499 ... 44144
E 67th St
800-1199 ... 44103
2300-2699 ... 44104
2900-3063 ... 44127
3681-3897 ... 44105
W 67th St ... 44102
E 68th Pl ... 44103
W 68th Pl ... 44102
E 68th St
1000-2299 ... 44103
2600-2899 ... 44104
3101-3199 ... 44127
4000-4100 ... 44105
4102-4398 ... 44105
W 68th St ... 44102
E 69th Pl ... 44103
W 69th Pl ... 44144
E 69th St
900-2299 ... 44103
2300-2899 ... 44104
3400-3499 ... 44127
3600-3799 ... 44105
W 69th St ... 44102
E 70th St
800-2299 ... 44103
2800-2899 ... 44104
3301-3359 ... 44127
3361-3499 ... 44127
W 70th St ... 44102
E 71st Pl ... 44104
W 71st Pl ... 44144
E 71st St
1000-2299 ... 44103
2300-3099 ... 44104
3400-3414 ... 44127
3500-4579 ... 44105
4580-5154 ... 44125
W 71st St
1800-3299 ... 44102
3851-3899 ... 44144
E 72nd Pl
900-1299 ... 44103
4901-4999 ... 44125
E 72nd St
600-1199 ... 44103
2800-2899 ... 44104
2901-3059 ... 44104
3300-3398 ... 44127
3400-3499 ... 44127
3500-4399 ... 44105
E 73rd Pl
1200-1299 ... 44103
3601-3649 ... 44105
E 73rd St
700-798 ... 44103
2500-3099 ... 44104
3400-3499 ... 44127
4201-4277 ... 44105
W 73rd St ... 44102
E 74th St
900-2299 ... 44103
2300-2399 ... 44104
3500-4199 ... 44105
W 74th St ... 44102
E 75th Pl
1300-2299 ... 44103
2826-2898 ... 44104
E 75th St
800-1999 ... 44103
2400-3020 ... 44104
3300-3499 ... 44127
3500-4000 ... 44105
4002-4198 ... 44105
W 75th St ... 44102

E 76th Pl ... 44103
E 76th St
800-898 ... 44103
900-2299 ... 44103
2300-2399 ... 44104
3400-3499 ... 44127
3500-4199 ... 44105
W 76th St ... 44102
E 77th St
800-2299 ... 44103
2300-3099 ... 44104
3600-4352 ... 44105
W 77th St ... 44102
E 78th Pl ... 44103
E 78th St
900-2299 ... 44103
2800-3051 ... 44104
3053-3099 ... 44104
3400-3499 ... 44127
3500-4199 ... 44105
W 78th St ... 44102
E 79th St
700-2299 ... 44103
2300-3299 ... 44104
3300-3360 ... 44127
3362-3398 ... 44127
4000-4199 ... 44105
W 79th St ... 44102
E 80th Pl ... 44103
W 80th Pl ... 44102
E 80th St
1100-2299 ... 44103
2500-3299 ... 44104
3301-3399 ... 44127
3500-3512 ... 44105
3514-4144 ... 44105
4146-4198 ... 44105
W 80th St ... 44102
E 81st Pl ... 44103
E 81st St
1100-2299 ... 44103
2500-3299 ... 44104
3500-4199 ... 44105
4800-4898 ... 44125
4900-4999 ... 44125
W 81st St ... 44102
E 82nd St
700-2299 ... 44103
2300-3299 ... 44104
3500-4199 ... 44105
W 82nd St ... 44102
E 83rd St
1100-2299 ... 44103
2300-3099 ... 44104
W 83rd St
1200-2299 ... 44102
5200-5298 ... 44129
E 84th St
1100-1920 ... 44103
1921-1999 ... 44106
1922-2298 ... 44103
2101-2299 ... 44103
2300-3099 ... 44104
4700-4999 ... 44125
W 84th St
1400-3399 ... 44102
5300-5498 ... 44129
E 85th St
1100-1299 ... 44108
1300-2399 ... 44106
4301-4499 ... 44105
4600-4999 ... 44125
W 85th St ... 44102
E 86th St
1100-1299 ... 44108
1300-2399 ... 44106
2400-2599 ... 44104
3900-3980 ... 44105
3982-4471 ... 44105
4473-4599 ... 44105
4600-5037 ... 44125
5039-5099 ... 44125
W 86th St ... 44102
E 87th St
1100-1299 ... 44108
1700-2399 ... 44106
2600-3099 ... 44104

3300-3399 ... 44127
W 87th St ... 44102
E 88th Pl ... 44106
E 88th St
501-597 ... 44108
599-799 ... 44108
801-899 ... 44108
1300-2399 ... 44106
3300-3499 ... 44104
3500-3599 ... 44105
4600-5299 ... 44125
W 88th St ... 44102
E 89th Pl ... 44108
E 89th St
1200-1299 ... 44108
1300-2399 ... 44106
2400-3499 ... 44104
3900-4099 ... 44105
W 89th St ... 44102
E 90th St
700-736 ... 44108
738-800 ... 44108
802-1298 ... 44108
1302-2399 ... 44106
2700-3299 ... 44104
4600-4999 ... 44125
W 90th St ... 44102
E 91st St
600-799 ... 44108
1302-1400 ... 44106
1402-1498 ... 44106
2800-3199 ... 44104
3500-4100 ... 44105
4102-4198 ... 44105
W 91st St ... 44102
E 92nd St
600-800 ... 44108
802-1098 ... 44108
1300-1499 ... 44106
2700-2999 ... 44104
W 92nd St ... 44102
E 93rd St
601-629 ... 44108
631-999 ... 44108
1300-2399 ... 44106
2401-2449 ... 44104
3501-3547 ... 44105
4600-5000 ... 44125
W 93rd St ... 44102
E 94th St
600-699 ... 44108
1300-1699 ... 44106
3100-3299 ... 44104
4100-4299 ... 44105
4600-5599 ... 44125
W 94th St
3100-3499 ... 44102
5600-5698 ... 44129
E 95th St
600-698 ... 44108
700-899 ... 44108
1300-2399 ... 44106
3701-3997 ... 44105
3999-4199 ... 44105
4800-4999 ... 44125
W 95th St ... 44102
E 96th St
600-799 ... 44108
1500-1998 ... 44106
2000-2199 ... 44106
2601-2669 ... 44104
2671-2799 ... 44104
3700-4299 ... 44105
4800-5599 ... 44125
W 96th St ... 44102
E 97th St
500-1199 ... 44108
1800-2399 ... 44106
2800-3199 ... 44104
3700-4199 ... 44105
4800-4999 ... 44125
W 97th St ... 44102
E 98th St
1000-1199 ... 44108
2800-3499 ... 44104
3560-3638 ... 44105
3640-4299 ... 44105

5100-5249 44125
W 98th St 44102
E 99th Pl 44104
E 99th St
500-1199 44108
1201-1299 44108
2800-3499 44104
3800-4299 44105
W 99th St 44102
E 100th St
700-1299 44108
2100-2350 44106
2800-2899 44104
3701-3997 44105
5200-5399 44125
W 100th St
1900-2299 44102
3000-3098 44111
E 101st St
500-1299 44108
1800-2399 44106
W 101st St
1400-2299 44102
3000-3199 44111
E 102nd St
500-1299 44108
2800-3499 44104
3801-4097 44105
4099-4199 44105
5200-5300 44125
5302-5398 44125
W 102nd St
1200-1599 44102
3500-3699 44111
E 103rd St
500-1299 44108
2100-2399 44106
2800-3499 44104
3500-3799 44105
3801-4099 44105
W 103rd St
1100-2299 44102
3000-3799 44111
E 104th Pl 44108
E 104th St
2800-3499 44104
3500-4199 44105
4500-5300 44125
5302-5398 44125
W 104th St
1200-1238 44102
1240-2299 44102
3000-3799 44111
E 105th St
400-412 44108
414-1299 44108
1300-2309 44106
2311-2399 44106
3200-3499 44104
3500-3799 44105
5200-5222 44125
W 105th St
1200-2299 44102
3000-3699 44111
E 106th St
401-549 44108
1400-2299 44106
2700-3399 44104
3401-3499 44104
3500-4199 44105
4800-4999 44125
W 106th St
1200-2299 44102
3000-3799 44111
E 107th St
500-699 44108
1300-2199 44106
4800-4999 44125
W 107th St
1400-1499 44102
3500-3698 44111
3700-3799 44111
E 108th St
400-1299 44108
1300-1398 44106
1400-2299 44106
2400-3499 44104
3500-4199 44105
4800-4999 44125
W 108th St 44102
E 109th St
400-799 44108
1300-1499 44106
1501-2099 44106
2500-2599 44104
3901-3931 44105
4800-4999 44125
E 110th St
400-498 44108
1301-1317 44106
2400-3499 44104
3500-4299 44105
4900-5099 44125
W 110th St
1201-1255 44102
3000-3300 44111
E 111th St
1000-1299 44108
1300-1599 44106
2500-3066 44104
3068-3098 44104
4100-4299 44105
4900-5399 44125
W 111th St
1200-1399 44102
3000-3399 44111
E 112th St
400-1299 44108
1300-1499 44106
2600-3399 44104
3500-4299 44105
5100-5199 44125
W 112th St
1200-1999 44102
3000-3299 44111
E 113th St
600-1299 44108
3300-3499 44104
3500-4199 44105
5000-5299 44125
E 114th St
400-1299 44108
1300-1499 44106
2600-3499 44104
3500-4399 44105
5000-5299 44125
W 114th St
1200-2299 44102
3000-3699 44111
E 115th St
400-1299 44108
1300-1312 44106
1314-2099 44106
2600-2999 44104
5000-5399 44125
W 115th St
1201-1259 44102
1261-1399 44102
3000-3299 44111
E 116th Pl 44106
E 116th St
1400-1499 44106
1501-1699 44106
2601-2747 44120
2749-3499 44120
3500-4399 44105
W 116th St
1201-1255 44102
1257-1699 44102
3000-3899 44111
E 117th St
400-800 44108
802-822 44108
1300-1999 44106
2700-3499 44120
3500-3799 44105
5000-5399 44125
W 117th St 44111
E 118th St
400-799 44108
1400-1699 44106
2700-3499 44120
3500-3725 44105
3727-3799 44105
W 118th St 44111
E 119th St
1800-1999 44106
2700-3499 44120
4100-4399 44105
5100-5399 44125
W 119th St
3100-3218 44111
3220-3599 44111
3950-3998 44135
4000-4099 44135
E 120th St
400-799 44108
1300-1999 44106
2700-2999 44120
3500-4199 44105
W 120th St
3000-3168 44111
3170-3699 44111
4000-4099 44135
E 121st St
2500-2598 44120
2600-3499 44120
3900-3999 44105
4001-4099 44105
W 121st St
3000-3299 44111
4200-4300 44135
4302-4498 44135
E 122nd St
1500-1599 44106
2600-2899 44120
W 122nd St 44111
E 123rd St
300-1299 44108
1300-1999 44106
2900-3499 44120
3800-4199 44105
W 123rd St
3200-3599 44111
4200-4299 44135
E 124th Pl 44106
E 124th St
300-1299 44108
1300-1499 44106
2400-2899 44120
3500-4399 44105
5301-5397 44125
5399-5499 44125
E 125th St
400-1099 44108
1100-1399 44112
2000-2019 44106
2700-3499 44120
W 125th St
3200-3599 44111
4600-4699 44135
4701-4799 44135
E 126th St
400-799 44108
1900-1999 44106
2400-3499 44120
3700-4399 44105
4400-4544 44105
4401-4599 44105
4546-4598 44105
5101-5299 44125
W 126th St
3200-3699 44111
4801-4899 44135
E 127th St
400-799 44108
2401-2409 44120
2411-2899 44120
3600-3648 44105
3650-4199 44105
W 127th St 44111
E 128th St
400-999 44108
2600-3499 44120
4200-4399 44105
5100-5199 44125
W 128th St
3200-3899 44111
4401-4499 44135
E 129th St
400-1099 44108
3500-3760 44105
3762-3798 44105
5300-5499 44125
W 129th St 44111
E 130th St
600-1099 44108
2600-3499 44120
3801-4097 44105
4099-4299 44105
W 130th St
3200-3999 44111
4000-4999 44135
5001-6479 44130
6481-7899 44130
E 131st St
100-1099 44108
3500-3899 44120
3900-4699 44105
4309-4397 44105
4399-4800 44105
4701-4899 44105
4802-4898 44105
5100-5499 44125
W 131st St
3201-3297 44111
3299-3469 44111
4300-4499 44135
E 132nd St
3100-3499 44120
5300-5499 44125
W 132nd St
3300-3899 44111
4300-4399 44135
E 133rd St
700-748 44110
1220-1722 44112
3500-3699 44120
4200-4299 44105
5200-5337 44125
W 133rd St
3400-3899 44111
4400-4499 44135
E 134th St
1000-1138 44110
1220-1499 44112
3100-3499 44120
4200-4299 44105
5300-5499 44125
W 134th St
3501-3597 44111
4200-4298 44135
E 135th St
1220-1499 44112
3100-3699 44120
4100-4199 44105
4800-5599 44125
5601-6039 44125
W 135th St
3300-3899 44111
4400-4599 44135
E 136th St 44105
3050-3899 44111
4400-4599 44135
E 137th St
801-899 44110
1220-1299 44112
3100-3499 44120
4200-4299 44105
W 137th St
3050-3899 44111
4200-4599 44135
E 138th St
3500-3699 44120
4000-4299 44105
5300-5398 44125
W 138th St
3050-3881 44111
3883-3899 44111
4300-4599 44135
E 139th St
800-999 44110
1300-1399 44112
3200-3699 44120
4000-4299 44105
5301-5497 44125
W 139th St
3050-3799 44111
4300-4899 44135
E 140th St
400-1161 44110
3200-3749 44120
3750-3999 44128
W 140th St
3100-3999 44111
4000-4599 44135
E 141st St
800-1199 44110
1220-1399 44112
3900-4499 44128
4800-4999 44125
W 141st St 44111
E 142nd St
400-499 44110
1220-1399 44112
3200-3749 44120
3750-4499 44128
4600-4799 44125
W 142nd St 44111
E 143rd St
400-1219 44110
1220-1399 44112
3200-3749 44120
3750-3750 44128
3751-3751 44120
3752-4585 44128
4587-4599 44128
W 143rd St
3600-3999 44111
4000-4499 44135
E 144th St
800-1199 44110
1220-1299 44112
3500-3749 44120
3750-4799 44128
W 144th St
3201-3281 44111
3283-3499 44111
4000-4599 44135
E 145th St
1000-1199 44110
1201-1219 44110
1220-1299 44112
3200-3499 44120
W 145th St
3450-3509 44111
3511-3599 44111
4100-4699 44135
E 146th St
300-1219 44110
1220-1299 44112
3200-3749 44120
3750-4499 44128
W 146th St
3000-3999 44111
4000-4799 44135
E 147th St
300-1199 44110
3200-3749 44120
3750-4699 44128
W 147th St
3500-3699 44111
4300-4799 44135
E 148th St
300-1199 44110
3900-4199 44128
W 148th St
3300-3700 44111
3702-3798 44111
4200-4799 44135
E 149th St
200-1099 44110
3200-3749 44120
3750-3916 44128
3918-3998 44128
W 149th St 44135
E 150th St
200-999 44110
3400-3499 44120
3900-4199 44128
W 150th St
3301-3397 44111
3399-3899 44111
3901-3999 44111
4000-4999 44135
E 151st St
200-399 44110
3500-3749 44120
3750-4200 44128
4202-4298 44128
W 151st St 44111
E 152nd St
300-1249 44110
1250-1298 44112
1300-1399 44112
3400-3499 44120
W 152nd St
3400-3899 44111
4200-4599 44135
4601-4799 44135
E 153rd St
3400-3749 44120
3750-4699 44128
W 153rd St
3101-3197 44111
3199-3299 44111
4200-4299 44135
4301-4399 44135
E 154th St
700-849 44110
851-899 44110
3400-3749 44120
3750-4499 44128
W 154th St 44135
E 155th St
700-899 44110
3750-3900 44128
3902-4198 44128
W 155th St
3000-3699 44111
4200-4499 44135
E 156th St
100-899 44110
4300-4499 44128
W 156th St 44135
E 157th St 44110
3200-3999 44111
4000-4799 44135
E 158th St
423-499 44110
4300-4499 44128
W 158th St
3300-3999 44111
4000-4799 44135
E 159th St 44110
W 159th St 44111
E 160th St
300-799 44110
4101-4197 44128
4199-4399 44128
W 160th St
3000-3999 44111
4000-4899 44135
E 161st St 44110
W 161st St 44135
E 162nd St
300-799 44110
4200-4699 44128
W 162nd St
3100-3999 44111
4201-4399 44135
E 163rd St
300-378 44110
4200-4399 44128
W 163rd St 44135
E 164th St
300-398 44110
4200-4399 44128
E 165th St 44110
W 165th St 44111
E 166th St 44110
W 166th St 44135
E 167th St
1000-1299 44110
4200-4399 44128
W 167th St 44135
E 168th Pl 44128
E 168th St 44110
W 168th St
3801-3999 44111
4190-4198 44135
4200-4599 44135
E 169th St
1000-1299 44110
4000-4150 44128
W 169th St 44111
E 170th Pl 44128
E 170th St 44110
W 170th St 44135
E 171st St
1000-1199 44119
1300-1399 44110
W 171st St 44135
E 172nd Pl 44128
E 172nd St
1100-1299 44119
1400-1599 44110
W 172nd St 44135
E 173rd St
1100-1299 44119
1400-1599 44110
4001-4097 44128
4099-4899 44128
W 173rd St 44135
E 174th Pl 44128
E 174th St
1000-1199 44119
1400-1599 44110
4500-4899 44128
W 174th St 44135
E 175th St
1100-1299 44119
1400-1499 44110
4000-4899 44128
E 176th St
1000-1299 44119
1400-1499 44110
3800-4899 44128
W 176th St
3700-4099 44111
4300-4499 44135
E 177th Pl 44128
E 177th St
1000-1200 44119
1202-1298 44119
3751-3873 44128
3875-4899 44128
E 178th St
900-1099 44119
4100-4800 44128
W 178th St 44111
E 179th St
900-1099 44119
1301-1399 44110
W 179th St 44111
W 180th St 44135
E 181st St 44128
W 181st St 44135
W 182nd St 44135
E 183rd St 44122
E 185th St 44119
E 185th St
1300-1500 44110
1502-1598 44110
W 185th St 44135
E 186th St
1200-1399 44110
3800-4299 44122
E 187th St
1200-1399 44110
4000-4299 44122
W 187th St 44135
E 188th St
801-899 44119
1200-1399 44110
3700-4299 44122
E 189th St 44122
W 189th St 44135
E 190th St
100-299 44119
3800-4098 44122
W 190th St 44135
E 191st St 44119
W 191st St 44135
E 192nd St 44119
W 192nd St
4200-4300 44126
4302-4398 44126
4400-4700 44135

4702-4898 44135
E 193rd St 44119
W 193rd St 44135
E 194th St 44119
W 194th St 44135
E 195th St 44119
E 196th St 44119
3900-4399 44126
4600-4698 44135
E 197th St 44119
W 197th St 44135
W 198th St 44135
E 200th St 44119
W 200th St 44135
W 202nd St
4200-4399 44126
4800-4899 44135
W 204th St 44126
E 207th St 44119
E 208th St 44119
W 208th St 44126
E 209th St 44119
E 210th St 44119
W 210th St 44126
E 211th St 44119
W 211th St 44126
E 212th St 44119
W 212th St 44126
E 213th St 44119
W 213th St 44126
E 214th St 44119
W 214th St 44126
W 215th St 44126
E 216th St 44119
W 217th St 44126
E 218th St 44119
W 219th St 44126
E 220th St 44119
W 220th St 44126
W 221st St 44126
W 222nd St 44126
W 223rd St 44126
W 224th St 44126
W 225th St 44126
W 226th St 44126
W 227th St 44126
W 228th St 44126
W 229th St 44126

COLUMBUS OH

General Delivery 43216

POST OFFICE BOXES MAIN OFFICE STATIONS AND BRANCHES

Box No.s
1 - 2994 43216
3001 - 3820 43210
5002 - 5009 43201
6001 - 6646 43206
6801 - 7277 43205
7301 - 7990 43207
8001 - 8474 43201
9001 - 9999 43209
10001 - 10860 43201
11301 - 11956 43211
12001 - 12834 43212
13001 - 13998 43213
14001 - 14982 43214
15001 - 15998 43215
16000 - 16974 43216
18013 - 18360 43218
20001 - 20989 43220
21001 - 21998 43221
23030 - 23998 43223
24001 - 24960 43224
26015 - 26992 43226
27001 - 27995 43227
28001 - 28998 43228
29001 - 29979 43229
30001 - 30988 43230
32001 - 32932 43232
43251 - 43299 43218
44001 - 44996 43204
72001 - 77700 43207
82001 - 82640 43202
83001 - 83652 43203
91000 - 91370 43209
132300 - 132550 43213
141101 - 141558 43214
151000 - 159020 43215
163001 - 165031 43216
180371 - 183990 43218
201001 - 201050 43220
211000 - 218909 43221
236001 - 236240 43223
247101 - 248840 43224
261051 - 267121 43226
272001 - 272120 43227
282001 - 282248 43228
292025 - 298238 43229
300745 - 307794 43230
328531 - 329256 43232
340001 - 359001 43234
360351 - 369099 43236
441001 - 441278 43204

NAMED STREETS

A Ave
1801-2099 43217
3100-3299 43207
Aaron Dr 43228
Abbey Ct 43213
Abbey Rd 43221
Abbey Orchard Ln 43240
Abbeyhill Dr 43085
Abbington Pl 43230
Abbot Ave & Pl 43085
Abbots Bluff Ct 43204
Abbots Cove Blvd 43204
Abbots Green Cir 43204
Abbots Lake Ct 43204
Abbots Loop Ct 43204
Abel Merril Rd 43221
Aberdeen Ave
1000-2499 43211
3700-3999 43219
Aberdeen Dr 43220
Abernathy Ln 43232
Abicos Dr 43085
Abingdon Dr 43224
Abington Rd
2200-2758 43221
2512-2586 43231
2588-2799 43231
2760-2780 43221
Abner Ave 43224
Abney Rd 43207
Abraham Woods Rd 43232
Abshire Ct 43231
Academy Ct E, S & W 43230
Academy Woods Dr 43230
Acarie Dr 43219
Access Rd 43217
Accomodation Ave 43211
Acela St 43235
Acevedo Ct 43235
Ackerman Rd 43202
Ackley Pl 43219
Acorn Ave 43207
Acree Ln 43228
Acres Dr 43207
Acropolis Way 43231
Acton Rd
1-699 43214
1000-1399 43224
Adair Rd 43227
Adalric Dr 43219
Adams Ave 43202
Adamson Dr 43230
Adanac Pl 43224
Adara Dr 43240
Adcock Dr 43232
Adda Ave 43231
Adderley Ave 43232
Addy Rd 43214
Adelbert Dr 43228
Adell Ct & Rd 43228
Adena Dr 43215
Adena Brook Ln 43214
Adena Point Ct 43221
Adin Trl 43235
Adirondack Ave 43231
Adner Ct 43220
Adonai Blvd 43219
Adrian Dr 43207
Advance Ave 43207
Advanced Business Center Dr 43228
Aeden Dr 43219
Affirmed Ct 43230
Afton Rd 43221
Agape Dr 43224
Agate Aly 43205
Agawam Cir 43224
Aggie Ct 43223
Agler Rd
200-298 43230
300-799 43230
1800-2899 43224
3000-3100 43219
3101-3199 43218
3102-4098 43219
3201-4099 43219
Aigen Ave 43207
Ainsley Ave 43230
Ainsworth Ave & Ct 43230
Ainwick Rd 43221
Airendel Ct & Ln 43220
Airpointe Dr 43219
Airport Dr 43219
Akeya Ct 43207
Akola Ave 43211
Akron Dr 43223
Aladdin Ct 43207
Aladdin Woods Ct 43212
Alan Schwarzwalder St 43217
Alane Ct 43224
Albany Brg 43230
Albany Dr 43232
Albany Chase 43230
Albany Gate 43230
Albert Ave 43224
Alberta St
3201-3399 43204
3500-3599 43228
Albion Way 43230
Albrook Dr 43228
Alburn Dr 43207
Alcantara Dr 43219
E & W Alcott Rd 43207
Alcoy Dr 43227
Alden Ave 43201
Alder Vista Dr 43231
Alderson Ct 43228
Alderwood Dr 43219
Aldgate St 43232
Aldrich Pl & Rd 43214
Aldworth Ln 43228
Alexander Aly 43206
Alexander Ln 43213
Alexandria Colony Ct E, N & S 43215
Alfie Pl 43213
Alfred Ct 43221
Alfreda Ln 43211
N & S Algonquin Ave 43204
Alice Rita St 43228
Alissa Ln 43213
Aljor Ct 43219
Alkire Mdw & Rd 43228
Alkire Glen Way 43228
Allanby Ct 43230
Allegheny Ave 43209
Allegiance Rd 43235
Allen Ave 43205
Allen Dr 43213
Allendale Dr 43227
Allenford Ct 43232
Alliance Way 43228
Allington Ln 43240
Allison Dr 43207
Allister Way 43235
Alliston Ct 43220
Alloway St E & W 43085
Allwood Ct & Dr 43231
Almond Ave 43203
Almont Dr 43229
Aloha St 43213
Alona Dr 43224
Alpena Rd 43232
Alpha Ct 43231
Alpine Dr 43229
Alps Ct 43230
Alrojo St 43085
Als Ct 43231
Alsace Rd 43232
Alshire Rd 43232
Alta View Blvd & Ct 43085
Alta View Village Ct 43085
Altair St 43240
Alton Ave 43219
Alton Darby Creek Rd & Spur 43228
Altos Ct 43231
Aluaton St 43207
Alum Creek Dr
500-598 43205
600-799 43205
900-1699 43209
1700-4700 43207
5001-5199 43207
6800-7000 43217
7002-7498 43217
Alumcrest Ln 43209
Alumview Dr 43209
Alvada St 43232
Alvason Ave 43219
Alvina Dr 43229
Alwine Rd 43224
Alyssum Ave 43207
Amalia Pl 43227
Amana Ct 43235
Amazon Pl 43214
Amber Clb 43219
Amber Ct 43232
Amber Crossing Dr 43232
Amberfield Dr 43232
Amberlea Dr E & W 43230
Amberly Pl 43220
Ambleside Ct & Dr 43229
Ambrosia Ave 43235
American Blvd 43223
American Beauty Ln 43240
Americana Ct 43229
Americus Aly 43201
Amesbury Dr 43230
Amesbury Rd 43227
Amesbury Way 43228
Amfield Ct 43230
Amherst Ave 43223
Amol Ln 43235
Ams Ct 43231
Amsterdam Ave 43207
Amur Dr 43235
Amwell Rd E 43207
Amwood St 43228
Amy Ln 43235
Anawanda Ave 43213
Anchor Dr E & W 43207
Andalus Ct & Dr 43230
Anderson Dr 43221
Andes Ct 43230
Andover Rd
1600-2039 43212
2040-2899 43221
Andover St 43085
Andrew Rd 43227
Andrew Hill Pl 43235
Andrus Ave & Ct E & W 43227
Andy Ter 43223
Andy Groom Blvd 43207
Angus Ct 43085
Anita St 43224
Ann St
600-1296 43206
1400-1799 43207
Anna Maria Dr 43224
Annadale Dr 43214
Annagladys Dr 43085
Annandale Ln 43235
Annarue Pl 43231
Annelane Blvd 43235
Annette St 43228
Annhurst Rd 43228
Anson Dr 43220
Anson St 43215
Antar Pl 43240
Antares Ave 43240
Antares Park Dr 43240
Antcliff Ct 43230
Antelope Way 43235
Anthony Ct 43230
Anthony Ct N 43213
Anthony Ct S 43213
Anthony Dr 43204
Antigua Dr 43235
Antler Ct 43230
Antrim Rd 43221
Antrim Ridge St 43235
Antwerp Rd 43213
Apley Pl 43231
Apollo Pl 43201
Appaloosa Ct 43221
Appian Way 43230
Appian Way Ct 43230
Apple St 43204
Apple Blossom Ln 43223
Appleby Dr 43228
Applefair Dr 43228
Applegate Ln 43213
Appleleaf Dr 43230
Appleridge Dr 43223
Appleton Ct 43232
Appleway Dr 43228
Applewick Dr 43228
April Ln
1500-1698 43209
3700-3899 43227
Aqua St 43229
Aqua Bay Dr 43235
Aqua Park Ave 43229
Aquaford Pl 43235
Aqueduct Ct 43221
Arabian Ct 43221
Aragon Ave 43227
Arapaho Ave & Ct 43085
Arbor Dr 43232
Arbor Lee Ct 43213
Arbor Village Dr 43214
Arborfield Pl 43219
Arborhill Dr 43229
Arbors Cir 43230
Arborview Dr 43229
Arborway Ct 43085
Arborwood Ct & Dr 43229
Arbrook 43228
Arbury Ct & Ln 43224
E Arcadia Ave
1-599 43202
700-799 43211
W Arcadia Ave 43207
Arcaro Ct & Dr 43230
Archdale Ln 43214
Archer St 43235
Archmere Sq E 43229
Archway Dr 43235
Arcola Rd 43207
Ardath Ct & Rd 43228
Arden Rd 43214
Arden Forest Ln 43223
Ardenrun Way 43219
Ardleigh Rd 43221
N & S Ardmore Rd 43209
Ardwick Rd 43220
Arendell Ct & Pl 43231
Argo Ln 43232
Argonne Ct 43232
Argus Rd 43227
Argus Green Ct 43227
Argyle Dr 43219
Ariel Dr 43232
Aries Dr 43230
Aries Brook Dr 43207
Arkwood Ave & Ct 43227
Arlingate Dr E 43220
Arlingate Dr N 43220
Arlingate Dr S 43220
Arlingate Dr W 43220
Arlingate Ln 43228
Arlingate Plz 43228
Arlington Ave
600-799 43211
1100-1399 43212
1400-1408 43211
1401-1449 43212
1410-1410 43212
1412-1418 43211
1420-1422 43212
1424-1428 43211
1430-1430 43212
1432-1440 43211
1450-1450 43212
1451-1650 43211
1481-1485 43212
1487-1630 43212
1632-1650 43212
1652-1672 43211
1653-1653 43212
1655-1661 43211
1663-1663 43212
1665-1675 43211
1680-1682 43212
1684-1799 43212
1800-1812 43211
1801-1813 43212
1814-1840 43211
1816-1918 43212
1841-1917 43212
1842-1850 43211
1919-2049 43212
2050-2499 43221
Arlington Centre Blvd 43220
Arlingtowne Ln 43221
Armada Rd 43232
Armor Hill Dr 43230
Armstrong St 43215
Armuth Ave 43219
Arnelle Ct & Rd 43228
Arness Ave 43207
Arnold Ave 43228
Arnold Pl 43235
Arnsby Rd 43232
Arrington Ln 43214
Arrowbend Ct 43229
Arrowhead Ct 43232
Arrowhead Dr 43223
Arrowood Ct & Loop E, N & W 43229
Arrowroot Ct 43085
Arroyo Ct 43231
Artane Pl 43219
Arthur Ct & Pl 43220
Arthur E Adams Dr 43221
Arturo Ct 43231
Aruba Ct & Dr 43230
Asbury Dr 43221
Asbury Ridge Ct & Dr 43230
Aschinger Blvd 43212
Ascot Dr 43229
Ash Dr 43235
Ash Hill Way 43219
E Asharalt St 43215
Ashberry Village Ct & Dr 43228
Ashbourne Pl & Rd 43209
Ashburnham Dr 43230
N Ashburton Rd 43213
S Ashburton Rd
1-699 43213
701-745 43213
758-1099 43227
Ashbury Rd 43231
Ashby Rd 43209
Ashcreek Ave 43219
Ashdowne Rd 43221
Asher Ct 43223
Asheville Park Dr 43235
Ashford Glen Ct & Dr 43230
Ashland Ave 43212
Ashler Ct 43235
Ashley Ave 43213
Ashley Ct 43230
Ashley Dr 43224
Ashley Meadow Dr 43219
Ashmead Dr 43230
Ashmore Rd 43220
Ashpath Cir 43213
Ashpoint St 43219
Ashridge St 43219
Ashtabula Ct 43210
Ashton Ct 43227
Ashton Rd 43227
Ashton Spg 43228
Ashton Woods Pl 43230
Ashtree Pl 43229
Ashwood Rd 43207
Ashworth Pl & St 43235
Askins Rd 43232
Aspen Rd 43229
Aspendale Dr 43235
Aspenspring Dr 43219
Aspenwood Ln 43235
Aston Martin Ct 43232
Astor Ave
2100-3049 43209
3050-4399 43227
5900-6199 43232
Astor Place Dr 43230
Astoria Ave 43207
Atcheson St 43203
Athalia Dr 43228
Athens St 43204
Atkinson Rd 43232
Atlanta Dr 43228
Atlantic Ave 43229
Atlas St 43228
Atlee Ct 43220
Atterbury Ave 43229
Attica Dr 43232
Atwater Dr 43229
Atwood Ter
2200-2869 43211
2870-3799 43224
Auburn Ave 43205
Auden Ave 43215
Audra Ct 43230
Audrey Rd 43224
Audubon Rd
2400-2899 43211
3000-3599 43224
Audubon Trl 43231
Augmont Ave 43207
Augusta Ave 43228
Augusta Glen Dr 43235
Augustwood Dr 43207
Aurelia Dr 43232
Austin Dr 43220
Author Pl 43203
Auto Mall Dr 43228
Autumn Pl 43223
Autumn Ash Ct 43230
Autumn Chase Dr 43232
Autumn Hill Ct & Dr 43235
Autumn Leaf Ct 43235
Autumn Rush Ct 43230
Autumn Village Ct & Dr 43223
Avalon Ave 43229
Avalon Pl 43219
Avalon Rd 43221
Avati Dr 43207
Avebury Ct 43220
Aven Dr 43227
Avendinc Ave 43223
Avenue Chateau Du Nord 43229
Avenwood Ct 43229
Aviator Ave 43228
Avignon Pl 43221
Avir Ct 43230
Avis St 43223
Avon Pl 43203
Avondale Ave
1-169 43222

170-399 43223
800-998 43212
1000-1099 43212
1101-1399 43212
Avonia Dr 43228
Avonwick Pl 43230
Aylesbury Dr 43230
Azelda St
2400-2869 43211
2870-3199 43224
B Ave
3100-3299 43207
6900-6999 43217
B Miller St 43217
Babble Dr 43207
Baccarat Dr 43228
Backbay Dr 43235
Bagley Rd 43232
Bahamas Dr 43230
Bailey Pl 43235
Bainbridge Pl 43228
Baintree Dr 43213
Bairsford Cir & Dr 43232
Baja Ln 43204
Baker Hill Rd 43207
Baker Ridge Dr 43228
Baldridge Rd 43221
Balford Sq E 43232
Balkan Pl 43231
Ballard Dr 43230
Ballycastle Dr 43235
Ballyvaughn Dr 43219
Balm St 43232
Balmoral Ct & Rd 43229
Balsam Lake Dr 43219
Balsamridge Rd 43229
Banbury Dr
300-499 43230
5300-5499 43235
Bancroft St
1900-2249 43219
2250-2499 43211
Bandera Ct 43232
Bandol Ct 43230
Bandshell Pl 43235
Baneberry Ave & Ct 43235
Bangor Ct 43235
N Bank Dr 43220
Bank St 43206
Bankview Dr 43228
Banner Ln 43224
Banningway Dr 43213
Bantann Dr 43228
Banwick Rd 43232
Bar Harbor Pl & Rd 43219
Barbara Ct 43227
Barberry Holw & Ln 43213
Barcher Rd 43207
Barclay Sq E, N, S & W 43209
Barden Ct 43230
Bardwell Rd 43219
Barkley Pl E & W 43213
Barkwillow Ln 43207
Barkwood Dr 43085
Barley Cir 43207
Barley Loft Dr 43240
Barleycorn Pl 43230
Barnes Dr E 43229
Barnett Ct E 43227
Barnett Ct S 43227
Barnett Ct W 43227
Barnett Rd
300-599 43213
800-1899 43227
Barney Ln 43235
Barnhill Ct 43230
Barnsley Ln 43085
Baroma Dr 43228
Baroness Way 43230
Baronne St 43221
Baronsmede Ct 43221
Barr St 43224
Barrett Ln 43229
Barrington Rd 43221
Barrington Club Dr 43220
Barrows Rd 43232
Barry Dr 43211
Barrydowne Dr 43230
Barrymede Ct 43220
Barrymore Ave 43219
Bartfield Dr 43207
Barthel Ave 43227
E & W Barthman Ave 43207
Bartle Dr 43207
Barton Pl 43209
Barwood Dr 43230
Bashan Dr 43228
Basia Dr 43204
Basil Dr 43227
Baskerville Dr 43213
Bass Ave 43207
Bassett Ave
400-599 43203
700-899 43219
Basswood Rd 43207
Bastille Pl 43213
Battle Creek Way 43228
Baudin St 43221
Baughman Ave 43211
Baumock Burn Dr 43235
Baxter Dr 43227
Bay Ct 43227
N Bay Dr 43231
Bay Club Cir 43228
Bay Meadows Ct 43221
Bay Run Dr 43228
Bay Village St 43232
Bayberry Cir 43207
Bayberry Ct 43220
Bayfield Ct & Dr 43229
Bayford Ct 43220
Baylor Ave 43219
Baynard Dr 43232
Baynes Dr 43232
Bayou Rd 43221
Bayshore Dr 43204
Bayswater Dr 43235
Bayview Pl 43230
Baywood Pl 43230
Baywood St 43213
Beachworth Ct & Dr 43232
Beacon Aly 43201
Beacon Run E 43228
Beacon Run W 43228
Beacon Hill Ct & Rd 43228
Beacontree Dr 43224
Beagle Blvd 43232
Beaker Pl 43213
Beal Dr 43232
Beaman Dr 43228
Bear Dr 43228
Bear Tooth Ct 43230
Beary Ave 43203
Beatrice Dr 43227
Beaucroft Ct 43231
Beaufort Ln 43214
Beaumont Ave 43229
Beaumont Rd 43221
E Beaumont Rd
1-799 43214
1800-2079 43224
2081-2099 43224
W Beaumont Rd 43214
Beautyview Ct 43214
Beaver Ave 43213
Beaver Head Ct 43230
Beaverbrook Ct & Dr 43230
E Beck St
1-99 43215
100-799 43206
W Beck St 43215
Beckenham Ct 43230
Becket Ave 43235
Beckley St 43230
Bedford Ave 43205
Bedford Rd 43212
Beech Dr 43235
Beech St 43206
Beech Hill Ave 43214
Beech Knoll Ave 43230
Beecham Ct 43220
Beechbank Rd 43213
Beechcreek Rd 43213
Beechcroft Rd 43229
Beecher Rd & Xing N 43230
Beechford Rd 43213
Beechlake Dr 43235
Beechlawn Rd 43213
Beechmill Ct 43213
Beechrun Rd 43213
Beechton Rd 43232
Beechtree Rd 43213
Beechview Dr E 43085
E Beechwold Blvd 43214
W Beechwold Blvd 43214
Beechwold Dr 43224
Beechwood Dr 43230
Beechwood Rd
64-868 43213
869-1399 43227
Beehive Ln 43230
Behm Rd 43207
Belcher Ct & Dr 43224
Belden Rd 43229
Belfast Dr 43227
Belford Ave 43207
Belgrave Dr 43220
Bella Dr 43085
Bella Via Ave 43231
Bellamy Pl 43213
Bellann Rd 43221
Bellbrook Pl 43085
S Belle St 43215
Belleek Ln 43219
Bellero Way 43219
Belleshire St 43229
Bellevue Ave 43207
Bellflower Ave 43204
Bellingham Ct 43085
Bellmeadow Dr 43229
Bellow Falls Pl 43228
Bellows Ave
600-786 43222
787-1199 43223
Bellrose Ln 43220
Belltowne Blvd 43213
Bellwood Ave & Ct 43209
Belmar Rd 43209
Belmead Ave 43223
Belmont Ave 43201
Belvedere Park 43228
Belvidere Ave 43223
Belvoir Blvd 43228
Beman Ct 43228
Bembridge Rd 43221
Ben Davis St 43217
Ben Dougan Ln 43229
Bench Ct 43230
Benchmark Dr 43219
Benchmark Park Dr 43220
Bendelow Dr 43228
Benderton Ct 43220
Benedetti Ave 43213
Benedict Way 43221
Benfield Ave 43207
Benham Ct & Dr 43232
Benie Ct 43232
Bennington Ave 43231
Bennington Hill Dr 43220
Bennington Woods Ct 43220
Benoit St 43228
Benson Dr 43227
Bent Tree Blvd 43235
Bentgate Ln 43230
Bentham Ct E 43219
Bentham Ct S 43219
Bentham Dr 43219
Bentler Dr 43232
Bentley Ln 43220
Benton St 43205
Benton Way 43230
Bentridge Ln 43230
Bentwick Ln 43230
Bentwood Cir 43235
Bentworth Ln 43230
Benvue Dr 43207
Beraliso Ave 43206
Berend St 43085
Berger Aly 43206
Berkeley Rd
300-869 43205
870-1499 43206
1550-1999 43207
Berkhard Dr 43223
Berkley Pointe Dr 43230
Berkshire Rd 43221
Bermuda Bay Dr 43235
Bernadette Rd 43204
Bernard Pl 43224
Bernard Rd 43221
Bernhard Rd
400-949 43213
950-1399 43227
Bernice Ln 43213
Berning Ct 43228
Berrancher Dr 43228
Berrell Ave
2000-2139 43219
2140-2999 43211
Berry Lane Ct 43231
Berry Ridge Ln 43230
Berrybush Dr 43230
Berryfield Dr 43230
Berryhill Ct 43230
Berryleaf Grv 43231
Berrypatch Dr 43230
Berryville Rd 43207
Berrywood Dr 43220
Berthstone Ct & Dr 43231
Bertram Dr & Pl 43230
Bertson Pl 43235
Berwick Blvd 43209
Berwick Sq 43232
Berwick Arms Pl 43227
Berwyn Rd 43221
Beth Ln 43211
Beth Ann Dr 43207
Bethel Rd
700-1019 43214
1020-3199 43220
Bethel Center Mall 43220
Bethel Park Dr 43235
Bethel Reed Park 43220
Bethel Sawmill Ctr 43235
Bethel Woods Dr 43220
Bethesda Ave 43219
Betsey Pl 43085
Betsy Dr 43227
Betsy Ross Rd 43207
Betty Ct 43231
Betz Rd 43207
Beulah Cir 43224
Beulah Rd
2500-2899 43211
3300-3999 43224
Beverly Pl
200-299 43085
2300-2499 43209
Beverly Rd 43221
Beverly Hills Dr 43213
Bevis Rd 43202
Bexford Pl 43209
Bexley Ct 43209
Bexley Park Rd
2300-3179 43209
3300-3398 43213
Bexton Loop 43209
Bexvie Ave 43227
Bibury Ct 43221
Bickford Ct & Ln 43230
Bickley Pl 43220
Bide A Wee Park Ave 43205
Bidlington Dr 43224
Bidwell Ln 43213
Biehl Aly 43206
Bienville St 43221
Big Bear Ct 43213
Big Ben Ln 43213
Big Pine Dr 43230
Big Red Way 43214
Big Sky Ct 43230
Big Timber Ct 43230
Big Tree Dr 43223
Big Walnutview Ct & Dr 43230
Bigby Hollow Ct & St 43228
Bill Of Rights Sq 43207
Billie Dr 43227
Billingsley Rd 43235
Billington Dr 43213
Billiton Ct 43220
Bimini Ct & Dr 43230
Binbrook Ct & Rd 43227
Bingham Ct 43235
Binns Blvd 43204
Birch Dr 43223
Birch Pl 43217
Birch Hollow Way 43231
Birchcreek Ln 43229
Birchcrest Rd 43221
Birchland Ct 43231
Birchmont Rd 43220
Birchtree Ct, Ln & Way 43232
Birchwood Dr 43228
Bird St 43230
Birdie Dr 43211
Birkdale Ct & Dr 43232
Birkewood St 43229
Birmingham Ct 43214
Birnam Ct 43221
Biscayne Ct 43230
Bishop Sq 43209
Bishopknight 43228
Bittersweet Ct 43230
Bixbywoods Ct 43232
Black And Gold Blvd 43211
Black Cherry Pl 43230
Black Gold Ave & Pl 43230
Black Walnut Dr 43230
Blackberry Aly 43206
Blackbird Ct 43219
Blackbottom Ct 43221
Blackgum Pl 43229
Blackoak Ave 43229
Blackstone Dr 43235
Blackthorne Pl 43224
Blaine Dr 43227
Blair House Ct 43235
Blairfield Dr 43214
E Blake Ave
1-299 43202
1200-1639 43211
1640-1899 43219
W Blake Ave 43202
Blakehope Dr 43219
Blanchester Ct 43229
Blandford Dr 43085
Blandings Ct 43085
Blandon Run 43230
Blarefield Dr 43231
Blatt Blvd 43230
Bleaker Ave 43232
Blendon Dr 43230
Blendon Bend Way 43231
Blendon Grove Way 43230
Blendon Park Dr 43230
Blendon Place Dr 43230
Blendon Point Dr 43230
Blendon Ravine Ct & Way 43230
Blendon Valley Dr 43230
Blendon View Ct 43230
Blendon Way Dr 43230
Blendon Woods Blvd 43231
Blendonbrook Ln 43230
Blendonridge Dr 43230
Blenheim Rd
1-699 43214
900-1099 43224
E Blenkner St
1-99 43215
100-599 43206
W Blenkner St 43215
Blind Brook Ct & Dr 43235
Blinnton Pl 43235
Bliss St 43219
Bloom Dr 43219
Bloomington Blvd 43228
Blossom Ave & Ct 43231
Blue Ash Pl & Rd 43229
Blue Coat Ln 43230
Blue Fox Ct & Ln 43235
Blue Heron Ln 43230
Blue Largo Ct 43230
Blue Meadow Ct 43231
Blue Moon Dr 43232
Blue Mountain Cir & Dr 43230
Blue Ridge Rd 43219
Blue River Ct 43230
Blue Spruce Cir, Pl & St 43231
Blue Tail Bend Dr 43230
Blue Top Dr 43232
Blueberry Hollow Rd 43230
Bluefield Dr 43207
Bluejay Dr 43235
Bluestem Ave 43230
Bluewing Ct 43235
Bluff Ave 43212
Bluff Bend Dr 43235
Bluff Crest Dr 43235
Bluff Ridge Dr 43235
Bluff Vista Dr 43235
Bluffpoint Ct & Dr 43235
Bluffstream Ct 43235
Bluffton Ct 43228
Bluffview Dr 43235
Bluffway Dr 43235
Bluhm Ct & Rd 43223
Blythe Rd 43224
Boardwalk St 43229
Bob O Link Bnd E & W 43229
Bobby Trl 43207
Bobcat Ave 43212
Boca Ct 43230
Bodman Dr 43219
Bogart Ln 43207
Bolenhill Ave & Ct 43229
Bolingbrook Dr 43228
Bolivar St 43203
Bolton Ave 43227
Boltonfield St 43228
Bon Air Dr 43230
Bonaire St 43213
Bonaventure Dr 43228
Bond Ave 43229
Bonham Ave 43211
Bonita Pl & Rd 43232
Bonne Cir 43207
Bonnett Ct 43232
Bonnie Brae Ln 43235
Bonnie Ridge Rd 43228
Bonnington Way 43230
Bonus Dr 43232
Boone St
500-699 43215
700-799 43203
Bootman Dr 43228
Booty Dr 43207
Border St 43207
Borel Ct 43230
Borror Dr 43210
Boscastle Ct 43214
Bosswood Dr 43230
Boston Ave 43209
Boston Common Pl 43232
Boston Ivy Pl 43228
Boston Ridge Dr 43219
Bostwick Rd 43227
Boswall Dr 43085
Bosworth Ct, Pl & Sq N, S & W 43229
Botsford Dr & Pl 43232
Boulder Ct 43214
Boulder Ln 43224
Boulder Creek Dr 43230
Boulder Crest St 43235
Boulder Dam Dr 43230
Bourbon St 43221
Bourke Rd 43229
Bow Dr 43230
Bowdoin Cir 43204
Bowerman Ct & St 43085
Bowery Bay Ln 43230
Bowley Brook Dr 43219
Bowling Green Pl 43230
Bowman Ave 43205
Boxelder Pl 43221
Boxford Ln 43213
Boxwood Dr 43229
Boyd Dr 43085
Boyleston Blvd 43224
Boynton Pl 43227
Boysenberry Ln 43228
Bracken Ct 43085
Bracken House Ct 43235
Brackenridge Ave 43228
Brackenwood Trl 43228
Brackley Rd 43220
Bradbury Ct 43231
Bradbury Ln 43232
Braddock Ct 43220
Bradenton Ct 43235
Bradford Ave & Rd 43220
Bradington Ct 43229
Bradley St 43201
Bradshire Dr 43220
Bradwell Dr 43207
Brady Dr 43229
Brady Commons Dr 43229
Braemar Dr 43220
Braemer Ct 43230
Brafferton Pl 43235
Bragg Dr 43207
Braiden Ct 43213
Bramble Brook Dr 43228
Bramblebush Ct 43224
Bramblewood Ct 43228
Brambury Cir 43228
Bramford Rd 43220
Branch St 43235
Branchwood St 43229
Brandenberry Ct & Dr 43228
Brandenbush Ct & Ln 43228
Brandigen Ln 43228
Brandon Ct 43213
Brandon Rd 43221
Brandon St 43224
Brandonbury Way 43232
Brandt Cir 43230
Brandy Dr 43232
Brandy Oaks Ln 43220
Brandywine Dr 43220
Branford 43232
Brant Rd 43230
Brassic Way 43213
Braunton Rd 43220
Brayton Ave 43232
Bread St 43230
Breathitt Ave & Pl 43207
Breckenridge Way 43235
Breezedale Pl 43213
Brehl Ave
1-349 43222
350-599 43223
Bremen St
2250-2500 43211
2502-2598 43211
2710-3699 43224
Brenda Dr 43207
Brendan Dr 43221
Brendel Dr 43235
Brennan Pl 43235
Brent Blvd 43228
Brentfield Pl 43228
Brentford Dr 43220
Brenthaven Dr & Pl 43228
Brenthurst Dr 43230
Brentnell Ave
700-2099 43219
2101-2109 43211
2111-2899 43211
Brenton Pl 43213
Brentwood Ct 43213
Brentwood Rd 43209
Brett Ct & Ln 43207
Bretton Pl 43211
Bretton Rd 43219

Bretton Woods Dr ... 43231
Brevoort Rd ... 43214
E & W Brewer St ... 43215
Brewster Dr ... 43232
Brexton Pl ... 43212
Brian Ct
2600-2699 ... 43204
4300-4499 ... 43207
Brianlane Blvd ... 43231
Briar Ct ... 43230
Briar Ridge Rd ... 43232
Briar Rose Ave ... 43231
Briarbank Dr ... 43235
Briarbush Ct & Dr ... 43207
Briarhurst Ct & Ln ... 43220
Briarmeadow Dr & Ln ... 43235
Briarwood Ave ... 43211
Briarwood Dr ... 43213
Brice Rd ... 43232
N Brice Rd ... 43213
Brice Outlet Mall ... 43232
Brichar Way ... 43204
Brick Ct ... 43230
Brickel St ... 43215
Bricker Blvd ... 43221
Bricker Hall ... 43210
Brickwall Dr N ... 43213
Bride Water Blvd ... 43235
Bridgemont Ct ... 43228
Bridgemore Dr ... 43232
Bridgeport Rd ... 43220
Bridgestone Dr ... 43219
Bridget Dr ... 43221
Bridgeton Dr ... 43220
Bridgeview Ct ... 43224
Bridgeview Dr ... 43224
Bridgeview Rd ... 43221
Bridgewalk St ... 43224
Bridgeway Ave ... 43219
Bridgeway Cir ... 43220
Bridgewood Ct ... 43229
Bridle Ct ... 43221
Bridle View Way ... 43240
Bridletree Way ... 43235
Bridlewood Blvd & Ct ... 43207
Bridlington Ct & Ln ... 43229
Briers Dr ... 43209
Briggs Rd
2300-2649 ... 43223
2650-2744 ... 43204
2746-3619 ... 43204
3620-4099 ... 43228
Briggs St ... 43206
Briggs Center Dr ... 43223
Briggston Ave ... 43204
Bright Star Ct ... 43228
Brighton Rd ... 43202
E Brighton Rd ... 43224
Brightwell Ln ... 43230
Brimfield Ct & Rd ... 43229
Brindley Pl ... 43230
N & S Brinker Ave ... 43204
Brinkley Ct ... 43235
Brinkton Dr ... 43231
Brinwood Ct & Pl ... 43232
Bristol Rd ... 43221
Bristol Way ... 43085
Bristol Commons Pl ... 43240
Bristol Woods Ct ... 43085
Briston Dr ... 43221
Britains Ln ... 43224
Britannia Dr W ... 43221
Britt Pl ... 43227
Brittany Ct E ... 43229
Brittany Ct W ... 43229
Brittany Ln ... 43220
Brittany Rd ... 43229
Brittingham Ct ... 43214
Britton Ave ... 43204
Brixham Rd ... 43204
Brixton Rd ... 43221
Brixton Park Ave ... 43235
E Broad St
2-122 ... 43215
124-700 ... 43215
702-720 ... 43215
721-1539 ... 43205
1540-1899 ... 43203
1900-3279 ... 43209
3280-7142 ... 43213
7144-7230 ... 43213
W Broad St
10-18 ... 43215
20-679 ... 43215
680-1516 ... 43222
1497-1499 ... 43223
1517-1601 ... 43222
1518-1594 ... 43222
1596-1600 ... 43223
1602-2269 ... 43223
2270-2279 ... 43204
2280-2298 ... 43223
2281-3509 ... 43204
2300-3508 ... 43204
3510-5660 ... 43228
Broad Pointe Pl ... 43213
Broadhurst Dr ... 43213
Broadland Ln ... 43213
Broadlawn Ave ... 43228
Broadleaf Ct & Ln ... 43224
N & S Broadleigh Rd ... 43209
Broadmeadows Blvd ... 43214
Broadmoor Ave
3100-3279 ... 43209
3280-3499 ... 43213
Broadview Ave ... 43212
Broadview Ct ... 43230
Broadview Rd ... 43230
Broadview Ter ... 43212
Broadway Ln & Pl ... 43214
Brocton Ct & Rd ... 43219
Brodbelt Ln ... 43215
Brodie Dr ... 43228
Brodribb Ct ... 43220
Broehm Rd ... 43207
Brofford Dr ... 43235
Brokaw Dr ... 43231
Broken Arrow Rd ... 43230
Broken Lance Dr ... 43219
Brome Dr ... 43221
Bromfield Ct ... 43232
Bromley Ave ... 43085
Bromsgrove Ct ... 43232
Bromton Ct ... 43232
Bronwyn Ave ... 43204
Brook Holw ... 43230
Brookbend Dr ... 43235
Brookcliff Ave ... 43219
Brookdown Dr ... 43235
Brookeville Ave & Ct ... 43229
Brookfield Rd & Sq N, S & W ... 43229
Brookforest Dr ... 43204
Brookhaven Dr E ... 43230
Brookhill Dr ... 43230
Brookhouse Ln ... 43230
Brookhurst Ave ... 43229
Brookie Ct ... 43214
Brookline Ave ... 43223
Brooklyn Ct ... 43229
Brooklyn Rd
2200-2339 ... 43229
2340-2699 ... 43231
Brookridge Dr ... 43235
Brookrun Dr ... 43204
Brooks Ave ... 43211
Brooks End Ct ... 43204
Brookshire Ct ... 43227
Brookside Blvd ... 43204
Brookside Ct ... 43228
Brookside Dr ... 43209
Brookside Oval ... 43085
Brookview Way ... 43221
Brookway Rd ... 43227
Brookwood Pl & Rd ... 43209
Broomwood Loop N & S ... 43230
Broughton Ave ... 43213
Brown Rd ... 43223
S Brown St ... 43228
Brownfield Ct & Rd ... 43232
Browning Ave ... 43209
Brownleaf Rd ... 43223
Brownlee Ave
2700-3029 ... 43209
3030-3199 ... 43227
Brownsfell Dr ... 43235
Bruce St ... 43207
Bruceton Ave ... 43232
Bruck St
700-1349 ... 43206
1350-2099 ... 43207
Bruckner Rd ... 43207
Brunson Ave ... 43203
Bruntsfield Rd ... 43235
Brush Ridge Ct ... 43228
Brust St ... 43206
Bryant Ave ... 43085
Bryden Aly ... 43205
Bryden Rd
600-699 ... 43205
700-708 ... 43215
701-2099 ... 43205
710-1998 ... 43205
2100-2999 ... 43209
Bryn Mawr Dr ... 43230
Brynhild Rd ... 43202
Brynwood Dr ... 43220
Bryson Rd ... 43224
Bucher St ... 43207
Buck Creek Dr ... 43207
Buck Rub Ct ... 43085
Buck Run Dr ... 43213
Buck Thorn Ln ... 43220
Buck Trail Ln ... 43085
Buckeye Cir ... 43217
Buckeye Dr W ... 43223
Buckeye Grv ... 43214
Buckeye Park Rd ... 43207
Buckingham St
300-398 ... 43215
700-832 ... 43203
834-898 ... 43203
Buckley Rd ... 43220
Buckman St ... 43232
Bucknell Rd ... 43213
Buckpoint Ln ... 43085
Bucks Aly ... 43202
Buckshot Ct ... 43085
Buckskin Ct ... 43221
Buckthorn Way ... 43230
Bucktrout Pl ... 43235
Buckwheat Ct ... 43207
Budd St ... 43228
Buechler Bnd ... 43228
Buena Vista Ave ... 43228
Buffalo Ct ... 43207
Buffalo Creek Ct ... 43223
Bufflehead Dr ... 43230
Bufford Ct ... 43231
Buggywhip Ln ... 43207
Bugle Ct ... 43230
Builders Pl ... 43204
Bulen Ave
500-909 ... 43205
910-1299 ... 43206
2500-2999 ... 43207
Bull Run Ct ... 43230
Bullitt Park Pl ... 43209
Bunker Ave ... 43228
Bunker Hill Blvd ... 43220
Burbank Dr ... 43220
Burbank Rd ... 43232
Burberry Ln ... 43228
Burdett Ct & Dr ... 43232
Burgandy Ln ... 43228
N & S Burgess Ave ... 43204
Burgoyne Ct & Ln ... 43220
Burkeshire Dr ... 43232
Burlawn Ct ... 43235
Burley Dr ... 43207
Burlington Ave ... 43227
Burnaby Dr ... 43209
Burnell Cir & Rd ... 43224
Burnham Dr ... 43228
Burnley Ct & Sq E, N & S ... 43229
Burr Ave & Ct ... 43212
Burrell Ave ... 43212
Burstock Ct & Rd ... 43206
Burt St ... 43203
Burton Ave ... 43207
Burwell Dr ... 43209
Busch Blvd & Ct ... 43229
Bushmill Falls Dr ... 43221
Bushwood Ln ... 43235
Business Park Dr ... 43204
Butler Ave ... 43223
Butler Farms Dr ... 43207
Butterfly Ct ... 43223
Buttermilk Ave ... 43235
Butternut Ct E & W ... 43229
Buttles Ave ... 43215
Buttonbush Ct & St ... 43230
Buttonwood Ct ... 43230
Buzick Dr ... 43207
Bycroft Rd ... 43206
Byers Cir E & W ... 43229
Byrd Dr ... 43219
Byron Ave ... 43227
Bywood Ln ... 43214
C Ave ... 43207
Cabin Ln ... 43230
Cable Ave ... 43222
Cabora Ln ... 43232
Cadbury Ct & Dr ... 43230
Cadell Rd ... 43232
Cadillac Ct ... 43232
Cadmus Dr ... 43228
Cailin Dr ... 43207
Caine Rd ... 43235
Cairngorm Dr ... 43221
Caladium Dr ... 43235
Calahan Rd ... 43207
Calais Dr ... 43221
Calais Way ... 43235
Calder Ct E ... 43221
Calderwood Dr ... 43231
Caldwell Pl ... 43203
Caleb Dr ... 43220
Calgary Ct & Dr ... 43229
E & W California Ave ... 43202
Calimero Dr ... 43224
Calkin Ln E & W ... 43230
Callahan Pl ... 43213
Callender Ave ... 43203
Callisto Dr ... 43240
Calum Ct ... 43235
Calumet St
2600-3349 ... 43202
3350-3699 ... 43214
Calveylee Ln ... 43232
Calvin Dr ... 43227
Calvington Ct ... 43230
Cam Ct ... 43230
Camaro Ave ... 43207
Camborne Rd ... 43220
Cambrian Ct & Dr ... 43220
Cambrian Commons Dr ... 43240
Cambridge Blvd
1100-1959 ... 43212
1960-2499 ... 43221
Cambridge Ct
800-899 ... 43085
4200-4299 ... 43224
Cambron Dr ... 43219
Camden Ave ... 43201
Camden Rd ... 43221
Camden Passage Dr ... 43230
Camden Yard Ct ... 43235
Camdenway Ct ... 43213
Camelback Dr ... 43228
Camelot Dr ... 43220
Cameron Ridge Dr ... 43235
Camp Chase Dr ... 43204
Campbell Ave
700-829 ... 43222
830-1299 ... 43223
Campus Pl ... 43201
E & W Campus View Blvd ... 43235
Camrose Ct ... 43230
Canaday Ct ... 43228
Canal Bay Way ... 43232
Canal Cove Way ... 43231
Canby Ct ... 43230
Cancouni Dr ... 43230
Candace Pl ... 43085
Candlewick Cir ... 43230
Candlewood Dr & Ln ... 43235
Canfield Dr ... 43230
Canford Pl ... 43230
Canice Ave ... 43219
Caniff Ct, Pl & Rd ... 43221
Cannington Ct & Dr ... 43229
Cannock Ln ... 43219
Cannon Dr ... 43210
Cannon Point Ct ... 43209
Cannonade Ct ... 43230
Cannongate Ct & Dr ... 43228
Canon Ridge Ct & Pl ... 43230
Canonby Pl ... 43223
Canopy Ln ... 43219
Cantara Pl ... 43232
Canter Ridge Ln ... 43085
Canterbury Ln ... 43221
Canterbury Rd ... 43221
Canterbury Way ... 43213
Cantering Pl E & W ... 43230
Canterwood Ct ... 43230
Cantigern Dr ... 43235
Canton Ave ... 43207
Canvasback Ln ... 43215
Canyon Dr N, NE & S ... 43214
Canyon Tree Dr ... 43229
Cap Ln ... 43085
Cape Charles Dr ... 43228
Cape Cod Ln ... 43235
Cape Henry Dr ... 43228
Capital St ... 43205
E Capital St ... 43215
W Capital St
1-679 ... 43215
1101-1199 ... 43222
Capital Park Ct ... 43224
Capitol Sq ... 43215
Capitol View Dr & Pl ... 43203
Capstone Way ... 43221
Captains Ct ... 43220
Carahan Rd ... 43229
Caralee Dr & Pl ... 43219
Carano Way ... 43240
Caravel Dr ... 43207
Carbondale Ct, Dr & Pl ... 43232
Carbone Dr ... 43224
Cardiff Rd ... 43221
Cardigan Ave
1900-2099 ... 43212
2200-2399 ... 43215
Cardinal Ct ... 43231
Cardinal Park Dr ... 43213
Cardington Ave ... 43229
Cardston Ct, Dr & Pl ... 43232
Cardwell Sq E ... 43229
Caren Ave ... 43085
Carex Ln ... 43228
Carey St ... 43224
Cargo Rd ... 43217
Caribou Trl ... 43235
Carilla Ln ... 43228
Carisbrook Rd ... 43221
Carleton Ct ... 43231
Carlford St ... 43232
Carlin Ct E & W ... 43230
Carlisle Ave ... 43224
Carliss Ave ... 43207
Carlton Ave ... 43227
Carmack Rd
1000-1099 ... 43210
2100-2199 ... 43221
2200-2298 ... 43210
2400-2498 ... 43221
2401-2497 ... 43210
2499-2599 ... 43210
Carmell Ct & Dr ... 43228
Carnation St ... 43207
Carnegie Cove Ct ... 43213
Carnforth Dr ... 43221
Caro Ln & Pl ... 43230
Carol Ave ... 43204
Carolann Ave ... 43207
Carolina Ave & Ct ... 43229
Caroline Ave ... 43209
Carolwood Ave ... 43227
Carolyn Ave ... 43224
Caroway Blvd ... 43230
Carpenter Rd ... 43230
Carpenter Rdg ... 43228
Carpenter St
200-739 ... 43205
740-788 ... 43206
790-999 ... 43206
Carriage Ln ... 43221
Carriage Hill Ln ... 43220
Carrie Ave ... 43205
Carrigallen Ln ... 43228
Carrimore Ln ... 43228
Carrington Ct ... 43085
Carrock Ct ... 43219
Carroll Rd ... 43219
Carrollton Dr ... 43223
Carrollton Club Cir ... 43219
Carron Dr ... 43220
Carruthers Dr ... 43235
Carson Michael Ave ... 43230
Carstare Ct & Dr ... 43227
Carter Ct ... 43204
Carteret Dr ... 43228
Cartwright Ln ... 43231
Carver Ct ... 43219
Cary Ln ... 43232
Carylake Cir ... 43240
Casa Mila ... 43219
Casado Dr ... 43213
Cascade Ct ... 43204
Cascade View Dr ... 43240
Case Rd ... 43224
W Case Rd ... 43235
N Cassady Ave
2-298 ... 43209
300-579 ... 43209
580-2799 ... 43219
S Cassady Ave
1-399 ... 43209
2500-2599 ... 43207
2601-2799 ... 43207
Cassady Ct N ... 43219
Cassady Ct S ... 43219
Cassady Ct W ... 43219
Cassady Pl ... 43219
Cassady Village Trl ... 43219
Cassandra Ln ... 43211
Cassill Ct & St ... 43220
N & S Cassingham Rd ... 43209
Cassini Dr ... 43240
Castle Pnes ... 43235
E Castle Rd ... 43207
W Castle Rd ... 43207
Castle Crest Dr ... 43085
Castle Pines Dr ... 43230
Castlebrook Dr ... 43229
Castleford Ln ... 43228
Castlegate Rd ... 43209
Castlerea Ct ... 43221
Castleton Rd ... 43220
Castlewood Rd ... 43230
Caswell Dr ... 43230
Catalina Ct ... 43204
Catalona Ct ... 43230
Catalpa Dr ... 43232
Catamaran Dr ... 43207
Catania Way ... 43232
Catbird Crossing Dr ... 43230
Catherine St ... 43223
Cathoway Ct ... 43240
Catkin Ct ... 43207
Cavan Ct ... 43221
Cayman Ln ... 43085
Cedar Aly
100-199 ... 43215
573-599 ... 43206
Cedar Dr ... 43232
Cedar Spgs ... 43228
Cedar St ... 43217
Cedar Crest Ln ... 43230
Cedar Rapids Dr ... 43228
Cedar Willow Dr ... 43229
Cedarbush Rd ... 43229
Cedarwood Rd ... 43207
Celina Rd ... 43228
Cenpac Ave ... 43213
Centab Dr ... 43203
Centauri Ave ... 43240
Center St ... 43213
Center Woods Dr ... 43214
Centner Ln ... 43232
N Central Ave ... 43222
S Central Ave
1-169 ... 43222
170-1699 ... 43223
Central Park Dr & Pl ... 43231
Century Dr ... 43211
Ceramic Dr ... 43214
Certaldo Dr ... 43219
Chacey Ln ... 43085
Chadbourne Dr ... 43220
Chadbyrne Dr ... 43235
Chadwick Dr ... 43224
Chadwood Dr ... 43230
Chadwood Ln ... 43235
Chaffin Rdg ... 43214
Chagrin Dr ... 43219
Chambers Ave ... 43223
Chambers Cir ... 43212
Chambers Rd ... 43212
Chambersburg Rd ... 43207
N Champion Ave ... 43203
S Champion Ave
1-779 ... 43205
780-1469 ... 43206
1470-3799 ... 43207
Chancel Dr ... 43235
Chancery Way ... 43219
Chandlee Pl ... 43230
Chandler Ave ... 43207
Chandler Dr ... 43213
Chaney Pl ... 43207
Channing Ter ... 43232
Channingway Blvd & Ct ... 43232
Channingway Center Dr ... 43232
Chante Ct ... 43219
Chanterwood Dr ... 43231
Chantilly St ... 43207
Chantry Ct ... 43220
Chantry Dr ... 43232
Chaparral Rd ... 43235
E Chapel St ... 43205
W Chapel St
300-679 ... 43215
681-739 ... 43222
741-799 ... 43222
Chapel Hill Ct ... 43228
Chapelfield Rd ... 43230
Chappel Chase ... 43232
Chaps Ct ... 43221
Chara Ln ... 43240
Charbert Ct ... 43232
Charbonnett Ct ... 43232
Chardon Rd ... 43220
Charecote Ln ... 43220
Charing Rd ... 43221
Charlbury Dr ... 43220
Charles St ... 43209
Charlesfield Dr ... 43230
Charleston Ave ... 43214
Charlesway Dr ... 43085
Charlotte Dr ... 43224
Charlotte Rd ... 43207
Charlton Ct ... 43229
Charmel Pl ... 43235
Charming Ct ... 43231
Charmingfare St ... 43228
Charnwood Ln ... 43085
Charter St ... 43228
Charter Oak Way ... 43219
Chartwell Rd ... 43220
N Chase Ave ... 43204

S Chase Ave 43204
Chase Rd 43214
Chateau Cir S 43221
Chateau Chase Dr 43235
Chateau Morse Ct & Dr 43231
Chatfield Park 43219
Chatfield Rd 43221
Chatford Dr & Sq 43232
Chatham Ln 43221
Chatham Rd 43214
Chatterly Ln 43207
Chattermark Dr 43207
Chatterton Rd 43232
Chaucer Ct 43085
Chaucer Dr 43221
Chaucer Ln 43220
Chaumonte Ave 43232
Chauncy Rd 43219
Cheaves Pl 43224
Checkrein Ave 43229
Chelford Ct & Dr 43219
Chelmsford Ct & Sq E, N & S 43229
Chelsea Ave 43209
Chelsea Ct 43232
W Chelsea Rd 43212
Chelsea Bridge Ln 43230
Chelsea Square Ave 43230
Cheltenham Rd 43220
Chelton Pl 43220
Chennin Dr 43230
Cherlyn Ct 43228
Cherokee St 43204
Cherry Dr 43215
Cherry Rd 43230
E Cherry St
456-500 43215
502-695 43215
700-1899 43205
W Cherry St 43215
Cherry Bottom Ct & Rd 43230
Cherry Bud Ct & Dr 43228
Cherry Chase Ct 43228
Cherry Creek Pkwy N & S 43228
Cherry Glen Rd 43228
Cherry Grove Ct 43228
Cherry Hill Ct E 43228
Cherry Hill Ct S 43228
Cherry Hill Ct W 43228
Cherry Hill Dr 43213
Cherry Hollow Rd 43228
Cherry Orchard Ln 43230
Cherry Park Dr 43230
Cherry Ridge Rd 43228
Cherry Way Dr 43230
Cherry Wood Pl 43230
Cherryberry Dr 43228
Cherryblossom Way 43230
Cherrybluff Ct 43230
Cherrydale Ave 43207
Cherryfield Ave & Pl 43235
Cherryhaven Dr 43228
Cherryhurst Dr 43228
Cherrymonte Dr 43228
Cherrystone Dr N & S 43230
Cherrywood Ct & Rd 43229
Chervil Dr 43221
Cheryl Ct 43219
Cherylane Blvd 43235
Chesapeake Ave 43212
Chesapeake Ct 43220
E Chesfield Dr 43204
Chesford Rd 43224
Cheshire Rd 43221
Cheshire Commons Ct 43229
Chester Rd
2480-2484 43221
2486-2799 43221
2501-2531 43231
2533-2649 43231
N & S Chesterfield Ct & Rd 43209
Chestershire Rd 43204
Chesterton Ln & Sq E, N & S 43229
E Chestnut St 43215
Chestnut Hill Dr 43230
Chestnut Oak Way 43228
Chestnut Ridge Dr & Loop 43230
Cheswick Rd 43231
Chetti Dr 43213
Chevington Rd 43220
Cheviot Ct & Dr 43220
Chevy Chase Ave & Ct 43220
Chicago Ave 43222
Chickory Ave 43230
Chickory Hollow Ct 43085
Chilcote Ave 43202
Childrens Dr 43205
Childrens Xrd 43215
Chiller Ln 43219
Chillicothe St 43207
Chillmark Dr 43230
Chilton Pl 43230
Chimes Ct 43235
Chimney Point Dr 43231
Chinaberry Dr
601-699 43230
6000-6299 43213
Chingford Rd 43232
Chinook Pl 43235
Chipman Dr 43232
Chippewa St 43204
Chipshot Ct 43228
Chiselhurst Pl 43220
Chittenden Ave
1-499 43201
800-1199 43211
Choctaw Ct & Pl 43085
Chopper Ln 43228
Chowning Ct 43220
Chowning Way 43213
Chreshem Ave 43230
Chris Perry Ln 43213
Chrisman Dr 43223
Christie Rd E 43207
Christina Ln 43230
Christine Blvd 43231
Christopher Wren Dr 43230
Christy Bloom Dr 43230
Chrisview Dr 43227
Chriswood Ct 43235
Chuckas Ct E & W 43230
Churchbell Way 43235
Churchill Ave 43214
Churchill Dr
600-699 43230
2800-2899 43221
Churchview Ln 43220
Cider Mill Ct & Dr 43204
Cimmaron Rd 43221
Cimmaron Sta 43235
Cindy Ave 43207
Cindy Ct 43232
Cindy Ellen Ct 43228
Cinna Dr 43228
Circle Ct 43224
Circle Dr 43220
Circle On The Grn 43235
Cirque Cir 43207
Ciscero Dr 43235
Citadel St 43230
Citation Ct 43230
Citizens Pl 43232
City Center Dr 43215
City Park Ave
400-599 43215
600-1329 43206
1330-1399 43207
Citygate Dr
2000-2300 43219
2301-2399 43218
2302-2424 43219
2401-2425 43219
Civic Center Dr 43215
Civitas Ave 43215
Clabber Rd 43207
Clairbrook Ave 43228
Clairmont Ct & Rd 43220
Clairpoint Ct & Way 43227
Clan Ct 43085
Clancy Ct 43230
Clara St 43211
Clare Dr 43228
Clarendon Ave & Ln 43223
Claretta Rd 43232
Clarfield Ave 43207
Claridon Rd 43231
Clarington Ct 43214
Clarion Ct 43220
Clark Ave 43223
Clark Pl 43201
Clark St 43230
Clark State Rd 43230
Clarkston Ave & Ln 43232
Claude Dr 43207
Claver Dr 43219
Clay Ct 43205
Clayborn Ct 43235
Claycraft Rd 43230
Clayford Dr 43204
Claypool Ct 43213
Clayridge Ln 43224
Clayton Dr 43085
Clear Creek Cir 43235
Clear Ridge Dr 43219
Clearbrook Ct 43220
Clearhurst Dr 43229
Clearview Ave
3300-3429 43221
3430-4099 43220
E Clearview Ave 43085
W Clearview Ave 43085
Clearwater Dr 43232
Clement Dr 43085
Clemson St 43230
Cleophus Kee Blvd 43211
Clermont Rd
2800-3049 43209
3050-3199 43227
Cleveland Ave
1-699 43215
800-1299 43201
1300-2709 43211
2710-4407 43224
4408-5562 43231
5563-5567 43229
5564-6858 43231
5601-6859 43231
6861-6899 43229
Cleveland Innis Plz 43224
Clevelawn Pl 43224
Cliff Ct 43204
Cliff Brook Ln 43228
Cliff Creek Dr 43228
Cliff Ridge Ct & Dr 43230
Cliff Springs Trl 43240
Cliffside Dr 43202
Cliffthorne Pl & Way 43235
Cliffview Dr 43230
Clifton Ave
1500-1799 43203
1800-1999 43219
2000-2499 43209
Clifton Ct 43203
Clifton Rd 43221
Clifton Park Cir E 43230
Clime Rd
2500-3509 43223
3510-4499 43228
Clime Rd N 43228
Cline St 43206
Clinton St
1-599 43202
701-797 43211
799-1399 43211
Clinton Heights Ave 43202
Clintonview St 43229
Clipper Ct 43231
Clipper Landing Dr 43228
Clipperway Ln 43221
Clock Ct 43230
Cloister Dr 43235
Clotts Rd 43230
Clovelly St 43240
Clovenstone Dr 43085
Clover Dr 43235
Cloverdale Ct & Ln 43235
Cloverknoll Ct 43235
Cloverleaf St E 43232
Cloverly Dr 43230
Club Ln 43230
Club Rd
2042-2078 43217
2080-2147 43217
2149-2161 43217
2200-2499 43221
Club House Dr 43211
Club Lane Dr 43219
Clubview Blvd N & S 43235
Clybourne Rd 43231
Clyde Pl 43227
Clydesdale Ave & Ct 43229
Clydeway Ct 43085
Coach Rd N 43220
Coachford Dr 43231
Coachman Rd 43220
Coatbridge Ln 43229
Cobalt Moon Xing 43240
Cobble Hl 43230
Cobblestone Dr 43220
Coburg Rd 43227
Cochrane Ave 43207
Code Pl 43207
Codet Rd
600-700 43230
702-798 43230
3700-3999 43219
Codrington Cir 43230
Cody Rd 43224
Coe Dr 43207
Coffey Rd 43210
Coghill Dr 43229
Coit Rd 43232
Colburn Ct 43085
Colby Ave 43227
Colchester Rd 43221
Coldspring Ct 43220
Coldstream Dr 43235
Coldstream Ln 43209
Coldwater Dr 43223
Coldwell Ct & Dr 43230
Cole Rd 43228
Cole St 43205
Coleman Dr 43235
Colerain Ave 43214
Coleridge Ct 43232
Colette Ct 43228
Colfax Ave 43224
Colgate Rd 43213
Colhasset Ln 43220
Colin Ct 43229
Colleen Ct 43221
College Ave 43209
N College Rd 43210
S College Rd 43210
College And Main 43209
College Hill Dr 43221
College Park Dr 43209
Collegiate Ct 43235
Collet Ct 43228
Collier Dr 43230
Collier Ridge Dr 43235
Collingdale Rd 43231
Collingswood Rd 43221
Collingville Way 43230
Collingwood Ave 43213
Collingwood Pointe Pl 43230
Collins Ave 43215
Collins Dr 43085
Collins Way 43085
Colonel Perry Dr 43229
Colonial Ave 43085
Colonial Ct 43229
Colonial Pkwy 43214
Colonial Commons Dr 43240
Colonial Way Cir 43235
Colony Ct
100-399 43230
700-899 43235
Colony Pl 43230
Colony Way 43235
Colony Hill Ln 43204
Colony Vista Ln 43204
Colton Ct & Rd 43207
Columbard Way 43230
N Columbia Ave
1-599 43209
600-699 43219
S Columbia Ave 43209
Columbia Pl 43209
Columbian Ave 43223
Columbine Ct 43230
Columbus Ave 43209
Columbus Ct 43209
Columbus Sq 43231
E Columbus St 43206
W Columbus St 43206
S Columbus Airport Rd 43207
Column Dr 43221
Colvin Rd 43232
Comet Rd 43232
Commander Ln 43224
Commerce Sq 43228
Commerce Loop Dr 43240
Commercial Ln 43232
Commission Dr 43230
Commodore St 43224
Commonwealth Park N & S 43209
Communications Pkwy 43214
Community Park Dr 43229
E Como Ave
1-699 43202
800-1199 43224
W Como Ave 43202
Compass St 43240
Compton Dr 43219
Comstock Dr 43232
Conant Dr 43229
Concord Ave 43212
Concord Ln 43224
Concord Pl 43206
Concord Rd 43212
Concord Hill Dr 43213
Concord Village Dr 43220
Concourse Dr & Loop 43229
Concrea Rd 43219
Condon Dr 43232
Conestoga Dr 43213
Confederation Dr 43207
Congress St 43232
Congressional Way 43235
Conneaut Ct 43224
Connecticut Ave 43229
Connell Aly 43215
Connie Ct 43227
Connors Grv 43213
Connors Point Dr 43220
Conover Pl 43227
Conrad Dr 43207
Constitution Pl 43235
Conway Dr 43227
Cook Cleland Ave 43217
E Cooke Rd
1-839 43214
840-2199 43224
W Cooke Rd 43214
Coolidge Ave 43228
Cooper Rd 43231
Cooper Bluff Dr 43231
Cooper Ridge Rd 43231
Copeland Rd 43212
Copper Glen St 43235
Copperfield Dr 43235
Coppertree Ln & Rd 43232
Coral Berry Dr 43235
Coral Tree Ct 43228
Corban Commons Dr 43219
Corbin St 43207
Corby Dr 43207
Cordell Ave
1400-1649 43211
1650-1799 43219
Cordero Ln 43230
Coriander Pl & St 43230
Corinne Creek Dr 43232
Cornelius St 43215
Cornell St 43219
Cornish Ct 43207
Coronation Ave 43230
Coronet Dr 43224
Corporate Dr 43231
Corporate Exchange Dr 43231
Corporate Hill Pkwy 43085
Corr Rd 43207
Corrugated Way 43201
Cortina Ct & Ln 43085
Cortney Ln 43229
Cortona Rd 43204
Corvair Ave & Blvd 43207
Corvette Ct 43232
Corwin Ave 43219
Cotswold Pl 43230
Cottage Ave 43205
Cottage St 43230
Cottingham Ct E & W 43209
Cottonwood Dr 43229
Cottrell Ct & Dr 43228
Coulter Ave 43207
Country Rd 43213
Country Club Rd
400-957 43213
959-1021 43213
1050-1599 43227
Country Corner Dr 43220
Countrybrook Dr E & W 43228
Courtland Ave 43201
Courtley Dr 43232
Courtney Pl 43235
Courtright Ct 43227
Courtright Ln 43232
Courtright Rd
1300-1899 43227
2000-3099 43232
Courtside Dr 43232
Cove Ave 43232
Cove Point Ct & Dr 43228
Coventry Ct 43232
Coventry Ct N 43232
Coventry Ct S 43232
Coventry Dr 43232
Coventry Ln 43232
Coventry Rd
1700-2059 43212
2060-2799 43221
Coventry Sq 43213
Cover Pl 43235
Covert Ct & Dr 43231
Covina Dr 43228
Covington Rd 43229
Cowton Dr 43228
Cozzins St 43215
Cradiso Ave 43217
Crafton Park 43221
Craig Ct 43204
Craigmore Ct 43231
Craigs Way 43221
Craigside Dr 43235
Cranberry Ct 43213
Crandall Dr 43085
Cranfield Pl 43213
Cranford Rd 43221
Cranwood Dr & Sq N, S & W 43229
Crater Lake Ln 43085
Crawdaddy Ln 43228
Crawford Dr 43229
Creek Dr 43231
Creek Ridge Ct 43230
Creek Run Dr 43231
Creekhaven Dr 43207
Creekhill Rd 43223
Creeks Bank Ln 43213
Creeksedge Dr 43209
Creekside Dr 43223
Creekside Plz 43230
Creekside Green Dr 43230
N Creekway Ct 43230
S Creekway Ct 43230
Creekway Dr 43207
Creekwood Ave 43223
Creighton Ct 43230
Crenshaw Dr 43230
Crescent Ct 43085
Crescent Dr 43204
Crescent Rd 43204
Cressing Ct & Pl 43227
Cressingham Ct 43214
Cresthill Dr 43221
Crestview Rd 43202
Crestway Dr 43235
Crestwood Ave 43227
Crevis Ln 43228
Cricket Pl 43231
Crimson Ct 43235
Crisfield Dr 43204
Criswell Dr 43220
Critchfield Rd 43213
Crocker Rd 43232
Croft Farm Dr 43235
Crompton Dr 43220
Cromwell Ave 43204
Cromwell Dixon St 43217
Crooked Mile Rd 43230
Cross Country Dr 43235
Cross Creek Dr 43204
Cross Keys Rd 43232
Cross Pointe Rd 43230
Crosscreek Dr 43232
Crossford St 43219
Crossgate Pl 43229
Crossgate Rd 43232
Crossing Crk N 43230
Crossing Crk S 43230
Crossing Ct 43231
Crossing Creek Way 43230
Crossing Hill Way 43219
Crossover Blvd 43235
Crosspointe Dr 43207
Crossroads Ctr 43232
Crossroads Plaza Dr 43219
Crosstree Ct 43221
Crosswind Dr 43228
Crosswoods Dr 43235
Croswell Rd 43214
Crowhurst Dr 43235
Crowley Rd 43207
Crown Ave 43207
Crown Crest Ln 43235
Crown Hill Ct 43230
Crown Park Ct 43235
Crown Plaza Dr 43235
Crown Point Dr 43220
Crown Ridge Blvd 43235
Crownwood Dr 43228
Crupper Ave 43229
Crusoe Dr 43235
Cryodon Blvd N & W 43232
Crystal Cay Ct 43230
Culbertson St 43215
Cullen Dr 43232
Cullman Rd 43207
Culpepper Ct 43207
Cumberland Dr 43213
Cumberland St 43219
Cumberland Woods Dr 43219
Cummington Ct, Pl & Rd 43213
Cunard Rd & Sq 43227
Curl Dr 43210
Curleys Ct 43235
Currency Dr 43228
Currier Dr 43207
Curtis St 43207
Curtis Lemay Ave 43217
Cushing Dr 43227
Custer Ct 43207
Cutlip Dr 43085
Cutter Ct 43235
Cuyahoga Ct 43210
Cyber Ave 43221
Cygnus Ln 43240
N Cypress Ave 43222

S Cypress Ave
1-169 43222
170-399 43223
Cypress Ln 43230
Cypress Chase 43228
Cypress Club Way 43219
Cypress Creek Ct & Dr 43228
Cypress Ridge Pl 43228
Cypresswood Ct & Rd 43229
Cyprus Ct 43207
D Ave 43207
Daffodil Dr 43230
Daglow Rd 43232
Dahlia Way 43235
Dahltry Ln 43220
Daily Rd 43232
Daisy Ln 43204
Daisyfield Dr 43219
Dakota Ave
1-169 43222
170-499 43223
Dale Ave
2100-3199 43209
3200-3399 43213
Dalehurst Rd 43219
Daleton Pl 43232
Dalewood Rd 43229
Dalmeny Ct 43220
Dana Ave
1-169 43222
170-599 43223
Dana Dr 43209
Danbury Pl 43235
Danby Dr 43211
Dancer Pl 43230
Dandelion Dr 43231
Dandridge Dr 43229
Dandy Brush Ln E & W 43230
Daner Rd 43213
Danforth Rd 43224
Danhurst Rd 43228
Daniel Burnham Sq 43215
Danmoor Rd 43232
Dans Ave 43207
Danvers Ct 43220
Danwood Dr 43228
Darby Ln 43229
Darbyhurst Rd 43228
Darcann Dr 43220
Darcy Rd 43229
Darfield Pl 43209
Darien Ave 43228
Dark Star Ave & Pl 43230
Darlington Rd 43220
Darracq Cir 43223
Dartmouth Ave 43219
Darwin Dr 43235
Dashshund Ct 43232
Datune Ct 43229
Daugherty Ave 43207
Daventry Ln 43230
Daventry Rd 43220
David Ct 43224
David Harris Ave 43217
Davis Ave 43207
S Davis Ave 43222
Dawes Dr 43207
Dawn Ct 43232
Dawnlight Ave 43211
N Dawson Ave 43219
S Dawson Ave 43209
Dawson Pl 43209
Dayton Ave 43202
Daytona Rd 43228
Deacon Cir 43214
Deanne Ln 43223
Dearborn Dr 43085
Dearborn Park Ln 43085
Deborah Ct 43229
Debra Ln 43230
Decaro House 43219
Dechant Ct & Rd 43229
Deckenbach Rd 43223
Decker Ct 43235
Declaration Dr 43230
Dedham St 43224
Deep Shadow Ct 43231
Deephollow Ct & Dr 43228
Deer Crossing Ct & Ln 43085
Deer Hollow Dr 43235
Deer Knoll Dr 43230
Deer Lake Ct & Way 43204
Deer Meadow Dr 43230
Deer Ridge Ln 43229
Deer Run Dr 43230
Deer Tail Ct 43230
Deerbrook Ln 43213
Deercreek Ct & Dr 43085
Deerfield Rd 43228
Deerlick Dr 43228
Deerwood Ave E 43230
Deewood Ct, Dr & Loop E, N, S & W 43229
Deffenbaugh Ct 43230
Defford Ct 43227
Defiance Dr 43210
Deforest Dr 43232
Dehner Dr 43227
Deignese Pl 43228
Dejoan Ct 43228
Delamere Ave 43220
Delancey St 43220
Deland Ave 43214
Delaney Dr 43207
Delashmut Ave 43212
Delavan Dr 43219
Delawanda Ave 43214
Delaware Ave
823-872 43215
900-1099 43201
Delbert Rd
1400-1799 43219
2200-2499 43211
Delcane Dr 43235
Delegate Dr 43235
Delgany St 43228
Delhi Ave 43202
Dell Ave 43211
Della Pl 43228
Dellfield Ln & Way 43230
Dellwin Ct 43231
Dellwood Ave 43227
Dellworth St 43232
Delmar Dr 43209
Delmont Ct 43235
Delno Ave 43224
Delport Way 43232
Delray Rd 43207
N Delta Dr 43214
Demaret Ln 43228
Deming Ave 43202
Demington Rd 43232
Demorest Rd
1-1299 43204
1300-1899 43228
Dempster Dr 43228
Denbigh Ct & Dr 43220
Denbridge Way 43219
Dendra Ln 43085
Denise Dr 43229
Denison Ave & Ct 43230
Denmark Rd 43232
Dennison Ave
601-757 43215
759-899 43215
900-1399 43201
Denos Ct 43220
Densmore Rd 43224
Denton Aly 43206
Denune Ave 43211
Denver Ave 43209
Denwood Ct & Dr 43230
Depauw Ct 43230
Deporres Dr 43219
Depot Dr 43228
Derby Rd 43221
Derby Hall 43210
Derbyshire Dr 43224
Dering Ave 43207
Derrer Ct & Rd 43204
Derrer Den Ln 43204
Derrer Estates Pl 43204
Derrer Field Dr 43204
Derrer Height Ln 43204
Derrer Hill Dr 43204
Derrer Hollow Way 43204
Derrer Meadow Ln 43204
Derrer Run Dr 43204
Derry Ct 43221
Desantis Ct & Dr 43214
Deserette Ct & Ln 43224
E Deshler Ave
1-1599 43206
3100-3899 43227
W Deshler Ave 43206
Detroit Ave 43201
Devaney Ct 43230
Devilling Ct 43235
Devlin Ct 43228
N Devon Rd
1800-2099 43212
2100-2199 43221
W Devon Rd 43212
Devonhill Ct & Rd 43229
Devonhurst Dr 43232
Devonshire Rd 43219
Devontry Ln 43220
Devton Dr 43228
Dewberry Rd 43207
Dewey Ave 43219
Dexham Ct 43224
Dexter Ave 43204
Dexter Ct 43207
Dexter Row 43221
Dexter Falls Rd 43221
Dial Dr 43213
Diamond Loch 43228
Diamond View Dr 43223
Diamondcut Dr 43231
Diana Pl 43231
Diane Pl 43207
Dibblee Ave 43204
Dick Ave 43201
Dickens Dr 43227
Dickson Dr 43228
Diem Ave 43219
Dierker Rd
4700-5100 43220
5102-5298 43220
5500-5799 43235
Dill St 43207
Dillingham Ct 43228
Dillmont Dr 43235
Dillon Dr 43227
Dillward Dr 43219
Dimson Dr E 43213
Dinard Way 43221
Dinon Dr 43221
Dinsmore Castle Dr 43221
Diplomacy Dr 43228
Directory Dr 43213
Discovery Dr 43085
Distribution Dr 43228
Diven Ct & Ln 43230
Dividend Dr 43228
Divot Pl 43211
Dixie Ct 43228
Dixon Aly 43206
Dixon Ct 43214
Dlyn St 43228
Dobson Sq E 43229
Dodd Dr 43210
E & W Dodridge St 43202
Doe Run 43223
Doeskin Ct 43085
Doewood Ct & St 43229
Dogwood Dr 43228
Dolan Pl 43228
Dolby Dr 43207
Dolle Ave 43211
Dollivor Dr 43235
Dolomite Ct & Dr 43230
Domain Dr 43230
E & W Dominion Blvd 43214
Don Eisele Rd 43217
Donahey St 43235
Donahue Ct 43235
Donalda Ct 43231
Doncaster Rd 43221
Dondondo Ave 43203
Donegal Ct 43228
Doney Ct & St 43213
Donington Rd 43220
Donlyn Ct 43232
Donna Dr 43220
Donnylane Blvd 43235
Donora Ln 43235
Dontante Ave 43205
Donwalter Ln 43235
Doone Rd 43221
Doral Ave 43213
S Dorchester Rd 43221
Doreen Ct 43221
Doren Ave 43223
Dorko Ct 43224
Dorothy Dr 43224
Dorris Ave 43202
Dorset Rd 43221
Dorsetshire Rd 43229
Dorsey Dr 43235
Dort Pl 43227
Dory Ln 43235
Doten Ave 43212
Doubletree Ave 43229
Douglas Dr 43230
S Douglass St 43205
Doulton Ct 43228
Dove Dr 43219
Dover Ave 43212
Dover Ct 43085
Dover Rd
2300-3099 43209
3200-3599 43204
Dovewood Dr 43230
Dow Ave 43211
Dowitcher Ln 43230
Downey Dr 43235
Downhill Dr 43221
Downing Dr 43232
Downing Way 43221
Downs St 43085
Downwing Ln 43230
Dragonfly Dr 43204
Drake Rd 43219
Drayton Park Ct 43212
Dresden St
2000-2098 43211
2100-2609 43211
2710-4399 43224
Drew Ave 43235
Drexel Ave 43207
N Drexel Ave
1-599 43209
600-899 43219
S Drexel Ave 43209
Driffield Ct 43221
Drifton Dr 43227
Driftwood Rd 43229
Druid St 43202
Drumbarton Ct 43235
Drumcliff Ct 43221
Drummond Ct 43214
Drury Ln 43235
Drysdale Sq N 43229
Dsw Dr 43219
Dubay Ave 43219
Dublin Fls 43221
Dublin Rd
700-920 43215
922-1600 43215
1602-1698 43215
2000-2599 43228
3120-3298 43221
3300-4938 43221
E Dublin Granville Rd
1-589 43085
590-2499 43229
2469-2471 43226
2500-3299 43231
W Dublin Granville Rd
1-400 43085
402-498 43085
500-1816 43085
1818-2310 43085
2311-3741 43235
3743-3749 43235
Ducat St 43207
Duchene Ln 43213
Duck Hollow Ct 43230
Ducrest Ct & Dr 43220
Duffield Dr 43227
Duffy St 43235
Duke Rd 43213
Dulcet Ln 43229
Dumont Ln 43235
Dunbar Dr 43224
Dunbarton Rd 43230
Dunbridge St 43224
Dunbrooke Ct 43228
Dunbury Dr 43228
E & W Duncan St 43202
Dunchurch Rd 43230
Dundee Ave, Ct & Pl 43227
E Dunedin Rd
1-599 43214
900-1899 43224
W Dunedin Rd 43214
Dunfield Ln 43232
Dunford Dr 43221
Dunhill St 43235
Dunkirk Dr 43219
Dunkle Dr 43223
Dunlane Ct 43228
Dunlap Rd 43229
Dunlavin Glen Rd 43221
Dunloe Pl & Rd 43232
Dunn Ct 43207
Dunne Dr 43207
Dunning Ct & Rd 43219
Dunoon Dr 43230
Dunraven Ct 43231
Dunstan Dr 43235
Dunster Ct 43230
Dunsworth Dr 43235
Dupler Ln 43207
Dupont Ave 43201
Duquesne Pl 43235
Durant Ave 43232
Durbin Rd 43213
Durbridge Rd 43229
Durham Dr 43207
Durness Ct, Dr & Pl 43235
Durrell Rd 43229
Durrow Dr 43228
Durwin Ave 43207
Dustins Way 43228
Dutton Pl 43227
Duvall Ln 43207
Duxberry Ave
900-1599 43211
1600-1699 43219
Dwight Ave 43228
Dyer Ln 43228
Dynasty Dr 43235
Dysart Ave 43219
E Ave 43207
Eagle Head Dr 43230
Eagle View Ct & Dr 43228
Eakin Rd
2000-2359 43223
2361-2465 43204
2467-3664 43204
3665-3999 43228
Earhart Ave 43228
Earl Ave
2000-2299 43211
3600-3899 43219
Early Ct 43207
Earncliff Dr 43219
Earnings Dr 43232
East Ave 43202
East St 43228
Eastapryl Dr 43209
Eastbrook Dr N & S 43223
Eastbury Woods Dr 43230
Eastcherry Ave 43230
Eastchester Ct & Dr 43230
Eastcleft Dr 43221
Eastern St 43207
Eastern Glen Dr 43219
Eastern Pine Rd 43232
Eastfield Dr 43223
Eastfield Dr N 43223
Eastfield Rd 43085
Eastgate Pkwy 43230
Eastham Way 43228
Easthaven Ct & Dr N & S 43232
Easthill Dr 43213
Eastland Dr 43232
Eastland Mall 43232
Eastland Rd 43085
Eastland Food Ct 43232
Eastland Square Dr 43232
Eastlea Dr 43214
Eastman Ave 43207
Eastmeadow Pl 43235
Eastminster Rd 43209
Eastmoor Blvd 43209
Eastmoreland Dr 43209
Easton Cmns 43219
Easton Loop E 43219
Easton Loop W 43219
Easton Oval 43219
Easton Pl 43221
Easton Sta 43219
Easton Way 43219
Easton Gateway Dr 43219
Easton Market 43219
Easton Square Pl 43219
Easton Town Ctr 43219
Eastpoint Dr 43232
Eastpointe Ridge Dr 43213
Eastview Ave 43212
Eastview Ct 43228
Eastview Dr 43085
Eastway Ct 43213
Eastwick Rd 43232
Eastwood Ave 43203
Eastworth Ct & Way 43085
Easy Ct 43231
Eaton Ave 43223
Eatonia Pl 43228
Ebner St 43206
Echele Dr 43240
Echo Ct & Rd 43230
Echo Hill Ct 43240
Echomoore Dr 43231
Echorock Dr 43231
Eddington Dr 43224
Eddystone Ave 43224
Eden Aly 43215
Eden Ave 43224
Edenbrook Ct 43221
Edenburgh Dr E & S 43219
Edencreek Ln 43207
Edendale Ct & Rd 43207
Edenhurst St 43224
Edgar Pl 43211
Edge Crk 43231
Edgecliff Dr 43235
Edgecreek Ln 43231
Edgefield Rd 43221
Edgehill Dr 43220
Edgehill Rd 43212
N Edgemont Rd 43212
Edgevale Rd
1-299 43209
2100-2799 43221
Edgeview Rd 43207
Edgeway Dr 43231
Edgewood Rd 43220
Edinburgh Ln 43229
Edington Rd 43221
Edinwick Way 43232
Edmonton Rd 43229
Edsel Ave & Ct 43207
Edson Dr N 43228
Edward St
300-699 43215
700-799 43203
Edwards Farms Rd 43221
Edwards Plantation Dr 43221
Edwin St 43223
Eel Ct 43235
Effingham Rd 43213
Effington Ln 43207
Efner Dr 43227
Ehring Rd 43211
Eiger Dr 43213
Eisenhower Rd
3000-3999 43224
5200-5399 43229
El Cid Ct 43204
El Greco Dr 43204
El Nino Dr 43204
El Paso Dr 43204
El Toro Dr 43204
Elaine Ct 43227
Elaine Pl N 43227
Elaine Pl S 43227
Elaine Rd
400-899 43213
900-1899 43227
Elaine Park Dr 43227
Elam Way 43228
Elan Ct 43220
Elana Ave 43230
Elbern Ave
2900-3199 43209
3200-4299 43213
Elco Dr 43224
Elda Ct & St 43203
Elder Ln 43227
Elderberry Ct 43220
Elderwood Ave 43227
Eldon Ave 43204
Eldorn Dr E 43207
Eldridge Ave 43203
Electra St 43240
Elgate Pl 43230
Elgin Rd 43221
Elginfield Rd 43220
Elim Estates Dr 43232
Elim Manor Ct 43232
Eliots Oak Rd 43228
Elite St 43231
Elizabeth Ave
500-749 43213
750-1199 43227
Elks Dr 43214
Elkton St 43207
Elkwood Pl 43230
Ella Ct 43231
Ellerdale Dr 43230
Ellery Dr 43227
Ellicot Ct 43223
Ellinger St 43235
Ellington Cir 43230
Ellington Rd 43221
Elliott Aly 43215
Elliott Ave 43204
Elliott St 43205
Ellis Pl 43204
Ellison St 43203
Ellsworth Ave
800-1549 43206
1900-1999 43207
Elm Ave 43209
Elm Dr 43235
Elm Pass 43213
Elm Rd 43217
Elm St 43213
Elm Bluff Way 43213
Elmer St 43223
Elmers Ct 43085
Elmhurst Ave 43231
Elmira Dr 43232
Elmore Ave & Ct E, S & W 43224
Elmreeb Dr 43219
Elmsbury Ct 43213
Elmwood Ave 43212
Elsinor Rd 43219
Elsmere St 43206
Elspeth Ct 43231
Elton Rd 43219
Elwood Ave 43207
Embassy Ct 43230

Emco Pl 43085
Emeline Ct & Dr 43204
Emerald Ave 43203
Emeraldcut Dr 43231
Emerius Dr 43219
Emerson Ave 43085
Emery Club Way 43219
Emig Rd 43223
Emil Ave 43207
Emmit Ave 43228
Emmons Ave 43219
Emory St 43230
Empire Dr N 43230
Emporium Sq 43231
Empress Ln 43235
Emrick Ct 43232
Emslie Dr 43224
En Joie Ct & Dr 43228
Enderly Dr 43219
Endicott Rd 43229
Enfield Rd 43209
Engadine Ave 43223
England Dr 43240
Englander Ct 43085
Engle Dr 43207
E Engler St
2-152 43215
154-699 43215
800-1400 43205
1402-1698 43205
Englewood Dr 43219
English Rd 43207
English Way 43201
Enterprise Ave 43228
Enterprise Dr 43230
Epsom Ct 43221
Equestrian Ct 43221
Equity Dr 43228
Eric Pl 43235
Erickson Ave
400-899 43213
900-1108 43227
Erickson Rd 43227
Erie Rd 43214
Ernie Hall Rd 43217
Errington Rd 43227
Esker Dr 43207
Esmond St 43202
Esplanade St 43221
Essex Ave
1100-1349 43201
1350-1499 43211
Essex Rd 43221
Estates Pl 43224
Estel Rd 43235
Esterbrook Rd 43229
Estes St 43207
Esther Dr 43207
Ethel Ave 43219
Ethel Rd 43207
Etna Rd 43213
Etna St
2800-3199 43209
3575-4249 43213
Eton Ct 43230
Eton Grv 43203
Etrick Dr 43220
Euclaire Ave 43209
Euclid Ave 43201
N Eureka Ave 43204
S Eureka Ave 43204
Eureka Blvd 43223
Eva Ln 43227
Evaline Dr 43224
Evangeline Dr 43235
Evans Way Ct 43228
Evansdale Rd 43214
Evanston Rd 43232
Evanswood Dr 43229
Evening St 43085
Evening Star Rd 43240
Everby Way 43232
Everest Way 43231
N & S Everett Ave 43213
Evergreen Cir 43085
Evergreen Rd 43207
Evergreen Ter 43228
Everson Rd E 43232
Everton Pl 43235
Everwood Ave 43214
Evinrude Ave 43229
Ewald Dr 43232
Ewing Aly 43201
Excalibur Pl 43235
Exchange Dr 43228
Executive Dr 43220
Exeter Rd 43213
Exmoor Rd 43221
Exploration Ct & Dr 43085
Express Dr 43230
Exton Ct 43230
F Ave 43207
Faber Ave 43207
Fabron Ave 43203
Faculty Dr 43221
Fahlander Dr N & S 43229
Fahy Dr 43223
Faincha Dr 43232
Faintint Rd 43213
Fair Ave
1000-1599 43205
2000-3179 43209
3180-3201 43213
3203-3499 43213
Fairbank Rd 43207
Faircrest Rd 43229
Fairfax Ave 43207
Fairfax Dr 43220
Fairfax Rd 43221
Fairfield Ave 43203
Fairfield Pl 43223
Fairgarth Cir 43207
Fairgate Ave & Pl 43206
Fairglade Ln 43224
Fairgrove Rd 43231
Fairhaven Rd 43229
Fairholme Rd 43230
Fairlane Rd 43207
Fairlawn Dr 43214
Fairlington Dr 43220
Fairmont Ave 43223
Fairmoor Pl & Rd 43228
Fairoaks Dr 43214
Fairport Dr 43213
Fairview Ave 43212
Fairway Blvd 43213
Fairway Cir 43213
Fairway Ct 43214
Fairway Dr
100-399 43214
7900-8499 43235
Fairway Oaks Dr 43213
Fairwind Dr 43235
Fairwood Ave
200-869 43205
870-1699 43206
1700-3299 43207
Faith Ave 43213
Falcon Bridge Dr 43232
Falcon Hunter Way 43230
Falkirk Pl 43229
Fall Brook Rd 43223
Fall Creek Ln 43235
Fall Water Ct 43220
Fallgate Ct 43235
Fallhaven Dr 43235
Falling Water Ln 43240
Fallis Rd 43214
Fallow Ct 43230
Falmouth Ct 43085
Fancyfree Ln 43231
Faneuil Hall Pl 43230
Fanwick Ct 43230
Far Hills Dr 43224
Farber Ct & Row 43221
Farberdale Dr 43223
Fareham Ct 43232
Farleigh Rd 43221
Farler Dr 43213
Farlook Ct 43231
Farm Creek Dr 43230
Farm View St 43232
Farmbrook Ln 43204
Farmers Dr 43235
Farmhurst Ct & Ln 43204
Farmington Dr 43213
Farmlane Dr 43085
Farms Dr 43213
Farmwood Pl 43230
Farnham Rd 43220
Farnsworth House 43219
Farrel Dr 43235
Farrington Dr 43085
Farthing Ln 43232
Farview Dr 43231
Fashion Mall Pkwy 43240
Fassett Ave 43201
Faunsdale Dr 43228
Faversham Dr 43228
Fawn Ct 43085
Fawn Meadow Ct 43085
Fawndale Pl 43230
Faycrest Rd 43232
Faye Dr 43230
Fayette Dr 43224
Faymeadow Ave & Ln 43229
Featherwood Dr 43228
Febor Ct 43204
Feder Rd 43228
Federal Pkwy 43207
Federated Blvd 43235
Felix Dr 43207
Fenceway Dr 43229
Fenchurch Way 43230
Fenimore Ct 43232
Fenlon St 43219
Fenstermaker Ln 43085
Fenton St 43224
Fenway Ct, Pl & Rd 43214
Fenwick Ct & Rd 43220
Fenwood Dr 43232
Fergus Rd 43207
Ferman Rd 43207
Fern Ave & Pl 43211
Ferndale Pl 43209
Fernhill Ave 43228
Fernleaf Ln 43235
Ferntree Rd 43219
Fernwood Ave 43212
Ferrell Pl 43204
Ferris Rd 43224
Ferris Park Dr 43224
Ficus Dr 43085
Fidelity Rd 43235
Fieldpointe Ct 43221
Fields Ave
1100-1349 43201
1350-1499 43211
Fieldstone Pl 43235
Fieser St 43206
Fiesta Ct 43229
Fiesta Dr 43235
Figian Sq 43207
Filco Dr 43207
Fincastle Ct 43235
Finch Shelter Dr 43235
Findley Ave 43202
Finland Ave 43223
Finstock Ct & Way 43230
Fiona Ln 43211
Firebush Ln 43235
Firefly Ct 43221
Firefox Dr 43213
Firestone St 43228
Firth Ave 43085
Firwood Dr & Pl 43229
Fish Hawk Lndg 43230
Fishburn Ct & St 43207
Fisher Pl 43221
Fisher Rd
2400-3529 43204
3530-3548 43228
3531-3549 43204
3550-5599 43228
Fisher Run Ct 43235
Fishinger Rd 43221
Fisk St 43224
Fitchburg Dr 43228
Fitz Henry Blvd 43214
Fitzroy Dr & Pl 43224
Flags Center Dr 43229
S Flanchig Ave 43204
Flanders Ct 43235
Flat Head Ct 43230
Flat Rock Ct 43235
Flat Rock Dr 43235
Flat Rock Run 43240
Fleet Rd 43232
Fleetrun Ave 43230
Fleetwood Dr 43229
Fleming Rd 43232
Fletcher St 43215
Flicker Dr 43230
Flint Rd 43235
Flint Ridge Dr 43230
Flint Run Pl 43235
Flint Valley Ct 43085
Flinthill Dr 43223
Flintlock Ln 43213
Flintwood Dr 43230
Flora Villa Dr 43085
Floral Ave 43223
Floral Cir S 43228
Florence Ave 43228
Flores Pl 43213
Florian Dr 43219
Floribunda Dr 43209
Floridale St 43235
Flowerdew Ln 43228
Floyd Dr 43232
Flynnhaven Ct 43221
Flynnway Dr 43085
Folger Dr 43227
Folkestone Ct & Rd 43220
Folkstone Rd 43220
Fondorf Dr 43228
Fontaine Rd 43232
Fontenay Ct 43235
Fontenay Pl 43220
Foos St 43222
Footemill Ln 43235
Footloose Dr 43231
Foraker Dr 43219
Ford St 43205
Fordham Rd 43224
Forest Ave 43214
Forest Dr 43223
Forest St 43206
Forest Trl 43230
Forest Ash Ln 43229
Forest Birch Ln 43229
Forest Cedar Ct 43229
Forest Creek Dr E 43223
Forest Creek Circle Dr 43223
Forest Edge Dr 43230
Forest Elm Ct & Ln 43229
Forest Green Ct 43232
Forest Hill Dr 43221
Forest Hills Blvd 43231
Forest Maple Ln 43229
Forest Oak Ln 43229
Forest Ridge Ct, Dr &
Pl 43235
Forest Village Ln 43229
Forest Willow Ct & Ln 43229
Forestview Dr 43213
Forestwood Dr 43230
Forestwood Rd 43229
Fornoff Rd 43207
Forsythe Ave 43201
Fortin Ct 43229
Fortner St 43207
Fortress Pl & Trl 43230
Fortstone Ln 43228
Fossil Dr 43204
Foster Ave
5300-5411 43214
5413-5543 43214
5545-5799 43085
Foster St 43214
Foundation Dr 43219
Founders Ct 43230
Founders Ridge Dr 43230
Fountain Ln 43213
Fountain Square Ct &
Dr 43224
Fountaine Dr 43221
Fountainview Ct 43232
Four Seasons Dr 43207
Fowler Dr 43224
Fox Dr 43220
Fox Ln 43085
Fox Chaple Dr 43232
Fox Glove Ln 43230
Fox Hollow Dr 43228
Fox Hunt Trl 43221
Fox Ridge Ct & St 43228
Fox River Run 43231
Fox Tail Dr 43230
Foxboro Ct & Ln 43235
Foxbury Ct 43228
Foxcroft Ct & Grn 43232
Foxfield Ct 43235
Foxmoor Pl 43235
Foxwood Dr 43230
Foxworth Dr 43231
Fraley Ct & Dr 43235
E Frambes Ave 43201
Framingham Cir 43224
Framington Dr 43224
Frances Ct 43230
Frances Pl 43201
Francine Ct 43232
Francinelane Dr 43235
Francis Ave 43209
Francis Scott Key
Way 43207
Francisco Ct, Pl & Rd 43220
Francisco Glen Dr 43220
Frank Rd
300-499 43207
500-2299 43223
E & W Frankfort Sq &
St 43206
Franklin Aly 43228
Franklin Ave
100-399 43085
500-695 43215
696-1899 43205
2500-2599 43223
Franklin Ct 43085
Franklin Ln 43229
Franklin Park S 43205
Franklin Park W 43205
Franklin Rd 43209
Franksway St 43232
Franshire E 43228
Frazier Rd E 43207
Frebis Ave & Ln 43206
Fred Taylor Dr 43210
Frederick St 43206
Fredericksburg Ave 43228
Freedom Crossing Rd 43235
Freedom Ridge Ct &
Dr 43230
Freeman Ave 43215
Freeway Dr E 43229
Fremont Ct & St 43204
French Dr 43228
French Creek Ct & Dr 43207
Frenchpark Ct & Dr 43231
Friar Ln 43221
Friars Green Ln 43213
Friend St 43235
Friendship Dr 43230
Frisbee Dr 43224
N Front St 43215
S Front St
1-640 43215
641-1299 43206
Frontenac Pl 43085
Frost Ave 43228
Frusta Dr 43207
Fuji Dr 43229
Fullen Rd 43229
Fuller Dr 43214
Fullerton Dr 43232
E Fulton St
34-598 43215
700-2099 43205
3200-4399 43227
Funston Ct & Pl 43232
Furnace St 43215
Fyffe Ct & Rd 43210
Gables Ct 43235
Gablewood Dr 43219
Gabriel Ct 43228
Gabrielle Elaine Dr 43228
Gadston Way 43228
Gadwall Rd 43230
Gaffney Ct 43228
Gafford Dr 43229
Gage St 43240
Gahanna Pkwy 43230
Gahanna Highlands Dr 43230
Gail Ave 43224
Gainsborough Ct 43220
Gairlock Dr 43228
Galaxie St 43207
Galecrest Dr 43207
Gallant Dr 43232
Gallatin Dr 43207
Gallery St 43230
Galli Ct 43228
Galliton Ct 43220
Galton Ct 43220
Galveston Dr 43228
Galway Crossing Dr 43221
Gamewood Dr 43230
Gannett Rd 43231
Ganson Dr 43224
Gardeau Ct 43223
Garden Dr 43085
Garden Rd
1-799 43214
800-1199 43224
Garden Rdg 43228
Garden Glen Ln 43228
Garden Heights Ave 43228
Garden Terrace Rd 43229
Gardenbrooke St 43235
Gardendale Dr W 43219
Gardenia Dr 43235
Gardenstone Dr 43235
Gardenway Ct 43230
N Garfield Ave 43203
S Garfield Ave 43205
Garling Ave 43223
Garmouth Ct 43221
Garnet Pl 43232
Garrard Dr 43207
Garrett Dr & Pl 43214
Garrison Dr 43085
Garston Ct 43230
Gartner Ct & Dr 43207
Garvey Rd 43229
Gary Dr 43207
Gary Dennis Dr 43229
Gary Ganue Dr 43228
Gary Lee Dr 43230
Garywood Ave 43227
Gatehouse Dr 43213
Gatehouse Ln 43235
E & W Gates St 43206
Gateside Ct 43230
Gatestone Ln 43235
Gateway Blvd 43228
Gateway Dr 43220
Gatewood Ct & Rd 43219
Gatwick Ct 43230
Gault St 43205
Gaver Ln 43223
Gavin Ln 43220
Gavinley Way 43220
E Gay St
1-499 43215
800-898 43203
900-1199 43203
W Gay St
1-679 43215
680-1099 43222
Gayle Dr
500-599 43230
2300-2999 43219
Gaylord Pl 43232
Gaynor Rd 43227
Geers Ave & Pl 43206
Gelbray Ave 43204
Gem Ln 43231
Gemini Pkwy & Pl 43240
W Gendinti St 43222
Genessee Ave
1000-2299 43211
3700-3999 43219
Geneva Ave 43223
Genevieve Dr 43219
Genoa Pl 43227
Gentry Ln 43232
George Page Jr Rd 43217
Georges Pl 43204
Georgesville Pl & Rd 43228
Georgesville Green Dr 43228
Georgesville Square
Dr 43228
Georgetown Dr 43214
Georgia Ave 43219
Georgian Dr 43228
Geormar Dr 43227
Gerald Ave 43211
Geraldine Ave 43219
Gerbert Rd
2100-2399 43211
2800-3699 43224
Gerling Blvd 43232
Gerrard Ave 43212
Gertrude Dr 43227
Gettysburg Rd 43220
Geyer Dr 43228
Gibbard Ave
500-1109 43201
1110-1699 43219
Gibbs Dr 43207
Gibbstone Dr 43204
Gibson Dr 43207
Gideon Ln 43219
Gifford Rd 43235
N & S Gift St 43215
Gilbert St
300-739 43205
740-1328 43206
1330-1330 43206
Gilby St 43230
Gilcrest Ave 43207
Giles Ct 43228
Gilhem Ct 43228
Gillespie Ct 43230
Gilligans Ct & Dr 43221
Gilman Rd 43228
Gilroy Rd 43227
Gilston Ct 43235
Gimbles Dr 43223
Gina Pl 43231
Ginger Pl 43230
Ginger Willow Ct 43228
Gingerclove Way 43213
Gioffre Woods Ln 43232
Giovanna Ave 43213
Girard Rd 43214
Gladden Rd 43212
Glade St 43085
Gladstone Ave
700-1299 43204
1700-1999 43211
Gladys Rd 43228
Glasgow Pl 43235
Glaston Pl 43232
Glen Cir & Dr 43085
Glen Cabin Ln 43230
Glen Cove Way 43204
Glen Echo Cir & Dr 43202
Glen Grove Ln 43231
Glenbar Ct & Dr 43219
Glenbriar Ct & St 43232
Glenbrook Dr 43232
Glenburn Ave & Pl 43214
Glencoe Rd 43214
Glencreek Rd 43223
Glenda Pl 43220
Glendale Ave 43212
Glendon Rd 43229
Glendora Rd 43207
Glendower Ave 43207

Glenellen Ct 43221
Glenfield Rd 43232
Glengarry Ct 43235
Glengate Dr 43232
Glengreen Ct 43229
Glenhaven Dr 43231
Glenhollow Ct 43235
Glenhurst Ct 43230
Glenlea Dr 43207
Glenmate Ct 43223
Glenmawr Ave
2300-2699 43202
4100-4699 43224
Glenmere Rd 43220
Glenmont Ave & Pl 43214
Glenmoor Dr 43228
Glenn Ave 43212
Glenoak Dr 43219
Glenrich Pkwy 43221
Glenridge Pl 43214
Glenshaw Ave & Pl 43231
Glenshire Dr 43219
Glenview Blvd 43204
N Glenwood Ave 43222
S Glenwood Ave
1-169 43222
170-499 43223
Glenwood Spring Ct 43228
Gleska Dr 43219
Gliddon Ct 43235
Globe St 43212
Gloria Ct 43231
Glorious Rd 43204
Glouchester Ave 43229
Godown Rd
4900-5199 43220
5200-6099 43235
Goethe St 43207
Gold Pl 43230
Golden Cloud Ln 43228
Golden Fern Ln 43228
Golden Leaf Ln 43223
Golden Springs Dr 43235
Goldengate Oval & Sq E, N, S & W 43224
Goldenrod Dr 43229
Goldmill Way 43204
Golf Green Dr 43224
Golfview Ct 43235
Golleang Rd 43227
Goodale Blvd 43212
E Goodale St 43215
W Goodale St 43215
Gordon Cir 43235
Gorham Dr 43223
Gorman Dr 43085
Gosbeak Cove Ln 43230
Goshawk Lndg 43230
Goshen Ct & Ln 43230
Gosling Way 43207
Gosling Gate Ln 43229
Gothic Ct 43230
N Gould Rd
1-579 43209
580-899 43219
S Gould Rd 43209
Governor Ct 43229
Governors Pl 43203
Governors Club Blvd 43219
Grace Ln 43220
Grace St 43204
Graceland Blvd 43214
Gracewood Ct 43229
Grafton Ave 43220
Graham St 43203
Graham House 43219
Gramercy St 43219
Gramford St 43240
Granada Hills Dr 43231
Granby St 43085
Grand Bahama Dr 43085
Grand Cayman Dr 43085
Grande Rue Cir 43229
Granden Rd 43214
Grandon Ave 43209
Grandover Dr 43207
Grandview Ave
600-860 43215
861-863 43212
862-864 43215
865-1699 43212
Granfield Ct 43230
Granite Pointe Dr 43213
Graniteway Ln 43229
N Grant Ave
1-33 43215
35-499 43215
800-1599 43201
S Grant Ave
1-411 43215
413-419 43215
500-899 43206
Grants Ln E & W 43228
Granville Sq 43085
Granville St
1-499 43230
1200-1699 43203
Grasmere Ave
1101-1897 43211
1899-2819 43211
2820-3499 43224
Grasmere Abbey Ln 43230
Grattan Rd 43227
Gravenhurst Ct 43231
Graves Dr 43207
Gray St 43201
Gray Gables Ln 43235
Gray Meadow Dr 43223
Graybeck Dr 43204
Graydon Blvd 43220
Grayfriars Ln 43224
Grayling Ct 43235
Grays Market Dr 43230
Grayson Dr 43207
Graystone Dr 43232
Great Brook Dr 43223
Great Hall Ct 43231
Great Lawn Way 43235
Great Oak Dr & Way 43213
Great Southern Blvd & Ct 43207
Great Western Blvd 43204
Great Woods Blvd 43231
Greatmoor St 43219
Grebus Rd 43207
Green Dr 43230
Green St 43228
N Green St 43222
S Green St 43222
Green Apple Ave 43229
Green Castle Ct 43221
Green Friar Dr 43228
Green Island Ct & Dr 43228
Green Jay Bnd 43230
Green Meadows Dr E 43230
Green Meadows Dr N 43230
Green Meadows Dr W 43230
Green Meadows St 43207
Green River Dr 43228
Green Springs Dr 43235
Green Trails Ct 43085
Greenbank Ct 43221
Greenbank Rd 43230
Greenbriar Ct 43085
Greenbrook Ct 43224
Greencamp Dr 43235
Greencrest Dr 43214
Greencroft Rd 43230
Greenery Dr 43207
Greenfield Dr 43223
Greenglade Ave 43085
Greenglen Ct 43229
Greenlawn Ave
49-99 43206
200-498 43223
500-1099 43223
Greenleaf Rd 43223
Greenock Ct & Rd 43228
Greenpine St 43232
Greenridge Rd 43235
Greensboro Ct & Dr 43220
Greensedge Way 43220
Greenside Ln 43235
Greensview Dr 43220
Greentree Ct 43220
Greenup Dr 43207
Greenvale Dr 43235
Greenville Rd 43223
Greenway Ave 43203
Greenway Ave N 43219
Greenway Ave S 43219
Greenwich St
500-5899 43085
2300-2709 43211
2710-3599 43224
Greenwold Ct 43235
E Greenwood Ave 43201
W Greenwood Ave 43201
Greenwood Ct 43213
Greenwood Pl 43213
Greenwood Rd 43213
Grenada Rd 43207
Grenadier Ct 43230
Grenadine Way 43235
N & S Grener Ave 43228
Grenerma Dr 43218
Grenoble Rd 43221
Grenville Dr 43231
N Gresham Rd 43204
Grey Cliff Ln 43221
Grey Fox Dr 43230
Grey Oaks Dr 43230
Greycliff Ln 43221
Greyhawk Cir 43240
Greyrocks Way 43235
Greystone Dr 43220
Greystone Village Dr 43228
Greythorne Pl 43230
Greywood Dr 43219
Griffen House Ct 43235
Griffith Ct 43235
Griggs Ave & Ct 43223
Griggsview Ct 43221
Grimes Dr 43204
Grimsby Rd 43227
Grinnell Dr 43231
Griswold St 43085
Grogan Ave 43211
Gromwell Dr 43221
Grosse Pt 43232
Grossgate Rd 43232
Groton Pl 43213
Grotto Ct 43235
Grove Cir 43230
Grove Dr 43230
Grove St
300-378 43215
380-499 43215
700-799 43203
Grove Hill Dr 43240
Grovedale Ct 43231
Groveport Rd 43207
Groveport East Rd 43207
Groves Rd 43232
Grovewood Dr 43207
N & S Grubb St 43215
Grunwell St 43201
Gudrun Rd 43202
Guernsey Ave 43204
Guildhall Dr 43209
N Guilford Ave 43222
S Guilford Ave 43223
Guilford Rd 43221
Guinevere Dr 43229
Gulf Stream Ct 43230
Gulliver Dr 43207
Gumwood Dr 43229
Gunderson Ct 43228
Gunston Dr 43232
Gustavus Ln 43205
Guston Pl 43230
Guthrie Ct & Rd 43207
Guyer St 43085
Gypsy Ln 43229
Habersack Ave 43207
Habitat Dr 43228
Hacket Dr 43232
Hackworth St 43207
Hadden Ln 43235
Haddon Rd 43209
Hadleigh Rd 43220
Hadley Dr 43228
Hafey Ave 43228
Hafton Rd 43204
Hafton Woods Ct & Dr 43204
Hager Ct 43230
Hagerman Dr 43235
N & S Hague Ave 43204
Haig Pt 43219
Haines Ave 43212
Haldy Ave 43204
Haldy Rd 43228
Hale Ct 43228
Halesworth Rd 43221
Halfhill Way 43207
Halifax Ct 43232
Halkirk St N & S 43229
Hall Ln 43230
Hall Rd 43228
Halleck Dr & Pl 43209
Halleyberry Dr 43230
Hallidon Ave 43203
Halligan Ave E 43085
Hallmark Pl 43085
Halloran Ct 43232
Hallridge Cir & Rd 43232
Hallworth Ave & Ct 43232
Halo St 43240
Halpern St 43230
Halsbury Cir 43230
Halsey Pl 43228
Halstead Rd 43221
Halstock Ct 43235
Haltonia Dr 43228
Hambrick St 43228
Hamden Way 43228
Hamilton Ave
1-97 43203
99-380 43203
382-598 43203
1600-2799 43211
2820-3299 43224
Hamilton Ct
400-599 43230
4420-4460 43232
Hamilton Ct E 43232
Hamilton Ct N 43232
Hamilton Ct S 43232
Hamilton Park 43203
N Hamilton Rd
1-402 43213
1-1000 43230
490-622 43219
624-646 43219
648-998 43219
1001-1097 43230
1002-1098 43230
1099-5999 43230
S Hamilton Rd
1-999 43213
1-499 43230
1000-1799 43227
2000-3700 43232
3702-4420 43232
Hamlet St
600-859 43215
860-1599 43201
Hamlin Pl 43227
Hammerton Dr 43228
Hammerwood Ct 43219
Hampshire Rd
1900-1999 43221
2800-3099 43209
Hampstead Dr & Ln N, S & W 43229
Hampton Ln 43220
N Hampton Rd 43213
S Hampton Rd
1-749 43213
750-1199 43227
2800-2999 43232
Hampton Woods Ct & Dr 43230
Hanbury Ct 43230
Hanby Sq E 43229
Hanford Sq & St 43206
Hanging Rock Ct 43230
Hanley St 43203
Hanna Dr 43211
Hannah Noble Way 43231
Hannaway Ln 43229
Hanning Dr 43207
Hanover St 43215
Hanover Hill Ct 43232
Hansen Ave 43224
Hanton Way 43213
Harbinger Cir E & W 43213
Harbor Blvd 43232
Harbor Bay Dr 43221
Harborough Dr 43230
Harborough Rd 43220
Harborton Dr 43228
Harbour Pointe 43231
Hard Rd 43235
Hardesty Ct, Dr & Pl E, N, S & W 43204
Harding Dr 43228
N Harding Rd 43209
S Harding Rd 43209
Hardtack Ct 43230
Hardwick Dr 43232
Hardy Way 43085
Hares Ear Dr 43230
Harland Ct & Dr 43207
Harley Dr 43202
Harlow Rd 43227
Harlton Ct 43221
Harmon Ave & Plz 43223
Harmony Ct & Dr 43230
Harmount Rd 43231
Harnet Ct 43231
Harold Pl 43211
Harper Rd 43204
Harpers Grove Ct 43223
Harr Ct 43231
Harran Ave 43235
Harrington Ct & Dr 43229
N & S Harris Ave 43204
Harrisburg Pike 43223
Harrison Ave
500-949 43215
950-1399 43201
Harrison Dr 43204
Harrison Rd 43204
Harrison Park Pl 43201
Harrow Blvd & Ct 43230
Harrow Gate Ct 43220
Harrowgate Dr 43230
Harshaw Dr 43207
Harston Ave 43207
Hart Rd 43223
N Hartford Ave 43222
S Hartford Ave 43222
Hartford Ct 43085
Hartford St 43085
Hartford Village Blvd 43228
Hartman St 43207
Hartney Dr 43230
Hartshorn St 43219
Hartwell Rd 43224
Hartwood Dr 43228
Harvard Ave 43203
Harvest Lane Ct 43213
Harvest Ridge Ct 43230
Harvester Ln 43229
Harvestwood Ln 43230
Harvey Ct 43219
Harwitch Rd 43221
Harwood Dr & Rd 43228
Haskell Dr 43219
Hastings Ln 43220
Hatfield Ct & Dr 43232
Hatherly Pl 43235
Hau Dr 43219
Haul Rd 43207
Havelock Ct 43230
Havencrest Ct 43220
Havendale Dr 43220
Havenhill Dr 43235
Havens Rd 43230
Havens Corners Rd 43230
N & S Havenwood Dr 43209
Haverford Ct & Rd 43220
Haversham Ct & Dr 43230
Haviland Dr 43207
Haviland Rd 43220
Hawkes Ave
1-169 43222
170-499 43223
Hawkeye Ct 43235
Hawksview Ct 43228
Hawksway Ct 43231
Hawthorne Ave 43203
Hawthorne Park 43203
Hawthorne St 43085
Haybrook Dr 43230
Hayden Ave 43222
Hayden Blvd 43221
Hayden Rd 43235
Hayden Falls Blvd & Dr 43221
Hayden Park Dr 43219
Hayden Run Plz 43235
Hayden Run Rd 43221
Haygate Pl 43230
Hayhurst St 43085
Haymarket Ct 43220
Haymarket Pl 43230
Haymore Ave N 43085
Hazelwood Pl & Rd 43229
Headford Ct 43231
Headington Pl 43230
Headley Rd 43230
Headley Heights Ct 43230
Healy Dr 43227
Heanchaw Rd 43224
Hearthstone Ave 43229
Heath Ct 43232
Heathcliff Dr 43209
Heather Ct 43230
Heather Ln 43229
Heather Rd 43230
Heatherfield Ave 43235
Heatherglen Dr 43221
Heatherhill Rd 43213
Heatherleaf Way 43231
Heathermoor Dr 43235
Heatherton Dr 43229
Heatherwood Dr 43213
Heathmoor Dr 43220
Heathmoor St 43235
Heathrowe Ct 43219
Heathside Ct 43235
Heathview St 43085
Heaton Pl & Rd 43229
Hebrides Dr 43232
Heckin Ct 43229
Hedera Ct 43235
Hedge Apple Dr 43223
Hedgebrooke Ave 43214
Hedgerow Rd 43220
Hedgewood Pl & Rd 43229
Hedley Pl 43230
Hegemon Crest Dr 43219
Heil Dr 43230
Heinzerling Dr 43223
Heischman Ave 43085
Heisley Dr 43207
Helen Ct 43201
Helen Dr 43232
Helen St 43223
Helena Ave 43219
Helenrose Ln 43230
Helmbright Ct & Dr 43230
Helmsdale Dr 43204
Helston Ct & Rd 43220
Hemingway Ct 43232
Hemlock Ave 43229
Hemlock St 43217
Hempwood Dr 43229
Hemston Ct & Dr 43230
Hemswell Ct 43227
Henderson Rd 43220
E Henderson Rd 43214
W Henderson Rd 43214
Henderson Heights Rd 43220
Henderson Miller Rd 43232
Henley Ave 43228
Henna Way 43228
Hennessey Ave 43085
Henrietta St 43215
Henry St 43215
Hensel Woods Ct & Rd 43230
Henthorn Rd 43221
E, N, S & W Heritage Dr 43213
Herman Ct & Rd 43230
Hermitage Rd 43230
Herndon Dr 43221
Heron Nest Ct 43240
Heron Pointe 43231
Heroncreek Blvd 43213
Herrick Rd 43221
Hess Blvd & St 43212
Heston Ct 43235
Hetter St 43228
Hewn Timber Ln 43230
Heyl Ave 43206
Heysham Dr 43221
Hialeah Ct 43221
Hiawatha St
2400-2869 43211
2870-3899 43224
Hiawatha Park Dr 43211
Hibbert Ave 43202
Hibbs Dr 43220
Hibernia Dr 43232
Hickman Rd 43224
Hickok Dr 43085
Hickory Grv 43214
E Hickory St 43215
Hickory Bluff Dr 43213
Hickory Brook Way 43213
Hickory Creek Ln 43229
Hickory Grove Ct 43085
Hickory Hill Dr & Pl 43228
Hickory Ridge Ln 43235
Hickory Run Dr 43204
Hickory Wood Dr 43228
Hidden Acres Ct 43224
Hidden Cove Way 43228
Hidden Gate 43228
Hidden Hollow Dr 43235
Hidden Ridge Ct & Dr 43230
Hidden Trail Way 43232
Hiddenspring Dr 43219
Hideaway Ct 43231
Higbee Dr E 43207
Higgs Ave 43212
High St 43085
N High St
1-905 43215
73-77 43230
79-176 43230
178-190 43230
906-1658 43201
1659-2139 43210
1660-2298 43201
2141-2299 43201
2300-3409 43202
3410-5569 43214
5570-7177 43085
7179-7299 43085
7201-7387 43235
7389-8696 43235
8698-8698 43235
S High St
1-47 43215
49-632 43215
62-70 43230
72-104 43230
106-124 43230
633-687 43206
634-688 43215
689-1314 43206
1315-4599 43207
4601-4799 43207
High Creek Dr 43223
High Cross Blvd 43235
High Grove Dr 43235
Highbluffs Blvd & Ct 43235
Highbrook Dr 43204
Highbury Cres 43230

Highcliff Ct 43231
Highcrest Ct 43224
Highfield Dr 43214
Highgate Ave 43085
Highgate Dr 43224
Highland Ave 43085
N Highland Ave 43204
S Highland Ave 43223
Highland Dr
600-799 43214
800-1199 43220
Highland Pl 43085
Highland St
719-830 43215
832-898 43215
900-1699 43201
Highland Ter 43085
Highland Way 43085
Highland Pointe Cir 43235
Highlawn Dr 43229
Highmeadow Ct & Dr 43230
Highpoint Dr 43221
Hightower Dr 43235
Highview Blvd 43207
Highview Dr 43235
Highview Lndg 43207
Highwall Way 43221
Higley Ct 43230
Hildreth Ave
1100-1499 43203
6700-6799 43229
Hiler Rd 43228
Hill Ave 43201
Hill Grove Ave 43223
Hillandale Ave 43229
Hillborn Dr 43085
Hillcreek Ct 43224
Hillcrest Ave 43207
Hillery Rd 43229
Hillgate Rd 43207
Hilliard Green Dr 43228
Hilliard Rome Rd E 43228
Hillman Rd E 43207
Hillpine Dr 43207
Hillsdale Dr 43224
Hillside Dr 43221
Hillstone St 43219
Hilltonia Ave 43223
Hilltop Ln 43228
Hillview Ct 43228
Hillview Dr 43220
Hilo Ln 43212
Hilock Ct, Pl & Rd 43207
Hilton Ave 43228
Hilton Corporate Dr 43232
Hines Rd 43230
Hingham Ln 43224
Hinkle Ave 43207
E & W Hinman Ave 43207
Hinsdale Ct 43085
Hinsel Dr 43232
Hirst Dr 43207
Historical Ave 43207
Hitesman Way 43214
Hoadley Dr 43228
Hobson Dr 43228
Hocking St 43215
Hodges Dr 43204
Hoffman Ave 43205
Hoffman Trace Dr 43213
Hoffman Valley Dr 43219
Hogan Way 43219
Hogans Run Rd 43221
Holbrook Dr 43232
Holburn Ave 43207
Hollingbourne Ct 43214
Hollister St 43235
Hollow Cove Ct 43231
Hollow Run Dr 43223
Holloway Ave 43223
Hollowcrest Ave 43223
Hollowwood Ave 43223
Holly Ave 43212
Holly Hill Dr 43228
Holly Ridge Rd 43219
Hollybriar Ct 43228
Hollybrier Dr 43230
Hollywood Pl 43212
Holsworth Dr 43219
Holt Ave 43219
Holt Rd 43228
Holt Run Dr 43228
Holton Ave 43223
Holtzman Ave 43205
Holyoke Ln 43231
Home Acre Dr
1100-1599 43229
2400-2999 43231
Homecroft Dr
2400-2999 43211
3300-3499 43224
Homestead Dr
2101-2149 43211
2151-2399 43211
3300-3699 43224
Homewood Ave 43223
Honey Creek Dr 43228
Honeylocust Dr 43228
Honeysuckle Blvd 43230
Honeytree Ct & Loop E,
N & W 43229
Honeywood Ct 43228
Honorata Dr 43213
Hope Ave 43212
Hope Pl 43223
Hopkins Ave 43223
Horint Rd 43214
W Horizons 43204
Horizons Dr 43220
Horned Grebe Ln 43230
Hornsby Dr 43240
Horton Pl 43228
Hosack St 43207
Hoseah St 43228
Hoskins Way 43213
Hostas Ln 43235
E & W Hoster St 43215
Houston Dr 43207
Hove Rd 43221
Howard Ave 43085
E Howard Rd 43207
Howard St 43201
Howey Rd
2100-2819 43211
2820-3299 43224
Howland Dr 43230
Hoxton Ct 43220
E & W Hubbard Ave 43215
Hubbell Rd 43232
Huber Ave 43211
Hudgins Ct 43228
E Hudson St
1-549 43202
550-2100 43211
2102-2198 43211
3000-3399 43219
W Hudson St 43202
Hudson Bay Way 43232
Hughes St 43203
Hull Aly 43215
Hull Farm Rd 43232
N & S Hulmac 43229
Humboldt Ct & Dr 43230
Hume Ct 43230
Hummingbird Ct N &
S 43229
Humphrey Ave 43223
Hunt Ave 43223
Hunter Ave
600-648 43215
650-808 43215
810-898 43215
900-1699 43201
Hunters Run 43230
Hunters Glen Dr 43230
Hunting Ln 43230
Hunting Brook Dr 43231
Huntington Dr 43207
Huntington Park Dr 43235
Huntington Park Ln 43215
Huntley Rd 43229
Huntly Dr 43227
Hunts Dr 43230
Hurd Rd 43207
Hurley Ct & St 43230
N & S Huron Ave 43204
Hutchinson Ave 43235
Hutchinson St 43085
Hutchinstone Rd 43232
Hutton Pl 43215
Huxley Ct & Dr 43227
Huy Rd 43224
Hyacinth Ln 43235
Hyatt Ct & Dr 43228
Hyland Ct 43213
Hythe Ct & Rd 43220
Ida Ave 43212
Ides Ct 43232
Idlewild Dr 43232
Ilene Rd 43232
Ilo Dr 43229
Imani Dr 43224
Imperial Dr 43230
Impound Lot Rd 43207
Inah Ave & Ct 43228
Inca Ct 43085
Inchcliff Rd 43221
Independence Rd 43212
Indian Head Ct 43224
Indian Hills Pl 43235
Indian Mound Ct & Rd 43213
Indian Run Ct 43235
Indian Springs Dr 43214
Indian Summer Dr 43214
Indian Village Rd 43221
Indiana Ave
2000-2239 43201
2240-2499 43202
Indianapolis Ave 43240
Indianola Ave
1200-2239 43201
2240-3299 43202
3300-5302 43214
5304-5398 43214
5400-5492 43085
5493-5519 43085
5494-5520 43085
5521-5799 43085
Indianwood Ct 43235
Indigo Way 43211
Industrial Center Dr 43207
Industrial Mile Rd 43228
Industry Dr 43204
Ingham Ave 43214
Ingleside Ave 43215
Ingleside Dr 43230
Inglis Ave 43212
Inkster Dr 43228
Inlet Dr 43232
Inn Rd 43232
Innbrook Pl 43235
E Innis Ave 43207
W Innis Ave 43207
Innis Rd 43224
Integrity Dr E 43209
Interchange Rd 43204
Intercontinental Dr 43228
Intermodal Ct N 43217
International Gtwy 43219
International St 43228
Internet Dr 43207
Inverary Dr 43228
Inverness Way 43221
Invicta Pl 43230
Inwood Pl 43224
Ione Ct 43235
Ipswick Cir 43224
Irene Pl 43222
Iron Ore Ct & Ln 43213
Ironclad Dr 43213
Irongate Ln 43213
Ironstone Dr 43231
Ironton Dr 43228
Ironwood Ct & Dr 43229
Ironwood Ridge Dr 43213
Iroquois Park Pl 43230
Irvine Ct 43228
Irving Way N & W 43214
Irving Schottenstein Dr 43210
Irvington Pl 43230
Irwin Ave 43207
Isabel Ave 43211
Isington Ct 43232
Island Ct 43214
Island Bay Dr 43235
Iswald Rd 43202
Ithaca Dr 43228
Iuka Ave 43201
Ivanhoe Ct 43220
Ivanhoe Dr 43209
Iverness Dr 43228
Ivorton Rd E 43207
Ivy Dr 43207
Ivy Brush Ct 43228
Ivyhill Loop N 43229
Ivyhurst Dr 43232
Ivywood Ln 43229
Jack Gibbs Blvd 43215
Jack Pine Ct 43224
Jack Russell Way 43232
Jackielane Dr 43235
Jackson Pike 43223
Jackson Rd 43223
Jackson St 43206
Jacob Close 43230
Jacqueline Ct 43232
Jae Ave 43213
Jaeger St 43206
Jahn Ct & Dr 43230
Jake Pl 43219
James Rd 43230
N James Rd
1-303 43213
305-399 43213
400-1599 43219
S James Rd
1-699 43213
700-1638 43227
2100-2299 43232
James Emmett Pl 43235
Jameson Dr 43232
Jamestown Ct
200-399 43228
4900-4999 43220
Jamestown Rd 43220
Jana Kay Ct 43207
Jane Ave 43219
Janet Cir 43209
Janet Dr 43224
Janice Pkwy 43223
Janice Marie Blvd 43207
Janis Dr 43227
Janitrol Rd 43228
Janwood Dr 43227
Jardin Pl 43213
Jared Ct & Pl 43219
Jason Dr 43227
Jasonway Ave 43214
Jay Pl 43235
Jed Ct 43227
Jefferson Ave
1-35 43215
37-199 43215
1400-2399 43211
E & W Jeffrey Pl 43214
Jemima Ln 43211
Jenera Pl 43232
Jenifer Pl 43219
E & W Jenkins Ave 43207
Jennie Dr 43230
Jennie Wren Ct N & S 43229
Jennifer Ct 43232
Jeri Ave 43219
Jermain Dr
1700-2199 43219
2200-2399 43211
Jermoore Rd 43207
Jerrie Mock Ave 43217
Jerry Lee Dr 43207
Jersey Dr 43204
Jervis Rd 43221
Jessamine Pl 43207
Jesse Dr 43207
Jessica Way 43230
Jessing Trl 43235
Jester Ln 43231
Jet Ln 43228
Jetstream Dr 43231
Jetway Blvd 43219
Jewett Dr 43229
Jillmarie Ct 43221
Joan Pl 43211
Joan Rd 43204
Jodilee Ct 43228
Joel Pl 43211
Joes Way 43223
Joes Hopper Rd 43230
John St 43222
John Circle Dr 43217
John G Mccoy Cir 43224
John Glenn Ave 43217
John H Mcconnell
Blvd 43215
John Herrick Dr 43210
John Michael Way 43235
Johnanne St 43229
Johnny Appleseed Ct 43231
Johnson St 43203
Johnston Rd 43220
Johnstown Rd 43219
E Johnstown Rd 43230
W Johnstown Rd 43230
Joi Ave 43219
Jonathan Dr 43207
Jonathan Noble Way 43231
N Jones Ave 43222
Jones Mill Rd 43229
Jonquil St 43224
Jonsol Ct 43230
Joos Ave 43229
Jordan Rd 43231
Jordana Dr 43230
Josaphat Way 43213
Josephine Ave 43204
Josephus Ln 43227
Joshstock Dr 43232
Joshua Run Rd 43232
Joslyn Pl 43085
Journal St 43228
Jousting Ln 43231
Joyce Ave
800-2249 43219
2250-2899 43211
Joyful St 43204
Jude Ct 43229
Judson Ct & Rd 43207
Judwick Dr 43229
Julia Ct 43230
Julian Dr 43227
Juliana Pl 43235
Julie Pl 43229
Junction Crossing Dr 43213
Juniper Ln 43230
Justice Ave 43229
Justin Rd 43227
K Of C Ct 43224
Kaderly Dr 43228
Kady Ln 43232
Kae Ave 43213
Kail Ave 43207
Kanard Ave 43228
E & W Kanawha Ave 43214
Kane Dr 43207
Kantian Dr 43219
Karen Ct 43204
Karenway Dr 43232
Kariba Dr 43207
Karl Ct 43229
Karl Rd
3000-4599 43224
4600-6799 43229
Karl St 43227
Karlslyle Dr 43228
Karney Pl 43230
Karon Dr 43219
Kasons Way 43230
Katherine Dr 43232
Katherines Ridge Ln 43235
Katherines Wood Dr 43235
Kathiwade Dr 43228
Kathy Run Ln 43229
Katie Dr 43221
Katies Way Ln 43085
Katrina Ln 43211
Kawanee Cir & Pl 43207
Keaton Dr 43231
Keats Ct 43235
Keble Ct 43228
Kedge Ln 43232
Kedleston Dr 43230
Keeler Ct & Dr 43227
Keeley St 43235
Keelson Dr 43232
Keeneland Ct 43230
Keep Pl 43204
Keeper Ct 43221
Keffer Rd 43224
Keilach Ave 43219
Keim Cir 43228
Kelburn Rd 43227
Kelenard Ave 43219
Kellen Dr 43230
Kellerman Ct 43228
N & S Kellner Pl & Rd 43209
Kellsford Ct 43235
E & W Kelso Rd 43202
Kelton Ave
200-869 43205
870-1499 43206
1700-1867 43207
1869-1999 43207
Keltonshire Ave 43229
Kelvin Ct 43085
Kelvinway Dr 43085
Kemper Rd 43219
Kempton Dr 43220
Kempton Run Ct & Dr 43235
Kenard Ct 43213
Kenaston Dr 43232
Kenbridge Dr 43219
Kenbrook Dr 43085
Kenbrook Common St 43220
Kenbrook Hills Dr 43220
Kenbury Pl 43220
Kenchester Ct & Dr 43220
Kendale Ct & Rd N &
S 43220
Kendall Pl 43205
Kendalwood Ct 43213
Kendra Ct 43220
Kenesaw Pl 43207
Kenfield Rd 43224
Kenilworth Ct 43230
Kenilworth Pl 43209
Kenilworth Rd 43219
Kenlawn St 43224
Kenley Ave 43220
Kenmont Pl 43220
Kenmore Rd
1400-1649 43211
1650-1799 43219
Kenmure Ct 43220
Kennedy Dr 43215
Kennerdown St 43229
Kennet Ct 43220
Kenneylane Blvd 43235
Kennington Ave 43220
Kenny Rd
1400-1899 43212
1900-1999 43210
2000-2300 43221
2301-2497 43210
2302-2498 43221
2499-2899 43210
2900-3649 43221
3650-4900 43220
4902-4998 43220
Kenny Centre Mall 43220
Kennybrook Blf & Ln 43220
Kenray Dr 43219
Kenridge Ct & Dr 43220
Kenross Dr 43207
Kensington Dr
602-648 43230
650-699 43230
2300-2499 43221
Kensington Pl E 43202
Kensington Pl W 43202
Kensington Way 43085
Kensingwood Dr 43230
Kent Cir 43213
Kent Rd 43221
Kent St 43205
Kentland Ct 43221
Kenton St 43205
Kentwell Rd 43221
Kentwood Pl 43227
Kenview Rd S 43209
Kenway Ct 43220
Kenwick Rd 43209
Kenwood Ln 43220
E Kenworth Rd 43224
W Kenworth Rd 43214
Kenwyn Ct 43220
Kenyon Rd 43221
Kenyon Brook Dr 43085
Kermit Ave 43207
Kerr St 43215
Kerrwood Dr 43231
Kerry Ct 43221
Kersey Ct 43221
Kershaw Dr 43207
Kertess Ave 43085
Kertzinger Cir 43230
Kessler St 43201
Keswick Ct & Dr 43220
Ketch Run 43219
Kettering Rd 43202
Kettle Way 43207
Kevin Ct 43204
Kevin Dr 43224
Key Pl 43207
Key Deer Dr 43085
Key West Ave 43219
Keyes Ln 43085
Keys View Ct 43085
Keystone Dr 43209
Kian Ave 43207
Kidron Ct 43232
Kiefer St 43215
Kilbourne Ave
2100-2570 43229
2571-2999 43231
Kilbourne Dr 43085
Kilbourne St 43215
Kilbourne Run Pl 43229
Kilbourne Run Rd 43231
Kilbride Ct 43221
Kilcary Ct 43220
Kilconnel Dr 43221
Kilcullen Dr 43221
Kildale Ct & Sq N, S &
W 43229
Kildare Pl 43228
Kildeer Ct 43231
Kilham Ct 43235
Kilkenny Dr 43221
Killington Ct 43221
Killowen Ct 43230
Kilmuir Dr 43221
Kilt Ct 43085
Kilwinning Pl 43221
Kimball Pl 43205
Kimberly Ave 43224
Kimberly Pkwy 43232
Kimberly Pkwy E 43232
Kimberly Pkwy N 43232
Kimberly Pkwy W 43232
Kimberly West Dr 43232
Kimberly Woods Dr 43232
Kimmel Rd 43224
Kimton Way 43228
Kinder Pl 43230
Kinderly Dr 43232
Kinerint Ave 43201
King Ave
1-9 43201
11-599 43201
601-699 43201
700-1999 43212
King Ct 43229
King Edward Ct E 43228

King George Ave 43230
Kingbird Dr 43230
Kingland Dr 43207
Kingpin Dr 43231
Kingry St 43211
Kings Ct 43212
Kings Cross Ct 43229
Kings Highland Dr S & W 43229
Kings Realm Ave 43232
Kingsbury Ct & Pl 43209
Kingsdale Ctr 43221
Kingsdale Ter 43220
Kingsford Rd 43204
Kingsgate Rd 43221
Kingshaven Pl 43232
Kingshill Dr 43229
Kingship Loop 43231
Kingsland Ave 43232
Kingslea Rd 43209
Kingsmill Ct & Pkwy 43229
Kingsrowe Ct 43209
Kingston Ave 43207
Kingston Ct 43220
Kingsway Dr 43221
Kinloch Castle Ct 43221
Kinnards Pl 43235
Kinnear Aly 43202
Kinnear Rd 43212
Kinnear Place Dr 43202
Kinneton 43228
Kinnia Dr 43219
Kinsale Head Dr 43221
Kinsey Dr 43224
Kinsman Ct & St 43207
Kinver Edge Way 43213
Kioka Ave
3100-3699 43221
3700-4099 43220
Kiowa Way 43085
Kipling Rd 43220
Kirby Ave 43223
Kirk Ave 43085
Kirkbridge Ct 43227
Kirkby Ct 43085
Kirkham Rd 43221
Kirkland Way 43231
Kirkley Rd 43221
Kirkwood Rd 43227
Kitchner Dr 43207
Klamath Falls Rd 43085
Kleiner Ave 43215
Kleinline Ln 43207
Klibreck Ct & Dr 43228
Knighthood Ln 43231
Knightlow Dr 43230
Knights Ave 43230
Knightsbridge Blvd 43214
Knightsway Ln 43232
Knob Hl E 43228
Knoll Ct & Dr 43230
Knollridge Ct 43229
Knollwood Dr E 43232
Knotty Knolls Dr 43230
Koebel Ave & Rd 43207
Kohr Blvd 43224
Kohr Pl 43211
Kola Way 43219
Kon Tiki Ct 43207
Kool Air Way 43231
Kornwal Dr 43232
E & W Kossuth St 43206
Kramer Ave 43212
Kramer Pl 43215
Kreber Ave 43204
Kresge Dr 43232
Krieger Ct & St 43228
Kristie Fls 43221
Kristin Ct 43231
Kriswood Ln 43228
Krumm Ave 43219
Kumler Dr 43213
Kutchins Pl 43205
Kyger Dr 43228
Kyle Ave 43207
Kyle Ct 43204

La Coste Ln 43228
La Rochelle Dr 43221
La Vista Dr 43204
Labelle Dr 43232
Labrador Ln 43232
Ladywell Ct 43085
Lafayette Ct 43213
Lafayette Dr 43220
Lafayette Pl 43212
E Lafayette St 43215
Laforge St 43228
Laguna Dr 43232
N Lake Ct 43231
Lake Bluff Ct & Dr 43235
Lake Club Ct, Dr, Pl, Sq & Ter 43232
Lake Crossing Ave 43213
Lake Knoll Ct 43230
Lake Park Dr 43232
Lake Pointe Dr 43219
Lake Ridge Dr 43085
Lake Shore Dr
700-899 43235
1100-2099 43204
Lakebrook Blvd 43235
Lakehill Ct 43229
Lakeland Ct 43231
Lakemere Way 43209
Lakes At Taylor Station Dr 43213
Lakes Circle Dr 43240
Lakeside Cir E 43085
Lakeside Cir W 43085
Lakeside Ct 43085
Lakeside Pl 43085
Lakeside St N 43232
Lakeside St S 43232
Lakeside Way 43085
E Lakeview Ave
1-299 43202
1600-1899 43224
W Lakeview Ave 43202
Lakeview Plaza Blvd 43085
Lakewood Dr 43231
Lakewood Rd 43209
Lakinhurst Dr 43220
Lamarque Ct 43232
Lamb Ave 43219
Lambeth Ct, Dr & Pl 43220
Lambourne Ave 43085
Lambs Creek Ct 43085
Lamby Ln 43213
Lamont Ave 43224
Lamson Ave 43207
Lancashire Rd 43219
Lancaster Ave 43207
Lancaster Ln 43229
Lance Ct 43204
Lancelot Rd 43227
Lancer Way 43213
Lancewood Dr 43230
Landers Ave 43207
Landings Loop 43085
Landmark Way 43219
Landon Dr 43209
Landou Way 43207
Landover Pl & Rd 43230
Landsburn Dr 43231
E Lane Ave 43201
W Lane Ave
1-699 43210
2-598 43201
600-698 43210
700-2220 43221
2222-2598 43221
Lane Rd 43220
Lane On The Lk 43235
Lane Woods Ct & Dr 43221
Lanercost Way 43220
Lanes End St 43220
Lang Dr 43230
Langdon Rd 43219
Langfield Dr
2800-2969 43209
2970-3099 43227
Langford Ct 43230

Langham Rd 43221
Langhorn Dr 43235
Langland Dr 43220
Langley Ave 43213
Langport Rd 43220
Langston Dr 43220
Langtry Ave 43207
Lanning Dr 43220
Lansdowne Ave 43230
Lansdowne St 43085
Lanshire Ct 43229
Lansing St 43206
Lansmere Ln 43220
Lantern Dr 43224
Laraine Ct 43232
Larch Ln 43219
Larcomb Ave 43223
Largo Ct 43230
Lark Dr 43219
Larkfield Dr 43085
Larkhall Ln 43229
Larkin Dr 43231
Larkstone Dr 43235
Larkwell Way 43232
Larkwood Pl & Rd 43229
Larrimer Ave 43085
Larry Ln 43230
Larry Pl 43227
Larwell Dr 43220
Las Vegas Blvd 43240
Lasky Ct 43230
Lateen Dr 43207
Latham Ct 43214
Lathrop St 43206
Latin Ln 43220
Latonia Ct & Rd 43232
Latta Ave 43205
Lattimer Dr 43227
Lauffer Rd 43231
Lauffer Ravines Dr 43231
Laura Dr 43230
Lauraland Dr E & S 43214
Laurel Ave 43223
Laurel Ln
181-185 43085
3900-3999 43232
Laurel Ridge Ct & Dr 43230
Laurel Valley Dr 43228
Laurelstone Pkwy 43228
Laurelwood Ct & Dr 43229
Lauren Pl 43235
Laurent Ct 43231
Lavender Ln 43207
Lavender Ridge Dr 43230
Lavoie Dr 43230
W Lawn Ave 43207
Lawndale Ave 43207
Lawnview Dr 43214
Lawrence Ave 43228
Lawrence Dr 43207
Laylon Dr 43229
Lazelle Rd
1-65 43235
67-274 43240
276-298 43235
300-664 43240
Lazelle Rd E 43235
N Lazelle St 43215
S Lazelle St
31-250 43215
252-298 43215
400-999 43206
Le Anne Marie Cir 43235
Le Marie Ct & Pl 43224
Leach Dr 43207
Leafapple Ln 43232
Leaflock Ct 43230
Leafridge Ln 43232
Lealand Way 43235
Leamington Ct 43213
Leamoor Dr 43235
Lear Rd 43220
Lear St 43206
Leather Stocking Trl 43230
Leatherwood Dr 43224
Leaview Ct & Dr 43235

Lechner Ave 43223
Ledge Ln 43221
Lee Ave 43219
Lee Chapel Ct 43085
Lee Ellen Pl 43207
Leeds Aly 43202
Leeds Rd 43221
Leenchal Dr 43235
Leesburg Ct E 43228
Legacy Ln 43228
Legare Ln 43230
Legend 43230
Legion Ln 43232
Legionary St 43207
Legislate Dr 43207
Lehman St 43206
Lehner Rd 43224
Leicester Pl 43235
Leighton Rd 43221
Leland Ave 43214
Lemery Dr 43213
Lemon Tree Ln 43230
Lemonwood St 43229
Lenappe Dr 43214
Lenker Dr 43240
Lennon Ct 43213
Lennox Ave 43228
Lennox Flats Dr 43212
Lenora Ave 43204
Lenore Ave 43224
Leon Ave 43219
Leona Ave 43201
Leonard Ave
700-820 43203
822-1399 43203
1800-2299 43219
Leontria Ave 43219
Lepage Ct 43229
Les Paul St 43235
Lesbrook Dr 43228
Lester Dr 43215
Letchworth Ave 43204
Levelgreen Dr 43219
Lewis Rd 43207
Lexington Ave
801-1067 43201
1069-1199 43201
1600-2599 43211
Lexmont Rd S 43228
Libby Dr 43207
Liberton Pl 43085
Liberty Pl 43223
Liberty St 43215
Liberty Commons Rd 43235
Liberty Isle Rd 43235
Library Park Ct 43215
Lidell Pl 43219
Lieb St 43214
Liegh Run Ct 43228
Lifestyle Blvd 43219
Lifford Ct 43221
Lightshine Ln 43235
Lila Way 43235
Lilacwood Ave 43229
Lilley Ave
400-869 43205
870-1499 43206
Lillian Ln 43227
Lily Pond Ct 43230
Lilyhill Ct 43085
Lilypark Dr 43219
Limberlost Ct 43235
Limestone Way 43228
Limited Pkwy 43230
Limpkin Dr 43230
Linbrook Blvd & Ct 43235
Linchara Rd 43220
E Lincoln Ave
1-659 43214
660-1099 43229
W Lincoln Ave 43085
Lincoln Cir 43230
Lincoln Rd 43212
E Lincoln St 43215
W Lincoln St 43215
Lincoln Park Ct 43228

Lincolnshire Rd 43230
Lindale Rd 43224
Lindbergh Blvd 43228
Lindbergh Dr 43223
Lindel Ct & Dr 43207
Linden Ave & Pl 43211
Linden Leaf Cir 43235
Lindendale Ct & Dr 43204
Lindenhaven Ct & Rd 43230
Lindenwood Rd N 43229
Lindhurst Rd 43220
Lindora Dr & Pl 43232
Lindsay Rd 43207
Lindsey Marie Ln 43235
Lindstrom Ct & Dr 43228
Line Way 43230
Linfield Pl 43219
Lingle Ln 43213
Link Ct & Rd 43213
Linkbury Ln 43221
Linkfield Dr 43085
Linnet Ave 43223
Lintner St 43230
Linton Blvd 43235
Linton Gardens Dr 43219
Linview Ave 43211
Linwood Ave
1-799 43205
800-1499 43206
1500-3699 43207
Linwood Dr 43230
Linworth Rd
5200-7201 43235
5785-5877 43085
5879-6699 43085
7203-7599 43235
Linworth Rd E 43235
Linworth Village Dr 43235
Lion Dr 43228
Lipton Rd 43232
Lis Ln 43227
Lisa Dr 43219
Lisa St 43231
Lisa Marie Rd 43229
Lisbon Dr 43232
Liscomb Rd 43207
Lisle Aly 43206
Lisle Ave 43207
Liston Ave 43207
Litchfield Ct & Rd 43235
Little Ave 43223
Little Ben Cir 43231
Little Brook Way 43232
Little Deer Ln 43213
Little Flower Ln 43213
Little Pine Dr 43230
Little Plum Ln 43227
Little Water Dr 43223
Littlebury Way 43230
Littlejohn Dr 43227
Littleleaf Ct & Ln 43235
Littler Ln 43228
Liv Moor Ct & Dr 43227
Live Oak Pl 43221
Liverpool Ct 43229
E Livingston Ave
1-197 43215
199-599 43215
600-1827 43205
1829-1879 43205
1874-1878 43209
1880-3039 43209
3041-3047 43227
3049-5000 43227
5002-5198 43227
5200-6185 43232
6187-6199 43232
W Livingston Ave 43215
Livingston Ct 43227
Lizzie Ln 43213
Llanfair Ct 43221
Llewellyn Ave 43207
Llewellyn Rd 43230
Lloret Ct 43228
Local Ln 43213
Loch Lomond Ln 43085

Loch Ness Ave 43085
Lochcarren Ct 43235
Lock Ave 43207
Lockberry Ave & Ct 43207
Lockbourne Rd
700-829 43205
830-1519 43206
1520-5199 43207
Lockbourne Industrial Pkwy 43207
Lockhurst Rd 43207
Lockwin Ave 43201
Lockwood Rd 43227
Locust St 43207
Locust Post Ln 43230
Lodge Ct 43228
Lodgelane Dr 43229
Loeffler Ave 43205
Loew St 43201
Lofton Pl 43230
Logan St 43204
Loganwood Rd 43229
Loggers Run Ct 43235
Logwood Ln 43228
Loire Ln 43221
Lola Way 43235
Lombard Rd 43228
London Dr 43221
London Court Dr 43221
London Groveport Rd 43217
London Plane Dr 43235
Londonderry Ave 43228
Lone Eagle St 43228
Lone Spruce Rd 43219
E Long St
1-640 43215
642-688 43215
690-1829 43203
1830-1999 43219
W Long St 43215
Longbow Ln 43235
Longbranch Ln 43213
Longeaton Dr 43220
Longfellow Ave 43085
Longfield Rd 43204
Longhill Rd 43220
Longhurst Dr E 43228
Longspur Dr 43228
Longstreth Park Pl 43230
Longton Dr 43221
E Longview Ave
1-699 43202
700-899 43224
W Longview Ave 43202
Longview Ct 43235
Longwood Ave 43223
Lonsdale Pl & Rd E, N & S 43232
Lookout Point Dr 43235
Loon Song Ct 43085
Loos Cir E & W 43214
Lorain Ct 43210
Loretta Ave 43211
Lorine Ct & Pl 43235
Loring Rd 43224
Lornaberry Ln 43213
Lorraine Ave 43235
Lou St 43231
Louden Ave 43204
Louis Ave 43211
Louis Dr 43207
Louise Ave 43213
Louisville Pl 43240
Louvaine Dr 43223
Love Dr 43221
Loveman Ave 43085
Lowell Dr 43204
Lowell Rd 43209
Lower Chelsea Rd 43212
Lower Green Cir 43212
Lowery Dr 43231
Lowestone Rd 43220
Lowland Ct 43204
Loxley Dr 43207
Loyola St 43221
Lucas St 43215

Luccis Ct 43228
Lucinda Ct 43232
Ludington Rd 43227
N & S Ludlow St 43215
Ludwig Dr 43230
Lummisford Ln E & N 43214
Lunar Dr 43214
Lundy St 43215
Lupo Ct 43224
Luxury Ln 43224
Lydie Ct 43085
Lyle Rd 43229
Lyman Ave 43205
Lymington Rd 43220
Lynanne Ct 43231
Lynbrook Rd 43235
Lyncroft Ct & Dr 43230
Lyndenhall Dr 43207
Lyngail Ct 43230
E Lynn St 43215
Lynnhaven Ct 43228
Lynnhaven Dr 43221
Lynnhurst Rd 43229
Lynnmore Dr 43235
Lynnwood Ln N 43228
Lynward Rd 43228
Lyon Dr 43220
Lyons Brook Ct 43085
Lyonsgate 43209
Lyra Dr 43240
Lytham Ct & Rd 43220
Lytton Ct & Way 43230
Mabry Mill Ct 43085
Mac Ct 43235
Macaldus Dr 43219
Macgregor Ave & Ct 43085
Macgregor West Ave 43085
Macintosh Dr 43230
Mackenzie Dr 43220
Mackinac Dr 43207
Maclam Dr 43204
Maclee Aly 43205
Macon Aly 43206
Macsway Ave 43232
Maddens Pointe Ln 43235
Madeline Dr 43232
Madison Ave 43205
Madison School Dr 43232
Maetzel Dr 43227
Magnolia Blossom Blvd 43230
Magoffin Ave 43207
Mahoning Ct 43210
Maidens Larne Dr 43221
Maidstone Dr 43230
Maier Pl 43215
E Main St
21-97 43215
99-528 43215
530-648 43215
651-749 43205
751-2099 43205
2100-3129 43209
3130-6310 43213
W Main St 43215
Maize Ct 43229
Maize Rd
3000-4639 43224
4640-4899 43229
Majestic Ct, Dr & Pl E, N & W 43232
Malabar St 43230
Malay Rd 43230
Malbec Dr 43230
Malden Way 43228
Maleka Ct 43235
Malibu Dr 43213
Malin Dr, Pl & St E & W 43224
Malka Ct 43232
Mall View Ct 43231
Mallard Crossing Way 43215
Mallards Lndg 43229
Mallards Marsh 43229
Mallcreek Ct 43223
Mallet Pl E & W 43230

N & S Mallway Dr ... 43221
Malo Dr ... 43207
Malton Ln ... 43085
Malvern Ave ... 43219
Malvern Rd ... 43221
Man O War Ct ... 43221
Manassas Ct ... 43207
Manchester Ave ... 43211
Mandeville Ct ... 43232
Manfeld Dr ... 43227
Mangersi Ave ... 43209
Manitoba Ct & Rd ... 43229
Mannboro Dr ... 43220
Manning Ave ... 43205
Manola Dr ... 43209
Manor Dr ... 43232
Manor Ln ... 43221
Manor Rd ... 43224
Manor Hill Ln ... 43219
Manor Park Dr ... 43228
Mansfield Ave ... 43219
Mansion Way ... 43221
Manville Ct ... 43231
Maple Bnd ... 43229
Maple Dr
1-599 ... 43228
700-799 ... 43235
Maple Rd ... 43217
Maple St ... 43223
Maple Canyon Ave ... 43229
Maple Glen Dr ... 43230
Maple Hedge Way ... 43219
Maple Hill Blvd ... 43235
Maple Shade Ct ... 43228
Maple Tree Ln ... 43232
Maple Valley Dr ... 43228
Maplebrook Ln ... 43235
Mapleleaf Blvd & Ct ... 43235
Mapleridge Dr ... 43232
Mapleway Ct, Dr & Ln ... 43204
Maplewood Aly ... 43203
Maplewood Ave ... 43213
Maplewood Ct E ... 43229
Maplewood Ct W ... 43229
Maplewood Dr
2000-2299 ... 43229
2500-5099 ... 43231
Maplewood Rd ... 43207
Mar Min Ct ... 43085
Mara Dr ... 43224
Marathon Ct ... 43230
Marbella Pl ... 43219
Marble Dr ... 43227
Marble Cliff Office Park ... 43215
Marblecliff Crossing Ct ... 43204
Marblehead Ct ... 43220
Marblevista Blvd ... 43204
Marblewood Dr ... 43219
Marburn Dr ... 43214
Marcella Dr ... 43230
Marcellus Dr ... 43219
Marchfield Way ... 43204
Marci Way ... 43228
Marcia Dr ... 43211
Marconi Blvd ... 43215
Marden Ct ... 43230
Mareco Pl E ... 43207
Margaret Ave & Pl ... 43219
Margate Rd ... 43221
Margo Rd ... 43229
Margraf Aly ... 43206
Marias Point Ln ... 43213
Marigold Ave ... 43207
Marilla Rd ... 43207
Marilyn Ln ... 43219
Marilyn Park Ln ... 43219
Marina Dr ... 43219
Marion Dr N ... 43207
Marion Pl ... 43227
Marion Rd ... 43207
Marita Ln ... 43235
Marjoram Dr ... 43230
Mark Ct & Pl ... 43204
E Market St ... 43203
Markham Rd ... 43207

Markhaven Ct & Dr ... 43235
E & W Markison Ave ... 43207
Markland St ... 43235
Markridge Ln ... 43231
Markview Rd ... 43214
Markwood St ... 43085
Marl Pl ... 43221
Marla Dr ... 43221
Marland Dr ... 43224
Marlboro Ave ... 43207
Marlborough Ct ... 43229
Marley Ct ... 43227
Marlin Dr ... 43232
Marlow Dr ... 43085
Marlowe Ct ... 43228
Marlyn Dr ... 43220
Marlyn Ln ... 43227
Marquis Ct ... 43230
Marrus Dr ... 43230
Marsala Ave ... 43228
Marsdale Ave ... 43223
Marsh Wren Dr ... 43230
Marsha Dr ... 43207
Marshall Ave ... 43207
Marshall Psge ... 43215
Marshlyn Ct ... 43220
Marston Rd ... 43219
Martell Dr ... 43229
Martha Ave ... 43223
Martha Ln ... 43213
Martin Ave ... 43222
Martin Luther King Jr Blvd ... 43203
Martindale Blvd ... 43214
Martinique Dr ... 43085
Martinsburg Dr ... 43207
Martlet Ave ... 43235
Marview Rd ... 43219
Marwick Rd ... 43232
Marwood Ct ... 43232
Mary Ave ... 43204
Maryland Ave
1500-1829 ... 43203
1831-1861 ... 43219
1863-2129 ... 43219
2130-3127 ... 43209
3129-3279 ... 43209
3280-3499 ... 43213
Masefield St ... 43085
Mason Pl ... 43235
Mason Village Ct & Dr ... 43232
Master Ct ... 43085
Masters Dr ... 43220
Mathena Way ... 43232
Mathews Ave ... 43207
Matthias Dr ... 43224
Mattox St ... 43228
Matuka Dr ... 43232
Maumee Bay Way ... 43232
Maureen Blvd N & S ... 43207
Maurine Dr ... 43228
Mautino Dr ... 43231
Mawyer Dr ... 43085
Maxfield Dr ... 43212
Maxim Ln ... 43235
Maxton Pl ... 43085
Maxview Pl ... 43232
Maxwell Pl ... 43228
Maxwelton Ct ... 43235
May Aly ... 43206
S May Ave ... 43215
May Ct ... 43235
Maybank Ct ... 43230
Maybrook St ... 43235
Maybury Pl & Rd ... 43232
Mayfair Blvd ... 43213
Mayfair Park Pl ... 43213
Mayfield Pl ... 43209
Mayflower Blvd ... 43213
Mayme Moore Pl ... 43203
E Maynard Ave
1-599 ... 43202
700-1599 ... 43211
1600-1899 ... 43219
W Maynard Ave ... 43202
Mayo Ct ... 43235

Maywood Rd ... 43232
Mcallister Ave
701-797 ... 43205
799-1999 ... 43205
4100-5099 ... 43227
Mcbane Ct & St ... 43220
Mcburney Pl ... 43085
Mccall Ct ... 43235
Mccallum Clb ... 43219
Mccampbell Rd ... 43085
Mccarley Dr E, S & W ... 43228
Mccarron Ct ... 43230
Mccartney Ln ... 43229
Mccarty Aly ... 43205
Mccauley Ct ... 43220
Mcclain Rd ... 43212
Mcclay Ave ... 43230
Mccleary Ct ... 43235
Mcclelland Ave ... 43211
Mcconnell Rd ... 43214
Mccord St ... 43085
Mccormick Blvd ... 43213
Mccoy Ave ... 43085
Mccoy Rd ... 43220
Mccoy St ... 43215
Mccraney Ln ... 43213
Mccutcheon Pl ... 43219
Mccutcheon Rd
2-98 ... 43230
100-799 ... 43230
2101-2297 ... 43219
2299-2680 ... 43219
2682-2798 ... 43219
3200-3899 ... 43230
Mccutcheon Crossing Dr ... 43219
Mcdannald Dr ... 43230
Mcdermot Ct ... 43228
Mcdole Ave ... 43207
Mcdonell Dr & Pl ... 43230
Mcdowell St ... 43215
Mcdowell Ridge Dr ... 43223
Mcfadden Rd ... 43229
Mcgaw Rd ... 43207
Mcgreegor St ... 43085
Mcguffey Rd
2100-2819 ... 43211
2820-3899 ... 43224
Mchenry Dr ... 43207
Mckahan Ave & Ct ... 43232
Mckee St ... 43215
Mckenna Ct ... 43221
Mckenna Creek Dr ... 43230
Mckinley Ave
800-1969 ... 43222
1970-3399 ... 43204
Mckitrick Blvd ... 43235
Mcmillen Ave ... 43201
Mcnaughten Ctr ... 43232
Mcnaughten Rd
1-1149 ... 43213
1150-1799 ... 43232
Mcnaughten Grove Ln ... 43213
Mcnaughten Place Ln ... 43213
Mcnaughten Woods Dr ... 43232
Mcnery Dr ... 43219
Mcpartlan Ct ... 43221
Mcspaden Ct ... 43228
Mcvey Blvd & Ct ... 43235
Meadow Ln ... 43207
Meadow Rd ... 43212
Meadow Beauty Ct ... 43230
Meadow Cove Pl ... 43230
Meadow Creek Dr ... 43235
Meadow Gold Dr ... 43223
Meadow Green Cir ... 43230
Meadow Hills Ct ... 43228
Meadow Lakes Dr ... 43219
Meadow Oak Dr ... 43235
Meadow Park Ave ... 43209
Meadow Spring Cir & Dr ... 43235
Meadow Valley St ... 43207
Meadow Village Dr ... 43235
Meadow Wood Ln ... 43228
Meadoway Park ... 43085

Meadowbank Dr ... 43085
Meadowbrook Cir ... 43085
Meadowbrook Dr ... 43207
Meadowcrest Dr & Pl ... 43228
Meadowdale Ave ... 43219
Meadowedge Dr ... 43230
Meadowhaven Blvd ... 43235
Meadowick Dr ... 43230
Meadowknoll Ln ... 43220
Meadowlark Ln ... 43214
Meadowlawn Dr ... 43219
Meadowleigh Way ... 43230
Meadows Blvd & Ct ... 43229
Meadowside Ct ... 43230
Meadowsweet Pl ... 43230
Meadowview Ct & Dr ... 43224
Meadwell Ct ... 43235
Meander Dr ... 43229
Mecca Rd ... 43224
Mechwart Pl ... 43230
Med O Mac Ln ... 43221
Medalist ... 43230
Medary Ave ... 43202
Medbrook Way N ... 43214
Medfield Way ... 43228
Medford Pl & Rd ... 43209
Medhurst Rd ... 43220
Medical Center Dr ... 43210
Medick Way ... 43085
Medina Ave
1901-1949 ... 43211
1951-2400 ... 43211
2402-2498 ... 43211
2710-3699 ... 43224
Medinah Ter ... 43235
Meditation Ln ... 43235
Mediterranean Ave ... 43229
Medoc Ct ... 43229
Medoma Dr ... 43204
Medway Ave
3100-3199 ... 43209
3400-4299 ... 43213
Medwin Pl ... 43230
Meek Ave ... 43222
Meekison Dr ... 43220
Meeklynn Dr ... 43235
Meeks Meadow Dr ... 43223
Meeting St ... 43220
Megan Dr ... 43221
Mehrman Way ... 43214
Meigs Dr ... 43207
Melbourne Pl ... 43085
Melbury Dr ... 43221
Meldrake Ct & St ... 43230
Melford Rd ... 43221
Melissa Ct ... 43230
Melissa Pl ... 43227
Melissa Dawn Dr ... 43207
Melkridge St ... 43219
Mellacent Dr ... 43235
Mellowbrook Ct & St ... 43232
Melony Ct ... 43231
Melrose Ave
400-699 ... 43202
700-2299 ... 43224
2300-2599 ... 43211
Melroy Ave ... 43227
Melva Ave ... 43224
Melville St ... 43219
Melwood Dr ... 43228
Melyers Ct ... 43235
Memory Ln N ... 43209
Mendes Ct ... 43235
Mendon Ct & Pl ... 43232
Menifee Ave ... 43207
Menlo Pl ... 43203
Menzola Dr ... 43228
Merbrook Rd ... 43235
Mercedes Ln ... 43232
Mercer Rdg ... 43228
Mercer St ... 43235
Mercury St ... 43240
Meredith Dr ... 43219
Merganser Run Dr ... 43215
Meridian Ct & Rd ... 43232
Meriline Ave ... 43207

N & S Merkle Rd ... 43209
Merlot Ln ... 43228
Merrick Rd ... 43212
Merrifield Pl ... 43220
Merrimac Ave ... 43222
Merrimar Cir E ... 43220
Merritt St ... 43207
Merriweather Dr ... 43221
Merry Ln ... 43229
Merry Oak Ct & Ln ... 43230
Merrydawn Dr ... 43221
Merryhill Dr ... 43219
Merrymount Ct ... 43232
Merston Dr ... 43235
Merton Dr ... 43229
Merwin Pl & Rd ... 43235
Merwin Hill Dr ... 43219
Merwood St ... 43235
Mesa Ridge Ln ... 43231
Metcalfe Ave ... 43207
Metro Ave ... 43203
Metropolitan Dr ... 43235
Metzger Pl ... 43213
Mews Ct ... 43212
Miami Ave ... 43203
Michael Ct ... 43204
Michael View Ct ... 43085
Michaela Ct ... 43235
Michelle Ct ... 43228
Michigan Ave
700-969 ... 43215
970-1599 ... 43201
Mid Dr ... 43085
Midcliff Dr ... 43213
Middle School St ... 43207
Middlebrook Ln ... 43235
Middlebury Ct & Dr E, N & W ... 43085
Middlecoff Ct ... 43228
Middlefield Ct & Dr ... 43235
Middlehurst Dr ... 43219
Middlemore Dr ... 43219
Middleport Dr ... 43235
Middlesex Rd ... 43220
Middleshire St ... 43229
Middletowne St ... 43214
Midgard Rd ... 43202
Midhurst Rd ... 43230
Midland Ave ... 43223
Midvale Rd ... 43224
Midway Ave ... 43207
Mifflin Blvd & St ... 43219
Migration Ln ... 43230
Miguel St ... 43213
Milan Dr ... 43230
Milden Rd ... 43221
Milepost Ct & Dr ... 43228
Milford Ave
400-699 ... 43202
1400-1899 ... 43224
2300-2599 ... 43211
Militia Ln ... 43230
Milk St ... 43230
Mill St ... 43230
N Mill St ... 43215
S Mill St ... 43215
Millay Aly ... 43215
Millbank Rd ... 43229
Millbourne Dr ... 43230
Millbrae Rd ... 43235
Millbrook Way ... 43219
Millcreek Ct & Ln ... 43220
Millcrest St ... 43235
Millennium Ct ... 43219
Miller Ave
100-829 ... 43205
830-1599 ... 43206
Millerbrook Ct ... 43224
Millerdale Rd ... 43209
Millersfield Dr ... 43232
Millerton St ... 43232
Millikin Ct ... 43228
Millikin Rd ... 43210
Millington Ct & Rd ... 43235
Millrace Dr ... 43207
Millside Dr ... 43230

Millstone Rd ... 43207
Millvale St ... 43232
Millview Ct & Dr ... 43207
Millwood Ct ... 43230
Millwood Dr ... 43221
Milt Caniff Blvd E & W ... 43217
Milton Ave
3200-3449 ... 43202
3450-5499 ... 43214
5500-5599 ... 43085
Milton Ct ... 43228
Miltwood Rd ... 43227
Milverton Way ... 43224
Mimosa Pl ... 43230
Mimring Rd ... 43202
Minck Dr ... 43219
Miner Ave ... 43223
Minerva Ave
800-2601 ... 43229
2602-2999 ... 43231
Minerva Lake Rd ... 43231
Minerva Park Pl ... 43229
Mink St ... 43203
Minnesota Ave
1100-2499 ... 43211
3700-3999 ... 43219
Mintwood Dr ... 43229
Minuteman Ct ... 43220
Minuteman Way ... 43217
Mira St ... 43240
Miranova Pl ... 43215
Miriam Dr E ... 43204
Mission Hills Ln ... 43235
Missouri Ave ... 43219
Missy Ln ... 43221
Mistletoe Ct & St ... 43230
Misty Way ... 43232
Misty Cove Ln ... 43231
Misty Dawn Dr ... 43240
Misty Hollow Ln ... 43228
Misty Oak Pl ... 43230
E Mithoff St ... 43206
Mitzi Dr ... 43209
Mix Ave ... 43228
Mobile Dr ... 43220
Mock Rd ... 43219
Mockingbird Ct N & S ... 43229
Modesta Rd ... 43213
Modoc Rd ... 43085
Mohawk St ... 43206
Mohican Ave ... 43224
E & W Moler Rd & St ... 43207
Molly Ln ... 43207
Monaco Ct ... 43230
Monarch Dr ... 43235
Moncrief Ave ... 43207
Monfort Ave ... 43232
Monmouth Ct
2400-2499 ... 43219
4500-4699 ... 43232
Monmouth Dr ... 43219
N Monroe Ave ... 43203
S Monroe Ave ... 43205
Monsono Dr ... 43240
Montague Ct ... 43220
Montaine Ave ... 43232
Montcalm Rd ... 43221
Montclair Dr ... 43219
Montego Blvd ... 43235
Monterey Ct ... 43207
Montgomery Ct ... 43210
Monticello Pl ... 43219
Monticello Hall Dr ... 43221
Montrose Ave ... 43209
Montrose Way ... 43214
Mooberry St ... 43205
Moon Rd ... 43224
Moon Glow Ct ... 43230
Moonlight Ln ... 43207
Moonmist Ct ... 43228
Moores Trail Rd ... 43228
Moorfield Dr ... 43230
Moorgate Dr ... 43235
Moorlane Dr ... 43085
Morality Dr ... 43231
Moravian St ... 43220

Moreland Dr W ... 43220
Morgan Ln ... 43230
Morning Ave ... 43212
Morning St
500-5599 ... 43085
5201-5499 ... 43214
Morning Glory Pl ... 43230
Morningside Dr ... 43202
E & W Morrill Ave ... 43207
Morris Ave
700-799 ... 43219
4600-4699 ... 43213
Morrison Ave ... 43205
Morrison Rd
100-400 ... 43213
300-398 ... 43230
400-691 ... 43230
402-698 ... 43213
693-999 ... 43230
700-998 ... 43230
1000-1199 ... 43230
Morrissey St ... 43232
Morse Rd
1-749 ... 43214
750-848 ... 43229
850-2469 ... 43229
2470-3599 ... 43231
3600-4038 ... 43219
4039-5600 ... 43230
Morse Xing ... 43219
Morse Centre Rd ... 43229
Morse Creek Dr ... 43224
Morse Creek Commons Dr ... 43224
Morse Ravine Dr ... 43224
Morsetowne Ct E, N, S & W ... 43224
Mosaic Ct ... 43230
Moss Ct ... 43214
Moss Oak Ave ... 43230
E Mound St
2-22 ... 43215
24-599 ... 43215
700-1899 ... 43205
2100-3100 ... 43209
3102-3198 ... 43209
3200-4499 ... 43227
W Mound St
1-300 ... 43215
302-398 ... 43215
801-897 ... 43223
899-2269 ... 43223
2270-3199 ... 43204
Moundcrest St ... 43232
Moundview Ave ... 43207
Mount Air Pl ... 43235
Mount Airyshire Blvd ... 43235
Mount Auburn Ct ... 43085
Mount Calvary Ave ... 43223
Mount Carmel Mall ... 43222
Mount Holyoke Rd ... 43221
Mount Hood Ct ... 43230
Mount Pleasant Ave ... 43201
Mount Royal Ave ... 43228
Mount Rushmore Ct ... 43230
Mount Vernon Ave
200-499 ... 43215
600-1599 ... 43203
Mountain Oak Rd ... 43219
Mountain Springs Ct ... 43230
Mountshannon Rd ... 43221
Mountview Rd
2800-3599 ... 43221
3600-4399 ... 43220
Mountville Ave ... 43232
Mouzon Dr ... 43232
Muffin Way ... 43207
Muirwood Dr ... 43232
Muirwood Village Dr ... 43228
Mulberry Dr ... 43235
Mulberry St ... 43219
Mulby Pl ... 43211
Muleady Ct ... 43221
Mulford Rd ... 43212
Mullens Ct ... 43228
Mullgrove Ct ... 43221
Mumford Ct & Dr ... 43220

Murphy Way 43235
Murray Ave
400-599 43204
800-899 43219
N & S Murray Hill Rd 43228
Murrayfield Dr 43085
Murrell Ave 43212
Musket Way 43228
Musket Ridge Dr 43223
Muskingum Ct
300-399 43230
2500-2699 43210
Muskingum Dr 43230
Mustang Ct 43221
Myers Rd 43232
Myron St 43213
Myrtle Ave 43211
Myrtle Valley Dr 43228
Mystic Ct 43224
Mystic Pines Dr 43230
Nace Ave 43223
Nafzger Dr 43230
E Naghten St 43215
Naiche Ct & Rd 43213
Nancy Ln 43227
Nanticoke 43219
Nantucket Ave 43235
Napoleon Ave & Ct 43213
Nash Trl 43228
Nashoba Ave 43223
Nashville Dr 43240
Nason Ave 43207
Nassau Dr 43232
Natalia Dr 43232
Natalie Rose Way 43235
Natchez Dr 43209
Nathan Ct & Dr 43204
Nathaniel Blvd 43232
Nationwide Blvd 43228
E Nationwide Blvd 43215
W Nationwide Blvd 43215
Nationwide Plz 43215
Naughten Pond Dr 43213
Naughten Ridge Ct 43213
Nautical Dr 43207
Navarre Rd 43207
Navigator Dr 43228
Navy Hill Dr 43230
Nayland Rd 43220
Nectar Ln 43235
Needletail Rd 43230
E & W Neff Ave 43207
Negley Ct & Rd 43232
Neil Ave
201-207 43215
209-929 43215
930-1584 43201
1585-1667 43210
1586-1668 43201
1669-2179 43210
2180-2319 43201
2320-3099 43202
Neilston St 43215
N Nelson Rd 43219
S Nelson Rd
1-999 43205
1501-1599 43206
Nelsonia Pl 43213
Neruda Ave 43215
Nestling Dr 43229
Netherlands Pl 43235
Nettle Dr 43221
Nevada Dr E & W 43207
Nevis Dr 43235
New Bond St 43219
New Dawn Ct & Ln 43228
E & W New England Ave 43085
New Haven Dr 43220
New London Dr 43231
New Market Center Way 43235
New Moon Dr & Pkwy 43223
New Village Rd 43232
New World Dr 43207
New York Ave 43201
Newburgh Dr 43219
Newbury Ct & Dr 43229
Newcastle Ct 43232
Newcomer Rd 43235
Newell Ct & Dr 43228
Newfield Rd 43209
Newhall Rd 43220
Newport Ct & Rd 43232
Newton Ct 43230
Newton St 43205
Newtown Dr 43231
Niagara Ct & Rd 43227
Niantic Dr 43224
Nicholas Ave 43204
Nicholas Dr
6200-6315 43235
6316-6318 43234
6316-6598 43235
6317-6599 43235
Nicholas Gln 43213
Nickerson Rd 43228
Nieles Edge Dr 43232
Nightfall Cir 43211
Niles Dr 43207
Nipigon Dr 43207
Nissi Dr 43219
Nixon Dr 43204
Noam Ct 43232
Nob Hill Ct & Dr N, S & W 43230
Nobility Dr 43231
E Noble St 43215
Noble Run Way 43229
Nobleshire Rd 43229
Noddymill Ln E & W 43085
Noe Bixby Rd
1-1200 43213
1201-3999 43232
Noelle Ct 43232
Nomination Ln 43207
Nona Rd 43207
Norahrow Dr 43085
Norbrook Dr 43220
Norcrest Dr 43232
Norcross Ct & Rd 43229
Noreen Ct & Dr 43221
Norham Rd 43235
Norhill Rd 43235
Norma Rd 43229
Norman Dr 43227
Normandy Ave 43215
Norris Dr 43224
North Blvd 43204
North Ct 43229
North St
1-199 43202
1-199 43230
5800-5899 43230
E North St 43085
W North St 43085
E North Broadway St
1-699 43214
700-1999 43224
W North Broadway St 43214
Northam Rd 43221
Northbridge Ln 43235
Northbrook Dr E & W 43085
Northcliff Dr & Loop E, N & W 43229
Northcrest Ave 43220
Northcrest Dr 43224
Northern Oaks Dr 43235
Northern Pine Pl & St 43231
Northern Woods Ln 43231
Northgap Dr 43229
Northgate Rd 43229
Northglen Dr 43224
Northgrove Ct 43229
Northigh Dr 43085
Northland Rd 43085
Northland Park Ave 43229
Northland Plaza Dr 43231
Northland Ridge Blvd 43229
Northland Square Dr E 43231
Northmoor Pl 43214
Northport Cir & Dr 43235
Northridge Rd
1-699 43214
800-1899 43224
Northshire Ln 43235
Northtowne Blvd, Ct & Pl 43229
Northview Ave 43219
Northview Ct 43228
Northview Dr 43209
Northway Dr 43235
Northwest Blvd
700-2039 43212
2040-3299 43221
Northwest Ct 43212
Northwind Ct 43235
Northwold Rd 43231
E & W Northwood Ave 43201
Northwoods Blvd, Ct & Dr 43235
Norton Ave 43212
Norton Ct 43228
Norton Ctr 43228
Norton Ln 43213
Norton Rd 43228
Norwalk Rd 43207
Norway Dr 43221
Norway Glen Ave 43230
Norwell Ct & Dr 43220
E & W Norwich Ave 43201
Norwood St 43224
Notre Dame Pl 43213
Nottingham Rd
1-199 43214
2100-2899 43221
Nottinghill Way 43230
Nottinghill Gate Rd 43220
Nourse Ave 43228
Nova Ct 43085
Nugent Dr 43220
Nursery Ln 43206
Nutcreek Ct 43224
Nuthatch Way 43235
Nuway Rd 43207
Oak Rd 43217
Oak St
100-299 43235
325-695 43215
700-1899 43205
Oak Breeze Dr 43207
Oak Brook Pl 43228
Oak Creek Dr 43229
Oak Creek Pl 43230
Oak Gale Ln 43230
Oak Hollow Ct 43228
Oak Knoll Dr 43231
Oak Mill Dr 43207
Oak Path Ln 43213
Oak Point Cir 43229
Oak Spring St 43219
Oak Village Dr 43207
Oakbourne Dr 43235
Oakcrest Rd 43232
Oakdale Ave 43204
Oakes Dr 43207
Oakfair Ave 43235
Oakfield Dr E 43229
Oakgrove Ct 43229
Oakhill Rd 43220
Oakhurst Ln 43235
Oakland Ave 43212
E Oakland Ave
1-252 43201
253-253 43202
254-254 43201
255-499 43202
3400-3499 43219
W Oakland Ave 43201
Oakland Park Ave
1-659 43214
660-2399 43224
Oakland Park Ct 43224
Oaklawn St 43224
N & S Oakley Ave 43204
Oakmeadows Dr 43085
Oakmont Dr 43232
Oakmount Rd 43221
Oakridge Ct, Pl & Rd 43221
Oaks Blvd 43228
Oaks Edge Dr 43230
Oakshade Dr 43230
Oakstone Dr 43231
Oakstream Ct 43235
Oakton Ln 43229
Oakview Dr
1300-1699 43235
4300-4399 43204
Oakway Ct & Dr 43228
Oakwind Dr 43207
Oakwood Ave
200-398 43205
400-779 43205
780-1479 43206
1480-3799 43207
Oberlin Ct N 43230
Oberlin Dr 43221
Oberlin Pl 43221
Oberlin St 43230
Obetz Ave & Rd 43207
Obetz Reese Rd 43207
Obrien Rd 43228
October Ridge Ct & Dr 43223
Odonnell Ct 43228
Of Lassiter St 43217
Officenter Pl 43230
N & S Ogden Ave 43204
Oglethorpe 43228
N Ohio Ave 43203
S Ohio Ave
1-740 43205
741-1469 43206
3700-3799 43207
Ohlen Ave 43211
Okell Rd 43224
Oklahoma Ave 43230
Old Cherry Bottom Rd 43230
Old Colony Ln 43209
Old Courtright Rd 43232
Old Farm Ct & Rd 43213
Old Forest Ct 43230
Old Forge Rd 43209
Old Foxe Ct 43235
Old Henderson Rd & Sq 43220
Old Hickory Dr 43223
Old Leonard Ave 43219
Old Livingston Ave 43232
Old Mill Dr 43230
Old Oak Trce 43235
Old Pine Dr 43230
Old Rathmell Ct 43207
Old Ravine Ct 43220
Old Redbud Ct 43235
Old Roberts Rd 43228
Old Shay Ct 43229
Old Trail Ct & Dr 43213
Old Tree Ave & Pl 43228
Old Village Rd 43228
E & W Old Wilson Bridge Rd 43085
Old Woods Rd 43235
Oldbridge Dr 43220
Olde Bailey Way 43213
Olde Cape St E 43232
Olde Colony Way 43213
Olde Coventry Rd 43232
Olde Hill Ct N & S 43221
Olde Orchard Ct & Dr 43213
Olde Ridenour Rd 43230
Olde Settler Pl 43214
Olde Towne Ave 43214
Oldentime Ct 43207
Oldham Rd 43221
Ole Country Ln 43219
Olen Ave 43224
Olen Dr 43085
Olenhurst Ct 43235
Olentangy Blvd
3500-5499 43214
5600-5873 43085
5874-6098 43085
5875-5999 43085
6100-6199 43085
Olentangy Pt 43202
Olentangy St 43202
Olentangy Forest Dr 43214
Olentangy River Rd
901-1097 43212
1099-2099 43212
2100-2491 43210
2492-3499 43202
3500-5090 43214
5091-5099 43235
5092-5100 43214
5101-5970 43235
5901-5997 43085
5972-5998 43235
5999-6531 43085
6532-6560 43085
6533-6561 43085
6562-6838 43085
6839-8599 43235
Olentangy Woods Dr 43235
Olenwood Ave 43085
Olgate Ln 43220
Olive St 43204
Oliver St 43231
Olivette Rd 43232
Olmstead Ave 43201
Olney Dr 43227
Olpp Ave 43207
Olympia Dr 43207
Olympia Fields Ct 43230
Omar Dr 43207
Ombersley Ln 43221
Omega Dr 43231
Onandaga Dr 43221
Onaway Ct 43228
Ong St 43223
W Ongaro Dr 43204
Onslow Ct & Dr 43204
Ontario St
2130-2399 43211
2401-2599 43211
2710-3699 43224
Open Meadows Dr 43228
Ophelia Ln 43211
W Oraincom Ave 43210
Orange Blossom Ct & Ln 43230
Orangeburg Ct & Dr 43228
Orchard Dr
1-19 43085
1-116 43230
21-199 43085
Orchard Ln
1-399 43214
4100-4399 43207
Orchard Glen Ct 43228
Orchard Hill Ct 43230
Orchard Knoll Ln 43235
Orchard Lake Dr 43219
Orchard Park Dr 43232
Orchid Pl 43235
Oregon Ave 43201
Orel Ave 43204
Oriole Pl 43219
Orion Pl 43240
Orlando Ct & Rd 43232
Orleans Dr 43224
Ormanton Dr 43230
Ormond Ave 43224
Ormsby Pl 43212
Orson Dr 43207
Orville Ave 43228
Orwell Dr 43220
Osborn Dr 43221
Oscar Aly 43206
Osceola Ave 43211
Osceola Dr 43224
Osgood Rd E 43232
Osimund Dr 43235
Ostia Dr 43219
Oswin Dr 43219
Ottawa Dr 43229
Otter Creek Ct 43235
Ottis Ct 43204
Outerbelt St 43213
N & S Oval Mall 43210
Overbrook Dr 43214
Overbrook Service Dr 43224
Overdale Dr 43220
Overlook Ave & Dr 43214
Overlook Ridge Dr 43219
Overstreet Way 43228
Overview Ct 43231
Owens St 43228
Owsley St 43207
Oxford Ct 43085
Oxford Dr 43220
Oxford Rd 43221
Oxford St
500-999 43085
1300-1499 43211
Oxfordshire Dr 43228
Oxley Rd
2-48 43228
50-308 43228
800-1300 43212
1302-1398 43212
E & W Pacemont Rd 43202
Pacherm Rd 43221
Pacific Ct 43085
Paddington Ct 43230
Page Rd 43207
Page St 43230
Painted Cliff Dr 43219
Paisley Pl 43085
Palace Ln 43230
Paladim Pl & Rd 43232
Palamino Dr 43207
Palisades Ave 43207
Palm St 43213
Palm Springs Dr 43213
Palmatum Dr 43230
Palmer Rd 43212
Palmer House Ct 43235
Palmer Park Cir N & S 43230
Palmetto St
2200-2299 43223
2300-2328 43204
2330-3499 43204
4600-5199 43228
Palmira Way 43231
Palmleaf Ct & Ln 43235
Palmwood St 43229
Palomar Ave 43231
Pambrook Ct 43213
Pamela Dr 43230
Pamella Dr 43207
Pamlico St 43228
Pamona Ct 43228
Pampas Ct 43235
Pannell Ave 43207
Panorama Dr 43230
Papin St 43228
Paragon Dr 43228
W Park Ave
1-169 43222
170-1399 43223
Park Blvd 43085
Park Ct
700-799 43230
2300-2399 43224
Park Dr
2-898 43209
1101-1197 43230
1199-1299 43230
Park Ln 43220
Park Rd
1-231 43235
233-689 43085
691-751 43085
753-899 43085
Park St 43215
Park City Ct 43230
Park Crescent Dr 43232
Park Front Ct 43215
Park Hill Dr 43209
Park Lane Ct & Dr 43231
Park Overlook Dr 43085
Park Plaza Dr 43213
Park Ridge Ct & Dr 43235
Park Row Dr 43235
Park Run Dr 43220
Park Village Dr 43235
Parkcove Dr 43230
Parkcrest Ln 43220
Parkdale Dr 43229
Parkedge Dr 43230
Parker Knoll Ln 43219
Parkfair Pl 43213
Parkford Ln 43229
Parkgate Rd 43229
Parkgreen Pl 43229
Parkinson Ln 43232
Parkland Dr 43230
Parkland Pl 43209
Parklane Ave 43231
Parklawn Blvd & Cir 43213
Parkleigh Rd 43220
Parkline Dr 43232
Parkshire Dr 43229
Parkside Ct 43230
Parkside Rd 43204
Parksley Ct 43204
N Parkview Ave 43209
S Parkview Ave 43209
Parkview Blvd 43219
N Parkview Blvd 43219
Parkview Dr
300-499 43202
1200-1299 43229
Parkviewlake Dr 43207
Parkville Ct & St 43229
Parkway N 43212
Parkway Dr 43212
N Parkway Dr 43221
S Parkway Dr 43221
Parkwest Dr 43228
Parkwick Dr & Sq 43228
Parkwood Ave
1-599 43203
700-2139 43219
2140-2599 43211
2800-2999 43224
Parliament Ave 43230
Parliament Dr 43213
Parma Ave 43204
Parr Pl 43232
Parrau Dr 43228
Parsiphony Pl 43235
Parsley Pl 43230
Parsons Ave
1-261 43215
263-599 43215
600-1407 43206
1408-4899 43207
Partlow Dr 43220
Partridge Pl 43231
Pasadena Ave 43228
Pasqual Ave 43213
Passage Ln 43219
Pate Ct 43235
Patenson Dr 43219
Pathfield Dr 43230
Patricia Dr 43220
Patricia Ln 43213
Patrick Ave 43231
Patrick Henry Ave 43207
Patriot Blvd 43219
E & W Patterson Ave 43202
Patton Ave 43219
Paul Dr 43211
Paul Tibbets St 43217
Paula Ct & Dr 43220
Pauley Ct 43235
Pauline Ave 43224
Paw Paw Rd 43229
Pawling Pl 43235
Pawnee Ct 43085
Payday Ln 43232
Payne St 43205
Payton Way 43235
Pazzi Chapel 43219
Peabody Ave 43223
Peace Pl 43209
Peach Blossom Ct 43204

Peach Tree Ct 43204
Peach Tree Rd 43213
Peadwalm Rd 43207
Peak Ridge Dr 43230
Peale Ct 43230
Peandowe Dr 43229
Pear Tree Ct 43230
Peardale Rd E & N 43229
N Pearl St
1-25 43215
27-899 43215
901-1097 43201
1099-1799 43201
2400-2699 43202
S Pearl St
161-317 43215
319-599 43215
600-1329 43206
1500-1800 43207
1802-1898 43207
Pearway Ln 43228
Peat Moss Dr 43235
Pebble Ln 43220
Pebble Brook Dr 43240
Pebble Way Ct 43235
Pebblelane Dr 43085
Pechman Ln 43213
Peekskill Dr 43219
Pegg Ave 43214
Pegg Ct 43214
Pegg Rd 43224
Pegwood Ct & Dr 43229
Pelden Ct 43231
Pelham Pl 43207
Pelican Pointe 43231
Pemberton Dr 43221
Pembroke Ave 43203
Pendennis Ct 43235
Pendent Ln 43207
Pendlestone Dr 43230
Pendleton Ct & Pl 43219
Penfield Ct & Rd E, S & W 43227
Penhurst Rd 43228
Pennfair St 43214
Penniman St 43232
Pennsylvania Ave
600-699 43215
900-1599 43201
Penny Ct 43230
Penny Ln 43230
Penny Ln E 43230
Penny Ln N 43230
Penny Ln S 43230
Penny Ln W 43230
Penny St 43201
Penrose Dr 43219
Pentland Pl 43235
Penwood Pl 43235
Penworth Dr 43229
Pepper Ct & St 43219
Peppercorn Pl 43230
Pepperell Dr 43235
Pepperridge Ct 43228
Percy Pl 43204
Perdue Ave
2200-2849 43211
2850-3099 43224
Peregrine Pass Dr 43230
Performance Way 43207
Perigeaux Way 43219
Perimeter Dr 43228
S Perimeter Rd 43217
Perinton Pl 43232
Perkins Ct 43229
Perlman St 43228
Permit Ct 43230
Perry Dr 43085
Perry Pl 43085
Perry St
900-980 43215
981-1571 43201
1583-1599 43210
Pershing Dr 43224
Persimmon Pl 43213
Peru Aly 43201

Pervience St 43223
Peters Aly & Ave 43201
Petersburg Rd 43207
Petiole Way 43207
Petrel Aly 43219
Petticoat Ct 43231
Petzinger Ct 43232
Petzinger Rd
2401-2497 43209
2499-2899 43209
3000-3999 43232
Pevensey Ct & Dr 43220
Pewter Ct 43230
Phale D Hale Dr 43203
Pheasant Run E & W 43228
Pheasantview Ct 43213
Phelps Rd 43207
Phillipi Rd 43228
Phillips St 43203
Phoenician Way 43240
Picadilly Ct 43230
Picard Rd 43227
Picayune St 43221
Piccadilly Pl 43229
Picket Post Ln 43220
Pickett Ln 43235
Pickforde Dr 43235
Pickwick Dr 43221
Piedmont Rd
1-599 43214
600-1899 43224
Piedmont Rd S 43224
Pierce Ave
400-899 43213
900-1399 43227
Pierce Dr 43223
Pimlico Dr 43230
Pin Oak Dr 43229
Pincay Pl 43230
Pincherry Ln 43085
Pine Dr 43207
Pine St 43217
Pine Bark Ln 43235
Pine Bluff Rd 43229
Pine Grove Ln 43232
Pine Knoll Ave 43229
Pine Meadow Ct 43085
Pine Needle Ct 43232
Pine Rise Ct 43231
Pine Siskin Dr 43230
Pine Trace Ct 43228
Pine Tree St N 43229
Pine Valley Rd 43219
Pine Way Dr 43085
Pine Wild Dr 43223
Pinebrook Rd 43220
Pinecliff Pl 43085
Pinecone Ct & Ln 43231
Pinecrest Dr 43229
Pinegrove Pl 43230
Pinehurst Ct 43223
Pineland Ct 43223
Pinellas Ct 43231
Pinemoor St 43229
Pinerock Pl 43231
Pinestone Dr 43223
Pineview Dr 43213
Pinewood Dr 43213
Pinewood Ln 43230
Piney Glen Dr 43230
Pingree Ct & Dr 43085
Pingue Dr 43085
Pinnacle Dr 43204
Pinney Dr 43085
Pinney Hill Ct 43085
Pinto Ct 43221
Pinwherry Ct 43221
Pinzon Pl 43235
Pioneer St 43085
Pioneers Ct 43085
Pipers Ln 43228
Pipers Meadow Dr 43228
Pipers Run Ct 43228
Pipestem Ct 43229
Pipestone Dr 43235
Piragua Dr 43207

Piscitelli Pl 43201
Pittsfield Dr 43085
Pittston Ct 43231
Place De La Concorde St S & W 43229
Placid Ave 43085
Plainview Ave 43223
Plainview Dr 43204
Plane Tree Dr E & W 43228
Planetree Ct 43235
Plank Pl 43204
Plankton Dr & Pl 43213
Plant Dr 43085
Plantation Lake Ct 43221
Planters Ct 43207
Plateau St 43207
Plaza Ctr 43228
Plaza Properties Blvd 43219
Pleasant Ridge Ave 43209
Pleasant Valley Dr 43220
Pleasant View Rd 43219
Pleasant Woods Ct 43230
Plesenton Dr 43085
Plover Ct 43228
Plum Rdg 43213
Plum St 43204
Plum Creek Dr 43219
Plum Orchard Dr 43213
Plum Tree Dr 43235
Plumrose Dr 43228
Plumway Ct & Dr 43228
Plumwood St 43229
Plymouth Ave
2400-3099 43209
3300-3699 43213
Plymouth Ct 43213
Plymouth Pl 43213
Plymouth St 43085
Plymouth Rock Ct 43230
Pocono Rd 43235
Poe Ave 43085
Polaris Pkwy 43240
Polaris Green Dr 43240
Polaris Lakes Dr 43240
Poling Ct & Dr 43224
Polley Rd 43221
Pollman Dr 43224
Polo Dr N 43229
Polo Club Dr 43230
Pomeroy Pl 43202
Pomola St 43204
Ponderosa Dr
3100-3299 43204
5200-5799 43231
Pontiac St
2200-2869 43211
2870-3199 43224
Poolside Dr 43224
E Poplar Ave 43215
W Poplar Ave 43215
Poplar Ct 43207
Poplar Dr 43204
Poplar St 43207
Poplar Bend Dr 43204
Poplarwood Rd 43229
Poppy Ln 43235
Poppyseed Ct 43207
Porsche Ct 43232
Port Rd 43217
Portage Dr 43235
Porter St 43223
Portland St
5000-5199 43220
5200-5499 43235
Portlock Dr 43228
Portman Rd 43232
Portobello Dr 43230
Possum Run Ct S & W 43224
Post Oak Ct & Ln 43228
Poste Ln 43221
Postle Blvd 43228
Postlewaite Rd 43235
Poth Rd 43213
Powder Mill Ln 43228

Powell Ave
2000-2899 43209
4000-4299 43213
N Powell Ave 43204
S Powell Ave 43204
N Powell Cir 43204
E Powell Rd 43240
Powhatan Ave 43204
Prairiecreek Way 43213
Prairiefire Ave 43230
Prairieview Dr 43235
Preakness Ct 43221
Preamble Ln 43207
Predmore Pl 43230
Premier Dr 43207
Prentis House Ct 43235
E & W Prescott St 43215
Preservation Ln 43230
Preserve Crossing Blvd E, N & W 43230
Presidential Dr 43212
Presidential Gtwy 43231
Preston Ave 43221
Preston Clb 43219
Preston Rd 43209
Preston Woods Ct & Rd 43235
Prestwick Ct 43220
Prestwick Dr 43232
Prestwick Green Dr 43240
Price Ave 43201
Price Rd 43230
Primrose Pl 43212
Primrose Trl 43231
Primrose Hill Dr 43230
Prince George Dr 43209
Prince Of Wales Dr 43230
Princess Pl 43231
N Princeton Ave 43222
S Princeton Ave
1-169 43222
170-599 43223
Priory Ct 43224
Proclamation Ct & Way 43207
Proctor Dr 43209
Procyon Ave 43240
NW Professional Plz 43220
Progress Ave 43207
Proprietors Rd 43085
Prospect St 43204
Prosperity Ln 43231
Providence Ave 43214
Providence Glen Dr 43219
Pulsar Pl 43240
Punta Aly 43201
Purdy Aly 43206
Puritan Ave 43219
Putney Dr 43085
Putter Ave 43211
Pyle Pl 43227
Pyrenees Ct 43230
Quail Crossing Dr 43207
Quail Haven Ct & Dr 43235
Quail Hollow Dr 43228
Quail Ridge St 43229
Quail Valley Ct 43085
Quaker Rd 43207
Quaker Ridge Ct 43230
Quality Pl 43215
Quantum Square Dr 43240
Quarry Pt, Trce & Vw 43204
Quarry Crest Dr 43204
Quarry Lake Dr 43204
Quarry Ridge Dr 43232
Quarry Valley Rd 43204
Quartermaster Rd 43217
Quay Ave & Ct 43212
Queen Ann Ct 43235
Queens Ct 43229
Queensbridge Dr 43235
Queensgate Ln 43235
Queensrowe Ct, Dr & Pl 43227
Queenswood Ct & Dr 43219
Quentin Blvd 43230

Quigley Rd 43227
Quinby Dr 43232
Quince Dr 43228
Quincy Dr 43232
Quitman Dr E & W 43230
R Ave 43207
Raccoon Dr 43230
Race St 43204
Racine Ave 43204
Radbourne Dr 43207
Radekin Rd 43232
Rader Aly 43206
Radio City Blvd 43235
Radnor Ave 43224
Raflin Ct & Dr 43231
Raft Ln 43207
Rainbow Park 43206
Rainier Ave 43231
Rainier Lake Dr 43231
Raintree Pl 43229
Rainwater Way 43228
Rakeford Dr 43231
Raleigh Dr 43228
Ralston St 43214
Ramble Branch Dr 43220
Ramblehurst Ct & Rd 43221
Ramblewood Ave & Ct 43235
Rami Ave 43240
W Ramlow Aly 43202
Rampart Rd 43207
Ramsdell Dr 43231
Ramsey Ct 43231
Ramsgate Rd 43221
Ranchwood Dr 43228
Rand Ave, Cir, Ct & Sq E & W 43227
Randan Dr 43207
Randell Rd 43228
Randmore Ct & Rd 43220
Randolph Ct 43085
Randy Ct 43232
Ranelle Dr 43204
Rankin Ave
1700-2139 43219
2140-2399 43211
Ransburg Ave 43223
Ransey Ct 43230
Ransom Oaks Dr 43228
Ranstead Ct 43220
Rantines Dr 43231
Raphael Dr 43232
Rarig Ave 43219
Raspberry Ct 43204
Raspberry Run Dr 43204
Raspberrybush Ct 43230
Rathbone Ave 43214
Rathmell Rd 43207
Ratify Blvd 43207
Ravenel Dr 43209
Ravenglass Ct 43221
Ravens Glen Dr 43221
Ravens Nest Ct 43235
Ravenswood Ct 43232
Ravine Cir 43085
Ravine Bluff Ct 43231
Ravine Pointe Dr 43231
Ravine Ridge Dr 43085
Ravine Run Ln 43235
Ravine View Ct 43231
Ravines Edge Ct 43235
Ray St 43204
Rayme Dr 43207
Raymond St 43205
Rayne Ln 43220
Raynor Ct & Dr 43219
Rea Ave 43223
Reaver Ln 43223
Rebecca St 43219
Red Apple Rdg 43232
Red Bend Ln 43230
Red Bird Ct 43232
Red Cherry Ct 43230
Red Clover Pl 43224
Red Coat Ln 43230
Red Fern Dr & Pl 43229
Red Hill Ct 43085

Red Leaf Ln 43223
Red Oak Ln 43224
Red Robin Rd 43229
Red Sunset Pl 43213
E Redbud Aly 43206
W Redbud Aly 43206
Redbud Dr 43228
Redding Rd 43221
Redfield Dr 43229
Redford Ave 43207
Redmond Rd 43228
Redmond Way 43230
Redroyal Ave 43230
Redwood Ct & Rd 43229
Reeb Ave 43207
Reece Ridge Dr 43230
Reed Rd
99-99 43220
3500-3599 43221
3600-5199 43220
5200-5399 43235
Reed St 43223
Reed Circle Dr 43224
Reedbury Ln 43220
Reedy Dr 43085
Reese Ave 43207
Refugee Ln 43207
Refugee Park 43207
Refugee Rd
1100-2699 43207
2900-3128 43232
3130-5999 43232
Regal Pl 43230
Regaldo Dr 43219
Regency Dr 43220
Regency Sq 43213
Regency Manor Cir 43207
Regent St 43219
Regents Rd 43230
Regents Hill Dr 43223
Regentshire Dr 43228
Regiment Ln 43207
Regina Ave & Ct 43204
Reinbeau Ct & Dr 43232
Reindeer Ln 43230
Reinhard Ave 43206
Reis Ave 43224
Reliance St 43085
N & S Remington Rd 43209
Remington Ridge Rd 43232
Rendezvous Ln 43207
Rendon St 43221
Renfro Rd 43232
Renick St 43223
Renner Rd 43228
Rennes Dr 43221
Rentra Dr 43228
Renwell Ln 43230
Renwick Ln 43230
Renwood Pl 43211
Representation Ter 43207
Republic Ave 43211
Research Rd 43230
Reserve Rd 43217
Reston Park Dr 43235
Restwood Ct 43204
Retriever Rd 43232
Revere Ct 43228
Revere Rd 43213
Revolutionary Dr 43207
Rexwood Dr 43230
Reymond Ct & Rd 43220
Reynard Rd 43232
Reynolds Ave 43201
Rhoads Ave
200-899 43205
1100-1198 43206
2300-2699 43207
Rhoda Ave 43212
Rice Ave 43230
E Rich St
1-699 43215
900-1999 43205
W Rich St
1-630 43215
632-678 43215

680-939 43222
940-1302 43223
1304-1498 43223
1341-1345 43222
1401-1499 43223
Richard Ct 43085
Richards Rd 43214
N & S Richardson Ave 43204
Richey Ln 43213
Richland Dr 43230
Richmond Ave 43203
Richmond Rd 43223
Richter Rd 43223
Richtree Rd 43219
Richwood Ave 43215
Rickenbacker Ave 43213
Rickenbacker Pkwy 43217
Rickenbacker Pkwy W 43217
Rickenbacker St 43223
Rickenbacker Angb Bldg 43217
Rickenbacker Hanger 43217
Ridenour Rd 43230
Ridge Ave 43204
Ridge Pl 43230
Ridge St
1001-1025 43215
1027-1199 43215
4700-4999 43207
Ridge Crest Dr 43230
Ridge Gap Rd 43221
Ridgecliff Rd 43221
Ridgedale Dr E & N 43085
Ridgerun Dr 43229
Ridgeview Rd 43221
Ridgeway Ave 43219
Ridgeway Pl 43212
Riding Club Ln 43213
Ridley Dr 43228
Rieber St 43085
Riegel Rd 43232
Riegelwood Ct & Ln 43204
Riga Aly 43201
Rigel Dr 43240
Rightmire Blvd 43221
Rightmire Hall 43210
Riley Ave 43085
Rimbey Ave 43230
Rinaldi Dr 43219
Ringling Ln 43230
Ripplebrook Rd 43223
Rising Way 43235
Rita Ct
1-199 43213
300-399 43230
Rita Joanne Ln 43230
Ritamarie Dr 43220
Rittenhouse Sq N 43220
Riva Pl 43230
Riva Ridge Blvd & Ct 43230
River Dr 43230
River Rd 43214
River St 43222
River Avon Cir 43221
River Look Dr 43219
River Oaks Dr 43228
River Park Dr 43220
River Place Ct & Dr 43221
River Rhone Ln 43221
River Run Trce 43235
River Seine St 43221
River Thames St 43221
River Trail Ct 43228
Riverbend Pl & Rd 43223
Riverbirch Dr N 43229
Riverbrook Dr 43221
Rivercliff Rd 43223
Rivercreek Bay Way 43232
Rivercrest Dr 43223
Riverdale Rd & Sq E & W 43232
E & W Riverglen Dr 43085
Riverhill Rd 43221
Riverlane Ct 43221
Rivermill Dr 43220
Rivermont Rd 43223

Riverpoint Ct 43223
Riverport Dr 43221
Riverrock Dr 43228
Rivers Edge Dr 43235
Rivers Edge Way 43230
Rivers End Rd 43230
Rivers Gate Way 43221
Riverside Dr
1800-1879 43212
1880-3199 43221
3200-3248 43221
3201-3281 43202
3250-3330 43221
3283-3389 43202
3332-3550 43221
3391-3399 43202
3552-3798 43221
3800-4298 43220
4300-4400 43220
4402-5248 43220
5250-5256 43214
5257-5271 43220
5258-5272 43214
5273-5310 43220
5311-5317 43214
5312-5318 43220
5319-5320 43214
5321-5339 43220
5322-5340 43214
5341-5429 43220
Riverside Plz 43215
Riverstone Dr 43228
Riverton Ct & Rd 43232
Rivertop Ln 43220
Rivervail Ct & Dr 43221
Riverview Cir 43202
Riverview Dr
500-899 43202
3600-4099 43221
Riverview Pl 43202
Riverview Park Dr 43214
Riverwatch Ln 43221
Riviera Ct
600-799 43207
1300-1399 43204
Roads End Pl 43209
Roanoke Ave 43207
Robbins Rd 43219
Robbins Way 43085
Robena Ln 43211
Roberson St 43201
Robert St 43224
Robert Paul Pl 43231
Roberts Pl 43207
Roberts Rd 43228
Robin Hill Ct E & W 43223
Robinhood Park 43227
Robinwood Ave 43213
Robmeyer Dr 43207
Roche Ct, Dr & Pl N, S & W 43229
Rochelle Pl 43232
Rochfort Bridge Dr E 43221
Rock Gln 43230
Rock Fence Dr 43221
Rock Glen Ct 43232
Rock Hill Rd 43213
Rockcastle Dr 43229
Rockchester Ln 43229
Rockcress Ct 43085
Rockdale Dr 43229
Rockford Dr 43221
Rockford Ln 43232
Rockhaven Pl 43235
Rockledge Dr 43223
Rockpointe Ct & Dr 43221
Rockport Ct, Ln, Rd & St 43235
Rockwell Rd 43207
Rockwell Way 43085
Rockwood Ct, Pl & Rd 43229
Rockwoods Pl 43085
Rocky Gln 43230
Rocky Rd 43223
Rocky Creek Dr 43230
Rocky Fork Blvd, Ct, Dr & Pl N & S 43230
Rocky Pine Loop N 43229
Rocky Rill Rd 43235
Rocky Way Ln 43223
Rodell Rd 43232
Rodeo Dr 43213
Rodger Rd 43207
Rodgers Ave 43222
Rodney Rd 43227
Roebuck Dr 43230
Roehampton Ct 43209
Roggie Ave 43207
Roland Dr 43223
Roll Call Dr 43207
Rolling Brook Ln 43232
Rolling Meadows Dr 43228
Rolling Rock Ct & Dr 43229
Rollingwood Dr 43219
Rolls Royce Ct 43232
Romnay Rd 43220
Romona Pl 43204
Ronald Dr 43207
Ronda Rd 43232
Rondel Rd 43231
Ronnie Ln 43223
Ronnie Way 43207
Ronson Ave & Way 43230
N & S Roosevelt Ave 43209
Root Pl & St 43207
Rosalie Cir 43235
Rosburg Dr 43228
N Rose Ave 43219
Rose Pl 43227
Rose Way 43230
Rose View Dr 43209
Rosebank Dr 43235
Rosebery Dr 43220
Rosebud Ct 43230
Rosebush Dr 43235
Rosedale Ave
2400-2599 43223
2600-2899 43204
2901-3099 43204
Roselawn Ave 43232
Roselea Pl 43214
Rosemary Pkwy 43214
Rosemont Ave 43223
Rosemont Pl 43214
Rosemore Ave 43213
Rosethorne Ave 43203
Rosewind Ct 43235
Rosewind Dr 43211
Rosewood Ave 43219
Rosland Dr 43207
Roslindale Dr 43235
Ross Ave 43219
Ross Rd
100-979 43213
980-1099 43227
Rosser Dr 43214
Rosslyn Ave 43214
Rossmoor Pl 43220
Roswell Dr 43227
Roth Ave 43228
Rotherham Rd 43232
Rothingham Ln 43229
Rotunda Ct & Dr 43232
Round Rock Dr 43219
Roundtable Ln 43235
Roundtop Rd 43207
Rover Ln 43232
Rowanne Ct & Rd 43214
Rowland Ave 43228
Rowles Dr 43235
Roxburgh Ct 43213
Roxbury Ct 43219
Roxbury Rd
1400-1851 43212
1853-1899 43212
2600-2780 43219
2782-2798 43219
Roxham Ct 43230
Roxmore Ct 43232
Royal Cres 43219
Royal Dr 43223
Royal Crest Ct 43235
E & W Royal Forest Blvd 43214
Royal Gold Dr 43240
Royal Hill Dr 43223
Royal Oak Dr 43229
Royal Palm Ct 43207
Royal Tern Xing 43230
N & S Roys Ave 43204
Royston Dr 43204
Ruby Ave 43227
Rubythroat Dr 43230
Rudon Ln 43204
Rudy Rd 43214
Rue De Brittany 43221
Rue De Fleur 43221
Rue Montmarte St 43229
Rue Royale St 43229
Ruff Ct 43230
Rugby Ct & Ln 43230
Ruhl Ave 43209
Ruma Rd 43207
Rumsey Rd 43207
Runaway Bay Dr 43204
Rundell Dr 43204
Running Fox Rd 43235
Runnymede Ln 43228
Runyon Rd 43227
Rush Ave 43214
Rushden Dr 43230
Rushing Way 43235
Rushmore Dr 43220
Ruskin Ave 43219
E & W Russell St 43215
Rustic Pl 43214
Rustic Bridge Rd 43214
Rustic Ledge Dr 43219
Rustic Woods Ln 43230
Ruston Ave 43230
Ruth Ct 43204
Rutherford Pl 43213
Rutherglen Dr 43235
Ruthton Rd 43220
Rutland Way 43085
Rutledge Dr N 43232
Ruxton Ln 43220
Ryan Ave 43223
S Ave 43207
Sabastian Ct 43213
Sabers Ln 43232
Sabin Cir 43230
Sable Crossing Dr 43240
Saddle Ridge Ln 43085
Saddlebrook Ct & Dr 43221
Saddlehorn Dr 43221
Saddlery Dr E & W 43230
Safford Ave
1500-2299 43223
2401-2499 43204
Safin Rd 43204
Sagamore Rd 43219
Sage Ct 43085
Sagecrest Dr 43229
Sagemeadow Ct 43235
Sagewood Ct 43235
Saint Agnes Ave 43204
Saint Albans Ct 43220
Saint Andre St 43085
Saint Ann Ln 43235
Saint Anthony Ln 43213
Saint Antoine St 43085
Saint Bernard Cir 43232
Saint Catherine St 43221
Saint Cecelia Dr 43204
Saint Christopher Ln 43213
Saint Clair Ave
100-699 43203
700-1299 43201
1344-1408 43211
1411-1499 43211
Saint Croix Dr 43085
Saint Elizabeth St 43221
Saint Francis Ln 43213
Saint Helena St 43221
Saint Jacques St 43085
Saint James Ct 43220
W Saint James Lutheran Way 43228
Saint John Ct 43202
Saint Johns Ct & Pl N 43230
Saint Joseph Ave 43204
Saint Jude Ave 43204
Saint Julien St 43085
Saint Kitts Dr 43085
Saint Laurent St 43085
Saint Lawrence Dr 43223
Saint Louis St 43221
Saint Margaret Ln 43213
Saint Marie St 43221
Saint Martins Ct 43230
Saint Mary Ct 43213
Saint Matthew Ave 43204
Saint Michelle St 43085
Saint Patrick Rd 43204
Saint Pauls St 43221
Saint Peter St 43221
Saint Phillip St 43221
Saint Pierre St 43085
Saint Rita Ln 43213
Saint Rosalie St 43221
Saint Rose St 43221
Saint Stephens Ct 43230
Saint Will St 43221
Salado Creek Dr 43219
Sale Rd 43224
Salem Dr 43228
Saling Ct & Dr 43229
Salisbury Rd 43204
Salt Lick Ln 43230
Salt Spring Ln 43207
Samada Ave 43085
Samick St 43235
Sampson Ave 43219
San Andres Pl 43230
San Bonita Dr 43235
San Diego Dr 43213
San Gabriel Dr 43213
San Jose Ln 43213
San Remo Dr 43204
Sanborn Pl 43229
Sanbridge Cir 43085
Sancroft Rd 43235
Sanctuary Ct 43235
Sanctuary Dr 43235
Sanctuary Pl 43230
Sanctuary Village Dr 43235
Sancus Blvd
7300-7501 43085
7503-7999 43085
8311-9599 43240
Sand Dollar Dr 43232
Sandals Ct 43235
Sandalwood Blvd, Ct & Pl 43229
Sandburr Dr 43230
Sandbury Blvd 43235
Sanders Dr 43213
Sanderson Ct & Dr 43228
Sandgate Rd 43229
Sandhurst Rd 43229
Sandlin Ave 43224
Sandman Dr 43235
Sandover Ct & Rd 43220
Sandra Ct 43230
Sandrell Dr 43228
Sandridge Ave 43224
Sandridge St 43207
Sandringham Ct & Dr 43220
Sandston Rd 43220
Sandstrom Dr 43235
S Sandusky St 43215
Sandy Lane Rd 43224
Sandy Ridge Dr 43204
Sandy Side Dr 43235
Sanford Dr 43235
Sanita Ct 43204
Sansom Ct 43220
Santa Barbara Ct & Dr 43213
Santa Catalina Ct 43213
Santa Clara 43213
Santa Maria Ct 43207
Santa Maria Ln 43213
Santa Michele Ct 43207
Santa Monica Dr 43213
Santa Rosa 43213
Santana St 43235
Saranac Dr 43232
Sarazen Ct 43228
Sargas St 43240
Sarin St 43240
Sassafras Rd 43229
Satinwood Dr 43229
Satterfield Rd 43235
Satyr Hl 43219
Saugus Cir 43224
Saulsbury Ct 43230
Saunderlane Rd 43235
Savannah Dr 43228
Savannah Grove Ln 43221
Saverio Ct 43235
Savern Pl 43230
Saville Ct & Row 43224
Sawatch Dr 43228
Sawbury Blvd & Ct 43235
Sawmill Rd
4000-4749 43220
4750-4776 43235
4751-4777 43220
4778-5000 43235
5002-7460 43235
Sawmill Place Blvd 43235
Sawmill Village Ct & Dr 43235
Sawtooth Oak Dr 43228
Sawyer Blvd 43203
Sawyer Rd
4200-4266 43219
4267-4299 43236
4268-5098 43219
4401-5099 43219
Saxon Ct 43232
Saxony Rd 43207
Say Ave 43201
Sayan Pl 43230
Scales Dr 43228
Scarborough Blvd & Sq 43232
Scarfield Ln 43235
Scarlet St 43227
Scarlett Ln 43207
Scenic Dr 43214
Scenic Bluff Dr 43231
Scenic View Cir 43240
Scepter Pl 43235
Schaaf Dr 43209
Schehl Dr 43219
Schenley Dr 43219
Scherers Ct 43085
Schiller Aly 43206
Schilling Ln 43223
Schillingwood Dr 43230
Schmidt Rd 43224
Schofield Dr 43213
School St 43215
Schoolcraft Ln 43235
Schoolhouse Ln 43228
Schooner Ct 43221
Schreiner St E & W 43085
E & W Schreyer Pl 43214
Schrock Ct 43229
Schrock Rd
200-459 43085
460-2499 43229
Schrock Hill Ct 43229
Schryver Rd 43207
Schultz Ave 43222
Schurtz Ave 43204
Schuster Way 43207
Schuylkill St 43220
Schwartz Rd
2800-3199 43232
3200-3399 43207
Schyler Ct & Way 43230
Science Blvd 43230
Sciotangy Dr 43221
Scioto Pkwy, Pl & Trce 43221
Scioto Darby Creek Rd 43221
Scioto Estates Ct 43221
Scioto Harper Dr 43204
Scioto Pointe Dr & Ln 43221
Scioto Station Dr 43204
Scioto View Ln 43221
Scioto Villa Ln 43207
Scotch Pine Ct 43231
Scotsfield Dr 43230
Scott Ct N 43228
Scott Ct S 43228
Scott Dr 43228
Scott Rd 43223
Scott St
500-552 43215
554-580 43215
582-678 43215
680-866 43222
868-1099 43222
Scott Glen Ct 43229
Scott Valley Dr 43223
Scottsbury Ct 43230
Scottsdale Ave 43235
Scottsford Pl 43235
Scottwood Rd
2400-2983 43209
2984-3599 43227
Scriven Ave 43228
Sea Harbor Dr 43230
Sea Pines Pl 43221
Seabell Ct 43230
Seabrook Ave 43227
Seabury Dr 43085
Seaford Ct & Dr 43220
Seaforth Pl 43232
Searles Ave 43223
Seasons Dr 43235
Seaton Ct & Ln 43229
Seattle Ave 43240
Seattle Slew Dr 43221
Secludedwood Ct 43230
Secor Ct 43224
Secrest Ave 43207
Secretariat Ct 43221
Securities St 43228
Sedalia Dr 43232
Sedan Ave 43207
Sedge Ln 43230
Sedgwick Ct 43235
Sedgwick Dr 43220
Sedgwick Rd 43235
Seeger St 43228
Seemic Cir 43203
Seeran Pl 43228
Sefton Park Dr 43235
Seigman Ave 43213
Seiler Ct 43223
Seisher Rd 43213
E, N, S & W Selby Blvd & Ct 43085
Selkirk Rd 43227
Sellers Ave 43214
Sells Ave 43212
Selwyn Ct 43235
Seminary Rdg 43235
Senator Ct 43204
Seneca Park Pl 43209
Sente Ln 43219
Sepich Ln 43232
Serene Pl 43231
Serenity Dr 43230
Serenity Ln 43085
Serran Dr 43230
Sertan Ave 43240
Sessil Ct 43230
Sessions Dr 43209
Sessis Dr & Ln 43085
Sestos Dr 43207
Setterlin Dr 43228
Severn Rd 43209
Seville Ave 43232
Sexton Dr 43228
Seymour Ave
400-869 43205
870-1399 43206
Shackleford Ct 43220
Shademont Ct 43235
Shadewood Ct 43230
Shadow Falls Ln 43231
Shadow Lake Cir 43235
Shadow Rock Dr 43219
Shadowbrook Dr 43235
Shadowland Ln 43213
Shadowstone Way 43221
Shady Ct 43229
Shady Brook Ln 43228
Shady Hill Ct & Dr 43221
Shady Lake Dr 43228
Shady Lane Ct & Rd 43227
Shady Ridge Dr 43231
Shady Spring Dr 43230
Shadycrest Rd 43229
Shadymere Ln 43213
Shadyside St 43213
Shadywood Rd 43221
Shagbark Rd 43230
Shaker Dr 43230
Shakerton Ln 43228
Shakespeare Garden Pl 43235
Shale Ridge Ct 43235
Shalers Dr 43228
Shallowford Ave 43235
Shalom Way 43219
Shamrock Dr 43227
Shana Dr 43232
Shanley Dr 43224
Shannon Ln 43235
Shannonbrook Dr 43221
Shapter Ave 43229
Shara Park Pl 43230
Sharbot Dr 43229
Shari Dr 43223
Sharon Ave 43214
Sharon Ct 43229
Sharon Rd 43231
Sharon Brook Ct 43229
Sharon Creek Ct 43229
Sharon Green Dr 43229
Sharon Hill Dr 43235
Sharon Mill Ct 43085
Sharon Park Ave 43214
Sharon Springs Dr 43085
Sharon Woods Blvd 43229
Sharrington Dr 43235
Sharwood Ct 43235
Shasta Ave 43231
Shattuck Ave
3200-3449 43221
3450-4099 43220
Shaula Dr 43240
Shawbury Ct E & W 43229
Shawnee Ave 43211
Sheffield Dr 43230
Sheffield Rd 43214
Sheila Pl 43232
Shelbourne Ln 43220
Sheldon Ave 43207
Sheldrake Ct 43085
Shell Ct E 43213
Shelley Ct 43235
Shellwick Ct 43235
Shelly Dr 43207
Shelton St 43223
Shenandoah Valley Dr 43207
Shepard St 43230
Sherborne Cres 43224
Sherborne Dr 43219
Sherbrooke Pl 43209
Sheridan Ave 43209
Sheridan St 43223
Sheridan Park Ct 43209
Sheringham Rd 43220
Sherman Ave 43205
Sherry Ct 43232
Sherwill Ct & Rd 43228
Sherwin Rd 43221
Sherwood Frst E 43228
Sherwood Frst N 43228
Sherwood Frst W 43228
Sherwood Rd 43209

Sherwood Forest Ct 43228
Sherwood Meadows Dr 43230
Sherwood Villa 43221
Shetland Ct 43085
Shetland St
6900-7001 43085
7002-7199 43235
Shields Pl 43214
Shilling Dr 43232
Shiloh Dr 43220
Shires Ct & Rdg 43220
Shirley Ln 43228
Shirlington Dr 43235
Shoemaker Ave 43201
Shook Rd 43217
Shoppers Ln 43228
Shore Blvd E 43232
Shore Blvd W 43232
E Shore Ct 43231
Shore Dr 43229
E Shore Dr 43231
Shore Line Ln 43221
Shoreham Rd 43220
Shorehill Ln 43235
Shoreline Ct & Dr 43232
Short St
100-198 43230
300-599 43215
601-799 43215
W Short St 43085
Shoupmill Dr 43230
Showcase Dr 43212
Shrewsbury Rd 43221
Shull Ave & Rd 43230
Shumaker Ln 43213
Shuster Ln & Rd 43214
Sibby Ln 43235
Sibley Ave 43227
Sidney St 43201
Sidway Ave 43227
Siebert St 43206
Sienna Ln N 43229
Sierra Dr 43230
Sierra Ridge Dr 43231
Sigler Ln 43230
Signal Dr 43232
Sigsbee Ave 43219
Silkwood Ct 43085
Silvaner Dr 43230
Silver Crk 43228
Silver Dr
2301-2697 43211
2699-2899 43211
2921-3299 43224
Silver Ln 43230
Silver Fox Dr 43235
Silver Oak Dr 43232
Silver Rod Ln 43230
Silver Springs Ln 43230
Silverado Dr 43228
Silverberry Ct 43228
Silverbrook Dr 43207
Silverglade Ct & Dr 43230
Silverleaf Ct 43235
Silverton Ct & Dr 43232
Silverwood St 43229
Simbury St 43228
Simpson Dr 43227
Sinclair Rd 43229
Singing Hills Ln 43235
Singletree Dr 43229
Sinsbury Dr E & N 43085
Sinsidee Ct 43228
Siphda Dr 43240
Sirius St 43240
Sisco Aly 43203
Sisk Ct 43219
Siskin Ave 43228
Six Point Ct 43085
N & S Skidmore St 43215
Skimmer Ln 43230
Skinner Ave 43230
Skipstone Pl 43221
Skylark Ln 43235
Skyline Dr 43235

Skyview Dr 43224
Skywae Dr 43229
Slade Ave 43235
Slate Hill Ct & Dr 43085
Slate Run Ct & Rd 43220
Slate Run Woods Ct 43220
Slatebrook Ln 43229
Slatey Hollow Ln 43220
Slaton Ct 43235
Sleaford Ave 43230
Slemmons Dr 43235
Slippery Rock Dr 43229
Smallwood Dr 43235
Smiley Rd 43221
Smith Ct 43207
Smith Pl 43201
Smith Rd
300-599 43228
1017-1699 43207
Smith Pines Dr 43230
Smokehill Dr 43228
Smoketree Ct 43235
Smokey Pl 43230
Smoky Meadow Ct & Dr 43235
Smoky Row Rd 43235
Snap Dragon Dr 43207
Snohomish Ave 43085
Snouffer Pl 43235
Snouffer Rd
1800-1962 43085
1963-2499 43085
1964-2498 43085
2601-2613 43235
2615-3899 43235
Snowbird Cir 43229
Snowmass Rd 43235
Snyder Ct 43231
Sobeck Rd 43232
Society Hill Ct 43219
Soft Wind Ct & Dr 43232
Solar Dr 43214
Soldano Blvd 43228
Soldier St 43232
Solera Dr 43229
Solitare Ln 43231
Somerford Rd 43221
Somerset Ct E 43227
Somersworth Ct & Dr 43219
Sommerfeld Pl 43201
Sonata Dr 43209
Songbird Dr 43229
Sonoma Ct 43229
Sophie St 43219
Soramill Ln 43085
Sorren Ct 43230
N Souder Ave 43222
S Souder Ave
1-449 43222
601-697 43223
699-799 43223
Souninco Ave 43212
South Aly 43230
South Blvd 43204
South Ln 43206
E South St 43085
W South St 43085
N & S Southampton Ave 43204
Southard Dr 43207
Southbridge Ln 43213
Southfield Dr 43207
Southgate Dr 43207
E & W Southington Ave 43085
Southminster Rd 43221
Southpark Dr 43230
Southpoint Blvd 43207
Southport Cir & Dr 43235
Southridge Dr 43224
Southview Ct & Dr 43235
Southwark Ln 43204
Southway Dr 43221
Southwind Ct & Dr 43230
Southwood Ave 43207
Sovereign St 43235

Spaatz Ave 43204
Spangler Rd 43207
Sparrow Ln 43235
Sparrow Hill Dr 43219
Spartan Dr 43209
Spectacle Dr 43230
Speedway Ln 43207
Spencer Ct 43228
Sperry Ave 43230
Spica Ave 43240
Spice Market N 43221
Spicewood Ct 43228
Spindler Rd 43228
Spire Ln 43232
Spirea Ave 43230
Splitrock Rd 43221
E Spring St
1-689 43215
690-1099 43203
W Spring St 43215
Spring Beauty Ct 43230
Spring Flower Ct 43230
Spring Grove Ln 43235
Spring House Ln 43229
Spring Lake Dr 43219
Spring Park Pl 43230
Spring Rock Cir 43229
Spring Run Dr 43229
Springboro Ln 43235
Springbrook Dr & Pl 43230
Springfield Chase 43228
Springhill Dr 43221
Springmont Ave 43223
Springs Dr 43214
Springside Dr 43230
Springston Ln 43235
Springtime Ct 43207
Springway Ct 43232
Springwood Dr 43224
Springwood Lake Dr 43230
Spruce Dr 43217
Spruce Dr E 43217
Spruce St 43215
Spruce Hill Dr 43230
Spruce Hollow Cir 43235
Spruce Needle Ct 43235
Spruce Pine Dr 43235
Spruce Tree Dr 43232
Sprucefield Dr & Rd 43229
Spruceview Ct 43231
Sprucewood Rd 43229
Spur Ln 43221
Spyglass Dr 43228
Squadron Dr 43207
Squires Ln & Rdg 43220
Squirrel Bnd 43220
Squirrel Ridge Dr 43219
Stacie Ln 43224
Stadium Dr 43202
E Stafford Ave 43085
W Stafford Ave 43085
Stafford Pl 43209
Staffordshire Rd 43229
Stag Pl 43230
Stalling Ct 43204
Stalywood Ct 43085
Stambaugh Ave 43207
Stanaford Pl 43207
Stanbery Ave & Dr 43209
Stanburn Rd 43235
Standhill Dr 43219
Stanford Rd 43212
Stanhope Dr 43221
Stanlake Ct 43235
Stanley Ave 43206
E Stanton Ave 43214
W Stanton Ave 43085
Stanwix Ct 43223
N & S Stanwood Rd 43209
Stapleford Dr 43230
N Star Ave 43212
N Star Rd
1661-1697 43212
1699-1899 43212
1901-2039 43212
2040-3199 43221

Star Check Dr 43217
Starbridge Ct 43235
Starbright Crossing Dr 43240
Stark Ct 43210
Starleaf Ln 43235
E & W Starr Ave 43201
Starrett Ct & Rd 43214
E State St 43215
W State St
1-679 43215
680-1499 43222
State House 43215
Station Rd 43228
Station St 43235
Stavely Ct 43232
Stedway Ct 43230
Steele Ave 43204
Steelwood Rd 43212
Stegner Rd 43207
Steiner St 43231
Steiner House 43219
Stella Ct 43215
Stelzer Rd
400-4115 43219
4116-4298 43230
Stemwood Dr 43228
Stenten St 43085
Stenton Ln 43230
Stephanie Ct 43232
Stephen Dr S & W 43204
Sterling Ave, Ln & Rd 43219
Sterling Silver Way 43240
Sternberger Pl 43214
Stetson Rd 43232
Stevenlane Blvd 43232
Stevens Ave 43222
Stevenson Ave 43085
Stewart Ave 43206
Stewart Pl 43214
Stiles Ave 43228
Stillbreeze Ct 43230
Stillponds Pl 43228
Stilson Ct 43235
Stilton Ave 43228
Stimmel Rd 43223
Stimmel St 43206
Stinchcomb Dr 43202
Stinson Ct & Dr 43214
Stirlingshire Ct 43219
Stirrup Ct 43221
Stock Rd 43229
Stockade Pl 43230
Stockbridge Rd 43207
Stockton Trail Way 43213
Stockwell Dr 43235
Stoddart Ave 43205
Stokey Ct 43230
Stokley Ct 43235
Stone Ave 43205
Stone Ct 43235
Stone Ridge Dr & Rd S 43213
Stone Ring Ct 43240
Stonebluff Dr 43232
Stonebridge St 43229
Stonebridge Crossing Dr 43221
Stonebrook Ct 43220
Stonebrook Ln 43229
Stonecastle Dr 43229
Stonecreek Ct 43224
Stonecrest Ct 43221
Stoneford Dr 43235
Stonegate Cir 43230
Stonegate Sq E 43224
Stonegate Sq N 43224
Stonegate Sq S 43224
Stonegate Sq W 43224
Stonegate Village Dr 43212
Stonehaven Ct, Dr & Pl N & S 43220
Stonehedge Rd 43231
Stonehenge Ct 43221
Stonehenge Dr 43224
Stonemason Way 43221
Stonemeadow Ave 43220

Stoneridge Dr & Ln 43230
Stonevista Ln 43221
Stonewater Dr 43221
Stoneway Dr 43229
Stonewood Ct 43235
Stoney Bridge Ln 43221
Stoney Creek Ct & Rd 43235
Stoneygate Ln 43221
Stornoway Dr E 43213
Strack Rd 43207
Stransberry Ct 43085
Stratford Dr 43220
Stratford Ln 43232
Stratford Way 43219
Strathaven Ct & Dr E, N & W 43085
Stratshire Ct, Ln & Pl 43230
Stratton Rd 43220
Strawberry Ct 43085
Strawberry Flds 43235
Strawberry Farms Blvd 43230
Strawberry Glade Dr 43230
Strawberry Hill Rd E & W 43213
Strawfield Dr 43230
Stream Pebble Dr 43240
Stresswood Ct 43085
Stretford Ln 43229
Striebel Ct & Rd 43227
Strimple Ave 43229
Stripes Ln 43207
Stroup Ln 43230
Struif Ct 43207
Stuart Ln 43085
Studer Ave
800-1509 43206
1510-2099 43207
Stunsail Ln 43221
Sturbridge Dr 43209
Sturbridge Rd 43228
N & S Stygler Rd 43230
Sudbury Rd 43221
Suffield 43232
Suffolk Rd 43221
Sugar Hill Pl 43230
Sugar Loaf Ct 43221
Sugar Plum St 43230
Sugarbush Blvd 43230
Sugarmaple Ct & Dr 43229
Sullivant Ave
540-679 43215
680-786 43222
787-1799 43223
1800-1810 43222
1801-2299 43223
1818-2298 43223
2300-3589 43204
3590-5200 43228
5202-5298 43228
Sumac Dr & Loop E, N & S 43229
Summer Breeze Dr 43223
Summer Hill Cir & Pl 43230
Summerdale Ln 43221
Summerduck 43219
Summerfern Ln 43213
Summerhill Ln 43221
Summerland Ct 43230
Summerside Dr 43085
Summerstone Dr 43230
Summertime Ct 43221
Summerview Dr 43085
Summerway Ct 43232
Summerwood Dr 43235
Summit Dr 43224
Summit St
760-899 43215
900-2239 43201
2240-3299 43202
4600-4698 43224
Summit Hollow Dr 43219
Summit Ridge Rd 43220
Summit Rock Pt 43235
Summit Springs Dr 43207
Sumption Dr 43230
Sun Flare Dr 43240

Sunapple Way 43232
Sunburst Dr 43207
Sunbury Ct E 43219
Sunbury Ct N 43219
Sunbury Ct W 43219
Sunbury Dr 43219
Sunbury Rd
400-698 43219
700-4799 43219
4800-5949 43230
Sunbury Sq 43219
Sunbury Ridge Dr 43219
Suncrest Dr 43223
Sundale Pl & Rd N, S & W 43232
Sundance Dr 43224
Sunderland Dr 43229
Sundridge Dr 43221
Sunflower Dr 43204
Sunglade Ct 43235
Sunleaf Ct 43235
Sunmark Ave 43232
Sunningdale Way 43221
Sunny Ct 43229
Sunny Glen Pl 43224
Sunny Hill Dr 43221
Sunny Vale Dr 43228
Sunnybrook Ct & Dr 43221
Sunnyside Ln 43214
Sunrise Ave 43212
Sunrise Lake Cir 43219
Sunset Blvd 43223
Sunset Cv 43202
Sunset Dr
2800-2898 43221
2901-2997 43202
2999-3099 43202
3300-3799 43221
Sunset View Ct 43207
Sunshine Pl 43232
Surface Rd 43228
Surfbird Dr 43230
Surrey Pl 43219
Surrey Hill Pl 43220
Surreygate Ct & Dr 43235
Sussex Ct & Dr 43220
Sutherland Dr 43207
Sutterton Dr 43230
Sutton Ave 43204
Sutton Place Dr 43230
Suwanee Rd 43224
Swallowfield St 43207
W Swan St
1-99 43215
701-799 43212
Swansea Rd 43221
Sweet Basil Dr 43213
Sweet Clover Ct 43228
Sweet Shadow Ave 43230
Sweet William Ct 43230
Sweetday St 43224
Sweetgum Pl 43229
Sweeting Ave 43229
Sweetwater Ct 43229
Swift Way 43235
Swingley Dr 43230
Switchback Trl 43228
Switzer Ave 43219
Sycamore Pl
600-699 43230
700-799 43206
E Sycamore St 43206
W Sycamore St
1-51 43206
53-129 43206
130-199 43215
Sycamore Knolls Dr 43219
Sycamore Mill Dr 43230
Sycamore Ridge Way 43230
Sycamore Turn Ln 43213
Sycamore Woods Ln 43230
N & S Sylvan Ave 43204
Symington Ave 43204
T Ave 43207
Tabernash Dr 43240
Tabon Ct 43230

Tacoma Rd 43229
Tadcaster Ln 43228
Taft Ave 43228
Tahoma St 43240
Talbert Ct & Dr 43232
Talbot Pl 43223
Talcott Ct & Dr 43204
Talford Ct & Rd 43232
Taliesin Pl 43219
Talisman Ct 43209
Tall Meadows Dr 43223
Tall Oaks Dr 43230
Tall Pine Ct 43223
Tall Timbers Ct 43228
Talmadge St 43203
Tamara Dr N & S 43230
Tamarack Blvd, Cir & Ct E, N & S 43229
Tamarin Dr 43235
Tami Pl 43230
Tammery Ct 43231
Tanager Dr 43230
Tangarey Ct 43235
Tanglewood Ct 43224
Tappan St 43201
Tara Ct 43224
Tarben Woods Ct & Dr 43230
Tarragon Way 43213
Tarrington Ln 43220
Tarryton Ct E 43228
Tartan Ln 43235
Tatersall Ct 43230
Tattler Rd 43230
Taunton Way 43228
Taurus Ave 43230
Tauton Ct 43221
Taylor Ave
1-560 43203
700-1500 43219
1502-1598 43219
2200-2499 43211
Taylor Rd 43230
Taylor Station Rd
2-198 43213
200-300 43213
302-398 43213
411-597 43230
599-1100 43230
1102-1398 43230
Taymouth Rd 43229
Tea Party Pl 43207
Teak Ct 43231
Teakwood Ct & Dr 43229
Tealwater Trail Dr 43207
Teardrop Ave 43235
Tech Center Dr 43230
Technology Dr 43230
Tecumseh Ave 43207
Tedco Dr 43223
Teddy Dr 43227
Teeway Dr 43220
Tegmen St 43240
Telford Dr 43229
Telham Ct & Dr 43204
Tellega Ave 43207
Teller St 43228
Tempest Dr 43232
Templar St 43232
Temple Ave 43211
Templeton Rd 43209
Tenabo Ave 43231
Tenagra Way 43228
Tenbrook Pl 43228
Tenby Dr 43240
Tendril Ct 43229
Tennyson Blvd 43232
Tennyson Ct 43235
Tera Alta Rd 43207
Teresa Sq 43207
Ternstedt Ln 43228
Terra Dr 43228
N Terrace Ave 43204
S Terrace Ave 43204
Terrace Dr 43212
Terrace Ln 43211

- Terrace Park Dr 43235
- Terran Way 43219
- Terrance Dr 43220
- Tessier Dr 43235
- Teter Ct 43220
- Teteridge Rd 43214
- Tetford Rd 43220
- Teton Ct & Rd 43230
- Tewksbury Rd 43221
- Thacker Ct 43204
- Thackeray Ave 43085
- Thada Ln 43229
- Thames Dr 43219
- Thayer Dr 43230
- The Old Poste Rd 43221
- The Strand 43219
- Thelma Dr 43207
- Theori Ave 43230
- Thimbleberry Rd 43207
- Thistle Ave 43230
- Thistledown Dr 43221
- Thistlewood Ct & Dr 43235
- Thoburn Rd 43221
- Tholderm Dr 43085
- Thomas Ave 43223
- Thomas Ln
  - 500-672 43214
  - 674-849 43214
  - 850-1099 43220
- Thomas Pl 43207
- Thomas Rd 43212
- Thomas Joseph Ln 43235
- Thompson Rd 43230
- Thompson St 43235
- Thorburn Pl 43230
- Thoreau Ct 43232
- Thornapple Cir & Dr E, N, S & W 43231
- Thornberry Dr 43231
- Thornburg Ct 43230
- Thorncroft Ct 43235
- Thorndale Ave 43207
- Thorndyke St 43232
- Thorne St 43085
- Thornell Way 43232
- Thornfield Ln 43235
- Thornford Ct 43235
- Thornham Dr 43228
- Thornstone Ct 43228
- Thornway Dr 43231
- Thornwood Pl 43212
- Thoroughbred Ct 43221
- Thoroughbred Dr 43217
- Three Oaks Ct 43230
- Threshing Ct 43230
- Thunderbird Ct 43228
- Thurber Dr E & W 43215
- Thurell Rd 43229
- Thurman Ave 43206
- Thurston Dr 43227
- Thyme Pl 43213
- Tiara Ave 43207
- Tibet Rd 43202
- E Tibet Rd 43211
- Tiehack Ct 43235
- Tiffany Ct 43209
- Tiffin St 43205
- Tiger Dr 43228
- Tiger Lilly Dr 43207
- Tillbury Ave 43220
- Tiller Ln 43231
- Tillicum Dr 43085
- Tillingham Dr 43228
- Tillinghast Dr 43228
- Tim Tam Ave 43230
- Timber Dr 43213
- Timber Oak Dr 43204
- Timber Range Ct 43231
- Timber Run Dr 43204
- Timber Valley Dr 43230
- Timber Way Dr 43085
- Timberbrook Ln 43228
- Timberland Dr 43230
- Timberline Rd 43220
- Timberman Rd 43212
- Timbers Dr 43230
- Timbers Edge Ln 43235
- Timberside Dr 43235
- Timbertrail Dr E 43224
- Timberwood Dr N & W 43228
- Timothy Ct & Dr 43230
- Tina Ct 43235
- Tinkers Creek Ln 43207
- Tinley Park 43232
- Tinsbury Ct 43235
- Tipple Dr 43207
- Tishman St 43228
- Tiverton Sq N 43229
- Tivoli Ct 43230
- Tobey Dr 43230
- Tobi Dr 43207
- Todd Ave & Pl 43207
- Toll Ln 43213
- Toll Gate Sq 43085
- E Tompkins St
  - 1-599 43202
  - 1300-1399 43211
- W Tompkins St 43202
- Tonbridge St 43085
- Toni St 43219
- Tonkens Ln 43219
- Topgallant Ct 43221
- Topsfield Rd 43228
- Torbert Way 43207
- Torch Ct 43230
- Torchwood Dr & Loop E, S & W 43229
- Tornes Rd 43213
- Toronado Blvd 43207
- E & W Torrence Rd 43214
- Torrey Hill Dr 43228
- Torwood Ct & Rd 43232
- Toweron Ln 43235
- Towers Ct 43227
- Towhee Dr 43230
- Town Rd 43213
- Town St 43230
- E Town St 43215
- W Town St
  - 1-23 43215
  - 25-679 43215
  - 700-1399 43222
  - 1400-1499 43223
- Town And Country Rd 43213
- Towncrier Ct & Pl 43230
- Towne Ct E 43230
- Towne Center Blvd 43219
- Townhouse Ln 43213
- Townsend Ave 43223
- Townsfair Way 43219
- Trabue Rd
  - 3100-3600 43204
  - 3601-3669 43228
  - 3602-3670 43204
  - 3671-5699 43228
- Trabue Run Rd 43204
- Trabue Woods Blvd & Ct 43228
- Tracer Rd 43232
- Traci Ct 43207
- Tracy Cir 43223
- Tradan Dr 43232
- Trade Rd 43204
- Trade Royal Xing 43230
- Trade Winds Dr 43204
- Trafalgar Ct 43230
- Trail Lane Ct 43231
- Trailway St 43211
- Tramont Ct 43228
- Tramore Sq 43235
- Tranquil Dr 43085
- Transamerica Ct & Dr 43228
- Traphill Ct 43235
- Trapp Dr 43230
- Travelo Blvd 43223
- Travers Ct 43224
- Travis Rd 43209
- Traymore Pl 43211
- Treadway Pl 43235
- Tree Knoll Ct 43219
- Tree Top Ln 43085
- Treehaven Ln 43204
- Treeridge St 43229
- Treeview Ct 43231
- Trellis Ln 43230
- Tremaine Ct & Rd 43232
- Tremont Ctr 43221
- Tremont Rd
  - 1500-2000 43212
  - 2001-3699 43221
- Trent Rd 43229
- Trenton Rd 43232
- Trentwood Rd 43221
- Tresham Ct & Rd 43230
- Trestle Ct 43204
- Trevitt St 43203
- Trevor Ct & Dr 43204
- Tri Corner Ct 43230
- Triad Ct 43235
- Trickle Creek Ln 43228
- Trifecta Ct 43230
- Trilby Ct 43230
- Trillium Ct 43230
- Trillium Xing 43235
- Trina Way 43209
- Trindel Way 43231
- Trinity Marsh 43228
- Triple Crown Ct & Ln 43221
- Tristram Pl 43231
- Triumph Way 43230
- Troon Trl 43085
- Trotter Dr 43207
- Trotterslane Dr 43235
- Trottersway Dr 43235
- Trowbridge Way 43229
- Troy St 43213
- Trumbull Ct 43210
- Truro Station Service Rd 43232
- Tuckaway Ct 43228
- Tucker Dr 43085
- Tudor Rd 43209
- E Tulane Rd
  - 1-599 43202
  - 700-899 43211
- W Tulane Rd 43202
- Tulip Hill Rd 43235
- Tuliptree Ave 43229
- Tuller St 43201
- Tulsa Dr 43229
- Tuppence Dr 43232
- Tupsfield Rd 43229
- Turcotte Ct & Dr 43230
- Turnbridge Ln 43230
- Turner Ct 43219
- Turnhart Pl 43240
- Turnock Gln 43230
- Turnstone Rd 43235
- Turpin Ln & Sq 43230
- Turtle Creek Dr 43235
- Tuscarawas Ct 43210
- Tuskegee Airmen Rd 43217
- Tussuck Ct 43085
- Tuttle Park Pl 43210
- Tuxford Ct 43085
- Tuxworth Ct & Dr 43232
- Tweed Ct 43085
- Tweedsmuir Dr 43221
- Twig Ct 43230
- Twin Creeks Dr 43204
- Twin Rivers Dr
  - 750-770 43215
  - 800-851 43216
  - 853-899 43216
- Twinview Way 43219
- Tyjon Cir 43235
- Tylor Dr 43232
- U Ave 43207
- Ulverston Dr 43230
- Umiak Dr 43207
- Underwood Farms Blvd 43230
- Union Ave 43223
- United Crossing Rd 43235
- Universal Rd 43207
- Upham Dr 43210
- Upholland Ln 43085
- Upland Dr 43229
- Upper Chelsea Rd
  - 1700-1949 43212
  - 1950-2099 43221
- Upper Green Cir 43212
- Upton Rd E 43232
- Upwoods Dr 43228
- Ural Ave 43213
- Urana Ave 43224
- Uranium Cir 43213
- Urban Dr 43229
- Urlin Ave
  - 800-910 43215
  - 911-1199 43212
- Uxbridge Ave 43230
- V Ave 43207
- Vadis St 43223
- Valcon Ave & Pl 43207
- Valerie Ln 43213
- Valley Ln E 43231
- Valley Ln S 43231
- Valley Rd 43231
- Valley Rdg 43228
- Valley Creek Dr 43223
- Valley Crest Dr 43228
- Valley Forge Dr 43229
- Valley Green Dr 43207
- Valley Park Ave 43231
- Valleydale Way 43231
- Valleyview Dr 43204
- Valleywood Ct & Dr 43223
- Valor Rd 43235
- Value Way Dr 43224
- Van Buren Dr 43223
- Van Heyde Pl 43209
- Van Pelt St 43220
- Vandalia Ct 43223
- Vanderberg Ave & Pl 43204
- Vanderbilt Dr 43213
- Vanelm St 43228
- Vanlear Ct & Rd 43229
- Vanschoor Dr 43219
- Vantage Dr 43235
- Vantage Point Dr 43224
- Varick St 43235
- Varsity Ave 43221
- Vasalboro Way 43204
- Vassar Pl 43221
- Vaughn St 43223
- Vause Rd 43217
- Vauxhall Dr & Pl 43204
- Vegas Ct 43228
- Velma Ave 43211
- Vendome Dr S 43219
- Venetian Ct & Way 43230
- Venice Dr 43207
- Venture Ct 43228
- Venturi House 43219
- Vera Pl 43204
- Verde Aly 43201
- Verdin Ct 43230
- Verdun Dr 43232
- Vermont Pl 43201
- Vernon Dr 43207
- Vernon Rd 43209
- Vernon L Tharp St 43210
- Veronin Ln 43232
- Vesta Ave 43211
- Via Da Vinci St 43229
- Viburnum Ln 43235
- Vicente Ct 43235
- Vicki Ct 43229
- Victor Ave 43207
- Victoria Park Ct & Dr 43235
- Victorian Ct 43220
- Victorian Gate Way 43215
- Victory Ct 43231
- Vida Ct 43228
- Vida Pl 43204
- Vida Way 43228
- Viewpointe Dr 43207
- Vilardo Ln 43227
- Villa Ct & Dr 43207
- Villa Capri 43235
- Villa Farnese 43219
- Villa Oaks Ct & Ln 43230
- Villa Pointe Dr 43213
- Villa Savoire 43219
- Villa Side Ln 43213
- Villabrook Dr 43235
- Village Blf 43235
- Village Ct 43212
- Village Dr 43214
- Village At Bexley Dr 43209
- Village Bluff Dr 43235
- Village Brook Way 43235
- Village Creek Dr 43209
- Village Park Ct & Dr 43228
- Village Ridge Ln 43219
- Village Woods Pl 43085
- Villamere Dr 43213
- Vine St 43215
- Vineshire Dr & Ln 43227
- Vinewood Ct & Dr 43229
- Vining Dr 43229
- Vining Lake Ct 43085
- Vinton Ave 43220
- Violet St 43204
- Viotis Dr 43228
- Virginia Ave 43212
- Virginia Cir E 43213
- Virginia Cir W 43213
- Virginia Dr 43207
- N & S Virginialee Rd 43209
- Vision Dr 43219
- Vision Center Ct 43227
- Vista Dr 43230
- Vista View Blvd 43231
- Vivian Ct 43230
- Vogel Ave 43203
- Volney Ave 43228
- Vulcan Ave 43228
- Wabash Ct N 43232
- Waddington Rd 43220
- Wade Rd 43232
- Wadsworth Ct & Dr 43232
- Wager St
  - 600-1399 43206
  - 1400-1599 43207
- Wagner St 43206
- Wagon Wheel Ln 43230
- Wagtail Rd 43230
- Wainfleet Ct 43221
- Wainwright Dr 43224
- Wait St 43207
- Wake Robins Edge St 43229
- Wakefern Pl 43224
- Wakefield Ct E & W 43209
- Wakeford St 43214
- Walbridge Dr 43230
- Walbridge St 43229
- Walburn Rd 43232
- Walcreek Dr E & W 43230
- Walcutt Ave 43219
- Walcutt Ct 43228
- Walcutt Rd 43228
- Waldeck Ave 43201
- Walden Dr 43229
- Walden Ravines 43221
- Waldo Pl 43220
- Waldorf Rd 43229
- Waldron St 43215
- Waldwick 43229
- Walford Ln & St 43224
- Walhalla Rd 43202
- Walhaven Ct & Rd 43220
- Walkath Dr 43227
- Walker Park Dr 43240
- N Wall St
  - 2-28 43215
  - 30-786 43215
  - 900-1499 43201
  - 2400-3399 43202
- S Wall St
  - 43-133 43215
  - 135-592 43215
  - 594-638 43215
  - 747-1015 43206
  - 1017-1027 43206
  - 1330-1899 43207
- Wallbury Ct 43228
- Wallcrest Blvd 43231
- Wallingford Ave 43231
- Walmar Dr 43224
- Walnut Dr
  - 1-199 43217
  - 700-899 43235
  - 3400-3499 43232
- Walnut St 43230
- E Walnut St
  - 382-498 43215
  - 500-699 43215
  - 1700-1999 43205
- W Walnut St
  - 24-298 43215
  - 300-599 43215
  - 600-999 43222
  - 2401-2499 43223
- Walnut Cliffs Dr 43213
- Walnut Creek Dr 43224
- Walnut Hill Blvd 43232
- Walnut Hill Park Dr 43232
- Walnut Ridge Dr 43224
- Walnut View Blvd 43230
- Walnut Woods Ct 43230
- Walsh Ave 43223
- Walshire Dr N 43232
- Walters St 43201
- Waltham Rd 43221
- Walton Aly 43205
- Wambli Dr 43219
- Wanda Lane Rd 43224
- Wango Ct 43221
- Warble Dr 43204
- Ward Rd 43224
- Wareham Rd 43221
- Warehouse Rd 43217
- Waridera Ave 43202
- Waring Way
  - 400-599 43213
  - 400-599 43230
  - 600-699 43230
- Warlock Ct 43230
- Warminster Dr 43232
- Warner Ln 43085
- N Warren Ave 43204
- S Warren Ave 43204
- Warren St 43215
- Warren Grimes St 43217
- Warrington Way 43235
- Washburn St 43213
- N Washington Ave
  - 1-299 43215
  - 800-999 43201
- S Washington Ave
  - 1-33 43215
  - 35-499 43215
  - 500-1230 43206
  - 1232-1298 43206
  - 1617-2099 43207
- Washington Blvd 43215
- Water Crest Ln 43209
- Water Oak Way 43228
- Waterbrook Ln 43209
- Waterbury Blvd & Ct 43230
- Waterfall Ln 43209
- Waterford Dr 43220
- Waterford Pointe Cir 43228
- Watergate Ct 43221
- Watergrass Hill Dr 43221
- Waterman Ave 43215
- Watermark Dr 43215
- Waterpoint Dr 43221
- Waterpointe Ct 43209
- Waters Edge Blvd 43209
- Waterside Ct 43209
- Watersilk Ct 43221
- Waterstone Ct 43235
- Watersway Ln 43213
- Watertower Dr 43235
- Watkins Rd
  - 1000-3459 43207
  - 3460-3699 43232
- Watling Rd 43230
- Watt Rd 43230
- Waveland Dr 43230
- Waverly Ct 43227
- N Waverly St 43213
- S Waverly St
  - 400-749 43213
  - 750-1199 43227
- Wavetree Ct 43235
- Waybaugh Dr 43230
- Waybourn Rd 43220
- Waycross St 43207
- Wayland Dr 43207
- Waymont Rd 43229
- N & S Wayne Ave 43204
- Weather Stone Ln 43235
- Weatherburn Pl 43085
- Weatherford Ln 43230
- Weathersfield Dr 43085
- E Weber Rd
  - 1-599 43202
  - 600-1779 43211
- W Weber Rd 43202
- Webster Dr 43232
- Webster Canyon Ct 43229
- Webster Park Ave 43214
- Wedge St 43211
- Wedgewood Dr 43228
- Weeping Willow Blvd & Ct 43207
- Weibel Ct 43224
- Weiler Ave 43207
- Weirton Ct & Dr 43207
- E & W Weisheimer Rd 43214
- Weiskopf Dr 43228
- E & W Welch Ave 43207
- Welcome Pl 43209
- Weldon Ave 43224
- Welistat Ave 43211
- Well Fleet Dr 43231
- Wellesley Dr 43221
- Wellesley Ln 43221
- Wellesley Rd 43209
- Welling Way 43085
- Wellingshire Blvd 43085
- Wellington Blvd 43219
- Wellington Rd 43221
- Wellington Willows Way 43213
- Wellington Woods Blvd & Ct 43213
- Wellsbourne Pl 43230
- Wellsleyglen Dr 43207
- Welsford Rd 43221
- Wenbury Rd 43220
- Wendcliff Dr 43231
- Wendell Ave 43222
- Wendler Blvd 43230
- Wendover Ct & Dr 43232
- Wendy Ln 43223
- Wendys Dr 43220
- Wenham Park 43230
- Wentworth Rd 43219
- Werling Pl 43219
- Werner Way 43085
- Wesbury Park Ave 43235
- Wesfall Ct 43228
- Wesley Blvd 43085
- Wesley Ct 43085
- Wesley Trl 43207
- Wesley Way 43214
- Wesleyan Dr 43221
- Wesliegh Run Dr 43228
- Wespot Dr 43203
- Wessel Dr 43235
- Wessex Ct 43232
- Wesson Dr 43232
- West St
  - 24-39 43228
  - 41-45 43228
  - 200-398 43215
  - 7900-7999 43235
- Westaire Ct 43232
- Westbay Dr 43231
- Westbelt Dr 43228
- Westborough Dr N & W 43220
- Westbourne Ave 43213
- Westbriar Ct 43228
- Westbridge Rd 43231

Westbrook Ct
600-799 43204
1100-1199 43085
Westbrook Dr 43223
Westbrook Pl 43085
Westbrook Village Dr 43228
Westbrooke Dr 43228
Westbury Dr
3200-3399 43221
5100-5299 43228
Westbury Ln N 43228
Westbury Ln S 43228
Westchester Ct 43085
Westcott Dr 43228
Westerdale Dr 43230
Western Ave 43212
Western Hill Ct & Rd 43223
Western Run Dr 43228
Westerpool Cir 43228
Westerville Rd
2600-2669 43211
2670-4300 43224
4301-5319 43231
Westerville Run Dr 43230
Westerville Woods Ct & Dr 43231
Westfield Dr 43223
Westford Pl 43219
N & S Westgate Ave 43204
Westgrove Dr 43228
Westhaven St 43228
Westhill Dr 43213
Westland Ave 43209
Westland Mall 43228
Westleton Ct 43221
Westmead Dr 43228
Westmeadow Dr 43223
Westmeath Dr 43221
Westmills Dr 43204
Westminster Dr 43221
Westmont Blvd 43221
N & S Westmoor Ave, Ct, Dr & Pl 43204
Westmoreland Ct 43220
Weston Pl 43214
Westover Rd 43221
Westphal Ave
200-899 43213
900-1499 43227
Westpoint Dr 43232
Westpointe Plaza Dr 43228
Westport Ct & Rd 43228
Westravine Ct 43228
Westridge St 43228
Westrun St 43207
Westshire Rd 43204
Westview Ave 43214
Westview Ct 43228
Westview Dr 43085
Westview Center Plz 43228
Westward Ave 43228
Westway Dr 43204
Westwick Rd 43232
Westwind Ln 43223
Westwood Ave 43212
Westwood Dr 43204
Westwood Rd 43214
Wetherburn Dr 43235
Wethersfield Pl 43085
Wetmore Rd
1-799 43214
800-1099 43224
Wetmore Rd E 43224
Wexford Rd 43221
Wexford Green Blvd 43228
Wexford Park Dr 43228
S Weyant Ave
1-749 43213
750-1499 43227
Weybridge Rd E, N, S & W 43220
Weyburn Ct & Rd 43232
Weydon Rd 43085
Weymouth Ln 43228
Wharton Ave 43223
N & S Wheatland Ave 43204
Wheaton Ct 43235
Whieldon Ln 43085
Whimpstone Ct 43235
Whimswillow Dr 43207
Whipple Aly 43215
Whippoorwill Ct N & S 43229
Whirlaway Cir & Ct 43230
Whisper Cove Ct 43230
Whisper Creek Ct & Dr 43231
Whispering Pines Ct 43085
Whitby Sq N 43229
Whitcombe Way 43228
S White Ash Dr 43204
White Bark Pl 43221
White Chapel Ct 43229
White Leaf Way 43229
White Oak Pl 43085
White Pine Ct 43229
White Swan Ct 43230
White Tail Dr 43230
White Tree Ct 43228
White Water Blvd 43085
White Willow Ln 43235
Whitehall Dr 43213
Whitehead Rd
2000-2299 43223
2300-3299 43204
Whitehurst Way 43219
Whitespire Dr 43230
Whitestone Dr 43228
Whitethorne Ave 43223
Whitewood Ct 43235
Whitley Dr 43230
Whitlow Rd 43232
Whitman Rd 43213
Whitney Ave 43085
Whitney Woods Ct 43213
Whitneyway Dr 43085
Whitson Dr 43230
E Whittier St 43206
W Whittier St
1-199 43206
200-498 43215
500-599 43215
Whitworth Way 43228
Wick Ct 43207
Wickersham Ln 43228
Wickford Rd 43221
Wickham Way 43230
Wickliffe Rd 43221
Wickliffe Woods Ct 43221
Wicklow Rd 43204
Widner Ct & St 43220
Wigan Ct 43230
Wigmore Dr 43235
Wilber Ave 43215
Wilce Ave 43202
Wilcox St 43202
Wild Ash Dr 43204
Wild Cherry Ln 43230
Wild Oats Dr 43204
Wildberry Ln 43213
Wildwood Ave 43219
Wildwood Ct 43230
Wildwood Rd 43231
Wilke Pl 43230
Wilkes Ct 43204
Willa Dr 43219
Willamont Ave 43219
Willard Ave 43212
William Lambert St 43217
Williams Ave 43212
Williams Rd 43207
Williams St
2201-2319 43201
2320-2399 43202
Willingford Ln 43230
Williwaw St 43085
Willoughby St 43235
E Willow St
1-99 43215
100-199 43206
Willow Bend Ln 43204
Willow Bluff Dr 43235
Willow Forge Dr 43220
Willow Glen Ln 43229
Willow Green Ct 43085
Willow Hollow Ct & Dr 43230
Willow Knoll Ave 43230
Willow Springs Dr 43219
Willoway Cir & Ct N, S & E 43220
Willowbrook Rd 43220
Willowburn Dr 43207
Willowcreek Cir 43213
Willowcreek Dr 43228
Willowcrest Dr 43229
Willowdale Ct 43229
Willowdown Ct 43235
Willowford Ln 43235
Willowick Cir, Dr & Sq 43229
Willowing Ct 43207
Willowmere Bnd 43228
Willowridge Rd 43228
Willowswitch Ln 43207
Willowtree Ln 43207
Willowwood Rd 43229
Wilmington Pl 43220
Wilmore Dr 43209
Wilshire Dr 43221
Wilshire Village Ct 43085
Wilson Ave
1-799 43205
800-1479 43206
1480-3399 43207
Wilson Dr
1-199 43085
800-899 43223
Wilson Rd 43228
N Wilson Rd 43204
S Wilson Rd 43228
E & W Wilson Bridge Rd 43085
Wilson Woods Dr 43204
Wilstone Ct 43240
Wilton Dr & Pl 43227
Wiltshire Rd
500-1199 43204
1300-1499 43223
Wimbeldon Blvd 43228
Wimbledon Rd 43220
Winberie Ct 43230
Winchester Ct & Pike 43232
Winchester Bend Dr 43232
Wind Gate Ct 43229
Wind Rush Ave 43213
Windbourne Ct & St 43230
Windchime Way 43213
Windermere Rd 43220
Windham Clb 43219
Windham Rd 43220
Winding Way 43220
Winding Brook Ct 43235
Winding Creek Dr 43223
Winding Field St 43223
Winding Hills Ct & Dr 43224
Winding Hollow Dr 43223
Winding Oaks Dr 43228
Winding Ridge Dr 43213
Winding Willow Way 43213
Winding Woods Blvd 43213
Windon Ave 43219
Windridge Ct 43232
Windridge Dr
2700-2799 43231
3000-3198 43232
3200-3399 43232
3401-3499 43232
Windrow Ct 43230
Windsong Ct 43235
Windsor Ave
1100-1399 43211
1500-1799 43219
Windsor Chase 43235
Windswept Way 43235
Windward Ln 43230
Windward Ln E 43230
Windward Way
700-899 43230
3600-3799 43204
Windward Way W 43230
Windy Creek Dr 43240
Winery Way 43230
Winesap Dr 43204
Winewood Dr 43230
Winfall Dr 43230
Winfield Rd 43220
Wingate Rd 43232
Wingfield St 43231
Winnard Ct & Dr 43213
Winner Ave 43203
Winningham Ln 43240
Winningwillow Dr 43207
Winona Dr 43235
Winsford Ct 43232
Winslow Dr
1900-2299 43207
4900-5199 43213
Winsome Way 43220
Winsor Woods Dr 43230
Winstead Rd 43235
Winston Ct E 43235
Winter Dr 43085
Winter Lane Park 43232
Wintercress Ct 43207
Wintergreen Blvd 43230
Winterset Dr 43220
Wintertime Dr 43207
Winthrop Rd 43214
Wintinto Ave 43219
Wisconsin Ave 43222
Wishing Well Ln 43213
Witham Ct 43230
Withers Ave 43223
Wittenberg St 43230
Wolf Run Dr 43230
Wolfe Ave 43213
Wollaster Ct 43220
Wollaston Ct 43228
Wood Ave 43221
Wood St 43207
Wood Lilly Ct 43230
Wood Run Blvd 43220
Wood Stork Ln 43230
Woodbay Dr 43230
Woodberry Pl 43230
Woodbine Pl 43202
Woodbriar Pl 43229
Woodbridge Dr 43231
Woodbridge Rd 43220
Woodbrie Ct 43230
Woodbrook Cir, Ct & Ln N, S & W 43223
Woodbury Ave 43223
Woodcliff Dr 43213
Woodcrest Rd 43232
Woodcroft Rd E 43204
Woodcutter Ave & Ln 43224
Woodduck Ct 43215
Woodduck Way 43229
Woodette Rd 43232
Woodfield Ct 43230
Woodford Ave 43219
Woodgate Ct 43229
Woodglen Ct & Rd 43214
Woodhall Rd 43220
Woodham Ln 43235
Woodhill Ct & Dr 43212
Woodhouse Ln 43085
Woodhurst Ct 43223
Woodingham Pl 43213
Woodland Ave
1-599 43203
900-2139 43219
2140-2849 43211
2850-3099 43224
Woodland Trail Dr 43231
Woodland Village Dr 43231
Woodlawn Ave 43228
Woodley Rd 43231
Woodloop Ln 43204
Woodman Dr 43085
Woodmark Run 43230
Woodmere Rd 43220
Woodmoor St 43229
Woodnell Ave 43219
Woodridge Dr 43213
E Woodrow Ave 43207
E Woodruff Ave 43201
W Woodruff Ave 43210
Woods Ln 43235
Woodsboro Dr 43228
Woodsedge Ct & Rd 43224
Woodsfield Dr 43214
Woodside Dr 43229
Woodside Lake Dr 43230
Woodside Meadows Pl 43230
Woodspath Ln 43232
Woodstock Rd 43221
Woodstone Ct 43231
Woodstream Ct & Dr 43230
Woodthrush Way 43229
Woodtown Dr 43230
Woodtree Ct 43230
Woodview Pl 43220
Woodville Ct & Dr 43230
Woodward Ave 43219
Woodway Rd 43207
Woody Hayes Dr 43210
Wooley Ave 43201
Woolwich Ct 43232
Worcester Ct & Dr 43232
Wordsworth Ct 43232
Worman Dr 43230
Worth Ave 43219
Worthington Mall 43085
Worthington St 43201
Worthington Ter 43214
Worthington Centre Dr 43085
Worthington Creek Dr 43085
Worthington Forest Pl 43229
Worthington Galena Rd 43085
Worthington Heights Blvd 43235
Worthington Ridge Blvd 43085
Worthington Row Dr 43235
Worthington Run Dr 43235
Worthington Trace Ln 43085
Worthington Woods Blvd 43085
Worthington Woods Loop Rd 43085
Wrangell Pl 43230
Wren St 43204
Wren Trce 43231
Wrexham Ave 43223
Wright Ave
1400-1499 43211
4200-4445 43213
4447-4599 43213
Wright Park 43213
Wright Brothers Ave 43217
Wrothston Dr 43228
Wyandotte Ave 43202
Wyandotte Cir 43230
Wyandotte Dr 43230
Wyandotte Rd 43212
Wyman Ct 43232
Wymore Dr & Pl 43232
Wyncote Rd 43232
Wyndburgh Dr 43219
Wyndham Ridge Dr 43207
Wynding Dr 43214
Wynds Ct & Dr 43232
Wynne Ridge Ct 43230
Wynwood Ave 43223
Wynwood Ct 43220
Wyoming Ln 43228
Wythe St 43235
Wyton Ct 43227
Xavier St 43230
N Yale Ave 43222
S Yale Ave
1-221 43222
222-599 43223
Yard St 43212
Yarmouth Ln 43228
Yaronia Dr N & S 43214
Yates Dr 43207
Yeager Ave 43228
Yeardley Trl 43209
Yearling Cir 43213
N Yearling Rd 43213
S Yearling Rd
1-77 43213
79-899 43213
900-1399 43227
Yellow Pine Ave 43229
Yellowbud Dr 43231
Yellowwood Dr 43229
Yeoman Ave 43201
Yew Dr 43228
Ymca Pl 43230
Yoder Ct 43230
Yolanda Dr 43207
York Ln N 43232
York Ln S 43232
York Rd 43221
York County Rd 43221
Yorkcliff Rd 43219
Yorkhull Ct & Ln 43229
Yorkland Ct & Rd 43232
Yorkshire Rd 43221
Yorkshire Terrace Dr 43232
Yorkshire Village Ln 43232
Yorktown Rd 43232
Yosemite Dr 43085
Youn Kin Pkwy N 43207
N & S Young St 43215
Youngland Dr 43228
Youngs Dr 43231
Youngs Grove Rd 43231
Younkin Circle Dr 43223
Yozuri Dr 43232
Yvette Ct 43223
Zach Ct & Dr 43219
Zachary Woods Ln 43232
Zander Ln 43230
Zane Trace Dr 43228
Zareba Dr 43207
Zebulon Ave 43224
Zeller Rd 43214
Zenner Dr 43207
Zephyr Pl 43232
Zettler Rd
1200-1999 43227
2000-2098 43232
Zettler Center Dr 43223
Ziegler Ave 43207
Zimmer Dr 43232
Zimpfer St 43206
Zistel St 43217
Zodiac Ave 43230
Zollinger Rd 43221
Zumstein Dr 43229

NUMBERED STREETS

E 1st Ave 43201
W 1st Ave
1-500 43201
501-599 43215
502-528 43201
1001-1129 43212
1131-1999 43212
1st St 43217
E 2nd Ave 43201
W 2nd Ave
1-532 43201
533-599 43215
534-698 43201
900-1499 43212
2nd St 43217
S 2nd St 43215
E 3rd Ave 43201
W 3rd Ave
1-609 43201
610-2099 43212
N 3rd St 43215
S 3rd St
1-599 43215
600-999 43206
1300-2299 43207
E 4th Ave
2-30 43201
1400-3099 43219
W 4th Ave 43201
N 4th St
1-860 43215
861-2235 43201
2236-2699 43202
4300-4699 43224
S 4th St
1-399 43215
400-1330 43206
1331-1331 43207
1332-1332 43206
1333-2599 43207
E 5th Ave
1-1109 43201
1110-5099 43219
W 5th Ave
1-699 43201
700-2067 43212
2200-2309 43215
2310-2320 43204
N 5th St
1-399 43215
1200-1599 43201
S 5th St
1-499 43215
500-899 43206
1300-2699 43207
E 6th Ave
1-349 43201
2600-3399 43219
W 6th Ave
100-499 43201
901-997 43212
N 6th St
1-851 43215
895-897 43201
S 6th St
1-121 43215
500-899 43206
1300-3441 43207
E 7th Ave
1-399 43201
2400-3599 43219
W 7th Ave
200-499 43201
1300-1599 43212
S 7th St 43207
E 8th Ave
1-699 43201
2900-3099 43219
W 8th Ave
1-471 43201
472-498 43210
473-499 43201
801-999 43212
S 8th St 43207
E 9th Ave
1-399 43201
2700-2999 43219
W 9th Ave
1-299 43201
300-498 43210
800-999 43212
N 9th St
1-199 43215
800-1199 43201
S 9th St
1-99 43215
500-799 43206
1900-1999 43207
E 10th Ave 43219
W 10th Ave
1-299 43201
300-457 43210
459-599 43210
800-999 43212
E 11th Ave
1-404 43201
406-410 43201
460-1098 43211
2800-3399 43219
W 11th Ave
1-299 43201
70-298 43210
800-999 43212
E 12th Ave
1-499 43201
700-1299 43211

1500-3299 43219
W 12th Ave 43210
E 13th Ave
1-499 43201
800-1200 43211
1202-1298 43211
2800-3299 43219
E 14th Ave
1-499 43201
900-1099 43211
2800-3099 43219
E 15th Ave
1-499 43201
900-1499 43211
W 15th Ave 43210
E 16th Ave
1-499 43201
900-1399 43211
1500-1899 43219
E 17th Ave
1-459 43201
460-1402 43211
1403-1447 43219
1404-1448 43211
1449-3699 43219
W 17th Ave 43210
N 17th St 43203
S 17th St
1-499 43205
600-1399 43206
1400-1599 43207
E 18th Ave
1-433 43201
435-459 43201
900-1499 43211
W 18th Ave 43210
N 18th St 43203
S 18th St
1-679 43205
680-1326 43206
1328-1398 43206
1600-1799 43207
E 19th Ave
200-499 43201
900-1499 43211
3100-3399 43219
W 19th Ave 43210
N 19th St 43219
S 19th St
1-199 43205
1400-2199 43207
E 20th Ave
300-499 43201
900-1499 43211
N 20th St
1-326 43203
325-327 43205
327-499 43203
328-498 43203
800-999 43219
S 20th St
1-299 43205
1600-1799 43207
E 21st Ave 43211
N 21st St
1-299 43203
800-999 43219
S 21st St 43205
E 22nd Ave 43211
N 22nd St
1-399 43203
800-999 43219
S 22nd St
1-739 43205
740-1499 43206
E 23rd Ave
1000-1599 43211
1700-1764 43219
N 23rd St 43219
E 24th Ave
1100-1599 43211
1600-1799 43219
E 25th Ave
1100-1549 43211
1550-1899 43219
E 26th Ave
900-1599 43211
1600-1899 43219

CUYAHOGA FALLS OH

General Delivery 44221

POST OFFICE BOXES MAIN OFFICE STATIONS AND BRANCHES

Box No.s
1 - 470 44222
110 - 235 44223
501 - 660 44222
707 - 4454 44223
5005 - 67354 44222

NAMED STREETS

Acorn Pl 44221
Adam Run Dr 44223
Adams Ave 44221
Aeries Way 44223
Aero Ave 44221
Akron Peninsula Rd 44223
Alameda Ave 44221
Albemarle Ave 44221
Albertson Pkwy 44223
Alderwood Way 44223
Aleah Ct 44223
Aloha Ln 44221
Americhem Way 44221
Anderson Rd 44221
Antoinette Dr 44223
Applejack Ln 44221
Apricot Ln 44221
Arcadia Ave 44221
Archdale Ave 44221
Archwood Pl 44221
Ardella Rd 44223
Ascot Ln & Pkwy 44223
Ash Ln 44223
Ashland Ave 44221
Atterbury St 44221
Audrena Ct 44221
Avery St 44221
Aycliffe Ln 44221
Bailey Rd 44221
Bancroft St 44221
Barnes Ave 44221
Baronsway Dr 44223
E & W Bath Rd 44223
Bath Heights Dr 44223
Beacon Hill Cir 44221
Beech St 44221
Beechwood Cir 44221
Bent Creek Trl 44223
Berk St 44221
Billman Pl 44221
Birchwood Ave 44221
Board Dr 44223
Bonnett Dr 44224
Brace Pl 44221
Briarwood Cir 44221
Bridgeview Cir 44223
Bristol Ln 44223
Broad Blvd
100-1099 44221
1100-2799 44223
Broadway St E 44221
Brook View Dr 44223
Brookpark Dr 44223
Brookpoint Ln 44223
Brookside Ln 44223
Brookside Rd 44221
Buchholzer Blvd 44223
Buckingham Gate Blvd 44221
Burnham Jump Dr 44223
Byrd Ave 44223
Caleb Ave 44221
Calvert Dr 44223
Camden Rue 44223
Cameo Ct & Ln 44221
Campbell St 44223
Carriage Hill Ln 44223
Carters Grove Dr 44224
Carters Grove Rd 44223
Cathedral Ln 44223
Cedar Hill Cir & Rd 44223
Cedar Woods Dr 44223
Center Ave 44221
Chaney Dr 44223
Charles St 44221
Chart Ave 44221
Chart Rd 44223
Chatam St 44221
Cheantow Rd 44223
Cherie Cercle 44223
Chestnut Blvd
100-1099 44221
1100-2699 44223
Christy Dr 44223
Clara St 44221
Clear Creek Dr 44223
Cliffside St 44221
Clover Ave 44221
Clyde Ave 44221
Cobblestone Ln 44223
Cochran Rd 44223
Collinwood Cir 44221
Concord Pl 44221
Continental Dr 44221
Cook St 44221
Cooper Dr 44223
Cora St 44221
Cox Dr 44223
Cramer Ct 44223
Crawford Cir 44223
Creek View Dr 44223
Creekside Trl 44223
Crest Ave 44223
Crestwood Cir 44223
Cross Creek Trl 44223
Crown Pointe Pkwy 44223
Crown Ridge Dr 44223
Curtis Ave 44221
Davis Ave 44221
Dawn Ter 44223
Deer Ridge Run 44223
Delmore St 44221
Deming St 44221
Devan Vale Dr 44223
Dominic Dr 44223
Dove Ln 44221
Drexmore Dr 44223
Dwight St 44221
Eakins Rd 44223
Earle Ct 44224
Eaton Ave 44221
Edison St 44221
Edwards Ave 44221
Eleanora Dr 44223
Elizabeth Ct 44221
Ellesmere Ave 44221
Elmwood St 44221
Emidio Cir 44223
Ensemble Dr 44223
Erie St 44221
Fairland St 44221
Fairview Pl 44221
Falls Ave
100-1099 44221
1100-2599 44223
Fickey Dr 44223
Fieldstone Ct 44223
Filmore Ave 44221
Firwood Ave 44221
Forest Edge Dr 44223
Forest Glen Dr 44221
Forestmeadow Dr 44223
Fox Trace Trl 44223
Foxglove Cir 44223
Francis Ave 44221
Franklin Ave 44221
Franklin Ct 44223
Frederick Ct 44223
Frederick Dr 44221
Front St 44221
Galaxy Ln 44221
Garden Ave 44221
Garfield Ave 44221
Gaylan Dr 44221
Gaylord Grove Rd 44221
Germaine St 44221
Giffels Dr 44221
Gilbert Ln & Rd 44221
Goldwood Dr 44221
Graham Rd
1-399 44223
400-999 44221
1000-1298 44224
Grant Ave
100-1099 44221
1100-1198 44223
1200-2599 44223
Grove Ave 44221
Haas Rd 44223
Haggarty Way 44223
Hampton Heights Dr 44223
Hampton Ledges Dr 44223
Hanover St 44221
Harding Rd 44223
Hardy Rd 44223
Hathaway Dr 44223
N Haven Blvd 44223
Hawthorne Rd 44221
Hayes Ave 44221
Heather Ct & Ln 44221
Heathrow Dr 44223
Hemlock Dr 44223
Hendon Cir 44221
Herbruck Ave 44223
E & W Heritage Dr 44223
Heron Crest Dr 44223
Heron Lakes Cir 44223
Hickory Cv 44223
N & S Hidden Valley Rd 44223
High St 44221
High Hampton Trl 44223
Highbridge Rd 44223
Highland Ave 44221
Highpoint Ln & Rd 44223
Highwood Dr 44223
Hillbrook Dr 44223
Hillcrest Dr 44221
Hillside St 44221
Hoch Dr 44221
Hoffman Rd 44223
Hollywood Ave & Cir 44221
Homewood Ave 44221
Horace Ave 44221
Howe Ave & Rd 44221
Huddleston Ave 44223
Hudkins Dr 44223
Hudson Dr 44221
Huff Dr 44223
Hunter Ave 44221
Hunter Pkwy 44223
Hunters Lake Dr E & W 44221
Insande Ave 44221
Iota Ave 44223
Ironwood St 44221
Issaquah St 44221
Jackson St 44221
James Ave 44221
Jefferson Ave
701-803 44221
805-899 44221
901-999 44221
1100-1999 44223
Jennings Ave 44221
Joan Of Arc Cir 44223
Johnson Ave 44221
Julian St 44221
Kathron Ave 44221
Keenan Ave 44221
Kellybrook Dr 44223
Kelsey Dr 44221
Kemppel Cir 44221
Kendall Cir 44221
Kennedy Blvd 44221
Keyser Pkwy 44223
Kilarney St 44221
Koir Dr 44224
Kube St 44223
Lakehurst Dr 44223
Lancaster St 44221
Larchdale Dr 44221
Laura Ct 44221
Lavender Ct, Ln & Way 44221
Leavitt Ave 44221
Ledge Rock Trl 44223
Lehigh Ave 44221
Leighton Ave 44221
Liberty St 44221
Lillis Dr 44223
Lincoln Ave
1-1099 44221
1100-1299 44223
Lindbergh Ave 44223
Lindley Rd 44223
Linwood Ave 44221
Liverpool St 44221
Lloyd St 44221
Loomis Ave 44221
Lourdes Dr 44223
Lynn Dr 44221
Madison Ave 44221
Magnolia Ave 44221
Main St 44221
Maitland Ave & Cir 44223
Maplecrest Ave 44221
Maplewood St 44221
Marc Dr 44223
Marcia Blvd 44223
Margaret Ave 44224
Marguerite Ave 44223
Marian Lake Blvd 44223
Marie Ave 44221
Markham Ave 44221
Maurice St 44221
May Ave 44221
Mayfield Rd 44221
Mcshane Dr 44221
Meadow Ln 44221
Meier Pl 44221
Meredith Ln 44223
Meriline St 44221
Michael Ln 44223
Michele Ruelle 44223
Middlestone Way 44223
Miller Ct 44221
Monroe Ave 44221
Montclair Dr 44224
Morrison Ave 44221
Moulton Ave 44221
Muffin Ln 44223
Munroe Falls Ave 44221
Murray Ave 44221
Myrtle Ave 44221
Nathan Ave 44221
Nestico Dr 44223
Newberry St 44221
Newcastle Ave 44221
Norma St 44223
Norona Dr 44224
Northampton Rd 44223
Northbrooke Cir 44223
Northland St 44221
Northmoreland Blvd 44221
Norwood St 44221
Notre Dame Ave 44221
Nutwood Ave 44221
Oak Park Blvd 44221
Oakwood Dr 44221
Ohio Ave 44223
Old Creek Ct 44223
Olive Pl 44221
Olympic St 44221
Oneida Ave 44221
Oneil Rd 44223
Orchard Ave 44221
Orchestra St 44223
Orlen Ave 44221
Orrville Ave 44221
Otis Ave 44221
Overbrook Rd 44221
Overlook Dr 44223
Owaisa Rd 44221
Paddison Ave 44223
Parkview Dr 44223
Parsons Dr 44223
Pauline Ct 44221
Pendleton St 44221
Penny Ct, Ln & Way 44221
Phelps Ave 44223
Phillips Dr 44223
Pierce Ave 44221
Pinebrook Trl 44223
Plensont Ave 44221
Plymouth Ln 44223
Portage Trl
100-1099 44221
1100-1999 44223
E Portage Trl 44221
Portage Trail Ext W 44223
Prange Dr 44223
Pratt Ave 44221
E & W Prescott Cir 44223
Prior Cir & Dr 44223
Prior Park Dr 44223
Prospect Ave 44221
Providence Blvd 44223
Purdue St 44221
Quail Hollow Cir 44224
Quartette Ln 44223
Queens Gate Cir 44221
Queensbury Cir 44224
Rainier St 44221
Ravenshollow Dr 44223
Reed Ave 44221
Reserve Dr 44223
Revere Dr 44223
Rexdale Dr 44221
Rice Rd 44223
Richmond Rd 44221
N Ridge Dr 44223
Ridgecrest Dr 44221
Ridgeline Dr 44223
Ritchie St 44221
River Rock Dr 44223
Riverfront Pkwy 44221
Riverway Rd 44221
Roanoke Ave 44221
Rockledge Trl 44223
Rocky Creek Ct 44223
Roosevelt Ave
200-1099 44221
1100-1299 44223
Rose Ave 44221
Roth Dr 44221
Royalwood Dr 44223
Rudolph Ave 44221
Ruggles Rd 44221
Russell St 44221
Ruth Ave 44221
Sackett Ave
100-1099 44221
1100-2700 44223
2702-2998 44223
Sandalwood Ln 44223
Saunders St 44221
Saxe Ave 44221
Scenic Valley Way 44223
Schiller Ave 44223
School Ave 44221
Schubert Ave 44221
Scott St 44223
Seafoam Cir & Ln 44221
Searl St 44221
Seasons Rd 44224
Seattle St 44221
Sedro St 44221
Seibel Dr 44221
Sequoia St 44221
Shadow Creek Dr 44223
Shannon Ave 44221
Shaw Ave 44223
Shirley Ann Dr 44221
Short Ave 44223
Sill Ave 44221
Silver Lake Ave
600-999 44221
1001-1099 44221
1101-1797 44223
1799-1999 44223
Silver Lake Cir 44223
Southport Ave 44221
Squires Bnd 44223
State Rd 44223
Steele Ct 44221
W Steels Corners Rd 44223
Stone St 44221
Stone Creek Trl 44223
Stow Ave 44221
Stuart Ave 44221
Suncrest Cir & Dr 44221
Susan Ln 44223
Sutton Dr 44221
Sweetbriar Dr 44221
Sylvan Rd 44221
Symphony St 44223
Tacoma St 44221
Taft Ave 44223
Talbot St 44221
Tallmadge Rd 44221
Tanglewood Trl 44223
Taylor Ave 44221
Tewksbury Cir 44221
Theiss Rd 44223
Thomas Ct 44221
Tifft St 44221
Timber Rdg 44223
Timber Brook Dr 44223
Timberline Trl 44223
Timothy Ave 44223
Treasch Dr 44223
Tudor Cir & St 44221
Tyler Ave 44221
Underwood St 44221
Union St 44221
Valencia Dr 44223
Valley Rd 44223
Valley View Dr 44223
Van Buren Ave 44221
Van Doren Dr 44221
Vancouver St 44221
Victor Ave 44221
Victoria St 44221
Viewpoint Ave 44221
Village Ct 44223
Vincent St 44221
Vision Ln 44223
Wadsworth Ave 44221
Walker Dr 44223
Washington Ave
25-1099 44221
1100-1299 44223
Weller Ct 44221
Wellingshire Cir 44221
Wetmore Rd 44223
White Marsh Cir 44223
Whitelaw St 44221
Wichert Dr 44221
Wild Ave 44221
Williams St 44221
Willis St 44221
Wilson St 44221
Win St 44223
Windham Cir 44223
Windsor St 44221
Winter Pkwy 44221
Woodbrook Rd & Trl 44223
Woodhaven Dr 44223
Woodward Rd 44221
Wyandotte Ave 44223
Yukon Rd 44224
Zorn Dr 44223

NUMBERED STREETS

2nd St
1300-1398 44221
1400-2099 44221
2054-2054 44222
2100-2998 44221
2101-2999 44221

3rd St 44221
4th Ct & St 44221
5th Ct & St 44221
6th St 44221
7th St 44221
8th St 44221
9th Ct & St 44221
10th St 44221
11th St 44221
12th St 44223
13th St 44223
14th St 44223
15th St 44223
16th St 44223
17th St 44223
18th St 44223
19th St 44223
20th St 44223
21st St 44223
23rd St 44223
24th St 44223
25th St 44223
26th St 44223
27th St 44223
28th St 44223

DAYTON OH

POST OFFICE BOXES MAIN OFFICE STATIONS AND BRANCHES

Box No.s
All PO Boxes 45390

NAMED STREETS

Aaron Dr 45440
Aaron Ln 45424
Aaron Nut Dr 45458
Abbey Ave 45417
Abbeywood Ct 45458
Abbott Dr 45420
Abby Loop Way 45414
Abercorn Ct 45458
Aberdeen Ave 45419
Abilene Ct 45431
Abingdon Rd 45409
Abington Green Ct 45459
Abraham Ct 45414
Abraham Lincoln Dr 45459
Academy Pl 45406
Academy View Ct 45458
Accent Park Dr 45417
Access Rd 45431
Acclivis Dr 45424
Ace Pl 45417
Acer Ct E & W 45458
Ackerman Blvd 45429
Acme Ct 45440
Acorn Dr 45419
Acosta St 45420
Acreview Ct & Ln 45429
Acro Ct 45459
Adair Ave 45405
Adams Cir 45459
Adams Pl 45440
Adams Rd 45424
Adams St 45410
Adamwald Ct 45459
Addison Ave 45405
Adelite Ave 45417
Adirondack Trl 45409
Adlon Ct 45449
Adrian Ct 45439
Adventure Dr 45420
Aenora Dr 45426
Aerial Ave
2600-2999 45419
3000-3799 45429
Aero Ave 45429
Afton Dr 45415

Agate Trl 45459
Agne Ct 45459
Air St 45404
Air City Ave 45404
Air Freight Rd 45433
Airstream Dr 45449
Airway Rd
4300-4874 45431
4876-4922 45431
4924-4924 45437
4926-6098 45431
Akron Pl 45404
Alameda Pl 45406
Alamo Ct 45417
Alaska St 45404
Albany St 45417
Albers Ave 45417
Alberta St
1-499 45410
500-698 45409
700-999 45409
1001-1199 45409
Albrecht Ave 45404
Albritton Dr 45417
Albrook Dr 45433
Alcott Dr 45406
Alda Ct 45459
Alden St 45405
N & S Alder St 45417
Aldersgate Rd 45440
Aldine Dr 45406
Aldrich Rd 45417
Alex Ct
1-199 45449
500-699 45440
N Alex Rd 45449
S Alex Rd 45449
Alex Trl 45440
E Alex Bell Rd 45459
W Alex Bell Rd
300-2999 45459
3000-3899 45449
Alexander Dr 45403
Alexis Ave 45431
Alfred Dr 45417
Algoma St 45415
Algonquin Pl 45402
Algood Pl 45429
Alhambra Ct 45416
Alice St
1900-1999 45410
2300-2398 45420
Alicia Rd 45417
Allanwood Ln 45432
Allegheny Ave 45432
Allen Pl 45449
Allen St 45410
Allen Ridge Dr 45458
Allenby Pl 45449
Allendale Dr 45409
Allenwood Ct 45420
Allerton Rd 45405
Alliance Pl 45404
Allison Ave 45415
Allwen Dr 45406
Almira Ave
200-299 45440
1900-1999 45406
Almond Ave 45417
Almont Pl 45424
Almore St 45417
Alp Ct 45424
Alpena Ave 45406
Alpine Way 45406
Alpine Rose Ct 45458
Alpwoods Ln 45459
Alston Woods Ct 45459
Alta Vista Dr 45420
Alter Rd 45424
Alton Ave 45404
Altrim Rd 45417
Alvarado Dr 45420
Alverno Ave 45410
Alvin Ave 45417
Alvira Ave 45414
Alwildy Ave 45417

Amanda Dr 45406
Amber Dr 45458
Amberley Dr 45406
Ambershire Dr 45458
Amberwood Dr 45424
Amble Way 45424
Ambridge Ln & Rd 45459
Ambrose Ct 45410
Amchar Ct 45458
Ames Ave 45432
Amesborough Rd 45420
Amherst Pl 45406
Amiens Ln 45459
Amos Pl 45459
Amsted Ln 45424
Amston Dr 45424
Amy Ct 45415
Anderson St 45410
Anderson Goodrich Ct 45402
Andes Dr 45432
Andover Ave 45449
Andrea Dr 45429
Andrew Rd 45440
Andrews St 45410
Angelita Ave 45424
Angiers Dr 45417
Anglers Ln 45414
Angora Way 45424
Anita Ct 45449
Anna St
1-499 45417
500-799 45402
Annabelle Dr 45429
Annandale Ln 45458
Annapolis Ave 45416
Anne Ln 45459
Annette Dr 45458
Anniston Dr 45415
Ansbury Dr 45424
Ansel Dr 45419
Ansonia Hunchbarger Rd 45390
Anthem Ct 45414
Antietam Ave 45417
N & S Antioch St 45402
Antler Pt 45459
Anton Ct 45458
Apache St 45424
Apex St 45424
Appaloosa Ct 45414
E Apple St 45409
W Apple St 45402
Apple Brook Ln 45458
Apple Park Ct 45458
Apple Springs Dr 45458
Apple Tree Ct 45417
Applebrook Ln 45458
Applecreek Rd 45429
Applehill Dr 45449
Appleridge Ct 45424
Appleseed Pl 45424
Appleton Pl 45440
Appletree Dr 45426
Applewood Ln 45429
April Lynn Ave 45458
Aqua Pl 45459
Aquilla Dr 45415
E Aragon Ave 45414
Arbor Ave 45420
Arbor Walk 45459
Arbor Glen Ct 45414
Arcadia Blvd
4000-4584 45420
4585-4999 45432
Archdeacon Ct 45439
Archer Pl 45458
Archmore Dr 45440
Archwood Dr 45406
Arcola Ave 45449
Arden Ave 45420
Ardery Ave 45406
N & S Ardmore Ave 45417
Arena Park Dr 45417
Arenel Dr 45449
Argella Ave 45410
Argonne Dr 45417

Argray Dr 45414
Argyle Ave 45410
Argyle St 45420
Ariadne Trl 45458
Arisa Dr 45449
Ark Ave 45416
Arlene Ave 45406
Arlington Ave 45417
Arlmont Cir 45440
Armen Ave 45432
Armeria Cir 45431
Armitage Ln 45414
Armold Rd 45390
Armor Pl 45417
Armstrong Ln 45414
Arn Dr 45458
Arnold Pl 45402
Arnold Rd 45433
Arrow Sheath Dr 45449
Arrowhead Dr 45440
Arrowhead Xing 45449
Arrowrock Ave 45424
Arrowview Dr 45424
Artesia Dr 45440
Arthur Ave 45414
Artic St 45424
Artz Rd 45424
Arundel Rd 45426
Arwa Dr 45440
Asahel Ct 45458
Ascot Ct 45429
Ash St 45433
Ash Hollow Ln 45458
Ashbrook Cir & Rd 45415
Ashburton Dr 45459
Ashbury Meadows Dr 45458
Ashbury Park Pl 45458
Ashbury Woods Dr 45458
Ashcraft Rd 45414
Ashcreek Dr 45458
Ashel Ct 45458
Ashford Dr 45459
Ashland Ave 45420
Ashley St 45409
Ashley Meadows Ct 45424
Ashmore Dr 45420
Ashpark Ct 45458
Ashton Cir 45429
Ashton Ln 45420
Ashview Ct 45424
Ashwood Ave 45405
Ashworth Ct 45459
Ashwyck Pl 45429
Aspen Ave 45404
Aspen Ridge Ct 45459
Aspenbrook Ct 45458
Astor Ave 45449
Atchison Rd 45458
Atha Ct 45424
Athens Ave 45406
Atherton Rd 45409
Atlantic Ave 45406
Atlas Dr 45406
Atterbury Ct 45459
Attwood Ct 45458
Atwood Pl 45431
Auburn Ave 45406
Auburndale Ave 45414
Audrey Pl 45406
Audubon Park 45402
Aullwood Rd 45414
Aurora St 45420
Austin Pl 45431
Austin Rd 45458
Auto Club Dr 45402
Autumn Pl 45414
Autumn Glen Ct 45458
Autumn Hills Dr 45426
Autumn Leaf Dr 45426
Autumn Meadows Dr 45424
Autumn Ridge Ct 45414
Autumn Wind Ct 45458
Autumn Woods Dr 45426
Autumngate Ln 45424
Avalon Ave 45409
Avalon Cir 45458

Avco Dr 45439
Averell Dr 45424
Avian Glen Ct 45424
Avingnon Way 45458
Avionics Cir 45433
Avis Ct 45406
Avocet Ct 45424
Avon Way 45429
Avondale Dr 45404
Aylesbury Ct 45424
Ayrshire Ct 45429
Azalea Dr 45417
Azara Dr 45431
Azure Way 45449
B St 45433
E & W Babbitt St 45405
Babson St 45403
Babylon St 45439
Back Bay Ct 45458
Backstretch Ct 45434
Bacon St 45402
Baileys Trl 45440
Bainbridge St
1-299 45402
300-399 45410
401-499 45410
Baker Ct 45426
Baker Rd 45424
Baldwin Dr 45459
Ballard Dr 45417
Ballauer Pl 45424
Balmoral Dr 45429
Balsam Dr 45432
Baltic St 45406
Baltimore St 45404
Bamboo Cir 45431
Banbury Rd 45459
Bancroft St 45417
Bandit Trl 45434
Bank St 45402
Banker Pl & St 45417
Banning Ct 45405
Bannock St 45404
Bantam Way 45434
Bantz Ct 45403
Bantz Dr 45440
Barbanna Ln 45415
Barbara Dr 45424
Barbara Lee Ln 45424
Barbarosa Dr 45416
Barbee Dr 45406
Barcelona Ave 45404
Bareback Trl 45434
Barker St 45402
Barksdale Ave 45431
Barley Dr 45415
Barling Ave 45404
Barnard Dr 45424
Barnett St 45402
Barney Ave 45420
Barnhart Ave 45432
Barnsley Pl 45459
Barnview Ct 45458
Baronsmere Ct 45415
Barr Cir 45459
Barr Rd 45390
Barrett Dr 45431
Barrington Dr 45415
Barryknoll St 45420
Barstow Ave 45403
Barth Ln 45429
Bartlett Ct 45424
Bartley Rd 45414
Barton Ave 45429
Bascombe Dr 45424
Basore Rd
4800-4899 45426
5000-5999 45415
Bassett Dr 45424
Basswood Ave 45405
E & W Bataan Dr 45420
Bates St 45402
Bath Rd 45424
Baton Rouge Dr 45424
Batsford Dr 45459
Battle Creek Rd 45433

Bauer Ave 45420
Bavaria Pl 45424
Bay Harbour Cir 45458
Bay Tree Ct 45424
Baylor Ct 45420
Bayport Dr 45458
Bayside Dr 45431
Bayview Ct 45424
Baywood St 45406
Beach Haven Ct 45424
Beacon Ct 45458
Beacon Light Ct 45458
Beacon Tree Ct 45424
Beaconview Dr 45424
Beaconwood Ct 45429
Beamsville Union City Rd 45390
Beardsley Rd 45426
Beatrice Dr
1-1199 45404
500-699 45390
1501-1599 45424
Beatty Dr 45416
Beaufort Run 45458
Beaulieu Ct 45405
Beaumonde Ln 45409
Beaumont Ave 45410
Beaushire Cir 45459
Beaver Ave 45429
Beaver Creek Ln 45429
Beaver Ridge Dr 45429
Beaver Valley Rd 45434
Beaver Vu Dr 45434
Beaverpark Dr 45434
Beaverton Dr 45429
Beavon Ave 45449
Beck Dr 45458
N & S Beckel St 45403
Becker Dr 45417
Beckett Ct 45459
Beckley Ave 45416
Beckman St 45410
Beckton Ct 45424
Bedford Ave 45402
Bedford Ct 45458
Beech Ct 45424
Beech St 45433
Beech Trl 45458
Beech Hill Rd 45419
Beech Tree Ct 45424
Beecham Dr 45424
Beechcomb Pl 45429
Beechcreek Dr 45458
Beecher Ave 45420
Beechknoll Pt 45458
Beechview Dr 45424
E & W Beechwood Ave 45405
Beejay Ct 45414
Beerman Ave 45417
Belcourt Dr 45417
Beldale Ave 45424
Belfast Dr 45440
Belfry Ct 45458
Bell St 45403
Bella Casa Dr 45449
Bellaire Ave 45420
Bellcreek Ln 45426
Belle Chase Dr 45424
Belle Isle Dr 45439
Belle Meadows Dr 45426
Belle Plain Dr 45424
Belleclaire Hl 45458
Bellefontaine Ave 45404
Bellefontaine Rd 45424
Belleglade Dr 45424
Belleterrace Pl 45458
Belleville Ln 45459
Bellevue Ave 45406
Bellewood Ave 45406
Bellfield St 45420
Bellflower St 45409
Bellingham Dr 45458
Belloak Dr 45440
Bellsburg Dr 45459
Bellview Ct 45424

Belmar Dr 45424
Belmont Ct & Pl 45424
Belmonte Park E & N 45405
Belmore Trce 45426
Belpre Pl 45403
Belton St 45417
Belvedere Ln 45416
Belvoir Ave 45409
Benchwood Rd 45414
Bender Ave 45417
Bending Willow Dr 45440
Benedict Rd 45424
Benerint Ave 45417
Benfield Dr 45429
Bengie Ct 45424
Benham Dr 45458
Benjamin Ct 45424
Benjamin Way 45458
Benn St 45402
Benning Pl 45417
Bennington Dr 45405
Bennington Way 45458
Benson Dr 45406
Bentgrass Ln 45458
Bentley St 45404
Bently Oak Dr 45458
Benton Ave 45406
Bentwood Ct 45429
Benzell Dr 45458
Berchman Dr 45424
Berea Pl 45404
Bergan Dr 45424
Bergerac Ct 45459
Berkley St 45409
Berkshire Rd 45419
Berna Ln 45429
Bernard Ct 45417
Bernie Dr 45415
Bernwald Ln 45432
Berquist Dr 45426
Berry Ave 45431
Berry Dr 45426
Berrycreek Dr 45440
Berryleaf Ct 45424
Berrywood Dr 45424
Bertram Ave 45406
Berwin Ave 45429
Berwyck Ave 45414
Beryl Trl 45459
Bessmer Dr 45426
Best St 45405
Betal Ct 45424
Beth Rd 45424
Beth Page Cir 45458
Bethania Ave 45404
Bethany Ct 45415
Bethany Commons Trl 45458
Bethany Village Dr 45459
Bethel Rd 45458
Bethpolamy Ct 45415
Bethune Cir 45417
Betsy Ross Cir 45459
Betty Ln 45449
Bexley Pl 45404
Bickmore Ave 45404
Biddison Ave 45426
Bidleman St 45410
Bidwell Ave 45417
Bierce Ave 45403
Big Bear Dr 45458
Big Bend Dr 45417
Big Hill Rd
700-999 45419
1000-1699 45429
1700-1899 45439
2900-2998 45419
3000-3199 45419
Big Horn Ct 45424
Big Oak Dr
700-799 45426
9100-9199 45458
Big Pine Rd 45431
Big Rock Rd 45431
Big Springs Ct 45424
Bigger Ln 45459

Bigger Rd
  4400-5999 45440
  6000-7999 45459
Billwood Rd 45431
Biltmore Pl 45431
Bimni Dr 45459
Bingham Ave 45420
Birch Ct 45390
Birch Dr 45414
Birch St 45433
Birch Bark Ct 45440
Birchbend Ct 45415
Birchbrook Ct 45458
Birchcreek Cir 45458
Bircher Ave 45403
Birchton Ct 45424
Birchview Ct 45424
Birchwood Ave 45405
Bird Dog Ct 45424
Birdland Ave 45417
Birdwood Cir 45449
Birdwood Rd 45440
Birkdale Pike 45458
Birkdale Hills Cir 45458
Birkdale Village Dr 45458
Biscayne Ct 45424
Bish Ave 45417
Bishop Dr 45449
Bit Pl 45449
Bittern Ct 45424
Bittersweet Dr 45429
Bizzell Ave 45459
Black Forest Dr 45449
Black Horse Ct 45458
Black Oak Dr 45459
Black Oak Pl 45424
Blackberry Rd 45431
Blackbirch Dr 45458
Blackfoot St 45424
Blackhawk Rd 45420
Blackleaf Ct 45458
Blackshear Dr 45424
Blacksmith Ln 45434
Blackstone Dr 45459
Blackwood Ave 45403
Blaine St 45402
Blairfield Pl 45426
Blairgowrie Cir 45429
Blairwood Ave 45417
Blairwood Dr 45426
Blake Ave 45414
Blakley Dr 45403
Blanche Dr 45449
Blanche St 45417
Blazing Ct 45431
Blenham Ct 45459
Bliss Pl 45440
Blocker Dr 45420
Blommel Ln 45410
Bloomfield Dr 45426
Blossom Heath Rd 45419
E & W Blossom Hill Rd 45449
Blossom Park Dr 45449
Blossom Wood Ct 45458
Blossomview Ct 45424
Blue Ash Rd 45414
Blue Bell Rd 45431
Blue Gate Cir 45429
Blue Rock Rd 45432
Blue Spruce Ct 45424
Blue Stone Ct 45440
Blueberry Ave 45406
Bluecrest Ave 45417
Bluefield Ave 45414
Bluehaven Dr 45406
Blueridge Dr 45415
Bluestream Ct 45459
Bluewood Ln 45458
Bluff Pl 45449
Bluffs Dr 45459
Bluffside Dr 45426
Bluffview Dr 45424
Blumen Ln 45439
Blythe Ct 45431
Bob White Pl 45431

Bobbie Pl 45429
Bobolink Pl 45414
Boca Ct 45426
Bodem Dr 45458
Boeing Ave 45433
Boesel Ave 45429
Bofield Dr 45429
Bogey Ct 45459
Boggs Ave 45416
Bohemian Ave 45406
Bohn Ct 45417
Bokay Dr 45440
Bolander Ave 45417
Boltin St
  2-2 45403
  4-163 45403
  400-499 45410
Bomarc St 45404
Bon Air Dr 45415
Bon Bon Dr 45390
Bond St 45405
Bong St 45433
Bonita Dr 45415
Bonner St 45410
Bonnie Rd 45440
Bonnie Ann Pl 45458
Bonnie Birch Ct 45459
Bonnie Villa Ln 45431
Bonnieview Ave 45431
E & W Bonsai Ct 45431
Bontralt Ave 45419
Boone Pl 45417
Bordeaux Dr & Way 45458
Bostelman Pl 45424
Boston Pl 45415
Bothwell Pl 45424
Botkins Rd 45424
Boulder Ave 45414
Boulder Creek Ct 45458
Boundbrook Dr 45459
Bourdeaux Way 45458
Bournemouth Ct 45459
Bowen St 45410
Bower Ave 45431
Bowie Dr 45417
Bowman Ave 45409
Box Elder Dr 45458
Boxwood Dr 45414
Boyce Rd 45458
Boyer St 45402
Bracken Pl 45459
Brad Cir 45410
Braddock St 45420
Bradfield Dr 45426
Bradford St 45410
Bradley Ln 45410
Bradstreet Rd 45459
Bradwood Dr 45405
Brady St 45409
Braewick Cir 45440
Braewood Trl 45459
Bragg Pl 45417
Brahms Blvd 45449
Brainard Dr 45440
Brainard Woods Dr 45458
Bralinch Dr 45431
Bramblewood Ct 45424
Bramley Ct 45414
Brampton Rd 45429
Brams Hill Dr 45459
S Branch Rd 45458
Branch Creek Ct 45458
Branchport Dr 45424
Brandon Rd 45414
Brandonview Ct 45424
Brandt Pike
  1000-4399 45404
  4400-9899 45424
Brandt St 45404
Brandtvista Ave 45424
Brandwynne Ct 45459
Brandy Ct 45458
Brandy Mill Ln 45459
Brantford Rd 45414
Brantly Ave 45404
Brantwood Ct 45414

Brassfield Cir 45459
Brattleboro Ct 45440
Braxton Pl 45459
Brazoria Pl 45440
Breckenridge Rd 45429
Breckenwood Dr 45424
Breenbrier Ct 45431
Breene Dr 45433
Breezewood Ave 45406
Breezy Hill Cir 45459
Brenau Ave 45429
Brendonwood Ln 45415
Brennan Dr 45404
Brenner Ave 45403
Brentlinger Dr 45414
Brenton Dr 45416
Brentshire Ct 45459
Brentwood Ct 45424
Brentwood Dr
  1200-1299 45406
  5200-5299 45424
Brett Dr 45433
Briar Pl 45405
Briar Heath Cir 45415
Briar Knoll Dr 45429
Briar Ridge Ct 45424
Briarcliff Rd 45415
Briarwood Ave 45403
Bricker Ave 45417
Brickstone Ct 45402
Brickwall Dr 45420
Bridge St 45402
Bridgeport Dr 45406
Bridget St 45417
Bridgewater Rd 45424
Bridle Ln N 45449
Bridlegate Way 45424
Bridlewood Trl 45458
Briedweng Ave 45420
Brigantine Way 45414
Briggs Rd 45459
Brigham Sq 45459
Bright Bounty Ln 45449
Brighton St 45404
Brightwood Ave 45405
Brilliant Way 45459
Brinsted Ave 45449
Brio Dr 45424
Bristol Dr 45458
Brittany Ct 45459
Brittany Hills Dr 45459
Britton Ave & Ct 45429
Broad Blvd 45419
Broad Oak Dr 45426
Broadacres Ave 45405
Broadbent Way 45440
Broadbush Dr 45426
Broadcast Plz 45417
Broadmead Ave 45404
Broadmoor Dr 45419
Broadripple Rd 45458
Broadstone Ct 45458
Broadview Blvd S 45419
N Broadway St 45402
S Broadway St
  1-499 45402
  500-1799 45417
Brock Ln 45415
Brock Cosmos Rd 45390
Broerman Rd 45414
Brohm Ln 45417
Broken Arrow Pl 45459
N & S Bromfield Rd 45429
Bromley Pl 45420
Bromwick Dr 45426
Bronson St 45417
Bronze Leaf Ct 45424
Brookbank Dr & Pl 45440
Brookburn Ct 45459
Brookdale Dr 45429
Brookfield Rd 45429
Brookgreen Ct 45458
Brookhaven Dr 45426
Brookhill Ln 45405
Brooklands Rd 45409
Brooklawn Ct 45429

Brookline Ave 45420
Brooklyn Ave
  100-599 45417
  600-899 45402
Brookmeadow Dr 45459
Brookmill Ct 45414
Brookmount Rd 45429
Brookpark Dr 45440
Brooks Rd 45390
Brooks St 45420
Brooks Bend Ct 45458
Brookside Dr
  300-599 45406
  2800-2899 45431
Brookston Rd 45426
Brookview Ave 45409
Brookway Rd 45459
Brookwood Ct 45405
Broom Ln 45404
Broomall St 45424
Broomsedge Dr 45431
Broughton Pl 45431
Brown Rd 45440
Brown St
  1-799 45402
  800-1999 45409
Brown Bark Dr 45431
Brown Deer Pl 45424
Brownell Rd 45403
Brownleigh Rd 45429
Brubaker Dr 45429
E & W Bruce Ave 45405
Brumbaugh Blvd
  3300-3499 45406
  3500-4499 45416
Brunswick Ave 45416
Brunswick Dr 45424
Brush Hill Ct 45449
Brushwood Ct 45415
Bruton Cir 45429
Bryant Ave 45414
Brydon Rd 45419
Bryn Mawr Dr
  900-1399 45402
  1400-1599 45406
Brynford Pl 45426
Buchanan Ave 45410
Buck Spring Cir 45459
Buckeye Cir 45433
Buckeye Ct 45424
Buckeye St
  2-198 45402
  5486-5518 45433
Buckingham Rd 45419
Buckleigh Way 45426
Buckman Dr 45424
Buckner Dr 45424
Buckner Rd 45433
Bucksport Ct 45440
Buel Ct 45433
Buell Ln 45424
Buena Vista Ave 45414
Bueno Ct 45431
Buffalo St 45432
Buffalo Gap Cir 45424
Bufort Blvd 45424
Buggy Whip Ln 45459
Buglers Sound 45458
Bulah Dr 45429
Bunche Dr 45417
Bungalow Rd 45417
Bunker Ct 45459
Bunker Hill Ct 45440
Bunnell Hill Rd 45458
Bur Del Dr 45429
Burbank Dr 45406
Burchcliff Cir 45449
Burchdale St 45440
Burchwood St 45426
Burgess Ave 45415
Burgoyne Dr 45405
Burgundy Ln 45459
Burke Way 45403
Burkhardt Ave
  1-800 45403
  802-998 45403

  4300-4690 45431
  4692-4698 45431
  4700-4799 45403
Burkhardt Rd 45431
Burleigh Ave
  200-699 45417
  700-1199 45402
Burlingame Commons 45426
Burlington Ave 45403
Burman Ave 45426
Burnet Isle Dr 45458
Burnham Ln 45429
Burning Bush Ln 45429
Burning Tree Dr 45440
Burns Ave
  1-299 45402
  300-322 45410
  323-399 45449
  324-498 45410
  401-499 45410
  500-604 45449
  606-698 45449
Burnside Dr 45439
Burr Oak Ct 45420
Burroughs Dr 45406
Bursley Ct 45449
E & W Burton Ave 45405
Burwood Ave 45417
Bus Stop Rd 45433
Bushnell Ave 45404
Bushwick Dr 45439
Business Center Ct 45410
Business Park Dr 45417
Buttercreek Cir 45458
Butternut Dr 45419
Butterwood Ct 45424
Byesville Blvd 45431
Byrd Ct 45458
Bywood Ct 45458
C St 45433
Cabell Ct 45424
Cabin Croft Ct 45424
Cable Ct 45458
Cactus Ct 45433
Cades Cv 45459
Cadet Cir 45424
Cadie Ave 45414
Cadiz Ct 45424
Cadman Dr 45424
Caho St 45410
Cain Ct 45417
Caisson St 45426
Cajun Ct 45424
Calais Ct 45459
Caldero Ct 45415
Caldwell Cir 45424
Calhoun St 45417
Calico Ct 45424
California Ave
  2500-2999 45419
  3000-3899 45429
Caliph Ct 45406
Callamere Dr 45424
Callamere Farms Dr 45424
Calm St 45417
Calmcrest Ct 45424
Calumet Ln 45417
Calvary Dr 45409
Calverda Dr 45458
Calvin Ave 45414
Camargo Dr 45415
Cambridge Ave
  1-199 45406
  200-699 45402
Cambridge Station Rd 45458
Camden Ave 45405
Camelia Pl 45429
Camelot Rd 45426
Cameo Ln 45424
Camerford Dr 45424
Cameron Rd 45459
Camino Pl E & W 45420
Camp Hill Way 45449
Campbell St 45417
Campus Dr 45406
Camrose Ct 45424

Canal St 45402
Canal Boat Ct 45402
Canary Ct
  2100-2199 45414
  8900-8999 45424
Candle Ridge Ct 45458
Candlelight Ln 45431
Candlestick Ln 45424
Candlewood Dr 45419
Candlewyck Ct 45459
Candy Ct 45424
Canfield Ave 45406
Cannonbury Ct 45429
Cannondale Ln 45424
Canova Ln 45431
Cantata Ct 45449
Cantella Ct 45429
Canterbury Dr 45429
Canton Pl 45404
Cantura Dr 45415
Canyon Rd 45414
Cape Cod Ct 45406
Capitol Pl 45420
Capitol Hill Ln 45459
Captains Brg 45458
Caracara Ct 45424
Caraway Ct 45424
Cardiff Pl 45424
Cardigan Rd 45459
Cardinal Ave 45414
Cardington Rd 45409
Carew Ave 45420
Caribe Pl 45424
Caribou Trl 45459
Carillon Blvd 45409
Carinthia Dr 45459
Carlin Dr 45449
Carlisle Ave
  400-498 45410
  500-899 45410
  1000-1499 45420
Carlo Dr 45429
Carlotta Dr 45404
Carlton Dr 45404
Carlyle Cir 45429
Carma Dr 45426
Carmel Ct 45458
E Carmel St 45390
Carmelita Dr 45424
Carmichael Pl 45420
Carmin Ave 45417
Carnation Rd 45449
Carnegie St 45406
Carol Pkwy 45440
E Caroline St 45390
Carousel Cir 45429
Carriage Dr 45415
Carriage Hall Ct 45459
Carriage Trace Blvd 45459
Carrick Dr 45458
Carrier Ave 45429
Carrilon Woods Dr 45458
Carrlands Dr 45429
Carroll Ave 45405
Carrollton Ave 45409
Carson Ave 45415
Carter Ave 45405
Carter Talbot Ct 45419
Carters Grove Rd 45459
Carthage Pl 45426
Cartwright Pl 45420
Caruso Ct 45449
Carver Pl 45417
Casa Grande Ct 45424
Casaba Ct 45417
Casper Ave 45416
Cass St 45402
Cassel Rd 45414
Casselberry Ct 45424
Castano Dr 45416
Castle Dr
  1-299 45429
  4800-4999 45424
Castlecreek Dr 45458
Castlecrest Dr 45424
Castlerock Trl 45459

Castleview Ct 45424
Castlewood Ave 45405
Catalina Ave 45416
Catalina Dr 45449
Catalpa Dr
  700-1299 45402
  1300-2999 45406
  3000-4699 45405
Catawba Ave 45424
Cathedral Ct 45458
Catherine Ave 45449
Catherine St 45402
Cathy Ln 45429
Catskill Ln 45432
Cattail Ct 45431
Cauley Pl 45431
Causeway Dr 45458
Cavanaugh Rd 45405
Caylor Rd 45439
Cayuga Ct 45424
Cecil Ct 45402
Cecilia Dr 45414
Cedar St 45449
N Cedar St 45390
Cedar Trl 45415
Cedar Bark Trl 45449
Cedar Bluff Cir 45415
Cedar Cove Dr 45459
Cedar Creek Cir 45459
Cedar Crest Trl 45459
Cedar Hill Dr 45424
Cedar Knolls Dr 45424
Cedar Pines Ct 45459
Cedar Ridge Rd 45414
Cedar Valley Ct 45414
Cedarbrook Cir 45415
Cedarcliff Cir 45414
Cedargate Pl 45424
Cedarhurst Ave 45402
Cedarlawn Dr 45415
Cedarleaf Ct & Dr 45459
Cedarview Ct 45459
Celestine St 45424
Celina St 45402
Celita Ct 45449
Cellarius Ct 45405
Celtic Dr 45432
Cemetery Dr 45459
Cemetery Rd 45429
Centennial Ct 45458
Center Park Blvd 45431
Center Point Dr 45459
Center Point 70 Blvd 45424
Centerbrook Ct 45458
Centerlawn Dr 45424
Centerplex Ln 45420
Centerridge Pt 45458
Centerville Business Pkwy 45459
Centerville Creek Ln 45458
E Centerville Station Rd 45459
Centerwood Ln 45429
Central Ave 45406
E Central Ave 45449
W Central Ave 45449
E Central Ln 45449
E Central St 45390
Central Park Ave 45409
Centre St 45403
Century Ln 45424
Chadbourne Dr 45424
Chadwick Dr 45406
Chain Ave 45417
Chalet Pl 45424
Chalmers St 45424
Chamber Plz 45402
Chamberlin Ave 45406
Chambers St 45409
Chambersburg Rd 45424
Chambrey Ct 45458
Chaminade Cir 45458
Champaign Ave 45424
Champion Ct 45424
Champion Oak Ct 45439
Champions Xing 45458

Chandler Ct 45420
Chandler Dr
400-499 45433
600-899 45426
Channing Ln 45416
Channingway Ct 45424
Chantilly Ln 45458
Chapel Ln 45431
Chapel St 45404
Chapin St 45429
Chaplen Dr 45426
Chardon Ct 45403
Chardonnay Dr 45459
Charing Ct 45424
Charity Cir 45424
Charlesgate Rd 45424
Charleston Blvd 45402
Charlesworth Dr 45424
Charleton Ave 45415
Charlotte Ct 45424
Charlotte Mill Dr & Rd 45439
Charlwood Ave 45432
Charnwood Dr 45424
Charter Pl 45458
Chartwell Dr 45459
Chase Dr 45458
Chase St 45433
Chateau Dr 45429
Chateauroux Dr 45459
Chatfield Pl 45424
Chatham Dr 45429
Chatlake Dr 45424
Chatsworth Dr 45424
Chaucer Rd 45431
Chaumont Ave 45458
Chauncy Pl 45424
Chedworth Dr 45458
Chee Ct 45429
Cheers Cir 45424
Chelsea Ave 45420
Cheltenham Dr 45459
Cherbourg Pl 45459
Cheri Lynne Dr 45415
Cherokee Dr
1-499 45417
1700-1799 45449
Cherry Dr
100-699 45405
711-797 45406
799-1099 45406
E Cherry St 45390
S Cherry St 45390
Cherry Blossom Dr & Pl 45449
Cherry Oak Dr 45440
Cherry Point Way 45449
Cherry Tree Ter 45458
Cherrycreek Dr 45458
Cherrygate Ct 45424
N & S Cherrywood Ave 45403
Cheryl Ct 45415
Chesapeake Ave 45417
Chesham Dr 45424
Cheshire Rd 45459
Chesney Ct 45458
Chess Wood Pt 45458
Chesterfield Cir 45431
Chestnut Cir 45433
Chestnut St 45433
N Chestnut St 45390
S Chestnut St 45390
Chestnut Hill Ln 45458
Cheswick Ct 45431
Chevington Ct 45459
Cheviot Cir 45424
Chevy Ln 45458
Cheyenne Ave 45424
Chicahominy Ave 45417
Chicamauga Ave 45417
Chickadee Ct 45458
Chidlaw Rd 45433
Childrens Plz 45404
Childs St 45417
Chilton Ln 45459
Chimney Cir & Ln 45440
Chinaberry Pl 45424
Chinook Ln 45420
Chipgate Ct 45424
Chipmunk Ct 45458
Chippendale Pl 45420
Chippewa Ave 45424
Chippingdon Dr 45424
Chipplegate Dr 45459
Chipstone Ct 45424
Chisolm Trl 45458
Choice Ct 45424
Chowning Cir 45429
Christopher Ave 45406
Christopher Dr 45458
Christy Ave 45431
Christygate Ln 45424
Chuck Wagner Ln 45414
Chukar Dr 45424
Chukka Dr 45458
Church St 45410
Churchill Downs Ct & Pl 45424
Churchland Ave 45406
Cicero Ct 45424
Cicilion Ave 45402
Cincinnati St
1-127 45402
129-199 45402
201-297 45417
299-1499 45417
Cindy Dr 45449
Circle Dr 45415
E Circle Dr
100-399 45449
700-798 45403
W Circle Dr
100-399 45449
600-699 45403
Circle Rd 45417
Circle Hill Ct 45424
Circle View Dr 45419
Circlewood Ln 45458
Citadel Dr 45424
Citation Ave 45420
Citrus Cir 45424
City Lights Dr 45402
City View Ter 45431
Civic Pl 45420
Claar Ave 45429
Claggett Dr 45414
Clagston Ct 45424
Claircrest Dr 45424
Clare Dr 45431
Claremont Ave 45403
Clarence Ave 45420
Clarence St 45410
Clarendon Dr 45440
Clareridge Ln 45458
Clarewood Ave 45431
N & S Claridge Dr 45429
Clarington Rd 45429
Clarissa Ave 45429
Clark Dr 45431
Clarkson Ave 45402
Classic Ct 45424
Claude Ave 45414
Claxton Glen Ct 45429
Clay St 45402
Claybeck Dr 45424
Claybourne Rd 45429
Clear Brook Dr 45440
Clear Springs Ct 45458
Clearlake Dr 45424
Clearwater Ct 45424
Clegg St 45417
Clematis Dr 45449
Clement Ave 45417
Clemmer St 45417
Cleveland Ave
3100-3198 45420
3401-3497 45410
3499-4299 45410
Cleverly Rd 45417
Cliff St 45405
Cliffanne Ct 45415
Cliffbrook Ct 45458
Cliffside Ct 45440
Cliffstone Dr 45424
Cliffview Ct 45459
Cliffwood Pl 45424
Clifton Dr 45417
Clifty Falls Rd 45449
Cline St 45409
N & S Clinton St 45402
Clintshire Dr 45459
Cloister Ln 45449
Cloud Ct 45424
Cloud Park Dr 45424
Cloudsdale Dr 45440
Clover St 45410
Cloverbrook Park Dr 45459
Clovercrest Ln 45458
Cloverfield Ave 45429
Cloverhill Ct 45440
Cloverwood Dr 45458
Clovis Ct 45417
Club Cir 45459
Club View Dr 45458
Clubhouse Dr 45449
Cluster Ave 45439
Clydesdale Ct 45458
Clyo Rd
4200-4299 45440
4300-7999 45459
8000-10699 45458
Coach Dr 45440
Coach Light Trl 45424
Coachman Dr 45458
Coachshire Ct 45459
Cobb Dr 45431
Cobb Run Ln 45415
Cobble Brook Dr 45458
Cobblecreek Dr 45458
Cobblegate Dr 45449
Cobbleskill Ct 45459
Cobblestone Ct 45431
Cobblestone Ln 45429
Cobblestone St 45432
Cobblestone Crossing Ct 45458
Cobblewood Ct 45458
Coburn Ct 45424
Coca Cola Blvd 45424
Coco Dr 45424
Cody Ct 45424
Coffman Ave 45426
Cohasset Dr 45424
Coker Dr 45440
Colameo Ct 45458
Colby Ln 45409
Colchester Ct 45458
Cold Spring Dr 45458
Cold Water Ct 45459
Coldwater Ct 45431
Colechester Ct 45459
Colegrove Dr 45424
Colemere Cir 45415
Coleraine Dr 45424
Coleridge Ave 45426
Coletown Lightsville Rd 45390
Colfax Ave 45419
Colgate Ave 45417
Colin Kelly Dr 45431
Colleen Ct 45415
College Dr 45420
College St 45402
College Hill Ct 45431
College Park Ave 45409
College View Dr 45417
Collett Pl 45406
Colley Pl 45420
Collins Ave 45420
Collins Ct 45439
Collinwood Ave 45405
Collopy Ct 45433
Cologne Pl 45424
Colombo Ct 45416
Colonel Glenn Hwy 45433
Colonial Ave 45419
Colonial Ln 45429
Colonial Village Ln 45406
Colony Way 45440
Colony Cove Ct 45459
Colorado Ave 45410
Colton Dr 45420
Columbine Pl 45405
Columbus St 45403
Colwick Dr 45420
Colwood St 45426
Comanche Dr 45420
Commerce Center Dr 45414
Commerce Park Dr 45404
Commercial St 45402
Commons Rd 45459
Communications Blvd 45433
Community Dr 45404
Como Ln 45402
Compark Rd 45459
Composite Dr 45420
Compton St 45404
Concept Ct 45458
Concerto Ct 45449
Concord St 45417
Concord Commons Dr 45459
Concorde Dr 45490
Concordia Cir 45440
Condominium Cir 45449
Condor Ct 45458
Cone Ct 45417
Cone Flower Dr 45431
Congaree Ct 45424
Congress Ct 45415
Congress Park Dr 45459
Conifer Cir 45431
Conifer Ln 45419
Conley St 45417
Connecticut Ave 45410
Conners St 45417
N & S Conover St 45402
Constance Ave 45409
Constantia Ave 45419
Constitution Dr 45415
Constitutional Ct 45440
Converse Rd 45390
Conway Rd 45431
Cooper Pl 45402
Cooper Pl E 45402
Cooper Pl W 45402
Cooper St 45433
Cooper Farm Rd 45415
Coover Mill Ct 45414
Copeland Ave 45406
Copley Cir 45424
N & S Copper Ct 45415
Copper Beech Ct 45459
Copper Pheasant Dr 45424
Copper Tree Ct 45424
Copperfield Dr 45415
Coppergate Ct & Dr 45414
Coppermill Pl 45429
Copperside Dr 45415
Coppersmith Ave 45414
Copperton Dr 45458
Coral Dr 45420
Coral Oak Cir 45440
Coral Ridge Ct 45449
Coralbells Ct 45449
Corby Way 45424
Cordell Dr 45439
Coretta Ct 45417
Corfu Ct 45424
Corinth Blvd 45410
Corkhill Dr 45424
Corkwood Dr 45424
Corlett Ct 45424
Corlington Dr 45440
Cornell Dr 45406
Cornell Ridge Dr 45406
Cornell Woods Dr E & W 45406
Cornerstone Ct 45458
Cornwall Dr 45415
Cornwallis Ct 45414
Corona Ave 45419
Coronado Cir 45424
Coronette Ave 45414
Corporate Way 45459
Corsair Ct 45404
Corsica Dr 45424
Cortez Dr 45415
Cortina Dr 45459
Corwin St 45410
Cory Dr 45406
Corydale Ct 45415
Cosler Dr 45403
Cosmo Ct 45432
Cosmos Dr 45449
Cosner Dr 45424
Costello St 45402
Cotswold Dr 45459
E Cottage Ave 45449
Cottage Ter 45420
Cottage Point Way 45449
Cotter Cir 45424
Cottingwood Ct 45429
Cotton Ct 45458
Cottonrose Dr 45431
Cottontail Ct 45431
Cottonwood Dr 45424
Cottonwood Rd
900-999 45419
1000-1099 45409
Coughlin Ct 45415
Coulson Dr 45417
Countess Ct 45459
Country Pl 45429
Country Brook Ct 45414
Country Club Dr 45417
Country Corner Ln 45458
Country Creek Way 45458
Country Haven Ct 45424
Country Manor Ln 45458
Country Squire Ct 45458
Country Walk Ct 45458
Country Wood Dr 45440
Countrydale Ct 45415
Court St 45402
Courter St 45417
Courthouse Plz 45402
Courtland Ave 45420
Courtney Dr 45431
Courtwood Ave
1000-1099 45417
3600-3699 45402
Courtyard Pl 45458
Coury Ln 45424
Cove Ct 45416
Covenant House Dr 45426
Coventry Rd
1400-1699 45410
1700-1999 45420
Covertside Dr 45459
Covina St 45431
Cowan Pl 45431
Cowart Ave 45417
Cox Rd 45390
Cozycroft Dr 45424
Crabtree Ln 45424
Craftmore Dr 45424
Craftsbury Ct 45440
Craig Dr 45420
Craigmont Ct 45424
Cranberry Pl 45431
Cranbrook Ct 45459
Crane St 45403
Cranford Dr 45459
Cransberry Dr 45449
Cranston Ct 45458
Cranwell Cir 45424
Crauder Ave 45409
Crawley Run 45458
Craycraft Ave 45424
Cree Ave 45424
N Creek Ln 45458
Creek Bed Ct 45424
Creek Bend Way 45458
Creek Landing Way 45458
Creek Stone Ct 45458
Creek Water Dr 45459
Creekmore Ct 45440
Creeknoll Ct 45424
Creekside St 45417
Creekview Cir 45414
Creekview Dr 45426
Creekway Trl 45440
Creighton Ave
500-999 45410
1000-1499 45420
Crenshaw Ln 45424
Crescent Blvd 45409
Crest Dr 45416
Crest Oak Pl 45414
Crestline Ct 45424
Crestmore Ave
500-598 45417
600-699 45417
700-999 45402
Creston Ave 45404
Crestridge Dr 45414
Crestview Rd 45431
Crestwell Pl 45420
Crestwood Ave 45431
Crew Cir 45439
Cricket Ln 45414
Cricket Woods Dr 45414
Crimson Creek Dr 45459
Crispy Dr 45440
Criswell Ct 45449
Crocus Dr 45417
Croftshire Dr 45440
Cromwell Pl 45405
Cronk Dr 45424
Crooked Creek Dr 45458
Cross Ln 45458
Cross St 45410
Cross Creek Cir 45429
Crossbrook Dr 45459
Crossland Ct 45404
Crossridge Dr 45429
Crossview Dr 45459
Crown Ave 45417
Crown Point Dr & Mdws 45458
Crownwood Ave 45415
Croyden Dr 45420
Crusader Dr 45449
Cruxten Dr 45424
Crystal Dr 45431
Crystal Point Dr 45459
Crystal Springs Ln 45429
Culpepper Ct 45459
Culver Ave
1800-2499 45420
2600-2899 45429
2900-2902 45420
2904-3099 45420
Culzean Dr 45426
Cumberland Ave 45406
Cummings Ct 45417
E Cunnington Ln 45420
Curlwood Ct 45424
Current Ct 45459
Curry Ln 45424
Curtis Dr 45431
Curundu Ave 45416
Cushing Ave 45429
Cushwa Dr 45459
Custer Pl 45417
Cutleaf Ct 45424
Cutlers Trce 45458
Cuyuse Ct 45414
Cynthia Ln 45429
Cypress Ct 45417
Cypress Dr 45414
Cypressgate Dr 45424
D St 45433
Dabel Ct 45459
Daffodil Cir 45449
Dahle Ct 45459
Dahlia Dr 45449
Daisy Ct 45420
Dakota St 45402
Dale Ridge Dr 45458
Daleview Ave 45405
Dalewood Pl 45426
Dallas Dr 45406
Dalmation Dr 45424
Damascus Dr 45424
Danado Dr 45406
Danan Cir 45429
Danbury Rd 45420
Dandridge Ave 45402
Danforth Pl 45431
Daniel St 45404
Danner Ave 45417
Dantanch Dr 45449
Dantande Ave 45406
Danube Ct 45420
Danz Ave 45420
Daphne Ln 45415
Darby Rd 45431
Darien Dr 45426
Darnell Dr 45431
Darron Ct 45432
Darst Ave 45403
Darst Rd 45440
Dartmoor Dr 45416
Dartmouth Dr 45406
Daruma Pkwy 45439
Darwin Ct 45429
Datchet Ct 45459
Davenport Ave 45417
Daventry Ct 45459
W David Pkwy 45429
E David Rd
1-1699 45429
1700-2299 45440
W David Rd 45429
David Allen Cir 45459
David Andrew Way 45458
Davidgate Dr 45424
Davis Ave 45403
Davis Rd 45459
Davue Cir 45406
Dawes Ave 45404
Dawn Dr 45419
Dawnridge Dr 45414
Dawnview Ave 45431
Dawnwood Dr 45415
Dayoh Pl 45417
Dayton Ave 45402
Dayton Christian School Rd 45419
Dayton Farmersville Rd 45417
Dayton Lebanon Pike 45458
Dayton Liberty Rd 45417
Dayton Park Dr 45414
Dayton Towers Dr 45410
Dayton View Pl 45402
Dayton Wire Pkwy 45404
Dayton Xenia Rd
1800-3290 45434
3501-3549 45432
3541-3541 45434
Daytona Pkwy 45406
Dayview Ave 45417
De De Ct 45449
Dean Pl 45420
Deanmont Pl 45459
Deanwood Ave 45410
Dearborn Ave 45417
Deauville Dr 45429
Debbie Ct 45415
Debra Ave 45420
Decatur Ave 45417
N & S Decker Ave 45417
Deeds Ave 45404
Deep Forest Ln 45458
Deer Bend Dr 45424
Deer Bluff Dr 45424
Deer Chase Dr 45424
Deer Creek Cir 45449
Deer Crossing Way 45458
Deer Face Ct 45458
Deer Garden Ln 45424
Deer Haven St 45424
Deer Hollow Dr 45424
Deer Knolls Dr 45424
Deer Meadows Dr 45424
Deer Park Cir 45429
Deer Park Pl 45424
Deer Path Ln 45415
Deer Plains Way 45424
Deer Ridge Dr 45424

Deer Run Rd 45459
Deer Valley Dr 45424
NW Deerfield Rd 45390
SE Deerfield Rd 45390
Deerfield St 45414
Deergate Dr 45424
Deergreen Ct 45424
Deering Ave 45406
Deerland St 45432
Deerview Ct 45458
Deerwood Ct 45424
Defoe Dr 45431
Del Ray Ave 45414
Delaine Ave
2900-2928 45419
2930-3019 45419
3020-3700 45429
3702-3910 45429
Delaney St 45420
Delano Pl 45420
Delavan Dr 45459
Delaware Ave 45405
Delba Dr 45439
Delbrook Dr 45405
Delco Dell Rd 45429
Delco Park Dr 45420
Delcourt Dr 45439
Deldelac Dr 45415
Delhi Dr 45432
Dell St 45404
Dell Ridge Dr 45429
Della Dr 45417
Dellhurst Dr 45429
Dellrose Ave 45403
N & S Delmar Ave 45403
Delmonte Ave 45419
Delno Dr 45406
Delor St 45402
Delphos Ave
2901-2997 45417
2999-3899 45417
3900-4099 45402
Delta Ave 45419
Delvue Dr 45459
Delynn Dr 45459
Demphle Ave 45410
Dencench Dr 45432
Denger Dr 45426
Denham Ct 45458
Denise Dr 45429
Denlinger Rd
3000-3399 45406
3401-3499 45406
3500-5880 45426
5882-5898 45426
Dennison Ave 45417
Denny Ln 45431
Denver St 45424
Depoy St 45424
Deptford Ave 45429
Derby Pl 45424
Derby Rd 45417
Derbyshire Dr 45417
Derwent Dr 45431
Descant Dr 45424
Desert Turtle Ct 45414
Deshler Pl 45405
Desmond St 45417
Desoto St 45426
Detrick St 45404
Detroit Ave 45416
Devay Ave 45458
Deville Dr 45415
Devon Ave 45429
Devonhurst Dr 45429
Devonshire Ave 45417
Devonshire Rd 45419
Devonwood Dr 45424
Dewberry Ct 45431
Deweese Pkwy 45414
Dewey Dr 45420
Dewitt Dr 45406
Dexter Ave 45419
Dial Dr 45424
Diamond Ave 45403
Diamond Dr 45458

N Diamond Mill Rd
1-999 45417
2500-5099 45426
Diamondback Dr 45414
Diana Dr 45449
Dickman Dr 45431
Dietzen Ave 45417
Dijon Ct 45458
Dimco Way 45458
Dinsmore Rd 45449
Dinwiddie Ct 45458
Dionne Ct 45459
Discovery Trl 45449
Display Ln 45429
Ditzel Ave 45417
Division Ave 45414
N Division St 45390
S Division St 45390
E Dixie Dr 45449
N Dixie Dr 45414
S Dixie Dr
1600-1798 45414
2201-2297 45409
2299-3000 45409
3002-3098 45409
Dobbin Cir 45424
Dobbs Dr 45440
Doddington Rd 45409
Dodge Ct 45431
Dodgson Ct 45404
Dody Cir 45440
Doe Xing 45459
Doe Run Ct 45440
Doe Run Pl 45424
Dog Leg Rd
6000-6369 45415
6400-9499 45414
Dogwood Ct 45417
Dogwood Trl 45429
Dolley Dr 45440
Dolores Ct 45415
Dominican Dr 45415
Dona Ave 45417
Donald Ave 45420
Donamere Cir 45459
Donegal St 45426
Donington Dr 45449
Donlaw Ave 45417
Donnybrook Dr 45459
Donson Cir & Dr 45429
Doolittle Dr 45431
Doornock Ct 45429
Dora Ave 45432
Dorchester Dr 45415
Dorf Dr 45439
Dorham Pl 45406
Doris Dr 45429
E Dorothy Ln
100-198 45419
200-1399 45419
1400-1800 45429
1801-1807 45420
1802-1808 45429
1809-1811 45420
1812-1898 45429
1813-3199 45420
1900-3198 45420
W Dorothy Ln
1-499 45429
600-799 45419
800-998 45409
1000-1500 45409
1502-1598 45409
Dorset Dr 45405
Dorsey Ct 45459
Dorshire Ct 45415
Douglas Ave 45403
Dovecrest Ct 45459
Dover St 45410
Dow St 45402
Dowden Ln 45420
Downey Ln 45426
Downing St 45414
Downs Ln 45402
Draher St 45417
Drake Ave 45405

Drayton Ct 45440
Dreamer Ct 45404
Dressler Ct 45410
Drew Way 45416
Drexel Ave 45417
Driftwood Cir 45415
Drill Ave 45414
Drowfield Dr 45426
Druewood Ln 45459
Druid Ln 45439
Drummer Ave 45403
Drury St 45403
Drycreek Cir 45458
Drywood Pl 45424
Duberry Pl 45459
Duck Row 45429
Duckview Ct 45458
Duffield Cir 45459
Duffy Ct 45431
Dugger Rd 45417
Duncan Ct 45426
Duncraig Dr 45426
Dundee Cir 45431
Dunhill Pl 45420
Dunmore Dr 45459
Dunn Pl 45416
Dunston Ln 45424
Dunwoody Ct 45420
Dupont Way 45433
Duquesne Ave 45431
Durand St 45414
Durban Rd 45459
Durham Dr 45459
Durner Ave 45417
Durning St 45417
Durwood Rd 45429
Duryea Ct 45424
Dushore Dr 45417
Dustin St 45402
Dutchess Ave 45420
N & S Dutoit St 45402
Dutton Ct 45458
Duxbury Cir 45440
Dwight Ave 45420
E St 45433
Eagle Cir 45429
Eagle Dr 45431
Eagle Creek Dr 45459
Eagle Feather Cir 45449
Eagle Nest Ct 45449
Eagle Pass Dr 45424
Eagle Ridge Dr 45459
Eagle Run Dr 45458
Eagle Stone Ct & Dr 45440
Eagle View Dr 45431
Eagle Watch Way 45424
Eagledale Cir 45429
Eagles Nest Cir 45429
Eagleview Dr 45429
Eaker St 45402
Earhart Pl 45420
Earl Ave 45404
Earlham Dr 45406
Earlington St 45424
Earlwood Dr 45414
Early Rd 45415
Early Spring Ct 45459
Earnshaw Dr 45429
East Dr
100-199 45458
500-950 45419
952-998 45419
Eastdale Dr 45415
Eastern Ct 45403
Eastgate Ave 45420
Eastman Ave 45432
Eastmoor Dr 45431
Easton St 45402
Eastpoint Ct 45459
Eastport Ave 45417
Eastview Ave 45405
Eastwey Ave 45410
Eastwood Ave 45403
Eccles Pl 45458
Echo Spring Trl 45429
Echo Wood Ct 45429

Echoing Oaks Cir 45414
Eckley Blvd 45449
Eda Dr 45449
Eddie St 45417
Eddington Ct 45459
Edelweiss Ct 45459
Edelweiss Dr 45458
Eden Ln 45431
Eden Meadows Way 45440
Edendale Rd 45432
Edenhill Ave 45420
Edenhurst Dr 45458
Edgar Ave 45410
Edgebrook Ct & Dr 45459
Edgecliff Dr 45402
Edgemere Way 45414
Edgemont Ave 45417
Edgepark Dr 45431
Edgewater Dr
2300-2491 45431
2493-2499 45431
5200-5499 45414
Edgewood Ave 45402
Edgeworth Ave 45414
Edinboro Ct 45431
Edinburgh Village Dr 45458
Edison St
1-799 45402
801-897 45417
899-4299 45417
4301-4499 45417
Edith St 45402
Edith Marie Dr 45431
Edmund St 45404
Edna St 45431
Edna Oaks Ct 45459
Edward Dr 45420
Edwards Dr 45433
N Edwin C Moses Blvd 45402
S Edwin C Moses Blvd
1-599 45402
601-1097 45417
1099-2399 45417
2401-2599 45417
Effingham Pl 45431
Egret Ct 45424
Eichelberger Ave 45406
Eileen Rd 45429
Eisenhower Dr 45431
El Kenna Ct 45458
El Morado Pl 45405
El Paso Ave 45406
Elaine St 45417
Elberon Ave 45403
Elcar Ct 45404
Elderberry Ave 45416
Elderwood Rd 45429
Eldorado Ave 45419
Eleanor Ave 45417
Elementary Dr 45449
Elgin Ave 45402
Elgin Roof Rd 45426
Elin Ct 45415
Elizabeth Pl 45417
Elizabeth St 45405
Elk Hollow Ln 45459
Elkhart Ave 45414
Elkins Ave 45417
Elkmont Ct 45414
Elkton Ave 45403
Ellen Dr 45417
Ellendale Ct 45431
Ellenwood Dr 45449
Ellington Rd 45431
Elliot Ave
3100-3799 45420
3801-3999 45420
4000-4599 45410
Ellis Ave 45415
Ellis Rd 45390
Ellsworth Dr 45426
Elm St 45426
E Elm St 45390
N Elm St 45449
S Elm St 45449

Elm Creek Cir 45458
Elm Grove Dr 45415
Elm Hill Dr 45415
Elmbrook Trl 45458
Elmdale Dr 45409
Elmer Ave 45417
Elmhurst Rd 45417
Elmira Dr 45439
Elmore St 45426
Elmridge Rd 45429
Elmshaven Dr 45424
Elmview Cir 45449
Elmway Dr 45415
Elmwood Ave E 45405
Elmwood Cir 45449
E Elmwood Dr 45459
W Elmwood Dr 45459
Elmwood Park Dr 45449
Elrod Ct 45439
Elru Dr 45415
Elsmere Ave 45406
Elverne Ave 45404
Elwood Ave 45402
Elyria Ln 45406
Elysee Cir 45458
Elysian Ct 45426
Elysian Way 45424
Elzo Ln 45440
Embassy Pl 45414
Embury Park Rd 45414
Emerald Ct 45403
N Emerald Dr 45431
S Emerald Dr 45431
Emerald Downs 45424
Emeraldgate Dr 45424
Emerson Ave 45406
Emery Dr 45414
Emmet St 45405
Emmons Ave
1400-1799 45410
1801-1899 45410
2100-2199 45420
Emory Ct 45424
Encanto Pl 45424
Encore Dr 45424
End St 45426
Endicott Rd 45424
Endover Rd 45439
Energy Dr 45414
Enfield Rd 45459
England Ave 45406
Engleka Ct 45417
English Ct 45414
English Bridle Ct 45458
Enid Ave 45429
Enigma Pl 45449
Enright Ave 45431
Ensley Ave 45414
Enterprise Ave 45420
Enxing Ave 45449
Epcot Ln 45414
E & N Eppington Dr 45426
Epworth Ave 45410
Erbaugh Ave 45417
Erbe Ave 45417
Erdiel Dr 45415
Eric Dr 45414
Erica Ct
4400-4499 45440
5900-5999 45414
Ericson Ave 45417
Ericsson Way 45426
Erie Ave 45410
Ernroe Dr 45417
Ernst Ave 45405
Eshbaugh Rd 45417
Esmeralda Ave 45406
Esquire Ave 45459
Essex Way 45429
Essington Cir 45459
Estates Ct & Dr 45459
Esther Ave 45431
Ethan Allen Ln 45459
Ethel Ave 45417
Etter Dr 45416
Eubanks Dr 45431

N Euclid Ave
100-1399 45402
1400-1599 45406
S Euclid Ave
1-751 45402
753-799 45402
800-1499 45417
Eugene Ave 45403
Eureka Dr 45419
Eva St 45410
Evans Ln 45459
Evanston Ave 45409
Evansville Ave 45406
Evelyn Dr 45409
Everett Dr
900-1299 45402
1301-1399 45406
Evergreen Ave 45402
Evergreen Cir 45424
Evergreen Park Ct 45458
Evergreen Woods Dr 45424
Evermur Dr 45414
Everview Cir 45459
Ewalt Ave 45420
Ewing St 45404
Exchange Dr 45439
Executive Blvd 45424
Executive Park Blvd 45431
Exeter Rd 45449
Expansion Way 45424
Factory Rd 45434
Fair Ln 45416
Fair Oaks Rd 45405
Fair Valley Rd 45414
Fairacres Dr 45429
Fairbanks Ave 45402
Fairchild St 45433
Fairfax Ave 45431
Fairford Ct 45414
N & S Fairgreen Ave 45416
Fairground Ave 45409
Fairgrove Way 45426
Fairhaven Ct 45419
Fairhill Ln 45440
Fairhurst Dr 45414
Fairmont Ave 45429
Fairpark Ave 45431
Fairport Ave 45406
Fairsmith St 45416
E Fairview Ave 45405
W Fairview Ave
1-699 45405
700-1399 45406
Fairway Dr 45409
Fairwind Ct 45458
Falcon Cir 45424
Falcon Ridge Ct 45458
Falke Dr 45432
Falkland Dr 45424
Falkmore Ct 45459
Fallen Oak Trce 45459
Falling Water Dr 45459
Falls Creek Ln 45458
Falmouth Ave
2100-3699 45406
3800-3999 45416
Fame Rd 45449
Fantasia Trl 45449
Far Hills Ave
2900-2999 45419
3000-5999 45429
6000-7499 45459
Faraday Ct 45416
Farlawn Ct 45429
Farley St 45402
Farmborough Dr 45424
Farmersvil W Carrolton Rd 45449
Farmersville Rd 45458
Farmside Dr 45420
Farnham Ave 45420
Farnsworth Dr 45449
Farr Dr 45404
Farrington Dr 45420
Faulkner Ave 45402
Fauna Way 45459

Fauver Ave
1500-1699 45410
1700-2499 45420
Fawn Run 45459
Fawn Lea Trl 45459
Fawn Willow Ct 45459
Fawnwood Rd 45429
Fayetta Ct 45424
Fayette Ct 45415
Feather Heights Ct 45440
Feather Wood Ln 45458
Federal St 45406
Federalist Dr 45440
Feedwire Rd 45440
Feldman Ave 45432
Felix Ct 45410
Felton Dr 45431
Fence Stone Ct 45458
Fenway Ct 45458
Fenwick Ct 45431
Fer Don Rd 45405
Ferellak Ave 45404
Ferguson Ave 45402
Fern Cir 45431
Fernbank Ct 45424
Fernbrook St 45440
Ferncliff Ave 45420
Ferndale Ave 45406
Ferngrove Dr 45432
Fernmont St 45440
Fernshire Dr 45459
Fernside Ct 45414
Fernwood Ave 45405
Fernwood Ct 45440
Fez Ln 45402
Ficus Cir 45431
Field Point Ct 45440
Fielding Dr 45403
Fields Ave 45420
Fieldson Rd 45459
Fieldstone Dr
100-299 45426
1400-1899 45414
Filbrun Ln 45426
Fillmore St 45410
Finch St 45415
N Findlay St
1-400 45403
402-448 45403
425-425 45404
445-445 45403
447-447 45404
449-599 45404
S Findlay St 45403
Fine Dr 45424
Finegan Dr 45424
Finger Lks 45458
Finland Dr 45439
Fir St 45433
Firegate Ct 45424
Fireside Dr 45459
Firethorn Ln 45458
Firwood Dr 45419
Fishburg Rd 45424
Fisher Dr 45424
Fisher Dangler Rd 45390
Fiske Ave 45417
Fitch St 45402
Five Oaks Ave 45406
Flagler St 45415
Flagstone Ct 45424
Flamingo Ct 45431
Flat Creek Ct 45424
Fleetfoot Ave 45417
Fleetwood Dr 45416
Fleming Ct 45458
Flemington Rd 45459
Flesher Ave 45420
Flicker Way 45424
Floral Ave 45405
Floral Home Ave 45404
Florence St 45403
Florida Dr 45404
Florrel Crest Ln 45415
Flory Ave 45405
Flotron Dr 45424

Flower Ave 45415
Flowerdale Ave 45429
Flowerstone Dr 45449
E & W Floyd Ave 45415
Fluhart Ave 45417
Flynn St 45416
Folkerth St 45403
Folkestone Dr 45459
Folsom Dr 45405
Fontano Dr 45440
Fontella Ct 45415
W Foraker Ave 45402
E Foraker St 45409
Forbes St 45433
Forent Ave 45417
Forest Ave 45405
Forest Run 45429
Forest Bend Dr 45429
Forest Brook Blvd 45459
Forest Creek Dr
2801-2899 45431
7400-7599 45459
Forest Crest Ln 45458
Forest Glen Ave 45405
Forest Green Ct 45414
Forest Grove Ave 45406
Forest Home Ave 45404
Forest Lawn Ct 45458
Forest Park Ct
1-99 45449
500-599 45405
Forest Park Dr 45405
Forest Park Mall Dr 45405
Forest Ridge Blvd 45424
Forest Walk Dr 45459
Forestdale Ave 45417
Forestdean Ct 45459
Forester Ct 45449
Forestview Dr 45459
Forrer Blvd
500-599 45419
800-1900 45420
1902-2098 45420
Forsythe Ave 45406
Fortman Dr 45417
Fortune Rd 45449
Foster Ave 45414
Fotip Ln 45406
Foulois Dr 45431
Founders Dr 45420
Fountain Ave 45405
Fountain Cir 45420
Fountain View Dr 45414
Fountainhead Dr 45424
Fourman Ct 45410
Fox Chase Ct 45459
Fox Grove Dr 45458
Fox Hollow Ct 45458
Fox Run Rd 45459
Fox Trace Ct 45424
Foxboro Dr 45416
Foxburrow Way 45458
Foxcroft Ct 45414
Foxdale Dr 45429
Foxgate Ct 45424
Foxglen Cir 45429
Foxhall Ct 45440
Foxknoll Dr 45458
Foxmoor Cir 45429
Foxridge Dr 45429
Foxshire Pl 45458
Foxton Ct 45414
Foxwood Ct 45424
Frances Ave 45417
Franciscan Ct 45459
Frank St 45409
Frankie Ln 45424
Franklin St 45402
E Franklin St 45459
N Franklin St 45390
W Franklin St 45459
Franlou Ave 45432
Fransican Way 45417
Frazer St 45417
Frederick Pike 45414
Fredericksburg Dr 45415
Fredonia Ave 45431
Free Pike
3900-4999 45416
5000-5499 45426
Freedom Dr 45431
Freeland Ave 45404
Freeman Rd 45459
Freeport Dr 45415
Freesia Dr 45431
French Ln
801-1097 45402
1099-1199 45402
1201-1499 45402
2200-2299 45417
Frericks Way 45409
Freshbrook Ct 45459
Freudenberger Ave 45417
Freyn Dr 45458
Friar Ln 45431
Friden Ct 45417
Frieda Ln 45429
Friendship Cir 45426
Fritchie Pl 45420
Frizell Ave 45417
Front St 45402
Frontier Ct 45458
Frytown Rd 45417
Fulmer Dr 45403
G St 45433
Gaddis Blvd 45403
Gainsborough Rd 45419
Gaiter Ln 45417
Galaxie Dr 45415
Gale St 45417
Galewood St 45420
Galileo Ave 45426
Gallatin Ct 45458
Gallery Ct 45458
Galt Ct 45414
Galvin Ave 45417
Galway Ct 45440
Gambit Sq 45449
Gamut Dr 45424
Gander Rd E 45424
Gant Dr 45414
Garaills Dr 45424
Garber Rd 45415
Gard Ave 45417
Garden Springs Ct 45429
Gardendale Ave 45417
Gardengate Dr 45424
Gardenia Dr 45449
Gardenside Dr 45414
Gardenview Pl 45429
Gardenwood Pl 45458
Gardner Rd 45429
N & S Garfield St 45403
Gargrave Rd 45449
Garianne Dr 45414
N & S Garland Ave 45403
Garnet Dr 45458
Garret St 45410
Garrison Ave 45429
Garrison Ct 45459
Garst St 45402
Garvin Rd 45405
Garwood Dr 45432
Gary Dr 45424
Gascho Dr 45410
Gate Manor Ct 45424
Gatekeeper Way 45458
Gates St 45402
Gatesland Ct 45459
Gateview Ct 45424
Gateway Cir 45440
Gateway Dr 45404
Gatewood Pl 45416
Gawain Cir 45449
Gay Dr 45420
Gaylord Ave 45419
Gaywood Pl 45414
Geary Pl 45424
Gebhart Rd 45458
Gebhart St 45410
Geis Rd 45416
Gem Ct 45459
Gem Stone Dr 45458
Genesee Ave 45406
Genesis Way 45417
Geneva Rd 45417
Gentle Wind Pt 45458
Gentry Ln 45424
Gentry Woods Dr 45459
George St 45410
George Wythe Commons 45459
Georgeland Trl 45459
Georgia Dr 45404
Georgian Dr 45429
Gerber Ct 45458
Gerhard St 45404
Gerlaugh Ave 45403
Germantown Pike
3700-6199 45417
6200-6500 45439
6201-6499 45417
Germantown St
800-999 45402
1000-3699 45417
Germantown Liberty Rd 45417
Germany Ln 45431
Gershwin Dr 45458
Gerstner Way 45402
N Gettysburg Ave
1-1999 45417
2000-3199 45406
S Gettysburg Ave
2-98 45417
100-2800 45417
2801-2999 45439
2802-2998 45417
Geyer St 45405
Geyser Ct 45424
Ghent Ave 45420
Ghirardelli Cir 45459
Gibbons Rd 45449
Gibson Ct 45410
Gilbert Ave 45403
Giles Ave 45404
Gilmore Ave 45417
Gilsey Ave 45417
Ginger Pl 45426
Gingko Cir 45431
Gipsy Dr 45414
Girard Ct 45405
Gladecress Cir 45431
Glaser Dr 45429
Glasgow Pl 45459
Glastonbury Ln 45459
Gleason Ave 45417
Gleason Dr 45424
Glen Arbor Ct 45459
Glen Helen Rd 45406
Glen Ivy Dr 45424
Glen Jean Ct 45459
Glen Martin Dr 45431
Glen Meadow Dr 45417
Glen Oaks Ct 45424
Glen Rock Rd 45420
Glen Vista Ct 45459
Glenada Ct 45449
Glenarm Ave 45420
Glenbeck Ave 45409
Glenbrier Pl 45459
Glenbrook Dr 45406
Glenburn Ct & Dr 45459
Glencoe Ave 45410
Glencroft Pl 45459
Glencross Dr 45406
Glendale Ave
1200-1399 45402
1400-1499 45406
Glendean Ave 45431
Glendon Ln 45440
Gleneagle Dr 45431
Glenfield Ct 45458
Glengarry Dr 45420
Glengate Ct 45424
Glenhaven Rd 45415
Glenheath Dr 45440
Glenhurst Dr 45414
Glenmere Ct 45440
Glenmina Dr 45440
Glenmore Ave 45409
Glenn Abbey Dr 45420
Glennelle Dr 45417
Glenova Ave 45414
Glenridge Blvd 45458
Glenridge Rd 45429
Glensdel Dr 45417
Glenside Ct 45426
Glenside Dr 45439
Glenstead Dr 45429
Glenstone Ct 45426
Glenview Rd 45426
Glenway Rd 45404
Glenwood Ave 45405
Glenwood Ct 45405
Glenwood Way 45440
Glenwyck Ct 45458
Glissade Dr 45424
Glo Ct 45424
Gloucester Ct 45440
Glouster Ave 45431
Glover Ave 45417
Gloxinia Ct 45449
Goal Post Dr 45458
Gold St 45402
Gold Finch Ct 45458
Gold Key Blvd 45415
Golden Meadows Ct 45404
Golden Oak Ct 45424
Golden Pheasant Ct 45424
Goldengate Dr 45459
Goldenrod Ct 45416
Golf St 45432
Golf Green Dr 45459
Golfview Ave 45406
Golfwood Dr 45449
Gondert Ave 45403
Good Samaritan Way 45424
Goodfield Pt 45458
Goodlow Ave 45417
Goodyear Dr 45406
Gordon Ave 45402
Gotham Ave 45406
Gothic Pl 45459
Governors Trl 45409
Governors Place Blvd 45409
Governors Square Dr 45458
Grace Ave 45420
Graceland Dr 45449
Graceland St 45459
Gracemore Ave 45420
Gracewood Dr 45458
Grady Ct 45409
Graf St 45402
Grafix Blvd 45417
Grafton Ave
1-799 45406
801-899 45406
900-1199 45405
Graham Pl 45417
Gramont Ave
1-499 45417
500-799 45402
Grand Ave 45426
E Grand Ave 45405
W Grand Ave
200-599 45405
600-699 45406
701-799 45406
800-2099 45402
Grand Oak Blvd 45426
Grand Oak Trl 45440
Grand Vista Dr 45458
Grandview Ave 45417
N Grandview St 45390
Granger Cir 45433
Granite Dr 45415
Grant Ave 45406
Grant St 45404
Grantland Dr 45429
Grants Trl 45459
Grants Hill Cir 45459
Grants Ridge Cir 45459
Grants View Ct 45459
Grants Walk Ln 45459
Grantwood Dr 45449
Granville Pl 45431
Grassland Way 45459
Grassy Creek Way 45458
Gray St 45410
Gray Goose Ct 45449
Gray Oak Dr 45426
Grayson St 45429
Graystone Dr 45417
Graywood Ct 45458
Greacian Ave 45426
Great Hill Dr 45414
Great Lakes Cir 45458
E & W Great Miami Blvd 45405
Great Oaks Dr 45403
Great View Cir 45459
Greeley Ave 45424
Green St 45402
Green Acres Dr 45414
Green Ash Ct 45459
Green Branch Dr 45459
Green Feather Ct 45449
Green Hollow Ct 45458
Green Knolls Dr 45424
Green Lee Ct 45424
Green Park Dr 45459
Green Springs Dr 45440
Green Timber Trl 45458
Green Tree Dr 45429
Green Turtle Dr 45414
Greenbank Ct 45415
Greenbay Dr 45415
Greenbelt Ave 45429
Greenbrier Dr 45406
Greenbrook Dr 45426
Greenbush Ct 45429
Greencastle St 45417
Greencrest Dr 45432
Greencroft Dr 45426
Greendale Dr 45429
Greenfield Way 45424
Greenhill Rd 45405
Greenhouse Dr 45419
Greenlawn Ave 45403
Greenleaf Dr 45417
Greenmanor Ct 45415
Greenmount Blvd 45419
Greenoak Ct 45440
Greenport Dr 45449
Greenridge Dr 45429
Greensboro Dr 45459
Greenside Ct 45458
Greenskeeper Way 45458
Greenspire Ct 45459
Greentree Pl 45424
E & W Greenview Dr 45415
Greenville Nashville Rd 45390
Greenwald St 45410
Greenway St 45417
Greenwich Village Ave 45406
Greenwood Ave 45410
Gregory St 45417
Grenfeld Pl 45420
Grenoble Dr 45459
Greta Ln 45458
Greydale Dr 45424
Greyfield Ct 45459
Greystone Cir 45414
Greystone Dr 45458
Grice Ln 45429
Gridley Dr 45432
Griffon Pl 45459
Grimes St 45402
Grist Mill Ct 45409
Gross Dr 45431
Grosse Point Pl 45415
Grosvenor Ave 45417
Groton Ct 45431
Grouse Ct
4100-4299 45430
5200-5399 45424
Grove Ave 45404
Grovebelle Dr 45424
Grovecreek Ct 45458
Grovehill Dr 45424
Groveland Ave 45417
Groveview Ave 45415
Gruner Ave 45405
Guadalupe Ave 45417
Guard Hill Pl 45459
Guenther Rd 45417
Guernsey Dell Ave 45404
Guilford Dr 45414
Gulfwood Ct 45458
Gullane Cir 45429
Gummer Ave 45403
Gump Pl 45426
Gunckel Ave 45410
Gurney Ct 45458
Guthrie Rd 45417
Gwinnett Cmns & Ln 45459
H St 45433
Haberer Ave 45417
Hackamore Trl 45459
Hackberry Pl 45458
Hacker Rd 45415
Hacker Farm Ln 45458
Hackett Dr 45417
Hackney Dr 45420
Hackview Ct 45424
Haddon Pl 45424
Hadley Ave 45419
Haer Dr 45414
Haerlin Ln 45417
Hagen Ave 45417
Hagerman Dr 45417
Haig Ave 45419
Halbert Ct 45459
Haldeman Ave 45404
Hale Ave 45419
Haley Dr 45458
Halford Ct 45440
Halidon Ct 45449
Hall Ave 45404
Halleck Ct 45433
Haller Ave 45417
Hallmark Ln 45440
N & S Halloway St 45417
Hallwood Ave 45417
Hallworth Pl 45426
Haloran Ln 45414
Halsey Dr 45431
Halstead Cir 45458
Halworth Rd 45405
Hamilton Ave 45403
Hamlet Dr 45440
Hamlin Dr 45414
Hammond Ave 45417
Hampshire Rd 45419
Hampstead Ct 45458
Hampton Rd
25-199 45459
2501-2525 45419
2527-2599 45419
Hancock Ave 45406
Handel Ct 45424
Haney Rd
3000-3399 45405
3500-4099 45416
Hanley Dr 45414
Hanna Ave 45417
Hannaford St 45439
Hannibal Ct 45417
Hanover Ave 45417
Haplin Dr 45439
N & S Harbine Ave 45403
Harbinger Ln 45449
Harbison St 45439
Harbor Ln 45459
Harbour Town Way 45458
Harding Ave 45414
Hardwicke Pl 45414
Hardwood Trl 45424
Harewood Ct 45459
Harker St 45404
Harlamert Dr 45449
Harlan Pl 45431
Harlou Dr 45432
Harold Dr 45406
Harper Ave 45410
Harpers Ferry Ct 45459
Harr Ct 45431
Harries St 45402
Harriet St 45417
Harrington Ave 45415
Harrison Ct 45459
Harron Ave 45417
Harrow Ct 45414
Harshman Rd 45424
Harshman St 45403
Harshmanville Rd 45424
Hart Rd 45390
Hart St 45404
Hartcrest Ln 45459
Hartford St 45417
Hartley Ct 45424
Hartwick Ln 45424
Harvard Blvd 45406
Harvest Ave 45429
Harvest Meadows Dr 45424
Harvey Ave 45419
Harwich Ct 45440
Harwood St 45429
Hasenstab St 45404
E & W Haskett Ln 45424
Haskins Ave 45420
Hassan Cir 45432
Hassler St 45420
Hastings Ct 45458
Hastings Dr 45440
N & S Hatfield St 45417
Hathaway Rd
2800-3019 45419
3020-3126 45429
3128-3198 45429
Hauk Dr 45405
N Haven Way 45414
Haven Hill Dr 45459
Haverfield Rd 45432
Haverhill Dr 45406
Haverstraw Ave 45414
Haviland Ave 45410
Havitshire Way 45458
Hawk Watch Way 45424
Hawker St 45410
Hawks Nest Ct 45458
Hawley Ct 45458
Hawn Cir 45419
Hawthorn St 45402
Haxton Dr 45440
S Hayden Ave 45431
Haynes St 45410
Hays St 45405
Hayward Ave 45414
Hazel Ave 45420
Hazelbrook Dr 45414
Hazelhurst Ct 45440
Hazelpark Pl 45406
Hazelridge Cir 45424
Hazelton Ave 45431
Hazelwood Ave 45419
Hazelwood Cir 45449
Hearthside Ct 45424
Hearthstone Dr 45410
Heartland Trce 45458
Heartsoul Dr 45417
Heathcliff Rd 45415
Heather Dr 45405
Heather Ln 45458
Heather Way 45424
Heather Hollow Dr 45415
Heatherdale Dr 45429
Heatherstone Dr 45417
Heatherton Dr 45426
Heatherwood Ct 45459
Heathshire Dr 45459
Heaton Ave 45410
Hebble Creek Rd 45433
Heck Ave 45417
Hedge Row Ct 45458
Hedge Run Ct 45415
N & S Hedges St 45403
Hedgestone Dr 45414
Hedgewood Dr 45406
Hedington Sq 45459

Heid Ave 45404
Heidi Ct 45459
Heikes Ave 45405
Heincke Rd 45449
Heiss Ave 45403
E Helena St
1-94 45405
96-98 45405
100-599 45404
W Helena St 45405
Helwig Dr 45424
Hemingway Rd 45424
Hemlock St 45433
Hemphill Rd 45440
Hemple Rd
6700-7499 45439
7500-8499 45417
Hempstead Mews 45459
Hempstead Station Dr 45429
Henderson Pl 45420
Hendon Ave 45431
Henrich Dr 45429
Henry St
1-99 45402
100-299 45403
Henshire Ct 45459
Hepburn Ave 45406
Herbert St 45404
Heritage Rd 45459
Heritage Lake Dr 45458
Heritage Park Blvd 45424
Heritage Point Dr 45409
Herman Ave 45404
Hermiston Ave 45404
Hermitage Ct 45459
Hermosa Dr 45416
Herraire Dr 45439
Herron Cir 45414
Herron Pl 45424
Hershey St 45405
Hertland Dr 45439
Hess St 45402
Hewitt Ave 45440
Hialeah Park 45424
Hiawatha Dr 45414
Hibberd Dr 45458
Hibiscus Ct 45459
Hickam Dr 45431
Hickory Dr 45426
Hickory St
100-699 45410
2251-2265 45433
Hickory Bark Dr 45458
Hickory Hill Dr 45417
Hickory Woods Trl 45432
Hickorydale Dr 45406
Hickorygate Ln 45424
Hickoryview Ct 45458
Hidden Cir 45458
Hidden Hills Dr 45459
Hidden Knolls Ct 45449
Hidden Landing Trl 45449
Hidden Meadows Dr 45459
Hidden Oaks Dr 45459
Hidden Ridge Ln 45459
Hidden Valley Ct 45429
Hidden Woods Ln 45406
Hide A Way Ln 45458
High St 45403
High Knoll Dr 45414
Highbury Rd 45424
Highcrest Ct 45405
Highfield Dr 45415
Highgate Dr 45429
Highgrove Pl 45429
Highland Ave 45410
Highland Grn 45429
Highland Ter 45429
Highland Hills Ave 45410
Highland Meadows Dr 45459
Highmeadow Ln 45415
Highridge Ave 45420
Highview Ave 45420
Highview Hills Rd 45417
Hilary Ave 45417
Hilgeford Dr 45424
S Hill Ct 45459
Hill St 45409
Hillary 45426
E Hillcrest Ave 45405
W Hillcrest Ave
1-299 45405
300-5199 45406
Hillerman Ln 45429
Hillgard St 45426
Hillgrove Ave 45415
Hillgrove Fort Recover Rd 45390
Hillgrove Southern Rd 45390
Hillgrove Woodington Rd 45390
Hillhaven Dr 45449
Hilliard Ave 45415
Hillmont Ave 45414
Hillpoint Ln 45414
Hillpoint St 45426
Hillrose Ave 45404
E Hills Ln 45432
Hillsdale Ave 45414
Hillside Ave 45429
Hillstone Pl 45424
Hilltop Dr 45415
Hillview Ave 45419
Hillview Ct 45426
Hillway Dr 45405
Hillwood Dr 45439
Hilton Dr 45409
Himes Ln 45429
Hinckley Ct 45424
Hingham Ln 45459
Historic Ct 45414
Hithergreen Dr 45429
Hitz Rd 45390
Hivling St 45403
Hobart Ave 45429
Hobson Way 45433
Hoch St 45410
Hochwalt Ave 45417
Hodapp Ave 45410
Hoffman Dr 45415
Hogue Ave 45414
Holbrook Dr 45424
Holes Creek Trce 45458
Holland Ave 45417
Hollencamp Ave 45417
Hollendale Dr 45429
Holler Rd 45417
Hollier Ave 45403
Hollins Way 45459
Hollister Ave 45417
Hollow Run 45459
Hollowbrook Dr 45458
Hollowview Trl 45459
Holly Ave 45410
Holly Bend Cir 45429
Holly Brook Ct 45458
Hollyhill Ct 45449
Hollywreath Ct 45424
Holmes Ave 45406
Holt St 45402
Holyoke Ave 45406
Home Ave
1100-1700 45402
1702-1798 45402
1800-3499 45417
3501-3599 45417
E Home Ave 45449
Home Ln 45402
Home Path Ct 45459
Homecrest Ave 45404
Homedale St 45449
Homeland Ct 45420
Homesite Dr 45414
Homestead Ave 45417
Homestretch Rd 45414
Homeview Dr 45415
Homewood Ave
200-298 45405
301-599 45405
601-697 45406
699-799 45406
Honey Hill Ln 45405
Honey Jay Ct 45458
Honeybee Dr 45417
Honeybrook Ave 45415
Honeycutt Cir 45414
Honeygate Dr 45424
Honeyleaf Way 45424
Honeysuckle Dr 45429
Honeywell Ct 45424
Honeywood Ct 45424
Hook Estate Dr 45405
Hoover Ave
2200-4199 45402
4200-6999 45417
Hopeland St 45417
Hopewell Ave 45417
Hopton Loop 45414
Horace St 45402
Horlacher Ave 45420
Horning Pl 45403
Hornwood Dr 45405
Horrell Rd 45426
Horseshoe Bnd 45458
Horseshoe Dr 45432
Horstman Dr 45429
N & S Horton St 45403
Howell Ave
1600-1799 45402
1800-2199 45417
Howie St 45417
Howland Pl 45424
Hoyle Pl 45439
Hubbard Ct & Dr 45424
Huber Rd 45424
Huberville Ave 45431
E Hudson Ave 45405
W Hudson Ave
1-299 45405
300-599 45406
Huffman Ave 45403
Hugh Dr 45459
Hughes Pl 45417
Hulbert St 45410
Hullway Ct 45417
Hulman Dr 45406
Humming Bird Ln 45458
Hummock Rd 45426
Humphrey Ave 45410
Hunter Ave 45404
Hunterglen Ct 45459
Hunters Crk 45459
Hunters Bluff Ct 45458
Hunters Brook Ct 45424
Hunters Halt Ct 45424
Hunters Ridge Rd 45431
Huntington Pl 45420
Huntsford Pl 45426
Huntsman Ct 45424
Huntsman Ln 45459
Huntsview Ct 45424
Huron Ave
100-599 45417
700-999 45402
Hurst Dr 45414
Hutchins Ct 45414
Hyacinth Ct 45449
Hyannis Port Dr 45458
Hyde Ave 45406
Hyde Park Dr 45429
Hydraulic Rd 45449
Hyfield Dr 45429
N & W Hyland Ave 45424
Hypathia Ave 45404
Hythe Cir 45459
Iams Ct 45426
Ibis Ct 45431
Ice Ave 45402
Ida Ave 45405
Idaho Falls Dr 45431
Iddings Ct 45405
Idle Hour Cir 45415
Idlewood Rd 45432
Idlywilde Blvd 45414
Ila Ct 45432
Ila Sue Ct 45390
Illinois Ave 45410
Image Dr 45414
Imo Dr 45405
Imogene Rd 45405
Imperial Blvd 45419
Imperial Rd 45449
Imperial Hills Dr 45414
Imperial Woods Rd 45459
Independence Dr 45429
Indian Ln 45416
Indian Trl 45449
Indian Bluff Cir 45424
Indian Club Cir 45449
Indian Creek Blvd 45449
Indian Head Rd 45459
Indian Hill Dr 45429
Indian Mound Dr 45424
Indian Runn Dr 45415
Indian Springs Ct 45458
Indian Summer Ct 45459
Indiana Ave 45410
Indianola Ave 45405
Indigo Trl 45459
Indigo Creek Cir 45458
Industrial Estates Dr 45409
Infirmary Rd
1-2999 45417
3000-3098 45439
3001-3599 45417
3100-3598 45417
3600-3999 45439
Ingersol Dr 45429
Ingleside Ave 45404
Ingomar Ave 45417
Ingram St 45417
Inner Mission Way 45459
Innovation Ct 45414
Innsbruck Dr 45459
Innsdale Pl 45424
Inpark Cir & Dr 45414
Intercity Dr 45424
Interlude Ln 45449
Interpoint Blvd 45424
Invention Dr 45426
Inwood Ave 45415
Iola Ave 45417
N & S Iona Ave 45417
Iowa Ct 45431
Ipsen Ct 45439
Irelan St 45440
Irmal Dr 45432
Irongate Park Dr 45459
Ironside Dr 45459
Ironwood Cir 45449
Ironwood Ct 45440
Ironwood Dr 45449
Iroquois Ave 45405
Iroquois Dr 45449
Irving Ave
201-797 45409
799-899 45409
901-925 45409
927-1299 45419
Irvington Ave 45415
N & S Irwin St 45403
Isaac Dr 45431
Isaac Prugh Way 45429
Isabela Cir 45458
Island Lake Ct 45458
Iver Ct 45459
Iverson Ct 45424
Ives Ct 45414
Ives Ln 45429
Ivy Ave 45417
Ivy Glen Cir 45424
Ivy Hill Cir 45449
Ivy Ridge Rd 45431
Ivycrest Ter 45429
Ivyton Ct 45440
Ivywood St 45420
Jackie Cir 45415
Jackson St
100-299 45402
301-499 45410
Jacquelyn Ct 45415
Jade Ct 45459
Jadik Way 45449
Jaime Rose Way 45459
Jameantr Dr 45430
James St 45410
James Bradford Dr 45459
N James H Mcgee Blvd
1-1799 45402
1800-4999 45417
S James H Mcgee Blvd 45402
James Hill Rd 45429
James Madison Trl 45440
Jamestown Cir 45458
Jameswood Cir 45429
Jana Cir 45415
Janice Pl 45415
Janine Ct 45424
Janney Rd 45404
Jansin Pl 45424
Jason Ave 45416
Jason Ln 45459
Jasper St 45409
Jassamine Dr 45449
Jay St 45410
Jaybee Ct 45429
Jean Dr 45415
Jeanette Ave 45458
Jeanette Dr 45432
Jeannie Ct 45415
N & S Jefferson St 45402
Jen Lee Dr 45414
Jenera Ln 45424
Jenkins Dr 45417
Jennagate Ln 45424
Jenny Ln 45459
Jennysim Pl 45415
Jergens Rd 45404
Jerome Ave 45417
N & S Jersey St 45403
Jessie St 45410
Jett Ave 45417
Jewelstone Dr 45414
Jimike Dr 45414
Joe St 45402
Joel Ct 45439
N Johanna Dr 45459
S Johanna Dr 45458
Johannsen Ave 45424
John St 45403
S John St 45390
John Adams Ln 45459
John Elwood Dr 45459
John Glenn Rd
1300-1699 45410
1700-2499 45420
John Hancock Ln 45459
Johnny Ct 45424
Johnsfield Ct 45459
Johnson Dr 45433
Johnson St 45410
E Johnson St 45390
Johnson Trl 45439
Jonathan Dr 45440
Jones St
1-99 45402
100-399 45410
Jonetta St 45424
Jonquil St 45417
Jordan Ave 45410
Joselin Rd 45432
Joseph Pl 45459
Joshire Pl 45458
Joshua Trl 45417
Josie St 45403
Joy Elizabeth Dr 45458
Joyce Dr 45439
Joyce Ann Dr 45415
Judith Dr 45429
Judy Ln 45405
Julia Ave 45405
Julian Pl 45458
N & S June St 45403
Juniper Dr 45432
Jupiter St 45404
K St
1-299 45409
2330-2711 45433
Kajean Ave 45439
Kalida Ave 45424
Kammer Ave 45417
Kane Ct 45431
Kantner Dr 45429
Kantwell Ln 45459
Kapp Dr 45424
Karen Dr 45429
Karlsridge Dr 45459
Karwin Dr 45406
Kastner Ave 45410
Kate Ave 45406
Katherine Ct 45424
Kathleen Ave 45405
Kathylee Ct 45416
Katy Dr 45459
Kauffman Ave 45433
Kautz Dr 45424
Kay Ct 45424
Kearney Ave 45402
Kearns Ave 45414
Keats Dr 45414
Keelboat Ct 45402
Keeler St 45424
Keenan Ave 45414
Keene Cir 45440
Keeneland Ct 45424
Keeneland Dr 45414
Keifer St 45404
Keith Dr 45449
Kelford Pl 45426
Kellenburger Rd 45424
Kelly Ave 45404
Kelsey Ct 45458
N & S Kelseys Ct & Way 45440
Kelton Pl 45424
Kemler Dr 45439
Kemper Ave 45420
Kenberry Pl 45414
Kencedge St 45402
Kencenco Dr 45459
Kendall Ave 45414
Kendon St 45414
Kenesaw Ave 45417
Kenilwood Ave 45424
Kenilworth Ave 45405
Kenmar St 45440
Kenmore Ave 45420
Kennebec Ave 45424
Kennedy Ave 45420
Kenneth Ave 45414
Kennywood Ln 45449
Kenosha Rd 45429
Kenrick Rd 45458
Kensington Dr
1401-1417 45440
1419-1499 45440
1601-1697 45406
1699-2299 45406
Kent Pl 45404
Kentfield Dr 45426
Kenton St 45402
Kentshire Dr
700-1399 45459
5600-5999 45440
Kentwood Rd 45417
Kenview Ave 45420
Kenwick Dr 45429
Kenwood Ave
200-399 45405
400-699 45406
Kenworthy Pl 45458
Kenyon Pl 45406
N Keowee St
2-98 45402
100-199 45402
301-697 45404
699-1699 45404
S Keowee St
100-200 45402
202-298 45402
600-700 45410
702-798 45410
Kepler Rd 45414
Kerry Ct 45449
Kershner Rd 45414
Kerwood Dr 45420
Kester Ave 45403
Keswick Cir 45426
Keswick Ln 45439
Ketcham St 45431
Kettering Square Dr N & S 45440
Keturah Dr 45417
Ketway Cir 45420
Ketwell Cir 45420
Ketwood Pl 45420
Kevin Dr 45432
Kevton Ct 45415
Key Cir 45424
Key West Dr 45424
Keystone Ave 45403
Keystone Club Dr 45439
Keystover Trl 45459
Kiefaber St 45409
Kildare Ave 45414
Kildare Pl 45426
Kilkenny Ct 45440
Killian Ct 45440
N & S Kilmer St 45417
Kim Ln 45420
Kimball Ct 45432
Kimbary Dr 45458
Kimberly Cir 45417
Kimberly Dr 45429
Kimbolton Ave 45431
Kimmel Ln 45417
Kimway Dr 45459
Kindred Sq 45449
King Ave 45420
King Arthur Dr 45429
King James Ct 45424
King Oak Ln 45415
King Richard Pkwy 45449
King Tree Dr 45405
Kingman Dr 45414
Kingrey Dr 45402
Kings Hwy 45406
N & S Kings Arms Cir 45440
Kings Cross Ct 45449
Kings Grant Psge 45459
Kings Mill Ct 45406
Kings Row Ave 45429
Kings Run Rd 45459
Kingsbury Dr 45424
Kingsford Dr 45426
Kingsley Ave 45406
Kingsley Park Dr 45429
Kingsridge Dr
7900-7999 45459
8000-8999 45458
Kingston Ave 45420
Kingswood Dr 45429
Kingview Ave 45420
Kinmont Rd 45414
Kinnard Ave 45402
Kipling Dr 45406
Kipp Ct 45416
Kirby Ln 45417
Kirk Lynne St 45403
Kirkham St 45417
Kirkstone Dr 45459
Kirkview Dr 45424
Kiser St 45404
Kiska Ave 45417
Kismet Pl 45424
E Kitridge Rd 45424
Kitts Hill Ct 45459
Kitty Ct 45424
Kittyhawk Dr 45403
Kittyhawk Commons Blvd 45424
Klee Ave 45403
Klepinger Rd
2401-3097 45406
3099-3199 45406
3201-3399 45406
3500-4299 45416
Kling Dr 45419
Kloss Pl 45424
Klyemore Dr 45424
Knecht Dr 45405

Knob Creek Dr 45417
Knobhill Dr 45424
Knollcrest Ct 45429
Knollcroft Rd 45426
Knollridge Dr 45449
Knollview Dr 45405
Knowlton Ct 45459
Knox Ave 45417
Koehler Ave 45414
Kolmar Ave 45432
Kolping Ave 45410
Korner Dr 45424
Kosmo Dr 45402
Koster Ln 45458
Kramer Rd 45419
Kratochwill St 45410
Krebs Ave 45419
Kresswood Cir 45429
Kristina Ct 45458
Kropf Dr 45424
Krug St 45417
Kruss Ave 45429
Kuder Pl 45424
Kuendinger Ave 45417
Kuglics Blvd 45433
Kumler Ave
700-1299 45402
1300-1599 45406
Kuntz Rd 45404
Kurtz Ave 45405
Kyle Ave 45429
Kylemore Ct 45459
L St
1-399 45409
2511-2609 45433
La Belle St 45403
La Crosse Ave 45414
La France Pl 45440
La Perre Dr 45431
La Plata Dr 45420
La Salle Dr 45417
Lac Lamen Dr 45458
Lacoda Ct 45424
Laconia Ave 45417
Ladera Trl 45459
Lago Mar 45458
Laguna Rd 45426
Lahm Cir 45433
Laird Ave 45420
Lairwood Dr 45458
Lake Center Dr 45426
Lake Forest Dr 45449
Lake Glen Ct 45459
Lake Pointe Way 45459
Lake Shore Pl 45420
Lake Tree Ct 45459
Lakebend Dr 45404
Lakeport Dr 45426
Lakeridge Ct 45417
Lakeside Dr 45417
Lakeview Ave 45417
Lakeview Dr 45459
Lakewood Dr 45420
Lamar St 45404
Lambert Ave 45414
Lambeth Dr 45424
Lammers Ave 45459
Lamont Dr 45429
Lamp Lighter Trl 45429
Lanbury Dr 45439
Lancashire Dr 45417
Lancaster Pl 45404
Lancelot Dr 45449
Lancer Ct 45424
Land Dr 45440
Landau Dr 45429
Lander Ln 45459
Landis Ct 45426
Landola Dr 45424
Landsend Ct 45414
Landview Ave 45449
Lane Garden Ct 45404
Lanewood Dr 45406
Langdon Dr 45459
Langford 45414
Langtree Ln 45458
Lansdale Ct 45414
N & S Lansdowne Ave 45417
Lansing Dr 45420
Lansmore Dr 45415
Lantern Way 45458
Lantern Glow Trl 45431
Lantern Hill Dr 45459
Lantz Rd 45432
Lanyard Ave 45426
Laramie Dr 45432
Larch Tree Ct 45424
Larchmont Dr 45417
Larchview Dr 45424
Larchwood Dr 45432
Larcomb Dr 45424
Lareta St 45426
Lariat Ct 45458
Larissa Ct 45414
Larkspur Dr 45406
Larkswood Dr 45417
Larona Rd 45426
Larriwood Ave 45429
Larue Dr 45429
Latchwood Ave 45405
Late Autumn Ct 45459
Latham St 45417
Lathrop St 45410
Latonia Ave 45439
Laura Ave 45405
Laurel Dr 45417
Laurel Ln
5900-6099 45424
7800-7999 45414
Laurel Fork Dr 45415
Laurel Hill Ct 45415
Laurel Oak Ct & Dr 45459
Laurel Ridge Dr 45414
Laurelann Dr 45429
Laureldale Rd 45429
Laurelhurst Ln 45459
Laurelview Dr 45424
Laurelwood Rd
700-999 45419
1000-3599 45409
Lausanne Dr 45458
Lavern Ave 45429
Lavon Ct 45415
Lawn St 45405
Lawncrest Ave 45417
Lawnview Ave 45409
Lawnwood Ave 45429
Lawrence Rd 45390
Lawrence St 45402
Lawver Ln 45431
Layton Dr 45406
Le Juene Dr 45405
Leacourt Dr 45410
Leafback Pl 45424
Leafburrow Dr 45424
Leafy Hollow Ct 45458
Leah Dr 45417
Lear St 45433
Leatherback Ct 45414
Leatherwood Pl 45424
Leawood Dr 45424
Ledgewood Pl 45449
Lee Dr 45417
Lee Ann Dr 45417
Leedale Dr 45417
Leeds Cir 45459
Leenerne Dr 45440
Leeper St 45424
Lefevre Cir & Dr 45429
Legend Way 45449
Legendary Way 45458
Lehar Pl 45424
Leibold Dr 45424
Leicester Dr 45459
Leila Ct 45449
Leising Rd 45432
Leisure Dr 45458
Leland Ave
300-699 45417
700-1099 45402
Lemans Blvd 45458
Lemans Ln 45424
Lemoyne Dr 45424
Lempco Ln 45415
Lenita Ave 45417
Lenox Dr 45429
Lensdale Ave 45417
Leo St 45404
Leonhard St 45404
Leonora Dr 45420
Leroy St 45402
Lesher Dr 45429
Leston Ave 45424
Lewisham Ave 45429
Lewiston Rd 45429
Lexington Ave 45402
Lexington Pl N 45424
Lexington Pl S 45424
Lexington Green Pl 45459
Lexow St 45419
Leycross Dr 45424
Leyden Ln 45424
Liberty Ln 45449
Liberty St
200-299 45402
8900-8999 45390
Liberty Bell Cir 45459
Liberty Ellerton Rd
1600-3799 45417
3800-3999 45439
Liberty Meadows Rd 45417
Liberty Tower 45402
Liberty Woods Ln 45459
Lido Pl 45420
Light St 45404
Lightbeam Dr 45458
Lighthouse Trl 45458
Lightning Ave 45433
Lilac Ave 45417
Lillian Dr 45404
Lily Ln 45414
Lima Pl 45404
Limberlost Trl 45429
Limerick Ln 45440
Limestone Ave 45417
Linchmere Dr 45415
E Lincoln St 45402
Lincoln Green Dr 45449
Lincoln Park Blvd 45429
Lincoln Woods Ct 45429
Lincrest Pl 45424
Linda Vista Ave 45405
Lindale Ave 45414
Lindbergh Blvd 45449
Linden Ave
1-699 45403
800-898 45410
900-3699 45410
3800-5099 45432
Linden Dr 45459
Linden Brook Dr 45458
Lindenhurst Dr 45459
Lindenwood Rd 45417
Lindner Ln 45458
Lindorph Dr 45404
Lindy Ct 45415
Linnbrook Dr 45406
Linsan Ct 45410
Linwald Ln 45459
Linwood St 45405
Lisa Ln 45414
Lisa Lee Ln 45415
Lisbon St 45429
Liscum Dr 45417
Lisle Pl 45402
Litchfield Ave 45406
Littell Ave 45419
Little Ct 45449
Little St 45410
Little Creek Ct 45424
Little Falls Dr 45458
Little John Cir 45459
Little Meadow Dr 45404
Little Richmond Rd
4000-4721 45417
4722-6999 45426
7000-7999 45417
8000-8999 45426
Little Sugar Creek Rd 45440
Little Turtle Ct 45414
Little Woods Ln 45429
Little Woods Rd 45419
Little Yankee Run 45458
Little York Rd 45414
Littlebury Ln 45458
Littrell Rd 45433
Live Oak Dr 45417
Livingston Ave
1-299 45403
400-499 45410
Livingstone Ave 45426
Lloyd Ave 45424
Lobata Pl 45416
Loblolly Dr 45424
Lobster Tail Ct 45458
Lockerbie Ln 45429
Lockheed Ave 45433
Lockland Pl 45404
Lockport Blvd 45459
Lockwood Dr 45424
Lockwood St 45415
Locus Bend Dr 45440
Locust Ct 45417
Locust Dr 45429
Locust St 45405
N Locust St 45449
Locust Camp Rd 45419
Locust Hill Rd 45459
Locustview Dr 45424
Locustwood Dr 45429
Lodell Ave 45414
Lodewood Dr 45458
Lodge Ave 45414
Lodgeview Dr 45424
Lodi Pl 45439
Loffer Ct 45449
Lofino Ct 45424
Lofty Oaks Ln 45415
Logan Ave 45431
Loganwood Dr 45458
Loggerhead Ct 45414
Logic Cir 45458
Logic Ct 45440
Logistics Ave 45433
Lois Cir 45459
Loma Linda Ln 45459
Lombard St 45403
Lombardy Ct 45449
Lome Ave 45417
Lone Pine Ln 45417
Lone Tree Dr 45424
Longbourne St 45417
Longbow Ln 45449
Longcreek Dr 45458
Longfellow Ave 45424
Longford Rd 45424
Longines Rd 45414
Longmore Ct 45424
Longridge Dr 45429
Longstreet Ln 45433
Longvale Dr 45417
Longworth St 45402
Lonoke Ave 45403
Lookout Ave 45417
Lookout Trl 45449
Loop Rd
1-6999 45459
1788-1790 45433
1822-1824 45433
2528-2690 45433
Lorain Ave 45410
Lorella Ave 45404
Lorenz Ave 45417
Loretta Dr 45415
Lori Ln 45449
Lori Sue Ave 45406
Lorien Woods Dr 45459
Lorimer St 45417
Loris Dr 45449
Lorna Ct 45420
Los Arrow Dr 45439
Lott Pl 45420
Lotus Dr 45417
Lotusdale Dr 45429
Lotz Rd 45429
Louella Ave 45417
Louelm Ave 45459
Lounsbury Dr 45417
Lourdes Ct 45410
Loveland Ct 45439
Lovell Ct 45424
Lovetta Ave 45429
Lowell Ct 45420
E Lower St 45390
Lower Valley Pike 45424
E & W Lowery Ave 45449
Lowes St 45409
Loxley Dr 45439
Loxwood Ln 45458
Loyala Chase Ln 45424
Lucas Dr 45458
Lucerne Ave 45410
Lucian Ave 45416
Lucille Dr 45404
N & S Ludlow St 45402
Ludwell Pl 45449
Lunceford Dr 45424
Luntshire Ct 45459
Luther Ave 45431
N Lutheran Church Rd
1-1999 45417
2000-3299 45426
Luton Ct 45424
Lutz Ave 45420
Lyleburn Rd 45417
Lyncreek Dr 45458
Lyndhurst Dr 45434
Lynell Dr 45429
Lynhurst Ave 45420
Lynn Ave 45406
Lynn Rae Cir 45458
Lynnaway Dr 45415
Lynnfield Dr 45429
Lynnhaven Dr 45431
Lynpark Ave 45439
Lynwood Ct 45390
Lyon St 45424
Lyons Dr 45459
Lyons Rd
600-999 45459
1000-1899 45458
Lyons Ridge Dr 45458
Lytle Ln 45409
E Lytle 5 Points Rd 45458
Lytton Pl 45432
Mabel Ave 45403
Macduff Dr 45426
Macgregor Dr 45426
Macintosh Cir 45426
Mack Ave 45404
Mackenzie Ct 45458
Mackoil Ave 45403
Macmillan Dr 45426
Macon Ave 45424
Macready Ave 45404
Macy St 45415
Mad River Rd
4501-4597 45429
4599-5399 45429
5400-7899 45459
Madden Pl 45420
Madden Hills Dr 45417
Madeira Ave 45404
Madison Ave 45426
Madison St 45402
Madison Square Pl 45414
Madisonwoods Dr 45417
Madora Ave 45426
Madrid Ave 45414
Maeder Ave 45417
Maefel Ln 45415
Magellan Ave 45426
Magnolia Ct 45417
Mahler Dr 45424
Mahogany Trl 45458
Maiden Pl 45417
Maidstone Ct 45458
Main St 45439
E Main St
100-899 45390
500-1199 45426
N Main St
2-20 45402
22-39 45402
40-98 45423
41-299 45402
100-348 45402
350-4899 45405
4900-9399 45415
S Main St
1-1 45402
3-900 45402
902-998 45402
1000-1700 45409
1702-1898 45409
W Main St 45449
Maitland Ave 45417
Majestic Dr 45417
Malabar Ct 45459
Malcom Dr 45420
Malden Ave 45417
Malibu Ct 45426
Malina Ave 45414
Mall Park Dr 45459
Mall Ring Rd 45459
Mall Woods Dr 45449
Mallard Dr 45424
Mallard Glen Dr 45458
Mallet Dr 45458
Mallet Club Dr 45439
Malone Ave 45429
Maltbie Rd 45458
Malton Ct 45424
Malvern Ave 45406
Manchester Rd 45449
Mandalay Dr 45416
Mandel Dr 45458
Mandrake Dr 45424
Manette Pl 45410
Mangas Rd 45390
Mangold Dr 45424
Mangrove Way 45431
Manhattan Ave 45406
Manor Ln 45429
Manor Pl 45406
Manorside Dr 45459
Mansfield Pl 45404
Mansion House Ct 45449
Mantell Ct 45440
Mantz Ave 45417
Manx Ct 45424
Maple Ave 45459
Maple St 45426
N Maple St 45390
Maple Green Ct 45414
Maple Hill Cir 45449
Maple Hill Dr 45449
Maple Hill Ter 45430
Maple Leaf Ct 45440
Maple Run Dr 45458
Maple Springs Dr 45458
Maplebrook St 45458
Maplecliff Ct 45415
Maplecreek Dr 45426
Maplecrest Dr 45409
Mapledale Dr 45432
Maplegate Ct 45424
Maplegrove Ave 45414
Maplehurst Ave 45402
Maplelawn Dr 45405
Mapleleaf Dr 45416
Mapleridge Pl 45429
Mapleside Dr 45426
Maplestone Ln 45458
Mapleton Dr 45459
Mapletrace Trl 45458
Mapleview Ave 45420
E & W Maplewood Ave 45405
Mar Ken Dr 45405
Maral Trl 45458
Marathon Ave
1-299 45405
300-499 45406
Marauder St 45433
Marblehead Dr 45431
Marbrook Dr 45429
Marburn Ave 45417
Marbury Ct 45424
Marcella Ave 45405
Marchester Dr 45429
Marchmont Dr 45406
Marco Ln 45458
Marcus Cir 45440
Marcy Rd 45449
Mardel Dr 45449
Mardell Dr 45459
Mardi Gras Dr 45424
Margaret St 45410
Margate Dr 45430
Mariam Ln 45458
Marianne Dr 45404
Maricarr Dr 45429
Marie Ave 45405
Marietta Pl 45404
Marigold Ct 45440
Marigold Dr 45449
Marilake Cir 45429
Marilyn Ave 45420
Marimont Dr 45410
Marina Dr 45449
Mariner Dr 45424
Maringo Dr 45424
Marino 45424
Mario Dr 45426
N & S Marion St 45417
Marjorie Ave 45404
Mark Ave 45424
Mark Dale Dr 45459
Mark Twain Ct 45414
Marker Ave 45414
S Market St 45390
Market Place Dr 45458
Markey Rd 45415
Markwell Pl 45416
Marlay Rd 45405
Marlboro Pl 45420
Marlette Dr 45424
Marlin Ave 45416
Marlowe St 45416
Marose Dr 45424
Marot Dr 45417
Mars Hill Dr 45449
Marscott Dr 45440
Marsh Creek Dr 45426
Marsha Ln 45417
Marsha Jeanne Way 45458
Marshall Rd
3200-5999 45429
6000-6499 45459
N Marshall Rd 45429
Marshfield St 45404
Marson Dr 45405
Marstead Cir 45429
Martel Dr 45420
Martha Ave
1-299 45458
500-599 45417
Martin Ave 45414
Martingale Ln 45459
Martins Dr 45449
Martz Ave 45403
Marvine Ave 45417
Marwyck Dr 45459
Mary Ave 45405
Mary Ellen Dr 45419
Mary Haynes Dr 45458
Marybrook Dr 45429
Marycrest Ln 45429
Maryknoll Dr 45429
Maryland Ave 45404
Marylew Ln 45415
Marylhurst Dr 45459
Mason St 45417
Matador St 45404
N & S Mathison St 45417
Matt Way 45424
Mattis Dr 45439
Mauford Dr 45424
Maughn Dr 45431

Maumee Ave 45414
Maverick Dr 45431
Mavie Dr 45414
Maxlin Rd 45429
Maxton Rd 45414
Maxwells Xing 45458
Maxwelton Ln 45459
Mayapple Ave 45432
Mayberry Pl 45415
Mayfair Rd 45405
Mayfield Ave 45429
Mayflower Ave 45420
Maylan Dr 45405
Maynard Ave 45415
Mayo Ave 45409
Mayrose Dr 45449
Mayview Dr 45416
Mayville Dr 45432
Maywood Ave 45417
Mcarthur Ave 45417
Mccabe Ave 45417
Mccall St
1501-1597 45402
1599-1999 45402
2000-3899 45417
Mccleary Ave 45406
Mcclellan Dr 45433
Mcclure Rd 45390
Mcclure St
1-156 45403
200-299 45410
Mccook Ave 45404
Mccormick Ave 45433
Mcdaniel Rdg 45424
Mcdaniel St 45405
Mcdonough St 45402
Mcdowell Pl 45433
Mcewen Rd
6500-7999 45459
8000-8999 45458
Mcewen Woods Ct 45458
Mcfadden Ave 45403
Mcfarlane Ct 45417
Mcfeely Petry Rd 45390
N & S Mcgee St 45403
Mcgrevey Ave 45431
Mcguerin St 45431
Mcintosh Ct 45449
Mckinley St 45403
Mckinney Ln 45458
Mclain St 45403
Mclin Dr 45417
Mcnary Ave 45417
Mcnay Ct 45426
Mcowen St 45405
W Mcpherson St 45405
Mcrae Ct 45417
Mcreynolds St 45403
Mcsmith Ln 45414
Mead St 45402
Meadow Dr 45416
Meadow Ln 45419
Meadow Green Ct 45414
Meadow Haven Pt 45458
Meadow Hawk Ct 45458
Meadow Park Dr 45440
Meadow Pond Ct 45458
Meadow Woods Ln 45458
Meadowbrook Ave 45415
Meadowcreek Dr 45458
Meadowcrest Ln 45440
Meadowcroft Rd 45429
Meadowdale Dr 45416
Meadowfields Ct 45458
Meadowgate Ct 45458
Meadows Mnr 45458
Meadowside Ln 45458
Meadowsweet Dr 45424
Meadowview Dr 45459
Meadowvista Dr 45424
Meandering Cv 45459
Medford St 45410
Medina Ct 45405
Meditation Ln 45449
Meehan Dr 45431
Meeker Rd 45414

Meeker Commons Ln 45414
Meeker Creek Dr 45414
Meeker Woods 45414
Meeting House Rd 45459
Meigs St 45402
Mel St 45404
Melba St 45402
Melberth Rd 45404
Melbourne Ave 45417
E & W Melford Ave 45405
Melgrove Ave 45416
Melinda Ct 45414
Mello Ave 45410
Melody Rd 45415
Melron Ct 45432
Melrose Ave 45409
Melvin Ave 45417
S Melvin Eley Ave 45390
Melwood Ave 45417
Memorial Rd 45433
Memory Ln 45414
Mendocino Ct 45424
Mendota Ct 45420
Mengel Dr 45429
Menlo Way 45424
Mentor Ave 45404
Mercedes Rd 45424
Mercer Ave 45402
Mercury Dr 45404
Meredith St 45402
Meridian St 45403
Meriline Ave
1401-1497 45410
1499-1700 45410
1702-1798 45410
1900-2199 45420
Merily Way 45424
Merrick Dr 45415
Merrill Rd 45414
Merrimac Ave 45405
Merrydale Ave 45431
Merryfield Ave 45416
Mershon Ave 45420
Mertland Ave
1-455 45431
471-800 45403
802-998 45403
Merwin Pl 45431
Mesmer Ave 45410
Metlic Dr 45424
Metro Gdns 45402
S Metro Pkwy 45459
Metzger Dr 45433
Meyer Ave 45431
Mia Ave 45417
N Miami Ave 45449
Miami Chapel Rd 45417
Miami Valley Dr 45459
Miamisburg Centerville Rd
300-800 45459
802-3098 45459
1127-1129 45449
1201-3099 45459
3500-3800 45449
3802-3898 45449
Michael Ave 45417
Michael Ln 45449
Michigan Ave 45416
Middle St 45402
Middle Park Dr 45414
Middlebury Rd 45432
Middlefield Ct 45414
Middlehurst Ln 45406
Middleport Dr 45459
Middy Dr 45433
Midforest Ct 45424
Midvale St 45420
Midway Ave 45417
Midwood Ave 45417
Mike Ct 45424
Milburn Ave 45404
Mildred Dr 45415
Milesburn Dr 45439
Milford Dr 45429
Military Blvd 45417

Mill Run Ct 45459
Mill Trace Ln 45458
Millard Rd 45426
Millbank Dr 45459
Millbridge Ct 45440
Millbrook Dr 45459
Millbrook Pl 45429
Millcreek Rd 45440
Miller Ave 45417
Miller Ln 45414
Miller Rd 45433
Millers Farm Ln 45458
Millerton Dr 45459
Millgate Ln 45458
Millhoff Dr 45424
Millicent Ave 45417
Millpark Dr 45458
Millridge Rd 45424
Millshire Dr
5800-5999 45440
6000-6199 45459
Millspring Pl 45424
Millstone Rd 45458
Millvale Rd 45405
Millwheel Dr 45458
Millwood Rd 45440
Milo Rd 45414
Milton St 45403
Mimi Dr 45414
Mimosa Dr 45459
Mineola Ct 45426
Mini Ct 45420
Minnesota Ave 45404
Minotaur Way 45458
Minstrel Dr 45449
Mintcreek Ct 45458
Mintwood Ave 45415
Mintwood Rd 45458
Minty Dr 45415
Miracle Ln 45406
Miriam Dr 45429
Mirimar St 45409
Mission Ct 45431
Missouri Ave 45410
Mistletoe Ct 45458
Misty Ln 45424
Misty Creek Dr 45458
Misty Morning 45429
Misty Oaks Ct 45415
Mistyview Dr 45424
Mitchell Dr
4851-4875 45433
5300-5499 45431
Moberly Pl 45424
Moccasin Way 45424
Modena St 45417
Modern Way 45426
Mohawk Trail Rd 45459
Mohegan Ave 45424
Mohican Ave 45429
Molane St 45416
Moler Ave 45420
Molly Ave 45426
Mona Cir 45440
Monaco Cir 45458
Monarch Rd 45458
Monda Ct 45440
Mondelet Ct 45429
Monitor Dr 45424
N & S Monmouth St 45403
Monohan Way 45433
Monroe Ave 45416
Montague Rd 45424
Montbello Cir 45440
Monte Carlo Way 45424
Monteray Ave 45419
Montevideo Dr 45414
Montezuma Pl 45440
Montgomery Square Dr 45440
Monticello Ave 45404
Montpelier Dr 45440
Montpellier Blvd 45459
Montrose Ave 45414
E & W Monument Ave 45402
Moon Ct 45404

Moorefield Dr 45424
Moorewood Cir 45415
Moorgate Ct 45458
Mooring Ln 45458
Moraine Ave 45406
Moraine Cir 45439
Moraine Ridge Ln 45429
More Ave 45403
Morehouse Ave 45417
Moreland Ave 45420
Morelawn Ct 45429
Morgan Ave 45417
Morgan Grey Ct 45458
Morley Ln 45424
Morning Glory Rd 45449
Morning Mist Cir 45426
Morning Sun Ct 45458
Morningside Blvd 45432
Morningstar Ct 45420
Morrell Dr 45424
Morris Ave 45417
Morrow Dr 45415
Morse Ave 45420
Morton Ave 45410
Mosby Ln 45433
S Moss Ave 45417
Moss Bank Ct 45458
Moss Hill Ct 45424
Mossoak Dr 45429
Mott Way 45424
Moulins Dr 45459
Mound St
1-399 45402
501-599 45417
Moundview Ct 45458
Mount Aetna St 45424
Mount Carmel St 45424
Mount Charles Dr 45424
Mount Clair Ave 45417
Mount Crest Ct 45403
Mount Everest St 45424
Mount Hood 45424
Mount Mansfield Dr 45424
Mount Mckinley Dr 45424
Mount Olive Ct 45426
Mount Ranier 45424
Mount Snow Dr 45424
Mount Vernon Ave 45405
Mount Washington Dr 45424
Mount Whitney St 45424
Mountain Trl 45459
Mountain Ash Ln 45458
Mountview Cir 45414
Mountville Dr 45440
Mourning Dove Ct 45458
Mozart Ave 45424
Mugavin Ct 45424
Muirfield Ct 45459
Muirfield Dr 45431
Mulberry Rd 45414
Mulford Ave 45417
Mullen Ct 45420
E & W Mumma Ave 45405
Mundale Ave 45420
Mundy Ct 45431
Munger Rd 45459
Munger Pointe Dr 45459
Munich Ave 45439
Murchison Ln 45431
Murdock Ave 45424
Muriel Ave 45429
Murphys Xing 45440
Murray Dr 45403
Murray Hill Dr 45403
Murrell Dr 45429
Mustang Rd 45433
Myron Ave 45416
Mystic Dr 45424
Naas Pl 45404
Nacoma Pl 45420
Nagle Ct 45430
Namboo Cir 45431
Nancy Ave 45417
Nantucket Lndg 45458
Nantucket Rd 45426
Napa Rdg 45458

Naples Dr 45424
Napoleon Dr 45429
Nash Ct 45439
Nassau St 45410
Natalie Ct 45416
Natchez Ave 45416
Nathan Pl
600-899 45409
900-1099 45410
Nathaniel St 45417
National Rd 45433
W National Rd 45414
Natoma Pl 45424
Nature Ct 45440
Naughton Dr 45424
Navajo Ave 45424
Navara Dr 45431
Navarre Ave 45424
Neal Ave
1-599 45405
600-999 45406
Nebraska Ave 45424
Necco Ave 45406
Necessity Pl 45449
Needmore Rd
1400-3599 45414
3600-3698 45424
3700-4799 45424
Neff Rd 45414
Negley Pl 45402
Nelapark Dr 45424
Nellie Ave 45410
Nelson Ave 45410
Neosha Ave 45417
Neptune Ln 45424
Nestle Creek Ln 45459
Netherdale Rd 45404
Netherland Dr 45431
Nettle Ct 45431
Neva Dr 45414
Nevada Ave 45416
Neville St 45424
New Carlisle Pike 45424
New England Ave 45429
New Horizon Pl 45420
New London Cir 45459
New York Way 45414
Newark Ave 45433
Newark Pl 45404
Newark St 45433
Newberry Ct 45432
Newborne Dr 45414
Newburg Ct 45458
Newcastle Dr 45420
Newell Cir & Dr 45440
Newgate Ave 45420
Newport Ave 45405
Newton Ave 45406
Neyer Ct 45424
Niagara Ave 45405
Nicholas Rd 45417
Nicholson Ct 45459
Nicole Ct 45420
Nicolet Ln 45429
Nielson Ct 45424
Night Hawk Trl 45458
Nightingale Pl 45420
Nightwind Ct 45424
Nike Ln 45404
Niles Pl 45404
Nill Ave 45420
Nimitz Dr 45431
Nina V Ln 45424
Ninebark Pl 45424
Niobe Pl 45420
Noble Ave 45417
Nobleton Cir 45440
Noel Ct 45410
Nogoso Cir 45431
Nolan Rd 45426
Nomad Ave 45414
Nona Dr 45426
Noranda Dr 45415
Nordale Ave 45420
Nordic Rd 45414
Norfolk Ave 45417

Norita Ct 45414
Norledge Dr 45414
E Norman Ave 45405
W Norman Ave
1-399 45405
400-699 45406
701-799 45406
Norman Blvd 45431
Norman Cross Ln 45459
Normancrest Ct 45459
Normandy Ln 45459
S Normandy Ln 45458
Normandy Creek Dr 45458
Normandy Ridge Rd 45459
Normdave Dr 45417
Normont Ct 45414
Norris Dr 45414
North Ave 45406
E North St 45390
North Trl 45414
Northam Dr 45459
N & S Northampton Ave 45417
Northbrook St 45426
Northcliff Dr 45431
Northcrest Dr 45414
Northcutt Pl 45414
Northdale Rd 45432
Northern Cir 45424
Northerton Ct 45414
Northfield Rd 45415
Northford Rd 45426
Northgarden Ave 45431
Northgate Ct 45416
Northlake Ct 45414
Northland Ct 45415
Northwest Pkwy 45426
Northwood Ave 45405
Norton Ave 45420
Norville Ct 45417
Norway Dr 45439
Norwell Dr 45449
Norwich Ln 45459
Norwood Ave 45402
Notre Dame Ave 45404
E & W Nottingham Rd 45405
Novi Dr 45414
Nowak Ave 45424
Nutmeg Ct 45459
Nutt Rd 45458
Nutwood Dr 45458
Nyack Ln 45439
Oak Ave 45439
S Oak Ct 45458
Oak St
1-199 45426
200-664 45410
666-698 45410
2381-2421 45433
E Oak St 45390
Oak Bend Cir 45440
Oak Branch Dr 45426
Oak Brook Dr 45458
Oak Creek Trl 45424
Oak Glen Ct 45459
Oak Grove Ave 45414
Oak Hill Ln 45459
Oak Knoll Dr 45419
Oak Manor Ct 45429
Oak Park Ave 45419
Oak Ridge Dr 45424
Oak Springs Ct 45424
Oak Tree Dr E & S 45440
Oak Valley Rd 45440
Oakbrooke Dr 45440
Oakcreek Dr 45429
Oakcrest Ave 45409
Oakcroft Cir 45440
Oakdale Ave 45420
Oakdell Ave 45432
Oakes Rd 45426
Oakfield Dr 45415
Oakgate Ct 45424
Oakham Dr 45426
Oakhaven Cir 45440
Oakhurst Pl 45414

Oakland Ave 45409
Oaklawn Ave 45410
Oakleaf Dr 45417
Oakley Ave 45419
Oakley Pl 45405
Oakmont Ave 45429
Oakmoor Ln 45459
Oakport Dr 45458
Oakridge Dr
1000-1199 45402
1200-4999 45417
Oakshire Pl 45440
Oakside Pl 45426
Oakton Cir 45440
Oakview Dr 45429
Oakvista Pl 45440
Oakwood Ct 45417
Oakwood Ln 45424
Obco Ct 45414
Obell Ct 45409
Oberer Dr 45404
Oberlin Ave 45417
Oberon Ct 45402
Obie St 45432
Obispee Ave 45415
Obrian Pl 45459
Observation Trl 45449
Ocala Ct 45459
Odin Ct 45439
Odlin Ave 45405
Office Park Dr 45439
Ogden Ave 45433
Oglethorpe Ct 45458
Ogletree Ct 45424
Oh In State Line Rd N & S 45390
Ohmer Ave 45410
Old Barn Rd 45415
Old Beech Ct 45458
Old Bridge Dr 45458
Old Church Ct 45429
Old Country Ln
1100-1499 45414
7700-7799 45424
Old Creek Ct 45458
Old Dayton Rd 45417
Old Denlinger Rd 45426
Old Dobbin Pl 45459
Old Dublin Ct 45415
Old Harbor Ct 45458
Old Harshman Rd 45431
Old Hickory Pl 45426
Old Lane Ave 45409
Old Orchard Ave 45405
Old Riverside Dr 45405
Old Salem Rd 45415
Old Spanish Trl 45459
Old Spring Ct 45458
Old Spring Valley Ct 45458
Old Stable Ln 45459
Old Stone Ct 45459
Old Tappan Way 45458
Old Troy Pike 45404
Old Vienna Dr 45459
Old Whipp Ct 45440
Old Yankee St 45458
Olde Farm Ln 45458
Olde Georgetown 45458
Olde Greenbrier Ln 45459
Olde Haley Dr 45458
Olde Sterling Way 45459
Olde Woods Ct 45458
Oldegate Ct 45424
Oldfield Pl 45417
Ole Quaker Ct 45458
Olena Ln 45458
Olentangy Dr 45431
Olive Rd
1-999 45417
1000-5599 45426
Olive Tree Dr 45426
Olmsted Pl 45406
Olson Dr 45420
Olt Rd 45417
Olympian Cir 45417
Omad Ct 45449

Ome Ave 45414
Omega Ave 45406
Onaoto Ave 45414
Oneida Ave 45414
Ontario Ave 45414
Onyx Way 45459
Open Way 45459
Opperman Ave 45431
S Orange St 45390
Orangewood Dr 45429
N Orchard Ave 45417
S Orchard Ave
  1-200 45417
  202-298 45417
  300-399 45402
Orchard Dr
  555-697 45419
  699-999 45419
  1800-2599 45426
Orchard Glen Dr 45449
Orchard Hill Dr 45449
Orchard Run Rd 45449
E & W Orchard Springs Dr 45415
Orchardview Ct 45458
Orchid Cir 45459
Oren Dr 45415
Orinoco St 45431
Orleans St 45417
Ormand Rd 45449
Orth Ave 45402
Orville St 45458
Osage Ave 45419
Osceola Dr 45417
Osmond Ave
  601-697 45417
  699-799 45417
  800-899 45402
Osprey Ct 45424
Ostrander Dr 45403
Oswalt Good Rd 45390
Otis Dr 45416
Ottawa St 45402
Ottello Ave 45414
Otterbein Ave 45406
Our Place Ln 45424
Outer Belle Rd 45426
Overbrooke Rd 45440
Overhill Ln 45429
Overland Trl 45429
Overture Dr 45449
Owendale Dr 45439
Owens Dr 45406
Owl Ct 45424
Oxford Ave
  1-1299 45402
  2700-2899 45406
Oxford Rd 45402
Ozark Ave 45432
Pablo Dr 45424
Pacemont Ave 45415
Pacer Ave 45424
Pacific Ct 45424
Packard Dr 45424
Paddington Rd 45459
Paddock Rd 45414
Pafford Rd 45405
Pagent Ln 45424
Pagoda Ct 45431
Paige Ave 45417
Painewood Pl 45458
Painted Turtle Dr 45414
Paisley St 45402
Palace Dr 45449
Palace Green Pkwy 45459
Paletz Ct 45424
Palisades Dr 45414
Palm Dr 45449
S Palmer Rd 45424
Palmer St 45405
Palmerston Ave 45417
Palmetto Ct 45459
Palmwood Dr 45426
Palomar Ave 45426
Palos Verdes Ct 45426
Pamela Ave 45415

Pamela Sue Dr 45429
Pamona Pl 45459
Panama Pl 45440
Pandora Dr 45431
Panorama Cir 45415
Paragon Rd
  6800-7590 45459
  7525-7525 45475
  7525-7525 45441
  7591-7999 45459
  7592-7998 45459
  8000-10499 45458
Paragon Commons Cir 45459
Paragon Mills Ln 45458
Paramount Ave 45424
Pardee Pl 45431
Parity Ln 45449
Park Dr 45410
S Park Ln 45458
Park Pl
  1-99 45426
  1100-1199 45449
Park Ter 45440
Park Center Dr 45414
Park Creek Dr 45459
Park Crest Ln 45414
Park Edge Dr 45458
Park End Dr 45415
Park Glen Dr 45417
Park Haven Pt 45458
Park Manor Dr 45410
Park Ridge Dr 45459
Park Villa Ct 45459
Parkbrook Dr 45458
Parkchester Rd 45459
Parkdale St 45429
Parkeast Ct 45458
Parker Ave 45402
Parkfield Pl 45416
Parkhill Dr 45406
Parkland Ave 45405
Parklawn Dr 45440
Parknoll Rd 45429
Parkside Dr 45458
Parkvale Dr 45439
Parkview Ave 45403
Parkview Ct 45458
Parkway Dr 45416
E & W Parkwood Dr 45405
Parliament Pl 45429
Parma Pl 45404
Parnell Ave 45403
Parran Dr 45420
Parrish Ct 45424
Parrot St 45410
Parsons Ave 45417
Partridge Run Cir 45429
Pascal Dr 45431
Passaic Ct 45424
Passport Ln 45414
Pathview Dr 45424
Pathway Ct 45420
Patricia Dr
  2100-2199 45429
  2200-2299 45420
Patrick Blvd 45431
Patrick St 45426
Patrick Henry Ln 45459
Patriot Sq 45459
Patriot Woods Ct 45458
N Patterson Blvd 45402
S Patterson Blvd
  1-1299 45402
  1300-2000 45409
  2002-2699 45409
  2900-2999 45419
Patterson Pkwy 45433
Patterson Rd
  401-421 45419
  423-999 45419
  1000-2720 45420
Patterson Village Dr 45419
Patton Ave 45417
Patty Lou Ave 45459
N Paul Laurence Dunbar St 45402

S Paul Laurence Dunbar St
  1-632 45402
  634-698 45402
  718-798 45417
  800-1299 45417
Pauley Woods Cir 45429
Pauline Ave 45420
Pawnee Pass 45458
Pawpaw St 45404
Pawtucket St 45417
Payne Ave
  4201-4697 45414
  4699-5199 45414
  5150-5150 45413
  5150-5150 45490
  5201-5699 45414
  5442-5698 45414
Payne Pl 45439
Payne Farm Ln 45458
Peach Blossom Dr 45458
Peach Grove Ave 45458
Peach Hill Dr 45458
Peach Leaf Dr 45458
Peach Orchard Dr 45449
Peach Orchard Pl 45449
Peach Orchard Rd 45419
Peach Tree Ave 45406
Peachcreek Rd 45458
Peachview Pl 45424
Peachwood Dr 45458
Pear St 45433
Pearhill Dr 45449
Pearson Rd 45433
E Pease Ave 45449
W Pease Ave 45449
Pease St 45402
Pebble Ct 45459
Pebblestone Dr 45458
Peck Ln 45459
Peerless Ln 45424
Pegram Way 45424
Pegwood Ct 45424
Pelbrook Farm Dr 45459
N & S Pelham Dr 45429
Pell Dr 45410
Pelway Dr 45459
Pelwood Dr 45459
Pemberton Ave 45417
Penbrooke Trl 45459
Pence Pl 45432
Penconda Dr 45458
Penhurst Pl 45424
Penn Ave 45432
Pennfield Rd 45458
Pennlyn Ave 45429
Pennswood Dr 45424
Pennsylvania Ave 45404
Pennway Pl 45406
Pennyston Ave 45424
Pennywell Dr 45424
Penridge Dr 45459
Penrod Ave 45417
Pentland Cir 45424
Pentley Pl 45429
Penwick Ct 45431
Peony Pl 45420
Pepper Dr 45424
Pepper Hill Dr 45429
Pepper Tree Ct 45424
E Peppermint St 45390
Pepperton Ct 45415
Peppervine Cir 45431
Pepperwood Dr 45424
Perrine St 45410
N & S Perry St 45402
Pershing Blvd
  1400-1699 45410
  1700-2199 45420
Persian Ct 45424
Peters Park & Pike 45414
Phantom Dr 45431
Pheasant Ct 45424
Pheasant St 45431
Pheasant Finch Dr 45424
Pheasant Hill Rd 45424

Pheasant Ridge Rd 45424
Pheasant Run Dr 45458
Pheasant Valley Rd 45424
Pheasant Wood Trl 45458
Phelps Cir 45433
Philadelphia Dr
  1000-1199 45402
  1200-2400 45406
  2402-2446 45406
  2448-2798 45405
  2800-4899 45405
  4900-6499 45415
N Philadelphia St 45403
S Philadelphia St 45403
Phillips Ave 45410
Phoenix Pl 45420
Phyllis Ave 45431
Piccadilly Ave 45406
Picket Pl 45433
Pickett Rd 45390
Pickford Dr 45432
Pico Dr 45439
Piedmont Ave 45416
Pierce St 45410
Pierpont Dr 45426
Pilgrim Rd 45414
Pimlico Dr 45459
Pimlico Pl 45424
Pin Oak Ct 45424
Pine St 45402
Pine Cone Dr 45449
Pine Frost Dr 45459
Pine Glen Ln 45424
Pine Green Dr 45414
Pine Meadow Ter 45431
Pine Needles Dr 45458
Pine Point Pl 45424
Pine Ridge Rd 45405
Pine Tree Ln 45449
Pine Valley Ct 45414
Pinebrook Ct 45458
Pinecastle Ct 45424
Pinecreek Dr 45458
Pinecrest Dr 45414
Pinecroft Ct 45424
Pinegate Way 45424
Pinegrove Dr 45449
Pinehill Ct 45431
Pinehill Dr 45424
Pinehurst Ave 45405
Pineland Trl 45415
Pineview Ct 45417
Pineview Dr 45424
Pinewood Cir 45426
Pinewood Pl 45459
Pinnacle Rd
  3300-3598 45417
  3401-3499 45439
  3501-3599 45417
  3600-3799 45439
  3800-4199 45417
  4200-4399 45439
  4400-4599 45417
  4600-5099 45439
  5100-5499 45417
Pinnacle Park Dr 45439
Pintail Ct 45424
Pinto Pt 45424
Pioneer St 45405
Piper Ln 45440
Piqua Pl 45402
Pitcairn Rd 45424
Pittsburg Ave 45406
Pittsfield St 45420
Placid Dr 45458
Plainfield Rd 45432
Plamor Cir 45459
Plantation Ln 45419
Planters Ave 45431
Plareenw Ave 45402
Platt Cir 45402
N & S Plaza Ave 45417
Pleadong Ave 45403
Pleasant Ave 45403
Pleasant Hill Ct & Dr 45459

N & S Pleasant Valley Ave 45404
Pleasant View Ave 45420
Plocher Ln 45403
Plum St 45433
Plumtree Path 45415
Plumwood Rd 45409
Plymouth Ave 45406
Pobst Dr 45420
Pocahontas St 45424
Pocatello Ave 45404
Pocono Dr 45424
Poe Ave 45414
Poinciana Dr 45459
Point Ave 45415
Pointview Ave 45405
Polen Cir & Dr 45440
Polk Blvd 45414
Pollard Way 45424
Pollock Rd 45403
Polo Ct 45458
Polo Park Dr 45439
Pomeranian Dr 45424
Pomeroy Ave 45417
Pompano Cir 45404
Pompton Ct 45405
Ponca Ct 45420
Pond St 45402
Pond Meadows Ct 45458
Pond Ridge Dr 45459
Ponderosa Ln 45415
Pondoray Pl 45440
Pondview Dr 45440
Pondway Rd 45419
Ponstone Pl 45424
Pontiac Ave 45417
Poplar Ct 45424
Poplar St
  1-199 45415
  2379-2380 45433
N Poplar St 45449
Poppa Dr 45424
Port Cir 45459
Porter Ave 45402
Porterfield Dr 45417
Portrait Dr 45415
Portsmouth Way 45459
Possum Run Ct & Rd 45440
Post Town Rd 45426
Potomac St 45403
Powell Ct & Rd 45424
Powers Ln 45440
Powhattan Pl 45420
Prague Ct 45458
Prairie Ct 45424
Prairie Creek Ct 45424
Preakness Pl 45459
Prelude Path 45449
Prentice Dr 45420
Prescott Ave 45406
Preserve Pl 45458
President Ct 45414
Presidential Way 45429
Preston Ave 45417
Price Hill Pl 45459
Primrose Dr 45449
Primrose Ln 45429
Prince Albert Blvd 45404
Prince Edward Way 45424
Princeton Dr 45406
Princewood Ave 45429
Priscilla Ave 45415
Pritz Ave
  200-399 45403
  400-1399 45410
Procuniar Dr 45424
Production Ct 45414
Profit Way 45414
Progress Ct 45424
Progress Rd 45449
Prospect Ave 45415
Prosperity Dr 45426
Prosser Ave 45409
Providence Rd 45426
Provincetown Rd 45459
Provincial Way 45458

Pruden Ave 45403
Prugh Ave 45417
Prystup Pl 45439
Pueblo Ave 45424
Pugliese Pl 45415
Pulaski St 45402
Purdue Dr 45420
Puritan Pl 45420
Pursell Ave 45420
Putterview Way 45458
Pyramid Ave 45414
Q St 45433
Quail Ln 45434
Quail Bend Cir 45429
Quail Bush Dr 45424
Quail Hill Ct 45424
Quail Hollow Rd 45459
Quail Run Dr 45458
Quailwood Trl 45458
Quaker Way 45458
Quaker Trace Ct 45414
Quality Ln 45449
Qualstan Ct 45429
Queen Anne Ct 45424
Queens Ave 45406
Queens Xing 45458
Queensbury Rd 45424
Queensview Ct 45429
N & S Quentin Ave 45403
Quiet Brook Trl 45458
Quiet Meadows St 45459
Quinby Ln 45432
Quincy Way 45417
N Quinella Way 45459
Quintessa Ct 45449
Quisenberry Dr 45424
Quitman St 45410
Quorn Ct 45458
R St 45433
Raab Ct 45416
Rachel Ct 45440
Radcliff Rd 45406
Radio Rd
  1300-1722 45403
  1724-1798 45403
  1800-1999 45431
Radvansky Ln 45424
E Rahn Rd
  1-1199 45429
  2000-3099 45440
W Rahn Rd
  1-1199 45429
  1200-1799 45459
Rahn De Vue Pl 45459
Rahndale Pl 45429
Rahway Ct 45415
E Railroad St 45390
Rainbow Dr 45420
Rainbrook Way 45424
Rainier Dr 45432
Raintree Rd 45459
Rainview Ct 45424
Rainwood Ct 45424
Rall Ave 45417
Ralliston Ave 45417
Ramah Ct 45458
Rambeau Dr 45449
Rambler Dr 45459
Ramblewood Dr 45424
Ramblingwood Ln 45458
Ramsdell Ct 45405
Ramsey Pl 45415
Ranch Hill Dr 45415
Randall Ave 45420
Randolph St 45417
Randy Dr
  300-399 45449
  2300-2399 45440
Randy Scott Dr 45449
Rangeley Ave 45403
Rangeview Dr 45415
Rausch Ave 45432
Ravelle Ct 45420
Raven Cv 45459
Ravenna Rd 45414
Ravenwood Ave 45406

Ravine View Ct 45459
Rawlings Dr 45432
Rawnsdale Rd 45440
Rawson Pl 45432
Ray St 45404
Raymond Ct 45424
Raymont Dr 45429
Reading Rd 45420
Rean Meadow Dr 45440
Reardon Dr 45420
Rebecca St 45402
Rector Ave 45414
Red Ash Ct 45458
Red Bud Cir 45449
Red Bud Trl 45409
Red Coach Rd 45429
Red Haw Rd 45405
Red Lion Ct 45440
Red Maple Dr 45433
Red Oak Ct
  1101-1111 45439
  5800-5999 45424
Red Oak Rd 45432
Red Pine Way 45458
Red River St 45417
Red Rock Ct 45440
Red Rock Ln 45417
Redbank Ln 45424
Redbarn Trl 45458
Redbay Dr 45424
Redbird Ct 45431
Redbluff Dr 45449
Redbud Ln 45433
Redbush Ave 45420
Redder Ave 45405
Redfern Ave
  1000-1099 45406
  1200-1299 45405
Redington Ct 45449
Redlands St 45402
Redleaf Ct 45432
Redmaple Ct 45424
Redmond Pl 45417
Redonda Ln 45416
Redway Cir 45426
Redwood Ave 45405
Redwood St 45433
Reeder Dr 45458
Reedsdale Rd 45432
Reese Ct 45458
Reeves Ct 45415
Regal Ave 45449
Regal Ct 45440
Regency Ridge Dr 45459
Regent St 45409
Regent Park Dr 45429
Regina Dr 45458
Reich St 45426
Reichert Rd 45439
Reigate Rd 45459
Reims Dr 45459
Reinwood Dr 45414
Reisinger Ave 45417
Reist Ave 45417
Relka Ave 45403
Rembrandt Blvd 45420
Remington Dr 45415
Remington Hill Rd 45458
Remmick Ln 45424
Rena Pl 45424
Renard Dr 45424
Rendale Pl 45426
Renee Dr 45440
Renfield Dr 45424
Renoir Pl 45431
Renolda Woods Ct 45429
Renshaw Ave 45439
Renslar Ave 45432
Renwood Dr 45429
Republic Dr 45414
Resaca Ave 45417
Research Blvd 45420
Residenz Pkwy 45429
Resik Dr 45424
Resinda Dr 45459
Resthaven Rd 45424

Reston Ct 45458
Retford Dr 45417
Revels Ave 45417
Revere Ave 45420
Revere Village Ct 45458
Reverie Ln 45449
Revlon Dr 45420
Rexford Ct 45414
Rexwood Dr 45439
Reynolds Way 45430
Rhapsody Dr 45449
Rhine Way 45458
Rhineview Ct 45459
Rhoads Center Dr 45458
Rice Pl 45424
Richard St 45403
Richard Oswald Ln 45426
Richfield Dr 45420
Richie Dr 45449
Richland Ave 45432
Richlawn Cir 45440
Richley Dr 45417
Richmond Ave
1-500 45406
502-598 45406
700-999 45405
1001-1299 45405
Richview Ct 45429
Richwood Dr 45439
Rider Ave 45417
Ridge Ave
1-199 45405
2601-2697 45414
2699-3999 45414
Ridge Creek Ct 45426
Ridge Gate Rd 45429
Ridge Line Ct 45458
Ridgebury Dr 45440
Ridgecrest Ave 45416
Ridgecrest Dr 45449
Ridgedale Rd 45406
Ridgefield Way 45459
Ridgeleigh Rd 45429
Ridgemore Ave 45429
Ridgepath Dr 45424
Ridgeview Ave 45409
Ridgeville Ct 45440
E Ridgeway Dr 45459
W Ridgeway Dr 45459
Ridgeway Ln 45417
Ridgeway Rd
3000-3799 45419
3800-4199 45429
Ridings Blvd 45458
Riegel St 45417
Riley St 45424
Ring Neck Dr 45424
Ringgold St 45403
Ringwalt Dr 45432
Rio Ln 45429
Rio Grande Ave 45426
Rio Vista Ct 45424
Rip Rap Rd
5500-5599 45414
5600-6700 45424
6702-7198 45424
Ripplecreek Ct 45458
Rising Spring Ct 45459
Risley Dr 45449
Rita St 45404
Ritchie Rd 45433
Ritchie St 45404
Rittenhouse Dr 45424
Riva Ridge Ave 45414
River Pl 45405
W River Rd 45417
River Corridor Dr 45402
River Downs Dr 45459
River Park Dr 45409
River Ridge Rd 45415
Riverbend Dr
1-99 45405
6300-6699 45415
Riverbrook Ct 45426
Rivercliff Ln 45449
Riverdale St 45405
Rivers Edge Blvd 45414
Riverside Dr 45405
Riverton Dr 45414
E Riverview Ave 45405
W Riverview Ave
1-497 45405
499-599 45405
601-799 45406
800-2999 45402
3000-3098 45406
3100-5100 45406
5102-5598 45406
Riverview Rd 45433
Riverview Ter 45402
Riviera Ct 45406
Road I 45433
Road Z 45433
Roamont Dr 45459
Roanne Ct 45458
Roanoke Ave 45419
Robb Ct 45417
Robbins Run Ct 45458
Robert Ct 45458
Robert St 45449
Robert Dickey Pkwy 45409
Robert Ulrich Ave 45415
Roberta Ln 45424
Robertann Dr 45420
Robeson Pl 45417
Robin Rd 45409
Robindale St 45424
Robinhill Ct 45416
Robinhood Dr 45449
Robinview Ct 45424
Robinwood Ave 45431
Robleigh Dr 45459
Rochelle Ave 45429
Rockcliff Cir 45406
Rockcreek Dr 45458
Rockdell Ct 45424
Rockford Ave 45405
Rockhill Ave 45429
Rockhurst Ave 45420
Rockingham Dr 45429
Rockland Dr 45406
Rockleigh Rd 45458
Rockport Ave 45417
Rockside Dr 45458
Rockview Ct 45424
Rockwell Ct 45420
Rockwell Dr 45414
Rockwood Ave 45405
Roejack Dr 45417
Roesch St 45417
Roger Ct 45406
Rogge St 45409
Rohrer Blvd 45404
Roland Cir 45406
Rolfe Ave 45414
Rolling St 45439
Rolling Glen Dr 45424
Rolling Meadows Dr 45459
Rolling Oak Dr 45459
Rolling Timber Trl 45429
Rolling Woods Trl 45429
Romaine Dr 45415
Roman Dr 45415
Rondeau Ridge Dr 45429
Rondowa Ave 45404
Rooks Rd 45458
Rooks Mill Ln 45458
Roop Pl 45420
Roosevelt Ave 45417
Rosa Linda Dr 45459
Rosalie Rd 45424
Rosamond Dr 45417
Rosary Cir 45404
Roscommon Way 45440
Rose Ln 45449
Rose Ter 45415
Rose Arbor Dr 45458
Rose Bower Ave 45429
Rose Glen Dr 45459
Rose Ridge Ct 45459
Rosebud Way 45415
Rosebury Dr 45424
Rosecliff Pl
6600-6699 45449
6701-6797 45459
6799-7099 45459
Rosecrest Dr 45414
Rosedale Dr
600-1299 45402
1300-1398 45406
1400-1475 45406
1477-1499 45406
Rosegarden Ct 45424
Rosehaven Cir 45429
Roselake Dr
300-699 45458
7400-7699 45414
Roseland Ave 45402
Rosemary Ave 45405
Rosemont Blvd
1400-1699 45410
1700-2499 45420
Roseview Dr 45432
Rosewood Dr 45415
Rosezita Ln 45459
Roslyn Ave 45429
Rosof Blvd 45406
Ross Ave 45414
Rossini Rd
2300-2499 45459
2500-2599 45449
Rossiter Dr 45417
Rossmore Ct 45459
Rothfield Dr 45424
Rott Ave 45403
Rousseau Dr 45424
Rover Ct 45439
Rowell Cir 45424
Rowena Dr 45415
Roxbury Rd 45417
Roxford Dr 45432
Roy Ave 45419
Royal Gtwy 45431
Royal St 45417
Royal Archer Dr 45449
Royal Birkdale Dr 45458
Royal Oak Dr 45429
Royal Palm Ct 45424
Royal Ridge Dr 45449
Royal Ridge Way 45429
Royalston Ave 45419
Royalwood Dr 45429
Ruanda Ct 45414
Rubicon Rd & St 45409
Rubyvale Ct 45417
Rucks Rd 45417
Rue Ct 45458
Rue Marseille 45429
Rue Royale 45429
Rugby Rd
1900-2899 45406
2900-2999 45405
Rulla Ct 45439
Rumford Way 45431
Rundell Dr 45415
Running Brook Trl 45449
Runnymede Rd 45419
Runyon Ave 45416
Rural Ln 45414
Rusby Ave 45449
Rush St 45417
Rushland Dr 45419
Rushton Dr 45431
Ruskin Rd 45406
Russell Ave 45420
Russell Dr 45431
Russet Ave
1600-1899 45410
1900-2300 45420
2302-2398 45420
Russett Ave 45404
Rustic Rd
1900-1999 45406
2000-2299 45405
2300-2399 45406
Rustic Creek Dr 45458
Rustic Oak Dr 45415
Rustic Park Trl 45458
Rustic View Dr 45431
Rustic Woods Dr 45424
Rustling Oak 45459
Rustling Oak Ct 45431
Rutgers Rd 45431
Ruth Ave 45417
Ruth Ann Dr 45426
Rutland Dr 45406
Rutledge Ave 45404
Ryburn Ave 45405
Rydale Rd 45405
Rye Dr 45424
Ryegrass Way 45431
Ryland Ct 45459
Rymark Ct 45415
Sabra Ave 45424
Sachs St 45403
Sacramento Ave 45409
Sacramento St 45433
Saddle Creek Trl 45458
Saddle Park Ct 45458
Saddle Ridge Cir 45424
Saddle River Dr 45458
Saddlewood Ave 45459
Safari Dr 45424
Safeway Dr 45414
Saffron Dr 45424
Saffron Ln 45431
Sagamon Ave 45429
Sagamore Ave 45404
Sage Ave 45417
Sage Meadow Ct 45458
Sahara Ct 45404
Sail Boat Run 45458
Saint Adelbert Ave 45404
Saint Agnes Ave 45402
Saint Anne Dr 45458
Saint Charles Ave 45410
N & S Saint Clair St 45402
Saint Dunston Ct 45449
Saint Etienne Ln 45459
Saint Francis Ct & Dr 45458
Saint James Ave 45406
Saint Johns Ave 45406
Saint Joseph Ave 45410
Saint Jude Ave 45403
Saint Laurent Cir 45459
Saint Leonards Way 45458
Saint Louis Ave 45405
Saint Michel Cir 45429
Saint Nicholas Ave 45410
Saint Paul Ave 45410
Saint Simons Ln 45458
Salem Ave
100-3999 45406
4000-4999 45416
5000-5899 45426
Salem Rdg 45458
Salem Bend Dr 45426
Salem Woods Dr 45426
Salidor Ct 45431
E & W Salinas Cir 45440
Salisbury Dr 45406
Salon Cir 45424
Salt Box Ct 45459
Samuel St 45403
San Antonio Ave 45433
San Fernando Rd 45424
San Jose St 45403
San Juan Ct 45424
San Marino St 45440
San Rae Dr 45419
Sancroft Dr 45424
Sand Lake Rd 45414
Sand Stone Ct 45440
Sand Trap Ln 45459
Sand Wedge Ct 45458
Sandalview Dr 45424
Sandalwood Dr 45405
Sandbury Dr 45424
Sander Ct 45403
Sanderson Dr 45459
Sandhurst Dr 45405
Sandpiper Ct & Ln 45424
Sandy Dr 45426
Sandyhill Dr 45459
Sandywood Dr 45440
Sanford Dr 45432
Sanibel Dr 45459
Saninced Dr 45429
Santa Anita Pl 45424
Santa Clara Ave 45405
Santa Cruz Ave 45410
Santa Fe Dr 45414
Santa Rosa Dr 45440
Sapphire Dr 45458
Sapphire Pt 45431
Sarah Freeman Dr 45458
Sarahs Way 45440
Saranac Cir & Dr 45429
Saratoga Pl 45424
Sassafras Ln 45431
Sassafras Pl 45405
Satellite Ave 45415
Saturn St 45404
Saundra Ct 45430
Savannah Ave 45417
Savina Ave 45415
Savoy Ave 45449
Sawmill Rd 45409
Sawtry Ln 45458
Sayebrooke Rd 45459
Saylor St 45416
Sayre Ave 45417
Scarborough Dr 45414
Scarborough Village Dr 45458
Scarlet Ridge Dr 45458
Scarsdale Dr 45440
Scatler Root Pl 45424
Scenic Dr 45414
Scenic Hls 45459
Scenic River Dr 45415
Scenicview Ct 45459
Schaeffer St 45404
W Schantz Ave 45409
Schatz Pointe Dr 45459
Schenley Ave 45439
Schervier Ct 45458
Schlatter Dr 45433
Schloss Ln 45439
School Dr 45414
Schoolgate Dr 45424
Schroeder Rd 45417
Schrubb Dr 45429
Schumaker Ct 45459
Schuster Rd 45433
Schuyler Dr 45429
Schwienfort Ave 45433
Schwinn Dr 45404
Scioto Ct 45420
Scofield Pl 45417
Scorthen Rd 45414
Scotsman Dr 45414
Scott St 45402
Scottsdale Dr 45420
Scottswood Rd 45417
Scranton St 45404
Sea Pines Ln 45458
Sea Turtle Dr 45414
Seaboard Dr 45414
Seabreeze Ct 45458
Seabrook Rd 45432
Seadelaw Dr 45434
Seagate Pl 45424
Seaman Dr 45424
Sears St 45402
Seashalm Ave 45410
Seashea Ave 45416
Seashenw Ave 45420
Sebring Dr 45424
Secrateriat Rd 45414
Sedgewick Dr 45424
Seeley Dr 45417
Seema Ct & Dr 45440
Segal Ct 45459
Seiber Ave 45405
Sekford Cir 45424
Selby Pl 45420
Selkirk Rd 45432
Selma Rd 45429
Selwood Cir 45424
Seminary Ave 45403
Seminary View Dr 45458
Semler St 45404
Semley Ct 45415
Semmes Ln 45424
Semmes Pl 45433
Senate Dr 45459
Senator Ln 45459
Seneca Dr 45402
Senna Ct 45431
Sennett Ave 45414
Sentinel Oak Dr 45458
Sentry Hill Ct 45440
Sequoia Ct 45419
Sequoia Dr 45431
Serene Pl 45424
Serpentine Dr 45424
Serrell Ln 45424
Serro Pl 45404
Sesame St 45424
Sessions Dr 45459
Seton Hill Pl 45459
Settlement Way 45414
Settlement House Rd 45458
Severn Ln 45459
Seybold Rd 45426
Shadbush Cir 45458
Shade Dr 45449
Shadeland Dr 45414
Shadetree Dr 45431
Shadow Lake Trl 45459
Shadow Oaks Pl 45440
Shadow Wynd Cir 45459
Shadowbrook Dr 45426
Shadowlawn Ave 45419
Shadows Glade 45426
Shadwell Dr 45416
Shady Cove Ln 45426
Shady Crest Dr 45429
Shady Hill Ln 45429
Shady Knoll Dr 45414
Shady Oak St 45424
Shady Water Ln 45459
Shadybrook Dr 45459
Shadybrook Ln 45449
Shadycreek Dr 45458
Shadycrest Dr 45431
E & W Shadyside Dr 45405
Shadywood Dr 45415
Shafor Blvd 45419
Shaftesbury Rd 45406
Shagbark Ct 45426
Shaker Ct 45458
Shakespeare Ave 45402
Shalamar Dr 45424
Shambord Cir 45429
Shamrock Ct 45424
Shane Dr 45424
Shank Ave 45426
Shank Rd
4800-5299 45439
5300-5799 45417
E Shannon Ave 45449
W Shannon Ave 45449
Shannon Ct 45440
Shannon St 45402
Share Dr 45432
Sharewood Ct 45429
Sharon Ave 45429
Sharp Rd 45432
Sharsted Cir 45424
Shasta Ave 45417
Shaunee Creek Dr 45415
Shaw Ave 45405
Shaw Farm Ln 45429
Shawhan Dr 45458
Shawnee Run 45449
Shawnee Trl 45458
Shawono Pl 45402
Sheba Ct 45424
Shedborne Ave 45403
Shedwick Ct 45426
Sheehan Rd 45458
Sheelah Ct 45420
Sheelin Ct 45415
Sheffield Rd 45449
Shelbourne Ln 45458
Shelby Ave 45419
Sheldon Dr 45459
Shell Ave 45415
Shellcross Dr 45424
Sheller Ave 45432
Shelley Dr 45406
Shelterglen Ct 45459
Sheltering Tree Dr 45449
Shelterwood Dr 45409
Shelton Dr 45429
Shenandoah Dr 45417
Shenandoah Trl 45449
Shepherdess Dr 45424
Sherbrooke Dr 45429
Sherer Ave 45414
Sherfield Dr 45426
Sheridan Ave 45403
Sheringham Ct 45429
Sherman St 45403
E Sherry Dr 45426
Sherwood Dr 45406
Sherwood St 45433
Sherwood Forest Dr 45449
Shetterly Ln 45440
Shields Ave 45433
Shiloh Dr 45415
Shiloh Springs Rd
1-1299 45415
1300-6999 45426
Shiloh View Dr 45415
Shire Ct 45414
Shirecliff Ct 45459
Shirley Ann Dr 45458
Shively Ct 45420
Shoop Ave
2-98 45417
100-499 45417
500-799 45402
Shore Dr 45424
Shore Woods Dr 45459
Shorham Ct 45426
Short St 45449
Shortcreek Cir 45458
Shoup Mill Rd
100-1099 45415
1300-1499 45414
Showalter Ct 45459
Showplace Dr 45424
Shroyer Rd
200-2999 45419
3000-4499 45429
Shull Rd 45424
Shuster Ave 45417
Siamese Ave 45424
Sidney Dr 45415
Sidneywood Dr 45449
E Siebenthaler Ave
1-599 45405
1300-2099 45414
W Siebenthaler Ave
1-699 45405
701-1199 45405
3101-3297 45406
3299-3799 45406
Siena St 45459
Sierra Cir E 45414
Sierra Mist Ct 45414
Signalfire Dr 45458
Signet Dr 45424
Silbury Ln 45429
Sillman Pl 45440
Silver Ln
601-699 45410
7300-7499 45414
Silver Arrow Dr 45424
Silver Bugle Ln 45449
Silver Lake Dr 45458
Silver Maple Ct 45458
Silver Oak St & Way 45424
Silver Pheasant Ct 45424
Silver Rock Ave 45414
Silver Spur Ct 45424
Silverberry Ave 45424
Silvercliff Dr 45449
Silvercreek Dr 45458

Silverdome Dr 45414
Silverleaf Dr 45431
Silvertree Ct & Ln 45459
Silverwood Dr 45429
Silverwyck Pl 45429
Simms St 45403
Simms Station Rd 45458
Singer Rd 45424
Singing Circle Dr 45414
Singing Hills Blvd 45414
Single Tree Ln 45459
Sinton Pl 45429
Skeel Ave 45433
Skeeter 45458
Skinner Dr 45426
Skylane Dr 45414
Skylight Cir 45458
Skyline Dr 45433
Skyros Dr 45424
Skyview Dr 45449
Slagle Rd 45458
Sleepy Hollow Ln 45414
Slipperywood Pl 45424
Slonaker Dr 45449
Smallwood Rd 45417
Smith St 45417
N Smith St 45449
S Smith St 45449
N Smithville Rd
1-299 45403
300-999 45431
S Smithville Rd
1-299 45431
300-1199 45403
1400-1799 45410
1800-3499 45420
Smugglers Way 45459
Snake Rd 45426
Snapping Turtle Ct 45414
Snow Hill Ave 45429
Snowbank Ct 45431
Snowbell Way 45458
Snowberry Cir 45431
Snowcloud Ct 45420
Snowlight Ct 45458
Snowshoe Trl 45449
Snyder Ct 45440
N Snyder Rd
1-1999 45417
2000-4399 45426
Soaring Heights Dr 45440
Social Row Rd 45458
Society Ct 45414
Softwood Ln 45424
Soldiers Home West Car Rd
1200-2999 45417
3000-3399 45439
Soliloquy Trl 45449
Soloman St 45426
Somerset Ave 45431
Somerset Ct 45458
Somerset Dr 45458
Somerville Dr 45424
Sonata Cir 45449
Sonia Cir 45449
Sonnet Pl 45424
Sonora Pl 45416
Sophista Way 45434
Sorrento Ct 45459
Sourwood Dr 45424
Sousa Pl 45420
South Blvd 45419
South Trl 45414
Southampton Dr 45459
Southard Ln 45449
Southbridge Ln 45459
Southbrook Dr 45459
Southbury Dr 45458
Southdale Dr 45409
Southern Blvd
3000-3399 45409
3400-4499 45429
4501-4699 45429
Southern Belle Ct 45458
Southford Ave 45429
Southlake Dr 45459
Southland Dr 45429
Southlea Dr 45459
Southlyn Dr 45409
Southmoor Cir NE 45429
Southpoint Dr 45459
Southshore Dr 45404
Southtown Blvd 45439
Southwind Dr 45459
Sovereign Ct 45414
Spaatz St 45433
Space Dr 45414
Spanish Villa Dr 45414
Sparkhill Dr 45414
Sparks St 45426
Sparrow Dr 45424
Sparrow Pond 45458
Spaulding Rd 45432
Speargrass Dr 45431
E Spearmint St 45390
Specialty Pl 45417
Speice Ave 45403
N & S Sperling Ave 45403
Spice Bush 45429
Spicewood Dr 45424
Spinnaker Way 45458
Spinning Rd
1-999 45431
1000-1299 45432
3420-3421 45433
Split Rail 45429
Split Rock Dr 45424
Spokane Dr 45424
Spoonbill Ct 45424
Sportscraft Dr 45414
Sprague St 45402
Spring St 45403
Spring Ash Dr 45458
Spring Falls Cir 45440
Spring Falls Dr 45449
Spring Farm Ct 45459
Spring Garden Pl 45431
Spring Glen Cir 45414
Spring Hollow Ct 45424
Spring Lake Cir 45449
Spring Ridge Pl 45458
Spring Rose Dr 45459
Spring Run Ln 45458
E & W Spring Valley Pike 45458
N Springboro Pike 45449
Springbrook Blvd 45405
Springcreek Dr 45405
Springdale Dr 45419
Springdawn Dr 45426
Springfield St
1-4299 45403
4300-5299 45431
5301-5699 45431
Springgate Ct 45424
Springhill Ave 45409
Springhill Rd
3000-3199 45434
6500-8799 45390
Springmeadow Ln 45426
Springmill Rd 45440
Springmont Ave 45420
Springport Way 45424
Springside Dr 45440
Springtree Ct 45459
Springview Cir 45426
Springway Dr 45415
Springwood Way 45440
Spritz Ln 45424
Spruce Way 45433
Spruce Pine Ct 45424
Sprucehill Ct 45424
Squire St 45449
Squire Hill Ct 45424
Squirrel Rd 45405
Stablehand Dr 45458
Stacey Rd 45417
Stadium Ave 45449
Stafford Ave 45405
Stafford Springs Pl 45458
Stagecoach Dr S 45458
Stainton Ave 45403
Stamford Pl 45459
Stanbridge Dr 45429
Stancrest Dr 45424
Standish Ave 45432
Stanford Pl 45406
Stanhill Pl 45424
Stanhope Ave 45406
Stanley Ave 45404
Stanley Mill Dr 45459
Stansel Cir 45458
Stanton Hall Ct 45429
Stanview Ave 45404
Stapleton Ct 45404
N Star Rd 45432
Star Valley Ct 45458
Starlight Cir 45415
Starr Ave 45417
Starr Pl 45420
N & S State Line St 45390
State Road 47 E & N 45390
State Road 502 45390
State Route 235 45424
State Route 4 45424
State Route 48 45458
State Route 571 45390
Statesboro Rd 45459
Station House Rd 45458
Stationview Ct 45458
Staudt Rd 45390
Staverton Dr 45459
Stayman Dr 45440
Stedman Ln 45431
Steele Ave 45410
Stefan Pl 45431
Stegman Ave 45404
Stein Way 45416
Steinbeck Way 45440
Steiner Ave 45417
Stephanie St 45458
Stephen Ct 45458
Sterling Pl 45459
E Stewart St
1-399 45409
700-1099 45410
W Stewart St
2-198 45409
300-1722 45417
1724-1848 45417
Still Meadow Ln 45458
Stillcreek Dr 45458
Stillcrest Way 45414
Stillmead Dr 45414
Stillwater Ct 45426
Stillwater Ln 45415
Stillwell Dr 45431
Stockbridge Dr 45424
Stocker Dr 45429
Stockholm Dr 45424
Stocksdale Rd 45390
Stockton Ave 45409
Stoddard Ave 45405
Stolz Ave 45417
Stone Ash Ct 45458
Stone Brook Ct 45458
Stone Lake Dr 45429
Stonebridge Rd 45419
Stonecreek Cir 45458
Stonecrest Dr 45424
Stonecrop Cir 45431
Stonegate Ct 45424
Stonehaven Rd 45429
Stonehedge St 45426
Stonehenge Ln 45429
Stonehouse Ct 45459
Stonehurst Dr 45424
Stonemead Way 45458
Stonemill Rd 45409
Stonequarry Rd 45414
Stoner Dr 45414
Stoner Rd 45390
Stonerock Ct 45458
Stonesboro Dr 45424
Stoneview Ct 45429
Stonewall Cir 45415
Stoney Creek Dr 45424
Stoneybrook Dr 45429
Stoneyridge Dr 45429
Stoneyview Ct 45424
Stonington Cir 45458
Stony Hollow Rd 45417
Stop 8 Rd 45414
Storck Dr 45424
Stormont Rd 45426
Storms Cir & Rd 45429
Stout St 45402
Stovall Dr 45424
Strader Dr 45426
Strand Ave 45417
Strasburg Ln 45459
Strathaven Dr 45424
Strathmoor Dr & Xing 45429
Stratsburg Dr 45417
Stratton Ct 45458
Strawberry Ct 45426
Strawberry Row 45417
Stream Park Ct 45458
Streamside Dr 45459
Streamview Ct 45458
E Stroop Rd 45429
W Stroop Rd
1-1299 45429
1500-2599 45439
2601-2699 45439
Stroud Ln 45458
Stubbs Dr 45426
Stuben Dr 45417
Stuckhardt Rd 45426
Student St 45449
Sturgis Ct 45424
S Suburban Rd 45458
Success Ln 45458
Successful Way 45414
Sudachi Dr 45414
Sudbury Dr 45420
Sue Ln 45415
Sue Ann Blvd 45415
Sue Anne Blvd 45405
Sue Eileen Ct 45424
Suffolk Ct 45420
Sugar Bend Trl 45458
Sugar Leaf Dr 45440
Sugar Maple Dr
2300-2399 45440
4881-4882 45433
4884-4884 45433
5100-5299 45440
Sugar Ridge Blvd 45440
Sugar Ridge Ln 45458
Sugarberry Dr 45431
Sugarberry Pl 45458
Sugarbrook Ct 45458
Sugarbush Pl 45458
Sugarcreek Pt 45458
Sugarside Ct 45458
Sugartree Dr 45414
Sulky Ct 45434
Sullivan Ct 45431
Sum Pl 45417
Sumac Ct 45417
Suman Ave 45403
Summer Breeze Ct 45429
Summer Park Way 45458
Summerdale Dr 45424
Summerford Pl 45458
Summergreen Dr 45424
Summit Glen Rd 45449
Summit Ridge Dr 45424
Summit Square Dr 45417
Sumner Ave 45429
Sumpter Ave 45414
Sun Prairie Ct 45424
Sunberry Ave 45431
Suncrest Dr 45414
Sundale Ave 45406
Sunderland Woods Ct & Dr 45458
Sunflower Ct 45458
Sunlight Ave 45417
Sunnington Grove Dr 45458
Sunny Crest Ln 45419
Sunny Ridge Rd N & S 45414
Sunnybrook Ct 45426
Sunnycliff Pl 45459
Sunnycreek Dr 45458
Sunnydale Pl 45429
Sunnyridge Ln 45429
Sunnyvale Cir 45424
Sunnyview Ave 45406
Sunray Rd 45429
E Sunrise Ave 45426
N Sunrise Ave 45426
S Sunrise Ave 45426
W Sunrise Ave 45426
Sunrise Pl 45402
Sunshine Ct 45403
Sunwick Pl 45459
Superba Ct 45403
Superior Ave
200-399 45406
500-1699 45402
Surrey Ct 45440
Surrey Gate Pl 45458
Surry Ridge Way 45424
Susan Dr
5200-5499 45415
8800-8999 45458
Susan Jane Ct 45406
Susannah Ave 45414
Suttercreek Cir 45459
Sutton Ave 45429
Suzanne Cir 45459
Swallow Dr 45415
N & S Swan Lake Dr 45424
Swango Dr 45429
Sweeney Dr 45458
Sweet Audrey Ct 45458
Sweet Briar Ln 45459
Sweet Shrub Cir 45458
Sweetbell Ct 45424
Sweetbirch Dr 45424
Sweetgum Pl 45424
Sweetleaf Dr 45424
Sweetman St 45402
Swinger Dr 45417
Swinging Gate Dr 45424
Swisher Ave 45417
Swiss Hill Ct 45459
Swissway Dr 45459
Sycamore Ave 45432
Sycamore St 45433
N Sycamore St 45390
S Sycamore St 45390
Sycamore Creek Ct 45459
Sycamore Hills Dr 45459
Sycamore Springs Ct 45458
Sycamore View Dr 45458
Sycamore Woods Blvd 45426
Sykes Cir 45433
Sykes Ct 45424
Sylmar Ct 45424
Sylvan Dr 45417
Sylvan Oak Dr 45426
Sylvandale Dr 45419
Sylvester Dr 45409
Symmes Ln 45424
Symphony Way 45449
Syracuse Ave 45405
Tabby Dr 45424
Tabor Ave 45420
Tacoma St 45410
Taffy Ct 45390
Taffy Ln 45459
Taft Ave 45417
Taggart St 45420
Tahitian Pl 45440
Tahoe Dr 45458
Tai Trce 45458
Tait Rd
100-999 45429
3401-3497 45439
3499-3999 45439
4300-4999 45429
Tait Circle Rd 45429
Taitwood Rd 45459
Takisa Cir 45415
Talawanda Trl 45429
Talbott Dr 45429
Talbott Rd 45433
Talbott Tower 45402
Talbrook Ct 45458
Talcott Trl 45426
Talisman Dr 45420
Tall Hickory Trl 45415
Tall Oaks Ct & Dr 45432
Tall Timber Trl 45409
Tall Trees 45429
Tallview Ct 45424
Talon Ridge Ct 45440
Tam O Shanter Way 45429
Tamarac Ln & Trl 45429
Tamarind Trl 45459
Tamerlane Rd 45429
Tammy Cir 45415
Tampa Ave 45417
Tanager Mdws 45426
Tanager Way 45449
Tangent Dr 45440
Tangletree Ct 45414
Tanglewyck Pl 45458
Tangy Ct 45414
Tanley Ct 45424
Tanner Dr 45424
Tantamount Ln 45449
Tapestry Ln 45426
Tara Way 45426
Tarnview Dr 45424
Tarryton Rd 45459
Tato St 45403
Tattersall Rd 45459
Tauber Dr 45458
Taunton Way 45424
Tavenshire Dr 45424
Tayfield Ct 45414
Taylor Ave 45402
Taylor St 45404
Taylorsville Rd 45424
Teaberry Dr 45424
Teagarden Cir 45449
Teakwood Ct 45424
Teal Way 45459
Technology Blvd 45424
Tecumseh St 45402
Tedbury Ct 45459
Telford Ave 45419
Tellamere Ct 45424
Tellea St 45424
Temple Ln 45431
Tennyson Ave 45406
Tenshaw Dr 45417
Terieris Ave 45409
Termarli Rd 45426
Terminal Ln 45424
Terrace Crk 45459
Terrace Park Dr 45429
Terrace View Ct 45424
Terrace Villa Dr 45459
Terraceview Trl 45431
Terre Linda Dr 45424
Terrence Ct 45449
N & S Terry St 45403
Terrygate Ct 45424
Terrylynn Ave 45439
Teton Ln 45417
Tewkesbury Dr 45424
Texas Ave 45404
Thatchwood Cir 45431
The Mall St 45402
Thelma Ave 45415
Theobald Ct 45410
Theodore Ave 45405
Thicket Walk 45429
Thimble Creek Dr 45426
Thistle Dr 45417
Thistlewood Ct 45424
Thomas Farm Ct 45458
Thomas Jefferson Ln 45459
Thomas Paine Pkwy 45459
Thompson Dr 45416
Thor St 45404
Thorain Ct 45416
Thoreau Ave 45424
Thornbury Dr 45459
Thorndale Dr 45429
Thornton Dr 45406
Thornwood Pl 45429
Thorpe Dr 45420
Thrush Ct 45458
Thruston Blvd E 45409
Thunderbird Ln 45449
Thunderhawk Ct 45414
Thundering Herd Pl 45415
Thurlow St 45433
Tiara Ct 45459
Tibbals Ct 45458
Tibet Dr 45424
Tica Ave 45424
Tice St 45458
Tidewater Dr 45424
Tiffany Dr 45420
Tiffin Pl 45404
Tifton Green Trl 45459
Tiger Dr 45424
Tilbury Rd 45424
Tilden Ct 45424
Tillers Rd 45433
Tillman Rd 45458
Tillotson Pl 45458
Timber Ln 45414
Timber Bend Pl 45424
Timber Brook Ln 45458
Timber Creek Ct 45458
Timber Hill Dr 45424
Timber Oak Cir 45440
Timber Park Dr 45458
Timber Walk Ct 45458
Timbercrest Dr 45424
Timbergate Trl 45424
Timberhawk Trl 45458
Timberidge Cir 45459
Timberlake Ct 45429
Timberlake Dr 45414
Timberlands Dr 45414
Timberlea Trl 45429
Timberlodge Trl 45458
Timberly Dr 45440
Timbertrail Ct 45458
Timberview Dr 45424
Timberwilde Dr 45440
Timberwyck Ct 45458
Timshel St 45440
Tina Ct 45424
Tip Top Ave 45410
Tipton Ct 45458
Titan St 45404
Titus Ave 45414
Tiverton Cir 45459
Tobin Rd 45390
Todd St 45403
Tomahawk Trl 45459
Tomberg St 45424
Tonga Dr 45414
Toni Ct 45424
Toni Dr 45417
Tony Stein Way 45404
Tonywood Cir 45449
Top O Rahn Ct 45459
Torch Ln 45417
Torlage Dr 45431
N & S Torrence St 45403
Torrey Ct 45417
Torreyson Ave 45429
Torrington Pl 45406
Tortuga Dr 45414
Totem Pole Ct 45449
Touchstone Ave 45417
Toulon Ct 45424
Toulouse Cir 45429
Touraine Cir 45440
Tours Ln 45459
Towanda Cir 45431
Tower Ln 45403
Towerview Rd 45429
Town St 45403
E & W Town And Country Rd 45429
Townhall Ct 45458
Townhouse Ct 45406

Townsend Pl 45431
Townsley Rd 45432
Trace Ct 45439
Tracy Dr 45414
Trade Winds Ave 45424
Trafalgar Ct 45459
Trail Stone Pt 45458
Trails End Dr 45429
Trailside Ct 45424
Trailview Dr 45414
Trailway St 45415
Trailwoods Dr 45415
Traine Dr 45429
Tranquil Trl 45459
Transportation Rd 45404
Travelo Dr 45424
Travis Dr 45431
Traymore Dr 45424
Treasury Dr 45429
Trebor Ln 45459
Tree View Dr 45459
Treeglen Way 45415
Treeland Ln 45458
Treeside Ct 45458
Treewick St 45433
Tremont Ave 45429
N & S Trenton St 45417
Trentwood Cir 45459
Treon Pl 45424
Triangle View Dr 45414
Tridelak Rd 45390
Trieschman Ave 45417
Trimbach Ln 45402
Trina Ave 45449
Trinity Ave 45409
Trinity Church Rd 45415
Tristan Ct 45449
Trone Ave 45406
Troon Trl 45429
Trotter Ct 45417
E & W Trotwood Blvd 45426
Trowbridge Way 45424
Troy Pike 45424
Troy St 45404
Troy Crest Ct 45424
Troy Manor Rd 45424
Troy Villa Blvd 45424
Trubee Ln 45432
Trudy Ave 45426
Trula Pl 45415
Truman Ct 45406
Trumpet Dr 45449
Trunk Dr 45431
Tubman Ave 45417
Tucson Dr 45417
Tudor Rd 45419
Tulip Dr 45449
Tulip Ln 45432
Tulip Tree Ct 45424
Tulipwoods Cir 45459
Turchin Pl 45424
Turf Club Ct 45439
Turfwood Ct 45424
Turnberry Village Dr 45458
Turnbridge Ln 45424
Turnbull Rd 45432
Turner Rd 45415
Turquoise Ct 45459
Turtle Creek Dr 45414
Turtle Dove Way 45459
Turtle Shell Dr 45414
Turtleback Dr 45414
Turtlebrook Ct 45414
Turtlehead Ct 45414
Tuscany Ct 45424
Tuscola Dr 45426
Tuttle Ave 45403
Tuxford Pl 45415
Tuxworth Rd 45458
Twain Pl 45420
Tweed Cir 45459
Twilight Hill Dr 45429
Twin Ln 45410
Twin Creek Dr 45426
Twin Fork Ct 45459
Twin Oaks Dr 45431
Twin Pine Ln 45449
Twin Woods Dr 45426
Twinbrook Ln 45429
Twinning Dr 45431
Tymill Ct 45415
Tyndale Ct 45424
Tyrol Trl 45459
Tyron Ave 45404
Tyronda Ln 45429
Tyson Ave 45417
Uehling Ln 45424
Uhl Ct 45420
Uhrig Ave 45406
Ula Dr 45414
Ulrich Ave 45406
Ultimate Way 45449
Underwood Rd 45431
Union Rd 45424
N Union Rd
1-1999 45417
2000-4999 45426
S Union Rd
1-3599 45417
3600-3698 45439
3601-3799 45417
3700-3798 45417
3800-3999 45439
Union City Elroy Rd 45390
Union Hill Cir 45449
Union Schoolhouse Rd 45424
Union Springs Ct 45458
Unity Pl 45420
University Pl 45406
Upham Rd 45429
N Upland Ave
1-799 45417
800-999 45402
S Upland Ave 45417
Upland Cir 45449
Upland Dr 45449
Uplands Camp Rd 45419
Upper Ave 45417
Upper Valley Rd 45424
Upson Pl 45409
Upton Pl 45417
Urban Ave 45429
Urbana Ave 45404
Utah Ct 45410
Utica Dr 45439
Utopia Pl 45431
Vagabond Ln 45424
Val Vista Ct 45406
Valais Ct 45458
Vale Dr 45420
Valemont Rd 45417
Valencia St 45404
Valentine Dr 45431
Valerie Dr 45405
Valerie Arms Dr 45405
Valewood Ln 45405
Valley Pike
2001-2097 45404
2099-2999 45404
3001-3199 45404
6500-7099 45424
Valley St
1-97 45404
99-2000 45404
2002-2098 45404
3200-4799 45424
Valley Forge Dr 45440
Valley Greene Dr 45440
Valley Oak Ct 45415
Valley Vista Way 45429
Valleybrook Pl 45459
Valleycrest Dr 45404
Valleyview Dr 45405
Valleywood Dr 45429
Van Buren St 45402
Van Cleve St 45402
Van Dorn Ln 45433
Van Kirk Rd 45390
N & S Van Lear St 45403
Van Meter St 45424
Van Patton Dr 45433
Van Wert Pl 45404
Vance Rd
2100-3299 45417
3300-3699 45439
Vancouver Dr 45406
Vandenburg Rd 45433
Vandergrift Dr 45431
Vanguard Ave 45417
Vaniman Ave 45426
Vanquil Trl 45449
Varney Ave 45420
Vassar Dr 45406
Vega Ct 45432
Velma Ave 45420
Ventnor Ave 45414
Ventura Ave 45417
Vera Pl 45429
Verdi Ct & Dr 45449
Verdon Pl 45426
Vermeer Dr 45420
Vermont Ave 45404
Verna Ct 45458
Vernadale Dr 45429
Vernell Dr 45449
Vernon Dr
900-1299 45402
1400-1499 45406
1501-1599 45406
Verona Rd 45417
Veronica Pl 45459
Versailles Dr 45459
Veterans Pkwy 45402
Vickers Pl 45449
Vicksburg St 45417
Vickwood Ln 45426
Vicky Dr 45417
Victor Ave 45405
Victoria Ave 45406
Victory Dr 45417
Vienna Pkwy 45459
Vienna Estates Dr 45459
Vienna Woods Trl 45459
Viewcrest Pl 45420
Viewell Ave 45414
Viewland Ter 45431
Viewmont Dr 45415
Viewpoint Dr 45459
Villa South Dr 45449
Villa Vista Pl 45458
N Village Dr 45459
S Village Dr 45459
Village Pkwy 45417
Village Green Dr 45414
Village Square Dr 45458
Villanova Dr 45429
Vina Villa Ave 45417
Vinal Ave 45417
Vincent Ave 45433
Vincent St 45405
Vine St 45409
N Vine St 45390
Vinemont Dr 45449
Vineyard Dr 45429
Vinita Dr 45429
Vintage Pl 45415
Vintage Green Way 45458
Vintage Lake Ct 45458
Vinton Pl 45431
Vinway Ct 45415
Viola Ave 45405
Virginia Ave
1-299 45410
300-399 45458
Virginia Lee Dr 45458
Vista Oak Trl 45459
Vista View Dr 45402
Vitek Dr 45424
Volk Dr 45415
Volkenand Ave 45410
Volkman Dr 45414
E & W Von Dette Cir 45459
Vondale Ct 45404
Voyager Blvd 45417
Vull St 45404
Wabash Ave
1200-1399 45405
1600-1699 45406
1800-1899 45405
Waco Ave 45449
Wadsworth Rd 45414
Wagner Rd
500-799 45390
4000-5099 45440
Wagon Wheel Dr 45431
Wagoner Ford Rd 45414
Wahsum Cir 45459
Wainscott Way 45414
Wainwright Dr 45431
Wake Ave 45431
Wake Forest Rd 45431
Wakefield Ave 45406
Wakeshire Ct 45426
Wakeview Ct 45424
Walbrook Ave 45405
Wald Ave 45404
Waldeck Pl 45405
Walden Ln 45429
Waldheim Ct 45459
Waldorf Dr 45415
Waldrun Ave 45404
Wales Dr 45405
Walford Dr 45440
E Wall St 45390
Wallace St 45402
Waller Mill Rd 45459
Wallingsford Cir 45458
Wallington Dr 45440
Walmac St 45424
Walnut Ct 45417
Walnut St 45402
N Walnut St
1-299 45449
100-599 45390
S Walnut St 45449
Walnut Walk 45429
Walnut Creek Ct 45459
Walnut Grove Dr 45458
Walnut Hill Pl 45410
Walnut Ridge Rd 45414
Walnut Valley Ln 45458
Walnut Wood Way 45415
Walshwood Ct 45424
Walsingham Ct 45429
Walston Ct 45426
Walters St 45404
Waltham Ave 45429
Walther Cir 45429
Walton Ave
100-699 45417
700-1099 45402
Wampler Ave 45405
Waneta Ave 45404
Wanlow Ln 45459
Warbler Way 45449
Warburton Dr 45426
Ward St 45417
E Ward St 45390
Ward Hill Ave 45420
Wardcliff Dr 45414
Warder St 45405
Wardmier Dr 45459
Wardway Dr 45426
Ware Ave 45410
Wareham Ct 45459
Warm Springs Ct 45458
Warner Ave 45404
Warner Robins St 45433
Warren St
101-197 45402
199-499 45402
500-699 45409
Warrendale Ave 45404
Warrington Pl 45419
Warrior Ct 45415
Warwick Pl 45419
Washburn Dr 45426
Washington Rd 45390
Washington St 45402
Washington Church
Rd 45458
Washington Colony Dr 45458
Washington Creek Ln 45458
Washington North Dr 45458
Washington Park Dr 45459
Washington South Dr 45458
Washington Villa Trce 45459
Washington Village Dr
7600-7999 45459
8000-8499 45458
Washington West Dr 45458
Washington Woods Dr 45459
Wasson Rd 45390
Watch Hill Ln 45458
E Water St 45390
Water View Way 45424
Waterbury Dr 45439
Waterbury Ridge Ln 45458
Waterbury Woods Ln 45458
Waterford Dr 45458
Waterfront Pl 45458
Watergate Dr 45424
Watergreen Ct 45424
Waterlily Dr 45431
Waterloo Rd 45459
Waters Edge Dr 45458
Waterton Ct 45426
Watertower Ln 45449
Waterview Ct 45414
Watervliet Ave 45420
Waterwyck Trl 45458
Watkins Pl 45417
Watkins Glen Dr 45458
Watson St 45417
Watson Way 45433
Watterson St 45417
Watts St 45403
Waverly Ave 45405
Waves Lndg 45459
Waving Willow Dr 45409
Wawona Rd 45402
Wax Wing Pt 45458
Wayland Ave 45420
Waymire Ave 45406
Wayne Ave
1-299 45402
300-2299 45410
2300-3999 45420
Wayne Estates Blvd 45424
Wayne Meadows Cir 45424
Wayne School Rd 45424
Waynedale Cir 45424
Waynegate Rd 45424
Waynetowne Blvd &
Ct 45424
Waywind Dr 45426
Weakley St 45417
Weathered Wood Trl 45459
Weatherfield Ct 45459
Weathersfield Dr 45440
Weaver St 45417
Webb St 45403
Webbshaw Dr 45458
Webster St
1-299 45402
500-698 45404
700-2199 45404
4300-7499 45414
Weddington Dr 45426
Wedge Creek Pl 45458
Wedgestone Ct 45458
Wedgewood Ave 45429
Weeping Willow Ct 45424
Weeping Willow Dr 45449
Wehner Rd 45429
Wehrly Ave 45419
Weidner Ln 45458
Weigold Ct 45426
Weir St 45449
Weiss Rd 45390
Weitzel Way 45433
Welcome Way 45433
Welford Dr 45434
Well Fleet Dr 45426
Weller Ave 45458
Weller St 45402
Wellesley Way 45459
Wellington Dr 45410
Wellington Pl 45424
Wellmeier Ave 45410
Wells Ave 45431
Wells Spring Pt 45458
Welsford Ct 45459
Wembley Cir 45459
Wenbrook Dr 45429
Wendell Ln 45431
Wendsbury Dr 45426
Wendy Way 45449
Wendy Sue St 45424
Weng Ave 45420
Wenrick Dr 45432
Wenston Ct 45429
Wentworth Ave 45406
Wenz Ct 45405
Wenzler Dr 45429
Wesley St 45403
Wesleyan Rd 45406
West Ave 45419
S West End Ave 45417
Westanna Dr 45426
Westbay Ct 45426
Westboro St 45417
Westbrook Rd 45415
Westbury Rd 45409
Westchester Ln 45416
Westcliff Ct 45409
Westcott Dr 45420
Westcreek Dr 45426
Westcrest Dr 45426
Westdale Ct 45402
Westerfield Dr 45458
Westerly Dr & Ln 45458
Westfall Dr 45414
Westfield Ave 45420
Westford Rd 45426
Westgate Dr 45429
Westgrove Dr 45426
Westhaven Dr 45429
Westland Dr 45426
Westlawn Dr 45440
Westledge Dr 45426
Westminster Pl 45419
Westmont Pl 45414
Westmore Ct 45416
Westmoreland Ct 45431
Weston Cir 45429
Westona Dr 45410
Westover Dr 45426
Westpark Rd 45459
Westport Dr 45406
Westridge Rd 45459
N & S Westview Ave 45403
Westwicke Pl 45459
Westwood Ave
100-599 45417
600-999 45402
Westwood Xing 45426
Wetherburn Dr 45459
Wexford Pl 45417
Weybridge Dr 45426
Weybright Ct 45440
Weyburn Dr 45426
Weymouth Ct 45426
Whalers Wharf 45458
Whaley Dr 45417
Wharton Dr 45426
Wheatfield Ct 45458
Wheatland Ave 45429
Wheatley Ave 45405
Wheaton St 45429
Wheeler Ave 45406
E Whipp Rd
1-1199 45459
1700-2600 45440
2602-2798 45440
W Whipp Rd 45459
Whipple Tree Dr 45458
Whippoorwill Ln 45459
Whisper Creek Dr 45414
Whispering Dr 45426
Whispering Meadow
Dr 45415
Whispering Oak Dr 45440
Whispering Pine Ln 45458
Whispering Willow Cir 45440
Whispering Woods Dr 45449
Whitaker St 45415
Whitcomb Pl 45459
White Allen Ave 45405
White Birch Rd 45458
White Oak Ct 45439
White Oak Dr 45420
White Oak Way 45424
White Spruce Cir 45424
White Water Ct 45414
Whitebrush Cir 45431
Whitehall Dr 45459
Whitehorse Ave 45420
Whites Corner Rd 45459
Whitestone Ct 45416
Whitetail Trl 45459
Whitewood Ct 45424
Whitlock Pl 45420
Whitmore Ave 45417
Whitney Pl 45420
Whittier Ave 45420
Whittington Dr 45459
Wick Ct 45429
Wicker Pl 45431
Wicklow Pl 45406
Wicksford Ct 45414
Widgeon Ct 45424
Wieland Way 45459
Wienburg Dr 45439
Wierfield Pl 45426
Wiesen Ln 45439
Wilberforce Pl 45417
Wilbur Ave 45405
Wilcke Way 45459
Wild Cherry Dr 45414
Wild Goose Way 45458
Wild Hickory Ln 45458
Wild Horse Dr 45458
Wild Ivy Way 45440
Wild Orchard Pt 45458
Wild Timber Ln 45429
Wild Willow Ct 45424
Wildcat Rd
500-899 45390
7600-8099 45424
8101-8499 45424
Wilderness Way 45459
Wildfire Ct 45458
Wilding Ave 45414
Wildoak Ct 45424
Wildrose Dr 45414
Wildview Dr 45424
Wildwood Ave 45417
Wiles Dr 45419
Wilfred Ave 45410
N & S Wilkinson St 45402
Will Rogers Pl 45420
Willamet Rd 45429
Willard St 45417
Willaston Dr 45431
Willet Way 45449
William Ln 45429
William St 45449
William Penn Ln 45459
N Williams St 45402
S Williams St
1-499 45402
501-599 45402
600-699 45417
Williamsburg Ln 45459
Williamson Dr 45416
Willow Ct 45433
Willow Dr 45426
Willow St 45404
Willow Walk 45415
Willow Branch Dr 45424
Willow Brook Ct 45424
Willow Brook Rd 45458
Willow Creek Dr
3700-4299 45415
6600-6899 45424
Willow Glen Ct 45431
Willow Hill Ct 45459
Willow Mist Dr 45424
Willow Oak Ct 45439
Willow Oak Ln 45458
Willow Park Ct 45458

Willow Springs Dr 45417
Willow Tree Ln 45424
Willow Twig Ln 45459
Willow Way Dr 45424
Willowbend Ct 45426
Willowbrook Way 45431
Willowburn Ave 45417
Willowby Ln 45459
Willowdale Ave 45429
Willowgate Ln 45424
Willowgrove Ave 45409
Willowhurst Dr 45459
Willowick Pl 45459
Willowmere Ct 45424
Willowmere Dr 45459
Willowpoint Ln 45459
Willowridge Dr 45414
Willowwood Dr 45405
Wilmar Cir 45417
Wilmette Ct 45459
Wilmington Ave 45420
Wilmington Pike
- 1500-2399 45420
- 2400-2999 45419
- 3000-3999 45429
- 4000-5499 45440
- 5500-7499 45459
- 7500-7899 45458

Wilmore St 45416
Wilson Dr 45402
Wilson Rd 45390
Wilson Park Dr 45449
Wilton Ave 45405
Wiltshire Blvd 45419
Wimbledon Cir 45420
Win Dr 45415
Winburn Ave 45420
Winchcombe Dr 45459
Winchester Dr 45429
Winchester Pl 45458
Wind Field Ct 45458
Windbluff Pt 45458
Windemere Dr 45429
Winden Ave 45419
Windham St 45404
Winding Cv 45459
Winding Way
- 1-599 45429
- 600-3399 45419

Winding Creek Trl 45429
Winding Green Way 45458
Winding Hollow Trl 45414
Winding Oak Cir 45424
Winding Ridge Dr 45415
Windjammer Pl 45458
Windlow Dr 45406
Windom Sq 45458
Windsor Ave
- 401-599 45449
- 900-1299 45402

Windsor Ct 45449
Windsor Dr 45434
Windsor Park Dr 45459
Windsor Ridge Dr 45424
Windwood Pt 45458
Windy Strm 45414
Windy Bluff Ct 45440
Windy Hill Ct 45459
Windy Hill Ln 45414
Winesap Ct 45449
Wing View Ln 45429
Wingreen Ave 45414
Winlock Ave 45404
Winnebago St 45404
Winners Cir 45404
Winnet Dr 45415
Winona Ave 45405
Winshire Ter 45440
Winslow Ct 45432
Winston Ave 45403
Winston Farm Ln 45458
Winston Woods Dr 45415
Winter Haven Ave 45415
Winter Hill Ct 45459
Winterberry Ct 45431
Wintergreen Pl 45424
S Wintergreen St 45390
Winters Rd 45459
Winters St 45417
Winterstone Ct 45458
Winterwood Dr 45424
Winthrop Pl 45459
Winton Dr 45419
Wire Dr 45414
Wisconsin Blvd 45417
Witherby Dr 45429
Witherspoon Dr 45440
Witherward Trl 45449
Withrow Way 45415
Wittelsbach Dr 45429
Wittenberg Ave 45417
Wolf Rd 45416
Wolf Creek Pike
- 4500-4884 45417
- 4885-10499 45426

Wolf Ridge Rd 45415
Wonderview Dr 45414
N Wood Creek Dr 45458
Wood Creek Rd 45426
Wood Dale Dr 45414
Wood Hollow Rd 45429
Wood Mill Trl 45459
Wood Trails Ct 45459
Wood Turtle Dr 45414
Woodbank Dr 45440
Woodbine Ave
- 3500-4575 45420
- 4576-5599 45432

Woodbluff Ln 45458
Woodbourne Trl 45459
Woodbriar Dr 45440
Woodbridge Ln 45429
Woodbrook Way 45430
E & W Woodbury Dr 45415
Woodcliffe Ave 45420
Woodcock Way 45424
Woodcove Way 45430
Woodcrest Ave 45405
Woodcroft Trl 45430
Wooden Shoe Ln 45459
Woodenbrook Ct 45430
Woodfield Pl 45459
Woodford Pl 45430
Woodgate Dr 45424
Woodglen Pt 45458
Woodgrove Ct 45458
Woodhaven Ave 45414
Woodhaven Dr 45429
Woodhill Rd 45431
Woodhills Blvd 45449
Woodhurst Ct 45430
Woodknolls Dr 45449
Woodlake Dr 45406
Woodland Ave 45409
Woodland Hills Blvd 45414
Woodledge Pt 45458
Woodley Rd 45403
Woodman Dr
- 1-999 45431
- 1000-1699 45432
- 1708-1708 45420
- 1710-3299 45420
- 3300-3999 45429
- 4000-4199 45440

N Woodman Dr 45431
Woodman Center Ct & Dr 45420
Woodman Park Dr 45432
Woodmore Dr 45414
Woodner Dr 45440
Woodpine Ct 45424
Woodpoint Ct 45424
Woodrow Ter 45410
Woodruff Dr 45405
Woodsdale Rd 45404
Woodsedge Ct 45449
Woodside Ave
- 3500-3598 45417
- 3600-3899 45402

Woodson Ct 45459
Woodson Dr 45414
Woodstone Dr 45426
Woodstream Ln 45458
Woodview Ct 45417
Woodville Dr 45414
N & S Woodward Ave 45417
Woodway Ave
- 2400-2699 45406
- 2700-2999 45405

Woodwell Dr 45440
Woodwyck Ct 45458
Woolery Ln 45415
Worchester Dr 45431
E & W Worley Ave 45426
Worth Rd 45390
E & W Wren Cir 45420
Wrencroft Cir 45459
Wrenford St 45409
Wrenside Ln 45440
Wrenview Ct 45424
Wright Ave 45433
N Wright Ave 45403
S Wright Ave 45403
Wright Brothers Ct 45458
Wright Patterson Afb 45433
Wright Way Rd 45424
Wroe Ave 45406
Wyandot St 45402
Wyburn Pl 45417
Wyckoff Cir 45458
Wycliffe Pl 45459
Wymore Pl 45459
Wyngate Dr 45429
Wynkoop Ct 45431
Wynora Ave 45404
Wynwood Ct 45431
Wyoming St
- 1-299 45409
- 300-2499 45410

Wyse Rd 45414
Wythe Ct 45406
Wythe Parish St 45459
Xenia Ave 45410
Yale Ave
- 1-200 45406
- 202-298 45406
- 600-699 45402

Yalecrest Dr 45417
Yankee St
- 6501-6597 45459
- 6599-7699 45459
- 8000-11299 45458

Yankee Cove Ct 45458
Yankee Park Pl 45458
Yankee Rose Ct 45458
Yankee Trace Dr 45458
Yankee Vineyards 45458
Yankee Woods Dr 45458
Yanks Ct 45458
Yardley Cir 45459
Yarmouth Dr 45459
Yates St 45403
Yearling Run S 45458
Yellow Locust Ln 45458
Yellowcreek Dr 45458
Yellowstone Ave 45416
Yeoman Ct 45449
Yergen Ct 45417
Yolanda Dr 45417
York Ave 45403
York Center Dr 45414
York Commons Blvd 45414
Yorkcliff Pl 45459
Yorkshire Dr 45414
Yorkshire Pl 45419
Yorktown Ct 45431
Young Rd 45390
Yount Dr 45433
Yucca Ct 45431
Yuma Pl 45402
Zach Pl 45459
Zachary Ln 45424
Zehler Ave 45409
Zeigler St 45402
Zengel Ct & Dr 45459
Zephyr Dr 45414
Zumbrum Rd 45390

NUMBERED STREETS

1st St 45433
S 1st St 45390
E 2nd St 45402
S 2nd St 45390
3rd St 45433
4th St 45433
5 Oaks Ave 45405
5th St 45433
6th St 45433
7 Gables Ave 45426
7 Pines Dr 45449
7th St 45433
8th St 45433
10th St 45433
11th St 45433
12th St 45433
13th St 45433

DUBLIN OH

General Delivery 43016

POST OFFICE BOXES MAIN OFFICE STATIONS AND BRANCHES

Box No.s
- 1 - 2089 43017
- 3001 - 5396 43016
- 5458 - 7778 43017
- 8000 - 8110 43016
- 9029 - 10209 43017
- 10009 - 10209 43016
- 109838 - 109838 43017

NAMED STREETS

Abbey Chapel Dr 43017
Abbey Church Rd 43017
Abbey Marie Ct 43017
Abbeyshire Ct 43016
Abbotsford Dr 43017
Abbotsford Way 43016
Aberdeen Ave 43016
Achill Dr 43017
Adare Ct 43016
Addinston Ct 43017
Aderholt Rd 43016
Adventure Dr 43017
Alan Moss Ct 43017
Alchester Mnr 43017
Alder Glen Ct 43017
Alderbrook Dr 43016
Alderridge Ct 43017
Aldridge Pl 43017
Aleshire Dr 43017
Alimoore Grn 43016
Allen Dr 43017
Amber Ln 43016
Amberfalls Ct 43016
Amberleigh Way 43017
Amston Dr 43017
Angeles Dr 43016
Anglesea Dr 43016
Anna Loop 43016
Anselmo Ct 43017
Ansonia Way 43017
Applecross Dr 43017
Arapahoe Pl 43017
Arborg Ct 43017
Arbory Hill Ct 43017
Archer Ln 43017
Ardaugh Ct 43017
Ardenlee Ct 43017
Ardmore Way 43016
Armistead Ln & Pl 43017
Armscote Rd 43017
Arran Ct 43017
Aryshire Ct & Dr 43017
Asherbrand Ln 43017
Asherton Blvd 43017
Ashford Rd 43017
Ashgate Ct 43017
Ashleigh Dr 43016
Ashleylynn Ct 43016
Ashlord Ct 43017
Ashworth Ct 43017
Aspen Pine Blvd 43016
Aston Way 43016
Athy Ct 43017
Atlin Ave & Ct 43017
Aubrey Loop 43016
Aullwood Ct 43017
Autumn Fern Dr 43016
Autumnwood Way 43017
Avaleen Cir N & S 43016
Avemore Ct 43017
Avery Rd
- 4800-6300 43016
- 6302-6398 43016
- 6400-8299 43017
- 8301-8899 43017

Avery Xing 43016
Avery Muirfield Dr
- 6601-6899 43016
- 6700-6798 43017

Avery Oak Dr 43016
Avocet Ct 43017
Avon Ct 43017
Avondale Ridge Ct & Dr 43017
Badenoch Dr 43017
Baffin Ct & Dr 43017
Balfoure Cir 43017
Ballantrae Cir, Loop & Pl 43016
Balloch Ct 43017
Ballybridge Dr 43017
Ballymead Blvd 43016
Balmoral Ct & Dr 43017
Banavie Ct 43017
Banbridge Ln 43016
Bandon Ct 43016
Bangle Ct 43016
Bannister Dr 43017
Banting St 43017
Bantry Ct 43016
Barassie Pl 43017
Bardston Ct & Dr 43017
Barney Dr 43016
Baronet Blvd 43017
Baronscourt Loop & Way 43016
Baronsmore Way 43016
Barrister Dr 43016
Barronsmore Way 43016
Barry Trce 43017
Barry Trace Ct & Dr 43017
Bartles Ave 43016
Baybridge Ln 43016
Baybrook Ln 43016
Baythorne Ct 43016
Bearclover Dr 43016
Beckley Ln 43017
Beech Wood Loop 43016
Beery Ln 43017
Beeswing Ct 43017
Belfield Ct 43017
Belfield Dr
- 4600-4804 43017
- 4806-4806 43017
- 4822-4898 43016

Belisle Ct 43017
Bellaire Ave & Ct 43017
Bellepoint Pl 43017
Bellow Valley Dr 43016
Beltain Ln 43016
Belvedere Green Blvd 43016
Bennett Ct 43017
Bennington St 43016
Berkshire Ct 43017
Berthold Pass Dr 43016
Betonywood Pl 43016
Bibury Ln 43016
Bidle Ct 43016
Birchton Ct & St 43017
Birgham Ct N & S 43017
Bishops Crossing Cir 43016
Bishops Retreat Pl 43017
Black Abbey Ct 43017
Black Hawk Ct 43017
Black Kettle Trl 43017
Black Willow Dr 43016
Blackjack Ct 43016
Blakeford Dr 43017
Blakemore Ln 43016
Blazer Pkwy
- 4801-4857 43017
- 4859-5503 43017
- 5505-6099 43017
- 5520-5522 43016
- 5550-6198 43017

Blessington Ct 43017
Blickling Dr 43017
Bloomfield Pl 43016
Blunden Rd 43016
Bobcat Way 43016
Bonaly Ct 43016
Bonanza Ln 43016
Bono Ct 43016
Bordeaux Ct 43016
Borge Way 43016
Boucher Rd 43016
Bow Falls Blvd 43016
Bowland Pl N & S 43016
Bowles Ct 43017
Boylston Ct 43016
Bradenton Ave 43017
Bradhurst Dr 43016
Braelinn Dr 43017
Braeside Ct 43017
Braids Ct 43017
Brampton Ct & St 43017
Brand Rd
- 4600-6299 43017
- 6300-7099 43016

Brandbury Pl 43017
Brandonway Ct & Dr 43017
Brandshire Ln 43017
Brandy Creek Dr 43016
Braxmar Pl 43017
Breen Cir 43016
Brelsford Ln 43016
Brenham Way 43017
Briardale Ct & Ln 43016
E & W Bridge St 43017
Bridle Path Ct & Ln 43017
Brigham Dr 43016
Bright Rd 43016
Brightington Dr 43017
Brighton Hill Ln 43016
Brigids Close Dr 43017
Brinsworth Dr 43016
Bristol Dr & Pkwy 43016
Bristol Bane Ct 43016
Britton Pkwy 43016
Britton Woods Dr 43016
Brock St 43017
Brodie Blvd 43017
Brolio Villa Dr 43016
Brookedge Ct 43017
Broome Dr 43016
Browning Ct 43017
Broxburn Ct 43017
Bryant Park Dr 43016
Bryne Ct 43017
Bryson Cove Cir 43016
Buckhannon St 43016
Buffalo Head Trl 43017
Bull Creek Dr 43016
Burleigh Dr 43017
Burnett Ln 43017
Burnside Ln 43016
Burrwood St 43016
Buttleston Dr 43016
Cabernet Ct 43016
Cabot Ct 43017
Cadmore Dr 43016
Cahill Ct 43016
Caithness Dr 43017
Calabria Pl 43016
Caldy Ct 43017
Calloway Ct 43017
Calvert Ct 43016
Calypso Cascades Dr 43016
Camberry Ct 43016
Cambrooke Ct 43016
Cambry Ln 43016
Camden Cir 43016
Camden Row Rd 43016
Cameo Dr 43016
Campbell Ln 43017
Campden Lakes Blvd 43016
Canaan Cir 43017
Canyon Creek Dr 43016
Cape Ct 43017
Cape Wrath Dr 43017
Caplestone Ln 43017
Cara Ct & Rd 43016
Caraway Ave 43016
Carberry Dr 43016
Cardin Blvd 43016
Cardinal Pl W 43017
Carinlough Pl 43016
Carlow Ct 43016
Carnegie Hall Blvd 43016
Carnoustie Cir & Ct 43017
Carrick Ct 43017
Carrigan Ridge Ct & Dr 43017
Carrowmoor Ct 43017
Carson Ct & Way 43017
Carson City Ln 43016
Cartgate Ct 43017
Cartney Ct 43017
Cartwright Ln E & N 43016
W Case Rd 43017
Cashel Ct 43017
Caspersan Ct 43017
Castlebar Ln 43017
Castlebay Dr 43017
Castleforbes Ct 43016
Castleknock Rd 43016
Castlestone Dr 43016
Catawba Pl 43017
Catmint Dr 43016
Cavalry Ct 43017
Cedar Branch Way 43016
Cedar Lake Dr 43016
Cedric Ln 43016
Celtic Ct 43017
Chaddington Dr 43017
Chaffinch Ct 43017
Chancery Dr 43016
Channel Ln 43016
Chapel Way Ct 43016
Charmonte Ct 43017
Charmwood Ct 43017
Chatelaine Dr 43017
Chatham Ct 43017
Chatterfield Dr 43017
Chedworth Park 43017
Chelsea Park Dr 43016
Cherrybridge Ln 43016
Cherylbrook Ln 43017
Chesley Ct & Rd 43017
Chetwood Pl 43017
Chippenham Dr 43016
Chippenhook Ct 43016
Chippewa Falls St 43016
Chiron Ct 43016
Christie Chapel Rd 43017
Claddaugh Ln 43016
Claire Ct 43017
Clark Ave & St 43017
Classics Ct 43017
Clayton Ct 43016
Clearfield Ln 43016
Cleeve Hl 43017
Clementine Way 43017
Clifton Ct 43016
Closeburn Ct 43017
Clove Mill Dr 43016
Clover Ct & Ln 43017
Clover Park Way 43016
Cobble Way 43017
Coffman Rd 43017
Colister Dr 43016

Collinford Dr 43016
Colt Ct 43017
Commerce Pkwy 43017
Common Good Ln 43016
Common Market Pl 43016
Concord Rd 43017
Conine Ct & Dr 43016
Conleth Cir 43017
Conley Ln 43016
Connolly Ct 43016
Conquistador Ct 43017
Coogan Pl 43016
Coopers Hawk Cir 43016
Cooperstone Dr 43017
Copper Creek Dr 43016
Copperhill Dr 43016
Copperview Dr 43016
Corazon Dr 43016
Corbins Mill Dr 43017
Corey Swirl Dr 43017
Corley Dr 43016
Cormorant Dr 43017
Corporate Center Dr 43016
Corsham Ct 43016
Cosgray Rd 43016
Country House Ln 43017
Courtier Ct 43017
Coventry Woods Ct & Dr 43017
Cowan St 43017
Crafton Ln 43016
Cragie Hill Ct 43017
Craginhall Ln 43017
Craigston Ct 43017
Crail Ct 43017
Craindow Ct 43017
Cramer Creek Ct 43017
Cranleigh Ct 43016
Cranston Dr & Way 43017
Craughwell Ln 43017
Crawley Dr 43017
Crescent Ridge Dr 43016
Creston Ct & St 43017
Crighton Dr 43016
Criterion Way 43016
Cromdale Dr 43017
Cross River Falls Blvd 43016
Crossbill Ct 43017
Crossgate Ct & Dr 43017
Crosshaven Dr 43016
Crosshaven Ln 43017
Crossing Ln 43016
Cruden Bay Ct 43017
Crystal Falls St 43016
Culross Ct 43017
Curragh Ct 43017
Curtis Knoll Dr 43017
Cutters Edge Ct 43016
Dale Dr 43017
Dalmore Ln 43016
Dalymount Dr 43016
Dan Sherri Dr 43016
Darby St 43017
Darry Ln 43016
Dartford Trce 43017
Dartshire Blvd 43016
Darylane Dr 43017
Dave Thomas Blvd 43017
Davenport Ln 43016
David Rd 43017
Davington Dr 43017
Deacon Ct & Dr 43017
Deer Run Dr 43017
Deercrest Ct 43016
Deeside Dr 43017
Delancy Park Dr 43016
Delburn Ave & Ct 43017
Delta Loop 43016
Dennison Ct 43017
Desert Ln 43016
Desmond Ct 43017
Devonwood Ct 43017
Din Eidyn Dr 43017
Dinglebay Ct 43017
Discovery Blvd 43017
Division St 43017
Dominick Ct 43017
Donatello Dr 43016
Donegal Cliffs Dr 43017
Donegan Way 43016
Donnally Ct 43016
Donnybrook Dr 43017
Doolin Dr 43016
Dornoch Ct 43017
Drake Rd 43017
Driscoll Ct 43016
Drumcally Ln 43017
Drury Rd 43016
Dry Creek Dr 43016
Drymen Ct 43017
Dublin Rd
- 4937-4937 43017
- 4939-5122 43017
- 5124-10898 43017
- 5191-5223 43016
- 5301-5321 43017
- 5375-5453 43016
- 5519-10899 43017

Dublin Arbor Ln 43017
Dublin Center Dr 43017
W Dublin Granville Rd 43017
Dublin Industrial Ln 43016
Dublin Park Dr 43016
Dublin Plaza Ln 43016
Dublin Village Dr 43017
Dublinshire Dr 43017
Duddingston Dr 43017
Dumfries Ct 43016
Dumfries Ct E 43016
Dumfries Ct W 43016
Dummerston Ct 43017
Dunabbey Loop 43017
Dunblane Ct 43017
Dundon Ct 43017
Dundrum Dr 43016
Dunglady Ct 43017
Dunheath Cir & Loop 43016
Dunkerrin Ct 43017
Dunlavin Way 43017
Dunleary Dr 43017
Dunleavy Ct 43016
Dunliam Pl 43017
Dunmere Ln 43017
Dunn Ct 43017
Dunniker Park Dr 43017
Dunnwood Ct 43017
Dunsinane Dr 43017
Dunskeath Ct 43017
Durkin Cir 43017
Durwood Ln 43016
Dyrham Park 43017
Eagle Ct 43016
Earlington Pkwy 43017
Earlsford Dr 43017
Earlston Ct 43017
Ebner Cir 43016
Ebonywood Ct 43017
Eckington Dr 43016
Eden Bridge Dr 43016
Edgebrook Dr 43017
Edgewood Cir & Dr 43017
Edinburgh Rd 43017
Egg Ct 43017
Eiterman Rd 43016
Elk River Dr 43016
Ellis Brook Dr 43016
Elmbridge Ln 43016
Elmfield Dr E & W 43016
Emberwood Rd 43017
Emerald Pkwy
- 4701-5097 43017
- 5099-5200 43017
- 5202-5298 43017
- 6000-6400 43016
- 6402-6598 43016

Emmet Row Ln 43017
Emmett Row Way 43017
Enfield Ct & Trce 43017
Enke Ct 43017
Ennishannon Pl 43016
Enterprise Ct 43016
Eppleworth Dr 43017
Erie Ct 43017
Erin Ln 43016
Erin Isles Ct 43017
Erin Woods Dr 43017
Ernest Way 43017
Essex Gate Dr N & S 43016
Essington Dr 43017
Falcon Ct 43016
Fallen Timbers Dr 43017
Falls Branch Dr 43016
Faulkner Way 43017
Fawnbrook Ct & Ln 43017
Fayborough Ct 43016
Fenian Ct 43017
Festival Ln 43017
Finbarr Ct 43017
Finlarig Dr 43017
Finnegan Ct 43017
Finsbury Dr 43016
Firehole Falls St 43016
Firenza Pl 43016
Fishel Dr N & S 43016
Fitzgerald Rd 43017
Fitzgibbon Ct 43017
Fitzwilliam Dr 43017
Flint Creek Ave 43016
Flynn Ct 43016
Flynn Ln 43016
Forest Knoll Ct & Dr 43017
Forest Run Ct & Dr 43017
Foresthaven Loop 43016
Forfar Ln 43017
Fossella Blvd 43016
Foxford St 43016
Franklin St 43017
Frantz Rd
- 5300-5498 43016
- 5500-5600 43017
- 5602-5698 43017
- 5700-5776 43016
- 5777-5799 43017
- 5778-5998 43016
- 5801-5999 43016
- 6001-6039 43017
- 6041-6045 43016
- 6047-6297 43017
- 6299-6300 43017
- 6302-6500 43017

Frawley Dr 43016
Friars Haven Dr 43017
Frobisher Ave 43017
Fulmar Dr 43017
Gabrielle Dr 43016
Gaelic Ct 43016
Gailes Ct 43017
Gairloch Ct 43017
Galway Dr 43017
Garden Grove Blvd 43017
Garden Hill Ln 43017
Gardengate Pl 43016
Gardenview Pl 43016
Garylane Dr 43017
Gavinton Ct 43017
Gillingham Way 43017
Gilmerton Ct 43017
Ginger Pl 43017
Gingrey Rd 43016
Girvan Lndg 43016
Glacier Ridge Blvd 43017
Gladesend Ct 43017
Glanmore Ct 43017
Glasgow Ct 43017
Glasin Ct 43016
Glassford Ct N & S 43017
Glen Meadow Ct 43017
Glen Tanar Ct 43017
Glen Village Dr 43016
Glenaire Dr 43017
Glenalmond Ct 43017
Glenamoy Cir 43017
Glenbarr Pl 43017
Glenbervie Ct 43017
Glencree Pl 43016
Glencullen Ct 43017
Glendavon Loop & Pl 43016
Glendon Ct 43016
Gleneagles Ct 43017
Glenfinnan Ct 43017
Glenliven Ct 43017
Glenloch Cir 43017
Glick Rd 43017
Gnarled Pine Dr 43016
Gold Leaf Ln 43016
Golden Pl 43017
Golden Cascade Dr 43016
Golden Rose Way 43017
Goose Falls Dr 43016
Gorden Farms Pkwy 43016
Gordon Way 43017
Grafton End 43016
Grand Dr 43016
Grandee Cliffs Dr 43016
Grandview Dr 43017
Grandwoods Cir 43017
Grange Hill Pl 43017
Grant Dr 43017
Grantham Ln 43016
Grassland Dr 43016
Graylake Ct 43016
Great Novel Ct 43017
Green Arbor Ln 43017
Greenbridge Loop N & S 43016
Greenland Pl 43016
Greenmont Dr 43016
Greenside Dr 43017
Greenstone Loop 43016
Greenstone Pt 43017
Greensway Loop 43016
Grey Abby Ct 43017
Grey Friar Way 43017
Guinness Ct 43017
Gullane Ct 43017
Gullway Bay Dr 43017
Gwynedd Ct 43016
Gylwyn Ct 43017
Haddington Ct & Dr 43017
Haddingtonshire Ln 43016
Haddler Ct & Dr 43016
Haddo Way 43017
Hagan Ct 43016
Halley Dr 43016
Hamden Ct 43017
Hampton Dr & Pl 43016
Hampton Green Pl 43016
Hanna Hills Dr 43016
Hanover Cir 43016
Hanover Square Dr 43016
Hansgrove Ct 43016
Hard Rd 43016
Harlan Ct 43017
Harmill Dr 43016
Harriott Rd 43017
Harvest St 43016
Harvest Oak Dr 43017
Hathaway Ave & Ct 43016
Hathaway Park Ct 43016
Haverhill Ct & Dr 43017
Havington Ct 43017
Hawick Ct N & S 43017
Hawks Nest Dr 43017
Hawksbury Ct 43017
Hawley Ct 43017
Hawthornden Ct 43017
Hayden Farms Rd 43016
Hayden Run Blvd 43016
Hayden Run Rd 43017
Haydens Crossing Blvd 43016
Haymaker Ln 43017
Heather Bluff Dr 43016
Heather Glen Blvd & Ct 43016
Heatherside Dr 43017
Heatherstone Cir, Ct & Loop 43017
Heatherwood Ct & Ln 43017
Heathstead Dr 43016
Henry David Ct 43016
Herald Square Pl 43016
Heritage Woods Ct 43016
Herring Run Way 43016
Hertford Ln 43017
Hewitt Pl 43017
Hichenco Dr 43016
Higgins Pl 43016
N & S High St 43017
Hildenboro Dr 43017
Hirth Rd 43016
Hitching Post Ct 43017
Hobbs Landing Dr E & W 43017
Holbein Dr 43016
Holiday Ln 43016
Holiston Ct 43016
Holly River Ave 43016
Hollyhead Dr 43017
Holyrood Ct 43017
Holywell Dr 43017
Honbury Ct 43017
Hopewell Ct & St 43017
Horseshoe Falls Dr 43016
Hospital Dr 43016
Hoss Ln 43016
Houchard Rd 43016
Hyland Dr 43017
Hyland Croy Rd 43016
Indian Hill Rd 43017
Indian Run Dr 43017
Inisheer Ct 43017
Inishmore Ln 43017
Inistork Ct & Dr 43017
Innisfree Ct & Ln 43017
Innovation Ct & Dr 43016
Inslee Rd 43016
Invergordon Ct 43017
Inverness Cir & Ct 43016
Inverurie Dr E & W 43017
Irelan Pl 43016
Iveswood Ct 43017
Ivy Branch Dr 43016
Ivygate Pl 43016
Ivystone Ct 43016
Ivyvine Blvd 43016
Jacana Dr 43017
Jacobsen St 43016
Jaymes St 43017
Jenmar Ct 43016
Jerome Rd 43016
Johntimm Ct 43017
Karrer Pl 43017
Karric Ln 43016
Karric Square Dr 43016
Kate Brown Dr 43017
Katesbridge Ct 43017
Kays Rd 43017
Keating Dr 43016
Keiler Ct 43017
Kellingsworth Way 43017
Kelly Dr 43016
Kendall Ridge Blvd & Loop 43016
Kendelmarie Way 43017
Kentfield Dr 43016
Kentigern Ct N & S 43017
Kenzie Ct & Ln 43017
Kestrel Way E & W 43017
Ketchum Ct 43017
Keystone Pine Way 43016
Kicking Bird Trce 43017
Kilbannan Ct 43017
Kilbannon Way 43016
Kilbirnie Ct 43017
Kilbrittain Ln 43017
Kildoon Ct 43017
Kilgour Pl 43017
Kilimanjaro Ct 43017
Killarney Ct 43017
Killary Ct & Dr 43016
Killie Ct 43017
Killilea Ct & Dr 43016
Killiney Ln 43016
Killochan Ct 43017
Kilmurry Ct 43017
Kingham Park 43017
Kingscote Ct 43017
Kingsmead Trce 43017
Kingstree Ct & Dr 43017
Kinross Ct 43017
Kinvarra Ct & Ln 43016
Kirkaldy Ct 43017
Kirkhill Ct 43017
Kirkwall Ct E & W 43017
Kittiwake Ct 43017
Laidon Ct 43017
Lake Placid Ln 43016
Lakehurst Ct 43016
Lakeshire Dr 43017
Lakeside Xing 43016
Lanark Ct 43017
Landsbury Ct 43017
Landview Dr 43016
Lanham Ct 43016
Lantos Rd 43016
Larbrook Ct 43017
Larchwood St 43016
Larne Dr 43016
Laurel Pine Ln 43016
Lea Ct 43017
Leatherlips Trl 43017
Leesville Way 43017
Leighlinbridge Way 43016
Leister Rd 43017
Leith Dr 43017
Leitrim Ct 43016
Lerwick Dr 43017
Leven Links Ct 43017
Lewis Ave 43017
Liberton Ct 43017
Libra Rd 43016
Lido Ct 43016
Liggett Rd 43016
Lilly Mar Ct 43017
Lime Creek Dr 43016
Limerick Ln 43017
Limestone Ridge Dr 43016
Linchmere Ln 43017
Lincoln Center Blvd 43016
Linden Ln 43016
Linke Ct 43017
Liscarroll Pl 43016
Lismore Ct 43017
Literary Ln 43017
Little Falls Dr 43016
Little Minch Ct 43017
Locbury Ln 43016
Loch Broom Cir 43017
Loch Dunne Pl 43016
Loch Leven Ct 43017
Loch Maree Ct 43017
Loch More Ct E & W 43017
Locherbie Ct 43017
Lockhart Ln 43017
Locust Hill Ln 43017
Lombard Way 43016
Longbenton Way 43017
Longbranch Dr 43017
Longford Dr 43016
Longleat Dr 43017
Longview Dr 43017
Lorne Scots Ave 43017
Lothian St 43016
Loughmoor Dr 43016
Luckstone Dr 43017
Lyme Ct 43016
Lynx Ln 43017
Lytfield Dr 43017
Macallan Ct E & W 43017
Macbeth Dr 43016
Macdermott Ct 43017
Macdonald Dr 43017
Macduff Pl & Way 43016
Macewen Ct 43017
Macintyre Dr 43017
Macken Ct 43016
Mackenzie Way 43017
Macneil Dr 43017
Macrenan Ln 43017
Madison Square Blvd 43016
Maidens Way 43017
Mallard Dr 43016
Mallard Mdws 43017
Manley Rd 43017
Manor Ct E & W 43017
Manor House Way 43017
Manteo Dr 43016
Marble Creek St 43016
Marion St 43017
Marist Ln 43017
Mark Ln 43016
Marlearl Dr 43017
Marmion Dr 43016
Marston Ln 43016
Martin Pl & Rd 43017
Maryhurst Dr 43017
Maxwell Way 43017
May Apple Ct 43016
Maynooth Dr 43017
Mcbride Ct 43016
Mccarthy Ct 43017
Mccotter Rd 43016
Mccrae Ct 43017
Mcdevitt Ct & Dr 43017
Mcdougal Ct 43017
Mcginty Ct 43017
Mcgrath Dr 43016
Mcgreevy Ct & Dr 43017
Mcinnis Rd 43016
Mcintyre Dr 43016
Mckitrick Rd 43016
Mcneven Ct 43017
Meadow Lark Ct 43016
Meadowhurst Way 43017
Meadowsglen Ct & Dr 43017
Meadowshire Ct 43017
Meaghan Dr 43016
Meath Ct 43016
Mediterra Pl 43016
Meehan Rd 43016
Melody Ln 43016
Melrue Ct 43016
Memorial Dr 43017
Merino Ct 43016
Mesa Falls St 43016
Mesquite Ct 43017
Metro Pl N & S 43017
Michaelkenney Ln 43017
Middle Falls St 43016
Middleboro Ct & Way 43017
Mill Bench Ct 43016
Mill Springs Ct & Dr 43016
Millbury Ave 43016
Millhouse Ln 43016
Millridge Cir & Pl 43017
Millrow Loop 43016
Milmichael Ct 43017
Missy Park Ct 43017
Mojave St 43017
Moliana Ct 43016
Monaghan Dr 43016
Monahan Ln 43016
Monifieth Ct 43017
Monsarrat Dr 43017
Montana Creek Dr 43016
Monterey Dr 43017
Monticello Ln 43016
Montridge Ln 43016
Moors Pl N & W 43017
Moray Ct 43017
Morlich Sq 43016
Morris Dr 43017
Morrisey Pl 43016
Mossy Creek Dr 43016
Mountjoy Ct 43017
Muirfield Ct, Dr & Pl 43017
Muirkirk Dr 43017
Muirloch Ct & Dr 43017
Muldoon Ct 43016
Mullane Ct 43016
Mulryan Dr 43016
Muncie Ct 43017
Murray Cir 43016
Myrick Rd 43016
Myrtlestone St 43016
Mystic Falls Dr 43016
Nadler Rd 43016
Nairn Ct 43017
Naples Ln 43016
Nassau Loop 43017
Natureview Ln 43017

Street	ZIP
Needham Dr	43017
Newbank Cir	43017
Newbridge Dr	43017
Newgate Ct & Rd	43017
Newgrange Dr	43016
Newkirk Ln	43016
Newtonmore Pl	43016
Nicholson Way	43017
Nolon Ct	43017
Noor Dr	43016
Noor Park Cir	43016
Norn St	43016
Norshire Ct	43016
North St	43017
Northcliff Blvd & Ct	43016
Northup Rd	43016
Oak Meadow Dr	43016
Oak Park Blvd	43016
Oak Wood Ct	43016
Oakbridge Ln	43016
Oakview Ave S	43016
Oconnell Ct	43017
Odessa Ln	43017
Oisin Ct	43016
Old Avery Rd	43016
Old Bridge Ln E & W	43016
Old Finglas Ct	43017
Old Oak Ln	43017
Old Pond Dr	43017
Old Prose Ct	43017
Old Spring Ct & Ln	43017
Old Wilcox Rd	43016
Olde Dublin Woods Dr	43016
Olde Sawmill Blvd	43016
Oldenburgh Way	43016
Olivia Ct	43016
Orchard Crest Ct	43016
Oshannon Rd	43016
Osweeney Ln	43016
Ottawa Pl	43017
Otter Ln	43016
N & S Oval St	43017
Paddock Falls Dr	43016
Palatas Pl	43017
Palmer Ct	43017
Park Mill Dr	43016
Parkbridge Ln	43016
Parkcenter Ave & Cir	43017
Parker Hill Ln	43017
Parkmoor Dr	43016
Parkridge Rd	43017
Parkside Xing	43016
Parkview Xing	43016
Parkwood Pl	43016
Parnell Ct	43017
Partridge Dr	43016
Passage Creek Dr	43016
Payton St	43016
Pebble Creek Dr	43017
Pebble Run Ln	43017
Penn Station Blvd	43016
Penneyroyal Pl	43017
Pennington Creek Dr	43016
Penrith Ct	43017
Pensworthy Dr	43016
Peregrine Pass	43016
Perimeter Dr	
5501-5687	43017
5689-6299	43017
6315-6325	43016
6329-6329	43017
6335-6397	43016
6399-6899	43016
Perimeter Lakes Dr	43017
Perimeter Loop Rd	43017
Perth Dr	43017
Pharoah Ct & Dr	43016
Pheasant Run Blvd	43016
Phoenix Park Dr	43016
Picardy Ct	43017
Pilar Ct	43017
Pintail Dr	43016
Pirthshire Cir, Ct & St	43016
Pisces Ct	43016
Pitlochry Ct	43017
Pleasant Dr	43016
Ponder St	43016
Pondloop Dr	43016
Ponset St	43017
Portofino Pl	43016
Post Rd	
5000-6334	43017
6336-6398	43017
6400-7200	43016
7202-7298	43016
Post Preserve Blvd	43016
Postlake Ct	43016
Pratolino Villa Dr	43016
Preston Mill Ct & Way	43017
Preswick Ct & Dr	43017
Primrose Ct	43016
Pueblo Ct	43017
Pyramid Falls Dr	43016
Quail Ct	43016
Quarry Ln	43017
Queens Park Dr	43016
Quetzal Dr	43017
Quin Abbey Ct E & W	43017
Rainbow Falls St	43016
Ravine Lk & Way	43016
Raymond Dr	43017
Raynor Ct	43017
Rays Cir	43016
Red Bay Ct	43016
Red Oak Ln	43016
Red Stone Loop	43016
Red Winesap Way	43016
Redan Ct	43017
Reddington Ct & Dr	43017
Redwater Dr	43016
Reflections Dr	43017
Renfield Dr	43017
Rensbury Ct	43016
Reserve Dr	43016
Rhapsody Dr	43016
Richens Dr	43017
Richgrove Ln	43016
Rimmer Ct & Dr	43017
Rings Rd	
4100-5499	43017
5500-7999	43016
Ringsend Ct	43016
River Forest Rd	43016
River Highlands Way	43017
River Knolls Pl	43016
Riverside Dr	
5430-6900	43017
6902-6998	43016
7000-8016	43016
8018-8098	43016
Riverside Glen Ct	43017
Riverside Green Dr	43017
N & S Riverview St	43017
Rob Roy Dr	43016
Robertson Ct	43017
Robinbrook Blvd	43017
Rockefeller Center Blvd	43016
Rockland Ct & Dr	43017
Romero Ct	43016
Roscoe Ct & Pl	43016
Roscommon Rd	43017
Rose Of Sharon Dr	43016
Rosegate Ct & Pl	43016
Roseto Villa Dr	43016
Rosewick Dr	43016
Ross Ave	43017
Ross Bnd	43016
Rossbury Ct	43017
Rothbury Ct	43017
Rothesay Ct & Dr	43017
Rothschild Ct	43017
Round Tower Ln	43017
Roundstone Loop & Pl	43016
Roundwood Ct	43016
Royal Arch Cascade Dr	43016
Royal Dublin Ct & Dr	43016
Royal Lytham Ct	43017
Royal Plume Dr	43016
Royalwood Dr	43017
Roycroft Ct	43017
Ruffed Grouse Cir	43016
Running Deer Pl	43017
Rush St	43017
Rushbury Dr	43017
Rushwood Dr	43017
Russell Fork Dr	43016
Rustic Falls Dr	43016
Ruth Ann Ct	43016
Saberly Ct	43016
Sable Ct	43016
Sachem Ct	43017
Sagestone Dr	43016
Saint Albans Pl	43017
Saint Andrews Dr	43017
Saint Anns Ct	43017
Saint Boswell Ct	43016
Saint Fillans Ct E & W	43017
Saint Mel Cir	43017
Salt River St	43016
Saltcoats Ct	43017
Saltergate Dr	43016
Samberly Rd	43016
Sanbrooke Rd	43016
Sandown Ln	43016
Sandwich Ct	43016
Sandy Rings Ln	43016
Sandymount Dr	43016
Santa Anita St	43016
Santori Ln	43016
Sarahurst Dr	43016
Sarbury Ct & Dr	43016
Satterbury Ct	43016
Satterton Cir	43016
Sawdust Ln	43017
Sawmill Rd	
5000-6357	43017
6359-6999	43016
7001-7467	43016
7469-8154	43016
8156-8198	43016
Sawmill Commons Ln	43016
Sawmill Forest Ave	43016
Sawmill Meadows Ave	43016
Sawmill Park Dr	43017
Sawmill Ridge Dr	43016
Saybrook Ct	43017
Scarlino St N & S	43016
Scenic Edge Blvd	43017
Scherers Pl	43016
Schoolcraft Dr	43017
Schoolway Ct	43016
Scioto Rd	43017
Scioto Crossing Blvd	43016
Scofield Ct	43016
Scotia Ct	43016
Scotscraig Ct	43016
Scotsman Ct	43016
Scottingham Dr	43016
Scribner Way	43017
Seay Ct	43017
Seddington Ct	43016
Seddon Dr	43016
Sedgebrook Ct	43016
Selbourne Ct	43016
Sells Mill Dr	43016
Selsdon Dr	43017
Sentinel Falls St	43016
Serenity Dr	43017
Sethwick Rd	43016
Settlers Pl	43017
Settlers Rd	43016
Severhill Ct & Dr	43016
Shadeview Ct	43016
Shadmill Ct	43016
Shady Nelms Dr	43017
Shaftsbury Ln	43017
Shamrock Blvd	43017
Shamrock Ct	43016
Shamrock Ln	43016
Shanagan St	43016
Shannon Glen Blvd	43016
Shannon Heights Blvd	43016
Shannon Park Dr	43016
Shannon Place Ln	43016
Sharlene Dr	43016
Shawan Falls Dr	43017
Shawnmont Ct	43016
Sheehan Ct	43016
Shefford Pl	43016
Shelbyville Pl	43016
Shelton Ct	43017
Shermont Rd	43016
Sherwington Ct	43016
Shier Ln	43016
Shier Rings Rd	43016
Shireton Dr	43016
Shropshire Cir	43016
Shuford Dr	43016
Silver Falls St	43016
Silver Pine Pl	43016
Silver Rose Ct	43016
Silver Saddle Ct	43016
Silver Woods Ln	43016
Silverton Way	43016
Simfield Rd	43016
Simmswood Ct	43016
Sixpenny Cir	43016
Skyridge Dr	43016
Slateshire Dr	43016
Smokymill Ct & Rd	43016
Snowdrop Ct	43016
Somerset Way	43017
Sonnington Dr	43016
Sorrento Ct	43016
Southby Ct	43017
Southwick Dr	43016
Sovron Ct	43016
Spencerton Way	43016
Spirowood St	43016
Spotted Tail Ct	43017
Spring River Ave	43016
Springburn Dr	43017
Springridge Ln	43016
Springview Ln	43016
Squirewood Ct	43016
Staircase Falls Dr	43016
Stanburn Rd	43016
Stancrest Rd	43016
Stanley Steemer Pkwy	43016
Stanwick Ct	43016
Starford Dr	43016
Starkeys Ct	43017
Starmont Ct	43016
State Route 161	43016
Statham Ct	43016
Stearns Rd	43016
Stein Ct	43017
Stepping Stone Ln	43016
Sterling Woods Ct	43016
Stillhouse Ln	43016
Stillmeadow Dr	43017
Stockport Cir	43016
Stockton Way	43016
Stokemont Ct	43016
Stokeswood Ct	43016
Stone Circle Way	43016
Stone Lake Dr	43016
Stonechat Loop	43017
Stonefence Ln	43017
Stonehenge Pkwy	43017
Stonehurst Dr	43016
Stoneleigh Ct	43016
Stonemill Ln	43017
Stoneridge Ln	43017
Stonewall Ct	43016
Stover Ct	43017
Stowbridge Rd	43016
Stowmont Ct	43016
Strasbourg Ct	43017
Stratford Pine Ln	43016
Strathaven Ct	43017
Strathburn Ct	43017
Strathcona Ave	43017
Strathern Ct	43017
Strathmoore Rd	43016
Strathmore Ln	43017
Stratingham Dr	43016
Stratton Ln	43017
Strome Ct	43017
Suffolk Dr	43016
Sullivan Dr	43016
Sully Pl	43016
Summer Dr	43016
Summerhouse Dr E & W	43016
Summitview Rd	43016
Sumner Loop	43016
Sunart Ct N & S	43017
Sunbridge Ln	43017
Sundown Ct	43017
Sunlight Ct	43016
Sunningdale Ln	43017
Surrywood Dr	43016
Sutcliff Ct	43016
Sutter Pkwy	43016
Swansford Dr	43016
Sweeny Ct	43017
Sweetwood Ct	43016
Swickard Ct	43016
Sycamore Ridge Blvd	43017
Sylvia Dr	43016
Sylvian Dr	43017
Tain Dr	43017
Talbrock Cir	43017
Talladega Dr	43016
Tamarisk Ct	43016
Tamworth Ct & Pl	43017
Tanera More Ct	43017
Tantallon Sq	43016
Tantalus Dr	43016
Tara Hill Dr	43017
Tarrin Ct	43016
Tartan Fields Dr	43017
Tartan Ridge Blvd & Ct	43017
Tarton Cir & Dr	43017
Tauzin Ln	43016
Tayport Dr	43017
Tayside Cir	43016
Telluride Pine Way	43016
Tenbury Dr	43017
Terrazza North Ct	43016
Terrazza South Ct	43016
Terre Prince Ct	43017
Terry Lee Ct	43016
Tevis Ann Ct	43016
Thatcher Dr	43017
Thornhill Ln	43017
Tibbermore Ct	43017
Tillinghast Dr	43017
Tillmore Sq	43016
Timber Mist Ct	43017
Timberview Dr	43017
Timble Falls Dr	43016
Times Square Blvd	43016
Tipperary Ct N & S	43017
Tonti Dr N	43016
Torwoodlee Ct	43016
Touraco Dr	43017
Tower Fls	43016
Townsend Rd	43016
Traceyton Dr	43017
Trade Royal Xing	43016
Trafalgar Ct, Ln & Loop	43016
Trailpath Dr	43016
Trails End Dr	43016
Tralee Dr	43017
Tramore Dr	43016
Traquair Pl	43016
Tripoli Ct	43016
Tromley Ct	43016
Troutbrook Dr	43017
Tuckahoe Ln	43016
Tuller Pkwy & Rd	43016
Tuller Ridge Dr	43016
Tully Ct	43016
Tullymore Dr	43016
Tumbling Creek Dr	43016
Turfway Dr	43016
Turin Hill Ct N & S	43017
Turkey Legs Ct	43017
Turnberry Ct & Ln N	43017
Turvey Loop E & W	43016
Tuscany Dr	43016
Tuswell Dr	43016
Tuttle Rd	43017
Tuttle Commons Blvd	43016
Tuttle Crossing Blvd	43016
Tuttle Mews Way	43016
Tuttles Brooke Dr	43016
Tuttles Creek Dr	43016
Tuttles Grove Blvd	43016
Tuttles Pointe Dr	43016
Tuttles View Dr	43016
Tuttles Woods Dr	43016
Tweedsmuir Ln	43017
Twin Falls Dr	43016
Twin Oaks Dr	43016
Twonotch Ct	43016
Tynecastle Loop	43016
Ulster Dr	43016
Union Square Blvd	43016
Upper Metro Pl	43017
Vail Pine Pl	43016
Valley Stream Dr	43017
Vally Down Rd	43017
Vandeleur Pl	43016
Varwyne Dr	43016
Ventura Way	43016
Venture Dr	43017
Vessey Ct	43016
Village Pkwy	43017
Villas Dr	43017
Vineyard Haven Dr & Loop	43016
Viningbrook Dr	43016
Vinings Blvd, Bnd, Grv, Rdg & Vw	43016
Vinington Pl	43016
Vintage Ln & Pl	43016
Violet Veil Ct	43016
Virginia City Ln	43016
Vista Ridge Dr	43017
Wabash River St	43016
Wakeshire Dr	43017
Walden Cir & Ct	43016
Wall St	43017
Wallsend Ct	43017
Walton Dr	43016
Wareham Dr	43016
Waterford Dr	43017
Watervale Dr	43016
Waxen Dr	43016
Wealthy Ln	43016
Welland St	43017
Wellington Ct	43016
Wellington Reserve Ct	43017
Wellspring Ct	43016
Wellston Ct	43017
Welsh Abbey Rd	43017
Wendy Trail Ln	43017
Westbury Ct & Dr	43016
Weston Cir & Ct	43016
Wexford Woods Dr	43016
Wexler Rd	43016
Whigham Ct	43016
Whitecraigs Ct	43017
Whitegate Ct	43016
Whittingham Dr	43017
Wichita Ct & Dr	43017
Wicklow Ct	43017
Wigeon Ct	43017
Wilcox Pl & Rd	43016
Wildcat Falls Dr	43016
Wildflower Trl	43017
Wilford Ln	43016
Willington Dr	43017
Willis Rd	43016
Willow Grove Ln & Pl E, N & S	43017
Willow Run Dr	43017
Willowcove Ct	43016
Wilton Loop	43017
Wilton Chase	43017
Wiltshire Ct & Dr	43016
Winberry Creek Dr	43016
Winchcombe Dr	43016
Winchell Ct	43017
Windsor Dr	43016
Windwood Dr	43017
Windy Hill Ct	43016
Wine Tavern Ln	43017
Winemack Ln & Loop	43016
Wings Livery Rd	43017
Winnipeg Dr	43016
Winnoch Ct	43017
Winslow Ct	43016
Winters Run Rd	43016
Wisdom Ln	43016
Wismer Cir	43016
Wisteria Cir & Ct	43016
Woerner Temple Rd	43016
Wolcott Ct	43017
Wood Duck Dr	43016
Woodsview Xing	43016
Workingham Dr	43017
Worsham Way	43016
Worsley Ct & Pl	43017
Wryneck Dr	43017
Wuertz Ct	43016
Wyandotte Woods Blvd	43016
Wyler Ct & Dr	43016
Wyndburne Dr	43016
Wyndle Ct	43016
Wynford Dr	
6000-6200	43017
6201-6201	43016
6202-6202	43017
6203-6399	43016
Wynwright Ct & Dr	43016
Yellow Wood Dr	43016
Zachariah Way	43016
Zachary Ct	43017
Zetland Ct	43017

EASTLAKE OH

POST OFFICE BOXES MAIN OFFICE STATIONS AND BRANCHES

Box No.s	
5001 - 6020	44095
7001 - 7600	44097
8017 - 8099	44095

NAMED STREETS

All Street Addresses 44095

NUMBERED STREETS

All Street Addresses 44095

ELYRIA OH

General Delivery 44035

POST OFFICE BOXES MAIN OFFICE STATIONS AND BRANCHES

Box No.s	
All PO Boxes	44036

NAMED STREETS

Street	ZIP
Abbe Rd	44054
Abbe Rd N	
200-1100	44035
Abbe Rd S	44035
N Abbe Rd	
5000-5399	44035
Academy Ct	44035
Adams St	
301-397	44035
399-1299	44035
33600-33999	44039
Adelbert St	44035
Adele St	44039

Street	ZIP
Alameda Dr	44035
Albert St	44039
Albrecht Rd	44035
Alden Ave	44039
Alexander Dr	44035
Alexis Dr	44035
Allen St	44035
Amanda Ct	44039
Amaryllis Dr	44035
Amber Way	44039
Ambler Dr	44035
Andress Ct	44035
Antioch Dr	44035
Antlers Trl	44039
Antoinette St	44035
Antrim Rd	44035
Apollo Dr	44035
Apple St	44035
Apple Creek Dr	44054
Arbor Ave	44054
Archer Rd	44039
Ardola Ct	44035
Arlington Ct	44035
Arrow Ct	44035
Artemas Ct	44035
Asbury Ln	
1-100	44035
102-298	44035
9300-9499	44039
Ashfield Ct	44035
Ashfield Way	44039
Ashland Ave & Ct	44035
Ashton Pl	44039
Ashwood Dr	44035
Aspen Ct	44035
Aspen St	44039
Atlantic Ave	44039
Auburn St	44035
Augdon Dr	44035
Augusta Dr	44035
Aurensen Rd	44039
Autumn Ln	44039
Avalon Dr	44039
Avon Belden Rd	44039
Baetz Ct	44035
Bagley Rd	44039
Bailey Ct	44039
Bainbridge Rd	44039
Baldwin Ave	44035
Bank St	44035
Barbara St	44035
Barkwood Dr	44054
Barres Ln	44035
Barres Rd	44039
Barrington Ct	44035
N Barton Rd	44039
Bath St	44035
Bauer Cir	44039
Bayberry Cir	44039
Bayberry Dr	44035
Bears Paw	44035
Bechtel Rd	44035
Bedford Ave	44035
Beebe Ave	44035
Beechwood Dr	44035
Behm Dr	44039
Bell Ave & Ct	44035
Bellfield Ave	44035
Belmar Ct	44035
Belmont Ave	44035
Belton Dr	44039
Bender Rd	44039
Bennett Dr	44035
Bentley Dr	44035
Berkeley Dr	44054
Berkley Rd	44039
Berkshire Ct	44039
Berkshire Dr	44054
Berkshire Rd	44035
Bernice St	44039
Berwick Ct	44035
Bethesda Cir	44035
Betty Ln	44035
Beverly Ct	44035
Birch St	44039
Birchbark Dr	44035
Birchwood St	44035
Bird	44035
Blackbird St	44035
Blaine St	44035
Blake St	44035
Blanchard Dr	44039
Blanche Ave	44035
Bliss Pkwy	44039
Bluebird Dr	44035
Bluffstone Cir	44039
Bohannon Ct	44035
Bolton Dr	44039
Bon Air Ave	44035
Bond St	44035
Boston Ave	44035
Boulder Dr	44039
Bowling Green Cir	44035
Brace Ave	44035
Bradford Dr	44035
Braemore Dr	44039
Brandemere Ct	44035
Brandtson Ave	44035
Brandywine St	44035
Breck Ct	44039
Breckenridge Oval	44035
E & W Breezeway Dr	44039
Brenthaven St	44035
Brian St	44039
Briar Lake Dr	44035
Briarcliff St	44035
Briarwood Ct	44035
Briarwood Dr	44039
Bridge St	44036
E Bridge St	44035
W Bridge St	44035
Bridgeport Dr	
100-299	44035
36104-36110	44039
36112-36155	44039
36157-36159	44039
Bridgestone Dr	44039
Briggs Cir	44039
Brittany Ln	44035
Broad Blvd	44039
Broad St	44035
E Broad St	44035
Broadway Blvd	44039
Brookfield Dr	44035
Brooklyn St	44035
Brookstone Ln	44039
Brookvalley Dr	44039
Browning Dr	44039
Brownstone Ln	44039
Bruce Ln	44035
Brunswick Dr	44035
Bryan Ct	44035
Buckeye St	44035
Buckingham Dr	44035
Bullocks St	44035
Bunker Hill Ln	44035
Burlington Dr	44039
Burns Ave	44035
Burns Rd	
100-299	44035
39100-39399	44039
Burr Oak Ct	44035
Burrell Dr	44054
Buttercup Ct	44039
Butternut Park Ct	44035
Butternut Ridge Rd	
10801-10897	44035
10899-42699	44035
36000-38299	44039
Byington Ct	44035
Cadet Dr	44039
Calann Dr	44039
Caldwell Ave	44035
California Ave	44035
Calista Dr	44039
Cambridge Ave	44035
Cambridge Dr	44039
Cameron Ct	44054
Campagna St	44035
Canary Dr	44035
Canterbury Ct & Rd	44035
Capital Ct	44035
Cardinal Dr	44035
Cardinal Ln	44039
Carl Dr	44035
Carlene Dr	44054
Carlisle Ave	44035
Carol Ln	44035
N & S Carolina Dr	44035
Caroline St	44035
Carolyn Dr	44039
Carriage Cir	44039
Carriage Ct	44035
Carrington Ct	44035
Cary Rd	44039
Cascade St	44035
Case Ave	44035
Case Rd	44039
Catawba Ct	44035
Cattail Run	44035
Cedar St	44035
Cedar Branch Cir	44039
Cedar Brook Dr	44035
Cedarville Ave	44054
Center St	44035
Center Ridge Rd	44039
Centurion Dr	44035
Chaddwyck Ln	44039
Chadwick Ct	44039
Chapel Ln	44039
Chapman Ave	44054
Chapman Ln	44035
Charles Ct	44035
Charles Rd	44039
Chase St	44035
Chatham Cir	44039
Chaucer Ct	
100-299	44035
35200-35399	44039
Chelsee Pl	44035
Chennault Dr	44039
Cherry Bottom Gln	44035
Chesapeake Ct	44035
Chesapeake Dr	44039
Cheshire Dr	44035
Chesterfield Dr	44039
Chestnut St	44035
Chestnut Commons Dr	44035
Chestnut Ridge Rd	
31600-36912	44039
36913-36919	44035
36914-36920	44039
36921-39599	44035
Chipper Dr	44039
Clark Dr	44039
Clark St	44035
Clear Creek Dr	44039
Clemens Ave	44035
Clemson Ct	44035
Cletus Dr	44039
Cleveland St	44035
Clinton Ave	44035
Clover Dr	44035
Coach Light Trl	44054
Cobblestone Cir	44039
Cobblestone Rd	44035
Colgate Ave	44035
College Heights Blvd	44054
College Park Dr	44035
Colley Cir	44039
Colonial Blvd	44039
Colony Dr	44035
Colorado Ave	44054
Columbia Ave	44035
Columbus St	44035
Commerce Ct	44035
Commodore Cir	44039
Concord Ave	44035
Condor Dr	44039
Connecticut Dr	44035
Cook Ct	44035
Cook Rd	44039
Cooley Cir	44039
Cooper Ave	44035
Cornell Ave	44035
Cornell Blvd	44039
Coronado Ct	44035
Cottage Cir	44039
Cottonwood Crst	44039
Country Meadow Way	44039
Countryview Way	44035
Court St	44035
Courtland St	44035
Cozy Meadow Ct	44039
Creekfield Ct	44035
Creekside Dr	44035
Creekside Ln	44039
Crehore Ct	44035
Crestlane Dr	44035
Crestview Dr	44035
Crestwood Dr	44039
Cumberland Ct	44035
Daisy Ln	44039
Dakota Dr	44039
Dana Pl	44039
Danforth Ct	44039
Dartmouth Cir	44035
David Dr	
100-199	44035
33800-33999	44039
Davis Dr	44039
Day St	44054
Dayton Ct	44035
Debbie Dr	44039
Deborah Dr	44039
Debra Dr	44035
Deer Xing	44035
Deer Lake Dr	44039
Deer Run Dr	44039
Deercreek Ct	44054
Deercrossing	44054
Deerfield Ct	44035
Deerfield Meadows Ct	44039
Deerspring Ct	44039
Defiance Ave	44035
Delaware Ave & Cir	44035
Dellefield Rd	44035
Demas Ave	44035
Denise Dr	44039
Denison Ave	44035
Denny Dr	44039
Depot St	
300-399	44035
8200-8358	44039
Detroit Rd	
4700-5598	44035
4701-5599	44054
Devonshire Ct	44035
Dewey Ave	44035
Dewhurst Rd	44035
Dewy Meadow Ct	44039
Diane Dr	44039
Dickens Cir	44039
Dilworth St	44035
Dodge Ave	44039
Dogwood Ln	44039
Donna Ave	44039
Dorchester Ave	44039
Dorset Ct	44035
Douglas Ave	44035
Dowd Rd	44035
Downing Ave	44039
Drake St	44039
Driftwood Ct	44035
Drury Way	44039
Duffey St	44035
Duke Ct	44035
Durkee Rd	44039
Dyke Ave	44039
Eady Ct	44035
Eagle Cir	44035
Eagles Glen Ct	44039
Earl Ct	44035
Earlene Ct	44035
East Ave	44035
Eastern Heights Blvd	44035
Eastview Ave	44039
Edge Meadow Ct	44039
Edgebrook Dr	44039
Edgecliff Cir E & W	44035
Edgefield Dr	44035
Edgehill Dr	44035
Edgewood Ct	44039
Edgewood St	44035
Edison Ct	44035
Edward Ave	44035
Edwin Ave	44039
Egret Dr	44035
Elbe St	44035
Elder St	44039
Elizabeth Ln	44039
Elizabeth St	44035
Elm St	44035
Elma Dr	44035
Elmwood St	44035
Elva Dr	44039
Elyria Ave	44035
Elyria St	44039
Elywood Dr	44035
Emerald Dr	44035
Emerald St	44039
Emerson Ct	44035
Emily Ln	44035
Englewood Ct	44039
Erie St	44035
Erin Ct	44035
Eschtruth St	44035
Essex Pl	44039
Ethel Ave & Dr	44035
Euclid St	
100-199	44035
36000-36299	44039
Evergreen Blvd	44039
Evergreen Pkwy	44054
Fackler Ave	44035
Fairacres Ave	44039
Fairfield Dr	44035
Fairfield Ln	44039
Fairlawn Ave	44035
Fairmount Ave	44035
Fairwood Blvd	44035
Falcon Ct	44039
Falcon St	44035
Fallhaven Cir	44039
Fallingwater Dr	44039
Fawn Ln	44039
Faxon Pl	44035
Fern Tree Ln	44039
Ferris State Ct	44035
Fieldstone Cir	44039
Fieldstone Dr	44035
Filbert St	44035
Filimore Ave	44035
Finch Dr	44035
Findlay Ct	44035
Finwood Ct	44035
Firecrest Cir	44039
Fitch Dr	44054
Floradale Ct	44035
Floral Ct	44035
Floraline St	44039
Ford Rd	44035
Forest St	
1-99	44035
34300-34399	44039
Forest Glen Way	44039
Forest Park Dr	44035
Forest Wood Dr	44039
Fortune Ct	44039
Foster Ave	44035
Fountain Cir	44039
Fowl Rd	44035
Fowlers Run	44039
Fox Chase Dr	44035
Fox Hill Ln	44035
Fox Hollow Cir	44039
Foxboro Dr	44039
Frances Blvd	44035
Frances St	44039
Frank Ct	44035
Franklin Ave	44035
Franklin Dr	44039
Freedom Ave	44039
Freedom Ct	44035
Freeland Dr	44039
Fremont St	44035
French Creek Rd	44054
Fresno Ct	44035
Fuller Ct & Rd	44035
Fullerton Rd	44035
Furnace St	44035
Gail Dr	44039
Galaxy Dr	44035
Garden St	44035
Garfield Ave	44035
Garfield Blvd	44054
Garford Ave	44035
Garrett Dr	44039
Garvin Ave	44035
Gate Moss Oval	44039
Gates Ave	44035
Gatestone Rd	44039
Gateway Blvd N & S	44035
Gatewood Dr	44039
Gem Cir	44039
George St	44035
Georgetown Ave	44035
Georgia Ave	44035
Gerhart	44035
Getz St	44035
Gilbert Ct	44039
Gina Dr	44039
Gladys Ave	44035
N Glen	44035
S Glen	44035
W Glen	44035
Glen Dr	44039
Glendale Ct	44035
Glendale Rd	44039
Gleneagle Dr	44035
Glenwood Ct	44039
Glenwood St	44035
Gloria Ave	44039
Glover Ct	44035
Golden Eagle Dr	44039
Goldenrod Cir & Ln	44035
Golfway Trl	44035
Grace Ave	44035
Grace Cir	44039
Grafton Rd	44035
Grandview Dr	44035
Granite Ln	44039
Grant Dr	44039
Grant St	44035
Greenbriar St	44035
Greenview Dr	44035
Greenview Trl	44039
Greenway Dr	44035
Greenwich Ave	44039
Greenwood Ct	44035
Gregory Ave	44039
Grist Mill Dr	44039
Griswold Rd	44035
Gulf Rd	44035
Gull Dr	44035
Hadaway St	
100-499	44035
35300-35499	44039
Haines St	44035
Hall Rd	44035
Halle Cir	44039
Hamilton Ave, Cir & St	44035
Hamker Ct	44039
Hammer Ct	44035
Hampton Dr	44035
Hancock Ln	44035
Handyside Dr	44039
Harbor Dr	44039
Harding Ave	44039
Hardwood Dr	44039
Harper Ave	44035
Harris Ct	44039
Harris Dr	44039
Harris Rd	44054
Harrison St	44035
Hartford Dr	44035
Harvard Ave	44035
Harvard Dr	44039
Harvest Ridge Way	44039
Harwood St	44035
Haven Dr	44035
Hawks Nest Ct	44039
Hawthorne Holw	44039
Hawthorne St	44035
Haydens Arbor	44035
Hayes Ave	44035
Hazel St	44035
Hazelwood Run	44039
Hazelwood St	44035
Heather Brook St	44035
Heather Woods Dr	44035
Hedgerow Park Dr	44039
Helen St	44035
Hemlock Dr	44035
Henkle Ct	44035
Henry St	44035
Heron Cir	44039
Hersey Cir	44039
Hickory Cir	44035
Hickory Ln	44035
Hickory Trl	44039
Hidden Hollow Ct	44039
Hidden Tree Cir	44039
Hiddenview Ct	44039
High St	44035
Highland Ct	44035
Highland Dr	44039
Highland Park Dr	44035
Hillcrest Ln	44035
Hilliard Rd	44035
Hillsdale Ct	44035
Hilltop Cir & Dr	44035
Hoag Dr	44035
Hodge Ct	44035
Hollis Dr	44035
Hollow Tree Oval	44039
Holly Ln	44035
Hollywood Blvd	44035
Home Crest Dr	44039
Homer Ct	44035
Homesite Ct	44035
Honeycut Dr	44039
Honeysuckle Ln	44039
Hope Ct	44035
Howard St	44035
Howe St	44035
Humphrey Cir	44039
Hunter Lake Dr	44039
Hunters Crossing Dr	44035
Huntington Cir	44035
Hurd Dr	44035
Huron St	44035
Ichabod Dr	44039
Idaho Ave	44035
Idlewood Dr	44035
Illinois Cir	44035
Imperial Ct	44035
Indian Hollow Rd	44035
Indiana Ave	44035
Infirmary Rd	44035
Inglewood Pl	44035
Innovation Dr	44035
Invacare Way	44035
Ira Dr	44039
Irondale St	44035
Ironwood Ct	44035
Island Dr	44039
Island Rd	44039
Jackson Ave	44035
Jade Cir	44039
James Rd	44039
Jamestown Ave	44035
Jason Dr	44039
Jay Dr	44039
Jaycox Rd	44039
Jean Ct	44035
Jefferson Ave	44039
Jefferson St	44035
Jerrol Ct	44039
Jewel Cir	44039
Joanne Ct	44039
Jordan Ct	44039
Joseph Ct	44039
Kaiser Ct	44035
Kansas Ave	44035
Kaplan Dr	44054
Katherine St	44039
Keep Ct	44035
Kelly Ct	44035
Kenmore Way	44039
Kennedy Ct	44035
Kenny Brook Ln	44035

Kensington Oval 44035
Kenssington Dr 44039
Kent Cir 44035
Kentucky Dr 44035
Kenwood St 44035
Kenyon Ave 44035
Kerstetter Way 44035
Kevin St 44054
Keys Dr 44035
Kildeer Ct & Ln 44035
King St 44035
Kingsbury Dr 44039
Kingston Ct 44054
Kingston Dr 44039
Kipling St 44035
Lafayette St 44035
Lagrange Rd 44035
Lake Ave 44035
Lake Breeze Rd 44054
Lakeside Dr 44039
Landings Edge Dr 44035
Lark Ln 44035
Larkmont Dr 44035
Larkstone Pl 44035
Laundon St 44035
Laura Ct 44035
Laurel Cir 44039
Lavender Ct 44039
Lawrence Ct 44035
Leafy Mill Ln 44039
Leann Ct 44054
Lear Nagle Rd 44039
Leavitt Rd 44035
Lee Ave 44039
Lee Ct 44035
Leo Bullocks Pkwy 44035
Leona St 44035
Leslie Ave 44039
Lesnick Ct 44035
Levi Ct 44039
Lewis St 44035
Lexington Ave 44035
Lexington Way 44039
Libby Ave 44035
Liberty Ct 44035
Liberty Pkwy 44039
Lilac Ln 44039
Lincoln Ave 44039
Lincoln Ct 44035
Linda Ln 44054
Lindsay Ct 44035
Linwood Ct 44035
Lisa Way 44039
Little Flower Cir 44039
Livermore Ln 44035
Locust St 44035
S Logan St 44035
Loman Ct 44039
Longbrook Dr 44039
Longfellow St 44035
Longford Ave 44035
Longson Ave 44035
Lorain Blvd 44035
Lorain Rd 44039
Louden Ct 44035
Louisiana Ave 44035
Lowell St 44035
Loyola Dr 44035
Luanne Dr 44039
Lucas Ct 44035
Lucille Dr 44035
Lydia Cir 44039
Lyman Ct 44039
Maddock Rd 44035
Madison Ave 44039
Madison St 44035
Main Ave 44039
Majestic Dr 44039
Mallard Cir 44039
Mallard Dr 44035
Mallard Run 44054
Malone Ave 44054
Manchester Ct 44035
Manchester St 44039
Manning Cir 44039
Manning Ct 44035
Manor Dr 44035
Maple Dr 44039
S Maple St 44035
Maplewood Cir 44054
Marcus Dr 44054
Mardun Ct 44039
Marigold Blvd 44039
Mark Ct 44039
Market Dr 44035
Marseilles Ave 44035
Marsh Pl 44039
Marshs Ln 44035
Martha Ct & Dr 44035
Maryland Ave 44035
Massachusetts Ave 44035
May St 44039
Mcarthur Dr 44039
Mckinley St 44039
Meadow Dr 44035
Meadow Creek Oval 44039
Meadow Lakes Blvd 44039
Meadow Lane Ct 44035
Meadow Moss Ln 44039
Meadowfield Ct 44039
Meander Ln 44035
Melvyn Ln 44035
Mendel Ct 44035
Mercury Dr 44035
Metcalf Rd 44035
Miami Ave 44035
Michael Ln 44035
Michigan Ave 44035
Middle Ave 44035
Middlebury Ct 44054
Midvale Dr 44035
Midway Blvd & Mall 44035
Mildred St 44039
Mill Stream Cir 44035
Millenium Ct 44039
Miller Ct 44035
Miller Dr 44039
Mills Rd 44039
Mills Creek Ln 44039
Mills Industrial Pkwy 44039
Millwood Cir 44039
Minott Ct 44039
Misty Meadow Trl 44039
Mitchell Dr 44039
Mockingbird Ln 44035
Monica Dr 44039
Monroe Ln 44039
Monroe St 44035
Montgomery Dr 44039
Monticello Cir 44035
Moran St 44035
Morgan Ave 44035
Morgan Cir 44039
Morning Glory Ln 44035
Mosswood Cir 44039
Mound St 44035
Mount Vernon Ct 44035
Mulberry Ln 44035
Mulberry Chase 44039
Murray Ridge Rd 44035
Mussey Ave 44035
Myrtle Ct 44035
Naples Dr 44035
Nash Ave 44035
Nebraska Ave 44035
Nelson St 44035
Nesthaven Way 44039
Neufer Ct 44035
New Hampshire Cir 44035
New Haven Ct 44054
New Jersey Cir 44035
New York Ave 44035
Newport Ct 44035
Nicoll Dr 44039
Nightengale Ct 44035
Nikki Ave 44039
Noah Ln 44039
Noll Dr 44039
North St 44035
Northfield Dr 44035
Northrup St 44035
Northview Cir 44039
Northwood Ct 44039
Northwood St 44035
Norwich Pl 44039
Notre Dame Cir 44035
Nottingham Dr 44035
Oak St
100-899 44035
35100-35199 44039
Oakdale Cir 44035
Oakhurst Cir 44039
Oakley Green Dr 44035
Oakwood Cir 44039
Oakwood Dr
800-1100 44035
1102-1198 44035
5300-5499 44054
Oakwood St 44035
Oberlin Rd 44035
Oberlin Elyria Rd 44035
Ohenry Cir 44039
Ohio St 44035
Old Abbe Rd 44054
Old Colorado Rd 44054
Olive Ave 44039
Olive St 44035
Oliver Ct 44035
Olivet Dr 44035
Opal St 44039
Orchard Ct
2000-2299 44054
41600-41799 44035
Orchard Ln 44039
Oriole Ct 44035
Oster Rd 44054
Otten Rd 44039
Overbrook Rd 44035
Overlook Ct & Way 44039
Oxford Ave 44035
Oxford Ct 44039
Paradise Dr 44035
Paradise Way 44039
Park Ave 44035
Park Pl 44035
Park Trl 44039
Park Meadow Ln 44035
Parkhurst Dr 44054
Parkview Ct & Dr 44035
Parmely Ave 44035
N Pasadena Ave 44035
Patricia Ave 44039
Patricia Ct 44035
Patton Dr 44039
Paula Blvd 44039
S Pearl Ave 44035
Pearl St 44039
Pebble Ct 44039
Pebble Creek Ln 44035
Pebble Lake Trl 44039
Pebblebrook Dr 44039
Pelican Lake Dr 44039
Pemberton Dr 44035
Pendince Rd 44039
Penfield Ave 44035
Pennsylvania Ave 44035
Pennsylvania Dr 44039
Penny Ln 44035
Penrose Ct 44035
Pepper Ridge Run 44039
Pepperdine Dr 44035
Peregrine Way 44039
Perry Ct 44035
Persons Ct 44035
Phillips Ct 44035
Pilgrim Ct 44039
Pin Oak Cir
100-499 44035
5300-5599 44054
Pine St 44035
Pine Branch Cir 44035
Pinehurst Ave 44035
Pineview Cir 44039
Pinewood Dr 44035
Pitts Blvd 44035
Plantation Pl 44039
Plas Dr 44035
Pleasant St 44039
W Point Dr 44039
Poplar St
401-497 44035
499-899 44035
35000-35999 44039
Portia Ct 44035
Potomac Dr & Ln 44035
Prairie Moon 44039
Pratt Blvd 44035
Predarri Rd 44035
Preston St 44035
Princeton Ave 44035
Princeton Dr 44039
Pronesti Ln 44035
Prospect St 44035
Purdue Ave 44035
Quail Ct 44039
Quail Dr 44035
Quails Nest Ln 44039
Queen Anne Cir 44035
Queens Ct 44035
Quincy St 44035
Race Rd 44039
Rachel Ln 44039
Railroad St 44035
Rain Tree Cir 44039
Raleigh Dr 44039
Rambler Ave 44035
Randall Rd 44035
Rauscher Ct 44035
Raven Cir 44035
Ravenway Dr 44035
Reading Way 44039
Reaser Ct 44035
Red Pine Way 44039
Redington Dr 44039
Redwood Ct 44039
Reed Rd 44039
Reeve Rd 44035
Regency Ct 44035
Regent Dr 44054
Reserve Way 44054
Reublin Ct 44035
Revere Ct 44035
Revere Dr 44039
Revere Ln 44035
Rhode Island Dr 44035
Rhonda Dr 44039
Richmond Ct 44035
N & W Ridge Rd & St 44035
Ridge Circle Ln 44035
Ridge Plaza Dr 44039
Ridgeview Blvd 44039
E River Rd
2200-4999 44054
9500-39199 44035
W River Rd N 44035
W River Rd S 44035
E River St 44035
Riverdale Ct 44035
Riveredge Dr 44035
Riverside Ct & Dr 44035
Riverside Homes 44035
Riverwood Dr 44039
Robert Ct 44039
Robert Ln 44035
Robin Dr 44035
Rock Creek Cir 44039
Rock Point Cir 44039
Rockfern Ave 44039
Rocky Run Ct 44039
Ronald Dr 44039
Roosevelt Ave
100-399 44035
5200-5599 44035
Root Rd 44039
Rose St 44039
Rosealee Ave 44035
Rosebelle Ave 44039
Rosemere St 44035
Rosewood Ct 44054
Rosewood Dr 44035
Rosewood St 44035
Rush St 44035
Russia Rd 44035
Rustic Rdg 44039
Rutgers Ct 44035
Ryan Ct 44035
Saint Andrews 44035
Saint Charles Pl 44035
Saint Clair St 44035
Salem Ave 44035
Samuel St 44035
Sandelwood Ave 44039
Sandlewood Dr 44035
Sandpiper Ave 44035
Sandpiper Ct 44039
Sandstone Ln 44039
Sandy Ln 44035
Sandy Ridge Dr 44039
Santa Fe Ct 44035
Savannah Dr 44039
Saw Mill Dr 44039
Saybrook Dr 44039
Schadden Rd 44035
Schafer Dr 44039
School St 44035
Schoolhouse Ln 44039
Schueller Blvd 44054
Scotch Pine Way 44039
Scott Ct 44035
Sederis Ln 44035
Seneca St 44035
Shady Ln 44039
Shady Moss Ln 44039
Shaker Blvd 44039
Shaw Dr 44039
Shawn Dr 44039
Shear St 44035
Shelly Ave 44039
Sheriff St 44035
Sherman St 44035
Sherwood Dr 44035
Sicily Dr 44039
Skylark Ct 44035
Skyline Dr 44035
Smith Ct
1-99 44035
5100-5199 44054
Soaring Ct 44039
Somerset Ct 44039
Sommer Way 44035
Sonesta Ave 44035
Song Bird St 44035
Songbird Ln 44039
Sourbrook Ln 44039
Southwood Dr 44035
Spencer Ct 44039
Sprague Rd 44039
Spring St 44035
Springbrook Cir 44035
Springdale Dr 44039
Springwood Ct 44039
Spruce St
100-399 44035
401-999 44035
35100-35199 44039
Spruce Pine Way 44039
Spyglass Dr 44035
Squire St 44035
Stafford Dr 44035
Stanford Ave 44035
Stang Rd 44035
Stargate Dr 44035
Starling Ct 44035
State St 44035
Steelton St 44035
Steinbeck Ct 44039
Stevens Ct 44035
Still Water Blvd 44035
Stone Creek Dr 44039
Stonebriar Ln 44039
Stonegate Cir 44039
Stonehedge Dr 44035
Stoney Brook Dr 44035
Stoney Lake Dr 44039
Stoney Meadow Dr 44039
Stoney Ridge Rd 44039
Stradford Ct 44039
Sturbridge Ct 44054
Sugar Ln 44035
Sugar Creek Ln 44039
Sugar Ridge Rd 44039
Sullivan Dr 44039
Summerset Dr 44035
Sumner St
200-399 44035
4500-4599 44054
Sun Meadow Ct 44039
Sunflower Ln 44039
Sunset Ct 44035
Sussex Dr 44035
Sweetbriar Ct 44039
Sycamore St
600-899 44035
35500-35599 44039
Syracuse Ct 44035
Taft Ave 44035
Tail Feather Dr 44039
Talon Way 44039
Tanager Ct 44039
Tannery St 44035
Tarry Ln 44035
Tattersal Ct 44035
Taylor Ct 44054
Taylor Pkwy
37800-38599 44039
38600-39499 44035
Taylor St 44035
Teal St 44035
Tedman Ct 44035
Telegraph Rd 44035
Temple Ct 44035
Tennessee Ave 44035
Ternes Ln 44035
Terrell Dr 44039
Thornwood St 44035
Tillotson St 44035
Timber Edge Dr 44039
Timber Ridge Dr 44035
Timberlane Dr 44035
Timothy St 44039
Topaz St 44039
Trails End Ct 44054
Transportation Dr 44054
Tree Moss Ln 44039
Tremont St 44035
Tucker Dr 44039
Tulane Ct 44035
Turner Blvd & St 44035
Tuscarawas St 44035
Twin Lakes Dr 44035
Tyler St 44035
Unionville Dr 44039
University Ave 44035
Valley Blvd 44035
Valley Forge Cir & Ln 44035
Vanderbilt Ct 44035
Vassar Ave 44035
Vermont Rd 44035
Vernon Hl 44039
Victoria Ct 44035
Victoria Ln 44039
Victory Ln 44039
Villanova Cir 44035
Virginia Ave 44035
Vista Ct 44035
Vista Lake Way 44039
Wainwright St 44039
Wakefield Run 44039
Walker Dr 44039
Wallace Blvd 44039
Walnut Ave 44054
Walnut Ct 44039
Walnut St 44035
Wanda St 44035
Warblers Ln 44039
Warden Ave 44035
Warren Ave 44035
Warwick Ct 44035
Washington Ave 44035
Washington Blvd 44039
Water St 44035
Waterford Cir & Dr 44035
Waters Edge Dr 44035
Watson Ave 44039
Waverly St 44035
Wayne St 44035
Weatherstone Dr 44039
Wedgewood Ave 44035
Weller Rd 44035
Wesley Ave 44035
Wesleyan Ct 44035
West Ave 44035
Westfield Dr 44039
Westin Way 44035
Westminister Ave 44039
Westminster Way 44035
Westmont Dr 44054
Westwood Dr 44039
Wheaton Dr 44054
Wheaton Pl 44039
White Ave & Ct 44035
White Oak Dr 44035
White Oak Way 44039
White Pine Way 44039
Whitman Blvd 44035
Wil Lou Ln 44039
Wilbur St 44035
Wilder Ave 44035
Wildlife Trl 44039
Wildwood Pl 44035
Williams St 44035
Willow Brook Ln 44039
Willow Haven Dr 44035
Willow Park Rd 44035
Willys Dr 44039
Wilshire Ct 44035
Winckles St 44035
Windbrook Ct 44035
Windemere Pl 44039
Windgate Dr 44035
Windsford Cir 44039
Windsor Dr
200-499 44035
5000-5138 44039
5140-5199 44039
Windward Dr 44035
Winson Cir 44039
Winthrop Dr 44035
Wisconsin Cir 44035
Wolf Ct 44035
Wood St
500-799 44035
35200-35799 44039
Woodbine St 44039
Woodbridge Ct 44039
Woodbury St 44035
Woodcrest Ct 44035
Woodford Ave 44035
Woodhaven Cir 44039
Woodhill Dr 44035
Woodland Ave 44035
Woodland Dr 44039
Woodland Way 44039
Woodlawn Dr 44039
Woodridge Ct 44039
Woodridge Dr 44035
Woodside Dr 44035
Woodsledge Dr 44039
Woodspring Cir 44039
Woodstone Cir 44039
Woodview Dr 44035
Wooster St 44035
Wren Cir 44035
Wren Haven St 44039
Wurst Ct 44035
Wyllys Dr 44039
Wynn Ave 44035
Xavier Ct 44039
Xavier St 44035
Yale Ave 44035
Yellowtail Ln 44039
York Cres 44039
Yorkshire Ct 44035
Yorktown Ln 44035
Yunker Ct 44035

NUMBERED STREETS

All Street Addresses 44035

EUCLID OH

POST OFFICE BOXES MAIN OFFICE STATIONS AND BRANCHES

Box No.s
17001 - 17538 44117
23002 - 23559 44123
32001 - 32714 44132
178000 - 178099 44117
328000 - 328099 44132

NAMED STREETS

Aaron Dr 44132
Alberton Rd 44123
Algonquin Rd 44117
Arbor Ave 44123
Ardwell Dr 44123
Arms Ave 44123
Babbitt Rd
201-297 44123
299-999 44123
1100-1599 44132
Ball Ave 44123
Beachland Dr 44123
Beachview Dr 44117
Beckford Ave 44123
Beech Dr 44132
Bennington Hamlet Cir 44123
Benton Ave 44132
Beverly Hills Dr 44117
Birch Ave 44132
Blackfoot Ave 44117
Blackstone Ave 44123
Bliss Ln 44123
Braeburn Park Dr 44117
Breckenridge Dr 44117
Briardale Ave
24101-24199 44123
25100-26599 44132
Brookdale Ln 44117
Bruce Ave 44123
Brush Ave 44132
Buckner Dr 44123
Buena Vista Dr 44117
Cameron Ave 44132
Caswell Ct 44132
Cedar Ct 44117
Century Corners Pkwy 44132
Champ Dr 44117
Chardon Rd 44117
Chatworth Dr 44117
Clearview Dr 44123
Colbourne Rd 44123
Concordia Dr 44117
Coolidge Dr 44132
Coulter Ave 44117
Crescent Dr 44117
Crystal Ave 44123
Dansy Dr 44117
Dawn Dr 44117
Deanna Ct 44123
Delaware Ct & Dr 44117
Devoe Ave 44123
Dille Rd 44117
Drakefield Ave
24701-24999 44123
25100-27199 44132
Eastbrook Dr 44132
Edgecliff Dr
19500-19599 44119
19601-19699 44119
20000-22799 44123
25500-27199 44132
27201-27299 44132
Effingham Blvd 44117
Elinore Ave 44132
Elmwood Dr 44123
Elsmere Dr 44117
Euclid Ave
18900-25599 44117
25601-25697 44132
25699-28099 44132
Euclid Square Mall 44132
Fairlawn Dr 44117
Farringdon Ave
23301-23697 44123
23699-24999 44123
25000-27199 44132
Fisher Rd 44117
Forest Dr 44117
Forestview Ave 44132
Fox Ave 44123
Fuller Ave 44123
Fullerwood Dr 44132
Garden Dr 44123
Gary Ave 44132
Gay St 44123
Genesee Rd 44117
Gilchrist Dr 44132
Gleashig Ave 44132
Glen Russ Ln 44117
Glenbrook Blvd 44117
Glenforest Rd 44123
Glenridge Rd 44117
Grand Blvd 44117
Green Oak Dr 44117
Greenwood Rd 44117
Hadden Rd 44117
Hall Ct 44132
Halle Dr 44132
Hartland Dr 44123
Hawthorne Dr 44117
Hemlock Dr 44132
Hickory Ct 44132
Hillandale Dr 44132
Hillcrest Dr 44117
Idlehurst Dr 44117
Ivan Ave 44123
Kapel Dr 44117
Karen Dr 44117
Kathy Dr 44117
Kennison Ave 44123
Kenwood Dr 44123
Knuth Ave 44132
Lake Edge Dr 44123
Lake Shore Blvd
18600-18698 44119
20000-24999 44123
25000-28299 44132
S Lake Shore Blvd 44123
N Lakeland Blvd 44132
Lakemont Ave 44123
Leslie Ave 44132
Linda Dr 44117
Lloyd Rd 44132
Luikart Dr 44123
Magnolia Dr 44132
Major Dr 44117
Mallard Ave 44132
Maplewood Ave 44123
Markbarry Ave 44132
Marsdon Dr 44132
Mavec Ave 44123
Maydale Ave 44123
Metro Dr 44132
Miami Rd 44117
Miller Ave 44123
Mills Ave 44132
Milton Dr 44123
Morris Ave 44123
Natona Rd 44117
Naumann Ave 44123
Nicholas Ave 44123
Noble Beach Dr 44123
North St 44117
Oak Ct 44132
Oakham Rd 44117
Oakhill Dr 44117
Oriole Ave 44132
Overlook Dr 44117
Pam Ct 44123
Paradise Ln 44123
Park Ct 44117
Parklane Dr 44132
Parkview Dr 44132
Parkwood Dr 44132
Pinehurst Dr 44117
Pontiac Dr 44117
Priday Ave 44123
Puritan Rd 44123
Rainesto Dr 44117
Rena Ct 44132
Richards Ave 44132
Roberts Ave 44123
Rockwell Dr 44117
Roger Dr 44123
Roseland Ave 44117
Russell Ave 44123
Sagamore Dr 44117
Saint Clair Ave
19001-19397 44117
19399-24099 44117
25500-25598 44132
Seabrooke Ave 44123
Seminole Rd 44117
Seneca Rd 44117
Shawnee Rd 44117
Sherwood Blvd 44117
Shirley Ave 44132
Shore Center Dr 44123
Shoreview Ave
24700-24998 44123
25100-27199 44132
Sidney Dr 44132
Spino Dr 44117
Stephen Ave 44123
Sulzer Ave 44132
Sunnycliff Dr 44123
Sycamore Dr 44132
Terindia Ave 44132
Tracy Ave 44123
Treadwell Ave 44117
Tremaine Dr 44132
Tungsten Rd
21600-22199 44117
25400-27799 44132
Upper Terrace Dr 44117
Upper Valley Dr 44117
Voelker Ave 44123
Walnut Dr 44132
Walworth Ave 44132
Wayne Ct 44123
Waynoka Rd 44117
Wells Ct 44132
Westbrook Dr 44132
Westport Ave 44123
Wildwood Ave 44123
Williams Ave 44123
Willow Dr 44132
Wilmore Ave 44123
N Wind Dr 44132
Wondergrove Dr 44132
Wyandotte Rd 44117
Yosemite Dr 44117
Zeman Ave
24700-24999 44123
25100-27199 44132

NUMBERED STREETS

E 191st St 44117
E 193rd St 44117
E 195th St 44117
E 196th St 44117
E 197th St 44119
E 199th St 44119
E 200th St 44119
E 200th St 44119
1000-1299 44117
E 201st St 44123
E 202nd St 44123
E 203rd St 44123
E 204th St 44123
E 204th St 44123
1400-1599 44117
E 205th St 44123
E 206th St 44123
E 207th St 44123
E 208th St 44123
E 209th St 44123
E 210th St 44123
E 211th St 44123
E 212th St 44123
1500-1599 44117
E 213th St 44123
E 214th St 44123
1500-1599 44117
E 215th St 44123
E 216th St 44123
E 217th St 44123
E 218th St 44123
E 219th St 44123
1301-1497 44117
E 220th St 44123
E 221st St 44123
E 221st St 44123
1300-2099 44117
E 222nd St
200-208 44123
1000-1599 44117
E 223rd St
800-999 44123
1800-1899 44117
E 224th St
1-999 44123
1900-2099 44117
E 225th St
900-999 44123
1800-1899 44117
E 226th St 44117
E 227th St 44117
E 228th St 44123
E 228th St 44123
1700-2099 44117
E 230th St
800-899 44123
1500-1799 44117
E 232nd St
200-999 44123
1700-1799 44117
E 233rd St
1-199 44123
1900-1998 44117
E 234th St 44117
E 235th St 44123
E 236th St 44123
1600-1698 44117
E 237th St 44123
E 238th St 44123
1700-1799 44117
E 239th St 44123
E 240th St 44123
1700-1799 44117
E 241st St 44123
E 242nd St 44123
E 243rd St 44123
E 243rd St 44123
1600-1799 44117
E 244th St 44123
E 245th St 44123
E 246th St 44123
E 248th St 44123
1400-1599 44117
E 249th St 44123
E 250th St 44132
1400-1599 44117
E 252nd St
1-199 44132
1400-1499 44117
E 253rd St 44132
E 254th St 44132
1500-1599 44117
E 255th St 44132
E 256th St 44132
E 257th St 44132
E 258th St 44132
E 260th St 44132
E 261st St 44132
E 262nd St 44132
E 263rd St 44132
E 264th St 44132
E 265th St 44132
E 266th St 44132
E 267th St 44132
E 270th St 44132
E 271st St 44132
E 272nd St 44132
E 273rd St 44132
E 274th St 44132
E 275th St 44132
E 276th St 44132
E 279th St 44132
E 280th St 44132
E 286th St 44132

FAIRFIELD OH

POST OFFICE BOXES MAIN OFFICE STATIONS AND BRANCHES

Box No.s
All PO Boxes 45018

NAMED STREETS

Abbot Dr 45014
Acme Dr 45014
Adams Cir 45014
Albemarle Dr 45014
Alec Dr 45014
Ambassador Ct & Dr 45014
Amherst Pl 45014
Ann Ct 45014
Annandale Dr 45014
Anthony Wayne Ave 45014
Antioch Dr 45014
Anzio Ct 45014
Apothecary Pl 45014
Applebury Pl 45014
N & S Applewood Ct & Dr 45014
Arcade Dr 45014
Arndt Ct 45014
Ascot Ct 45014
Ashley Briar Dr 45014
Astro Pl 45014
Auberger Dr 45014
Augusta Blvd 45014
Bach Ln 45014
Bacher Sq 45014
Bandelier Ct 45014
Banker Dr 45014
Banyon Ct & Dr 45014
Barkley Ct 45014
Bartel Dr 45014
Bassett Pl 45014
Becker Dr 45014
Beech Ave 45014
Beechwood Dr 45014
Bellavista Dr 45014
Bellbrook Ct 45014
Bellwood Ct 45014
Benchway Ct 45014
Bennett Dr 45011
Bent Tree Dr 45014
Benzing Dr 45014
Bibury Rd 45014
Bill Williams Dr 45014
Billy Cir 45014
Birch Dr 45014
Blackburn Ave 45014
Blackwell Ct & Dr 45014
Blair House Pl 45014
Bobmeyer Rd 45014
Boehm Ct & Dr 45014
Bohlke Blvd 45014
Bookbinder Pl 45014
Bordeaux Way 45014
Boymel Dr 45014
Bracken Pl 45014
Bradley Dr 45014
Braintree Ct 45014
Brians Ln 45014
Briarcliff Ct 45014
Brick House Ln 45014
Brittany Ln 45014
Broadview Dr 45014
Brockton Dr 45014
Brook Ct 45014
Bruce Dr 45014
Brushback Ct 45014
Bruton Parish Way 45014
Buck Ct 45014
Buckhead Dr 45014
Burgundy Pl 45014
By Pass 4 45014
Caddys Ct 45014
Calumet Way 45014
Camelot Cir, Ct & Dr 45014
Canary Ln 45014
Capitol Hill Dr 45014
Cardinal Ave 45014
Caribou Ct 45014
Carlin Ct 45014
Carlsbad Ct 45014
Carousel Cir 45014
Casa Loma Dr 45014
Casey Ct 45014
Castleton Dr 45014
Cavalier Ct 45014
Cedar Breaks Ct 45014
Cedarwood Dr 45014
Celadon Ave 45014
Central Dr 45014
Chablis Ct 45014
Chad Ln 45014
Chamois Dr 45014
Chapel Hill Dr 45014
Charlene Ave 45014
Charter Oak Dr 45014
Chateau Way 45014
Chatfield Dr 45014
Cherry Hill Dr 45014
Cherry Mill Ct 45014
Cheryl Dr 45014
Chesapeake Way 45014
Chesterfield Ct 45014
Chloe Dr 45014
Chowning St 45014
Christa Ct 45014
Christine Dr 45014
Cinchris Dr 45014
Cincinnati Brookville Rd 45014
Circle Dr 45014
Citadel Dr 45014
City Center Ln 45014
Claiborne Ct 45014
Clara Bea Ln 45014
Clemmer Dr 45014
Clemson Ct 45014
Clifford Dr 45014
Clifton Pl 45014
Clubhouse Ln 45014
Clyde Ct 45014
Coachmont Dr 45014
Cody Ct 45014
Cog Hill Dr 45014
Cogswells Grant 45014
Cole Dr 45014
Coltan Ct 45014
Commercial Dr 45014
Concord Mill Pl 45014
Congress Hill Ln 45014
Connie Ct 45014
Constitution Dr 45014
Coolbrook Dr 45014
Corporate Ct 45014
Corydale Dr 45014
Cosway Ct 45014
Countrydale Ct 45014
Creech Ln 45014
Creekside Dr 45014
Crestview Ave & Dr 45014
Crestwind Ct 45014
Crestwood Ln 45014
Criswell Ln 45014
Cross St 45014
Crossbow Dr 45014
Crystal Dr 45014
Cunagin Dr 45014
Cypress Ln 45014
W Dalton Ct & Dr 45014
Damon Ct 45014
Dan Ct 45014
Danbury Ln & Rd 45014
Danforth Dr 45014
Danube Ct & Dr 45014
Darby Ct 45014
Darby Heath 45014
David Pl 45014
Ddc Way 45014
Dee Alva Dr 45014
Deis Dr 45014
Delcrest Ct & Dr 45014
Dellbrook Dr 45014
Dennison Dr 45014
Depauw Dr 45014
Desales Ct 45014
Devon Ct 45014
Devonian Dr 45014
Distribution Cir & Dr 45014
Dixie Hwy 45014
Doe Ct 45014
Donald Dr 45014
Donbar Dr 45014
Doral Dr 45014
Doris Jane Ave 45014
Dorshire Dr 45014
Dow Ct 45014
Dubonnet Dr 45014
Duffy Ct 45011
Dunleith Ct 45014
Dusk Ct 45014
Eastgate Dr 45014
Edinburg Ct & Ln 45014
Edmorr Way 45014
Edna Ct 45014
Eland Ct 45014
Elda Dr 45014
Elk Ct 45014
Elm Hill Ln 45014
Embassy Dr 45014
Emerald Lake Dr 45014
Epps St 45014
Erding Ct 45011
Essex Orchard Station Dr 45014
Ethan Ct 45014
Evalie Dr 45014
Evans Ct 45011
Ewing Dr 45014
Factory Dr 45014
Fairdale Dr 45014
Fairfield Ave & Cir 45014
Fairfield Business Ctr 45014
Fairfield Commons Dr 45014
Fairgreen Cir 45014
Fairview Hill Ct 45014
Fairwood Ct 45014
Fall River Ct 45014
Fawn Dr 45014
Fenwick Dr 45014
Finch St 45014
Firestone Ct & Dr 45014
Flaig Dr 45014
Fleming St 45014
Fox Hollow Ct 45014
Friars Grn 45014
N Frieda Dr 45014
Gail Ave 45014
Gamay Ln 45014
Garrett House Ln 45014
Gelhot Dr 45014
Genevieve Pl 45014
Georgetown Rd 45014
N & S Gilmore Ct, Dr & Rd 45014
Glade Ct 45014
Glenmary Trce 45014
Glenna Dr 45014
Glenwood Ct 45014
Gloucester Dr 45014
Golfview Ct 45014
Gorsuch St 45014
Governors Ct & Dr 45014
Grand Teton Ct 45014
Gray Rd 45014
Green Dr 45014
Green Oak Ct 45014
Greenbriar Dr 45014
Greenwich Dr 45014

- Gregorian Dr 45014
- Griffin Ln 45014
- Groh Ln 45014
- Guenther St 45014
- Hagen Ct 45011
- Hallmark Ct 45014
- Hamilton Cleves Rd 45014
- Hannah View Dr 45014
- Happy Valley Ct & Dr 45014
- Hardell Dr 45014
- Harrowgate Hill Ln 45014
- Hassfurt Dr 45011
- Hazelwood Ct & Dr 45014
- Heffron Dr 45014
- Henesy Ln 45014
- Heritage Knoll Ter 45014
- Hexagon Dr 45014
- Hiawatha Ct 45014
- Hicks Blvd 45014
- Hicks Manor Ln 45014
- Hidden Hills Ct & Dr 45014
- Highcliff Ct 45014
- Highknoll Ct 45014
- Highridge Ct 45014
- E Highwood Dr 45014
- Hill Ave 45014
- Holden Blvd 45014
- Holiday Dr 45014
- Holliston Park Cir 45014
- Hollyhock Ct 45014
- Holyoke Ct 45014
- Homeward Way 45014
- Honeysuckle Pl 45014
- Horizon Ct 45014
- Horning Dr 45014
- Huber Trace Ct 45014
- Huhlhauser Rd 45014
- Hunter Ct & Rd 45014
- Ibex Dr 45014
- Independence Pl 45014
- Industry Dr 45014
- Ironwood Ct 45014
- Iroquois Ave 45014
- Ivanhoe Dr 45014
- Ivy Ln 45014
- Iwata Dr 45014
- Jamesfield Ct 45014
- Jamestown Pl 45014
- Jamie Dr 45011
- Janice Dr 45014
- Jefferson Ct 45014
- Jeffrey Pl 45014
- Joe Nuxhall Way 45014
- John Goode Way 45014
- John Gray Rd 45014
- Josie Ct 45014
- Joyce Park Dr 45014
- Judy Dr 45014
- Jupiter Ct & Dr 45014
- Kay Dr 45014
- King Arthur Ct 45014
- Kings Arms Way 45014
- Kings Ridge Sq 45014
- Kingsbury Rd 45014
- Kingsmont Ct & Dr 45014
- W Knoll Ct 45014
- Knollridge Ct 45014
- Knollwood Ct 45014
- Kohn Dr 45014
- Kolb Dr 45014
- Kraus Ln 45014
- La Forge Pl 45014
- Lake Circle Dr 45014
- Lake Cumberland Dr 45014
- Lake Erie Dr 45014
- Lake Huron Dr 45014
- Lake Manor Dr 45014
- Lake Mead Dr 45014
- Lake Michigan Dr 45014
- Lake Superior Dr 45014
- Lake Tahoe Ct 45014
- Lakeside Dr 45014
- Lamonte Dr 45014
- Lamplighters Ct 45014
- Lancaster Dr 45011
- Lark St 45014
- Larry Ln 45014
- Laurie Ct 45014
- Lauryn Meadows Ct 45014
- Layhigh Rd 45014
- Le Saint Dr 45014
- Lelia Ln 45014
- Leslie Dr 45014
- Levy Dr 45014
- Leway Dr 45014
- Lighthouse Dr 45014
- Limestone Dr 45014
- Lindale Dr 45014
- Linden Ct 45014
- Lindenwood Ln 45014
- Linwood Ave 45014
- Littlebrook Dr 45014
- Lohr St 45014
- Lombardy Dr 45014
- Long St 45014
- Loren Ln 45011
- Louise Ave 45014
- Ludwell Ln 45014
- Mack Rd 45014
- Mackview St 45014
- Magie Ave 45014
- Main St 45014
- Mantinte Dr 45014
- Maple Ridge Ct 45014
- Marcel Ct & Dr 45014
- Mardel Ct 45014
- Marlene Dr 45014
- Marsh Dr 45014
- Martha Ln 45014
- Matthew Pl 45014
- May Ave 45014
- Mccormick Ln 45014
- Mcgreevy Dr 45014
- Meadow Ct 45014
- Meadowlawn Way 45014
- Meadowview Ct 45014
- Mendingwall Way 45014
- Merlin Dr 45014
- Mesa Verda Ct 45014
- Miamidale Dr 45014
- Michael Ln 45014
- Mikehill Dr 45014
- Milky Way Ct 45014
- Millbrook Ct 45014
- Milona Ct 45014
- W Minster Dr 45014
- Mississippi Dr 45014
- Moeller Dr 45014
- Monastery Dr 45014
- Monica Dr 45014
- Moonbeam Ct 45014
- Morning Glory Dr 45014
- Morningside Dr 45014
- Mosswood Pl 45014
- Mount Vernon Dr 45014
- Muhlhauser Rd 45014
- Muirfield Ct 45014
- Muriel Ct 45014
- Murray Pl 45014
- Muskopf Ct, Dr & Rd 45014
- Myrtle Dr 45014
- Nantucket Ct 45014
- Napoli Ct 45014
- Narrow St 45014
- Nathanial Ln 45014
- Neptune Way 45014
- New Briton Cir 45014
- Newcomb Dr 45014
- Newkirk Dr 45011
- Nicholas Ct 45014
- Nickey Ct 45011
- Nicolson Cir 45014
- Niemoeller Dr 45011
- Nilles Rd 45014
- Northpointe Dr 45014
- Northview Cir 45014
- Nottingham Pl 45014
- Oak Creek Ct 45014
- Oak Knoll Ct 45014
- Oak Valley Dr 45014
- Oakbrook Ct & Dr 45014
- Oaktree Dr 45014
- Oberlin Dr 45014
- Office Park Dr 45014
- Old Duxbury Ct 45014
- Old Gilmore Rd 45014
- Old Tower Ct 45014
- Olde Station Ct 45014
- Olde Winton Ct & Ln 45014
- Olin Ct 45014
- Oliver Knoll Ct 45014
- Orchardglow Close 45014
- Ordinate Dr 45014
- Oriole St 45014
- Osborne Dr 45014
- Overlook Ct 45014
- Palm Springs Dr 45014
- Palmer Ct 45014
- Palmetto Dr 45014
- Panda Blvd 45014
- Park Pl 45014
- Park Meadows Dr 45014
- Parkland Hills Dr 45014
- Parkway Ct 45014
- Parliament Ct 45014
- Patricia Dr 45014
- Patterson Blvd 45014
- Pauline Dr 45014
- Peachtree Ct 45014
- Pebble Beach Ct 45014
- Pinehurst Ct 45014
- Pineview Ct 45014
- Pinnacle Peak 45014
- Planet Ct & Dr 45014
- Pleasant Ave 45014
- Pleasant Creek Ct 45014
- Pleasantdale Ter 45014
- Plover Ave 45014
- W Point Pleasant Cir 45014
- Polo Springs Ct 45014
- Polo Woods Ct 45014
- Ponderosa Dr 45014
- Port Ct 45014
- Port Union Rd 45014
- Potomac Dr 45014
- Primrose Ct & Ln 45014
- Production Dr 45014
- Profit Dr 45014
- Providence Dr 45014
- Quality Blvd 45014
- Raleigh Ct 45014
- Ramblewood Dr 45014
- Ramey Ln 45014
- Ramona Ln 45014
- Randolph Ct 45014
- Randy Dr 45014
- Red Oak Ct & Dr 45014
- Redford Ct 45014
- Redstart Dr 45014
- Redwood Dr 45014
- Remington Ct 45011
- Republic Dr 45014
- Reserve Ct 45014
- Resor Rd 45014
- Reswin Dr 45014
- Retha Dr 45014
- Richard Dr 45014
- Ricky Ct & Dr 45014
- Ridge Dr 45014
- Riegart Sq 45014
- Rita Mae Dr 45014
- E River Cir & Rd 45014
- River Valley Ct 45014
- Riverbend Ct 45014
- Robert E Lee Dr 45014
- Robin Ave 45014
- Roesch Blvd 45014
- Rolling Hills Blvd 45014
- Rosewood Pl 45014
- Ross Rd 45014
- Royal Manor Pl 45014
- Sable Dr 45014
- Saint Andrews Ct 45014
- Saint James Ct 45014
- Saint Lawrence Dr 45014
- Saint Thomas Ct 45014
- Salem Dr 45014
- Sammy Dr 45014
- Sando Dr 45014
- Sandstone Dr 45014
- Sandy Ln 45014
- Saturn Dr 45014
- Schiering Dr 45014
- Schroeder Ct & Dr 45011
- E & W Scioto Dr 45014
- Scottwood Dr 45014
- Security Dr 45014
- Senate Dr 45014
- Seward Rd
  - 7800-8999 45011
  - 9100-9899 45014
- Shady Ln 45014
- Shearwater Dr 45014
- Shenandoah Dr 45014
- Sherry Ln 45014
- Sherwood Dr 45014
- Shoal Meadows Ct 45014
- Sigmon Way 45014
- Simons Ln 45014
- Sioux Dr 45014
- Sir Lancelot Ln 45014
- Skydale Dr 45014
- Skylark Dr 45014
- Slade Dr 45014
- Sosna Dr 45014
- Southgate Blvd 45014
- Southhall Pl 45014
- Southview Dr 45014
- Southwind Dr 45014
- Spandrel Dr 45014
- Springbok Dr 45014
- Spruce Hill Dr 45014
- Spyglass Hill Ct 45014
- Stablegate Ct 45014
- Stadium St 45014
- Stardust Ct 45014
- N & S Staunton Dr 45014
- Stockton Rd 45014
- Stone Hill Dr 45014
- Stone Meadow Ct 45014
- Stone Mill Rd 45014
- Stonegate Ct 45014
- Stonewall Ln 45014
- E & W Stonington Dr 45014
- Story Dr 45014
- Suffolk Ct 45014
- Summit Ct 45014
- Sunflower Dr 45014
- Sunnyside Dr 45014
- Sunrise Ct 45014
- Sunshine Dr 45014
- Suwannee Dr 45014
- Symmes Rd 45014
- Tallawanda Dr 45014
- Tammy Ln 45014
- Tedia Way 45014
- Terrace Ct 45014
- Thrush Ave 45014
- Thunderbird Ln 45014
- N & S Timber Hollow Dr 45014
- Timberscent Cir 45014
- Tina Lee Dr 45014
- Today Dr 45014
- Tolley Wood Dr 45014
- Tollgate Ct 45014
- Tomahawk Ave 45014
- Town Ct 45014
- Trappist Walk 45014
- Travelle Ter 45014
- Tuckahoe Ct 45014
- E & N Turtle Creek Dr 45014
- Twilight Dr 45014
- Twin Lakes Dr 45014
- Union St 45014
- Union Centre Blvd 45014
- Valley Ct 45014
- Valley Forge Dr 45014
- Van Cleves Pl 45014
- Varsity Ct 45014
- Vassar Ct 45014
- Venice Blvd 45014
- Venus Ln 45014
- Vernon Ct & Pl 45014
- Veterans Dr 45014
- View Ct & Dr 45014
- Village Dr 45014
- Vinnedge Ave 45014
- Vinnedge Ct 45014
- Vinnedge Rd 45011
- Viola Ct 45014
- Vonderhaar Ct 45014
- Wabash Dr 45014
- Wade Mill Rd 45014
- Walker Ln 45014
- Walter Ave 45014
- Walther Dr 45014
- Waterbury Pl 45014
- Waterfront Ct 45014
- Weaver St 45014
- Weber Dr 45014
- Weiser Ct 45011
- Wellesley Pl 45014
- Wesleyan Ct & Dr 45014
- Wessel Dr
  - 400-699 45014
  - 700-798 45014
  - 700-702 45018
  - 701-799 45014
- Westwood Dr 45014
- Weymouth Pl 45014
- Whispering Hills Dr 45014
- Whitmore Ln 45014
- Whitney Ln 45014
- Wildwood Dr 45014
- Wilhelm Ct 45014
- Wilkens Ct 45014
- William Hensley Dr 45014
- Williamsburg Way 45014
- Wiltshire Blvd 45014
- Winchester Pl 45014
- Windage Dr 45014
- Windermere Ln 45014
- Winding Trails Ct 45014
- Winkler Dr 45011
- Winton Rd 45014
- Winton Meadows Ct 45014
- Wittenburg Dr 45014
- Woodbrook Ct 45014
- Woodcreek Dr 45014
- Woodland Park Dr 45014
- Woodmont Ct 45014
- Woodmoss Dr 45014
- Woodridge Blvd 45014
- Woodsfield Ct 45014
- Woodside Dr 45014
- Woodstock Dr 45014
- Woodtrail Dr 45014
- Wren Ave 45014
- Wyoming Ave 45014
- Wythe Ct 45014
- Yellowdale Dr 45014
- Yellowstone Dr 45014
- Yorktown Ct & Dr 45014
- Yosemite Dr 45014
- Zack Ct 45014

FINDLAY OH

- General Delivery 45839

POST OFFICE BOXES MAIN OFFICE STATIONS AND BRANCHES

Box No.s

- All PO Boxes 45839

NAMED STREETS

- Abbey Ln 45840
- Aberdeen Dr 45840
- Adams St 45840
- Alexis Pl 45840
- Allen Ave 45840
- Alpine Dr 45840
- Amelia Ave 45840
- Anna St 45840
- Apple Aly 45840
- Arapaho Dr 45840
- Arbors Pkwy E 45840
- Arizona Dr 45840
- Arrowhead Dr 45840
- Ash Ave 45840
- Ash Ridge Ln 45840
- Ashbury Ln 45840
- Autumn Dr 45840
- Avalon Ter 45840
- Avondale Rd 45840
- Baker Way 45840
- Baldwin Ave 45840
- Balsley Ave 45840
- Bank St 45840
- Barnett St 45840
- Bay Hill Dr 45840
- Bay Tree Dr 45840
- Bear Creek Ct 45840
- Beech Ave 45840
- Beecher St 45840
- Beechmont Dr 45840
- Beechwood Rd 45840
- Bell Ave 45840
- Bennett St 45840
- Bent Tree Dr 45840
- Bentbrook Dr 45840
- Bentley Ct 45840
- Bernard Ave 45840
- E & W Bigelow Ave 45840
- Birch Ct 45840
- Birchaven Ln 45840
- Bishop Ln 45840
- Bitterbrush Ln 45840
- Bittersweet Dr 45840
- Blaine St 45840
- N & S Blanchard Ave & St 45840
- Bliss Ave 45840
- Blue Bonnet Dr 45840
- Bluestone Dr 45840
- Bolton St 45840
- Bonnie Ln 45840
- Braemar Dr 45840
- Brand Manor Dr 45840
- Breckenridge Rd 45840
- Breezewood Ct 45840
- Brenda Ct 45840
- Brentwood Ct 45840
- Briarcliff Dr 45840
- Bright Rd 45840
- Bristol Dr 45840
- Broad Ave 45840
- Broadway St 45840
- Brook Lawn 45840
- Brookfield Cir, Dr & Hts 45840
- Brookhaven Rd 45840
- Brookside Dr 45840
- Brookstone Dr 45840
- Brookview Ct & Trl 45840
- Brookwood Dr 45840
- Brush Creek Dr 45840
- Burberry Ct 45840
- Burson Dr 45840
- Byal Ave 45840
- Byrnwyck Dr 45840
- Cain Ridge Ln 45840
- California Ave 45840
- Camden Dr 45840
- Camelot Ln 45840
- Candlewick Dr 45840
- Canterbury Dr 45840
- Capital Ln 45840
- Carey Ave 45840
- Carlee Ln 45840
- Carlin St 45840
- Carnahan Ave 45840
- Cedar Ave 45840
- Center St 45840
- Central Ave 45840
- Chagrin Vly 45840
- Chapel Dr 45840
- Charles Ave 45840
- Chase Rd 45840
- Chateau Cir, Ct & Dr 45840
- Cherokee Dr 45840
- Cherry Ln & St 45840
- Chestnut Ln 45840
- Christina Ct 45840
- Church Hill Dr 45840
- Cimmaron Ct 45840
- E & W Circle Dr 45840
- Claudia Ln 45840
- Clearbrook Cir & Dr 45840
- Clifton Ave 45840
- Clinton Ct & St 45840
- Cobblestone Dr 45840
- College St 45840
- Colonel Dr 45840
- Colorado Ave 45840
- Colt Dr 45840
- Commerce Pkwy 45840
- Concord Ct 45840
- Congress Dr 45840
- Connell Ave 45840
- Cord St 45840
- N & S Cory St 45840
- Cottonwood St 45840
- Country Club Dr 45840
- Country Creek Dr 45840
- Countryside Dr 45840
- County Road 139 45840
- County Road 140 45840
- County Road 161 45840
- County Road 169 45840
- County Road 172 45840
- County Road 173 45840
- County Road 18 45840
- County Road 180 45840
- County Road 193 45840
- County Road 212 45840
- County Road 214 45840
- County Road 216 45840
- County Road 220 45840
- County Road 223 45840
- County Road 236 45840
- County Road 248 45840
- County Road 252 45840
- County Road 26 45840
- County Road 313 45840
- County Road 330 45840
- County Road 37 45840
- County Road 40 45840
- County Road 45 45840
- County Road 54 45840
- County Road 7 45840
- County Road 75 45840
- County Road 8 45840
- County Road 84 45840
- County Road 86 45840
- County Road 9 45840
- County Road 95 45840
- County Road 97 45840
- County Road 99 45840
- Court Ruelle 45840
- Courtney Ln 45840
- E & W Cove Ct 45840
- Coventry Dr 45840
- Covington Ave 45840
- Cranberry Ln 45840
- E & W Crawford St 45840
- Cross Ave 45840
- Crosshill Dr 45840
- Croy Dr 45840
- Crystal Ave & Ln 45840
- Crystal Glen Blvd & Ct 45840
- Crystal Meadows Ct 45840
- Cunningham Dr 45840
- Cynthia Ct 45840
- Cypress Ave & Lk 45840
- Dakota Dr 45840
- Dalores Dr 45840
- Davis St 45840
- Dayton Ave 45840
- Decker Ave 45840
- Deer Creek Dr 45840
- Deer Lake Dr 45840
- Deer Landing Dr 45840
- Deer Ridge Dr 45840

Deer Run Rd 45840
Deer Trail Ct 45840
Deer Valley Cir, Ct & Ln 45840
Defiance Ave 45840
Delaware Ave 45840
Delmonte Dr 45840
Delwood Ave 45840
Distribution Dr 45840
Dogwood Dr 45840
Dold Dr 45840
Dorney Plz 45840
Douglas Pkwy 45840
Doune Dr 45840
Drake Ave 45840
Driftwood Dr 45840
E & W Dundee Dr 45840
Dunn Ave 45840
Durrell St 45840
E Eagle Dr & St 45840
Eagle Hill Ct 45840
Eagle Ridge Dr 45840
Early Dr 45840
East St 45840
Eastern Woods Pkwy 45840
Eastowne Park Row 45840
Eastshore Dr 45840
Eastview Dr 45840
Eben Ave 45840
E & W Edgar Ave 45840
Edgehill Rd 45840
Edgemont Dr 45840
Edgewood Dr 45840
Edinborough Dr 45840
Edith Ave 45840
Eggleston Dr 45840
Eisenbrandt Ave 45840
Elizabeth St 45840
Ellis Ave 45840
Elm St 45840
Elwood St 45840
Ely Ave 45840
Elyria St 45840
Emma St 45840
Enterprise Ave 45840
Esther Ln 45840
Eton Pl 45840
Evergreen Dr 45840
Expressway Dr 45840
Fair St 45840
Fairfield St 45840
Fairlawn Pl 45840
Fairmont Dr 45840
Fairview Dr 45840
Fairway Rd 45840
Falcon Lndg 45840
Fawn Dr 45840
Ferndale Ave 45840
Fernwood Dr 45840
Filmore St 45840
Findlay St 45840
Firestone Dr 45840
Fishlock Ave 45840
Flag City Dr 45840
Fleetwood Ave 45840
Flintlock Ct 45840
Floral Ave 45840
Foraker Ave 45840
Forest Ct, Ln & Park 45840
Forest Edge Dr 45840
Forest Lake Dr 45840
Forest Trail Dr 45840
Fostoria Ave & Rd 45840
E & W Foulke Ave 45840
Fox St 45840
Fox Hound Dr 45840
Fox Run Cir & Rd 45840
Foxbury Ln 45840
Foxfire Ln 45840
Foxmoor Rd 45840
Foxtail Dr 45840
Foxwood Dr 45840
France St 45840
Frank St 45840
Franklin Ave 45840
Frazer St 45840

Fremont Ave 45840
E & W Front St 45840
G St 45840
Garfield Ave 45840
Gay Ave 45840
Gayle Ln 45840
Geffs Ave 45840
George St 45840
Glen Rd 45840
Glen Haven Ct & Dr 45840
Glen Meadow Dr 45840
Glencoe Dr 45840
Glendale Ave 45840
Gleneagle Dr 45840
Glengerry Dr 45840
Glenmar Pkwy 45840
Glenn Ave 45840
Glenwood St 45840
Glessner Ave 45840
Gold Dr 45840
Golden Eagle Dr 45840
Goldenrod Ln 45840
Grace Blvd 45840
Graceland Ave 45840
Grand Ave 45840
Grant Blvd 45840
Gray St 45840
Greenacre Dr 45840
Greendale Ave 45840
Greenfield Dr 45840
Greenlawn Ave 45840
Greenwood St 45840
Greystone Ct & Dr 45840
H St 45840
Haley Wood Dr 45840
Hampton Dr 45840
Hancock St 45840
E & W Hardin St 45840
Harmon St 45840
Harrington Ave 45840
Harrison St 45840
Harvard Ave 45840
Hawthorne Rd 45840
Hazelwood Dr 45840
Heartland Ct 45840
Heathbrook Ct 45840
Heather Dr 45840
Heather Downs Dr 45840
Heatherview Ct 45840
Heatherwood Dr 45840
Hedgewyck Dr 45840
Hemphill Blvd 45840
Hickory Ln 45840
Hickory Grove Ct 45840
E & W High St 45840
High Point Ln 45840
Highland Dr 45840
Hilary Ln 45840
N, S & W Hill Cir & Trl 45840
Hillcrest Ave 45840
Hillshafer Dr 45840
Hillstone Dr 45840
Hilltop Dr 45840
Hilton Ave 45840
E & W Hobart Ave 45840
Hogan Dr 45840
Hollow Tree Dr 45840
Hollybrook Dr 45840
Homestead Dr 45840
Honeytree Ct 45840
Hope Ln 45840
Howard St 45840
Hulick St 45840
Hull Ave 45840
Hunters Creek Dr 45840
Hunters Gate Dr 45840
Huntington Dr 45840
Hurd Ave 45840
Huron Rd 45840
Imperial Ln 45840
Independence Dr 45840
Indian Lake Dr 45840
Industrial Dr 45840
Inglewood Ave 45840
Innisbrook Dr 45840

Interchange Ave 45840
Interstate Ct & Dr 45840
Inverness Dr 45840
Ironwood Dr 45840
Ithica Ct 45840
Ivy Ct & Ln 45840
Jacob Dr 45840
Jacobs Ave 45840
Jadlos Dr 45840
James Ct 45840
Jamie Dr 45840
Jefferson St 45840
Jennifer Ln 45840
Jessica Dr 45840
Joy St 45840
Juno Dr 45840
Jurnee Dr 45840
Karen Ct 45840
Katarina Ln 45840
Kathryn Ct 45840
Keith Pkwy 45840
Kellybrooke Ct 45840
Kennison Dr 45840
Kennsington Dr 45840
Kenwood Ct 45840
Kingswood Dr 45840
Kirk Dr 45840
Kirkwood Ct 45840
Knollwood Dr 45840
La Plas Dr 45840
Lagrange St 45840
N Lake Ct 45840
Lake Cascade Pkwy 45840
Lakebend Dr 45840
Lakebrook Dr 45840
Lakeland Dr 45840
Lakeside Ct & Dr 45840
Lakeview Pkwy 45840
Lakewood Dr 45840
Laquineo St 45840
Larkins St 45840
Laurel Ln 45840
Lawn Ave 45840
Leiser Ave 45840
Lesa Ave 45840
Lester Ave 45840
Lexington Ave 45840
Liberty St 45840
Lilac Ln 45840
E & W Lima Ave & St 45840
Lime St 45840
E & W Lincoln St 45840
Lincolnshire Ln 45840
Linden Ave 45840
Lippincott Ave 45840
Livery Cir 45840
Lockwood Rd 45840
Locust St 45840
Logan Ave 45840
Londonderry Dr 45840
Lonetree Dr 45840
Longmeadow Ln 45840
Lotze St 45840
Lye Creek Dr 45840
Lynn St 45840
Lynshire Ln 45840
Madison Ave 45840
Magnolia Dr 45840
Mahogany Trl 45840
E Main St 45840
E Main Cross St 45840
W Main Cross St
200-300 45840
229-229 45839
301-2299 45840
302-2198 45840
Manor Hill Rd 45840
Maple Ave 45840
Maplewood Dr 45840
Marathon Blvd & Way 45840
Marcelle Ave 45840
Marilyn Dr 45840
Marion Dr 45840
Markle St 45840
Marshall St 45840
Mary St 45840

Marys Glen Ct 45840
Massillon St 45840
Mcconnell St 45840
Mckinley St 45840
Mcmanness Ave 45840
E & W Mcpherson Ave 45840
W Meade Ave 45840
Meadowbrook Dr 45840
Meadowood Dr 45840
Meadowview Dr 45840
Medical Blvd & Dr S 45840
Meeks Ave & Ct 45840
E & W Melrose Ave 45840
Merriweather Dr 45840
Middle Ct 45840
Midland Ave 45840
Midwest Ct 45840
Milestone Dr 45840
Milton Ct & St 45840
Misty Oaks Dr 45840
Mohican Rd 45840
Mona Ln 45840
Monroe Ave 45840
Monto Ln 45840
Morey Ave 45840
Morrical Blvd 45840
Morse St 45840
Moulton Dr 45840
Mound St 45840
Muirfield Dr 45840
Nancy Ln 45840
National Ct 45840
Nebraska Ave 45840
Nevada Ln 45840
Newberry Dr 45840
Newell St 45840
Nicklaus Dr 45840
Norcrest St 45840
Normandy Dr 45840
North Ct 45840
Northcliff Dr 45840
Northgate Blvd & Ct 45840
Northparke Dr 45840
Northridge Rd 45840
Northtowne Dr 45840
Northview St 45840
Norwood Ave 45840
Nottingham Pl 45840
Nutmeg Ln 45840
Oak Ave 45840
Oak Shade Ln 45840
Oakdale Dr 45840
Oakland Ave 45840
Oakmont Dr 45840
Oakwood Dr 45840
Oakwoods Ln 45840
Oklahoma Ct 45840
Old Mill Rd 45840
Olive St 45840
Olney Ave 45840
Olympic Ct & Dr 45840
Omaha Dr 45840
Orchard Ln 45840
Oregon Dr 45840
Osborn Ave 45840
Oxford Dr 45840
Paige Ln 45840
Palm Dr 45840
Palmer Dr 45840
Paradise Ln 45840
Park Ave & St 45840
Parkside Pl 45840
Parkview Dr 45840
Parkway Dr 45840
Parkwood Dr 45840
Patriot Dr 45840
Payne Ave 45840
E & W Pearl St 45840
Pebble Beach Ct 45840
Pebblestone Dr 45840
Penbrooke Dr 45840
Penrose Dr 45840
Pepper Pike 45840
Pershing St 45840
Perth Dr 45840

Pheasant Run Ln & Pl 45840
Piedmont Ct 45840
Pierce Dr 45840
E & W Pine Ave 45840
Pinehurst Dr 45840
Pinewood Ct & Dr 45840
Plaza St 45840
Plum Creek Dr 45840
Plumwood Dr 45840
E Point Dr 45840
Portz Ave 45840
Prentiss Ave 45840
Prierree Dr 45840
Production Dr 45840
Prospect Ave & St 45840
Putnam St 45840
Quail Lake Rd 45840
Queenswood Dr 45840
Ra Nik Ct 45840
Rector Ave 45840
Red Hawk Ct & Dr 45840
Redfox Rd 45840
Redwood Dr 45840
Reimund Ct 45840
Remington St 45840
Rettig Rd 45840
Richard Ave 45840
Ridgeview Dr 45840
Rilla Rd 45840
Ringle Rd 45840
Ritchey Dr 45840
River St 45840
River Birch Ct 45840
Robinhood Ave 45840
Rockwell Ave 45840
Rockwood Dr 45840
N Romick Pkwy 45840
Rosemont Dr 45840
Rosewood Ave 45840
Rum Run 45840
Rush Creek Ct 45840
Rutherford Ave 45840
Saddlebrook 45840
Saint Andrews Ct & Dr 45840
E & W Sandusky St 45840
Santee Ave 45840
Saratoga Dr 45840
E & W Sawmill Bnd, Cv & Rd 45840
Scarlet Oak Dr 45840
Scenic View Dr 45840
Scott Ave & Ct 45840
Selby St 45840
Seneca Ave 45840
Shadow Ridge Rd 45840
Shady Ln 45840
Shaffer St 45840
Shawnee Forest Dr 45840
Sheffield Dr 45840
Sheridan Ave 45840
Sherman Dr 45840
Sherry St 45840
Sherwood Ave & Rd 45840
Shinkle St 45840
Shore Dr 45840
Sierra Ct 45840
Silver Creek Dr 45840
Silver Lake Dr 45840
Silver Pine Ln 45840
Silverstone Dr 45840
Silverwood Dr 45840
Skateway Dr 45840
Skye Dr 45840
E & W Skyeview Dr 45840
Smith St 45840
Smokies Way 45840
Snow Trail Dr 45840
Soldiers Dr 45840
South Ct & St 45840
Southcliff Dr 45840
Southshore Dr 45840
Southwood Ave 45840
Speedway Dr 45840
Springbrook Dr 45840
Springlake Dr 45840

Springmill Rd 45840
Spyglass Dr 45840
Stadium Dr 45840
Stall Dr 45840
Stanford Pkwy 45840
Stanley Ave 45840
State St 45840
E & W State Route 12 45840
State Route 235 45840
State Route 37 45840
State Route 568 45840
State Route 613 45840
State Route 68 45840
State Route 698 45840
Sterling Ct 45840
Sterling Hill Dr 45840
Still Meadows Ct 45840
Still Waters Dr 45840
Stonecliff Ct & Dr 45840
Stonecrop Dr 45840
Stonehedge Ct & Dr 45840
Stonehill Dr 45840
Strathaven Dr 45840
Strong Ave 45840
Sugar Maple Ct 45840
Summit St 45840
Sunhaven Rd 45840
Sunset Dr 45840
Sunwood Ave 45840
Surrey Dr 45840
Sutton Pl 45840
Sweetwater Rd 45840
Swing Ave 45840
Sycamore Dr 45840
Sylvan Cv 45840
Tanglewood Dr 45840
Tappan St 45840
Tarra Oaks Dr 45840
Tawa Creek Dr 45840
Taylor St 45840
Technology Dr 45840
Tecumseh Dr 45840
Terrace Dr & Ln 45840
Thimbleberry Dr 45840
Thornapple Ln 45840
Thornwood Dr 45840
Tiffin Ave 45840
Tiki St 45840
Timberstone Dr 45840
Timberview Ct & Dr 45840
Timberwood Dr 45840
Tioga Ave 45840
Torrey Pines Dr 45840
Township Road 10 45840
Township Road 100 45840
Township Road 101 45840
Township Road 107 45840
Township Road 108 45840
Township Road 109 45840
Township Road 123 45840
Township Road 125 45840
Township Road 128 45840
Township Road 130 45840
Township Road 135 45840
Township Road 136 45840
Township Road 139 45840
Township Road 142 45840
Township Road 145 45840
Township Road 168 45840
Township Road 173 45840
Township Road 174 45840
Township Road 179 45840
Township Road 180 45840
Township Road 182 45840
Township Road 190 45840
Township Road 201 45840
Township Road 202 45840
Township Road 204 45840
Township Road 205 45840
Township Road 207 45840
Township Road 208 45840
Township Road 209 45840
Township Road 212 45840
Township Road 213 45840
Township Road 215 45840
Township Road 227 45840

Township Road 228 45840
Township Road 229 45840
Township Road 230 45840
Township Road 232 45840
Township Road 233 45840
Township Road 234 45840
Township Road 236 45840
Township Road 237 45840
Township Road 240 45840
Township Road 242 45840
Township Road 243 45840
Township Road 244 45840
Township Road 245 45840
Township Road 246 45840
Township Road 25 45840
Township Road 251 45840
Township Road 253 45840
Township Road 254 45840
Township Road 255 45840
Township Road 292 45840
Township Road 295 45840
Township Road 296 45840
Township Road 37 45840
Township Road 40 45840
Township Road 43 45840
Township Road 44 45840
Township Road 45 45840
Township Road 48 45840
Township Road 49 45840
Township Road 50 45840
Township Road 51 45840
Township Road 53 45840
Township Road 58 45840
Township Road 67 45840
Township Road 72 45840
Township Road 73 45840
Township Road 74 45840
Township Road 76 45840
Township Road 77 45840
Township Road 79 45840
Township Road 80 45840
Township Road 81 45840
Township Road 82 45840
Township Road 83 45840
Township Road 84 45840
Township Road 89 45840
Township Road 94 45840
Township Road 95 45840
Township Road 98 45840
NW Township Road 99 45840
Treetop Ct & Dr 45840
Trenton Ave 45840
Turnberry Dr 45840
Tyler St 45840
E & W Us Route 224 45840
Utah Ave 45840
Ventura Dr 45840
Veterans Ln 45840
Villa S & W 45840
Vincent St 45840
Waddle St 45840
Wagner Way 45840
E & W Wallace St 45840
Walnut Ct & St 45840
Wanda Way 45840
Warrington Ave 45840
Washington Ave & St 45840
Waterford Way 45840
E Watermark Dr 45840
Weatherby Ct 45840
Wedgewood Dr 45840
Wellington Pl 45840
N & S West St 45840
Westchester Dr 45840
Western Ave 45840
Westfield Dr 45840
Westgate Dr 45840
Westland Dr 45840
Westmoor Rd 45840
Westshore Dr 45840
Westview Dr 45840
Westwood Rd 45840
White Birch Dr 45840
White Tail Run 45840
Whitespire Ct 45840

Wildwood Rd 45840
Williams St 45840
Willow Dr 45840
Willow Wood Ave 45840
Willowick Dr 45840
Wilson St 45840
Winchester Ct 45840
Windermere Dr 45840
Windsong Dr 45840
Windsor Pl 45840
Windstone Ct & Dr 45840
Winfield Ave 45840
Winter Pine Dr 45840
E, N & S Winter Woods Dr 45840
Winterberry Dr 45840
Winterhaven Dr 45840
Winthrop Dr 45840
Wolf Run 45840
Woodcliff Dr 45840
Woodhaven Pl 45840
E Woodland Trl 45840
Woodley Ave & Ter 45840
Woodridge Cres 45840
Woods Dr 45840
Woodside Dr 45840
Woodstock Ct 45840
Woodworth Dr 45840
Wyandot St 45840
Wyoming Trl 45840
Yarrow Ct 45840
E & W Yates Ave 45840
Yorkshire Dr 45840

NUMBERED STREETS

All Street Addresses 45840

HAMILTON OH

General Delivery 45011

POST OFFICE BOXES MAIN OFFICE STATIONS AND BRANCHES

Box No.s
1 - 5003 45012
13001 - 13660 45013
15001 - 15222 45015
137173 - 137180 45013

NAMED STREETS

S A St 45013
Abbot Run Ct 45011
Abilene Ct 45013
Acer Ct 45013
Adler Ave 45011
Ainsley Ln 45013
Alana Ct & Pl 45011
Alberta Dr 45013
Alberton Ave 45013
Alert New London Rd 45013
Alexander Dr 45013
Alexis Ct 45013
Alfreda Dr 45013
Algonquin Dr 45013
Allen Ave 45015
Allison Ave 45011
Allstatter Ave
1300-1399 45011
1800-2199 45015
Alpine Ct 45011
Alpine Dr 45013
Alsace Ln 45011
Alston Ave 45015
Alton Cir & Rd 45013
Amanda Ct 45013
Amarillo Dr 45013
Amberly Dr 45013
Amy Ct 45013
Amy Lynne Cir 45011
Anchor Dr 45011
Andover Ave 45015
Andrea Ct 45013
Andrew Ave 45015
Angie Ct 45011
Ann Elise Ct 45011
Annie Lou Dr 45013
Anthony Dr 45011
Apex Ct 45011
Appaloosa Ct 45011
Appletree Dr 45011
Arbor Ct 45013
Arbor Springs Dr 45013
Arch St 45013
Archery Ln 45011
Arlington Ave 45015
Armistead Dr 45013
Armo Ave 45013
Arrowhead Ct 45013
Arroyo Ridge Ct 45011
Ash Way 45011
Ashby Ct 45011
Ashe Knl 45011
Ashley Brook Dr 45013
Ashton Cir 45011
Ashview Ln & Pl 45011
Ashwood Knolls Dr 45011
Aspen Dr 45011
Aspen Valley Dr 45011
Aspenwood Dr 45011
Aston Ct 45011
Auburn Ln 45013
Audubon Dr 45011
Augspurger Ave & Rd 45011
Autumn Walk 45013
Autumn Hill Ln 45011
Avion Ave 45015
Avon Dr 45013
Azel Ave 45013
N & S B St 45013
Bab Ln 45013
Baccarat Dr 45013
Back Trail Ct 45011
Baffin Dr 45011
Bailey St 45011
Bainbridge Ct 45011
Baker Dr 45011
Baldwin Ct 45013
Balford Ct 45011
Bank Ave 45015
Baraboo St 45011
Barbara Ave 45013
Barbary Dr 45013
Barker Dr 45011
Barnard Ave 45013
S Barnum St 45011
Barrington Dr 45013
Bassett Trl 45011
Bayberry Ct & Dr 45011
Beagle Ct & Dr 45011
Beal Ave 45013
Beatrice Ln 45013
Beaty Ln 45011
Beaver Ct 45011
Beck Ct 45011
Beckett Dr & St 45011
Bedford Ave 45015
Beech Knoll Ln 45011
Beeler Blvd 45013
Beissinger Rd 45013
Bell Rd 45013
Belle Ave 45015
Belle Reeve Ct 45011
Belmar Ct 45013
Belmont Ave 45015
Bender Ave 45011
Benninghofen Ave 45015
Bentbranch Ln 45011
Berger Ct 45013
Berkley Dr 45013
Berkshire Ct 45013
Berry Blossom Ct 45011
Berrywood Ct 45011
Beth Ln 45013
Betsy Ross Ct & Dr 45011
Betty Dr 45013
Beverly Ct & Dr 45013
Bevington Ln 45013
Bicentennial Ct 45015
Billy Cir 45013
Bilstein Blvd 45015
Bingham St 45011
Birchley Dr 45011
Biscayne Dr 45013
Bishop Ave 45015
Black Rd 45013
Black Oak Dr 45011
Black Squirrel Trl 45011
Blackberry Cir & Ct 45011
Blackfoot Ct 45011
Blue Gill Ct 45013
Blue Heron Dr 45011
Blue Jacket Dr 45013
Blue Ridge Dr 45011
Blueberry Dr 45011
Bluegrass Ct 45011
Bluewood Knl 45011
Bobmeyer Rd 45015
Boehm Farm Rd 45013
Boeing Ct 45015
Bohne Dr 45013
Bonacker Ave 45011
Bond Ave 45011
Booth Ave 45011
Boulder Dr 45013
Boyle Rd 45013
Boysenberry Dr 45011
Bramble Ct 45011
Brandy Ct 45011
Brater Ct 45013
Breckenridge Ln 45011
Bremen St 45011
Brenda Dr 45013
Briar Hill Ct 45011
Briarwood Dr 45013
Bridgeport Dr 45013
Bridgeton Manor Ct & Dr 45011
Bridgewater Ln 45011
Brightwaters Ct 45011
Bristol Ct 45013
Bristol View Dr 45013
Brittany Ct 45013
Brofield Dr 45011
Bromley Dr 45011
Brook Hollow Ct 45011
Brookcrest Dr 45013
Brooke Hill Ct 45011
Brooke Meadows Ct 45011
Brooks Rd 45013
N Brookwood Ave 45013
Broshear Dr 45011
Brough Ave 45015
Brown Farm Dr 45013
Brunner Rd 45013
Bryant Ln 45013
Buckeye Aly & St 45011
Buckthorn Knl 45011
Buell Rd 45013
Buffalo Dance Dr 45011
Burns Rd 45014
Butler Ave & St 45011
Buttonwood Ct 45011
N & S C St 45013
Cabernet Ct 45011
Cadillac Dr 45013
Cain Ave 45011
Calan Ct 45013
Caldwell St 45011
Caledonia Ct 45013
Calusa Dr 45011
Cambridge Dr 45013
Camden Ct 45011
Cameron Pl 45013
Campbell Ave & Dr 45011
Canal Rd 45011
Canastota Dr 45011
Canyon Pass Dr 45011
Canyon Ridge Dr 45011
Capitol Cres 45013
Cardiff Ct 45011
Cardome Dr 45013
Cari Ln 45013
Carlisle Ave 45013
Carlton Dr 45015
Carmen Ave 45013
Carol Ct 45013
Carol Woods Dr 45013
Caroldon St 45013
Caroline Faye Ct 45011
Carriage Ct 45013
Carriage Hill Ln 45013
Carriage Oak Way 45011
Carrington Way 45011
Carrousel Blvd 45011
Carter Cir & Ter 45011
Carthel Dr 45011
Carver Pl 45011
Carya Ct 45013
Cassandra Ct 45011
Cassidy Pass Dr 45011
Cassinelli Way 45011
Castle Pines Ct 45013
Castlewood Way 45011
Catawba Ct 45011
Cathedral Ln 45013
Cathleen Ct 45011
Cavalcade Dr 45011
Cedar Ln 45013
Cedar Brook Ct 45011
Cedar Grove Ct 45011
Cedar Hill Dr 45011
Cedar Lake Ct 45011
Celtis Ct 45013
Center St 45011
Central Ave 45011
Cereal Ave 45013
Cessna Ct 45015
Chablis Dr 45011
Chamberlin Ct & Dr 45013
Chancery Pl 45011
Chandler Way 45011
Chapel Rd 45013
Chapman Rd 45011
Charfield Ln 45011
Charlberth Dr 45013
Charles St 45011
N & S Charlestown Ct 45013
Charleton Ct 45011
Charlotte Dr 45013
Charlton Ct 45013
Chase Ave 45015
E Chase Run 45011
W Chase Run 45011
Chateauguay Dr 45011
Chelsea Ct 45011
Cherokee Dr 45013
Chestnut St 45011
Chestnut Oak Ct 45011
Cheyenne Ct 45011
Chickadee Dr 45011
Chickasaw Dr 45013
Chippewa Dr 45013
Choctaw Ln 45011
Christian Rd 45013
Christina Dr 45013
Christopher Ct 45011
Churchill Ct 45011
Churchill St 45013
Cincinnati Brookville Rd 45013
Circle Ln 45013
Citation Dr 45011
Clarion Ct 45011
Clark St 45011
Clawson Ridge Ct 45011
Clear Water Dr 45011
Clearcreek Dr 45013
Clearview Pl 45011
Clearview Lake Dr 45011
Cleveland Ave 45013
Clinton Ave 45015
Cloe Ln 45013
Clovernook Dr 45013
Clovis Dr 45011
Clyde Ct 45011
Coach House Way 45011
Coach Light Cir 45011
Cobblestone Way 45011
Cochran Rd 45013
Cody Dr 45013
Cody Brook Dr 45011
Cody Pass Dr 45011
Coleman Dr 45013
Colonial Dr 45013
Colonial Lake Dr 45013
Colonial Orchard Ct 45011
Colony Ter 45013
Colorado River Trl 45011
Columbia Rd 45013
Columbus Dr S & W 45013
Commerce St 45013
Commerce Center Dr 45011
Concord Ave & St 45015
Conley Bottom Ct 45011
Conner Dr 45013
Connor Ct 45011
Conover St 45011
Constance Ave 45013
Convair Dr 45015
Coral Dr 45011
Coral Way 45013
Coralie Ave 45013
Corkwood Knl 45011
Corliss Ave 45011
Cornell Ave 45011
Corwin Ave 45015
Cory Ct 45013
Cotswold Ln 45013
Cottage View Ct 45011
Cotton Run Rd 45011
Cottonwood Dr 45013
Cottonwood Knl 45011
Country View Dr 45011
Court St
1-99 45011
105-107 45012
105-225 45011
227-229 45011
231-399 45011
Courtney Dr 45013
Cove Ct 45013
Coventry Ct 45011
Covered Wagon Estates Ln 45013
Covington Rd 45011
Craig Dr 45013
Cranberry Ct 45011
Cranbrook Dr 45011
Crawford Dr 45015
Creek Lake Ct 45011
Creekside Dr & Way 45011
Creekside Meadows Dr 45011
Crescent Rd 45013
Crest Manor Dr 45011
Crockett Pass 45011
Crooked Tree Cir 45011
Cross Creek Ct & Ln 45011
Crosscreek Ct 45011
Crowfoot Dr 45011
Crown Pointe Dr 45011
Crows Nest Ct 45013
Crowthers Dr 45013
Cumberland Dr 45011
Cumberland Lake Ct 45011
Cunningham Ct 45011
Curnie Dr 45013
Curtis Dr 45013
Cypress Hill Dr 45011
N & S D St 45013
Dakota Ct 45011
Dale Rd 45013
Dan Patch Ct 45011
Danielle Ct 45013
Daniels Xing 45011
Darcie Dr 45011
Darlington Rd 45011
Darrtown Rd 45013
Dartmouth Ct 45011
Davis Rd 45013
Dawn Dr 45011
Dawnee Dr 45013
Dayspring Dr 45015
Dayton St & Trl 45011
Decamp Rd 45013
Dedham Dr 45011
Deer Vly & Xing 45011
Deer Cross Ln 45011
Deer Hill Dr 45013
Deer Ridge Ct 45011
Deerfield Cir 45013
Del Rio Dr 45013
Delphia Dr 45011
Delta Dr 45015
Denby Ct 45013
Dennis Ln 45013
Depot Rd 45013
Derby Dr 45011
N & S Derexa Dr 45011
Devanshae Ct 45013
Dewberry Ct 45011
Dexter Ct 45013
Diana Dr 45013
N & S Dick Ave 45013
Dickinson Trl 45011
Dixie Hwy
1400-2199 45011
2200-3199 45015
3201-3999 45015
Dixon Dr 45011
Donna Ave 45013
Donna Marie Dr 45013
Dorsey Dr 45011
Douglas Ln 45013
Dover Pl 45013
Drew Dr 45011
Dry Leaf Ct 45011
Dry Run Dr 45013
Dunston Pl 45013
Dunwoody Rd 45013
Dust Commander Ct & Dr 45011
N & S E St 45013
Eagle Creek Cir & Dr 45011
Eagle Dance Dr 45011
Eagle Point Dr 45011
Eagles View Dr 45013
East Ave 45011
Eastfield Ct 45011
Eastridge Dr 45011
N & S Eastview Pkwy 45011
Eaton Ave & Rd 45013
Echo Point Ct 45013
Echo Springs Dr 45011
Eden Park Dr 45013
Edgeton Ct 45013
N & S Edgewood Ave 45013
Edgeworth Dr 45011
Edison Ave 45011
Edisto Dr 45011
Edmonton Pl 45013
Edwards Ave 45013
Edwood Dr 45011
Elaine Ave 45011
Elbe Ave 45015
Elbert Dr 45011
Elderberry Ct 45011
Elenor Dr 45011
Elissa Dr 45011
Elizabeth Dr 45013
Elk Fairways Dr 45011
Elk Green Ct 45011
Elk Meadows Ct 45011
Elk Run Dr 45011
W Elkton Rd
116-166 45011
1100-2699 45013
2700-5599 45011
Ellen Cir 45011
Elliott Ave 45011
Ellsworth Ct 45013
Elm St 45011
Elm Leaf Ct 45011
Elmo Ave 45015
Elmont Ave 45013
Elmwood Rd 45013
Elora Ln 45011
Elsmere Ct 45013
Elvin Ave 45013
Elvin Ln 45011
Emerson Ave 45013
Emery Ave 45011
Englewood Dr 45011
Enterprise Dr 45015
Eric Ln 45011
N & S Erie Hwy 45011
Erwin Marie Ln 45011
Essex Ct 45013
Ethel Dr 45011
Eureka Dr 45011
Excalibur Ct & Ln 45011
Exchange St 45013
Exeter Ave 45015
N & S F St 45013
N & S Fair Ave 45011
Fairborn Ct & Dr 45013
Faircrest St 45011
Fairfax Ave 45015
Fairfield Ridge Dr 45011
Fairgrove Ave 45011
Fairham Rd 45011
Fairhaven Dr 45013
Fairoaks Ct 45011
Fairridge Ln 45011
Fairview Ave 45015
E & W Fairway Ct & Dr 45013
Fairway Eleven Ct 45011
Fairways Dr 45011
Fairy Dr 45013
Fall Wood Dr 45011
Fallert Ave 45015
Far Crest Ct 45011
Farmington Dr 45013
Fatima Pl 45013
Fawn Run Ln 45011
Fayetta Dr 45011
Fear Not Mills Rd 45011
Fenton Rd 45013
Fenton St 45011
Fern Ln 45013
Fern Valley Way 45011
Ferndale Ln 45011
Fernway Dr 45011
Fiat Ct 45011
Ficus Ct 45013
Field Glen Ct 45011
Fitton Ave 45015
Flagler Ct 45013
Flamingo Dr 45013
Fletching Cir 45011
Florence Dr 45011
Florence Ln 45013
Forest Ave 45015
Forest Trl 45011
Forest Hill Ln 45011
Forest Knoll Ln 45011
Forest Park Dr 45011
Foster Ave 45015
Four Mile Creek Rd 45013
Fox Ave
1-199 45011
1000-1099 45015
Fox Den Ct 45013
Fox Lake Ct 45011
Fox Run Dr 45013
Foxhound Dr 45011
Foxwood Pl 45011
Francis St 45011
Franklin St 45013
Franklin Trl 45011
Freeman Ave 45015
Front St
919-1151 45011
2800-2899 45013
2901-2999 45013
S Front St 45011
Furlong Way 45011
Fye Rd 45013
S G St 45013
Garden Ave 45011
Gardner Rd 45013
Garfield Ave 45015
Garner Rd 45013

Street	ZIP
Garnet Ave	45013
Gates Rd	45013
Gateway Dr	45011
Gatewood Ct	45013
Gene Ave	45013
Gephart Rd	45011
Gerald Ln	45015
N & S Gersam Ave	45013
Gilday Ct	45013
Gilmore Ave	45011
Gilmore Rd	45011
N Gilmore Rd	45015
Glen Abby Ct	45011
Glen Hollow Dr	45011
Glen Springs Dr	45011
Glenbrook Dr	45013
Glencross Ave	45013
Glenmont Dr	45011
Glenn Dr	45011
Glenn Moor Dr	45011
Glenway Dr	45013
Gloria Ln	45013
Golden Bell Way	45011
Golden Oak Dr	45013
Golf Club Ln	45011
Golfview Dr	45013
Gollenso Ave	45015
Goodman Ave	45013
Goos Rd	45013
Gordon Ave	45013
Gordon Smith Blvd	45013
Gorham Dr	45011
Govenors Hill Ct & Dr	45013
Grand Blvd	45011
Grandin Ridge Dr	45011
Grandview Ave	45013
Grant Cir & Ln	45011
Gray Ave	45013
Graybirch Knl	45011
Greatus Dr	45011
Green Crest Dr	45011
Green Knoll Cir	45011
Greenacres Ct	45013
Greenlawn Rd	45011
Greenlea Dr	45013
Greens Way	45011
Greensward Dr	45011
Greenway Pl	45013
Greenwood Ave	45011
Greer Ct	45013
Gregory Ct & Ln	45013
Grey Elk Ct	45011
Griesmer Ave	45015
Griffin Ct	45011
Griffis Lake Dr	45011
Grimsby Ln	45011
Gristmill Dr	45011
Grove Ave	45015
Grove Ter	45011
Hackberry Ct	45011
Haldimand Ave	45013
Hales Ln	45011
Hamel Dr	45013
Hamilton Ave & Trl	45011
Hamilton Cleves Rd	45013
Hamilton Eaton Rd	
2000-4699	45011
4701-4749	45013
4750-4750	45011
4751-5899	45013
4752-5898	45013
Hamilton Enterprise Park Dr	45011
Hamilton Mason Rd	45011
Hamilton Middletown Rd	45011
Hamilton New London Rd	45013
Hamilton Princeton Rd	45011
Hamilton Richmond Rd	45013
Hamilton Scipio Rd	45013
Hamilton View Dr	45013
Hammond Blvd	45015
Hampshire Ct & Dr	45011
Hancock Ave & Trl	45011
Hanover Ct	45013
Hanover Dr	45011
Hanover Pl	45013
Hanover St	45011
Hanover Way	45013
Happy Ct	45011
Harbour Landings Dr	45011
Harmon Ave	45011
Harris Rd	45013
Harrison Ave	45013
Hartford Dr	45013
Harvard St	45015
Harvest Ave	45011
Harvey Ct	45013
Hastings Ave	45011
Hatherly Dr	45013
Haven Ave	45013
Havenwood Ct	45011
Haverford Dr	45011
Haverhill Dr	45013
Haverland Dr	45015
Hawkins Rd	45011
Hawthorn Dr	45013
Hawthorn Knl	45011
Hayes Ave	45015
Hazel Nut Dr	45011
Headgates Rd	45011
Hearthside Ct	45011
Hearthwood Dr	45011
Heathrow Ct & Dr	45013
Heathwood Ln	45013
Heaton St	45011
Hedge Ln	45011
Hedgington Ct	45013
Heitsman Dr	45013
Helen Ave	45011
Helma Ave	45013
Henry Ln	45013
Henry St	45011
Hensley Ave	45011
Herd Ct	45013
Herman Ave & Rd	45013
Hermay Dr	45013
Hichitee Ct	45011
Hickory St	45011
Hickory Glen Dr	45011
Hickory Hollow Dr	45013
Hickory Trail Pl	45011
Hickory View Dr	45011
Hickory Woods Dr	45013
Hidden Hollow Dr	45011
Hidden Oaks Ln	45011
Hieb Ln	45011
High St	
1-1399	45011
1401-1599	45011
2800-2900	45013
2902-2998	45013
High Saddle Ct	45011
Highland Ave	
1-299	45011
700-1199	45013
Highland Pl	45013
Highpoint Blvd & Ct	45011
Hilda Ave	45015
Hill Ave & Rd	45015
Hillcrest Dr	45013
Hillgale Ln	45011
Hine Rd	45013
Historic Crescent Dr	45013
History Bridge Ln	45013
Hoadley Ave	45015
Hogan Dr	45013
Hogue Rd	45013
Hollin Ln	45013
Hollow Ridge Dr	45011
Hollowtree Ct	45013
Hollowview Ct	45011
Holly Berry Ct	45011
Hollyberry Ln	45011
Hollytree Ct	45011
Holmes Ct	45013
Home Ave	45013
Hooven Ave	45015
Horizon Dr	45013
Horse Trail Ct	45013
Horseshoe Bend Rd	45011
Hoskins Cir	45011
Howell Ave	45011
Howman Ave	45011
Huckleberry Ln	45011
Hudson Ave	45011
Hueston St	45013
Huffman Rd	45013
Hughes Ct	45013
Hughes Glen Ct	45011
Hughes Ridge Ln	45011
Hughes Woods Ln	45011
Hunt Ave	45013
Hunter Ave	45013
Hunters Moon Ct	45011
Hunting Horn Ct	45011
Huntington Ct	45013
Huntsman Way	45011
Hurm St	45011
Huron Ct	45011
Hussey Rd	45013
Huston Rd	
3300-3600	45013
3602-5098	45013
3701-3799	45015
3801-5099	45013
Hyde Park Ct & Dr	45013
Imlay Ave	45015
Impala Pl	45013
Imperial Dr	
300-399	45013
4500-4899	45011
Independence Cres	45013
Indian Ct	45011
Indian Creek Trl	45013
Indian Hill Ct	45011
Indian Meadows Dr	45011
Indian Trace Dr	45011
Innsbrooke Ln	45011
Irene Ave	45011
Irma Ave	45011
Iron Kettle Ct & Dr	45011
Isabella Ln	45013
Island Lake Dr	45013
Ivy Ct	45011
Ivywood Ct & Dr	45011
Jackson Rd	45011
Jackson St	45013
Jacksonburg Rd	45011
Jacobs St	45011
Jade Ct	45013
James Ct	45013
James Pl	45011
James Rd	45013
Jamil Ct	45011
Jasper Ct	45011
Jay Drew Dr	45013
Jay Phillips Ct	45013
Jayfield Ct & Dr	45011
Jeff Scott Ct & Ln	45013
Jenkins Rd	45013
Jennifer Dr	45013
Jenny Marie Ct	45011
Jerdon Ln	45013
Jeremy Ct	45013
Jerome St	45011
Jerri Ter	45013
Jesse Dr	45013
Jessies Way	45011
Jimmy Stewart Dr	45013
Joan Dr	45013
Jocelyn Dr	45011
Jodphur Ct	45011
Joe Nuxhall Blvd	45011
John St	45011
John Jacob Ct	45011
John Wayne Dr	45011
Jones Ln	45011
Joshua Ct	45013
Journal Sq	45011
Judith Dr	45011
Julias Rose Ct	45011
Juneberry Ct	45011
Justin Pl	45013
Kahn Ave	45011
Kailyn Ct	45013
Karen Ln	45013
Karriwood Dr	45013
Katherine Manor Ct	45011
Kathy Ct	45013
Keeneland Dr	45011
Kelly Ct	45013
Kelly St	45011
E Kelly St	45011
Kelly Marie Ct	45011
Kelso Ct	45011
Kendrick Ct	45011
Kenneth Ave	45013
Kensington Dr	45013
Kenton Ave	45013
Kenwood Dr	45015
S Kenworth Ave	45013
Kenyon Dr	45015
Kerry Ct	45013
Keshena Ct & Dr	45011
Keystone Ct	45011
Kiesland Ct	45015
Kimberly Dr	45011
King Ave	45015
Kingsley Ct	45011
Kingston Dr	45013
Kinsinger Rd	45013
Kiowa Ct	45011
Kirchling Rd	45013
Kirk Ave	45011
Klenk Pl	45013
Knapp Dr	45013
Knightsbridge Dr	45011
Kristine Dr	45011
Krucker Rd	45013
Kyles Station Rd	45011
La Grange St	45013
Lagonda Ave	45013
Lake Crest Dr	45011
Lake Front Ct	45013
Lake Vista Ct	45011
Lakebrook Ct	45011
Lakepoint Ct	45011
Lakerun Ct	45011
Lakeside Dr	45013
Lakeview Ct	45011
Lakewood Ct & Dr	45011
Lakota Ridge Dr	45011
Landis Cir	45013
Landmark Cres	45013
Lane St	45011
Lanes Mill Rd	45013
Lansing Ct	45011
Laredo Dr	45013
Laura Ct	45013
Laura Jean Dr	45013
Laurel Ave	45015
Laverna Ct	45013
S Lawn Ave	45013
Lawrence Ave	45013
Lawson Ave	45013
Layhigh Rd	45013
Leah Ct	45013
Leah Ann Ct	45013
Leeds Ln	45011
Lees Ford Ln	45011
Leeward Ct	45011
Lehmann Trl	45013
Lenox Ave	45015
Leo Dr	45013
Leona Ct	45013
Leonard Ave	45013
Leslie Lee Ct	45011
Lesourdsville West Chester Rd	45011
Lester Ave	45011
Lexington Dr	45013
Liberty Ave	45013
Liberty Bell Dr	45011
Liberty Fairfield Rd	45011
Liberty Falls Dr	45011
Liberty Farms Ct	45011
Liberty Knoll Dr	45011
Liberty Ridge Dr	45011
Liberty Square Dr	45011
Liberty Woods Ct & Dr	45011
Lilac Ct	45011
Lilliedale Ln	45015
Lincoln Ave	45011
Linda Ln	45011
Linden St	45013
Lindley Way	45011
Links Ln	45011
Linn St	45011
Lisa Dr	45013
Lisa Renee Dr	45013
Little Turtle Ct	45013
Livingston Ct & Dr	45013
Lockwood Ave	45011
Logan Ave	45015
Loganberry Ct	45011
Logsdon Rd	45011
Logsdons Meadow Dr	45011
Logsdons Woods Dr	45011
London Ridge Trl	45013
Long Dr & St	45011
Long Pine Ct	45011
Longbow Dr	45011
Longhorn Dr	45013
Longview Dr	45011
Longwood Ct	45011
Lookout Ct	45011
Lora Ln	45013
Loraine Cir	45011
Lorinda Dr	45011
Lovelace Dr	45011
Luann Ct	45013
Ludlow St	45011
Lulu Ave	45011
Lurmer Dr	45011
Madeline Pl	45013
Madison Ave	45015
Madmans Dr	45013
Maidstone Ct	45011
Main St	45013
Mainring St	45011
Maple Ave	45011
Maple Ct	45013
Maple Crest Ct & Dr	45011
Maplewood Rd	45013
Marcia Ave	45013
Margaret Ave	45015
Marian Dr	45013
Mariners Way	45011
Mark Ave	45013
Market St	45011
Marlou Dr	45013
Marriott Ct	45011
Martha Ln	45013
Martin Ave	
1-99	45011
800-899	45013
Martin Dr	45013
N & S Martin Luther King Jr Blvd	45011
Mary Elaine Dr	45013
Mary Jane Dr	45013
Mason Aly	45013
Maud Hughes Rd	45011
Mavern Ave	45013
Mayflower Ter	45013
Mcbride Ct	45011
S Mckinley Ave	45013
Mclean St	45011
Mcwhorter Dr	45013
Meadow Dr	45013
Meadow Breeze Dr	45011
Meadow Creek Ct	45011
Meadow Falls Dr	45011
Meadow Spring Ct	45011
Meadow Vista Ct	45011
Meadowood Way	45013
Meadowside Ct	45011
Medford Ct	45011
Megan Dr	45011
Meier Ln	45011
Melbourne Dr	45011
Mellwood Dr	45011
Melrose Pl	45011
Melvin Cox Ave	45011
Mercedes Dr	45011
Merle Ave & Ct	45013
Merlin Way	45011
Mesa Pl	45011
Meyer Way	45011
Miami Ave & St	45011
Miami Way Dr	45013
Michael Ave	45013
Midarie Dr	45011
Mill Rd	45011
Mill St	45013
Mill Creek Ct	45011
Mill Crest Ct & Dr	45011
Mill Pond Ct & Dr	45011
Mill View Ct	45011
Millers Manor Ct	45011
Millers Run Ct	45011
Millikin Rd	45011
Millikin St	45013
Millville Ave	45013
Millville Oxford Rd	45013
Millville Shandon Rd	45013
Milton St	45015
Mimosa Ct	45013
Mindy Dr	45011
Minor Ave	45015
Minster St	45011
Minton Rd	45013
Missy Ct	45013
Mitchell Ave	45013
Mogul Ln	45011
Mollie Dr	45013
S Monument Ave	45011
Moore Rd	45013
Morey Ave	45011
Morgan Ln	45013
Morgan Ross Rd	45013
Morganthaler Rd	45011
Morman Rd	45013
Morris Ave	
1-299	45011
3100-3299	45015
Morris Rd	45011
Morrow Trl	45013
Moselle Dr	45011
Moser Ct	45013
Mosketti Ct	45013
Mosler Ave	45011
Mosley Dr	45013
Mossy Grv	45013
Mostow Dr	45011
Mountview Ct	45011
Mourning Dove Ln	45011
Muhlhauser Rd	45011
Murphy Cir	45013
Nadir Ct	45011
Nancy Ln	45013
Natchez Dr	45013
Nature Trl	45011
Neal Blvd	45011
Nelson St	45013
New Haven Rd	45013
New London Rd	45013
Nicholas Ln	45013
Nichole Ct	45013
Nichols Rd	45013
Noble Ave	45015
Noelle Dr	45013
Normandy Ct & Dr	45013
North St	45011
Northampton Ln	45011
Northland Dr	45011
Northwood Ter	45013
Norvel Ln	45011
Noyes Ave	45015
Nugent Rd	45013
Oak St	45013
Oak Creek Trl	45011
Oak Grove Ct	45011
Oak Spring Dr	45011
Oak Vista Ct	45011
Oakdale Dr	45013
Oakland Gardens Ct	45011
Oakmeadow Ln	45011
Oakmont Ave	45013
Oakridge Dr	45011
Oakview Ct & Ter	45011
Oakwood Dr	45013
Office Park Dr	45013
N & S Ohio Ave	45013
Old Line Ln	45011
Old Mill Ct	45011
Old Oxford Rd	45013
Old Republic Path	45013
Old Stone Ct	45011
Olde Woods Dr	45011
Olinger Dr	45011
Olympus Ct & Dr	45013
Onedia Ct	45011
Opal Dr	45013
Orchard Dr	45013
Orient Way	45013
Osage Dr	45011
Osprey Pointe Dr	45011
Ouray Ct	45011
Outpost Dr	45013
Owen St	45011
Oxford St	45013
Oxford Circle Ct	45013
Oxford Middletown Rd	45013
Oyler Dr	45013
Paddys Run Rd	45013
Paducah Ave	45011
Paige Dr	45013
Palatine Ave	45011
Palomino Ln	45011
Pan Am Way	45015
Park Ave	45013
Parkamo Ave	
1200-1899	45011
1900-2199	45015
Parkside Ct	45011
Parkview Ave	45013
Parkwood Ln	45011
Parliament Pl	45011
Parrish Ave	
1081-1197	45011
1199-1899	45011
1900-2199	45015
Pater Ave	
1200-1399	45011
1800-2199	45015
Patriot Cres	45013
Patton Ave	45015
Pawnee Ct	45011
Peak Dr	45011
Peakview Ct	45011
Pearl St	45013
Pearl Crest Dr	45011
Pearle Ln	45013
Pebble Brook Ln	45011
Pebble Ridge Ct	45011
Pembroke Dr	45015
Penelope Dr	45011
Penn Ln	45011
Pennington Way	45011
Pennsylvania Ave	45011
Pepperwood Ct	45013
Peregrine Way	45013
Pershing Ave	45011
W Persimmon Dr	45013
Petty Dr	45013
Pheasant Trail Ct	45011
Piccadilly Dr	45013
Pickney Trl	45011
Pierson Rd	45013
Pimlico Ct	45011
Pine St	45011
Pine Valley Dr	45013
Pinecrest Ln	45013
Pineview Ct	45013
Pinnacle Ct	45011
Piper Pl	45015
Platanus Dr	45011
Plateau Dr	45013
Plaza Dr	45013
Pleasant Ave	45015
Pleasant Ridge Dr	45011
Pleasant View Dr	45011
Poets Way	45011
Pond Ridge Cir	45013
Pond Run Cir	45013
Pond View Ct	45011
Poplar St	45011
Porsche Dr	45011

Port Ln 45011
Power Ave 45015
Prairie Ln 45013
Preakness Ln 45011
Prescott Ct 45011
Preserve Ln 45011
Princeton Holw, Pl, Rd, Rdg, Trce & Trl 45011
Princeton Glendale Rd 45011
Privet Ct 45011
Progress Ave 45013
Prospect Ln 45013
Providence Ridge Dr 45011
Prytania Ave 45013
Pueblo Dr 45013
Pumpkin Ridge Ct 45013
Puthoff St 45013
Putnam Ave 45015
Pyramid Hill Blvd 45013
Quapaw Ct 45011
Queen Mary Ln 45013
Queenswood Ct 45011
Quercus Dr 45013
Quincy Dr 45013
Quiver Ct 45011
Race St 45011
Rachaels Run 45011
Rachel Dr 45013
Rachels Vw 45011
Rahfuse Dr 45013
Ramon Dr 45013
Ramsey Ct & Dr 45013
Randall Dr 45011
Random Ct & Dr 45013
Random Oaks Ln 45013
Ranlyn Dr 45013
Raspberry Rdg 45011
Raven Crst & Ct 45011
Raven Valley Dr 45011
Ravena Dr 45011
Ray Combs Ave 45011
Read Trl 45011
Rebecca Rdg 45013
Red Ash Ct 45011
Red Bird Ln 45011
Red Bud Ln 45013
Red Coat Dr 45011
Red Fox Run 45011
Redbay Knl 45011
Redbud Dr 45013
Redstone Dr 45011
Redwing Ct 45013
Reflection Pt 45011
Regina Pl 45013
Reiff Dr 45013
Reigart Rd 45011
Reily Millville Rd 45013
Reister Dr 45013
Rentschler Estates Dr 45011
Reservoir St 45011
Revere Dr 45013
Rhea Ave 45013
Richard Dr 45015
Richwood Ave & Cir 45013
Ridgefield Rd 45013
Ridgelawn Ave 45013
Ridgeview Dr 45011
Ridgewood Ave 45013
Rigdon St 45011
Ringling St 45011
Rippling Lake Ct 45011
E Ritter St 45011
Riva Ridge Dr 45011
River Rd 45015
River Ridge Dr & Ln 45011
Riverdowns Ct 45011
Riverfront Plz 45011
N & S Riverside Dr 45011
N & S Riverview Dr 45015
Roanoke Dr 45013
Robert Ct 45015
Robert Dr 45013
Roberta Dr 45013
Robina Ln 45013
Robinson Rd 45013
Rochester Ave 45011
Rochester Hills Dr 45011
Rock Springs Dr 45011
Rockdale Rd 45011
Rockford Dr 45013
Rockyhill Dr 45013
Rollingsfjord Dr 45011
Rosary Cir 45013
Rose Ave & Dr 45015
Rose Lea Ave 45011
Roseville Dr 45013
Ross Ave & Rd 45013
Ross Estates Dr 45013
Ross Hanover Rd 45013
Ross Millville Rd 45013
Ross Trails Dr 45013
Rossgate Ct 45013
Rost Hill Dr 45013
Roundhill Dr 45013
Rowe Ct 45015
Roy Rogers Dr 45011
Royale Dr 45011
Rutledge Ct 45013
Rutledge Trl 45011
Ryan Ct 45011
Saddle Horn Dr 45013
Saint Albans Way 45011
Saint Clair Ave 45015
Saint Clair St 45011
Salman Rd 45013
Salvatore Pl 45013
Samantha Ct 45011
San Angelo Dr 45013
Sanctuary Pl & Rdg 45011
Sand Hill Ct 45011
Sand Ridge Ct 45011
Sandalwood Ter 45011
Sanders Dr 45013
Sandyhills Dr 45013
Sanibel Ln 45011
Santa Maria Pl 45013
Sara Ct 45011
Sarasota St 45011
Saratoga Ct & Dr 45011
Sauterne Dr 45011
Savitz Dr 45011
Schafer Knoll Ct 45011
Schaffers Run Ct & Dr 45011
Schenk Ave 45015
Schlichter Dr 45015
Schloss Ln 45013
School Rd 45013
Schroder Ln 45013
Schueler Dr 45013
Schwartz Dr 45013
Scott Ave 45013
Scott Ln 45015
Sebastian Ln 45011
See Ave
1400-1899 45011
1900-1999 45015
Selu Dr 45011
Semlar Ave 45015
Serenity Ct 45011
Serenity Hill Ln 45013
Service Ln 45011
Seven Mile Ave 45011
Shademore Ln 45011
Shadow Creek Dr 45011
Shadow Ridge Ct 45011
Shady Rd 45013
Shady Creek Way 45011
Shady Meadows Dr 45011
Shafor Dr 45011
Shanda Ct 45013
Shandon Dr 45013
Shank Rd 45013
Shannon Dr 45011
Sharkey Ct 45013
Sharon Ln 45013
Sharps Ridge Ct 45011
Shawn Trl 45013
Shawnee Dr 45013
Sheerin Dr 45013
Sheila Ct 45013
Sheraton Ct 45013
Sherman Ave 45013
Sherman Oaks Dr 45013
Sheryl Ct 45013
Shirley Ave 45011
Shore Acres Ct 45011
Short St 45011
Shoshoni Ct 45011
Shrewsbury Ct 45011
Shuler Ave 45011
Shultz Dr 45013
Siaron Way 45011
Silax Dr 45013
Silver Ln 45013
Silver Creek Ct 45011
Silver Fox Run 45011
Silver Stone Ct 45011
Singer Ave 45011
Sipple Ave 45011
Sipps Ln 45013
Sir Douglas Dr 45013
Sir Edward Dr 45013
Sir Lawrence Dr 45013
Sir Martin Dr 45013
Sirena Dr 45013
Sky Meadow Dr 45013
Smalley Blvd 45013
Smith Rd 45013
Snow Hill Dr 45011
Snow Valley Ln 45011
Snowbird Dr 45011
S Snowmass Dr 45011
Sohngen Ct 45013
Somerset Dr 45011
Somerton Ct 45013
Sophora Knl 45011
Sorbus Dr 45013
South St 45011
Southern Hills Blvd 45013
Southwood Dr 45013
Sparks Ln 45011
Spring Lake Dr 45011
Spring Meadows Dr 45011
Spring Orchard Ln 45013
Springbrook Dr 45011
Springcrest Dr 45011
Springleaf Dr 45011
Springmeadow Dr 45011
Springvale Dr 45013
Springview Dr 45011
Springwood Ct 45011
Spyglass Rdg 45013
Squaw Valley Dr 45011
Stable Ct 45011
Stafford Dr 45013
Stahlheber Rd 45013
Stallings Ln 45011
Stamford Ct 45011
Standen Dr 45015
Stanton Ct 45011
Stapleton Ct 45011
Starr Ave 45013
State Rd 45013
State Route 127 Rd 45013
Stephanie Dr 45013
Stephens St 45011
Stereo Ln 45013
Stewart St 45011
Stillington Dr 45011
Stillwater Ln 45011
Stillwell Rd 45013
Stillwell Beckett Rd 45013
Stirrup Ct 45013
Stockbridge Ln 45011
Stone Creek Ct & Dr 45011
Stone Meadow Dr 45011
Stone Mill Ct & Way 45011
Stone Trace Ln 45011
Stone Valley Ct 45011
Stonehaven Dr 45011
Stonelake Way 45011
Stony Brook Dr 45011
Stony Ridge Ct 45011
Stout Ave 45011
Stratton Ct 45011
Strawberry Ct 45011
Streamside Ct 45011
Sugar Maple Run 45011
Sugar Valleys Pl 45011
Sugartree Ct 45011
Summer St 45013
Summer Stone Ct 45011
Summerdale Ln 45011
Summerville Ln 45011
Summit Ridge Ct 45011
Sunnybrook Ct 45013
Sunset Ct 45013
Sunset Dr 45013
Sunset Ln 45011
Sunset Ridge Ln 45011
Sunview Dr E & W 45013
Susan Dr 45013
Sutherland Ct 45013
Sweet Gum Dr 45013
Sycamore St 45011
Sycamore Woods Ln 45011
Sylvia Dr 45011
Symmes Ave & Rd 45015
Tabor Ln 45013
Taft Pl 45013
Tallawanda Ct 45011
Tallowtree Knl 45011
Tally Ho Trl 45011
Tammy Rae Ct 45011
Tanbark Dr 45011
Tantivy Ter 45011
Tara Brooke Ct & Way 45011
Tari Ct & Ln 45013
Tarragon Ct 45011
Tatum Ln 45013
Tawny Ln 45013
Tay Berry Dr 45011
E Taylor School Rd 45011
W Taylor School Rd 45013
Taylor Trace Ln 45011
Teakwood Dr 45011
Tebbe Ln 45013
Tecumseh Dr 45013
Telford Ct 45011
Teresa Ct 45013
Teresa Ann Dr 45013
Thackara Pl 45013
Thall Dr 45013
Theodore Ave 45011
Thinnes Ct 45013
Thomas Blvd 45013
Thoreau Dr 45013
Thornhill Dr 45013
Tiffany Ct 45013
Tiffin Ave 45015
Timber Hill Dr 45013
Timbercreek Dr 45013
Timberhill Dr 45013
Timberman Ave & Rd 45013
Timmy Dr 45011
Todd Pl 45011
Tolbert Rd 45011
Tonya Trl 45011
Tracy Ln 45013
Tradewinds Ct 45011
Trails Run Ct 45011
Trailview Ct 45013
Treadway Trl 45011
Treaty Ct 45013
Treiber Rd 45011
Trenton Rd 45011
Trenton Oxford Rd
1300-1399 45013
2700-4999 45011
Tri County View Dr 45011
Tribe Ct 45013
Trotters Way 45013
Trudy Ln 45013
Tuley Rd 45015
Tulipwood Dr 45013
Tuscarora Ct 45011
Tuskegee Dr 45013
Twinberry Ct 45011
Twinbrook Ct & Dr 45013
Tyler Point Dr 45011
Tylers Ridge Ct 45011
Tylersville Rd
2600-2999 45015
3000-3098 45011
3100-4199 45011
Union Ave 45011
University Blvd
1300-1699 45011
1900-2299 45015
Urban St 45013
Urmston Ave 45011
Utica Ave 45011
Vailsgate Ct 45011
Valley Falls Ct 45011
Valleyview Dr 45013
Van Buren Ct & Dr 45011
Van Gordon Rd 45011
Van Hook Ave 45015
Vance Ct 45015
Vanda Ave 45013
Vanderveer Ave 45011
Verelang Rd 45013
Verlyn Ave 45013
Victor Ct 45013
E & W Victory Dr 45013
Vidourek Dr 45011
Village St 45011
Vincent Dr 45011
Vine St 45011
Virginia Ave 45013
Vista Dr 45011
Vizedom Rd 45013
Vonnie Vale Ct 45011
Waco Ct 45013
Waco Way 45015
Wade Ct 45013
Wagon Wheel Dr 45013
Walden Creek Ct 45011
Walden Ponds Cir 45011
Walkers Ct 45011
Wallace St 45011
Walliswood Ct 45011
Walnut Dr 45011
Walnut St
100-1199 45011
700-999 45013
Walnut Creek Dr 45011
Walnut Grove Rd 45013
Walthan Ct 45013
Wanda Way 45011
Wardlow Dr 45011
Warr Ct & Ln 45013
Warrington Rd 45011
Warvel Rd 45013
Warwick Ave & Rd 45013
Washburn Rd 45013
N Washington Blvd 45013
NW Washington Blvd 45013
S Washington Blvd 45013
Washington Dr 45011
Washington St 45011
Wasserman Rd 45013
Water St 45013
Water Creek Ct 45011
Waterfowl Ln 45011
Waterpoint Ln 45013
Waters Way 45013
Waterview Ct 45013
Watoga Dr 45011
Waverly Dr 45013
Wayne Ave 45013
Wayne Milford Rd 45013
Waynes Trace Rd 45011
Wayside Cir 45013
Weathered Oaks Ct & Ln 45011
Webster Ave 45013
Weeping Willow Dr 45011
Wehr Rd 45011
Weigel Ln 45015
Weinman Dr 45013
Weller Ave 45015
Wellington Ct 45013
Welliver Dr 45011
Welsh Ave 45011
Welsh Ln 45013
Wembley Ct 45011
Wencella Dr 45013
Wesley Way 45011
Wessel Dr 45015
Westbourne Ct 45011
Westbrook Dr 45013
Western Ave 45013
Westfield Ave 45013
Weston Ct 45011
Westridge Dr 45013
Westview Ave 45013
Westwind Ave 45011
Wexford Way 45011
Wheelright Cres 45013
Whippoorwill Dr 45011
Whirlaway Dr 45011
Whispering Brook Ct 45011
Whispering Woods Ln 45013
Whitaker Ave 45011
Whitcomb Dr 45011
White Path Ln 45011
Wichita Dr S 45013
Wild Flower Ct 45011
Wildbranch Rd 45011
Wildwood Ct 45013
Wilks Ln 45011
Willer Way 45011
Willey Rd 45013
Williams Ave 45015
Williams St 45011
Willow Ave 45013
Willow Bend Dr 45011
Willow Brooke Dr 45011
Willow Dale Ct 45011
Willow Ridge Ct & Dr 45011
Willow View Ct 45011
Wills Way 45011
Wilson St
1-99 45013
100-199 45011
Winding Creek Blvd 45011
Windlake Ct 45011
Windsor Dr 45013
Windy Hl 45013
Windy Knoll Dr 45013
Windy Meadows Dr 45011
Windy Ridge Ct 45011
Winford Ave 45011
Winslow Dr 45013
Winston Dr 45013
Winter Hill Dr 45011
Wisconsin St 45011
Withrow Rd 45011
Wittman Way 45013
Wood Ct 45011
Wood Valley Dr 45011
Woodberry Dr 45011
Woodbine Rd 45013
Woodbury Ct 45013
Woodfield Ct 45011
Woodford St 45013
Woodlawn Ave 45015
Woodmansee Way 45011
Woodridge Dr 45013
Woodrow St 45013
Woodview Ln 45013
Wrenwood Dr 45013
Wulzen Ave 45015
Wyngate Ct 45011
Yamassee Dr 45011
W Yard St 45013
York Ave 45011
Zenith Ct 45011
Zilpha Ct 45011
Zimmerman Ave 45015
Zoar St 45013
Zoellners Pl, Rdg & Way 45011

NUMBERED STREETS

All Street Addresses 45011

KENT OH

General Delivery 44240

POST OFFICE BOXES MAIN OFFICE STATIONS AND BRANCHES

Box No.s
All PO Boxes 44240

NAMED STREETS

Aarons Way 44240
Ada St 44240
Adamle Dr 44240
Addie St 44240
Admore Dr 44240
Adrian Ave 44240
Akron Blvd 44240
Algonquin Pl 44240
Allen Dr 44240
Allerton St 44240
Alpha Dr 44240
Alta St 44240
Anita Dr 44240
Anna Ave 44240
Arcadia Rd 44240
Aries Ct 44240
Artemis Dr 44240
Arthur Rd 44240
Ash Ct 44240
Ashton Ln 44240
Aspen Ct 44240
Athena Dr 44240
Avondale St 44240
Basswood Dr 44240
Beal Dr 44240
Beaver Cir 44240
Beech Dr 44240
Beechmont Place Dr 44240
Beechwold Dr 44240
Benjamin Ct 44240
Berkeley St 44240
Beryl Dr 44240
Biltz Rd 44240
Birchwood Cir & Dr 44240
Birkner Dr 44240
Blessing Ln 44240
Bobolink Cir 44240
Bowman Dr 44240
Boydell Rd 44240
Brady St 44240
Brady Lake Rd 44240
Brentwood Ave 44240
Bridge St 44240
Brimfield Dr & Plz 44240
Brookdale Ln 44240
Brookview Dr 44240
Brower Tree Ln 44240
Bruce Dr 44240
Bryce Rd 44240
Bull Dr 44240
Burnett Rd 44240
Burns Ct 44240
Burr Oak Dr 44240
By Ln 44240
Cambridge Ct & Dr 44240
W Campus Center Dr 44240
Caranor Rd 44240
Carl Dr 44240
Carlisle Ct 44240
Carlton Rd 44240
Carol Dr 44240
Carthage Ave 44240
Cascades Blvd 44240
Catlin Ct 44240
Cedar St 44240
Cedarwood Dr 44240
Chadwick Rd 44240
Chapman Dr 44240
Chauncey Ln 44240
Chelton Dr 44240
Cherry Ln & St 44240

Cherry Hollow Ln 44240
Cherrywood Rd 44240
N & S Chestnut Dr & St 44240
Chiarucci Dr 44243
Chippewa Pl 44240
Choctaw Pl 44240
Church St 44240
Cindy Cir 44240
Circle Dr 44240
Clarkview Cir 44240
Clearfield Dr 44240
Cline Rd 44240
Clio St 44240
Clyde Ave 44240
Coffeen St 44240
Colleen St 44240
E & W College Ave, Ct & St 44240
Columbus St 44240
Comanche Pl 44240
Costley Ct 44240
Cottage Gate Dr 44240
Countryview Dr 44240
Court St 44240
Courtland Dr 44240
Covington Oval 44240
E & W Crain Ave 44240
Creekside Dr 44240
Crescent Ln 44240
Crestview Cir 44240
Cricket Ln 44240
Crossfield Cir 44240
Crystal Pkwy & St 44240
Cunningham Dr 44243
Currie Hall Pkwy 44240
Cuyahoga St 44240
Cypress St 44240
Cyprus Cir 44240
Dale Dr 44240
Dansel St 44240
Davey Ave 44240
Davidson St 44240
E & W Day St 44240
Dayton Ave 44240
Dean Ct 44240
Deer Path 44240
Deer Trace Dr 44240
Deidrick Rd 44240
Deleone Dr 44240
Delores Ave 44240
Denise Dr 44240
N & S Depeyster St 44240
Devon Pl 44240
Diagonal Rd 44240
Dodge St 44240
Dollar Lake Dr 44240
Dominion Dr 44240
Doramor St 44240
Dorchester Dr 44240
Duffield Rd 44240
Dussel Rd 44240
Earl Ave 44240
Easlan Ct 44240
Eastway Dr 44243
Eckwood Dr 44240
Edgewater Cir 44240
Edgewood Dr 44240
Edson Rd 44240
Elizabeth Ct 44240
Ella St 44240
E & W Elm Dr & St 44240
Elma St 44240
Elmhurst Ct 44240
Elmwood Dr 44240
Elno Ave 44240
Emich Dr 44240
Enterprise Way 44240
E & W Erie St 44240
Erin Dr 44240
Ernlee Dr 44240
Estes Dr 44240
Evergreen Dr 44240
Fairchild Ave 44240
Fairview Dr 44240
Fairwood Rd 44240
Fawn Cir 44240
Ferguson Rd 44240
Fieldstone Dr 44240
Fleeter Ct 44240
Forest Dr 44240
Forest Brook Cir 44240
Forest Hill Dr 44240
Fountain Dr 44240
Frances Dr 44240
N & S Francis St 44240
Franklin Ave 44240
Fraternity Cir 44240
Gale Dr 44240
Gardenview St 44240
Garrett St 44240
Garth Dr 44240
Gate Post Ln 44240
Gemberling Dr 44240
Gemini Ct 44240
Gill Dr 44240
Ginkgo Ct 44240
Glad Blvd 44240
Glen Park Dr 44240
Glenview Ct 44240
Golden Oaks Dr 44240
Gougler Ave 44240
Governors Cir 44240
Grace Dr 44240
Graham Ave 44240
E & W Grant St 44240
Greenbriar Pkwy 44240
Greenhaven Ct 44240
Greenwood Ave 44240
Grove Ave 44240
E & W Hall St 44240
Hampton Rd 44240
Hanover Dr 44240
Harold Ave 44240
Harris St 44240
Harvey St 44240
Hastings Dr 44240
Heather Cir 44240
Hemlock Dr 44240
Hickory Ln 44240
Hickory Mills Cir 44240
High St 44240
Highland Ave 44240
Highpoint St 44240
Highridge Ln 44240
Highway View Dr 44240
Hissom Ln 44240
Hodgeman Ln 44240
Holiday Dr 44240
Hollister Dr 44240
Holly Dr 44240
Honeychuck Ln 44240
Horning Rd 44240
Howe Rd 44240
Hudson Rd 44240
Hughey Dr 44240
Indian Valley Dr 44240
Indiana Ave 44240
Indonti Dr 44243
Irish Rd 44240
Irma St 44240
Ivan Dr 44240
Ivanhoe Dr 44240
Jacobs Ln 44240
Jameson Dr 44240
Janet Ct 44240
Janik Dr 44243
Jessie Ave 44240
Johnson Rd 44240
Johnston Dr 44243
Jones St 44240
Joyanne Ct 44240
Judson Rd 44240
Karg Industrial Pkwy 44240
Kelso Rd 44240
Kent Rd & St 44240
Keswick Dr 44240
Kevin Dr 44240
Kimberly Dr 44240
King St 44240
King Meadow Trl 44240
Knoll Rd 44240
Lake Blvd & St 44240
Lake Martin Dr 44240
Lake Rockwell Rd 44240
Lake Roger Dr 44240
Lake Royale Blvd 44240
Lake Shore Blvd 44240
Lakeview Ct 44240
Lakewood Cir 44240
Lancaster Ln 44240
Laurel Dr 44240
Lawndale Dr 44240
Lawrence Ct 44240
Ledge Ct 44240
Leebrick Dr 44243
Leonard Blvd 44240
Libra Ct 44240
Lightning Ln 44240
N & S Lincoln St 44240
Linden St 44240
Loblolly Ct 44240
Lock St 44240
Longcoy Ave 44240
Longmere Dr 44240
Loop Rd
1-21 44243
23-31 44243
1300-1499 44240
Lor Ron St 44240
Loraine Dr 44240
Louise Ave 44240
Lowell Dr 44240
Lower Dr 44240
Luce St 44240
Luther Ave 44240
Lynn Rd 44240
Lynwood Dr 44240
Mae St 44240
E & W Main St 44240
Majors Ln 44240
Mallard Cir 44240
Manchester St 44240
N & S Mantua St 44240
Maple St 44240
S Marigold Ln 44240
Marilyn Dr 44240
Marteney Ave 44240
Martha Rd 44240
Martinel Dr 44240
Marvin St 44240
Mason Ave 44240
Mckinney Blvd 44240
Mctaggart Blvd 44240
Meadow Dr 44240
Meadow Park Dr 44240
Meadowview Rd 44240
Meloy Rd 44240
Meredith St 44240
Merrill Ave & Rd 44240
Michaels Dr 44240
Michigan Ave 44240
Middlebury Rd 44240
Midway Dr 44243
Mill Creek Dr 44240
Miller Ave 44240
Mockingbird Dr 44240
Mogadore Rd 44240
Mohawk Pl 44240
Mohican Pl 44240
Morley Dr 44240
Morris Rd 44240
Morrow Rd 44240
Mulberry Ct 44240
Munroe Falls Kent Rd 44240
Myrna Blvd 44240
Nathan Dr 44240
Nature Wood Cir 44240
Needham Ave 44240
Neville Dr 44240
Newcomer Rd 44240
Newton Rd 44240
Nicholas Dr & Way 44240
North Blvd 44240
Northeast Ave 44240
Norwood St 44240
Nottingham Cir 44240
E & W Oak St 44240
Oak Hill Dr 44240
Oakwood Dr 44240
Oakwood Estates Dr 44240
Ohio Ave 44240
Old Forge Rd 44240
Olmsby Dr 44240
Olympus Dr 44240
Orchard St 44240
Overbrook Rd 44240
Overholt Rd 44240
Overlook Dr & Rd 44240
Pachitt Rd 44240
Park Ave 44240
Parliament Dr 44240
Parmalee Dr 44240
Parsons Dr 44240
Paulus Dr 44240
Pawnee Pl 44240
N & S Pearl St 44240
Pebblebrook Ln 44240
Pelham Ln 44240
Pembroke Dr 44240
Perie Wood Ln 44240
Perry St 44240
Petrarca Dr 44243
Phillip Dr 44240
Picadilly Ct 44240
Pin Oak Dr 44240
Pine Dr & St 44240
Pineview Dr 44240
Pioneer St 44240
Pit Rd 44240
Plant Dr 44240
Pleasant Ave 44240
Pleasant Lakes Dr 44240
Plum Dr & St 44240
Poplar Ln 44240
Portage Blvd & St 44240
Powdermill Rd 44240
Powell Rd 44240
Primrose Ln 44240
Progress Blvd 44240
N & S Prospect St 44240
Queenstown Rd 44240
Raintree Trl 44240
Rambling Trl 44240
Randall Dr 44240
Ranfield Rd 44240
Ravenna Rd 44240
Red Fern Cir 44240
N & S Reeves St 44240
Rellim Dr 44240
Revere St 44240
Rhodes Rd 44240
Ridge View Dr 44240
Ridgecrest Dr 44240
River Rd & St 44240
River Bend Blvd 44240
River Edge Dr 44240
River Park Dr 44240
River Trail Dr 44240
Riverside Ct 44240
Robert Dr 44240
Roc Marie Ave 44240
Rockwell St 44240
Rohrer Ave 44240
Rollins Cir 44240
Roosevelt St 44240
Rose Ct 44240
Rosewood Dr 44240
Roy Marsh Dr 44240
Rugg St 44240
Rustic Bridge Dr 44240
Rustic Knoll Dr 44240
Saint Clair Ave 44240
Sanctuary View Dr 44240
Sandlewood Dr & Oval 44240
Sandy Lake Rd 44240
Sassafras Ct 44240
E & W School St 44240
Schoolview Dr 44240
Scorpio Ct 44240
Seasons Rd 44240
Selnik Rd 44240
Senhauser Dr 44243
Shady Lakes Dr 44240
Shaw Dr 44240
Shawnee Dr 44240
Sheppard Dr 44240
Sheri Dr 44240
Sherman Rd & St 44240
Sherman Wood Dr 44240
Shorewood Cir 44240
Short Ave & St 44240
Silver Meadows Blvd 44240
Simon Ln 44240
Sioux Pl 44240
Skyline Dr 44240
Skyview Dr & Ln 44240
South Blvd 44240
Spaulding Dr 44240
Spell Rd 44240
Spruce Ct 44240
Standing Rock St 44240
Starr Ave 44240
State Route 261 44240
State Route 43 44240
State Route 59 44240
Statesman Pl 44240
Steele St 44240
Stein Ct 44240
Stewart Lake Rd 44240
Stillwood Dr 44240
Stinaff St 44240
Stonewater Dr 44240
Stow St 44240
Stratford Dr 44240
Stratton St 44240
Sugar Maple Dr 44240
E & W Summit Rd & St 44240
Summit Gardens Blvd 44240
Sunnybrook Rd 44240
Sunrise Dr 44240
Sunset Way Blvd & Cir 44240
Suzanne Dr 44240
E & W Swan Lake Cir 44240
Sylvan Dr 44240
Tallmadge Ave & Rd 44240
Tart Cherry Ln 44240
Temple Ave 44240
Terrace Dr 44243
Thorndale Dr 44240
Timber Mill Dr 44240
Tonkin Ct 44240
Town Square Dr 44240
Towner Dr 44240
Treeview Cir 44240
Troyer Dr 44240
Tudor Ln 44240
Turtle Bay Cir 44240
Twin Hills Rd 44240
University Dr 44240
University Esplanade 44243
Valley View Ct 44240
Valleyview Dr 44240
Verner Rd 44240
Verona Dr 44240
Vfw Pkwy 44240
Vine Ct & St 44240
Virginia Ave 44240
Vista Cir 44240
Walden Dr 44240
Walnut Rd & St 44240
Walters St 44240
Walton Rd 44240
Waring St 44240
N & S Water St 44240
Waterford Pointe Dr 44240
West Blvd & St 44240
Westminster Ln 44240
Westshore Dr 44240
Westview Rd 44240
Whetstone Dr 44240
Whitehall Blvd 44240
Whitestone Rd 44240
Whitewood Dr 44240
Whittier Ave 44240
Williams Dr 44243
E Williams St 44240
W Williams St 44240
N & S Willow St & Way 44240
Willow Ridge Cir 44240
Willyard Ave 44240
Wilson Ave 44240
Windward Ln 44240
Windy Hill Dr 44240
Wolcott Ave 44240
Woodard Ave 44240
Woodglen St 44240
Woodhill Dr 44240
Woods Trl 44240
Woodside Dr 44240
Woodway Rd 44240
Wrens Hollow Cir 44240
Wunderlich Ave 44240
Yacavona St 44240
Yellowwood Cir 44240

NUMBERED STREETS

All Street Addresses 44240

LIMA OH

General Delivery 45802

POST OFFICE BOXES MAIN OFFICE STATIONS AND BRANCHES

Box No.s
1 - 2000 45802
3001 - 3207 45807
4501 - 5680 45802

NAMED STREETS

Abnaki Trl 45805
Ada Rd 45801
Adak Ave 45805
Adamlee Pl 45801
Adams St 45801
Adgate Rd 45805
Agerter Rd
5100-5499 45805
5800-7899 45806
Airport Dr 45804
E Albert St 45804
Alexandria Dr 45805
Algonkin Trl 45805
Alix Dr 45807
Allentown Rd
1201-1211 45805
1213-3299 45805
3300-9299 45807
Allison Dr 45805
Alton Ave 45804
Amanda Lakes Dr 45805
Amaryllis St 45807
E Amblewood Cir 45806
Amherst Rd 45806
Amy Dr 45807
Ann Way 45805
Aqua Dr 45807
Arapaho Trl 45805
Arcadia Ave 45805
Arlington Dr 45805
Armstead Pl 45804
Arrowhead Trl 45806
Arthur Ave 45805
Ash Dr 45806
E & W Ashton Ave 45801
Ashwood Ave 45801
Aspen Dr 45805
Aster St 45807
Atalan Trl 45805
S Atlantic Ave 45804
Auglaize County Line Rd 45806
Augusta Dr 45805
Austin Ct 45805
Autumn Blaze Dr 45801
Autumn Leaves Ct 45805
Autumn Ridge Dr 45801
Axminster Ter 45805
B St 45804
Bahama Dr 45801
Balyeat Dr 45805
Barnsbury Dr 45804
Baton Rouge 45805
Baty Rd 45807
Baxter St 45807
N Baxter St 45801
S Baxter St 45801
Bay Circle St 45801
Bayberry Dr 45806
Baywood Dr 45805
Beaumont Pl 45805
Bechtol Rd 45801
Beech Ct 45807
Beechwood Pl 45807
Beeler Rd 45806
Beery Rd 45807
Bel Aire Pl 45805
Bellefontaine Ave
700-899 45801
900-1499 45804
Bellefontaine Rd 45804
Bellwood Dr 45805
Belmont Ave 45804
Belvidere Ave 45801
Benham Dr 45805
Bentwood Dr 45805
Bentz Rd 45805
Bermuda Dr 45801
Berryhill Rd 45801
Berryman Blvd 45805
Bible Rd 45801
Bice Rd 45806
Bikini Dr 45801
Billymack Rd 45807
Birch Crest Dr 45804
Birelist Rd 45806
Biscayne Dr 45801
Bittersweet Dr 45807
Black Dr 45805
Blackburn Dr 45805
Blackhawk Pl 45806
Bliss Rd 45807
Blue Jacket Ct 45806
Blue Jay Ct 45806
Bluebird Cir 45807
E & W Bluelick Rd 45801
Bluff Oak Trl 45807
Bonnieview Dr 45801
Boundry Rd 45806
Bowman Rd
1001-1297 45804
1299-2699 45804
2700-5199 45806
Bowsher Rd 45806
Boxwood Dr 45804
Boyer St 45801
Braburn Ct 45806
Bradfield Dr 45804
Bradford Ave 45805
Branson Ave 45804
E & W Breese Rd 45806
Breezewood Ln 45805
Brendonwood Dr 45801
Brenneman Rd 45807
Brentlinger Rd 45801
Briargrove Ln 45806
Briarwood Ct 45806
Brice Ave
600-899 45801
900-1399 45805
Bridle Trl 45807
Bristol Ave 45804
Britt Ave 45806
S Broadway St 45804
Brookgrove Ct 45807
Brookhaven Dr 45805
Brookhill Ln 45807
Brookshore Dr 45801
Brookview Ct 45801

Brookwood Dr 45801
Brower Rd 45801
Bryn Mawr Ave 45804
Buckeye Rd 45804
Buckingham Dr 45807
Buckland Holden Rd 45806
E Buckskin Trl 45807
Bunker Dr 45805
Bur Oak Trl 45807
Burch Ave 45801
Burden Dr 45801
Burlington Pl 45805
Burntwood Dr 45805
Bussert Rd 45807
Buttercup Dr 45807
C St 45804
Cable Ct 45805
N Cable Rd
100-398 45805
400-2100 45805
2102-2198 45805
2200-5499 45807
S Cable Rd 45805
Calumet Ave
100-199 45801
200-699 45804
Cam Ct 45805
Cambria St 45807
Cambridge Pl 45804
Camden Pl 45806
Cameron Ln 45805
Camp Ave 45805
Campus Dr 45804
Canary Rd 45801
Candy Ln 45805
Canterbury Dr 45805
Canyon Dr 45804
Cardinal Ct 45806
Caribou Cir 45806
Carlisle Ave 45804
N Carlisle St 45806
S Carlisle St 45806
Carlos Ln 45804
Carlton Pl 45804
Carol Ann St 45801
Carolina Ave 45805
Carolyn Dr 45807
Carriage Ln 45807
Castle Green Dr 45805
Catalpa Ave 45804
Catawba Trl 45806
Cedar St 45804
Cedarwood Dr 45807
Celia Pl 45801
Center St 45806
N Center St 45801
N Central Ave 45801
S Central Ave
100-239 45801
241-309 45801
355-2699 45804
Central Point Pkwy 45804
Cessna Ave 45807
Chaldela Rd 45801
Chancellor Dr 45807
Chandler Dr 45805
Chapel Hill Dr 45805
E & W Chapman Ave & Rd 45801
Charledon Ave 45804
N Charles St
100-999 45805
1000-1999 45801
S Charles St 45805
Charwood Dr 45805
Chateau Dr 45805
Cherie Ave 45807
Cherokee Dr 45807
Cherry Blossom Ct 45807
Cheshire Cir 45804
Chester Pl 45801
Chesterton Dr 45805
Chestnut St 45804
Chestnut Oak Trl 45807
Chevy Chase Blvd 45804
Chicago Dr 45804

Chickadee Pl 45807
Chipman Ave 45805
Chris Ln 45806
Christopher Dr 45801
Circle Dr 45806
E & W Circular St 45804
Citabria Dr 45807
Clayton Dr 45806
Clement Dr 45806
Cletus Pkwy 45805
Clifford Dr 45805
Clinton Way 45805
Close Ave 45805
Clover Ave 45801
Clover Ridge Dr 45807
Clubview Dr 45805
Clum Rd 45806
Clyde Ave 45804
Coakley Dr 45807
N Cole St
100-114 45805
116-1199 45805
1200-3699 45801
3700-5499 45807
S Cole St 45805
College Ave & Park W 45805
N Collett St 45805
S Collett St
200-600 45805
602-616 45805
700-999 45804
Collingwood Blvd 45801
N & S Collins Ave 45804
Colonial Ln 45805
Colony Trl 45804
Columbia Dr 45805
Commerce Pkwy 45804
Commercial Ave 45805
Commonwealth Ave 45806
N Conant Rd 45807
N & S Concept Dr 45807
Concord Dr 45806
Concord Pl 45805
N Cool Rd
300-624 45801
626-4999 45801
5000-5299 45807
S Cool Rd
100-198 45801
200-634 45801
1000-2699 45806
Coon Rd 45806
Coons Ln 45806
N Copus Rd 45807
S Copus Rd
100-264 45807
266-298 45807
300-1199 45805
Cornell Dr 45805
Cortlandt Ave 45801
Cotner Rd 45807
Cottonwood Dr 45805
Country View Cir 45801
Couples Ln 45805
Crabb Rd 45806
Crayton Ave 45805
Creek Xing 45804
Cremean Rd 45807
Creps Rd 45806
Crestview Dr 45801
Crestwood Dr 45805
Crites Pl 45807
Cumberland Dr 45804
Cuttler Ln 45805
Cuyahoga Dr 45806
Cynthia Dr 45801
Cypress Ave 45806
Dabill Pl 45805
Daisy Ln 45807
N & S Dale Dr 45805
N & S Dana Ave 45804
Daniels Ave 45805
Danny Dr 45801
Darrell Dr 45806
Dawn Dr 45804
Daytona Dr 45801

Dean Ave 45804
Debbie Dr 45807
Deborah St 45801
Deep Cut Rd 45806
Deer Run 45807
Deercreek Cir 45804
Deerfield Dr 45805
Defiance Trl N 45807
Delaware Ave 45801
Delong Rd 45806
Delphos Ave
700-799 45801
801-899 45801
901-1199 45805
Detroit St 45804
Devonshire Dr 45804
N & S Dewey Ave 45804
Dickson Rd 45806
Diller Rd 45807
Dingledine Ave 45804
N Dixie Hwy
100-109 45806
111-299 45806
1700-4299 45801
4300-6099 45807
S Dixie Hwy
101-103 45806
105-5399 45806
400-599 45806
1400-3699 45804
3700-4799 45806
Doe Ct 45807
Dogleg Rd 45807
Dogwood Dr 45805
Dove Ct 45806
Dughill Rd 45806
Dupler Ave 45806
Dutch Hollow Rd 45807
Eagles Pt E & W 45805
Early Ave 45801
East Rd 45807
Eastern Ave 45804
Eastom Cir 45804
N & S Eastown Rd 45807
Eastpark Dr 45804
Eastwood Dr 45804
Edgewood Dr 45805
Edna Dr 45807
Edsel Ave 45801
E Edwards St 45801
Elida Rd
1352-1398 45805
1400-3299 45805
3300-6800 45807
Elijah Pkwy 45805
N Elizabeth St
100-299 45806
100-1999 45801
S Elizabeth St
100-210 45801
212-317 45801
319-399 45801
500-999 45804
Ellen Dr 45806
Ellison Dr 45805
E Elm St
100-200 45801
202-418 45801
500-2299 45804
W Elm St
126-198 45801
200-799 45801
800-3299 45805
3300-5099 45807
Elmire Dr 45806
Elmview Ct 45805
Elmview Dr 45806
Elmwood Pl 45801
Emerald Ln 45805
Emma Pkwy 45806
Erie St 45804
Ernest Dr 45805
Ertel Ave 45801
Essex Dr 45804
Estate Dr 45805
Esther Blvd 45805
Euclid Ave 45804

E Eureka St 45804
W Eureka St
108-118 45804
120-299 45804
500-999 45801
Evergreen Dr 45806
Ewing Ave 45801
Fairfield Dr 45805
Fairgreen Ave 45805
Fairlane Dr 45806
Fairview Ave 45804
Fairway Dr 45805
W Falls Rd 45805
Farmdale Ave 45801
Faurot Ave
500-999 45801
1000-1099 45805
Fawn Ct 45807
Fawnwood Dr 45804
Faze Rd 45801
Feeman Ave 45805
Fenway Dr 45804
N & S Fernwood Dr 45805
Fett Ave 45801
Fetter Rd 45801
Fieldstone Rd 45807
Finch Ct 45806
Finch Rd 45807
Findlay Rd 45801
Fisher Rd 45801
Flanders Ave 45801
Florence Ave 45804
E & W Ford Ave 45801
Forest Dr 45805
Fort Amanda Rd
1200-1498 45804
1500-2699 45804
2700-2742 45805
2744-6299 45805
6300-8899 45806
Fort Shawnee Ave 45806
Fort Shawnee Industrial Dr 45806
Fox Run 45805
Fox Creek Dr 45805
Fox Hollow Dr 45804
Foxfield Ct 45804
Frail Rd 45806
Franklin St 45804
Franks Dr 45807
Fraunfelter Rd N & S 45807
Freyer Rd 45807
Friar Ln 45805
Fulton Rd 45805
Gaithersburg Dr 45805
Gala Ct 45806
Galvin Ln 45805
Gannon Dr 45807
Garden Blvd 45805
Gardenview Cir 45801
Garfield Ave 45805
Garford Ave 45804
Garland Ave 45804
N & S Gay St 45806
Geneva Ln 45807
George Bingham Dr 45807
Georgian Ave 45806
Glen Arbor Ter 45805
Glenn Ave 45804
Glenrary Rd 45805
N & S Glenwood Ave 45805
Gloria Ave 45805
Gloucester Pl 45804
Golden Ln 45807
Gomer Rd 45807
Gracely Dr 45801
Grady Ave 45807
Graham Pl 45805
Graham Rd 45806
E & W Grand Ave 45801
Grant St 45801
Greely Chapel Rd
900-2699 45804
2700-6599 45806
Greenbriar Ct 45804
Greenbriar St 45806

Greendale St 45801
Greenglen Ave 45805
Greenlawn Ave 45804
N Greenlawn Ave 45807
S Greenlawn Ave
102-102 45807
104-299 45807
1000-1098 45804
Greens Rd 45805
Greentree Cir 45806
Gregory Ln 45807
Griffiths Dr 45807
Grimmwood Dr 45806
Grove Ave 45801
Groves Rd 45805
Grubb Rd N 45807
S Grubb Rd 45806
Gull Ct 45806
Hadsell Rd 45801
Haida Trl 45805
Hall Dr 45806
Haller St 45801
Hampton Ct 45805
Hanover Dr 45805
Hansom Ln 45806
Hanthorn Rd 45806
E Hanthorn Rd 45804
W Hanthorn Rd 45804
Harding Hwy
1500-5899 45804
5900-8999 45801
Harper Ave 45807
Harrington Rd 45801
Harris Rd 45807
Harrison Ave 45804
Harrod Rd 45806
Hartford Ct 45805
Hartman Rd 45807
Hartzler Rd 45805
Harvard Ave 45804
Harvest Way 45807
Harwood Ln 45806
Hastings Ave 45806
Hauss Rd 45806
Hawthorne Dr 45805
Hazel Ave
400-799 45801
901-997 45805
999-1699 45805
Heather Rd 45804
Heathway Ln 45801
Hefner Dr 45801
Heindel Ave 45804
Helen Ave 45801
Hemlock Ave 45806
Henry St 45807
Heritage Dr 45804
Herman St 45804
Hermitage Ln 45806
Herr Rd 45801
Hiawatha Trl 45806
Hickory Pl 45807
Hickory St 45806
Hickorywood Ln 45805
Hide Away Dr 45806
E High St
100-599 45806
100-999 45801
1000-1699 45804
W High St
101-107 45801
109-700 45801
201-201 45806
203-409 45806
411-499 45806
702-898 45801
900-2299 45805
2900-2999 45807
High Ridge Rd 45805
Highland Ave 45804
Highland Lakes Dr 45801
Hill St 45804
Hillcrest Dr
300-399 45807
1800-1999 45805
Hillsdale Ave 45805

Hillville Rd 45807
Hofferbert Rd 45807
Hokan Trl 45805
Hollar Ave 45805
Holly St 45804
Hollyhock Ave 45807
Holmes Ave 45804
Homestead Ave 45804
Homestead Dr 45807
Homeward Ave 45805
Honeysuckle Bnd 45807
Hook Waltz Rd E & W 45807
Hope St 45804
Hopewell St 45801
Hopi Trl 45805
Houx Pkwy 45804
Howard St 45807
Hubbard Pl 45804
Huffer Rd 45807
Hughes Ave 45804
E & W Hume Rd 45806
Hummingbird St 45807
Huntington Dr 45806
Huntleigh Dr 45806
Hurley Pl 45804
Huron Pl 45806
Idlewild Dr 45805
Ilata Ave 45805
Independence Rd 45801
Indian Hill Dr 45806
Industry Ave 45804
Industry Avenue Ct 45804
Inwood Dr 45806
Irvin Rd 45807
Ivy Dr 45807
N Jackson St 45801
S Jackson St
100-198 45801
200-499 45804
Jacobs Ave 45801
N & S Jameson Ave 45805
Jane Pkwy 45806
Jared Pl 45805
Jean Ct 45805
N Jefferson St 45801
Jenny Pl 45805
Jo Jean Rd 45806
Johns Ave 45807
Jonathan Dr 45806
Jones Rd 45807
Joyce Ln 45806
Judith St 45801
S Judkins Ave 45805
Jules Dr 45805
Julian Ave 45801
Juliette Dr 45805
June Dr 45805
Juneau Dr 45805
Juniper Ave 45806
Karen Ave 45801
Karif Cir 45805
Kell Dan Ave 45806
Kemp Rd N 45807
S Kemp Rd 45806
N & S Kenilworth Ave & Ter 45805
Kenmore St 45801
Kenny Lee Dr 45807
Kensington Cir 45804
Kent Ave 45801
Kenyon Dr 45805
Keresan Trl 45805
Kerr Rd 45806
E & W Kibby St 45804
E & W Kildare Ave 45801
Kimberly Dr
2100-2599 45805
2600-2899 45807
King Ave 45805
King Arthur Ct 45805
Kingsbury Ct 45804
Kingston Ave 45804
Kingswood Dr 45804
Kiowa Trl 45805
E & W Kiracofe Ave 45807
Kirkland Dr 45801

Kissing Hollow Dr 45801
Kitamat Trl 45805
Kitchen Rd 45807
Knollwood Dr 45801
Koch Dr 45806
Koneta Dr 45806
Koop Rd
2400-2798 45805
2801-2897 45807
2899-2999 45807
Kruse Aly 45807
Kunneke Ave 45805
Lady Bird Ln 45801
Lafayette St 45804
Lake St 45804
Lake Circle Dr 45801
Lake Ridge Dr 45804
Lakeshore Dr 45806
Lakeside Dr 45804
Lakewood Ave 45805
Lancewood Pl 45805
E & W Lane Ave 45801
Lanes End 45805
Laney Ave 45804
Langans Ln 45804
Lansing Ln 45805
Lark Ave 45801
Larkspur Dr 45807
Larry St 45801
Latham Ave 45805
Lavina Ave 45806
Lawnwood Dr 45805
Leatherwood Rd 45807
Lee Ann Dr 45801
Leffler Dr 45806
Leist Ave 45805
Leland Ave 45805
Lennox Ave 45804
Lenore St 45804
N & S Leonard Ave 45804
Lester Ave 45801
Lewis Blvd 45801
Liberty St 45801
Liberty Commons Pkwy 45804
Lilac Ln 45806
Lilly Dr 45807
Lincoln Ave 45805
E Lincoln Hwy
100-198 45807
200-2600 45807
2602-2698 45807
7400-8199 45801
W Lincoln Hwy 45807
Linden St 45804
Linfield Ln 45806
Live Oak Trl 45807
Lloyd Rd 45807
Lobo St 45807
Loch Loman Way 45805
Loescher Rd 45801
Logan Ave 45801
London Dr 45805
Long Rd 45807
Lorain Dr 45805
Loretta Pl 45805
Lost Creek Blvd 45804
Lowell Ave 45805
Lucille Dr 45801
Lutz Rd 45801
Lyn Grove Dr 45806
Lynn Park 45805
Lyre Bird Ln 45801
Lytle Ln 45806
Mackenzie Dr 45805
Madden Rd 45806
Madison Ave 45804
Magnolia Ln 45806
Mahoning Dr 45806
E Main St
100-106 45806
100-699 45807
108-699 45806
700-799 45807
N Main St 45801

- S Main St
  - 101-141 45801
  - 143-299 45801
  - 301-331 45801
  - 400-2699 45804
- W Main St
  - 100-208 45807
  - 100-409 45806
  - 210-218 45807
  - 411-599 45806
- Makin Dr 45804
- Makley Dr 45805
- Malibu Dr 45807
- Mandalay Pl 45805
- Mandolin Dr 45801
- Maple Dr & Ln 45805
- Maple Leaf Dr 45804
- Maplewood Dr 45805
- Maplewood Ln 45806
- Marcella Ln 45806
- Marciel Dr 45807
- Marian Ave 45801
- E Market St
  - 100-717 45801
  - 719-999 45801
  - 1000-1699 45804
  - 716 1/2-716 1/2 45801
- W Market St
  - 119-129 45801
  - 131-799 45801
  - 801-897 45805
  - 899-2799 45805
  - 2800-2999 45807
- Marlboro Dr 45805
- Martin Ct 45806
- Masters Ct 45805
- Maumee Dr 45806
- Mayberry Rd 45807
- Mcbride Rd 45807
- Mcclain Rd
  - 1301-1587 45804
  - 1589-3799 45804
  - 3800-5899 45806
- N & S Mcclure Rd 45801
- Mccullough St 45801
- N Mcdonel St 45801
- S Mcdonel St
  - 101-125 45801
  - 127-420 45801
  - 422-444 45801
  - 600-899 45804
- E & W Mckibben St 45801
- Mckinley St 45801
- Mcpheron Ave & Rd 45804
- Meadow Ln 45806
- Meadow Glen Dr 45807
- Meadow View Dr 45805
- Meadowbrook Blvd 45806
- Meadowbrook Dr 45801
- Meadowlands Dr 45805
- Medical Dr 45804
- Mehaffey Rd 45801
- Melrose St 45801
- Memorial Arc 45801
- Merit Ave 45805
- Merlin Ave 45805
- N Metcalf St 45801
- S Metcalf St
  - 100-530 45801
  - 532-534 45801
  - 565-1499 45804
- Metzger Rd 45801
- Mews Rd 45805
- Miami Pl 45806
- Michael Ave 45804
- E & W Michigan Ave 45801
- Mickelson Ln 45801
- Milburn Ave 45804
- Miller Ave 45801
- Millia Dr 45806
- Mills Rd 45806
- Milton Ave 45805
- Miramonte Dr 45806
- Mirror Lake Dr 45801
- Mobel Ave 45804
- Mohawk Ct 45806
- Molly Ave 45801
- Monticello Ave 45804
- Morning Glory Dr 45807
- Morning Sun Dr 45805
- Morris Ave 45805
- Mound Rd 45805
- Mount Holyoke Ave 45804
- Mount Vernon Pl 45804
- Mowery Rd
  - 4700-4799 45806
  - 4900-5899 45801
- Mudsock Rd 45806
- Muirfield Pl 45805
- Mullen Ave 45801
- N & S Mumaugh Rd 45804
- E & W Murphy St 45801
- Murray Rd 45801
- Musket Cir & Trl 45804
- Muskingum Trl 45806
- Musser Dr 45807
- Myrtle Oak Trl 45807
- Nancy Sue Dr 45806
- N Napoleon Rd
  - 100-4999 45801
  - 4900-6099 45807
- S Napoleon Rd 45801
- National Rd 45806
- Neely Rd 45807
- Neff Rd 45807
- Nesbitt St 45807
- Neubrecht Rd 45801
- New Haven Dr 45806
- New Sterling Rd 45801
- N & S Nixon Ave 45805
- Norfolk St 45806
- E North St
  - 100-399 45807
  - 117-119 45801
  - 121-999 45801
  - 401-499 45807
  - 1000-1299 45804
- W North St
  - 100-499 45806
  - 100-800 45801
  - 100-100 45807
  - 102-300 45807
  - 302-302 45807
  - 802-898 45801
  - 900-1199 45805
- Northbrook Dr 45805
- E & W Northern Ave 45801
- Northlea Dr 45801
- Northplace 45806
- Northwestern Dr 45805
- Northwold St 45801
- Northwoods Dr 45804
- Norval Ave 45804
- Nova St 45804
- Nye St 45801
- Oak St 45804
- S Oak St 45806
- Oak Ter 45805
- Oak Creek Ln 45806
- Oak Hill Ct 45805
- Oak Woods Dr 45805
- Oakland Ave 45801
- Oakland Pkwy
  - 1200-2299 45805
  - 2900-2999 45807
- Oakview Ct 45804
- Oakwood Ln 45806
- Oakwood Pl 45804
- E & W Oconnor Ave 45801
- Odema Dr 45806
- Ohio St 45804
- Old Delphos Rd 45807
- Old State Route 12 45807
- Olentangy Dr 45806
- Olympia Cir 45805
- Onalee Dr 45806
- Ontario St 45804
- Orchard Dr 45807
- Orena Ave 45804
- Oriole Ct 45806
- Oriole Trl 45807
- Osman Rd 45806
- Ottawa Rd
  - 4100-5499 45801
  - 5500-8499 45807
- Oval Dr 45801
- Oxford Ave 45804
- Palm Ct 45807
- Palmer Dr 45801
- Pangle St 45801
- Paradise Pl 45801
- Parakeet Pl 45801
- S Park Ave 45801
- Park Cir 45805
- Parkview Dr 45806
- Parkway St 45805
- Partridge Ct 45806
- Partridge Pl 45801
- Patricia Dr 45801
- Patton Ave 45805
- Paul St 45804
- Pawnee Dr 45806
- Peachtree Pl 45805
- Peacock Dr 45805
- E Pearl St 45801
- N & S Pears Ave 45805
- Pebble Creek Dr 45801
- Pecan Ave 45806
- W Pennsylvania Ave 45801
- Penny Lee Dr 45805
- N & S Perry St 45804
- Perry Chapel Rd 45804
- Persimmon Ave 45806
- Pheasant St 45807
- Pickwick Pl 45805
- N Pierce St 45801
- S Pierce St
  - 129-197 45801
  - 199-400 45801
  - 402-458 45801
  - 500-899 45804
- Pierre Pl 45805
- Pilgrim Trl 45804
- Pin Oak Ct 45805
- Pine Run 45801
- N Pine St 45801
- S Pine St
  - 100-199 45801
  - 200-799 45804
- Pine Grove Way 45805
- Pine Haven Dr 45804
- Pine Lake Dr 45805
- Pine Shore Dr 45806
- Pinewood Cir 45804
- Pioneer Rd 45807
- Piper Cub Dr 45807
- Piquad Rd 45807
- Plainfield Dr 45805
- Plaza Way 45801
- Pleasant View Ave 45805
- Plum Cir & St 45807
- Plymouth Dr 45805
- Pocahontas Ave 45806
- Poinsettia Dr 45806
- Poling Rd 45807
- Ponderosa Ln 45805
- Pondview Ct 45804
- Poulston Pl 45805
- Powers Ave 45801
- Prairie Rose Dr 45807
- Primrose Ln 45807
- S Primrose Pl 45805
- Pro Dr
  - 1501-1531 45805
  - 1533-1656 45805
  - 1658-1698 45805
  - 2700-3199 45806
- Prospect Ave 45804
- Prosperity Rd 45801
- Providence Cir 45801
- Putters Ln 45805
- Quail Dr 45806
- Queens Ln 45805
- Queensbury Dr 45804
- Quilna Dr 45806
- Quince Ct 45807
- Racers Way 45805
- Radcliffe St 45804
- Rainbow Dr 45801
- Raleigh Creek Dr 45806
- Ramsey Rd 45807
- Ravine Ct 45805
- Ream Rd 45806
- Rebecca Dr 45805
- Red Oak Cir & Dr 45806
- Red Ridge Rd 45807
- Red Wing Ct 45806
- Redbud Ln 45806
- Redd Rd 45807
- Reed Rd 45804
- Reen Dr 45805
- Reese Ave 45804
- Reichelderfer Rd 45806
- Reinell Ave 45805
- Reppert Rd 45801
- Reservoir Rd
  - 1300-1899 45804
  - 1901-2199 45804
  - 2201-2397 45801
  - 2399-2899 45801
  - 2901-3899 45801
  - 4100-4899 45806
  - 4900-8599 45801
- Rhodes Ave 45805
- Rice Ave 45805
- Richard Dr 45806
- Richie Ave
  - 700-899 45801
  - 900-1199 45805
- Richlieu Dr 45805
- Ridge Rd 45807
- Ridge Crest Cir 45801
- Ridge Run Cir 45805
- Ridgehill Ln 45805
- Riley St 45805
- River Rd 45806
- River Trl 45807
- River Bend Dr 45807
- River Grove Dr 45807
- River Ridge St 45807
- Riverview Dr 45805
- Riverwalk Blvd 45806
- Road 17 S 45807
- Road 17u 45807
- E Robb Ave 45801
- W Robb Ave
  - 101-197 45801
  - 199-1299 45801
  - 1300-1999 45805
- N & S Roberts Ave 45804
- Robin Dr 45805
- Robinhood Dr 45805
- Roger St 45807
- Roosevelt Ave 45804
- Roschman Ave 45804
- Rose Ave 45806
- N & S Rosedale Ave 45805
- Rosewood Dr 45805
- Rosewood Ln 45806
- Rountree St 45805
- Roush Rd 45801
- Royal Oak Dr 45805
- Rue Dr 45806
- N & S Rumbaugh Rd 45801
- Running Oak Trl 45807
- Runyan Ave & Ct 45801
- Rupert Ct 45804
- Ruskin Ct 45806
- Russell Ave 45801
- Ruth Ave 45801
- Saddlebrook Dr 45807
- Saint Andrews Blvd 45804
- Saint Clair Ave 45801
- Saint Johns Ave 45804
- Saint Johns Rd
  - 1500-3699 45804
  - 3700-19999 45806
- Saint Matthews Dr 45806
- Sandalwood Ln 45806
- Sandpiper St 45801
- Sands Rd 45805
- Sandusky Rd 45801
- Sandy Ln 45806
- Sandy Point Rd 45807
- Santa Fe Rd 45806
- Sara Lee Ave 45806
- Saratoga Ave 45804
- Schooler Rd 45806
- Scioto Dr 45806
- N Scott St 45801
- S Scott St 45804
- Seandinc Dr 45805
- Sellers Rd 45806
- Seminole Trl 45805
- Seneca Ave & Dr 45806
- Sequoia Ave 45806
- N Seriff Dr 45807
- S Seriff Dr 45807
- S Seriff Rd 45805
- Shadowood Dr 45805
- Shady Woods Dr 45804
- Shagbark Dr 45806
- Shalloway Dr 45806
- Sharlene Dr 45807
- Sharon Pl 45805
- Sharon Rose Dr 45807
- Shawnee Rd
  - 100-399 45806
  - 700-2399 45805
  - 2400-5699 45806
- N Shawnee St 45804
- S Shawnee St 45804
- Shawnee Industrial Dr 45804
- Shearin Ave 45801
- Sheffield Ln 45805
- Shelly Pl 45805
- Shenk Rd 45807
- Sheridan Dr 45805
- Sherman Ave 45801
- Sherrick Rd 45807
- Sherry Lee Dr 45807
- Sherwood Ct & Dr 45805
- Shiloh Dr 45801
- Shock Ave 45805
- N Shore Dr 45801
- S Shore Dr 45804
- W Shore Dr 45805
- Shoreline Dr 45805
- Shores Ln 45807
- Shoreview Dr 45805
- Shorewood Ln 45806
- Short St 45806
- Shoshone Trl 45805
- S Side Dr 45807
- Silver Maple Dr 45804
- Silver Stream Ct 45805
- Simons Ave 45804
- Sinclair Ave 45806
- Singleton Ave 45805
- Sky Hawk Dr 45807
- Slabtown Rd
  - 1500-4699 45801
  - 4700-6499 45807
- Smead Ave 45804
- Smith Ave 45801
- Snowberry Ln 45806
- Sorenstam Ln 45801
- Southgate Blvd 45806
- Southland Pl 45805
- Southwood Dr 45805
- Spartan Way 45801
- Spencer Cir & Dr 45806
- Spencerville Rd
  - 1701-1797 45805
  - 1799-6299 45805
  - 6300-8299 45806
- N Spring Ct 45805
- E Spring Ln 45805
- S Spring Ln 45805
- E Spring St 45801
- W Spring St
  - 115-297 45801
  - 299-799 45801
  - 800-2499 45805
- Spring Blossoms Ct 45805
- Spring View Dr 45805
- Springbrook Dr 45801
- Springhill Dr 45805
- Spruce Dr 45807
- Squire Ln 45805
- Stadler Rd 45807
- Stahley St 45806
- Stanton Ave 45801
- E State Rd
  - 100-599 45807
  - 600-1899 45801
  - 1900-2240 45807
  - 2242-6149 45807
  - 6151-6199 45807
- W State Rd 45807
- W State St 45805
- State Route 196 45806
- State Route 198 45806
- Statesman Pkwy 45806
- Stearman Dr 45807
- Steeple Chase 45807
- Stemen St 45807
- Steven Dr 45807
- N & S Stevick Rd 45807
- Stewart Rd
  - 1200-5499 45801
  - 5500-8599 45807
- Stonecrest Pl 45807
- Stoneybrook Dr 45805
- Stonywood Dr 45801
- Streamview Dr 45804
- Struthmore Dr 45806
- E Sugar St 45806
- N Sugar St 45801
- S Sugar St 45804
- W Sugar St 45806
- Sugar Creek Rd
  - 2900-5899 45807
  - 5900-6699 45801
  - 6700-6899 45807
  - 6900-8699 45801
- Sugar Tree Dr 45804
- Summer Breeze Ct 45805
- Summer Rambo Ct 45806
- Summit St 45801
- Sunderland Rd 45806
- Sunnydale St 45807
- Sunnymeade Ln 45804
- Sunrise Ave 45806
- Sunrise Dr 45805
- Superior Ct 45801
- Surrey Ln 45807
- Susan Ln 45806
- Susan Ann Dr 45807
- Swallow Ct 45806
- Swaney Rd 45801
- Sweetbriar Ave 45806
- Sweger Rd 45807
- Sycamore St 45807
- Symphony St 45801
- Taft Ave 45804
- Tahoe Pl 45805
- Tall Oaks Ave 45805
- Tanglewood Ln 45805
- Tara Ct 45805
- Tawa Dr 45806
- Taylor Ave 45801
- Techwood Pl 45805
- Teresa Ave 45807
- N Thayer Rd
  - 100-4299 45801
  - 4300-5299 45807
- S Thayer Rd 45806
- Thomas Dr 45806
- Thorndyke Dr 45801
- Thrush Ct 45806
- Tillamook Trl 45805
- Timberfield Dr N 45807
- Timberlane Dr 45805
- Timberstone Dr 45807
- Timothy Dr 45807
- Tingle Ave 45801
- Tiqua Trl 45805
- Tolowa Trl 45805
- Tonkawa Trl 45805
- Town Sq 45801
- Town St 45807
- Townline Rd 45806
- Township Road 200 45806
- Trebor Dr 45805
- Tremont Ave 45801
- Trinchaw Ave 45804
- Trolley Ave 45805
- Troyer Rd 45807
- Tucumseh Trl 45806
- Tudor Rd 45807
- Tupelo Ave 45806
- Turner Ave 45804
- Tuscarawas Trl 45806
- N Union St 45801
- S Union St
  - 100-108 45801
  - 110-300 45801
  - 302-398 45801
  - 600-2699 45804
- University Blvd 45805
- Valley Way 45804
- Van Buren St 45807
- Vanness Ave 45804
- Vassar Ave 45804
- Vera Way 45805
- Victoria Ln 45805
- Victory Ave 45801
- E & W Vine St 45804
- Virginia Ave 45801
- Wakashan Trl 45805
- Wales Ave 45805
- Walmar Ave 45805
- Walnut Ct 45805
- Walter St 45806
- N Wapakoneta Rd 45807
- S Wapakoneta Rd
  - 148-210 45807
  - 212-699 45807
  - 700-2899 45805
  - 2900-20999 45806
- Ward Ave 45804
- Ward St 45807
- Wardhill Ave 45805
- Warren Ave 45801
- Warsaw Rd 45806
- N & S Washington St 45801
- S Water St 45806
- W Water St 45801
- Waterview Cir 45804
- Watkins Rd 45807
- Watt Ave 45801
- N & S Waverly St 45806
- E Wayne St
  - 101-123 45801
  - 125-701 45801
  - 1000-1100 45804
  - 1102-1198 45804
- W Wayne St
  - 100-106 45801
  - 108-899 45801
  - 900-2399 45805
- Wayside Dr 45805
- Weadock Ave 45804
- Weger Ave 45807
- Weldon Dr 45806
- Wellesley Dr 45804
- Wellontr Rd 45807
- Wells Dr 45804
- Wenatchie Trl 45805
- Wendell Ave 45805
- Wentz Rd 45807
- N West St
  - 100-5199 45801
  - 5201-5399 45801
  - 5500-8499 45807
- S West St
  - 122-202 45801
  - 204-208 45801
  - 210-450 45801
  - 500-699 45804
- Westbrook Dr 45801
- Westerly Dr 45805
- Western Ohio Ave 45805
- Westfield Dr 45805
- Westimber Ct 45805
- N & S Westwood Dr 45805
- Whalen St 45806
- Whippoorwill Ave 45807
- White Oak Ln 45805
- Whitehall Dr 45805
- Wicker Ln 45805
- Wilbur Dr 45805
- Wildbrook Ln 45807

Wildwood Ave 45807
Wildwood Pt 45805
Willard Ave 45804
Williams St 45801
Willow Dr 45807
Willow Oak Trl 45807
Wilshire Dr 45805
Wilson Ave 45805
Windsor Dr 45805
Winghaven Dr 45805
Winston Ct 45804
Winterberry Dr 45805
Wintergreen Dr 45805
Wolfe Rd 45807
Wonderlick Rd 45805
Wonnell Rd 45806
Wood St
100-199 45804
201-299 45806
Woodford Ter 45805
Woodhaven Ln 45806
Woodland Dr 45805
N & S Woodlawn Ave 45805
Woodridge Dr 45806
Woodrow Dr 45805
Woods Dr 45801
Woodward Ave
500-799 45805
800-899 45801
901-1099 45801
Wren Ave 45807
Wrestle Creek Rd 45806
Wyandot Dr & St 45806
Wyngate Ct 45805
Wynnwood Ct 45801
Yakima Trl 45805
Yale Ave 45804
Yellowood St 45806
Yew Ln 45806
Yoakam Rd 45806
Yoder Rd 45806
Yorkshire Cir & Dr 45804
Zeits Ave 45804
Zerkle Rd 45806
Zion Church Rd 45807
Zurmehly Rd 45806

NUMBERED STREETS

All Street Addresses 45804

LORAIN OH

General Delivery 44052

POST OFFICE BOXES MAIN OFFICE STATIONS AND BRANCHES

Box No.s
1 - 992 44052
1001 - 1360 44055
3001 - 8049 44052
8000 - 8201 44055

NAMED STREETS

Ada Ave 44055
Adams St 44052
Alabama Ave 44052
Albany Ave 44055
Alexander Ave 44052
Allison Ave 44052
Almadien Dr 44053
Amherst Ave 44052
Andover Ave 44055
Andress Ct 44055
Andrews Pl 44052
Antler Xing 44053
Apple Ave 44055
Appleseed Dr 44053
Archwood Ave 44052
Arianna Ave 44052
Arizona Ave 44052
Arkansas Ave 44052
Arrowhead St 44052
Ashland Ave
100-3099 44052
3200-5799 44053
Astor Ln 44053
Atlas Dr 44052
Augusta Ave 44052
Baldwin Blvd 44053
Bascule Dr 44052
Basswood Dr 44053
Baumhart Rd 44053
Bayberry Rd 44053
Beavercrest Dr 44053
Beech Ave 44052
Bellflower Dr 44053
Bellow Dr 44053
Belmont Dr 44053
Berkshire Blvd 44055
Birch Ct 44053
Black River Cir 44055
Black River Rd 44052
Black Walnut Trce 44053
Blossom Dr 44052
Blush Ct 44053
Bond Ave 44055
Boxwood Dr 44053
Brad Friedels Future Stars 44053
Brenner Dr 44053
Briarwood Dr 44053
Bridge Dr 44052
Broadway
101-297 44052
Broadway
299-2799 44052
2800-3599 44055
3600-5999 44052
S Broadway 44053
Brooks Ct 44053
Brookview Dr 44053
Brownell Ave 44052
Buck Horn Blvd 44053
Buckingham Dr 44052
Buttercup Ln 44053
C St 44052
Caferro Ave 44055
California Ave 44052
Cambridge Ave 44053
Camden Ave 44055
Camden Blvd 44053
Canterbury Ct 44053
Canton Ave 44055
Cardinal Ct 44053
Carek Ct 44055
Carmelita Ct 44052
Caroline Ave 44055
Carr Pl 44053
Carrie Dr 44055
Cedar Dr 44052
Central Dr 44052
Chalmers Ct 44052
Charles Dr 44053
Charleston Ave 44055
Chelsea Dr 44055
Cherrywood Dr 44053
Chestnut Ct 44053
Chris Ave 44052
Church Dr 44053
City Hall Pl 44052
Clark Ct 44053
Clearview Dr 44053
Clement Dr 44053
Cleveland Ave 44055
Cleveland Blvd 44052
Clifton Ave 44055
Clinton Ave 44055
Clovelly Dr 44053
Collins Dr 44053
Colony Ct 44053
Colorado Ave 44052
Columbo Ln 44055
Concord Dr 44052
Connecticut Ave 44052
Cooper Foster Park Rd E & W 44053
Coopers Ln & Trl 44053
Cornell Pl 44052
Cottonwood Dr 44053
Courtyard Dr 44053
Cranberry Ln 44053
Crehore St 44052
Cromwell Dr 44052
Crossing Trl 44053
D St 44052
Dakota Ave 44052
Dale Ave 44055
Dallas Ave 44055
N & S Danley Sq 44052
Dannie Dr 44053
Day Dr 44052
Dayton Ave
3000-3198 44055
3200-3599 44055
3600-3899 44052
Debra Dr 44053
Deer Run Dr 44053
Deer Trail Ln 44053
Delaware Ave 44052
Denison Ave 44055
Denver Ave 44055
Devore Ct 44052
Dewitt St 44055
Didrickson Dr 44053
Doe Xing 44053
Dorado St 44052
Dorwood Dr 44053
Douglas Ct 44053
Driftwood Dr 44052
Dunton Rd 44053
Duxbury Pl 44053
E St 44052
Eagle Ave 44055
Eagles Nest Dr 44053
East Ave
2100-2299 44052
2300-2499 44055
Eastlawn St 44052
Eastman Dr 44053
Edgewood Dr 44053
Edith St 44053
Elfleda St 44055
Elyria Ave
1700-2299 44052
2300-5299 44055
5301-5499 44055
Emerald Dr 44053
Erhart Dr 44053
E Erie Ave 44052
W Erie Ave
100-2399 44052
2400-8199 44053
8201-8309 44053
Estelle Ave 44052
Euclid Ave 44052
Evelyn Ave 44052
Evergreen Ct 44052
F St 44052
Factory St 44055
Fairbanks Ct 44053
Fairless Dr 44055
Fairway Dr 44053
Falbo Ave 44052
Falereen Ave 44052
Fallow Way 44053
Farr Ave 44055
Fields Way 44053
Fiesta Ct 44053
Fillmore Ave & Cir 44052
Fir Ct 44053
Fleming Ave 44055
Floral Dr 44055
Florida Ave 44052
Forest Ln 44053
Forest Hill Dr 44053
Frances Dr 44053
Franke Dr 44053
Frankfort St 44055
Freedom Pl 44053
Freshwater Dr 44052
Frontage St 44053
Fulmer Rd 44053
Fulton Rd 44055
G St 44052
Garden Ave 44052
Garfield Ave 44055
Garfield Blvd 44052
Gargasz Dr 44053
Gary Ave 44055
Georgia Ave 44052
Gettysburg Dr 44053
Glantz Dr 44055
Glen Oaks Blvd 44055
Globe Ave 44055
Gloucester Dr 44053
Goble Dr 44055
Goldenrod Ln 44053
Grace St
900-999 44055
2500-2799 44053
Grant Ave 44055
Grant St 44052
Greenbriar Ln 44053
Greenfield Pl 44052
Gregus Ave 44055
Grenoble Dr 44053
Grove Ave 44055
H St 44052
Haddam Dr 44052
Hafely Dr 44052
Hamilton Ave 44052
Hancock St 44052
Harborview Blvd 44052
Harriet St 44055
Harrison Ave 44055
Harvard Dr 44055
Hawk Ln 44053
Hawthorne Ave 44052
Hecock Ave 44052
Henderson Dr 44052
Henry Ct 44053
Herbert Dr 44053
Heron Dr 44053
Hickory Hill Ave 44052
Hidden Creek Dr 44053
High Ct 44055
Highland Park Blvd 44052
Hillgrove Dr 44053
Hillsdale Ave 44052
N & S Hogan Dr 44053
Homewood Dr 44055
Hoover Blvd 44053
Idaho Ave 44052
Idlewood Pl 44052
Illinois Ave 44052
Independence Dr 44053
Indiana Ave 44052
Industrial St 44055
Industrial Parkway Dr 44053
Infinity Ln 44053
Iowa Ave 44052
Ironwood Dr 44053
Ivanhoe Dr 44053
Jackson St 44052
Jaeger Rd 44053
Jamestown Pl 44053
N & S Jefferson Blvd & St 44052
Jenee Dr 44053
Jones Dr 44053
Josephine St 44052
Jude Ct 44052
Kansas Ave 44052
Kay Ave
1100-1399 44053
3000-3199 44053
Kelly Pl 44052
Kentucky Ave 44052
Kenyon Ave & Ct 44053
Kimberly Ct 44053
King Ave 44055
Kingsbury Ct 44053
Kingsway Dr 44052
Kneirim Dr 44053
Kolbe Rd 44053
Kyra Ln 44053
Lake Pl 44052
Lakeside Ave 44052
Lakeview Ave 44053
N Lakeview Blvd 44052
S Lakeview Blvd 44052
Lakeview Dr 44052
Larkmoor St 44052
Laura Dr & Ln 44053
Laurel Rd 44055
Leavitt Rd
1000-3099 44052
3200-5999 44053
N Leavitt Rd 44052
Lehigh Ave 44052
Lemonwood Ct 44053
Leroy St 44052
Lexington Ave
800-2599 44052
2600-3599 44055
3600-3899 44052
Liberty Ave 44055
Lincoln Ave E 44052
Lincoln Blvd 44055
Lincoln Dr 44052
Lincoln St 44052
Linda Dr 44053
Lindenwood Dr 44053
Livingston Ave
1700-2499 44052
3200-3599 44055
3700-3799 44052
Long Ave 44052
Longbrook Rd 44053
Longfellow Pkwy 44052
Lorain Ave 44055
Lorain Dr 44052
Loretta Ct 44053
Louis Ave 44055
Louisiana Ave 44052
Lovett Pl 44052
Lowell Ave 44055
Lucinda Ct 44053
Maddock St 44055
Madison Ave 44053
Magnolia Dr 44053
Maine Ave 44052
Mallard Creek Run 44053
Manhattan Dr 44053
Maple Dr 44052
Maple Rd 44055
Marie Ave 44052
E & W Marina Pkwy 44052
Mark Dr 44052
Marshall Ave
2300-2498 44052
2500-3099 44052
3500-4499 44052
Martin Dr 44053
Martins Run Dr 44053
Maryland Ave 44052
Massachusetts Ave 44052
Maurer Dr 44053
Mayfield St 44055
N & S Mayflower Dr 44053
Mckinley Ave 44055
Mckinley St 44052
Meadow Ln 44055
E & W Meadow Farm Ln 44053
Meadow Lark Dr 44053
Meadowbrook Dr 44053
Meariank Dr 44053
Meister Rd
700-1199 44052
1200-4799 44053
Miami Ave 44053
Michigan Ave 44052
Middle Ridge Rd 44053
Mildred Ave 44052
Mills Dr 44053
Mississippi Ave 44052
Missouri Ave 44052
Mohawk Dr 44055
Montana Ave 44052
Montgomery Dr 44053
Morningside Way 44053
Nantucket Dr 44053
Narragansett Blvd 44053
Nebraska Ave 44052
Nevada Ave 44052
New Hampshire Ave 44052
New Jersey Ave 44052
New Mexico Ave & Ct 44052
Nichols Ave 44053
Norfolk Ave 44055
Normandy Dr 44053
North Dr 44053
Oak Branch Cir 44053
Oak Point Ests & Rd 44053
Oak Tree Dr N & S 44053
Oakcrest Dr 44053
Oakdale Ave
1700-2599 44052
2600-3599 44055
3600-3999 44052
Oakhill Blvd 44053
Oakwood Ave 44055
Oberlin Ave
100-3199 44052
3200-5999 44053
Ohio Ave 44052
Old Lake Rd 44053
Omaha Ave 44055
Oneil Blvd 44055
Orchard Ave 44055
Orchard Hill Blvd 44053
Oroszy Ave 44052
Osborn Ave 44052
Oxford Dr 44053
Packard Dr 44055
Paine St 44052
Palm Ave 44055
Palm Springs Dr 44053
Park Dr 44052
S Park Dr 44053
W Park Dr 44053
Park Square Dr 44053
Parkside Cir E & W 44053
Parkview Ave 44052
Parkway Dr 44053
Pearl Ave 44055
Pennsylvania Ave & Ct 44052
Perry Ct 44053
Pheasant Dr 44053
Pickett Rd 44053
E Pier 44052
Pin Oak Dr 44053
Pine Hollow Blvd 44055
Plant St 44055
Plymouth Dr 44053
N Pointe Pkwy 44053
Pole Ave
1700-3099 44052
3200-3299 44053
Poplar Dr 44053
Postage Due St 44053
Pridenwo Ave 44055
Primrose Way 44053
Princess Anne Ct 44052
Province Ct 44053
Pueblo Dr 44053
Queen Anne Ave 44052
Quincy Adams Ct 44053
Randall St 44052
Randolph Dr 44053
Red Hill Dr 44052
Redbud Pl 44053
Reeves Ave 44052
Regina Ave 44052
Reid Ave
400-2599 44052
2600-3599 44055
3600-3999 44052
Reinwald Rd 44053
Reserve Cir & Trl 44053
Revere Pl 44053
N Ridge Rd E 44055
N Ridge Rd W 44053
W Ridge Rd 44053
Ridgeland St 44055
Ridgewood St 44055
Rita Dr 44053
W River Rd 44055
River Industrial Park Rd 44052
Riverside Dr 44055
Riverview Ln 44055
Robinhood Dr 44053
Roe Ln 44053
Rolling Ave 44055
Roosevelt Ave 44055
Root Rd 44052
Rosecliff Dr 44053
Rosecrest Dr 44053
Rosemont Ct 44053
Russell Ave 44055
Saint James Blvd 44053
Santina Way 44053
School St 44055
Seneca Ave 44055
E & W Serenity Ln 44053
Shaffer Dr 44053
Shawnee Dr 44055
Sheffield Ctr 44055
Sherrie Ln 44053
Sherwood Dr 44053
Shore Dr 44053
Six Point Ln 44053
E & W Skyline Dr 44053
Smith Ave 44052
Spaulding Ct 44053
Spruce Ct 44052
Squire St 44055
Squirrel Nest Dr 44053
Stag Horn Ln 44053
Stanford Ave 44053
Sterling Rd 44052
Stevens St 44053
Stonepath St 44052
Streator Pl 44052
Sunset Blvd 44052
Surf Ave 44053
Sycamore Dr 44053
Tacoma Ave 44055
Taft Ave 44055
Tait St 44053
Talbot Ln 44055
Tanglewood Dr 44053
Temple Ave 44053
Terminal Dr 44053
Texas Ave 44055
Timber Walk 44053
Timberview Dr 44053
Toledo Ave 44055
Tower Blvd
600-1199 44052
1200-2399 44053
Tranquility Ln 44053
Tressa Ave 44052
Urban Cir N & S 44053
Utica Ave 44052
Valleyview Dr 44053
Vardon Dr 44053
Vassar Ave 44053
Velvet Horn 44053
Vermont Dr 44052
Victoria Dr 44053
Victory Ave 44053
Viewcrest Ct 44053
Vincent Ave 44055
Vine Ave 44055
Vineyard Dr 44053
Wallace Ln 44053
Walnut Ct 44053
Wanda Dr 44053
Washington Ave 44052
Watson Ct 44053
Waverly Pl 44052
Werner Ct 44052
Westminster Dr 44053
Westview Ct 44052
Westwood Dr 44053
Wheatley Ave 44053
Whispering Pines Pl 44053
White Tail Ln 44053
Williamsburg Dr 44053
Willow Ave 44055

Wilson Ave 44055
Wilson Dr 44052
Wilson St 44052
Windsor Ct 44053
Winger Dr 44053
Winter Foe Trl 44053
Wood Ave 44055
Woodcrest Ct 44053
Woodstock Dr 44053
Woodward Ave 44055
Woodworth Dr 44053
Yale Dr 44055
York Dr 44053
Yorktown Ct & Rd 44053

NUMBERED STREETS

W 1st St 44052
W 2nd St 44052
W 4th St 44052
W 5th St 44052
W 6th Ct & St 44052
7 Pines Dr 44053
W 7th Ct & St 44052
E & W 8th 44052
E & W 9th 44052
E & W 10th 44052
W 11th St 44052
W 12th St 44052
W 13th St 44052
W 14th St 44052
W 15th St 44052
W 16th St 44052
W 17th St 44052
E & W 18th 44052
E & W 19th Ct & St 44052
E & W 20th 44052
E 21st St 44052
W 21st St
  100-2399 44052
  2400-3199 44053
E & W 22nd 44052
E 23rd St 44055
W 23rd St 44052
W 24th St 44052
W 25th Pl 44052
E 25th St 44055
W 25th St 44052
E 26th St 44055
W 26th St 44052
W 27th Pl 44052
E 27th St 44055
W 27th St
  100-599 44055
  600-1298 44052
  1300-1999 44052
E 28th St 44055
  100-599 44055
  1200-1899 44052
E 29th St 44055
  100-599 44055
  800-2099 44052
E 30th St 44055
W 30th St
  100-699 44055
  701-797 44052
E & W 31st 44055
E 32nd St 44055
  100-599 44055
  600-799 44052
E 33rd St 44055
W 33rd St
  100-699 44055
  700-799 44052
  1200-1799 44053
E 34th St 44055
W 34th St
  100-699 44055
  700-799 44052
  1200-1499 44053
E 35th St 44055
  100-499 44055
  1200-1699 44053
E 36th St 44055
  100-799 44052
  1700-2299 44053
E 37th St 44055
  100-1199 44052
  1200-2799 44053
E 38th St 44055
  100-1199 44052
  1200-2799 44053
E 39th St 44055
  100-299 44052
  1200-2799 44053
E 40th St 44055
W 40th St 44053
E 41st St
  100-699 44052
  1701-1897 44055
W 41st St 44053
W 42nd Pl 44052
E 42nd St
  200-599 44052
  1800-2599 44055
W 42nd St 44053
E 43rd St 44052
W 43rd St 44053
E 44th St 44052
W 44th St 44053
W & E 45th Pl & St 44052
E 46th St 44052
E 47th St 44052
E 48th St 44052
E 38 St 44055

MANSFIELD OH

General Delivery 44901

POST OFFICE BOXES MAIN OFFICE STATIONS AND BRANCHES

Box No.s
1 - 1999 44901
2001 - 2358 44905
2500 - 2867 44906
3001 - 3339 44904
3501 - 4009 44907
5001 - 5760 44901
7001 - 7254 44905
8051 - 8051 44906
8075 - 8078 44907
8101 - 8197 44901
8501 - 8683 44906
9001 - 9178 44904

NAMED STREETS

Abbeyfeale Rd 44907
Abbott Dr 44905
Abington Dr 44906
Abri Ln 44905
Acker Dr 44905
Adams Rd 44903
N Adams St 44902
S Adams St 44902
Addeline Dr 44904
Agate Ave 44907
Airport Rd 44903
Albert Ave 44903
Algire Rd 44904
All American Dr 44903
Allison Ave 44903
Alpine Dr 44906
Alta West Rd 44903
Altamont Ave 44902
Altman Dr 44903
Amber Ave 44907
Amoy East Rd 44903
Amoy Ganges Rd 44903
Amoy West Rd 44903
Anderson Rd 44903
Andover Rd 44907
Anglewood Dr 44903
Angus Dr 44903
Annadale Ave 44905
Annfield Dr
  600-799 44905
  900-1199 44903
Antibus Pl 44902
Antionette Dr 44903
Apple Ln 44905
Arbor Ave 44906
E & W Arch St 44902
Arlington Ave 44903
Armstrong St 44906
Arnold Ave 44903
Arnold Dr 44906
Arthur Ave 44903
Ashland Rd
  1-199 44902
  200-2999 44905
Ashwood Dr 44906
Aspen Ct 44906
Aspira Ct 44906
Atcheson Ave 44903
Atenway St 44902
Atherton Ave 44903
Auburn St 44902
Auer Blvd 44907
E & W Augustine Ave 44902
Aurelia Ave 44906
Ausdale Ave 44906
Austin Rd 44903
Autumn Dr 44907
Avalon Dr 44906
Averill Ave 44906
Avon Dr 44904
Bahl Ave 44905
Bailey Dr 44904
Baird Pkwy 44903
Baldwin Ave 44906
Balgreen Dr 44906
Bally Row 44906
Banyon Ln 44907
Barbara Ln 44905
Barberry Dr 44904
Barker St 44904
Barnard Ave 44903
Barnes Ave 44905
Barr Rd 44904
Bartley Ave
  1-99 44906
  100-499 44903
Bass Dr 44903
Bauer Rd 44903
Beadiank Rd 44905
Beal Rd
  800-1199 44905
  1200-2099 44903
Bechtel Ave 44905
Becky Dr 44905
Beech Dr 44906
Beechdale Dr 44907
Beechwood Dr 44907
Beethoven St 44902
Bell Rd 44904
Bell St 44903
Bella Vista St 44904
Bellaire Dr 44907
Bellview Dr 44905
Bellville North Rd 44904
Bellwood Dr 44904
Belmar Dr 44907
Belmont Ave 44906
Bendix St 44905
Benedict Ave 44906
Benjamin St 44904
Bennett St 44903
Bennington Dr 44904
Bentley St 44902
Benton St N & S 44903
Bentwood Ct 44903
Berkshire Rd 44904
Berlyn Ct 44907
Bertram Ave 44907
Beryl Ave 44907
Betner Dr
  600-684 44904
  685-899 44907
Betzstone Dr 44907
Beymiller St 44902
Bigelow Rd 44907
Birchlawn Blvd 44907
Bird Cage Walk 44902
Biscayne Cir & Dr 44903
Bissman Ct 44903
Blair Ave 44903
E Blanche St 44902
W Blanche St
  1-90 44907
  91-199 44903
Bloomingrove Rd 44903
Blue Cedar Dr 44904
Blue Locust Dr 44905
Blust Ave 44903
Blymyer Ave 44903
Boals Ave 44905
Bonair Ave 44905
Bonham Dr 44905
Bonnie Dr 44905
Bonterid Rd 44903
Boston Ave 44906
Boughton Ave 44903
Bowen Rd 44903
Bowers Rd 44903
Bowers St 44902
Bowland Rd 44907
Bowman St 44903
Bowman Street Rd 44903
Boyle Rd 44906
Brace Ave 44905
Braden Ln 44907
Bradford Ave 44902
Brae Burn Rd 44907
Branchwood Dr 44905
Brandywine Dr 44904
Breezeway Dr 44904
Brenda Dr 44907
Brentwood Rd 44907
Breton Dr 44904
Briarwood Rd 44907
Brickman Ave 44906
Bridgewater Way N & S 44906
Brinkerhoff Ave 44906
Broadview Ave 44903
Broken Oak Ct 44904
Brooker Pl 44902
Brookfield Dr 44907
Brookpark Dr 44906
Brookwood Way N & S 44906
Brown Rd 44903
Brownwood Rd 44907
Brubaker Creek Rd 44903
Brushwood Dr 44907
Bryden Rd 44903
Brymwood Dr 44904
Bryne Gear Dr 44903
Bryonaire Rd 44903
Buckeye Ave 44906
Buckingham Ave 44903
Buckthorn Ct 44907
Buffalo St 44902
Bulkley Ave 44903
Burger Ave 44906
Burgraff Dr 44905
Burkwood Rd 44907
Burnese Ave 44903
Burnison Rd 44903
Burns St 44903
Burton Ave 44906
Bush Pl 44902
Bushnell St 44902
Butternut Ct 44906
Butternut Pl 44903
Cairns Rd 44903
Caldwell Ave 44905
Caldwell St 44906
Cambridge Ct 44904
Camden Ct 44904
Cameo Ln 44903
Cameron Ave 44902
Candlewood Trl 44905
Canteberry Ln 44906
Cape Cod Dr 44904
Cappellar Ct 44903
Carl Rd 44906
Carls Ln 44905
Carol Ln 44907
Carpenter Rd 44903
Carter Dr 44906
Carter Ln 44903
Castor Rd 44904
Cecilwood Dr 44907
Cedar St 44903
Cedar Creek Cv 44904
Cedar Locust Dr 44905
Cedar Ridge Pl 44903
Cedarbrook Ct 44906
Cedarlawn Ct 44906
Cedarwood Dr 44904
Central Ave 44905
Champion Rd 44905
Chandler Pl 44903
Chapelwood Blvd 44907
Chapman Ct, Ln & Way 44904
Charles Ct 44904
Charles Rd 44903
Charles St 44903
Charletta Dr 44903
Charolais Dr 44903
Charvid Ave 44905
Charwood Rd 44907
Chelsea Dr 44904
Chendern Rd 44907
Cherokee Dr 44903
Cherry St 44905
Cherry Hill Rd 44907
E & W Chesrown Rd 44903
Chester Ave 44903
Chestnut Ct 44906
Chestnut St E 44902
Chestnut St W 44902
Chevy Chase Rd 44907
Chew Rd 44903
Chilton Ave 44907
Church St E & W 44904
Circle Dr E & W 44905
City View Dr 44905
Clairmont Ave 44903
Clark Ct 44906
Clearfork Dr 44904
Clearview Cir 44905
Clearview Dr 44904
Clearview Rd 44907
Cleveland Ave 44902
Clever Ln 44904
Cliffbrook Dr 44907
Cliffside Dr 44904
Cliffwood Dr 44904
Clifton Ave & Blvd 44907
Cline Ave 44907
Cloverdale Dr 44903
Cloverleaf Ct 44904
Coachman Rd 44905
Cole Ave 44902
Coleman Rd 44903
Collins Dr 44903
Colonial Dr 44903
Columbia Ave 44903
Conard Rd 44903
Conchemco St 44905
Concord Ave 44906
Connor Dr 44905
Constance Ct 44906
E Cook Rd
  1-299 44907
  400-499 44903
W Cook Rd
  1-999 44907
  1000-2299 44906
Cookton Grange Rd 44903
Cotter Rd 44903
Coul St 44902
Country Club Dr 44906
County Road 1688 44903
County Road 20 44904
County Road 37 44904
County Road 47 44904
County Road 50 44903
County Road 57 44904
County Road 59 44904
Courtwright Blvd 44907
Craigston Dr 44903
Crall Rd 44903
Cranberry Ct 44905
Crandal Rd 44906
Crawford Ave N 44905
Crescent Rd 44907
Crestline Ave 44903
Crestview Ave 44907
Crestwood Dr 44905
Cricket Ln 44906
Crider Rd 44903
Crimson Rd 44903
Crouse St 44902
Crowell Dr 44903
Crystal Spring St 44903
Cunning Dr 44907
Curtis Dr 44907
Cypress Dr 44903
Daisy St 44903
Dale Ave 44902
Danwood Ave 44907
Darby Ct & Dr 44904
Darbydale Rd 44905
Darralet Rd 44904
Dartmouth Dr 44904
Davey Ave 44903
Davids Ln 44905
Davidson St 44907
Davis Rd 44907
Dawson Ave 44906
Day Rd 44903
Dean Rd 44906
Deborah Ct 44904
Deer Creek Ln 44903
Deer Run Rd 44906
Delaware Ave 44904
Delph Ave 44906
Delwood Dr 44905
Denman Rd 44904
Denzler Cir 44903
Detroit Ave 44905
Devon Rd 44904
Devonshire Ln 44907
Devonwood Rd 44907
Deweese Pl 44903
Dewey Ave
  400-549 44902
  550-554 44905
  555-557 44902
  556-698 44905
  559-699 44905
N Diamond St
  2-54 44902
  56-199 44902
  200-202 44901
  200-202 44903
  201-399 44902
  204-398 44902
  500-500 44901
S Diamond St
  7-51 44902
  53-616 44902
  617-899 44907
Dianewood Dr 44903
E Dickson Ave 44902
W Dickson Ave 44903
Dickson Pkwy 44907
Dillon Rd 44906
Dina Ln 44903
Dirlam Ct 44906
Dirlam Ln 44904
Distl Ave 44902
Distribution Dr N 44905
Dogwood Cir 44903
Dolan Ct 44903
Donal Dr 44907
Donald Ct 44903
Donnawood Dr 44903
Dorothy Dr 44903
Douglas Ave 44906
Dougwood Dr 44904
Dream Dr 44907
Dresden Dr 44905
Dudley Ave 44903
Duke Ave 44905
Dunbilt Ct 44907
Dyas Dr 44905
Eagle Dr 44904
Eagle Point St 44903
Earick Rd 44903
Eastlawn Ave 44905
Eastview Dr 44905
Eaton St 44905
Eckert Rd 44904
Eckstein Rd 44903
Edgewood Rd 44907
Educational Pl 44902
Edwards Ave 44902
Eisenhower Ave 44904
Elderberry Ct & Dr 44907
Eleanor Ave 44906
Elizabeth St 44902
Ellen Ave 44904
Elm St 44902
Elmleaf Cir 44904
Elmridge Rd 44907
Elmwood Dr 44906
Elmwood Pl 44904
Emerald Ave 44907
Emerson Dr 44904
Emery Ct 44906
Emma Ln 44903
Empire Rd 44906
Erhart St 44905
Erie St 44906
Ernsberger Rd 44903
Esley Ln 44905
Essex Cir & Rd 44904
Estate Ct 44906
Euclid Ave 44903
Evans Ave 44907
Evelyn Ave 44907
Everett Ln 44906
Evergreen Ave W 44905
Evline Dr 44904
Executive Ct 44907
Expressview Dr 44905
Fair St 44902
Fairfax Ave 44906
Fairlawn Ave 44903
Fairoaks Blvd 44907
Farmbrook Dr 44904
Farmdale Rd 44905
Fenway Blvd 44904
Fern Ave 44903
Ferndale Rd 44907
Fike Dr 44906
Fir Dr 44906
Five Points East Rd 44903
Fleetwood Rd 44905
Fleming Falls Rd
  400-1220 44905
  1222-2499 44903
Flint St 44902
Floral Ct 44903
Florence Ave 44907
Flowers Rd 44903
Ford Ave 44902
Ford Rd N 44905
Ford Rd S 44905
Ford St 44902
Forest Dr 44905
Forest St 44903
Forest Hill Rd 44907
S Foster St N 44902
Fox Rd 44904
Fox Run St 44903
Foxcroft Cir & Rd 44904
France St 44903
Frank Rd 44903
N & S Franklin St 44902
Franklin Church Rd 44903
Frederick Ct 44906
Frederick St 44904
Freedom Ct 44904
Freeway Cir 44903
Frey Dr 44903
Front St 44903
Frontier Trl 44905
Fuhrer Ave 44904

Fuller Ct 44903
Gadfield Rd 44903
Galaxie Dr 44903
Galaxy Ct & Dr 44903
Galewood Ave 44904
Ganges Five Points Rd 44903
Gare Ave 44905
Garfield Pl 44903
Garver Rd 44903
Gary Dr 44903
Gass Rd 44904
Gatewood Dr 44907
Geary Rd 44906
Gem Ave 44907
George Ave 44907
Georgia Ln 44903
Gerald Ave 44903
Gerke Ave 44903
German Church Rd 44904
Gettings Pl 44903
Getz Blvd 44907
Gfrer Rd 44903
Gibson Ave 44907
Gilbert Ave 44907
Gimbel Dr 44903
Ginger Ln E 44905
Gladys Ave 44904
Gladysfield Dr 44903
Glenbeck Ln 44906
Glendale Blvd 44907
N Glenn Ave S 44902
Glenwood Blvd 44906
Glenwood Hts 44903
Glessner Ave 44903
Gloria Ct 44905
Goldenwood Ave 44904
Gordon Pl 44902
Gordon Rd 44905
Grace St
201-247 44902
249-354 44902
355-1699 44905
Graham Rd
1300-1670 44903
1671-2199 44904
Grandridge Ave 44907
Grandview Ave, Ct & Ter 44903
Grange St 44904
Granite St 44902
Grant St 44903
Grasmere Ave & Cir 44906
Gray Ct 44903
Greenbriar Dr 44907
Greendale Ave 44902
Greenfield Dr 44904
Greenlawn Ave 44902
Greenlee Rd 44907
Greenwood Ave 44907
Greibling Rd 44906
Grimes Rd 44903
Grover St 44903
Grubb Rd 44904
Gruber Ave 44907
Hagerman Rd 44904
Hahn Rd 44906
Halcyon Dr 44906
Hale Rd 44905
Hammond Ave 44902
Hampton Dr 44907
Hampton Rd 44904
Hanley Rd W
541-597 44904
E Hanley Rd 44903
1-540 44903
Hanna Rd 44906
Hanover Rd 44904
Harding Ave & Rd 44906
Harker St 44903
Harlan Rd 44903
Harmon Ave 44903
Harold Ave 44906
Harrington Memorial Rd 44903
Harris Pl 44902

Harter Ave 44907
Harvard Ave 44906
Harwood Dr 44906
Hastings Newville Rd 44903
Haviland Ct 44903
Hawthorne Ln 44907
Haywood Dr 44903
Hazelwood Dr 44905
Hecht Rd 44903
Hedeen Dr 44907
Hedges St 44902
Heidi Ln
400-499 44903
500-699 44904
Heineman Blvd 44903
Helen Ave 44903
Helena Dr 44904
Hemlock Ave & Pl 44903
Henry St 44907
Heritage Trl 44905
Herman Ave 44903
Herring Ave 44906
Herring St 44903
Hess Cir & Ln 44907
Hickory Ct 44904
Hickory Ln 44905
Hidden Oak Trl 44906
High St 44903
Highland Ave
500-799 44903
800-899 44906
Highlook Dr 44904
Highridge Ct & Rd W 44904
Hill Ave 44903
Hillcrest Dr 44904
Hillcrest St 44907
Hillgrove Ave 44907
Hillside Cir 44907
Hoff Dr 44903
Hoffer Ave 44902
Hoffman Ave 44906
Holiday Dr & Hl 44904
Holly Dr 44903
Hollywood Ln 44907
Holzworth Dr 44903
Home Ave 44902
Home Rd N 44906
Home Rd S
1-197 44906
1100-1799 44904
Honey Locust Dr 44905
Honeysuckle Dr 44905
Hoover Rd
558-598 44905
600-999 44905
1000-1299 44903
S Horning Rd 44903
Hout Rd 44905
Howard St 44903
Hulit Rd 44903
Hull Rd 44903
Hunters Rdg 44904
Hunters Ridge Ct 44904
Huntington Dr 44906
N Illinois Anx 44905
Illinois Ave N 44905
Illinois Ave S
1-399 44905
400-899 44907
Impala Dr 44903
Indiana Ave 44905
Industrial Dr 44904
Industrial Pkwy 44903
Interstate Cir 44903
Inwood Dr 44903
Ironwood Dr 44903
Jade Ave 44907
James Ave 44907
Jamestown Dr 44906
Jane Ave 44905
Jeanette Ave 44902
Jefferson St 44903
Jeffrey Ln 44907
Jennings Ave 44907
Johns Ave 44903

Johns Park Entrance St 44903
Joselyn Ave 44904
Josephine Ave 44904
Joy Lynn Ln 44903
Junction St 44902
Karlson Dr 44904
Keefer Rd 44903
Keller Dr 44905
Kenmore Dr 44906
Kennedy Dr 44904
Kent Rd 44904
Kentland Dr 44906
Kentucky Ave 44905
Kentwood Dr 44903
Kenwood Cir 44906
Kimberwick Ct & Rd 44904
King St 44903
Kings Corners Rd E & W 44904
Kings Pointe Dr 44903
Kingston Dr 44906
Kingwood Pl 44906
Kinkel Ave 44907
Kirkwood Dr 44904
Kline Rd 44903
Knapp Rd 44907
Knight Pkwy 44903
Kochheiser Rd 44904
Koogle Rd 44903
Lafayette Ave 44902
Laird Ave 44905
Lakecrest Dr
2200-2399 44903
2600-2799 44904
Lakefront Dr 44905
Lakeside Dr 44904
Lakeview Dr 44904
Lakewood Dr
1-299 44904
2100-2399 44905
Lamberton Ave 44907
Lantz Rd 44906
Lantz St 44905
Larchwood Rd 44907
Lasalle St 44906
Lascerne Cir N & S 44906
Laurelwood Rd 44907
Laver Rd 44905
Lawn Ave 44907
Lawnsdale St 44903
Ledgewood Ct 44906
Ledgewood Dr 44905
Lee Ln 44905
Lehigh Ave 44905
Lehnhart Dr 44907
Lenox Ave 44906
Leppo Ln 44907
Leppo Rd 44903
Lester Ct 44903
Lexbrook Trl 44907
Lexdale Ln 44907
Lexington Ave
1-2449 44907
2450-2899 44904
Lexington Ontario Rd
1-3 44904
20-22 44904
209-1500 44903
1502-1598 44903
1600-2399 44904
2401-2599 44904
N Lexington Springmill Rd 44906
S Lexington Springmill Rd
188-198 44906
200-834 44906
835-1499 44903
1700-2599 44904
Lexington Steam Corners Rd 44904
Lexpark Dr 44907
Lexview Cir 44907
Lexwood Rd 44907
Liberty St 44905

Library Ct 44902
Lida St 44903
Lilac Ct E & W 44907
Lily St 44903
Lincoln Ave 44902
Lincoln Park Blvd 44905
Lincoln Terrace Dr 44905
Lind Ave 44903
Linda Ln 44907
Lindaire Ln E 44906
E, W, N & S Linden Cir & Rd 44906
Lindsey Rd 44904
Linn Rd 44903
Linwood Pl 44906
Lipizzan Dr 44904
Locust Ln 44907
Logan Rd 44907
Lohr Rd 44903
London Dr 44905
Longview Ave E 44903
Longview Ave W
1-499 44903
500-1599 44906
Loran Ter 44903
Lorkay Dr 44905
Louis St 44903
Louise Ave 44903
Lucas Dr 44903
Lucas Rd
970-998 44905
1000-1303 44905
1304-1600 44903
1602-1750 44903
Lukes Dr 44905
E & W Luther Pl & St E 44902
Lutz Ave
1-99 44904
2600-2800 44903
2802-2898 44903
Machangt Rd 44906
Madison Ave
300-399 44902
400-448 44905
450-599 44905
Madison Rd 44905
Magnolia Dr 44903
E Main St 44904
N Main St
1-25 44902
27-899 44902
900-4278 44903
4280-4298 44903
S Main St
1-392 44902
393-2400 44907
W Main St 44904
Malabar Ln 44907
Malajora Rd 44905
Malone Rd 44907
Manchester Rd 44903
Manner Dr 44905
Mansfield Ave 44902
Mansfield Adario Rd 44903
Mansfield Lucas Rd
500-768 44907
778-798 44903
800-2398 44903
Mansfield Washington Rd 44903
Maple Dr 44905
Maple Ln 44906
Maple Pl 44907
Maple St
1-199 44904
500-842 44906
844-898 44906
Maple Locust Dr 44905
Mapledale Ave 44903
Marcella Ave 44903
Marcus St 44903
Marianna Cir & Dr 44903
Marion Ave
1-668 44903
669-1499 44906
1501-1599 44906

Marion Avenue Rd N 44903
Marlette St 44905
Marlin Dr 44905
Marlow Pl & Rd 44906
Marquis Ave 44907
Marshall Ave 44902
Martha Ave 44905
Marwood Dr 44904
Mary Ct 44906
Mason St 44902
Massa Ave 44907
Matthes Dr 44906
Maumee Ave 44906
Max Walton Dr 44903
Maxwell Dr 44906
Maxwell Rd 44904
Mayer Dr 44907
Mayfair Dr 44905
Mayfair Rd 44904
Mayflower Dr 44905
Mcbride Rd 44905
Mccarrick Pkwy 44903
Mcclintock Rd 44906
Mccullough Blvd 44907
N Mcelroy Rd E 44905
Mcnaul Rd 44903
Mcpherson St 44903
Meadowdale Dr 44907
Meadowood Dr 44903
Melody Ln 44905
Melrose Dr 44905
Mendota St 44903
Micah Pl 44902
Michael Dr 44905
Michigan Ave 44905
Middle Bellville Rd 44904
Midland Dr 44903
Miley Dr 44907
N & S Mill St 44904
Mill Run Rd 44904
Miller St 44902
Millsboro Rd
600-979 44903
980-2199 44906
2201-2499 44906
Millsboro Rd E 44903
Millsboro Rd W 44903
Milton Ave 44904
Minerva Ave 44902
Mock Rd 44904
Mohican Trl 44904
Molly Ct 44905
Monterey Dr 44907
Morgan Ave 44905
Morgan Dr 44904
Moritz Ln 44903
Morningside Dr 44906
Morrison Ave 44904
Mount Zion Rd 44903
Muirfield Dr 44903
N Mulberry St 44902
S Mulberry St
1-181 44902
182-299 44903
Muskie Dr 44903
Muth Rd 44903
Myers Ave 44902
Myers Ln 44903
Myers Rd 44903
Nancy Ave 44904
Nantucket Dr 44904
S Nasua Dr 44904
National Pkwy 44906
Needham Rd 44904
Neff Rd 44906
Neil Cir N & S 44903
Nestor Dr 44906
E & W Newlon Pl 44902
Newman St 44902
Newport Ct 44904
Noblet Rd 44903
Norfolk Dr 44904
Norris Rd 44905
North St 44905
Nottingham Ct 44904

Oak St
1-199 44902
200-899 44907
2400-2499 44903
Oak Creek Dr 44903
Oak Hill Pl 44902
Oak Ridge Ct 44906
Oak Run Ct 44906
Oakdale Dr 44905
Oakenwaldt St 44905
Oakleaf Dr E & W 44904
Oakwood Dr 44906
Ohio St 44903
Ohio Brass Rd 44902
Old Bowman St 44903
Old Mill Run Rd 44906
Old Stone Ct 44904
Olivesburg Rd
600-1768 44905
1769-4399 44903
On A Way Ave 44906
Opal Dr 44907
Orange St
100-417 44902
418-600 44905
602-698 44905
Orchard Dr 44903
Orchard Dr E 44904
Orchard Dr W 44904
Orchard St 44903
Orchard Park Rd 44904
Orweiler Rd 44903
Osbun Rd 44903
Oswalt Rd 44903
Otterbein Dr 44904
Outer Dr 44905
Overdale Dr 44907
Overlook Rd 44907
Owens Rd 44904
Oxford Ave 44906
Oxford Rd 44904
Pacific St 44905
Paddock Dr 44906
Painter Ave 44907
Palomar Dr 44906
Paradise View St 44905
Paragon Pkwy 44903
Park Ave E
1-300 44902
301-2100 44905
Park Ave W
1-289 44902
290-1344 44906
1346-1398 44906
W Park Blvd 44906
Park Dr 44906
Park St N 44902
Park St S 44902
Parker St 44906
Parkview St 44903
Parkway Dr 44906
Parkwood Blvd 44906
Parkwood Rd 44905
Parnell Dr 44903
Parry Ave 44905
Partridge Ct 44904
Pat Ln 44906
Patriot St 44905
Patton Ave 44902
Paul Blvd 44907
Pavonia Rd 44903
Pavonia East Rd 44903
Pavonia North Rd 44903
Pavonia South Rd 44903
Pavonia West Rd 44903
Pawnee Ave 44906
Paxford Pl 44906
Peaceful Path 44907
Peach Pl 44905
Pear Pl 44905
Pearce Dr 44903
Pearl Ave 44907
Pearl St 44902
Pembroke Blvd 44904
Penn Ave 44903
Pennsylvania Ave 44905

Penny Ln 44904
Perch Dr 44903
Peterson Rd 44903
Pheasant Trl 44904
Pike Dr 44903
Pin Oak Trl 44906
Pine Grove Ct 44906
Pinecrest St 44906
Pinehurst Dr 44903
Pinewood Cir 44903
Pinkney Rd 44903
Piper Rd 44905
W Piper Rd 44903
Pittinger Rd 44903
Plainview Rd 44907
Pleasant Ave 44903
Pleasant Valley Rd 44903
Plum Pl 44905
Plymouth St 44904
Pollock Pkwy 44905
Pomerene Rd 44906
Pond Rd 44906
Poplar St 44903
Possum Run Rd 44903
Poth Rd 44906
Preakness Dr 44906
Prescott St 44903
Priar Rd 44906
Princeton Ct 44904
Pristerm St 44902
Prospect St E 44902
W Prospect St 44907
Province Ln 44906
Pugh Rd 44903
Pulver Rd 44903
Pulver List Rd 44905
Purdy St 44902
Quail Run Ct 44904
Quincy St 44902
Rachel Rd 44907
Radio Ln 44906
Rae Ave 44903
E & W Raleigh Ave 44907
Rambleside Dr 44907
Ramsey Dr 44905
Ranchwood Dr 44903
Randall Rd 44907
Random Dr 44904
Randy Ave 44905
Rayfield Dr 44905
Raymond Ave 44903
Reba Ave 44907
Red Oak Dr & Trl 44904
Redman Ave 44905
Redwood Rd 44907
Reed Rd 44903
Reed St
200-699 44903
1000-1200 44906
1202-1298 44906
Reform St 44902
Reformatory Rd 44905
Reiser Dr 44905
Rembrandt St 44902
Remy Ave 44902
Resthaven Dr 44903
Rhein Ave 44903
Rhodes Ave 44906
Richard Ct & Dr 44905
Richland Ave 44903
Richland Mall 44906
Richland Shale Rd 44903
Richwood Dr 44904
Ridge Rd N & S 44905
Ridgewood Blvd 44907
Rippling Brook Dr 44904
Ritter Rd 44904
Riva Ridge Dr 44904
River Dr 44906
Robinhood Ln 44907
Robinson Rd 44903
S Rock Rd 44903
Rockwell Dr 44907
Rocky Rill Ct 44904
Roger Ln 44902
Rolling Meadows Dr 44904

Rome South Rd 44903
Rose Ave 44903
Rosedale Ave 44905
Rosedale Dr 44906
Ross Rd
  7200-8999 44904
  9100-9600 44903
  9602-9798 44903
Rowland Ave 44903
Royal Oak Ct, Dr &
Trl 44906
Ruby Ave 44907
Rudy Rd 44903
Running Brook Way 44903
Rupp Rd 44903
Russell Rd 44903
Rustic Ln 44907
Ruth Ave 44907
Sabo Dr 44905
Sackman St 44903
Saint Andrews Ct 44903
Saint Clair St 44903
Saint James Rd 44904
Salem Rd 44904
Sandy Ct 44904
Sandy Ln 44903
Saratoga Ct 44904
Sassafras Cir & Dr 44905
Satinwood Cir & Dr 44903
Sautter Dr 44904
Sawmill Pl 44904
Sawtooth Pl 44904
Sawyer Pkwy 44903
Saxton Rd 44907
Scarletts Way 44906
Scenic Dr 44907
Schmidt Ct 44902
Schmidt Rd 44904
Scholl Rd 44907
Schulties Dr 44903
Scott Ln & Rd 44903
Seminole Ave 44906
Sequoia Ln 44904
Shad Dr E & W 44903
Shadowood Ln 44903
Shady Ln 44906
Shaffner Blvd 44907
Sharon Rd 44907
Shauck Rd 44904
Sheets Dr 44903
Sheirer Rd 44903
Shelaire Dr 44903
Shelley Dr 44903
Shepard Rd 44907
Sherbrook Rd 44907
Sheridan Ave 44903
Sherman Ave 44906
Sherman Pl 44903
Sherman Rd 44903
Sherwood Dr 44904
Short St 44904
Silver Ln 44906
Silvercrest Dr 44904
Sites Rd 44903
Sites Lake Dr 44903
Skyline Dr 44903
Skyline Rd 44905
Sloane Ave 44903
Small Ave 44902
Smart Rd 44903
Smith Ave 44905
Smokewood Dr 44903
Snodgrass Rd 44903
Snyder St 44902
Somerset Ct & Dr 44906
Sowers Pl 44904
Spayer Ln 44903
Sprang Pkwy 44903
Spring St
  200-399 44902
  400-499 44905
  500-599 44902
Springbrook Dr 44906
Springlake Dr 44905
Springmill Rd 44903
Springmill St
  300-338 44903
  340-800 44903
  801-1220 44906
Springmill North Rd 44903
Springmill West Rd 44903
Spruce St 44902
Sprucewood Cir & Dr ... 44903
Stadium St 44906
Stafford Dr 44904
Stage Rd 44905
Stander Ave 44903
Stark St
  400-490 44903
  492-498 44903
  600-699 44906
Starlight Ter 44904
State St 44907
State Route 13 44904
State Route 181 44903
State Route 314
  7400-9652 44904
State Route 314
  9654-9798 44903
  401-1197 44903
  2-98 44903
State Route 42 44903
State Route 42 S 44904
State Route 430 44903
State Route 546 44904
State Route 603 44903
State Route 97
  1-2999 44904
  3001-3199 44904
  6860-6898 44903
  6900-7500 44903
  7502-7998 44903
Steeple Chase Dr 44906
Steltz Ln 44906
Sterkel Blvd 44907
Stevens Ct 44903
Stewart Ave N 44906
Stewart Ave S 44906
Stewart Ln 44907
Stewart Rd N
  1-1199 44905
Stewart Rd S 44905
N Stewart Rd
  1200-2499 44903
Stimens Dr 44907
Stiving Rd 44903
Stocking Ave 44903
Stone Rd 44906
Stone Ridge Ave 44903
Stonewood Dr 44904
Stoney Ridge Ct 44904
Stoodt Ct 44902
Straub Rd E
  1-199 44907
  300-399 44903
Straub Rd W
  1-399 44907
  400-1100 44904
  1102-1198 44904
Sturges Ave
  2-44 44902
  46-89 44902
  90-415 44903
  416-499 44907
Suburban Dr 44903
Summerview Ct 44904
Summit Ct 44906
Summit Dr 44903
Summit Hl 44903
Summit St 44906
Sungate Dr 44903
Sunnydale Ave 44905
Sunnyslope Dr 44907
Sunrise Dr 44906
Sunset Blvd 44907
Sunset Dr 44905
Superior Ave 44902
Surrey Rd 44902
Sussex Ct E & W 44904
Swanger Ave 44902
Swarn Pkwy 44903
Sweetbriar Dr 44903
Sycamore St 44903
Tamarac Dr 44904
Tamiami Ter 44904
Tangee Pl 44906
Tarzana Ln 44906
Taurus Ct 44904
Taylor Rd 44903
Taylortown Rd 44903
Temple Ct W 44903
E Temple Ct 44902
Templeton Ter 44904
Terman Rd 44907
Terrace Dr 44905
Texter Rd 44904
Thistle Ct & Dr 44907
Tiffany Dr 44907
Timber Rd 44905
Timbercliff Dr 44907
Timmerman Rd 44903
Timothy Ln 44905
Tingley Ave 44905
Tommy Ln 44903
Tonawanda Dr 44906
Topaz Ave 44907
Torch St 44905
Touby Ct 44902
Touby Ln 44903
Touby Rd 44903
Tower Dr 44906
Township Road 1419 44903
Township Road 235 44904
Township Road 29 44904
Township Road 45 44904
Township Road 49 44904
Township Road 50 44904
Township Road 53 44904
Township Road 54 44904
Township Road 55 44904
Township Road 56 44904
Townview Cir E 44907
Tracy St 44903
Trails End Dr 44903
Trease Rd
  1-283 44904
  284-699 44903
Tremont St 44903
Trenton Ct 44904
N Trimble Rd 44906
S Trimble Rd
  1-1200 44906
  1201-1317 44907
  1202-1318 44906
  1319-1399 44907
Trolley Dr 44905
Trout Dr 44903
Troy Dr 44905
Truxell Dr 44906
Tudor St 44906
Tulipwood Dr 44906
Twin Lakes Dr 44903
Twin Yokes Dr 44904
Twins Ln 44905
Twitchell Rd 44903
Unity Dr 44905
University Dr 44906
Vale Ave 44902
Valley Ct 44905
Valley Dale Ave 44905
Valley Hi Dr 44904
Valley View Rd 44905
Van Buren St 44905
Vanderbilt Rd 44904
Vantilberg Rd 44903
Vennum Ave 44903
Vernon Rd 44905
Vicksburg Dr 44904
Victory St 44905
Vincennes Ct 44904
Vine St
  201-299 44902
  300-599 44905
Virginia Ave 44906
Virginia Ln 44905
Voegele St 44903
Vonhof Blvd 44905
Wade Dr 44906
Wagon Wheel E 44905
Wahl Dr 44904
Walcrest Dr 44903
Walfield Dr 44904
Walker Ave E 44905
Walker Ave N 44905
Walker Ave S 44905
Walker St 44906
Walker Lake Rd
  1000-1599 44906
  2366-3099 44903
Wallace Rd 44903
Walnut Dr 44904
Walnut Dr N 44904
Walnut St 44904
N Walnut St 44902
S Walnut St 44902
Walnut Creek Trl 44906
Walter Ave 44903
Warden Ave 44905
Waring Ave 44902
Warner Ave 44905
Warren Rd 44906
Washington Ave 44903
Washington North Rd 44903
Washington South Rd 44903
Wayne St 44902
Wayne St N 44905
Wedgewood Dr 44903
N & S Weldon Ave 44902
Weller Ave 44904
Wellington Ave 44906
Wellsley Dr 44904
Wempless Ave 44902
Wesley Ave 44905
Westbrook Ave 44906
Western Ave 44906
Westgate Dr 44906
Westover Ct & Ln 44906
Westview Blvd 44907
Westwood Ave 44906
Wheatrow Ave 44903
Whippoorwill Ln 44906
White Oak Ct 44906
White Pine Dr 44904
Whitehall St 44904
Whitetail Dr E & W 44904
Whitnauer Dr 44904
Whittier Rd 44907
Wildwood Dr 44907
Wiles Rd 44903
Wilging Dr 44907
Wilging Rd 44903
Will Dr 44903
E & W Williams Ave 44902
N & S Willis Ave 44902
Willow Dr 44905
Willow Ln 44904
Willow St 44903
Willow Hill Rd 44904
Willow Park Dr 44903
Willowbrook Dr 44907
Willowick Rd 44907
Wilmar Ave 44903
Wilmington Pt 44904
Wimbledon Dr 44906
Winchester Rd 44907
Winding Way 44907
Windsor Rd 44905
Winners Cir N & S 44906
Winterberry Pl 44905
Winwood Dr 44907
Wittmer Rd 44903
Woerth Ave 44902
Wolf Rd 44903
Wolf School Rd 44903
Wolfe Ave 44907
Wolford Rd 44903
Wood St
  1-402 44903
  403-599 44907
Woodcrest Dr 44905
Woodhill Rd 44907
Woodland Ave 44903
Woodland Rd
  500-799 44906
  800-984 44907
  986-1199 44907
Woodmont Rd 44905
Woodridge Dr 44906
Woodruff Rd 44904
Woodside Blvd 44904
Woodside Ct 44904
Woodside Dr 44906
Woodview Ave 44907
Woodville Rd
  400-1289 44907
  1300-2299 44903
Woodward Ave 44903
Wyandotte Ave 44906
Yale Ave 44905
Yale Dr 44907
Yoha Dr 44907
York St W 44904
Yorkshire Rd 44904
Yorktown Dr 44906
Yorkwood Rd 44907
Zachary Way 44903

NUMBERED STREETS

1st Ave 44904
  101-499 44902
E 1st St 44902
W 1st St 44902
2nd Ave
  1-99 44904
  200-499 44902
E 2nd St 44902
W 2nd St 44902
3rd Ave 44905
E 3rd St 44902
W 3rd St
  1-200 44902
  201-549 44903
  550-899 44906
4th Ave 44905
E 4th St 44902
W 4th St
  1-54 44902
  55-67 44903
  56-68 44902
  69-589 44903
  590-799 44906
5th Ave 44905
E 5th St 44902
W 5th St
  1-200 44902
  201-201 44903
  203-499 44903
6th Ave 44905
E 6th St 44902
W 6th St
  1-201 44902
  202-522 44903
7th Ave 44905
8th Ave 44905
9th Ave 44905

MARION OH

General Delivery 43302

POST OFFICE BOXES MAIN OFFICE STATIONS AND BRANCHES

Box No.s
All PO Boxes 43301

NAMED STREETS

All Street Addresses 43302

MASSILLON OH

General Delivery 44646

POST OFFICE BOXES MAIN OFFICE STATIONS AND BRANCHES

Box No.s
1 - 1620 44648
2001 - 2060 44646
4800 - 4817 44648

NAMED STREETS

Aaronwood Ave NE &
NW 44646
Abbey Glen St NE 44646
Abbington St NW 44646
Abraham Ave NW 44647
Acadia St NW 44646
Albrecht St SW 44647
Albright St SE 44646
Alden Ave NW 44647
Alexandria Blvd SE 44646
Allen Ave NW 44647
Almond Pl SE 44646
Alpha St NW 44647
Amanda St SW 44647
Amberwood Cir NE 44646
Amesbury Cir NW 44646
Amherst Ave & Rd NE &
NW 44646
Amvale Ave NE 44646
Andette Ave NW 44647
Andrew Ave NE 44646
N & S Answick Cir 44646
Anthony Ave SW 44647
Appleknoll St NW 44646
Aramis St NW 44646
Arapahoe Rd SE 44646
Arch Ave SE 44646
Arlington Ave NW 44646
Arthur St SE 44646
Ashmede Court Cir
NW 44646
Ashton Ave NW 44646
Ashwell Ave SW 44646
Aster St NW 44647
Athens Ave NW 44646
Auburn Ave NW 44647
Audubon St NW 44646
Augusta Cir & Dr 44646
Austin Ave NW 44646
Autumn St NW 44647
Avis Ave NW 44646
Avon Pl SE 44646
Babylon Ave SW 44646
Bahama Ave NW 44646
Bailey St NW 44646
Bakerwood Dr SW 44647
Bald Eagle Cir NW 44646
Baldauf Ct NE 44646
Ballinger Ave SE 44646
Banyan St NW 44646
Barbara St SW 44647
Barbie Ave SW 44646
Barkman Ave NW 44647
Barrington Cir SE 44646
Barrs Rd SW 44647
Bayberry St NW 44646
Bayer Cir NW 44646
Beatty St NW
  8200-9099 44646
  9200-9499 44647
Beaumont Ave NW 44647
Bebb Ave SW 44647
Beckman St SE 44646
Beechcreek St NW 44646
Beechtree Cir NE 44646
Beiner Pl NE 44646
Belle Ave NW 44646
Bellevue Ave SW 44647
Belmere Ave NW 44647
Bennington Ave NE 44646
Benson St SW 44647
Bent Creek Cir SW 44647
Bentley Ct NW 44646
Bermuda St NW 44646
Bernard Ave SW 44647
Bernower Ave SW 44646
Beryl St NW 44646
Bethann Ave SW 44647
Beverly Rd NE 44646
Big Indian Dr SW 44646
Birchcrest St NW 44646
Bison St NW 44647
Bittersweet Dr NE 44646
Blempton Rd NW 44646
Blossom Cir NW 44646
Blue Heron Cir NW 44646
Blue Thistle Cir NW 44646
Bluff St SE 44646
Bonnie Brae Dr NW &
SW 44647
Borden Ave SW 44647
Boron St NW 44646
Bostic Blvd SW 44647
Bowling Green Dr SE 44646
Boyds Cors NW 44647
Bradford Rd NE 44646
Braewick Cir NW 44646
Bramblebush St NW 44646
Bramblewood Cir NE 44646
Brenner Ave NW 44647
Bretz St NW 44646
Briar Hill St SW 44646
Briardale Dr NW 44646
Bricker Rd NW 44646
Bridgeton Ave & St NE &
NW 44646
Brightleaf Ave NW 44647
Brighton Cir NW 44646
Broadhaven Ave NW 44646
Broadland St NW 44646
Brockton Ave NW 44646
Brook Ave NW 44646
Brooke Hollow St NW 44646
Brookwood St NE 44646
Brotherly Ave NW 44647
Brown Bear Cir NW 44646
Brunnerdale Ave NW 44646
Brunswick Cir NW 44646
Bryce Cir NW 44646
Buckingham Cir NW 44646
Buckley Cir NW 44646
Buckwalter Dr SW 44646
Bunker Hill St NW 44646
Bunyan Cir NW 44646
Burd Ave NE 44646
Burton Ave NE & NW 44646
Byron Ave SW 44647
Cable Ct NW 44647
Cadbury St NW 44646
Cambridge Ave NW &
SE 44646
Campbell Cir NE 44646
Campus Dr SW 44647
Canal Pl NW 44647
Candell Ave SW 44646
Candleberry St NW 44646
Canford Ave NW 44646
Canter St NW 44646
Caraway Cir NW 44646
Carie Hill Cir NW 44646
Caritas Cir NW 44646
Carlene Ave SW 44647
Carlyle St NE & NW 44646
Carmela Cir NW 44647
Carmont Ave NW &
SW 44647
Carnation St NE 44646
Carnegie Ave NW 44646
Carolina St NW 44646
Caroline St NW 44646
Carolwood Ave NW 44646
Carriage Hill St NW 44646
Carson Ave NW 44647
Carters Grove Cir NW 44646
Carver St NW 44647

Case Western Dr SE 44646
Castello Cir NW 44646
Castle West Cir NW 44647
Catalina Ave NW 44646
Cayuga St NW 44647
Cedar Knoll St NW 44646
Cedarcrest Ave SW 44646
Cedarhill Cir NE 44646
Celina St NW 44646
Central Ct SE 44646
Chablis Dr NW 44646
Chadwick St NW 44646
Champion Ave NW 44646
Championship Cir SE 44646
Charldon Ave SW 44646
Charles Ave SE & SW 44646
Chauncey St NW 44647
Chelsea St NW 44646
Cherry Rd NE 44646
Cherry Rd NW
1-199 44646
200-1599 44647
1601-2759 44647
Cherrywood Cir NW 44646
Cheryl Ln NW 44646
Chester Ave SE 44646
Chestnut Ave NE 44646
Cheverton Cir NW 44646
Chevron Cir SW 44646
Chippendale St NW 44646
Chittenden Cir NE 44646
Cincinnat St SE & SW 44646
Cinderella St NW 44646
Cinwood St NW 44646
Citadel Ave NW 44646
City Hall St SE 44646
Claremont Ave NW 44647
Clark St SW 44646
Clearbrook Rd NW 44646
Clearview Dr NE 44646
Clearway St NW 44647
Clementz St SW 44647
Cleveland St SW 44647
Cliff St NW 44647
Cliffside Ave NW 44646
Clifton Court Cir NW 44646
Cloverdale Cir NE 44646
Cloverleaf St NW 44647
Cloverleaf St SE 44646
Club House Cir NW 44646
Clyde Ave & Ct NW & SW 44647
Colina Vista St NW 44646
Collingswood Cir NW 44646
Colonial Pkwy NE 44646
Colton St NW 44646
Columbia Ave NW 44646
Commerce Dr SW 44646
Commons Dr NW 44646
Commonwealth Ave NE 44646
Concord St NW 44646
Concord Hill Cir NE 44646
Condor Cir NW 44646
Connecticut Ave & St SE & SW 44646
Conover St NW 44646
Cook Ct SW 44647
Coolidge Ave SE 44646
Cooper Ave SW 44646
Cornell St NE 44646
Corniche St NW 44646
Corundite Rd NW 44647
Country St NW 44646
Country Club Cir NW 44647
Courtland Ave NW
2100-2299 44647
5700-5999 44646
Coventry Rd NE 44646
Cranford St NW 44646
Crescentview Dr SW 44646
Crest Cir NW 44647
Cricket Cir NW 44646
Crimson St NW 44647
Cross Creek Cir SW 44647
Crown Point St NW 44646

Crystal Lake Rd NW 44647
Culverne St NW 44647
Curley Ct SE 44646
Cyprus Dr SE 44646
Cyril Ave SW 44647
Dakota St NW 44646
Dale St NW 44646
Dale Hollow Cir NW 44646
Dalecrest St NW 44646
Danner St NE 44646
Daphne Cir NW 44646
Darby Dr NW 44646
Dartmouth Ave NW 44646
Darwin St SW 44646
David Ave NE 44646
David Canary Dr SW 44647
David Dodson Dr SE 44646
Davis Cir NW 44647
Daytona St NW 44646
Deanne Cir NW 44646
Deerfield Ln NE 44646
Deerford Ave & St NW & SW 44647
Deermont Ave NW & SW 44647
Delaware Ave NE 44646
Delford Ave NW 44646
Delmont Ave NW 44647
Delray Ave NW 44646
Denmont Ave SW 44646
Dewalt St SE 44646
Dexter Rd NE 44646
Diamond Ct SE 44646
Dielhenn Ave SE 44646
Dogwood Dr NE 44646
Doral Cir SE 44646
Dorchester Court Cir NW 44646
Dovershire Ave NW 44646
Drexel St NW 44646
Dromoland Cir NW 44646
Drummond Dr NW 44646
Duane Ave NW 44647
Dublin Ridge Cir NW 44646
Duke Cir SW 44646
Duncan St SW 44647
Dupont St NW 44646
Durham Cir NW 44646
Dwight Ave SE 44646
Eagle View Cir NW 44646
Eagles Cir SE 44646
Earl Rd NW 44647
Eastbrook St 44646
Eastlynn Ave NW 44646
Eastwood Ave NE 44646
Easy St NW 44646
Eden Ave NW 44646
Edgar Pl NW 44647
Edgewater Ave NW 44646
Edgewood Ave SW 44646
Edmund Court Cir NW 44646
Edward Ave SW 44647
Edwin Ave SE 44646
Eileen Ave SW 44646
Elden Rd NW 44647
Eldridge Ave SW 44646
Elizabeth Ave NW 44646
Elm Ct NE 44646
Elmbreeze St NW 44646
Elmford Ave SW 44646
Emily Cir NW 44647
Enterprise Pl SE 44646
Equestrian St NW 44646
Erb Ct SW 44647
Erica Cir NW 44646
Erie Ave NW
1700-3999 44646
4000-4469 44647
4471-4499 44647
Erie Ave SW 44646
Erie St N 44646
Erie St S
1-334 44646
333-333 44648
335-4199 44646
336-4298 44646

Ertle Ave NE 44646
Esquire St NW 44646
Euclid St SW 44647
Evangel Ave NW 44647
Fairgrove Ave SW 44646
Fairland St NW 44647
Fairlawn Ave SW 44646
Falcon Cir NW 44646
Fallen Oak Cir NE 44646
Fan Ct NW 44646
Fasnacht Cir NW 44646
Fay St SE 44646
Fayette Ave NW 44646
Federal Ave NE 44646
Federal Ave NW 44647
Finefrock Rd SW 44647
Finley Pl SW 44647
Fire Bush Dr NW 44647
First National Plz NW 44647
Floral St SW 44646
Floyd Ct NW 44647
Foch St NW 44646
Fontana St NW 44646
Forbes Ave NW 44646
Ford St NW 44647
Forest Ave SE 44646
Forest Glen Ave NW 44647
Forest Ridge St NW 44646
Forest Trail Ave NW 44647
Forty Corners Rd NW 44647
Fox Ct NW 44647
Frances Pl NW & SW 44647
Franklin Rd NE 44646
Freeman Ave NW 44646
Fries St SE 44646
Fulmer St NW 44647
Fulton Dr NW 44647
Gage St SW 44647
Gail Ave NE 44646
Galena St NW 44646
Garnell St NW 44647
Gauntlet St SW 44646
Geiger Ave SW 44647
Genoa Ave NW & SW 44646
Gentry St NW 44646
George Red Bird Dr SE 44646
Georgia St NW 44646
Gettysburg Cir NW 44647
Gi Ante St NW 44646
Gibson Ave SE 44646
Gill Ct NE 44646
Glacier Ave NW 44646
Gladdis St SW 44647
Gladys St NW 44646
Glasgow Cir NW 44646
Glen Pl & St NW & SW 44647
Glen Elm Cir NW 44646
Glenarden Cir NW 44646
Glenbrook Ave NW 44646
Glendevan St NW 44646
Glenpointe Cir NW 44646
Glenwood Ave SE 44646
Gnau Ave SW 44646
Golden Eagle Rd NW 44646
Goldenrod Cir NW 44646
Goodyear St NW 44646
Gordon Ave NW 44647
Graber St SW 44646
Gray Ct NE 44646
Gray Ridge Ave SE 44646
Grayson Green St NW 44646
Great Court Cir NW 44646
Green Ave SW 44647
Green Oaks Cir NW 44646
Greenbrier Cir NE 44646
Greendale Ave SW 44647
Greenford Ave SW 44646
Greenpark St NW 44647
Greenridge Dr NE 44646
Greentree Pl SE 44646
Greenway Trail St NW 44647
Greenwich Blvd NW 44646
Griffith Ave SW 44647
Groose Ave NW 44646

Grosvenor Ave NW 44647
Grouse Cir NW 44646
Guy St NW 44647
Haag Ave SW 44646
Hadleigh Ave SW 44646
Hale Pl SE 44646
Hall Ct SE 44646
Hamilton Ave NE 44646
Hankins Rd NE & NW 44646
Harcrest Ave SW 44646
Hardin St NW 44646
Harding Ave NW & SW 44646
Harlequin Cir NW 44646
Harmon Pl NE 44646
Harmony St NW & SW 44647
Harold Ave SE 44646
Harris Pl SE 44646
Harsh Ave SE & SW 44646
Harvard Ave NE 44646
Harvest Cir NE 44646
Hawthorne Ave NE 44646
Hayes Ave NE 44646
Hazel Pl SE 44646
Hazelbrook St SW 44646
Healy St NE 44646
Hearth Cir NW 44646
Heatherview St NW 44646
Hedge Ct NE 44646
Heidelberg Ave SE 44646
Heiman Pl SW 44647
Helena Ave NW 44646
Hemlock St NW 44647
Hess Rd NW 44647
Hewitt Ave NW 44646
Hickory Ave NE 44646
High Mill Ave NW
4400-5399 44647
5400-6899 44646
Highbrook Ave NW 44647
Highland Ave SE & SW 44646
Highlander Ave & St 44647
Highsaddle Ave NW 44646
Highton St SW 44646
Hill Run Cir NW 44646
Hills And Dales Rd NE & NW 44646
Hillside Pl SW 44647
Hilton St NW 44646
Hinderer Ave SW 44646
Hobart Ave NE 44646
Hocking St NW 44646
Holodale St SW 44646
Hostetter Pl SW 44647
Houston St NW & SW 44647
Hoverland Ave NW 44646
Howard Ave NW 44647
Howell Pl NW 44647
Hunters Way SW 44647
Hunters Chase St NW 44646
Huron Rd SE 44646
Hyatt Ave NW 44646
Hyde Park Blvd NW 44646
Ideal Ct SE 44646
Idlecrest Ave SW 44647
Independence St SE 44646
Indian River Rd SW 44646
Indiana Ave NE 44646
Indorf Ave SW 44647
Industrial Ave SW 44647
Ingall Ave NW 44646
Inwood Dr NW 44646
Ironwood Cir NE 44646
Irvington Ave NE 44646
Isle Cir NW 44646
Jackson Ave NW 44646
Jackson Ave SW 44646
Jackson St SW 44646
Jamberan Ave NW 44646
James Ave NW 44647
James Duncan Plz 44646
Jane St NW 44646
Janice St NE 44646
Jefferson Rd NE 44646

Jeffrey Ave NW 44646
Jenny Cir SW 44647
Jimmie St SW 44646
John Carroll Dr SE 44646
Johnson St SE 44646
Jolynn St NE 44646
Jormay Ave NW 44647
Joshua St NW 44647
Julian St NW 44646
Karen Ave NW 44647
Karn Ave SW 44647
Kathy Ln NW 44646
Kaylynn St SE 44646
Kaymont Ave SE 44646
Kayview St SW 44647
Kaywood St NW 44647
Kelford St NW 44646
Kelly St SW 44646
Kellydale St NW 44646
Kendal Ave NE 44646
Kenny St SW 44646
Kensington St NW 44646
Kenwood Cir NW 44646
Kenyon Ave NW & SW 44647
Kenyon Creek Ave NW 44647
Keswick Court Cir NW 44646
Keuper Blvd NE 44646
Kilkenny Cir NW 44646
Killeen St NW 44646
Kimmens Rd SW 44647
Kinloch Court Cir NW 44646
Kipling Ave NW 44646
Kiski Ave NW 44647
Kitzmiller St SW 44646
Klick St SW 44646
Klingston St NW 44646
Knight St NW 44646
Knolls Ave SW 44646
Kolpwood Ave NW 44646
Korman Ave NE 44646
Kracker St NW 44646
Lachelle Ave SW 44646
Lafayette Dr NW 44647
Lake Ave NE 44646
Lake Ave NW
1-48 44646
49-399 44647
Lake Trl NE 44646
Lake Bluff Dr NW 44646
Lake Creek Cir NW 44647
Lake Vista Cir NW 44646
Lakeridge St NW 44647
Lakeshore Cir NW 44646
Lanedale St NW 44647
Lassen Cir NW 44646
Laura St NW 44646
Lauren Ave NW 44646
Lauren Cir NW 44647
Laurenbrook Ln NE 44646
Lauri Jo Ln SW 44647
Lavenham Ave SW 44646
Lawn Ave SW 44647
Lawnwood St NW 44647
Lawton St SE 44646
Ledgewood Blvd NE 44646
Lee Ave NW 44647
Leecrest St NW 44646
Lennox Ave NE 44646
Leonard Ave NW & SW 44646
Lewis Pl NE 44646
Liberty Ct SW 44647
Lighthouse Cir NW 44646
Lilac Cir NW 44646
Lillian Gish Blvd SW 44647
Limbach Pl SW 44647
Lincoln Way E 44646
Lincoln Way NW 44647
Lincoln Way W 44647
Linda Ln SW 44647
Lindbergh Ave NE 44646
Linden St NW 44647
Link St NW & SW 44647
Linway Ave NW 44646

List St NW 44646
Lochwood St SW 44647
Locke Ave NW & SW 44646
Longbrook St SW 44646
Longford Ave NW 44646
Longlynn St SW 44646
Longview St SW 44646
Lords Lake Cir NW 44646
Lori Ave NE 44646
Lorin Pl SW 44647
Loriwood Cir NW 44646
Lorraine Ave NW 44646
Lorwood St NW 44646
Louisa Marie Ave NW 44646
Lutz Ave NW 44646
Lynch St SW 44646
Lyndale Ave NW 44647
Lynndell St NW 44647
Maclaren Ave NW 44646
Mader Ct NE 44646
Main Ave W 44647
Malabu Ave NW 44646
Mallard Cir NW 44646
Malone Ave SE 44646
Manchester Ave NW & SW 44647
Maple Ave SE 44646
Margaret St NW 44646
Margilee Dr SW 44647
Marion Ave NW & SE 44646
Mariwood Ave NW 44646
Marjory Dr SW 44647
Mark Ross Ave SW 44647
Marlyn Pkwy NE 44646
Marta St SW 44646
Mary Lou St NW 44646
Mason St SW 44646
Massachusetts Ave SE 44646
Massillon Marketplace Dr SW 44646
Masters Point Cir SE 44646
Mathias Ave NE 44646
Mayflower Ave NW 44647
Maytime St NW 44646
Mccadden Ave NE 44646
Mcdonald Cir SE 44646
Mckinley Ave SW 44647
Meadowbrook Rd SW 44647
Meadowcrest St NW & SW 44647
Meadowlawn St SW 44646
Meadows Ave NW 44647
Meadowside St NW 44647
Meadowwind Ln NE 44646
Meadowwood St NW 44646
Medill Ave NE 44646
Meiner Ct NE 44646
Merino Cir NE 44646
Mesa Cir NW 44646
Miami Ave NW 44647
Michael Cir NW 44647
Milburn Rd NE 44646
Mill Creek Run NE 44646
Mill Race St NW 44647
Mill Ridge Path NE 44646
Millennium Blvd SE 44646
Millersburg Rd SW 44647
Millstone Ln NE 44646
Milmont St NW 44646
Milton Ave NE 44646
Minuteman Ave NW 44646
Moffitt St SW 44647
Mohican Ave SE 44646
Mollane St NW 44646
Monroe St NW 44647
Mont Clair Blvd NW 44646
Montaque Ave NW 44646
Montrose Ave NW 44646
Morton Rd SW 44647
Mossglen Cir NE 44646
Mossy Oaks Ave NW 44646
Mount Union Ave SE 44646
Mudbrook Rd NW 44646
Muffly Rd SW 44647
Nancy Anna Ave NW 44646

Navarre Rd SE & SW 44646
Nave Rd SE & SW 44646
Neale Ave SW 44647
Nearwood St NW 44646
Nettlecreek Ave NW 44646
Newport Ave NW 44646
Nicholas Cir NW 44647
Niles St SW 44647
Nish Ave NW 44646
Noble Pl NW 44647
Noble Loon St NW 44646
Nobleman Cir NW 44646
Nordic Cir NW 44646
Norma Ave NW 44646
North Ave NE 44646
North Ave NW 44647
Northcrest St NW 44647
Northwood St NW 44646
Norwich Ave NW 44646
Nottingham St NW 44646
Nova Dr SE 44646
Nutmeg Cir NE 44646
Oak Ave SE & SW 44646
Oak Bluff Rd NE 44646
Oak Hill Cir & Dr 44646
Oak Manor Ave NE 44646
Oak Trail St NE 44646
Oakcrest Ln NE 44646
Oakdale St NW 44646
Oakview St NW 44646
Oakwood Ave NE 44646
Oberlin Ave SW 44647
Ocala Ave NW 44646
Ogle Pl SE 44646
Ohio Ave NE & NW 44646
Ohio State Dr SE 44646
Ohlman Ct NE 44646
Old Bridge Ave NW 44646
Old Church Ave NW 44646
Old Forest St NW 44646
Olivewood Cir NE 44646
Ontario St NW 44646
Onyx Ave NW 44646
Opal St NW 44646
Orange St NW 44647
Orchard Ave NE 44646
Orchard Hill Cir 44646
Ordell Ave SW 44647
Orrville St NW 44647
Osage Ave SE 44646
Overlook Ave SW 44647
Overmont Ave SW 44646
Oxford Ave NE & NW 44646
Oxford Chase Cir NW 44646
Page St NW 44647
Par Four Cir SE 44646
S Park Dr NW 44646
Parkbrook St NW 44647
Parkford St NW 44646
Parkland Ave SW 44646
Parknoll St SW 44646
Parkview St NE 44646
Parsons Court Cir NW 44646
Partridge St NW 44646
Patriot Pl SW 44647
Paul E Brown Dr SE 44646
Paulding St NW 44646
Pearl Ave & Pl 44646
Pebble Beach Dr SE 44646
Pebble Chase Cir NE 44646
Penn Ave SE 44646
Pennberthy Pl NE 44646
Perlee St NW 44646
Perry Ave SW 44647
Perry Dr NW 44646
Pershing Ave NW 44646
Persia Cir SW 44646
Peyton St NW 44646
Pheasant Grove Ave NW 44646
Phillips Rd NE 44646
Pigeon Run Rd SW 44647
Pike Ave SW 44647
Pin Oak St NW 44647
Pine St SE 44646
Pine Knoll Ave NW 44646

Pine Meadow Cir NW .. 44646
Pinehills Dr SW 44646
Pinehurst Ave NW 44646
Pinelane St NW 44646
Pinewood Ave SW 44646
Piperglen Ave NW 44646
Pirates Cove St NW 44646
Plymouth St NW 44646
Plymouth Knoll Ave NW 44646
W Pointe Cir NW 44647
Pond St SW 44647
Pondera St NW 44646
Poplar St NW 44647
Portage St NW 44646
Postal Pl SE 44646
Prairie Cir NE 44646
Prescot Ave NW 44646
Princehorn Cir NW 44647
Princeton Ave NW....... 44646
Priscilla Ave NW 44647
Prospect Dr SE 44646
Prosway Ave SW....... 44646
Proudley Ave SW 44646
Providence Rd NE 44646
Province Dr NW.......... 44646
Puritan Cir NW 44647
Putney Court Ave NW .. 44646
Quail Hollow St NW 44646
Queen Anne Dr NW 44647
Rachel Cir NW 44646
Radcliff Ave NW 44646
Raleigh St NW 44646
Ranier Ave NW 44646
Rapid Falls St NW 44647
Rawson Ave SE......... 44646
Rayanna St NW 44646
Raymond Cir NW 44647
Raymond Ct NE 44646
Raynell St NW 44647
Red Fox Dr NW 44646
Red Oak Cir NW 44646
Red Panda Cir NW...... 44646
Regency Dr NW 44646
Relda Cir SW 44647
Reservoir Dr NE......... 44646
Revere Ave NW 44647
Rhode Island Ave SE .. 44646
Richard Ave SW 44647
Richville Dr SE & SW .. 44646
Ridgecrest Dr NE & NW 44646
Rio Grande Cir SE 44646
River Crest St NW 44647
River Ridge Cir NW 44647
Riverside Dr NW 44647
Riviera Ave NW 44646
Roanoke St NW 44646
Rob St NW 44646
Rodman Ave NE 44646
Roger Ave NW 44646
Rohr Ave NW 44646
Rohrland St NW 44647
Rohrway Ave NW 44647
Rolling Acres Cir E & W 44647
Rolling Green Ave NW . 44646
Rolling Lea Cir W 44647
Rolling Park Dr N & S .. 44647
Rolling View Cir 44647
Rolling Village Ln 44647
Ron Cir NW 44646
Rondale Cir NW 44646
Rondale St SW 44647
Roni St SW 44646
Roosevelt St NE 44646
Rose Ave SE 44646
Rosefield Cir NW 44646
Roseland Ave NW 44647
Roselawn Ave SW 44646
Roslyn Ave NE 44646
Rotch Ave NE 44646
Round Top Cir NW 44646
Roush St NW 44646
Rowford Ave SW 44646
Rowmont Ave SW 44646
Roxbury Ave NW 44646
Ruby Ave NW 44647
Rudy St SW 44647
Russ Ranch St NW 44646
Russell Blvd SE 44646
Rustic Ridge Cir NW 44646
Ruth Ave, Ln & Pl 44646
Ryder Ave & St 44647
Sally St SW 44647
Sandbridge St NW 44646
Sandbrook St NW 44646
Sanders Ave SW 44647
Sandy Ave NE 44646
Sarbaugh St SW 44647
Sawgrass Cir SE 44646
Sawmill Trl NE 44646
Schrock Pl SW 44647
Schuler Ave NW 44647
Scotsbury St NW 44646
Scotsbury Glen St NW . 44646
Scotslanding Cir NW ... 44646
Scott Pl NW 44647
Scottwood Pl NE 44646
Sedwick Ave NW 44646
Seifert Ct NW 44646
Seneca St NE & NW ... 44646
Serenity Dr NW 44647
Seymour St NW 44646
Shady Crest Ave NW ... 44646
Shady Knoll Ave NW ... 44646
Shady Stone St NW 44646
Shady Trail St NW 44647
Shadyview Ave NW 44646
Shaefer St NW 44647
Shaw Ave NE 44646
Shawnee Ave SE 44646
Sheffield Ave NE 44646
Sheila St NW 44646
Shelby St NW 44646
Sheri Ave NE 44646
Sherlin Ave NW 44646
Sherman Cir NE 44646
Sherwood Ave NW 44646
Shirlie Ave SW 44646
Shoreway Cir NW 44646
Shriver Ave SE 44646
Sickels Cir SE 44646
Silver Creek Cir NW 44647
Simsbury Cir NW 44646
Sinclair St SW 44647
Singer St NW 44647
Singingbrook Ave NW .. 44646
Sippo Ave & Blvd NE & NW 44646
Sippo Creek St NW 44646
Sippo Reserves Dr NW 44647
Skyland Ave NW 44646
Smithview Ave NW 44647
Snively Ave NW 44646
Snowy Owl Cir NW 44646
Snyder Pl SW 44647
Soames Dr NW 44646
Sonia Ave NW 44647
South Ave SE & SW 44646
Southview Cir NW 44646
Southway St SW 44646
Sparrow Ridge Ave NW 44646
Spindle St NW 44646
Spring Hill Ln NE 44646
Springhaven Cir NE 44646
Springhill Ave NE 44646
Spruce Ave SW 44646
Stahl Ave NW 44646
Stanbury Cir NW 44646
Standish Cir & St 44647
Stanton Ave NW 44647
Stanwood Rd SW 44647
Star Cir SW 44646
Starbrook St NW 44646
Stardale Ave SW 44646
Starr Ridge St SE 44646
State Ave NE 44646
State Ave NW
1-99 44646
300-399 44647
Sterlilite St SE 44646
Sterling Place Cir NW .. 44646
Stevie Ave SW 44646
Stewart Ave NW & SW 44646
Stockton Rd NW 44646
Stonehenge Ave NW ... 44646
Stoner Ave NE 44646
Stratford Ave NE & NW 44646
Strausser St NW 44646
Stuart St NW 44646
Stuhldreher St NW 44646
Stump Ave SW......... 44646
Summerdale Ave NW .. 44646
Sundale St NW 44646
Sunmont St NW 44646
Sunnybrook St NW & SW 44647
Sunset Pl SE........... 44647
Sunshine Cir NW 44647
Susan St SW 44647
Suwannee St NW 44646
Suzette Ave NW 44647
Sweetbriar Cir NW 44646
Sweetleaf Cir NW 44647
Tabor St SW 44646
Taggart Ave & St NE & NW 44646
Tahiti St NW 44646
Tammie Ct NE 44646
Tanglewood Dr NE 44646
Tansy Cir NW 44646
Tanya Ave NW 44646
Tarpon St NW 44646
Taylor St SW........... 44647
Tennyson Ave & St NE & NW 44646
Terry Ave NE 44646
Teton Cir NW 44646
Thackeray Ave NW..... 44646
Thames Court Cir NW .. 44646
Thomas Blvd NW 44647
Thomas Cir NE 44646
Thorne Ave NE & NW .. 44646
Thornridge Rd NW 44646
Tiffin Cir SE 44646
Tillman St NW 44646
Timber Wolf Cir NW 44646
Timbercrest St NW 44646
Timberidge Ave NW 44646
Timberline Cir NE 44646
Timothy Cir SW 44647
Topaz St NW 44646
Trail Head Cir NW 44647
Traphagen St NW 44646
Tremont Ave SE 44646
Tremont Ave SW 44647
Treyburn Ave NW 44646
Trillium Cir NE 44646
Triple Crown Cir SE 44646
Trockenw St SW 44647
Turning Leaf Ave NW .. 44647
Twin Oaks St NE....... 44646
Tylers Mill Ln NE 44646
Underhill Dr SE 44646
Uniondale St NW 44646
University Dr SE 44646
University Commons Dr SE 44646
Upland Ave SW 44647
Urban Ct SW........... 44647
Urbana Ave SE 44646
Ute Ave SE 44646
Utopia Cir NW 44647
Valerie Ave NE & NW ... 44646
Valeside Ave & St NE & NW 44646
Valleyside Cir NE 44646
Valleywood Ave NE 44646
Vantage Hill Ave NW ... 44646
Vega St SW 44647
Ventura Cir NW 44646
Venture Cir SE 44646
Vermont Ave SE 44646
Verna Ct SE 44646
Veterans Blvd SE 44646
Viceroy Dr SW 44647
Villarose Ave NW 44647
Vindell Ave NW 44647
Vine St NW 44646
Vinette Pl NE 44646
Vintage Ave NW 44646
Virginia St SE 44646
Vista Ave SE 44646
Vogel Ave NE 44646
Vonnie Dr SW 44647
Vorys Ave SW 44647
Wabash Ave SW 44647
Wagon Trail St NE 44646
Wagoner St NW 44647
Wales Ave & Rd NE & NW 44646
Wall Pl & St SE & NW 44646
Wallace Ave SE 44646
Walnut Rd SE 44646
Walnut Rd SW
100-199 44646
401-597 44647
599-1699 44647
Walter St NW 44646
Walterson Ave NW 44646
Warmington Rd SE 44646
Warren St SW 44647
Warrington Rd NW 44646
Warwick Ave NW 44646
Washington St NW 44647
Water Ave NW 44647
Wattova Rd NW 44646
Weatherston St NW 44646
Webb Ave SW 44647
Webster Ave NW 44647
Weirich Blvd NW 44647
Wellesley St NW 44646
Wellington Cir NW 44646
Wellman Ave SE 44646
Wendling Ave NW 44647
Westbury Cir NW 44646
Westdale St SW 44646
Westhaven Dr SW 44647
Westland Ave NW & SW 44646
Westlynn Ave NW 44646
Westminster Cir NW 44646
Westmont Ave SW 44646
Westwood St SW 44646
Wetmore Ave SE 44646
Wheaton Cir NE 44646
Wicliff Ave NE.......... 44646
Wild Fox Run Ave NW . 44646
Wildflower Ln NE 44646
Wildridge Dr NW 44646
Wildwood Cir SW 44646
Willard Ave NE 44646
Williams Ave NE 44646
Willow Ave NE 44646
Willowlane Ave NW 44646
Willwood St NW 44646
Wilmington Ave SE 44646
Wilson Ave SE 44646
Windamere Ave NW 44646
Windsong Cir NE 44646
Windsor Rd NE 44646
Windward Trace Cir NW 44646
Windy Ln NW 44646
Windy Hill Cir NW 44646
Winrich St NW 44646
Winslow Ave NW 44647
Winterhills Cir NW 44646
Wittenberg Ave SE 44646
Wood Creek Cir NW ... 44647
Woodbine Cir NE 44646
Woodbridge Cir NW 44646
Wooded Point Cir NW .. 44646
Woodforest St NW 44647
Woodland Ave SE 44646
Woodrich St SW 44646
Woodruff Ave NW 44647
Woodstock Cir NW 44646
Woodstone Ave NW 44647
Woodvale Cir NW 44646
Woodview Dr NE 44646
Wooster St NW 44647
Woutat Cir SW 44647
Wray St NE 44646
Wrexham Ave SW 44646
Wright State Dr SE 44646
Wyoming Pl NE 44646
Xavier Dr SE 44646
Yale Ave NE 44646
Yorkshire St NW 44646
Young Ave NW 44647
Young St SE 44646
Zern Ave SW 44646
Zion Cir NW 44646

NUMBERED STREETS

1st St NE 44646
1st St NW
1-499 44647
500-699 44646
1st St SE 44646
1st St SW
1-199 44647
200-699 44646
2nd St NE 44646
3rd St NE 44646
3rd St NW 44647
3rd St SE 44646
4th St NE 44646
4th St NW 44647
4th St SE 44646
4th St SW 44647
5th St NE 44646
5th St NW 44647
5th St SE 44646
5th St SW 44647
6th St NE 44646
6th St NW 44647
6th St SE 44646
6th St SW 44647
7th St NE 44646
7th St SW 44647
8th St NE 44646
8th St SE 44646
8th St SW 44647
9th St NE 44646
9th St SE 44646
9th St SW 44647
10th St NE 44646
10th St SE 44646
10th St SW 44647
11th St NE 44646
11th St SE 44646
11th St SW 44647
12th St NW
1-499 44647
2700-3599 44646
12th St SE 44646
12th St SW 44647
13th St SE
1-1399 44647
3700-4399 44646
14th St NW 44647
14th St SE 44646
14th St SW 44647
15th St NW 44647
15th St SE 44646
15th St SW 44647
16th St NE 44646
16th St SE 44646
16th St SW 44647
17th St NE 44646
17th St NW 44647
17th St SW 44647
18th St NE 44646
18th St NW 44647
18th St SE 44646
19th St NE 44646
19th St NW 44647
19th St SE 44646
20th St NW 44647
20th St SE 44646
20th St SW 44647
21st St NW 44647
21st St SE 44646
22nd St NW 44647
22nd St SE 44646
22nd St SW 44647
23rd St NE 44646
23rd St NW 44647
23rd St SE 44646
23rd St SW 44647
24th St NW 44647
24th St SE 44646
24th St SW 44647
25th St NW 44647
25th St SE 44646
26th St NW 44647
26th St SE 44646
27th St NE 44646
27th St NW 44647
27th St SE 44646
28th St NW 44647
29th St NW 44647
30th St NW 44647
32nd St NW 44647

MEDINA OH

General Delivery 44256

POST OFFICE BOXES MAIN OFFICE STATIONS AND BRANCHES

Box No.s
All PO Boxes 44258

NAMED STREETS

Aaron Dr 44256
W Abbey Dr 44256
Abbeyville Rd 44256
Aberdeen Ln 44256
Acorn Cir 44256
Alameda Ct 44256
Alber Dr 44256
Alden Ct 44256
Aldo Dr 44256
Alexandria Ln 44256
Alfred Oval 44256
Allard Rd 44256
Alyssa Ln 44256
Amy Trl 44256
Andrews Rd 44256
Antler Trl 44256
Arbor Ct & Xing 44256
Argyle Ln 44256
Arielle Ct 44256
Arlyne Ln 44256
Asherbrand Dr 44256
Ashford Ct 44256
Ashwood Ln 44256
Autumn Run Dr 44256
Autumn Tree Dr 44256
Avery Ln 44256
Avon Lake Rd 44256
Bachtell Rd 44256
Bagdad Rd 44256
Bainbridge Dr 44256
Baker Rd 44256
Ballash Rd 44256
Ballou Rd 44256
Bambeck Rd 44256
Bar Harbor Blvd 44256
Barnhill Dr 44256
Barrington Dr 44256
Bath Rd 44256
Baxter St 44256
Bayberry Dr 44256
Beach Rd 44256
Beachler Rd 44256
Bear Swamp Rd 44256
Beck Rd 44256
Beechwood Dr 44256
Bella Rosa Ct 44256
Belmont Ct 44256
Bent Oak Cir 44256
Bentwood Trl 44256
Benwick Dr 44256
Berkshire Dr 44256
Bilney Ct 44256
Birch Hill Dr 44256
Bishop Ct & St 44256
Black Bird Way 44256
Blake Ave 44256
Blakeslee Blvd 44256
Blanot St 44256
Blue Heron Trce 44256
Bluebell Pkwy 44256
Boardman Aly 44256
Bolivar Aly 44256
Boneta Rd 44256
Bonnie Ct 44256
Booth Bay Dr 44256
Bowman Ln 44256
Boxelder Dr 44256
Braddocks Lndg 44256
Bradley Ct 44256
Bradway St 44256
Branch Rd 44256
Brandywine Dr 44256
Brenelle Ln 44256
Brenton Ln 44256
Bridgehampton Dr 44256
Bridgeport Dr 44256
Bridle Ct 44256
Brimfield Dr 44256
Bristol Ln 44256
N & S Broadway St 44256
Broken Fence Dr 44256
Brompton Dr 44256
Bronson St 44256
Brook Run Dr 44256
Brookfield Dr 44256
Brookland Dr 44256
Brookledge Dr 44256
Brookpoint Dr 44256
Brownstone Ln 44256
Brynmar Ln 44256
Brynwood Dr 44256
Buehlers Dr 44256
Bunker Hl 44256
Burgundy Bay Blvd E, N & W 44256
Burnhill Dr 44256
Burntwood Dr 44256
Burrow Ct 44256
Butterfly Cir 44256
Cambridge Dr 44256
Canterbury Ln 44256
Cantwell Trl 44256
Cardinal Dr 44256
Carlton Rd 44256
Carriage Ln 44256
Carrick Dr 44256
Carsten Rd 44256
Carsten Woods Ln 44256
Carter Dr 44256
Carver Dr 44256
Catherines Overlook Dr 44256
Catmere Dr 44256
Cedar St 44256
Cedarwood Ln 44256
Central Park Ln 44256
Century Oak Cir 44256
Chadwick Ln 44256
Champagne Shrs 44256
Champion Creek Blvd .. 44256
Champions Way 44256
Chandler Ct 44256
Chapel Cir 44256
Chapman Ln 44256
Charleton Dr 44256
Chatham Rd 44256
Chaucer Dr 44256
Chestnut Cor 44256
Chestnut Hill Dr 44256
Chippewa Rd 44256
Church Rd 44256

Street	ZIP
Churchill Way	44256
Circle Dr	44256
Clay Mountain Dr	44256
Cloverdale Ave	44256
Clubhouse Pointe Dr	44256
Cobblefield Dr	44256
Cobblestone Park Dr	44256
Coddingville Rd	44256
Colinas Dr	44256
Colonial Ct	44256
Columbia Rd	44256
Commerce Dr	44256
Concord Dr & Knls	44256
Conestoga Ln	44256
Continental Dr	44256
Cook Rd	44256
Coon Club Rd	44256
Cornell Ct	44256
Cornwallis Ct	44256
Country Club Dr	44256
Countryside Dr	44256
N Court St	
100-104	44256
106-304	44256
301-303	44258
305-1299	44256
306-1298	44256
S Court St	44256
Coventry Ct	44256
Coventry Lakes Dr	44256
Coventry Park Ln	44256
Coverdale Way	44256
Covington Ln	44256
Creative Living Way	44256
W Creek Dr	44256
Creekside Chase Dr	44256
Crimson King Ct	44256
Crooked Creek Cir	44256
Crossbow Cir	44256
Crosswind Ct	44256
Crown Pointe Dr	44256
Curtis St	44256
Cynthia Dr	44256
Damon Dr	44256
Dan Rd	44256
N & S Danbury Cir	44256
Dartford Ln	44256
Dawn Ct	44256
Day Lilly Ln	44256
Debbie Dr	44256
Debra Ct	44256
Deepwood Dr	44256
Deer Lake Dr	44256
Deer Run Dr	44256
Deer Tail Dr	44256
Deerview Ln	44256
Delmar Ct	44256
Derby Dr	44256
Devon Path	44256
Diamond Creek Dr	44256
Dogleg Trl	44256
Dogwood Trl	44256
Douglas Ln	44256
Dover Dr	44256
Druerie Ln	44256
Dunbar Cir	44256
Dunsha Rd	44256
Eagle Dr	44256
Eagles Nest Ln	44256
East St	44256
Eastgate Dr	44256
Eastlake Rd	44256
Eastpointe Dr	44256
Eden Ln	44256
Edinburgh Dr	44256
Egypt Rd	44256
Elizabeth Way	44256
Ellington Ct	44256
N & S Elmwood Ave	44256
Elyria Rd	44256
Emerald Lakes Dr	44256
Emerald Run Rd	44256
Enfield Cir	44256
English Turn Dr	44256
Enterprise Dr	44256
Equestrian Trl	44256
Erhart Rd	44256
Erhart Northern Rd S	44256
Essex Ln	44256
Exchange Park Dr	44256
Fairfax Dr	44256
Fairhaven Oval Dr	44256
Fairway Dr	44256
Falcon Ridge Dr	44256
Falling Oaks Dr	44256
Farmcote Cir	44256
Farmington Cir	44256
Fawn Run	44256
Fawn Haven Dr	44256
Fawn Lake Dr	44256
Fawndale Dr	44256
Featherstone Dr	44256
Fenn Rd	44256
Fennec Pointe Cir	44256
Fennway Blvd	44256
Fixler Rd	44256
Flowering Woods Dr	44256
Foote Rd	44256
Forest Dr	44256
Forest Hills Dr	44256
Forest Lake Dr	44256
Forest Meadows Dr	44256
Forest Ridge Cir	44256
Forest Run Cir	44256
Foskett Rd	44256
Foundry St	44256
Fox Glen Dr	44256
Fox Haven Dr	44256
Fox Meadow Dr	44256
Foxborough Dr	44256
Foxford Ct	44256
Foxglove Dr	44256
Franklin Dr	44256
Frantz Rd	44256
Frederick St	44256
Freedom Ct	44256
Freeport Dr	44256
E & W Friendship St	44256
Friendsville Rd	44256
Frith Ct	44256
Furlong Dr	44256
Garden Lake Ct	44256
Gary Kyle Ct	44256
Gates Mills Blvd	44256
Gateway Dr	44256
Gayer Dr	44256
Genny Dr	44256
Gentry Dr	44256
Gladden Pl	44256
Glen Eagles Dr	44256
Glenmoore Way	44256
Glenshire Ln	44256
Glenwell Cir	44256
Gloucester Dr	44256
Gold Crest Dr	44256
Grand Canyon Dr	44256
Grand Teton Dr	44256
Grande Blvd	44256
Grande Shops Ave	44256
Granger Rd	44256
Granger Willows Dr	44256
Grant St	44256
Grassy Branch Dr	44256
Great Smokey Cir	44256
Green Ash Trl	44256
Greenfield Dr	44256
Greenleaf Way	44256
Greentree Cir	44256
Greenview Dr	44256
Greenwood Ct	44256
Grey Dr	44256
Grove Ln	44256
Grovewood Ln	44256
Guilford Blvd	44256
Gunnison Ct	44256
Hadam Hls	44256
Halifax Ln	44256
Halle Dr	44256
Hamilton Rd	44256
Hamlin Rd	44256
Hampden Ct	44256
Hampshire Dr	44256
Hanover Dr	44256
Harding St	44256
Hardwood Hollow Rd	44256
Harger Ln	44256
Harmon Ct	44256
N & S Harmony St	44256
Hartford Dr	44256
Hastings Dr	44256
Haury Rd	44256
Hearthstone Way	44256
Heather Ln	44256
Heather Glen Dr	44256
Heathery Cir	44256
Hedgewood Dr	44256
Heritage Dr	44256
Hickory Grove Ave	44256
Hickorycreek Dr	44256
Hidden Acres Dr	44256
Hidden Falls Dr	44256
Hidden Lake Dr	44256
Hideaway Dr	44256
High Meadow Ct	44256
High Point Dr	44256
Highland Dr	44256
Highland Green Dr	44256
Highland Meadows Dr	44256
Hilltop Point Cir	44256
Hillview Way	44256
Hollow Ln	44256
Hollyhock Ln	44256
E & W Homestead St	44256
Honeystone Cir	44256
Hood Rd	44256
Hounds Run Dr	44256
Howard St	44256
Huffman Rd	44256
Hunters Trl	44256
Hunters Field Dr	44256
Hunting Run Rd	44256
N & S Huntington St	44256
Huntley Dr	44256
Hus Cir	44256
Imagine Ln	44256
Independence Dr	44256
Indian Wells Dr	44256
Indoe St	44256
Industrial Pkwy	44256
Irondale Dr	44256
Irvine Oval	44256
Island Creek Dr	44256
Ivandale Dr	44256
Ivy Hill Ln	44256
Jackson St	44256
Jamestown Pl	44256
Jason Oval	44256
Jasper Ln	44256
N & S Jefferson St	44256
Jenna Ct	44256
Jessie Ann Cir	44256
Joanna Ln	44256
Joeys Ln	44256
Jonathan Ct	44256
Joshua Way	44256
Jumper Knoll Dr	44256
Kapok Dr	44256
Kellsway Ct	44256
Kelly Ln	44256
Kempton Oval	44256
Kennard Rd	44256
Kennebank Ln	44256
Kennedy Rd	44256
Kenner Cir & Dr	44256
Kensington Dr	44256
Kings Ct	44256
Kingsbury Rd	44256
Knots Lndg	44256
Koons Ave	44256
La Salle St	44256
Lafayette Rd & St	44256
Lake Rd	44256
Lake Dawn Dr	44256
Lake Forest Trl	44256
Lake Ridge Dr	44256
Lakeshore Walk	44256
Lakeview Dr	44256
Lakeview Glen Dr	44256
Lampson Rd	44256
Lancaster Dr	44256
Lance Rd	44256
Lang Farm Dr	44256
Larkens Way	44256
Larkspur Ct	44256
Laurel Glens Dr	44256
Lauren Oval	44256
Lavender Ln	44256
Lawrence St	44256
Ledge Rd	44256
Ledgewood Dr	44256
Leisure Ln	44256
Leslie Ln	44256
Lester Rd	44256
Lexington Ridge Dr	44256
E & W Liberty St	44256
Lincoln Ave	44256
Linda Dr	44256
Lindenwood Ln	44256
Lindsey Oval	44256
Lipke Ct	44256
Lisa Oval	44256
Livia Ln	44256
Logans Run	44256
Londonderry Ln	44256
Lonesome Pine Trl	44256
Longview Rd	44256
Longwood Dr	44256
Lovell Ln	44256
Loyal Ln	44256
Lundys Ln	44256
Mackensey Cir	44256
Maggie Marie Blvd	44256
Mahogany Cir	44256
Maidstone Ln	44256
Majestic Cir	44256
Malibu Dr	44256
Mallard Bay	44256
Mallet Hill Ct	44256
Mallory Ct	44256
Malloy Ct	44256
Manchester Ct	44256
Manor Glen Dr	44256
Maple St	44256
Maple Heights Dr	44256
Maplewood Farm Dr	44256
Marilyn Way	44256
Marks Rd	44256
Marla Ct	44256
Marshall Ct	44256
Martin Ct	44256
Masons Rest Dr	44256
Matthew Ln	44256
Mayapple Dr	44256
Mccarren Dr	44256
Meadow Gtwy	44256
Meadow Lake Dr	44256
Meadow Oaks Trl	44256
Meadowlark Ln	44256
Meadowood Dr	44256
N & S Medina Rd & St	44256
N Medina Line Rd	44256
Melody Ln	44256
Merimack Cir	44256
W Mill St	44256
Millbury Dr	44256
Miller Dr	44256
Miner Dr	44256
Mint Hill Dr	44256
Montauk Pointe	44256
Monterey Dr	44256
Montview Dr	44256
Montville Dr	44256
Montville Lakes Blvd	44256
Montville Trails Dr	44256
Morning Glory Ln	44256
Morning Song Dr	44256
Muir Tap Dr	44256
Mulberry Bend Dr	44256
Myers Rd	44256
Neff Rd	44256
Nettleton Rd	44256
New Haven Dr	44256
Newell Ln	44256
Newfield Cir	44256
Nichols Rd	44256
E Normandy Park Dr	44256
E & W North St	44256
Northampton Dr	44256
Northford Ct	44256
Northland Dr	44256
Norwalk Rd	44256
Norwegian Wood Dr	44256
Nottingham Dr	44256
Oak St	44256
Oakbrooke Dr	44256
Octagon Dr	44256
Odesa Dr	44256
Okey Ct	44256
Old Farm Trl	44256
Old Hickory Ln	44256
Old Lyme Ct	44256
Olde Stone Dr	44256
Orchard Ln	44256
Overlook Dr	44256
Palker Rd	44256
Paradise Rd	44256
Paramount Dr	44256
W, N & S Park Blvd, Dr & Ln	44256
Parkview Dr	44256
Parnham Dr	44256
Partridge Cir	44256
Patrick Dr	44256
Patriots Way	44256
Pearl Rd & St	44256
Pebble Ct	44256
Pennyroyal Cir	44256
Perian Ct	44256
Pheasant Run Dr	44256
Pierce Rd	44256
Pilgrim Dr	44256
Pimlico Cir	44256
Pine St	44256
Pine Hill Dr	44256
Pine Lake Dr	44256
Pine Tree Ct	44256
Pine Valley Dr	44256
Pinehurst Dr	44256
Pinewood Dr	44256
Pioneer Way Dr	44256
Pleasant Valley Dr	44256
Plum Creek Pkwy	44256
Plymouth St	44256
Poe Rd	44256
Pondsford Dr	44256
Port Centre Dr	44256
Portside Dr	44256
Portsmouth Cir	44256
Potomac Ct	44256
Preserve Run Cir	44256
Primrose Path	44256
N & S Progress Dr	44256
S Prospect St	44256
Providence Dr	44256
Public Sq	44256
Puffin Pointe Dr	44256
Quail Roost Dr	44256
Quincy Ct	44256
Racoa Pl	44256
Rathburn Dr	44256
Ravine Woods Dr	44256
Raymond Way	44256
E & W Reagan Pkwy	44256
Red Maple Ct	44256
Red Oak Cir	44256
Red Tail Ct	44256
Reeves Ln	44256
Regal Brook Dr	44256
Reid Hill Rd	44256
Remsen Rd	44256
Reserve Dr	44256
Reserve Commons Dr	44256
Retreat Dr	44256
Revere Cir	44256
Richard Dr	44256
Ridge Dr & Rd	44256
Ridgeline Dr	44256
Ridgestone Way	44256
Ridgetop Ct	44256
Ridgeview Dr	44256
Ridgewood Rd	44256
Ridley Way	44256
Rimrock Rd	44256
Ritz Ct	44256
Rivendale Dr	44256
River Forest Dr	44256
River Oaks Dr	44256
River Styx Rd	44256
Riverrock Way	44256
Robert Gary Ct	44256
Rock Maple Dr	44256
Rockport Dr	44256
Rocky Hollow Dr	44256
Rocky Mountain Dr	44256
Rolling Meadows Dr	44256
Rollingwood Dr	44256
Rosemont Way	44256
Roshon Dr	44256
Royal Brook Dr	44256
Rubystone Ln	44256
Rustic Hills Dr	44256
Rustic Lake Dr	44256
Rustic Valley Dr	44256
Ryan Rd	44256
Ryeland Cir	44256
Sacramento Blvd	44256
Salem Ct	44256
Salems Way	44256
Sandview Dr	44256
Sandy Ln	44256
Sapphire Ct	44256
Sarah Ln	44256
Saratoga Trl	44256
Sassafras Dr	44256
Savannah Trl	44256
Scenic Way	44256
Secrest Cir	44256
Secretariat Ct	44256
Seeley Dr	44256
Sequoia Dr	44256
Seven Bridges Rd	44256
Seymour Dr	44256
Shady Brooke Run	44256
Shagbark Trl	44256
Shaker Dr	44256
Shale Ct	44256
Sharon Copley Rd	44256
Shencene Rd	44256
Shoreline Cir	44256
Shorewood Dr	44256
Shurell Pkwy	44256
Sierra Cir	44256
Silver Maple Ln	44256
Silver Ridge Trl	44256
Silverstone Ln	44256
Simon Ln	44256
Sleepy Hollow Rd	44256
E & W Smith Rd	44256
Smokerise Dr	44256
Snowberry Ln	44256
Soapstone Dr	44256
South Dr & St	44256
Southampton Dr	44256
Southport Dr	44256
Sovereign Ln	44256
Spencer Lake Rd	44256
Spieth Rd	44256
N & S Spring Grove St	44256
Springbrook Dr	44256
Spruce St	44256
Squires Ct	44256
Standing Oak Dr	44256
Starlight Cir	44256
State Rd	44256
State Route 57	44256
Station Rd	44256
Steeple Chase Way	44256
Sterling Lake Dr	44256
Stiegler Rd	44256
Stillwater Dr	44256
Stillwood Dr	44256
Stockbridge Dr	44256
Stoll Dr	44256
Stone Rd	44256
Stonebrooke Ln	44256
Stonegate Dr	44256
Stoneycreek Cir	44256
Stonington Dr	44256
Stony Hill Rd	44256
Stratton Dr	44256
Strawberry Ln	44256
W Sturbridge Dr	44256
Styx Hill Rd	44256
Substation Rd	44256
Sugarhill Dr	44256
Sugarhouse Ln	44256
Summer Lake Dr	44256
Summerwind Dr	44256
Sunburst Dr	44256
Sunhaven Dr	44256
Sunrise Oval	44256
Sunset Dr	44256
Sunset Cove Dr	44256
Sutton Ln	44256
W Sweet Briar Dr	44256
Sycamore Tree Dr	44256
Tahoe Dr	44256
Talbot Dr	44256
Tall Trees Trl	44256
Tanglewood Dr	44256
Tara Way	44256
Tatiana Trl	44256
Technology Ln	44256
Thomas Lincoln Pkwy	44256
Tidewater Cv	44256
Timber Trl	44256
Timber Creek Dr	44256
Tompkins Rd	44256
Torbay Dr	44256
Torington Dr	44256
Tory Ln	44256
Toucan Dr	44256
Tower Rd	44256
Trails End Dr	44256
Trails Lake Dr	44256
Treetop Cir	44256
Tremain Pl	44256
Triple Crown Dr	44256
Trystin Tree Dr	44256
Turnberry Dr	44256
Twelve Oaks Cir	44256
Twin Fawn Ct	44256
Twin Oaks Blvd & Cir	44256
Ty Dr	44256
Tyndale Ln	44256
E & W Union St	44256
Upland Ridge Dr	44256
Valley Dr	44256
Valley View Dr	44256
Van Buren Way	44256
Vandemark Rd	44256
Veraway Ct	44256
Victor Dr	44256
Victoria Cir	44256
View Point Dr	44256
N & S Vine St	44256
Vineyard Dr	44256
Wadsworth Rd	44256
Wagon Trl	44256
Walena Dr	44256
Walnut Dr	44256
Walnut Hollow Dr	44256
Walter Rd	44256
Warwick Ct	44256
E & W Washington St	44256
Waterbury Dr	44256
Watercourse Dr	44256
Waterloo Ln	44256
Waterside Dr	44256
Watkins Rd	44256
Wayside Dr	44256
Wedgewood Rd	44256
Wellington Dr	44256
Westbranch Dr	44256
Westfield Rd	44256
Westfield Landing Rd	44256
Westgrove Ct	44256
Westland Dr	44256
Westview Ct	44256
Westwood Dr	44256

Wexford Ct 44256
S Weymouth Rd 44256
Weymouth Woods Dr 44256
White Oak Cir 44256
Wilbur Rd 44256
Wildflower Ln 44256
Wildwood Ct & Dr 44256
Williamsburg Ct 44256
Willow Bend Dr 44256
Willow View Dr 44256
Wilmington Dr 44256
Wimbleton Dr 44256
Wind Field Dr 44256
Windchime Dr 44256
Windem Dr 44256
Windfall Rd 44256
Winding Woods Trl 44256
Windmill Ct 44256
Windsong Dr 44256
Winner Cir 44256
Winston Cir 44256
Winterberry Ln 44256
Wisteria Ln 44256
Wolff Rd 44256
Woodberry Dr 44256
Woodglen Cir 44256
Woodhaven Dr & Ln 44256
Woodlake Dr 44256
Woodland Dr 44256
Woodland View Dr 44256
Woodlark Trl 44256
Woodling Way 44256
Woodshire Ln 44256
Wooster Pike 44256
Worchester Ln 44256
Wren Way 44256
Wycliffe Dr 44256
Yellowstone Dr 44256
Yesterday Ln 44256
Yorkshire Dr 44256
Yorktown Dr 44256
Yosemite Dr 44256
Young Ave 44256

MENTOR OH

General Delivery 44060

POST OFFICE BOXES MAIN OFFICE STATIONS AND BRANCHES

Box No.s
All PO Boxes 44061

NAMED STREETS

Abbeyshire Way 44060
Abby Ct 44060
Acacia Ave 44060
Adams Ct 44060
Adkins Rd 44060
Agard Ct 44060
Aileen Dr 44060
Alder Ct 44060
Alfred Dr 44060
Allegheny Dr 44060
Allen Troy Ct 44060
Allendale Dr 44060
Ambleside Dr 44060
Ambrose Dr 44060
Anaconda Ave 44060
Anchor Ct 44060
Andover Dr 44060
Andrea Dr 44060
Andrews Rd 44060
Angelina Cir 44060
Anna Ct 44060
Antoinette Dr 44060
Appleton Ct 44060
Applewood Ct 44060
Arbor Glen Pl 44060
N Arden Dr 44060
Argee Dr 44060
Arrowood Ct & Dr 44060
Ashley Ln 44060
Ashton Ct 44060
Ashwood Trl 44060
Aspen Ct 44060
Aspenwood Ct 44060
Aster Dr 44060
Avon Dr 44060
Azalea Ln 44060
Baker Ave 44060
Baldwin Rd 44060
Bar Harbour Ln 44060
Barbara Dr 44060
Barberry Hill Dr 44060
Barkwood Ct 44060
Barnaby Ln 44060
Barnswallow Ln 44060
Barry Ct 44060
Bartley Ln 44060
Barton Dr 44060
Basswood Ln 44060
Bauer Ln 44060
Bay Point Cv 44060
Bay Ridge Ct 44060
Baythorne Dr 44060
Beacon Dr 44060
Beaumont Dr 44060
Beaver Creek Dr 44060
Becker Ave 44060
Beech Dr 44060
Beechwood Dr 44060
Belglo Ln 44060
Belle Meadow Rd 44060
Bellflower Ct & Rd 44060
Belvedere Dr 44060
Berkshire Dr 44060
Bernard Dr 44060
Bernwood Ct 44060
Biltmore Rd 44060
Birch Ln 44060
Birchwood Dr 44060
Birdie Ln 44060
Bishop Ct 44060
Blackbrook Rd 44060
Blossom Dr 44060
Blue Bell Ct 44060
Blue Heron Way 44060
Blue Ridge Dr 44060
Bluejay Ln 44060
Booth Rd 44060
Bosley Cv 44060
Boyer Ln 44060
Brainard Ct 44060
Braintree Ln 44060
Brambleside Ln 44060
Bramblewood Pl 44060
Brandywine Dr 44060
Brayes Manor Dr 44060
Brenel Dr 44060
Brentwood Rd 44060
Brewer Ct 44060
Briarcliff Ct 44060
Briarwood Dr 44060
Brichford Rd 44060
Bricker Ct 44060
Bridgeport Ln 44060
Bridle Ct 44060
Brighton Rd 44060
Brimfield Dr 44060
Bringman Ct 44060
Brittany Ct 44060
Broadmoor Cir & Rd 44060
Brookfield Dr 44060
Brookhaven Dr 44060
Brookridge Ln 44060
Brooks Blvd 44060
Brooksdale Rd 44060
Brookside Cir 44060
Brownell Dr 44060
Browning Ct 44060
Brownstone Ct 44060
Bryson Dr 44060
Buchanan Ct 44060
Buckboard Ln 44060
Buckeye Ln 44060
Buckhill Ct 44060
Buckhurst Pl 44060
Buckthorn Dr 44060
Buena Vista Dr 44060
Bunker Cv 44060
Burridge Ave 44060
Bushnell Ct 44060
Butternut Ln 44060
Button Rd 44060
C J Ct 44060
Cabot Ct 44060
Cabriolet Ave 44060
Cadle Ave 44060
Cambridge Park Dr 44060
S Camelot Dr 44060
Campbell Rd 44060
Candlewood Ct 44060
Cannon Ridge Dr 44060
Canterbury Ln 44060
Canterwood Trl 44060
Captains Ct 44060
Cardinal Dr 44060
Carlton Ct 44060
Carmen Pl 44060
Carnegie St 44060
Carole Dr 44060
Carolyn Dr 44060
Carriage Cir 44060
Carriage Hills Dr 44060
Carrington Dr 44060
Carter Blvd 44060
Case Ave 44060
Cat Tail Ct 44060
Catalpa Cir 44060
S Cedarwood Rd 44060
Center St 44060
Chablis Ct 44060
Chagrin Dr 44060
Chairmans Ct 44060
Chambers Ct 44060
Champaign Dr 44060
Channing Ln 44060
Chapelway Dr 44060
Chardonwood Dr 44060
N & S Chariot St 44060
Charmar Dr 44060
Chase Dr 44060
Checquers Ct 44060
Cherry St 44060
Cherry Blossom Dr 44060
Cherrystone Dr 44060
Cherrywood Cir 44060
Cheshire Ct 44060
Chestnut St 44060
N & S Chestnut
Commons Dr 44060
Chillicothe Rd 44060
Christopher Ct 44060
Churchill Sq 44060
Civic Center Blvd 44060
Clearair Dr 44060
Clearmont Dr 44060
Cliffwood Ct 44060
Clifton Ct 44060
Clopton Ct 44060
Clover Ave 44060
Club Ct 44060
Cobblestone Ln 44060
Cole Dr 44060
College Park Dr 44060
Collins Rd 44060
Colonial Dr 44060
Colony Ct 44060
Colt Dr 44060
Comanche Trl 44060
Comet Ct 44060
Commerce Dr 44060
Concord Dr 44060
Concord Point Ct 44060
Conestoga Trl 44060
Connecticut Colony Cir 44060
Connie Dr 44060
Conover Ct 44060
Constantine Ct 44060
Coolidge Ct 44060
Cooper Ln 44060
Corduroy Rd 44060
Cornell Ln 44060
Cornwall Ct 44060
Coronada Dr 44060
Corporate Blvd 44060
Cottonwood Ct 44060
Country Ct 44060
Country Scene Ln 44060
Cranberry Ln 44060
Creekwood Dr 44060
Crimson Ct 44060
Cross Creek Dr 44060
Crossfield Ave 44060
Crown Ct 44060
Culver Blvd 44060
Cumberland Ct & Dr 44060
Curberry Dr 44060
Curtiss Ct 44060
Cypress Cir 44060
Dahlia Dr 44060
Daisy Ct 44060
Daleford Dr 44060
Dallas Dr 44060
Dalton Ct 44060
Danbury Ct 44060
Darby Ct 44060
Dartmoor Rd 44060
Davis Dr 44060
Dawn Pl 44060
Dawson Blvd 44060
Debonaire Dr 44060
Deborah Ct 44060
Deepwood Blvd 44060
Deer Holw & Rdg 44060
Deer Wood Ct 44060
Deerborn Ave 44060
Dellhaven Ave 44060
Demshar Dr 44060
Dennison Ct 44060
Devonshire Ct 44060
Diamond Centre Dr 44060
Division Dr 44060
Dogwood Ln 44060
Dolphin Rd 44060
Donald Dr 44060
Doncaster Ct 44060
Doral Dr 44060
Dorchester Ln 44060
Dorrwood Dr 44060
Dovegate Cir & Dr 44060
Driftwood Dr 44060
Dublin Ln 44060
Duckworth Ln 44060
Duke Ct 44060
Dunbar Dr 44060
Durham Ct 44060
Dwayne Ct 44060
Eagles Nest Rd 44060
East Ave 44060
Eastmoor Rd 44060
Easton Way E & W 44060
Eastway Dr 44060
Eaton Cir 44060
E Echo Dr 44060
Edgehill Rd 44060
Edgewood Rd 44060
Edmund Cir 44060
Edson Rd 44060
Edward St 44060
Eldon Ct 44060
Eleanor Ct 44060
Elizabeth Ct 44060
Ellie Pl 44060
Ellington Pl 44060
Elm St 44060
Elmwood Rd 44060
Emerald Ct 44060
Emery Cir 44060
Enfield Dr 44060
Enterprise Dr 44060
Equestrian Ct 44060
Eric Dr 44060
Erie Dr 44060
Essex Dr 44060
Esther St 44060
Evergreen Dr 44060
Executive Ct 44060
Fairfax Dr 44060
Fairhaven Ct 44060
Fairlawn Dr 44060
Fairview Ave 44060
Farley Dr 44060
Farmingdale Ln 44060
Farmington Ct 44060
Farnham Dr 44060
Fawn Ct 44060
Faye Ln 44060
Fenwood Ct 44060
Fern Dr 44060
Fieldstone Ct 44060
Fillmore Ct 44060
Findley Dr 44060
Fireside Ct 44060
First St 44060
Firwood Rd 44060
Foothill Rd 44060
Foraker Ct 44060
Forbes Ct 44060
Ford Dr 44060
Forest Ln & Rd 44060
Forestview Ave 44060
Forsythe Ln 44060
Fortuna Dr 44060
Fox Hill Trl 44060
Fox Hollow Ln 44060
Foxmill Rd 44060
Foxwood Ct 44060
Francis St 44060
Frederick Dr 44060
Freeport Ln 44060
French Blvd 44060
Frontier Dr 44060
Gabriel Ct 44060
Galaxie Dr 44060
Gallowae Ct 44060
Gamekeeper Ct 44060
Garden Ln 44060
Garfield Rd 44060
Gatewood Dr 44060
Georgeanne Ct 44060
Georgetown Dr 44060
Georgie Ct 44060
Glen St 44060
Glen Arbor Ct 44060
Glencairn Ct 44060
Glenn Lodge Rd 44060
Glenwood Dr 44060
Goldenrod Dr 44060
Goldfinch Ct 44060
Goodell Ct 44060
Gosling Way 44060
Governors Pl 44060
Grace Ct & Dr 44060
Granada Dr 44060
Grant St 44060
Graystone Ln 44060
Green Oak Ave 44060
Green Valley Dr 44060
Greenridge Ct 44060
Gregory Ct 44060
Grenway Dr 44060
Gristmill Dr 44060
Griswold Rd 44060
Grove Ave 44060
Grovewood Dr 44060
Hackberry Dr 44060
Hackney Ct 44060
Hallnorth Dr 44060
Hamilton Dr 44060
S Hampton Ct 44060
Hansom Pl 44060
Harbor Dr 44060
Harbor Creek Dr 44060
Harborside Lndg 44060
Harding St 44060
Harley Ln 44060
Harrison St 44060
Hart Rd & St 44060
Harvest Home Dr 44060
Hathaway Dr 44060
Havenhurst Ct 44060
Haverford Blvd 44060
Hawk Ave 44060
Hawthorne Dr 44060
Hayes Blvd 44060
Headlands Rd 44060
Heather Hill Dr 44060
Heidi Ct 44060
Heisley Rd 44060
Hemingway Ln 44060
Hendricks Rd 44060
Hickory St 44060
Hidden Glen Dr 44060
Hidden Hollow Dr 44060
Hidden Valley Ct 44060
Highbridge Ct 44060
Highgate Ct 44060
Highland Ct 44060
Hillcrest Ave 44060
Hilltop Dr 44060
Hilo Farm Dr 44060
Hobby Horse Ln 44060
Hodgson Rd 44060
Holden Ct 44060
Holly Dr 44060
Holly Park Dr 44060
Hollycroft Ln 44060
Homewood Dr 44060
Hoose Rd 44060
Hoover Ct & Dr 44060
Hopkins Rd 44060
Howell Dr 44060
Hoyt Ct 44060
Hudson Ave 44060
Hulls Cv 44060
Hunting Hill Dr 44060
Hyde St 44060
Idlewood Dr 44060
Ilsley Sq 44060
Independence Dr 44060
Indigo Trl 44060
Industrial Park Blvd 44060
Inland Shores Dr 44060
Inverness Ct 44060
Iroquois Trl 44060
Ivan Pl 44060
Ivana Ct 44060
Ivy Ct & Dr 44060
Jackie Ct 44060
Jackson St 44060
Jamesway Ct 44060
Jane Dr 44060
Jasani Ct 44060
E & W Jefferson Dr 44060
Jenther Dr 44060
Jeremy Ave 44060
Jody Lynn Dr 44060
Johnnycake Ridge Rd 44060
Jordan Dr 44060
Jovanna Ct 44060
Julian Ct 44060
Juniper Ct 44060
Justin Way 44060
Katherine Ct 44060
Kathleen Dr 44060
Kellogg Creek Dr 44060
Kelly Dr 44060
Kennedy Ct 44060
Kenyon Ct 44060
Kephart Dr 44060
Kimberly Dr 44060
King Memorial Rd 44060
Kings Hollow Ct 44060
Kingston Ct 44060
Kingwood Dr 44060
Kirkwood Dr 44060
Kittery Ln 44060
Knightsbridge Ln 44060
Knollwood Ridge Dr 44060
Lafayette Dr 44060
Lake Rd 44060
Lake Overlook Dr 44060
Lake Shore Blvd 44060
Lakeview Dr 44060
Lakewood Ct 44060
Lambton Ct 44060
Lancaster Dr 44060
Lanmark Dr 44060
Larkspur Dr 44060
Lasalle Ln 44060
Lauren J Dr 44060
Lawnfield Dr 44060
Leah Ct 44060
Lenore Dr 44060
Liberio Ct 44060
Liberty St 44060
Light House Ct 44060
Lincoln Dr 44060
Linden St 44060
Lindsay Dr 44060
Links Rd 44060
Lione Dr 44060
Lismore Ln 44060
Litchfield Dr 44060
Little Mountain Rd 44060
Lockwood Dr 44060
Longhorn Rd 44060
Longview Ave 44060
Lori Jean Dr 44060
Lorrey Pl 44060
Lorrich Dr 44060
Louise Dr 44060
Low Ridge Ln 44060
Lucretia Ct 44060
Luoem Trl 44060
Lupine Dr 44060
Lynford Way 44060
Magnolia Dr 44060
Maiden Ln 44060
Maidstone Dr 44060
Malabar Ct 44060
Mallard Ct 44060
Mandinti Dr 44060
Manor Dr 44060
Manor Gate Way 44060
Manry Ct 44060
Mansfield Ct 44060
Mansion Blvd 44060
Maple St 44060
Mapledale Rd 44060
Maplegrove Ln 44060
Maplewood Rd 44060
Marigold Rd 44060
Marine Pkwy 44060
Marion Dr 44060
Marjory Dr 44060
Market St 44060
Markwood Dr 44060
Marshview Ln 44060
Martinique Dr 44060
Mary Ln 44060
Matthew Ct 44060
Mckinley St 44060
Meadowbrook Dr 44060
Meadowdale Dr 44060
Meadowlake Ct 44060
Meadowlawn Dr 44060
Megan Ct 44060
Meister Rd 44060
Meldon Dr 44060
Melody Ln 44060
Meloria Ln 44060
Melshore Dr 44060
Memory Ln 44060
Mentor Ave & Rd 44060
Mentor Harbor Blvd 44060
Mentor Hills Dr 44060
Mentor Park Blvd 44060
Mentorwood Dr 44060
Mercantile Dr 44060
Mersey Ct 44060
Metric Dr 44060
Miami Rd 44060
Michael Dr 44060
Middlesex Rd 44060
Midland Rd 44060
Milford Ln 44060
Milton Dr 44060
Mitchells Mill Rd 44060
Monmouth Ct 44060
Monroe Ct 44060
Monterey Bay Dr 44060
Mooreland Ave 44060

Morley Rd ... 44060
Mount Vernon Ct ... 44060
Mountain Ash Dr ... 44060
Mountain Park Dr ... 44060
Mountain View Dr ... 44060
Moving Way ... 44060
Munson Rd ... 44060
Murphys Ln ... 44060
Murray Ave ... 44060
Musket Dr ... 44060
Nancy Dr ... 44060
Nearing Circle Dr ... 44060
New Castle Dr ... 44060
New Concord Dr ... 44060
Newell Creek Dr ... 44060
Newhouse Ct ... 44060
Newton Dr ... 44060
Noble Ct ... 44060
North Rd ... 44060
Norton Pkwy ... 44060
Norwood Dr ... 44060
Nottingham Dr ... 44060
Nowlen St ... 44060
Oak St ... 44060
Oakdale Rd ... 44060
Oakridge Dr ... 44060
Ocean Pt ... 44060
Ohio St ... 44060
Old Heisley Rd ... 44060
Old Johnnycake Ridge Rd ... 44060
Old Village Ln ... 44060
Olde Farm Ln ... 44060
Olde Field Ct ... 44060
Olde Meadows Ct ... 44060
Omega Ct ... 44060
Orchard Rd ... 44060
Orchid Ave ... 44060
Oriole Ct ... 44060
Orvos Ct ... 44060
Osborne Dr ... 44060
Overton Dr ... 44060
Oxford Glen Dr ... 44060
Packard Ct ... 44060
Paddock Ct ... 44060
Page Dr ... 44060
Palisades Pkwy ... 44060
N Palmerston Dr ... 44060
Park St ... 44060
Parker Dr ... 44060
Parkwood Rd ... 44060
Parmalee Dr ... 44060
Partridge Ct ... 44060
Patriot Ct ... 44060
Patterson Dr ... 44060
Pear Tree Ln ... 44060
Pekin Ct ... 44060
Penshurst Dr ... 44060
Pepperwood Ct ... 44060
Perennial Ln ... 44060
Perkins Dr ... 44060
Pheasant Run Ln ... 44060
Pilgrim Dr ... 44060
Pinecone Dr ... 44060
Pinehill Dr ... 44060
Pinehurst Dr ... 44060
Pineneedle Dr ... 44060
Pinetree Dr ... 44060
Pinewood Ct ... 44060
Plains Rd ... 44060
Plaza Blvd ... 44060
Pleasantvale Ct ... 44060
Pleasantview Trl ... 44060
Polk Ct ... 44060
Poplar Ln ... 44060
Port Royal Ct ... 44060
Prairie Grass Ln ... 44060
Presley Ave ... 44060
Preston Hill Ct ... 44060
Primavera Dr ... 44060
Primrose Dr ... 44060
Princeton Ct ... 44060
Production Dr ... 44060
Progress Pkwy ... 44060
Prospect St ... 44060
Puritan Dr ... 44060
Quail Point Ln ... 44060
Rambler Dr ... 44060
Ramblewood Dr ... 44060
Raymond Dr ... 44060
Red Oak Dr ... 44060
Redwood Ct ... 44060
Reedhurst Ln ... 44060
Reef Rd ... 44060
Remington Dr ... 44060
Reynolds Rd ... 44060
Richards Dr ... 44060
Richwood Dr ... 44060
Ridgeside Dr ... 44060
Ridgeview Trl ... 44060
Ridgeway Dr ... 44060
Rippling Brook Ln ... 44060
Robinwood Dr ... 44060
Rockingham Rd ... 44060
Rockport Ln ... 44060
Rockwell Ct ... 44060
Rockwood Ct ... 44060
Roosevelt Ave ... 44060
Rosebud Dr ... 44060
Rosedale Dr ... 44060
Roselawn Dr ... 44060
Rosemary Ln ... 44060
Rosewood Ln ... 44060
Royale Oak Ct ... 44060
Rushton Dr ... 44060
Ruth St ... 44060
Rutland Dr ... 44060
Ryan Dr ... 44060
Sable Ct ... 44060
Saint Charles Pl ... 44060
Saint Clair Ave ... 44060
Saint James Dr ... 44060
Saint John Ct ... 44060
Saint Peters Way ... 44060
Salida Rd ... 44060
Salt Lick Ct ... 44060
Sanctuary Dr ... 44060
Sand Dune Ct ... 44060
Sandbridge Ct ... 44060
Sandtree Ln ... 44060
Sarah Ct ... 44060
Savannah Dr ... 44060
Saw Grass Ct ... 44060
Schaeffer St ... 44060
Scottsdale Cir ... 44060
Sea Pines Dr ... 44060
Seaton Pl ... 44060
Seminole Trl ... 44060
Seneca Rd & Trl ... 44060
Sequoia Ct ... 44060
Settlers Ct ... 44060
Shady Ln ... 44060
Shamrock Dr ... 44060
S Shandle Blvd ... 44060
Shannon Ln ... 44060
Sharon Dr ... 44060
Sharonlee Dr ... 44060
Sheltered Cv ... 44060
Shenandoah Ct ... 44060
Sherwood Dr ... 44060
Silver Ct ... 44060
Silver Beech Ln ... 44060
Silvermound Dr ... 44060
Sir Roberts Ct ... 44060
Sittingbourne Dr ... 44060
Skylineview Dr ... 44060
Snell Dr ... 44060
Snowberry Ct ... 44060
Southgrove Rd ... 44060
Southland Dr ... 44060
Southwood Dr ... 44060
Sperry Rd ... 44060
Spinach Dr ... 44060
Spinnaker Ct ... 44060
Spring Blossom Dr ... 44060
Spring Gardens Dr ... 44060
Spring Valley Dr ... 44060
Springhouse Ln E & W ... 44060
Springwood Ct & Dr ... 44060
Spruce Ln ... 44060
Starburst Rd ... 44060
Station St ... 44060
Steeplechase Dr ... 44060
Sterling Ct ... 44060
Stirrup Ct ... 44060
Stockbridge Rd ... 44060
Stone Hollow Rd ... 44060
Stone Jug Ln ... 44060
Stone Mill Dr ... 44060
Stoneybrook Ln ... 44060
Stratford Cir ... 44060
Stratton Ct ... 44060
Sugarbush Dr ... 44060
Sunflower Ct ... 44060
Sunnyvale Ct ... 44060
Sunrise Ct ... 44060
Sunset Dr ... 44060
Surrey Ct ... 44060
Sutherland Ct ... 44060
Suwanee Dr ... 44060
Sweet Hollow Dr ... 44060
Sweetgum Trl ... 44060
Sycamore Rd ... 44060
Sylvan Ln ... 44060
Sylvia Dr ... 44060
Taft St ... 44060
Talbot Cir ... 44060
Tall Oaks Dr ... 44060
Tamarin Ct ... 44060
Tammany Ct ... 44060
Tanager Ct ... 44060
Tanbark Trl ... 44060
Tea Rose Dr ... 44060
Terrace Park Dr ... 44060
Texas Ave ... 44060
Thatchum Ln ... 44060
Theresa Ln ... 44060
Thistlewood Dr ... 44060
Thomas Ct ... 44060
Thunderbird Dr ... 44060
Tiffin Ct ... 44060
Timberidge Ct ... 44060
Tina Dr ... 44060
Tinman Rd ... 44060
Tipperary Ln ... 44060
Tortugas Ln ... 44060
Townsend Ct ... 44060
Trailwood Ct ... 44060
Traymore Ct ... 44060
Trian Ct ... 44060
Trillium Ln ... 44060
Trimble Ct ... 44060
Trotter Ln ... 44060
Troy Ct ... 44060
Truman Ct ... 44060
Tulip Ln ... 44060
Tunbridge Dr ... 44060
Twilight Dr ... 44060
Twin Creek Ct ... 44060
Twinbrook Rd ... 44060
Tyler Blvd
- 7400-8599 ... 44060
- 8600-8600 ... 44061
- 8601-9099 ... 44060
- 8602-9298 ... 44060

Union St ... 44060
E & W Valleyview Ct ... 44060
Van Buren Ct ... 44060
Victoria Dr ... 44060
Villa Marina Ct ... 44060
Village Dr ... 44060
Vintage Ct ... 44060
Wake Robin Rd ... 44060
Walcott Way ... 44060
Walden Ct ... 44060
Walnut St ... 44060
Warrendale Dr ... 44060
Warrington Ln ... 44060
Washington Ave ... 44060
Waterford Ln ... 44060
Wayside Dr ... 44060
N Weatherby Dr ... 44060
Weathersfield Dr ... 44060
Weathervane Ct ... 44060
Weber Dr ... 44060
Wedgewood Dr ... 44060
Welk Ct ... 44060
Welland Dr ... 44060
Wentworth Ln ... 44060
West Rd ... 44060
Westmoor Rd ... 44060
Westport Dr ... 44060
Weymouth Dr ... 44060
Whalers Cv ... 44060
Wheatfield Ln ... 44060
Wheeler Ct ... 44060
White Rd ... 44060
White Oak Dr ... 44060
White Pine Ct ... 44060
Whitetail Run Ln ... 44060
Whitethorn Dr ... 44060
Wild Flower Way ... 44060
Wilderness Dr ... 44060
Wildwood Dr ... 44060
Wilkenson Cir ... 44060
William St ... 44060
Willow Ln ... 44060
Willow Run Dr ... 44060
Willowbrook Dr ... 44060
Wilson Dr ... 44060
Windham Dr ... 44060
Windmill Ln ... 44060
N & S Winds Dr ... 44060
Windsor Ln ... 44060
Winfield Dr ... 44060
Winterberry Ln ... 44060
Wintergreen Ln ... 44060
Winthrop Ct ... 44060
Wixford Ln ... 44060
Woodbury Ct ... 44060
Woodcreek Dr ... 44060
Woodland Pl ... 44060
Woodridge Ln ... 44060
Woods Edge Ct ... 44060
Woodside Rd ... 44060
Woodvale Ct ... 44060
Wooster Ct ... 44060
Worthington Ln ... 44060
Wren Ct ... 44060
Wyant Dr ... 44060
Yellowbrick Rd ... 44060
Yellowwood Dr ... 44060
Yorkshire Dr ... 44060
Yorktown Ct ... 44060
Yorkwood Ct ... 44060
Zinnia Ct ... 44060

MIAMISBURG OH

General Delivery ... 45343

POST OFFICE BOXES MAIN OFFICE STATIONS AND BRANCHES

Box No.s
All PO Boxes ... 45343

NAMED STREETS

Aberfield Ln ... 45342
Ainsworth Ct ... 45342
Albright Rd ... 45342
Aldora Dr ... 45342
N & S Alex Rd ... 45342
Alexandersville Rd ... 45342
Allister Cir ... 45342
Alma Ave ... 45342
Almedia Ct & Dr ... 45342
Althea Dr ... 45342
Amelia Ct ... 45342
Anthony Ln ... 45342
Appleblossom Dr ... 45342
April Ct ... 45342
Arboridge Ln ... 45342
Arlis Ln ... 45342
Arrow Ridge Ct ... 45342
Arthur Ave ... 45342
Asbury Ct ... 45342
Ashley Dr ... 45342
Audene Ct ... 45342
Augusta Rd ... 45342
Austin Blvd ... 45342
Austin Springs Blvd ... 45342
Automation Way ... 45342
Autumn Haze Trl ... 45342
Autumn Plank Ln ... 45342
Ayer Pl ... 45342
Aylesworth Ln ... 45342
Bakersfield Ct ... 45342
Ballinshire Ct ... 45342
Bambridge Dr ... 45342
Bannon Ct ... 45342
N & S Bayberry Dr ... 45342
Bear Creek Rd ... 45342
Beauview Ln ... 45342
Beldon Ct ... 45342
Belvo Rd ... 45342
Belvo Estates Ct & Dr ... 45342
Benavides St ... 45342
Bending Branch Ln ... 45342
Benner Rd ... 45342
Bentree Ct ... 45342
Bermuda Dr ... 45342
Berwick Ct ... 45342
Beth Ln ... 45342
Beth Ann Way ... 45342
Birch Run Ct ... 45342
Blackbird Ct ... 45342
Blackmoat Pl ... 45342
Blanche Dr ... 45342
Blanton Dr ... 45342
Bluebird Ct ... 45342
Bluegrass Ct ... 45342
Bonniebrook Dr ... 45342
Boss Ct ... 45342
Boyer Dr ... 45342
Bradshire Rd ... 45342
Branch Ln ... 45342
Branch Lane Ct ... 45342
Brandonhall Dr ... 45342
Bridle Path Ct ... 45342
Britwell Ct ... 45342
Broadleaf Cir ... 45342
Broken Woods Dr ... 45342
Brookshire Ln ... 45342
Brookstream Ct ... 45342
Buckeye St ... 45342
Bugleboy Ct ... 45342
Burnside Dr ... 45342
Byers Rd ... 45342
Byers Ridge Dr ... 45342
Cabbage Key Dr ... 45342
Cambray Ct ... 45342
Camp Trl ... 45342
Canal St ... 45342
Canincot Rd ... 45342
Canterchase Dr ... 45342
Capstone Cir ... 45342
Captiva Bay Dr ... 45342
Carloway Ct ... 45342
Carlwood Dr ... 45342
Carole St ... 45342
Carolyn Cir & Dr ... 45342
Carriage Ln ... 45342
Carrington Ln ... 45342
Case Ave & Ct ... 45342
Casilla Ct ... 45342
Castleton Ct ... 45342
Catalina Dr ... 45342
Cedar Ln ... 45342
Cedar Ridge Ct ... 45342
Center St ... 45342
E & W Central Ave ... 45342
Chaffman Ct ... 45342
Chautauqua Rd ... 45342
Chelman Dr ... 45342
Cherry Hill Dr ... 45342
Cherry Stone Ct ... 45342
Chestnut Sq ... 45342
Chestnut Hill Ln ... 45342
Chris Ln ... 45342
Church Dr ... 45342
Cimarron Cir & Ln ... 45342
Cincinnati Pike ... 45342
Cinnamon Ridge Ct ... 45342
Clarion Ct ... 45342
Clearbrook Ct ... 45342
Clearcreek Franklin Rd ... 45342
Clemens Ct ... 45342
N & S Cliff Swallow Ct ... 45342
Cloverleaf Ln ... 45342
Cobblestone Ct ... 45342
Cogswell Ct ... 45342
Coldstream Ct ... 45342
Cole Ave ... 45342
Coleman Rd ... 45342
Colinda Ct ... 45342
Colson Ct ... 45342
Commons Dr ... 45342
Contemporary Ln ... 45342
Cook Ln ... 45342
Copper Creek Ct ... 45342
Corporate Pl ... 45342
Cotinga Way ... 45342
Cottage Ave ... 45342
Country Path Trl ... 45342
Country Pond Trl ... 45342
Countryside Ln ... 45342
Cozy Ln ... 45342
Crains Creek Rd ... 45342
Crains Run Rd ... 45342
Cranbrook Ct ... 45342
Crayton Ct ... 45342
Crimson ... 45342
Cromer Blvd ... 45342
Crosley Ct ... 45342
Cross Pointe Dr ... 45342
Cross Village Dr ... 45342
Crow Ct ... 45342
Cudgell Dr ... 45342
Curtis Dr ... 45342
Cybelle Ct ... 45342
Dalton Ct ... 45342
Danielle Ln ... 45342
Darlene Ct ... 45342
David Dr ... 45342
Dayket Cir ... 45342
Dayton Cincinnati Pike ... 45342
Decker Ct & Dr ... 45342
Dee Ave ... 45342
Deer Foot Way ... 45342
Delbarton Ave ... 45342
Dellingham Ct ... 45342
Diana Ave ... 45342
Dorothy Ave ... 45342
Dorset Woods Ct ... 45342
Dorval Ave ... 45342
Douglas Dr ... 45342
Drake Ct ... 45342
Draycott Ct ... 45342
Dunaway St ... 45342
Dunes Dr ... 45342
Dunraven Pass ... 45342
Dunshire Ct ... 45342
Eagle Down Ct ... 45342
Eagle Mountain Dr ... 45342
Earl Blvd & Ct ... 45342
Early Dr E & W ... 45342
Eastbrook Dr ... 45342
Eastover Ln ... 45342
Edgerton Dr ... 45342
El An Ja Dr ... 45342
Elwyn Pl ... 45342
Emily Beth Dr ... 45342
English Oak Ct ... 45342
Equestrian Dr ... 45342
Esther Ave ... 45342
Ethel Ave ... 45342
Evangeline Dr ... 45342
Evans Ave ... 45342
Exchange Place Blvd ... 45342
Fairway Ct ... 45342
Fairwood Ct & Dr ... 45342
Falling Leaf Ln ... 45342
Farmersville W Carrollton Rd ... 45342
Farmington Rd ... 45342
Farmview Ct ... 45342
Faversham Rd ... 45342
Feather Ct ... 45342
Featherston Ct ... 45342
Ferndown Dr & Rd ... 45342
E & W Ferry St ... 45342
Fiesta Ln ... 45342
Fitzooth Ct & Dr ... 45342
Floyd Ave ... 45342
Forestedge Ln ... 45342
Foundry St ... 45342
Fountain Abbey Pl ... 45342
Four Seasons Trl ... 45342
Fox Glove Way ... 45342
Foxhill Dr ... 45342
Foxhound Dr ... 45342
Foxwood Ct ... 45342
Franklin Ave ... 45342
Friar Tuck Ct ... 45342
Galaton Ct ... 45342
Game Creek Ct ... 45342
Gamewell Dr ... 45342
Gander Creek Dr ... 45342
Gas Light Ct ... 45342
N & S Gebhart Church Rd ... 45342
Genetta Dr ... 45342
Germantown Pike ... 45342
Gillen Ln ... 45342
Gladwin Ct ... 45342
Glen Orchard Ct ... 45342
Golden Arrow Ct & Dr ... 45342
Goodwin Pl ... 45342
Gordon Ct ... 45342
Granite Peak Way ... 45342
Graystone Ct ... 45342
Green Apple Rd ... 45342
Greenfinch Dr ... 45342
Greenview Dr ... 45342
Greenway Ct ... 45342
Gressbach Ct ... 45342
Grove Park ... 45342
Halstead Crk ... 45342
Hambletonian Ct ... 45342
Harnam Ct ... 45342
Hastings Ave ... 45342
Hatteras Ct ... 45342
Heartwood Ct ... 45342
Heather Renee Ct ... 45342
N Heincke Rd ... 45342
S Heincke Rd
- 1-299 ... 45342
- 240-242 ... 45343
- 300-1498 ... 45342
- 301-1499 ... 45342

Helmet Pl ... 45342
Hemlock Ln ... 45342
Hemple Rd ... 45342
Heritage Glen Dr ... 45342
Herlihy Dr ... 45342
Hickory Glenn Dr ... 45342
Hidden Creek Rd ... 45342
Hidden Meadows Dr ... 45342
Highland Village Ln ... 45342
Highlander Ave ... 45342
Highpoint Dr ... 45342
Highridge Ct ... 45342
Hill Ave ... 45342
Hillgate Ct ... 45342
Hillview Ave ... 45342
Hollow Oak ... 45342
Hollowcreek Ct & Dr ... 45342
Hollyhill Dr ... 45342
Hoover Ave ... 45342
Hunt Dr ... 45342
Imperial Crown Blvd ... 45342
Industry Ln ... 45342
Infirmary Rd ... 45342
Innovation Ct & Dr ... 45342
Jamaica Rd ... 45342
Jamestown Dr ... 45342
Jandor Pl ... 45342
Jane Ave ... 45342
Jeannie Way ... 45342
Jefferson St ... 45342
Jena Ct ... 45342
Jessi Ln ... 45342
Joann St ... 45342
Johnson Ave ... 45342

Justin Ct 45342
Kathy Ln 45342
Kehm St 45342
Keithshire Ct 45342
Kelly Marie Ct 45342
Kercher St 45342
Kimberly Ct 45342
King Bird Ln 45342
King Harry Pl 45342
King Richard Pkwy 45342
Kirkley Hall Dr 45342
Kirkwall Ct 45342
Kiwi Ct 45342
Knollview Ct 45342
Kodiak Run Dr 45342
Kohnle Dr 45342
Krischel Dr 45342
Landing Way 45342
Lang St 45342
Las O Las Dr 45342
Lawrence Ave 45342
Lea Ave 45342
Lea Castle Pl 45342
Leeds Ct 45342
Leis Rd 45342
Leiter Rd 45342
Limerock St 45342
Limestone Way 45342
Lincolnshire Rd 45342
Lindamede Ln 45342
E Linden Ave 45342
Lindenborough Ct 45342
E & N Lindsey Ave 45342
Lion Heart Dr 45342
Little John Ct 45342
E & W Lock St 45342
Lonesome Oak 45342
Lonesome Pine Dr 45342
Loop St 45342
Lord Fitzwalter Dr 45342
Louis St 45342
Lower Germantown Rd 45342
Lower Miamisburg Rd 45342
Lyncris Ln 45342
Lyons Rd 45342
Lyons Gate Way 45342
Maddux Dr 45342
Magnolia Cir 45342
Maid Marion Ct 45342
N & S Main St 45342
Mals Way 45342
Manning Rd 45342
Manton Dr 45342
E Maple Ave 45342
Maple Row Dr 45342
Maria Ct 45342
Marketplace Dr 45342
Marquis Dr 45342
Marsha Dr 45342
Marwood Ct 45342
Mary Ln W 45342
Mary Francis Ct 45342
Maue Rd 45342
Mays Ave 45342
E & W Mcguire Cir & St 45342
Mckinley Ct 45342
Meadowview Dr 45342
Mears Dr 45342
Medlar Rd 45342
Medlar Woods Ct 45342
Mellow Dr 45342
Merry John Dr 45342
N & S Miami Ave 45342
Miami Village Dr 45342
Miamisburg Centerville Rd 45342
Miamisburg Springboro Rd 45342
Michelle Ct 45342
Mockingbird Ln 45342
Monarch Ln 45342
Monica Dr 45342
Montgomery St 45342
Moon Ct 45342
Moondust Ct 45342
Moore Ave 45342
Motter Ln 45342
Mound Ave & Rd 45342
Muzette Ct 45342
Myna Ln 45342
Nancy Dr 45342
Nashua Ln 45342
Nassau Dr 45342
Nestling Dr 45342
Nettie Dr 45342
Nettle Creek Ct 45342
Nettleton Park 45342
New Yorker Blvd 45342
Newfield Ct 45342
Newmark Dr 45342
Nicholson Rd 45342
Nila Gay Ct 45342
Nogales Trl 45342
North Dr 45342
Northpointe Dr 45342
Nottingham Pl 45342
Nouvelle Dr 45342
Nunnery Dr 45342
Oak Knoll Cir 45342
Oak Ridge Blvd 45342
Oakbark St 45342
Oakwood Village Blvd 45342
Old Byers Rd 45342
Old Lantern Ct 45342
Old Main St W 45342
Old Osprey Cir 45342
Old Timber Ct 45342
Opal Ave 45342
Orchard Hill Dr 45342
Oriole Ct 45342
Overcliff Ct 45342
Overland Trl 45342
Paget Dr 45342
Painter Pl 45342
Panjab Ct 45342
Park Ave 45342
Parkwyn Dr 45342
Peacock Ln 45342
E & W Pearl St 45342
Pecos Ct 45342
Pellston Way 45342
Pendle Pt 45342
Pennyroyal Rd 45342
Pewter Hills Ct 45342
Phyllis Ave 45342
Pin Oak Ct 45342
Pine Forest Dr 45342
Pine Knoll Ct 45342
Pinebrooke Ct 45342
Pinecastle Ave 45342
Pinemount Cir & Dr 45342
Pinnacle Rd 45342
Pipestone Dr 45342
Plum St 45342
Plumage Ct 45342
Pomona St 45342
Powell Ave 45342
Precision Ct 45342
Prestige Pl 45342
Prestige Plaza Dr 45342
Promenade Way 45342
Puplefinch Ln 45342
Purplefinch Ln 45342
Queen Eleanor Ct 45342
Queensway Dr 45342
Range Ave 45342
Raton Pass 45342
Red Deer Ln 45342
Richard St 45342
S River Rd 45342
N & S Riverview Ave 45342
Robinhood Dr 45342
Rockcastle Ct 45342
Rolling Greens Trl 45342
Rosalind Dr 45342
Rosefinch Way 45342
Rosetta Ave 45342
Rosewell St 45342
Rosina Dr 45342
Rotellini Dr 45342
Royal Arms Ct 45342
Royal Ridge Dr 45342
Russell Ct 45342
Saddlebrook Ln 45342
Sagebrook Dr 45342
Sagewood Dr 45342
Saint Andrews Trl 45342
Sally Cir 45342
Sapling Ct & Dr 45342
Sawgrass Dr 45342
Sawtooth Pass 45342
Saxony Rd 45342
School St 45342
Schroeder St 45342
Secretariat Cir 45342
Seibert Ave 45342
Sennett St 45342
Shana Ct 45342
Shelley Ct 45342
Shepard Rd 45342
Sherwat Cir 45342
Sherwood Forest Dr 45342
Sierra Ridge Dr 45342
Simonton Ave 45342
Sir Guy Ct 45342
Sir Lockesley Dr 45342
Snowy Spruce Ct 45342
Soldiers Home Miamisburg Rd 45342
Soldiers Home W Carrollton Rd 45342
Somerset Dr 45342
South Dr & St 45342
Southpointe Dr 45342
Spring Blossom Trl 45342
Spring Valley Rd 45342
Springboro Pike 45342
Springhaven Dr 45342
Springpointe Cir 45342
Springwater Ln 45342
Stanford Ridge Ct 45342
Starting Gate Ct 45342
Steeplechase Dr 45342
Stephens St 45342
Sterling Ln 45342
Stinton Ln 45342
Stout Will Ct 45342
Stutely Pl 45342
Sue Ave 45342
Sulky Trl 45342
Summer Wind Trl 45342
Sunair Ct 45342
Sundance Dr 45342
Sunflower Dr 45342
Sunset Ave 45342
Suttman St 45342
Swallow Ct 45342
Swaying Pine Ct 45342
E & W Sycamore Lndg, St, Ter & Vly 45342
Sycamore Cove Cir 45342
Sycamore Glen Dr 45342
Sycamore Hill Ct 45342
Sycamore Ridge Ct 45342
Sycamore View Ct 45342
Sycamore Woods Dr 45342
Sydneys Bend Dr 45342
Tall Timbers Ct 45342
Tamworth Cir 45342
Taos Dr 45342
Tarpon Bay Dr 45342
Tartan Cir 45342
S & W Tech Blvd 45342
Technical Dr 45342
Telluride Ln 45342
Terrington Way 45342
Thayer Ave 45342
Thelma Ave 45342
Tivoli Ct 45342
Toucan St 45342
Towering Pine Dr 45342
Towson Blvd 45342
Trailing Oak 45342
Trails Way 45342
Tranquil Dr 45342
Tree Top Ct N & S 45342
Trish Ct 45342
Turtledove Way 45342
Twilight Dr 45342
Uhlwood Dr 45342
Umbreit Ct 45342
S Union Rd 45342
Upper Miamisburg Rd 45342
Upper River Rd 45342
Upperton Dr 45342
Valcourt St 45342
Valette Cir E 45342
Vanguard Blvd 45342
Vantage Pl & Pt 45342
Vaughn Rd 45342
Vicki Ln 45342
Villa Way 45342
Village Tree Ct 45342
Village View Ct 45342
Villagewood Ct 45342
Vista Ridge Dr 45342
Warwick Dr 45342
Washington Church Rd 45342
Waterbridge Ln 45342
Watermark Ct 45342
Waterstone Blvd 45342
Waterway Ct 45342
Wedgefield Ct 45342
Western Ave 45342
Westknoll Ct 45342
Whisper Dr 45342
Whispering Tree Dr 45342
White Cedar Dr 45342
White Pine Ct 45342
White Walnut Ct 45342
Wild Ginger Way 45342
Wileray Dr 45342
Williams St 45342
Wilson Park Dr 45342
Windsong Ct 45342
Windsor Village Dr 45342
Winters End Trl 45342
Wise Dr 45342
Wood Rd 45342
Wood Thrush Ct 45342
Woodchuck Ct 45342
Woodedge Ct 45342
Woodenbrook Dr 45342
Woodlawn Ave 45342
Woodridge Dr 45342
Woods View Ct 45342
Yale Ave 45342
Yorkridge Ct 45342
Zeck Rd 45342

NUMBERED STREETS

All Street Addresses 45342

MIDDLETOWN OH

General Delivery 45042

POST OFFICE BOXES MAIN OFFICE STATIONS AND BRANCHES

Box No.s
1 - 698 45042
701 - 1000 45044
1001 - 42664 45042
44704 - 44988 45044
420381 - 428810 45042

RURAL ROUTES

02, 04 45042
01, 03, 05, 06 45044

NAMED STREETS

Aaron Dr 45044
Aberdeen Dr 45042
Ada Dr 45042
Adria Ct 45044
Aeronca St 45042
Airport Dr 45042
Airy View Dr 45044
Alameda Cir 45044
Alamo Rd 45042
Alder Ct 45044
Alex Way 45044
W Alexandria Rd 45042
Aljen Rd 45042
Alpine Aster Ct 45044
Ambergreen Ct 45044
Amberley Ct 45044
Amberley Ter 45042
Amity Ln 45044
Amsterdam Dr 45044
Anderson Dr 45044
Andrew St 45044
Anne Rd 45044
Antrim Ct 45042
Apple Knoll Ln 45044
Apple Ridge Ct 45044
Appleton Ct 45044
April Cir 45042
Arbor Ct 45044
Arbor Pointe Dr 45042
Arcadia Dr 45042
Ardmore Dr 45042
Arlington Ave 45044
Armco Dr 45042
Arnold Dr 45044
Asbury Ct 45044
Ascot Glen Ct 45044
Ash Creek Ct 45044
Ashbrook Trl 45044
Ashcroft Ct 45042
Ashdale Ct 45044
Ashley Ter 45042
Ashlyn Ct 45044
Ashmont Pl 45044
Askew St 45044
Aspen St 45042
Aster Ct 45044
Atco Ave 45042
Auburn St 45042
Audrey Ct 45042
Audubon Dr 45044
August Ave 45044
Autumn Dr 45042
Autumn Creek Dr 45044
Autumn Oak Dr 45044
Ava Ct 45044
Avalon Dr 45042
Bahama Dr 45044
Baker Ct 45044
Balsam Dr 45044
Baltimore St 45044
Bannon Ct 45042
Barbara Ct & Dr 45044
Barberry Ln 45044
Barnitz St 45042
Batsey Dr 45044
Bavarian St 45044
Baybrook Ct 45044
Beatrice Dr 45044
Beck Rd 45042
Becky Dr 45044
Beech St 45042
Beechwood Ln 45042
Bellemonte St 45042
Belvidere Ave 45044
Belvoir Cir 45044
Ben Harrison St 45044
Bendel Dr 45044
Bentwood Dr 45042
Berkshire Pl 45044
Bernice St 45044
Bertha Ave 45044
Berwick Ln 45042
Beth Ann Ct 45044
Beth Anne Ct 45044
Bethany Rd 45044
Beverly Ln 45042
Bexhill Dr 45044
Bexley Dr 45042
Birch Creek Ct 45044
Blair Ct 45042
Bluebird Ct 45044
Bluffs Dr 45044
Bobby Dr 45042
Bonita Dr 45044
Boxwood Ln 45044
Boylston St 45044
Bradford Dr 45044
Brady Ct 45044
Brandon Ln 45042
Brandywine St 45044
N Breiel Blvd
1-2099 45042
2-10 45044
22-2098 45042
S Breiel Blvd 45044
Brell Dr 45042
Brent Dr 45044
Brentwood St 45044
Brian Ct 45044
Bridgewood Dr 45044
Brightfield Ct 45044
Brittany Pl 45044
N Broad St 45042
S Broad St 45044
Brookfield Dr 45044
Brookhaven Dr 45044
Brookside St 45042
Brookview Dr 45044
Brown St 45044
Browning St 45042
Browns Run Rd 45042
Bryant St 45042
Buckeye Dr 45044
Buckingham Ct 45044
Buena Ave 45044
Bunker Ln 45042
Burbank Ave 45044
Burton Dr & Rd 45044
Butler Warren Rd 45044
Buttercup Ct 45042
Byron St 45042
Callisto Dr 45044
Calloway Ct 45044
Calumet Ave 45044
Cambridge Dr 45044
Cambridge Trl 45044
N & S Canal Rd & St 45044
Canterbury Ct 45044
Caprice Dr 45044
Cardinal Ct 45044
Cardnia Ct 45044
Carlow Cir 45042
Carmody Blvd 45044
Carmody Pl 45044
Carol Ann Ln 45044
Carolina St 45044
Carriage St 45044
Carroll Ave 45044
Carroll Lee Ln 45044
Carson Rd 45044
Cartman Ct 45044
Casper St 45042
Castle Hill Dr 45044
Catalina Ct 45044
Catalpa Dr 45042
Cedar Gate Ct 45044
Cedar Glen Way 45042
Cedar Ridge Ct 45044
Cedarcrest Dr 45044
Cedarview Ct 45044
Cedarwood Ct 45042
Celestial Ave 45042
Celestial Cir 45044
Centennial St 45044
Centerview Ct 45044
Central Ave 45044
Chalkstone 45044
Chandler Dr 45042
Chandler Xing 45044
Charles St 45042
Charleston Woods Dr 45044
Cherokee Ln 45044
Cherry St 45044
Cherry Laurel Dr 45044
Cherry Mill Ct 45044
Cheshire Cir 45042
Chestnut St 45042
Chestnut Woods Ct 45044
Chris Ct 45042
Chris Ln 45044
Chrisman Ln 45042
Christel Ave 45044
Church St 45042
Churchill Manor Ct 45044
Cimmeron Dr 45044
Cincinnati Dayton Rd 45044
Circle Dr 45044
Circle Pkwy 45042
Circle Ginny 45044
Circle Kelly Jo 45044
City Centre Mall 45042
Clarendon Ave 45042
Clark Blvd 45044
Clark St 45042
Clayton Ave 45042
Cleveland St 45044
N Clinton St 45042
S Clinton St 45044
Cloister Cliffs Dr 45042
Clover Ln 45044
Cobblers Trl 45044
Colbrook Ct 45044
Coles Rd 45044
Columbia Ave 45042
Colyn Ct 45044
Concord Ave 45044
Conifer Dr 45044
Coral Bell Ct 45044
Cordia Ct 45044
Corlee Ln 45042
Corta Via 45044
Cotton Run Rd 45042
Cougar Path 45044
Countryside Trl 45044
Court Donegal 45042
Court Edmun 45044
Court Louise 45042
Crawford St 45044
Creekview Dr 45044
Crescent Blvd 45042
Crest Cir & Dr 45042
Cribbs St 45044
Croydon Ln 45042
Curryer Rd 45042
Curtis St 45044
Cypress Ln 45044
Dairy Ln 45042
Dalewood Dr 45042
Daniel Ct 45044
Dantawood Ln 45044
Darl Dr 45042
Darlene Ter 45044
Dartford Way 45044
Davidson St 45044
Davinci Dr 45042
Dawson Dr 45044
Dazey Dr 45044
Deer Crk & Run 45042
Deer Run Rd 45044
Delano Dr 45044
Delaware Ave 45044
Derbyshire Ct 45044
Devon Dr 45044
Diamond Loop 45044
Dickens Ave 45044
Dickey Rd 45042
Diver Ln 45044
Dix Rd 45042
Dixie Hwy 45044
Donham Dr & Plz 45042
Dorothy Ln 45044
Dorset Dr 45044
Douglas St 45044
Dover Ave 45044
Driftwood St 45042
Dubois Ct 45044
Dusty Trl 45044
Dutchland Blvd & Pkwy 45044

Street	ZIP
Dutchview Ct	45044
Eaglestone Ct	45044
Earl Ave	45044
East St	45044
Eastline Dr	45044
Easton Ave	45044
Eaton Ave & Dr	45044
Eck Rd	45042
Edam Ct	45044
Eddington St	45044
Edgewater Dr	45042
Edgewood St	45044
Edison Dr	45044
Edith Dr	45042
Eisenhower Pl	45042
El Camino Dr	45044
El Paso Ave	45044
Eldora Dr	45042
Eldorado Dr	45044
Elk Creek Rd	45042
W Elkton Gifford Rd	45042
Ellen Dr	45042
Elliott Dr	45044
Ellis Way	45044
Elm St	45044
Elm Creek Ct	45044
Elman Ct & Dr	45044
N Elmer Dr	45042
S Elmer Dr	45044
Elmgrove Ter	45044
Elmo Pl	45042
Elmwood Ln	45044
Elsmere St	45042
Elwood St	45042
Emerald Way	45044
Emerick Rd	45042
Emerson Rd	45042
Emi Dr	45044
English Oaks Sta	45044
Enoch Dr	45042
Enterprise Dr	45044
Erie Ave	45042
Erika Ct	45042
Ernestine Dr	45042
Essex Mill Ter	45044
Ethel Ct	45044
Euclid Ct & St	45044
Eunice Dr	45042
Evelyn Dr	45042
Evergreen Dr	45044
Evergreen Ln	45044
Evergreen St	45042
Fairfield Ave	45044
Fairmount Ave	45044
Fernwood St	45044
Fielders Way	45042
Fiesta Way	45044
Finley St	45044
Firman Cir	45042
Fisher Ave	45042
Flemming Rd	45042
Flora Ln	45042
Florence St	45044
Follmers Ct	45042
Forest Ave	45044
Forest Glen Dr	45042
Forest Oaks St	45042
Forest Pond Dr	45044
Forrer St	45044
Fox Trot Ct	45044
Foxstone Ct	45044
Foxtail Ln	45044
Foxwood Ct	45044
Francis Dr	45044
Franklin St	45042
Franklin Madison Rd	45042
Franora Ln	45042
Frazer Dr	45042
Freedom Ct	45044
Front St	45042
Frontier Ct	45044
Fulton Ln	45044
Gage Dr	45042
Galloway Dr	45044
Galway Cir	45042
Garden Ave	45044
Gardner Pl	45042
Garfield St	45044
Garver Rd	45044
Gem Stone Dr	45044
Genesis Ct	45044
Georgetown Ln	45042
Gerber Dr	45042
Germantown Rd	45042
Gerry St	45042
Gideon Dr & Rd	45044
Gingerich Rd	45042
Ginny Ct	45044
Girard Ave	45044
Gladys Dr	45044
Glen Ln	45042
Glencoe St	45042
Gleneagle Ln	45042
Glenmore Dr	45042
Glenn Ave	45044
Goldendawn Way	45044
Goldfinch Ct	45044
Goldman Ave	45044
Golfview Rd	45042
Granada Ave	45044
Grand Ave	45044
Granny Smith Ln	45044
Graydon Dr	45042
Green Lake Dr	45044
Green Meadow Dr	45044
Green Oval Dr	45044
Greenbush Rd	45042
E Greenfield Dr	45044
Greentree Rd	45044
Greenview Dr	45044
Greenwood Ct	45044
Greenwood Dr	45044
Greenwood Rd	45042
Gretel Ct	45044
N Grimes St	45042
Grove St	45044
Groveland St	45042
Hailey	45044
Halifax Ct & Dr	45044
Hamilton Rd	45044
Hamilton Lebanon Rd	45044
Hamilton Middletown Rd	45044
Hampshire Trl	45044
Hampton Pl	45042
Hankins Rd	45044
Hannah Dr	45044
Hansbrinker Ct & Dr	45044
Harbor Cove Ct	45044
Harden Ave	45044
Harkie St	45044
Harlan St	45044
Harrison St	
1-299	45042
3100-3299	45044
Hawthorne St	45042
Hawthorne Reserves Dr	45044
Hayden Dr	45042
Heather Springs Dr	45044
Heatherway St	45042
Heatherwood Ct	45042
N Heinkel Rd	45042
S Heinkel Rd	45044
Helton Dr	45044
Hemlock Ct	45044
Hendrickson Rd	45044
Henrick Dr	45044
Henry Ave	45042
Heritage Trail Dr	45044
Hetzler Rd	45042
Hickory Ave	45044
Hickory Holw	45042
Hickory Knoll Dr	45044
Hickory Pointe Dr	45044
Highland St	45044
N Highview Dr	45042
S Highview Rd	45044
Hill Ave	45044
Hill St	45042
Hinkle Rd	45042
Holloway Dr	45044
Holly Ave	45044
Hollybrook Dr	45044
Hollytree Dr	45044
Hollyview Ln	45042
Hood Ave	45044
Hook Dr	45042
Hoover Ct	45042
Hope Dr	45042
Hoskins Ln	45042
Howard Ave	45044
Howe Rd	45042
Hughes St	45042
Hummingbird Cir	45044
Hunting Creek Dr	45044
Huntington St	45042
Hursh Rd	45042
Iglehart St	45042
Illinois Ave	45042
Inland Dr	45042
Ivory Ln	45044
Jackie Dr	45042
Jackson Ln	45044
Jackson St	45042
Jacksonburg Rd	45042
Jacoby Ave	45044
Jamison Way	45044
Jason Ct	45044
Jeanette St	45044
Jefferson Ave	45042
Jennifer Ct	45044
Jessica Ct	45044
Jewell St	45042
Joann Ln	45042
Joanne Dr	45044
Jodee Dr	45042
Johns Rd	45044
Jonathan Way	45044
Joshua Cir	45044
Joy Dr	45044
Judy Dr	45044
Juniper Cir	45044
Justess Ln	45044
Kalbfleisch Rd	45042
Kanaugua Pl	45044
Karen Dr	45042
Karincrest Dr	45044
Kay Dr	45042
Keays Ave	45044
Keister Rd	45042
Kelsey Trl	45044
Kempton Ct	45044
Kenec Dr	45044
Kenridge Dr	45042
Kensington Ct, St & Trl	45044
Kent Ct	45044
Kenway Pl	45044
Kenwood Dr	45042
Kilkerry Ct & Dr	45042
Kimball Ct	45044
Kings River Ct	45044
Klare Ct	45042
Knoll Ln	45044
Krach Ct	45044
Kreiger St	45042
Kunz Ave	45044
Kyle Ct	45042
Kyles Ln	45044
Kyles Station Rd	45044
Kyles Station Meadows Dr	45044
Lacy Ct	45044
Lafayette Ave	45044
Lakeview Dr	45044
Lakota Ln	45044
Lakota Meadows Dr	45044
Lakota Pointe Ln	45044
Lakota Woods Dr	45044
Lamberton Ct & St	45044
Lamneck St	45044
Lancashire Trl	45044
Lantana Dr	45044
Larkspur Ln	45044
Laurel Ave	45044
Laurel Lake Ct	45044
Lawn Ave	45044
Lefferson Rd	45044
N Leibee St	45042
S Leibee St	45042
Leichty Ave	45042
Leland Ct	45042
Lenrose Rd	45042
Lesley Ln	45042
Lewis St	45044
N & S Liberty Ct, Dr, Ln & St	45044
Liberty One Dr	45044
Liberty Park Dr	45044
Liberty Pass Dr	45044
Liberty Plaza Dr	45044
Liberty View Ct	45044
Limerick Ln	45042
Lincoln St	45044
Lind St	45042
Linden Ave	45044
Lindsey Ct	45044
Lindy Dr	45044
Linn Ln & Rd	45044
Lisa Ln	45042
Litchfield Ln	45042
Locust St	45044
Logan Ave	45044
Logistics Way	45044
Lois Ln	45044
Londonderry Dr	45042
Long Ln	45044
Longfellow St	45042
Longford Ct & Dr	45042
Longhunter Chase Dr	45044
Lopane Ave	45044
Loretta Dr	45044
Lorraine Dr	45042
Louis Pl	45044
Lowell St	45044
Lucky Ln	45044
Lylburn Rd	45044
Lynch Ln	45044
Macintosh Ln	45044
Made Dr	45044
Madison St	45044
Magnolia Dr	45042
Mahogany Ct	45044
N Main St	45042
S Main St	45044
Mallard Ct	45044
Malvern St	45042
Manchester Ave	45042
Manchester Ct	45044
Manchester Mnr	45042
Manchester Rd	45042
Manhattan St	45044
Manitee St	45044
Maple St	45044
Maple Creek Dr	45044
Maple Leaf Ct	45044
Marcie Dr	45042
Marguerite Ct	45042
Marie Dr	45044
Marisa Dr	45044
Marken Ct	45044
N Marshall Rd	45042
S Marshall Rd	45044
Marts Rd	45042
Mary Etta St	45042
Marymont Ct	45042
Maud Hughes Rd	45044
May Ave	45042
Maybelle Dr	45042
Mcgee Ave	45044
Mcguire Ave	45044
Mckinley St	45042
Mcknight Dr	45042
Meadow Ave	45044
Meadowlark Dr	45044
Meadowood Dr	45044
Melissa Xing	45044
Melrose Ln	45044
Miami Ave	45042
Michael Rd	45042
Michelle Ln	45044
Michigan Ave	45044
Middlemoor Ln	45042
Middletown Eaton Rd	45042
Middletown Germantown Rd	45042
Middletown Oxford Rd	45042
Midway St	45042
Mill Rd	45042
Millbrook Dr	45042
Miller Rd	45042
Millikin Rd	45044
Milton Ct & Rd	45042
Mindy Mnr	45044
Minnesota St	45044
Moder Ln	45042
Mohawk St	45044
Monarch Dr	45044
Monroe St	45042
Mont Cir & Dr	45042
Moore Rd	45042
Moore St	45044
Moorman Pl	45042
Morgan St	45044
Mosiman Rd	45042
Mother Teresa Ln	45044
Mount Vernon St	45044
Mulberry St	45044
Murphy Ct	45044
Myers Rd	45042
Myrtle Ln	45044
Navaho St	45044
Nelbar St	45042
Nelson Rd	45042
Netherland Ct & Dr	45044
Newgate Pl	45044
Niderdale Way	45042
Niederlander Ln	45044
Nightingale Dr	45044
Nixon Ct	45042
No Mans Rd	45042
Nora Ave	45044
Norfolk Ct	45044
North Ave	45042
Northbrook Ln	45044
Norwich Ct	45044
Oak Manor Dr	45044
Oak Trail Ln	45042
Oakcroft Cir	45042
Oaklawn Dr	45044
Oaks Cir & Ct	45042
Oakview Dr	45042
Oberon Dr	45044
Ocala Dr	45044
Ogden Dr	45044
Ohio Ave	45042
Old Middletown Germantown Rd	45042
Oleander Ct	45044
Omaha St	45044
Oneka Ave	45044
Onyx Ct	45044
Opal Dr	45044
Ora Ln	45042
Orchard St	45044
Orlando Ave	45042
Ottawa St	45044
Otter Creek Dr	45044
Oxford Ave	45042
Oxford State Rd	45044
Panama Ave	45042
Panther Dr & Run	45044
Paradise Cv	45044
Park Dr	45044
Park Ln	45042
Park St	45044
Parkview Ave	45044
Paul Ln	45044
Paullin Dr	45042
Peaceful Way	45044
Pearl St	45044
Pebble Crk	45044
Penfield Ave	45044
Pennswood Dr	45044
Penny Ln	45044
Perry Ave	45042
Pershing Ave	45044
Philadelphia Ave	45044
Phillip Ct	45044
Pine St	45044
Pine Cone Ct	45044
Pinta Ave	45044
Pioneer Ct	45044
Plain St	45042
Plum St	45042
Plymouth St	45044
Poe St	45044
Poinciana Rd	45042
Poplar St	45044
Poppy Dr & Ln	45044
Prairie Ct	45044
Preble County Line Rd	45042
Preblewood Dr	45042
Primrose Ln	45044
Princeton Ave	45042
Princeton Rd	45044
Prospect Ave	45044
Puma Ct	45044
Quail Run Rd	45042
Queen Ave	45044
Rachel Ln	45042
Rainwood Ct	45044
Raymond Dr	45042
Rayview St	45044
Red Pine Dr	45044
Redbud Dr	45042
Redmont Ct	45044
Regent Dr	45044
Reinartz Blvd	45042
Renee Dr	45042
Reynolds Ave	45044
Richardson Dr	45042
Richmond St	45044
Ristaneo Dr	45042
River Birch Ct	45044
River Trail Dr	45042
Riverchase Dr	45042
Riverview Ave	45042
Riviera Dr	45042
Rocky Rd	45042
Roden Park Dr	45044
Rodeo Dr	45044
Ronald Dr	45042
Roosevelt Ave, Blvd & Pkwy	45044
Rosedale Rd	45042
Rosemont Ct	45042
Rosewood Ct	45042
Roslyn Dr	45044
Ross St	45044
Rotterdam Ct	45044
Roxbury Ct	45042
Royal Fern Ct	45044
Royal Garden Ct	45044
Roycroft Dr	45042
Ruby Ln	45044
Rufus St	45044
Run Way	45042
Rusmar Ct	45042
Safari Dr	45044
Safe Haven Way	45042
Saint Andrews Ct	45042
Saint Andrews Cross	45044
Salzman Rd	45044
Sandra Lee Ln	45042
Sandric Ln	45044
Santa Barbara Dr	45042
Santa Fe Rd	45044
Sawyer Ave	45042
Sawyers Mill Dr	45042
Saybrook Dr	45044
Scarborough Ct	45042
Schirm Dr	45044
Schlade Ct	45044
Schoolview Dr	45044
Schroff Dr	45042
Schul Rd	45042
Scott St	45042
Selden Ave	45044
Seneca St	45044
Serena Way	45044
Serenity Lake Dr	45044
Severn Pl	45044
Shadow Hill Rd	45042
Shafor St	45042
Shannon Way	45042
Sharon Ct	45042
Shartle St	45042
Shawna Ct	45044
Shawnray Dr	45044
Sheffield Rd	45042
Sheffield St	45044
Shelburne Ct	45044
Shelby Ln	45044
Sheldon Rd	45042
Shelley St	45042
Sheridan Ave	45044
Sherman Ave	45044
Short St	45042
Shotten Rd	45042
Shurz Rd	45042
Sierra Rd	45042
Silver Skate Dr	45044
Sir Gregory Way	45044
Sloebig Rd	45042
Smith Ave	45044
Snapdragon Ln	45044
Sols Cir	45042
Somerville Jacksonburg Rd	45042
Sophie Ave	45042
Sora Ln	45044
Sorg Pl	45042
Spencer Ln	45042
Spring Garden Dr	45044
Spring Grove Ln	45044
Spring Mountain Ln	45044
Spruce Creek Dr	45044
Stanley St	45044
State Route 4	45042
S State Route 503	45042
Staton St	45044
Stellar Ct	45044
Stepping Stone	45044
Stolz Dr	45042
Stone Path Ct & Dr	45042
Stone Ridge Ln	45044
Stonebrook Ct	45044
Stonefort Dr	45044
Stoneham Ct	45044
Stonehenge Blvd	45044
Stonerun Pl	45044
Stoney Pt	45044
Stonington Dr	45044
Stratford Dr	45042
Streamstone Dr	45044
Streebee Rd	45042
Stubbs Rd	45042
Summerfield Ct	45044
Summerlin Blvd	45044
Summitt Dr	45042
Sunrise View Cir	45044
Sunset Pl & St	45042
Superior Ave	45044
N Sutphin St	45042
S Sutphin St	45044
Sutton Brooke Ct	45044
Sweet Briar Ct	45044
Sycamore Ter	45044
Tall Oaks Dr	45044
Talton Dr	45042
Tara Oaks Dr	45044
Tarrimore Cir	45044
Taylor Ave	45044
Taylor Lake Ln	45044
Terhune Dr	45044
Terrace Dr	45044
Terry Dr	45042
Texas Ave	45042
The Alameda	45044
Theresa Ct	45044
Thistle Ln	45044
Thomas Rd	45042
Thorn Hill Ln	45042
Timber Trail Dr	45044
Timberline Dr	45042
Tipperary Ct & Dr	45042
Todds Trl	45044
Todhunter Rd	45044
Tory Ln	45044
Towne Blvd	45044

Tracy Ln 45044
Trafalgar Ct 45044
Trafford Ct 45044
Tranquillity Trce 45044
Tree Ridge Ct 45044
Tree View Dr 45044
Treeside Dr 45044
Tremont Ct 45044
Trenton Franklin Rd 45042
Trine St 45044
Trinity Dr 45044
Trinity Pl 45042
Trinity Shore Cir 45044
Tulip Ct & Ln 45044
Tullis Dr 45042
Twin Cove Dr 45044
Twin Oaks Dr 45042
Tytus Ave 45042
Union Rd 45044
N University Blvd 45042
S University Blvd 45044
Vail Ave 45042
Valley View Dr 45044
Valleybrook Dr 45044
Van Ave 45042
Van Trump Rd 45042
Vance St 45044
Vancouver St 45044
Vanderveer St 45044
Vannest Ave 45042
Verbena Ln 45044
N Verity Pkwy 45042
S Verity Pkwy 45044
Vermont St 45044
Victoria Ave & Pl 45044
Victory Garden Ln 45044
Villa Ct 45044
Vincent Ct 45042
Vine Ave & St 45042
Vinny Dr 45044
Waite St 45044
Wakefield Dr 45044
Walton Ct 45042
Waneta St 45044
Warrenton Ct 45044
Washington St
700-799 45042
1001-1199 45044
Wayne Ave 45044
Waynebrook Dr 45044
Weatherwood Dr 45042
Weaver Ave 45044
Webber Ave 45042
Webster St 45042
Wedekind Dr 45042
Wedgewood Ter 45044
Weeping Cherry Ct 45044
Wellington Rd 45044
Welney Run 45044
Westheimer Dr 45044
Westmeath Ct 45042
Westminster Ct 45044
Westmont Ln 45044
Westover Ct 45044
Whisman Dr 45042
White Birch Ln 45044
Whittier St 45042
Wicklow Dr 45042
Wicoff St 45044
Wilbraham Rd 45042
Wildwood Rd 45042
Wilhelmina Dr 45044
Willow Creek Dr & Run 45044
Willowknoll Cir 45042
Wilma St 45042
Wilmore Dr 45042
Wilshire Dr 45044
Wilson St 45044
Windham Ct 45044
Winding Oaks Dr 45044
Windmill Dr 45044
Windridge Ct 45042
Windsor Ave, Rd & Trl 45044
Winesap Ln 45044
Winfield Ln 45042
Winona Dr 45042
Winsford Ct 45044
Winter Hazel Dr 45044
Winton St 45044
Wisteria Ct 45044
Woodburn Ave 45042
Woodcreek Dr 45042
Woodcrest Dr 45044
Wooden Shoe Ct & Dr 45044
Woodgate Ct & Way 45044
Woodhall Ct 45042
Woodland Ct 45044
Woodland Trace Ct 45044
Woodland View Dr 45044
Woodlawn Ave 45044
Woodmere Ct 45044
Woodridge Dr 45044
Woodsedge Dr 45044
Woodside Blvd 45044
Woodstone Ct 45044
Woodwind Ct 45044
Worchester Pl 45044
Wrenn Ct & St 45042
Wright Dr 45044
Wyandot Ln 45044
Yale Dr 45042
Yankee Rd 45044
Yankee Estates Dr 45044
Yarrow Ct 45044
Yoakum Ct 45044
Yorkshire Dr 45044
Young St 45044
Zachery Dr 45042

NUMBERED STREETS

All Street Addresses 45044

NEWARK OH

General Delivery 43055

POST OFFICE BOXES MAIN OFFICE STATIONS AND BRANCHES

Box No.s
All PO Boxes 43058

NAMED STREETS

Abby Dr 43055
Adams Ave 43055
Alcon Dr 43055
Alford Dr 43055
Allen St 43055
Allston Ave 43055
Alma Ave 43055
Alpine Blvd 43055
Alta Dr 43055
Amesbury Ln 43055
Amy Ln 43055
Andover St 43055
Andrea Ct 43055
Annette Ave 43055
Anthony Dr 43055
Aqueduct Ave 43055
Arbor Ct & Park 43055
Arcade Anx & Pl 43055
N & S Arch St 43055
Arlington Ave 43055
Arrow St 43055
Arthur Ave 43055
Ashford Ln 43055
Auburn Dr 43055
E & W Audrey Dr 43055
Augusta Dr 43055
Bachmann Ave 43055
Baker Blvd, Dr & Rd 43055
Ballard Ave 43055
Banks Hollow Rd NE 43055
Barbara Ave 43055
Barclay St 43055
Bates St 43055
Beacon Rd 43055
Beechwood Rd 43055
Belle Vista Ave 43055
Belmont Ave 43055
Berkley Dr 43055
Berwyn Ln 43055
Bessie Ln 43055
Blakeley Pl 43055
Blueberry Ct 43055
Bodle Rd 43055
Bolen Ave, Ct & Rd 43055
Bolton Ave 43055
Boner St 43055
Bow St 43055
Bowers Ave 43055
Boxwood Dr 43055
Boyleston Ave 43055
Bracken Moor Dr 43055
Bradford Cir 43055
Breef Ct 43055
Brennan St 43055
Brenthill Dr 43055
Brenton Dr 43055
Brentview Dr 43055
Brentwood Dr 43055
Briarhill Dr 43055
Briarwood Dr & Ln 43055
Brice Ct & St 43055
Bristol Downs Rd 43055
Brittany Hls E 43055
Broad St 43055
Brooke Way 43055
Brookside Dr 43055
Bryn Mawr Cir & Dr 43055
Buckeye Ave 43055
Buckingham St 43055
N & S Buena Vista St 43055
Builders Dr 43055
Burch Dr 43055
Burt Ave 43055
Butler Rd 43055
Calash Ct 43055
Calburn St 43055
Cambria St 43055
Camden Dr 43055
Camp St 43055
E & W Canal St 43055
Canterbury Ct 43055
Cardiff Rd 43055
Carlee Cir N & S 43055
Carlyle Ct 43055
Carolina Dr 43055
Carriage Ct 43055
Case Ave 43055
Catalina Dr 43055
Catt Rd NE 43055
N & S Cedar St 43055
Cedar Run Rd 43055
Cedarcrest Ave 43055
Centennial Rd 43055
N Center Dr 43055
S Central Ave 43055
N & S Chalfant Rd 43055
E & W Channel St 43055
Charles St 43055
Chatham Rd 43055
Chelsea Rd 43055
Cherry St 43055
Cherry Bend Dr 43055
Cherry Bottom Dr 43055
Cherry Grove Dr 43055
Cherry Valley Rd 43055
Cherrywood Dr 43055
Chester Dr 43055
Chestnut St 43055
Chestnut Hills Rd 43055
E Church St
1-71 43055
70-70 43058
72-168 43055
73-125 43055
W Church St 43055
Churchill Downs Rd 43055
Clarendon St 43055
Claygate Ln 43055
Clearview Dr 43055
Cleveland Ave 43055
Clinton St 43055
Cloe Creek Rd 43055
Clover Ct 43055
Cobble Stone Ct 43055
Coffman Rd 43055
Columbia St 43055
Commodore St 43055
Compton Rd 43055
Conley Ave 43055
Conn Dr 43055
Conrad St 43055
Constitution Ct & Dr 43055
Coolidge Ct 43055
Cooper Ave 43055
Cottage St 43055
Cottonwood Dr 43055
Counter Dr 43055
Country Club Dr 43055
Country Side Dr 43055
Courthouse Sq 43055
Courtney Dr 43055
Coventry Cir 43055
Craig Pkwy 43055
Cranwood Dr 43055
Crawford Ln & Rd 43055
Creeks Edge Dr 43055
Crestview Woods Ct & Dr 43055
Crilly St 43055
Crimson Dr 43055
Crocus Ct 43055
Crosley Dr 43055
Crystal Ct 43055
Cumberland St 43055
Curtis Ave 43055
Cypress Dr 43055
Cypress Bend Dr 43055
Dana Rd 43055
Daniel Ave 43055
Danielle Dr 43055
Darla Dr 43055
Darlene Dr 43055
Daugherty Cir 43055
Davis Ave 43055
Day Ave 43055
Dayton Rd NE 43055
Decrow Ave 43055
Deer Trce 43055
Deer Run Rd 43055
Deerfield Dr 43055
Delmar Ave 43055
Deo Dr 43055
Derby Downs Rd 43055
Dewey Ave 43055
Dickerson St 43055
Dietrich Ct & St 43055
Ditmore Stroll 43055
Dogwood Dr & Ln 43055
Donn Rd 43055
Donovan Dr 43055
Doral Dr 43055
Downey Ave 43055
Drexel Ave 43055
Dry Creek Rd 43055
Duane Dr 43055
Dumont St 43055
Dustin Ct 43055
Dutch Ln NE & NW 43055
Earl Dr 43055
Earlinglow Ct 43055
East St 43055
Eastern Ave 43055
Easy St 43055
Echo Ct & Dr 43055
Ecology Row 43055
Eddy St 43055
Eddyburg Rd NE 43055
Edgehill Rd 43055
Edgemont Rd 43055
Edgewood Dr 43055
Edison St 43055
Edith Dr 43055
Edwards St 43055
Eisenhower Ct 43055
El Rancho Dr NE 43055
Elcar Ave 43055
Eleanor Pkwy 43055
Elizabeth St 43055
Ellis Dr 43055
Elm Dr 43055
Elma Dr 43055
Elmod Ave 43055
Elmwood Ave 43055
Emerald Ct 43055
Emerson St 43055
Empire Dr 43055
English Ave 43055
Eric Dr 43055
Erin Ln 43055
Essex St 43055
Essex Downs Rd 43055
Estates Dr 43055
Euclid Ave 43055
Eutreva Dr 43055
Evans Blvd & St 43055
Evansdale Ave 43055
Evanwood Dr NE 43055
Everett Ave 43055
Evergreen St 43055
Executive Ct & Dr E, N, S & W 43055
Fairbanks Ave 43055
Fairfield Ave & Dr 43055
Fairlawn Ave 43055
Fairmont Ave 43055
Fallsburg Rd NE 43055
Faye Dr 43055
Fern St 43055
Fielde Dr 43055
Flamingo Dr 43055
Fleek Ave 43055
Fleming Dr 43055
Florence St 43055
Flory Ave 43055
Flowers Dr 43055
Floyd Boyer Rd 43055
Forest Cir 43055
Forry St 43055
Fox Chase Dr 43055
Fox Grove Ct 43055
Fox Run Cir 43055
Franklin Ave 43055
Frasure Dr 43055
N Front St 43055
N & S Fulton Ave 43055
Gainor Ave 43055
Garden Ave 43055
Garfield Ave 43055
Garrett Pkwy 43055
Garrick St 43055
Gary Ct 43055
Gay St 43055
Gilbert St 43055
Gladys Ave 43055
Glenbrook Dr 43055
Gleneagles Dr 43055
Glenmore Ave 43055
Glenn St 43055
Glenridge Dr 43055
Glyn Dennis Dr 43055
Glyn Evans Ct 43055
Glyn Jones Ct 43055
Glyn Morgan Ct 43055
Glyn Owen Ct 43055
Golden Dr 43055
Goosepond Rd 43055
Grafton Rd 43055
Grandview Rd 43055
Grant St 43055
Granville Rd & St 43055
Green Meadow Dr 43055
Green Wave Dr 43055
Greenfield Ave 43055
Greenland Cir & Dr 43055
Greenwood Loop 43055
Greer Dr E & W 43055
Gregory Dr 43055
Grove St 43055
Grumms Ln NE 43055
Guardian Ct 43055
Guckert Ave 43055
Gunnison St 43055
Hainshill Dr 43055
Hainsview Dr 43055
Hall Ave 43055
Hamilton Ave 43055
Hammond Ct 43055
Hampton Rd S 43055
Hancock St 43055
Hantines Rd 43055
Harchedan Rd 43055
Harding Ct 43055
Harlech Dr 43055
Harris Ave 43055
E & W Harrison St 43055
Hatfield Ln 43055
Haver Hill Rd 43055
Hawkes Ave 43055
Hawthorne Ln 43055
Hazel Bark Dr 43055
Hazel Dell Rd 43055
N & S Hazelwood Ave 43055
N & S Heather Dr 43055
Heide Ct 43055
Heidi Way 43055
Hemlock Pl 43055
Henderson Ave 43055
Hickman Rd NE 43055
High St 43055
Highbanks Valley Ct & Dr 43055
Highland Blvd 43055
Highpoint Dr 43055
Hill St 43055
Hillandale Dr 43055
Hillcrest St 43055
Hills Rd 43055
Hillside Dr 43055
Hilltop Dr NE 43055
Hillview Cir E & W 43055
Hilly Rd 43055
Hofacker Hill Rd 43055
Hollander St 43055
Hollar Ln 43055
E & W Holliday St 43055
Homewood Ave 43055
Hoover Rd & St NE 43055
Horns Hill Rd 43055
Horseshoe Dr 43055
Houdeshell Rd 43055
Howell Ct & Dr 43055
Hudson Ave 43055
Hull St 43055
Hunt St 43055
Hunter St 43055
S & W Hunters Ct & Dr 43055
Idaho Ave 43055
Idlewilde Ave 43055
Independence Ct & Dr 43055
Indian Ln 43055
Indiana St 43055
Iron Ave 43055
Irwin Ave 43055
Isabel Ave 43055
Isabelle Rd 43055
Ivy St 43055
Jackson Blvd 43055
James Rd & St 43055
Jamestown Ct 43055
Jason Ct 43055
Jean Ct 43055
Jefferson Rd & St 43055
Jenna Dr 43055
Jeremy Ct 43055
Jin Joe Dr NE 43055
Jobes Rd NE 43055
John St 43055
Johnson Ave 43055
Jonathan Ln 43055
Jones Ave & St 43055
Judith Ln 43055
Jutlew Rd 43055
Karen Pkwy 43055
Keller Ln 43055
Kelley Ln 43055
Kemp St 43055
Ken Mar Ln 43055
Kenarbre Dr 43055
Kenbrook Ave 43055
Kennedy St 43055
Kenwell Dr 43055
Keny Park Ct 43055
Kibler Ave 43055
Kiley Xing 43055
Kim Ave 43055
King Ave, Ct & Rd 43055
Kingsbury Ct 43055
Knollwood Dr 43055
Kozy Ave 43055
Krebs Ct & Dr 43055
Kreider Blvd 43055
Kreig St 43055
Kropf Ave 43055
Lafayette Rd 43055
Laird Way 43055
N Lake Dr 43055
Lake Drive Rd 43056
Lakeview Dr 43055
Lambs Ln 43055
Lansbury Ct 43055
Larkspur Dr 43055
Lateglow Ct 43055
Laverne Dr 43055
Lawnview Ave 43055
Lawrence St 43055
Lee Ave 43055
Lemae Ave 43055
Leonard Ave 43055
Leslie Dr 43055
Lewie Dr 43055
Lewis Ln 43055
Lexington Ave 43055
Liberty Ave 43055
Licking Springs Rd 43055
Licking Valley Rd 43055
Lillian Ct 43055
Lincoln Dr 43055
Linden Ave 43055
Linwood Ave 43055
Lisa Cir 43055
Little Fawn Dr 43055
Livingston Rd NE 43055
E & W Locust St 43055
Log Pond Dr 43055
Logan Ave 43055
London Hollow Rd NE 43055
Londondale Pkwy 43055
Londonderry Ln 43055
Loper Rd NE 43055
Lorimer Dr 43055
Lorraine Ave NE 43055
Lundys Ln 43055
Lynn St 43055
E & W Madison Ave & Dr 43055
Magnolia Ave 43055
Maholm St 43055
E, N, S & W Main Pkwy & St 43055
Mallard Cir & Dr 43055
Manning St 43055
Manor Dr 43055
Maple Ave & Ln NE 43055
Maple Grove Ave 43055
Maplewood Rd 43055
Margaret St 43055
Margery Dr 43055
Marion Ct & Rd 43055
Marion Manor Woods 43055
Mark Ave, Cir & Dr 43055
E & W Market St 43055
Marlyn Dr 43055
Marne Dr & Rd 43055
Martinsburg Rd 43055
Mary Ann Furnace Rd 43055
Mary Jean Dr NE 43055
Maxola Ave 43055
Mccown Rd 43055
Mcintosh Dr 43055
Mckinley Ave 43055

Mckinney Xing 43055
Mcmillen Dr 43055
Meadow Ct, Dr & Ln ... 43055
Meadowbrook Dr 43055
Meadowland Dr 43055
Meggin Melanne Ln 43055
Melanie Ct 43055
Mellars Ln 43055
Merchant St 43055
Merry Wood Dr 43055
Messimer Dr 43055
Meyers Dr 43055
Midway Dr 43055
Mikes Ln 43055
Mill St 43055
Miller Ave & St 43055
Millie Ln 43055
Milner Rd 43055
Misty Glenn Dr 43055
Modern Way 43055
Mohawk St 43055
Moloviste Ave 43055
Monroe Ave & St 43055
Montgomery Ave, Pl & Rd 43055
Morgan Ave & Run 43055
Morgan Bryan Dr 43055
N & S Morris St 43055
Moull St 43055
Mound Ct & St 43055
Moundbuilders Rd 43055
Moundview Ave 43055
Mount Vernon Rd 43055
Mulberry St 43055
Myrtle Ave 43055
Nancy Ln 43055
Nathaniel Ave 43055
E & W National Dr 43055
Naughtingham Rd 43055
Neal Ave 43055
Neibarger Ln 43055
Neptune St 43055
New Haven Ave & Ct .. 43055
New Home Dr 43055
Newton Ave & Rd 43055
Normandy Ct & Dr 43055
E & W North Ave & St NE & NW 43055
Northcutt Dr 43055
Northern Songs Ln 43055
Northpointe Ln 43055
Northtowne Ct 43055
Norton Ave 43055
E & W Oak St 43055
Oakland Blvd 43055
Oakwood Ave 43055
Obannon Ave 43055
Ohio St 43055
Olde Creek Dr 43055
Olympic Ct 43055
Opossum Hollow Rd 43055
Orchard St 43055
Oregon Ave 43055
Osborn Rd 43055
Oxford Downs Rd 43055
Painter Run Rd 43055
Parana Dr 43055
N & S Park Ave & Pl ... 43055
Park Ridge Ct & Ln 43055
Park Trails Ct & Dr 43055
Parker Ave & Dr 43055
Parkview Rd 43055
Parkway Dr 43055
Parsons Ln 43055
Patrick Dr E 43055
Patton Rd & St 43055
Paul Ave 43055
Paul Revere Dr 43055
Pearl St 43055
Pembroke Ct & Rd 43055
Penn Rd 43055
Penney Ave 43055
Pershing Ave 43055
Persimmon Dr 43055
Pewter Dr 43055
Pheasant Run Dr 43055
Philmont Ave 43055
Pierce Ave 43055
Pierson Blvd & Dr 43055
Pimlico Ave 43055
N & S Pine St 43055
Pine Ridge Rd 43055
Pinehurst Ct 43055
Pineview Trl 43055
Pinewood Trl 43055
Pleasant St 43055
Pleasant Crest Ct 43055
Pleasant Hill Rd 43055
Pleasant Valley Dr 43055
Plymouth Pl 43055
Pond Dr 43055
Poole Dr 43055
W Poplar Ave 43055
Porter Rd NE 43055
E & W Postal Ave 43055
Pound St 43055
Preston Pl & Rd 43055
Price Rd NE 43055
Priest Ln 43055
Prior Ave 43055
Prospect St 43055
Purity Rd NE 43055
Quail Creek Dr 43055
E & W Quail Run Ct & Dr 43055
Queens Dr N & S 43055
N & S Quentin Rd 43055
Race St 43055
W Railroad St 43055
Rainrock Rd 43055
Ramona Ave 43055
Randy Dr 43055
Ravine Bluff Dr 43055
Red Fox Ct 43055
Reddington Rd S 43055
Reddington Village Ln .. 43055
Reform Rd 43055
Regal Ave 43055
Renae Dr 43055
Residence Dr 43055
Resonant Dr 43055
Reverie Pl 43055
Reynolds Rd 43055
Rice St 43055
Richards Rd 43055
Ridge Ave 43055
Ridgefield Rd 43055
Ridgelawn Ave 43055
Ridgepoint Dr 43055
Riggs Rd 43055
Riley Rd & St NE 43055
Ritz Ave 43055
River Rd 43055
River Bend Ct 43055
Riverdale Rd 43055
Riverside Dr 43055
Riverview Dr 43055
Robbins Dr 43055
Roberts Ave 43055
Robin Ln 43055
Robinhood Dr 43055
Robinson Dr 43055
Rock Haven Rd 43055
Rocky Fork Dr & Rd ... 43055
Rocky Ridge Rd 43055
Roe Ave 43055
Roger Rd NE 43055
Roosevelt Ct 43055
Rose Ave 43055
Rosebud Ave 43055
Rosehill Ave 43055
Rugg Ave 43055
Ruggland Ter 43055
Russell Ave 43055
Russett Ln 43055
Sabrecutt Dr 43055
E & W Saint Clair St ... 43055
Saint Joseph Rd 43055
Sandalwood Dr 43055
Santa Anita Ave 43055
Saratoga Ave 43055
Saxony Dr 43055
Scenic Dr 43055
Schaffner Dr 43055
Scheffler St 43055
Schuler St 43055
Scioto Way 43055
Selby St 43055
Seneca Dr 43055
Senior Dr E & W 43055
Seroco Ave 43055
Seven Hills Rd 43055
Shalimar Dr 43055
Shamps Ct 43055
Shamrock Ln 43055
Sharon Cir 43055
Sharon Glyn Dr 43055
Sharon Valley Rd NE ... 43055
Sharon View Dr 43055
Shaw Ct & Dr 43055
Shawnee St 43055
Shelbourne Pl 43055
Sherman Ave 43055
Sherwick Rd 43055
Sherwood Dr E 43055
Sherwood Downs Rd E 43055
Sheryl Lynn Dr 43055
Shide Ave 43055
E & W Shields St 43055
Shoreham Dr 43055
Showman St 43055
Shultz Walk 43055
Simms St 43055
Sinalda Ave 43055
Sisal St 43055
Skyline Dr 43055
Smith Chapel Rd 43055
Smithfield Dr 43055
Smoketown Rd 43055
Snowdon Dr 43055
Snyder Rd 43055
Soliday Rd NE 43055
Southern Ct 43055
Speedway Dr 43055
Spencer St 43055
Sportsman Club Rd 43055
Spring Dr & St NE 43055
Spring Valley Dr 43055
Stanberry St 43055
Stanhope Dr 43055
Stanwick Ct 43055
Star Ave 43055
Stare Rd 43055
State St 43055
Steele Ave 43055
E & W Stevens St 43055
Stewart Rd & St 43055
Stone House Ct, Pl & Way 43055
Stone Ridge Way 43055
Stonewall Dr 43055
Stonington Cir & Pl ... 43055
Storybook Ln 43055
Stratford Woods Dr 43055
Summer St 43055
Summit St 43055
Sunny Ln 43055
Sunnyside Dr 43055
Sunrise Dr 43055
Sunset Dr NE 43055
Surrey Dr 43055
Surrey Downs Rd 43055
Sutton Pl 43055
Swans Rd NE 43055
Swansea Rd 43055
Swern Ln 43055
Swisher Rd 43055
Taft Ave 43055
Tall Oaks Dr 43055
Tamarack Rd 43055
Tammy Cir 43055
Target St 43055
Taylor Ave & Ln 43055
Techniglas Rd NE 43055
N & S Terrace Ave & Ct 43055
Terry Dr 43055
Thomas Ave 43055
Tigre Dr 43055
Timber Hearth Ct 43055
Timberland View Dr 43055
Tinon Ln 43055
Toboso Rd 43055
Tower Ct 43055
Towne Krier Ct 43055
Trail Ct 43055
Trask Ave 43055
Trentwood Dr 43055
Troy Ct 43055
Truman Ct 43055
Tupelo Ln 43055
E & W Turkey Run Dr .. 43055
Turnberry Ct 43055
Turner Rd 43055
Tuscarawas St 43055
Twin Pines Ct & Trl 43055
Tyler Ln 43055
Union St 43055
University Dr 43055
Upland View Ct 43055
Upson Downs Rd 43055
S Utah Ave 43055
Valentina Ln 43055
Valley Blvd, Dr & St W & NE 43055
Valley View Dr NE 43055
Van Tassell Ave 43055
Van Voorhis St 43055
Velma Ave & Ct 43055
N Vernon Ave 43055
Vesper Dr 43055
E, N & W Village Dr & Pkwy 43055
Village Green Ct 43055
Vine St 43055
Violet Ct 43055
Vista Ct 43055
Vogel St 43055
Waldo St 43055
Walhalla Rd 43055
Walker St 43055
Wallace Pl & St 43055
E & W Walnut Ln & St 43055
Washington St 43055
Water St 43055
Waterworks Rd 43055
Wayne Ave & Dr 43055
Weaver Blvd 43055
S Webb St 43055
Wehrle Ave 43055
Weiant Ave 43055
Welcome Rd 43055
Wellington Ave 43055
Wells Ave 43055
Welsh Hills Rd 43055
Welsh View Dr 43055
Wesley Ave 43055
Western Ave 43055
Westgate Ave & Dr 43055
N & S Westmoor Ave .. 43055
Weston 43055
Westwood Dr 43055
Whispering Way 43055
N & S Wild Turkey Dr .. 43055
Wildflower Dr 43055
Wilkin St 43055
Wilkins Run Rd NE 43055
N & S Williams St 43055
Willowood Rd 43055
Willrich Dr 43055
Wilmington Ct 43055
Wilson St 43055
Wilwood Ave 43055
Wince Rd 43055
N Wing St 43055
Wintermute Ave 43055
Wolfe Den Rd 43055
Wolford Rd 43055
Woodlawn Ave 43055
Woodridge Dr 43055
Woods Ave 43055
Woods Run Dr 43055
Woodswalk Dr 43055
Wrens Cross Ln 43055
Wright Dr & St 43055
Wynnewood Dr 43055
Wyoming St 43055
Yorkshire Dr 43055
Young Ave 43055
Zelora Ave 43055

NUMBERED STREETS

All Street Addresses 43055

OREGON OH

POST OFFICE BOXES MAIN OFFICE STATIONS AND BRANCHES

Box No.s
All PO Boxes 43616

NAMED STREETS

All Street Addresses 43616

PERRYSBURG OH

General Delivery 43551

POST OFFICE BOXES MAIN OFFICE STATIONS AND BRANCHES

Box No.s
All PO Boxes 43552

NAMED STREETS

A St 43551
Abbey Rd 43551
Adams Ct 43551
Amberwood Dr 43551
Apex Ln 43551
Appaloosa Ct 43551
Apple Creek Dr 43551
Applewood Ct & Dr 43551
Arbor Ct 43551
Arrow Ln 43551
Arrowhead Dr 43551
Ashbury Dr 43551
Ashington Dr 43551
Ashwood Ct 43551
Aspen Dr 43551
Atterbury Ln 43551
Ault Rd 43551
Austin Ct 43551
Avenue Rd 43551
Ayers Rd 43551
B St 43551
Baker Dr 43551
Ballantree Ct 43551
Ballybay Ct 43551
Barlow Xing 43551
Basswood Dr 43551
Bates Rd 43551
Bay Trace Dr 43551
Bayer Rd 43551
Belmont Ct 43551
Belmont Farm Rd 43551
Belmont Lake Rd 43551
Belmont Meadows Ln .. 43551
Bennett Ranch Blvd ... 43551
Berkshire Dr 43551
Beverly Ct 43551
Bexford Dr 43551
Bexley Dr 43551
Bexton Dr 43551
Birch Dr 43551
Birchcrest Dr 43551
Birchdale Rd 43551
Bishopswood Ln 43551
Black Oak Ct 43551
Blackhorse Ct 43551
Blue Harbor Ct 43551
Blue Jacket Rd 43551
Boston Bay Rd 43551
Bostwick Rd 43551
E & W Boundary St 43551
Bradner Rd 43551
N & S Bramblewood Rd 43551
Brentfield Rd 43551
Briarwood Cir 43551
Bridgeton Ln 43551
Bridgeview Dr 43551
Bridgewood St 43551
Brigham Dr 43551
Brittany Rd 43551
Broad St 43551
Broadmoor Rd 43551
Broadstone Rd 43551
E Broadway Rd 43551
Brockway Dr 43551
Brookfield Ln 43551
Brookhaven Blvd 43551
Brookside Dr 43551
Brookview Ct 43551
Brookwoode Rd 43551
Buck Rd 43551
Burlingwood Dr 43551
C St 43551
Callander Ct 43551
Candyce Ct 43551
Cape Cod Ln 43551
Cardiff Rd 43551
Carnoustie Ct & Rd 43551
Carol Ln 43551
Carolin Ct 43551
Carolina Dr 43551
Carrington Blvd 43551
Carronade Dr 43551
Castlebar Dr 43551
Catawba Dr 43551
Cedar Ct 43551
Cedar Park Blvd 43551
Cedar Ridge Ct 43551
Cedarwood Ln 43551
Champlin Dr 43551
Chapel Creek Dr 43551
Chapelgate Ct 43551
Chappel Dr 43551
Charlemont Rd 43551
Chatham Way 43551
Cherbourg Ln 43551
Cherry St 43551
Chesterton Dr 43551
Chippewa Ln 43551
Chrysler Dr 43551
Civic Dr 43551
Cliffwood Rd 43551
Clover Ln 43551
Cobbler Ct 43551
Coe Ct 43551
Colony Ct 43551
Commerce Dr 43551
Commodore Way 43551
Connor Lake Cir 43551
Coopers Hawk Rd 43551
Corner Brook Ct 43551
Coventry Ct 43551
Craig Dr 43551
Cranden Ct & Dr 43551
Creekside Ct 43551
Cricket Ln 43551
Cross Ridge Rd & Way 43551
Crossfields Rd 43551
D St 43551
Darcey Ct 43551
Deer Run 43551
Deerwood Ct 43551
Deimling Rd 43551
Delaware Dr 43551
Desmond Pl 43551
Dexter Falls Rd 43551
Dixie Hwy 43551
Dogwood Dr & Ln 43551
Doncogan Ct 43551
Douglas Rd 43551
Dowling Rd 43551
Dr Mcauleys Ct 43551
Dunbridge Rd 43551
Durham Cir & Dr 43551
Duxbury Ct & Ln 43551
E St 43551
Eaglecrest Rd 43551
Eastbrook Dr 43551
Eckel Rd 43551
Eckel Junction Rd 43551
Edgewater Dr 43551
Edgewood Dr 43551
Edinborough Cir 43551
Elizabeth Dr 43551
Elk Ct 43551
Ella St 43551
Elm St 43551
Emerald Lakes Dr 43551
Evergreen Ct 43551
Exeter Rd 43551
F St 43551
Fallen Oak Cir 43551
Falling Waters Ln 43551
Farewell Dr 43551
Fawn Cir 43551
Findlay St 43551
Flagship Dr 43551
Ford Rd 43551
Fort Meigs Blvd, Ct & Rd 43551
Fox Run 43551
Fox Cove Dr 43551
Fox Creek Dr 43551
Fox Hunt Dr 43551
Fox View Ct 43551
Foxhill Ln & Rd 43551
Foxton Ct 43551
Fremont Pike 43551
E & W Front St 43551
Garfield Dr 43551
Genoa Rd 43551
Georgia Rd 43551
Gerdes Rd 43551
Glades Dr 43551
Glenchester Rd 43551
Gleneagles Rd 43551
Glenwood Rd 43551
Gloria St 43551
Goldenrod Ln 43551
Golf Creek Ln 43551
Grand Bank Way 43551
Grassy Creek Dr 43551
Green Meadows Dr 43551
Green Ville Dr 43551
Gregory Dr 43551
Grogan Dr 43551
H St 43551
Hamilton Dr 43551
Hanley Rd 43551
Harold St 43551
Harrison Rd 43551
Haskins Rd 43551
Hawksbury Ln 43551
Hazel Rd 43551
Heatherford Dr 43551
Heathermoor Ln 43551
Heilman Ave 43551
Helen Dr 43551
Hickory St 43551
Hickory Hill Dr 43551
Hickson Dr 43551
Hidden Ridge Dr 43551
Highview Ln 43551
Holbrook Ct 43551
Holiday Ln 43551
Hollenbeck Dr 43551
Hollister Ln 43551
Holly Ln 43551
Homestead Dr 43551
Horseshoe Bend Dr 43551

Hufford Rd 43551
Hull Prairie Rd 43551
Hulls Trace Dr 43551
Hunters Run 43551
Huron Ct 43551
Indian Creek Dr 43551
Indian Wells Ln 43551
E & W Indiana Ave 43551
Iron Trail Rd 43551
J St 43551
Jacqueline Pl 43551
Jefferson St 43551
John F Mccarthy Way 43551
Kenhurst Ln 43551
Kensington Ln 43551
Kenton Trl 43551
Kettle Run Ct 43551
Kingsborough Ct 43551
Kingsgate Ct 43551
Kingsview St 43551
Kirkshire Dr 43551
Knollwood Dr 43551
E & W Lake Ct, Dr & Rd 43551
Lake Meadows Dr 43551
Lake Winds Dr 43551
S Lakes Dr 43551
Lakevue Dr 43551
Latcha Rd 43551
Laurel Ln 43551
Lawrence Dr 43551
Lem Ct 43551
Lemoyne Rd 43551
Leroy St 43551
Levis Commons Blvd 43551
Lexington Dr 43551
Libbey Rd 43551
Lighthouse Dr & Way 43551
Lime City Rd 43551
Limerick Blvd 43551
Lincoln Blvd 43551
Linden Ln 43551
Lindsay Dr 43551
Lisa Ln 43551
Little Creek Dr 43551
Lober Dr 43551
Locust St 43551
Logan Ln 43551
Lones Dr 43551
Loomis Dr 43551
Louisiana Ave
100-1206 43551
1205-1205 43552
1208-1498 43551
1301-1499 43551
Lowry Dr 43551
Loyer Ln 43551
Luckey Rd 43551
Lunitas Ln 43551
M St 43551
Mallard Rd 43551
Mandell Rd 43551
Manor Dr 43551
Maple St 43551
Margaret Pl 43551
Marie Pl 43551
Mark Ln 43551
Marsh Hawk Rd 43551
Mary Lou Ct 43551
Maumee Western Reserve Rd 43551
Maurice Pl 43551
Mccallister Dr 43551
Mccarty Dr 43551
Mccutcheonville Rd 43551
Mckinley Dr 43551
Meadowbrook Dr 43551
Meadowpond Dr 43551
Meadowwood Dr 43551
Miami Rd 43551
Miamis Ln 43551
Michael Owens Way 43551
Mill Rd 43551
Millcroft Rd 43551
Miller Rd 43551
Mingo Dr 43551
Mission Hill Dr 43551
Mohawk Dr 43551
Monarch Ct 43551
Morgan Pl 43551
Morningside Dr 43551
Moser Ln 43551
Mulberry St 43551
N St 43551
Nawash Dr 43551
Neiderhouse Rd 43551
New England Ln 43551
Niagara Ln 43551
Nora Dr 43551
Normandy Rd S & W 43551
O St 43551
Oak St 43551
Oak Haven Ct 43551
Oak Knoll Dr 43551
Oak Meadow Dr E & W 43551
Oakmead Dr 43551
Oakmont Dr 43551
Ogill Dr 43551
Old Trail Rd 43551
Olde Orchard Dr 43551
Olde Trail Dr 43551
Orchard St 43551
Oregon Rd 43551
Osage Ct 43551
Osprey Ct 43551
Ottawa Ln 43551
Ottekee Dr 43551
Otusso Dr 43551
Ovitt Rd 43551
Oxborough Dr 43551
P St 43551
Pargillis Rd 43551
Parkview Dr 43551
Parliament Pl 43551
Partridge Ln 43551
Pauly Dr 43551
Pearkenn Rd 43551
Pemberville Rd 43551
Pepperwood Ct 43551
Perry Dr 43551
Pheasant Dr 43551
Pin Oak Ct 43551
Pine St 43551
Pinewood Ct 43551
Plum St 43551
Ponderosa Rd 43551
Portside Cir 43551
Prairie Crossing Ln 43551
Prairie Farms Rd 43551
Prairie Lake Dr 43551
Prairie Rose Dr 43551
Preston Pkwy W 43551
Prestonwood Rd 43551
Professional Dr 43551
Progress Dr 43551
Quail Rd 43551
Queensland Blvd 43551
Ramblehurst Dr 43551
Rapids Rd 43551
Recker Rd 43551
N & S Redhawk Dr 43551
Reitz Rd 43551
Reserve Dr 43551
Rice St 43551
N & S Ridge Dr 43551
Ridge Cross Rd 43551
Ridge Lake Ct 43551
Ridgewood Cir 43551
Riva Ridge Ct 43551
E & W River Rd 43551
River Oaks Dr 43551
River Ridge Way 43551
River View Pl 43551
Riverbend Ct E & W 43551
Rivercrest Dr 43551
Riverford Dr 43551
Rivers Edge Dr 43551
Riverview Ct 43551
Riverwood Ct 43551
Roachton Rd 43551
Roberts Ave 43551
Rockledge Cir & Dr 43551
Rockthorn Ct 43551
Rocky Rd 43551
Rocky Harbour Dr 43551
Roosevelt Blvd 43551
Running Brook Dr 43551
Rutledge Ct 43551
Saddle Horn Dr 43551
Saddlebrook Blvd & Ct 43551
Sagebrush Ct 43551
Saint Andrews Rd 43551
Saint Martins Dr 43551
Sandalwood Rd E & W 43551
Sandstone Dr 43551
Sandusky Pl & St 43551
Sandy Glen Dr 43551
Scarlet Oak Dr 43551
Schaller Dr 43551
Scheider Rd 43551
Schroeder Rd 43551
Secor Woods Ln 43551
Sedgefield Rd 43551
Seminary Rd 43551
Seneca Creek Ct 43551
Sergen Rd 43551
N & S Shannon Hills Dr 43551
Shawnee Dr 43551
Shearwood Dr 43551
Sheffield Rd 43551
Shelbourne Rd 43551
Sheringham Rd 43551
Sherman Pl 43551
Silver Creek Dr 43551
Silver Maple Dr 43551
Simmons Rd 43551
Somerset Rd 43551
E & W South Boundary St 43551
Southpoint Rd 43551
Southwood Dr 43551
Spring Mill Ln 43551
Spring Trace Dr 43551
Stable Creek Dr 43551
Starbright Blvd 43551
Starcrest Rd 43551
Stargate Rd 43551
Starlawn Rd 43551
Starlight Rd 43551
Starridge Ct 43551
Steeple Chase Ln 43551
Sterlingwood Ln 43551
Stillwater Dr 43551
Stirling Ct 43551
Stone Creek Ct 43551
Stonecroft Dr 43551
Stonefence Dr 43551
Stonehaven Dr 43551
Stony Ridge Rd 43551
Strail Rd 43551
Stratford Ln 43551
Streamview Dr 43551
Sun Air Blvd 43551
Sun Trace Dr 43551
Sunflower Ct 43551
Sussex Rd 43551
Sutton Pl 43551
Swift Current Ct 43551
Sycamore Ln 43551
Tecumseh Ct 43551
Thistledown Ln 43551
Thompson Rd 43551
Tilayne Dr 43551
Timber Ridge Ct 43551
Timberbrook Ct 43551
Timbercreek Ct 43551
Tonbridge Ct 43551
Tracy Rd 43551
Tracy Creek Dr 43551
Trails End Dr 43551
Tricia Ct 43551
Trinity Ct 43551
Triumph Ln 43551
Truman Rd 43551
Turnbridge Dr 43551
Turnbury Ln 43551
Turtle Creek Dr 43551
Twin Lakes Rd 43551
Twinbrook Dr 43551
Twining Ct 43551
Valley Ln 43551
Valley Bend Ct 43551
Valley Bluff Dr 43551
Valleybrook Blvd 43551
Village Square Dr 43551
Wagoner Dr 43551
Walbridge Rd 43551
Walnut St 43551
Warns Dr 43551
Washington St 43551
Water St 43551
Waterbury Cir 43551
Waterford Dr 43551
Watermill Ln 43551
Waters Edge Dr 43551
Waterstone Ln 43551
Waterview Dr 43551
Welling Rd 43551
Wentworth Ct 43551
Westbrook Dr 43551
Wethersfield Rd 43551
E & W Wexford Dr 43551
Whispering Way 43551
White Rd 43551
White Oak Dr 43551
Whitehall Dr 43551
Whitehorse Ct 43551
Whiteside Dr 43551
Whitewater Dr 43551
N & S Wilkinson Way 43551
William Dr 43551
Williams Rd 43551
Willow Ln 43551
Willowbend Rd 43551
Wilson St 43551
Windford Dr 43551
Winding Brook Rd 43551
Winding River Ct 43551
Winds Dr 43551
Windsor Ct 43551
Windy Trace Dr 43551
E & S Winners Cir 43551
Wolf Creek Ct 43551
Wood Creek Ct & Rd 43551
Wood Sorrel Ln 43551
Woodland Ave & Pl 43551
Woodleigh Ct 43551
Woodmont Dr & Way 43551
Woods Edge Rd 43551
Woods Hole Rd 43551
Woodstream Rd 43551
Woodview Dr 43551
Wyandot Pl 43551
Zoar Dr 43551

NUMBERED STREETS

All Street Addresses 43551

SANDUSKY OH

General Delivery 44870

POST OFFICE BOXES MAIN OFFICE STATIONS AND BRANCHES

Box No.s
All PO Boxes 44871

NAMED STREETS

A St 44870
E & W Adams St 44870
Adrian Cir 44870
Alex Ct 44870
Alexandrias Dr 44870
E & W Algonquin Trl 44870
Alpine Dr 44870
Anderson St 44870
Angels Way 44870
Angels Pointe Dr 44870
Anita Dr 44870
Ann Dr 44870
Arthur St 44870
Ashburn Dr 44870
Aspen Run Rd 44870
Atlantic Ave 44870
Autumn Ridge Ln 44870
Avondale St 44870
Baltimore St 44870
Bardshar Rd 44870
Barker St 44870
Barrett Rd 44870
Bauer Ave 44870
Bay Breeze Dr 44870
Bay Shore Dr & Est 44870
Bayshore Ct & Rd 44870
E, W & N Bayview Dr & Ln 44870
Beatty Ave & Ln 44870
Bell Ave & St 44870
Bellevue Ave 44870
Bennett Ave 44870
E Beverly Dr 44870
Bimini Dr 44870
E & W Birchwood Ct & Dr 44870
E & W Boalt St 44870
Boardwalk Blvd 44870
E & W Bogart Rd 44870
Bone Creek Dr 44870
Boston Rd 44870
Botay Rd 44870
Brandon Blvd 44870
Broadway St 44870
Brown St 44870
Buchanan St 44870
Buckeye Ln 44870
Buckingham St 44870
Butler St 44870
C St 44870
Cable St 44870
Caldwell St
2000-2221 44870
2220-2220 44871
2222-2398 44870
2223-2399 44870
Cambridge Cir 44870
Camp St 44870
Campbell St 44870
Carbon Ave 44870
Carly Ln 44870
Carr St 44870
Carroll Ave 44870
Castalia Ave 44870
Catalina Dr 44870
E & W Cayuga Trl 44870
Cedar Brook Ln 44870
Cedar Point Dr & Rd 44870
E & W Cedarwood Dr 44870
Cement Ave 44870
Center St 44870
Central Ave & St 44870
Chalet Dr 44870
E & W Cherokee Trl 44870
Chickasaw Trl 44870
Church St 44870
Clark Rd 44870
Clay St 44870
Cleveland Rd 44870
Clinton St 44870
Clyde Ave 44870
Cold Creek Blvd 44870
Columbus Ave 44870
Columbus Crystal Rock Ave 44870
Comanche Trl 44870
Conner Way 44870
Cove Dr & St 44870
Cove Park Blvd 44870
W Cowdery St 44870
Creekside Cir 44870
Crossings Rd 44870
Crosstree Ln 44870
Crystal Rock Ave 44870
Curran St 44870
Dallas Ave 44870
Decatur St 44870
Deerpath Dr 44870
E & W Delaware Trl 44870
Denver Ave 44870
N Depot St 44870
Dewey St 44870
Dewitt Ave 44870
Didion Dr 44870
Dietrick St 44870
Dill Ave 44870
Division St 44870
Dixie Ave 44870
Dixon Dr 44870
Doerzbach Ave 44870
Donair Dr 44870
Dor Dr 44870
Dorn Dr 44870
Douglas Dr 44870
Dutch Ln 44870
E St 44870
Eagles Nest Cir 44870
Eastwood Dr 44870
Edgewater Ave 44870
Electric Ave 44870
Elm St 44870
Erie Blvd & St 44870
F St 44870
Fairmont Ln 44870
Fairview Ave 44870
Fairway Ln 44870
Fallen Timber Dr 44870
E & W Farwell St 44870
Ferndale Dr 44870
Ferry Ln 44870
Filmore St 44870
Finch St 44870
Fisher Ave 44870
E & W Follett St 44870
Force Ave 44870
E, N, S & W Forest Dr 44870
Fox Rd & St 44870
Fox Run Trl 44870
Foxborough Cir 44870
Franklin St 44870
Frantz St 44870
Fremont Ave 44870
Fulton St 44870
Fun Dr 44870
Gabriels Pl 44870
Galloway Rd 44870
Garfield Ave 44870
Gartland Ave 44870
General Dr 44870
George St 44870
Gilcher Ct 44870
Gildona Dr 44870
Ging St 44870
Grand Pass 44870
Grant Ave & St 44870
Greenbrier Ln 44870
Greenfield Dr 44870
Greentree Ln 44870
Hancock St 44870
Harbor Blvd 44870
Harbour Pkwy 44870
Harbourside Dr 44870
Harris Rd 44870
Harrison St 44870
Hartford Ave 44870
Hasting Dr 44870
Hayes Ave 44870
Helina Dr 44870
Hendry St 44870
Heritage Dr 44870
Heron Creek Dr 44870
Heywood Rd 44870
High St 44870
Highland Dr 44870
Hinde Ave 44870
Hoffman Dr 44870
Hollyrood Rd 44870
Homegardner Rd 44870
Homestead St 44870
Horseshoe Ave 44870
Howard Dr 44870
Hull Rd 44870
Hunters Way 44870
Huntfield Dr 44870
Huntington Ave & Pl 44870
Huron Ave & St 44870
Indiana Ave 44870
Industrial Pkwy 44870
E & W Iroquois Trl 44870
Jackson Ext & St 44870
Jay St 44870
Jeanette Ct & Dr 44870
E & W Jefferson St 44870
John St 44870
Johnson St 44870
Judy Ln 44870
Julianne Cir & Dr 44870
Kalahari Dr 44870
Karl Ann Dr 44870
Kay Cir 44870
Kelley Ln 44870
Kevin Dr 44870
King St 44870
Kingsley Cir E 44870
Kirkwood Ter 44870
Knupke St 44870
Lake Ct & St 44870
S Lake Wilmer Dr 44870
Lakecrest Pkwy 44870
Lakeland Dr 44870
Lakeside Park 44870
Landsrush St 44870
Lane St 44870
Lane C 44870
Lane D 44870
Langston Pl 44870
E, N, S & W Larchmont Dr 44870
Lasalle St 44870
Laurel Ln 44870
Lauren Ct 44870
Lawrence St 44870
Lima Sandusky Rd 44870
Lin Cir 44870
Lincoln St 44870
Linden Ct 44870
Linden Way Dr 44870
Lindsley St 44870
Linwood Ave 44870
Lisbon Cir 44870
Loch Lomond Ln 44870
Lockwood Ave 44870
Lurie Ln 44870
Lynn Dr 44870
E & W Madison St 44870
Mall Dr N 44870
Maple Ave 44870
Maple Oxford Township Ave 44870
Marina Point Dr 44870
E & W Market St 44870
Marlboro St 44870
Marlenkay Pl 44870
Marquette St 44870
Marrissee Dr 44870
Marshall Ave 44870
Martin Ave & Dr 44870
Martins Point Rd 44870
Mason Rd 44870
Matthes Ave 44870
Mccartney Rd 44870
Mcdonough St 44870
Mcewen St 44870
Mckelvey St 44870
Mckinley St 44870
Meadow Dr & Ln 44870
Meadowlawn Dr 44870
Meigs St 44870
Melody Ln 44870
Melville St 44870
Memphis Ave 44870
E & W Menominee Trl 44870

Merriweather Rd 44870
E & W Miami Trl 44870
Michaels Cir 44870
Michigan Ave 44870
Milan Rd 44870
Mill Pond Dr 44870
Miller Rd 44870
Mills St 44870
Milne St 44870
Mohawk Path 44870
E & W Mohegan Trl 44870
E & W Monroe St 44870
Monticello Ln 44870
Morningside Ct 44870
Mulberry Dr 44870
Nantucket Dr 44870
Neil St 44870
Neill Dr 44870
Neilson Ave 44870
Newberry Ave 44870
Niagara St 44870
Niagra Dr 44870
Norbert Pl 44870
Normandy Ct 44870
Northwest Rd 44870
Norwood Ave 44870
Oakland Ave 44870
Oakmont Ln 44870
E & W Ogontz St & Trl 44870
Ohio St & Ter 44870
Old Mill Pl 44870
Old Railroad Rd 44870
E & S Oldgate St 44870
Olds St 44870
E Oneida Trl 44870
Ontario St 44870
Osborn Dr 44870
E & W Osborne St 44870
Palmer Dr 44870
E & W Parish St 44870
E & W Park Ln & St 44870
Parker Dr 44870
Parkland Dr 44870
Parkview Blvd 44870
Patten Tract Rd 44870
Paxton Ave 44870
Pearl St 44870
Pease Ln 44870
Pebble Ln 44870
Pelton Park Ln 44870
Pemington Pl 44870
Pennsylvania Ave 44870
E & W Perkins Ave 44870
Perry St 44870
Peterson Ln 44870
Pierce St 44870
Pinewood Dr 44870
Pioneer Trl 44870
Pipe St 44870
Pleasant Ave 44870
Pleasantview Pl 44870
Plum Brook Cir 44870
Plum Brook Creek Dr 44870
Polk St 44870
Poplar St 44870
Porter St 44870
Portland Ave & Rd 44870
Portside Dr 44870
Potawatomi Trl 44870
Prairie Rd 44870
Prospect St 44870
Providence Dr 44870
Putnam St 44870
Quail Hollow Cir & Ln 44870
Quarry Lakes Dr 44870
Ramada Dr 44870
Randall Dr 44870
Ransom Rd & St 44870
Reese St 44870
Remington Ave 44870
Rhode St 44870
Richmond Cir 44870
River Ave 44870
Rockwell St 44870
Rods Dr 44870
Roosevelt St 44870
Sadler St 44870
Sagamore St 44870
Saint Clair St 44870
Saint James Pl 44870
Sandusky Ave & St 44870
Sandusky Mall Blvd 44870
Sandy Acres Dr 44870
Sanford St 44870
Scheid Rd 44870
Schenk Rd 44870
Schiller Ave 44870
Scott St 44870
Scottley Dr 44870
Seavers Way 44870
Seminole Trl 44870
E & W Seneca St & Trl 44870
Shady Ln 44870
E & W Shawnee Trl 44870
Sheffield Way 44870
Shelby St 44870
Sherman St 44870
E & W Shoreline Dr 44870
E & W Shoreway Dr 44870
Skadden Rd 44870
Sloane St 44870
Snow Ct 44870
South Ave, Pass & St 44870
Spencer Ave 44870
Springdale Dr 44870
Spruce St 44870
E & W Sprucewood Dr 44870
Stacey Rd 44870
Stahlwood Dr 44870
State Route 99 44870
Stoll Ave 44870
Stone St 44870
E & W Stoneplace Dr 44870
E & W Stoneway Dr 44870
Stonewood Dr 44870
Stonyridge Dr 44870
Strouse Ln 44870
E & W Strub Rd 44870
Sunset Dr, Ln & Plz 44870
Superior St 44870
Susan Ln 44870
Sweetbriar Dr 44870
Sycamore St 44870
Sycamore Line 44870
Tall Oaks Ln 44870
Taylor Rd & St 44870
Taylorbrook Cir 44870
Terrace Ct 44870
Thicket Rd 44870
Thomas St 44870
Thorpe Dr 44870
Tiffin Ave 44870
Timber Ln 44870
Timber Commons Dr 44870
Timber Lake Ln 44870
Townsend St 44870
Tremper Ave 44870
E & W Tuscarawas Trl 44870
Tyler St & Way 44870
Valley Ln 44870
Van Buren St 44870
Venetian Dr 44870
Venice Rd 44870
Venice Heights Blvd 44870
Vine St 44870
Wade Blvd 44870
Wagner Ave 44870
Wahl Rd 44870
Walnut Creek Ln 44870
Walnut Ridge Ln 44870
Walt Lake Trl 44870
Wamajo Dr 44870
Ward St 44870
Warren St 44870
E & W Washington Ct, Row & St 44870
E & W Water St 44870
Waverly Rd 44870
Wayne St 44870
Weihur Dr 44870
Westwind Dr 44870
Westwood Dr & Way 44870
Whispering Pines Ln 44870
White Tail Run 44870
Wilbert St 44870
Wildman St 44870
Willow Dr 44870
Wilson St 44870
Windamere Ln 44870
Windcrest Ct 44870
Windham Pl N & S 44870
Windswood Way 44870
Windward Cir 44870
Winnebago Ave 44870
Wintinte St 44870
Wood Rd 44870
Woodland Trl 44870
Woodlawn Ave 44870
Woodridge Dr 44870
Wyndham Ln 44870
Zachary Dr 44870

NUMBERED STREETS

All Street Addresses 44870

SPRINGFIELD OH

General Delivery 45501

POST OFFICE BOXES MAIN OFFICE STATIONS AND BRANCHES

Box No.s
All PO Boxes 45501

RURAL ROUTES

02, 03, 04, 05, 06, 07, 08 45502

NAMED STREETS

A Ave 45502
Abbey Ave 45505
Aberdeen Dr 45506
Aberfelda Ct & Dr 45504
Abington Pl 45503
Acreview Ave 45502
Adaway Trl 45502
Adlyn Rd 45505
Airpark Dr 45502
Alameda Dr 45503
Alamo Ave 45503
Albemarle Rd 45504
Alden Ave 45503
Allen Dr 45505
Allison Ave 45506
Allium Ct 45505
Alpha Rd 45504
Alta Rd 45503
Amanda St 45506
Amarillo Ave 45503
Amelia St 45506
Amherst Rd 45504
Andaric Ave 45505
Andover Ave 45503
Anita Dr 45504
Anoka St 45503
Anson Pl 45502
Antrim Ln 45503
Apollo Ave 45503
Appian Way 45503
Apple Hl 45504
Apprentice Dr 45504
Arbor Ln 45503
Archer Dr & Ln 45503
Ardmore Rd 45504
Argonne Ave & Ln 45503
N Arlington Ave 45503
S Arlington Ave 45505
Armsgate Rd 45503
Arthur Rd 45502
Ash Dr 45504
Ashbrook Dr 45502
Ashbury Ln 45502
Ashlar Dr 45503
Ashley Cir & Dr 45503
Ashton Ln 45503
Assurant Way 45505
Attleboro Ave 45503
Aubree Ln 45502
E Auburn Ave
1-99 45506
100-699 45505
W Auburn Ave 45506
Audubon Park Dr 45504
Augusta Ave 45503
Austin Ave 45503
Auston St 45502
Autumn Ln 45503
Autumn Creek Dr 45504
Avenue A 45504
Avenue B 45504
Avenue C 45504
Avery Cir 45503
Avodire St 45504
Avondale Ave 45503
Bahia Dr 45503
Baker Rd 45504
Baldwin Ave 45505
Baldwin Ln 45502
Ballentine Pike 45502
Ballydoyle Dr 45503
Balsam Dr 45503
Baltimore Pl 45504
Banes Rd 45502
Barclay St 45505
Barker Dr 45505
Bassett Dr 45506
Basswood Dr 45504
Bay St 45505
Beacon St 45505
Beard Dr & Rd 45502
Beatrice St 45503
N Bechtle Ave 45504
S Bechtle St 45506
Beech Dr 45504
N Bell Ave 45504
S Bell Ave 45506
Belleaire Ave 45503
Bellefair Ave 45506
Bellevue Ave & Pl 45503
N Belmont Ave 45503
S Belmont Ave 45505
Benin Dr 45504
Benjamin Dr 45502
Bentley Dr 45504
Berger Ave & Pl 45503
Berkley Rd 45504
Berwick Dr 45503
Betty Jean Ct 45503
Beverly Ave 45504
Bexley Ave 45503
Bicentennial Ave 45503
Biel St 45505
Bill Edwards Dr 45504
Billings Dr 45505
Birch Rd 45503
Birchwood Ct 45502
N Bird Rd 45503
S Bird Rd 45505
Biscayne Dr 45503
Blaine Ave 45503
E & W Blee Rd 45502
Blithe Rd 45503
Blue Sky Dr 45502
Bock St 45503
Boda St 45503
Bolin Ave 45502
Bonita Ave 45503
Bosart Rd 45503
Bostic St 45506
Bowman Rd
1-1199 45505
1200-1499 45502
Bradford Dr 45503
Brandyleigh Ln 45506
Brannan Dr E & W 45502
Brantford Ct 45503
Braytonburne Dr 45503
Breezewood St 45502
Brenda Kay Ct 45503
Brendle Trce 45503
Brennan Ln 45506
Brent Dr E & W 45505
Brentwood Dr 45503
Brewster Ct 45503
Briarwood Ter 45504
Brighton Rd 45504
Bristol Dr 45503
Brixton Dr E 45503
N & S Broadmoor Blvd 45504
Broadview Dr 45505
Broadway Rd 45502
Broadway St 45504
Broken Trail Dr 45502
Brookdale Dr 45502
Brookhollow Dr 45504
Brookshire Ln 45502
Brookside Dr 45503
Brookston Dr 45502
Brust Dr 45505
Buck Creek Ln 45502
Buckeye St 45505
Buckthorn Ct 45502
Buffenbarger Rd 45502
Burchill St 45503
N Burnett Rd 45503
S Burnett Rd 45505
Burrwood Dr 45503
Burt St 45505
Burton Dr 45503
Buxton Ave 45505
Cabot Dr 45503
Calais Dr 45503
Caldwell St 45503
Calhoun Dr 45505
California Ave 45505
Cambridge Dr 45503
Camelot Dr 45503
Cameron Ave & Ln 45503
Campbell Dr 45503
Candace Dr 45504
Canterbury Dr 45503
Cape Cod Dr 45505
Caplinger Dr 45504
Capri Cir 45505
Cardinal Rd 45502
Carillion Dr 45503
Carlisle Ave 45504
Carona St 45503
Carousel Dr 45503
Carriage Ln 45505
Carson Ln 45503
Casey Cir & Dr 45503
E Cassilly St
1-199 45504
200-799 45503
W Cassilly St 45504
Catawba Ave 45503
Catherine St 45505
Cattail Pt 45502
Cavins Dr 45503
E Cecil St
1-199 45504
200-899 45503
Cedar St 45504
Cedar Hills Ave 45504
Cedarview Dr 45503
S Center Blvd 45506
Center St 45505
N Center St 45502
S Center St
1-199 45502
200-1350 45506
Central Aly 45503
Central Ave 45505
Champion Ave 45503
Chapman Ln 45503
Chapter Ct 45504
Charles St 45505
S Charleston Pike 45502
Chatham Pl 45505
Cheadona Ave 45506
Cherokee Dr 45506
Cherry Dr 45506
Cherry Ln 45504
Chestnut Ave 45503
Cheviot Hills Dr 45505
Cheyenne Ave 45503
Chick Ln 45505
Chickasaw Ave 45502
Chico Ct 45502
Chippendale Dr 45503
Christopher Dr 45505
Church Ave & Ln 45505
Circle Dr 45503
N Clairmont Ave 45503
S Clairmont Ave 45505
Clarion Dr 45503
E Clark St 45506
W Clark St
1-99 45506
101-1899 45506
104-118 45502
120-138 45506
140-150 45502
200-1898 45506
Clay St 45505
Clayton Ave 45502
Cleve Ave 45505
Cleveland Ave 45503
Cliff St 45504
Cliff Park Rd 45504
Clifton Ave 45505
Cobb Ave 45506
Coffin Station Rd 45502
Colaw St 45505
Colby Ln 45505
Cold Springs Rd 45502
E College Ave
1-199 45504
200-499 45503
W College Ave 45504
Collier Rd
2000-2799 45506
2800-2899 45502
Colonial Dr 45504
Colony Ln 45503
E Columbia St
1-199 45502
200-899 45503
W Columbia St
1-149 45502
151-199 45502
200-3399 45504
Columbus Rd 45503
Commandry Ct 45504
Commerce Cir & Rd 45504
Concord Ave 45504
Conestoga St 45503
Conowoods Dr 45503
Conrad Ct & Dr 45502
Consistory St 45504
Cook St 45506
Cookston Ave 45503
Cora St 45503
Corlington Dr 45506
Cornell St 45503
Cortland Dr 45505
Corwin Cir 45502
Corwin Ln 45503
Cottage Ave 45506
Cottage Dr 45506
Cottage Pl 45503
Cottingham Rd N & S 45506
Cottonwood Dr 45504
Council Ct 45504
Country Side Ct 45503
E & W County Line Rd 45502
Court St 45506
Covina Dr 45504
Covington Dr 45503
Crabill Rd 45502
Craig Rd 45502
Cranchen Rd 45504
Crandall Ln 45503
Creekwood Ct 45504
Crescent Dr 45504
Crescent Pt 45503
Crescent Hill Rd 45502
Crest Dr 45502
Crestview Dr 45504
Crist Rd 45502
Critter Ct 45502
Croft Rd 45503
Cropper St 45503
Crossgate Ct 45505
Crystal Ln 45502
Cullen Ave 45503
Cumberland Dr 45506
Curtis Dr 45503
Cypress St 45505
Dakota Ave 45504
Dale Ave 45503
Damascus Ave 45506
Danbury Rd 45505
Darien Ln 45505
Darnell Rd 45504
Dartmouth Rd 45504
Darwin Ave 45504
Dawn Ln 45503
Dayton Ave & Rd 45506
Dayton Springfield Rd 45502
Deardorf Ave 45506
Deer Run Rd 45504
Deercreek Dr 45502
Deerfield Trl 45503
Delaware Ave
100-299 45503
1700-1999 45506
2700-2799 45503
Delcourt Dr 45506
Dellwood Dr 45505
Delmar Cir & Dr 45503
Delrey Rd 45504
Delta Rd 45505
Denise Ave 45502
Derby Rd 45503
Derr Rd 45503
Detrick Jordan Pike 45502
Devon Dr 45503
Dialton Rd 45502
Dibert Ave 45506
Dogwood Dr 45504
Donnelly Ave 45503
Donnels Creek Ln 45502
Dorchester Dr 45506
Doris Dr 45505
Dorothy Ln 45505
N Douglas Ave 45503
S Douglas Ave 45505
Dover Rd 45504
Dowden St 45503
E & W Downey Dr 45504
Dredge Rd 45502
Drew Ct 45503
Drexel Ave 45505
Driscoll Ave 45506
Duncan St 45505
Dunhollow Dr 45503
Dunnwood Ln 45503
Dunseth Ln 45503
Duquesne Dr 45506
Dwight Rd 45503
E Ave 45502
Eagle Ct 45505
Eagle City Rd
1-399 45502
800-1599 45504
East Ct & St 45505
Eastgate Rd 45503
Eastham St 45503
Eastmoor Dr 45505
Eastridge Ave 45503
Eastwood Dr 45504
Ebersole Rd 45502
Echo Dr 45502
Echo Hills Ave 45502
Eden Ave 45506

- Edenwood Dr 45504
- Edgar Ave 45506
- Edgewood Ave 45503
- Edna Ln 45503
- Edwards Ave 45503
- Egmont Ave 45503
- Ehrhart Dr 45502
- Eichelberger Ln 45505
- El Camino Dr 45503
- Elaina Dr 45503
- Elbron Rd 45505
- Elder St 45505
- Elderwood Rd 45504
- Eldora Dr 45503
- Elizabeth Ct 45503
- Elk Ave 45505
- Ellsworth Ave 45505
- Elm Dr 45504
- Elm St 45503
- Elmore Dr 45505
- Elmsford St 45506
- Elmwood Ave 45505
- Elwood Ln 45506
- Emerald Ct 45503
- Emery Ave 45504
- Emery St 45503
- Emmanuel Way 45502
- Englewood Rd
  - 1-199 45504
  - 200-400 45503
  - 402-498 45503
- Enon Rd 45502
- Eric Dr 45502
- Erie Ave 45505
- Erika Dr 45503
- Erter Dr 45503
- Essex St 45505
- Estle Rd 45502
- Eton Ct 45503
- E Euclid Ave
  - 1-99 45506
  - 100-799 45505
- W Euclid Ave 45506
- E & W Eva Cir 45504
- Evans Ave 45504
- Evergreen Dr 45504
- F Ave 45502
- Faculty Ct 45504
- Fair St 45506
- Fairfield Pike
  - 1300-1599 45506
  - 1600-5499 45502
- Fairview Ave
  - 100-199 45504
  - 2500-2599 45503
- Fairway Dr 45504
- Falkirk Dr 45502
- Falmouth Ave 45503
- Farlow St 45503
- Farnam St 45506
- Faux Satin Dr 45504
- Feese Pl 45505
- Fellowcraft Ave 45504
- Ferncliff Ct & Pl 45504
- Ferndale Ln 45503
- Fernway Pl 45503
- Fieldbrook Dr 45502
- Fisher St 45502
- Fletcher Chapel Rd 45502
- Floral Ave
  - 1-199 45504
  - 200-399 45503
- N Florence St 45503
- S Florence St 45505
- Flowerdale Rd 45504
- Floyd Dr 45502
- Foley Cir 45503
- Folk Ream Rd 45502
- Fontaine Ln 45502
- Forest Dr
  - 200-599 45505
  - 4800-5599 45506
- Forest Edge Ave 45503
- Forrest Ave 45505
- N Foster St 45503
- S Foster St 45505
- N Fostoria Ave 45503
- S Fostoria Ave 45505
- Fotler St 45504
- N Fountain Ave
  - 1-199 45502
  - 200-1199 45504
- S Fountain Ave
  - 1-199 45502
  - 200-2199 45506
- N Fountain Blvd 45504
- Fowler Rd 45502
- Fox St 45503
- Fox Hollow Rd 45502
- Fox Ridge Dr E 45503
- Foxboro Rd 45503
- Franklin St 45506
- Fraternal Cir 45504
- N Freeman St 45503
- S Freeman St 45505
- Fremont Ave 45505
- Front St 45503
- Fruitland Rd 45503
- Fulton Ave 45505
- Gable St 45505
- Gallagher St 45505
- Galway Dr 45503
- Gardena Ct 45503
- Garfield Ave 45504
- Garland Ave 45503
- Garlough Rd 45502
- Gateway Blvd 45502
- Gay St 45503
- Gazaway Ct 45505
- Georgia Ave 45505
- Gerald Dr 45505
- Geron Dr 45505
- Gladden Ave 45503
- Glendale Ave & Dr 45504
- Glenmore Dr 45503
- Glenn Ave 45505
- E & W Glenwood Ave 45506
- Glouster St 45503
- Goldfinch Bnd 45502
- Golfview Dr 45502
- Gonder St 45503
- Goodwin Ave 45504
- Gordon Rd 45504
- Gordon Hill Dr 45502
- Gothic St 45503
- Graham St 45502
- Granada Dr 45503
- Granby Ave 45503
- E Grand Ave
  - 1-99 45506
  - 100-799 45505
- W Grand Ave 45506
- Grandview Dr 45503
- Grange Ave 45504
- Grange Hall Rd 45504
- Grant Rd 45502
- Grant St 45504
- Grayson Dr 45502
- Green Acres Dr 45504
- Greenbrier Ave 45503
- Greenfield Ave 45505
- Greenknoll Dr 45502
- N Greenmount Ave 45503
- S Greenmount Ave 45505
- Greenoak Ct 45503
- Greenwich Cir 45504
- Greenwood Ave 45503
- Grey Stone Xing 45504
- Greystone Dr & Ln 45503
- Gridley Ct 45505
- Groop Rd 45504
- Grossepoint 45503
- Grover St 45505
- Grube St 45503
- Gruen Dr 45505
- N & S Hadley Rd 45505
- Hagan Rd 45502
- Halifax Ct 45503
- Hampton Pl
  - 117-148 45504
  - 150-152 45504
  - 200-499 45503
- N Hampton Rd
  - 300-1199 45504
  - 2400-6499 45502
- Hampton Trl 45502
- N Hampton Donnelsville Rd 45502
- Hanson Ct & Rd 45504
- E & W Harding Rd 45504
- Harford St 45503
- Harris Ln 45503
- Harrison St 45505
- Harshman Blvd 45504
- Harshman Rd 45502
- Hartford Dr 45503
- Harvard Rd 45504
- Harvest St 45502
- Hatcher Dr 45503
- Haucke Ave 45506
- Haven Hill Rd 45502
- Haverhill St 45503
- Hawthorne Rd 45504
- Hazelbrook Ave 45506
- Heard Ave 45506
- Hearthstone Dr 45502
- Heartland Ct 45503
- Heather Glen Ct 45503
- Heathers Down Dr 45502
- Heatherwood Ave 45503
- Hedge Dr 45504
- Hedgely Rd 45506
- Heide Rd 45506
- Helena Ct & Dr 45503
- Hemlock Dr 45506
- Henderson Ct & Dr 45503
- Hennessy Ave 45505
- Henry St 45503
- Hensel Ave 45505
- Heritage St 45503
- Heron Rd 45502
- Hiawatha Ave 45504
- Hickory Dr 45503
- High St 45505
- E High St
  - 1-199 45502
  - 200-3649 45505
- W High St
  - 1-199 45502
  - 200-1999 45506
- Highland Ave 45503
- Highlander Ln 45502
- Highview Ave 45505
- Hillcrest Ave 45504
- Hilldale Rd 45505
- Hilliard St 45506
- Hillside Ave 45503
- Hilltop Ave 45503
- Hinkle Rd 45505
- Hiser Ave 45503
- Hodge Rd 45502
- Holiday Dr 45505
- Holland Cir 45503
- Hollwood Rd 45502
- Holly Dr 45504
- E Home Rd
  - 1-199 45504
  - 200-2599 45503
- W Home Rd 45504
- Home Orchard Dr 45503
- Homestead Ave 45503
- Hometown St 45504
- Homeview Ave 45505
- Hominy Ridge Rd 45502
- Honeysuckle Dr 45505
- Hoppes Ave 45503
- Hornwood Dr 45504
- Horseshoe Ln 45502
- Howard St 45503
- N Hubert Ave 45503
- S Hubert Ave 45505
- Hughes Ct 45503
- Hummingbird Way 45502
- Huron Ave 45505
- Hustead Rd 45502
- Hyannis Dr 45503
- Hyer Ave 45504
- Imperial Blvd & Dr 45503
- Indiana Ave 45505
- Innisfallen Ave 45506
- Iowa Ave 45506
- Ipswich St 45503
- Ironwood Dr 45504
- Iroquois St 45506
- Irwin Ave 45505
- N Isabella St 45504
- S Isabella St 45506
- E Jackson Rd 45502
- W Jackson Rd 45502
- N Jackson St 45504
- S Jackson St 45506
- Jacksonville Rd 45504
- James St 45503
- Jasper St 45503
- W Jefferson St 45506
- Jenny Ct 45504
- Jenson Dr 45503
- Jensvold Rd 45502
- Jeremy Ave 45502
- Jessica Ct 45504
- E John St
  - 1-99 45506
  - 100-1299 45505
- W John St 45506
- E & W Johnny Lytle Ave 45506
- Johnson Ave 45505
- Johnson Rd 45502
- W Johnson St 45506
- Jordan Dr 45503
- Josephine St 45505
- Joshane St 45502
- Judy Ln 45505
- Juniper Dr 45503
- Kaffenbarger Ct 45504
- Kaffenbarger Dr 45502
- Kappel Dr 45503
- Karr St 45503
- Kay Ave 45502
- Keene Ave 45503
- Keifer Ave 45504
- Keller Ave 45504
- Kelley Ave 45502
- Kenerly St 45502
- Kenilworth Ave 45505
- N Kensington Pl 45504
- S Kensington Pl
  - 1-199 45504
  - 200-399 45503
- Kenton St 45505
- Kentucky Ave 45505
- Kenwood Ave 45505
- Kerns Rd 45502
- Kewbury Rd 45504
- Kildeer Dr 45502
- Kilkenny Ct & Dr 45503
- Kimberly Cir, Ct & Dr 45503
- King Tree Ln 45506
- Kingsgate Ct 45503
- Kingsgate Rd
  - 1000-1499 45503
  - 1900-1998 45502
- Kingsreach Ln 45504
- Kingswood Dr E 45503
- Kinnane Ave 45505
- Kinsman Ave 45504
- Kittyhawk Ave 45503
- Kizer Ln 45502
- Klobdenz Ave 45504
- Knickerbocker Ave 45506
- Knight Ter 45504
- Knobs End Ct 45502
- Knollwood Rd 45502
- Koa Dr 45504
- Kohl Ave 45503
- Kramer Rd 45505
- Lafayette Ave 45505
- Lagonda Ave 45503
- Lajunta Ave 45503
- Lakeview Ct 45503
- Lakota Ln 45502
- Lamar Dr 45504
- Landor Rd 45503
- N Lannert Ave 45504
- S Lannert Ave 45506
- Lansdowne Ave 45505
- Larch St 45503
- Larchmont Ave 45503
- Laredo St 45503
- Lark Ln 45502
- Latimer Dr 45503
- Laura Ln 45502
- Laurel St 45503
- Lawnview Ave 45505
- Lawrenceville Dr 45504
- Laybourne Rd 45505
- Leander Dr 45504
- E Leffel Ln 45505
- W Leffel Ln 45506
- Lehigh Dr 45503
- Lehman Rd 45502
- Leland Dr 45505
- Leon Ln 45502
- Lexington Ave 45505
- Liberty Ave 45506
- E Liberty St
  - 1-99 45506
  - 100-599 45505
- W Liberty St 45506
- N Light St 45504
- S Light St 45506
- Lilac Dr 45503
- Limba Dr 45504
- Limerick Rd 45502
- N Limestone St
  - 1-149 45502
  - 150-198 45501
  - 151-199 45502
  - 200-2799 45503
- S Limestone St
  - 1-199 45502
  - 200-3599 45505
- Lincoln Ave & Park S 45505
- Lincoln Park Cir 45505
- Lindair Dr 45502
- Lindeman Dr 45503
- Linden Ave 45505
- Lindsey Rd 45503
- Linmuth Ct & Dr 45503
- Linn St 45506
- Linwood Ave 45505
- Lisa Ct 45504
- Little Pl 45504
- Locust Dr 45504
- Logan Ave 45505
- Lohnes Ave 45504
- Lone Wolf Ave 45502
- Lonesome Dove Ln E & W 45505
- Loney Ct 45503
- Longford Close E 45503
- Longview Dr 45504
- Lost Rd 45504
- Lost Arrow Ct 45504
- Lowell St 45503
- Lower Valley Pike
  - 3100-5625 45506
  - 5626-6399 45502
- Lowman St 45505
- N Lowry Ave 45504
- S Lowry Ave 45506
- Lucas Dr 45506
- Ludlow Ave 45505
- Lyle Ave 45505
- Lynnhaven St 45503
- Mad River Rd 45502
- E Madison Ave
  - 1-199 45504
  - 200-799 45503
- Madrid Ct & St 45502
- Magnolia Blvd 45503
- Maiden Ln 45504
- E Main St
  - 1-199 45502
  - 200-2899 45503
- W Main St
  - 1-199 45502
  - 200-2599 45504
- Malaga Cir 45502
- Malden Ave 45504
- Malibu St 45503
- Mallard Ave 45503
- Manete St 45502
- Manhattan Blvd 45504
- Mansfield Ave 45505
- Maple Grove Rd 45504
- Maplewood Ave 45505
- Marbella Ave 45502
- Marinette Dr 45503
- Marlo Rd 45504
- Marshall Rd 45503
- Martin Dr 45502
- Mary St 45505
- Maryland Ave 45505
- Mason St 45503
- Masonic Dr 45504
- Master St 45504
- Maumee Dr 45502
- Mavor St 45505
- May St 45505
- Mayfair Dr 45505
- Mayflower Pl 45506
- Mayhill Rd 45504
- Mccain Ave 45506
- Mccord St 45503
- E Mccreight Ave
  - 1-97 45504
  - 99-199 45504
  - 200-899 45503
- W Mccreight Ave 45504
- Mcgillivray Ave 45503
- Mckinley Ave 45505
- Mead Ln 45506
- Meadow Cir 45506
- Meadow Ln 45505
- Meadow Wood Dr 45505
- Meadowbrook Dr 45506
- Meadowgate Dr 45502
- Mechanicsburg Rd
  - 1800-3349 45503
  - 3350-7299 45502
- Medford Dr 45503
- Medical Center Dr 45504
- Meenach Ln 45505
- Meissen Dr 45502
- Memorial Dr 45505
- Memorial Pl 45504
- Merrimont Ave 45503
- Merritt St 45503
- Merrydale Rd 45503
- Mesa Ln 45503
- Meyer Ct 45503
- Miami Aly & St 45506
- Michigan Ave 45505
- Middle St 45503
- Middle Urbana Rd
  - 2500-3999 45502
  - 4000-4999 45503
  - 5000-6906 45502
- Midfield St 45503
- Midland Pl & Rd 45503
- Midvale Rd 45504
- E & W Mile Rd 45503
- Miller Rd 45502
- Miller St 45506
- Mills Rd 45502
- Milton Carlisle Rd 45504
- Mindy Ct 45502
- Mingo Ln 45502
- Miracle Mile 45503
- Mitchell Blvd 45503
- Mitchell Rd 45502
- Mobile St 45503
- Mohawk Dr 45502
- Monaco Dr 45506
- Monroe St
  - 1-99 45506
  - 100-499 45505
- Montclair Dr 45503
- Montego Dr 45503
- Monterey Ave 45504
- Montgomery Ave 45506
- Moore St 45503
- Moorefield Ct 45502
- Moorefield Rd
  - 1-999 45502
  - 1000-1999 45503
  - 2000-6499 45502
- Moorlands Dr 45506
- Morgan St 45503
- Morningside Cir 45502
- Morris Rd 45502
- Morton Dr 45505
- Moss Point Ln 45504
- Mound St 45505
- Mount Joy St 45505
- Mount Vernon Ave 45503
- E Mulberry St
  - 1-99 45506
  - 100-299 45505
- W Mulberry St 45506
- Mumma Ct 45503
- Mumper Rd 45502
- Murphy Ct 45503
- N Murray St 45503
- S Murray St 45505
- Myers Rd 45502
- Mystic Ln 45503
- Nagley St 45505
- Nantucket St 45503
- Narra Pl 45504
- National Pl 45503
- E National Rd 45505
- W National Rd 45504
- Nauset St 45503
- Navajo St 45502
- Neon St 45503
- Neosha Ave 45505
- Nettlewood Ln 45502
- Nevada Rd 45503
- New Carlisle Pike 45504
- New Castle Ln 45503
- New Haven St 45503
- Noble Ave & Ter 45504
- Noel Dr 45506
- North Dr 45504
- E North St
  - 1-99 45504
  - 100-599 45503
- W North St 45504
- Northbourne Dr 45506
- E Northern Ave
  - 1-99 45504
  - 200-899 45503
- W Northern Ave 45504
- Northfield Blvd 45503
- Northfield Ct 45502
- Northgate Dr & Rd 45504
- Northlawn Dr 45503
- Northmoor Dr 45503
- Northparke Dr 45503
- Northpoint Rd 45503
- Northridge Dr 45504
- Northwood Dr 45504
- Norwood Ave 45506
- Oak St 45505
- Oak Knoll Dr 45504
- Oakdale Rd 45503
- Oakland Ave 45503
- Oakland Ct 45505
- Oakleaf Ave 45506
- Oakmont Ct 45502
- Oakridge Dr 45504
- Oaksmere St 45503
- Oakwood Pl 45506
- Oakwood Rd 45502
- Oakwood Village Dr E 45503
- Obenchain Aly 45506
- Obenchain Ave 45503
- Oconnor Ln 45504
- Oesterlen St 45503
- Ogden Rd 45503
- Ohio Ave 45505
- Old Arthur Rd 45502
- Old Clifton Rd 45502
- Old Coach Rd 45505
- Old Columbus Rd
  - 1-3999 45503
  - 4000-6499 45502
- Old Farm Ln 45503
- Old Mill Rd
  - 1-1499 45506

1500-4999 ... 45502
Old Oak Ln ... 45503
Old Route 70 ... 45502
Old Selma Rd ... 45505
Old Springfield Rd ... 45502
Oldham Dr ... 45503
Olds Ave ... 45503
Oletha Ave ... 45505
Olive St ... 45503
Olympic St ... 45503
Omega Ave ... 45504
Oneida Dr ... 45502
Ontario Ave ... 45505
Outerview Dr ... 45502
Overholser Rd ... 45502
Overlook Dr ... 45504
Owl Ave ... 45503
Oxford Dr ... 45506
Oxtoby St ... 45505
Oyler Dr ... 45504
Paldao Ct ... 45504
Paradise Ln ... 45502
Park Ave ... 45503
Park Pl ... 45504
Park Rd ... 45504
Parker Ct ... 45504
Parker St ... 45503
Parkridge Dr ... 45506
E Parkwood Ave ... 45506
W Parkwood Ave ... 45506
Parkwood Cir ... 45504
Parnell Pl E ... 45503
Parr Dr ... 45503
Party Ln ... 45504
Patrick Rd ... 45503
Pauline St ... 45503
Peach Blossom Ct ... 45502
Peacock Rd ... 45502
Pembrook Rd ... 45504
Penn St ... 45505
Penny Pike ... 45502
Penrose Ave ... 45505
Pepper Ave ... 45503
Perkins Dr ... 45505
E & W Perrin Ave ... 45506
Perry St ... 45504
Peshek Ln ... 45506
Petre Rd ... 45502
Pheasant Run ... 45503
Phoenix Cir & Dr ... 45503
Pine St ... 45505
Pine Tree Pl ... 45504
Pinehurst Dr ... 45502
Pinewood Ave ... 45502
Piney Branch Cir & Dr ... 45503
Piqua Pl ... 45506
E & S Pitchin Rd ... 45502
Planters Grv ... 45503
Plateau Dr ... 45502
Plattsburg Rd ... 45505
E Pleasant St
1-99 ... 45506
100-2099 ... 45505
W Pleasant St ... 45506
N Plum St ... 45504
S Plum St ... 45506
Plum Tree Ct ... 45503
Pompano St ... 45506
Pond Dr ... 45505
Poplar Dr ... 45504
Portage Path ... 45506
E Possum Rd ... 45502
W Possum Rd ... 45506
Power St ... 45503
Prairie Ave ... 45505
Prairie Rd ... 45502
Prairie Bluff Ave ... 45502
Preston Dr ... 45506
Prestwick Village Cir ... 45503
Primm Dr ... 45503
Prince Cir ... 45503
Princess Ct ... 45506
Progress Rd ... 45505
Prospect Cir & St ... 45503
Prosperity Dr ... 45502
Prosser Rd ... 45503

Providence Ave ... 45503
Pumphouse Rd ... 45503
Pythian Ave ... 45504
Qu Wood Rd ... 45506
Quail Haven Ct ... 45504
Quailhollow Ct ... 45502
Quality Ln ... 45505
Quincy Rd ... 45505
Quinlan Ct ... 45503
Ra Mar Dr ... 45502
N Race St ... 45504
S Race St ... 45506
Radewonuk Ave ... 45502
Raffensperger Ave ... 45505
Railroad St ... 45505
Ramsey Ln ... 45502
Randall Dr ... 45503
Randee Ln ... 45502
Ravenwood Dr ... 45504
Raydo Cir ... 45506
Reading Dr ... 45505
Reames Ave ... 45505
Reaper Ave ... 45503
Rebecca Dr ... 45503
Rebert Pike
1258-2200 ... 45506
2201-5999 ... 45502
Red Bud Ln ... 45504
Red Coach Dr ... 45503
Red Oaks Cir ... 45506
Redbud Ln ... 45504
Redmond Rd ... 45505
Redwood Blvd ... 45503
Redwood Dr ... 45504
Reed Ave ... 45505
Regan Ln ... 45503
Regent Ave ... 45503
Regula Ave ... 45502
Renee St ... 45502
Reno Ln & Rd ... 45503
Rensselaer St ... 45503
Revels St ... 45503
Rhea Ln ... 45502
Rhonemous St ... 45506
Rice St ... 45505
Richard Ave ... 45503
Richmoor Rd ... 45503
Ridge Rd
200-399 ... 45503
1800-3999 ... 45502
Ridge Mall Dr ... 45504
Ridgeview Cir, Ct & Ln
E, N & S ... 45504
Ridgeway Dr ... 45506
Ridgewood Rd E ... 45503
Ridgewood Rd W
4300-5544 ... 45503
5545-5999 ... 45502
Riley Rd ... 45502
Rittal Pl ... 45504
N River Rd ... 45502
Riverside Dr ... 45504
Roberts Ave ... 45503
Robin Rd ... 45503
Robin Hood Ct ... 45505
Robinson Dr ... 45506
Rocket Ave ... 45505
Rockford Dr ... 45503
Rockrun Way ... 45504
Rockview Dr ... 45504
Rockway Ave ... 45506
Rocky Point Rd ... 45502
Rodgers Dr ... 45503
Ronald Rd ... 45503
Ronda Ct ... 45502
Roosevelt Dr
1-199 ... 45504
200-499 ... 45503
Roosevelt Pl ... 45503
Roscommon Dr ... 45503
Rose Aly ... 45506
E Rose St ... 45505
W Rose St ... 45506
Rosedale Ave ... 45506
Roseland Ave E & W ... 45503
Rosewood Ave ... 45506

Ross Ln ... 45502
Rosswood Ln ... 45502
Rouge Pl ... 45504
Rubsam St ... 45504
Runyan Ave ... 45503
Russell Ave ... 45506
Rutland Ave ... 45505
Ryan Ct & Rd ... 45503
Ryland Dr ... 45503
Saddlebrook Run ... 45502
Saint Andrews Ct ... 45502
Saint Clair Ct ... 45505
Saint George Pl ... 45505
Saint James Ct ... 45502
Saint Paris Pike ... 45504
Saint Paul Ave ... 45504
Salem Ave ... 45505
Sandalwood Ave ... 45502
Santa Monica Ave ... 45503
Sapele Dr ... 45504
Sarah Leigh Ave ... 45502
Sassafras Dr ... 45504
Satinwood Cir ... 45504
Sawgrass Ct ... 45502
Sawmill Ct ... 45503
Saybrook Ln & Rd ... 45505
Scanlon Ln ... 45503
Scarboro St ... 45506
Schiller St ... 45505
Scioto St ... 45506
Scotsdale Dr ... 45504
Scott St ... 45505
Secretariat Dr ... 45503
Section St ... 45505
Security Dr ... 45503
Seever St ... 45506
Selma Rd
100-3130 ... 45505
3131-6499 ... 45502
Seminole Ave ... 45506
Seneca Rd ... 45502
Seymour Ln ... 45503
Shadeland Dr ... 45503
Shadla Rd ... 45505
Shady Ln ... 45504
Shady Oak Ct ... 45502
N Shaffer St ... 45504
S Shaffer St ... 45506
Shaler Rd ... 45502
Shank Rd ... 45502
Shannon Ave ... 45504
Share St ... 45505
Shawnee Ave ... 45506
Shawnee Blvd ... 45504
Shawnee Park Dr ... 45506
Sheaff Rd ... 45504
Sheffield Dr ... 45506
Shelby Dr ... 45504
Sheridan Ave ... 45505
Sherman Ave ... 45503
Sherwood Park Dr ... 45505
Shinchel Rd ... 45502
Short St ... 45503
Shoup St ... 45503
Shrine Rd
300-1699 ... 45504
1700-3999 ... 45502
Sierra Ave ... 45503
Sigler St ... 45506
Signal Hill Rd ... 45504
Simon Ct ... 45503
E & W Singer St ... 45506
Sintz Rd ... 45504
Skinner Ln ... 45504
Skylark Rd ... 45502
Skyline Ln ... 45505
Snow Owl Ct ... 45503
Snowhill Blvd ... 45504
Snyder St ... 45504
Snyder Domer Rd ... 45502
Snyderville Rd ... 45502
South Dr ... 45504
Southbury St ... 45505
E Southern Ave
1-99 ... 45506
100-1099 ... 45505

W Southern Ave ... 45506
Southern Pkwy ... 45506
Southfield Ave ... 45505
Southgate Ave ... 45506
Southwest Ct ... 45504
Southwood Dr ... 45504
E & W Sparrow Rd ... 45502
Sparta Dr ... 45503
Spence Rd ... 45502
N Spring St ... 45502
S Spring St
1-199 ... 45502
400-599 ... 45505
Spring Falls Ave ... 45502
Spring Meadow Dr ... 45503
Springfield Jamestown
Rd ... 45502
Springfield Xenia Rd
2300-2999 ... 45506
5500-6500 ... 45502
6502-6502 ... 45502
Springmont Ave ... 45506
Spruce Dr ... 45504
Stanford Pl ... 45503
Stanton Ave ... 45503
Stanway Ave ... 45503
N Star Dr ... 45504
W State St ... 45506
State Route 55 ... 45502
Stephen Ln ... 45505
Stevison Dr ... 45503
Stiles Aly ... 45505
Stone Bridge Dr ... 45504
Stone Crossing Ln ... 45503
Stonecroft Dr ... 45502
Stonehaven Dr ... 45503
Stoneridge Dr ... 45503
Stoney Creek St ... 45504
Stott Rd ... 45502
Stoughton Pl ... 45504
Stowe Dr ... 45505
Stratford Pl ... 45504
Student Ave ... 45503
Stump Ln ... 45506
Sturbridge St ... 45503
Sturgeon St ... 45506
Sudbury St ... 45503
Sullivan Rd ... 45502
Summer St ... 45505
Summit St ... 45503
Sun Valley Dr ... 45505
Suncrest Dr ... 45503
Sundance St ... 45502
Sundown Rd ... 45503
Sunnyland Blvd ... 45506
Sunnyside Pl ... 45504
Sunrise Cir & Dr ... 45502
Sunset Ave ... 45505
Sunset Dr ... 45504
Superior Ave ... 45505
Sweetbriar Ln ... 45505
N Sycamore St ... 45503
S Sycamore St
1-29 ... 45503
30-199 ... 45505
Tackett Ln ... 45505
Tackett St ... 45503
Tacoma St ... 45503
Talisman Cir ... 45503
Tamarack Ave ... 45502
Tanager Rd ... 45505
Tanglewood Dr ... 45504
Tarimore Dr ... 45506
Tarryton Ln ... 45503
Tavenner Ave ... 45503
Taywell Ct & Dr ... 45503
Tecumseh Ave ... 45503
N Tecumseh Rd ... 45504
S Tecumseh Rd
1-1499 ... 45506
1500-6499 ... 45502
Temple St ... 45502
Tener Pl ... 45502
Terrace Dr ... 45503
Texas Ave ... 45505
Thackery Rd ... 45502

The Post Rd ... 45503
Thomas Dr ... 45503
Thomaston Trl ... 45503
N Thompson Ave ... 45504
S Thompson Ave ... 45506
Thor Dr ... 45503
Thrasher St ... 45503
Thrawn Rd ... 45503
Tibbetts Ave ... 45505
Tiffany Ln ... 45502
Timberline Dr ... 45504
Timberline Trl ... 45503
Timberview Ave ... 45502
Tioga Ct ... 45502
Titus Ln ... 45502
Titus Rd
100-399 ... 45505
400-1799 ... 45502
Todd Ave ... 45505
Tollhouse Rd ... 45504
Torrence Dr ... 45503
Towerwood Dr ... 45503
Trails End ... 45503
Tree Line Ave ... 45502
Tremont Ln ... 45502
Tremont City Rd ... 45502
Trent Close ... 45503
Trenton Pl ... 45504
Trimmer Ln ... 45502
Trinity Dr ... 45503
Tritle Trl ... 45503
Troehler Rd ... 45505
Trotwood Cir ... 45503
Troy Rd
1600-3669 ... 45504
3671-3699 ... 45504
4000-7999 ... 45502
Tudor Cir ... 45503
Tulane Ct & Rd ... 45503
Turner Dr E & W ... 45504
Tuttle Rd ... 45503
S Tuttle Rd ... 45505
Twitchell Rd ... 45502
Universal Dr ... 45504
Uplands Dr ... 45506
Upper Valley Pike
1-1799 ... 45504
2200-2449 ... 45502
2450-3499 ... 45504
3500-5799 ... 45502
Urbana Rd
2800-3199 ... 45503
3201-3299 ... 45503
3300-6999 ... 45502
Vada Ln ... 45503
Vale Rd ... 45504
Valley Dr ... 45504
Valley St ... 45506
Valley Loop Rd ... 45504
Valley View Dr ... 45503
Van Buren Ave ... 45505
Vananda Ave ... 45506
Venice Dr ... 45503
Ventura Ave ... 45503
Veronia Dr ... 45505
Versailles Ct ... 45502
Vester Ave ... 45503
Victorian Ln & Way ... 45503
Victory Dr ... 45505
Victory Rd ... 45504
Villa Rd ... 45503
Village Rd ... 45504
Vine St ... 45505
Vineyard St ... 45503
Virginia Ave ... 45505
Vista Dr ... 45506
Wabash Ct & Dr ... 45503
Walker St ... 45505
Walnut St ... 45505
Walnut Ter ... 45504
Walnut Grove Ln ... 45504
Walter St ... 45506
Walters Way ... 45502
Waltham Ave ... 45503
Waltin Ln ... 45503
Warbler Rdg ... 45503

E & W Ward St ... 45504
Warder St
1-99 ... 45504
200-1999 ... 45503
Warren Dr ... 45503
Washington Pl ... 45505
E Washington St ... 45502
W Washington St
1-199 ... 45502
300-1999 ... 45506
Water St ... 45503
Wayne Ave ... 45503
Weber Rd ... 45503
Wedgewood Cir ... 45503
Weimers Section ... 45505
Wellington Dr ... 45506
Wellsford Dr ... 45503
Wendover St ... 45506
Wenova Dr ... 45502
West Dr ... 45504
Westboro Ave ... 45503
Westchester Park Dr ... 45504
Westcliff Ct ... 45502
N Western Ave ... 45504
S Western Ave ... 45506
Westgate Rd ... 45504
Westmont Cir & Dr ... 45503
Westview Ave ... 45502
Westwood Dr ... 45504
Weybridge Dr ... 45503
Wheel St ... 45503
Whispering Wind Dr ... 45504
White Cliffs Ct ... 45503
White Oak Dr ... 45504
Whitestone Rd ... 45504
Wickford Pl ... 45503
Wildflower Dr ... 45504
Wildwood Dr ... 45504
Wiley Ave ... 45506
Wilkes Dr ... 45503
Willard Ave ... 45505
N William St ... 45504
S William St ... 45506
Williamson St ... 45503
Willis Ave ... 45505
Willoughby Ave ... 45502
Willow Dr ... 45505
Willow Rd ... 45502
Willow Chase Cir ... 45502
Willow Chase Ct ... 45502
Willow Chase Dr ... 45503
Willow Gate Dr ... 45503
Willow Lakes Dr ... 45502
Willow Ridge Ct ... 45502
Willowbrook Dr ... 45503
Willowdale Rd ... 45502
Wilson Ave ... 45505
Winding Trl ... 45503
Windsor Ave ... 45505
Windwood St ... 45503
Windy Ridge Dr ... 45502
Winfield Dr ... 45503
Winton Pl ... 45503
Wisconsin Ave ... 45506
Wispering Wind Dr ... 45504
N Wittenberg Ave
1-199 ... 45502
200-699 ... 45504
S Wittenberg Ave
1-199 ... 45502
200-1899 ... 45506
E Wittenberg Blvd ... 45506
W Wittenberg Blvd ... 45506
Woodale Ave ... 45503
Woodbine Ave ... 45503
Woodbridge Ln ... 45505
Woodedge Ave ... 45504
Woodford Dr ... 45503
Woodhaven Ct ... 45503
Woodland Dr ... 45503
Woodlawn Ave ... 45504
Woodrow Dr ... 45504
Woods Dr ... 45506
Woodside Ave ... 45503
Woodthrush Rd ... 45502
Woodview Dr ... 45504

Woodward Ave ... 45506
Woonsocket St ... 45503
Wrenview Dr ... 45502
Wrenwood Rd ... 45505
Wyandot Dr ... 45502
Wyndover St ... 45503
Wynn Rd ... 45502
Yale St ... 45502
Yeazell Rd ... 45502
N Yellow Springs St ... 45504
S Yellow Springs St ... 45506
York St
100-199 ... 45503
200-2899 ... 45505
Yorkshire Ct ... 45503
Young Ave ... 45502
Yuma Dr ... 45502
Zachary Ave ... 45502
Zeller Dr ... 45503
Zerkle Rd ... 45502
Zimmerman St ... 45503
Zischler St ... 45504

NUMBERED STREETS

E & W 1st ... 45504
E & W 2nd ... 45504
E 3rd St ... 45504
200-599 ... 45503
W 3rd St ... 45504
4th Ave ... 45505
5th St ... 45504

STEUBENVILLE OH

General Delivery ... 43952

POST OFFICE BOXES MAIN OFFICE STATIONS AND BRANCHES

Box No.s
1 - 1856 ... 43952
2001 - 2620 ... 43953
4001 - 9999 ... 43952

RURAL ROUTES

01, 07 ... 43952
02, 03, 04, 05, 06 ... 43953

NAMED STREETS

Aberdeen Rd ... 43953
Adams St ... 43952
Airport Rd ... 43953
Alexander Mnr E & W ... 43952
Alfred Dr ... 43953
Aliceland Dr ... 43953
Alter St ... 43952
Alvarado Blvd ... 43952
Americana Cir ... 43953
Amos Ln ... 43953
Anart St ... 43953
Andrews Dr ... 43953
Anina St ... 43953
Anthony Dr ... 43953
Arden Ave ... 43952
Argonne Ave ... 43952
Arlington Ave ... 43952
Arnil St ... 43952
Arrow Rd ... 43952
Ash St ... 43952
N & S Avalon Dr &
Ests ... 43953
Avery Ave ... 43952
Backbone Ridge Rd ... 43952
Balinert Dr ... 43953
Bantam Ridge Ct &
Rd ... 43953
Barbara Ave ... 43952

Beaumont Pl 43953
Beechwood Blvd & Dr 43953
Bel Aire Ter 43952
Bell St 43953
Belle Ave 43953
Belleview Blvd 43952
S Bend Blvd 43952
Bennett Blvd 43953
Benson Ln 43952
Benton St 43952
Beverly Ln 43953
Bradley Ave 43953
Brady Ave & Cir 43952
Brandywine Cir E 43953
Braybarton Blvd 43952
Brenda Cir 43953
Brentwood Blvd 43953
Bristol Ave 43952
Brittany Dr 43953
Broadview Pl 43953
Broadway Blvd 43952
Brockton Rd 43953
Brondos Ave 43952
Bryden Rd 43953
Buchanan Rd 43953
Buckeye St 43952
Buena Vista Blvd 43952
Butte St 43952
N & S Byron Dr 43953
Cadiz Rd 43953
Canterbury Blvd 43952
Canton Rd
100-1089 43953
1090-1099 43952
Capital St 43952
Caraplace 43953
Caravel Pl 43953
Cardinal St 43952
E & W Carlton Rd 43953
Carnegie St 43952
Cathy Dr 43953
Cedar Ave 43952
Center Ave 43952
Central Ave & Ct 43952
Cervo Trce 43952
Chase Rd 43953
Chauncey St 43952
Cherry Ave & Dr 43952
Chestnut St 43952
Christopher Ave 43953
E & W Church St 43953
Churchman Cir 43953
Circle Dr 43953
Claire Ave 43952
Claremont Ct 43952
Clashman Ln 43952
Cleveland Ave 43952
Clinton Ave 43952
Colonial Dr 43952
Columbia Ave 43952
Columbus Cir 43952
N & S Commercial St 43952
Concord Dr 43953
Connie St 43952
Country Club Dr 43953
County Road 26 43953
County Road 28 43953
County Road 43 43952
County Road 45 43952
County Road 56 43952
N & S Court St 43952
Crabbe Blvd 43952
Crawford Ave 43953
Crescent Ave 43952
Crestline Dr 43952
Cross St 43953
Cross Creek Rd 43953
Cunningham Dr 43952
Cunningham Ln 43953
Dana Lynn Dr 43953
Darlington Rd 43952
David St 43952
Day Circle Dr 43953
Dean Martin Blvd 43952
Deerfield Dr 43952
Delwood St 43952

Detmar Rd 43953
Devonshire Rd 43952
Digregory Ave 43952
Dock St 43952
Doral Dr & St 43953
Douglas Ave 43953
Dresden Ave 43952
Dunbar Ave 43952
Dusty Ln 43952
Earl Dr 43953
Edgar Ave & Way 43952
Edgewood Dr 43953
Edgewood Pl 43952
Efts Ln 43953
Eisenhower Rd 43953
Ekey St 43953
El Villa Way 43953
Elaine St 43952
Eldorado Dr 43953
Elk St 43952
Ellsworth Ln 43952
Ellsworth St 43953
Elm St
1-107 43952
108-112 43953
109-399 43952
114-114 43952
116-148 43953
150-498 43952
Emmett Way 43952
Estelle Ave 43952
Etta Ave 43952
Euclid Ave 43952
Eugene St 43952
Eve Dr 43952
Everett Way 43952
Evergreen Terrace Dr 43953
Fairmont Ave 43952
Fairview Way 43952
Fairway Dr 43953
Fellows Dr 43953
Fernwood Rd 43953
Floyd St 43953
N Forest Ave 43952
S Forest Ave 43952
Forest Ct 43952
Forest St 43952
Forestview Dr 43953
Foster Pl 43952
Franciscan Way 43952
Franklin Ave 43952
Frostview Dr 43953
Gambill Rd 43952
Garden Dr 43953
Garden Acres 43953
Garfield Ave 43952
Garrett Ave 43952
George St 43952
Girard Ave 43952
Glendwell Rd 43952
Glenn St 43952
Goulds Rd 43953
Grafton Ext & Rd 43953
Gramercy Pl 43952
Granard Pkwy 43952
Grandview Ave 43952
Grandview Dr 43953
Grant St 43952
Greenbrier Ct 43953
Greenfield Ave 43952
Greenwich Ave 43952
Grove St 43953
Gumps Ln 43953
Gundrum Court Rd 43953
Hamilton Pl 43952
Harding Ave 43952
Harmony Dr 43953
Harold St 43952
Harvard Ave & Blvd 43952
Hawthorne Ct 43952
Hazelwood Dr 43953
Hemlock Pl 43952
Henry Ave & Ln 43952
Herald Sq 43952
Hermenia Ave 43952
Hiddenwood Dr 43953

S High St 43952
Highland Ave 43952
Higler Ave 48953
Hill Ave 43952
Hillary Sq 43952
S Hollywood Blvd 43952
Homewood Ave 43952
Howard Dr 43952
Huggins Dr 43952
Hughes Ln 43952
Iva Way 43952
Jacks Ln 43952
Jackson Dr 43953
Jackson Pl 43952
Jeanette Ave 43952
Jefferson St 43952
Jeffrey St 43953
Jewett Rd 43952
John Hood Rd 43952
John Scott Hwy 43952
Johnson Rd 43952
Joyce St 43952
Juanita St 43952
Karen Pl 43953
Keagler Dr 43953
Kendall Ave 43952
Kenwood Rd 43953
Kilgore St 43952
Kings Dr 43952
Kingsdale Rd 43952
Kingston Ave 43952
La Belle Ave & Ct 43952
S Labelle Ct 43952
Lacy Dr 43952
Lafayette Blvd 43952
Laila Ct 43953
N & S Lake Erie St 43952
Lamar Dr 43953
Langley Ave 43952
Laurel Hills Dr 43952
Laurel Woods St 43953
Lauretta Dr 43952
Lawson Ave 43952
Leonard Ave 43953
Levinson Aly 43952
Lewis St 43952
Lexington Dr 43953
Lincoln Ave, Blvd & Pl 43952
Linda Way 43952
Linden Ave 43952
Linduff Ave 43952
Linmar Ave 43953
Locust Ave 43952
Locust Blvd 43953
Locust St 43952
Logan St 43952
Long St 43953
Longford Dr 43952
Longvue Dr 43953
Lovers Ln 43953
Lovers Lane Cir 43953
Ludlow Ave 43952
Luray Dr 43953
Madison Ave 43952
Main St
100-899 43953
900-1099 43952
Majestic Cir 43952
Mall Dr 43952
Malone Ave 43953
Maple Way 43952
Maplewood Ave 43953
Maplewood Dr 43952
Maplewood Way 43952
Margaret St 43952
Marion Pl 43953
Market St 43952
Marsh Aly 43952
Marshall Rd 43953
Martha Pl 43952
Mary Ave & St 43952
Maryland Ave 43952
Maxwell Ave 43952
May Ln 43953
Mccauslen Mnr 43952
Mcconnell Ave 43952

W Mcconnell Ave 43953
Mccook Rd 43952
Mcdowell Ave 43952
Mckee St 43952
Mckinley Ave 43952
Mcneal St 43952
Meadow Dr 43952
Meadow Ln 43953
Meadow Rd 43953
Meadowbrook Dr 43953
Mears Ave 43952
Melinda Dr 43953
Melvin St 43953
Mercer Ave 43952
Meridian Way 43953
Merryman Ave 43952
Michaelangelo Ct 43953
Mildred St 43953
Milhorn Ln 43952
Milky Way 43953
Miller Rd 43952
Moreland Dr 43952
Morningside Dr 43953
Morningside Woods Dr 43953
Morrow Dr 43952
Mount Calvary Ln 43952
Murphy Ave
1-199 43953
200-399 43952
Myers Ave 43952
Myers Dr 43953
Nancy St 43952
Nature Way 43952
Nedra Ave 43952
Negley Ave 43952
Nelson Dr 43952
Nevada Dr 43952
Nimitz Ave 43953
Normandy Dr 43953
Norris St 43952
North St 43953
Norton Pl 43952
Oakgrove Ave 43952
Oakland Way 43952
Oakmont Ave 43952
Ohio St 43952
Old State Route 7 43952
Olive Dr 43953
Oliver Pl 43953
Opal Blvd 43952
Orchard Ave 43952
Orchard Pl 43953
Orchard St
100-399 43953
1100-1199 43952
Oregon Ave 43952
Orlando Mnr 43953
Overlook Dr 43953
Oxford Blvd 43952
Paddy Mud Rd 43952
Park Dr 43953
Park St 43952
W Park St 43953
Parkdale Rd 43952
Parkview Cir 43952
Parkview Dr 43953
Patton Ave 43953
Paul Ave 43953
Paul St 43952
Pekruhn Ct 43952
Pembroke Rd 43953
Penfield Rd 43953
Pennsylvania Ave 43952
Pershing Ave 43952
Peto Ln 43952
Phillips Ln 43952
Pico St 43952
Pine Ln 43953
Pine St 43952
Pine Valley Dr 43953
Pioneer Dr 43953
Pittsburgh St 43952
Pleasant St 43953
Plum St 43952
Porco Strada Rd 43952
Portland Blvd 43952

Potter Ave 43952
Pottery Rd 43952
Powell Ave 43952
Powells Ln 43953
Preston Rd 43953
Princeton Ave 43952
Prospect Ave 43952
Railroad Ave 43952
Rainbow Dr 43953
Randolph Ln 43953
Ravine St 43952
Red Donley Plz 43952
Reichart Ave 43953
Renee Dr 43953
Reserve Ave 43953
Rex Ave 43953
Reynolds Ave 43952
Richland St 43952
Ridge Ave 43952
Rinker Rd 43953
Risdon St 43952
Riverview Ave 43952
Roberts Ln 43952
Roberts St 43953
Rockdale St 43952
Roosevelt Ave 43952
Rosemont Ave 43952
Ross St 43952
Ross Park Blvd 43952
Rosslyn Blvd 43952
Rosswell Ave 43952
Russell Dr 43953
Rustic Rd 43952
Sabina Dr 43953
Saint Andrews Dr 43953
Saint Charles Dr 43952
Saint Joseph Dr 43952
Sams Way 43953
Scenic Dr 43953
Schenley Ave 43952
School St
100-120 43953
121-199 43952
200-299 43953
Scioto Dr 43953
Scott St 43952
Sealock Ave 43952
Selma Dr 43953
Seven Creeks Rd 43952
Sewickley Ave 43952
Shady Ave 43952
Shaffer Trailer Ct 43953
Sharmont Dr 43952
Sheffield Ave 43952
Sherman Ave 43952
Shirley Cir 43952
Short St 43952
Sinclair Ave
1200-1500 43952
1502-1598 43952
1701-1797 43953
1799-1899 43953
Skyline Cir 43953
Skyview Dr 43953
Slack St 43952
Smith Ave 43952
Snug Hbr 43953
Solter Rd 43953
South St 43952
Southeast Dr 43953
Spencer Ave 43952
Spring Ave 43952
Springdale Ave 43953
Squirrel Hl 43953
Squirrel Hill Rd 43953
Stanton Blvd & St 43952
Stardust Dr 43953
Starkdale Rd 43953
Starkey Blvd 43953
State St 43952
State Route 213 43952
State Route 43 43952
State Route 7 43952
Steele Ave 43952
Steuben Woods Dr 43953
Stevens St 43953

Stewart St 43952
Stratford Blvd 43952
Stuart Dr 43953
Summit Ave 43952
Sunny Acres Dr 43953
Sunset Blvd
1400-4599 43952
4600-4699 43953
Sunshine Park Rd 43953
Superior St 43952
Susan Cir & Dr 43953
Swick Ln 43952
Talbott Dr 43953
Target Rd 43953
Technology Way 43952
Tera Mnr 43953
Teresa Dr 43953
Terminal Rd 43952
Terrace Ave 43952
Terrace Dr 43953
S Terrace Dr 43953
Terri Ave 43952
Thomas St 43953
Town St 43952
Township Road 166 43953
Township Road 167 43953
Township Road 281 43952
Township Road 375 43952
Township Road 378 43952
Township Road 380 43952
Township Road 381 43952
Township Road 382 43952
Township Road 384 43952
Township Road 418 43952
Township Road 45c 43952
Township Road 460 43952
Township Road 506 43952
Township Road 582 43952
Township Road 675 43952
Township Road 676 43952
Township Road 677 43952
Township Road 678 43952
Township Road 682 43952
Township Road 683 43952
Trantrel Ave 43952
Troy Dr & Pl 43953
Tweed Ave 43952
Two Acre Dr 43953
Two Ridge Rd 43953
Union Ave 43952
University Blvd 43952
Valleyview Ave 43952
Vernon Ave 43952
Villa Dr 43953
Vireo Dr 43953
Virginia Ave 43952
Walden Ave 43952
Walnut Ave 43952
Walnut St 43953
Ward Dr 43953
Ward Pl 43952
Warren Ln 43953
Washington St 43952
Water St 43952
N & S Webster Ave 43952
Welday Ave
100-118 43953
115-117 43952
119-140 43952
142-144 43952
Wellesley Ave 43952
Wells St 43952
Westmont Ln 43953
Westview Ave 43952
Westwood Dr 43953
White Oaks Dr 43953
Whitehall Pl 43953
Whitehaven Blvd 43952
Wildens Ave 43953
Wildon Ave 43952
Wilkins St 43952
Williams Blvd 43953
Williams Pl 43952
Williams St 43952
Wilma Ave 43952
Wilshire Blvd 43952

Wilson Ave
1000-1199 43952
3400-3699 43953
Wilson Pl 43952
Winks Way 43953
Winters Dr 43953
Woodland Ave 43952
Woodland Park 43953
Woodlawn Ct & Rd 43952
Woodmont Ave 43952
Woodridge Dr 43953
Woodvue Ln 43953
Yale Pl 43952
Yorktown St E & W 43953

NUMBERED STREETS

All Street Addresses 43952

STRONGSVILLE OH

POST OFFICE BOXES MAIN OFFICE STATIONS AND BRANCHES

Box No.s
8000 - 8040 44149
8005 - 8064 44136
49100 - 49699 44149
360001 - 368099 44136

NAMED STREETS

Abigail Ln 44149
Acacia Dr 44136
Academy Dr 44149
Adams Dr 44149
Admiralty Dr 44136
Akita Ct 44136
Alameda Dr 44149
Albion Rd
13000-17200 44136
17202-17298 44136
19000-22299 44149
22301-22999 44149
Alpine Cir 44136
Altis Ct 44149
Antler Ln 44136
Apple Ln 44149
Applebrook Cir 44136
Applewood Ln 44149
Araglin Ct 44149
Arlington Dr 44149
Ascoa Ct 44149
Ash Dr 44149
Ashford Ct 44149
Ashley Cir 44149
Ashwood Dr 44149
Aspen Cir 44136
Atlantic Rd 44149
Autumn Oval 44149
Badger Den Ln 44136
Ballymore St 44149
Balmoral Ct 44136
Barbara Dr 44136
Barton Dr 44149
Basswood Cir 44136
Baywood Ln 44136
Bear Creek Ln 44136
Bears Paw Ln 44136
Beaver Cir 44136
Beech Cir 44136
Beech Creek Trl 44149
Beechwood Ln 44149
Belhaven Pl 44149
Benbow Rd 44149
E & W Bend Dr 44136
Bennington Dr 44136
Bent Tree Ct & Dr 44136
Bentley Ln 44136
Benwood Ct 44149
Berkshire Cir 44149

Bernice Dr 44149
N & S Bexley Cir & Dr 44136
Big Creek Pkwy 44149
Birchwood Ln 44149
Bishop Ln 44149
Bittersweet Ct 44136
Blackberry Cir 44136
Blazey Trl 44136
Blazing Star Dr 44136
Blodgett Creek Trl 44149
Blue Point Dr 44136
Blue Spruce Dr 44149
Bluffside Pl 44136
Bob White Cir 44136
Bonnie Ln 44136
Boston Rd
4200-4898 44149
13000-19098 44136
19100-21200 44149
21202-22998 44149
Bowman Dr 44149
Bradford Ct 44149
Bradgate Ln 44149
Brady Ln 44149
Braemar Way 44149
Brandywine Dr 44136
Breckenridge Ln 44149
Briar Bush Ln 44149
Briarwood Ln 44149
Brick Mill Run 44136
Bridge Path 44136
Bridgecreek Cir 44136
Bridle Trl 44136
Brigadoon Way 44149
Bristol Ln 44149
Britannia Ct 44149
Brittany Pl 44136
Brookfield Pl 44149
Brookline Oval 44136
Brookstone Way 44149
Broxton Dr 44149
Brushwood Ln 44136
Bryn Mawr Blvd 44136
Buccaneer Creek Ln 44149
Bunker Hill Dr 44136
Burgandy Dr 44149
Burlwood Dr 44136
Burnham Dr 44149
Butternut Cir 44149
Calderdale Ln 44136
Calumet Cir 44149
Cambridge Oval 44136
Camden Cir & Dr 44136
Canterbury Dr 44136
Cardinal Cir 44149
Carlton Ct 44149
Carlyle Dr 44149
Carmel Oval 44136
Carol Dr 44136
Cartwright Pkwy 44136
Castlemaine Cir 44149
Castlereagh Ln 44136
Castletown Dr 44136
Castlewood Dr 44149
Cedar Branch Trl 44149
Cedar Creek Dr 44149
Celianna Dr 44149
Century Oak Dr 44136
Chandler Grn 44136
Chapman Cir 44136
Charter Ln 44149
Chase Moor 44136
Chatham Ct 44136
Chatman Dr 44149
Cheerful Ln 44136
Cherry Stone Ln 44136
Cherry Tree Dr 44136
Cheryl Dr 44136
Chestnut Dr 44149
Chestnut Oak Ln 44149
Chevy Chase 44136
Chitanne Rd 44149
Christopher Ct 44149
N & S Churchill Way 44149
Circle Rdg 44136
Clare Ct 44149
Clear Brook Cir 44149
Cliffside Dr 44136
Clinton Cir 44136
Clipper Cove Dr 44136
Co Moor Blvd 44149
Colebright Rd 44136
Colleen Ct 44149
Collier Dr 44136
Colony Ct 44136
Commerce Pkwy 44149
Commons Oval 44136
Compass Point Dr 44136
Concord Dr 44136
Cook Ave 44136
Coopers Run 44149
Corinth Ct 44149
Coronet Dr 44149
Cortland Way 44149
Cottonwood Trl 44136
Council Blf 44136
Country Way 44136
Country Meadows Ln 44149
Countryside Dr 44136
Court Cir 44136
Courtland Dr 44149
Crab Apple Ct 44136
Craig Dr 44149
Creek Bend Ct 44136
Creek Moss Ln 44136
Creek Stone Cir 44149
Creekside Dr 44149
Creekwood Ln 44136
Cricket Ln 44149
Cross Trl N & S 44136
Cross Creek Oval 44136
Crown Point Pkwy 44136
Crystal Creek Dr 44149
Currier Dr 44136
Cypress Ave 44136
Darice Pkwy 44149
Dawn Ct 44136
Decatur Dr 44136
Deer Path Dr 44136
Deer Ridge Cir 44136
Deer Run Ln 44149
Deerfield Dr 44136
Delaware Dr 44136
Dell Dr 44149
Dell Ridge Ct 44149
Delmont Ave 44136
Derby Ct 44149
Dewitt Dr 44136
Diane Cir 44149
Doe Cir 44136
Dogwood Ct 44136
E Donegal Ln 44136
Dorchester Cir 44136
Doria Ct 44149
Dow Cir 44136
Downers Grove Ct 44136
Drake Rd
13000-18999 44136
19000-22299 44149
Driftwood Ct 44149
Durian Cir 44136
Eagles Nest Cir 44136
Eastland Rd 44149
Eastwind Ct 44149
Echo Dr 44149
Edgebrook Dr 44149
Edgehill Oval 44149
Eldorado Trl 44136
Elizabeth Cir 44136
Ellis Way 44136
Ellsworth Dr 44136
Elm Dr 44136
Emerald Edge Pl 44136
Ennis Dr 44149
Erin Cir 44149
Essex Dr 44136
Ethel Dr 44149
Evelyn Ct 44136
Evergreen Dr 44149
Fair Rd 44149
Fair Isle Way 44149
Fair Meadow Pl 44149
Fairfax Ln 44136
Fairfield Pl 44149
Fairtree Dr 44149
Fairwinds Dr 44136
Falling Leaves Rd 44136
Falling Water Rd 44136
Falmouth Dr 44136
Fawn Cir 44136
Fawn Meadow Ln 44136
Fence Row Dr 44149
Fern Canyon Dr 44136
Fernwood Cir 44136
Fetterman Dr 44149
Fetzer Dr & Rd 44136
Fieldstone Pt 44149
Foltz Pkwy 44149
Forest Park Dr 44136
Forest Point Pl 44136
Forestview Dr 44136
Forestwood Dr 44149
Fountain Ct 44136
Fox Grv 44149
Fox Hollow Dr 44136
Fox Hunt Dr 44136
Foxe Dr 44149
Framingham Oval 44136
Fullers Ln 44149
Gary Dr 44136
Gate Post Rd 44149
Georgetown Ct 44136
Gifford Ct 44136
Glen Cairn Way 44149
Glenbrook Dr 44136
Glencreek Ln 44136
Glendale Ave 44136
Glenmar Way 44149
Glenwood Ln 44149
Gold Rush Dr 44136
Golden Star Dr 44136
Grand Prairie Ln 44136
Great Oak Ln 44136
Great Oaks Ln 44149
Greenbrier Dr 44136
Greenfield Pl 44149
Greenwich Dr 44136
Greenwood Dr 44136
Greystone Pt 44149
Grosse Pointe Oval 44136
Grouse Run Pl 44149
Groveside Dr 44136
Hamilton Ct 44136
Hampton Pl 44136
Hampton Chase 44136
Handle Rd 44149
Harbour View Oval 44136
Harper Rd 44149
Hartford Dr & Trl 44136
Harvest Oval 44136
Hastings Ct 44136
Hawks Lookout Ln 44136
Hawthorn Ln 44149
Hazelwood Ave 44149
Hazen Dr 44149
Hearthstone Dr 44136
Heather Ln 44149
Heatherwood Ct 44149
Hemlock Cir 44149
Heritage Trl 44136
Hickory Pl 44149
Hickory Branch Trl 44136
Hidden Meadows Ln 44136
Hidden Woods Ln 44136
High Pt 44136
High Point Club Blvd 44136
Highland Park 44136
Hillcliff Cir 44149
Hollo Oval 44149
Hollowrun Pl 44149
Holly Cir 44149
Homestead Park Dr 44136
Horseshoe Ln 44149
Howe Rd 44149
Hunt Rd 44136
Hunters Pointe Dr 44136
Hunting Meadows Dr 44136
Huntington Park Dr 44136
Idlewood Trl 44149
Imperial Pkwy 44149
Indianhead Ln 44136
Inglewood Ct 44136
N & S Inlet Dr 44136
Ionia Ct 44149
Ivywood Trl 44149
Iyami Ct 44136
Jacque Rd 44136
James Way Dr 44149
Jamestown Cir 44136
Janette Ave 44136
Jasmine Ct 44136
Jefferson Ct 44149
Jerry Coe Ln 44149
Jonathan Dr 44136
Julie Cir 44136
Juniper Ct 44136
Kelsey Ln 44149
Kensington Ct 44136
E & W Kerry Pl 44136
Kettering Oval 44136
Killians Grv 44149
King Coe Ln 44149
Kingswood Ct 44149
Knowlton Pkwy 44149
Kortz Cir 44136
Kronos Ct 44149
Kylemore Dr 44149
N Laguardia Pkwy 44136
Lake Circle Dr 44136
Lake Meadows Dr 44136
Lakeforest Dr 44136
Lakeview Cir 44136
Lanier Ave 44136
Laurelbrook Oval 44136
Laurell Cir 44136
Lauren Way 44136
Leana Ct 44149
Leawood Oval 44136
Ledgepoint Pl 44136
Ledgeside Dr 44136
Lenox Dr 44136
Lexington Ln 44136
Lincolnshire Blvd 44136
Lismore Ct 44136
Little Brook Way 44149
Litto Dr 44136
Logan Ct 44136
Long Boat Cir 44136
Lorraine Dr 44136
Lucerne Ln 44149
Lunn Rd 44136
Lymans Ln 44149
Lyon Ln 44149
Main St 44149
Mallard Cir 44136
Maple Cir 44136
Maple Branch Trl 44149
Maple Brook Trl 44136
Marks Rd 44149
Martins Ln 44149
Mataire Ln 44136
Meadow Ln 44136
Meadow Trl 44136
Meadowgrass Rd 44136
Meadownorth Ct 44136
N & S Meadows Cir 44136
Meadows Edge Ln 44136
Meadowsouth Ct 44136
Melissa Ln 44136
Mill Hollow Ln 44136
Miller Ct 44149
Misty Lake Dr 44136
Mohawk Dr 44136
Montclare Blvd 44136
Monterey Pine Dr 44136
Morar Cir 44136
Morgan Ct 44149
Morning Star Dr 44136
Morris Dr 44136
Moss Point Rd 44136
Moss Ridge Cir 44136
Mulberry Cir 44136
Nanci Dr 44136
Nantucket Row 44136
Needlewood Cir 44149
Niagara Dr 44136
Nicole Cir 44136
Nob Hl 44136
North Trl 44149
Northpointe Cir 44136
Northrup Ln 44149
Northview Dr 44136
Northwood Trl 44149
Oak Bark Trl 44149
Oak Branch Trl 44149
Oak Hollow Ln 44149
Oak Leaf Dr 44136
Oak Trail Ct 44149
Oakhurst Ln 44149
Oakland Park Dr 44136
Oakwood Pl 44149
Old Oak Dr 44149
Olde Creek Trl 44149
Olde Orchard Rd 44136
Olde Surrey Ct 44136
Olde Towne Trl 44136
Oliver Dr 44149
Olympus Ct & Way 44149
Ordner Dr 44136
Osage Dr 44149
Otani Ct 44136
Overland Park Dr 44149
Oxbow Path 44149
Oxford Dr 44149
Oxford Oval 44136
Paddock Cir 44136
Pamela Dr 44149
Panorama Pkwy 44136
Park Pt 44136
Park Cliff Rd 44136
Park Lane Dr 44136
Park Moss Ave 44136
Park View Cir 44136
Parkwood Ln 44136
Partridge Dr 44149
Peachtree Dr 44149
Pearl Rd 44136
Pearlview Dr 44136
Pebble Brook Ln 44149
Pebblestone Ct 44136
Pembrooke Oval 44136
Penny Pines Cir 44136
Pepper Grass Cir 44136
Peppercreek Dr 44136
Pepperwood Ct 44136
Pheasant Run Pl 44136
Pheasant Trail Pl 44136
Pierce Dr 44149
Pin Oak Dr 44136
Pine Lakes Dr 44136
Pine Needle Trl 44149
Pine Tree Pl 44136
Pinebrook Oval 44136
Pineview Cir 44149
Pinewood Dr 44149
Pinnacle Pt 44136
Pioneers Creek Cir 44136
Pirates Cove Cir 44136
Placid Cv 44136
Pleasant Ridge Pl 44136
Plum Brook Ln 44136
Plymouth Row 44136
Point Overlook Pl 44136
Polo Club Dr 44136
Pomeroy Blvd 44136
Porters Ln 44149
Potomac Dr 44136
Prairie Meadows Pl 44136
Priem Rd 44149
Princeton Cir 44136
Progress Dr 44149
Prospect Rd 44149
Quail Hollow Dr 44136
Rabbit Run Dr 44136
Raccoon Trl 44136
Rainier Ct 44136
Ranchwood Dr 44149
N & S Red Oak Dr 44136
N & S Red Rock Dr 44136
Regency Dr 44149
Resting Mdws 44136
Richards Dr 44149
Ridge Creek Rd 44136
Ridge Point Cir 44136
Ridgecliff Cir 44136
Ridgeline Ct 44136
Ringneck Cir 44136
River Moss Rd 44136
River Ridge Rd 44136
Robindale Dr 44136
Rock Creek Cir 44149
Rosalee Ln 44136
Rosewood Ln 44136
Royal Oak Dr 44136
Royalton Rd
13001-18699 44136
18701-18999 44136
19000-22999 44149
Rudy Dr 44149
Ruggiero Dr 44136
Rustic Holw 44136
Ruth Dr 44136
Saddle Horn Cir 44149
Saddlebrook Ln 44149
Sagamore Cir 44136
N & S Salem Row 44136
Sand Creek Cir 44149
Sandalwood Ln 44149
Sandy Spring Oval 44136
Saratoga Trl 44136
Sassafras Dr 44149
Savannah Ct 44136
Scarlet Oak Trl 44149
Scenic Pt 44149
Scotch Pine Way 44149
Scott Dr 44149
Scottsdale Dr 44136
Seashins Rd 44136
Selby Cir 44136
Serenity Dr 44136
Settlers Run 44136
Settlers Trl 44136
Settlers Way 44149
Seven Oaks Dr 44136
Shagbark Trl 44149
Shale Brook Ct & Way 44149
Shandon Ct 44149
Shenandoah Rdg 44149
Sherbrooke Oval 44136
Sherwood Dr 44149
Shireen Dr 44149
Shurmer Rd 44136
South Dr & Trl 44149
Southpark Ctr 44136
Southporte 44136
Southview Ct & Ln 44136
Southwind Ct 44149
Spinnaker Cir 44136
W Sprague Rd
13001-17499 44136
22001-22999 44149
Springfield Cir 44149
Spruce Dr & Pt 44149
Spyglass Hill Dr 44136
Squirrel Hollow Ln 44136
Stafford Dr 44149
Stag Thicket Ln 44136
Stamford Ct 44136
Stapleton Dr 44136
Steeplechase Ln 44149
Stelfast Pkwy 44149
Sterling Way 44149
Steven David Dr 44149
Stillbrooke Dr 44136
Stone Creek Oval 44149
Stoneridge Trl 44136
Stony Point Dr 44136
Stoughton Dr 44149
Stratford Cir 44149
Strongsville Blvd 44149
Summer Place Dr 44149
Sun Meadow Trl 44149
Suncliff Pl 44136
Suncrest Ct 44136
Sunridge Cir 44136
Sunset Dr 44136
Sunwood Oval 44136
Sycamore Cir 44136
Tahoe Cir 44136
Tanbark Ln 44149
Tawny Brook Ln 44149
Temple Dr 44149
Thatchers Ln 44149
The Blf 44136
Timber Creek Cir 44136
Timber Edge Pl 44136
Timber Lake Dr 44136
Timber Oak Ct 44149
Timberline Dr 44136
Tomson Dr 44149
Tracy Ln 44136
Tradewinds Dr 44136
Trails Lndg 44136
Trails Edge Ct 44136
Trailside Pl 44136
Tramore Ln 44149
Trapper Trl 44149
Treasure Isle Cir 44136
Trenton Ave & Oval 44136
Trillium Trl 44149
Trotwood Park 44149
Turkey Meadow Ln 44136
Twelve Oaks Cir 44136
Valley Creek Dr 44136
Valleybrook Ln 44149
Versailles Dr 44136
Village Green Dr 44149
Vincennes Pl 44136
Wakefield Cir 44149
Walking Stick Way 44136
Walnut Dr 44149
Walnut Creek Dr 44149
Watercress Rd 44149
Waterfall Rd 44149
Waterford Pkwy 44149
Webster Rd 44136
Wedgewood Ln 44149
Wellington Ct 44136
Wesley Dr 44136
Westbrooke Ln 44149
Westfield Ln 44136
Westminster Dr 44149
Weston Pt 44136
Westwind Ct 44149
Westwood Dr
18700-18998 44136
19000-22999 44149
Westwood Park Blvd 44149
Weymouth Ln 44136
Wheelers Ln 44149
Whispering Pines Cir 44136
White Bark Dr 44149
N & S White Oaks Dr 44136
Whitemarsh Ln 44149
Whitney Rd
13000-17999 44136
18100-18298 44149
18300-18900 44149
18902-19498 44149
Wildwood Ln 44149
Williamsburg Oval 44136
Willow Cir 44136
Willow Ln 44149
Willow Wood Dr 44136
Wilma Dr 44136
Wilmington Dr 44136
Winchester Ct 44136
Windcliff Rd 44136
Winding Trl 44149
Windsor Dr 44136
Windsor Castle Ln 44149
Windward Way 44136
Wolf Dr 44136
Wolf Run Cir 44136
Wolzhaven Ave 44149
Woodberry Ln 44149
Woodbriar Cir 44136
Woodfield Trl 44149
Woodhaven Dr 44149
Woodhurst Dr 44149
Woodlawn Ct 44149

Woodleaf Rd 44136
Woodridge Cir 44136
Woodrun Dr 44136
Woodshire Dr 44149
Woodside Ct 44136
Woodside Xing N 44149
Woodside Xing S 44149
Woodstock Run 44149
Woodview Cir 44149
Worthington Park Dr 44149
Wynnewood Pl 44149
Yager Dr 44149
Yarrow Pl & Trl 44149
Yorktown Oval 44136

NUMBERED STREETS

All Street Addresses 44136

TOLEDO OH

General Delivery 43601

POST OFFICE BOXES MAIN OFFICE STATIONS AND BRANCHES

Box No.s
1 - 1080 43697
30 - 30 43614
315 - 1079 43699
1311 - 2372 43603
2441 - 2999 43606
2453 - 3497 43607
4401 - 4986 43610
5001 - 5355 43611
5401 - 5938 43613
5620 - 5660 43614
6401 - 6998 43612
7000 - 7004 43623
8000 - 8399 43605
8401 - 8990 43623
9001 - 9952 43697
10000 - 10099 43699
11411 - 11466 43611
12011 - 12285 43612
12400 - 12670 43606
13001 - 13370 43613
14801 - 14801 43614
20001 - 20176 43610
23001 - 23332 43623
30001 - 30534 43603
50401 - 50634 43605
64010 - 64010 43612
70511 - 70656 43607
80001 - 80776 43608
118001 - 118116 43611
140001 - 148004 43614
350001 - 355010 43635
810015 - 820064 43699

NAMED STREETS

A St 43608
Abbotswood Dr 43615
Abbott Ave 43614
Aberdeen Ave 43614
Abygail Trl 43611
Academy Ave 43606
Acklin Ave 43620
Acoma Dr 43623
Acorn Dr 43615
Acton Dr 43615
Adams St 43604
Addington Rd 43607
Addison Ave 43607
Adelaide Dr 43613
Adelbert St 43615
Adella St 43613
Adrian St 43611
Advantage Dr 43612
Airedale Ave 43623
Airline Ave 43609
Airport Hwy
1700-3599 43609
3600-5999 43615
Akron St 43605
Albany St 43611
Albar Dr 43623
Albert St 43605
Albion St
2200-2499 43606
2500-3099 43610
3200-3298 43606
Alcott St 43612
Alden Ct 43609
Aldringham Rd 43606
Alexandria Dr 43606
E Alexis Rd 43612
W Alexis Rd
1-1699 43612
1700-3299 43613
3300-4699 43623
Algonquin Pkwy 43606
Alisdale Dr 43606
Alldays Ave 43607
Allenby Rd 43607
Allendale Dr 43611
Allison Ave 43605
Almeda Dr 43612
Almon Ave 43614
Alpena St 43611
Althea Ln 43623
Altonbrough Dr 43617
Alva St 43612
Alvin St 43607
Alvison Rd 43612
Amanda Cir 43615
Amara Dr 43615
Amber Ct 43608
Amberwood Ln 43617
Ambia St 43610
Amelia St 43607
American Rd E 43612
Amesbury Rd 43612
Amherst Dr 43614
Amsden Ave 43613
Amsterdam Rd 43607
Ancil Rd 43615
Ancona Dr 43623
Anderson Pkwy
3300-3540 43606
3541-3799 43613
Anderson St 43619
Andora Dr 43609
Andover Ave 43612
E & W Andrus Rd 43619
Angel Ave 43611
Angela Pl 43608
Angelwood Dr 43615
Anglebrook Ct 43611
Angola Rd 43615
Ann Dr 43613
Ann Rose Ct 43611
Annabelle Dr 43612
Apple Ave 43609
Apple Crk 43612
Appledore Pl 43606
Applegate Dr 43615
Applewood Dr 43615
Applewood Ln 43619
April Dr 43614
Apsley Blvd 43617
Arbor Dr 43619
Arcadia Ave
200-329 43608
330-799 43610
Arch St 43605
Archwood Ln 43614
Arco Dr 43607
Arden Pl 43605
Argyle St 43607
Aria Dr 43608
Ariel Ave 43623
Arklow Dr 43615
Arletta St 43613
Arlington Ave
1601-1697 43609
1699-2199 43609
2200-2498 43614
2500-3399 43614
Armada Dr 43623
Arnelle Dr 43606
Artis Pl 43605
N & S Arvilla Dr 43623
Asbury Dr 43612
Ascot Ave 43607
Ash St 43611
Ashborne Pl 43606
Ashbrook Dr 43614
Ashdale Ct 43612
Ashland Ave
1900-1999 43604
2000-2399 43620
Ashwood Ave 43608
Aspen Dr 43615
Asta Ct 43613
Astor Ave 43614
Atkins St 43605
Atlantic Ave 43609
Atwell Rd 43613
Atwood Rd 43615
Auburn Ave 43606
Audubon Pl 43606
Aurora L Gonzalez Dr 43609
Austin St 43608
Austin Bluffs Ct 43615
Autumn View Ct 43614
Avalon Pl 43611
Avatar Ct 43615
Avondale Ave
100-799 43604
800-3299 43607
3301-3499 43607
Avonhurst Rd 43623
Ayers Ave 43606
B St 43608
Baden St 43609
Bahiamar Rd 43611
Bailey Rd 43619
Bainbridge Rd 43623
Baker St 43608
Bakewell St 43605
Baldwin Pl 43610
Bales Rd 43613
Balfe St 43609
Balkan Pl 43613
Balsum Ct 43615
Baltimore St 43612
Bampton Ave 43614
Banbury Dr 43615
E Bancroft St
1-599 43620
700-1299 43608
W Bancroft St
13-97 43620
99-799 43620
801-825 43620
827-1899 43606
1900-1998 43607
2001-2699 43607
2700-2798 43606
2800-3299 43606
3300-4199 43606
4200-4400 43615
4402-4498 43615
4500-6021 43615
6020-6020 43635
6022-7498 43615
6023-7499 43615
7500-9099 43617
Bandore Rd 43615
Bangor St 43605
Baninewo Dr 43615
Banks St 43609
Bannockburn Dr 43623
Banquot Way 43615
Bapst Ave 43615
Barbara Dr 43623
Barcelona Dr 43615
Barclay Dr 43609
Barendt Rd 43617
Barker St 43605
Barlow St 43605
Barnstable Dr 43613
Baron Steel Ave 43607
Baronial Plaza Dr 43615
Baronsmede Dr 43615
Baronswood Cir 43615
Barrington Dr 43606
Barrows St 43613
Barry Dr 43617
S Barstow Ave 43623
Bartley Pl 43609
Bassett St 43611
Basswood St 43605
Batavia St 43620
Bateman St 43605
Bates Rd 43610
Baxter St 43606
Bay View Ct 43611
Bayard Ave 43606
Baybrook Ln 43623
Beach St 43619
Beachcraft Dr 43619
Beachwood Dr 43615
Beacon St 43620
Beaconsfield Ct 43623
Beaufort Ave 43613
Beaumont Dr 43608
Bedford Ln 43619
Bedford Woods Dr 43615
Beecham St 43609
Beecher Ave 43615
Beechway Blvd 43614
Belfair Ct 43623
Bell Ave 43607
Bellaire Dr 43611
Belle Aire Ct 43607
Belle Glade Dr 43617
Bellevista Dr 43612
Bellevue Rd
3100-3499 43606
3532-4399 43613
Belmar Ave 43612
Belmont Ave
100-799 43604
800-1799 43607
Belpre Dr 43611
Belt St 43605
Belvedere Dr 43614
Belvoir Dr 43613
Ben Lomond Ct 43607
W Benalex Dr 43612
Bender Dr 43609
Benedict St 43605
Bennett Rd 43612
Benore Rd 43612
Bensch Dr 43614
Bent Tree Dr 43617
Bentley Blvd 43606
Bentwood Dr 43615
E & N Benwick Rd 43613
Berdan Ave
700-796 43610
798-798 43610
800-898 43612
900-1618 43612
1700-3199 43613
Berg St 43604
Beringer Ave 43619
Berkeley Dr 43612
Berkshire Pl 43613
N Berlin Ave 43605
Bernath Ct & Pkwy 43615
Berry St 43605
Berwick Ave 43612
Betag St 43605
Beverly Dr 43614
E, N & S Beverly Hills Dr 43614
Bexford Pl 43606
Bexley Rd 43613
Bieber Dr 43619
Big Stag Cir 43617
Bigelow St
1700-1899 43613
2000-2099 43606
Bihl Ave 43619
Birch Dr 43614
Birchall Rd 43612
Birchard St 43605
Birchdale Dr 43623
Birchtree Dr 43623
Birchwood Ave 43614
Birchwood Ln 43619
Birckhead Pl 43608
Birdie Dr 43615
Birdsall Rd 43612
Birkdale Rd 43615
Birmingham Ter 43605
Birnham Wood Dr 43615
Biscayne Dr 43612
Bishop St 43606
Bishopsgate Dr 43614
Bismark St 43604
Bittersweet Dr 43614
Black Oak Dr 43615
Blackburn Rd 43615
Blackstone Dr 43608
Blackthorn Dr 43614
Blaine St 43606
Blair Ct 43604
Blairmont Ave 43614
Blake Pl 43614
Blanchard St 43608
Blessing Dr 43612
Bloomfield Ave 43607
Bloomfield St 43609
Blossman Rd
5900-6299 43617
6300-6399 43615
6400-7099 43617
Blucher St 43607
Blue Rock Ct 43615
Blue Spruce Ct 43615
Bluff St 43606
Blum St
700-799 43604
800-1399 43607
Boalt St 43609
Bobolink Ln 43615
Bobwhite Dr 43619
Bodette Ave 43613
Bogar St 43605
Bogart St 43607
Boles Dr 43605
Bonaparte Dr 43615
Bond St 43605
Bonfield Dr 43609
Bonnie Brae Cir 43606
Bonnie Brook Rd
4200-4299 43606
4300-4499 43615
Bonsels Pkwy
5600-5899 43615
5900-6299 43617
Bonwood Dr 43623
Boody St 43609
Boone St 43605
Booth Ave 43608
Boothbay Dr 43615
Bordeaux Rue 43619
Boshart Way 43606
Boston Pl 43610
Botkins Dr 43605
Bow St 43609
Bowen Rd
3500-3599 43606
3600-4999 43613
E Bowen Rd 43613
W Bowen Rd 43613
Bowlus Ave 43607
Bowman St 43609
Bowood Rd 43617
Bowser Dr 43613
Boxhall Rd 43612
Boxwood Rd 43613
Boyd St 43615
Boydson Dr 43623
Bradford Dr 43614
Bradmore Dr 43612
Bradner Rd 43619
Brame Pl 43613
Branbury Rd 43612
Brancaster Rd 43615
Branch Dr 43623
Brand Whitlock Homes 43604
Brandel Cir 43615
Brandon Rd 43615
Branleigh Dr 43612
Brant Ct & Rd 43623
Brantford Rd 43606
Breckenridge Dr 43623
Breezeway Dr 43613
Brenda Dr 43614
Brendamar Ct 43611
Brenner Ct 43611
Brent Dr 43611
Brentford Ct 43609
Brentwood Ave 43610
Brentwood Dr 43619
Brest Dr 43614
Bretton Pl 43606
Brewster St 43607
Brian Ln 43619
Briar Ln 43614
Briarcrest Rd 43623
Briarwood Ln 43615
Bricker Ave 43608
Bridgeview Dr 43611
Bridlewood Dr 43614
Bridlington Dr 43623
Brierheath Ave 43614
Brigham St 43608
Brighton Ave 43609
Brigitte Dr 43614
Brim Dr
1600-1699 43612
1700-1999 43613
Brinton Dr 43612
Bristol Ct 43623
Britainia Ct 43617
Brittany Rd 43615
Broadstone Rd 43615
Broadway St
1-699 43604
800-2799 43609
2800-2998 43614
E Broadway St
100-1770 43605
1772-1898 43605
1900-2999 43619
Brock Dr
2900-3399 43613
3500-3699 43623
Brockton Dr 43623
Brodywood Dr 43615
Broer Ave 43607
Brogan Dr 43614
Bromfield Cir 43623
Bromley Dr 43623
Brompton Ct 43615
Bromwich Ln 43615
Bronson Ave & Pl 43608
Bronx Dr 43609
Brook Cliffe Rd 43614
Brook Point Rd 43611
Brookdale Rd 43606
Brooke Park Dr 43612
Brookfield Dr 43623
Brookford Dr 43614
Brookhurst Rd 43623
Brooklawn Dr 43623
Brookley Blvd 43607
Brooklynn Park E 43615
Brookridge Ct 43615
Brookridge Dr 43613
Brookside Rd
3300-3398 43606
3400-4299 43606
4300-4699 43615
Brookview Dr 43615
Brookwood Ave 43604
Brophy Dr 43611
Brothan Dr 43614
Brott Rd 43613
Brown Ave 43607
Brownlee Dr 43615
Brownstone Blvd 43614
Brummel St 43605
Brunswick Dr 43606
Brussels St 43613
Bryant Ct 43610
Bryn Mawr Dr 43606
Brysen Ave 43609
Buchanan Dr 43623
Buckeye St
300-1299 43611
2700-3499 43608
Buckingham St 43607
Bucklew Ct & Dr 43613
Bucks Run Ct 43617
Buell Ave 43613
Buffalo St 43604
Burbank Dr 43607
Burdette St 43613
Burger St 43605
Burgoyne Dr 43612
Burke Glen Rd 43607
Burlingame Dr 43615
Burnett Pl 43610
Burnham Ave 43612
Burnham Green Rd 43615
Burningtree Dr 43623
Burr St 43605
Burr Oaks Dr 43613
Burroughs Dr 43614
Burton Ave 43612
Burwell Dr 43609
Bush St 43604
Butler St 43605
Butterfield Dr 43615
Butternut Ln 43615
Buxton Dr 43614
N Byrne Rd 43607
S Byrne Rd
1-499 43615
500-1099 43609
1101-1197 43614
1199-3199 43614
Byrneport Dr 43609
Byrneway Dr 43614
C St 43608
Cable St 43614
Cadillac Ct 43610
Caledonia St 43605
California Blvd 43612
Calla Ln 43615
Calumet Ave 43607
Calvert Pl 43614
Calverton Rd 43607
Calyx Ln 43623
Camberly Dr 43615
Cambrian Rd 43623
Cambridge St 43610
Camden St 43605
Cameron Ln 43623
Cameron Cove Ct 43623
Camille Dr 43614
Camp St 43605
Campanile Ct 43615
Campbell St 43607
Campus Rd 43606
Canada Southern Ave 43612
Canal Ave 43609
W Candlestick Ct E 43615
Canevin Dr 43623
Cannons Park Rd 43617
Canterbury Ct 43606
Canton Ave
1600-1999 43604
2000-2199 43620
Cape Ln 43615
E & W Capistrano Ave 43612
Capital Commons Dr 43615
Caple Blvd 43619
Capri Dr 43611
Capshore Dr 43611
Caravelle Dr 43623
Carbon St 43605
Cardiff Ct 43606
Cardinal St 43606
Carlingfort Dr 43623
Carlton St 43609
Carlyle St 43605
Carmelle Ct 43614
Carnation Dr 43615

Carol Ln 43615
Caroline Ave 43612
Carpenters Ct 43619
Carriage Dr 43615
Carriage Hill Dr 43606
Carrie Creek Ln 43617
Carrie Pine Ln 43617
Carrietowne Ct 43615
Carrietowne Ln
6500-6699 43615
6700-6748 43617
6750-6899 43617
Carrington St 43615
Carroll Pl 43609
Carskaddon Ave
2900-3199 43606
4500-4522 43615
4524-4899 43615
Cartagena Dr 43623
Carthage Rd 43612
Carvelle Dr 43619
Carver Blvd 43607
Cason Ave 43615
Cass Rd 43614
Cassandra Dr 43611
Castener St 43612
Castle Blvd 43610
Castle Ridge Rd 43617
Castlerock Dr 43615
Castleton Ave 43613
Castlewood Dr 43613
Caswell Ave 43609
Catalina Dr 43615
Catawba St 43612
Cavalear Dr 43606
Cavendish Dr 43623
Caxton Ln 43613
Cecelia Ave 43608
Cedar Rdg 43612
Cedar Creek Dr 43619
Cedar Creek Ln 43617
Cedar Valley Dr 43619
Cedarbrook Ct & Dr 43615
Cedardale Ct 43623
Cedarhurst Rd 43613
Celesta Dr 43612
Centennial Rd 43617
Center St 43609
E Central Ave 43608
W Central Ave
2-151 43608
200-1299 43610
1401-1497 43606
1499-4100 43606
4101-4197 43606
4102-4298 43606
4199-4245 43606
4247-4299 43606
4300-5098 43615
4301-5099 43615
5100-6399 43615
6400-8299 43617
Central Grv 43614
Central Park W 43617
Chadbury Ln 43614
Chadwick Dr 43614
Chalice Way 43613
Challedon Ct 43615
Chalmette Dr 43611
Champe Rd 43615
Champion St 43609
Champlain St
700-1699 43604
1800-2098 43611
2100-2200 43611
2202-2998 43611
Chancery Rd 43617
Chaney Dr 43615
Chantilly Rue 43619
Chapel Ct & Dr 43615
Chapin St 43609
Char Ming Ave 43615
Chardonnay Dr 43615
Charles St 43609
Charlestown Ave 43613
Charlevoix Ct 43607

Charlotte St 43613
Charmaine Dr 43614
Chase St 43611
Chatfield Dr 43615
Chatham Ct 43620
Chatham Vly 43615
Chatsworth Rd 43614
Chelmsford Ln 43614
Chelmsley Ct 43615
Chelsea Ct 43615
Cheltenham Rd 43606
Cherokee Rd 43613
Cherrington Rd 43623
Cherry St
100-900 43604
902-998 43604
1000-3399 43608
3400-3499 43610
Cherry Creek Ln 43615
Cherry Hill Ct 43619
Cherry Hill Rd 43615
Cherry Valley Rd 43607
Cherry Wood Ln 43615
Cherrylawn Dr 43614
Cheryl Ln 43606
Chesapeake Ln 43619
Chesbrough St 43605
Cheshire Woods Rd 43617
Chester St 43609
Chesterton Dr 43615
Chestnut St
300-999 43604
1500-3499 43608
Chestnut Hill Rd 43606
Chevy Chase Ln 43614
Cheyenne Blvd 43614
Chicago St 43611
Chicory Dr 43615
Chippendale Ct 43615
Chippewa Rd 43613
Chipplegate Rd 43614
Chollett Dr 43606
Chorus Ln 43615
Christian Ave 43613
Christie Blvd & St 43606
Christopher Ct 43614
Chriswood Rd 43617
Chrysler Dr 43608
Church St 43605
Cincinnati St 43611
Cinnamon Teal Ct 43617
Circle Dr 43607
Circleview Dr 43615
Circular Rd 43614
N & S Citation Rd 43615
City Park Ave
1-74 43609
75-97 43604
76-98 43609
99-1299 43604
Clara Ave 43612
Claradale Rd 43614
Claredale Rd 43613
Clarendon Dr 43607
Clareridge Dr 43623
Clarewood Dr 43623
Clarion Ave 43615
Clark St 43605
Claudia Dr 43614
Clawson Ave 43623
Claxton St 43615
Clay Ave 43608
Claybourne Dr 43614
Clayton St 43604
Clegg Dr 43613
Cleveland St 43611
Cliange St 43620
Clifford St 43611
Clifton Blvd & Rd 43607
Clinton St 43607
Cloister Ct & Rd 43617
Clover Ln 43623
Clover Ridge Ct 43623
Cloverdale Rd 43612
Clyde St 43605
Clymena St 43612

Coeli Dr 43612
Coining Dr 43612
Colburn St 43609
Colby Dr 43614
Coldstream Rd 43623
Colfax St 43606
Colgate Rd 43623
Colima Dr 43609
N Colleen Ct 43614
College Dr 43607
Collingwood Blvd
301-697 43604
699-1999 43604
2000-2499 43620
2500-3399 43610
3400-3499 43608
Collins St 43610
Collins Park Ave 43605
Collinway St 43606
Collomore Rd 43615
Colonial Ct 43620
Colony Dr 43614
Colony Oaks Dr 43617
Colony Woods Dr 43617
Colorado St 43605
Colton St 43609
Columbia St 43620
Columbus St 43611
Comet Ave 43623
Commerce Park Blvd 43619
Commercial Blvd 43619
Commonwealth Ave 43612
Compton Ct 43615
Concord St 43612
Condley Dr 43608
Cone St 43606
Coney Ct 43605
Conference Dr 43614
Congress St 43609
Connelsville Ave 43615
Conrad Ave 43607
Consaul St 43605
Constitution Ave 43604
Continental Blvd 43607
Cook Dr 43615
Coolidge Pkwy 43613
Copland Blvd 43614
Copley Dr 43615
Copper Creek Ln 43615
Coral Ave 43623
Corbin Rd 43612
Cordova St 43609
Corey Rd
3100-3999 43615
4100-4298 43623
4300-5199 43623
Corey Creek Rd 43623
Corinth St 43609
Cornell Dr 43614
Coronada Dr 43615
Corry Ave 43614
Corydon Dr 43613
Cotswold Rd 43617
Cottage Ave 43608
Council St 43606
Counter St 43608
Country Trce 43615
E Country Club Pkwy 43614
Country Creek Ln 43615
Country Squire Ln 43615
Country View Ln 43615
Courtland Ave 43609
Courville Ave 43623
N & S Cove Blvd 43606
Coventry Ave 43607
Covert Rd 43617
Coveview Dr 43611
Covington Ct 43615
Cowan St 43613
S Coy Rd 43619
Coyne Ave 43605
Crabb Rd 43612
Cragmoor Ave 43614
Craig St 43605
Craigwood Rd 43612
Cranbrook Dr 43615

Crane Ln 43604
Crane Way 43619
Cranford Dr 43614
Cranston Dr 43615
Crary Dr 43613
E & W Crawford Ave 43612
S Creek Ln 43615
Creek Run Dr 43614
Creekside Ave 43612
Creekview Dr 43611
Creekwood Ln 43614
Crescent St 43605
E & W Crest Dr 43614
Cresthaven Ln 43614
Creston St 43605
N & S Crestridge Rd 43623
Crestwood Rd 43612
Cribb St 43612
Crittenden Ave 43609
Crompton Cir 43607
Cropthorne Dr 43623
Crossbough Dr 43614
Crossfields Rd 43623
Crosshaven Ln 43614
Crossleigh Ct 43617
Crosswell Pl 43607
Croton Dr 43607
Crystal St 43605
Cuba St 43615
Cullen Ln 43611
Cumberland Pl 43610
Cummings Ave 43609
Curson Dr 43612
Curtice Rd 43619
Curtis St 43609
Custer Dr 43612
Cuthbert Rd 43607
Cutter St 43605
Cynabare Ct 43611
Cypress Ave 43623
Cypress Ln 43612
Cypress Colony Dr 43617
Cypress Creek Ln 43615
Cyril St 43605
D St 43608
Dahlia Cir & Dr 43611
Dale St 43609
Daleford Dr 43614
Daleview Ct 43614
Dalling Dr 43619
Dalton Rd 43612
Damascus Dr 43615
Dana St 43609
Danberry St 43609
Daniels Ave 43609
Darewood Dr 43623
Darlene Dr 43615
Darlington Rd 43606
Darrel Rd 43612
Darrow Ave 43607
Dartmoor Dr 43612
Dartmouth Dr 43614
E & W Dauber Dr 43615
Dave Oberlin Dr 43605
Davewood Dr 43623
David Dr 43612
Davida Dr 43612
Davids Crk 43611
Davis St 43609
Dawn Rd 43612
Dawson St 43605
Day St 43623
Daytona Dr 43612
Deal Ave 43605
Dean Ave 43608
Deane Dr 43613
Deanville Rd 43617
Dearborn Ave 43605
Dearden Pl 43612
Debra Ct 43615
Decatur St 43609
Deepwood Ln 43614
Deer Park Ct 43614
Deer Trail Ct & Dr 43615
Deerpath Ln 43614
Deerpointe Dr 43617

Deerwood Ln 43615
Deigle Dr 43615
Deland Dr 43612
E Delaware Ave 43608
W Delaware Ave
1-1199 43610
1200-1499 43606
Delence St 43605
Deline Dr 43615
Dellwood Ct & Dr 43613
Delmond Ave 43605
Delmonte Dr 43615
Denby St 43615
Denise Dr 43614
Dennis Ct 43604
Dennison Rd 43615
Densmore Dr 43606
Denver Ave 43605
Depot St 43604
Deptford Ln 43615
Derby Rd 43615
Derbyshire Ct & Rd 43615
Deshler Ave 43605
N Detroit Ave
200-1799 43607
1800-2399 43606
2400-2499 43620
2500-3499 43610
3500-3599 43608
3600-3698 43612
3700-6299 43612
S Detroit Ave
100-899 43609
900-4800 43614
4802-4898 43614
Detwiler Dr 43611
Devilbiss Ct 43623
Devinci Dr 43615
Devon Pl 43610
Devon Hill Rd 43606
Devonshire Rd 43614
Dewey St 43612
Dewlawn Dr 43614
Dexter St 43608
Dianne Ct 43623
Dickens Dr 43607
Digby St 43605
Dikway Dr 43614
Dillrose Dr 43619
Discovery Way 43604
Division St 43604
Dix Ln 43609
Dixie Dr 43611
Dixon Ave 43613
Dogwood Ln 43623
Dolores Ave 43607
Donegal Dr 43623
Donerail Dr 43623
Donnelly Rd 43623
N & S Dorcas Rd 43615
Dorchester Dr 43607
Dorelark St 43608
Dorian Ct & Dr 43614
Doris St 43606
Dority Rd 43615
Dorr St
400-799 43604
801-1097 43607
1099-2599 43607
2600-3198 43606
2601-4499 43607
3200-4498 43607
4500-7599 43615
7600-9099 43617
Doty Dr 43613
Douglas Rd
2200-3599 43606
3600-6210 43613
Dove Ln 43604
Dover Pl 43605
Downing Ave 43607
Doyle St 43608
Drexel Dr 43612
Driftwood Rd 43614
Drouillard Rd 43619
Drummond Rd
2200-3499 43606
3600-4499 43613
Dry Creek Rd 43619
Dryden Dr 43612
Dublin Pl 43614
Dubois Rd 43615
Dulton Dr 43615
Duncan Rd 43613
Dundas Rd 43606
Dundee St 43609
Dunderry Ln 43615
Dunham St 43609
Dunkirk Rd 43606
Dunloe Ct 43615
Dunstans Ln 43617
Dunwood Ct 43609
Dura Ave 43612
Durango Dr 43609
Durham Ct 43623
E St 43608
Eagle Ln 43604
Eaglebrook Rd 43615
Earl St
200-299 43619
400-1199 43605
Earlwood Ave 43605
Eastbrook Dr 43613
Eastedge Dr 43614
Easterly Ct 43605
Eastern Ave 43609
Eastgate Rd
1100-1399 43615
1400-2699 43614
Eastpointe Dr 43619
Eastway St 43612
Eastwick Dr 43614
Eaton Dr 43614
Eberle Dr 43615
Echo Rd 43613
Eddington Ct 43615
Eden Ct 43607
Eden East Dr 43619
Edgar St 43613
Edgebrook Blvd 43615
Edgebrook Dr 43613
Edgedale Cir 43613
Edgehill Rd 43615
Edgemont Rd 43611
Edgevale Rd 43606
Edgewater Dr & Park 43611
Edgewood Dr 43612
Edinborough Dr 43606
Edison St 43611
Edna St 43609
Edwin Dr 43609
Eggeman Ave 43612
Egger Rd 43615
Eileen Rd 43615
Eisenhower Dr 43619
El Centro Dr 43615
Elaine Dr 43613
Elbon St 43608
Elder Dr 43608
Eldora Dr 43613
Eldred Ave 43609
Eleanor Ave 43612
Elgin Ave 43605
Elizabeth St 43604
Elk Ridge Rd 43619
Elkhorn Ln 43617
Elks Run 43617
Ellenridge Ln 43606
Elleric Rd 43619
Elliott Ave 43606
Ellis Ave 43605
Elm Pl 43613
Elm St
200-999 43604
1100-3699 43608
Elm Tree Ct 43619
Elmdale Ct 43609
Elmdale Rd
1-299 43607
500-550 43609
552-700 43609
702-798 43609
Elmer Dr 43615

Elmhurst Rd 43613
Elmlawn Dr 43614
Elmont Rd 43615
Elmore St 43605
Elmridge Rd 43613
Elmview Dr 43613
Elmway Dr 43614
Elmwood Ave 43606
Elsie Ave 43613
Elsmere Ave 43605
Elton St 43608
Elysian Ave 43607
Emden Oaks Ln 43623
Emerald Ave
300-599 43604
600-998 43609
Emerson St 43605
Emery St 43609
Emkay Dr 43606
Emma St 43609
Emmajean Rd 43607
Emmick Dr 43606
Engel Blvd 43611
Enright St 43608
Enterprise Blvd 43612
Erawa Dr 43614
N Erie St
14-16 43604
18-1799 43604
1800-3799 43611
S Erie St
1-413 43604
415-499 43604
601-625 43609
627-900 43609
902-998 43609
Escott Ave 43614
Essex St 43605
Essex Gate Way 43615
Estateway Rd 43607
Estero Pl 43623
Esther St 43605
Eton Rd 43615
Euclid Ave 43605
Evans St 43606
Evansdale Ave 43607
Evanston Ct 43610
Everett St 43608
Evergreen Ct 43610
Evergreen Rd
1800-1899 43607
2100-2599 43606
2600-3199 43606
Eversham Ct 43617
Everwood Rd 43613
Evesham Ave 43607
Ewing St 43607
Executive Pkwy 43606
Exmoor 43615
N & S Expressway Dr 43608
F St 43608
Fair Oaks Dr 43613
Fairbanks Ave 43615
Fairfax Rd 43613
Fairfield Dr
4700-4999 43623
6000-6640 43619
Fairgreen Dr 43613
Fairhaven Dr 43623
Fairlawn Ave 43607
Fairmont St 43605
Fairview Dr 43612
Falcon Rd 43607
Falla Ct 43613
Fallbrook Rd 43614
Fallen Leaf Dr 43615
Falloden St 43607
Falmouth Rd 43615
Fanning Dr 43614
Fantasy Dr 43615
Far Hills Rd 43623
Farkas Rd 43605
Farm View Ct 43615
Farmington Rd 43623
Farnham Rd 43607
Farnstead Dr 43619

Farragut Ave 43613
Farrington Rd 43606
Fassett St 43605
N Favony Ave 43615
Fawn Crst 43617
Fawn Hollow Rd 43617
N Fearing Blvd 43607
S Fearing Blvd 43609
Federal St 43605
Federman St 43609
Felice Dr 43615
Fellows Ave 43608
Felt St 43605
Fenwick Dr 43623
Fern Dr 43613
Fernhill Rd 43607
Fernwood Ave
  500-799 43604
  800-2099 43607
Ferris Ave 43608
Field Ave 43609
Fielding Ave 43615
Finch St 43609
Finchley Ct 43617
Finchwood Ln 43617
Fir Ln 43613
Firethorne Dr 43615
Firlawn Dr 43614
Fitch Rd 43613
Fitchland Ave 43606
Fitkin St 43613
Flag St 43619
Flaire Dr 43615
Flamingo Pl 43623
Flanders Rd 43623
Flanders Hill Ct 43623
Fleet Rd 43615
Fleming Dr 43612
Flint Dr 43614
Floex Dr 43615
E & W Florence Ave 43605
Florita Dr 43615
Flormar Ct 43612
Floyd St 43620
Flynn Ct 43615
Folkstone Rd 43614
Foraker Ave 43609
Ford Ave 43612
Fordway St 43606
Foredale Ave 43609
Forest Ave
  600-1799 43607
  1800-2199 43606
Forest Bend Ct 43615
Forest Green Dr 43615
Forest Grove Dr 43623
Forest Hill Ct & Dr 43623
Forest Scene Dr 43614
Forestlawn Rd 43623
Forestvale Rd 43615
Forestview Dr 43615
Forrer St 43607
Forsythe St 43605
Fortune Dr 43611
Foster Ave
  1200-1599 43606
  1900-1999 43607
Fostoria Rd 43619
Foth Dr 43613
E & W Foulkes St 43605
Fox Run 43623
Fox Borough Ct 43614
Fox Hill Dr 43623
Foxbourne Rd 43614
Foxbrook Ct 43611
Foxchapel Rd 43607
Foxcroft Rd 43615
Foxfire Ct 43615
Foxglove Rd 43623
Frampton Dr 43614
Francis Ave 43609
Frank St 43609
Franklin Ave
  1800-1999 43604
  2000-2499 43620
  2500-2699 43610
  3000-3098 43608
  3100-3499 43608
Fredelia Dr 43623
Frederick St 43608
Fredonia Ave 43608
E Freedom Dr 43619
N Freedom Dr 43619
S Freedom Dr 43619
Freedom St 43605
Freeman St 43606
Frelinso St 43604
Fremont St 43605
Frenchmens Rd 43607
Frey Rd 43619
Friars Ln 43615
Friarton Cir 43617
Friedly Dr 43623
Fries Ave 43609
Front St 43605
Frontenac St 43607
Fryer Ave 43615
Fullington Rd 43614
Fulton St
  2000-2098 43620
  2100-2499 43620
  2500-3099 43610
Funston St 43612
Futura Dr 43612
Gage Rd 43612
Galahad Dr 43613
Galena St 43611
Gallatin Rd 43606
Gallier Dr 43611
Gany Mede Dr 43623
Garden Ln 43607
Garden Trl 43614
Garden Estates Dr 43623
Garden Lake Ct, Dr,
Pkwy & Pl 43614
Garden Park Dr 43613
Garden Ridge Dr 43614
Gardengate Pl 43614
Gardner Ave 43619
Garfield Pl 43605
Garland Ave 43609
Garrison Rd 43613
Gasser St 43606
Gateway Dr 43614
Gawil Ave 43609
Gay St 43613
Geer Ln 43615
Genesee St 43605
Geneva Ave 43609
George St
  200-299 43619
  700-1099 43608
George Hardy Dr 43605
Georgedale Rd 43613
Georgetown Ave 43613
Georgia Ave 43613
Gessner St 43605
Giant St
  1700-1999 43613
  2000-2221 43606
Gibbons St 43609
Gibley Park Rd 43617
Gibralter Heights Dr 43609
Gibson Dr 43612
Giger Dr 43611
Gilbert Rd 43614
Gilhouse Rd 43623
Gill St 43605
Gilliotte St 43613
Ginger Trl 43623
Ginger Hill Ln & Rd 43623
Ginger Tree Ln 43623
Girard St 43605
Gladstone Ave 43608
Glann Rd 43607
Glanzman Rd 43614
S Glass Bowl Dr 43606
Glaston Oaks Ct 43617
E & S Glastonberry Ct &
Rd 43613
Glen Arbor Dr 43614
Glen Ellyn Dr 43614
Glen Oaks Dr 43613
Glen Valley Dr 43614
Glenbrier Rd 43614
Glenbrook Dr 43614
Glencairn Ave 43614
Glencoe St 43605
Glencove Dr 43609
Glencrag Way 43615
Glendale Ave 43614
Glendel Ln 43614
Glenfield Ln 43614
Glenford Dr 43614
Glengary Rd 43617
Glengate Dr 43614
Glenloch Way 43615
Glenmere Way 43615
E Glenn St 43613
Glenridge Dr 43614
Glenrock Ct 43615
Glenross Pl 43619
Glenton Dr 43614
Glenview Rd 43614
Glenway St 43607
Glenwood Ave
  1700-1799 43604
  1901-1997 43620
  1999-2499 43620
  2500-3499 43610
Globe Ave 43615
Gloria Ct 43614
Gloucester Dr 43615
Glynn Dr 43614
Goddard Rd 43606
Golden Rd 43615
Golf Ln 43614
Golf Creek Dr 43623
Golfgate Dr 43614
Goodale Ave 43606
Goodhue Rd 43615
Goodrich Ave 43619
Goodwill Rd 43613
Goodwin Ave 43605
Goodwood Ave 43612
Gordon St 43609
Gorney Pl 43608
Gould Rd 43612
Gould St 43619
Government Ctr 43604
Graceway Dr 43606
Gracewood Rd 43613
Gradolph St 43612
Gradwohl Rd 43617
Grafton Ave 43609
Graham St 43605
W Gramercy Ave 43612
Grand Ave
  1001-1097 43606
  1099-1699 43606
  1700-1910 43607
Grandview Ct 43614
Granite Cir 43617
Granite Ln 43615
Grantley Rd
  3500-3599 43606
  3600-4499 43613
Grantwood Dr 43613
Granville Ct 43615
Gray Fox Curv 43617
Grayling Pl 43623
Grecourt Dr 43615
Green Glen Rd 43614
Green Meadow Ct 43614
Green Valley Dr 43614
Greenacre Rd 43615
Greenbriar Rd 43607
Greenbrook Ct 43614
Greencrest Ln 43614
Greene St 43609
Greenfield St 43605
Greengate Dr 43614
Greenhills Rd 43607
Greening Rd 43607
Greenlawn Ct & Dr 43614
Greenridge Dr & Ln 43615
Greenrose Ct 43614
Greenview Dr 43606
Greenway St 43607
Greenwich Ln 43611
Greenwood Ave 43605
Grelyn Dr 43615
Gretna Green Ave 43607
Greystone Pkwy 43615
Gribbin Ln 43612
Griffin St 43609
Grimes Golden Dr 43611
Grimsby Pl 43606
Groesbeck St 43604
Gronlund Cir 43614
Grosse Point Pkwy 43611
W Grove Pl 43620
Groveland Rd
  2300-2499 43613
  2801-2899 43606
Guardian Dr 43615
Gunckel Blvd 43606
Hackett Rd 43610
Haddington Dr 43623
Haddon Rd 43623
Hageman Rd 43619
Hagley Rd 43612
Hagman Rd 43612
Hakes Rd 43619
Hal Dr 43615
Halfway Ct 43612
Halifax Rd 43606
Hallgate Ave 43612
Halstead St 43605
Hamilton St
  100-799 43604
  800-1799 43607
Hammond Dr 43611
Hampsford Cir 43617
Hampton Ave 43609
Hancock Ave 43615
Hannaford Dr 43623
Hanover St 43609
Hanson St
  700-999 43619
  1000-1099 43605
E Harbor Dr 43611
Harbord Dr 43623
Hardale Blvd 43606
Harding Ave 43619
Harding Dr 43609
Hardwood Ct 43612
N Harefoote Rd 43615
Harford Rd 43612
Hargo Rd 43606
Hargrave Rd 43615
Harlan Rd 43615
Harleau Pl 43610
Harley Rd
  3300-3599 43606
  3600-3799 43613
Harmony Ln 43615
Harold Ave 43615
Harold Ct 43608
Harrington Dr 43612
Harrington St 43615
Harris St 43613
Harrison St 43609
Harrow Rd 43615
Harschel Dr 43623
Hartman St 43608
Hartwell Ave 43607
Harvard Blvd 43614
Harvest Ln 43623
Harvey St 43608
Hastings Ave 43607
Hasty Rd 43615
Hathaway St 43605
Haughton Dr 43606
Hausman St 43608
N Haven Ave 43612
N Haven Rd 43615
S Haven Rd 43615
Havencrest Ct 43611
Havenhurst Ave &
Blvd 43614
Havenwood Dr 43614
Haverhill Dr 43612
Havre St 43609
Hawk St 43612
Hawkins Ave 43607
N Hawley St 43607
S Hawley St 43609
Hawthorne Rd & St 43606
Hayden St 43605
Hayes Rd 43615
Hazelhurst Ave 43612
Hazeltine 43615
Hazelwood St 43605
Hearthstone Pl 43613
Heather Gate Blvd 43614
Heather Hills Rd 43614
Heatherbank Rd 43614
Heatherbrook Dr 43614
Heathercove Pl 43614
Heatherdale Dr 43609
Heatherdowns Blvd 43614
Heathergreen Ct 43614
Heatherlake Pl 43614
Heatherlawn Dr 43614
Heatherton Dr 43614
Heathervalley Pl 43614
Heatherwood Dr 43614
Heatherwyck Ct 43614
Heathfield Rd 43614
Heathshire Dr 43607
Hecla Ct 43611
Heffner St 43605
Heidelberg Rd 43615
E Heights Dr 43613
Helen Dr 43615
Helene Ct 43623
Helmond Ct 43611
Hemlock Dr 43614
Hempstead Rd 43606
Hendalis St 43604
Hendon St 43606
Heritage Ct 43612
Herman Pl 43623
Hermosa Ave 43607
Herst Rd 43613
Hess Rd 43615
Heston St 43607
Heysler Rd 43617
Hickory St 43605
Hidden Pines Way 43623
Hidden Ridge Rd 43615
Hidden Valley Dr 43615
Hiddenbrook Dr 43613
Hiddenwood Ct 43615
Hiett Ave 43609
Higgins St 43608
High St 43609
High Oaks Blvd 43623
High Pines Dr 43615
Highland Ave 43610
Highland Green Dr 43614
Highpoint Dr 43615
Higley St 43612
Hilary Ln 43615
Hildebrand Ave 43604
Hill Ave
  2100-4399 43607
  4400-6799 43615
Hill River Dr 43615
Hillandale Rd 43606
Hillcrest Ave 43612
Hillcroft Dr 43615
Hillside Ave 43609
Hilltop Blvd 43607
Hilltop Ln 43615
Hillwood Dr 43608
Hillwyck Dr 43615
Hilton Dr 43615
Hinde Rd 43607
Hingham Ln 43615
Hinsdale Dr 43614
Hippo Way 43609
Hirzel St 43605
Hoag St
  200-1799 43607
  1800-1999 43606
Hobart St 43609
Hoehler Dr 43606
Hoffman Rd 43611
Hogan Ave 43615
Hogarth Rd 43615
Hoiles Ave 43612
Holbrook St 43607
Holifield Dr 43623
N Holland Sylvania Rd
  1-9 43615
  11-3899 43615
  4000-4699 43623
S Holland Sylvania Rd 43615
Holliday Dr 43611
Hollow Creek Dr 43617
Holly Glenn Dr 43612
Holly Hill Dr 43614
Holly Valley Dr 43612
Hollywood Ave
  2200-2299 43606
  2300-2499 43620
Holman Rd 43615
Holmes St 43605
Holstein Rd 43617
Holyoke Dr 43606
Homan Dr 43615
Home Ln 43623
Homeland Dr 43611
Homer Ave 43608
Homerdale Ave 43623
Homeside Ave 43612
Homestead St 43605
Homewood Ave 43612
Honeymaple Ln 43623
Hood St 43610
Hoops Dr 43611
Hopewell Pl 43606
Hopkins Ct 43607
Horace St 43606
Horseshoe Dr W 43615
Horton St 43620
Hospital Dr 43614
House Of Stuart Ave 43607
Howard St 43609
Howland Ave 43605
Huberdale Ct 43605
E & W Hudson St 43608
Hughes Blvd & Dr 43606
Hull St 43605
Humboldt St 43604
Hunker Rd 43605
Hunters Green Dr 43623
Hunters Trail Dr 43607
Hunting Creek Rd 43615
Huntingfield Blvd 43615
Huntley Rd 43606
Hurd St 43605
Hurley Ct & Dr 43614
Huron Ct 43611
N Huron St 43604
S Huron St 43604
Hyatt Ln 43604
Hyde Pl 43610
Ida Dr 43613
Idaho St 43605
Idlewood Dr 43615
Ilger Ave 43606
Imani Cir 43604
Imlay St 43612
Imperial Blvd 43623
Imperial Dr
  4300-4417 43615
  4418-4899 43623
Independence Rd 43607
Indian Rd
  3300-4299 43606
  4000-4021 43606
  4023-4099 43606
  4300-4599 43615
Indian Knoll Dr 43607
Indian Oaks Ln 43617
Indian River Rd 43607
Indian Trail Ln 43617
Indiana Ave
  1-799 43604
  800-1799 43607
Indianola Dr 43614
Industrial St 43605
Ingomar Ave 43609
Inlands Ct 43615
Innisbrook Rd 43606
Innovative Dr 43619
Inverdale Ave 43607
Inverness Ave 43607
Inwood Dr 43606
Ira Rd 43605
Irma Pl 43612
Ironwood Ave 43605
Irving St 43620
Irvington Pl 43606
Isabella St 43606
Isha Laye Way 43606
Isherwood Ave 43606
Island Ave 43614
Islington St 43610
Ivanhill Rd 43615
Ivy Pl 43613
Jackman Rd
  3100-3499 43613
  3500-4700 43612
  4702-4798 43612
  4800-6199 43613
  6201-6215 43613
Jackson St 43604
James Gate Dr 43615
Jamesford Dr 43617
Jamestown Dr
  500-699 43607
  2400-2499 43619
Jamesway Dr 43606
Jamie Ln 43611
Jamieson Dr 43613
Jan Ct 43613
Jasik Dr 43611
Jason St 43611
Jay St 43605
Jean Rd 43615
Jeannette Ave 43608
Jeep Pkwy 43610
Jefferson Ave 43604
Jennings Dr 43615
Jermain Dr 43606
Jervis St 43609
Jessie St 43605
Joann Dr 43612
Jodore Ave 43606
Joel Ave
  200-299 43619
  1100-1199 43610
Joelle Dr 43617
Joffre Ave 43607
John Q Carey Dr 43605
Johnson St 43607
Joseph St
  1900-1999 43619
  3000-3099 43611
Joyce Ln 43615
Judge Dr 43615
Juhasz St 43605
Juliet Dr 43614
Junction Ave 43607
June Dr 43614
Juniper Dr 43614
Jutland St 43613
Kalida Dr 43612
Kane St 43612
Karen St 43623
Karendale Dr 43614
Katherine Ave 43613
Kathy Ln 43623
Kearsdale Rd 43623
Kedron St 43605
Keefer Dr 43615
Keemont Dr 43613
Keen Ave 43611
Keeshin Pl 43612
Keil Rd 43607
Kelker St 43617
Kelley Ave 43613
Kellogg Rd 43615
Kelsey Ave 43605
Kemper Ave 43609
Kendale Dr 43606
Kenilworth Ave
  1-99 43608

200-499 43610
Kenmore Ave 43609
Kennerly Dr 43612
N & S Kennison Dr 43609
Kensington Rd 43607
Kent St 43620
Kenwood Blvd 43606
Kenyon Dr 43614
Kepler Rd 43612
Kerr St 43623
Kershaw Ave
3400-3499 43606
3540-3999 43613
Ketcham Ave 43608
Ketner Ave 43613
Kettering Dr 43612
Ketukkee Trl 43611
Kevin Pl 43610
Key St 43614
Keygate Dr 43614
Kildare Dr 43615
Kimball Ave 43610
Kimberly Dr 43615
Kimberton Dr 43614
Kincora Dr 43612
Kinder Rd 43615
King Rd 43617
King St 43607
King Arthur Ct 43613
Kings Cv 43619
Kings Hollow Ct 43617
Kings Park Rd 43617
Kings Pointe Rd 43617
Kingsbury Ave 43612
Kingsford Dr 43614
Kingsgate Rd 43606
Kingsley Ct 43607
Kingsmoor Dr 43613
Kingston Ave 43605
Kingswood Trail Dr 43615
Kinsale Ct 43615
Kipling Dr 43612
Kirby Pl 43608
Kirk St 43614
Kirkland Rd 43615
Kirkwall Rd 43606
Kitchener Dr 43615
Klondike St 43607
Knapp St 43604
Kneer Dr 43614
Knights Hill Ln 43614
Knightsbridge Dr 43614
Knightswood Ln 43617
Knoll Ave 43615
Knollcrest Rd 43611
Knower St 43609
Knox St 43605
Koch Dr 43615
Koehler Ave 43613
Kopernik Ave 43607
Kosciusko St 43608
Kossuth St 43605
Kress St 43610
Krieger Dr 43615
Kristi Lynne Ln 43617
Kuhlman Dr 43609
Kury Ave 43607
Kyle St 43611
Kylemore Rd 43606
La Jolla Dr 43615
Laburnum Ln 43604
Lachapelle Dr 43611
Laclede Rd 43612
Lafayette St 43604
Lagrange St
200-298 43604
300-999 43604
1000-3500 43608
3502-3598 43608
3701-3797 43612
3799-4499 43612
Lainar Dr 43606
E & W Lake St 43608
Lake Pointe Dr 43614
Lake Shore Ave 43609
Lake Vista Dr 43614
Lakehurst Dr 43619
Lakepointe Dr 43619
Lakeside Ave 43611
Laketon Ter 43619
Lakewood St 43605
Lambert Dr 43613
Lampwick Pl 43614
Lamson St 43620
Lancaster Ave 43615
Lancelot Rd 43623
Lane Ave 43606
Langdon St 43609
Laning Rd 43615
Lansdowne Rd 43623
Lape Kala Way 43606
Lapier St 43611
Larc Ln 43614
Larch Rd 43617
Larchmont Pkwy 43613
Larchway Ct & Rd 43613
Larchwood Ln 43614
Lark Ave 43613
Larkhall Dr 43614
Larkhaven Dr 43623
Larkin Dr 43609
Larkspur Ln 43615
Lasalle St 43611
E Laskey Rd 43612
W Laskey Rd
2-498 43612
500-1699 43612
1700-3299 43613
3300-4999 43623
Latonia Blvd 43606
Lauderdale Dr 43615
Laurel Ave 43614
Laurel Hill Pl 43614
Laurel Oak Ln 43615
Laurel Valley Dr 43614
Lauren Ln 43619
Laurentide Ln 43614
Lawndale Dr 43619
Lawnview Ave 43607
Lawrence Ave
1300-1799 43607
1800-2099 43606
2101-2199 43606
2300-2499 43620
2500-3099 43610
Lawrin Dr 43623
Lawton Ave
2300-2399 43606
2400-2499 43620
Leach Ave 43605
Leamington Ave 43613
Leander Dr 43615
Lear Dr 43619
Lebanon St 43605
Ledyard Ave 43606
Lee St 43605
Lehman Ave 43611
Leicester Rd 43617
Leisure Dr 43615
Leith Dr 43614
Leland Ave 43609
Lemert St 43605
Lemon Crk 43612
Lemoyne Rd 43619
Lenox St 43620
Lenticel Dr 43623
Leonard St 43605
Lerado Rd 43623
Lester Ave 43619
Letchworth Pkwy 43606
Levis Sq 43604
Lewis Ave 43612
Lexham Rd 43615
Lexington Ave 43606
Leybourn Ave 43612
Liberty St 43605
Library Cir 43614
Licking St 43605
Lighthouse Dr 43611
Lima Ave 43613
Lincoln Ave
500-699 43604
800-1599 43607
E & W Lincolnshire Blvd 43606
Lincolnshire Woods Ct & Rd 43606
Linda Dr 43612
Lindbergh Dr 43615
Linden Ln 43615
Linden Pl 43609
Linden Green Dr 43614
Lindsay Ave 43610
Linmore St 43605
Lint Ave 43612
Linwood Ave
1900-1999 43604
2000-2098 43620
Lisa Ln 43611
Live Oak Dr 43613
Liverpool Ct 43617
Livingston Dr 43613
Loch Lomond Ave 43607
N Lockwood Ave 43612
Locust St
200-999 43604
1300-2699 43608
Lodge Ave 43609
Logan St 43604
Lois Ct 43613
Lombard Ave 43614
E & S London Sq 43606
London Ridge Ct 43615
Londonderry Ln 43615
Long Winter Ln 43614
Longdale Ave 43605
Longwood Dr 43615
Lookover Ct 43612
Lorain St 43609
Lorle St 43606
Lost Creek Dr 43617
Lott Ct 43605
Lotus Ave 43609
Louie St 43609
Louis St 43619
Lowe Rd 43612
Lowell Dr 43610
Loxley Rd 43613
Luann Ave 43623
Lucas St
1-699 43604
1201-1297 43607
1299-1399 43607
Lucien St 43605
Luddington Dr 43615
Luscombe Dr 43614
Lutaway Dr 43614
Lyceum Pl 43613
Lyman Ave 43612
Lynbridge Ln 43614
Lynbrook Dr 43614
Lynn Park Dr 43615
Lynnhaven Dr 43609
Lyric Ln 43615
Mabel St 43612
Macarthur Dr 43619
Macauley Ct 43607
Machen St 43620
Macklyn Dr 43615
Mackow Dr 43607
Macomber St 43606
Madeleine St 43605
Madison Ave 43604
Maeterlinck Ave 43614
Magnolia St 43604
Magyar St 43605
Maher St 43608
Main St 43605
Majestic Dr 43608
Malabar Dr 43611
Malcolm Rd 43615
Malden Ave 43623
Malerrai Dr 43614
Mallett St 43612
Mallory Ct 43623
Manchester Blvd 43606
E Manhattan Blvd
1-2100 43608
2102-2298 43608
2800-3600 43611
3602-3898 43611
W Manhattan Blvd 43608
Manila St 43607
Manoa Ln & Rd N 43615
Manorwood Rd 43612
Mansfield Rd 43613
Mantey Ln 43623
Maple Ln 43615
Maple St 43608
Maple Colony Dr 43617
Mapleview Dr 43623
Mapleway Dr 43614
Maplewood Ave
2000-2298 43620
2300-2499 43620
2500-3499 43610
Marcella Ct 43607
March Dr 43614
Marcy St 43605
Mardone Dr 43615
Marengo St 43614
Marie St 43619
Marin Dr 43613
Marine Rd 43609
Marion Ct & St 43609
Maritime Plz 43604
Mark St 43608
Market St 43604
Markham Ct 43615
Markway Rd 43606
Marlaine Dr 43606
Marlboro St 43609
Marlow Rd 43613
Marmion Ave 43607
Marne Ave 43613
Marquette Pkwy 43612
Marriat Rd 43615
Marsrow Ave 43615
Martha Ave 43612
Marthal Rd 43607
Martin Ave 43612
Martin Ln 43604
Martin Luther King Jr Dr 43604
Marvin Ave 43606
Marvindale Dr 43606
Marwood Ave 43607
Mary Ave 43619
Maryann Pl 43614
Marybrook Dr 43615
Maryland Ave 43605
Maryland Pl 43619
Mason St
200-299 43619
800-2099 43605
Massillon St 43605
Mathers Ave 43615
Mathews Rd 43619
Matlack Ave 43613
Matson St 43606
E Matzinger Rd 43612
Maumee Ave 43609
Maxwell Rd
3400-3599 43606
3600-3999 43613
May Ave 43614
Mayberry St 43609
Mayfair Blvd 43612
Mayfield Dr 43612
Mayo St 43611
Mayport Dr 43611
Mayville Pl 43620
Maywood Ave 43608
Mcclinton Nunn Homes St 43604
Mcclure Rd 43612
N Mccord Rd
1-3099 43615
3100-3999 43617
Mcdonald St 43612
Mcgregor Ln
3000-3299 43613
3300-4299 43623
Mckain Dr 43623
Mckeever St 43613
Mckinley Ave 43605
Mckivett Dr 43615
Mcnerney Dr 43619
Mctigue Dr 43615
Meadow Ln 43623
Meadow Creek Ct 43614
Meadow Rue Dr 43614
Meadowbrook Ct 43606
Meadowchase Ln 43615
Meadowcroft Ln 43615
Meadowhill Ct 43614
Meadowlake Dr 43617
Meadowland Trl 43615
Meadowlark Ave 43614
Meadowrise Ct 43611
Meadowvale Dr 43613
Meadowview Ln 43619
Meadowwood Dr 43606
Mechanic St 43605
Medcorp Dr 43608
Medford Dr 43614
E Medical Loop 43614
Meijer Dr 43617
Mel Simon Dr 43612
Melamad Ct 43609
Melington Dr 43610
Melleray Ct 43615
Mellwood Ave & Ct 43613
Melody Ln 43615
Melrose Ave 43610
Melva Ct 43611
Melvin Dr 43615
Mentor Dr 43608
Mercer Ct & St 43609
Mercereau Pl 43607
Merle St 43623
Merrimac Blvd 43606
Merriweather Rd 43623
Merry Ln 43615
Metcalf Rd 43615
Meteor Ave 43623
Mettler St 43608
Miami St 43605
Micham Rd 43615
Michele Dr 43614
N Michigan St
1-1799 43604
1800-2999 43611
S Michigan St 43604
Middlebury Ln 43612
Middlesex Dr 43606
Midland Ave 43614
Midlawn Dr 43614
Midvale Ave 43605
Midway Plaisance St 43607
Midwest Ave 43613
Midwood Ave 43606
Milan St 43605
Milburn Ave 43606
Miles Ave 43606
Milford St 43605
Mill St 43609
Mill Run Ct 43623
Millard Ave 43605
Millbury Rd 43619
Miller Rd 43619
N Miller St 43607
S Miller St 43609
Millicent Ave 43615
Milrose Ln 43617
Milroy St 43605
Milstead Dr 43606
Milton St 43605
Miner Rd 43615
Minerva St 43605
Miramar Dr 43614
Misty Ln 43619
Mitchell St 43609
Mockingbird Ln 43623
Moffat Rd 43615
Mona Ln 43613
Monac Dr 43623
Monarch Pl 43619
Monroe St
1-2399 43604
2400-2699 43620
2700-4354 43606
4356-4398 43613
4400-4599 43613
4600-5499 43623
Mont Royal Dr 43608
Montain Rd 43615
Montcalm St 43607
Montebello Rd 43607
Monterey Ct 43609
Montrose Ave 43607
Moore St 43608
Moorish Ave 43604
Morack Dr 43615
Moran Ave 43607
Moravan St 43605
Morgan St 43619
Morning Glory Ln 43614
Morningside Dr 43612
Morrell Dr 43613
Morris St 43604
Morrison Dr 43605
Morrow Rd 43615
Morton St 43609
Mosher St 43605
Moss Crk 43612
Moss St 43608
Mott Ave 43605
Mound Ave 43614
Mount Vernon Ave 43607
Mourning Dove Ct 43617
Mozart St 43609
Muirfield Ave 43614
Mulberry St
300-999 43604
1601-1697 43608
1699-3499 43608
Murnen Rd 43623
Murray Dr 43613
Myers St 43609
Myrtle St 43605
Nagy St 43605
Nancy Dr 43607
Nannette Dr 43614
Nantuckett Dr 43623
Naomi Dr 43623
Naples Dr 43615
Nash Rd 43613
Nathan Dr 43611
National Ave 43609
Navarre Ave 43605
Nearing Ave 43608
Nebraska Ave
300-398 43604
400-799 43604
800-4199 43607
5000-5198 43615
5200-7599 43615
7600-8400 43617
8402-8998 43617
Neise Ave 43605
Nela Pkwy 43615
Nelson Ave 43609
Nesslewood Ave 43610
Nevada St 43605
New Towne Square Dr 43612
New West Rd 43617
New York Ave 43611
Newbury St 43609
Newhart Cir 43615
Newport Ave 43613
Newton St 43604
Nicholas St 43609
Noble St 43608
Norcross Dr 43619
Norma Pl 43619
North St 43620
Northbrook Dr 43623
Northbrook Ln 43612
Northcroft Ln 43611
Northdale Dr 43612
Northeast Dr 43612
E & W Northgate Pkwy 43612
Northgrove Pl 43611
Northlawn Ct & Dr 43612
Northmoor Rd
4100-4299 43606
4300-4499 43615
Northover Rd 43613
Northridge Dr 43611
Northridge Ln 43612
Northshire Dr 43611
Northshore Dr 43611
Northtowne Ct 43612
Northtowne Dr 43611
Northview Ln 43612
Northville Dr 43612
Northwood Ave
2600-3399 43606
3400-3599 43613
Northwyck Dr 43611
Norton Pl 43615
Norval Ct 43609
Norwalk St 43605
Norwich Rd 43615
Norwood Ave
400-799 43604
800-1899 43607
Norwood Ct 43604
Notting Hill Rd 43617
Nottingham Ter 43610
Nukar Dr 43615
N Oak Ct 43623
S Oak Ct 43623
Oak St
1-1899 43605
1900-1999 43619
Oak Alley Ct 43606
Oak Creek Ln 43615
Oak Forest Dr 43614
Oak Glen Dr 43613
Oak Grove Pl 43613
Oak Hill Ct 43614
Oak Park Dr
600-999 43617
1001-1199 43617
3900-3999 43623
Oak Tree Pl 43623
Oakcrest Rd 43623
Oakdale Ave 43605
Oakfield Dr 43615
Oakhaven Rd 43615
E & W Oakland St 43608
Oaklawn Ave 43605
Oaklawn Dr 43614
Oakmont St 43605
E Oakridge Dr 43623
Oaks Edge Dr 43617
Oakside Rd 43615
Oakway Dr 43614
Oakwood Ave
401-497 43604
499-799 43604
800-2599 43607
Oatis Ave 43606
Obrien St 43604
Oconnell St 43608
Ogden Ave 43609
Ogontz Ave 43614
Ohio St 43611
Old Farm Ct 43612
Old Lyme Dr 43623
Old Mill Rd 43615
Old Saybrook Dr 43623
Old Stone Ct 43614
Old Trail Dr 43619
Olde Brookside Rd 43615
Olde Curtice Rd 43619
Oldellak Dr 43623
Oldenburg Dr 43611
Oldham Dr 43613
Olimphia Rd 43615
Olin Dr 43613
Oliver St
100-599 TOLEDO 43604
600-799 43609
Olivewood Ave 43605
Olson St 43612
Omar Ave 43612
Oneida St 43608

Onondaga Ave 43611
N Ontario St
1-19 43604
21-1799 43604
1800-3199 43611
S Ontario St 43604
Opal Pl & St 43614
Opportunity Dr 43612
Oram Rd 43619
Orange St 43604
Orchard Ave 43619
Orchard Pl 43619
Orchard Rd 43606
Orchard St 43609
Orchard Hills Blvd 43615
Orchard Lakes Ct & Pl 43615
Orchard Trail Dr 43606
Orchard Tree Ln 43617
Oregon Rd
400-2999 43619
1600-1699 43605
3001-30699 43619
Orkney Dr 43606
Orlando Dr 43613
Orleans Dr 43614
Ormond Dr 43608
Orono Dr 43614
Orville Ct 43619
Orville Dr 43612
Ostrich Ln 43604
Oswald St 43605
Otis St 43604
Otjen Rd 43623
Ottawa Dr 43606
Ottawa St 43604
S Ottawa Cove Dr 43611
Ottawa River Rd 43611
Ottawa Trail Dr 43611
Otto St 43608
Overbrook Dr 43614
Overland Pkwy 43612
Overlook Blvd 43607
Overly Ct 43611
Owen Rd 43619
Owen St
1700-1899 43605
1900-1999 43619
Oxbridge Dr 43614
Oxford St 43606
Ozark Rd 43613
Packard Rd 43612
Pacquin Ln 43614
Paddington Dr 43623
Page St
1-300 43620
302-498 43620
700-1499 43608
Page Lindsay Ln 43615
Pageland Dr 43611
Paine Ave 43605
Paisley Rd 43615
Palmer St 43608
Palmetto Ave 43606
Palmwood Ave
500-799 43604
800-1899 43607
Panama St 43605
Paradise Ave 43613
Paranins Rd 43617
Parc Rue 43619
Park Ln 43615
N Park Ln 43614
S Park Ln 43614
Park Rd 43606
E Park St 43608
W Park St 43608
Park Center Ct 43615
Park Forest Dr 43614
Park Ridge Ln 43614
Parkcliff Ln 43615
Parkdale Ave 43607
Parker Ave 43605
Parkglen Ct 43615
Parkside Blvd 43607
Parkstone Dr 43615
Parkview Ave 43606
Parkwood Ave
1800-1898 43604
1900-1999 43604
2000-2499 43620
2500-3399 43610
Parliament Sq 43617
Parnell St 43605
Parrakeet Ave 43612
Partridge Ln 43623
Pasadena Blvd 43612
Pashanch Ave 43607
Patmore Ct 43607
Patriot Dr 43611
Pautucket Rd 43615
Pawnee Rd 43613
Paxton St 43608
Peabody Ave 43614
Peak Ave 43612
Pearinta St 43609
E & W Pearl St 43608
Peck St 43608
Pelee St 43607
Pelham Rd 43606
Pemberton Dr 43606
Pemberville Rd 43619
E & W Pembridge Dr 43615
Pembroke Rd 43606
Pemwood Ct 43615
Pendleton Rd 43623
Penelope Dr 43623
Penn Rd 43615
Pennelwood Dr 43614
Pennfield Rd 43612
Penoyer Rd 43605
Penridge Rd 43615
Penrose Ave & Ct 43614
Pensou Rd 43606
Pepperell Pl 43612
Percentum Rd 43617
Pere St 43609
Peregrine Dr 43619
Perivale Park Rd 43617
Perlawn Dr 43614
Pernell Pl 43615
Perry Ave 43605
Perry St 43604
Pershing Dr 43613
Perth St 43607
Peru St 43612
Petee Rd 43611
Pheasant Dr 43619
Pheasant Ln 43615
Pheasant Hollow Dr 43615
Pheasant Run Ct 43619
Phillips Ave
300-999 43612
3500-3598 43608
Philmar Dr 43623
Photos Dr 43613
Pickard Dr 43613
Pickfair Dr 43615
Piddock Rd 43613
Piedmont Dr 43615
Piero Ave 43615
Pilgrim Rd 43607
Pin Oak Dr 43615
Pine Rdg 43612
Pine Creek Dr 43617
Pine Grove Ct 43615
Pine Knoll Dr 43617
Pine Ridge Rd 43615
Pine Tree Ct 43606
Pine Valley Ln 43615
Pine View Dr 43617
Pinebrook Pkwy 43615
Pinecrest Dr 43623
Pinecroft Ct & Dr 43615
Pinedale Dr 43613
Pinehurst Dr 43613
Pinelawn Dr 43614
Pinestead Dr 43623
Pineway Dr 43614
Pinewood Ave
100-799 43604
800-1699 43607
Piney Pointe Dr 43617
Pingree Rd 43612
Pintail Ln 43619
Piper Dr 43619
Pitt St 43612
Plainview Dr 43615
Planet Ave 43623
Plantation Dr 43623
Platt St 43605
E Plaza Blvd 43619
Pleasant Pl 43609
Plum Grove Ln 43615
Plum Leaf Ln 43614
Plum Tree Ct 43606
Plumbrook Dr 43623
Plumcreek Rd 43615
E & W Plumer St 43605
Plumey Rd 43619
Plymouth St 43605
E & W Poinsetta Ave 43612
Point Pleasant Way 43611
W Pointe Dr 43619
Polk Pl 43608
Polonia Ct 43607
Pomeroy St 43608
Pontiac St 43611
Pool St 43605
Poplar St 43605
Port Sylvania Dr 43617
Portsmouth Ave 43613
Post St 43610
Post Oak Rd 43617
Potomac Dr 43607
Potomac Ln 43619
Potter St 43605
Powhattan Pkwy 43606
Prairie Ave 43614
Pratt St 43605
Prentice Ave 43605
Prescott St 43620
President Dr 43611
Prestler Rd 43615
Price St 43605
Primrose Ave
1300-1699 43612
1700-1899 43613
Princeton Dr 43614
Proctor Pl 43610
Progress Ave 43612
Prospect Ave 43606
Prosperity Rd 43612
Prouty Ave 43609
Provincetowne Dr 43613
Pulaski St 43607
Putnam St
1900-1999 43604
2000-2499 43620
Quail Run Dr 43615
Quaker Rdg 43615
Quast Ln 43623
Queen St 43609
Queen Annes Ct 43617
Queensberry Ct 43623
Queensbury Rd 43617
Queensdale Rd 43614
Queenswood Blvd 43606
Quincy St 43605
Quinton Ave 43623
Radcliffe Dr 43609
Raddatz Dr 43612
Radford Dr 43614
Radisson Ave 43614
Ragan Woods Dr 43614
Rainswood Dr 43615
Raintree Ln 43611
Raleigh Dr 43606
Rall Rd 43617
Rall St 43605
Ralph St 43609
Ralphwood Dr 43613
Ralston Cir 43615
Ramblewood Dr 43619
Rambo Ln 43623
Ranch Dr 43607
Randon Dr 43611
Ranger Dr 43619
Rathbun Dr 43606
Ratteree Dr 43611
Raven Dr 43612
Ravenwood Blvd 43614
Ravenwood Dr 43619
N & S Ravine Pkwy 43605
Ravine Park Village St 43605
Rawson Dr 43619
Ray St 43606
Raymer Blvd 43605
Raynor Dr 43615
Recamper Dr 43613
Rector St 43615
Red Bud Dr 43619
Red Oak Dr 43615
Redberry Ct 43617
Redfox Dr 43611
Redington Woods Rd 43615
Redondo Ave 43607
Redwood Ave 43609
Reed St 43605
Reen Dr 43613
Rega Dr 43623
Regency Ct 43623
Regency Dr 43615
Regents Park Blvd
6600-6699 43615
6700-7399 43617
Regina Pkwy 43612
Regis Dr 43623
Reineck Dr 43605
Reinwood Dr 43613
Remington St 43605
Renaissance Pl 43623
Renwyck Dr 43615
Reo St 43615
N & S Republic Blvd 43615
Research Dr 43614
Residence Dr 43606
Reva Dr 43619
Revere Dr 43612
Revilla Dr 43619
Revillo Ct 43613
Rex St 43611
Rexton Ridge Cir 43617
N Reynolds Rd 43615
S Reynolds Rd
1-1 43615
3-1499 43615
1501-1599 43615
1700-2599 43614
2601-2625 43614
Richards Rd
1-2099 43607
2100-2199 43606
N Richardson Dr 43608
Richford St 43605
Richlawn Dr 43614
Richmand Dr 43619
Richmond Rd 43607
Richwood St 43614
Ridge Ln 43619
Ridgedale Rd 43613
Ridgewood Ave 43608
Ridgewood Pl 43619
Ridgewood Rd 43606
Ridgewood Trl 43617
Rinker Pt 43619
Ritter Ave 43619
Riva Ridge Rd 43615
Rivard Rd 43615
River Pl 43611
River Rd 43614
Rivercrest Ave 43605
Riverhills Ln 43623
Riverside Ct 43611
Riverview Ct 43614
Riviera Dr 43611
Roanoke Rd 43613
Roanwood Dr 43613
Roberta Dr 43614
Robin Rd 43623
Robinhood Ln 43623
Robinwood Ave
2000-2499 43620
2500-2800 43610
2802-2998 43610
Rochelle Rd 43615
Rochester Pl 43619
Rock Ct 43608
Rockcress Dr 43615
W Rocket Dr 43606
Rockingham St
1-99 43608
100-499 43610
E & W Rockridge Cir 43606
Rocksberry Ave & Ct 43614
Rockspring Rd 43614
Rockwood Pl 43610
Roff St 43609
Rogers St 43605
Rohr Dr 43613
Rolandale Ave 43623
Rolland Dr 43612
Rollins Rd 43612
Romaker Rd 43615
Rommany Dr 43613
Romona Dr 43614
Ronaldo Rd 43615
Rondeau St 43615
Rood St
200-299 43619
2100-2399 43613
Roosevelt Ave & Cir 43607
Rosalind Pl 43610
Rose Ct 43614
Rose Acres Dr 43615
Rose Arbor Dr 43614
Rose Garden Dr 43623
Rose Glenn Dr 43615
Rose Hill Dr 43615
Rose Point Ct 43611
Rose Tree Ct 43606
Roseann Dr 43611
Roseanna Dr 43615
Rosedale Ave 43606
Rosedale Dr 43619
Roselawn Dr 43611
Rosemar Rd 43611
Rosemary St 43614
Rosetta St 43612
Roseview Dr 43613
Rosewood Ave
2200-2299 43606
2300-2499 43620
Ross St
800-899 43607
2400-2429 43619
2431-2499 43619
Rounding River Ln 43611
Roundtree Dr 43615
Rowland Rd 43613
Royal Ave 43619
Royal Haven Dr 43614
Royalton Rd 43612
Royce Rd 43615
Royer Dr 43619
Royer Rd 43623
Royton Rd 43614
Roywood Rd 43613
Rozelle Dr 43612
Rubicon Dr 43608
Rudford Dr 43615
Rudgate Blvd 43623
Rugby Dr 43614
Rulo Rd 43613
Runnymede Rd 43623
Rushland Ave
3400-3599 43606
3600-3999 43613
Ruskin Dr 43607
Russell St 43608
Ruth Ave 43613
Ruthanne Dr 43611
Ruthdale Ave 43605
Ruxton Rd 43612
Ryan Ct 43614
Ryan Pl 43619
Ryan Rd 43614
Ryan Ridge Pl 43614
Ryder Rd 43607
Rye Mill Ct 43611
Ryewyck Ct & Dr 43614
Sabra Rd 43612
Sadalia Rd 43623
Saddle Ridge Ln 43615
Saddlebrook Ct 43615
Saddlecreek Rd 43623
Saddlewood Dr 43613
Sagamore Rd 43606
Sahr Dr 43619
Saillond Ave 43610
Saint Andrews Blfs 43615
Saint Andrews Rd 43607
Saint Aubin Dr 43615
Saint Bernard Dr
3100-3399 43606
3400-3599 43613
Saint Charles Rd 43615
N Saint Clair St 43604
S Saint Clair St
1-298 43604
300-598 43604
435-435 43601
501-599 43604
600-899 43609
Saint Clement Ct 43613
Saint James Ct 43609
Saint James Woods Blvd 43617
Saint John Ave 43608
Saint Lawrence Dr 43605
Saint Louis St 43605
Saint Marys St 43609
Saint Roberts Ln 43617
Saint Thomas Ct 43617
Salem St 43609
Sallaken St 43604
Sampson St 43612
San Joaquin Dr 43615
San Jose Dr 43615
San Juan Dr 43612
San Lin Dr 43611
San Paulo Dr 43612
San Pedro Dr 43612
San Rafael Ave 43607
Sandalwood Ave 43614
Sanders Dr 43615
Sandown Rd 43615
Sandra Ct & Dr 43613
Sandralee Dr 43612
Sandringham Dr 43615
Sandusky St 43611
Sanford St 43606
Santa Maria Dr 43614
Sarasota Dr 43612
Sassafras Ln 43615
Satin Leaf Dr 43615
Satinwood Ct & Dr 43623
Saturn Dr 43615
Sawyer Rd 43615
Saxon Ln 43615
Scarlet Oak Dr 43615
Scarsborough Rd 43615
Scarsbrook Cir 43611
Schley St 43612
Schneider Rd 43614
Schomberg St 43605
Schroeder Ct & St 43613
Schuyler Rd 43612
Schwartz Rd 43611
Scioto 43615
Scotsmoore Ln 43607
Scott St 43620
Scottwood Ave
1900-2499 43620
2500-3199 43610
Seadwa St 43611
Seagate 43604
Seagert Dr 43623
Seagull Ln 43611
Seaman St 43605
Searles Rd 43607
Seckinger Ct & Dr 43613
Secor Rd
600-1499 43607
1500-1698 43606
1501-1799 43607
1700-1798 43607
1800-3699 43606
2201-2299 43606
3700-5999 43623
6000-6199 43613
Secretariat Rd 43615
Sefton Rd 43623
Segur Ave 43609
Seiss Ave 43612
Selkirk St 43605
Selma St 43613
Semoff Dr 43613
Seneca St 43608
Sentry Hill Rd 43615
Sequoia Rd 43617
Seymour Rd 43615
Shade Tree Dr 43615
Shadow Ln
700-1199 43615
1900-1999 43619
Shadow Lake Ct & Dr 43623
Shadowlawn Dr 43609
Shadowood Ln 43614
Shady Dr 43612
Shady Grv 43623
Shadylawn Dr 43614
Shaftsbury Dr 43615
Shakespeare Ln 43615
Shale Ln 43615
Shallowford Dr 43611
Shamley Green Dr 43623
Shamrock Dr 43615
Shannon St 43604
Sharon Dr 43619
Shasta Dr 43609
Shawn Ter 43615
Shawnee Rd 43613
Shea St 43609
Sheffield Ct 43623
Sheffield Pl 43619
Sheila Dr 43613
Shelbourne Ave 43613
Sheldon St 43605
Shellbrook Ln 43614
Shenandoah Rd 43607
Shepard St 43604
Shepler St 43609
Sheraton Rd
4100-4299 43606
4300-4499 43615
Sherbrooke Rd
2600-3499 43606
3501-3597 43613
3599-3899 43613
Shereton Pl 43615
Sheri Ln 43614
Sheridan St 43604
Sherman St
300-499 43620
700-1299 43608
1301-1429 43608
Sherwood Ave 43614
Sherwood Forest Manor Rd 43623
Shetland Rd 43617
Shieldwood Rd 43617
Shinnecock Hls 43615
Shirley Ave 43607
Shoal Crk 43615
Shooters Hill Rd 43617
Shorebridge Dr 43611
Shoreham Ln 43612
Shoreland Ave 43611
Short St 43619
Shortford Dr 43614
Sibley Rd 43615
Siegel Ct 43605
Sierra Ct 43607
Sigsher Dr 43615
Silver Dr 43612
Silver Creek Rd 43613
Silverdale Dr 43612
Silverpine Ct 43615
Silverside Dr 43612
Sims Dr 43615
Sinclair St 43605
Sisson Dr 43605

Street	ZIP
Skagway Dr	43619
Skelly Rd	43623
Skye Dr	43615
Skyview Dr	43612
Slater St	43612
Sloan Dr	43615
Smead Ave	
1500-1799	43607
1800-2299	43606
Smith St	43604
Snowden Dr	43623
Somerset St	43609
South Ave	
1-3499	43609
3500-6399	43615
Southaire Dr	43615
Southard Ave	43604
Southbriar Rd	43607
Southbridge Rd	43623
Southcrest St	43609
Southdale Rd	43612
Southern St	43615
Southgate Circle Dr	43615
Southlawn Dr	43614
Southmoor Dr	43609
Southover Rd	43612
Southpoint Rd	43615
Southview Dr	43609
Southway Ct	43614
Southwood Rd	43614
Southwyck Blvd	43614
Spencer St	43609
Spicer Rd	43612
Spieker Ter	43605
Spielbusch Ave	43604
Spring St	43608
Spring Grove Ave	43605
Spring Hollow Dr	43615
Spring Mill Ct	43615
Spring Rye Ct	43617
Spring Water Dr	43617
Springbrook Dr	
4300-4698	43615
4700-4880	43615
4882-4898	43615
30800-30999	43619
Springburn Dr	43615
Springdale Ave	43613
Spruce Ln	43614
Squirrel Bnd	43617
Stableside N & S	43615
Staghorn Dr	43614
Stahlwood Ave	43613
Stamford Dr	43614
Stanbery Ct	43612
Standing Timbers Ct & Ln	43623
Stanhope Dr	43606
Stanley Ct	43608
Stannard Dr	43613
Stanton St	43609
Stanwix Dr	43614
Starr Ave	43605
State St	43604
E & W State Line Rd	43612
Statesville Dr	43623
Stateview Dr	43609
Steadman St	43605
Stebbins St	43609
Steel St	43605
Steeple Chase Cir	43615
Steeplebush Dr	43615
Steffens Ave	43623
Stengel Ave	43614
Sterling St	43609
Stickney Ave	
300-999	43604
2401-2797	43608
2799-3999	43608
4000-5800	43612
5802-6098	43612
Stillman St	43605
Stillwater Dr	43615
Stirrup Ln	43613
Stitt St	43605
Stock Ave	43623
Stockbridge Dr	43612
Stockdale Ave	43607
Stoneham Rd	43615
Stoneleigh Dr	43617
Storrs St	43609
Strang Cir & Dr	43623
Stratford Pl	43620
Strathmoor Ave	43614
Stratton St	43605
Strauss Ave	43606
Streatham Ct	43615
E & W Streicher St	43608
Stroehlein Ave	
1800-1899	43605
1900-1999	43619
Strotz Dr	43612
Sturbridge Rd	43623
Suder Ave	43611
Sugar Creek Ln	43615
Sugarberry Ln	43615
Sugarmaple Ln	43623
Sulgrave Dr	43623
Sullivan Dr & Rd	43613
Sulphur Spring Rd	43606
Summerdale Ave	43605
Summerfield Rd	43623
N Summit St	
21-101	43604
103-1149	43604
1151-1499	43604
1801-2097	43611
2099-6299	43611
S Summit St	43604
Sumner St	43609
Sunforest Ct	43623
Sunnybrook Dr	43615
Sunnylawn Dr	43614
Sunnyside Dr	43612
Sunset Blvd	43612
Sunwood Dr	43623
N Superior St	
100-198	43604
200-1500	43604
1502-1698	43604
1800-1999	43611
S Superior St	43604
Surrey Rd	43615
Susan Ln	43612
Sussex Pl	43607
Sutton Pl	43623
Suzanne Dr	43612
Swan Ln	43604
Swan Creek Dr & Ln	43614
Swanbrook Ct	43614
Sweetbriar Ct	43615
Sweetwater Ct	43614
Swift Ave	43615
Swiler Dr	43606
Swiss Garden Rd	43612
Sycamore St	43604
Sylvan Ave	43606
Sylvan Ridge Ct & Dr	43623
E Sylvania Ave	43612
W Sylvania Ave	
1-1699	43612
1700-3299	43613
3300-6399	43623
Sylvester St	43605
Tadmore Dr	43605
Talbot St	43613
Tall Oaks Rd	43614
Tall Pines Dr	43615
Talmadge Ct	43623
Talmadge Rd	
2200-3099	43606
3100-3999	43606
4037-5799	43623
Talmadge Green Rd	43623
Talmadge Woods	43623
Talwood Ln	43606
Tamarack Dr	43614
Tampa Ave	43615
Tanglewood Dr	43614
Tantara Rd	43623
Tappan Ave	43612
Tara Way	43615
Tarkington Ave	43614
Tarrytowne Dr	43613
Tavistock Dr	43623
Teal Dr	43615
Tecumseh St	
100-799	43604
800-1799	43607
Tedrow Rd	43614
Tejon Rd	43623
Telegraph Rd	43612
Teletowne Dr	43612
Telstar Dr	43607
Templar Rd	43613
Tennyson Pl	43620
Terminal Rd	43612
Terrace Dr	43611
Terrace Downs St	43614
N Terrace View St	43607
Terramar Rd	43611
Terri Rue	43619
Terry Dr	43613
Tetherwood Dr	43613
Thad St	43609
Thatcher Dr	43606
Thayer St	43609
The Blfs	43615
Thelma Dr	43613
Thobe Rd	43615
Thoman Pl	43613
Thomas St	43609
Thorn Lea Dr	43617
Thornapple Dr	43614
Thornbrook Trl	43611
Thornbrough Dr	43617
Thornhill Dr	43614
Thornridge Dr	43614
Thornton Ave	43612
Thornwood Dr	43609
Thousand Oaks Dr	43613
Thunder Hollow Dr	43615
Thurston St	43605
Thyssenkrupp Pkwy	43619
Tibaron Ln	43615
Tiffany Square Dr	43607
Tiffin St	43605
Tillimon Trl	43623
Timber Creek Dr	43615
Timberlake Ct	43619
Timberlane Dr	43615
Timberlawn Rd	43614
Timbers Edge Blvd	43617
Timberside Dr	43615
Timberview Dr	43619
Tiverton Ave	43615
Toledo Ave	43609
Torgler Ave	43611
Torisdale Ct	43611
Toronto Ave	43609
Torquay Ave	43615
Torrance Dr	43612
Torrey Hill Dr	43606
Torrington Dr	43615
Tottenham Rd	43617
Tourville Dr	43612
Towne Ct	43613
Townley Rd	43614
Townsend Dr	43615
Tracewood Dr	43617
Tractor Rd	43612
Tracy Rd	43619
Tracy St	43605
Trailwood Ct	43615
Tralger Dr	43612
Transport St	43612
Transverse Dr	43614
Travis Dr	
1500-1699	43612
1700-1899	43613
Tredwell St	43605
Treelawn Dr	43614
Treetop Ct	43615
Tremain Dr	43620
Tremainsville Rd	43613
Trent St	43612
Trenton Ave	43606
Trimble Rd	43613
Trinity Dr	43606
Triple Crown Ln	43615
Trotter Rd	43617
Trowbridge St	43606
Troy St	43611
True St	43607
Truxton Place Dr	43615
Tudor St	43612
Tulane Ave	43611
Tully Ave	43614
Tunnel St	43609
Turnbridge Cir & Rd	43623
Turnbrook Dr	43623
Turner Ave	43607
Turret Green Dr	43607
Twin Oaks Dr	43615
Twining St	43608
Tyler St	43612
Underhill Rd	43615
Underwood Ave	43607
Union St	43619
Unity Ct	43614
Unity Walk	43620
N University Ave	43607
University Blvd	43614
University Hills Blvd	43606
Upton Ave	
900-2199	43607
2200-3099	43606
3100-4199	43613
Utah St	43605
Utica St	43608
Utopia St	43606
Vail Ave	43623
Valbon Ct	43615
Valencia Dr	43623
Valentine St	43605
Valerian Ct	43615
Valeway Dr	43613
Vallejo Dr	43615
Valleston Pkwy	43607
Valley Brook Dr	43615
Valley Forge Dr	43613
Valley Park Dr	43623
Valley Ridge Ct	43614
Valley Stream Rd	43615
Valley View Dr	43615
Valley Way Dr	43614
Valleycrest Ct	43614
Valleywood Dr	43605
Van Buren Ave	43605
Van Dusen Way	43606
Van Fleet Pkwy	43615
Van Wormer Dr	43612
Vance St	
1-799	43604
800-1799	43607
Vandalia St	43611
Vanderbilt Rd	43615
Vaness Dr	43615
Varland Ave	43605
Vassar Dr	43614
Venice Dr	43619
Ventura Dr	43615
Vermaas Ave	43612
Vermont Ave	
1800-1899	43604
2200-2299	43620
Verna Dr	43615
Vernice Dr	43612
Viancoma Dr	43613
Victoria Pl	43610
Victory Ave	43607
Viking St	43605
Villa Dr	
2600-2800	43617
2802-2898	43617
2900-3199	43614
S Village Dr	43614
W Village Dr	43614
Village Ln	43614
Village Loop	43606
Villamar Rd	43611
Vinal St	43605
Vinchara Ave	43612
Vine St	43604
Vineyard Ct	43607
Vineyard Rd	43623
Vinton St	43609
Violet Rd	43623
Viramar Rd	43611
Virginia St	
500-800	43620
802-898	43620
900-999	43606
1001-1099	43606
Virginia Lake Rd	43614
Vista Dr	43615
Vistamar Rd	43611
Vogel Dr	43613
Vosper Ct	43614
Wabash St	43604
Wade St	43604
Waggoner Blvd	43612
Waite Ave	
1500-1799	43607
1800-2099	43606
Wakefield Dr	43623
Walbridge Ave	43609
Walbridge Rd	43619
Walden Ave	43605
Walden Pond Dr	43606
Waldmar Rd	43615
Waldorf Dr	43611
Wales Rd	43619
Walker Ave	43612
Wall St	43610
Wallace Blvd	43611
Wallingford Dr	43612
Wallwerth Dr	43612
Walnut Cir	43615
Walnut Ln	43612
Walnut St	
300-999	43604
1300-2600	43608
2602-2698	43608
Walsh St	43609
Waltham Rd	43619
Wamba Ave	43607
Wanamaker Dr	43613
Ward St	43609
Wardell St	43605
Ware St	43619
Warehouse Rd	43615
Warner Ave	43615
Warren St	
1900-1999	43604
2000-2499	43620
Warrington Rd	43612
Warsaw St	43608
Warwick Ave	43607
Wasaon St	43609
Washington St	43604
Water St	43604
Water Point Ct	43611
N & S Watercrest Dr	43614
Waterford Ct & Pl	43623
Waterworks Dr	43609
Watkins Dr	43614
Watova Rd	43614
Watson Ave	43612
Waverly Ave	43607
Waybridge Rd	43612
Wayman Palmer Ct	43620
Wayman Palmer Dr	43606
Wayne St	43609
Wealdstone Rd	43617
E & W Weber St	43608
Wedgewood Ct	43615
Weiler Ave	43604
Weirwood Dr	43607
Welker Ave	43613
Wellesley Dr	43606
Wellington St	43607
Wells St	43604
Wembley Ter N & W	43617
Wendell St	43609
Wendover Dr	43606
Wenz Rd	43615
Wernert Ave	43613
Wersell Ave	43608
Wesleyan Dr	43614
West Cir	43615
Westacre Ln	43615
Westbank Rd	43614
Westbourne Rd	43623
Westbrook Dr	43613
Westbury Ct	43609
Westcastle Dr	43615
Westchester Rd	43615
Westedge Dr	43614
Western Ave	43609
Westgate Rd	43615
N & S Westhaven Rd	43615
Westland Ave	
3100-3199	43606
3300-3999	43613
Westland Gardens Rd	43615
Westmar Ct	43615
Westmeyer St	43614
Westmonte Rd	43607
Westol Dr	43606
Weston St	43609
Westowne Ct	43615
Westway St	43612
N Westwood Ave	
1-1299	43607
1500-1598	43606
1600-1700	43606
1702-1718	43606
1720-2098	43607
S Westwood Ave	
112-298	43607
300-799	43609
801-899	43609
Wetzler Rd	43612
N Wheeling St	43605
S Wheeling St	43619
Whillons St	43605
Whispering Pines Dr	43617
White St	43605
White Oak Dr	43615
White Tail Ct	43617
Whiteacre Rd	43615
Whitechapel Dr	43614
Whiteford Rd	43623
Whiteford Center Rd	43613
Whitegate Dr	43607
Whitehall Rd	43606
Whitehouse Dr	43611
Whiteway Rd	43606
Whitewood Ln	43617
Whiting Ave	43609
Whitlock Ave	43605
Whitmer Dr	43613
Whitney Ave	43606
Whittemore St	43605
Whittier St	43609
Wichita Rd	43613
Wickford Point Dr	43607
Wicklow Rd	43606
Wild Oaks Dr	43615
Wildwood Blvd & Rd	43614
Wiler Ln	43611
Wilford Dr	
2200-3099	43615
3100-3599	43617
Willamont Rd	43612
Willard St	43605
E Willcrest Dr	43615
Willesden Green Rd	43617
Williams St	43604
Williamsdale Dr	43609
Williamsville Ave	43609
Willis Blvd	43623
Williston Rd	43619
Willow Ave	43605
Willow Crk	43612
Willow Brook Ln	43611
Willow Lane Dr	43615
Willow Run Dr	43607
Willowhill Ln	43615
Willowood Ct	43615
Willowvale Dr	43615
Willys Pkwy	43612
Wilmore Dr	43614
Wilmot St	43605
Wilshire Ave	43614
Wilson Pl	43608
Wilson St	43619
Wilton St	43609
Wimbledon Park Blvd	43617
Winchester Rd	43613
Wind Breeze Dr	43615
Windamar Rd	43611
Windbrook Ct	43611
Windermere Blvd	43608
Windgate Dr	43615
Winfield Rd	43610
Winnette Dr	43614
Winona Ave	43605
Winona Dr	43613
Winsted Dr	43606
Winston Blvd	43614
Winterfield Ct	43607
Winterset Dr	43614
Winthrop St	43620
Wise St	43619
Wissman Rd	43615
Wolf Creek Ct	43619
Woodbine Dr	43614
Woodbriar Dr	43623
Woodbridge Rd	43615
Woodbrook Rd	43617
Woodford St	43605
Woodfox Dr	43611
Woodhaven Dr	43612
Woodhill Rd	43615
Woodhurst Dr	43614
Woodlake Dr	43617
Woodland Ave	
300-799	43604
800-1699	43607
Woodlawn Dr	43612
Woodley Ct & Rd	43606
Woodlore Dr	43614
Woodmeadow Dr	43617
Woodmere Ct	43615
Woodmont Rd	
3500-3599	43606
3600-4499	43613
Woodmore St	43605
Woodridge Dr	43623
Woodrow Blvd	43608
E Woodruff Ave	43604
W Woodruff Ave	
112-524	43604
526-640	43604
800-899	43620
900-1699	43606
1900-1999	43607
Woods Ave	43623
Woods Edge Ct	43615
Woodsdale Ave	43609
Woodsdale Park Dr	43614
Woodside Trl	43623
Woodstock Ave	43607
Woodview Dr	43623
Woodville Rd	
400-1799	43605
2500-5999	43619
Woodward Ave	43608
Woolcut Ln	43615
Woonsocket Rd	43615
Worley Pl	43608
Worth St	43605
Worthington St	43605
Wreford Ct	43614
Wrenwood Rd	43623
Wright Ave	43609
Wright Dr	43617
Wychwood St	43613
Wyckliffe Pkwy	
3300-3599	43606
3600-3799	43613
Wylie Ave	43609
Wyman St	43609
Wyndale Ct & Rd	43613
Wyndhurst Rd	43607
Wyndwood Dr	43623
S Wynn Rd	43619
Wynnewood Dr	43613
Yale Dr	43614
Yambor St	43605

Yarmouth Ave 43623
Yaryan Dr 43614
Yates St 43608
Yellowstone Dr 43613
Yermo Dr 43613
Yondota St 43605
York St 43605
Yorkshire Dr 43615
Yosemite Dr 43614
Zachary Rd 43623
Zale Pl 43614
Zelpha Dr 43615
Zenda St 43607
Zepplin Ct 43619
Zone Ave 43617

NUMBERED STREETS

1st St 43605
2nd St 43605
3rd St 43605
4 Seasons Dr 43615
4th St 43605
5th St 43605
6th St 43605
10th St 43604
S 11th 43604
12th St 43604
  1700-1998 43604
  2000-2199 43620
13th St 43604
N 13th St
  1800-1999 43604
  2100-2199 43620
S 13th St 43604
14th St 43604
N 14th St
  1800-1800 43604
  1802-1999 43604
  2000-2199 43620
S 14th St 43604
S 15th 43604
16th St 43604
17th St 43604
18th St 43604
19th St 43604
20th St 43604
21st St 43604
S 22nd 43604
23rd St 43604
101st St 43611
102nd St 43611
103rd St 43611
104th St 43611
105th St 43611
106th St 43611
107th St 43611
108th St 43611
109th St 43611
110th St 43611
111th St 43611
112th St 43611
113th St 43611
114th St 43611
115th St 43611
116th St 43611
117th St 43611
118th St 43611
119th St 43611
120th St 43611
121st St 43611
122nd St 43611
123rd St 43611
124th St 43611
125th St 43611
126th St 43611
127th St 43611
128th St 43611
129th St 43611
130th St 43611
131st St 43611
132nd St 43611
133rd St 43611
134th St 43611
135th St 43611
136th St 43611
137th St 43611
138th St 43611
139th St 43611
140th St 43611
141st St 43611
142nd St 43611
145th St 43611
146th St 43611
147th St 43611
148th St 43611
149th St 43611
282nd St 43611
283rd St 43611
284th St 43611
285th St 43611
286th St 43611
287th St 43611
288th St 43611
289th St 43611
290th St 43611
291st St 43611
292nd St 43611
293rd St 43611
294th St 43611
295th St 43611
296th St 43611
297th St 43611
298th St 43611
299th St 43611
301st St 43611
302nd St 43611
303rd St 43611
304th St 43611
305th St 43611
306th St 43611
307th St 43611
308th St 43611
309th St 43611
310th St 43611
311th St 43611
313th St 43611
314th St 43611
315th St 43611
316th St 43611
317th St 43611
318th St 43611
319th St 43611
320th St 43611
321st St 43611
322nd St 43611
323rd St 43611
324th St 43611
325th St 43611
326th St 43611

WADSWORTH OH

General Delivery 44281

POST OFFICE BOXES MAIN OFFICE STATIONS AND BRANCHES

Box No.s
All PO Boxes 44282

NAMED STREETS

All Street Addresses 44281

NUMBERED STREETS

All Street Addresses 44281

WARREN OH

General Delivery 44481

POST OFFICE BOXES MAIN OFFICE STATIONS AND BRANCHES

Box No.s
1 - 1998 44482
2001 - 2490 44484
3001 - 3698 44485
4001 - 5005 44482
8501 - 8952 44484

NAMED STREETS

A Dr NE 44484
Abbington Dr NW 44481
Ada Ave SE 44484
Adams Ave NW 44483
Adelaide Ave NE 44483
Adelaide Ave SE
  100-699 44483
  700-1699 44484
Adrian Dr SE 44484
Airport Rd NW 44481
Albert St NE 44483
Aleesa Dr SE 44484
Allenwood Dr SE 44484
Allison Ave NW 44483
Allyson Dr SE 44484
Althea Ave NW 44483
Altura Dr NE 44484
Alva Ave NW 44483
Amber Dr SE 44484
American Way NE 44484
Anderson Ave NE 44484
Anderson Anthony Rd NW 44481
Andrews Dr NE 44481
Angel Ct NW 44481
Anna St NW 44481
E & W Apricot Dr 44485
Arbor Ave SE 44484
Aris St NW 44485
Arlington Ave NW 44483
Arnold Dr SW 44483
Arthur Dr NW 44485
Asbury Dr NW 44485
Ashalloc St SW 44485
Ashwood Ave & St 44483
N Aspen Ct 44484
S Aspen Ct 44484
Aspen Dr NW 44483
Aspinwall Ave NE 44483
Athens Dr SE 44484
Atlantic St NE & NW 44483
Atwood St NW 44485
Augusta Pl NE 44484
Austin Ave NW & SW 44485
Autumn Dr NW 44485
Avalon Dr SE 44484
Avon Ct NE 44483
B Dr NE 44484
Bacher Rd SW 44481
Bailey Ct NE 44481
Baker Ave SW
  600-899 44481
  1200-1899 44485
Bane St SW 44485
Bank St NE 44483
Barder Ave SE 44484
Basil Pl SE 44484
Basswood Ave NE 44483
Bay Hill Dr NE 44484
Bayberry Dr NE 44484
Bazetta Rd NE 44481
Beachwood Ave NE 44483
Beal St NW 44485
Beaver Creek Dr SW 44481
Beck St SE 44484
Beechcrest St NW 44485
Beechwood St NE 44483
Beechwood St SW 44485
Bellcrest Ave SW 44485
Belle St SE
  1200-1399 44484
  2001-2099 44483
Bellwood Dr SE 44484
Belmont Ave NE & NW 44483
Belvedere Ave NE 44483
Belvedere Ave SE
  100-699 44483
  700-1699 44484
Bennett Ave NW 44485
Benton St SE 44484
Berkshire Dr SE 44484
Beverly St NW 44485
Bingham Ave NW 44485
Birch Run Dr NE 44483
Birchwood Ave NE 44483
Bittersweet Dr NE 44484
Black Oak Dr NE 44484
Blair Ave & Dr NE & NW 44483
Blakely Cir SW 44485
Blossom Ln SW 44485
Blue Winged Dr SE 44484
Blueberry Ln SW 44485
Bock Ct SW 44485
Bolin Ave SE 44484
Bon Air Ave NW 44485
Bond Ave NW 44483
Bonnie Dr SW 44485
Bonnie Brae Ave NE 44483
Bonnie Brae Ave SE 44484
Boston Ave SE 44484
Bradford Ln NE 44484
Bradford St NW 44485
Brandywine Rd SE 44484
Brentwood Ave NE 44484
Brewster Dr SE 44484
Brianna Way NW 44481
Briarbrook Ct & Dr 44484
Bridle Ln NE 44483
Brier St SE 44484
Brighton Ave NE 44483
Bristol Champion Townline Rd NW 44481
Brittainy Oaks Trl NE 44484
Broadacres Dr SE 44484
Broadway Ave SE 44484
Bronze Rd NE 44483
Brookhollow Dr SW 44481
Brookside Dr NW 44483
Brookwood St NE 44484
Bruce Dr SE 44484
Brucewood Dr SE 44484
Brunstetter Rd SW 44481
Brunswick Ave SW 44485
Bryan Pl NW 44485
Buckeye St NW 44485
Buena Vista Ave NE 44483
Burnett East Rd SW 44481
Burning Oaks Dr NE 44484
Burton St SE 44484
Butler Rd NE 44483
C Dr NE 44484
Cain Dr NE 44484
Caleb Dr NW 44485
Calla Ave NW 44483
Cambridge Ct NE 44484
Campbell Pl NE 44481
Candace Ave SE 44484
Candlelight Dr SE 44484
Canvasback Dr SE 44484
Caprice Dr SW 44481
Cardiff Ln SE 44484
Cardiff Lane Ext SE 44484
Cardinal Dr SW 44481
Carlton Dr NW 44485
Carolewood Cir NW 44483
Carolina Ave SE 44484
Carriage Hill Dr NE 44484
Carroll Ave NW 44483
Casale Ct NW 44485
Castillion Dr NE 44484
Castle Rock Dr NE 44484
Catalpa St SE
  2800-2998 44483
  3200-3299 44484
N & S Catawba Dr 44481
Celestial Dr NE 44484
Center St E & W 44481
Central Parkway Ave SE
  100-499 44483
  600-2599 44484
Chalfonte Dr & Pl 44484
Champion Ave E & W 44483
Chapel Hill Ct N 44483
Charles Ave NE & SE 44483
Chatham Ct NE 44484
Cherry Ave NW 44485
Cherry Hill Dr NE 44484
Chester Ave SW 44481
Chestnut Ave NE 44483
Chestnut Ave SE 44483
Chestnut Cir SE 44484
Chevelle Dr SE 44484
Chinnock Pl NE 44483
Chipola Ct SE 44484
Choctaw St SW 44485
Citadel Dr NE 44483
Clarence St SE 44484
Clearview Ave NW 44483
Clearview St NW 44485
Clearwater St NW 44485
Clemmens Ave NW 44485
Clermont Ave NE 44483
Cleveland Ave E 44483
Cleveland Ave SW 44485
Cleveland Ave W 44483
Clifton Dr NE 44484
Clovercrest Dr NW 44483
Cloverlane Ave NW 44483
Coit Dr NW 44485
Coleridge Ave NW 44483
Colonial St SE 44484
Colt Ct SW 44485
Columbia Pl SE 44484
Commerce Ave NW 44485
Commonwealth Ave NE 44483
Comstock St NE & NW 44483
Copeland Ave NW 44483
Coral Dr NE 44484
Cornwall Ave SW 44485
Cottage Ct SE 44483
Cottage Pines Dr SW 44481
Country Trl & Way NW & SW 44481
Country Club Dr & Ln 44484
Country Pines Dr SW 44481
Coventry Ave NE 44483
Craig Ave NW 44483
Cranberry Ct & Ln NE 44483
Cranbrook Cir & Dr 44484
Cranwood Dr SW 44485
E & W Creekside Ct 44484
Crescent Dr NE 44483
Crestview Ave SE 44484
Crestwood Dr NW 44485
Crosby Ave SE 44484
Cross Dr SW 44481
Cross Creek Dr NW 44483
Crosswinds Ct NE 44484
Curtis Ave SE 44484
D Dr NE 44484
Dalton Dr NW 44481
Damon Ave NW 44483
Dana St NE 44483
Danbury Ct NW 44481
Dantanin Rd SW 44481
Darlington Rd NE & SE 44484
Dartmoor Dr NE 44483
Davis Ave SW 44485
Dawson Dr SE 44484
Deer Creek Ln NE 44484
Deer Run Dr NW 44483
Deerfield Ave SW 44485
Deforest Rd SE 44484
Delaware Ave NW & SW 44485
Dell Ave SW 44485
Demura Dr SE 44484
Den Jean Dr NE 44483
Denison Ave NW 44485
Depot St NW 44485
Desota Ave NW 44483
Devon Dr SE 44484
Dickey Ave NW 44485
Dietz Rd NE 44483
Dilley Rd NW 44485
Dillon Dr SE 44484
Dodge Dr NW 44485
Dogwood Dr SW 44481
Donora Ave NE 44483
Doral Dr SE 44484
Doris Jean Dr NW 44483
Douglas St NE & NW 44483
Dove Dr SW 44481
Dover St SW 44485
Downs Rd NW 44481
Draper Ave SE 44484
Drexel Ave NW 44485
Duffus Rd NE 44484
Duke Ave SE 44484
Dunstan Dr NW 44485
Durst Dr NW 44483
Durst Clagg Rd NE 44481
E Dr NE 44484
Eagle Trace St NE 44484
Earl Dr NW 44483
East Ave SE 44484
Eastland Ave SE
  100-499 44483
  600-1599 44484
Eastpoint Heights Dr SE 44484
Eastwind Dr NE 44484
Echo Lake Dr NE 44484
Edgehill Ave SE 44484
Edgewater Pines Dr SW 44481
Edgewood St NE 44483
Educational Hwy NW 44483
Edward St NW 44483
Edwards Ct NE 44483
Eldon Dr NW 44483
Elizabeth Ave SE 44484
Elizabeth Dr SW 44481
Ellsworth Ave NW 44483
Ellsworth Bailey Rd SW 44481
Elm Ct & Rd 44483
Elmhill Dr NW 44485
Elmwood Ave NE 44483
Emerson Ave NW 44483
Englesson Dr NW 44485
Englewood St NE 44484
Enterprise Dr NW 44481
Ernest Lyntz Rd SW 44481
Estabrook Ave NW 44485
Esther Ave NW 44483
Euclid Pl NE 44483
Evaline St SE 44484
Evergreen Ave SE 44484
Ewalt Ave NE 44483
Fairfield Ave NE 44483
Fairgreen Ave & St NE & NW 44483
Fairhill Dr NE 44484
Fairlane Dr NW 44483
Fairlawn Heights Dr SE 44484
Fairmount Ave NE 44483
Fairview Ave SE 44484
Fairway Ct, Dr & Pl 44483
Falcon Trak NE 44484
Fawn Trl NE 44483
Federal St NE & NW 44483
N & S Feederle Dr 44484
Fern Ct 44484
Ferncliff Ave NW 44483
Ferndale Ave SW 44485
Firestone Dr SE 44484
Flora Ct SE 44484
Flory Ave SE 44484
Folsom St NW 44483
Fonderlac Dr SE 44484
Ford Ave NW 44485
Forest St NE & NW 44483
Forest Glen Rd SW 44481
Forest Hills Dr NE 44484
Forest Pointe Ct SE 44484
Forest Springs Dr SE 44484
Foster Dr NE 44483
Fox Hound Run NE 44484
Fox Ridge Cir SE 44484
Francis Ave SE 44484
Franklin Ct SE 44483
Franklin St SE
  100-199 44481
  200-499 44483
Franklin St SW 44481
Franwae Dr SW 44481
Freeman St NW 44483
Fremont Ave NE 44483
Front St SW 44485
Fuller Ave NW 44485
Fuller Dr NE 44484
Fulton St SE & SW 44483
Garden St NW 44485
Garfield Dr NE 44483
Genesee Ave NE 44483
Genoa Ave NW 44483
George Pl SW 44485
Gertrude Pl & St 44483
Gladstone Rd SW 44481
Glen Oaks Dr NE 44484
Glendola Ave NW 44483
Glenn Dr NE 44483
Glenwood St NE 44483
Goldner Ln SW 44481
Golf Dr NE 44483
Gordon Rd NW 44485
Grady Ave NW 44483
Grandview St SE
  1300-1599 44484
  2000-2099 44483
  2101-2699 44483
Grant St SE 44483
Grassy Pt NW 44481
Greenfield Oval NW 44483
Greenfield St NW 44485
Greenlawn Ave NW 44483
Greenleaf Ave NE 44484
Greenmont Dr SE 44484
Gretchen Dr NE 44483
Grissom Dr NE 44483
Griswold St NE 44483
Griswold Street Ext NE 44483
Grove Ave NW 44483
Guarnieri Dr NE 44483
Hall St NW 44483
Hallock Young Rd SW 44481
Halsey Dr NE 44483
Hamilton St SW 44485
Harmon Ave NW 44483
Harrison St NE 44483
Hartman Ave NW 44485
Harvard Dr SE 44484
Harvest Dr NE 44481
Harvey Ave SE 44484
Hawks Lndg NE 44484
Hawthorne Ave NW 44483
Hawthorne Ln NE 44484
Hayes Ave SW 44485
Haymaker Ave NW 44485
Hazelwood Ave SE
  100-699 44483
  700-2199 44484
Hearranc Ave SE 44484
Heath Dr NW 44481
Heather Ln NW 44485
Heatherwood Dr SE 44484
E Heights St SE 44484
Heiser Pl SE 44484
Helmick Dr SW 44481
Heltzels Ct NE 44484
Hemlock Ave SW 44485
Henn Pkwy SW 44481
Henn Hyde Rd NE 44484
Hewitt Gifford Rd SW 44481
Hickory Ct NE 44483
Hickory Ln SW 44481
Hidden Hills Dr SE 44484
Hidden Lakes Dr NE 44484
Hidden Trail Dr NW 44483
Hidden Valley Dr NE 44484
High St NE
  100-499 44481
  500-1299 44483
  8200-8699 44484

High St NW
100-104 ... 44481
106-200 ... 44481
202-298 ... 44481
2100-3999 ... 44483
Highland Ave SW
200-2199 ... 44485
2200-8299 ... 44481
Highland Ct SW ... 44485
Highland Terrace Blvd ... 44484
Highlawn Ave SE ... 44484
Hightree Ave & Cir ... 44484
Hilda Dr SE ... 44484
Hillsdale Dr NW ... 44485
Hillside Dr SE ... 44484
Hillview Dr NE ... 44484
Hiram Ave NW ... 44483
Hiram Pl SE ... 44484
Hoffman Cir NE ... 44483
Hoffman Norton Rd NW ... 44481
Hogan Ln NE ... 44484
Hollywood St NE ... 44483
Holmes Ave NW ... 44483
Homewood Ave SE
100-599 ... 44483
700-1699 ... 44484
Hood St SW ... 44481
Housel Dr SW ... 44481
Howland Springs Blvd & Rd ... 44484
Howland Terrace Blvd ... 44484
Howland Wilson Rd NE & SE ... 44484
Hoyt St SW ... 44485
Hudson St NW ... 44483
Huffman Dr SW ... 44481
Hummel Dr NW ... 44483
Hunt Club Trl NE ... 44484
Hunter St NW ... 44485
Hunters Trl SE ... 44484
Hunters Hollow Dr SE ... 44484
Huntington Dr NW ... 44481
Huntley Dr SE ... 44484
Iddings Ave NE & SE ... 44483
Idylwild St NE & NW ... 44483
Imperial Dr SW ... 44481
Ina Dr SW ... 44481
Independent Dr NE ... 44484
Indian Trl SW ... 44481
Industrial Trce SW ... 44481
Inverrary Dr SE ... 44484
Iowa Ave NW ... 44485
Irene Ave NE ... 44483
Ivanhoe St NE ... 44483
Jackson St SW ... 44485
James St SE ... 44484
Janet Dr NE ... 44483
Jay St SW ... 44481
Jeanette Dr SE ... 44484
Jefferson St SW ... 44485
Jesse Ave NE ... 44483
Johnnycake Rd SE ... 44484
Johnson Plank Rd NE ... 44481
Jonathan Ln NW ... 44483
Juanita Ave NW ... 44483
Judyth St SE ... 44484
Julia Dr SW ... 44481
Justice Dr SW ... 44481
Kale Adams Rd SW ... 44481
Karl Ave SW
600-799 ... 44481
900-1999 ... 44485
Kenilworth Ave NE ... 44483
Kenilworth Ave SE
100-599 ... 44483
700-1699 ... 44484
Kenmore Ave NE ... 44483
Kenmore Ave SE
100-699 ... 44483
700-1299 ... 44484
Kensington Ln NE ... 44484
Kensington St NW ... 44485
Kenwood Dr SW ... 44485
Kenworthy Ave SW ... 44485
Kenyon Dr SE ... 44484

Keri Dr SW ... 44485
Kettering St SE ... 44484
Kibler Toot Rd SW ... 44481
Kimberly Dr NE ... 44483
Kimblewick Ln NE ... 44484
Kincaid East Rd NW ... 44481
King Graves Rd NE ... 44484
Kings Dr SW ... 44481
Kingston Ct ... 44484
Kinsman St NW ... 44483
Knickerbocker Dr NE ... 44484
Knox Ave NW ... 44483
Kuszmaul Ave NW ... 44483
Lafayette St NE ... 44483
Laird Ave NE ... 44483
Laird Ave SE
100-499 ... 44483
500-799 ... 44484
Lake Shore Ter SW ... 44481
Lakeside Way SW ... 44481
Lamphier Pl NE ... 44483
Lancer Ct NW ... 44485
Landsdowne Ave NW ... 44485
Lane Dr SW ... 44483
Lane West Rd SW ... 44481
Larchmont Ave NE ... 44483
Lauder Ave E & NW ... 44483
Laurel Ct NE ... 44483
Laurelwood Dr SE ... 44484
Lawrence Ave NE ... 44483
Layer Rd SW ... 44481
Leavitt Dr NW ... 44485
N Leavitt Rd NW ... 44485
S Leavitt Rd SW ... 44481
Lener Ave SW ... 44485
Leslie Dr NW ... 44483
Lexie Ln SE ... 44484
Lexington Ave NW ... 44485
Lilac Pl NW ... 44485
Linda Dr NW ... 44485
Linden Ave NE ... 44483
Linden Ave SE ... 44483
N Linden Ct ... 44484
S Linden Ct ... 44484
Livingston Cir NW ... 44483
Locust Dr SW ... 44481
Lodwick Dr NW ... 44485
Logan Ave NE & SE ... 44483
Longfellow Ct NE ... 44483
Longhill Dr SE ... 44484
Longview Dr NE ... 44484
Lori Dr SW ... 44485
Louise Ave NW ... 44483
Louise Ct NW ... 44481
Loveless Ave SW ... 44485
Lovers Ln NW ... 44485
Lowell Ave NE ... 44483
Lucetta St SE ... 44484
Lydia Dr SW ... 44481
Lyle Rd SW ... 44485
Lynn Dr NE ... 44481
Lynn Pl NW ... 44483
Lyntz Townline Rd SW ... 44481
Lynwood Dr NW ... 44485
Mabel Pl SW ... 44485
Madison Ave NW ... 44483
Mae Dr SW ... 44481
Mahoning Ave NW
200-5999 ... 44483
6000-7199 ... 44481
Mahoning Ct NW ... 44483
Main Ave SW
100-499 ... 44481
500-1599 ... 44483
1600-2199 ... 44485
2300-4299 ... 44481
Main Street Ext SW ... 44481
Malibu Dr SW ... 44481
Maple St SW ... 44485
Maplewood St NE ... 44483
E Market St
100-899 ... 44481
900-3199 ... 44483
3200-10499 ... 44484

W Market St
101-197 ... 44481
199-1099 ... 44481
1100-3499 ... 44485
Marlin Pl NW ... 44483
Marquis Dr SW ... 44481
Marshall Ave E & W ... 44483
Martha St NE ... 44483
Martin St SW
400-581 ... 44483
583-599 ... 44483
600-699 ... 44485
Martin Luther King Blvd SW ... 44485
Marwood Dr SE ... 44484
Mary Dr NE ... 44483
Mary Dr SW ... 44481
Maryland St NE & NW ... 44483
Mason St NW ... 44485
Masters Ct NE ... 44484
Masters Rd NW ... 44485
Mauro Cir SE ... 44484
Maxwell Ave NW ... 44485
Mayflower Rd SE ... 44484
Mayflower St NW ... 44483
Maywood St NW ... 44485
Mazda Ave NE ... 44483
Mckinley St NE ... 44483
Mcmyler St NW ... 44485
Meadow Ln NE ... 44483
Meadowbrook Ave SE
100-499 ... 44483
600-1499 ... 44484
Meadowview Cir NW ... 44483
Meadowview Dr NW ... 44481
Mellgren Dr SW ... 44481
Melrose Ct NW ... 44485
Melwood Dr NE ... 44483
Mercer Ave & Pl ... 44483
Merriweather St NW ... 44485
Micawber Rd NE ... 44484
Michelle Ave SW ... 44485
Miles Ave NW ... 44483
Mill St NE ... 44483
Millard St SW ... 44481
Miller St SW ... 44485
Miller Graber Rd SW ... 44481
Millikin Pl NE ... 44483
Milton St SE ... 44484
Mines Rd SE ... 44484
Mistletoe Dr SE ... 44484
Moncrest Dr NW ... 44485
Monroe St NW ... 44483
Montclair St NE ... 44483
Montgomery Ave NW ... 44485
Monticello Ave NW ... 44485
Muirfield Dr SE ... 44484
Muirwood Dr NE ... 44484
Mulberry Ave NW ... 44485
Muth Rd SW ... 44481
Myrtle Ave NW ... 44483
Nevada Ave NW & SW ... 44485
New Dr SW ... 44481
Newton Falls Bailey Rd SW ... 44481
Newton Tomlinson Rd SW ... 44481
Nezbar Dr NW ... 44481
Niblock Ave NW ... 44485
Nicklaus Dr NE ... 44484
Niles Rd SE
700-899 ... 44483
1100-3999 ... 44484
Niles Cortland Rd NE & SE ... 44484
Nocturne Ave NE ... 44483
Noel Dr ... 44481
North Rd NE ... 44483
North Rd SE ... 44484
North St NW ... 44483
Northfield Ave NW ... 44485
Northgate Dr NE ... 44484
Northwest Blvd NW ... 44485
Northwood Dr SE ... 44484
Northwoods Ct NE ... 44483

Norwood St NW ... 44485
Nottingham St NW ... 44485
Nutley Ave NE ... 44483
Nutwood Ave NW ... 44483
Oak Cir & St ... 44485
Oak Hill Dr NW ... 44481
Oak Hollow Dr NW ... 44481
Oak Knoll Ave NE ... 44483
Oak Knoll Ave SE
100-699 ... 44483
700-1699 ... 44484
Oak Tree Ln SE ... 44484
Oakdale Dr NW ... 44485
Oaklawn Ave SE ... 44484
Oakview Dr ... 44481
Oakview Dr NE ... 44484
Oakwood Dr SE ... 44484
Ogden Ave NW ... 44483
Ohio Ave NW ... 44485
Old Colony Rd NW ... 44481
Old Farm Trl NE ... 44484
Old Orchard Rd SE ... 44484
Old Wagon Ln NE ... 44484
Ole Time Ln NW ... 44481
Olian Ave NW ... 44485
Olive Ave NE ... 44483
Orange Ct NE ... 44483
Orange Dr SW ... 44485
Orchard Ave SE ... 44484
Orchard Ct SE ... 44484
Orchard Pl NE ... 44483
Oregon Ave NW ... 44485
Oriole Pl SW ... 44485
Orleans Ave SW ... 44485
Orlo Dr NW ... 44485
Overland Ave NE ... 44483
Overlook Ave SE ... 44484
Overlook Dr NE ... 44483
Overlook Dr NW ... 44483
Pacific Pl NW ... 44483
Packard St NW ... 44483
Paige Ave NE ... 44483
Pallette Dr NE ... 44484
Palm Ave NW ... 44483
Palmer Cir NE ... 44484
Palmyra Rd SW
800-2099 ... 44485
2101-2111 ... 44485
2110-2110 ... 44481
2112-7499 ... 44481
Panther Ave NE ... 44483
N Park Ave
100-198 ... 44481
200-599 ... 44481
600-4600 ... 44483
4602-4898 ... 44483
S Park Ave
100-299 ... 44481
300-699 ... 44483
W Park Dr SW ... 44485
N Park Avenue Ext ... 44481
Parkman Rd NW
100-3000 ... 44485
3001-3002 ... 44481
3003-3003 ... 44485
3004-3058 ... 44481
3005-3029 ... 44481
3029-3029 ... 44485
3031-3039 ... 44481
3041-3041 ... 44485
3043-6199 ... 44481
3060-3060 ... 44485
3062-3110 ... 44481
3110-3110 ... 44485
3112-3118 ... 44481
3120-3120 ... 44485
3122-6198 ... 44481
Parkman Rd SW ... 44485
Parkwood Dr NW ... 44485
Pat Ann Dr NW ... 44483
Patchen Ave SE ... 44484
Paulo Dr NE ... 44483
Pawnee St SW ... 44485
Paxton St SW ... 44485
Peace Ave NW ... 44483
Peach Ln SW ... 44485
Pearl St SW ... 44485

Peerless Ave SW ... 44485
Pegotty Ct & Dr ... 44484
Penn Ave NW & SW ... 44485
Perkins Dr NW ... 44483
Perkins Jones Ct & Rd ... 44483
Perkinswood Blvd NE ... 44483
Perkinswood Blvd SE
100-799 ... 44483
800-1399 ... 44484
Pershing St SW ... 44485
Pew Ct NE ... 44481
Pheasant Run Rd SE ... 44484
Phillips Dr SW ... 44485
Phoenix Rd NE ... 44483
Pierce Rd NW ... 44481
Pin Oak Ln NW ... 44481
Pine Ave NE ... 44481
Pine Ave SE
100-199 ... 44481
201-299 ... 44481
300-2000 ... 44483
2002-2098 ... 44483
Pinehurst Dr SE ... 44484
Pineside Ln NE ... 44481
Pineview Dr NE ... 44484
Pintail Dr SE ... 44484
Pioneer Ct NW ... 44481
Plaza Ave NE ... 44483
Pleasant Dr NW ... 44483
Pleasant Park Ct NW ... 44481
Pleasant Valley Dr NE ... 44483
Pleasant Valley Dr SW ... 44481
Plymouth Pl NE ... 44483
Pond Ln SW ... 44481
Portal Dr NE ... 44484
Porter St NE ... 44483
Post Rd NW ... 44483
Potter Ct SE ... 44481
Prentice Rd NW ... 44481
Prier Pl NE ... 44483
Pritchard Ohltown Rd SW ... 44481
Prospect Ave NW ... 44483
Quail Hollow Cir SE ... 44484
Quail Run Dr NW ... 44483
Quarry Ln NE ... 44483
Queens Dr SW ... 44481
Raccoon Dr NE ... 44483
Rachel Dr SW ... 44481
Radtka Dr SW ... 44481
Raglan Cir, Dr & Ext ... 44484
Railroad Ave NE ... 44483
Randolph St NW ... 44485
Ratliff Ave NW ... 44485
Ravenwood Dr SE ... 44484
Ravine Ct SW ... 44481
Raymond Ave NW ... 44483
Raymond St NW ... 44483
Red Fox Run Dr NW ... 44485
Red Oak Dr NE ... 44484
Redwood Ave NE ... 44483
Reeves Rd NE ... 44483
Refractories Dr NW ... 44483
Regal Dr NW ... 44485
Rellim Ave NW ... 44483
Reo Blvd & Ct ... 44483
Republic Ave NW ... 44483
Republic Ave SE ... 44484
Research Pkwy NW ... 44483
Reuther Dr SW ... 44481
Rex Blvd NW ... 44483
Richard Dr NW ... 44483
Richwood St SW ... 44485
Ridge Ave SE ... 44484
Ridge Run Dr NW ... 44481
Ridgelawn Ave SE ... 44484
Risher Rd SW
2100-2799 ... 44485
2800-4199 ... 44481
N River Rd NE
1-3199 ... 44483
3200-4699 ... 44484
N River Rd NW ... 44483
River Glen Dr NE ... 44484

Riverside Dr NW ... 44483
Riverview St NW ... 44485
Riviera Ct SE ... 44484
Roanoke Ave SW ... 44485
Roberts Ave NW ... 44485
Roberts Ln NE ... 44483
Robinwood Dr SW ... 44481
Rock Dr SW ... 44481
Rogers Ave SE ... 44484
Rolling Meadows Dr NE ... 44484
Roman St SE ... 44484
Roosevelt St NW ... 44483
Rose Pl SW ... 44485
Rosedale Ave NW ... 44483
Rosegarden Dr NE ... 44484
Roselawn Ave NE ... 44483
Rosenbaum St SW ... 44481
Roseway Ave SE ... 44484
Rosewood Dr NE ... 44484
Royal Troon Dr SE ... 44484
Rustic Run Rd SW ... 44481
Sabrina Ln NW ... 44483
Saddle Ridge Cir SE ... 44484
Saint Andrews Pl NE ... 44484
Saint Clair Dr NE ... 44483
N Salem Warren Rd ... 44481
Salt Springs Rd ... 44481
Sandberg Way NW ... 44483
Sandpiper Trl SE ... 44484
Sarah Ave NW ... 44483
Saratoga Ave SW ... 44485
Sarkies Dr NE ... 44483
Sassafras Ln SW ... 44485
Sawgrass St NE ... 44484
Schenley Ave NE ... 44483
School St NW ... 44483
Scott St NE ... 44483
Sealy Ct NW ... 44483
Seater Rd NW ... 44485
Sedgewick St NE ... 44483
Selkirk Bush Rd SW ... 44481
Seneca Ave NE ... 44481
Severn Ct SE ... 44483
Sferra Ave NW ... 44483
Shadowood Ln SE ... 44484
Shady Ave NW ... 44483
Shady Ln NE ... 44484
Shady Lane Cir NE ... 44483
Shaffer Dr NE ... 44484
Shaffer Rd NW ... 44481
Shalom Ave NW ... 44483
Shepard Dr NE ... 44483
Shepherds Way NE ... 44484
Sheridan Ave NE ... 44483
Sherwood Dr NE ... 44484
Shirley Ln NW ... 44483
Sidells Ct NE ... 44483
Silver Fox Dr SW ... 44481
Silver Fox Ln NE ... 44484
Singing Hills Dr NE ... 44484
Sleepy Hollow Dr NE ... 44484
Smith Pl NE ... 44483
Solar Dr NW ... 44485
Somerset St SE ... 44484
South St SE
101-197 ... 44483
199-2899 ... 44483
8100-8999 ... 44484
South St SW ... 44483
Southern Blvd NW ... 44485
Southwest Blvd SW ... 44485
Southwind Dr NE ... 44484
Southwood Dr SE ... 44484
Sparks Dr SW ... 44485
Spring St SW ... 44485
Spring Creek Holw NE ... 44484
Spring Pines Dr SW ... 44481
Spring Run Rd NE ... 44484
Springbrook Dr NE ... 44484
Springwood Trce SE ... 44484
Spruce Trl SW ... 44481
Spyglass Ct SE ... 44484
Squires Ln NE ... 44484
Squirrel Hill Dr NE ... 44484
Stafford Ave NE ... 44483

Stanley St SE ... 44484
Stans Way SE ... 44484
Starlite Dr NW ... 44485
State Rd NW
100-899 ... 44483
900-3299 ... 44481
State Route 305 Rd NW ... 44481
Steele St SW ... 44485
Stephens Ave NW ... 44485
Stetson Dr NE ... 44484
Stewart Ave NW ... 44483
Stewart Cir NW ... 44485
Stewart Dr NW ... 44485
Stiles St NW ... 44485
Stillwagon Rd SE ... 44484
Stone Ridge Dr SE ... 44484
Stonecreek Ln NE ... 44484
Stonehenge Ave NE ... 44483
Stoneybrook Dr SE ... 44484
Sugar Pines Dr SW ... 44481
Summerdale Ave NW ... 44483
Summerfield Ln NE ... 44483
Summit St NW
301-397 ... 44483
399-499 ... 44483
600-1200 ... 44485
1202-1298 ... 44485
Sunnybrook Dr SE ... 44484
Sunnyfield Ave NW ... 44481
Sunnyside Dr NW ... 44483
Sunset Dr NE ... 44483
Sunview Dr NE ... 44484
Superior St NW ... 44483
Supreme St NE ... 44483
Surfwood Cir SW ... 44485
Surrey Rd SE ... 44484
Surrey Point Cir & Dr ... 44484
Sussex St SE ... 44484
Sutton Pl NE ... 44484
Swallow St SW ... 44485
Sweetbrier St SW ... 44485
Sycamore Ln SW ... 44481
Sylvan St NW ... 44485
Tait Rd SW ... 44481
Tanya Ave NW ... 44485
Taylor St NW ... 44485
Templeton Rd NW ... 44481
Terra Alta St NE ... 44483
Thai Dr SW ... 44481
The Grn NE ... 44484
Thistle Pl SE ... 44484
Thomas Rd SE ... 44484
Thorn Ct NE ... 44483
Thorn Dr NE ... 44484
Thornwood Ave & St ... 44483
Tidewater St NE ... 44483
Tiffany Dr NE ... 44483
Timberlane Dr NE ... 44484
Tod Ave NW ... 44485
Tod Ave SW
100-198 ... 44485
200-2899 ... 44485
2900-8999 ... 44481
Tod Pl NW ... 44485
Torrey Pines St NE ... 44484
Towson Dr NW ... 44483
Transylvania Ave SE ... 44484
Trefeathen Dr NE ... 44484
Trentwood Dr SE ... 44484
Tridalto Ave NE ... 44483
Trinity Way ... 44481
Trumbull Ave NE ... 44483
Trumbull Ave SE
100-499 ... 44483
600-1399 ... 44484
Truxton St NE ... 44483
Tulip Ct SW ... 44485
Turnberry Ct NE ... 44484
Turnberry Ln NW ... 44481
Union St SW ... 44485
University St NE ... 44483
Utica Ct NW ... 44485
Valacamp Ave SE ... 44484
Valley Ave SW
1400-1699 ... 44483

1700-1999 44485
Valley Cir NE 44484
Valley Dale Dr NW 44485
Van Wye St SE 44484
Venice Heights Dr NE 44484
Vermont Ave NW & SW 44485
Vernon Ave NW 44483
Verona St NW 44483
Victoria St SW 44485
Victoria Ter SE 44484
Vine Ave NE & SE 44483
Viola St SW 44485
Virginia Ave SE 44484
Virginia Ave SW 44481
Virginia Dr NW 44483
Wainwood Dr SE 44484
Wal Mart Dr NE 44483
Walker Ave NW 44483
Wallace St SE 44484
Walnut Ct SW 44483
Ward St NW 44485
Warrenton Dr NW 44481
Warwick Rd SE 44484
Washington St NE & NW 44483
Waverly Ave & Dr NE & NW 44483
Webb Ave SW 44485
Weilacher Rd SW 44481
Weir Rd NE 44483
Welcker Dr NE 44483
West Ave NW 44483
Westchester Dr SE 44484
Westgate Dr NE 44484
Westover Dr SE 44484
Westview Dr NE 44483
Westview St SW 44481
Westwind Dr NE 44484
Westwood Dr NW 44485
Wheelock Dr NE 44484
Whispering Mdws NE 44483
Whispering Pines Dr SW 44481
White Ct SW 44485
White Oak Dr NE 44484
Whittier Pl NE 44483
Wick St SE 44484
Wilderness Ct SW 44481
Wildwood Dr NE 44483
Will Anna Ct NW 44481
Willard Ave NE 44483
Willard Ave SE
100-699 44483
700-2199 44484
Williams St NW 44481
Williams St SE 44484
Williamsburg St NW 44485
Willow Dr NE 44484
Willow Dr SE 44484
Willow Dr SW 44485
Willow Brook Dr NE 44483
Willow Creek Dr SE 44484
Wilson Ave NE & NW 44483
Wimber Ave NE 44483
Windsor Pl 44483
Windsor Trce NE 44484
Wood Ave SW 44485
Wood Lenhart Rd SW 44481
Woodbine Ave SE
100-699 44483
700-3699 44484
Woodhill Cir & Ct 44484
Woodland St NE
700-2899 44483
8200-8399 44484
Woodland Grove Ave NW 44483
Woodridge Way SW 44481
Woodrow Ave NW 44483
Woodside Dr NW 44483
Woodview Ave SW 44485
Wreyford Ave NW 44483
York Ave NW & SW 44485
Yorkshire Ct NE 44484
Youngs Run Dr NW 44483
Youngstown Rd SE 44484

NUMBERED STREETS

1st St SE 44484
1st St SW 44485
2nd St SW 44483
3rd St SW
200-899 44483
1700-1799 44485
4th Dr SW 44485
4th St SW
100-999 44483
1600-1799 44485
5th St SW 44485
6th St SW 44485
7th St SW 44485
8th St SW 44485
27th St SW 44481
28th St SW 44481

WEST CHESTER OH

General Delivery 45069

POST OFFICE BOXES MAIN OFFICE STATIONS AND BRANCHES

Box No.s
8729ST - 8729ST 45071
1 - 1896 45071
8001 - 8474 45069
8702 - 8728 45071
8705 - 8726 45069
8750 - 8750 45071
8750 - 90092 45069

NAMED STREETS

Aaron Ct 45241
Absaroka Ct 45069
Acorn Ct 45241
Acredale Dr 45069
Adena Ct 45069
Adena Hills Ct 45069
Airy Ct 45069
Albritton Ct & Pl 45069
Alexander Ct 45069
Allegheny Dr 45069
Allen Rd 45069
Allencrest Dr 45069
Allendale Dr 45069
Amber Ln 45069
Amberwood Ct 45241
Ambleside Dr 45241
Amy Beth Dr 45069
Amy Marie Dr 45069
Andria Ct 45069
Anna Ct 45069
Anvil Ct 45069
Apache Way 45069
Apple Blossom Ln 45069
Applewood Dr 45069
Appomatox Ct 45069
E & W Arbor Ct, Ln & Ter 45069
Arborcrest Ct 45069
Arborview Dr 45069
Ash Hill Ct 45069
Ashbrook Dr 45069
Ashford Glen Ct 45069
Ashley Dr 45011
Ashley Hall Ct 45069
Ashley Oaks Ct 45069
Ashtree Dr 45069
Ashwood Dr 45069
Aster Park Dr 45011
Atchison Ct 45069
Auburn Ave 45241
Autumn Ln 45069
Autumn Glen Dr 45069
Autumn Woods Ln 45069
Avenel Ct 45069
Aviation Way 45069
Bach Dr 45069
Banbridge Ct 45069
Bannerwood Dr 45069
Bardean Dr 45069
Barge Ct 45069
Barkwood Dr 45069
Baron Ct 45069
Barret Rd 45069
Barrister Ct 45069
Basin St 45069
Basswood Dr 45069
N Bay Pl 45241
Bayer Dr 45069
Baytree Ct 45069
Beaver Brk 45069
Beckett Rd 45069
Beckett Center Dr 45069
Beckett Park Dr 45069
Beckett Pointe Dr 45069
Beckett Ridge Blvd 45069
Beckett Station Ct & Dr 45069
Belmont Park Ct 45069
Bennington Dr 45241
Bent Tree Dr 45069
Berkshire Ct 45069
Bermuda Trce 45069
Berry Hill Dr 45241
Bertwood Ct 45069
Birch Hollow Ln 45069
Birchstone Ct 45069
Birchwood Dr 45069
Birkdale Dr 45069
Black Hawk Ct 45069
Blackstone Ct 45069
Blossom St 45011
Blue Fox Run 45069
Blue Spruce Ct 45069
Bluebird Ct & Dr 45069
Bobtail Ct 45069
Bodford Dr 45069
Bolingbroke Dr 45241
Bonnie Dr 45069
Boxwood Ct 45241
Braemer Ln 45069
Brandy Wine Ln 45241
Brantford Ct 45069
Breakers Pt 45069
Breezewood Ct 45069
Bridgeford Ct 45069
Bridle Ct 45069
Brigantine Ct 45069
Brighton Ln 45069
Bromyard Ave 45241
Brook Knoll Dr 45069
Brookdale Dr 45069
Brookfield Dr 45069
Brookridge Dr 45069
Brookside Ave 45069
Brookstone Dr 45069
Brown Ct 45011
Brownstone Ct & Dr 45241
Brucehills Dr 45069
Brushwood Dr 45069
Buckhorn Dr 45069
Bulrush Ct 45069
Burlington Dr 45069
Burning Bush Ct 45241
Business Center Way 45246
Butler Warren Rd 45069
Butler Warren Line Rd 45241
Butterfly Way 45069
Butterwood Dr 45241
Canal Way 45069
Candlelight Ter 45069
Candy Ln 45069
Cannon Ct 45069
Cannon Knoll Ct 45069
Canvas Canopy 45069
Canyon Pass Dr 45011
Cape Cod Ct 45069
Cardinal View Way 45069
Cardington Pl 45069
Carey Woods Ln 45069
Carnegie Way 45246
Cascade Dr 45069
Cascara Dr 45069
Caseys Xing 45069
Castle Pines Ln 45069
Castlebridge Ct 45069
Castlerock Ln 45069
Cattail Ln 45069
Cecelia Ct 45241
Cedar Creek Dr 45069
Cedar Falls Ln 45069
Centre Park Dr 45069
Centre Pointe Dr 45069
Chadwick Ct 45069
Champions Ln 45069
Chantilly Dr 45069
Chappell Crossing Blvd 45069
Chappellfield Dr 45069
Charlemont Ct 45069
Charming Mnr 45069
Charter Cup Ln 45069
Charter Oak Ct 45069
Charter Park Dr 45069
Chateau Ct 45069
Chatham Ct 45069
Chattanooga Dr 45069
Cherry Lane Farm Dr 45069
Cherrywood Ln 45069
Chessie Dr 45069
W Chester Ct, Pt & Rd 45069
W Chester Towne Ctr 45069
Chestershire Dr 45241
Chesterwood Blvd 45069
Chestnut Hill Ct & Ln 45069
Chicamauga Ct 45069
Chinook Dr 45069
Christine Ave & Dr 45241
Churchview Ln 45069
Cincinnati Columbus Rd
8401-8457 45069
8459-9199 45069
9100-9198 45241
9200-9210 45069
9200-9598 45241
9201-9599 45069
9600-10201 45241
Cincinnati Dayton Rd
7100-7198 45069
7201-7397 45069
7399-8731 45069
8730-8730 45071
8732-9998 45069
8733-9999 45069
Cindy Dr 45069
Cindy Lou Dr 45069
Cinnamon Woods Dr 45069
Circle Freeway Dr 45246
Civic Centre Blvd 45069
Clarinbridge Ct 45069
Clawson Ct 45069
Clearbrook Dr 45069
Clearmeadow Dr 45069
Cliffwood Ct 45241
Cloverhill Ct 45069
Club Ln 45069
Clubhouse Ct 45069
Coachford Dr 45069
Coachlight Way 45069
Coachman Dr 45069
Cobblestone Walk 45069
Colegate Way 45011
College Dictionary 45069
Colonial Mill Mnr 45069
Columbia Cir 45011
Commanche Dr 45069
Commerce Park Dr 45246
Commercial Dr 45014
Congress Ct 45069
Coppernail Way 45069
Cornell Ln 45011
Cottonwood Dr 45069
Country Way 45069
Country Club Ln 45069
Country Green Ct 45069
Country Oaks Sta 45069
Course View Dr 45069
Cox Ln & Rd 45069
Coyote Ct 45069
Creativity 45069
Creek Bend Dr 45069
Creekside Ct 45069
Creekstone Ln 45241
Creekwood Cir 45069
Crescent Park Dr 45069
Crescentville Rd 45069
E Crescentville Rd 45246
W Crescentville Rd 45246
Crestfield Dr 45069
Cresthaven Ave 45069
Crestmont Dr 45069
Crestridge Dr 45069
Crossbridge Dr 45069
Cypresstree Cir 45069
Danbury Ct 45069
Darlene Dr 45069
Daycrest Dr 45246
Debbie Dr 45069
Deer Path 45069
Deer Hollow Dr 45069
Deer Track Rd 45069
Deer Walk Ct 45069
Delview Dr 45069
Desert Spring Ct 45069
Desoto Dr 45069
Destination Ct 45069
Devitt Dr 45246
Devonshire Dr 45069
Devonwood Dr 45069
Dimmick Ct 45069
Dimmick Rd
6500-6854 45069
6856-7487 45069
7488-8399 45241
Discovery Dr 45069
Doc Dr 45069
Dockside Way 45069
Doe View Dr 45069
Doerfler Ct 45069
Dogwood Ct 45069
Donegal Dr 45069
Dorchester Ct 45069
Dorset Dr 45241
Dorsetshire Dr 45069
Douglas St 45069
Dove Ln 45069
Dover Ct & Dr 45069
Drawbridge Ct 45069
Duane Dr 45241
Dublin Ct 45069
Dudley Dr 45069
Dues Dr 45246
Duff Ct & Dr 45246
Dukes Dr 45069
Dundee Dr 45069
Dunmore Ct & Dr 45069
Eagle Ln 45069
Eagle Creek Ct 45069
Eagle Nest Ct 45069
Eagle Ridge Ct & Dr 45069
Eagles Wing Dr 45069
Eaglet Dr 45069
Eagleview Dr 45069
Eastbrook Dr 45069
Easton Ct 45069
Eastview Dr 45241
Eastwind Way 45069
Edgecliff Cir 45069
Edgeridge Dr 45069
Edgeview Dr 45069
Eleventh Hour Ln 45069
Elkwood Dr 45069
Ell Char Ct 45241
Emberwood Ct 45069
Emerald St 45069
Emery Ct 45069
Erie Cir 45069
Esther Dr 45069
European Jaunt 45069
Evergreen Ct 45069
Excello Ct 45069
Exchequer Ct 45069
Executive Ct 45069
Fairview Ave 45241
Fairwind Dr 45069
Falcon Ln 45069
Fallen Timbers Dr 45069
Falling Waters Ct 45069
Fallingwoods Ln 45241
Fallsridge 45069
Farm Acre Dr 45069
Farmcrest Dr 45069
Farmgate Dr 45069
Farmmeadow Ct 45069
Farr Ct 45246
Fawn Ct 45069
Fawnview Ct 45069
Fence Row 45069
Ferdinand Dr 45069
Fieldstone Ct 45069
Finchnest Way 45069
Firebird Dr 45014
Fireplace Ct 45069
Fireside Ct 45069
Fitzroy Ct 45241
Flagstone Way 45069
Floer Dr 45069
Floral Ave 45069
Forest Hills Ct 45069
Forestview Ct & Dr 45069
Forge Bridge Dr 45069
Founders Row 45069
Fountains Blvd 45069
Fox Chase Dr 45069
Fox Cub Ct 45069
Fox Glove Ln 45069
Fox Hill Ct 45069
Fox Hunt Ct 45069
Fox Knoll Ct & Dr 45069
Fox Plum Dr 45069
Fox Sedge Way 45069
Foxboro Dr 45069
Foxdale Ct 45069
Foxview Pl 45069
Fredericksburg Dr 45069
Friar Tuck Dr 45069
Fruitwood Dr 45069
Furrow Ct 45069
Gail Sue Dr 45069
Galewind Way 45069
Galway Ct 45069
Gano Rd
6300-6499 45069
6500-6599 45241
Gary Lee Dr 45069
W Gate Park 45069
Gatewood Ct 45241
Gina Dr 45069
Glades Dr 45011
Glen Arbor Dr 45069
Glen Meadow Dr 45069
Glen Moor Dr 45069
Glen Oaks Ct 45069
Glen Trace Ln 45069
Glenhaven Ct 45241
Glenn Farms Dr 45069
Glenn Knoll Dr 45069
Glenngate Ct 45069
Glennsbury Ct 45069
Glennshire Ct 45069
Glennstone Ct 45069
Glenridge Ct 45069
Global Way 45069
Golay Ave 45241
Goldcrest Dr 45069
Goldfinch Cir, Ct & Way 45069
Goldpark Dr 45011
Golf Crest Dr 45069
Golfview Ct 45069
Goodsite Dr 45011
Grace Meadows Way 45069
Granby Way 45069
Graystone Ct 45069
Great Waters Ln 45069
Green Valley Ct 45069
Green View Ct 45069
Greenwillow Cir 45069
Gregg Dr 45069
Gregory Creek Ln 45069
Grey Fox Dr 45069
Grinn Dr 45069
Grove St 45069
Guard St 45069
Guildford Dr & Ln 45069
Gulfstream Ct 45069
Haden Ln 45069
Hadley Dr 45069
Halifax Ct 45069
Hamilton Mason Rd 45069
Hampstead Ct 45241
Hance Ln 45069
Happiness Way 45069
Harbor Cove Dr 45069
Harbour Town Dr 45069
Hare Dr 45069
W Hartford Ct 45069
Harwood Ct 45014
Hastings Pt 45069
Haystack Way 45069
Hazeltine Blvd 45069
Hearthstone Ct 45241
Heathcock Ct 45241
Heather Ann Dr 45069
Heatherhill Dr 45069
Hedgerow Dr 45069
Heritage Dr 45069
Heritagespring Dr 45069
Heron Dr 45069
Hialeah Dr 45069
Hickory Hill Ln 45241
Hidden Knoll Ct 45069
Hidden Mill Ct 45069
Hidden Ridge Dr 45069
Hidden Trace Dr 45069
Highfield Ct 45069
Highland Greens Dr 45069
Highland Pointe Dr 45069
Highridge Dr 45069
Hillsdale Ln 45069
Hollow Oak Ct 45069
Holly Hill Ln 45069
Holly Leaf Cir 45241
Hollyhock Ct 45069
Hollywood Ct & Dr 45069
Homan Dr 45069
Honeysuckle Ln 45069
Honeywood Dr 45241
Hopewell Dr 45069
Hopi Dr 45069
Hummingbird Ln 45069
Hunters Trl 45069
Hunters Ridge Dr 45069
Huntington Cir 45069
Huntsman Ln 45069
Ikea Way 45069
Illumination 45069
Indian Trl 45069
Indian Pond Ct 45241
Indian Ridge Dr 45069
Indian Springs Dr 45241
Innovation Pl 45011
Inter Ocean Dr 45246
International Blvd 45246
Interstate Dr 45246
Inverary Ct 45069
Inverness Ct 45069
Iris Dr 45241
Ironside Ct 45069
Ironwood Way 45069
Ivory Hills Dr 45069
Jabberoo 45069
Jacquemin Dr 45069
Jane Ct 45241
Jasmine Trl 45241
Jean Dr 45069
Jeannes Ct 45069
Jeannes Creek Ln 45069
Jeff Ct 45241
Jennifer Lynn Ct 45069
Jerry Ct & Dr 45069
Jims Ct 45069

Joan Dr 45069
John St 45069
Jolena Ct 45241
Jonathan Ct 45069
Joseph James Dr 45246
Julie Marie Dr 45069
Julies Cv 45069
Junction Pl 45069
Kates Way 45069
Kearny Ct 45069
Keehner Ct & Dr 45069
Keehner Ridge Ct 45069
Keel Boat Ct 45069
Kelly Ct 45241
Keltner Dr 45069
Kendal Ln 45069
Kennesaw Dr 45069
Kenneth St 45069
Kildare Ct 45069
Kilkenny Dr 45069
Kimberly Ann Ct 45069
Kindlewood Dr 45069
Kingfisher Ln 45069
Kingland Dr 45069
Kinglet Dr 45069
Kingsfjord Ct 45069
Kingsgate Way 45069
Kingswood Dr 45069
Kirkcaldy Dr 45069
Kirkwood Dr 45069
Knights Knoll Ct 45069
Knoll Crest Ct 45069
Kohls Ct 45069
Kristen Dr 45069
Lackawana Ct 45069
Lady Anne Dr 45069
W Lake Dr 45069
Lake Lakota Cir 45069
Lake Meadow Ct 45069
Lake Park Dr 45069
Lake Ridge Dr 45069
Lake Shore Dr 45069
Lake Spring Dr 45069
Lakeland Ct 45069
Lakenoll Dr 45069
Lakes Edge 45069
Lakeside Dr 45069
Lakewood Cir 45069
Lakota Ct & Dr W 45069
Lakota Hills Dr 45069
Lakota Plaza Dr 45069
Lakota Springs Dr 45069
Lakota Trail Dr 45069
Landings Dr 45069
Landmark Ct 45069
Laray Dr 45069
Larchwood Dr 45241
Larrywood Dr 45069
Lawndale Dr 45069
Lawrence Dr & Rd 45069
Le Saint Ct & Dr 45014
Leaf Back Dr 45069
Leatherwood Dr 45069
Leblanc Way 45069
Leeds Point Ct 45069
Leemel Dr 45069
N & S Legare Ct 45069
Legendary Ln 45069
Leisure Ct 45241
Leopard Ln 45069
Lesourdsville West Chester Rd 45069
Liberty Cir & Way 45069
Liberty Centre Dr 45069
Liberty Grand Dr 45069
Lighthouse Ln 45069
Lindfield Dr 45069
Live Oak Dr 45069
Locust St 45069
Logans Ridge Dr 45069
Lois Dr 45241
Londondale Dr 45069
Long Meadow Dr 45069
Lowery Ln 45069
Lupine Dr 45241
Luster Dr 45069
Lynn Ave 45069
Lyonhil Dr 45069
Maddox Dr 45069
Mallard Dr 45069
Manassa Ct 45069
Manor Dr 45069
Maple Rdg 45069
Marcus Ct 45069
Marie Ct 45241
Mark Twain Ct 45069
Marketplace Dr 45069
Marsh Willow Ct 45069
Martins Way 45069
Mary Beth Dr 45069
Mary Lee Ln 45069
Mathes Dr 45069
Maud Hughes Rd 45069
Mccarthy Ct 45069
Mccauly Rd 45241
Meadow Hills Dr 45241
Meadow Ridge Dr 45241
Meadowbrook Ct 45069
Meadowlark Ct & Dr 45069
Meadowview Dr 45069
Medinah Ct 45069
Meeting St 45069
Mellowtone Ct 45069
Meridian Way 45069
Merryman Way 45069
Michelle Pt 45069
Middleshire Ct 45069
Mill Creek Cir 45069
Mill Rock Rd 45069
Millrace Way 45069
Millstone Cir 45069
Millwheel Way 45069
Mimosa Ln 45069
Minuteman Way 45069
Miranda Pl 45069
Misty Way 45069
Misty Shore Dr 45069
Moatbridge Ct 45069
Monarch Ct 45069
Monticello Dr 45069
Montreal Ct 45241
Mosteller Ln 45069
Muhlhauser Rd
4400-5199 45011
5201-5299 45011
5800-6299 45069
6301-6399 45011
Murtaugh Ln 45069
Near Dr 45246
Neida Dr 45069
New Brunswick Dr 45241
New Castle Dr 45069
New England Ct 45069
New Market Ct 45069
Neway Dr 45011
Nighthawk Ln 45069
Noel Ct 45069
Nordan Dr 45069
Norfolk Dr 45069
O Leary Dr 45241
Oak Creek Ct 45069
Oak Leaf Cir 45241
Oakleaf Ln 45069
E Observatory 45069
Oceola Ln 45069
Office Park Dr 45069
Old Crow Ct 45069
Old English Dr 45069
Old Forest Ln 45069
Old Shaw Way 45069
Old Stable Ct 45069
Old Station Dr 45069
Old Walnut Dr 45069
Oldgate Dr 45069
Olympia Fields Ct 45069
Oraderm Dr 45069
Orchard Ct 45069
Oregon Pass 45069
Ottawa Ln 45069
Overglen Dr 45069
Overland Park Ct 45069
Owl Nest Dr 45069
Paddington Ct 45069
Paige Ct 45069
Pam Ct 45069
Park Place Cir 45069
Park Ridge Ct 45069
Parktown Dr 45069
Parliament Ct 45069
Partridge Cir 45069
Patriot Dr 45069
Patti Cir 45069
Paul Dr 45069
Paul Manors Dr 45069
N Pavillion 45069
Pelican Dr 45069
Pepper Pike 45069
Pepperwood Dr 45069
Peter Pl 45246
Petersburg Ln 45069
Pheasant Hill Dr 45069
Pilgrim Ct 45069
Pine Needle Ct 45069
Pine Vista Ct 45069
Pinecastle Ct 45069
Pinemill Dr 45069
Pinetree Cir 45069
Pinevalley Dr 45069
Pinewood Ln 45241
Pinnacle Point Dr 45069
Pinter Ct 45069
N Pisgah Dr 45069
Placid Dr 45241
Plantation Dr 45069
Planters Ln 45069
Pleasure Dr 45069
Plowshare Way 45069
Plumwood Ct 45241
Polo Trail Pl 45069
Pons Ln 45069
S Port Dr 45069
Port Union Rd 45011
Port Union Rialto Rd 45069
Prairie Lake Blvd 45069
Preserve Pl 45069
Primary Colors 45069
Prince Wilbert Way 45069
Princess Ct 45069
Princeton Glendale Rd
7600-7898 45011
7900-7970 45011
8100-8300 45069
8301-8399 45011
8302-8998 45069
8601-8799 45069
8801-8997 45011
8999-9626 45011
9701-9735 45246
9737-10006 45246
10008-10132 45246
Princeton Square Cir 45246
Pros Dr 45069
Providence Woods Ct 45069
E Provident Dr 45246
Ptarmigan Ct 45069
Pullbridge Ct 45069
Pullman Ct 45069
Putters Cir 45069
Putting Green Ln 45069
Quail Hollow Ct 45069
Quail Meadow Ln 45069
Quail Run Dr 45069
Quailwood Ct 45069
Quaker Ct 45069
Quaker Ridge Ct 45069
Quebec Ct 45241
Queen Ann Ct 45069
Queens Ct 45069
Quentin Ct 45069
Quiet Time Pl 45069
R E Smith Dr 45069
Raintree Cir 45241
Ramblingridge Dr 45069
Ravenwood Dr & Way 45069
Red Bluff Ln 45069
Red Cedar Dr 45069
Red Fox Dr 45069
Red Mill Dr 45069
Red Pheasant Way 45069
Regal Ln 45069
Regency Ct 45069
Renwick Ct 45069
Revere Ct & Run 45069
Rialto Rd 45069
Rialto Ridge Dr 45069
Richmond Dr 45069
Rickhaven Ct 45069
Ridge Meadow Ct 45069
Ridgecrest Dr 45069
Ridgemont Dr 45069
Ridgetop Dr 45069
Rite Track Way 45069
Robert E Lee Ln 45069
Rock Port Way 45069
Rocky Pass 45069
Rodney Ct 45241
Rokeby Ct 45241
Rolling Meadows Dr 45069
Rollingwood Way 45069
Rose Mallow Dr 45069
Rosewood Dr 45069
Roundhouse Dr 45069
Rozelle Ct 45069
Runabay Ct 45069
Running Deer Dr 45069
Rupp Farm Dr 45069
Rushwood Ct 45241
Ruth Ct 45069
Saddle Ct 45069
Sage Meadow Ct 45069
Saint Andrews Dr 45069
Saint Ives Pl 45069
Saint Leger Ct 45069
Saint Matthew Dr 45069
San Mateo Dr 45069
Sandpiper Ct 45069
Santa Anita Ct 45069
Sawgrass Dr 45069
Saxony Dr 45069
Saxton Dr 45069
Schoolhouse Ct 45069
Schulze Dr 45069
Schumacher Park Dr 45069
Scioto Ct 45069
Scott Glen Ct 45069
Sea Mist Ct 45069
Sea Pines Pl 45069
Seaboard Ln 45069
Seabury Ct 45069
Secret Creek Ct 45069
Seedling Way 45069
Selkirk Dr 45069
Semaphore Ct 45069
Seminary St 45069
Seminole Dr 45069
Sennet Pl 45069
E Senour Dr 45069
Sequoia Ct 45069
Service Center Dr 45069
Shadetree Dr 45069
Shady Hollow Ln 45069
Shady Knoll Cir 45069
Shady Tree Dr 45069
Shady Well Ct 45069
Shadybrook Dr 45069
Shadyside Ln 45241
Shaggy Bark Dr 45069
Shaker Ct 45069
Shaker Run Ln 45069
Shamrock Ct 45069
Shasta Dr 45069
Shawnee Ln 45069
Shenandoah Ct 45069
Shepherd Ln 45069
Shepherd Farm Dr 45069
Shiloh Ct 45069
Shirley Dr 45069
Shoal Creek Ct 45069
N Shore Dr 45069
Short Line Ct 45069
Siebert Ct 45069
Silver Fox Ct 45069
Silverwood Ct 45069
Skyline Dr 45069
Sleepy Hollow Dr 45069
Smith Rd 45069
Somersby Ct 45069
Sonya Ln 45241
Southampton Ln 45069
Spellmire Dr 45246
Spikerush Ln 45069
Spinningwheel Ct 45069
Spring Ave 45241
Spring Garden Ct 45069
Spring Valley Ct 45069
Spruce Hill Cir 45069
Spruce Run Dr 45069
Sprucewood Ct & Ln 45241
Squire Ct 45069
Squirrel Hollow Rdg 45069
Staffordshire Ct 45069
Standers Knl 45069
Station Rd 45069
Steamboat Way 45069
Steeplechase Way 45069
Steleta Dr 45069
Sterling Dr 45241
Stillmeadow Dr 45069
Stirrup Ct 45069
Stone Dr 45241
Stone Harbour Ln 45069
Stonebarn Dr 45069
Stonewall Dr 45069
Stonewood Ct 45241
Stonyford Ct 45069
Strathaven Dr 45069
Stuart Ct 45069
Summerbridge Way 45069
Summerhill Dr 45069
Summit Ave 45241
Sun Lin Ct 45069
Sunburst Dr 45241
Sundance Cir 45069
Sunderland Way 45069
Sunny Ln 45241
Surrey Ct 45069
Surrey Brook Pl 45069
Susan Springs Dr 45069
Sussex Ct & Dr 45069
Sutton Pl 45011
Suzi Cir 45069
Sweetwater Br 45069
Switchback Ln 45069
Sylvan Ave 45241
Taffy Dr 45069
Tall Timber Dr 45241
Talltree Way 45069
Tamarack Ter 45241
Tamarron Pl 45069
Tammy Dr 45069
Tanager Dr 45069
Tanager Woods Ct 45069
Tanglewood Ln 45069
Tara Dr 45069
Tarragon Ct 45069
Tasselberry Dr 45069
Tawna Dr 45069
Taylor Ridge Dr 45069
Tennyson Ct & Dr 45069
Tepperwood Dr 45069
Terraqua Dr 45241
Tessa Ct 45241
Thames Ct 45069
Thistlewood Dr 45069
Thornwood Ct 45241
Threshing Ct 45069
Thunderbird Ln 45014
Timber Dr 45241
Timberchase Ct 45069
Timberdale Dr 45069
Timberjack Way 45069
Timberline Dr 45241
Timbermist Ct 45241
Timbernoll Dr 45069
Timberoak Trl 45241
Timberrail Ct 45069
Timbertree Way 45069
Timberview Ct & Dr 45241
Timberwolf Ct 45069
Timberwood Dr 45069
Todd Creek Cir 45069
Toddy Dr 45069
Tollbridge Ct 45069
Topeka Ln 45069
Topridge Dr 45069
Torrington Ln 45069
Town Centre Dr 45069
Towpath Ln 45069
Trade Port Dr 45011
Trailwoods Ct 45069
Tranquility Ct 45069
Transportation Way 45246
Traverse Ct 45069
Trestle Dr 45069
Triangle Dr 45011
Trillium Ct 45241
Tucker Dr 45069
Tuliptree Cir 45069
Turfway Trl 45069
Turnberry Ct 45069
Twin Cove Ct 45069
Twin Creek Trce 45069
Twin Valley Ct 45241
Tylers Cir, Ter, Way & Xing 45069
Tylers Corner Pl 45069
Tylers Creek Dr 45069
Tylers Estates Dr 45069
Tylers Hill Ct 45069
Tylers Knoll Dr 45069
Tylers Meadow Dr 45069
Tylers Place Blvd 45069
Tylers Reserve Dr 45069
Tylers Valley Dr 45069
Tylersville Rd
4200-4799 45011
4800-5598 45069
5600-8099 45069
8101-8399 45069
Tylersville Square Dr 45069
Union Park 45069
Union Centre Blvd
6001-6027 45014
7300-7498 45014
7900-8698 45069
8700-9200 45069
9202-9398 45069
Union Centre Dr 45069
Union Centre Pavilion Dr 45069
University Ct & Dr 45069
Us Grant Ct 45069
Vadith Ct 45069
Vegas Cir & Ct 45069
Ventle Dr 45069
Verdant Dr 45069
Vicksburg Dr 45069
Victory Ct 45069
View Pl 45069
Village Center Ave 45069
Voice Of America Centre Dr 45069
W Voice Of America Park Dr 45069
Wabash Way 45069
Wakeshire Dr 45069
Walnut Rdg & St 45069
Walnut Creek Ct & Dr 45069
Walnutwood Dr 45241
Water Front Dr 45069
Waterbury Ct 45069
Waterford Ct 45069
Waterleaf Ln 45069
Watermark Ct 45069
Waterpark Dr 45069
Weatherby Ct 45069
Weatherly Ct 45069
Weathervane Way 45069
Wellness Way 45069
Wells Xing 45069
Welsford Ct 45069
Welsley Trce 45069
Wendel Dr 45241
Westberry Ct 45069
Westchester Park Ct 45069
Westsand Ct 45069
Wetherington Dr 45069
Wethersfield Dr 45069
Wexford Way 45241
Wheatland Meadow Ct 45069
Whisper Way 45069
Whispering Run Ct 45069
Whispering Willows Way 45069
Whispering Woods Dr 45069
Whistle Stop Ct 45069
White Hill Ln 45069
Whitehall Cir E & W 45069
Whitehaven Ct 45069
Whitehorse Ct 45069
Whitehouse Ct 45069
Whitetail Cir 45069
Wildbrook Ct 45069
Wilderness Trl 45069
Wildridge Dr 45069
Willet Ln 45069
Willoughby Ct 45069
Willow Crest Ln 45069
Willow Oak Dr 45069
Willow Run Ct 45069
Willowood Ct & Dr 45241
Windbrook Trl 45069
Windcrest Dr 45069
Winding Creek Way 45069
Windisch Rd 45069
Windrift Dr 45241
Windsong Way 45069
Windwood Dr 45241
N Windwood Dr 45069
Windy Ct 45069
Windy Harbor Way 45069
Windy Knoll Dr 45241
Winged Foot Dr 45069
Winterberry Pl 45241
Wintergreen Dr 45069
Wise Ave & Ct 45069
Woodbine Ave 45241
Woodbridge Ln 45069
Woodcliff Ct 45069
Woodglen Dr 45069
Woodland Cir 45069
Woodland Hills Dr 45011
Woodlark Ln 45069
Woodreed Dr 45069
Woods Edge Ct 45069
Woodsong Dr 45069
Woodthrush Ln 45069
Woodward Dr 45069
Woody Hollow Dr 45241
Wunnenberg Way 45069
Wyndtree Dr 45069
Wynstone Ct 45069
Yacht Haven Way 45069
Yorkshire Dr 45069
Zaring Dr 45069
Zebra Ct 45069

NUMBERED STREETS

All Street Addresses 45069

WESTERVILLE OH

General Delivery 43082

POST OFFICE BOXES MAIN OFFICE STATIONS AND BRANCHES

Box No.s
All PO Boxes 43086

NAMED STREETS

Abba Dr 43081
Abbeycross Ln 43082
Abbotsbury Ct & Dr 43082
Abby Gate Ave & Ct 43081

Aberfeldy Ct 43082
Abington Ct 43082
Abney Ct 43082
Acapulco Pl 43081
Acillom Dr 43081
Acorn Ct 43082
Adcock Rd 43082
Africa Rd 43082
Ainsley Dr 43082
Albany Grn, Grv, Ln, Mdw, Run, Trce & Xing 43081
Albany Bend Dr 43081
Albany Brooke Dr 43081
Albany Reserve Dr 43081
Albany Springs Dr 43081
Albany Terrace Way 43081
Albany Way Dr 43081
Albanyview Dr 43081
Alberta Pl 43082
Albion Pl 43082
Alice Dr 43081
Alkyre Run 43082
Allview Ct & Rd 43081
Alston Grove Dr 43082
Alumwood Dr 43081
Amanda Ridge Ct 43082
Amber Rock Rd 43081
Amesbury Ct 43082
Amity Moor Rd 43081
Amy Glenn 43081
Amy Lu Ct 43082
Anacala Ct 43082
Anderson Park Ct & Ln 43081
Andrew Ave 43081
Andrews Dr E & W 43082
Annandale Ct 43082
Annarose Run 43081
Annelise Ln 43081
Apache Cir & St 43081
Apple St 43082
Apple Ridge Pl 43081
Applewood Ln 43081
Apricot Pl 43082
Arcadia Blvd 43082
Arnett Ct & Rd 43081
Arnold Aly 43081
Arundel Ave 43081
Ash Ct 43081
Ash Rock Cir 43081
Ashbrooke Dr 43082
Asherton Grove Dr 43081
Ashford Ct & Dr 43082
Ashford Ridge Rd 43081
Ashington Pl 43081
Augusta Dr 43082
Augusta Woods Ct & Ter 43082
Autumn Branch Rd 43081
Autumn Creek Cir 43081
Autumn Crest Ct
1000-1099 43081
6300-6499 43082
Autumn Lake Ct 43081
Autumn Lake Dr 43082
Autumn Meadows Dr 43081
Autumn Park Ct 43081
Autumn Tree Pl 43081
Autumn Woods Dr 43081
Aylesbury Ct & Dr 43082
Babbington Ct 43081
Bader Ct & Rd 43081
Baker Lake Ct & Dr 43081
Balboa Ct, Pl & Rd 43081
Bald Eagle Ct 43082
Baldwin Ct 43082
Baltimore Ave 43081
Baltusrol Ct 43082
Baneberry Dr 43082
Bangasi Rd 43081
Baranof E & W 43081
Barcelona Ave 43081
Bardon Dr 43082
Barlow Rd 43081
Barony Village Dr 43081
Barrington Ct & Dr 43082
Bashaw Dr 43081
Batavia Ct & Rd 43081
Bay Dr 43082
Bay Forest Dr 43082
Beachside Dr 43081
Bears Paw Ct 43081
Beauty Rose Ave 43081
Beddingfield Pl 43081
Bedford Ct 43082
Beech Ln 43081
Bell Classic Dr 43081
Belle Haven Ct & Pkwy 43082
Belle Meade Ct & Pl 43081
Bellefield Ave 43081
Bellerive Pl 43082
Bellfrey Ct, Dr & Ln 43082
Belpre Pl E & W 43081
Benderson Dr 43082
Benon Rd 43082
Benpatrick Ct 43081
Bentley Pl 43082
Bering Ct 43081
Beringer Dr 43082
Berkeley Pl N & S 43081
Berkshire Commons Dr 43082
Bernadine Ct 43081
Bethany Dr 43081
Bevelhymer Rd 43081
Big Rock Ct & Dr 43082
Big Walnut Rd 43082
Bilberry Ln 43081
Birch St 43082
Birchwood Ln 43081
Birkland Ln 43081
Birmingham Rd 43081
Bishop Dr 43081
Bitternut Ln 43081
Bitterroot Dr 43081
Black Walnut Dr 43082
Blackgum Way 43081
Blackhawk Cir 43082
Blackhawk Forest Dr 43082
Blackmore Ct 43081
Blackoak Cir 43081
Blacksmith Dr 43081
Blendon Dr 43081
Blendon Chase Dr 43081
Blendon Pond Dr 43081
Blue Bonnet Ct 43081
Blue Cloud Ln 43081
Blue Fescue Dr 43082
Blue Hen Pl 43081
Blue Heron Ct & Dr 43082
Blue Juniper Dr 43082
Blue Sail Dr 43081
Blue Sky Ct 43081
Bluebird Ct 43081
Bluestone Ct 43081
Bobby Ln 43081
Boehm Ct 43081
Bogota Dr 43081
Bolamo Ct & Dr 43081
Bombay Ave 43081
Bookmark Ct 43081
Bowermoss Dr 43082
Braet Rd 43081
Bramblewood Ct 43081
Brandywine Dr 43081
Branscom Blvd 43081
Brassie Ave & Cir 43081
Braxton Pl E & W 43081
Brayford Dr 43081
Braymoore Dr 43082
Brazzaville Rd 43081
Breakers Ct 43082
Breezewood Ct 43081
Brelsford Woods Dr 43081
Breshly Way 43081
Bretton Pl 43082
Brewton Dr 43081
Briarwood Ct 43081
Bricklin St 43081
Bridgeford Dr 43081
Bridgewater Ct 43081
Bridwell Ln 43081
Brimley Pl 43081
Brisbane Ave 43081
Broad St 43081
E & W Broadway Ave 43081
Brockwell Dr 43081
Broken Bow Ct 43081
Bromfield Dr 43082
Brook Run Ct & Dr 43081
Brookpoint Pl 43081
Brooksedge Blvd 43081
Brooksedge Plaza Dr 43081
Brookstone Blvd 43081
Brookstone Dr 43082
Brownstone Ct 43081
Bruce Ct 43081
Brule Ct 43081
Brush Creek Dr 43081
Bryan Dr 43081
Buck Run Trl 43082
Buckeye Ct & St 43081
Buckhorn Ct 43081
Buckland Dr 43081
Buckstone Pl 43082
Buenos Aires Blvd 43081
Buffalo Run 43081
Bullfinch Dr 43081
Bulrush Ct 43082
Bunch Flower Ct 43082
Bunch Line Ln 43081
Bunker Hill Ct 43081
Bunstine Dr 43081
Bunting Ct 43081
Buoy Ct 43082
Burbank Pl 43082
Burns Ct 43081
Burns Dr 43081
Burns Dr N 43081
Burntwood Way 43081
Burson Springs Ct 43082
Burwood Ct 43081
Button Bush Ln 43082
Buxley Dr 43081
Cactus Ct 43081
Cairo Rd 43081
Caldwell Dr 43082
Calebs Creek Way 43081
Caledonia Dr 43081
Cali Glen Ln 43082
Callaway Ct 43082
Camargo Ct 43082
Cambria Way 43081
Camellia Ct 43081
Cameron Crossing Dr 43081
Cameron Ellis Dr 43081
Canberra Ct 43081
Canmore Ct 43082
Cantebrick Dr 43082
Canterbury Ct 43082
Capilano Ct 43082
Caplinger Ave 43081
Caracas Dr 43081
Carlatun St 43081
Carmichael St 43081
Carnation Dr 43081
Carousel Ct 43081
Carthage Ct & Dr 43081
Castile Ln 43081
Catawba Ave & Ct 43081
Caterney Dr 43081
Cattail Run 43081
Cautela Dr 43081
Cavenway Pl 43081
Cedar Row Blvd 43081
Cedar Trace Blvd 43081
Cedar View Blvd 43081
Cedardale Dr 43081
Center St 43081
Center Green Dr 43082
Center Village Rd 43081
Centerpark Dr 43082
N Central Ave & Dr 43081
Central College Rd 43081
Ceramic Pl 43081
Chambers Dr 43082
Champaign Ct 43082
Champions Dr 43082
Chandler Ct & Dr 43082
Chanticleer Ct 43082
Charles Rd 43082
Charleston Way Dr 43081
Charlotte Way Ave 43081
Charmar Dr 43082
Charring Cross Dr S 43081
Charterhouse Ct 43081
Chase Mills Dr 43081
Chaseley Ct 43081
Chateau Ln 43082
Chatham Ridge Rd 43081
Chelsea Ln 43081
Chelton Pl 43082
Cherokee Dr 43081
Cherokee Rose Dr 43081
Cherri Park Sq 43081
Cherrington Ct & Rd 43081
Cherry St 43081
Cherry Ravine Ct 43081
Chertsey Ct 43081
Chestnut Ave 43082
Chetenham Dr 43081
Cheyenne Ct & Dr 43081
Chickadee Ct & Pl 43081
Chiddingstone Ln 43082
Chimney Rock 43081
Chinkapin Way 43081
Chuckleberry Ln 43081
Circle Ct 43081
Clancy Way 43082
Clapham Ct 43081
Clear Stream Way 43081
Clear Water Dr 43082
Clearfork Ln 43081
Clearview Ave 43082
Cleveland Ave NW 43081
N Cleveland Ave
50-54 43081
56-120 43081
122-158 43081
300-600 43082
602-610 43082
7760-7798 43081
S Cleveland Ave 43081
Clover Ln 43081
Cloverleaf Rd 43081
Club Dr
900-998 43081
5000-5429 43082
5431-5599 43082
Club Ridge Rd 43081
Club Trail Dr 43081
Cobblestone Ave E 43081
Cobdon Ave 43081
Cochran Aly 43081
Cogswell Ct & St 43081
Coldstream Ct 43082
E & W College Ave, Ct & Pl 43081
College Crest Rd 43081
Collegeview Rd 43081
Colleton Dr 43082
Collier Dr 43082
Collingwood Dr
600-799 43081
6400-6899 43082
Cologne Pl 43081
Colonial Pl 43082
Colony Dr 43081
Colston Dr 43081
Colt Ct 43081
Commerce Park Dr 43082
Commonwealth Dr 43082
Compton Ct 43082
Concord Ct & Sq 43081
Congressional Dr 43082
Conifer Ct & Dr 43081
Connorwill Dr 43081
Cooper Rd 43081
Cooper Colony Dr 43081
Cooper Meadows Rd 43081
Cooper Woods Dr 43081
Copeland Mill Rd 43081
Copenhagen Dr 43081
Corbin Ct 43081
Cornell Ct 43081
Cornerstone Ct 43081
Cornhill Ct 43081
Coss Cir 43081
Country Meadow Ct 43082
County Brook Ln 43081
County Line Rd 43081
County Line Rd W 43082
Course Dr 43081
Covan Dr 43082
Coventry Ct 43081
Covington Meadows Ct & Dr 43082
Covington Springs Ct 43082
Cranbrook Ln 43081
Crawford Ct 43082
Crazy Horse Ln 43081
Creek Ln 43081
Creek Run Ct 43081
Crenton Dr 43081
Crescent Ct & Dr 43081
Crescent Ridge Blvd 43081
Cresswood Pl 43081
Crimson Maple Ln 43082
Crimsonrose Run 43081
Crooked Tree Ct 43081
Cross Club Dr 43081
Cross Country Dr & Loop E, S & W 43081
Cross Wind Dr & Loop 43081
Crosshaven Ct 43081
Crossings Dr 43082
Crosskirk Dr 43082
Crosslake Ct 43081
Crowles Ave 43081
Crystal Ct 43082
Cubbage Rd 43081
Cumbleside Ln 43082
Cypress Ct & Dr 43082
Dahlgreen Dr 43081
Dajana Ave 43081
Dakar Rd E & W 43081
Daleview Dr 43081
Damson Pl 43082
Danann Dr 43081
Danbridge Way 43081
Danbury Dr 43081
Daniel Dr 43081
Danvers Ave 43081
Dark Shadow Ct 43081
David Sq 43081
Day Ct 43081
Deagle Dr 43081
Deansboro Dr 43081
Debbie Dr 43081
Deer Trl 43082
Deer Forest Pl 43081
Deer Run Ct, Pl & Rd 43081
Deercreek Rd 43081
Deerskin Dr 43081
Delaware Ct & Dr 43081
Delcastle Dr 43081
Dellhaven Dr 43081
Dempsey Rd 43081
Denman Ct 43081
Derringer Dr 43081
Directors Ct 43081
Dogwood Ln 43082
Dolly Ct 43081
Donmac Dr 43081
Doral Ct 43082
Dorchester Dr 43082
Dorchester Sq N 43081
Dorchester Sq S 43081
Double Eagle Dr 43081
Drakewood Rd 43081
Drindel Dr 43081
Dristor Dr 43081
E Dublin Granville Rd 43081
Dunaway Ln 43082
Duncans Glen Dr 43082
Duvall Dr 43082
Eagle Harbor Dr 43081
Eagle Trace Dr 43082
Eaglesham Dr 43081
Eaglesnest Ct & Dr 43081
Early Meadow Rd 43082
East St 43081
Eastwind Ct & Dr 43081
Eastwood Ave 43081
Echo Spring Dr 43081
Eden Valley Dr 43081
Edge Of Vlg 43081
Edilyn Ct 43081
Edinvale Ln 43082
Egret Ct 43082
Elcliff Dr 43081
Electric Ave 43081
Elgin Ct 43082
Ellerby Pl 43081
Elm Ct 43082
Elmwood Pl 43081
Enclave Blvd 43081
English Oak Ct & Dr 43081
Enterprise Dr 43081
Erie Ave 43082
Essen Pl 43081
Everett Ct 43082
Executive Ct & Pkwy 43081
Executive Campus Dr 43082
Fairdale Ave 43081
Fairford Ct 43081
Fairlawn Ct 43081
Fairview Ave 43081
Fairway Lakes Dr 43081
Falco Dr 43081
Falcon Chase Dr 43082
Fallgold Ln 43082
Fallsburg Dr 43081
Fallside Ln 43081
Fallston Ct 43081
Fancher Rd 43082
Farmeadow Dr 43082
Farrington Dr 43081
Farthing Ct & Dr 43081
Fawn Ct 43081
Ferndale Pl 43082
Fielding School Rd 43081
Finn Glen Dr 43081
Firestone Pl 43082
Firewater Ln 43081
Fisher Pond Dr 43082
Fishermans Dr 43082
Flagstone Sq 43081
Flanders Field Dr 43081
Fleur Dr 43081
Flintrock Ct & Dr 43081
Flintstone Dr 43081
Flour Ct 43082
Fogle Ct 43082
Follensby Dr 43081
Forest Glen Rd 43081
Forest Grove Ave 43081
Forest Highland Ct 43082
Forest Rise Dr 43081
Forest View Ct 43081
Fortunegate Dr 43081
Four Seasons Dr 43082
Fox Haven Ct 43082
Fox Run Ct 43081
Fox Run Dr 43082
Fox Run Rd 43081
Foxglove Pl 43082
Foxhound Ln 43081
Foxmeadow Dr 43081
Foxtrail Cir, Ct & Pl E & W 43081
Franklin Ave 43081
Frasier Rd 43082
Freeman Rd 43082
Freeport Ct 43081
Freshman Dr 43081
Freshwater Ct 43082
Frost Rd 43082
Fultonham Dr 43081
Gainey Ct 43082
Ganton Pl 43082
Garand Dr 43081
Garden View Dr 43082
Garnier Ave & Pl 43081
Garrett Ct 43082
Gateshead Ct & Way 43081
Gemstone Sq E & W 43081
Genoa Farms Blvd 43082
Gentlewind Dr 43081
Gerwig Ct 43082
Gibson Pl 43081
Gillen Way 43082
Glacier Pass 43081
Gladale Dr 43081
Glaslyn Way 43081
Glass Dr 43081
Glastonbury Ct 43081
Glen Rock Dr 43081
Glenabby Dr 43081
Glenacre Dr 43081
Glenmore Way 43082
Glenview Ct 43081
Glenwood Dr 43081
Golden Wheat Ln 43082
Goldfinch Dr 43081
Goldsmith Dr 43081
Gorsuch Rd 43082
Gosfield Gate Ct & Rd 43081
Gossamer Ct 43081
Grackle Ln 43081
Gradington Dr 43081
Granby Pl E 43081
Grand Strand Ave 43081
Grangefield Ct 43081
Granite Dr 43082
Graphic Way 43081
Grasshopper Ln 43081
Grasslands Ct 43082
Grassmere Dr 43082
Grayburn Ct 43081
Green Acres Dr 43081
Green Cook Rd 43082
Green Crest Dr 43081
Green Knoll Dr 43081
Green Meadows Dr N & S 43081
Green Ravine Dr 43081
Greenery Ct 43082
Greenhurst Dr 43082
Greenscape Blvd 43081
Grindstone Rd 43082
Grisham St 43082
Grist Run Ct & Rd 43082
Groton Dr 43081
N & S Grove St 43081
Gurgun Ln 43081
Hackberry Dr 43081
Haddam Pl E & W 43081
Haig Point Ct 43082
N Hamilton Ave & Rd 43081
Hampton Cv & Park E, N & W 43081
Hanawalt Rd
3101-3499 43082
3600-3698 43082
8200-8399 43081
Hanby Ave 43081
Harbin Ct & Pl 43081
Harbor View Dr 43082
Harbour Town Cir 43082
Harbridge Ct 43081
Harlem Rd
5353-5355 43082
5357-6667 43082
6669-6783 43082
6785-6785 43081
6787-6788 43081
6789-6799 43082
6790-6790 43081
6858-6860 43082
6866-6880 43081
6882-6927 43081
6928-6930 43082
6929-6935 43081
6941-6943 43082
6948-6952 43081
6954-6959 43081
6960-6998 43082
6961-6999 43081
7000-7002 43081

7000-7006 43082
7008-7168 43082
7170-7238 43082
7240-7240 43081
7242-7338 43082
7373-7597 43081
7599-8399 43081
8401-9199 43081
Harrogate Ct & Loop E, N & W 43082
Hartfordshire Ln 43081
Harvest Wind Dr 43082
Harwick St 43081
Hastings Ct 43082
Hatch Rd 43082
Hatcher Ln 43081
Haussman Dr & Pl 43081
Havelock St 43082
Havendale Dr 43082
Hawksbeard Dr 43082
Hawksnest Ct 43082
Hawthorne Pt 43082
Hawthorne Valley Dr 43082
Heathcock Ct 43081
Heatherbrooke Way 43081
Heatherdown Dr 43081
Heckert Rd 43081
Helenhurst Ct 43081
Hemingway Pl 43082
N & S Hempstead Ct & Rd 43081
Hemstead Rd 43082
Henschen Cir 43082
Hepplewhite Ct & St 43081
Heritage Pl 43082
Hermitage Dr 43082
Heron Ct 43082
Hiawatha Ave 43081
Hibiscus Ct 43081
Hickory Ln 43081
Hickory View Ct 43081
Hidden Cove Ct 43082
Hideaway Woods Dr 43081
High Rock Dr 43081
High Timber Dr 43082
Highbridge Pl 43082
Highbrook Ct 43081
Highland Forest Pl 43082
Highland Hills Dr 43082
Highland Lakes Ave & Pl 43082
Highlander Dr 43081
Highplains Ct 43081
Hightop Dr 43081
Hightree Dr 43081
Hillcrest Dr 43081
Hillegas Farm Dr 43082
Hillsdowne Rd 43081
Hilmar Ct & Dr 43082
Hoff Rd 43082
Hollandia Ct & Dr 43081
Hollow Log Ln 43081
Hollytree Ln 43081
E & W Home St 43081
Honey Ct 43081
Honors Ct 43082
Hoover Ct 43082
Hoover Gate Ln 43082
Hoover Lake Ct 43081
Hoover Reserve Ct & Dr 43081
Hooverview Dr 43082
Howell Ct & Dr 43081
Huber Village Blvd 43081
Hudson Reserve Way 43081
Hunt Club Rd N & W 43082
Hunter Pl 43082
Huntland Ln 43081
Huron Ct 43082
Idana Ct 43081
Illinois Ave & Ct 43081
Indian Ct 43082
Inglewood Dr 43081
Inkwell Ct 43081
Inlet Ct 43082
Innisbrook Ct 43082
Intek Way 43082
Interlachen Ave 43082
Inverness St 43082
Ipswich St 43081
Isle Ct 43082
Israel St 43081
Ivydale Dr 43081
Ivyside Sq 43082
Jacquelin Ct 43082
Jamesport Dr 43081
Jasper Rock Rd 43081
Jean Ct 43082
Jeffries Ct 43082
Jennette Dr 43081
Jennis Rd 43081
Jessamine Ct 43081
Jobar Ct 43081
Jourdon Dr 43081
Judy Ct 43081
Julian Dr 43082
Juniper Ave 43081
Kalu Pl 43081
Kanpur Pl 43081
Karen Ct 43081
Karikal Ct & Dr 43081
Katherines Way 43082
Kean Rd 43082
Keats Pl 43082
Keene Dr 43081
Keethler Dr N & S 43081
Kellerman Dr 43082
Kenmore Ct 43081
Kennebec Pl E & W 43081
Kentonhurst Ct 43082
Kenwood Pl 43082
Kepwick Dr 43081
Ketterington Ln 43082
Keyham Terrace Dr 43082
Kienle Ave 43081
Killarney Ct 43082
Kim Ct E & W 43081
Kimberly Ct 43082
Kimothy Dr 43081
King Arthur Blvd & Ct 43081
Kingfisher Ct & Dr 43082
Kingsmead Rd 43082
Kirklington Cir 43081
Kitty Dr 43081
Knebworth Ct 43081
Knights Way 43082
Knollbrook Dr 43081
Knotting Woods Dr 43081
S Knox St 43081
Kristin Ct 43081
La Casa Ct 43082
La Paz Pl 43081
Lafayette Dr 43081
Lahinch Ct 43082
Laird Ln 43082
Lake Dr & Pt 43082
Lake Forest Blvd 43081
Lake Forest Way 43082
Lake Harbor Ct 43081
Lake Run Cir 43081
Lake Shore Ave 43082
Lake Trail Dr 43082
Lake Valley Dr 43082
Lakegrove Ct 43081
Lakeland Dr 43081
Lakeloop Dr 43081
Lakemont Dr 43081
Lakes Club Dr 43082
Lakeside Ct 43082
Lakeside Dr 43082
Laketree Ct E & W 43081
Lakeway Ct E & W 43081
Lakota Dr 43081
Lambright St 43081
Lance Ct 43081
Lancelot Ln 43081
Landings Ct & Loop E, N, S & W 43082
Lanetta Ln 43082
Langton Cir 43082
Langwell Dr 43082
Latrobe St 43081
Laureen Ct 43081
Laurel Dr 43081
Laurel Oak Ct 43081
Laver Ln 43082
Lawn Pl 43081
Lawrence Rd 43081
Lawson Ct & Dr 43081
Lazelle Rd 43081
Lazelle Woods Dr 43081
Leacrest Pl E & W 43081
Leapsway Dr 43081
Ledbury Ct 43081
Lee Rd & Ter 43081
Legacy Ct & Dr 43082
Legends Ct 43082
Leighton Ct 43082
Leighway Dr 43081
Lewis Center Rd 43082
Lexington Ct 43081
Leydorf Ln 43082
Libbet Dr N & S 43081
Liber Ct 43081
Liberty Ln 43081
Liege Pl 43081
Lighthouse Ct 43082
Lightwind Ct 43081
Lima Dr 43081
Limerock Dr 43081
Linabary Ave 43081
E & W Lincoln St 43081
Linda Ct 43081
Lindsey Ct 43082
Linksview Cir 43082
Linncrest Dr 43081
Lisbon Pl 43081
Little Leaf Ct & Ln 43082
Little Rock Rd 43082
Little Turtle Way W 43081
Liverpool Pl 43081
Llewellyn Ave 43081
Locust Ct 43082
Logan Ave 43081
Long Cove Ct 43082
Longbow Ct 43082
Longrifle Ct & Rd 43081
Longshadow Dr 43081
Lookout Ridge Dr 43081
Lori Ln 43081
Lorna Pl 43081
Lower Lake Dr 43082
Loxmoor Ln 43081
Luke Ct 43081
Lynbrook Ln 43082
N Lyndale Dr 43081
Lyndsey Ct 43082
Lynette Pl N & S 43081
Lynmouth Dr 43081
Lynnfield Dr 43081
Lynx Ct & Dr 43082
Macintosh Way 43081
Madrid Dr 43081
Maebelle Way 43081
Magnolia Pl 43081
Maidstone Ct 43082
E & W Main St 43081
Mainsail Dr 43081
Maisa Ct 43082
Makassar Dr 43081
Mallard Dr 43082
Managua Dr 43081
Manchester Way Dr 43082
Manila Dr & Pl 43081
Manitou Dr 43081
Manor Ridge Ct 43082
Maple Hill Ct & Dr 43082
Maple Rock Dr 43081
Maplebrooke Dr E 43082
Maplerun Ln 43081
Mapleside Pl 43082
Mardela Dr 43081
Margaret Dr 43082
Marie Lou Dr 43081
Mariemont Dr E 43081
Marjorie Ct 43081
Mark Pl 43081
Market Exchange Dr 43081
Markworth Ct 43081
Marlene Dr 43081
Marsh Blue Ct 43082
Marshfield Dr 43081
Martin Grove Ct 43081
Mary Ave 43081
Massey Dr 43081
Matthew Ave & Ct 43081
Maxtown Rd & Xing 43082
Mccorkle Blvd
501-597 43082
599-618 43082
617-617 43086
619-799 43082
620-798 43082
Mcjessy Dr 43081
Meacham Run Ct 43081
Meadcrest Ct 43082
Meadow Glen Dr N & S 43082
Meadowood Ln & Pl 43082
Mealla Rd 43081
Medalist Ct 43082
Medallion Dr E & W 43082
Medinah Ct 43082
Meldelly Dr 43082
Melinda Dr 43081
Mentor Dr 43081
Merlin Dr 43081
Merriss Ct 43081
Metzger Cres 43081
Mexico Ave 43081
Michael Ave 43081
Michigan Ct 43082
Midfield Dr 43082
Mikayla Dr 43082
Mike Ct 43081
Milford Ave 43082
Mill Crossing Dr 43082
Mill Wind Ct & Dr 43082
Miller Paul Rd 43082
Millfield Ave 43081
Millstone Sq 43081
Mingo Ln 43081
Mission Hills Pl 43082
Mist Flower Ln 43082
Moccasin Dr & Pl 43081
Mockernut Ln 43081
Mohawk Ave 43081
Mohican Way 43081
Monica Ct 43082
Monna Ct 43081
Monroe Ln 43081
Montchanin Ct 43082
Montevideo Rd 43081
Montford Rd E 43081
Montreal Pl 43081
Moonlight Ct 43081
Morello Pl 43082
Mosaic Way 43082
Moss Rd 43082
Mossman Ave 43081
Mount Row 43081
Mount Royal Ave 43082
Mountainview Dr 43081
Mulberry Way N 43082
Munich Pl 43081
Murmac Ln 43081
Murnane St 43081
Myrtle Dr 43081
Nadine Pl N & S 43081
Naples Pl 43081
Nash Ave & Pl 43081
Natalie Ct N & S 43081
Nature Trl 43082
Nautilus Pl 43082
Navajo Dr 43081
Neilston Crossing Dr 43081
New Albany Condit Rd
5000-5198 43082
5200-5854 43082
5856-6336 43082
7760-8499 43081
Newark Ave 43081
Newfields Ln 43081
Niagara Reserve Dr 43081
Nicole Dr 43081
Nighthawk Ct 43082
Nightshade Dr 43082
Nightshadow Dr 43081
Nineteen Rock Xing 43081
Nordley Vlg 43081
North St 43081
Northbridge Ct 43081
Northchurch Ln 43082
Northfield Rd 43082
Northgate Ct 43081
Northgate Way 43082
Norway Ln 43081
Nottingham Ct 43081
Nottinghamshire Ln 43081
Nutmeg Ct 43081
Oak Bluff Ct 43081
Oak Hill Dr 43081
Oak Ridge Pl 43082
Oak Shadow Dr 43082
Oak Tree Ct 43081
Oakmont Pl 43082
Oakwind Ct 43081
Oakwood Ct 43081
Oakwood Ln 43081
Oakwood Pt 43082
Office Pkwy 43082
S Old 3c Hwy 43082
Old Coach Rd 43081
Old County Line Rd 43081
Old Dover Rd 43082
Old Field Ct 43082
Old Head Ct 43082
Old Providence Ln 43081
Olde English Ct & Dr 43082
Olde Mill Ct & Dr 43082
Olde North Church Rd 43081
Olde Richmond Ln 43081
Olde Worthington Ct & Rd 43082
Olga Ct 43082
Olgelbay Dr 43082
Olivia Michael Pl 43081
Olympic Way 43082
Oneida Ave 43081
Orchard Ln 43081
Ormsbee Ave 43081
Oslo Dr 43081
Oswald St 43081
Ottawa Ave 43081
N & S Otterbein Ave 43081
Otterbein College 43081
Owl Creek Dr 43081
Oxbow Rd 43082
Ozem Gardner Way 43081
Paddlecreek Dr 43082
Paddlewheel Ct & Dr 43082
Palermo Pl 43081
Panama Dr 43081
Pannelly Pl 43081
Parchment Dr 43081
Paris Blvd & Ct E & N 43081
E & W Park Rd & St 43081
Park Bend Ct & Dr 43082
Park Club Dr 43081
Park Meadow Dr & Rd 43081
Park Place Dr 43081
Park Trail Dr 43081
Parkmoor Dr 43082
Parkview Ave 43081
Pasque Ct 43081
Patricia Ln 43082
Patricia Ann Ln 43082
Patti Ct & Dr 43081
Paul Rd 43082
Pavilion Landing Pl 43082
Pawnee Dr 43081
Peach St 43082
Peachtree Cir 43082
Peachtree Ct 43081
Pebble Beach Pl 43082
Pelham Ct & Dr 43081
Pelican Pl 43081
Penbrook St 43082
Pennyroyal Pl 43082
Pepper Ct 43082
Peppergrass Ct 43082
Peppermill Dr 43081
Perkins Ln 43082
Philadelphia Dr 43081
Piermont Ct 43082
Pierpont Dr 43081
Pimpernel Pl 43082
Pin Oak Ct 43081
Pine Creek Dr 43081
Pine Hollow Dr 43082
Pine Lake Dr 43081
Pine Needle Dr 43082
Pine Post Ln 43081
Pine Tree Ct 43082
Pine Valley Ln 43082
Pine View Rd 43081
Pine Wild Dr 43082
Pinebrooke Dr & Ln 43082
Pinehaven Dr 43082
Pinehurst Pointe 43082
Pintail Ct 43082
Pittsford Dr 43081
Pleasant Ave 43081
E & W Plum St 43081
Pocowillis Ct 43082
Poe Pl 43082
Pointe Pl 43082
Pointview Dr 43081
Polaris Pkwy 43082
Polaris Crossing Blvd 43081
Polaris Woods Blvd 43082
Pond View Dr 43081
Poplar Ridge Dr 43081
Porlock Pl 43081
Portrait Cir 43081
Potawatomi Dr 43081
Potomac Ave & Ct 43082
Powderhorn Ln 43081
Prairie Fire Ct 43082
Presidents Cup Dr 43082
Prince William Ln 43081
Progressive Way 43082
Prosen Dr 43081
Prospect Ln 43082
Prusok Ct 43081
Puddington Ct 43081
Pueblo Ct 43082
Purplefinch Ct 43081
Quail Hollow Way 43082
Quartz Creek Dr 43081
Quicksilver Dr 43081
Quince Ct 43081
Quinn Ct 43081
Rackenford Ln 43081
Rackley Way 43081
Radcliff Dr 43082
Raintree Ct 43081
Ramonford Ct 43081
Rangoon Dr 43081
Ravine Dr 43081
Ravines Way 43082
Rebecca Ave 43081
Red Bank Rd 43082
Red Barn Ct 43081
Red Bluff Ln 43082
Red Maple Pl 43081
Redsail Ct 43081
Regency Dr 43082
Rene Ct 43081
Reno Rd 43081
Reston Ct 43082
Retreat Ln 43082
Richert Ct 43081
Ridge Lake Ct 43082
Ridge Row Rd 43081
Ridge View Dr 43081
Ridgemoor Ln 43081
Ridgewood Ave 43082
Rigdemoor Ln 43081
Rising Rock Dr 43081
River Trce 43081
Riverlake Ct 43081
Riviera Ct 43082
Robinhood Cir 43082
Robins Rd 43082
Rochester Way 43081
Rock Run Dr 43081
Rockbourne Ct & Dr 43082
Rockbridge Rd 43081
Rockingham Ct 43081
Rocky Junction Pl 43081
Rocky Moor Pl 43081
Rocky Ridge Landings Dr 43081
Rocy Terrace Ln 43081
Rolling Ridge Way 43082
Rookery Way 43082
Rosaberry Run 43081
Rose Ct 43081
Rose Hedge Dr 43081
Rosebay Ct 43081
Rosedale Dr 43082
Rousham St 43082
Royal Ct 43081
Royal Birkdale Dr 43082
Royal County Down 43082
Ruckmoor Dr 43082
Rufford St 43082
Ruihley Way 43081
Rundlet Ct 43081
Running Brook Dr 43081
Rushka Ct 43081
Russell St 43081
Russett Ct 43082
Ruth Amy Ave 43081
Ruttington Ln 43082
Ryder Cup 43082
Ryedale Ln 43081
Saddle Ln E 43081
Saddle Lane Ct 43081
Saddlewood Dr 43082
Sagebrush Ct 43081
Saigon Dr 43081
Sailing Ct 43082
Saint Andrews Cir & Dr 43082
Saint Clair Ave 43081
Saint George Ave 43082
Saint Medan Dr 43082
Saint Thomas Dr 43081
Salem Dr 43082
Sanctuary Dr 43082
Sancus Blvd 43081
Sand Broad Ct 43081
Sand Spurrey Ct 43082
Sanderling Ln 43081
Sanders Way 43082
Sandimark Pl 43081
Sandpiper Ct 43082
Sandstone Loop E 43081
Sanibel Ave & Ct 43081
Santiago Dr 43081
Sassafras Way 43081
Sawgrass Way 43082
Saxman Pl 43081
Saybrook Dr 43082
Scarlet Ct 43081
Scenic Club Dr 43081
Schleppi Rd 43081
Schoolside Dr 43081
Schott Rd 43081
E & W Schrock Rd 43081
Scioto Ct 43082
Scissortail Loop 43081
Scituate Ct 43081
Scott Ct 43081
Scottsdale Ct 43082
Sea Shell Ct & Dr 43082
Seafield Ct 43082
Seager Dr 43081
Seagull Ct 43082
Seaside Ct 43082
Seckel Ct & Dr 43082
Sedgemoore Dr 43081
Seminole Ave 43081
Seminole Way 43082
Seneca Ave 43081
Sentry Ln 43081
Shadow Dr 43081
Shadow Creek Dr 43082
Shady Oaks Pl 43082
Shagbark Dr 43081

Sharelane 43082
Sharps Ct 43081
Sherbrook Dr 43082
Shiloh Spring Dr 43082
W & N Shore Ct & Dr 43082
Showy Ct 43081
Shreven Dr 43081
Sierra Dr 43082
Silver Frost Rd 43081
Silver Lake Ct 43082
Silverleaf Oak Ct 43081
Silverthorne Rd 43081
Sioux Dr 43081
Sipeston Ln 43081
Six Pence Cir 43081
Slane Ridge Dr 43082
Slater Rdg 43082
Smiley Ct 43081
Smoke Burr Dr 43081
Smoketalk Ln 43081
Smothers Rd 43081
Snead Way 43082
Snowhill Ct 43081
Soft Rush Dr 43082
Softwood Ct 43081
Solitude Dr 43081
Somerset Ave 43082
Somerton Dr 43082
Sorensen Pl 43082
Sorrento Blvd & Ct 43082
South St 43081
Southbluff Dr 43082
Sowerby Ln 43081
Spikerush Ct 43082
Spohn Dr 43081
Spring Brk E 43081
Spring Brk W 43081
N Spring Rd
1-215 43081
216-298 43082
300-700 43082
702-798 43082
S Spring Rd 43081
Spring Brook Ct 43081
Spring Creek Dr 43081
Spring Hollow Ct & Ln 43082
Spring Run Dr 43082
Spring Valley Rd 43081
Springfield Ct & Dr 43081
Springhurst Ct 43081
Springtree Ct & Ln 43081
Springview Dr 43082
Springwood Pl 43082
Spruce Ln 43082
Spyglass Ct 43082
Staffington Dr 43081
Starbuck Ct 43081
Starlight Ln 43082
N State St
1-269 43081
271-285 43081
300-899 43082
901-925 43082
S State St
1-261 43081
260-260 43086
263-999 43081
280-798 43081
State Route 3 43082
Steeplebush Ave 43082
Steeplechase Ln 43081
Steffan Ct 43081
Steinbeck Way 43082
Sterling Ct 43082
Sterling Glen Dr 43081
Stillwater Ave & Cv 43082
Stires Ln 43081
Stockholm Rd 43081
Stone Ridge Ct 43081
Stone Trace Cir 43081
Stonefield Dr 43082
Stoner Aly 43081
Stoneshead Ct 43081
Storington Rd 43081
Stormcroft Ave 43081
Storrow Dr 43081
Straiton Sq 43082
Strand Rd 43081
Stratfordchase Dr 43081
Strawpocket Ln 43081
Stroud Ct 43081
Sudeley Ct 43081
Sugar Ct 43082
Sugarberry Ct 43081
Sugarmaple Ct & Dr 43082
Summertree Ln 43081
S Summit St 43081
Sunbury Rd 43082
N Sunbury Rd 43081
S Sunbury Rd 43081
Sunbury Lake Dr 43082
Sunlawn Dr 43081
Sunlight Ct 43081
Sunningdale Dr 43082
Sunset Dr 43081
Suntree Dr 43081
Sunwood Pl 43081
Superior Ct 43082
Surf Ct 43082
Susan Ave 43081
Sutterton Ln 43081
Swanton Ct 43081
Sweetbriar Ln 43081
Sweetgum Way 43081
Syracuse Ln 43081
Tacoma Ln 43082
Talia Ct 43081
Tallowwood Dr 43081
Talltree Ct 43081
Talon Cir 43082
Talon Ct 43081
Tami Sue Ct 43082
Tammerlane Ct 43081
Tansy Ln 43081
Tarrycrest Dr 43081
Tassel Ct 43081
Tawny Ln 43081
Taylor Way 43082
Teasel Dr 43082
Telluride Blf 43081
Temperance Point Pl & St 43082
Terry Jill Ln 43082
Thetford Ct 43081
Thirlwall Ct 43081
Thornbush Dr 43082
Thornwood Dr 43082
Thrasher Loop 43081
Three Forks Dr N & S 43081
E & W Ticonderoga Dr 43081
Tidewater Ct 43082
Timberbank Dr & Ln 43081
Timberlake Dr 43081
Tipton Ct 43081
Tomahawk Ln 43081
Torrey Pines Ave 43082
Totten Springs Dr 43082
Tottenham Blvd 43082
Tournament Ave 43081
Tournament Dr 43082
Tradewind Ct & Dr 43081
Trails End 43082
Tralee Ln 43082
Travis Pointe Ct 43082
Tree Bend Ct & Dr 43082
Treebrook Ln 43081
Treeline Dr 43082
Trelawny Ln 43081
Treva Ct 43081
Treven Way 43081
Triesta Pl 43081
Triton Ct 43081
Troon Pl 43082
Troy Ct 43081
Trumhall Ave 43081
Turnberry Dr 43082
Turnwood Dr 43081
Turtle Sta 43081
Tussic St 43082
Twin Lakes Ct 43082
Ulry Ct & Rd 43081
Under Brook Ct 43081
University St 43081
Upper Albany Crossing Dr 43081
Upper Cambridge Way 43082
Upper Lake Cir 43082
Valley Forge Ct 43081
Valley Quail Blvd N & S 43081
Valley Wood Ct 43081
Valleyview Ct & Dr 43081
Vancouver Dr 43081
Varadero Dr 43081
Varick Ln 43082
Venture Dr 43081
Via Alvito Dr 43082
Vickers Ct & Dr 43081
Victoria Ct 43082
Vienna Ct & Dr 43081
Viewland Ct 43081
Village Mdw & Mews 43081
Village Green Dr & Loop 43082
Vincent Ct 43081
N & S Vine St 43081
N Virginia Ln 43081
Virginia Lane Ct 43081
Wackeman Ct 43081
Wake Dr 43082
Wallasey Dr 43081
Wallean Dr 43081
Wallpepper Ct 43082
E & W Walnut St 43081
Walnut Fork Dr 43081
Walnut Hull Dr 43082
Walnut Ridge Ln 43081
Walsingham Ct 43081
Warbling Ln 43081
Warner Blf & Rd 43081
Warner Meadows Dr 43081
Warner Park Dr 43081
Warner Ridge Rd 43081
Warner Springs Dr 43081
Warner View Ln 43081
Washington Square Ct 43081
Water Willow Ct 43082
Waterport Dr 43081
Waterton Ct & Dr 43081
Waterwood Dr 43082
Watten Ln 43081
Waxwing Ct 43082
Weathered Oak Ct 43082
Weatherwood Ct 43082
Wedgewood Ct & Ter 43082
Welwyn Dr 43081
Wena Way 43081
Wensley Ct & Ln 43082
Wentworth Ct 43082
Wesley Way 43082
N West St
1-216 43081
218-300 43081
308-340 43082
342-399 43082
401-8469 43082
S West St 43081
Westar Blvd & Xing 43082
Westbury Woods Ct 43081
Westdale Ave 43082
Westerview Dr 43081
Westerville Plz, Rd & Sq 43081
Westerville Crossing Dr 43081
Westgreen Ln 43082
Westray Dr 43081
Westridge Ct 43081
Wetherby Ln 43081
Weyant St 43081
Whilehaven Ct 43081
Whipple Pl 43081
Whisperwood Ct 43081
Whistlewood Ln 43081
White Cloud Ct 43081
White Oak Ln 43082
Whitehead St 43081
Whitetail Ln 43082
Whithorn Ct 43081
Whitmore Ct 43082
Whitney Ln 43081
Wild Mint Ct 43082
Wild Pine Dr 43082
Wild Rose Ln 43082
Wilder Ct 43082
Wildflower Ln 43081
Wildindigo Run 43081
Wildwood Dr 43081
Wilkens Ct 43081
Willet Ln 43081
Willoughby Ct 43082
Willow Ct 43081
Willow Bend Ct & Ln 43082
Wilmot Ct 43081
Windcroft Dr 43082
Windemere Cir, Dr & Pl 43082
Winding Rock Dr 43081
Windorf Dr 43081
Windsor Village Dr 43081
Windstar Dr 43082
Windy Bluff Ct 43081
Winebrook Dr 43081
Winesap Pl 43082
Winfield Meadows Dr 43082
Winfree Dr 43081
Wingstem St 43082
E Winmar Pl 43081
Winsholen Ct 43081
E Winter St 43081
Winter Hill Ct 43081
Winterburg Way 43081
Wintersong Ln 43081
Witherbee Dr 43081
Witheridge Way 43081
Witherspoon Way 43081
Wood St 43081
Woodbend Dr 43082
Woodcreek Ln 43082
Woodgate Ln 43082
Woodglen Rd 43081
Woodington Rd 43081
Woodlake Ct & Dr 43081
Woodlawn Ave 43081
Woodmont Ct 43081
Woodsedge Ln 43081
Woodshire Dr 43081
Woodthrush Dr 43081
Woodvale Ct 43081
Woodview Rd 43081
Worthington Ct & Rd 43082
Worthington Club Dr 43081
Worthington Crossing Dr 43081
Worthington Galena Rd 43081
Worthington Lake Dr 43081
Worthington Park Blvd 43081
Wren Ave 43081
Wycliffe Pl 43082
Wycombe Ct 43081
Wyndale Dr 43081
Wyndham Park N & S 43082
Yellowhammer Dr 43081
Yoest Dr 43081
Yulia Ct 43081

WILLOUGHBY OH

General Delivery 44094

POST OFFICE BOXES MAIN OFFICE STATIONS AND BRANCHES

Box No.s
All PO Boxes 44096

NAMED STREETS

A T Hill Pl 44094
Abbotts Mill Dr 44094
Adkins Rd 44094
Aimee Ln 44094
Airport Pkwy 44094
Alpenrose Dr 44094
W Alpine Dr 44094
Amber Ct 44094
Amber Wood Dr 44094
Amelia Ave 44094
Andrews Pl 44094
Andrews Ridge Way 44094
Angela Dr 44094
Anna Dr 44094
Apollo Pkwy 44094
Appaloosa Trl 44094
Applewood Dr 44094
Aquarius Pkwy 44094
Arbor Dr 44094
Arborhurst Ln 44094
Arcadia Cir 44094
Arlington Dr 44094
Arthur St 44094
Ascot Pl 44094
Ash Rd 44094
Aspen Wood Ln 44094
Atwood Pl 44094
Avenel Ct 44094
Avondale Rd 44094
Bar Hbr 44094
Barber Ave 44094
Barnes Ct 44094
Barristers Ct 44094
N Bay Ct & Dr 44094
Bayshire Trl 44094
Beachview Rd 44094
Beacon Dr 44094
Beech St 44094
Beechwood Dr 44094
Beidler Rd 44094
Beldelis Rd 44094
Bell Rd 44094
Bellevue Dr 44094
Ben Hur Ave 44094
W Bend Dr 44094
Berkshire Hills Dr 44094
Bethany Ct 44094
Billings Rd 44094
Biltmore Pl 44094
Birchwood Dr 44094
Blair Ln 44094
Blueberry Hill Dr 44094
Bluff Rd 44094
Booth Rd 44094
Boyd Ct 44094
Bramble Ct 44094
Bretton Ct 44094
Briar Hill Dr 44094
Bridlehurst Trl 44094
Brighton Path 44094
Brookline Pl 44094
N Brooks Dr 44094
Brookstone Ln 44094
Brown Ave 44094
Buckeye Ave 44094
Bunker Ln 44094
Burrard Ct & Ln 44094
Callahan Ct 44094
Campbell Rd 44094
Canyon Ct 44094
Cardinal Dr 44094
Carl Ct 44094
Carriage Ln 44094
Casabona Pl 44094
Cascade Ct 44094
Center St 44094
Chagrin Mills Ct 44094
Chapin Falls Ln 44094
Charlesderry Rd 44094
Cheltenham Dr 44094
Cherokee Trl 44094
Chestnut Blvd 44094
Chestnut Hill Dr 44094
Chillicothe Rd 44094
Christina Dr 44094
Church St 44094
Clairidge Dr 44094
Clark Ave & Ct 44094
Cliff Ct 44094
Clocktower Dr 44094
Clover Cir 44094
Code Ave 44094
Colonial Blvd 44094
Comanche Trl 44094
Commerce Cir 44094
Community Dr 44094
Congressional Ln 44094
Conley Dr 44094
Coudry Dr 44094
Courtland Dr 44094
Courtney Ln 44094
Crary Lane Dr 44094
Creawood Frst 44094
Crestwood Ave & Dr 44094
E Cross Creek Dr 44094
Crossbrook Ave 44094
Crown Ct 44094
Daisy Ln 44094
Deer Creek Dr 44094
Deerfield Pl 44094
Delta Cir 44094
Depot St 44094
Dewey Rd 44094
Drury Ln 44094
Eagle Rd 44094
Eagle Creek Ct 44094
Eagle Mills Rd 44094
Eagles Nest Ln 44094
Eaglewood Dr 44094
Edgewood Ln 44094
Edward Walsh Dr 44094
Eisenhower Dr 44094
Eldo St 44094
Elm St 44094
Elmwood Dr 44094
Emerald Glen Ct 44094
Emsley Ct 44094
English Turn Ln 44094
Ericson Ln 44094
Erie Rd 44094
Erie St
3700-4039 44094
4040-4198 44094
4040-4040 44096
4041-4199 44094
Euclid Ave 44094
Euclid Chardon Rd 44094
Fairidge Rd 44094
Fairview Ave 44094
Far Bar Rd 44094
Farmbrook Ln 44094
Fawn Hill Pl 44094
Figgie Dr 44094
Firestone Way 44094
Florence Rd 44094
Foothills Blvd 44094
Forest Dr 44094
Forest Edge Dr 44094
Forestdale Dr 44094
Fox Run Dr 44094
Foxhill Dr 44094
Foxwood Trl 44094
Franklyn Blvd 44094
Gaitside Trl 44094
Gale Rd 44094
Garden Rd 44094
Gardenside Dr 44094
Garfield Rd 44094
Gildersleeve Cir & Dr 44094
Giuliano Dr 44094
Glen Park Rd 44094
Glenbrook Rd 44094
Glenbury Ln 44094
Glenn Ave 44094
Glenstone Dr 44094
Glenwood Ave 44094
Gold Rush Dr 44094
Grace Woods Dr 44094
Grand Pl 44094
Grandview Dr 44094
Granite Dr 44094
Green Cir 44094
Grove Ave 44094
Halle Farm Dr 44094
Hamann Pkwy 44094
Hampton Ct 44094
Harlow Dr 44094
Harmondale Dr 44094
Harmony Ln 44094
Hartshire Dr 44094
Harvard Dr 44094
Hastings Ave 44094
Haven Ct 44094
Hayes Ave 44094
Heath Rd 44094
Heathergreen Ct 44094
Hemlock Ridge Dr 44094
Heritage Ct 44094
Hickory Ln 44094
Hickory Hill Ct 44094
Hidden Valley Dr 44094
High Point Ln 44094
Highgate Bluff Ln 44094
Highland Ct & Dr 44094
Hillcrest Rd 44094
Hillsover Dr 44094
Hillward Dr 44094
Hobart Rd 44094
Hodgson Rd 44094
Hughes Ave 44094
Hurricane Dr 44094
Indian Pointe Dr 44094
N Industrial Pkwy 44094
Iroquois Trl 44094
Ivy Ct 44094
Jessica Cv 44094
Jet Center Pl 44094
Johnnycake Ridge Rd 44094
Jordan Dr 44094
Joseph St 44094
Joseph Lloyd Pkwy 44094
Kaiser Ct 44094
Karen Isle Dr 44094
Kellogg Ct 44094
Kelsey Ct 44094
Kennedy Pkwy 44094
Kilarney Rd 44094
Killdeer Rd 44094
Kimberly Dr 44094
King Edward Ct 44094
Kirtland Rd 44094
Kirtland Chardon Rd 44094
Kirtland Lakes Blvd 44094
Kyle Cv 44094
Lake Shore Blvd 44094
Lakebrook Dr 44094
Ledgestone Ct 44094
Ledgewood Dr 44094
Leeward Ln 44094
Liberty Ln 44094
Lincoln Ave 44094
Lisle Ct 44094
N & S Locust Dr 44094
Longview Dr 44094
Lonsdale Pl 44094
Loreto Ridge Dr 44094
Lost Nation Rd 44094
Lyons Ave 44094
Madison Ave 44094
Maple St 44094
Maplegrove Rd 44094
Marble Ln 44094
Margaret Walsh Ct 44094
Markell Rd 44094
Martin Rd 44094
Mary Clarke Dr 44094
Mckinney Ave 44094
Melody Ln 44094
Melrose Farms Dr 44094
Mentor Ave 44094
Metcalf Rd 44094
Millwood Ln 44094
Misty Hollow Ln 44094
Mohegan Trl 44094
Monterey Dr 44094
Mooreland Ave 44094
Mountainview Dr 44094
Murray Ave 44094
Nan Linn Dr 44094

Nantucket Dr 44094
Newport Cv 44094
Nicklaus Pl 44094
Ninadell Ave 44094
Noble Ct 44094
North Ln 44094
Northridge Dr 44094
Oak Hill Ln 44094
Oak Ridge Dr 44094
Oak Tree Dr 44094
Oakdale Ave 44094
Oakwood Dr 44094
Ocean Reef 44094
Old Willoughby Dr 44094
Orchard Ave, Dr & Rd 44094
Overlook Dr 44094
Palmetto Dr 44094
Palomino Trl 44094
Park Ave 44094
Parklawn Dr 44094
Parkview Ln 44094
Parkway Blvd 44094
Parkwood Dr 44094
Partridge Trl 44094
Peach Blvd 44094
Pebble Ct 44094
Pelton Rd 44094
Pheasant Ln 44094
Piccadilly Sq 44094
Pinecrest Pl 44094
Pinehurst Dr 44094
Pineview Ln 44094
Pinnacle Ct 44094
Plains Ct 44094
Polo Park Dr 44094
Poplar Dr 44094
Prelog Ln 44094
Preserve Dr 44094
Prospect St 44094
Ptarmigan Ct 44094
Public Sq 44094
Quail Cir 44094
Quarry View Ln 44094
Quartz Ct 44094
Raccoon Hill Dr 44094
Ramona St 44094
Ranch Rd 44094
Reading Ave 44094
Red Tail Ln 44094
Redwood Dr 44094
Reeves Rd 44094
Regency Woods Dr 44094
Ridge Rd 44094
Ridgeview Ln 44094
Ridgeway Ln 44094
River St 44094
River Bend Dr 44094
Riverside Dr 44094
Riverwood Way 44094
Robin Ln 44094
Robinhood Dr 44094
Rocking Horse Trl 44094
Rockwood Dr 44094
Rollin Rd 44094
Roselawn Ave 44094
Royal Dr 44094
Russellhurst Dr 44094
Saint Clair St 44094
Sandridge Ln 44094
Saxon Dr 44094
Seneca Pl 44094
Shadowbrook Dr 44094
Shadowrow Ave 44094
Shankland Rd 44094
Sharpe Ave 44094
Sheerwater Ln 44094
Shepherds Gln 44094
Sherwin Rd 44094
Shetland Ct 44094
Sierra Dr 44094
Signature Cir 44094
Singlefoot Trl 44094
Skiff St 44094
Skytop Ln 44094
Smith Rd 44094
Smugglers Cv 44094
Som Center Rd 44094
South Ln & St 44094
E & W Spaulding St 44094
Sperry Rd 44094
N Springer Dr 44094
St Johns Bluff Ln 44094
N Star Rd 44094
State Route 306 44094
Steve Guard Ct 44094
Stevens Blvd 44094
Stillman Ln 44094
Stone Ridge Dr 44094
Stonebridge Dr 44094
Strawberry Ln 44094
Strumbly Pl 44094
Strumbly Glen Rd 44094
Sturbridge Ln 44094
Sugarhouse Hill Ct 44094
Summerwood Ct 44094
Summit St 44094
Sunset Trl 44094
Sutton Ln 44094
Tamarac Blvd 44094
Thorne Ave 44094
Tibbetts Rd 44094
Timber Ridge Ln 44094
Timbercreek Dr 44094
Timothy Ln 44094
Tioga Trl 44094
Topps Industrial Pkwy 44094
Trafalgar Sq 44094
Tudor Dr 44094
N & S Turtle Trl 44094
Union St 44094
Valley View Oval 44094
Vine St 44094
Vista Cir 44094
Waite Hill Rd 44094
Waldamere Ave 44094
Walkers Ln 44094
Waterford Dr 44094
Wells Fleet Cir 44094
Western Pkwy 44094
Westminster Ln 44094
Weston Ct 44094
Westover Dr 44094
Westwood Dr 44094
White Oak Rd 44094
Wilbert Dr 44094
Wildwood Ct 44094
Willodale Dr 44094
Willoughby Pkwy 44094
Willoughcroft Rd 44094
Willow Creek Pl 44094
Wilson Ave 44094
Windermere Dr 44094
Windsor Ave 44094
Wisner Rd 44094
Wood Rd & St 44094
Woodcroft Ct 44094
Woodhawk Ln 44094
Woodhill Rd 44094
Woodlake Dr 44094
Woods Way Dr 44094
Woodside Ave 44094
Worrell Rd 44094
Wrens Ln 44094
Wrenwood Dr 44094
Wright St 44094
York Ct 44094
Zackary Ct 44094

NUMBERED STREETS

All Street Addresses 44094

YOUNGSTOWN OH

General Delivery 44501

POST OFFICE BOXES MAIN OFFICE STATIONS AND BRANCHES

Box No.s
1 - 1893 44501
1902 - 2078 44506
2101 - 2299 44504
2300 - 2497 44509
2502 - 2799 44507
2801 - 3099 44511
3101 - 3994 44513
4000 - 4995 44515
5001 - 5594 44514
5601 - 5960 44504
6000 - 6896 44501
8000 - 8004 44513
8665 - 8718 44507
9001 - 9952 44513
11101 - 11280 44511
14001 - 14700 44514
15100 - 15178 44515
60001 - 60177 44506
90101 - 90212 44509

NAMED STREETS

Abbott St 44515
Aberdeen Ave 44502
Academy Dr 44505
Acatello Pl 44514
Acton Ave 44515
Ada St 44510
Adams St 44505
Adelaide St 44506
Afton Ave 44512
Alameda Ave
200-599 44504
701-797 44510
799-1199 44510
Alamo Pl 44502
Alanson Ave 44515
Albert St
300-730 44506
731-1700 44505
1702-1798 44505
Alburn Dr 44512
Alden Ave 44505
Aldrich Rd 44515
Alexander St 44502
Algonquin Dr 44514
Alice St 44502
Alissa Pl 44512
Allegro Ln 44502
Allen Dr 44512
Allen Rd 44505
Allendale Ave 44511
Allerton Ct 44505
Alma Ct 44509
Almon Ave 44505
Almont St 44510
Almyra Ave 44511
Alpine St 44502
Alverne Dr 44514
Amberly Dr 44511
Ambert Ave 44502
Amberwood Ct & Trl 44512
Ameritech Blvd 44509
Ames Ct 44505
Amherst Ave 44512
Amhurst Dr 44505
Anderson Dr 44511
N Anderson Rd 44515
S Anderson Rd 44515
Andrea Ln 44512
Andrews Ave
100-199 44503
200-1199 44505
1201-1399 44505
Angiline Dr 44512
Anna Dr 44509
Annawan Ln 44512
Annetta Ave 44515
Anoka Ln 44511
Ansel Ct 44505
Anthos Ct 44512
Apache Ln 44514
Applecrest Ct & Dr 44512
Applegate Rd 44505
Appleridge Cir & Dr 44512
Applewood Blvd 44512
Aquadale Dr 44512
Aravesta Ave 44512
Arbor Cir 44505
Arcadia Ave 44505
Arch St
1000-1299 44506
1600-1899 44505
Arden Blvd 44511
Ardendale Ln 44512
Ardenwood Pl 44515
Ardmore Dr 44505
Argo St 44509
Argonne Dr 44515
Argyle Ave 44512
Arkwright Ave 44502
Arlene Ave 44512
Arlington St
300-699 44502
700-799 44510
Arrel Rd 44514
Arrow St 44505
Arrowae Dr 44511
Artmar Dr 44515
Ascot Ct 44511
Ash St 44507
Ashley Ave 44509
Ashley Cir 44515
Aspen Dr 44515
Aspen Ln 44514
Athens Dr 44515
Atkinson Ave 44505
Atlanta Ave 44515
Atlantic Ct 44514
Atoka Rd 44511
Auburn Hills Dr 44512
E & W Auburndale Ave 44507
Audubon Ln 44514
Audubon Rd 44514
Audubon St 44505
Augusta Dr 44512
Augusta St 44506
Augustine St 44505
Aurora Cir & Dr 44505
Austin Ave 44509
Autumnwood Trl 44514
Avalon Ct 44515
Avery Ave 44502
Avon St 44505
E Avondale Ave
1-399 44507
500-899 44502
W Avondale Ave 44507
Ayers St 44506
Aylesboro Ave 44512
Ayrshire Dr 44511
Backwater Cv 44515
Bailey St 44506
Bainbridge Ave 44511
Baker St
2700-2899 44505
5300-5499 44515
Baldwin St 44505
Balsam Ct 44507
Banbury Dr 44511
Bancroft Ave 44514
Bangor Ct 44511
Bank St 44506
Barbie Dr 44512
Barkley Ave 44515
Barrington Ct & Dr 44515
Barth Dr 44505
Basil Ave 44514
Bassett Ln 44505
Bauker Ln 44505
Baxter Ave 44509
Bay Meadow Ct 44515
Baylor Ave 44515
Baymar Dr 44511
Beachwood Dr 44505
E & N Beacon Dr 44515
Beard Rd 44514
Bears Den Ct & Rd 44511
Beaver Dr 44515
Beck St 44510
Becky Ct 44512
Beech Ave 44512
Beechcrest Ave 44515
Beechwood Dr
1-199 44512
2400-5999 44514
Beechwood Pl 44502
Beechwood Trl 44514
Bel Aire Ln 44514
Belden Ave 44502
Belgrade St 44505
Belle Ave 44515
N & S Belle Vista Ave 44509
Belleview Ave
1000-1198 44502
1200-1300 44507
1302-1598 44507
Bellfield Ave 44502
Belmar Dr 44505
Belmont Ave
100-198 44503
200-799 44502
900-1999 44504
2001-2197 44505
2199-5999 44505
Belmont Ct 44502
Bendemeer Ct, Dr & Way 44514
Benford Ln 44505
Benita Ave
1-199 44505
200-218 44504
220-299 44504
Bennington Ave 44505
Bentley Ave 44505
Benton St 44515
Bentwillow Ct & Ln 44511
Benwood Ave 44502
Berklee Dr 44514
Berkley Ave 44505
Berkshire Dr 44512
Bernadette Ave 44509
Bernard Ave 44502
Berwick Ave 44505
Bessemer St 44509
Bev Rd 44512
N & S Beverly Ave 44515
Beverly Hills Dr 44505
Bexley Dr 44515
Billingsgate Ave 44511
Birch St 44507
Birch Hill Dr 44509
Birch Trace Dr 44515
Birchcrest Dr 44515
Birchwood Dr 44515
Biscayne Ave 44505
Bishop Rd 44514
Bishop Woods Ct 44514
Bissell Ave 44505
Black Friar Ln 44511
Black Oak Ct & Ln 44511
N Blaine Ave
1-199 44506
300-499 44505
S Blaine Ave 44506
Blair Ave 44505
Blount St 44505
Blue Bird Ln 44512
Blue Ridge Dr 44514
Bluebell Trl 44514
Boardman Blvd 44512
E Boardman St 44503
W Boardman St 44503
Boardman Canfield Rd
1-408 44512
407-407 44513
409-1599 44512
410-1598 44512
Boardman Poland Rd
2-98 44512
100-999 44512
1000-1999 44514
Boardwalk Dr 44514
Bob O Link Dr 44511
Bob White Ct 44511
Boggess St 44502
N & S Bon Air Ave 44509
Bonnell Dr 44512
Bonnie Pl 44512
Bonnie Brae Ave 44511
Borden St 44505
Border Ave 44512
E Boston Ave
1-399 44507
500-1499 44502
W Boston Ave
1-199 44507
300-699 44511
Botsford St 44514
Bott St 44505
Boulder Creek Dr 44515
Bouquet Ave 44509
Bowman Ave 44515
Bradley Ln 44504
Brainard Dr 44512
Brandomyne Ave 44511
Brandon Ave 44514
Brandt Pl 44512
Brandywine Dr 44511
Brantford Dr 44509
Breaden St 44502
Breeze Knoll Dr 44505
Breezewood Dr 44515
Brentwood Ave 44511
Briarwood Ct 44514
Briarwood Ln 44511
Brickley Ave 44509
Bridge St 44509
Bridgewood Dr 44512
Brighton St 44505
Bristlewood Dr 44512
Brittain St 44502
Broad Blvd 44505
Broadview Ave 44509
Broadway Ave
1-199 44505
200-298 44504
300-499 44504
Broadway St 44510
Brockton Dr 44511
N & S Brockway Ave 44509
Brookfield Ave 44512
Brookline Ave 44505
Brooklyn Ave 44507
Brookstone Pl 44514
Brookwood Rd 44512
Browning Ave 44505
Brownlee Ave 44514
N & S Bruce St 44506
Bruno St 44509
Brunswick Pl & Rd 44511
Bryant Ave 44505
Bryant Dr 44511
Bryn Mawr Ave 44505
Bryson St
600-799 44502
800-1699 44505
Buchanan Dr 44512
Buckeye Cir 44502
Buckeye Ct 44505
Buena Vista Ave 44512
Bundy Ave
1000-3399 44509
3600-3799 44515
Burbank Ave 44509
Burford St 44505
Burgess Lake Dr 44514
Burgess Run Rd 44514
Burkey Rd 44515
Burlington St 44510
Burma Dr 44511
Burnett St 44502
Burning Tree Ln 44505
Burr Oaks Ct 44515
Burton Ave 44515
Burton St 44505
Butler Ave 44509
Byron St 44506
Cabot St 44509
N & S Cadillac Dr 44512
Cain St 44511
Caledonia St 44502
E California Ave 44512
Calla Rd E & W 44514
Callaway Cir 44515
Calvary Ct 44515
Calvin Ct & St 44510
Cambridge Ave 44502
Camden Ave 44505
Camella Dr 44514
Cameron Ave 44502
Campbell St 44502
Canavan Dr 44514
Candy Woods Dr 44514
Canfield Rd 44511
N & S Canfield Niles Rd 44515
Cannon Rd 44515
Canterbury Ln 44512
Canton St 44502
Cantwell Ave 44505
Caplende Ave 44504
Capri Ct 44514
Car St 44506
Carbone St 44505
Cardinal Dr 44505
Caribou Dr 44512
Carlin Dr 44515
Carlisle Ave 44511
Carlotta Dr 44504
Carlton Ave 44505
Carnegie Ave 44515
N Carolina Pl 44514
Caroline Ave 44506
Carroll St 44502
Carson St 44505
Carter Cir 44512
Cascade Dr 44511
Cassius Ave 44505
Castalia Ave 44505
Castle Ct 44511
Catalina Ave
300-599 44504
800-1199 44510
Catarina Pl 44514
Catherine St 44505
Cathy Way 44512
Cathy Ann Dr 44512
Cavalcade Dr 44515
Cedar Ln 44505
Cedar St 44502
Cedar Way 44512
Celesta Pl 44514
Celeste Cir 44511
Cennerma St 44510
Centennial Dr 44514
Center Rd 44514
N Center St 44506
S Center St 44506
Centervale Ave 44512
Central Ave 44515
Central Sq 44503
Cerni Pl 44515
Chablis Ln 44514
Chadwick Ln 44515
E Chalmers Ave 44507
W Chalmers Ave
1-299 44507
300-699 44511
N & S Champion St 44503
Champlain Ave 44502
Chaney Cir 44509
Chapel Hill Dr 44511
Chapman St 44502
Chardonnay Ln 44514
Charles Ave 44512
Charlestown Pl 44515
Charlotte Ave 44506
Chatham Ln 44505
Chattanooga Ave 44514
Chaucer Ln & Way 44511
Cheriwood Ct 44512
Cherokee Dr 44511
Cherry St 44506
Cherry Blossom Trl 44514
Cherry Hill Ave 44509
Cherry Hill Pl 44514
Cherrywood Dr 44512
Chester Dr 44512
Chesterton Dr 44514

- Chestnut Ln 44512
- N Chestnut St 44503
- Chestnut Hill Dr 44511
- Chianti Crk 44514
- Chicago Ave
  - 1-299 44507
  - 300-499 44511
- Choice Ct 44505
- Christine Ln 44511
- Christopher Dr 44514
- Churchill Hubbard Rd 44505
- Cider Mill Xing 44515
- Circle Dr 44514
- Citation Ct 44515
- City View Ct 44502
- Clarencedale Ave 44512
- Claridge Dr 44511
- Clark St 44505
- Clarkins Dr 44515
- Clay St 44506
- Claybourne Ave 44512
- Clearmount Dr 44511
- Clearwater Cv N & S 44515
- Cleveland St
  - 1-200 44507
  - 202-298 44507
  - 300-599 44511
- Cliffview Dr 44514
- Clifton Dr 44512
- Clifton St 44510
- Clingan Rd 44514
- Clingan St 44505
- Clinton St 44506
- Cloister St 44505
- Clovermeade Ave 44514
- Clyde St
  - 200-799 44510
  - 2101-2197 44514
  - 2199-2499 44514
- Cobblers Run 44514
- Coblentz Dr 44514
- Cohasset Dr 44511
- Coitsville Hubbard Rd 44505
- Colby Ave 44505
- Coleman Dr 44511
- Colfax St 44511
- Colgate Ave 44515
- Colleen Dr 44512
- College Ln & St 44514
- Collingwood Pl 44515
- Collins Ave 44515
- Colonial Dr 44505
- Colonial Estates Dr 44514
- Columbia St 44510
- Colwyn Ct 44512
- Comanche Trl 44511
- Commerce Dr 44514
- E Commerce St 44503
- W Commerce St 44503
- S Commons Pl 44514
- Commonwealth Ave 44505
- Compass West Dr 44515
- Compton Ln 44502
- Concord Ave 44509
- Connecticut Ave
  - 1900-1998 44509
  - 2000-3599 44509
  - 3600-3700 44515
  - 3702-3798 44515
- Cook Ave 44512
- Cool St 44509
- Cooper St 44502
- Coral St 44510
- Coral Sea Dr 44511
- Corby Dr 44509
- Cordova Ave 44504
- Cornell Ave 44507
- Cornell St 44502
- Corning Ave 44505
- Cornwall Ave 44505
- Coronado Ave 44504
- Cortland Ave 44514
- Cottage Grove Ave 44507
- Council Rock Ave 44506
- Country Ln 44514
- Country Trl 44515
- Country Club Ave 44514
- Country Club Dr 44505
- Country Green Dr 44515
- Country Ridge Ave 44515
- Countryside Dr 44515
- Court St 44505
- Court Way 44512
- Courtway Aly 44512
- Cove Pl 44511
- Cover Dr 44514
- Covington Cv 44515
- Covington St 44510
- Cowden Rd 44514
- Crabwood Ct & Dr 44515
- Craiger Ave 44502
- Craiglee Ave 44506
- Cranberry Crk & Ln 44512
- Cranberry Run Dr 44512
- Cranbrook Ct & Dr 44511
- Crandall Ave
  - 200-491 44504
  - 700-1099 44510
- Craven St 44510
- Creed Ave 44515
- Crescent St 44502
- Crestline Pl 44512
- Creston Dr 44512
- Crestview Dr 44512
- Crestwood Blvd 44505
- Cricket Dr 44511
- Crimson Ct 44515
- Crimson Trl 44512
- Crofton St 44505
- Cromwell St 44505
- Cross Cv & Dr 44515
- Crossroad Dr 44514
- Crum Rd 44515
- Crumrine St 44505
- Crystal Dr 44512
- Cuddy Ave 44505
- Cumberland Cir & Dr 44515
- Curry Pl 44504
- Curtis Ave 44505
- Custer Ave 44502
- Dade Ave 44505
- Daffodil Trl 44514
- Dailey Ave 44505
- Dalderiv Ave 44505
- Dale St 44505
- Danbury Dr 44512
- Danzig Ct 44502
- Darlington Ave 44505
- Darwin St 44505
- Datson Ave 44505
- David Ct 44511
- Davis Ln 44510
- Day Ct 44505
- Dayton Ave 44509
- Daytona Dr 44515
- De Gaulle Ct 44512
- Dean Ave 44505
- Dearborn St 44510
- Debartolo Pl 44512
- Deborah Ct 44511
- Decamp Rd 44511
- Decatur St 44506
- Deer Creek Ct 44515
- Deer Run Dr 44512
- Deerpath Dr 44512
- Dehoff Dr 44515
- E Delason Ave 44507
- W Delason Ave
  - 1-299 44507
  - 300-699 44511
- Delaware Ave
  - 1-199 44514
  - 600-1099 44510
  - 1800-1899 44514
- Delmar St 44505
- Demorest St 44505
- E Dennick Ave 44505
- W Dennick Ave
  - 1-199 44505
  - 200-299 44504
- Denver Ave 44505
- Denver Dr 44514
- Deopham Green Dr 44515
- Depauw Ave 44515
- Desoto Ave 44502
- Detroit Ave 44502
- Devon Ave 44505
- Devonshire Dr 44512
- E Dewey Ave
  - 1-499 44507
  - 500-999 44502
- W Dewey Ave
  - 1-199 44507
  - 300-699 44511
- Diana Dr 44514
- Dickson St 44502
- Dignan St 44505
- Division St 44509
- Division Street Ext 44510
- Dobbins Rd 44514
- Dogwood Dr 44511
- Dogwood Ln 44505
- Donald Ave 44509
- Donation Ave 44505
- Doncaster Dr 44511
- Donmar Ln 44511
- Doral Dr 44514
- Dorothy Ave 44502
- Dorset Ave 44509
- Douglas Ave 44502
- Dover Rd 44511
- Drake Ave 44505
- Dravis Dr 44515
- Driftwood Ln 44515
- Drummond Ave 44506
- Dryden Ave 44505
- Dudley Ave 44505
- Duke Cir 44515
- Dunbar St 44515
- Duncan Dr 44514
- Duncan Ln 44505
- Dundee St 44505
- N Dunlap Ave 44509
- S Dunlap Ave 44509
- Dunlap Rd 44515
- Dupont St 44510
- Dutton Dr 44502
- Eagle Trce 44512
- E Earle Ave 44507
- W Earle Ave
  - 100-299 44507
  - 300-699 44511
- Early Rd 44505
- East Dr 44505
- Eastbrooke Trl 44514
- Eastlawn Ave 44505
- Eastview Dr 44505
- Eastway Dr 44505
- Eastwind Pl 44515
- Eddie St 44509
- Eden Ln 44509
- Edenridge Dr 44512
- Edgar Ave 44505
- N & S Edgehill Ave 44515
- Edgewater Dr
  - 1-99 44514
  - 1-299 44515
  - 2200-2499 44514
- Edinburgh Dr 44511
- Edna St 44514
- Edwards St
  - 1-1299 44502
  - 1300-1599 44511
- Eigen St 44515
- Eisenhower Dr 44512
- Elberen St 44509
- Elbertus Ave 44507
- Eldora Dr 44511
- Eleanor Ave 44509
- Eliot Ln 44505
- Elizabeth St 44506
- Elk St 44505
- Ella Ave 44506
- Ellenwood Ave 44507
- Elm St
  - 1-99 44514
  - 200-399 44503
  - 700-799 44502
  - 800-2599 44505
- Elm Trace St 44515
- Elmland Ave 44514
- Elmwood Ave
  - 3600-3700 44505
  - 3601-3631 44515
  - 3633-3835 44515
  - 3702-3839 44505
  - 3837-3899 44515
  - 3900-4299 44515
- E Elmwood Ave 44515
- W Elmwood Ave 44515
- Elva Ave 44512
- Elwood St 44515
- Emerald St 44505
- Emerson Pl 44504
- Emery Ave 44507
- Emmett St 44506
- Erie St
  - 600-1099 44502
  - 1200-3799 44507
  - 3900-5699 44512
- Erskine Ave 44512
- Essex St 44502
- Estates Cir 44511
- Euclid Ave 44506
- Euclid Blvd
  - 1-299 44505
  - 3900-4799 44512
- Eugene Ct 44511
- Evans Ave 44515
- N & S Evanston Ave 44509
- Evelyn Rd 44511
- Everett Ave 44514
- E Evergreen Ave 44507
- W Evergreen Ave
  - 1-199 44507
  - 201-299 44507
  - 300-699 44511
- Evergreen Dr 44514
- Ewing Rd 44512
- Excellence Dr 44505
- Excelsior Ave 44506
- Fairfax St 44505
- Fairfield Dr 44512
- Fairgreen Ave
  - 200-499 44504
  - 500-999 44510
- Fairlawn Ave
  - 17-38 44512
  - 20-33 44505
  - 35-37 44505
  - 40-98 44512
- Fairmeadow Dr 44515
- Fairmont Ave 44510
- Fairview Ave 44502
- Fairview Rd 44515
- Fairway Dr 44505
- Fairweather Trl 44514
- Falcon Dr 44515
- Falls Ave 44502
- Farnbauer Ct 44506
- Fawn Ct 44512
- E & W Federal St 44503
- Felicia Ave 44504
- Ferdinand Rd 44511
- Ferncliff Ave
  - 1-99 44512
  - 400-599 44514
- Ferndale Ave 44511
- Fernwood Ave 44509
- Fieldstone 44514
- Filmore Ave 44505
- Fincastle Ln 44514
- Finland Rd 44515
- Finnley Ave
  - 2700-3899 44511
  - 4700-5199 44512
- Fitch Blvd 44515
- Fithian Ave 44502
- Fitzgerald Ave 44515
- Flagler Ln 44511
- Fleming St 44510
- Flintridge Dr 44515
- Flo Lor Dr 44511
- Flontong Dr 44511
- Flora Ln 44511
- Florence Ave 44509
- Florencedale Ave 44505
- E Florida Ave
  - 1-399 44507
  - 500-1499 44502
- W Florida Ave 44507
- Florist Ave 44505
- Ford Ave
  - 400-799 44502
  - 800-998 44504
  - 1000-1799 44504
- Forest Ave 44514
- N Forest Ave 44506
- S Forest Ave 44506
- Forest Garden Dr 44512
- Forest Glen Ave 44505
- Forest Green Dr 44515
- Forest Hill Ave 44514
- Forest Hill Dr 44515
- Forest Hill Rd 44512
- Forest Lake Dr 44512
- Forest Park Dr & Pl 44512
- Forest Ridge Dr 44512
- Forest View Dr 44505
- Foster St
  - 300-799 44502
  - 1100-1599 44510
- Fountain St 44502
- Fountain Square Dr 44515
- N & S Four Mile Run Rd 44515
- Four Seasons Trl 44514
- Fox Holw 44512
- Fox Chase 44515
- Fox Crossing Ct 44515
- Fox Hunt Ct 44515
- Fox Run Dr 44512
- Foxridge Dr 44512
- Foxwood Ct 44514
- Francisca Ave 44504
- Franco Ct 44512
- Franklin Ave 44502
- Frederick Dr 44505
- Frederick St 44515
- Fredericksburg Dr 44512
- Fredrick Douglas Pl 44505
- Freeman Ct 44502
- Fremont Ave 44511
- Friendship Ave 44512
- E & W Front St 44503
- Frontier Dr 44514
- Frost Ave 44505
- Frostwood Dr 44515
- N & S Fruit St 44506
- Funston Dr & St 44510
- Gaither Ave 44507
- Garden Gate Ct 44512
- Garden Place Dr 44514
- Garden Valley Ct & Dr 44512
- Gardenridge Ct 44512
- Gardenview Dr 44512
- Gardenwood Dr & Pl 44512
- Garfield St 44502
- N Garland Ave
  - 1-799 44506
  - 800-1799 44505
- S Garland Ave 44506
- Garver Dr 44512
- Genesee Dr 44511
- Geoffrey Trl 44509
- George St 44502
- Georgetown Pl 44515
- Gertrude Ave 44512
- Gertrude Pl 44507
- Gerwig Ave 44505
- Gibson St 44502
- Gilbert Dr 44512
- Gillian Ln 44511
- Glacier Ave 44509
- Glacier Heights Rd 44509
- Glacierview Dr 44509
- Gladstone St 44506
- Gladwae Dr & Pl 44511
- W Glen Dr 44512
- Glen Oaks Dr 44511
- Glen Park Rd 44512
- E Glenaven Ave 44507
- W Glenaven Ave
  - 1-199 44507
  - 201-299 44507
  - 300-599 44511
- Glenbrook Rd 44512
- Glendale Ave 44512
- N & S Glenellen Ave 44509
- Glenmere Dr 44511
- Glenmont St 44510
- Glenmore St 44505
- Glenridge Rd 44512
- Glenwood Ave
  - 201-297 44502
  - 299-1299 44502
  - 1300-3899 44511
  - 3900-8699 44512
- Glenwoods Ct 44512
- Gluck St 44505
- Goldie Rd 44505
- Goleta Ave
  - 1800-2399 44504
  - 2400-2998 44505
  - 3000-3199 44505
  - 3201-3299 44505
- Golfview Ave 44512
- Goodlow Ave 44510
- Grace St 44504
- Granada Ave
  - 200-300 44504
  - 302-498 44504
  - 500-598 44505
  - 600-699 44505
- Grandview Ave 44506
- Granite St 44502
- Grant St 44502
- N & S Gray Ave 44505
- Greeley Ln 44505
- Green St 44506
- Green Acres Dr 44505
- Green Bay Dr 44512
- Green Garden Dr 44512
- Green Glen Dr 44511
- Green Grass Way Ln 44515
- Green Meadow Pl 44514
- Greenfield Dr 44512
- Greenwood St 44509
- Gregory Ave 44511
- Greyledge Pl 44511
- Greystone 44514
- Griffith St 44510
- Griselda Ave 44511
- Griswold Dr 44512
- Grove St 44505
- Grover Dr 44512
- Guadalupe Ave 44504
- Guss St 44505
- Gypsy Ln
  - 1-197 44505
  - 199-200 44505
  - 202-202 44505
  - 203-497 44504
  - 499-537 44504
  - 538-598 44505
  - 600-1100 44505
  - 1102-1598 44505
- Hadley Ave 44505
- Halbert Dr 44514
- Halleck St 44505
- Halls Heights Ave 44509
- Hamilton Ave 44514
- Hammaker St 44510
- Hamman Dr 44511
- Hampton Ct 44509
- Hampton Hall 44514
- Handels Ct 44512
- Hanley Ave 44505
- Hanover St 44505
- Harlem St 44510
- Harmon Ave 44502
- Harold Ave 44515
- Harper Ave 44515
- Harrington Ave 44512
- Harrison St 44505
- Harrow Ln & Pl 44511
- Harry St 44506
- N & S Hartford Ave 44509
- Hartzell Ave 44509
- Harvard Blvd 44514
- Harvard Pl 44515
- Harvard St 44510
- E Harvest Ridge Dr 44515
- Harvest Run Trl 44514
- Haskell Ave 44515
- Hasty Rd 44515
- Havenwood Dr 44512
- Haviland Dr 44505
- Hawn St 44506
- Hawthorne St 44502
- Hayden Dr 44511
- Hayes Ave 44502
- Hayman St 44510
- N & S Hazel St 44503
- Hazeltine Ave 44506
- N Hazelwood Ave 44509
- S Hazelwood Ave 44509
- Hazelwood Dr 44505
- Heasley St 44507
- Heather Ln 44511
- Heather Creek Run 44511
- Heatherbrae Dr 44514
- N Heights Ave 44504
- S Heights Ave 44502
- W Heights Ave 44509
- Helena Ave 44512
- Hemlock Ct 44515
- Hendricks Rd 44515
- E & W Henry St 44502
- Herielan St 44507
- Heritage Trl 44514
- Hermosa Dr 44511
- Heron Bay Dr 44514
- Herons Blvd & Cir 44515
- Hickory Ct 44505
- Hickory Ln 44515
- Hickory St 44506
- Hickory Hill Dr 44514
- E High Ave
  - 1000-1098 44506
  - 1100-1399 44506
  - 1400-1498 44505
  - 1500-2100 44505
  - 2102-2198 44505
- E High Ct 44505
- High St 44502
- Highland Ave
  - 1500-1800 44510
  - 1802-1998 44510
  - 2600-3199 44514
- Highlawn Ave 44509
- Hill Dr 44514
- Hill St 44505
- Hillcrest Ave 44505
- Hillman St
  - 500-1299 44502
  - 1300-3899 44507
- Hillman Way 44512
- Hillsdale Ave 44509
- Hilltop Dr 44514
- Hilltop St 44506
- Hilton Ave 44507
- Himrod Ave 44506
- N Hine St 44506
- Hiram St 44502
- Hitchcock Rd 44512
- Hoffman St 44502
- Hogue St 44502
- Holbrook Rd 44514
- Hollacks Dr 44515
- Holland Ave 44505
- Hollywood Ave 44512
- Holyoke Dr 44514
- Homestead Ave 44502
- Homestead Dr 44512
- Homestead Rd 44505
- Homewood Ave 44502
- Hood St 44515
- Hopkins Rd 44511
- Houston Ave 44505
- Howard St
  - 1-199 44515

3900-4399 44512
4401-4499 44512
Howe St 44505
Howell Dr 44514
Hubbard Ct & Rd 44505
Hudson Ave 44511
Hudson Dr 44512
Hughes St 44502
Humbolt Ave 44502
Hummingbird Hill Dr 44514
Hunter Ave 44502
Hunters Ct 44512
Hunters Cv 44512
Hunters Gln 44512
Hunters Hl 44514
Hunters Rdg 44512
Hunting Valley Dr 44512
E Huntington Cir, Ct & Dr 44512
Huntmere Ave 44515
E Hylda Ave 44507
W Hylda Ave
1-199 44507
300-599 44511
Ida Dr 44514
Idaho Rd 44515
Idlewood Ave 44511
Idlewood Rd 44515
Idora Ave 44511
Illinois Ave 44505
Impala Dr 44515
Imperial St 44509
Indian Trl 44514
Indian Creek Dr 44514
Indiana Ave 44505
E Indianola Ave
1-499 44507
500-1699 44502
W Indianola Ave
1-199 44507
300-999 44511
Indianola Rd 44512
Industrial Rd 44509
Inglenook Pl 44511
N & S Inglewood Ave 44515
Ingram Dr 44512
Innovation Pl 44509
Innwood Dr 44515
Interstate Blvd 44515
Intertech Dr 44509
Inverness Ave 44502
Iona St 44502
Irene Ave
501-599 44509
6600-6699 44515
Irma Ave 44514
Irma St 44502
Irving Pl 44502
Island Dr 44514
Ivanhoe Ave 44502
Ives St 44505
Ivy Hill Dr 44514
Jachentr Dr 44512
N & S Jackson St 44506
Jacobs Rd 44505
Jaguar Dr & Pl 44512
James St 44514
Jamestown Ct 44515
Jaronte Dr 44512
Jasper Ct 44514
Javit Ct 44515
Jean St 44502
Jeanne Lynn Ave 44514
Jefferson Ct 44505
Jefferson St 44510
Jennette Dr 44512
Jennifer Dr 44514
Jo Ann Ln 44505
Jochman Ct 44514
John St 44502
Johnson St 44502
Johnston Pl 44514
Jonathan Ln 44511
Jones St 44502
Joseph St 44502
Josephine St 44505
Joyce Ann Dr 44511
Juanita Ave 44504
E Judson Ave
1-399 44507
500-799 44502
W Judson Ave
1-99 44507
300-699 44511
Julian St 44502
Junior Ave 44511
Karago Ave 44512
Karen Ct 44511
Karl St 44505
Katahdin Dr 44514
Katherine Ave 44505
Kay Ct 44505
Kendis Cir 44505
Kenmar Ct 44515
Kenmore Ave
1-299 44507
300-599 44511
Kennedy Ave 44506
Kenneth St 44505
Kensington Ave 44505
Kentwood Dr 44512
Kenyon Ave 44505
Keogh Ave 44505
Kerry Ln 44514
Kerrybrook Dr 44511
Kerrybrooke Trl 44514
Keystone Ave 44505
N & S Kimberly Ave 44515
Kimmel St 44505
Kincaid Rd 44509
King Ave 44514
King St 44502
Kingston Ln 44511
Kiowa Dr 44511
Kirk Rd
2000-4399 44511
4400-5499 44515
Kirkhaven Dr 44511
Kirkwood St 44506
Kirtland Ave 44505
Kirwan Dr 44515
Kist Pl 44502
Kiwana Dr 44512
Kiwatha Rd 44511
Kleber Ave 44515
Knapp St 44505
Knob Ct 44505
Knollwood Ave 44514
Knox St 44502
Kreidler Rd 44514
Krieger Ln 44502
Kroeck Ave 44515
Labelle Ave 44507
E Laclede Ave
1-499 44507
700-799 44502
W Laclede Ave
1-299 44507
300-999 44511
Laclede Ct 44502
Lafayette St 44510
Laird Ave
1-99 44509
400-599 44514
Lake Ave 44515
Lake Dr 44511
Lake Rd 44511
Lake Park Rd 44512
Lake Shore Dr 44511
Lakeside Dr 44509
N & S Lakeview Ave 44509
Lakewood Ave 44502
Lakewood Cir 44505
Lamar Ave 44505
Lancaster Dr 44511
N & S Lane Ave 44506
Lansdowne Blvd
1-399 44506
400-2799 44505
Lansing Ave 44506
Lanterman Ave 44511
Lanterman Rd 44515
Larkridge Ave 44512
Lasalle Ave 44502
Lauderdale Ave 44505
Laurel St 44505
Laurelwood Pl 44515
Laurie Dr 44511
Laverne Dr 44511
E & W Lawrence St 44506
Leadville Ave 44509
Leah Ave 44502
Lealand Ave 44514
Lee Ave 44502
Lee Dr 44514
Lee St 44514
Lee Lynn Ct 44514
Lee Run Rd 44514
Leharps Dr 44515
Leighton Ave 44512
Lemans Dr 44512
Lemont Dr 44514
Lemoyne Ave 44514
Lenox Ave 44502
Leo Ave 44509
Leopard Way 44505
Lexington Ave
300-400 44504
402-498 44504
500-999 44510
Lexington Pl 44515
Leyton Dr 44509
E Liberty Rd & St 44505
Liesken Ln 44511
Lightner Pl 44514
Lilac St 44502
Lilburne Dr 44505
N Lima Rd 44514
Lincoln Ave
1-299 44503
300-699 44502
Lincoln Park Dr 44506
Linden Ave 44505
Linger Pl 44514
Linwood Ave 44511
Little Johns Pl 44511
Little North Rd 44505
Livingston St 44506
Lloyd Ave 44505
Loch Heath Ln 44511
Lockwood Blvd
3900-5199 44511
5200-7199 44512
Locust Ave 44512
Locust Ln 44514
Logan Ave & Way 44505
Logan Arms Dr 44505
Logan Gate Rd 44505
Loguidice Ave 44506
Lois Ct 44502
Loma Vista Dr 44511
Lombardy Ct 44502
London Ct & Dr 44515
Longview Ave 44512
Lora Ave 44504
Lorentz St 44505
Loretta Ave 44505
Loretta Dr 44512
Lost Creek Dr 44512
Lost Tree Dr 44512
Lou Ida Blvd 44515
Louise Rita Ct 44511
Loveland Rd 44502
N & S Loveless Ave & Ct 44506
Lowell Ave 44512
Lucerne Ln 44511
E Lucius Ave
1-399 44507
500-899 44502
W Lucius Ave 44507
Lucy St 44512
Lundy Ln 44512
Luteran Ln 44514
Luther Rd 44514
Lyden Ave 44505
Lynhaven Rd 44511
Lynn Ave 44514
Lynn St 44512
Lynn Mar Ave 44514
Lynridge Dr 44512
Lyon Blvd 44514
Mabel St 44502
Macachee Dr 44511
Macarthur Dr 44512
Mackey St 44505
Madera Ave 44504
Madison Ave
1-199 44505
200-299 44504
301-499 44504
500-699 44502
700-799 44510
801-999 44510
Madison Rd 44505
Madonda Dr 44512
Madrid Dr 44515
Magnolia Ave 44505
Mahoning Ave
500-1099 44502
1300-1398 44509
1400-3599 44509
3600-7199 44515
N Main St
1-399 44514
37-47 44515
49-300 44515
302-322 44515
400-999 44514
S Main St
1-215 44514
39-39 44515
41-299 44515
217-221 44514
300-599 44514
Mallard Ct 44515
Manchester Ave 44509
Manhattan Ave 44509
Manley St 44505
Manning Ave 44502
W Manor Ave 44514
Mansell Dr 44505
Maple Ave
1-199 44515
300-999 44512
4300-4398 44515
4400-4499 44515
Maple Dr
1-299 44512
300-399 44514
Maple Leaf Dr 44515
Maple Ridge Dr 44512
Maple Trace Ct 44515
Maplecrest Dr 44515
Maplecroft Rd 44514
Maplewood Ave & Ct 44505
Maramont Dr 44512
Maranatha Ct & Dr 44505
Marble St 44502
March Ave 44505
Marcia Dr 44515
Margaret St 44510
Mariner Ave 44505
Marinthana Ave 44512
E Marion Ave 44507
W Marion Ave
1-199 44507
201-299 44507
300-499 44511
Marion Dr 44514
Market Ct 44503
Market St
1-399 44503
500-1299 44502
1300-3899 44507
3900-8599 44512
Marlin Ave 44502
Marlindale Ave 44512
Marlyn Pl 44512
Marmion Ave
200-399 44507
501-797 44502
799-899 44502
Marshall St 44502
Martin Luther King Jr Blvd
400-498 44502
500-799 44502
800-998 44510
801-1299 44502
1000-1298 44502
1300-3199 44510
3201-3299 44510
Marwood Cir 44512
Mary Pl 44515
Mary St 44507
Mary Ann Ln 44511
N & S Maryland Ave 44509
Marylyn Ave 44505
Massachusetts Ave 44514
Mathews Rd
100-999 44512
1100-2099 44514
Matta Ave 44509
Maureen Dr 44511
Mayfield Ave 44509
Mayfield Dr 44512
Mayflower Dr 44512
Maywood Dr 44512
Mcbride St 44505
Mccartney Rd 44505
Mcclure Ave 44505
Mcclurg Rd 44512
Mccollum Rd 44509
Mcfarland Ave 44511
Mcguffey Rd 44505
Mchenry St 44506
Mckay Ct 44512
Mckinley Ave 44509
E Mckinley Way 44514
W Mckinley Way 44514
Mcquiston St 44505
Meadow Ln
1-99 44514
1100-1199 44512
1200-1300 44514
1302-1398 44514
2700-4099 44511
7700-7799 44514
Meadow St 44505
Meadowbrook Ave
1-1199 44512
1500-2099 44514
Meadowbrooke Trl 44514
Meadowlark Ln 44511
Meadowood Cir 44514
Meander Dr & Run 44515
Meander Glen Dr 44515
Medford Ave 44514
N & S Medina St 44506
Megan Cir 44505
Mehlo Ln 44509
Melbourne Ave 44512
Melrose Ave
1-499 44512
4400-4499 44515
9100-9398 44514
Melvina St 44505
Mercer St 44502
Mere Ct 44512
Meredyth Ln 44511
N Meridian Rd 44509
S Meridian Rd
1-1000 44509
1001-1097 44511
1002-1098 44509
1099-3697 44511
3699-3699 44511
Meriline Ave 44505
Merrill Rd 44505
Miami St 44505
Michael Dr 44511
Michigan Ave
1-9 44514
11-99 44514
800-899 44504
Michigan Blvd 44505
Middle Dr 44505
Middletown Rd E 44514
Midgewood Dr 44512
Midland Ave 44509
E Midlothian Blvd
1-399 44507
500-2100 44502
2102-2798 44502
W Midlothian Blvd
1-99 44507
300-1999 44511
Midwood Cir 44512
Milan St 44510
Mildred St 44515
Mill Creek Blvd & Dr 44512
Mill Run Dr 44505
Mill Trace Rd 44511
Millard St 44505
Miller St
300-399 44507
400-799 44502
Millet Ave 44509
Millicent Ave 44505
Milton Ave 44509
Miltonia Ave 44505
Mineral Springs Ave 44511
Mistletoe Ave 44511
Misty Ridge Trl 44514
Mogg Ct 44502
Mohawk Ave 44502
Moherman Ave 44509
Mona Ln 44509
Monaca Ave 44511
Montclair Ave 44511
Monterey Ave 44509
N & S Montgomery Ave 44506
Monticello Blvd & Dr 44505
Montrose Ave 44512
Montrose Cir 44512
E Montrose St 44505
W Montrose St 44505
Moorefield Ave 44515
Moraine Dr 44509
Morningside Dr & Pl 44514
Morse Pl 44514
Mosier Pl 44510
Mount Vernon Ave 44502
Moyer Ave 44512
Mulberry Ln 44512
Mulberry Walk 44514
Mumford Cir, Ct & Dr 44505
Murdock St 44506
Murray Hill Dr 44505
Myron Ave 44505
E Myrtle Ave
1-499 44507
501-697 44502
699-799 44502
W Myrtle Ave
1-299 44507
300-599 44511
Myrwood Ln 44511
Nadyne Dr 44511
Nair St 44505
Nantucket Dr 44515
Nashua Dr & Pl 44515
Nassau Ct 44511
Navajo Pl 44514
N & S Navarre Ave 44515
Neilson Ave 44502
Nellbert Ln 44512
Nelson Ave 44505
Neosho Rd 44511
Nesbitt St 44514
Neshoba Dr 44511
Nevada Ave 44512
New Ct 44502
New Rd 44515
New England Blvd 44512
New Hampshire Ct & Pl 44515
New York Ave 44505
Newbern Cir 44502
Newport Dr 44512
Newton Ave 44512
Nisonger Dr 44512
Noel Dr 44509
Norman Ave 44506
Normandy Dr 44511
Norquest Blvd 44515
North Ave 44502
Northgate Ave 44505
Northlawn Ave 44512
Northlawn Dr 44505
Northview Blvd 44504
Northwood Ave
2800-3399 44505
3600-3699 44511
Norwick Dr 44505
Norwood Ave
200-499 44504
600-1199 44510
Notre Dame Ave 44515
Nottingham Ave 44511
Nova Ln 44514
Oak Ave 44512
Oak Dr 44514
Oak Ln 44505
Oak Park 44505
Oak St 44506
Oak Hill Ave
1-97 44502
99-1299 44502
1300-2699 44507
Oak Knoll Dr 44512
Oak Street Ext 44505
Oak Trace St 44515
Oakcrest Ave 44515
Oakenert St 44506
Oakland Ave 44510
Oakland Dr 44505
Oakleigh Ave 44515
Oakley Ave 44512
Oakridge Dr 44512
Oakwood Ave
1601-1697 44509
1699-3599 44509
3600-3899 44515
3701-3703 44505
3705-3722 44505
3901-4099 44515
Oberlin Pl 44515
Oden Ave 44515
Ohio Ave
1-99 44514
800-2599 44504
Ohio Trl 44505
Ohio Works Dr 44510
Ohltown Rd 44515
Oklahoma Ave 44502
Old Farm Trl 44515
Old Furnace Rd 44511
Old Harbour Pl 44511
Old Orchard Ln 44511
Old Oxford Ln 44512
Old Shay Ln 44512
Olde Charted Trl 44514
Olde Stone Xing 44514
Olde Winter Trl 44514
Oles Ave 44514
Olive St 44505
Olivette Ct 44502
Olson Ave 44509
Oneta Ave 44509
Oran Dr 44511
Orange Ave 44502
Orchard Ave 44505
Orchard Dr 44514
Orchard Pl 44502
Oregon Ave 44509
Oregon Trl 44512
Oriole Dr 44505
Orkney Ave 44515
Orlo Ln 44512
Orrin Ave 44505
N & S Osborn Ave 44509
Otis St 44510
Ottawa Dr 44511
Outlook Ave 44504
Outlook St 44514
W Oventana St 44503
Overbrook Ave 44505
Overhill Rd 44512
Overland Ave
500-1299 44502

1300-1899 44511
Overlook Ave 44509
Oxford St 44510
Oyster Bay Dr 44512
Pacifica Dr 44514
Paisley St 44511
Palestine Ave 44512
Palisades Dr 44514
Palmarie Dr 44514
Palmer Ave 44502
Palmetto Dr 44511
Palo Verde Dr 44514
Pamela Ct 44514
Paris Dr 44515
Park Ave
100-199 44505
201-297 44504
299-400 44504
401-437 44514
402-438 44504
439-599 44514
700-899 44510
Park Dr 44505
Park Harbour Dr 44512
Park Heights Ave 44506
Park Hill Dr 44502
Park Place Dr 44514
Park Vista Dr 44505
Parkcliffe Ave 44511
Parker St 44505
Parkgate Ave 44515
Parkland Ave 44512
Parkland Ct 44514
E & W Parkside Ct & Dr 44512
Parkview Ave 44511
Parkway Dr 44514
Parkwood Ave
500-1099 44502
4000-4199 44505
Parmalee Ave 44510
Parnell St 44502
Partridge Park Dr 44514
Pasadena Ave
1-499 44507
500-999 44502
Pathendi Ave 44509
Patricia Ave 44511
Patterson Ct 44511
Paulin Dr & Rd 44514
Pawnee Pl 44514
Paxton Rd 44512
Payne Ct 44506
Payton Dr 44505
Peachtree Ct 44514
Peacock Dr 44511
Pearce Ave 44511
N & S Pearl St 44506
Pearson Cir 44512
Peddlers Ct 44514
Pembrook Rd 44515
Pembrooke Pl 44512
Penn Ave 44506
Pennsylvania Ave
800-899 44504
7200-7249 44514
7251-7299 44514
Penny Ln 44515
Penny Lane Ct 44515
Pepsi Pl 44502
Perdulla Ln 44514
Performance Pl 44502
Perry St 44506
Pershing St 44510
Petrie St 44502
Pheasant Ct & Dr 44512
N & S Phelps St 44503
E Philadelphia Ave
1-399 44507
500-999 44502
W Philadelphia Ave 44507
Philrose Ln 44514
Pierce Dr 44511
Pike St 44502
Pimlico Dr 44515
Pine Hollow Dr 44502
Pine Trace St 44515
Pine Tree Ln 44512
Pinebrook Ct 44515
Pinecrest Ave 44515
Pinegrove Ave 44515
Pinehill Dr 44514
Pinehurst Ave 44512
Pineridge Ct 44515
Pineview Ave 44511
Pineview Dr 44515
Pinewood Ct 44515
Pinewood Dr 44512
Pioneer Dr 44512
Placid Blvd 44515
Playhouse Ln 44511
Plazaview Ct 44505
Plum St 44502
Plymouth Dr 44512
Plymouth St 44502
Pointview Ave 44502
Poland Ave 44502
Poland Mnr 44514
Poland Center Dr 44514
Poland Struthers Rd 44514
Poland Village Blvd 44514
Polley Dr 44515
Polo Blvd 44514
Poplar Ave 44515
Poplar St 44510
Porter Ave 44505
N & S Portland Ave 44509
Potomac Ave
200-399 44507
3800-3999 44515
Powder Mill Run 44505
Powers Ave 44505
Powers Way 44502
Powersdale Ave 44502
Preserve Blvd 44514
Presidential Ct & Dr 44512
Prestwick Dr 44512
Price Rd 44509
E Princeton Ave 44507
W Princeton Ave
1-199 44507
300-699 44511
199 1/2-199 1/2 44507
N & S Prospect Ave & St 44506
Purdue Ave 44515
Pyatt St 44502
Quail Ct 44512
Quebec Ave 44511
Queen St 44506
Quentin Dr 44511
Quill Ct 44515
Quinn St 44506
N & S Raccoon Rd 44515
Radcliffe Ave 44515
E & W Radio Rd 44515
Raintree Run 44514
Randall Ave 44505
Randolph St 44509
Ranier Ave 44512
Ranquest Ln 44515
Raupp Ave 44512
Ravenna Ave 44505
E Ravenwood Ave 44507
W Ravenwood Ave
1-99 44507
300-699 44511
Ravine Dr 44505
Ravine Pl 44514
Ravine Rd 44505
E Rayen Ave
1-199 44503
200-399 44505
W Rayen Ave
1-299 44503
300-1299 44502
Raymond St 44510
Red Apple Dr 44515
Red Fox Ct & Dr 44512
Red Grouse Ct 44511
Red Maple Ln 44514
Red Tail Hawk Ct & Dr 44512
Redfern Dr 44505
Redgate Ln 44511
Redondo Rd 44504
Redwood Trl 44512
Reel Ave 44511
Regal Dr 44515
Regent St 44507
Regis Ave 44505
Renwick Dr 44514
Republic Ave 44505
Reserve Ct & Dr 44514
Reta Ln 44512
Revere Ave 44505
Rexford Rd 44511
Rheims Ave 44515
Rhoda Ave 44509
Rhode Island Dr 44515
Riblett Ave 44509
Riblett Rd 44515
Richards Dr 44505
Richland Ave 44509
Richmond Ave 44505
N & S Richview Ave 44509
Ridelind Ave 44502
Ridge Ave 44502
Ridgefield Ave 44512
Ridgelawn Ave 44509
Ridgely Ct & Park 44514
Ridgeview Ave 44515
Ridgeview Ln 44514
Ridgewood Dr 44512
Ridgewood Rd 44502
Ridley Ave 44505
Rigby St 44506
Risher Rd 44511
Rita St 44515
Riverside Ct 44514
Riverside Dr
1-199 44514
4000-4199 44511
N & S Roanoke Ave 44515
Robert Frost Dr 44511
Robin Hood Dr 44511
Robinwood Ave 44510
Robinwood Ln 44512
Rocco St 44509
Roche Ave 44505
Roche Way 44512
Rockdale Ave 44512
Rockland Dr 44512
Rockview Ave 44502
E & W Rockwell Rd 44515
Rockwood Dr 44505
Rogers Rd 44511
Romaine Ave 44512
Rome Dr 44515
Ron Ln 44505
Ron Park Pl 44512
Ronjoy Pl 44512
Ronlee Ln 44512
Roosevelt Dr 44504
Rose Pl & St 44506
Rose Lynn Pl 44514
Rosedale Ave 44511
Rosehedge Ct & Dr 44514
Rosemont Ave 44515
Rosewae Dr 44511
Rosewood Ave 44505
Rosewood Dr 44512
Rosewood Ln 44505
Roslyn Ave & Dr 44505
Rowland St 44510
Roxbury Ave 44502
Roy St 44509
Royal Palm Dr 44512
Ruby Cts 44515
Runnemede Dr 44512
Rush Blvd
2100-3799 44507
3900-4599 44512
Rush Cir 44512
Russell Ave
100-199 44515
400-599 44514
1900-2499 44509
Ruth Cir 44505
Rutland Ave 44515
Rutledge Dr 44505
Sable Ct 44512
Sabrina Dr 44512
Sackville St 44506
Saddlebrook Dr 44512
Saginaw Dr 44514
Sahara Trl 44514
Saint Albans Dr 44511
Saint Andrews Dr 44505
Saint Louis Ave
1-299 44507
300-699 44511
Salearin Rd 44514
Salinas Trl 44512
Salt Springs Rd
401-497 44509
499-3499 44509
3600-3699 44515
Sampson Dr & Rd 44505
Samuel Ave 44502
San Pedro Ct & Dr 44511
Sandalwood Ct & Ln 44511
Sandburg Dr 44511
Santa Fe Trl 44512
Santa Monica Cir & Dr 44505
Sarah St 44510
Saranac Ave 44505
S & W Saratoga Ave 44515
Scheetz St 44509
N Schenley Ave 44509
S Schenley Ave
1-1099 44509
1200-1598 44511
1600-4099 44511
School St 44502
Sciota Ave 44512
Scioto St 44505
Scotland Ave 44512
E Scott St 44505
W Scott St 44502
Sedonia Ln 44509
Seifert Ave 44505
Selkirk Ave 44511
Selma Ave 44504
Sena Ln 44514
Seneca St 44510
Sequoya Dr 44514
Shadeland Dr 44512
Shadow Creek Dr 44512
Shadow Oak Dr 44515
Shady Rd 44505
Shady Glen Trl 44514
Shady Run Rd 44502
Shadyside Dr 44512
Shalisma Dr 44509
Shannon Ave 44505
Sharlene Dr 44511
Sharon Dr 44512
Sharrott Rd 44514
Shaw Ave 44505
Shawbutte St 44514
Shawnee Trl 44511
Sheban Dr 44511
Sheffield Dr 44515
Shehy St 44506
Shelbourne Dr 44511
Shelby Rd 44511
Sheldon Ave 44512
S Shendow St 44501
Shepherds Rdg 44514
Sheridan Rd
1-197 44514
199-399 44514
3200-3899 44502
3900-6399 44514
Sherwood Ave 44511
Shetland Ln 44514
Shields Rd
1-499 44512
800-1198 44511
1200-1499 44511
Shirley Rd 44502
S Shore Dr 44512
Shorehaven Dr 44512
Shores Dr 44514
Short St 44504
Shutrump Ct 44515
Sierra Dr 44511
Sierra Madre Trl 44512
Sigle Ln 44514
Signature Cir & Dr 44515
Silica Rd 44515
Silliman St 44509
Silver Fox Dr 44512
Silver Meadow Ln 44512
Simon Rd 44512
Sinter Ct 44510
Skywae Dr 44511
Smith St
200-399 44502
6500-6699 44515
Smithfield St 44509
Smithsonian Ave 44505
Somerset Dr 44505
South Ave
1-99 44503
2-98 44501
700-3799 44502
3900-8399 44512
8400-10599 44514
Southbrooke Trl 44514
Southern Blvd
2800-3899 44507
3900-8599 44512
Southward Dr 44515
Southwestern Run 44514
Southwind Trl 44514
Southwoods Ave 44512
Sparkhill Ave 44505
Spartan Dr 44512
Spitler Rd 44514
Spring Cmn 44503
E Spring St 44502
W Spring St 44502
Spring Garden Ct & Dr 44512
Spring Hill Trl 44514
Spring Meadow Cir 44515
Spring Park Dr 44512
Springdale Ave 44505
Springfield Rd 44514
Sprucewood Ct & Dr 44515
Squires Ct 44505
Squirrel Hill Ct & Dr 44512
Staatz Dr 44511
Stacey St 44505
Stadium Dr 44512
Stadler Ave & Ct 44512
Stafford Ave 44512
Stafford St 44506
Stambaugh Ct 44502
Stanford Ave 44515
Stansbury Dr 44510
Stanton Ave 44512
Stanton St 44505
Star St 44505
Stark Dr 44515
State St 44506
Staunton Dr 44505
Steel St 44509
Stephens St 44509
Sterling Ave 44515
Stewart Ave 44505
Stiles Ave 44505
Stillson Pl 44512
Stocker Ave 44505
Stoner Ave 44514
Stones Throw Ave 44514
Stoney Creek Ct & Dr 44512
Stoney Ridge Dr 44515
Stonington Dr 44505
Straley Ln 44511
Stratford Rd 44512
Stratmore Ave 44511
Strausbaugh Ave 44505
Struthers Rd 44514
Struthers Coitsville Rd 44505
Struthers Liberty Rd 44505
Stuart Ave 44512
Sturbridge Pl 44514
Sugar Cane Dr 44512
Sugar Creek Dr 44512
Sugartree Dr 44512
Summer St 44511
Summerland Trl 44514
Suncrest Ct & Dr 44514
Sunnybrooke Dr 44511
Sunset Blvd
3700-3799 44502
3900-4099 44512
Sunshine Ave 44505
Superior St 44510
Susan Cir 44511
Suzylinn Ave 44512
Swallow Hollow Dr 44514
Sycamore St 44505
Sylvia Ln 44511
Tacoma Ave 44505
Taft Ave 44502
Tala Dr 44514
Talbot Dr 44505
Tall Oaks Ln 44511
Tam O Shanter Dr 44514
Tamarisk Trl 44514
Tampa Ave 44502
Tangent St 44502
Tanglewood Dr
1300-1699 44505
6700-6899 44512
Tanner Ln 44515
Tara Ct & Dr 44514
Tarrytown Rd 44515
Taylor St 44502
Teakwood Dr 44512
Teamster Dr
1200-1299 44502
1300-1999 44510
Temple St 44510
Terra Bella Dr 44505
Terrace Dr 44512
Terraview Dr 44512
Thacher Ln 44515
Thalia Ave
1000-1299 44512
1500-2099 44514
The Ledges 44514
Theodore Ave 44505
Thorne St 44502
Thornhill Rd 44505
Thornton Ave 44505
Thunderbird Ct & Dr 44514
Thurber Ln 44509
Tiffany Blvd S 44514
Timber Ln 44511
Timberbrooke Trl 44514
Timbercrest St 44505
N & S Timberidge Dr 44515
Timothy Ln 44511
Timothy Knoll Ln 44514
Tioga Ave 44511
Tippecanoe Ave 44509
Tippecanoe Rd 44511
Tippwood Ct 44512
Tod Ave
700-999 44502
7700-8399 44512
Tod Ln
1-199 44505
200-699 44504
Tonti Ct 44506
Townsend Ave 44505
Tracey Ln 44509
Tracy Dr 44512
Trailwood Dr 44512
Traymore Ct & Dr 44511
Trenholm Rd 44512
Trenton Ave 44507
Trotter Dr 44512
Trotwood Dr 44512
N Truesdale Ave 44506
S Truesdale Ave 44506
Truesdale Rd 44511
Truman Ave 44505
Trumbull Ave & Ct 44505
Trussit Ave 44505
Tudor Ln 44512
Tulane Ave 44515
Turin St 44510
Turnberry Dr 44512
N & S Turner Rd 44515
Tuscany Crk, Ct & Dr 44514
Tuxford Ct 44515
Twin Oaks Ct 44514
Tyrell St 44509
Uber Ave 44506
Union St 44502
Unity Rd 44514
University Plz 44502
Upland Ave
1-199 44505
200-299 44504
Upton Rd 44509
Utilis Ave 44511
Valerie Dr 44502
Valiant Dr 44514
Valla St 44505
Valley St
200-299 44505
900-1299 44506
Valley View Dr 44512
Van Dr 44514
Van Dyke St 44505
Vassar Ave 44515
Vaughn Ave 44505
Velma Ct 44512
Venloe Dr 44514
Ventura Dr 44505
Vermont Ave 44512
Vernette Ave 44515
Vernon St 44506
Verona Ave 44506
Vestal Rd 44509
Via Atillio 44514
Via Bellagio 44514
Via Cassia 44514
Via Mount Carmel Ave 44505
Via Siena 44514
Viall Rd 44515
Victor Ave 44505
Victor Ct 44515
Victoria Rd 44515
Victoria St 44510
Victoria East Rd 44515
Victory Hill Ln 44515
Vienna Ave 44505
Village Cir 44514
Vindicator Sq 44503
Vineland Pl 44512
E Viola Ave 44515
W Viola Ave 44515
Viola St 44505
Virginia Ave 44510
Virginia Dr 44515
Virginia Trl 44505
Vittoria Ave 44505
Vollmer Dr 44511
Volney Rd 44511
Wabash Ave 44502
Waggaman Cir 44512
Wakefield Ave 44514
Walden Ct 44509
Walker Ct 44514
Walker Mill Rd 44514
Wallace St 44502
Walnut St 44512
N Walnut St
1-299 44503
300-599 44505
601-899 44505
S Walnut St
1-99 44501
2-198 44503
Walnut Trce 44515
Wampum Dr 44511
Wardle Ave 44505
Warren Ave 44514
E Warren Ave 44507
W Warren Ave
1-299 44507
300-799 44511
Warren Ct 44507

Warren Pl 44507
Warwick Ave 44505
Waseka Ln 44512
Washington Blvd 44512
Washington Square Dr . 44515
Water St 44514
Watt St
1-99 44503
200-499 44505
Waverly Ave 44509
Wayne Ave 44502
Wayside Dr 44502
Weathered Wood Trl ... 44514
E Webb Rd 44515
W Webb Rd 44515
Webb St 44505
Webster Ave 44512
Wedgewood Dr 44511
Wellington Ave 44509
Wells Ct 44502
N & S Wendover Ave & Cir 44511
Wendy Ln 44514
Werner St 44502
Wesley Ave 44509
N West Ave 44502
S West Ave 44502
West Blvd 44512
Westchester Dr 44515
Western Pl 44515
E & W Western Reserve Rd 44514
Westfield Dr 44512
Westgate Blvd 44515
Westhampton Dr 44515
Westminster Ave 44515
Westmont Dr 44515
Weston Ave 44514
Westport Cir & Dr 44511
Westview Dr 44512
Westwind Pl 44515
Westwood Dr 44515
Whippoorwill Ln 44511
Whippoorwill Way 44505
Whirlaway Cir 44515
White Beech Ln 44511
White House Ln 44512
Whitman Ln 44505
Whitney Ave N & S 44509
Whittier Ct 44514
Wick Ave
1-399 44503
500-699 44502
700-1799 44505
Wick Oval 44502
N & S Wickliffe Cir 44515
Wilbur Ave 44502
Wilcox Rd 44515
Wilcox St 44509
Wilda Ave 44512
Wildfern Dr 44505
Wildflower Ln 44514
Wildwood Dr
1-899 44512
6000-6898 44514
Wilkinson Ave 44509
Wilkoff St 44515
Willard St 44505
Williams St 44502
Williamson Ave
1-499 44507
501-517 44502
519-799 44502
Willis Ave
1-299 44507
300-699 44511
Willow Ct 44505
Willow Dr 44512
Willow St 44506
Willow Crest Ave 44515
Wilma Ave 44512
Wilmette Ln 44505
Wilshire Dr 44511
Wilson Ave 44506
Wilton Ave 44505
Winchester Ave 44509
Windel Way 44512
Windemere Dr & Pl 44514
Windham Ct 44512
Windpoint Trl 44514
Windsor Ave 44502
Windsor Rd 44512
Winfield St 44505
Wingate Rd 44514
Winged Foot Dr 44512
Winona Dr 44511
Winston Ave 44509
Winter Ridge Ct 44515
Winterberry Dr 44512
Winterpark Ave 44515
Winthrop Dr 44515
Winton Ave 44505
Wirt Blvd 44510
Wiseman St 44507
Withers Dr 44512
Wolcott Dr 44512
Wolosyn Cir 44514
Wood Ave 44512
E Wood St 44503
W Wood St
1-199 44503
200-300 44502
302-398 44502
Woodbine Ave E & W .. 44505
Woodcrest Ave 44505
Woodfield Ct 44512
Woodford Ave 44511
Woodgate St 44515
Woodhurst Dr 44515
E Woodland Ave 44502
W Woodland Ave 44502
Woodland Cir 44514
Woodland Dr 44514
Woodland Trce 44515
Woodlawn Ave 44514
Woodleigh Ct & Ln 44511
Woodmere Dr 44515
Woodridge Ct & Dr 44515
Woodrow Ave 44512
Woodside Ave 44505
Woodview Ave 44512
Woodward Ave 44514
N Worthington St 44510
S Worthington St 44502
Wyandot Ln 44502
Wychwood Ln 44512
Wydesteel Ave 44505
Wymer Ct 44507
Wyndclift Cir & Pl 44515
Yakata Dora Dr 44511
Yarmouth Ln 44512
Yellow Creek Dr 44514
Yolanda Dr
1000-1599 44515
1600-1699 44511
York Ave 44512
N & S Yorkshire Blvd ... 44515
Yorktown Ln 44515
Youngstown Hubbard Rd 44505
Youngstown Pittsburgh Rd 44514
Youngstown Poland Rd 44514
Yvonne Dr 44505
Zander Dr 44511
Zedaker St 44502
Zents Ave 44505

NUMBERED STREETS

1st St 44515
1500-1699 44509
2nd St
1-99 44514
1500-1699 44509
3rd St
1-299 44515
1500-1699 44509
5th Ave
1-100 44503
102-198 44503
200-400 44502
402-798 44502
801-833 44504
835-2399 44504
2400-5199 44505
5th St 44514
5th Avenue Ct 44504
76 Dr 44515

ZANESVILLE OH

General Delivery 43701

POST OFFICE BOXES MAIN OFFICE STATIONS AND BRANCHES

Box No.s
All PO Boxes 43702

NAMED STREETS

All Street Addresses 43701

NUMBERED STREETS

All Street Addresses 43701

Oklahoma

People QuickFacts	Oklahoma	USA
Population, 2013 estimate	3,850,568	316,128,839
Population, 2010 (April 1) estimates base	3,751,357	308,747,716
Population, percent change, April 1, 2010 to July 1, 2013	2.6%	2.4%
Population, 2010	3,751,351	308,745,538
Persons under 5 years, percent, 2013	6.9%	6.3%
Persons under 18 years, percent, 2013	24.6%	23.3%
Persons 65 years and over, percent, 2013	14.3%	14.1%
Female persons, percent, 2013	50.5%	50.8%
White alone, percent, 2013 (a)	75.4%	77.7%
Black or African American alone, percent, 2013 (a)	7.7%	13.2%
American Indian and Alaska Native alone, percent, 2013 (a)	9.0%	1.2%
Asian alone, percent, 2013 (a)	2.0%	5.3%
Native Hawaiian and Other Pacific Islander alone, percent, 2013 (a)	0.2%	0.2%
Two or More Races, percent, 2013	5.8%	2.4%
Hispanic or Latino, percent, 2013 (b)	9.6%	17.1%
White alone, not Hispanic or Latino, percent, 2013	67.5%	62.6%
Living in same house 1 year & over, percent, 2008-2012	82.1%	84.8%
Foreign born persons, percent, 2008-2012	5.5%	12.9%
Language other than English spoken at home, pct age 5+, 2008-2012	9.2%	20.5%
High school graduate or higher, percent of persons age 25+, 2008-2012	86.2%	85.7%
Bachelor's degree or higher, percent of persons age 25+, 2008-2012	23.2%	28.5%
Veterans, 2008-2012	322,008	21,853,912
Mean travel time to work (minutes), workers age 16+, 2008-2012	21	25.4
Housing units, 2013	1,682,256	132,802,859
Homeownership rate, 2008-2012	67.5%	65.5%
Housing units in multi-unit structures, percent, 2008-2012	15.1%	25.9%
Median value of owner-occupied housing units, 2008-2012	$110,800	$181,400
Households, 2008-2012	1,439,292	115,226,802
Persons per household, 2008-2012	2.53	2.61
Per capita money income in past 12 months (2012 dollars), 2008-2012	$24,046	$28,051
Median household income, 2008-2012	$44,891	$53,046
Persons below poverty level, percent, 2008-2012	16.6%	14.9%

Business QuickFacts	Oklahoma	USA
Private nonfarm establishments, 2012	90,954	7,431,808
Private nonfarm employment, 2012	1,305,183	115,938,468
Private nonfarm employment, percent change, 2011-2012	3.5%	2.2%
Nonemployer establishments, 2012	266,586	22,735,915
Total number of firms, 2007	333,797	27,092,908
Black-owned firms, percent, 2007	3.1%	7.1%
American Indian- and Alaska Native-owned firms, percent, 2007	6.3%	0.9%
Asian-owned firms, percent, 2007	2.0%	5.7%
Native Hawaiian and Other Pacific Islander-owned firms, percent, 2007	0.0%	0.1%
Hispanic-owned firms, percent, 2007	2.3%	8.3%
Women-owned firms, percent, 2007	25.3%	28.8%
Manufacturers shipments, 2007 ($1000)	60,681,358	5,319,456,312
Merchant wholesaler sales, 2007 ($1000)	48,074,682	4,174,286,516
Retail sales, 2007 ($1000)	43,095,353	3,917,663,456
Retail sales per capita, 2007	$11,931	$12,990
Accommodation and food services sales, 2007 ($1000)	5,106,585	613,795,732
Building permits, 2012	11,930	829,658

Geography QuickFacts	Oklahoma	USA
Land area in square miles, 2010	68,594.92	3,531,905.43
Persons per square mile, 2010	54.7	87.4
FIPS Code	40	

(a) Includes persons reporting only one race.
(b) Hispanics may be of any race, so also are included in applicable race categories.
FN: Footnote on this item for this area in place of data
NA: Not available
D: Suppressed to avoid disclosure of confidential information
X: Not applicable
S: Suppressed; does not meet publication standards
Z: Value greater than zero but less than half unit of measure shown
F: Fewer than 100 firms
Source: US Census Bureau State & County QuickFacts

Oklahoma

3 DIGIT ZIP CODE MAP

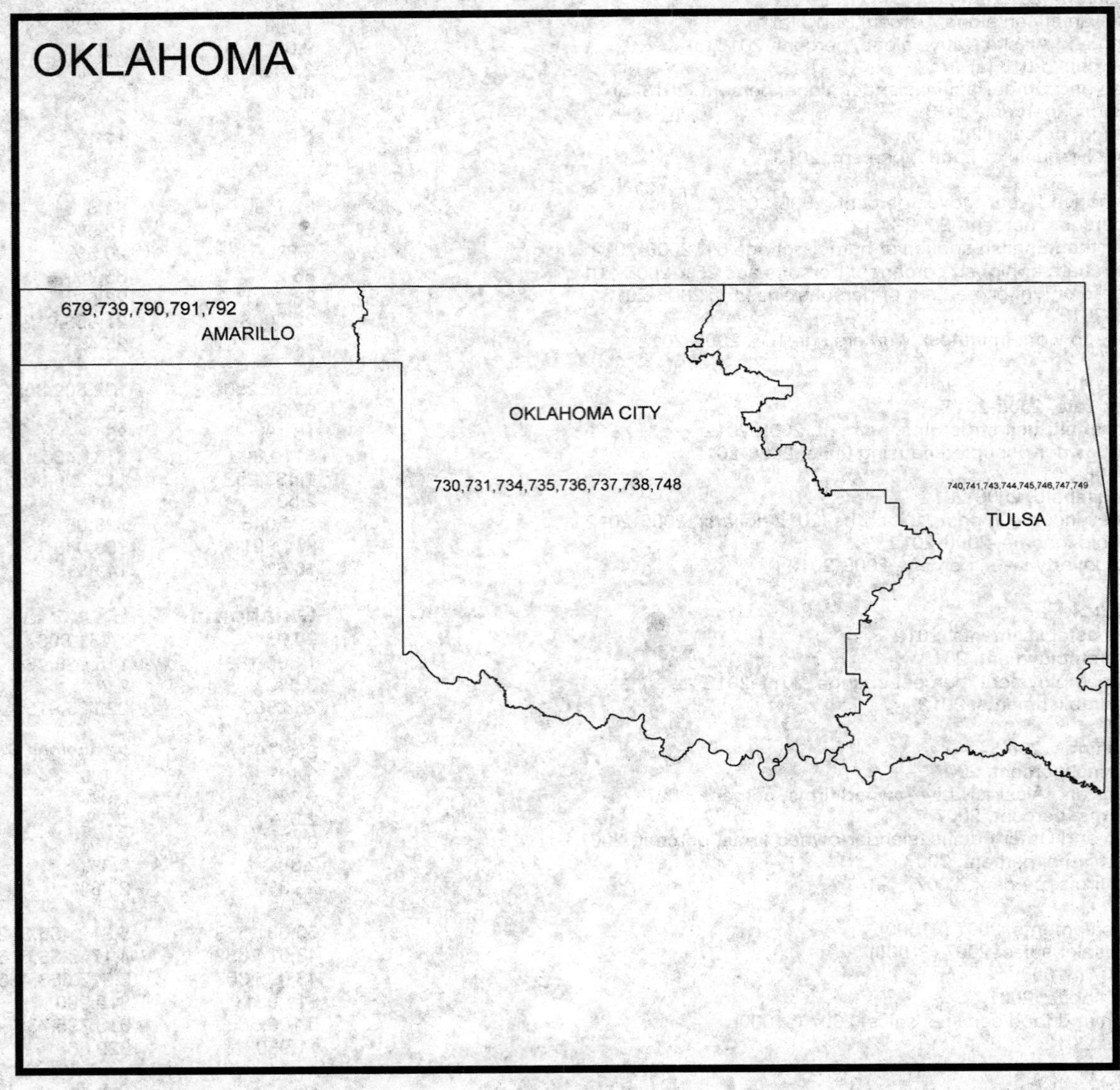

Oklahoma

(Abbreviation: OK)

Post Office, County — ZIP Code

Places with more than one ZIP code are listed in capital letters, See pages indicated.

Achille, Bryan 74720
ADA, Pontotoc (See Page 3081)
Adair, Mayes 74330
Adams, Texas 73901
Addington, Jefferson 73520
Afton, Ottawa 74331
Agra, Lincoln 74824
Albany, Bryan 74721
Albert, Caddo 73001
Albion, Pushmataha 74521
Alderson, Pittsburg 74522
Alex, Grady 73002
Aline, Alfalfa 73716
Allen, Pontotoc 74825
ALTUS, Jackson (See Page 3081)
Altus Afb, Jackson 73523
Alva, Woods 73717
Amber, Grady 73004
Ames, Major 73718
Amorita, Alfalfa 73719
Anadarko, Caddo 73005
Antlers, Pushmataha 74523
Apache, Caddo 73006
Arapaho, Custer 73620
Arcadia, Oklahoma 73007
ARDMORE, Carter (See Page 3081)
Arkoma, Le Flore 74901
Armstrong, Bryan 74726
Arnett, Ellis 73832
Asher, Pottawatomie 74826
Ashland, Hughes 74570
Atoka, Atoka 74525
Atwood, Hughes 74827
Avant, Osage 74001
Avard, Woods 73717
Bache, Pittsburg 74501
Baker, Beaver 73950
Balko, Beaver 73931
Barnsdall, Osage 74002
BARTLESVILLE, Washington (See Page 3081)
Battiest, Mccurtain 74722
Bearden, Okfuskee 74859
Beaver, Beaver 73932
Beggs, Okmulgee 74421
Bennington, Bryan 74723
Bernice, Ottawa 74331
Bessie, Washita 73622
Bethany, Oklahoma 73008
Bethel, Mccurtain 74724
Bethel Acres, Pottawatomie 74801
Big Cabin, Craig 74332
Billings, Noble 74630
Bing, Pontotoc 74820
Binger, Caddo 73009
Bison, Garfield 73720
Bixby, Tulsa 74008
Blackburn, Pawnee 74058
Blackwell, Kay 74631
Blair, Jackson 73526
Blanchard, Mcclain 73010
Blanco, Pittsburg 74528
Blocker, Pittsburg 74529
Bluejacket, Craig 74333
Boise City, Cimarron 73933
Bokchito, Bryan 74726
Bokoshe, Le Flore 74930
Boley, Okfuskee 74829
Boswell, Choctaw 74727
Bowlegs, Seminole 74830
Bowring, Osage 74056
Boynton, Muskogee 74422
Bradley, Grady 73011
Braggs, Muskogee 74423
Braman, Kay 74632
Bray, Stephens 73055
Bridgeport, Caddo 73047
Bristow, Creek 74010
BROKEN ARROW, Tulsa (See Page 3082)
Broken Bow, Mccurtain 74728
Bromide, Johnston 74530
Buffalo, Harper 73834
Bunch, Adair 74931
Burbank, Osage 74633
Burlington, Alfalfa 73722
Burneyville, Love 73430
Burns Flat, Washita 73624
Butler, Custer 73625
Byars, Mcclain 74831
Byng, Pontotoc 74820
Byron, Alfalfa 73722
Cache, Comanche 73527
Caddo, Bryan 74729
Calera, Bryan 74730
Calumet, Canadian 73014
Calvin, Hughes 74531
Camargo, Dewey 73835
Cameron, Le Flore 74932
Canadian, Pittsburg 74425
Caney, Atoka 74533
Canton, Blaine 73724
Canute, Washita 73626
Capron, Woods 73717
Cardin, Ottawa 74335
Carmen, Alfalfa 73726
Carnegie, Caddo 73015
Carney, Lincoln 74832
Carrier, Garfield 73727
Carter, Beckham 73627
Cartwright, Bryan 74731
Cashion, Kingfisher 73016
Castle, Okfuskee 74833
Catoosa, Rogers 74015
Cement, Caddo 73017
Centrahoma, Coal 74534
Central High, Stephens 73055
Centralia, Craig 74301
Chandler, Lincoln 74834
Chattanooga, Comanche 73528
Checotah, Mcintosh 74426
Chelsea, Rogers 74016
Cherokee, Alfalfa 73728
Chester, Major 73838
Cheyenne, Roger Mills 73628
CHICKASHA, Grady (See Page 3084)
Choctaw, Oklahoma 73020
Chouteau, Mayes 74337
Cimarron City, Logan 73028
CLAREMORE, Rogers (See Page 3084)
Clarita, Coal 74535
Clayton, Pushmataha 74536
Clearview, Okfuskee 74880
Cleo Springs, Major 73729
Cleora, Ottawa 74331
Cleveland, Pawnee 74020
Clinton, Custer 73601
Coalgate, Coal 74538
Colbert, Bryan 74733
Colcord, Delaware 74338
Cole, Mcclain 73010
Coleman, Johnston 73432
Collinsville, Tulsa 74021
Colony, Washita 73021
Comanche, Stephens 73529
Commerce, Ottawa 74339
Concho, Canadian 73022
Connerville, Johnston 74836
Cookson, Cherokee 74427
Cooperton, Kiowa 73564
Copan, Washington 74022
Cordell, Washita 73632
Corn, Washita 73024
Cornish, Jefferson 73456
Council Hill, Muskogee 74428
Countyline, Stephens 73425
Covington, Garfield 73730
Coweta, Wagoner 74429
Cowlington, Haskell 74941
Coyle, Logan 73027
Crawford, Roger Mills 73638
Crescent, Logan 73028
Cromwell, Seminole 74837
Crowder, Pittsburg 74430
Cushing, Payne 74023
Custer City, Custer 73639
Cyril, Caddo 73029
Dacoma, Woods 73731
Daisy, Atoka 74540
Dale, Pottawatomie 74851
Davenport, Lincoln 74026
Davidson, Tillman 73530
Davis, Murray 73030
Deer Creek, Grant 74636
Del City (See Oklahoma City)
Delaware, Nowata 74027
Depew, Creek 74028
Devol, Cotton 73531
Dewar, Okmulgee 74431
Dewey, Washington 74029
Dibble, Mcclain 73031
Dill City, Washita 73641
Disney, Mayes 74340
Dougherty, Murray 73032
Douglas, Garfield 73733
Dover, Kingfisher 73734
Drummond, Garfield 73735
Drumright, Creek 74030
Duke, Jackson 73532
DUNCAN, Stephens (See Page 3086)
DURANT, Bryan (See Page 3086)
Durham, Roger Mills 73642
Dustin, Hughes 74839
Eagle City, Dewey 73658
Eagletown, Mccurtain 74734
Eakly, Caddo 73033
Earlsboro, Pottawatomie 74840
EDMOND, Oklahoma (See Page 3087)
El Reno, Canadian 73036
Eldorado, Jackson 73537
Elgin, Comanche 73538
ELK CITY, Beckham (See Page 3092)
Elmer, Jackson 73539
Elmore City, Garvin 73433
Elmwood, Beaver 73932
Empire City, Stephens 73533
ENID, Garfield (See Page 3092)
Erick, Beckham 73645
Erin Springs, Garvin 73052
Etowah, Cleveland 73068
Eucha, Delaware 74342
Eufaula, Mcintosh 74432
Fair Oaks, Rogers 74015
Fairfax, Osage 74637
Fairland, Ottawa 74343
Fairmont, Garfield 73736
Fairview, Major 73737
Fallis, Lincoln 74881
Fanshawe, Le Flore 74935
Fargo, Ellis 73840
Farris, Atoka 74525
Faxon, Comanche 73540
Fay, Dewey 73646
Felt, Cimarron 73937
Finley, Pushmataha 74543
Fittstown, Pontotoc 74842
Fitzhugh, Pontotoc 74843
Fletcher, Comanche 73541
Foraker, Osage 74652
Forest Park, Oklahoma 73121
Forgan, Beaver 73938
Fort Cobb, Caddo 73038
Fort Coffee, Le Flore 74959
Fort Gibson, Muskogee 74434
Fort Sill, Comanche 73503
Fort Supply, Woodward 73841
Fort Towson, Choctaw 74735
Foss, Washita 73647
Foster, Stephens 73434
Fox, Carter 73435
Foyil, Rogers 74031
Francis, Pontotoc 74844
Frederick, Tillman 73542
Freedom, Woods 73842
Ft Towson, Choctaw 74735
Gage, Ellis 73843
Gans, Sequoyah 74936
Garber, Garfield 73738
Garvin, Mccurtain 74736
Gate, Beaver 73844
Geary, Blaine 73040
Gene Autry, Carter 73436
Geronimo, Comanche 73543
Gerty, Hughes 74531
Glencoe, Payne 74032
Glenpool, Tulsa 74033
Golden, Mccurtain 74737
Goldsby, Mcclain 73093
Goltry, Alfalfa 73739
Goodwell, Texas 73939
Gore, Sequoyah 74435
Gotebo, Kiowa 73041
Gould, Harmon 73544
Gowen, Latimer 74545
Gracemont, Caddo 73042
Grady, Jefferson 73569
Graham, Carter 73437
Grand Lake Towne, Mayes 74349
Grandfield, Tillman 73546
Granite, Greer 73547
Grant, Choctaw 74738
Greenfield, Blaine 73043
GROVE, Delaware (See Page 3093)
Guthrie, Logan 73044
Guymon, Texas 73942
Haileyville, Pittsburg 74546
Hallett, Pawnee 74034
Hammon, Roger Mills 73650
Hanna, Mcintosh 74845
Harden City, Pontotoc 74871
Hardesty, Texas 73944
Harmon, Ellis 73832
Harrah, Oklahoma 73045
Hartshorne, Pittsburg 74547
Haskell, Muskogee 74436
Hastings, Jefferson 73548
Haworth, Mccurtain 74740
Haywood, Pittsburg 74501
Headrick, Jackson 73549
Healdton, Carter 73438
Heavener, Le Flore 74937
Helena, Alfalfa 73741
Hendrix, Bryan 74741
Hennepin, Carter 73444
Hennessey, Kingfisher 73742
Henryetta, Okmulgee 74437
Hickory, Pontotoc 74865
Hillsdale, Garfield 73743
Hinton, Caddo 73047
Hitchcock, Blaine 73744
Hitchita, Mcintosh 74438
Hobart, Kiowa 73651
Hodgen, Le Flore 74939
Hoffman, Okmulgee 74437
Holdenville, Hughes 74848
Hollis, Harmon 73550
Hollister, Tillman 73551
Hominy, Osage 74035
Honobia, Le Flore 74549
Hooker, Texas 73945
Hopeton, Woods 73746
Horntown, Hughes 74848
Howe, Le Flore 74940
Hoyt, Haskell 74440
Hoyt, Haskell 74472
Hugo, Choctaw 74743
Hulbert, Cherokee 74441
Hunter, Garfield 74640
Hydro, Caddo 73048
Idabel, Mccurtain 74745
Indiahoma, Comanche 73552
Indianola, Pittsburg 74442
Inola, Rogers 74036
Isabella, Major 73747
Jay, Delaware 74346
Jefferson, Grant 73759
Jenks, Tulsa 74037
Jennings, Pawnee 74038
Jet, Alfalfa 73749
Johnson, Pottawatomie 74801
Jones, Oklahoma 73049
Kansas, Delaware 74347
Kaw, Kay 74641
Kaw City, Kay 74641
Kellyville, Creek 74039
Kemp, Bryan 74747
Kendrick, Lincoln 74079
Kenefic, Johnston 74748
Kenton, Cimarron 73946
Keota, Haskell 74941
Ketchum, Mayes 74349
Keyes, Cimarron 73947
Kiamichi, Le Flore 74549
Kiefer, Creek 74041
Kingfisher, Kingfisher 73750
Kingston, Marshall 73439
Kinta, Haskell 74552
Kiowa, Pittsburg 74553
Knowles, Beaver 73844
Konawa, Seminole 74849
Krebs, Pittsburg 74554
Kremlin, Garfield 73753
Lahoma, Garfield 73754
Lake Aluma, Oklahoma 73121
Lamar, Hughes 74850
Lambert, Alfalfa 73728
Lamont, Grant 74643
Lane, Atoka 74555
Langley, Mayes 74350
Langston, Logan 73050
Laverne, Harper 73848
Lawrence Creek, Creek 74044
LAWTON, Comanche (See Page 3093)
Lebanon, Marshall 73440
Leedey, Dewey 73654
Leflore, Le Flore 74942
Lehigh, Coal 74556
Lenapah, Nowata 74042
Leon, Love 73441
Leonard, Tulsa 74043
Lequire, Haskell 74943
Lexington, Cleveland 73051
Lima, Seminole 74884
Lindsay, Garvin 73052
Loco, Stephens 73442
Locust Grove, Mayes 74352
Logan, Harper 73848
Lone Grove, Carter 73443
Lone Wolf, Kiowa 73655
Longdale, Blaine 73755
Lookeba, Caddo 73053
Loveland, Tillman 73553
Loyal, Kingfisher 73756
Lucien, Noble 73757
Luther, Oklahoma 73054
Macomb, Pottawatomie 74852
Madill, Marshall 73446
Manchester, Grant 73758
Mangum, Greer 73554
Manitou, Tillman 73555
Mannford, Creek 74044
Mannsville, Johnston 73447
Maramec, Pawnee 74045
Marble City, Sequoyah 74945
Marietta, Love 73448
Marland, Noble 74644
Marlow, Stephens 73055
Marshall, Logan 73056
Martha, Jackson 73556
Mason, Okfuskee 74859
Maud, Pottawatomie 74854
May, Harper 73851
Maysville, Garvin 73057
Mazie, Mayes 74337
Mc Millan, Marshall 73446
MCALESTER, Pittsburg (See Page 3095)
Mccurtain, Haskell 74944
Mcloud, Pottawatomie 74851
Mead, Bryan 73449
Medford, Grant 73759
Medicine Park, Comanche 73557
Meeker, Lincoln 74855
Meers, Comanche 73558
Meno, Major 73760
Meridian, Logan 73058
MIAMI, Ottawa (See Page 3095)
Midwest City (See Oklahoma City)
Milburn, Johnston 73450
Milfay, Creek 74046
Mill Creek, Johnston 74856
Millerton, Mccurtain 74750
Milo, Carter 73401
Minco, Grady 73059
Moffett, Sequoyah 74946
Monkey Island, Ottawa 74331
Monroe, Le Flore 74947
Moodys, Cherokee 74444
Moore (See Oklahoma City)
Mooreland, Woodward 73852
Morris, Okmulgee 74445
Morrison, Noble 73061
Mounds, Creek 74047
Mountain Park, Kiowa 73559
Mountain View, Kiowa 73062
Moyers, Pushmataha 74557
Muldrow, Sequoyah 74948
Mulhall, Logan 73063
Muse, Le Flore 74949
MUSKOGEE, Muskogee (See Page 3095)
Mustang, Canadian 73064
Mutual, Woodward 73853
Nardin, Kay 74646
Nash, Grant 73761
Nashoba, Pushmataha 74558
New Lima, Seminole 74884
Newalla, Cleveland 74857
Newcastle, Mcclain 73065
Newkirk, Kay 74647
Nichols Hills (See Oklahoma City)
Nicoma Park, Oklahoma 73066
Ninnekah, Grady 73067
Noble, Cleveland 73068
Norge, Grady 73018
NORMAN, Cleveland (See Page 3097)
North Enid, Garfield 73701
North Miami, Ottawa 74358
Nowata, Nowata 74048
Oakhurst, Tulsa 74050
Oakland, Marshall 73446
Oaks, Delaware 74359
Oakwood, Dewey 73658
Ochelata, Washington 74051
Octavia, Mccurtain 74957
Oilton, Creek 74052
Okarche, Kingfisher 73762
Okay, Wagoner 74446
Okeene, Blaine 73763
Okemah, Okfuskee 74859
OKLAHOMA CITY, Oklahoma (See Page 3100)
Okmulgee, Okmulgee 74447
Oktaha, Muskogee 74450
Olustee, Jackson 73560
Omega, Kingfisher 73764
Oologah, Rogers 74053
Optima, Texas 73945
Orienta, Major 73737
Orlando, Logan 73073
Osage, Osage 74054
Oscar, Jefferson 73561
Overbrook, Love 73453
Owasso, Tulsa 74055
Paden, Okfuskee 74860
Panama, Le Flore 74951

Panola, Latimer 74559
Paoli, Garvin 73074
Paradise Hill, Sequoyah 74435
Park Hill, Cherokee 74451
Pauls Valley, Garvin 73075
Pawhuska, Osage 74056
Pawnee, Pawnee 74058
Peckham, Kay 74647
Peggs, Cherokee 74452
Pensacola, Craig 74301
Peoria, Ottawa 74363
Perkins, Payne 74059
Pernell, Garvin 73433
Perry, Noble 73077
Pharoah, Okfuskee 74880
Picher, Ottawa 74360
Pickens, Mccurtain 74752
Piedmont, Canadian 73078
Pittsburg, Pittsburg 74560
Platter, Bryan 74753
Pocasset, Grady 73079
Pocola, Le Flore 74902
PONCA CITY, Kay
(See Page 3113)
Pond Creek, Grant 73766
Pontotoc, Pontotoc 74820
Pooleville, Carter 73401
Porter, Wagoner 74454
Porum, Muskogee 74455
Poteau, Le Flore 74953
Prague, Lincoln 74864
Preston, Okmulgee 74456
Proctor, Adair 74457
Prue, Osage 74060
PRYOR, Mayes
(See Page 3114)
Purcell, Mcclain 73080
Putnam, Dewey 73659
Quapaw, Ottawa 74363
Quinton, Pittsburg 74561
Ralston, Pawnee 74650
Ramona, Washington 74061
Randlett, Cotton 73562
Ratliff City, Carter 73481
Rattan, Pushmataha 74562
Ravia, Johnston 73455
Red Oak, Latimer 74563
Red Rock, Noble 74651
Redbird, Wagoner 74458
Reed, Greer 73554
Renfrow, Grant 73759
Rentiesville, Mcintosh 74459
Reydon, Roger Mills 73660
Ringling, Jefferson 73456
Ringold, Mccurtain 74754
Ringwood, Major 73768
Ripley, Payne 74062
Rocky, Washita 73661
Roff, Pontotoc 74865
Roland, Sequoyah 74954
Roosevelt, Kiowa 73564
Rose, Mayes 74364
Rosedale, Mcclain 74831
Rosston, Harper 73855
Rubottom, Carter 73463
Rufe, Mccurtain 74755
Rush Springs, Grady 73082
Ryan, Jefferson 73565
S Coffeyville, Nowata 74072
Saint Louis, Pottawatomie 74866
Salina, Mayes 74365
Sallisaw, Sequoyah 74955
Sand Springs, Tulsa 74063
SAPULPA, Creek
(See Page 3114)
Sasakwa, Seminole 74867
Savanna, Pittsburg 74565
Sawyer, Choctaw 74756
Sayre, Beckham 73662
Schulter, Okmulgee 74460
Seiling, Dewey 73663
Selman, Harper 73834
SEMINOLE, Seminole
(See Page 3115)
Sentinel, Washita 73664
Shady Grove, Pawnee 74020
Shady Point, Le Flore 74956
Shamrock, Creek 74068
Sharon, Woodward 73857
Shattuck, Ellis 73858
SHAWNEE, Pottawatomie
(See Page 3115)
Shidler, Osage 74652
Silo, Bryan 74701
Skedee, Pawnee 74058
Skiatook, Tulsa 74070
Slaughterville, Cleveland 73051
Slick, Creek 74071
Smith Village, Oklahoma 73115
Smithville, Mccurtain 74957
Snow, Pushmataha 74567
Snyder, Kiowa 73566
Soper, Choctaw 74759
Southard, Blaine 73770
Sparks, Lincoln 74869
Spaulding, Hughes 74848
Spavinaw, Mayes 74366
Spencer, Oklahoma 73084
Spencerville, Choctaw 74760
Sperry, Tulsa 74073
Spiro, Le Flore 74959
Sportsmen Acres, Mayes 74361
Springer, Carter 73458
Sterling, Comanche 73567
Stidham, Mcintosh 74461
Stigler, Haskell 74462
STILLWATER, Payne
(See Page 3116)
Stilwell, Adair 74960
Stonewall, Pontotoc 74871
Strang, Mayes 74367
Stratford, Garvin 74872
Stringtown, Atoka 74569
Strong City, Roger Mills 73628
Stroud, Lincoln 74079
Stuart, Hughes 74570
Sugden, Jefferson 73573
Sulphur, Murray 73086
Summit, Muskogee 74401
Sweetwater, Roger Mills 73666
Swink, Choctaw 74761
Taft, Muskogee 74463
TAHLEQUAH, Cherokee
(See Page 3118)
Talala, Rogers 74080
Talihina, Latimer 74571
Taloga, Dewey 73667
Tatums, Carter 73487
Tecumseh, Pottawatomie 74873
Temple, Cotton 73568
Terlton, Pawnee 74081
Terral, Jefferson 73561
Terral, Jefferson 73569
Texhoma, Texas 73949
Texola, Beckham 73668
Thackerville, Love 73459
The Village, Oklahoma 73120
Thomas, Custer 73669
Tinker Afb, Oklahoma 73145
Tipton, Tillman 73570
Tishomingo, Johnston 73460
Tom, Mccurtain 74740
Tonkawa, Kay 74653
Tribbey, Pottawatomie 74878
Tryon, Lincoln 74875
Tullahassee, Wagoner 74454
TULSA, Tulsa
(See Page 3119)
Tupelo, Coal 74572
Turpin, Beaver 73950
Tuskahoma, Pushmataha 74574
Tussy, Carter 73488
Tuttle, Grady 73089
Twin Oaks, Delaware 74368
Tyrone, Texas 73951
Union City, Canadian 73090
Valley Park, Rogers 74017
Valliant, Mccurtain 74764
Velma, Stephens 73491
Vera, Washington 74082
Verden, Grady 73092
Vernon, Mcintosh 74845
Vian, Sequoyah 74962
Vici, Dewey 73859
Village, Oklahoma 73120
Vinita, Craig 74301
Vinson, Harmon 73571
Wade, Bryan 74723
WAGONER, Wagoner
(See Page 3126)
Wainwright, Muskogee 74468
Wakita, Grant 73771
Walters, Cotton 73572
Wanette, Pottawatomie 74878
Wann, Nowata 74083
Wapanucka, Johnston 73461
Wardville, Pittsburg 74576
Warner, Muskogee 74469
Warr Acres
(See Oklahoma City)
Warwick, Lincoln 74881
Washington, Mcclain 73093
Washita, Caddo 73005
Watonga, Blaine 73772
Watson, Mccurtain 74963
Watts, Adair 74964
Waukomis, Garfield 73773
Waurika, Jefferson 73573
Wayne, Mcclain 73095
Waynoka, Woods 73860
Weatherford, Custer 73096
Webb City, Osage 74652
Webbers Falls, Muskogee 74470
Welch, Craig 74369
Weleetka, Okfuskee 74880
Welling, Cherokee 74471
Wellston, Lincoln 74881
Welty, Okfuskee 74833
West Siloam Springs,
Delaware 74338
Westville, Adair 74965
Wetumka, Hughes 74883
Wewoka, Seminole 74884
Wheatland, Oklahoma 73097
White Oak, Craig 74301
Whitefield, Haskell 74472
Whitesboro, Le Flore 74577
Wilburton, Latimer 74578
Willow, Greer 73673
Wilson, Carter 73463
Winchester, Okmulgee 74421
Wister, Le Flore 74966
Woodlawn Park, Oklahoma 73008
WOODWARD, Woodward
(See Page 3126)
Wright City, Mccurtain 74766
Wyandotte, Ottawa 74370
Wynnewood, Garvin 73098
Wynona, Osage 74084
Yale, Payne 74085
Yarnaby, Bryan 74741
Yeager, Hughes 74848
YUKON, Canadian
(See Page 3126)

ADA OK

General Delivery 74820

POST OFFICE BOXES MAIN OFFICE STATIONS AND BRANCHES

Box No.s
All PO Boxes 74821

RURAL ROUTES

01, 02, 03, 04, 05, 06, 07, 08, 09, 10 74820

HIGHWAY CONTRACTS

64 74820

NAMED STREETS

All Street Addresses 74820

NUMBERED STREETS

N & W 1st Pl & St 74820
SW, E, N & W 2nd Pl & St 74820
E & W 3rd 74820
E & W 4th 74820
NE, W & E 5th Ave & St 74820
E & W 6th 74820
W & E 7th Ave, Pl & St 74820
E & W 8th 74820
E & W 9th Ave & St 74820
NW, SE, E, NE & W 10th St 74820
E 11th St 74820
E 12th Ave 74820
E 12th St
100-200 74820
131-131 74821
201-2999 74820
202-2998 74820
W 12th St 74820
E & W 13th Ave & St 74820
E, S & W 14th Pl & St 74820
E & W 15th 74820
E & W 16th 74820
E & W 17th 74820
E & W 18th 74820
W 19th St 74820
E & W 20th 74820
E & W 21st 74820
E & W 22nd 74820
W 23rd St 74820
W 24th St 74820
E 26th St 74820
E 30th St 74820
E 32nd St 74820
W 33rd St 74820

ALTUS OK

General Delivery 73521

POST OFFICE BOXES MAIN OFFICE STATIONS AND BRANCHES

Box No.s
All PO Boxes 73522

RURAL ROUTES

01, 02, 03, 04 73521

NAMED STREETS

All Street Addresses 73521

NUMBERED STREETS

All Street Addresses 73521

ARDMORE OK

General Delivery 73401

POST OFFICE BOXES MAIN OFFICE STATIONS AND BRANCHES

Box No.s
A - E 73402
1 - 2606 73402
5001 - 6058 73403

RURAL ROUTES

01, 02, 03, 04, 05, 06, 07 73401

HIGHWAY CONTRACTS

60, 70, 71, 72 73401

NAMED STREETS

All Street Addresses 73401

NUMBERED STREETS

1st Ave NW 73401
1st Ave SE 73401
1st Ave SW
100-299 73401
208-208 73403
208-208 73402
301-1799 73401
400-1798 73401
2nd Ave NE 73401
3rd Ave NE 73401
4th Ave NE 73401
5th Ave NW 73401
6th Ave NE 73401
7th Ave NE 73401
8th Ave NE 73401
9th Ave NE 73401
10th Ave NE 73401
11th Ave NE 73401
12th Ave NE 73401
13th Ave NE 73401
14th Ave NW 73401
15th Ave & Pl 73401
16th Ave NW 73401

BARTLESVILLE OK

General Delivery 74003

POST OFFICE BOXES MAIN OFFICE STATIONS AND BRANCHES

Box No.s
E - R 74005
1 - 2572 74005
3001 - 4078 74006
3338 - 9000 74005

RURAL ROUTES

03, 05, 07 74003
01, 02, 04, 06, 07 74006

NAMED STREETS

Aaron St 74003
Abbey Rd 74006
Acorn Dr 74003
SE Adams Blvd
100-1299 74003
2100-6999 74006
SW Adams Blvd 74003
SE Adams Rd 74006
NW & SW Adeline Ave 74003
Admiral Ct 74006
NW Aledo Dr 74003
Allen Ct 74006
Allen Rd 74003
Amherst Dr 74006
Apple Alley St 74003
Arbor Dr 74006
S Armstrong Ave 74003
Ashbrook Dr 74006
Ashford Ct & Dr 74006
Ashton Ln 74006
Aspen 74006
Audubon Ct 74006
Autumn Cir & Ct 74006
Avalon Rd 74006
NE & SE Avondale Ave 74006
N & S Barbara Ave 74006
Barlow Ct, Dr & Pl 74006
Barnett Ave, Ct & Pl 74006
Bartles Rd 74006
Baylor Ct, Dr & Pl 74006
Beacon Ct 74006
Beck Dr 74006
Beecher Ln 74006
Belmont Rd 74006
Berryhill Ln 74003
NE & SE Bison Rd 74006
Blackstone Ct 74006
Blake Cir 74006
Boardwalk Cir & Ct 74006
Bonnie Lee Ct & Ln 74006
Boston Ave 74006
Bow Dr 74006
Bowring Rd 74003
Bradbury Ct 74006
Braddock Rd 74006
Bradley Pl 74006
Brentwood Rd 74003
Briar Dr 74006
Briarwood Dr 74006
Bridgett Ct 74006
Bridle Rd 74006
Brighton Ln 74006
S Brinerli Ave 74003
Brock Dr 74006
Brookhollow Ct & Ln 74006
Brookline Dr & Pl 74006
Brookside Pkwy 74006
Bryce Cir 74006
Buckskin Ct 74006
N & S Bucy Ave 74003
Burlingame Pl & Rdg 74006
Bynum Rd 74006
Cambridge Ct 74006
Camden Ct 74006
Camelot Ct & Dr 74006
Candlestick Ct 74006
Canterbury Ct 74006
Canyon View Dr 74003
Cara Lee Ln 74006
Carlyle Rd 74003
Carol Rd 74003
Carole Ct 74006
Carolyn Pl 74003
NW & SW Cass Ave 74003
Castle Ct & Rd 74006
Caterank Dr 74006
Cedar Ct & St 74006
Centre Rd 74003
Chapel Hill Ct & Rd 74006
Charleston Dr 74006
Cherokee Ave & Pl 74003
Cherokee Hills Cir, Ct, Dr & Pl 74006
Cherry Ln 74003
Chestnut Ct 74003
Chestnut Hl 74006
N, S, E & W Cheyenne Ave & Pl 74003
N & S Chickasaw Ave 74003
Chickering Ct 74006
Chisholm Cir 74006
N & S Choctaw Ave 74003
N & SE Cholwell Ave 74006
NW Chouteau 74003
Church Ct 74006
Churchill Dr 74006
Circle Dr 74006
Circle Mountain Rd 74003
Claremont Dr 74006
Clark Rd 74006
Clear Creek Loop 74006
Clear Ridge Ct 74006
Clearview Dr 74006
Clipper Ct 74006
College View Dr 74003
Colony Ct, Dr, Pl & Way 74006
Colorado Ave 74003
N & S Comanche Ave 74003
Concord Dr 74006
Cooper Ct 74006
Cornell Dr 74006
Cottonwood Ln 74003
Country Ln, Pl & Rd 74003
Country Club Rd 74006
County Road 2001 74003
County Road 2003 74003
County Road 2015 74003
County Road 2017 74003
County Road 2019 74003
County Road 2105 74003
County Road 2107 74003
County Road 2131 74003
County Road 2137 74003
County Road 2145 74003
County Road 2146 74003
County Road 2175 74003
County Road 2189 74003
County Road 2197 74003
County Road 2365 74003
County Road 2415 74003
County Road 2425 74003
County Road 2427 74003
County Road 2491 74003
County Road 2562 74003
County Road 2570 74003
County Road 2571 74003
County Road 2600 74003
County Road 2610 74003
County Road 2656 74003
County Road 2660 74003
County Road 2676 74003
County Road 2678 74003
County Road 2680 74003
County Road 2682 74003
County Road 2684 74003
County Road 2686 74003
County Road 2690 74003
County Road 2691 74003
County Road 2692 74003
County Road 2696 74003
County Road 2702 74003
County Road 2704 74003
County Road 2706 74003
County Road 2708 74003
County Road 2712 74003
County Road 2732 74003
County Road 2740 74003
County Road 2804 74003
County Road 2904 74003
County Road 3001 74003
County Road 3002 74003
County Road 3004 74003
County Road 3006 74003
County Road 3007 74003
County Road 3009 74003
County Road 3013 74003
County Road 3022 74003
County Road 3102 74003
County Road 3103 74003
County Road 3104 74003
County Road 3233 74003
County Road 3235 74003
County Road 3237 74003
County Road 3239 74003
County Road 3309 74003
County Road 3425 74003
County Road 3503 74003
County Road 3505 74003
County Road 3550 74003
County Road 3551 74003
Coventry Ct & Ln 74006
Cr 2001 74003
Cr 2145 74003
Cr 2175 74003
Cr 2617 74003
Cr 2670 74003
Cr 2684 74003
Cr 2690 74003
Cr 2706 74003
Cr 2732 74003
Cr 3002 74003
Cr 3007 74003
N & S Creek Ave 74003
Crescent Dr 74006
Crestland Dr 74006
Crestview Dr 74003
Crestwood Cir 74003
Crown Dr 74006
Cudahy St 74003
Cumberland Dr 74003
N Cummings Ave 74006
Cypress Cir 74006
Dale Pl 74006
Dana Dr 74006
Dartmouth Dr 74006
David Dr 74006
Debbie Ln & Pl 74006
NE & SE Debell Ave 74006
Deerfield Cir & Pl 74006
SE Delaware Ave 74003
Denver Pl & Rd 74003
Dewey Ave & Pl 74003
Dogwood Ct 74006
Dorchester Dr 74006
Dorsett Ct & Dr 74006
Douglas Ln 74003
Dover Ct 74006
W & E Durham Dr & Rd 74006
East Cir, Ct, Dr & Pl 74006
NE Edge Hill Dr 74006
Edgewood Ave & Ct 74006
Edna Mae Ln 74003
S Elm Ave 74003
NE & SE Elmhurst Ave & Ct 74006
Essex Ln 74006
Eton Dr 74006
Evergreen Ct & Dr 74006
Fairview Rd 74006
Fairway St 74003
N, NE & S Fenway Ave, Cir, Ct & Pl 74006
Fleetwood Ct, Dr & Pl 74006
SE Fordham Dr 74006
Forrest Park Rd 74003
Fox Hollow Ct 74006
E Frank Phillips Blvd 74006
SE Frank Phillips Blvd 74003
SW Frank Phillips Blvd 74003
Fremont Rd 74006
Gap Rd 74003
Garden Dr 74003
Gary Ave 74006
Georgetown Cir, Ct & Dr 74006
Glen Ct 74006
Glynnwood Dr & Ln 74006
Grandview Pl & Rd 74006
SE Green Country Rd 74006
Greenleaf Ct 74006
Greenwood Ct 74006
Greystone Ave & Pl 74006
Grove Ln & St 74003
Guinn Ln 74006
Hampden Rd & Sq 74006
Harned Ct, Dr & Pl 74006
Harriman Cir 74006
Harris Dr 74006
Harvard Ct & Dr 74006
Harvey Rd 74006
Harwood Dr 74003
Hawken Ln 74003
Hawthorne Ct 74006
Hazel Ct & Rd 74006
Hazlette Ln 74003
Heidi Ct 74006
Henrietta Ave 74006
NW Henry Ave 74003
E & W Hensley Blvd 74003
Herrick St 74003
S Hickory Ave 74003
Highland Dr 74003
S Highway 123 74003
SW Highway 123a 74003
Hill Dr 74006
Hillcrest Dr 74003
SE Hillsboro Rd 74006
Hillsdale Dr 74006
Hillside Dr 74006
SE Hilltop Dr 74006
Holly Ln 74003
NE Home Ave 74006
Homestead Dr 74006
NE & SE Howard Ave 74006
Hudson Lake Rd 74003
Huntington Dr 74006
Idaho Ave 74006
Ilma Dr 74003
Indiana St 74006
Industrial Blvd 74006
International Blvd & Dr 74006
Interurban Dr 74006
Inwood Dr 74003
Jack Ln 74003
Jacquelyn Ln 74006
Jefferson Ct, Pl & Rd 74006
NW Jennings Ave 74003
SW Jennings Ave
601-613 74003
615-797 74003
615-615 74005
799-1799 74003
N & S Johnstone Ave & Pl 74003
Jupiter Ct 74006
Kane Hill Dr 74006
Kansas Ln 74006
NE & SE Katherine Ave 74006
N & S Kaw Ave 74003
S Keeler Ave 74003
Kensington Ct & Way 74006
SE Kentucky Pl & St 74006
Kenwood Ct, Dr & Rd 74006
Kevin Ct 74006
King Dr 74006
Kings Cir & Ct 74006
Kingston Ct & Dr 74006
Kristin Ln 74006
Kyle Ct & Rd 74006
Lahoma Dr 74003
Lakeview Ct & Dr 74006
Larchmont Dr 74003
Lariat Dr 74006
Larkspur Dr 74006
Laurel Pl 74003
Lauren Ct 74006
Lee Dr 74003
Legacy Ct 74006
Leisure Ln 74006
Lester Ave 74006
Lewis Dr 74006
Limestone Ct & Rd 74006
Lincoln Pl & Rd 74006
Lindenwood Dr 74003
Locust Rd 74006
London Ln 74006
Longridge Ln 74006
Loris Ln 74006
NW Lupa St 74003
Lynn Rd 74006
Lynnwood Ct 74006
Macklyn Ct, Ln & Pl 74006
N & S Madison Blvd & Pl 74006
Manning Rd 74006
Manor Dr 74006
S Maple Ave 74003
N Margarite Ave 74003
Mars Ct 74006
Martin Ln & Pl 74006
Maryland St 74006
Maudie Ln 74003
May Ln 74006
Mckinley Rd 74006
Mcnamara St 74003
Meadow Dr & Ln 74006
Meadow Lane Pl 74006
Meadowbrook Ln 74003
Meadowcrest Ct & Dr 74006
Meadowlark Ave & Pl 74006
Melmart Dr 74006
Melody Ln 74006
Melrose Dr 74006
Mercedes Ave 74003
Mercury Ct 74006
Mesa Ave 74006
Michigan St 74006
Middle Path Rd 74003
Milford Dr 74006
Mill St 74003
Millway St 74006
Mimosa Ln 74006
Minnesota St 74006
SE Mission Ct, Dr & Rd 74006
Mistletoe Ln 74003
Mockingbird Ln 74003
Monticello Ct & Dr 74006
Montrose Ct & Dr 74006
Moonlight Dr 74006
Morgan Ave 74006
NE & SE Morningside Ave 74006
N & S Morton Ave 74003
E Mountain Cir, Dr & Rd 74003
Mulberry Ln 74003
NE & SE Myers Ave 74006
NE Nebraska Ave, Ct & St 74006
Neptune Ct 74006
North Rd 74006
Nottingham Dr 74006
Nova Ave 74006
Nowata Pl & Rd 74006
S Oak Ave 74003
Oak Rd 74006
Oak Park Rd 74003
Oakdale Dr & Pl 74006
Oakridge Ct & Dr 74006
Ohio St 74006
Okesa Rd 74003
SW Oklahoma Ave 74003
SE Orchard Ln 74006
N & S Osage Ave 74003
Osage Moon Rd 74003
Oxford Ct 74006
SE Paddock Ct 74006
Palmetto 74003
N Park Ave 74003
S Park Ave 74003
SE Park Ln 74006
N Parkhill Ct, Dr, Ln, Loop & Pl 74006
Parkview Dr 74003
Parkway St 74003
Parsons Dr 74006
Pathfinder Ct 74006
Pecan Pl 74003
N & S Penn Ave 74003

Penny Ln 74006
Pepper Grass Ct 74006
Philson Farm Rd 74006
Pine Ave 74006
Pleasant View Ct & Dr 74003
Polaris Dr 74006
Pr 2696 74003
Prairie Heights Dr 74006
Prairie Ridge Ct & Dr 74006
Price Rd 74006
Princeton Dr 74006
Private Road 2676 74003
Private Road 2698 74003
Private Road 2705 74003
Private Road 3250 74003
Putnam Dr 74006
Quail Ct, Dr & Pl 74006
Quail Ridge Loop & Rd 74006
N & S Quapaw Ave 74003
Quarry Park Dr 74006
NE & SE Queenstown Ave 74006
Rabbit Ridge Rd 74006
Rachel Ln 74006
Radar Hill Rd 74003
Ramblewood Rd 74003
Ranch Ct & Rd 74003
Ravenwood Ct & Dr 74006
Redbud Ln 74006
Redhawe Ct 74006
Redwood Ln 74003
Regency Rd 74006
Renick Ln 74006
Revere Way E & W 74006
Revere Way Ct 74006
SE Rice Creek Rd & Way 74006
Richmond Dr 74006
Ridge Ct & Rd 74006
Ridgecrest Ct 74006
Ridgewood Rd 74006
Roanoke Ridge Rd 74006
Robin Ave 74006
Rockdale Rd 74006
NE & SE Rockwood Ave 74006
N & S Rogers Ave 74003
Rolling Hills Ct, Dr & Pl 74006
Rolling Meadows Ct & Rd 74006
Roman Cir & St 74006
NE & SE Roselawn Ave, Ct & Pl 74006
Rushmore Cir & St 74006
Saddle Ln 74006
Sagebrush Dr 74006
Sandstone Dr 74006
N & S Santa Fe Ave & Pl 74003
Saturn Ct 74006
Sawgrass Dr & Pl 74006
N & S Seminole Ave 74003
N & S Seneca Ave 74003
Shady Grove Ct 74006
Shannon Ave & Dr 74006
S Shawnee Ave 74003
Sheridan Rd 74006
Short Ave 74003
E Silas St 74003
Silver Lake Dr, Pl, Rd & Vw 74006
Sirocco Pl 74003
Skyline Dr & Pl 74006
Smysor Dr 74006
Sooner Rd 74003
Sooner Park Dr & Rd 74006
Southport Dr & Loop 74006
Southview Ave 74003
Split Rock Rd 74003
Spring Rd 74003
N & S Spruce Ave 74006
Staats Dr & Pl 74006
Stanford Dr 74006
Stanley Ln 74006
N Star Ct 74006
Starboard Ct 74006
Starlight Ct 74006
Starview Cir 74006
State St 74006
State Highway 123
1000-7798 74003
State Highway 123
7800-16152 74003
16154-16400 74006
16401-16499 74003
16401-16599 74006
16402-16698 74006
16601-16697 74003
16699-16789 74003
16790-16798 74006
16791-16799 74003
Steeper Dr 74006
Stonehenge Dr 74006
Stoneridge Ct 74006
Stonewall Dr 74006
Summers Ave 74006
Summit Rd 74006
N & S Sunset Blvd 74003
Sunshine Ct 74006
Sunview Ct & Pl 74006
Surrey Ct & Ln 74006
Swan Dr 74006
Talbot Cir 74006
Talimena Ct 74006
Tallgrass Trl 74006
Tanglewood Ct 74006
Taylor Dr & Ln 74006
Terrace Dr 74006
Terri Ct & Dr 74006
Texas Cir 74003
N Theodore Ave 74003
Theresa Ln 74006
Toledo Rd 74006
Tower Cir & Ct 74006
Trail Ct & Dr 74006
Trail Ridge Ct 74006
Trolley 74006
Turkey Creek Rd 74006
Turner Pl 74003
Turtle Crk 74006
Tuxedo Blvd 74003
E Tuxedo Blvd 74003
Us Highway 60
400-9199 74003
399501-400497 74006
400499-403999 74006
Us Highway 75 74006
Utah Ave 74006
Valley Rd 74003
Valley View Ct 74006
Velma Dr 74006
Venus Ct 74006
Vermont St 74006
Versailles Pl 74006
SE Vicksburg St 74006
N & S Virginia Ave 74003
Vista Dr 74006
Warwick Ct 74006
NE & SE Washington Blvd & Pl 74006
Waterford Ct 74006
SW Watson Ave 74003
SE Waverly Ave 74003
Wayland Ct 74006
Wayside Dr 74006
Westcliff Dr 74003
Westview Dr 74003
Whippoorwill Ct 74006
Whiteway Ct 74006
Whitney Ct, Ln & Pl 74006
Wildwood Ct 74006
Wiley Post Rd 74003
Will Rogers Rd 74003
Willhite Dr 74006
Williamsburg St 74006
Willow Ave 74006
Willow Creek Dr 74006
Willow Park Dr 74006
Willowood Dr 74006
NE & SE Wilshire Ave 74006
Wilson Rd 74006
Winding Way 74006
Windsor Way 74006
Windstone Ct & Dr 74006
NE Wisconsin St 74006
Woodland Loop & Rd 74006
N Woodrow Ave 74003
Woodville Rd 74006
Woolaroc Ranch Rd 74003
Wright Rd 74006
N & S Wyandotte Ave 74003
Yale Dr & Pl 74006
Yorktown Ln 74006
Yorman Rd 74006
NE & SE Young Ave 74006

NUMBERED STREETS

W 1st St 74003
E & W 2nd 74003
E 3rd St 74003
E 4th St
100-1299 74003
3101-3199 74006
W 4th St 74003
E & W 5th 74003
W 6th St 74003
E & W 8th 74003
E & W 9th 74003
E & W 10th 74003
E & W 11th 74003
E & W 12th Pl & St 74003
E & W 13th 74003
W & E 14th Pl & St 74003
14th Street Loop 74003
SW, E & W 15th Pl & St 74003
E & W 16th Pl & St 74003
E 17th St 74003
W & E 18th Pl & St 74003
W 19th St 74003
E & W 20th 74003
E 21st St 74003
E 22nd St 74003
E 23rd St 74003
W 1300 Rd 74006
W 1400 Rd 74003
W 1500 Rd 74006
W 1600 Rd
393600-393799 74003
399800-400099 74006
W 1788 Dr 74006
W 1800 Rd 74006
W 1900 Rd 74006
W 1960 Dr 74006
W 1970 Dr 74006
W 1980 Dr 74006
W 2010 Dr 74006
W 2050 Dr 74006
W 2100 Rd
393000-393899 74003
401700-403999 74006
W 2110 Dr 74006
W 2137 Dr 74006
W 2140 Dr 74006
W 2150 Dr 74006
W 2155 Dr 74006
W 2200 Rd 74006
W 2225 Dr
393200-393299 74003
402900-402999 74006
W 2240 Dr 74006
W 2300 Rd
393000-393399 74003
397001-397097 74006
W 2330 Dr 74006
W 2340 Dr 74006
W 2380 Dr 74006
W 2400 Rd 74006
W 2437 Rd 74006
W 2460 Dr 74006
W 2480 Dr 74006
W 2500 Rd 74006
W 2550 Rd 74006
W 2578 Way 74006
W 2600 Rd 74006
W 2650 Dr 74006
N 3937 Dr 74003
N 3930 Rd 74003
N 3935 Rd 74003
N 3945 74006
N 3946 Rd 74003
N 3940 Rd 74003
N 3945 Rd
12401-13899 74003
N 3950 Rd 74006
21100-22199 74003
22700-22899 74006
3962 Dr & Rd 74006
N 3960 Rd 74006
N 3965 Rd 74006
N 3967 Rd 74006
N 3974 Ln 74006
N 3982 Dr 74006
N 3985 Dr 74006
N 3980 Rd 74006
N 3996 Dr 74006
N 3998 Dr 74006
N 3990 Rd 74006
N 4000 Rd 74006
N 4011 Dr 74006
N 4013 Dr 74006
4015 Dr & Rd 74006
N 4010 Rd 74006
N 4028 Dr 74006
4025 Dr & Rd 74006
N 4020 Rd 74006
N 4037 Dr 74006
N 4032 Dr 74006
N 4034 Dr 74006
N 4035 Dr 74006
4030 Dr & Rd 74006
N 4040 Rd 74006

BROKEN ARROW OK

General Delivery 74012

POST OFFICE BOXES MAIN OFFICE STATIONS AND BRANCHES

Box No.s
1 - 3940 74013
140001 - 141476 74014

RURAL ROUTES

06, 08, 09, 16, 18, 21, 22, 25, 37 74011
01, 19, 20, 24, 27, 28, 29, 32, 33, 35, 38, 43 74012
02, 03, 04, 05, 07, 10, 11, 12, 13, 14, 15, 17, 23, 26, 30, 34, 39, 40, 44 74014

NAMED STREETS

W Albany Dr 74012
E Albany St
100-1299 74012
1301-1999 74012
2501-2799 74014
W Albany St 74012
W & E Albuquerque Pl & St 74011
Angus Dr 74014
Archdale Dr 74014
Arkansas St 74014
N Ash Ave 74012
S Ash Ave
100-3399 74012
4001-4297 74011
4299-8299 74011
S Ash Ct
2201-2697 74012
2699-3399 74012
5000-5799 74011
S Ash Dr 74011
S Ash Pl
1600-3399 74012
4300-8299 74011
Ashton Dr 74014
N Aspen Ave 74012
S Aspen Ave
500-3499 74012
3601-4097 74011
4099-5299 74011
Aspen Cir 74014
Aspen Ct 74014
S Aspen Ct 74012
S Aspen Pl 74011
N Aster Ave 74012
S Aster Ave
100-3599 74012
3700-3899 74011
N Aster Ct 74012
S Aster Ct 74012
N Aster Pl 74012
S Aster Pl 74012
W & E Atlanta Ct, Pl & St 74012
E Aurora St 74014
W & E Austin Pl & St 74011
Bass Pro Dr 74012
W & E Baton Rouge Cir & St 74011
N Battle Creek Dr 74012
N Beech Ave 74012
S Beech Ave
300-3299 74012
4000-8299 74011
N Beech Cir 74012
S Beech Ct 74012
E Berkeley St 74014
E Biddle St 74014
N Birch Ave 74012
S Birch Ave
501-597 74012
599-3099 74012
4000-4098 74011
4100-8299 74011
S Birch Pl
700-999 74012
4000-4399 74011
Birmingham Cir, Pl & St 74011
W & E Boise Cir, Pl & St 74012
E & W Boston Ct, Pl & St 74012
Briarwood Ave, Cir & Ct 74011
W Broadway Ave 74012
W Broadway Cir 74012
W Broadway Ct 74012
W Broadway Pl 74012
E Broadway St
100-599 74012
6300-7899 74014
W Broadway St 74012
Buena Vista Cir 74014
S Bushnell Blvd 74014
N Butternut Ave 74012
S Butternut Ave
100-1900 74012
1902-2098 74012
3700-4699 74011
4701-4799 74011
N Butternut Cir 74012
N Butternut Ct 74012
N Butternut Pl 74012
S Butternut Pl 74012
W & E Canton Ct, Pl & St 74012
Carlyle Dr 74012
N Cedar Ave 74012
S Cedar Ave
200-3099 74012
4000-7299 74011
S Cedar Ct
2900-2999 74012
4300-4399 74011
S Cedar Pl 74011
Cedar Ridge Rd 74011
Charleston Ct, Pl & St 74011
W & E Charlotte Ct & St 74011
N Chestnut Ave 74012
S Chestnut Ave
100-598 74012
600-3599 74012
3600-3998 74011
4000-5399 74011
S Chestnut Ct 74011
Chestnut Dr 74014
E Cheyenne Cir 74014
Cibola Dr 74014
N Circle Dr 74012
Clearview Dr 74014
W & E College Ct & St 74012
S Collins St 74014
S Colony St 74014
W Commercial Ct 74012
E Commercial Pl 74014
E Commercial St
100-599 74012
4800-7999 74014
W Commercial St 74012
W & E Concord Cir, Pl & St 74012
Coronado Dr 74014
Cortez Dr 74014
E Cottonwood St 74014
N Cypress Ave 74012
S Cypress Ave
300-2099 74012
4400-4699 74011
S Cypress Ln 74012
S Cypress Pl 74012
W Dallas Ct 74012
E Dallas Pl 74014
E Dallas St
100-899 74012
2400-2498 74014
2500-7899 74014
W Dallas St 74012
N Date Ave 74012
S Date Ave
200-398 74012
400-3099 74012
4000-8299 74011
S Date Pl 74011
Dawn Cir 74014
W & E Decatur Pl & St 74011
E & W Delmar St 74012
S Delucca St 74014
S Dennis Blvd 74014
N Desert Palm Ave 74012
S Desert Palm Ave
100-1999 74012
4300-4499 74011
S Desert Palm Ct 74012
S Desert Palm Ln 74012
S Desert Palm Pl 74012
W & E Detroit Pl & St 74012
Doewood Cir 74011
N Dogwood Ave 74012
S Dogwood Ave
101-297 74012
299-3599 74012
3600-8599 74011
S Dogwood Blvd 74011
S Dogwood Ct 74011
Dogwood Dr 74014
S Dogwood Pl
1800-3599 74012
3700-3999 74011
E & W Dover Pl & St 74012
Durham Ct, Pl & St 74011
Eagle Pass Ct & St 74011
E & W Edgewater Pl & St 74012
W El Dorado St 74011
W El Paso Ct 74012
E El Paso Pl 74014
W El Paso Pl 74012
E El Paso St
100-499 74012
2500-7899 74014
W El Paso St 74012
N Elder Ave 74012
S Elder Ave
400-3399 74012
3401-3599 74012
7201-7897 74011
7899-8499 74011
S Elder Blvd 74011
S Elder Cir 74012
S Elder Ct 74012
N Elder Pl 74012
E & W Elgin Pl & St 74012
N Elm Ave 74012
S Elm Ave
1600-3099 74012
4100-7599 74011
S Elm Ct 74012
N Elm Pl 74012
S Elm Pl
100-198 74012
200-3399 74012
3600-8299 74011
S Elm St 74011
E & W Elmira Pl & St 74012
Emmitsburg Pl & St 74014
N Eucalyptus Ave 74012
S Eucalyptus Ave
1600-1699 74012
4300-4499 74011
N Eucalyptus Ct 74012
S Eucalyptus Ln 74012
SW Expressway Dr 74012
Fair Oaks Rd 74014
Fairmont Pl & St 74014
Fairway Cir, Ct, Dr & Pl 74011
W & E Fargo Ct, Dr, Ln, Pl & St 74012
S Fawnwood Ct 74011
N Fern Ave 74012
S Fern Ave
300-1399 74012
1401-1999 74012
4000-7599 74011
N Fern Ct 74012
S Fern Pl
300-1599 74012
4100-4199 74011
N Fir Ave 74012
S Fir Ave
200-298 74012
300-3399 74012
8500-8599 74011
S Fir Blvd 74011
S Fir Ct
600-699 74012
3600-3799 74011
N Fir Pl 74012
S Fir Pl
1500-1999 74012
7200-7398 74011
7400-8099 74011
N Firewood Ave 74012
S Firewood Ave
200-299 74012
4300-4499 74011
N Firewood Ct 74012
W & E Florence Ct & St 74011
E Forest Ridge Blvd 74014
S Forrest Rd 74011
E Fort Worth Dr 74012
E Fort Worth Pl
600-699 74012
6400-7599 74014
W Fort Worth Pl 74012
E Fort Worth St
100-1399 74012
2400-7799 74014
W Fort Worth St 74012
W Fradiang St 74012
E & W Fredericksburg Ct & St 74011
W Freeport Cir 74012
E Freeport Pl
600-699 74012

7700-7798 74014
7800-7999 74014
W Freeport Pl 74012
E Freeport St
100-1599 74012
8100-8399 74014
W Freeport St 74012
E & W Fulton Pl & St 74012
S Gafford Blvd 74014
E Galveston Dr 74012
E Galveston Pl 74014
W Galveston Pl 74012
E Galveston St 74014
W Galveston St 74012
N Gardenia Ave 74012
S Gardenia Ave
1700-2899 74012
7200-8599 74011
S Gardenia Ct 74012
S Gardenia Pl 74012
S Garnett Rd
6100-9700 74012
9702-9998 74012
10101-10297 74011
10299-14999 74011
Gary Pl & St 74012
E Gillette St 74014
E & W Glendale St 74011
W Glenwood Cir, Ct &
St 74011
Gordon St 74014
E & W Granger Pl &
St 74012
E Greeley Pl 74014
E Greeley St 74012
W Greeley St 74012
Gulfport Cir, Pl & St 74011
N Gum Ave 74012
S Gum Ave
300-2099 74012
4000-7899 74011
N Gum Ct 74012
N Gum Pl 74012
S Gum Pl
1500-1599 74012
4000-4099 74011
4101-7399 74011
Hansen Rd 74014
S Hanson Rd 74014
Harp Blvd 74014
W & E Hartford Pl &
St 74012
Haskell Dr 74014
S Hawthorn Ave 74011
Hawthorne Ave & Dr 74014
E & W Helena Pl & St 74012
N Hemlock Ave 74012
S Hemlock Ave
300-2799 74012
8100-8199 74011
8201-8399 74011
N Hemlock Cir 74012
N Hemlock Ct 74012
S Hemlock Ct 74012
S Henry St 74014
E Herrianc St 74014
N Hickory Ave 74012
S Hickory Ave
300-2599 74012
4000-7599 74011
Hickory Cir 74014
S Hickory Cir 74012
N Hickory Ct 74012
S Hickory Ct
2500-2599 74012
7800-7899 74011
N Hickory Dr 74012
Hickory Ln 74014
N Hickory Pl 74012
S Hickory Pl
200-2399 74012
4300-4399 74011
S Highland Ave 74014
Highland Dr 74014
N Highland Dr 74012
S Highland Pl 74014
E & S Highway 51 74014
Hillcrest Dr 74014
E Hillside Dr
201-1097 74012
1099-1999 74012
2001-2399 74012
3900-3998 74014
Honolulu Pl & St 74012
Hot Springs Ct, Pl &
St 74011
E Houston Dr 74012
W Houston Pl 74012
E Houston St
300-1799 74012
3400-3499 74014
W Houston St 74012
E Hudson St 74014
W & E Huntsville Ct, Pl
& St 74011
Hycrest Dr 74014
Idyllwyld St 74011
E & W Imperial St 74011
W & E Indianapolis Pl &
St 74012
E Indianola St 74014
W Indianola St 74012
N Indianwood Ave 74012
S Indianwood Ave
100-2499 74012
8100-8300 74011
8302-8398 74011
W Inglewood St 74011
W & E Iola Pl & St 74012
N Ironwood Ave 74012
S Ironwood Ave
801-997 74012
999-2399 74012
4000-7599 74011
N Ironwood Ct 74012
N Ironwood Pl 74012
Irvington Pl & St 74014
E & W Ithica Pl & St 74012
W Jackson Cir 74012
W Jackson Ct 74012
E Jackson Pl
801-899 74012
2700-7599 74014
W Jackson Pl 74012
E Jackson St
100-599 74012
2701-7499 74014
7501-7599 74014
W Jackson St 74012
E Jacksonville St 74012
E & W Jasper Pl & St 74011
Jefferson Cir, Pl & St 74011
E Jersey St 74014
Johanna Blvd 74014
E Johnson St 74014
Joliet Ct & St 74012
N Joshua Ave 74012
S Joshua Ave
100-2699 74012
8300-8399 74011
S Joshua Cir 74011
E Joy Ave 74014
E & W Juneau Pl &
St 74012
N Juniper Ave 74012
S Juniper Ave
1300-1598 74012
1600-3299 74012
4000-8199 74011
8201-8299 74011
N Juniper Ct 74012
S Juniper Ct 74012
N Juniper Pl 74012
S Juniper Pl
800-3299 74012
4300-8199 74011
N Kalanchoe Ave 74012
S Kalanchoe Ave
101-297 74012
299-2399 74012
8300-8499 74011
S Kalanchoe Pl 74012
E Kansas St
100-899 74012
2800-2899 74014
2901-2999 74014
E Kenosha St
100-2399 74012
2400-6499 74014
6501-7599 74014
W Kenosha St 74012
W & E Kent Cir, Ct, Pl &
St 74012
Kenwood Ave & Dr 74012
W Keywest St 74011
Kilby Dr 74014
King Ct & St 74014
E & W Kingsport Ct &
St 74011
W Knollwood St 74011
W Knoxville Pl 74012
E Knoxville St
100-299 74012
2600-7599 74014
W Knoxville St 74012
Lamb Ter 74014
E Lansing Ave 74014
W Lansing Cir 74012
E Lansing Pl 74014
W Lansing Pl 74012
E Lansing St
1000-1299 74012
7901-7997 74014
7999-8599 74014
W Lansing St 74012
E & W Laredo Pl & St 74012
Lariat Cir 74014
N & S Laurel Ave &
Pl 74012
Laver Ct & St 74014
W Lincoln Pl 74012
E Lincoln St 74014
W Lincoln St 74012
N Lions Ave 74012
S Lions Ave
800-3299 74012
4000-7599 74011
N Lions Ct 74012
S Lions Ct 74012
N Lions Dr 74012
N Lions Pl 74012
W & E Little Rock Pl &
St 74011
Los Angeles Cir, Pl &
St 74011
W Louisville Pl 74012
E Louisville St
1101-1199 74012
2700-2798 74014
2800-7599 74014
W Louisville St 74012
Luther Dr 74012
S Lynn Lane Rd
5601-5697 74012
5699-10000 74012
10002-10098 74012
10100-11800 74011
11802-11898 74011
Lynwood Cir & Ln 74011
E Madison Ave 74014
E Madison Pl 74012
W Madison Pl 74012
E Madison St
100-599 74012
8000-8509 74014
8511-8599 74014
W Madison St 74012
N Magnolia Ave 74012
S Magnolia Ave 74012
Magnolia Ct 74011
N Magnolia Ct 74012
S Magnolia Pl 74012
N Main St 74012
S Main St
100-1700 74012
1701-2099 74012
1701-1701 74013
1702-2098 74012
N Maple Ave 74012
S Maple Ave
1600-3299 74012
4000-7700 74011
7702-7898 74011
N Maple Pl 74012
S Maple Pl
1100-3299 74012
5300-5499 74011
E Mason Dr 74012
Meadow Crest Cir &
Dr 74014
Meadow Lark Ln 74014
Meadowood Ave, Cir &
Dr 74011
W Memphis Pl 74012
E Memphis St
1000-1200 74012
1202-1398 74012
2800-7599 74014
W Memphis St 74012
W Miami St 74011
E & W Midway St 74012
Millwood Cir & Rd 74011
S Mimosa Ave 74011
E & W Mobile Ave, Pl &
St 74011
Mockingbird Ln 74014
E & W Montgomery Pl &
St 74012
E Montpelier Ct 74014
E Montpelier St 74014
W Montpelier St 74012
S Murphree Dr 74014
N Narcissus Ave 74012
S Narcissus Ave
800-3199 74012
3201-3299 74012
3700-5499 74011
N Narcissus Ct 74012
S Narcissus Ct 74012
S Narcissus Pl
1500-3199 74012
4700-4799 74011
W Nashville Ct 74012
W Nashville Pl 74012
E Nashville St 74014
W Nashville St 74012
E & W Natchez St 74011
S Nedra Ave 74014
New Haven Pl & St 74014
E New Orleans Pl 74011
W New Orleans Pl 74011
E New Orleans St
200-599 74011
3100-6800 74014
6802-8098 74014
W New Orleans St 74011
E Norman Ave 74014
W Norman Cir 74012
E Norman Ct 74012
E Norman Pl
100-199 74012
2700-2999 74014
E Norman St 74014
W Norman St 74012
N & S Nyssa Ave, Ct &
Pl 74012
N Oak Ave 74012
S Oak Ave
200-3199 74012
3600-7399 74011
7401-7499 74011
N Oak Ct 74012
N Oak Pl 74012
S Oak Pl
2500-2799 74012
7300-7499 74011
7501-7899 74011
Oak Grove Rd 74014
E Oakland Ave 74014
W Oakland Cir 74012
E Oakland Pl 74014
W Oakland Pl 74012
E Oakland St 74014
W Oakland St 74012
W Oakridge Ct 74012
Oakridge Dr 74014
E Oakridge St 74014
W Oakridge St 74012
Oakwood Dr 74011
E & W Ocala St 74011
N Olive Ave 74012
S Olive Ave
100-200 74012
202-1598 74012
4400-4500 74011
4502-4698 74011
W Omaha Pl 74012
E Omaha St
200-799 74012
801-2199 74012
4100-4299 74014
W Omaha St 74012
S Oneta Rd 74014
Orange Ave & Cir 74011
W & E Orlando Cir, Ct,
Pl & St 74011
Osage Cir 74014
N Palm Ave 74012
S Palm Ave
1900-1999 74012
2001-2099 74012
3800-3898 74011
3900-4399 74011
N Palm Ct 74012
S & W Park Ave, Cir, Ct
& Pl 74011
E Pasadena St 74011
E Pawhuska St 74014
Peach Ave & Cir 74011
N Pecan Ave 74012
S Pecan Ave 74012
Pecan Cir 74011
S Pecan Ct 74012
S Pecan Pl 74012
W Pensacola Ct 74011
Pensacola Dr 74014
E Pensacola St 74011
W Pensacola St 74011
E Perkins St 74014
W & E Phoenix Ct, Pl &
St 74011
Pin Oak Ln 74014
N & S Pine Ave & Pl 74012
Pittsburg Cir, Ct, Pl &
St 74012
Plymouth Cir, Pl & St 74012
N Poplar Ave 74012
S Poplar Ave
100-3200 74012
3202-3298 74012
3700-5100 74011
5102-5498 74011
W Princeton Cir 74012
E Princeton Ct 74014
W Princeton Ct 74012
W Princeton Pl 74012
E Princeton St
1900-2399 74012
2500-5499 74014
W Princeton St 74012
W & E Quanah Ct, Pl &
St 74011
W & E Quantico Ct, Pl &
St 74011
W Queens Pl 74012
E Queens St
1900-2399 74012
2400-2498 74014
2500-2699 74014
W Queens St 74012
W Quincy Cir 74012
W Quincy Ct 74012
E Quincy Pl 74014
E Quincy St 74012
W Quincy St 74012
S Quinoa Ave 74011
E & W Quinton St 74011
Raleigh Ct & Pl 74011
N Redbud Ave 74012
S Redbud Ave
400-2699 74012
3900-7499 74011
S Redbud Ct 74012
Redbud Ln 74014
N Redbud Pl 74012
S Redbud Pl
100-2499 74012
4600-4699 74011
E Redoak St 74014
N Redwood Ave 74012
S Redwood Ave
301-497 74012
499-1000 74012
1002-2498 74012
4100-4399 74011
S Redwood Cir 74012
N Redwood Ct 74012
S Redwood Pl
200-2499 74012
4200-4299 74011
E Reno Ct 74012
E Reno Pl 74012
E Reno St
1100-2399 74012
2500-2999 74014
3001-3099 74014
W Reno St 74012
Retana Ave & Pl 74011
W & E Richmond Ct, Pl
& St 74012
River Ridge Rd 74014
W & E Roanoke Ct, Pl &
St 74011
Robson Cir 74014
E Rochester St 74011
Rockport Pl & St 74012
Rosewood Dr 74014
S Royal Dublin Ln 74011
W San Antonio St 74012
E & W San Diego St 74011
W Sandusky St 74012
E Santa Fe St 74014
W Seattle Blvd 74012
E Seattle Ct 74012
E Seattle Pl 74012
E Seattle St
300-2299 74012
2800-2899 74014
W Seattle St 74012
S Sequoia Ave 74011
Shadowood Ave 74011
S Shelby Ln 74014
Sherwood Ln 74011
E & W Shreveport St 74011
E Sidney Ave 74014
E Sisemore St 74014
South Park Blvd & St 74012
Spring Creek Dr & Ln 74014
Spring Lake Cir & Dr 74014
N & S Spruce Ave 74012
St Andrews Cir 74011
S State Highway 51 74014
Stone Wood Cir & Dr 74012
Streator Dr 74014
Swan Dr 74014
N Sweet Gum Ave 74012
S Sweet Gum Ave
500-2499 74012
4100-4399 74011
S Sweet Gum Pl
100-399 74012
3801-3899 74011
N Sycamore Ave 74012
S Sycamore Ave
100-2699 74012
3600-7599 74011
S Sycamore Ct 74012
S Sycamore Pl
100-399 74012
3800-7599 74011
E Tacoma Ct 74012
E Tacoma St
800-1699 74012
2500-3099 74014
W Tacoma St 74012
S Tamarack Ave
400-498 74012
500-3499 74012
3700-4399 74011
S Tamarack Pl 74011
Timberlane Ct & St 74011
W & E Toledo Cir, Ct, Pl
& St 74012
S Townsend Ave 74014
E Trenton St 74014
W Trenton St 74012
E & W Tucson St 74011
Twin Oaks Dr, Pl & St 74011
W Ulysses St 74012
N Umbrella Ave 74012
S Umbrella Ave
1100-3499 74012
4000-4099 74011
N Umbrella Cir 74012
S Umbrella Cir 74012
S Umbrella Ct 74012
S Umbrella Pl 74012
E & W Union Ct, Pl &
St 74011
E & W Uniontown St 74012
Urbana Ct & St 74012
Utica Ave, Cir, Ct, Pl &
St 74011
W Vail Pl 74012
E Vail St 74014
W Vail St 74012
W & E Van Buren Ct &
St 74011
E Vancouver Cir 74012
E Vancouver Ct 74012
E Vancouver St
800-1399 74012
2400-3199 74014
W Vancouver St 74012
Vandalia Cir & St 74012
Vandever Blvd & Ct 74012
W & E Vicksburg Ct, Pl
& St 74011
Village Ave & Pl 74012
W & E Waco Ct, Pl &
St 74011
S Wagon Trail Rd 74014
N Walnut Ave 74012
S Walnut Ave
100-2700 74012
2702-2998 74012
3800-4399 74011
S Walnut Pl 74011
E Warren Ave 74014
S Warwick St 74014
W Washington Cir 74012
E Washington Pl 74012
W Washington Pl 74012
E Washington St
100-500 74012
502-598 74012
4200-4299 74014
W Washington St 74012
Wesley Dr 74012
Whipperwill Ln 74014
E & W Wichita Ct &
St 74012
N Willow Ave 74012
S Willow Ave
700-898 74012
900-3499 74012
3700-4399 74011
S Willow Pl 74012
Willow St 74014
Willow Springs Ct 74011
E & W Winston Cir, Ct &
St 74011
S Winwood Ln 74014
W Woodbury 74012
E Woodbury St 74014
Wright Ave & Pl 74014
W Xenia St 74012
E Yakima St 74012
E Yazoo 74011
S Yellow Pine Ave 74011
N Yellowood Ave 74012
S Yellowood Ave
100-1999 74012
3700-4099 74011
S Yellowood Pl 74012
Yuma Cir, Ct, Dr & St 74011
W Zillah St 74012

NUMBERED STREETS

S 1st Pl
400-2899 ... 74012
4300-6399 ... 74011
N 1st St ... 74012
S 1st St
100-3599 ... 74012
6501-6597 ... 74011
6599-8499 ... 74011
N 2nd Pl ... 74012
S 2nd Pl ... 74011
N 2nd St ... 74012
S 2nd St
300-1699 ... 74012
4300-8499 ... 74011
S 3rd Ct ... 74011
N 3rd Pl ... 74012
S 3rd Pl ... 74011
N 3rd St ... 74012
S 3rd St
900-1699 ... 74012
1701-1799 ... 74012
4300-8399 ... 74011
N 4th St ... 74012
S 4th St
200-298 ... 74012
300-1799 ... 74012
4201-4297 ... 74011
4299-8499 ... 74011
S 5th Cir ... 74011
S 5th Pl ... 74012
N 5th St ... 74012
S 5th St
100-1799 ... 74012
6300-8699 ... 74011
N 6th Pl ... 74012
S 6th Pl ... 74012
N 6th St ... 74012
S 6th St
300-2799 ... 74012
7300-8499 ... 74011
8501-8599 ... 74011
N 7th Pl ... 74012
N 7th St ... 74012
S 7th St
300-2699 ... 74012
7700-8699 ... 74011
N 8th Pl ... 74012
N 8th St ... 74012
S 8th St
300-899 ... 74012
8300-8799 ... 74011
N 9th St ... 74012
100-3199 ... 74012
8501-8599 ... 74011
N & S 10th ... 74012
N & S 11th ... 74012
N & S 12th Pl & St ... 74012
S 13th Pl ... 74011
N 13th St ... 74012
S 13th St
2400-2799 ... 74012
5900-5998 ... 74011
6000-8299 ... 74011
N 14th Pl ... 74012
S 14th Pl
2600-2699 ... 74012
8200-8399 ... 74011
N 14th St ... 74012
S 14th St
2400-2599 ... 74012
3701-5897 ... 74011
5899-8199 ... 74011
S 15th Pl ... 74012
3700-6199 ... 74011
N 15th St ... 74012
S 15th St
2400-2599 ... 74012
3600-8199 ... 74011
S 16th Ct ... 74012
N 16th Pl ... 74012
S 16th Pl ... 74012
E 16th St S ... 74014
N 16th St ... 74012
S 16th St ... 74012
N & S 17th ... 74012
N & S 18th Pl & St ... 74012
N 19th Pl ... 74012
E 19th St S ... 74014
N 19th St ... 74012
N 20th St ... 74012
E 21st Pl S ... 74014
E 21st St S ... 74014
N 21st St ... 74012
N 22nd St ... 74012
E 23rd St S ... 74014
N 23rd St
600-1199 ... 74014
1201-2499 ... 74014
2200-2298 ... 74012
2400-2498 ... 74014
S 23rd St ... 74014
E 24th St S ... 74014
E, N & S 25th Pl & St
S ... 74014
N, E & S 26th Ct, Pl &
St S ... 74014
N & S 27th ... 74014
S, E & N 28th Ct, Pl &
St S ... 74014
N & S 29th Pl & St ... 74014
N & S 30th Pl & St ... 74014
E, N & S 31st Pl & St
S ... 74014
E, N & S 32nd Pl & St
S ... 74014
N, E & S 33rd Ct, Pl &
St S ... 74014
E, N & S 34th Pl & St
S ... 74014
E, N & S 35th Pl & St
S ... 74014
E, N & S 36th Pl & St
S ... 74014
E & N 37th Ct, Pl & St
S ... 74014
38th Pl & St ... 74014
39th Pl & St ... 74014
40th Pl & St ... 74014
E & N 41st Pl & St S ... 74014
42nd Pl & St ... 74014
43rd Ct, Pl & St ... 74014
44th Pl & St ... 74014
E 45th St S ... 74014
E 46th St S ... 74014
47th Pl & St ... 74014
E & S 48th S ... 74014
S & E 49th Ct, Pl & St
S ... 74014
E & S 50th Ct, Pl & St
S ... 74014
E 51st St ... 74012
E 51st St S ... 74014
E & N 52nd S ... 74014
N 53rd St ... 74014
E 54th St S ... 74014
E 55th St S ... 74014
E 56th St S ... 74014
E 57th St S ... 74014
58th Pl & St ... 74014
E 59th St S ... 74014
E 60th St S ... 74014
E 61st Pl ... 74012
E 61st Pl S ... 74014
E 61st St ... 74012
E 61st St S ... 74014
E 62nd Pl ... 74012
E 62nd St ... 74012
E 62nd St S ... 74014
N 62nd St ... 74014
S 62nd St ... 74014
S 63rd Pl ... 74014
E 63rd St ... 74012
E 63rd St S ... 74014
S 63rd St ... 74014
E 64th St ... 74012
E 64th St S ... 74014
S 64th St ... 74014
E 65th St S ... 74014
66th Cir, Ct & St ... 74014
S 67th Cir ... 74014
E 67th Pl S ... 74014
E 67th St ... 74012
E 67th St S ... 74014
N 67th St ... 74014
S 67th St ... 74014
E 68th Ct S ... 74014
E 68th St ... 74012
E 68th St S ... 74014
N 68th St ... 74014
S 68th St ... 74014
69th Cir, Pl & St ... 74014
70th Pl & St ... 74014
E 71st Pl S ... 74014
E 71st St ... 74012
E 71st St S ... 74014
S 71st St ... 74014
E & S 72nd S ... 74014
E & S 73rd S ... 74014
E & S 74th S ... 74014
E & S 75th S ... 74014
E & S 76th Pl & St S ... 74014
S & E 77th Pl & St S ... 74014
N, E & S 78th Pl, St &
Ter S ... 74014
E, N & S 79th Ct, Pl &
St S ... 74014
E & N 80th Pl & St S ... 74014
E 81st St S ... 74014
E & N 82nd S ... 74014
E & N 83rd Pl & St S ... 74014
E & N 84th S ... 74014
E & N 85th S ... 74014
E & N 86th Pl & St S ... 74014
E 87th St S ... 74014
E 88th St S ... 74014
89th Pl & St ... 74014
90th Pl & St ... 74014
E 91st Pl S ... 74014
E 91st St ... 74012
E 91st St S ... 74014
92nd Ct, St & Ter ... 74014
E 93rd Ct S ... 74014
E 93rd Pl S ... 74014
E 93rd St ... 74012
E 93rd St S ... 74014
E 94th St ... 74012
E 94th St S ... 74014
E 95th St S ... 74014
E 96th St ... 74012
E 96th St S ... 74014
E 97th St ... 74012
E 97th St S ... 74014
E 98th St S ... 74014
E 99th St S ... 74014
E 101st Pl S ... 74014
E 101st St ... 74011
E 101st St S ... 74014
E 102nd St S ... 74014
103rd Pl & St ... 74014
E 104th St S ... 74014
E 105th St S ... 74014
106th Pl & St ... 74014
E 107th St S ... 74014
E 108th St S ... 74014
E 109th St S ... 74014
E 110th St S ... 74014
E 111th Pl S ... 74014
E 111th St ... 74011
E 111th St S
11700-11799 ... 74011
20300-20498 ... 74014
20500-25500 ... 74014
25502-25598 ... 74014
112th Pl & St ... 74014
E 113th St S ... 74014
S 114th East Ave
6100-6399 ... 74012
12800-13299 ... 74011
E 114th Pl S ... 74014
E 114th St ... 74011
E 114th St S ... 74014
S 115th East Ave ... 74012
S 115th East Ave ... 74012
12301-12399 ... 74011
115th Pl & St ... 74014
S 115th East Pl ... 74012
S 116th East Ave ... 74012
S 116th East Ave ... 74012
12101-12197 ... 74011
12199-13199 ... 74011
E 116th St S ... 74014
S 117th East Ave
6100-6199 ... 74012
12801-12997 ... 74011
12999-13299 ... 74011
S 117th East Ct ... 74011
S 117th East Pl ... 74011
S 118th East Ave
6100-6299 ... 74012
13200-13299 ... 74011
E 118th St ... 74011
E 118th St S ... 74014
S 119th East Ave ... 74011
E 119th St S ... 74014
S 120th East Ave ... 74012
12700-12799 ... 74011
S 120th East Pl ... 74011
E 120th St S ... 74014
S 121st East Ave ... 74011
E 121st St S
11501-12297 ... 74011
19300-25299 ... 74014
S 122nd East Ave ... 74011
E 122nd St S
15301-15399 ... 74011
19300-23999 ... 74014
123rd East Ave & Pl ... 74011
E 123rd Pl S
11600-11698 ... 74011
22201-22299 ... 74014
S 124th East Ave ... 74011
125th East Ave & Pl ... 74011
S 126th East Ave ... 74011
126th Pl & St ... 74014
S 127th East Ave ... 74011
E 127th St S ... 74011
S 128th East Ave ... 74011
E 128th Pl S ... 74011
E 128th St S
11800-16799 ... 74011
19401-19497 ... 74014
S 129th East Ave
6201-6397 ... 74012
10401-10497 ... 74011
10499-15099 ... 74011
15101-15199 ... 74011
E 129th St S
11901-12597 ... 74011
19900-20198 ... 74014
E 130th St S ... 74011
E 131st Pl S ... 74014
E 131st St S
12100-19100 ... 74011
19102-19198 ... 74011
19400-23800 ... 74014
23802-24098 ... 74014
132nd Pl & St ... 74011
S 133rd East Ave ... 74011
133rd Pl & St ... 74011
E 134th St S ... 74011
E 135th St S ... 74011
S 136th East Ave ... 74012
E 136th St S ... 74011
S 137th East Ave ... 74011
E 137th St S ... 74011
E 138th St S
12300-12898 ... 74011
22400-22499 ... 74014
S 139th East Ave ... 74011
S 140th East Ave ... 74011
S 141st East Ave ... 74011
E 141st St ... 74011
E 141st St S ... 74014
S 143rd East Ave ... 74011
S 145th East Ave ... 74012
11000-12198 ... 74011
12200-12700 ... 74011
12702-13098 ... 74011
E 151st St S
11600-11699 ... 74011
19500-20198 ... 74014
S 152nd East Ave ... 74011
S 154th East Ave ... 74011
S 161st East Ave ... 74011
E 161st St S ... 74014
S 163rd East Ave ... 74011
S 168th East Ave ... 74011
E 171st St S ... 74014
S 177th East Ave ... 74011
S 185th East Ave ... 74011
S 186th East Ave ... 74011
S 187th East Ave ... 74012
S 188th East Ave ... 74012
13800-13898 ... 74011
S 189th East Ave ... 74011
S 190th East Ave ... 74012
S 193rd East Ave ... 74014
S 194th East Ave ... 74014
195th East Ave, Ct &
Pl ... 74014
S 196th East Ave ... 74014
S 197th East Ave ... 74014
198th East Ave & Pl ... 74014
S 199th East Ave ... 74014
S 200th East Ave ... 74014
S 201st East Ave ... 74014
S 202nd East Ave ... 74014
S 203rd East Ave ... 74014
S 204th East Ave ... 74014
205th East Ave & Pl ... 74014
206th East Ave & Pl ... 74014
S 207th East Ave ... 74014
S 208th East Ave ... 74014
S 209th East Ave ... 74014
S 210th East Ave ... 74014
S 211th East Ave ... 74014
S 212th East Ave ... 74014
S 213th East Ave ... 74014
S 214th East Ave ... 74014
S 215th East Ave ... 74014
S 216th East Ave ... 74014
S 217th East Ave ... 74014
S 218th East Ave ... 74014
S 219th East Ave ... 74014
S 221st East Ave ... 74014
222nd East Ave & Pl ... 74014
S 223rd East Ave ... 74014
S 224th East Ave ... 74014
S 225th East Ave ... 74014
S 226th East Ave ... 74014
S 227th East Ave ... 74014
S 228th East Ave ... 74014
S 229th East Ave ... 74014
S 230th East Ave ... 74014
S 231st East Ave ... 74014
S 232nd East Ave ... 74014
S 233rd East Ave ... 74014
S 234th East Ave ... 74014
235th East Ave & Pl ... 74014
S 236th East Ave ... 74014
S 237th East Ave ... 74014
S 238th East Ave ... 74014
S 239th East Ave ... 74014
S 240th East Ave ... 74014
S 241st East Ave ... 74014
S 244th East Ave ... 74014
S 245th East Ave ... 74014
S 246th East Ave ... 74014
S 248th East Ave ... 74014
S 249th East Ave ... 74014
S 250th East Ave ... 74014
S 251st East Ave ... 74014
S 252nd East Ave ... 74014
S 253rd East Ave ... 74014
S 254th East Ave ... 74014
S 255th East Ave ... 74014
S 256th East Ave ... 74014
257th East Ave & Pl ... 74014
258th East Ave, Ct &
Pl ... 74014
S 259th East Ave ... 74014
S 260th East Ave ... 74014
S 261st East Ave ... 74014
S 262nd East Ave ... 74014
S 263rd East Ave ... 74014
S 264th East Ave ... 74014
S 265th East Ave ... 74014
S 266th East Ave ... 74014
S 267th East Ave ... 74014
S 268th East Ave ... 74014
S 270th East Ave ... 74014
S 273rd East Ave ... 74014
S 275th East Ave ... 74014
S 277th East Ave ... 74014
S 281st East Ave ... 74014
S 282nd East Ave ... 74014
283rd East Ave & Pl
E ... 74014
S 284th East Ave ... 74014
S 285th East Pl ... 74014
S 286th East Ave ... 74014
S 287th East Ave ... 74014
S 288th East Ave ... 74014
S 289th East Ave ... 74014
S 290th East Ave ... 74014
S 292nd East Ave ... 74014
S 293rd East Ave ... 74014
S 294th East Ave ... 74014
S 295th East Ave ... 74014
S 296th East Ave ... 74014
S 297th East Ave ... 74014
S 298th East Ave ... 74014
S 300th East Ave ... 74014
S 301st East Ave ... 74014
S 302nd East Ave ... 74014
S 303rd Ct ... 74014
S 304th East Ave ... 74014
S 305th East Ave ... 74014
309th East Ave & Pl ... 74014
310th East Ave & Pl ... 74014
S 311th East Ave ... 74014
S 321st East Ave ... 74014
S 329th East Ave ... 74014
S 330th East Ave ... 74014
S 333rd East Ave ... 74014
S 334th East Ave ... 74014
S 335th East Ave ... 74014
S 336th East Ave ... 74014
S 337th East Ave ... 74014
S 353rd East Ave ... 74014
S 360th East Ave ... 74014
S 369th East Ave ... 74014
S 385th East Ave ... 74014

CHICKASHA OK

General Delivery ... 73018

POST OFFICE BOXES MAIN OFFICE STATIONS AND BRANCHES

Box No.s
All PO Boxes ... 73023

RURAL ROUTES

01, 02, 03, 04, 05, 06 ... 73018

NAMED STREETS

All Street Addresses ... 73018

NUMBERED STREETS

All Street Addresses ... 73018

CLAREMORE OK

General Delivery ... 74017

POST OFFICE BOXES MAIN OFFICE STATIONS AND BRANCHES

Box No.s
All PO Boxes ... 74018

RURAL ROUTES

03, 04, 05, 09, 10, 12,
14, 15, 16, 19 ... 74017
01, 02, 06, 07, 08, 11,
13, 15, 16, 17, 20 ... 74019

NAMED STREETS

Academy St ... 74017
E Acorn Rd ... 74017
E Airpark Rd ... 74019
Alaska St ... 74017
Alawhe Dr ... 74019
Alliance Dr ... 74019
E Allsup Ave ... 74019
Amah Pkwy ... 74019
E & S Amber Ct & Dr ... 74019
E & S Anderson Dr &
Way ... 74017
Andre Cir ... 74017
S Andreas Rd ... 74019
Andy Payne Blvd &
Cir ... 74017
E Apple Ln ... 74019
Archer Ct & Dr ... 74017
S Arlene Dr ... 74019
Arlington Ct ... 74019
Arrowood Dr ... 74019
S Ash Ct ... 74019
S Ash Rd ... 74019
S Ash St ... 74017
W Ash St ... 74017
S Ash Valley Ln ... 74017
E Aspen Dr ... 74019
E Aspenwood Dr ... 74019
Avian Ave ... 74017
E Aztec ... 74017
Back Nine Dr ... 74017
E Barbara Blvd ... 74019
E Battenfield Dr ... 74019
S Bellmon St ... 74019
Belvedere Dr ... 74019
Berry Pickin Ln ... 74019
W Bert St ... 74017
W Berwick ... 74017
S Beulah Cv ... 74019
S & E Big Valley Blvd,
Dr, Ln & Pl ... 74017
E Birch St ... 74017
W Birch St ... 74017
S Birch Hollow Way ... 74017
E Birchwood Dr ... 74019
Birdie Ct ... 74019
E & S Biswell Dr ... 74019
E Black Jack Dr ... 74019
Blackberry Blvd ... 74019
E Blackwell St ... 74019
E Blue Jay Ln ... 74017
E & W Blue Starr Dr ... 74017
S Blue Stem ... 74017
Bogey Ct ... 74019
E Bolen Rd ... 74019
N Boling St ... 74017
Bon Terre St ... 74017
E Bond Dr ... 74017
E Boysen Dr ... 74019
S Brady St ... 74017
Branch Rd ... 74017
S Brandon Terrace Dr ... 74019
S & E Brendan Blvd &
Cir ... 74017
Briar Dr ... 74019
Bristol Rd ... 74017
E Brit Dr ... 74019
S Brittany Dr ... 74019
Brook Ln ... 74017
S Brook Ln ... 74019
W Brooks St ... 74017
Brookside Dr ... 74017
Brookview Ct ... 74017
E Brookview Dr ... 74019
E Browning Ave ... 74019
S Bryanwood Dr ... 74019
Buckingham Dr ... 74017
Bunker St ... 74019

Burma Dr 74019
S Cactus Rd 74019
Calen Dr 74019
Callaway Dr 74019
Camden St 74017
S Camel Dr 74019
Canary Ln 74017
S Candlestick Ln 74019
Canyon Rd 74017
S Canyon Rd 74019
S Canyon Creek Rd 74017
E & S Canyon Oaks Blvd, Cir, Ct, Ln, Pl, Rd & Way 74017
E & S Canyon View Dr 74019
Carefree Dr 74019
Castle Pines Cir 74019
S Cedar Ave 74017
Cedar Dr 74017
E Cedar Dr 74019
S Cedar Dr 74019
S Cedar Ln 74019
S Cedar Rd 74017
Cedar Spgs 74017
E Cedar St 74019
S Cedar St
13000-13399 74017
23100-23899 74019
W Cedar St 74017
E Cedar Creek Rd 74019
E & S Cedar Ridge Rd 74019
S Cedercrest Dr 74017
N, S & W Chambers Ave, Ct, Pl, Ter & Trl 74017
Charlestown Cir 74017
N Cherokee Ave 74017
S Cherokee Ave
100-499 74017
1700-2099 74019
S Cherokee Pl 74019
S Cherokee St 74017
Cherokee Park Dr 74017
N Cherrington Ave 74017
E Cherry Ln 74019
E Cherrywood Dr 74019
S Cherrywood Dr 74017
E Cherye Ln 74017
E Chestnut Dr 74019
N & S Chickasaw Ave & Pl 74017
N & S Choctaw Ave, Ct & Pl 74017
Christmas Ln 74017
N Cieda Dr 74017
Circle Dr 74019
E & W Claremore St 74017
E Claude St 74019
Clayton Ave & Rd 74019
Clear Creek Ct 74017
E Clearview Rd 74019
W Clint St 74017
E Clover Creek Dr 74017
Club St 74019
N Clubhouse Rd 74017
S Cody Trce 74019
Coeur D Alene St 74019
Cog Hill Ct 74019
College Park Rd 74017
Colonial Dr 74019
S Colt Ave 74019
E Colt Dr 74017
Columbia Crest Cir & Dr 74019
Comet Pl & St 74017
S Concord Cir & Dr 74019
E Cook Ln 74019
Cornerstone Ave, Cir, Ln & Pl 74017
Cottonwood Ave 74019
Cottonwood Ln 74017
Cottrell Dr 74019
E Country Dr & Vw 74017
W Country Club Rd
300-998 74017
1000-1599 74017
1601-1699 74017
1800-5199 74019
5201-8999 74019
Country Ridge Ct & Ln 74019
E Country Road Dr 74019
Countryside Dr 74019
E & S Courtney Ln 74019
Covey Ct 74019
Covey Trail Cir 74017
Cowell Pl & St 74017
Coyote Dr 74017
Coyote Trl 74019
S & E Coyote Hills Dr, Ln & Rd 74017
Creek Bank Trl 74019
S Creekside Dr 74017
Creekwood Ct & Trl 74017
E Crest Dr 74017
Crestview Cir 74017
E Crestview Dr 74019
E Crestview Rd 74019
S Crystal Lake Dr 74019
S Cypress St 74017
Cypress Pt Cir 74017
E Daisy Ln 74017
E Dakota Rd 74017
W Danny St 74017
N & S Davis Ave 74017
S Dawn Ter 74019
E Deano Pl 74019
SW Deer Trl 74019
Deer Creek Rd 74017
S Desert Trl 74019
E & S Diana Cir, Ct & Dr 74019
W Diane St 74017
S Dickerson Dr 74017
S Dog Creek Rd 74017
E Dogwood Ct 74019
S Dogwood Ct 74019
S Dogwood Dr 74017
E Dogwood Ln 74019
S Dogwood Pl 74019
S Dogwood Rd 74019
E Dogwood St 74017
S Dogwood St 74017
S Dollar Dr 74019
W Doris St 74017
N Dorothy Ave 74017
N Douglas Dr 74017
S Dove Ave 74017
Dove Dr 74019
W Driftwood Dr 74017
Drivers Ln 74017
E Duck Pond 74017
Duck Pond Dr 74019
Duck Pond Ln 74019
Dunlap Gap 74017
Dunnwood Rd 74019
W Dupont St 74017
S Durango Dr 74019
Eagle Ct
3300-3399 74019
17000-17299 74017
Eagle Dr 74017
Earthside Cir & Dr 74017
S Eastwood Dr 74019
Easy St 74017
Echelon Dr 74019
E Echo Dr 74019
Echo Canyon Pl & Rd 74019
W Eddy St 74017
S & E Edgewater Cir, Cv & Rd 74017
E Edwards St 74019
El Anderson Blvd 74017
E Eldorado Rd 74019
SW Elk Trl 74019
S Elm Pl 74017
E Elm Rd 74019
S Elm Rd 74019
E Elm St 74019
S Elm St
13200-13299 74017
25000-25299 74019
E Engelmann St 74019
S Ethel St 74019
W Evergreen Ln 74017
Fairway St 74019
S Faith Ln 74017
Fall Ct & Ln 74017
E Falletti Ave 74017
S Falyn Rd 74019
S Faulkner Ave 74019
N Faulkner Dr 74017
N Faulkner Pl 74017
Fern Ct & Pl 74019
S & E Fern Valley Dr & Rd 74019
S, E & N Fieldstone Ct & Dr E, N, S & W 74017
E First Pl 74017
E First St 74019
Flint Rd 74019
NE Flintlock Dr 74017
N & S Florence Ave & Pl 74017
Forest Hill Dr 74017
Forest Park Dr 74017
Forest Ridge Pkwy 74017
Forrest Glenn Rd 74019
E Fourth St 74017
Fox Run Dr
1400-1499 74019
15000-15499 74019
Foxen Dr 74019
S Foxfire Ln 74019
S Foyil Acres 74017
Fred Swan Ln 74017
Frederick Rd 74019
Freedom Dr 74017
S Frisco Dr 74017
E & W Fry Ct, Pl, St & Ter 74017
Fulham St 74019
Gallo Dr 74019
E George St 74017
S Giftland Dr 74017
Glencoe Cir 74017
E & S Glenwood Dr 74019
W Graham St 74017
Grand Meadow Dr & Rd 74017
S Grand View Rd 74017
Grande Point Pkwy 74017
E Green Country Dr 74019
Greenbrier Cir & Ct 74017
Greenleaf St 74017
E & S Greenway Dr 74019
S Gregory Dr 74019
E Gum St 74017
E Hackamore Rd S 74019
Hackberry Ln 74017
S Hager St 74019
Hahn Dr 74019
E Hampton Rd 74019
E Hansford Rd 74019
Harbour Town Pl 74019
S Hariston St 74019
W Haskell St 74017
Hawthorne Dr 74019
S Heartwood Dr 74019
E Heather Dr 74019
Helt Rd 74017
Henderson Rd 74017
Heritage Dr 74019
Heritage Hills Pkwy 74019
Hickory Dr 74019
E Hickory Dr 74019
Hickory Ln 74019
S Hickory Pl 74019
Hickory St 74017
S Hickory St 74019
E Hickory Bluff Dr 74019
S & E Hickory Hollow Pl & Rd 74019
E Hickory Meadow Dr 74019
High Cir 74017
Highfill Mdws 74019
Highland Ct & Dr 74017
E Highway 20
4200-9899 74019
E Highway 20
13400-13999 74017
14400-21699 74019
E Highway 266 74019
E Highway 28a 74017
S Highway 66
1700-3498 74019
11200-19199 74017
23000-26699 74019
E Highway 88 74017
N Highway 88 74017
S Highway 88
400-19199 74017
21700-24899 74019
Highwood Ct, Dr & Pl 74017
E & S Hill Dr 74019
Hillcrest Dr & Rd 74019
Hillside Ct 74019
Hilltop Ct, Dr & Ln 74017
NE & S Hisaw Dr 74017
Holiday Ln 74017
E & S Holliday Dr 74019
Hollingshead Rd 74019
Hollow Ln 74017
Holly Rd 74019
Holly Creek Rd 74017
S Honeycreek Ln 74019
Honeysuckle Ln 74019
E & S Hootycreek Rd 74019
E Horizon St 74019
Hubbard Rd 74019
Hummingbird Ln 74017
Humphries Cir 74019
E Hunter Ln 74019
Hunters Ct 74019
N Industrial Blvd 74017
Inola St 74017
N & S J M Davis Blvd 74017
N Jay St 74017
S Jewell Dr 74019
John Burrows Dr 74017
W Jordan St 74017
S Juniper St 74019
N Kansas Ave 74017
S Karla St 74019
N Kates Ave 74017
Kay Pl & St 74017
E & S Keetonville Rd 74019
Kelly Ct 74017
King Rd 74019
S Kingsbury Rd 74019
E Kingsridge Rd 74017
S Kingston Cir 74019
S Kiowa Rd 74017
S Klamath 74017
Knight Ln 74019
Ky Ave 74017
Kylie Ct 74019
E & S Lake Dr 74017
E Lake Country Dr 74017
S Lake Forest Dr 74017
S Lakeview Pl 74019
S Lakeway Rd 74019
Lakewood Ct 74017
N & S Lang St 74017
Lanora Ave 74017
S Lariat Ct 74019
Lariat Ln 74017
Laurel Ln 74017
S Laurel St 74019
Lavira Ave & Pl 74017
N Lee St 74017
E Leland Ave 74017
S Leola Ln 74019
Lexington Rd 74017
Liberty Ln 74019
W Lillian St 74017
S Limestone Dr 74019
S Lindley Dr 74019
E Lindy Ln 74019
S Lisa Ln 74017
Lisa Way 74019
S Little Fox Dr 74019
N Louisville Ave 74017
E, N & W Lowry Ln & Rd 74017
S Lucky Duck 74017
Lynn Cir 74019
N Lynn Riggs Blvd 74017
S Lynn Riggs Blvd
200-1700 74017
1702-1708 74017
1710-1998 74019
2000-2099 74019
E Magnoliawood Dr 74019
Maiden Ln 74017
E Main St 74019
S Malcom Rd 74019
Mallard Lake Rd 74019
E Maple Ave 74019
S Maple Ave 74017
E Maple Ct 74019
E Maple Dr 74019
E Maple Ln 74019
S Maple St 74017
Maplewood Dr 74017
Marblehead Dr 74019
Marian Ave 74017
E Marlar Rd 74019
S Marlene Dr 74019
S Maryland Ave 74017
E Mayberry Ave 74017
NE Mayes Rd 74019
S Maywood Dr 74017
Mcclellan Ave 74017
E & N Mccloud Ave & St 74017
N Mcfarland Pl 74017
E & N Meadow Ln & Rd 74017
S & E Meadow Circle Dr & Rd 74019
E Meadow Lake Rd 74019
S Meadow Ranch Rd 74019
S Meadow Ridge Rd 74019
S Meadow View Rd 74017
Meadow Wood Pl 74017
Meadowlark Ln 74017
S Meadowview Ct 74019
Medical Pkwy 74017
E & S Melody Ct, Dr, Ln & Rd 74019
Memorial Dr 74017
Mesa Dr 74017
Midway Rd 74019
Military Dr 74017
N Miller Dr 74017
Mingo Ct 74017
Mirage Dr & Ln 74019
N Missouri Ave 74017
S Missouri Ave
100-599 74017
1000-2099 74019
S Missouri Ct 74019
S Missouri Pl 74019
E Misty Dr 74019
E & S Misty Morning Pl 74019
Mockingbird Ln 74017
Mockingbird Ln E 74019
Mockingbird Ln W 74019
E Modoc St 74017
Monique Cir 74017
S Montgomery Dr 74019
E Montgomery Rd 74017
S & E Mony Cir & Trl 74019
N & S Moore Ave 74017
S Moretz Ave 74017
E Morgan Rd 74019
Morning Glory Ln 74019
Mountain Ln 74019
Mulberry Ln & Mdw 74019
Mullinax Rd 74019
Murphy Ct 74017
N Muskogee Ave 74017
S Muskogee Ave 74017
N Muskogee Pl 74017
S Muskogee Pl 74017
Navajo Rd 74017
Neel Dr & Rd 74017
S Newport Rd 74019
N & S Nome Ave 74017
S Normal Ave 74017
Northaven Rd 74017
E Northglen 74017
Northlake Dr 74017
E Northlea 74017
E Northpark 74017
E Northshire 74017
Norway Ct 74019
E Oak Ave 74017
S Oak Ave 74017
Oak Dr 74019
E Oak Dr 74019
Oak Ln 74017
E Oak Ln 74019
E Oak St
9500-10099 74017
11500-11799 74019
N Oak St 74017
S Oak St
12001-12097 74017
12099-13299 74017
25000-25199 74019
W Oak St 74017
E Oaklawn Dr & Pl 74017
NE, E & S Oakridge Cir, Dr & Way 74017
Odie 74019
N, S & W Oklahoma Ave, Pl & St 74017
S Old Highway 88 74017
S Oqeche 74019
S Orange Cv 74019
N Osage Ave 74017
N Oseuma Ave 74017
Overlook Trl 74019
N & S Owalla Ave 74017
Owalla Valley Dr 74017
Oxford Ln 74019
S Painted Pony Ln 74019
E Palm Tree Rd 74019
E Pamela Rd 74019
Par Ct 74019
S Par Lane Rd 74017
Paradise Ct, Ln & Pkwy 74017
E Park St 74017
Park Crest Ct 74017
Parkland Ave 74017
Parkwood Cir, Ct & Dr 74017
E & W Patti Page Blvd 74017
E Payne St 74017
E Peachtree St 74019
S Pecan Ct 74019
Pecan Ln 74017
E Pecan Ln 74019
E Pecan St 74017
S Pecan St 74019
Pecan Chase Cir 74017
Pecan Ridge Cir, Ct & Pl 74017
S Perdue Ave 74017
Persimmon Ct 74019
Pheasant Cir 74019
Pheasant Dr 74019
S Pheasant Ln 74017
E Pin Oak Ln 74019
Pine Ave & St 74017
S Pinto Ln 74019
S Plainview Ave 74019
S Pleasant View Dr 74019
S & E Pony Lake Cir & Dr 74019
S Poplar St 74017
Poser Pl & Rd 74019
S Potter Cir 74019
E Powder Dr 74017
E Powell St 74017
S Prairie Meadow Dr 74017
S Prairie Meadows St 74017
E Prairie View Dr 74019
W Preparatory St 74017
E & S Pueblo Rd 74017
E & S Quail Ave, Rd & Run 74017
Quail Creek Rd 74017
S Quail Meadow Dr 74017
Quail Ridge Rd 74019
S Quail Run Ct 74017
SW Quail Run Ct 74019
SW Quail Run Dr 74019
Quail Valley Dr 74017
W Quarles St 74017
E Quarterhorse Dr 74019
S Quinton Way 74017
W Ramm Rd 74017
E & S Ranch Rd 74019
Ratliff Dr 74017
S Rauquel Rd 74019
S & E Rawhide Dr, Ln & Rd 74017
S Ray Davis Rd 74019
S Reavis Rd 74017
Reavis Xing 74019
S Red Oak Dr 74019
Red Rock Ranch Rd 74017
E Redbud Dr 74019
E Redbud St 74017
S Redbud St 74017
E Remington Ave 74019
S Remington Ct 74019
E Remington Rd 74017
E Renee Rd 74019
Ridge Ave & Rd 74017
S Ridgefield Cir 74019
S Ridgemont Dr 74017
Ridgeview 74017
Ridgeview Ct 74017
S Ridgeview Ct 74019
Ridgeview Dr 74017
S Ridgeview Dr 74019
Ridgeview Ln 74017
E Ridgeview Ln 74019
Ridgeview Pl 74017
S Ridgeview Rd 74019
E Ridgeview Way 74019
S Ridgewood Dr 74019
River Bend Dr 74019
E River Ranch Rd 74019
S Riverbirch Rd 74019
Riverwood Ct & Dr 74019
Robin Rd 74017
E Robin Way 74019
Rockcrest Dr 74019
Rockhill Rd 74017
Rockport Dr 74019
S & E Rocky Ridge Dr, Ln, Pl, Rd & St 74019
Rodeo Dr 74017
S Rogers Dr 74019
E Rogers Post Rd 74019
E & S Rose Glen Blvd, Ct, Dr & Pl 74019
S Roselake Dr 74019
Rosewood Cir & Ct 74017
Russell Dr 74017
Rutter Rd 74017
E Sageeyah Rd 74017
S & E Salem Cir & Dr 74019
E Savage Dr 74017
Savanna Ct 74019
S & E Scherry Cir, Ct & Ln 74019
W School Ct 74017
E School Rd 74019
W School St 74017
E Second St 74019
N & S Seminole Ave 74017
E Sequoyah Park Dr 74017
Shade Tree Ct & Pl 74019
E Shadowbrook Rd 74017
Shadowlake Ct, Dr & Ln 74017
E Shadowview Dr 74017
Shady Cir & Ln 74019
Shady Lane Dr 74019
E & S Shannon Dr 74019
E Shasta St 74017
S Shelly Rd 74019

S Shepherd Dr 74019
S Shetland Ln 74019
E & S Shiloh Rd 74019
Silverado Rd 74019
Silverwood Rd 74019
Singletree Ln 74019
N & S Sioux Ave 74017
Skylark Cir 74019
E & S Skyline View Dr & Rd 74019
Smith Cir 74017
E Sonora Rd 74019
Southaven Rd 74019
E Southern Hills Rd 74019
Southpark Ave 74017
E Southpark Rd 74019
S Southridge Dr 74019
S Southview Dr 74019
E Spotted Horse Dr 74019
Spring Ln 74017
Spring Creek Ct 74019
Spring Creek Ln
8500-8599 74019
18700-18999 74017
S Spruce Ln 74017
E Sprucewood Dr 74019
E Star St 74017
Stirrup St 74017
E & S Stone Creek Dr 74017
Stonebridge Pkwy 74019
Stonehaven Dr 74017
Stonehedge Ct & Dr 74017
W Strain St 74017
E & W Stuart Roosa Dr 74017
Summer Ln 74017
E Summer Ln 74019
Summerhill Ln 74017
Summerset Ct 74019
Summit Dr
1800-1899 74017
22801-22897 74019
22899-22999 74019
S Summit Trl 74019
S Sundance Dr 74019
E & S Sunny Dr & Ln 74019
S Sunny Lake Rd 74019
S Sunrise Dr & Rd 74017
S & W Sunset Dr 74017
E Swan Dr 74019
E Sycamore Ave 74019
E Sycamore St 74017
Tall Pine Ln 74017
E Tanner Dr 74019
Tee Rd 74019
Terry St 74017
E Third St
10200-10799 74019
17100-17399 74017
E Thomas Dr 74017
Timber Rdg 74017
E Timber Trl 74019
E Timber Ridge Rd 74019
E Timbercreek Ln 74019
Timberlake Dr 74017
E Timberline Pl 74019
Tims Ln 74019
Tower Ln 74019
Trailwood Dr 74017
S Trinity 74017
Tulip Ct 74019
E Turner Dr 74019
E Turtle Dr 74019
S Turtle Run 74017
S Twin Oaks Dr 74019
University Dr 74017
Upland Dr 74017
Valentine Ln 74017
S Valeview Ave 74017
S Valley Dr 74019
Valley Pkwy 74019
Valley View Dr 74017
Valley West Dr 74019
Vantage Ct 74019
E Verdigris Dr 74019
Vest Dr 74017
S Veterans Pkwy 74017
Village Ct 74017
Vintage Trace Dr 74019
S Walnut Ln 74019
E Walnut Rd 74017
S Walnut Rd 74017
Walnut St 74017
Walnut Hill Ln 74019
Warehouse Rd 74019
Weber Rd 74017
N & S Weenonah Ave 74017
S Wells Ranch Rd 74019
S & E Wesson Ave & Ct 74019
Westin Park Ln 74019
E Weston Ln 74019
Westwind Ct 74017
Westwood Dr 74017
N & S Wewoka Ave 74017
Wild Fawn Rd 74019
Wildwood Ln & Pl 74019
E & W Will Rogers Blvd, Cir, Ct & Pl 74017
Williams Ct 74017
E Willow Dr 74019
N Willow Dr 74017
N Willow Pl 74017
E Willow Rd 74019
S Willow Rd 74019
E Willow St 74017
S Willow St 74019
Willow Tree Ct 74019
E Winchester Ave 74019
S Winchester Ct 74019
E Winchester Dr 74017
Winter Ln 74017
Wolf Run Ct & Dr 74019
Woodcrest Dr 74017
Woodland Rd 74019
Woodmere Rd 74017
Woodridge Dr 74019
Woods Ct, Dr & Ln 74017
N & S Wortman Ave & Pl 74017
S Wrangler 74019
Yonkipin Dr 74019
E Yorkshire Ave 74017

NUMBERED STREETS

E & W 1st 74017
W & E 4th Pl & St S 74017
E 5th St 74017
E & W 6th 74017
E & W 7th 74017
E & W 8th 74017
E 9th Pl S 74017
W 9th Pl S 74017
E 9th St 74017
E 9th St S 74017
W 9th St
100-399 74017
400-898 74017
400-400 74018
401-899 74017
W 9th St S 74017
E & W 10th S 74017
E & W 11th S 74017
E & W 12th Pl & St 74017
E & W 13th Pl & St S 74017
14th Pl & St S 74017
E & W 15th 74017
W & E 16th Pl & St 74017
E 17th St 74017
W 17th St 74017
W 17th St S 74019
E 18th St 74017
W 18th St 74017
W 18th St S 74019
W 19th St 74017
W 19th St S 74019
W 20th St 74017
W 20th St S 74019
21st N 74017
W 22nd St 74017
23rd Pl & St 74017
W 24th St N 74017
E 103rd St N 74019
E 106th St N 74019
E 108th St N 74019
E 110th St N 74019
E 111th St N 74019
E 116th St N 74019
E 119th 74019
E 121st 74019
E 122nd 74019
E 124th St N 74019
E 126th St N 74019
E 135th St N 74019
N 197th East Ave 74019
N 198th East Ave 74019
N 202nd East Ave 74019
N 204th East Ave 74019
N 205th East Ave 74019
N 206th East Ave 74019
N 207th East Ave 74019
N 209th East Ave 74019
E 350 Rd 74017
E 355 Rd 74017
E 357 Rd 74017
E 360 Rd 74017
E 370 Rd 74017
E 380 Rd 74017
E 390 Rd 74017
E 394 Rd 74017
E 395 Rd 74017
400 Cir & Rd 74017
E 405 Rd 74017
407 Cir & Ct 74017
S 4077 Rd 74019
S 4074 Rd 74019
S 4076 Rd 74019
S 4079 Rd 74019
S 4080 Rd 74019
S 4092 Rd 74019
S 4094 Rd 74019
S 4090 Rd 74019
E 410 Rd 74017
S 4102 Rd 74017
S 4109 Rd 74019
S 4106 Rd 74019
S 4100 Rd
15200-17199 74017
19800-25899 74019
S 4110 Rd 74019
S 4112 Rd 74019
S 4111 Rd 74019
S 4116 Rd 74019
S 4110 Rd
15700-16799 74017
20500-27099 74019
S 4126 Rd 74019
S 4120 Rd
19500-19999 74017
20000-27899 74019
S 4133 Rd 74017
S 4131 Rd 74017
S 4130 Rd
15500-16399 74017
21100-26999 74019
S 4140 Rd 74019
S 4151 Rd 74019
S 4150 Rd
9000-18999 74017
22055-25399 74019
S 4162 Rd 74017
S 4168 Rd 74017
S 4160 Rd
9000-19199 74017
21500-22899 74019
S 4177 Pl 74017
E 417 Rd 74017
S 4178 Rd 74019
S 4176 Rd 74017
S 4170 Rd
7001-7297 74017
S 4175 Rd
7300-7800 74017
21000-21499 74019
S 4170 Rd
21200-25899 74019
4187 Pl & Rd 74017
S 4185 Rd 74017
S 4182 Rd 74017
S 4183 Rd 74019
S 4180 Rd
6900-20499 74017
20500-24999 74019
S 4192 Rd 74017
S 4194 Rd 74017
S 4195 Rd 74017
S 4196 Rd 74017
S 4197 Rd 74017
S 4193 Rd 74019
S 4190 Rd
9400-19899 74017
20000-24399 74019
E 420 Rd 74017
S 4205 Rd 74017
S 4203 Rd 74017
S 4200 Rd
7500-9098 74017
19400-21999 74019
S 4212 Rd 74017
S 4215 Rd 74019
S 4210 Rd
11400-18999 74017
19000-21099 74019
E 422 Rd 74017
S 4226 Rd 74017
S 4220 Rd
11000-18599 74017
18800-20999 74019
S 4233 Rd 74017
S 4237 Rd 74017
S 4239 Rd 74017
S 4235 Rd 74017
S 4230 Rd
12500-17999 74017
18400-22999 74019
S 4240 Rd
14500-15999 74017
17200-20999 74019
N 425 74019
S 425 74019
E 425 Rd 74017
N & S 4250 74019
430 Pl & Rd 74017
E 435 Rd 74017
E 436 Rd 74017
438 Pl & Rd 74017
E 440 Rd 74017
E 442 Rd 74017
E 445 Rd 74017
E 446 Rd 74017
E 450 Rd 74017
E 453 Rd 74017
E 454 Rd 74017
E 455 Pl 74017
E 456 Rd 74017
E 458 Rd 74017
E 460 Rd
9400-20499 74017
20500-21899 74019
462 Pl & Rd 74017
E 463 Rd 74017
E 465 Rd
14300-14899 74017
20200-20299 74019
E 470 Pl 74017
E 470 Rd
4500-5699 74019
8400-17499 74017
19200-20999 74019
E 472 Rd 74019
E 473 74017
E 474 Rd 74019
E 475 Rd 74019
E 477th Pl 74019
E 480 Rd
500-699 74017
5600-6699 74019
7500-8099 74017
8100-9498 74019
8101-15899 74017
13500-15798 74017
16800-21999 74019
E 484 Rd
4800-5000 74019
5002-16998 74019
14701-14999 74017
16701-16999 74019
E 485 Rd 74019
E 486 Rd 74019
E 488 Rd 74019
E 489 Rd 74019
E 490 Rd 74019
E 492 Rd 74019
E 495 Rd 74019
E 496 Rd 74019
E 500 Rd 74019
E 505 Rd 74019
E 510 Rd 74019
E 520 Rd 74019
E 521 Rd 74019
E 523 Rd 74019
E 525 Rd 74019
E 527 Rd 74019
E 530 Rd 74019
E 534 Rd 74019
E 535 Rd 74019
E 538 Rd 74019
E 540 Rd 74019
E 542 Rd 74019
E 550 Rd 74019
E 560 Rd 74019
E 66 Pines Rd 74017

DUNCAN OK

General Delivery 73533

POST OFFICE BOXES MAIN OFFICE STATIONS AND BRANCHES

Box No.s
All PO Boxes 73534

RURAL ROUTES

01, 02, 03, 04, 05, 06, 07, 08 73533

NAMED STREETS

All Street Addresses 73533

NUMBERED STREETS

All Street Addresses 73533

DURANT OK

General Delivery 74701

POST OFFICE BOXES MAIN OFFICE STATIONS AND BRANCHES

Box No.s
All PO Boxes 74702

RURAL ROUTES

01, 02, 03, 04, 05 74701

HIGHWAY CONTRACTS

62, 63 74701

NAMED STREETS

Aaron Ct 74701
Acorn Trail St 74701
Ada St 74701
E & W Alabama St 74701
Albert Pike Rd 74701
Allison Way 74701
Alma Dr 74701
Anna Dr 74701
Apple Ln 74701
E & W Arkansas St 74701
Armstrong Rd 74701
Arrowhead Ln 74701
Asberry St 74701
Avalanche Rd 74701
Baltimore St 74701
E & W Beech St 74701
Bella Dr 74701
Benjamin Dr 74701
Bentlee Rd 74701
Benttree 74701
Beretta Blvd 74701
Berne Blvd 74701
Berry St 74701
Berrywood Ln 74701
Big Lots Rd 74701
Blackjack Rd 74701
Blades Cir 74701
Blake Ln 74701
Blanchard Rd 74701
Blue Main St 74701
Bo Ct 74701
E & W Bourne St 74701
Brandi Ln 74701
Braudrick Ln 74701
Briarcreek Dr 74701
Briarwood Ave & Pl 74701
Brittney Dr 74701
Brooke Ln 74701
Brookhaven 74701
Brookline Dr 74701
Brookside Dr 74701
Brothers Way 74701
Bryan Dr & Rd 74701
Bryant St 74701
Buck Trl 74701
Buckeye Rd 74701
Buffalo Crossing Rd 74701
Bunker Dr 74701
Burkett Ln 74701
Bushnell Ln 74701
Butlan Cir 74701
Butterfield Trl 74701
Byers Rd 74701
Cale Switch Rd 74701
Cardinal Ln & Pkwy 74701
Carl Albert Dr 74701
Carol Cir 74701
Caroline Ct 74701
Carriage Point Dr 74701
Casey Ln 74701
Castle Ct 74701
Cavender Ln 74701
E & W Cedar St 74701
Cedar Ridge Cir 74701
Cemetery Rd 74701
Cessna Dr 74701
Chad Ln 74701
Chaparral Dr 74701
Cheek Ln 74701
Cherry Ln 74701
Chestnut Ln 74701
Chittamwood Rd 74701
Choctaw Rd 74701
Christy Ln 74701
Chubley Rd 74701
Chuckwa Dr 74701
Church Rd 74701
Ciara Dr 74701
Clark Dr 74701
Claymill Ln 74701
Colonel Phillips Rd 74701
Colt Dr 74701
Commercial Ln 74701
Cooper School Rd 74701
Corinne Dr 74701
Cornell Dr 74701
Country Club Rd 74701
Covington Rd 74701
Coxsey Rd 74701
Coyote Trl 74701
Creekwood Dr 74701
Crepe Myrtle Ln 74701
Crestview Ave & Ln 74701
Criswell Dr 74701
Crooked Oak Dr & Pl 74701
Crystal Ln 74701
Cypress Rd 74701
Daisy St 74701
Daisy Mae Ln 74701
Dakota St 74701
Dallas St 74701
Dana Dr 74701
E Davis Rd 74701
Dawna St 74701
Dead End Rd 74701
E Deb Meade Rd 74701
Deer Run 74701
Delivery Ln 74701
Denison St 74701
Dentwood Ct 74701
Devault Ln 74701
Dixon St 74701
Donna Sue Pl 74701
Eagle Loop Rd 74701
Eaglelake Dr 74701
Easy St 74701
Ed F Davis Rd 74701
E & W Elm St 74701
W End St 74701
Engles Dr 74701
Englewood Dr 74701
Enterprise Dr 74701
W Eppler Dr 74701
Estelle St 74701
E & W Evergreen St 74701
Fairway Dr 74701
Falcon Dr 74701
Farmer Rd 74701
Felice Ln 74701
Fisher Station Rd 74701
Fisherman Ln 74701
Flamingo Rd 74701
E Florida St 74701
Folsom Rd 74701
Forest Ln 74701
Forrest Cir 74701
Fort Mcculloch Rd 74701
Four Seasons Dr 74701
Frances St 74701
Frank Ln 74701
Gail Farrell Dr 74701
Gainer St 74701
Gamco Pl 74701
Gapwedge 74701
Gary Ln 74701
Gates Ave 74701
E & W Georgia St 74701
Gerlach Dr 74701
Gershwin Dr 74701
Glen St 74701
Grand Ave 74701
Granny Teel Rd 74701
Grant Ave 74701
Greenbriar 74701
Greens Rd 74701
Haley Rd 74701
Hamby Ln 74701
Hardrock Ln 74701
Hardy Dr 74701
Harmony Dr 74701
Haworth Rd 74701
Haynie Rd 74701
Heritage Dr 74701
Hickory Dr & Pl 74701
Hickory Hollow Rd 74701
Hickory Ridge Rd 74701
Highland Dr 74701
Highroad 74701
Highway 48 N 74701
S Highway 69 74701
E & W Highway 70 74701
Highway 78 S 74701
Hill St 74701
Hillcrest Ave & Ct 74701

Hillcrest Heights Dr 74701
Hilltop Hollow Rd 74701
Holcomb Ave 74701
Hollis Roberts Dr 74701
Honeysuckle Rd 74701
S Hoover Rd & St 74701
Horton Ln 74701
Houston St 74701
Hunnicutt Ln 74701
Ike St 74701
Indian Rd 74701
Indian Terrace Ln 74701
Industrial Ln 74701
Isabella Ct 74701
Jerry St 74701
Jim Mac Rd 74701
Joan St 74701
Jodi St 74701
Joe Bullard Dr 74701
John Jct 74701
Johnson St 74701
E Jones St 74701
Joshua 74701
Julia Ln 74701
Kade Ct 74701
Kande Ln 74701
Karr Rd 74701
Katherine St 74701
N Katy St 74701
Kay St 74701
Kelly Dr 74701
Kernel Ln 74701
Kimber Ln 74701
Kimberly Rd 74701
Klayton Ct 74701
Knight Dr 74701
Kolten Dr 74701
Lacey Dr 74701
Lahoma Cir 74701
Lake Durant Rd 74701
Lakeshore Dr 74701
Lakeview Dr 74701
Larkspur Ln 74701
Laura Dr 74701
Lavola St 74701
Lear St 74701
Lee Ave 74701
Lenore St 74701
Lionel Ln 74701
W Litatera St 74701
Little John Dr 74701
W Liveoak St 74701
E & W Locust St 74701
Lois Ln 74701
N & S Lone Oak Rd 74701
Lorrie Ln 74701
W Lost St 74701
W Louisiana St 74701
Lynn Haven Dr 74701
Lynnwood St 74701
Madeline Dr 74701
Madison St 74701
E Main St 74701
W Main St
1-1224 74701
1223-1223 74702
1225-4999 74701
1226-4998 74701
Mallard Dr 74701
N & S Malone Dr 74701
Maple St 74701
Marie Dr 74701
Market Sq 74701
Martin Cir 74701
Mason Ct & St 74701
Matney Sumner Rd 74701
Matthew Dr 74701
Maxey Dr 74701
Mayapple Cir 74701
Mayhew St 74701
Mccarty Rd 74701
Mcclure Rd 74701
N & S Mclean Dr & Rd 74701
Meadow Ln 74701
Meadowlark Ln 74701
Meadows Dr 74701
Meagan Ave & Ct 74701
Megan 74701
Melissa St 74701
Michelle St 74701
Mills Dr 74701
Minor St 74701
E & W Mississippi St 74701
Misty Cir & Ln 74701
Mitchel Dr 74701
W Mockingbird Ln 74701
Monterrey St 74701
Montgomery St 74701
Mooney Dr 74701
Moore Ln 74701
Moreland Ave 74701
E & W Mulberry St 74701
Nails Crossing Rd 74701
Nelson Rd 74701
Northridge Dr 74701
Oak Ct, Ln & St 74701
Oak Hills Dr 74701
Oakridge Dr 74701
Oilmill Ave 74701
Old Highway 70 74701
Olive St 74701
Olivia Ave 74701
One Well Rd 74701
Oneida St 74701
Osage St 74701
Osprey 74701
Overland Dr 74701
Papa Hall Rd 74701
Parker Ln 74701
Parkland Dr 74701
Parkview Dr 74701
Parkway Cir 74701
Pawnee Dr 74701
Pearl St 74701
Pecan Pl & St 74701
Pecan Acres Dr 74701
Peppernut Ln 74701
Perfect Dr 74701
Pheasant Run 74701
N Philadelphia Rd 74701
Pickett Ln 74701
E & W Pine St 74701
Pipeline Rd 74701
N & S Pirtle Rd 74701
W Plum St 74701
Poltico Rd 74701
E & W Poplar St 74701
Portman Ln 74701
Presley 74701
Preston Wood 74701
Provisional Dr 74701
Quail Creek Rd 74701
Quail Ridge Cir & Rd 74701
Radio Rd 74701
Red Bud Ln 74701
Red Fox Rd 74701
Red Oak Dr 74701
Reid St 74701
Remington Cir 74701
Remington East Cir 74701
Remington North Cir 74701
Remington South Cir 74701
Remington West Cir 74701
N & S Risner Rd 74701
River Crest Ln 74701
Roadrunner Ct & Dr 74701
N & S Roberta Rd 74701
Roberts Ln & Rd 74701
Robin Rd 74701
Robin Hood Dr & Pl 74701
Robinson 74701
E Rodeo Rd 74701
S Rodgers Ln 74701
Rogers Cir 74701
Rolling Lane Dr 74701
Rolling Wood Hills Dr 74701
Roosevelt Ave 74701
Roping Ln 74701
Routh St 74701
Ruby Lee 74701
Ruger Dr 74701
Sam Hill Ln 74701
Sandpiper Cir 74701
Sandstone Rd 74701
Sandtrap Dr 74701
Sandwedge 74701
Sandy Hill Ln 74701
Sawmill Rd 74701
Scott St 74701
Shadow Wood Ln 74701
Shady Ln 74701
Shady Creek Rd 74701
Shamrock Ln 74701
Shawna Dr 74701
Shell Ln 74701
Shields Rd 74701
Shirley St 74701
Silo Rd 74701
Silver Valley Rd 74701
Silverado Dr 74701
Simons Rd 74701
Six Springs Dr 74701
Skyline Dr 74701
Sleepy Hollow Dr 74701
Smith St 74701
Smithville Ln 74701
Sooners Rd 74701
Springfield Court St 74701
Stage Coach Ave 74701
Star Rd 74701
State Road 199 74701
State Road 48 74701
State Road 70 E 74701
State Road 78 74701
Stone Rd 74701
Stonebriar Cir 74701
Stonebrook Cir & Way 74701
Stonecreek Dr 74701
Summit Cir 74701
Sunnymeadow Dr 74701
Sunnyside Rd 74701
Sunshine Ln 74701
Swan Ln 74701
Sweet Briar Rd 74701
W Sycamore St 74701
Tandy Walker Rd 74701
Ten Acres Dr 74701
W Tennessee St 74701
Texas St 74701
Thomas Way 74701
Three Mile Rd 74701
Thunder Rdg 74701
Timberline Dr 74701
Todd Cir 74701
University Blvd & Pl 74701
Us Highway 70 74701
Valley Trl 74701
Valley View Dr 74701
Van St 74701
Vanmeter Ln 74701
W Virginia St 74701
Waco St 74701
Wagon Trl 74701
Waldron Dr 74701
Walker Hill Rd 74701
W Walnut Rd & St 74701
W Ward Rd 74701
N Washington Ave 74701
N Washington Place Rd 74701
Washita St 74701
Weak Bridge Rd 74701
Weatherby Way 74701
Wendell Dr 74701
Wesley St 74701
West St 74701
Western Mdws 74701
Westside Dr 74701
Westwood St 74701
Widow Moore Ln 74701
Wildwood Dr 74701
W Willow St 74701
Wilson St 74701
Winchester Way 74701
Windsor Dr 74701
Woodland Cir 74701
Woodland Springs Dr 74701
Woodlawn St 74701
Worley St 74701
Yellowbrick Rd 74701

NUMBERED STREETS

All Street Addresses 74701

EDMOND OK

General Delivery 73034

POST OFFICE BOXES MAIN OFFICE STATIONS AND BRANCHES

Box No.s
1 - 9120 73083
30001 - 32100 73003

RURAL ROUTES

17, 18, 27, 30, 43, 46, 61 73003
02, 12, 15, 25, 29, 34, 39, 48, 50, 53, 56, 57, 59, 65, 66, 70 73012
09, 11, 16, 20, 22, 26, 36, 37, 41, 42, 44, 49, 52, 55, 62, 63, 69, 71, 73 73013
01, 08, 10, 23, 31, 32, 47, 72 73025
05, 06, 07, 13, 14, 19, 24, 28, 33, 35, 40, 45, 51, 54, 58, 64 73034

NAMED STREETS

Abbey Cir & Pl 73034
Aberdeen Rd 73025
Abierto Dr 73012
Abigail Ct 73003
Abilene Ave 73003
Acoma Pl 73013
Acorn Dr 73025
Ada Sage Ln 73003
Adagio Ln 73012
Adam Ct 73003
Adams Trl 73012
Admiral St 73013
Adobe Dr 73013
Aerial Rd 73012
Aerie Dr 73013
Affirmed Dr 73025
Agua Dr 73012
Ainsley Ct 73034
N Air Depot Blvd
1-6899 73034
11600-12199 73013
S Air Depot Blvd
1-99 73034
1600-3699 73013
13600-14799 73034
Albany Dr 73003
Alberto Pl 73012
Alexa Ave 73034
Alexanders Trl 73012
Allegheny Dr 73013
Allen Rd 73034
Allens Trl 73012
Allergando Ln 73012
Allie Dr 73012
Allie Brooke Dr 73034
Allora Dr 73012
Alyssum Ct 73034
Amanda Dr & Ln 73034
Amber Run 73013
Amberfield Dr 73034
Amberwood Cir 73003
Amberwood Ct 73003
Amberwood Pl 73013
Amberwood Rd 73003
Amesbury Lake Dr 73013
Anadarko Pl 73013
Andalucia Dr 73012
Angie Kaye Ln 73013
Anita Ln 73034
Ann Arbor 73013
Antelope Cir & Trl 73012
N Antler Way 73012
Antler Farms Dr 73013
Apache Dr 73013
Apache Trl 73003
Apian Way 73003
Apollo Cir & Rd 73003
Appalachian Trl 73003
Appaloosa Trl 73012
Apple Tree Dr 73012
Apple Valley Rd 73034
Applebrook Dr 73012
Appleway St 73013
Applewood Dr
6400-6899 73034
16900-16999 73012
Aquarius Rd 73003
Arapaho Rd 73013
Arbor Ln 73012
Arbor Chase 73013
Arbor Valley Dr 73025
Arbuckle Dr 73025
Arbuckle Hts 73013
N & S Arcadian Oaks Dr 73034
S & W Aries Rd 73003
Arrowhead Cir, Ct & Dr 73013
Arthurs Cir 73012
Ascot Cir 73034
Ash Grove Cir & Rd 73003
Ashe Brooke Pl 73034
Ashe Creek Dr 73034
Ashe Spring Dr 73034
Ashe Wood Dr 73034
Ashebriar Ln 73034
Ashebury Way 73034
E & N Ashecroft Cir & Dr 73034
Asheforde Pl 73034
Asheforde Oaks Blvd 73034
Ashehollow Ln 73034
Ashelynne Ct 73034
Asheton Ct 73034
Ashford Grv 73013
Ashley Cir 73025
Ashley Dr 73003
N Ashley Dr 73025
W Ashley Dr 73025
Ashley Trl 73025
Ashton Hill Cir 73034
Ashwood Ct 73025
Aspen Trl 73012
Astoria Bridge Ct 73034
Atchley Dr 73034
Auburn Ct 73012
Auburn Ln 73013
Auburn Xing 73012
Auburn Meadows Dr 73012
Augusta Ave 73034
Aurora Dr & Pl 73013
Autumn Rd 73013
Autumn Creek Dr 73003
Autumn Sage Dr 73034
Autumnwood Ct 73003
Autumnwood Dr 73012
Avalon Ln & Pl 73034
Avery Cir 73025
Avondale Cir 73013
E Ayers St 73034
Backhorn Rd 73012
Baffy Ct 73025
Bailey Cir 73025
Baird Dr 73013
Bald Cypress Cv 73013
Balmoral Ct & Dr 73034
Bandera 73013
Bandit Pt 73025
Bank Side Cir 73012
Banner Ave & Ct 73013
Barbara Dr 73013
Barberry Ct & Rd 73013
Barcas Rd 73012
Barnstable Ct 73012
Barracho Dr 73012
Barrett Pl 73003
Barrington Dr 73012
Barrington Ln 73034
Barrington Hills Ln 73012
Basking Ridge Trl 73013
Bassie Rd 73025
N & S Baumann Ave 73034
Bavarian Dr 73034
Bay Bridge Ct 73034
Bay Hill Pl 73034
Bayliner Launch 73013
Bayonne Bridge Ct 73034
Beacon Hill St 73034
Beagle Cir 73003
Beano Bnd 73034
Beaver Cir 73034
Beaver Creek Rd 73025
Beavers Bnd 73034
Bebida Way 73012
Bedford Cir
2600-2699 73034
16900-16999 73012
Bedford Dr 73012
Belcaro Bnd & Dr 73034
Bell Oak Rd 73013
Bell Tolls Ter 73034
Bella Mira Ln 73013
Bella Sera Dr 73034
Bella Terra Way 73034
Bella Vista Dr 73013
Bella Vista St 73025
Belle Air Ave 73013
Belmar Ct & Dr 73025
Belmont Cir & Dr 73034
Bending Oak Ct 73013
Benson Rd 73013
Bent Cedar Trl 73034
Bent Trail Cir & Rd 73012
Bent Tree Dr 73034
Bent Twig Cir & Rd 73013
Benton Rd 73034
Bergamo Blvd 73034
Berkley Dr 73034
Berkshire Dr 73034
Berryhill Cir & Ct 73034
Berrywood Cir & Dr 73034
Beverly Dr 73013
Big Cedar Ave 73012
Big Cypress Dr 73013
Big Horn 73012
Big Piney Ln 73012
Big Sky Dr 73025
Bigbee Dr 73003
Billy Ct, Dr, Ln & Pl 73034
Bip Pkwy 73025
Birch Ln 73034
Birchfield Dr & Rd 73012
Birdneck 73025
Birdsong 73003
Birkdale Dr 73025
Bison Dr 73034
Black Hawk Cir 73012
Black Hawk Dr 73012
Black Hawk Rd 73025
Black Walnut Cir 73012
Blackberry Rd & Rdg 73034
Blackbird Ln 73034
Blackhawk Trl 73034
Blackhorn Dr 73012
Blackjack Ln 73034
N & S Blackwelder Ave 73034
Blake Ct 73003
E Blanch Ave 73034
W Blanch Ave 73003
Blanch Ln 73025
Blevins Blvd 73013
Blossom Ct 73012
Blue Atlas Ct 73012
Blue Bird Cir 73034
Blue Bird Ln 73025
W Blue Cedar Rd 73025
Blue Fox Dr 73025
Blue Gramma Trl 73034
Blue Heron Cv & Pt 73034
Blue Jay Ct 73034
Blue Jay Dr
2200-2399 73012
15200-15699 73013
Blue Mesa Dr 73013
Blue Oak Way 73034
Blue Quail Pass 73013
Blue Ridge Dr 73003
E Blue Ridge Rd 73034
N Blue Ridge Rd 73034
Blue Sage Rd 73034
Blue Spruce Rd 73025
Blue Wister Cv 73013
Bluegrass Ln 73003
Bluff Cir 73013
Bluff Creek Dr 73012
Bob White 73034
Bob White Dr 73025
Bobcat Cir 73034
Bobwhite Ln 73034
Bobwhite Trl 73025
Bodega Way 73003
Bodegon Rd 73012
Bogie Rd 73012
Bonaire Dr & Pl 73013
Bond St 73034
Bonito Way 73012
Bonney Dr 73034
Boomer Trl 73034
Boreal Ct 73012
Boucher Dr 73034
Boulder Ct 73003
Boulder Bridge Way 73034
N Boulevard
1-1199 73034
N Boulevard
4700-4799 73025
S Boulevard
1-1499 73034
1500-3999 73013
N Boulevard St 73003
E Bowman Ave 73034
W Bowman Ave 73003
Bozeman Trl 73003
Bracken Ct 73034
Brackendale Ln 73003
Brad St 73003
Bradbury Cir 73012
N Bradbury Dr 73034
S Bradbury Dr 73034
Bradford Pl 73012
Bradford Way 73003
Bradford Farms Ln 73025
Bramblewood 73034
Branden Ln 73003
Brandon Ln 73034
Branson Valley Ct 73025
Brass Dr 73012
Brasswood Blvd & Pkwy 73013
Bravada Ct & Dr 73013
Bravado Pl 73013
Braxton Way 73034
Brayhill Ct & Rd 73003
Breckenridge Dr 73013
Breezy Hill Rd 73025
Brenner Pass 73013
Brenton Ct 73013
Brenton Dr 73012
Brenton Hills Ave 73013
Brentwood Dr 73013
Brett Dr 73013
Brewster Ln 73012
Briar Bend Trl 73012
Briar Forest Cir & Ct 73025
Briar Meade Cir & Rd 73025
Briarwood 73034
Briarwood Dr 73034
N Briarwood Dr 73025
Briarwood Pl 73034

NW Briarwood Rd 73025
Briarwyck 73013
Bridgeview Blvd & Pl 73003
Bridle Ct 73025
Bridle Ridge Cir 73012
N & S Bridlewood Dr 73034
Bridlington Dr 73012
Bright Angel Trl 73003
Brighton Dr 73003
Bristle Cone Cir, Dr & Way 73012
Bristol Ct & Ln 73034
Bristol Park Blvd 73013
Brittany Ln 73003
Brittany Paige Dr 73034
Brixton Ct & Rd 73034
N Broadway
1-199 73034
200-6898 73034
200-200 73083
201-6899 73034
S Broadway
1-1499 73034
1500-3999 73013
10100-14699 73034
Broadway Ct 73013
Broadway Ext 73013
E & S Broken Bow Cir, Ct & Rd 73013
Bronte Way 73034
Bronze Ln 73012
Brook Frst 73034
Brook Hill Dr 73013
Brookdale Ave 73034
Brooke Ave 73013
Brooke Ct 73003
Brookhaven Ct & Dr 73034
Brookshire Ct 73012
Brookside Ave 73034
Brookside Ct 73025
Brookview Ln 73034
Brookwood Cir, Ct, Dr & Pl 73034
Brownwood Ln 73034
Brush Creek Dr 73034
Bryan Dr 73003
N Bryant Ave
1-6899 73034
12400-14399 73013
S Bryant Ave
1-1499 73034
1500-3999 73013
10900-14699 73034
Buckhead Path 73034
Buckhorn Dr 73034
Buckingham Way 73034
Buckland Rd 73034
Buffalo Pass 73034
Buffalo Ridge Rd 73025
Bull Run 73034
Bunting Cir 73013
Bunting Ct 73034
Bunting Ln 73034
Bur Oak Dr 73012
Burkett Cir 73013
Burnham Ct 73025
Burning Spring Rd 73013
Burning Wood Rd 73013
N & W Burns Rd 73025
Burton Pl 73013
Butte Rd 73025
Butterfield Dr 73013
Butterfield Trl 73003
Butterfly Blvd 73012
Butterfly Creek Blvd 73013
Butternut Pl 73013
Cactus Cir, Ct & Dr 73013
Cade Ct 73012
Cadence Way 73025
Caines Hill Rd 73034
Cale Dr 73013
Caliburn Pkwy 73034
Calle Way 73012
Calm Waters Way 73034
Cambria Ct 73013
Cambridge Way 73013
Camden Way 73013
E Campbell St 73034
W Campbell St 73003
Canaan Creek Rd 73034
E & N Canary Cir, Ct, Dr & Pl 73034
Candleberry Dr 73012
Candlewood Dr 73034
Cantera Creek Dr 73013
Canterbury Dr 73013
Canton Ln 73012
Canyon Rd 73034
Canyon Bridge Ln 73034
Canyon Creek Pl 73012
Canyon Crest Dr 73025
Canyon Oak Dr 73025
Canyon Park Cir 73013
Canyonwood Ln 73012
Capitol Dr 73003
Capri Ct 73034
Capri Dr 73034
Capri Ln 73013
Capri Pl 73034
Capulet Dr 73013
Cardinal 73034
Cardinal Cir 73013
Cardinal Dr 73013
Cardinal Ln 73013
Cardinal Nest Dr 73013
Cardinal Ridge Dr & Ln 73034
Carfax Rd 73034
N & W Caribou Ct & Dr 73012
Carillo Rd 73012
Carlingford Way 73013
Carlton 73034
Carlton Dr 73012
Carlton Way 73012
Carmel Valley Pl & Way 73025
N & W Carol Cir & Dr 73003
Carriage Way 73013
Carriage Bluff Ct 73003
Carriage House Rd 73013
Carriage Park Ln 73003
Carrick Ct 73034
Casa Blanca 73025
Cascade Dr 73025
Cascata Dr 73013
Cascata Way 73034
Case Ln 73034
Casero Dr 73012
Caseys Ct 73025
Casi Ct 73034
Castellina Ct 73034
Castle Rd 73034
Castle Creek Dr 73034
Castle Rock 73003
Castleton Ave 73034
Catalina Dr 73013
Cattail Cir 73013
Cattle Dr 73034
Cavallo Rd 73013
Cave Creek Pt 73034
Caveat Ct & Dr 73025
Cedar Dr 73012
Cedar Ln 73034
Cedar Rdg 73025
Cedar Trl 73034
Cedar Vw 73013
Cedar Creek Dr & Ter 73034
Cedar Crest Dr 73003
Cedar Farm Rd 73025
Cedar Lake Dr 73034
Cedar Meadow Ln 73003
Cedar Mountain Ave, Dr & Rd 73034
Cedar Oak Dr 73013
Cedar Oaks Ter & Trl 73034
Cedar Pointe Cir, Ct & Ln 73003
Cedar Ridge Dr 73025
Cedar Ridge Rd
1200-2099 73013
22100-22228 73025
22230-22899 73025
Cedarbend Ct 73003
Cedarwood Dr 73012
Celtic Cir & Ct 73025
Centennial Blvd 73013
Central Ct 73034
Century Dr 73013
Cerrado Cir 73012
Chadwicke Dr 73013
Chain Bridge Ct 73034
Chaparral Ln 73013
Chaparral Ridge Rd 73034
Chappel Ridge Ln & Rd 73013
Charla Dr 73012
Charleston Rd 73025
Charlton Rd 73003
N Charter Oak Cir 73034
W Charter Oak Cir 73034
E Charter Oak Rd 73034
W Charter Oak Rd
100-3999 73034
4300-4498 73025
4500-15799 73025
Chartrand Ave & Ct 73034
Chartres Cir 73034
Chateau Ln 73034
Chaumont 73034
Chelham Ln 73034
Chelsea Dr 73013
Cherokee 73013
Cherry Creek Rd 73034
Cherry Hollow Rd 73013
Cherryvale Rd 73003
Chestermere Cir 73012
Chestnut Ct 73025
Chestnut Ln 73034
Chestnut Oak Dr 73012
Cheval Pointe Dr 73034
Cheyenne Dr 73013
Cheyenne Villa Cir 73013
Chickasaw Dr 73013
Chickasha Cir 73013
Chimney Hill Ct & Rd 73034
Chinaberry Ln 73013
Chipper Ln 73025
Chisholm Cir 73025
Chisholm Trail Blvd 73012
N Chisholm Trail Blvd 73025
W Chisholm Trail Blvd 73025
Chiswick Rd 73034
Choctaw Dr & Ln 73013
Chowning Ave 73034
Churchill Rd 73034
Cinnamon Dr 73003
Cinnamon Ridge Rd 73025
Circle Gln 73025
Circle Bend Ct & Pl 73034
Citation Dr 73025
Claremont Blvd 73013
Clay Dr 73013
Claybridge Cir 73012
N Clayton Rd 73034
Clear Creek Cir 73034
Clear Creek Dr 73013
Clear Midnight Dr 73034
Clearwater Cir 73003
Cleaton Dr 73012
Cleek Ct 73025
E Clegern Ave 73034
W Clegern Ave 73003
Clegern Dr 73034
Clemson Ct 73013
Clermont Ct & Dr 73003
Cliffgate Dr 73003
Clifford Farms Rd 73012
Clipper Xing 73013
Cloudview Pl 73003
Clove Hill Pl 73012
Clover Glen Dr 73013
Clubhouse Rd 73013
Coachlight Dr 73013
Coachman Rd 73013
Cobalt Ave 73012
Cobalt Cv 73013
Cobblestone Cir & Ct 73034
Coffee Creek Ln 73034
E Coffee Creek Rd 73034
W Coffee Creek Rd 73025
Coffey Cir 73013
Coffey Ridge Rd 73025
Cogswell Cir 73013
Cola Dr 73012
Colchester Dr & Ter 73034
E Colcord Ave 73034
W Colcord Ave 73003
Coldbrook Cir & Ln 73003
Coleman Ct 73034
Coles Rd 73013
N & S College St 73034
Collingwood Ln 73013
Colonia Bella Dr 73013
Colonial Ln 73013
Colony Ct & Dr 73003
Colt Dr 73034
Coltrane Pl 73034
N Coltrane Rd
100-6700 73034
6702-6768 73034
12300-13999 73013
S Coltrane Rd
201-297 73034
299-1499 73034
1500-4699 73013
10700-14799 73034
Columbia Ct 73003
Comfort Dr 73013
Concord Cir, Ct & Ln 73003
Coneflower Rd 73013
Conifer Ln 73012
Connie Ln 73034
Conquistador Ct 73025
Conridge Dr 73034
Constitution Ave 73013
N & S Cooke Trl 73034
Cooper Cir 73025
Coopers Hawk Ct 73003
Copeland Way 73025
Copper Cove Dr 73013
Copper Creek Dr 73012
Copper Oaks Dr 73025
Copper Rock Dr 73025
Copperfield Ct & Dr 73003
Cordillera Way 73012
Cordova Ct 73034
Corjil Ln 73013
Coronado Dr 73013
Coronado Bridge Ct 73034
Corral Pl 73012
Cottage Ln 73013
Cottonwood 73025
Cottonwood Ct 73012
N Council Rd
15100-15999 73013
16800-21899 73012
22200-24899 73025
S Council Rd 73025
Council Bluff Dr 73013
Country Club Dr & Ter 73025
E & N Country Oaks Rd 73034
Country Side Trl 73012
Countryside Ct 73013
Countrywood Ln 73012
N County Line Rd 73012
S County Line Rd 73025
W County Road 72 73012
Courtney Ln 73013
Cove Wood Cir 73025
Covell Ln 73034
E Covell Rd 73034
W Covell Rd
300-1499 73003
2500-4899 73012
Covell Village Dr 73003
Coventry Ct 73012
Coverton Way 73012
Covey Run Dr & Ln 73034
Covington Mnr 73012
Cowan Dr 73025
Coyote Pt & Trl 73034
Coyote Pass Dr 73012
Crab Apple Pl 73012
Crab Orchard Dr 73025
Craig Blvd 73003
Cranbrook Rd 73012
Crane Way 73013
Creek Cir 73013
N Creek Dr 73034
Creek Bank Dr & Rd 73003
Creek Bend Rd 73003
Creek Heights Dr 73013
S & W Creek Side Dr 73012
Creek Spur Rd 73003
Creek View Dr
1-99 73003
15400-15699 73013
Creek Vista Cir 73013
Creekwood 73025
Crest Vly 73012
Crest Glen Rd 73013
Crest Ridge Dr 73012
Crested Owl Dr 73013
Crestmere Ln 73025
Crestmont Ln 73025
Creston Way 73012
Crestview 73012
Cricket Holw 73034
Cricklewood Ct 73012
Crimson Bluff Way 73034
Crimson Oak Ln 73012
Cristo Pass 73025
Cristobal Blvd 73012
Crockett Ln 73034
Cross St 73034
Cross Creek Rd
1700-1799 73012
3600-3799 73003
Crossbow 73034
Crossfield Ct & Dr 73025
Crossing Dr & Way 73013
Crossland Ct 73003
N & S Crosstimber Dr & Trl 73034
Crosstrails 73003
Crosswinds Trl 73013
Crown Dr 73034
Crown Colony Ct, Ln & Rd 73034
Crown Feathers Dr 73013
Crusader Ave 73025
Crystal Crk 73034
Crystal Trl 73013
Crystal Creek Pl 73034
W Crystal Springs Cir 73012
Cumberland Dr 73034
Currant Dr 73012
Cypress Ct 73013
Cypress Holw 73034
Cypress Creek Rd & Way 73034
Cyrus Cir 73013
Dalemead Way 73012
Dalton Cir 73034
E Danforth Rd 73034
W Danforth Rd
100-2299 73003
2300-3199 73012
Danforth Farms Blvd 73012
Dardanelle Pass 73025
Darlington Ct & Ln 73013
Darril Rd 73025
N Darwin Rd 73034
Dauphin Ave 73034
W Davis Dr 73025
Daybright Dr 73013
Dayflower Ln 73013
De Vita Rd 73003
Deason Dr 73013
Deborah Ln 73034
Deep Fork Pt 73013
Deer Ct 73013
Deer Ln 73034
Deer Vly 73034
Deer Xing 73025
Deer Creek Dr 73025
Deer Creek Holw 73012
Deer Creek Rd 73012
Deer Haven Ct 73025
Deer Hollow Dr 73012
Deer Park Dr 73003
Deer Path Rd 73025
Deer Ridge Dr 73034
Deer Run Rd 73034
Deer Springs Cir 73012
Deer Trail Dr 73025
Deer View Xing 73034
Deerbrook Ct 73003
Deerfield Dr 73034
Deermont 73034
Deerwood Ct & Trl 73034
Del Mar Dr 73013
Del Norte Dr 73003
Del Simmons Dr 73003
Dena Dr 73003
Denham Cir 73034
Dennis St 73003
Depel Dr 73034
Derby Run Dr 73034
Devon Dr 73034
Devonshire Ct 73034
Dickinson Ct 73013
Diego Pl 73012
Diplomat Dr 73034
Dixie Ln 73013
Dodge Trl 73003
Doe Trl 73012
Dogwood Dr 73013
Dogwood Ln 73034
Doningham Ct & Dr 73034
Donner Trl 73003
Dooley Farms Ln 73003
Doral Dr 73034
Dornoch Dr 73034
Douglas Ave 73012
Douglas St 73034
Dove Ct 73034
Dove Crossing Dr 73034
Dover Dr 73034
Dovetail 73034
Downing Ct 73034
Dr Tom Rd 73034
Driftwood Ct 73034
Driftwood Dr 73013
Dripping Springs Dr 73034
Driver Ln 73025
Duckhawk Ct 73003
Dudley Ct 73013
Duncan Dr 73025
Dundee Ct & Ter 73025
Dunes Cir 73003
Dupont 73034
Durango Way 73034
Durbin Park Rd 73012
Durham Ct 73013
Durland Dr 73012
Dustin Dr 73003
Dustin Ln 73013
Dutch Forest Ln & Pl 73013
Duxsford Ct 73034
Eagle Dr 73034
Eagle Ln
2100-2199 73034
3200-3299 73013
Eagle Crest Rd 73013
Eagle Pass Ln 73013
Earl A Rodkey Dr 73003
Early Dawn Dr 73034
East Dr 73034
N Eastern Ave 73013
N & S Easy St 73012
Easy Street Ct 73012
Eaton Pl 73034
Echo Dr 73034
Echo Rdg 73012
Echo Trl 73013
Echohollow Trl 73025
N Ecker Dr 73013
Edge Rd 73034
Edgemont 73013
Edgewater Ln 73013
Edgewood Dr 73013
Edinburgh Dr 73013
W Edmond Rd
200-2299 73003
2301-2397 73012
2399-3199 73012
Edmond Gardens Dr 73013
E Edwards St 73034
W Edwards St 73003
Egrets Ldg 73012
El Greco Dr 73012
El Zorro 73034
Elizabeth Ln 73025
N Elk Ln 73012
Elk Horn Rd 73034
Ella Ct 73034
Elm 73034
Elmtree Ln 73013
Elmwood Dr 73013
Elmwood Ln 73034
Elwood Dr 73013
Emerald Brook Ct 73003
Emily Way 73025
Englewood Ln 73013
English Oak Ln 73012
Enterprise Dr 73013
Enz Dr 73034
Equestrian Ct 73034
Eric Ln 73034
Erinblu Pl 73003
Ernest Ct 73013
Essex Ct 73013
Estancia Cir 73034
Evan Ct 73013
Evan Shaw Ct 73013
N Everest Ave 73013
Everett Dr 73013
Everglade Ln 73013
Evergreen Ct 73025
N Evergreen Dr 73025
W Evergreen Dr 73025
Evergreen St 73003
Evermay Dr 73013
Everwood Dr 73012
Every Ct 73034
Explorer Dr 73012
Faculty Row 73034
Fair Meadow Dr 73003
Fair Winds Way 73013
Faircloud Ct, Cv, Dr & Ln 73034
Fairfax Dr 73034
Fairfield Dr 73012
Fairhill Ave 73013
Fairmont Ln 73013
Fairview Farm Blvd & Rd 73013
Fairway Dr 73025
Falcon Ln & Rdg 73034
Falkland Ter 73034
Fall Creek Dr 73013
Falling Sky Dr 73034
Farm Cove Rd 73013
Farmington Cir & Way 73012
Fawn Trl 73034
Fawn Valley Ln 73003
Feliz Dr 73012
Fenmoor Ln 73012
Fenwick Blvd 73012
Fernwood Dr 73034
Fieldshire Dr 73012
Filly Dr 73012
N Filly Ln 73034
S Filly Ln 73034
Findhorn Dr 73034
Firelane Rd 73003
Firetree Ln 73003
Firewheel Rd 73013
First Light Ln 73034
Fisher Rd 73013
Fisher Hill Rd 73013
Flagstone Ln 73003
Flint Ridge Rd 73003
Florence Dr 73034
Flowered Meadows Way 73012
Folcroft Rd 73013
Folkstone 73034

Fontella Ln 73034
Ford Ct 73034
Forest Rd 73025
Forest Creek Dr 73034
Forest Fox Rd 73034
Foss Dr 73025
N Fossil Creek Dr 73012
Fountain Vw 73013
Fountain Creek Dr 73034
Four Winns Strait 73013
Fox Bend Trl 73034
Fox Bluff Ct 73034
Fox Cove Ct 73034
Fox Den 73034
Fox Hill Dr & Ter 73034
Fox Hole Rd 73034
Fox Hunt Ln 73003
Fox Lake Ln 73034
Fox Pass Rd 73034
Fox Prowl Ln 73012
Fox Ridge Dr 73034
Fox Run Trl 73034
Fox Tail Dr 73034
Fox Trail Rd 73034
Fox View Ct 73034
Foxfire Rd 73003
Foxwood Cir 73034
Francis Ln 73034
Fredrick Dr 73003
Freedom Rd 73025
Freeman Dr 73025
Fremont Bridge Ct 73034
French Park Dr & Pl 73034
Fretz Ave 73003
N Fretz Ave 73003
S Fretz Ave 73013
Fretz Dr 73003
Friar Ct 73013
Frisco Way 73012
Frisco Bridge Blvd 73034
Frontier Cir 73025
Frontier Ln 73034
Fruited Plain Ln 73012
Gallant Fox Ct & Dr 73025
Garcia Ave 73003
Garden Vis 73034
Garden Creek Ln 73012
Garden Hill Cir & Dr 73034
Garden Ridge Dr 73013
Garden Ridge Rd 73012
Garrett Dr 73013
Gateway Dr 73013
Gathering Leaves Way 73034
Gaycliffe Ter 73003
Gebron Dr 73003
Geeta Rd 73003
S & W Gemini Rd 73003
Geneva Dr 73025
Gentry Cir 73034
George St 73003
Georgetowne Rd 73034
Georgia St 73034
Gettysburg Rd 73013
Glacier Ln 73003
Gladstone Cir & Ln 73012
Glen Cove Dr 73003
N & W Glen Eagle 73025
Glen Hollow Rd 73034
Glen Oaks Pl 73013
Glendale Cir & Dr 73034
Gleneagles Ct & Dr 73013
Glenlake Dr 73013
Glenmark Ct & Dr 73013
Glenmere Ct & Dr 73003
Glenn Dr 73034
Glenn Brook Ln 73034
W Glenn Trail Dr 73025
Glenolde Pl 73003
Glenridge Dr 73013
Glenrock 73012
Glenville Ct 73013
Glenway Cir 73034
Glenwood Cir & Ln 73034
Godhania Rd 73003
Gold Dr 73012
Gold Circle Dr 73025
Gold Fields Trl 73003
Gold Post Rd 73025
Golden Ln 73012
Golden Eagle Dr 73013
Golden Elm Cir 73012
Golden Hawk Ln 73012
Goodnight Trl 73003
Grace Ann Ct 73013
Graces Cir & Ter 73025
Gracie Dr 73025
Graeber 73025
Granada Ln 73034
N & S Grand Fork Dr 73003
Grand National Dr 73034
Grand Parke Dr 73013
Grandview Ter 73013
Granite Pl 73012
Grassmere Way 73012
Gray Fox Cir, Dr &
Run 73003
Grayson Dr 73013
Great Hampden Rd 73034
Green Canyon Dr 73013
Green Leaf Cir & Ln 73013
Green Meadow Ln 73012
Green Meadows Ct &
Dr 73025
Green Oaks Way 73034
Green Springs Dr 73012
Green Wood Gln 73025
Greenbriar Ave 73034
Greenery Ln 73012
Greenfern Ln 73034
Greenfield Dr 73012
Greenmore Dr 73034
Grey Hawk Ln 73012
Grey Hawk Rd 73003
Grey Owl Blvd 73013
Greystone Ct 73034
Griffin Blvd 73034
Griffin Cove Ct 73012
Griffin Gate Dr 73012
Griffin Park Blvd 73012
Grove Hill Ter 73012
Groveton Blvd 73012
Gulmor Dr 73034
Gwendolyn Ln 73034
Habben Way 73034
Hackberry Trl 73034
Hadwiger Ave 73034
Halbrooke Cir & Rd 73012
Halifax Cir 73034
Hampton Ct 73034
Hamptonridge Rd 73034
Hanover Dr & Ln 73034
Harding Ave, Ct & Pl 73013
Hardwick Ln 73034
Hardwick Rd
2800-3099 73034
15900-16099 73013
Hardwood Pl 73012
Hardy Dr 73013
Harness Ct 73012
Harness Creek Ct 73034
Harper Creek Trl 73034
Harrier Hawk 73003
Harris Dr 73013
Hartford Dr 73003
Harts Mill Rd 73013
Harvest Ct & Ln 73003
Harvestyme Ln 73025
N Harvey Ave 73013
Harward Ct 73013
Haslemere Ln 73012
Hatterly Ln 73013
Havenshire Ln 73034
Hawk Cliff Pl 73025
Hawkeye Pass 73034
Hawks Lndg 73003
Hawks Ridge Ln 73012
Hawks Tree Ln 73012
Hawks View Ct 73012
Hawthorne Ln & Pl 73003
Hawthorne Branch Dr 73012
Hazelhurst 73013
Heather Ct 73013
Heatherstone Rd 73034
Heavenfield Ct & Dr 73034
Heavenly Dr 73012
N Hefner Rd 73013
NW Heidelberg Rd 73012
N Heidi Dr 73012
Helts Hvn 73034
Hemingway Dr 73013
Henderson Dr 73013
Heritage Blvd 73025
Heritage Cir 73013
Heritage Ct 73025
Heritage Pl 73013
Heritage Green Cir, Rd &
Trl 73003
Hesston St 73034
Hiburn Cir 73034
Hickory Ln 73034
Hickory Rdg 73013
Hickory Bend Cir & Ln 73013
Hickory Creek Ln 73034
Hidden Creek Ct 73034
Hidden Hills Dr 73034
Hidden Hollow Cir &
Dr 73034
Hidden Lake Dr 73034
Hidden Prairie Cir &
Way 73013
Hidden Valley Rd 73013
High Mdw 73003
High Pt 73025
High St 73003
High Range Ln 73034
High Sierra Blvd 73013
Highland Blvd 73025
Highland Arbors Dr 73034
Highland Hills Dr 73034
Highland Park Rd 73012
Highlander Ridge Dr 73012
Highlands Lndg 73013
Highridge 73003
Highwater Cir 73034
N Highway 77 73012
W Hill Rd 73012
Hill Valley Way 73012
Hillcrest Dr & Ln 73025
Hillsdale Dr 73013
Hillside Cir 73034
Hillside Ln 73025
Hillside Rd 73034
Hilltop Rd 73034
Himalaya Rdg 73013
Hoffman Rd 73013
Hogan Ct 73013
Hollie Chappell Dr 73034
Hollow Brook Dr 73025
Hollow Glen Rd 73013
Hollowbrook 73012
Hollowdale Cir, Ct &
Ln 73003
Holly Ct & Dr 73034
Holly Burn Cir 73012
Holly Green Cir 73013
Holly Hill Dr 73034
Holly Hill Rd 73003
Hollycrest Ln 73025
Homecoming Dr 73013
Homestead Dr 73013
Homesteaders Pl &
Rd 73012
Honey Creek Dr 73034
Horse Shoe Bnd 73034
Horse Trail Rd 73012
N Horseshoe Rd 73012
N Hortense Ave 73003
N Howard Ct & St 73003
Huckleberry Rd 73012
N Huffines Rd 73012
Humber Bridge Ct 73034
Hummingbird Ln 73034
Hunt Club Ct 73034
Hunter Dr 73013
Hunter Pl 73003
Hunter Creek Dr 73012
Hunters Ct 73034
Hunters Path 73034
Hunters Trl 73025
Hunters Way 73034
Hunters Creek Rd 73003
Hunters Glen Cir 73012
Hunters Path Cir 73034
Hunters Pointe 73034
Hunters Pointe Rd 73003
Hunters Ridge Rd 73034
Hunters Spring Dr 73025
Hunting Hawk Cir 73013
Huntington Dr 73012
Huntsman Ct & Rd 73003
Huntwick Dr 73034
E Hurd St 73034
W Hurd St 73003
Hutton Dr, Lndg &
Way 73034
Hyde Parke Dr 73013
E I 35 Frontage Rd
200-1098 73034
1100-1299 73034
3400-3598 73013
3600-3700 73013
3702-4298 73013
N I 35 Frontage Rd 73034
W I 35 Frontage Rd
1000-1499 73034
1701-2697 73013
2699-4699 73013
E I 35 Service Rd 73034
Idabel Bridge Cir 73034
Idlewild Trl 73025
Illuvia De Oro Rd 73012
Indian Grass Ct 73013
Indian Hill Rd 73034
Indian Springs Dr 73003
Indians Springs Rd 73013
Industrial Blvd 73034
Inland Harbor Dr 73013
Integris Pkwy 73034
Interurban Way 73034
Inverary Dr 73025
Inwood Cir 73013
Irish Ln 73003
Iron Ln 73012
Iron Bridge Ct 73034
Iron Fire Ct 73013
Iron Horse Pass 73034
Iron Ridge Rd 73013
Iron Tree Ln 73013
Ironrock Dr 73012
Ironwood Ct 73003
Irvine Ct, Dr & Ter 73025
Island Dr 73034
Ivy Glenn Ct 73034
Ivy Ridge Ct 73034
Ivy Wood Rd 73034
Jabez Rd 73013
N & S Jackson St 73034
Jaclyns Trl 73012
Jacobs St 73034
James Creek Trl 73034
James Thomas Ct 73013
Jamestown Cir 73003
Jamin Paul Cir 73013
Jannas Trl 73012
Janos Cir 73003
Janson Dr 73003
Jarrell Ln 73034
Jasmine Pl 73003
Jeannes Trl 73012
Jefferson Ct & St 73034
Jeffersons Garden Ct 73013
Jeffery Dr 73013
Jennifer Ave 73003
Jennifer Ln 73025
Jessica Ln 73034
Jessica Pl 73003
Jessie James Dr 73034
Jills Trl 73012
Jills Garden Dr 73013
Jim Robison Dr 73013
John Deere Ave 73034
John Rausch Ln 73003
Joni Deanne Ct 73034
Jordan Ave 73013
Joseph Dr 73003
Josiah Pl 73013
Julies Trl 73012
Julies Trail Cir 73012
Juliet Dr 73013
Juneberry Ct 73012
Juniper Dr 73013
Juno Cir 73003
Jupiter Cir, Ct & Rd 73003
Kamber Ter 73003
Kambers Ln 73025
Kamran Ct 73013
Karen Dr 73013
Kasey 73034
Katherine Ct 73013
Kathy Ln 73034
Katie Ln 73012
Katie Michelle Blvd 73034
Katie Ridge Dr 73013
Katy Ln 73025
Kay Hill Ln 73003
Kayly Ct 73013
Kelley Pointe Pkwy 73013
Kellogg Dr 73034
Kelly Ave 73025
N Kelly Ave
1-4099 73003
4700-6499 73025
14600-15099 73013
S Kelly Ave
1-1499 73003
1600-4099 73013
10600-14699 73025
Kelly Lakes Dr & Pass 73025
Kelly Park Rd 73003
Kelsey Dr 73013
Kemble Ln 73012
Kendal Ct 73003
Kendre Ct 73025
Kennedy Ave 73034
Kenneth Dr 73034
Kensington Ter 73034
Kenswick Ct 73034
Kentucky Way 73034
Kenwood Ct 73034
Kerry Layne 73034
Kestral Way 73013
Kestral Lake Dr 73013
Kestral Park Ct 73013
Ketch Dr & Pl 73003
Kevins Way 73025
Keystone Cir 73025
Kian Pl 73013
Kiawah Cir 73025
Kickingbird Ln & Rd 73034
Kierland Ct 73012
Kiley Way 73034
Kimberly Dr 73003
Kimberwick Cir 73034
Kingfisher Way 73012
Kings Ct, Rd & Xing 73013
Kingsley Rd 73012
Kingston Blvd & Ct 73034
Kingwood Dr 73013
Kinross Cir 73012
Kiowa Rd 73013
Kirkland Rdg 73013
Kitty Cir 73034
Kittyhawk Ln 73034
Knights Bridge Rd 73034
Korie Dr 73013
Kristy Dr 73003
Kurdson Way 73013
La Cruz Ave 73003
La Due Ln 73013
La Paloma Ln 73012
Labelle Rue 73034
Lacebark Ln 73013
Ladbrooke Pl 73012
Ladera Ln 73034
Laguna Dr 73013
S Lake Dr 73012
Lake Front Dr 73034
Lake Shadows Ct &
Dr 73012
Lake Vista Rd 73034
Lakeshire Ridge Ct &
Way 73034
Lakeshore Dr 73013
Lakeside Cir 73012
Lakeview Ct 73003
Lakeview Rd 73025
Lakeview Trl 73003
Lakewood Dr 73034
Lakewood Ridge Rd 73013
Lambeth Cir & Dr 73003
Lamond Hill Ave 73034
Lamplight Ln 73013
Lamplighter Ln 73034
Lancaster Cir, Ct & Dr 73012
Landmark Rd 73012
Landon Ct & Dr 73013
Lanes Turn 73003
Lapwing Rd 73003
Laquinta Cir & Dr 73025
Laras Ln 73025
Lariat Cir 73003
Lariat Trl 73012
Larkspur Ct & Ln 73003
Las Meninas Dr 73012
Laurel Dr & Pl 73003
Laurel Oak Dr 73012
Lauren Ln 73025
Lauri Ln 73013
Lavender Ln
3000-3099 73013
3100-3200 73012
3202-3298 73012
Layne Ct 73013
Lazo Dr 73012
Lazy Brook Trl 73013
Lea Ct 73013
Lead Ln 73012
Leaning Willow 73025
Leatherwood Cir 73025
Leaves Of Grass Ln 73034
Leawood Ct, Dr & Pl 73034
Ledge Ln 73013
Ledgemont Dr 73013
Leesa Ln 73013
Legacy Cir & Dr 73025
Lenrose Ln 73013
Leo Rd 73003
S & W Lexington Way 73012
Lexy Ln 73034
Libby Ln 73012
Lil Ln 73013
Lilac Dr 73034
Lillehammer Dr 73034
N & W Lily Ln 73025
E Lincoln Ave 73034
N Lincoln Blvd 73013
Linda Ln 73013
Lindhurst Rd 73034
Lindsay Ln 73025
Lindy Ter 73025
Lisa Ln 73013
Little Chisholm Cir 73012
Little Horn Rd 73034
Little Leaf Ct & Ln 73012
Little Timber 73025
N & S Littler Ave & Pl 73034
Liveoak Dr 73034
N & S Lockeport Dr 73003
Lockhart Dr 73013
Locust Ln 73013
Locust Grove Ln 73012
Lois Lynn Ln 73003
Lolo Trl 73003
Lone Oak St & Way 73003
Lone Tree Trl 73034
Lonetree Dr 73025
Long Trl 73012
Long Branch Ln 73034
Long Spur Trl 73034
Long Trail Ct 73012
Longford Way 73013
Longhorn Dr 73003
Longmeadow Ct & Ln 73003
Lonsdale Dr 73034
Lookout Cir & Pt 73034
Lorenta Cir 73013
Lost Creek Dr 73013
Lost Forest Dr 73034
Lost Rock Trl 73012
Lost Trail Rd 73012
Louis Scott St 73003
Loutain Ct 73013
Low Mdw 73003
Lucy Ln 73012
Lupine Ln 73012
Lytal Ln & Ter 73013
N Macarthur Blvd
15100-16399 73013
16600-21799 73012
22500-24799 73025
S Macarthur Blvd 73025
Madder Dr 73013
N & S Madison St 73003
Magnolia 73025
Magnolia Ln 73013
Magnolia Way 73034
E Main St 73034
W Main St 73003
Mallard Ave 73003
Mallard Ln 73034
Malvern Ct 73034
Man O War Ct & Dr 73025
Manchester Ave 73034
Manner Park Ave 73034
Manzori Pass 73034
Maple Ln 73034
Maple Ridge Ln & Rd 73013
Maplelake Dr 73013
Marbella Dr 73012
Marbleleaf Dr 73013
Maria Cir 73034
Mariah Hbr 73013
Marigold Ln 73013
Marilyn Ave 73013
Marilyn Williams Dr 73003
Marjayoun Way 73034
Mark Rd 73003
Marked Tree Cir & Dr 73013
Marla Ln 73034
Mars Cir & Rd 73003
Marsh Hawk Ct 73012
Marshall Dr 73013
Marston Dr 73034
Martin Dr 73034
Martina Ln 73034
Martinique 73025
Mary Lee Ln 73034
Mashie Cir 73025
Mason Hills Dr 73034
Maverick Rd 73034
N May Ave
15100-16499 73013
16500-21799 73012
22200-24699 73025
S May Ave 73025
Mccartney Ln 73034
Mcdonald Dr 73034
Mckenzie Cir 73025
Mcraines Rd 73013
Meadow Ln 73013
Meadow Bend Ave 73012
Meadow Hill Dr 73034
Meadow Lake Dr 73003
Meadow Mist Cir 73012
Meadow Rock Trl 73034
Meadow View Cir &
Rd 73013
Meadow Vista Dr 73013
Meadowlark Ter 73034
Meadows Crossing Dr 73012
Meaghan Leigh Dr 73034
Medical Center Dr 73034
Medical Park Blvd 73013
Megans Way 73034
Melanie Way 73025
Melinda Ln 73013
Meline Dr 73034
Melody Ct 73012
Melody Dr 73012
Melody Ln 73013
Melville Ln 73012
E Memorial Rd 73013

Memory Ln 73013
Mendoza Dr 73013
Mercury Cir 73003
Mercury Ln 73012
Mercury Rd 73003
N Meridian Ave
18300-21399 73012
22300-24899 73025
S Meridian Ave 73025
Meritage Dr 73034
Meriweather Rd 73003
Merlot Cir 73012
Mesa Rd 73012
Mesa Trl 73025
Mesquite Ln 73034
Metro Plaza Blvd 73013
Michael Dr 73013
Michael Rd 73025
Mickerad Dr 73012
Mid Iron Ln 73025
Middleberry Rd 73013
Midway Ct 73034
N Midwest Blvd
1-6799 73034
13900-14399 73013
S Midwest Blvd 73034
Midwest Ln 73034
Milan Ct 73034
Milanese Ave 73013
Miles Dr 73034
Military Ave 73012
Mill Creek Rd 73025
Mill Hollow Rd 73012
Millies Trl 73012
Miracle Way 73025
Miramonte Cir 73003
Miranda Dr 73025
Mirano Ln 73034
Mission Dr & Rd 73034
Mission Hills Cir 73025
Mission Ridge Dr 73025
W Mission Springs Dr 73012
E & N Mistletoe Ct & Ln 73034
Misty Glen Dr 73025
Misty Park Dr 73013
Mockingbird Ln 73034
Mohawk Ct 73013
Mohawk Trl 73003
Mollie Rausch Ln 73003
Monarch Ln 73013
Monarchos Dr 73025
Montague Dr 73013
Montclair Dr 73013
Monterey Pl 73013
Montmatre Ct 73012
Montoro Way 73012
Moon Daisy Dr 73013
Moorgate Ln 73012
Morgan Trl 73012
Morley Ln 73012
Morning Dove Ln 73025
Morning Sky Ln 73012
Morning Song Dr 73012
Morning Star 73034
Morning Woods Pl 73034
Morningside Dr 73013
Morrison Trl 73012
Mount Vernon Pl 73013
E, N & S Mountain View Cir, Ln & Rd 73034
Muirfield Dr 73025
Muirfield Pl 73013
Mulberry Cir 73034
Mulholland Dr 73012
Mustang Trl 73012
Myra Ct 73013
Myrtle Ave 73034
Myrtle Dr
800-1199 73034
13100-13299 73013
Nandina Cir 73013
Nantucket Ave, Ln & Rd 73013
Napa Cir & Rdg 73013
Napa Valley Rd 73013

Naples Way 73034
Napol Ave 73034
Napoleon Ln 73025
Narrows Bridge Cir 73034
Natchez Rd & Trl 73012
Native Dancer Dr 73025
Nature Ln 73034
Nay Ave & Cir 73034
S & W Neptune Rd 73003
New Bond Cir 73034
New Canaan Rd 73034
New Haven Ct 73013
New Stem Rd 73003
Newbrook Dr 73003
Newport Dr 73013
Newport Bridge Dr 73034
Nez Perce Trl 73003
Niblick Way 73025
Nicholas Ct 73034
Nickel Ln 73012
Nighthawk Ct, Dr & Hl 73034
Nightingale Ln 73034
Nimrod Rd 73003
E & N Noble Dr 73034
Nora Dr 73034
Norma Ln 73034
Normal Hl 73034
Normandy Rd 73013
Northampton Ct 73013
Northbrook Ave 73034
Northern Dancer Dr 73025
Northgate Ter 73013
Northpark Ct 73012
Northwestern Dr 73034
Northwood Blvd 73013
Northwood Dr 73034
Northwood Ln 73013
Notting Hill Way 73012
Oak Ave 73034
Oak Dr 73034
E Oak Pl 73025
E & N Oak Cliff Dr 73034
Oak Creek Dr & Ter 73034
Oak Forest Dr & Rd 73025
Oak Heritage Trl 73025
Oak Hollow Dr 73013
Oak Leaf Rd 73013
Oak Springs Ct, Dr & Ln 73034
Oak Summit Rd 73025
Oak Tree Cir, Dr & Rd 73025
Oak Valley Cir & Ter 73025
Oak View Rd 73025
Oakcrest Dr 73012
Oakdale Farm Cir & Rd 73013
Oakdale Forest Ct & Rd 73013
Oakdale View Dr 73013
Oaklawn Ct 73013
E & N Oakleaf Dr 73034
Oaklee Way 73013
Oakmond Rd 73013
Oakmount Dr 73013
N Oakridge Cir, Dr & Rd 73034
Oakshire Dr 73012
Oakwood Dr 73013
Oakwood Creek Rd 73034
Ochoa Dr 73012
Oconee Creek Dr 73013
October Dr 73034
Okalee Ln 73013
Old Barn Rd 73025
Old Bugle Rd 73003
Old Country Cir 73034
Old Country Rd
12100-12299 73034
12300-12699 73013
Old Creek Rd 73034
Old Elm Ln 73013
Old English Rd 73003
Old Farm Ln & Rd 73013
Old Field Rd 73012
Old Georgetowne Rd 73013
Old Hickory Dr 73013

Old Ivy Cir 73013
Old Lake Ln 73013
Old Oak Dr 73013
Old Olive Way 73013
Old Pond Rd
2200-2499 73034
17300-17699 73012
Old River Trl 73013
Old Timbers Dr 73034
Olde Smt 73034
Olde Bridge Rd 73034
Olde Depot Dr 73034
Olde Edmond Dr 73034
Olde North Pl 73034
Olde Ridge Rd 73012
Olde School Pt & Rd 73012
Olde Towne Rd 73034
Olde Village Cir & Way 73013
Olde Waterfront 73034
Ole Barn Rd 73025
Olive Branch Ct 73012
Opal Ln 73012
Open Range Rd 73034
Open Trail Rd 73034
Orchard Ave 73012
Orchard Trl 73025
Orchard Vw 73025
Orchard Hill Dr 73025
Oregon Trl 73003
Orozco Cir 73012
Osage Dr 73013
Osceola Trl 73013
Osprey Cir 73012
Otter Dr 73013
Otter Creek Dr 73012
Outabounds Dr & Way 73034
Outer Banks Way 73034
Overland Way 73012
Owens Ave 73013
Owl Creek Dr 73034
Oxford Ave, Dr & St 73013
Ozark Dr 73034
Ozark Trl 73003
Pacheadw Dr 73034
Pacific Crest Trl 73003
Pacific Grove Dr 73003
Paddock Ln 73013
Padova Pt 73034
Pagoda Ct 73012
Painted Desert Dr 73034
Palazzo Pt 73034
Palermo Cir & Dr 73034
Palladium Ln 73012
Palm Ave 73013
Palm Beach Cir 73025
Paloma Ct 73012
Palomino Dr 73034
Panther Way 73013
Paper Birch Ct 73012
Park Pl & Rd 73034
Park Hollow Ln 73003
Park Lake Rd 73013
Park Lane Dr 73003
Park View Pl 73003
Parkgrove Dr 73012
Parkhurst Cir 73034
Parkhurst Rd
3700-5698 73034
5700-6099 73034
16600-16999 73012
Parkhurst Ter 73003
Parkside Dr 73012
Partridge Ln 73034
Patterson Dr 73013
Pawnee 73013
Pawnee Dr 73013
Pawnee Xing 73034
Pawtucket Ln 73012
Peachtree Ct 73025
Peacock Dr 73012
Pebble Ter 73034
Pebble Creek Blvd 73003
Pecan Pl 73013
Pecan Grove Pl 73034
Pecan Hollow Ter 73013

Pembroke Dr & Ln 73003
Penn Grove Dr 73003
Penn Place Dr 73025
Pennington Ave & Cir 73012
N Pennsylvania Ave
15400-16399 73013
16401-16499 73013
16500-20899 73012
22100-24599 73025
S Pennsylvania Ave 73025
Pepperdine Ave 73013
Pepperdine Dr 73012
Pershing Cir 73034
Persimmon Creek Dr 73013
Perth Dr 73013
Petaluma Pl 73013
Pheasant Run 73012
Pheasant Crest Rd 73034
Pheasant Pointe Dr 73034
Pheasant Ridge Trl 73034
Piedra Dr 73012
Pienza Pt 73034
Pin Oak 73013
S Pine 73034
Pine Crk 73034
Pine Dr 73034
Pine Frst 73012
Pine Trl 73012
Pine Vly 73012
Pine Cone Dr 73012
Pine Oak Cir 73034
Pine Oak Dr
700-1499 73034
1500-2199 73013
Pine Oak Pl 73034
Pine Ridge Cir 73034
Pine Ridge Rd 73025
Pine View Ter 73003
Pinehurst 73034
Pinehurst Trail Dr 73012
Pinnacle Ln 73003
Pinon Pl 73013
Pintail Pl 73003
Pinto Trl 73012
Pioneer Cir 73012
Placid Dr 73025
Plantation Way 73013
Platinum Ln 73012
Pleasant Cove Ln 73013
Pleasant Oaks Cir & Dr 73034
Pleasant Ridge Ct & Rd 73012
Pleasant Wood Ln 73034
Plum Grv 73012
Plumtree Ln 73034
Plymouth Xing 73013
Pointe Manor Ln 73013
Pointe Oak Cir 73013
Pollock Dr 73025
Polo Club Ct 73034
Pompeya Ln 73013
Pond Walk Ct 73012
Ponderosa Pne 73012
Pondince Dr 73013
Pony Express Trl 73003
N Portland Ave
13100-13199 73025
16500-20699 73012
24301-24499 73025
S Portland Ave 73025
Portofino Pl 73034
Posados Dr 73012
Positano Dr 73013
Post Oak Ln 73034
Powderhorn Trl 73034
Prairie Ave 73013
Prairie Pt 73034
Prairie Run 73034
Prairie Dog Dr 73034
Prairie Dunes Way 73003
Prairie Falcon Pt 73034
Prairie Hay Trl 73012
Prairie Hill Ct 73003
Prairie Run Dr 73013
Prairie Sky Way 73012

Prairie View Rd 73034
Pranter Ln 73013
Prescott Ave & Pl 73013
Preserve Pl 73034
Preston Pl 73013
Prestwick Cir 73012
Primrose Ter 73013
Princeton Ave 73034
Princeton Ln 73013
Progressive Dr 73034
Promontory Rd 73013
Prospect Ct 73034
Providence Ave 73012
Providence Cir 73003
Providence Ct 73003
Pruett Dr 73003
Ptarmigan Ln 73012
Pueblo 73013
Puget Sound Dr 73034
Purple Martin Ln 73034
Putter Pl 73025
Quail Holw 73012
Quail Run 73025
Quail Crossing Way 73034
Quail Ridge Cir & Rd 73034
Quail Roost Dr 73034
Quail Run Dr 73034
Queens Cir 73034
R Rd 73034
Rabbit Run 73034
Raccoon Cir 73034
Rail Dr 73025
Railroad Dr 73013
Raineys Blvd 73025
Raintree Ln & Rd 73013
Rainwater Trl 73012
Raliegh Cir & Ct 73003
Ramblewood Ter 73034
Rambling Rd 73025
Ranch Dr 73013
Ranch House Rd 73034
Randall Rd 73034
E & S Randolph Rd 73013
S Rankin St
200-1299 73034
1600-3299 73013
Rankin Ter 73013
Raquel Rd 73003
Rasheed Rd 73003
Raspberry Trl 73034
Rastro Dr 73012
Raton 73013
Ravello Ct 73013
Raven Cir 73034
Real Quiet Cir 73025
Recycle Trl 73034
Red Admiral Way 73013
Red Bird 73012
Red Bud Ct 73013
Red Bud Ln 73034
Red Bud Pl 73013
Red Canyon Rd 73013
Red Cedar Dr 73025
Red Cedar Ln 73034
Red Clover Ct 73013
Red Coach Rd 73013
Red Deer Xing 73034
Red Eagle Pass 73013
Red Elm Ct & Dr 73013
Red Fern 73034
Red Fox Rd 73034
Red Fox Trail Rd 73034
Red Hawk Cir 73012
Red Hill Ln 73013
Red Oak Dr 73034
Red Oak Ln 73034
Red Oak Ter 73003
Red Prairie Dr 73025
Red River Cir 73025
Red River Ct 73034
Red Rock Lake Rd 73013
Red Tailed Hawk Way 73012
Redbud Holw 73034
Redbud Ln
2700-2899 73025
3800-4199 73034

E Redbud Ln 73034
S Redbud Ln 73034
Redbud Canyon Dr & Trl 73034
Redbud Creek Dr 73034
Redcliff Ln 73003
Redhawk Ln 73034
Redland Dr 73003
Redmont Ct & Trce 73034
Redrock Cir 73034
Redrock Dr 73003
Redstem Way 73013
Redstone Ave 73013
Redtail Hawk 73003
Redvine Rd 73034
Redwood Ln 73013
Regis Ct 73034
Remington Rd 73034
Rena Dawn Ln 73013
Renaissance Blvd 73013
Resto Ln 73012
Reveille Rd 73013
Reynolds Rd 73013
Rhett Ln 73025
Rhode Island Ave 73013
Rhonda Ln 73013
Rich Earth Ln 73012
Richard Dr 73003
Richfield Ln 73013
Richland Ave, Cir & Dr 73012
Richmond Rd 73034
Rickasha Dr 73025
Ricks Ct & Trl 73012
Riders Mark 73025
Ridge Rd 73034
N Ridge Rd 73025
E & S Ridge Pointe Cir & Dr 73034
Ridge View Ln 73025
Ridgecrest Dr 73034
Ridgecrest Rd 73013
Ridgeview Dr 73034
Ridgewood Dr
2900-3899 73013
17000-17399 73012
Ridgewood Ln 73034
Righto Way 73034
Riley Rdg 73025
Rim Rd 73013
Rimridge Rd 73025
Rimrock Rd 73034
Ripple Creek Ln 73012
Rising Star Ln 73034
Riva Rdg 73025
Riva Ridge Cir & Ct 73025
Rivanna Way 73034
Riven Rock Rd 73034
River Birch Ct 73034
River Chase Ct & Dr 73025
River Downs Dr 73034
River Lark Ln 73012
River Oaks Rd 73013
Riverbirch Ln 73012
Riverglen Way 73013
Riverwood Ln 73034
Road Not Taken 73034
Roaring Fork Trl 73034
Rob Ln 73003
Roberts Rd 73013
Robey Dr 73034
Robin Rd 73034
Robin Hill Rd 73003
Robin Ridge Ln 73012
Roblee 73025
Robtrice Ct 73034
Rock Canyon Rd 73025
E & N Rock Circle Dr 73034
Rock Creek Dr 73034
N Rock Creek Pl 73034
Rock Creek Rd 73013
Rock Dove Land 73034
Rock Hollow Rd 73034
Rockbrook Dr 73034
Rockford Ln 73034
Rockport Rd & Way 73013

Rockridge Cir 73034
N Rockwell Ave
15400-15698 73013
15700-16499 73013
16500-21999 73012
22000-24899 73025
S Rockwell Ave 73025
Rockwood Ct & Dr 73013
Rocky Mountain Dr 73013
Rocky Mountain Way 73003
N & W Rockypoint Dr 73003
Roff Ave 73012
Rogers Dr 73013
Rolling Creek Rd 73034
Rolling Hill Way 73012
Rolling Hills Ter 73012
Rollingwood Dr 73034
Romeo Dr 73013
Rondo Dr 73012
Roosevelt St 73034
Rose Holw 73012
Rose Creek Dr 73012
Rose In Bloom Way 73034
Rosedale Dr 73013
Rosewood Ln 73013
Round Barn Rd 73034
Roundup Rd 73034
Roxburgh Ct 73013
Royal Way 73034
Royal Crest Ln 73013
Royal Troon Dr 73012
Royale Ct 73025
Ruffin Cir & Ct 73025
Rugosa Rose Dr 73012
Ruidosa Dr 73034
Running Branch Rd 73013
Running Deer Ct 73013
Running Deer Trl 73025
NW Rush Creek Rd 73025
Rushing Mdws 73013
Rushing Springs Trl 73013
Rustic Rd 73034
Rustic Creek Ter 73013
Ryan Ct & Way 73003
Saber Ln 73034
Saddle Rd 73034
Saddle River Dr 73012
Saddleback Dr 73034
Saddlecreek Way 73012
Sagewood Dr 73013
Sahoma Ter 73013
Sailboat Bridge Way 73034
S Saint Blvd 73034
Saint Andrews Dr 73025
Saint Annes Dr 73034
Saint Christopher Dr 73003
Saint Croix Dr 73025
Saint Fergus Dr 73034
Saint James Dr 73034
Saint Johns Way 73034
Saint Lucia Dr 73025
Salem Ave & Ct 73003
Salem Creek Pl & Rd 73013
Salvador Rd 73012
Salvo Bridge Ct 73034
Sams Dr 73025
San Clemente Dr 73013
San Fidel Ln 73003
San Juan Ave 73003
San Marco Ln 73034
San Mateo Ct 73012
San Miguel Cir 73013
San Nicolas Dr 73013
San Simeon Dr 73003
Sand Plum Cir 73025
Sand Plum Dr 73025
Sand Plum Dr N 73025
Sand Plum Ln 73003
Sand Springs Trl 73013
Sandhurst Cir & Dr 73034
Sandia Cir 73012
Sandpiper Dr 73034
Sandsage Dr 73034
Sandy Ln 73034
Sandy Creek Trl 73013
Sandys Cir 73025

N Santa Fe Ave
700-898 ... 73003
900-2999 ... 73003
4200-6199 ... 73025
13900-14098 ... 73013
14100-16399 ... 73013
16401-16499 ... 73013
S Santa Fe Ave
200-1499 ... 73003
3200-3299 ... 73013
10600-14799 ... 73025
Santa Fe Cir ... 73012
S Santa Fe Dr ... 73003
N Santa Fe St ... 73003
Santa Fe Ter ... 73012
Santa Fe Trl ... 73025
Santa Fe Crossings Dr ... 73013
Sara Hill Rd ... 73034
S & W Sarah Rd ... 73025
Saratoga Way & Xing ... 73003
Sarava Dr ... 73025
Savannah Ln ... 73003
Savona Ln ... 73034
Savoy Cir ... 73003
Sawgrass Ct & Rd ... 73034
Sawmill Rd ... 73034
Scarab Inlt ... 73013
Scarborough Dr ... 73012
Scarlet Cir ... 73025
Scarlet Oak Ct & Ln ... 73012
Scissortail Dr ... 73013
Scissortail Ln ... 73034
Scissortail Landing Dr ... 73012
Scotch Pne ... 73012
Scotland Way ... 73013
Scott Dr & St ... 73013
Scrambler Ln ... 73025
Scrub Oak Rd ... 73034
Sea Biscuit Dr ... 73025
Sea Ray Channel ... 73013
Seattle Slew Ct ... 73025
Secretariat Ln ... 73025
Sedonia Ct ... 73034
Segovia Cir ... 73034
Seminole Dr ... 73013
Seminole Creek Cir ... 73013
Seminole Pointe Pl ... 73013
Sequoyah Dr ... 73013
Sequoyah Pl ... 73003
Sequoyah St ... 73003
Settlers Dr ... 73034
Seville Dr ... 73034
Shades Bridge Rd ... 73034
Shadow Ct ... 73013
Shadow Creek Dr ... 73034
Shadow Hawk Ln ... 73012
Shadow Lake Dr ... 73025
Shadow Mountain Dr ... 73013
Shadow Valley Dr ... 73034
Shadow Wood Dr ... 73034
Shady Ct & Ln ... 73003
Shady Glen Cir & Ct ... 73025
Shady Run Ct ... 73025
Shady Tree Dr ... 73034
Shady Tree Ln ... 73013
Shady Tree Pl ... 73013
Shadybrook Ln ... 73013
Shalamar Rd ... 73013
Shamrock Dr ... 73003
Shannon Cir ... 73034
Shannon Dr ... 73025
Shannon Ln ... 73034
Shannon Way ... 73034
Shawnee Ave ... 73012
Sheffield Ave ... 73034
Sheffield Blvd ... 73013
Shelburne Dr ... 73034
Shelby Cir ... 73034
Shelly Cir & Ln ... 73034
Shelton Pl ... 73034
Sherry Ln ... 73003
Sherrywood Rd ... 73034
Sherwood Ln ... 73034
Sherwood Green Ln ... 73034
Shilestone ... 73012
Shiloh Frst, Ln, Pl, Rdg & Ter ... 73034
Shiloh Valley Rd ... 73034
Shilstone Way
2000-2199 ... 73013
18700-19199 ... 73012
Shirley Ln ... 73003
Sholom Rd ... 73013
Shore Dr ... 73003
Shorerun Dr ... 73012
Shorewood Ln ... 73003
N Short ... 73025
Short Dr ... 73034
Short Grass Rd ... 73034
Shortgrass Cir & Rd ... 73003
Shorthorn Ln ... 73034
Siena Dr ... 73034
W Sierra Springs Dr ... 73012
Signal Ridge Dr ... 73013
Silent Sun Cir ... 73034
Silver Charm Ln ... 73025
Silver Crest Dr ... 73025
Silver Eagle Trl ... 73013
Silver Fox Dr ... 73003
Silver Oaks Dr ... 73025
Silver Spur Ct ... 73034
Silver Stone Dr ... 73013
Silverado Dr ... 73013
Silvercliffe Ct & Dr ... 73012
Silverfield Ln ... 73025
Silverhawk Way ... 73012
Silvertree Ln ... 73013
E Simmons Rd ... 73034
W Simmons Rd
100-3699 ... 73034
4300-19399 ... 73025
Simon Ave ... 73003
E Simpson Rd ... 73034
W Simpson Rd
100-3599 ... 73034
4500-9499 ... 73025
Sims Ave ... 73013
Singingwood Rd ... 73013
Sisken Ct ... 73003
Sky Blue Ct ... 73012
Sky Run Dr ... 73013
Skylark Ct ... 73034
Skylers Dr ... 73012
Skyline Blvd ... 73025
Skyline Dr ... 73003
Skyridge Dr ... 73025
Skyview Rd ... 73034
Slash Pine Dr ... 73013
Slate Bridge Rd ... 73034
Sleepy Hollow Rd ... 73034
Smiling Hill Blvd, Cir & Ct ... 73013
Smithurst Rd ... 73013
Smoking Oak ... 73025
Smoky Hill Trl ... 73034
Smoky Hollow Rd ... 73013
N Smythe Ave ... 73034
Snake Dr ... 73013
Snowy Owl Dr ... 73013
Somerset Ave ... 73013
Sonador Dr ... 73013
Sonatina Dr ... 73012
Songwood Dr ... 73003
Sonny Blues Pl ... 73034
Sonoma Ct & Dr ... 73013
Sonoma Lake Blvd ... 73013
Sonoma Park Dr ... 73013
Sonora ... 73013
Sonya Way ... 73013
Sooner Cir ... 73034
Sooner Ct ... 73034
Sooner Pl ... 73034
N Sooner Rd
1-6800 ... 73034
6802-6898 ... 73013
10900-12199 ... 73013
S Sooner Rd ... 73034
Sorghum Rd & Run ... 73034
E Sorghum Mill Rd ... 73034
W Sorghum Mill Rd ... 73025
South Ave ... 73013
Southbend Rd ... 73034
Southerly Rdg ... 73025
Southerly Farms Blvd ... 73025
Southern Pl ... 73013
Southern Oaks Dr ... 73034
Southridge Dr ... 73013
Southwestern Dr ... 73034
Spacious Sky Ct ... 73012
Sparrow Hawk ... 73003
Sparrow Hawk Ln ... 73012
Sparrowhawk Ln ... 73012
Spavinaw Ln ... 73025
Spectacular Bid Ave ... 73025
Spence Ct ... 73034
Spinnaker Pt ... 73013
Spirit Wood Ln ... 73025
Split Fence Ln ... 73034
N & W Spoon Ct & Ter ... 73025
Sportsman Rd ... 73012
Spring Hill Dr ... 73013
Spring Manor Ct & Dr ... 73025
Springer Run ... 73012
Springhill Rd ... 73013
Spyglass Hill Rd ... 73034
Squirrel Tree Pl ... 73034
Staci Ln ... 73025
Stafford Rd ... 73012
Stag Trl ... 73012
Stagmoor Cir & Rd ... 73034
Stamford Ct ... 73034
Stampede Dr ... 73034
Starboard Cv ... 73013
Starling Path ... 73034
Starwood Trl ... 73025
N State St ... 73003
S State St
100-999 ... 73003
1500-1799 ... 73013
Steeplechase Dr & Rd ... 73034
Stephanie Ct ... 73034
Stepping Stone Trl ... 73013
Sterling Dr ... 73012
Sterling Creek Dr ... 73013
Sterling Pointe Way ... 73003
Sterlington ... 73013
Stetson Dr ... 73034
Steve Douglas Dr ... 73034
Steven Ct & Dr ... 73013
Stevens Rd ... 73034
Sticks Trl ... 73034
Still Hollow Rd ... 73034
Still Meadow Rd ... 73013
Still Moon Cir ... 73013
Still Water Ln ... 73013
Stillmeadows Dr ... 73013
Stirrup Ln ... 73034
Stone Brg ... 73034
Stone Canyon Cir ... 73034
Stone Creek Xing ... 73034
Stone Cress Ct ... 73012
Stone Crest Cir & Dr ... 73034
Stone Hill Dr ... 73034
Stone Oak Rd ... 73012
Stone Point Cir ... 73034
Stone Ridge Dr ... 73034
Stone Trail Dr ... 73034
Stone Valley Cir & Dr ... 73034
Stonebridge Blvd ... 73013
Stonebrook Ln, Rd & Way ... 73003
Stonecreek Way ... 73025
Stonecroft Cir ... 73034
Stonegate Pl ... 73025
Stonehenge Ct & Dr ... 73034
Stonepoint Dr ... 73034
Stoney Ridge Rd ... 73034
Stoney Spring Rd ... 73013
Stony Trl ... 73034
N & S Story St ... 73003
Stratford Pl ... 73012
Stratmore Way ... 73012
Stratton Dr ... 73013
Strawberry Ln ... 73034
Strayfox Xing ... 73012
Strayhorn ... 73034
Stubblefield Ln ... 73012
Sugar Loaf Dr ... 73013
Sugarberry Cir ... 73034
Sumac Cir ... 73013
Sumac Dr ... 73012
Summer Dr ... 73025
Summer Cloud Dr ... 73013
Summer Grove Ave ... 73012
Summer Hollow Ln ... 73013
Summer Oak Dr ... 73013
Summer Set Trl ... 73012
Summer Way Ln ... 73013
Summerfield Dr ... 73012
Summerhaven Way ... 73013
Summit Dr & Pl ... 73034
Summit Lake Blvd ... 73012
Summit Oak Dr ... 73034
Summit Parke Dr ... 73013
Summit Ridge Dr ... 73025
Sun River Ct ... 73012
Sun Valley Ln ... 73034
Sunburst Ct ... 73012
Sundance Ln ... 73034
Sunflower Dr ... 73013
Sunny Brook Cir, Ct, Dr & Pl ... 73034
Sunny Hollow Rd ... 73012
Sunnyside Pl ... 73003
Sunset Cir ... 73025
Sunset Dr ... 73003
Surrey Rd ... 73013
Sutton Pl ... 73012
Swallowtail Rd ... 73013
Swan Lake Ct & Rd ... 73003
Sweetbriar Ct ... 73034
Sweetwater ... 73012
Swisher Pl ... 73012
Switchgrass Rd ... 73013
Sycamore Ln ... 73034
Taber Ln ... 73003
Table Rock Dr ... 73025
Tacoma Bridge Ct ... 73034
Tahlequah Dr & Pl ... 73013
Tahoe Dr ... 73013
Talavera Ln ... 73012
Tall Grass Cir & Ct ... 73012
Tall Oaks Ct & Trl ... 73025
Talon Rd ... 73013
Tamarac Ct ... 73003
Tambor Dr ... 73012
Tambos Trl ... 73013
Tanbark ... 73034
Tangle Vine Dr ... 73034
Tanglewood Cir ... 73034
Tanglewood Dr ... 73013
Taos ... 73013
Taurus Dr ... 73003
Teakwood Ln & Rd ... 73013
Teal Pl ... 73003
Technology Dr ... 73013
Tedessa Turn ... 73034
Teesdale Rd ... 73013
Teeside Blvd ... 73034
Tenbears Rd ... 73034
Terra Pl ... 73012
Terra Trl ... 73034
Terra Vita Dr ... 73034
Terrazza Xing ... 73034
Territories Dr ... 73034
E Thatcher St ... 73034
W Thatcher St ... 73003
Thayer Cir ... 73012
The Ranch Rd ... 73034
Thomas Ct ... 73012
Thomas Dr ... 73003
Thomas Trl ... 73003
Thompson Rd ... 73013
Thompson Trl ... 73034
Thorn Briar Rd ... 73034
Thornbrook Blvd ... 73013
Thornhill Blvd ... 73012
Thorton Ln ... 73012
Thousand Oaks Dr ... 73034
N Three Creeks Dr ... 73012
Three Stars Rd ... 73034
Thrush Cir ... 73034
Thunder Pass ... 73034
Thunderbird Blvd ... 73013
Thunderwind Cir ... 73034
Thurlow Pl ... 73034
Tifton Ct & Dr ... 73012
Tiger Maple Ct ... 73012
E & N Timber Ln & Trl ... 73034
Timber Ridge Ct, Dr & Rd ... 73034
Timber Wolf Trl ... 73034
Timbercreek Cir ... 73034
Timberdale Dr & Ter ... 73034
Timberlake Ave ... 73034
Timberlake Cir ... 73034
Timberlake Dr ... 73025
Timberline Pl ... 73013
Timberline Trl ... 73034
Timberview Dr ... 73013
Timberwind Rd ... 73034
Timberwolf Way ... 73034
Timothy Way ... 73034
Tomahawk Rd ... 73013
Tommys Ranch Rd ... 73034
Tonka Trl ... 73012
Torres Rd ... 73003
Toscana Ct ... 73012
Touchmark Ct & Dr ... 73003
Tower Bridge Ct ... 73034
Tracys Ter ... 73013
Traditions Blvd & Dr ... 73013
Trail Creek Rd ... 73012
N & S Trail Ridge Rd ... 73012
Trailhead Dr ... 73034
Trails End Rd ... 73034
Trailwood Rd ... 73034
Tranquil Pasture Ln ... 73012
Travers Ct ... 73003
Travis Cir ... 73013
Tredington Ct & Way ... 73034
Trenton Dr ... 73012
Treviso Trl ... 73034
Trolley Trl ... 73034
Troone Ct & Dr ... 73025
Trophy Dr ... 73012
Tudor Ln ... 73003
Tulip Trl ... 73025
Tullahoma Dr ... 73034
Turkey Run Dr ... 73025
Turtle Holw ... 73013
Turtlecreek Rd ... 73013
Tuscan Ln ... 73003
Tuscany Plz ... 73025
Tuscany Way ... 73034
Twelve Oaks ... 73025
Twin Grove Cts ... 73025
Twin Ridge Dr & Rd ... 73034
Twisted Oak Ln ... 73013
N & S University Dr ... 73034
Vail Dr ... 73013
Val Ct ... 73013
Val Genes Rd ... 73003
Valderama Way ... 73012
Vallejo Pl ... 73013
Valley Crst ... 73012
Valley Ct ... 73012
Valley Ln ... 73012
Valley Park ... 73025
Valley Pl ... 73012
Valley Rdg ... 73025
Valley Brook Dr ... 73034
Valley Creek Cir & Rd ... 73034
Valley Forge Ln ... 73013
Valley Ridge Dr ... 73034
Valley View Ln & Rd ... 73034
Vance Dr ... 73013
Vandivort Pl ... 73034
Vanishing Trl ... 73013
Vaquero Ct ... 73034
Vea Dr ... 73012
Vellano Ln ... 73034
Veneterra Vw ... 73034
Venezia Cir & Ln ... 73034
Ventana Blvd ... 73012
Venus Cir ... 73003
Vermejo Dr ... 73012
Verona Cir, Ct & Way ... 73034
Via Bella ... 73013
Via Esperanza ... 73013
Via Serena ... 73013
Via Sierra ... 73013
Victoria Dr & Pl ... 73003
Victory Rd ... 73003
Viento Dr ... 73012
Viewmont Ct, Dr & Rd ... 73003
Village Cir ... 73013
Village Pkwy ... 73003
Village Common Dr ... 73013
Village Garden Dr ... 73012
Village Green Dr ... 73013
Villagio Dr ... 73012
Villas Creek Ct & Dr ... 73003
Vintage Ct & Dr ... 73013
Vista Ave ... 73012
Vista Cir ... 73025
Vista Ln ... 73034
Vista Hill Dr ... 73025
Vista Valley Ln ... 73025
Visto Dr ... 73012
Vivace Ct & Dr ... 73012
Vulcan Cir ... 73003
Wade Martin Rd ... 73034
Wagon Rd ... 73025
Wagonwheel Cir & Rd ... 73034
Wain Bridge Ave ... 73012
Wake Forest Rd ... 73034
Wakefield Rd ... 73034
Wales Green Ave ... 73012
Walking Sky Rd ... 73013
N & S Walnut St ... 73003
Walnut Cove Rd ... 73013
Wanetta Ave ... 73013
War Admiral Ct ... 73025
Warwick Pl ... 73013
Washington St ... 73034
Washita Trl ... 73003
Water Oak Cir ... 73012
Waterfront Rd ... 73013
Waterloo Cir ... 73034
W Waterloo Ct ... 73025
E Waterloo Rd ... 73034
W Waterloo Rd ... 73025
E Waterloo Industrial Rd ... 73034
E & N Waterloo Wood Dr ... 73034
Waters Welling Way ... 73013
Waterscape Bay ... 73013
Waterwood Pkwy ... 73034
Wayne Ave ... 73034
E Wayne St ... 73034
W Wayne St ... 73003
Wb Meyer Pkwy ... 73025
Weathers Rd ... 73025
Weathers Brook Ln ... 73025
Wedge Ct ... 73025
Weeping Willow Way ... 73034
Wellington Way ... 73012
Wellsburg Ct ... 73013
Wendell Dr ... 73013
Wendy Ln ... 73013
Wescott Cir ... 73034
N Western Ave
2000-3399 ... 73012
13800-16499 ... 73013
16500-22099 ... 73012
22800-24799 ... 73025
S Western Ave ... 73025
Western Vista Dr ... 73013
Westland Dr ... 73013
Westmoreland Dr ... 73034
Westridge Cir & Dr ... 73013
Westwood Ln ... 73013
Wheatley Way ... 73034
Whimbrel Ln ... 73012
Whipporwill Ct ... 73013
Whirlaway ... 73025
Whisper Creek Dr ... 73034
Whisper Glen Dr ... 73034
Whisper Oak Dr ... 73034
Whispering Creek Ct & Dr ... 73013
Whispering Heights Dr ... 73013
Whispering Oak Dr ... 73034
Whispering Oak Rd ... 73025
White Fox Cir ... 73034
White Hawk Dr ... 73012
White Magnolia Ln ... 73013
White Pine Cir & Trl ... 73012
Whitehawk Rd ... 73003
Whitehouse Cir & Ln ... 73003
Whiteoak Rd ... 73034
Whitetail Ct ... 73012
W Whitetail Dr ... 73012
Whitetail Run ... 73013
Whitman Ct ... 73003
Whitwell Cir ... 73034
Wickersham Dr ... 73013
Wicklow Dr ... 73013
Wickshire Cir ... 73013
Wilbur Way ... 73034
Wild Creek Dr ... 73013
Wild Plum Ct & Ln ... 73025
Wild Rose Trl ... 73034
Wild Wind Rd ... 73003
Wilderness Rd ... 73025
Wildhorse Dr ... 73003
Wildmeadow Ct & Dr ... 73003
Wildwood Rd & Ter ... 73034
Wilford Way ... 73013
Williams Dr ... 73034
Willis Way ... 73034
Willment Pl ... 73034
Willow Cir ... 73013
Willow Crk ... 73034
Willow Bend Dr ... 73003
Willow Creek Rd ... 73013
Willow Oak Ln ... 73012
Willow Ridge Pl ... 73003
Willow Way Cir ... 73013
Willowbrook Ln ... 73034
Willowood Rd ... 73034
Wilson Dr ... 73034
Wilson Rd ... 73013
Wimbledon Rd ... 73003
Winchester Dr ... 73034
Wind Dr ... 73013
Wind Call Ln ... 73034
Wind Crest Way ... 73013
Windbreak Cir ... 73025
Windham Cir ... 73034
Windhill Ave ... 73034
Winding Crk ... 73012
Winding Ln ... 73003
Winding Trl ... 73025
Winding Creek Cir ... 73034
Winding Park Dr ... 73013
Winding Ridge Rd ... 73034
Windmere Dr ... 73034
Windmill Rd ... 73013
Windover Dr ... 73013
Windrush Pl ... 73013
Windsong ... 73034
Windward Way ... 73013
Winners Cir
1000-1099 ... 73025
3600-3799 ... 73034
Winning Colors Dr ... 73025
Winterwood Dr ... 73025
Wishon Dr ... 73025
Wishon Acres ... 73025
Wister Pass ... 73025
Wolf Creek Cir ... 73034
Wolf Creek Dr ... 73012
Wood Way ... 73034
Wood Creek Ln ... 73013
Wood Duck Cir & Dr ... 73013
Woodbridge Cir ... 73012
Woodbury Cir, Dr & Rd ... 73034
Woodchuck Ct ... 73034
Woodcreek Rd ... 73034
Woodcrest Ln ... 73034
Woodford Ct & Way ... 73034
Woodhill Rd ... 73025
Woodhollow Trl ... 73012
Woodland Blvd ... 73034
Woodland Dr ... 73025

Woodland Rd 73013
Woodland Creek Ct & Dr 73034
Woodridge Cir 73025
W Woodridge Ct 73025
Woodridge Trl 73034
Woodruff Cir & Rd 73013
Woods And Sons Ave 73034
Woodshadow Rd 73003
Woodside Cir & Dr 73013
Woodsorrel Rd 73012
Woodview Ln 73013
Woodvine Dr 73012
Woody Ln 73003
Woody Creek Ct 73034
Woody Creek Dr 73012
Worthington Ln 73013
Wren Ct 73034
Wright Cir 73013
Wright Way 73034
Wynchase Dr 73013
Wynn Cir & Dr 73013
Wynstone Ct & Dr 73034
Yearling Way 73012
Yellow Sky Cir 73013
Yellow Woods Way 73034
Yellowstone Ln 73003
York Dr 73034
Yorkshire Ct & Dr 73013
Yosemite Pl 73003
Yucca Dr 73013
Zinc 73012
Zion Pl 73003

NUMBERED STREETS

E 1st St 73034
W 1st St 73003
E 2nd St 73034
W 2nd St 73003
E 3rd St 73034
W 3rd St 73003
E 4th St 73034
W 4th St 73003
E 5th St 73034
W 5th St 73003
E 6th St 73034
W 6th St 73003
E 7th St 73034
W 7th St 73003
E 8th St 73034
W 8th St 73003
E 9th St 73034
W 9th St 73003
W 10th Pl 73003
E 10th St 73034
W 10th St 73003
E 10th Street Plz 73034
E 11th St 73034
E 12th St 73034
E 13th St 73034
E 14th St 73034
E & W 15th 73013
W 18th St 73013
E 19th St 73013
E 21st St 73013
E 22nd St 73013
E 23rd St 73013
E 26th St 73013
27th Pl & St 73013
E 28th St 73013
E 29th St 73013
E 30th St 73013
E 31st St 73013
E 32nd St 73013
E 33rd St 73013
W 33rd St
1-500 73013
502-1998 73013
801-1999 73013
801-801 73083
E 35th St 73013
37th Ct & St 73013
E 40th St 73013
E 44th St 73013
NE 109th St 73013
NE 111th St 73013
NE 113th St 73013
NE 116th St 73013
NE 117th Ct 73013
NE 119th Pl 73013
NE 121st St 73013
NE 122nd St 73013
NE 123rd St 73013
NE 124th St 73013
NE 125th St 73013
NE 126th St 73013
NE 129th St 73013
NE 130th St 73013
131st Ct, Pl & St 73013
NE 132nd St 73013
NE 133rd St 73013
NE 134th Cir 73013
NE 135th St 73013
NE & NW 137th 73013
NW & NE 138th Cir, St & Ter 73013
NW 139th Street Pkwy 73013
NE & NW 139th 73013
140th Terrace Cir & Ct 73013
NE & NW 140th Pl, St & Ter 73013
NE & NW 141st Cir, Ct & St 73013
NE & NW 142nd Cir, Ct & St 73013
NE & NW 143rd 73013
144th Cir, St & Ter 73013
145th Cir, Ct, St & Ter 73013
146th Ct, St & Ter 73013
147th St & Ter 73013
148th St & Ter 73013
149th St & Ter 73013
NW & NE 150th Ct, Pl, St & Ter 73013
151st Cir, Pl, St & Ter 73013
152nd St & Ter 73013
153rd Ct, St & Ter 73013
154th Ct, St & Ter 73013
155th Cir, Pl, St & Ter 73013
156th Cir, Pl, St & Ter 73013
157th Cir, Ct, Pl, St, Ter & Way 73013
158th Cir, St & Ter 73013
159th Cir, Pl, St & Ter 73013
160th Pl, St & Ter 73013
161st Cir, Pl, St & Ter 73013
162nd Cir, Ct, St & Ter 73013
163rd Cir, Ct, St & Ter 73013
164th Cir, St & Ter 73013
165th Ct, St & Ter 73012
166th Ct, St & Ter 73012
167th Cir, Ct & St 73012
168th Ct, St & Ter 73012
NW 169th St 73012
170th Ct, St & Ter 73012
171st Pl, St & Ter 73012
172nd Cir, Pl, St & Ter 73012
173rd Cir, St & Ter 73012
174th Cir, Ct & St 73012
175th Ct & St 73012
176th Ct, Pl, St & Ter 73012
177th Ct, St & Ter 73012
NW 178th St 73012
179th Cir, Ct, St & Ter 73012
NW 180th St 73012
181st St & Ter 73012
182nd St & Ter 73012
183rd Ct, St & Ter 73012
184th Ct, St & Ter 73012
NW 185th St 73012
186th St & Ter 73012
187th Cir, Pl, St & Ter 73012
188th St & Ter 73012
NW 189th St 73012
190th Ct & Pl 73012
191st St & Ter 73012
192nd St & Ter 73012
193rd Cir & St 73012
194th Cir, St & Ter 73012
195th Cir, Pl, St & Ter 73012
196th Pl, St & Ter 73012
197th Cir, St & Ter 73012
NW 198th St 73012
NW 199th St 73012
NW 201st St 73012
NW 203rd St 73012
NW 206th St 73012
NW 210th St 73012
NW 215th St 73012
NW 220th St 73025
NW 222nd St 73025
NW 234th St 73025
NW 235th St 73025
NW 238th St 73025

ELK CITY OK

General Delivery 73644

POST OFFICE BOXES MAIN OFFICE STATIONS AND BRANCHES

Box No.s
All PO Boxes 73648

RURAL ROUTES

01, 02, 04, 05 73644

NAMED STREETS

All Street Addresses 73644

NUMBERED STREETS

All Street Addresses 73644

ENID OK

General Delivery 73701
General Delivery 73705

POST OFFICE BOXES MAIN OFFICE STATIONS AND BRANCHES

Box No.s
1 - 6254 73702
9001 - 9040 73705
10001 - 10894 73706

RURAL ROUTES

04, 05, 06, 15 73701
02, 03, 07, 08, 09, 10, 11, 12, 13, 15 73703

NAMED STREETS

S A St 73703
Abby Rd 73701
Acorn Trl 73703
N & S Adams St 73701
Addington 73701
N & S Adolpha Cir 73703
Alamo Rd 73703
E Allen Rd 73701
Alpine Pl 73703
Amy Ln 73701
Anna Belle Ln 73703
Antelope Dr 73701
Applewood 73701
Appomattox 73703
Arapaho Dr 73703
Arlington Dr & Pl 73703
Arrowhead Dr 73703
S Arthur St 73703
Asbury Cir 73703
E Ash Ave 73701
W Ash Ave 73701
W Ash St 73703
Aspen Dr 73703
Atkinson Dr 73701
B Ct 73703
S Baker St 73701
Bana Dr 73703
Banner Dr & Rd 73703
Barn Swallow Rd 73703
Barnes Ct 73703
Bass Dr 73703
Bear Run 73703
Beaver Trl 73703
E Beech Ave 73701
Belle Crossing Dr 73703
Bereenco Rd 73705
Beverly Dr 73703
E & W Birch Ave 73701
Birchwood St 73703
Black Ave 73703
Blackjack St 73703
W Blaine Rd 73703
Bland Dr 73703
Bluebird Ln 73703
Bluestem Dr 73701
Bluestem Rd 73703
Bob White Ln 73703
Bobcat 73703
Bobolink 73703
Books St 73703
N & S Boomer Rd 73703
Brandywine 73703
Breckinridge Rd 73701
Briar Creek Rd 73703
Briar Ridge Rd 73703
Briarwood Dr 73703
Bridge Crk 73703
Bridlewood 73701
E Broadway Ave 73701
W Broadway Ave
100-999 73701
1000-2999 73703
Brooks Dr 73701
Brookside Dr 73703
Brookwood St 73703
S Brown Pkwy & Rd 73705
Bryan Dr 73701
N & S Buchanan St 73703
Buckboard Ln 73703
Buffalo Dr 73701
W Buffalo Rd 73703
Buggy Whip Ln 73703
Bunker Hill St 73703
Bunny Trl 73701
N & S Burdel Ln 73703
C Ct 73703
Cactus Flts 73703
Calico Ln 73703
California 73701
E Cambridge Ave 73701
Camelot Dr 73703
Canary Ln & Pl 73703
Candlestick 73703
Candlewood Cir 73701
Cansler Dr 73703
Canterbury Rd 73703
Cardinal Pl 73703
Caribou Cir 73703
Carlisle Ct 73703
E Carrier Rd 73701
W Carrier Rd
300-999 73701
1100-10699 73703
Cascade St 73703
Caton Pl 73703
W Cedar 73703
E Cedar Ave 73701
W Cedar Ave 73701
Cedar Ridge Dr 73703
Cellar Door Ln 73703
Centennial Ct 73703
E Centennial Rd 73701
W Centennial Rd
300-899 73701
5500-5599 73703
N Central St 73701
Champlin Ct 73703
Channel St 73705
Chantell St 73703
Chaparral Run 73703
Chelsea Ct 73703
E Cherokee Ave 73701
W Cherokee Ave
100-999 73701
1000-5399 73703
E Cherry Ave 73701
W Cherry Ave
100-999 73701
1000-1199 73703
E Chestnut Ave 73701
W Chestnut Ave
100-499 73701
1000-10200 73703
10202-11998 73703
Cheyenne Ave 73703
Chickadee Ln 73703
Chickasaw Dr 73703
Chisholm Crk 73701
Chisholm Ln 73703
Chisholm Trl 73701
Choctaw St 73701
N & S Cimarron Dr 73703
Circle Dr 73703
Clairemont 73703
Clark Dr 73703
N & S Cleveland St 73703
Club House Dr 73703
Cogdal Dr 73703
Coletta Dr 73703
Colorado Ave 73701
W Colorado Ave 73703
E & W Columbia Ave 73701
Comanche Trl 73703
S Commerce St 73703
Commercial Cir 73703
Compound 73703
Concord Pl 73703
Constitution Ave 73703
Continental Pl 73703
N & S Coolidge St 73703
E Cornell Ave 73701
Cottontail Ln 73703
E & W Cottonwood Ave & Ln 73701
Cougar Ln 73703
Country Club Dr 73703
County Road 840 73703
Coventry Rd 73703
S Covered Wagon Trl 73701
Coyote Trl 73703
Craftsman Dr 73703
Creekdale 73703
Creekside Dr 73701
Crestview 73703
Crestwood 73701
Cumberland Trl 73703
Cumberlin Rd 73703
E Cypress Ave 73703
D Ct 73703
Dagenhart Rd 73705
Dalton Ct 73703
Dana Dr 73703
Danika Dr 73703
Dans Ct 73703
Danvere 73703
Daves Dr 73703
N Davis St 73701
Day Break Ln 73703
Dean Ave & Cir 73703
Deer Run 73703
Deerfield Ave 73703
Delaware 73701
W Delta Dr 73703
Demla Ct 73703
Denim Ln 73703
Dogwood Ln 73703
Don Kroll St 73701
Dona Kaye Dr 73701
Dorr Dr 73703
Double Tree Ln 73703
Douglas 73701
Dover Pl 73703
Drewstead 73703
Driftwood 73703
Durango Rd 73703
Dwelle Dr 73701
E Ct 73703
Eagle Ln 73703
Edgewater Dr 73703
Edgewood Dr 73703
Edwards St 73703
N Eisenhower St 73703
Elam Rd 73705
Elk Run 73703
E Elm Ave 73701
W Elm Ave
100-999 73701
1000-2899 73703
Elm Pl 73703
Elmwood Cir 73703
N Emerson St 73701
Enterprise Blvd 73701
E Eucalyptus Ave 73701
N & S Eufaula Dr 73703
Evandale Dr 73703
Everitt Dr 73703
Failing Dr 73701
Fair Dr 73703
Falcon Crst 73703
N & S Ferguson St 73701
Field Dr 73703
Fields St 73705
N & S Fillmore St 73703
Fisher Rd 73705
Flintridge Rd 73703
Florence St 73703
Forest Trl 73703
Forestridge Dr & Pl 73701
W Forrest Ave 73703
E Forrest St 73701
Fountain Head Dr 73703
Fountain Lake Ave 73703
Fowler St 73703
E Fox Dr 73701
W Fox Dr 73703
Foxcroft 73703
Francis St 73703
Franklin Cir & Dr 73703
W Frantz Ave 73701
Freeland Dr 73701
Gannon Ave 73703
N & S Garfield St 73703
N & S Garland Rd 73703
Gingham Ln 73703
Glenhaven Dr 73703
N Glenwood Dr 73703
Goad St 73705
Goldfinch Ln 73703
N Gore St 73701
Gott Rd 73705
Graham Ave 73703
N & S Grand St 73701
N & S Grant St 73703
Grayridge Rd 73703
Grays Peak 73701
W Great Lakes Rd 73703
Green Olive St 73701
N & S Greenleaf Ct & Dr 73703
Greenwood Pl 73703
Greg Dr 73703
Gritz St 73705
Grizzly Ln 73703
E & W Hackberry Ave 73701
Hampton Ct 73703
Hancock Ave 73703
N & S Harding St 73703
Harpers Fry 73703
N & S Harrison St 73703
E Harvard Ave 73701
Harvest Dr 73701
N & S Hayes St 73703
Haystack Ln 73703
Heather Rdg 73703
Helen Cir 73703
E & W Hemlock Ave 73701
Hennessey St 73701
Hereford Dr 73703
Heritage Trl 73703
Heritage Garden Ct 73703
E & W Hickory Ave 73701
Highland Dr 73701
N & S Highway 132 73703
W Highway 412 73703
N Highway 81 73701
Hillcrest Dr 73701
Hillsboro Dr 73703
Hillside Dr 73701
Hilltop Dr 73701
Hite Blvd 73703
N Hobart Rd 73703
Homestead Rd 73703
E & S Honey Dale St 73701
N & S Hoover St 73703
S & W Hudson Dr 73703
Hummingbird Ln 73703
Hunters Hill Dr 73703
Huron St 73703
Hurst Dr 73703
E & W Illinois Ave 73701
N & S Imo Rd 73703
N & S Independence St 73701
W Indian Cir, Dr & Ter 73703
E & W Indiana Ave 73701
Industrial Dr 73701
E & W Iowa Ave 73701
N & S Jackson St 73701
Jaguar Ln 73703
W James Ave 73703
N & S Jane Ln 73703
N & S Jefferson Pl & St 73701
Jenny Ln 73703
N & S Johnson St 73703
K L Dr 73703
Kansas Ave
200-500 73701
502-598 73701
2300-2399 73703
Katie Ln 73701
Kaw St 73703
Kb Johnson St 73701
Kelly Rd 73703
N Kennedy St 73701
Kenwood Blvd 73701
W Keowee Rd 73703
Kesterfield Blvd 73703
N & S Keystone Dr 73703
Kimbra Dr 73703
King St 73703
Kingwood 73701
Kiowa St 73703
Kline Cir 73701
Kremlin St 73701
Kylie Ln 73703
N & S La Mesa Dr 73703
E Lake Hellums Rd 73701
W Lake Hellums Rd
200-699 73701
1100-6999 73703
Lake Trail Dr 73701
Lakeshore Dr 73703
S Lakeside St 73701
Lakeview Dr 73701
Lakewood Dr 73703
Lantern Ln 73703
Larkspur Ln 73703
Last Chance 73703
Laurel Pl 73703
Legacy Ct 73703
Lehr St 73703
Leona Mitchell Blvd 73701
Lexington Pl 73703
Liberty Ln 73703
Lieb Way 73703
Lilac Dr 73701
Lilac Pl 73703

N & S Lincoln Dr & St . 73703
Linda Cir ... 73703
Linwood Rd ... 73701
Lisa Ln ... 73703
Lisas Way ... 73703
Live Oak St ... 73703
E Locust Ave ... 73701
W Locust Ave
100-699 ... 73701
1800-1999 ... 73703
N Logan Rd ... 73703
London Ln ... 73703
Long Br ... 73703
Longbranch ... 73703
E Longhorn Trl ... 73701
S & W Longview Dr ... 73703
Lookout Dr ... 73701
Lorean Dr ... 73703
Lovell Ln ... 73703
Lynn Ln ... 73703
N & S Madison St ... 73701
Magnolia St ... 73701
E Maine Ave ... 73701
W Maine Ave
100-999 ... 73701
1000-3299 ... 73703
N Malone St ... 73701
Manchester Dr ... 73703
E Maple Ave ... 73701
W Maple Ave
100-999 ... 73701
1000-2499 ... 73703
Maple Leaf Cir ... 73703
Maplewood Cir ... 73703
Margaret Cir ... 73703
E Market St ... 73701
Marlboro Dr ... 73703
Martin Ave ... 73701
Marymount ... 73703
Mason Dr ... 73703
Matthew Dr ... 73701
Mayberry St ... 73703
Mcaffrey Ave ... 73705
Mclaflin Dr ... 73701
Mcgill Dr ... 73703
N & S Mckinley St ... 73703
N Meadowbrook Dr ... 73701
Meadowlark Ln ... 73703
Memorial Dr ... 73701
Mercer Dr ... 73701
Merrimac ... 73703
Merritt Ave ... 73705
Mesquite Dr ... 73701
S Michael Rd ... 73703
Midway St ... 73701
Mill Run ... 73703
Mimosa St ... 73701
Minco Rd ... 73701
W Minnie Ave ... 73703
N & S Mission Rd ... 73703
Mistletoe ... 73701
Mocking Bird Ln ... 73703
Mohawk St ... 73703
Monitor ... 73703
N & S Monroe St ... 73701
Monterey Dr ... 73703
Monticello Pl ... 73703
E & W Moore St ... 73701
Morningside Pl ... 73701
Morris Ln ... 73703
Mosher Dr ... 73703
Mt Vernon Rd ... 73703
E & W Mulberry St ... 73701
Munger Dr ... 73703
Myriah Ln ... 73703
W Nagel Ave ... 73701
Nancy Dr ... 73701
Natchez Trace Rd ... 73703
National Rd ... 73703
Navajo St ... 73703
Navy Blue St ... 73701
W Neilson Dr ... 73703
Nicholas Oaks Dr ... 73703
Nightengale Ln ... 73703
Norman Rd ... 73703
Northgate Dr ... 73703

Northlake Ln ... 73703
Nottingham Rd ... 73703
E Oak Ave ... 73701
W Oak Ave
100-999 ... 73701
1200-3699 ... 73703
Oak Trl ... 73703
Oak Bridge Ln ... 73703
Oak Leaf Cir ... 73703
Oak Ridge Pl & Rd ... 73703
Oakcrest Ave ... 73703
Oakdale Dr ... 73703
Oakhill Cir ... 73703
N & S Oakwood Ct &
Rd ... 73703
E Ohio Ave ... 73701
Okarche ... 73701
E Oklahoma Ave ... 73701
W Oklahoma Ave
100-999 ... 73701
1000-3499 ... 73703
S Old Trl ... 73703
Old Mallard Rd ... 73703
Old Post Cir, Ln & Rd .. 73703
E Olive St ... 73701
Orleans Ave ... 73701
Osage Ave ... 73703
Ottawa St ... 73701
Overland Trl ... 73703
E Owen K Garriott Rd .. 73701
W Owen K Garriott Rd
100-999 ... 73701
1200-11899 ... 73703
E Oxford Ave ... 73701
W Oxford Ave
100-899 ... 73701
1200-1599 ... 73703
W Palm St ... 73701
E Paradise Ln ... 73701
Paris Pl ... 73703
W Park Ave
200-999 ... 73701
2500-2599 ... 73703
E Park St ... 73701
Parker Dr ... 73701
Parker St ... 73703
Parkway St ... 73703
Parkwood Ave ... 73703
Partridge Ln ... 73703
Paseo Dr ... 73701
Patrick Henry Pl ... 73703
Pawhuska Ave ... 73703
Pawnee St ... 73703
Pebble Dr ... 73703
Perry Ave ... 73703
Pheasant Run Dr ... 73703
Philadelphia Pl ... 73703
E Phillips Ave ... 73701
W Phillips Ave
100-999 ... 73701
1000-9499 ... 73703
Picketwire Cir ... 73703
N & S Pierce St ... 73703
Pin Oak Ave ... 73703
E Pine Ave ... 73701
W Pine Ave
100-999 ... 73701
1000-3099 ... 73703
Pine Cone Ln ... 73703
Pinto Ln ... 73701
Pioneer Trl ... 73701
Plantation ... 73703
Pocasset ... 73701
N & S Polk St ... 73703
Ponca Ave ... 73703
Ponderosa Dr ... 73703
Pontiac Dr ... 73703
E Poplar Ave ... 73701
W Poplar Ave
200-799 ... 73701
1100-1599 ... 73703
Prairie Rd ... 73703
Prairie Rose Ln ... 73701
Pride Dr ... 73703
E Princeton Ave ... 73701
Prospect Ave ... 73703

Providence Dr ... 73703
Psc Box ... 73705
E Purdue Ave ... 73701
W Purdue Ave
100-999 ... 73701
1500-13199 ... 73703
Quail Ln & Trl ... 73703
Quail Creek Dr ... 73703
Quail Ridge Rd ... 73703
Quailwood Dr ... 73703
Quannah Dr ... 73703
Quapaw St ... 73701
N & S Quincy St ... 73701
S Raleigh Rd ... 73701
Ramona Dr ... 73703
Rampart St ... 73703
Ranch Cir ... 73703
E Randolph Ave ... 73701
W Randolph Ave
100-999 ... 73701
1100-5399 ... 73703
Raven Rdg ... 73703
Red Cedar St ... 73701
Red Rock Cir ... 73703
Redbird Ln ... 73703
Redbud Dr ... 73701
Redpath Dr ... 73703
Redwood ... 73701
Reiter Cir ... 73701
Remington Ct ... 73703
Revere Rd ... 73703
Richard Rd ... 73701
W Richland Ave ... 73703
Ridge Pl ... 73701
Ridgedale Dr ... 73703
Ridgeview Ave ... 73703
Ridgeway Dr ... 73701
Ridgewood ... 73701
N & S Rimrock Rd ... 73703
Ritchie Ave ... 73703
E Robertson Rd ... 73701
W Robertson Rd
100-298 ... 73701
300-899 ... 73701
1800-6599 ... 73703
Robin Rdg ... 73703
Rock Island Blvd ... 73701
Rockcrest St ... 73701
Rockwood Rd ... 73703
Rogers Ter ... 73703
Rolling Oaks Dr ... 73703
Roman Nose Dr ... 73703
S Roosevelt St ... 73703
Rosanne St ... 73703
Rose Tree Ln ... 73703
Rosewood Cir ... 73703
E Rupe Ave ... 73701
W Rupe Ave ... 73703
W Rush St ... 73701
Sac Dr ... 73701
N & S Saddle Rd ... 73703
Sage Dr ... 73701
Salisbury Rd ... 73703
Sand Creek Dr ... 73701
Sand Creek Rd ... 73703
Sand View Dr ... 73703
Sandhill ... 73703
Sandpiper St ... 73703
Sandridge St ... 73703
Sandy Dr ... 73703
Santa Fe Ln ... 73703
Sara Dr ... 73703
Sawyer St ... 73705
Saybrook Dr ... 73703
Scarlett ... 73703
Scissortail Ln ... 73703
Scott Rd ... 73705
E Second Pine St ... 73701
Seminole St ... 73703
Seneca Ave ... 73703
Sequoyah Dr ... 73703
Seven Pines Dr ... 73703
Shadowood Dr ... 73703
Shady Ln ... 73701
Shady Oaks ... 73703
Shenandoah ... 73703

Sherry Cir ... 73703
Sherry Lee Ave ... 73703
Sherwood Dr ... 73703
Sheryl Ann ... 73703
Shiloh Ave ... 73703
Shirley Dr ... 73701
Silver Meadow Ln ... 73703
Single Tree Ln ... 73703
Sioux Ave ... 73703
Skyline Pl ... 73703
Skyview Cir ... 73703
Sleepy Hollow Cir &
Dr ... 73703
Sombrero Cir ... 73703
Sonata Cir ... 73703
Songbird Ln ... 73701
S Sooner Trl ... 73703
Sooner Trend ... 73701
E Southgate Rd ... 73701
W Southgate Rd
500-999 ... 73701
1100-11899 ... 73703
Split Rail Rd ... 73703
Spring Ridge Rd ... 73703
Spring Valley Ln ... 73701
E Spruce Ave ... 73701
W Spruce Ave
400-699 ... 73701
1100-1399 ... 73703
St Andrews Cir & Ct ... 73703
Stagecoach ... 73703
Stahl St ... 73701
E Stanford Ave ... 73701
Starlight Cir ... 73703
E & W State Ave ... 73701
E Steele St ... 73701
Stonewall Ct ... 73703
Stratford Dr ... 73703
Stull Ct ... 73703
Suggett Ave ... 73703
Sun Rise Dr ... 73703
Sundown Cir ... 73703
Sunnybrook Cir & Ln ... 73703
Sunset Ave & Plz ... 73703
Sunshine Cir ... 73703
Surrey Ln ... 73703
N & S Taft St ... 73703
Tahlequah Pl ... 73703
Tamarack Cir ... 73703
Tanglewood Dr & St ... 73703
Tara Ln ... 73703
N Taylor St ... 73703
Texoma Dr ... 73703
The Trails West Loop .. 73703
Thistledown Rd ... 73703
Thompson Ave ... 73705
W Thompson Ave
400-999 ... 73701
1000-1899 ... 73703
Thousand Oaks ... 73703
Timberlane ... 73703
Timberwood ... 73701
Tory Cir ... 73703
Twilight Ave ... 73703
Twisted Oak Ave ... 73703
N & S Tyler St ... 73703
Union Rd ... 73703
N & S University Ave &
Blvd ... 73701
Unruh Dr ... 73703
N Us Highway 81 ... 73701
Utah Ave ... 73701
Valley Crest St ... 73703
Valley Forge Dr ... 73703
Valley View Rd ... 73701
N Van Buren Byp ... 73701
N Van Buren St ... 73703
S Van Buren St ... 73703
Vance Afb ... 73705
Ventris Dr ... 73703
Vicksburg ... 73703
Village Dr ... 73703
E & W Vine St ... 73701
Vinita Ave ... 73703
Violet Rose St ... 73701
E Wabash Ave ... 73701

W Wabash Ave
100-999 ... 73701
1000-1499 ... 73703
Wagon Trl ... 73703
E Walker St ... 73701
S & W Wallace Dr ... 73703
W Waller Dr ... 73703
E Walnut Ave ... 73701
W Walnut Ave
100-899 ... 73701
1000-2899 ... 73703
N & S Washington St .. 73701
Waterford Ct ... 73703
N & S Watson St ... 73703
Waurika ... 73701
Wedgewood Rd ... 73703
W Wellesly St ... 73701
Wellington Ave ... 73703
Wesley Ln ... 73703
Westchester Dr ... 73703
Western Dr ... 73703
Westminster Dr ... 73703
Westwind ... 73703
Westwood Rd ... 73703
Weycroft ... 73703
E Wheat Capital Rd ... 73701
W Wheat Capital Rd
600-700 ... 73701
702-898 ... 73701
9300-11999 ... 73703
Wheatland St ... 73703
N & S Wheatridge Rd .. 73703
Whippoorwill Ln &
Way ... 73703
Wilderness Cv & Rd ... 73703
Wildoak Cir & Dr ... 73701
Wildwood Dr ... 73703
Will Rogers Dr ... 73703
Williamsburg ... 73703
Willow Pl ... 73701
E Willow Rd ... 73701
W Willow Rd
100-999 ... 73701
1000-13099 ... 73703
Willow Run ... 73703
Willow Creek Cir ... 73703
Willow Lake Ln ... 73703
Willow Spring Dr ... 73703
W Willowbrook Dr ... 73703
Willowmere Pt & Rd ... 73703
Wilshire Dr ... 73703
N & S Wilson St ... 73703
Winchester Ave ... 73703
Windmeer Ave ... 73701
Windmill Ln ... 73703
Woodbriar Sq ... 73703
Woodchuck Rd ... 73703
Woodland Trl ... 73703
Woodlands Dr ... 73703
Woodmoor Rd ... 73703
Woolwine St ... 73703
Wren Ln ... 73703
W Wynona Ave ... 73703
W Yale Ave ... 73701
Yellow Pine St ... 73701
E York Ave ... 73701
W York Ave
100-999 ... 73701
1000-1499 ... 73703
Yorkshire Dr ... 73703
Young Rd ... 73705
Yucca Dr ... 73701
Zachary Ln ... 73703

NUMBERED STREETS

All Street Addresses ... 73701

GROVE OK

General Delivery ... 74344

POST OFFICE BOXES MAIN OFFICE STATIONS AND BRANCHES

Box No.s
6501 - 7318 ... 74344
450001 - 453340 ... 74345

RURAL ROUTES

01, 02, 03, 04, 05, 06,
07, 08, 10 ... 74344

NAMED STREETS

All Street Addresses ... 74344

NUMBERED STREETS

All Street Addresses ... 74344

LAWTON OK

General Delivery ... 73501

POST OFFICE BOXES MAIN OFFICE STATIONS AND BRANCHES

Box No.s
708A - 708A ... 73502
1 - 5000 ... 73502
6001 - 8040 ... 73506
10001 - 10120 ... 73501
555060 - 888050 ... 73506

RURAL ROUTES

01, 02, 03, 06 ... 73501
04, 05, 07, 08 ... 73505
01 ... 73507

HIGHWAY CONTRACTS

60, 61, 64 ... 73507

NAMED STREETS

SW A Ave
1-2299 ... 73501
2301-2397 ... 73505
2399-2699 ... 73505
2701-2799 ... 73505
SE Aberdeen Ave ... 73501
SW Abilene Dr ... 73501
NE Abshere Rd ... 73507
Addiebeth ... 73507
SW Airport Industrial
Rd ... 73501
NW Alan A Dale Ln ... 73505
NW Aldwick Ave ... 73505
NW Allison Ln ... 73505
Allison Rd ... 73507
NW Allison Rd ... 73507
SE Alta Ln ... 73501
SE Andover Ave ... 73501
NW Andrews Ave
1100-2099 ... 73507
6300-6398 ... 73505
6400-8000 ... 73505
8002-8098 ... 73505
SW Angelwood Dr ... 73505
Angus Cir, Pl & St ... 73507
NW Apache Dr ... 73507
SW Applewood Ln ... 73505
SW Arbuckle Ave ... 73501
SW Ard St ... 73505
NE Arlington Ave ... 73507
NW Arlington Ave
1-2199 ... 73507
2700-3899 ... 73505
NE Arlington Dr ... 73507
Arnold Ct ... 73505
NW Arrowhead Dr ... 73505
NW Ash Ave
1100-1999 ... 73507
5100-7399 ... 73505
SW Ashbrook Ave ... 73505
NW Ashbury Way ... 73505
NW Ashby Ave ... 73505
NW Ashley Ct ... 73505
NW Atlanta Ave ... 73505
SW Atom Ave ... 73505
SW Atterbury Dr ... 73505
NW Austin Dr ... 73505
Autumn Dr & Ln ... 73507
SE Avalon Ave ... 73501
SE Avondale Ln ... 73501
SE B Ave ... 73501
SW B Ave
1-2299 ... 73501
2400-2699 ... 73505
NE Babbit St ... 73507
SW Bainbridge Ave ... 73505
NW Baldwin Ave
1101-1197 ... 73507
1199-2099 ... 73507
7000-8099 ... 73505
Baltimore Ave & Cir ... 73505
SE Barclay Rd ... 73501
SE Baseline Rd ... 73501
SW Baseline Rd
1000-2599 ... 73501
4000-5399 ... 73505
Baylee Creek Cir & Trl . 73501
SW Baywood Dr ... 73505
SE Beaver View Rd ... 73501
Becontree Dr & Pl ... 73505
Bedford Cir & Dr ... 73501
NW Beechwood Dr ... 73505
NE Bel Air Cir ... 73507
NE Bell Ave ... 73507
NW Bell Ave
1-2199 ... 73507
2300-3899 ... 73505
NE Bell Dr ... 73507
NE Bellevue Cir ... 73507
SW Belmont Ave ... 73501
NW Bent Tree Cir ... 73505
Berkshire Ct & Way ... 73501
NW Bessie Ave
1200-1599 ... 73507
2100-2199 ... 73505
SW Beta Ave ... 73505
NE Bethel Rd
1-8899 ... 73507
2-98 ... 73501
100-8898 ... 73507
SE Bethel Rd ... 73501
NW Bingo Rd ... 73507
NW Birch Ave
1100-1199 ... 73507
6100-6499 ... 73505
NW Birch Pl ... 73505
NW Birchwood Pl ... 73505
SE Bishop Est ... 73501
SE Bishop Rd ... 73501
SW Bishop Rd
1-1699 ... 73501
2200-8599 ... 73505
Bittersweet Ln ... 73507
NW Black Mesa Dr ... 73505
NW Blackstone Trl ... 73505
Blue Beaver Rd ... 73507
NE Blue Sage Ln ... 73507
NE Bly Ln ... 73507
SW Boatsman Ave ... 73505
NE Bob White Rd ... 73507
SW Boyles Landing
Rd ... 73505
SW Bradbury Cir ... 73505
SW Bradford Ln ... 73505
NE Bradford St ... 73507
Bradley Ct ... 73505
NW Brady Way ... 73505
SW Brandon Ln ... 73505
Breckinridge Dr ... 73507
NW Brent Cir ... 73505
SW Brentwood Blvd ... 73505
NE Brentwood Cir ... 73507
NE Brentwood Dr ... 73507
Brian Pl ... 73507

NE Briarcliff Cir 73507
NW Briarcreek Dr 73505
NW Briarwood Ave 73505
Brigadoon Pl & Way 73501
Brighton Cir, Ct, Dr & Pl 73501
SW Brimwood Dr 73505
NW Britni Cir 73505
Brookehaven Pathway .. 73505
SW Brookline Ave 73505
SE Brown St 73501
Brownwood Rd 73507
NE Buckingham Ln 73507
NW Buffalo Dr 73505
NW Burgess Rd 73507
SW Burk Rd 73505
NW Burr Oak Dr 73507
SW Butterfield Dr 73501
SE C Ave 73501
SW C Ave
1-2099 73501
2400-2699 73505
SE Caber Cir 73501
Cache Rd 73505
NE Cache Rd 73507
NW Cache Rd
600-2100 73507
2101-2197 73505
2102-2198 73507
2199-13699 73505
NW Cache Road Sq 73505
SE Camden Way 73501
SE Camelot Dr 73501
Cara Rd 73507
NE Carlson Rd 73507
Carrie Rd 73507
NW Carroll Ave 73505
NW Carroll Dr 73507
SE Carter Pl 73501
NE Carver Ave 73507
NW Castle Rock Pl 73505
SW Castlestone 73505
Cedar Mountain Rd 73507
NW Cedarwood Dr 73505
NW Cedric Cir 73505
NW Central Dr 73507
Central Mall 73501
Century Oaks Ln 73505
Charles Whitlow Ave ... 73501
Charlotte Dr 73507
SE Chat Rd 73501
Chaucer Cir, Dr & Way 73507
Cherokee Ave & Cir 73505
NW Cherry Ave
1100-1999 73507
3800-6499 73505
NW Cherry Cir 73505
Cheryl Blvd, Cir & Pl ... 73505
NW Chesley Dr 73505
NW Chestnut Ln 73505
Cheswick Ave & Pl 73505
NW Cheyenne Ave 73505
NW Cheyenne Cir 73505
NW Cheyenne Dr
1-699 73507
6200-6299 73505
NW Chibitty Rd 73507
NW Chimney Creek Dr 73505
SW Chisholm Trail Blvd 73501
NW Chosin Rd 73507
SE Churchill Way 73501
Cimarron Cir, Pl & Trl .. 73507
SE Clover Ln 73501
Coachman Dr & Pl 73501
SW Cody Pl 73501
Cole Creek Dr 73507
NE Colonial Dr 73507
NE Columbia Ave 73507
NW Columbia Ave
1-2199 73507
2500-6599 73505
NW Comanche Dr 73507
NW Commerce Cir 73507
NW Compass Dr 73505
NW Concho Rd 73505
SE Conquistador Acres 73501
SE Coombs Rd 73501
SW Coombs Rd
600-1099 73501
2200-10999 73505
Copper Mountain Dr 73507
SW Coral Ave 73505
SW Coralwood Dr 73505
SW Cornell Ave 73505
SW Cornish Ave 73505
NE Coronado Blvd 73507
SE Cortez Ave 73501
NW Cottonwood Dr 73505
SW Country Club Dr ... 73505
NW Country Meadow Rdg 73505
Cox Rd 73507
NW & NE Creek Pl & Rd 73507
NW Creek Hollar Dr 73505
NW Creekside Ct 73505
Crescent Ridge Dr 73505
SW Crestview Dr 73505
NW Crestwood Dr 73505
NW Crosby Ave 73507
Crosby Park Blvd & Cir 73505
NE Cross Rd 73507
NW Crossland Cir 73505
NW Crusader Dr 73505
Crystal Hills Dr & Pl ... 73505
NW Currell Dr 73505
Curts Dr 73507
NE Cypress Ln 73507
NW Cypress Ln 73505
SE D Ave 73501
SW D Ave
1-2099 73501
2400-2699 73505
SW Daun 73505
NE Dearborn Ave 73507
NW Dearborn Ave
1-2199 73507
3800-6199 73505
NW Debracy Ave 73505
NW Deer Run Trl 73505
Deerfield Rd 73507
Delta Ave & Cir 73505
NW Denver Ave 73505
SE Devonshire Dr 73501
NW & SW Deyo Mission Rd 73505
NW Dogwood Ln 73505
SW Doolittle Ave 73505
SE Dorchester Dr 73501
SW Douglas Ave
100-2199 73501
2300-2399 73505
NE Dove Ln 73507
SW Dove Creek Blvd ... 73505
SE Dover Dr 73501
NW Downy 73505
SW Dr Elsie Hamm Dr . 73505
SW Drakestone Blvd ... 73505
SE Drexel Dr 73501
SW Driftwood Dr 73505
NE Dunlop St 73507
NW Dunstan Ln 73505
SW E Ave
1-2299 73501
2300-2699 73505
NW Eagle Rd 73507
NW Eagle Mountain Rd 73507
NE Eastlake Dr 73507
NW Echo Rd 73505
NW Edgemere Cir 73505
SE Edinburgh Ln 73501
SW Edinburough Dr 73505
SW Edward Cir 73505
NW Eisenhower Dr 73505
NW Elk Dr 73505
Ellsworth Ave & Cir 73501
NW Elm Ave
1100-2099 73507
5100-6699 73505
NW Elm St 73505
SE Elmhurst Ln 73501
SW Embassy Cir 73505
NW Enclave Blvd 73505
SW Englewood Dr 73505
NE English St 73507
Erwin Ln 73505
Estates Cir 73507
NE Euclid Ave 73507
NW Euclid Ave
1-1999 73507
2700-6699 73505
SW Evans Ave 73505
SE F Ave 73501
SW F Ave
1-2299 73501
3500-3599 73505
Faircloud Cir & Dr 73505
Fairway Villa Dr & Pl ... 73505
NW Farkenco Ave 73507
SW Fenwick Ave 73505
NW Ferris Ave
1-2299 73507
2600-6699 73505
NW Ferris Pl 73505
NE Fieldcrest 73507
Fitzroy Pl 73505
NE Flower Mound Rd .. 73507
SE Flower Mound Rd .. 73501
NW Floyd Ave
1600-2099 73507
4300-4899 73505
NE Flycatcher Ln 73507
NW Folkstone Way 73505
SE Footman Ln 73501
SE Ford Rd 73501
SW & NW Forest Ave, Cir, Ln & Pl 73505
NW Fort Sill Blvd 73507
Foster Dr 73507
Foxfire Rd 73507
SW Franklin Ave 73505
Franks Ct 73505
SE French Rd 73501
NW Friar Tuck Ln 73505
SE Fullbright Ln 73501
NE Fullerton St 73507
SW G Ave
1-1699 73501
2300-2698 73505
2700-4600 73505
4602-4998 73505
SE Gant Rd 73501
NE Garden Ln 73507
SW Garfield Ave 73501
SW Gaylord Ave 73505
NE Georgetown Ave 73507
SW Georgia Ave
1100-1699 73501
2300-2399 73505
SW Gilbert Gibson Rd .. 73501
SE Glasgow Ave 73501
NW Glendale Dr 73507
SW Glenhaven Ave 73505
NW Glenn Ave
1900-1999 73507
5300-5799 73505
5801-5899 73505
SE Glennbrook Ln 73501
Goldenrod Way 73507
SE Goodin Rd 73501
NW & SW Goodyear Blvd 73505
E Gore Blvd 73501
W Gore Blvd
100-2299 73501
2300-7500 73505
7502-7998 73505
SW Grand Ave 73501
Gray Hawk Dr 73507
Gray Warr Ave & Pl 73505
NW Graysons Mountain Dr 73505
NW Great Plains Blvd .. 73505
SW Green Terrace Blvd 73505
NW Greenmeadow Dr .. 73507
SW Greenwich Dr 73505
NW Grensted Ln 73505
SE H Ave 73501
SW H Ave
1-1699 73501
2300-4999 73505
NE Haddington Pl 73507
SW Hampshire Cir 73505
NW Hampton Ct 73505
Hankins Dr 73505
SE Hardin Ave 73501
SW Hasty Way 73505
NW Havenshire Cir 73505
SE Heather Ln 73501
Heatherstone Cir & Dr .. 73505
NW Heinzwood Cir 73505
Heritage Dr & Ln 73507
NE Heritage Creek Dr .. 73507
Hickory Ln & Pl 73505
SW Highland Ave 73501
NE Highlander Cir 73507
N Highway 277 73507
S Highway 277 73501
Highway 62 W 73505
SE Hillcrest Ave 73501
NW Hillcrest Dr 73505
NW Hilliary Rd 73507
NW Hilltop Dr 73507
NW Hillview Dr 73505
Holly Rd 73507
NW Homestead Dr 73505
NW Hoover Ave
1200-2099 73507
2100-4999 73505
NW Horton Blvd 73505
Humberson Dr 73507
NW Hunter Rd 73505
SE Huntington Cir 73501
SE I Ave 73501
SW I Ave
1-1699 73501
2300-4699 73505
NE Independence Ave .. 73507
SE Indiana Ave 73501
SE Interstate Dr 73501
SW Inwood Cir 73505
NW Ironpin Cir 73507
NW Irwin Ave
1100-1198 73507
1200-2099 73507
6300-6499 73505
NW Ivanhoe Pl 73505
SE J Ave 73501
SW J Ave
300-1699 73501
2300-4699 73505
SE James Rd 73501
SE Jarman Ave 73501
SW Jefferson Ave
300-2199 73501
2300-4199 73505
Jesse L Davenport St .. 73501
NW Julie St 73505
NW Junipers Ln 73507
K Ave & Cir 73505
SE Katie Ln 73501
NW Kensington Pl 73505
Ketch Creek Cir, Dr, Pl & Way 73507
NW Keystone Dr 73505
Kimberlys Way 73507
Kimiko Ln 73507
SE Kincaid Ave 73501
NW King Rd 73507
NW King Richard Ave .. 73505
Kingsbriar Cir, Dr & Pl .. 73507
NW Kingsbury Ave
1100-2099 73507
7000-7799 73505
NW Kingswood Rd 73505
NW Kinyon Ave
1700-1999 73507
3100-5899 73505
NW Kiowa Dr 73507
Kirk Ave 73507
NW Kirkley Pl 73505
SW Koch St 73505
NW Lady Marna Ave ... 73505
NW Laird Ave 73507
NE Lake Ave 73507
NW Lake Ave
1100-2199 73507
3800-3899 73505
Lake Rd 73507
E Lake Rd 73507
Lake Crest Cir & Dr 73507
NW Lake Front Dr 73505
NW Lake Ridge Dr 73505
SW Lake Unity Dr 73505
Lakeland Dr 73507
NE & NW Lakeview Cir, Dr & Pl 73507
NW Lakewood Dr 73505
SW Lana Ln 73505
NE Lancaster Ln 73507
SE Lancelot Ln 73501
NW Lancet Ln 73505
Landmark Cir & Rd 73507
Landon Ln 73507
SE Larrance St 73501
SE Larriat Ave 73501
SE Lasso Loop 73501
SW Latham Ave 73505
NE Lawrie Tatum Rd ... 73507
NW Lawton Ave
1201-1297 73507
1299-2099 73507
7200-8099 73505
Lawtonka Cir & Rd 73507
Lazy Cir 73507
SE Lee Blvd 73501
SW Lee Blvd
1-2199 73501
2300-12599 73505
NW Legacy Dr 73505
NW Leona Cir 73505
NW Liberty Ave
1700-1999 73507
2800-5899 73505
NW Lincoln Ave
1100-2099 73507
2100-6199 73505
NW Lindy Ave
1400-2099 73507
2100-4999 73505
NW Locksley Ln 73505
NW Logan Ave 73507
SE Lomond Ln 73501
NW Longview Ave 73507
Lora Ln 73507
Lost Bridge Rd 73507
Louis K Jones 73507
NW Lynn Cir 73507
SW Lynnwood Ave 73505
NE Macarthur Cir 73507
NW Madische Rd 73507
NE Madison Ave 73507
Mae Ave 73507
SW Magnolia Ave 73501
NE Maine St 73507
SW Majestic Oak Blvd .. 73505
SW Malcom Rd 73505
SW Manning Ave 73501
NW Maple Ave
1100-1799 73507
6100-6599 73505
NW Maple Dr 73505
NW Marion Ave 73507
SW Mark Edwards Dr .. 73505
Marshall Dr 73505
NE Mayflower Ave 73507
NW Mcclung Rd 73507
NW Mcclung Acres 73507
NW Mccracken Rd 73507
NW Mcintosh Rd 73507
SW Mckinley Ave 73501
NW Meadowbrook Dr ... 73505
NE, E & W Meadowlark Ln & Rd 73507
Medicine Creek Dr 73507
NW Meers Porter Hl 73507
Melodie Ln 73507
NE Mesa Verde Rd 73507
SW Mesquite Dr 73505
NW Micklegate Blvd 73505
Mieling Cir & Dr 73501
NW Millcreek Rd 73505
NW Miller Rd 73507
SE Mills Ave 73501
NW Mimosa Ln 73507
NW Mission Blvd 73507
NW Mobley Ave 73507
NW Mockingbird Rd 73507
SW Monroe Ave
300-2199 73501
2400-2499 73505
NE Montfort Dr 73507
NW Montgomery Dr 73507
Montgomery Sq 73501
NW Morford Dr 73507
NW Morningside Dr 73507
NW Morrocco Rd 73505
NE Mossy Oak Cir & Dr 73507
NW Motif Manor Blvd ... 73505
Mount Marcy 73507
Mount Pinchot 73507
Mount Scott Cir 73507
Mount Sheridan Rd 73507
Mountain Ridge Dr & Ln 73507
NE Mountain View Rd .. 73507
NE Muse Cir 73507
SW N H Jones Ave 73501
SW Neal Blvd 73505
SW New York Ave
1100-1699 73501
2400-2499 73505
NW Nob Hill Dr 73505
NW Norman Cir 73505
SW Normandy Ave 73505
NW North Dr 73507
Northwood Ave & Pl ... 73507
Norwick Ave & Pl 73505
NW Nottingham Rd 73505
NW Oak Ave
1100-2199 73507
3400-6599 73505
SW Oak Cliff Ave 73505
NW Oak Dale Dr 73505
SW Oak Pointe Blvd ... 73505
SW Oak Tree Dr 73505
SW Oakland Ln 73505
SW Oakley 73505
SW Oakmont 73505
SW Oklahoma Ave
1200-1699 73501
3400-3499 73505
NE Oriole Dr 73507
SW Overland Dr 73501
Oxford Ave, Dr & Pl 73505
NW Ozmun Ave
1100-1999 73507
2100-4999 73505
NW Paint Rd 73507
NW Palomino Rd 73505
SW Pamela Ln 73505
Paradise Valley Dr & Est 73507
SE Park Ave 73501
SW Park Ave
200-1699 73501
2400-6199 73505
SW Park Pl 73505
Park Rd 73507
SW Parkgrove Dr 73505
SW Parkridge Blvd 73505
NW Parkview Blvd 73507
SW Parkway Dr 73505
Parkwood Cir, Ln & Pl .. 73505
NE Patterson Ave 73507
SE Pebble Creek Rd ... 73501
SW Pecan Pl 73505
SW Pecan Rd
700-1199 73501
4500-13299 73505
NW Pecan Creek Dr ... 73505
SW Pecan Lake Cir 73505
SW Pecan Meadow Dr 73505
NW Pecan Valley Dr ... 73505
NE Penland Rd 73507
SW Pennsylvania Ave
1100-1699 73501
2300-2399 73505
NW Pershing Dr 73507
E, NE & W Pheasant Ln & Way 73507
Pinchot Rd 73507
Pine Creek Cir 73507
SE Pinewood Dr 73501
NE Pioneer Blvd 73507
NW Pleasant View Rdg 73505
NE Plymouth Rock Ave 73507
Poko Mtn 73507
NW Pollard Ave
1600-1999 73507
2100-4999 73505
SW Powell Ct 73505
SE Powers Rd 73501
SE Prairie Vw 73501
NW Prentice Ave 73507
SW Preston Trl 73505
SE Prestwick Dr 73501
Quail Pl 73507
Quail Creek Cir, Dr & Rd 73507
NE Quail Run Blvd 73507
Quanah Mountain Rd ... 73507
Quannah Parker Trl & Trwy 73505
SW Railroad St 73501
Ranch Dr 73507
SW Ranch Oak Blvd ... 73501
SE Randolph Rd 73501
NW Rebecca Ter 73505
NW Red Bud Rd 73507
NW Red Elk 73505
NW Red Elk Dr 73507
NE Red Hawk Ln 73507
SW Red Oak 73505
SE Redbud Pl 73501
NW Redwood Ln 73505
NW Reed Rd 73507
SW Rex Madeira Rd ... 73501
NW Rhoades Rd 73507
NE Richmond St 73507
Ridge Road Cir & Pl ... 73505
NW Ridgecrest Dr 73505
NW Ridgeview Way 73505
SW River Bend Rd 73505
NW Robinhood Dr 73505
Robinson Rd 73507
Rogers Ln 73507
NE Rogers Ln 73507
NW Rogers Ln
300-998 73507
2100-3498 73505
3500-11599 73505
NW Rolando Rd 73505
Rolling Hills Dr & Pl ... 73505
SW Roosevelt Ave 73501
SW Rosemary Way 73505
NW Rotherwood Dr 73505
NW Rowena Ter 73505
NW Runyon Rd 73505
SW Salinas Dr 73501
SW Sandra Cir 73505
NW Sandy Trail Cir & Ln 73505
NW Santa Fe Ave 73505
SW Sapp Cir 73505
NW Saxon Cir 73505
NW Scenic Ridge Dr ... 73505
NE Scissortail Dr 73507
NE Scottsdale Cir 73507
NW Seaton Pl 73505
Sedalia Ave & Pl 73501
NW Sequoyah Dr 73507

NW Shadow Lake Rd .. 73505
NW Shadybrook Dr 73505
Sharon Rd 73507
Sharps Ln 73501
Shelter Creek Cir & Dr . 73507
NW Shelter Lake Dr 73505
NW & SW Sheridan
Rd 73505
NW Sherwood Dr 73505
NW Shroyer Rd 73507
Silcott Cir & Pl 73507
Silver Creek Cir 73505
SE Simpson St 73501
NW Sir Brian Ave 73505
NE Skyline Cir 73507
SE Skyline Dr 73501
NE Skyline Pl 73507
SE Skyline Rd 73501
NW Smith Ave
1100-2099 73507
2100-4999 73505
Snowmass Rd 73507
NE Spencer Rd 73507
NW Springhollow Ln &
Rd 73505
NW Sprucewood Dr 73505
SE Stafford St 73501
State Highway 115 73507
State Highway 49 73507
State Highway 58 73507
N State Highway 65 73507
S State Highway 65 73501
NW Steeple Ridge Dr .. 73505
SW Sterling Dr 73501
NW Still Water Trl 73507
NW Stone Hill Dr 73505
NW Stonebridge Ct 73505
NW Stonebrook Dr 73505
Stonegate Dr & Pl 73505
NW Stoney Point Rd 73507
SW Stradford Ave 73505
NE Stratford Cir 73507
SE Sullivan Dr 73501
SW Summit Ave
200-1699 73501
3000-6299 73505
NW Sun 73505
SW Sun Valley Dr 73505
SW Sunflower Ln 73505
SE Sungate Blvd 73501
SE Sunnymeade Dr 73501
Sunnyside Dr & Ln 73501
SE Sunnyside Acres 73501
Sunset St 73507
SW Superior Cir 73505
Surrey Ln & Pl 73501
Surreywood Cir & Pl 73505
NW Tackle Box Rd 73507
NW Taft Ave 73507
Tanglewood Cir & Ln ... 73505
NW Tango Rd 73505
SE Tattershall Way 73501
NW Taylor Ave
1100-2099 73507
6300-8099 73505
NW Taylor Lndg 73505
NW Templeton Ter 73505
SW Tennessee Ave
1100-1699 73501
3300-3699 73505
SW Tennessee St 73505
NW Terrace Hills Blvd .. 73505
SW Texas Ave
1-1699 73501
2300-3499 73505
NW Thornbury Dr 73505
Thurman Dr 73507
Timber Creek Dr 73507
SE Tinney Rd 73501
SW Tinney Rd
1300-2099 73501
4000-6099 73505
Tomlin Cir & Pl 73505
NW Tonbridge Pl 73505
NE Tortoise Dr 73507
SE Tower Rd 73501
NE Townley Rd 73507
NE Trail Rd 73507
SE Trail Rd 73501
Travers Cir & Ln 73507
SE Trenton Rd 73501
SW Trevor Cir 73505
SW Tulane Ave 73505
NE Turtle Creek Dr 73507
NE Turtle Dove Ln 73507
SW Tyler Ave 73505
SW University Dr 73505
Vail Mountain Dr 73507
NW Valley Ridge Dr 73505
NE Valley View Rd 73507
NW Valleybrook Dr 73505
Valleyview Dr 73507
Valor Ave 73505
SW Victoria Blvd 73505
NE Viking Ln 73507
NE Village Dr 73507
NW Village Green Dr ... 73505
NW Vista Ridge Dr 73505
Wahnetah Ln 73507
NW Walding Ave 73507
Wall Mountain Trl 73507
SE Wallock St 73501
SE Walnut Creek Rd ... 73501
SE Warwick Way 73501
SE Washington Ave 73501
SW Washington Ave
200-2199 73501
2400-2599 73505
Washita Dr 73507
NE Water Edge Dr 73507
Water Ski Dr 73501
NW Waterford Dr 73505
SW Waterstone Pl 73505
NW Welch Rd 73507
NW Welco Ave 73505
SW Wendy Dr 73505
NW Wentwood Hill Dr .. 73505
NW Wesley Ave 73505
NW Westaire Cir 73505
SW Westchester Cir 73505
NW Westmont Cir 73505
SW White Ave 73505
Wichita Dr 73507
NW Wichita Dr 73505
Wichita Ridge Dr 73505
NW Wild Plum Rd 73507
Wildwood Rd 73507
NW Wilfred Dr 73505
NW Williams Ave
1100-2099 73507
2200-6199 73505
SE Willow Ln 73501
NW Willow Pl 73505
NE Willow Way 73507
NW Willow Creek Dr ... 73505
NW Willow Springs Dr .. 73505
NW Willow Tree Cir 73505
NW Willow Wood
Loop 73505
SE Wilshire Ter 73501
Wilson Ln 73505
SW Winchester Ave 73505
NW Winding Creek Rd . 73505
NW Windledge Cir 73505
NW Windmere Cir 73505
NE Windridge Ln 73507
Windyhollow 73505
NE Winfield Cir 73507
SW Wisconsin Ave 73501
NE Wisteria 73507
Wistoria St 73507
SW Wolf Ave 73505
NW Wolf Rd 73507
SW Wolf St 73505
NW Wolfcreek Blvd 73505
Woodland Cir, Dr & Pl .. 73505
SE Woodlawn Rd 73501
SW Woodlawn Rd 73505
NW Woodridge Dr 73507
SW Woodstock Ave 73505
Wyatt Lake Dr 73505
NW Wycliffe Ln 73505
Yorkshire 73507

NUMBERED STREETS

NW 1st St 73507
SE 1st St 73501
SW 1st St 73501
NW 2nd St 73507
SE 2nd St 73501
SW 2nd St 73501
NW 3rd St 73507
SE 3rd St 73501
SW 3rd St 73501
NW 4 Mile Rd 73507
NW 4th St 73507
SE 4th St 73501
SW 4th St 73501
NW 5th Pl 73507
NW 5th St 73507
SW 5th St 73501
NW 6th St 73507
SE 6th St 73501
SW 6th St 73501
NW 7th St 73507
SE 7th St 73501
SW 7th St 73501
NW 8th St 73507
SW 8th St 73501
NE 9th St 73507
NW 9th St 73507
SW 9th St 73501
NW 10th St 73507
SW 10th St 73501
SW 11th St 73501
NW 12th St 73507
SW 12th St 73501
NW 13th St 73507
SW 13th St 73501
SW 14th Pl 73501
NW 14th St 73507
SW 14th St 73501
NE 15th St 73507
NW 15th St 73507
SE 15th St 73501
SW 15th St 73501
NW 16th St 73507
SW 16th St 73501
NW 17th St 73507
SW 17th St 73501
NW 18th St 73507
SW 18th St 73501
NW 19th St 73507
SW 19th St 73501
NE 20th St 73507
NW 20th St 73507
SW 20th St 73501
NW 21st Pl 73505
NW 21st St 73507
SW 21st St 73501
NE 22nd St 73507
NW 22nd St
700-799 73507
1400-2899 73505
2901-2999 73505
SW 22nd St 73501
SW & NW 23rd Pl &
St 73505
SW & NW 24th Pl &
St 73505
SW 25th Pl 73505
NE 25th St 73507
NW 25th St 73505
SW 25th St 73505
SW 26th Pl 73505
NE 26th St 73507
NW 26th St 73505
SW 26th St 73505
NE 27th St 73507
NW 27th St 73505
SW 27th St 73505
NW & SW 28th 73505
NE 29th St 73507
NW 29th St 73505
SW 29th St 73505
NW & SW 30th 73505
NE 31st St 73507
NW 31st St 73505
NW 32nd St 73505
NW & SW 33rd Pl &
St 73505
NW & SW 34th 73505
NW 35th Pl 73505
NE 35th St 73507
NW 35th St 73505
SW 35th St 73505
NE 36th St 73507
NW 36th St 73505
SE 36th St 73501
SW 36th St 73505
NW & SW 37th 73505
NW 38th Pl 73505
NE 38th St 73507
NW 38th St 73505
SE 38th St 73501
SW 38th St 73505
NW & SW 39th 73505
NW 40th St 73505
SE 40th St 73501
SW 40th St 73505
NE 41st St 73507
NW 41st St 73505
SE 41st St 73501
SW 41st St 73505
NW & SW 42nd 73505
NE 43rd St 73507
NW 43rd St 73505
SW 43rd St 73505
NE 44th St 73507
NW 44th St 73505
SW 44th St 73505
NW 45th Pl 73505
SW 45th Pl 73505
NE 45th St 73507
NW 45th St 73505
SE 45th St 73501
SW 45th St 73505
NW 46th Pl 73505
NE 46th St 73507
NW 46th St 73505
SW 46th St 73505
NW 47th Pl 73505
NW 47th St 73505
SE 47th St 73501
SW 47th St 73505
NE 48th Pl 73507
NE 48th St 73507
NW 48th St 73505
SW 48th St 73505
NW & SW 49th 73505
NW & SW 50th 73505
NE 51st St 73507
NW 51st St 73505
SW 51st St 73505
NW 52nd Cir 73505
NE 52nd St 73507
NW 52nd St 73505
SW 52nd St 73505
NW & SW 53rd 73505
NW & SW 54th 73505
NW & SW 55th 73505
NW & SW 56th 73505
NW 57th St 73505
NW 58th St 73505
NW 59th St 73505
NE 60th St 73507
NW 60th St 73505
SE 60th St 73501
SW 60th St 73505
NE 61st St 73507
NW 61st St 73505
SW 61st St 73505
NE 62nd St 73507
NW 62nd St 73505
SW 62nd St 73505
SW & NW 63rd Pl &
St 73505
NW & SW 64th 73505
NW 65th St 73505
NW & SW 66th Cir &
St 73505
NW & SW 67th 73505
NW & SW 68th 73505
NW & SW 69th 73505
NW & SW 70th 73505
NW & SW 71st 73505
NW & SW 72nd 73505
73rd Pl & St 73505
NW & SW 74th Pl &
St 73505
NE 75th St 73507
NW 75th St 73505
SE 75th St 73501
SW 75th St 73505
NW & SW 76th 73505
NW & SW 77th 73505
NW & SW 78th 73505
NW & SW 79th 73505
NW & SW 80th 73505
NW & SW 81st 73505
NW & SW 82nd 73505
SW 83rd St 73505
SW 84th St 73505
SE 90th St 73501
NW & SW 97th 73505
SE 105th St 73501
NW & SW 112th 73505
NE 120th St 73507
SE 120th St 73501
NE 124th St 73507
SW 127th St 73505
NE 135th St 73507
SE 135th St 73501
NE 150th St 73507
SE 150th St 73501
NE 165th St 73507
SE 165th St 73501
NE 180th St 73507
SE 180th St 73501
SE 195th St 73501
NE 210th St 73507
SE 210th St 73501

MCALESTER OK

General Delivery 74501

POST OFFICE BOXES MAIN OFFICE STATIONS AND BRANCHES

Box No.s
All PO Boxes 74502

RURAL ROUTES

01, 02, 03, 04, 05, 06,
07, 08, 09 74501

HIGHWAY CONTRACTS

75 74501

NAMED STREETS

All Street Addresses 74501

NUMBERED STREETS

All Street Addresses 74501

MIAMI OK

General Delivery 74354

POST OFFICE BOXES MAIN OFFICE STATIONS AND BRANCHES

Box No.s
All PO Boxes 74355

RURAL ROUTES

01, 02, 03, 04, 05 74354

NAMED STREETS

All Street Addresses 74354

NUMBERED STREETS

All Street Addresses 74354

MUSKOGEE OK

General Delivery 74401

POST OFFICE BOXES MAIN OFFICE STATIONS AND BRANCHES

Box No.s
All PO Boxes 74402

RURAL ROUTES

01, 03, 04, 10 74401
02, 05, 06, 08, 09, 11 .. 74403

NAMED STREETS

E, N, S & W Aberdeen
St 74403
Admiral St 74403
Altamont St 74401
Anderson Dr 74403
N & S Anthony Rd &
St 74403
Arline St 74401
Arthur St 74401
Ash St 74403
Augusta St 74403
E Augusta St 74403
W Augusta St 74401
Austin St 74401
Avondale St 74403
Azalea Dr 74401
Azalea Park Dr 74401
N & S B St 74403
Bacon Ct & Rd 74403
S Bacone St 74403
Baltimore Ave & St 74403
Barclay Rd 74403
Barnett Dr 74403
Baugh St 74403
Beacon St 74403
Beaver Rd 74403
Beckman Dr & Rd 74401
Bel Aire Pl 74403
Belmont Rd 74403
Beth Ann Dr 74403
Betty Jane Ln 74403
W Biggs St 74401
Blue Jay Ln 74403
Blue Ridge Ct 74403
Bona Villa Dr 74403
Bonnie Ave 74403
Booker St 74401
Border Ave 74401
Boston St 74401
Boxcar Rd 74403
Bradford Ct 74403
Branson Park Dr & Pl .. 74403
Brewer St 74401
E Broadway St 74403
W Broadway St 74401
Brockway St 74403
Buford St 74403
Burbank St 74403
Butler St 74403
N & S C St 74403
Caddo St 74401
Callahan St 74403
Callery Dr 74403
N & S Camden Pl &
St 74403
Camelot Ct 74403
Canadian St 74403
Canterbury Ave & St ... 74403
Capitol Pl 74401
Cardinal Cir & Rd 74403
Carlton Way 74403
Carodobo St 74403
Carolyn St 74401
Carroll St 74401
Carver Ave 74401
Cary Pl 74403
Center Ln 74403
Chandler Rd 74403
Chaucer St 74403
Chelsea Ln 74403
Cheri St 74401
N & S Cherokee Dr, Ln
& St 74403
Cherry Pl & St 74403
Chestnut St 74403
Chicago St 74401
Chickasaw Dr 74403
W Chimney Mountain
Rd 74401
Choctaw St 74403
Christy Dr 74403
E Cincinnati Ave 74403
W Cincinnati Ave 74401
Circle Dr 74403
Club Estates Dr 74403
Club House Dr 74403
Club View Dr 74403
Cobblestone Cir, Ct &
Dr 74403
E & W Coburn Cir 74401
Coldwater Crk 74403
Collier St 74403
Colonial Pl 74403
Colorado St 74403
Columbus St 74401
Cooda Rd 74403
Coody St 74401
Cook St 74403
N & S Country Club
Cir, Ct, Dr, Pl & Rd 74403
Court St 74401
Coyote Pass 74403
Coyote Pass Ct 74403
Crabapple Ct 74403
N & S Crabtree Rd 74403
Creek St 74403
Crest Ct 74401
Crestview 74403
Crestview Ave 74401
Crestwood Dr 74403
Cromwell Ave, Pl & St .. 74403
Cumberland Dr 74403
N & S D St 74403
Daisy St 74403
Dakota Ave & Pl 74403
Dal Tile Rd 74401
Damson Ct 74403
Daniel Blvd 74403
Daniel Rogers Dr 74403
Davenport St 74403
N & S David Ct & Ln ... 74403
E Davis Field Rd 74403
W Davis Field Rd 74401
Dayton St 74403
Debby Jane Ln 74403
Deer Run 74403
Deer Run Cir & Ct 74403
Delaware St 74403
Denison St 74401
Denver St 74401
Doering Ln 74403
Don Cayo Dr 74403
Dorchester Ave 74403
Douglas St 74401
Dover Rd 74403
Drexel Pl 74403
Dublin Rd 74403

Dunbar St 74401
N & S E St 74403
Eaglecrest Dr 74401
Eastpoint Dr 74403
Eastside Blvd 74403
Eco Friendly Dr 74401
N & S Edmond Pl & St 74403
Elberta Ct & St 74403
Elbow Ln 74403
Elgin St 74401
Elizabeth St 74401
Elliott St 74403
Ellsworth St 74403
Elm St 74401
Elm Grove Rd 74403
Elmeda St 74403
Elmira St 74403
Elmwood Ln 74403
Elton Dr 74403
Elwell Rd 74401
Emporia St 74401
Enid St 74403
Erie St 74403
Estelle Ave 74401
Euclid St 74401
Eufaula Ave & St 74403
Evelyn St 74401
Even Par Ave 74401
Everett Ct 74403
N & S F St 74403
Faculty Row 74403
Fairfax Dr 74403
Fairmont St 74401
Fairway Dr 74403
Farris St 74403
Felix St 74403
Fenwick Pl 74403
Fern Mountain Dr & Rd 74401
Findlay St 74401
Fite St 74403
Foltz Ln & Pl 74403
W Fondulac St 74401
Fort Davis Dr & Pl 74403
Fox Ln 74403
Foxcroft Cir & Dr 74403
Francis St 74401
E Frankfort St 74403
E Frankie Ln 74403
Fredonia St 74403
Fremont St 74401
N & S G St 74403
Galahad Ct 74403
Galveston St 74403
Garland St 74401
Gawf Ct, Ln, Pl & Rd 74403
Geneva St 74403
Georgetown St 74401
Georgia Ave, Pl & St 74403
Gibson St 74403
Gilcrest 74401
Girard St 74401
Grand Ave 74403
Grandview Blvd, Cir & Ct 74403
Grandview Park Blvd 74403
Grant St 74403
Gulick St 74403
N & S H St 74403
Haddock Dr 74401
Hamilton St 74403
E Hancock St 74403
W Hancock St 74401
Harold Abitz Dr 74403
Harold Scoggins Dr 74403
Harrell Ave 74401
Harris Ave 74403
E Harris Rd 74403
W Harris Rd 74401
Harris St 74403
Harrison St 74403
Hartford St 74401
Haskell Blvd & St 74403
E Hayes St 74403
Helena Dr 74403
Heritage Pl 74403
Hiawatha Dr & Pl 74401
Hickory Creek Rd 74403
High Oaks St 74401
Highway 16 W 74401
Highway 64 S 74403
Hill St 74401
Hillcrest 74403
Hilldale Springs Cir & Dr 74403
Hilltop Ave, Ln & Pl 74403
E Holden St 74403
W Holden St 74401
Honor Heights Dr 74401
Horn St 74403
Houston St 74403
Howard St 74401
S Hunt Loop 74403
Hyde Park Ave 74403
S I St 74403
Illinois St 74403
Independence St 74403
Indiana St 74403
Indianapolis St 74401
Inman St 74401
Iola St 74401
Irving St 74403
N J St 74403
Jackson St 74401
Jeannie Ln 74403
Jeannie Lane Ct 74403
Jefferson Ct & St 74403
Jeffrey Dr 74403
Jennifer Ave & Ln 74403
Jennings St 74403
Joliet St 74403
Jonathan Pl 74403
Joplin St 74401
N & S Junction St 74401
N & S K St 74403
Kaad St 74401
E Kalamazoo St 74403
W Kalamazoo St 74401
Kankakee St 74403
Kansas Ave 74403
Katy St 74401
Keaton St 74401
Keats St 74403
Keetoowah Trl 74403
Kelancha St 74401
Kelley Dr 74403
Kendall Blvd 74401
Kent Dr 74403
Kentucky St 74403
Kershaw Cir & Dr 74401
Kimberlea Dr 74403
Kimberlea Park Dr 74403
W Kindell St 74401
Kingsbury Dr 74403
Kingston St 74403
Kingsway St 74403
Kinney St 74403
Kinsley St 74401
N & S L St 74403
Lampton St 74403
Lancelot Ct 74403
Lawrence St 74403
Leathers Ln 74401
Lee St 74403
Lenapah St 74401
Lenox Dr 74403
Lexington St 74403
Lincoln St 74401
Linda Ln 74401
W Lindsey St 74401
Live Oak St 74403
Locust St 74403
Louisiana St 74403
Love St 74401
Lowry St 74401
N & S M St 74403
Madison St 74403
N Main St
100-4699 74401
6300-6399 74403
S Main St 74401
Manila St 74403
Manitou St 74403
Maple St 74403
Margaret Lynn Ln 74403
Marietta St 74401
Market St 74403
Martin St 74401
E Martin Luther King St 74403
W Martin Luther King St 74401
Maryland 74401
Maxey Dr 74403
Mayer Ln 74403
Mayes St 74401
Mccloud St 74403
Meadowbrook Dr 74401
Meadowlane Ct, Dr & Pl 74401
Meadowlark Cir 74403
Michael Ave, Ct & Rd 74403
Military Blvd 74401
N Mill St 74401
Miller St 74401
Millis Rd 74403
Mississippi Ave 74403
Missouri St 74403
Mockingbird Ln 74401
Monta Ave & Pl 74403
Moody Dr 74401
Mount Calvary St 74401
Mulberry St 74403
Murrow Cir 74403
Muskogee Dr 74401
N & S N St 74403
Nashville St 74403
Nebraska St 74403
Nelson Dr 74403
Neosho Ave 74403
North St 74403
N & S O St 74403
Oak St 74401
Oak Park Ln 74401
Okay Rd 74403
Oklahoma St 74401
E Okmulgee Ave 74403
W Okmulgee Ln 74401
E Okmulgee St 74403
W Okmulgee St
1-600 74401
525-525 74402
601-6399 74403
602-6398 74401
Oktaha Rd 74401
Old Bacone Rd 74403
Old Shawnee Rd 74403
Old Taft Rd 74401
Orchard Pkwy 74403
Osage St 74403
Out Of Bounds Dr 74403
Oxford Ln 74403
N & S P St 74403
Palm Ave 74401
Palmer Dr 74403
Park Ave 74401
Park Blvd 74401
Park Cir 74403
Park Pl 74401
Park Pl N 74403
Patterson St 74403
E Peak Blvd 74403
W Peak Blvd 74401
Peggy Ln 74403
Peoria St 74401
Persimmon Dr 74401
Phoenix Dr 74401
Phoenix Village Rd 74403
Pickens St 74401
Pin Oak Rd 74403
Pine St 74401
Poplar St 74403
Poplin Ave 74403
Port Pl 74403
Porter Ave 74403
Prairie Dog Rd 74403
Pratt St 74403
Prentani St 74403
Putter Pl 74403
Quail Run 74403
Queens Rd 74403
N & S R St 74403
Ramona Dr 74401
Ransom St 74403
Rector St 74401
Redbird Ln 74403
Reeves St 74401
Regency Pl 74403
Ridge St 74403
Risser Ave & Pl 74403
River Bend Pl & Rd 74403
River Oaks Dr 74403
River Ridge Rd 74403
N Robb Ave 74401
Robertson St 74401
Robin Ln 74403
Robison St 74403
Rockefeller Dr 74401
Rodman Cir 74403
Rolling Oaks Dr, Ln, Pl & Trl 74401
Roosevelt St 74401
Royal Oak Dr 74403
Ruth St 74403
Rutherford St 74403
N S St 74403
Sabre St 74403
Sadler Rd 74401
Saint Andrews Ct 74403
Sallie St 74403
Sally Brown Rd 74403
Samuel Dr 74403
Sandow St 74401
Sarah Ln 74403
Scott Dr 74403
Seminole St 74403
Severs St 74403
Sharon St 74403
W Shawnee Byp 74401
E Shawnee Rd 74403
W Shawnee St 74401
Shefield 74403
Shelby Cir & Ct 74403
Sherwood Ct & Ln 74403
Silverwood Ln 74403
Skyview Dr 74403
E Smith Ferry Rd 74403
W Smith Ferry Rd 74401
Solomon St 74403
Southern Heights Dr 74401
W Southside Blvd 74401
Spaulding Blvd & Ct 74403
Spring Creek Rd 74401
Spruce St 74401
State St 74401
State College Dr 74403
Stonecreek Ct & Dr 74403
Summit St 74403
Sunset St 74403
Sunset Ridge Dr 74403
Suroya St 74403
Sycamore St 74403
N T St 74403
Tahlequah St 74401
Talladega St 74401
Tamaroa St 74401
Tanglewood Ct & Ln 74403
Tantalum Pl 74403
Tennyson St 74401
N & S Terrace Blvd, Pl & St 74401
Texas St 74403
Timberline Rd 74403
Tollett Rd 74401
Topeka St 74401
Tower Hill Blvd 74401
Trenton Rd 74403
Trumbo St 74403
Tull Ave, Pl & St 74403
Turner Cir, Dr, Pl & St 74403
University St 74403
N & S Utah Ct & St 74403
Valhalla Dr 74403
Verdigris Ave 74403
Virgil Matthews Dr 74401
N & S Virginia St 74403
Wall St 74401
Walnut St 74403
Ward St 74403
Warrior St 74401
Warwick Dr 74403
N Washington St
400-498 74403
601-699 74403
2300-2499 74401
2501-2799 74401
S Washington St 74403
Wauhilah Dr 74401
Wewoka St 74401
Wildair St 74403
Williams Ave 74401
Willoughby St 74403
Windsor Dr 74403
Wiswell St 74403
Wolfe Paw Ct 74403
Wood St 74403
Woodbine 74403
E, N & S Woodland Cir & Rd 74403
N & S York St 74403
York Village Dr 74403

NUMBERED STREETS

S & W 1st W 74401
N 2nd St 74401
N & S 3rd 74401
N 4th St 74401
S 4th St 74401
S 4th St E 74403
N & S 5th 74401
N 6th St 74401
S 6th St 74401
S 6th St E 74403
S 6th St W 74401
N 7th St 74401
S 7th St 74401
S 7th St E 74403
W 7th St S 74401
N 8th St 74401
S 8th St 74401
S 8th St E 74403
N 9th St 74401
S 9th St 74401
S 9th St E 74403
N 10th St 74401
S 10th St 74401
S 10th St E 74403
N 11th St 74401
N 11th St W 74401
S 11th St 74401
S 11th St E 74403
N 12th St 74401
N 13th St 74401
N 13th St W 74401
S 13th St 74401
S 13th St E 74403
N & S 14th 74401
N 15th St 74401
E 16th St S 74403
N 16th St 74401
N 16th St W 74401
S 16th St 74401
W 16th St N 74401
17th W 74401
E 18th St S 74403
N 18th St 74401
N 18th St W 74401
E 19th St S 74403
N 19th St 74401
W 19th St S 74401
E 20th St S 74403
N 20th St 74401
N 20th St E 74403
S 20th St E 74403
W 20th St N 74401
W 20th St S 74401
N 21st St 74401
N 21st St W 74401
S 21st St 74401
S 21st St E 74403
W 21st St N 74401
E 22nd St S 74403
N 22nd St 74401
N 22nd St W 74401
S 22nd St 74401
W 22nd St N 74401
N 23rd St E 74403
N 23rd St W 74401
S 23rd St 74401
W 23rd St N 74401
S 24th Pl W 74401
E 24th St S 74403
N 24th St 74401
N 24th St W 74401
S 24th St 74401
S 24th St W 74401
W 24th St N 74401
S 25th Pl 74401
N 25th St 74401
N 25th St E 74403
S 25th St E 74403
W 25th St N 74401
S 26th Pl 74401
E 26th St S 74403
N 26th St 74401
S 26th St 74401
W 26th St N 74401
W 26th St S 74401
S 27th Pl 74401
E 27th St S 74403
N 27th St 74401
S 27th St 74401
W 27th St N 74401
W 27th St S 74401
S 28th Pl 74401
E 28th St S 74403
N 28th St 74401
S 28th St 74401
S 28th St E 74403
W 28th St N 74401
N, S & W 29th W & N 74401
E 30th St S 74403
S 30th St 74401
S 30th St E 74403
S 30th St W 74401
W 30th St S 74401
E 31st St S 74403
S 31st St 74401
S 31st St E 74403
E 32nd St S 74403
N 32nd St 74401
S 32nd St 74401
S 32nd St E 74403
S 32nd St W 74401
W 32nd St N 74401
N 33rd St 74401
N 34th St 74401
S 34th St 74401
S 34th St E 74403
W 34th St N 74401
E 35th St S 74403
N 35th St 74401
S 35th St 74401
S 35th St E 74403
S 35th St W 74401
W 35th St N 74401
E 36th St S 74403
N 36th St 74401
S 36th St 74401
E 37th St S 74403
N 37th St 74401
S 37th St 74401
S 37th St E 74403
W 37th St S 74401
N & S 38th 74401
S & W 39th Pl & St S 74401
S 40th Pl 74401
N 40th St 74401
N 40th St W 74401
S 40th St 74401
S 40th St E 74403
S 40th St W 74401
W 40th St N 74401
N & S 41st 74403
S 42nd St E 74403
N 43rd St E 74403
S 43rd St 74401
S 43rd St E 74403
W 43rd St S 74401
N & S 44th 74401
E 45th St S 74403
N 45th St 74401
N 45th St E 74403
N 45th St W 74401
S 45th St E 74403
W 45th St S 74401
N 46th St 74401
N 46th St E 74403
W 46th St S 74401
E 47th St S 74403
N & S 48th W 74401
N 49th St 74401
E 50th St N 74403
S 50th St W 74401
E 51st St S 74403
N 51st St 74401
S 51st St W 74401
N 52nd St 74401
N 52nd St W 74401
S 52nd St E 74403
S 52nd St W 74401
E 53rd St S 74403
N 53rd St 74401
W 53rd St S 74401
S 54th Pl 74401
E 54th St S 74403
N 54th St 74401
N 54th St W 74401
S 54th St 74401
S 54th St W 74401
E 55th St S 74403
N 55th St W 74401
S 55th St 74401
S 55th St E 74403
E 56th St S 74403
N 57th St W 74401
S 58th Pl E 74403
E 58th St N 74403
E 58th St S 74403
S 58th St E 74403
W 58th St S 74401
S 58th East Cir 74403
E 59th St N 74403
E 59th St S 74403
N 59th St W 74401
W 59th St S 74401
W 60th Pl S 74401
E 60th St N 74403
N 60th St W 74401
S 60th St E 74403
W 60th St N 74403
W 60th St S 74401
E 61st St S 74403
S 61st St E 74403
S 61st St W 74401
W 61st St S 74401
E 62nd St N 74403
E 62nd St S 74403
N 62nd St 74401
S 63rd St E 74403
S 63rd St W 74401
W 63rd St N 74401
N 64th St W 74401
S 64th St E 74403
S 64th St W 74401
W 64th St S 74401
E 65th St N 74403
S 65th St E 74403
W 65th St S 74401
S 66th Pl W 74401
S 66th St E 74403
W 66th St S 74401
E 67th St S 74403
S 67th St E 74403
W 67th St S 74401
E 68th St S 74403
S 68th St E 74403
W 68th St S 74401
W 69th St S 74401
S 70th St E 74403

S 70th St W 74401
W 70th St 74401
W 70th St S 74401
S 71st St E 74403
S 71st St W 74401
S 72nd St E 74403
W 72nd St S 74401
E 73rd St S 74403
S 73rd St E 74403
S 73rd St W 74401
W 73rd St S 74401
N & S 74th 74401
75th Pl & St 74403
N 76th Cir E 74403
E 76th St S 74403
N 76th St E 74403
W 76th St S 74401
N 77th St W 74401
S 77th St E 74403
S 77th St W 74401
W 77th St S 74401
N 78th St W 74401
S 78th St E 74403
W 78th St S 74401
N 79th St E 74403
N 79th St W 74401
S 79th St E 74403
S 79th St W 74401
S 80th St E 74403
E 81st St S 74403
N 81st St W 74401
S 81st St E 74403
N 82nd St W 74401
E 83rd St S 74403
W 83rd St S 74401
N & S 84th 74401
S 85th St E 74403
S 85th St W 74401
S 87th St E 74403
S 88th St W 74401
S 89th St W 74401
E 93rd St S 74403
W 93rd St S 74401
E 94th Pl S 74403
N 94th St W 74401
S 94th St W 74401
N 101st St W 74401
S 102nd St W 74401
N & S 104th 74401
E 105th St S 74403
E 106th St S 74403
E 111th St S 74403
S 112th St W 74401
E 113th St S 74403
S 114th St W 74401
E 116th St S 74403
E 117th St S 74403
E 118th St S 74403
E 123rd St S 74403
E 125th St S 74403
E 127th St S 74403
E 128th St S 74403
E 133rd St S 74403

NORMAN OK

General Delivery 73069
General Delivery 73072

POST OFFICE BOXES MAIN OFFICE STATIONS AND BRANCHES

Box No.s
All PO Boxes 73070

RURAL ROUTES

02, 03, 04, 06, 08, 09, 15, 30 73026
16, 31, 32 73069
11, 26, 27, 28, 29, 30, 31 73071
05, 07, 10, 12, 14, 17, 18, 19, 20, 21, 22, 23 73072

NAMED STREETS

A St 73071
Abbey Dr 73071
Abbotsford 73072
Abe Martin Dr 73071
Aberdeen Ct 73072
Abilene Cir 73072
Acacia Ct 73072
Accipiter St 73072
E Acres St
100-399 73069
400-899 73071
W Acres St 73069
N & W Adkins Hill Rd 73072
Adney Cir 73026
Agape Ln 73026
Aiken Ct 73071
S Air Depot Blvd 73071
Akerman Dr 73026
Aladdin St 73072
Alameda Dr 73026
Alameda Plz 73071
Alameda St
200-399 73069
400-2499 73071
3601-3697 73026
3699-20399 73026
Alameda Park Dr 73071
Albany Pl 73071
Alderbrook Ct 73072
Alex Plaza Dr 73071
Alexander Ct 73072
Allen Rd 73072
Allenhurst St 73071
Allspice Run 73026
Alpine Cir & Dr 73072
American Legion Rd 73026
Americana Ct 73069
Amhurst Ave 73071
Andover Dr 73071
Andrea St 73072
Angel Ter 73026
Angus Dr 73069
Aniol Ave 73071
Ann Arbor Dr 73069
Ann Branden Blvd 73071
Annalane Dr 73072
Annie Ct 73069
E Apache St
300-399 73069
400-999 73071
W Apache St 73069
Apex Ct 73072
Applewood Ln 73026
Arapaho Dr & Rd 73026
Arbor Dr 73071
Arkansas St 73071
Arrowhead Cir 73026
Asbury Ct & Pl 73071
Ash Ct & Ln 73072
Ashland Ct 73071
Ashley Cir 73069
Ashton Ct 73072
Ashwood Ln 73071
Askew St 73071
Asp Ave
600-999 73069
1400-1598 73072
1600-2799 73072
Aspen Cir & Ln 73072
Astor Dr 73072
Atchison Dr 73069
Atlanta Cir 73071
Atterberry Dr 73071
Atwood Dr 73069
Auburn Ct 73071
Audrey Cir 73026
Augusta Dr 73072
Aussie Ct 73072
Austin Rd 73026
Avon Dr 73072
Avondale Dr 73069
Aztec Dr 73026
B St 73071
Bailey Ct
100-199 73072
500-599 73026
Bailey Ln 73026
Bains Ln 73026
Baker St 73072
Bald Eagle Ct & Dr 73072
Ballard Dr 73026
Balmoral Ct 73072
Baltic Ave 73026
Banbury Ct 73072
Bankers Ave 73072
Bannister Ct 73072
Baradind Dr 73071
Barainti Ave NE 73026
Barb Ct & Dr 73071
Barbary Dr 73072
Barbour Ave & St 73069
Barkley Ave, Cir & St 73071
Barley Ct 73072
Barn Owl St 73072
Barnhill Rd 73026
Baron Dr 73071
Barrington Dr 73071
Barry Switzer Ave 73072
Bart Conner Ct & Dr 73072
Barton St 73072
Barwick Ct & Dr 73072
N Base Ave 73069
Bass Ct 73072
Bates Ct & Way 73071
Baycharter St 73071
Bayland Dr 73026
Beacon Ave & Cir 73071
Beal St 73069
Bear Mountain Dr 73069
Beaumont Dr, Sq & St 73071
Beaurue Dr 73069
Beckett Ct 73072
Bedford Ln 73072
Beechwood Dr 73072
Belhaven Cir 73072
Belknap Ave 73072
Bellingham Ln 73072
Bellwood Cir 73026
Bellwood Dr 73072
Belmar Blvd & Cir 73071
Belmont Dr 73072
Belt Line Dr 73072
Benny Bruce St 73026
Benson Dr 73071
Bent Oaks Cir 73072
Bentbrook Pl 73072
Bentwood Rd 73026
Bergen Peak Dr 73069
Berry Cir 73072
N Berry Rd 73069
S Berry Rd
100-1099 73069
1200-3299 73072
Berry Farm Ct & Rd 73072
Bert Ln 73026
Beth Dean Dr 73072
Bethany Oaks Dr 73071
Bethel Rd 73026
Beverly Hills St 73072
Big Jim Cir & Rd 73026
Bill Carrol Dr 73071
Billy P Dr 73072
Biloxi Dr 73071
Biltmore Ct 73071
Bingham Pl 73072
Birch Dr 73072
Birmingham Dr 73071
Bishop Dr 73072
Bishops Ct & Dr 73072
Bismarc Ct & Ln 73072
Bixler Cir & Ct 73026
Black Bear Trl 73072
Black Hawk Dr 73072
Black Horse Rd 73072
Black Locust Ct & Pl 73071
Black Mountain Way 73069
Black Oaks Cir 73071
Blackberry Rd 73026
Blackburn Ave 73026
Blackjack Trl 73026
Blessing Ct 73071
Blue Ct & Ln 73026
Blue Creek Dr & Pkwy 73026
Blue Hills Ct & Ln 73026
Blue Jay Rd 73026
N Blue Lake Dr 73069
Blue Ridge Dr 73026
Blue Sage Ct & Rd 73072
Bluebird Dr 73026
Bluestem 73069
Bluestem Cir 73072
Boardwalk 73069
Bob Busch Dr 73072
Bob White Ave 73072
Bois De Arc Cir 73071
Bonita Cir 73072
Bonnybrook St 73071
Boomer Ave 73072
Boulder Ct 73072
Boulevard Du Lac 73071
Bowling Green Ct & Pl 73071
Boxwood Ave 73072
E Boyd St
100-499 73069
500-1799 73071
9700-10799 73026
W Boyd St 73069
Braden Dr 73072
Bradford Brk 73072
Branchwood Ct & Dr 73072
Branderwood St 73072
Brandies Ct 73071
Brandon Cir 73071
Brandywine Ln 73071
Breakwater Dr 73026
Breckenridge Ct 73072
Brenda Cir 73026
Brentwood Dr 73069
Bretford Way 73071
Brian Cir 73026
Briar Meadow Rd 73071
Briar Patch Way 73071
Briarcliff Ct & Rd 73071
Briarcreek 73071
Briarcrest Cir & Dr 73072
Bridge Creek Dr 73026
Bridgeport Rd 73071
Briggs St 73072
Bright St 73072
Brighton Ct 73072
Bristol Dr 73072
Brittany Ct 73072
Broad Ln 73069
Broad Acres Dr & Rd 73072
Broadway 73069
Broadwell Oaks Dr 73071
Broce Ct & Dr 73072
Brompton Dr 73072
Brookdale Dr 73072
Brookfield Dr 73072
Brookford Dr & Sq 73072
Brookhaven Blvd 73072
Brookhollow Rd 73072
Brookline Pl 73072
E Brooks St
100-499 73069
500-1399 73071
W Brooks St 73069
Brookside Dr 73072
Brookview 73072
Broone Dr 73071
Brownfield St 73026
Brownwood Ln 73072
Bruckner Dr 73071
Bruehl Ln 73026
Brunswick Ln 73072
Brush Creek Rd 73026
Bryant Cir 73026
Bryarwood Dr & Pl 73069
Buchanan Ave 73069
Buckhorn Cir & Dr 73072
Buckingham Dr 73072
Buckskin Pass 73026
Bud Wilkinson Dr SW 73069
Buena Vista Cir 73071
Bull Run St 73071
Bumgarner Ave 73026
Burgundy Ct 73071
Burkshire Ter 73072
Burlington Dr & Pl 73072
Burlwood Rd 73026
Burning Tree 73071
Burnt Oak St 73071
E & W Burr Oak Rd 73072
Burton Dr 73026
Butler Dr 73069
By Dr 73072
C St 73071
Cabella Ct 73072
Cabin Rd 73026
Caddell Ln 73069
Caddo Ln 73072
Calais Ct 73072
Calla Lily Ln 73069
Calvin Dr 73069
Calypso Cove Ave 73026
Cambridge Dr 73069
Camden Way 73069
Camelia St 73071
Camelot Dr 73069
Camino Real Dr 73026
Campus Crest Dr 73072
Canadian River Rd 73072
Canadian Trails Dr 73072
Candlewood Dr 73071
Cannon Dr 73072
Canonbury Cir & Rd 73072
Canterbury Ave & St 73069
Canyon Oaks Ct 73071
Cara Jo Dr 73071
Caracara Dr 73072
Cardinal Ln 73026
Cardinal Creek Blvd 73072
Carey Dr 73069
Caribou Ct 73071
Carling St 73071
Carlisle Cir 73069
Carnoustie Dr 73072
Carol Ave 73026
Carolyn Ct 73071
Carolyn Ridge Rd 73071
Carriage Ln 73069
Carrie Ln 73026
Carrington Ct & Ln 73072
N & S Carter Ave 73071
Cash Rd 73026
Castlebay St 73071
Castlerock Rd 73072
Castlewood Dr 73072
Castro St
100-399 73069
400-499 73071
Cate Center Dr 73072
Cavecreek St 73071
Cedar Creek Ct & Dr 73071
Cedar Hill Rd 73072
Cedar Lane Rd 73071
E Cedar Lane Rd
400-1599 73072
4800-17899 73026
Cedar Ridge Dr 73072
Cedarbrook Ct & Dr 73072
Cedarcrest St 73071
W Center Rd 73072
Central Pkwy 73071
Chadwick Ct & Dr 73071
Chalmette Dr 73071
Chamberlyne Way 73072
Chambers St 73071
Chamblee Dr 73071
Chandelier Dr 73069
Chaparral Rd 73026
Chapel Ln 73026
Chapel St 73071
Chardonnay Ln 73071
Charing Cross Ct 73072
Charles St 73069
Charles David Dr 73026
Charleston Ct 73071
Charleston Rd 73069
Charlie Cir 73026
Charlotte Ct 73071
Chateau Dr 73069
Chatham Ct 73072
Chatham Hills Rd 73071
Chaucer Dr 73069
Chautauqua Ave
200-999 73069
1000-3499 73072
Checkerboard Cir 73026
Chelsea Ct & Dr 73072
Cherokee Ln 73071
Cherry Creek Dr 73072
Cherry Laurel Dr 73072
Cherry Stone St 73072
Cherrystone Cir 73072
Chestnut Ln 73072
Cheswick Ct 73072
Cheyenne Way 73071
Cheyney Ct 73071
Chickasha St 73071
Chilmark Dr 73071
Chisholm Trl 73071
Chloe Ln 73026
Christine Dr 73072
Chukkar Ct 73072
Churchill Downs Dr 73069
Cimarron Dr 73071
Cinderella Ave 73072
Cindy Ave 73071
Cinnamon Cir 73026
City View Ct 73071
Claremont Dr 73069
Classen Blvd & Cir 73071
Claudia Dr 73071
Clayton Cir 73026
Clear Bay Ave 73026
Clearview Dr 73072
Clearwater Dr 73071
Clement Dr 73069
Cliffside Ct 73072
Clingmans Dome Rd 73069
Clinkenbeard Rd 73026
Cloudcroft 73072
Cloverdale Ln 73071
Coach Ct 73071
Coalbrook Dr 73071
Cobble Cir 73072
Cobblestone Creek Dr 73072
N & S Cockrel Ave 73071
Colchester Ct 73072
College Ave
300-899 73069
900-1699 73072
Collier Dr 73069
Collins Ct 73026
Colony Dr 73072
Columbia Cir & Ct 73071
Comanche Rd 73026
E Comanche St
100-399 73069
400-999 73071
W Comanche St 73069
Commerce Dr 73071
Concho Dr 73026
Concord Ct, Dr & Pl 73071
Conestoga Dr 73072
Conference Dr 73069
Congress St 73072
Connelly Ln 73072
Constellation St 73072
E & W Constitution St 73072
Conway Dr 73071
S Cook Ave 73071
Cooper Ct 73071
Coopers Hawk Dr 73072
Copperfield Dr 73072
Corbett Dr 73072
Cord Cir 73072
Cordova Ct 73072
Corky Dr NE 73026
Coronado Ave 73071
Corvette Dr
1500-1699 73072
2300-2399 73026
Cotswold Cmns, Dr & Sq 73072
Cottonwood Rd
2000-2399 73071
7200-7899 73072
Country Club Dr & Ter 73072
Countrywood Est 73026
Cove Hollow Ct 73072
Coventry Ln 73072
Covington Ct & Way 73072
Coyote Trl 73026
Crail Dr 73072
N & S Crawford Ave & Ct 73069
N & S Creekdale Dr 73072
Creekside Ct, Dr & Ln 73071
Creekview Pl & Ter 73071
Creekwood Ct 73072
Creighton Ct & Dr 73071
Crest Ct & Pl 73071
Crestland Dr 73071
Crestmont Ave & St 73069
Creston Way 73071
Crickett Ln 73026
Cripple Creek Dr 73071
Cristo Ct 73071
Crocker St 73026
Crooked Oak Cir & Dr 73026
Cross Center Dr 73072
Crossroads Blvd & Ct 73072
Crown Point Ave 73072
Cruce St 73069
Cruden Dr 73072
Crystal Bnd 73069
Crystal Cir 73069
Crystal Ct
100-199 73069
4100-4199 73072
Crystal Brook Cir 73026
Crystal Lake Rd 73072
Crystal Spring Ct & Dr 73072
Cupid Ct 73026
Cynthia Cir 73072
Cypress Ave 73072
Cypress Lake Dr 73072
D St 73071
Da Vinci St 73069
Daffodil Ct 73026
Daisy Ln 73071
Dakota St 73069
E & W Dale St 73069
Dalewood Pl & Ter 73071
Dalston Cir 73072
Damann Ln 73026
Danfield Dr & Ln 73072
Daniel Ct 73072
Dare Ln 73026
Dartmouth Ct 73071
N & S Darwin Cir & St 73026
David Ct 73071
David L Boren Blvd 73072
Davinbrook Dr 73072
Dawn Cir 73072
E & W Daws St 73069
Day Dr 73026
Daybreak Dr 73071
Dayflower Ln 73069
Debarr Ave 73069
Debbie Lynn Ln 73072
Dee Ann Dr 73069
Deep Fork Cir & Dr 73026
Deer Chase Cir & Dr 73071
Deer Run Dr 73071
Deerfield Dr 73026
Deerhurst Dr 73072
Delancey Dr 73071
Delaware Ln 73071
NW Della St 73072
Dellingham Ln 73072
Dena Dr 73071
Denison Cir & Dr 73069
Deonne Cir 73072

Derby Cir & Dr 73069
Derek Ln 73069
Desert Willow Ter 73071
Desiree Dr 73071
Deskin Dr 73069
Devon Ct 73072
Devonshire Dr 73071
Dewey Ave 73072
Diamond Dr 73026
Diana Dr 73071
Dixon St 73026
Doe Ridge Ct 73026
Dogwood Dr 73026
Dollina Ct & Dr 73069
Don Ray Cir & Rd 73026
Donna Dr 73071
Dorchester Dr 73069
Dornoch Ln 73072
Double C Dr 73069
S Douglas Blvd 73026
Douglas Dr 73069
Dove Crossing Dr 73072
Dove Hollow Ln 73072
Dover St 73071
Dragonfly Rd 73071
Drake Ct 73072
Drake Dr 73071
Drawbridge Ln 73072
Driftwood Cir & Dr 73026
E Duffy St
100-399 73069
400-499 73071
W Duffy St 73069
Duke Dr 73026
Dummy Record 73071
Dunford Ln 73026
Dunham Dr 73071
Durango Cir 73072
Durham Pl 73071
Durham Place Ct 73071
Dustin Dr 73071
Duvall Dr 73072
E St 73071
Eagle Cliff Dr 73072
Eagle Nest Dr 73071
Eagle Owl Dr 73072
Eaglerock Ln 73069
S Eastern Ave 73069
Eastgate Dr 73071
Eaton Dr 73072
Eccell Ct 73072
Echo Trl 73072
Ed Noble Dr & Pkwy 73072
Eddington St 73069
Eden Ct 73072
Edge Brook Ln 73071
Edgemere Dr 73071
Edgewater Ct 73071
Edgewood Ter 73026
Edinburg Dr 73071
Edwards Ct & Dr 73072
Egret Ln 73071
Eisenhower Rd 73069
El Cerito 73026
El Dorado Dr 73026
Elf Owl Ct 73072
Elie St 73072
Elk Cir 73071
Elk Horn Rd 73071
Elm Ave
400-899 73069
900-1799 73072
Elmcrest Dr 73071
Elmhurst Dr 73071
Elmwood Dr & St 73072
Emberwood Dr 73072
Emelyn St
200-299 73069
300-399 73071
Emerald Ct & Way 73072
English Elm Ln 73069
Enid St 73071
Enterprise Dr 73026
Erie Ave 73071
Escalon Dr 73072
Escort Ln 73026

Essex Ct 73069
Estate Dr 73072
Estates Dr 73072
Estell Ln 73026
E Eufaula St
100-399 73069
400-999 73071
W Eufaula St 73069
Evans Ln 73026
Evening Star Ct 73071
Evergreen Cir 73072
Evesham Ct 73072
Eyre Cir 73026
F St 73071
Fairfield Dr 73072
Fairlawn Dr 73071
Fairsted Ct 73071
Fairway Ct & Dr 73069
Falco Concolor Dr 73072
Falcon Ct 73069
Farm Hill Rd 73072
Farmer St 73072
Farmington Ave 73072
Fawn Cir 73026
Fawn Run Xing 73071
Fay Ave 73069
Fenwick Ct 73072
Ferrill Ln 73069
Ferrill St
200-299 73069
400-499 73071
N Fields St 73072
Fillmore Ave 73072
Finch St 73071
N & S Findlay Ave 73071
Fireside Cir & St 73072
Fischer Dr 73026
Fishermans Pt 73026
Five Oaks St 73071
Flaming Oaks Cir & Dr 73026
Fleetwood Dr 73072
Flint Ridge Cir, Ct & Dr 73072
N Flood Ave 73069
S Flood Ave
100-999 73069
1000-1199 73072
Flora Dr 73026
Floyd Ave 73026
Floyd Cox Dr 73026
Foreman Ave & Cir 73069
Forest Cir 73069
Forest Dr 73069
Forest Rd 73026
Forest Glenn Cir 73071
Forest Oak Cir 73071
Forest Road Cir 73026
Forister Ct 73069
Fort Dr 73072
Fortuna Dr 73072
Foster Dr 73071
Fountain St 73071
Fountain Gate Cir, Ct & Dr 73072
Fountain View Dr 73072
Fox Croft Rd 73026
Foxborough Ct 73072
E Frank St
100-399 73069
400-899 73071
W Frank St 73069
Franklin Ct 73026
Franklin Dr 73072
E Franklin Rd
100-3099 73071
3700-15399 73026
6600-1-6600-4 73026
W Franklin Rd
100-2599 73069
3000-7199 73072
Frederick Dr 73071
Fritzlan Rd 73072
Frontier Cir 73026
Frost Ln 73071
Ga Zump Dr 73069

Gallant Way 73072
Gander Ln 73026
Garfield Ave 73072
Garland Ct 73072
Garnet Rd 73026
Garrison Dr 73069
Garver St 73069
Gatewood Dr 73069
George Ave 73072
George L Cross Ct & Dr 73069
Geronimo Dr 73026
Ginger Dr 73026
Gini Lee Ln 73071
Glad Ln 73026
Glasgow Dr 73072
Glen Eagles Ct 73072
Glen Ellen Cir 73071
Glen Oaks Ct & Dr 73071
Glenbrook Dr 73072
Glencliff Dr 73071
Glenn Cir 73026
Glenn Bo Dr 73071
Glenoak Rd 73026
Glenwood St 73069
Glisten Ct & St 73072
Gloucester Ln 73072
Goddard Ave 73069
Goertzen Dr 73026
Golden Eagle Dr 73072
Golden Oaks Cir & Dr 73072
Golden Pond Dr 73072
Goldfinch Ct 73071
Goodman Ln 73026
Gordon Cir 73026
Goshawk Cir & Dr 73072
Grand Canyon Dr 73026
Grand View Ave 73072
Grange Hill Way 73072
Grant Rd 73071
Grassland Cir & Dr 73072
E Gray St
100-399 73069
400-799 73071
W Gray St
100-200 73069
129-129 73070
201-799 73069
202-798 73069
Great Oaks Dr 73071
Green Field Cir 73072
Green Hills Ct & Dr 73072
Green Meadow Cir 73072
Green Ridge Rd 73026
Green Turf Cir 73026
Green View Cir 73072
Greenbriar Ct & Dr 73072
Greens Pkwy 73072
Greenway Cir 73072
Greenwood Ct & Dr 73072
Greystone Ct & Ln 73072
Grickle Dr 73069
Griffin Dr 73071
Grill Ave 73071
Grover Ln 73069
Guilford Ct & Ln 73072
Guinn Ave 73072
Gullane Dr 73072
Gyrfalcon Ct & Dr 73072
H E Black Dr 73072
Hackney Wick Ct & Rd 73072
E & W Haddock St 73069
Hal Muldrow Dr 73069
Halifax Way 73069
Hallbrooke Ct & Dr 73071
Halley Ave & Cir 73069
Halray Dr 73071
Hamden Ave 73069
Hammer Dr 73026
Hampton Ct 73072
Hanging Elm Dr 73071
Hannibal Dr 73026
Hanover Dr 73072
Harbor Dr 73071
Hardin Dr 73072

Harold Way NE 73026
Harriett Rd 73069
Harrington Ct 73069
Harrogate Dr 73072
Hartford Dr 73072
Hartman Dr 73069
Harvard Rd 73072
S Harvey Ave 73072
Harwich Ct 73071
Hatterly Ln 73072
Havasu Dr 73071
Havenbrook Cir & St 73072
Haverford Ct 73071
Haverhill Cir 73071
Hawkesbury Park 73072
Hawks Nest Dr 73072
Hawthorne Ct 73072
Hayes St 73069
E Hayes St
100-399 73069
800-899 73071
W Hayes St 73069
Hayfield Rd 73026
Haynes Ln 73072
Hazelwood Dr 73071
Healthplex Dr & Pkwy 73072
Hearthstone 73072
Heather Glen Dr & Ter 73072
Heatherfield Ln 73071
Heatherhill Ct & Dr 73072
Helm Ct 73071
Hemphill Dr 73069
Hempstead Ct 73071
Henderson Ct 73069
Hensley Rd 73026
Henson Ct 73026
Heritage Place Dr 73072
Hermes Ct 73026
Heron Dr 73071
Hickory Rd 73026
Hickory Bend Dr 73026
Hickory Hill Rd 73026
Hidden Hill Rd 73072
Hidden Hollow Rd 73026
Hidden Lake Dr 73069
High Cir 73071
High Meadows Dr 73071
High Point Ct 73072
High Trail Rd 73071
High Valley Rd 73072
N Highland Dr 73026
Highland Gln 73069
Highland Pkwy 73069
Highland Ter 73069
Highland Hills Cir & Dr 73026
Highland Lake Dr 73026
Highland Ridge Dr 73069
Highland Village Dr 73069
Highway 9 73071
Hillcrest Dr 73071
Hillside Dr 73072
Hilltop Cir & Dr 73026
Hillview Dr 73072
Hillwood Cir 73026
E & W Himes St 73069
Hoffman Dr 73026
Holliday Dr 73069
Hollister Trl 73071
Hollow Tree Ter 73071
Holly Cir 73026
Hollywood Ave 73072
Homeland Ave 73072
Homestead Ct 73072
Hood Ct 73072
Hoover St 73072
Hope Valley Dr 73026
Horizon View Ct 73071
Houston Ave 73071
Huettner Ct & Dr 73069
E Hughbert St
100-399 73069
400-899 73071
W Hughbert St 73069
Hughes Cir 73072
Humming Fish Dr 73069

Hunter Dr 73071
Hunters Glen Rd 73026
Hunters Hill Cir & Rd 73072
Hunting Horse Trl 73071
Huntington Way 73069
Huntleigh Ct 73072
Huron St 73071
Idaho St 73071
E Imhoff Rd
1400-1598 73071
1600-2799 73071
12400-19599 73026
W Imhoff Rd 73072
Imperial Dr 73026
E Indian Hills Rd
100-2599 73071
3600-12899 73026
W Indian Hills Rd
100-2899 73069
3600-7299 73072
Indian Point Cir 73026
Industrial Blvd 73069
Inglewood Dr 73071
Innsbrook Ct 73072
E Interstate Dr 73072
N Interstate Dr
101-6499 73069
300-6498 73072
S Interstate Dr 73072
W Interstate Dr 73072
Intrepid Cir 73072
Inverness Ct 73072
Inwood Dr 73072
Iowa St 73069
Ironhorse Cir 73072
Irvine Dr 73072
Isabella Rd 73072
Isim Rd 73026
Ithaca Dr 73071
Ives Way 73072
Jackson Dr 73071
Jade St 73026
Jaffa Cir 73026
James Dr & Ln 73072
James Dean Dr 73072
Jami Dr 73071
Jansing Dr 73069
Jason Dr 73071
Jazzman Dr 73071
Jean Marie Dr 73069
Jefferson St 73072
Jenkins Ave
500-799 73069
1301-1597 73072
1599-4799 73072
Jennifer Cir 73071
Jessie Dr 73072
Joe Keeley Dr 73072
Joe Taylor Cir & St 73072
John Saxon Blvd 73071
E Johnson St
100-299 73069
600-799 73071
W Johnson St 73069
Jona Kay Ter 73069
N & S Jones Ave 73069
Jonquil Ln 73026
Jordan Cir 73071
Joseph Cir 73072
Journey Pkwy 73072
Jubilee St 73072
Julia Ave 73069
Junction 73026
Juniper Ln 73069
Justice Ct 73072
Justin Dr 73071
Kansas St 73069
Kara Ct 73071
Kasey Dr 73026
Kathy Lynn Dr 73072
Keith St
100-399 73069
400-499 73071
Kellogg Dr 73072
Kensal Rise Cir & Pl 73072
Kensington Rd 73072

Kent St 73072
Kenwood Dr 73071
Kestrel Ct 73071
Keystone Ln 73072
Kiamichi Ct & Rd 73026
Kilby Ave 73072
Kimball Dr 73071
Kimberlee Ct 73026
Kindle Ln 73072
Kings Ct & Rd 73072
Kings Canyon Rd 73071
Kings Land Rd 73072
Kingsbury Dr 73072
Kingston Rd 73071
Kingswood Dr 73071
Kiowa Way 73071
Knights Bridge St 73072
Knob Hill Cir & Ct 73072
Knollwood St 73071
Kunkel Ave 73026
Kyle Dr 73026
La Dean Dr 73069
Ladbrook St 73072
Ladybank Ln 73072
Lafayette Dr 73071
Lago Ranchero Dr 73026
Lago Vista Rd 73026
N Lahoma Ave 73069
S Lahoma Ave
200-999 73069
1000-1199 73072
Lairds Woods Cir 73026
S Lake Blvd 73071
E Lake Dr 73071
Lake Rd 73026
Lake Front Cir 73069
Lake Front Dr 73072
Lake Grove Ct 73069
Lake Ridge Rd 73026
Lakecrest Dr 73071
Lakehurst Dr 73071
Lakeshore Cir 73026
Lakeside Dr 73026
Lakeview Cir 73026
Lakewood Dr
700-999 73072
1200-1899 73026
Lamar Dr & Rd 73072
Lamp Post Rd 73072
Lancaster Cir 73069
Landrun Ave 73072
Landsaw Dr 73026
Landsdowne Ct & Dr 73072
Langley Ct & Dr 73071
Laramie Rd 73026
Larkhaven St 73071
Las Colinas Ln 73072
Laurel Dr 73072
Laurelbrook Ct 73072
Lauriston Dr 73072
Laws Dr 73072
Lawter Ln 73026
Leaning Elm Dr 73071
Lee Ave 73069
Leeds Ln 73071
Lenox Dr 73069
Leopard Lily Dr 73069
Lerkim Cir & Ln 73069
Leslie Ln 73069
Lewis St 73026
Lexington Ave & St 73069
Libby Ln 73072
Libby Lou Ln 73026
Lilac Ln 73026
Lilly Cir & Ln 73026
Lincoln Ave & Grn 73072
Lindale Ave & Cir 73069
Linden Ave 73072
Lindenwood Ln 73071
Lindsey Dr 73072
E Lindsey St
100-198 73072
200-699 73069
700-3399 73071
3600-19899 73026

W Lindsey St
400-498 73069
500-2399 73069
2900-2999 73072
Lindsey Plaza Dr 73071
Line Dr 73071
Linfield Ct 73071
E Linn St 73071
W Linn St 73069
Litchfield Ln 73072
Little Axe Dr 73026
Little Pond Rd 73026
Little River Dr 73026
Little River Rd 73071
Little Sandy Rd 73026
Live Oak Dr 73072
Lochinver Dr 73069
Lochwood Dr 73071
Locust St 73072
Logan Dr 73069
Lohman Cir 73069
Lois Ln 73026
Lois St 73071
Lola Rd 73026
Loma Dr 73072
Lone Oak Dr 73071
Long Cir 73071
Long Lake Pl 73026
Lora Lea Ln 73026
Lorings Cir & Rd 73072
Louise Ln 73071
E Louisiana St 73071
Love Letter Ln 73026
Lower Lake Dr 73072
Lucas Ct 73026
Luke Ln 73072
Lynn Rd 73026
Lynnbrook Cir 73072
Lynnwood Cir 73072
Lyon Dr 73072
Lyrewood Ln 73072
Lyric St 73071
Macdonnell Dr 73069
Macy St 73071
Madison St 73069
Madra 73071
Maggie Cir 73072
Magnolia St 73072
Mahogany Run 73072
E Main St
100-399 73069
400-1499 73071
W Main St
100-2699 73069
3201-3297 73072
3299-5399 73072
Majesty Ct 73072
Manchester Ct 73072
Manchester Ln 73026
Manor Dr 73072
Manor Hill Ct & Dr 73072
Maple Ave 73072
Maple Ln 73069
Marbel Dr 73069
Margaret Dr 73069
Marian Dr 73069
Marigold Trl 73072
Marina Rd 73026
Mark Cir 73026
Market Pl 73072
Marshall Ave 73072
Marston Ct 73072
Martingale Dr 73072
Mary Ln 73026
Marymount Rd 73071
Mason St 73026
Mathis Fox Ln 73069
S May Ave 73072
Mayes Dr 73072
Mayfair Dr 73072
Mccall Dr 73072
Mcclelland Dr 73026
Mccomb Rd 73026
Mccullough 73069
Mcfarland St 73069

Mcgee Dr
600-1199 73069
1200-2999 73072
Mckee Dr 73026
Mckenzie Rd 73026
Mckinley Ave 73072
Mckown Dr 73072
Mcnamee St 73069
Mcsha Pl 73072
Meadow Ave 73072
Meadow Park Dr 73069
Meadow Ridge Cir & Rd 73072
Meadowbrook Dr 73072
Meadowood Blvd 73071
Melba Ln 73072
Melisa Dr 73071
Melody Ln 73026
Melrose Ct & Dr 73069
Memphis Dr 73071
N & S Mercedes Dr 73069
Merchant Dr 73069
Meridian Dr 73071
Merkle Dr 73069
Merlin Cir 73072
Merrymen Grn 73072
Merrywood Ln 73069
Mesquite Rd 73026
Middlefield Ct 73072
Midland Dr 73072
Midway Dr 73072
Midwest Blvd 73026
Milford Pl 73072
Millbrook Dr, Pl & Sq 73072
Millbury Ct & Rd 73071
Miller Ave & Ln 73069
Mimosa Dr 73069
Missouri St 73071
Mistletoe Rd 73026
Misty Lake Ct 73071
Misty Ridge Dr 73071
N & S Moa Cir 73026
Mobile Cir 73071
Mockingbird Ct & Ln 73071
Mohawk Rd 73026
Monitor Ave 73072
Monnett Ave 73069
Monomoy Ct 73071
Monroe Ct 73071
Montclair Ct 73071
Monterey Dr 73072
Montgomery Cir 73071
Monticello Rd 73072
Montrose Cir & Ct 73072
Moonbeam Dr 73026
Moonlight Dr 73026
Moorehead Cir 73026
Moorgate Cir & Dr 73072
Morain Ct 73072
Morgan Dr 73069
Morland Ave 73071
Morning Dew Trl 73072
Morning Glory Dr 73026
Morningside Dr 73071
Morren Dr 73071
Morrison Cir & Ct 73072
E Mosier St
100-399 73069
800-899 73071
W Mosier St 73069
Motelena Cir & Ct 73072
Mount Vernon Dr 73071
Mount Williams Dr 73069
Mountain Brook Dr 73072
Mountain Oaks Dr 73071
Muldrow Ct 73069
Murphy St 73072
Mystic Isle 73026
Nailon Dr 73072
Nancy Lynn Ter 73069
Nantucket Blvd 73071
Napoli Ct 73069
Nashville Dr 73071
Natchez Dr 73071
Nathan Dr 73069
National Dr 73069

Navajo Rd 73026
Nebraska St 73069
Nelson Ln & Rd 73026
Ness Cir & Dr 73069
Newberry Rd 73026
Newbury Dr 73071
Newman St 73071
Newport Dr 73072
Newton Dr 73069
Nicole Cir, Dr & Pl 73072
Night Hawk Dr 73072
Norman Center Ct 73072
Normandie Dr 73072
Norris Cir 73026
Northcliff Ave 73071
Northcrest Dr 73071
Northern Hills Ln & Rd 73071
Northglenn Ln 73071
Northhampton Ct & Dr 73072
Northridge Rd 73072
Northwest Blvd 73072
Northwich Dr 73072
Nottingham Cir 73072
Nutmeg Dr 73026
O J Talley Cir 73072
Oak Forest Dr 73071
Oak Grove Dr 73026
Oak Tree Ave 73072
Oakbrook Dr
700-999 73072
4900-4999 73026
Oakcliff Rd 73071
Oakcreek Dr 73071
Oakcrest Ave 73071
Oakhill Dr 73071
Oakhollow Dr 73071
Oakhurst Ave & Cir 73071
Oakmeadows Dr 73071
Oakridge Cir & Dr 73026
Oakside Dr 73071
Oakview Dr 73071
Oakvista Cir 73071
Oakwood Dr 73069
Oklahoma Ave 73071
Okmulgee St 73071
Old Central Dr 73071
Old Farm Rd 73072
Olde Brook Ct 73072
Olde Oak Ct 73026
Oliphant Ave 73026
Oliver St 73071
Olmstead Ct 73071
Omega St 73071
Onyx Ave 73026
Orchard Ln 73072
Oriole Ct & Dr 73071
Orr Dr 73071
Osage Rd 73026
Osage Way 73071
Osborne Dr 73069
Osprey Dr 73072
Outpost Cir 73072
Overton Dr 73071
Owl St 73071
Oxford Way 73072
Paddock Cir 73072
Page Cir & St 73069
Painted Bird Ln 73071
Painted Forest Rd 73071
Palmer Cir 73069
Palomino Way 73071
Pamela Cir 73071
N Park Ave 73069
Park Dr 73069
Park Pl 73071
Park Hollow Ct 73071
Parkland Way 73069
Parkridge Dr 73071
Parkside Rd 73072
Parkview Ter 73072
Parsons St 73069
Paso De Vaca Dr 73026
Pathway Cir 73072
Paul Ct 73071
Pawnee Rd 73026
Paxton Ct 73069

Peach Tree Ln 73071
Pebble Beach Dr 73072
Pebble Creek Rd 73072
Pecan Ave 73072
Pecan Vly 73069
Pecos Dr 73026
Pelham Cir & Dr 73071
Pembroke Dr 73072
Pendleton Ct & Dr 73072
S Penn Ave 73072
Pennington Ct 73072
Penrith Pl 73072
Peppertree Ct & Pl 73071
Peregrine Dr 73072
Persimmon Ct 73072
Perth Dr 73069
Peter Pan St 73072
N & S Peters Ave 73069
Pheasant Run Ct & Rd 73072
N Pickard Ave 73069
S Pickard Ave
100-1199 73069
1200-2799 73072
Pimlico Dr 73072
Pin Oak Cir 73072
Pinafore Dr 73072
Pine Cove Ct 73071
Pine Hill Rd 73072
Pine Ridge Rd 73026
Pine Tree Cir & Ln 73072
Pinebrooke Ct 73072
Pinecrest Ct & St 73071
Pinehurst Dr 73072
Pinelake Ct & St 73071
Pinewood Dr 73072
Piney Oak Dr 73072
Pinon Ct 73072
Pioneer Cir & St 73072
Pleasant Grv 73072
Pleasant Hill Ln 73026
Pleasant Valley Cir & Dr 73072
Pocasset Cir 73071
Point Fowler Ave 73026
Polo Ridge Cir 73072
Pomelo Cir 73071
N & S Ponca Ave 73071
Poplar Ln 73072
Poppy Ln 73069
N & S Porter Ave 73071
Portland Ct & St 73072
E & W Post Oak Rd 73072
Potomac Dr 73072
Pottawatomie Rd 73026
Prairie Ln 73026
Prairie Dunes Ct 73072
Presidio Cir & Dr 73072
Preston Ct 73072
Prestwick St 73072
Princeton Cir 73071
Prospect Ct 73071
Pullin Ln 73069
Pyle St 73071
Quail Dr 73072
Quail Creek Cir & Dr 73026
Quail Hollow Ct & Dr 73072
Quail Ridge Rd 73072
Quail Run Cir 73072
Quail Springs Dr 73072
Quality Ave 73071
Quanah Parker Trl 73071
Queensbury Ct 73072
Queenston Ave 73071
Quidnet Rd 73071
Raintree Cir 73072
Raleigh Cir 73071
Rambling Oaks Dr 73072
Rampart Rd 73071
Ramsey Ct & St 73071
Ranch Rd 73026
Rancho Dr 73071
Ranchwood Ter 73072
Rangeline Rd 73071
Ravenscourt Ln 73072
Ravenwood Ln 73071

Reagan Cir 73071
Rebecca Ln 73072
Red Bird Ln 73072
Red Bud Dr 73026
Red Fern Ln 73026
Red Fish Rd 73069
Red Oaks Dr 73072
Red Rock Rd 73026
Redwing Dr 73026
Redwood Cir & Dr 73071
Reed Ave 73071
Regal Run Dr 73072
Regent St 73069
Reginald Dr 73072
Regis Ct 73071
Reid Pryor Rd 73072
Remington Ct & St 73072
Remington Place Rd 73072
Renaissance Dr 73071
Research Park Blvd 73069
Resh Ct 73072
Reynolds Ct 73069
Reynolds Lake Dr 73026
Rhoades Ct & Dr 73072
E Rich St
100-399 73069
500-999 73071
W Rich St 73069
Richard Ln NE 73026
Richardson Dr 73071
Richmond Dr 73071
Rider Hill Dr 73026
E & W Ridge Rd 73069
Ridge Bluff Ct & Dr 73071
Ridge Lake Blvd 73071
Ridgecrest Cir & Ct 73072
Ridgefield Dr 73069
Ridgeline Cir & Dr 73072
Ridgemont Cir 73071
Ridgeway Pl 73072
Ridgewood Dr 73072
Riggs Rd 73026
Ringwood St 73069
Ripple Ave 73072
Rising Hill Dr 73071
River Oaks Dr 73072
River View Dr 73071
Rivercross Ct 73072
Rivermont Ct 73072
Riverside Dr 73072
Riverwalk Ct & Dr 73072
Riviera Dr 73072
Robin Hood Ln 73072
Robin Ridge Dr 73072
E Robinson St
200-399 73069
400-3099 73071
3600-20399 73026
W Robinson St
300-2699 73069
3200-7299 73072
E Rock Creek Rd
600-3399 73071
3601-4097 73026
4099-19099 73026
W Rock Creek Rd
600-1299 73069
3100-7599 73072
Rock Creek Trl 73072
Rock Hollow Dr 73071
Rock Ridge Ct 73071
Rockingham Dr 73071
Rockland Rdg 73026
Rockwood Ln 73071
Rodeo Trl 73072
Rogers Cir 73071
Rolling Hills St 73072
Rolling Meadows Pl 73072
Rolling Stone Dr 73071
Rolling Woods Dr 73072
Rose Ct 73072
Rose Rock Hl 73026
Rosebrook Ct 73072
Rosedale Dr 73069
Rosemont Dr 73072
Roserock Dr 73026

Rosewood Dr 73069
Ross Dr 73071
Rowena Ln 73069
Royal Oak Dr 73069
Ruby Ln 73072
Rudolph Ln 73026
Rue De Montserrat 73071
Running Deer Rd 73026
Russell Cir 73071
Rustic Hills St 73072
Rye Rd 73072
Saddleback Blvd 73072
Saint Andrews Ct 73072
Saint Clair Cmn & Dr 73072
Salem Ct 73072
Saliangt Dr 73072
Salsbury St 73069
Sam Gordon Dr 73072
Sand Hill Ct 73026
Sandalwood Dr 73071
Sandpiper Ln 73071
Sandstone Cir & Dr 73071
Santa Fe Ave 73072
N Santa Fe Ave 73069
S Santa Fe Ave
100-699 73069
3900-3999 73072
Santa Rosa Ct 73071
Saratoga Dr 73072
Sawgrass Dr 73072
Scarlet St 73072
Schooner Dr 73072
Schulze Dr 73071
Scott Dr 73069
Scotts Blf 73072
Sebastiani Cir 73071
Sedona Dr 73071
Seminole Rd 73026
Sequoyah Trl 73071
Sequoyah Trails Dr 73071
Sexton Dr 73026
Shadow St 73071
Shadow Creek Ct 73072
Shadow Crest Ct 73072
Shadow Grove Ct 73072
Shadow View Ct 73072
Shadowhill St 73071
Shadowlake Rd 73071
Shadowridge Dr 73072
Shady Ln 73069
Shadybrook Dr 73072
Shadywood Pl 73026
Sharpish Way 73069
Shawnee St 73071
Sheffield Cir & Dr 73071
Shelby Ct 73071
Sherburne Ct & Rd 73072
N & S Sherry Ave 73069
Sherwood Dr 73071
Shiloh Dr 73071
Shona Way 73069
Shoreline Cir & Dr 73026
Shoreridge Ave 73072
Short A Rosa 73026
Short Stop Way 73071
Shrill Ct & St 73071
Siena Springs Dr 73071
Sierra St 73071
Sierra Vista Way 73071
Silver Chase 73026
Silver Creek Cir 73071
Silverado Way 73026
Silverton Cir 73072
Silverwood Ct 73072
Sinclair Dr 73071
Sky Ct 73026
Skye Ridge Dr 73069
Skylane Dr 73071
Skylark Ct 73069
Skyler Way 73072
Skyline Dr 73071
Skyview Ln 73026
Slater Dr 73071
Sleepy Hollow Rd 73069
Sloane St 73072
Smalley Cir & Dr 73071

Smoking Oak Ct, Pl & Rd 73072
Snowy Owl Cir & Dr 73072
Sonia Dr 73072
Sonoma Park Dr 73071
Sooner Dr 73072
S Sooner Rd 73071
Southcliff 73072
Southcourt Dr 73072
Southcrest Dr 73071
Southern Heights Ave 73072
Southern Hills Cir 73072
Southern Shores Dr 73026
Southlake Dr 73072
Sparkle St 73072
Sparrow Rd 73072
Sparrow Hawk Dr 73072
Spencer Cir 73026
Spoonwood Dr & Rd 73071
Spotted Owl Cir 73072
Spring Mill Rd 73069
Spring View Dr 73026
Springer Dr 73069
Springlake Dr 73072
Springwood St 73072
Spruce Dr 73072
Spyglass Dr 73072
Stable Dr 73072
Stafford Dr & Sq 73072
Stansbury Cir & Rd 73072
Stanton Dr 73071
Starbrook Ct 73072
Stardust Ln 73026
Starlight Dr 73026
Starshine Dr 73071
N State Dr 73071
State Highway 9 73072
E State Highway 9
2800-3599 73071
E State Highway 9
3600-19799 73026
W State Highway 9 73072
NW Steed Dr 73072
Steeplechase Dr 73072
Stelens Ct 73071
Stella Rd 73026
Stephan Rd 73026
Stephenson Pkwy 73072
NW Sterling St 73072
N Stewart Ave 73071
S Stewart Ave 73071
Stewart Dr 73026
Stinson St 73072
Stone Well Ct & Dr 73072
Stonebridge Ct & Dr 73071
Stonebrook Dr 73072
Stonegate Dr 73072
Stonehaven Dr 73072
Stonehenge Ln 73026
Stonehurst St 73072
Stoneleigh Pl 73072
Stonewood Cir & Rd 73026
Stoney Brook Dr 73072
Storm King Rd 73026
Stratford Ln 73072
Stubbeman Ave 73069
Sturtz Cir 73072
Sumac Dr 73071
Summer Dr 73071
Summerfield Ct 73072
Summit Bnd 73071
Summit Cir 73072
Summit Way 73071
Summit Crest Ln 73071
Summit Crossing Pkwy 73071
Summit Hill Ct & Rd 73071
Summit Hollow Dr 73071
Summit Lakes Blvd 73071
Summit Park Ct 73071
Summit Ridge Ct 73071
Summit Terrace Dr 73071
Summit View Ct 73071
Sunbelt Dr 73026
Sunburst St 73069
Suncrest Dr 73072

Sundance Ct 73072
Sundown Dr 73069
Sunflower Cir & St 73072
Sunnydale Rd 73026
S Sunnylane Rd 73071
Sunrise Cir & St 73071
Sunset Dr 73069
Sunvalley Dr 73026
Superior Ave 73071
Surrey Dr & Pl 73071
Sussex Pl 73072
Swan Hollow Dr 73072
Sweetheart Cir 73026
Sycamore Rd & St 73072
E Symmes St
100-299 73069
400-999 73071
W Symmes St 73069
Tahoe Dr 73071
Tall Oaks Cir 73072
Tallywood Dr 73026
Tanglewood Ct 73072
Tara Ln 73069
Tarkington Dr 73026
Tarman Cir 73071
Tatge Cir 73026
Taurus Rd 73026
Taylor Dr 73072
Tayport St 73072
Teakwood Cir & Dr 73071
Technology Pl 73071
Tecumseh Dr 73069
E Tecumseh Rd
1200-3599 73071
3600-17999 73026
10321-1-10321-9 73026
W Tecumseh Rd
200-2999 73069
3100-6899 73072
Tecumseh Meadows Ct, Dr & Way 73069
Tecumseh Ridge Cir, Ct & Rd 73069
Tee Cir & Dr 73069
Telstar Ct & St 73069
Tenkiller Ln 73071
Teresa Dr 73071
Terra Ct 73069
Terrace Pl 73069
Terrace Rdg 73026
Terrace Park Trl 73069
Terry Dr 73069
Terryton Dr 73071
Teton Cir, Ct, Ln & Oval 73072
Texas St 73071
Thistlewood Dr 73072
Thompson Dr 73069
Thornebrook Dr 73069
Thorton Dr & St 73069
Thunder Rdg 73072
Thunderbird Dr 73069
Thunderbird Rdg 73026
Tiffany Dr 73071
Tiffin Ave 73071
Timber Shadows Dr 73069
Timbercrest Ct, Pl & St 73071
E & W Timberdell Rd 73072
Timberidge Cir & Dr 73072
N & S Timberline Dr 73026
Timberwind Dr 73072
Timberwood Ct 73071
Tioga Cir 73071
Tisbury Rd 73071
Toberman Dr 73069
Tobin Cir 73026
Tollie Dr 73071
E Tonhawa St
100-399 73069
400-499 73071
W Tonhawa St 73069
Topaz Ln 73026
Topeka St 73069
Torrans Ln 73026
Torrey Pines Rd 73072

Town Park Rd 73072
Townhouse Cir 73069
Towry Dr 73069
Tracy Cir 73026
Trailpine Ct 73072
Trailridge Dr 73072
Trails Ct 73072
Trails End 73026
Trailview Ct & Dr 73072
Trailwood Dr 73069
Tree Line Dr 73071
Trenton Rd 73069
Trevor Ct 73072
Triad Village Dr 73071
Trinidad Dr 73072
Trisha Ln 73072
Troon St 73072
Trophy Dr 73072
Tropicana Ave 73071
Trout Ave 73069
Truffula Cir 73069
Tudor Cir 73072
Tuffy Ln 73026
Tufts Ln 73069
Tulip Cir 73026
Tulsa St 73071
Turkey Run 73026
Turnberry Dr 73069
Turnbridge Ct 73072
Turtle Creek Dr & Way 73071
Tuscany Dr 73072
Twin Acres Dr 73071
Twin Tree Dr 73071
Twisted Oak Cir & Dr 73071
W Two Lakes Ave 73072
Tyler Dr 73071
Uncle Bill Ln 73026
N & S University Blvd 73069
Upper Lake Dr 73072
Utah Ave 73069
Valkyrie St 73026
Valley Brk 73071
Valley Dr 73026
Valley Holw 73071
Valley Mdw 73071
Valley Ridge Rd 73072
Valley View Rd 73069
Valley Vista St 73072
Van Buren St 73072
Vanessa Dr 73071
Venice Ct 73071
Venture Dr 73069
Vermillion St 73026
Verreaux Ct & Dr 73072
Via Cir 73071
Vicksburg Ave, Cir & Ct 73071
Victoria Dr 73072
Victory Ct & Dr 73072
E & W Vida Way 73069
E View Dr 73071
Villa Dr 73071
Village Dr 73071
Vincent St 73072
Vine St 73072
Vinita Dr 73071
Virginia St 73071
Vista Dr 73071
Vista Springs Dr 73026
Wabash Cir 73026
Wadsack Dr 73072
Wake Forest Ln 73071
Wakefield Ct 73072
Wall St 73069
Walnut Pl & Rd 73072
Walnut Hill St 73072
Walnut Ridge Rd 73026
Wandering Oaks Ct & Ln 73026
War Bird Dr 73071
Warrington Cir & Way 73072
Warwick Ct & Dr 73072
Washington Dr 73069
Water Front Cir 73072
Water View Ct 73071
Waterfront Dr 73071
Waterleaf Dr 73069
Waterwood Dr 73072
Watkins Rd 73072
Wauwinet Way 73071
Waverly Ct & Dr 73072
Wayside Dr 73072
Weatherford Dr 73071
N & S Webster Ave 73069
Wellesley Ct & Pl 73071
Wellington Pl 73072
Wellington Lake Dr 73026
Wellman Dr & Way 73072
Wellsite Dr 73069
Welston Cir 73071
Wembleton Cir 73072
Westbrooke Ter 73072
Westbury Ct 73072
N & S Westchester Ave & Cir 73069
S Western Ave 73072
Western View Dr 73072
Westfield Cir 73071
Westheimer Dr 73069
Westlakes Dr 73072
Westlawn Dr 73069
S Westminster Rd 73026
Westpark Dr 73069
Westport Dr 73069
Westridge Ter 73069
Westside Dr 73069
Westwood Dr 73069
Wewoka Dr 73071
Wexford Ct 73072
Weymouth Ct, Pl & Way 73071
Wheatland Dr & Pl 73071
Wheaton Dr 73071
Whippoorwill Dr
1300-1499 73071
31900-32499 73072
Whispering Pines Cir & Dr 73072
White St 73069
White Feather Rd 73026
White Oaks Dr 73071
Whitebrook St 73026
Whiteoak Cir 73071
Whitmere Ct & Ln 73072
Wichita Dr 73071
Wilcox Dr 73069
Wild Horse Trl 73072
Wilderness Dr 73071
Wildfire Dr 73026
Wildwood Ct & Ln 73071
Wilkenson Dr 73026
Wilkinson Ct 73069
William Pereira 73072
Williams Cir 73071
Willige Dr 73072
Willow Ln 73072
Willow Bend Rd 73072
Willow Branch Rd 73072
Willow Brook Ln 73069
Willow Creek Cir & Dr 73071
Willow Grove Dr 73072
Willow Rock Ct & Rd 73072
Willow Springs Rd 73072
Willoway Dr 73072
Willowcliff Ct 73071
Willowisp Dr 73072
Willowood Way 73026
Willowpoint Dr 73072
Willowrun Cir 73072
Wilmington Ct 73071
Wilshire Ave 73072
Wilson St 73072
Winchester Cir 73072
Wind Hill Rd 73071
Windbrook Dr & Sq 73072
Windchime Dr 73071
Windermere Dr 73072
Windham Ct 73071
Winding Creek Cir 73071
Winding Oaks Ln 73026
Winding Ridge Cir & Rd 73072
Windjammer St 73072
Windmill Cir 73072
Windover Dr 73072
Windrush Cir 73072
Windsor Way 73069
Windward Ct 73072
Winners Cir 73072
Winston Dr 73072
Wl Mayhew Dr 73071
Wood Castle St 73072
Wood Dale Ave 73026
Wood Hollow St 73071
Wood Valley Rd 73071
Woodbine Cir 73072
Woodbriar Dr 73071
Woodcreek Ct & Dr 73071
Woodcrest Cir 73071
Woodcrest Dr 73071
Woodcrest Way 73026
Woodcrest Creek Dr 73071
Woodlake Dr 73071
Woodland Dr 73072
Woodland Oaks Ct 73026
Woodrow Ct 73072
Woods Ave & Cir 73069
Woodsboro Ct & Dr 73072
Woodside Dr 73071
Woodsong Dr 73071
Woodstock Ct 73072
Woodvale Ave 73026
Woodview Dr 73071
Wooster St 73071
Worthington Dr 73072
Wren St 73069
Wyandotte Way 73071
Wyckham Pl 73072
Wylie Rd
500-1199 73069
1200-1399 73072
Wyndham Pl 73072
Yarmouth Rd 73071
York Dr 73069
Yorkshire Ter 73072
Yorktown Cir 73071
Yosemite Dr 73071
Yucca Rd 73026
Zachary Ln 73072

NUMBERED STREETS

W 1st St 73072
2nd St 73071
8 A St 73026
8th Ave NE 73071
8th Avenue Ave & Cir NE 73071
9th Ave NE 73071
12th Ave NE
100-2500 73071
2502-5498 73071
3201-3201 73072
3401-5499 73071
12th Ave NW
2600-5999 73069
12th Ave SE
100-1899 73071
3100-4799 73072
NW 12th Ave
100-2299 73072
SW 12th Ave 73072
13th Pl 73072
22nd Ave & St NE 73071
23rd Ave & St 73071
24th Ave NE 73071
24th Ave NW
100-6299 73069
24th Ave SE
100-4499 73071
4600-4799 73072
24th Ave SW
100-1199 73069
1200-2399 73072
NW 24th Ave
300-900 73072
26th Ave NE 73071
26th Ave NW 73069
26th Dr SW 73069
28th Ave NE 73071
28th Ave NW 73069
SE 32nd St 73072
34th Ave SW 73072
SE 35th St 73072
36th Ave NE 73026
36th Ave NW
100-199 73072
200-200 73070
201-6499 73072
400-6498 73072
36th Ave SE 73026
36th Ave SW 73072
SE 37th St 73072
38th Ave NE 73026
SE 38th Cir 73071
SE 38th St 73072
SE 39th Cir 73071
SE 40th St 73072
4100-4499 73071
4900-5499 73072
SE 41st St 73071
43rd Pl & Ter 73072
SE 44th St 73072
48th Ave NE 73026
48th Ave NW 73072
48th Ave SE 73026
48th Ave SW 73072
58th Ave NE 73026
60th Ave NE 73026
60th Ave NW 73072
60th Ave SE 73026
66th NE & SE 73026
68th NE & SE 73026
72nd Ave NE 73026
72nd Ave NW 73072
72nd Ave SE 73026
75th Ave SE 73026
79th Ave NE 73026
80th NE & SE 73026
81st Ave NE 73026
82nd Ave SE 73026
84th NE & SE 73026
86th Ave & Cir NE 73026
88th Ave NE 73026
89th Cir 73026
90th Ave SE 73026
91st Ave & Cir NE 73026
92nd Cir 73026
94th Cir 73026
96th NE & SE 73026
98th NE & SE 73026
1 St 73071
100th Ave NE 73026
101st Ave NE 73026
103rd Ave NE 73026
108th NE & SE 73026
110th NE & SE 73026
112th Ave NE 73026
113th Ave NE 73026
120th NE & SE 73026
124th Ave SE 73026
132nd NE & SE 73026
134th Ave SE 73026
136th Ave SE 73026
138th Ave SE 73026
139th Ave SE 73026
140th Ave SE 73026
142nd Ave SE 73026
143rd Ave SE 73026
144th NE & SE 73026
SE 149th St 73026
156th NE & SE 73026
SE 164th St 73071
8200-11999 73026
SE 167th St 73026
SE 168th Ave & St NE & SE 73026
SE 170th St 73026
SE 175th St 73026
SE 177th St 73026
SE 179th St 73071
8000-10999 73026
180th NE & SE 73026
189th Ave NE 73026
192nd NE & SE 73026
3 St 73071
308th St 73072
310th St 73072
311 Rd 73026
315th St 73072
319th St 73072
320th St 73072
323rd St 73072

OKLAHOMA CITY OK

General Delivery 73102
General Delivery 73105
General Delivery 73106
General Delivery 73109
General Delivery 73112
General Delivery 73114
General Delivery 73117
General Delivery 73118
General Delivery 73119
General Delivery 73120
General Delivery 73123
General Delivery 73129
General Delivery 73137
General Delivery 73142
General Delivery 73147
General Delivery 73148
General Delivery 73153
General Delivery 73155
General Delivery 73159
General Delivery 73170
General Delivery 73195

POST OFFICE BOXES MAIN OFFICE STATIONS AND BRANCHES

Box No.s
1 - 4120 73101
7000 - 7000 73153
11000 - 11856 73136
12001 - 12998 73157
13001 - 14999 73113
15001 - 15824 73155
16001 - 16476 73113
17401 - 17636 73136
18101 - 18998 73154
19001 - 19976 73144
20000 - 21912 73156
22000 - 23992 73123
24000 - 24990 73124
25008 - 25991 73125
26010 - 26967 73126
32002 - 32964 73123
36001 - 36690 73136
42001 - 42880 73123
44000 - 44500 73144
45501 - 46100 73145
52000 - 53594 73152
54001 - 54994 73154
55480 - 55840 73155
57000 - 58240 73157
60001 - 61360 73146
70999 - 70999 73153
74911 - 76572 73147
82001 - 83456 73148
94001 - 96996 73143
108800 - 108850 73101
138800 - 138899 73113
238800 - 238811 73123
248800 - 248899 73124
258800 - 258899 73125
268800 - 269097 73126
270001 - 272610 73137
458000 - 458000 73145
528800 - 528804 73152
540001 - 548817 73154
568801 - 568803 73156
700001 - 700440 73107
720001 - 731944 73172
890001 - 898802 73189
950001 - 950920 73195
1812899 - 1848699 73154
9545800 - 9640800 73143

RURAL ROUTES

19 73111
16, 26, 65, 73 73114
19, 91 73117
02, 66 73120
04, 19 73121
22, 60 73127
03, 84 73128
08 73129
28, 43, 64 73130
01, 58, 73 73131
45 73132
37, 49 73134
38, 50, 67, 81 73135
19 73141
18, 20, 27, 30, 40, 59, 62, 98 73142
08 73149
12, 17, 43 73150
21 73151
23, 54, 80 73160
13, 20, 41, 46, 56, 63 73162
09, 10, 14, 69, 96 73165
06, 95 73169
07, 11, 25, 29, 32, 34, 35, 51, 52, 55, 61, 71, 72, 74, 75, 82, 83, 85, 87, 88 73170
05 73173
24, 48, 90 73179

NAMED STREETS

A Ave 73145
A St 73165
Aaron Dr 73132
Abbey Ln 73130
Abbey Rd 73120
Abbeywood 73170
Abbotts Way 73142
Abram Ross Ave 73117
Acacia Rd 73170
Acadia Ct 73142
Ace Dr 73127
Acoma Dr 73160
Acorn Dr 73151
Acre View Dr 73151
S Acres Dr 73130
Acropolis St 73120
Adair Blvd 73110
N Adams Ave 73127
Addie Ln 73165
S Adeline Ave 73115
Admiral Ct & Dr 73162
Admiralty Way 73116
S Agnew Ave
200-1100 73108
1101-1101 73148
1102-2998 73108
1103-2999 73108
3100-5600 73119
5602-5998 73119
5701-5999 73119
5701-5701 73144
S Agnew Pl 73119
Air Cargo Rd
5600-6399 73159
6500-6598 73195
Air Depot Blvd 73145
N Air Depot Blvd
100-899 73110
901-1499 73110
1200-1298 73110
2000-7699 73141
7900-8999 73151
S Air Depot Blvd
101-197 73110
199-2999 73110
6000-7300 73135
7302-8598 73135
12700-13998 73165
14000-16399 73165
Air Guard Dr 73179
Airey Cir & Dr 73145
S Airline Dr 73119
Akin Dr 73149
Alan Ln
1200-1499 73130
5000-5099 73135
NE Alaniant St 73104
Albany Ave 73111
Albert Dr 73130
Alderham Ave 73170
Aldersgate Cir 73151
Alethea Dr 73160
Alexandria Dr 73142
Alexis Ct 73139
Alicia Dr 73130
Alicia Springs Ct 73165
S Allen Dr 73139
N Allen Ln 73127
N Allen St 73107
S Allen St 73107
Allenhurst Ave 73114
SW Allereda St 73159
Alliance Blvd & Ct 73128
N Allison Dr 73112
Allison Ln
500-699 73160
9000-9399 73151
Almond Dr 73170
Almond Valley Dr 73165
Alpine Dr & Ter 73109
Alta Dr 73179
Altadena Ave 73112
Alturas Cir & Ct 73120
Aluma Valley Dr 73121
Alviola Ave 73110
Alyssa Ln 73160
Ambassador Rd 73169
Amber Rd 73170
Amber St 73160
Amelia Ave 73112
Amelia Earhart Dr 73159
American Ln 73135
American Indian Blvd 73129
Amhurst Pl 73112
Amy Ct 73160
Amy Way 73162
Anahiem Ct 73139
Anchor Dr 73107
Anderson Dr 73149
N Anderson Rd 73130
S Anderson Rd
1700-2999 73130
3200-8999 73150
9100-16399 73165
Andover Ct
1300-2299 73120
11500-11599 73130
Andrea Ct 73160
Andrea Reve Pl 73160
N Andrews Dr 73127
Anduin Ave 73170
Angela Cir 73115
Angela Dr
4000-4399 73115
9000-9199 73130
Angela Francis Pl 73160
N Anita Dr 73127
S Anita Dr 73128
N Anita Pl 73127
N Ann Dr 73107
N Ann Arbor Ave
1-3099 73127
3100-6399 73122
3900-5099 73122
6400-6699 73132
7300-7699 73132
10700-11599 73162
S Ann Arbor Ave
300-2999 73128
3000-3346 73179
3348-3398 73179
N Ann Arbor Pl
1900-2025 73127

2027-2099 73127
3500-3817 73122
3819-3899 73122
N Ann Arbor Ter 73132
Anns Pl 73160
Anthony Ave 73128
Anthony Cir 73110
S Apollo Dr 73129
Apple Dr & Way 73130
Apple Blossom Cir 73160
Apple Estates Rd 73160
Apple Tree Ln 73160
Apple Valley Dr 73120
E Apple Valley Rd 73151
Applegate Dr 73160
Applegrove Cir 73130
Appleton Way 73142
Applewood St 73160
Apricot Ct 73127
Aragon Ln 73170
E Arbor Dr 73110
Arbor Lake Dr 73170
Arbor Rose Ct & Rd 73170
Ardyce Dr 73112
Arlington Dr 73132
Armstrong St 73160
Arnold Ave 73160
Arnold Dr 73110
Arnold St 73145
S Arrow Dr 73129
S Arrow Wood Dr 73129
Arrowhead Dr, Ln, Ter & Way 73120
Artesia Pl 73139
Arthur Ave 73142
Arthur Dr 73110
N Asbury Ave 73132
Asbury Ct 73162
Asbury Dr 73162
N Asbury St 73122
Ashbury Cir & Ct 73170
Ashby Ter 73149
Asher Ct 73160
Ashewood Dr 73151
Ashley Dr
600-799 73160
1500-2599 73120
Ashley Pl 73120
Ashling Dr 73118
Ashton Dr 73160
N Ashton Pl 73117
Ashton Ter 73130
Ashwood Ln 73160
Askew Dr 73110
Aspen Ct 73160
Aspen Dr
1300-1799 73160
5301-5499 73118
Aspen Pl 73132
Aspen Creek Dr 73170
Aspen Hills Dr 73132
Astoria Blvd 73122
Astoria Dr 73160
Atalon Dr 73160
Athens Ave 73107
Atkinson Dr & Plz 73110
Augusta Dr 73160
Aurea Ln 73142
Aurelia Rd 73121
Aurora Ct 73107
N Austin Ave 73127
Autumn Dr 73160
Autumn Ln 73170
N Autumn Rd 73151
Autumn Leaves 73170
Auzela Cir 73160
Ava Ave 73149
Avalon Ct 73120
Avalon Ln
6200-6399 73118
6400-6499 73116
Avenel Dr 73160
S Avenida Ave 73119
N Avery Ave 73141
S Avery Ave 73130
N Avery Dr 73160
S Avery Dr 73160
N Avery Pl 73160
S Avery St 73160
Avian Way 73170
Avila Ln 73170
Avondale Ct & Dr 73116
Azalea Ave 73132
Azurewood Dr 73135
B St 73165
Babb Dr 73110
Bacardy Pl 73162
Baer Dr 73160
Bailey Dr 73162
Bainbridge Rd 73114
Baird St 73160
Bald Cypress Dr 73120
Baldwin Ave 73160
Baldwin Dr 73142
Ballad Dr 73130
Banbury Ln 73170
Bannockburn Pl 73142
Banyan Ln 73162
Barbara Pl 73111
Barbour St 73160
Barcelona Dr 73170
Barclay Rd 73120
Barclay St 73160
Barkwood Ln 73135
N Barnes Ave
1100-2399 73107
3100-6299 73112
11400-11799 73120
S Barnes Ave
1000-2899 73108
3000-5699 73119
6500-9699 73159
N Barnes Cir 73112
S Barnes Pl 73119
S Barnes Rd 73150
Barnes Ter 73170
Barnhill Cir 73162
Barnsteeple Ct 73142
Baron St 73150
N Barr Ave
3700-4299 73122
6600-6999 73132
Barren Oak Dr 73150
Barryton Rd 73120
Barrywood Dr 73120
N Bartell Rd 73121
Bartlett Dr 73131
Bartley Springs Rd 73165
Barton Dr 73120
Barton Pl 73170
Basinger St 73150
Bass Pro Dr 73104
Basswood Canyon Rd 73162
S Bates Ave 73128
N Bath Ave
100-1300 73117
1302-1598 73117
1700-2098 73111
2100-2399 73111
Bath Cir 73117
Bath Ct 73117
Baxter Dr 73120
Bay Ct 73159
Bay Ridge Dr 73165
Bayberry Dr 73162
S Bea St 73150
N Beach Ave 73110
Beacon Dr
500-599 73127
3800-4399 73179
Beacon Pl 73127
Beacon Hill Rd 73135
Beals Pl 73108
Bean Blossom Dr 73111
Bear Canyon Dr 73162
E Beard Dr 73110
Beaulaine Pl 73114
Beaux Jangles Rd 73170
Beaver Creek Rd 73162
Beck Dr 73127
Becker Pl 73115
Bedford Dr 73116
Beechwood Ave 73149
Beechwood Dr 73115
Beechwood Way 73160
Beil Ter 73109
Bel Air Pl 73120
Belaire Dr 73110
Belford Ave 73116
Bell Ave 73142
Bell Dr 73110
S Bell Dr 73110
Bell Fountaine Dr 73160
Bell Gardens Dr 73170
Bella Vista Dr 73110
N Bella Vista Dr 73110
Bella Vista Ln 73131
Bellaire Cir & Dr 73160
Belle Dr 73112
Belle Isle Blvd 73118
Beller Pl 73160
Bellevidere Dr 73117
Belleview Dr & Ter 73112
Bellhurst Ave 73162
Bellmon Ave 73149
Bellmont Ave 73130
E Bellview Dr 73130
NE Benconde St 73141
Bennie Ter 73135
Bent Creek Dr 73135
Bent Tree Dr 73130
Bent Wood Dr 73169
Bentley Dr 73169
Benttree Cir 73120
Bergamo Ln 73170
Berkley Ave 73116
Berkley Cir 73162
Berkley Ct
6900-6999 73116
9600-9699 73162
Berkley Ter 73162
Berkshire 73130
Berkshire Way 73120
Bermuda Cir 73170
Bernadine Ln 73159
Bernard Blvd 73117
Berry Ln 73130
N Berry St 73127
S Berryman Rd 73150
Berrywood Dr 73151
Berwyck Dr 73160
Beth Ct 73120
Beth Dr 73120
W Bethel Rd 73160
Betty Ln 73110
Bevenshire Rd 73162
Beverly Dr & Ter 73105
Big Oak Dr 73110
Bigwood Dr 73135
S Bill Ave 73129
Bill Atkinson Dr 73139
N Billen Ave
1100-2299 73107
4500-5999 73112
S Billen Ave 73159
Biltmore Dr 73173
Bingham Ct 73132
SE Binkley St 73129
SW Binkley St
1000-1299 73109
1300-2499 73119
Birch Dr 73170
Birch St 73108
Birch Bark Ln 73120
Bird Dr 73121
Birdnest Ct 73173
S Birdsong Ln 73150
Biscay Ct 73159
Bishop Bobby L Williams Dr 73111
Bishops Gate 73162
Bismarc Dr 73115
Bizzel Ave 73110
Black Jack Ln 73160
Black Jack Ridge Rd 73150
Black Oaks Dr 73165
Blackberry Run 73112
Blackberry Patch Cir 73170
Blackbird Dr 73145
Blackjack Ln 73150
Blackjack Rd 73131
N Blackwelder Ave
200-3099 73106
3200-4900 73118
4902-5098 73118
10900-11299 73120
S Blackwelder Ave
1-199 73106
300-2899 73108
3000-5900 73119
5902-5998 73119
6000-8199 73159
9200-10499 73139
10500-14899 73170
Blackwood Blvd 73132
Blaine Ct 73160
N Blake Dr 73130
Blanca Mesa Dr 73142
Blanchett Dr 73169
E Blossom Dr 73110
Blue Bell Ave 73162
Blue Bonnet Dr 73159
Blue Bonnet Pl 73128
Blue Canyon Cir 73142
Blue Haven Ct 73162
Blue Moon Ave 73162
Blue Ridge Ln & Rd 73160
Blue Sage Rd 73120
Blue Sky Dr
500-10999 73130
11600-11999 73162
Blue Spruce Ct 73162
Blue Spruce Dr 73130
Blue Spruce Rd 73162
Blue Stem Blvd 73160
Blue Stem Cv 73162
Blue Stem Dr 73162
Blue Stem Pl 73162
Blue Stem Back Rd 73162
Blue Stem West Rd 73162
Blueberry Dr 73165
Bluebird Ct 73110
Bluebird Dr 73110
Bluebird Rd 73179
Bluegrass Ct 73160
Bluejay Ct 73160
Blueridge Ct 73162
W Blueridge Dr 73110
Bluewater Cir & Rd 73165
Blueway Ave 73162
Bluff Creek Dr 73162
Boardwalk Ave 73160
Boardwalk Blvd 73162
Bocage Dr, Ln & Pl 73142
Bodega Dr 73170
S Bodine Dr 73135
E & W Boeing Dr 73110
Bolton Pl 73110
Bomarc Cir & Dr 73115
Bonaparte Blvd 73110
Bonnie Dr 73162
NW Bontria St 73142
Boone Ct 73120
Borum Pl 73110
Boulder Ridge Way 73130
Bourbon St 73128
E Bouse Dr 73110
N & S Bouziden Dr & Pl 73160
Bovee Rd 73165
Box Canyon Rd 73142
Box Turtle Way 73130
Boxwood Ct 73170
N Boyd St 73141
Boykin Dr 73110
Brack Pl 73130
Braden Ct 73120
Bradford Dr 73160
Bradford Pl 73130
Bradfred Dr 73110
N Bradley Ave 73127
Bradley Cir 73110
Bradley Pl 73127
Bramblebush Ct 73151
S Branch St 73115
Brandon Pl 73142
Brandt Ct & Dr 73120
Brandy Ln 73170
Brandywine Ln 73116
Braniff Dr 73105
Braniger Way 73132
Brantwood Cir 73142
Brasier Rd 73165
N Brauer Ave
600-2299 73106
10900-11299 73114
S Brauer Ave 73106
Brawdy Dr 73150
Brayden Dr 73160
Breakers Ln 73128
Breakers West Blvd 73128
Breccia Rd 73170
Breckenridge Dr 73115
Bree Ln 73170
E Breezeway St 73149
Breezewood Dr 73135
S Brent Cir & Dr 73170
Brentco Dr 73115
Brentford Ave, Pl & Ter 73132
S Brentwood Dr 73139
Brentwood Mnr 73169
Brentwood Rd 73116
W Brett Dr 73110
Brettshire Way 73142
Brian Ct 73160
Briar Hollow Dr & Ln 73170
N Briarcliff Cir & Dr 73170
Briarcreek Dr 73162
Briarcrest Dr 73110
Briarhill Dr 73160
Briarlake Ct & Mnr 73170
Briarlane Rd 73115
Briarwood Dr 73130
S Briarwood Dr 73135
Briarwood Ln 73116
Briarwood St 73160
Brice Dr 73160
Brickstone Ct 73142
Bright Prairie Cir 73142
Brighton Ave 73120
Brighton Ct 73130
Brightside Dr 73110
Brinley Way 73142
N & S Bristow Ave 73160
Brittany Ct 73160
Britton Cir 73120
E Britton Rd
200-999 73114
1000-1098 73131
1100-5599 73131
5700-7999 73151
W Britton Rd
100-300 73114
301-301 73113
301-1499 73114
302-1498 73114
1500-3299 73120
5700-8299 73132
W Broadlawn Ln 73122
Broadmoor Ave 73132
N Broadview Cir & Dr 73127
N Broadway
1-1 73102
N Broadway
20-100 73102
10701-10701 73114
Broadway Ave 73170
N Broadway Ave
1-1099 73102
1100-2399 73103
400-5999 73109
6300-10399 73139
10500-14799 73170
Broadway Cir 73170
N Broadway Cir 73103
Broadway Ct 73170
N Broadway Dr 73103
S Broadway Dr 73139
Broadway Ext
5800-5899 73118
6400-7899 73116
9000-13499 73114
N Broadway Pl 73103
S Broadway Pl 73109
N Broadway St 73160
S Broadway St 73160
Broadway Ter 73160
S Brock Dr
2301-2397 73108
2399-2400 73108
2402-2898 73108
3100-3699 73119
Brockton Pl 73162
Broderson Cir 73119
Brody Dr 73160
Bromley Ct 73159
Bronze Medal Rd 73160
S Brook Dr 73165
Brook Ln 73130
Brook Hollow Dr 73150
Brookdale Dr 73115
Brookdale St 73135
Brookend Ct 73120
Brookhaven 73150
Brookhaven Pl 73118
Brookhollow Ct & Rd 73120
N Brookline Ave
1200-3099 73107
3100-6199 73112
7200-7399 73116
S Brookline Ave
1200-1498 73108
1500-2599 73108
3700-5199 73119
7200-10099 73159
10900-14099 73170
S Brookline Pl 73159
Brooklyn Ave 73160
Brookmill Ct 73159
Brookridge Dr 73132
Brookshire Dr 73162
Brookside Dr
100-199 73160
3300-3599 73110
6200-8299 73132
Brookside Ter 73160
Brookstone Ct 73160
Brookwood Dr
500-899 73139
9000-9199 73130
Broughton Ct 73132
Brown Ave 73162
Brown Dr
900-999 73110
4000-4099 73145
Brown Oaks Dr 73127
Browne Stone Rd 73120
N Brunson St 73112
S Brunson St 73119
Brush Arbor Dr 73160
Brush Creek Rd 73120
Brutus Blvd 73165
Bryan Dr 73160
N Bryant Ave
300-2099 73160
500-1599 73117
1701-1797 73121
1799-7600 73121
2101-3099 73160
7602-7798 73121
7900-12199 73131
S Bryant Ave
200-11299 73160
1200-4399 73115
4500-4799 73135
4900-5399 73129
6200-8899 73149
Bryant Ct 73122
Bryant Pl 73115
S Bryant Ter 73160
Bubbling Springs Ct 73150
Buccaneer Dr 73159
Buchanan Pl 73165
Buckboard Ln 73130
Buckeye Ct 73170
Buckingham Pl 73110
Buckwood Rd 73165
S Buddy Ln 73119
Buena Vista Ave 73110
Building Tinker Fld 73145
Burk Dr & Way 73115
Burlingame Ave 73120
Burlingame Dr 73110
Burnham Pl 73132
Burning Oaks Dr & Rd 73150
Burnt Oak Rd 73120
Burntwood Dr 73135
Burr Oaks Pl & Rd 73105
N Bush Blvd 73112
Bush Creek Way 73117
NW Buthorth St 73116
Butler Pl 73118
Butler St 73160
Buttercup Cir 73170
Button Ave 73160
Buttonfield Ave 73160
Buttonwood Ave 73160
Buttram Rd 73120
S By Pass Ter 73119
S Byers Ave
100-199 73104
600-698 73129
700-5599 73129
6300-6999 73149
Byrd Dr 73110
Byron Ave 73112
Byron Ct 73111
Byron Pl 73112
Bywater Rd 73170
C Ave 73145
C St 73165
C A Henderson Blvd 73139
S Cabin Rd 73169
N Caddo Ct 73132
Cadiz Ct 73170
Cadorna Strada 73170
Cadwell Ave 73170
Caffery Dr 73150
Cagle St 73160
Cairo Ave 73111
Calais Cir 73142
S Caldwell Dr 73130
Caleb St 73179
Caledonia Way 73142
Caliber Dr 73134
E California Ave
1-699 73104
2100-2399 73117
W California Ave
400-799 73102
800-999 73106
2300-2899 73107
Calistoga Dr 73170
Callahan Cir & Dr 73121
Callie Dr 73131
Calm Water Dr 73135
Calm Wind Dr 73170
Calvia Ct 73173
S Camay Ave 73159
Cambridge Ct
1000-1099 73160
2600-2899 73116
Cambridge Dr 73110
Cambridge Rd 73130
Camden Ct 73162
Camden Way 73116
Camellia Rd 73170
Camelot 73160
Camelot Ct 73120
Camelot Dr
2000-2099 73130
2700-12299 73120
Camelot Pl 73120
Cameron Ct 73112
Cameron St 73160
Camille Ave 73149
E Campbell Dr 73110
W Campbell Dr 73110
Campbell Pl 73108
Campbell Rd 73111
Camrose Ct 73159
Candlewood Dr 73132
Candy Ln 73115

Candy Tuft Ln 73162
Canna Ln 73132
Canterbury Ln 73130
Canterbury Pl 73116
Canterbury Rd 73130
Cantle Cir, Ct & Rd 73120
Canyon Dr
5401-5499 73118
6200-6399 73105
Canyon Rd 73120
Canyon Lakes Dr 73142
Canyon Trail Dr 73135
SW Caplerri St 73170
W Captains Dr 73162
Cardan Pl 73160
E Cardinal Dr 73121
N Cardinal Dr 73121
E Cardinal Pl 73130
Carey Pl
1800-2199 73106
3100-3299 73160
SW Caridenw St 73119
Carlisle Ct & Rd 73120
Carlton Ct 73130
Carlton Way 73120
Carnelian Way 73170
Carol Cir 73160
N Carol Dr 73141
N Carol Ln 73127
Carol Ann Pl 73160
Carolyn Dr 73110
Carpenter Dr 73110
Carriage Way 73142
Carrick Ln 73162
Carrie Ct 73120
N Carrie Ln 73117
Carrington Pl 73131
E Carroll Cir 73150
E Carroll Ln 73110
Carter Ct 73170
S Carter Ct 73159
Carter Dr 73129
Carverdale Dr 73117
Casa Linda 73139
Casady Ln 73120
Cascata Strada 73170
Cashion Pl 73112
Casper Dr 73111
Cass Ave 73160
Cassidy Ct 73130
Castle Rd 73162
Castle Row 73127
Castle Bay Cv 73115
Castle Creek Cir 73165
Castlerock Ct 73142
Castlerock Rd 73120
Catalina Dr 73139
Catalpa Ln 73130
Cates Way 73139
Cathy Ln 73110
Caton Pl 73130
Cavalier St 73160
Cayman Ln 73170
Cecelia St 73121
Cecilia Dr & Pl 73162
Cedar Crk 73169
Cedar Ct 73110
N Cedar Dr 73130
Cedar Ln
200-499 73160
8700-8899 73110
Cedar Trl 73131
Cedar Bend Dr 73130
Cedar Brook Dr 73160
Cedar Creek Ter 73131
Cedar Crest Rd 73169
Cedar Hill Pl 73110
Cedar Hollow Rd 73162
Cedar Lake Ave &
Blvd 73114
Cedar Park Dr 73120
Cedar Ridge Dr 73110
Cedar Ridge Rd 73162
Cedar Springs Ln &
Rd 73120
Cedar Tree Rd 73120
Cedar Valley Dr, Rd &
Ter 73170
W Cedarbrook Ln 73170
N Cedardale Dr 73127
NW Cedgeriv St 73107
Celina Dr 73130
SE Centanti St 73160
Centennial Ct 73116
Center Dr 73110
S Center Ln 73165
Center St 73120
Central Ave 73122
N Central Ave
200-499 73104
2200-2399 73105
S Central Ave 73129
Central Park Dr 73105
Century Blvd 73110
Century Dr
400-598 73160
600-799 73160
11600-12099 73162
Chad Rd 73135
Chadbrooke Pl 73142
NW Chamindo St 73106
Champion Ln 73160
Channing Sq 73102
Chapel Hill Rd 73120
Char Ln 73110
Chardonnay Dr 73170
Charing Cross Rd 73120
Charity Ln 73121
Charlene Dr 73132
N Charles Ave 73130
Charlie Christian Ave 73104
S Charlotte Dr 73159
W Charlotte Dr 73139
Charter Ave 73108
Charwood Ct 73139
Charwood Dr 73139
Charwood Ln 73135
Chase End Ct 73142
Chateau Dr 73160
Chateaux Rd 73142
Chatfield Cir 73179
Chatham Rd 73132
Chaucer Dr 73120
Chaucer Crescent St 73130
Checkerbloom Dr 73165
Cheek Pl 73115
Chelsea Chase 73170
Chelsey Ln 73132
Chennault Dr 73145
N Cherokee Ct, Dr,
Lndg,
Plz & Xing E & W 73132
N Cherry Ave 73121
Cherry Ln
1600-1999 73115
2400-2499 73130
N Cherry Ln 73127
Cherry Pl 73127
Cherry Hill Ln
4000-4299 73120
4500-4999 73135
Cherrywood Dr
100-299 73110
200-300 73160
302-398 73160
Chesterfield Ln 73173
Chesterfield Pl 73179
Chesterton Pl 73120
N Chestnut Ave 73160
S Chestnut Ave 73160
Chestnut Dr 73119
Chestnut Ridge Ct &
Rd 73120
Chetwood Dr 73115
Chevy Chase Dr 73110
Cheyenne Ct & Rd 73132
Chianti Cir 73120
N Chicago St 73112
Chidlaw Ct & Dr 73145
Childrens Ave 73104
Chisholm Ct 73127
Chisholm Pl 73173
Chisholm Rd 73173
N Chisholm Rd 73127
Chisholm Trl 73114
Chisholm Trail Ln 73160
Chisholm Village Dr 73114
Choctaw Ridge Rd 73130
Christie Dr 73110
Christina Ct 73160
N Christine Dr 73130
Christmas Dr 73169
Christon Ct 73118
Christopher Todd Dr 73160
Chumley Ln 73135
Church Way 73139
Churchill Pl 73120
Churchill Rd 73165
Churchill Way 73120
Cielo Ter 73149
Cimarron Dr 73162
Cimarron Estate Dr 73121
Cinder Dr 73135
Cinderella Dr 73129
S Cindy Ln 73110
Cindy Rd 73132
Cindy Brook Ln 73160
Cinnamon Teal Dr 73132
Circle Dr 73122
City Ave 73160
City Office Bldg 73102
SW Clacheri St 73128
Clarence Ct 73142
Claridge Ct 73118
Clarisa Dr 73160
Clary Dr
1900-2298 73110
4000-4299 73129
N Classen Ave 73160
S Classen Ave 73160
N Classen Blvd
100-3099 73106
3100-6299 73118
6500-7799 73116
8000-10099 73114
Classen Cir 73118
N Classen Ct 73118
Classen Dr
1100-1399 73103
1400-1699 73106
Classic Dr 73165
Clayton Dr 73132
Clear St 73165
Clear Creek Rd 73160
Clearbrook Rd 73120
Clearwater Dr 73179
S Clegern St
3000-3299 73109
9900-10099 73139
Clendon Way
3800-4499 73115
4500-4799 73135
Clermont Pl 73116
Cliff Rose Dr 73162
Cliffe Hollow Dr 73162
Clipper St 73107
Clover Ln 73131
Clover Rd 73160
Cloverlawn Ct & Dr 73135
Cloverleaf Ln 73170
E & N Clyde Ave 73121
Coachlight Dr 73110
Cobblestone Ct &
Pkwy 73142
Coble St 73135
Coburg Ave & Pl 73170
S Coburn Rd 73150
E & W Coe Dr 73110
Colcord Dr 73102
Cold Fire Rd 73170
Coldstream Dr & Ln 73169
Colebrook Dr 73120
S Coleman Dr 73179
Coletta Dr 73120
Colfax Pl 73112
College 73121
College Ave 73106
N College Ave 73132
N College St 73122
Collin Dr 73129
Colony Ln 73112
Colton Dr 73127
Coltrane Pl 73121
N Coltrane Rd
1701-2197 73121
2199-7899 73121
7900-11999 73131
Columbia Dr 73134
Columbine Way 73142
Comanche Ave & Ct 73132
Commerce Park Dr 73132
Commodore Ln 73162
Commonwealth Pl 73159
Condor Dr 73170
Condor Ter 73162
Connaught Ct 73132
Connie Dr 73115
Cook Ave 73145
Cooke Way 73179
N & S Cooley Dr 73127
N Cooper Ave 73118
Copper Trails Ln 73170
Coral Creek Ln 73165
Corbett Dr 73115
Corbin Cir & Dr 73160
Cord Ave 73132
Core Ave 73170
Cork Rd 73162
Corn Flower Pl 73120
Cornell Pkwy 73108
Cornwall Pl 73120
Corona Dr 73149
Corrine Dr 73111
Corso Strada 73170
Cosby Ln 73165
Cottage Park Dr 73110
Cottingham Rd 73142
Cottonwood Dr 73160
N Cottonwood Dr 73130
S Cottonwood Dr 73170
Couch Dr 73102
N Council Rd
1-2199 73127
5100-9299 73132
9400-12299 73162
12700-15099 73142
S Council Rd
1-99 73127
100-198 73128
200-2999 73128
3100-5999 73179
6400-10399 73169
10600-11999 73173
12001-12699 73173
Council Heights Rd 73179
Country Clb 73160
Country Dr
11300-11699 73170
14500-14899 73165
W Country Dr 73170
Country Ln
200-11699 73130
12800-13499 73165
Country Pl 73131
Country Club Cir 73110
N Country Club Dr 73116
S Country Club Dr 73159
W Country Club Dr 73116
N Country Club Pl 73116
Country Club Ter 73110
Country Edge Dr 73170
Country Hollow Rd 73142
Country Place Rd
100-199 73130
1600-1699 73131
County Line Rd 73128
S County Line Rd
3500-5299 73179
6000-8899 73169
10500-12199 73173
County Office Bldg 73102
Courier Dr 73169
Courtyards Ct 73149
Cove Hollow Rd 73132
Coventry Ln & Park 73120
Coventry Manor Dr 73128
Covey Creek Dr 73142
Covington Ln
900-999 73130
6000-6199 73132
Cowan Pl 73160
Cox Ave 73149
Coyote Trl 73165
Coyote Creek Rd 73165
Coywood 73142
Crabtree Cv 73110
Craford Ct 73159
Crafton Ct 73159
Cragg Dr 73150
Craig Dr 73160
Creek Ct 73135
Creek Meadow Dr 73151
Creekmore Dr 73179
Creekridge Dr 73141
Creeks End Cir 73131
Creekside Dr 73131
Creekvale Rd 73165
Creekwood 73165
Creekwood Dr 73135
Creekwood Ter 73135
SE Crellea St 73149
Crescent Cir
600-799 73110
15600-15699 73165
Crest Cir 73130
Crest Dr 73130
Crest Pl
4700-4799 73117
11400-11498 73131
11500-11699 73131
Crestline Ct, Dr & Ter 73132
Crestmont Dr 73132
Crestmoor Dr 73160
Creston Dr 73111
Crestview Dr 73105
Crick Hollow Ct 73170
Cricket Ct 73162
Cricket Canyon Rd 73162
Crimson Ln 73127
N Cromwell Ave 73112
Crooked Creek Ln 73160
Crooked Creek Rd 73117
Crosby Blvd 73110
Crosby Dr
200-399 73115
4900-5199 73135
N Cross Ave
1700-2399 73107
5100-5199 73112
N Cross St 73110
Cross Timbers Dr 73160
Cross Vine Ct 73170
Crossgate Dr 73170
Crossroads Blvd &
Mall 73149
Crow Cir 73132
Crown Dr 73150
Crown Point Rd 73132
Croydon Ct 73120
Croydon Rd 73130
Crystal Dr 73160
Crystal Gardens Dr &
Pl 73170
Crystal Park Ave 73139
Crystal Springs Rd 73160
Culbertson Dr 73105
Cumberland Dr 73116
Cumberland Ln 73162
Cummings Dr 73107
Cunningham Dr 73135
E Curtis Dr 73110
W Curtis Dr 73110
Curtis Ter 73132
Cynthia Dr 73130
Cypress Ct
3300-3399 73170
4700-4799 73162
Cypress Cv 73110
Cypress Dr 73170
Cypress Grv 73162
Cypress Ln 73162
D Ave 73145
D St 73165
Dahoon Dr 73120
S Daisy Dr 73159
Dakota Dr 73160
Dale Dr 73160
Dalea Dr 73142
N & S Dallas Ave 73160
Dalton Dr 73162
Daman Pl 73159
Damron Dr 73110
Dana Beth Dr 73165
Danfield Dr 73149
Danielle Ter 73160
Danish Dr 73132
S Danner Dr 73159
Dansmere Ave 73170
Darla Dr 73135
Darryl Ln 73165
S Daugherty Ave 73108
S David Dr 73159
David Rd 73160
David Ter 73141
S Davidson Rd 73130
Davinbrook Dr 73118
N Davis Ave
500-2099 73127
8900-9099 73132
Davis Cir 73110
Davis Ct 73162
Davis St 73162
Dawn Cir 73135
Dawn Dee Rd 73150
Dawn Marie Dr 73112
Dawson Cir & Ct 73142
Day Lilly Ln 73120
Dayton Cir, Dr & Ln 73160
Dean Pl 73117
Dean A Mcgee Ave
100-499 73102
800-899 73106
Debar Cir 73132
S Debbie Ln 73110
S Deborah Dr 73129
Debra Ct 73132
Decker Dr 73160
Decon Ave 73132
Deep Creek Rd 73131
Deepwood Creek Dr 73142
Deer Ct & St 73165
Deer Meadow Dr 73150
Deerberry Ln 73150
Deerfield Cir & Ct 73142
Deerwood Cir 73142
Deerwood Ct 73142
Deerwood Dr 73142
Deerwood Trl 73130
S Dees Dr 73150
Del Rd 73115
Del Aire Dr & Pl 73115
Del Arbole Dr 73110
Del Casa Cir 73110
Del Creek Rd 73117
Del Crest Dr 73115
Del Haven Dr 73115
Del Mar Gdn 73107
Del Porte Dr 73115
Del Rancho Dr 73115
Del Rey Cir & Dr 73110
Del View Dr 73115
Delia St 73110
Delmar Cir 73160
Delmar Rd 73115
Delta Pl 73115
Delwood Dr 73115
Dena Ln 73132
Denise Rd 73165
S Denning Ave 73169
Denniston Dr 73107
NW Denteren St 73118
Dentwood Ter 73115
Denver Cir 73160
Derby Dr 73130
Derby Way 73173
Derrick Cir 73170
Desert Willow Ct 73160
Desiree Pl 73160
N Detroit St 73112
Devonbrook Ct 73130
Devonshire St 73116
Devore Dr 73162
N Dewey Ave
500-1099 73102
1100-2899 73103
3300-5499 73118
11800-12299 73114
S Dewey Ave
1-99 73102
500-5499 73109
6000-10499 73139
Diane Dr
3200-3299 73112
6200-6299 73118
Dik Dik St 73110
N & S Dillon Ave 73160
S Dimple Dr 73135
N Ditmer Rd 73127
Doble Rd 73165
Dodd Dr 73130
N Dodson Ter 73111
Doe Rd 73165
Dogwood Ct 73160
Dogwood Dr
4000-4099 73110
7100-7199 73150
Dogwood Rd 73150
N Donald Ave
1400-2899 73127
5500-5899 73122
Donley Dr 73127
Donna Ct 73162
S Donna Ln 73150
N Donnelly Ave 73107
Donning St 73162
Dons Rd 73165
Doolittle Ave 73145
Doons Dr 73142
Doral Ct 73142
Dorchester Dr
1400-1499 73114
1500-1999 73120
2600-2899 73120
Dorchester Pl 73120
Dorchester Rd 73130
Doriath Way 73170
Doris Ave 73115
Doris Dr 73162
Doris Pl 73162
N Doris St 73127
Dornick Cir 73162
Dornick Dr 73162
N Dornick Dr 73121
Dorothy Dr
1400-1598 73170
1600-1999 73170
10300-10899 73162
Dorset Dr
7600-7799 73116
8000-12499 73120
Dorsey St 73131
Double Springs Dr 73150
Dougherty Pl 73179
N Douglas Ave 73106
S Douglas Ave
2300-5999 73109
6000-10499 73139
11800-11899 73170
N Douglas Blvd
100-1699 73130
1700-2400 73141
2402-2998 73141
S Douglas Blvd
100-2999 73130
3000-5799 73150
E Douglas Dr 73110
S Douglas Dr 73139
W Douglas Dr 73110
S Douglas Pl 73139
Doulton Cir 73142
Dourdan Ct 73142
Dove Holw 73110
Dove Creek Rd 73165

Dove Tree Ln 73162
Dover Cir 73162
Dover Dr 73162
Dover Rd 73130
Dow Dr 73116
Downing St 73120
Downsview Ln 73142
Drakestone Ave 73120
Draper Dr 73110
Draper Ln 73165
S Drexel Ave
1100-1198 73108
3800-5599 73119
6000-10100 73159
10102-10198 73159
12900-16099 73170
N Drexel Blvd
1300-2999 73107
3100-3299 73112
3300-3300 73107
3301-6399 73112
3304-6398 73112
6600-7199 73116
N Drexel Cir 73112
NW Drexel Ct 73107
S Drexel Pl 73159
Drinkwater Dr 73111
Dripping Springs Ln 73150
Drury Ln 73116
Drywater Dr 73170
Duane Dr 73132
Dublin Rd 73120
Duffner Dr 73118
S Duke Ave 73169
Dulane Cir 73132
Dumas Ave & Ln 73119
Dummy Record
73110-73110 73110
Dummy Record
73131-73131 73131
73146-73146 73145
Dunbar Ct 73162
Duncan Dr 73107
Durham Dr 73162
S Durland Ave
600-5199 73129
6300-6499 73149
Durland Way 73114
Dyer Dr 73160
N & S E K Gaylord
Blvd 73102
Eagle Cir 73135
Eagle Dr
700-1599 73160
1601-1999 73160
2200-2298 73115
2300-2799 73115
Eagle Ln 73162
N Eagle Ln
800-3099 73127
8600-9299 73132
11000-11399 73162
S Eagle Ln
200-499 73128
3000-3399 73179
7500-7799 73169
Eagle Creek Way 73117
Eagle Hill Dr 73162
Eagle Wood Dr 73150
Eagles Lndg 73135
Eagles Cove Ave 73170
S East Ave 73129
East Dr
800-999 73105
4900-5699 73145
Eastbourne Ln 73132
Eastbrook Dr & Ter 73115
N Eastern Ave
100-2800 73160
2802-3698 73160
8000-13699 73131
S Eastern Ave
100-9400 73160
1100-5999 73129
6000-8799 73149
9402-9598 73160
Eastern Pl 73131

Eastgate Dr 73162
Eastlake Cir & Dr 73162
Eastman Dr
3300-3699 73112
4600-4999 73122
Eastmoor Ct 73160
Eastridge Cir 73160
Eastridge Dr
1900-2099 73141
13100-13399 73170
Eastridge Pl 73141
S Eastside Dr 73165
Eastvalley Rd 73170
Eastwood Cir
1700-1799 73160
3300-3499 73115
6500-6799 73132
N Easy St 73150
Eberle Dr 73160
Echo Glen Cir 73142
S Eckroat St 73129
Eddie Dr 73110
Eden Cir, Ct & Dr 73135
Edenborough Dr 73132
Edgebrook Rd 73132
Edgemere Ct 73118
Edgemont Cir 73162
N Edgewater Dr 73116
Edgewood Dr 73110
Edgewood St 73160
Edinburg Way 73115
Edington Ct 73118
Edison Dr 73120
Edna Rd 73165
Edwards Ave 73111
Edwin Rd 73165
S Eggleston Ave 73109
El Toro Dr 73129
Elaine Dr 73130
Eland St 73110
Elisabeth Anne Ter 73160
Elizabeth Cv & Dr 73130
Elk Canyon Ct & Rd 73162
Ella Ln 73160
Ellen Ln 73132
Ellis Ave 73160
N Ellison Ave 73106
S Ellison Ave 73108
Elm Dr 73115
Elm St 73110
Elm Creek Dr 73160
Elm Creek Rd 73165
Elmhurst Ave 73120
Elmhurst Dr 73130
Elmhurst St 73160
Elmo Way 73160
Elmview Dr 73115
Elmwood Ave 73116
Elmwood Ct 73160
Elmwood Forest Dr 73151
Elrond Dr 73170
Elton Ave 73111
S Embassy Ter 73169
Ember Ln 73130
Ember Glow 73160
Embers Dr & Pl 73135
S Emco Dr 73129
Emerald Dr 73150
Emerald Island Dr 73142
Emerwood Ct & Rd 73160
Emilie Grace Ln 73160
Emily Ln 73130
Emma Ct 73165
Emma Dr 73130
Empire Blvd 73129
W End Ave 73160
Endicott Dr 73165
Endor Cir, Ct & Dr 73170
Englewood Rd 73115
N & S English St 73160
Enterprise Ave, Dr, Pl &
Way 73128
Entrance Rd A 73145
S Envoy Rd 73169
Epperly Dr
2000-4499 73115
5600-5698 73135
5700-5999 73135
E & W Ercoupe Ct &
Dr 73110
Eric Cir 73160
Eric Ct 73135
Eric Dr 73135
Eric Field Pl 73142
Erin Pl 73120
Erryn Ln 73135
Eskridge Dr 73114
Essex Ave & Ct 73120
Estell Dr 73160
Estelle Ct 73135
Estelle Manor Cir 73135
Esther Ave 73130
Ethan Ln 73160
Eton Ave 73122
E Eubanks St
600-899 73105
1700-1800 73111
1802-1898 73111
NW Eubanks St 73118
W Eubanks St 73112
NE Euclid St 73117
Evanbrook Ter 73135
Evanhale Rd 73127
Evans Ct 73160
N Evans Dr 73121
Evans Ln 73150
N Everest Ave
600-1499 73117
1700-6700 73111
6702-6898 73111
S Everest Ave 73129
Everett Ct 73111
Everett Dr 73104
Everglade Ct 73128
Evergreen Cir 73110
Evergreen Ct 73162
Evergreen Canyon Rd 73162
Evie Dr & Pl 73160
Exchange Ave 73108
Exeter Ct 73159
Exmoor Cir 73142
NW Expressway
1401-1597 73118
NW Expressway
1599-1999 73118
2100-3699 73112
3701-3999 73112
4000-4499 73116
4500-7999 73132
5500-5899 73132
8000-8999 73162
E & W Fairchild Dr 73110
W Fairfield Ave 73116
Fairfield Greens Dr 73110
Fairlane Dr 73110
N Fairmont Ave 73111
S Fairmont Ave 73129
E Fairview Dr 73115
S Fairview Dr 73159
W Fairview Dr 73159
Fairway Ave 73170
Fairway Dr 73160
Faith Anne Pl 73179
Falcon Dr 73145
N Falcon Dr 73127
Falcon Pl 73162
SW Falernew St 73173
Falling Leaf Ter 73160
Farm Rd 73160
Farra Dr & Rd 73107
Fawn Ln 73165
Fawn Canyon Dr 73162
Fawn Hill Rd 73173
Fawn Lily Rd 73128
Featherstone Rd 73120
Federal Ct 73135
Felix Pl 73110
Fendrych Dr 73165
Fennel Rd 73128
Fenwick Pl 73116
Fernwood Dr 73130
S Fields St 73150

Fiesta Ct 73127
Finchley Ln 73120
Finley Dr 73130
Finley Rd 73120
Fire Light Dr 73160
Firethorn Dr 73115
Fishermans Rd 73162
Flagstone Ct 73142
Flair Dr 73159
Flame Lily Rd 73128
Flaming Lips Aly 73104
Flamingo Ave
500-1899 73127
10500-10699 73162
Flamingo Way 73127
Flannery Dr 73110
Flatt Cir 73165
Fleetwood Dr 73127
Fleming Cir 73160
Fleshman Dr 73160
Flicker Rdg 73160
Flight Line Dr 73179
Flint Ct 73165
N Florida Ave
2100-2999 73106
3200-5799 73118
10900-11599 73120
Flower Wood Dr 73120
N Flynn Ave
1700-2399 73107
3800-3999 73112
N Fonshill Ave
300-1599 73117
2100-3299 73111
Fontana Dr 73116
Fontana Ln 73115
N & W Fordson Dr 73127
Forest Ln
7500-8099 73150
10000-10199 73130
Forest Cove Cir 73130
Forest Dale Dr 73151
Forest Glade Dr 73151
Forest Hollow Ct 73151
Forest Meadow Dr 73151
E & N Forest Park Dr &
Ter 73121
Forest Tree Ln 73150
Forman Dr 73170
Forrest Spring Dr 73173
Fossil Creek Ln 73134
Foster Dr 73135
Foster Pl 73110
Foster Rd 73129
Fountain Blvd 73170
Fountain Grass Rd 73128
Four Oclock Dr 73128
Fox Ave 73160
Fox Ct 73111
S Fox Dr 73110
Fox Holw 73131
Fox Creek Dr 73131
Fox Fair Holw 73130
Fox Forest Cir 73142
Fox Hill Way 73173
Fox Hollow Rdg 73131
Fox Run Dr & Way 73142
Foxfire St 73160
Foxglove Ct & Ln 73120
Foxhorn Cir 73130
S Foxmor Dr 73165
N Fradindo Ave 73131
N Francis Ave
400-2599 73106
3100-4500 73118
4502-6198 73118
9300-12099 73114
S Francis Ave
200-5999 73109
6000-6399 73139
N Frankford Ave 73112
Frankie Ln 73165
Franklin St 73145
Frazier Dr 73105
N Fred Jones Ave 73106
Frederick Dr
1200-1299 73139
1300-1399 73159
Frederick J Douglas
Dr 73117
Freedom Ave 73135
Freeman Dr 73160
Fremont Dr 73120
French Ct 73121
E & S Friendly Ln &
Rd 73130
S Fritts Blvd 73160
E Frolich Dr 73110
Frontier Dr 73128
Frostwood Ter 73115
Fruit Orchard Pl 73170
Fruitful Dr 73130
Frye Ln 73135
Futurity Dr 73130
Gabriel Ct & Dr 73160
Gadwall Rd 73179
Gaelic Glen Ct & Dr 73142
Gaillardia Blvd, Cir, Dr,
Ln, Pkwy & Pl 73142
Gaillardia Corporate Pl 73142
Gaines St 73135
Galahad Cir 73132
Galaxie Dr & Ter 73132
Gale 73160
Galering Rd 73195
Galway Ct 73159
Garden Ct 73170
Garden Dr 73170
Garden Pl 73112
Gardenview Dr 73110
N Gardner Ave 73127
S Gardner Dr 73150
Garland Ave 73111
Garland St 73160
S Garnada Ln 73165
N Garnett St 73114
Garr Pl 73165
Garrett Rd 73121
S Garrett St 73139
Garrett Cole Dr 73130
Gaston Ct 73170
Gateshead Dr 73170
Gateway Plz 73110
Gateway Ter 73149
Gateway Gardens Dr 73165
N Gatewood Ave 73106
Gayle Dr 73130
Gaylon Cir 73170
Gaylord Dr 73162
N Geary Ave 73104
Gee Dr 73165
Gemini Blvd 73179
General Pershing Blvd 73107
General Senter Dr 73110
SE Genereli St 73165
S Genessee Ave 73129
Gentry Dr 73142
S George Dr 73165
Georgia Ave 73120
N Georgia Ave
3801-3897 73118
3899-5799 73118
8500-9199 73114
S Georgia Pl 73129
S Georgia Ter 73129
N Geraldine Ave
2400-3099 73107
3100-3999 73112
Gerenuk St 73110
Gerrie St 73130
N Gibson Ave 73127
Gill Dr 73110
Gilliam 73170
S Gilson Way 73179
Gina Cir & Pl 73115
Ginger Ave 73160
Givens Dr 73110
Glade Ave
400-1299 73127
8000-8699 73132
11300-11699 73162
Gladstone Ter 73120
Gladys Dr 73165

Glearrai Dr 73145
Glen Dean Cir 73119
Glen Ellyn St 73111
Glenbrook Ct 73118
Glenbrook Dr 73118
Glenbrook Ter 73116
Glencove Pl 73132
S Glendale Rd 73130
Glendover Ave & Ct 73162
Glenhaven Dr 73110
Glenhaven Villas Ct 73110
Glenhurst Blvd 73162
Glenmanor Cir & Dr 73110
S Glenn Ave 73115
S Glenn St 73129
N Glenoaks Dr 73110
N Glenvalley Dr 73110
Glenwood Ave
1100-1599 73116
7900-8699 73114
Glenwood Dr 73160
Glenwood Plz 73110
Glimmer Cir 73165
Global Pkwy 73110
Godlin St 73141
N Goff Ave 73107
S Goff Ave
2100-2999 73108
3100-4299 73119
Goforth Dr 73165
Gold Field Pl 73128
Gold Medal Dr 73114
Goldbeck St 73165
Golden Astor Ln 73142
Golden Leaf Dr 73160
Golden Oaks Rd 73127
Goldenrod Ln
1800-2099 73130
10200-10499 73162
10500-10599 73130
Goldleaf Ln 73131
Goldsborough Rd 73130
Goodger Dr 73112
Goodman Ln 73129
Goodrich Dr 73170
Gordon Cooper St 73107
Goshen Dr 73120
Gossamer Way 73165
S Gould St 73129
S Grace Dr 73159
Grace Way 73170
Grace Pointe Dr 73170
Graham Ave & Cir 73127
Gramercy Dr 73139
Gramercy Park Pl 73142
Granada Blvd 73111
Granada Dr 73173
E Grand Blvd 73129
N Grand Blvd
1100-3099 73107
3100-5498 73112
5500-6399 73112
6500-6699 73116
6701-6799 73116
NE Grand Blvd
1100-1699 73117
1700-5599 73111
5601-5799 73111
NW Grand Blvd
100-1099 73118
2300-2422 73116
2423-2497 73116
2424-2498 73116
2499-3399 73116
5800-6299 73118
6400-7099 73116
S Grand Blvd 73108
SE Grand Blvd 73129
SW Grand Blvd
100-1299 73109
1300-2899 73119
NE Grand Cir 73111
NW Grand Cir 73116
NW Grand Ct 73116
Grand Dr 73116
Grand Mnr 73130

Grande Mesa Ter 73162
Grandmark Dr 73116
Grandview Pl 73116
Grandview Rd 73130
Granger St 73118
Granite Dr 73179
Grape Arbor Ter 73170
Grapevine Dr 73130
Grapevine Trl 73170
Grayson Pl 73142
Great Plains Walk 73107
Green Apple Dr & Pl 73160
Green Cedar Ln & Ter 73131
Green Meadow Ln 73132
Green Valley Dr 73120
Green Valley Rd 73151
Green Wing Ct 73120
Greenbriar Pkwy & Pl 73159
Greenbriar Chase 73170
Greenbrier Ter 73115
Greenlawn Ave 73170
Greenlea Chase E &
W 73170
Greenvale Rd 73127
Greenview Dr 73135
Greenway Dr 73132
N Greenway Dr 73127
Greenway Ter 73115
Greenwick Dr 73162
Greenwood Dr 73110
Greenwood Ln 73132
Greer Way 73132
Gregg Dr 73169
Grey Fox Run 73131
Greystone Ave
7100-7199 73116
8300-12299 73120
N Greystone Cir 73120
Greystone Ct 73120
Greystone Ter 73120
Griffin Ctr 73150
Grimsbey Ct 73159
Grissom Dr 73130
N Grove Ave
2800-2999 73127
3100-3499 73122
3700-6299 73122
6400-6999 73132
11000-11599 73162
N Grove Pl 73127
E Grumman Dr 73110
N Guernsey Ave 73103
Guilford Ln 73120
N & W Gun Hill Way 73132
Guy Dr 73110
Gwendolyn Ln 73131
H Ave 73145
Hackberry Rd 73120
Haile St & Ter 73121
Haindl Dr 73129
Halaby Dr 73169
Halbrook Manor Ln 73169
Hales Dr 73112
Hallbrook Mnr 73169
Hallmark Cir 73139
N Hamilton Dr 73112
Hamlet Rd 73159
N Hammond Ave
2500-3099 73127
4600-4698 73122
4700-6399 73122
7200-7399 73132
N Hammond Cir 73132
Hampshire Ln 73179
N Hampton Ave 73111
Hampton Dr
800-3399 73115
11500-11599 73130
Hand Rd 73130
Hanna Dr 73115
Hanover Way 73132
Harbor Dr 73162
Harden Ct & Dr 73118
Hardin Dr 73111
Hardy Dr 73179
Hargis Ln 73160

Harli Ln 73170
W & E Harlow Ave & Pl 73127
Harmon Ave 73179
Harmon Cir 73160
Harmon Dr 73135
E Harmon Dr 73110
N Harmon Dr 73122
W Harmon Dr 73110
Harmony Dr
  3700-3899 73160
  9000-9999 73130
Harold Ct & Dr 73110
Harper Ave 73131
N & S Harr Dr 73110
Harrell Dr 73165
Harriet St 73131
Harrington Dr 73160
Harris Ave 73107
Harrison Ave 73104
Harrison Blvd 73141
S Harrison Dr 73150
Harroz Ln 73110
Harry Dr 73149
N Hartford St 73112
Hartline Dr 73115
Hartsdel Dr 73115
N Harvard Ave
  200-2999 73127
  3800-6399 73122
  4700-4799 73122
  6400-6899 73132
Harvard Dr 73122
S Harvard Dr 73128
Harvest Cir 73170
Harvest Hills Rd
  7900-8299 73132
  9900-10499 73162
Harvest Hills South Blvd 73132
Harvest Moon Ave 73162
Harvest Moon Rd 73132
Harvest Time Ln 73162
N Harvey Ave
  200-999 73102
  1001-1099 73102
  1200-2899 73103
  5300-5498 73118
  6001-6199 73118
  6800-7699 73116
  8200-8899 73114
S Harvey Ave
  200-5910 73109
  5912-5998 73109
  6000-10399 73139
  10500-14799 73170
Harvey Cir 73139
S Harvey Ct 73109
N Harvey Pkwy
  2900-3099 73103
  3100-5099 73118
N Harvey Pl
  6600-7699 73116
  7900-8599 73114
S Harvey Pl
  6400-6999 73139
  13800-13899 73170
Harwich Manor St 73132
Hasley Dr 73120
Hasley Pl 73114
N Hassett Rd 73131
Hasswell Dr 73170
Hastings Rd 73130
S Hattie Ave
  3200-5999 73129
  6100-6198 73149
Haven Cir 73130
Haven Dr 73130
Haven Pl 73120
Haven Way 73120
W Havenwood Dr 73110
Haverhill Pl 73120
Hawk Dr 73150
Hawkins Dr 73169
Hawthorn Dr 73120
Hawthorne Dr 73110
Hawthorne Ln 73162

Hay Stack Ln 73170
Hayden Ln 73112
Hazelwood Dr 73110
Hazelwood St 73160
Heather Ln 73160
Heather Wood Ct & Dr 73160
Heathfield Ln 73173
Hedge Dr 73110
Hedgewood Dr 73160
E Hefner Rd
  100-399 73114
  1000-5299 73131
  7200-7799 73151
W Hefner Rd
  100-1399 73114
  1500-2399 73120
  2304-2304 73156
  2400-4098 73120
  2401-4099 73120
  5700-7799 73162
  7800-7998 73162
  7800-7800 73172
  7801-7999 73162
Hefner Pointe Dr 73120
Hefner Village Blvd, Cir, Ct, Dr, Pl & Ter 73162
Helm Dr 73130
Helm Pkwy 73149
Helm St 73118
Hemingford Ct & Ln 73120
Hemingway Dr 73118
Hemlock Cir 73162
Hemlock Ln
  3400-3499 73120
  4600-4799 73162
Hemstead Pl 73116
Henderson Dr 73139
Henley Ave, Pl & St 73131
S Henney Rd
  7300-8899 73150
  11100-11298 73165
  11300-12699 73165
  12701-12799 73165
S Henrietta Ave 73115
SW Hentrens St 73169
Hepler Dr 73150
Herbert Dr 73130
Heritage Cir 73160
Heritage Pl 73110
Heritage Oaks Dr 73120
Heritage Park Dr & Rd 73120
Heritage Square Rd 73120
SW Herleara St 73109
Heron Ct 73179
Heron Ln 73170
Hertz Quail Springs Pkwy 73134
Hester St 73114
Heyman St 73108
Hickory Ln 73110
N Hickory Ln 73160
S Hickory Ln 73160
Hickory Creek Blvd 73170
Hickory Hollow Dr 73142
Hickory Sign Post Rd 73116
Hickory Stick Rd 73120
Hicks Ln 73129
Hidden Canyon Rd 73165
Hidden Creek Way 73117
Hidden Forest Blvd 73142
Hidden Hollow Ln 73151
Hidden Lake Cir 73160
Hiddleston Cir 73135
N High Ave 73117
S High Ave 73129
High Meadow Ct 73170
High Meadow Dr 73120
High Meadow Ln 73160
Highfield Ct 73159
S Highland Ave 73110
Highland Dr 73160
N Highland Dr
  1300-1399 73117
  1700-1799 73111
  1801-2599 73111

N Highland Pl 73116
Highland Rd 73110
S Highland Rd 73110
Highland Park Blvd 73120
S Highland Park Dr 73129
Highlander Dr 73160
Highley Dr 73111
Highline Blvd 73108
Highside Ct 73120
Highview Dr 73151
Hill Rd 73170
E Hill St
  1-999 73105
  1600-1699 73111
W Hill St
  400-1099 73118
  2900-3099 73112
Hill Cross Ct 73159
Hillahay Dr 73170
Hillcrest Ave 73160
N Hillcrest Ave 73116
S Hillcrest Dr 73159
S Hillcrest Ter 73159
Hillers Rd 73132
Hillridge Dr 73141
Hills Cir & Dr 73160
Hillside Dr 73115
Hilltop Ct 73110
Hilltop Dr
  900-999 73160
  5800-6399 73121
Hilltop Ln 73169
Hilltop Rd
  3200-3299 73110
  6000-9799 73145
  14301-14497 73165
  14499-14899 73165
Hillview Dr 73150
Hinchey Ln 73179
Hisel Rd 73115
S Hiwassee Rd
  6100-8999 73150
  9000-9398 73165
  9400-16399 73165
Hobbiton Ct 73170
Holden Dr 73145
Holiday Pl 73112
Holland 73131
Holli Ln 73165
S Holliday Ave 73115
Hollow Oak Dr 73160
Hollow Rock Rd 73120
S Holly 73169
N Holly Ave 73127
Holly Dr 73110
Holly Ln 73110
Holly Brooke Ln 73135
Hollyhock Dr 73142
E & N Holman Ct & Pl 73110
Holmboe Ave 73114
Holoway Dr 73110
Homa Ave 73111
Homestead Rd 73165
Honey Tree Ln 73151
Honeysuckle Ln 73130
Honeysuckle Rd 73159
N Hood St 73111
Hope Dr 73160
Horsepen Rd 73173
Horseshoe Bnd 73169
E Horseshoe Ln 73160
Horseshoe Rd 73162
N Howard Ave 73160
S Howard Ave 73160
Howard Dr
  1-1599 73115
  9900-9999 73162
Hoyt Ave 73114
S Huddleston Dr 73135
Hudiburg Cir 73108
Hudiburg Dr 73110
N Hudson Ave
  1-397 73102
  399-1000 73102
  1002-1098 73102
  1100-3099 73103
  3100-5499 73118
  6700-7799 73116
  7900-11599 73114
S Hudson Ave
  100-199 73102
  300-4899 73109
  6700-10499 73139
  14200-14999 73170
Hudson Dr 73150
Hudson Pl 73110
Hughson Ave 73141
Hummingbird Cir & Ln 73162
Hunter Blvd 73179
Hunterfield Ave 73179
Hunters Run 73130
Hunters Glen Ct 73160
Hunters Hill Rd 73127
Hunting Hill Ln 73116
Huntington Ave 73116
Huntington Rd 73130
Huntleigh Ct & Dr 73120
Huntly Dr 73115
Hurst Ct 73114
Hyde Park Dr 73162
SE I 240 St 73150
E I 240 Service Rd
  1-1699 73149
  3000-3398 73135
  3400-6899 73135
  6901-6999 73135
  11200-12499 73150
W I 240 Service Rd
  1-1299 73139
  1300-2899 73159
I 35 Service Rd 73160
N I 35 Service Rd
  801-2797 73160
  2799-2899 73160
  2901-2997 73111
  2901-3399 73160
  2999-3399 73111
  3401-5199 73111
  7300-7398 73121
  8300-12299 73131
S I 35 Service Rd
  601-8997 73160
  601-601 73153
  1600-4700 73129
  4702-5598 73129
  4801-5599 73129
  4801-4801 73143
  6000-8999 73149
  8999-9599 73160
  9601-9699 73160
E I 40 Service Rd 73150
W I 40 Service Rd
  3700-4499 73108
  4700-4998 73128
  5000-9599 73128
E I 44 Service Rd
  200-299 73105
  301-599 73105
  1201-2699 73111
N I 44 Service Rd 73112
W I 44 Service Rd
  2100-3099 73112
  3022-3022 73157
  3100-3298 73112
  3101-3299 73112
Ians Pl 73160
N Idaho St 73117
SE Idell Dr 73165
N & W Idylwild Dr 73110
Ina Mae Ave 73115
N Independence Ave
  1100-3099 73107
  3100-6399 73112
  6800-7199 73116
S Independence Ave
  1800-2799 73108
  3101-3797 73119
  3799-5599 73119
  6200-8699 73159
  13800-14199 73170
E Indian Dr 73110
Indian Creek Blvd 73120

Indian Creek Ct 73120
Indian Creek Dr 73130
Indian Creek Pl 73120
N Indiana Ave
  100-2999 73106
  3100-4699 73118
  13400-13599 73134
S Indiana Ave
  1200-2999 73108
  3000-3499 73119
  6400-6598 73159
  6600-9699 73159
  14600-14899 73170
S Indiana Pl 73119
Indigo Rd 73159
Industrial Blvd
  100-399 73160
  401-599 73160
  8500-8799 73145
Ingram Dr 73162
Inland Rd 73132
Inman Dr 73127
Innsbrook Ln 73142
Interpace St 73135
Interstate 35 Frontage Rd 73160
S Interstate 44 Service Rd
  4201-4399 73119
  11300-11599 73173
  11601-11999 73173
  14100-14499 73170
Inverness Ave 73120
N Ione Dr 73122
S Irving Dr 73160
N Irving St 73117
S Irving St 73129
Isaac Dr 73130
Island View Dr 73162
Itio Blvd 73129
S Ivanhoe St 73129
Ivy Ter 73165
Ivy Hill Dr 73170
SW Jachelan St 73125
Jacinth Ct 73170
Jack Dr 73132
Jacks Ave 73149
N Jackson Dr 73130
Jacob Dr 73160
E & W Jacobs Dr 73110
Jacqui Ln 73165
Jade Way 73135
Jadesdale Cir 73170
James Dr
  1300-1399 73119
  4100-4199 73145
E James Ter 73141
James L Dennis Dr 73162
S Jamie Dr 73170
Jan Cir 73115
S Janet St 73150
N & S Janeway Ave & Cir 73160
January Pl 73160
E & W Jarman Dr 73110
Jasmine Ln
  1000-1199 73110
  12700-12999 73142
Jason Dr 73135
Jason Ryan Cir 73160
Jasper Ave 73170
Jaycie Cir 73130
Jaymel Ln 73170
Jean Rd 73130
Jeanie Ct 73130
Jed Ln 73165
Jefferson Dr 73160
Jefferson Ln 73134
Jeffery Dr 73115
Jeffrey Laird Pl 73160
Jennifer Dr 73165
Jennifer Pl 73130
Jenny Ln 73135
Jenny St 73165
Jeri Pl 73162
S Jernigan Blvd 73128

Jersey Rd 73130
Jesse Trl 73150
Jet Dr 73110
Jetty Ct 73159
Jewell 73165
Jo Ann Dr 73119
Joan Dr 73130
Jobe Ave 73130
Jody 73149
S Jody Way 73165
Joel Mcdonald Dr 73134
Joes Dr 73149
John Fourteen Ave 73170
W John Kilpatrick Tpke 73114
John Robert Dr 73135
John Ryan Dr 73165
Johnnie Ter 73149
Johnny Bench Dr 73104
Johnston Dr 73119
Jones Ave 73145
Jones Blvd 73135
Jones Pl 73110
Jones Taber Rd 73150
N Jordan Ave
  1100-1300 73117
  1302-1498 73117
  1700-3699 73111
S Jordan Ave 73129
Jordan Dr 73160
Joshua Dr 73131
Joshua Ln 73165
Judy Dr 73115
Judy Ter 73160
Julie Ct 73127
Julie Dr 73160
Julie Pl 73127
Julie St 73165
Julies Trl 73160
N June Ave 73112
June Ln 73115
Juniper Ave 73130
Juniper Cir 73110
Jupiter Pl 73129
Jury Ln 73160
Justin Pl 73110
Kaden Rd 73132
Kaeylee Ln 73115
Karen Dr
  1600-1999 73115
  15800-15999 73165
S Karen Dr 73135
Karen Ln 73110
S Karen St 73135
Karla Ln 73132
Karsten Creek Dr 73160
Kasbaum Ln 73150
N Kate Ave
  500-1699 73117
  1900-2098 73111
  2100-2699 73111
S Kate Ave 73129
NE Katherine Pl 73114
Kathleen Dr 73110
Kathryn Way 73162
Kathy Ct 73120
S Kathy Dr 73135
Katie Cv 73131
Katie Beth Cir & Ln 73170
Katie Ridge Dr 73160
Kavel Dr 73127
N Kaye Dr 73141
Kaylee Way 73132
Kear Dr 73165
Keats Pl 73120
Keen Oaks Dr & St 73150
Keisa Cir 73139
Keith Ct
  1501-1697 73160
  1699-1799 73160
  3700-3799 73135
Keith Dr 73135
Kel Dr 73127
N Kelham Ave
  500-1499 73117
  1501-1699 73117
  1700-2399 73111
S Kelham Ave 73129
N Kelley Ave
  500-702 73117
  701-701 73136
  701-701 73152
  704-1498 73117
  801-1499 73117
  1800-1998 73111
  2000-7500 73111
  7502-7698 73111
  8000-13499 73131
  14300-14599 73114
S Kelley Ave
  3300-3699 73129
  6000-6699 73149
Kelly Cir 73130
Kelly Dr 73160
Kelsi Dr 73160
Ken Rd 73165
Kendra Dr 73110
Kenilworth Rd
  900-1299 73114
  1300-1499 73120
Kenley Way 73142
Kennington Ln 73150
Kenny Cir 73132
Kensington Ct 73132
Kensington Dr 73160
N Kensington Rd 73132
W Kensington Rd 73132
Kent Dr
  2600-3199 73120
  9600-9799 73130
Kentish St 73132
N Kentucky Ave
  300-3099 73106
  3100-4299 73118
S Kentucky Ave
  1000-2999 73108
  3000-5899 73119
  6000-9099 73159
S Kentucky Pl 73108
Kenyon Dr 73127
Keri Cir 73170
E & W Kerr Dr 73110
Kerry Ln 73120
Ketch St 73107
Kevin Dr 73129
E Key Blvd 73110
N Key Blvd 73110
Key Pl 73112
Keystone Cir & Rd 73114
Kim Ct 73120
Kim Dr 73115
Kim Marie Ln 73132
Kimberling Dr 73160
Kimberly Rd 73132
Kimberlyn Rd 73162
Kindling Ln 73135
N King Ave 73130
King Dr 73110
Kings Cir 73162
Kings Ct
  700-1299 73160
  3700-4299 73121
Kings Mnr 73160
Kings Rd 73160
NE Kings Row 73121
Kings Way 73120
Kings Court Cir 73160
Kings Manor Ct 73132
Kingsbridge Dr 73162
Kingsbrook Rd 73142
Kingsbury Ln 73116
Kingsgate Dr
  10000-10499 73159
  10900-12699 73170
Kingsgate Ln 73170
Kingsgate Rd 73159
S Kingsgate Rd 73159
Kingsgate Ter 73170
Kingsley Ln 73128
Kingsridge Dr 73170
Kingsridge Rd 73132
Kingsridge Ter 73170

Kingston Rd 73122
Kingston Way 73120
Kingswick Dr 73162
Kingswood Cir 73170
Kinkaid Dr 73119
Kirby Dr 73160
E & W Kittyhawk Dr 73110
Kiva Ct 73135
N Klein Ave 73106
S Klein Ave
200-399 73108
2700-5999 73109
6100-10399 73139
Kleiner Ave 73169
Klipspringer St 73110
Knight Hill Rd 73142
Knight Island Dr 73142
Knight Lake Dr 73132
Knightsbridge Rd 73132
Knollwood Ter 73160
Knottingham 73130
Knox Dr 73115
Koch Dr 73130
Koelsch Dr 73117
Korie Cir 73160
Kovelda Dr 73165
Krauss Rd 73121
Kristie Dr 73115
Kristie Ln 73130
Kristin Ct 73170
Kristina Pl 73162
S Krowse Dr 73115
Kudu St 73110
E Kuhl Ter 73149
Kyle Ct 73160
Kyle Dr 73170
Kyle Robert Ln 73160
Kylie Dr & Pl 73160
Kysela Dr & St 73170
N Lackey St 73107
Ladd Cir 73160
Ladera Cir 73160
Ladonna Dr 73170
Lafayette Dr 73119
Lago Dr 73160
Lago Strada 73170
N Laird Ave
500-799 73104
2400-7199 73105
8501-8599 73114
S Laird Ave 73129
N Lake Ave 73118
Lake Ln 73162
Lake Aluma Dr 73121
N & W Lake Front Dr .. 73132
S Lake Hefner Dr
3700-4499 73116
4800-4899 73132
Lake Hefner Pkwy 73120
Lake Hickory Dr 73165
Lake Oaks Dr 73165
Lake Park Dr 73170
Lakeaire Dr 73132
Lakecrest Dr
700-2599 73170
9000-9799 73159
Lakehurst Dr 73120
Lakeland Rd & Ter 73162
Lakepointe Dr 73116
Lakeridge Cir & Run 73170
NE Lakerlin St 73111
Lakeshore Dr 73120
W Lakeshore Dr 73132
Lakeside Cir 73120
Lakeside Dr
2000-2099 73130
2600-10899 73120
S Lakeside Dr 73179
W Lakeside Dr 73127
Lakeview Dr 73160
N Lakeview Dr 73127
S Lakeview Dr 73165
W Lakeview Dr 73127
W Lakeview Pl 73127
N Lakeway Cir & Dr 73132
Lakewood Cir 73132

Lamar Dr 73115
Lamp Post Ln 73120
Lancaster Cir 73132
Lancaster Ln 73116
Lance Dr
4800-4999 73150
8100-8499 73132
Lancelot Pl 73132
Lancer Ln 73132
Lanceshire Cir 73162
Lanceshire Ln 73135
Lancet Ct & Ln 73120
N Land Ave
1300-2899 73107
3600-3899 73112
S Land Ave
2600-2799 73108
4900-5599 73119
6200-10199 73159
12000-13699 73170
S Land Ct 73170
N Land Pl 73112
Land Run Rd
2700-2899 73160
13900-14099 73170
Land Rush St 73107
Landing Rd 73132
Lands End Ct 73159
Lanesboro Dr 73120
Laneway Cir & Dr 73159
Lanie Ln 73160
Lansbrook Ct 73132
Lansbrook Ln
6200-9399 73132
9400-9499 73162
Lansdowne Ln 73120
Lapis Ln 73170
Larchmont Ln 73116
Lariet Ln 73115
Larimore Ln 73151
Larissa Ln 73112
Larkin Ln 73130
Larkspur Ln 73159
Larkspur Rd 73160
Larkwood Dr 73115
Lasley Dr 73127
Latham Ct 73132
S Laura Dr 73179
N Laura Ln 73151
Laura Kate Ct 73130
Laurel Dr 73162
Laurel Ln 73130
Laurel Rd 73162
Laurel Valley Ct 73142
Lauren Dr 73160
Lauren Ln 73110
Laurie Ln 73142
Laurin Ln 73142
Laverne St 73135
Lawn Dr 73115
Lawrence Dr 73145
N Lawson Ave 73130
S Lawson Ave 73130
Lawson Ln 73132
Lawton 73160
Lawton Dr 73159
Lazy Ln 73115
Le Richardson Cir 73121
Leaf Dr 73160
Leafcrest Dr 73160
Leafhurst Rd 73160
Leafring Cir 73173
Leaning Elm Ct & Rd .. 73120
Leatherwood Cir 73165
N Lee Ave
1-1099 73102
1100-3099 73103
3700-5099 73118
10900-11899 73114
S Lee Ave
400-5999 73109
6400-6499 73139
Lee Ln 73120
N Lee Pl 73114
Leftwich Dr 73165
Legacy Ct 73170

Legacy Crossing Dr 73169
Legacy Hill Rd 73170
Lehenbaur Ln 73165
Leisure Ct & Dr 73110
Lejean Dr 73130
N Lela St 73127
S Lenora St 73129
N Lenox Ave 73116
Lenox Ct 73118
Leoma Ln 73150
Leonard Ln 73110
Leonhardt Dr 73115
Lerida Ln 73173
N Leroy Dr 73127
Leslie Dr 73115
Leslie Beachler Ln 73130
Lester Ln 73139
Leverich Ct 73160
Levescy Rd 73150
Lewis Ln
1900-1999 73160
5001-5099 73121
Lexi Ct 73130
Lexington Dr 73173
N Libby Ave
1400-1599 73127
4000-4299 73122
4300-4799 73122
6400-7099 73132
S Libby St 73170
S Liberty Ave 73119
Liberty Crk 73165
Liberty Dr 73160
Liberty Pkwy 73110
NW Liberty St 73107
Liberty Oak 73165
Liberty Trails Blvd 73135
Life Style Dr & Ln 73127
Lighthouse Ct 73159
S Lightner Ln 73179
W, E & N Lilac Ct &
Ln 73110
Lilly Ln 73135
Lilly Garden Ln 73170
Lincenes Dr 73115
NW Linchita St 73122
N Lincoln Ave 73160
N Lincoln Blvd
1-897 73104
899-1399 73104
1401-1699 73104
1700-6599 73105
9700-11699 73114
S Lincoln Blvd
1-99 73104
101-199 73104
600-698 73129
701-799 73129
Lincoln Sq 73135
Lincolnshire Rd 73159
Linda Ave 73112
Linda Ln
1900-1999 73160
2000-2899 73115
SE Linda Ln 73149
Lindee Ln 73179
Linden St 73108
W Lindley Ave 73107
Lindon Dr 73170
N Lindsay Ave
400-1699 73104
1700-4399 73105
8500-10199 73114
S Lindsay Ave
1600-5999 73129
6300-6699 73149
Lindsey Ln 73160
N Linn Ave
1-2499 73107
3700-5899 73112
10900-10999 73120
S Linn Ave
2300-2899 73108
3000-5599 73119
6000-10099 73159
10500-11699 73170
Linwood Blvd 73106

Linwood Diagonal 73106
Lions Park Pl 73110
Lippert Ln 73162
Lisa Ln 73115
Little Ln 73160
Little Pond Dr 73162
Little River Cir 73160
Live Oak Dr 73110
Lloyd Ave & Dr 73130
Loch Ln 73115
E & W Lockheed Ct &
Dr 73110
Lockhoma Ln 73160
N & S Locust Dr & Ln .. 73110
Loftin Dr 73130
E Lois Ln 73150
Lois Arlene Cir 73160
Lolly Ln 73160
Lombardy Ln 73112
Lombardy Rd 73118
London Ln 73110
London Way 73132
Long Beach Dr 73139
Long Lake Blvd 73170
Long Meadow Rd 73162
Longridge Rd 73115
Longview Dr 73162
Lonnie Ln 73170
Loren Dr 73160
Lorene Ave 73130
Lorien Way 73170
Lost Creek Dr 73160
N Lottie Ave
100-1499 73117
1501-1599 73117
1700-6599 73111
6601-6699 73111
12100-12199 73131
Lotus Ave 73130
Lou Anna Pl 73130
Louisburg Dr 73162
Louise Ave 73106
Love Dr 73135
Lowery Ln 73132
S Lowery St 73129
Lowrie Ln 73159
Loyd Ln 73160
Lucas Dr 73150
Lullaby Ln 73130
Lunow Dr 73135
Lurk Ln 73142
S Lyman Rd 73150
Lyndon Cir & Rd 73120
Lynn Ln 73120
Lynn Fry Blvd 73130
Lyon Blvd 73112
N Lyon Blvd 73107
N Lyons Dr 73111
Lyrewood Cir, Ct, Ln &
Ter 73132
Lyric Ln 73130
Lysander Pl 73128
Lytle Dr 73127
S Mable Ave 73129
Macalpine St 73160
N Macarthur Blvd
2-8 73127
10-3099 73127
3100-3399 73122
3400-6399 73122
6400-9399 73132
9500-12299 73162
12300-14399 73142
S Macarthur Blvd
200-2899 73128
3200-5999 73179
6100-9699 73169
13500-15600 73173
15602-15798 73173
Macarthur Dr 73110
N Macarthur Ter 73132
Macarthur Park Ln 73127
E Mack Dr 73130
Mackel Dr 73170
Mackelman Dr 73135
Mackenzie Dr 73160

Mackinac Island Dr 73142
Macomber Way 73130
Macys Pl 73160
Madeline Ln 73160
Madera St & Ter 73129
Madison Ave
4000-4199 73160
11000-11299 73130
E Madison Ave 73105
Madison Ct 73160
E Madison St 73111
Madison Place Dr 73160
S Madole Blvd 73159
Madrid Cir 73170
Maehs Cir, Dr, Ln, Pl &
Ter 73162
Magdalena Dr 73119
S Magerus St 73128
Magnolia Ln 73110
Magnolia Park 73120
N Magnolia St 73117
S Magnolia St 73129
Mahler Pl 73120
Maiden Ln 73142
Main St 73115
E Main St
1-399 73104
100-2299 73160
8401-8497 73110
8499-8899 73110
9500-9699 73130
W Main St
100-1099 73160
100-699 73102
701-799 73102
800-1899 73106
2100-2799 73107
Major Ave 73120
Malaga Way 73173
Mallard Dr 73115
Mallorca Dr 73173
N Mallory St 73121
N Maloney Dr & St 73121
Mamosa Dr 73142
Manchester Dr 73120
Manchester Ln 73127
N Maney St 73112
Manhattan Dr 73160
NE Maninerl St 73117
Manns Dr 73111
S Manor Cir 73139
N Manor Dr 73107
Mansfield Ave & St 73115
Mantle Ave 73132
Mantle Ct 73162
Mantle Dr 73162
Mantle Ln 73162
Maple Dr 73110
Maple Grv 73120
Maple Ln 73170
Maple Hollow Ct 73120
Maple Leaf Dr 73170
Maple Ridge Ct & Rd .. 73120
Maple Valley Dr 73170
Marathon Dr 73160
Marbella Dr
11300-11999 73173
16900-16999 73170
Marblewood Dr 73179
Marforio Pl 73170
Margaret 73150
S Margene Dr 73130
S Maricle Way 73165
Marie St 73131
Marilyn Dr 73160
N Marilyn Dr 73121
Marilyn St 73105
N Marion Ave 73106
S Marion Ave 73130
Mark Cir 73160
Mark Dr 73115
S Mark Dr 73165
Mark St 73130
Mark Trl 73141
Mark Wood St 73130
Market Dr 73114

N Markwell Ave
100-899 73160
600-2199 73127
8900-8999 73132
11100-11399 73162
S Markwell Ave
100-298 73160
300-399 73160
400-498 73128
500-599 73128
N Markwell Ct 73162
N Markwell Dr 73162
N Markwell Pl 73127
Marlboro Ln 73116
Marlow Dr 73110
Marlow Ln
6000-6099 73132
11900-11999 73165
E Mars St 73141
Marsh Ln 73170
Marsh St 73130
E Marshall Dr 73110
Marston Cir 73120
N Martin Luther King Ave
900-1699 73117
1700-7299 73111
7301-7499 73111
S Martin Luther King
Ave 73117
Mary Ave 73127
Mary Ann Cir & Ln 73150
Mary Claire Dr 73162
Marydale Ave 73130
Marywood Cir 73135
Mashburn Blvd 73162
Mason Dr
500-699 73129
4100-4199 73112
S Mason Dr 73150
Masons Dr 73142
N Massachusetts Ave .. 73117
Massey Ter 73150
Mattern Dr 73118
Matthews Ave 73162
S Matthews Pl 73115
E & N Maxwell Dr 73121
N May Ave
1-2999 73107
3001-3099 73107
3100-6399 73112
6400-7899 73116
7900-13699 73120
13700-15399 73134
S May Ave
1-199 73107
200-2999 73108
3000-5799 73119
5801-5999 73119
6000-9699 73159
9701-10099 73159
10500-16699 73170
May Park Cir & Dr 73159
Mayberry Ln & Pl 73142
Maybrook Dr 73159
N Mayfair Dr 73112
Maynord Cir 73110
Maypole Ct 73159
N Mayside Dr 73127
Mayview Cir & Ct 73159
S Maywood Ln 73150
W Mcarthur Dr 73110
Mcauley Blvd
4200-4499 73120
13900-13999 73134
14001-14099 73134
Mcclaren St 73160
N Mccormick St 73127
Mccracken Dr 73115
Mcdonald Dr 73130
Mcgregor Dr 73130
Mcintosh Ave 73130
N Mckee Blvd 73132
N Mckinley Ave
1-3099 73106
3100-4900 73118
4902-4998 73118
8000-11299 73114

S Mckinley Ave
1100-2299 73108
2300-5899 73109
6000-10399 73139
10600-10699 73170
S Mckinley Ct 73139
Mckinley Pl 73108
S Mckinley Pl 73139
E Mckinney Ln 73150
Mckittrick Dr 73160
Mclaughlin Dr 73170
S Mclemore Dr 73159
Mcmechan Pkwy 73105
N Mcmillan Ave
1100-1899 73127
8500-8999 73132
Mcnarney Ave 73145
Mcnickle St 73145
Mead Cir & Ln 73170
S Meade Pl 73130
Meadow Ln
100-199 73110
3500-3799 73160
N Meadow Ln 73110
SW Meadow Cliff Dr 73159
Meadow Creek Ln 73165
Meadow Crest Dr 73170
Meadow Land Dr 73160
Meadow Lark Ln
1800-1999 73130
3600-3699 73120
8400-8599 73132
10600-10799 73130
Meadow Run Dr 73160
Meadowbrook Dr
100-199 73160
3300-3699 73110
Meadowgreen Dr 73110
Meadowlake Farms Dr . 73170
Meadowoak Dr 73110
N Meadowood Dr 73110
Meadowpark Dr 73110
Meadowridge Dr 73110
Meadows Dr 73120
Meadowvale Dr 73110
Meadowview Dr 73115
NW Meancenw St 73127
Medina Ln 73170
Meeker Dr 73120
Meench Dr
2100-2199 73170
4700-4799 73115
Megan Cir 73170
Megan Dr 73135
Mehl Dr 73108
Melcat Dr 73179
Melinda Ln 73130
Mellow Hill Dr 73120
Melody Dr 73130
Melrose Dr 73160
Melrose Ln 73127
S Melrose Ln 73109
Melton Ct 73162
Melton Dr 73132
Memorial Cir 73142
E Memorial Rd
1-100 73114
102-798 73114
201-299 73131
301-799 73114
1100-1999 73131
W Memorial Rd
1-1399 73114
1600-2899 73134
2901-4499 73134
3000-3398 73120
3700-3798 73134
4000-4498 73120
4500-7600 73142
7602-7898 73142
Memorial Park Dr 73134
W Memorial Park Dr 73120
Memory Ln 73112
Mercury Rd 73145
N Meridian Ave
1-1599 73107
1600-1699 73127

1700-3099 ... 73107
3100-6399 ... 73112
4301-5099 ... 73112
6400-6899 ... 73116
10900-13599 ... 73120
13800-13899 ... 73134
S Meridian Ave
1-199 ... 73107
300-2999 ... 73108
3000-5399 ... 73119
6600-6699 ... 73159
11200-15999 ... 73173
N Meridian Ct
2600-2899 ... 73127
3100-3499 ... 73122
N Meridian Pl
2700-2799 ... 73127
5800-6099 ... 73122
11600-11799 ... 73162
SE Merreens St ... 73135
Messenger Ln ... 73160
S Meta Ave ... 73119
N Meta St ... 73107
Metlock Ln ... 73160
Metropolitan Ave ... 73108
Meyers Pl ... 73111
Michael Ct ... 73132
Michael Dr ... 73115
W Michael Dr ... 73110
Michael Pl ... 73115
Michell Dr ... 73141
Michelle Ct ... 73160
Michelle Ln ... 73127
Michelle Rd ... 73165
N Michigan St
1700-1999 ... 73121
5100-5299 ... 73111
Mickey Rd ... 73115
S Mickey Mantle Dr ... 73104
Mid America Blvd
400-499 ... 73110
7900-8199 ... 73135
E Mid America Blvd ... 73110
W Mid America Blvd ... 73110
Middlesex Dr ... 73120
Midfield Cross St ... 73159
Midridge Dr ... 73141
N Midwest Blvd
100-1599 ... 73110
1401-1499 ... 73110
1700-6099 ... 73141
S Midwest Blvd
100-298 ... 73110
300-2999 ... 73110
6200-6499 ... 73145
10900-13398 ... 73165
13400-15799 ... 73165
15801-16399 ... 73165
Milam Ct ... 73111
Milano Ln ... 73120
Milano Rd ... 73173
Mildred Ave ... 73105
Miles Ln ... 73132
N Military Ave
2500-3000 ... 73106
3002-3098 ... 73106
3100-3198 ... 73118
3200-5899 ... 73118
7900-10899 ... 73114
NE Military Cir ... 73111
Military Ct ... 73118
Mill Hollow Ct ... 73131
Millbrook Ln ... 73162
N Miller Ave
3700-6299 ... 73112
11000-11799 ... 73120
S Miller Ave
500-2399 ... 73108
3000-4699 ... 73119
10500-11599 ... 73170
N Miller Blvd ... 73107
S Miller Blvd ... 73159
Miller Cir ... 73162
N Miller Pl ... 73112
S Miller Pl ... 73108
Miller St ... 73145
Millstone Dr ... 73179
Milrace Ln ... 73132
E Mimosa Dr ... 73110
Mindy Ln ... 73130
N Minnie Ln ... 73127
Minute Man Dr ... 73179
Miramar Blvd ... 73111
N Miramar Blvd ... 73117
N Missouri Ave
500-1699 ... 73117
1700-6699 ... 73111
S Missouri Ave ... 73129
Mistletoe Ave ... 73115
Mistletoe Ct ... 73142
Mistletoe Dr ... 73142
Misty Ln ... 73160
Misty Glen Cir ... 73142
Misty Hollow Dr ... 73110
Misty Hollow Ln ... 73151
Mitchell Ave ... 73145
N Mitchell Dr ... 73110
W Mitchell Dr ... 73110
Mobile Dr & Way ... 73107
Mobility Dr ... 73179
Moccasin Ln ... 73170
Mockingbird Ln ... 73110
Moiselle St ... 73110
Monarch Pass ... 73162
Monica Dr ... 73115
Monica Ln ... 73160
Monroney Dr ... 73110
Montclair Dr ... 73115
Montclaire Dr ... 73130
Monte Dr & Pl ... 73119
Monte Cavallo Cir ... 73170
Montego Ter ... 73170
Monterey Dr ... 73139
Monticello Ct ... 73111
Monticello Dr ... 73134
Montrose Dr ... 73115
E Moon St ... 73141
Moon Beam Dr ... 73162
N Moore Ave
600-2799 ... 73160
1800-2299 ... 73141
S Moore Ave ... 73130
Moore Estates Dr ... 73149
Moose St ... 73110
Moraine Ave ... 73130
N Morgan Dr ... 73160
S Morgan Dr ... 73160
N Morgan Rd ... 73127
S Morgan Rd
300-1999 ... 73128
3000-5799 ... 73179
Moritz Ct ... 73162
Morning Glory Dr ... 73159
Morning Glory St ... 73160
Morning Song Dr ... 73150
Morning View Rd ... 73131
E & W Morningside Dr ... 73110
N Morris Dr ... 73121
Morris Ln ... 73112
Morrison Ln ... 73130
Morton Ave ... 73128
Moseley Rd ... 73141
Mosteller Dr ... 73112
N Moulton Ct ... 73127
N Moulton Dr ... 73127
S Moulton Dr ... 73179
Moultrie Ave ... 73112
Mount Pleasant Dr ... 73110
Mulberry Ln ... 73116
Mundell St ... 73145
Munser St ... 73115
Murcielago Ct ... 73170
N Murphy ... 73121
Murray Ct ... 73165
Murray Dr ... 73110
SW Murray Dr ... 73119
Musgrave Blvd ... 73114
Mustang St ... 73115
N Mustang Plant Rd ... 73127
Muzny Ln ... 73135
N Myers Ter ... 73141
Myriad Gdns ... 73102
E, W & N Myrtle Dr & Ln ... 73110
Mystic Pl ... 73150
N Ave ... 73145
Nabors Dr ... 73145
N Nail Pkwy ... 73160
Nancy Rd ... 73131
Nancy Jane Ct ... 73160
Nathan Ln ... 73160
National Ave & Blvd ... 73110
Nawassa Dr ... 73130
Nazih Zuhdi Dr ... 73105
N Nebraska Ave
500-1399 ... 73117
1700-5099 ... 73111
S Nebraska Ave ... 73129
Necia St ... 73160
Neighbors Ln ... 73115
Nelson Park Cir & Pl ... 73160
Nemaha ... 73160
Neptune Dr ... 73116
N Nesbitt Ave
2800-3099 ... 73107
3200-3599 ... 73112
New Haven Ct ... 73160
New London Ave ... 73160
Newberry Rd ... 73141
Newcastle Blvd ... 73108
Newcastle Rd
3500-4499 ... 73119
6000-7299 ... 73179
7500-7799 ... 73169
Newey Ave ... 73150
Newey Cir ... 73110
Newman Cir & Dr ... 73162
Newport Ave
900-1099 ... 73160
4100-4199 ... 73112
Newport Dr ... 73115
Newport St ... 73112
Nichols Rd
7000-7099 ... 73116
7100-7399 ... 73120
7400-9999 ... 73120
Nichols Gate Cir ... 73116
Nicholson Dr ... 73162
N Nicklas Ave
1400-1599 ... 73127
3700-4299 ... 73122
6400-6499 ... 73132
S Nicklas Ave ... 73128
W Nicklas Ave ... 73132
Night Hawk Ct ... 73145
Nighthawk Ln ... 73160
Nightshade Dr ... 73170
Nile Ave ... 73114
Nimitz Blvd ... 73112
Nittany Cir & Dr ... 73120
Noah Pkwy ... 73132
Noble Dr ... 73115
S Noma Rd ... 73150
Norcrest Dr ... 73121
Norham Ct ... 73118
Norman Ave
2400-2699 ... 73127
6200-6399 ... 73122
N Norman Ave ... 73160
S Norman Ave ... 73160
Norman Rd ... 73122
N Norman Rd ... 73132
N Norman St ... 73122
Normandy St ... 73111
Normandy Ter ... 73142
Norrington Ln ... 73120
North Ct ... 73111
North Pl ... 73107
North St ... 73108
Northampton Pl ... 73120
Northern Hills Rd ... 73121
Northgate Ave ... 73162
Northlake Dr ... 73142
Northland Rd ... 73120
Northridge Dr ... 73132
Northridge Rd ... 73160
Northridge Ter ... 73132
E Northrup Dr ... 73110
Northstar Dr ... 73142
Northview Dr ... 73142
Northway Ct, St & Ter ... 73162
Norwich Ct ... 73132
Norwood Pl ... 73120
Notting Hill Dr ... 73160
N Nottingham Way ... 73160
Nottoway Dr ... 73130
Novona Pl ... 73170
Oak Ave ... 73130
Oak Dr ... 73170
Oak Ln
1600-1699 ... 73127
14500-14798 ... 73165
Oak St ... 73110
Oak Cliff Dr ... 73130
Oak Cliff St ... 73170
Oak Creek Dr
600-1199 ... 73160
9100-9199 ... 73130
S Oak Creek Dr ... 73109
N Oak Grove Dr ... 73110
Oak Hill Dr
1000-1199 ... 73110
8300-8899 ... 73150
Oak Hollow Dr ... 73130
Oak Hollow Rd ... 73120
Oak Manor Dr & Ter ... 73135
Oak Park Dr & Ter ... 73130
Oak Tree Dr, Ln & Ter ... 73130
Oak Valley Dr ... 73110
Oak Valley Rd ... 73135
Oakbrook Dr ... 73115
Oakcliff Dr ... 73135
Oakcliff Rd ... 73120
Oakdale Dr ... 73127
Oakgrove Dr ... 73173
Oakhill Dr
1400-1699 ... 73127
8700-8799 ... 73150
Oakhill Ln ... 73127
Oakhurst Dr ... 73110
Oakland Cir ... 73142
N Oaklawn Ave ... 73121
Oakleaf Ln ... 73131
Oakmont Cir & Dr ... 73131
Oakmont Valley Dr ... 73131
Oakridge Dr ... 73110
N Oaks Ave ... 73110
Oaks Way ... 73131
Oaks Crossing Rd ... 73165
Oakside Dr ... 73160
Oaksplinter Ln ... 73173
N Oakview Dr ... 73110
Oakview Rd ... 73165
Oakwood Dr
1-99 ... 73121
9100-9199 ... 73130
S Oakwood Ln ... 73150
Oakwood St ... 73160
Oakwood East Blvd ... 73130
Ocama Blvd ... 73110
Odom Rd ... 73139
Odom Way ... 73170
Oelke Dr ... 73110
Ohara Ln ... 73130
N Oklahoma Ave
1-699 ... 73104
701-1399 ... 73104
2400-3099 ... 73105
9500-11599 ... 73114
S Oklahoma Ave
1-299 ... 73104
2300-4499 ... 73129
Oklahoma Tower ... 73102
Old Brompton Rd ... 73132
Old Bryant ... 73160
Old Colony Rd ... 73130
Old Farm Cir ... 73120
Old Farm Pl ... 73120
Old Farm Rd
4100-4299 ... 73120
4500-4599 ... 73162
Old Forest Ln ... 73131
Old Glory Ln ... 73135
Old Hickory Ln ... 73116
Old Mill Rd
800-1198 ... 73160
1200-2799 ... 73160
11600-12199 ... 73131
Old Orchard Ln ... 73132
Old Pond Ct ... 73160
N & S Olde Bridge Rd ... 73160
Olde Copper Creek Rd ... 73160
Olde Harwick Cir & Dr ... 73162
Olde Tuscany Rd
9100-10499 ... 73169
10500-10999 ... 73173
Olde Warwick Dr ... 73162
Oldwick Cir ... 73162
N Olie Ave
1800-2399 ... 73106
3200-3799 ... 73118
6400-6799 ... 73116
7900-9399 ... 73114
S Olie Ave
2300-5199 ... 73109
6300-8999 ... 73139
S Olie Pl ... 73109
NW Oliver St ... 73107
Olivia Ln ... 73149
Olivine Ter ... 73170
E Ollie Ave ... 73130
Olympia Dr ... 73165
Olympic Dr ... 73160
N Omaha Ave ... 73116
Ontario Way ... 73139
Orange Dr ... 73130
Orchard Blvd ... 73130
Orchard Dr ... 73110
Orlando Rd ... 73120
Orleans Ct ... 73170
NE Orlie Dr ... 73121
S Osborne Way ... 73165
S Otella Ave ... 73128
Otterson Dr ... 73112
Outabounds Ct & Ln ... 73116
Outlet Shoppes Dr ... 73128
N Outpost Dr ... 73141
SW Oveneran St ... 73179
N & NE Overbrook Dr ... 73121
Overcourt Mnr ... 73132
Overhead Dr ... 73128
Overholser Ct & Dr ... 73127
Overland Dr ... 73115
Oxford Ct ... 73130
Oxford Way ... 73120
Oxlow Ct & Rd ... 73159
Paddington Ave ... 73142
Paddle Wheel Pl ... 73170
N Page Ave
1101-1699 ... 73117
1701-2199 ... 73111
Palamino Dr ... 73121
W Palm Pl ... 73128
Palmer Dr ... 73110
Pam Pl ... 73115
Pamalos Trl ... 73173
Pamona Ct ... 73139
Pamplona Way ... 73173
Panda Way ... 73165
Pantheon Cir ... 73170
SE Paralinc St ... 73129
Paramount Dr ... 73162
Park Ave ... 73102
Park Cir ... 73111
Park Ln ... 73111
Park Pl ... 73110
E Park Pl
1-799 ... 73104
1300-3399 ... 73117
2400-2499 ... 73160
N Park Pl ... 73160
W Park Pl
1-99 ... 73103
1000-2099 ... 73106
2100-4199 ... 73107
2400-2499 ... 73160
4500-4799 ... 73127
Park Glenn Dr ... 73160
Park Hill Rd ... 73142
Park Manor St ... 73116
Park Vista Dr ... 73115
Parke Ave & Pl ... 73130
Parke Ridge Ln ... 73130
Parker Dr
800-899 ... 73127
3000-3499 ... 73135
Parker Rd ... 73127
Parkland Pl ... 73142
Parklawn Dr ... 73110
Parkridge Dr ... 73132
E Parkridge Dr ... 73141
Parkridge Ter ... 73132
Parkside Ct & Dr ... 73160
S Parkview Ave ... 73119
N Parkview Cir ... 73170
Parkview Dr
1000-1199 ... 73110
2100-2199 ... 73170
Parkway Cir ... 73130
Parkway Dr ... 73160
Parkway Commons Dr ... 73134
Parkwood Ct ... 73160
Parkwood Ln ... 73132
Parkwoods Ct, Ln & Ter ... 73110
Parrianc Dr ... 73130
Partnership Dr ... 73131
Partridge Rd ... 73120
Paschall Ct ... 73132
Paseo ... 73103
Paseo Del Vita ... 73131
NW Passage ... 73132
Pat Ave ... 73149
Pat Murphy Dr ... 73112
N Pate Ave ... 73112
Pathway St ... 73160
Patricia Ave ... 73127
Patricia Dr ... 73130
Patrick Ct ... 73130
Patrick Dr ... 73127
N & S Patterson Dr ... 73160
Patti Pl ... 73120
Paul Dr ... 73160
Pauline Renee Dr ... 73160
W Peach St ... 73110
Peachtree Ave ... 73121
Peachtree Dr ... 73122
Peachtree Ln ... 73130
Peacock Cir ... 73130
Pear St ... 73130
Pearl Way ... 73115
Pearson Dr ... 73110
Pebble Ln ... 73132
Pecos Dr ... 73139
N & W Peebly Dr ... 73110
S Peggy Lou Dr ... 73165
Pelham Dr ... 73120
Pembroke Ter ... 73116
Pendell Dr ... 73116
N Peniel Ave ... 73132
N Peniel St ... 73127
S Peniel St ... 73128
Penn Ln ... 73160
Penn Pl ... 73118
N Penn Plz ... 73120
Penn Place Office Tower Ave ... 73118
Pennington Cir ... 73130
Pennington Way ... 73116
N Pennsylvania Ave
1-3099 ... 73107
3100-6199 ... 73112
6400-6699 ... 73116
9200-13699 ... 73120
13700-14999 ... 73134
S Pennsylvania Ave
1-17 ... 73107
19-99 ... 73107
900-2999 ... 73108
3000-5999 ... 73119
6000-9202 ... 73159
9201-9201 ... 73189
9204-10498 ... 73159
9301-10499 ... 73159
10500-17199 ... 73170
N Pennsylvania Pl ... 73120
Penny Dr ... 73110
S Penny Dr ... 73173
Penny Ln ... 73127
Penrith Ln ... 73114
Pentree Dr ... 73149
Pepper Tree Pl ... 73120
Pepperdine ... 73130
Peppertree Ln ... 73110
Peppertree Pl ... 73142
Pepperwell Oaks Dr ... 73165
Peregrine Dr ... 73170
Perimeter Rd ... 73145
Perimeter Center Dr & Pl ... 73112
N Perrine Dr ... 73141
Persimmon Dr ... 73120
Petrie Dr ... 73165
Pettee Ave ... 73108
Pheasant Cv & Ln ... 73162
Philbrook Dr ... 73109
N Phillips Ave
400-1699 ... 73104
2000-4299 ... 73105
8500-9299 ... 73114
S Phillips Ave
1200-5699 ... 73129
6300-6699 ... 73149
Phillips St ... 73160
Phinney Dr ... 73110
Picadilly Cir ... 73132
Picasso Dr ... 73170
Piccadilly Cir ... 73160
Pickford Ct & Ln ... 73159
Picnic Ln ... 73127
Pin Oak Rd ... 73170
Pinckney Ct ... 73162
NW Pindered St ... 73103
Pine Ave
2300-2999 ... 73128
3900-4099 ... 73115
N Pine Ave ... 73130
Pine Bluff Dr ... 73142
Pine Creek Dr ... 73130
Pine Ridge Rd ... 73120
Pinefield ... 73149
Pinehurst Dr ... 73130
Pinehurst Rd ... 73120
Pineridge Rd ... 73130
Pinewick Dr ... 73162
Pinewood Cir ... 73160
Pinewood Ct
700-799 ... 73160
1300-1399 ... 73110
Pinewood Dr
500-1805 ... 73160
1807-1899 ... 73160
8300-8499 ... 73135
Pinewood Forest Cir ... 73151
Pinnacle Pt ... 73170
S Pinto Pass ... 73179
Pioneer Ln ... 73160
Pioneer St ... 73107
Pittsburgh Ave ... 73120
NW Plachann St ... 73134
Placid Dr ... 73131
Placker Pl ... 73159
Planet Ct ... 73110
Plato Pl ... 73107
N Platt Cir ... 73170
Platt Ln ... 73160
Plaza Dr ... 73160
Plaza Ter ... 73120
Pleasant Dr
500-899 ... 73170
3300-3499 ... 73110
Pleasant Acres Dr ... 73150
Pleasant Valley Rd ... 73151
NE Plum Creek Cir ... 73131
Plum Hollow Dr ... 73142
Plum Thicket Pl & Rd ... 73162
Plumb Ct & Dr ... 73130
Plymouth Ct ... 73159
Plymouth Ln ... 73120
Pointon Rd ... 73150

Pole Rd
2000-9799 73160
7400-8099 73149
Pond Rd 73145
Pond Meadow Dr 73151
Ponderosa Blvd 73142
Pony Rd 73134
Poplar Dr 73160
N Poplar Ln 73130
Port Rush Dr 73160
N Porter Dr 73116
N Porter Pl 73117
N Portland Ave
100-3099 73107
3100-6399 73112
6400-7099 73116
11101-11197 73120
11199-12299 73120
13900-14699 73134
S Portland Ave
200-2999 73108
3100-3198 73119
3200-4200 73119
4202-5798 73119
6000-6499 73159
10700-10899 73173
11400-12699 73170
Portofino Strada 73170
Portsmouth Ct 73159
N Post Rd
100-1699 73130
1700-3100 73141
3102-3598 73141
S Post Rd
200-2999 73130
3100-7999 73150
15000-16399 73165
Post Oak Ln 73160
N Post Oak Rd 73105
Postside Ln 73132
Potter Ct 73130
Powell Rd 73165
Prado Dr 73170
Prairie Ln
3900-4399 73115
10500-10799 73162
14101-14397 73165
14399-14999 73165
Prairie Field Ln 73160
Prairie Grass Rd 73120
Prairie Ridge Rd 73135
Prairie Rose Ct & Rd 73120
Prairie View Ln 73142
E & W Pratt Dr 73110
Preakness Rd 73173
N Preston Dr 73122
Preston Hills Dr 73142
Price Dr
1100-1199 73160
11500-11899 73170
SE Pridendi St 73150
S Priellia Ave 73139
Primrose Ln 73159
Prince George St 73110
Princess Ln 73115
NW Prindend St 73162
Procter Pl 73110
Promise Ln 73135
N Prospect Ave 73111
S Prospect Ave 73129
Prosper Dr 73151
Pruitt Dr 73170
Pulchella Dr & Ln 73142
N Purdue Ave 73127
Purdue Ct 73127
Purdue Dr 73128
N Purdue Pl 73127
S Purdue St 73179
Putnam Heights Blvd 73118
Pybas Ln 73115
S Quadrum Dr 73108
Quail Cir 73120
Quail Ct 73120
Quail Dr 73121
Quail Creek Rd 73120
Quail Plaza Dr 73120
Quail Pointe Dr 73134
Quail Ridge Dr 73160
Quail Run Cir 73160
Quail Run Dr 73160
Quail Run Rd
10500-10699 73130
10800-10999 73150
Quail Springs Pkwy 73134
Quailbrook Dr 73134
Quaker Dr 73120
N Quapah Ave
100-2399 73107
4900-6299 73112
S Quapah Ave
2500-2598 73108
3300-3699 73119
Quapah Cir 73112
N Quapah Pl 73112
Quartz Pl 73170
Queen Anne Ave 73114
Queens Dr 73160
Queens Gate Rd 73132
Queens Towne 73130
Queensbury Rd 73160
Queensland Ct 73130
Queenstown Rd 73116
Queenswick Ct & Dr 73162
Quiet Storm 73170
Raceway Ln 73169
Rachel Ct 73170
S Rachel Ct 73159
Railroad 73130
Railway Dr 73114
Rain Tree Dr 73160
Raindust Dr 73170
Raintree Dr 73150
Raintree Rd 73120
N & S Ramblin Oaks
Dr 73160
Rambling Rd 73132
Rambridge Dr 73162
Rancho Dr 73119
E Ranchwood Cir 73160
W Ranchwood Ct 73139
E Ranchwood Dr 73160
W Ranchwood Dr 73139
S Ranchwood Manor
Dr 73139
Randall Dr
200-300 73110
302-398 73110
600-999 73160
Randel Rd 73116
Randels Way 73121
Randi Rd 73132
S Randie 73150
N Randolph Ave 73141
Randwick Dr 73162
W Ranger Ln 73179
Rankin Rd 73120
Rapcon Rd 73145
Raptor Ct 73145
Rausch Ln 73135
Raven Ave 73132
Raven Cir 73145
Rawlings Ave 73145
N Ray Ave 73121
Ray Dr 73135
Rayburn Ave 73149
Rayburn Dr 73165
Raymond King Dr 73165
Red Apple Cir & Ter 73160
Red Cedar Cir & Dr 73131
Red Hawk Ln 73170
Red Maple Ln 73170
Red Oak Cir 73160
Red Oak Rd 73120
Red Oak Way 73162
Red Plum Dr 73160
Red Rock Cir 73120
Red Rock Dr 73165
Red Rock Ln 73116
Red Rock Rd 73120
Redbird Cir 73110
Redbud Ct 73160
N Redbud Dr
700-1199 73110
1800-1900 73121
1902-2198 73121
NE Redbud Dr 73117
Redbud Ln 73120
Redbud Ridge Rd 73162
Reding Dr 73119
N Redmond Ave
2500-2899 73127
5001-5897 73122
5899-6199 73122
N Redmond Ct
2900-2999 73127
6100-6299 73122
Redstone Ct 73142
Redwood Cir 73160
Redwood Ter 73110
Reed Dr 73116
Reed Pl 73110
N Reeder Ave 73122
N Reeves Ave 73127
Reeves Ct 73122
Reeves Rd 73165
N Reeves St 73122
Regal Ln 73162
Regal Rd 73150
Regal Vintage Rd 73170
N Regatta Dr 73127
Regency Blvd 73160
Regency Ct 73120
Regency Pl 73160
Regent St 73162
Regina Ave 73169
S Regina Ave 73179
Regina St 73160
Reiss Ct 73118
Reiter Dr 73130
Remington Ave 73130
Remington Pl 73111
Remington Rd 73170
Remington Way 73134
Rempe Farm Rd 73173
Renita Ct & Way 73160
E Reno Ave
100-999 73104
1000-5599 73117
5600-8300 73110
8275-8275 73140
8301-8899 73110
8302-8898 73110
9000-12499 73130
12501-12599 73130
W Reno Ave
1-799 73102
900-1899 73106
2100-4022 73107
4024-4498 73107
4025-4025 73125
4027-4027 73127
4029-4029 73125
4031-4499 73107
4500-4900 73127
4901-10599 73127
4901-4901 73137
4902-10598 73127
Renwick Ave 73128
Republic Ave 73110
Republic Cir 73110
Republic Dr 73135
Research Pkwy 73104
Reserve Rd 73145
Rev J A Reed Jr Ave 73117
N Rhode Island Ave
300-699 73117
701-799 73117
2100-6900 73111
6902-7698 73111
S Rhode Island St 73129
Rhythm Rd 73130
N Richards Ave 73130
Richaven Rd 73162
Richmond Dr 73165
Richmond Sq 73118
Rick Rd 73170
E & W Rickenbacker
Dr 73110
N Rickey Dr 73111
Rickwood Cir 73160
Ricky Ln 73130
Riddell Cir 73179
Ridge Spgs 73132
Ridge Manor Ln 73150
Ridgedale Cir 73170
Ridgefield Dr 73150
Ridgehaven Dr 73110
Ridgemont Dr 73165
Ridgeview Cir 73120
Ridgeview Ct 73120
Ridgeview Dr 73120
Ridgeview Rd 73130
Ridgeway Dr
900-1499 73160
4700-4799 73115
Ridgeway Rd 73131
Ridgewood Dr 73160
E Ridgewood Dr 73110
N Ridgewood Dr 73110
W Ridgewood Dr 73110
Ridglea Ct 73115
Rifle Range Rd 73121
Rita Rd 73160
Ritter Rd 73162
Rivendell Dr 73170
River Bend Blvd 73132
River Birch Dr 73130
River Oaks Dr 73142
W River Park Dr 73108
Rivergate Ln 73132
N & S Riverside Dr 73160
S Riverview Rd 73173
Riverwalk Dr 73160
Riverwind Dr 73130
Riviera Dr 73112
Riviera Ln 73128
Roadrunner Ave 73139
Robert Ave 73165
Robert S Kerr Ave
1-97 73102
99-599 73102
601-799 73102
800-899 73106
Robin Dr 73151
Robin Rd 73110
E Robin Rd 73130
Robin Hill Ln 73150
Robin Ridge Rd 73120
N Robinson Ave
1-1000 73102
700-1299 73170
1002-1098 73102
1100-3099 73103
3100-3198 73118
3200-6200 73118
6202-6298 73118
6800-7899 73116
7900-10699 73114
S Robinson Ave
400-5999 73109
2100-2299 73170
6300-9499 73139
12900-14799 73170
Robinson Ct 73170
S Robinson Dr 73139
Robinwood Ln 73131
Robinwood Pl 73120
Robison Rd 73165
Roby Rd 73151
Rochdale Ave 73114
Rock Pl 73160
Rock Ter 73165
Rock Canyon Rd 73142
Rock Creek Cir 73132
W Rock Creek Rd 73120
Rock Creek Way 73120
Rock Crest Rd 73162
Rock Hollow Rd 73120
Rock Hollow St 73160
Rock Island Cir 73111
Rock Meadows Cir 73142
Rock Ridge Ct, Pl &
Rd 73120
Rockback Ct 73132
Rockefeller Rd 73169
Rockhampton Ave 73179
N Rockwell Ave
100-198 73127
200-1699 73127
6700-9399 73132
9600-12299 73162
12300-14699 73142
S Rockwell Ave
2-198 73127
200-1399 73128
6100-10399 73169
11300-12598 73173
12600-14399 73173
N Rockwell Dr 73132
S Rockwell St 73179
Rockwell Ter 73162
Rockwood Ave 73170
S Rockwood Ave
901-905 73108
907-1599 73108
5300-5699 73119
Rocky Way 73162
Roefan Rd 73130
N Roff Ave
1100-3099 73107
3100-5999 73112
7000-7099 73116
S Roff Ave 73119
Rohan Ct & Rd 73170
Rolfe Ave 73117
E Rolla Ter 73141
Rolling Ln 73110
Rolling Green Ave 73132
Rolling Lane Cir 73110
Rolling Meadows Blvd 73110
Rolling Stone Rd 73120
Rolling Terrace Dr 73165
Roman Rd 73122
Roosevelt St 73150
Rooster Rd 73165
Rose Dr 73170
E Rose Dr 73110
N Rose Dr 73110
W Rose Dr 73110
Rose Rock Dr 73111
Rosebay Ct & Pl 73142
Rosedale Dr 73162
Rosehaven Dr 73162
S Roselawn Ave 73130
Rosemeade Ct 73162
Rosewood Ct 73110
Rosewood Dr 73110
Rosewood Ln 73120
Rosewood St 73160
N Ross Ave
1100-2399 73107
3100-6299 73112
6400-6799 73116
11600-11799 73120
S Ross Ave
100-199 73107
300-398 73108
3200-5999 73119
7500-10099 73159
10800-11599 73170
Rossmore Ct & Pl 73120
S Rotary Dr 73108
Rouen Ct 73142
Rowlett Ave 73150
Roxboro Ave & Dr 73162
Roxbury Blvd & Ter 73132
Royal Ave
500-999 73130
4200-4299 73108
Royal Dr 73150
Royal Ln 73135
Royal Creek Cir & Rd 73135
Royal Oak Dr 73135
Royal Ridge Rd 73135
Royalwood Cir 73115
Rozell Dr 73131
Rubeye Redbud Cir 73134
Ruby Ln 73130
Ruff Rd 73150
W Rulane Dr 73110
Rumsey Rd 73132
Runway Rd 73135
Rushing Rd 73132
Rushmore 73162
Russell Dr 73110
Russell M Perry Ave 73104
Rustic Creek Rd 73165
Rustic Ridge Ave 73142
Rusty Rd 73107
Ruth Dr 73130
Ruth St 73121
Ryan Ct 73135
Ryan Dr 73135
Ryan Rd 73160
Ryan Rhodes Dr 73150
Ryecroft Rd 73162
Rylee Dr 73179
Sable St
6600-6799 73110
14600-14899 73165
Sabra Lee Ln 73142
Sachs Ave 73160
Sacramento Dr 73139
Saddle Ridge Rd 73131
Saddleback Dr 73150
S Sage Ave 73109
Sage Trail Cir 73179
Sahara Dr 73162
Saint Andrews Dr &
Ter 73120
Saint Ann Dr 73162
Saint Bernard St 73141
Saint Cecil 73160
Saint Charles Ave 73162
N Saint Charles Ave 73127
Saint Charles Cir 73160
Saint Charles St 73160
N Saint Charles St 73122
Saint Christopher Dr 73120
N Saint Clair Ave
1100-2399 73107
3700-4699 73112
6500-6999 73116
S Saint Clair Ave
2100-2999 73108
3200-3298 73119
3300-4100 73119
4102-4298 73119
Saint Elmo Ct 73139
Saint George Ave 73160
Saint George Cir 73160
Saint George Dr
3700-3799 73112
4300-4499 73120
Saint George Pl 73160
Saint George Way 73110
Saint Gregory Dr 73120
Saint James Cir 73110
Saint James Pl 73179
Saint John Ave 73160
N Saint John Ave 73110
Saint Johns Dr 73120
Saint Johns Pl 73142
N Saint Luke Ave 73141
N Saint Mark Ave 73141
Saint Marys Cir & Pl 73132
Saint Mathews Dr 73110
Saint Michael Ct 73139
Saint Michel Cir 73151
Saint Patrick Dr
4300-4499 73120
10100-10399 73130
S Saint Paul Ave 73130
N Saint Peter Ave 73141
Saint Thomas Ave 73160
Saint Thomas Dr 73120
Saintsbury Ct 73132
Sally Ct 73160
Salsbury Ln 73132
Samantha Ct 73162
Samantha Ln 73160
San Juan Trl 73160
San Leon Ct 73160
San Lorenzo Dr 73173
San Sebastian Dr 73173
Sand Oak St 73127
Sand Plum Dr 73160
Sanderling Rd 73179
Sandlewood Dr 73132
S Sandman St 73150
Sandpiper Ct 73170
Sandpiper Rd 73132
Sandra Dr 73110
Sandringham Dr 73170
Sandstone Ter 73170
Sandy Ln
1900-1999 73127
9600-9699 73131
N Santa Fe Ave
100-2700 73160
2400-2899 73103
2702-3598 73160
3100-6300 73118
6302-6398 73118
6400-7499 73116
11600-13699 73114
S Santa Fe Ave
700-1598 73160
1100-5999 73109
1600-3299 73160
6300-10399 73139
10500-17699 73170
Santa Fe Plz 73102
Santa Rosa Dr 73139
Sapphire Ln 73150
N Sapulpa Ave
1700-2299 73107
5100-5999 73112
Sara Ct 73130
Sarah Ln
2000-2099 73160
2700-2899 73131
2901-2999 73131
Saratoga 73142
Sauna Ln 73165
Saw Mill Rd 73170
Sawgrass Rd 73162
Saxon Dr 73132
Scenic Meadow Rd 73173
Schooner St 73107
Schooner Way 73160
Schroeder Ln 73121
Schwartz Dr 73165
Scirocco Cir 73135
Scott Dr 73160
Scott Rd 73165
S Scott St 73115
Sea Smoke 73131
Seabrook Ct 73142
Seadog Dr 73142
Seamans Way 73142
Sean Ct 73110
Sears Ter 73149
Sedona Dr 73142
Seiter Ln 73165
Seminole Ct, Rd &
Ter 73132
Senate Dr 73162
Sendera Lakes Dr 73160
Sentry Blvd 73145
Sequoyah Ave, Cir, Ct &
St 73160
Serenade Dr 73130
Serrano Dr 73170
N & S Service Rd 73160
Servon Dr 73170
Seven Oaks Cir 73142
N Sewell Ave 73118
Shadowlake Dr 73159
Shadowridge Ct & Dr 73159
Shadowview Dr 73159
Shady Ln 73131
Shady Creek Ln 73160
Shady Glade Ln 73151
Shady Glen Rd 73162
Shady Grove Rd 73160
Shady Lane Ct 73131
Shady Oaks Cir 73150
Shady Ridge Rd 73150
Shady Trail Ln 73120
N Shadybrook Ct, Dr &
Pl 73110
N Shadynook Way 73141
N Shadyway Dr 73110
N & W Shadywood Dr 73110

Shaftsbury Rd 73132
Shalimar Ct 73135
Shalimar Dr
800-1599 73115
4500-5799 73135
S Shallow Brook Dr 73129
Shallow Lake Ct 73159
NW Shamersi St 73112
Shamrock Cir & Rd 73131
S Shane Blvd 73160
Shannon Ave 73162
N Shannon Ave 73132
Shannon Dr
1600-1799 73130
3300-3899 73160
10100-10299 73165
10300-10399 73130
Shapard Dr 73130
Sharon Dr 73160
S Sharon St 73159
Sharry Ln 73111
N Shartel Ave
100-1099 73102
1100-2999 73103
3100-5299 73118
5300-5300 73154
5300-6198 73118
5301-6199 73118
6400-7099 73116
9100-11799 73114
11801-12099 73114
S Shartel Ave
600-5899 73109
6000-10299 73139
11200-11399 73170
S Shartel Pl 73109
Shasta Ln 73162
N Shawnee Ave
1100-2299 73107
5500-6299 73112
6400-7099 73116
S Shawnee Ave 73119
Shearer Cir 73160
Shearwater Ct 73179
Sheffield Rd 73120
Sheffield St 73130
Shelby Ln 73130
Shell Dr 73130
Shelly Ct 73160
Shepherd Mall 73107
E Sheridan Ave 73104
W Sheridan Ave
101-397 73102
399-799 73102
800-1899 73106
2100-2799 73107
Sheringham Dr 73132
Sherman Ave & Ter 73111
Sherrie Elaine Dr 73170
NE Sherwell Dr 73130
S Sherwood Ave 73159
Sherwood Ct
200-299 73160
11500-11599 73130
Sherwood Dr
400-599 73160
11301-11399 73165
Sherwood Ln 73116
N Shields Blvd 73160
S Shields Blvd
2600-5999 73129
6000-8999 73149
9000-9899 73160
Shilling Shore Ct 73132
Shiloh Blvd 73179
Shire Ln 73170
Shirley Ln 73116
Shorehan Ct 73170
Shoreline Dr 73132
Shoreside Dr 73170
N Short St 73110
Showalter Dr 73110
Shroyer Dr 73170
Shull Ave 73111
Sidney Dr 73160
Sierra Rd 73162
Signature Blvd & Cir 73142

Silks Dr 73130
Silo Ridge Rd 73170
Silver Ln 73120
Silver Xing 73132
Silver Ash St 73160
Silver Glade Rd 73120
Silver Lake Dr 73162
N & S Silver Leaf Dr 73160
Silver Maple 73160
W Silver Meadow Dr 73110
Silver Medal Dr 73160
Silver Sun Dr 73162
Silverleaf Ln 73131
Silvermoon Dr 73162
Silvertree Dr 73120
W Silverwood Dr 73110
Simmons Dr 73115
Ski Dr 73162
Skip Cir 73115
Skylark Ct 73162
Skylark Dr 73127
Skylark Ln 73162
Skylark Rd 73162
Skylark Ter 73162
S Skyline Dr 73129
Skyway Ave 73162
S Sleepy Hollow Dr 73150
Slim Dr 73130
Small Oaks 73110
Smith Blvd 73112
Smith Ct 73145
Smithfield Ln 73173
Smitty Rd 73165
Smoking Oak Cir 73160
Smoking Oaks Dr 73150
Smoking Tree St 73160
Snowberry Dr 73165
E Snyder Ct 73149
Socrates St 73107
Softwind Ave 73128
Somerset Pl 73116
Sonata Ct 73130
Songbird Ln 73130
S Sonic Ln 73129
Sonoma Lakes Blvd 73160
Sooner Dr 73165
N Sooner Rd
201-897 73117
899-1200 73117
1202-1698 73117
1700-7399 73141
7900-10499 73151
S Sooner Rd
100-1799 73110
1801-2399 73110
2800-2898 73165
2900-3900 73165
3401-3499 73165
3902-4098 73165
4400-4499 73115
5100-5898 73135
5900-8999 73135
9000-13800 73165
13802-15698 73165
Sooner Lake Cir & Dr 73165
S Sooner Road Pl 73165
Sorrento Dr 73120
Sorrento Ln 73170
South Dr 73119
Southcreek Rd 73165
Southern Creek Dr 73165
Southern Hills Dr 73160
Southern Oaks Dr 73130
Southern View Dr 73165
Southlake Dr 73159
N Southminster St 73160
Southridge Dr & Ter 73159
Southshore Dr 73162
Southwind Ave & Ct 73179
Southwood Dr 73170
Sovereign Row 73108
Spaatz Ct 73145
S Spaceland St 73129
Sparrow Dr 73165
Sparta St 73107

N Spencer Rd
1000-1699 73110
1700-2299 73141
N Spinnaker Ln 73116
Spitler Dr 73150
Spitz Dr 73135
Spiva Dr 73115
N Spring Dr 73127
Spring Creek Dr 73130
Spring Creek Rd
200-499 73117
11300-11499 73162
Springbrook Dr 73132
Springcreek Cir, Ct, Dr & Pkwy 73170
Springfield Dr 73149
Springhollow Ct & Rd 73120
Springlake Dr
1600-1898 73111
1900-1999 73111
3400-3699 73105
3700-4499 73111
Springwood Dr 73120
S Spruce Ave 73128
Spruce St 73160
Spur Dr 73130
Spyglass Rd 73120
St Claire 73170
St Croix Cir 73170
St Lukes Ln 73142
Staci Ln 73129
Stacy Ct 73162
Stacy Ln 73150
Stadium Rd 73160
Staff Dr 73145
Stagecoach Trl 73114
Stahl Dr 73110
N Standish Ave 73117
Stanford Ct 73132
N Stanley Ave
4300-4799 73122
6600-7099 73132
W Stanley Draper Dr 73165
Stansbury Pl 73162
Stansell Dr 73110
Stanton L Young Blvd
600-999 73104
1000-1099 73117
E Star St 73141
NE Stardust Ln 73130
Starling Rd & Way 73179
Starwood Dr & Ln 73121
State Ave 73162
N State St 73122
Staton Dr 73111
N Steanson Dr 73112
E & W Steed Dr 73110
S Steele St 73109
Steeple Chase Cir & St 73131
Steeple Ridge Rd 73150
Stefanie Ln 73160
E Stella Rd 73165
Stepping Stone Ln 73170
Steppingstone Ct 73170
N Sterling Ave
1100-2999 73127
4000-4299 73122
4300-4799 73122
Sterling Ct 73122
N Sterling Ct 73127
N Sterling Dr
5800-6399 73122
6400-6499 73132
Sterling Canyon Dr 73165
S Steve Ave 73129
Steve Dr 73165
Stevens Dr 73110
Stevenson Cir 73121
Stewart Ct 73111
Stickney Pl 73170
N Stiles Ave
900-1599 73104
1900-4899 73105
S Stiles Ave
2300-5099 73129

6100-7599 73149
Still Hollow Dr 73162
Stillwind Dr 73170
Stinchcomb Ave & Dr 73132
Stiver Dr 73110
Stone Brook Ct 73120
Stone Creek Dr 73165
Stone Creek Rd 73130
Stone Hollow Xing 73130
Stone Manor Dr 73142
Stone Meadows Dr 73170
Stonecrest Ln 73142
N & S Stonecrop Dr 73110
Stonegate 73130
Stoneham Ave 73120
Stonehaven Dr 73115
Stonehedge Ave & Ln 73170
Stoneleigh Ct 73132
Stonemill Rd 73131
Stoneridge Ct 73130
Stoneridge Dr 73160
Stoneridge Ln 73130
Stoneview Dr 73170
N Stonewall Ave
600-898 73117
900-1499 73117
1700-6099 73111
S Stonewall Ave 73129
N Stonewall Dr 73111
Stonewood Dr 73135
Stonybrook Ct & Rd 73120
Stonycreek Dr 73132
Stori Ln 73150
N Stout Cir 73170
Strait Dr 73121
Straka Rd 73165
Straka Ter 73139
SW Straka Ter 73159
Straka Farm Rd 73173
Stratford Dr 73120
Stratford Pl 73160
Strawberry Hl 73130
S Stults Ave 73119
Sturbridge Rd 73162
N Styll Rd 73112
NE Success St 73111
Sudbury Dr 73162
Sudbury Ln 73135
Sudik Dr 73165
Sue Ct 73120
Sulgrave Mnr 73132
Sulzburger St 73108
Summer Hill Dr 73160
Summerwind Ave & Ct 73179
Summit Dr 73162
Summit St 73112
Summit Ridge Dr 73114
E Sun St 73141
Sun Country Dr 73130
Sun Drop Ct, Ln & Pl 73128
Sun Tree Cir 73160
Sundance Mountain Rd 73162
W Sundown Dr 73127
Sunny Ct 73135
Sunny Pointe Ln 73135
Sunny Slope Dr 73160
Sunnybridge Ct 73132
Sunnybrook Ln 73128
Sunnydale Dr 73135
Sunnylane Cir 73115
Sunnylane Pl 73115
N Sunnylane Rd
100-999 73117
100-1499 73160
S Sunnylane Rd
200-16899 73160
200-4400 73115
4402-4498 73115
4500-8899 73135
Sunnymeade Pl 73120
Sunnyview Dr
4200-4299 73115
4500-4799 73135
Sunrise 73160
Sunrise Blvd 73120

Sunrise Dr 73160
Sunset Blvd 73120
Sunset Dr
800-899 73105
2001-2099 73160
Sunset Ln
1600-1699 73127
3000-10399 73120
Sunset St 73160
Suntane Cir & Rd 73115
Sunvalley Dr 73110
Sunway 73127
Superior Ave 73149
E Surrey Ln 73130
Surrey Pl 73120
Susan Ln 73120
Sussex Rd 73130
Suttle Ct 73135
Sutton Cir 73160
Sutton Pl 73132
Sutton Hill Rd 73142
Swanhaven Dr 73170
Sweet Berry Rd 73170
N Sweetgum Ave 73127
Sweetgum St 73160
Sycamore Ave 73128
Sycamore Ct 73160
Sycamore Dr
1000-3599 73110
3100-3299 73160
Sylena Way 73170
Sylvester Dr 73162
Symphony Ln 73130
Syracuse St 73160
N Tabor Ave 73107
N Tacoma St 73112
Talbot Ct 73162
Talbot Canyon Rd 73162
Tall Oaks Dr
1000-1199 73110
6700-6799 73127
Tall Trees Way 73131
Talver Ln 73170
Tamace Dr 73170
Tamarisk Dr
3900-4499 73120
4500-4799 73142
Tammy Cir 73132
Tangleroot Way 73173
Tanglewood Dr 73115
Tara Dr
1200-1399 73130
1400-1599 73160
1601-1799 73160
Tarantino Dr 73173
Tarragona Dr 73173
Tasha Cir 73160
Tate Dr 73115
Tatum Ln 73165
Taylor Paige Dr 73130
Taylor Wayne Ln 73165
Teak Ct 73160
Teal Dr 73115
Tealwood Dr 73120
Technology Dr 73134
E Teddy Dr 73149
Teddy Rd 73179
Tedford Way 73116
Teka Cir 73139
N Tela Dr 73127
N & S Telephone Rd 73160
Templet Dr 73127
Tempo Dr 73115
Tenkiller Ct & Pl 73165
Teresa Cir 73111
Teresa Dr 73160
Teresa Ter 73111
Terminal Dr 73159
Terrace Dr 73127
Terrace Lawn Dr 73129
N Terry Ave 73111
Terry Way 73115
S Terry Joe Ave 73129
Teton Rd 73162
S Texas Ave 73130
Texoma Dr 73119

Texoma Pl 73165
Thames St 73142
E Thayer St 73130
Thiemer Sq 73130
Thistle Trl 73170
Thomas Ave 73115
Thomas Dr
2500-2699 73160
3900-4199 73115
Thomas Pl 73107
S Thomas Rd 73179
Thompkins Cir, Ct, Ln & Pl 73162
Thompson Ave 73105
Thompson Dr
100-199 73160
1600-1899 73110
Thorn Burn Pl 73179
Thorn Ridge Rd 73120
Thornburn Pl 73179
Thornhill Dr 73170
E & N Thornton Dr 73110
Thousand Oaks Dr 73127
Three Oaks Cir & Dr 73130
Thunder Dr 73102
Thunderbird Dr 73120
Tiffany Cir 73132
Tiffany Dr
3500-3799 73160
8400-8599 73132
Tilbury Ct 73162
E Tiller Dr 73110
Tilman Dr 73132
Tim Dr 73141
Timber Ct 73165
Timber Ln
600-699 73127
5400-5699 73111
S Timber Ln 73130
N Timber Rd
400-1699 73130
1700-1899 73141
Timber Xing 73141
Timber Oak Dr 73151
Timber Ridge Rd 73130
Timber Valley Dr 73151
Timbercrest 73142
Timbers Dr 73165
E Timberview Dr 73130
Timberwood Ln 73135
Timmons Dr 73110
Timothy Ln 73135
Tina Dr 73110
Tinker Dr 73110
Tinker Rd 73135
Tinker Diagonal
3000-5599 73115
Tinker Diagonal
5600-6499 73110
6501-6799 73110
Tinker Diagonal St 73129
Tivoli Ter 73170
Todd Way 73170
Toledo Dr 73170
N Tompkins Dr 73127
Tony Ceasar Ave & Ln 73130
Tortoise Cir 73130
Tottingham Rd 73120
Tower Cir 73160
Tower Dr 73160
Tower Rd 73145
Towers Ct 73111
Town View Dr 73149
S Townley Dr 73129
Townsend Ct 73130
S Townsend Pl 73115
Towry Ct 73165
E Towry Dr 73110
N Towry Dr 73110
Tracy Dr
8700-9199 73132
12400-12999 73165
S Trafalgar Dr 73139
Trail Oaks Dr 73120
Trail Ridge Rd 73114

Trapp Dr 73115
Traub Pl 73110
Traviness Trl 73170
Travis Ct 73130
Treadwell Dr 73112
Treat Dr 73110
Treeline Ct 73165
Treemont Ln 73162
Trellis Ct 73107
Trenton Rd 73116
Trevi Ct 73116
Triana Dr 73170
Trigg Dr 73115
Trina Dr 73115
Triple Rrr Rd 73165
N Trosper Dr 73141
Trosper Pl 73115
Trosper Rd 73110
Trout St 73120
Truitt 73160
Trumball Cir 73142
Tucker Ln 73150
Tudor Dr 73160
Tudor Pl 73160
Tudor Rd
2700-3099 73127
3100-3399 73122
N Tulsa Ave
600-2299 73107
3200-6399 73112
S Tulsa Ave 73108
Tulsa Cir 73107
N Tulsa Dr 73107
S Tulsa Dr 73170
Tumilty Ave, Cir & Ter 73130
N Tunbridge Rd 73130
Turbine Dr 73145
Turley Pl 73110
Turnberry Ln 73170
N Turner Ave 73160
S Turner Ave 73160
Turner Dr 73110
Turtle Crk 73160
Turtle Back Dr 73130
Turtle Creek Ct, Dr & Rd 73170
Turtle Dove Dr 73132
Turtle Lake Ct 73165
Turtle Lake Pl 73165
Turtle Lake Rd 73160
Turtle Pond Ct 73142
Turtlewood Blvd & Dr 73130
Turtlewood River Rd 73130
Tuscan Rd 73170
Tuscany Blvd
2300-2399 73120
2700-2799 73134
Tuscany Dr 73170
Tuscany Ranch Rd 73173
Tuscany Ridge Rd 73130
Tuttington Cir 73170
N & S Tuttle St 73107
Twelve Oaks Rd 73120
Twilight Dr 73110
Twin Circle St 73160
Twin Creek Dr 73131
Twin Fawns 73173
Twin Lake Dr 73165
Twin Lakes Cir 73132
Twin Leaf Ct 73110
Twining Dr 73145
Twisted Oak Dr 73130
Twisted Oak Pl 73120
Twisted Oak Rd 73120
Twisted Trail Rd 73150
Two Bridge Dr 73131
Two Forty Pl 73139
Tyanne Blvd 73117
Tyler Ln 73170
Tyson Ct 73130
N Umbrian Rd 73132
Union Cir 73135
United Founders Blvd 73112
N University Ave 73114
Upper Pond Ct 73142
Uptown Dr 73110

Urban League Ct 73105
Urschel Ct 73132
N Utah Ave
1200-3099 73107
3100-6299 73112
S Utah Ave 73108
N & W Utica Dr 73120
Vail Cir 73114
Vail Ct 73162
Vail Dr 73162
Val Verde Dr 73142
Valley Way 73150
N Valley View Dr 73127
Valleyside Cir 73151
Vanaman Rd 73145
Vanchald Dr 73110
Vandenberg St 73145
Vandiver Dr 73142
Veda Dr 73121
Veneto Cir 73120
Venice Blvd 73112
N Venice Blvd 73107
Ventura Ct 73139
S Ventura Dr 73135
Ventura Ln 73165
Vera Pl 73115
Verbena Ln 73142
Vermeer Dr 73160
N Vermont Ave
1100-3099 73107
3200-6299 73112
S Vermont Ave
1-199 73107
200-2699 73108
2701-2799 73108
Verna Marie Dr 73110
N Vernon Rd 73121
Verona Strada 73170
Verrelac Dr 73151
Versailles Blvd 73116
Veterans Ln 73115
Vfw Dr 73115
Via Del Vis 73131
NW Viansou St 73132
Vick Cir 73115
Vicki Dr 73170
Vickie Dr 73115
N Vickie Dr 73117
Victor Ct 73130
N Victoria Dr 73120
S Victoria Dr 73159
Victoria Pl 73120
Victorian Dr 73160
N Viewpoint Dr 73110
N Villa Ave
1-3099 73107
3200-6399 73112
10900-11299 73120
S Villa Ave
100-199 73107
2000-2799 73108
3000-5700 73119
5702-5898 73119
6000-6098 73159
6100-9599 73159
11300-12699 73170
S Villa Pl
3800-3999 73119
8800-8999 73159
Villa Lante Cir 73170
Villa Prom 73107
Village Ave 73130
Village Dr 73120
Village Ln 73170
Village Oaks Dr 73130
Village South Dr 73139
N Vincent St 73114
N Vine St 73121
Vinehaven Blvd 73170
SW Vinerlea St 73108
Vineyard Blvd 73120
Vineyard Rd 73173
Vintage Farms Rd 73170
Violet Ct 73127
N Virginia Ave
100-3099 73106
3100-4799 73118
4801-5799 73118
11900-12099 73120
S Virginia Ave
1-99 73106
2400-2899 73108
3100-3399 73119
8600-8999 73159
15100-15699 73170
N Virginia Dr 73107
Virginia Ter 73159
Vitoria Dr 73170
Vixen Ln 73131
Vixen Way 73142
Volterra Way 73170
S Voorhees Dr 73135
Wagon Cir 73170
Wagon Boss Rd 73170
Wagon Wheel Rd 73173
Wakefield St 73149
Walden Ave 73179
Walden Estates Dr 73179
N Walerain Ave 73102
N Walker Ave
1-1099 73102
1100-3099 73103
3100-5499 73118
8000-12199 73114
S Walker Ave
100-198 73102
200-5999 73109
6100-9499 73139
10600-11999 73170
Wall Cir 73160
N Wall St 73122
Wallace Ave 73162
N Walnut Ave
200-1399 73104
1800-4799 73105
S Walnut Ave 73129
Walnut Ct 73160
Walnut Ln
6100-6199 73132
9800-9899 73130
Walnut Creek Dr 73142
Walnut Hollow Dr 73162
Walters Ave 73162
Waltz Way 73130
Wandering Way 73170
N Warren Ave
700-3099 73107
3100-6399 73112
6400-6499 73116
N Warren Pl 73107
Warriner Cir & Way 73162
Warringer Ct 73162
Warrior Cir & Ct 73121
Warwick Dr
2500-2899 73116
12100-12299 73162
Warwick Place Dr 73162
NE Washenne St 73121
N Washington Blvd
1400-1599 73117
1700-2099 73121
Washington Cir 73160
Washington Sq 73135
Water Crest Ct & Dr 73159
Water Leaf Ct 73110
Water Plant Rd
10700-10899 73130
13700-13799 73165
NW Waterana St 73114
Waterford Blvd 73118
Watermark Blvd 73134
Watermill Rd 73131
Waters Edge Way 73135
Waterside Dr 73170
Waterview Ct & Rd 73170
N Waterwood Cir, Ct, & Way 73132
Watts Dr 73110
Waverly Ave
7100-7199 73116
7200-7400 73120
7402-8498 73120
8500-10099 73120
Way Cross Rd 73162
Wayfield Ave 73179
Wayfield Cir 73142
S Webster Dr 73130
Webster St 73160
Wedgewood Dr 73179
Wedgewood Creek Dr 73179
Weedn Ct 73160
Wegner Way 73162
Welch Dr 73139
NE Weliante St 73105
Well Oak Cir 73127
Wellington Ave 73120
Wellington Ln 73160
Wellington Way 73115
Wellington Parke 73115
Wentworth Ct & Pl 73170
Wesley Cir
100-199 73160
10700-10799 73151
West Dr 73145
Westbrook Dr 73162
Westbury Dr 73130
Westbury Glen Blvd 73179
Westchester Dr
900-1299 73114
1300-2399 73120
2300-2499 73160
Westcourt 73142
Westend Ave 73160
N Western Ave
1-2799 73106
3100-3398 73118
3400-6399 73118
6400-7699 73116
7900-13100 73114
13102-13698 73114
S Western Ave
1-97 73106
99-199 73106
200-5999 73109
6000-10499 73139
10500-17399 73170
Western Heights Ave 73179
Western Heights Dr 73127
Western View Dr 73162
Westgate Rd 73162
Westhaven Dr 73169
Westlake Blvd 73142
Westlake Dr 73162
Westlake Rd 73165
Westlane 73142
Westlawn Pl 73112
Westline Dr 73108
N Westminster Dr 73141
Westminster Ln 73165
Westminster Pl 73120
N Westminster Rd 73130
S Westminster Rd
100-2699 73130
3100-8999 73150
9100-16499 73165
S Westminster Way 73150
N Westmont St 73118
Westmore Dr 73170
N Westmoreland Ave 73130
Westover Ave 73162
Westpark Dr & Pl 73142
Westpoint Blvd 73179
N Westridge St 73122
Westrock Dr 73132
Westway 73142
Westwood Ave 73108
Westwood Cir 73127
Westwood Ct 73127
Westwood Dr 73127
Westwood Ln 73169
Wexford Ave 73179
Weyland Loop 73145
Wheat Pl 73170
Wheatland Dr 73169
Wheeler Ct
2900-2999 73127
6800-6899 73110
Wheeler Plz 73110
N Wheeler St 73127
E Whipper Will St 73141
Whippoorwill Rd 73120
Whispering Trl 73130
Whispering Grove Dr 73169
Whispering Hollow Dr 73142
Whispering Oak Dr 73130
Whispering Oak Rd 73127
Whispering Oaks Blvd 73160
Whispering Oaks Dr 73165
S Whitbourne Pl 73170
White Dr 73145
White Cedar Ct & Dr 73160
White Cross Rd 73150
White Fences 73131
White Hawk Ln 73170
White Night Ct 73170
N White Oak Ave 73130
White Oak Rd 73160
White Oak Canyon Rd 73162
Whitecap Ln 73127
Whitechapel St 73162
Whitefield Cir 73142
Whitehall Blvd 73162
Whitehall Ct 73132
Whitehall Dr 73132
Whitehaven Rd 73120
Whitney Way 73131
Wickliff St 73111
Wilburn Dr 73127
Wild Honey Ct 73179
Wildewood Dr, Plz & Ter 73105
Wildfire St 73160
Wileman Way 73162
Wilkerson Cook Ln 73165
Wilkinson Ct 73160
Wilkinson Dr 73160
N Wilkinson Dr 73130
Will Rogers Pkwy 73108
Will Rogers Rd 73110
N Willard Ave 73105
William Penn Blvd 73120
Williams Ct 73142
Williams Dr
400-699 73160
701-799 73160
1300-1499 73119
N Williams St 73112
Williamson Farms Blvd 73173
Williamsport Ave 73120
Willingham Way 73160
Willis Dr 73150
Willow Ln 73170
Willow Way 73162
Willow Bend Ave 73165
Willow Bend Blvd 73160
Willow Branch Rd 73120
Willow Brook Dr 73110
Willow Brook Rd 73120
Willow Brook St 73160
Willow Cliff Rd 73122
Willow Creek Blvd 73162
Willow Creek Dr 73110
Willow Grove Rd 73120
Willow Pine Dr 73160
Willow Reed Dr 73165
Willow Ridge Dr 73130
Willow Springs Ave & Dr 73112
Willow Wind Ct & Dr 73130
Willowcrest Ln 73170
Willowridge Dr 73122
E Wilshire Blvd
100-799 73105
1200-2300 73111
2302-2698 73111
3500-3898 73121
3900-5499 73121
5600-7899 73141
W Wilshire Blvd
2-98 73116
100-3299 73116
1500-1899 73116
5701-5797 73132
5799-8899 73132
N Wilshire Ct 73132
Wilshire Ter 73116
Wilshire Hills Dr 73132
Wilshire Ridge Dr 73132
Wilson Blvd 73160
Wilson Dr 73110
Wilson Pl 73135
Wilton Ln 73120
Wimberley Creek Dr 73160
Wimbledon Rd 73130
Winchester Dr 73162
Wind Chime Dr 73120
Wind Flower Pl 73120
Windemere Dr 73117
N Windermere Dr 73160
Windgate East Rd 73179
Windgate West Rd 73179
Winding Creek Ct & Rd 73160
Winding Hollow Rd 73151
Winding Meadow Ln 73132
Winding Oaks Dr 73151
Winding Trail Rd 73170
Winding Vine Ln 73170
Windmill Ct 73162
Windmill Pl 73162
Windmill Rd
3300-3499 73165
11000-12299 73162
Windmill Farms Rd 73130
Windover Cv 73130
Windrun Pl 73179
Windscape Ave & Ct 73179
Windsong Dr 73130
Windsong Way 73120
N Windsor Ave 73122
Windsor Blvd 73122
N Windsor Blvd 73127
Windsor Pl 73116
N Windsor Pl 73127
Windsor Rd 73130
Windsor Ter 73122
N Windsor Ter 73127
Windsor Way 73110
Windstop Ct 73170
N Windsurf Way 73127
Windswest Ct 73179
Windtree Dr 73122
Windway Ave 73162
Windy Hill Rd 73179
Windy Hollow Dr 73110
Winelake Dr 73170
Wineview Dr 73170
Winfield Dr 73162
Winfield Ln 73160
Wingspread Dr 73159
Winoma Dr 73142
Winston Rd 73120
S Winston Way
6800-10399 73139
10500-10799 73170
Winter Dr 73112
Wireless Way 73134
N Wisconsin Ave
200-1399 73117
4900-5400 73111
5402-5498 73111
Wister Ln 73150
Wisteria Dr 73142
Wisteria Way 73170
S Wofford Ave 73115
Wolfe Dr 73145
Wonga Dr 73130
Wood Dr 73150
Wood Crest St 73160
Wood Duck Dr 73132
Wood Hollow Ct & Ln 73160
Woodbend Dr & Ln 73135
Woodbine Cir & Ter 73160
Woodbriar Cir, Ct, Ln & Pl 73110
Woodbridge Rd 73162
Woodbrier Dr 73122
N & W Woodbrook Rd 73132
Woodcreek Ct 73122
Woodcreek Dr 73122
Woodcreek Rd 73110
N & W Woodcrest Dr 73110
Woodcutter Dr 73150
Woodedge Dr 73115
Woodfield St 73149
Woodhollow Rd 73121
Woodhue Dr 73135
Woodlake Dr 73132
Woodland Blvd 73105
Woodland Dr
400-999 73130
4300-5099 73105
Woodland Way 73127
Woodland Hills Dr 73131
W Woodlane Dr 73110
Woodlawn Dr 73160
Woodlawn Pl 73118
Woodman Dr 73110
Woodmont Dr 73135
Woodnoll St 73121
Woodridden 73170
Woodridge Ave 73132
Woodrock Ct 73130
Woodrock Dr 73169
Woodrock Pl 73130
Woodrow Ct 73169
Woods Ave 73160
Woods Dr 73111
Woods Way 73160
Woodside Dr 73110
Woodsmoke Ln 73131
Woodstock Rd 73160
Woodvale Dr 73110
Woodview Dr
4700-4899 73115
9700-9798 73165
9800-10499 73165
Woodview St 73160
Woodward Ave 73160
N Woodward Ave
1100-2899 73107
4700-5099 73112
6700-6799 73116
S Woodward Ave
2300-2899 73108
3100-5199 73119
Woodward Dr 73116
Wrexham Ct 73162
Wright Dr 73129
Wyfield Ave 73179
Wyndemere Ct & Spgs 73160
N & S Wyndemere Lakes Dr 73160
Yale Dr 73162
Yellow Rose Ln 73150
York Way 73162
Yorkshire Ave 73160
Yorkshire Cir 73160
Yorkshire Dr 73130
Yorkshire Ln 73142
E Young Rd 73130
Youngs Ave 73159
S Youngs Ave 73159
N Youngs Blvd
1100-2999 73107
3100-5999 73112
S Youngs Blvd
900-2999 73108
3100-5799 73119
7600-7698 73159
7700-8999 73159
9001-9299 73159
S Youngs Ln 73159
S Youngs Pl
3900-5599 73119
12500-12599 73170
Yule Dr 73160
Zachary Dr 73160
Zachry Cir 73110
Zandra Ave 73130
Zebra St 73110
N Zedna Dr
3000-3099 73107
3500-3699 73112

NUMBERED STREETS

SW 1st Pl 73160
1st St 73145
NE 1st St
100-3199 73160
200-499 73104
1000-1099 73117
NW 1st St
100-198 73160
200-1099 73160
900-1899 73106
2300-2799 73107
4500-8899 73127
SE 1st St 73160
SW 1st St 73160
NW 1st Ter 73107
NE 2nd Pl 73130
NE 2nd St
1-999 73104
100-2199 73160
1400-5598 73117
8800-8899 73110
9700-9799 73130
NW 2nd St
101-197 73160
1100-1899 73106
2200-2699 73107
5900-10099 73127
SE 2nd St
100-199 73129
100-1899 73160
5600-5699 73110
SW 2nd St
100-1099 73160
200-1099 73109
1200-3599 73108
8500-8699 73128
NE 3rd Pl 73130
NE 3rd St
1-999 73104
100-1599 73160
1300-1498 73117
9100-10599 73130
NW 3rd St
300-399 73160
1100-1899 73106
2300-4099 73107
4500-8399 73127
4021-25-4021-25 73107
SE 3rd St
100-2299 73160
200-299 73129
5601-5697 73110
9700-10999 73130
SW 3rd St
100-1099 73160
400-1199 73109
1300-4499 73108
4501-4597 73128
NW 4th Dr 73106
SW 4th Pl 73160
4th St 73145
NE 4th St
100-2899 73160
200-999 73104
1300-2698 73117
8800-8999 73110
9600-10799 73130
NW 4th St
1-699 73102
800-1899 73106
2300-4499 73107
5000-9799 73127
SE 4th St
1-2699 73129
100-3499 73160
5400-5599 73115
6000-6199 73110
9000-9699 73130
SW 4th St
100-1099 73160
100-999 73109
2300-2399 73108
5901-5999 73128
SW 4th Ter 73128
SE 5th Ct 73160
NW 5th Pl 73127
5th St 73145
NE 5th St
100-999 73104

100-1699 73160
1100-1298 73117
8600-8799 73110
9700-10799 73130
NW 5th St
100-400 73102
305-305 73101
305-305 73146
401-799 73102
600-1099 73160
800-1899 73106
5000-5198 73127
SE 5th St
200-2999 73160
700-999 73129
5600-6899 73110
SW 5th St
1-299 73109
100-999 73160
300-398 73125
301-1099 73109
2700-2899 73108
4025-4029 73125
5510-5698 73128
NE 5th Ter 73117
NW 5th Ter 73127
SE 6th Cir 73160
NW 6th Pl
1000-1099 73160
1100-1499 73170
6th St 73145
NE 6th St
1-999 73104
100-1699 73160
1001-1397 73117
9500-9599 73130
NW 6th St
1-799 73102
800-898 73106
900-1099 73160
900-1899 73106
6700-9799 73127
SE 6th St
300-2799 73160
600-699 73129
6000-6299 73110
9000-9699 73130
SW 6th St
1-999 73109
100-999 73160
NE 6th Ter 73160
NW 6th Ter 73127
NE 7th Cir 73160
SE 7th Cir 73160
SE 7th Ct 73160
NW 7th Pl
1000-1099 73160
1100-1399 73170
8001-8001 73127
NE 7th St
1-899 73104
100-3499 73160
1000-1999 73117
9800-10799 73130
NW 7th St
1-799 73102
600-1099 73160
800-2099 73106
1100-1199 73170
4400-4499 73107
7100-8399 73127
SE 7th St
1400-2799 73160
5600-6200 73110
SW 7th St
100-699 73160
100-899 73109
4900-5099 73128
NW 7th Ter 73127
SE 8th Ct 73160
SE 8th Pl 73129
NE 8th St
1-999 73104
100-2399 73160
1000-1298 73117
NW 8th St
1-799 73102

600-1099 73160
800-1999 73106
1200-1399 73170
3700-4422 73107
4500-10399 73127
SE 8th St
200-2799 73160
2100-2499 73129
5700-6299 73110
SW 8th St
100-999 73160
1900-2999 73108
5901-7997 73128
NW 8th Ter 73127
SE 9th Cir 73160
NE 9th Ct 73160
SE 9th Ct 73160
NE 9th St
1-99 73104
100-3699 73160
1300-3199 73117
NW 9th St
1-699 73102
800-1099 73160
800-1999 73106
1200-1499 73170
3700-4099 73107
4500-6499 73127
SE 9th St
500-2899 73129
700-2899 73160
4000-4199 73115
5800-6299 73110
10800-10899 73130
SW 9th St
100-699 73160
1700-3099 73108
NW 10th 73127
NW 10th Cir 73170
NE 10th Ct 73160
SE 10th Ct 73160
SE 10th Pl
2400-2499 73160
3900-4099 73115
NE 10th St
1-999 73104
100-2399 73160
1000-1298 73117
7000-8999 73110
9000-10999 73130
NW 10th St
1-699 73103
800-2099 73106
900-1099 73160
1100-1217 73170
2100-4499 73107
4500-10599 73127
SE 10th St
400-2899 73160
500-2499 73129
3900-4199 73115
5800-6299 73110
10100-10499 73130
SW 10th St
1-699 73109
100-999 73160
1701-1797 73108
NW 10th Ter 73127
NE 11th Cir 73160
NE 11th Pl 73160
NE 11th St
1-399 73104
100-2199 73160
1300-3399 73117
9300-9699 73130
NW 11th St
2-298 73103
800-2099 73106
1200-1299 73170
2100-4499 73107
4500-9699 73127
SE 11th St
500-2499 73129
1000-2899 73160
3900-4199 73115
5800-6299 73110
SW 11th St
100-1099 73160

100-699 73109
1300-3699 73108
5100-5899 73128
NW 11th Ter 73107
SE 12th Ct 73160
NW 12th Pl 73127
NE 12th St
1-99 73104
100-3799 73160
1100-3399 73117
8600-8999 73110
9300-10499 73130
NW 12th St
1-500 73103
100-1099 73160
502-598 73103
801-897 73106
1101-1199 73160
1200-1599 73170
2100-4499 73107
4500-10499 73127
SE 12th St
500-2599 73129
600-698 73160
3900-5399 73115
5700-5799 73110
10300-10499 73130
SW 12th St
100-1099 73160
200-699 73109
1300-3699 73108
6001-6099 73128
NE 13th Pl 73130
NW 13th Pl
1200-1599 73170
9500-9699 73127
NE 13th St
1-999 73104
1100-3399 73117
2100-2599 73160
8800-8999 73110
9101-9297 73130
NW 13th St
1-799 73103
800-2099 73106
1000-1099 73160
2100-4499 73107
4600-8299 73127
SE 13th St
500-2599 73129
800-2599 73160
4300-4499 73115
SW 13th St
100-1099 73160
300-499 73109
1300-3699 73108
NE 14th Pl 73117
NW 14th Pl
1000-1099 73160
1200-1499 73170
9500-9599 73127
SE 14th Pl 73115
SW 14th Pl 73108
NE 14th St
1-899 73104
500-2699 73160
1000-3399 73117
9300-9499 73130
NW 14th St
100-799 73103
800-1099 73160
900-2099 73106
2100-4499 73107
6900-9599 73127
SE 14th St
500-999 73129
800-1999 73160
3100-3299 73115
10001-10097 73130
SW 14th St
100-1099 73160
200-399 73109
1300-3099 73108
NW 14th Ter 73127
SW 15th Pl 73108
NE 15th St
100-999 73104

600-2399 73160
1000-3399 73117
8500-8999 73110
NW 15th St
100-799 73103
600-1099 73160
800-2099 73106
1200-1298 73170
2100-4499 73107
4600-10599 73127
SE 15th St
200-2899 73129
800-1913 73160
3100-5599 73115
5600-8999 73110
9000-11999 73130
SW 15th St
1-499 73109
100-1099 73160
1200-4499 73108
4600-9799 73128
NE 16th Pl 73104
NW 16th Pl 73107
NE 16th St
1-97 73104
300-699 73160
901-999 73104
1000-4299 73117
7700-8899 73110
9000-10999 73130
NW 16th St
1-799 73103
600-899 73160
800-2099 73106
2100-3700 73107
3621-3621 73147
3701-4499 73107
4500-8499 73127
SE 16th St
300-1499 73129
1200-1905 73160
3100-4399 73115
8000-8099 73110
SW 16th St
100-1099 73160
1100-3099 73108
9600-9799 73128
NE 16th Ter
1400-2299 73117
4200-4499 73121
NW 16th Ter 73107
NE 17th Ct 73160
NE 17th St
600-999 73105
900-1099 73160
1000-2999 73111
3000-3399 73121
8500-10999 73141
NW 17th St
100-799 73103
500-899 73160
800-2099 73106
2100-4499 73107
4900-5200 73127
SE 17th St
1-1499 73129
1400-1999 73160
4300-4799 73115
8400-8499 73110
10100-10199 73130
SW 17th St
700-899 73160
1100-3599 73108
9600-9799 73128
SW 17th Ter 73160
NE 18th Ct 73160
NW 18th Pl 73160
SE 18th Pl 73115
NE 18th St
100-2399 73160
200-999 73105
1000-2999 73111
3000-4299 73121
7800-10999 73141
NW 18th St
100-799 73103
600-1099 73160

800-2099 73106
2100-4499 73107
4800-8299 73127
SE 18th St
200-2299 73129
1500-1999 73160
3000-4799 73115
8400-8499 73110
SW 18th St
1100-3499 73108
4600-9799 73128
NW 18th Ter 73127
NE 19th Cir 73121
NE 19th Pl 73160
NE 19th St
200-1199 73160
600-999 73105
1000-2899 73111
3000-4299 73121
9000-10999 73141
NW 19th St
100-799 73103
600-1099 73160
800-2099 73106
1200-1399 73170
2100-4499 73107
4500-4598 73127
SE 19th St
1-1499 73129
100-3099 73160
3000-4999 73115
10300-10499 73130
SW 19th St
100-1099 73160
1100-1199 73170
1100-4499 73108
NE 19th Ter 73160
NW 19th Ter 73127
SE 19th Ter 73129
NE 20th Pl 73160
NE 20th St
400-1299 73160
700-999 73105
1000-2699 73111
3100-4599 73121
8300-8699 73141
NW 20th St
100-799 73103
600-1099 73160
800-2099 73106
2100-4499 73107
4700-8099 73127
SE 20th St
100-1499 73129
3000-4999 73115
SW 20th St
1100-1298 73170
1101-1199 73108
1101-1199 73170
1201-1299 73108
1201-1299 73170
1300-1499 73108
1500-1799 73170
2100-3599 73108
4600-5999 73128
NW 20th Ter 73127
NE 21st Ct 73160
NE 21st Pl 73160
SE 21st Pl 73115
NE 21st St
100-799 73160
200-999 73105
1001-1397 73111
1399-2699 73111
3301-3399 73121
9800-10499 73141
100-799 73103
600-1099 73160
800-2099 73106
2100-4399 73107
1-1299 73129
3000-4699 73115
10400-10599 73130
200-299 73109
600-699 73160
900-1000 73108
1002-1098 73108

1100-1299 73170
1300-1399 73170
1300-1499 73108
1500-1899 73170
2100-4499 73108
5700-9799 73128
NW 21st Ter 73107
SW 21st Ter 73128
SE 22nd Cir 73115
NE 22nd St
1000-2699 73111
1100-1399 73160
9100-9199 73141
NW 22nd St
1-799 73103
600-1099 73160
800-2099 73106
2100-4499 73107
SE 22nd St
100-2999 73129
3300-4899 73115
SW 22nd St
1-1299 73109
600-699 73160
1000-1499 73170
1300-4399 73108
5900-9399 73128
SW 22nd Ter 73128
SW 23rd Pl 73108
NE 23rd St
1-999 73105
100-1302 73160
1000-2799 73111
1304-1398 73160
2800-4599 73121
5900-10999 73141
NW 23rd St
1-799 73103
800-1099 73160
800-2099 73106
2100-4499 73107
4500-8799 73127
SE 23rd St
1-1699 73129
200-399 73160
3700-4799 73115
10100-10499 73130
SW 23rd St
1-1299 73109
600-699 73160
1000-1799 73170
1300-4499 73108
4700-5198 73128
SE 23rd Ter 73129
SE 24th Cir 73129
NW 24th Pl 73127
NE 24th St
1-899 73105
900-1299 73160
1200-2899 73111
NW 24th St
100-799 73103
800-1099 73160
800-1599 73106
2500-4499 73107
4700-8399 73127
SE 24th St
100-1299 73129
200-299 73160
3200-5099 73115
SW 24th St
1-1299 73109
600-699 73160
1000-1899 73170
1300-4099 73108
9100-9399 73128
SW 24th Ter 73128
SW 25th Cir 73170
NE 25th Ct 73160
NW 25th Pl 73127
NE 25th St
700-899 73105
1000-1098 73160
1100-1198 73111
1100-1999 73160
1200-2799 73111
NW 25th St
100-799 73103

800-2099 73106
1000-1099 73160
2100-4399 73107
4700-5199 73127
SE 25th St
1-1999 73129
200-299 73160
3800-4799 73115
SW 25th St
2-4 73109
600-999 73160
1000-1499 73170
1300-4499 73108
5200-9599 73128
SE 25th Ter 73115
SE 26th Cir 73129
NE 26th Ct 73160
NE 26th St
1-999 73105
1001-1397 73111
1100-1999 73160
1399-2499 73111
9700-9999 73141
NW 26th St
100-799 73103
1000-1099 73160
1100-2099 73106
2100-4499 73107
4500-6099 73127
SE 26th St
100-1199 73129
100-2999 73160
3600-4799 73115
8700-8799 73110
10600-10799 73130
SW 26th St
1-1299 73109
600-699 73160
1300-1600 73108
1700-1799 73170
2100-4099 73108
4800-9599 73128
SW 27th Pl 73108
NE 27th St
1-999 73105
100-1399 73160
1000-2499 73111
9000-9999 73141
NW 27th St
100-799 73103
100-1199 73160
1100-2099 73106
2100-4499 73107
4500-6099 73127
SE 27th St
1-1599 73129
100-2999 73160
3400-4799 73115
10800-10899 73130
SW 27th St
1-1299 73109
200-899 73160
1300-4099 73108
5400-9600 73128
NE 27th Ter 73160
NE 28th St
1-999 73105
900-999 73160
1000-2100 73111
9400-9499 73141
NW 28th St
100-799 73103
900-1099 73160
1100-2099 73106
2100-4299 73107
4500-6499 73127
SE 28th St
1-799 73129
200-299 73160
4300-4501 73115
4500-4500 73155
4502-4798 73115
4601-4797 73165
8701-8799 73110
11000-11499 73130
SW 28th St
1-1299 73109

100-1899 73160
1300-4099 73108
5000-9599 73128
SW 29th Cir 73160
SE 29th Ct 73165
SW 29th Pl 73119
NE 29th St
1-999 73105
1000-1098 73111
1100-1199 73160
1100-2099 73111
3000-4499 73121
9700-9799 73141
NW 29th St
100-699 73103
900-1099 73160
1100-2099 73106
2100-4199 73107
4500-5899 73127
SE 29th St
1-2900 73129
200-299 73160
2902-2998 73129
3100-5599 73115
6101-7197 73110
9000-11899 73130
SW 29th St
1-1299 73109
1300-4499 73119
4500-9099 73179
SW 29th Ter 73128
SW 30th Cir 73160
NW 30th Ct 73160
SE 30th Ct 73165
SW 30th Ct 73160
NW 30th Pl 73122
SW 30th Pl 73179
NE 30th St
1-999 73105
900-999 73160
1200-1398 73111
1400-1700 73111
1702-2598 73111
3000-5099 73121
9600-9898 73141
100-2099 73118
2100-4499 73112
4500-5899 73122
8500-8799 73127
1-2999 73129
200-299 73160
3100-3199 73165
3200-3298 73115
3200-3298 73165
9701-9799 73150
100-1299 73109
200-1899 73160
1300-2899 73119
2100-2299 73170
9100-9699 73179
NW 30th Ter 73112
SW 30th Ter 73179
SE 31st Cir 73165
SE 31st Ct 73165
NW 31st Pl 73122
SE 31st Pl 73165
NE 31st St
1-999 73105
1400-1699 73111
1700-2099 73160
3900-4799 73121
NW 31st St
100-2099 73118
2100-4499 73112
4500-5899 73122
SE 31st St
1-1399 73129
4300-4599 73115
9701-9799 73150
SW 31st St
100-1299 73109
1300-1699 73119
1600-1899 73160
1900-2099 73170
2100-4299 73119
9400-9599 73179
NW 31st Ter
2000-2099 73118

4100-4299 73112
4900-5899 73122
SW 31st Ter 73160
NW 32nd Pl
4400-4499 73112
4500-4699 73122
NE 32nd St
600-999 73105
1000-2099 73160
1201-1397 73111
4200-4299 73121
NW 32nd St
100-1999 73118
900-921 73160
2100-4499 73112
4500-5899 73122
SE 32nd St
1-899 73129
3200-3399 73165
11600-11999 73150
SW 32nd St
100-1299 73109
200-1799 73160
1300-1699 73119
2000-2099 73170
2100-4399 73119
9400-9799 73179
NW 32nd Ter 73118
SW 32nd Ter 73179
NW 33rd Dr 73122
NE 33rd St
600-899 73105
1200-1699 73111
3700-5099 73121
NW 33rd St
200-2099 73118
900-999 73160
2100-4299 73112
4500-5899 73122
SE 33rd St
1-899 73129
300-499 73160
3200-3399 73165
4300-4699 73115
SW 33rd St
100-1299 73109
1300-4499 73119
1600-1799 73160
2000-2022 73170
4500-9699 73179
NW 33rd Ter 73122
NE 34th St
100-699 73105
1200-1799 73111
1700-1899 73160
4100-4499 73121
NW 34th St
200-2099 73118
800-999 73160
2100-4299 73112
4500-5999 73122
SE 34th St
1-1299 73129
100-2799 73160
3000-5100 73165
9700-9799 73150
SW 34th St
200-1299 73109
401-797 73160
1300-4499 73119
7600-9799 73179
NE 34th Ter 73105
NE 35th Pl 73111
NW 35th Pl 73112
SW 35th Pl 73160
NE 35th St
600-999 73105
1500-1799 73111
NW 35th St
200-2099 73118
800-999 73160
2100-3299 73112
4600-5999 73122
SE 35th St
1-799 73129
800-999 73160
4300-4699 73115

9700-9798 73150
SW 35th St
100-1299 73109
500-1699 73160
1300-2899 73119
8300-9799 73179
SW 35th Ter 73179
NE 36th St
1-999 73105
1000-2600 73111
3000-4899 73121
6700-7799 73141
NW 36th St
200-298 73118
2100-4499 73112
4500-5500 73122
SE 36th St
800-999 73160
2100-2799 73129
9100-9799 73150
SW 36th St
600-999 73160
3300-4499 73119
4600-9900 73179
NW 36th Ter
500-999 73118
2400-2799 73112
SW 36th Ter 73179
NW 37th Pl 73112
SW 37th Pl 73119
NE 37th St
1-799 73105
1200-1500 73111
5000-5098 73121
NW 37th St
500-2099 73118
2100-3299 73112
4500-5898 73122
SE 37th St
1-1699 73129
900-999 73160
4300-4699 73115
12100-12299 73150
SW 37th St
600-999 73160
800-1299 73109
1400-3899 73119
8300-8599 73179
SW 38th Cir 73179
SW 38th Pl 73160
NE 38th St
1-999 73105
1101-1197 73111
4500-5199 73121
NW 38th St
300-2099 73118
2100-4499 73112
4800-5999 73122
SE 38th St
1-2699 73129
600-898 73160
4300-4699 73115
SW 38th St
201-297 73109
800-1799 73160
1300-3899 73119
5500-8299 73179
NE 38th Ter 73105
SW 38th Ter
500-599 73160
9000-9099 73179
NE 39th St
400-799 73105
1200-1699 73111
8000-8098 73141
NW 39th St
300-2099 73118
2100-4499 73112
4500-5999 73122
SE 39th St
1-1699 73129
2500-2899 73160
4300-4699 73115
SW 39th St
1-1299 73109
200-999 73160
1600-3899 73119

8400-9599 73179
NE 39th Ter 73105
NW 39th Ter 73112
SW 39th Ter 73119
SW 40th Pl
3000-3899 73119
4100-4199 73160
NE 40th St
100-499 73105
1300-1499 73111
NW 40th St
200-2099 73118
2100-3799 73112
4700-5999 73122
SE 40th St
1-2899 73129
2100-2299 73160
4300-4499 73115
SW 40th St
1-1299 73109
200-298 73160
1500-3899 73119
SW 40th Ter 73109
SE 41st Pl 73165
NE 41st St
600-699 73105
4400-4499 73121
NW 41st St
1-297 73118
2200-3599 73112
5400-5899 73122
SE 41st St
1-1499 73129
4100-4899 73115
SW 41st St
1-1299 73109
100-999 73160
1500-3899 73119
NE 41st Ter 73111
NW 42nd Cir 73112
SW 42nd Ct 73160
NW 42nd Pl 73118
NE 42nd St
1-999 73105
1000-1198 73111
4300-4499 73121
NW 42nd St
1-1999 73118
2200-4099 73112
4501-4697 73122
SE 42nd St
1-2099 73129
4100-4799 73115
10800-10999 73150
SW 42nd St
1-1199 73109
800-999 73160
1300-3899 73119
8500-8599 73179
NW 42nd Ter 73112
SE 42nd Ter 73115
NW 43rd Cir 73112
NW 43rd Pl 73112
NE 43rd St 73111
NW 43rd St
400-1699 73118
2100-4499 73112
4500-4599 73122
SE 43rd St
1-1099 73129
4100-4799 73115
9700-9999 73150
SW 43rd St
1-1299 73109
300-1099 73160
1300-3899 73119
SW 44th Cir 73179
NW 44th Ct 73112
SW 44th Ct 73179
SE 44th Pl 73150
NE 44th St
1-299 73105
1200-1999 73111
NW 44th St
2-98 73118
2400-4499 73112
4500-5399 73122

SE 44th St
1-2999 73129
3000-5499 73135
9200-11911 73150
SW 44th St
1-1299 73109
300-799 73160
1300-4499 73119
5300-9799 73179
NW 45th Pl 73112
SE 45th Pl 73135
NE 45th St 73111
NW 45th St
400-2099 73118
2100-4499 73112
5300-5899 73122
SE 45th St
1-2999 73129
3500-4899 73135
10100-10399 73150
SW 45th St
100-1299 73109
300-1099 73160
1300-3299 73119
NW 45th Ter
3300-3399 73112
5400-5599 73122
SE 45th Ter 73135
SW 45th Ter 73179
NW 46th Ct 73122
NW 46th Dr 73122
SW 46th Pl
2700-2899 73119
8400-8799 73179
NE 46th St
1-599 73105
1200-1699 73111
5300-5599 73121
NW 46th St
400-2099 73118
2200-4499 73112
4500-5899 73122
SE 46th St
1-2899 73129
3400-6299 73135
SW 46th St
100-1299 73109
1300-3399 73119
8900-8999 73179
NW 46th Ter
400-499 73118
5400-5599 73122
SW 46th Ter 73119
SW 47th Cir 73179
SE 47th Pl 73129
NE 47th St
1-199 73105
1200-1799 73111
NW 47th St
400-2099 73118
2100-4499 73112
5000-5899 73122
SE 47th St
200-2999 73129
3300-6299 73135
10400-10499 73150
SW 47th St
500-1299 73109
1600-3399 73119
8000-8199 73179
SE 47th Ter 73129
NW 48th Cir 73112
SE 48th Pl
1500-1599 73129
3700-3799 73135
NE 48th St
1-499 73105
1100-1899 73111
4300-5499 73121
NW 48th St
400-2099 73118
2200-4499 73112
5700-5799 73122
SE 48th St
200-2799 73129
3400-6499 73135

SW 48th St
300-1299 73109
1500-3599 73119
8400-8999 73179
SE 48th Ter 73135
SW 49th Cir 73179
NW 49th Pl 73112
NE 49th St
900-999 73105
1800-1899 73111
NW 49th St
400-1599 73118
2200-4499 73112
5900-6199 73122
SE 49th St
300-2799 73129
4200-6299 73135
9100-11499 73150
SW 49th St
100-1299 73109
2100-3399 73119
SE 49th Ter
1500-1599 73129
4200-4399 73135
SW 50th Pl 73109
NE 50th St
1-999 73105
1100-2799 73111
2800-2998 73121
2801-2899 73111
3000-5599 73121
5600-6599 73141
NW 50th St
1-1299 73118
2100-4499 73112
4500-6199 73122
7301-8699 73132
SE 50th St
200-2799 73129
4500-6299 73135
SW 50th St
1-1299 73109
2100-3399 73119
SE 50th Ter 73135
NW 51st Pl 73112
NE 51st St
1-199 73105
1500-1899 73111
5300-5499 73121
NW 51st St
400-1199 73118
2400-4299 73112
5800-5899 73122
SE 51st St
1-2799 73129
3000-6399 73135
10100-10999 73150
SW 51st St
300-1299 73109
1300-3499 73119
SE 51st Ter 73135
SW 52nd Pl 73119
NE 52nd St
1-199 73105
1201-1297 73111
5400-5499 73121
NW 52nd St
600-798 73118
2200-4499 73112
5900-5999 73122
SE 52nd St
1-1799 73129
3700-6399 73135
SW 52nd St
400-1199 73109
1300-3299 73119
8800-8999 73179
SW 53rd Ct 73179
NW 53rd Dr 73118
NE 53rd St
1-199 73105
1300-1999 73111
5300-5599 73121
NW 53rd St
700-1299 73118
3400-4499 73112
5800-5899 73122

SE 53rd St
200-499 73129
4200-6699 73135
SW 53rd St
1-1299 73109
2200-3199 73119
NW 53rd Ter 73122
NW 54th Cir 73112
NW 54th Dr 73118
NW 54th Pl 73122
SW 54th Pl 73119
NE 54th St
1300-1999 73111
5400-5599 73121
NW 54th St
200-799 73118
2200-4499 73112
5800-5899 73122
SE 54th St
200-499 73129
3000-5299 73135
10000-10399 73150
SW 54th St
1-1299 73109
1300-3699 73119
8900-8999 73179
NW 55th Pl 73112
NE 55th St
1100-1999 73111
4300-5599 73121
NW 55th St
1100-1199 73118
2200-4499 73112
6000-6199 73122
SE 55th St
1-2500 73129
3000-6599 73135
10000-11299 73150
SW 55th St
1-1299 73109
2100-3099 73119
6700-9199 73179
NW 55th Ter 73112
SE 55th Ter 73135
SE 56th Cir 73135
SE 56th Ct 73135
NW 56th Pl 73112
NE 56th St
1300-1899 73111
5400-5599 73121
NW 56th St
701-1097 73118
2200-4499 73112
5800-5899 73122
SE 56th St
1-2999 73129
3000-6299 73135
SW 56th St
1-1299 73109
1300-3099 73119
5200-5499 73179
NW 56th Ter
1800-2099 73118
2100-4499 73112
SE 57th Cir 73135
SW 57th Pl 73119
NW 57th St
700-1199 73118
2200-4499 73112
4600-6199 73122
SE 57th St
1-2999 73129
3000-6599 73135
10000-10499 73150
SW 57th St
1-1299 73109
2200-3099 73119
5300-8799 73179
NW 58th Cir 73112
SW 58th Cir 73179
NW 58th Pl 73112
SE 58th Pl 73135
NE 58th St 73111
NW 58th St
800-1199 73118
2200-4299 73112
4600-6599 73122

SE 58th St
200-1899 73129
4900-6199 73135
SW 58th St
700-1299 73109
1300-2599 73119
5200-5399 73179
NW 58th Ter
3700-3999 73112
5600-5699 73122
NW 59th Cir 73112
NW 59th Ct 73122
NW 59th Pl 73112
SE 59th Pl 73135
SW 59th Pl 73159
NE 59th St
300-499 73105
1100-1299 73111
NW 59th St
1-197 73118
2100-4499 73112
4600-6099 73122
SE 59th St
1-2899 73129
3000-6799 73135
7200-8899 73145
9700-13899 73150
SW 59th St
1-1299 73109
1300-3200 73119
6300-6398 73179
NW 59th Ter
3700-4399 73112
4600-4899 73122
SW 59th Ter 73179
SE 60th Ct 73149
NW 60th Pl 73112
SE 60th Pl 73149
SW 60th Pl 73159
NE 60th St
300-499 73105
3300-3399 73121
NW 60th St
100-198 73118
2100-4499 73112
4500-6099 73122
SE 60th St 73149
SW 60th St
900-1299 73139
1300-3099 73159
SE 60th Ter 73149
SW 60th Ter 73139
NW 61st Pl
3000-3299 73112
5000-5099 73122
NE 61st St 73105
NW 61st St
200-799 73118
2100-4299 73112
4600-6799 73122
SE 61st St
200-1799 73149
5700-6300 73135
SW 61st St
900-1299 73139
1300-3299 73159
6201-6299 73169
NW 61st Ter 73112
SW 61st Ter
500-599 73139
1300-2299 73159
NW 62nd Cir 73122
NW 62nd St
101-197 73118
2100-4199 73112
4600-6099 73122
8300-8499 73132
SE 62nd St 73149
SW 62nd St
1-1299 73139
1300-3299 73159
NW 62nd Ter
4000-4199 73112
4700-5999 73122
SW 62nd Ter 73139
SW 63rd Pl
400-499 73139
2500-2699 73159
NE 63rd St
1-999 73105
1000-2800 73111
3000-3098 73121
5600-7699 73141
NW 63rd St
1-4499 73116
4500-6000 73132
6001-6001 73123
6001-7099 73132
SE 63rd St 73149
SW 63rd St
400-1299 73139
1300-3299 73159
5700-5899 73169
NW 63rd Ter 73132
SW 63rd Ter 73139
SW 64th Pl 73139
NE 64th St
1-999 73105
1101-1199 73111
NW 64th St
1-4099 73116
5400-5899 73132
SE 64th St
300-1599 73149
12000-12299 73150
SW 64th St
400-1299 73139
1400-3299 73159
5900-6299 73169
NW 64th Ter 73132
SW 64th Ter
1-299 73139
3000-3099 73159
NW 65th Pl 73132
SW 65th Pl 73159
NE 65th St
1-999 73105
4600-4799 73121
NW 65th St
1-3899 73116
4600-4899 73132
SE 65th St 73149
SW 65th St
1-1299 73139
1400-3299 73159
NW 65th Ter 73116
NE 66th St
1-999 73105
1500-1698 73111
5600-7399 73141
NW 66th St
200-3899 73116
5400-5899 73132
SE 66th St
300-1799 73149
5900-6099 73135
SW 66th St
1-1299 73139
1300-3299 73159
6100-6199 73169
NW 67th Ct 73132
NW 67th Pl 73132
SW 67th Pl 73139
NE 67th St
1-999 73105
1101-1197 73111
4500-4699 73121
NW 67th St
100-3899 73116
5400-5598 73132
SE 67th St
200-2299 73149
3100-6099 73135
SW 67th St
500-1199 73139
1300-4599 73159
NW 68th Pl 73132
NE 68th St
700-999 73105
1000-1198 73111
NW 68th St
800-4099 73116
4800-4899 73132
SE 68th St
700-999 73149
5900-5999 73135
10800-10999 73150
SW 68th St
100-1099 73139
1300-3199 73159
6100-6199 73169
NW 68th Ter 73132
NW 69th Cir 73132
SW 69th Ct 73139
NE 69th St
700-999 73105
1200-1999 73111
NW 69th St
700-3899 73116
4700-8499 73132
SE 69th St
200-2222 73149
5900-5999 73135
12500-12999 73150
SW 69th St
1-1099 73139
1300-2699 73159
NW 69th Ter 73116
SW 69th Ter 73139
NE 70th Ct 73121
NE 70th St
1-999 73105
1200-1398 73111
5000-5399 73121
5800-7399 73141
NW 70th St
200-4099 73116
4600-8699 73132
SE 70th St
200-999 73149
5701-5897 73135
10800-13899 73150
SW 70th St
500-1299 73139
1400-2699 73159
SE 71st Cir 73150
SW 71st Cir 73159
NW 71st Pl 73116
SE 71st Pl 73150
NE 71st St
700-999 73105
2801-2897 73111
5800-6899 73141
NW 71st St
200-3699 73116
5800-5999 73132
SE 71st St
500-999 73149
5900-6099 73135
12300-13999 73150
SW 71st St
500-799 73139
1300-3299 73159
SE 71st Ter 73150
SW 71st Ter 73159
NW 72nd Cir 73132
NW 72nd Ct 73132
NW 72nd Pl 73132
NW 72nd St
900-3699 73116
4700-8999 73132
5500-5999 73132
SE 72nd St 73149
SW 72nd St
700-1299 73139
1300-3299 73159
8000-8099 73169
NE 73rd St 73105
NW 73rd St
900-3199 73116
4700-8799 73132
SE 73rd St
600-699 73149
12200-14199 73150
NW 73rd Ter 73132
NW 74th St
900-999 73116
4700-8999 73132
SE 74th St
5701-6297 73135
6299-6600 73135
6602-6698 73135
9900-14399 73150
SW 74th St
1300-1398 73159
1400-3399 73159
6500-8899 73169
NW 75th St
1000-1099 73116
4700-8499 73132
SE 75th St 73150
SW 75th St
2600-2799 73159
8500-8699 73169
SE 76th Pl 73150
NW 76th St 73132
SW 76th St
2100-2899 73159
8500-8699 73169
NW 77th Pl 73132
SW 77th Pl
1100-1299 73139
1300-2499 73159
NW 77th St 73132
SE 77th St 73135
SW 77th St
900-998 73139
2100-2899 73159
7801-7897 73169
SE 77th Ter 73150
SW 77th Ter
1100-1224 73139
1300-1699 73159
SE 78th St 73135
SW 78th St 73159
NW 78th Ter 73132
SW 78th Ter
1100-1299 73139
1400-1699 73159
NE 79th Pl 73114
NW 79th St
100-1399 73114
8200-8399 73132
SE 79th St
100-899 73149
4500-6299 73135
13500-13799 73150
SW 79th St
300-410 73139
2100-2899 73159
NW 79th Ter 73132
SE 79th Ter 73135
SW 79th Ter 73159
NW 80th St
100-1399 73114
6900-8999 73132
SE 80th St
4500-6299 73135
11000-12399 73150
SW 80th St
200-599 73139
1500-2899 73159
8700-8999 73169
SE 81st Cir 73135
SW 81st Pl 73159
NE 81st St 73114
NW 81st St
100-1399 73114
5900-8199 73132
SE 81st St 73135
SW 81st St
700-1299 73139
1300-2899 73159
8700-8799 73169
SE 81st Ter 73135
NW 82nd Cir 73132
SE 82nd Cir 73135
SW 82nd Cir 73159
SE 82nd Pl 73135
NE 82nd St 73131
NW 82nd St
100-1399 73114
5600-9000 73132
SE 82nd St
500-1399 73149
5000-5899 73135
SW 82nd St 73159
NW 83rd Pl 73132
SE 83rd Pl 73135
NE 83rd St 73114
NW 83rd St
200-1399 73114
5600-8999 73132
SE 83rd St
501-511 73149
5000-5899 73135
SW 83rd St
100-1199 73139
1300-3299 73159
NW 83rd Ter 73132
NW 84th Pl 73132
SE 84th Pl 73135
NE 84th St
600-999 73114
5900-5999 73151
NW 84th St
200-1499 73114
6200-8999 73132
SE 84th St
800-899 73149
4600-4998 73135
SW 84th St
900-1199 73139
1300-1398 73159
8100-8399 73169
SE 84th Ter 73135
SW 85th Cir 73169
NW 85th Pl 73132
NE 85th St
601-899 73114
1500-1599 73131
NW 85th St
200-1399 73114
5601-5997 73132
SE 85th St 73135
SW 85th St
500-899 73139
1600-3299 73159
NW 85th Ter 73132
SE 85th Ter 73135
SW 85th Ter 73139
NW 86th Pl 73132
SE 86th Pl 73135
NE 86th St 73131
NW 86th St
200-1099 73114
5700-8800 73132
SE 86th St
800-899 73149
4300-6199 73135
SW 86th St 73159
SE 86th Ter 73135
SW 87th Cir 73169
NW 87th St
200-1199 73114
5700-8799 73132
SE 87th St
1-99 73149
4300-6099 73135
SW 87th St
100-399 73139
1400-2899 73159
NW 87th Ter 73132
SE 87th Ter 73135
NE 88th St 73131
NW 88th St
200-1599 73114
5800-8799 73132
SE 88th St
1-899 73149
5000-6099 73135
SW 88th St
1000-1099 73139
2800-2899 73159
SE 88th Ter 73135
NW 89th St
200-1599 73114
5800-8599 73132
SE 89th St
1-2999 73149
3100-6300 73135
10200-14599 73150
SW 89th St
1-1299 73139
1300-3299 73159
6100-8899 73169
SE 89th Ter
2400-2899 73160
3900-4999 73135
SW 90th Pl 73159
NE 90th St 73131
NW 90th St
200-1499 73114
5800-8799 73132
SE 90th St
2700-2899 73160
5101-5199 73165
SW 90th St
1400-2999 73159
6500-7099 73169
NW 90th Ter 73132
NW 91st St
200-1499 73114
8200-8899 73132
SE 91st St 73160
SW 91st St
1-1299 73139
2300-2899 73159
SE 92nd Cir 73160
SW 92nd Cir 73169
SW 92nd Ct 73159
SW 92nd Pl 73139
NE 92nd St 73131
NW 92nd St
200-1499 73114
8200-8999 73132
SE 92nd St 73165
SW 92nd St
200-1299 73139
2300-3299 73159
6600-7099 73169
SE 92nd Ter 73160
NE 93rd Pl 73131
SW 93rd Pl 73159
SE 93rd St 73160
SW 93rd St
1-1299 73139
1300-3299 73159
SE 94th Cir 73160
SW 94th Ct 73159
NE 94th St 73151
NW 94th St
200-1499 73114
6500-7899 73162
SE 94th St
2100-2999 73160
13000-13699 73165
SW 94th St
900-1399 73139
2300-3299 73159
NW 94th Ter 73162
SW 94th Ter 73159
NE 95th St 73151
NW 95th St
200-1499 73114
6500-6699 73162
SE 95th St
2600-3299 73160
11000-13999 73165
SW 95th St
1000-1299 73139
1300-3299 73159
6500-7099 73169
SW 96th Ct 73159
NE 96th St 73131
NW 96th St
100-1499 73114
6500-6699 73162
SE 96th St 73160
SW 96th St
1000-1299 73139
1300-3299 73159
SE 97th Ct 73165
SW 97th Ct 73159
NE 97th St 73114
NW 97th St
200-1499 73114
6500-6599 73162
SE 97th St
300-2999 73160
4400-11499 73165
SW 97th St
1-1299 73139
2300-3199 73159
NE 97th Ter 73151
NE 98th Cir 73151
NE 98th St
600-699 73114
2000-2799 73131
7000-7099 73151
NW 98th St
900-1499 73114
6500-8299 73162
SE 98th St 73165
SW 98th St
1-1299 73139
2600-2699 73159
7600-7999 73169
SW 99th Pl 73139
NE 99th St 73131
NW 99th St
400-1499 73114
8200-8499 73162
SE 99th St 73165
SW 99th St
1-1299 73139
1300-3299 73159
SW 99th Ter 73139
SW 100th Cir 73139
SW 100th Ct 73139
NE 100th Pl 73131
SW 100th Pl 73159
NE 100th St 73131
NW 100th St
500-1499 73114
6900-8499 73162
SW 100th St
1-1299 73139
2300-3299 73159
SW 100th Ter 73139
NE 101st St
1300-1399 73131
6400-7399 73151
NW 101st St
700-1399 73114
5700-8499 73162
SW 101st St
1-1299 73139
2300-2599 73159
7600-7999 73169
NE 102nd St 73114
NW 102nd St
500-1599 73114
5700-8499 73162
SW 102nd St
1-1199 73139
2200-3299 73159
SW 102nd Ter 73159
NW 103rd Pl 73162
SW 103rd Pl
500-699 73139
3100-3299 73159
NE 103rd St 73151
NW 103rd St
900-1499 73114
5600-8999 73162
SW 103rd St
1-1299 73139
2300-3299 73159
NW 103rd Ter 73162
SW 103rd Ter
1000-1099 73139
2300-2499 73159
NE 104th Pl 73151
SW 104th Pl 73139
NE 104th St 73151
NW 104th St
300-1599 73114
7400-8999 73162
SE 104th St
3100-4099 73160
4401-4497 73165
SW 104th St
1-1299 73139
1400-3100 73159
6200-6498 73173
6501-7497 73169
8000-8098 73173

8001-8099 73169
8100-8199 73173
8301-8899 73169
NW 104th Ter 73114
SW 104th Ter 73159
SE 105th Ct 73165
SW 105th Ct 73170
SW 105th Pl 73170
NE 105th St 73151
NW 105th St
300-1499 73114
7300-8799 73162
SW 105th St
1200-3199 73170
7100-8899 73173
NW 105th Ter
1200-1499 73114
7200-8799 73162
SW 105th Ter 73170
SW 106th Pl 73170
NE 106th St
1-499 73114
7100-7399 73151
NW 106th St
400-1599 73114
5400-8999 73162
SE 106th St
4100-4199 73160
10500-13998 73165
14000-14299 73165
SW 106th St 73170
SW 106th Ter 73170
SW 107th Cir 73170
SW 107th Pl 73170
NE 107th St 73151
NW 107th St
1200-1499 73114
5400-8799 73162
SE 107th St 73165
SW 107th St
900-3199 73170
8100-8899 73173
NW 107th Ter 73162
SW 107th Ter 73170
SW 108th Pl 73170
SE 108th St
3800-4299 73160
4500-14199 73165
14201-14299 73165
SW 108th St 73170
NW 108th Ter 73162
SW 108th Ter 73170
SW 109th Ct 73173
NW 109th Pl 73162
SW 109th Pl 73170
NW 109th St
600-999 73114
2300-2799 73120
5200-8999 73162
SE 109th St 73165
SW 109th St
1000-3299 73170
6200-7999 73173
NW 109th Ter
2700-2799 73120
8300-8399 73162
NW 110th Ct 73162
SW 110th Pl 73170
NW 110th St
600-1099 73114
2400-2799 73120
5200-8999 73162
SE 110th St 73165
SW 110th St 73170
NW 110th Ter 73162
SW 110th Ter 73170
SW 111th Cir 73170
NW 111th Ct 73162
SW 111th Ct 73173
SW 111th Pl 73170
NW 111th St
200-1299 73114
2300-2799 73120
5200-8999 73162
SE 111th St 73165
SW 111th St 73170
NW 111th Ter 73162
SW 112th Pl 73170
NW 112th St
500-1299 73114
2300-2799 73120
5400-8999 73162
SE 112th St
3900-4299 73160
11800-11999 73165
SW 112th St
600-2899 73170
7300-7499 73173
NW 112th Ter
2300-3399 73120
8000-8599 73162
NW 113th Ct 73162
NW 113th Pl
2200-2499 73120
7500-7899 73162
SW 113th Pl 73170
NW 113th St
400-899 73114
2100-2699 73120
5300-8999 73162
SW 113th St
600-2799 73170
3800-4200 73173
NW 113th Ter 73162
SW 113th Ter 73170
NW 114th Cir 73162
NW 114th St
200-899 73114
2100-2799 73120
5300-8999 73162
SE 114th St 73165
SW 114th St 73170
NW 114th Ter
2500-2599 73120
7300-7499 73162
NW 115th Ct 73114
NW 115th Pl 73120
SW 115th Pl 73170
NE 115th St
400-499 73114
2000-3699 73131
NW 115th St
400-1499 73114
1700-3599 73120
5200-8999 73162
SE 115th St 73165
SW 115th St 73170
NW 115th Ter 73120
NW 116th Ct 73114
NW 116th Pl 73162
SW 116th Pl 73170
NE 116th St 73131
NW 116th St
400-1199 73114
2500-2599 73120
5500-8899 73162
SE 116th St 73165
SW 116th St 73170
NW 116th Ter
600-899 73114
3500-3599 73120
8700-8999 73162
SW 116th Ter 73170
NW 117th Ct 73162
SW 117th Pl 73170
NE 117th St 73131
NW 117th St
600-899 73114
2100-2899 73120
5200-8399 73162
SE 117th St 73165
SW 117th St 73170
NW 117th Ter 73162
NW 118th Cir
2621-2633 73120
5200-5499 73162
SW 118th Pl 73170
NE 118th St 73131
NW 118th St
300-899 73114
2100-2642 73120
4500-8599 73162
SE 118th St 73165
SW 118th St
2200-2499 73170
7100-7499 73173
NW 118th Ter 73120
NW 119th Cir 73162
NW 119th Ct 73120
SW 119th Pl 73170
NE 119th St 73131
NW 119th St
200-899 73114
2200-2799 73120
4200-8899 73162
SE 119th St 73165
SW 119th St
500-3799 73170
4000-8999 73173
NW 119th Ter
2200-2399 73120
5200-5499 73162
SW 119th Ter 73170
NW 120th Cir
2300-2334 73120
5600-5699 73162
SW 120th Cir 73170
NW 120th Ct 73162
SW 120th Pl
3100-3199 73170
4900-4999 73173
NE 120th St 73131
NW 120th St
200-799 73114
2200-2799 73120
5200-8899 73162
SW 120th St 73170
NW 120th Ter
800-899 73114
2600-2799 73120
SW 120th Ter
500-2599 73170
4800-4999 73173
NW 121st Cir
2405-2413 73120
5600-5699 73162
SW 121st Ct 73170
SW 121st Pl
500-1399 73170
4900-4999 73173
NE 121st St 73131
NW 121st St
200-699 73114
2300-2799 73120
5200-8899 73162
SW 121st St
500-3199 73170
4500-4899 73173
NW 121st Ter
600-899 73114
8800-8899 73162
SW 121st Ter 73170
NW 122nd Cir 73142
SW 122nd Ct 73170
SW 122nd Pl 73170
NE 122nd St
1-799 73114
900-1399 73131
NW 122nd St
100-1499 73114
1800-4199 73120
5600-8299 73142
SE 122nd St 73165
SW 122nd St
1300-2499 73170
4500-4999 73173
NW 122nd Ter 73162
SW 122nd Ter
2200-2299 73170
4900-5099 73173
NW 123rd Cir 73142
SW 123rd Ct 73170
NW 123rd Pl 73120
SW 123rd Pl 73170
NW 123rd St
1500-1599 73120
5200-8699 73142
SW 123rd St
1300-3499 73170
4800-6799 73173
NW 123rd Ter 73142
NW 124th Cir 73142
NW 124th Ct 73142
SW 124th Ct 73170
SW 124th Pl
500-599 73170
4700-5199 73173
NW 124th St
1500-1599 73120
5200-8699 73142
SW 124th St
1300-3699 73170
4800-5099 73173
NW 124th Ter 73142
SW 124th Ter 73170
NW 125th Ct 73142
NW 125th Pl 73142
SW 125th Pl
1300-2899 73170
4700-5199 73173
NW 125th St
1500-3899 73120
5509-5597 73142
SW 125th St
2300-3199 73170
6800-6999 73173
SW 125th Ter 73170
NW 126th Ct
1500-1599 73120
5200-5299 73142
SW 126th Ct 73173
SW 126th Pl
1300-1399 73170
4700-5199 73173
NW 126th St
1400-1699 73120
5400-8699 73142
SE 126th St 73165
SW 126th St
900-3499 73170
4700-5199 73173
SW 126th Ter
3500-3699 73170
4800-4900 73173
NW 127th Cir 73142
SW 127th Ct 73170
NW 127th Pl 73142
SW 127th Pl 73170
NW 127th St
1600-1699 73120
5500-8699 73142
SW 127th St
2900-3699 73170
4700-4999 73173
NW 128th Cir 73142
NW 128th Pl 73142
SW 128th Pl 73170
NW 128th St 73142
SE 128th St 73165
SW 128th St
1000-3699 73170
4700-6999 73173
NW 128th Ter 73142
NW 129th Cir 73142
NW 129th Ct 73142
NW 129th Pl 73142
NW 129th St 73142
SW 129th St
200-3100 73170
3102-3198 73170
4700-4999 73173
SW 129th Ter 73170
NW 130th Cir 73142
SW 130th Ct 73170
NW 130th Pl 73142
SW 130th Pl 73170
NW 130th St 73142
SW 130th St
1000-3699 73170
4800-4999 73173
NW 130th Ter 73142
NW 131st Cir 73142
NW 131st Ct 73142
NW 131st St 73142
SW 131st St 73170
NW 131st Ter 73142
SW 131st Ter 73170
NW 132nd Cir 73142
NW 132nd Pl 73142
SW 132nd Pl 73170
NW 132nd St
1-399 73114
5300-7599 73142
SW 132nd St 73170
NW 132nd Ter 73142
NW 133rd Pl 73142
SW 133rd Pl 73170
NW 133rd St 73142
SW 133rd St 73170
NW 133rd Ter 73142
NW 134th St 73142
SE 134th St 73165
SW 134th St
200-4099 73170
4100-7500 73173
7502-7698 73173
NW 134th Ter 73142
SW 134th Ter 73170
NW 135th Cir 73142
SW 135th Cir 73170
NW 135th Pl 73142
SW 135th Pl 73170
NE 135th St 73131
NW 135th St
3300-3400 73120
5700-6498 73142
SW 135th St 73170
NW 135th Ter 73142
SW 135th Ter 73170
SW 136th Cir 73170
NW 136th Ct 73142
NW 136th Pl 73142
SW 136th Pl 73170
SW 136th St 73170
SW 136th Ter 73170
SW 137th Ct 73170
SW 137th Pl 73170
NW 137th St 73134
SE 137th St 73165
SW 137th St 73170
SW 137th Ter 73170
NW 138th St 73134
SW 138th St 73170
SW 138th Ter 73170
SW 139th Ct 73170
NW 139th St 73142
SE 139th St 73165
SW 139th St
1-3299 73170
7100-7199 73173
NW 140th St
2200-2799 73134
8300-8499 73142
SW 140th St 73170
SW 140th Ter 73170
NW 141st Cir 73142
SW 141st Pl 73170
NW 141st St 73142
SE 141st St 73165
SW 141st St 73170
SW 141st Ter 73170
NW 142nd St
1900-2099 73134
8300-8499 73142
SE 142nd St 73165
SW 142nd St 73170
NW 143rd St 73134
SW 143rd St 73170
NW 143rd Ter 73142
NW 144th Pl 73134
NW 144th St 73134
SE 144th St 73165
SW 144th St 73170
NW 144th Ter 73134
NW 145th St 73134
SE 145th St 73165
SW 145th St 73170
NW 146th St
4100-4299 73134
8001-8499 73142
SW 146th St 73170
NW 146th Ter 73134
NW 147th St 73134
SE 147th St 73165
SW 147th St 73170
NW 147th Ter 73142
NW 148th St 73134
SE 148th St 73165
SW 148th St 73170
NW 148th Ter 73134
SW 149th Pl 73170
NW 149th St
2900-4299 73134
8100-8299 73142
SE 149th St 73165
SW 149th St
500-4299 73170
4900-5300 73173
5302-5698 73173
SE 150th Ct 73165
NW 150th St
2000-2798 73134
2800-4399 73134
5301-7497 73142
7499-8899 73142
SW 150th St 73170
NW 150th Ter 73134
SW 151st Cir 73170
SE 151st St 73165
SW 151st St 73170
SE 152nd Ct 73165
SW 152nd Pl 73170
SE 152nd St 73165
SW 153rd St 73170
SE 154th Ct 73165
SW 154th Ct 73170
SW 154th Pl 73170
SE 154th St 73165
SW 154th St 73170
SW 155th Ct 73170
SW 155th Pl 73170
SE 155th St 73165
SW 155th St 73170
SW 156th Ct 73170
SW 156th Pl 73170
SE 156th St 73165
SW 156th St
500-1099 73170
5100-5198 73173
5200-5299 73173
SW 157th Cir 73170
SE 157th Pl 73165
SE 157th St 73165
SW 157th St 73170
SE 158th St 73165
SW 158th St 73170
SW 158th Ter 73170
SE 159th St 73165
SW 159th St
500-699 73170
4600-5199 73173
SW 159th Ter 73170
SW 160th Ct 73170
SE 160th St 73165
SW 160th St 73170
SE 161st Ct 73165
SW 161st St 73170
SE 162nd St 73165
SW 162nd St 73170
SE 163rd Ct 73165
SW 163rd St 73170
SE 164th St 73165
SW 164th St 73170
SW 164th Ter 73170
SW 168th St 73170
SW 169th St 73170
170th St & Ter 73170
171st Ct & St 73170
172nd Cir & St 73170
SW 173rd St 73170
SW 174th St 73170
SW 175th Ter 73170

PONCA CITY OK

General Delivery 74601

POST OFFICE BOXES MAIN OFFICE STATIONS AND BRANCHES

Box No.s
All PO Boxes 74602

RURAL ROUTES

01, 04, 05, 07, 08, 09 74601
02, 03, 05, 07, 09 74604

NAMED STREETS

A St 74604
Aa St 74604
Academy Rd 74604
Acoma Pl 74604
Adams Rd 74604
E Adobe Rd 74604
W Adobe Rd 74601
E & W Albany Ave 74601
E Alma Ave 74601
Ames Ave 74604
Ann Ave 74604
N & S Ash St 74601
Ashbury Rd 74604
Ashley Pl 74604
Austin Rd 74601
Autumn Rd 74604
Avon Ave 74604
B St 74604
B J Rd 74604
Bainbridge Ave 74604
Bales Ln 74604
Barclay Pl 74601
Bass Dr 74604
Bell Rd 74604
Bellflower Ave 74604
N Beralist St 74601
Berkshire Dr 74604
Bermuda Dr 74604
Big Hill Rd 74604
Big Snake Rd 74604
N & S Birch St 74601
Blackard Ln 74604
Blake Dr 74604
Blue Elk Dr 74601
Blue Jay Ln 74604
Bluebird Ln 74604
Bluestem Rd 74604
Bobwhite Rd 74604
Bonnie Dr 74601
S Bonnie Rd 74604
Bowman Rd 74604
Bradbary Ln 74601
Braden School Rd 74604
Braden School 8 Rd 74604
Bradley Ave 74604
E Bradley Ave 74601
W Brake Rd 74601
Brentwood Dr 74601
Briar Ridge Rd 74604
Bridge Ave 74604
E & W Broadway Ave 74601
E & W Brookfield Ave 74601
Broughton Rd 74601
Buffalo Dr 74601
Burgundy Pl 74604
Burr Oak St 74604
C St 74604
Cadet Rd 74604
Cains Mhp Rd 74604
Calvert Dr 74601
Canary Dr & Pl 74601
Candace Dr 74604
Canterbury Ave 74604
Cardinal Rd 74604
Catfish Dr 74604
Cedar Ln & St 74604
Cedar Valley Rd 74604
E Central Ave
100-1299 74601
1400-1798 74604
1800-2599 74604
W Central Ave 74601
Chapel Hill Rd 74604
Checkstand Rd 74604
E & W Cherry Ave 74601
E & W Chestnut Ave 74601
Christmas Tree Ln 74604
Christy Ln 74604
Chuck Dr 74604

Church St 74604
City View Rd 74604
Clarke St 74601
Cleary Dr 74604
E & W Cleveland Ave 74601
Clifton Ln 74604
E Coleman Rd
  700-1499 74601
  1600-9299 74604
W Coleman Rd 74601
E & W Comanche Ave 74601
Cookson Dr 74604
Cooley Ave 74601
Coon Creek Cv 74604
Coppercreek 74604
Copperfield Ave & Cir 74604
Coronado St 74604
Cory Rd 74601
W County Line Rd 74601
County Rd 190 74601
County Rd 240 74601
County Road 230 74601
County Road 6301 74604
Cowboy 74601
E & W Cowboy Hill Pl & Rd 74601
Cowskin Dr 74601
Crawford Ave 74604
Crown St 74604
D St 74604
Dakota 74601
Dalewood Ln 74604
Darr Park Dr 74601
De Soto St 74604
Dean Ave 74604
Deer Pl 74604
Denoya Rd 74604
E & W Detroit Ave 74601
E Dixie Ave 74601
Donahoe Dr 74601
Donald Ave 74604
Donner Ave & Pl 74604
W Doolin Ave 74601
Dove Dr & Ln 74604
Dover Dr 74604
Doyle Keirn Ave 74601
Drake Dr & Ln 74604
E Drummond Ave 74601
Duane Ave 74604
E St 74604
Eagle Rd 74601
Eagle Nest 74601
Edgewood Dr 74604
Edwards Ave 74601
El Camino St 74604
Elm Ave 74604
N Elm St 74601
S Elm St 74601
Elmwood Ave 74601
E & W Emporia Ave 74601
N & S Enterprise Rd 74604
Fa Lan Heights Rd 74604
Fa Lan Ridge Rd 74604
Fairview Ave 74601
Fairway Ln & Pl 74604
Fawn Ln 74604
Fern Dr 74604
Field Crest Dr 74604
Fields Rd 74604
Fieldstone Trl 74604
Fishermans Bend Rd 74604
Fleming Rd 74604
N & S Flormable St 74601
Forest Rd 74604
Foster Ave 74601
Fouad Dr 74604
E & W Fountain Rd 74601
Four Wheel Dr 74604
Fox Xing 74604
S Franklin St 74601
Frazier Rd 74604
E & W Fresno Ave 74601
Frontier Ave 74604
E Furguson Ave
  600-1098 74601
  1100-1499 74601
  3300-8599 74604
W Furguson Ave 74601
Garden St 74601
Garden View Dr 74604
E & W Gary Ave 74601
George Braden Rd 74604
Gibson Pl 74601
Ginger Dr 74604
Glasgow Rd 74604
Glendale Ave 74601
Glenmore Pl 74601
Glenside Ave 74601
Goldenrod Ave 74604
E Grand Ave
  100-499 74601
  402-402 74602
  500-1398 74601
  501-1399 74601
  1500-1599 74604
W Grand Ave 74601
Gray Ave 74601
Green Meadow Dr 74604
Greenbriar Ct 74604
Greenbriar Rd 74601
Greenwood Ave 74601
Guinn Rd 74604
Hall Blvd 74601
Hampton Dr 74601
Hanna Dr 74604
Hargraves Rd 74604
E Hartford Ave
  100-198 74601
  200-1299 74601
  1400-9899 74604
W Hartford Ave 74601
Harth Ave 74601
Harvest Rd 74601
Hathaway St 74604
Havenwood Rd 74604
E & W Hazel Ave 74601
Hazen Rd 74604
N & S Heather Rdg 74604
Hiawatha Cir & Dr 74604
Hickory Ln 74604
High Pointe Dr 74604
E & W Highland Ave 74601
S Highway 177 74604
Highway 60 74604
E Highway 60
  700-998 74601
E Highway 60
  2700-3899 74604
  3901-64699 74604
W Highway 60 74601
N Highway 77 74601
N Highway 77 Access Rd 74601
E Hillcrest Dr 74604
SW Hillside Ave & Rd 74601
Hilltop Dr 74604
Hoddy Rd 74604
Holbrook St 74604
Holmes Rd 74604
Homestead N 74604
Honeywood St 74604
Houseman Rd 74604
E Houston Ave 74601
Howard St 74604
E Hubbard Rd
  700-1499 74601
  1500-8799 74604
W Hubbard Rd 74601
Hubbs Estate Rd 74604
Hudson Dr 74601
Hummingbird Ln 74604
E Hunt Rd 74604
Hunters Inn Rd 74604
Huntington Pl 74604
Indian Spgs 74604
N & S Indian Hill Rd 74604
Indian Hills Rd 74604
Industrial Blvd 74601
N & S Irving St 74601
Jamison Rd 74604
Jane St 74601
Joe St 74601
Joe Colby Rd 74604
John St 74601
John B Hayes Rd 74601
Jones Rd 74604
Juanito Ave 74604
Jupiter Pkwy 74601
Kay Dr 74604
N & S Keeler Rd 74604
Keeler 10 Rd 74604
Kelley Ave 74604
Kildare Rd 74604
Kimball Rd 74604
Kingston Rd 74604
Klufa Rd 74604
Knight Rd 74604
E Knight Rd 74604
Knight St 74601
Knox Rd 74604
Kygar Rd 74604
Kyme Dr 74604
L A Cann Dr & Rd 74604
Laila Pl 74604
E Lake Dr 74604
Lake Rd 74604
N Lake St 74601
S Lake St 74601
Lakeview Dr 74604
Lansbrook Rd 74601
Larchmont Ave 74604
Larkspur Dr 74604
Larue Rd 74604
Lazear Rd 74604
Leatherman Rd 74604
Lechtenburg Rd 74604
Lee Ave 74604
Leisure Ln 74604
Lemon Tree Ln 74604
Leslie Ln 74604
Lewis Dr 74604
E & W Liberty Ave 74601
Lil Acres Rd 74604
S Lincoln St 74601
Linwood St 74601
Little Ln 74601
SW Longview Blvd 74601
N Longwood Rd 74604
Lonnie Ave 74601
Lora Ave 74601
E Madison Ave 74601
E Maple Ave 74601
Maple St 74604
Marland Dr 74601
Martha Ave 74601
E Mary Rd 74604
Mary St 74601
May Ave & St 74604
Mccord Rd 74604
Mcenany Rd 74604
Mcfadden Dr 74601
Mcfadden Cove Rd 74604
Mcgee Ln 74604
Mcgraw Dr 74601
Mckinley Pl 74601
Mcnew Rd 74604
Meadow Ln 74604
Meadowbrook Dr & St 74604
Melrose Dr 74604
Memory Ln 74601
Merrifield Rd 74604
Michael Dr & Ln 74604
SW Miller Ave & Ln 74601
Mistletoe Dr 74604
N & S Misty Isle Rd 74604
Mockingbird Dr & Ln 74604
Moneytree Dr 74604
Monterey St 74601
Monument Rd 74604
Nazarene Church Rd 74601
Nightengale Ln 74604
Noel Ln 74604
W North Ave 74601
Nottingham Cir & Dr 74604
N & S Oak St 74601
Oak Place Rd 74604
Oakdale Rd 74604
N & S Oaken Gate Rd 74604
E & W Oakland Ave 74601
Oakridge Rd 74604
Oakwood St 74604
E Oklahoma Ave
  100-1299 74601
  1400-1699 74604
W Oklahoma Ave 74601
Old Country Rd 74604
E Old River Rd 74604
Olivewood Ct 74604
N & S Olympia St 74601
Oneill Ln 74604
Orchard Ln 74604
Oriole St 74601
Osage Ln 74604
N Osage St 74601
S Osage St 74601
E & W Otoe Ave 74601
E & W Overbrook Ave 74601
Overcrest Rd 74604
Overlook Rd 74604
Oxford Dr 74604
S P St 74601
N & S Palm St 74601
E Park Ave 74601
W Park Ave 74601
Park Pl 74604
Parkview Ln 74601
Patton Dr 74601
Paul Rd 74604
N & S Peachtree St 74601
N & NE Pecan Pl & Rd 74604
Perch Ln 74604
S Perry St 74601
Pike Ln 74604
N & S Pine St 74601
Pioneer Rd 74604
N, NE & S Pleasant View Pl & Rd 74601
E & W Ponca Ave & Dr 74601
Pond Rd 74604
Poplar Ave 74601
Potomac Dr 74601
Prairie View Dr 74604
N & S Prentice Rd 74604
Princeton Ave
  1100-1300 74601
  1302-1398 74601
  1401-1597 74604
  1599-1899 74604
  1901-1999 74604
Private Road 6952 74604
E Prospect Ave
  300-1299 74601
  1301-1399 74601
  1500-8899 74604
W Prospect Ave 74601
Prospect Rd 74604
S Prospect Rd 74604
N & S Q St 74601
Quail Ln 74604
Quail Ridge Rd 74604
Quarterhorse Ln 74604
Queens Ave 74604
N & S R St 74601
Rainbow Dr 74604
Raintree St 74604
Ramblewood St 74604
N & S Ranch Dr 74601
Ray Rd 74604
Reaves Rd 74604
Red Hawk Ln 74601
Red Oak Dr 74604
Redbird Dr 74601
Redbud Dr 74604
Reddick Rd 74604
Reveille Dr 74604
Rhgato Acres Rd 74604
Rice St 74604
Richardson Rd 74604
Richway Dr 74601
Ridge Dr 74604
Ridge Creek Rd 74604
Riggs Dr 74601
River St 74604
River Ridge Dr 74604
SW Riverside Ave 74601
Riverview Dr 74604
Riverview Pl 74601
E Riverview Rd 74601
W Riverview Rd 74601
Riviera Dr 74601
Road Runner Dr 74604
Robin Rd 74604
N & S Rock Cliff Rd 74604
Rockview Rd 74604
Rocky Ridge Pl & Rd 74604
Roosevelt Ave 74601
Rose Ln 74604
Rosedale Dr 74604
Rustic Rd 74604
N & S S St 74601
Santa Fe St 74601
Scissortail Ln 74604
E Scott Ave 74601
Seeley Rd 74604
E Seventy Rd 74604
Shady Pl 74601
Shamrock Cir 74601
Shannon Rd 74601
Sharon Pl 74604
Shasta Ave 74604
Sherman Ln 74604
Sherwin Ave 74604
Shirlee Ave
  1000-1299 74601
  1400-1699 74604
N & S Silverdale Ln 74604
Skinner Ln 74604
Skylark Rd 74604
Sneed Rd 74604
Sooner Ln 74604
Souligny Rd 74601
E South Ave
  201-397 74601
  399-1399 74601
  1400-9499 74604
W South Ave 74601
Spring Rd & Vlg 74604
Spring Village Ct 74604
Springwood St 74604
Stangeland Rd 74604
Stardust Ln & Trl 74604
Starting Point Dr 74601
N & S Stephens St 74601
Stolhand Rd 74604
Stoneridge Rd 74604
Sugar Maple Dr 74604
Summer Field Ave 74604
Summers Pl 74604
E Summit Ave 74601
W Summit Ave 74601
Summit St 74604
Sunny Ln 74601
N & S Sunset St 74601
Sweigart Rd 74604
Sykes Blvd 74601
N & S T St 74601
Talmer Pl & Rd 74604
Tanglewood Cir 74604
Tanglewood Stables Rd 74604
Tapp Rd 74604
Temple Pl 74604
Throop Blvd 74601
Throop Blvd 74601
Timberline 1st 74604
Timberline 2nd 74604
Timberline Mobile Home Park Rd 74604
Todd Dr 74604
E Tower Rd
  700-1100 74601
  1102-1298 74601
  1600-9699 74604
W Tower Rd 74601
Trio Ln 74604
Turkey Crk 74604
Turner St 74604
Turquoise Pl 74604
N & S U St 74601
N & S Union St 74601
Us Highway 60 74604
Valley Cir 74604
Valley Rd 74601
Valleyview Dr 74604
Victory St 74604
Village Cir 74601
Viola Ave 74601
Virginia Ave 74601
N & S W St 74601
Walker Rd 74604
E Walnut Ave
  100-498 74601
  500-1099 74601
  1500-1599 74604
W Walnut Ave 74601
Walters Rd 74604
Warwick Rd 74601
S Washington St 74601
NW & S Waverly Rd & St 74601
Wellington Rd 74604
Westbury Rd 74601
Whippoorwill Rd 74604
W White Eagle Dr & Rd 74601
Whitlock Ln 74604
Whitworth Ave 74601
Wilde Rd 74604
Wildwood Ave 74604
Willow Ave 74604
Willow Springs Rd 74601
Willow Wood Pl 74604
Windsor Rd 74601
Winter Green Ave 74604
E Woodbury Rd 74601
Woodcreek Rd 74604
Woodcrest 74604
E, N & NE Woodland Rd 74604
Woodmont Cir 74604
Woodmoor Pl 74604
Woodridge Dr 74604
Woodthrush Rd 74604
Wren Dr & Pl 74601
Yale Ave 74604
Young Ave 74601

NUMBERED STREETS

N & S 1st 74601
N & S 2nd 74601
N & S 3rd 74601
N & S 4th 74601
S 5 Mile Rd 74604
N & S 5th 74601
N & S 6th 74601
N & S 7 Mile 74604
N & S 7th 74601
N & S 8 Mile 74604
N & S 8th 74601
N & S 9 Mile 74604
9th Ave 74604
N 9th St 74601
S 9th St 74601
10th Ave 74604
N 10th St 74601
S 10th St 74601
11th Ave 74604
N 11th St 74601
S 11th St 74601
N & S 12th 74604
N & S 13th 74601
N & S 14th 74601
85th Rd 74604
S 11 Mile Rd 74604
E 20 74604
E 30 74604
E 40 Rd 74604
N 40 Rd 74601
E 45 74604
60 Rd 74604
65 Rd 74604
E 70 74604
E 80 74604
E 85 Rd 74604
E 90 74604

PRYOR OK

General Delivery 74361

POST OFFICE BOXES MAIN OFFICE STATIONS AND BRANCHES

Box No.s
All PO Boxes 74362

RURAL ROUTES

01, 02, 03, 04 74361

HIGHWAY CONTRACTS

65, 68, 70 74361

NAMED STREETS

All Street Addresses 74361

NUMBERED STREETS

All Street Addresses 74361

SAPULPA OK

General Delivery 74066

POST OFFICE BOXES MAIN OFFICE STATIONS AND BRANCHES

Box No.s
All PO Boxes 74067

RURAL ROUTES

01, 02, 04, 05, 06, 07, 08, 09, 10 74066

NAMED STREETS

N & S Adams St 74066
E & W Anderson Ave 74066
W Andrew Ave 74066
W Appaloosa Dr 74066
Apple Pl & St 74066
Arcadia Ln 74066
E Arch Ave 74066
Ashton Rd 74066
Belle Ln 74066
Bennett Rd 74066
Beverly Dr 74066
N & S Birch St 74066
E & W Bird St 74066
S Bixby St 74066
Blackjack Rd 74066
N & S Boyd Cir, Pl & St 74066
Brenner Rd 74066
Briarwood St 74066
Brittany Ct 74066
Brittin Ln 74066
Brook Ln 74066
N Brown St 74066
Bruce Ave 74066
E & W Bryan Ave 74066
Buford Ave 74066
N & S Burnett St 74066
E & W Burnham Ave 74066

Burroughs Rd 74066
Cardinal Cir 74066
E Carriage Rd 74066
Castle Creek Dr 74066
S & W Cedar Dr, Ln & St 74066
Cedar Creek Cir 74066
Challenger St 74066
S Chestnut 74066
S Cheyenne Rd 74066
Circle Dr 74066
Clearview Cir 74066
E & W Cleveland Ave 74066
E Cobb Ave 74066
S Codi St 74066
Colleen Dr 74066
Colonial Dr 74066
Columbia Ave & St 74066
Concord Cir 74066
Cordova Ct 74066
Cornelius Ct 74066
Cornerstone Ct 74066
Cottonwood Rd 74066
W Country Rd 74066
Countrywood Way 74066
E & W Courtney Ave & Cir 74066
Creekside Dr 74066
E Crestview Dr 74066
Cross Timbers Blvd 74066
Custer St 74066
E & W Davis Ave & Dr 74066
N Dawn Ln & Pl 74066
E Denton Ave 74066
E & W Dewey Ave 74066
S Diane St 74066
W Dickey Rd 74066
N & S Division St 74066
Dogwood Ln & Pl 74066
Donna St 74066
Dripping Springs Dr 74066
Dugans Rd 74066
Dusty Trl 74066
Echo Rd 74066
Edgewood Ln & Trl 74066
Eisenhower St 74066
N Elizabeth St 74066
N & S Elm St 74066
Emily Cir 74066
E & W Fairlane Ct, Dr & Pl 74066
E Fairview Ave 74066
E & W Falcon Cir & Dr 74066
E & W Fern Ave 74066
E Fife Ave 74066
Foreacre Cir & Dr 74066
Forest St 74066
Forest Lake Dr 74066
Foxwood Ct & Dr 74066
Franklin Rd 74066
Frankoma Rd 74066
Freedom Ave & Rd 74066
Frontier Rd 74066
Gail Ln 74066
Galaxy Pl & Rd 74066
N Gammil Ct 74066
Gano Rd 74066
W Garfield Ave 74066
S Garrett St 74066
Glendale Rd 74066
E Glenpool Ave 74066
Glidden Ave 74066
E & W Goodykoontz Ave 74066
E & W Gordon Ave 74066
N Gore St 74066
Gowdy Rd 74066
N Graham 74066
Grandview Ave 74066
Grant St 74066
Gray Ave & St 74066
E Grayson Ave 74066
Green Hill Dr 74066
Grisham Ave 74066
S Grove St 74066
Gunner Loop 74066
E Haskell Ave 74066
E & W Hastain Ave & Pl 74066
S Hawthorne St 74066
W Heights Dr 74066
Henshaw Ave 74066
Heywood Hill Rd 74066
S Hiawatha St 74066
W, N & S Hickory Dr & St 74066
Hickory Bluff Rd 74066
Hickory Hill Rd 74066
E & W Highway 117 74066
E Highway 166 74066
W Highway 33 74066
S & W Highway 66 74066
S Highway 75 74066
S Highway 75a 74066
Highway 97 N 74066
E Hill Ave 74066
Hillside Dr 74066
E & W Hilton Rd 74066
E & W Hobson Ave 74066
N Hodge St 74066
W Houston St 74066
W Howard St 74066
Hunters Hl 74066
E Illinois 74066
S Independence St 74066
Industrial Rd 74066
E & W Jackson Ave N & S 74066
E James Ave 74066
N Jennetta St 74066
N Johannas St 74066
W Johnson Dr & St 74066
Jolin 74066
E Jones Ave 74066
S Kathy Ln & St 74066
W Keeling Ave 74066
Kevin Ln 74066
W King St 74066
Kings Crest Dr 74066
Kingsway St 74066
Lakeside Dr 74066
E & W Lakeview Cir, Ct & Dr 74066
W Larkspur Ln 74066
S Lasiter Ave 74066
W Laura St 74066
Laurel Oaks Cir & Rd 74066
Laury Ln 74066
N Leah St 74066
E & W Lee Ave & Cir 74066
Lense Iv Ct 74066
N Leonard St 74066
Lexington Rd 74066
Liberty Bell Ln 74066
E & W Lincoln Ave 74066
W Linda Ln & St 74066
N & S Linden St 74066
Lindsay Ln 74066
Lindsey Dr 74066
E & W Line Ave, Pl & St 74066
S Loblolly 74066
Lone Star Rd 74066
Longhorn Ave, Cir & Ct 74066
Luker Ln 74066
Lynn Ln 74066
Mabelle Dr 74066
N Main St 74066
S Main St
1-499 74066
410-410 74067
500-16098 74066
501-16099 74066
Mandy Ct 74066
N Mann St 74066
N & S Maple St 74066
W Mary Lynn Dr 74066
S Mason Rd 74066
Maybelle Dr 74066
Mayfield St 74066
Mcdonald Rd 74066
E & W Mckinley Ave 74066
E Mcleod Ave 74066
Melinda Rd 74066
Melissa Cir 74066
S Mesa Cir & Rd 74066
Midcrest Cir 74066
W Mike Ave 74066
E & W Mill Ave 74066
N & S Mission St 74066
N & S Moccasin Blf, Ln, Pl & St 74066
W Mockingbird Ln 74066
E Moman Ave 74066
E & W Monterey Ave 74066
Mose Meadows Rd 74066
W, N & S Mounds Ct & St 74066
E Murphy Ave 74066
E, W & S Muskogee Ave & St 74066
Mustang Cir 74066
Nafcoat Ln 74066
New Sapulpa Rd 74066
W Newburg Ave 74066
W Norma St 74066
Northaven Ave & Ct 74066
W Nunley Ave 74066
N & S Oak St 74066
W Oak Leaf Dr 74066
S Oakwood Cir 74066
W Obrien Cir 74066
S & W Oklahoma Ave & St 74066
E & W Okmulgee Ave 74066
W Orleans Ave 74066
Overcrest Ln 74066
S Overlook Dr 74066
W Ozark Trl 74066
E & W Paige Ave 74066
Panther Ln 74066
N & S Park St 74066
Patrick Pl 74066
Patriot Ln 74066
Patton St 74066
N Pearson Dr 74066
E & W Perkins Ave 74066
E Pfendler Ave 74066
S Pinehill Rd 74066
Pinto Ln 74066
Pioneer Rd 74066
W, N & S Poplar Ct & St 74066
E & W Portland St 74066
S Postoak Rd 74066
Quail Run Ln 74066
S Quenath St 74066
W Quickel Dr 74066
Raintree Cir 74066
Ranger Rd 74066
E & W Ray Ave & Ln 74066
Regency Ln 74066
Ridge Rd 74066
Ridge Oak Ln & Rd 74066
Ridge Pointe Dr 74066
Ridgeview Dr, Rd & St 74066
N & S Ridgeway St 74066
Rockcrest Ln 74066
Rockwood Dr & Ln N 74066
Rockwood North Cir 74066
Rodgers Rd 74066
W Roosevelt Ave 74066
E, W & N Ross Ave & St 74066
Royal Oak Ln 74066
N & S Ruble St 74066
Sahoma Lake Rd 74066
S Scott St 74066
Seminary Ave 74066
Shadow Cir & Ln 74066
S Shaw Dr 74066
Sherlyn Ln 74066
Sherman 74066
Simmental Ln 74066
Skyline Cir 74066
W Southfork Rd 74066
E & W Speer Ave 74066
N Spocogee St 74066
W Springdale Ave 74066
S Spruce St 74066
Stagecoach Dr 74066
Stanfield Rd 74066
Starling Ct 74066
State Highway 75a 74066
S Stephanie St 74066
W Strauss Rd 74066
Summercrest Ct 74066
Sunset Dr, Hl & Ln 74066
Surrey Ln 74066
E & W Taft Ave 74066
E Tamah Ln 74066
E & W Teel Rd 74066
E Teresa Ave 74066
Terrace Dr 74066
Terrill Cir 74066
E & W Thompson Ave & Rd 74066
Thunderbird Ln 74066
W Tiger Ln 74066
Timber Hill Dr 74066
Timberlake Dr 74066
Timberton Rd 74066
Tracie Ln 74066
Trail Ridge Rd 74066
E University Ave 74066
Valley Rd & Vw 74066
Valwood Ln 74066
S Vancouver Ave 74066
Via Los Robles St 74066
Victory Ln 74066
S Waco Ave 74066
N Wallace St 74066
N & S Walnut Dr & St 74066
E Washington Ave 74066
Watashe Ln 74066
E, N & S Watchorn Ave & St 74066
N & S Water St 74066
S Webb Pl 74066
E & W Wells Blvd 74066
Westgreen Way 74066
Westland Dr & Rd 74066
S Whitehouse Dr 74066
S Wickham Rd 74066
Wildwood Cir 74066
S & W Willow Ln 74066
S Woodbine Dr 74066
Woodland Ave & Rd 74066
Woodmere Ln 74066
Woodview Ln 74066
S Yukon Ave 74066

NUMBERED STREETS

All Street Addresses 74066

SEMINOLE OK

General Delivery 74868

POST OFFICE BOXES MAIN OFFICE STATIONS AND BRANCHES

Box No.s
All PO Boxes 74818

RURAL ROUTES

01, 02, 03, 04, 05 74868

NAMED STREETS

All Street Addresses 74868

NUMBERED STREETS

All Street Addresses 74868

SHAWNEE OK

General Delivery 74801

POST OFFICE BOXES MAIN OFFICE STATIONS AND BRANCHES

Box No.s
All PO Boxes 74802

RURAL ROUTES

04, 05, 06, 09, 11 74801
01, 02, 03, 07, 08, 10, 12 74804

NAMED STREETS

Abigail Dr 74801
Acme Rd
3001-5397 74804
5399-15299 74804
16500-16699 74801
16701-16899 74801
E Ada St 74801
Airport Dr 74804
E Alice St 74801
Alma Ln 74801
Amber Rdg 74801
American Way 74804
Amy Ave 74804
Angel Ln 74801
Angie Ln 74801
E Anna St 74801
Apache 74801
Apple Rd 74801
Aquarius 74804
Arapaho Dr 74801
Archery Range Rd 74801
Ariana St 74804
Ashley Dr 74804
Aspen Dr
1-99 74801
1000-1099 74804
Aspen Pl 74804
Augusta Ct & Dr 74801
Austin Dr 74801
Autumn Ln 74804
N Aydelotte Ave
200-699 74801
2100-4499 74804
S Aydelotte Ave 74801
Aydelotte Cir 74801
E & W Ayre St 74801
Baker St 74801
Bankhead Ln 74804
E Bannock St 74801
Barnard Ln 74801
Barnes Rd 74804
N Beard Ave
100-1399 74801
1401-1499 74801
1500-3400 74804
3402-3898 74804
S Beard Ave 74801
Beccon Rd 74804
Beckley St 74804
Belcher Rd 74801
N Bell Ave
100-699 74801
1700-3299 74804
3301-3799 74801
S Bell Ave 74801
Bella Vista Ln 74804
Belle Brook Cir 74804
W Benedict St 74801
Benson Park Rd & Spur 74801
Bent Tree Rd 74804
E Bentley St 74801
Berkshire Pl 74804
Bethel Rd
5000-5598 74804
5600-14099 74804
15100-15298 74801
15300-19499 74801
Bettie Sue Dr 74804
Big Sky Dr 74804
Bingham Cir & Ct 74804
Birdie Ln 74804
Bison Rd 74804
Blaine Rd 74804
Blaise Dr 74804
Blue Cedar Cir 74804
E & W Bluff St 74801
Bob Crouch Dr & Rd 74801
Bobolink 74804
N Bonita Ave
500-700 74801
702-1098 74801
2000-2299 74804
Boomer Rd 74804
Bradford Ct 74804
E Bradley St 74801
Brangus Rd
5100-14899 74804
15301-15397 74801
15399-19999 74801
Brenna Ct 74804
Brentwood Pl 74804
Briarwood St 74804
Bridlewood Ct 74804
Bristow Ln 74801
N Broadway Ave
100-1499 74801
1500-2900 74804
2902-2998 74804
S Broadway Ave 74801
Brook Holw 74804
Brookridge 74804
Brownstone Way 74804
N Bryan Ave
101-197 74801
199-1499 74801
1600-6099 74804
S Bryan Ave 74801
N Bryan Rd 74804
Bryant Via 74804
Buck Dr & Rd 74801
Buckthorne Cir 74804
Burlison Rd 74801
Burning Wood Dr 74804
E & W Burns St 74801
Burr Dr 74801
Bush Creek Dr 74801
Butler Dr 74804
Butterfly Dr 74804
Cabin Trl 74804
E California 74801
Calle Laventa 74804
Camaron Dr 74804
Cambridge Ct & Dr 74804
Camelot Ct 74804
E & W Cammack Cir & St 74804
Candlewood Dr 74804
Capricorn 74804
Cardinal Ln 74804
Carmin Dr 74804
Carol Dr 74804
Carol Ln 74801
Castle Creek Pl & St 74804
Castle Rock Ln 74804
Cedar Ln 74801
Cedar Bend Ct 74804
Cedar Creek Dr 74804
Cedar Ridge Rd 74804
N Center Ave
100-1499 74801
1500-1698 74804
1700-1899 74804
1901-1999 74804
S Center Ave 74801
E Chandler Cir, Dr & St 74801
N Chapman Ave
300-1399 74801
2100-4499 74804
S Chapman Ave 74801
Charles Dr 74804
Charleston Loop & Pt 74801
Checotah Ln 74801
Cherokee St 74801
Chevy Chase 74804
Cheyenne Dr 74801
E & W Chicago St 74804
Chickasaw Dr 74801
Choctaw Rd 74801
Churchill 74804
Citizen Place North Rd 74801
Clark Cir 74804
Clearpond Ln & Rd 74801
N Cleveland Ave 74801
Club House Dr 74801
Cobblestone Dr 74804
Coffman 74801
Coker Rd
5200-14099 74804
15000-19699 74801
Comanche Cir & Dr 74801
Concord Blvd 74804
Cook Ave 74801
Copper Creek Ln 74804
Cottage Dr 74804
Cottage Park Ln 74804
Cotton Tail Dr 74804
Country Club Rd 74801
E Country Grove Dr 74804
Cow Trail Dr 74801
Creek Dr & Rd 74801
Crest Dr 74801
Crimson Ln 74804
Crooked Oak Ct & Dr 74804
Crosslin Rd
5000-14799 74804
15600-17899 74801
Crown Pt 74804
Cuyler Dr 74804
Cypress Dr 74804
Dakota Dr 74801
Daley Ln 74801
Dany Ln 74801
E Darrow St 74801
David Dr 74804
Dawson Ln 74804
Dee Dee Dr 74804
Deer Valley Dr 74804
Del Rancho Ct & Ln 74804
Delaware Dr 74801
Dennis Blvd 74804
Derek Rd 74804
E & W Dewey St 74801
E Dexter St 74801
W Dill St 74801
S Dixon Ave 74801
Donald Dr 74804
Donna Ln 74801
N Dorothy Ave
500-699 74801
2000-2299 74804
Doug Dr 74804
Dougherty Dr 74804
N Douglas St 74801
Doyle Dr 74801
N & S Draper Ave 74801
Drummond Rd
13200-14999 74804
15300-19299 74801
E Drummond St 74801
W Drummond St 74801
Dukes Realm 74804
E & W Dunbar St 74801
E Dunlop Rd 74804
Dustin Cir 74804
Eagle Rd 74804
Earl Dr 74804
N Eastern Ave 74801
Eckel Rd 74801
Econtuchka Rd 74804
S Eden Ave 74801
E Edwards St 74801
Elberta Ave 74804
E & W Elizabeth St 74804
Ella Ln 74804

Ellis Dr 74804
N Elm Ave
201-297 74801
299-599 74801
1500-1898 74804
Emerald Ct 74804
E & W Emmett St 74804
English Dr 74804
Enterprise Ct 74804
Eric Dr 74804
Eugene Dr 74804
Fairview Ln 74804
Faith Blvd 74804
Falencol Rd 74801
E & W Farrall 74801
Father Joe Murphy Dr 74804
Fawn Trl 74804
E Fay St 74801
E & W Federal St 74804
Fischer Dr 74804
N Florence Ave 74801
Flossie Hattler Rd 74801
W Ford St 74801
E & W Forrest St 74801
Fountain Lake Dr 74804
Fox Run 74804
Frank Ln 74801
Frank Buck Dr 74804
E & W Franklin Cir, Dr & St 74804
Frosty Acres 74801
Gabriel 74804
Gaddy Rd
12700-13899 74804
14800-19499 74801
Galway Ct 74804
Garden Oaks Dr 74804
Garretts Lake Rd 74804
Gayla 74804
Gemini 74804
Geneva Way 74801
E & W Georgia St 74804
W Gilmore St 74804
N Gilpin Ave 74804
Gina Ln 74804
Glenbrook Dr 74804
Glory Ln 74804
Gordon Cooper Dr 74801
Grace Ct 74804
Gracelann 74804
Granada Dr 74804
Grand Casino Blvd 74804
E Grant Rd & St 74801
Gray Dove Dr 74804
Graystone Pl 74801
Green Cedar Ct 74804
Greenfield Dr 74801
Gregory Ln 74804
Gretchin 74804
Hampton Ln 74804
Happy Vly 74804
Hardesty Dr 74804
Hardesty Rd 74801
Harmony Ln 74804
N Harrison 74804
N Harrison Ave 74801
S Harrison Ave 74801
Harrison Rd
10800-11599 74804
19000-19799 74801
N Harrison St 74804
Hart Ave & Rd 74801
E & W Hayes St 74801
Hazel Dell Rd 74804
Henson Ct 74804
Heron Ln 74804
E Hickman St 74804
E Hickory 74804
W Hickory 74804
Hickory Dr 74804
Hickory Holw 74801
Hickory Hollow Rd 74804
Hidden Pointe Rd 74804
N High Ave 74801
E & W Highland St 74801
S Highway Dr 74804
Highway 102
6400-14899 74804
Highway 102
15300-19399 74801
Highway 177
5800-14599 74804
18400-18499 74801
Highway 3 74801
Hill Rd 74804
Hillcrest Dr 74801
N Hobson Ave 74801
Homer Lane Rd 74801
Hornbeck Rd 74801
Hughes Cir 74804
Hunters Hill Dr & Rd 74801
Hunters Ridge Dr 74804
Huntington Ct 74801
Hurford Ave 74801
Hyatt Ct 74804
Independence St 74804
Industrial Dr 74804
Ingram Rd 74801
W Interstate Pkwy 74804
Inverness Cir 74801
N Ione Ave
500-699 74801
2000-2299 74804
2301-2311 74804
J M Ln 74801
Jack Rabbit Dr 74804
Jackie Ln 74801
Jade Ln 74801
James Ray Rd 74801
Janeway Pl 74804
Janice Ln 74801
Jarrot Dr 74801
E Jefferson Cir, Pl & St 74801
Jenny Dr 74804
Jericho Rd 74801
Joellen Dr 74804
John C Bruton Blvd 74804
Johnson Rd 74804
Jon Flowers Dr 74801
Jonco Rd 74804
Jones Rd 74801
Juel Dr 74804
Kaross Rd 74801
Katelyn 74801
Katie Rd 74804
Keller Pl 74804
Kelli Ln 74801
Kellye Green St 74804
Ken Del Dr 74804
N & S Kennedy Ave 74801
Kensington Pl 74804
Kent Rhoad 74804
Kethley Rd 74804
N Kickapoo Ave
101-197 74801
199-1499 74801
1500-11699 74804
S Kickapoo Ave 74801
Kickapoo Spur St 74801
Kim Ct 74804
N Kimberly Ave 74801
Kin Ville Ct & Rd 74804
N Kinerend Ave 74801
Kingfisher Ln 74804
Kings Rd
12701A-12701B 74804
5800-14300 74804
14302-14598 74801
16000-20399 74801
Kingsbury Ln 74801
Kiowa 74801
E & W Kirk St 74801
Konnor Ln 74801
Kraig Dr 74801
Kristin Rd 74804
Ladonna Dr 74801
Lady Ln 74804
Lake Est 74801
Lake Ln 74804
Lake Rd 74801
Lake Shore Dr 74804
Lakeside Cir & Ct 74801
Lakeview Cir 74804
Lancet Cir & Ct 74804
Lantana Cir & Ct 74804
Larkens Pl 74801
E & W Larry Rd 74804
Laverne Ave 74801
Lee Ann Ln 74804
N Leo Ave
100-900 74801
902-1298 74801
1500-2098 74804
2100-10999 74804
11001-11099 74804
S Leo Ave 74801
Leo Sun St 74804
Liberty Cir & St 74804
Libra St 74804
Lilly Valley St 74804
Limestone Dr 74804
Limousin Ln 74804
S Lincoln Ave 74801
S Lindale Ave 74801
W Locust St 74801
Lone Oak Cir 74804
Lori Ln 74804
N Louisa Ave
100-1499 74801
1500-1999 74804
S Louisa Ave 74801
Lynette St 74804
M Laine St 74801
Macarthur St 74804
Madeline Dr 74801
Maggies Pl 74801
Magnino Rd 74801
Magnolia Hills Ln 74801
E & W Main St 74801
Manchester Dr 74804
Manuel Dr 74801
E Margaret St 74801
Margaret Manor Dr 74804
Marie Dr 74804
Mark St 74801
N Market Ave
100-1499 74801
1500-4199 74804
S Market Ave 74801
Marys Rd 74801
Mason Dr 74804
Matt St 74801
Mays Addition Rd 74804
Mcdonald Dr 74804
N Mckinley Ave
100-1599 74801
2001-2399 74804
S Mckinley Ave 74801
N Mead Ave 74801
Meadowbrook Ln 74801
Meadowheath 74804
Meadowood Dr 74804
Meadows Ln 74804
Medical Park Dr 74804
Medinah Dr 74801
Melanie Ln 74801
Melissa 74801
Mesa Verde 74801
Mia 74804
E & W Midland Ct & St 74804
Mikish Dr 74801
Milstead Cir 74801
E Milton St 74801
N Minnesota Ave
100-1499 74801
1500-2299 74804
S Minnesota Ave 74801
Minnesota Cir 74804
Moccasin Trl 74804
Mockingbird Ln & Rd 74804
Mohican Cir & Dr 74801
Mojave Dr 74801
Monroe Dr 74804
Monticello Dr 74804
Moon Lake Cir 74804
Moonchild St 74804
E Morgan St 74801
Morning Side Ct 74804
Muirfield Dr 74801
Mullins Dr 74804
Musson Rd 74801
Nail Rd 74801
Nan Katherine Ln 74801
Navajo Cir 74801
Nickens Rd 74801
Nix Allen Ln 74801
Northridge Rd 74804
Northwood Dr 74804
Norwich Ct 74804
Nottingham Cir & Pl 74804
Ns 3500 Rd 74804
O Susanna 74804
S Oak Ave 74801
Oak Dr 74804
Oak St 74801
Oak Arbor Ln 74804
Oak Grove Ct 74804
Oak Hill Rd 74804
Oak Hollow Rd 74804
Oak Pond 74804
E & W Oakland St 74801
Oakmont Cir 74801
Oakridge Dr 74804
Oaks Ct 74804
Oakwood Dr
1-11 74801
12-12 74801
13-99 74801
14-98 74801
W Ohio St 74801
N Oklahoma Ave
100-1499 74801
1500-3499 74804
S Oklahoma Ave 74801
Old Highway 270 74804
Old Towne Trl 74804
Oldewood Pl 74804
Orchard Dr 74804
Orlando Ct & Dr 74804
Orville Rd 74801
Osage Ave & Dr 74801
Overland Ct
100-199 74804
900-1099 74801
Owen Rd 74801
Palmer Dr 74804
Pam Dr 74804
N Park Ave
101-197 74801
199-1499 74801
1500-2999 74804
3001-3299 74804
S Park Ave 74801
Park Dr 74801
E Parker St 74801
Parkview Dr 74804
N Patchin Ave 74801
Patterson Rd 74804
Peach Tree 74801
Pecan Rdg 74804
Pecan Crossing Dr 74804
Pecan Grove Rd 74804
Pecan Ridge Pl 74804
N Pennsylvania Ave
300-1399 74801
1500-1999 74804
S Pennsylvania Ave 74801
Penny St 74804
Perry Rd 74801
N & S Pesotum Ave 74801
N Philadelphia Ave
100-1499 74801
1500-1798 74804
1800-1999 74804
S Philadelphia Ave 74801
Pierre Taron Rd 74804
E Pine St 74801
Pine Ridge Rd 74804
Pinehurst Ct 74801
Piney Rdg 74801
Pinkston Rd 74804
Pond Vw 74801
Ponds Ln 74804
Pontotoc Ave 74801
Pool Ct, Ln & Pl 74801
W Poplar St 74801
Post Oak Rd 74801
Post Office Ln & Nck 74801
N Pottenger Ave
100-899 74801
901-1199 74801
2000-4499 74804
S Pottenger Ave 74801
Prairie Rdg 74804
Primrose Ln 74804
E & W Pulaski St 74804
Quail Rdg 74804
Quail Hollow Rd 74804
Quailwood Dr 74804
Rachel Dr 74804
Rain Tree Dr 74804
Ranch Rd 74804
Rangeline 74801
Raymond 74801
Red Oak Rd 74804
Red Rock Rd 74804
Redbud Ln & Rd 74801
E Remington Cir & St 74801
Rene Pl 74804
Rhonda Ln 74804
N Rice Ave 74804
N Rich Ave 74804
Rickey Rd 74801
N Rickey Rd 74804
Ridge Crest Dr 74804
E & W Ridgewood St 74801
River Rd 74801
River Bend Dr 74804
River Birch Dr 74804
Robby Rd 74804
Robert Rd 74804
Robin Rd 74804
Robinette St 74801
Robinwood Cir & Pl 74801
S Rock Creek Dr & Rd 74801
Rock Hollow Rd 74804
Roland Rd 74801
N Roosevelt Ave 74801
E & W Rosa St 74804
Rose Dr 74804
Rose Ln 74801
Rustic Oak Dr 74804
S Ruth Ave 74801
Saint John Rd 74801
Saint Louis St 74801
W Santa Fe St 74801
Saratoga St 74804
Savanna Pl & Sq 74804
Scenic Dr 74804
Scotlyn Dr 74801
Scott Cir 74804
E Scott St 74801
Seneca Dr 74801
Sequoyah Blvd 74801
Serenada Ct & Ln 74804
Seth Ln 74801
E & W Severn St 74801
E Seymour St 74801
Shamrock Cir 74804
Sharon Rd 74801
N Shawnee Ave
100-999 74801
1500-1599 74804
Shawnee Mall Dr 74804
Shawnee Mission Dr 74804
Sherry Ln 74801
Shorty Dr 74804
Siara Dr 74804
Simco Pl 74804
Sir Jake 74804
Skyview 74801
Sleepy Hollow Rd 74801
W Slover St 74801
Smoking Tree 74804
Sonata Ln 74804
Sooner Rd 74804
Spring Brook Rd 74804
Springhill Rd 74801
Spruce Cir 74804
Stage Coach Dr 74804
Star Lisa Ln 74801
Steven Dr 74804
Stevens Rd
12500-12598 74804
12600-13899 74804
16500-18999 74801
Stonebrook Dr 74804
Strawberry Ln 74801
Summit Dr 74801
Sunrock Dr 74801
Sunset Blvd 74804
Sunset Trl 74801
Surrey Dr 74804
Susan Dr 74804
Sutton Ct 74804
Sweet Grass Ct 74804
Sweetwood Rd 74801
Tanglewood Ln 74804
Tanner Rd 74804
Tawana Dr 74804
Teal Dr 74804
N Tenbrook Ave 74801
N & S Tennessee Ave 74801
Terra Ln 74804
Terrell Rd 74801
Thomas Glenn Rd 74801
Thompson Dr 74801
Thunder Rd 74801
Tiffany Ln 74801
Timber Rd 74804
Timber Creek Cir, Dr & Way 74804
Timber Dale Dr 74804
Timber Pond 74804
Timbers Blvd 74804
Tincup Dr 74804
Tonya Rd 74801
Traditional Way 74804
Traditional Way Ct 74804
Tribalway Dr 74801
Trinity Dr 74804
Troon Cir 74801
N Tucker Ave
100-1599 74801
1601-1699 74801
2000-3100 74804
3102-3198 74804
Turkey Knob St 74804
Turnberry Cir 74801
Turtle Bay 74801
Twilight Ln 74804
Tyler Ln 74801
N Union Ave
101-197 74801
199-1499 74801
1500-4999 74804
S Union Ave 74801
W University Pkwy & St 74804
Valley Ln 74804
Valley Rim Ct 74804
Valley View Blvd 74801
Valley View Dr 74804
Valley View Rd
5600-14799 74804
15000-15799 74801
15801-16299 74801
Vera Ln 74801
View St 74804
Virgie 74804
Vista Del Sol St 74804
Vivian Ter 74804
Waco Rd 74801
Walker Cir 74804
Walker Rd 74801
E & W Wallace St 74801
E & W Walnut St 74801
N Washington Ave 74801
Waunda Dr 74801
E Wayne St 74801
Westech Rd 74804
Westgate Dr 74804
Westlake Rd 74801
Weston Rd 74804
W Wheeler St 74801
Whipowill 74801
Whispering Meadows Rd 74804
Whispering Oak Dr 74804
Whispering Pine Blvd 74804
E Whittaker St 74801
Wildwood 74804
W Wiley St 74804
Willow Brk 74804
Willowcreek Rd 74801
E Wilson St 74804
Windmill Ridge Dr 74804
Windsor Ct & Pl 74804
Winged Foot Way 74801
Wolf Trl 74804
Wolverine Rd 74804
W Wood St 74801
Woodbridge Dr 74804
Woodcrest 74804
N Woodland 74801
Woodstock 74804
Yellowbird 74801

NUMBERED STREETS

E & W 7th Cir & St 74801
E & W 9th 74801
E & W 10th 74801
E & W 11th 74801
13th St 74801
W 32nd St 74804
W 33rd St 74804
E & W 34th 74804
E & W 35th 74804
W 36th St 74804
W 37th St 74804
W 38th St 74804
E & W 39th 74804
E 40th St 74804
E 41st St 74804
E 42nd St 74804
45th St 74804

STILLWATER OK

General Delivery 74074

POST OFFICE BOXES MAIN OFFICE STATIONS AND BRANCHES

Box No.s
All PO Boxes 74076

RURAL ROUTES

01, 04, 05, 06, 08 74074
01, 02, 03, 07, 08, 09 74075

NAMED STREETS

S Abbey Ln 74074
S Acorn Ln 74074
S Adams St 74074
Admiral Ave & Rd 74074
S Aetna St 74074
Aggie Dr 74074
E, N & W Airport Ln & Rd 74075
N Airport Industrial Access Rd 74075
Alamo 74075
E Alcott Ave 74074
Aloysius Dr 74074
N Amanda Ln 74075
Amethyst Ave 74075
Andy Kay Ln 74075
Appleway Ln 74074
W Arapaho Ave 74075

Arbor Cir 74074
N Arrington Ct 74075
S Arrington Dr 74074
Arrington Pl 74074
N Arrington St 74075
Arrowhead Dr & Pl 74074
Ash St 74074
Ashbury St 74074
Ashford Ct 74074
S Ashton Ave 74074
E Audene Dr 74075
S August St 74074
Austin Ct 74074
W Avery Ln 74075
Avondale St 74074
E Baker Ct 74075
S Barnes Ct 74074
N Barrett Ct 74075
N Benjamin St 74075
S Benjamin St 74074
W Bennett Dr 74075
S Berkshire Dr 74074
N Berry Ct 74075
S Berry St 74074
S Berry Creek St 74074
N Bethel Rd 74075
S Bethel Rd
400-499 74075
2200-3799 74074
Billingslea Ct 74074
Birchwood Ct 74075
Black Copper Rd 74075
S Black Oak Dr 74074
Blackfield Trl 74074
Blackjack 74074
S Blair St 74074
S Blakely St 74074
Blue Duck Ln 74074
S Blue Ridge St 74074
Bluebird Trl 74074
S Bluestone St 74074
N Boardwalk 74075
W Bonfire Trl 74074
N Boomer Rd 74075
S Boomer Rd 74074
Boomer Lake Station Dr 74075
S Boulder Creek Dr 74074
Boyles Ct 74075
Braxton Ln 74074
E Breckenridge Dr 74075
Brentwood Dr 74075
S Briarcliffe St 74074
Briarcreek Dr & Ter 74074
N Briarwood St 74075
Bridlewood Dr 74074
W Bristol Ave 74074
Bristol Road Ave 74074
N Britton Ct & Dr 74075
Broderick 74075
Bronco Dr 74075
E & W Brooke Ave 74075
N & W Brooke Hollow Ct 74075
Brookside Ct 74075
Brown Ave 74075
Brown Rock Rd 74074
Brumley 74074
N Brush Creek Rd 74075
S Brush Creek Rd
100-198 74075
200-499 74075
700-8799 74074
S Bryan Ct 74074
S Buckingham Rd 74075
N Burdick St 74075
S Burdick St 74074
Burr Oak St 74074
E & W Burris Rd 74075
Cabin Ct & Rd 74074
Callie Ln 74074
S & W Cambridge Ct & Dr 74074
Camden Ct 74074
E Camden Ln 74075
S Campbell Ct 74074
Candy Ln 74075
Canter Ct 74075
W Canterbury St 74074
W Cantwell Ave 74075
Canyon Ct 74075
E Canyon Pass 74074
S Canyon Rd 74074
N Canyon Rim Dr 74075
Casey Ln 74074
E Cedar Ct & Dr 74075
W Cedar Crest Trl 74074
Cedar Hill Dr 74074
Cedar Ridge Ln 74074
Cedardale Ln 74075
Celia Ln & St 74074
Champion Pl 74074
Chandler St 74074
Chapel Hill Rd 74074
S Charles Dr 74074
W Charleston Ct 74074
Charolais Cir 74075
Charring Cross 74074
W & N Chatburn Dr, Ln, Pl & Ter 74075
Chateau Ct, Dr & Pl 74075
E Checkers Ln 74075
W Cherokee Ave 74075
Cherry Ln 74075
S Chester St 74074
W Cheyenne Dr 74075
W Chickasaw Ln 74075
Chiquita Ct 74075
Chisholm 74075
W Choctaw Ln 74075
S Chuckwagon Ln 74074
E Cimarron Dr 74075
N Cimarron Hl 74075
E Cimarron Ln 74075
Cimarron Plz 74075
S Cimarron Rd 74074
E Cimarron Hill Ct 74075
Cindy Ln 74075
Circle Arrow Trl 74075
Classen Ct 74075
Clayton Ln 74075
S Cleveland St 74074
Coaches Building 74075
Colby Lance St 74074
Collins Ct 74074
E & W Connell Ave & Ct 74075
E Copper Canyon Ave 74075
N Copper Mountain Dr 74075
Copperfield 74074
Copperhead Ln 74075
S Cottontail Ln 74075
N Cottonwood Rd
100-199 74074
2100-3599 74075
S Cottonwood Rd 74074
S Council Crk 74074
Country Ln 74075
Country Club Ct 74074
W Country Club Dr 74074
N Country Club Rd 74075
S Country Club Rd 74074
S Country Side Dr 74074
County Road 160 74075
County Road 175 74075
County Road 180 74075
County Road 190 74075
County Road 200 74075
County Road 210 74075
W Coventry Dr 74074
S Cowboy Ct 74074
N Cowboy Canyon Rd 74075
S Coyle Rd 74074
Coyote Run 74075
N Craft Rd 74075
Crazy Horse 74075
S & W Creekside Ct & Dr 74074
N Crescent Dr 74075
E Crested Butte Dr 74075
Crestview Ave & Ct 74074
Crestwood Cir, Ct & Dr 74075
S Culpepper Dr 74074
W Cypress Mill Ave 74074
N Dakota 74075
E Dalton Ave 74075
Dapple Gray Ln 74075
Darryl Dr 74075
Davinbrook Ln 74075
N Davis Ct 74075
W Deanita Ln 74075
S Deer Crk 74074
W Deer Crk 74074
Deer Fld 74074
Deer Rdg 74075
Deer Trl 74074
Deer Creek Rd 74075
W Deer Crossing Dr 74074
Deer Pointe 74075
Deer Ridge Ln 74075
Deer Run Ct 74074
E Dell Ave 74075
W Dells Ave 74075
N Denver Ct 74075
S Denver Ct 74074
N Denver St 74075
S Denver St 74074
S Devin Lea St 74074
Devon St 74074
W Devonshire Rd 74074
N Diamond Vly 74075
Diamond Ridge Run 74075
Diamond Valley Rd 74075
Dobbs Ln 74075
Dobi Ln 74075
Doe Run 74075
N Donaldson Dr 74075
Doolin Ct & Ln 74074
Doral Ln 74074
S Doty St 74074
N Drury Ln 74075
S Drury St 74074
Dry Bean Trl 74074
N Dryden Cir 74075
N Dryden Ct 74075
N Dryden St 74075
S Dryden St 74074
S Dublin Dr 74074
N Duck St 74075
S Duck St 74074
E Duke Ave 74075
N Duncan St 74075
S Duncan St 74074
N Durango Pl 74075
S Durham Ct 74074
W Eagle Creek Ave 74074
S Eagle Summit Dr 74074
Eagles Ln 74074
Eastern Ave 74075
Eastgate St 74074
E Echo Mountain Dr 74075
Eden Chapel Ln 74074
Edgemoor Dr 74074
N & S Edna Dr 74075
S Ellen Ct 74074
E & W Elm Ave 74075
Elmwood Cir & Dr 74075
S Elvin Dr 74074
Emma Ln 74075
Enchanted Ln 74075
Equine Dr 74074
Erica Ave & Ln 74074
E & W Eskridge Ave & Pl 74075
S Eunice St 74074
Evergreen 74075
Expo Cr E & S 74075
Eyler Ln 74075
W Fagan Ln 74074
Fairfield Dr 74074
S Fairgrounds 74074
N Fairgrounds Rd 74075
S Fairgrounds Rd 74074
S Fairway Dr 74074
Falls Dr 74075
Fawn Ln 74075
S Fawn St 74074
Fawn Creek Rd 74074
S Fern St 74074
Fiddlers Hl 74074
Fiddlers Hill St 74074
W Forest Trail Ct 74074
Forrest Hills Dr 74074
S & W Fountain View Ct & Dr 74074
Fouquet Dr 74074
S & W Fox Ledge Dr & Ln 74074
W Frances Ave 74075
E & W Franklin Ave & Ln 74075
E Frazier Ct 74075
E Frontier Dr 74075
Furman Ln 74075
Gallagher Iba Arena 74075
W Garden Pointe Dr 74074
N Garfield St 74075
S Garfield St 74074
W Georgia Ave 74075
Germaine Ct 74074
E & W Glencoe Rd 74075
Glenwood Ct & Dr 74075
Golden Oaks Dr 74075
W Golf Dr 74075
W Graham Ave 74075
N Grandview Ct 74075
S Grandview Ct 74074
N Grandview St 74075
S Grandview St 74074
S Gray St 74074
S Green Valley Dr 74074
Greenbriar Ct 74075
E & N Greenvale Cir & Ct 74075
Gregory Ln 74074
Greystone St 74074
Gunsmoke 74074
S Hackleman Rd 74074
S Hafner St 74074
Haley Ln 74074
S Hall St 74074
W & E Hall Of Fame Ave 74075
E Hanson Cir & St 74075
E & W Harned Ave 74075
S Hart Dr 74074
N Hartford St 74075
S Hartford St 74074
E & W Hartman Ave 74075
W Hartwood Ave 74074
S Harvest Ln 74074
Harvest Rd 74075
Hat Creek Xing 74075
Helena Hts 74074
S Henderson St 74074
S Hester St 74074
S Hickory Ct 74074
Hidden Oaks Dr 74074
Hidden Trails Dr 74074
S Hideaway Ln 74074
S Highland Ct 74074
W Highpoint Dr 74075
N Hightower St 74075
S Hightower St 74074
E Highview Ave 74075
W Highway 51 74074
S Hill Ln 74074
W Hillcrest Ave 74075
Hillside Ct & St 74074
N Hoke St 74075
N & S Hoppy Rd 74075
E Horizon Dr 74075
S Hunters Cir 74074
N Hunters Rdg 74075
Hurst Ln 74074
N Husband Ct 74075
W Husband Ct 74075
N Husband Pl 74075
S Husband Pl 74074
N Husband St 74075
S Husband St 74074
S Iba Dr 74074
Idlewild Acres 74074
S Ingalls Rd 74074
S Ingalls Main 74074
S Ingalls Oak 74074
S Ingalls Oak Main 74074
S Ingalls Walnut St 74074
S Innovation Way 74074
S Isabell Pointe Dr 74074
Ivy Ct 74075
Ja Linda Lou Ct 74074
N Jackson Pl 74075
Jacquelyn Ter 74075
W James Pl 74075
S James Creek Ct 74074
Janes Ct 74075
N Jardot Rd 74075
S Jardot Rd 74074
S Java St 74074
N Jefferson St 74075
S Jefferson St 74074
Jesse Ln 74074
Jordan 74074
Judy Dr 74075
E Kara Dr 74074
Karr Ct 74075
N Karsten Crk 74075
S Karsten Crk 74074
Katy Ct 74075
Katys Way 74075
Kc Ct 74075
S Keats Dr 74074
Keely Ct 74075
Keller Ct & Dr 74075
S Kelly St 74074
W Kelly Sue Dr 74074
E Kelsey Ln 74075
Kenslow Dr 74074
S Kings St 74074
Kinnick Rd 74074
Kirby Ln 74074
E & W Knapp Ave 74075
N Knoblock St 74075
S Knoblock St 74074
Kody Ct 74075
E Krayler Ave 74075
Kyle Ct 74075
Lake Mdws 74075
E & W Lakehurst Dr 74075
W Lakeridge Ave 74074
W Lakeshore Dr 74075
E, N & W Lakeview Ct & Rd 74075
N Land Run Dr 74075
S Lane Pl 74074
W Lapoint Ct 74074
E Lauren Ln 74075
S Legendary Ln 74074
S Leigh St 74074
E Leisure Ln 74075
Leland Ct 74075
N Lewis St 74075
S Lewis St
100-900 74074
809-809 74076
901-1499 74074
902-1498 74074
E & W Liberty Ave, Cir & Ct 74075
Lilly Ln 74074
N Lincoln St 74075
S Lincoln St 74074
E Linda Ave 74075
W Lisa Cir 74075
Live Oak Ln 74074
W Loma Verde Ln 74074
E & W Lone Chimney Rd 74075
Lone Creek Trl 74075
E Lone Wolf Ave 74075
S Longview Dr 74074
Loper Ave 74074
Lori Cir 74075
Lost Acres Rd 74075
E Loveland Dr 74075
S Lowry St 74074
Lydia Ln 74074
Lyndsey Ct 74074
Lynn Ln 74075
Macy Ln 74075
S Macy Ln 74074
Macy Lynn 74074
N Madison Ct 74075
N Main St 74075
S Main St 74074
E & N Manning Ct & St 74075
S Mansfield Dr 74074
E & W Maple Ave & Ct 74074
S Mar Vista St 74074
E Marcus Ave 74075
E Marie Dr 74075
N Marine Rd 74075
Mark Cir 74075
S Marshall St 74074
E & W Matthews Ave 74075
Mavrick Ln 74075
S Mcbride 74074
S Mcdonald St 74074
E & W Mcelroy Pl & Rd 74075
S Mcfarland St 74074
W Mcmurtry Rd 74075
W Meadow Ave 74074
N Meadow Ln 74075
E Meadow Brook Ln 74075
N Meadow Park Cir 74075
Medford Rd 74075
S Mehan Rd 74074
Melissa Ln 74075
S Melrose Dr 74074
S Memorial Dr 74074
Memory Ln 74075
W Mercedes Ln 74075
S Meridian 74074
Mesa Cir 74074
Middlefork Rd 74075
E & W Miller Ave 74075
Misty Mountain Ln 74074
Mockingbird Ln 74074
N Mockingbird Ln 74075
E Mohawk Ave 74075
N Monroe St 74075
S Monroe St 74074
W Montera 74074
S Monticello Dr 74074
E & W Moore Ave 74075
S Mound St 74074
S Murphy St 74074
Murray Ct 74074
N Nancy Lee Dr 74075
E & W Newman Ave 74075
Noble Rd 74075
N Norellon St 74075
Norrie Ln 74074
E Norris Dr 74075
S Norris Prairie Ln 74074
W Northgate Dr 74075
Oak Creek Dr 74074
Oak Forrest Cir 74074
S Oak Knoll Ct 74074
Oak Trail Dr 74074
Oakcrest Ct & Rd 74075
S Oakdale Dr 74074
Oakfield Ct 74074
Oakridge Dr 74074
Oakwood Dr 74074
W October Trce 74074
Old Bumpy Rd 74074
W Old Forest Ave 74074
N & S Old Highway 51 74075
S Old Pond Ct & Dr 74074
S Orchard St 74074
W Osage Dr 74075
W Owens Ct 74075
S Oxford Dr 74074
S Palmetto St 74074
N Park Cir 74075
N Park Dr 74075
S Park Dr 74074
Park Pl 74075
N Parker Ln 74075
N Parkview Ct 74075
Parkway Dr 74075
N Payne St 74075
S Payne St 74074
Peaceable Acres 74075
E Peachtree Ave 74074
Pearl Snap Trl 74074
Pecan Dr 74075
Pecan Rd 74074
Pecan Hill Ct & St 74075
Pecan Lake Ct 74074
S Pennsylvania St 74074
Perfect Dr 74074
N Perkins Rd 74075
S Perkins Rd 74074
S Perry St 74074
S Persimmon St 74074
W Pheasant Rdg 74074
W Pheasant Ridge Ave 74074
Pickles Gap 74074
S Pine St 74074
Pinewood Cir 74074
Pinto Dr 74074
Pioneer St & Trl 74074
S Pioneer Trail St 74074
Pleasant Oaks St 74074
N Poe Rd 74075
Poplar St 74074
Post Oak Ct, Dr & Pl 74075
Poultry Sciences 74075
N Prairie Rd 74075
S Prairie Rd 74074
Prescot Dr 74074
Preston Ave, Cir & Ln 74075
Primrose Ln 74074
Private Dr 74075
Quail Creek Farms 74074
Quail Ridge Ct & St 74074
E Raintree Ave 74074
N Ramsey St 74075
S Ramsey St 74074
Ranch Ave 74075
Randolph Ct 74075
Range W 74074
N Range Rd 74075
S Range Rd 74074
S Ransom Dr 74074
Rattlesnake Dr 74074
Red Rose Dr 74074
S Red Wagon Rd 74074
E & W Redbud Ct & Dr 74075
N Redlands Rd
200-218 74074
220-1498 74075
1500-7999 74075
S Redlands Rd 74074
S Redwood Dr 74074
Reese Lndg 74075
S Richfield Ct 74074
E & W Richmond Pl & Rd 74075
N Richmond Hill Rd 74075
S Ridge Dr 74074
E Ridgecrest Ave 74075
Ridgewood Dr 74074
S Ridings Ct 74074
N Ripley Rd 74075
S Ripley Rd
100-499 74075
1300-3599 74074
N Ritter Rd 74075
N Rock Ct 74075
S Rock Hollow Ct 74074
S Rocky Rd 74074
S Rocky Ridge St 74074
Rockys Ln 74075
E & N Rogers Dr 74075
Roka Rdg 74075
S Ropers Ln 74074
N Rose Rd 74075
S Rose Rd
100-399 74075
1100-1500 74074

1401-1499 74075
1502-1998 74074
1601-1999 74074
S Rose Hollow Ln 74074
N Running Bear St 74075
S Russell Ct 74074
W Rutledge Dr 74075
Sable Oaks Ln 74075
S Saddle Rock Rd 74074
E Saddlebrook Dr 74075
Sage Rd 74074
W Sandplum Dr 74074
Sangre Bnd 74075
N Sangre Rd 74075
S Sangre Rd 74074
W Santa Fe Ct 74074
Sassy Ln 74074
S Savannah Dr 74074
S Sawgrass St 74074
S Scissortail Dr 74074
E & W Scott Ave 74075
N Seadog Rd 74075
W Seminole Dr 74075
S Serenity Ln 74074
Serenity Creek Trl 74074
Shadow Creek Ln 74074
S Shalamar Dr 74074
N Shallow Brk 74075
Shamrock Ln 74075
Sharon Ln 74074
Sherman Lake Dr 74074
W Sherwood Ave 74074
Shiloh St 74074
W Shiloh Creek Ave 74074
S Shinnery Oak Ct 74074
S Shumard Dr 74074
Sierra Ln 74074
S Silverdale Dr 74074
Simpson Cir 74074
Skyline Ln & St 74075
Sleepy Holw 74074
Southern Oaks 74074
Southwinds Ln 74075
Spring Creek Cir, Dr &
Ln E & W 74074
S Springdale Dr 74074
S Springfield St 74074
W Springhill Ct 74074
S Squires St 74074
S Squires Landing
Blvd 74074
N Stallard St 74075
S Stallard St 74074
S Stanley St 74074
N Star Dr 74075
Starr Vly 74075
State Ln & St 74075
S Stokes Rd 74075
Stone Pt 74074
Stone Ledge Trl 74074
W & N Stonecrest Ave &
Ct 74075
E Stonegate Ave 74074
Stoneridge Dr 74074
N Stoney Crk 74075
S Stoneybrook St 74074
Student Un 74075
Summer Hill Ct 74074
W Summerlin Ct 74074
Summit Cir 74075
Summit Ridge Dr 74074
S Sumner Ln 74074
Sunny Ln 74074
Sunnybrook Ct & Dr 74075
Sunrise Ave & Dr 74075
Sunset Ave & Dr 74074
S Surrey Dr 74074
Susan Pl 74075
Susie Q Ln 74074
W Swim Ave 74075
Sycamore Dr & Ln 74075
Sycamore Valley Dr 74074
Tan Tara St 74074
Tanglewood Cir 74074
N Taylor Ln 74075
S & W Teal Ct & St 74074
N Telluride St 74075
N & S Terrill Dr 74075
Territory Ln 74075
Thatcher Hall 74075
The Cedars 74075
E & W Thomas Ave 74075
Thunder Rd 74074
Tiftin Trl 74075
Timber Creek Trl 74074
Timbercrest Ct & Dr 74075
Timberlake Dr 74075
Timberline Dr 74074
Tobacco Rd 74075
Topaz Ave 74075
Tower Park Dr 74075
W Trenton Ave & Ct 74074
Trophy Ln 74075
Turtle Pond Ct 74074
E & W Tyler Ave 74075
N Union Rd 74075
S Union Rd
200-499 74075
600-10199 74074
W University Ave 74074
University Cir 74074
N University Pl 74075
S University Pl 74075
University Mailing
Svcs 74075
Usda 74075
W Ute Ave 74075
N Vail St 74075
Valley Rd 74075
Valley Ridge Dr 74075
Valley Springs Ln 74075
Valley View Rd 74075
Vena Ln 74075
Villa 74074
W Village Ct 74074
W Villas Ct 74074
E Virginia Ave 74075
W Virginia Ave
100-199 74075
3000-8899 74074
S & W Walking Vista Ct & Ln 74074
S Walking Trail Dr 74074
S Walnut Cir, Crk &
St 74074
N Warren Dr 74075
N Washington Rd 74075
N Washington St 74075
S Washington St 74074
Wedgewood Ct 74075
Wedgewood Dr 74075
S Wedgewood Dr 74074
N West St 74075
S West St 74074
S West Oaks 74074
S West Point Rd 74074
Westbrook Ct & Dr 74074
N Western Rd 74075
S Western Rd 74074
Westpark Ct 74074
S Westridge St 74074
S Westwood Dr & Ln 74074
N Wheatley Ln 74075
White Oak Dr 74074
Whitney Ct 74075
Wicklow St 74074
E Wild Turkey Rd 74075
S Wild Turkey Pass
Dr 74074
Wildwood Ct & Dr 74075
N Wildwood Acres Cir,
Ct & Dr 74075
N Wiley St 74075
E & W Will Rogers Dr 74075
E Willham Dr 74075
N William Ct 74075
S Williamsfield Dr 74074
N Willis St 74075
S Willis St 74074
Willow W 74074
N Willow Dr 74075
Willow Rdg 74074
Willow Park Cir & Ln 74074
Windmill Ct & Dr 74075
Windsor Cir & Dr 74074
Windy Acres 74074
E Winter Park Dr 74075
S Woodcrest Dr 74074
Woodlake Dr 74075
Woodland Ct & Dr 74074
Woodland Trails Dr 74074
S Woodstone Dr 74074
Wooten Cir & Ln 74074
Wright Dr 74075
Yellow Brick Dr 74074
York Rd 74074
Yorkshire Dr 74074
E & W Yost Rd 74075
N Young St 74075
E Zachary Ln 74074

NUMBERED STREETS

W 1st Ave 74074
E 2nd Ave 74074
W 2nd Ave 74074
S 2nd Ct 74074
E 2nd St 74075
E 3rd 74075
E 3rd Ave 74074
W 3rd Ave 74074
W 3rd Pl 74074
E & W 4th 74074
E & W 5th Ave & Pl 74074
E 6th Ave
100-3399 74074
3400-3899 74075
3900-13099 74074
W 6th Ave 74074
E & W 7th Ave & Pl 74074
E & W 8th Ave & Ct 74074
E & W 9th Ave & Ct 74074
E & W 10th 74074
E & W 11th Ave, Ct &
Pl 74074
E & W 12th 74074
E & W 13th 74074
E & W 14th 74074
E & W 15th 74074
E & W 16th 74074
E & W 17th 74074
E & W 18th Ave, Ct &
Pl 74074
E & W 19th Ave & St 74074
W 20th St 74074
21st Ave & Ct 74074
S & W 22nd Ave & Ct 74074
W 23rd Ave 74074
W 24th Ave 74074
W 25th Ave 74074
E & W 26th 74074
E & W 27th Ave & Ct 74074
W 28th Ave 74074
29th Ave & Ct 74074
W 30th Ave 74074
31st Ave & Ct 74074
E & W 32nd 74074
E & W 33rd 74074
W 35th Ave 74074
E 36th Ave 74074
37th Ave & St 74074
W 40th St 74074
E & W 44th Ave & St 74074
E 45th St 74074
46th Ave & St 74074
W & E 47th Ave & St 74074
W 49th Ave 74074
E 50th Ave 74074
W 53rd St 74074
E & W 56th Ave & St 74074
E 57th Ave 74074
W 58th St 74074
E & W 60th 74074
E 63rd St 74074
E 64th St 74074
E 65th St 74074
E 66th St 74074
E 67th St 74074
W & E 68th Ave & St 74074
E 70th St 74074
E 71st Ave 74074
E & W 80th 74074
E 84th Ave 74074
E 85th St 74074
E 86th Ave 74074
E 92nd Ave 74074

TAHLEQUAH OK

General Delivery 74464

POST OFFICE BOXES MAIN OFFICE STATIONS AND BRANCHES

Box No.s
All PO Boxes 74465

RURAL ROUTES

02, 03, 04, 05, 06, 07,
08, 09, 10 74464

HIGHWAY CONTRACTS

11, 61 74464

NAMED STREETS

W Abby Ln 74464
W Abel 74464
Academy St 74464
N Acuff Ave 74464
Agni Way 74464
Airport Pkwy 74464
Alder Way 74464
Alice Davis Dr 74464
W & E Allen Cir, Rd &
St 74464
Amber Way 74464
N Amelia Ct 74464
Amity Ln 74464
Anderson Ave 74464
E & W Arden St 74464
Arizona Ln 74464
Arnold Price Dr 74464
N Ash Ave 74464
E Ashley Ln 74464
Aspen Dr 74464
Bailey Blvd 74464
W Baird Ln 74464
N Baker Ave & Rd 74464
S Bald Hill Rd 74464
E Balentine Rd 74464
E Ballentine Rd 74464
Baron Cir & Dr 74464
Basin Ave 74464
Bean St 74464
E Beaverson Rd 74464
E Belcher Ln 74464
N Bells Rd 74464
N Ben George Rd 74464
W Benton Rd 74464
Berry St 74464
Beth Ave 74464
Bill John Ave 74464
W Billie Davis Dr 74464
Billies Ln 74464
Birch Ln 74464
S Black Jack Dr 74464
S Black Valley Rd 74464
N & S Bliss Ave 74464
N Blue Springs Rd 74464
Bluebird Ln 74464
N & S Bluff Ave 74464
Bois Darc 74464
E Boone St 74464
Boudinot Ct 74464
E Brandon Dr 74464
N Brandy Lynn Ln 74464
Brenda Ave 74464
Brentwood Dr 74464
Brewer Ave 74464
Briar Ln 74464
N Briggs Flat Rd 74464
E Bright Star Dr 74464
N Britton Rd 74464
Brooklynn Ave 74464
N Brookside Ave 74464
Bryan Blvd 74464
N & S Bryant Ave &
Rd 74464
W Burchett Rd 74464
S Burnt Cabin Rd 74464
Bushyhead St 74464
Butler Rd & St 74464
Byrd St 74464
W Calista Dr 74464
Callie Ave 74464
Cambridge Cir 74464
Camelot Dr 74464
S Campbell Rd 74464
E Canyon View Dr 74464
Carol St 74464
W Carr Ln 74464
N & S Cary Ln 74464
Cathy Ave 74464
Cecilia Dr 74464
N & S Cedar Ave, Pl &
St 74464
Chance Dr 74464
Chapman Ave 74464
Chase Ave 74464
N & S Cherokee Ave 74464
E Cherrie St 74464
Cherry Springs Dr 74464
E & W Chickasaw St 74464
E & W Choctaw St 74464
Circle St 74464
Clay Rd & St 74464
Clayton Dr 74464
W Clenerad Rd 74464
E Clover Cir 74464
W Clyde Maher Rd 74464
E Cobbs Corner Rd 74464
Coffee Hollow Rd 74464
N & S College Ave &
Ct 74464
Commercial Rd 74464
S Coos Thompson Rd 74464
Corn St 74464
Country Cir & Ln 74464
Covington Pl 74464
Coy St 74464
Crafton Pl & St 74464
Creek Dr 74464
Creekside Dr 74464
S Cresent Valley Rd 74464
Crestview 74464
Crestwood Ave & Dr 74464
Cross Timbers Rd 74464
Crystal Ln 74464
Cypress Ln 74464
Daisy Dr 74464
Dale Ave 74464
Daniel Stern Dr 74464
N Darrell Ave 74464
N Davis Rd 74464
N Davis Ranch Ln 74464
Day Ln 74464
N Deer Clan Dr 74464
E & W Delaware St 74464
E Diedrick Ln 74464
Diffee Dr 74464
E Dixie Pkwy 74464
Dogwood Dr 74464
Don Ave 74464
N Douglas Ave 74464
E & W Downing St 74464
W Dusty Ave 74464
Earl St 74464
N & S East Ave 74464
Echota Ave 74464
Elada Dr 74464
E Elephant Rock Rd 74464
Elizabeth Ave 74464
W Ellis Rd 74464
N Elm Grove Rd 74464
S Epp Wagers Rd 74464
Essary Ave 74464
Eubanks 74464
Evans St 74464
N Farm Ln 74464
S Felts Dr 74464
Forest Ridge Dr 74464
S Forrest Dr 74464
Fowler Rd 74464
W Fox St 74464
Francis Ave 74464
N Fred Smith Rd 74464
Frye St 74464
E Fuller St 74464
Garden Rd 74464
Garden Lake Dr 74464
Garner Ave 74464
Gary St 74464
Gee Ga Lee Lee 74464
Gerri Dr 74464
W Gideon Rd 74464
Glover Ave 74464
Goingsnake St 74464
W Golf Course Rd 74464
Gourd Ln 74464
Graham Ave 74464
N Grand Ave 74464
Grandview Dr & Rd 74464
Green Country Dr 74464
Greenhaw Cir 74464
Greentree Dr 74464
Greenwood Dr 74464
Griffin Ave 74464
N Grover Ln 74464
Guinn Ave 74464
E Hanging Rock Rd 74464
E Harbison Dr 74464
Harris Cir 74464
N, S & E Harrison Ave &
St 74464
Hensley Dr 74464
N Heritage Ln 74464
S Hickory Dr & Ln 74464
W Hickory Nut Rdg 74464
Hicks St 74464
Highland Dr 74464
N Highway 10 74464
Highway 51 74464
Highway 62 74464
Highway 82 74464
Highway 82a 74464
Highway 82b 74464
Highway 82c 74464
S Highway View Dr 74464
Hillcrest Ave 74464
Hillside Ave 74464
Hilltop Cir 74464
E Hogner St 74464
Holiday Dr 74464
S Holloway Ave 74464
N Houston St 74464
Hugh Ave 74464
Ida Ln 74464
N Iredelle Way 74464
S J F Davis Ln 74464
Jackson Ave 74464
James St 74464
Jamestown Dr & St 74464
Janet St 74464
N Jarvis Rd 74464
Jay Ln 74464
Jeanette Ln 74464
Jeffery St 74464
Jo St 74464
Joe Carroll St 74464
E Johnson Ln 74464
N & W Jones Ave &
Rd 74464
Judy Ln 74464
S Jules Valdez Rd 74464
Kaufman Ave 74464
Kay Ln 74464
W & E Keetoowah Cir,
Ct & St 74464
Kelly St 74464
N Kennedy Ln 74464
Kim St 74464
S Kindle Ave 74464
Kingston Pl 74464
Kupsick St 74464
Lakes Dr 74464
Lamer Ave 74464
S Lamons Rd 74464
N Lane Ave 74464
E Lane School Rd 74464
Larry Ave 74464
Lauren Ave 74464
E Lawrence St 74464
S Lee Ave 74464
N Legion Dr 74464
N, S & E Lena Ave &
Ln 74464
Leoser St 74464
N Lewis Ave 74464
Lexington Ave & Ct 74464
N Limbsey Ln 74464
W Lisa Dr 74464
W Lisa Ann Dr 74464
Lloyd Ln 74464
N & S Logan Dr 74464
W Lois Ln 74464
Lola St 74464
W Louellen St 74464
E Love Ln 74464
E Lowe Dr 74464
W Maggie Rd 74464
Magnolia St 74464
Mahaney Ave 74464
Main Pkwy 74464
S Manard Rd 74464
N Mandy Rd 74464
Mankiller Cir 74464
N & S Maple Ave &
Pl 74464
Marvin St 74464
Mathis Park Dr 74464
May Ave 74464
Mayberry Dr 74464
N Mccrary Rd 74464
Mckie St 74464
Mcspadden Ct 74464
Meadow Creek Dr 74464
W Meadow View Ln 74464
Meadows Cir 74464
Michael St 74464
Mike Ave 74464
Mill St 74464
Miller Dr 74464
Mimosa Ln 74464
Minor St 74464
N & S Mission Ave 74464
Missionary Cir 74464
N & S Moccasin Ave 74464
S Mockingbird Ln 74464
Monroe St 74464
E & W Morgan St 74464
S Morris Ave 74464
W Mossy Oak Ln 74464
Mountain Dr 74464
Mountain View Dr 74464
W Mud Valley Rd 74464
W Mulberry Ln 74464
E & W Murrel Rd 74464
E Murrell Rd 74464
E & W Murrell Home
Rd 74464
N Muskogee Ave 74464
S Muskogee Ave
100-1100 74464
1101-18099 74464
1101-1101 74465
1102-18098 74464
S Muskogee Pl 74464
N Nadine Dr 74464
S Nalley Rd 74464
Nola Ave 74464
E Normal St 74464
North St 74464
W Northlake Dr 74464
Northpark Dr 74464

Northside Ct 74464
Notty Acres 74464
Nsu Dr 74464
N & S Oak Ave 74464
Oak Hill Cir & Ln 74464
N Oakdale Dr 74464
N Oakleaf Ln 74464
Oakridge Dr 74464
N Oaks Rd 74464
Oakwood Dr 74464
N Oklahoma Ave 74464
S Old Highway 62 74464
Old River Rd 74464
N Old Toll Gate Rd 74464
S Owens Ave 74464
W Ozark 74464
Pamela St 74464
S Park Ave 74464
S Park Hill Rd 74464
Parker St 74464
Pat St 74464
N Pathfinder St 74464
Patriot Way 74464
Patti Cir 74464
Patti June St 74464
Pebbles Ln 74464
Pecan Rd 74464
Pecan Creek Cir 74464
Pendleton St 74464
S Phoenix Ave 74464
S Pin Oak Dr 74464
N Pine Ridge Dr 74464
Plaza Dr 74464
Plaza South St 74464
E Post Grove St 74464
E Powell Rd 74464
E Power Ln 74464
N Primrose Ln 74464
S Putnam Ave 74464
Quail Ridge Dr 74464
Ranch Acres Dr 74464
S Rand Ave 74464
Ransten St 74464
E Rayne St 74464
Reasor St 74464
E Red Fuller Rd 74464
W Red Oak St 74464
Redbird 74464
Redbud Ln 74464
N Redtail Hawk Dr 74464
Redwood Pl 74464
Remington Pl 74464
N Rice Rd 74464
Richmond Cir 74464
Ridge Dr & St 74464
River Bend Dr 74464
N Rivercrest Ln 74464
Riverview Dr 74464
W Robin Dr 74464
S Rocky Top Ln 74464
E Rogers Dr 74464
Rolling Hills Dr 74464
Roosevelt Ave 74464
Rosewood Pl 74464
W & E Ross Ave, Byp,
Pl & St 74464
N Round Hollow Rd 74464
Rozell Ave 74464
Rubber Rd 74464
Russell Ave 74464
Samuel St 74464
S Sandstone Ave 74464
Sandy Cir 74464
Sasha Ln 74464
Scarlett Dr 74464
W Selu Ln 74464
Seminary Ave 74464
S Seminole Ave 74464
E & W Seneca St 74464
Sequoyah St 74464
Sequoyah Club Dr 74464
W Seth Ln 74464
W Shady Grove Rd 74464
E & W Shawnee Cir, St
& Ter 74464
Shelley Cir 74464

E Shepherd Rd 74464
Sheryl St 74464
Short St 74464
Skill Center Cir 74464
Skipper Dr 74464
Sleepy St 74464
N Sleepy Hollow Ln 74464
E & W Smith St 74464
Songbird Dr 74464
E Sonny Ln 74464
Sooner Dr 74464
E & W South St 74464
W Southern Oaks St ... 74464
W Southlake Dr 74464
Southland Dr 74464
Southridge Cir, Pl &
Rd 74464
N Spears Rd 74464
Spring St 74464
Stan Watie Dr 74464
S Stanley Ln 74464
N & S State Ave 74464
E Steely Hollow Rd 74464
Stephens Dr 74464
Stick Ross Mountain Cir
& Rd 74464
N Still Hill Ln 74464
W Stone Chapel Rd 74464
Stonebrook Dr 74464
E Summerfield St 74464
Summerset Pt 74464
Summit Ave 74464
Summit Ridge Ct & Dr . 74464
Sunrise Ridge Dr 74464
Sunset Rd 74464
N Swannanoa Rd 74464
Sycamore Dr 74464
Talley Dr & St 74464
Tanglewood Dr 74464
Tarkington St 74464
E Taylor Dr 74464
S Teehee Dr 74464
E Thompson Dr 74464
Tim St 74464
S Timber Trl 74464
Timbers Ln 74464
Tommye Ln 74464
W Tray Rd 74464
N Trent St 74464
Trimble Ave 74464
E Turk St 74464
Turney Ave 74464
Turpin Ln 74464
N Tye Ln 74464
N Tyler St 74464
University Dr 74464
Utah Dr 74464
Valley Ave 74464
Valley Acre Ln 74464
Valley View Rd 74464
Victor St 74464
S Vina Ave 74464
N Vinita Ave 74464
Vo Tech Dr 74464
N Wakins St 74464
N Walkingstick St 74464
W Walnut Ln 74464
Wanetah Dr 74464
E Ward St 74464
N & S Water Ave 74464
W Webb St 74464
N Webster Rd 74464
W Wedgewood Dr 74464
S Welling Rd 74464
S West Ave 74464
S Westwood Dr 74464
Wheeler Cir & St 74464
E Whipperwill Rd 74464
White Ave 74464
W Whitley Rd 74464
Whitney Ln 74464
S Whittmore Dr & Ln ... 74464
Wilcox Cir 74464
Williams St 74464
E & W Willis Rd 74464
Willow Ave 74464

Wilson Ave 74464
Windchester Dr 74464
N Windle Ln 74464
Windwood Cir 74464
E Winsett Ln 74464
W Wisteria Ln 74464
S Woodall Dr 74464
N & W Woodard Ave &
Rd 74464
Woodhaven Ave 74464
E Woodland Ln & Rd .. 74464
Woodlawn Ave 74464
Workman Ct 74464
York St 74464
W Youngbird St 74464
Zion St 74464

NUMBERED STREETS

All Street Addresses 74464

TULSA OK

General Delivery 74103

POST OFFICE BOXES MAIN OFFICE STATIONS AND BRANCHES

Box No.s
1 - 10 74102
2 - 271 74101
201 - 300 74102
320 - 320 74159
321 - 880 74101
500 - 871 74102
921 - 1440 74101
1300 - 1300 74102
1471 - 1769 74101
1770 - 1770 74102
1801 - 3692 74101
2187 - 3878 74102
4101 - 4999 74159
6001 - 6496 74148
6504 - 6770 74156
8008 - 8531 74101
9151 - 9965 74157
14001 - 14578 74159
21001 - 22452 74121
27002 - 27968 74149
33001 - 35994 74153
48501 - 48676 74148
50000 - 50994 74150
52001 - 52960 74152
54002 - 55772 74155
59001 - 59001 74159
74182 - 74182 74102
150001 - 150370 74115
330007 - 330432 74133
470001 - 477200 74147
480681 - 481258 74148
501002 - 501136 74150
520941 - 521500 74152
570971 - 571510 74157
580001 - 583899 74158
690001 - 699000 74169
700001 - 707909 74170

RURAL ROUTES

08 74106
05, 09, 30 74107
01 74108
03 74115
03, 14 74116
82 74117
08 74126
06, 28 74127
08 74130
13, 16, 30 74131
05, 07, 17, 29, 32 74132
04, 18, 19, 22, 24, 41,
43, 44, 45, 51, 52, 56 .. 74133
36, 37, 80, 81 74134
02, 11, 40, 46, 47, 50,
53, 54, 58, 60, 61, 63,
64, 65 74137
57, 79 74146

NAMED STREETS

Aberdeen Pkwy E &
W 74132
E Admiral Blvd
700-799 74120
801-1699 74120
2000-2899 74110
2901-3299 74110
4100-6200 74115
6202-8898 74115
10100-16699 74116
W Admiral Blvd 74127
E Admiral Ct
2500-3299 74110
3300-9299 74115
12300-12399 74116
E Admiral Pl
1400-1699 74120
2401-2797 74110
2799-3299 74110
3300-9500 74115
9502-9598 74115
9700-17699 74116
Airport Way 74132
N Allegheny Ave 74115
S Allegheny Ave
200-1499 74112
3200-4399 74135
8300-11999 74137
S American Plaza St
E 74135
E Apache St
200-699 74106
626-626 74148
626-626 74149
626-626 74156
701-1699 74106
1000-1698 74106
1700-3199 74110
3300-7799 74115
11300-14199 74116
W Apache St
1-299 74106
1200-2328 74127
2330-3700 74127
3702-4098 74127
E Archer Pl 74116
W Archer Pl 74127
E Archer St
1-299 74103
300-1099 74120
1101-1699 74120
1701-1797 74110
1799-3299 74110
3300-6800 74115
6802-9198 74115
12001-12007 74116
12009-12399 74116
W Archer St
1-499 74103
900-6799 74127
N Atlanta Ave
1-3499 74110
4700-4799 74130
S Atlanta Ave
1-1799 74104
3100-6099 74105
6600-6698 74136
6700-7499 74136
8600-8799 74137
N Atlanta Ct
1500-3499 74110
5900-6099 74130
S Atlanta Ct 74105
N Atlanta Pl 74110
S Atlanta Pl
1100-1799 74104

2100-2199 74114
3400-6099 74105
6601-6697 74136
6699-7000 74136
7002-7298 74136
8600-8799 74137
E Ba Frontage Rd 74145
S Baltimore Ave 74119
Beechcraft Dr 74132
N Birmingham Ave
1-3799 74110
5400-5498 74130
5500-6299 74130
S Birmingham Ave
1-1899 74104
2501-2599 74114
3100-6099 74105
6600-7399 74136
S Birmingham Ct
2100-2199 74114
7000-7499 74136
N Birmingham Pl
100-3499 74110
4700-6299 74130
S Birmingham Pl
1100-1299 74104
2300-3099 74114
3800-6099 74105
6900-7399 74136
N Boston Ave
100-400 74103
402-498 74103
901-1097 74106
1099-2599 74106
4600-6299 74126
S Boston Ave
1-297 74103
299-599 74103
600-1999 74119
2101-2197 74114
2199-2800 74114
2802-2898 74114
4700-5699 74105
S Boston Ct
2900-3099 74114
3100-3199 74105
N Boston Pl
1100-2899 74106
2901-4499 74106
4600-5099 74126
S Boston Pl
2500-3099 74114
3100-5799 74105
N Boulder Ave
100-499 74103
2700-2899 74106
4600-6399 74126
S Boulder Ave
200-599 74103
601-797 74119
799-1899 74119
W Bowen Pl 74127
N Braden Ave 74115
S Braden Ave
900-1499 74112
2400-3099 74114
3200-4999 74135
7100-8099 74136
8400-11900 74137
11902-12098 74137
S Braden Pl
3600-4399 74135
9100-9300 74137
9302-10998 74137
W Brady Pl 74127
E Brady St
1-299 74103
300-399 74120
11100-17699 74116
W Brady St
1-199 74103
900-7299 74127
Bratton Rd 74126
Briar Ridge Ln 74131
Broken Arrow Expy 74145
E Cameron St
5100-5199 74115

10900-11199 74116
W Cameron St
100-199 74103
1300-7399 74127
N Canton Ave
800-2499 74115
6700-6798 74117
S Canton Ave
900-2099 74112
3700-4399 74135
6800-7799 74136
8400-11999 74137
S Canton Pl 74137
W Canyon Rd 74131
S Carestow Ave 74112
N Cargo Rd 74115
S Carson Ave 74119
S Carthage Ave 74119
S Cedar Ave 74107
Cessna Dr 74132
Charles Page Blvd 74127
N Cheyenne Ave
1-599 74103
600-2799 74106
4600-6599 74126
S Cheyenne Ave
200-499 74103
800-898 74119
900-1999 74119
N Cheyenne Pl 74126
N Cincinnati Ave
200-399 74103
1100-1128 74106
1130-4599 74106
4601-5197 74126
5199-7399 74126
S Cincinnati Ave
100-599 74103
600-698 74119
700-2099 74119
2100-2398 74114
2400-3099 74114
3100-5699 74105
N Cincinnati Ct 74106
N Cincinnati Dr 74106
N Cincinnati Pl
1400-4499 74106
4600-4999 74126
5001-5099 74126
S Cincinnati Pl 74119
Civic Ctr 74103
Clean Air Dr 74116
N Clerrens Ave 74115
N College Ave 74110
S College Ave
1-1999 74104
2300-2599 74114
4900-4999 74105
7100-7899 74136
8200-11499 74137
S College Ct 74137
S College Pl
7300-7899 74136
8200-10199 74137
N Columbia Ave
1-3800 74110
3802-4098 74110
6300-6398 74130
6501-6599 74130
S Columbia Ave
1-1899 74104
1901-1999 74104
2100-2599 74114
4100-5999 74105
6700-7399 74136
S Columbia Cir 74105
S Columbia Ct
5100-5599 74105
7300-7399 74136
N Columbia Pl
100-2599 74110
5000-5099 74130
S Columbia Pl
1200-1799 74104
2300-2899 74114
3400-5899 74105
7100-7299 74136

N Corsair Ave 74115
Country Club Dr 74127
N Darlington Ave 74115
S Darlington Ave
200-2099 74112
2100-2799 74114
2801-3099 74114
3200-4999 74135
6501-7097 74136
7099-8099 74136
8600-11099 74137
N Darlington Pl 74115
S Darlington Pl
2100-2198 74114
2200-2299 74114
4200-4299 74135
Dawson Rd
2400-2699 74110
2701-3299 74110
3500-5299 74115
N Delaware Ave 74110
S Delaware Ave
300-1999 74104
2201-2297 74114
2299-2999 74114
3300-5999 74105
6800-6899 74136
8400-11699 74137
N Delaware Blvd 74110
S Delaware Ct
2100-2399 74114
5500-5599 74105
9700-9799 74137
N Delaware Pl 74110
S Delaware Pl
1100-2099 74104
2200-2800 74114
2802-2898 74114
3100-5899 74105
6900-7099 74136
8200-10399 74137
N Denver Ave
100-599 74103
600-2799 74106
4601-5597 74126
5599-6399 74126
S Denver Ave
100-599 74103
600-1799 74119
N Denver Blvd 74106
N Denver Pl
2200-2499 74106
5000-5098 74126
N Detroit Ave
100-199 74120
1100-4499 74106
4600-5799 74126
S Detroit Ave
100-1800 74120
1802-1998 74120
2100-3099 74114
3100-4999 74105
5001-5399 74105
N Detroit Pl 74106
S Detroit Pl 74105
N Dunintan Ave 74106
Eagles Nest 74132
W Easton Ct 74127
E Easton Pl 74115
W Easton Pl 74127
E Easton St
1000-1699 74120
2901-3097 74110
3099-3299 74110
3300-7799 74115
7801-7999 74115
W Easton St 74127
Ecker Ln 74126
Edinburgh Ct 74132
W Edison St
500-599 74103
1300-7299 74127
N Elgin Ave
1-299 74120
301-499 74120
500-898 74106
900-4399 74106

4600-5999 ... 74126
S Elgin Ave ... 74120
N Elgin Pl ... 74106
Ellanced Ctr ... 74172
N Elwood Ave
1-99 ... 74103
1501-1597 ... 74106
1599-2399 ... 74106
4600-5798 ... 74126
5800-6599 ... 74126
S Elwood Ave
600-1699 ... 74119
3600-5399 ... 74107
6600-9099 ... 74132
N Erie Ave
100-3199 ... 74115
6300-6499 ... 74117
S Erie Ave
500-1799 ... 74112
2500-2599 ... 74114
3200-4299 ... 74135
6400-8099 ... 74136
8600-11999 ... 74137
12001-12099 ... 74137
N Erie Pl ... 74115
S Erie Pl
1700-1799 ... 74112
2101-2197 ... 74114
2199-2299 ... 74114
10600-10899 ... 74137
N Evanston Ave
500-4699 ... 74110
4701-4799 ... 74110
5900-6099 ... 74130
S Evanston Ave
100-1999 ... 74104
2200-2799 ... 74114
3200-5899 ... 74105
6700-7900 ... 74136
7902-8098 ... 74136
8200-10299 ... 74137
S Evanston Cir ... 74136
S Evanston Ct ... 74105
N Evanston Pl ... 74110
S Evanston Pl
4700-5799 ... 74105
9200-10299 ... 74137
W Fairview St
100-198 ... 74106
200-599 ... 74106
600-2599 ... 74127
N Falcon Ave ... 74115
Fantacy Ln ... 74131
N Florence Ave ... 74110
S Florence Ave
1-1999 ... 74104
2100-2899 ... 74114
3100-5899 ... 74105
6500-7999 ... 74136
8100-10399 ... 74137
S Florence Ct ... 74105
S Florence Dr ... 74114
N Florence Pl ... 74110
S Florence Pl
1100-1999 ... 74104
2100-2599 ... 74114
3100-4899 ... 74105
6100-6199 ... 74136
8100-9199 ... 74137
Forest Blvd ... 74114
Foxbriar Dr ... 74132
Foxtail Ln ... 74132
N Frankfort Ave
1100-4599 ... 74106
4600-6299 ... 74126
S Frankfort Ave ... 74120
N Frankfort Ct ... 74106
N Frankfort Pl
1400-4599 ... 74106
4900-6299 ... 74126
Frankoma Rd ... 74131
S Frisco Ave
200-299 ... 74103
1200-1599 ... 74119
7700-7999 ... 74132
S Frontage Rd ... 74107
N Fulton Ave ... 74115
S Fulton Ave
1-2099 ... 74112
3200-5099 ... 74135
6100-8099 ... 74136
8600-11899 ... 74137
S Fulton Cir ... 74136
S Fulton Ct ... 74135
S Fulton Pl
2100-2599 ... 74114
4700-4799 ... 74135
7300-7799 ... 74136
S Galveston Ave
1200-1499 ... 74127
3600-4300 ... 74107
4302-4598 ... 74107
7700-7799 ... 74132
S Galveston Ct ... 74132
N Garnett Rd ... 74116
S Garnett Rd
1-2099 ... 74128
2100-3099 ... 74129
3100-6099 ... 74146
N Garrison Ave
2100-4399 ... 74106
4600-6399 ... 74126
6401-6599 ... 74126
N Garrison Ct ... 74126
N Garrison Pl
2100-4399 ... 74106
4600-6099 ... 74126
N Gary Ave ... 74110
S Gary Ave
200-1999 ... 74104
2200-2899 ... 74114
3100-5699 ... 74105
6100-8099 ... 74136
8200-9499 ... 74137
S Gary Ct ... 74105
Gary Dr ... 74131
S Gary Dr ... 74114
N Gary Pl ... 74110
S Gary Pl
500-1999 ... 74104
2100-2298 ... 74114
2300-2899 ... 74114
3100-5999 ... 74105
7200-8099 ... 74136
10300-10399 ... 74137
N & S Gilcrease Museum
Rd ... 74127
N Gillette Ave
1-2999 ... 74110
5600-6299 ... 74130
S Gillette Ave
2-98 ... 74104
100-1599 ... 74104
5400-5499 ... 74105
Glenn Ln ... 74131
Glenside Ln ... 74131
E Globemaster St ... 74115
W Golden Ave ... 74106
W Golden St ... 74127
N Granite Ave ... 74115
S Granite Ave
3500-4699 ... 74135
6600-7899 ... 74136
9700-12099 ... 74137
S Granite Ct ... 74136
S Granite Pl
4700-4799 ... 74135
7500-7599 ... 74136
11400-11412 ... 74137
11414-11422 ... 74137
11424-11498 ... 74137
Greendale Rd ... 74131
N Greenwood Ave
2-98 ... 74120
100-399 ... 74120
500-1699 ... 74106
S Greenwood Ave ... 74120
N Greenwood Pl ... 74106
N Guthrie Ave ... 74103
S Guthrie Ave
200-299 ... 74103
1200-1298 ... 74119
1300-1499 ... 74119
7600-8099 ... 74132
S Guthrie Ct ... 74132
S Guthrie Pl ... 74107
Hackberry Ct ... 74132
S Hanger Rd ... 74132
N Harivent Ave ... 74116
N Hartford Ave
1500-1598 ... 74106
1600-4599 ... 74106
4600-5599 ... 74126
N Hartford Pl
3100-3199 ... 74106
5400-5599 ... 74126
N Harvard Ave ... 74115
S Harvard Ave
100-1999 ... 74112
2101-2107 ... 74114
2109-3099 ... 74114
3100-5699 ... 74135
6300-8099 ... 74136
8100-11499 ... 74137
S Harvard Ct
2500-2599 ... 74114
5600-5799 ... 74135
S Harvard Pl
2500-2599 ... 74114
7500-7598 ... 74136
7600-7799 ... 74136
11200-11299 ... 74137
E Haskell Pl
1000-1199 ... 74106
1801-1997 ... 74110
1999-2200 ... 74110
2202-2298 ... 74110
3300-7300 ... 74115
7302-9698 ... 74115
W Haskell Pl ... 74127
E Haskell St
1000-1699 ... 74106
1700-2900 ... 74110
2902-3298 ... 74110
3300-7299 ... 74115
W Haskell St
500-599 ... 74106
1700-2499 ... 74127
Hazel Blvd ... 74114
Heavy Traffic Way ... 74127
Hillwood Dr ... 74131
S Houston Ave
200-1499 ... 74127
5201-5216 ... 74107
6700-6999 ... 74132
S Houston Ct ... 74132
N Hudson Ave ... 74115
S Hudson Ave
1-2099 ... 74112
2700-3099 ... 74114
3100-5899 ... 74135
6100-8099 ... 74136
8600-11599 ... 74137
S Hudson Ct ... 74137
S Hudson Pl
2100-2600 ... 74114
2602-2998 ... 74114
4200-6099 ... 74135
6100-7999 ... 74136
9700-11799 ... 74137
S Indarl Ave ... 74128
E Independence Pl ... 74115
W Independence Pl ... 74127
E Independence St
100-1699 ... 74106
2301-2397 ... 74110
2399-3200 ... 74110
3202-3298 ... 74110
3300-5314 ... 74115
5313-5313 ... 74158
5315-9699 ... 74115
5316-7898 ... 74115
10700-11399 ... 74116
W Independence St ... 74127
S Indian Ave
1200-1399 ... 74127
4900-4999 ... 74107
7300-7899 ... 74132
N Indianapolis Ave ... 74115
S Indianapolis Ave
100-1999 ... 74112
2200-2299 ... 74114
3300-5999 ... 74135
6100-7500 ... 74136
7502-7798 ... 74136
8300-9699 ... 74137
S Indianapolis Pl
5900-5999 ... 74135
6200-6499 ... 74136
8300-8399 ... 74137
N Iroquois Ave
1000-1098 ... 74106
1100-4599 ... 74106
4600-7500 ... 74126
7502-7598 ... 74126
S Iroquois St ... 74120
N Irvington Ave ... 74115
S Irvington Ave
1800-1899 ... 74112
2101-2397 ... 74114
2399-2799 ... 74114
2801-3099 ... 74114
3200-6099 ... 74135
6100-8099 ... 74136
9800-10699 ... 74137
10701-10799 ... 74137
S Irvington Ct ... 74135
S Irvington Pl ... 74135
Jack Bates Ave ... 74132
S Jackson Ave
800-1198 ... 74127
1200-1399 ... 74127
1700-4599 ... 74107
4601-4811 ... 74107
7100-7499 ... 74132
N Jamestown Ave ... 74115
S Jamestown Ave
100-1999 ... 74112
2100-2799 ... 74114
2801-2899 ... 74114
3100-6099 ... 74135
6200-8099 ... 74136
8100-11099 ... 74137
S Jamestown Pl ... 74136
Janis Ln ... 74131
E Jasper St
1300-1598 ... 74106
1600-1699 ... 74106
1700-2799 ... 74110
3300-7899 ... 74115
W Jasper St
200-599 ... 74106
2100-3199 ... 74127
John Hope Franklin
Blvd ... 74106
N Johnstown Ave
4100-4599 ... 74106
4800-6599 ... 74126
N Joplin Ave ... 74115
S Joplin Ave
1-397 ... 74112
399-1899 ... 74112
2300-2398 ... 74114
2400-3099 ... 74114
3100-6099 ... 74135
6100-8099 ... 74136
8600-11499 ... 74137
S Joplin Ct ... 74135
S Joplin Pl
3000-3099 ... 74114
3500-5299 ... 74135
9700-11099 ... 74137
N Kenosha Ave
1000-4599 ... 74106
5100-6099 ... 74126
S Kenosha Ave ... 74120
E King Pl
1000-1098 ... 74106
1301-1399 ... 74106
1700-2799 ... 74110
3300-7899 ... 74115
E King St
400-1599 ... 74106
1601-1699 ... 74106
2400-2800 ... 74110
2802-3098 ... 74110
3300-7899 ... 74115
15700-15799 ... 74116
W King St ... 74106
S Kingston ... 74137
N Kingston Ave ... 74115
S Kingston Ave
1-1899 ... 74112
3200-6099 ... 74135
6100-7799 ... 74136
8200-12099 ... 74137
N Kingston Ct ... 74115
N Kingston Pl ... 74115
S Kingston Pl
7600-7699 ... 74136
12000-12099 ... 74137
N Knoxville Ave ... 74115
S Knoxville Ave
1-1999 ... 74112
2401-2499 ... 74114
3100-5999 ... 74135
6100-7599 ... 74136
8701-9597 ... 74137
9599-11099 ... 74137
S Knoxville Pl
4800-4999 ... 74135
6900-6999 ... 74136
N Lakewood Ave
1-99 ... 74115
6900-7599 ... 74117
S Lakewood Ave
2-198 ... 74112
200-2099 ... 74112
3200-6099 ... 74135
6100-8099 ... 74136
8600-12099 ... 74137
S Lakewood Ct ... 74137
S Lakewood Pl
5400-5499 ... 74135
8100-9899 ... 74137
N Lansing Ave
1000-1198 ... 74106
1200-3999 ... 74106
6000-6599 ... 74126
S Lansing Ave ... 74120
N Lansing Pl ... 74106
E Latimer Ct
400-699 ... 74106
1700-2799 ... 74110
5300-9199 ... 74115
W Latimer Ct ... 74127
E Latimer Pl
100-298 ... 74106
300-1100 ... 74106
1102-1198 ... 74106
1700-3199 ... 74110
3300-9199 ... 74115
15700-15899 ... 74116
15901-16099 ... 74116
W Latimer Pl ... 74127
E Latimer St
101-397 ... 74106
399-1500 ... 74106
1502-1598 ... 74106
2701-3097 ... 74110
3099-3199 ... 74110
3201-3299 ... 74110
3300-9599 ... 74115
10500-16399 ... 74116
W Latimer St
1-499 ... 74106
501-599 ... 74106
1700-1999 ... 74127
Laufen Dr ... 74117
N Lawton Ave ... 74127
S Lawton Ave
1-1399 ... 74127
3600-5399 ... 74107
Lear Jet Ln ... 74132
N Lewis Ave
1-4599 ... 74110
4600-7299 ... 74130
S Lewis Ave
1-2099 ... 74104
2100-2799 ... 74114
3101-3597 ... 74105
3599-6099 ... 74105
6100-8099 ... 74136
8100-9099 ... 74137
S Lewis Ct ... 74105
N Lewis Pl ... 74110
S Lewis Pl
1100-1699 ... 74104
3100-5565 ... 74105
5567-5599 ... 74105
S Lincomea Ave ... 74119
Loch Ness Cir & Ln ... 74132
E Loraderl St ... 74146
N Louisville Ave ... 74115
S Louisville Ave
1-1500 ... 74112
1502-1998 ... 74112
2101-2397 ... 74114
2399-2800 ... 74114
2802-3098 ... 74114
3100-5899 ... 74135
6100-8099 ... 74136
8100-11699 ... 74137
S Louisville Pl
100-199 ... 74112
5900-5999 ... 74135
11400-11499 ... 74137
S Lynn Lane Rd ... 74108
N Madison Ave
1-99 ... 74120
800-3299 ... 74106
5400-5898 ... 74126
5900-6599 ... 74126
S Madison Ave
200-1799 ... 74120
2100-3099 ... 74114
3100-5799 ... 74105
5801-6099 ... 74105
N Madison Pl ... 74106
S Madison Pl
700-799 ... 74120
3500-6099 ... 74105
6100-6399 ... 74136
S Madwasto Ave ... 74107
S Main Ave ... 74119
N Main St
101-197 ... 74103
199-499 ... 74103
600-2900 ... 74106
2902-4598 ... 74106
4600-6499 ... 74126
S Main St
300-599 ... 74103
600-1799 ... 74119
2200-2299 ... 74114
N Maplewood Ave ... 74115
S Maplewood Ave
500-1900 ... 74112
1902-2098 ... 74112
2100-2598 ... 74114
2600-2899 ... 74114
3600-5899 ... 74135
6100-7699 ... 74136
8500-11499 ... 74137
S Maplewood Pl ... 74137
Marilyn Ln ... 74131
N Marion Ave ... 74115
S Marion Ave
500-1499 ... 74112
2100-2298 ... 74114
2300-2499 ... 74114
3200-6099 ... 74135
6100-8099 ... 74136
8200-11699 ... 74137
S Marion Pl
2700-2799 ... 74114
5100-6099 ... 74135
E Marshall Ct
200-299 ... 74106
5300-5599 ... 74115
E Marshall Pl
200-699 ... 74106
1700-1999 ... 74110
5300-9199 ... 74115
E Marshall St
101-397 ... 74106
399-1699 ... 74106
1700-2799 ... 74110
3300-9499 ... 74115
10700-17299 ... 74116
W Marshall St
200-528 ... 74106
1000-2099 ... 74127
N Martin Luther King Jr
Blvd
200-399 ... 74103
1100-4599 ... 74106
4601-4697 ... 74126
4699-6599 ... 74126
E Mathew Brady St
1-299 ... 74103
300-399 ... 74120
11100-11299 ... 74116
W Mathew Brady St
1-199 ... 74103
900-4699 ... 74127
N Maybelle Ave ... 74127
S Maybelle Ave
1900-4999 ... 74107
8100-8599 ... 74132
Meadowside Ln ... 74131
N Memorial Dr ... 74115
S Memorial Dr
1-1999 ... 74112
2100-3099 ... 74129
3100-5800 ... 74145
5802-6098 ... 74145
6100-11099 ... 74133
S Michael Dr ... 74132
Midland Ave & Pl ... 74106
N Mingo Rd
1-4599 ... 74116
4600-5899 ... 74117
S Mingo Rd
1-1099 ... 74128
3100-6099 ... 74146
6100-10099 ... 74133
N Mingo Valley Expy ... 74116
N Mintine Ave ... 74110
Mohawk Blvd
1700-3099 ... 74110
3300-4900 ... 74115
4902-6798 ... 74115
E Mohawk Blvd
101-197 ... 74106
199-1699 ... 74106
8800-9498 ... 74117
9500-9599 ... 74117
E Mohawk Rd ... 74117
Montclair Ave ... 74104
E Mustang St ... 74115
N New Haven Ave ... 74115
S New Haven Ave
100-1499 ... 74112
2801-3099 ... 74114
3100-5999 ... 74135
6100-7999 ... 74136
8200-11899 ... 74137
S New Haven Pl ... 74135
New Sapulpa Rd ... 74131
Newblock Park Dr ... 74127
S Newport Ave
1100-1799 ... 74120
4900-5700 ... 74105
5702-6098 ... 74105
6300-6599 ... 74136
E Newton Ct
2600-2799 ... 74110
5500-8099 ... 74115
W Newton Ct ... 74127
E Newton Pl
200-699 ... 74106
701-1599 ... 74106
1900-2799 ... 74110
5500-9599 ... 74115
10800-17199 ... 74116
W Newton Pl ... 74127
E Newton St
100-199 ... 74106
201-1699 ... 74106
1900-2600 ... 74110
2602-2698 ... 74110
3301-3397 ... 74115
3399-9499 ... 74115
10800-10998 ... 74116
11000-16899 ... 74116
W Newton St
1-197 ... 74106
199-581 ... 74106

583-599 ... 74106
1000-2799 ... 74127
N Nogales Ave ... 74127
S Nogales Ave
1-499 ... 74127
1700-4899 ... 74107
S Nogales Ave W ... 74132
N Norfolk Ave
100-199 ... 74120
700-3299 ... 74106
5200-6599 ... 74126
S Norfolk Ave
100-1799 ... 74120
1801-2099 ... 74120
2100-2599 ... 74114
3500-5599 ... 74105
N Norfolk Pl ... 74126
S Norfolk Ter ... 74114
N Norwood Ave ... 74115
S Norwood Ave
301-497 ... 74112
499-1200 ... 74112
1202-1298 ... 74112
2400-3099 ... 74114
3200-5799 ... 74135
7400-7699 ... 74136
8600-11999 ... 74137
N Norwood Pl ... 74115
Oak Rd ... 74105
Oak Fairway ... 74131
Oak Field Dr ... 74131
Oak Forest Ln ... 74131
Oak Lake Ln ... 74131
Oak Leaf Dr
4400-4899 ... 74132
4900-5198 ... 74131
5200-5399 ... 74131
5401-5499 ... 74131
Oak Line Dr ... 74131
Oak Meadow Dr ... 74131
Oak Timber Dr ... 74131
N Oakcliff Dr ... 74126
E Oklahoma Pl
200-398 ... 74106
400-600 ... 74106
602-698 ... 74106
1700-3299 ... 74110
6200-9599 ... 74115
16100-16599 ... 74116
W Oklahoma Pl ... 74127
E Oklahoma St
200-1699 ... 74106
1700-2799 ... 74110
4301-4997 ... 74115
4999-9199 ... 74115
15400-17699 ... 74116
W Oklahoma St
200-299 ... 74106
1200-2499 ... 74127
Old Bridge Ln ... 74132
Old North Rd ... 74127
N Olympia Ave ... 74127
S Olympia Ave
1-999 ... 74127
1700-5499 ... 74107
6800-8599 ... 74132
One Williams Ctr ... 74172
N Osage Ave ... 74106
N Osage Dr
600-1399 ... 74106
3201-3397 ... 74127
3399-4199 ... 74127
4500-4599 ... 74106
4600-7699 ... 74126
N Oswego Ave ... 74115
S Oswego Ave
500-1499 ... 74112
2101-2197 ... 74114
2199-2699 ... 74114
3200-6099 ... 74135
6100-7500 ... 74136
7502-8098 ... 74136
8200-12099 ... 74137
N Oswego Pl ... 74115
S Oswego Pl
2100-2699 ... 74114
7600-7999 ... 74136
10200-11099 ... 74137
S Oswego Ter ... 74114
S Oventone Ave ... 74131
N Owasso Ave
2-98 ... 74120
800-2599 ... 74106
2601-2799 ... 74106
5900-6099 ... 74126
S Owasso Ave
400-1999 ... 74120
2100-2699 ... 74114
3100-5899 ... 74105
6300-6399 ... 74136
N Owasso Pl ... 74126
S Owasso Pl
2100-2499 ... 74114
6300-6399 ... 74136
N Oxford Ave ... 74115
S Oxford Ave
1100-1198 ... 74112
4600-5499 ... 74135
6600-7899 ... 74136
8500-11999 ... 74137
S Oxford Pl ... 74137
E Pack ... 74116
Park Rd ... 74115
W Parkway Blvd ... 74127
S Patton Ave ... 74107
W Pearthes St ... 74127
N Peoria Ave
1-199 ... 74120
201-599 ... 74120
700-4599 ... 74106
4600-7599 ... 74126
S Peoria Ave
100-1900 ... 74120
1902-2098 ... 74120
2100-2398 ... 74114
2400-3099 ... 74114
3100-6099 ... 74105
6100-6999 ... 74136
8200-8899 ... 74132
S Peoria Pl ... 74105
N Phoenix Ave
1-1599 ... 74127
4900-5199 ... 74126
5201-6899 ... 74126
S Phoenix Ave
1-799 ... 74127
1700-3699 ... 74107
8500-8599 ... 74132
S Phoenix Pl ... 74132
E Pine Pl
301-497 ... 74106
499-1199 ... 74106
3700-6599 ... 74115
W Pine Pl ... 74127
E Pine St
100-1699 ... 74106
1700-3299 ... 74110
3300-9699 ... 74115
9700-17599 ... 74116
W Pine St ... 74127
Piper Dr ... 74132
N Pittsburg Ave
1300-2799 ... 74115
6900-7599 ... 74117
S Pittsburg Ave
100-1499 ... 74112
2200-3099 ... 74114
3300-6099 ... 74135
6200-7499 ... 74136
8100-12399 ... 74137
S Pittsburg Ct ... 74135
S Pittsburg Pl ... 74135
Point Dr ... 74131
Post Oak Dr ... 74126
S Pradongs Ave ... 74129
E Prendert St ... 74114
N Quaker Ave
500-599 ... 74120
700-3899 ... 74106
6300-6499 ... 74126
6501-6599 ... 74126
S Quaker Ave
500-1899 ... 74120
2900-3099 ... 74114
4300-4398 ... 74105
4400-5699 ... 74105
6200-6899 ... 74136
S Quaker Rd ... 74105
N Quanah Ave ... 74127
S Quanah Ave
1-799 ... 74127
3600-3699 ... 74107
N Quebec Ave ... 74115
S Quebec Ave
200-1499 ... 74112
2400-2699 ... 74114
3200-6099 ... 74135
6100-8099 ... 74136
8100-11999 ... 74137
S Quebec Pl
7600-7699 ... 74136
10300-11099 ... 74137
E Queen Pl
700-799 ... 74106
2100-2198 ... 74110
W Queen Pl ... 74127
E Queen St
500-1299 ... 74106
2500-3098 ... 74110
3100-3199 ... 74110
6000-6098 ... 74115
6301-6799 ... 74115
W Queen St
2-198 ... 74106
200-300 ... 74106
302-398 ... 74106
1200-1899 ... 74127
N Quincy Ave
1-99 ... 74120
700-2799 ... 74106
5900-6599 ... 74126
S Quincy Ave
100-1899 ... 74120
3300-6099 ... 74105
6200-6698 ... 74136
6700-7299 ... 74136
S Quincy Pl ... 74105
N Raniangt Ave ... 74130
W Reading Ct ... 74127
E Reading Pl
4000-7299 ... 74115
12900-12999 ... 74116
W Reading Pl ... 74127
E Reading St
200-1599 ... 74106
2101-2197 ... 74110
2199-2299 ... 74110
3300-7999 ... 74115
W Reading St ... 74127
S & E Regal Blvd, Ct & Pl ... 74133
S Regency Dr ... 74131
S Richaris Ave ... 74145
N Richmond Ave ... 74115
S Richmond Ave
200-1499 ... 74112
2100-2899 ... 74114
3400-6099 ... 74135
6100-7999 ... 74136
8100-11799 ... 74137
S Richmond Pl
6800-6899 ... 74136
10200-10799 ... 74137
Ridgeview St ... 74131
N Ridgeway St ... 74131
Riva Ridge Rd ... 74132
Riverside Dr
1300-1399 ... 74127
1501-1697 ... 74119
1699-1999 ... 74119
2300-2398 ... 74114
2701-2799 ... 74114
3201-4097 ... 74105
4099-4199 ... 74105
4201-4699 ... 74105
Riverside Pkwy
7100-7799 ... 74136
7801-7999 ... 74136
8300-9999 ... 74137
W Riverview Dr ... 74107
N Rockford Ave
1-100 ... 74120
102-198 ... 74120
600-2799 ... 74106
4600-6599 ... 74126
S Rockford Ave
200-1799 ... 74120
2201-2299 ... 74114
3400-3498 ... 74105
3500-6099 ... 74105
6600-6799 ... 74136
S Rockford Dr ... 74105
S Rockford Pl
4100-5799 ... 74105
6600-6899 ... 74136
S Rockford Rd ... 74114
Rolling Oaks Cir & Dr ... 74107
N Rosedale Ave
1-2299 ... 74127
4800-5299 ... 74126
S Rosedale Ave
1-299 ... 74127
2101-3399 ... 74107
Royalwood Way ... 74131
N Sabre Ave ... 74115
N Saint Louis Ave
700-2899 ... 74106
4600-6599 ... 74126
S Saint Louis Ave
400-2099 ... 74120
2100-2699 ... 74114
3800-5799 ... 74105
6700-7799 ... 74136
S Saint Louis Pl ... 74136
S Sanchana Ave ... 74137
N Sandusky Ave ... 74115
S Sandusky Ave
1-1499 ... 74112
2100-3099 ... 74114
3100-5999 ... 74135
6200-7599 ... 74136
7601-8099 ... 74136
8100-12099 ... 74137
N Sandusky Pl ... 74115
S Sandusky Pl ... 74137
N Santa Fe Ave ... 74127
S Santa Fe Ave
1-199 ... 74127
3300-6000 ... 74107
6002-6098 ... 74107
N Santa Fe Pl ... 74127
S Santa Fe Pl ... 74107
S Scorings Ave ... 74132
S Searthen Ave ... 74108
E Seminole Pl ... 74106
W Seminole Pl ... 74127
E Seminole St
100-498 ... 74106
500-1600 ... 74106
1602-1698 ... 74106
2100-3099 ... 74110
3101-3299 ... 74110
7400-7599 ... 74115
10700-10799 ... 74116
W Seminole St
200-299 ... 74106
301-399 ... 74106
900-1999 ... 74127
Shadywood Dr ... 74131
Shari Ln ... 74131
N Sheridan Rd ... 74115
S Sheridan Rd
1-31 ... 74112
33-2099 ... 74112
2100-3099 ... 74129
3100-6099 ... 74145
6100-11099 ... 74133
Silver Oak Cir, Ct, Dr, Pl & Ter ... 74107
E Skelly Dr
100-3199 ... 74105
3301-4197 ... 74135
4199-6099 ... 74135
6101-6399 ... 74135
6500-6600 ... 74145
6602-7898 ... 74145
7701-8097 ... 74129
8099-9199 ... 74129
10700-12599 ... 74128
12601-12899 ... 74128
14800-16599 ... 74116
W Skelly Dr ... 74107
W Skyline Dr ... 74107
S Sleepy Hollow Dr ... 74136
E Smindo St N ... 74117
Smith Cir ... 74131
Southwest Blvd
1500-5800 ... 74107
5802-6798 ... 74107
7300-7698 ... 74131
7700-7799 ... 74131
State Farm Blvd ... 74146
Sulzer Way ... 74131
Summit Dr ... 74131
Sunset Dr ... 74114
Swan Dr ... 74120
N Tacoma Ave ... 74127
S Tacoma Ave
1-199 ... 74127
3601-4597 ... 74107
4599-4799 ... 74107
4801-4999 ... 74107
N Tacoma Pl ... 74127
W Tecumseh Pl ... 74127
E Tecumseh St
200-999 ... 74106
1900-3299 ... 74110
5300-6399 ... 74115
6401-6499 ... 74115
11300-11400 ... 74116
11402-11798 ... 74116
W Tecumseh St
201-297 ... 74106
299-300 ... 74106
302-398 ... 74106
1000-2399 ... 74127
Terrace Dr
1300-1499 ... 74104
1423-1423 ... 74159
Terwilleger Blvd
2100-2699 ... 74114
3600-3899 ... 74105
Tiger Switch Rd ... 74116
Timberlane Rd ... 74136
N Toledo Ave ... 74115
S Toledo Ave
1-1299 ... 74112
2100-2899 ... 74114
3100-5599 ... 74135
6800-7999 ... 74136
8001-8099 ... 74136
8100-12099 ... 74137
S Toledo Ct ... 74137
N Toledo Pl ... 74115
S Toledo Pl ... 74135
N Trenton Ave
1-99 ... 74120
101-599 ... 74120
700-4599 ... 74106
4600-7599 ... 74126
S Trenton Ave
100-1799 ... 74120
2401-2597 ... 74114
2599-3099 ... 74114
3301-3497 ... 74105
3499-5699 ... 74105
6100-7799 ... 74136
S Trenton Ct ... 74136
S Trenton Pl ... 74136
N Troost Ave
800-3199 ... 74106
4600-6299 ... 74126
S Troost Ave
400-1799 ... 74120
2200-3099 ... 74114
3200-5199 ... 74105
6100-6699 ... 74136
6701-6799 ... 74136
N Troost Pl ... 74106
S Troost Pl ... 74105
Tucker Dr ... 74104
Tulsa Mountain Ranch Rd ... 74126
Turkey Creek Rd ... 74126
N Union Ave ... 74127
S Union Ave
1-99 ... 74127
1700-5999 ... 74107
6100-9699 ... 74132
N Union Pl ... 74127
S Union Pl ... 74107
N Urbana Ave ... 74115
S Urbana Ave
1-1499 ... 74112
2100-2699 ... 74114
3100-6099 ... 74135
7200-7899 ... 74136
8200-11099 ... 74137
S Urbana Pl
7500-7599 ... 74136
8800-9399 ... 74137
E Ute Pl
200-300 ... 74106
302-598 ... 74106
5500-5999 ... 74115
W Ute Pl ... 74127
E Ute St
200-1699 ... 74106
2000-2098 ... 74110
2100-2699 ... 74110
2701-2999 ... 74110
3300-5999 ... 74115
10501-10597 ... 74116
10599-10799 ... 74116
W Ute St ... 74127
N Utica Ave
1-1899 ... 74110
1901-3199 ... 74110
2000-2044 ... 74106
4600-6600 ... 74130
6602-6898 ... 74130
S Utica Ave
100-198 ... 74104
200-1999 ... 74104
2100-3099 ... 74114
3100-6099 ... 74105
6100-7999 ... 74136
S Utica Cir ... 74136
N Utica Pl ... 74130
S Utica Pl
2200-2299 ... 74114
6600-6950 ... 74136
6952-6956 ... 74136
Utica Sq
1700-2099 ... 74114
2032-2032 ... 74152
Valley Cir ... 74131
N Vancouver Ave ... 74127
S Vancouver Ave
4300-5799 ... 74107
6100-6499 ... 74132
S Vancouver Pl ... 74107
N Vandalia Ave ... 74115
S Vandalia Ave
1-1299 ... 74112
2100-2699 ... 74114
4000-5299 ... 74135
7401-7599 ... 74136
8300-11799 ... 74137
N Vandalia Pl ... 74115
N Victor Ave
1-2399 ... 74110
4601-6197 ... 74130
6199-7599 ... 74130
S Victor Ave
100-1799 ... 74104
2700-2899 ... 74114
3100-5899 ... 74105
6100-7999 ... 74136
S Victor Ct ... 74105
E & W Victoria St ... 74106
E Viper St ... 74115
E Virgin Ct ... 74115
E Virgin Pl ... 74115
E Virgin St
200-1699 ... 74106
1700-2799 ... 74110
2801-3299 ... 74110
3300-6800 ... 74115
6802-6998 ... 74115
W Virgin St ... 74127
N Waco Ave ... 74127
S Waco Ave
4000-4298 ... 74107
4300-5799 ... 74107
6100-8299 ... 74132
N Warainey Ave ... 74126
S Warindal Ave ... 74105
Waverly Dr ... 74104
Webb Dr ... 74131
Westway Rd ... 74131
N Wheeling Ave
1-2899 ... 74110
4801-6097 ... 74130
6099-6499 ... 74130
S Wheeling Ave
1-2099 ... 74104
3000-3099 ... 74114
3300-5899 ... 74105
7100-8099 ... 74136
N Wheeling Pl ... 74110
S Whintriv Ave ... 74104
Whirlpool Dr ... 74117
Whitetail Cir & Ln ... 74132
N Wild Mountain Rd ... 74127
Wilshire Dr ... 74106
N Winston Ave ... 74115
S Winston Ave
900-1499 ... 74112
2200-2899 ... 74114
3100-5699 ... 74135
7400-7699 ... 74136
8400-11499 ... 74137
S Winston Ct ... 74137
S Winston Pl
7400-7599 ... 74136
8600-8799 ... 74137
Woodridge Cir ... 74131
E Woodrow Ct ... 74110
E Woodrow Pl
1-1699 ... 74106
1700-1798 ... 74110
1800-3299 ... 74110
3300-4599 ... 74115
W Woodrow Pl
200-300 ... 74106
302-398 ... 74106
1400-2399 ... 74127
E Woodrow St
200-599 ... 74106
1700-3299 ... 74110
3500-5299 ... 74115
W Woodrow St ... 74127
Woodward Blvd
1-3099 ... 74114
3100-3199 ... 74105
N Xanthus Ave
1-2599 ... 74110
4800-6599 ... 74130
S Xanthus Ave
1-2099 ... 74104
3300-5499 ... 74105
N Xanthus Pl
2200-2498 ... 74110
2500-3299 ... 74110
6101-6197 ... 74130
6199-6299 ... 74130
S Xanthus Pl ... 74104
N Xenophon Ave ... 74127
S Xenophon Ave
3700-5699 ... 74107
6100-7899 ... 74132
E Xyler St
200-699 ... 74106
701-1399 ... 74106
1800-3299 ... 74110
3300-6099 ... 74115
W Xyler St ... 74127
N Yale Ave
1-3299 ... 74115
5800-7199 ... 74117
S Yale Ave
1-1999 ... 74112
2200-2999 ... 74114
3100-6099 ... 74135
6100-8099 ... 74136
8100-11899 ... 74137
S Yale Pl ... 74136

N Yorktown Ave
1-3199 74110
4600-6299 74130
S Yorktown Ave
1-2099 74104
2101-2497 74114
2499-3099 74114
3200-6099 74105
6100-6911 74136
6910-6910 74170
6912-6998 74136
6913-6999 74136
8100-8341 74137
8343-8399 74137
S Yorktown Ct
4800-4899 74105
8200-8399 74137
N Yorktown Pl
1600-2800 74110
2802-2898 74110
4800-4998 74130
S Yorktown Pl
1500-1599 74104
3500-6099 74105
6200-6299 74136
E Young Ct 74115
E Young Pl
200-1699 74106
1700-2099 74110
4200-7599 74115
7601-7799 74115
E Young St
100-1699 74106
1701-1797 74110
1799-3200 74110
3202-3298 74110
3600-5499 74115
W Young St
301-397 74106
399-400 74106
402-498 74106
1300-5699 74127
N Yukon Ave 74127
S Yukon Ave
2100-5799 74107
7900-8299 74132
N Yukon Cir 74127
N Zenith Ave 74127
S Zenith Ave
3900-4599 74107
9200-9299 74132
N Zenith Pl 74127
E Zion Ct 74106
E Zion Pl
200-599 74106
601-1099 74106
5300-6399 74115
E Zion St
200-1599 74106
2000-2099 74110
3900-6099 74115
W Zion St 74106
N Zunis Ave
1-3299 74110
4701-5197 74130
5199-6199 74130
S Zunis Ave
1-2299 74104
2600-2699 74114
2701-2799 74114
3100-5699 74105
6100-6799 74136
S Zunis Ct 74105
S Zunis Pl
3100-5499 74105
6700-6700 74136
6702-6799 74136
S Zurich Ave
400-599 74112
7000-7099 74136

NUMBERED STREETS

E 1st Ct 74108
E 1st Pl
800-899 74120
2800-2899 74104
16400-19799 74108
E 1st St
1-299 74103
300-900 74120
1700-1798 74104
3700-9299 74112
10600-12399 74128
16200-18900 74108
W 1st St
100-399 74103
601-797 74127
E 2nd Pl
3700-4499 74112
11700-11799 74128
16500-19318 74108
W 2nd Pl 74127
E 2nd St
1-299 74103
300-1699 74120
1700-3299 74104
3600-8899 74112
10100-11999 74128
16100-20599 74108
W 2nd St
1-599 74103
600-5999 74127
E 3rd Pl
8900-9399 74112
18100-18599 74108
E 3rd St
1-99 74103
300-1699 74120
1700-3299 74104
3300-7899 74112
9700-11999 74128
16100-20599 74108
W 3rd St
1-199 74103
600-6999 74127
E 4th Pl
1500-1699 74120
1800-3211 74104
3300-9099 74112
9700-12799 74128
13000-19599 74108
W 4th Pl 74127
E 4th St
1-199 74103
400-1699 74120
2300-3299 74104
3300-9199 74112
9700-11499 74128
13500-16098 74108
W 4th St
1-199 74103
333-333 74101
333-333 74150
1000-7228 74127
E 4th Ter 74112
E 5th Ct
1300-1599 74120
1601-1699 74120
5900-5999 74112
E 5th Pl
1000-1399 74120
2200-3299 74104
3300-8899 74112
9700-9899 74128
E 5th St
1-200 74103
400-1699 74120
1700-2999 74104
4300-9299 74112
9700-11500 74128
13200-13299 74108
W 5th St
13-97 74103
3300-7399 74127
E 6th St
1-299 74119
300-1699 74120
1700-2999 74104
3300-9199 74112
10100-11799 74128
13200-19298 74108
19300-20099 74108
W 6th St
1-599 74119
5000-6499 74127
E 7th Pl
1900-2099 74104
11500-11899 74128
E 7th St
1-99 74119
301-997 74120
1700-3299 74104
3300-9299 74112
9700-12799 74128
13001-19097 74108
W 7th St
1-599 74119
600-7899 74127
E 8th St
100-299 74119
401-997 74120
999-1699 74120
1700-3299 74104
3300-9199 74112
11500-11999 74128
W 8th St
100-299 74119
3900-6499 74127
E 9th St 74112
W 9th St
1-197 74119
700-6199 74127
E 10th St
300-1320 74120
1322-1631 74120
1633-1699 74120
2200-2699 74104
6500-9599 74112
W 10th St 74127
E 11th Ct 74128
E 11th Pl
1100-1199 74120
2500-2599 74104
3700-9099 74112
10700-11099 74128
14600-14699 74108
W 11th Pl 74127
E 11th St
1-99 74119
300-1699 74120
1700-1706 74104
3300-9599 74112
9700-12899 74128
12900-13098 74108
W 11th St
100-599 74119
600-6161 74127
E 12th Pl
2000-2399 74104
3500-3699 74112
9800-9899 74128
14300-14899 74108
E 12th St
1-99 74119
300-398 74120
2000-3199 74104
3300-9099 74112
9700-12099 74128
13400-18099 74108
W 12th St
200-599 74119
600-5699 74127
E 13th Pl
1700-2799 74104
4400-4699 74112
9700-12899 74128
E 13th St
1101-1297 74120
1700-3099 74104
3300-9299 74112
9900-12899 74128
13300-17899 74108
W 13th St
200-500 74119
600-799 74127
E 14th Ct 74128
E 14th Pl
1700-2799 74104
4400-6999 74112
10700-12499 74128
W 14th Pl
300-599 74119
600-699 74127
E 14th St
1300-1699 74120
1700-3199 74104
3300-8999 74112
9700-12899 74128
12900-17699 74108
W 14th St
200-299 74119
600-7799 74127
E 15th Ct 74112
E 15th Pl
2500-2699 74104
6900-7999 74112
10800-12599 74128
14600-15199 74108
E 15th St
1-299 74119
1000-1699 74120
1700-3299 74104
3301-3497 74112
9701-10797 74128
13600-17999 74108
W 15th St
100-599 74119
600-7799 74127
E 16th Pl
1800-2799 74104
8900-8999 74112
10700-12499 74128
13000-13199 74108
W 16th Pl 74119
E 16th St
1-299 74119
1100-1599 74120
1701-1797 74104
3300-9499 74112
9900-12699 74128
13000-13199 74108
W 16th St
200-299 74119
7200-8199 74127
E 17th Ct 74108
E 17th Pl
200-299 74119
1000-1699 74120
1800-2699 74104
5401-8897 74112
10600-11799 74128
12900-13299 74108
W 17th Pl 74119
E 17th St
1-199 74119
1100-1699 74120
1700-3299 74104
3300-9199 74112
10800-11298 74128
12900-12998 74108
W 17th St
200-399 74119
1100-1199 74107
7400-7999 74127
E 18th Ct 74108
E 18th Pl
10600-12699 74128
12900-14299 74108
E 18th St
1-299 74119
300-1399 74120
2100-2699 74104
5700-8999 74112
10600-12599 74128
12900-15099 74108
W 18th St
200-299 74119
7700-8099 74127
E 19th Pl 74128
E 19th Pl 74112
13600-14098 74108
E 19th St
101-197 74119
300-1599 74120
1700-3299 74104
3500-8899 74112
10800-10998 74128
14100-14199 74108
W 19th St
200-299 74119
800-899 74107
E 20th Pl
6900-7599 74112
12000-12599 74128
W 20th Pl 74107
E 20th St
200-299 74119
300-1599 74120
2000-2699 74104
5200-7499 74112
10600-12599 74128
W 20th St 74107
E 21st Ct 74129
E 21st Pl
1100-5899 74114
6500-12199 74129
W 21st Pl 74107
E 21st St
1-6299 74114
6500-6544 74129
12900-14899 74134
W 21st St
2-198 74114
701-1597 74107
E 22nd Pl
1500-5899 74114
7300-12099 74129
W 22nd Pl 74107
E 22nd St
1-5899 74114
7800-12799 74129
W 22nd St
1-99 74114
1100-1298 74107
1300-6399 74107
E 23rd Pl
8500-10098 74129
10100-11699 74129
13700-14499 74134
W 23rd Pl 74107
E 23rd St
2100-6099 74114
8100-12899 74129
12900-13399 74134
W 23rd St 74107
N 23rd West Ave 74127
4000-4899 74107
7900-7999 74132
E 24th Pl
200-6399 74114
8500-12899 74129
13600-14199 74134
W 24th Pl 74107
E 24th St
2-98 74114
6500-12899 74129
12900-12998 74134
W 24th St 74107
N 24th West Ave 74127
S 24th West Ave
4100-5399 74107
7600-7699 74132
N 24th West Pl 74127
S 24th West Pl 74107
E 25th Ct 74114
E 25th Pl
2100-5999 74114
6500-12399 74129
12900-12999 74134
E 25th St
1-5999 74114
8500-12599 74129
12900-12999 74134
W 25th St 74107
N 25th West Ave 74126
S 25th West Ave
500-599 74127
2500-2698 74107
2700-4900 74107
4902-5098 74107
E 26th Ct
100-199 74114
6500-9099 74129
E 26th Pl
1-6299 74114
6500-11099 74129
E 26th Pl N
2-98 74106
1700-2699 74110
4300-6399 74115
W 26th Pl N 74106
E 26th St
1-5999 74114
9101-9597 74129
13600-14200 74134
W 26th St 74107
E 26th Ter 74114
N 26th West Ave 74127
S 26th West Ave
3500-3598 74107
7100-8099 74132
E 27th Ct 74129
E 27th Ct N 74106
E 27th Pl
200-5999 74114
6500-12599 74129
13000-13899 74134
E 27th Pl N
200-699 74106
6200-6299 74115
W 27th Pl 74107
E 27th St
200-5999 74114
6500-12699 74129
12900-13999 74134
E 27th St N
100-998 74106
1700-2799 74110
11400-11699 74116
W 27th St 74107
W 27th St N
2-298 74106
2000-2099 74127
N 27th West Ave 74127
3600-5099 74107
6400-9299 74132
E 28th Ct 74129
E 28th Ct N 74115
E 28th Pl
4100-4399 74114
6600-12599 74129
12900-13999 74134
E 28th Pl N 74115
E 28th St
200-6299 74114
6500-12399 74129
13000-13899 74134
E 28th St N
200-799 74106
1700-1898 74110
W 28th St 74107
W 28th St N 74106
N 28th West Ave 74127
S 28th West Ave
3600-5099 74107
6100-9099 74132
N 28th West Pl 74127
S 28th West Pl 74132
E 29th Ct 74129
E 29th Pl
100-1299 74114
9000-11200 74129
13200-13899 74134
E 29th Pl N
2200-2799 74110
3900-3999 74115
E 29th St
200-5799 74114
6500-6698 74129
13100-13899 74134
E 29th St N
200-299 74106
1800-1898 74110
3700-6199 74115
W 29th St 74107
W 29th St N 74127
N 29th West Ave 74127
S 29th West Ave
3300-5099 74107
6100-6999 74132
S 29th West Pl 74132
E 30th Pl
1000-6299 74114
7400-12299 74129
13200-13799 74134
E 30th Pl N
2400-2600 74110
3300-3799 74115
E 30th St
1200-6399 74114
6500-12499 74129
12900-13899 74134
E 30th St N
200-598 74106
2200-2700 74110
3300-7499 74115
W 30th St 74107
W 30th St N 74127
N 30th West Ave
1-299 74127
5300-5399 74126
S 30th West Ave
4300-6099 74107
6300-7900 74132
7902-7998 74132
E 31st Ct
1200-1299 74105
4100-4199 74135
7900-8199 74145
12600-12700 74146
12900-13199 74134
E 31st Pl
100-2299 74105
3900-4699 74135
7300-8599 74145
11401-12097 74146
13100-13799 74134
E 31st Pl N
1600-1699 74106
1700-2199 74110
E 31st St
108-898 74105
3300-6399 74135
6500-9499 74145
9700-12899 74146
12900-18600 74134
E 31st St N
400-799 74106
2001-2199 74110
W 31st St 74107
W 31st St N 74127
N 31st West Ave 74127
3600-6099 74107
6200-10099 74132
E 32nd Ct 74134
E 32nd Pl
1000-2899 74105
3300-6199 74135
6700-9299 74145
11400-12499 74146
13100-13899 74134
700-899 74106
901-999 74106
2100-2299 74110
3300-3799 74115
E 32nd St
1200-2999 74105
3300-6399 74135
6700-6998 74145
7000-9099 74145
10101-10197 74146
10199-12599 74146
12601-12799 74146
12900-14899 74134
500-599 74106
1700-3299 74110
3300-3999 74115
13100-13199 74116
N 32nd West Ave 74127
S 32nd West Ave
3600-5999 74107
6400-7099 74132
S 32nd West Pl 74107
E 33rd Ct
5700-5999 74135
10600-12699 74146
E 33rd Pl
100-2699 74105

8200-9000 74145
10000-12500 74146
13300-14999 74134
W 33rd Pl 74107
E 33rd St
1200-3199 74105
3300-5399 74135
7000-9099 74145
9700-12599 74146
12900-14899 74134
E 33rd St N
201-297 74106
2100-2300 74110
3500-3599 74115
W 33rd St 74107
W 33rd St N 74127
N 33rd West Ave 74127
S 33rd West Ave
1-499 74127
1900-6099 74107
6100-10099 74132
E 34th Pl 74146
W 34th Pl 74107
E 34th St
100-3299 74105
3900-4899 74135
8200-9699 74145
10100-12800 74146
12900-14999 74134
E 34th St N
200-698 74106
2500-3299 74110
5300-5599 74115
W 34th St 74107
W 34th St N 74127
N 34th West Ave 74127
S 34th West Ave
100-199 74127
3800-3898 74107
3900-5199 74107
6100-8499 74132
E 35th Ct 74135
E 35th Ct N 74106
E 35th Pl
100-2899 74105
4100-5399 74135
12900-15099 74134
E 35th Pl N 74106
W 35th Pl 74107
W 35th Pl N 74127
E 35th St
100-2899 74105
3400-5999 74135
8100-9099 74145
11300-12899 74146
12900-15098 74134
E 35th St N 74106
W 35th St 74107
N 35th West Ave 74127
S 35th West Ave
100-199 74127
4001-4097 74107
4099-5799 74107
6100-7399 74132
E 36th Ct 74105
E 36th Pl
900-2899 74105
3700-4199 74135
10900-12199 74146
E 36th Pl N 74106
W 36th Pl 74107
E 36th St
900-2700 74105
3300-6299 74135
9001-9397 74145
10601-10897 74146
12901-12997 74134
E 36th St N
300-1599 74106
1900-1998 74110
3300-6499 74115
11300-15399 74116
W 36th St 74107
W 36th St N
1-99 74106
900-4099 74127
N 36th West Ave 74127

S 36th West Ave
100-199 74127
4400-5399 74107
7200-9399 74132
S 36th West Pl 74127
E 37th Ct
9100-9200 74145
9202-9498 74145
9800-9899 74146
E 37th Pl
900-2899 74105
3700-4999 74135
8200-9299 74145
9800-12899 74146
14200-14299 74134
E 37th Pl N 74106
W 37th Pl 74107
E 37th St
901-917 74105
919-3299 74105
3300-5599 74135
8101-8197 74145
8199-9399 74145
9401-9699 74145
9700-12799 74146
13100-14399 74134
701-797 74106
799-1399 74106
2500-2599 74110
W 37th St 74107
N 37th West Ave 74127
S 37th West Ave
100-599 74127
3400-5700 74107
E 38th Pl
100-3199 74105
4500-5199 74135
8600-9499 74145
11300-11798 74146
13500-13599 74134
W 38th Pl 74107
E 38th St
1000-3199 74105
3300-6199 74135
6801-6897 74145
9700-12599 74146
13200-14499 74134
E 38th St N
700-1399 74106
2900-2998 74110
W 38th St 74107
W 38th St N 74127
N 38th West Ave 74127
400-599 74127
4100-5799 74107
E 39th Ct N 74110
E 39th Pl
2700-2799 74105
3700-5399 74135
9400-9499 74145
10000-12599 74146
13000-13599 74134
E 39th Pl N 74106
E 39th St
100-3199 74105
3300-5499 74135
8600-9499 74145
10000-12899 74146
12900-13599 74134
E 39th St N
500-600 74106
4900-5199 74115
W 39th St 74107
N 39th West Ave
1-799 74127
3800-5599 74126
S 39th West Ave
400-765 74127
767-799 74127
4100-6099 74107
6100-9099 74132
E 40th Pl
3600-4399 74135
8800-9499 74145
13200-13599 74134
E 40th Pl N
400-599 74106

2800-2899 74110
W 40th Pl 74107
E 40th St
2400-2800 74105
3400-4799 74135
6500-9499 74145
9800-12399 74146
13000-13599 74134
E 40th St N 74106
W 40th St 74107
W 40th St N 74127
N 40th West Ave 74126
S 40th West Ave
400-599 74127
4100-6099 74107
6300-9099 74132
E 41st Pl
1300-1599 74105
4000-4199 74135
10200-10299 74146
13300-18299 74134
E 41st Pl N
600-799 74106
2800-2899 74110
W 41st Pl 74107
E 41st St
101-197 74105
3300-6399 74135
6500-6698 74145
9700-12899 74146
16300-17298 74134
E 41st St N
2501-2697 74110
4800-5299 74115
W 41st St 74107
W 41st St N
100-499 74106
3400-3699 74127
N 41st West Ave
1-97 74127
6100-7299 74126
S 41st West Ave
1-599 74127
3200-5699 74107
6100-9099 74132
W 42nd Ct 74107
E 42nd Pl
100-1399 74105
4000-4199 74135
7400-7799 74145
10200-10398 74146
18000-18799 74134
E 42nd Pl N
500-799 74106
2200-2899 74110
W 42nd Pl
2100-3398 74107
3408-3408 74157
3410-6198 74107
E 42nd St
200-3199 74105
4000-5499 74135
6500-6599 74145
9700-10499 74146
13100-18899 74134
E 42nd St N
500-799 74106
2800-2899 74110
9300-9399 74115
W 42nd St 74107
N 42nd West Ave 74127
100-499 74127
6100-6599 74132
E 43rd Ct 74105
E 43rd Pl
100-1599 74105
3700-3799 74135
10400-10499 74146
12900-18699 74134
W 43rd Pl 74107
E 43rd St
300-1999 74105
3700-6299 74135
8700-8800 74145
9900-10198 74146
12900-18799 74134

E 43rd St N
200-799 74106
2100-2899 74110
11500-11699 74116
W 43rd St 74107
W 43rd St N 74127
N 43rd West Ave 74127
S 43rd West Ave
100-799 74127
4100-5799 74107
6100-9499 74132
E 44th Ct 74105
E 44th Pl
2400-3199 74105
9801-9897 74146
17400-17699 74134
E 44th Pl N
1-99 74106
2701-2797 74110
W 44th Pl 74107
E 44th St
1-3299 74105
3700-5999 74135
6500-8599 74145
10200-11199 74146
13100-18699 74134
E 44th St N
1-399 74106
2700-2899 74110
9300-9399 74115
W 44th St 74107
N 44th West Ave 74127
S 44th West Ave
100-599 74127
1800-1999 74107
6100-7999 74132
8001-8099 74132
E 45th Ct 74105
W 45th Ct 74107
E 45th Pl
200-2999 74105
3700-4099 74135
9800-9898 74146
9900-9999 74146
10001-10199 74146
17400-17699 74134
500-599 74106
601-699 74106
2800-2899 74110
W 45th Pl 74107
E 45th St
1300-3199 74105
3201-3299 74105
3300-5999 74135
10800-10899 74146
10901-11299 74146
12901-12997 74134
12999-17599 74134
1-99 74106
2700-2999 74110
W 45th St 74107
N 45th West Ave 74127
S 45th West Ave
300-599 74127
4100-5699 74107
6100-9399 74132
W 46th Ct 74107
N 46th West Ave 74127
300-599 74127
6100-9399 74132
E 47th Pl
1800-2899 74105
3300-5999 74135
6800-9599 74145
9700-10399 74146
16200-16599 74134
E 47th Pl N
500-1399 74126
2201-2397 74130
W 47th Pl 74107
W 47th Pl N 74126
E 47th St
1-3299 74105
3700-5899 74135
6500-9199 74145
9914-10099 74146
16200-18899 74134

E 47th St N 74126
W 47th St 74107
W 47th St N 74126
N 47th West Ave 74127
S 47th West Ave
300-799 74127
2500-4599 74107
8400-8599 74132
E 48th Pl
1000-3199 74105
3500-5599 74135
6800-9499 74145
16200-19299 74134
E 48th Pl N 74126
W 48th Pl 74107
E 48th St
300-3199 74105
3600-6399 74135
6500-9399 74145
10101-10999 74146
16200-18899 74134
E 48th St N
500-1599 74126
1700-1998 74130
W 48th St 74107
W 48th St N 74126
N 48th West Ave 74127
S 48th West Ave
300-599 74127
3900-5000 74107
5002-5598 74107
8900-9099 74132
E 49th Ct N 74126
E 49th Pl
1100-1599 74105
3600-3699 74135
7300-9199 74145
16200-18999 74134
E 49th Pl N 74126
W 49th Pl 74107
W 49th Pl N 74126
E 49th St
101-997 74105
3600-6299 74135
7300-9499 74145
10201-10297 74146
16200-19199 74134
E 49th St N
1-197 74126
2000-2799 74130
W 49th St 74107
W 49th St N 74126
N 49th West Ave 74127
S 49th West Ave
1-1099 74127
1800-6099 74107
6101-6197 74131
6199-9199 74131
E 50th Ct N 74126
W 50th Ct N 74126
E 50th Pl
1400-1599 74105
6800-9499 74145
10101-10299 74146
16400-19099 74134
E 50th Pl N
1-1299 74126
1701-1897 74130
W 50th Pl N 74126
E 50th St
1400-1799 74105
5800-6199 74135
6500-9299 74145
10200-10298 74146
16300-19099 74134
E 50th St N
1-1299 74126
1900-2199 74130
W 50th St 74107
W 50th St N 74126
N 50th West Ave 74127
300-699 74127
6200-6599 74131
E 51st Ct 74145
E 51st Pl
1-1999 74105
2001-2199 74105

3701-3897 74135
3899-6111 74135
6110-6110 74153
6112-6134 74135
6113-6199 74135
6700-6799 74145
11300-11399 74146
E 51st Pl N 74126
E 51st St
1900-2198 74105
2200-3199 74105
3300-6156 74135
6158-6198 74135
6500-9599 74145
9700-12699 74146
12900-13499 74134
13501-14499 74134
1300-1699 74126
1700-3199 74130
W 51st St 74107
N 51st West Ave 74127
S 51st West Ave
300-1299 74127
3700-4099 74107
9100-9200 74131
9202-9398 74131
E 52nd Pl
1400-2299 74105
3801-3997 74135
7000-7599 74145
E 52nd Pl N 74126
W 52nd Pl 74107
E 52nd St
1-2799 74105
3900-6199 74135
6701-6797 74145
10000-12599 74146
E 52nd St N 74126
W 52nd St 74107
W 52nd St N 74126
N 52nd West Ave 74126
2600-2699 74107
8400-8499 74131
E 53rd Pl
1-1499 74105
4100-4200 74135
6700-7799 74145
W 53rd Pl 74107
E 53rd St
1-2799 74105
3800-6499 74135
6600-6998 74145
E 53rd St N 74126
W 53rd St 74107
W 53rd St N 74126
N 53rd West Ave 74127
S 53rd West Ave
100-1199 74127
2700-2899 74107
S 53rd West Pl 74131
E 54th Pl
1-1699 74105
7600-7699 74145
E 54th Pl N 74126
E 54th St
1-2599 74105
3300-3598 74135
6600-9599 74145
9700-10199 74146
E 54th St N
200-1699 74126
1700-2799 74130
W 54th St 74107
S 54th West Ave
400-1099 74127
2900-3099 74107
8200-8499 74131
E 55th Ct 74105
E 55th Pl
1300-2799 74105
4600-4699 74135
7200-9599 74145
9700-11000 74146
E 55th Pl N
400-699 74126
9600-9699 74117
W 55th Pl 74107

E 55th St
1000-2799 74105
3300-6099 74135
6500-9599 74145
12100-12799 74146
E 55th St N 74126
W 55th St 74107
W 55th St N 74126
S 55th West Ave
400-599 74127
3600-3999 74107
E 56th Ct
1600-2999 74105
4600-4699 74135
E 56th Pl
100-2999 74105
3300-6399 74135
6500-8999 74145
W 56th Pl 74107
E 56th St
1100-2799 74105
3600-6099 74135
6800-9399 74145
10900-11199 74146
E 56th St N
100-1699 74126
1700-3199 74130
3500-10099 74117
W 56th St 74107
W 56th St N 74126
S 56th West Ave
400-1199 74127
5900-6099 74107
8100-8198 74131
8200-8499 74131
E 57th Pl
100-2999 74105
3400-6399 74135
6500-6899 74145
E 57th Pl N 74126
W 57th Pl 74107
E 57th St
100-3299 74105
3400-6399 74135
6500-9399 74145
E 57th St N 74126
S 57th St 74131
W 57th St 74107
W 57th St N 74126
N 57th West Ave
900-3999 74127
5200-6600 74126
6602-6898 74126
S 57th West Ave
400-1199 74127
2200-6099 74107
6100-6799 74131
E 58th Ct 74145
E 58th Pl
3100-3199 74105
3400-5999 74135
6700-9299 74145
E 58th St
100-3199 74105
3300-6399 74135
6500-9299 74145
9700-9898 74146
E 58th St N 74126
S 58th St 74131
W 58th St 74107
W 58th St N 74126
N 58th West Ave 74127
S 58th West Ave
5801-5897 74107
6100-7799 74131
E 59th Ct 74105
E 59th Pl
1500-2199 74105
3700-4499 74135
7300-9299 74145
E 59th Pl N
200-1599 74126
2001-2099 74130
E 59th St
1500-3299 74105
3400-4699 74135
6800-9299 74145

9800-10099 74146
E 59th St N
100-1499 74126
2400-2499 74130
S 59th St 74131
W 59th St 74107
W 59th St N 74126
S 59th West Ave
100-999 74127
2100-6199 74107
E 60th Ct 74105
E 60th Pl
1500-2699 74105
3900-5999 74135
6600-9099 74145
11300-11399 74146
E 60th Pl N 74126
W 60th Pl N 74126
E 60th St
1001-1097 74105
3400-6299 74135
6500-9299 74145
11300-12298 74146
E 60th St N
801-897 74126
2300-2398 74130
W 60th St 74107
W 60th St N 74126
S 60th West Ave
400-499 74127
3700-6100 74107
E 61st Ct 74136
E 61st Ct N 74130
E 61st Pl
1700-5899 74136
6900-7399 74133
E 61st Pl N 74130
W 61st Pl 74132
W 61st Pl N 74126
E 61st St
900-6299 74136
6501-7497 74133
E 61st St N
200-1399 74126
2000-3099 74130
S 61st St 74131
W 61st St
2400-4699 74132
4900-9599 74131
W 61st St N 74126
S 61st West Ave
400-1199 74127
2200-5999 74107
6001-6099 74107
6600-6799 74131
E 62nd Cir 74133
E 62nd Ct 74133
E 62nd Pl
3400-5899 74136
6900-8999 74133
E 62nd Pl N
1-199 74126
1900-2099 74130
W 62nd Pl N 74126
E 62nd St
1300-6299 74136
6900-10200 74133
E 62nd St N
500-599 74126
1700-1898 74130
S 62nd St 74107
W 62nd St
1700-3999 74132
4900-6899 74131
W 62nd St N 74126
S 62nd West Ave 74127
E 63rd Ct 74133
W 63rd Ct N 74126
E 63rd Pl
4100-5799 74136
7300-8299 74133
W 63rd Pl N 74126
E 63rd St
1000-5899 74136
6900-10499 74133
E 63rd St N
1-1699 74126
1700-2399 74130
S 63rd St 74131
W 63rd St
1700-3799 74132
4900-6799 74131
W 63rd St N 74126
N 63rd West Ave 74126
S 63rd West Ave
500-999 74127
2100-6099 74107
6401-7197 74131
7199-7699 74131
E 64th Pl
1000-6099 74136
6900-8499 74133
W 64th Pl 74132
W 64th Pl N 74126
E 64th St
1000-5899 74136
7200-9499 74133
E 64th St N 74126
W 64th St
1800-4599 74132
4900-6600 74131
W 64th St N 74126
S 64th West Ave
1-899 74127
4200-6099 74107
E 65th Pl
2600-5799 74136
6600-8399 74133
E 65th Pl N
1-397 74126
1700-1799 74130
W 65th Pl 74132
W 65th Pl N 74126
E 65th St
3100-5799 74136
6501-6597 74133
E 65th St N
1300-1324 74126
1700-1799 74130
S 65th St 74131
W 65th St
1900-3399 74132
4900-5799 74131
W 65th St N 74126
S 65th East Pl 74133
N 65th West Ave 74127
6500-7699 74126
S 65th West Ave
1-1499 74127
2200-5999 74107
6001-6099 74107
6600-7999 74131
W 66th Cir 74132
E 66th Ct
1500-2699 74136
7000-7399 74133
E 66th Pl
1000-3799 74136
6700-8699 74133
W 66th Pl
2500-2800 74132
4900-5599 74131
E 66th St
1500-4499 74136
6500-11199 74133
E 66th St N
600-1699 74126
1700-3099 74130
3400-6699 74117
W 66th St
1700-2999 74132
4900-5600 74131
N 66th East Ave 74115
S 66th East Ave
1-499 74112
2800-2999 74129
4600-6099 74145
6500-10799 74133
S 66th East Pl 74129
N 66th West Ave 74126
S 66th West Ave
5600-5999 74107
7700-7799 74131
E 67th Ct
1500-6399 74136
9100-9199 74133
E 67th Pl
1500-6399 74136
7300-10699 74133
E 67th Pl N 74126
E 67th St
1000-4899 74136
6501-6597 74133
E 67th St N 74126
S 67th St
6001-6099 74107
6201-6697 74131
W 67th St
400-3299 74132
6900-6999 74131
W 67th St N 74126
N 67th East Ave 74115
S 67th East Ave
1-1599 74112
2100-2999 74129
3100-5899 74145
6201-6597 74133
6599-10499 74133
S 67th East Pl
5100-5399 74145
5401-5499 74145
9800-10099 74133
N 67th West Ave 74126
S 67th West Ave
200-299 74127
2500-5699 74107
7900-8599 74131
E 68th Pl
1400-4399 74136
7300-7499 74133
W 68th Pl 74132
E 68th St
1500-5099 74136
7400-11100 74133
E 68th St N 74126
S 68th St
5900-6099 74107
6200-6299 74131
W 68th St
400-2999 74132
5700-6599 74131
W 68th St N 74126
N 68th East Ave 74115
S 68th East Ave
1-2099 74112
3100-5999 74145
6700-10799 74133
S 68th East Pl
1700-1799 74112
5200-5699 74145
7500-10599 74133
N 68th West Ave 74126
S 68th West Ave
3401-3433 74107
3435-5999 74107
7600-7698 74131
7700-7799 74131
S 68th West Ct 74107
W 69th Ct 74132
E 69th Pl 74136
W 69th Pl 74132
E 69th St
2100-4399 74136
6500-6698 74133
E 69th St N 74126
S 69th St
5901-5999 74107
6500-6600 74131
W 69th St
3000-3099 74132
6300-8499 74131
W 69th St N 74126
N 69th East Ave 74115
S 69th East Ave
1-2099 74112
2900-3099 74129
3100-5899 74145
6700-10999 74133
S 69th East Ct 74133
S 69th East Pl
2000-2099 74112
6100-9199 74133
N 69th West Ave 74126
S 69th West Ave
400-599 74127
2500-5999 74107
S 69th West Ct 74107
E 70th Ct 74136
E 70th Pl 74136
W 70th Pl N 74126
E 70th St
2500-4399 74136
7000-7499 74133
W 70th St 74132
N 70th East Ave 74115
S 70th East Ave
1-499 74112
501-1499 74112
3100-5899 74145
6300-10799 74133
S 70th East Ct 74133
S 70th East Pl
5100-5599 74145
5601-5699 74145
7700-8199 74133
N 70th West Ave
100-599 74127
6200-6899 74126
S 70th West Ave 74107
N 70th West Pl 74127
E 71st Ct 74133
W 71st Ct 74132
E 71st Pl
1500-5900 74136
6900-7099 74133
E 71st St
1300-6199 74136
6500-11299 74133
E 71st St N
1100-1599 74126
1700-1799 74130
S 71st St 74131
W 71st St
2-198 74132
4900-5998 74131
W 71st St N 74126
N 71st East Ave 74115
S 71st East Ave
1-2099 74112
4800-5399 74145
6700-10599 74133
N 71st West Ave 74127
S 71st West Ave
100-699 74127
3400-5999 74107
E 72nd Ct 74136
E 72nd Pl
2400-5799 74136
6600-8799 74133
W 72nd Pl 74132
E 72nd St
1700-6499 74136
6900-6999 74133
E 72nd St N
1300-1398 74126
1700-1799 74130
W 72nd St
2600-3299 74132
8200-8298 74131
N 72nd East Ave 74115
S 72nd East Ave
1-499 74112
2801-2997 74129
2999-3099 74129
4100-6099 74145
6100-10199 74133
S 72nd East Pl
4600-4699 74145
6300-7799 74133
N 72nd West Ave
100-599 74127
6300-6399 74126
S 72nd West Ave
200-699 74127
3300-6000 74107
6002-6098 74107
8300-8399 74131
E 73rd Pl
1500-5399 74136
6600-7299 74133
E 73rd St
1700-5599 74136
6500-11099 74133
E 73rd St N
401-597 74126
1700-2199 74130
W 73rd St
400-3699 74132
7400-7699 74131
W 73rd St N 74126
N 73rd East Ave 74115
S 73rd East Ave
1-1499 74112
2100-2899 74129
3101-3197 74145
3199-6099 74145
6200-9599 74133
S 73rd East Pl 74133
N 73rd West Ave
700-998 74127
1000-1200 74127
1202-1698 74127
5200-7299 74126
S 73rd West Ave
400-699 74127
3300-4999 74107
5001-5099 74107
7500-8298 74131
8300-8499 74131
E 74th Ct
2500-2599 74136
8100-8300 74133
8302-8499 74133
E 74th Pl
1600-4399 74136
8100-10799 74133
E 74th St
1500-6299 74136
6500-10999 74133
W 74th St 74132
N 74th East Ave 74115
S 74th East Ave
2-398 74112
400-2099 74112
2100-3099 74129
3100-6099 74145
6401-6497 74133
6499-10999 74133
S 74th East Ct 74145
S 74th East Pl 74145
N 74th West Ave 74126
S 74th West Ave
400-1599 74127
3900-3999 74107
S 74th West Cir 74107
S 74th West Ct 74107
S 74th West Pl 74107
E 75th Ct
1500-2999 74136
6700-6999 74133
E 75th Pl
1400-5899 74136
10900-11199 74133
E 75th Pl N
1600-1698 74126
1700-1798 74130
E 75th St
1500-6300 74136
6700-10799 74133
E 75th St N
1200-1699 74126
1700-1899 74130
W 75th St 74131
N 75th East Ave 74115
S 75th East Ave
400-2099 74112
2100-2799 74129
5100-6099 74145
6100-6598 74133
6600-9799 74133
S 75th East Pl 74145
S 75th West Ave
1500-1699 74127
3400-4099 74107
E 76th Ct 74136
E 76th Pl
2900-6399 74136
9100-9299 74133
E 76th St
1500-6299 74136
6500-6698 74133
6700-10999 74133
E 76th St N 74117
W 76th St 74131
N 76th East Ave 74115
S 76th East Ave
400-1599 74112
2100-2199 74129
3100-6099 74145
6300-6598 74133
6600-10399 74133
S 76th East Pl 74129
N 76th West Ave 74126
S 76th West Ave 74107
E 77th Ct 74133
E 77th Pl
2900-6399 74136
7000-9099 74133
W 77th Pl 74132
E 77th St
1500-6499 74136
6900-9499 74133
W 77th St
401-511 74132
513-3099 74132
6000-6599 74131
N 77th East Ave 74115
S 77th East Ave
400-2099 74112
2100-3099 74129
5300-5899 74145
6600-11099 74133
S 77th East Ct 74133
S 77th East Pl 74133
S 77th West Ave
1400-1699 74127
6200-7799 74131
E 78th Ct 74133
E 78th Pl
2900-6399 74136
6600-9599 74133
W 78th Pl 74132
E 78th St
2900-6399 74136
6501-6597 74133
6599-8699 74133
W 78th St
400-3099 74132
5000-7799 74131
N 78th East Ave 74115
S 78th East Ave
101-397 74112
399-1599 74112
2100-2299 74129
4800-5899 74145
6500-10199 74133
S 78th East Pl 74145
N 78th West Ave 74126
S 78th West Ave
1600-1799 74127
4100-4399 74107
6100-8099 74131
E 79th Pl
1600-6099 74136
6800-7900 74133
7902-8698 74133
W 79th Pl 74132
E 79th St
3100-6399 74136
6600-10199 74133
W 79th St 74132
S 79th East Ave
400-1799 74112
2600-2799 74129
3100-5899 74145
8000-9999 74133
S 79th East Pl 74145
S 79th West Ave 74127
E 80th Pl
2900-2998 74136
7600-9299 74133
W 80th Pl 74132
E 80th St
3200-5999 74136
6800-10199 74133
W 80th St
600-3299 74132
7100-7599 74131
N 80th East Ave 74115
S 80th East Ave
101-397 74112
399-599 74112
2100-2999 74129
5700-5800 74145
5802-5998 74145
6300-8799 74133
N 80th West Ave 74126
S 80th West Ave 74131
E 81st Pl
2800-3799 74137
3801-4299 74137
6800-8599 74133
E 81st St
100-899 74132
1600-6199 74137
6600-11199 74133
W 81st St
1-4299 74132
6000-9999 74131
S 81st East Pl
5800-5899 74145
6500-6599 74133
N 81st West Ave 74127
S 81st West Ave
1500-1999 74127
4500-5899 74107
8100-8999 74131
S 81st West Pl 74131
E 82nd Ct 74137
E 82nd Pl
2800-6199 74137
7000-10099 74133
E 82nd Pl S 74133
E 82nd St
2800-4499 74137
6800-8599 74133
W 82nd St
1700-4299 74132
5400-8499 74131
S 82nd East Ave
1900-1999 74112
2200-2399 74129
3200-5699 74145
6300-10499 74133
N 82nd West Ave 74126
E 83rd Ct 74137
E 83rd Pl
2800-3298 74137
3300-4299 74137
6500-11099 74133
11101-11199 74133
E 83rd St
2101-2797 74137
2799-4599 74137
6800-11199 74133
W 83rd St 74132
S 83rd East Ave
400-1499 74112
2200-2499 74129
4600-5699 74145
6500-7498 74133
7500-10999 74133
S 83rd East Cir 74133
S 83rd East Pl 74145
S 83rd West Ave 74107
E 84th Pl 74137
7300-10899 74133
W 84th Pl 74132
E 84th St
2800-6099 74137
6500-11199 74133
W 84th St
800-4699 74132
4900-8799 74131
S 84th East Ave
1700-1999 74112
2200-2399 74129

5600-5699 74145
6300-10999 74133
S 84th East Cir 74133
S 84th East Pl 74133
E 85th Ct 74137
W 85th Ct S 74132
E 85th Pl
3100-3799 74137
9700-11199 74133
W 85th Pl 74132
E 85th St
2800-5199 74137
6500-9899 74133
W 85th St
900-4899 74132
4900-8599 74131
N 85th East Ave 74115
S 85th East Ave
1-1999 74112
2100-2699 74129
3100-5699 74145
6300-11099 74133
S 85th East Pl 74133
S 85th West Ave 74107
E 86th Pl 74137
6500-7199 74133
E 86th St
3100-6199 74137
6500-8999 74133
9001-9199 74133
W 86th St 74132
S 86th East Ave
2800-2898 74129
3800-5099 74145
6101-6197 74133
S 86th East Cir 74133
S 86th East Ct 74133
S 86th East Pl
3000-3099 74129
7500-10599 74133
S 86th West Ave 74107
E 87th Ct 74133
E 87th Pl
3100-4899 74137
6500-9208 74133
9210-9298 74133
E 87th St
2301-2797 74137
2799-5999 74137
6800-9299 74133
W 87th St 74132
S 87th East Ave
400-1499 74112
2100-3099 74129
3800-5999 74145
6100-6198 74133
6200-11099 74133
S 87th East Pl 74133
S 87th West Ave 74131
E 88th Ct 74137
9101-9199 74133
E 88th Pl
4900-5299 74137
6600-9299 74133
E 88th St
2500-6399 74137
6600-9099 74133
W 88th St 74132
S 88th East Ave
2800-2899 74129
3100-5699 74145
6200-6398 74133
6400-11099 74133
S 88th East Cir 74133
S 88th East Pl
3100-3899 74145
6400-9899 74133
9901-10099 74133
S 88th West Ave 74131
E 89th Ct 74137
E 89th Pl
3000-6399 74137
6500-7799 74133
E 89th St
2800-6499 74137
6500-9100 74133
9102-9298 74133
W 89th St 74132
N 89th East Ave 74115
S 89th East Ave
1-197 74112
199-1700 74112
1702-1998 74112
2600-2699 74129
3100-6099 74145
6200-11099 74133
S 89th East Pl
4800-5099 74145
6200-8699 74133
S 89th West Ave
5500-5999 74107
6800-8699 74131
E 90th Ct 74137
E 90th Pl
3000-4499 74137
7100-9299 74133
E 90th St
2800-5599 74137
6500-9299 74133
W 90th St 74132
S 90th East Ave
400-799 74112
2600-2999 74129
3001-3099 74129
3200-6000 74145
6002-6098 74145
6100-10599 74133
S 90th East Ct 74133
S 90th East Pl
6000-6099 74145
6300-6499 74133
E 91st Ct
5200-5299 74137
7100-7299 74133
E 91st Pl
3100-6299 74137
6700-7098 74133
E 91st St
801-899 74132
2700-6299 74137
6500-10599 74133
W 91st St
700-4599 74132
5000-5599 74131
N 91st East Ave 74115
S 91st East Ave
1-1899 74112
2100-2699 74129
3700-5899 74145
6300-11099 74133
S 91st East Ct 74133
N 91st East Pl 74115
S 91st East Pl 74129
E 92nd Ct 74133
E 92nd Pl
2900-2999 74137
6700-9399 74133
E 92nd St
4900-5599 74137
6900-9399 74133
W 92nd St 74132
N 92nd East Ave 74115
S 92nd East Ave
100-398 74112
2100-2699 74129
3201-3697 74145
6600-10399 74133
S 92nd East Cir 74133
S 92nd East Ct 74133
S 92nd East Pl
3800-3899 74145
7700-9099 74133
E 93rd Ct 74137
E 93rd Pl
2900-4699 74137
7300-9399 74133
E 93rd St
2700-6299 74137
6600-9499 74133
W 93rd St
4400-4499 74132
5500-5598 74131
N 93rd East Ave 74115
S 93rd East Ave
300-598 74112
600-2099 74112
2900-2999 74129
3200-5699 74145
6500-10999 74133
S 93rd East Pl 74133
E 94th Ct 74137
E 94th Pl 74137
E 94th St
2900-3298 74137
3300-5699 74137
7500-9099 74133
N 94th East Ave 74115
S 94th East Ave
400-1799 74112
2601-2697 74129
2699-3099 74129
3400-5599 74145
7400-10899 74133
S 94th East Ct 74133
S 94th East Pl
4900-5999 74145
10100-10899 74133
E 95th Ct 74133
E 95th Pl
2900-6499 74137
8500-9599 74133
E 95th St
2900-5399 74137
6500-9299 74133
N 95th East Ave 74115
S 95th East Ave
900-1099 74112
2900-2999 74129
3400-5699 74145
7400-10899 74133
S 95th East Ct 74133
N 95th East Pl 74115
S 95th East Pl 74133
E 96th Ct 74137
E 96th Pl
3300-4299 74137
6700-9899 74133
E 96th St
6300-6499 74137
8800-8898 74133
8900-9399 74133
N 96th East Ave 74115
S 96th East Ave
2200-2799 74129
3400-3999 74145
7400-10799 74133
S 96th East Ct 74129
N 96th East Pl 74115
S 96th East Pl
2500-2899 74129
10201-10697 74133
E 97th Ct 74137
E 97th Pl
2800-5999 74137
7801-9197 74133
9199-9299 74133
E 97th St
3600-6199 74137
6500-9999 74133
W 97th St 74132
N 97th East Ave 74117
S 97th East Ct 74128
S 97th East Pl 74128
S 97th West Ave 74131
E 98th Pl 74137
7700-10099 74133
E 98th St
3300-6399 74137
6800-10299 74133
S 98th East Ave
500-1299 74128
2700-2999 74129
3700-4099 74146
8300-9999 74133
S 98th East Pl 74133
E 99th Pl
3700-3999 74137
6600-10699 74133
E 99th St
3300-6299 74137
6500-10899 74133
S 99th East Ave
500-1499 74128
2100-2198 74129
2200-2399 74129
3700-5999 74146
6100-7298 74133
7300-10099 74133
S 100th East Ave
2300-2399 74129
2401-2899 74129
3800-5999 74146
8200-9799 74133
E 100th Ct 74133
E 100th Dr 74133
E 100th Pl
3300-6299 74137
6700-10799 74133
S 100th East Pl
4400-4599 74146
8200-10099 74133
E 100th St
3500-6399 74137
6900-10799 74133
S 101st East Ave
1-1699 74128
1701-1799 74128
2100-3099 74129
3100-5499 74146
6200-9799 74133
E 101st Pl
2900-5899 74137
7700-9199 74133
S 101st East Pl
2300-2499 74129
3200-3299 74146
E 101st St
2800-6399 74137
6500-9699 74133
W 101st St 74132
S 102nd East Ave
200-699 74128
2100-2399 74129
3200-4799 74146
6301-9597 74133
9599-9799 74133
E 102nd Pl
2800-5799 74137
9100-9699 74133
E 102nd St
2900-6399 74137
6700-9199 74133
S 102nd St 74133
S 103rd East Ave
200-1499 74128
2100-2699 74129
3600-3798 74146
3800-5200 74146
5202-5498 74146
6300-6399 74133
E 103rd Pl
2800-5599 74137
6500-9499 74133
E 103rd St
2800-5899 74137
6600-9699 74133
S 104th East Ave
1-599 74128
2100-2899 74129
4100-5599 74146
6100-6799 74133
E 104th Pl
3500-5799 74137
8600-9099 74133
E 104th St
2800-6099 74137
6600-9599 74133
N 105th East Ave
1100-1899 74116
5600-5699 74117
S 105th East Ave
1200-1299 74128
4200-4298 74146
4300-4499 74146
6700-6800 74133
6802-6898 74133
E 105th Ct 74133
E 105th Pl
4200-5499 74137
8700-8799 74133
E 105th Pl S 74133
N 105th East Pl 74116
S 105th East Pl 74128
E 105th St
3300-6399 74137
6600-8799 74133
E 105th St S 74133
N 106th East Ave 74116
S 106th East Ave
1-1899 74128
2100-2999 74129
3300-3598 74146
7400-10099 74133
E 106th Pl
5401-5497 74137
5499-6199 74137
6500-6900 74133
6902-7898 74133
E 106th Pl S 74133
N 106th East Pl 74116
S 106th East Pl
1-1899 74128
3600-3699 74146
6400-6599 74133
E 106th St
4200-6199 74137
6500-9099 74133
E 106th St S 74133
N 107th East Ave 74116
S 107th East Ave
100-1999 74128
2100-2999 74129
3600-5999 74146
6200-10099 74133
E 107th Pl
3500-5599 74137
8300-8399 74133
E 107th Pl S 74133
E 107th St
3700-6499 74137
6600-8899 74133
E 107th St S 74133
N 108th East Ave 74116
S 108th East Ave
1-2099 74128
2200-2699 74129
3100-5499 74146
7400-10099 74133
E 108th Pl 74137
E 108th Pl S 74133
S 108th East Pl 74128
E 108th St
3700-6499 74137
6600-8399 74133
E 108th St S 74133
N 109th East Ave 74116
S 109th East Ave
200-1999 74128
2100-2800 74129
2802-2898 74129
3400-4400 74146
4402-4898 74146
6300-9099 74133
E 109th Pl
4500-6099 74137
6500-9499 74133
S 109th East Pl
1-199 74128
8200-8299 74133
E 109th St
3300-6099 74137
6600-9599 74133
S 110th East Ave
1100-1899 74128
2400-2600 74129
2602-2698 74129
3400-5199 74146
6300-8499 74133
E 110th Ct 74133
E 110th Pl
3400-5999 74137
8400-8899 74133
S 110th East Pl 74128
E 110th St
3500-6399 74137
7400-9399 74133
N 111th East Ave 74116
S 111th East Ave
2-98 74128
100-1999 74128
2001-2099 74128
2400-2498 74129
2500-3099 74129
3400-3499 74146
3501-4499 74146
6300-8499 74133
E 111th Pl 74137
E 111th St
3600-5899 74137
7700-7799 74133
N 112th East Ave 74116
S 112th East Ave
400-1699 74128
2500-2799 74129
2801-2899 74129
3300-3900 74146
3902-4498 74146
6300-8599 74133
112th Pl & St 74137
113th Pl & St 74137
S 114th East Ave
1700-2099 74128
2700-2799 74129
3100-3700 74146
3702-3798 74146
114th Pl & St 74137
S 115th East Ave
1500-1700 74128
1702-1798 74128
2700-2999 74129
3100-3999 74146
115th Pl & St 74137
S 115th East Pl 74129
S 116th East Ave
300-1999 74128
2201-2697 74129
2699-3099 74129
3100-6099 74146
116th Pl & St 74137
S 116th East Pl
2700-2799 74129
3300-3499 74146
S 117th East Ave
100-1999 74128
2100-2799 74129
3100-3899 74146
117th Dr, Pl & St S 74137
S 117th East Pl 74128
S 118th East Ave
200-1699 74128
2200-2799 74129
3300-6000 74146
6002-6098 74146
118th Blvd, Dr, Pl & St
S 74137
S 119th East Ave
1-1899 74128
2200-2799 74129
3300-3899 74146
119th Pl & St 74137
S 119th East Pl 74128
N 120th East Ave 74116
S 120th East Ave
200-2099 74128
2101-2697 74129
2699-2799 74129
3300-3899 74146
120th Ct & St 74137
S 120th East Pl
1-99 74128
3200-3298 74146
3300-3699 74146
N 121st East Ave 74116
S 121st East Ave
1300-1599 74128
1601-1699 74128
2100-3099 74129
3100-3899 74146
3901-3999 74146
S 121st East Pl
2900-2999 74129
3600-3799 74146
S 122nd East Ave
1-1699 74128
2500-2999 74129
3200-5699 74146
S 122nd East Pl 74146
S 123rd East Ave
600-1900 74128
1902-2098 74128
2400-2999 74129
3600-4000 74146
4002-4098 74146
S 123rd East Pl
100-298 74128
300-1499 74128
3900-3999 74146
S 124th East Ave
1100-1899 74128
2201-2397 74129
2399-3099 74129
3100-3899 74146
S 125th East Ave
1100-2000 74128
2002-2098 74128
2100-2999 74129
3300-5399 74146
5401-5499 74146
N 125th East Pl 74116
N 126th East Ave 74116
S 126th East Ave
1500-1598 74128
1600-1899 74128
2200-2899 74129
3100-3198 74146
3200-3399 74146
N 126th East Pl 74116
N 127th East Ave 74116
S 127th East Ave
400-1699 74128
2200-2499 74129
3200-3299 74146
3301-4099 74146
S 127th East Pl 74146
N 128th East Ave 74116
S 128th East Ave
1200-1298 74128
1300-1899 74128
2400-2499 74129
3101-3197 74146
3199-3799 74146
3801-3899 74146
N 128th East Pl 74116
S 128th East Pl 74129
N 129th East Ave 74116
S 129th East Ave
1-2099 74108
2100-2298 74134
2300-2921 74134
2920-2920 74169
2923-6099 74134
3100-5998 74134
S 129th East Pl 74134
S 130th East Ave
400-1899 74108
2100-4200 74134
S 130th East Pl 74134
S 131st East Ave
600-1900 74108
1902-1998 74108
2200-4499 74134
S 131st East Pl
1600-1699 74108
2900-2999 74134
S 132nd East Ave
500-1399 74108
2200-4599 74134
S 132nd East Ct 74108
S 132nd East Pl
1800-1899 74108
4500-4600 74134
4602-4698 74134
S 133rd East Ave
1100-1899 74108
2200-4499 74134
S 133rd East Pl 74134

134th East Ave & Pl ... 74134
S 135th East Ave
1100-1198 ... 74108
1200-1500 ... 74108
1502-1598 ... 74108
2500-2598 ... 74134
2600-4599 ... 74134
4601-4699 ... 74134
S 135th East Pl ... 74134
136th East Ave & Pl ... 74134
S 137th East Ave
1500-1799 ... 74108
2100-2398 ... 74134
S 137th East Pl ... 74134
S 138th East Ave
700-1899 ... 74108
2400-3399 ... 74134
S 138th East Pl ... 74134
S 139th East Ave
1200-1899 ... 74108
2400-3399 ... 74134
S 139th East Pl ... 74134
S 140th East Ave
1500-1999 ... 74108
2400-3399 ... 74134
N 141st East Ave ... 74116
1100-1999 ... 74108
2400-3399 ... 74134
S 142nd East Ave
700-1899 ... 74108
3300-3899 ... 74134
N 143rd East Ave ... 74116
S 143rd East Ave
1200-1299 ... 74108
3300-3899 ... 74134
144th East Ave & Pl ... 74134
N 145th East Ave ... 74116
100-1999 ... 74108
3101-3299 ... 74134
S 146th East Ave ... 74108
N 147th East Ave ... 74116
100-199 ... 74116
3100-3299 ... 74134
148th East Ave & Pl ... 74134
N 149th East Ave ... 74116
S 149th East Ave
1100-1299 ... 74108
3101-3297 ... 74134
S 150th East Ave ... 74134
N 151st East Ave ... 74116
S 151st East Ave
1600-1899 ... 74108
3300-3499 ... 74134
S 151st East Pl ... 74134
N 153rd East Ave ... 74116
N 154th East Ave ... 74116
N 155th East Ave ... 74116
N 156th East Ave ... 74116
S 156th East Ave ... 74108
N 157th East Ave ... 74116
S 157th East Ave ... 74108
N 158th East Ave ... 74116
N 159th East Ave ... 74116
N 160th East Ave ... 74116
N 161st East Ave ... 74116
S 161st East Ave ... 74108
S 161st East Pl ... 74108
N 162nd East Ave ... 74116
100-499 ... 74108
4700-4899 ... 74134
N 163rd East Ave ... 74116
100-299 ... 74108
4800-5099 ... 74134
S 164th East Ave
100-199 ... 74108
4800-5099 ... 74134
S 164th East Pl ... 74108
N 165th East Ave ... 74116
S 165th East Ave ... 74134
N 166th East Ave ... 74116
S 166th East Ave
1-199 ... 74108
4700-4799 ... 74134
S 166th East Pl ... 74134
N 167th East Ave ... 74116
S 167th East Ave
100-799 ... 74108
4600-5099 ... 74134
S 167th East Pl ... 74134
N 168th East Ave ... 74116
1-199 ... 74108
4700-5099 ... 74134
N 169th East Ave ... 74116
100-1299 ... 74108
4700-4799 ... 74134
N 170th East Ave ... 74116
S 170th East Ave ... 74134
N 171st East Ave ... 74116
N 172nd East Ave ... 74116
S 172nd East Ave ... 74134
N 173rd East Ave ... 74116
1100-1599 ... 74108
4600-4799 ... 74134
N 174th East Ave ... 74116
S 174th East Ave ... 74134
S 175th East Ave ... 74134
176th East Ave & Pl ... 74134
177th East Ave & Pl ... 74134
S 178th East Ave ... 74134
S 179th East Ave
1100-1199 ... 74108
4600-4799 ... 74134
S 180th East Ave ... 74134
S 181st East Ave
200-1799 ... 74108
4100-4799 ... 74134
S 182nd East Ave
200-399 ... 74108
4200-4999 ... 74134
S 183rd East Ave ... 74108
S 184th East Ave
200-299 ... 74108
4200-4299 ... 74134
S 184th East Pl ... 74108
S 185th East Ave
1-499 ... 74108
4100-4999 ... 74134
S 186th East Ave
300-499 ... 74108
4400-4900 ... 74134
187th East Ave & Pl ... 74134
S 188th East Ave
1-99 ... 74108
4201-4697 ... 74134
4699-4899 ... 74134
4901-5099 ... 74134
S 189th East Ave
1-299 ... 74108
4600-4900 ... 74134
S 190th East Ave
300-499 ... 74108
4100-4798 ... 74134
4800-4899 ... 74134
4901-5099 ... 74134
S 191st East Ave
300-399 ... 74108
4800-4999 ... 74134
S 192nd East Ave
300-399 ... 74108
4800-4999 ... 74134
S 193rd East Ave ... 74108
S 194th East Ave ... 74108
S 195th East Ave ... 74108
S 196th East Ave ... 74108
S 197th East Ave ... 74108
S 198th East Ave ... 74108
S 199th East Ave ... 74108
S 200th East Ave ... 74108
S 201st East Ave ... 74108
S 204th East Ave ... 74108
S 205th East Ave ... 74108

WAGONER OK

General Delivery ... 74467

POST OFFICE BOXES MAIN OFFICE STATIONS AND BRANCHES

Box No.s
All PO Boxes ... 74477

RURAL ROUTES

01, 02, 03, 04, 05 ... 74467

NAMED STREETS

All Street Addresses ... 74467

NUMBERED STREETS

All Street Addresses ... 74467

WOODWARD OK

General Delivery ... 73801

POST OFFICE BOXES MAIN OFFICE STATIONS AND BRANCHES

Box No.s
All PO Boxes ... 73802

RURAL ROUTES

01, 02, 03, 04, 05 ... 73801

NAMED STREETS

All Street Addresses ... 73801

NUMBERED STREETS

All Street Addresses ... 73801

YUKON OK

General Delivery ... 73099

POST OFFICE BOXES MAIN OFFICE STATIONS AND BRANCHES

Box No.s
All PO Boxes ... 73085

RURAL ROUTES

01, 02, 03, 04, 05, 06, 07, 08, 09, 10, 11, 12, 13, 14, 15, 16, 17, 18, 19, 20, 21, 22, 23, 24, 25, ... 73099

NAMED STREETS

Abbeywood Pl ... 73099
Abby Ln ... 73099
Aberdeen Dr & Ln ... 73099
Abigail Ln ... 73099
Abigale Dr ... 73099
Abilene Way ... 73099
Acadia Ct ... 73099
Agate Dr ... 73099
Albert Ln & St ... 73099
N Alberts Dr ... 73099
Aldwin Ter ... 73099
Alexander Way ... 73099
Aline St ... 73099
Allen St ... 73099
Allie Hope Ln ... 73099
Alliyah Ct ... 73099
Ally Way ... 73099
Amanda Dr ... 73099
Ambleside Dr ... 73099
Ames Cir ... 73099
Amethyst Cir ... 73099
Andrew Dr ... 73099
Annawood Dr ... 73099
Apache Gate Dr ... 73099
Arcadia Dr ... 73099
Argos Rd ... 73099
Arlington Dr ... 73099
Arrowhead Dr ... 73099
Artena Ct ... 73099
Arthur St ... 73099
Asbill Ave ... 73099
Ash Ave ... 73099
Asher St ... 73099
Ashford Dr ... 73099
Ashley Ter ... 73099
Aspen Dr ... 73099
Aspen Creek Ter ... 73099
Augusta Cir ... 73099
Austrian Pine Pl ... 73099
W Avant Dr ... 73099
Avignon Ln ... 73099
Azalea Pl ... 73099
Azalea Hill Dr ... 73099
Banff Cir, Ct & Way ... 73099
N Banner Rd ... 73099
Bar Harbor Cir ... 73099
E & W Bass Ave ... 73099
Beachcomber Dr ... 73099
W & E Beam Ave & Dr ... 73099
Bear Xing ... 73099
Beaver Bend Ln ... 73099
Beckman Ct ... 73099
E & W Beech Ave ... 73099
Belisle Ave ... 73099
Bellgate Dr ... 73099
Belmonte Ct & Pl ... 73099
Ben Ct ... 73099
Bentham Ct, Pl & Way ... 73099
Big Cedar Ln & Trl ... 73099
Big Horn Canyon Rd ... 73099
Big Sky Cir ... 73099
Biggs Cir ... 73099
Birch Ave ... 73099
Birch Creek Ave ... 73099
Birdie Ct ... 73099
Birkenhead Ct & Rd ... 73099
Bishop Rock Pl ... 73099
Bison Cir ... 73099
Blake Run Rd ... 73099
Blue Quail Rd ... 73099
Bluegrass Ln ... 73099
Bobwhite Rd ... 73099
Bois D Arc Dr ... 73099
Bonnycastle Dr & Ln ... 73099
Boston Trl ... 73099
Bradford Ter & Way ... 73099
Bradgate Dr ... 73099
Brampton Way ... 73099
Branch Line Rd ... 73099
Brandon Pl ... 73099
Brian Ln ... 73099
N Briarwood St ... 73099
Bridle Path ... 73099
Brighton Pl ... 73099
Bristol Ct ... 73099
W Britton Rd NE ... 73099
W Broadway St ... 73099
Brody Ct ... 73099
Brookhurst Blvd ... 73099
Brookstone Lakes Dr ... 73099
Bryce Canyon Ct ... 73099
Buckingham Ct, Ln & Pl ... 73099
Burning Sky Ct ... 73099
Busheywood Dr ... 73099
Byron Cir ... 73099
Caboose St ... 73099
Cactus Ct & Rd ... 73099
Calliope Ct ... 73099
Camber St ... 73099
Cambridge Dr ... 73099
Camden Way ... 73099
Camelot Dr ... 73099
Cameo Dr ... 73099
Cameron ... 73099
Canadian Ct ... 73099
Candy Lane Cir ... 73099
Canteberry Dr ... 73099
Canton Trl ... 73099
Canyon Rd ... 73099
Canyon Creek Dr ... 73099
Cara Ln ... 73099
Caravel Dr ... 73099
Cardiff Cir & Pl ... 73099
Carlisle Crossing Dr ... 73099
Carlsbad Ct ... 73099
Carnie Cir ... 73099
Caroline Dr ... 73099
Carriage Dr ... 73099
Castle Rock Ct & Rd ... 73099
Castlebury Mansion ... 73099
Catamaran Dr ... 73099
Cedar Ave ... 73099
Cedarburg Ct ... 73099
Celtic Cir ... 73099
N & S Cemetery Rd ... 73099
Centennial Farm Ln ... 73099
Chadsford Ln ... 73099
Champlain Ct ... 73099
Chancellor Ct & Dr ... 73099
Charles Ct ... 73099
Charleston Way ... 73099
Chase Cir & Way ... 73099
Chateau Ave ... 73099
Cherokee Dr ... 73099
Cherokee Gate Dr ... 73099
E Cherry Ave ... 73099
Cherry Point Ln ... 73099
Cherrywood Ln ... 73099
Cheshire Ct ... 73099
Chester Ter ... 73099
Chestnut Dr ... 73099
Chestnut Creek Dr ... 73099
Chickasaw Ln ... 73099
Chimney Hill Rd ... 73099
Chisholm Pl, Rd, Spur, Trl & Vly ... 73099
N Chisholm Hill Rd ... 73099
Chisholm Valley Rd ... 73099
Choctaw Pl ... 73099
Choctaw Gate Dr ... 73099
Christian Ln ... 73099
Chukar Rd ... 73099
Church St ... 73099
Churchill Rd ... 73099
Cimarron Rd NW ... 73099
Cimarron Creek Dr ... 73099
Cinderwood Cir & Dr ... 73099
Clair Ct W ... 73099
Clay Dr ... 73099
Clear Crk ... 73099
Coachman Rd ... 73099
Colechester Ct ... 73099
Coles Creek Ln ... 73099
Commerce ... 73099
Commons Cir ... 73099
Comrade Ln ... 73099
Conestoga Dr ... 73099
Cooper Ln ... 73099
S Cornwell Dr ... 73099
Cottontail Rd ... 73099
Cottonwood Dr ... 73099
Cottonwood Creek Ave ... 73099
N Countyline Rd ... 73099
Cove Dr ... 73099
Coxwald Pl ... 73099
Coyote Ct & Dr ... 73099
Creek Dr ... 73099
Creekwood Dr ... 73099
Cripple Creek Rd ... 73099
Crop Cir ... 73099
Crown Dr ... 73099
Cumberland Mansion ... 73099
Cypert Rd ... 73099
E Cypress Ave ... 73099
N & S Czech Hall Cir, Pl & Rd ... 73099
Dacia Pl ... 73099
Dale Ln ... 73099
Dana Dr ... 73099
Danbury Pl ... 73099
Dartmouth St ... 73099
Daryl Dr ... 73099
Daughety Dr ... 73099
Davis Ave ... 73099
Dawn Ave ... 73099
Deer Crk ... 73099
Deer Creek Ct ... 73099
Deer Ridge Blvd ... 73099
Del Mar Dr ... 73099
Del Rio Dr ... 73099
Delp Dr N ... 73099
Delphi Cir ... 73099
Demotte Dr ... 73099
Denmark St ... 73099
Derail St ... 73099
Desert Trl ... 73099
Devon Pl & St ... 73099
Dianna Dr ... 73099
Dickens Ave ... 73099
Doe Run Dr ... 73099
Dogwood Creek Ave ... 73099
Dome Dr ... 73099
Dorchester Ct & Dr ... 73099
Dover Ct & Dr ... 73099
Dover Mansion ... 73099
Drakes Way ... 73099
Driftwood Cir ... 73099
Drover Ln ... 73099
Durango Cir ... 73099
Durkee Rd ... 73099
Dusty Trl ... 73099
Earl Ave ... 73099
N East Dr ... 73099
Eastblake Pl ... 73099
Eastblake Landing Rd ... 73099
N & S Eastgate Dr ... 73099
Eastridge Dr ... 73099
Eastview Cir, Ct & Dr ... 73099
Edinburg Ct & Dr ... 73099
Elk Run & St ... 73099
Elk Creek Dr ... 73099
Ellison St ... 73099
Ellsworth Ave ... 73099
Elm Ave ... 73099
Empress Cir ... 73099
Eric Cir ... 73099
Erinova Dr ... 73099
Ethan Ln ... 73099
Euclid St ... 73099
Evening Dr ... 73099
Evening Star Ct ... 73099
Everglade Ct ... 73099
Excalibur Ct ... 73099
NW Expressway ... 73099
Exter Ave & Cir ... 73099
Fairbanks St & Way ... 73099
Fairfax Cir, Ct, Ln & Ter ... 73099
Fairways Ave ... 73099
Falling Springs Ln ... 73099
Fawn Run Dr ... 73099
Fay Ave ... 73099
Fiddler Rd ... 73099
Fiddlesticks Ln ... 73099
Firefork Ave ... 73099
First Place Blvd ... 73099
Flagman St ... 73099
Flint Dr ... 73099
Folkstone Dr ... 73099
Footmans Ct ... 73099
NE & W Foreman Rd ... 73099
Forrest Ridge Way ... 73099
W, N & S Frisco Dr & Rd ... 73099
Frisco Ranch Dr ... 73099
W Funston ... 73099
Galatian Way ... 73099
Garden Dr & Grv ... 73099
Garrison Ln ... 73099
Garth Brooks Blvd
1-899 ... 73099
900-900 ... 73085
900-1798 ... 73099
901-1799 ... 73099
Gemstone Cir ... 73099
Geneva Rea Ln ... 73099
Georgian Way ... 73099
Glacier Rd ... 73099
Gladstone Cir ... 73099
Glascow Dr & Ter ... 73099
Glass Ave ... 73099
Glen Dr ... 73099
Glenda Dr ... 73099
Glenwood Dr ... 73099
Golden Creek Ct ... 73099
Golden Pond Dr ... 73099
Goodman St ... 73099
Goya Cir ... 73099
Grace Cir ... 73099
Graham ... 73099
Grainer St ... 73099
E & W Grand Teton Ct ... 73099
Granite Ct ... 73099
Greenfield Ave, Ct & Dr ... 73099
N & S Greengate Dr ... 73099
Greenway Ave, Cir & Ct ... 73099
Greenwood Dr ... 73099
Gregg Ct ... 73099
N & W Gregory Pl, Rd & Ter ... 73099
Guilford Pl ... 73099
Hackberry Creek Ave ... 73099
Hackney Ln ... 73099
W Hale St ... 73099
Hamlet Cir & Ln ... 73099
Hampton Cir ... 73099
Harold Dr ... 73099
Harrogate Dr ... 73099
Harvest Dr & Trl ... 73099
Hastings Ave ... 73099
Hawksbury Rd ... 73099
Health Center Pkwy ... 73099
Heather Ter ... 73099
Heather Glen Dr ... 73099
Heathrow Way ... 73099
Hebron Ct ... 73099
W Hefner Rd ... 73099
Heritage Mansion ... 73099
Hickory Ave ... 73099
Hickory Hill St ... 73099
Highway 66 St ... 73099
Hilltop Mansion ... 73099
Hobo ... 73099
Hodges Ter ... 73099
Holly Ave & Ct ... 73099
Hollyhead Ter & Way ... 73099
Hollyrock Ct & Dr ... 73099
Hope Ln & Ter ... 73099
Horizon Blvd ... 73099
Hunter Jackson Dr ... 73099
Hunton Ter ... 73099
Hutton Rd ... 73099
Hyacinth Hollow Dr ... 73099
I 40 Service Rd ... 73099
Industrial Dr ... 73099
Inla St ... 73099
W Interstate 40 Hwy ... 73099
Inverleith Cir ... 73099
Irish Ln ... 73099
James Ln ... 73099
Janeen St ... 73099
E & W Janice Ave ... 73099
Janus ... 73099
Jaxon Ct ... 73099
Jay Dr ... 73099
Jay Matt Dr ... 73099
Jb St ... 73099
Jensen Ln ... 73099
John F Kroutil Dr ... 73099
John Wedman Blvd ... 73099
Jordan Pl ... 73099
Joseph Way ... 73099
Josephine Ct ... 73099
Justin Dr & Ln ... 73099
Kaelyn Ln ... 73099
Kali Ave ... 73099
Karla Ct ... 73099
Karly Ln W ... 73099

Katelyn Ct 73099
Kathleens Xing 73099
Katy Line Ct & Dr 73099
Kay Rdg 73099
Kearny Ln 73099
Keith St 73099
Kendal Ave, Ct & Pl 73099
Kendall Ln 73099
Keswick Ln 73099
N & S Kimbell Rd 73099
Kimberly Ln 73099
Kings Canyon Dr 73099
Kingsgate Ct, Rd & Ter 73099
Kingsridge Dr 73099
Kingston Dr & Pl 73099
Kingsway Ave & Ct 73099
Kirk Dr 73099
Klondike Dr 73099
Korbyn Dr 73099
Kouba Dr 73099
Kyles Cir 73099
Lake Dr 73099
Lakeshore Dr 73099
Lancaster Dr 73099
Lancelot Dr 73099
Land Run Ln 73099
Landmark Dr & Rd 73099
Lankestar Pl & Way 73099
Laramie Rd 73099
Larkdale Dr 73099
Larry Ave 73099
Laurel Creek Dr 73099
Leeds Dr 73099
Legate 73099
Leicester Dr 73099
Leigh Cir 73099
Lexington Ln 73099
Liberty Ct 73099
Liberty Mesa Ct 73099
Limestone Pl 73099
Linda Ln 73099
Linn Ln 73099
Loch Ln & Loop 73099
Lochwood Cir, Dr, Ln & Pl 73099
Lois Ln 73099
Loren Pl 73099
Lost Lake Ln 73099
Lucky Ln 73099
Mabel C Fry Blvd 73099
Mackenzie Way 73099
Magnolia Blossom Ct & Ln 73099
E & W Main St 73099
Maindale Dr 73099
Majestic St 73099
Makaila Way 73099
Mamus Ln 73099
Manor Rd 73099
Maple St 73099
Marathon Ln 73099
Mariner Dr 73099
Mark Ave 73099
Mark J Ave 73099
Market Ave 73099
Markley Ln 73099
Marrgate Dr 73099
Mathew Dr 73099
Maxi Ct 73099
Mayer Dr 73099
Mcarthur St 73099
Mcconnell Dr 73099
Mclain Ave 73099
E & W Meade Dr 73099
Meadow Lake Dr 73099
Meadow Run Ct 73099
Melina Dr 73099
W Memorial Rd 73099
E Mesa Verde St 73099
Middlesbrough Ln 73099
Mill Springs Ct 73099
Miller Dr 73099
Millspaugh Way 73099
Mirage St 73099
Monarch Ct 73099
Monticello Ct 73099
Montreal Dr 73099
Monument Ln 73099
Moose St 73099
N Morgan Cir & Rd 73099
Morgan Creek Rd 73099
Morgan Trace Rd 73099
Morningside Dr 73099
Morningstar Dr 73099
Mulberry Creek Ave 73099
Mulbury Mansion 73099
N & S Mustang Rd 73099
Mustang Creek Cir 73099
Napa 73099
Natasha Way 73099
Nathan Way 73099
Newgate Dr 73099
Noble Ct 73099
Noel Dr 73099
Norton Cir 73099
Norway Ave & Ct 73099
Norwich Cir & Pl 73099
Nottingham Pl 73099
Novak Cir 73099
O Casey St 73099
W Oak Ave & Dr 73099
Oak Creek Dr 73099
Oakdale St 73099
Oakwood Dr 73099
Oasis Ln 73099
Okie Ridge Rd 73099
Old Home Pl 73099
Old Mill Ln 73099
E & W Olympic Dr 73099
Osborn Ln 73099
Oswego Dr 73099
Ottawa Pl 73099
Out West Trl 73099
Overholser Dr 73099
Owen Ave 73099
Paisley Ct & Rd 73099
Palais Ave 73099
Palm Ave 73099
Palo Verde Ct & Dr 73099
Pamela Ln 73099
Park Ave & Dr 73099
E & W Parkland Dr 73099
Parsons Dr 73099
Partridge Run Rd 73099
Pascali Ct 73099
Patco Ave 73099
Patco Spur Ave 73099
Paul Ave 73099
Pawnee Cir, Dr & Pl ... 73099
Pecan Grv W 73099
Periwinkle Dr 73099
Pettijohn 73099
N Piedmont Rd 73099
Pikes Peak Rd 73099
Pine Ave 73099
Pine Creek Ave 73099
Pinty Riv 73099
Pistache Ln 73099
E & W Platt Dr 73099
Plaza Dr 73099
Pointe Parkway Blvd ... 73099
Poplar Ave 73099
Prairie Hill Ln 73099
Prairie Twyne Dr 73099
Preston Park Dr 73099
Professional Cir 73099
Prue Sand 73099
Pumpkin Cir 73099
Queensboro Pl 73099
Queensbury Ct & Dr 73099
Raintree Mansion 73099
Ralph Ct 73099
Rambling Rose 73099
Ramsey Ct & Rd 73099
Rancho Estates Blvd ... 73099
Ranchoak Ct & Dr 73099
N & S Ranchwood Blvd 73099
Randy Ct 73099
Rebekah Rd 73099
Rebel Ridge Ct 73099
Red Rock Canyon Ln .. 73099
Redbud St 73099
Redbud Creek Ave 73099
Redwood Ave 73099
Redwood Creek Dr 73099
Regal Rd 73099
Regatta Rd 73099
Regiment Way 73099
Remuda East St 73099
Remuda West St 73099
W Reno Ave 73099
N & S Richland Rd 73099
Richmond St 73099
Ridgegate Rd 73099
Ridgeway Dr 73099
River Birch Dr & Ln 73099
River Mesa Dr 73099
Robin Cir 73099
Roche Dr 73099
Rochefort Ln 73099
Rock Creek Rd 73099
Rockbridge Ct 73099
Rockbridge Mill Ln 73099
Rockgate Dr 73099
Rocky Ct & Rd 73099
Rolling Hills Rd 73099
Ronald St 73099
Rookhaven Ln 73099
Rose Creek Ln 73099
Rosemoor Ct 73099
Royal Ln 73099
Royal Coach Dr 73099
Royce Pl 73099
Ruby Ave 73099
Runner St 73099
Russell Dr 73099
Rustler Ln 73099
Rutland Ter 73099
Ryder Dr 73099
Sagamore Dr 73099
Sage Brush Pl & Rd ... 73099
Sahoma Trl 73099
Saint Helens Dr 73099
Saint James Ct & Pl ... 73099
Sally Ct 73099
Sand Trap Way 73099
Sandstone Dr 73099
Sandy Cir 73099
N & S Sara Rd 73099
Sardis Way 73099
Savage Rd 73099
Savanah Pl 73099
Savannah Ave 73099
Savannah River Way ... 73099
Scarlet Blvd 73099
Scissortail Dr 73099
Scully Rd 73099
Seaward Cir 73099
Selborne Pl 73099
Seminole Ln 73099
Sennybridge Ct & Dr ... 73099
Sequoia Park Dr 73099
Settlers Way 73099
Shady Creek Ln 73099
Shamrock Cir 73099
Shandon Way 73099
Shedeck Pkwy 73099
Shell Ln 73099
N Shell Creek Rd 73099
Shelly Rd 73099
Sherri Ln 73099
Shimmering Ct 73099
Signalman 73099
Silver Maple Dr 73099
Silver Ridge Rd 73099
Silver Springs Ln 73099
Skelly Cir 73099
Sky Ray Ct 73099
Skyland Dr 73099
Skytrail Ct 73099
Skyward Cir 73099
Smoking Oaks Dr 73099
E Snowmass Dr 73099
Somers Pointe Blvd 73099
Somerville Dr 73099
Southgate Dr 73099
Spence Rd 73099
Spindle Ridge Dr 73099
Spring Creek Dr 73099
Spring Meadows Rd 73099
Spring Valley Cir & Ln .. 73099
Spruce Ave & Dr 73099
Squire Ln 73099
Squire Mansion 73099
Stable Rock 73099
Stacy Lynn Ln 73099
Stag Horn Dr 73099
Stanley Station St 73099
State Highway 4 73099
Stebbins 73099
Stefano Cir 73099
Steve Ct 73099
Stirrip Way 73099
Stockdale Pl 73099
Stone Ln 73099
Stone Creek Blvd 73099
Stonebridge Cir, Ct & Dr 73099
Stonemill Blvd 73099
Stony Brook Ln 73099
Sudbury Rd 73099
Sue Anthony 73099
Summerhill Ln 73099
Summerton Pl 73099
Sundance Dr 73099
Sundance Ridge Rd 73099
Sunflower Dr 73099
Sunridge Dr 73099
Sunrise Dr 73099
W Sunshine Rd 73099
Sunward Cir 73099
Surrey Ln 73099
Surrey Hills Blvd 73099
Sweetwater Dr 73099
Swingman Ct & Rd 73099
Switzerland Ave 73099
Sycamore St 73099
Sycamore Creek Ave ... 73099
Sylvan Sand 73099
Tahoe Ln 73099
Tall Grass Dr 73099
Tanglewood Ct & Dr 73099
Tara Plantation Dr 73099
Taylor Ln 73099
Tea Rose Dr 73099
Teagen Ln 73099
Teakwood Ave 73099
Tecumseh Dr 73099
Tenkiller Ct 73099
Tesh Dr 73099
Thompson Ave 73099
Thompson Farm Ln 73099
Thornberry Ln 73099
Tilted Mesa Ct 73099
Timber Rdg & Xing 73099
Tipi 73099
Tomahawk Dr 73099
Topaz Cir 73099
Tori Pl 73099
Torre Pines Ct & Ln 73099
Trails Head Dr & Way .. 73099
Travertine Cir 73099
Trenton Ter 73099
Trevor Dr 73099
Trinity Industrial Ct 73099
Tucson Dr 73099
Tulip Dr 73099
Tumbleweed Dr & Rd .. 73099
Turtle Creek Dr 73099
Twilight Ter 73099
Twin Oaks Dr 73099
Utah Ave 73099
W & E Vail Ct & Dr 73099
Valley Rd 73099
Valley Forge Dr 73099
E & W Vandament Ave 73099
Vanguard Dr 73099
Velletri Ave 73099
Vick Cir 73099
Vickery Ave 73099
Vickie Dr 73099
Victoria Dr 73099
Villa Ave 73099
Vine St 73099
Vineyard Rd 73099
Vintage Park Ln 73099
Viola Dr 73099
Volare Dr 73099
Von Elm Ave & Pl 73099
E & W Wagner Rd 73099
Wagner Lake Dr 73099
Walnut Ave 73099
Walsh Ln 73099
Walter St 73099
War Eagle Ln 73099
Waterford Ln 73099
Wayne Cutt Ave 73099
Westbury Ct & Ter 73099
Westend Pointe Dr 73099
Westgate Dr 73099
Westglen Dr 73099
Westmark Dr 73099
Westminster Ln 73099
Westport Blvd 73099
Westridge Ct & Dr 73099
Westview Dr 73099
Wheatfield Ave 73099
White Tail Trl 73099
Wicket Pl 73099
Wickford Pl 73099
Wilcox Ln 73099
William Ave 73099
E Willow Pl & Run 73099
Willowood Dr 73099
W Wilshire Blvd 73099
Wimberley Dr 73099
Wimberley Creek Dr 73099
Winding Creek Rd 73099
Windsor Ct 73099
Windward Way 73099
Winnipeg Dr 73099
Wolf Ln 73099
Woodchuck Rd 73099
Woodgate Dr 73099
Woodlawn Dr 73099
Wrand Dr & Rd 73099
Wyatt Way 73099
Yellowstone Dr 73099
Yosemite Park 73099
Yuhoma Dr 73099
N & S Yukon Ave & Pkwy 73099
Zion Park 73099

NUMBERED STREETS

All Street Addresses 73099

Oregon

People QuickFacts	Oregon	USA
Population, 2013 estimate	3,930,065	316,128,839
Population, 2010 (April 1) estimates base	3,831,073	308,747,716
Population, percent change, April 1, 2010 to July 1, 2013	2.6%	2.4%
Population, 2010	3,831,074	308,745,538
Persons under 5 years, percent, 2013	5.9%	6.3%
Persons under 18 years, percent, 2013	21.8%	23.3%
Persons 65 years and over, percent, 2013	15.5%	14.1%
Female persons, percent, 2013	50.5%	50.8%
White alone, percent, 2013 (a)	88.1%	77.7%
Black or African American alone, percent, 2013 (a)	2.0%	13.2%
American Indian and Alaska Native alone, percent, 2013 (a)	1.8%	1.2%
Asian alone, percent, 2013 (a)	4.1%	5.3%
Native Hawaiian and Other Pacific Islander alone, percent, 2013 (a)	0.4%	0.2%
Two or More Races, percent, 2013	3.5%	2.4%
Hispanic or Latino, percent, 2013 (b)	12.3%	17.1%
White alone, not Hispanic or Latino, percent, 2013	77.5%	62.6%
Living in same house 1 year & over, percent, 2008-2012	82.1%	84.8%
Foreign born persons, percent, 2008-2012	9.8%	12.9%
Language other than English spoken at home, pct age 5+, 2008-2012	14.7%	20.5%
High school graduate or higher, percent of persons age 25+, 2008-2012	89.2%	85.7%
Bachelor's degree or higher, percent of persons age 25+, 2008-2012	29.2%	28.5%
Veterans, 2008-2012	333,395	21,853,912
Mean travel time to work (minutes), workers age 16+, 2008-2012	22.4	25.4
Housing units, 2013	1,684,035	132,802,859
Homeownership rate, 2008-2012	62.5%	65.5%
Housing units in multi-unit structures, percent, 2008-2012	23.2%	25.9%
Median value of owner-occupied housing units, 2008-2012	$246,100	$181,400
Households, 2008-2012	1,512,718	115,226,802
Persons per household, 2008-2012	2.48	2.61
Per capita money income in past 12 months (2012 dollars), 2008-2012	$26,702	$28,051
Median household income, 2008-2012	$50,036	$53,046
Persons below poverty level, percent, 2008-2012	15.5%	14.9%

Business QuickFacts	Oregon	USA
Private nonfarm establishments, 2012	107,549	7,431,808
Private nonfarm employment, 2012	1,363,523	115,938,468
Private nonfarm employment, percent change, 2011-2012	1.6%	2.2%
Nonemployer establishments, 2012	261,156	22,735,915
Total number of firms, 2007	348,154	27,092,908
Black-owned firms, percent, 2007	1.2%	7.1%
American Indian- and Alaska Native-owned firms, percent, 2007	1.2%	0.9%
Asian-owned firms, percent, 2007	3.6%	5.7%
Native Hawaiian and Other Pacific Islander-owned firms, percent, 2007	0.2%	0.1%
Hispanic-owned firms, percent, 2007	3.3%	8.3%
Women-owned firms, percent, 2007	29.8%	28.8%
Manufacturers shipments, 2007 ($1000)	66,880,653	5,319,456,312
Merchant wholesaler sales, 2007 ($1000)	51,910,777	4,174,286,516
Retail sales, 2007 ($1000)	50,370,919	3,917,663,456
Retail sales per capita, 2007	$13,494	$12,990
Accommodation and food services sales, 2007 ($1000)	7,555,764	613,795,732
Building permits, 2012	10,608	829,658

Geography QuickFacts	Oregon	USA
Land area in square miles, 2010	95,988.01	3,531,905.43
Persons per square mile, 2010	39.9	87.4
FIPS Code	41	

(a) Includes persons reporting only one race.
(b) Hispanics may be of any race, so also are included in applicable race categories.
FN: Footnote on this item for this area in place of data
NA: Not available
D: Suppressed to avoid disclosure of confidential information
X: Not applicable
S: Suppressed; does not meet publication standards
Z: Value greater than zero but less than half unit of measure shown
F: Fewer than 100 firms
Source: US Census Bureau State & County QuickFacts

3 DIGIT ZIP CODE MAP

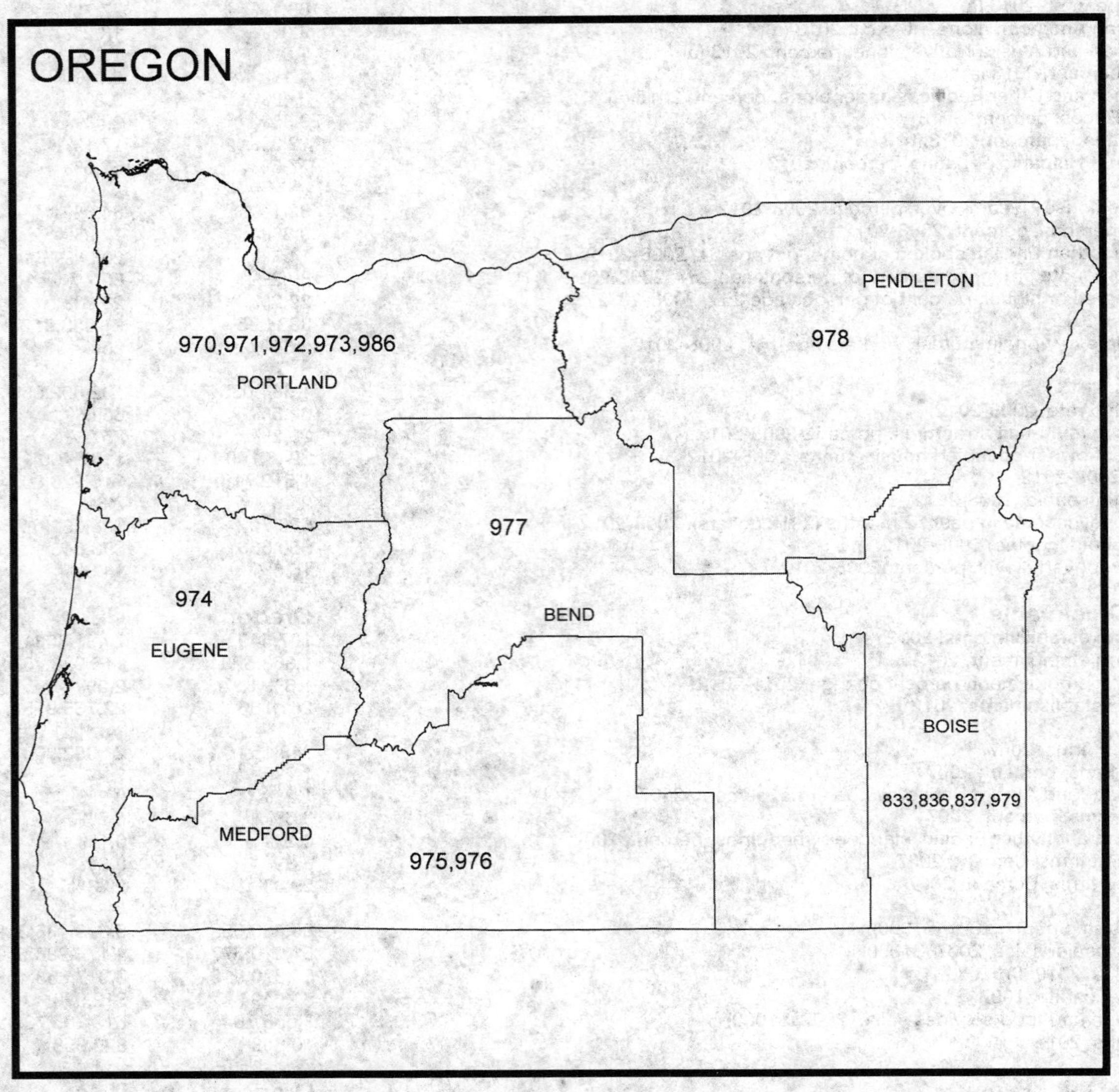

Oregon

(Abbreviation: OR)

Post Office, County — ZIP Code

Places with more than one ZIP code are listed in capital letters, See pages indicated.

Adair Village, Benton 97330
Adams, Umatilla 97810
Adel, Lake 97620
Adrian, Malheur 97901
Agness, Curry 97406
ALBANY, Linn
(See Page 3132)
Allegany, Coos 97407
Aloha
(See Beaverton)
Alsea, Benton 97324
Alvadore, Lane 97409
Amity, Yamhill 97101
Antelope, Wasco 97001
Applegate, Jackson 97530
Arch Cape, Clatsop 97102
Arlington, Gilliam 97812
Arlington, Gilliam 97861
Arock, Malheur 97902
Ashland, Jackson 97520
Ashwood, Jefferson 97711
Astoria, Clatsop 97103
Athena, Umatilla 97813
Aumsville, Marion 97325
Aurora, Marion 97002
Azalea, Douglas 97410
Baker City, Baker 97814
Bandon, Coos 97411
Banks, Washington 97106
Banks, Washington 97109
Bates, Grant 97817
Bay City, Tillamook 97107
Beatty, Klamath 97621
Beaver, Tillamook 97108
Beaver, Tillamook 97112
Beavercreek, Clackamas 97004
BEAVERTON, Washington
(See Page 3133)
BEND, Deschutes
(See Page 3137)
Birkenfeld, Columbia 97016
Blachly, Lane 97412
Blodgett, Benton 97326
Blue River, Lane 97413
Bly, Klamath 97622
Boardman, Morrow 97818
Bonanza, Klamath 97623
Boring, Clackamas 97009
Boring, Clackamas 97089
Bridal Veil, Multnomah 97010
Bridgeport, Baker 97819
Brightwood, Clackamas 97011
Broadbent, Coos 97414
Brogan, Malheur 97903
Brookings, Curry 97415
Brooks, Marion 97305
Brothers, Deschutes 97712
Brownsville, Linn 97327
Burns, Harney 97720
Butte Falls, Jackson 97522
Buxton, Washington 97109
Camas Valley, Douglas 97416
Camp Sherman, Jefferson 97730
Canby, Clackamas 97013
Cannon Beach, Clatsop 97110
Canyon City, Grant 97820
Canyonville, Douglas 97417
Carlton, Yamhill 97111
Cascade Locks, Hood River 97014
Cascadia, Linn 97329
Cave Junction, Josephine 97523
Cave Junction, Josephine 97531
Cayuse, Umatilla 97801
Central Point, Jackson 97502
Charleston, Coos 97420
Chemult, Klamath 97731
Cheshire, Lane 97419
Chiloquin, Klamath 97624
Chiloquin, Klamath 97639
Christmas Valley, Lake 97641
Ckenzie Bridge, Lane 97413
Clackamas, Clackamas 97015
Clackamas, Clackamas 97086
Clatskanie, Columbia 97016
Cloverdale, Tillamook 97112
Coburg, Lane 97408
Colton, Clackamas 97017
Columbia City, Columbia 97018
Condon, Gilliam 97823
Coos Bay, Coos 97420
Coquille, Coos 97423
Corbett, Multnomah 97019
Cornelius, Washington 97113
Cornelius, Washington 97123
CORVALLIS, Benton
(See Page 3142)
Cottage Grove, Lane 97424
Cove, Union 97824
Crabtree, Linn 97335
Crane, Harney 97732
Crater Lake, Klamath 97604
Crawfordsville, Linn 97336
Crescent, Klamath 97733
Crescent Lake, Klamath 97733
Creswell, Lane 97426
Crooked River, Jefferson 97760
Crooked River Ranch, Jefferson 97760
Culp Creek, Lane 97434
Culver, Jefferson 97734
Curtin, Lane 97424
Dairy, Klamath 97625
Dale, Umatilla 97880
Dallas, Polk 97338
Damascus, Clackamas 97009
Damascus, Clackamas 97015
Days Creek, Douglas 97429
Dayton, Yamhill 97114
Dayville, Grant 97825
Deadwood, Lane 97430
Deer Island, Columbia 97054
Depoe Bay, Lincoln 97341
Detroit, Marion 97342
Dexter, Lane 97431
Diamond, Harney 97722
Diamond Lake, Klamath 97731
Dillard, Douglas 97432
Donald, Marion 97020
Dorena, Lane 97434
Drain, Douglas 97435
Drewsey, Harney 97904
Dufur, Wasco 97021
Dundee, Yamhill 97115
Dunes City, Lane 97439
Durkee, Baker 97905
Eagle Creek, Clackamas 97022
Eagle Point, Jackson 97524
Echo, Umatilla 97826
Eddyville, Lincoln 97343
Elgin, Union 97827
Elkton, Douglas 97436
Elmira, Lane 97437
Enterprise, Wallowa 97828
Estacada, Clackamas 97023
EUGENE, Lane
(See Page 3144)
Fairview, Multnomah 97024
Fall Creek, Lane 97438
Falls City, Polk 97344
Fields, Harney 97710
Florence, Lane 97439
Forest Grove, Washington 97116
Fort Klamath, Klamath 97626
Fort Rock, Lake 97735
Fossil, Wheeler 97830
Foster, Linn 97345
Fox, Grant 97856
Frenchglen, Harney 97736
Friend, Wasco 97021
Gales Creek, Washington 97117
Gardiner, Douglas 97441
Garibaldi, Tillamook 97118
Gaston, Washington 97119
Gates, Marion 97346
Gearhart, Clatsop 97138
Gervais, Marion 97026
Gilchrist, Klamath 97737
Gladstone, Clackamas 97027
Glendale, Douglas 97442
Gleneden Beach, Lincoln 97388
Glenwood, Washington 97116
Glide, Douglas 97443
Gold Beach, Curry 97444
Gold Hill, Jackson 97525
Government Camp, Clackamas 97028
Grand Ronde, Polk 97347
Granite, Baker 97877
GRANTS PASS, Josephine
(See Page 3148)
Grass Valley, Sherman 97029
Greenhorn, Baker 97877
Greenleaf, Lane 97430
GRESHAM, Multnomah
(See Page 3150)
Haines, Baker 97833
Halfway, Baker 97834
Halsey, Linn 97348
Hammond, Clatsop 97121
Happy Valley, Clackamas 97015
Happy Valley, Clackamas 97086
Harbor, Curry 97415
Harper, Malheur 97906
Harrisburg, Linn 97446
Hebo, Tillamook 97122
Helix, Umatilla 97835
Heppner, Morrow 97836
Hereford, Baker 97837
Hermiston, Umatilla 97838
HILLSBORO, Washington
(See Page 3152)
Hines, Harney 97738
Hood River, Hood River 97031
Hubbard, Marion 97032
Huntington, Baker 97907
Idanha, Marion 97350
Idleyld Park, Douglas 97447
Imbler, Union 97841
Imnaha, Wallowa 97842
Independence, Polk 97351
Ione, Morrow 97843
Ironside, Malheur 97908
Irrigon, Morrow 97844
Island City, Union 97850
Jacksonville, Jackson 97530
Jamieson, Malheur 97909
Jasper, Lane 97438
Jefferson, Marion 97352
John Day, Grant 97845
Jordan Valley, Malheur 97910
Joseph, Wallowa 97846
Junction City, Lane 97448
Juntura, Malheur 97911
Keizer, Marion 97303
Keizer, Marion 97307
Keno, Klamath 97627
Kent, Sherman 97033
Kerby, Josephine 97531
Kimberly, Grant 97848
King City, Washington 97224
Kinzua, Wheeler 97830
KLAMATH FALLS, Klamath
(See Page 3154)
La Grande, Union 97850
La Pine, Deschutes 97739
Lafayette, Yamhill 97127
Lake Grove, Clackamas 97035
LAKE OSWEGO, Clackamas
(See Page 3155)
Lakeside, Coos 97449
Lakeview, Lake 97630
Langlois, Curry 97450
Lawen, Harney 97720
Leaburg, Lane 97489
Lebanon, Linn 97355
Lexington, Morrow 97839
Lincoln City, Lincoln 97367
Logsden, Lincoln 97357
Lonerock, Gilliam 97823
Long Creek, Grant 97856
Lorane, Lane 97451
Lostine, Wallowa 97857
Lowell, Lane 97452
Lyons, Linn 97358
Madras, Jefferson 97741
Malin, Klamath 97632
Manning, Washington 97125
Manzanita, Tillamook 97130
Mapleton, Lane 97453
Marcola, Lane 97454
Marion, Marion 97392
Marylhurst, Clackamas 97036
Maupin, Wasco 97037
Mayville, Wheeler 97830
Mckenzie Bridge, Lane 97413
Mcminnville, Yamhill 97128
Mcnary, Umatilla 97882
Meacham, Umatilla 97859
MEDFORD, Jackson
(See Page 3157)
Medical Springs, Baker 97814
Mehama, Marion 97384
Merlin, Josephine 97532
Merrill, Klamath 97633
Metolius, Jefferson 97741
Midland, Klamath 97634
Mikkalo, Gilliam 97861
Mill City, Linn 97360
Milton Freewater, Umatilla 97862
Milwaukie
(See Portland)
Mitchell, Wheeler 97750
Molalla, Clackamas 97038
Monmouth, Polk 97361
Monroe, Benton 97456
Monument, Grant 97864
Moro, Sherman 97039
Mosier, Wasco 97040
Mount Angel, Marion 97362
Mount Hood Parkdale, Hood River 97041
Mount Vernon, Grant 97865
Mulino, Clackamas 97042
Murphy, Josephine 97533
Myrtle Creek, Douglas 97457
Myrtle Point, Coos 97458
Nehalem, Tillamook 97131
Neotsu, Lincoln 97364
Neskowin, Tillamook 97149
Netarts, Tillamook 97143
Netarts Bay, Tillamook 97143
New Pine Creek, Lake 97635
Newberg, Yamhill 97132
Newport, Lincoln 97365
Newport, Lincoln 97366
North Bend, Coos 97459
North Plains, Washington 97133
North Powder, Union 97867
Norway, Coos 97458
Noti, Lane 97461
Nyssa, Malheur 97913
O Brien, Josephine 97534
Oak Grove
(See Portland)
Oakland, Douglas 97462
Oakridge, Lane 97463
Oceanside, Tillamook 97134
Odell, Hood River 97044
Ontario, Malheur 97914
Ophir, Curry 97464
Oregon City, Clackamas 97045
Oretech, Klamath 97601
Otis, Lincoln 97368
Otter Rock, Lincoln 97369
Oxbow, Baker 97840
Pacific City, Tillamook 97135
Paisley, Lake 97636
Paulina, Crook 97751
Pendleton, Umatilla 97801
Philomath, Benton 97370
Phoenix, Jackson 97535
Pilot Rock, Umatilla 97868
Pleasant Hill, Lane 97455
Plush, Lake 97637
Port Orford, Curry 97465
PORTLAND, Clackamas
(See Page 3159)
Post, Crook 97752
Powell Butte, Crook 97753
Powers, Coos 97466
Prairie City, Grant 97869
Prescott, Columbia 97048
Princeton, Harney 97721
Prineville, Crook 97754
Prospect, Jackson 97536
Rainier, Columbia 97048
Redmond, Deschutes 97756
Reedsport, Douglas 97467
Remote, Coos 97458
Rhododendron, Clackamas 97049
Richland, Baker 97870
Rickreall, Polk 97371
Riddle, Douglas 97469
Riley, Harney 97758
Ritter, Grant 97856
Rivergrove, Clackamas 97034
Riverside, Malheur 97917
Rockaway, Tillamook 97136
Rockaway Beach, Tillamook 97136
Rogue River, Jackson 97537
Rose Lodge, Lincoln 97367
ROSEBURG, Douglas
(See Page 3169)
Rufus, Sherman 97050
Saginaw, Lane 97424
Saint Benedict, Marion 97373
Saint Helens, Columbia 97051
Saint Paul, Marion 97137
SALEM, Marion
(See Page 3171)
Sandy, Clackamas 97055
Scappoose, Columbia 97056
Scio, Linn 97374
Scotts Mills, Marion 97375
Scottsburg, Douglas 97473
Seal Rock, Lincoln 97376
Seaside, Clatsop 97138
Selma, Josephine 97538
Seneca, Grant 97873
Shady Cove, Jackson 97539
Shaniko, Wasco 97057
Shedd, Linn 97377
Sheridan, Yamhill 97378
Sherwood, Washington 97140
Siletz, Lincoln 97380
Silver Lake, Lake 97638
Silverton, Marion 97381
Sisters, Deschutes 97759
Sixes, Curry 97476
South Beach, Lincoln 97366
South Mountain, Malheur 97910
Sprague River, Klamath 97639
Spray, Wheeler 97874
SPRINGFIELD, Lane
(See Page 3178)
Stanfield, Umatilla 97875
Stayton, Marion 97383
Sublimity, Marion 97385
Summer Lake, Lake 97640
Summerville, Union 97876
Sumpter, Baker 97877
Sunriver, Deschutes 97707
Sutherlin, Douglas 97479
Sweet Home, Linn 97386
Swisshome, Lane 97480
Talent, Jackson 97540
Tangent, Linn 97389
Tenmile, Douglas 97481
Terrebonne, Jefferson 97760
The Dalles, Wasco 97058
Tidewater, Lincoln 97390
Tigard
(See Portland)
Tillamook, Tillamook 97141
Tiller, Douglas 97484
Timber, Washington 97144
Timberline Lodge, Clackamas 97028
Toledo, Lincoln 97391
Tolovana Park, Clatsop 97145
Trail, Jackson 97541
Troutdale, Multnomah 97060
Tualatin, Washington 97062
Turner, Marion 97392
Tygh Valley, Wasco 97063
Ukiah, Umatilla 97880
Umatilla, Umatilla 97882
Umpqua, Douglas 97486
Union, Union 97883
Unity, Baker 97884
Vale, Malheur 97918
Veneta, Lane 97487
Vernonia, Columbia 97064
Vida, Lane 97488
Waldport, Lincoln 97394
Wallowa, Wallowa 97885
Walterville, Lane 97489
Walton, Lane 97490
Wamic, Wasco 97063
Warm Springs, Jefferson 97761
Warren, Columbia 97053
Warrenton, Clatsop 97146
Wasco, Sherman 97065
Wedderburn, Curry 97491
Welches, Clackamas 97067
West Linn, Clackamas 97068
West Stayton, Marion 97325
Westfall, Malheur 97920
Westfir, Lane 97492
Westlake, Lane 97493
Weston, Umatilla 97886
Westport, Columbia 97016
Wheeler, Tillamook 97147
White City, Jackson 97503
Wilbur, Douglas 97494
Wilderville, Josephine 97543
Willamina, Yamhill 97396
Williams, Josephine 97544
Wilsonville, Clackamas 97070
Winchester, Douglas 97495
Winchester Bay, Douglas 97467
Winchestr Bay, Douglas 97467
Winston, Douglas 97496
Wolf Creek, Josephine 97497
Wood Village, Multnomah 97060
Woodburn, Marion 97071
Yachats, Lincoln 97498
Yamhill, Yamhill 97148
Yoncalla, Douglas 97499
Zigzag, Clackamas 97049

ALBANY OR

General Delivery 97321

POST OFFICE BOXES MAIN OFFICE STATIONS AND BRANCHES

Box No.s
All PO Boxes 97321

NAMED STREETS

NW Abraham Ln 97321
Adah Ave NE 97322
Airport Rd SE 97322
Alameda Ave NE 97322
Alandale Ave SW 97321
Alco St NE & SE 97321
NW Alder Ave 97321
NE Alexander Ln 97321
Allbee Ln SE 97322
NW Alpine Mdw 97321
Altamont Ave & Dr 97322
Amanda Ln NE 97321
Anderson Pl SE 97322
NW Angelo Jay Dr 97321
Anne Ct SE 97322
Antelope Cir & Ct 97321
NE & NW Anthony Ln & Pl 97321
NW Arlington Dr 97321
Arnold Rd NE 97321
Arroyo Ridge Dr 97321
Arthur Dr SW 97321
Ash St SE 97322
Ashley Dr & Loop 97321
Aspen Cir SE 97322
NW Augusta Ct 97321
Avalon Ave & Ct 97322
Aviation Way 97322
Azalea Ave SE 97322
Aztec Loop NE 97321
Bain Ct SE 97322
Bain St NE 97321
Bain St SE 97322
Baker St NE 97321
Balboa Pl SE 97322
Barker Ct NE 97321
Bartley Ct, Dr & Pl 97322
NW Beaumont Ln 97321
Beaver Ct SW 97321
Becca Ct SE 97322
Becker Cir SE 97322
Beehallow Ln NW 97321
Beehollow Ln NW 97321
Belden Ln NW 97321
Bellaire Ct NE 97322
Belmont Ave & Loop 97321
Bentley Ct & Dr 97322
NW Benton Dr & Pl NW 97321
Bernard Ave NE 97322
Berry Dr NE 97322
Beta Dr SW 97321
Bethel Loop SW 97321
Black Bear Ave & Ct 97321
Black Dog Rd NE 97321
Bloom Ln NW 97321
NW Blossom Ln 97321
Blue Ox Dr SE 97322
NW Bluff Pl 97321
Bobcat Ave SW 97321
Bond Rd NE 97322
Bonnie St SW 97321
Boston Ct & St 97322
Bradley St SE
400-599 97321
800-899 97322
Bramblewood Ct & Ln 97321
Breakwood Cir SE 97322
Breezy Way NE 97322
NW Brianna St 97321
NW Briarwood Pl 97321
Brice Ct SW 97321
Bridle Springs St SE 97322
Bridlewood Loop SE 97322
Brighton Way SE 97322
Broadalbin St NW & SW 97321
Broadway St NW 97321
Brookside Ave SE 97322
Bryant Dr & Way 97321
Buena Vista Dr & Rd NW 97321
Burkhart St NE 97321
Burkhart St SE
100-699 97321
800-3899 97322
Cabrillo Pl SE 97322
Calapooia St SW
100-1799 97321
3000-3098 97322
NW Camala Dr 97321
NW Camela Dr 97321
Cameron Ct & St 97322
Campbell Ct SW 97321
Canal Ave SE 97322
Canterbury St SE 97322
Canyon Ct 97321
Caribou Ct & Dr 97321
Carrol Pl SW 97321
NW Cascade Falls Ct 97321
NW Cascade Heights Dr 97321
Castillo Dr NE 97321
Casting St SE 97322
Cedar Cir SE 97322
NW Cedar Ln 97321
Cedarwood Ct SE 97322
Center St SE 97322
Century Dr NE 97322
Chapman Ct & Pl 97321
Charlotte St NE 97322
Chartwell St SE 97322
Chase Loop SW 97321
NW Cheri Pl 97321
NE Cherry Ln 97321
Chestnut Ct & St 97322
Chi Ct SE 97322
Chicago Ct SE 97322
Chicago St NE 97321
Chicago St SE
100-699 97321
800-3899 97322
Chinook Ct & Dr 97321
NW Christmas Tree Ln 97321
Christopher Ave SE 97322
Church Dr SW 97321
Churchill Downs St SE 97322
Circle Dr SE 97322
City View Pl SW 97321
Claremont St NE 97322
Clay Ct SE 97322
Clay Pl SE 97322
Clay St SE
200-399 97321
800-5399 97322
Clearwater Ct & Dr 97321
Cleveland St NE 97321
Cleveland St SE
100-799 97321
1200-1399 97322
Clover St NE 97322
Clover Ridge Ct & Rd 97322
Cloverdale Dr & Pl 97321
NW Cluster Oak Ave NW 97321
Coho Ave SW 97321
College Loop SE 97322
College Park Dr SW 97322
Collingwood St SE 97322
Columbus Pl SE 97322
Columbus St NE 97321
Columbus St SE
200-599 97321
800-34399 97322
E & S Commercial Way 97322
Concord Ct & St 97322
Conser Rd NE 97321
Cooper Dr NE 97321
Coquille Ct & Ln 97321
Cordova Pl SE 97322
Cortez Pl & Way 97322
NW Cottonwood Ln 97321
Cougar Ave, Ct & Dr 97321
NE Country Vlg 97321
NW Country Club Ln 97321
NW Countryman Cir & Pl NW 97321
Cowboy Ave SE 97322
Cox St SE 97322
Cox Creek Ln SE 97322
Creekside Dr NE 97322
Creel Ave SE 97322
Crescent Dr SW 97321
Crest Loop & Pl 97321
NW Creswell Ln 97321
Cricket Ln NE 97322
Crittenden Loop & St SW 97321
Crocker Ln NW 97321
Curtis St NE 97322
Cushman Rd SW 97321
Cyrus Rd NE 97322
NW Daemon Pl 97321
NW Daffodil Ln 97321
Dale St SE 97322
David Ave NE 97322
Davidson Ct SE 97322
Davidson St NE 97321
Davidson St SE
119-197 97321
199-399 97321
700-5499 97322
Deer Run Dr & St 97321
Del Monte Pl SE 97322
Del Rio Ave, Ct & Pl 97322
Denton Pl SE 97322
Denver St NE & SE 97322
Derby St SE 97322
NW Desert Pine St 97321
Dever Conner Rd NE 97321
Devon Pl SE 97322
Dian Ave NE 97322
Dogwood Ave SE 97322
NW Dogwood Ln 97321
Dolores Way SE 97322
Douglas St SE 97322
Dover Ave NW 97321
Drew Pl SW 97321
NW Dumbeck Ave 97321
Dunlap Ave NE 97322
Durillo Pl SE 97322
NW Eagle View Dr 97321
NW Eagles Nest Cir 97321
NW Eagles Ridge Ln 97321
Earl Ave NE 97322
Eastiner SE 97322
Easy Ave SW 97321
Ebenger St SW 97321
Echo Springs Pl SE 97322
Edgemont St SE 97322
Edgewater Dr NE 97322
Edgewood Dr & Pl 97321
Ehlen Dr SW 97321
Eicher Rd SE 97322
Eleanor Ave NE 97322
Elena St NE 97321
NW Eliza Ct 97321
Elk Cir SW 97321
Elk Run Dr SW 97321
Ellingson Rd SE & SW 97322
Ellsworth St SW 97321
Elm St SW 97321
NW Embassy Pl 97321
NW Emerald Oaks Pl 97321
Empire Ct, St & Way 97322
Engle Rd SE 97322
NW Erin Crst 97321
Ermine Ct SE 97322
Ermine St SE
100-499 97321
700-5399 97322
Essex Ave & Ct 97321
NW Estate Ln 97321
Evergreen Ln & St NE & SE 97322
Excor Rd SW 97321
Expo Pkwy NE 97322
NW Fairbank Pl 97321
Fairlane St NE 97322
Fairmont Dr NE 97322
NE Fairway Dr 97321
Falcon St SW 97321
NW Fawn Ridge Dr 97321
NW Ferguson Dr 97321
Fern Pl SW 97321
Ferry St NW 97321
Ferry St SW
100-1299 97321
1600-1698 97322
1700-3399 97322
Fescue St SE 97322
Fir Pl & St NE 97322
Fir Oaks Ct, Dr & Pl 97321
NW Fircrest Dr 97321
Firwood Cir & Pl 97322
NW Fisher Loop 97321
Flame Tree Ln NW 97321
N Folsom Rd 97322
Fox Dr NE 97322
Foxglove Loop SE 97322
Foxwood Ct SE 97322
Franklin Ave SE 97322
Freedom Ct SE 97322
Freitag Rd NE 97322
Front Ave NE 97321
Fry Rd SE 97322
Fulton Ct SE 97322
Fulton Pl SE 97322
Fulton St SE
100-499 97321
600-2699 97322
Gale St NW 97321
Gatewood Pl SE 97322
Geary Cir SE 97322
Geary Pl SE 97322
Geary St NE 97321
Geary St SE
100-799 97321
800-4899 97322
Gerig Dr SE 97322
NW Gibson Way 97321
NW Gibson Hill Rd 97321
NW Gilmour Ln 97321
Glendale St SE 97322
NW Glenwood Ave 97321
Goldfinch Loop SE 97322
Goldfish Farm Rd SE 97322
Goltra Rd SE 97322
Gore Dr SE 97322
Grace Ave NW 97321
Grand Prairie Rd SE 97322
Grand Ridge Dr NW 97321
NW Grandview Dr 97321
NE Granite Ave 97321
NE Green Ct 97321
Green Acres Ln & Loop 97321
Grenz Ln NE 97322
Groshong Rd NE 97321
Groves Ct SE 97322
Gusty Ave & Ct 97322
Hafez Ln NE 97322
Hancock Ct SE 97322
Hannah Ave SE 97322
NW Happy Dr 97321
Harber Rd NE 97322
NW Harder Ln 97321
Harnisch Dr NE 97321
Harrison St NE & SE 97321
Harvard Ave SE 97322
Harvest Dr SW 97321
Haydens Loop 97321
NE Heather Ct 97321
Hemlock Pl SE 97322
Heritage Way SE 97322
Heron Loop SE 97322
NW Heron Point Ct 97321
Hickory St NW 97321
Higbee Rd NE 97322
Highway 20 SE 97322
NW Highway 20 97321
Highway 226 SE 97322
Highway 34 SE 97322
Highway 34 SW 97321
Highway 99e NE 97322
Hill St SE
100-799 97321
900-3899 97322
NE Hill St 97321
Hillcrest Pl & St 97321
Hoefer Dr NE 97321
Holiday St SW 97321
NW Holly Pl 97321
Hollyburn Ave NE 97322
Honey Sign Dr SE 97322
NW Honeywood Dr 97321
Hood St SE 97322
Hop St SW 97321
Horn Ln SE 97322
Horseshoe Dr SW 97321
Horseshoe Lake Cir & Ct 97321
Houston St NE 97322
Howard Dr SE 97322
Hummingbird St SE 97322
NW Hurleywood Dr 97321
Idlewood Pl SE 97322
NW Independence Hwy 97321
Industrial Way SW 97322
Iris Ln SE 97322
Isaac Ave SE 97322
Jackson St NE 97321
Jackson St SE
100-351 97321
352-398 97321
353-799 97321
400-798 97321
800-3399 97322
Jasmine Ln 97322
Jefferson Ct SE 97322
Jefferson Pl SE 97322
Jefferson St NE 97321
Jefferson St SE
100-699 97321
800-2499 97322
Jessicas Ct SE 97322
Jon St SW 97321
NW Jones Ave 97321
NW Jordan Dr 97321
Juan Way SE 97322
NW Juniper Ln 97321
Kamph Dr NE 97322
NW Karstens Ln 97321
NE Katelyn Way 97321
Kathryn Ave NE
3000-3199 97321
3400-3499 97322
Kennel Rd SE 97322
Kenworthy Rd NE 97322
Kerrisdale Dr SE 97322
Kestrel Ln SE 97322
Killdeer Ave SE 97322
NE Kindsey Ln 97321
Kingfisher Ct SE 97322
NW Kingston Way 97321
Kizer Ave NE 97322
NW Knollwood Dr 97321
Knox Butte Ave NE 97321
Knox Butte Rd E 97322
Kodiak Ave SW 97321
Kouns Dr NW 97321
NE Lafayette Pl 97321
Lafayette St SE
500-599 97321
1100-3799 97322
NE Lafayette St 97321
Lake St SE 97321
Lakewood Dr SW 97321
Lamb Dr SW 97321
Lanier St SW 97321
Lansing Ave SE 97322
NW Lariat Dr 97321
Laura Ln SE 97322
NW Laura Vista Dr NW 97321
Laurel Pl & Way 97321
NW Laurel Heights Dr 97321
NW Laurel Oaks Dr 97321
Laurelhurst Dr NE 97322
Lauren Ave NE 97321
NW Lawnridge St SW 97321
Lawrence Ave SW 97321
Lehigh Way SE 97322
NE Levi Ln 97321
NW Lew St NW 97321
Liberty St SW 97321
Lickskillet Rd NE 97322
NW Lincoln St SW 97321
Linn Ave NE 97321
Linn Ave SE 97322
NW Linnview Ln 97321
Linnwood Dr NE 97322
Lochner Rd SE 97322
Lockwood Pl SE 97322
Locust Ave & Pl 97322
Lone Oak Ln SW 97321
NW Lone Tree St 97321
Looney Ln SW 97321
Luckiamute Ln NE 97321
Lukas Ct SE 97322
Lynx Ave SW 97321
Lyon Ct SW 97322
Lyon Pl S 97322
Lyon St N 97321
Lyon St S 97321
Lyon St SE 97322
Lyon St SW 97322
Mackinaw Ave SE 97322
Madison St NE 97321
Madison St SE
100-799 97321
800-3799 97322
Madrona Pl & Way 97322
NW Maier Ln 97321
Main St NE 97321
Main St SE
100-799 97321
800-2699 97322
NE Malachi Way 97321
Mallard Cir SW 97321
Manor St NE 97322
Maple St SW 97321
Marilyn St NE 97322
Marion St SE 97322
NW Mariposa Dr 97321
Marten Ave SW 97321
Mary Kay Ave NE 97321
Mason Rd NE 97322
Mason St SE 97321
NE Mayview Dr 97321
Meadow Ct NE 97322
Meadow Pl SE 97322
Meadow Rd SW 97321
NW Meadow Wood Dr 97321
Meadowlark Ct SE 97322
Meadowview St SE 97322
Meeker Hill Rd NE 97322
Megan Ave & St 97321
NW Merrill Pl 97321
Mesa Ct 97321
NW Metge Ave 97321
Midway Dr SE 97322
Mike St SW 97321
Millbrook Pl SE 97322
Miller Ln & Pl 97321
Millersburg Dr NE 97321
Millstream Pl NE 97322
NW Mint Ave 97321
NW Mirada Dr & St NW 97321
Montanya St SW 97322
Montclair Dr NE 97322
NE Montgomery Pl 97321
Montgomery St NE 97321
Montgomery St SE
100-799 97321
1200-1299 97322
Monticello St SE 97322
Moose Run Dr SW 97321
Moraga Ave & Pl 97322
Morningstar Rd NE 97321
Morse Ave & Ln 97321
Mount Vernon St SE 97322
E & S Mountain View Dr & Pl SE & NE 97322
Muirfield Ave NW 97321
Muller Dr SE 97322
Murder Creek Dr NE 97322
NW Murphy Ln 97321
National Way SW 97322
Neely Rd NE 97322
NE Nehalem Ave 97321
Nelson Loop & Pl 97321
Noah Ave SE 97322
NW North Albany Rd 97321
NW North Heights Dr 97321
NE North Nebergall Loop 97321
NW North View Ln 97321
Northwood Dr NE 97322
Oak St NE 97321
Oak St SE
100-199 97321
1000-3899 97322
NW Oak Glen St 97321
Oak Grove Dr, Loop & Way 97321
NW Oak Hills Dr 97321
Oak Ridge St NW 97321
Oakmont Loop NE 97322
Oakville Rd SW 97321
Oakwood Ave SE 97322
NE Obsidian Ave 97321
Old Bridge Dr SE 97322
Old Highway 34 SE 97322
Old Oak Dr SE 97322
Old Salem Rd NE 97321
NW Olivia Cir 97321
Olson Rd SE 97322
Onyx St NE 97322
Opal St NE 97322
Oranda St SE 97322
Orchard Ln SW 97321
NW Orchard Heights Ave 97321
Orleans Rd SW 97321
Orsborn Way SE 97322
Otter Ct SW 97321
Oxford Ave & Ct 97322
N Pacific Blvd, Hwy & Pl SE, SW & NE 97321
NW Paddington Dr & Pl NW 97321
Page Ct SE 97322
NW Palestine Ave 97321
Palm Harbor Dr NE 97321
Panorama Dr NE 97322
Paradise Ln SE 97322
NW Park Pl & Ter SW 97321
NW Parker Ln & Pl NE 97321
Parkside Rd NE 97322
Parkwoods Dr NE 97322
Patrick Ct & Ln 97321
NW Paula Ave 97321
NE Peachtree Ln 97321
NW Peacock Ln 97321
Penn St SW 97321
NW Penny Ln 97321
NW Penrose Ave 97321
Peoria Rd SW 97321
Perfect Ln SW 97321
Periwinkle Cir SE 97322
Peterson Ln NE 97322
NW Picadilly Cir 97321
NW Picardy Ln 97321
Piedmont Pl SW 97321
Pine Ln SE 97322
Pine St NE 97321
Pine St SE
100-799 97321
2700-3899 97322
Pine Meadow Dr SE 97322

Pineview Dr & Pl 97321
Pirtle Dr SW 97321
Pitt St SE 97322
Plagmann Dr NE 97322
N Pointe Dr NW 97321
Ponderosa Dr SW 97321
NW Poplar St 97321
Powell St SE 97322
NW Powers Ave 97321
Prairie Pl SE 97322
Price Rd SE 97322
NW Primrose St 97321
NW Pulver Ln & Pl
NW 97321
NE Putter Pl 97321
Quail Ave & Ct 97322
NW Quailwood Dr 97321
NW Quarry Rd 97321
Queen Ave SE 97322
Queen Ave SW
100-699 97322
700-2399 97321
Queen Anne Pl SE 97322
Quince St NW 97321
NE Rachel Ct 97321
Railroad Ct SE 97322
Railroad St SE
100-799 97321
2800-3199 97322
NW Rainwater Ln 97321
Raleigh Ct SE 97322
Ramona Pl & Way 97322
Ranch Ct & Dr 97321
Ranchero Ave SE 97322
Ravenwood Ct & Dr 97321
NW Raymond Ct 97321
Red Bridge Rd SE 97322
Red Oak St NW 97321
Redwood St SE 97322
Revere St SE 97322
NW Ridders Ln 97321
Ridge Ave NE 97322
NW Ridgecrest Ave 97321
Ridgeview Ln & Pl 97321
NW Riverbow Ave 97321
Riverside Dr SW 97321
Robinhood Ln NW 97321
NW Rondo St 97321
NE Rosa Ln 97321
Rosehill Ave SE 97322
Rosemarie St NE 97321
NW Ryals Ave 97321
Rye St SE 97322
Ryunkin St SE 97322
Sable Ct 97321
Salem Ave SE 97321
Salmon Ct & Run 97321
San Felicia Ave SE 97322
San Pedro Ave NW 97321
Santa Maria Ave NE 97322
Santiam Hwy SE
1100-1965 97321
1966-36099 97322
Santiam Way NE 97322
Santiam Bluffs Rd NE 97322
NW Sarah Ave 97321
NW Sarah Maria Ct 97321
Scenic Dr & Way 97321
NW Scenic Wood Pl 97321
Scott Ave NE 97322
Scravel Hill Rd NE &
SE 97322
Sedgewick Pl SE 97322
Sedona Rd 97321
Seven Mile Ln SE 97322
NW Shady Ln 97321
Shady Bend Rd NE 97322
Shady Oak Rd NE 97322
NW Shannon Dr 97321
Sherman St NE
100-299 97321
Sherman St SE
100-799 97321
900-2699 97322
NE Sherman St
1300-1603 97321

NW Sherwood Pl 97321
N & S Shore Dr 97322
Shortridge Pl & St 97322
Siletz Ln NE 97321
Siltcoos Ct & Ln 97321
Sitka Ct SW 97321
Siuslaw Ave & Ct 97321
Skyline Dr & Ter 97321
Snyder Rd SE 97322
Somerset Ave & Dr 97322
NE South Nebergall
Loop 97321
NW South View Dr 97321
NW Sox Ln 97321
NW Sparks Ave 97321
NW Spencer Mountain
Dr 97321
Spicer Dr SE 97322
Spicer Wayside SE 97322
Spring Ave NE 97322
NW Springhill Dr 97321
NE Springwood Dr 97321
Spruce St SW 97321
NW Spyglass Ct 97321
Squire Pl & St 97321
Steckley Dr NE 97321
Stellmacher Dr SW 97321
NW Stone Ridge Ave 97321
Stormy St NE 97322
Stutzman Dr SE 97322
Summercrest St SE 97322
Summerfield Ct SW 97321
Summerhill Ln & Pl 97321
Sun Pl SE 97322
Sundale Pl SE 97322
NW Sunny Ln NW 97321
Sunnyview Dr NE 97322
Sunset Dr NE 97322
NW Sunset Ridge Dr 97321
Supra Dr SW 97321
Swank Dr SE 97322
Takena St SW 97321
Tamarack Ct SW 97321
Tangent Dr SE 97322
Tangent Dr SW 97321
Tapper Ln SE 97322
NW Teak Loop 97321
Tec Labs Way SW 97321
Teddy Ave NE 97322
Tennessee Rd SE 97322
NW Terra Lynda Dr 97321
NW Terrace Dr 97321
Terri Ln NE 97321
Texas St SW 97321
NW Thorn Dr 97321
Thornton Lake Dr & Pl 97321
Thoroughbred Ave SE 97322
Three Lakes Rd SE 97322
Thurston St NE 97321
Thurston St SE
100-599 97321
800-3799 97322
Timber St SE 97322
Timber Ridge St NE 97322
Toni St NE 97321
Tracy Ct SW 97321
Trinity St NE 97322
Troon St NW 97321
Trudell Ct SE 97322
Tudor Pl & Way 97322
Turnidge Rd NE 97321
NW Turning Leaf St 97321
NW Twins Ln 97321
Twister Ave NE 97322
Tyson Pl SW 97321
Umatilla Ct, Pl & St 97321
Umpqua Ln NE 97321
Union St SE 97322
Valley View Dr NW 97321
NW Veilleux Ln 97321
Viewcrest Dr NE 97322
Vine St SW 97321
Violet Ave & Ct 97321
NW Vista Pl 97321
Walden Cir SE 97322
NW Walker Ln 97321

Walnut Dr SW 97321
Walnut St SW
400-2099 97321
2400-2599 97322
Warwick Ct & Pl 97321
Washington St SW
200-1499 97321
1600-2199 97322
Water Ave NE & NW 97321
Waterford St SE 97322
Waverly Dr NE 97321
Waverly Dr SE
100-399 97321
600-2899 97322
Wayside Ct SE 97322
Weldon Ct & Pl 97322
NW West Thornton Lake
Dr NW 97321
Westcott Ave SE 97322
Western St SE 97322
Western Way NE 97321
NW Westminster Way 97321
Westpark Ct SE 97322
Westwood Pl SE 97322
Wheeler St SE 97322
Whirlwind Dr NE 97321
NW Whispering Oaks
Pl 97321
NW White Oak Ave
NW 97321
NW Whitecliff Dr 97321
NW Whitmore Dr 97321
NW Widmer Pl 97321
NW Wildwood Dr 97321
Wilford Ct & Pl 97321
Willamette Ave NE 97321
Willamette Ave SE 97322
Willetta Pl & St 97321
Willow Way NE 97322
Willoway Dr SW 97321
Wilt Ct SE 97322
Windmill Ln SW 97321
Windsar Pl SE 97322
Windy Ave NE 97322
NW Winn Dr 97321
Winners Circle Ave
SE 97322
Winton Ct SE 97322
NW Wishram Dr 97321
NW Woodcrest Ave 97321
Woods Rd NE 97321
Woodward Dr NE 97322
Wright Pl SE 97322
Yellowstone Pl NE 97321
Yih Ln NE 97322
Yosemite Pl NE 97322
NE Zuhlke Ln 97321

NUMBERED STREETS

1st E & W 97321
2nd Ave SE
100-1999 97321
3900-4099 97322
2nd Ave SW 97321
3rd SE & SW 97321
4th SE & SW 97321
5th SE & SW 97321
6th SE & SW 97321
7th Ave SE
100-1799 97321
2700-2799 97322
7th Ave SW 97321
8th Ave SE 97321
8th Ave SW 97321
9th Ave SE 97322
9th Ave SW 97321
10th Ave SE 97322
10th Ave SW 97321
11th Ave SE 97322
11th Ave SW 97321
12th Ave SE 97322
12th Ave SW 97321
NW 12th Ave 97321
13th Ave NW 97321
13th Ave SE 97322
13th Ave SW 97321
NE 13th Ave 97321
14th Ave SE 97322
14th Ave SW 97321
NE 14th Ave 97321
NW 14th Ave 97321
15th Ave SE 97322
15th Ave SW 97321
16th Ave SE 97322
16th Ave SW 97321
NE 16th Ave 97321
16th Pl SE 97322
17th Ave SE 97322
17th Ave SW 97321
NW 17th Ave 97321
18th Ave SE 97322
18th Ave SW
200-299 97322
700-999 97321
NW 18th Ave 97321
NW 18th Ct 97321
18th Pl SE 97322
19th Ave SE 97322
19th Ave SW
500-599 97322
700-999 97321
NW 19th Ave 97321
19th Pl SE 97322
20th Ave SE 97322
20th Ave SW
400-599 97322
900-999 97321
NW 20th Ave 97321
NW 20th Loop 97321
20th Pl SE 97322
21st Ave SE 97322
21st Ave SW 97321
21st Ct SE 97322
21st Pl SE 97322
21st St SE 97322
NW 21st St 97321
22nd Ave SE 97322
22nd Ave SW
300-599 97322
800-999 97321
22nd Ct SE 97322
22nd Pl SE 97322
22nd St NW 97321
23rd Ave NW 97321
23rd Ave SE 97322
23rd Ct SE 97322
23rd Pl SE 97322
24th Ave NW
3300-3399 97321
24th Ave SE 97322
24th Ave SW 97321
NW 24th Ave
3100-3499 97321
24th Ct SE 97322
25th Ave SE 97322
25th Ave SW
400-599 97322
1100-1799 97321
NW 25th Ave 97321
25th Ct SE 97322
NW 25th St 97321
26th Ave SE 97322
26th Ave SW 97321
NW 26th Ave 97321
26th Ct SE 97322
27th Ave SE 97322
27th Ave SW 97321
28th Ave SE 97322
28th Ave SW 97321
28th Pl SE 97322
29th Ave SE 97322
29th Ave SW
100-899 97322
900-1199 97321
29th Ct SE 97322
30th Ave SE 97322
30th Ave SW 97322
30th Ct SE 97322
30th Pl SE 97322
30th Pl SW 97321
31st Ave SE 97322
32nd Ave & Ct 97322
33rd Ave SE 97322
33rd Ave SW 97321
34th SE & SW 97322
35th Ave SE 97322
36th Ave SE 97322
36th Ave SW
800-899 97322
1000-1399 97321
36th Ct SE 97322
36th Pl SE 97322
37th Ave SE 97322
37th Ave SW 97321
38th Ave SE 97322
39th Ave SE 97322
39th Ave SW 97321
40th Ave SE 97322
41st Ave & Pl 97322
43rd Ave & Pl 97322
44th Ave SE 97322
45th Ct SE 97322
47th Ave SE 97322
48th Ave SE 97322
49th Ave SW 97321
51st Ave SW 97321
53rd Ave SE 97322
53rd Ave SW 97321
54th Ave NE 97321
54th Ave SE 97322

BEAVERTON OR

General Delivery 97005

POST OFFICE BOXES MAIN OFFICE STATIONS AND BRANCHES

Box No.s
ZZ - ZZ 97075
8C - 8C 97076
688C - 688C 97076
1417C - 1417C 97076
2209C - 2209C 97076
1 - 772 97075
500 - 500 97076
801 - 2279 97075
1600 - 2100 97076
2301 - 2458 97075
3000 - 4050 97076
4017 - 4017 97075
4119 - 4250 97076
4121 - 4250 97075
4300 - 4600 97076
4675 - 4675 97075
4700 - 4810 97076
4848 - 4848 97075
4850 - 4875 97076
4901 - 4901 97075
4950 - 4985 97076
5001 - 5999 97006
6001 - 7476 97007

NAMED STREETS

SW Abbott Ln 97007
SW Abelia Pl 97008
SW Ace Ter 97078
NW Acorn Pl 97006
NW Adlington Ln 97006
NW Adwick Dr 97006
SW Agate Ct 97007
SW Alabaster St 97007
SW Alameda Ln 97007
SW Alan Blumlein
Way 97005
SW Albert Ct 97007
NW Albion Ct 97006
NW Aldea Ter 97006
SW Alderview Ct 97007
Alderwood Ct & Dr 97003
SW Aldrich Ct 97007
SW Alexander St 97003
SW Alger Ave
5100-5999 97005
6101-6199 97008
SW Alibhai St 97005
Alice Ct & Ln 97008
SW Alicia Pl 97003
SW Allen Blvd
9301-9397 97005
9399-14499 97005
14600-14799 97007
Almond Ct & St 97003
SW Almonte Ct 97007
Aloha Ct & St 97003
SW Alpine Dr 97008
SW Althea Ln 97078
NW Altishin Pl 97006
SW Alton St 97003
SW Alvina Pl 97078
SW Alvord Ln 97007
NW Amber View Ln 97006
NW Amberbrook Dr 97006
Amberglen Ct & Pkwy 97006
NW Amberwood Dr 97006
SW Amicus Ter 97007
SW Amy Ln 97007
SW Anderson St 97078
SW Angel Ave 97005
SW Angie Ln 97003
SW Angora Ln 97008
SW Anna Ct 97006
SW Annadel St 97078
SW Annamae Ln 97003
SW Anne St 97008
SW Annie Ln 97078
Anthony Ct & Dr 97003
NW Anzalone Dr 97006
SW Appaloosa Pl 97008
SW Appian Ct 97078
SW Applegate Dr 97007
SW Appletree Pl 97078
SW Appy Ct 97007
SW Aquaduct Ct 97008
SW Arabian Dr 97008
SW Arago Pl 97007
SW Aragon St 97005
SW Aralia Pl 97008
SW Arbela Ct 97008
Arborcrest Ct & Way 97003
SW Arbutus Dr 97007
NW Arcadia Ct 97006
SW Arctic Dr 97006
NW Arizona Dr 97006
NW Arletta Pl 97006
SW Arrowwood Dr 97005
Artesian Ct & Dr 97006
SW Ashcroft Ln 97003
Ashland Dr & Pl 97006
SW Aspen St 97005
SW Aten Rd 97007
SW Athena Ct 97003
NW Audrey Dr 97006
SW Audubon St 97003
Augusta Ct, Dr, Ln, Pl &
St 97003
SW Augustine Ct 97007
SW Auklet Loop 97007
Autumn Dr & Ln 97007
NW Autumn Ridge Dr 97006
NW Autumncreek Way 97006
NW Avery Park Way 97006
SW Avocet Ct 97007
SW Avon Ct 97078
NW Avondale Dr 97006
SW Azalea Ct 97008
SW Back Court Pl 97003
SW Baker St
11500-11999 97008
17000-17399 97007
SW Balsam Ave 97005
NW Bandon Ct 97006
SW Bany Rd 97007
Barberry Dr, Ln & Pl 97008
Barcelona Ct, Ln &
Way 97007
SW Barclay Ct 97005
Barkton Ct & St 97006
SW Barlow Ct
13901-13997 97008
13999-14399 97008
15100-15199 97007
SW Barlow Pl 97008
SW Barlow Rd 97008
Barnard Ct & Dr 97007
SW Barrows Rd 97007
NW Bartley Ct 97006
SW Basalt Ct 97007
SW Baseline Rd
15800-16498 97006
16500-20699 97006
21000-21199 97003
21200-21599 97006
SW Bay Meadows Ct 97008
SW Bayberry Dr 97007
SW Beard Rd 97007
SW Beaver Ct 97003
SW Beavercrest Ct 97008
SW Beaverdam Rd 97005
SW Beaverton Creek
Ct 97003
SW Beaverton Hillsdale
Hwy 97005
SW Beaverwood Ct 97008
SW Becket Ct 97007
SW Beckman Pl 97003
SW Becky Ct 97007
SW Beech Dr 97005
SW Beechwood Ave 97005
Bel Aire Dr & Ln 97008
SW Bella Pl 97005
SW Bella Ter 97003
SW Bellavista Ct 97007
NW Belle Pl 97006
Belmont Dr & Ter 97008
SW Benaroya Ct 97007
SW Benji Ct 97003
SW Benton Ln 97007
SW Berger Ct 97078
SW Bergs Ct 97003
SW Berkeley Ln 97003
SW Bermuda Ct 97078
NW Bernard Pl 97006
SW Bernhardt Dr 97007
SW Bernice Ln 97008
Berryhill Ct & Ln 97008
SW Berthold St 97005
SW Beryl Ct 97007
Bethany Blvd & Ct 97006
SW Bethel Ct 97007
Betts Ave 97075
SW Betts Ave 97005
SW Betts Ct 97008
SW Bettys Pl 97003
SW Beverly Ct 97005
SW Beverly Beach Ct 97007
SW Biggi Ter 97005
SW Biles Ln 97003
SW Bingo Ln 97006
SW Birch Ave 97005
Black Bird Dr & St 97007
SW Black Quartz St 97007
SW Blackbear Ct 97006
SW Blackberry Ln 97007
SW Blackstone Dr 97007
Blaine Ct, Dr, St &
Ter 97003
Blakeney Ct & St 97008
Blamon Ct & St 97078
SW Blanco Pl 97007
SW Blanton St 97078
NW Blaze Ter 97006
SW Blue Bill Ln 97007
SW Blue Goose Ln 97007
SW Bluebell Ln 97008
Blueridge Ct, Dr & St 97006
SW Bluestone Ct 97007
NW Bobcat Pl 97006
SW Bobolink St 97007
Bobwhite Cir & Pl 97007
SW Bonanza Ct 97007
Bonneville Loop & Pl 97006
SW Bonnie Brae Ct 97005

SW Bonnie Brae Dr 97008
SW Bonnie Brae St
13410-13498 97005
13500-14499 97005
14500-14598 97007
14600-14899 97007
SW Bonnie Meadow Ln 97003
SW Booker Ct 97003
SW Boones Bend Dr 97008
SW Boston Way 97006
Boucher Ct & Pl 97003
SW Boulder Ln 97007
SW Bowerman Dr 97005
SW Brackenwood Ln 97003
SW Bradley Pl 97008
SW Brady Ct 97007
SW Breccia Dr 97007
SW Breckenridge Ln 97007
SW Brendon Ct 97005
NW Brentford Ter 97006
SW Briarcliff Cir 97008
NW Briarcreek Way 97006
Brickstone Ct & Ln 97006
NW Bridgeway Ln 97006
SW Bridle Hills Dr 97007
SW Bridletrail Ave 97008
SW Brigadoon Ct 97005
Briggs Ct & Rd 97005
Brighton Ct & Way 97007
SW Brightwood Ct 97003
SW Brightwood St 97005
SW Brisk Ln 97007
Bristol Ct & Ln 97007
SW Britetree Cir 97007
Broad Oak Blvd, Ct & Dr 97007
SW Broadway St 97005
SW Brockman St 97008
NW Broken Top Dr 97006
NW Bronson Rd 97006
SW Brookfield Ln 97003
SW Brookings Ln 97007
Brooklawn Ct & Pl 97003
Bruce Ct, Dr & Ln 97008
SW Bryan Way 97007
SW Bryant St 97003
SW Bryce Ct 97007
SW Bucher Ave 97008
SW Buckingham Pl 97007
SW Buckskin Ter 97008
SW Bunker Oak Rd 97006
SW Burkwood Ln 97003
SW Burlington Dr 97006
Burlwood Ln & St 97005
Burnett Ct & Ln 97008
SW Burnsridge Ct 97007
Burntwood Ct & Way 97007
SW Butner Ct 97005
SW Butner Rd
12400-13700 97005
13702-13798 97005
13800-14100 97006
14102-14198 97006
SW Butte Ln 97008
SW Butterfly Ct 97007
SW Butternut Dr 97007
SW Butternut Pl 97078
SW Butternut St 97078
SW Bygones Ct 97007
SW Caballero Ct 97008
SW Cabot St 97005
NW Cadbury Ave 97006
SW Cady Ln 97005
SW Calaveras Ct 97007
SW Caldera Ct 97007
SW Calico Ct 97008
SW Camas St 97003
Cambray Pl & St 97006
Cambridge Ct & Dr 97078
SW Camden Ln 97008
NW Camelback Ln 97006
SW Camelia St 97005
SW Campion Ct 97008
SW Canby Ct 97007
SW Canseco Ct 97007

SW Canter Ct 97008
NW Canvasback Way 97006
SW Canvasback Way 97007
SW Canyon Rd 97005
SW Canyon Wren Way 97007
SW Cape Meares Ct 97007
SW Capri Ct 97005
SW Capriole Pl 97008
SW Capstone Ct 97007
SW Cardinal Loop 97007
SW Cardinal Ter 97008
SW Carlin Blvd 97078
SW Carlsbad Dr 97007
SW Carmina Ln 97005
SW Carol Glen Pl 97007
SW Carolwood Dr 97007
SW Carousel Ct 97005
SW Carr St 97008
SW Carriage Way 97008
SW Carrollon Dr 97007
SW Carson Ct 97078
SW Cascade Ave 97008
SW Cascade Dr 97003
Cascadia Ct & St 97078
SW Cashew Way 97006
SW Casilda Ct 97007
SW Caspian Ct 97008
SW Cassandra Ln 97007
SW Castle Ct 97007
SW Castle Dr
18500-18799 97007
20500-20699 97078
SW Castlewood St 97005
SW Catbird Ln 97007
SW Cathedral Dr 97007
SW Cavalier Ct 97008
NW Cedar Falls Loop 97006
SW Cedar Grove Ln 97003
SW Cedar Hills Blvd 97005
Celebrity Ct, Ln & St 97078
SW Center St 97005
NW Challis Pl 97006
SW Champlin Ln 97007
SW Chandelle Ct 97078
NW Chaparral Ter 97006
SW Chaps Ct 97008
SW Chariot Ct 97008
NW Charlais St 97006
Charlene Ct & St 97003
SW Charles Ter 97007
SW Charlotte Dr 97007
SW Chatelain Dr 97003
SW Chelan Pl 97008
SW Cherry Ave 97005
SW Cherry Blossom Ct 97008
Cherryhill Ct, Dr & Ln 97008
SW Cheryl Ln 97008
SW Cheshire Ct
11700-11799 97008
20500-20599 97078
SW Cheshire Rd 97008
Chestnut Ave, Ln & Pl 97005
SW Chevy Pl 97008
SW Chianti Pl 97078
SW Chiara Pl 97003
SW Chickadee Ter 97007
SW Chris St 97078
SW Chrisben Ct 97007
SW Christopher Dr 97003
SW Christy Ave 97005
SW Chukar Ter 97007
SW Cicero Ct 97007
SW Cindy St 97008
SW Cinnabar Ct 97007
SW Cirrus Dr 97008
Citation Dr & Pl 97008
Citrine Loop & Way 97007
Clarion Ct & St 97003
SW Clark Hill Rd 97007
SW Clearwater Ct 97006
NW Cleary Ct 97006
SW Cleveland Bay Ln 97008
SW Clifford St 97008
SW Cloverdale Way 97003

SW Clydesdale Ter 97008
SW Coach Ct 97008
SW Cobalt Ln 97007
SW Cobb Ln 97007
Coburg Ct & Ln 97006
Cody Ln & St 97007
SW Coe Way 97007
SW Colleen Ct 97007
Colony Ct & Ln 97005
SW Colt Ct 97008
Combine Ct & St 97008
SW Commons Ct 97005
SW Commonwealth Ln 97005
SW Compass Dr 97005
Compton Dr & Way 97006
SW Concord Way 97006
SW Cone Pl 97006
SW Conestoga Dr 97008
Connemara Pl & Ter 97008
SW Conor Cir 97006
SW Constance St 97007
NW Continental Pl 97006
SW Cooper Mountain Ln 97007
SW Cooper Ridge Ct 97007
SW Cooperhawk Ct 97007
SW Cooperidge Ct 97007
SW Copper Ct 97007
SW Coral Bell Ct 97008
Cormorant Ct & Dr 97007
SW Cornelian Way 97007
NW Cornell Rd 97006
SW Cornhusker Ave 97008
SW Corona Ln 97003
NW Corridor Ct 97006
SW Corrine St 97007
SW Corsica Ct 97008
Cottontail Ln & Pl 97008
Cougar Ct & Ln 97008
SW Cougar Ridge Dr 97008
NW Covent Garden Pl 97006
SW Coventry Pl 97007
NW Craig Dr 97006
SW Cranberry Ct 97007
SW Crater Loop 97008
SW Creekside Pl 97008
SW Crescent St 97005
SW Cresmoor Dr 97008
SW Crestview Pl 97008
Crestwood Ct & Dr 97008
SW Cricket Ct 97003
SW Crisp Dr 97007
SW Cross Bill Ter 97007
Cross Creek Ave & Dr 97078
SW Crossview Ct 97003
NW Crosswater Ter 97006
SW Crystal St 97008
SW Cumberland Way 97006
SW Curry Ct 97006
SW Cutter Pl 97008
SW Cyber Ct 97008
SW Cynthia Ct 97008
SW Cynthia Ln 97007
SW Cynthia St
9601-9697 97008
9699-10399 97008
10401-10499 97008
16400-17299 97007
Cypress Ln & St 97005
SW Daisy Dr 97007
Dale Ave & Cir 97008
SW Dalton Pl 97078
SW Daly Ln 97005
SW Dana Ct 97003
SW Daniel Rd 97078
SW Danielle Ave 97008
SW Daphne Ct
12600-12799 97005
14700-15199 97007
SW Daphne St 97008
SW Dapplegrey Loop 97008
SW Darlene Ct 97078
SW Dartmoor Ct 97008
NW David Ct 97006
SW Davies Rd
8301-8497 97008
8499-10600 97008
10602-13698 97008
11101-11599 97007
12001-13499 97008
SW Davis Rd 97007
SW Dawson Way 97005
SW Declaration Way 97006
SW Deepwell Ct 97078
SW Deer Ln 97008
SW Deer Oak Ln 97008
SW Deercrest Ln 97007
SW Del Mar Ct 97008
NW Delamere Ter 97006
SW Deline Ct 97007
SW Deline St
15300-15400 97007
15402-15498 97007
18300-20899 97078
SW Deloris Ln 97007
Delta Ct & Dr 97006
SW Denfield St 97005
SW Denney Rd 97008
SW Derby St 97005
SW Derrill Pl 97003
NW Derrington Ct 97006
NW Desert Canyon Dr 97006
SW Devon Ln 97006
SW Devonshire Dr 97005
SW Devonwood Ave 97006
SW Diamond St 97007
SW Diamond View Way 97007
NW Diamondback Dr 97006
SW Diane Pl 97005
SW Dillan Dr 97006
SW Dipper Ln 97007
SW Division St
14801-14839 97007
14841-17299 97007
18000-18499 97078
NW Dogwood Ct 97006
SW Dolin Ct 97003
SW Doma Ln 97003
SW Dominie Ct 97078
SW Domino St 97005
SW Donald Ct 97078
NW Donin Ct 97006
SW Donna Ct 97078
NW Dorado Ln 97006
SW Dori Ct 97008
SW Dorothy Dr 97003
SW Downing Ct 97006
SW Downing Dr 97008
SW Downing St 97006
SW Doyle Pl 97003
SW Driftwood Pl 97005
SW Duchess Way 97008
SW Duncan Ln 97005
SW Dunlin Pl 97007
SW Dunsmuir Ln 97007
SW Durant Pl 97008
SW Durell Ct 97003
NW Dustin Ln 97006
NW Dutch Ln 97006
SW Dutton Ct 97078
Eagle Ct & Ln 97008
SW Eaglecrest Ter 97007
SW Eaker Pl 97007
SW East Ave 97005
NW Eastbrook Ct 97006
NW Eastmoreland Ct 97006
Eastway Ct & Pl 97006
SW Eaton Ct 97003
SW Ebberts Ct 97008
SW Ecola Pl 97007
SW Ecole Ave 97005
SW Edgemont St 97003
SW Edgemoor Ave 97005
NW & SW Edgeway Dr 97006
Edgewood Ct & St 97005
NW Edward Ct 97006
SW Edwards Pl 97078
SW Eggert Way 97078
SW Egret Ave & Pl 97007
SW Eider Ave 97007

NW Eider Ct 97006
SW Eirwen St 97003
SW El Rancho Ct 97007
NW Elaine Ct 97006
SW Electric St 97005
NW Elizabeth Ct 97006
NW Elk Run Dr 97006
NW Elkton Ct 97006
SW Ella Pl 97003
SW Ellerson St
16200-16599 97007
16601-16699 97007
18901-19097 97078
19099-19199 97078
SW Ellerson Ter 97007
SW Elliott Pl 97003
SW Ellis Ct 97078
SW Elm Ave 97005
SW Elmhurst Ave 97005
SW Elmonica Pl 97006
Emerald Ct & St 97007
NW Emerald Canyon Dr 97006
SW Emerald View St 97007
NW Emily Ln 97006
SW Enduro Pl 97078
SW Equestrian Ln 97008
SW Erica Pl 97008
SW Erickson Ave
4501-5097 97005
5099-5900 97005
5902-5998 97005
6000-6299 97008
Erin Ct, Pl & Ter 97003
SW Escalon Pl 97008
SW Essen Ct 97078
SW Estuary Dr 97006
SW Euclid Ln 97003
Everett Ct & Pl 97007
NW Evergreen Pkwy 97006
SW Evergreen St 97005
SW Ewen Dr 97003
SW Exmoor Pl 97008
SW Fagan Ct 97003
Fairfield Ct, Pl & St 97005
SW Fairmount Dr 97005
Falcon Ct & Dr 97007
Fall Ave, Ct & Pl 97006
Fallatin Ct & Loop 97007
SW Fallbrook Pl 97008
SW Falling Leaf Ct 97003
SW Fannowood Ln 97008
SW Far Vista Dr 97005
SW Farmington Rd
12500-13198 97005
13200-14200 97005
14202-14498 97005
14500-20199 97007
20200-20299 97078
20400-20798 97007
20800-24599 97007
NW Farmstead Ct 97006
SW Farrin Ct 97003
NW Faye Ct 97006
NW Feldspar Way 97007
SW Fernshire Ln 97003
SW Ferrelo Pl 97007
NW Fieldcrest Way 97006
SW Fielding Ct 97008
NW Fieldstone Dr 97006
SW Filbert Ave 97005
SW Finch St 97007
SW Fir Ct 97008
SW Fircrest Ct 97008
NW Firestone Ct 97006
SW Firview Pl 97007
SW Firwood Ct 97008
SW Fisher Ave 97008
SW Flagstone Dr 97007
SW Flicka Pl 97008
SW Flicker Ct 97007
SW Florence St 97078
SW Florendo Ln 97007
SW Foothill Dr 97005
NW Forest Ave 97006
SW Forest Dr 97007

SW Forest Pl 97007
SW Forest Glenn Ct 97008
SW Forest Ridge Pl 97007
NW Forestel Loop 97006
SW Forsythia Pl 97008
SW Fossil Ln 97007
SW Foster Ln 97078
SW Fountain Grove Ter 97078
SW Fox Ln 97008
NW Foxborough Cir 97006
SW Foxglove Pl 97008
SW Foxtrot Ter 97008
SW Frammy Way 97003
SW Frances St 97003
SW Frank Ct 97007
SW Franklin Ave 97005
NW Franson Way 97006
SW Frenwood Way 97005
SW Friendly Ln 97007
SW Fritz Pl 97003
SW Fulmar Ter 97007
Furlong Ct & Way 97005
NW Gables Creek Ln 97006
SW Gadwall Ln 97007
SW Gage Ln 97006
SW Galena Way 97007
SW Gallop Ct 97008
SW Galloway Ct 97008
SW Garibaldi Ct 97007
SW Garnet Ct 97007
NW Garswood Ter 97006
SW Gary Ln 97003
SW Gassner Rd 97007
Gateway Ct, Pl & St 97006
SW Gault Ct 97008
SW Gavin Ct 97006
Gearhart Ct & Dr 97007
SW Gem Ln 97005
SW Gemini Dr 97008
SW Gemstone Ct 97007
SW Genoa Ct 97078
SW Gentry Ln 97005
SW George Ct 97078
SW Georgene Ct 97007
SW Georgetown Way 97006
SW Georgia Ct 97003
NW Gianola Ct 97006
NW Gibbs Dr 97006
SW Gibraltar Ct 97007
SW Gillenwater Pl 97078
SW Gilmore Ct 97078
NW Gina Way 97006
SW Gingham Ln 97008
NW Glacier Ln 97006
SW Glen Oak Pl 97007
SW Glen Park Ct 97003
SW Glenbrook Rd 97007
Gleneden Ct & Dr 97007
SW Glenhaven St 97005
NW Glenlakes Pl 97006
Glenn Ct & Dr 97008
NW Gold Canyon Ln 97006
SW Golden Gate Way 97078
SW Goldeneye Ct 97007
SW Goldfinch Ter 97007
SW Goldstone Pl 97007
SW Goldview Way 97007
SW Goshawk St 97007
SW Grabhorn Rd 97007
SW Gracie St 97006
SW Granada Dr 97007
SW Granite Ct 97007
SW Graphite Ter 97007
SW Grayling Ln 97007
SW Grebe Ln 97007
SW Green Ln 97008
SW Green Slope Rd 97007
NW Greenbrier Pkwy 97006
SW Greenleaf Pl 97005
SW Greensboro Way 97078
SW Greenway 97008
SW Greenwood St 97005
SW Gregory Dr 97006
NW Greyhawk Dr 97006
SW Greystone Ct 97006

SW Griffin Pl 97008
SW Griffith Dr 97005
SW Grosbeak Ter 97007
SW Grove Ln 97007
Gull Ct, Dr & Pl 97007
SW Hackamore Ct 97008
SW Hackett Ln 97078
SW Hagg Ln 97078
SW Halite Ct 97007
SW Hall Blvd
3501-3597 97005
3599-5999 97005
6000-8724 97008
8726-8738 97008
SW Hall Ct 97005
SW Halter Ter 97008
SW Hamlin Ct 97007
SW Hammond Ter 97007
SW Hancock Way 97006
Hanson Ln & Rd 97008
SW Hargis Rd
13500-14499 97008
16500-16899 97007
SW Harlequin Dr 97007
SW Harmony Pl 97078
SW Harness Ln 97008
NW Harriet Ct 97006
SW Hart Dr 97007
SW Hart Pl 97008
SW Hart Rd
12400-14200 97008
14202-14398 97008
14500-18899 97007
SW Hart Way 97007
SW Harvest Ct 97005
SW Harvey Way 97003
SW Havencrest St 97005
SW Hawkeye Ln 97078
SW Hayden Dr 97007
Haystack Dr & Pl 97008
SW Hazel St 97005
NW Hazelgrove Ct 97006
SW Hearth Ct 97007
SW Heath Pl 97008
Heather Ct & Ln 97008
SW Heceta Ct 97007
SW Hedlund Ln 97007
SW Heights Ln 97007
Heightsview Ct & Dr 97007
SW Heiser St 97006
SW Henderson Ct 97007
Hennig Ct & St 97003
NW & SW Henry Dr & St 97005
SW Heritage Ct 97003
NW Heritage Pkwy 97006
SW Heritage Pkwy 97006
NW Heritage Ter 97006
SW Heron Cir 97007
SW Heron Ct 97007
SW Heron Pl 97007
NW Heron Way 97006
SW Hewitt Pl 97008
Hialeah Dr & Pl 97008
SW Hickory Ln 97007
SW Hidden Ct 97003
SW Hideo Ct 97003
SW High Hill Ln 97007
SW Highgate Ter 97078
SW Hill Pl 97008
SW Hillary Pl 97007
Hillcrest Ct & Pl 97008
Hiteon Ct, Dr, Ln & Pl 97008
SW Hocken Ave 97005
NW Hodes Dr 97006
SW Hoffert Pl 97078
SW Holland Ln 97008
SW Hollis Ct 97078
NW Holly St 97006
SW Hollyridge Ln 97005
SW Hollywoods Ct 97078
SW Homestead Ln 97008
SW Honeywood Dr 97003
SW Hoodoo Ct 97007
SW Hoodview Pl 97008
SW Horizon Blvd 97007

SW Horse Tale Dr 97007
SW Horseshoe Way 97007
SW Horton Way 97006
SW Hudgik Ct 97003
SW Hunter Ln 97007
NW Hunters Dr 97006
SW Hurrell Ln 97006
NW Hyde Park Ln 97006
Hyland Ct, Ter & Way 97008
SW Hyland Park Ct 97008
SW Hyland Way Ct 97008
SW Ibis Ter 97007
SW Illinois Ln 97007
SW Imperial Ct 97003
SW Imperial Dr 97008
SW Imperial Ln 97003
SW Imperial Pl 97003
SW Imperial St 97003
SW Independence Way 97006
SW Indian Hill Ln 97008
SW Indigo Ter 97007
SW Inglis Dr 97007
SW Ingrid Ter 97007
SW Innovation Ct 97003
SW Inverness Way 97007
SW Iris Ct 97008
SW Iron Horse Ln 97008
SW Ironstone Pl 97007
Island Cir & Ter 97006
SW Ivory St 97007
Ivy Glen Ct, Dr & St 97007
SW Jacktown Rd 97078
SW Jaden Dr 97003
SW Jaeger Ter 97007
Jamieson Ct & Rd 97005
SW Janell Ct 97003
SW Janet Pl 97078
Jann Ct, Dr & Pl 97003
SW Jasmine Pl 97003
Jasper Dr & Ln 97007
SW Jay Ct 97003
SW Jay St
15500-15799 97006
17300-21899 97003
SW Jaylee St
15100-15799 97007
18200-20599 97078
NW Jeanne Ct 97006
NW Jeffrey Pl 97006
SW Jenine Ln 97008
SW Jenkins Rd
12701-12997 97005
12999-14300 97005
14302-14498 97005
15500-15798 97006
15800-16299 97006
NW Jenne Lake Ct 97006
SW Jennett Ct 97008
SW Jeremy St 97007
SW Jersey Ct 97078
SW Jesse Ct 97007
Jessica Ct & Way 97006
SW Jette Ln 97003
SW Joann Ct 97003
SW Jody St 97005
SW Johnson St 97003
NW Joscelyn St 97006
SW Jourdan Ct 97003
SW Juanita Pl 97008
SW Juliann Ln 97007
SW Juniper Ter 97008
NW Jupiter Hills Ct 97006
SW Kalyca Way 97003
SW Kamalyn Pl 97005
SW Kamen Pl 97078
SW Kandrea Ct 97078
SW Karl Braun Dr 97005
SW Kathy Ct 97007
SW Katie Rose Ter 97078
NW Katsules Pl 97006
SW Kattegat Dr 97006
SW Kaufman Dr 97007
SW Kavitt Ln 97078
SW Kaylynn Ln 97006
SW Keas Ct 97008

SW Keena Ct 97007
SW Keiko St 97007
SW Kelly View Loop 97007
SW Kemmer Rd 97007
SW Kemmer View Ct 97007
SW Kendall Ln 97003
SW Kennedy St 97005
SW Kenneth Ct 97006
SW Kentucky Pl 97008
SW Kenwood Ct 97006
SW Kestrel Ct 97007
NW Kevin Ct 97006
SW Keylock Ln 97003
SW Keystone Ct 97007
NW Kian Ln 97006
Kilchis Ct & St 97007
SW Kiley Way 97006
SW Killpack Ln 97005
SW Kim Pl 97078
SW Kimber Pl 97007
Kimberly Ct & Dr 97008
SW Kimmel Ct 97007
SW Kimy Ter 97078
SW King Blvd 97008
SW Kingbird Dr 97007
SW Kingfisher Ln 97007
SW Kinnaman Rd 97078
NW Kino Springs Pl 97006
SW Kirby Ln 97007
Kirkwood Ct & St 97006
SW Kirsten Ct 97005
SW Kittiwake Ct 97007
SW Kiwanda Ln 97007
SW Knowlton Rd 97005
SW Kobbe Dr 97007
SW Koehler Rd 97007
SW Kolding Ln 97007
SW Koll Pkwy 97006
SW Kost Ln 97078
NW Kotrik Pl 97006
SW Kristin Ct 97003
NW La Paloma Ln 97006
SW La Paz Ct 97007
SW Laducer Pl 97078
SW Laird Pl 97007
NW Lakeridge Ct 97006
Lakeway Ct & Ln 97006
SW Lamb Ct 97007
NW Lancashire Ct 97006
SW Lancaster Way 97078
SW Lancewood St 97008
SW Landon Ln 97006
SW Lansford Ct 97007
Lantana Ct & Pl 97008
SW Lanterna Pl 97003
Larch Dr, Ln & Pl 97005
SW Lark Ln 97007
SW Larkcrest Ln 97003
SW Larkspur Pl 97008
SW Lars Ter 97003
SW Larson St 97005
SW Lassie Ter 97003
SW Latigo Cir 97008
SW Latitude Way 97005
SW Laurel Rd 97005
SW Lava Ct 97007
SW Lawrence Way 97006
SW Lawton St 97003
SW Leann Ct 97007
Ledgestone Ct & Dr 97007
SW Lee Ave 97005
SW Leeds Ct 97078
Leewood Dr & Ln 97003
NW Legend Trail Pl 97006
NW Lehman Pl 97006
SW Lela Ln 97003
SW Leland Dr 97007
Lenore Ct & Dr 97003
SW Leonardo Ln 97007
SW Lexington Ln 97007
SW Lexington Way 97006
SW Liberty Bell Dr 97006
SW Lido Ct 97078
SW Lillian Ct 97007
SW Lily Pl 97008
SW Limestone Ct 97003

Linda Ct & Ln 97006
SW Lindenwold Ct 97005
Linette Ct & Way 97007
SW Lisa Ct 97006
SW Lisa Dr 97006
SW Lisa Ln 97005
SW Lisa St 97006
SW Lisbon Ct 97078
SW Little Ct 97078
SW Liz Pl 97007
SW Lloyd Ave 97005
SW Lodestone Dr 97007
SW Logan St 97005
SW Lois St 97003
SW Loma Vista St 97007
SW Lombard Ave
4000-4098 97005
4100-5999 97005
6100-6800 97008
6802-6998 97008
NW Lonerock Ln 97006
Longacre Ct & St 97003
NW Longbow Ln 97006
SW Longhorn Ln 97008
SW Longspur Ter 97007
SW Lookout Ter 97008
SW Loon Dr 97007
SW Lori Way 97007
SW Lorna Ter 97007
SW Lotus Ln 97003
SW Lotus Blossom Pl 97008
SW Loxley Dr 97007
SW Lucas Oaks Ln 97007
SW Ludwig St 97078
SW Luelling Pl 97008
SW Lundgren Ter 97005
SW Luree St 97003
NW Lydia Pl 97006
NW Lyndel Ln 97006
SW Lynmar Pl 97078
SW Lyon Ct 97078
SW Mabel St 97006
SW Macorey Ct 97008
SW Mad Hatter Ln 97008
Madeline Pl & St 97078
SW Madison Ct 97008
NW Madras Ct 97006
Madrid Ct & Dr 97078
SW Magnolia Pl 97008
SW Magpie Ln 97007
SW Main Ave
4501-4597 97005
4599-5999 97005
6001-6097 97008
6099-6199 97008
6201-6399 97008
SW Mallard Dr 97007
SW Manchester Pl 97007
SW Mandy Ct 97007
SW Manor Way 97078
SW Maple Ave 97005
SW Maplecrest Ct 97008
SW Mapleoak Ln 97003
SW Marcile Ln 97007
NW Marcola Ct 97006
SW Maria Ct 97007
SW Marimar St 97078
SW Mario Ct 97003
SW Marjorie Ln 97008
SW Marko Ln 97007
SW Marlee Ln 97078
Marlin Ct & Dr 97007
SW Marne Ct 97007
SW Marseilles Dr 97007
Marsuda Ter & Way 97006
SW Martin St 97078
SW Martingale Ct 97008
SW Martini Ct 97078
SW Marty Ln 97003
SW Marylyn Pl 97008
SW Mason Ln 97006
SW Masters Loop 97078
SW Matheny Dr 97008
SW Matthew Ct 97007
NW Maudsley Ct 97006
Maverick Ct, Pl & Ter 97008

SW Max Ct 97078
SW Mayberry Pl 97007
SW Mayfair Ct 97005
SW Mayfield Ave 97005
SW Mayjohn Ct 97007
SW Mcalpin Pl 97007
SW Mcbride Pl 97005
SW Mccamley Rd 97005
SW Mcclarey Dr 97007
SW Mcgwire Ct 97007
SW Mcinnis Ln 97078
SW Mckay Ct 97008
SW Mcknight Ln 97006
SW Mcmillan St 97005
SW Meader Way 97008
NW & SW Meadow Dr 97006
Meadow Grass Ct & Dr 97006
Meadowbrook Ct & Way 97078
SW Meadowlark Ln 97007
SW Medallion Ln 97007
Melinda Dr & St 97007
SW Melnore Ct 97003
Melody Ct & Ln 97006
SW Menlo Dr
4800-5900 97005
5902-5998 97005
6000-6298 97008
SW Mercer Ter 97005
SW Merganser Ln 97007
NW Merganser Way 97006
SW Meridian St 97005
Merlo Ct, Dr & Rd 97003
SW Merrill Ln 97005
SW Merry Ln 97008
SW Mesa Ct 97008
NW Mesa View Ln 97006
SW Metz St 97008
SW Mica Ln 97007
SW Mickey Ct 97007
SW Middlesex Way 97006
SW Middleton Ct 97007
NW Midlake Ln 97006
SW Midline St 97003
NW Milburn St 97005
SW Military Ln 97007
NW Mill Creek Dr 97005
SW Millennium Ter 97007
SW Miller Hill Rd 97007
SW Millerglen Dr 97007
SW Millikan Way
12201-12997 97005
12999-13499 97005
13501-14525 97005
14601-15200 97003
15202-15998 97003
SW Mindi Ter 97003
SW Minnie Ct 97007
NW Miriam Way 97006
NW Mission Oaks Dr 97006
SW Misty Ct 97007
SW Mobile Ln 97003
Mockingbird Ct & Way 97007
SW Mohican St 97006
SW Moline Ct 97006
SW Moniker Pl 97078
SW Monson St 97003
SW Monte Verdi Blvd 97007
SW Monte Vista Dr 97007
Monticello Ct & St 97008
NW Moon Valley Ter 97006
Moonstone Ln & Ter 97007
SW Moore St 97003
SW Moorhen Way 97007
SW Moraine Ct 97007
Morgan Ct & Dr 97008
SW Morganfield Ter 97078
SW Morlock Ct 97008
NW Moro Pl 97006
SW Morrison St 97005
SW Morse Ln 97003
SW Mortondale Ln 97006
SW Mount Adams Dr 97007
SW Mount Hood Dr 97007
SW Mourning Dove Pl 97007

SW Mueller Dr 97078
NW Muirfield Ct 97006
SW Muirfield St 97003
SW Muledeer Dr 97007
SW Murphy Ct 97078
SW Murphy Ln
11800-11999 97008
20600-22399 97078
SW Murphy St 97078
SW Murray Blvd
2-298 97005
300-5400 97005
5402-5898 97005
6035-6191 97008
6193-11498 97008
Murray Scholls Dr & Pl 97007
SW Murre Ter 97007
SW Murrelet Dr 97007
SW Nadina Ct 97005
SW Nafus Ln 97007
SW Nancy Ln 97007
SW Nantucket Ln 97006
Naples Ct & St 97078
SW Navarre Ln 97007
SW Nazaneen Dr 97006
SW Nehalem Ln 97007
Neptune Ct, Ln & Ter 97007
Netarts Ct & Pl 97007
SW New Forest Dr 97008
SW New Plymouth Ln 97007
SW Newbury Ct 97007
Newcastle Dr & Pl 97078
SW Newport Pl 97007
NW Newstead Ter 97006
NW Nick Way 97006
SW Nicota Ct 97003
SW Night Heron Ln 97007
SW Nighthawk Dr 97007
SW Nightingale Ct 97007
SW Niks Dr 97003
SW Nimbus Ave 97008
SW Noah Ln 97078
SW Noble St 97078
NW Noelle Way 97006
SW Nora Rd 97007
SW Normandy Pl 97005
SW Norris Ter 97007
NW Northumbria Ln 97006
Norwalk Dr & Pl 97006
Norwich Cir, Ct & St 97006
SW Novato Ln 97078
SW November Ct 97003
SW Nutcracker Ct 97007
NW Nyssa Ct 97006
SW Nyssen St 97003
SW Oak Ct
16100-16399 97007
19800-20099 97078
SW Oak Pl 97005
SW Oak St
16500-18199 97007
19000-19799 97078
NW Oak Creek Dr 97006
NW Oak Knoll Pl 97006
NW Oakhills Dr 97006
NW Oakmont Loop 97006
SW Oakville Ct 97078
SW Oakwood Ct 97003
SW Oakwood Dr 97008
SW Oakwood St 97005
SW Obsidian St 97007
SW Octavia Ln 97007
SW October Ct 97003
NW Okanogan St 97006
SW Olaf Ter 97003
SW Old Oak Dr 97007
SW Oliver Ter 97078
SW Olivia Pl 97007
SW Olson Ct 97078
SW Onassis Pl 97007
SW Onita Ct 97006
SW Onyx Ct 97007
SW Opal Dr 97007
NW Ordonez Pl 97006

Oregon Jade Ct, Ln & Ter 97007
SW Oregon Trail Ln 97006
SW Oriole Cir 97007
NW Orion Greens Ct 97006
SW Orlov Ct 97078
SW Osprey Ct 97007
SW Osprey Dr
14301-14499 97008
14501-14777 97007
14779-14999 97007
SW Oster Ct 97078
SW Otter Ln 97008
SW Outlook Ln 97007
Overton Ct & Dr 97006
Oviatt Dr & St 97007
SW Oxbow Ter 97008
SW Oystercatcher Ln 97007
Pacer Ct & Dr 97008
SW Pacific Ave 97005
NW Pacific Grove Dr 97006
SW Pacifica Ct 97006
SW Packard Ln 97008
NW Paddington Dr 97006
SW Paddock Ct 97008
SW Padova Ct 97003
SW Page Ct 97007
NW Painted Mountain Dr 97006
Paisley Ct & Dr 97006
SW Palatial Pl 97006
NW Palmbrook Dr 97006
SW Palmer Way 97007
NW Palo Verde Pl 97006
SW Palomino Pl 97008
Palouse Ct & St 97006
SW Pamela Ct 97003
SW Pams Ct 97003
NW Park Ct 97006
NW Park Ridge Way 97006
SW Parker Ct 97078
SW Parkin Ln 97003
NW Parkview Dr 97006
SW Parkview Loop 97008
SW Parkway 97005
SW Pars Pl 97078
SW Partridge Loop 97007
SW Parvenu Pl 97006
SW Pasquinade Pl 97006
SW Pastern Pl 97008
SW Pasture Ln 97008
SW Pate Ct 97003
SW Patience Ln 97003
NW Patricia Ann Pl 97006
SW Paul Ct 97003
SW Peach Ln 97008
SW Pearl St 97005
SW Pearson Ct 97008
SW Pebble Ct 97007
NW Pebble Beach Way 97006
Pecan Ct & St 97003
SW Pegg Ct 97005
SW Peggy Ct 97003
SW Pelham Ct 97008
SW Pelican Way 97007
SW Peninsula Ct 97006
SW Peppermill Ct 97007
SW Percheron Ln 97003
SW Perfecta Ave 97005
SW Peridot Way 97007
Perimeter Dr & Pl 97006
NW Perl Way 97006
NW Persimmon Pl 97006
SW Pete Dr 97078
Petrel Ct & Ln 97007
Pheasant Ct, Dr & Ln 97003
SW Philadelphia Way 97006
SW Picadilly Ln 97007
Pike Ln & St 97078
SW Pimlico Ter 97008
SW Pine St 97005
SW Pinecrest Ct 97008
SW Pinehurst Dr 97005
SW Pinewood Way 97078
SW Ping Ct 97003

Pintail Ct & Loop 97007
Pinto Ct & Ter 97008
NW Pioneer Ct 97006
SW Pioneer Ln 97008
NW Pioneer Rd 97006
NW Pioneer Park Way 97006
SW Pipit Ct 97007
SW Platinum Pl 97007
SW Pleasant Valley Rd 97007
SW Pleasanton Ln 97003
SW Plumeria Way 97078
SW Plymouth Way 97006
SW Pointe Forest Ct 97003
SW Polo Ct 97008
SW Polsky Rd 97005
SW Pommel Ct 97008
SW Pomona Dr 97007
SW Pony Pl 97008
SW Portsmouth Pl 97006
SW Postrio Ct 97007
SW Prairie Ter 97008
SW Premier Ct 97003
NW Prescott Pl 97006
SW Princess Ave 97008
SW Pronghorn Ln 97007
Prospect Ct, Ln, Pl & St 97078
SW Puffin Ct 97007
SW Pumice Ln 97007
SW Quail Ln 97007
SW Quarry Rd 97007
NW Quatama Rd 97006
SW Queen Ln 97008
SW Quinn Ct 97003
Quint Ct & Ter 97008
SW Quintessa Ct 97078
SW Rachelle Ct 97078
SW Radford Ln 97078
SW Raintree Dr 97008
SW Ramble Ct 97007
NW Ramona Dr 97006
SW Rancher Ln 97008
SW Rankin Ct 97003
NW Rapid St 97006
SW Raven Ct 97007
SW Ravenswood St 97078
SW Ravine Dr 97007
SW Rawhide Ct 97008
SW Rebecca Ln 97008
SW Red Bird St 97007
SW Red Haven Dr 97008
SW Red Maple Ln 97007
SW Red Oak Ln 97078
Red Rock Ct & Way 97007
SW Red Sunset Ln 97007
NW Red Wing Way 97006
SW Redbud Way 97007
NW Redelfs Way 97006
SW Redstart Way 97007
SW Redstone Dr 97007
SW Redwing Ter 97007
Regal Ct & Ln 97003
SW Regatta Ln 97006
SW Reid Ct 97008
SW Remington Dr 97007
SW Remudo Ln 97008
SW Reusser Ct 97007
SW Richard Ct 97007
SW Richmond Way 97006
SW Riddle Ct 97007
SW Rider Ln 97007
SW Ridgecrest Dr 97008
SW Ridgepath Ln 97005
Ridgetop Ct & Ln 97006
SW Ridgeview Ter 97008
Rigert Ct, Rd & Ter 97007
SW Riggs Rd 97078
SW Riley Ct 97005
SW Rita Dr 97005
SW Riviera Pl 97078
SW Roan Ct 97008
SW Robbins Dr 97008
SW Robert Ln 97078
SW Rochester Dr 97008
Rock Ct, Dr & Rd 97003

SW Rock Cress Ct 97008
SW Rocklynn Pl 97005
NW Rockne Way 97006
SW Rockport Ln 97006
SW Rockridge Ct 97003
NW Rockspring Ln 97006
SW Rockwood Ct 97007
SW Rodeo Pl 97008
SW Roger Ln 97078
SW Rogue River Ter 97006
NW Rogue Valley Ter 97006
Rolling Hill Dr & Ln 97006
SW Rollingwood Dr 97008
SW Romal Ct 97008
NW Romane Pl 97006
SW Ronald Ct 97006
SW Rosa Dr 97078
SW Rosa Pl 97007
SW Rosa Rd
16000-16699 97007
17900-23699 97078
SW Rose Ln 97005
SW Rose Biggi Ave 97005
SW Rose Petal Ln 97003
SW Rose Quartz St 97007
SW Rosebud Ct 97078
NW Roseburg Ter 97006
SW Rosedale Ct 97007
SW Rosedale Rd 97078
SW Rosemount St 97078
SW Roth Dr 97078
SW Royal Woodlands Dr 97005
NW Roydon Ter 97006
Ruby Ct & St 97007
SW Ruth Ct 97007
SW Rydell Pl 97007
SW Sabin St 97008
SW Saddle Dr 97008
SW Saddlebrook Ct 97003
SW Sage Pl 97008
SW Sagehen St 97007
SW Sahnow Dr 97003
SW Saint John Vianney Way 97078
SW Saint Marys Dr
4400-4498 97078
4401-4499 97007
SW Salal Ct 97008
Salix Ct, Pl & Ter 97006
SW Salix Ridge St 97006
SW Samantha Ln 97006
SW Samaritan Ct 97003
SW Samedy Ct 97003
SW Sammy Dr 97003
SW San Mateo Ter 97003
SW Sandalwood Ave 97005
NW Sandelie Ct 97006
SW Sanderling Ct 97007
SW Sandhill Loop 97007
NW Sandpines Ln 97006
SW Sandpiper Ln 97007
Sandra Ct & Ln 97003
SW Sands Ln 97078
Sandstone Ct & Pl 97007
SW Santa Anita Ct 97008
SW Santa Rosa Ct 97078
SW Santolina Pl 97008
SW Santoro Dr 97007
Sapphire Dr & Ln 97007
SW Sarah Ellen Ct 97078
SW Sarala St 97007
SW Saratoga Ln 97008
SW Satterberg Rd 97007
SW Savannah Pl 97078
SW Savaria Ct 97005
NW Schendel Ave 97006
SW Schiffler Pl 97005
NW Schmidt Way 97006
SW Scholls Ferry Rd
6601-6697 97008
6699-8699 97008
8701-13775 97008
13700-14798 97007
14800-22199 97007
SW Scottie Pl 97078

NW Scottsdale Dr 97006
SW Scout Dr 97008
Secretariet Ct, Ln & Ter 97008
NW Sedgewick Ct 97006
NW Sedona Ln 97006
SW Sellwood Ln 97078
SW Selvarosa Ct 97003
Seminole Ct & Dr 97006
SW September Ln 97003
SW Serah St 97007
SW Settler Way 97008
SW Sexton Mountain Ct 97008
SW Sexton Mountain Dr
14000-14298 97008
14300-14499 97008
16000-16400 97007
16402-16498 97007
SW Sexton Mountain Rd 97007
NW Shadow Hills Ln 97006
NW Shady Fir Loop 97006
SW Shady Meadow Ct 97007
SW Shadypeak Ln 97007
SW Shallowbrook Ln 97007
SW Shannon Ct 97008
SW Sharoaks Dr 97003
SW Shaw St 97078
SW Shawmut Dr 97007
Shearwater Ct, Loop & Pl 97007
NW Sheffield Ave 97006
SW Shelby Ct 97007
SW Sheldrake Way 97007
SW Shelley Ct 97078
SW Shelly St 97078
SW Shelton St 97078
SW Shem Ter 97078
SW Sheridan Ct 97008
SW Sherwood Pl 97005
SW Shetland Ct 97008
SW Shire Ct 97003
Shorewood Ct & Dr 97006
NW Sidewinder Pl 97006
SW Sienna Ln 97007
Sierra Ct & Ln 97007
SW Siler Ridge Ln 97007
SW Siletz Ct 97007
SW Silver Pl 97008
NW Silver Creek Pl 97006
NW Silverado Dr 97006
SW Singletree Dr 97008
SW Sire Ter 97008
NW Siskiyou St 97006
SW Sister Ln 97003
SW Sitkum Pl 97006
Skiver Ct, Dr & St 97078
SW Skyline Woods Ln 97007
SW Smokette Ln 97003
NW Snoqualmie St 97006
SW Snowgoose Pl 97007
SW Snowshoe Ln 97008
SW Snowy Owl Ln 97007
NW Somerset Dr 97006
SW Somes Ln 97078
SW Sonia Ln 97007
SW Sora Ct 97007
SW Soren Ct 97007
SW Sorrento Rd 97008
SW Sosa Pl 97003
Southview Ct, Pl, St & Ter 97078
Spaniel Ct, Pl & St 97008
SW Sparrow Loop 97007
SW Spellman Dr 97007
SW Spencer Ave 97005
SW Spinnaker Dr 97005
SW Spirea St 97008
SW Spratt Way 97078
SW Springdale Ct 97007
SW Springfield Ln 97007
SW Springfield St 97078
Springwater Ct & Ln 97006
SW Spruce Ave 97005
SW Spur Ct 97008

NW Spyglass Dr 97006
SW Squire Dr 97007
SW Stacey St 97003
Stallion Ct & Dr 97008
SW Star Jasmine Pl 97008
SW Starbuck Ln 97078
SW Stark St 97006
SW Starling Ln 97007
NW Station Pl 97006
SW Steamboat Dr 97008
SW Steele Way 97006
Steeplechase Cir & Ct 97008
SW Stepping Stone Dr 97003
SW Stillwell Ln 97008
Stirrup Ct, Pl & St 97008
SW Stoddard Dr 97078
SW Stokesay Ln 97078
SW Stone Ridge Cir 97007
SW Stonecreek Dr 97007
Stonehedge Ct & Ln 97006
SW Stott Ave 97005
SW Strathmoor St 97007
SW Stratus St 97008
SW Strickland Dr 97007
SW Strowbridge Ct 97008
SW Stubblefield Way 97003
NW Sue Ct 97006
SW Suffolk Ct 97008
Sugar Plum Ct & Ln 97007
SW Sumac Ct
17000-17400 97007
17402-17498 97007
19600-19699 97078
SW Sumac Ln 97007
SW Sumac St 97007
NW Summer Falls St 97006
SW Suncrest Ln 97007
NW Sunningdale Dr 97006
SW Sunnyhill Ln 97005
SW Sunshine Ct 97005
SW Sunstone Loop 97007
Surrey Ct & St 97006
SW Susan Ln 97003
SW Sussex St 97008
SW Sutherland Way 97006
SW Swan Ct 97007
SW Sweet Gum Ct 97078
SW Swift Ave 97007
NW Swire Ln 97006
NW Sydney St 97006
SW Taft Ct 97007
SW Takena Ct 97003
NW Talkingstick Way 97006
SW Tall Tree Pl 97007
SW Tallac Way 97007
Talus Ct, Pl & Way 97007
SW Tammy Ct 97078
SW Tanager Ter 97007
NW Tanasbrook Ct 97006
SW Tanner Ln 97006
SW Tapadera St 97008
NW Tara St 97006
SW Tara Meadows Ct 97078
Taralynn Ave & Pl 97005
NW Targhee Pl 97006
Tarpan Ct & Dr 97008
NW Tatum Ranch Pl 97006
SW Taurus Pl 97007
SW Tea Party Cir 97008
SW Teal Blvd
11000-11699 97007
14000-14499 97008
14500-15299 97007
SW Teddi Rose Ct 97003
Telluride Ct & Ter 97007
Telshire Dr, Ln & Ter 97006
SW Templar Pl 97008
Tennessee Ln & Pl 97008
NW Tennyson Ln 97006
SW Tephra Ter 97007
SW Terman Rd 97005
SW Terra Linda St 97005
SW Tesoro Ct 97003
SW Teufel Hill Ave 97007
SW Thatcher Dr 97008
SW Theodore Way 97006

SW Theresa Ct 97007
SW Thiessen Pl 97003
SW Thoroughbred Pl 97008
SW Thunderegg Ct 97007
SW Thunderhead Way 97008
SW Tia Ter 97007
SW Tierra Del Mar Dr 97007
SW Tiger Lilly Ln 97008
SW Tile Flat Rd 97007
SW Tillamook Pl 97007
Timberland Dr & Pl 97007
Timberline Ct & Dr 97008
SW Tobias Way 97003
NW & SW Todd St 97006
Topaz Ct & Ln 97007
NW Tork Pl 97006
NW Torrey Pines Ct 97006
SW Touchstone Ter 97007
SW Towhee Ln 97007
NW Town Center Dr 97006
SW Trachsel Dr 97003
SW Tracy Ann Ct 97007
NW Trafalgar Ln 97006
Trail Ct & Pl 97008
NW Trailwalk Dr 97006
SW Tranquility Ter 97003
SW Trapper Ter 97008
SW Treehouse Ln 97078
SW Trelane St 97003
NW Tremaine Ct 97006
SW Tremont Way 97007
SW Trenton Ct 97006
Trigger Ct & Dr 97008
SW Trillium Ave 97008
SW Trillium Ct 97008
SW Trillium Ln 97007
NW Tripton Ct 97006
SW Tropicana Ave 97005
SW Trotter Pl 97008
SW Trout Creek Ln 97006
SW Troutman Ln 97003
SW Tualatin Valley Hwy
13401-13897 97005
13899-13999 97005
14001-14499 97005
14500-21699 97003
21701-21899 97003
SW Tualaway Ave 97005
SW Tucker Ave 97005
SW Tuckerwood Ct 97008
NW Tucson St 97006
SW Tulip Ct 97008
SW Tupelo Ln 97008
SW Turin Ct 97078
NW Turnberry Ter 97006
SW Turning Leaf Dr 97003
SW Turnstone Ave 97007
Turquoise Ct & Loop 97007
SW Turtledove Ln 97007
NW Twin Oaks Dr 97006
SW Tyrone Ter 97003
NW Union Hills Ter 97006
SW Uphill Pl 97007
SW Vale Ct 97008
SW Valiant Dr 97007
Valley Ave & Cir 97008
SW Valley Forge Way 97006
NW Valsetz Ct 97006
SW Vance Ln 97078
SW Vandermost Rd 97007
SW Vanguard Ln 97007
SW Vendla Park Ln 97003
SW Venice Ct 97078
SW Vermont St 97078
SW Verona Ct 97003
SW Veronica Pl 97008
SW Veta St 97003
SW Vicki Ln 97007
SW Victoria Ln 97078
Vienna Ct & Dr 97078
SW Viking Ct
13100-13299 97005
16400-18799 97007
SW Viking St 97007
Village Cir, Ct, Ln & Pl 97007

Vincent Ct & St 97078
SW Vino Pl 97078
SW Vinwood Ter 97078
SW Violet Ct 97008
SW Vista St 97003
NW Von Neumann Dr 97006
SW Vulcan Ct 97007
SW Wagner Ln 97007
SW Wagonwheel Ct 97008
Wakem Ln & St 97003
SW Wakkila Ter 97007
SW Walden Ln 97008
NW Walker Rd 97006
SW Walker Rd
10000-13999 97005
14001-14099 97005
14100-16599 97006
SW Wallingford Way 97006
SW Walquin Ct 97078
Walton Ct & St 97006
SW Warbler Way 97007
SW Washington Ave 97005
SW Washington Ct 97078
SW Washington Dr 97078
SW Watercrest Ct 97006
NW Waterfield Ct 97006
NW Waterhouse Ave 97006
Waterleaf Ln & St 97006
SW Watermark Ln 97006
SW Watershed Ln 97007
SW Waterthrush Ter 97007
SW Watson Ave 97005
Waxwing Pl & Way 97007
SW Wedgefield Ln 97078
NW Weible Way 97006
SW Weir Rd
13000-14100 97008
14102-14498 97008
14500-17060 97007
Welch Ct & Ter 97008
SW Wembley Pl 97005
SW Wentworth Ter 97078
SW Western Ave 97005
SW Westgate Dr 97005
SW Westland Ln 97003
SW Westside Dr 97078
NW Westway St 97006
Westwind Ct, Dr & Ln 97078
SW Westword St 97078
NW Weybridge Way 97006
SW Wheaton Ln 97007
SW Wheeler Ct 97078
NW Wheelock Pl 97006
SW Whisper Ct 97008
SW Whispering Fir Dr 97007
Whistling Ct & Way 97008
SW Whistling Swan Ln 97007
SW White Bird St 97007
NW White Fox Dr 97006
NW White Mountain Ter 97006
SW White Oak Ln 97007
SW Whitetail Ln 97007
SW Whitford Ln 97008
SW Whitley Way 97006
SW Why Worry Ln 97008
SW Widgeon Ct 97007
NW Widgi Creek Ct 97006
SW Wildcat Ln 97007
SW Wildhorse Way 97008
SW Wilkens Ln 97008
NW Wilkins St 97006
SW Willamette Valley Ct 97007
SW Willet Ter 97007
SW Williams Dr 97005
SW Williamsburg Way 97006
Willow Creek Ct, Dr, Pl & Ter 97003
NW Willow Glen Pl 97006
SW Willowview Ter 97003
Wilson Ave, Ct & Dr 97008
Windjammer Ct & Way 97005
Windmill Dr & Pl 97008

Windrose Ter 97003
Windstone Ct & St 97006
SW Winery Ln 97007
NW Winged Foot Ter 97006
SW Winona Ln 97078
SW Winslow Dr 97007
SW Winston Ct 97007
Winter Ct & Ln 97008
SW Winterfield Ln 97003
SW Winterhawk Ln 97007
SW Wisteria Pl 97008
SW Wolds Dr 97007
SW Wood Duck Pl 97007
SW Woodard Ct 97007
SW Woodberry Ct 97007
NW Wooded Way 97006
NW Woodmere Ct 97006
SW Woodruff Ct 97007
SW Woodwind Ct 97007
SW Wrangler Pl 97008
SW Wright Ct 97078
SW Wright St
16100-17899 97007
18700-20899 97078
SW Wyngate St 97078
SW Wynwood Ave 97005
SW Yamhill Ct 97006
SW Yeager Ln 97078
Yearling Ct, Pl & Way 97008
NW Yellowstone Ct 97006
SW Yocom Ln 97007
York Pl & St 97003
NW Yorktown Dr 97006
NW Yosemite Ter 97006
SW Zabaco Ter 97078
SW Zackwood Ct 97078
SW Zenith Pl 97078
SW Zion Ct 97007
SW Zoe Ln 97003
SW Zurich Ct 97078

NUMBERED STREETS

SW 1st St 97005
SW 2nd St 97005
SW 3rd St 97005
SW 4th St 97005
SW 5th St 97005
SW 6th St
11600-11698 97005
14500-14899 97007
SW 7th St 97005
SW 8th St 97005
SW 9th St 97005
SW 10th St 97005
SW 11th St 97005
SW 12th St 97005
SW 13th St 97005
SW 14th St 97005
SW 17th St 97008
SW 18th St 97008
SW 19th St 97008
20th Ct & St 97008
SW 21st St 97008
SW 22nd St 97008
SW 23rd St 97008
SW 24th St 97008
27th Ct & St 97008
SW 28th Ct 97008
SW 29th Ct 97008
31st Ct & St 97008
SW 32nd St 97008
SW 33rd Pl 97008
SW 96th Ave 97005
SW 98th Ave 97005
SW 98th Ct 97008
SW 99th Ave 97005
SW 99th Pl 97008
SW 100th Ter
4141-4193 97005
7000-7199 97008
SW 101st Ave
4400-4498 97005
7201-7297 97008
SW 101st Ct 97005

SW 102nd Ave
3700-4299 97005
7200-7599 97008
SW 103rd Ave
3301-3397 97005
3399-4400 97005
4402-4598 97005
7000-8099 97008
SW 103rd Ct 97005
SW 104th Ave
3500-3599 97005
6800-7399 97008
SW 105th Ave 97008
SW 106th Ave 97005
SW 107th Ave 97005
SW 108th Ave 97005
SW 109th Ave 97005
SW 110th Ave 97005
SW 110th Ct 97008
SW 111th Ave 97008
SW 112th Ave 97008
SW 113th Ave 97005
SW 114th Ave 97005
SW 116th Ave 97005
SW 116th Ter 97008
SW 117th Ave 97005
SW 118th Ave 97005
SW 119th Ave 97005
120th Ave & Pl 97005
121st Ave & Pl 97005
SW 122nd Ave 97005
SW 123rd Ave
2700-3599 97005
6501-6699 97008
SW 124th Ave
3100-3599 97005
6001-6097 97008
SW 125th Ave
3200-3298 97005
3300-3599 97005
9001-9497 97008
9499-10000 97008
10002-10098 97008
SW 125th Pl 97008
SW 126th Ave 97005
SW 126th Ct 97008
SW 127th Ct 97008
SW 129th Ter 97008
SW 130th Ave
1-699 97005
6000-10599 97008
SW 131st Ave
1-400 97005
7400-8055 97008
SW 132nd Ave 97005
SW 133rd Ave
200-499 97005
8000-8298 97008
SW 133rd Pl 97008
SW 134th Ave 97005
SW 135th Ave
1300-1399 97005
7800-10899 97008
SW 136th Ave
600-799 97005
7201-7397 97008
7399-7899 97008
7901-7999 97008
SW 136th Pl 97008
SW 137th Ave 97006
SW 137th Pl 97008
SW 138th Ave 97006
SW 139th Ave 97006
1600-5099 97005
7900-7999 97008
SW 139th Way 97005
SW 140th Ave
1-599 97006
7200-7799 97008
SW 140th Ct 97008
NW 140th Pl 97006
SW 140th Pl 97008
SW 141st Ave
300-599 97006
3700-3898 97005
3900-5999 97005
7500-10499 97008

SW 141st Pl 97008
SW 142nd Ave
1-299 97006
4300-4699 97005
6801-7097 97008
7099-7499 97008
7501-7999 97008
SW 142nd Ct
5400-5599 97005
7500-7699 97008
SW 142nd Pl 97008
SW 143rd Ave 97006
NW 144th Ave 97006
SW 144th Ave
1-599 97006
1700-4100 97005
4102-4198 97005
10101-10257 97008
10259-10299 97008
SW 144th Pl 97008
NW 145th Ave 97006
SW 146th Ter 97007
NW 147th Pl 97006
SW 147th Pl 97006
NW 147th Ter 97006
SW 147th Ter 97007
SW 148th Ave
1-100 97006
4200-4499 97078
6001-6097 97007
SW 148th Ct 97007
NW 148th Pl 97006
SW 148th Ter
400-499 97006
4800-8498 97007
SW 149th Ave
101-399 97006
4800-9299 97007
SW 149th Ct 97007
SW 149th Pl 97007
SW 149th Ter
400-499 97006
10100-10299 97007
NW 150th Ave 97006
SW 150th Ave
1-699 97006
5900-5998 97007
6000-6299 97007
SW 150th Ct 97007
SW 150th Pl 97007
SW 151st Ave 97007
NW 151st Pl 97006
SW 151st Pl 97007
NW 152nd Ave 97006
SW 152nd Ave
1-99 97006
4800-10499 97007
SW 152nd Ct 97007
NW 153rd Ave 97006
SW 153rd Ave 97007
SW 153rd Dr 97003
NW 153rd Pl 97006
SW 153rd Pl 97007
NW 154th Ave 97006
SW 154th Ave 97007
NW 154th Pl 97006
SW 154th Pl 97007
SW 154th Ter
3001-3099 97003
7100-7353 97007
7355-7405 97007
155th Ave, Ct & Ter 97007
NW 156th Ave 97006
SW 156th Ave
4564-4698 97078
6800-6898 97007
6900-7299 97007
NW 156th Pl 97006
SW 156th Pl 97007
SW 157th Ave 97007
NW 157th Pl 97006
SW 157th Pl 97007
NW 158th Ave 97006
SW 158th Ave
700-1799 97006
4900-12399 97007
12401-12499 97007
SW 158th Pl 97007
SW 158th Ter 97007
SW 159th Ave 97078
SW 159th Ct 97007
NW 159th Pl 97006
SW 159th Pl
4470-4499 97078
8000-8499 97007
NW 159th Ter 97006
NW 160th Ave 97006
SW 160th Ave
1000-1399 97006
4000-4999 97078
5000-9999 97007
NW 160th Ct 97006
SW 160th Ter 97007
NW 161st Ave 97006
SW 161st Ave 97007
SW 161st Ct 97007
SW 161st Dr 97007
NW 161st Pl 97006
SW 161st Pl
4600-4699 97078
6100-7299 97007
NW 161st Ter 97006
SW 161st Ter
4901-4999 97078
7100-7199 97007
SW 162nd Ave
1000-1299 97006
5400-5599 97007
SW 162nd Ct 97078
SW 162nd Dr 97007
SW 162nd Pl
4200-4699 97078
6100-8399 97007
NW 162nd Ter 97006
SW 163rd Ave
900-999 97006
4400-4599 97078
5000-9999 97007
NW 163rd Ct 97006
NW 163rd Pl 97006
SW 163rd Pl 97007
NW 163rd Ter 97006
SW 164th Ave
4100-4399 97078
9400-9599 97007
SW 164th Ct 97007
SW 164th Pl
4400-4599 97078
6100-8799 97007
NW 164th Ter 97006
SW 164th Ter
4600-4899 97078
6000-7200 97007
7202-7298 97007
SW 165th Ave
4000-5099 97078
5100-9699 97007
SW 165th Ct 97007
NW 165th Pl 97006
SW 165th Pl 97007
NW 166th Ave 97006
SW 166th Ave
500-999 97006
4700-5099 97078
5100-9799 97007
SW 166th Ct 97007
NW 166th Dr 97006
SW 166th Pl 97007
NW 166th Ter 97006
SW 166th Ter 97007
NW 167th Ave 97006
SW 167th Ave
1-899 97006
4100-5099 97078
5100-6099 97007
NW 167th Pl 97006
SW 167th Pl
800-999 97006
6700-9899 97007
NW 167th Ter 97006
SW 168th Ave 97007
NW 168th Pl 97006
SW 168th Pl
4800-4898 97078
4900-5099 97078
5101-5199 97078
6700-9799 97007
SW 168th Ter 97007
NW 169th Ave 97006
SW 169th Ave 97007
SW 169th Ct 97006
NW 169th Pl 97006
SW 169th Pl
301-367 97006
369-499 97006
6795-6797 97007
6799-9799 97007
SW 170th Ave
801-899 97006
1000-1098 97003
3801-3877 97078
5300-5398 97007
NW 170th Dr 97006
NW 170th Pl 97006
NW 171st Ave 97006
SW 171st Ave
1-899 97006
5900-9499 97007
SW 171st Dr 97007
NW 171st Pl 97006
SW 171st Pl
200-299 97006
2400-2599 97003
4100-4200 97078
7500-8299 97007
SW 171st Ter 97003
SW 172nd Ave
2-132 97006
3300-3599 97003
3800-4698 97078
5400-7499 97007
SW 172nd Ct 97003
NW 172nd Pl 97006
SW 172nd Pl 97007
NW 172nd Ter 97006
SW 172nd Ter 97007
NW 173rd Ave 97006
SW 173rd Ave
1-600 97006
2951-3599 97003
3900-5300 97078
5900-7300 97007
SW 173rd Ct 97003
NW 173rd Pl 97006
SW 173rd Pl 97007
NW 173rd Ter 97006
SW 173rd Ter 97003
NW 174th Ave 97006
SW 174th Ave
1400-3699 97003
3901-4097 97078
5900-7299 97007
NW 174th Pl 97006
SW 174th Pl
700-999 97006
5000-5099 97078
6700-7999 97007
NW 174th Ter 97006
SW 174th Ter
500-599 97006
5101-5197 97078
8058-8286 97007
SW 175th Ave
1-499 97006
1200-3399 97003
4000-5200 97078
6500-11999 97007
NW 175th Pl 97006
SW 175th Pl
627-707 97006
6300-7899 97007
SW 175th Ter
800-999 97006
7300-7499 97007
NW 176th Ave 97006
SW 176th Ave
2800-3499 97003
5600-9299 97007
NW 176th Ct 97006
NW 176th Pl 97006
SW 176th Ter
900-1499 97003
4600-4699 97078
7900-7999 97007
SW 177th Ave
4000-4800 97078
4802-4898 97078
5700-6599 97007
NW 177th Pl 97006
SW 177th Pl
3100-3199 97003
6300-6899 97007
SW 177th Ter 97003
NW 178th Ave 97006
SW 178th Ave
1200-1330 97003
1332-3699 97003
3800-3899 97078
NW 178th Pl 97006
SW 178th Pl
900-1370 97003
1372-2198 97003
6500-7199 97007
NW 179th Ave 97006
SW 179th Ave
800-1199 97003
4300-4599 97078
5700-7299 97007
SW 179th Ct 97003
SW 179th Pl 97007
SW 179th Ter 97003
NW 180th Ave 97006
SW 180th Ave
4300-5699 97078
6600-6999 97007
SW 180th Ct 97003
SW 180th Pl
3000-3299 97003
7000-9199 97007
SW 180th Ter
2500-2599 97003
3900-4099 97078
7300-7399 97007
NW 181st Ave 97006
SW 181st Ave
1000-1399 97003
1401-2771 97003
7600-8599 97007
SW 181st Pl 97007
NW 182nd Ave 97006
SW 182nd Ave
1100-3399 97003
3401-3599 97003
4200-5699 97078
6900-9199 97007
SW 182nd Pl
3900-4099 97078
7600-8299 97007
SW 182nd Ter 97007
NW 183rd Ave 97006
SW 183rd Ave 97078
SW 183rd Ct 97078
SW 183rd Pl
1100-2699 97003
2701-2799 97003
7300-7499 97007
SW 183rd Ter
4300-4399 97078
6100-6299 97007
SW 184th Ave
3900-5599 97078
6800-8399 97007
SW 184th Dr 97007
SW 184th Loop 97007
SW 184th Pl
1100-1199 97003
7000-7499 97007
SW 184th Ter 97003
NW 185th Ave 97006
SW 185th Ave
701-1197 97003
3600-3699 97078
3800-3800 97006
3800-3800 97007
3800-5998 97078
6200-6298 97007
SW 186th Ave
2001-2099 97003
2200-2498 97003
4000-4098 97078
4100-4699 97078
7800-8496 97007
SW 186th Pl
2600-2699 97003
5300-5398 97078
5400-5651 97078
SW 186th Ter 97078
NW 187th Ave 97006
SW 187th Ave
1500-3499 97003
4001-4097 97078
4099-5452 97078
5454-5454 97078
8000-8388 97007
SW 187th Dr 97078
SW 187th Pl
5700-6099 97078
7300-7399 97007
NW 188th Ave 97006
SW 188th Ave
3600-5499 97078
6700-7199 97007
SW 188th Ct
2200-2336 97003
2338-2398 97003
6201-6297 97078
6299-6399 97078
SW 188th Pl
4800-5099 97078
7300-7399 97007
SW 189th Ave
2000-2331 97003
2333-2399 97003
5100-5299 97078
6601-6697 97007
6699-8099 97007
SW 189th Ct 97078
SW 189th Pl 97078
NW 189th Way 97006
SW 190th Ave 97078
8500-9399 97007
SW 190th Ct 97007
NW 191st Ave 97006
SW 191st Ave
500-3000 97003
3002-3098 97003
3900-5999 97078
7000-8499 97007
SW 191st Ct
900-999 97003
5100-5699 97078
SW 191st Pl 97007
SW 191st Ter 97003
NW 192nd Ave 97006
SW 192nd Ave
1375-1377 97003
3900-6599 97078
6601-6697 97007
SW 192nd Ct 97003
SW 192nd Pl
100-399 97006
4400-4599 97078
9300-9399 97007
NW 193rd Ave 97006
SW 193rd Ave 97078
SW 193rd Ct 97003
NW 193rd Pl 97006
SW 193rd Pl
2000-2099 97003
5100-5199 97078
SW 194th Ave
501-1397 97003
5600-5999 97078
SW 194th Ct
200-599 97006
4400-4999 97078
SW 194th Pl
2000-2099 97003
3700-5199 97078
8700-8999 97007
SW 194th Ter 97007
SW 195th Ave
100-198 97006
1900-2956 97003
4000-5699 97078
6801-6897 97007
SW 195th Ct
500-699 97003
4000-4899 97078
SW 195th Pl
5100-5199 97078
7400-8499 97007
SW 195th Ter 97078
SW 196th Ave
1400-2999 97003
3500-6799 97078
SW 196th Ct 97003
SW 196th Pl 97007
SW 196th Ter 97007
SW 197th Ave
700-898 97003
900-3199 97003
4200-5699 97078
SW 197th Pl
500-599 97006
4800-4899 97078
7300-7399 97007
SW 198th Ave
400-599 97006
1700-3399 97003
3500-6899 97078
SW 198th Pl 97003
SW 199th Ave
400-599 97006
900-998 97003
8000-8199 97007
SW 199th Ct
1100-2299 97003
6600-6799 97078
SW 199th Pl
2700-2999 97003
6000-6199 97078
SW 199th Ter 97003
SW 200th Ave
301-397 97006
399-599 97006
4401-4497 97078
4499-4899 97078
SW 200th Ct 97003
SW 200th Pl
4000-5499 97078
7200-7299 97007
SW 201st Ave
299-599 97006
600-798 97003
800-2699 97003
4400-6999 97078
SW 201st Ct 97078
SW 202nd Ave
3000-3099 97003
3800-5899 97078
SW 202nd Pl
200-599 97006
6200-6299 97078
SW 202nd Ter
700-898 97003
6900-6948 97078
SW 203rd Ave
200-599 97006
1400-2699 97003
3800-6599 97078
SW 203rd Ct 97078
SW 203rd Pl
600-1199 97003
6200-6299 97078
SW 204th Ave
1100-1198 97003
1200-2600 97003
2602-2698 97003
5001-5077 97078
5079-7099 97078
7100-7899 97007
SW 204th Pl 97078
SW 204th Ter 97006
SW 205th Ave
300-599 97006
3800-6299 97078
SW 205th Ct 97078
SW 205th Pl
1400-2300 97003
2302-2398 97003
6800-6999 97078
SW 205th Ter
1200-1399 97003
7500-7699 97007
NW 206th Ave 97006
SW 206th Ave
1-168 97006
700-898 97003
5500-5899 97078
SW 206th Ct 97078
SW 206th Pl
700-2599 97003
4200-7199 97078
NW 207th Ave 97006
SW 207th Ave
301-325 97006
327-599 97006
2800-3099 97003
5500-6699 97078
SW 207th Ct 97078
SW 207th Pl
717-1199 97003
5000-5099 97078
SW 207th Ter 97003
NW 208th Ave 97006
SW 208th Ave
101-399 97006
1300-2299 97003
6800-6921 97078
SW 208th Ct 97078
NW 208th Ln 97006
NW 208th Pl 97006
SW 208th Pl
900-1199 97003
6000-6199 97078
7486-7575 97007
NW 208th Ter 97006
SW 208th Ter 97078
NW 209th Ave 97006
SW 209th Ave
1100-3199 97003
3300-7198 97078
3301-3599 97007
3601-7199 97078
SW 209th Ct 97003
NW 209th Ln 97006
SW 209th Pl 97003
SW 210th Ct 97003
NW 210th Ln 97006
SW 210th Pl 97003
NW 210th Way 97006
SW 211th Ave
300-599 97006
700-1499 97003
1501-3199 97003
6500-6899 97078
SW 211th Ct 97003
SW 211th Pl 97003
SW 212th Ave 97006
SW 212th Ct 97003
SW 213th Ave
1094-1599 97003
5800-6899 97078
SW 213th Pl 97003
214th Ave & Pl 97003
SW 215th Ave 97003
NW 215th Ter 97006
216th Ave & Pl 97003
217th Ave, Ct & Pl 97003
218th Ct, Dr, Pl & Ter 97003
SW 229th Ave 97078
SW 240th Pl 97078

BEND OR

General Delivery 97701

POST OFFICE BOXES MAIN OFFICE STATIONS AND BRANCHES

Box No.s
1 - 2418 97709

1921 - 4958 97707
5001 - 9838 97708

NAMED STREETS

Aaron Way 97702
Abbey Rd 97701
Aberdeen Dr 97702
Abilene Ct 97701
Acorn Ct & Way 97701
NW Adams Pl 97701
Addie Triplett Loop 97702
NE Addison Ave 97701
Admiral Way 97702
NE Adrian Ct 97701
Agate Rd 97702
Ahha Ln 97702
SE Airpark Dr 97702
SE Airstrip Dr 97702
Aladdin Ct 97701
Alan A Dale Ct 97702
NW Albany Ave 97701
Alcor Pl 97701
NE Alden Ave 97701
SE Alden Ave 97702
Alder Ln 97701
Alderwood Cir 97702
NE Aldrich Ave 97701
Alexandrite Dr 97702
Alfalfa Market Rd 97701
Allen Rd 97701
NW Allen Rd 97701
SW Allen Rd 97702
Alopex Ln 97702
NE Alpenglow Pl 97701
NE Alpenview Ln 97701
Alpine Dr 97702
Alpine Ln
24800-25499 97701
60948-60999 97702
Alpine Trl 97701
NE Alpine Peaks Pl 97701
Alpine Ridge Pl 97701
Alstrup Rd 97702
Alta View Cir 97702
Altair Ct 97701
NE Altura Dr 97701
SE Amanda Ct 97702
Ambassador Dr 97702
Amber Ct & Way 97701
Amber Meadow Dr 97702
Amberwood Pl 97702
Ambrosia Ln 97702
American Ln & Loop 97702
Amethyst St 97702
Amherst Pl 97701
NW Anderson Ct 97701
NW Anderson Ranch Rd 97701
Angel 97702
NE Angela Ave 97701
Angler Ave 97701
NE Angora Ct 97701
Anika Ln 97701
Anker Ln 97702
Ann Margaret Dr 97701
Anne Ln 97702
Anson Pl 97701
Antelope Dr 97707
Antler Rd 97702
Antler Point Dr 97702
Apache Rd 97702
NE Apple Creek Ln 97701
April Ann Ct 97701
Arago Cir 97701
Arapaho Ln 97702
SE Arborwood Ave 97702
NW Archie Briggs Rd 97701
Arid Ave 97701
NW Arizona Ave 97701
SE Armour Rd 97702
Arnold Market Rd 97702
Arntz Ct 97702
Arrow Ave 97702
Arrow Wood Dr & Pl 97702
Arrowhead Dr 97701
NW Arrowleaf Ct 97701
Arroyo Ct 97701
Ascha Rose Ct 97702
Ashford Dr 97702
Ashwood Dr 97702
Aspen Ln 97702
Aspen Pl 97707
Aspen Meadows Dr 97702
Aspen Ridge Dr 97702
Aspen Rim Ln 97702
Aspenwood Rd 97702
Aster Ln 97702
Astro Pl 97702
NE Atherton Ct 97701
Athletic Club Dr 97702
August Ln 97702
Auklet Dr 97707
SW Aune St 97702
NE Aurora Ave 97701
NW & SW Austin Ct & Rd 97701
SE Autumnwood Ct 97702
Avery Ln 97702
Avocet Dr 97707
Avonlea Cir 97702
Avro Pl 97701
NW Awbrey Rd 97701
NW Awbrey Glen Dr 97701
NW Awbrey Point Cir 97701
Azalia Ave 97702
NE Azure Dr 97701
Azusa Rd 97707
Bacchus Ct & Ln 97702
Bachelor Ln & Way 97701
Bachelor View Rd 97702
Back Alley Rd 97702
Badger Rd 97702
Badlands Ranch Dr 97701
Bailey Rd 97701
NE Bain St 97701
Bainbridge Ct 97702
Baker Rd 97702
Bakersfield Rd 97707
NW Balitch Ct 97701
Ball Butte Ct 97702
Ballantrae Ct 97702
NW Baltimore Ave 97701
Bandley Rd 97707
Baneberry Ave 97702
SE Banewood Ct 97702
Banff Dr 97702
Baptist Way 97702
Barbara Way 97701
Barleycorn Ln 97702
Barlow Trl 97702
NE Baron Ct 97701
NE Baroness Pl 97701
Barr Rd 97701
NE Barrett Ct 97701
NE Barrington Ct 97701
Barrows Ct 97702
Bartlett Ln 97701
Barton Crossing Way 97701
Barton View Pl 97701
Basket Flower Pl 97702
Baskin Ct 97701
Bass Ln 97701
Bates St 97707
Bayou Dr 97702
SE Baywood Ct 97702
Beall Dr 97701
Bear Dr & Ln 97707
NE Bear Creek Rd 97701
Bear Paw Ln 97707
Bearing Dr 97701
Bearwallow Rd 97701
Beaufort Ct 97701
Beaumont Dr 97701
Beaver Dr 97707
Beaver Ln 97701
Beaver Pl 97707
Becker Rd 97701
Becky Ct 97701
Bedford Pl 97701
Bedrock Ct 97701
Bee Tree Ln 97701
Belknap Dr 97701
NE Bellevue Dr 97701
Bellflower Pl 97702
Belmore Loop 97702
Bemis Ln 97701
SE Benaiah Cir 97702
Bench Leg Rd 97707
Bend Rd 97701
NE Bend River Mall Dr 97701
Benham Rd 97702
Bennett Rd 97701
NE Bennington Way 97701
NW Bens Ct 97701
NE Berg Ln & Way 97701
Besson Rd 97707
Beth Ave 97702
Beverly Ln 97707
Big Bear Ct 97702
Big Buck Ln 97707
Big Eddy Cir 97702
Big River Dr 97707
Big Sage Way 97701
Big Sky Trl 97702
Bighorn Ct 97702
Bill Martin Rd 97701
Billadeau Rd 97702
Bilyeu Ct & Way 97701
Birch Ln 97701
Birchwood Dr 97702
Birdsong Ln 97701
Bivouac Rd 97707
Black Duck Rd 97707
NW Black Hawk Ave 97701
Black Horse Ln 97701
NW Black Pines Pl 97701
Black Powder Ln 97701
SE Black Ridge Pl 97702
Black Rock Ln 97701
Blackfoot Trl 97702
Blacksmith Cir 97702
Blacktail Ln 97707
Blakely Ct & Rd 97702
Blanca Dr 97701
Blue Bush Ct 97701
Blue Eagle Rd 97707
Blue Heron Dr 97707
Blue Lake Loop 97702
Blue Ridge Ln 97702
Blue Sky Ln 97702
NE Bluebell Ln 97701
NE Bluebird Ct 97701
SW Bluff Dr 97702
Blurton Ct 97702
NE Bobbie Ct 97701
Bobcat Rd 97702
Bobwhite Ct 97701
NW Bond St 97701
SW Bond St 97702
SW Bonnett Way 97702
Bonny Brg 97702
Boones Borough Ct & Dr 97701
NW Bordeaux Ln 97701
Borden Dr 97702
Borealis Ln 97702
NE Boston Pl 97701
Boulder Ct & Rd 97701
Boulderfield Ave 97701
Bounty Lake Ct 97702
Bowery Ln 97701
Boyd Ct 97701
NE Boyd Acres Rd 97701
Bozeman Trl 97702
Brad St 97701
SW Bradbury Way 97702
Bradetich Loop 97701
NE Bradford Ct 97701
Brahma Ct N & S 97701
NW Braid Dr 97701
Branding Iron Ct 97701
Brandis Ct 97701
NE Brandon Ct 97701
Brandywine Rd 97701
Brant Ct 97701
Brant Dr 97707
Brasada Way 97702
Brass Dr 97702
NW Bratton Ln 97701
Breckenridge 97702
Breezy Way 97701
SE Breitenbush Ln 97702
Brenda Dr 97707
Brentwood Ave 97702
NE Brian Ray Ct 97701
Brianne Pl 97702
SE Briarwood Ct 97702
NW Brickyard St 97701
Bridge Creek Dr 97702
Bridgecliff Dr 97702
SE Bridgeford Blvd 97702
Bridle Ln 97701
Brightenwood Cir & Ln 97702
Brighton Cir 97702
Brightwater Dr 97701
Brinson Blvd 97701
Bristol Way 97702
Britta St 97701
Brittle Bush St 97702
NW Broadway St 97701
Brock Ln 97702
Brody Ln 97701
NW Brogan 97701
NW Broken Arrow Rd 97701
NE Broken Bow Dr 97701
Broken Top Dr 97702
Bronco Ct 97701
Bronco Ln 97702
Bronze St 97701
Bronze Meadow Ln 97702
SE Bronzewood Ave 97702
Brookhollow Dr 97702
Brooklyn Ct & Pl 97701
NW Brooks St 97701
Brooks Scanlon Logging Rd 97701
Brookside Loop & Way 97702
Brookstone Ln 97701
SW Brookswood Blvd 97702
Brosterhous Rd 97702
Brown Trout Pl 97702
Browning Dr 97707
Bruce Ave 97701
Brumby Ln 97701
NE Brush Ct 97701
Brushline Ct 97701
SW Bryanwood Pl 97702
NW Bryce Canyon Ln 97701
Buck Dr 97701
Buck Canyon Rd 97702
Buckshot Pl 97702
Buckskin Ct 97701
NE Buckwheat Ct 97701
Bufflehead Rd 97707
Builders Ct 97701
Bull Springs Rd 97701
Bullblock Rd 97702
Bunchgrass Ct & Pl 97701
Bungalow Ct & Dr 97701
Bunker Hill Ct 97702
NE Burgess Pl 97701
NE Burks Ct 97701
NE Burnside Ave 97701
SE Business Way 97702
Butcher Ln 97701
NE Butler Market Rd 97701
Butt Riggin Rd 97702
Butte Ranch Rd 97702
Butterfield Trl 97702
Buttermilk 97702
Button Brush Ave 97702
Byers Ave & Ct 97701
Byram Ct & Rd 97701
NW Cabernet Ln 97701
Cabin Ct & Ln 97702
NW Cabot Lake Ct 97701
NE Cackler Ln 97701
Caddisfly Way 97701
Cady Way 97701
Cairn Ct 97701
NE Caldwell Ct 97701
Caleb Pl 97702
Calgary Dr, Ln & Loop 97702
Calico Ct 97707
Calico Rd 97702
Calvin Way 97702
Cambridge Ct 97702
Camden Pl 97702
Camellia St 97702
Camelot Pl 97702
Camp Site 97707
E Campbell Ct & Rd 97702
Campion Pl 97701
NW Campus Village Way 97701
Canal View Dr 97702
NW Candlelight Pl 97701
NE Canoe Ct 97701
Canoe Camp Dr 97707
Canterbury Ct 97702
Canvasback Dr 97707
Canyon Park Dr & Pl 97701
Canyon View Loop 97701
Capella Pl 97702
Caribou Dr 97707
Carl St 97701
NW Carlon Ave 97701
Carly Ln 97701
Carm Ln 97702
Carmen Loop 97702
Carnelian Ln 97701
Carolyn Ct 97701
NE Carrie Ln 97701
Carrington Ave 97707
NE Carson Way 97701
Carson Creek Ct 97702
Cartmill Dr 97702
Casa Ct 97701
E, W & NW Cascade Pl & Way 97701
Cascade Estates Dr 97701
NW Cascade View Dr 97701
Cascade Village Dr 97701
SE Case Dr 97702
Casey Pl 97701
Casper Dr 97707
Cassin Dr 97701
NE Castle Ave 97701
SE Castlewood Dr 97702
Cathy Ct 97701
Cayuse Crater Ct 97702
Cedar Ln 97701
Cedarwood Rd 97702
Celestial Dr 97707
NW Celilo Ln 97701
Centennial Ct & St 97702
Central St 97701
S Century Dr 97707
SW Century Dr 97702
Cephus Ct 97701
SE Cessna Dr 97702
NW Chamberlain St 97701
SW Chamberlain St 97702
Chamomile Pl 97702
NW Champanelle Way 97701
NW Champion Cir 97701
SW Chandler Ave 97702
NE Chanel Ct 97701
Chaney Rd 97701
Chaparrel Ct & Dr 97701
Chapman Ln 97707
Charbonneau 97701
NW Chardonnay Ln 97701
Charity Ln 97702
NE Charleston Ct 97701
Charleswood Ln 97702
Chase Rd 97702
Chasing Cattle Ln 97701
Chelsea Ct & Loop 97701
Cherokee Ln 97701
Cherokee Rd 97702
Cherry Tree Ln 97702
Cherrywood Ln 97702
Chewacan Ct 97702
Cheyenne Rd 97702
NW Chianti Ln 97701
Chickadee Ln 97701
Chickasaw Way 97702
Chicory Ave 97702
Chief Paulina Dr 97707
Chikamin Dr 97702
Chilliwack Way 97702
Chiloquin Dr 97701
China Hat Rd 97702
Chip Shot Ln 97702
Chisholm Trl 97702
Chivas Pl 97702
Chloe Ln 97702
Choctaw Rd 97702
NE Christina Ln 97701
Christmas Rdg 97702
Christopher Ct 97702
Chuckanut Dr 97702
SW Chukar Ln 97702
Cimarron Dr 97701
Cinder Ln 97702
Cinder Butte Rd 97702
Cindy Ct 97701
Cinnabar Ct 97702
Circle St 97707
Cirrus Ct 97702
NW City Heights Dr 97701
NW City View Dr 97701
Clairaway Ave 97702
Claremont Ct 97702
Clarion Ave 97702
NW Clark Ct 97701
Clausen Rd 97701
NE Clay Ave 97701
Clay Pigeon Ct 97702
Clear Night Dr 97702
Clear View Ct 97702
Clearmeadow Ct 97702
NW Clearwater Dr 97701
SE & SW Cleveland Ave 97702
SE Cleveland Square Loop 97702
NE Cliff Dr 97701
Cliffrose Dr 97702
Cline Falls Rd 97701
Cloverdale Rd 97701
NW Clubhouse Dr 97701
Clyde Ln 97701
Cob St 97702
NE Cobble Creek Ave 97701
Cobblestone Pl 97702
Cody Rd 97701
Cody Jr Rd 97701
NW Coe Ct 97701
Coffee Ct 97702
NE Coho St 97701
Cole Rd 97701
NW College Way 97701
NW Collett Way 97701
NW Collette Way 97701
NE Collier Ct 97701
Collins Rd 97701
NW Colonial Dr 97701
NW Colorado Ave 97701
SW Colorado Ave 97702
Colt Ln 97701
NW Colter Ave 97701
NW Columbia St 97701
SW Columbia St 97702
Columbine Ln 97702
NW Colver Ct 97701
Comanche Ln 97702
NE Comet Ct 97701
Comet Dr 97707
Comet Ln 97701
NE Comet Ln 97701
NW & SW Commerce Ave 97701
NE Community Ln 97701
NW Compass Ln 97701
Concho St 97702
Concorde Ln 97701
Cone Flower St 97702
Conger Ct 97701
NW Congress St 97701
Conifer Ave 97702
Connarn Rd 97701
NE Conners Ave 97701
NW Conrad Dr 97701
NW Constellation Dr 97701
Cook Ave 97701
Cooley Rd 97701
Cooper Dr 97707
SE Cooper Pl 97702
SW Cooper Rd 97701
SW Cooper St 97701
Copernicus Ave 97702
Copperfield Ave 97702
Cordata Pl 97701
Cori Way 97701
Corona Ln 97701
Corporate Pl 97701
Corral Rd 97702
Corsica Ln 97702
NW Cottage Pl 97701
NW Cotton Pl 97701
Cottonwood Dr 97702
Cottonwood Rd 97707
Couch Market Rd 97701
Cougar Trl 97701
SE Cougar Peak Dr 97702
Coulter Ln 97702
Country Club Dr 97702
Country Squire Rd 97701
Country View Ln 97701
SW County Line Rd 97701
Couples Ln 97702
NE Courtney Dr 97701
NW Cousins Pl 97701
Coventry Cir 97702
Covey Ct 97701
Covey Ln 97702
Covina Rd 97707
NE Covington Ln 97701
Cox Ln 97701
Coyote Dr 97702
Coyote Trl 97701
Coyote Run Ln 97701
NE Cradle Mountain Way 97701
NW Craftsman Dr 97701
Craig Pl 97702
Crane Dr 97707
Crater Rd 97702
NE Craven Rd 97701
SE Craven Rd 97702
Cree Cir 97702
Creekstone Loop 97702
Crescent Ct 97702
Crest View Ln 97702
Crested Ct 97701
Crested Butte Ln 97702
SW Crestline Dr 97702
NE Crestridge Dr 97701
Crestview Ct & Dr 97701
NE Cretia Ct 97701
Cricketwood Rd 97701
NW Criterion Ln 97701
Crockett Way 97702
NE Crocus Way 97701
Crofoot Ct 97701
NE Cromwell Ct 97701
Crooked Rocks Rd 97701
Crosby 97701
Cross Ct & Rd 97701
SW Crosscut Ct 97702
NW Crossing Dr 97701
Crosswinds Rd 97701
SW Crowell Way 97702
NE Cruise Loop 97701
Crusher Ave 97701
NW Cruzatte Ln 97701
Crystal Ct 97701
Crystal Ln 97702
Crystal Creek Ct 97702
Crystal Mountain Ln 97702
NE Crystal Springs Dr 97701
Cultus Dr 97702
Cultus Ln 97701
Cultus Lake Ct 97702
Cultus Mountain Ct 97702
NW Cumberland Ave 97701
Cumulus Ln 97702

Curlew Dr 97707
Currant Way 97702
Currier Dr 97702
NE Curtis Dr 97701
NE Cushing Dr 97701
SE Cutlass Pl 97702
SW Cyber Dr 97702
Cyprus St 97702
NE Daggett Ln 97701
Daisy Ln 97702
Dakota Dr 97701
Dakota Trl 97702
Dale Rd 97701
NE Dalton St 97701
Daly Estates Dr 97702
Damascus Ln 97701
Daniel Ct & Rd 97701
Daniel Duke Way 97701
Dantili Rd 97701
Daphne Ct & Dr 97701
Darby Ct 97702
Darin Ln 97707
Darla Pl 97702
Darnel Ave 97702
Dartmouth Ave 97702
NW Davenport Ave 97701
SE Davis Ave 97702
Davis Lake Loop 97702
NE Dawson Dr 97701
Daylily Ave 97702
Dayspring Dr 97702
Dayton Rd 97701
De Haviland Ct & St 97701
Dea Dr 97701
Dean Swift Rd 97701
NE Deborah Ct 97701
NW Debron Ln 97701
NE Decatur Ct 97701
Decoy Ct 97702
Dee Dr 97701
Deer Ln 97701
Deer Run Rd 97707
Deer Trail Rd 97701
Deer Valley Dr 97702
Defiance St 97702
NE Dekalb Ave 97701
Del Coco Ct 97702
NW Delaware Ave 97701
Delicious St 97701
SE Dell Ln 97702
NE Delmas St 97701
NE Dempsey Dr 97701
NW Denali Ln 97701
Denning Dr 97702
NE Dennis Ct 97701
NE Derek Dr 97701
Derringer Dr 97707
Deschutes Pl & Rd 97701
Deschutes Market Rd 97701
Deschutes Pleasant Ridge Rd 97701
NE Desert Ct 97701
Desert Oasis Ct 97702
Desert Sage Ct & St 97701
Desert Skies Pl 97702
Desert Stream Pl 97702
NE Desert Willow Ct 97701
Desert Woods Dr 97702
Destiny Ct 97701
Devils Lake Dr 97702
Devon Cir 97702
NE Diablo Way 97701
Diamond Rd 97702
Diamond Forge Rd 97701
Diamond Lake Dr 97702
Diamond T Rd 97701
Diana Ln 97707
Dickens Ct 97701
Dickey Rd 97701
Dione Way 97701
Dipper Ln 97707
SW Disk Dr 97702
NE Division St 97701
NW Division St 97701
SE Division St 97702
SW Division St 97702
NW Divot Dr 97701
Dixon Loop 97701
Doanna Way 97702
Dobbin Ct & Rd 97702
NE Doctors Dr 97701
Dodds Rd 97701
Doe Ln 97701
NE Dogwood Dr 97701
Don St 97701
Don Jr Ln 97701
Donkey Sled Rd 97702
Donna Ln 97701
SW Donovan Ave 97702
Dooley Mountain Ct 97702
Dorchester E & W 97702
NW Dorion Way 97701
SE Dorrie Ct 97702
Double Peaks Dr 97701
Double R Way 97701
Double Tree Ct 97702
Douglas Ln 97701
SE Douglas St 97702
Dove Ln 97702
Dover Ln 97702
Dovewood Pl 97702
Downey Rd 97707
NW Drake Rd 97701
Driftwood Ln 97702
NE Drost Dr 97701
NW Drouillard Ave 97701
Drover Way 97702
Dry Canyon Ave 97702
Dryer Ct 97702
Duck Call Ln 97702
NW Duffy Dr 97701
Duke Ln 97702
Dulin Dr 97701
Dunbar Ct 97702
Duncan Ln 97702
NW Duniway Ct 97701
Dusty Loop 97701
Dusty Dirt Rd 97701
Dutchman Ct 97702
NW Dwight Ct 97701
NE Dyer Dr 97701
Dylan Loop 97702
Eagle Rd 97701
East St 97701
NW Eastes St 97701
Eastmont Dr 97701
Eastview Dr 97701
NE Eastwood Dr 97701
Eaton Ln 97702
Echo Hollow Rd 97702
Eclipse Dr 97707
NE Eddie Ct 97701
Edelweiss 97702
NE Edgecliff Cir 97701
NE Edgewater Dr 97701
SE Edgewater Ln 97702
NE Edgewood St 97701
Edmonton Dr 97702
Edro Pl 97702
Eena Ct 97702
Egret Dr 97707
Egypt Dr 97701
Eider Rd 97707
NW Eighteenth Fairway Pl 97701
El Dorado Trl 97701
Elaine Ln 97702
Elder Ln 97701
Elder Ridge St 97702
NW Element Pl 97701
NW Elgin Ave 97701
NE Elizabeth Ct 97701
Elizabeth Ln 97702
NE Elk Ct 97701
Elk Dr 97707
Elk Ln 97701
Elkai Woods Dr 97702
Elkhorn St 97702
SE Elkwood Ct 97702
SW Ellenhurst Pl 97702
Ellie Ln 97701
NW Elliot Ct 97701
Elm Ln 97701
Elmwood Pl 97702
Elsinore Rd 97707
Emerald Pl 97702
NE Emerson Ave 97701
Emigrant Cir & Dr 97702
Emily Ct 97701
SW Emkay Dr 97702
Empire Ave 97701
Enati Ct 97702
Enterprise Dr 97707
Erickson Rd 97701
NW Erin Ct 97701
NE Evelyn Ct & Pl 97701
Evening Star Ln 97702
NW Evergreen St 97701
Fairey Ct 97701
Fairfield Dr 97702
NE Fairmont Ct 97701
Fairway Dr 97702
NW Fairway Heights Dr 97701
Fairway Ridge Ln 97702
SE Fairwood Dr 97702
NE Faith Dr 97701
NW Falcon Rdg 97701
Falcon Pointe Ln 97702
Fall Creek Loop 97702
Fall River Dr 97707
Farenuff Pl 97701
NW Farewell Dr 97701
Fargo Ln 97702
Faridend Rd 97702
Farview Dr 97701
Faugarwee Cir 97702
Fawn Ln 97701
NW Fawn Run Ln 97701
Fazio Ln 97701
NW Federal St 97701
Fennic Ct 97702
Ferguson Ct & Rd 97702
NW Fernie Ct 97701
Ficco Ct 97701
NE Fieldstone Ct 97701
Filly Ct 97702
Finchwood Dr 97702
Findlay Ln 97701
S Fir Ln & St 97701
Fir Crest Knl 97702
Firerock Rd 97701
Fireside Trl 97702
Fisher Lake Ln 97702
Fishhawk Loop 97702
NW Fishwick Ct 97701
NW Fitzgerald Ct 97701
NW Flagline Dr 97701
NE Flagstone Ave 97701
Fletcher Ln 97701
Flint Ln & Rd 97702
Flintlock Ct 97701
Florence Dr 97701
NW Florida Ave 97701
NE Flower Ct 97701
NW Floyd Ln 97701
NW Foley Ct 97701
Fontana Rd 97707
NE Forbes Rd 97701
Ford Rd
25400-25499 97702
27600-27899 97701
33500-33599 97702
Forest Ln 97707
SW Forest Grove Dr 97702
Forest Meadow Pl 97702
SW Forest Ridge Ave 97702
Forest Service Rd 97701
NW Fort Clatsop St 97701
NW Fort Mandan Way 97701
Fort Rock Rd 97701
Fort Thompson Ln 97701
NE Forum Dr 97701
Foster Ln 97702
Foster Rd 97707
Fox Hills Dr 97702
Foxborough Ln 97702
Foxglove Loop 97702
NW Foxwood 97701
NE Francis Ct 97701
NE Frank Mcclean Ct 97701
Franke Ln 97702
NE & NW Franklin Ave 97701
NW Frazer Ln 97701
Fred Meyers Rd 97701
Freedom Pl 97701
Fremont Rd 97701
NW French Ct 97701
Fresca St 97701
NW Fresno Ave 97701
Friar Tuck Ln 97702
Frontier Way 97702
Fryrear Rd 97701
Fryrear Ranch Rd 97701
NE Full Moon Dr 97701
Futurity Ct 97701
Gadwall Dr 97707
Gaines Ct 97702
Galen Rd 97702
Galileo Ave 97702
Gallop Ct & Rd 97701
NW Galveston Ave 97701
NW Gander Ct 97701
Garcia Rd 97701
SE Gardenia Ave & Ct 97702
SW Garfield Ave 97702
Garnet St 97702
Garrison Dr 97702
NW Gasoline Aly 97701
Gatehouse Ln 97707
SE Gatewood Pl 97702
Geary Dr 97702
Gemini Way 97702
NE Genet Ct 97701
Gentry Loop 97701
George Millican Rd 97701
NW Georgia Ave 97701
NE Georgianne Ct 97701
Gerking Market Rd 97701
Ghost Tree Ln 97701
Gibson Dr 97702
Gibson Air Rd 97701
Gift Pl & Rd 97701
NW Gilchrist Ave 97701
NW Gill Ct 97701
Gillette Rd 97701
Gina Ln 97707
Gist Rd 97701
NE Glacier Ridge Rd 97701
Glacier View Dr 97701
NW Glassow Dr 97701
NW Glen Rd 97701
Glen Falls Pl 97701
Glen Vista Rd 97701
NW Glenbrooke 97701
SE Glencoe Pl 97702
Glendale Rd 97707
SW Gleneagles Way 97702
SE Gleneden Pl 97702
SE Glengarry Pl 97702
Glenn Maroe Ct 97701
NE Glenshire Pl 97701
SE Glenwood Dr 97702
Gloucester Ln 97701
Gold Crest Ln 97707
Gold Spur Way 97701
Golden Eye Dr 97707
Golden Gate Pl 97702
Golden Lake Ct 97702
Golden Meadow Loop 97702
Goldenrain Dr 97702
Goldenrod Ln 97702
Goldenwood Ct & Loop 97702
NW Golf Course Dr 97701
NW Golf View Dr 97701
Golf Village Loop 97702
NW Goodwillie Ct 97701
Goose Creek Ct 97702
Gooseberry Pl 97702
NW Gordon Rd 97701
Gorge View St 97702
Gosney Rd 97702
Gothard Way 97707
Graham Ln 97701
Grand Targhee Dr 97702
Grand Teton Dr 97702
Grande Loop 97701
Grandview Dr 97701
Granite Dr 97702
NE Grant Cir 97701
Grassland Ct 97702
Gray Squirrel Dr 97707
Gray Wolf Ln 97707
Grayson Way 97702
NW Great Pl 97701
NE Great Horned Pl 97701
Greatwood Loop 97702
Grebe Rd 97707
NE & NW Greeley Ave 97701
Green Lakes Loop 97702
NW Greenbriar 97701
NW Greenleaf Way 97701
Greenmont Dr 97702
NE & NW Greenwood Ave 97701
Greg Ct 97701
NW Greyhawk Ave 97701
Gribbling Rd 97701
Grimm Rd 97707
Groff Rd 97702
Gross Dr & Ln 97707
Guadalupe Way 97707
Guinevere Ct 97702
Gull Dr 97707
Gunwood Ln 97702
Guss Way 97707
Hackleman Ct 97702
Hakamore Dr 97701
NW Hale Ct 97701
NW Haleakala Way 97701
Haley Creek Pl 97702
Half Mile Ln 97701
Halfway Rd 97701
NE Hall Cir 97701
Halley St 97702
NE Halston Ct 97701
Hamby Rd 97701
Hamehook Rd 97701
Hamilton Ln 97702
Hammock Ct 97702
NE Hampton Ln 97701
Hanes Rd 97702
Hardy Rd 97701
Harlequin Dr 97707
SE Harley Ln 97702
NW Harmon Blvd 97701
Harmony Ln 97701
Harper Rd 97701
NW Harriman St 97701
Harrington Loop Rd 97701
Harris Way 97701
NW Hartford Ave 97701
Harvard Ct & Pl 97702
Harvest Ln 97701
NE Harvey Ln 97701
Hashknife Rd 97707
NW Hastings Pl 97701
NW Havre Ct 97701
Hawes Ln 97702
Hawk Ct 97702
Hawkin Pl 97701
Hawkview Rd 97701
NE & NW Hawthorne Ave 97701
SW Hayes Ave 97702
NW Healy Ct 97701
Hearthstone Ln 97702
Heath Ct 97702
NE Heather Ct 97701
NE Heavenly Dr 97701
Heidi Ct 97707
Heidi Ln 97702
Heierman Dr 97707
Helbrock Dr 97707
SE Helen Ln 97702
Hemlock Ct 97707
Hemlock Ln 97701
NW Hemmingway St 97701
Hereford Ave 97701
Heritage Ave 97702
Hermosa Rd 97707
Heron Loop 97702
Herschel Ct 97702
SE Heyburn St 97702
Hiawatha Ln 97702
Hicrest Pl 97701
Hidaway Hills Ct 97701
NE Hidden Brook Pl 97701
NE Hidden Valley Dr 97701
SE Hiddenwood Pl 97702
Hideaway Ln 97701
High Desert Ct & Ln 97701
NW High Lakes Loop 97701
High Lead Dr 97702
High Meadow Cir 97702
High Mowing Ln 97701
High Ridge Dr 97701
High Standard Dr 97701
NE Higher Ground Ave 97701
Highland Rd 97701
Highway 20 97701
N Highway 97 97701
S Highway 97
59800-61399 97702
S Highway 97
61396-91396 97708
61400-61598 97702
61401-61599 97702
NW Hill St 97701
SW Hill St 97702
NW Hill Point Dr 97701
Hiller Dr 97702
NW Hillpine Ct 97701
Hillridge Rd 97702
NW Hillside Park Dr 97701
Hilltop Pl 97701
SW Hillwood Ct 97702
Hilmer Creek Dr 97702
NW Hilton Ct 97701
Hitching Post Ln 97702
NW Hixon Ave 97701
SW Hobart Pl 97702
NE Hobbs Ct 97701
NE Holliday Ave 97701
Hollinshead Ct & Dr 97701
SE Hollis Ln 97702
NE Hollow Tree Ln 97701
Holly Ct 97702
Hollygrape St 97702
Homestead Way 97707
Honeysuckle Ln 97702
Honkers Ct & Ln 97702
NW Hood Pl 97701
NE Hoona Dr 97701
Hoopskirt Ct 97701
NE Hope Dr 97701
Hopi Rd 97702
Hopper Rd 97701
NW Horizon Dr 97701
Horizon Ridge Pl 97701
Horse Butte Rd & Trl 97702
Horse Ridge Frontage Rd 97701
Horsell Rd 97701
Horseman Ln 97701
Hosmer Lake Dr 97702
NW Hosmer Lake Dr 97701
Hubble St 97702
Huckleberry Pl 97702
NE Huettl Ln 97701
Hufflepuff Ct 97702
Hughes Rd 97701
Hummingbird Ln 97702
Hunnell Rd 97701
NW Hunter Pl 97701
Hunters Cir 97701
Huntington Rd 97707
Hurita Pl 97702
Hurst Ln 97702
Husky Ln 97707
NE Hyatt Ct 97701
Hyde Ln 97701
NW Idaho Ave 97701
Idanha Ct 97701
Illahee Dr 97702
Imperial Ave 97701
Imwalle Ct 97701
Independence Way 97701
Indian Summer Cir & Rd 97702
Indigo Ln 97707
NE Indigo Ln 97701
Indio Rd 97707
SW Industrial Way 97702
NE Innes Ln 97701
Innes Market Rd 97701
Innsbruck Ct 97702
NW Iowa Ave 97701
NE Iris Way 97701
SE Ironwood Cir & Ct 97702
Iroquois Cir 97702
NE & NW Irving Ave 97701
NE Isabella Ln 97701
NE Isaiah Dr 97701
Island Loop Way 97707
NW Ithaca Ave 97701
J D Estates Dr 97701
J W Brown Rd 97701
Jacinto Rd 97707
NW Jack Lake Ct 97701
Jack Pine Rd & Way 97707
NE Jackdaw Dr 97701
Jacklight Ln 97702
NE Jackson Ave 97701
NW Jacksonville Ave 97701
Jade Ct 97702
SW James Dr 97702
James Ln 97701
Jamie Way 97707
Jamison St 97701
Jan Dr 97701
Janalee Pl 97702
Jasmine Pl 97702
Jason Dr 97701
Jasper Pl 97702
Jayhawk Ln 97702
Jeffers Ct 97701
NW Jefferson Ct & Pl 97701
Jenay Ct 97702
NE Jennie Jo Ct 97701
Jennings Rd 97702
Jericho Rd 97701
Jessica Ct 97702
NW Jewell Way 97701
Jill Ave & Ct 97701
Jillian Ln 97707
Joan Ct 97702
Joe Neil Rd 97701
NE John Ct 97701
NW John Fremont St 97701
Johnson Rd 97701
Johnson Ranch Rd 97701
NE Jonahs Ct 97701
Jonathon Ct 97701
NE Jones Rd 97701
Joshua Ct 97701
Journey Ave & Dr 97701
Julias Trl 97701
NW Juniper Ln, Rd & St 97701
Juniperhaven Ave 97702
Justice Ct & Ln 97701
K Barr Rd 97701
Kaci Ln 97702
Kalamata Loop 97701
Kandi Ct 97701
NW Kansas Ave 97701
Karch Dr 97702
SE Karena Ct 97702
Kasserman Dr 97707
Katie Dr 97701
NE Kayak Loop 97701
SE Kayla Ct 97702
NE & NW Kearney Ave 97701
NE Keats Dr 97701
Keelally Ct 97702
NW Keenan Ct 97701

Keith Ct 97701
Keller Ct 97702
Kelly Ct 97701
NW Kelly Hill Ct 97701
Kemple Dr 97702
Kentucky Rd 97701
NW Kenwood Ct 97701
Kenzie Ave 97702
Kepler St 97702
Kevin Dr 97701
Keystone Ct 97702
Keyte Ln & Rd 97701
NW Kidd Pl 97701
Kiger Gorge Way 97702
Kilbourne Loop 97701
Kildonan Ct 97702
Killdeer Dr 97707
Killowan Dr 97702
NE Kim Ln 97701
Kimberly Ct 97702
Kindle Rock Loop 97702
King Arthur Ct 97702
King David Ave 97702
King Hezekiah Way 97702
King Jehu Way 97702
King Jeroboam Ave 97702
King Josiah Pl 97702
King Richard Ct 97702
King Saul Ave 97702
King Solomon Ct & Ln 97702
King Zedekiah Ave 97702
Kingfisher Dr 97707
Kings Ln 97702
Kingsberry Ct 97702
Kingsburg Rd 97707
NW Kingston Ave 97701
Kiowa Dr 97701
Kiowa Rd 97702
NW Kirkaldy Ct 97701
Kiwa Ln 97701
Klahani Dr 97702
Klippel Rd 97701
Knight Rd 97701
Knightsbridge Pl 97702
SW Knoll Ave 97702
Knott Rd 97702
Knoxville Blvd & Ct 97701
Kobe St 97702
Kodiak Ct 97701
Kodiak Ln 97707
Kohfield Rd 97701
Kona Dr 97702
Kramer Ln 97702
Kretch Ct 97701
Kristen St 97702
Kristin Ct 97701
Kuhlman Rd 97701
Kwinnum Dr 97702
NW Labiche Ln 97701
Ladera Rd 97702
Lady Bug Ln 97707
NE & NW Lafayette Ave 97701
Laguna Rd 97707
Laidlaw Ln 97701
E Lake Dr 97702
NW Lake Pl 97701
NW Lakemont Dr 97701
NE Lakeridge Dr 97701
NW Lakeside Pl 97701
Lakeview Dr 97702
Lamoine Ln 97701
Lana Way 97702
Lancaster St 97701
Lance Rd 97701
Lancelot Ave 97702
Lane Knolls Ct 97702
NE Lansing Ct 97701
NE Lapointe Ct 97701
NE Larado Way 97701
NE Laramie Way 97701
NE Larch Dr 97701
Lariat Ln 97701
Larkin Ct 97702
Larkspur Loop 97702
Larkview Rd 97701
Larkwood Dr 97702
Larsen Rd 97702
Larsen Brook Ln 97702
Latigo Ct 97701
NE Laurel Oak Dr 97701
Laurel Springs Ln 97702
SW Laurelhurst Way 97702
SE Laurelwood Pl 97702
NW Lava Ln & Rd 97701
Lava Flow Ln 97701
Lavacrest St 97701
NE Lavender Way 97701
NW Lawrence Ct 97701
Layton Ave 97701
Lazy River Dr 97707
Ledgestone Ct 97701
SE Lee Ln 97702
NW Lemhi Pass Dr 97701
NE Lena Pl 97701
NW Lepage Pl 97701
NE Lesley Pl 97701
NW Lewis St 97701
NW Lexington Ave 97701
NE Libby Pl 97701
Liberty Ln 97701
NE Lilac Ct 97701
Lily Way 97702
Limelight Dr 97702
Limestone Ave 97701
SE Lincoln Ln 97702
NW Lindsay Ct 97701
Linfield Ct 97702
NW Links Ln 97701
NE Linnea Dr 97701
NW Linster Pl 97701
Linton Loop 97702
Lisa Ln 97707
Lithic Ct 97701
Little John Ln 97702
Little River Ct & Dr 97707
Lively Ln 97707
Livengood Way 97702
Livingston Dr 97701
Lloyd Way 97707
NW Locke Ct 97701
NE Locksley Dr 97701
Loco Rd 97701
Lodgepole Dr 97702
Lodgepole Ln 97707
Log Bridge Dr 97707
Log Cabin Ln 97707
Logan Ave 97701
NW Loggan Ct 97701
SE Logsden St 97702
Lois Way 97702
NW Lolo Dr 97701
Loma Vista Dr 97701
Lone Cow Dr 97702
Lonesome Pine Rd 97707
SW Long Creek Ln 97702
NE Longfellow Ct 97701
Longhorn Ct 97701
SW Longview St 97702
Lookout Dr 97701
S Loop Pl 97701
Lora Ln 97702
Lorrin Pl 97702
Los Serranos Dr 97701
Lost Lake Dr 97702
Lost Rider Loop 97707
Lost Valley Ct 97702
SE Lostine Cir 97702
NE Lotno Dr 97701
NE Lotus Dr 97701
NW Louisiana Ave 97701
Lowe Ln 97701
Lower Meadow Dr 97701
NW Lower Village Rd 97701
Loy Ln 97702
Lucia St 97702
NE Lucinda Ct 97701
NW Lucus Ct 97701
Lunar Dr 97707
Lupine Ave 97701
Lydia Dr 97701
Lyman Pl 97701
NE Lynda Ln 97701
Lynn Way 97701
Lynx Ln 97702
Lynx Rd 97707
Lyon Ct 97702
Lyra Dr 97701
Lysander Pl 97701
NE Lytle St 97701
NE Mable Ct 97701
Macalpine Loop 97702
NE Madison Ave 97701
Magnolia Ln 97702
Mahogany St 97702
Mahsie Ct 97702
Maid Marian Ct 97702
Mainline Rd 97702
Majestic Ct & Loop 97701
Majestic View Ct 97702
NE Majesty Ln 97701
NE Maker Way 97701
Mallard Dr 97707
Mammoth Dr 97702
Manchester Ave & Ct 97701
Manhae Ln & Loop 97702
SE Manley Pl 97702
Manzanita Ct 97701
Manzanita Ln 97702
Maple Dr 97707
Mare Ct 97702
NE Marea Dr 97701
Margaret Ln 97701
SW Maricopa Dr 97702
Marigold Ln 97702
Mariner Dr 97701
NE Marion Pl 97701
Mariposa Ln 97701
NE Mark Ct 97701
Marken Pl & St 97701
Marlboro Dr 97701
Marlece Ln 97702
Marlin Ct 97701
Marsh Rd 97701
Marsh Hawk Rd 97707
Marsh Orchid Ct & Dr 97701
NE Marshall Ave 97701
Martee Ln 97701
Marten Ln 97707
Martingale Cir 97701
Mary Way 97701
NE Mary Rose Pl 97701
NE Mason Rd 97701
NW Massey Dr 97701
Mathers Rd 97701
NE Matson Rd 97701
Maverick Ct & Ln 97701
Mayberry Ct 97702
Mayfield Dr 97707
NE Mays Ave 97701
Mazama Pl 97702
Mcardle Rd 97702
NW Mccann Ave 97701
NE Mccartney Dr 97701
Mcclain Dr 97701
Mcclellan Ln & Rd 97702
Mcconnell Dr 97701
NW Mccook Ct 97701
NW Mccready Dr 97701
NW Mcdermott Pl 97701
Mcgilvray Rd 97702
Mcgrath Rd 97701
NW Mckay Ave 97701
SE & SW Mckinley Ave 97702
NE Mclaughlin Pl 97701
Mcmullin Dr 97702
NW Meadow Ct 97701
Meadow Ln 97701
NE Meadow Ln 97701
Meadow Way 97707
Meadowbrook Dr 97702
NE Medical Center Dr 97701
Medicine Hat Ln 97702
Meeks Trl 97702
NE Meerkat Ave 97701
Megan Ct 97701
NW Meissner Ct 97701
NE Meister Pl 97701
Mel Ct 97702
NW Meldrum Ct 97701
Melinda Ct 97701
Melody Ln 97702
NW Melville Dr 97701
NE Mendenhall Dr 97701
Merced Rd 97707
NW Merchant Way 97701
Mercury Pl 97701
Merganser Ct & Dr 97707
NW Merlot Ln 97701
Merriewood Ct & Ln 97702
Merritt Ct 97702
NE Mesa Ct 97701
Mesa Verde Ct & Pl 97701
Meteor Dr 97707
NW Metke Pl 97701
Metolius Dr 97702
Meulink Dr 97702
Meyer Dr 97702
Miday Way 97701
Miles Ct 97702
Milky Way 97707
Mill Rd 97701
SW Mill Pond Pl 97702
Mill Terrace Pl 97702
SW Mill View Way 97702
Millbrook Ln 97702
Millcrest Pl 97702
SE Miller Ave 97702
NE Milltown Ln 97701
Milo Ave 97702
NW Milton Ct 97701
NW Milwaukee Ave 97701
Mimosa Dr 97701
SE Minam Ave 97702
Minaret Cir 97702
Mini Ln 97702
Mink Ct 97707
NW Minnesota Ave 97701
Minnetonka Cir & Ln 97702
Mira Cir 97701
Miramar Dr 97702
Mirror Lake Pl 97702
Mission Rdg 97702
NE Mistletoe Ct 97701
Misty Ln 97702
Mock Rd 97701
Mockingbird Ln 97707
Modoc Ln 97702
Mohawk Cir & Rd 97702
NE Monroe Ln 97701
Montana Way 97701
Montara Dr 97701
NE Monte Vista Ln 97701
NE & NW Monterey Ave & Mews 97701
NW Monterey Pines Dr 97701
Monticello Dr 97701
Montrose Pass St 97702
Moon Mountain Ct 97702
NE Moonglow Ct 97701
Moonlight Ct 97702
NE Moonlight Dr 97701
Moonstone Ln 97701
NW Moore Ct 97701
Moorman Ln 97701
SE Moorwood Ct 97702
Moraine Ct 97702
NW Morelock Ct 97701
SW Morgan Loop & Rd 97701
Morning Tide Pl 97702
Morningstar Ct & Dr 97701
Morningwood Ct & Way 97701
Morrill Rd 97701
NW Morris Ct 97701
SE Morton Ct 97702
Moss Rock Dr 97701
Mount Bachelor Ct & Dr 97702
Mount Faith Pl 97702
Mount Hope Ln 97702
Mount Vista Dr 97702
Mountain Breezes Ct 97702
Mountain Goat Ln 97707
Mountain High Loop 97702
NE Mountain Oak Ln 97701
Mountain Sheep Ln 97707
Mountain View Ct 97707
Mountain View Dr 97701
NE Mountain Willow 97701
Mountaineer Way 97702
Mt Hood Dr & Pl 97701
Mt Jefferson Pl 97701
Mt Mcloughlin Ln 97701
Mt Shasta Ct & Dr 97701
Mt Thielsen Dr 97701
NW Mt Washington Dr 97701
SW Mt Washington Dr 97702
NW Mueller Ave 97701
Mule Deer Ln 97707
Munson St 97707
Murphy Rd 97702
Murray Rd 97701
Mustang Ct 97701
SE Mustang Pl 97702
Mustang Rd 97701
Mutt Ct 97701
SE Myrtlewood St 97702
SW Nancy Way 97702
Narnia Pl 97702
NW Nashville Ave 97701
Nasu Pl 97701
Nasu Park Loop 97701
NE Nates Pl 97701
NE Nathan Dr 97701
Navajo Cir & Rd 97702
Nawadaha Way 97702
NE Neff Rd 97701
Neighbors Dr 97702
NE Neil Way 97701
Nels Anderson Pl & Rd 97701
Nelson Rd 97701
Nest Pine Dr 97707
Newbedford Cir 97702
Newberry Dr 97702
Newcastle Dr 97702
Newcomb Rd 97701
Newhall Pl 97701
Newport Ave & Hls 97701
NW Newport Hills Dr 97701
News Ln 97702
Niagara Ct 97701
Nicklaus Dr 97701
Nicole Ct 97701
Nicolette Dr 97701
NW Nightfall Cir 97701
Nighthawk Rd 97702
NE Nikki Ct 97701
Nino Ct 97701
Nisika Ct 97702
Noe Dr & St 97701
Nolan Ct 97701
NW Nordeen Way 97701
NW Nordic Ave 97701
NE North Civet Ct 97701
NE North Pilot Butte Dr 97701
NW Northcliff 97701
NE Northview Dr 97701
NE & NW Norton Ave 97701
Norwalk Rd 97707
Norwood Ct 97701
Notch Rapids Ct 97702
Nova Loop 97701
Nugget Ave & Pl 97702
NE Nuttail Ct 97701
NE O B Riley Rd 97701
NE Oakley Ct 97701
Oakview Dr 97701
Oakwood Pl 97702
Oasis Pl 97702
Obernolte Rd 97701
Obie Way 97701
NW Obrien Ct 97701
Obsidian Ave & Rd 97702
Oceanspray Way 97702
Ochoco Cir 97702
NE Ocker Dr 97701
Oconnor Way 97701
Odell Lake Dr 97702
NW Ogden Ave 97701
Ogles Rd 97701
Okanagan Ln 97702
NW Okane Ct 97701
Old Bend Redmond Hwy 97701
Old Deschutes Rd 97701
Old Red Rd 97702
Old Rock House Rd 97702
Old Wood Rd 97707
Olivia Ct 97701
NE & NW Olney Ave & Ct 97701
NW Olympic Ct 97701
Omer Dr 97701
NW Oneil Pl 97701
Onyx St 97702
Opal Dr & Ln 97702
NW Ordway Ave 97701
NW Oregon Ave 97701
Oriole Ln 97701
Orion Dr 97702
Osage Rd 97702
Osprey Ct & Rd 97707
Osprey Nest Pl 97702
NE Otelah Pl 97701
SW Otter Way 97702
Otter Run Ln 97701
Outback 97702
NW Outlook Vista Dr 97701
Over Under Ct 97701
NW Overlook Dr 97701
Overton Pl 97701
Overtree Rd 97701
Overturf Ave & Ct 97702
Ox Spur Ct 97701
Oxbow Ln 97701
Oxnard Rd 97707
NE Pacific Crest Dr 97701
NW Pacific Park Ln 97701
Paddle Ct 97702
Painted Ridge Loop 97702
Painters Ct 97701
SE Paiute Way 97702
Paladin Dr 97701
NW Palisades Dr 97701
Palla Ln 97701
NE Palmer Dr 97701
SE Palmwood Ct 97702
Paloma Dr 97701
Pam Pl 97702
NW Panama St 97701
NW Panorama Dr 97701
Paradise Aly 97701
Paramount Dr 97701
Park Pl & Way 97701
Park Commons Dr 97701
Park Vista Cir 97702
Parker Ln 97701
NE Parkridge Dr 97701
Parkside Pl 97702
NE Parkview Ct 97701
Parkway Ln 97701
Parkwood Ct 97702
Parr Ln 97702
Parrell Rd 97702
Pasadena Rd 97707
Patriot Ln 97701
NE Patterson Cir 97701
NE Paula Dr 97701
Paulina Ln 97702
Pawnee Ln & Rd 97702
Peacock Ln 97701
Peak Ave 97702
SW Peak View Pl 97702
Peale St 97701
Pearl Ln 97701
Pecoraro Loop 97701
NW Pee Wee Ct 97701
Peerless Ct 97701
Pelican Dr 97701
SE & SW Pelton Pl 97702
NW Pence Ln 97701
Penhollow Ln 97702
NE Penn Ave 97701
Penny Ln 97701
Peony Pl 97702
NW Peoples Ct 97701
NW Perlette Ln 97701
Perrigan Dr 97702
NW Perspective Dr 97701
Peterman Ln 97701
Peterson Ridge Rd 97701
Pettigrew Ct & Rd 97702
Peyton Pl 97707
Pharaoh Ct 97701
Pheasant Cir, Ct & Ln 97701
Philly Ave 97702
NW Phils Loop 97701
Phoenix Way 97701
NW Pickett Ct 97701
Pikes Ct 97701
NE Pikes Peak Rd 97701
SE Pilatus Ln 97702
NW Pilot View Ct 97701
Pima Rd 97702
Pine Dr 97702
Pine Holw 97702
Pine Ln 97701
Pine Cone Dr 97702
Pine Knoll Cir 97701
Pine Mountain Rd 97701
Pine Vista Dr 97702
Pinebrook Blvd 97702
NW Pinecrest Ct 97701
Pinehaven Ave 97702
Pinehurst Rd 97701
Pinewood Ave 97707
NE Pinewood Dr 97701
Pinewood Rd 97702
NE Pinnacle Pl 97701
NW Pinot Ct 97701
Pintail Dr 97707
Pioneer Loop 97701
SE Piper Dr 97702
SE Pitts Dr 97702
Piute Cir 97702
Plainview Ct & Rd 97701
Plateau Dr 97701
Platinum Dr & Way 97702
Pleasant View Ct 97707
Pocahontas Ln 97702
Poe Sholes Dr 97701
Pohaku Rd 97701
SE Polaris Ct 97702
NW Polarstar Ave 97701
Pond Meadow Ave & Ct 97702
Ponderosa Loop 97701
Ponderosa St 97702
Ponderosa Cascade Dr 97701
Pony Ave 97701
Pony Express Way 97707
Poplar St 97702
Poppy Pl 97702
Porcupine Dr & Rd 97702
Porter Pl 97702
NW Portland Ave 97701
NE Post Ave 97701
Postage Due St 97702
Powder Mountain Ct 97702
Powderhorn Dr 97701
Powell Ln 97707
NW Powell Butte Hwy & Loop 97701
SW Powerhouse Dr 97702
Powers Rd 97702
NW Prairie Pl 97701
NW Precision Ln 97701
SW Prestwick Pl 97702
Prince John Ct 97702
NW Princess Ct 97701
Princeton Loop 97702
NE Professional Ct 97701
Promise Pl 97701
Promontory Ct & Dr 97701
Prong Horn Dr 97707

Pronghorn Club Dr ... 97701
Pronghorn Estates Dr ... 97701
NW Proshop Dr ... 97701
Prospector Loop ... 97702
NE Providence Dr ... 97701
NW Puccoon Ct ... 97701
Puffin Dr ... 97701
Pumice Butte Rd ... 97702
NE Purcell Blvd ... 97701
NE Purser Ave ... 97701
NW Putnam Ln & Rd ... 97701
Quail Dr & Ln ... 97701
SW Quail Butte Pl ... 97702
E & W Quail Haven Dr ... 97701
Quail Pine Loop ... 97702
Quail Ridge Rd ... 97701
Quail Run Pl ... 97701
Quartz Hill Rd ... 97707
Quay Ct ... 97702
Quebec Ct & Dr ... 97702
S Queens Dr ... 97702
NE Quiet Canyon Dr ... 97701
NE Quiet Ridge Ln ... 97701
NW Quiet River Ln ... 97701
NE Quimby Ave ... 97701
NW Quincy Ave ... 97701
NW Quinn Creek Loop ... 97701
R U Guelfi Rd ... 97707
Rabbitbrush Dr ... 97701
NE Rachel Ct ... 97701
Radcliffe Cir ... 97702
NW Rademacher Pl ... 97701
Rae Rd ... 97702
Rafters Ct ... 97702
Rail Dr ... 97707
SE Railroad St ... 97702
NW Rainbow Ct ... 97701
Rainbow Lake Trl ... 97702
NW Rainbow Ridge Dr ... 97701
NE Rainier Dr ... 97701
Raintree Dr ... 97702
NE Raleigh Ct ... 97701
NE Rambling Ln ... 97701
SE Ramsay Rd ... 97702
Ranch Village Ct & Dr ... 97701
Rancho Rd ... 97702
Randall Ct ... 97702
Range Pl ... 97702
Ranger Way ... 97702
Rani Way ... 97707
Rastovich Rd ... 97702
Raven Ct & Ln ... 97701
NE Ravenwood Dr ... 97701
Rawhide Dr ... 97702
NW Rawlins Ct ... 97701
Raymond Ct ... 97701
Rebecca Ln ... 97701
Red Band Rd ... 97701
Red Bear Ln ... 97707
Red Fox Ln ... 97707
Red Meadow Ct ... 97702
NE Red Oak Dr ... 97701
NE Red Rock Ln ... 97701
Red Sky Ln ... 97702
NE Redbay Ln ... 97701
NW Redfield Cir ... 97701
NE Redrose Ct ... 97701
Redside Ct ... 97701
Redwing Ln ... 97702
Reed Ln ... 97702
Reed Market Rd ... 97702
NW Regency St ... 97701
NW Remarkable Dr ... 97701
Remington Dr ... 97707
Remuda Ln ... 97701
Renee Ct ... 97701
Repine Dr ... 97701
Research Rd ... 97701
NW Reserve Camp Ct ... 97701
Reservoir Rd ... 97701
NE & NW Revere Ave ... 97701
SE Rice Way ... 97702
Richard Way ... 97707
Richardson Rd ... 97701
NE Richmond Ct ... 97701
Rickard Rd ... 97702
Ridge Dr & Hts ... 97702
Ridge Falls Pl ... 97702
Ridgecrest Rd ... 97701
Ridgefield Dr ... 97701
Ridgeview Ct, Dr & Pl E & W ... 97702
Ridgewater Ct & Loop ... 97702
Ridgewood Dr ... 97701
Rigel Way ... 97702
Rim Lake Ct ... 97702
Rimfire Rd ... 97702
NW Rimrock Ct, Dr & Rd ... 97701
Rincon Ave ... 97702
Ring Bearer Ct ... 97702
Ritz Pl ... 97702
River Rd ... 97701
River Bend Dr ... 97702
River Bluff Trl ... 97702
River Loop Dr E & W ... 97707
River Point Ct ... 97707
NW River Trail Pl ... 97701
River Woods Cir & Dr ... 97702
NW Riverfront St ... 97701
NW Rivermist Dr ... 97701
NW Riverside Blvd ... 97701
Riverstone Dr ... 97701
Riverview Ave ... 97701
SE Riviera Dr ... 97702
NW Roanoke Ave ... 97701
Roats Ln ... 97702
Robal Ln & Rd ... 97701
NW Robert Way ... 97701
Robin Ave ... 97701
NE Robin Ct ... 97701
Robin Ln ... 97707
Robin Hood Ln ... 97702
NE Robinson St ... 97701
Robinwood Pl ... 97702
Rocca Way ... 97702
SW Rochambeau Rd ... 97701
Rocher Way ... 97701
Rock Bluff Cir & Ln ... 97702
Rock Canyon Rd ... 97701
NE Rock Chuck Dr ... 97701
Rock Island Ln ... 97701
Rock Park Dr ... 97701
Rock Springs Ct & Rd ... 97701
Rocking Horse Ct & Rd ... 97702
NW Rocklyn Rd ... 97701
NE Rockridge Dr ... 97701
Rockway Ter ... 97702
NW Rockwood Ln ... 97701
Rocky Top Ct ... 97702
Rodeo Ct & Dr ... 97701
Rogers Rd ... 97701
Roland Pl ... 97701
Rolen Ave ... 97702
Roller Coaster Ct ... 97702
Romaine Village Way ... 97702
SE & SW Roosevelt Ave ... 97702
Roper Ln ... 97701
Ropp Ln ... 97702
Rorick Dr ... 97701
NE Rosemary Dr ... 97701
Rosemead Rd ... 97707
NE Rosewood Dr ... 97701
NE Ross Rd ... 97701
Roughrider Ln ... 97702
Rowallan Ct ... 97702
NE Roxy Pl ... 97701
NE Royal Ct ... 97701
Royal Oak Cir ... 97701
Ruby Pl ... 97702
SE Ruby Peak Ln ... 97702
Rudi Rd ... 97701
NE Rumgay Ln ... 97701
NW Runyun Ct ... 97701
Russell Dr ... 97701
Rustic Ln ... 97702
Rustic Canyon Rd ... 97702
Rusticate Rd ... 97702
NE Saber Dr ... 97701
NW Sacagawea Ln ... 97701
Sacramento Rd ... 97707
Saddle Dr ... 97701
NE Saddle Rock Ct ... 97701
Saddleback Dr, Ln & Pl ... 97701
Sage Ct ... 97701
Sage Canyon Ct ... 97701
Sage Creek Dr ... 97702
Sage Ranch Rd ... 97701
Sage Stone Loop ... 97702
Sagebrush Ln ... 97701
Sager Loop ... 97702
Saghali Ct ... 97702
NW Saginaw Ave ... 97701
Saint Cloud Ct ... 97701
Saint George Ct ... 97702
Sally Ct & Ln ... 97702
Salmonberry Ct ... 97702
NE Salvia Way ... 97701
NW Sample Ct ... 97701
NE Sams Loop ... 97701
NW Sand Lily Way ... 97701
NE & NW Sandalwood Dr & Loop ... 97701
Sandpiper Rd ... 97707
NE Sandy Dr ... 97701
Santa Cruz Ave ... 97701
Sapphire Ln ... 97702
Sarah Dr ... 97702
NE Saranac Pl ... 97701
NW Sargent Way ... 97701
Saros Ln ... 97701
Saskatoon Ln ... 97702
Satterlee Way ... 97707
Savage Dr ... 97707
NE Savannah Dr ... 97701
Sawtooth Mountain Ln ... 97702
NW Sawyer ... 97701
Sawyer Reach Ct & Ln ... 97701
NW Sawyer Trail Pl ... 97701
Scale House Rd ... 97702
Scalehouse Ct & Loop ... 97702
NW Scandia Loop ... 97701
NE Scarlet Ct ... 97701
Scarlet Sage Way ... 97702
Scaup Dr ... 97707
Scenic Dr ... 97701
NW Scenic Heights Dr ... 97701
Schaeffer Dr ... 97701
Schibel Rd ... 97701
Schmidt Rd ... 97701
School House Rd ... 97707
SE Scott St ... 97702
Scotts Bluff Pl ... 97702
Scottsdale Dr ... 97701
NW Sean Ct ... 97701
Seaton Loop ... 97702
NE Sedalia Loop ... 97701
Sedonia Ln ... 97702
Selkirk Mountain Way ... 97702
Seminole Cir ... 97702
SE Sena Ct ... 97702
Serenity Way ... 97701
Service Rd ... 97701
Seventh Mountain Dr ... 97702
NE Seward Ave ... 97701
NE Shadow Brook Pl ... 97701
SE Shadowood Dr ... 97702
SE Shady Pines Pl ... 97702
Shahala Ct ... 97702
Shalimar Ct ... 97702
NE Shane Ln ... 97701
Shaniko Ln ... 97701
Shannon Ct ... 97702
NE Sharkey Ter ... 97701
Sharp Dr & Pl ... 97707
NW Shasta Pl ... 97701
Shaw Rd ... 97702
Shawnee Cir ... 97707
SE Shea Ct ... 97702
NE Shelley Way ... 97701
Shepard Pl & Rd ... 97701
NE Sheridan Ave ... 97701
Sherman Rd ... 97701
Sherwood Ct ... 97702
Shetland Loop ... 97701
NW Shevlin Rdg ... 97701
NW Shevlin Crest Dr ... 97701
SW Shevlin Hixon Dr ... 97702
NW Shevlin Meadow Dr ... 97701
NW Shevlin Park Rd ... 97701
NW Shields Dr ... 97701
NW Shiraz Ct ... 97701
Shire Ln ... 97702
NE Shirley Ct ... 97701
Sholes Rd ... 97702
Shoshone Cir & Rd ... 97702
Sidewinder ... 97702
NE Sierra Ct & Dr ... 97701
NW Silas Dr & Pl ... 97701
Silver Ct ... 97702
NW Silver Buckle ... 97701
Silver Cloud Ct ... 97702
Silver Fox Dr ... 97707
SW Silver Lake Blvd ... 97702
Silver Sage St ... 97702
Silver Tip Ct ... 97702
Silverado Dr ... 97701
Silverado Valley Ave & Ln ... 97702
SE Silvis Ln ... 97702
Silvis Rd ... 97701
Simon Rd ... 97701
SW Simpson Ave ... 97702
Sioux Ln ... 97702
Sirocco Ln ... 97701
Sisemore Rd ... 97701
NW Sisemore St ... 97701
SW Sisemore St ... 97702
Skene Trl ... 97702
Sky Harbor Dr ... 97702
SE Skylark Dr ... 97702
Skyline Dr ... 97701
Skyline Ranch Rd
19100-19199 ... 97701
61200-61299 ... 97702
63100-63399 ... 97701
NW Skyline Ranch Rd ... 97701
Skyline View Dr ... 97702
NW Skyliner Summit Loop ... 97701
NW Skyliners Rd ... 97701
Skyview Ln ... 97702
Skywagon Dr ... 97701
Skyway ... 97702
NW Slagsvold ... 97701
Slalom Way ... 97702
SW Sleepy Ct ... 97702
Smith And Wesson Ct ... 97701
NE Smoke Stack Ln ... 97701
Smokey Butte Dr ... 97701
Smokey Ridge Rd ... 97701
Snap Shot Loop ... 97702
Snow Cap Pl ... 97701
Snow Cap Rd ... 97707
Snow Creek Ln & Rd ... 97701
Snow Goose Ct & Rd ... 97707
Snow Peaks Dr ... 97701
NE Snow Willow ... 97701
Snowberry Pl ... 97702
NE Snowbird Ct ... 97701
Snowbrush Dr ... 97702
Snowcap Ct ... 97701
Snowmass ... 97702
NE Soaring Ct ... 97701
Sockeye Pl ... 97701
Soda Springs Dr ... 97702
Soft Breeze Ct ... 97701
Soft Tail Dr & Loop ... 97702
Solar Dr ... 97707
Solitude Ln ... 97702
Solstice Ct & Dr ... 97701
Someday Way ... 97701
Somerset Dr ... 97702
Sonata Way ... 97702
Songbird Ln ... 97702
NW Sonora Dr ... 97701
NE Sonya Ct ... 97701
Sorrento Pl ... 97702
South Rd ... 97701
Sparrow Ct ... 97702
Sparrow Hawk Cir ... 97701
Spencer Wells Rd ... 97701
Spencers Crossing Ln ... 97702
Spikerman Ct ... 97707
Spinnaker St ... 97701
Splashy Rapids Ct ... 97702
Splendor Ln ... 97702
Sprig Ct ... 97702
NE Spring Creek Pl ... 97701
Spring River Dr, Loop & Rd ... 97707
NE Spring Water Pl ... 97701
Springcrest Dr ... 97702
SE Springer Ct ... 97702
Springtree Ct ... 97702
Spunky Dr ... 97701
NW Squirreltail Loop ... 97701
NW St Helens Pl ... 97701
NW Staats St ... 97701
Stacy Ln ... 97701
Stafford Loop ... 97702
Stag Dr ... 97701
Stagestop Dr ... 97707
NE Stalker Ct ... 97701
Stanley Way ... 97701
NW Stannium Rd ... 97701
NE Stanton Ave ... 97701
Star Cir & Way ... 97701
Star Ridge Ct ... 97701
Star Thistle Ln ... 97701
Stardrift Dr ... 97702
Starfire Ridge Ct ... 97702
Starlight Dr ... 97702
Starling Dr ... 97701
SW Starshine Ln ... 97701
NW Starview Dr ... 97701
Starwood Dr ... 97701
NW State St ... 97701
Steamboat ... 97702
Steens Ln ... 97702
Steens Mountain Ct & Loop ... 97702
NW Steidl Rd ... 97701
Stellar Dr ... 97707
Stem Pl ... 97701
Stenkamp Rd ... 97701
Stevens Rd ... 97702
Stirling Dr ... 97702
Stone Wall Ct ... 97701
Stonebrook Dr & Loop ... 97701
Stonegate Dr ... 97702
NW Stonehill Dr ... 97701
NW Stonepine Dr ... 97701
NW Stoneridge ... 97701
Stonewood Dr ... 97702
Stony Ridge Rd ... 97701
Stormy Ln ... 97701
NW Stover ... 97701
SE Stratford Ct ... 97702
NW Strath Way ... 97701
Strawberry Mountain Ct ... 97702
Strawline Rd ... 97702
Strickler Ave ... 97701
Stub Pl ... 97701
Stud Ct ... 97702
NE Studio Rd ... 97701
Sturgeon Rd ... 97701
Sue Rd ... 97701
SE Suffolk Pl ... 97702
Sugar Mill Loop ... 97702
Sugarbush Ln ... 97702
Sum View Dr ... 97702
SW Summer Lake Dr ... 97702
Summer Shade Dr ... 97702
NW Summerfield ... 97701
NW Summerhill Dr ... 97702
Summerwalk Pl ... 97702
Summerwood Way ... 97702
NW Summit Dr ... 97701
Sun Ct ... 97707
SE Sun Ln ... 97702
Sun Country Dr ... 97707
Sun Meadow Way ... 97702
NW Sun Ray Ct ... 97701
Sunbeam Ln ... 97701
Sunbrook Dr ... 97702
Sunburst Ct ... 97702
Sunburst St ... 97701
Sunderland Way ... 97701
Sunflower Ln ... 97702
Sunglow Ct ... 97701
Sunny Breeze Ln ... 97702
Sunridge Dr ... 97702
Sunrise Cir ... 97701
Sunset Dr & Pl ... 97701
Sunset View Dr ... 97702
Sunshine Way ... 97702
SE Sunwood Ct ... 97702
Superior Ct ... 97702
Supreme Ct ... 97702
Sutherland Ct ... 97702
Suttle Lake Ct ... 97702
Swalley Rd ... 97701
Swallows Nest Ln ... 97701
Swan Rd ... 97707
Swarens Ave ... 97702
Sweetgrass Dr & Ln ... 97702
Switchback Ct ... 97701
NE Sycamore Ct ... 97701
Sydney Harbor Dr ... 97702
Sylvan Loop ... 97701
SE & SW Taft Ave ... 97702
NE Tahoe Ct ... 97701
Tailblock Rd ... 97702
NW Talapus Ct ... 97701
Tall Mountain Cir ... 97702
Tall Pine Ave ... 97702
SW Tall Timber Ct ... 97702
Tall Tree Ct ... 97702
NE Talon Ct ... 97701
Talus Pl ... 97701
Tam Lake Ct ... 97702
Tam Mcarthur Loop ... 97702
Tamar Ln ... 97702
Tamarack Rd ... 97707
Tamoli Ln ... 97701
Tan Oak Pl ... 97707
Tanglewood Rd ... 97701
Tango Creek Ave ... 97701
SW Tanner Ct ... 97702
Tanya Dr ... 97702
Taos Ct ... 97702
Tapadera St ... 97702
Tara Ln ... 97702
Taralon Pl ... 97702
Targee Dr ... 97702
NE Taurus Ct ... 97701
NE Taylor Ct ... 97701
SE Teakwood Dr ... 97702
Teal Rd ... 97702
SE Tee Ct ... 97702
Tekampe Rd ... 97702
NE Telima Ln ... 97701
Telluride Dr ... 97702
SE Tempest Dr ... 97702
Ten Barr Trl ... 97701
Ten Barr Ranch Rd ... 97701
Ten Peaks Ct ... 97701
Tennessee Rd ... 97701
SW Tenos Ct ... 97702
NW Terra Meadow Dr ... 97701
Terrace Ln ... 97702
Terrango Ave ... 97701
Terry Dr & Ln ... 97701
Teton Ct & Ln ... 97702
SE Textron Dr ... 97702
SW Theater Dr ... 97702
Thimbleberry Way ... 97702
Tholstrup Dr ... 97707
Thomas Dr ... 97702
NE Thompson Dr ... 97701
Thornhill Ln ... 97701
NW Three Sisters Dr ... 97701
Thunder Rd ... 97702
Thunderbird ... 97702
NE & NW Thurston Ave ... 97701
Tiberon Pl ... 97702
NE Tierra Rd ... 97701
NE Tiffany Ln ... 97701
Timberline ... 97702
Timberline Ct ... 97701
Timland Ln ... 97701
NW Tin Pan Aly ... 97701
Todd Rd ... 97701
Todd Lake Ct ... 97702
NW Todds Crest Dr ... 97701
Tokatee Lake Ct ... 97702
Tomahawk St ... 97702
NE Tombstone Way ... 97701
Top Knot Ln ... 97701
Topaz Ct ... 97702
Topwater Ct ... 97701
Torkelson Rd ... 97701
Torrance Rd ... 97707
NW Torrey Pines Dr ... 97701
NW Torsway St ... 97701
SW Touchmark Way ... 97702
Tourmaline Ln ... 97701
NW Toussaint Dr ... 97701
NW Tower Rock Rd ... 97701
Town Ct & Dr ... 97701
NE Tracker Ct ... 97701
Trader Ln ... 97707
Trail Scout ... 97707
Trailblazer Ln ... 97702
Trailmere Cir ... 97707
Trap Ct ... 97702
Travelers Pl ... 97702
Travis Rd ... 97702
Tree Duck Rd ... 97707
Treeland Ct ... 97707
NW Trenton Ave ... 97701
Triple Knot Rd ... 97702
Tristar Dr ... 97701
Tristen Way ... 97701
SW Troon Ave ... 97702
Trout Ln ... 97701
SE & SW Truman Ave ... 97702
Trumpeter Ln ... 97707
NE Tucson Way ... 97701
Tulip Way ... 97702
NW Tumalo Ave ... 97701
Tumalo Cir ... 97702
Tumalo Pl ... 97701
Tumalo Rd ... 97701
Tumalo Reservoir Rd ... 97701
Tumalo Rim Ct & Dr ... 97701
Tumbleweed Ct & Dr ... 97701
SW Turnberry Pl ... 97702
Turquoise Rd ... 97702
Turret Ct ... 97701
Tuscany Dr ... 97702
Tuscarora Ln ... 97702
Tweed Rd ... 97701
NE Tweet Pl ... 97701
NW Twilight Dr ... 97701
Twin Bridges Rd ... 97701
NE Twin Knolls Dr ... 97701
Twin Lakes Loop ... 97702
Twin Rivers Ct & Dr ... 97707
Tyler Rd ... 97701
NE Ulysses Dr ... 97701
Umatilla Cir ... 97702
NW Underhill Pl ... 97701
NE Underwood Ave ... 97701
NW Union St ... 97701
Upland Rd ... 97707
NW Upper Rim Pl ... 97701
SW Upper Terrace Dr ... 97702
SE Urania Ln ... 97702
Ute Ln ... 97702
NW Utica Ave ... 97701
NW & NE Vail Ave & Ln ... 97701
Vail Run Ct ... 97702
Valentine St ... 97701
Valeview Dr ... 97701
SE Valleywood Pl ... 97702
Vancouver Ln ... 97702
Vandervert Rd ... 97707
SW Vantage Pointway ... 97702
Varco Rd ... 97701
NW Vardon Ct ... 97701
Vassar Pl ... 97702

Vega St 97702
SE Velocette Ln 97702
Velvet Ct 97707
SE Ventura Pl 97702
Venture Ln 97707
NW Vermont St 97701
NE Veronica Ln 97701
Veryl Ct 97702
Via Bonita 97702
Via Diamante 97701
NW Via Palazzo 97701
Via Sandia 97702
Via Sierra 97702
Via Toscana 97701
SE Vickie Ct 97702
NW Vicksburg Ave 97701
NE Victor Pl 97701
Victoria Ln 97702
Victory Loop 97702
View Ln 97701
Viking Ave & Ct 97701
NE Village Ct 97701
Village Ln 97702
Village Office Ct 97702
Villano Pl 97702
SE Vine Ln 97702
Vintage Ln 97701
Violet Ln 97702
SE Virginia Rd 97702
Vista Bonita Dr 97701
Vogt Rd 97701
Volare Ln 97702
Voltera Pl 97702
SE Waco Dr 97702
Wagon Trl 97707
Wagon Master Way 97707
Wagon Tree Ct 97702
Wagontire Way 97701
NE Wakefield Pl 97701
Waldron Trl 97701
Walker Rd 97701
NW Wall St 97701
SW Wall St 97702
Wallace Rd 97701
NE Waller Dr 97701
Walsenberg Pl 97702
Walter Ct 97702
Walton Rd 97701
Wandalea Dr 97701
Wapiti Ct 97702
Wapiti Way 97701
Warbow Pl 97701
Ward Rd 97702
NE Warner Pl 97701
Wasatch Mountain Ln 97702
Water Fowl Ln 97702
Watercourse Way 97701
Watercress Way 97701
Waterfall Ln 97702
Waterfront Ct 97702
NE Watson Dr 97701
NE Watt Way 97701
Waugh Rd 97701
NE Waverly Ct 97701
Weatherby Ct 97701
NE Webster Ave 97701
Wecoma Ct 97702
NE Weddell St 97701
NE Weeping Willow Dr 97701
Weinhard Ct 97702
NW Welcome Ct 97701
Wellington St 97701
Wells Rd 97707
NE Wells Acres Rd 97701
West St 97701
NW West Hills Ave 97701
Westcampbell Rd 97702
SW Westpine Pl 97702
Westridge Ave 97702
Westview Dr 97702
NW Wethered Ct 97701
Wetland Ct 97702
Wharton Ave 97701
SW Wheeler Pl 97702
NE Whisper Ridge Dr 97701

Whistle Punk Rd 97702
White Dove Ln 97702
White Horn Ln 97701
White Pass Ct 97702
White Peaks Ct & Dr 97702
White Rock Loop 97701
Whitecliff Cir 97702
Whitehaven Cir & Ln 97702
Whiteoak Pl 97707
Whitetail Ln 97707
Whitetail St 97702
Whitewing Ct 97701
Whitney Pl 97702
Whitstone Cir 97702
Whittier Dr 97707
NW Whitworth Way 97701
NE Wichita Way 97701
Wickiup Rd 97702
Widgeon Dr 97707
NE Wiest Way 97701
Wild Buckwheat Ct 97701
Wild Goose Ln 97702
Wild Horse Trl 97701
NW Wild Meadow Dr 97701
Wild Rapids Dr 97702
NE Wild Rivers Loop 97701
Wild Rose Ln 97702
NW Wild Rye Cir 97701
Wild Water Ct 97702
SE Wildcat Dr 97702
Wilderness Way 97702
Wildwood Dr 97702
Will Scarlet Ln 97702
SW Willard Rd 97701
NW William Clark St 97701
Williamson Blvd & Ct 97701
Willopa Ct 97702
Willow Ct 97707
SE Willow Ln 97702
Willow Creek Ct & Loop 97702
NW Wilmington Ave 97701
SE & SW Wilson Ave 97702
Winchester Dr 97707
SE Wind Rider Ln 97702
SE Windance Ct 97702
Windflower Way 97702
NW Windham Loop 97701
Windsong Ln 97702
Windsor Ct & Dr 97702
NW Windwood Way 97701
NE Windy Knolls Dr 97701
Windy Ridge Rd 97702
NE Windy Tree Ct 97701
Winnebago Ln 97702
NW Winslow Dr 97701
Winston Ct & Loop 97701
Winter Park Ln 97702
Winter Wren Loop 97702
NE Wintergreen Dr 97701
Wishing Well Ct & Ln 97701
Witch Tree Rd 97707
Witherspoon Pl 97701
Wolcott Pl 97701
Wolf St 97707
Wood Ave 97701
Wood Duck Ct & Dr 97707
Woodbridge Pl 97701
NE Woodbury Ct 97701
Woodbury Ln 97702
Woodhaven Ave 97702
SE Woodland Blvd 97702
Woodridge Ct & Ln 97701
Woodriver Dr 97702
Woodruff Pl 97702
Woods Valley Pl 97702
Woodside Ct, Loop, Pl & Rd 97702
Woodside North Dr 97702
NE Worthington Ct 97701
Wrangler Pl 97701
Wrenwood 97702
Wright Point Way 97707
NE Wyatt Ct 97701
SE Wye Ln 97702
NW Wyeth Pl 97701

Yakwahtin Ct 97702
NE Yale Ave 97701
Yampa Pl 97701
Yarrow Ln 97702
SW Yates Dr 97702
Yellow Leaf St 97702
Yellow Pine Loop 97707
NE Yellow Ribbon Dr 97701
NW Yellow Tail 97701
NE Yellowstone Ln 97701
Yeoman Rd 97701
SE Yew Ln 97702
NE & NW York Cir & Dr 97701
NW Yosemite Dr 97701
Young Ave 97701
Yucca Ct 97701
Yukon Ln 97702
NE Zachary Ct 97701
Zagt Ln 97707
SE Zeller Ln 97702
Zircon Dr 97702
Zodiak Ln 97701
NE Zoe Ave 97701
Zuni Cir & Rd 97702

NUMBERED STREETS

NE & NW 1st Ave & St 97701
2nd Ave 97701
2nd St 97701
NE 2nd St 97701
NW 2nd St 97701
SE 2nd St 97702
3rd Ave 97701
3rd St 97701
NE 3rd St 97701
NW 3rd St 97701
SE 3rd St 97702
4th Ave 97701
4th St 97701
NE 4th St 97701
NW 4th St 97701
SE 4th St 97702
5th St 97701
NE 5th St 97701
NW 5th St 97701
SE 5th St 97702
NE 6th St 97701
NW 6th St 97701
SE 6th St 97702
7th St 97701
8th St 97701
NE 9th St 97701
NW 9th St 97701
SE 9th St 97702
NE & NW 10th 97701
NE & NW 11th Pl & St 97701
NW 11th Green Pl 97701
NE & NW 12th 97701
SW 13th Pl 97702
NE 13th St 97701
NW 13th St 97701
SE 13th St 97702
SW 13th St 97702
NE & NW 14th 97701
15th St 97702
NE 15th St 97701
NW 15th St 97701
SE 15th St 97702
SW 15th St 97702
NE 16th St 97701
SE 16th St 97702
SW 16th St 97702
NW 17th St 97701
SW 17th St 97702
NW 17th Tee Pl 97701
NW 18th Pl 97701
18th St 97701
NW 18th St 97701
SW 18th St 97702
19th St 97701
SW 19th St 97702
27th St 97701
NE 27th St 97701
SE 27th St 97702
61st St 97701
73rd St 97701
74th Ln 97701
76th St 97701
78th St 97701
85th Pl & St 97701
89th St 97701
92nd St 97701
93rd Pl & St 97701
94th St 97701
97th St 97701

CORVALLIS OR

General Delivery 97333

POST OFFICE BOXES MAIN OFFICE STATIONS AND BRANCHES

Box No.s
All PO Boxes 97339

NAMED STREETS

SW A Ave 97333
Acacia Dr & Pl 97330
Acey Pl & Way 97330
NW Acorn Ridge Dr 97330
Adair Frontage Rd 97330
Adams Ave 97331
SW Adams Ave 97333
Adams Hall 97331
Ag Life Sciences Bldg 97331
SW Agate Ave 97333
Airport Ave & Pl 97333
NW Alder Creek Dr 97330
SE Aldrin Pl 97333
SE & SW Alexander Ave & Pl 97333
SW Allen St 97333
NW Alta Vista Dr 97330
NW Amanda Pl 97330
SW Amberwood Ave 97333
Andrews Ln 97330
NE Angelee Pl 97330
Angelica Dr & Pl 97330
NW Anjni Cir 97330
NW Antelope Pl 97330
Antler Dr 97330
NW Appaloosa Ln 97330
Apperson Hall 97331
NW Apple Tree Pl 97330
NW Arbol Pl 97330
SW Arbor Grove Dr 97333
NW Arboretum Rd 97330
Arena Rd 97330
NW Armstrong Way 97330
NE & NW Arnold Ave & Way 97330
Arnold Complex 97331
Arnold Service Ctr 97331
NW Arrowood Cir 97330
Arthur Ave, Cir & Pl 97330
Asbahr Ave & Pl 97330
NW Ashwood Dr 97330
NW Aspen St 97330
SW Aster St 97333
SE Atwood Ave 97333
Audene Dr & Pl 97330
Audrey Ln 97333
Autumn Pl & St 97330
Avalon Dr & Pl 97330
SW Avena Pl 97333
SW Avery Ave 97333
SW Avery Park Dr 97333
NE Azalea Dr 97330
NW Aztec Ave 97330
SW B Ave 97333
Baker Ln 97333

Ballard Hall 97331
SW Balsam Dr 97333
Banks Ln 97333
SW Banyon Cir 97333
NW Barbara St 97330
NE Barberry Dr 97330
SW Barley Hill Dr 97333
SE Barton Ln 97333
Batcheller Hall 97331
Bates Hall 97331
SE Bayou Pl 97333
SE Bayshore Cir 97333
SW Beals Ave 97333
NW Beaver Pl 97330
Beaver Creek Rd 97333
NW Beca Ave 97330
SE Becker Dr 97333
NW Beechwood Pl 97330
Beef Barn Rd 97330
Belden Creek Rd 97330
NW Belhaven Dr 97330
SE Bell Ave 97333
Bellfountain Rd 97333
NE Belvue St 97330
Benton Anx 97331
Benton Hall 97331
Beth Ln 97330
Bethel Pl & St 97333
Bexell Hall 97331
NW Big Oak Pl 97330
NE Birch Ln 97330
SW Birdie Dr 97333
SW Birdsong Dr 97333
NW Bittersweet Pl 97330
NW Blacktail Trail Dr 97330
Blake Dr 97330
Blaze Dr 97330
Bloss Hall 97331
Bloss Hall Apt Rd 97331
NW Blue Grouse Pl 97330
Blue Heron Rd 97330
NW Bluebell Pl 97330
SW Blueberry Dr 97333
Bluerock Ln 97333
SW Bluestem Pl 97333
NW Bonney Dr 97330
SE Booneville Dr 97333
NE Boulder Pl 97330
S Boundary Rd 97330
Box Elder St 97330
Boxwood Dr & Pl 97330
Brenneman Ln 97330
Brewster Ln 97333
SE Bridgeway Ave 97333
NW Britta Pl 97330
SW Brooklane Dr 97333
SE Brookside Way 97333
NW Brownly Heights Dr 97330
Bruce Rd 97333
NW Bruno Pl 97330
NW Bryant St 97330
NW Buchanan Ave 97330
Buchanan Rd 97330
SW Buckwheat Ave 97333
SW Bunchberry Ave 97333
Bundy Rd 97330
NW Bunting Dr 97330
Burgundy Dr & Pl 97330
NE Burke Pl 97330
NE Burris St 97330
NW Buttercup Dr 97330
Butterfield Dr & Pl 97333
Buxton Hall 97331
NE Byron Pl 97330
SW C Ave 97333
NW Cabernet Pl 97330
Callahan Hall 97331
NW Calloway Dr 97330
NW Camas Pl 97330
NE Cambridge Cir 97330
NW Camellia Dr 97330
SW Campus Way 97331
NW Canary Pl 97330
NE Canterbury Cir 97330
NW Canyon Dr 97330

NW Cardinal Dr 97330
Cardwell Hill Dr 97330
NE Carmen Pl 97330
NW Carpathian Dr 97330
SE Carroll Dr 97333
SW Cascade Ave 97333
Cascade Hall Anx 97331
NW Cassia Pl 97330
SW Cattle Dr 97333
Cauthorn Hall 97331
Cedar Ln 97330
SE Centerpointe Dr 97333
NW Century Dr 97330
Ch2m Hill Alumni Ctr 97331
NW Chaparral Dr 97330
Chapel Dr 97333
SE Chapman Pl 97333
NW Charlemagne Pl 97330
SE Charlotte Pl 97333
NW Charmyr Vista Dr 97330
SE Charter Pl 97333
NW Chenille Pl 97330
SW Cherry Ave 97333
NE Cherry Ln 97330
SE Chester Ave 97333
SW Chestnut Dr 97333
SW Chickadee St 97333
Childcare Ctr 97331
NW Chinaberry Pl 97330
NW Chinook Dr 97330
NW Chinquapin Pl 97330
SW Chintimini Ave 97333
NW Chipmunk Pl 97330
NW Christine St 97330
NW Christopher Pl 97330
NW Churchill Way 97330
NE & NW Circle Blvd & Pl 97330
NW Clarence Cir 97330
SE Clearwater Dr 97333
NW Cleveland Ave 97330
NW Clover Pl 97330
NW Clubhouse Pl 97330
Coas Administration Bldg 97331
Coffin Butte Rd 97330
SW Coho St 97333
SW Cole Pl 97333
SE Collins Pl 97333
NE Colorado Lake Dr 97333
NE Columbia Ave 97330
SW Commons Way 97333
W Complex 97331
NW Concord Dr 97330
NE & NW Conifer Blvd & Pl 97330
NE Conroy Pl 97330
Conser Dr, Pl & St 97330
SW Convill Ave 97333
NW Conway Ln 97330
NW Coolidge Way 97330
SE Coral Reef Pl 97333
Cordley Hall 97331
Cori Ct 97330
SE Corliss Ave 97333
NW Cornell Ave 97330
NW Coronado St 97330
NW Council Tree Ln 97330
NW Country Ct 97330
Country Club Dr, Pl & Way 97333
NW Country Hills Dr 97330
Covell Hall 97331
NW Covey Run Rd 97330
SE Craig Ave 97333
NE Crane Ln 97330
NW Crescent Valley Dr 97330
Crest Dr & Pl 97330
Crisp Dr 97333
NW Crocus Pl 97330
Cronn Dr 97333
Crop Science Bldg 97331
SE Crystal Cir 97333
SE Crystal Lake Dr 97333
SW Cummings Ave 97333

SE Currier St 97333
Cutler Ln 97333
NW Cypress Ave 97330
SW D Ave 97333
SW Dakota Ave 97333
Dale Dr & Pl 97330
Daphne Ct 97330
NW Davis Meadows Pl 97330
NW Daylily Ave 97330
Daystar Dr 97330
Dearborn Hall 97331
SW Dearmond Dr 97333
SE Deborah Pl 97333
SE Debord St 97333
Decker Rd 97333
SW Decker Ridge Rd 97333
NW Deer Pl 97330
NW Deer Run St 97330
SW Deerhaven Dr 97333
SW Delwood Ave 97333
SE Denman Ave 97333
SE Dennis St 97333
SW Deon Dr 97333
SW Deschutes St 97333
NW Diamond Pl 97330
NE Diane Pl 97330
NW Dimple Hill Rd 97330
Division Pl & St 97330
NW Dixon St 97330
Dixon Recreation Ctr 97331
SE Dockside Dr 97333
NW Dogwood Dr 97330
SW Donovan Pl 97333
NE Dorchester Way 97330
SE Dorothy Ave 97333
Dorr Rd 97333
Douglas Ave & Pl 97330
NW Draper Pl 97330
NW Dream Pl 97330
SW Dresden Ave 97333
Dryden Hall 97331
NW Duchess Pl 97330
SW E Ave 97333
Earl Ln 97330
SE Eastgate Cir 97333
SW Easy St 97333
NE Ebony Ln 97330
Ece 97331
SW Edgeing Dr 97333
SE Edgewater St 97333
NW Edgewood Dr 97330
Education Hall 97331
SW El Rancho Ave 97333
NW Elder St 97330
NE Electric Rd 97333
Elizabeth Dr & Pl 97330
NW Elks Dr 97330
NE Elliott Cir 97330
Elmwood Dr & Pl 97330
NW Emperor Dr 97330
SW Englewood Ave 97333
NW Ermine Pl 97330
Estaview Cir, Dr & Pl 97333
Eureka Rd 97333
SE Everglade St 97333
NW Evergreen St 97330
Ewelty Way 97330
NE Fair Acres Dr 97330
Fair Oaks Dr & Pl 97330
Fairbanks Hall 97331
Fairhaven Ct & Dr 97333
NW Fairlawn St 97330
SW Fairmont Dr 97333
NW Fawnee Dr 97330
Fern Rd 97333
Fernwood Cir & Pl 97330
NW Fillmore Ave 97330
Finley Rd 97333
Finley Hall 97331
Finley Refuge Rd 97333
NW Fir Ridge Pl 97330
Firefern Pl & St 97330
NW Fireweed Pl 97330
Firwood Dr & Pl 97330
NE Flintlock Pl 97330

Foothill Dr & Pl … 97330
NW Forest Dr … 97330
Forest Research Lab … 97331
Forest Springs Ln … 97330
NW Forestgreen Ave … 97330
Forestry Sciences Lab … 97331
NE Four Acre St … 97330
NW Fox Pl … 97330
Foxtail Pl & St … 97330
NW Frazier Creek Rd … 97330
NE Freeman Ln … 97333
NW Fremont Ave … 97330
NW Fritz Pl … 97330
NW Fuchsia Dr … 97330
Furman Hall … 97331
SE Gagnon St … 97333
NE Garden Ave … 97330
NW Garfield Ave … 97330
Garryanna Dr, Pl & St … 97330
SW Gerold St … 97333
Gilbert Hall … 97331
Gilkey Hall … 97331
Gill Coliseum … 97331
Gilmore Hall … 97331
NW Ginseng Pl … 97330
NE Glacier Way … 97330
Gladys Valley Ctr … 97331
Gleeson Hall … 97331
NW Glen Eden Dr … 97330
NW Glen Ridge Pl … 97330
SE Glenn St … 97333
NW Glenridge Dr … 97330
Glenwood Dr & Pl … 97330
NW Goldenrod Pl … 97330
Goldfinch Dr & Pl … 97330
SW Golf View Dr … 97333
NW Gonzalez Ave … 97330
SE Goodnight Ave … 97333
SE Goodpark Ave … 97333
Govier Pl … 97330
SW Grand Oaks Dr … 97333
NW Grandview Dr … 97330
NE Granger Ave … 97330
Grant Ave, Cir & Pl … 97330
SW Grass Heights Dr … 97333
NW Greeley Ave … 97330
Green Cir & Pl … 97330
Greenberry Rd … 97333
NW Greenbriar Pl … 97330
SE Greenmore Pl … 97333
Greenwood Ave & Pl … 97330
Grimsley Rd … 97333
SW Grove St … 97333
Guerber Ln … 97333
NW Gumwood Ave … 97330
Halsell Hall … 97331
SW Hanson St … 97333
NW Happy Valley Dr … 97330
NW Harman Ln … 97330
NW Harmony Ln … 97330
NW Harrison Blvd … 97330
Harvey Ln … 97330
Hathaway Dr & Pl … 97333
NE Haugen Rd … 97330
NW Havengreen Pl … 97330
SW Hawkeye Ave … 97333
Hawley Hall … 97331
NW Hawthorn Pl … 97330
NW Hayes Ave … 97330
NW Hazel Ave … 97330
NW Heather Dr … 97330
SW Helen Ave … 97333
Helm Dr … 97330
NW Hemlock Ave … 97330
Henderson Rd … 97333
SW Herbert Ave … 97333
NW Heron Pl … 97330
Hibiscus Dr … 97330
Highland Dr & Pl … 97330
NW Highland Dell Dr … 97330
Highland Terrace Ave & Pl … 97330
NE Highway 20 … 97330
Highway 34 … 97333
NE & NW Highway 99 … 97330
Highway 99w
27300-31699 … 97333
38000-38599 … 97330
SW Hil Wood Pl … 97333
NW Hillcrest Dr … 97330
SW Hillside Dr … 97333
SW Hilltop Dr … 97333
SW Hillview Ave … 97333
NW Hobart Ave … 97330
SW Hoffman Ave … 97333
Holder Ln … 97333
Holiday Ln … 97333
NE Holly Ln … 97330
NE Holly Acres St … 97330
NE Holly Oak Pl … 97330
SW Hollyhock Cir … 97333
Honeysuckle Dr & Pl … 97330
NW Hood View Cir … 97330
NW Hope Dr … 97330
SW Hopkins Ave … 97333
Horning Ln … 97333
NW Houston Pl … 97330
SW Hout St … 97333
Hovland Hall … 97331
Huckleberry Dr & Pl … 97330
Hull Pl … 97333
NW Hummingbird Dr … 97330
NE Hundred Oak Ln … 97330
NW Huntington Dr … 97330
Hurlburt Rd … 97333
Hyacinth Ct … 97333
Hyslop Rd … 97330
SW Inavale Way … 97333
NW Independence Hwy … 97330
NW Inger Pl … 97330
SE Ireland Ln … 97333
NW Ironwood Ave … 97330
SW Ivy Pl … 97333
NE Jack London St … 97330
NW Jackson Ave … 97330
SW Jackson St … 97331
NW Jackson Creek Rd … 97330
James Ave & Pl … 97330
Jameson Dr & Pl … 97330
SW Janet Way … 97333
NW Janssen St … 97330
NW Jasmine Pl … 97330
Jasper Pl & St … 97330
NW Jean Pl … 97330
NW Jeanice Pl … 97330
SW Jefferson Ave
200-298 … 97333
300-1099 … 97333
1200-1599 … 97331
1601-1799 … 97331
SW Jefferson St … 97333
SW Jefferson Way … 97331
Johns Pl … 97330
NW Johnson Ave … 97330
NW Jon Pl … 97330
NW Jonquil Pl … 97330
SE Joy Ln … 97333
NW Joy Lyn Pl … 97330
NW Juniper Pl … 97330
NW Kainui Dr … 97330
NW Kari Pl … 97330
NE Karlene Ave … 97333
SW Kellarle St … 97333
Kelley Engineering … 97331
SW Kendra St … 97333
NE Kenny Dr … 97330
Kerr Administration Bldg … 97331
NW Kestrel Hill Ln … 97330
Kidder Hall … 97331
SE Kiger Island Dr … 97333
Kinderman Dr & Pl … 97330
NW Kinglet Pl … 97330
NW Kings Blvd … 97330
SW Kings Blvd … 97331
NW Kings Pl … 97330
NE Kirsten Pl … 97330
Kiwi Ln … 97330
NW Kleinschmidt Pl … 97330
NW Kline Pl … 97330
Knollbrook Ave & Pl … 97333
La Sells Stewart Ctr … 97331
Lab Animal Resource Ctr … 97331
Lakeside Dr … 97333
NE Lancaster St … 97330
Lance Pl & Way … 97330
SW Langton Pl … 97331
Langton Hall … 97331
NW Lantana Dr … 97330
NW Larch Ave … 97330
NW Lark Pl … 97330
NW Larkspur Pl … 97330
NW Lathrop Ln … 97330
NE Laurel Dr … 97330
NW Lavender Cir … 97330
NE Lawndale Pl … 97330
NW Lawrence Ave … 97330
NW Legacy Pl … 97330
SW Leland Pl … 97333
SW Leonard St … 97333
NW Leprechaun Ln … 97330
NW Lessie Pl … 97330
NW Lester Ave … 97330
NW Lewisburg Ave … 97330
Lilly Ave & Pl … 97333
Lincoln Ave & Ct … 97333
SE Linda St … 97333
NW Linden Ave … 97330
SE Linn Dr … 97333
NW Linnan Cir … 97330
Linville Ln … 97333
NW Lisa Pl … 97330
Live Oak Dr & Pl … 97330
Llewellyn Rd … 97333
NW Locke Cemetery Rd … 97330
NW Locust St … 97330
NE Logsdon Rd … 97330
NE Londonberry Way … 97330
SW Long Ave … 97333
SW Longhill St … 97333
SW Lookout Dr … 97333
Loren Ln … 97333
NW Lorri Pl … 97330
NE Lorvik Pl … 97330
SW Lostine Pl … 97333
SW Lowe St … 97333
NW Lowrie Ln … 97330
NW Lupine Pl … 97330
NW Lyman Dr … 97330
NW Lynwood Cir … 97330
SW Madison Ave … 97333
SW Madison Way … 97331
NW Madrone Way … 97330
NW Magnolia Dr … 97330
Magruder Hall … 97331
NW Mahonia Pl … 97330
SE Maley Rd … 97333
NE Manchester St … 97330
NW Manzanita Pl … 97330
NW Maple Ave … 97330
Maple Tree Ct & Dr … 97333
NE Marcus Harris Ave … 97330
NW Margarita Pl … 97330
NW Marigold Pl … 97330
SE Marion Ave … 97333
SE Maritime St … 97333
NW Marshall Dr … 97330
SE Marshland Ave … 97333
SW Martin St … 97333
Maser Dr & Pl … 97330
SE Mason Pl … 97333
Maxine Ave & Cir … 97330
SW May Ave … 97333
SW May Way … 97331
SE Mayberry Ave … 97333
NW Mazama Dr … 97330
NW Mc Dougal Cir … 97330
Mcalexander Fieldhouse … 97331
Mcdonald Cir & Pl … 97330
SW Mckenzie Ave … 97333
NW Mckinley Dr … 97330
Mcnary Complex … 97331
Mcnary Service Ctr … 97331
SW Meadow Flower Dr … 97333
SE Meadow Lark Dr … 97333
NW Meadow Ridge Pl … 97330
NW Meadow View Dr … 97330
NW Meadowgreen Pl … 97330
SE Melody Ln … 97333
Memorial Pl & Un … 97331
NW Menlo Dr … 97330
SW Meridian Pl … 97333
NE Merloy Ave … 97330
NW Merrie Dr … 97330
Merryfield Hall … 97331
NE Meyer Ln … 97330
SE Micah Pl … 97333
NW Michelle Dr … 97330
SE Midvale Dr … 97333
Milam Hall … 97331
Milne Computer Ctr … 97331
NW Mink Pl … 97330
NE Minnesota Ave … 97330
NW Mirador Pl … 97330
NE Mistletoe Cir … 97330
NW Mitchell Dr … 97330
SW Mobile Pl … 97333
NW Molly Ct … 97330
NW Monroe Ave … 97330
SW Monroe Ave
100-998 … 97333
1600-2598 … 97331
SW Monroe Way … 97331
Monterey Dr & Pl … 97330
Moreland Hall … 97331
NW Morgan Pl … 97330
NE Morning St … 97330
NW Morning Glory Dr … 97330
SW Morris Ave … 97333
NW Moselle Pl … 97330
Moss Rock Dr … 97330
Motor Pool Bldg … 97331
Mountain Laurel Cir & Pl … 97330
NW Mountain View Dr … 97330
NE Mulberry Dr … 97330
NW Mulkey Ave … 97330
SW Mulligan Pl … 97333
NW Myrtlewood Way … 97330
SW Nash Ave … 97333
Nash Hall … 97331
SE Natland Pl … 97333
Naval Armory … 97331
SW Neer Ave … 97333
Neuman Rd … 97333
NE Newcastle Pl … 97330
Newton Rd … 97333
Niagara Dr & Pl … 97330
SW Nicole Dr … 97333
NW Nightingale Pl … 97330
NE Noble Ave … 97330
Norwood Dr & Pl … 97330
Nutcracker Ln … 97333
NW Oak Ave … 97330
NW Oak Creek Dr … 97330
Oak Creek Bldg … 97331
SW Oak Shade Ave … 97333
NW Oakdell Pl … 97330
Oakview Dr … 97333
SW Oetjen Ave … 97333
Old River Rd … 97333
Oleander Ave & Pl … 97330
NW Orchard Ave
2700-3400 … 97330
3401-3401 … 97331
3402-3498 … 97330
3405-3499 … 97330
SW Orchard Ave … 97331
SW Orchid Cir … 97333
Oregon State Univ … 97333
Oregon State University … 97331
NW Osprey Pl … 97330
Otana Dr & Pl … 97333
SE Outrigger Pl … 97333
NW Overlook Dr … 97330
Owen Hall … 97331
NE Owl Pl … 97333
NW Oxbow Dr … 97330
NE Oxford Cir … 97330
NW Panorama Dr … 97330
SW Par Pl … 97333
SE Park Ave … 97333
SE Park Pl … 97333
SW Park Ter … 97331
Partridge Dr & Pl … 97333
NE Pax Pl … 97330
Payne Rd … 97333
NW Peavy Arboretum Rd … 97330
Peavy Hall … 97331
NW Pendleton Pl … 97330
SW Peony St … 97333
SE Peoria Rd … 97333
NW Peppertree Pl … 97330
Peterson Rd … 97333
NE Pettibone Dr … 97330
Pharmacy Bldg … 97331
NE Pheasant Ave … 97330
SW Philomath Blvd … 97333
SW Pickford St … 97333
NW Pielared St … 97330
NW Pierce Way … 97330
NE Pilkington Ave … 97330
NE Pin Oak St … 97330
NW Pinecone Way … 97330
SW Pinehurst Pl … 97333
NW Pinewood Pl … 97330
NW Pinot Pl … 97330
NE Pinot Gris Dr … 97330
NW Pintail Pl … 97330
SW Pioneer Pl … 97331
Plageman Bldg … 97331
SW Pleasant Pl … 97333
Pleasant Hill Dr … 97333
Plowshares Rd … 97330
SW Plumley St … 97333
NE Plymouth Cir … 97330
SW Plymouth Dr … 97333
Poling Hall … 97331
NW Polk Ave … 97330
NW Ponderosa Ave … 97330
SW Poplar Pl … 97333
NW Poppy Dr … 97330
Powderhorn Dr & Pl … 97330
Powell Ave & Pl … 97333
SE Powells Rd … 97333
SW Prairie Ave … 97333
SE Primrose Rd … 97333
NW Princess St … 97330
NW Professional Dr … 97330
NE Purple Vetch Ln … 97330
NE Quail Run Rd … 97333
SE Quayside St … 97333
NW Queens Ave … 97330
SW Quietcreek Dr … 97333
Radiation Ctr … 97331
NW Raintree Dr … 97330
SW Ralph Miller Ln … 97331
NW Ramona Ln … 97330
SW Randall Way … 97333
NW Raven Pl … 97330
SW Redtop Pl … 97333
SW Redwood Ln … 97333
SW Reed Pl … 97333
NW Reiman St … 97330
NE Rennie Pl … 97330
SW Research Way … 97333
SW Reservoir Ave … 97333
NW Rhoda Way … 97330
NW Ribier Pl … 97330
Richardson Hall … 97331
SE Richland Ave … 97333
Ridgewood Dr & Pl … 97330
Rifle Range Rd … 97330
Rivendell Ln … 97330
SE Rivergreen Ave … 97333
NW Robin Pl … 97330
NW Robin Hood St … 97330
SE Roche Ln … 97333
NE Rodeo Dr … 97330
Rogers Hall … 97331
NW Rolf Pl … 97330
NW Rolling Green Dr … 97330
NW Romancier Dr … 97330
Roosevelt Dr & Pl … 97330
SW Rose Pl … 97333
SW Roseberry St … 97333
NW Rosemarie Pl … 97330
Rosewood Dr & Pl … 97330
Ross Ln … 97333
SW Roth St … 97333
Royal Oaks Dr & Pl … 97330
NW Russell Pl … 97330
SE Ryan St … 97333
SW Sackett Pl … 97331
Sackett Hall … 97331
SE Safe Harbor St … 97333
SW Sagebrush Dr … 97333
NW Samaritan Dr … 97330
SW Sandalwood St … 97333
NE Santiam Ln … 97330
NW Satinwood St … 97330
SE Schooner Ave … 97333
SW Scott St … 97333
SE Seaport Cir … 97333
Seavy Ave, Cir & Pl … 97330
SW Secher Ln … 97333
Seed Laboratory … 97331
NW Seneca Pl … 97330
NW Sequoia Ave … 97330
SE Shady Oak Dr … 97333
SW Shamrock Ln … 97333
NW Shasta Ave … 97330
NW Shattock Pl … 97330
Shepard Hall … 97331
Sherwood Pl & Way … 97330
NW Shiloh Pl … 97330
NW Shooting Star Dr … 97330
SE Shoreline Dr … 97333
NW Short Ave … 97330
Silktassel Ct & Dr … 97330
NW Silverbelle Pl … 97330
NW Siskin Dr … 97330
NW Sisters Pl … 97330
NW Sitka Pl … 97330
NW Skillings Dr … 97330
NW Skipanon Dr … 97330
NW Skyline Dr … 97330
SW Skyview Ave … 97333
Smith Loop … 97333
Snell Hall … 97331
NW Snowberry Pl … 97330
NW Snowbrush Dr … 97330
Soap Creek Rd … 97330
Social Science Hall … 97331
NW Solar Pl … 97330
NW Somerset Dr … 97330
NW Sonja Pl … 97330
NE Sorrel Pl … 97330
NW Souza Pl … 97330
NW Sparrow Pl … 97330
NW Spring St … 97330
NW Spring Creek Dr … 97330
NW Spruce Ave … 97330
NW Spurry Pl … 97330
SW Stadium Ave … 97333
Stage Stop Ln … 97330
SE Stahlbush Island Rd … 97333
SW Stamm Pl … 97333
SE Standish Ave … 97333
SW Stanford St … 97333
NW Starker Ave … 97330
Starr Creek Rd … 97333
NW Starview Dr … 97330
NE Steele Ave … 97330
SE Steller Dr … 97333
SE Sternwheeler Dr … 97333
Stewart Pl & St … 97330
SE Stone St … 97333
SW Stopp Pl … 97333
Stout Ln … 97333
Strand Ag Hall … 97331
NE Strawberry Ln … 97330
NW Sulphur Springs Rd … 97330
NW Sumac Dr … 97330
Summerfield Dr & Pl … 97333
NW Sundance Cir … 97330
NE Sunflower Dr … 97330
NW Sunnybrook Ave … 97330
NE Sunrise St … 97333
SW Sunset Dr … 97333
NW Sunview Dr … 97330
NW Survista Ave … 97330
NW Swallow Dr … 97330
NW Swan Pl … 97330
NW Sycamore Ave … 97330
NW Sylvan Dr … 97330
NW Taft Ave … 97330
NW Takena Dr … 97330
NW Tamarack Dr … 97330
Tampico Rd … 97330
NW Tanager Dr … 97330
NW Tanya Pl … 97330
NW Taylor Ave … 97330
NW Teal Pl … 97330
SW Technology Loop … 97333
Tenax Pl … 97330
Terra Cir & Ln … 97333
NW Terracegreen Pl … 97330
The Valley Library … 97331
NW Thistle Pl … 97330
SE Thompson St … 97333
NE Thousand Oak Dr … 97330
SE Three Mile Ln … 97333
NW Thrush Pl … 97330
NW Tigress Dr … 97330
NW Tillicum Pl … 97330
SW Timber Ridge Dr … 97333
NE Timberline Dr … 97330
SW Timian St … 97333
SW Titleist Cir … 97333
NE Todd Dr … 97330
NW Tokay Pl … 97330
NW Tonka Dr … 97330
NE Toqua Ave … 97333
NW Towhee Dr … 97330
Traffic Services … 97331
SW Trellis Dr … 97333
Trillium Ln … 97330
SW Trophy Pl … 97333
SW Tunison Ave … 97333
SE Twin Maple Ln … 97333
SW Twin Oaks Cir … 97333
Twinberry Pl & St … 97330
Tyler Ave & Pl … 97330
NW University Pl … 97330
Valley Football Ctr … 97331
NW Valley View Dr … 97330
Valtones … 97331
NW Van Buren Ave … 97330
NE Vandenberg Ave … 97330
NE Velle St … 97333
Venell Ln … 97333
SE Vera Ave … 97333
NW Veracruz Pl … 97330
NW Veronica Pl … 97330
SE Vica Way … 97333
SE Viewmont Ave … 97333
Villa Dr & Pl … 97333
NW Village Green Pl … 97330
NE Vine Ave … 97330
NW Vineyard Dr … 97330
NE Vinifera St … 97330
NE Vintage St … 97330
NW Viola Pl … 97330
NW Virginia Pl … 97330
NW Vista Pl … 97330
Wake Robin Ave & Pl … 97333
SW Waldo Pl … 97331
Waldo Hall … 97331
NE & NW Walnut Blvd, Ct & Pl … 97330
NW Waneta Dr … 97330
NW Wapato Pl … 97330
NW Warbler St … 97330
SW Washington Ave … 97333
SW Washington Way … 97331
SW Watenpaugh Ave … 97333
SW Waterleaf Ave … 97333
NW Wayland St … 97330
SW Weatherford Pl … 97331
Weatherford Hall … 97331

SW Weltzin Ave ... 97333
Weniger Hall ... 97331
NE Weslinn Dr ... 97333
West Hills Pl & Rd ... 97333
SW Western Blvd
100-1700 ... 97333
1701-2099 ... 97331
1702-4198 ... 97333
2501-4199 ... 97333
NW Westview Pl ... 97330
NW Westwood Pl ... 97330
SW Whitby Ave ... 97333
White Fir Ln ... 97330
SE White Oak Rd ... 97333
SE White Pine Rd ... 97333
SW Whiteside Dr ... 97333
NW Widgeon Pl ... 97330
Wiegand Hall ... 97331
NW Wild Iris Ln ... 97330
NW Wild Rose Dr ... 97330
NW Wildview Pl ... 97330
Wiles Rd ... 97330
Wilkinson Hall ... 97331
NE Willamette Ave ... 97330
SW Willamette Ave ... 97333
SW William Way ... 97333
NE William R Carr St ... 97330
SW Willow Ave ... 97333
Wilson Hall ... 97331
SW Windflower Dr ... 97333
SW Winding Way ... 97333
NW Windsor Pl ... 97330
NW Wintercreek Dr ... 97330
SE Winterfield Pl ... 97333
NW Wintergreen Pl ... 97330
Wisteria Pl & Way ... 97330
NW Witham Dr ... 97330
NW Witham Hill Dr ... 97330
Withycombe Hall ... 97331
NE Wolcott St ... 97333
SW Wolverine Dr ... 97333
Womens Bldg ... 97331
NE Woodcrest Ave ... 97330
Woodland Dr & Pl ... 97330
Woodlane Dr ... 97333
NW Worden Cir ... 97330
Writsman Creek Dr ... 97330
NW Wynoochee Dr ... 97330
Yvette Ln ... 97330
SE Zedwick St ... 97333
Zeolite Hills Rd ... 97330
NW Zinfandel Ln ... 97330
NW Zinnia Pl ... 97330

NUMBERED STREETS

NW 1st St ... 97330
SW 1st St ... 97333
NE 2nd St ... 97330
NW 2nd St ... 97330
SW 2nd St
100-400 ... 97333
311-311 ... 97339
401-699 ... 97333
402-698 ... 97333
NE 3rd St ... 97330
NW 3rd St ... 97330
SE 3rd St ... 97333
SW 3rd St ... 97333
NW 4th St ... 97330
SW 4th St ... 97333
NW 5th St ... 97330
SW 5th St ... 97333
NW 6th St ... 97330
SW 6th St ... 97333
NW 7th St ... 97330
SW 7th St ... 97333
NW 8th St ... 97330
SW 8th St ... 97333
NW 9th St ... 97330
SW 9th St ... 97333
NW 10th St ... 97330
SW 10th St ... 97333
NW 11th St ... 97330
SW 11th St ... 97333
NW 12th St ... 97330
NW 13th Pl ... 97330
NW 13th St ... 97330
SW 13th St ... 97333
NW 14th Pl ... 97330
NW 14th St ... 97330
SW 14th St ... 97333
NW 15th St ... 97330
SW 15th St
500-600 ... 97331
601-697 ... 97333
602-698 ... 97331
699-1299 ... 97333
NW 16th St ... 97330
SW 16th St ... 97333
NW 17th Pl ... 97330
NW 17th St ... 97330
SW 17th St
600-612 ... 97331
614-698 ... 97331
621-697 ... 97333
699-799 ... 97333
NW 18th St ... 97330
NW 19th St ... 97330
20th Pl & St ... 97330
NW 21st St ... 97330
NW 23rd St ... 97330
25th Pl & St ... 97330
NW 26th St ... 97330
SW 26th St
100-799 ... 97331
1100-1299 ... 97333
27th Pl & St ... 97330
NW 28th St ... 97330
29th Pl & St ... 97330
NW 30th St ... 97330
SW 30th St ... 97331
NW 31st St ... 97330
NW 32nd St ... 97330
NW 33rd St ... 97330
NW 34th St ... 97330
NW 35th St ... 97330
SW 35th St
100-198 ... 97331
101-197 ... 97333
502-502 ... 97331
600-698 ... 97333
601-601 ... 97331
605-605 ... 97333
800-844 ... 97331
850-1698 ... 97333
851-899 ... 97331
1201-1699 ... 97333
NW 36th St ... 97330
SW 36th St ... 97333
SW 37th St ... 97333
45th Pl & St ... 97333
47th Pl & St ... 97333
SW 49th St ... 97333
NW 53rd St ... 97330
SW 53rd St ... 97333
SW 54th St ... 97333
SW 55th St ... 97333
SW 56th St ... 97333
SW 57th St ... 97333
NW 60th St ... 97330
SW 66th St ... 97333
SW 69th St ... 97333
SW 71st St ... 97333
SW 72nd St ... 97333

EUGENE OR

General Delivery ... 97440

POST OFFICE BOXES MAIN OFFICE STATIONS AND BRANCHES

Box No.s
1A - 1U ... 97440
F2 - F2 ... 97408
B - H ... 97408
1 - 1995 ... 97440
2001 - 2998 ... 97402
3001 - 3999 ... 97403
5001 - 5968 ... 97405
8001 - 8559 ... 97408
10001 - 14020 ... 97440
21001 - 26558 ... 97402
30001 - 30175 ... 97403
40001 - 42300 ... 97404
50001 - 51618 ... 97405

NAMED STREETS

A St ... 97405
Abbie Ln ... 97401
Abby Rd ... 97408
Aberdeen St ... 97402
Acacia Ave ... 97408
Acorn Park St ... 97402
Adams Aly ... 97405
Adams St
43-45 ... 97402
47-1299 ... 97402
1900-2999 ... 97405
N Adams St ... 97402
Adelman Loop ... 97402
Adkins St ... 97401
Admiral St ... 97404
Aerial Way ... 97402
Aerie Park Pl ... 97405
Agate Aly ... 97403
Agate St
1301-1797 ... 97403
1799-2799 ... 97403
3100-3699 ... 97405
Ainsley Ln ... 97402
Air Cargo Way ... 97402
Airport Rd ... 97402
Alameda St ... 97404
Alban St ... 97402
Alberta Ln ... 97404
Aldabra St ... 97402
Alder Aly
1001-1799 ... 97401
2212-3438 ... 97405
3440-3452 ... 97405
3454-3468 ... 97405
Alder St
900-1008 ... 97401
1010-1899 ... 97401
1900-4299 ... 97405
Alderbrook Ln ... 97404
Alderbury St ... 97402
Alderwood St ... 97404
Alexander Loop ... 97401
Alexandra Ct ... 97404
Alfaretta Dr ... 97401
Alladin Way ... 97404
Allane Ln ... 97402
Allbritain Ln ... 97405
Allea Dr ... 97404
Almaden Aly ... 97402
Almaden St
100-1199 ... 97402
2600-2899 ... 97405
Alphonse Ave ... 97402
Alpine Loop ... 97405
Alta Vista Ct ... 97403
Altura St ... 97404
Alva Park Dr ... 97402
Alyndale Dr ... 97404
E & W Amazon Dr ... 97405
Amazon Parkway Ct ... 97405
Amberland Ave ... 97401
Amesbury Ave ... 97404
Amherst Way ... 97408
Amirante St ... 97402
E & W Anchor Ave ... 97404
Andersen Ln ... 97404
Andover St ... 97404
Andrea Ave ... 97402
Antelope Way ... 97401
Anthony Way ... 97404
Antigua Dr ... 97408
Anton Ct ... 97402
Apple Dr ... 97404
Appletree Ct & Dr ... 97405
Applewood Ln ... 97408
Arbor Ave ... 97402
Arbor Dr ... 97404
Arcadia Dr ... 97401
Archie St ... 97402
Archwood St ... 97404
Arden Pl ... 97405
Ardendale Ln ... 97405
Argon Ave ... 97404
Arlie Rd ... 97405
Arline Way ... 97403
Arlington Ave ... 97408
Armitage Rd ... 97408
Armstrong Ave ... 97404
Arnold Ave ... 97402
Arondo Ct ... 97401
Arrowhead St ... 97404
Arrowsmith St ... 97402
Arthur Ct ... 97405
Arthur Pl ... 97402
Arthur St
1100-1781 ... 97402
1783-1799 ... 97402
1800-2399 ... 97405
N Arthur St ... 97402
Ascot Dr ... 97401
Ash St ... 97402
Ashbury Dr ... 97408
Ashford Dr ... 97405
Ashley Ct ... 97402
Ashley Ln ... 97402
Ashley Loop ... 97405
Assumption St ... 97402
Astove Ave ... 97402
Atticus Way ... 97404
Auction Way ... 97402
Audel Ave ... 97404
Augusta St ... 97403
Austin St ... 97408
Austin Way ... 97402
Autumn Ave ... 97404
Ava St ... 97404
Avalon St ... 97402
Avengale Dr ... 97408
Awbrey Ln ... 97402
Ayers Rd ... 97408
Azalea Ave & Dr ... 97404
Azure St ... 97401
B St ... 97405
Babcock Ln ... 97401
Backlund Pl ... 97401
Baden Way ... 97402
Bailey Ave ... 97402
Bailey Ln ... 97401
Bailey Hill Loop ... 97405
Bailey Hill Rd
1-1799 ... 97402
1800-1898 ... 97405
1900-87099 ... 97405
Bailey View Dr ... 97405
Baker Blvd ... 97403
Balboa St ... 97408
Balfour St ... 97408
Bampton Ct ... 97404
Banner St ... 97404
Banover St ... 97404
Banton Ave ... 97404
Bar M Dr ... 97401
Barbados Dr ... 97408
Barber Dr ... 97405
Bardell Ave ... 97401
Barger Dr ... 97402
Barker Rd ... 97402
Barnwell Ln ... 97405
Barrett Ave ... 97404
Barrington Ave ... 97401
Barstow Ave ... 97404
Barton Dr ... 97404
Battle Creek Rd ... 97402
Bauer Ct & Ln ... 97404
Baxter St ... 97402
Baywood St ... 97404
Be Ell Pl ... 97405
E Beacon Dr ... 97404
Bean St ... 97402
Beaver St ... 97404
Bedford Way ... 97401
Beebe Ln ... 97404
Beech Pl & St ... 97405
Belair Dr ... 97404
Bell Ave ... 97402
Belle Terra Dr ... 97408
Belmont St ... 97404
Bendix Ave ... 97401
Benjamin St ... 97404
Bennett Ln ... 97404
Benson Ln ... 97408
Benson Rd ... 97402
Bent Tree Ln ... 97405
Bentley Ave ... 97405
Beringer Ct ... 97404
Berkshire St ... 97401
Berntzen Rd ... 97402
Berry Ln ... 97404
Berry Hill Way ... 97405
Berrywood Dr ... 97404
N Bertelsen Rd ... 97402
S Bertelsen Rd
1-1700 ... 97402
1702-1798 ... 97402
1800-2499 ... 97405
Berwin Ln ... 97404
Best Ln ... 97401
Bethel Dr ... 97402
Bethesda St ... 97402
Betty Ln ... 97404
Betty Niven Dr ... 97405
Beymer Rd ... 97405
Birch Ln ... 97403
Birchwood Ave ... 97401
Black Oak Rd ... 97405
Blackberry Ln ... 97408
Blackburn St ... 97405
Blackfoot Ave ... 97404
Blacktail Dr ... 97405
Blair Blvd ... 97402
Blanton Rd ... 97405
Blanton Heights Rd ... 97405
Blazer Ave ... 97404
Bloomberg Rd ... 97405
Blossom St ... 97405
Blue Boy Ln ... 97404
Blue Heron Ln ... 97402
Blue Heron Way ... 97405
Blue Spruce Dr ... 97405
Boardwalk Ave ... 97401
Bobby Doerr Way ... 97402
Bobcat Ln ... 97405
Bobolink Ave ... 97404
Bodenhamer Rd ... 97402
Boehringer Rd ... 97402
Boeing Dr ... 97402
Bogart Ln ... 97401
Bon Vue Dr ... 97402
Bond Ln ... 97401
Bonnie Heights Rd ... 97402
Bonnie View Dr ... 97408
Boods Rd ... 97405
Boomer Rd ... 97402
Borders Dr ... 97404
Boresek Ln ... 97404
Boston Ln ... 97402
Bowmont Dr ... 97405
Bowtie Ave ... 97404
Boyce St ... 97404
Brackenfern Rd ... 97403
Bradbury Ln ... 97405
Bradford Ct ... 97404
Bradley Dr ... 97401
Brae Burn Dr ... 97405
Braeman Vlg ... 97405
Braewood Ln ... 97405
Bramblewood Ln ... 97404
Branch Rd ... 97402
Breezewood Ave ... 97405
Brentwood Ave ... 97404
Brett Loop ... 97404
Brewer Ave ... 97401
Briana Ln ... 97404
E Briarcliff Dr & Ln ... 97404
Briars St ... 97404
Brickley Rd ... 97401
Bridges Ln ... 97402
Bridgewater Dr ... 97402
Briggs Hill Rd ... 97405
Brighton Ave ... 97405
Brightstar Ln ... 97405
Bristol St ... 97403
Brittania Pl ... 97405
Brittany St
1500-1699 ... 97402
1800-2599 ... 97405
Broadview St ... 97405
E Broadway ... 97401
W Broadway
3-39 ... 97401
W Broadway
41-598 ... 97401
600-2399 ... 97402
W Broadway Aly ... 97402
Brockton Pl ... 97404
Broken Oak Loop ... 97405
Brookhaven Way ... 97401
N Brooklyn St ... 97403
Brookside Dr ... 97405
Brookview Dr ... 97401
Brookwood St ... 97405
Brotherton Ave ... 97404
Brower Ave ... 97402
Brown Ln ... 97402
Bruce Way ... 97408
Bryceler Dr ... 97405
Buck St
1201-1297 ... 97402
1299-1726 ... 97402
1728-1798 ... 97402
1800-2199 ... 97405
Buckhorn Ln ... 97405
Buckingham Ave ... 97401
Buckskin Dr ... 97402
Buff Way ... 97401
Burke St ... 97402
Burlington Dr ... 97405
Burlwood St ... 97404
Burnett Ave ... 97402
Bushnell Ln ... 97404
Bushy Tail Trl ... 97405
Butte Ln ... 97401
Butterfly Ln ... 97405
Butterfly Creek Ln ... 97404
Byron St ... 97404
C St ... 97405
Cabernet Ln ... 97404
Cabriole Ct ... 97401
Cal Young Rd ... 97401
Calgary St ... 97408
Calistoga Ct ... 97402
Calla St ... 97404
Calumet Ave, Cir & Way ... 97404
Calvin St ... 97401
Camas Ln ... 97405
Cambon St ... 97402
Cambridge Oaks Dr ... 97401
Camelot Ave ... 97404
Cameo Dr ... 97405
Camrose St ... 97404
Candlelight Dr ... 97402
Cannon Ct ... 97405
Canoe Ridge Way ... 97408
Canterbury St ... 97404
Cantrell Rd ... 97402
Canyon Dr ... 97405
Cap Ct ... 97402
Cape Hatteras Dr ... 97408
Capital Dr ... 97403
Caprice Way ... 97404
Carbona St ... 97404
Cardiff St ... 97402
Carlton St ... 97401
Carmel Ave ... 97401
Carol Ave ... 97402
Carolyn Dr ... 97402
Carriage Dr ... 97408
Carson ... 97403
Carthage Ave ... 97404
Cascade Ct & Dr ... 97402
Cassidy Ln ... 97405
Cassinia Ct ... 97404
Castelloe Ave ... 97405
Castrey St ... 97404
Catalina St ... 97402
Cecil Ave ... 97402
N Cedar St ... 97402
Cedar Brook Dr ... 97402
Cedar Ridge Dr ... 97401
Celeste Way ... 97408
Centennial Blvd, Loop & Plz ... 97401
Center Way ... 97405
Central Blvd ... 97403
Central Rd ... 97402
Century Dr ... 97402
Chad Dr ... 97408
Chambers Aly ... 97402
Chambers St
301-397 ... 97402
399-1700 ... 97402
1702-1798 ... 97402
1800-3600 ... 97405
3602-3698 ... 97405
Champagne Ln ... 97404
Chancellor Ln ... 97402
Chandler Ave ... 97403
Chapel Dr ... 97404
Chapman ... 97403
Chapman Dr ... 97404
Chapman Heights Rd ... 97402
Chardonnay Ln ... 97404
Charles Way ... 97402
Charlet Dr ... 97402
Charlottes Way ... 97405
Charnelton Aly
1101-1174 ... 97401
1176-1998 ... 97401
2100-2548 ... 97405
Charnelton St
400-698 ... 97401
700-1899 ... 97401
1900-3099 ... 97405
Chasa St ... 97401
Chase St ... 97402
Chateau Meadows Dr ... 97401
Chaucer Ct & Way ... 97405
Chelsea Ln ... 97405
Cherokee Dr ... 97402
Cherry Ave ... 97404
Cherry Dr ... 97401
Cherry Grove St ... 97403
Cherry Hill Ln ... 97405
Cherry Ridge Rd ... 97402
Cheryl St ... 97408
Chesapeake Dr ... 97408
Cheshire Ave
202-358 ... 97401
600-2899 ... 97402
358 1/2-358 1/2 ... 97401
E Cheshire Ave ... 97401
Chestnut Dr ... 97404
Chevy Chase Ln & St ... 97401
Chezem Rd ... 97405
Childers Rd ... 97402
Chimney Rock Ln ... 97404
Christensen Rd ... 97405
Christian Way ... 97408
Chuckanut St ... 97408
Chula Vista Blvd ... 97403
Churchill St ... 97405
Cimarron Pl ... 97405
Cinderella Loop ... 97404
Cindy St ... 97404
Cinnamon Ave ... 97404
City View St
1145A-1155A ... 97402
Clairmont Dr ... 97404
N Clarey St ... 97402
Clark St
300-499 ... 97401
600-1099 ... 97402
Classic Pl ... 97401
Clear Lake Rd ... 97402
Cleo Ave ... 97402
Cleveland Pl ... 97402
Cleveland St
100-167 ... 97402

1800-2599 97405
N Cleveland St 97402
Cline Rd 97405
Clinton Dr 97401
Cloudburst St 97402
Club Dr 97402
Club Rd 97401
Club Way 97401
Coachman Dr 97405
Cobblestone Ln 97402
Coburg Rd
1-2299 97401
2501-2697 97408
2699-92899 97408
92901-93199 97408
N Coburg Rd 97408
Coburg Bottom Loop Rd 97408
N & S Coburg Industrial Way 97408
Coburghills Dr 97408
Cody Ave 97402
Coetivy Ave 97402
Colby Ct 97401
Cold Springs Way 97405
N & S Coleman Rd & St 97408
College View Rd 97405
Collin Ct 97404
Colony Oaks Dr 97405
Colony Pond Dr 97401
Colt Dr 97401
Colton Way 97402
Columbia Aly & St 97403
Columbine St 97404
Commerce St 97402
Commercial St 97402
Commodore St 97404
Commons Dr 97401
Compton St 97404
Comstock Ave 97408
Concord St
1401-1497 97403
1499-1799 97403
1801-1899 97403
3401-3497 97402
3499-4699 97402
N Concord St 97403
Cone Ave 97402
Conestoga Way 97401
Conger St 97402
Constantine Pl 97405
Cooperstown Ave 97408
Copping St 97404
Coraly Ave 97402
Corinthian Ct 97405
Corliss Ln 97404
Cornell Way 97405
Cornwall Ave 97404
Corona St 97404
Cortland Ln 97404
Corum Ave 97401
Corvette Ln 97404
Corydon St 97401
Cosmoledo St 97402
Cottonwood Pl 97404
Cougar Ln 97402
Country Ln 97401
Country Club Pkwy & Rd 97401
Country View Dr 97408
Countryside Ln 97404
County Farm Rd 97408
Courtney Pl 97405
Coventry Way 97405
Covey Ln 97401
Coyote Creek Rd 97402
Craftsman Way 97408
Craigmont Ave 97405
Creekside Way 97408
Crencou Rd 97408
Crenshaw Rd 97401
Crescent Ave 97408
Crescent Ridge Ln 97405
Crest Dr 97405
Crest View Dr 97405
Cresta De Ruta St 97403
Crimson Ave 97408
Crocker Ln & Rd 97404
Cross Pl & St 97402
Crossley Ln 97402
E & W Crossroads Ln 97408
Crow Rd 97402
Crown Ave 97402
Crowther Dr 97404
Cubit St 97402
Cumberland Dr 97408
Curtis Ave 97401
Custer Ct 97404
D St 97405
Daffodil Ct 97404
Dahlia Ln 97404
Dakota St 97402
Dale Ave 97408
Dalewood St 97404
Dalton Dr 97404
N & S Danebo Ave 97402
Daniel Dr 97404
Danna Ct 97405
Dapple Ct & Way 97401
Darlene Ln 97401
Darrien 97408
Dartmoor Dr 97401
David Ave 97404
Davis St 97402
Day Ln 97402
Day Island Rd 97401
Dayna Ln 97408
Dean Ave 97404
Debrick Rd 97401
Dee Ct 97402
Deer Valley Dr 97405
Deerbrush Way 97405
Deertrail Rd 97405
Deerwood Dr 97405
Del Monte Ave 97405
Del Rio St 97405
E Delaney St 97408
Delay Dr 97404
Dellwood Dr 97405
Delmar Pl 97401
Delores Ct 97402
N Delta Hwy 97408
Delta St 97404
Delta Oaks Dr 97408
Delta Pines Dr 97408
Demarco Ave 97402
Derbyshire Ln 97405
Devon Ave 97408
Devonshire Dr 97405
Devos St 97402
Dewey St 97402
N Diamond St 97408
Diamond Ridge Loop 97408
Diane St 97401
Dibblee Ln 97404
Dillard Loop & Rd 97405
Dillard Access Rd 97405
Dilley Ln 97405
Division Ave 97404
E & W Dixon St 97408
Doane Pl & Rd 97402
Doble Dr 97402
Dogwood Dr 97405
Dola St 97402
Don Juan Ave 97408
Donald St 97405
Donegal St 97404
Donnalee Rd 97402
Donner Pl 97401
Donohoe Ave 97402
Donovan Dr 97401
Dorchester Ln 97404
Dorris St 97404
Douglas Dr
2300-2399 97405
28800-28899 97402
Douthit Ln 97408
Dove Ln 97402
Dover Dr 97404
Downing St 97408
Doyle St 97404
Driftwood Dr 97402
Drummond Dr 97405
Dry Creek Rd 97404
Dublin Ave 97404
Duck Horn Dr 97404
Duke Ct 97401
Duke Snider Ave 97402
Dukhobar Rd 97402
Dulles Ave 97401
Durbin St 97405
Durham Ave 97404
Eagles Aerie Rd 97405
Earlasue St 97405
Eastgate Ln 97404
Eastway Dr 97405
Eastwood Ln 97401
Easy Acres Dr 97405
Eaton Dr 97403
Eaton Ln 97402
Echo Ln 97404
Echo Hollow Rd 97402
Ed Cone Blvd 97402
Eddystone Pl 97404
Edendale Ln 97405
Edgewater Dr
2500-2999 97401
27900-28299 97402
Edgewood Dr 97404
Edison St 97402
Edna Way 97402
Edwards Dr 97404
Egge Rd 97408
El Camino St 97405
El Centro Ave 97405
El Manor Ave 97405
El Roble Ave 97405
Elanco Ave 97408
Eldale Dr 97402
Eldon Schafer Dr 97405
Eldridge Ave 97405
Elinor St 97403
Elizabeth St 97402
Elk Ave 97403
Elk Ridge Dr 97402
Elkay Dr 97404
Elkhorn Dr 97408
Ellen Ave 97405
Ellie Ln 97401
Ellis Ct 97405
Ellsworth St 97402
Elm Dr 97404
Elmira Rd 97402
Elsena Dr 97401
Elwing Ave 97401
Elwood Ct & Dr 97401
Elysium Ave 97401
Em Ray Dr 97405
Emerald Aly 97403
Emerald Pl 97405
Emerald St
1800-2899 97403
3000-3799 97405
N Emerald St 97408
Emerald Park Dr 97404
Emerenta Ave 97404
Emily Ln 97404
Empire Park Dr 97402
Empress Ave 97405
Enchantment Dr 97402
E & W Enid Rd 97402
Erickson Rd 97402
Erin Way 97408
Escalante St 97404
Essex Ln 97403
Estate Dr 97405
Eugene Ctr 97401
Everest Loop 97402
Evergreen Dr 97404
Excaliber Ln 97402
Excalibur Ln 97402
Executive Pkwy 97401
Exeter Ave 97404
Exmoor Pl 97401
Eyrie Ln 97402
Fair Oaks Dr 97401
Fairfield Ave 97402
Fairmount Blvd 97403
Fairway Dr 97404
Fairway Loop 97401
Fairway View Dr 97401
Farm House Dr 97401
Fawn Hills Dr 97405
Fayette Ave 97404
Federal Ln
1-399 97404
30000-30099 97402
Federal Pl 97404
Fee Ct 97404
Fell Pl 97401
Fenster St 97401
Fergus Ave 97402
Ferndale Dr 97404
Ferry Aly 97401
Ferry Ln 97401
Ferry St
200-698 97401
700-1899 97401
2800-4299 97405
Fetlock Ct 97401
Fetters Loop 97402
Field Stone Ct 97404
Fieldcress Rd 97403
Figueroa St 97402
Filbert Ave 97404
Fillmore St
400-598 97402
600-1099 97402
1801-3399 97405
Finch Ln 97401
Fir Ln
100-199 97404
1100-1299 97405
Fir Acres Dr 97401
Fir Butte Rd 97402
Fir Cove Ln 97405
Fircrest Dr 97403
Firestone Dr 97402
Firland Blvd 97405
Firview St 97402
Firwood Way 97401
Fisher Rd 97402
Flagstaff St 97402
Flintlock St 97408
Flintridge Ave 97401
Floral Hill Dr 97403
Florence Rd 97405
Foch St 97402
Foothill Dr 97405
Forest Blvd 97405
Forest Ln 97402
Forest Hill Ln 97405
Formac Ave 97404
Forrester Way 97401
Fountain Ct 97402
Four Oaks Grange Rd 97405
Fox Hollow Rd 97405
Fox Meadow Rd 97408
Foxboro Ln 97405
Foxglenn Ave 97405
Foxglove Ave 97404
Foxridge Ln 97405
Foxtail Dr 97405
Frank Parrish Rd 97405
Franklin Blvd
800-898 97403
900-5100 97403
5102-5598 97403
86160-86999 97405
Frederick Ct 97405
Freedom Ln 97408
Fremont Ave
700-899 97404
35000-35999 97405
Friendly Aly 97405
Friendly St
1600-1698 97402
1700-1899 97402
1900-3099 97405
3101-3111 97405
Frigon Ave 97402
Frogs Leap Ln 97404
Frontier Dr 97401
Fuller Ave 97402
Fulvue Dr 97405
Funke Rd 97408
Futura St 97404
Galaway Ct 97401
N Game Farm Rd 97408
Garden Ave 97403
N Garden Way 97401
S Garden Way 97401
Garden Valley Rd 97405
Gardenia Pl & Way 97404
Garfield Aly 97402
Garfield Pl 97402
Garfield St
2-198 97402
200-1799 97402
1800-2999 97405
N Garfield St 97402
Garnet St 97405
Garryana Ln 97402
Garth Ln 97404
Gas Lamp St 97402
Gay St 97408
Gentry Rd 97402
George Ct 97401
Gerald Ave 97404
Geyser Peak Pl 97402
Gibralter Loop 97405
Gilbert St 97402
Gilham Rd
1400-2000 97401
2002-2198 97401
2400-4199 97408
Gimpl Hill Rd 97402
Ginger Ave 97404
Ginkgo Way 97404
Gipson St 97404
Glen Mar Ave 97405
Glen Oak Dr 97405
Glenfiddich Way 97405
Glenhaven Rd 97402
Glenn Ellen Dr 97402
Glenwood Blvd & Dr 97403
Glory Dr 97404
Goble Ln 97402
Goldberry Ln 97404
Golden Ave 97404
Golden Eagle Dr 97402
Golden Gardens St 97402
Goodpasture Loop 97401
Goodpasture Island Rd 97401
Goodyear St 97402
Goose Cross Ln 97404
Gossler Rd 97405
Gould Ave 97402
Grace Dr 97404
Graham Dr 97405
N Grand St 97402
Grand Cayman Dr 97408
Grand View Dr 97405
Grant Aly 97402
Grant St
500-698 97402
700-1799 97402
1800-3499 97405
Green Ln 97404
Green Acres Rd 97408
Green Hill Rd 97402
Green Island Rd 97408
Green Oaks Dr 97402
Green Villa Ln 97404
Greenbriar Dr 97402
Greenfield Ave 97404
Greenleaf Ave 97404
Greentree Way 97405
Greenview St 97401
Greenwich Ave 97404
Greenwood St 97404
Greg Way 97404
Greiner St 97405
Grimes St 97402
Grizzly Ave 97404
Grove Ct & St 97404
Grumman Dr 97402
Gypsy Ln 97402
Hackamore Way 97401
Haig St 97402
Halderson Rd 97402
Hallett St 97402
Hallmark Ln 97405
Hamble Ave 97403
Hambletonian Dr 97401
Hamilton 97403
Hamilton Ave 97404
Hamlet Ln 97402
Hamm Rd 97405
Hammer Ln 97404
Hammock St 97401
Hampshire Ln 97404
Hampstead Ln 97405
Hampton Rd 97405
Hampton Way 97401
Hancock Dr 97404
Hanover St 97402
Hansen Ln 97404
Happy Ln 97401
Hardy Ave 97404
Harlow Rd 97401
Harold St 97402
Harpers Ct 97401
Harriett St 97402
Harris Aly
1829-1875 97403
1932-1974 97405
1976-2699 97405
2701-2999 97405
Harris Pl 97405
Harris St
1800-1899 97403
1900-3499 97405
N & S Harrison St 97408
Harry Taylor Rd 97405
Harshels Ct 97404
Harvard Dr 97405
Harvest Loop 97402
Harvey Ave 97404
Hastings St 97404
Hathaway Ave 97401
E Hatton Ave 97404
Haven St 97402
Hawkins Ln 97405
Hawks Lndg 97405
Hawthorne Ave
1-399 97404
3100-3198 97402
3200-4499 97402
Hayes Aly 97402
Hayes St
900-1799 97402
1800-2599 97405
Hazel Ct 97401
Hazel Dell Rd 97402
Heath Dr 97402
Heather Way 97405
Heathman Dr 97402
Heathrow Dr 97402
Heins Ct 97402
Heitzman Way 97402
Helen St 97404
Hemlock St 97404
Henceforth Ln 97402
Henderson Ave 97403
Hendricks Rdg 97403
Hendricks Hill Dr 97403
Henry Ct 97402
Herald Ln 97405
Heritage Ave 97404
Heritage Oaks Dr 97405
Herman Rd 97408
Herman St 97404
Heywood Ave 97404
Hickory Ave 97401
Hicks Ln 97405
Hidden Ln 97405
Hidden Hill Rd 97402
Hidden Meadows Dr 97405
Hideaway Ct 97401
N & S Hideaway Hills Rd 97405
Hideaway Hills Branch Rd 97405
High Aly
317-1297 97401
1299-1729 97401
1731-1799 97401
2400-2442 97405
2601-2699 97405
High St
100-1859 97401
1861-1899 97401
2432-2576 97405
2578-4599 97405
1858 1/2-1868 1/2 97401
Highbury Ln 97402
Highland Dr 97403
Highland Oaks Dr 97405
Highway 58 97405
Highway 99 N 97402
Highway 99 S 97405
Hileman Ln 97404
Hillaire St 97402
E & W Hillcrest Dr 97404
E & W Hilliard Ln 97404
W Hillside Dr 97405
Hillview 1 97408
Hillview 2 97408
Hilo Dr 97404
Hilton Dr 97402
Hilyard Aly 97401
Hilyard St
800-898 97401
900-1899 97401
1900-4499 97405
Hionda Ave 97405
Hiwan Ct 97405
Hodsdonsdale Ln 97402
Hodson Ln 97404
Holeman Aly & Ave 97404
Hollis Ln 97402
Hollow Way 97402
Holly Ave 97408
Hollyhock Ln 97404
Hollyview Ave 97404
Homestead Pl 97401
Honeycomb Dr 97404
Honeysuckle Ln 97401
Honeywood St 97408
Honolulu Ave 97404
Hoover Ln 97404
Hope Loop 97402
Horizon Rd 97405
Horn Ln 97404
E Howard Ave 97404
Hoya Ln 97405
Hoyt Ave 97404
Hubbard Ln 97403
Huey Ln 97402
Hughes St 97402
Hummingbird Ln 97405
Hunington Ave 97405
Hunsaker Ln 97404
Hunters Glen Dr 97405
Huntley Ct 97408
Hyacinth St 97404
Hyde Ln 97402
Impala Ave 97404
Imperial St 97405
Inavale St 97403
Indian Dr 97408
Ingalls Way 97405
Inglewood Ave 97401
Innsbrook Way 97402
Inspiration Point Dr 97405
Interior St 97402
Inwood Ln 97405
Ione Ave 97401
Iowa St 97402
Iron Horse Rd 97402
Ironwood St 97401
Irving Ct 97404
Irving Rd
1-1099 97404
1101-1399 97404
1500-2399 97402
Irvington Dr 97404
E & W Irwin Way 97402
Isabelle St 97402

Ivanhoe Ave 97404
Ivy Ave 97404
Ivy Glen Dr 97402
Izaak Walton Rd 97405
Jackies Ln 97404
Jackson St
200-1291 97402
1293-1845 97402
1900-2799 97405
N Jackson St 97402
Jacobs Dr & Ln 97402
Jacquelyn St 97402
James Ln 97404
Janelle Way 97404
Janisse St 97402
Jarding Rd 97405
Jasmine St 97404
Jason St 97404
Jay St 97402
Jayhawk Ct 97405
Jayne St 97404
Jean Ct 97402
Jefferson Aly
70-82 97402
1557-1571 97402
2041-2175 97405
2200-2299 97401
N Jefferson Aly 97402
Jefferson St
2-698 97402
700-1899 97402
1900-2999 97405
N Jefferson St 97402
Jeffrey Way 97402
Jenny Ln 97402
Jeppesen Ave 97401
Jeppesen Acres Rd 97401
Jerry St 97402
Jerusalem Rd 97402
Jessen Dr 97402
Jessie Ln 97405
Jill Ave 97404
Jonquil Ave 97404
Jordan Dr 97402
Josephine St 97404
Josh St 97402
Judkins Rd 97403
Judy Ave 97402
Juhl St 97402
Julia Loop 97404
Justine Ct & Ln 97404
Kaiser Ave 97402
Kalmia St 97404
Kamapheema Pl 97405
Karyl Ave 97405
Katy Ln 97404
Keeler Ave 97401
Keiper Ave 97404
Keith Way 97401
Keller St 97404
Kellmore St 97402
Kelly Ln 97404
Kelso St 97402
Kelsy Ln 97402
Ken Neilsen Rd 97402
Kendra St 97404
Kenmore St 97402
Kent Ln 97404
Kentwood Dr 97401
Kervon Ct 97405
Kestrel Ln 97405
Kevington Ave 97405
Key Ct 97405
Kildare St 97404
Kimberly Cir & Dr 97405
Kimwood Pl 97401
Kincaid Aly 97405
Kincaid St
1101-1197 97401
1199-1200 97401
1202-1598 97401
1800-1899 97403
1900-4299 97405
King Arthur Ct 97402
King Edwards Ct 97401
Kingfisher Way 97401

Kings North St 97401
Kings West St 97401
Kingsbury Ave 97404
Kingsley Rd 97401
Kingston Way 97401
Kingswood Ave 97405
Kinney Loop 97408
Kinsrow Ave 97401
Kintyre St 97402
Kinwood Rd 97402
Kirsten St 97404
Kismet Way 97405
Kistler Ln 97402
Klamath Ct & St 97404
Kloutz Rd 97405
Knapp Ln 97404
Knave St 97404
Knight 97403
Knight Ave 97404
Knob Hill Ln 97405
Knoop Ave 97402
Knoop Ln 97404
Knox Rd 97408
Kodiak St 97401
Koinonia Rd 97405
Kokkeler Rd 97402
Kona St 97403
Korbel St 97404
Kourt Dr 97404
Kristen Ct 97401
La Casa St 97402
La Darrah St 97404
La Porte Dr 97402
Labona Dr 97404
Lady Slipper Loop 97405
Lake Dr 97404
Lake Cove Ave 97408
Lake Creek Ave 97408
Lake Crest Dr 97408
Lake Forest Dr 97405
Lake Glenn Dr 97408
Lake Grove Dr 97408
Lake Harbor Dr 97408
Lake Isle Ct, Dr & Ter 97401
Lake Park Dr 97404
Lake Shore Dr 97408
Lake Wind Dr 97408
Lake Wood Dr 97408
Lakeland Way 97408
Lakemont Dr 97408
Lakeside Dr 97401
Lakeview Dr
1900-2599 97408
90100-90399 97402
Lakewood Ct 97402
Lamar Ln 97401
S Lambert St 97405
Lamplite Ln 97402
Lancaster Dr 97404
Lancelot Way 97402
Lancer Ln 97405
Landmark Ln 97402
Lanes Turn Rd 97408
Langers Ln 97402
Langton St 97402
Lansdown Rd 97404
Lanson Ln 97404
Lantana Ave 97404
Larch St 97405
Lariat Dr 97401
Lariat Meadows Dr 97401
Lariat Mesa 97401
Larksmead Ln 97404
Larkspur Ave & Loop 97401
Larkwood St 97405
Larson Rd 97405
Lasater Blvd 97405
Lassen St 97402
Latour Ln 97402
Laughlin Rd 97405
Laurel Hill Dr 97403
Laurelhurst Dr 97402
Laurelwood Ln 97403
Laveta Ln 97402
Law Ln 97401
Lawing Way 97402

Lawrence Aly
52-60 97401
1385-1755 97401
2401-2499 97405
2572-2588 97405
Lawrence St
1-1899 97401
1901-2097 97405
2099-3799 97405
N Lawrence St 97401
Lazy Ave 97404
Le Bleu Rd 97405
Lea Ave 97404
Lea Mac Cir 97402
Leahy Dr 97405
Leatherwood Dr 97405
Leda Way 97402
Legacy St 97402
Leghorn Ave 97402
Leigh St 97401
Lemery Ln 97405
Lemming Ave 97401
Lemuria St 97402
Lenore Dr & Loop 97404
Lenox Rd 97404
Leo Harris Pkwy 97401
Leona Ct 97402
Leonards Way 97404
Leopold Dr 97402
Lester Ave 97404
Lewis Ave 97402
Lexington Ave 97403
Leyton Ln 97404
Liberty St 97402
Lillian St 97401
Lily Ave 97408
Limerick Ave 97404
Lincoln Aly 97401
N Lincoln Aly 97401
Lincoln St
2-298 97401
300-1899 97401
1900-3299 97405
E Lincoln St 97408
Linda Ave 97401
Lindley Ln 97401
Lindner Ln 97404
Link Rd 97402
Linnea Ave 97401
Linwood St 97404
Lipinsky Ln 97402
Little John Ln 97401
Littlewood Ln 97404
Living Learning Ctr 97403
Livingston Ave 97402
Lobelia Ave 97404
Lochmoor Pl 97405
Lockheed Dr 97402
E Locust St 97408
Lodenquai Ln 97404
Logan St 97402
Loma Linda Dr & Ln 97405
Lombard St 97404
London Ct 97402
E & W Lone Oak Ave,
Loop & Way 97404
Long Island Dr 97401
Longview St 97403
Loop Ln 97405
Lorane Hwy 97405
Lorane Orchard Rd 97405
Lord Byron Pl 97408
Lorella Ave 97401
Loretta Way 97404
Los Altos Ln 97405
S Louis Ln 97405
Louis St 97402
Louvring Ln 97402
Loy Ave 97404
Ludgate Dr 97402
Luella St 97401
Lund Dr 97404
Lusk Rd 97405
Lydick Way 97401
Lynn Ln 97404
Lynnbrook Dr 97404

Mackin Ave 97404
Maclay Dr 97404
Macy St 97408
Madera St 97402
Madison Aly 97402
Madrona Dr 97403
Maesner St 97404
Mahalo Dr 97405
Mahe Ave 97402
Mahlon Ave 97401
Mahonia Ln 97404
Malabar Dr 97403
Malibu Way 97405
Mallory Ln 97401
Manchester Dr 97401
Manchester Ln 97405
Mangan St 97402
Manihi Dr 97404
Manzana Ln & St 97404
Manzanita St 97405
Maple Dr 97404
Maple St 97402
E Maple St 97408
Mar Loop 97401
Maranta St 97404
Marcella Dr 97408
Marche Chase Dr 97401
Marci Ln 97405
Marcum Ln 97402
Margaret St 97401
Marie Ln 97408
Marion Ln 97404
Marjorie Ave 97408
Market St 97402
Marlboro Ln 97405
Marlow Ln 97401
Marlow Rd 97405
Marquet Way 97401
Marquise Way 97408
Marshall Ave 97402
Martha Ct 97401
Martin St 97405
Martin Luther King Jr
Blvd 97401
Martingale St 97401
Martinique Ave 97408
Marvin Dr 97404
Mary Ln 97405
Mary Lee Ln 97402
Matt Dr 97408
Matthews Rd 97405
Maverick Ave 97404
Maxwell Rd 97404
Mayfair Ln 97404
E Maynard Ave 97404
Mayola Ln 97402
Maywood Ave 97404
Mcbeth Rd 97405
Mccarty Way 97402
Mcclelland Way 97402
Mcclure Ln 97404
Mcdonald Ct 97405
Mcdougal Ln 97402
Mckendrick St 97405
Mckenna Dr 97401
E & W Mckenzie St 97408
Mckenzie View Dr 97408
Mckinley Ct 97402
Mckinley St
500-1709 97402
1711-1799 97402
1801-2099 97405
N Mckinley St 97402
Mclean Blvd & Ct 97405
Mcmillan Aly & St 97405
Mcmorott Ln 97402
Mcmorran St 97403
Mcnaull Dr 97405
Mctavish Ln 97402
Mcvay Hwy 97405
Meadow Ln 97402
Meadow Butte Loop 97401
Meadow Pointe Ln 97408
Meadow View Dr 97408
Meadowvale Ct 97401
Mecca Ave 97404

Medina St 97401
Megan Way 97402
Mehr Ave 97402
Melanie Ln 97404
Melrose Loop 97402
Melvina Way 97404
Memory Ln 97404
Meredith Ct 97404
Merewether St 97401
Meriau Ln 97404
Merlin Way 97402
Merlot Ave 97404
Merrill Ct 97404
Merry Ln 97404
Merryman Rd 97402
Merryvale Rd 97404
Mesa Ave 97405
Metolius Dr 97408
Mia Ln 97401
Miami Ln 97403
Michael Ln 97405
Midland Brg 97404
Miles Way 97404
Mill Aly 97401
Mill St
4595A-4599A 97405
201-1097 97401
1099-1899 97401
2800-4599 97405
E Mill St 97408
N & S Miller St 97408
Millers Hilltop Rd 97405
Millrace Dr 97403
Milo Way 97404
Milton Ln 97404
Mimi St 97404
Mimosa Ave 97405
Minda Dr 97401
Minick Ln 97405
Minnesota St 97402
Mint Ave 97404
Mira Ct 97402
Miramar St 97405
Miramonti Dr 97405
Mirror Pond Way 97408
Mission Ave 97403
Mississippi Ave 97403
Mist Ct 97402
Mistletoe St 97402
Mlawa Dr 97402
N & S Modesto Dr 97402
Molly Ln 97404
Mondavi Ln 97402
Monroe Aly 97405
Monroe St
1-1899 97402
1900-3999 97405
N Monroe St 97402
Montara Way 97405
Montecello Dr 97404
Monterey Ave & Ln 97401
Montieth Ln 97402
Montreal Ave 97408
Monya Ln 97402
Moon Lee Ln 97403
Moon Mountain Dr 97403
Moonshadow 97405
Moore St 97404
Morely Loop 97402
Morgan Pl 97401
Morning View Dr 97405
Morningside Dr 97401
Morse St 97402
Moss Aly & St 97403
Mountain Ter 97408
Mountain Ash Blvd 97405
Mountain Quail Ln 97405
Mountain View St 97401
Mt Baldy Ln 97405
Mt Valvue Ln 97402
Mulinex Ave 97402
Murdock Rd 97405
Murin St 97402
Murnane St 97402
Murry Dr 97405
Musket St 97408

My De Ct 97401
Myers Rd 97401
W Myoak Dr 97404
Myrna Ave 97404
Mystic Ln 97405
Nadine Ave 97404
Naismith Blvd 97404
Nantucket Ave 97404
Naomi Ct 97401
Napa Creek Dr 97404
Napa Valley Ln 97404
Natchez Ct 97404
Natoma St 97404
Nebraska St 97402
Nectar Way 97405
Needham Rd 97405
Nelson Ln 97408
Neslo Ln 97405
Newcastle St 97404
Newton Pl 97405
Nirvana St 97401
Nixon St 97403
Noah St 97402
Nob Ct 97405
Norbert Ln 97401
Norkenzie Rd
1401-1497 97401
1499-2300 97401
2302-2398 97401
2400-2999 97408
Norman Ave 97404
Normandy Way 97405
North Way 97402
Northampton 97404
Northhill Ranch Rd 97402
Northridge Way 97408
Northrup Dr 97402
Northview Blvd 97405
Norwich Ave 97408
Norwood St 97401
Nottingham Ave 97404
Nueve St 97402
Nugget Way 97403
Nursery Ct 97402
Oak Aly
943-1513 97401
1957-2799 97405
Oak Ct 97405
Oak Dr 97404
Oak St
500-672 97401
674-1899 97401
1900-4299 97405
Oak Crest Rd 97408
Oak Grove Dr 97403
Oak Hill Dr 97402
Oak Hill Cemetery Rd 97402
Oak Leaf Dr 97404
Oak Patch Rd 97402
Oak Springs Ln 97408
Oakdale Dr 97402
Oakfern Rd 97403
Oakhurst Ct 97402
Oakleigh Ln 97404
Oakmont Way 97401
Oakview Ave 97402
Oakville Xing 97402
Oakway Ctr, Rd & Ter 97401
Oakwood Dr 97402
Obie St 97402
Ocean St 97402
Ogle Ave 97402
Ohio St 97402
Oland Ln 97405
Old Coburg Rd 97408
Old Dillard Rd 97405
Old Lorane Hwy 97405
Old Willamette Hwy S 97405
Olive Aly 97401
Olive St
500-1899 97401
1900-3499 97405
Olympic Cir 97402
Ono Ave 97404
Onyx Aly 97403
Onyx Pl 97405

Onyx St
1801-1847 97403
1849-2999 97403
3000-3999 97405
Opal Ln 97405
Oralling St 97405
Orchard Aly & St 97403
Oroyan Ave 97404
Orr Ln 97405
Oscar St 97402
Overbrook Ln 97405
Overpark Arc 97401
Owen Loop N & S 97402
Owl Rd 97405
Owosso Dr 97404
Oxbow Way 97401
Oxford Ct 97404
Pacific Ave 97402
Paddock Dr 97405
Paget Ave 97405
Paige Ave 97405
Paiute Ln 97408
Palace St 97404
Palmer Ave 97401
Palomino Dr 97401
Pam St 97402
Panda Loop 97401
Panorama Dr 97405
Paradise Ct 97401
Parish St 97401
Park Ave 97404
N Park Ave 97404
E Park St 97401
S Park St 97401
W Park St 97401
Park Ter 97404
Park Forest Dr 97405
Park Grove Dr 97408
Park Hills Dr 97405
Park Ridge Ln 97405
Park View Dr 97408
Park Wood Dr 97408
Parker Pl 97402
Parkside Dr & Ln 97403
Parliament St 97405
Parnell Dr 97404
Parsons Ave 97402
Patricia St 97404
Patterson Aly 97401
Patterson Ct 97405
Patterson St
900-1880 97401
1882-1898 97401
1901-2197 97405
2199-4099 97405
Pattison St 97402
Paula Ct 97404
Payne Dr 97402
Peaceful Valley Rd 97405
Pearl Aly 97401
Pearl St
200-1899 97401
1900-2798 97405
2800-4599 97405
E Pearl St 97408
Peascod Dr 97402
E & W Peebles Rd 97405
Peets Ct 97402
Peever St 97401
Peppermint Ln 97408
Peppertree Dr 97402
Perdue Loop 97401
Peregrine St 97404
Perini St 97405
Perleran St 97402
Pershing St 97402
Petzold Rd 97402
Phantom St 97440
Philip St 97402
Pickens Rd 97402
Pierce St 97405
N Pierce St 97404
Pine Canyon Dr 97405
Pine Forest Dr 97405
Pine Grove Rd
85100-85999 97405

86000-86999 97402
Pine Ridge Pl 97402
Pine View Ct 97405
Pinecrest Dr 97405
Pinerock Dr 97403
Pinewood Ter 97405
Pinto Way 97401
Pioneer Ct 97401
Pioneer Pike 97401
Pioneer Rd 97405
Piper Ln 97401
Piper Sonoma St 97404
Pitchford Ave 97402
Plancoun St 97403
Playway Rd 97402
Plearadw St 97401
Plentywood Ln 97404
Plumtree Dr 97402
Polar Ave 97401
Polaris Ct 97402
Polk Aly 97402
Polk St
100-164 97402
166-1799 97402
1801-1899 97402
1900-2799 97405
N Polk St 97402
N Pond Ln & Rd 97401
Pool St 97401
Poplar St 97404
W Port St 97402
Portland Aly & St 97405
Potter Aly
1862-1898 97403
2000-2098 97405
2757-2763 97405
Potter Pl 97405
Potter St
1800-1889 97403
1891-1899 97403
1900-3999 97405
4001-4083 97405
Powder River Dr 97408
Powderhorn St 97408
Powell Rd & St 97405
Powerline Rd 97408
Powers St 97402
Prairie Rd 97402
Praise Ln 97405
Prall Ln 97405
Pranz Pl 97402
Praslin St 97402
President St 97401
Preston St 97401
Prestwich Pl 97401
Primrose St 97402
Prince Ln 97402
Princess Ave 97405
Princeton Dr 97405
Prospect Dr 97403
Providence St 97401
Provincial Way 97401
Pruett Rd 97405
Quail Meadow Way 97408
Quailridge Ln 97404
Quaker St 97402
Quarry Ln 97402
Quebec St 97408
Queens Way 97401
Queens East St 97401
Quest Dr 97402
Quiet Ln 97404
Quince St 97404
Raber Rd 97402
Railroad Blvd 97402
Rainbow Valley Rd 97402
Rainier Dr 97402
Ranch House Rd 97405
Ranchwood Dr 97401
Randall St 97401
Randy Ln 97405
Ransom Ct 97401
Rasor Ave 97404
Rathbone Rd 97402
Raven Oaks Dr 97402
Ravenwood Dr 97401
Red Cedar Ct 97402
Reding Ave 97402
Redrock Way 97404
Redtail Ln 97405
Regal Ct 97401
Regency Dr 97401
Regent Ave 97401
Regina St 97402
Renne St 97402
Restwell Rd 97402
Revell St 97404
Reynolds Dr 97402
Rhine Way 97404
Richard Ave 97402
Richmond St 97402
S Ridge Dr 97405
Ridgefield St 97404
Ridgeline Dr 97405
Ridgemont Dr 97405
Ridgetop Dr 97405
Ridgeview Rd 97408
Ridgeway Dr 97401
Ridgewood Dr 97405
Ridgley Blvd 97401
Riggs St 97401
Riley Ln 97402
Rio Glen Dr 97401
Rio Vista Ave 97404
Risden Pl 97404
River Ave & Rd 97404
River Loop 1 97404
River Loop 2 97404
River Pointe Dr &
Loop 97408
Riverbend Ave 97408
Rivercrest Dr 97404
Riverplace Dr 97401
Riverview St 97403
Riverwalk Loop 97401
Riverwood Dr 97401
Riviera 97402
Roan Dr 97401
Roanoke Ave 97408
Robbie St 97404
Robert St 97402
Roberts Ct & Rd 97408
Robin Ave 97402
Robin Hood Ave 97401
Rockridge Ct, Dr &
Loop 97405
Rockwood St 97405
Rocky Ln 97401
Roland Way 97401
Rollie Loop 97405
Rombauer Rd 97402
Rome Ln 97404
Roosevelt Blvd 97402
Roper Rd 97402
Rose Ct 97401
Rose Ln 97403
Rosebay St 97402
Rosemary Ave 97404
Rosemont Way 97401
Rosetta Ave 97404
E Rosewood Ave 97404
Ross Ln 97404
Rossmore St 97404
Rosy Turn 97404
Roundup Dr 97401
Royal Ave 97402
Royalann Ln 97405
Royster Rd 97402
Ruby Ave 97404
Rupp St 97402
Ruskin St 97402
Russet Dr 97401
Rustic Ct 97408
Rustic Pl 97401
Ruth Ln 97402
Rutledge St 97402
Ryan St 97404
Sabrena Ave 97404
Saddle Pl 97401
Sage St 97404
Saint St 97401
Saint Croix St 97408
Saint Lucia St 97408
Saint Thomas St 97408
Salista Pl 97405
Sally Way 97401
Salty Way 97404
Sam Reynolds St 97402
Sanborn Ave 97404
Sand Ave 97401
Sand Trap Ln 97408
Sanders St 97404
Sandra Ln 97404
Sandstone Way 97402
Sandy Dr 97401
Sanford Rd 97402
Santa Anita Ct 97401
Santa Clara Ave 97404
Santa Rosa St 97404
Santiago Ct 97404
Sarah Ln 97408
Saratoga St 97405
Sarvis Berry Ln 97405
Satre St 97401
Saville Ave 97404
Saxon Way 97405
Scandia St 97402
Scenic Dr 97404
Scharen Rd 97405
Schnorenberg Ln 97405
Scottdale St 97404
Sean St 97402
Seavey Way 97405
Seavey Loop Rd 97405
Sedona Dr 97404
Seely Ln 97405
Selby Way 97408
Sells View Dr 97402
Seneca Ave 97403
Seneca Rd 97402
N Seneca Rd 97402
Senger Ln 97405
Serena Way 97404
Seymore St 97405
Shadow View Dr 97408
Shadow Wood Dr 97405
Shalar Ct 97405
Shamrock Ave & Ct 97404
Shane Ct 97405
Shane Dr 97405
Shannon St 97404
Sharon Way 97401
N & S Shasta Loop 97405
Shasta View St 97405
Shaughnessy Ln 97401
Sheffield Ct 97402
Sheldon Village Loop 97401
Shelton Ave 97405
Shelton Mcmurphey
Blvd 97401
Shenstone Dr 97404
Sheraton Dr 97401
Sherwood Pl 97401
Shields Ave 97405
Shiloh St 97401
Shire Ct 97401
Shirley St 97404
Shore Ln 97402
Shoreline Way 97401
Sierra St 97402
Siesta Ln 97402
Silhouette St 97402
Silver Ln 97404
Silver Lea Ct 97404
Silver Meadows Dr 97404
Silver Oak Dr 97402
Silverado Trl 97404
Silvercrest Dr 97405
Silverwater Ln 97402
Simmons Rd 97405
Simonsen Rd 97405
Sisters Loop 97405
Sisters View Ave 97401
N & S Skinner St 97408
Skip Ct 97404
Skipper Ave 97404
Sky Park Ct & Way 97405
Skybluff Dr 97405
Skyhawk Way 97405
Skylark Ln 97401
Skyline Blvd 97403
Skyline Park Loop 97405
Skyridge Dr 97405
Skyview Ln 97405
Small Ln 97405
Smith Ln 97408
Smithoak St 97404
Snell St 97405
Snelling Dr 97408
Snowberry Rd 97403
Solar Heights Dr 97405
Solar Peak Dr 97405
Soloman Loop 97405
Somerset Ct 97405
Sonoma Dr 97404
Sony Loop 97404
Sorrel Way 97401
South St 97401
Southpointe Dr 97405
Southridge Ct 97405
Southview Dr 97405
Souza Ct & St 97402
Sparrow Ct 97401
Spearmint St 97404
Spencer Ct 97405
Spencer Creek Dr &
Rd 97405
Spencer Glenn Dr 97405
Spencer Hollow Rd 97405
Spencers Crest Dr 97405
Spires Ln 97402
Spirit Valley Dr 97405
Spooky Hollow Dr 97405
Sprague Rd 97408
Sprague St 97405
Spring Blvd
2200-2899 97403
3400-4699 97405
Spring Creek Dr 97404
Spring Knoll Dr 97405
Spring Meadow Ave 97404
Spring Terrace Dr 97405
Springwood Dr 97404
Spur Pl 97401
Spyglass Dr 97401
Squire Dr 97402
St Andrews Dr 97401
St Charles St 97402
St Clair Ln 97405
St Helena St 97402
St Kitts Ave 97408
Stafford Ct 97405
Stagecoach Rd 97402
Stags Leap Ct 97404
Stallings Ln 97408
Stansby Way 97405
Stapp Dr 97408
Stark Ct & St 97404
Startouch Dr 97405
Stephens Dr 97404
Sterling Dr 97404
Sterling Woods Dr 97408
Stevens Ln 97404
Stevi Shay Ln 97404
Stewart Rd 97402
Stillman Ave 97404
Stone Creek Dr 97404
Stonecrest Dr 97401
Stonegate St 97401
Stonehaven St 97404
Stonehenge Ln 97402
Stonewood Dr 97405
Stoney Ridge Rd 97405
Stony Brook Way 97408
Storey Blvd 97405
Stratford St 97404
Strathmore Pl 97405
Strayer Pl 97405
Strome Ct 97404
S Stuart St 97408
Stults Ave 97404
Suburban Ave 97404
Suffolk Ct 97401
Sugarpine Cir 97402
Summer Ln 97404
Summerfield Ave 97402
Summerville Rd 97405
Summit Ave 97403
Summit Sky Blvd 97405
Summit Terrace Dr 97405
Suncatcher Way 97405
Suncrest Ave 97405
Sundance Ln 97402
Sundance St 97405
Sundial Rd 97405
Sundown Dr 97402
Sunny Dr 97404
Sunnyside Dr 97404
Sunnyview Ln 97405
Sunridge Dr 97405
Sunrise Blvd 97405
Sunset Aly 97403
Sunset Dr 97403
Sunset Vw 97405
Sunset Way 97402
Sunshine Acres Dr &
Pl 97401
Suntrek Dr 97403
Sunview St 97404
Surrey Ln 97402
Susan St 97404
Sussex St 97401
Sutherlin Ln 97405
Suzanne Way 97408
Svarverud Rd 97405
Swain Ln 97404
Sweet Gum Ln 97401
Sweetbriar Ln 97405
Sweetwater Ln 97404
Swenson Ln 97404
Sycamore St 97402
Sylvan St 97403
Symphony Dr 97404
Tabor St
1700-2399 97401
2600-2699 97408
Taft St 97402
Tahsili St 97405
Taito St 97404
Talisman St 97405
Talon St 97408
Tandy Turn 97401
Taney St 97402
Tanner Park Dr 97405
Tarpon St 97401
Tarton Pl 97404
Tatum Ln 97404
Taylor Ct 97402
Taylor St
101-197 97402
199-1799 97402
1800-2899 97405
Taz Ln 97404
Teague Loop 97405
Tempa St 97404
Tennyson Ave 97408
Teralee Ln 97402
Terra Linda Ave 97404
Terrace Trl 97405
Terrace View Dr 97405
Terresa Ave 97408
Territorial Hwy
80300-84699 97405
84800-86099 97402
N Terry St 97402
Thames St 97405
Theona Dr 97402
E Thomas St 97408
Thomas Judson Rd 97405
Thomason Ln 97404
Thornberry St 97401
Throne Dr 97402
Thunder Cloud Dr 97405
Thunderbird St 97404
Tiara St 97405
Tiburon Ln 97405
Tigertail Rd 97405
Tilden St 97404
Timber Ln 97405
Timberbrook Way 97405
Timbercrest Rd 97405
Timberline Dr 97405
Tipton Ave 97404
Tivoli Ave 97404
Todd St 97405
Tomahawk Ln & Pl 97401
Torr Ave 97408
Torrington Ave 97404
Tradition Aly 97402
Trail Ave 97404
Trailside Loop 97405
Trap Ln 97401
Travis Ave 97404
Treehill Loop 97405
Trevon St 97402
Tribute Way 97402
Trillium St 97405
Triple Oaks Dr 97408
Troy Way 97402
Tulip St 97408
Turnberry Ct 97401
Turnbull Ln 97401
Twin Buttes Rd 97405
Twin Elms Dr 97408
Tyinn St 97402
Tyler Aly 97402
Tyler St
500-1899 97402
1900-2746 97405
2748-2798 97405
Tyson Ln 97404
University St
1800-2799 97403
2801-2999 97403
3000-3999 97405
University Of Oregon 97403
Unthank Ave 97402
Valhalla St 97401
Valley Butte Dr 97401
Valley Forge Dr 97408
Valley River Ctr, Dr &
Way 97401
Van Ave 97401
Van Buren Aly 97405
Van Buren St
1-1799 97402
1900-3299 97405
3301-3499 97405
N Van Buren St 97402
Van Duyn Rd 97408
Van Duyn St 97401
E Van Duyn St 97408
N Van Duyn St 97401
W Van Duyn St 97408
Van Fossen Ct 97404
Van Ness St 97403
Ventura Ave 97405
Verbena Dr 97404
Verdehill Dr 97403
Vernal St 97401
Vernon Way 97401
Veronica Ln 97404
Victoria Ln 97404
Victorian Way 97401
Videra Dr 97405
View Ln 97405
Vilhauer Rd 97405
Village Ave 97402
Village Plaza Loop 97401
Villard Aly & St 97403
Vincent St 97401
Vine Maple St 97405
Vineyard Hill Dr 97402
Vintage Way 97408
Vintner Ln 97404
Violet Ln 97404
Virgil Ave 97404
Vista Heights Ln 97405
Wagner St 97402
Waite St 97402
Wakefield Ct 97404
Wales Dr 97402
Wallis St 97402
Walnut Aly 97403
Walnut Ave 97404
Walnut Ln 97401
Walnut St 97403
Walton Ln 97408
Ward Ln 97402
Ware Ln 97404
Warren St 97405
Warrington Ave 97404
Warwick Ln 97401
Washington Aly
1300-1672 97401
1677-1699 97401
1800-1898 97402
2001-2023 97405
2386-2428 97405
Washington St
1-697 97401
699-1899 97401
1900-2014 97405
2016-2999 97405
N Washington St 97401
Water St 97408
Waterbrook Way 97408
Waterford Way 97401
Waterstone Dr 97404
Watkins Ln 97405
Watson Dr 97404
Waverly St 97401
Webster St 97404
Wedgewood Dr 97404
Welcome Way 97402
Wellington St 97402
Wendell Ln 97405
Wendover St 97404
Westbrook Way 97405
Westec Dr 97402
Wester St 97408
Western Dr 97401
Westfall Ct 97401
Westleigh St 97405
Westover Dr 97403
Westward Ho Ave 97401
Westwood Ln 97401
Whisper Ln 97401
Whitbeck Blvd 97405
White Oak Dr 97405
Whiteaker St 97405
Whitney Ln 97402
Whitten Dr 97405
Why Worry Ln 97405
Wickham Ct 97404
Wide Site St 97402
Wilbur Ave 97402
Wild Turkey Way 97402
Wildish Ln 97408
Wildrose Ln 97402
Wildwood St 97401
Wildwood Creek Rd 97405
Wilkes Dr 97404
Wilkie St 97402
Wilkins Rd 97408
Willa St 97404
Willagillespie Rd 97401
Willakenzie Rd 97401
Willamette Aly
1403-1523 97401
1525-1529 97401
1531-1797 97401
2101-2199 97405
2402-2478 97405
Willamette St
301-397 97401
399-499 97401
501-1899 97401
520-1898 97401
520-520 97403
520-520 97440
1900-4899 97405
4901-5299 97405
N Willamette St 97408
S Willamette St
84800-85999 97405
90900-91099 97408
Willhi St 97402
Williams St 97402
Williamsburg Way 97401
Willona Dr & Park 97408
Willow Ave 97404

Willow Creek Cir & Rd 97402
Willow Springs Dr 97404
Willowbrook St 97404
Willowdale Dr 97402
Wills Ct 97405
Wilmington Ct 97408
Wilshire Dr & Ln 97405
Wilson Ct 97402
Wilson Dr 97405
Wilson St 97402
Wimbledon Ct 97401
Winchester Way 97401
Windsor Cir E & W 97405
Windward Pl 97402
Winery Ln 97404
Wingate St 97408
Winnebago St 97408
Wintercreek Ct & Dr 97405
Wisconsin St 97402
Wisteria St 97404
Wolf Meadows Ln 97408
Wood Ave 97402
Wood Duck Way 97401
Woodacres Dr 97401
Woodcutter Way 97405
Wooden Way 97404
Woodhill Dr 97405
Woodland Dr 97403
Woodland Acres Ln 97402
Woodlawn Ave 97403
Woodleaf Ln 97405
Woodridge Dr 97405
Woodruff St 97402
Woodsboro St 97402
Woodsia Ln 97405
Woodside Dr 97401
Woodson Ct, Loop & St 97405
Woodstone Pl 97405
Wylie Creek Dr & Pl 97401
Wyndham Ct 97408
Y Way 97405
Yogi Way 97404
York St 97404
Yorkshire Ave 97405
Zachary Ln 97405
Zane Ln 97404
Zarzamora Ln 97405
Zinfandel Ln 97404
Zinnia St 97404
Zoe Ave 97404
Zumwalt St 97402

NUMBERED STREETS

W 1st Ave
300-398 97401
600-4199 97402
1st St 97405
W 2nd Aly 97402
E 2nd Ave 97401
W 2nd Ave
301-499 97401
700-798 97402
800-2200 97402
2202-2298 97402
2nd St 97405
E 3rd Aly 97401
W 3rd Aly 97402
E 3rd Ave 97401
W 3rd Ave
301-349 97401
351-426 97401
428-498 97401
800-1500 97402
1502-3598 97402
W 3rd Pl 97402
W 4th Aly
331-497 97401
717-739 97402
741-1258 97402
1260-1356 97402
E 4th Ave 97401
W 4th Ave
1-97 97401
99-499 97401
600-1500 97402
1502-3698 97402
W 5th Aly 97402
E 5th Ave 97401
W 5th Ave
1-39 97401
41-499 97401
600-4300 97402
4302-4398 97402
W 6th Aly
236-240 97401
772-1188 97402
E 6th Ave 97401
W 6th Ave
3-97 97401
99-400 97401
402-498 97401
600-698 97402
700-4230 97402
4232-4298 97402
W 7th Aly
332-362 97401
642-1098 97402
E 7th Ave 97401
W 7th Ave
2-98 97401
600-4299 97402
W 7th Pl 97402
W 8th Aly
2-404 97401
733-933 97402
E 8th Ave 97401
W 8th Ave
27-97 97401
600-1999 97402
W 8th Pl 97402
W 9th Pl 97402
W 10th Aly 97402
E 10th Ave 97401
W 10th Ave
2-54 97401
56-599 97401
600-1899 97402
1901-2199 97402
W 10th Pl 97402
E 11th Aly 97401
W 11th Aly
362-486 97401
603-649 97402
E 11th Ave 97401
W 11th Ave
52-120 97401
600-28500 97402
E 12th Aly 97401
W 12th Aly
101-297 97401
852-930 97402
E 12th Ave 97401
W 12th Ave
147-591 97401
600-3999 97402
E 13th Aly 97401
W 13th Aly 97402
E 13th Ave
1-899 97401
1222-1372 97403
W 13th Ave
1-39 97401
601-697 97402
W 13th Pl 97402
E 14th Aly 97401
E 14th Ave
1-800 97401
3500-3599 97403
W 14th Ave
112-278 97401
1100-3399 97402
W 14th Ct 97402
W 14th Pl 97402
E 15th Aly 97401
E 15th Ave
1-49 97401
1301-1697 97403
W 15th Ave
2-70 97401
600-3499 97402
W 15th Ct 97402
E 16th Aly 97401
E 16th Ave
100-799 97401
2600-2698 97403
W 16th Ave
63-113 97401
600-3499 97402
W 16th Ct 97402
W 16th Way 97402
E 17th Aly 97401
E 17th Ave
30-72 97401
1600-4096 97403
W 17th Ave
1-579 97401
800-3399 97402
W 17th Ct 97402
E 18th Aly
301-717 97401
1472-1478 97403
E 18th Ave
50-58 97401
901-909 97403
W 18th Ave
1-554 97401
600-4099 97402
W 18th Pl 97402
E 19th Aly 97405
W 19th Aly 97405
E 19th Ave
2-64 97401
900-4100 97403
W 19th Ave
1-37 97401
600-1199 97402
1600-3199 97405
W 19th Pl 97405
E 20th Ave
17-39 97405
1100-1499 97403
1501-4399 97405
W 20th Ave 97405
E 21st Ave
662-698 97405
700-1099 97405
1101-1197 97403
1199-3899 97403
W 21st Ave 97405
E 22nd Aly 97405
E 22nd Ave
600-710 97405
712-1084 97405
1086-1098 97405
1100-3796 97403
3798-4098 97403
3795 1/2-3799 1/2 97403
W 22nd Ave 97405
E 23rd Ave
1-1099 97405
1101-1199 97403
1201-1799 97403
W 23rd Ave 97405
W 23rd Pl 97405
E 24th Aly 97403
E 24th Ave
1-21 97405
1100-1198 97403
W 24th Ave 97405
E 24th Pl 97405
W 24th Pl 97405
E 25th Ave
44-92 97405
1100-2000 97403
2002-3698 97403
W 25th Ave 97405
E 25th Pl 97405
W 25th Pl 97405
E 26th Ave
84-1050 97405
1052-1098 97405
1100-2799 97403
W 26th Ave 97405
W 26th Pl 97405
E 27th Ave
11-47 97405
49-1051 97405
1053-1099 97405
1100-2099 97403
W 27th Ave 97405
W 27th Pl 97405
E 28th Ave
1-97 97405
99-1074 97405
1076-1098 97405
1100-1999 97403
W 28th Ave 97405
W 28th Pl 97405
E 29th Ave
69-77 97405
79-999 97405
1100-2299 97403
W 29th Ave 97405
E 29th Pl
90-98 97405
1200-1299 97403
W 29th Pl 97405
E & W 30th 97405
E & W 31st 97405
32nd Aly & Ave 97405
E 33rd Ave 97405
E & W 34th Aly, Ave & Pl 97405
E & W 35th Ave & Pl 97405
E & W 36th Ave & Pl 97405
E & W 37th 97405
E & W 38th 97405
E & W 39th Ave & Pl 97405
E & W 40th 97405
E 41st Ave 97405
E 42nd Ave 97405
E 43rd Ave 97405
E & W 44th 97405
E 46th Ave 97405
E 47th Ave 97405
E 48th Ave 97405
E 49th Ave 97405
E 50th Ave 97405
W 52nd Ave 97405
E 53rd Ave 97405

GRANTS PASS OR

General Delivery 97526

POST OFFICE BOXES MAIN OFFICE STATIONS AND BRANCHES

Box No.s
376A - 376A 97528
1 - 2778 97528
5001 - 6000 97527

NAMED STREETS

A St 97526
Abby Ln 97527
SW Aberdeen Way 97526
SW Abilene Way 97526
Acacia Ln 97527
SW Acres Rd 97527
Adele Dr 97526
Adeline Dr 97527
Agape Way 97527
Agee Dr 97526
NE Agness Ave 97526
Alan Lee Rd 97527
Alanita Ln 97527
SW Alder St 97526
Alderbrook Ln 97527
Alexander Ln 97527
Alimossy Ln 97527
SW Allen Creek Rd 97527
SE Allenwood Dr 97527
Allman Way 97526
Almar Rd 97527
Alpine Cir 97526
Amber Ln 97527
NW Amelia Dr 97526
Ament Rd 97526
SE American Way 97526
Anastasia Ct 97527
NE Anderson St 97526
Andy Griffith Dr 97527
Angler Ln 97527
SW Anique Ln 97526
Anita Dr 97526
Ann Roy Dr 97527
Anna Way 97526
Annabelle Ln 97527
Anthony Pl 97527
Appaloosa Ln 97526
Apple Ln 97527
N Applegate Ave & Rd 97527
Arbor Ridge Dr 97527
SW Arch Ct 97527
Ardath Dr 97526
SW Argo Ln 97527
Arms Way 97527
Arnold Ave 97527
Arroyo Dr 97527
Artlin Rd 97526
Ashbrook Ln 97527
SE Ashley Pl 97526
Ashwood Dr 97526
Aspen Way 97527
Assembly Cir 97526
Auby Way 97527
Aunt Bea Way 97527
Aurora Ave 97526
NE Ausland Dr 97526
Autumn Ln 97527
SE Autumn Blaze Dr 97527
Avalon Pl 97527
Avenue De Teresa 97526
Averill Dr 97526
Axtell Dr 97527
Azalea Dr 97526
Aztec Ct 97527
NE & NW B St 97526
Bailey Dr 97527
NE Baker Dr 97526
Ball Ct 97526
SW Ballinger Dr 97526
SW Balsam Rd 97526
Bandy Way 97526
Bannister Ln 97526
Barbara Dr 97526
Barney Fife Blvd 97527
Bartlett Ln 97527
Bastian Rd 97526
Bayard Dr 97527
Bayou Pl 97526
NE Bea Villa Vw 97526
NE Beacon Dr 97526
Becky Springs Dr 97527
Beechwood Dr 97526
Belindy Cir 97527
Bella Vista Way 97526
SE Belle Aire Dr 97526
NW Bellevue Pl 97526
Bellewood Dr 97527
Belmont Pl 97526
Ben Aire Cir 97527
Bennett Ln 97527
Bentley Dr 97526
NW Berry Ln 97526
SW Betty Ln 97526
NE Beverly Dr 97526
Bickford Dr 97527
SE Big Leaf Ln 97527
Big Pine Dr 97526
Bill Baker Way 97527
NW Birch St 97526
NW Bishop St 97526
NW Black Oak Dr 97526
Black Oak St 97527
Black Pine Dr 97527
Blackhorse Dr 97526
Blackwell Dr 97527
Blake Ct 97527
SW Blenda Ct 97526
NW Blossom Dr 97526
SE Blue Bird Dr 97526
Blue Chip Ln 97527
Blue Heron Ct 97526
Blue Jay Ln 97527
Blue Moon Ln 97527
Blue Spruce Ln 97527
Blue Water Ln 97527
Bluebell Ln 97527
Bluegrass Pl 97526
Board Shanty Rd 97527
Bolt Mountain Rd 97527
Bolt View Rd 97527
NE Bonney Doon Ln 97526
Bonnie Ln 97527
NW & SW Booth St 97526
Boundary Ln & Rd 97527
Bower Ln 97527
Bowhill Rd 97526
Boyer Rd 97526
Boynton Dr 97527
Bradley Ct 97527
Brandy Ln 97527
Breezy Ln 97527
Brentwood Dr 97526
Brett Way 97526
Briarwood Way 97526
SW Bridge St 97526
Bristow Rd 97527
Brittany Ct 97527
Brock Ln 97527
Brooke Ln 97527
Brookhurst Way 97527
Brookside Blvd 97526
Brookstone Hills Dr 97526
SW Brownell Ave 97526
NE Bryce Ct 97526
SW Bryn Ct 97526
Buckhorn Dr 97526
Buckskin Rd 97526
NW Buddy Ln 97526
Buena Vista Ln 97527
Bull Creek Rd 97527
Bummer Creek Ln 97526
NW Bunnell Ave 97526
SW Burgess St 97526
Burnette Rd 97527
NW Burns Ave 97526
Burton Dr 97527
Bushnell Way 97527
NW Butler Ave 97526
Buttercup St 97527
Buysman Way 97526
NE & NW C St 97526
NW Caddis Pl 97526
SE Cadet Ct 97527
SW Cal Allen Ln 97527
California St 97526
Calvert Dr 97526
Cambridge Dr 97526
SE Camelot Dr 97526
Cameo Ct 97527
Cameron Cir 97526
Camp Joy Rd 97527
NE Campus Dr 97526
Campus View Dr 97527
Canaan St 97527
Canal Ave 97527
Candlelight Ln 97527
NW Candler Ave 97526
NE Candy Ln 97526
Canyon Dr 97527
Canyon Oak Dr 97526
NW Canyon View Dr 97526
NE Carla Way 97526
Carnahan Dr 97527
NW Carol Dr 97526
Carolann Way 97526
Carolbrooke Ln 97527
Carriage Rd 97526
Carrollwood Dr 97527
Carson Dr 97527
Carter Dr 97526
Carton Way 97526
SE Casey Pl 97526
Cashmere Dr 97527
Casita Dr 97527
Castle Creek Rd 97526
Catalpa Dr 97526
Cathedral Way 97526
Catherine Way 97526
NE Cedar Ln 97526
Cedar Heights Dr 97526
Cedar Springs Dr 97527
Cedar Valley Dr 97526
SW Central Ave 97526
Century Cir 97527
Chace Mtn 97526
Chace Mountain Rd 97526
Chambers Ln 97526
Chaparral Dr 97526
Cheney Creek Rd 97527
Cherokee Ln 97526
SE Cherry Ln 97526
Cheslock Rd 97527
Chestnut Ln 97526
Cheyenne Dr 97527
Chinook Park Ln 97527
Chipley Rd 97526
SE Christie Pl 97526
NE Churchill St 97526
Cienaga Ln 97526
Cindy Ln 97526
Claibourn St 97527
Clara Ave 97527
SE Clarey Ave 97526
NW Clarke St 97526
Claudia Way 97527
Clear Sky Dr 97526
SW Clementine Pl 97527
Clewis Ln 97526
Cliffside Dr 97527
Cline Dr 97527
E Cloverlawn Dr 97527
NE Clyde Pl 97526
Clydesdale Dr 97526
Coach Dr 97527
Coed Pl 97527
Coho Ct 97527
Colin Rd 97527
Colleen Ct 97527
College Dr 97527
Colonial Dr 97526
Colorado Ln 97527
E Columbia Crst 97526
Columbia Crest Dr 97526
Comet Ct 97527
Commerce Way 97526
Concord Ct 97527
Conestoga Dr 97527
Conger Ln 97527
Conifer Dr 97527
NW Conklin Ave 97526
NW Constitution Cir 97526
NW Cooke Ave 97526
NE Cooper Dr 97526
NW Copeland Ln 97526
Copper Dr 97527
Corbin Dr 97527
Coriander Way 97527
Corporate Way 97526
SW Cottonwood St 97526
Country Aire Dr 97526
Coutant Ln 97527
Covey Ln 97527
Creeks Rd 97526
NW Creekside Dr 97526
NW Crescent Dr 97526
Crestview Loop 97527
Cricket Ln 97527
Crossbow Ln 97527
NW Crown St 97526
NE Croxton Ave 97526
Crume Dr 97526
Crystal Dr 97527
Crystal Springs Rd 97527
Cullison Ln 97527
Culver Dr 97527
Cumberland Dr 97527
Currie Ln 97526
Curtis Dr 97527
SW Cypress St 97527
NE & NW D St 97526
Daily Ln 97527

Daisy Ln 97527
Dakota Ln 97526
Daleo Dr 97527
Damon Ct 97527
SW Dan Cir 97526
Darin Dr 97527
Darneille Ln 97527
Darrell Cir 97527
SW David Dr 97527
Dawn Dr 97527
Dawn Allan Dr 97527
NW Dawnhill Ct 97526
De Woody Ln 97527
NE Dean Dr 97526
Dearing Way 97527
Debra Ln 97527
Debrick Way 97526
Deer Haven Ln 97527
Deerhorn Dr 97527
Dell Rd 97527
Dellwood Dr 97526
Delsie Dr 97527
Demaray Dr 97527
Denton Trl 97527
Denver Ave 97526
Deodara Ct 97527
SW Derek Ln 97527
Detrick Dr 97527
Devon Dr 97527
Devonshire Way 97527
NE Dewey Dr 97526
Dexter Way 97527
Diamond Way 97526
Diane Dr 97526
NW & SW Dimmick St 97526
Dinkle Ln 97527
SW Division St 97526
Dogwood Dr 97526
SW, NE & NW Dolores Ave, Dr, Ln, St & Way 97527
Donaldson Rd 97526
Doneen Ln 97526
NW Donna Dr 97526
NW Donovan Ct 97526
Doris Ann Ln 97527
Dorry Ln 97527
Douglas Dr 97527
NW Dover Dr 97526
Dowell Rd 97527
Drury Ln 97527
NE Duane Dr 97526
NE Dudley Dr 97526
Duke Ct 97527
Dunlap Ln 97527
Dustin Way 97526
Dutcher Creek Rd 97527
Dutchy Way 97527
Dyer Rd 97527
NE & NW E St 97526
Eagle Ridge Dr 97526
Eagle View Dr 97527
Eagle Vista Dr 97526
SW Eastern Ave 97526
SW Eastwood Ln 97527
Easy St 97527
Eclipse Ln 97527
Eden Dr 97526
Edgewater Dr 97527
Edwards Way 97526
Egret Ct 97526
El Camino Way 97526
El Conejo Dr 97526
Elaine Dr 97527
Elberta St 97526
SE Elderberry Ln 97527
NE Elida Dr 97526
NE Eliza Dr 97526
NE Elizabeth Pl 97526
Elk Ln 97527
Elkhorn Dr 97527
SE, NW & SW Elm Ln & St 97526
SW Elmer Nelson Ln 97527
Elrod Ln 97527
NE Emerald Way 97526
Emily Way 97527

Eric Loop & Way 97526
SW Erica Dr 97526
Erin Dr 97527
S Espey Rd 97527
Estates Ln 97527
Esther Ln 97527
Euclid St 97527
NW Eunice Ave 97526
NE Evans St 97526
NE & NW Evelyn Ave 97526
Evergreen Ave 97527
Evon Cir 97527
Ewe Creek Rd 97526
SE Excalibur Dr 97526
NE & NW F St 97526
Fahey Way 97527
Fairfield Ln 97526
Fairgrounds Rd 97527
NE Fairview Ave 97526
Fairway Dr 97527
NE Fall Dr 97526
Fall Run Dr 97526
Favill Ln & Rd 97526
Fawn Dr 97526
Felicia Ln 97527
Felkner Rd 97527
SE Fern St 97526
Ferry Rd 97526
NE Fetzner St 97526
Fielder Ln 97526
Finley Bend Dr 97526
Fir Canyon Rd 97527
Fire Mountain Way 97526
Firwood Dr 97527
Fish Hatchery Rd 97527
Flaming Rd 97526
NE Flint St 97526
Florence Ln 97527
SW Florer Dr 97527
Flower Ln 97527
NE Foothill Blvd 97526
SW Ford St 97526
Forest Ln 97527
Forest Glen Dr 97526
Forestview Dr 97527
NE Foster Way 97526
SW Foundry St 97526
SW Fountain Cir 97527
Foxwood Dr 97527
Frances Way 97526
Frankham Rd 97527
NW Franklin Blvd 97526
Freedom Cir 97527
Frontier Ln 97526
Fruitdale Dr 97527
NW & SW Fry St 97526
SE & SW G St 97526
G I Ln 97527
Gaffney Way 97527
Gailmar Cir 97526
Galaxy Way 97527
SW Garden Meadow Dr 97527
Garden Terrace Rd 97527
SW Garden Valley Way 97526
Gardendale Ln 97527
Garnet Ln 97526
Gayle Way 97527
SE Gene Ln 97526
Genevieve Dr 97527
Genverna Gln 97527
George Tweed Blvd 97527
NW Gilbert Way 97526
SE Gladiola Dr 97526
Glen Dr 97526
Glen Crest Way 97527
Glenbe Dr 97526
Glenoak Ln 97526
E & W Glenwood St 97527
Gold Ct 97527
Gold River Ln 97527
Golden Aspen Dr 97527
Golden Park Dr 97527
Gordon Way N & S 97527
NE Grable Dr 97526

SW Grandview Ave & Ln 97527
Grange Rd 97526
Granite Hill Rd 97526
NW & SW Grant St 97526
Grants Pass Pkwy & Rd 97526
Gray Ave 97527
Gray Eagle Dr 97526
Gray Wolf Dr 97526
Grays Creek Rd 97527
SE Green Briar Ln 97526
Greenash Dr 97527
NE Greenfield Dr 97526
Greens Creek Rd 97527
Greentree Loop 97527
SW Greenwood Ave 97526
Gregg Cir 97527
Griffin Rd 97527
Grouse Creek Rd 97526
Gunnell Rd 97526
Guth Rd 97526
SE & SW H St 97526
Hacienda Way 97526
Hales Way 97526
Half Moon Cir 97527
SW Hall St 97526
Hamilton Ln 97527
Hampden Rd 97526
Hampshire Cir 97526
Hampton Way 97526
Hannah Way 97527
Hansen Dr 97526
W Harbeck Rd 97527
Harmony Cir 97527
Harpazo Ln 97527
Harper Loop 97527
Harris Rd 97526
Hartley Ln 97527
Hartman Ln 97527
Harvard Way 97527
SW Harvest Dr 97527
SE Harvey Dr 97526
Hasis Dr 97526
Haviland Dr 97527
Hawk Dr 97527
Hawksdale Dr 97526
NW Hawthorne Ave 97526
Haylees Way 97526
Hazelwood Dr 97527
SW Heather Dr 97526
NW Heathwood Pl 97526
NE Hefley St 97526
NW Heidi Ln 97526
Helgeson Ln 97527
Helms Rd 97527
Hemlock Ln 97527
Henderson Ln 97527
NE Heritage Dr 97526
SE Herrick Ln 97526
Hessar St 97527
NW Hewitt Ln 97526
Hickory Ln 97527
Hidden Pine Dr 97526
Hidden Valley Rd 97527
Hieglen Loop 97526
SW High St 97526
High Ridge Ter 97526
NW Highland Ave 97526
Highland Ranch Rd 97526
Highway 238 97527
Highwood Ln 97527
Hill Top Dr 97527
NE & NW Hillcrest Dr & Ln 97526
Hillpark Pl 97526
NW Hillside Dr 97526
Hilltop Vw 97527
Hillview Dr 97527
Himrich Dr 97527
Hitching Post Rd 97526
Hixson Dr 97527
Hoffman Way 97526
Holbrook Way 97526
Homewood Rd 97527
Honeycutt Dr 97526

Honeylocust Dr 97527
Honeylynn Ln 97527
Hope Ln 97527
Hornet Ln 97527
Horseshoe Dr 97526
Howard Pl 97526
Hubbard Ln 97527
SW Hudson Ln 97526
Hugo Rd 97526
Hull Dr 97526
Humanity Way 97526
Humberd Ln 97527
Humphrey Ln 97527
SW Hungry Hill Dr 97527
Hunt Ln 97526
Hussey Ln 97527
Hyde Park Rd 97527
SE & SW I St 97526
Ichabod Ln 97527
Idle Ct 97527
Incline Dr 97527
Independence Dr 97527
NE Industry Dr 97526
SE Inman Ln 97526
E & W Intervale Rd 97527
Irena Rd 97526
Iris Ln 97526
SW Ironwood Dr 97526
Isabella Ln 97526
SW Isham St 97526
SE & SW J St 97526
Jack Creek Rd 97526
Jackpine Dr 97526
NE Jackson St 97526
Jaime Ln 97526
SW Jamee Kay Ln 97527
Jasmine Dr 97526
Jason Way 97527
Jasper Ln 97527
SE Jaylen Dr 97527
Jaynes Dr 97527
Jeffrey Ct 97527
Jems Riffle Rd 97527
Jenkins Ave 97527
SW Jenn Way 97527
NE Jennifer Way 97526
Jeramy Way 97527
Jerome Prairie Rd 97527
SE Jerrine St 97527
Jesinghaus Rd 97527
Jess Way 97526
Jewett Creek Rd 97527
Jillana Ter 97527
Jody Ln 97527
SE Joel Dr 97527
NE John Dr 97526
Johnmark Cir 97527
Johnson Dr 97527
Jonathon Ln 97526
E & W Jones Creek Rd 97526
SW Jordan St 97526
NE Josephine St 97526
Joshua St 97526
SW Judson St 97526
SW Judy Ln 97526
NW Juliet Ln 97526
Jumpoff Joe Creek Rd 97526
SW Juniper Dr 97526
SE & SW K St 97526
Kadee Ln 97527
Kaneeta Ln 97526
Karral Dr 97527
SW Kathleen Cir 97526
Kayleigh Way 97526
Keen Rd 97527
Keeta Way 97526
Keldan Ln 97527
Kellenbeck Ave 97527
Kelly Way 97527
Ken Canyon Rd 97526
Kendall Dr 97527
Kendallbrook Way 97527
Kenwood St 97527
Kevin Dr 97527
Key Way 97527

Kids Way 97526
Kilborn Dr 97526
Kimberly Way 97526
Kings Way 97526
Kingsbury Dr 97526
Kingsgate Way 97527
Kingsley Dr 97526
NW Kinney St 97526
SW Kinsington Ct 97526
Kip Ct & Ln 97526
NW Knight Ct 97526
Knights Xing 97527
SE Kodie Ln 97527
Kokanee Ln 97527
Kolkana Way 97526
Kroner Dr 97527
Kruger Ln 97527
SE Krystin Pl 97526
Kubli Rd 97527
SW Kurtz Ln 97526
SE & SW L St 97526
Ladeana Way 97527
SW Lafayette Dr 97527
Laine Ct 97527
Lakeview Dr 97526
Lance Dr 97526
Landau Ln 97527
Landsiedel Ln 97527
Lappland Dr 97527
SW Larch Rd 97526
Lark Ellen Way 97527
Larkin Rd 97527
Larkspur Ct 97527
NW Lassen Way 97526
Lathrop Ln & Rd 97526
Laubach Ln 97527
Lauer Way 97526
NE Laura Ct 97526
Laurel Ave 97527
SW Laurel St 97526
Laureldale Ln 97527
Laurelridge Pl 97526
Lawless Ln 97527
NW Lawnridge Ave 97526
Le Karen Dr 97526
Leaning Pine Ln 97526
Leavitt Ln 97527
SW Lee Ln 97526
Lee Joy Dr 97526
Lee Roze Ln 97527
SE Lela Ln 97526
Lelith Ln 97527
Lenella Ln 97526
Leonard Rd 97527
SW Leonard St 97526
Lewis Ave 97527
Lexington Ct 97527
SE Liberty Dr 97526
Lilac Ln 97527
SE Lillian Ct 97527
Limpy Creek Rd 97527
Lincoln Rd 97526
Lind Rd 97527
Linda Lee Ln 97527
E & W Linda Vista Rd 97527
SE Linden Ln 97527
Lindy Ln 97526
Lisa Ln 97527
Lissy Way 97526
S Livingston Way 97526
Lloyd Dr 97526
Locust Way 97527
Lois Ln 97527
Long Acres Rd 97527
Lonnon Rd 97527
NW Loughridge Ave 97526
SW Louise Cir 97526
Lovitt Ln 97527
SW Lowe Ct 97527
Lower River Rd 97526
Loy Birch Dr 97526
Luba St 97527
Luzon Ln 97527
NE Lynda Ln 97526
NW Lynel Ct 97526
NW Lynwood Pl 97526

SE & SW M St 97526
Macnew Ln 97527
Madeline Way 97527
NE Madrone St 97526
Madrone Ridge Dr 97527
SE Maice Ct 97527
Majestic Dr 97527
SW Major St 97526
Mallory Heights Dr 97526
Malone Way 97527
NE & NW Manzanita Ave 97526
Maple Ln 97527
NE Maple St 97526
N & S Marble Dr 97526
Marble Mountain Rd 97527
Marcus Way 97527
Marcy Loop Rd 97527
Mardan Dr 97527
Marie Dr 97526
Marilee Row 97527
Marion Ln 97527
SE Marjean Ln 97526
Mark Brandt Dr 97526
SE Marlen Dr 97527
Marlsan Rd 97526
SW Martin Park Ln 97526
SW Mary Ave 97526
Mary Harris Way 97526
Mary Lynn Ln 97527
Mayfair Ln 97527
Mayfield Dr 97527
Mccarter Ln 97527
Mcdonald Ln 97527
Mckenzie Ridge Rd 97526
Mcvay Ln 97526
NE Mead St 97526
Meadow Gln 97527
Meadow Ln 97526
Meadow Lark Ln 97526
Medart Ln 97527
NE Meier Dr 97526
Melinda Way 97526
Melissa Ln 97526
NE Memorial Dr 97526
Mendi Way 97527
SW Mercury Ln 97526
Meridian Way 97527
Merlin Rd 97526
Mesman Dr 97527
Messinger Rd 97527
NW Michelle Way 97526
NE & NW Midland Ave 97526
Midway Ave 97527
SE Milbank Rd 97526
NE & SE Mill St 97526
Mimosa Way 97527
Mina Ln 97526
Mini Ln 97527
Mint Ln 97527
Missouri Flat Rd 97527
Mist Cir 97527
SW Mistybrook Dr 97526
Molly Ln 97527
Monica Dr 97526
Monroe Way 97527
Monteflora Ter 97526
Monterico Rd 97526
Montgomery Ln 97527
S Monument Dr 97526
Moon Glo Dr 97527
Moon Mountain Rd 97526
Moonbeam Ln 97527
Morewood Ln 97526
NE & NW Morgan Ln 97526
Morris Ln 97527
Moss Ln 97527
Mossflower Ln 97527
Mossy Oak Dr 97526
Mount Baldy Rd 97527
Mountain Fir Rd 97527
Mountain Greens Ln 97526
Mountain Home Dr 97527
Mountain Paradise Dr 97526
Mountain Pine Dr 97526

Mountain Springs Dr 97527
Mountain View Pl 97527
Mulberry Ct 97527
Murphy Ln 97527
Murphy Creek Rd 97527
Mystic Dr 97527
SE N St 97526
Nancy Pl 97527
Naples Dr 97527
NW Native Run Loop 97526
Naturescape Rd 97527
Neamar Dr 97527
Nebraska Ave 97527
Needlewood Dr 97526
Neila Ct & Ln 97527
Neill Rd 97527
Nelson Way 97526
New Hope Rd 97527
Newby Dr 97527
Nick Way 97527
Nicklaus Ln 97526
NE Noble Hts 97526
NW North Hill Dr 97526
Norwood Ln 97527
Nottingham Way 97527
Nunnwood Ln 97527
Nursery Ln 97527
SW Oak St 97526
NE Oak Dale Dr 97526
Oak Ranch Rd 97526
Oak View Dr 97527
Oakhill Ln 97527
Oakmont Dr 97526
Oakridge Dr 97526
Ojai Ave 97527
Old Highway 99 97526
Old Oak Cir 97526
NE Olive St 97526
NW Olmar Dr 97526
NE Olson Dr 97526
Omaha Dr 97527
Ootz Ln 97527
Opal Ln 97526
Opie Pl 97527
Orangewood Dr 97526
NW Orchard St 97526
NE Oregon Ave 97526
SE Oriole St 97526
Orofino Rd 97526
Osprey Dr 97526
Osprey Glen Ln 97526
Osprey Vista Dr 97526
SW Otis Ln 97527
SW Otter Ct 97527
NE Outlook Ave 97526
Overland Dr 97527
NW Oxford Cir 97526
Oxyoke Rd 97526
Pacific Crest Dr 97527
Palomino Dr 97526
Palos Verdes Dr 97526
Panoramic Loop 97527
Pansy Ln 97527
Paradise Gardens Rd 97527
Pardee Ln 97527
E & W Park St 97527
SE Park Plaza Dr 97527
Parkdale Cir & Dr 97527
NW Parker Dr 97526
Parkhill Pl 97527
S Pass Rd 97526
Pass Creek Rd 97526
Patrick Rd 97527
Patriot Ln 97527
Pauldine Way 97527
Pavillian Dr 97526
NW Pawn Way 97526
Peaceful Valley Ln 97527
Pearce Park Rd 97526
Pearl Dr 97527
Peckerwood Ln 97527
Peco Rd 97526
Penny Ln 97527
Penwheel Ln 97527
NE Pepperwood Dr 97526
SE Perry St 97526

Pesterfield Pl 97526
Phillips Ln 97527
W Pickett Creek Rd 97527
NE Piedmont Ave 97526
Pine Ct 97527
SW Pine St 97526
Pine Dell Ln 97526
Pine Ridge Dr 97527
Pinecrest Dr 97526
N Pinnon Rd 97526
Pintail Ct 97527
NE Pioneer Way 97526
Playford Ln 97527
NW Pleasant View Dr 97526
Pleasantville Way 97526
Plumlee Way 97527
Plummer Ave 97527
Plumtree Ln 97526
Ponderosa Ln 97527
NW Ponderosa St 97526
Pony Ln 97526
Pooh Ln 97526
Poplar Dr 97527
Poppy Ln 97527
Porter Ln 97527
Portland Ave 97526
SE Portola Dr 97526
Potts Way 97526
Prairie Ln 97527
NE Primrose Pl 97526
SW Princess Cir 97527
SW Princeton Pl 97527
SE Priscilla Ln 97526
NW Prospect Ave 97526
Providence Way 97526
Pruden Dr 97526
Pruitt Pl 97527
Pyle Dr 97527
Quail Ln & Xing 97526
NW Queens Way 97526
R J Dr 97526
Rainbow Dr 97526
Rainwood Ln 97527
SW Ramsey Ave 97527
Rancho Vista Dr 97526
Randy Dr 97527
SW Ravenwood Dr 97527
Raydean Dr 97527
Raywood Cir 97527
Red Fox Ln 97526
SE Red Maple Ln 97527
Red Mountain Dr 97526
Red Oak Ln 97527
Red Rock Ln 97527
Red Spur Dr 97527
Reddy St 97527
Redfin Ln 97527
Redland Dr 97527
Redwood Ave, Cir & Hwy 97527
Redwood Vista Ln 97527
Reel Ln 97527
NW Regent Dr 97526
Regina Way 97527
Rhonda Dr 97527
SW Rhumba Dr 97526
Richland Dr 97526
NE Riddle Dr 97526
NE Ridge Rd 97526
Ridgecrest Dr 97527
Ridgefield Rd 97527
Riessen Rd 97526
Ringuette St 97527
Rio Mesa Dr 97527
Rio Vista Ln 97527
Rivaway Ln 97527
S River Cir, Ln & Rd 97527
River Heights Way 97527
SW River Oaks Pl 97526
River Vista Dr 97527
Riverbanks Rd 97527
Rivercrest Dr 97527
SE Riverside Ave 97526
Roan Dr 97526
Robert Ave 97527
Robertson Crst & Ln 97527
Robertson Bridge Rd 97526
Robinson Rd 97527
Robmar Ln 97527
SW Rock Ct 97526
Rockingham Pl 97527
Rockinghorse Dr 97527
Rockwood St 97527
SE Rogers Ct 97526
SE Rogue Blvd & Dr 97526
Rogue Manor Pl 97527
Rogue Ridge Dr 97527
Rogue Riffle Dr 97526
SW Rogue River Ave 97526
Rogue River Hwy 97527
SE Rogue View Ln 97526
Roguelea Ln 97526
Rolling Hills Dr 97527
Ronstadt Way 97526
NW Rook Dr 97526
SE Rose Pl 97526
NE Roseana Dr 97526
Rosebank Way 97526
SE Rosemary Ln 97526
E & W Rosewood St 97527
Roslington Ln 97527
Rossier Ln 97527
Rounds Ave 97527
SE Roundtable Dr 97526
NE Royal Dr 97526
Royal View Ln 97527
Ruby Dr 97527
Russell Rd 97526
Rustic Canyon Dr 97526
Rusty Spur 97526
Ryan Ct 97527
Saddle Ln 97526
NW Salisbury Dr 97526
Sallsten Rd 97527
Salmon Cir 97527
SW Sams Cir 97526
San Francisco St 97526
Sand Creek Rd 97527
Sandlewood Dr 97526
NW Sandy Dr 97526
Sapphire Ct 97527
Saradan Ln 97527
Saratoga Way 97526
NW Sarum Cir 97526
Sasha Ct 97527
NE & NW Savage St 97526
W Savage Creek Rd 97527
NE & NW Scenic Dr 97526
Schaefers Ln 97526
NE School St 97526
N & S Schoolhouse Creek Rd 97526
Schroeder Ln 97527
W Schutzwohl Ln 97527
Scolaire Dr 97526
Scotch Pine Dr 97527
Scott Dr 97527
Scoville Rd 97526
Seclusion Loop 97526
Sequoia Ct 97527
Serenity Ln 97526
Shadow Ln 97526
Shadow Hills Dr 97526
Shadow Mountain Way 97527
Shady Ln 97527
Shamrock Ln 97527
Shan Creek Rd 97527
Shane Way 97527
Shannon Ln 97526
Sharon Dr 97527
NW Shelly Cir 97526
NE Sherman Ln 97526
Sherry Ln 97527
Sherwood Ln 97527
Shetland Dr 97526
Shimmer Ln 97527
Shire Ln 97526
Shoemaker Way 97527
Short St 97527
Shorthorn Gulch Rd 97526
Siebert Way 97527
Sierra Way 97526
Sierra Lodge Dr 97527
SW Silver Maple Way 97526
NE Silverwood Pl 97526
NW Sinclair Dr 97526
Siskiyou Rd 97527
SW Sisters Way 97526
Sky Way 97527
Sky Crest Dr 97527
Skylark Ln 97527
Skyline Dr 97527
Slagle Creek Rd 97527
Sleepy Hollow Loop 97527
Sloan Mountain Ln 97527
Smokey Ln 97527
Sockeye Cir 97527
Softwood Way 97526
Soldier Creek Rd 97526
Solitude Ln 97527
NE Sommer Dr 97526
Southgate Way 97527
SE Southpark Dr 97527
Southridge Way 97527
Southside Rd 97527
NE Sovereign Ave 97526
Space View Dr 97526
Sparrow Cir 97527
NE Spaulding Ave 97526
SW Spring St 97526
Spring Mountain Rd 97526
Springbrook Dr 97527
NW Springwood Pl 97526
Sprinkle Way 97527
SW Spruce St 97526
Spyglass Ln 97527
Squirrel Ln 97527
Stanford Way 97527
Stanvira Way 97526
N Star Ct & Dr 97527
Star Crest Dr 97527
NE Star View Ln 97526
Starburst Dr 97527
NW Starlite Pl 97526
Steelhead Ln 97527
NE Steiger St 97526
Stellar Ct 97527
Sterling Dr 97527
Stewart Rd 97526
Stone Canyon Rd 97527
Stone Fly Ct 97526
Stoneridge Dr 97527
Storey Ln 97527
Stringer Gap Rd 97527
SW Sturgeon Ct 97527
NW Sue Cir 97526
Summer Ln 97526
Summit Loop 97527
Sun Glo Dr 97527
Sun Oak Way 97526
Sunburst Dr 97527
Sunburst Way 97526
NW Sunday Dr 97526
Sunflower Ln 97527
Sunhill Dr & Ter 97526
Sunny Cir 97527
Sunny Slope Dr 97527
Sunrise Dr 97526
NW Sunset Dr 97526
NE Sunset Ln 97526
Sunset Way 97527
NW Sunview Pl 97526
SW Sunwood Way 97526
Surrey Dr 97526
SW Susan Ln 97526
Suzanne Ct 97527
Swarthout Cir & Dr 97527
Sweetbriar Cir 97527
Sycamore Dr 97526
Tacoma St 97526
Tahoe Cir 97527
NE Talbott Dr 97526
Tamara Cir 97526
Tamarac Ln 97527
Tami Rd 97526
Tanager Way 97527
NW Tara Ln 97526
SW Tater Way 97527
Teakwood Dr 97526
Tech Way 97526
Teel Ln 97527
Templin Ave 97526
NE Terrace Dr 97526
NE Terry Ln 97526
Thelma Way 97527
Thelma Lou Ln 97527
Thomas Cir & Ter 97527
NW Thompson Way 97526
Thornberry Dr 97526
Three Pines Rd 97526
Tiffany Way 97526
Timber Ln 97526
Timberridge Rd 97527
Tina Way 97526
Tipton Rd 97527
Tobin Ct 97527
NE Tokay Hts 97526
SW Topaz Ln 97526
Tori Ln 97527
Torrey Pines Rd 97527
Tower Heights Dr 97527
Towne St 97527
Tracy Dr 97527
Trevor Way 97526
Triller Ln 97527
SW Trinity Way 97527
Trolley Ln 97526
Trollview Rd 97527
SE Trooper Way 97527
Trout Cir 97527
Tunnel Creek Rd 97526
Tunnel Loop Rd 97526
SE Turnage Ct 97527
Turtle Ln 97527
Tussey Ln 97527
Twilight Ln 97527
Twisted Pines Dr 97527
Tyee Ct 97527
Union Ave 97527
University Rd 97527
Upper River Rd 97526
Upper River Road Loop 97526
Valle Vista Dr 97527
N Valley Dr 97526
Valley Rogue Way 97526
NW Valley View Dr 97526
NW Van Dyke Pl 97526
SE Vance Dr 97527
S Vannoy Creek Rd 97526
Venture Pl 97526
Verna Ln 97527
Veronique Pl 97527
SW Versappen Ln 97526
NE Vertical Dr 97526
SW Vicki Ln 97526
NE Victoria St 97526
NE View Dr 97526
E View Pl 97527
Village Ln 97527
NW Vine St 97526
SE Vine Maple Ln 97527
SW Viola Dr 97526
Virginia Ln 97527
Vista Dr 97527
SW Wagner Meadows Dr 97526
Wagon Rd 97526
Wagon Wheel Dr 97527
Walker Rd 97527
Wallace Ln 97527
Walnut Ave 97527
NW Washington Blvd 97526
SE Waterman Ln 97526
SW Waterstone Dr 97527
Watson Dr 97527
Waverly Dr 97526
SW Webster Rd 97526
Wedgewood Dr 97526
Weekly Dr 97527
Weeping Willow Ct 97527
Wen Dover Cir 97526
NW Wendy Way 97526
NE Wesley Ln 97526
NE Westbrook Way 97526
Westerly Ct 97527
SW Western Ave 97526
Westhills Dr 97526
SW Westholm Ave 97526
Westlake Dr 97526
Westmont Dr 97526
Westridge Dr 97526
Westview Dr 97527
Westwood Dr 97527
Wetherbee Dr 97527
NE Wharton Dr 97526
Whippletree Ln 97526
Whispering Dr 97527
Whispering Pines Ln 97527
Whispering Willow Dr 97527
White Fir Dr 97526
White Horse Dr 97527
Whiteridge Rd 97527
Whitestone Dr 97527
Wilderville Ln 97527
Wildrose Ln 97527
SW Wildwood Ave 97526
Willamette St 97526
Williams Hwy 97527
NW Williamsburg Dr 97526
Williamson Loop 97526
Willow Ct & Ln 97527
Willow Creek Ln 97527
Wilma Ln 97526
Wilmar Ave 97527
Wilson Ln 97526
NW Windsor Dr 97526
Wineteer Ln 97527
Winona Rd 97526
Winston Dr 97526
Wisteria Ln 97526
Wolf Ln 97527
Wolf Song Dr 97526
NW Woodbrook Dr 97526
Woodbury Ln 97527
NW Woodcrest Cir 97526
Woodlake Dr 97527
Woodland Park Rd 97527
Woodlawn Cir 97526
Woodrow Way 97527
E & W Woodside St 97527
NW Woodson Dr 97526
Worden Way 97527
Work Ln 97527
NW Wrightwood Cir 97526
Wylie Ln 97527
SE Wyndham Way 97527
Yale Ct 97527
Yearly Way 97527
SW Yellowtail Ln 97527
SE Yorktown Rd 97527
Your Way 97527
SW Yucca Dr 97527
SW Zane Grey Ct 97527

NUMBERED STREETS

NW 2nd St 97526
NW & SW 3rd 97526
NW & SW 4th 97526
NW & SW 5th 97526
NE 6th St 97526
NW 6th St
130-148 97526
132-132 97528
132-132 97527
200-1998 97526
SE 6th St 97526
SW 6th St 97526
NE & SE 7th 97526
NE & SE 8th 97526
NE & SE 9th 97526
NE & SE 10th 97526
NE & SE 11th 97526
NE & SE 12th 97526

GRESHAM OR

General Delivery 97030

POST OFFICE BOXES MAIN OFFICE STATIONS AND BRANCHES

Box No.s
All PO Boxes 97030

NAMED STREETS

Acacia Ave, Dr, Ln & Pl 97080
Alder Ct, Dr & St 97030
SE & SW Alder Ridge Rd 97080
SE Altman Rd 97080
SE Ambleside Dr 97080
SE Anderson Ave 97080
SE Anderson Ln 97080
NE Anderson Rd 97030
SE Anderson Rd 97080
NW Angeline Ave 97030
SW Angeline Ave 97080
NW Angeline Ct 97030
SW Angeline Ct 97080
Ankeny St & Ter 97030
Antelope Hills Dr & Pl 97080
SE Arrow Creek Ln 97080
SE Ash St 97030
SE Atherton Ave 97080
NW Aubrey Ln 97030
Augusta Loop, Pl & Way 97080
NW Ava Ave 97030
Avondale Ct & Way 97080
Baker Ave, Cir, Ln, Pl & Way 97080
Barn Owl Ln & Way 97080
NE Barnes Ave 97030
SE Barnes Ave 97080
NE Barnes Ct 97030
NE Barnes Ln 97030
SE Barnes Rd 97080
NW Battaglia Ave 97030
SW Battaglia Ave 97080
SW Battaglia Pl 97080
SE Baxter Rd 97080
NE Beech Ave 97030
SE Beech Ave 97080
NE Beech Ct 97030
NE Beech Dr 97030
NE Beech Pl 97030
SE Beech Pl 97080
NW Bella Vista Ave 97030
SW Bella Vista Ave 97080
NW Bella Vista Ct 97030
NW Bella Vista Dr 97030
SW Bella Vista Ln 97080
NW Bella Vista Pl 97030
SW Bella Vista Pl 97080
NW Bergeron Ct 97030
Bethesda Dr & Pl 97080
Binford Ave, Pl & Way 97080
SW Binford Lake Pkwy 97080
NW Birdsdale Ave 97030
SW Birdsdale Ct 97080
SW Birdsdale Dr 97080
SW Birdsdale Pl 97080
SW Blaine Ave 97080
SW Blaine Ct 97080
NW Blaine Ln 97030
SW Blaine Pl 97080
SE Bluff Rd 97080
SW Border Way 97080
SW Brittany Dr 97080
Brixton Ave, Ct, Dr & Pl 97080
Brooklyn Ct & Pl 97030
Bryn Mawr Ln, Pl & Way 97030
NW Burnside Ct 97030
SE Burnside Ct 97030
NE Burnside Rd 97030
NW Burnside Rd 97030
SE Burnside Rd 97080
SE & SW Butler Rd 97080
SE Callister Rd 97080
SE Carl St 97080
SE Carpenter Ln 97080
NW Cascade Ct 97030
SE Cedar Creek Pl 97080
SE Centurion Ave 97080
NE Centurion Ct 97030
NE Centurion Dr 97030
SE Centurion Ln 97080
NE Centurion Pl 97030
SE Centurion Way 97080
Chase Loop & Rd 97080
SW Chastain Ave 97080
NW Chastain Ct 97030
SW Chastain Ct 97080
SW Chastain Dr 97080
NW Chastain Pl 97030
SW Chastain Pl 97080
SE Cheldelin Rd 97080
SE Cherry Park Rd 97030
NW Civic Dr 97030
SE Clare Rd 97080
SE Clark Rd 97080
SE Clay Ct 97030
NE Cleveland Ave 97030
SE Cleveland Ave 97080
SE Cleveland Dr 97080
SE Clinton St 97030
SE Clorinco Ave 97080
NE Cochran Ave 97030
NE Cochran Dr 97030
SE Cochran Dr 97080
SE Cochran Rd 97030
SE Condor Ave 97080
NE Condor Dr 97030
SE Condor Dr 97080
SE Condor Pl 97080
SE Cottrell Rd 97080
Couch Ct & St 97030
NW Council Dr 97030
Country Club Ave & Ct 97030
SE Crystal Springs Blvd 97080
SE Darling Ave 97080
SW Day Ct 97080
NW Day Dr 97030
Deer Creek Pl & Way 97080
NE Dexter Ave 97030
NE Dexter Ct 97030
SE Dexter Ln 97080
NE Dexter Pl 97030
SE, NE & NW Division Dr & St 97030
SE Dodge Park Blvd 97080
Dogwood Ln & Way 97080
SE Douglas Pl 97080
SE Dowsett Ln 97080
SW Duniway Ave 97030
SE Durango Pl 97080
Eagle Ave & Ln 97080
Earl Ave & Ct 97030
SW Eastman Ave 97080
SW Eastman Ct 97080
NW Eastman Pkwy 97030
SW Eastman Pkwy 97080
NW Eastwood Ave 97030
SW Eastwood Ave 97080
SW Eastwood Ct 97080
SW Eastwood Pl 97080
SE Edgewood Pl 97080
NE El Camino Dr 97030
SE El Camino Dr 97080
NW Eleven Mile Ave 97030
SW Eleven Mile Ave 97080
NW Eleven Mile Ct 97030
SW Eleven Mile Dr 97080
SW Elk Ln 97080
NE Elliott Ave 97030
SE Elliott Ave 97080

SE Elliott Dr 97080
NE Elliott Pl 97030
SE Elliott Pl 97080
SE Elsa St 97080
Emerald Ave & Ln 97080
SW Equestrian Dr 97080
NE Evelyn Ave 97030
SE Evelyn Ave 97080
SE Evelyn Ct 97080
SE Evelyn Pl 97080
NW Fairview Dr 97030
NW & SE Fariss Rd 97030
NE Fleming Ave 97030
SE Fleming Ave 97080
NE Fleming Ter 97030
NW Florence Ave 97030
SW Florence Ave 97080
NW Florence Ct 97030
SW Florence Ct 97080
SW Florence Pl 97080
SE Foster Rd 97080
Foxglove Dr & Way 97080
NE Francis Ave 97030
SE Francis Ave 97080
NE Francis Ct 97030
NE Francis Pl 97030
SE Francis Rd 97080
SE & SW Gabbert Rd 97080
NW Giese Ave 97030
SW Giese Loop 97080
SW Giese Pl 97080
SE Giese Rd 97080
Glacier Ave, Ct & Ln 97080
NE Glisan St 97030
SE Grace St 97080
NE Greenway Dr 97030
SE Greenway Dr 97080
SE Greenway Ln 97080
NE Greenway Pl 97030
NE Hacienda Ave 97030
SE Hacienda Ave 97080
SE Hacienda Cir 97080
NE Hacienda Ct 97030
SE Hacienda Ct 97080
NE Hacienda Ln 97030
SE Hacienda Ln 97080
SE Hacienda Loop 97080
NE Hacienda Pl 97030
NE Hale Ave 97030
SE Hale Ave 97080
SE Hale Ct 97080
NE Hale Dr 97030
SE Hale Dr 97080
NE Hale Pl 97030
SE Hale Pl 97080
SE Hale Way 97080
SE Harris Pl 97080
NW Hartley Ave 97030
SW Hartley Ave
  1-899 97030
  1600-2399 97080
SW Hartley Dr 97080
SE Hawthorne St 97030
SW Heiney Rd 97080
Hickory Pl & Way 97080
SW Highland Dr 97080
Hillyard Ct & Rd 97080
NE Hogan Dr 97030
NE Hogan Pl 97030
SE Hogan Rd 97080
SW Hollybrook Ter 97080
SE Homan Rd 97080
Honors Dr & Pl 97080
NE Hood Ave 97030
SE Hood Ave 97080
NE Hood Ct 97030
NE Hood Pl 97030
SE Hood Way 97080
Hosner Rd & Ter 97080
SE Inverness Ave 97080
Ironwood Ln, Pl & Way 97080
SE Ivon Ct 97030
SW Ivory Loop 97080
SE Jackson Rd 97080
Jasmine Ave & Way 97080
SE Jeanette St 97080
SW Junction Pl 97080
NE Juniper Ave 97030
SE Juniper Ave 97080
NE Juniper Ct 97030
SE Juniper Ct E 97080
SE Juniper Ct W 97080
SE K W Anderson Rd 97080
SE Kane Ave 97080
NE Kane Dr 97030
SE Kane Dr 97080
SE Kay Pl 97080
SE Keller Ave 97080
NE Kelly Ave 97030
SE Kelly Ave 97080
NE Kelly Pl 97030
Kingfisher Ave & Ln 97080
SE Knapp St 97080
NE La Mesa Ave 97030
SE La Mesa Ave 97080
NE La Mesa Ct 97030
SE La Mesa Ct 97080
NE La Mesa Ln 97030
SE La Mesa Ln 97080
NE La Mesa Pl 97030
SE La Mesa Pl 97080
SW Lake Pl 97080
SE Lambert Cir 97080
Larch Ln & Way 97080
NE Laura Ave 97030
SE Laura Ave 97080
SE Laura Dr 97080
SE Laura Ln 97080
SE Laura Pl 97080
NE Liberty Ave 97030
SE Liberty Ave 97080
SE Liberty Ct 97080
SE Liberty Pl 97080
SW Lillyben Ave 97080
SW Lillyben Ct 97080
NW Lillyben Pl 97030
SW Lillyben Pl 97080
NE Linden Ave 97030
SE Linden Ave 97080
SE Linden Ct 97080
NE Linden Pl 97030
SE Linden Pl 97080
NW Linneman Ave 97030
SW Linneman Ave 97080
SW Linneman Ct 97080
SW Linneman Dr 97080
SW Lovhar Dr 97080
SE Lovrien Ave 97080
NE Lovrien Pl 97030
SE Lovrien Pl 97080
SE Lusted Rd 97080
N Main Ave 97030
S Main Ave 97080
SE Main Ct 97030
SE Main Dr 97030
SE Main St 97030
SE Mally Rd 97080
NE Maple Ave 97030
SE Maple Cir 97080
NE Maple Ct 97030
SE Maple Loop 97080
SE Maple Pl 97080
SE Margaret St 97080
SE Marsha Ln 97080
SW Mawrcrest Ave 97080
SW Mawrcrest Ct 97080
NW Mawrcrest Dr 97030
SW Mawrcrest Dr 97080
NW Mawrcrest Pl 97030
SW Mawrcrest Pl 97080
SE Mckinley Rd 97080
SE Mcnutt Rd 97080
SE Meadow Ct 97080
NE Meadow Pl 97030
NW Mignonette Ave 97030
SE Mignonette Ct 97080
NW Miller Ave 97030
SW Miller Ct 97080
SW Miller Dr 97080
SW Miller Pl 97080
SE Miller Rd 97080
SE Mimosa Dr 97080
NE Morlan Ave 97030
SE Morlan Ave 97080
SE Morlan Pl 97080
SE Morlan Way 97080
Morrison Ct, St & Ter 97030
SE Mount Hood Hwy 97080
Myers Dr & Pl 97080
SW Myrtle Ave 97030
Myrtlewood Ave, Ln, Pl & Way 97080
SW Nancy Ave 97030
SW Nancy Cir 97030
SW Nancy Ct
  600-699 97030
  1300-1399 97080
SW Nancy Dr 97080
NW Nancy Pl 97030
SW Nancy Pl 97080
Night Heron Ave, Pl & Way 97080
NW Norman Ave 97030
SW Norman Ct 97080
SE Oak St 97030
SE Old Woods Loop 97080
SE Olvera Ave 97080
NE Olvera Ct 97030
SE Olvera Pl 97080
NW Orchard Ave 97030
SW Orchard Ave 97080
SW Orchard Ct 97080
NW Orchard Pl 97030
SW Orchard Pl 97080
SE Orient Dr 97080
SE Orland St 97080
Osprey Ave & Loop 97080
NW Overlook Ave 97030
NW Overlook Ct 97030
SW Overlook Ct 97080
Oxbow Dr, Pkwy & Ter 97080
NE Palmblad Dr 97030
SE Palmblad Dr 97080
SE Palmblad Pl 97080
SE Palmblad Rd 97080
SE Palmquist Rd 97080
NE Paloma Ave 97030
SE Paloma Ave 97080
NE Paloma Ct 97030
SE Paloma Ct 97080
SE Paloma Dr 97080
SE Paloma Pl 97080
SE Paloma Ter 97080
SE Park Dr 97080
SE Paropa Ave 97080
NE Paropa Ct 97030
SE Paropa Ct 97080
SE Paropa Ln 97080
SE Paropa Pl 97080
NE Paropa Way 97030
Pheasant Ave & Way 97080
SE Phoebe Ct 97080
SW Phyllis Ave 97080
NW Phyllis Ct 97030
SW Phyllis Ct 97080
SW Phyllis Dr 97080
SW Phyllis Pl 97080
SE Pipeline Rd 97080
SE Pleasant Home Rd 97080
SW Pleasant View Ave 97030
SW Pleasant View Dr 97080
Postage Due St 97080
E Powell Blvd
  1-197 97030
  199-1799 97030
  1800-2599 97080
W Powell Blvd 97030
W Powell Loop 97030
SE Powell Valley Rd 97080
NE Pralista St 97030
SE Proctor St 97080
Quail Dr & Ln 97080
NE Red Sunset Dr 97030
Redfern Ave & Pl 97080
SE Regner Rd 97080
NE Rene Ave 97030
SE Rene Ave 97080
SE Richey Rd 97080
NW Riverview Ave 97030
SW Riverview Ave 97080
SW Riverview Ct 97080
NW Riverview Pl 97030
SW Riverview Pl 97080
NW Riverview Way 97030
NE Roberts Ave 97030
SE Roberts Ave 97080
NE Roberts Ct 97030
SE Roberts Dr 97080
NE Roberts Pl 97030
SE Robin Cir 97080
NE Robin Ct 97030
SE Robin Ct 97080
SE Robin Ln 97080
SE Robin Pl 97080
NE Robin Way 97030
SE Robin Way 97080
SW Rodlun Rd 97080
SE Roork Rd 97080
Rosefinch Dr & Pl 97080
NW Royal Ave 97030
SW Royal Ave 97080
SW Royal Ct
  200-299 97030
  1300-1399 97080
SW Royal Pl 97080
SW Royal Way 97080
SE Rugg Rd 97080
SE Saint Andrews Pl 97080
SE & NW Salmon Ct, Dr & St 97030
SE Salquist Rd 97080
SW Sandlewood Ave 97080
SW Sandlewood Ln 97080
SW Sandlewood Loop 97030
SW Sandlewood Pl 97080
NE Scott Ave 97030
SE Scott Ave 97080
NE Scott Ct 97030
NE Scott Dr 97030
NW Shattuck Way 97030
SE Short Rd 97080
NW Sleret Ave 97030
SW Sleret Ave 97080
NE Spruce Ave 97030
SE Spruce Ave 97080
SE Spruce Ct 97080
NW Stanley Ave 97030
SE Stapleton Loop 97080
SE Stark St 97030
SE Stone Rd 97080
SE Taylor Ct 97030
Teal Ave & Dr 97080
SW Tegart Ave 97080
SE Telford Rd 97080
SE Teton Dr 97080
Thomas Ct, Pl & Way 97080
SE Tibbetts Ct 97030
NW Towle Ave 97030
SW Towle Ave 97080
NW Towle Ct 97030
NW Towle Ter 97030
SE Troutdale Rd 97080
NW Victoria Ave 97030
SW Victoria Ct 97080
SW Victoria Ln 97080
SW Victoria Pl 97080
NE Victory Ave 97030
View Ave, Ct & Pl 97030
SW View Crest Dr 97080
Village Squire Ave & Ct 97030
SE Virginia Ave 97080
NE Vista Ave 97030
SE Vista Ave 97080
SE Vista Ter 97080
NE Vista Way 97030
SE Vista Way 97080
NW Wallula Ave 97030
SW Wallula Ave 97080
SW Wallula Ct 97080
SW Wallula Dr 97080
Walters Dr & Loop 97080
SE Welch Rd 97080
SE Wendy Ave 97080
SE Wendy Ct 97080
SE Wendy Dr 97080
NE Wendy Ln 97030
SE Wendy Ln 97080
SE Williams Ave 97080
SE Williams Dr 97080
NE Williams Rd 97030
SE Williams Rd 97080
SW Willow Pkwy 97080
SW Willowbrook Ave 97080
NW Willowbrook Ct 97030
SW Willowbrook Ct 97080
SW Willowbrook Dr 97080
SW Willowbrook Pl 97080
NW Wilson Ave 97030
SW Wilson Ct 97080
SE Wk Anderson Rd 97080
NW Wonderview Ave 97030
SW Wonderview Ave 97080
NW Wonderview Ct 97030
SW Wonderview Ct 97080
NW Wonderview Dr 97030
SW Wonderview Dr 97080
SW Wonderview Pl 97080
Woodland Dr & Way 97080
SE Yamhill St 97030

NUMBERED STREETS

NW 1st Ct 97030
SE 1st Ct 97080
SW 1st Ct 97080
NW 1st Dr 97030
SE 1st Pl 97080
NE 1st St 97030
NW 1st St 97030
SE 1st St 97080
SW 1st St 97080
SE 1st Ter 97080
NW 2nd Cir 97030
NE 2nd Ct 97030
SW 2nd Ct 97080
SW 2nd Dr 97080
SE 2nd Pl 97080
NE 2nd St 97030
NW 2nd St 97030
SE 2nd St 97080
SW 2nd St
  1701-1797 97080
  3300-3699 97030
NW 2nd Ter 97030
SE 2nd Ter 97080
SE 3rd Ct 97080
SW 3rd Dr 97080
NE 3rd St 97030
NW 3rd St 97030
SE 3rd St 97080
SW 3rd St
  2200-2499 97080
  3700-3999 97030
  4001-4299 97030
NW 3rd Ter 97030
NE 4th St 97030
NW 4th St 97030
SE 4th St 97080
SW 4th St
  200-2399 97080
  3700-3999 97030
SE 4th Ter 97080
NE 5th Ct 97030
NW 5th Ct 97030
SW 5th Ct
  600-1599 97080
  3601-3697 97030
NE 5th Dr 97030
SW 5th Dr 97030
SW 5th Pl 97080
NE 5th St 97030
NW 5th St 97030
SE 5th St 97080
SW 5th St 97080
NW 6th Ct 97030
SW 6th Ct 97080
NW 6th Dr 97030
NW 6th Pl 97030
SW 6th Pl 97080
NE 6th St 97030
NW 6th St 97030
SE 6th St 97080
SW 6th St
  200-599 97080
  3700-3899 97030
NE 6th Ter 97030
NE 7th Ct 97030
NW 7th Ct 97030
SW 7th Ct
  2000-2199 97080
  3700-3899 97030
NW 7th Pl 97030
NE 7th St 97030
SE 7th St 97080
SW 7th St
  300-799 97080
  3900-4199 97030
NE 8th Ct 97030
NW 8th Ct 97030
SE 8th Ct 97080
SW 8th Dr 97080
NE 8th Pl 97030
NE 8th St 97030
NW 8th St 97030
SE 8th St 97080
SW 8th St
  700-1099 97080
  3700-4199 97030
SE 9th Ct 97080
SW 9th Ct
  2100-2299 97080
  3800-4199 97030
  4900-4999 97080
SW 9th Pl 97080
NE 9th St 97030
NW 9th St 97030
SE 9th St 97080
SW 10th Ct 97080
NE 10th Dr 97030
NW 10th Dr 97030
SE 10th Dr 97080
SW 10th Dr 97080
NE 10th St 97030
SE 10th St 97080
NE 10th Ter 97030
SE 10th Ter 97080
NW 11th Dr 97030
NW 11th St 97030
SE 11th St 97080
SW 11th St 97080
NE 11th Way 97030
SE 11th Way 97080
NW 12th Ct 97030
SE 12th Ct 97080
SW 12th Ct 97080
NW 12th St 97030
SE 12th St 97080
SE 12th Way 97080
SE 13th Ct 97080
SW 13th Ct 97080
NE 13th St 97030
NW 13th St 97030
SE 13th St 97080
SW 13th St 97080
NE 13th Ter 97030
SE 13th Ter 97080
SE 14th Ct 97080
SW 14th Ct 97080
NW 14th Dr 97030
SW 14th Dr 97080
NE 14th Ln 97030
NW 14th Pl 97030
SE 14th Pl 97080
NW 14th St 97030
SE 14th St 97080
SW 14th St 97080
NW 15th Ct 97030
SE 15th Ct 97080
SW 15th Ct 97080
SE 15th Dr 97080
NE 15th Ln 97030
SE 15th Ln 97080
SE 15th Loop 97080
NE 15th St 97030
NW 15th St 97030
SE 15th St 97080
SW 15th St 97080
SE 15th Ter 97080
SW 16th Cir 97080
NE 16th Ct 97030
SE 16th Ct 97080
SW 16th Ct 97080
SE 16th Dr 97080
SE 16th Loop 97080
SW 16th Pl 97080
NE 16th St 97030
NW 16th St 97030
SE 16th St 97080
SW 16th St 97080
NE 16th Way 97030
NW 17th Ct 97030
SE 17th Ct 97080
SW 17th Ct 97080
SE 17th Loop 97080
SW 17th Pl 97080
NE 17th St 97030
NW 17th St 97030
SE 17th St 97080
SW 17th St 97080
SE 17th Ter 97080
SE 18th Cir 97080
NE 18th Ct 97030
NW 18th Ct 97030
SE 18th Ct 97080
SW 18th Ct 97080
SE 18th Ln 97080
SW 18th Pl 97080
NE 18th St 97030
NW 18th St 97030
SE 18th St 97080
SW 18th St 97080
SW 18th Ter 97080
SW 19th Ct 97080
SE 19th Dr 97080
SW 19th Dr 97080
NE 19th St 97030
NW 19th St 97030
SE 19th St 97080
SW 19th St 97080
SW 19th Ter 97080
SE 20th Ct 97080
SW 20th Ct 97080
NE 20th Dr 97030
NE 20th St 97030
NW 20th St 97030
SE 20th St 97080
SW 20th St 97080
SE 20th Ter 97080
SE 21st Ct 97080
SW 21st Ct 97080
SE 21st Dr 97080
SE 21st Pl 97080
NE 21st St 97030
SE 21st St 97080
NW 21st Ter 97030
SE 21st Ter 97080
SW 21st Ter 97080
NE 22nd Ct 97030
SE 22nd Ct 97080
SW 22nd Ct 97080
SE 22nd Dr 97080
SW 22nd Dr 97080
NE 22nd St 97030
NW 22nd St 97030
SE 22nd St 97080
SW 22nd St 97080
SW 22nd Ter 97080
NW 23rd Ave 97030
NW 23rd Ct 97030
SE 23rd Ct 97080
SW 23rd Ct 97080
SW 23rd Dr 97080
NE 23rd Pl 97030
NE 23rd St 97030
NW 23rd St 97030
SE 23rd St 97080
SW 23rd St 97080
SE 23rd Ter 97080

SW 23rd Ter 97080
NE 24th Ct 97030
SE 24th Ct 97080
SW 24th Ct 97080
SE 24th Dr 97080
SW 24th Dr 97080
NE 24th St 97030
NW 24th St 97030
SE 24th St 97080
SW 24th St 97080
SE 24th Ter 97080
SW 24th Ter 97080
NE 25th Ct 97030
SW 25th Ct 97080
SW 25th Dr 97080
NE 25th St 97030
NW 25th St 97030
SE 25th St 97080
SW 25th St 97080
SE 26th Ct 97080
SW 26th Ct 97080
SE 26th Dr 97080
SE 26th Pl 97080
NE 26th St 97030
SE 26th St 97080
SW 26th St 97080
SE 27th Ct 97080
SW 27th Ct 97080
NE 27th Dr 97030
SW 27th Dr 97080
NE 27th St 97030
SE 27th St 97080
SW 27th St 97080
NE 27th Ter 97030
NE 28th Ct 97030
SE 28th Ct 97080
SW 28th Ct 97080
SE 28th Dr 97080
NE 28th St 97030
SE 28th St 97080
SE 28th Ter 97080
SW 28th Ter 97080
NE 29th Ct 97030
SW 29th Ct 97080
NE 29th Dr 97030
SW 29th Dr 97080
NE 29th St 97030
SE 29th St 97080
SE 29th Ter 97080
SE 29th Way 97080
NE 30th Ct 97030
SW 30th Ct 97080
NE 30th Dr 97030
SW 30th Dr 97080
NE 30th Ln 97030
SE 30th St 97080
SW 30th St 97080
SE 30th Way 97080
SE & SW 31st Ct, St & Ter 97080
SE & SW 32nd Ct, St & Ter 97080
SE 33rd Ct 97080
NE 33rd St 97030
SE 33rd St 97080
SW 33rd St 97080
SE 33rd Way 97080
SW 34th Ct 97080
NE 34th St 97030
SE 34th St 97080
SW 34th Ter 97080
SE 34th Way 97080
NE 35th St 97030
SW 35th St 97080
NE 36th Ct 97030
SW 36th St 97080
37th Cir & Ter 97080
NE 38th Dr 97030
SE 38th Dr 97080
SW 38th Loop 97080
SE & SW 40th St & Ter 97080
SE & SW 41st Ct & St 97080
SE 46th Dr 97080
SE 47th Cir 97080
SE 48th Ter 97080
SE 49th Cir 97080
SE 170th Ave 97080
SE 172nd Ave 97080
SE 181st Pl 97030
SE 182nd Ave
2501-2597 97030
2599-4300 97030
4302-4398 97030
6500-7699 97080
SE 184th Pl 97030
SE 185th Ave 97030
SE 186th Pl 97030
SE 187th Pl 97030
SE 190th Ave 97030
SE 190th Dr 97080
SE 191st Pl 97030
SE 204th Pl 97030
205th Ave, Dr & Pl 97030
SE 207th Ave 97030
SE 208th Ave 97030
SE 209th Ave 97030
SE 210th Ave 97030
211th Ave & Ct 97030
SE 212th Ave 97030
213th Ave & Pl 97030
SE 214th Ave 97030
215th Ave & Way 97030
SE 216th Ave 97030
NW & SE 217th 97030
NE & SE 218th 97030
219th Ave & Ln 97030
NE & SE 220th 97030
SE 221st Ave 97030
NE & SE 223rd 97030
SE 224th Ave 97030
SE 225th Ave 97030
SE 226th Ave 97030
SE 236th Ct 97030
SE 238th Ave 97030
SE 240th Ct 97030
SE 241st Ct 97030
SE 242nd Ave
401-499 97030
7600-8199 97080
NE 242nd Dr 97030
SE 247th Ave 97080
SE 252nd Ave 97080
SE 257th Ave 97080
SE 262nd Ave 97080
SE 267th Ave 97080
SE 282nd Ave 97080
SE 298th Ave 97080
SE 301st Ave 97080
SE 302nd Ave 97080
SE 307th Ave 97080
SE 314th Ave 97080
SE 32 Nd St 97080
322nd Ave & Pl 97080

HILLSBORO OR

General Delivery 97123

POST OFFICE BOXES MAIN OFFICE STATIONS AND BRANCHES

Box No.s
All PO Boxes 97123

NAMED STREETS

NW Adagio Way 97124
NW Adams Ave 97124
SW Adams Ave 97123
NE Addison Ct 97124
Aerie Ave & Way 97123
NE Airport Rd 97124
SE Albertine St 97123
SW Albertson Rd 97123
SE Alder Ct 97123
NE Alder St 97124
NW Alder St 97124
SE Alder St 97123
NE Aldercreek Pl 97124
NE Alex Way 97124
SE Alexander St 97123
Alexandria Pl & St 97124
NE Alexis Ct 97124
SE Alika Ave 97123
NW Allie Ave 97124
Aloclek Dr & Pl 97124
NW Alphorn Ln 97124
NE Amanda Pl 97124
NE Amber Ave 97124
NW Amberwood Dr 97124
NE Andover St 97124
Angela Ln & St 97124
NE Anna Ave 97124
SE Anthony St 97123
SE Apollo Way 97123
SE Arbor Ct 97123
NE Archer Ct 97124
SE Ariel St 97123
SE Arlington Loop 97123
SW Armco Ave 97123
NE Arrington Rd 97124
NE Arrowwood St 97124
NW Arroyo Pl 97006
SE Ash St 97123
NE Ashberry Dr 97124
NW Ashford Cir 97124
NE Ashmont St 97124
NE Ashton Way 97124
SE Aspen Ct 97123
SE Aster Ct 97123
NE Atlantic Pl 97124
SE & SW Augusta Ct & Ln 97123
NE Aurora Dr 97124
Austin Ct & Dr 97123
NE Autumn Rose Way 97124
NE Autumnwood Ter 97124
SE Averi Ct 97123
NE Ayrshire Dr 97124
Azalea Ln & St 97124
NE Azores Ct 97124
SE Bacarra St 97123
SW Bachelor Blvd 97123
NW Badertscher Rd 97124
NW Bagley Rd 97124
NW Bailey Ave 97124
SW Bailey Ave 97123
SW Bald Peak Rd 97123
Baldwin Dr & St 97124
Barberry Ct & Dr 97124
W, SE & SW Baseline Rd & St 97123
Beach Ct & Rd 97124
NE Beacon Ct 97124
Beaumead Ln & St 97124
NW Beeler Dr 97124
NE Belknap Ct 97124
SE Belle Oak Ave 97123
SE Belmont Ct 97123
NW Bendemeer Rd 97124
NW Bennett St 97124
SE Bentley St 97123
SE Beverly Ln 97123
SE Bianca St 97123
NW Bidwell Rd 97124
NW & NE Birch Ave & St 97124
NE Birchaire Ln 97124
Birchwood Cir, Dr, Ln, Pl, Rd & Ter 97124
SE Birdhouse Way 97123
NE Birkshire Ct 97124
NW Bishop Rd 97124
NE Blacktail Way 97124
SE Blackwell Way 97123
SE Blaine St 97123
SE Blanchard St 97123
SE Bliss Ct 97123
SE Blossom St 97123
SE Blue Bird Dr 97123
SE Bluebonnet Ct 97123
SW & SE Borwick Rd & St 97123
SE Bradley Ct 97123
SE Brauner Pl 97123
NE Brennan Ln 97124
SE Brent St 97123
SE Brian St 97123
SW Bridges Rd 97123
SE Bridgeside Way 97123
SW Brighton Ln 97123
NE Brighton St 97124
SE Brodiaea Ct 97123
Brogden Ct & St 97124
SE Bronte Way 97123
Brookhill Ln & St 97124
Brookside St & Ter 97123
SE Brookwood Ave 97123
SW Brookwood Ave 97123
NE Brookwood Pkwy 97124
NW Brookwood Pkwy 97124
SW Browns Dr 97123
SW Bryanna Ct 97123
SW Buckhaven Rd 97123
NE Buena Vista St 97124
SW Burkhalter Rd 97123
SE Bush St 97123
NE & NW Butler St 97124
SE Buttercup Ct 97123
NE Caddis Dr 97124
NE Caden Ave 97124
SW Cady Rd 97123
NE Cafe Way 97124
NE Callan Ct 97124
NE Cambrey Ct 97124
SE Camellia Ct 97123
SW Camelot Ln 97123
NW Camp Ireland St 97124
SW Campbell Rd 97123
NE Campbell St 97124
Campus Dr & Way 97124
SE Camwal Dr 97123
Canard Ct & Dr 97124
NE Candlewood Pl 97124
NE Carillion Dr 97124
NE Carlaby Way 97124
NE Carole Ct 97124
SW Casavant Dr 97123
SE Cascade Ct 97123
NW Casper Pl 97124
NE Castlewood Ct 97124
NE Catherine Ct 97124
NW Cavens Ln 97124
SE & SW Cedar Dr & St 97123
SE Cedar Park Ct 97123
SE Celebration Ct 97123
NW Celtis Ln 97124
NW Century Blvd 97124
SE Century Blvd 97123
SE Century Ct 97123
NE Chancellor Ct 97124
Charlois Ct & Dr 97124
SW Chehalem Way 97123
SE Chelsea Ln 97123
NE & NW Cherry Dr & Ln 97124
NE Chesapeake St 97124
SE Chesney St 97123
NE & NW Chestnut St 97124
NW Clara Ln 97124
NE Clarendon St 97124
SW Clark Hill Rd 97123
SE Clearbrook St 97123
SE Clematis Ct 97123
SW Cloudrest Ln 97123
SE Clover Ct 97123
NW Cody Ct 97124
NW Coffey Ln 97124
SW Colby Ln 97123
NW Colonnade Dr 97124
SE Columbine Ct 97123
SE Columbus Ave 97123
NW Connell Ave 97124
SW Connell Ave 97123
SE Conrad Ct 97123
SW Cook Rd 97123
SE Coot Way 97123
NE Copper Beech Dr 97124
NW Cornelius Pass Rd 97124
SW Cornelius Pass Rd 97123
NE & NW Cornell Rd 97124
SE Cornutt St 97123
NW Cornwall Ln 97124
NE Corona Ct 97124
NE Corral Ct 97124
NE Cory St 97124
SW Cougar Hill Ln 97123
SE Covington St 97123
SE Creek Ct 97123
NE Creeksedge Dr 97124
SE Crestview Dr 97123
NE Crimson Pl 97124
NE Crocus Ct 97124
NW Croeni Rd 97124
Currin Dr & Ln 97123
NE Curtis Ct 97124
SE Cypress St 97123
SE Daffodil Pl 97123
NW Dale St 97124
NE Damsel Dr 97124
NE Danbury Ave 97124
NE Darby St 97124
SE Daren Dr 97123
NE & NW Darnielle Dr & St 97124
NE Daventry St 97124
NE Davis Ct 97124
SE Davis Ct 97123
SW Davis Ct 97123
SE Davis Rd 97123
SW Davis Rd 97123
SW Davis St 97123
NE Dawson Creek Dr 97124
NE Debra Ct 97124
SE Decade Ct 97123
NW Decora Ln 97124
NE Deer Run St 97124
SE Del Rio Ct 97123
NE Delsey Rd 97124
NW Dennis Ave 97124
SW Dennis Ave 97123
NE Dereck Ln 97124
NW Dick Rd 97124
NW Dierdorff Rd 97124
SE Discovery St 97123
NW Dogwood St 97124
NW Domaine Pl 97124
NW Doncaster Ter 97124
NW Donegal Pl 97124
NE & NW Donelson Rd & St 97124
NW Dorchester Way 97124
SE Dove St 97123
SE Dowery Ln 97123
SW & SE Drake Ct, Ln, Rd & St 97123
SE Duke Dr 97123
SW Dumas Rd 97123
NE Dunbar Ct 97124
Duncan Dr & Ter 97123
SE Dylan Way 97123
NE Eaglenest Ct 97124
SW Easystreet Ln 97123
NW Ebberts Ave 97124
NE Edgefield St 97124
NW Edinburg Dr 97124
NE Edison St 97124
SW Egger Rd 97123
SE Eileen Ln 97123
NE Elam Young Pkwy 97124
SE Elina Ave 97123
NW Elm St 97124
SE Elm St 97123
SW Elsinore Ln 97123
NW Emma Way 97124
SE Englewood Dr 97123
SW Enschede Dr 97123
SE Enterprise Cir 97123
NE Enyeart Pl 97124
SE Eric St 97123
NE Ernest St 97124
NE Estate Dr 97124
SE Estelle Ct 97123
NE Evening Star Dr 97124
Evergreen Pkwy & Rd 97124
NW Farm Park Dr 97124
NE Farmcrest St 97124
SW Farmington Rd 97123
NE Farnham St 97124
NE Feather Ct 97124
SW Fernhollow Ln 97123
SW Finnigan Hill Rd 97123
NW Fir St 97124
SE Fir Grove Loop 97123
SE Firwood Crest Ln 97123
NW Five Oaks Dr 97124
SE Flanders Ln 97123
NW Ford Ln 97124
NE & NW Forest Ln & St 97124
NW Forest Creek Dr 97124
SW Forest Park Rd 97123
SE Foxglove Ct 97123
SW Foxtail Pl 97123
SE & SW Frances Ct & St 97123
NW Freeman Ave 97124
SW Freeman Ave 97123
NW Freeman Ct 97124
SE Frewing Rd 97123
SE Gadroon St 97123
SE Gail Ct 97123
NW Galliard Loop 97124
NW Garibaldi St 97124
Geraldine Ct & Dr 97124
SE Gerhard Dr 97123
NW Germantown Rd 97124
SE Gettman Ter 97123
SE Gladys St 97123
NE Glen Ellen Dr 97124
SE Glen Meadows Way 97123
NW Glencoe Rd 97124
NE Glencoe Oaks Pl 97124
NW Glencory St 97124
SE Glendale Ct 97123
NW Gloucester Way 97124
SE Goboes Ct 97123
Golden Rd & St 97123
SE Golden Rod Ct 97123
NE Goldie Dr 97124
SW Grabel Rd 97123
SE Grace St 97123
NE Grant St 97124
Green Ct & St 97123
Greenridge Pl & Ter 97124
NE Greensword Dr 97124
SE Greenview Ct 97123
NE Griffin Oaks St 97124
NW Grossen Dr 97124
Groveland Dr & Rd 97124
SW Guenther Rd 97123
NE Guston Ct 97124
NE Gwen Ct 97124
Hacienda Ct & St 97123
NE Hampton Ct 97124
Handel Ave & Pl 97123
NE Hannah Ct 97124
Hanover Ct & St 97123
SE Hardwood Ln 97123
Hare Ave & Way 97123
NE Harewood Pl 97124
NE Harnish St 97124
NE Harrow St 97124
NE Harvest St 97124
NW Harvest Moon Dr 97124
SE Harwell Way 97123
NE Hawthorne Ave 97124
NW Hayden Ct 97124
NE Hayes St 97124
NE Haystack St 97124
SE Heathcliff Ln 97123
SE Heather Ct 97123
Heike Ct & St 97123
SW Heikes Dr 97123
Helene Ct & St 97123
NW Helvetia Rd 97124
Hemlock Ct & St 97123
SW Herd Ln 97123
NE Herrold Ct 97124
NW Hertel St 97124
NE Hidden Creek Dr 97124
SW Hideaway Ln 97123
SE High St 97123
SE Highcreek Ln 97123
SE Highfield Ave 97123
Hillaire Ct & Dr 97124
SW Hillecke Rd 97123
SW Hillsboro Hwy 97123
NE Hillwood Dr 97124
SE Hollow St 97123
SW Holly Hill Rd 97123
SE Hollyhock Ct 97123
SE Homestead Ct 97123
SE Honeysuckle Pl 97123
NE Hood St 97124
NE Horizon Loop 97124
NW Hornecker Rd 97124
NW Huffman St 97124
Hyde Cir & St 97124
NE Iberian Ln 97124
SE Ide St 97123
NE Idyl Way 97124
Imagine Way 97123
NW Imbrie Dr 97124
SE Imlay Ave 97123
NW Inverness Dr 97124
NW Iona Ct 97124
NE Irene Ct 97124
NE Ironcreek Ter 97124
SE Ironwood Ave 97123
SE Irwin Ct 97123
NE & NW Jackson St 97124
NW Jackson Quarry Rd 97124
NE Jackson Road Loop 97124
NE & NW Jackson School Rd 97124
NE Jackson Village Loop 97124
NW Jacobson Rd 97124
SE Jacquelin Dr 97123
NE Jamie Dr 97124
NW Jarrell Rd 97124
NW Jason Ct 97124
NE Java Way 97124
Jean Ct & Ln 97123
NE Jefferson St 97124
SE Jess Ct 97123
NE Jessica Loop 97124
Joanne Cir & Ct 97124
John Olsen Ave & Pl 97124
SW Johnson Ct 97123
NW Johnson Rd 97124
SE Johnson St 97123
SW Johnson St 97123
Josephine Ct, Dr & St 97124
NE Joyce Ct 97124
NE Kalahari Ridge Ave 97124
NE Karen Ct 97124
SE Karlson Ct 97123
SE Karpstein Pl 97123
NE Kaster Dr 97124
NE Kathleen Ct 97124
NE Kathryn St 97124
NE Katie Dr 97124
NE Kelly Ct 97124
NE Kennedy Ln 97124
SE Kensington St 97123
NE Kettering St 97124
SE Kingston Ct 97123
SE Kingswood Ave 97123
NE Kinney St 97124
NE Kinsale Ct 97124
NE Kirra St 97124
SW Kleier Dr 97123
SE Kobus Way 97123
NE Kristie Ct 97124
NE La Carter Ln 97124
NE Lagos Ct 97124

NE Lange Ct 97124
SE Langwood St 97123
NE Larena Pl 97124
SW Larkins Mill Rd 97123
SE Larkspur Ct 97123
SE & SW Larson Ct & Rd 97123
NE Latte Way 97124
Laura Ct & St 97124
SE & SW Laurel Ct & Rd 97123
NE Laurelee St 97124
SW Laurelview Rd 97123
Laurelwood Dr & Rd 97123
NE Lauren Ct 97124
SW Lazy River Pl 97123
SE Leander St 97123
NW Ledum Ln 97124
NW Leisy Rd 97124
NE & NW Lenox St 97124
SW Lepley Ln 97123
SW Lews Rd 97123
SE Lexington Dr 97123
SE Libby Ct 97123
Lilac Ct & St 97124
NE & NW Lincoln Ct & St 97124
NE Linden St 97124
SE Lindsay Ln 97123
Lindsey Ct & Dr 97124
NW Linnea Dr 97124
NE Lisbon Way 97124
Little Valley Ave & Way 97123
SE Littlegem St 97123
NE Lockheart Ln 97124
NW Logie Trl 97124
SE & SW Lois St 97123
Lone Oak Pl & St 97123
SW Loney Ln 97123
SE Lonny Ct 97123
NE Lorena Ct 97124
NE Lorie Dr 97124
NE Lovell St 97124
SW Lukas Rd 97123
SE Luna Way 97123
SE Lupine Ct 97123
Madera Ct & St 97123
SE Madison St 97123
SW Madrona Ridge Dr 97123
SE Madsen Ct 97123
NE Maidstone St 97124
E & W Main St 97123
W Main Street Ext 97123
SE Mair St 97123
NW Malia Ln 97124
NW Manchester Way 97124
NW Mandi St 97124
SW Manna Dr 97123
SW Mannsland Pl 97123
SE & SW Maple Ct & St 97123
SE Margaret Ln 97123
NE Margeaux Pl 97124
SE Marigold Ct 97123
Marina Ct & St 97124
SE Mariner Way 97123
SE Marinette Ave 97123
SE Mariposa Ct 97123
SE Marla Pl 97123
NW Marshall Dr 97124
SE Marston Ave 97123
NE Maryann Ct 97124
NE Maureen St 97124
NW Mauzey Rd 97124
SE Maxwell St 97123
SE Maya Ct 97123
NE Mcbride Ln 97124
SW Mccormick Hill Rd 97123
SW Mcfee Pl 97123
NE Mcmurtry Pl 97124
SW Mcnay Rd 97123
Meadow Ct & Ln 97124
NE Meadowgate Ct 97124
SE Meadowlark Dr 97123
SE Meadowview Way 97123

NW Meek Rd 97124
SW Meeker Ter 97123
SE Meier Ct 97123
NW Meier Rd 97124
SE Mel Ct 97123
NE Melinda Ct 97124
SW Melott Rd 97123
SW Melvista Dr 97123
NE & NW Merle Ct & Dr 97124
SE Merriweather Dr 97123
SW Midway Rd 97123
NE Miller St 97124
NE & NW Milne Ct, Rd & St 97124
SE & SW Minter Bridge Rd 97123
NE Mocha Way 97124
NW Moda Way 97124
NW Molini Ter 97124
NE Molly St 97124
Montego Dr & St 97123
NE Montgomery St 97124
NE Moon Rise Dr 97124
SE Moonlight Ave 97123
NE Moore Ct 97124
SE Morgan Rd 97123
SW Morilon Ln 97123
NE Morning Sun Dr 97124
SE Moscato Ct 97123
SW Mount Olive Pl 97123
NW Mullerleile Rd 97124
NE Naomi Ct 97124
NE Natalie St 97124
SE Nathan Ct 97123
SE Nazomi Ave 97123
NE Nelly St 97124
SW Neugebauer Rd 97123
NW Nicholas Ct 97124
NE Nicki Ct 97124
SE Nicklaus Ct 97123
SE Noland St 97123
SE Nordlund Ct 97123
SE Northwood Way 97123
NE Nova Ave 97124
SE Oak Ct 97123
NW Oak Dr 97124
SE Oak St 97123
SW Oak St 97123
SE Oak Crest Dr 97123
SE Oak Glen Way 97123
SW Oak Grove Ln 97123
SE Oakhurst St 97123
SE Oakleaf St 97123
NE Ocean Loop 97124
NE & NW Oelrich Rd 97124
NW Old Cornelius Pass Rd 97124
NW Old Pass Rd 97124
NE Oleander Ln 97124
NE Olerich Rd 97124
SE Olivewood St 97123
Olympic Ct & St 97124
SW Orchaedia Dr 97123
SW Orchid Hill Ln 97123
NE Orenco Gardens Dr 97124
NE Orenco Station Pkwy 97124
SW Ornduff Rd 97123
NW Overlook Dr 97124
SE & SW Ozark Ct & Ln 97123
NW Padgett Rd 97124
SE Paladin Ln 97123
NW Palazza Way 97124
SE Palmer Ct 97123
SE Palmire Ct 97123
NE Palomar Ct 97124
NE Park Pl 97124
NE Parks Edge Cir 97124
NE Parkside Dr 97124
NE Parkwood St 97124
SW & SE Patricia Ave & Ln 97123
SE Patterson St 97123

SE Paula Jean Ct 97123
SW Peaks View Dr 97123
NW Pederson Rd 97124
SE Pegasus St 97123
SE Pelton Ct 97123
NE Penny Way 97124
SE Pepperwood Way 97123
NE Pershing Ln 97124
SW Pheasant Ln 97123
NW Phillips Rd 97124
NE Phoenix St 97124
Pine Ct, St & Way 97123
NW Pinefarm Pl 97124
SE Pinewood Ave 97123
SW Pinot Pl 97123
SE Pipers Dr 97123
SW Pit Rd 97123
NE Platt St 97124
SE Player Ct 97123
SE Polaris Way 97123
SE Popes Pl 97123
SE Portlandia Ave 97123
NE Porto Way 97124
NE Poynter St 97124
SE Preston Ct 97123
SE Primrose Ct 97123
NW Progress Ct 97124
NW Pubols Rd 97124
SE Pueblo St 97123
Quail Cir & Way 97123
SE Quail Pointe Ct 97123
NW Quatama Rd 97124
NW & NE Queens Ct & Ln 97124
NW Rachel St 97124
SE Radcliff Ct 97123
SW Rainbow Ln 97123
SE Rancho St 97123
Ray Cir & Ct 97124
SW Raynard Rd 97123
SE Redberry Pl 97123
NE Redspire Ln 97124
SE Redwood St 97123
Reedville Creek Ct & Dr 97123
NE Regan Ct 97124
NE Retford Ave 97124
NW Rickey Ter 97124
NE Ridge Dr 97124
SW Ridge View Dr 97123
NE Ridgestone Ct 97124
SE Ripplewood Ave 97123
SE & SW River Rd 97123
SE Roanoke Ct 97123
SE Robin Cir 97123
SW Robinson Rd 97123
NE Rockridge Pl 97124
NW Rockton Dr 97124
NE Rocky Brook St 97124
NE Rogahn St 97124
SW Rogol Dr 97123
NE Ronler Way 97124
SE Rood Ct 97123
SE & SW Rood Bridge Dr & Rd 97123
SW Rosa Rd 97123
SE Rose Petal Pl 97123
NE Rosebay Dr 97124
SE Rosebud Way 97123
SE Rosespring Dr 97123
SE Rosewood St 97123
NE Rothbury Ave 97124
SE Roundelay St 97123
SW Rowell Rd 97123
SE Royalstar Ave 97123
SE Royce Ct 97123
NW Rubus Ln 97124
Russell Ct & St 97123
SE Sacha Pl 97123
NE Saddle Ct 97124
NW Sadie Ct 97124
NE Saida Ln 97124
NE Saint Jean Pl 97124
SE San Marino Ave 97123
SE Sandalwood St 97123
SE Satinwood St 97123

SE Scarlet Pl 97123
NW Schaaf Rd 97124
NE Schoeler Cir 97124
SW Scholls Ferry Rd 97123
NW Scotch Church Rd 97124
NW Scott St 97124
NE Sequoia Ct 97124
NE Setting Sun Dr 97124
NW Sewell Rd 97124
SE Shadowbrook Pl 97123
NE Shaleen St 97124
SE Shamrock Ln 97123
Shannon Ct, Dr & St 97124
SE Shega Ct 97123
NE Shelly Ct 97124
NE Sherborne St 97124
NE & NW Shute Rd 97124
SE Sierra St 97123
SE Sigrid St 97123
NE Silo Dr 97124
Silver Fox Ave & Way 97123
NE Simmental St 97124
SE Singing Woods Dr 97123
NE Skipton St 97124
NE Skylar St 97124
NE Sloan Way 97124
SE Smith Dr 97123
NE Snell Ct 97124
SE Snowberry Ct 97123
NE Southbrook Ct 97124
SW Southwind Dr 97123
SE Spoonbill Ct 97123
SE & SW Spring Dr & St 97123
NW Spring Meadows Way 97124
SE Springwood Pl 97123
SE Spruce St 97123
Stable Ct & Dr 97124
NE Stanchion Ct 97124
SE Stargazer Pl 97123
SE Starling Pl 97123
SE Stella Ct 97123
NE Stephanie Ct 97124
SE Sterling Ln 97123
SE Stewart Ct 97123
SW Stickney Dr 97123
NE Stile Dr 97124
NE Stonebriar Ln 97124
NE Stonewater St 97124
NE Stoneybrook St 97124
SW Straughan Rd 97123
SW Strawberry Hill Dr 97123
Stucki Ave & Pl 97124
NE Sturgess Ave 97124
SE Summerwood Pl 97123
NE Sunburst Ave 97124
NE Sundance Ct 97124
NW Sunday Dr 97124
NW Sunderland Dr 97124
NE Sundown Ct 97124
SE Sunflower Ct 97123
SE Sunnybrook Dr 97123
NE Sunrise Ln 97124
SW Sunrise Peaks Ln 97123
SE Sussex Ct 97123
NW Svea Dr 97124
SE Sweet Meadow Ln 97123
SE Sweetbay St 97123
SE Sycamore St 97123
SE Tamango St 97123
SE Tamora Ave 97123
SE Tanager Cir 97123
NW Tanasbourne Dr 97124
NE Tandem Way 97124
SE Teakwood St 97123
Terry Cir & Ct 97124
SE Thistle Ct 97123
Thomas Ct & St 97124
SE Thornapple St 97123
NW Thorncroft Dr 97124
SE Thrush Ave 97123
NW & NE Tiffany Ln & St 97124
SW Tile Flat Rd 97123
SE Timberlake Dr 97123

NE Timothy Ln 97124
Tina Ct & St 97124
NE Tipton Ct 97124
NE Tralee Ct 97124
NW Tree Haven Dr 97124
NE Treena St 97124
NW Treglown Ct 97124
SE Trellis Pl 97123
NE Trisha Dr 97124
NE Truman Ln 97124
SE & SW Tualatin Valley Hwy 97123
SE Tumblestone Dr 97123
NE Tunbridge St 97124
NE Turner Dr 97124
SW Turner Ln 97123
SE Turner Creek Dr 97123
SE Twelve Oaks St 97123
Val Ct & St 97124
NE Valarie Ct 97124
NW Valley Vista Rd 97124
SW Vanderschuere Rd 97123
NW Venetian Dr 97124
SE Verbena Pl 97123
NW Victory Ln 97124
NW Viewpoint Pl 97124
SW Viewridge Ln 97123
SE Villa St 97123
SE Village Ct 97123
NE Vinings Way 97124
NE Vino Ct 97124
SW Vintage Dr 97123
SE Virginia St 97123
SW Vista Hill Dr 97123
NE Waco Ct 97124
NW Wagon Way 97124
NE Walbridge St 97124
SE & SW Walnut Ct & St 97123
SE & SW Washington Ct & St 97123
SE Water Lily St 97123
SE Wedgewood Ave 97123
NE Weeping Willow Way 97124
SW Weiland Pl 97123
NE Weller Ct 97124
SE Wenlock Ave 97123
NW Wessex Ter 97124
NW West Union Rd 97124
SE Westcott Ln 97123
SE Westerland St 97123
NW Western Way 97124
NW Westmark Dr 97124
NE Wetherby St 97124
SE White Oak Ave 97123
Whitewood Dr & Ter 97124
SW Whitmore Rd 97123
SE Wicker Ct 97123
NE Wilcox St 97124
SE Wildflower Pl 97123
SW Wildhaven Ln 97123
NW Wildwood St 97124
Willow Ct, Dr & St 97123
NE Willowgrove St 97124
NE Windrow St 97124
SE & SW Witch Hazel Rd 97123
SE Wohler St 97123
SE Woll Pond Way 97123
SW Wolsborn Ave 97123
Wonder Way 97123
SW Wood St 97123
SE Woodrow Ln 97123
NE Woodsong St 97124
NE Woodview Dr 97124
NW Wren Rd 97124
SE Wrenfield St 97123
NE Wrenwood Ln 97124
SE Wynnwood Dr 97123
SE Yellowbird Ave 97123
SE Yew Wood Ln 97123
NW Yonia Ct 97124
SE Yulan Way 97123
NW Yungen Rd 97124
NE Zachary St 97124

NE Zander Ct 97124
NW Zimmerman Ln 97124
NW Zion Church Rd 97124

NUMBERED STREETS

N 1st Ave 97124
S 1st Ave 97123
NE 1st Ct 97124
NW 1st Ct 97124
NE 1st Dr 97124
NE 1st Pl 97124
NW 1st Pl 97124
NE 2nd Ave 97124
NW 2nd Ave 97124
SE 2nd Ave 97123
NE 2nd Ct 97124
NW 2nd Ct 97124
NE 2nd Dr 97124
NE 2nd Pl 97124
NE 3rd Ave 97124
NW 3rd Ave 97124
SE 3rd Ave 97123
NE 3rd Ct 97124
NE 3rd Pl 97124
NE 4th Ave 97124
NW 4th Ave 97124
SE 4th Ave 97123
NE 4th Ct 97124
NE 4th Pl 97124
NW 4th Way 97124
NE 5th Ave 97124
SE 5th Ave 97123
NE 5th Avenue Dr 97124
NE 6th Ave 97124
NW 6th Ave 97124
SE 6th Ave 97123
NE 6th Avenue Dr 97124
NE 7th Ave 97124
NW 7th Ave 97124
SE 7th Ave 97123
NE 7th Pl 97124
NE 8th Ave 97124
NW 8th Ave 97124
SE 8th Ave 97123
NE 8th Ct 97124
NW 8th Ct 97124
NW 8th Avenue Dr 97124
NE 9th Ave 97124
NW 9th Ave 97124
SE 9th Ave 97123
NW 9th Ct 97124
NE 9th Dr 97124
NE 9th Pl 97124
NE 10th Ave 97124
NW 10th Ave 97124
SE 10th Ave 97123
NE 10th Pl 97124
NW 10th Avenue Ct 97124
NE 11th Ave 97124
SE 11th Ave 97123
NE 11th Ct 97124
SE 11th Pl 97123
NE 11th Way 97124
NE 11th Street Dr 97124
NE 12th Ave 97124
SE 12th Ave 97123
SE 12th Ct 97123
NE 12th Way 97124
NE 13th Ave 97124
SE 13th Ave 97123
SE 13th Ct 97123
NE 13th Dr 97124
NE 13th Pl 97124
NE 13th Way 97124
NE 14th Ave 97124
SE 14th Ave 97123
NE 14th Pl 97124
NE 14th Way 97124
NE 15th Ave 97124
SE 15th Ave 97123
NE 15th Ct 97124
NE 16th Ave 97124
SE 16th Ave 97123
NE 16th Ct 97124
NE 17th Ave 97124

SW 17th Ave 97123
NE 18th Ave 97124
SE 18th Ave 97123
NE 18th Ct 97124
19th Ave & Ct 97124
SE 20th Ave 97123
SE 20th Ct 97123
NE 20th Dr 97124
NE 20th Pl 97124
SE 20th Pl 97123
NE 21st Ave 97124
SE 21st Ave 97123
SE 21st Ct 97123
SE 21st Pl 97123
NE 22nd Ave 97124
SE 23rd Ave 97123
NE 23rd Ct 97124
NE 24th Ave 97124
SE 24th Ave 97123
NE 25th Ave 97124
NE 25th Ct 97124
SE 25th Ct 97123
SE 25th Pl 97123
SE 26th Ave 97123
NE 26th Ct 97124
NE 27th Ct 97124
NE 28th Ave 97124
SE 28th Ave 97123
SE 28th Pl 97123
SE 29th Ave 97123
NE 29th Ct 97124
SE 29th Ct 97123
NE 30th Ave 97124
SE 30th Ave 97123
SE 30th Ct 97123
NE 31st Ct 97124
SE 31st Ct 97123
NE 32nd Ave 97124
SE 32nd Ave 97123
SE 32nd Ct 97123
SE 33rd Ave 97123
NE 33rd Ct 97124
SE 33rd Ct 97123
NE 34th Ave 97124
SE 34th Ave 97123
NE 34th Ct 97124
SE 34th Ct 97123
NE 34th Pl 97124
SE 35th Ave 97123
NE 35th Ct 97124
SE 35th Ct 97123
NE 36th Ave 97124
SE 36th Ave 97123
NE 37th Ave 97124
SE 37th Ave 97123
NE 38th Ave 97124
SE 38th Ave 97123
NE 38th Ct 97124
SE 38th Ct 97123
NE 39th Ave 97124
SE 39th Ave 97123
NE 39th Ct 97124
SE 39th Ct 97123
SE 39th Loop 97123
NE 40th Ave 97124
SE 40th Ave 97123
SE 40th Ct 97123
NE 41st Ave 97124
SE 41st Ave 97123
SE 42nd Ave 97123
NE 42nd Ct 97124
SE 42nd Pl 97123
SE 42nd Way 97123
NE 43rd Ave 97124
SE 43rd Ave 97123
SE 43rd Ct 97123
44th Ave, Ct & Way 97123
45th Ave & Ct 97123
NE 47th Ave 97124
SE 47th Ave 97123
NE 47th Pl 97124
SE 47th St 97123
NE 48th Ave 97124
SE 48th Ave 97123
SE 48th Pl 97123
NE 48th Way 97124

Street	ZIP
NE 49th Ave	97124
SE 49th Ave	97123
SE 49th Ct	97123
NE 49th Pl	97124
NE 49th Way	97124
SE 50th Ave	97123
NE 50th Way	97124
NE 51st Ave	97124
SE 51st Ave	97123
NE 52nd Ave	97124
SE 52nd Ave	97123
NE 52nd Ct	97124
SE 52nd Ct	97123
SE 52nd Pl	97123
NE 53rd Ave	97124
SE 53rd Ave	97123
NE 53rd Ct	97124
SE 53rd Ct	97123
NE 54th Ave	97124
SE 54th Ave	97123
NE 54th Ct	97124
SE 54th Ct	97123
NE 54th Way	97124
NE 55th Ave	97124
SE 55th Ave	97123
SE 55th Ct	97123
SE 55th Pl	97123
NE 56th Ave	97124
SE 56th Ave	97123
NE 56th Ct	97124
SE 56th Ct	97123
SE 56th Pl	97123
NE 57th Ave	97124
SE 57th Ave	97123
SE 57th Ct	97123
NE 58th Ave	97124
SE 58th Ave	97123
NE 58th Ct	97124
SE 58th Ct	97123
NE 58th Pl	97124
SE 59th Ave	97123
SE 59th Ct	97123
SE 59th Ln	97123
NE 59th Pl	97124
NE 60th Ave	97124
SE 60th Ave	97123
NE 60th Ct	97124
SE 60th Ct	97123
NE 60th Pl	97124
NE 61st Ave	97124
SE 61st Ave	97123
NE 61st Ct	97124
SE 61st Ct	97123
SE 61st Dr	97123
SE 61st Ln	97123
NE 61st Pl	97124
SE 61st Pl	97123
NE 61st Ter	97124
NE 61st Way	97124
SE 61st Way	97123
NE 62nd Ave	97124
SE 62nd Ave	97123
SE 62nd Ln	97123
NE 62nd Pl	97124
NE 63rd Ave	97124
SE 63rd Ave	97123
NE 63rd Ct	97124
SE 63rd Dr	97123
SE 63rd Ln	97123
NE 63rd Pl	97124
SE 63rd Pl	97123
NE 63rd Way	97124
SE 63rd Way	97123
NE 64th Ave	97124
NE 64th Ct	97124
SE 64th Ct	97123
NE 64th Ln	97124
NE 64th Pl	97124
NE 64th Ter	97124
NE 64th Way	97124
NE 65th Ave	97124
SE 65th Ave	97123
NE 65th Ct	97124
SE 65th Ln	97123
SE 65th Pl	97123
NE 66th Ave	97124
SE 66th Ave	97123
SE 66th Ct	97123
SE 66th Way	97123
SE 67th Ave	97123
68th Ave, Ct & Pl	97123
69th Ave & Ct	97123
NE 70th Ave	97124
SE 70th Ave	97123
SE 70th Ct	97123
NE 71st Ave	97124
SE 71st Ave	97123
SE 71st Ct	97123
SE 71st Pl	97123
NE 72nd Ave	97124
SE 72nd Ave	97123
SE 72nd Ct	97123
NE 72nd Pl	97124
SE 72nd Way	97123
NE 73rd Ave	97124
SE 73rd Ave	97123
SE 73rd Ct	97123
NE 74th Ave	97124
SE 74th Ave	97123
SE 74th Way	97123
NE 75th Ave	97124
SE 75th Ave	97123
SE 75th Ct	97123
NE 76th Ave	97124
NW 185th Ave	97124
NW 188th Ave	97124
NW 194th Ter	97124
NW 195th Ave	97124
NW 211th Ter	97124
NW 212th Pl	97124
NW 214th Pl	97124
NW 215th Ave	97124
SW 224th Ave	97123
NW 225th Ave	97124
NW 226th Ave	97124
SW 226th Ave	97123
NW 227th Ave	97124
NW 228th Ave	97124
NW 229th Ave	97124
SW 229th Ave	97123
NW 230th Ave	97124
NW 231st Ave	97124
SW 231st Pl	97123
SW 234th Ave	97123
NW 235th Ave	97124
NW 242nd Ave	97124
SW 247th Ave	97123
NW 253rd Ave	97124
NW 254th Ave	97124
NW 264th Ave	97124
268th Ave & Pl	97124
NW 271st Ave	97124
NW 273rd Ave	97124
NW 281st Ave	97124
NW 312th Ave	97124
NW 313th Ave	97124
NW 316th Pl	97124
NW 317th Ave	97124
SW 319th Pl	97123
SW 321st Pl	97123
325th Ave & Pl	97123
SW 329th Ter	97123
SW 331st Ave	97123
NW 334th Ave	97124
NW 336th Ave	97124
NW 338th Ave	97124
NW 341st Ave	97124
SW 345th Ave	97123

KLAMATH FALLS OR

Street	ZIP
General Delivery	97601

POST OFFICE BOXES MAIN OFFICE STATIONS AND BRANCHES

Box No.s	ZIP
JA - JR	97602
E - X	97601
1 - 5277	97601
7102 - 8200	97602
11001 - 13001	97601

NAMED STREETS

Street	ZIP
A St	97601
Abbott Mountain Way	97601
Abilene Ave	97601
Academy Ave	97601
Acosta Ave	97601
Adams St	97601
Addison St	97601
Adelaide Ave	97603
Agate St	97601
Airport Way	97603
Airway Dr	97603
N Alameda Ave	97601
S Alameda Ave	97603
Alandale St	97603
Algoma Rd	97601
Alisa Ln	97601
Allyn St	97603
Alma Alley St	97601
Almond St	97601
Alpin St	97601
Alpine Dr	97603
Alt Ct & Way	97603
Altadena Dr	97603
Altamont Dr	97603
Alva Ave	97603
Amber Ave	97603
Amberview Ln	97603
American Ave	97603
Anchor Way	97601
Anderson Ave & Rd	97603
Andrew Dr	97603
Angela Ct	97601
Angle St	97601
Ankeny St	97603
Antler Dr	97603
Apogee Way	97601
Appaloosa Ct	97603
Applegate Ave	97601
Applewood St	97603
Arant Pl & Rd	97603
Arlington Dr	97601
Armour Ave	97601
Arnel Rd	97601
Arnold Ave & St	97603
Arrowhead Rd	97601
Arroyo Ct	97603
Arthur St	97603
Asheradw St	97601
Ashland St	97601
Ashley Ct	
2100-2199	97603
22501-22599	97601
Aspen St	97601
Aster Ln	97601
Auburn St	97601
Ault St	97601
Aurora Ct & Dr	97603
Austin St	97603
Autumn Ave	97601
Autumn Dr	97603
Autumn Gold Dr	97601
Avalon Pl & St	97603
Bald Eagle Ct	97601
Balsam Dr	97601
Barnes Way	97603
Barney Ct	97601
Barry Ave & Dr	97603
Bartlett Ave	97603
Basin View Ct & Dr	97603
Bay St	97603
Bear Valley Dr	97603
Beat Ln	97603
Beaver Ave & St	97601
Beckton Ave	97603
Bedfield Rd	97603
Bel Aire Dr	97603
Bellm Dr	97603
Ben Gay Rd	97603
Ben Kerns Rd	97601
Benchwood Ave	97603
Benson Ave	97601
Berkeley St	97601
Best View Dr	97601
Beta Ln	97603
Beverly Dr	97603
Biehn St	97601
Big Buck Ln	97601
Big Fir Ln	97601
Big O Way St	97601
Big Pine Way	97601
Birch St	97601
Birddog Dr	97603
Bisbee St	97603
Bismark St	97601
Black Bear Ct	97601
Blackberry Ct	97603
Blue Gill Rd	97603
Blue Mountain Dr	97601
Blue Pool Way	97603
Blue Sage Ln	97603
Blue Wing St	97603
Bly St	97601
Boardman Ave	97603
Bong St	97603
Boone Cir	97603
Booth Rd	97603
Boulder Ln	97603
Boyd Ct & Pl	97603
Braymill Dr	97601
Breitenstein Ln	97601
Brentwood Dr	97603
Briana Dr	97603
Briarwood Ln	97601
Bristol Ave & Ct	97603
N & S Broad St	97601
Broadmore St	97603
Brooke Dr	97603
Brooklyn Ave	97603
Broyles Ave	97601
Bryant Ave & Ct	97603
Bryant Williams Dr	97601
Buck Ln	97601
Buck Rd	97603
Buck Island Dr	97601
Buena Vista St	97601
Buesing Rd	97603
Burns St	97603
Burton Flat Rd	97601
Bush St	97601
Butte St	97601
C St	97601
Cable St	97601
Cabria St	97603
Calhoun St	97601
California Ave	97601
Calimesa Way	97601
Cambridge Ct	97603
Camp Day Ln & Pl	97601
Campus Dr	97601
Canby St	97601
Cannon Ave	97603
Carlon Way	97603
Carlson Dr	97603
Carlyle St	97601
Caroline St	97603
S Carroll St	97601
Casa Way	97603
Cascade Ln & Way	97601
Cedar St	97601
Cedar Trl	97603
Cedar Way	97601
Cedar Ridge Rd	97601
Cemetary Rd	97603
Centurion Ct	97603
Century Ct & Dr	97601
Cerswell Ranch Rd	97601
Chambers Ln	97603
Chantal Ave	97601
Charter Isle Blvd	97601
Chelsea St	97601
Cherry Way	97603
Cherry Blossom Ln	97601
Chestnut Ln	97601
Cheyne Ave & Rd	97603
Chilly Valley Ln	97603
Chin Rd	97603
Chin Tolk St	97601
Chinchalla Way	97603
Choke Cherry Ct & Ln	97603
Christine Ln	97603
Church Hill Dr	97603
Cinnamon Teal Dr	97601
Clairmont Dr	97601
Cleveland Ave	97601
Climax Ave	97603
Clinton Ave	97603
Clover St & Way	97601
Clover Creek Rd	97601
Clovis Ct & Dr	97603
Coli Ave	97601
Collier Ln	97603
Colt Rd	97603
Commercial St	97601
Community Ave	97601
Como Way	97601
Conger Ave	97601
Cook St	97601
Coolidge St	97601
Coopers Hawk Rd	97601
Coos Ta St	97601
Cormorant Ct & Loop	97601
Coronado Way	97603
Cortez St	97601
Corvallis St	97601
Cottage Ave	97603
Cougar Butte	97601
Cougar Ridge Rd	97603
Country Ln	97603
Cove Point Rd	97601
Covina Ct	97603
Crater St	97601
Crawley Ln	97603
Cregan Ave	97601
Crescent Ave	97601
Crest St	97603
Crestdale Way	97603
Creswell Ranch Rd	97601
Crosby Ave	97603
Cross Rd	97603
Cross St	97601
Crossbill Dr	97601
Crystal Springs Rd	97603
Crystal Terrace Dr	97601
Cypress Ave	97601
Daggett Ave	97601
Dahlia St	97601
Dakota Ct	97603
Damont St	97601
Daniel Way	97603
Darrow Ave	
2000-2599	97601
2601-2899	97603
Darwin Pl	97603
Dawn Ct & Dr	97603
Day Dr	97603
Dayton St	97603
Dead Indian Rd	97601
Dead Indian Memorial Dr	97601
Debbie Dr	97601
Dehlinger Ln	97603
Del Fatti Ln	97603
Del Moro St	97601
Delap Rd	97601
Delaware Ave	97603
Delta St	97601
Dennis Dr	97603
Denver Ave & Park	97603
Derby Pl & St	97603
Devonridge Dr	97601
Dewitt Ct	97601
Diamond St	97601
Diane Dr	97603
Dipper Ln	97601
Ditchrider Rd	97603
Division St	97601
Dixon St	97601
Dolores Ave	97601
Donald St	97601
Donegal Ave	97603
Doty St	97601
Douglas Ave	97601
Dove Hollow Dr	97603
Dover Ave	97601
Dowitcher Rd	97601
Driftwood Dr	97603
Duffy Ave	97601
Dugout Ln	97601
Dunlin Ln	97601
Eagle Ct	97601
Eagle Claw Dr	97603
Eagle Ridge Rd	97601
Earle St	97601
East St	97601
Eastmount St	97603
Eastside Byp	97603
Eastwood Dr	97603
Easy St	97601
Eb Way	97601
Eberlein Ave	
2000-2599	97601
2600-6799	97603
Echo Way	97601
Eden Ct	97601
Edison Ave	97603
El Cerrito Way	97603
Elder Way	97603
Elderberry Ln	97601
N & S Eldorado Ave	97601
Elk St	97601
Elliott Rd	97603
Elm Ave & St	97601
Emerald St	97601
Engleman Spruce Way	97601
Erie St	97601
Erskine Cir	97601
Esi Way	97601
Esplanade Ave	97601
Estate Dr	97603
S Etna Rd	97601
Etna St	97603
S Etna St	97603
Euclid Ave	97601
Eulalona Ct	97601
Evergreen Dr	97603
Ewauna St	97601
Ezell Ave	97603
F St	97601
Fairchild Ave	97603
Faircliff Ln	97603
Fairhaven St	97601
Fairmount St	97601
Fairway Dr	97601
Falcon Dr	97601
Fargo St	97603
Fawn Ave	97601
Ferndale Pl	97603
Ferrier Ave	97601
Fieldcrest Rd	97603
Finch Ct	97601
Finley Ct	97603
Fir St	97601
Flag Ct	97603
Flint St	97601
Flowers Ln	97601
Foothills Blvd	
2600-2899	97603
2901-3099	97601
4100-4199	97601
4500-4599	97603
Forest Park Ln	97601
Fox Sparrow Dr	97601
Freight Road Ln	97601
Fremont St	97601
Frieda Ave	97603
Front St	97601
Frontage Rd	97601
Fugar Way	97601
Fulton St	97601
Gage Rd	97601
Galpin Ln	97603
Garden Ave & Cir	97601
Gardena Pl	97603
Gary St	97603
Gatewood Dr	97603
Gearhart Ct	97601
Gentile St	97603
George Nurse Way	97601
N Georgia St	97601
Gettle St	97603
Ginger Ln	97601
Glenridge Way	97603
Glenwood Dr	97603
Golden Ct & Trl	97603
Gordon St	
400-599	97601
3700-3799	97603
Grace Dr	97601
Gracile Ct	97603
Grand Ave	97601
Granite St	97601
Grant St	97601
Grape St	97601
Greenbriar Dr	97603
Greensprings Dr	97601
Gregory Dr	97603
Grenada Way	97603
Greylock Way	97601
Griffith Ln	97603
Grosbeak Dr	97601
Ground Ct	97603
Hager Ln & Way	97603
Hal Ct	97603
Hamaker Ln	97601
Hamaker Mountain Rd	97601
Hammer St	97603
Hanks St	97601
Harbor Isle Blvd	97601
Harbor View Dr	97601
Harbor Vista Blvd	97601
Harlan Dr	97603
Harmony Ln	97601
Harpold Rd	97603
Harrier Dr	97601
Harriette Dr	97601
Harriman Ave	97601
Hart Ct	97601
Harvard St	97601
Harvey Dr	97603
Haskins Ave	97601
Havencrest Ct & Dr	97603
Hawkins St	97601
Hawthorne St	97601
Heather St	97601
Helm St	97601
Henley Rd	97603
Henry St	97601
Herbert St	97601
Heritage Ct	97603
Hickory Ln	97601
Hidden Valley Rd	97603
High St	97601
Highland Way	97603
Highway 140 E	97603
Highway 140 W	97601
Highway 39	97603
Highway 66	97601
Highway 97 S	97603
N Highway 97	97601
Highway Contract 34	97601
Hill Rd	97603
Hill St	97601
Hillcrest Rd	97603
Hilldale St	97603
N Hills Dr	97603
Hillside Ave	97601
Hilton Dr	97603
Hilyard Ave & Ct	97603
Hogue Dr	97601
Holabird Ave	97601
Holbrook St	97601
Holliday Rd	97601
Holly Ave	97601
Home Ave	97601
Homedale Rd	97603
Homer Dr	97603
Homestead Ln	97601
Honey Locust Dr	97601
Hope St	97601
Horal Ave	97603
Horned Lark Dr	97601
Horseshoe Way	97601
Hosanna Way	97603

Hotchkiss Dr 97601
Howard Ln 97601
Hughes St 97601
Hunter Ct 97603
Hunters Ridge Rd 97601
Huron St 97601
Idaho St 97601
Independence Ave 97603
Ioof Cemetery Rd 97603
W Iowa St 97601
Iron St 97601
Island Circle Dr 97601
Ivan Ln 97603
Ivory St 97603
J F Goeller Way 97601
Jacks Way 97603
Jade Ter 97601
Jake Ct & Rd 97601
James Martin Ct 97601
Jana Dr 97603
Jasma Ln 97601
Jay St 97601
Jefferson St 97601
Jeffrey Ln 97603
Jennifer Ln 97603
Jensen Ln 97603
Jesse Ct 97603
Jewell Ter 97601
Joe Wright Rd 97603
Johns Ave 97603
Johnson Ave & Dr 97601
Jordon Jct 97603
Judy Ct 97603
Juniper Way 97603
K St 97601
Kane St 97603
Kann Springs Ln 97603
Kat Ta St 97601
Katie Ln 97603
Kellal Ln 97603
Keller Ct & Rd 97603
Kelley Dr 97603
Kelsey Ln 97603
Keno Ct 97601
Keno Terrace Dr 97601
Keno Worden Rd 97603
Kerns Swamp Rd 97601
Kestrel Rd 97601
Kid Ln 97603
Kiln St 97601
Kimberly Ct & Dr 97603
Kincheloe Ave 97603
Kingbird Ct 97601
Kings Way 97603
Klamath Ave 97601
Knightwood Dr 97603
Knollcrest Rd 97603
Kress Dr 97603
La Habra Way 97603
La Jolla Ct 97603
La Marada Way 97603
La Wanda Dr 97601
N & S Laguna St 97601
Lake Ridge Dr 97601
Lakeport Blvd 97601
Lakeridge Ct 97601
Lakeshore Dr 97601
Lakeview Ave 97601
Lakewoods Dr 97601
Lakey St 97603
Lancaster Ave 97601
Larch Ln 97601
Lark St 97601
Larry Pl 97603
Last St 97601
Laurel St 97601
Laurelwood Dr 97603
Lava Ln 97603
Laverne Ave 97603
Lavey St 97601
Lawanda Dr 97601
Lawrence St 97601
Lefever St 97603
Leighton Ave 97603
Leland Dr 97603
Leroy St 97601
Lewis St 97601
Lexington Ave 97601
Liberty Ave 97603
Lincoln St 97601
Linda Vista Dr 97601
Lindberg St 97601
Lindley Way 97601
Link St 97601
Lippencott Ave 97601
Lisa Rd 97603
Llanada St 97601
Lockford Dr 97603
Lodi St 97603
Logan Dr & St 97603
Loma Linda Dr 97601
Lombard Dr 97603
Lombardy Ln 97603
Longacre Ln 97601
Longlake Rd 97601
Lookout Ave 97601
Lorrayne Pl 97603
Lost River Rd 97603
E & W Lowell St 97601
Lower Klamath Lake
Rd 97603
Lupine Ln 97603
Lynnewood Blvd 97601
Lyptus Ln 97601
Lytton St 97601
M St 97601
Mack Ave 97603
Madera Dr 97603
Madison St 97603
Mahan Ave 97601
Main St 97601
Majestic St 97601
Mallard Ln 97603
Mallory Dr 97603
Mann Rd 97603
Manzanita St 97601
Maple St 97601
Maplewood Ct & Dr 97603
Mar St 97601
Margie Ln 97601
Marian Ct 97603
Marina Dr 97601
Mariposa Dr 97601
Marius Dr 97603
Market St 97601
Markgraf Ln 97603
Marsh Hawk Dr 97601
Martin St 97601
Maryland Ave 97603
Mason Ln 97601
Massart St 97601
Mathers St 97601
Matney Rd & Way 97603
Maywood Dr 97603
Mazama Dr 97603
Mc Cormick Rd 97601
Mcclellan Dr 97603
Mcconnell Cir 97603
Mccourt St 97601
Mcguire Ave 97603
Mckale St 97601
Mckinley St 97601
Mclaughlin Ln 97601
Mclean St 97601
Meadow Glen Loop 97603
Meadowbrook Ct 97601
Meadowbrook Ln
13900-14199 97601
14200-14299 97603
N & S Meadows Ct &
Dr 97603
Melanie Ct 97601
Melrose St 97601
Mels Pl 97603
Memorial Dr 97601
Memorie Ln 97603
Menlo Way 97601
Merganser Rd 97601
Merlin Way 97601
Merrill Pit Rd 97603
Merryman Dr 97603
Mesa Ct, Dr & St 97601
Metro St 97603
Michersi Ave 97603
Michigan Ave 97601
Mickshelly Cir 97603
Midland Rd 97603
Milbert Ave 97603
Mill St 97601
Miller Ave 97603
Miller Island Rd 97603
Miracle Dr 97603
Mitchell St 97601
Modoc St 97601
Monclaire St 97601
Monrovia Way 97603
Montelius St 97601
Monterey Dr 97603
Montevilla Dr 97603
Morningside Ln 97603
Mortimer St 97601
Mountain Lakes Dr 97601
Mountain View Blvd 97601
Mourning Dove Dr 97601
Moyina Way 97603
Mt Pitt St 97601
Mt Whitney St 97601
Murrelet Rd 97601
Mustang Rd
4000-4799 97601
15400-15499 97603
Myrtlewood Dr 97603
N St 97601
Naoma St 97603
Natasha Way 97601
Nevada St 97601
New Way 97601
Newcastle Ave 97601
Newlun Dr 97603
Nickolas Dr 97603
Nile St 97603
Norgold Ln 97603
Northern Heights Blvd 97601
Northhills Dr 97603
Northridge Rd 97601
Northwood Ct 97603
Nosler St 97601
Nu K Sham St 97601
Oak Ave 97601
Oconner Rd 97603
Octavia Ave 97601
Odessa St 97601
Ogden St 97603
Ohio Ave 97601
Old Fort Rd 97601
Old Midland Rd 97603
Old Wagon Rd 97601
Olson Mountain Ct 97601
Oneil Dr 97601
Onyx Ave, Dr & Pl 97603
Opal Ave 97601
Orchard Ave & Way 97601
W Oregon Ave 97601
Oregon Ash Cir 97601
Orindale Rd 97601
Orpine Ct 97603
Osprey Ln 97601
Overland Dr 97603
Owens Ln 97603
Owens St 97601
Oxbow St 97603
Pacific Ln 97603
Pacific Ter 97601
Paint Horse Way 97601
Painter St 97601
Palomino Ct 97603
Paper Birch Way 97601
Paragon Way 97601
Paramont St 97603
Park Ave 97601
Parula Rd 97601
Pat Dr 97601
Patterson St 97603
Payne Aly 97601
Peace Pipe Ln 97601
Peach St 97601
Pear St 97603
Pearl Ave 97601
Pearson Butte Trl 97603
Peck Dr 97603
Peggy Ave 97601
Pelican St 97601
Pelican Bay St 97601
Pelican Butte Rd 97601
Pepperwood Ct & Dr 97603
Peregrine Hts 97601
Perry St 97603
Pershing Way
2400-2499 97601
2501-2599 97601
2600-3099 97603
Pierce St 97601
Pine St 97601
Pine Grove Rd 97603
Pine Tree Dr 97603
Piney Ct 97601
Pinnacle Pl 97603
Pinole Ln 97601
Pinto Ct 97603
Pioneer Rd 97601
Pipit Ct 97601
Pleasant Ave 97601
Plum Ave 97601
Plum Bush Ct & Dr 97603
Plum Hill Rd 97601
N & S Poe Valley Rd 97603
Pointer Dr 97603
Ponderosa Dr, Ln & Pl 97601
Portland St 97601
Powell Rd 97601
Preddy Ave 97603
Prescott St 97601
Primrose Ln 97601
Princeton St 97601
Prospect St 97601
Puckett Ln & Rd 97601
Push Kin St 97601
Quail Ln 97603
Quail Park Cir 97601
Quail Point Ct & Dr 97601
Quail Ridge Dr 97601
Quarry St 97601
Radcliffe Ave 97601
Rae St 97601
E & W Rainbow Rd 97601
Ramirez Rd 97603
Rand Way 97603
Ravenwood Dr 97601
Raymond St 97603
Reber Rd 97603
Reclamation Ave
2000-2599 97601
2600-2899 97603
Red Barn Rd 97601
Red Bud Dr 97601
Redding St 97603
Redfern Ln 97603
Redondo Way 97603
Redstart Rd 97601
Redtail Dr 97601
Redwood Dr 97601
Reeder Rd 97603
Regency Dr 97603
Reiling Rd 97603
Richmond St 97601
Rickenbacker Ave 97601
N Ridge Dr 97601
W Ridge Dr 97601
Ridge Rd 97603
Ridgecrest Dr 97601
Ridgewood Dr 97603
Rio Vista Way 97603
River Edge Rd 97601
Riverside Dr 97601
Riverview Ln 97601
Roberta Dr 97603
Robins Nest Ln 97601
Rock Dove Ct 97601
Rockinghorse Ln 97603
Rocky Point Rd 97601
N & S Rogers St 97601
Roosevelt St 97603
Rosaria Pl 97603
Rose St 97601
Rosemont Ct 97603
Roseway Dr 97601
Round Lake Rd 97601
Ruger Rd 97601
Runnels Ln 97601
Running Y Rd 97601
Russell St 97603
Ruth Ct & Dr 97603
Saddle Butte Dr 97601
Sage Way 97603
Saint Andrews Cir 97601
Sanderling Rd 97601
Sarah Cir 97603
Sargent Ave 97601
Sari Dr 97601
Sayler Rd 97603
Schaupp Rd 97603
Schell St 97603
Schiesel Ave 97603
Schilling Cir 97603
Schooler Ct 97603
Scotch Pine Rd 97603
Scott St 97601
Scotts Valley Dr 97601
Scottsbluff Rd 97601
Selma St 97603
Sequoia St 97601
Seutter Pl 97603
Shadow Ln 97601
Shady Pine Rd 97601
Shallock Ave 97601
Shamrock Ln 97603
Shasta Way
2200-2599 97601
2600-6799 97603
6801-6899 97603
Shawna Ct 97603
Sheldon St 97601
Shelley St 97601
Sherwood Dr 97603
Shield Crest Dr 97603
Short Rd 97603
Sierra Ct 97601
Sierra Pl 97603
Sierra Heights Dr 97603
Simmers Ave 97603
Simpson Canyon Rd 97601
Sing Rd 97601
Siskin Ln 97601
Siskiyou St 97601
Sjodin Ln 97603
Skiway Dr 97601
Skycrest Dr 97601
Skyline Dr 97603
Skyridge Dr 97603
Skyview Cir 97601
Sloan St 97601
Small Ct 97603
Snowgoose Ln 97601
Snowpack Cir 97601
Soquel St 97601
Sora Loop 97601
Sorrel Ct 97603
Southgate Dr 97603
Southshore Ln 97601
Southside Expy 97603
Southview Dr 97603
Spinaker Isle N 97601
N & S Spring St 97601
Springcrest Way 97603
Springlake Rd 97603
Spruce Ave 97601
St Andrews Cir 97603
St Francis St 97601
Stagecoach Pl & Rd 97601
Stanford St 97601
Starlit Ct 97603
State St 97603
Stebbins Ave 97601
Steens Dr 97601
Stinson Way 97603
Stoneridge Dr 97601
Stukel Ave 97601
Sturdivant Ave 97603
Sue Dr 97601
Sumac Ave & Ct 97603
Summerfield Way 97603
Summers Ln 97603
Summit St 97603
Sunnyside Dr 97601
Sunrise Ct 97601
Sunset Ct 97603
Sunset Beach Rd 97601
Sunset Ridge Rd 97601
Sunshine Pl 97603
Swallow Ct 97601
Swan Ct 97603
Swan Lake Rd 97603
Sycamore Dr 97603
Sylvia Ave 97603
Tacoma Ave 97603
Tamarack Ave 97601
Tamera Dr 97603
Taylor Rd 97603
Terrace Ave 97601
Thicket Ct 97601
Thomas Dr 97603
Thompson Ave 97603
Thrall St 97601
Thrush Ln 97601
Tiffany St 97601
Timber Cir 97601
Timber Ridge Loop 97601
Timberline Ln 97601
Tingley Ln 97603
Toboggan Cir 97601
Tony Ct 97603
Topper Ave 97601
Torrey St 97601
Towhee Ln 97601
Town Center Dr 97601
Township Rd 97603
Traverse St 97601
Travis Way 97603
Trinity St 97601
Troubador Trl 97601
Tuckers Xing 97603
Tunnel St 97601
Turner Ct 97603
Turnstone Dr 97601
Twin Pines Ln 97603
Uerlings Ave 97601
Uhrmann Rd 97601
Union St 97601
Unity St 97603
Upham St 97601
Upland Dr 97603
Vale Rd 97603
Valencia Way 97603
Valhalla Ave 97603
Valinda Way 97603
Valley Ct 97603
Valleyview Ln 97601
Valleywood Dr 97603
Van Camp St 97601
Van Ness Ave 97601
Vandenberg Rd 97603
Varney Creek Rd 97601
Ventura Dr 97603
Venture Ct 97601
Verda St 97601
Verda Vista Ct, Dr &
Pl 97603
Verdick Dr 97603
Vermont St 97603
Villa Dr 97603
Vincent Dr 97603
Vine Ave 97601
Vista Way 97601
Waban Way 97601
Wade Cir 97601
Waggoner Ct 97603
Wagner St 97603
Walker Mountain Rd 97603
Wall St 97601
Walnut Ave 97601
Walton Dr 97603
Wantland Ave
1900-2599 97601
2801-2899 97603
Warring St 97601
Washburn Way
600-4299 97603
4500-4599 97601
4800-10999 97603
Washington St 97601
Watson St 97603
Waxwing Ct 97601
Webber Rd 97603
N & S Wendling St 97601
Wesgo Dr 97603
Westbrook Dr 97603
Western St 97603
Westgate Dr 97603
Westridge Dr 97601
Westside Rd 97601
Westview Dr 97603
Weyerhaeuser Rd 97601
White Ave 97601
White Goose Dr 97603
Wiard St 97603
Wicket Ct 97603
Wigwam Way 97601
Wild Plum Aly, Ct &
Dr 97601
Wilderness Ct & Way 97601
Wildland Dr 97601
Wildwood Ln 97603
Wilford Ave 97601
Willet Way 97601
N & S Williams Ave 97601
Willie Lown Ln 97601
Willmott Ave & Ct 97603
Willow Ave & St 97601
Windsor St 97603
Winema Dr 97603
Winona Way 97603
Winter Ave 97603
Winterfield Way 97603
Wocus Rd, St & Way 97601
Wolf St 97601
Wong Rd 97603
Worden Ave 97601
World Mark Loop 97601
Wright Ave 97603
Wyatt Ln 97601
Yale St 97601
Yonna St 97601
Zeb Way 97601

NUMBERED STREETS

N 1st St 97601
N 2nd St 97601
N & S 3rd 97601
N & S 4th 97601
N & S 5th 97601
N 6th St 97601
S 6th St
101-197 97601
199-2599 97601
2601-2697 97603
2699-7599 97603
N & S 7th 97601
N & S 8th 97601
N & S 9th 97601
N 10th St 97601
N & S 11th 97601
N 12th St 97601

LAKE OSWEGO OR

General Delivery 97034

POST OFFICE BOXES MAIN OFFICE STATIONS AND BRANCHES

Box No.s
780B - 780B 97034
810B - 810B 97034
840B - 840B 97034
870B - 870B 97034

1 - 1072 97034
1101 - 2436 97035

NAMED STREETS

A Ave 97034
Abelard St 97035
Adams Ct 97035
Adrian Ct 97034
Alber Spring Ct 97034
Albert Cir 97035
Alder Cir 97034
Allen Rd 97035
Allison Pl 97035
Alpine Way 97034
Alto Park Rd 97034
Alyssa Ter 97035
Amber Ln & Pl 97034
Amberwood Cir & Ct 97035
Amherst Ct 97035
Andrews Rd 97034
Anduin Ter 97034
Aquinas St 97035
Arbor Ln 97035
Arrowhead Ct 97034
Arrowwood Ave 97035
Ash St 97034
Ashley Ct 97035
Aspen Ct & St 97034
Astor Ave 97035
Atherton Dr 97034
Atwater Ln & Rd 97034
Auburn Ct & Ln 97035
Avery Ln 97035
B Ave 97034
Babson Pl 97035
Baleine St 97035
Bangy Rd 97035
Banyon Ln 97034
Barrington Ct 97035
Bartok Pl 97035
Barton Rd 97034
Bass Ln 97034
Bay Creek Dr 97035
Bay Point Dr 97035
Bay View Ln 97034
Bayberry Rd 97034
Beasley Way 97035
Becket St 97035
Bedford Ct 97034
Bella Terra Dr 97034
Belmore Ave & Ct 97035
Benfield Ave & Ct 97035
Bergis Rd 97034
Bergis Farm Dr 97034
Bernard St 97035
Bernini Ct 97035
Berwick Ct & Rd 97034
Bickel Ct 97035
Bickner St 97034
Bilford Ln 97035
Birdbill Ct 97035
Black Forest Ct 97035
Blazer Trl 97035
Bloch Ter 97035
Blue Heron Ct, Dr, Rd & Way 97034
Boca Ratan Dr 97034
Bolivar St 97035
Bonaire Ave 97035
Bonita Rd 97035
Bonniebrae Dr 97034
Boones Way 97035
Boones Ferry Ln & Rd 97035
Botticelli St 97035
Bradbury Ct 97035
Braeden Ct 97035
Bree Ct 97034
Brian Ct 97034
Brianne Ct 97035
Briarwood Rd 97035
Bridge Ct 97034
Briercliff Ln 97034
Britten Ct 97035
Brook Ct 97035
Brookhurst Ct & Dr 97034
Brookside Rd 97035
Bryant Rd
16200-17900 97035
17902-17998 97035
18100-19299 97034
Buck Brush Ln 97035
Buckingham Ter 97034
Bullock St 97034
Burma Rd 97035
Burnham Rd 97034
C Ave 97034
Cabana Ln 97034
Cabana Pointe 97034
Cambridge Ct 97035
Camden Ln 97035
Camelot Ct 97034
Cameo Ct 97034
Camincou Rd 97034
Campus Way 97034
Canal Cir 97035
Canal Rd
3900-4199 97034
17900-19698 97035
Canal Woods Ct 97034
Candlewood Ct 97035
Canyon Ct & Dr 97034
Capilano Ct 97034
Cardinal Ct, Dr & Pl 97034
Carlson Ct 97034
Carman Dr 97035
Carnegie Ave 97035
Carrera Ln 97034
Cascara Ln 97035
Casey Ct 97034
Cedar Ct, Rd & St 97034
Cellini Ct 97035
Centerpointe Dr 97035
Centerwood St 97035
Central Ave 97035
Cervantes Cir 97035
Chad Dr 97034
Chandler Pl & Rd 97034
Chapin Way 97034
Chapman Way 97035
Charles Cir 97035
Charleton Ct 97035
Chatham Ct 97035
Chelsea Dr & Ln 97035
Cherry Cir, Ct & Ln 97034
Cherry Crest Ave & Dr 97034
Cheryl Ct 97034
Childs Ct 97035
Childs Rd
1500-4199 97034
4201-4299 97034
4900-7299 97034
Chinook Ct 97035
Church St 97034
Churchill Downs 97035
Clairmont Ct 97035
Clara Ct 97034
Clara Ln 97035
Cloverleaf Rd 97034
Cobb Way 97035
Coho Ln 97034
Colby Ct 97035
Collins Way 97035
Coltsfoot Ln 97035
Condolea Ct, Dr, Ter & Way 97035
Conifer Dr & Ter 97034
Cornell Ct & St 97034
Cortez Ct 97035
Country Club Ct & Rd 97034
Country Commons 97034
Country Woods Ct 97035
Coventry Ct 97035
Creekside Ter 97035
Crest Dr 97034
Crestfield Ct 97034
Crestline Ct & Dr 97034
Crestview Dr 97034
Cumberland Pl & Rd 97034
D Ave 97034
Da Vinci St 97035
Daniel Way 97035
Dapplegrey Ln 97034
Davis Ln 97035
Dawn Ave 97035
Deemar Way 97035
Deer Oak Ave & Cir 97035
Deerbrush Ave 97035
Deerfield Ct 97035
Del Prado St 97035
Delenka Ln 97034
Dellwood Dr 97034
Denney Ct 97035
Denton Dr 97035
Depot St 97035
Devon Ln 97034
Devonshire Dr 97035
Diamond Head Rd 97034
Diane Dr 97035
Division Ct 97035
Dogwood Ct & Dr 97035
Dolph Ct 97034
Don Lee Way 97035
Doris Ave & Ct 97035
Douglas Cir & Way 97035
Dove Ct 97035
Dover Way 97034
Duncan Dr 97035
Dunmire Dr 97035
Durham St 97034
Dyer St 97034
E Ave 97034
Eagle Crest Dr 97035
Eastridge Ln 97034
SW Eastside Rd 97034
Eastview Ct 97034
Edenberry Ct & Dr 97035
Edens Edge Dr 97034
Edgecliff Ter 97034
Edgemont Rd 97035
Edgewood Ct & St 97035
Eena Rd 97034
Egan Way 97034
El Greco St 97035
Eleanor Ct 97035
Elk Rock Rd 97034
Ellis Ave 97034
Englewood Ct & Dr 97034
Erasmus St 97035
Erickson St 97034
Erin Ct 97035
Essex Ct 97034
Evergreen Rd 97034
F Ave 97034
Fairmont Rd 97034
Fairway Rd 97034
Falstaff St 97035
Fern Pl 97034
Fernbrook Cir, Ct, St & Way 97035
Fernwood Cir & Dr 97034
Fielding Rd 97034
Fieldstone Ct & Dr 97035
Fir Ln & Rd 97034
Fir Grove Ct 97035
Fir Ridge Rd 97035
Fircrest Ct & Dr 97034
Firwood Rd 97035
Foothills Dr & Rd 97034
Ford Pl 97035
Forest Meadows Way 97034
Fosberg Rd 97035
Fox Run 97034
Frost Ln & St 97035
Fruitwood Ct 97035
Furnace St 97034
G Ave 97034
Gabrielle Ct 97035
Galen St 97035
Galewood St 97034
Gans St 97034
Garibaldi St 97035
Gary Ln 97034
Gassner Ln 97035
Gershwin Ct 97035
Gimley Ct 97034
Glacier Lily St 97035
Gleason Dr 97034
Glen Eagles Ct, Pl & Rd 97034
Glen Haven Rd 97034
Glenmorrie Dr, Ln & Ter 97034
Glenwood Ct 97034
Golden Ln 97035
Goodall Ct & Rd 97034
Goya St 97035
Graef Cir 97035
Grand Oaks Dr 97035
Grandview Ct 97034
Green Acres Ln 97034
Greenbluff Dr 97034
Greenbrae Ct & Dr 97034
Greenbrier Rd 97034
Greenridge Ct & Dr 97035
Greensborough Ct 97035
Greentree Ave, Cir & Rd 97034
Greenwood Rd 97034
Greystoke Dr 97035
Grouse Ter 97035
Hallberg Ct 97035
Hallinan Cir, Ct & St 97034
Hallmark Dr 97035
Hampton Ct 97035
Harrington Ave 97035
Hartford Pl 97035
Harvard Ct 97035
Harvey Way 97035
Hastings Ct, Dr & Pl 97035
Haven St 97035
Hawthorne Dr 97034
Hazel Rd 97034
Headlee Ln 97034
Heather Ann Ct 97034
Heathrow Ln 97034
Hedge Nettle Ct 97035
Hemlock St 97034
Heritage Ct & Ln 97035
Hiawatha Ct 97035
Hidalgo St 97035
Hidden Bay Ct 97035
Hide A Way Ct & Ln 97034
Highland Dr 97034
Hill Way 97035
Hillshire Dr 97034
Hillside Ct, Dr, Ln & Way 97034
Hilltop Rd 97034
Hobbit Ct 97034
Hofer Ct 97034
Holly Springs Rd 97035
Holy Names Ct, Dr & Pl 97034
Hoodview Ln 97034
Horseshoe Curv 97034
Hotspur St 97035
Hunter Ct 97035
Icarus Loop 97035
Independence Ave 97035
Indian Trl 97034
Indian Creek Ave, Ct, Dr & Way 97035
Indian Springs Cir & Rd 97035
Inverurie Rd 97035
Iron Mountain Blvd 97034
Ivy Ct & Ln 97034
Jean Rd & Way 97035
Jefferson Pkwy 97035
Jenifers Way 97035
Jewell Ln 97035
Johnson Ter 97034
Juarez St 97035
Kara Ln 97035
Kelok Rd 97034
Kenny St 97035
Kennycroft Way 97035
Kenola Ct 97034
Kenwood Rd 97034
Kerr Pkwy 97035
Kilchurn Ave 97035
Kilkenny Dr & Rd 97034
Kimball Ct & St 97035
Kimberly Cir 97035
Kingsgate Rd 97035
Knaus Rd 97034
Koawood Dr 97034
Koderra Ave 97035
Kokanee Ct 97034
Kristi Way 97035
Kruse Way 97035
Kruse Oaks Blvd 97035
Kruse Way Pl 97035
La Mesa Ct 97035
Laburnum Way 97034
Ladd St 97034
Lake Bay Ct 97034
Lake Forest Blvd 97035
Lake Forest Dr 97034
Lake Front Rd 97034
Lake Garden Ct 97034
Lake Grove Ave 97035
Lake Haven Dr 97035
Lake Shore Rd 97034
Lakeridge Dr 97034
Lakeview Blvd & Ct 97035
Lakewood Rd 97034
Lamont Ct & Way 97035
Lanewood St 97034
Langford Ln 97035
Larch St 97034
Laurel St 97034
Leafy Ln 97034
Lee St 97034
Leonard St 97034
Leslie Ct & Ln 97034
Lexington Ct 97034
Lilli Ln 97034
Lily Bay Ct 97035
Lindsay Ct 97035
Livingood Ln 97034
Longfellow Ave 97035
Lookout Ct 97034
Lords Ln 97035
Lorna Ln 97035
Lothlorien Way 97034
Lowenberg Ter 97034
Lower Dr 97035
Lower Boones Ferry Rd 97035
Lower Meadows Dr 97035
Luce Ln 97035
Lund St 97034
Madrona St 97035
Majestic Ct 97035
Manchester Dr 97035
Mandi Ln 97035
Maple Cir & St 97034
Mapleleaf Ct & Rd 97034
Mardee Ave 97035
Maree Ct 97035
Marjorie Ave 97034
Marlin Ave & Ct 97035
Marquis Ct 97034
Marylbrook Dr 97034
Marylcreek Dr 97034
Marylhaven Pl 97034
Marylshire Ln 97034
Marylview Ct 97034
Masaryk St 97035
Matthew Ct 97034
Mayors Ln 97034
Mcduff Ct 97035
Mcewan Rd 97035
Mcnary Pkwy 97035
Mcvey Ave 97034
Meadow Grass St 97035
Meadowcreek Ct 97035
Meadowlark Ct 97035
Meadowlark Ln 97034
Meadows Dr 97034
Meadows Rd 97035
Megan Pl 97034
Megly Ct 97035
Melissa Dr 97034
Mellon Ave 97035
Melrose Pl & St 97035
Mercantile Dr 97035
Meridian Ct & Rd 97035
Middlecrest Rd 97034
Milburn Ct 97034
Minnehaha Ct 97035
Mirkwood Dr 97034
Monroe Pkwy 97035
Montauk Cir 97035
Monticello Dr 97035
Moria Ct 97034
Morning Sky Ct 97034
Morningview Cir, Ln & Pl 97035
Mount Jefferson Ter 97035
Mountain Cir 97035
Mountain View Ln 97035
Mozarteum Ct 97035
Mulholland Dr 97035
Murwood Ct 97035
Nansen Smt 97035
Neff Park Ln 97035
Nelson Ct 97034
Newcastle Dr 97035
Nicole Ln 97035
Nokomis Ct 97035
Nola Ct 97035
Northpoint Rd 97034
Northshore Cir, Pl & Rd 97034
Northview Ct 97035
Nottingham Pl 97035
Nova Ct 97035
Oak St & Ter 97034
Oak Knoll Ct 97034
Oak Meadow Ct, Dr & Ln 97034
Oakhurst Ln 97034
Oakridge Ct & Rd 97035
Obrien St 97034
Offenbach Pl 97035
Old Gate Rd 97034
Old River Dr & Lndg 97034
Olson Ave & Ct 97034
Orchard Dr & Way 97035
Orchard Hill Ln, Pl, Rd & Way 97035
Orchard Springs Rd 97035
Oriole Ln 97035
Oswego Smt 97035
Oswego Glen Ct 97034
Oswego Pointe Dr 97034
Oswego Shore Ct 97034
Othello St 97035
Overlook Cir, Dr & Ln 97034
Oxford Dr 97034
Pacific Hwy 97034
Palisades Crest Dr 97034
Palisades Lake Ct 97034
Palisades Terrace Dr 97034
Parelius Cir 97034
Park Rd 97034
Park Forest Ave & Ct 97034
Parker Rd 97035
Parkhill St 97035
Parkview Dr 97035
Parrish St 97034
Partridge Dr & Ln 97035
Patton Rd 97034
Peacock Pl 97035
Pearcy St 97034
Pebble Beach Ct 97035
Perch Ct 97034
Pericles 97035
Peters Rd 97035
Pfeifer Ct, Dr & Way 97035
Phantom Bluff Ct 97034
Pheasant Run 97035
Phyllis Ct 97035
Pilkington Rd 97035
Pimlico Ter 97035
Pine St 97034
Pine Valley Rd 97034
Pioneer Ct 97034
Piper Ct 97034
Polonius St 97035
Poplar Way 97034
Preakness Ct 97035
Prestwick Rd 97034
Princeton Ct 97035
Provincial Hill Dr & Way 97035
Quail Ct 97034
Quarry Rd 97035
Queens Park Rd 97035
Rachel Ln 97035
Rainbow Dr 97035
Ray Ridge Dr 97034
Reao Ct 97035
Rebecca Ln 97035
Red Cedar Way 97035
Red Leaf St 97035
Redfern Ave 97035
Redwing Ct & Way 97035
Redwood Ct 97034
Reese Rd 97035
Regency Ct 97035
Rembrandt Ln 97035
Ridge Lake Dr 97034
Ridge Pointe Dr 97034
Ridgecrest Dr 97034
Ridgetop Ct 97035
Ridgeview Ct & Ln 97034
Ridgeway Rd 97034
Ridgewood Ln & Rd 97034
Rivendell Ct & Rd 97034
River Bend Ln 97034
River Edge Ct & Ln 97034
River Run Dr 97034
River Woods Pl 97034
Rivers Edge Dr 97034
Riverside Dr 97034
Riverwood Ln 97035
Robb Pl 97034
Rockinghorse Ln 97034
Rockwood Ct 97035
Rogers Rd 97035
Roosevelt Ave 97035
Rosalia Way 97035
Rosecliffe Ct, Dr & Pl 97034
Rosemary Ln 97034
Rosewood St 97035
Royal Ct 97035
Royal Oaks Dr 97035
Royce Way 97034
Rye Rd 97034
Sabina Ct 97035
Sage Hen Cir & Way 97035
Saint Clair Dr 97034
Saint Helens Cir 97035
Sandalwood Ct 97035
Sandpiper Cir, St & Way 97035
Sarah Hill Ln 97035
Scarborough Dr 97034
Schalit Way 97035
Schukart Ln 97034
Scott Ct 97034
Sequoia Ct 97035
Seville Ave 97035
Shakespeare St 97035
Shelby Ct 97035
Shepherds Ct & Ln 97035
Sher Ln 97034
Sherbrook Pl 97034
Sherwood Ct 97034
Shireva Ct & Dr 97034
Sibelius Ct 97035
Siena Dr 97034
Sierra Ct 97035
Sierra Vista Dr 97035
Siletz Ct 97035
Silver Ct 97035
Skyland Cir & Dr 97034
Snowberry Ct 97035
Snowbrush Ct 97035
Southshore Blvd
300-3600 97034
3602-3698 97034
3700-4399 97034
Southview Rd 97034
Southwood Ct & Dr 97035
Spinosa 97035
Spring Ln 97035
Springbrook Ct 97034

Spruce St 97034
Stafford Rd 97034
Stampher Rd 97034
N & S State St 97034
Stephanie Ct 97035
Sterling Way 97035
Stewart Glenn Ct 97035
Stonebridge Way 97034
Stonehurst Ct 97034
Streamside Ct & Dr 97035
Summer Pl 97035
Summer Woods 97035
Summit Ct & Dr 97034
Summit Ridge Ct 97035
Sunbrook Dr 97035
Suncreek Dr 97035
Sundeleaf Dr 97034
Sundew Ct 97035
Sundown Ct 97034
Sunningdale Ct & Rd 97034
Sunny Hill Dr 97034
Sunrise Ct 97035
W Sunset Dr 97035
Suntree Ln 97035
Sunwood Ct 97035
Sycamore Ave 97035
Sydni Ct 97035
Sylvan Ct 97034
Tamara Ct 97035
Tamarack Ln 97035
Tamaway Dr 97034
Tanager Dr 97035
Tanglewood Dr 97035
Tara Pl 97035
Taylors Crest Ln 97035
Tempest Dr 97035
Terrace Dr 97034
Terry Ave & Ct 97035
The Grotto 97035
Thoma Rd 97034
Thunder Vista Ln 97035
Timbergrove Ct & St 97035
Timberline Dr 97034
Tippecanoe Ct 97034
Tolkien Ln 97034
Touchstone Ct & Ter 97035
Tracy Ave 97035
Tree St 97035
Treetop Ln & Way 97034
Trillium Ct 97035
Trillium Woods 97035
Troon Rd 97034
Trout Way 97034
Tualamere Ave 97035
Tualata Ave, Ct & Ln 97035
Tualatin St 97035
Twin Creek Ct & Ln 97035
Twin Fir Ct & Rd 97035
Twin Points Rd 97034
Tyndall Ct 97034
Uplands Dr 97034
Upper Dr 97035
Upper Boones Ferry Rd 97035
Upper Cherry Ln 97034
Upper Devon Ln 97034
Vale Ct 97034
Vermeer Dr 97035
Verte Ct 97034
Victoria Ct 97035
View Ct 97034
View Lake Ct 97034
Viewcrest Ln 97034
Viewpoint Ln 97034
Village Dr 97034
Village Park Ct & Ln 97034
Virginia Way 97035
Walking Woods Dr 97035
Wall St 97034
Waluga Dr 97035
Warren Ct 97035
Washington Ct 97035
Waxwing Cir, St & Way 97035
Wayside Ln 97034
Wayzata Ct 97035
Weidman Ct 97034
Wells St 97034
Wembley Ct & Pl 97034
Wembley Park Rd 97034
Wesley Ct 97035
West Rd 97035
Westbay Rd 97035
Westcott Ct 97035
Westfield Ct 97035
Westlake Dr 97035
Westminster Dr 97034
Westpoint Rd 97034
Westridge Dr 97034
Westview Cir, Ct & Dr 97034
Westward Ho Rd 97034
Wheatherstone 97035
White Oaks Dr 97035
Wight Ln 97035
Wilbur St 97034
Wildwood St 97035
Willow Ct & Ln 97035
Wilmot Way 97035
Windfield Loop 97035
Windsor Ct 97034
Winthrop Ct 97035
Wolf Berry Ct 97035
Wood Duck Cir, St & Way 97035
Wood Thrush Cir, St & Way 97035
Woodcrest Ln 97035
Woodhill Ct 97035
Woodhurst Pl 97034
Woodland Ter 97034
Woodside Cir 97035
Woodsman Ct 97034
Woodway Ct 97035
Worthington St 97034
Wren Ct & St 97034
Yarmouth Cir 97034
Yates St 97034
Yorick St 97035
York Rd 97034
Yorkshire Ct & Pl 97035
Zivney Ln 97034

NUMBERED STREETS

1st St 97034
2nd St 97034
3rd St 97034
4th St 97034
5th St 97034
6th St 97034
7th St 97034
8th St 97034
9th St 97034
10th St 97034
19th Ave 97035
12400-12999 97034
SW 21st Ct 97035
SW 22nd Ave 97035
27th Pl 97035
35th Ct & Pl 97034
63rd Ave 97035
65th Ave 97035

MEDFORD OR

General Delivery 97501

POST OFFICE BOXES MAIN OFFICE STATIONS AND BRANCHES

Box No.s
All PO Boxes 97501

NAMED STREETS

Acacia Way 97504
Academy Pl 97504
Acorn Way 97504
Adams Cir 97504
Adams Ln 97501
Admiral Way 97504
Aerial Heights Dr 97504
Aero Way 97504
Agate St 97501
Airport Rd 97504
Aitken Way 97504
Alamar St 97501
Alameda St 97504
Alba Dr 97504
Albert St 97501
Albion Ln 97501
Alcan Dr 97504
Alder St 97501
Alder Creek Dr 97504
Aldersgate Rd 97504
Alderwood Dr 97504
Alex Way 97501
Alexis Way 97501
Alice St 97501
Alley Ln 97501
Allison Way 97501
Alma Dr 97501
Almond St 97504
Aloha Ave 97504
Alpine Ct 97504
Alta Ave 97501
Amaryllis St 97501
Amber Cir 97504
Amblegreen Dr 97504
Amblewood Cir 97504
American Way 97504
Amerman Rd 97504
Amhurst Way 97504
Amy St 97504
Anderson Butte Rd 97501
Andover Way 97501
Andrew Dr 97501
Andrews Rd 97501
Angel Crest Dr 97504
Anita Cir 97504
Annapolis Dr 97504
Annettes Way 97504
Antilles Ln 97501
Anton Dr 97501
Apache Dr 97501
Applegate Ln 97501
Appleton Cir 97504
Applewood Cir 97501
Arbor Dr 97501
Arcadia St 97501
Archer Dr 97501
Arctic Cir 97504
Arden Cir 97504
Ardmore Ave 97504
Argonne Ave 97504
Argyle Ct 97501
Arlington Dr 97501
Armory Dr 97501
Arnold Ln 97501
Arnold Palmer Way 97504
Arnwood St 97501
Arrowhead Dr 97504
Arrowpoint Ct 97504
Arthur Ave 97501
Ashbrook Cir 97501
Asher Dr 97504
Ashford Way 97504
Ashland Ave 97501
Ashwood Ct 97504
Aspen St 97501
Auburn Way 97504
Augusta Ct 97504
Austin St 97501
Automation Way 97504
Autumn Park Dr 97504
Avalon Dr 97501
Avenel Ct 97504
Aviation Way 97504
Avion Dr 97504
Avocado Ln 97504
Aztec Ave & Cir 97501
Bailey Ave 97501
Balsum Way 97504
Banner Ct 97504
Barbara Jean Way 97504
Barclay Rd 97504
Barlynn St 97501
N & S Barneburg Rd 97504
Barnes Ave 97504
E Barnett Rd
200-429 97501
431-499 97501
901-1097 97504
1099-4499 97504
W Barnett St 97501
Barons Ave 97501
Barry Cir 97501
N & S Bartlett St 97501
Bayberry Dr 97501
Beall Ln 97501
Bear Creek Orch 97501
Beatty St 97501
Bedford Cir 97504
Beekman Ave 97501
Bel Abbes Ave 97504
Bel Air Ct 97504
Belknap Rd 97501
Bell Ct 97504
Bellinger Ln 97501
Belmont St 97501
Bennett Ave 97504
Bens Ln 97501
Benson St 97501
Bentley Ct 97504
N & S Berkeley Way 97504
Bermuda Dr 97504
Berrydale Ave 97501
Bessie St 97504
Bethany Ct 97504
Beverly Dr 97504
Bianca Ct 97504
Biddle Rd 97504
Birkshire Ct 97504
Birmingham St 97501
Black Oak Dr 97504
Blackhawk Dr 97501
Blackpine Dr 97504
Blackthorn Dr 97504
Bliss St 97501
Blossom Ct 97501
Blue Blossom Dr 97504
Bluebonnet Ave 97504
Boardman St 97501
Bon Bon Cir 97504
Bonita Ave & Cir 97504
Bora Bora Way 97504
Bordeaux Ave 97504
Bowmont Cir 97504
Bradbury St 97504
Bradford Way 97504
Brae Dr 97501
Brannon Dr 97504
Brentcrest Dr 97501
Brentwood St 97504
Brian Way 97501
Briarwood Ln 97504
Bridgeport Dr 97504
Bridgewater Way 97501
Brighton Cir 97504
Bristol Dr 97504
Britt Ave & Dr 97501
Broad St 97501
Broadview Ave 97501
Brock Way 97501
Bromley St 97504
Bron Cir 97504
Brook Ct 97504
Brookdale Ave 97504
Brookhurst St 97504
Brookside Dr 97504
Brown Ridge Ter 97504
Bryant St 97501
Bryson Way 97504
Buena Vista Dr 97501
Bullock Rd 97504
Bundy St 97504
Burgundy Cir 97504
Burl Crest Dr 97504
Burrell Rd 97501
Burton Dr 97504
Business Park Dr 97504
Cadet Dr 97504
Calhoun Rd 97501
Callaway Dr 97504
Calle Vista Dr 97504
Cambridge Cir 97504
Camellia Ave 97504
Camina Dr 97504
Camino Claire St 97504
Camino Viejo Rd 97501
Camp Baker Rd 97501
Campbell Rd 97504
Campus Dr 97504
Canal St 97501
Candice Cir 97504
Candlis Point Ct 97504
Canon St 97501
Canterbury Ln 97504
Canterwood Dr 97504
Canyon Ave 97504
Caperna Dr 97504
Capital Ave 97504
Cardinal Ave 97504
Cardley Ave 97504
Carlson Dr 97501
Carly Cir 97504
Carmel Cir 97504
Carol Rae 97501
Carolyn Cir 97504
Carpenter Hill Rd 97501
Carriage Dr 97501
Carrington Ave 97504
Cascadia Cir 97504
Cashmere Cir 97504
Casino Rd 97501
Castlewood Dr 97504
Catherine St 97501
Cedar Ln & St 97501
Cedar Links Ct & Dr 97504
Center Dr 97501
N & S Central Ave 97501
Centurion Cir 97504
Century Way 97504
Cerene Dr 97501
Cerritos Ave 97504
Chancery Cir 97504
Chandler Egan Dr 97504
Chantal Ct 97504
Char Way 97501
Charlaine St 97501
Charles Ln & Way 97501
Charleston Way 97501
Charlotte Ln 97501
Charlotte Ann Rd 97501
Cheltenham Way 97504
Cherry Ln 97504
Cherry St 97501
Cherry Bark Ln 97501
Cherrywood Dr 97504
Cheshire Way 97501
Chestnut St 97501
Chevy Way 97504
Cheyenne St 97501
Chico St 97501
Circlewood Dr 97501
Cirrus Dr 97504
Citation Way 97504
Clairmont Ct 97504
E & W Clark St 97501
Clearsprings Dr 97501
Clearview Ave 97501
Clearwater Dr 97501
Cleopatra Cir 97504
Cliffrose Cir 97504
Cliffwood Ct 97504
Cloie Anne Ct 97504
Cloudcrest Dr 97504
Clover Ln 97501
Coal Mine Rd 97504
Cody St 97504
Coghill Ln 97501
Coker Butte Rd 97504
Coleman Creek Rd 97501
Colinwood Ct & Ln 97501
College Way 97504
Colman Ct 97501
Colonial Ave 97504
N & S Columbus Ave 97501
Comice Dr 97504
Commanche Dr 97501
Commerce Dr 97504
Commercial Ct 97501
Compton Way 97501
Concord Way 97504
Congress Way 97504
Connell Ave 97501
Constitution Dr 97504
Coquette St 97504
Cordelia Way 97501
Corning Ct 97504
Corona Ave 97504
Cottage St 97504
Cottonwood Ave 97504
Country Club Dr 97504
Country Park Ln 97504
Court St 97501
Courtney Cir 97504
Coventry Cir 97504
Covina Ave 97504
Cox Ln 97501
Crater Lake Ave & Hwy 97504
Creek Mont Dr 97504
Creek View Dr 97504
Creekside Cir 97504
Crestbrook Rd 97504
Creston Ct 97504
Crews Rd 97501
Crown Ave 97504
Croxley Ln 97501
Crystal Dr 97504
Crystal Hts 97501
Crystal Mountain Ave 97504
Crystal Springs Dr 97504
Cummings Ln 97501
Cunningham Ave 97501
Cypress Point Dr 97504
Dahlia Way 97501
Dakota Ave 97501
Dale St 97501
Dalton St 97501
Dan Ave 97501
Dane Dr 97501
Danville Ln 97501
Dark Hollow Rd 97501
Darla Mae 97501
Darlene Dr 97501
Darlington St 97501
Darrell Dr 97501
David Ln 97504
De Barr Ave 97501
De Hague Rd 97501
Dearborn Ln 97504
Deer Pointe Ct 97501
Deer Ridge Dr 97504
Deer Trail Ln 97501
Dellwood Ave 97504
Delmar Way 97504
Delta Waters Rd 97504
Derek Dr 97504
Derry Ct 97504
Destiny Ln 97501
Devils Garden Rd 97504
Devonshire Pl 97504
Diamond St 97501
Diana Ct 97501
Disk Dr 97501
Dixie Ln 97501
Doctors Park Dr 97504
Dodson Rd 97504
Dogwood Dr 97501
Donaldson Way 97501
Donna Lee Dr 97504
Doral Cir 97504
Douglas St 97501
Dove Ln 97501
Dover Rdg 97504
Dragon Tail Pl 97504
Driftwood Pl 97501
Dry Creek Rd 97504
Duell Ave 97501
Duncan Dr 97504
Dunthorpe Dr 97504
Dusk Cir 97501
Eads St 97501
Eagle Trace Dr 97504
Earhart St 97501
Easthills Ct 97504
Eastover Ter 97504
Eastridge Dr 97504
Eastwood Dr & Ln 97504
Easy St 97504
Eaton Dr 97504
Eden Ct 97504
Edgemont Dr 97504
Edgevale Ave 97504
Edgewater Dr 97504
Edgewood Dr 97504
Edmond Way 97504
Edwards St 97501
Effie St 97504
Ehrman Way 97501
El Dorado Dr 97504
Elaine Way 97501
Elisa Ct 97504
Elk St 97501
Ellen Ave 97501
Ellendale Dr 97504
Elliott Ave 97501
Elm Ave & St 97501
Elmwood Ct 97504
Eloquence Ave 97504
Emerald Cir 97501
Englemann Ln 97501
Englesea Way 97504
Eric Ct 97504
Erie St 97504
Erin Way 97501
Eston Ct 97501
Eucalyptus Dr 97504
Euclid Ave 97504
Eureka Cir 97504
Evans Cir 97504
Evenbrook Dr 97504
Evening Ridge Ter 97504
Excel Dr 97504
Experiment Station Rd 97501
Fair Oaks Dr 97504
Fairbanks St 97504
Fairfax St 97504
Fairfield Dr 97504
Fairlane Dr 97501
Fairmount St 97501
Fairview Dr 97504
Fairway Cir 97504
Fairweather Dr 97501
Falcon Ridge Ter 97504
Fallbrook Ln 97504
Fallen Leaf Dr 97501
Far West Ave 97501
Farmington Ave 97504
Farr St 97501
Fawn Hills Cir 97504
Fern Valley Rd
101-199 97501
4200-5299 97504
Fernwood Dr 97504
Fieldbrook Ave & Ct 97504
Fieldstone Dr 97504
Fijian Way 97504
Filmore Dr 97504
Finch Ln 97501
Finley Ln 97501
Fiona Ln 97501
N & S Fir St 97501
Fire Station Spur 97504
Fisher Ave 97504
Flintridge Ave 97504
Florence Ave 97504
Flower St 97504
Fontaine Cir 97504
N & S Foothill Rd 97504
Ford Dr 97504
Fordham Ct 97504
Forelle Ave 97504
Forest Ave 97501
Forest Hills Dr 97504

Forest Ridge Dr 97504
Fortune Dr 97504
Fox Run 97504
Foxwood Dr 97504
Franklin Ct 97501
Franquette St 97501
Fredrick Dr 97504
Freedom Way 97504
N & S Front St 97501
Gabriel Way 97501
Garden Dr 97504
Garden Springs Cir 97504
Gardenbrook Ct 97504
Gardendale Ave & Cir 97504
Gardner Way 97504
Garfield St 97501
Garland Pl 97501
Gary Dr 97504
Gayety Ln 97504
Gaylee Ave 97501
Gene Cameron Way 97504
Genessee St 97504
Geneva St 97504
Georgia St 97501
Gibbs Ct 97501
Gilman Rd 97504
Ginger Way 97501
Girard Cir & Dr 97504
Glairgeau Cir 97501
Glen Oak Ct 97504
Glengrove Ave 97501
E & W Glenwood Rd 97501
Glory C Rd 97501
Golden Ln 97504
Golf View Dr 97504
Gould Ave & Cir 97504
Grand Ave 97504
Grandview Ave 97504
Grant Ave 97501
Granville Ct 97504
N & S Grape St 97501
Gravenstein Way 97501
Greenbrae Dr 97504
Greenbrook Dr 97504
Greenfield Ct 97504
Greenridge Dr 97504
Greenway Cir & Dr 97504
Greenwich Dr 97501
Greenwood St 97504
Grey Eagle Dr 97501
Grey Oak Ct 97501
Greystone Ct 97504
Griffin Ln 97501
W Griffin Creek Rd 97501
N & S Groveland Ave 97504
Grumman Dr 97504
Halsey St 97501
Halvorsen St 97501
Hamilton St 97501
Hammer Ct 97501
Hampton Way 97501
Hancock Ave 97501
Hanover Cir 97504
Happy Valley Dr 97501
Harbrooke Rd 97504
Harding Ct 97501
Harrisburg Dr 97501
Harrison Ave 97504
Hart St 97501
Hartell St 97504
Harvard Pl 97504
Hathaway Dr 97504
Havana Ave 97504
Haven St 97501
Hawaiian Ave 97504
Hawk Rd 97501
Hawk Gulch Ln 97501
Hawthorne St 97504
Hayden Pl 97504
Hayes Ave 97501
Hazel Ave 97501
Heartwood Ct 97504
Heather Ct 97504
Heathrow Way 97504
Heber Ln 97501
Hedy Jayne 97501
Hemlock Dr 97504
Hempstead St 97501
Henderson Way 97504
Henredon Way 97504
Heritage Way 97504
Herman Ave 97501
Herrin Ln 97501
Herrington Way 97504
Hidden Springs Dr 97504
Hidden Valley Ct 97504
Hidden Village Pl 97504
High Oak Dr 97504
High Prairie Dr 97504
Highbury Dr 97501
Highcrest Dr 97504
Highgate St 97501
Highland Dr 97504
Highway 238 97501
Hill Way 97504
Hillcourt St 97504
Hillcrest Rd 97504
Hillcrest Park Dr 97504
Hilldale Ave 97504
Hillhouse Ave 97504
W Hills Ter 97501
Hilton Rd 97504
Hobert St 97504
Hogan Ave 97504
N & S Holly St 97501
Hollyburn Rdg 97504
Hollyhock Dr 97504
Hollywood Ave 97501
Holmes Ave 97501
Homeview Dr 97501
Hondeleau Ln 97504
Honeysuckle Ave 97504
Honor Dr 97504
Hoover Park Dr 97504
Horizon Ln 97504
Horton Cir 97501
Hospitality Way 97504
Howard Ave 97501
Howard St 97504
Howell Ave 97501
Hoyt Ln 97501
Hughes Rd 97504
Hull Rd 97501
Humphrey St 97501
Huntington Ln 97504
Husker Butte Ln 97504
Hutchins Cir 97504
Hyacinth Ave 97501
Hybiscus St 97504
Independence School Rd 97501
Inglewood Dr 97504
Ingrid St 97501
Inner Cir 97504
Innsbruck Rdg 97504
International Way 97504
Inverness Dr 97504
Iowa St 97501
Ipson Dr 97501
Iris Cir 97504
Isabel Dr 97501
Island Pointe Dr 97504
N & S Ivy Cir & St 97501
J St 97501
Jack Nicklaus Rd 97504
Jackson Dr 97504
E Jackson St
100-499 97501
600-2199 97504
W Jackson St 97501
Jade Cir 97504
Janes Rd 97501
Janney Ln 97501
Jantzer Ct 97504
Jasmine Ave 97501
Jason Way 97504
Jasper St 97501
Jeanette Ave 97501
Jenero Ct 97504
Jennah Ln 97501
Jennie Way 97504
Jerome Ln 97504
Jessica Cir 97504
Jet Dr 97501
Johnson St 97504
Jolisa St 97501
Joseph St 97501
Joy Cir & St 97504
Juanipero Way 97504
Juanita Ave 97504
Jubilant Ave 97504
Judy Way 97501
Juniper Rdg 97504
Kaitlin Ln 97501
Kala Renee 97501
Kamerin Ln 97501
Karges Way 97504
Kari Cir 97504
Katie Mae Dr 97501
Kaufman Way 97501
Kaye St 97501
Keene Dr 97504
N & S Keene Way Dr 97504
Keith Ave 97504
Kelly St 97501
Kennet St 97501
Kensington Sq 97504
Kenwood Ave 97501
Kenyon St 97501
Kerrisdale Ridge Dr 97504
Kerry Dr 97504
Kevin Way 97504
Key Dr 97501
Kime Dr 97501
King St 97501
Kings Hwy 97501
Kingsgate Cir 97504
Kingsley Dr 97504
Kingswood Dr 97501
Knowles Rd 97501
Knutson Ave 97504
Kona Cir 97504
Kraig Ave 97501
Krissy Dee 97501
Kristen Dr 97504
Kyle St 97501
Kylee Ann 97501
La Costa Cir 97504
La Loma Dr 97504
La Mesa St 97504
La Mirada Dr 97504
Lake Village Dr 97504
Lara Ct 97504
Larkspur Ave 97504
Lars Way 97501
Larson Creek Dr 97504
Larue Dr 97504
Laurel Ln & St 97501
Laurelcrest Dr 97504
Laurelwood Dr 97501
Lausanne Cir 97504
Lawnridge St 97504
Lawnsdale Rd 97504
Lawnview Dr 97504
Lawrence Ave 97504
Layla Dr 97501
Lazy Creek Dr 97504
Le Roy Cir 97501
Lear Way 97504
Leland St 97501
Lenora Dr 97504
Leonard Ave 97504
Levi Cir 97504
Lewis Ave 97501
Lexington Dr 97504
Liberty St 97501
Lillian St 97501
Lincoln St 97501
Lindero Ave 97504
Lindley St 97504
Link Dr 97501
Lisa Cir 97504
Littrell Dr 97504
Loal St 97501
Locust St 97501
London Cir 97504
Lone Oak Dr 97504
Lone Pine Rd 97504
Louise Ave 97501
Lowry Ln 97501
Lozier Ln 97501
Lucky Ln 97501
Lyman Ave 97504
Lynn Ave 97501
Lynnwood Ave 97504
Maaike Dr 97504
Mace Rd 97501
Madrona Ln & St 97501
Mae St 97504
Magenta Cir 97504
Magnolia Ave 97501
E Main St
1-499 97501
500-2599 97504
W Main St 97501
Mallard Ln 97504
Manchester Dr 97501
Manzanita St 97501
Manzanita Heights Dr 97504
Maple St 97501
Maple Leaf Ct 97504
Maple Park Dr 97501
Margaret Rose 97501
Marie St 97504
Marigold Ln 97504
Marilee St 97501
Mariposa Ter 97504
Marissa Cir 97504
Market St 97504
Marsh Ln 97501
Marshall Ave 97501
Martin Dr 97501
Mary Pl 97501
Mary St 97504
Mary Bee Ln 97504
Mason Way 97501
Matt Loop 97501
Matthews Pl 97504
Mayette St 97504
E Mcandrews Rd
1-499 97501
1201-1297 97504
1299-3099 97504
W Mcandrews Rd 97501
Mckenzie Dr 97501
Mclaughlin Dr 97504
Mcphearson Ln 97504
Mcquire Way 97504
Meadow Creek Dr 97504
Meadow View Dr 97504
Meadows Ln 97501
Meals Dr 97501
Medford Ctr 97504
Medford Heights Ln 97504
Medical Center Dr 97504
Mel Lowe Ln 97501
Melissa Cir 97504
Mellecker Way 97501
Melody Ln 97501
Menlo Ct 97504
Merion Ct 97504
Merriman Rd 97501
Micah Cir 97504
Michael Park Dr 97504
Middleford Aly 97501
Midway Rd 97501
Milford Dr 97501
Milhoan Dr 97504
Miller Ct 97504
Milligan Way 97504
Mindy Sue 97501
Minear Rd 97501
Minnesota Ave 97504
Mira Mar Ave 97504
Miracle Ln 97504
Mistletoe St 97501
Misty Ln 97501
Mitchellen Pl 97504
N & S Modoc Ave 97504
Monarch Ln 97504
Monroe St 97501
Montara Dr 97504
Montclair Ter 97504
Monte Vista Dr 97504
Montego Pl 97504
Montelimar Dr 97504
Monterey Dr 97504
Moon Ter 97504
Morningside St 97501
Morrison Ave 97504
Morrow Rd 97504
Mountain Glen Ct 97504
Mountain View Dr 97504
Mt Echo Dr 97504
Mt Pitt Ave 97501
Murphy Rd 97504
Murray Ave 97501
Murry Hill Ct & Ter 97504
Myers Ct & Ln 97501
Myrtle St 97504
Nadia Way 97504
Nansen Dr 97504
Narregan St 97501
National Dr 97504
Navarro Springs Ave 97504
Nebula Way 97504
Nellie Ettinger Ln 97504
Nettie Way 97504
Neville Ln 97501
Newcastle St 97501
Newtown St 97501
Niantic St 97501
Nieto Way 97504
Nita Lynne 97501
Nobility Dr 97501
Nome Ct 97504
Nordic Ct 97504
Normil Ter 97504
Northbrook Cir 97504
Northcrest Cir 97504
Northridge Ter 97501
Northwood St 97504
Nottingham Cir 97504
Oak St 97501
Oak Crest Way 97501
Oak Grove Rd 97501
Oak Tree Cir 97504
Oak View Cir 97504
N & S Oakdale Ave & Dr 97501
Oakleaf Pass Dr 97504
Oakmont Way 97504
Oakwood Dr 97504
Obispo Dr 97504
Ogara St 97501
Ohare Pkwy 97504
Old Cherry Ln 97504
Oleander St 97504
Olwell Way 97504
Olympic Ave 97504
Omaha Ave 97501
Omni Cir 97501
Oneida Cir 97504
N & S Orange St 97501
Orangewood Dr 97504
Orchard Home Ct & Dr 97501
Orchard View Ter 97504
Oregon Ave & Ter 97504
Orinda Cir 97504
Overcup St 97501
Owen Dr 97504
Oxford Pl 97504
N & S Pacific Hwy 97501
Page St 97504
Palm St 97501
Palmyra St 97504
Paloma Ave 97504
Panorama Dr 97504
Papago Dr 97504
Park Ave 97501
Park Ridge Dr 97504
Parkdale Ave 97501
Parkhill Pl 97504
Parkview Ct 97504
Parkway Dr 97504
Parsons Dr 97501
Patrick St 97504
Patriot Way 97504
Paul Cir 97504
Pauline Pl 97501
Paulita Dr 97504
Pawnee St 97501
Payne Rd 97504
N & S Peach St 97501
Peachwood Ct 97501
Pear Tree Ln 97504
Pearl St 97504
Pearl Eye Ln 97504
Pearwood Dr 97501
Pebble Way 97504
Pebble Beach Ct 97504
Peebler Way 97501
Pembroke Cir 97504
Pendleton Dr 97501
Pennington Dr 97504
Pennsylvania Ave 97501
Pepper St 97501
Pepperwood Dr 97504
Perri Pl 97504
Perrydale Ave & Ct 97501
Petunia St 97504
Pheasant Ln 97504
N Phoenix Rd 97504
Piazza Dr 97501
Picadilly Cir 97504
Piedmont Ter 97504
Pierce Hts & Rd 97504
Pine St 97501
Pine Ridge Dr 97504
Pinebrook Cir 97504
Pinecrest Ct 97504
Pinecroft Ave 97501
Pinedale St 97504
Pinetop Dr 97504
Pineview Ct 97504
Pinnacle Dr 97504
Pinner Ln 97501
Pioneer Rd 97501
Pippin Cir 97504
Placid Cir 97504
Pleasant St 97504
Plum St 97501
Pointe View Ct 97504
Polar Cir 97504
Pomona Way 97504
Poplar Dr 97504
Poppie Cir 97504
Poppywoods Dr 97504
Portland Ave 97504
Posse Ln 97501
Powell St 97504
Prescott St 97504
Princeton Way 97504
Progress Dr 97504
Provincial St 97504
W Prune St 97501
Purdue Ln 97504
Putnam St 97501
Quail Run 97504
Quail Hollow Dr 97504
Quail Point Cir & Ter 97504
Quartz St 97501
Queen Anne Ave 97504
Queens Dr 97501
Queensbury Ln 97501
Quince St 97501
Rachel Way 97504
Ramada Ave 97504
Randolph St 97504
Reager St 97501
Reanna Way 97501
Red Hawk Dr 97504
Redbud Ln 97504
Reddy Ave 97504
Reed Ln 97501
Regal Ave 97501
Regency Ct 97504
Renault Ave 97501
Republic Way 97504
Richmond Ave 97504
Ridge Way 97504
Ridgepine Way 97501
Ridgeview Dr 97504
Ridgeway Cir 97504
Rimrock Cir 97504
Rio St 97501
Riverrock Way 97504
N & S Riverside Ave 97501
Roberts Rd 97504
Robin Way 97504
Rockwood Ct 97504
Rocky Road Dr 97504
Rogue Valley Manor Dr 97504
Rolling Meadows Ln 97504
Rome Beauty Ln 97501
Rose Ave & Ln 97501
Rosedale Ter 97504
Rosemont Ave 97504
Rosewood St 97504
N Ross Ct, Ln & St 97501
Rossanley Dr 97501
Roundelay Cir 97504
Roundgate Dr 97501
N Roxy Dr 97504
Roxy Ann Pl & Rd 97504
Roxy Ann Heights Dr 97504
Royal Ave & Ct 97504
Royal Crest Rd 97504
Ruby Dr 97504
Ruhl Way 97504
Ruskin Dr 97504
Ruth Dr 97504
Ryan Dr 97504
Saddle Ridge Dr 97504
Sage Rd 97501
Saginaw Dr 97504
Saint Andrew Way 97504
Saling Ave 97504
Salishan Ct 97504
Salyer St 97501
Samike Dr 97501
Samoan Way 97504
San Juan Dr 97504
San Marcos Dr 97504
Sandberg Ct 97504
Sandlewood Dr 97501
Sandpiper Dr 97501
Sandra Pl 97504
Sandstone Dr 97501
Sandy Ter 97504
Santa Barbara Dr 97504
Sarah Way 97501
Saratoga Dr 97501
Satellite Dr 97504
Scarlett Cir 97504
Scheffel Ave 97504
Scholarship Way 97501
Scott St 97504
Scottsdale Cir 97504
Seckel Ct & St 97504
Senate Way 97504
Seneca Ave 97501
Sequoia Cir 97501
Serenity Dr 97504
Seroba Cir 97501
Seventh Fairway Dr 97504
Severson Dr 97504
Seville Cir 97504
Shadow Wood Dr 97501
Shafer Ln 97501
Shamrock Dr 97504
Shaniko Ct 97504
Shannesy Dr 97504
Shannon Dr 97504
Shanteal Pl 97504
Sharman Way 97504
Shasta Dr 97504
Shawna Dr 97504
Sheffield Ct 97504
Shelby Dr 97504
Sheldon Ave 97501
Shelterwood Cir 97504
Sheraton Ct 97504
Sherbrook Ave 97504
Sherman St 97504
Sherry Ave 97501
Sherwood Park Dr 97504
Sidney Way 97504
Sieber Ln 97501
Sienna Ct 97504

Sierra Vista Ln 97501
Signature Ct 97504
Silky Oaks Ln 97501
Silver Palm Cir & Dr 97504
Silverado Cir 97504
Silverbirch Ct 97504
Silvercrest Ct 97504
Siskiyou Blvd 97504
Skeeters Ln 97504
Sky Park Dr 97504
Skyhawk Rdg 97504
Skyline Dr 97504
Skyview Dr 97501
Smith St 97504
Smithbury St 97501
Smokethorn Way 97504
Snowcrest Dr 97504
Solano Cir 97504
Somerset Cir 97504
Songbird Ln 97504
Sonnet Ln 97504
Sonya Cir 97504
South Way 97504
E South Stage Rd 97501
Southport Way 97504
Southview Ter 97504
Southvillage Dr 97504
Souvenir St 97501
Sparrow Way 97501
Sparta Way 97504
Spencer St 97504
Spicewood Ct 97504
Spring St 97504
Spring Hills Dr 97504
Spring Valley Dr 97501
Springbrook Ct & Rd 97504
Spruce Way 97501
Spyglass Ct 97504
St Augustine Dr 97504
St Charles Way 97504
St Clair St 97504
St Frances Dr 97504
St Thomas Way 97504
Stacie Way 97504
S Stage Rd 97501
Stanford Ave 97504
Stanley Ave 97504
Star Lite Ln 97501
Stardust Way 97504
Stark St 97504
Starling Ln 97501
Starwood Ct 97501
S State Rd 97501
State St 97504
Stearns Way 97501
Steelhead Run 97504
Sterling Point Ct & Dr 97504
Stevens St 97504
E & W Stewart Ave 97501
Stillwater Ct 97504
Stockel Ct 97504
Stonebrook Dr 97504
Stonefield Way 97501
Stonegate Dr 97504
N & S Stoneham Cir 97504
Stowe Ave 97501
Strasburg St 97504
Stratford Ave 97504
Summer Glen Dr 97501
Summerwood Dr 97504
Summit Ave 97501
Summitridge Cir 97504
Sun Oaks Dr 97504
Sunburst Ct 97504
Sundial Dr 97501
Sundown Rd 97501
Sunnyview Ln 97501
Sunrise Ave 97504
Sunset Ave, Ct & Dr 97501
Sunshine Ln 97501
Sunwood Dr 97501
Superior Ct 97504
Surrey Dr 97501
Sutter Ave 97504
Suzanna St 97504
Swayze Ln 97501
Sweet Rd 97501
Sweet Home Pl 97504
Swing Ln 97501
Sycamore Way 97504
Syringa Dr 97501
Tabby Ln 97504
Table Rock Rd
1900-1998 97501
2000-3099 97501
3101-3199 97501
3300-3699 97504
Taft St 97501
Tahitian Ave 97504
Tamara Cir 97504
Tamarack Dr 97504
Tan Oak Dr 97504
Tanglewood Ln 97501
Tara Cir 97504
Tawn Cheree 97501
Taylor St 97504
Temple Dr 97504
Tennessee Dr 97501
Terminal Loop Pkwy 97504
Terrace Dr 97504
Terrel Dr 97501
Terri Dr 97504
Theater Aly 97501
Thomas Rd 97501
Thomasville Dr 97504
Thorn Oak Dr 97501
Thrasher Ln 97504
Tiffany St 97504
Timothy Ave 97504
Tivoli Dr 97501
Todd Cir 97501
Tonia Cir 97504
Toralon Dr 97501
Torrey Pines Dr 97504
Tower E 97504
Town Centre Dr 97504
Tracy Ln 97501
Trinity Way 97501
Tripp St 97504
Union Ave 97501
United Way 97501
Upland Pl 97504
Upper Dr 97504
Valley View Dr 97504
Vancouver Ave 97504
Vashti Way 97501
Vawter Rd 97501
Velia St 97504
Veranda Park Dr 97504
Verde Pl 97504
Vernada Pl 97501
Veronica Way 97501
Vick Ln 97501
Victoria Ct 97504
Victory Ln 97501
View Pl 97504
Viewcrest Dr 97504
Viewpoint Dr 97504
Village Cir 97504
Village Center Dr 97504
Vineyard Ter 97504
Violet Dr 97501
Virginia Ave & St 97501
Vista Pointe Dr 97504
Vivian St 97501
Voorhies Rd 97501
Voss Rd 97501
Wabash Ave 97504
Wailea Ct 97504
Walnut St 97501
Warren Way 97501
Washburn Ln 97501
Washington St 97501
Waterbury Way 97504
Waterford Ct 97504
Waters Edge Way 97504
Waverly Way 97504
Welch St 97501
Wellington Dr 97504
Westerlund Dr 97504
Western Ave 97501
Westfall Cir 97504
Westfield Way 97501
Westin Heights Ln 97504
Westminster Dr 97504
Westport Cir 97504
Westview Ct 97504
Westwood Dr 97501
N & S Wexford Cir 97504
Wheat Ridge Dr 97504
White Oak Cir & Dr 97504
Whitman Ave & Pl 97501
Whitney Ter 97504
Whittle Ave 97504
Wildflower Cir & Dr 97504
Wildwood Cir 97504
Wildwood Dr 97501
Wilkshire Dr 97504
Willamette Ave 97504
Williams Ct 97504
Williamsburg Cir 97501
Willig Way 97501
Willow Way 97501
Willow Glen Way 97504
Willowbrook Dr 97501
Willowdale Ave 97501
Wilson Pl 97504
Wimbley St 97501
Winchester Ave 97501
Windermere Dr 97504
Windgate St 97504
Windsong Way 97504
Windsor Ave 97504
Windward Dr 97501
Winema Way 97501
Winslow Park Cir & Dr 97504
Winter Nell Cir 97504
Withington St 97501
Wolf Run Dr 97504
Woodbriar Dr 97504
Woodbridge Dr 97504
Woodland Dr 97501
Woodlark Dr 97501
Woodlawn Dr 97504
Woodrow Ln 97504
Woodside Dr 97501
Woodstock St 97501
Worchester Dr 97501
Wren Ct 97501
Wyatt Dr 97501
Yale Dr 97504
Yellowstone Ave 97504
Yorktown Ln 97501
Young Ct 97504
Yucca St 97504
Yukon Ave 97504
Yvonne Rd 97504

NUMBERED STREETS

W 2nd St 97501
E & W 3rd 97501
E & W 4th 97501
E & W 5th 97501
E & W 6th 97501
E 8th St
100-199 97501
601-699 97504
W 8th St 97501
E 9th St
201-299 97501
600-698 97504
700-1216 97504
1218-1298 97504
W 9th St 97501
E 10th St
101-121 97501
200-298 97501
801-997 97504
999-1312 97504
1314-1398 97504
W 10th St 97501
E 11th St
101-107 97501
109-115 97501
117-199 97501
1000-1299 97504
W 11th St 97501
E & W 12th 97501
E & W 13th 97501
W 14th St 97501

PORTLAND OR

NAMED STREETS

SE A St 97222
NW Abbey Rd 97229
NW Abby Ct 97229
SW Abercrombie Pl 97225
NW Aberdeen Dr 97229
SW Abernathy Ct 97221
SE Abernethy Ln 97267
NW Abernethy Rd 97229
SW Abernethy St 97239
SW Abigail Ct 97219
SE Acorn Ct 97267
SE Ada Ave 97267
SE Ada Ln
2500-2600 97267
2602-2698 97267
4600-4999 97222
NW Adams St 97229
SE Adams St 97222
SE Adamson Ct 97222
SW Addie Ln 97223
SE Addie St 97267
SW Adele Dr 97225
SW Adina Ct 97224
Admiral Ct & St 97221
NW Adrian St 97229
N Adriatic Ave 97203
SW Aerie Dr 97223
SW Afton Ln 97224
SW Agate Ln 97239
NE Ainsworth Cir 97220
NE Ainsworth Ct
4100-4138 97211
4140-4198 97211
5000-5199 97218
N Ainsworth St 97217
NE Ainsworth St
1-4199 97211
4200-6299 97218
NE Air Cargo Rd 97218
NE Airport Way
7000-7639 97218
7640-7640 97238
7641-8199 97218
7700-8198 97218
8201-8497 97220
8499-12199 97220
12200-18099 97230
NE Airtrans Way 97218
NE Airway Cir 97218
SW Akilean Ter 97223
NE Alameda Dr 97212
NE Alameda St
1900-4199 97212
4200-7799 97213
NE Alameda Ter 97212
SE Alarenti St 97214
N Alaska Pl 97217
N Alaska St
3600-3999 97217
4001-4299 97203
NW Albemarle Ter 97210
NE Alberta Ct
3300-4199 97211
4200-5199 97218
N Alberta St 97217
NE Alberta St
1-3299 97211
4200-8000 97218
8002-8098 97218
8200-9199 97220
SE Alberta St 97206
SW Alberta St 97223
N Albina Ave
2100-4099 97227
4100-8499 97217
8501-8699 97217
SE Alchar Dr 97222
SW Alcott Ave 97225
Alden Ct & St 97223
SE Alder Ct
3000-3299 97214
14300-16799 97233
SE Alder Pl 97222
SE Alder St
1-97 97214
99-4199 97214
4200-8199 97215
8200-11999 97216
12600-18099 97233
SW Alder St
221-295 97204
297-528 97204
530-598 97204
606-606 97205
608-1638 97205
1640-1736 97205
7600-7899 97224
NW Alder Grove Ln 97229
SE Alder Hill Loop 97267
Alderbrook Cir, Ct, Dr & Pl 97224
SE Aldercrest Ct 97267
SE Aldercrest Ln 97222
SE Aldercrest Rd
3200-5699 97222
5700-5898 97267
5900-6299 97267
SW Alderidge Dr 97225
NW Alderview Dr 97231
SE Alderway Ave 97267
NE Alderwood Dr 97218
NE Alderwood Rd
6700-6998 97218
7000-7400 97218
7402-7498 97218
8300-9199 97220
9201-9599 97220
NW Alexandra Ave 97210
NW Alfalfa Dr 97229
SW Alfred Ct 97219
SW Alfred St
3801-3997 97219
3999-6499 97219
6500-6800 97223
6802-6898 97223
SW Alice St 97219
SE Alii Ct 97267
N Allegheny Ave 97203
SE Allen Rd 97267
SW Allen Rd 97223
NW Allenbach Pl 97229
NW Ally Elizabeth Ct 97229
N Alma Ave 97203
SW Aloma Way 97223
SE Alpenglade Ct 97267
NW Alpenglow Way 97229
NW Alpine Ter 97210
SW Alpine Ter 97225
SW Alpine Vw 97224
SW Alpine Crest Way 97224
SW Alpine View Ct 97224
NW Alsace Ln 97229
N Alta Ave 97203
NW Alta Ln 97229
SW Alta Mira Cir 97239
SE Alta Verde Dr 97266
SW Alta Vista Pl 97201
Altadena Ave & Ter 97239
SW Altadina Ct 97219
NE Alton Ct 97230
NE Alton St
5700-6299 97213
9900-10199 97220
14200-14298 97230
14300-15599 97230
NW Alvada St 97229
SW Alyne Ln 97223
SW Alyssa Ln 97225
SW Amanda Ct 97224
NE Ambassador Pl 97220
SW Amber Ln 97225
SW Ambiance Pl 97223
SE Amelia Ct 97267
SW Ames Ln 97224
SW Ames Way 97225
NW Amethyst Ct 97229
N Amherst St 97203
NW Amity Ln 97229
NW Anastasia Dr 97229
Anchor St & Way 97217
SE Ancona Ct 97267
NW Andalusian Way 97229
Anderegg Dr & Loop 97236
NW Anderson St 97229
SE Andhop Ct 97266
SE Andover Pl 97202
NE Andra Pl 97230
NW Andrew Pl 97229
SW Andrew Ter 97224
NW Andria Ave 97229
SE Andys Ct 97267
SE Angel Ln 97267
SE Angela Way 97222
Angus Ct & Pl 97224
SE Ankeny Cir 97233
SE Ankeny Ct 97233
SE Ankeny St
532-606 97214
608-4099 97214
4300-6199 97215
8700-12199 97216
13000-17199 97233
SW Ankeny St
1-117 97204
119-232 97204
703-717 97205
720-720 97205
Ann Ct, Pl & St 97223
SW Anna Ct 97223
Anna Eve Dr 97267
SE Anna Marie Ct 97267
NW Annette Ct 97229
SE Anspach St 97267
SE Antigua Ave 97267
SW Anton Dr 97223
NW Appellate Way 97229
SE Appenine Way 97222
SE Apple St 97222
SW Apple Way 97225
NW Applegate Ln 97229
SE April Cir 97267
SW April Ln 97224
Arborcrest Ct & Way 97225
SW Arboretum Cir 97221
NW Arborview Dr 97229
SW Arbre Ct 97223
NW Arcadia St 97229
NW Arcadian Ln 97229
SW Arden Rd 97201
SE Arden St 97222
SW Ardenwood St 97225
SW Ardmore Ave 97205
NE Argyle Dr 97211
N Argyle St 97217
NE Argyle St 97211
NW Argyle Way 97229
NW Ariel Ter 97210
SE Arista Dr
13200-13298 97222
13300-13899 97222
13900-18199 97267
SE Arista Ln 97267
SW Arkenstone Dr 97224
SW Arlene Ln 97224
N Arlington Pl 97217
SW Arlington Ter 97224
N Armour St 97203
SW Arnold St 97219
SE Arnold Way 97236
SW Arnold Heights Ter 97219
NW Arnott Ln 97229
Arranmore Ct, Pl & Way 97223
SW Arrow Wood Dr 97223
SW Arrow Wood Ln
5300-5999 97225
6000-6399 97223
SW Arrowood Dr 97219
SW Artesa Ct 97225
SW Arthur Ct 97223
SW Arthur St 97201
SW Arthur Way 97221
SW Ascension Dr 97223
SW Ascot Ct 97225
SE Ash Ave 97267
SW Ash Ave 97223
NW Ash Ct 97231
SE Ash Ct
6300-6400 97215
6402-6630 97215
11300-11499 97216
12300-12499 97222
SW Ash Dr 97223
SE Ash Pl 97215
NW Ash St
8300-10199 97229
14600-14899 97231
SE Ash St
300-498 97214
500-4199 97214
4200-8199 97215
8200-12199 97216
12200-13199 97233
13600-13700 97222
13702-13798 97222
18100-19599 97233
SW Ash St 97204
SW Ash Creek Ct 97223
SW Ash Creek Dr 97219
NW Ash Creek Ln 97229
SW Ash Creek Ln 97219
NE Ashante Dr 97211
SW Ashbury Ln 97223
NW Ashby Ct 97229
Ashdale Ct & Dr 97223
SE Asherali Ave 97266
SW Ashford St 97224
NW Ashland Dr 97229
SW Ashley Ct 97224
SW Ashley Dr 97224
NE Ashley St 97211
SE Ashton Ln 97267
SW Ashwood Ct 97223
NW Aspen Ave 97210
SE Aspen St 97222
SW Aspen Ridge Dr 97224
SE Aspen Summit Dr 97266
SE Asti Ct 97222
SE Aston Loop 97236
N Astor St 97203
SE Astor St 97267
NW Astoria Dr 97229
Athena Pl & St 97229
NW Athens Dr 97229
SW Atlanta St 97223
N Atlantic Ave 97217
N Attu St
3800-3999 97217
4000-4099 97203
SE Augusta Ct 97206
SW Augusta Ter 97224
Aurora Pl & St 97229
SE Austin St 97267
SE Autumn Ridge Ter 97267
SW Autumn View St 97224
NW Avalon Dr 97229
NW Avamere Ct 97229
SW Aventine Ave 97219
SW Aventine Circus 97219
NW Avignon Ln 97229
NW Avocet Ln 97229
Avon Ct, Pl & St 97224
NW Avondale Ct 97229
SW Aynsley Way 97224
SE Azalea Ct 97267
SE Azalea Dr 97267
Azalea Pl 97224
SE B St 97222
SE Babbler St 97267
NW Bailey St 97231
SW Bailey Trce 97223
SW Baird St 97219
SW Baker Ln 97224

SE Baldock Way 97267
SE Baldry St 97236
N Baldwin St 97217
NE Baldwin St 97211
SE Balfour St 97222
N Ballast St 97217
SW Balmer Cir 97219
SE Balmoral Ct 97267
N Baltimore Ave 97203
SW Bambi Ln 97223
SW Bancroft Ct
123-135 97239
137-201 97239
3500-3699 97221
SW Bancroft St
-109--716 97239
-15--107 97239
-718--720 97239
12-526 97239
528-534 97239
4000-4098 97221
4100-6499 97221
SW Bancroft Ter 97239
SW Bancroft Way 97225
SE Bandon Ln 97267
NW Banff Dr 97229
N Bank St 97203
NW Bannister Dr 97229
SE Bantam Ct 97267
NW Banyon Pl 97229
SE Barba St 97222
SW Barbara Ln 97223
Barbara Welch Ln & Rd 97236
SW Barbur Blvd
2801-3097 97201
3099-3199 97201
3201-3297 97239
3299-4600 97239
4602-4998 97239
7200-11399 97219
NW Barclay Ter 97231
SW Bard Way 97224
SW Barnes Ct 97225
NW Barnes Rd
4200-4899 97210
12200-12398 97229
12400-12500 97229
12502-12798 97229
SW Barnes Rd
4900-5300 97221
5302-6498 97221
6500-9800 97225
9802-12038 97225
NW Barnsley Ct 97229
SW Barnum Dr 97223
N Barr Ave 97203
NW Barrett Way 97229
Barrington Pl & Ter 97224
SW Barrow Ln 97221
SW Barrows Rd 97223
NW Bartha Ln 97229
SE Bartholomew Ct 97266
NW Bartholomew Dr 97229
N Basin Ave 97217
SW Basswood Ct 97223
SE Bauer St 97236
NW Bauer Woods Dr 97229
N Bayard Ave 97217
SW Baylor St 97223
NW Bayonne Ln 97229
SW Beagle Ct 97223
NE Beakey St 97212
SE Bearspaw St 97236
SE Beatrice St 97222
NE Beaumont St 97212
SW Beaver Ave 97239
Beaverton Ave & Ct 97239
SW Beaverton Hillsdale Hwy
1827-2517 97239
2519-3435 97239
3437-3467 97239
3504-3538 97221
3540-6499 97221
6500-9099 97225
9101-9219 97225
NW Beck Rd 97231
SW Becker Dr 97223
Beckman Ave & Ter 97222
SW Becky Lange Ct 97223
SW Bedford St 97224
SW Bedford Glen Loop 97224
NE Beech Ct 97230
N Beech St 97227
NE Beech St
1-1500 97212
1502-1598 97212
4200-8199 97213
8200-11199 97220
12200-15899 97230
SE Beech St 97222
SW Beef Bend Rd 97224
SW Beemer Ln 97224
SW Belford Ct 97224
NW Belgrave Ave 97210
N Belknap Ave 97217
SE Bell Ave
9201-9299 97206
9300-10399 97222
SW Bell Ct 97223
NE Bell Dr 97220
NW Belle Ct 97229
NE Bellevue Ave 97211
SW Bellflower St 97224
SE Belmont Dr 97236
SE Belmont St
101-497 97214
499-4199 97214
4200-6999 97215
Belmore Hts & St 97236
SW Belvidere Pl 97225
NW Benburb Ln 97229
SW Benchview Pl 97223
SW Benchview Ter
13200-13999 97223
14000-14399 97224
NW Benfield Dr 97229
SW Benham Ct 97225
SW Benish St 97223
NW Benjamin Ct 97229
NE Benjamin St 97220
SW Bennington Dr 97205
NW Benny Dr 97229
Benson Ct, Ln & St 97229
SW Bently Ct 97219
SW Benz Farm Ct 97225
Benz Park Ct & Dr 97225
SW Berea Dr 97223
SE Berghammer St 97267
N Berkeley Ave 97203
SE Berkeley Pl 97202
SE Berkeley Way 97202
Berkshire Pl & St 97225
SW Berlisou Ave 97204
NW Bermar Ln 97229
SW Bernard Dr 97239
NW Bernietta Ct 97229
N Bersour Ave 97203
NW Bertani St 97229
SW Bertha Ave 97239
SW Bertha Blvd
1001-1097 97219
1099-1506 97219
1508-1698 97219
2202-2432 97239
2434-2926 97239
2928-3450 97239
SW Bertha Ct 97239
NE Beryl Ter 97220
SE Beta St 97222
NW Bethany Blvd 97229
NW Beuhla Vista Ter 97210
SW Beveland Rd 97223
SE Beverly Ln 97222
Bevington Ave & Ct 97267
SW Bexley Ln 97224
SE Bidwell St 97202
Big Fir Cir & Ct 97229
SW Bigleaf Dr 97223
NE Billingher Dr 97220
SE Bilquist Cir 97267
SE Bilsher Ct 97267
SW Binddale Ct 97224
SE Birch Ave 97267
SE Birch St 97214
SW Birch St 97223
SW Birch Hill Ln 97224
SW Birchwood Rd 97225
NW Birdie Ln 97229
SW Birdshill Ct 97223
SW Birdshill Rd 97219
Birdsview Ln & St 97224
SE Birk St 97222
NW Birkendene St 97229
SE Bixel Way 97267
SW Black Diamond Way 97223
Black Walnut St & Ter 97224
SE Blackberry Cir 97236
NW Blackcomb Dr 97229
NW Blackfield Ln 97229
NW Blackhawk Dr 97229
SW Blackoaks Ln 97224
SW Blackstone Ln 97239
NW Blacktail Dr 97229
NW Blackthorne Ln 97229
NW Blakely Ln 97229
N Blandena St 97217
NW Blandy Ter 97229
SE Blanton St 97267
SE Blatner Pl 97267
N Bliss St 97203
N Bloss Ave 97203
SE Blossom Ave 97267
SW Blue Gum Ct 97223
NE Blue Heron Ct 97211
NE Blue Heron Dr 97211
SW Blue Heron Pl 97223
NW Blue Pointe Ln 97229
SW Blue Spruce Ct 97224
SE Bluebird St 97222
NW Bluegrass Pl 97229
SE Bluerock Ct 97267
SW Bluestem Ln 97223
SE Bluff Rd 97222
Boardman Ave & Ct 97267
SE Bob White St 97222
NE Boehmer St 97220
SW Bohmann Pkwy 97223
SE Boise Ct 97236
SE Boise St
901-997 97202
999-4199 97202
4200-8199 97206
9101-9197 97266
9199-12100 97266
12102-12198 97266
12200-12799 97236
SW Bomar Ct 97223
SW Bonanza Way 97224
SW Bonaventure Ln 97224
SW Bond Ave 97239
SW Bond St 97224
SW Bonita Rd 97224
SE Bonnie Way 97267
SW Boones Ferry Rd
8900-12299 97219
18101-18147 97224
18149-18499 97224
NW Bordeaux Ln 97229
SW Borders St 97223
SW Borsch Ln 97219
N Borthwick Ave
2301-2497 97227
2499-4099 97227
4100-8499 97217
8501-8599 97217
SE Boss Ln 97222
N Boston Ave 97217
SW Boundary Ct 97239
SW Boundary St
-21--55 97239
-4--19 97239
2-20 97239
22-2999 97239
3001-3499 97239
3500-6499 97221
6500-6699 97225
SW Bouneff St 97223
N Bowdoin St 97203
SE Bowman St 97222
Bowmont Ln & St 97225
SW Boxelder St 97223
SW Boxwood Ct 97223
SE Boyd St 97222
SW Bradbury Ct 97224
N Bradford St 97203
SW Bradley Ln 97224
NW Brady Ln 97229
SE Brae St 97222
SW Brae Mar Ct 97201
SW Braeburn Ln 97224
SE Bramble Ct 97267
NW Brandberry Dr 97229
N Brandon Ave 97217
NW Brandt Pl 97229
SW Brandyshire Ct 97224
NW Brassie Pl 97229
SW Bray Ln 97224
SW Braydon Ct 97224
NE Brazee Ct
2700-2900 97212
2902-2998 97212
13500-14599 97230
NE Brazee St
400-3252 97212
3254-4198 97212
4200-6199 97213
6201-6399 97213
8200-12099 97220
12200-15199 97230
SW Breeze Ct 97225
SE Brehaut St 97222
SE Brekke Ct 97222
SE Brenda Ave 97267
SW Brenden Ln 97223
SE Brendon Ct 97267
SW Brenne Ln 97225
SE Brentwood Ct 97267
SW Brentwood Ct 97224
SW Brentwood Dr 97201
SW Brentwood Pl 97224
SW Brentwood St 97225
SW Bretton Ct 97224
NW Brewer Ln 97229
SW Brewer St 97210
SE Brewster Pl 97267
Breyman Ave & Ct 97219
SW Brianne Way 97223
SE Briar Ct 97267
SW Briar Ln 97225
SE Briarfield Ct 97222
NW Briarwood Dr 97231
SW Briarwood Pl 97223
NW Bridge Ave 97231
SW Bridgeport Rd 97224
N Bridgeton Rd 97217
NE Bridgeton Rd 97211
SW Bridgeview Ct 97223
NW Bridle Ln 97229
Bridlemile Ct & Ln 97221
NW Brie Ct 97229
SW Brier Ln 97223
SW Brier Pl 97219
SE Brigadoon St 97267
SE Briggs St
12900-13899 97222
13900-14099 97267
SW Brightfield Cir 97223
NW Brighton Ln 97229
SE Brightwood Ave 97267
SE Brigid Pl 97267
SW Brim Pl 97223
NW Brimpton Ct 97229
SW Bristlecone Way 97223
N Bristol Ave 97203
SW Brittany Dr 97223
NW Brittney Ct 97229
SE Britton Ave 97267
SW Broadleaf Dr 97219
SW Broadmoor Pl 97223
SW Broadmoor Ter 97225
NW Broadway 97209
SW Broadway
123-197 97205
SW Broadway
199-1225 97205
1227-1239 97205
1307-1317 97201
1319-2021 97201
2023-2121 97201
NE Broadway Ct
7000-7199 97213
13300-13399 97230
SW Broadway Dr 97201
N Broadway St 97227
NE Broadway St
15-27 97232
29-4199 97232
4200-7200 97213
7202-7898 97213
8200-12199 97220
12900-15900 97230
15902-15998 97230
NW Brocket Ter 97229
NW Bronson Rd 97229
NW Bronson Creek Dr 97229
NW Bronson Crest Loop 97229
SW Brook Ct 97223
SW Brooklet Pl 97224
SW Brookline Ln 97224
SE Brooklyn Ct
10100-10998 97266
11000-11099 97266
13200-13399 97236
SW Brooklyn Ln 97224
SE Brooklyn St
1001-1597 97202
1599-4199 97202
4201-4297 97206
4299-7399 97206
8201-8297 97266
8299-11599 97266
14300-18199 97236
SW Brookridge St 97225
NW Brooks Rd 97231
SW Brooks Bend Pl 97223
SW Brookside Ave 97223
SW Brookside Ct 97223
SE Brookside Dr
4500-5299 97222
11200-12199 97266
12200-12399 97236
SW Brookside Dr 97225
SW Brookside Pl 97223
NW Brookstone Ct 97229
NW Brookview Way 97229
SE Brookwood Ave 97213
Broughton Ct & Dr 97217
SE Brownlee Rd 97267
N Bruce Ave 97203
NW Brugger Rd 97229
SW Brugger St 97219
NE Bryant Ct 97211
N Bryant St 97217
NE Bryant St
1-4199 97211
5900-6299 97218
NE Bryce St 97212
SE Bryn Mawr Ct 97267
NW Brynwood Ln 97229
N Buchanan Ave 97203
SW Bucharest Ct 97225
NW Buckboard Dr 97229
SW Buckfield Ln 97224
SW Buckingham Ave 97201
SW Buddington St 97219
Buena Vista Dr & Pl 97201
SW Buffalo Pl 97223
N Buffalo St 97217
NE Buffalo St
1-4199 97211
4400-5099 97218
Buford Ct & Ln 97236
SW Bugle Ct 97224
SW Bull Mountain Rd 97224
NW Bullfinch Pl 97229
SW Bulrush Ln 97223
SE Bunnell St 97267
Burbank Ave & Pl 97225
Burgard St & Way 97203
Burgundy Ct & St 97224
NW Burkhardt Ct 97229
NW Burkhart Dr 97229
SW Burlcrest Dr 97223
SW Burlheights St 97223
SW Burlingame Ave
6200-6699 97239
6700-6798 97219
6800-8199 97219
SW Burlingame Pl 97239
SW Burlingame Ter 97239
N Burlington Ave 97203
NW Burlington Ct 97231
NW Burlington Dr 97231
NW Burnett St 97229
Burnham Ct & St 97223
NW Burning Tree Ct 97229
W Burnside Rd 97210
E Burnside St
7903A-7903C 97215
230-414 97214
416-4199 97214
4200-8199 97215
8200-12199 97216
12200-19699 97233
19701-19999 97233
W Burnside St
18-52 97209
54-2099 97209
2100-2499 97210
NW Burntknoll Ct 97229
N Burr Ave 97203
N Burrage Ave 97217
SW Burton Dr 97221
NW Burton St 97229
SE Bush Pl 97236
SE Bush St
801-897 97202
899-2199 97202
4701-4797 97206
4799-8199 97206
8201-8297 97266
8299-12199 97266
12200-17199 97236
SE Bush Ter 97236
N Butler St 97203
SW Butner Rd 97225
NE Buxton St 97232
SE Bybee Blvd
1400-4199 97202
4200-8199 97206
8300-8699 97266
12200-12499 97236
SE Bybee Ct 97236
SE Bybee Dr 97236
Bybee Lake Ct & Rd 97203
NW Byrne Ter 97229
Byron Ct & Dr 97267
SE C St 97222
Cabernet Ct & Dr 97224
SW Cable Ave 97201
Cache Creek Ln 97224
SW Cactus Dr 97205
SW Caddy Pl 97223
NE Cadet Ave 97220
SW Caesar Ter 97224
SW Caffall Ln 97224
SW Cafield Ct 97223
NW Caitlin Ter 97229
Caldew Dr & St 97219
SW Calearia Ave 97225
N Calhoun Ave 97203
SW California St 97219
NW Calumet Ter 97210
N Calvert Ave 97217
NW Calypso Ter 97229
N Cambridge Ave 97203
SW Cambridge Dr 97224
SE Cambridge Ln 97222
SW Camelot Ct 97225
SW Camelot Ln 97219
NE Cameron Blvd 97230
SW Cameron Ct 97223
SW Cameron Rd 97221
SW Camille Ter 97223
SW Camino Dr 97224
NE Campaign St
4200-5199 97218
9400-11099 97220
SE Campanario Rd 97222
N Campbell Ave 97217
SW Campbell Ct 97239
SE Campbell St 97222
SE Camplan Ct 97267
SW Campus Dr 97239
SW Canby Ct 97219
SW Canby Ln 97223
SW Canby St
-2--6 97219
-8--299 97219
5-13 97219
15-6499 97219
6500-6999 97223
7001-7199 97223
NE Canchent St 97232
SE Candy Ln 97267
NW Cannes Dr 97229
SW Canning St 97201
SE Cannon St 97236
NW Cannon Way 97229
SW Canterbury Ln
2900-3000 97205
3002-3098 97205
4701-4797 97219
4799-5099 97219
10300-10398 97224
10400-10900 97224
10902-10998 97224
NW Canterwood Way 97229
NW Canton St 97229
SW Canyon Crst 97225
SW Canyon Ct
5401-6397 97221
6399-6499 97221
6500-6599 97225
SW Canyon Dr 97225
SW Canyon Ln 97225
SW Canyon Rd
2201-2299 97201
4001-4033 97221
6600-6698 97225
6700-10000 97225
10002-10024 97225
SW Canyon Ter 97225
SW Canyonridge Ct 97224
SE Capistrano Ct 97222
SW Capitol Hwy
6001-6097 97239
6099-6629 97239
6630-6648 97219
6650-11599 97219
SW Capitol Hill Rd 97219
SW Capulet Ln 97224
SW Caraway Ct 97219
SW Cardinal Ln 97224
SE Cardinal St 97267
Cardinell Dr & Way 97201
N Carey Blvd 97203
SW Carey Ln 97219
NW Caribou Ct 97229
NW Carl Ct 97229
SW Carl Pl 97239
SE Carla Ct 97267
NW Carlton Ct 97229
SE Carlton St
1300-4100 97202
4102-4198 97202
4201-4797 97206
4799-8199 97206
12000-12199 97266
12200-14099 97236
SE Carmel Ct
10300-10399 97222
16800-16899 97267
SW Carmel Ct 97223
SW Carmel St 97224
SW Carmen St 97223
SE Carnation St 97267
SE Carol Ave 97267
SW Carol Ann Ct 97224
SW Caroland Rd 97223

SW Carole Ct 97224
SW Carolina Ct 97224
SW Carolina St 97239
SW Caroline Dr 97225
SE Carrie Lyn Ln 97222
SW Carson St 97219
SE Carson Corner Ct ... 97267
SW Carter Ln 97201
SE Caruthers Ct 97233
SE Caruthers St
110-208 97214
210-4100 97214
4102-4198 97214
4800-4999 97215
9700-10099 97216
12400-19099 97233
SW Caruthers St 97201
SE Casa Del Rey Dr ... 97222
SE Casa Verde Ct 97267
SW Cascade Ave 97223
SW Cascade Dr 97205
SW Cascade Ter 97205
NE Cascades Pkwy 97220
SW Case Ct 97223
NW Casey Dr 97229
SW Cashmur Ln 97225
SE Cassie Ct 97267
N Castle Ave
3900-3998 97227
4000-4099 97227
4100-4299 97217
SW Castle Ridge Ln 97219
SE Castle Rock Ct 97267
SW Catalina Dr 97223
SE Catalina Ln 97222
N Catlin Ave 97203
SW Catlin Crest Dr 97225
SE Catlyn Woods Dr ... 97267
SW Cattail Ct 97223
SE Causey Ave 97222
Cavalier St & Way 97267
Caxton Ct & Ln 97229
N Cecelia St 97203
SW Cecilia Ter 97223
SE Cedar Ave 97267
NW Cedar Ln 97229
SW Cedar Ln 97225
NW Cedar St 97231
SE Cedar St 97222
SW Cedar St
2300-2400 97205
2402-2498 97205
7500-8199 97225
NW Cedar Falls Dr 97229
NW Cedar Forest Ln ... 97229
NW Cedar Hills Blvd ... 97229
SW Cedar Hills Blvd 97225
SE Cedar Ridge Ct 97222
NW Cedar Ridge Dr 97229
NW Cedar View Ln 97229
SE Cedarcrest Dr 97222
SW Cedarcrest St 97223
SW Cedarwood Ln 97225
SE Celeste Ct 97267
SW Celeste Ln 97225
SW Centennial Block ... 97204
N Center Ave 97217
SE Center Ct 97266
SE Center St
901-1097 97202
1099-3899 97202
4200-8199 97206
9200-9298 97266
9300-10800 97266
10802-10998 97266
12400-12598 97236
12600-15000 97236
15002-15098 97236
SW Center St 97223
NE Center Commons Way 97213
N Center Court St 97227
NW Centine Ln 97229
NW Central Ct 97229
NW Central Dr 97229
N Central St 97203

Century Oak Cir & Dr .. 97224
NE Cesar E Chavez Blvd
1-97 97232
99-1299 97232
1301-1699 97232
1701-1797 97212
1799-4099 97212
4100-6500 97211
6502-6598 97211
SE Cesar E Chavez Blvd
1-2499 97214
2501-2697 97202
2699-8299 97202
SW Champion Pl 97225
SW Champlain Dr 97205
SW Chandler Dr 97224
NW Channa Dr 97229
N Channel Ave 97217
NW Chanticleer Dr 97229
Chapel Ct & Ln 97223
NW Chapin Dr 97229
SW Char Ct 97224
SW Chardonnay Ave ... 97224
SE Chardonnay Ct 97267
SE Charles St 97222
N Charleston Ave 97203
SW Charleston Dr 97224
SW Charleston Ln 97224
NW Charlton Rd 97231
SW Charming Way 97225
N Chase Ave 97217
SW Chase Ln 97223
SW Chateau Ln 97224
N Chatham Ave 97217
SW Chaucer Ct 97224
Chautauqua Blvd & Pl .. 97217
NW Cheerio Ln 97229
SW Chehalem Ave 97239
SW Chehalem Ct 97223
SW Chelmsford Ave 97201
SW Chelsea Loop 97223
SW Chelsea Pl 97223
SE Chelsea St 97222
Cheltenham Ct, Dr & St 97239
Chemeketa Ct & Ln 97229
NW Chemult Pl 97229
SE Cherry Ct 97267
SW Cherry Dr 97223
SE Cherry Blossom Dr . 97216
SE Cherry Hill Ln 97267
SW Cherrywood Ln 97224
SW Chesapeak Ave 97239
SW Chesterfield Ln 97224
SW Chestnut Dr 97219
NW Chestnut Ln 97231
SE Chestnut St 97267
SW Chestnut St
501-597 97219
599-999 97219
7500-7598 97223
7600-8300 97223
8302-8398 97223
N Chicago Ave 97203
SW Chicory Ct 97223
SW Childs Rd 97224
NW Chiloquin Ct 97229
Chimney Ridge Ct & St 97223
SW Chinn Ln 97224
NW Chipmunk Ln 97229
SW Chirp St 97224
Chloe Ln 97229
NW Christine Ct 97229
SE Christopher Ct 97267
N Church St 97217
NE Church St
400-1399 97211
4800-5799 97218
Churchill Ct & Way 97224
NW Cider Ln 97229
NW Cinder Ct 97229
SE Cinderella Ct 97222
SE Circle Ave 97236
NW Circle A Dr 97229
NE Clackamas Ct 97230

SE Clackamas Rd 97267
NE Clackamas St
301-597 97232
599-3499 97232
4900-8199 97213
8500-11699 97220
12600-19499 97230
SE Clackamas St 97222
NE Clackamas Ter 97230
NW Claire Ct 97229
SE Clara St 97267
SW Clara Mae Way 97219
SE Clare Ct 97267
NE Claremont Ave 97211
NW Claremont Dr 97229
SW Claremont Ter 97225
N Clarendon Ave 97203
SW Claridge Dr 97223
N Clark Ave 97227
NW Clark Ave 97231
NW Clarno Ct 97229
SE Clatsop Ct 97266
SE Clatsop St
501-697 97202
699-2499 97202
6100-7499 97206
8201-9717 97266
9719-10149 97266
10151-10199 97266
13301-16199 97236
SE Clay Ct 97233
SE Clay St
8921A-8921B 97216
49-117 97214
119-3799 97214
3801-3999 97214
4200-8199 97215
8200-10999 97216
13300-18199 97233
SW Clay St
104-210 97201
212-1720 97201
1722-1730 97201
5800-5999 97221
SE Claybourne St
1400-3799 97202
7200-8199 97206
8500-9899 97266
12300-14099 97236
SE Clayson Ave 97267
Clear Hills Dr & Ter 97225
Clearview Pl & Way 97223
NW Cleek Pl 97229
NW Cleetwood Ave 97231
SW Clemell Ave 97239
NW Clement Ln 97229
NE Cleveland Ave
3500-4099 97212
4100-7099 97211
NE Cliff St 97220
SW Clifton St 97201
SW Cline St 97219
SE Clinton Ct
11301-11499 97266
12500-15699 97236
SE Clinton St
401-997 97202
999-4199 97202
4200-8000 97206
8002-8098 97206
8200-12199 97266
14500-14698 97236
14700-17599 97236
SW Clinton St 97223
SW Cloud Ct 97224
SW Club Meadow Ln ... 97225
SW Club Mission Cir ... 97224
NW Clubhouse Dr 97229
Clydesdale Ct & Pl 97223
SE Clydie Ct 97206
SW Cole Ln 97224
NW Coleman Dr 97229
N Colfax St 97217
NE Colfax St 97220
SW Colin Ct 97223
SE Colina Vista Ave 97267
NW College Dr 97229

SW College St 97201
SW Collina Ave 97219
Collins Ct & St 97219
N Colonial Ave
3700-3798 97227
3800-4099 97227
4100-4799 97217
SE Colony Cir 97267
SW Colony Ct 97224
SW Colony Dr
400-799 97219
15800-16299 97224
SW Colony Pl 97224
Colony Creek Ct & Pl .. 97224
SE Colt Dr 97202
SW Colton Ln 97224
NW Columbia Ave 97229
N Columbia Blvd
201-217 97217
219-2631 97217
2633-3899 97217
4000-4498 97203
4500-12699 97203
NE Columbia Blvd
1-4199 97211
4200-8199 97218
8400-8799 97220
8801-9199 97220
N Columbia Ct 97203
NE Columbia Ct 97211
NW Columbia St 97231
SW Columbia St
1-1 97258
101-197 97201
199-1799 97201
N Columbia Way 97203
NW Columbine Ln 97229
NE Colwood Way 97218
Colyer Pl & Way 97224
NW Comadrona Ln 97229
N Commerce St 97217
N Commercial Ave
2600-2698 97227
2700-4099 97227
4100-7700 97217
7702-8198 97217
SW Commercial St 97223
SW Commonwealth Ave 97201
Comus Ct, Pl & St 97219
N Concord Ave
3900-4099 97227
4100-7499 97217
SE Concord Ct 97267
SE Concord Rd 97267
NW Concordia Ct 97229
NW Condenda Ave 97210
SW Condor Ave 97239
SW Condor Ln 97239
NW Condor Pl 97229
SW Condor Way 97239
N Congress Ave 97217
NW Connery Ter 97229
NW Connett Meadow Ct 97229
SE Connor Ln 97266
SW Connor Pl 97224
SE Conway St 97222
SE Cook Ct 97222
SW Cook Ct 97224
SW Cook Ln 97223
N Cook St 97227
NE Cook St 97212
SE Cook St 97267
SE Cooke Rd 97267
SW Cooper Ln 97224
SE Cooper St
3600-4199 97202
4200-8199 97206
8901-8997 97266
8999-9400 97266
9402-9498 97266
12700-14299 97236
SW Copel St 97225
NW Copeland St 97229
SW Copper Creek Dr ... 97224
SW Copper Hill Ln 97224

SE Cora Dr 97202
SE Cora St
900-4199 97202
4200-8199 97206
8400-11899 97266
12400-13999 97236
SW Coral St 97223
NW Corazon Ter 97229
SW Corbett Ave
2600-2698 97201
2700-2899 97201
2901-3099 97201
3200-6600 97239
6602-6698 97239
6700-7699 97219
SW Corbett Ln 97219
SW Corbett Hill Cir 97219
SW Corby Dr 97225
SE Cordova Ct 97267
SE Corey Ln 97267
NW Corinthian St 97229
NW Cornelius Pass Rd 97231
SW Cornell Pl 97223
NW Cornell Rd
2600-6499 97210
6701-7897 97229
7899-12700 97229
12675-12675 97291
12702-14998 97229
12801-14199 97229
NE Cornfoot Rd 97218
SE Cornish Ct 97267
SW Cornutt St 97224
SE Cornwell St 97206
SW Corona Ave 97201
SW Coronado St 97219
SE Corsage Ave 97267
NW Corso Ln 97229
SW Cortland Ln 97224
SW Corylus Ct 97224
SE Cottonwood Ct 97267
SW Cottonwood Ln 97223
SE Cottonwood St 97267
NE Couch Ct
11101-11197 97220
11199-11299 97220
15100-16999 97230
NE Couch Ln 97230
NE Couch St
300-398 97232
400-4099 97232
4101-4199 97232
4200-8199 97213
8700-11999 97220
12500-20199 97230
NW Couch St 97209
SW Council Crest Dr ... 97239
NW Country Dr 97229
NW Country Club Dr ... 97229
NW Country Woods Ln 97231
NW Countryridge Dr 97229
NW Countryside Ct 97229
NW Countryview Way ... 97229
NE Courier Ct 97218
N Court Ave
4000-4098 97227
4100-4299 97217
N Courtenay Ave 97203
SE Courtney Rd 97222
NW Cove Ct 97229
SE Covell St 97222
SW Cowles Ct 97223
SE Cozy Dr 97222
NW Crady Ln 97229
N Cramer St 97217
NE Cramer St 97211
SW Crane Ct 97223
NE Crane St 97211
N Crawford St 97203
Creekshire Dr & Pl 97223
NW Creekside Dr 97229
SE Creekside Dr 97267
SW Creekside Dr 97224
NW Creekview Dr 97229
SE Creighton Ave 97267

SW Creightonwood Pl .. 97219
NW Cresap Ln 97229
SW Cresmer Dr 97223
SE Crest Ct 97236
Crestdale Ct & Dr 97225
SW Crestline Ct 97224
SW Crestline Dr 97219
NW Creston Rd 97231
SW Crestridge Ct 97224
SE Crestview Ave 97267
SW Crestview St 97223
NW Crestview Way 97229
SE Crestwood Dr 97267
SW Crestwood Dr 97225
SW Crestwood Ln 97225
SW Crestwood St 97223
SE Creswain Ave 97267
SW Crickhollow Ct 97224
SW Crist Ct 97223
SE Criterion Ct 97222
SW Criterion Ter 97224
SW Cromwell Ct 97223
SW Cross Ave 97201
NW Crosshaven St 97229
NW Crossing Dr 97229
SE Crosswhite Way 97206
SE Crown Ct 97267
SW Crown Ct 97224
SW Crown Dr 97224
Crown Plz 97201
SE Crystal Ct 97236
NE Crystal Ln 97218
SE Crystal Ln 97267
SE Crystal St 97236
SW Crystal St 97223
NW Crystal Creek Ln ... 97229
SE Crystal Lake Ln 97222
SE Crystal Springs Blvd
2801-2997 97202
2999-4199 97202
4200-8100 97206
8102-8198 97206
8600-9099 97266
9101-9151 97266
14100-14399 97236
SE Crystal Springs Ct .. 97206
SE Crystal View Dr 97266
SW Cullen Blvd 97221
NE Cully Blvd
3800-4099 97213
4100-5999 97218
NW Culpepper Ter 97210
NW Cumberland Rd 97210
SW Curran Daniel Ln ... 97225
SW Curry St 97239
N Curtis Ave 97217
SE Cushman Ct 97267
SW Cushman Ct 97223
Custer Dr, St & Way ... 97219
N Cutter Cir 97217
SE Cypress Ave
2001-2097 97214
2099-2299 97214
7000-8099 97267
8101-8299 97267
SW Cypress Ln 97224
NW Cyrus Ln 97229
D Pl & St 97222
SW Da Vinci Ln 97224
Dagmar Ct & Rd 97267
SW Dahlia Ct 97223
SW Dakota St
-200--502 97239
-504--699 97239
2401-2499 97239
3500-4199 97221
NW Dale Ave 97229
NW Dallas Pl 97229
NW Dalton Ranch Ln ... 97229
Damascus Ct & St 97229
SW Damirs Ct 97223
N Dana Ave 97203
SE Dana Ave 97267
SW Danbush Ct 97223
NW Dane Ln 97229
SE Danica Ct 97267

SE Danna Ct 97267
SW Daphne Ave 97219
SE Daphne Ct 97222
SW Daphne Pl 97219
SW Darmel Ct 97224
SW Dartmouth St 97223
SW Dauer Ct 97223
Davenport Ct, Ln & St .. 97201
NE David Cir 97230
SE Davies Ct 97267
SW Davies Ct 97223
NE Davis Ct 97230
SW Davis Ln 97224
NE Davis St
317-397 97232
399-4199 97232
4200-7099 97213
8300-8398 97220
8400-11999 97220
12600-19899 97230
NW Davis St
1-1799 97209
1801-1863 97209
2101-2147 97210
2149-2199 97210
SW Dawn Ct 97224
SW Dawns Ct 97223
NW Dawnwood Dr 97229
SW Dayton Building 97204
NE Dean St 97211
SE Deardorff Rd 97236
N Decatur St 97203
NW Decatur Way 97229
SW Deeann Ct 97224
NW Deejay Ln 97229
SE Deer Creek Ln 97222
SW Deerberry 97224
NW Deerbrook Ct 97229
NW Deercreek Ct 97229
Deerfield Dr & Way 97229
NW Deerfoot Ln 97229
SW Deergrove Ln 97224
SE Deerhaven Dr 97266
SE Deering Ct 97222
NW Deette Dr 97229
SW Dekalb St 97224
SW Dekorte Ter 97224
N Dekum St 97217
NE Dekum St 97211
SE Del Dr 97267
SW Del Monte Dr 97224
SE Del Rey Ave 97267
SW Delaney Pl 97225
N Delaware Ave 97217
Dellwood Ave, Ct & Pl .. 97225
SW Delmont Ave 97225
SE Denny Ave 97222
N Denver Ave 97217
N Depauw St 97203
SE Derdan Ct 97222
SE Derry Ln 97267
SW Derry Dell Ct 97223
NW Deschutes Dr 97229
SE Deswell St 97267
SE Determan Ct 97267
N Detroit Ave 97217
SW Devon Ln 97219
NW Devoto Ln 97229
SW Dewberry Ln 97223
SE Dewey Ct 97222
SW Dewitt St 97239
NW Diamond Dr 97229
SE Diamond Ln 97267
N Dickens St 97203
Dickinson Ct, Ln, Pl & St 97219
SW Dickson St 97224
NW Dingo Dr 97229
NW District Ct 97229
SE Division Ct 97266
SE Division Pl 97202
SE Division St
801-835 97214
900-998 97202
1000-4199 97202
4200-8199 97206

8200-12199 97266
12200-18199 97236
N Dixon St 97227
NW Doane Ave 97210
SW Doe Ln 97223
SE Dogwood Ln 97267
SW Dogwood Ln 97225
SW Dogwood Pl 97225
NW Dogwood St 97229
SE Dohn Ct 97267
SE Dolinda St 97267
SW Dolph Ct 97219
SW Dolph Dr 97219
SW Dolph St
600-698 97219
700-1899 97219
8700-9099 97223
N Dolphin St 97217
NW Dominion Dr 97229
NW Donegal Ct 97229
SW Donner Way 97239
SW Donner Way Ct 97239
SE Dontindi Ave 97215
SW Dorburn Pl 97224
NW Dorena St 97229
SW Dosch Ct 97221
SW Dosch Rd 97239
SW Dosch Park Ln 97239
Doschdale Ct & Dr 97239
SW Doschview Ct 97239
SW Douglas Dr 97219
NW Douglas Pl 97229
SW Douglas Pl 97205
SW Douglas St 97225
SE Douglas Fir Ct 97267
SE Dove St 97222
SW Dover Ct
5200-5599 97225
10800-10999 97224
SW Dover Ln 97225
SW Dover Loop 97225
NW Dover St 97210
SW Dover St
6300-6499 97221
6500-6899 97225
Down Ct & Way 97267
Downs View Ct & Ter 97221
SW Dozier Way 97224
SE Drake St 97222
SE Drefshill St 97222
NW Dresden Pl 97229
N Drew St 97203
SE Drew St 97222
N Dribble Dr 97227
SW Driftwood Ct 97224
NW Driver Pl 97229
N Druid Ave 97203
N Drummond Ave 97217
NW Drury Ln 97231
NW Dublin Ct 97229
SW Duchilly Ct 97224
SE Duckey Ln 97267
NE Duddleson St 97220
SE Duke Ct 97236
SE Duke St
1400-1500 97202
1502-1698 97202
4900-8199 97206
8200-8298 97266
8300-9999 97266
13100-14899 97236
Dumar Ln & St 97229
SE Dunbar Dr 97236
NW Dunbar Ln 97231
NE Dunckley St 97212
SW Dune Grass Ln 97224
NE Durham Ave 97211
SW Durham Ln 97224
SW Durham Rd 97224
NW Durrett St 97229
SE Dustin Dr 97267
N Dwight Ave 97203
SE Dwyer Dr 97222
NE Dyer St 97220
SE Eagle St 97222
NW Eagleridge Ln 97229

SW Eagles Nest Ln 97239
SW Eagles View Ln 97224
SE East Ave 97267
NW East Rd 97229
SE East View Ct 97236
SE Eastbrook Dr 97222
SE Eastmoor Ter 97225
SE Eastridge Ct 97236
SE Eastridge St 97236
SW Eastridge St 97225
SE Eastwood Ct 97267
N Easy St 97203
NW Echo Ct 97229
SE Echo Way 97267
SE Eckler Ave 97222
SE Ed Anna Ct 97267
SW Eden Ct 97223
NW Edgebrook Pl 97229
SW Edgecliff Rd 97219
SW Edgefield Ter 97223
NE Edgehill Pl 97212
SW Edgemont Pl 97239
N Edgewater Ave 97203
SW Edgewater Ct 97223
NE Edgewater Dr 97211
NW Edgewood Dr 97229
NW Edgewood Pl 97229
SW Edgewood Rd 97201
SW Edgewood St
8800-9599 97223
11800-13199 97225
N Edison St 97203
SE Edison St 97222
NW Eggers Ct 97229
Eikrem Ln 97267
SE El Camino Way 97267
El Centro Ct & Way 97267
Elaina Ct & Ln 97229
SE Elderberry Ln 97267
SW Elderbrook Pl 97225
SE Eldorado Ct 97267
SW Eldorado Dr 97224
SE Eldorado St 97267
SW Eleanor Ln 97221
SW Electric St 97223
SW Elemar Ct 97224
SW Elena Ln 97223
SW Elise Ct 97224
Elizabeth Ct & St 97201
SE Elk St 97222
NW Elk Meadow Ln 97229
NW Elk Run Dr 97229
NW Elkcrest Ct 97229
SE Ella Ave 97267
NW Elliot Rd 97231
SE Elliott Ave 97214
SE Ellis St
1500-4199 97202
4200-8199 97206
8400-10599 97266
12200-14499 97236
SW Ellman Ln 97224
SW Ellson Ln 97223
SW Elm Ln 97221
SW Elm St 97201
SW Elmhurst St 97223
N Elmore Ave 97217
SW Elmwood St 97223
NW Eloise Ln 97229
NE Elrod Dr 97211
NE Elrod Rd 97218
Elrose Ct & St 97224
SE Elsasser Ln 97266
SE Elsewhere Ln 97222
SE Elston Ct 97267
SW Elton Ct 97223
NW Elva Ave 97231
SW Elysium Ave 97219
NW Ember Ln 97229
N Emerald Ave 97217
SE Emerald Dr 97267
N Emerson Ct 97217
NE Emerson Ct 97218
N Emerson Dr 97217
N Emerson St 97217

NE Emerson St
1-4199 97211
4200-7199 97218
8700-9199 97220
NW Emmaus Ln 97231
SE Emmert Ct 97233
SW Empire Ter 97224
N Endicott Ave 97217
NW Energia St 97229
NW Engleman St 97229
English Ct & Ln 97201
SW Enna Ct 97224
N Ensign St 97217
Equestrian Dr & Way 97236
SE Eric St 97222
SW Ericwood Ln 97221
NE Erin Way 97220
SW Ernst Rd 97225
SW Errol St 97223
SW Erste Pl 97223
SW Esau Pl 97223
SW Eschman Way 97223
N Esperanza Ct 97203
SW Esquiline Circus 97219
SW Essex Dr 97223
NW Esson Ct 97229
SE Estella Ave 97267
SW Esther Ct 97223
NW Ethan Dr 97229
SW Eton Ct 97225
SE Eton Ln 97222
SW Eucalyptus Pl 97223
NE Euclid Ave 97213
NE Eugene Ct 97230
NW Eugene Ln 97229
NE Eugene St
8200-12099 97220
12900-15799 97230
15801-15899 97230
SE Eunice St 97222
SW Evan Ct 97223
SW Evans St 97219
SW Evelyn St 97219
SW Evendenw Ave 97219
NW Evensong Pl 97229
NE Everett Ct
10600-10799 97220
15701-15897 97230
15899-18999 97230
NE Everett Ln 97230
NE Everett Pl 97220
NE Everett St
600-3299 97232
4700-8199 97213
8700-11699 97220
14600-19699 97230
NW Everett St
100-2081 97209
2104-2122 97210
2124-2331 97210
2333-2353 97210
SW Everett Ter 97223
SE Evergreen Ave 97222
SE Evergreen Ct 97236
SE Evergreen Dr 97236
SE Evergreen Ln 97267
SW Evergreen Ln 97205
NW Evergreen St 97229
SE Evergreen St
1950-1958 97222
1960-2562 97222
2564-2570 97222
3900-4199 97202
4200-7699 97206
13000-13098 97236
SW Evergreen Ter 97205
SW Excalibur Pl 97219
N Exeter Ave 97203
SE Exeter Dr 97202
NW Express Ave 97210
SE Ezgoin Ln 97236
NE Failing Ct 97230
N Failing St 97227
NE Failing St
1-47 97212
49-4199 97212

4200-8199 97213
9800-10199 97220
13100-14499 97230
NW Fainerri Rd 97231
SE Fair Oaks Dr 97222
SW Fair Ridge Way 97223
SW Faircrest St 97225
SW Fairfax Pl 97225
NW Fairfax Ter 97210
N Fairhaven Ave 97203
SW Fairhaven Ct 97223
SW Fairhaven Dr 97221
SW Fairhaven Ln 97221
SW Fairhaven St 97223
SW Fairhaven Way 97223
SW Fairmoor St 97225
Fairmount Blvd & Ln 97239
Fairoaks Ave, Ln &
Way 97267
N Fairport Pl 97217
Fairvale Ct & Dr 97221
SW Fairview Blvd
2700-3199 97205
4000-4198 97221
4200-4700 97221
4702-4898 97221
SW Fairview Ct 97223
SW Fairview Ln 97223
SW Fairview Pl 97223
SW Fairview Circus 97221
NE Fairway Dr 97211
SW Fairway Dr 97225
SW Falcon St 97219
SW Falcon Rise Dr 97223
NW Falconridge Ln 97229
SE Falentow Ave 97267
SW Falkland Ct 97223
NW Fall Creek Pl 97229
SW Falling Creek Ct 97219
NW Falling Waters Ln 97229
NE Faloma Rd 97211
SW Fanno Creek Ct 97224
SW Fanno Creek Dr
7801-7897 97224
7899-8399 97224
13800-13899 97223
13900-14099 97224
14101-14193 97224
SW Fanno Creek
Loop 97224
SW Fanno Creek Pl 97224
NE Fargo Cir 97230
NE Fargo Ct
11700-12199 97220
15600-16499 97230
NE Fargo Pl 97230
N Fargo St 97227
NE Fargo St
1-699 97212
10200-10298 97220
10300-12199 97220
16200-16499 97230
SE Farr Dr 97267
N Farragut St 97217
NE Farragut St 97211
SE Farthes Ave 97206
SW Fast Pl 97223
N Fathom St 97217
NW Fawnlily Dr 97229
NW Faxon Ter 97229
NE Fazio Way 97211
SW Feiring Ln 97223
N Fenwick Ave 97217
SE Feradia Ave 97202
SE Fern Ave 97206
SW Fern St
2700-2899 97201
13500-14899 97223
SW Fern Hollow Ct 97224
SE Fernridge Ave 97222
SW Fernridge Ter 97223
NW Ferry Rd 97231
NW Fescue Ct 97229
N Fessenden St 97203
Fieldcrest Dr & St 97222
NW Filbert St 97229

SE Filbert St 97222
SW Filmont Ave 97225
SW Findlay Rd 97224
SW Finis Ln 97224
NW Finzer Ct 97229
SE Fir Ave 97206
SW Fir Loop 97223
SW Fir St 97223
SW Fir Grove Ln 97225
SW Fir Lane Ter 97223
SE Fircrest Ct
14100-14199 97236
16700-16899 97267
SE Fircrest St 97236
SE Firenze Ln 97206
NW Fireweed Ter 97229
SW Firlock Way 97223
SW Firtree Dr 97223
SE Firwood St 97222
SW Fischer Rd 97224
N Fiske Ave 97203
Fitzwilliam Ct & Dr 97224
NE Flachela Ave 97230
NE Flanders Ct 97230
NE Flanders St
600-898 97232
900-4199 97232
4200-8099 97213
8700-11699 97220
12400-19899 97230
NW Flanders St
101-297 97209
299-2099 97209
2100-2399 97210
NE Flanders Way 97230
SE Flat Tail Ln 97267
SE Flavel Ave 97206
SE Flavel Ct 97266
SE Flavel Dr
4500-9299 97206
15700-16199 97236
SE Flavel St
1100-4199 97202
4200-8099 97206
8101-8199 97206
8200-8298 97266
8300-11999 97266
12001-12199 97266
12200-13499 97236
NW Fleetwood Dr 97229
NW Fleischner St 97229
N Flint Ave 97227
SE Flora Dr 97222
SE Floral Ct 97267
NE Floral Pl 97232
SE Floral Pl 97214
Florence Ct & Ln 97223
SW Florentine Ave 97223
Florida Ct & St 97219
SE Floss St 97222
NW Flotoma Dr 97229
SE Flower Ave 97267
SW Flower Ct 97221
SW Flower Pl 97221
SW Flower St
-214--236 97239
-317--333 97239
1500-1599 97239
4000-6499 97221
SW Flower Ter 97239
NW Foley Ct 97229
NW Folkenburg Rd 97231
SW Fonner St 97223
SW Fonner Pond Pl 97223
SW Foothill Dr 97225
SW Foran Ter 97224
N Force Ave 97217
SW Ford Street Dr 97201
NW Forest Ln 97229
SW Forest Ln 97223
NW Forest Spring Ln 97229
NW Forest View Way 97229
SW Foresta Ter 97225
SW Foriella Ave 97224
Fortune Ave & Ct 97203
Foss Ave & Ct 97203

SE Foster Pl
11800-12199 97266
13500-13899 97236
SE Foster Rd
4900-5099 97206
5010-5010 97286
5100-8198 97206
5101-8199 97206
8200-12199 97266
12200-16399 97236
SW Fountainwood Pl 97224
SE Foushee Way 97267
Fowler Ave & Ct 97217
N Fox St 97203
NW Fox Hollow Ct 97229
SW Foxfield Ct 97225
SE Foxfire St 97222
SW Foxwood Ct 97224
SW Fradeen Ln 97225
SE Fragrance Ave 97267
NW Francesca Dr 97229
SE Francis Ave 97267
SE Francis St
2600-4199 97202
4200-8199 97206
9200-10700 97266
10702-10798 97266
13100-17399 97236
NW Franklin Ct 97210
SE Franklin Ct 97236
SE Franklin St
601-697 97202
699-4199 97202
4200-7699 97206
7701-7899 97206
8200-8399 97266
8401-11099 97266
15100-15598 97236
15600-16999 97236
SW Franklin St 97223
SW Fraser Ave 97225
NW Frazier Ct 97229
SW Freeman Ct 97219
SE Freeman Rd 97222
SW Freeman St 97219
SE Freeman Way 97222
NE Fremont Ct
11200-11699 97220
13500-14999 97230
NE Fremont Dr 97220
N Fremont St 97227
NE Fremont St
1-4100 97212
4102-4198 97212
4200-8199 97213
8200-12199 97220
12300-16499 97230
NW French Ln 97229
Frewing Ct & St 97223
NW Front Ave
2000-2500 97209
2502-2598 97209
2601-2697 97210
2699-6600 97210
6602-7298 97210
10801-10897 97231
10899-11199 97231
SW Fuji Ct 97224
SE Fuller Rd 97222
Fullner Ct & Pl 97229
Fulton Park Blvd & Pl 97219
SE Furat Ct 97222
SE Furnberg St 97222
SW Gaarde St
10800-12099 97224
12500-12699 97223
SW Gable Pkwy
6401-6499 97221
6500-6598 97225
6600-7299 97225
SW Gable Park Rd 97225
SE Gaibler Ln 97236
SW Gaines Ct 97221
SW Gaines St 97239
SE Gaitgill Ct 97267
SW Gala Ct 97223
SW Gale Ave 97239

SW Galeburn St 97219
NW Gales Ridge Ln 97229
NW Galice Ln 97229
SW Gallin Ct 97223
SW Gallo Ave 97223
N Gammans Pl 97217
NW Gannet Ter 97229
N Gantenbein Ave
1900-4099 97227
4100-11099 97217
Garden Ln & Pl 97223
SW Garden Home Rd
3800-6499 97219
6500-9499 97223
SW Garden Park Pl 97223
Garden View Ave & Pl 97225
SW Gardner Ct 97224
NE Garfield Ave
3500-3598 97212
3600-4099 97212
4100-7099 97211
NW Gargany St 97229
Garland Ct, Ln & Way 97267
SE Garnet Way 97267
SE Garrett Cir 97222
SW Garrett Ct 97223
SE Garrett Dr 97222
SW Garrett St 97223
SE Gary Ln 97267
SW Gaston Ave 97239
NW Gatto Ct 97229
N Gay Ave 97217
SE Gayle Ct 97267
SW Gayle Ln 97225
SW Gearin Ct 97223
SW Genesis Loop 97223
N Geneva Ave 97203
SW Geneva St 97223
Gentle Woods Ct & Dr 97224
SW Georgian Pl 97201
SW Gerald Ave 97201
NW Gerber Ter 97229
NW Germantown Rd 97231
NW Gerritz Ter 97229
NE Gertz Cir 97211
NE Gertz Ct 97211
N Gertz Rd 97217
NE Gertz Rd 97211
SW Gibbs St 97239
SE Gideon St 97202
N Gilbert Ave 97203
NW Gilbert Ln 97229
N Gilbert Pl 97203
NE Gile Ter 97212
NE Gilham Ave 97213
SE Gilham Ave 97215
SE Gill St 97267
SW Gillcrest Ct 97221
NW Gilliam Ln 97229
NW Gillihan Rd 97231
SE Ginny Ln 97267
SE Gino Ln 97222
N Girard St 97203
SW Glacier Lily Cir 97223
SE Gladstone Ct
9900-9998 97266
13000-13199 97236
SE Gladstone Dr 97236
SE Gladstone St
2201-2297 97202
2299-4199 97202
4200-8199 97206
9200-12099 97266
12200-15399 97236
NE Glass Plant Rd 97220
SW Glastonbury Ln 97224
SW Glaze Ct 97223
SW Glen Rd 97219
SE Glen Echo Ave 97267
SE Glencoe Rd 97222
SW Glencreek Ct 97223
NE Glendoveer Ct 97230
NW Glendoveer Dr 97231
NW Gleneagles Pl 97229
SW Glenhaven St 97225
NE Glenn Widing Dr 97220

NW Glenridge Dr ... 97229
SW Glenview Ave ... 97225
SW Glenwood Ct ... 97223
SE Glenwood St
1400-4199 ... 97202
4200-8199 ... 97206
8300-9699 ... 97266
13000-13599 ... 97236
NE Glisan St
408-898 ... 97232
900-4199 ... 97232
4200-8199 ... 97213
8200-12199 ... 97220
12200-20199 ... 97230
NW Glisan St
201-307 ... 97209
309-2067 ... 97209
2069-2075 ... 97209
2100-2122 ... 97210
2124-2376 ... 97210
2378-2386 ... 97210
NW Gloaming Ln ... 97229
N Gloucester Ave ... 97203
SW Godwin Ct ... 97223
N Going Ct ... 97217
NE Going Pl ... 97220
N Going St ... 97217
NE Going St
1-4199 ... 97211
4200-8199 ... 97218
8200-9199 ... 97220
NW Goldenweed Dr ... 97229
NE Golf Court Rd ... 97211
SW Golf Creek Dr ... 97225
SW Gonzaga St ... 97223
SE Gordon Ct ... 97267
NW Gordon St ... 97210
SE Gordon St ... 97267
SW Gordona Ct ... 97223
SW Gordy Pl ... 97223
SW Grace Ln ... 97225
NW Graf St ... 97229
NE Graham Pl ... 97213
N Graham St ... 97227
NE Graham St
1-699 ... 97212
14800-15199 ... 97230
NE Grand Ave
1-13 ... 97232
15-1699 ... 97232
1800-4099 ... 97212
4100-4198 ... 97211
4200-7099 ... 97211
SE Grand Ave
3-2399 ... 97214
2539-2597 ... 97202
2599-8099 ... 97202
SE Grandview Ct ... 97267
SW Grandview Ln ... 97224
SW Grant Ave ... 97223
SE Grant Ct
3400-4099 ... 97214
8900-11199 ... 97216
13600-14999 ... 97233
SW Grant Ct ... 97223
SE Grant Ln ... 97233
SE Grant St
600-602 ... 97214
604-4199 ... 97214
4800-7999 ... 97215
9300-12199 ... 97216
13000-18999 ... 97233
SW Grant St ... 97201
SW Graven St ... 97224
N Gravenstein Ave ... 97217
SW Gravenstein Ln ... 97224
N Greeley Ave
3000-3098 ... 97227
3100-3199 ... 97227
4700-4998 ... 97217
5000-7499 ... 97217
SW Green Ave ... 97205
SE Green Ct ... 97267
NW Green Ln ... 97231
NE Green Tee Ct ... 97230
SW Green Valley Ter ... 97225
NW Green View Ln ... 97229
SE Green Vista Dr ... 97222
NW Greenbriar Ter ... 97210
SW Greenburg Rd ... 97223
SW Greenfield Dr
12800-13299 ... 97223
14200-15799 ... 97224
SW Greenhills Way ... 97221
SW Greenhouse Ln ... 97225
SW Greening Ln ... 97224
SW Greenland Dr ... 97224
SW Greenleaf Ct
4100-4199 ... 97221
15600-15699 ... 97224
SW Greenleaf Dr ... 97221
NW Greenleaf Rd ... 97229
SW Greenleaf Ter ... 97224
SW Greenridge Pl ... 97224
SW Greens Way ... 97224
SW Greens Way Ct ... 97224
SW Greenspark Ln ... 97224
SW Greensward Ln ... 97224
Greenview Ave & Dr ... 97267
SW Greenway Ave ... 97201
N Greenwich Ave ... 97217
SW Greenwich Dr ... 97225
NW Greenwood Dr ... 97229
SW Greenwood Dr ... 97223
SW Greenwood Rd ... 97219
SW Grelare ... 97258
NE Grelarre St ... 97220
SW Grenwolde Pl ... 97201
SW Griffin Dr ... 97223
SW Grimson Ct ... 97224
SE Grogan Ave ... 97222
Grove Ct & Loop ... 97222
SW Grover Ct ... 97221
SW Grover St
-18--320 ... 97239
127-897 ... 97239
899-999 ... 97239
1001-1299 ... 97239
3500-3800 ... 97221
3802-3898 ... 97221
NW Guam St ... 97210
SE Guido Bocci Dr ... 97222
Guilford Ct & Dr ... 97222
SW Gunther Ln ... 97219
NW Hackney Dr ... 97229
SE Hager Ln ... 97267
SE Haig Dr ... 97236
SE Haig St
600-3799 ... 97202
4500-6099 ... 97206
16100-16999 ... 97236
N Haight Ave
3500-4099 ... 97227
4100-11099 ... 97217
SW Haines St ... 97219
SW Halcyon Ter ... 97223
SE Hale St ... 97222
SW Hall Blvd
8725-8745 ... 97223
8747-13999 ... 97223
14010-14072 ... 97224
14074-15999 ... 97224
SW Hall St
401-497 ... 97201
499-1511 ... 97201
1513-14241 ... 97201
1402-1-1402-1 ... 97201
1406-1-1406-1 ... 97201
1408-1-1408-1 ... 97201
1410-1-1410-1 ... 97201
1412-1-1412-1 ... 97201
1414-1-1414-1 ... 97201
1416-1-1416-1 ... 97201
1418-1-1418-1 ... 97201
1420-1-1420-1 ... 97201
1422-1-1422-1 ... 97201
1424-1-1424-1 ... 97201
N Halleck St ... 97217
SW Hallmark Ter ... 97223
NE Halsey St
200-4099 ... 97232
4101-4199 ... 97232
4200-8099 ... 97213
8200-12199 ... 97220
12200-12298 ... 97230
12300-19999 ... 97230
NE Hamblet St ... 97212
NW Hamel Dr ... 97229
SW Hamilton Ct
-455--455 ... 97239
-470--470 ... 97239
15-19 ... 97239
21-3435 ... 97239
3500-4818 ... 97221
4820-4838 ... 97221
6700-6799 ... 97225
SW Hamilton St
-14--225 ... 97239
-227--239 ... 97239
-4--12 ... 97239
100-102 ... 97239
104-3440 ... 97239
3601-3697 ... 97221
3699-6499 ... 97221
6500-6599 ... 97225
6601-6625 ... 97225
SW Hamilton Ter ... 97239
SW Hamilton Way
6100-6499 ... 97221
6500-6599 ... 97225
Hamlet Ct & St ... 97224
N Hamlin Ave ... 97217
SE Hampshire Ln ... 97267
SW Hampshire St ... 97205
SW Hampshire Ter ... 97224
SW Hampton Ct ... 97223
NW Hampton Ln ... 97229
SW Hampton St ... 97223
NE Hancock Ct
6600-6699 ... 97213
11200-11299 ... 97220
15200-16899 ... 97230
SW Hancock Ct ... 97223
NE Hancock Dr ... 97220
N Hancock St ... 97227
NE Hancock St
1-4100 ... 97212
4102-4198 ... 97212
4200-6999 ... 97213
8200-12199 ... 97220
12600-16199 ... 97230
16201-17299 ... 97230
SE Hanna Harvester Dr ... 97222
SE Hannah Ln ... 97266
SW Hansen Ln ... 97224
N Hantando Ave ... 97227
SE Hanwood Ln ... 97267
NW Harbor Blvd ... 97231
NW Harbor Ln ... 97229
SW Harbor Pl ... 97201
SW Harbor Way ... 97201
N Harborgate St ... 97203
NW Harborton Dr ... 97231
N Harbour Dr ... 97217
SW Harcourt Ter ... 97224
N Harding Ave ... 97227
NW Harding Ct ... 97229
NW Hardy Ave ... 97231
SE Harlene St ... 97222
SE Harlow St ... 97222
SE Harmon Ct ... 97267
Harmony Dr & Rd ... 97222
SE Harney Ct
3300-3499 ... 97222
9200-9499 ... 97266
SE Harney Dr ... 97206
SE Harney St
100-598 ... 97202
600-2899 ... 97202
4200-8199 ... 97206
8200-8899 ... 97266
14100-14399 ... 97236
SE Harold Ave ... 97267
SE Harold Ct
3300-3398 ... 97202
3400-3599 ... 97202
4000-4199 ... 97267
SE Harold St
1500-4099 ... 97202
4101-4199 ... 97202
4200-8199 ... 97206
9200-12199 ... 97266
12200-14299 ... 97236
SE Harrison Ct
7100-7499 ... 97215
13500-17499 ... 97233
SE Harrison St
604-608 ... 97214
610-4199 ... 97214
4200-7999 ... 97215
8200-11599 ... 97216
13000-18099 ... 97233
SW Harrison St ... 97201
SW Hart St ... 97223
SE Hartcliffe Ct ... 97267
NW Hartford St ... 97229
N Hartman St ... 97203
SE Hartnell Ave ... 97267
NW Hartung Ct ... 97229
NW Hartwell Pl ... 97229
N Harvard St ... 97203
Harvest Ln & St ... 97229
NW Harvest Hill Dr ... 97229
SE Harvey St ... 97222
NW Haskell Ct ... 97229
NE Hassalo Ct ... 97230
N Hassalo St ... 97227
NE Hassalo St
300-4199 ... 97232
4200-7799 ... 97213
8200-10899 ... 97220
12300-19599 ... 97230
NW Hataya Ct ... 97229
SW Hathaway Ter ... 97223
N Haven Ave ... 97203
SE Haven Ln ... 97266
SW Havencrest St ... 97225
SE Hawk Ct ... 97236
NW Hawk Pl ... 97229
SW Hawk Ridge Rd ... 97224
NW Hawkins Blvd ... 97229
SW Hawks Beard St ... 97223
SE Hawthorne Blvd
5048-B-5048-B ... 97215
101-397 ... 97214
399-4199 ... 97214
4200-8199 ... 97215
8200-9399 ... 97216
SE Hawthorne Ct ... 97233
SW Hawthorne Ln ... 97225
SE Hawthorne St
11400-11699 ... 97216
15900-16099 ... 97233
SW Hawthorne Ter ... 97201
N Hayden Bay Dr ... 97217
N Hayden Island Dr ... 97217
N Hayden Meadows Dr ... 97217
SE Hayward Way ... 97267
SE Haze Ct ... 97267
SE Hazel Ave ... 97206
SE Hazel Pl ... 97222
SE Hazel St
1700-1899 ... 97214
3800-3999 ... 97222
SW Hazel Hill Dr ... 97224
Hazelcrest Ter & Way ... 97224
NE Hazelfern Pl
400-4199 ... 97232
4200-4399 ... 97213
SW Hazelfern Rd ... 97224
SW Hazeltine Ln ... 97224
NW Hazeltine St ... 97229
SW Hazeltree Ter ... 97224
SW Hazelvern Way ... 97223
SW Hazelwood Loop ... 97223
SE Heart Pl ... 97267
SW Hearthside Ct ... 97223
SE Heather Ct ... 97222
SW Heather Ct ... 97223
SW Heather Ln ... 97201
SE Heather Faye Way ... 97267
NW Heathman Ln ... 97229
NW Heckman Ln ... 97229
SE Hector St ... 97222
SW Hedlund Ave ... 97219
SW Heidi Ct ... 97224
SE Heights Ct ... 97267
NW Helen Ln ... 97229
SE Helena St ... 97222
SE Hemlock Ave ... 97214
SE Hemlock St ... 97222
SW Hemlock St ... 97223
SE Henderson Ct ... 97206
SE Henderson Dr ... 97266
SE Henderson St
3600-4199 ... 97202
4200-8099 ... 97206
8101-8199 ... 97206
8700-11200 ... 97266
11202-11398 ... 97266
12200-12499 ... 97236
SE Henderson Way ... 97236
N Hendricks St ... 97203
NW Henninger Ln ... 97229
NW Henry Ct ... 97229
SE Henry Ct ... 97236
SE Henry Pl ... 97206
SE Henry St
1200-4099 ... 97202
4301-4597 ... 97206
4599-8099 ... 97206
8101-8199 ... 97206
9200-10899 ... 97266
13800-13999 ... 97236
NW Henson Ct ... 97229
N Heppner Ave ... 97203
SW Herb Way ... 97223
N Hereford Ave ... 97203
NW Hermosa Blvd ... 97210
SW Hermoso Way ... 97223
SE Heron Glen Way ... 97267
NW Herrin Ct ... 97229
SW Hessler Dr ... 97239
SW Hewett Blvd ... 97221
SE Hi Lite Dr ... 97267
NW Hibbard Dr ... 97229
SW Hickman Ln ... 97223
SE Hickory Ct ... 97267
SE Hickory St ... 97214
SW Hicrest Ave ... 97225
SW Hidden Creek Pl ... 97223
SW High St ... 97201
SE High Meadow Loop ... 97236
SW High Tor Dr ... 97224
NW Highcroft Ct ... 97229
NW Highland Ct ... 97229
SW Highland Ct ... 97224
SW Highland Dr ... 97224
SW Highland Pkwy ... 97221
SW Highland Rd ... 97221
N Highland St ... 97217
NE Highland St ... 97211
NW Hildago Ln ... 97229
SW Hilen Ct ... 97219
SW Hill Ct ... 97223
SE Hill Rd ... 97267
SE Hill St ... 97222
SW Hill St ... 97223
NE Hill Way ... 97220
SE Hill Terrace Ct ... 97267
SW Hill View St ... 97224
NW Hillcourt Ln ... 97229
Hillcrest Dr & Pl ... 97201
SW Hillcroft Ave ... 97225
SW Hilldale Ave ... 97225
NW Hiller Ln ... 97229
SE Hillgrove Ct ... 97267
SW Hillsboro St ... 97239
SW Hillsdale Ave ... 97239
SW Hillshire Dr ... 97223
SE Hillside Ct ... 97222
SE Hillside Dr ... 97267
SW Hillside Dr ... 97221
SE Hillside Ln ... 97267
SW Hillside Ter ... 97223
NW Hilltop Dr ... 97210
SW Hilltop Ln ... 97221
SW Hillview Ct ... 97223
SW Hillview St ... 97223
SW Hillview Ter ... 97225
Hillwood Ave & Cir ... 97267
NW Hilton Head Ter ... 97229
SW Himes St ... 97239
SW Hindon Ct ... 97223
N Hodge Ave ... 97203
SW Hoffman Ave ... 97201
NW Hogan St ... 97229
NW Hoge Ave ... 97231
NW Holbrook Ct ... 97229
NW Holcomb Dr ... 97229
SE Holgate Blvd
1201-1297 ... 97202
1299-4199 ... 97202
4200-7999 ... 97206
8001-8199 ... 97206
8200-12199 ... 97266
12200-14199 ... 97236
NE Holladay Ct ... 97230
NE Holladay Pl ... 97230
NE Holladay St
1-3399 ... 97232
6000-8199 ... 97213
8200-12099 ... 97220
12600-12698 ... 97230
12700-19999 ... 97230
NE Holland Ct ... 97211
N Holland St ... 97217
NE Holland St ... 97211
SW Hollow Ln ... 97223
NW Holloway Dr ... 97229
SE Holly Ave ... 97222
SE Holly Ct ... 97267
SW Holly Ln ... 97223
SE Holly St ... 97214
NW Holly Springs Ln ... 97229
NE Hollyrood Ct ... 97212
SE Hollywood Ave ... 97222
NE Holman Pl ... 97218
N Holman St ... 97217
NE Holman St
1-4199 ... 97211
4200-8199 ... 97218
10600-11499 ... 97220
N Holmes Ave ... 97217
SW Homar Ave ... 97201
SE Home Ave ... 97222
SW Home St ... 97224
SW Homestead Dr ... 97239
SW Homewood St ... 97225
SW Hood Ave
3101-5497 ... 97239
5499-6299 ... 97239
7500-10699 ... 97219
SE Hood Ct ... 97267
SE Hood St ... 97267
SW Hoodview Dr ... 97224
SW Hoodvista Ln ... 97224
SW Hooker St ... 97201
SW Hoops Ct ... 97223
NW Hopedale Ct ... 97229
N Houghton St
2700-3699 ... 97217
4200-6399 ... 97203
SW Howard Dr ... 97223
SE Howard St ... 97267
SW Howards Way ... 97201
SW Howatt St ... 97225
Howe Ln & St ... 97222
NW Howell Park Rd ... 97231
NE Hoyt Ct ... 97230
NE Hoyt St
2000-2060 ... 97232
2062-4199 ... 97232
4200-7599 ... 97213
9000-10799 ... 97220
12200-20099 ... 97230
NW Hoyt St
300-398 ... 97209
400-700 ... 97209
701-799 ... 97208
702-1898 ... 97209
715-715 ... 97228
901-2067 ... 97209
2100-2399 ... 97210
8901-8999 ... 97229
NE Hoyt Ter ... 97230
Huber Ct & St ... 97219
SW Huddleson St ... 97219
N Hudson St ... 97203
SE Hugh Ave ... 97267
Hull Ave & Ct ... 97267
SE Hult St ... 97266
N Humboldt St ... 97217
NE Humboldt St
900-1399 ... 97211
8200-9099 ... 97220
9101-9199 ... 97220
Hume Ct & St ... 97219
Humphrey Blvd & Ct ... 97221
Humphrey Park Crst & Rd ... 97221
N Hunt St
4252A-4252C ... 97203
701-2397 ... 97217
2399-3599 ... 97217
4101-4197 ... 97203
4199-5099 ... 97203
SW Hunt Club Dr ... 97223
SW Hunt Club Ln ... 97223
SW Hunt Club Pl ... 97219
SW Hunt Club Rd ... 97223
SE Hunter Ct ... 97222
SW Huntington Ave
900-2299 ... 97225
10800-10999 ... 97223
Huntwood Ct & Pl ... 97224
SW Hunziker St ... 97223
N Huron Ave ... 97203
N Hurst Ave ... 97203
NW Huserik Dr ... 97229
SE Hymie Way ... 97267
N Ida Ave ... 97203
SW Idaho Dr ... 97221
SW Idaho St
-205--608 ... 97239
-610--612 ... 97239
1900-3399 ... 97239
5000-6099 ... 97221
SW Idaho Ter ... 97221
NW Idanha St ... 97229
NW Illahe St ... 97229
SW Illinois St
2700-2798 ... 97239
2800-3499 ... 97239
3500-5999 ... 97221
N Image Canoe Ave ... 97217
NW Imnaha Ct ... 97229
NE Imperial Ave ... 97232
SW Imperial Ave ... 97224
SE Imperial Ct ... 97222
SW Imperial Ct ... 97225
SW Imperial Dr ... 97225
NW Imperial Ter ... 97210
Ina Ave & Pl ... 97267
NW Industrial St ... 97210
SW Inez St ... 97224
Inglewood Ct, Pl & St ... 97225
SE Inglis Ct ... 97267
NW Innisbrook Pl ... 97229
SE Insley Ct ... 97202
SE Insley Pl ... 97266
SE Insley St
1600-4199 ... 97202
4200-7699 ... 97206
8225-8397 ... 97266
8399-11799 ... 97266
14100-14199 ... 97236
SW Intermark St ... 97225
SE International Way ... 97222
N Interstate Ave
1500-2098 ... 97227
2100-4099 ... 97227
4200-8499 ... 97217
N Interstate Pl ... 97217
SW Inverness Ct ... 97219
NE Inverness Dr ... 97220
SW Iowa St
-103--435 ... 97239
-21--101 ... 97239
1800-3199 ... 97239
3500-5100 ... 97221
5102-5498 ... 97221
SE Irina Ct ... 97206
SE Irina Rd ... 97267

SE Irina Way 97267
SE Iris Ct 97267
SE Iris St 97267
N Iris Way 97203
SW Iron Mountain
Blvd 97219
NW Ironwood Ln 97229
SW Ironwood Loop 97223
NE Irving Ct 97230
NE Irving St
1400-3499 97232
4400-7699 97213
9000-9899 97220
12700-17499 97230
NW Irving St
501-597 97209
599-2099 97209
2100-2399 97210
2401-2499 97210
8600-8698 97229
8700-8800 97229
8802-8898 97229
SE Isabella Ct 97266
N Island Cove Ln 97217
NW Ithaca Ct 97229
SW Ivana Ct 97223
N Ivanhoe St
6900-8499 97203
8420-8420 97231
8420-8420 97283
8500-10098 97203
8501-10099 97203
SE Ivon 97266
SE Ivon Ct 97236
SE Ivon St
301-397 97202
399-4199 97202
4200-6699 97206
16800-16999 97236
SW Ivy Ln 97225
N Ivy St 97227
NE Ivy St 97212
NW Ivybridge St 97229
NW Jack Ln 97229
SE Jack Rd 97222
SE Jack St 97222
SW Jackie Ct 97224
NW Jackson Ln 97229
SE Jackson St 97222
SW Jackson St 97201
SW Jacob Ct 97224
SW Jade Ave 97225
SE Jade Ct 97267
SE Jade High 97267
SW James Ct 97223
N James St 97203
SW James St 97223
NW James Arthur Ct 97229
SW Jamieson Rd 97225
SW Jan Tree Ct 97219
Jantzen Ave & Dr 97217
Jantzen Beach Ave &
Ctr 97217
SW Janzen Ct 97224
N Jarrett St 97217
NE Jarrett St
1-3299 97211
4200-5199 97218
13200-14099 97230
NW Jasmine Ln 97229
SE Jay St 97267
SE Jazmin Ln 97267
NW Jean Ln 97229
NE Jeanette Ct 97230
SW Jefferson Ave 97223
SE Jefferson Ct 97267
SE Jefferson St
1801-1997 97222
1999-4499 97222
7800-7999 97267
SW Jefferson St
1-2199 97201
2201-2255 97201
5500-5699 97221
SW Jenna Ct 97223
NW Jenne Ave 97229
SE Jenne Ln 97236

SE Jenne Rd 97236
NW Jennifer Pl 97229
SE Jennings Ave 97267
SE Jennings Crest Ln 97267
SW Jenshire Ln 97223
Jerald Ct & Way 97221
Jericho Ct & Rd 97229
N Jersey St 97203
NW Jessamine Way 97229
SE Jesse Ln 97266
SE Jessica Erin Ln 97267
NE Jessup Ct 97218
N Jessup St 97217
NE Jessup St
1-3999 97211
5200-5799 97218
NW Jewell Ln 97229
NE Jewell St 97230
SE Jewett Dr 97267
SE Jo Ct 97267
SE Jobes Ct 97222
SW Joe Ct 97223
SW Joelle Ct 97223
N John Ave 97203
SW John Ct 97223
SW Johnson Ct 97223
NW Johnson Rd 97231
SE Johnson Rd
13300-13700 97222
13702-13798 97222
14000-15199 97267
NW Johnson St
1000-1098 97209
1100-2099 97209
2100-2499 97210
8500-8599 97229
SW Johnson St 97223
SE Johnson Creek Blvd
3200-5399 97222
5401-5499 97222
5500-8199 97206
SE Johnston Dr 97236
N Johnswood Dr 97203
SE Jola Ln 97222
NW Jolie Pl 97229
SW Jonagold Ter 97224
SW Jonathan Ct 97219
NW Jonathon Pl 97229
NE Jonesmore St 97213
N Jordan Ave 97203
NW Jordan Ln 97229
SE Jordan St 97222
SW Jordan Way 97224
SW Jordy Ct 97224
NW Joseph Ct 97229
SW Joshua St 97219
NW Joss Ave 97229
NW Joy Ave 97229
SW Jubilee Ct 97224
SW Julia Ct 97221
SW Julia Pl 97224
SW Julia St
-233--233 97239
4501-4605 97221
4607-4900 97221
4902-4998 97221
SE Juliano Ct 97236
SE Julie Ln 97267
SE Julie Pl 97236
SW Juliet Ter 97224
N Juneau St
3800-3999 97217
4000-4299 97203
NE Junior St 97211
SE Juniper Dr 97267
SE Juniper St 97222
SE Jupiter Ct 97267
NW Justus Ln 97229
Kable Ln & St 97224
Kahneeta Ct & Dr 97229
NW Kaiser Rd
3700-3798 97229
3800-7899 97229
8000-10099 97231
NW Kalama St 97229
SW Kalay Ct 97223

N Kalmar St 97203
SW Kameron Way 97223
SW Kanan Dr 97221
SW Kanan St
1800-2200 97239
2202-2498 97239
5300-5599 97221
SW Karen St 97223
NW Karey Ct 97229
SW Kari Ln 97219
SW Karla Ct 97239
SW Karley Ct 97223
SW Karol Ct 97223
SE Karry Ave 97267
Kaslin Ct & Way 97267
SW Katherine Ln 97225
SW Katherine St 97223
NW Kathleen Dr 97229
SE Kathryn Ct 97222
SE Katie Ct 97267
SE Kay St 97267
SE Kayla Ct 97222
NW Kaylee St 97229
SE Keanu Ct 97267
NW Kearney St
900-2099 97209
2100-2499 97210
8700-12499 97229
NW Keenan Pl 97229
SW Keerins Ct 97223
NW Keeton Park Ln 97229
SE Kehrli Dr 97222
SE Kellogg Ave 97267
SE Kellogg Ct 97267
N Kellogg St 97203
SE Kellogg Creek Dr 97222
SW Kelly Ave
3204A-3204C 97239
2700-2800 97201
2802-2898 97201
3200-3298 97239
3300-6299 97239
7400-9699 97219
NW Kelly Cir 97229
SE Kelly Ct 97236
SW Kelly Ln 97223
SE Kelly St
1155-2597 97202
2599-4099 97202
4101-4199 97202
4500-6899 97206
8200-12199 97266
12200-18099 97236
Kelsi Ct & Ter 97223
SW Kelso Ct 97224
SE Kelvin St 97222
NW Kenai Ct 97229
SE Kendall Ct 97236
NW Kennedy Ct 97229
SE Kennedy Ct 97267
SE Kens Ct 97267
SW Kensington Rd 97223
SW Kent Ct 97224
SW Kent Pl 97224
SE Kent St 97222
SW Kent St 97224
SW Kenton Dr 97224
NW Kenzer Ct 97229
NW Kenzie Ln 97229
N Kerby Ave
2001-2297 97227
2299-4099 97227
4100-8599 97217
8601-10099 97217
SW Keri Ct 97224
SE Kern Ct 97267
SW Kerr Ct 97224
SW Kessler Ln 97224
SE Key Ct 97267
SE Keystone Dr 97267
N Killingsworth Ct 97217
NE Killingsworth Ct
600-816 97211
818-858 97211
6200-6499 97218
N Killingsworth St 97217

NE Killingsworth St
1-4199 97211
4200-8199 97218
8300-10999 97220
N Kilpatrick St
900-998 97217
1000-3999 97217
4000-4499 97203
NE Kilpatrick St 97211
N Kimball Ave 97203
SW Kimberly Dr 97224
NW Kimble Ct 97229
NW King Ave 97210
SW King Ave 97205
NW King Rd 97231
SE King Rd 97222
SW King Arthur St 97224
SW King Charles Ave 97224
SE King George Ct 97267
SW King George Dr 97224
SW King Henry Pl 97224
SW King James Pl 97224
SW King Lear Way 97224
SW King Richard Dr 97224
SW Kingfisher Way 97224
SW Kings Ct 97205
SE Kingsley Rd 97267
SE Kingsridge Ct 97267
SE Kingston Ave 97267
SW Kingston Ave 97205
SW Kingston Pl 97223
SW Kingsview Ct 97223
Kiska Ct & St 97217
NW Kiwanda Dr 97229
NE Klickitat Ct 97230
NE Klickitat St
1401-1597 97212
1599-4100 97212
4102-4198 97212
4200-8199 97213
8300-11799 97220
15000-16499 97230
Klipsan Ct & Ln 97223
SE Knapp Cir 97266
SE Knapp Ct 97236
SE Knapp Dr 97236
SE Knapp Ln 97266
SE Knapp St
1300-4199 97202
4200-6299 97206
8300-11299 97266
12300-12999 97236
SE Knight St
1301-1397 97202
1399-3900 97202
3902-3998 97202
4200-8199 97206
9600-10799 97266
13400-14299 97236
SW Knightsbridge Dr 97219
NW Knightsview Ln 97229
SE Knoll Ct 97267
SW Knoll Dr 97223
SE Knoll Ridge Ter 97267
SW Knollcrest Dr 97225
NW Knollview Dr 97229
NE Knott Ct 97230
N Knott St 97227
NE Knott St
1-97 97212
99-4199 97212
4200-4299 97213
8400-12199 97220
12300-15799 97230
N Knowles Ave 97217
NW Koa Ct 97229
NW Kollenborn Ln 97229
SW Koski Dr 97223
SW Kostel Ln 97224
SW Koven Ct 97224
Kraft Loop & Pl 97223
SW Kreick Pl 97224
SE Krieger Ln 97266
NW Krislynn Ter 97229
SE Kristin Ct 97267
SW Kroese Loop 97224
NW Kronan Ct 97210

SE Kronberg Ave 97267
SW Kruse Ridge Dr 97219
SE Kuehls Way 97267
Kuehn Ct & Rd 97222
NW Kyla Ln 97229
NW Kyle Pl 97229
SE La Bonita Way 97267
NW La Cassel Crest
Ln 97229
SE La Crescenta Way 97267
SE La Cresta Dr 97222
SE La Jolla St 97222
SW La Mancha Ct 97224
SE La Marquita Way 97267
SE La Mesa Way 97267
SE La Paz St 97267
SE La Rue Ct 97267
SW La View Dr 97219
SW Labbe Ave 97221
SE Label Ln 97206
SW Laber Ct 97221
SW Laber Rd
6301-6397 97221
6399-6499 97221
6800-6898 97225
6900-7100 97225
7102-7198 97225
SE Lacour Ct 97267
SE Ladd Ave 97214
SE Ladd Ct 97267
NE Laddington Ct
201-397 97232
399-4199 97232
4200-4299 97213
SW Lady Apple Ln 97224
SW Lady Marion Dr 97224
SE Lafayette Ct 97202
SE Lafayette St
1200-2199 97202
4900-8199 97206
8300-8999 97266
16400-16999 97236
N Lagoon Ave 97217
NW Laidlaw Rd 97229
SE Lake Rd
2000-2298 97222
2300-6799 97222
6900-8000 97267
8002-8198 97267
SW Lake St 97223
NW Lakeshore Ct 97229
SE Lakeside Dr 97222
SW Lakeside Dr 97224
NW Lakeview Dr 97229
SW Lakeview Ter 97223
SW Lakewood Ct 97223
SE Lakewood Dr 97222
NW Lambert St 97229
SE Lambert St
700-4199 97202
4200-8199 97206
8200-8899 97266
NW Lamonde Ter 97229
SE Lamphier St 97222
SE Lamplighter Ave 97222
N Lancaster Ave 97217
SW Lancaster Rd 97219
SW Lancaster St 97219
SW Lancelot Ln 97219
Landau Pl & St 97223
NW Landing Dr 97229
SW Landing Dr 97239
SW Landing Sq 97239
SW Landmark Ln 97224
SW Lane Ct 97221
SW Lane St 97239
SW Lanewood St 97225
NW Langley Ct 97229
SW Langtree St 97224
NW Langworthy Ter 97229
SW Lanier Ln 97224
NW Lansbrook Ter 97229
SW Lansdowne Ln 97223
Lapine St & Way 97229
SW Lara St 97223
SW Laralest St 97205

SE Larch Ave 97214
SW Larch St 97223
NW Lariat Ct 97229
SE Lark Ave 97267
SE Lark St 97222
NW Lark Meadow Ter 97229
SE Larlerid St 97216
N Larrabee Ave 97227
NW Larry Ct 97229
NW Larson Rd 97231
NE Las Brisas Ct 97230
SE Laugardia Way 97267
Laura Ave & St 97222
SE Laurel Ln 97267
SE Laurel St
2440-2472 97267
2474-2899 97267
5700-6099 97222
SW Laurel St
1600-2199 97201
7500-8099 97225
8101-8299 97225
SW Laurel Glen Ct 97224
Laurel Leaf Ln & Ter 97225
NE Laurelhurst Pl
1-4199 97232
4200-4399 97213
SE Laurelhurst Pl 97214
SW Laurelwood Ave 97225
SW Laurelwood Ct 97225
SE Laurelwood Dr 97267
SW Lauren Ln 97223
SE Laurie Ave
13000-13799 97222
13900-15300 97267
15302-15398 97267
SE Laurie Ct 97267
SE Laurie Pl 97222
NW Laurinda Ct 97229
Laurmont Ct & Dr 97223
SE Lava Dr 97222
SE Lavender St 97214
NE Lawrence Ave 97232
NW Le Mans Ct 97229
N Leadbetter Rd 97203
SW Leah Ct 97219
SW Leah Ter 97224
NW Leahy Rd 97229
SW Leahy Rd 97225
N Leavitt Ave 97203
SE Lee Ave 97267
SE Lee Ln 97233
NW Lee St 97229
SW Lee St 97221
SE Lee Anna Way 97236
SW Leeding Ln 97223
SW Legacy Oak Way 97223
SW Lehman St 97223
SE Lei Ct 97267
NW Leighbrook Rd 97229
SW Leiser Ln 97224
SE Lena Ave 97222
SE Lennon Ct 97236
NW Lennox Ln 97231
NE Lenore St 97211
SE Leona Ln 97267
N Leonard St 97203
SE Leone Ln 97222
SW Leslie Ct 97224
SW Leslie St 97223
Lesser Rd & Way 97219
NE Levee Rd 97211
N Leverman St 97217
N Lewis Ave 97227
NW Lewis Ln 97229
SW Lewis Ln 97223
SE Lexington Ct 97206
SE Lexington St
700-4199 97202
4200-7499 97206
10100-12199 97266
NW Lianna Way 97229
NE Liberty Ct 97211
Liberty Ctr 97232
N Liberty St 97217
NE Liberty St 97211

NE Liberty Ter 97211
Licyntra Ct & Ln 97222
SW Liden Dr 97223
SE Liebe Ct 97266
SE Liebe St
3700-4199 97202
4200-5899 97206
8200-12199 97266
NW Lightning Ridge
Dr 97229
NE Lija Loop 97211
NW Lilac Ct 97231
SE Lilac Dr 97267
NW Lilium Dr 97229
SE Lillian Ave 97267
SE Lillian Ct 97267
SE Lillian Way 97236
NW Lilywood Dr 97229
SW Lincoln Ave 97223
SE Lincoln Ct
8900-11699 97216
12400-12498 97233
12500-17299 97233
SE Lincoln St
500-4199 97214
4200-4298 97215
4300-7999 97215
8400-8898 97216
8900-12199 97216
12200-18599 97233
SW Lincoln St
245-307 97201
309-331 97201
333-741 97201
10300-10399 97223
SE Linden Ct 97267
SE Linden Ln
13100-13198 97222
13200-13899 97222
13900-15499 97267
SE Linden Pl 97222
SW Linden Rd 97225
SE Lindenbrook Ct 97222
NW Linder St 97229
NW Lindy Ln 97229
SE Lindy St 97206
Linmere Dr & Ln 97229
SE Linn St 97202
SE Linwood Ave 97222
SE Lisa Ln 97267
NW Listel Ln 97229
SE Little Creek Ln 97267
SW Litz Ct 97223
SW Lizzie Ct 97223
SE Llewellyn St 97222
NE Lloyd Blvd 97232
Lloyd Ctr 97232
SE Lloyd St 97222
SW Lobelia St 97219
SE Locust Ave 97214
SW Locust St 97223
SW Lodi Ln
4900-5099 97221
8500-8799 97224
SE Loeffelman Rd 97222
NW Logan Ct 97229
SW Logan Ct 97219
SW Logan St 97219
NW Logie Trail Rd 97231
SE Logus Rd 97222
NW Lois Elaine Ter 97229
SE Lola Ln 97267
SW Lola Ln 97223
SW Lomax Ter 97223
NE Lombard Ct 97211
NE Lombard Pl 97211
N Lombard St
8641A-8641C 97203
1-3999 97217
4001-4097 97203
4099-15799 97203
15801-15999 97203
NE Lombard St 97211
N Lombard Way 97203
NW Lombardy Dr 97229
SW Lomita Ave 97223
NW Lomita Ln 97210

NW Lomita Ter 97210
SW London Ct 97223
SE Lone Oak Ln 97267
NW Lone Rock Dr 97229
SE Long St
1301-1397 97202
1399-4199 97202
4200-7899 97206
9701-9797 97266
9799-11499 97266
12200-13299 97236
SW Longstaff St 97223
N Longview Ave
3700-4099 97227
4100-4299 97217
SW Lookout Dr 97224
SW Loop Dr 97221
SE Lora St 97233
SE Loren Ln 97267
SW Lorenzo Ln 97223
NW Loriann Dr 97229
N Loring St 97227
NW Lorraine Dr 97229
SE Lost Meadow Ln 97267
NW Lost Park Dr 97229
NW Lost Springs Ter ... 97229
N Lotus Beach Dr 97217
N Lotus Isle Dr 97217
SE Lou Ann Ct 97267
SE Lounsberry Ln 97206
NW Lovejoy Ct 97229
NW Lovejoy St
900-2099 97209
2100-2198 97210
2200-2699 97210
8500-13299 97229
N Lovely St 97203
SW Lowell Ct 97221
SW Lowell Ln 97239
SW Lowell St
-108--699 97239
-12--106 97239
4900-5199 97221
SW Lower Boones Ferry Rd 97224
NW Loy Ct 97229
SE Lucas Ct 97267
NW Lucerne Ct 97229
SW Lucille Ct 97223
SW Lucille St 97219
NW Lucy Reeder Rd ... 97231
SE Luella Ln 97267
SW Lukar Ct 97223
SW Luke Ln 97223
SE Lupine St 97267
Luradel Ct, Ln & St 97219
NW Luray Ter 97210
NW Luray Circus 97210
NW Lusanne Ct 97229
SE Luther Rd 97206
NW Luzon St 97210
SE Lydia Ct
10600-10699 97266
12600-12799 97236
SW Lyle Ct 97221
NW Lynch Ln 97229
SW Lynn St 97223
SW Lynnfield Ln 97225
SW Lynnridge Ave 97225
SW Lynnvale Dr 97225
SW Lynwood Ter 97225
N M L King Blvd 97217
NE M L King Blvd
5-17 97232
19-1610 97232
1803-4099 97212
4100-9099 97211
9101-9199 97211
SE M L King Blvd
5-197 97214
199-1801 97214
1803-1805 97214
2500-3299 97202
SE Mabel Ave 97267
SW Macadam Ave
6140A-6140C 97239
3400-3498 97239
3500-6699 97239
6700-8399 97219
8401-8499 97219
SW Macbeth Dr 97224
SE Macduffee Ct 97233
NW Mackay Ave 97231
SE Mackie Ln 97222
NW Macleay Blvd 97210
N Macrum Ave 97203
SE Macs Pl 97222
NW Mactavish Ln 97231
SE Madeira Dr 97222
SE Madison Ct 97233
SW Madison Ct 97221
SE Madison Dr 97216
SE Madison St
5-5 97214
7-2799 97214
2807-2815 97222
2825-2825 97214
2835-2889 97222
2905-2949 97214
2906-2906 97222
2910-2924 97214
2990-3098 97222
3100-3234 97222
3236-3236 97222
3255-3263 97214
3265-4199 97214
4200-8199 97215
8200-11999 97216
12201-12297 97233
12299-17199 97233
SW Madison St
101-121 97204
101-101 97207
123-432 97204
434-538 97204
710-1714 97205
1716-2374 97205
2376-2390 97205
SE Madison Way 97233
SE Madrona Ct 97267
SE Madrona Dr 97222
SE Madrona Ln 97267
NE Madrona St 97211
SE Mae Hazel Ln 97222
NE Magda Ln 97230
SE Magnolia St 97267
Mahama Pl & Way 97229
SE Mahany Ct 97267
SE Mailwell Dr 97222
SE Main Ct 97233
SE Main St
50-52 97214
54-4099 97214
4101-4199 97214
4200-8199 97215
8400-9299 97216
9300-9898 97222
9900-9999 97222
10000-11131 97216
11133-12199 97216
11200-11298 97222
11222-11222 97269
11500-12198 97216
12200-18199 97233
100-300 97204
302-426 97204
620-948 97205
950-2188 97205
2190-2226 97205
5700-5798 97221
12000-12098 97223
12100-12699 97223
SW Majestic Ln 97224
NW Majestic Sequoia Way 97229
SW Malcolm Ct 97225
SE Malcolm St 97222
SW Malcolm Glen St ... 97225
SE Malden Ct
7700-8199 97206
8601-11697 97266
11699-11899 97266
SE Malden Dr 97206
SE Malden St
700-4199 97202
4200-8199 97206
10100-11399 97266
NW Malhuer Ave 97229
NW Malia Ln 97229
SE Mall St
900-4199 97202
5200-7199 97206
11700-11899 97266
12500-14099 97236
SE Mallard Ct 97267
SW Mallard Ct 97223
SE Mallard Way 97222
NE Mallory Ave
3501-3597 97212
3599-4099 97212
4100-7499 97211
7501-8199 97211
SW Mallow Ter 97223
SE Maloy Ln
13601-13697 97222
13699-13899 97222
13900-14099 97267
NE Maltby St 97212
SE Manchester Pl 97202
SW Mandamus Ct 97223
SE Manewal Ln 97267
SE Manley St 97236
NW Mann Rd 97231
NW Manor Dr 97210
NW Manresa Ct 97229
Manzanita Ct & St 97223
NW Manzoni St 97229
SE Maple Ave 97214
SE Maple Ct 97222
SW Maple Ct 97223
SW Maple Dr 97225
SE Maple Ln
13200-13899 97222
13900-14399 97267
SW Maple Ln
2400-2498 97225
2500-2999 97225
5001-5031 97221
SE Maple St
1400-3299 97267
3301-3399 97267
5700-5999 97222
NW Maple Hill Ln 97229
SW Maplecrest Ct
500-1099 97219
13200-13299 97223
SW Maplecrest Dr 97219
SE Maplehurst Rd 97222
Mapleleaf Ct & St 97223
SW Mapleridge Dr 97225
SW Mapleview Ln 97224
SE Maplewood Ct 97222
SW Maplewood Dr 97223
SW Maplewood Rd 97219
SW Mara Ct 97224
SE Marcia Ct 97267
SW Marcia Dr 97223
NW Marcia St 97210
SW Marconi Ave 97205
NW Marcotte Rd 97229
NW Marguerite Ln 97229
SW Mariah St 97225
SE Marian St 97267
SW Maricara St 97219
SW Marie Ct 97223
SE Marie St 97236
SE Marigold St 97267
SW Marigold St 97219
SW Marilyn Ct 97224
NW Marina Way 97231
N Marine Dr
1-35 97217
37-4199 97217
5101-5297 97203
5299-8199 97203
8201-8399 97203
NE Marine Dr
1-2999 97211
3001-4199 97211
4300-7899 97218
7901-7999 97218
8201-9599 97220
10400-12198 97220
12501-13797 97230
13799-20099 97230
NE Mariners Loop 97211
NW Maring Dr 97229
SE Marion St 97202
SW Marion St 97223
SW Marissa Dr 97223
SE Mark Kelly Ct 97267
SE Market Ct 97233
SE Market Dr 97216
SE Market St
120-612 97214
614-3799 97214
3801-3899 97214
4901-4997 97215
4999-8199 97215
8400-12199 97216
12200-18099 97233
SW Market St 97201
SW Market Street Dr ... 97201
NW Marlborough Ave ... 97210
SW Marlow Ave 97225
SW Marquam Hill Rd ... 97239
NW Marsden Pl 97229
NW Marshall Ct 97229
NW Marshall St
700-1098 97209
1100-2063 97209
2065-2077 97209
2201-2311 97210
2313-2567 97210
2569-2575 97210
8500-8698 97229
8700-13999 97229
SE Martenson Ct 97267
SE Martha Ct 97222
SW Martha Ct 97239
SW Martha St
1501-1597 97239
1599-2199 97239
2201-2299 97239
4500-4598 97221
4600-5499 97221
9200-9599 97224
SW Martha Ter 97239
SE Martin Ct 97206
SE Martins Ct 97236
SW Martins Ln 97239
SE Martins St
1200-4000 97202
4002-4198 97202
4200-4798 97206
4800-8199 97206
10100-12199 97266
13800-16099 97236
16101-16299 97236
NW Marvin Ln 97229
NE Marx Dr 97220
NE Marx Pl 97220
NE Marx St
10100-12040 97220
12042-12198 97220
12200-12999 97230
SE Mary Ct 97222
SE Mary Pl 97223
SE Mary Ann Ln 97267
Mary Failing Ct & Dr ... 97219
SE Mary Jean Ct 97266
N Maryland Ave 97217
NW Marylee Ct 97229
Marylhurst Ct & Dr 97229
SE Mason Cir 97222
NE Mason Ct
4900-5199 97218
16800-16899 97230
SW Mason Ct 97224
SE Mason Ln 97222
N Mason St 97217
NE Mason St
1-3299 97211
4200-7799 97218
7801-8099 97218
9600-11100 97220
11102-11198 97220
14900-16799 97230
SE Mason Hill Dr 97222
N Massachusetts Ave
3700-4099 97227
4100-4299 97217
SW Matador Ln 97224
N Mather Pl 97217
NE Mathison Pl 97212
SE Matilda Dr 97267
NW Matomandy Ct 97229
SW Matthew Park St ... 97224
SW Maui Ct 97223
SW Maus St 97219
SE May St 97222
NW Maybrook Ave 97231
NW Mayer Ct 97229
SW Mayfield Ave 97225
SW Mayfield Pl 97225
NW Mayfield Rd 97229
SW Mayo St 97223
SW Maypark Ct 97225
SW Mayview Way 97223
SW Mayway Dr 97225
NW Maywood Dr 97210
NE Maywood Pl 97220
SW Mazama Pl 97224
SE Mcallister Ct 97267
SE Mcbride St 97222
SE Mcbrod Ave 97222
SE Mccabe Ct 97267
SE Mccartney Ln 97267
NW Mcchesney Ct 97229
N Mcclellan St 97217
NE Mcconnell Rd 97211
N Mccosh St 97203
N Mccoy Ct 97203
NW Mcdaniel Rd 97229
SW Mcdonald St 97224
SW Mcdonnell Ter 97239
SE Mceachron Ave 97222
NW Mcenery Ln 97229
SE Mcewan Rd 97224
SW Mcfarland Blvd 97224
NW Mcgrath Ct 97229
NW Mcgregor Ter 97229
SW Mcintosh Ter 97224
N Mckenna Ave 97203
NW Mckenna Dr 97229
SW Mckenna Pl 97223
SW Mckenzie St 97223
SE Mckinley Rd 97236
NW Mclain Way 97229
SE Mcloughlin Blvd
2727-2997 97202
2999-8399 97202
8400-13899 97222
13900-19120 97267
19122-19198 97267
SW Mcmillan St 97225
NW Mcmullen Ave 97229
NW Mcnamee Rd 97231
SE Mcnary Rd 97267
SW Meade Ct 97225
SW Meade St
-102--104 97201
-106--650 97201
-16--100 97201
26-116 97201
118-246 97201
248-338 97201
9900-9999 97225
NE Meadow Dr 97211
NE Meadow Ln 97211
SW Meadow Ln 97225
SW Meadow St 97223
SW Meadowbrook Dr ... 97224
SE Meadowcrest Ct 97222
SE Meadowgreen Dr ... 97267
SE Meadowland Ct 97236
NW Meadowlands Ter .. 97229
SE Meadowlark Ln 97267
SW Meadowood Way .. 97224
NW Meadowridge Dr ... 97229
N Mears St 97203
SW Medwyn Ter 97219
SW Megan Ter 97223
NW Mehama Ct 97229
NE Meikle Pl 97213
NW Meisner Dr 97229
SE Melania Ct 97266
SE Meldrum Ave 97267
NW Melinda Ave 97210
SE Mellmer Ln 97267
SW Melnore St 97225
NW Melody Ln 97229
SE Melody Ln 97222
N Melrose Dr 97227
NW Melrose Dr 97229
SW Melville Ave 97239
SW Memory Ln 97225
NW Mendenhall St 97229
Menefee Dr & Ln 97239
N Menlo Ave 97203
SW Menlor Ln 97223
Menzies Ct & Dr 97217
SE Mercers Way 97267
SW Merestone Ct 97223
SE Merganser Ct 97267
NE Merges Dr 97212
Meridian Ridge Ct & Dr 97210
SW Merlin Ct 97219
SW Merlin Pl 97223
SW Merlyne Ct 97224
NW Merranti St 97208
SW Merridell Ct 97225
Metolius Ct & Dr 97229
SW Metta Ter 97223
SW Meyer Ln 97224
SE Meyers St 97267
NE Michael Ct 97230
SE Michael Dr 97222
NE Michelle Ct 97220
SW Michelle Ct 97223
N Michigan Ave
3200-4099 97227
4100-6999 97217
N Middle Shore St 97217
NE Middlefield Rd 97211
Midea Ct & Ln 97225
SW Midmar Pl 97223
SW Midvale Rd 97219
N Midway Ave 97203
NW Midway St 97231
NW Mikalo Ct 97229
Milan Ln & St 97223
NW Milazzo Ln 97229
NW Milburn St 97229
NW Milcliff St 97229
NW Mildred St 97210
SE Mildred St 97267
SW Miles Ct
2400-6399 97219
6500-6899 97223
SW Miles Pl 97219
SW Miles St 97219
Military Ct, Ln & Rd 97219
SE Mill Ct
10100-12199 97216
12200-18099 97233
SE Mill Loop 97233
NW Mill Rd 97231
SE Mill St
616-620 97214
622-3799 97214
4900-4998 97215
5000-8199 97215
8200-9999 97216
12200-18699 97233
SW Mill St
424-696 97201
698-700 97201
702-950 97201
6000-6299 97221
NW Mill Creek Dr 97229
NW Mill Pond Rd 97229
NW Mill Ridge Rd 97229
SW Mill Street Ter 97201
NW Millbrook St 97229
NW Millcrest Pl 97229
SW Millen Dr 97224
SW Miller Ct 97224
NW Miller Rd 97229
SW Miller Rd 97225
SE Miller St 97202
Miller Hill Ct, Dr & Pl ... 97229
NW Millford St 97229
NW Millicomo Ct 97229
SE Millmain Dr 97233
NW Mills St 97231
NW Millstone Way 97229
SW Millview Ct 97223
SW Milon Ln 97225
SE Milport Rd 97222
NE Milton Ct 97230
SW Milton Ct 97224
NE Milton Pl 97230
NE Milton St
3700-3899 97212
5700-6299 97213
8200-8999 97220
13200-15399 97230
SE Milwaukie Ave 97202
SE Milwaukie Expy 97222
SW Miner Way 97225
N Minerva Ave 97203
SE Minerva Ln 97267
NE Mingerel Ave 97213
SE Miniview Ct 97267
N Minnesota Ave 97217
SW Mint Pl 97223
SE Mintone Dr 97222
SW Mira Ct 97223
NE Mirimar Pl 97232
N Mississippi Ave
2400-2498 97227
2500-4099 97227
4100-8299 97217
N Missouri Ave
3300-3498 97227
3500-4099 97227
4100-7100 97217
7102-8198 97217
SW Mistletoe Dr
13700-13799 97224
13800-14499 97223
SE Mitchell Ct
6600-7399 97206
12900-13099 97236
SW Mitchell Ct
2600-3299 97239
14000-14199 97223
SW Mitchell Ln 97239
NW Mitchell St 97229
SE Mitchell St
4101-4199 97202
4200-8199 97206
9200-10899 97266
12900-14199 97236
SW Mitchell St
-19--35 97239
-37--47 97239
-5--17 97239
21-997 97239
999-3399 97239
3701-4997 97221
4999-5299 97221
SW Moapa Ave 97219
N Mobile Ave 97217
SW Moet Ct 97224
N Mohawk Ave 97203
SW Molly Ct 97223
SE Molt St 97267
SW Monaco Ln 97224
SW Monica Ct 97223
N Monroe St 97227
NE Monroe St 97212
SE Monroe St 97222
SW Montage Ln 97223
SW Montague Way 97224
N Montana Ave
3700-4099 97227
4100-8300 97217
8302-8398 97217
Montara Ct, Dr & Loop 97229
SW Montclair Dr 97225
NW Monte Vista Ter 97210
SE Montego Bay St 97267

N Monteith Ave 97203
SW Monterey Ln 97224
SW Monterey Pl 97225
SE Montgomery Dr 97222
SW Montgomery Dr 97201
SW Montgomery Pl 97201
SW Montgomery St 97201
NW Montreux Ln 97229
SW Moody Ave
-305--315 97201
2700-2988 97201
2990-3000 97201
3002-3098 97201
3101-3497 97239
3499-3900 97239
3902-4198 97239
SE Moon Ave 97267
SW Moonridge Pl 97225
SW Moonshadow Ct 97223
N Moore Ave 97217
SE Moores St 97222
SE Moreland Ln 97202
NW Moresby Ct 97229
NW Moretti Ter 97229
NW Morgan Ln 97229
NW Morgan Rd 97231
N Morgan St 97217
NE Morgan St 97211
SE Morgan Hill Ln 97267
SW Morgen Ct 97223
SE Morning Glory Ct 97267
Morning Hill Ct & Dr 97223
SW Morningstar Dr 97223
SW Morocco Dr 97224
NE Morris Ct
10200-10299 97220
12700-16099 97230
NE Morris Pl 97230
N Morris St 97227
NE Morris St
1-3699 97212
6800-7699 97213
10201-10297 97220
10299-12099 97220
12200-15999 97230
16001-16099 97230
SE Morris St 97206
SE Morrison Ct
6300-6399 97215
6401-6499 97215
14901-16797 97233
16799-17899 97233
SE Morrison St
66-212 97214
214-4199 97214
4200-8199 97215
8200-12199 97216
12800-16799 97233
SW Morrison St
50-118 97204
120-521 97204
523-545 97204
617-797 97205
799-2038 97205
2040-2050 97205
8600-10199 97225
SE Morse Ct 97267
NW Mortensen Ter 97229
NE Morton St 97211
SW Moss St
600-3500 97219
3502-5098 97219
9300-9499 97223
SW Mount Adams Dr 97239
SW Mount Hood Ln 97239
SE Mount Royale Ct 97267
SE Mount Scott Blvd 97266
SW Mount Vista Ct 97224
SW Mountain Ridge Ct 97224
SE Mountain View Dr 97215
SW Mountain View Ln 97224
NW Mountain View Rd 97231
SW Mozart Ter 97225
SW Mt View Ln 97224
SW Muirwood Dr 97225
SE Mulberry Ave 97214
SE Mulberry Dr 97267
SW Mulberry Dr 97224
SE Mullan St 97222
SW Multnomah Blvd
1601-1797 97219
1799-6299 97219
6301-6499 97219
6501-6697 97223
6699-6791 97223
6793-6999 97223
NE Multnomah Ct 97230
NE Multnomah Dr 97230
NE Multnomah St
101-197 97232
199-4199 97232
4700-8199 97213
8200-11699 97220
12200-19999 97230
NE Multnomah Ter 97230
SW Murdock Ct 97224
SW Murdock Ln 97224
SW Murdock Pl 97224
NW Murdock St 97229
SW Murdock St 97224
Murlea Dr & Ln 97229
Murray Blvd & Rd 97229
SE My Way Ct 97267
SW Myrtle Ave 97224
SW Myrtle Ct 97201
SW Myrtle Dr 97201
SE Myrtle St 97222
SW Myrtle St 97201
Nacira Ct, Ln & Pl 97223
Naef Ct & Rd 97267
Naegeli Ct & Dr 97236
SW Naeve St 97224
SW Nahcotta Dr 97223
NW Naito Pkwy 97209
SW Naito Pkwy
1-900 97204
902-1038 97204
1401-1697 97201
1699-2200 97201
2202-2898 97201
3223-3419 97239
NW Naomi Ln 97229
SE Nase Ct 97222
N Nashton St 97203
SE Nature Way 97267
NW Neakahnie Ave 97229
SW Nebraska St
-205--616 97239
-618--618 97239
1900-3231 97239
3233-3239 97239
5000-5999 97221
NW Necanicum Way 97229
Needham Ct & St 97222
SE Nehalem Ct 97236
SW Nehalem Ct 97239
SE Nehalem St
500-4199 97202
4200-7199 97206
14400-16199 97236
NW Nela St 97210
NW Nelscott St 97229
SW Nemarnik Dr 97224
Neskowin Ave & Pl 97229
N Nesmith Ave 97227
NW Nestucca Dr 97229
Nevada Ct, St & Ter 97219
NW New Hope Ct 97229
N New York Ave 97203
N Newark St
2500-3799 97217
4500-6099 97203
NW Newberry Rd 97231
SW Newby Ter 97239
N Newcastle Ave 97217
N Newell Ave 97203
N Newman Ave 97203
NE Newport St 97230
SW Newton Pl 97225
NW Newton Rd 97231
NW Niblick Pl 97229
SE Nicholas Ct 97266
NW Nichwana Ct 97229
SW Nicol Rd
5500-5798 97225
6300-6398 97223
NW Nicolai St 97210
SW Nicole Ln 97224
SW Nicoli Pl 97224
NW Nightshade Dr 97229
SW Nimbus Ave 97223
SW Nipa Ct 97223
Nixie 97208
SE Nixon Ave 97222
NW Nolana Ct 97229
SE Norbert Dr 97222
SW Nordic Dr 97223
NW Norfolk Ct 97229
SW Norfolk Ct 97224
SW Norfolk Ln 97224
Norma Cir & Rd 97267
SW Norse Ln 97225
NW North Rd 97229
SW North Dakota St 97223
N North Portland Rd
10000-12099 97203
12100-12499 97217
Northgate Ave & Ct 97219
Northridge Ct & Dr 97222
NW Northrup St
1001-1097 97209
1099-2099 97209
2100-2699 97210
13101-13197 97229
13199-13499 97229
SW Northshire St 97225
NW Northshore Ct 97229
SW Northvale Way 97225
SE Northview Dr 97222
SW Northview Dr 97223
SW Northwood Ave 97239
NW Nottage Dr 97229
SW Nottingham Dr 97201
SW Nova Ct 97223
SW Novare Pl 97223
SE Oak Ct 97267
SW Oak Ln 97223
NW Oak St 97229
SE Oak St
201-201 97214
203-4199 97214
4200-5699 97215
9000-10499 97216
10800-11199 97222
11700-12199 97216
13900-18499 97233
SW Oak St
71-317 97204
319-551 97204
553-555 97204
601-797 97205
799-899 97205
901-999 97205
6501-6597 97223
6599-9300 97223
9302-9698 97223
SW Oak Way 97223
NW Oak Creek Dr 97229
SW Oak Creek Dr 97219
SE Oak Glen Ct 97267
SE Oak Grove Blvd 97267
NW Oak Island Rd 97231
SW Oak Meadow Ln 97224
NW Oak Shadow Ct 97229
Oak Shore Ct & Ln 97267
SW Oak Valley Ter 97224
SW Oakenshield Ct 97224
SW Oakhill Ln 97224
SE Oakhurst Ct 97267
SE Oakland Ave 97267
NW Oakley Ct 97229
SW Oakmont Pl 97224
NW Oakpoint Way 97229
NW Oakridge Dr 97229
SW Oaks Ln 97224
SE Oaks Park Way 97202
SW Oaktree Ln 97224
SE Oakwood Ave 97267
NW Oatfield Ct 97229
SE Oatfield Ct 97267
SE Oatfield Rd
12100-13899 97222
13900-17599 97267
SE Oatfield Hill Rd 97267
N Oatman Ave 97217
NW Oats Ter 97229
N Oberlin St 97203
SW Obrien St 97223
SE Ochoco St 97222
NW Oconnor Dr 97229
NW Oday Pl 97229
NW Odell Ct 97229
NW Odeon Ln 97229
SW Odino Ct 97224
Oetkin Dr, Rd & Way 97267
SE Ogden Ct
5900-5999 97206
12100-12199 97266
SE Ogden Dr 97236
NW Ogden St 97231
SE Ogden St
1400-4199 97202
4200-8199 97206
11200-11399 97266
NW Old Cornelius Pass Rd 97231
NW Old Germantown Rd 97231
SE Old Orchard Ct 97267
SW Old Orchard Ln 97225
SW Old Orchard Pl 97224
SW Old Orchard Rd 97201
NW Old Quarry Rd 97229
SW Old Scholls Ferry Rd
5700-5999 97225
6000-6599 97223
NW Old Skyline Blvd
8001-8097 97229
8099-8299 97229
9200-9399 97231
SW Oleson Rd
4700-5999 97225
6300-9200 97223
9202-9298 97223
N Olin Ave 97203
NW Olivares Ter 97229
SE Olive Ave 97267
SE Olsen St 97222
N Olympia St 97203
NW Olympic Dr 97229
N Omaha Ave 97217
SW Omara St 97223
SE Omark Dr 97222
SW Oneill Ct 97223
NE Oneonta St 97211
SW Onnaf Ct 97224
SW Ophelia St 97219
SE Orange Ave 97214
NW Orchard Dr 97229
SW Orchard Ln 97219
SE Orchid Ave 97267
SW Orchid Ct 97219
SW Orchid Dr 97219
SW Orchid Pl 97219
SW Orchid St
600-6499 97219
6500-6699 97223
NE Oregon St
1-797 97232
799-3499 97232
4400-8199 97213
9000-11399 97220
11401-11699 97220
12200-17999 97230
18001-18099 97230
N Oregonian Ave 97203
NW Origami Ct 97229
SW Orinda Way 97225
SE Oris Ln 97222
SE Ormae Rd 97267
SW Ormandy Way 97221
SE Orville Ave 97267
SW Osage St 97205
NW Osprey Pl 97229
N Oswego Ave 97203
SW Othello Ter 97224
SE Otty St 97222
SE Our Ct 97222
SW Ouzel Ln 97224
SW Overgaard St 97224
SE Overland St 97222
N Overlook Blvd
3700-4099 97227
4100-4399 97217
SE Overlook Ln 97267
N Overlook Ter
3900-4099 97227
4100-4199 97217
NW Overton St
900-906 97209
908-2099 97209
2100-2799 97210
12900-13699 97229
SE Owls Rest Ct 97267
NW Owyhee Ct 97229
SW Oxalis Ter 97223
NW Oxbridge Dr 97229
SW Oxford Ave 97225
SE Oxford Ln 97222
SE P Jays Ct 97267
NE Pacific Ct 97230
NE Pacific Dr 97230
SW Pacific Hwy
11415-11417 97223
11419-13999 97223
14000-17299 97224
N Pacific St 97227
NE Pacific St
1901-2197 97232
2199-3499 97232
4800-7799 97213
8200-11699 97220
12700-19399 97230
NE Pacific Ter 97230
SW Pag Pl 97223
N Page St 97227
SE Pagoda Ct 97267
NW Pagosa Ln 97229
SW Palater Rd 97219
Palatine Ct & St 97219
SW Palatine Hill Rd 97219
SW Palermo Ln 97223
SW Pallay Ct 97219
SW Palm Pl 97223
SE Palm St 97214
SE Palmetto St 97267
SW Pamela St 97219
SE Pamrick Ln 97267
SW Panorama Pl 97225
SE Pappas Loss Ct 97267
NW Par Ct 97229
SW Par 4 Dr 97224
Paradise Ct & Dr 97267
SE Pardee Dr 97236
SE Pardee St
1500-4199 97202
4200-6999 97206
8500-12199 97266
NW Park Ave 97209
SE Park Ave 97222
SW Park Ave
300-326 97205
328-1299 97205
1300-1599 97201
1601-2073 97201
NW Park Pl 97229
SW Park Pl 97205
SE Park Rd 97267
SE Park St 97222
SW Park St 97223
SW Park Way 97225
SE Park Entrance St 97267
NW Park Ridge Ln 97229
NW Park View Blvd 97229
NW Park View Ln 97229
SE Park View Ter 97222
N Parker Ave 97217
Parkhill Dr & Way 97239
SW Parkland Ter 97224
Parkside Dr & Ln 97205
SW Parkview Ave 97225
SE Parkview Cir 97267
SW Parkview Ct 97221
SW Parkwest Ln 97225
SW Parkwood Dr 97225
Parmenter Ct & Dr 97267
NW Parnell Ter 97229
SW Parrway Dr 97225
SW Parsons Ct 97219
Pasadena Dr & St 97219
NW Paseo Ter 97229
Pathfinder Ct & Way 97223
SE Patricia Ct 97267
NW Patrick Ln 97229
SW Patrick Pl 97239
SW Patrick Way 97239
SE Patsy Ave 97267
SW Patti Ln 97224
SW Patton Ct 97201
SW Patton Ln 97201
SW Patton Rd
2501-2597 97201
2599-2899 97201
2901-3499 97201
3500-6399 97221
NW Paulina Dr 97229
NW Paulson Ln 97229
NW Pauly Rd 97231
N Pavilion Ave 97217
NW Paxton Ct 97229
NW Payne Dr 97229
SW Peaceful Ln 97239
SW Peachtree Dr 97224
SW Peachvale St 97224
SE Peacock Ln 97214
SW Peak Ct 97224
NE Peerless Pl 97232
SE Pembroke Ct 97222
SW Pembrook St 97224
NW Pender Pl 97229
SW Pendleton Ct 97221
SW Pendleton St
-16--212 97239
-214--218 97239
-220--424 97239
1400-1999 97239
2001-2099 97239
3800-5699 97221
5701-5799 97221
N Peninsular Ave 97217
SW Penn Ct 97223
SW Pennie Ln 97224
NW Pennington Pl 97229
SW Pennoyer St 97239
Pennywood Ct & Dr 97222
SW Pennywort Ter 97224
NW Penridge Rd 97229
NW Pentland St 97229
SE Penzance St 97222
SW Peppertree Ln 97224
NW Peregrine Pl 97229
SW Periander St 97201
Permian Ct & Dr 97229
SE Pershing Ct 97236
SE Pershing St 97202
SE Persons Ct 97267
SW Peters Rd 97224
NW Pettygrove St
1400-1598 97209
1600-2000 97209
2002-2098 97209
2100-2799 97210
13100-13899 97229
SW Peyton Rd
6300-6399 97219
6500-6899 97223
SW Pfaffle St 97223
SE Pheasant Ct 97222
N Philadelphia Ave 97203
SE Phillips Creek Ln 97222
SW Picard Ct 97223
SW Picasso Pl 97223
SW Pickleweed Ln 97224
Picks Ct & Way 97224
N Pier Park Pl 97203
N Pierce Ave 97203
SE Pierce St 97222
Pihas Ct & St 97223
SE Pilgrim Ct 97267
SW Pilips Ln 97223
SE Pine Ct
6800-6899 97215
10900-11499 97216
14200-15199 97233
SE Pine Ln 97267
SE Pine St
309-527 97214
529-4199 97214
4200-8199 97215
8700-12199 97216
13300-19899 97233
SW Pine St
50-200 97204
202-331 97204
333-445 97204
600-698 97205
6600-8699 97223
SE Pine Cone Ln 97267
SE Pine Creek Way 97267
SW Pine Crest Way 97224
SW Pine View St 97224
Pinebrook Ct & Dr 97224
SE Pinehurst Ave 97267
SE Pinelane St 97267
SE Pineridge Ct 97236
SW Pineridge Ct 97225
Pinnacle Ct & Dr 97229
NW Pinon Hills Ter 97229
SW Pinot Ct 97224
SE Pinot Rd 97267
NW Pioneer Rd 97229
SW Piper Ter 97223
SW Pipit Ln 97224
SW Pippen Ln 97224
SW Pitic Ln 97223
NW Pittock Dr 97210
N Pittsburg Ave 97203
NW Placido Ct 97229
NW Plainview Rd 97231
SW Plantation Ter 97223
SE Platt Ave 97236
SW Pleasantview Ct 97224
SW Plum Cir 97219
SW Plum Ct 97219
SE Plum Dr 97222
SW Plum Dr 97219
SW Plum St 97219
SW Plum Ter 97223
SE Plymouth Ct 97267
NW Poehler Ter 97229
Pointer Rd & Way 97225
N Polk Ave 97203
SW Pollard Ln 97224
Pomona Ct & St 97219
SW Ponderosa Pl 97223
Pondosa Ct & Dr 97229
SE Poplar Ave 97214
SW Poplar Ln 97225
SE Poplar Pl 97267
SE Poppy St 97267
N Port Center Way 97217
NE Portal Way 97230
SW Porter St
-10--46 97201
-48--50 97201
-52--110 97201
16-118 97201
10300-10499 97225
SW Portia Ln 97224
SE Portland Ave 97267
NE Portland Hwy 97218
NE Portland Boulevard Ct 97211
SW Portola Ave 97225
N Portsmouth Ave 97203
SE Posey St 97267
Postage Due St 97267
NW Potters Ct 97229
SE Powell Blvd
600-1499 97202
1410-1410 97242
1500-4198 97202
1501-4199 97202

4200-8199 97206
8200-12099 97266
12101-12199 97266
12200-17499 97236
SE Powell Ct
11201-11297 97266
11299-11599 97266
12300-12598 97236
SE Powell Butte Pkwy 97236
SE Powell View Ct 97236
SW Power Ct 97225
SW Powers Ct 97219
N Powers St 97203
NW Powhatan Ter 97210
NW Praline Ln 97229
NW Preakness Ter 97229
SE Premier Ct 97267
NE Prescott Ct 97230
NE Prescott Dr 97230
N Prescott St 97217
NE Prescott St
1-4199 97211
4200-8199 97218
8200-12199 97220
SW Preslynn Dr 97225
NW Preston Ct 97229
NW Primino Ave 97229
SE Primrose Ave 97267
SW Primrose St 97219
SW Prince Albert St 97224
SW Prince Edward Ct 97224
SW Prince Phillip Ct 97224
SW Princeton Ln 97223
N Princeton St 97203
NW Priscilla Ct 97229
SE Progress Ct 97267
NW Promenade Ter 97229
NW Prominence Ct 97229
SW Prospect Dr 97201
NW Pumpkin Ct 97229
NW Purvis Dr 97229
SW Quail Creek Ln 97223
NW Quail Hollow Dr 97229
SW Quail Post Rd 97219
NW Quarry Rd 97231
SE Queen Rd 97222
SW Queen Anne Ave 97224
SW Queen Elizabeth St 97224
SW Queen Mary Ave 97224
SW Queen Victoria Pl 97224
NW Queens Dr 97210
SW Quelle Pl 97223
SE Quiet Meadows Dr 97267
NW Quimby St
1300-1398 97209
1400-1899 97209
1901-1999 97209
2100-2198 97210
2200-3499 97210
NW Quinault Ct 97229
SW Quinault Ct 97219
NW Quinn Ct 97229
SW Raab Rd 97221
NW Racely Ct 97229
SW Racely Pl 97224
SE Rachel Ln 97236
SW Radcliff St 97219
Radcliffe Ct, Ln & Rd 97219
SE Raelyn Ter 97267
SE Rafaela Ln 97222
NE Raillant Ave 97212
SE Railroad Ave 97222
Rainbow Cir & Ln 97222
NW Rainier Ave 97231
NW Rainier Ter
400-498 97210
4600-4899 97229
NW Rainmont Rd 97229
SE Raintree Ct 97267
SE Rajessa Ct 97236
SW Raleigh Ct 97223
NW Raleigh St
1300-1999 97209
2100-3499 97210
3501-3599 97210

Raleighview Ct & Dr 97225
SW Raleighwood Ct 97221
SW Raleighwood Ln 97225
SW Raleighwood Way 97225
SW Ralston Dr 97239
SW Rambler Ln 97223
SE Ramona Ct
11400-11499 97266
14000-14099 97236
SE Ramona St
1300-1398 97202
1400-4199 97202
4200-8199 97206
8201-8397 97266
8399-11999 97266
12001-12199 97266
12200-13999 97236
N Ramsey Blvd 97203
NW Ramsey Dr 97229
NW Ramsey Crest Dr 97229
SE Rancho Ave 97267
NE Randall Ave 97232
NW Randall Ln 97229
N Randolph Ave 97227
SW Range Ter 97223
SE Ranstad Ct 97222
SW Raphael Ln 97224
NW Rapidan Ter 97210
SW Raptor Pl 97223
SW Rask Ter 97224
SE Raspberry Ct 97267
SW Ravensview Dr 97201
SW Ray Ln 97219
SE Raymond Ct
6800-7999 97206
8201-8297 97266
8299-8700 97266
8702-11498 97266
12900-13099 97236
SE Raymond St
2400-4199 97202
4201-8199 97206
8600-12199 97266
12200-14199 97236
SE Rayna Ct 97267
SW Raz Ct 97223
SW Rebecca Ter 97223
NW Red Cedar Ct
12900-12999 97229
14800-15399 97231
SW Red Cedar Way 97223
SW Red Hawk Ct 97224
NW Redding Ln 97229
NW Redfox Dr 97229
SW Redoaks Ln 97224
SW Redondo Ave 97239
SE Redwood Ave
12000-12399 97222
13900-14299 97267
SW Redwood Ln 97224
NW Reed Dr 97229
NW Reed St 97210
Reed College Pl 97202
NW Reeder Rd 97231
SE Reedway Ct 97236
SE Reedway Pl 97236
SE Reedway St
1401-1497 97202
1499-4199 97202
4200-8199 97206
8700-12199 97266
12200-14499 97236
NW Reeves St 97229
SW Refectory Pl 97224
SW Regal Dr 97225
Regency Pl & Ter 97225
SW Regent Ter 97224
SE Regents Cir 97222
NE Regents Dr 97212
SE Regents Dr 97222
SW Regina Ln 97223
SW Reiling St 97224
NW Reindeer Dr 97229
SW Rembrandt Ln 97224
NW Remembrance Ct 97229
SE Renada St 97267
SW Renee Dr 97225

N Reno Ave 97203
SE Renton Ave 97222
SE Reserve Loop 97267
NW Reuben Ln 97229
N Revere St 97227
NW Rex Ct 97229
SE Rex Dr 97206
SE Rex St
900-1098 97202
1100-4199 97202
4200-4499 97206
10000-10899 97266
SE Reynolds St 97202
SW Rhett Ct 97224
SE Rhine Ct 97236
SE Rhine St
901-1097 97202
1099-1899 97202
1901-3799 97202
7900-8199 97206
8201-8297 97266
8299-8399 97266
13600-16999 97236
SW Rhino Way 97239
NW Rhodes Ln 97229
SE Rhodesa St 97222
SE Rhone Ct 97236
SE Rhone St
700-2799 97202
2801-2899 97202
4200-8199 97206
8200-12100 97266
12102-12198 97266
12500-17199 97236
SW Rhus Ct 97224
SW Rice Ct 97223
NW Rich Ct 97229
N Richards St 97203
Richardson Ct, Dr & St 97239
SW Richenberg Ct 97239
SW Richey Ln 97223
N Richmond Ave 97203
SE Rickshire Ln 97267
SW Ridge Dr 97219
NW Ridge Rd 97229
SW Ridgefield Ln 97223
SW Ridgemont St 97225
NW Ridgemoor Ct 97229
Ridgetop Ct & St 97229
SW Ridgeview Ln 97219
SW Ridgeway Dr 97225
SW Ridgewood Ave 97225
NE Ridgewood Dr 97212
NW Riesling Ct 97229
SE Riesling Rd 97267
NW Riggs Dr 97229
SE Rim Rock Ln 97267
Rinearson Dr & Rd 97267
SE Rio Vista St 97222
NW Rio Vista Ter 97210
Risley Ave & Ct 97267
SW Rivendell Dr 97224
SE River Dr 97267
SW River Dr
1800-2099 97201
10500-10799 97224
SW River Ln 97224
SW River Pkwy
-301--399 97201
2001-2097 97201
2099-2199 97201
3500-3799 97239
SE River Rd
11900-13899 97222
13900-19499 97267
SW River Sq 97201
N River St 97227
SW River Walk 97201
SE River Bluff Ct 97267
SE River Crest Ln 97267
River Drive Ct & Ln 97267
River Forest Ct, Dr, Ln, Pl & Rd 97267
SE River Glen Ct 97267
NE River Point Cir 97211
SE River Ridge Dr 97222

SW Riverdale Rd 97219
N Rivergate Blvd 97203
SW Riveridge Ln 97239
SW Riverpoint Ln 97239
NW Riverscape St 97209
SW Riverside Dr 97219
SW Riverside Ln 97239
NE Riverside Pkwy 97230
SW Riverside St 97219
NE Riverside Way 97211
NW Riverview Dr 97231
NE Riverview Ln 97230
SE Riverway Ln 97222
SW Riverwood Ln 97224
SW Riverwood Pl 97224
SW Riverwood Rd 97219
SW Riviera Dr 97224
SE Riviere Dr 97267
SW Rivington Dr 97201
NW Roanoke Ln 97229
NW Roanoke St 97210
SW Robert Ct 97219
SW Robert Gray Ln 97225
SE Roberta Ln 97222
N Roberts Ave 97203
SE Robhil Dr 97222
SW Robillard Dr 97224
Robin Ct & Rd 97267
SE Robinette Ct 97267
NW Robinia Ln 97229
SW Robins Crest Dr 97201
N Rochester St 97203
NW Rock Creek Blvd 97229
NW Rock Creek Cir 97229
NW Rock Creek Ct 97229
NW Rock Creek Dr 97229
NW Rock Creek Rd 97231
NW Rock Creek Way 97229
SW Rockingham Dr 97223
SW Rockrose Ln 97223
SE Rockvorst St 97222
NW Rockwell Ln 97229
SE Rockwood St 97222
SE Rocky Ln 97267
Rocky Butte Ln & Rd 97220
SW Rocky Mountain Ct 97224
NE Rodney Ave
1901-1997 97212
1999-4099 97212
4100-7699 97211
NE Rodney Ct 97211
Roethe Ln, Pl & Rd 97267
SE Rofini Ct 97267
SW Romeo Ter 97224
NW Rondos Dr 97229
NW Roosevelt St 97210
SE Roots Rd 97267
N Rosa Parks Way 97217
NE Rosa Parks Way 97211
SE Rosanne St 97267
NW Rosaria Ave 97231
SW Rosario Ln 97224
SW Rose Ln 97201
NE Rose Pkwy 97230
SE Rose St 97267
SW Rose Garden Way 97205
NE Rose Parkway Ct 97230
SW Rose Vista Dr 97223
SW Roseberry Ln 97224
SE Rosebrier Ct 97267
NW Rosefinch Ln 97229
N Roselawn St 97217
NE Roselawn St
400-4199 97211
4800-7299 97218
SW Rosemary Ln 97223
NW Roseway Ave 97231
SW Rosewood Way 97225
SW Roshak Rd
13000-13098 97223
13100-13599 97223
15500-16035 97224
16100-16299 97223
SE Roslyn St 97222

N Ross Ave 97227
SW Ross St 97224
NW Rossetta St 97229
SW Roswell Ave 97201
SE Roswell St 97222
SW Rosy Ct 97223
NE Roth St 97211
SW Round Hill Way 97221
SE Round Oaks Ct 97267
SW Roundtree Ct 97219
SW Roundtree Dr 97223
SW Roxanne Ct 97223
SW Roxbury Ave 97225
NW Royal Blvd 97210
NE Royal Ct
400-4100 97232
4102-4198 97232
4200-4699 97213
SW Royal Ct 97224
SW Royal Oak Ct 97223
NW Royal Rose Ct 97229
SW Royal Villa Dr 97224
Royalty Ct & Pkwy 97224
NW Rubicon Ln 97229
SE Ruby Dr 97267
SW Ruby Ter 97219
Rudy Ct & St 97222
NW Runnymeade Ct 97229
SE Rupert Dr 97267
SE Rural Ct 97236
SE Rural St
1300-4199 97202
4200-7700 97206
7702-7798 97206
8700-9199 97266
SE Ruscliffe Ln 97222
SE Rusk Rd 97222
NE Russell Ct
10300-10699 97220
14600-14699 97230
NE Russell Pl
8700-8899 97220
15600-15699 97230
N Russell St 97227
NE Russell St
2-198 97212
200-699 97212
8200-12199 97220
12200-16699 97230
N Russet St
1-3799 97217
4100-4198 97203
NE Russet St 97211
SW Rustica Ter 97225
SW Rustling Leaves Pl 97223
SE Ruth Ct 97267
SW Rutland Ter 97205
SE Ryan Ave 97222
SE Ryan Ct 97222
NW Ryan St 97229
NW Ryegrass St 97229
SW Rystadt Ln 97225
NE Sacramento Dr 97230
NE Sacramento St
1-699 97212
5200-7799 97213
8200-12199 97220
13200-17799 97230
SW Sage Ter 97223
NW Saint Andrews Dr 97229
SE Saint Andrews Dr 97202
SW Saint Clair Ave 97205
NW Saint Helens Ave 97229
SW Saint Helens Ct 97201
NW Saint Helens Rd
2201-2297 97210
2299-8099 97210
8100-25299 97231
SW Saint James Ln 97224
SW Saint John Pl 97223
N Saint Johns Ave 97203
N Saint Louis Ave 97203
N Salem Ave 97203
Salishan Dr & Pl 97229
SE Salmon Ct
4500-4699 97215

9300-9399 97216
12400-12899 97233
SE Salmon St
100-106 97214
108-4100 97214
4102-4198 97214
4200-8199 97215
9200-11799 97216
12200-17199 97233
SW Salmon St
25-299 97204
301-515 97204
709-709 97205
711-2116 97205
2118-2148 97205
5700-6199 97221
9100-9399 97225
NW Saltzman Ct 97229
NW Saltzman Rd
401-597 97229
599-4999 97229
5900-6499 97210
10501-10597 97229
10599-11299 97229
NW Salvia Ct 97229
SW Sam Jackson Park Rd
2800-2899 97201
3000-3099 97239
3101-3299 97239
SE Sampson Ct 97267
NW Samuel Dr 97229
SE San Marcos Ave 97267
SE San Marino Ave 97267
NE San Rafael Dr 97230
NE San Rafael St
1-699 97212
10500-12199 97220
12400-20099 97230
SE Sancorad Ave 97233
SW Sandburg St 97223
SE Sandra Ave 97267
SW Sandridge Dr 97223
Sandview Ln & St 97222
NE Sandy Blvd
1300-3999 97232
4000-4199 97212
4200-8199 97213
8200-12199 97220
12300-13098 97230
13100-20099 97230
SE Sandy Blvd 97214
NE Sandycrest Ter 97213
SW Santa Monica Ct 97221
SW Santa Monica St 97239
SW Santana Pl 97225
NW Santanita Ter 97210
Santiam Ct & Dr 97229
NW Sarah Ln 97229
SE Sarah Ln 97267
N Saratoga St 97217
NE Saratoga St 97211
NW Sargent Ln 97231
SW Sattler St 97224
NW Sauvie Island Rd 97231
SE Savanna St 97267
NE Savier St
1400-1741 97209
1743-2099 97209
2100-3499 97210
NW Savoy Ln 97229
SE Sawtooth St 97236
NW Sawyer Ct 97229
Scarlett Dr & Pl 97224
SW Scenic Dr 97225
Scenic Drive Ct & Ter 97225
SW Schaeffer Ln 97224
SW Scheckla Dr 97224
NW Scheel Ter 97229
SE Schiller Ct 97266
SW Schiller Rd 97225
SE Schiller St
1501-1797 97202
1799-4199 97202
4200-7999 97206
8200-12199 97266
12200-13999 97236

SW Schiller Ter 97225
N Schmeer Rd 97217
N Schofield St 97217
SW Scholls Ferry Ct 97221
SW Scholls Ferry Rd
2141-2597 97221
2599-4005 97221
4007-4023 97221
4300-5999 97225
6000-8788 97223
8790-12930 97223
SW Schollwood Ct 97223
SW School St 97223
SE Schroeder Ave
13701-13797 97222
13799-13899 97222
13900-14000 97267
14002-14098 97267
SE Schroeder Ln 97267
NE Schuyler Ct 97230
NE Schuyler St
100-198 97212
200-3599 97212
7800-8198 97213
8200-11599 97220
12500-15899 97230
NW Science Park Dr 97229
SW Scoffins St 97223
SW Scott Ct 97223
SE Scott Dr 97215
SE Scott St 97222
SE Scottish Ct 97267
SW Scotts Bridge Dr 97223
N Scouler Ave 97217
SE Scrutton Ln 97267
SW Sean Michael Pl 97225
SW Seaview Ln 97223
SW Sebastian Ln 97224
Seblar Ct, Dr & Ter 97210
SW Seca Ct 97223
N Sedro St 97203
SE Segway Dr 97236
SW Selling Ct 97221
SE Sellwood Blvd 97202
SE Sellwood St 97222
SW Semler Way 97221
NE Senate St
3600-3900 97232
3902-4198 97232
4200-4399 97213
N Seneca St 97203
SE Sequoia Ave 97222
SW Sequoia Pkwy 97224
SE Sequoia Pl 97222
SE Sequoia St 97267
Serena Ct & Way 97224
NW Sethrich Ln 97229
N Sever Ct 97203
SW Sevilla Ave 97223
Seward Ave & Ct 97217
SW Seymour Ct
-200--299 97239
3200-3299 97239
3901-3997 97221
3999-5899 97221
SW Seymour Dr 97239
SW Seymour St
-121--121 97239
-20--40 97239
15-2197 97239
2199-3499 97239
3500-6499 97221
6500-6599 97225
SE Shadow Ct 97267
NW Shadow Ln 97229
Shady Ct, Ln & Pl 97223
SE Shadybrook Dr 97267
NW Shadywood Ln 97229
SW Shaker Pl 97225
SW Shakespeare St 97224
NW Shaniko Ct 97229
SW Sharon Ln 97225
SW Shattuck Rd 97221
NE Shaver Cir 97213
N Shaver St 97227
NE Shaver St
1-4099 97212

4101-4199 97212
4200-6299 97213
9700-12199 97220
12400-14599 97230
SW Shawn Pl 97223
SE Sheela Ct 97267
SW Sheffield Ave 97201
SW Sheffield Cir 97223
SE Shell Ln 97222
NW Shelsam Ter 97229
NW Sheltered Nook Rd 97231
NW Shenandoah Ter 97210
NW Shepherd St 97231
SW Sheridan Ct 97221
SW Sheridan St
401-599 97201
6100-6299 97225
NW Sherlock Ave 97210
SE Sherman Ct
11401-11497 97216
11499-11699 97216
13900-17599 97233
SE Sherman Dr 97233
SE Sherman St
800-4099 97214
4301-4697 97215
4699-7999 97215
9800-10399 97216
12200-17399 97233
SW Sherman St 97201
SE Sherrett St
701-797 97202
799-2299 97202
2800-3599 97222
6200-7499 97206
8200-8500 97266
8502-8598 97266
SE Sherrianne Ct 97222
NW Sherry Ct 97229
SE Sherry Ln 97222
NW Sherry St 97229
SW Sherwood Dr 97201
SW Sherwood Pl
2600-2632 97201
2634-3261 97201
3262-3500 97239
3502-3598 97239
SW Shilo Ln 97225
SW Shirley Ln 97223
SW Shore Dr 97223
NW Shoreline Way 97229
SW Shoreview Pl 97223
SW Shoue Dr 97224
SW Shrope Ct 97223
NW Sichel Ct 97229
NW Sicily Ave 97229
NW Sickle Ter 97229
SE Sierra Vista Dr 97267
SE Silver Leaf Ln 97267
NW Silver Ridge Loop 97229
SE Silver Springs Rd 97222
SE Silverleaf Ct 97222
NW Silverleaf Dr 97229
N Simmons Rd 97203
NW Simnasho Dr 97229
NE Simpson Ct 97218
N Simpson St 97217
NE Simpson St
400-3899 97211
4200-6499 97218
9901-10297 97220
10299-11299 97220
NE Siskiyou Ct 97230
NE Siskiyou St
700-798 97212
800-3500 97212
3502-3598 97212
4200-7999 97213
8001-8199 97213
8200-8598 97220
8600-12099 97220
12200-12298 97230
12300-16199 97230
SW Sitka Ct 97223
N Skidmore Ct 97217
N Skidmore St 97217
NE Skidmore St
1-4199 97211
4200-7999 97218
8001-8199 97218
8601-8697 97220
8699-11499 97220
N Skidmore Ter 97217
N Sky St 97203
SE Sky View Ct 97267
NW Skycrest Pkwy 97229
Skyhar Ct & Dr 97223
SE Skyhigh Ct 97267
NW Skyline Blvd
100-299 97210
300-398 97229
400-8399 97229
8401-8499 97229
8500-19199 97231
SW Skyline Blvd 97221
NW Skyline Ln 97210
NW Skyline Crest Rd 97229
NW Skyline Heights Dr 97229
NE Skyport Way 97218
Skyview Ct & Dr 97231
SW Slavin Rd 97239
NW Slocum Way 97229
Smith Ct & St 97203
SW Snapdragon Ln 97223
SE Snider Ave 97222
SW Snoopy Ct 97223
SW Snow Brush Ct 97223
SE Snowberry St 97222
NW Snowden Ct 97229
NW Snowlily Dr 97229
SW Snyder Pl 97221
Solano Ct & Ln 97229
SE Somewhere Dr 97222
SW Sonne Pl 97223
SW Sonnet Way 97224
SW Sophia Ln 97224
NW Sophie Ct 97229
SW Soprano Ln 97225
SW Sorrel Dock Ct 97223
South Dr & Rd 97229
N South Shore Ave 97217
NE South Shore Rd 97211
SE Southgate St 97222
SW Southridge Dr 97219
SE Southview Ave 97267
SW Southview Pl 97219
SW Southwood Dr 97219
SE Sparrow St 97222
NW Spartan Way 97229
SE Spaulding Ave 97267
NW Spencer St 97229
SW Spindler Ct 97224
SE Spokane St 97202
NW Spoon Pl 97229
SE Sporri Ln 97267
SE Spray Ave 97267
NW Spring Ave 97229
SW Spring Ct 97225
SW Spring Ln 97225
SW Spring St 97201
SW Spring Crest Dr 97225
Spring Garden Ct & St 97219
SW Springbrook Ln 97223
NE Springbrook St 97230
NW Springville Ct 97231
NW Springville Ln 97229
NW Springville Rd
8701-9097 97231
9099-9599 97231
10800-11498 97229
11500-17699 97229
17701-18399 97229
SE Springwater Dr 97206
SW Springwood Dr 97223
SE Spruce Ave 97214
SW Spruce St 97223
NW Spruceridge Ln 97229
SW St Andrews Ln 97224
N Stafford St
1-1099 97217
4601-4799 97203
NE Stafford St 97211
SW Stahl Dr 97223
NW Stalder Ln 97229
N Stanford Ave 97203
SW Stanford Ct 97223
SW Stanhope Ct 97201
SE Stanley Ave
9000-9299 97206
9300-12099 97222
12101-12399 97222
SE Stanley Ct 97222
SW Stanley Ct 97219
SE Stanley Pl 97206
NE Stanton Ct 97230
NE Stanton Pl 97230
N Stanton St 97227
NE Stanton St
1-4099 97212
4101-4131 97212
4230-4398 97213
4400-7699 97213
11700-12099 97220
12101-12199 97220
12200-16199 97230
SE Stanvick Ct 97267
SW Stardust Ln 97223
NW Starflower Dr 97229
NW Stark Ct 97229
SE Stark St
17439A-17439B 97233
1-197 97214
199-4199 97214
4200-8199 97215
8200-12199 97216
12200-20199 97233
SW Stark St
100-198 97204
200-599 97204
625-797 97205
799-1224 97205
1226-1234 97205
W Stark St 97229
N Starlight Ave 97217
SW Starview Dr 97224
NW Starview Pl 97229
SE Steele St
2600-2698 97202
2700-4199 97202
4200-7999 97206
8700-11199 97266
12200-14400 97236
14402-14498 97236
SE Steen Ct 97222
SW Stellers Jay Ln 97224
SE Stephanie Ct 97222
SW Stephen Ln 97225
SE Stephens Cir 97233
SE Stephens Ct 97233
SE Stephens Pl 97233
SE Stephens St
300-598 97214
600-3899 97214
6000-7999 97215
8301-8797 97216
8799-11699 97216
12200-18699 97233
Stephenson Ct & St 97219
SE Sterling Cir 97267
NW Sterling Ct 97229
SW Steve St 97223
SW Steven Ct 97223
SW Stewart St 97223
NW Stimpson Ln 97229
N Stockton Ave 97203
SE Stohler Rd 97267
NW Stoller Dr 97229
NW Stone Mountain Ln 97229
NW Stonebridge Dr 97229
Stonebrook Ct & Dr 97239
SW Stonecrest Ln 97219
SE Stratford Ave 97267
SW Stratford Ct 97224
SW Stratford Loop 97224
SW Strathfell Ln 97221
SE Strawberry Ln 97267
Streamside Ct & Dr 97219
SW Stringer Ln 97224
N Strong St 97203
SW Stuart Ct 97224
NE Stuart Dr 97212
SE Stuart Ln 97267
SE Stubb St 97222
NW Sue St 97229
NW Suffolk St 97210
NW Sugarberry Ter 97229
NW Sumida Ln 97229
SW Summer St 97223
Summer Crest Dr & Pl 97223
SW Summer Lake Dr 97223
Summerfield Ct, Dr & Ln 97224
SE Summerland Ct 97267
NE Summerplace Dr 97230
Summerview Ct & Dr 97224
SW Summerville Ave 97219
SW Summerwood Dr 97223
NW Summit Ave 97210
NW Summit Ct 97210
SW Summit Dr 97201
SW Summit Ridge St 97224
Summit View Ct & Dr 97225
NW Summitview Dr 97229
N Sumner St 97217
NE Sumner St
1-4199 97211
4200-7199 97218
8200-11999 97220
12001-12037 97220
SE Sun Ave 97267
Sun Meadow Ct & Ter 97267
NE Sunderland Ave 97211
SW Sundew Dr 97223
SE Sundial Ct 97222
Sundown Ln & Way 97229
NW Sunningdale Dr 97229
SE Sunny Slope Rd 97267
SE Sunnyside Dr 97222
SE Sunridge Ln 97267
SE Sunrise Ct 97267
NW Sunrise Ln 97229
SW Sunrise Ln 97224
SE Sunrise St 97236
SW Sunset Blvd 97239
NW Sunset Cir 97229
SE Sunset Ct 97267
SW Sunset Dr 97239
SW Sunset Hwy 97225
SE Sunset Ln 97206
NW Sunset View Ter 97229
SW Sunstead Ln 97225
N Superior St 97203
NW Supreme Ct 97229
NW Sussex Ave 97210
N Suttle Rd 97217
NE Suttle Rd 97211
SW Sutton Pl 97223
SW Suzanne Ct 97223
Swain Ave & Ct 97267
SE Swanson Ln 97267
SW Sweeney Pl 97223
SW Sweeney St
-202--248 97239
4701-4897 97221
4899-5199 97221
Sweetbriar Ct, Dr & St 97221
Sweetgale Ct & Ln 97229
SW Swendon Loop 97223
N Swenson St 97203
Swift Ct, St & Way 97203
NW Swiss Ln 97229
SW Sycamore Pl 97223
SW Sylvan Ct
7100-7399 97225
16300-16399 97224
NW Sylvania Ct 97229
SW Sylvania Ct 97219
NW Sylvania Ln 97229
SW Sylvania Ter 97219
N Syracuse St 97203
SE Tacoma St 97202
NW Taennler Ct 97229
N Taft Ave 97203
SE Taggart Ct
5201-7497 97206
7499-7699 97206
11000-11099 97266
15900-15999 97236
SE Taggart St
400-4199 97202
4200-8000 97206
8002-8066 97206
9100-10399 97266
12500-16999 97236
SW Takena Ct 97224
NW Talamore Ter 97229
Talbot Pl & Rd 97201
SW Tallwood Dr 97223
SW Talon Ln 97223
NW Talon Ter 97229
SE Talwood Ln 97267
SE Tamarack Ave 97214
SE Tamarack Ct 97267
SE Tamarack Way 97267
NW Tamarron Pl 97229
SW Tamaway Ln 97223
SE Tambara Ct 97222
NE Tamera Ln 97220
SW Tamera Ln 97223
NW Tamoshanter Way 97229
SW Tangela Ct 97223
SW Tangent St 97201
SW Tanoak Ct 97223
SW Tara Ct 97221
SE Tarbell Ave 97267
SW Tarleton Ct 97224
SW Tarlow Ct 97221
SE Taylor Ct
4900-8199 97215
8201-8297 97216
8299-8400 97216
8402-8498 97216
12900-14899 97233
SW Taylor Ct
5700-5799 97221
9800-9899 97223
12000-12299 97225
SW Taylor Ln 97224
SE Taylor St
11814A-11814B 97216
45-77 97214
79-4199 97214
4200-8199 97215
8200-12099 97216
13600-17199 97233
SW Taylor St
55-519 97204
521-545 97204
700-796 97205
798-1740 97205
1742-2124 97205
5700-6099 97221
6101-6199 97221
9000-10699 97225
SW Taylors Ferry Ct 97219
SW Taylors Ferry Rd
-201--699 97219
1-197 97219
199-6499 97219
6500-8999 97223
NW Teakwood Pl 97229
SW Tearose Way 97223
SW Tech Center Dr 97223
SE Teddy Ln 97267
NW Tee Ct 97229
SW Tempest Way 97224
SE Tenino Ct
4600-5199 97206
9200-9599 97266
SE Tenino Dr 97206
SE Tenino St
500-598 97202
600-4199 97202
4200-7299 97206
8900-9099 97266
13700-14699 97236
NW Terlette Ave 97209
SW Terlyn Ct 97221
NW Terminal St 97209
Terminal 4 97203
SW Terrace Dr 97201
SE Terrace Trails Dr 97266
SW Terrace Trails Dr 97223
NW Terraceview Ct 97229
Terraview Ct & Dr 97224
SW Terreton Pl 97223
SW Terri Ct 97225
N Terry St 97217
SW Terwilliger Blvd
2501-2599 97201
3301-5697 97239
5699-5999 97239
6001-6499 97239
6701-6797 97219
6799-12099 97219
12101-12699 97219
SW Terwilliger Pl
800-899 97239
10100-10699 97219
Terwilliger Plz 97201
SE Tessa St 97233
Tewkesbury Ct & Dr 97224
Texas Ct & St 97219
SW Thelen Ln 97219
SE Thelma Cir 97267
Thiessen Ct & Rd 97267
SW Thistlebrook Ct 97224
SE Thomas Ct 97222
SW Thomas Ct 97221
SW Thomas St
-108--114 97239
-116--118 97239
-120--130 97239
4900-5198 97221
5200-6100 97221
6102-6398 97221
SE Thomas Smith Rd 97267
NE Thompson Ct 97230
SE Thompson Ct 97222
NW Thompson Rd
6100-6499 97210
6600-6698 97229
6700-11999 97229
12001-13899 97229
SE Thompson Rd 97222
N Thompson St 97227
NE Thompson St
1-4099 97212
4101-4199 97212
4200-8199 97213
8200-12099 97220
13700-16499 97230
SE Thorburn St 97215
SW Thorn St 97223
SE Thornapple Ln 97267
SE Thornton Dr 97267
SW Thornwood Dr 97224
SE Thorville Ave 97267
SW Thunder Ter 97223
NW Thunder Crest Rd 97229
N Thunderbird Way 97227
SW Thurlow Dr 97225
NW Thurman St
4040A-4040B 97210
1500-1598 97209
1600-1799 97209
1801-2099 97209
2101-2197 97210
2199-4041 97210
4043-4099 97210
SW Thurston Ln 97224
SE Tiara Dr 97267
SE Tibbetts Ct 97266
SE Tibbetts St
1800-1898 97202
1900-4099 97202
4101-4199 97202
4201-4397 97206
4399-8199 97206
10800-12199 97266
12200-18199 97236
SW Tichner Dr 97205
SE Tidwells Way 97267
SW Tiedeman Ave 97223
Tigard Dr & St 97223
NW Tigon Ln 97229
SE Tikki Ct 97267
NE Tillamook Ct 97230
NW Tillamook Dr 97229
N Tillamook St 97227
NE Tillamook St
1-4199 97212
4200-8199 97213
8200-11099 97220
12800-16599 97230
SW Tillie Ln 97224
SW Timara Ln 97224
NW Timber Ridge Ct 97229
SW Timberline Dr 97225
NW Timberview Ln 97229
N Time Oil Rd 97203
SW Timothy Pl 97223
SE Tindall Cir 97202
N Tioga Ave 97203
SW Tippitt Pl 97223
SW Titan Ln 97224
NW Tivoli Ln 97229
N Todd St 97203
SW Todd St 97225
Toketee Ct & Dr 97229
SW Toland St 97223
SE Tolman St
1201-1397 97202
1399-3900 97202
3902-4198 97202
4600-4698 97206
4700-8199 97206
8300-8899 97266
8901-9099 97266
NW Tolovana St 97229
SW Toma Ct 97225
N & NE Tomahawk Island Dr 97217
SW Tony Ct 97223
SW Tookbank Ct 97224
SE Topaz Ave 97267
SE Torbank Rd 97222
SW Torchwood St 97223
SW Torland St 97223
SW Torr Ln 97221
Torrey View Ct, Dr & Ln 97229
SE Totem Peak Ln 97267
SW Tower Way 97221
SE Towhee Ct 97267
NW Townsend Ct 97229
NE Tracey Ln 97230
SW Tracy Pl 97223
SE Tracy Suzanne Ct 97267
NW Tradewind St 97229
NW Trail Ave 97229
SW Trail Ct 97219
NW Trakehner Way 97229
SE Tranquil Ct 97267
NE Transport Way 97218
SW Treehill Ct 97224
SW Treeview Ct 97224
SW Tremont St 97225
N Trenton Pl 97203
N Trenton St
2500-3799 97217
4301-4397 97203
4399-5199 97203
NW Trevino St 97229
SW Trevor Ln 97224
SW Trillium Ln 97219
SW Trillium Creek Ter 97225
SE Trilva Jean Ct 97267
NW Trinity Pl 97209
SE Trolley Ln 97267
SE Trolley Line Ln 97267
SE Trona Ln 97222
Troon Dr & Way 97229
NW Trowbridge Dr 97229
SW Troy St 97219
N Trumbull Ave 97203
SW Tryon Ave 97219
SW Tryon Hill Rd 97219
NW Tualatin Ave 97229
SW Tualatin Ave 97239
SW Tualatin Dr 97224
NW Tuality Way 97229
NW Tudor Ln 97229

- NW Tullamore Ct 97229
- NW Tullamorrie Way 97229
- NW Tumalo Ct 97229
- SW Tunnelwood St 97221
- SW Turnagain Dr 97224
- SE Tuscany Ct 97267
- SW Tuscany St 97223
- SE Tuscany Way 97267
- NW Tustin Ranch Dr 97229
- SW Twelve Oaks Ct 97224
- NW Twilight Ter 97229
- SW Twin Park Pl 97223
- NW Twinflower Dr 97229
- SW Twombly Ave 97239
- NW Twoponds Dr 97229
- SW Tybalt Pl 97224
- N Tyler Ave 97203
- NW Tyler Ct 97229
- N Tyndall Ave 97217
- Tyrol Cir & St 97239
- NW Ukiah St 97229
- SE Umatilla St
  - 500-698 97202
  - 700-4199 97202
  - 4400-4499 97206
  - 4501-7399 97206
- SW Underhill Rd 97219
- SW Underwood Dr 97225
- N Union Ct 97217
- N University Ave 97203
- NW Unrath Pl 97229
- N Upland Dr 97203
- SW Upland Dr 97221
- SW Uplands Dr 97223
- SW Upper Dr 97201
- SE Upper Aldercrest Dr 97267
- SW Upper Boones Ferry Rd 97224
- SW Upper Cascade Dr 97205
- SW Upper Drive Pl 97201
- SW Upper Hall St 97201
- NW Upshur St
  - 1700-1798 97209
  - 1800-1899 97209
  - 1901-1999 97209
  - 2101-2497 97210
  - 2499-2999 97210
- NW Upton Ct 97229
- NW Uptown Ter 97210
- NE Us Grant Pl 97212
- SW Us Veterans Hospital Rd 97239
- Vacuna Ct & St 97219
- NW Vale St 97229
- SW Valenta Ct 97223
- SW Valeria View Dr 97225
- NW Valle Vista Ter 97210
- Vallevue Ct & Pl 97229
- SW Valley View Ct 97225
- SW Valley View Dr 97225
- NW Valley View Ln 97231
- SE Valley View Rd 97267
- SW Valona Way 97219
- NW Valros Ln 97229
- N Van Buren Ave 97203
- N Van Houten Ave 97203
- Van Waters Ct & St 97222
- NW Vance Dr 97229
- N Vancouver Ave
  - 1600-1898 97227
  - 1900-4099 97227
  - 4100-11099 97217
- N Vancouver Way 97217
- NE Vancouver Way 97211
- N Vanderbilt St 97203
- NW Vardon Pl 97229
- SW Varns St 97223
- NW Vaughn Ct 97229
- NW Vaughn St
  - 1801-1897 97209
  - 1899-2099 97209
  - 2101-2197 97210
  - 2199-3499 97210
- SW Venezia Ter 97223
- Ventura Ct, Dr & Pl 97223
- SW Venus Ct 97223
- NE Vera St 97213
- SE Verbena Pl 97213
- SW Verde Ter 97223
- NW Verde Vista Ter 97210
- SW Vermont Ct 97223
- SW Vermont St
  - -100--600 97219
  - -602--698 97219
  - 100-6200 97219
  - 6202-6498 97219
  - 6500-7799 97223
- SE Vernelda St 97267
- Vernie Ave & Ct 97222
- NW Vernon Ct 97229
- SW Versailles Ln 97224
- NW Vesper Pl 97229
- SE Vest Ln 97222
- Vesta Ct & St 97219
- NW Vetter Dr 97229
- SE Victor St 97266
- N Victory Blvd 97217
- SW View Ct 97224
- SW View Pl 97205
- SW View Ter 97224
- SE View Acres Rd 97267
- SE View Meadows Ln 97267
- SW View Point Ter
  - 4641A-4641C 97239
  - 3801-3997 97239
  - 3999-6300 97239
  - 6302-6698 97239
  - 7400-9699 97219
- SW Viewcrest Ct 97224
- SE Viewcrest Dr 97267
- SW Viewmont Dr 97225
- Viewmount Ct & Ln 97223
- SW Viewpoint Ct 97224
- NW Village Cir 97229
- Village Glenn Cir, Ct & Dr 97223
- NW Village Heights Dr 97229
- SW Village Park Ln 97223
- N Villard Ave 97217
- SW Villeann Ave 97239
- N Vincent Ave 97217
- SW Vincent Pl 97239
- NW Vincola Ter 97229
- SE Vineyard Ave 97267
- SW Vineyard Ct 97223
- SE Vineyard Ln 97267
- SE Vineyard Rd 97267
- SE Vineyard Way 97267
- SE Vintage Pl 97267
- SW Viola St 97224
- SW Viredarl St 97221
- SW Virginia Ave
  - 6621A-6621C 97239
  - 5901-6097 97239
  - 6099-6622 97239
  - 6624-6698 97239
  - 6700-7499 97219
  - 7501-7599 97219
- SW Virginia Pl 97219
- SW Vista Ave
  - 700-1199 97205
  - 1400-2699 97201
- SE Vista Ct 97267
- SW Vista Dr 97225
- NW Vista Ln 97231
- SE Vista Ln 97267
- SW Vista Pl 97225
- SE Vista Sunrise Ct 97267
- SW Vista View Ct 97224
- SE Vivaldi Cir 97222
- SE Vivian Ln 97222
- N Wabash Ave 97217
- SE Wabash Ave 97222
- SE Wagner Ln 97267
- SW Wagoner Pl 97224
- SW Wahkeena Ct 97224
- NW Wahkeena Ln 97229
- Wake Ct & St 97222
- SW Wakefield St 97225
- NW Waker Dr 97229
- SE Walden Way 97267
- Waldron Dr & Rd 97222
- NE Walker Ct 97211
- SW Walker Rd 97225
- NE Walker St 97211
- SW Walking Woods Dr 97219
- N Wall Ave 97203
- Wallace Rd & Way 97267
- Wallowa Ct & Pl 97229
- NW Wallula Ct 97229
- NW Walmer Dr 97229
- SW Walnut Ln
  - 7800-7899 97225
  - 13535-14340 97223
- SW Walnut Pl 97223
- SE Walnut St 97267
- SW Walnut St 97223
- SW Walnut Ter 97223
- Walnut Creek Ct & Way 97223
- Walta Vista Ct & Dr 97267
- NW Walters Ln 97229
- NW Waltuck Ct 97229
- Wanda Ct & Dr 97267
- NW Wapato Ave 97231
- SW Wapato Ave 97239
- NW Wapato Dr 97231
- Wapinitia Ln & Pl 97229
- NE Ward St 97220
- NW Wardway St 97210
- SW Wareham Cir 97223
- SW Warner Ave 97223
- SE Warnock Ln 97267
- N Warren St 97203
- SW Warrens Way 97221
- NW Warrenton Ter 97210
- SW Warwick Ave 97225
- NE Wasco Ct 97230
- NE Wasco St
  - 401-1697 97232
  - 1699-3899 97232
  - 4700-8199 97213
  - 8200-10699 97220
  - 12300-19899 97230
- N Washburne Ave 97217
- SE Washington Ct 97233
- SW Washington Dr 97223
- SE Washington Pl 97222
- SW Washington Pl 97225
- SE Washington St
  - 61-85 97214
  - 87-1927 97214
  - 1928-1998 97222
  - 1929-1935 97214
  - 2000-2399 97222
  - 2604-2702 97214
  - 2704-2717 97214
  - 2720-2722 97222
  - 2724-2756 97222
  - 2758-2836 97222
  - 2809-2901 97214
  - 2903-2945 97214
  - 2947-2955 97214
  - 3000-3200 97222
  - 3202-3316 97222
  - 3303-3321 97214
  - 3323-3405 97214
  - 3406-3406 97222
  - 3407-4125 97214
  - 3416-3420 97214
  - 3426-3426 97222
  - 3436-4132 97214
  - 4200-8099 97215
  - 8200-11899 97216
  - 13000-17899 97233
- SW Washington St
  - 200-512 97204
  - 514-550 97204
  - 601-601 97205
  - 603-1321 97205
  - 1323-1337 97205
  - 9000-11099 97225
- SW Washington Square Rd 97223
- SW Washouga Ave 97239
- SW Wastoner Sq 97201
- SE Water Ave 97214
- SW Water Ave
  - 2301-2597 97201
  - 2599-3099 97201
  - 3200-4699 97239
- SE Water Edge Way 97267
- SW Water Parsley Ln 97224
- NW Waterford Way 97229
- Watkins Ave & Pl 97223
- SE Watson Pl 97267
- N Watts St 97217
- SE Waverleigh Blvd 97202
- SE Waverly Ct 97222
- SE Waverly Dr 97222
- SW Waverly Dr 97224
- SW Waverly Pl 97225
- N Wayland Ave 97203
- SE Waymire St 97222
- NW Wayne Ln 97229
- SW Webber Ln 97224
- SE Webber St 97202
- NE Webster Ct 97218
- SE Webster Ln 97267
- SE Webster Rd 97267
- N Webster St 97217
- NE Webster St
  - 400-3899 97211
  - 5400-5499 97218
  - 8200-9199 97220
- SW Wedgewood St 97225
- Weedman Ct & St 97222
- SE Weeks Ct 97267
- N Weidler St 97227
- NE Weidler St
  - 1-3299 97232
  - 4200-4399 97213
  - 8400-11399 97220
  - 12600-15799 97230
- SE Weiko Way 97222
- SE Welcome Ave 97214
- N Weldello Ave 97217
- N Wellesley Ave 97203
- SW Wellington Ave 97225
- SW Wellington Pl 97223
- NW Wells Ct 97229
- Wells Fargo Ctr 97201
- NW Welsh Dr 97229
- SW Wendover Ter 97223
- NW Wendy Ln 97229
- NW Wenmarie Dr 97229
- NW Werburgh Ln 97229
- NW Werner Ln 97229
- NW West Rd 97229
- SW West Haven Dr 97225
- SW West Point Ave 97225
- SW West Point Ct 97201
- SW West Slope Dr 97225
- NW West Union Rd 97229
- Westanna Ave & Ct 97203
- NW Westbrook Way 97229
- SW Westbury Ter 97223
- SW Westdale Ct 97221
- SW Westdale Dr 97221
- SW Westdale St 97225
- SW Westfield Ave 97225
- SE Westfork St 97206
- SW Westgate Dr 97221
- SW Westgate Way 97225
- Westlawn St & Ter 97229
- SW Westlund Ct 97224
- SW Westminster Dr 97224
- SW Westmoor Way 97225
- Westover Cir, Rd, Sq & Ter 97210
- SW Westridge Ter 97223
- N Westshore Dr 97217
- SE Westview Ave 97267
- SW Westwood Ct 97239
- SW Westwood Dr
  - 500-1799 97239
  - 3000-3199 97225
- SW Westwood Ln 97239
- SW Westwood Vw 97239
- SW Wexford Pl 97223
- N Weyerhaeuser Ave 97203
- NW Wheatfield Way 97229
- Wheeler Ave & Pl 97227
- SE Where Else Ln 97222
- Whipple Ave & Ln 97267
- NW Whistler Ln 97229
- Whistlers Ln & Loop 97223
- N Whitaker Rd 97217
- SW Whitaker St 97239
- NE Whitaker Way 97230
- SE Whitcomb Dr 97222
- SW White Ct 97225
- SW White Cedar Pl 97223
- SE White Lake Rd 97222
- SE White Oak Ave 97213
- SW White Pine Ln 97225
- SW Whitehall Ln 97223
- SW Whiteoaks Ln 97224
- Whitford Dr & Ln 97223
- SW Whitfurrows Ct 97224
- NW Whitman Ct 97229
- NW Whitney Ave 97231
- NE Wiberg Ln 97213
- Wichita Ave & Ct 97222
- NW Wickiup Way 97229
- NW Wilark Ave 97231
- SW Wilbard St 97219
- N Wilbur Ave 97217
- Wild Rose Ct & Ln 97267
- SW Wilderland Ct 97224
- SE Wildlife Estates Dr 97267
- SW Wildwood St 97224
- SE Wildwoods Ct 97267
- NW Wiley Ln 97229
- SE Wiley Way 97267
- NE Wilkes Rd 97230
- SE Wilkinson Ct 97267
- SE Willamette Ave 97222
- N Willamette Blvd
  - 1500-2919 97217
  - 2921-3999 97217
  - 4001-4997 97203
  - 4999-10099 97203
- SE Willamette Dr 97267
- N Willamette Ln 97203
- SE Willard St 97222
- NW Willbridge Ave 97210
- N Williams Ave
  - 1100-1498 97227
  - 1500-4099 97227
  - 4100-11099 97217
- N Willis Blvd
  - 1500-3999 97217
  - 4000-4098 97203
  - 4100-5799 97203
- SE Willow Ln 97267
- SW Willow Ln 97225
- NE Willow St 97213
- SE Willow St 97222
- SW Willow Point Ln 97224
- SW Willow Top Ln 97224
- SW Willow Wood Ct 97223
- SW Willowbottom Way 97224
- SW Willowmere Dr 97225
- SW Wills Pl 97223
- SE Wills Way 97267
- SE Wilma Cir 97222
- SW Wilmington Ln 97224
- SE Wilmot St 97267
- SE Wilshire Ct 97267
- NW Wilshire Ln 97229
- SE Wilshire St 97267
- SW Wilshire St 97225
- NW Wilson St
  - 3135A-3135C 97210
  - 2000-2099 97209
  - 2100-3299 97210
- SW Wilton Ave 97223
- SW Wimbledon Ct 97224
- NE Win Sivers Dr 97220
- N Winchell St
  - 600-3899 97217
  - 3901-3999 97217
  - 4001-4499 97203
- NE Winchell St 97211
- SW Winchester Ave 97225
- SW Winchester Pl 97225
- NW Winchester Ter 97210
- NW Wind Ridge Dr 97229
- SW Windemere Loop 97225
- SW Windham Ter 97224
- N Windle St 97203
- SE Windmill Ln 97267
- SW Windsong Ct 97223
- SE Windsor Ct 97206
- SW Windsor Ct
  - 4800-5799 97221
  - 10500-10699 97223
- SW Windsor Pl 97223
- SW Windwood Way 97225
- SE Windy Ln 97267
- NW Winema Ct 97229
- SE Wing St 97206
- N Winning Way 97227
- NE Winona St 97211
- Winsor Ct & Dr 97222
- NW Winston Dr 97210
- NW Winter Ln 97210
- Winter Lake Ct & Dr 97223
- NW Winter Park Ter 97229
- SW Wintergreen St 97223
- SW Winterview Dr 97224
- SW Winthrop Ave 97225
- SE Winworth Ct 97222
- NW Wismer Dr 97229
- NE Wistaria Dr
  - 3700-4199 97212
  - 4200-5399 97213
- SE Wister St 97222
- SW Withywindle Ct 97224
- NW Wood Ave 97231
- SE Wood Ave 97222
- SE Wood Ct 97222
- SW Wood Pkwy 97219
- SW Wood Pl 97224
- SW Wood Duck Pl 97223
- NW Wood Rose Loop 97229
- SW Woodard Ln 97223
- SE Woodcock Ave 97267
- NW Woodcreek Ct 97229
- SW Woodcrest Ave 97224
- SE Woodhaven St 97222
- SW Woodhue St 97224
- NW Woodland Ct 97229
- SE Woodland Way 97267
- SW Woodlawn Ct 97223
- Woodlee Heights Ave & Ct 97219
- NW Woodrose Dr 97229
- N Woodrush Way 97203
- SW Woods Ct 97221
- SW Woods St
  - 25-97 97201
  - 99-120 97201
  - 122-336 97201
  - 1001-1299 97239
  - 3500-3599 97221
  - 10400-10599 97225
- SW Woods Creek Ct 97219
- SW Woodshire Ln 97223
- SE Woodside Ave 97267
- SW Woodside Dr 97225
- NW Woodside Ter 97210
- SE Woodstock Blvd
  - 2800-3198 97202
  - 3200-4199 97202
  - 4200-8199 97206
  - 8200-10299 97266
- SE Woodstock Ct 97266
- SE Woodward Ct
  - 13800-14698 97236
  - 14700-15700 97236
  - 15702-17298 97236
  - 17201-17299 97236
  - 17201-17225 97266
- SE Woodward Pl 97266
- SE Woodward St
  - 501-597 97202
  - 599-4199 97202
  - 4200-8199 97206
  - 11200-11499 97266
  - 12500-17199 97236
- SW Woodward Way 97225
- SW Woody End St 97224
- Woolsey Ave & Ct 97203
- SW Worchester Pl 97223
- SE Worthington Ln 97267
- SE Wren St 97222
- SW Wright Ave 97205
- SW Wrightwood Ct 97224
- N Wygant St 97217
- NE Wygant St
  - 1-3299 97211
  - 4200-8199 97218
  - 8200-11499 97220
- SW Wyndham Ln 97221
- SW Wynwood Ave 97225
- NE Yacht Harbor Dr 97217
- SW Yale Pl 97223
- N Yale St 97203
- SE Yamhill Cir 97233
- SE Yamhill Ct 97215
- SE Yamhill St
  - 50-58 97214
  - 60-4199 97214
  - 4200-8199 97215
  - 8200-11900 97216
  - 11902-11998 97216
  - 13500-19699 97233
- SW Yamhill St
  - 53-527 97204
  - 529-555 97204
  - 600-798 97205
  - 800-2183 97205
  - 2185-2185 97205
  - 5900-6099 97221
- SW Yarrow Way 97223
- SE Yearling Ln 97267
- NW Yellowberry Way 97229
- NW Yeon Ave 97210
- SE Yew St 97267
- NW Yoncalla Ct 97229
- NE Yoristri St 97218
- NW York St
  - 2001-2099 97209
  - 2100-2399 97210
- NW Yorkshire Ln 97229
- Yukon St 97216
- SE Yukon St
  - 1300-2199 97202
  - 9600-10699 97266
- NW Yvonne Ln 97229
- SW Zander Ct 97223
- NW Zermatt Ct 97229
- N Ziegler Ave 97203

NUMBERED STREETS

- All Street Addresses 97211

ROSEBURG OR

- General Delivery 97470

POST OFFICE BOXES MAIN OFFICE STATIONS AND BRANCHES

Box No.s

- All PO Boxes 97470

NAMED STREETS

- Acorn Dr 97470
- Adams Loop 97471
- Addy Ln 97471
- Aerie Ln 97471
- Agape Ct 97471
- W Agee St 97471
- NE Airport Rd 97470
- Akin Ln 97471
- NE Alameda Ave 97470
- W Alamosa Ct 97471
- Alayne Ave 97471
- NE Alder St 97470
- NW Almira St 97471

Street	ZIP
NW Almond Ave	97471
Aloha Ct	97471
W Alpha St	97471
Alpine Dr	97471
W Altamont St	97471
Alyssa Ct	97471
E & W Amanda Ct & St	97471
Amber Ln	97471
Anderson Ln	97470
Andorra Dr	97471
NW Andrea St	97471
E & W Angela Ct	97471
Angelcrest Ct	97471
W Ann Ave	97471
Antelope Ln	97471
NW Apache Dr	97471
Apple Blossom Ln	97471
Apricot Ln	97471
Arcadia Dr	97471
Armande Loop	97471
Art Mill Ln	97471
Ash St	97471
NW Ashley Ave	97471
Aspen Ct	97471
Athena Ln	97470
Atkinson Ct	97470
NE Atlanta St	97470
Austin Rd	97471
Autumn Ave	97471
NW Avery St	97471
NW Aviation Dr	97470
NW Avoy Ct	97471
SE Azalea St	97470
Bailey Dr	97471
Balboa Ave	97471
Balder Ln	97470
W Ballf St	97471
SE Balsam Ave	97470
Bamboo Ln	97471
N & S Bank Dr & Rd	97470
NE Barager Ave	97470
Barberry Ln	97471
NE Barnes Ave	97470
Barron Ct	97471
NW Basco Ave	97471
W Basil St	97471
Basswood Ln	97471
NW Beacon St	97470
Beattie Ln	97471
NW Beaumont Ave	97471
Beaver Ln	97471
Beaver State Rd	97471
Becker Rd	97471
Beech St	97471
Bel Air Ct	97471
Belden St	97471
Bell Ranch Ln	97470
NE Bellview Ct	97470
Bellwood Ln	97471
Belmont Ave	97471
W Berdine St	97471
Berry Loop Ln	97471
W Bertha Ave	97471
NE Beulah Dr	97470
Beverly Ct	97471
Big Bend Rd	97471
W Birch Ct	97471
Birdie Ln	97471
NW Black Ave	97471
Black Oak Dr	97471
Blacktail Ln	97470
Blake Ave	97471
SE Blakeley Ave	97470
Blands Ln	97471
NE Bloomfield Ct	97470
Boardwalk Way	97471
Boatwatch Ln	97470
Bobwhite St	97471
W Bodie St	97471
NE Bogard St	97470
Bonifacio Ln	97471
SE Booth Ave	97470
NE Boston St	97470
Bourne St	97471
W Bowden St	97470
W Bradford Ave	97471
Bradley Ct	97470
Bramble Way	97470
Branding Iron Ln	97471
Brandy Ln	97471
Braunda Dr	97471
Breezy Ln	97470
NW Brent Ct	97471
Brentridge Dr	97471
Brittney Ave	97471
NW Broad St	97471
NW Broadway St	97471
W Broccoli St	97471
SE Brockway Ave	97470
Bronco Dr	97471
NE Brooklyn Ave	97470
W Brown Ave	97471
Broyhill Ln	97471
Brozio Rd	97471
Brumbach Rd	97470
SE Brush Ave	97470
Bryant Ln	97471
Buckhorn Rd	97470
Buell Ln	97471
Buena Vista Ln	97471
Buffalo Ln	97471
Bunting Ct	97471
Burdette Dr	97471
SE Burke Ave	97470
Burkhart Rapids Ln	97471
Busenbark Ln	97471
Butte Creek Ln	97470
Buzz Mountain Ln	97471
SE Byrd Ct	97470
NW Cabrillo Ct	97471
Cactus Ln	97471
Cal Henry Rd	97471
NW Calkins Ave	97471
Callahan Dr & Rd	97471
Callahan View Way	97471
Calypso Ln	97470
NE Cambrian Ct	97470
NE Camelot Ct	97470
Cameron Ave	97471
Camino Francisco Ave	97471
Camino Nina Ave	97471
Candy Ln	97471
Cannon Ave	97471
NW Canterbury Dr	97471
Capital Ln	97471
Capitola Ct	97471
W Cardinal St	97471
NW Carl Ave	97471
Carlton Ln	97471
Carmel Ct	97471
NE Carmen St	97470
Carnes Rd	97471
Carolyn Ct	97470
Carriage Ln	97471
Carrin Layne Ct	97471
W Carroll Ct	97471
Carson Ln	97471
SE Cascade Ct	97470
Cascara Ln	97471
W Casey St	97470
Cashew Ln	97471
NE Caskey Ct	97470
NE Casper St	97470
SE Cass Ave	97470
Castle Ave	97471
W Catherine Ave	97471
Cattle Dr	97470
NW Cecil Ave	97470
NE Cedar St	97470
Cedar Ridge Ct	97471
Cedar Tree Dr	97471
Cedrus Ln	97471
Cegavske Ln	97470
Centennial Dr	97471
W Center St	97471
NE Central St	97470
SE Chadwick St	97470
NW Chambers Dr	97471
Champagne Ct & Dr	97471
Champagne Creek Dr	97471
Chandler Dr	97471
NE Channon Ave	97470
W Chapman Ave	97470
Char St	97471
Chardonnay Way	97471
Charter Oaks Dr	97471
W Chateau Ave	97471
Cherokee Ave	97471
NW Cherry Dr	97471
NE Chestnut Ave	97470
NE Cheston Ct	97470
Chewaucan Ln	97471
SE Chinaberry Ave	97470
Chinkapin Ct	97470
Christensen Ln	97471
NW Christie Ct	97471
NE Church Ave	97470
Cinbar Dr	97471
Circle Dr	97471
Circle Star Ln	97470
SE Claire St	97470
Clarice Ln	97470
Clarks Branch Rd	97470
Clearview Dr	97471
SE Clearwater Ct	97470
Clellon Ct	97471
Cleveland Hill Rd	97471
Cleveland Loop Dr	97471
Cleveland Park Rd	97471
Cleveland Rapids Rd	97471
Cloake St	97471
Cloudcrest Ct	97471
NE Clover Ave	97470
Clover Leaf St	97471
Club Ave	97470
Clyde William Ln	97471
SE Cobb St	97470
W Cochrane Ct	97471
NE College St	97470
Colonial Rd	97471
SE Colorado St	97470
Colton Ln	97470
Columbia Loop Rd	97471
Colvin St	97471
Colwell Hill Ln	97471
NE Commercial Ave	97470
Coos Bay Wagon Rd	97471
W Copper Ct	97471
E & W Cordelia Ct	97471
W Corey Ct	97470
Cornerstone St	97471
Corona Loop Rd	97471
Coronado Dr	97471
SE Corrine Ave	97470
Corvallis Ave	97471
Country Ln	97471
Country Hill Dr	97471
SE Court Ave	97470
Coyote Ln	97471
Crawford Ln	97471
Creekside Ct	97471
Crescent Aly & St	97470
NW Crest Ct	97471
W Crestview Ave	97471
Cross Creek Dr	97471
NW Crouch St	97471
Croxton Ln	97471
Croy Park Ln	97471
Crystal Springs Ln	97471
NE Cummins St	97470
Currier Ave	97470
N Curry Rd	97471
Dairy Loop Rd	97471
Daisy Ln	97471
Danita Ln	97470
Dark Horse St	97471
Darley Dr	97471
Davis Ln	97470
Davis Creek Way	97470
Dawson Rd	97470
NW Daysha Dr	97471
NE Dee St	97470
Deer Creek Dr & Rd	97470
Deer Fern Way	97470
Del Castillo Ln	97471
Del Mar Dr	97471
Del Rio Rd	97471
NW Delridge Ave	97471
Delus Dr	97470
NE Delynne Ct	97470
NE Denn Ave	97470
NE Denver St	97470
Depriest St	97471
Dewey Ln	97470
Diamond Lake Blvd & Hwy	97470
SE Dickey Ct	97470
SE Dillard Ave	97470
NE Dixon St	97470
Dixonville Rd	97470
Dobie Ct	97470
Dodson View Rd	97471
Doerner Rd	97471
Doerner Cutoff Rd	97471
NW Dogwood St	97471
NW Domenico Dr	97471
Donruss Dr	97471
Doris St	97471
NE Dorwin Ave	97470
SE Dos Gatos Ct	97470
Douglas Ave	97470
SE Downey Ave	97470
Doyle Ln	97471
Dusty Ln	97471
Dwight Ln	97471
Eagle Dr	97471
SE Eagles Rest Ave	97470
SE Eastwood St	97470
Echo Dr	97470
Echo Canyon Ln	97471
SE Eddy St	97470
NW Eden St	97470
NW Edenbower Blvd	
2400-2999	97471
3200-3300	97470
3302-3498	97470
NE Edenbower St	97470
Edna Ave	97471
NW El Dorado St	97471
W Elaine Ave	97471
Elbridge Ln	97471
Elgarose Rd	97471
W Elizabeth St	97471
SE Ella St	97470
NW Ellan St	97470
NW Elliot St	97471
NW Ellis St	97471
W Elm St	97471
NE Emerald Dr	97470
Emery Ln	97471
Emils Way	97471
NE Erie St	97470
Erin Ct	97471
Ervin Ave	97471
W Esperanza Ct	97471
NW Esquire Dr	97471
Estacata Pl	97471
NW Estelle St	97471
NW Ethel Ct	97471
NW Evans Ave	97471
Evelyn St	97471
NW Excello Dr	97471
NE Exchange Ave	97470
W Fair St	97471
Fairacres Ln	97470
W Fairhaven St	97471
Fairhill Dr	97471
NW Fairmount St	97470
Fairway Village Ln	97471
Fawn Dr	97470
Felt St	97471
Fescue Ln	97470
W Filbert Ave	97471
NW Finch Ct	97471
W Finlay Ave	97471
W Fir St	97471
Fir Ridge Ln	97471
SE Fisher Dr	97470
Fisher Rd	97471
Fisk Ln	97471
NE Flagg St	97470
NE Flagstaff St	97470
Flangas Ave	97471
NE Fleser Ave	97470
SE Flint St	97470
SE Floed Ave	97470
NW Flora Ave	97471
Florence Ln	97471
SE Florida Ave	97470
Flournoy Valley Rd	97471
NE Follett St	97470
W Foothill Dr	97471
Forest Hills Ln	97471
Forest View Ln	97471
Forgotten Ln	97471
Foster Ln	97470
Four Seasons Dr	97470
SE Fowler St	97470
Fox Ln	97471
Fox Hill Ln	97470
Fox Hollow Ln	97471
W Francis St	97471
Frear St	97471
Freedom Ln	97470
Freeman Ave	97471
NE Freemont Ave	97470
W Fromdahl Dr	97471
Frontier Ln	97470
Fuchsia Ln	97471
SE Fullerton St	97470
NE Fulton St	97470
Gale St	97471
NW Garden Ln & St	97471
Garden Grove Dr	97471
NE Garden Valley Blvd	97470
NW Garden Valley Blvd	
100-174	97470
176-469	97470
471-499	97470
700-774	97471
776-2199	97471
Garden Valley Rd	97471
NE Gardiner St	97470
NE Garrecht St	97470
W Gary Ave	97471
Gateway Rd	97470
Gelding Ln	97471
Gem Dr	97471
General Ave	97470
Geneva Ct	97471
Gentry Way	97471
Georginna Dr	97471
SE Germond Ave	97470
W Gilbert Ave	97471
SE Giles St	97470
Glenda Ave	97470
Glengary Loop Rd	97470
Glenmar Dr	97471
SE Glenn St	97470
Glenwood Ct	97471
Glide Transfer Rd	97470
W Goedeck Ave	97471
NW Goetz St	97471
SE Golden Eagle Ave	97470
Golding St	97471
NE Gordon Ave	97470
Grace Ct	97471
Graham St	97470
NE Grandview Dr	97470
Grange Rd	97471
NE Granite Ridge St	97470
NE Grant Ave	97470
Grant Smith Rd	97471
Grassy Ln	97470
Grayson St	97471
Green Ave	97471
Green Siding Rd	97471
Green Vista Ln	97471
Greenhill Dr	97471
Greenley St	97471
Grouse Butte Ln	97470
NW Grove St	97471
Gypsy Ln	97471
W Haggerty St	97471
Hagle Ln	97470
Halfmile Rd	97471
NE Hall Ave	97470
SE Hamilton St	97470
Hanna St	97471
E Happy Valley Rd	97471
Harlan St	97471
Harmony Dr	97471
Harris Hills Dr	97471
W Harrison St	97471
W Harvard Ave	
300-599	97470
700-1699	97471
1700-1798	97470
1701-3199	97471
1800-3198	97471
3200-3299	97470
3300-3499	97471
Harvest Ln	97471
NW Harvey Ave	97471
Hatfield Dr	97470
Hawkeye Ln	97471
Hawks Mountain Rd	97470
SE Hawthorne Dr	97470
Hayes Eden Ln	97471
SE Haynes Ave	97470
W Hazel St	97471
Healy Rd	97471
Heartwood Ln	97471
Heather Ln	97471
Heatherwood Ln S	97471
Heavens Gate Ln	97471
Hebard Ave	97471
Hemlock Ln	97471
SE Henry St	97470
Heritage Loop & Way	97471
Hermosa Way	97471
Hess Ln	97471
Hewitt Ave	97470
Heydon Rd	97471
Hi Lo Ln	97471
W Hickory St	97471
NW Hicks St	97470
Hidden Valley Ln	97471
NW Highland Dr & St	97470
Highland Vista Ln	97471
NW Hill Ave	97471
Hillcrest Dr	97471
SE Hillside Dr	97470
NE Hillview Ct	97470
Hitchman Ln	97471
Holgate St	97471
NE Hollis St	97470
NW Holly Ave	97471
W Homewood Ct	97471
Honey Ln	97471
Hooker Rd	97470
Hoot N Holler Ln	97470
SE Hoover Ave	97470
Hope Ave	97470
NW Hopper St	97471
SE Houck Ave	97470
NE Housley Ave	97470
NE Hughes St	97470
Hughwood Ave & Ct	97471
Hummingbird Ln	97471
Hunter Ct	97471
Hunter Hill Ln	97471
Huntley Ave & St	97470
Huntley Creek Ln	97470
Hutchins Dr	97471
SE Ichabod St	97470
NE Imbler Ave	97470
Impala Dr	97470
Impossible Ln	97471
Independence Ln	97471
W Indianola St	97471
Industrial Dr	97471
Ingram Dr	97471
Irongate Ln	97471
Isabell Ave	97470
NE Ivan St	97470
SE Ivy Dr	97470
SE J R Ln	97470
Jackie Ave	97471
NE & SE Jackson St	97470
Jacob Hale Way	97471
NE Jacobson St	97470
Jade Dr	97471
Jamie Loop	97471
W Jay Ave	97471
Jeep Ln	97471
NW Jefferson St	97471
NW Jeffery St	97471
NW Jennifer Ct	97471
Jensen Ct	97471
Jerrys Dr	97470
Jesse Ln	97470
Jessica Way	97471
Jessica Lynn Ln	97471
Jewel Dr	97471
NE Joanne Dr	97470
Joe Ave	97471
NE John St	97470
NE Johnson St	97470
Jones Rd	97471
Jonni Ln	97471
Jordan Ln	97471
Joseph St	97470
Julia Ln	97471
Julina Ln	97471
W Juniper Ct	97471
NE Junker Ave	97470
Juno Ln	97471
SE Kane St	97470
SE Kansas Ave	97470
Karenza Ln	97471
Karma Ln	97470
Karuk Ln	97471
Kathleen Ct	97470
NE Katrina Ct	97470
W Keady Ct	97471
NW Keasey St	97471
Keeler Ct	97471
Kellisha Ln	97471
NW Kelsay Ct	97471
Kendall St	97471
NE Kennedy Loop Dr	97470
NE Kenneth Ford Dr	97470
Kent Ln	97471
W Kenwood St	97471
Kermanshah Ct & St	97471
Kerr St	97470
Kester Rd	97470
Kestrel Ln	97471
W Killdeer St	97471
NW Kimberly Ct	97471
Kincaid Dr	97470
NE Kirby Ave	97470
Kiss Ct	97471
Klahowya Ln	97471
NE Klamath Ave	97470
NW Kline St	97471
NE Knoll Ave	97470
Kohala Ct	97471
NW Kring St	97471
Krista Ln	97471
E & W Kristen Ct	97471
Kristi Lee Ln	97471
Krohn Ln	97471
Kylee St	97471
La Canada Dr	97471
La Donna Ln	97471
La Vista Dr	97471
Labrie Rd	97471
Lad Ln	97471
Lady Slipper Ln	97470
Laguna Ct	97471
Laid Back Ln	97471
NE Lake St	97470
Lakewood Ct	97471
Lakey Acres Ln	97471
NW Lamont Ave	97471
NW Lanaias Way	97471
Lancaster Ave	97471
Lance St	97471
Landers Ave	97471
SE Lane Ave	97470
W Langenberg Ave	97471
Lapp Ln	97471
Lark Ln	97471
Larson Rd	97471
SE Laurel Ct	97470
Laurel Dr	97471
Laurel Oaks Dr	97471
NE Laurel Spring Dr	97470

W Laurelwood Ct 97470
Laurie Ln 97471
Lazy Ln 97471
NW Le Mans St 97471
Lee Love Ln 97471
Leiken Ln 97470
SE Leland St 97470
NW Lester St 97471
Light Ct 97471
NW Lila Ct 97471
W Lilburn Ave 97470
Lillian Ln 97471
NE Lincoln St 97470
NW Lindell Ave 97471
Linnell Ave 97471
Little Branch Ln 97471
Little Pheasant Ln 97470
Little Springs Rd 97471
Little Valley Rd 97471
Littlebrook Ln 97471
NW Littlewood Ct 97471
Live Oak Ct 97470
Lockwood Rd 97471
Lohr Ln 97471
SE Lois Dr 97470
Loma Vista Dr 97471
NE Lombardy Dr 97470
Lone Oak Ct 97471
Lone Pine Ln 97470
Long Meadows Ln 97471
Longhorn Ln 97471
Longshot Ln 97471
Lookingglass Rd 97471
Loredo Dr 97471
W Lorraine Ave 97471
Louise Ln 97470
Lower Garden Valley Rd 97471
W Luellen Dr 97471
Lupine Ln 97471
NW Luth St 97471
NW Lynwood St 97471
M St 97471
Madeleine Ave 97471
NE Madison Ave 97470
W Madrone St 97470
NE Magali St 97470
SE Magnolia Dr 97470
SE Main St 97470
NW Makah Ct 97471
NE Malheur Ave 97470
Manderville Ln 97471
Manor Loop 97471
NE Manzanita Ct 97470
W Maple St 97471
Maplewood Ln 97471
Maria Ln 97471
Marilyn St 97470
NE Marlene Dr 97470
SE Marsters Ave 97470
NW Martin Ave 97471
Mary Ann Ln 97470
Marys View Rd 97471
Matthew Lee Ct 97471
Mattie K Ln 97471
Maywood Ct 97471
SE Mcclellan Ave 97470
Mckee Ln 97471
Mckya Ct 97471
Mclain Ave 97471
Mclain West Ave 97471
Meadow Ave 97470
Meadow View Rd 97471
Meadowbrook St 97471
Meadowlark Ave 97471
SW Medford Ave 97471
NW Medical Loop 97471
NW Medical Park Dr 97471
Melba St 97470
Melody Ln 97471
Melon Ln 97471
NW Meloy Ave 97470
Melqua Rd 97471
Melrose Rd 97471
Melrose Heights Ln 97471
Melrose Terrace Ln 97471
Melton Rd 97470
NW Mercy Dr 97471
NW Mercy Hills Dr 97471
NW Merle Ave 97471
Merlot Way 97471
Metolius Ln 97471
SE Metzger Ct 97470
SE Micelli St 97470
NE Miguel St 97470
W Military Ave 97471
SE Mill St 97470
SE Miller Ave 97470
Millsview Ln 97471
Minnesota Blvd 97471
Mirror Ln 97471
Mistletoe Hill Ln 97471
Misty Ln 97471
Mobridge Ave 97470
Molalla Ct 97470
Monique Ln 97471
Monta Vista Ln 97471
Monte Dr 97471
NE Monterey Dr 97470
NW Moore Ave 97471
Moorea Dr 97471
W Moose Dr 97471
NW Moritz Ct 97471
Morning Crest Ct 97471
Morning Glory Ln 97471
NE Morris St 97470
SE Morton Dr 97470
SE Mosher Ave 97470
NW Motah St 97471
Mountain Dr 97471
NW Mountain View Dr 97471
Mt Gurney Ln 97471
Mulberry Ln 97471
NW Mulholland Dr 97470
NW Munson Ct 97470
SE Murray Ct 97470
Museum Dr 97471
Musical Ln 97471
Myers Ln 97471
W Myrtle Ave 97471
W Myrtlewood Ct 97471
Nandy Dr 97471
NE Nash St 97470
Natures Ln 97470
NW Navajo Ave 97471
W Nebo St 97471
Nehalem Loop 97471
W Neill Ave 97471
NE Neptune Ln 97470
Nestucca Ln 97470
NE Neuner Dr 97470
W Nevada Ct 97471
NW Newcastle St 97471
NE Newport St 97470
NE Newton Creek Rd 97470
Nighthawk Ln 97471
Nob Hill Rd 97471
NE Norma Jean Dr 97470
Normandy Ave & Ct 97471
Northpark Ln 97470
Nugget St 97470
O C Brown Rd 97470
O Neal Ln 97470
SE Oak Ave 97470
Oak Way 97471
Oak Creek Dr 97470
Oak Hill Rd
1-199 97471
200-299 97470
300-8199 97471
Oak Tree Rd 97471
SE Oakbriar Ave 97470
NE Oakland Ave 97470
Oakley Rd 97471
Oakridge Ave 97471
Oakview Dr 97471
Oar Ln 97471
NE Odell Ave 97470
NW Oerding Ave 97471
SE Ohio Ave 97470
Old Barn Ct 97471
Old Del Rio Rd 97471
Old Garden Valley Rd 97471
Old Highway 99 N 97470
Old Highway 99 S 97471
W Old Melrose Rd 97471
Old Settlement Ln 97471
Oleson Ln 97471
Oleta Ct 97471
NW Olive Ln 97471
Oliver Ln 97470
Olivia Ln 97470
Orchard Ln 97471
Orchard Hill Ln 97471
SE Orcutt Ave 97470
W Oriole Dr 97471
Osage Dr 97471
Oscar Dr 97470
NE Oswego Ave 97470
Othello Ave 97471
NW Otie St 97470
SE Overlook Ave 97470
Owyhee Ln 97471
Palisade Dr 97471
Palmdale Ave 97471
Palomino Ave 97471
Palos Verdes Dr 97471
Panda Ln 97471
Paradise Ln 97471
Paradise Point Ln 97471
S Park Ct 97471
N Park Ln 97470
NW Park St 97470
NW Parkdale Ave 97471
NE Parker Rd 97470
NE Parkview Ct 97470
SE Parkwood Dr 97470
SE Parrott St 97470
SE Parrott Creek Rd 97470
Pasadena Ct 97471
NW Patricia St 97471
NE Patterson St 97470
NW Pawnee Ct 97471
Pear Tree Ln 97471
SE Pearce Rd 97470
Pecan Ln 97471
Pegasus Ln 97471
NE Peggy Ave 97470
Peppertree Ct 97471
Pheasant Ct 97471
W Pilger St 97471
SE Pine St 97470
Pine Meadows Ln 97471
Pinnacle Ln 97471
Pinot Noir Way 97471
Pippin Ave 97471
SE Pitzer St 97470
Pixie Ave 97471
Plarrank Rd 97470
NW Plateau Dr 97471
Platinum Dr 97471
Pleasant Ave 97470
Pleasant View Loop 97471
Plum Nearly Ln 97471
NE Polk St 97470
Pomona St 97470
Ponderosa Dr 97471
Pony Ln 97471
NE Poplar St 97470
Poppy Ln 97471
NE Porter St 97470
Portland Ave 97471
NE Post St 97470
Poteet Ave 97471
Preschern Ln 97471
NW Primrose Ln 97471
W Princeton Ave 97471
NE Privado Ct 97470
Promise Ave 97470
Quail Ln 97471
Quarry Rd 97470
Quincetree Ct 97471
Quincy Ave 97470
NW Rachel Ave 97471
Rachel Lynn Ct & Way 97471
Raelene Ct 97470
W Rainbow St 97471
Rainbow Ridge Ave 97471
NW Ralinda Ter 97471
Ramblin Ln 97471
SE Ramp St 97470
NW Randall Ct 97471
NE Raspberry Way 97470
SE Rast Ct 97470
Raven Ln 97471
NE Reagan Dr 97470
Recreation Ln 97470
Redtail Ridge Ln 97471
Redwood Dr 97470
SE Reservoir Ave 97470
Reston Rd 97471
Rex St 97471
SE Rice Ave 97470
Ridenour St 97470
NE Ridge Ave 97470
Ridgecrest Dr 97471
W Ridgeview Ct 97471
Ridgewood Dr 97471
SE & NE Rifle Range Rd & St 97470
Rio Nes Ln 97470
Rio Verde Ln 97471
Rio Vista Ln 97471
N River Dr 97470
River Bend Rd 97471
River Club Dr 97471
River Forks Park Rd 97471
River Place Dr 97471
River Ridge Ave 97471
NW Riverfront Dr 97471
Riversdale Valley Way 97471
Rivershore Dr 97470
W Riverside Dr 97470
NW Riverview Dr 97471
Roband Ln 97471
Roberlee Ln 97471
SE Roberts Ave 97470
Roberts Creek Rd
100-1599 97471
1800-10199 97470
Roberts Mountain Rd 97471
Robin St 97470
NE Rocky Dr 97470
Rocky Point Ln 97471
NE Rocky Ridge Dr 97470
Rogers Rd 97471
Rolling Hills Rd 97471
SE Rose St 97470
NE Roseland Ave 97470
Rosemary Ave 97471
W Rosemond Ave 97471
Rosewood Dr 97471
NE Ross Ave 97470
Rowan St 97471
NE Rowe Ave 97470
Royal Oaks Dr 97471
NE Ruby Ct 97470
Ruby May Way 97471
Russell Ave 97470
SE Rust Ct 97470
NW Rutter Ln 97470
Ryan Heights Ln 97470
Ryland Dr 97471
Sable Dr 97470
Saddlebutte Ln 97470
Sage Ln 97471
W Salida Ct 97471
Salix Ct 97470
Salmon St 97471
San Souci Dr 97471
W Sanders Ave 97471
SE Sanford Ave 97470
Santa Barbara Ct 97471
Santa Maria Ct 97471
Santa Rosa Ct 97471
Santiam Ln 97471
Sara Ln 97470
Savanna Ln 97471
S Savoy Ct 97471
NE Sawyers Ln 97470
NE Scofield Ave 97470
Seabiscuit Loop 97471
Sean Ln 97471
NW Sellwood St 97471
W Selmar Ct 97471
Serena Way 97471
Serene Ln 97471
Serenity Ln 97471
Seven Springs Ln 97471
Shadow Ranch Ln 97470
Shady Dr 97471
Shaffer Ct 97471
Shakemill Rd 97470
NE Shale Ct 97470
NE Shambrook Ave 97470
NW Shantel St 97471
SE Sharon Ave 97470
W Sharp Ave 97471
W Shasta Ave 97471
Shelton Ln 97470
W Shenandoah St 97471
SE Sheridan St 97470
W Sherwood Ave 97471
Shobu Ln 97471
SE Short St 97470
Sidney Dr 97470
Sierra Dr 97471
W Silver Ct 97471
Silver Maple St 97471
Silverado Ct & St 97471
Silvercrest Dr 97471
Sinclair Ln 97471
Single Tree Ln 97470
Singleton Rd 97470
Sisters Ln 97471
NW Skylee Dr 97471
Sleepy Ln 97471
Slope St 97470
Snowberry Rd 97471
Songbird Ct 97470
Southbank Dr 97470
Southgate Rd 97471
Southridge Way 97470
NW Southwater Dr 97471
Speedway Rd 97471
NE Spencer Ct 97470
Spike Ct 97470
Spirit Ln 97471
Sprague Ct 97471
NW Spray Ct 97471
Spring Ave 97470
SE Spruce St 97470
Spur Dr 97471
NE Spyglass Loop 97470
NW Stacie Ct 97471
W Stanton St 97471
SE Starmer St 97470
NE Steele Ct 97470
Steinhauer Rd 97471
Stella Ct & St 97471
SE Stellars Eagle St 97470
Stengar Ln 97471
NE & SE Stephens St 97470
Sterling Dr 97470
Stevenson Ln 97471
Stewart Ct 97471
NE Stewart Pkwy 97470
NW Stewart Pkwy
900-3099 97471
3500-3599 97470
3601-3899 97470
NW & W Stewart Park Dr 97471
Stillwater Rd 97470
Stocks Ln 97470
SE Stone Ave 97470
Stonehenge Ln 97470
Stonewood Ct 97471
Strader Rd 97470
Stratford Ln 97471
Strawberry Mountain Ln 97470
Strickland Canyon Rd 97471
SE Strong Ave 97470
Sue Ellen Ln 97470
Summer Ln 97471
N Summerwood Ct & St 97471
SE Summit Dr 97470
Summit Ridge Ln 97471
NW Sunberry Dr 97471
Sunburst Ct 97471
Sundance Ct 97471
Sunrise Ln 97471
NE Sunset St 97470
Sunset Loop Dr 97470
Sunshine Rd 97470
W Susan St 97471
Swan Hill Rd 97471
NW Sweetbrier Ave 97471
Sycan Ct 97471
SE Sykes Ave 97470
Sylvan Ln 97471
Taber Ln 97471
Taft Dr 97470
NE Tahoe Ave 97470
W Tanager St 97471
Tanglewood Ln 97471
Tannhauser Ave 97471
W Tarragon Dr 97471
NE Taylor St 97470
Teal Ln 97471
Temple Brown Rd 97470
SE Templin Ave 97470
SE Terrace Dr 97470
SE Thompson St 97470
Tillicum Ln 97471
Timberlake Ave 97470
Tinkers Ln 97471
Tipton Rd 97471
W Toby Ct 97471
NE Todd St 97470
Topaz Ln 97471
Touchstone Ln 97471
Tranquil Ln 97471
Trask Ct 97470
NW Troost St 97471
Trout Loop 97471
NW Trust St 97471
Tucson Ct 97471
Turken Ln 97470
Turkey Crick Ln 97471
Twilight Ave 97471
Twin Springs Ln 97470
NW Ulrich Ct 97471
N Umpqua Hwy 97470
W Umpqua St 97471
Umpqua College Rd 97470
Umpqua View Dr 97471
W Union St 97471
Upper Camp Loop Rd 97470
Upper Cleveland Rapids Rd 97471
NW Utah Dr 97471
Val Vista Ln 97471
NW Vale Ct 97471
NW Vallejo Dr 97471
Valley Rd 97471
NW Valley View Dr 97471
Van Horn Ln 97470
NW Van Pelt Blvd 97471
Vanessa Way 97471
NE Ventura St 97470
NW Veronica Ct 97471
NW Veterans Way 97471
Victoria Ct 97471
N View Dr 97470
NE Vine St 97470
Vineyard Ln 97471
SE Virginia Ct 97470
NE Vista Fe Ct 97470
SE Waite Ave 97470
SE Waldon Ave 97470
Walker Ct 97471
NE Walnut St 97470
Walter Ct 97471
Wanda Dr 97471
NW Wanell St 97471
NE Ward Ave 97470
Warewood Terrace Ct 97471
W Warren Ct 97471
SE Washington Ave 97470
Waterback Ln 97470
SE Watson St 97470
NW Watters St 97471
Wenaha Ln 97471
NE West Ave 97470
Westridge Ln 97471
Westview Dr 97471
Westwood Ln 97471
Weyerhaeuser Dr N 97470
W Wharton St 97471
NW Whipple Ave 97471
Whispering Pines Way 97471
Whistlers Ln 97470
Whistlers Park Rd 97470
White Fir Way 97471
White Oak Ln 97471
Whitetail Ln 97471
NW Wide Ave 97471
Wilbur Rd 97470
Wild Goose Ln 97470
Wild Iris Ln 97470
Wild River Dr 97470
Wild Turkey Ln 97471
SE Wildwood Ave 97470
Wilene Ct 97471
Willamina Ct & Ln 97470
NE Willow St 97470
Wilson Collins Rd 97471
NE Winchester St 97470
Windchime Ln 97471
Winery Ln 97471
Winngate Ct 97471
NE Winter St 97470
Winter Creek Ln 97471
W Winter Ridge Dr 97471
NW Witherspoon Ave 97471
Wood Duck Ln 97471
Woodberry Ln 97471
Woodoak Dr 97471
Woodrose Ln 97471
Woodruff Rd 97471
Woodruff Mountain Rd 97471
W Woodside Ave 97471
SE Woodward Ave 97470
Woodwillow Dr 97471
Wulff Ln 97471
W Yale Ave 97471
Yew Ln 97471
Yoder Ln 97471
Yokum Dr 97470
Youngs Ln 97471
NW Youngwood Ct 97471
NE Yount Ave 97470
Zachary Dr 97470
Zeigler Ct 97471
Zephyr Ct 97471
Zeus Ln 97470

SALEM OR

General Delivery 97301

POST OFFICE BOXES MAIN OFFICE STATIONS AND BRANCHES

Box No.s
1 - 1114 97308
1020 - 1020 97302
1430 - 2920 97308
3000 - 4780 97302
5001 - 6158 97304
7000 - 8210 97303
9001 - 9295 97305
12001 - 15138 97309
17000 - 18736 97305

NAMED STREETS

A St NE 97301
Aaron Ct NE 97301
Abbey Ln SE 97317
Abbie Ave SE 97306
Abbot Ln NE 97305
Aberdeen St S 97302

Street	ZIP
Abiqua Ct SE	97317
Abrams Ave NE	97301
Acacia Dr S	97302
Academy St NE	97301
Acorn Ln S	97302
Acorn Hill Ct SE	97317
Acts Way NE	97317
Adam Ct NE	97303
Adams St SE	97301
Adams Ridge Dr S	97306
Adamson Ln SE	97306
Addison Ct & Dr	97302
Adell Ln NE	97301
Aden Pl NE	97305
Adobe St SE	97317
Aerial Way SE	97302
Aetna St SE	97317
Agate Dr SE	97317
Aggas Way NE	97303
Ahrens Rd SE	97317
Airport Rd SE	97301
Akin Ct SE	97317
Alameda St NE	97301
Alana Ave SE	97302
Alaska St SE	97317
Albert Dr SE	97302
Albert Ln NE	97305
Alberta Ave NE	97301
Albion Ct SE	97302
Alder Dr NE	97303
Alderbrook Ave SE	97302
Aldercrest Ct S	97306
Aldine Ct & Dr	97303
Aldous Ave S	97302
Aldrich Ct NW	97304
Aldridge Dr N	97303
Alesia Ct SE	97306
Alex Ave & Ct	97302
Alexa Ln SE	97317
Alexander Ln SE	97306
Alexander St NE	97301
Alexandra Way SE	97317
Alexis Ln N	97303
Alice Ave S	97302
Alina Ave SE	97306
Allen Ct NE	97301
Allendale Way NE	97303
Alliance Ct NE	97303
Allison Ct SE	97302
Almond Ln NW	97304
Aloha Ct S	97302
Alpha St SE	97306
Alpine Ave NW	97304
Alpine Lakes St SE	97317
Alta View Dr S	97302
Altamont St NW	97304
Altimont Dr NW	97304
Alvarado Ter S	97302
Alvina St SE	97306
Amanda Way SE	97317
Amber St NE	97301
America Way SE	97317
Amethyst St SE	97306
Amherst Ct NE	97305
Ammon St NW	97304
Amy Ln NE	97303
Anaconda Dr S	97302
Anchor Ct NE	97305
Andrea Ct SE	97302
Andrea Dr NW	97304
Andresen St SE	97306
Andrew Ave NW	97304
Andyman Ct SE	97302
Angels Way SE	97317
Angie Way NE	97303
Angie Marie Way NE	97305
Angle Dr NE	97317
Anita Dr NE	97301
Ankeny Crest Ln S	97306
Ankeny Heights Ln S	97306
Ankrum Ln NE	97305
Anna Ln SE	97306
Anne Ct NE	97305
Anneka Loop SE	97302
Annette Ct NE	97301
Annie Ln S	97306
Antelope Ct NE	97305
Antigua Ln SE	97317
Antler St NE	97301
Antonia Ave NE	97301
Anunsen Ct NE	97301
Apache Ct SE	97317
Appaloosa Ct SE	97317
Appeal Ct S	97306
Apple Ct NE	97303
Apple Blossom Ave N & NE	97303
Apple Tree Ln SE	97317
April Ct & St	97301
Aqua St SE	97317
Arabian Ave & Ct	97317
Arbon St NE	97301
Arbordale Dr SE	97317
Arborwood Ct NE	97303
Arcade Ave NE	97303
Archer Ct NW	97304
Argyle Dr S	97302
Arithmetic Dr SE	97302
Arizona Ave NE	97305
Arlene Ave SE	97302
Arleta Ave & Pl	97303
Arnold St NE	97303
Arrow St NW	97304
Arrow Point Ct NE	97303
Arrowood Ct SE	97317
Arroyo Ridge Ct & Dr	97304
Arthur Way NW	97304
Ascot Ln NE	97303
Ash Ave SE	97302
Ashdown Ct SE	97317
Ashford Way N	97303
Ashland Ct NW	97304
Ashwood Ct SE	97302
Aspen Way NE	97317
Aster St NW	97304
Astoria St & Way	97305
Athens St SE	97306
Atlantis Ave SE	97306
Aubrey Ln NE	97303
Auburn Rd NE	
3750-3868	97301
3870-4999	97301
5000-5499	97317
Audobon Ave SE	97302
Augusta St SE	97306
Augusta National Dr S	97302
Aumsville Hwy SE	97317
Autumn Chase Way NE	97305
Autumn Leaf Ct N	97303
Avalon Ave SE	97306
Avens Ave NE	97301
Azalea Dr S	97302
B St NE	97301
Babcock St & Way	97317
Baber Ct SE	97317
Bachelor Ln NW	97304
Bailey Ct & Rd	97303
Bair Rd NE	97303
Baker St NE	97301
Bald Eagle Ave NW	97304
Baldwin Ave, Ct & Pl	97301
Ballymeade St SE	97306
Ballyntyne Rd S	97302
Ballyntyne Creek Ln S	97302
Balm Ct NE	97301
Balm St S	97302
Baloo Ln SE	97317
Balsam Dr S	97302
Bambi Ave NE	97301
Bandit Ct NE	97301
Bandon Ct NW	97304
Bannock Ct SE	97317
Banter Ct NE	97301
Banyan Ct NW	97304
Banyonwood Ave NW	97304
Barbara Ave NE	97303
Barbara Way NE	97305
Barbaresco St S	97306
Barberry St NW	97304
Barcelona Ct & Dr	97317
Barker St NE	97301
Barkstone Ct SE	97306
Barley Ct NE	97305
Barlow Ave NW	97304
Barnabas St NW	97304
Barnes Ave & Ct	97306
Barnick Rd NE	97303
Barrett St S	97302
Barrington Ave & Ct	97302
Bartell Dr NW	97304
Bartlett Dr SE	97302
Bartlett Hill Ct & Dr	97304
Basil St NE	97317
Basin Ct & St	97306
Bass Ln SE	97317
Bassett St NW	97304
Basswood Ct & St	97304
Bastille Ave & Ct	97306
Bates Dr NE	97301
Bates Rd S	97306
Batting St NE	97303
Battle Creek Rd SE	
4300-4999	97302
5000-5999	97306
6000-7899	97317
Battle Creek Heights Ln SE	97317
Battle Creek Hollow Ln SE	97317
Bavarian Way SE	97317
Baxter Ct & Rd	97306
Bay Club Ct SE	97306
Bayberry Ct SE	97306
Bayne St NE	97305
Bayonne Ct & Dr	97317
Bayview Way NE	97301
Beach Ave NE	97301
Beach Ln NW	97304
Beacon Ct & St	97301
Beaumont St NW	97304
Beaver Loop NW	97304
Beaver Pond Ct NE	97305
Beaverbrook Ct SE	97317
Beck Ave SE	97317
Becky Way NE	97301
Beebe St NE	97303
Beechwood Ct & St	97306
Begonia Dr NW	97304
Belaire Dr NW	97304
Belinda Ct SE	97306
Belknap Springs St SE	97306
Bell Rd NE	97301
Bella Terra Ave SE	97306
Bella Vista Way S	97306
Belle Pond Way S	97306
Belle Vista Ct S	97302
Bellevue St SE	97301
Bellflower Ct & St	97306
Belmont St NE	97301
Belvedere St NW	97304
Ben Vista Dr S	97302
Benevan Ct NE	97303
Benham Ave SE	97317
Benjamin Ave NW	97304
Benji Ct NE	97301
Bent Grass Ct NE	97303
Benton Ct NE	97305
Bergman Pl SE	97317
Berkshire Ct SE	97306
Bermuda Ln NE	97301
Berndt Hill Dr S	97302
Berry St SE	97302
Best Rd NW	97304
Beth St NE	97301
Bethany Ln SE	97317
Bethel Rd SE	97317
Bethel Heights Rd NW	97304
Betty Ln SE	97306
Beutler Dr NE	97305
Bever Dr NE	97303
Beverly Ave NE	97305
Bieber St NE	97301
Biegler Ln S	97302
Big Rock Ct SE	97306
Bigland Ln S	97306
Bill Frey Dr NE	97301
Billie Ln SE	97317
Bills Ln S	97306
Biltmore Ave	97306
Bingtree Ct NE	97303
Birch Ave N	97303
Birchwood Ct N	97303
Birdhill Dr S	97302
Bison Ct NE	97305
Bistrika Ln NE	97301
Bittern St NE	97301
Black Sheep Way NE	97303
Blackberry Ln NE	97305
Blackbird Ct NE	97301
Blackcherry Ct SE	97317
Blackhawk Ct SE	97317
Blacktail Deer Ct NW	97304
Blaine Ct NE	97301
Blair Ct NE	97301
Blanche Ln NE	97305
Blarney Stone Ct NE	97303
Blazer Ln SE	97317
Blazing Star Ct NE	97305
Blessing Ln NE	97305
Blier Ave NE	97301
Blossom Ct, Dr & St	97305
Blossom Lake Way SE	97317
Blue River Dr SE	97306
Blue Sky Ct SE	97317
Bluebell Ave SE	97306
Blueberry Ln NE	97305
Bluegrass St SE	97317
Bluestem St NE	97303
Bluff Ave & Ct	97302
Boardwalk Ave NE	97303
Boaz Ln NW	97304
Bobbie Ct N	97303
Bobs Ct S	97306
Boehmer St S	97306
Bohannon Ct & St	97305
Boice St S	97302
Bolf Ter N	97303
Bolin Ct N	97303
Bolivar Ct SE	97317
Bolliger Ct NE	97305
Bolton Ter S	97302
Bonanza Dr NE	97305
Bond Ct NE	97303
Bonham Ave S	97302
Bonneville Ave NE	97303
Bonnie Ct & Way	97304
Bonzi Ln SE	97317
Boone Rd S	97306
Boone Rd SE	
100-2799	97306
3200-3999	97317
Borsberry Ln SE	97306
Boston Ct S	97302
Boulder Dr SE	97317
Boulder Creek St SE	97317
Boulder Ridge Ct NW	97304
Boulder Ridge Ct SE	97317
Boundary Dr S	97306
Bow Ct SE	97306
Bowden Ln N	97303
Bowen Pl SE	97317
Bower Ct SE	97317
Box Berry Ave & Ct	97305
Boxwood Ln SE	97302
Bradford Loop SE	97302
Bradley Dr SE	97302
Brady Ct NE	97301
Bramble Ct NE	97305
Brandon Ave, Ct & St	97303
Breanna Ln NE	97305
Breckenridge St NW	97304
Bren Loop NE	97305
Brenna Ave NE	97301
Brenner St NE	97301
Brentwood Dr SE	97306
Brewster Ave & Ct	97302
Breyman St NE	97301
Breys Ave NE	97301
Brian Ct NE	97303
Briana Ct NW	97304
Briar Ct SE	97317
Briarwood Cir N	97303
Briarwood St NW	97304
Bridgeport Ave SE	97306
Bridlewood Way S	97306
Bright Ct NE	97303
Brightwood Ct S	97302
Brink Ave & Ct	97317
Brittany Way NE	97301
Broadmore Ave NE	97301
Broadview Ct & Ln	97304
Broadway St NE	
900-2799	97301
2800-3200	97303
3202-3298	97303
Brock Loop S	97302
Brogan Ave NE	97305
Broken Arrow Loop NW	97304
Broken Top Ave NE	97303
Broken Wheel Ct NW	97304
Brokenridge Dr SE	97317
Bronco Dr SE	97317
Bronec Ln N	97303
Brookhollow Ct NE	97303
Brooklake Rd NE	
1700-4299	97303
4300-8199	97305
Brooks Ave NE	
2500-3599	97301
3600-4399	97303
Brookside Ave NW	97304
Brookvale Ave SE	97306
Brookwood St S	97306
Brown Rd NE	97305
Brown Island Rd S	97302
Browning Ave S & SE	97302
Bruce St NE	97301
Brunner Ct NE	97303
Brush College Rd NW	97304
Brushwood Ct SE	97317
Bryan St S	97302
Bryce St SE	97306
Buchholz Ct N	97303
Buckboard Ct SE	97317
Buckhorn Ct SE	97317
Buckskin Ct NE	97305
Buddie Ln NE	97305
Buena Crest Ln NE	97303
Buffalo Ct & Dr	97317
Bundy Ave & Ct	97303
Bunker Ln S	97306
Bunker Hill Rd S	97306
Bunker Ridge Rd S	97306
Burbank St N	97303
Burgundy Ave & Ct	97303
Burley Hill Dr & Loop	97304
Burlington Ct, Loop & St	97305
Burlwood Loop SE	97317
Burma Ct NE	97301
Burnett Ln & St	97317
Burning Tree Dr S	97302
Burns Ave NE	97305
Burntwood Ct SE	97317
Burton Pl SE	97317
Bush St S & SE	97302
Buster Ln SE	97317
Butler Pl SE	97306
Butte Ct SE	97317
Buttercup Ave & Ct	97305
Butterfly Ave NW	97304
Buttonwood Ct SE	97306
Byers St S	97302
Byram St NE	97301
C St NE	97301
C J Way S	97306
Cabin Ct SE	97306
Cabos Way SE	97317
Cade Ave & St	97303
Cadmus Ct NE	97301
Cains Pl SE	97306
Caleb St NE	97303
Calico St NW	97304
Calmar Ct NE	97301
Calvert Ct SE	97302
Camas Ct NE	97305
Cambridge Dr SE	97302
Camden St NE	97303
Camellia Dr S	97302
Camelot Ct NE	97301
Camelot Dr S	97306
Cameo St NW	97304
Camishaun Ct NE	97305
Campbell Dr SE	97317
Campus Ct & Loop	97305
Camry Ct NE	97301
Canary Ct NE	97301
Candalaria Blvd S	97302
Candi Pl NE	97301
Candis Ave NE	97301
Candlewood Ct NE	97303
Candlewood Dr NE	
1000-1399	97303
1500-1699	97301
Candy Flower Ct SE	97306
Caneberry Ct NE	97303
Cannon St SE	97302
Canterbury Dr S	97302
Canvas Back Ct SE	97302
Canyon Ct NE	97305
Canyon St SE	97317
Capistrano Ct NE	97305
Capitol St NE	97301
Capitol St SE	
790-799	97301
1500-1899	97302
Caplinger Rd SE	97317
Cara Ct NW	97304
Caradon Ct NW	97304
Cardinal St NW	97304
Caribou Ct NW	97304
Carilor Ct NE	97303
Carla Ct SE	97302
Carleton Way NE	97301
Carmel Dr SE	97317
Carmelcrest Ct SE	97306
Carmelle Ct NE	97305
Carmen Ave N	97303
Carnelia St SE	97306
Carnoustie Ln S	97302
Carolina Ave NE	97305
Caroline St S	97302
Carpenter Pl NW	97304
Carriage Ct NE	97301
Carson Dr SE	97317
Carter Ave NW	97304
Carver Ct NE	97317
Cascade Dr NW	97304
Cascade Hwy NE	97317
Cascade Hwy SE	97317
Cascade Pl SE	97317
Cascade View Ln SE	97306
Cascadia Industrial St SE	97302
Cascara Loop S	97302
Casey Ln SE	97317
Casper Dr & Loop	97303
Castle Dr NE	97301
Castle Glen Ln N	97303
Castle Lake Ct N	97303
Castle Pines Cir & Dr	97303
Catalina St SE	97306
Catchum Ln SE	97317
Cater Ct & Dr	97303
Cathlamet Ct NW	97304
Catterlin St NE	97301
Causey Ln SE	97317
Cavalier Dr S	97302
Cayuse Cir SE	97306
Cecilia St SE	97306
Cedar Ave N	97303
Cedar Ct N	97303
Cedar Way SE	97302
Cedar Bluff Cir N	97303
Cedar Falls Ct NE	97303
Cedar Hill Ct S	97306
Cedarcrest Ct & Dr	97306
Celeen Ave SE	97302
Centennial Ct SE	97302
Centennial Dr NW	97304
Centennial Dr SE	97302
Center St NE	
300-398	97301
400-4999	97301
5000-5499	97317
5501-5699	97317
Centurian Ct S	97302
Century Ct & Dr	97302
Cerise Ave NW	97304
Chadbourne Ln NE	97301
Chakarun Ln SE	97306
Chambers Ave S	97302
Chameleon Ct NE	97305
Champion Hill Rd SE	97306
Championship Dr S	97302
Champlain Ct & Dr	97304
Chan St S	97306
Chandelle Ct NE	97301
Chandler Dr S	97302
Chandy Way S	97302
Chaney Way SE	97302
Chaparral Dr SE	97302
Chapman Ct & St	97306
Chapman Hill Dr NW	97304
Char Cir NW	97304
Chardonnay Loop NE	97303
Charity Ave NE	97305
Charlene St S	97306
Charles Ave S	97302
Charleston Dr SE	97317
Charmalee Ct NE	97305
Charolais St NE	97303
Charter Pl NE	97301
Chase Ave SE	97302
Chatham St SE	97302
Chatnicka St NW	97304
Chatter Ln SE	97306
Chauncey Ct & St	97302
Chehalis Ct, Dr & Pl	97303
Chelan St NE	97303
Chelsea Ave NW	97304
Chemawa Loop NE	97303
Chemawa Rd N	97303
Chemawa Rd NE	
600-2999	97303
3101-3597	97305
3599-3999	97305
Chemawa Way N	97303
Chemeketa St NE	97301
Cherie Ct SE	97306
Cherokee Dr S	97302
Cherokee Trail Ln S	97306
Cherry Ave NE	
4350A-4350A	97303
2300-3299	97301
3200-4399	97303
Cherry Bark Ct SE	97317
Cherry Blossom Dr NW	97304
Cherry Hill Ct NW	97304
Cherrybloom Ct SE	97317
Cherrybud Ct SE	97317
Cherrylawn Ct NE	97303
Cherrytree Ct SE	97317
Cherrywood Ct SE	97306
Cheryl Ct NE	97305
Cheryl Lynn Way NE	97305
Cherylee Dr S	97302
Chester Ave NE	97301
Chestnut St NW	97304
Chetco Ct NE	97303
Cheviot Way S	97302
Cheyenne Ct NW	97304
Chicago St NE	97303
Chickadee Ct NE	97301
Chiefs Ct NE	97305
Childs Ave NE	97301
Chinook Ct SE	97317
Chippewa Ct SE	97317
Chrisman Ln SE	97317
Chrissy Ct S	97306
Christen St S	97302
Christina St NW	97304
Christopher St NW	97304
Christy Ct SE	97317
Chukar Ct & Pl	97304
Church St NE	97301

Church St SE
100-198 97301
200-799 97301
1500-2999 97302
Churchdale Ave N & NE 97303
Churchill Ave SE 97302
Cimarron Ct SE 97306
Cindercone Ct SE 97306
Cindy Pl SE 97306
Cinnamon Hill Ct & Dr 97306
Cinnamon Teal St SE 97306
Cinnibar St SE 97306
Circuit Rider Ln S 97302
Cirrus Ct NW 97304
Citation Dr NE 97301
Citrus Pl NW 97304
Claggett St NE 97303
Clara Ct NE 97301
Clarence Ct SE 97302
Clarissa Ln S 97302
Clark Ave NE 97303
Clarmar Dr NE 97301
Clarmount Ct & St 97304
Classic Way S 97306
Classico Ct SE 97306
Claude St SE 97301
Clausen Acres Ln NE 97303
Claxter Ct NE 97301
Claxter Rd NE
1800-1899 97303
1900-2899 97301
Clay St NE 97301
Clearlake Ct & Rd 97303
Clearview Ave & Ct 97303
Clearwater Ave NE 97301
Cleveland Ave NW 97304
Cloud Dr S 97302
Cloudburst Ave NW 97304
Cloudview Dr S 97302
Clover Valley Ct NE 97317
Cloverleaf Ln NE 97303
Club House Dr SE 97306
Clydesdale Dr SE 97317
Coates Dr SE 97317
Coates Crest Way SE 97317
Cobalt Ct & Loop 97306
Cobb Ln S 97302
Cobbler Ct NW 97304
Coburn St S 97302
Cockspur Ct SE 97317
Coco St SE 97317
Coho Ave & Ct 97304
Colby Ln SE 97317
Cole Rd S 97306
Colgan Ct SE 97302
Colleen St NE 97305
College Dr NW 97304
College Park Pl SE 97317
Collins St NW 97304
Coloma Ct SE 97306
Coloma Dr SE 97302
Colonial Ave NE 97301
Colony Ct SE 97302
Colorado Dr NW 97304
Colson Ct SE 97302
Colt Ln NE 97301
Colton Ln NE 97305
Columbia St NE 97301
Columbine Ct NE 97305
Comber Ct NE 97305
Comfort Valley Way NE 97305
Commanche Ct NW 97304
Commercial St NE 97301
Commercial St SE
100-799 97301
800-4999 97302
5000-6399 97306
Compton Ln SE 97306
Concomly Rd S 97306
Concord St NE 97301
Conifer St NE 97317
Connecticut Ave & St 97317
Connector St S 97302
Connemara Ct SE 97317
Conner St NW 97304
Conrad St NE 97305
Conser Way NE 97305
Constitution Ave SE 97302
Continental Cir SE 97306
Cooke St S 97302
Cooley Dr NE 97305
Coolidge Dr SE 97317
Copper Creek Loop NE 97305
Copper Glen Ct & Dr 97302
Coral Ave NE 97305
Corbett Ct NE 97301
Cord Ln SE 97306
Cordon Rd NE
100-1399 97317
2900-5499 97305
Cordon Rd SE 97317
Corina Dr SE 97302
Corki Ct SE 97302
Cornerstone Ct NE 97301
Cornucopia St NW 97304
Coronado Ct NW 97304
Coronation Ct NE 97301
Corredale Ct & St 97302
Corum Ct NW 97304
Cottage St NE 97301
Cottage St SE
101-197 97301
199-200 97301
202-298 97301
1500-2999 97302
Cottontail Ct NE 97305
Cottonwood Ct S 97306
Cottonwood St NE 97317
Cougar Ct SE 97317
Council Ct NE 97305
Countess Ct NE 97301
Country Dr S 97302
Country Ln NE 97305
Country Club Dr S 97302
Country Glen Ave NE 97303
Countryside Ct & Dr 97305
Court St NE 97301
Courtlyn St NE 97303
Courtney Ln SE 97302
Cousteau Dr & Loop 97302
Coventry Ct NW 97304
Covey Ln NE 97317
Covington St NE 97305
Cowboy Ln NE 97305
Cowrie Ct NW 97304
Coyote Ct SE 97317
Crabgrass St NE 97301
Craftsman Loop N 97303
Craig Ln SE 97317
Crampton Dr N 97303
Cranberry Ct NE 97303
Cranston St SE 97317
Crater Ave N 97303
Crawford St SE 97302
Creek Ct NW 97304
Creekside Dr SE 97306
Crenshaw Dr & Loop 97303
Crescent Dr NW 97304
Crestbrook Dr NW 97304
Crestdale Ct NE 97305
Cresthill Ave NW 97304
Crestmont Cir S 97302
Creston Ln NE 97305
Crestview Ct & Dr 97302
Crestwood Ct NE 97303
Cricket Ct S 97302
Crimson Ct NE 97301
Crimson Cap Ln NE 97303
Croisan Creek Rd S 97302
Croisan Mountain Ct & Dr 97302
Croisan Ridge Way S 97302
Croisan Scenic Way S 97302
Crooked River Ave NW 97304
Crooked Stick Loop SE 97306
Cross St SE 97302
Cross Creek Ln SE 97317
Crossler Ct S 97306
Crosswater St NE 97303
Crouchen St NW 97304
Crowley Ave SE 97302
Crown Ct NE 97301
Crozer St NW 97304
Cryla Way S 97306
Crystal Ave NE 97305
Crystal Ct SE 97306
Crystal Springs Ct & Ln 97303
Cuckoo Ct NW 97304
Cultus Ave & Ct 97306
Culver Dr SE 97317
Culver Ln S 97302
Cumberland Ct SE 97306
Cummings Ln & Pl 97303
Cumulus Ct NW 97304
Cunningham Ln S 97302
Currant Ln NE 97305
Cushman Ln N 97303
Cutter Ct SE 97317
Cynthia Ct & St 97303
Cypress St NE 97301
D St NE 97301
Dahlia Way NW 97304
Dain Dr SE 97317
Daisy Ln NW 97304
Dakota Ct SE 97306
Dakota Rd SE
3800-4999 97302
5000-5099 97306
Daleview Rd SE 97317
Dalke Ct NE 97305
Dalke Ridge Ct & Dr 97304
Dan Ave NW 97304
Danalee St NE 97301
Dancers Ct SE 97302
Daniel St S 97306
Danielle Ln NE 97303
Danwood Ln NE 97303
Darcy St SE 97306
Darina Way NE 97305
Dark Forest Pl NE 97305
Darlene St NE 97305
Darlersi Rd NW 97304
Darling St SE 97317
Davcor St SE 97302
Dave St S 97302
Davidson St SE 97302
Davis Rd S 97306
Dawn St NE 97301
Dean Ct SE 97317
Dean St NE 97301
Deana St NE 97301
Dearborn Ave N & NE 97303
Debbie Way NE 97301
Debra Ct NW 97304
Dee Ct N 97303
Deepwood Ln NW 97304
Deepwood Loop NE 97305
Deepwood Pl NE 97305
Deer Lake Ct SE 97317
Deer Park Dr SE 97317
Deer Run Ave S 97302
Deerfield Ct & Dr 97302
Deerhaven Dr NE 97301
Deerhorn Ct NE 97305
Deering Dr NW 97304
Deerskin St NW 97304
Deerwind Ave & Ct 97304
Del St NW 97304
Del Webb Ave NE 97301
Delaney Rd SE
1600-2499 97306
3300-4699 97317
Delaplane St NE 97303
Delight St N 97303
Dell Villa Dr SE 97302
Della Way NE 97303
Delmar Dr N 97303
Delphinium Pl NE 97305
Delta Ct & Dr N & NE 97303
Demaris Ln SE 97317
Denise Ct & St 97306
Dennis Ln N 97303
Dennis Ray Ave NE 97303
Denny Ct N 97303
Denver Ave & Pl 97301
Deon Ln SE 97317
Depot Ct SE 97317
Derby Ct SE 97317
Derksen Hill Rd SE 97317
Derting Ln SE 97317
Deschutes Rd SE 97317
Desert Deer Ave NW 97304
Desiree Ct SE 97302
Devon Ave SE 97306
Devonshire Ave & Ct 97305
Dewpointe St SE 97306
Diamond Ct NE 97305
Diamond Peak Ct NW 97304
Dian Ave NW 97304
Diane Ln S 97306
Dianne Dr SE 97302
Dice Ln N 97303
Dietz Ave NE 97303
Discovery Pl NE 97317
Dishion Ct SE 97317
Distinctive Ct S 97306
Division St NE 97301
Dixie Ave NE 97301
Dixon St NE 97303
Doaks Ferry Rd NW 97304
Doe Ct NW 97304
Dogwood Ct & Dr 97302
Doloris Ct NE 97305
Dolphin Ave NE 97305
Dome Rock Ct SE 97306
Donahue Ct NE 97303
Donald St NE 97301
Donalyn Ln & St 97301
Donna Ave NE 97301
Donnan Pl NE 97303
Doogan Ct SE 97306
Dorado Ct NW 97304
Doral Dr SE 97306
Dorcas Dr N 97303
Dorchester Dr S 97302
Dorfs Ave NE 97301
Doris Ave & Loop 97302
Dorothy St NE 97301
Dorrance Loop & St 97305
Dorval Ave NW 97304
Dory Ct N 97303
Doug Fir Ln S 97302
Doughton St S 97302
Douglas Ave SE 97302
Dove Ave & Ct 97301
Dover Ave NE 97305
Dovetail Ct NE 97305
Dovich Ln SE 97317
Downs St S 97302
Dragon Fly Ct SE 97306
Drake Ct NE 97301
Draper St NE 97301
Dreamerie Ln NE 97303
Drew Ct & St 97305
Drexler Ln NE 97303
Driftwood Ct NE 97305
Drury Ln S 97306
Drysdale Ct & St 97303
Duane Dr S 97302
Dublin Ave S 97302
Duch Ln SE 97317
Duchess Ct NE 97301
Duck Inn Rd NE 97305
Duckhorn Ln NE 97303
Dudley Ave SE 97302
Duffield Heights Ave SE 97302
Duke Ct NE 97301
Dunbar Ave SE 97306
Duncan Ave NE 97301
Duniway Ct SE 97306
Dunlin Ct NE 97303
Dunsmere St SE 97317
Duplex Ct & Dr 97302
Durango Ct SE 97306
Durbin Ave SE 97317
Dustin Ct NE 97305
Dusty Pl NE 97305
Dutch Oven Ave NW 97304
Dutchman St NE 97305
Dwan Ct N 97303
Dwight Dr S 97302
E St NE 97301
Eagle Ct NE 97305
Eagle Cap St SE 97317
Eagle Crest Rd NW 97304
Eagle Eye Ave NW 97304
Eagle Feather Ct & St 97304
Eagle Nest St NW 97304
Eagle Ridge Ave NW 97304
Eagle View Dr NW 97304
Eagles Claw Ave NW 97304
Eagles Wing St NW 97304
Eaglet Ct & St 97304
Earhart St S 97302
Earle Ave NE 97301
East Ave NE 97301
Eastbrook Ct NE 97305
Eastlake Ct & Dr 97306
Eastland Ave & Pl 97317
Eaststar Ct NE 97305
Eastview Dr NE 97305
Eastwind Ct N 97303
Ebony Ln NE 97305
Echo Ct & Dr 97304
Eddy Ave & Ct 97301
Edelweis Ln SE 97306
Eden St SE 97317
Eden Way NW 97304
Edgecrest Ct SE 97306
Edgehill Ct S 97306
Edgewater St NW 97304
Edgewood Ave NE 97301
Edina Ln NE 97301
Edith Ave NE 97305
Edmond Ln NE 97305
Edmunson Dr SE 97317
Edward Dr SE 97302
Edwin Ct NE 97305
Effie Ln NE 97305
Egret Ave SE 97306
Eider Ave SE 97306
Eileen St NE 97301
Eisenhower Ct & Dr 97304
Ekonie Ln S 97306
El Cedro Loop & St 97305
El Dorado Ct & Loop 97302
El Rancho Ave NE 97305
El Segundo Ave NE 97303
Elderberry Dr S 97302
Eldin Ave NE 97301
Eldin Ave SE 97317
Electric Ave & St 97302
Elf Ave SE 97302
Elizabeth St N 97303
Elk Ct SE 97317
Elk River St NW 97304
Elkhorn Ct & Dr 97317
Elkins Way SE 97306
Ella Ln NE 97305
Ellen Ct & Ln 97304
Ellie Ct NE 97303
Elliot St NW 97304
Ellis Ave & Way 97301
Ellisons Way SE 97317
Elm St NW 97304
Elma Ave NE 97301
Elma Ave SE 97317
Elma Ct NE 97301
Elmhurst Ave S 97306
Elmwood Dr S 97306
Elmwood St NE 97305
Elser Ct & Dr 97302
Elsie Ct NE 97301
Elvira St N 97303
Embassy Way NE 97305
Emerald Dr NW 97304
Emery Ln NE 97303
Emily Ave NW 97304
Emmett Dr NW 97304
Emmons Dr & St 97301
Empire St NW 97304
Empress Way NE 97305
Enclid St NE 97305
Engel Ave & Ct 97304
Englewood Ave NE 97301
Enterprise Dr NE 97305
Eola Dr NW 97304
Equestrian Loop S 97302
Eric Ct NW 97304
Erika Ave NE 97303
Erin Way N 97303
Erixon St NE 97301
Espana Ave N 97303
Essex St SE 97317
Estate Ct NW 97304
Esther Ave SE 97302
Etomina Ln S 97306
Etta Dr NE 97305
Eugene Ct NE 97303
Eureka St SE 97306
Eva Ct NE 97305
Evans Ave, Ct & St 97303
Evanston St NE 97305
Eve Ct NE 97303
Evelyn Ave NE 97301
Everett Dr & Ln 97306
Evergreen Ave & Ct 97301
Everwood St NE 97303
Evie Jean St NE 97305
Ewald Ave S & SE 97302
Exmoor Ct SE 97317
Exodus St SE 97306
Explorer Cir & Pl 97303
Fabry Rd SE 97306
Fair Oaks Way NW 97304
Fairbanks Ct & St 97306
Faircrest Ct SE 97306
Fairfax Ct S 97302
Fairfield Ave & Ct 97306
Fairgrounds Rd NE 97301
Fairhaven Ave NE 97301
Fairmount Ave S 97302
Fairview Ave SE 97302
Fairview Industrial Dr SE 97302
Fairway Ave SE 97306
Faith Ave NE 97305
Falcon Ct & Rd 97305
Falcon View Way NE 97305
Fall Creek Ct & Dr 97306
Fanny Ct & Way 97301
Faragate St S 97302
Fargo Ln SE 97317
Farm Field Ave NE 97305
Farmland Ln NE 97303
Faro Ln SE 97317
Farrell Ave NE 97301
Fawk St SE 97302
Fawn St NW 97304
Faymar Dr NE 97303
Feather Cloud St NW 97304
Feather Fire Ave NW 97304
Feather Sky St NW 97304
Feddern Ln NE 97305
Felina Ave NE 97301
Fellowship Ave & Way 97305
Felton St S 97302
Fenmere Way SE 97317
Fenwick Ct N 97303
Ferguson St NW 97304
Fern Ct NE 97305
Fern Dr S 97302
Fernbrook Ct S 97306
Ferndell St NE 97301
Fernwood Ct NW 97304
Ferry St SE 97301
Fiddlers Ln SE 97317
Field Of Dreams Way NE 97303
Fieldcrest Ct S 97306
Fieldview St NE 97303
Filbert Ave NE 97303
Filbert Creek Ln SE 97317
Fillmore Ave NW 97304
Fillmore Ct NW 97304
Fillmore St N 97303
Finale Ct NE 97301
Finch Ct NE 97301
Fir Ln NW 97304
Fir Pl SE 97306
Fir St S 97302
Fir Cone Dr & Ln 97303
Fir Dell Ct SE 97306
Fir Dell Dr SE 97302
Fir Gardens St NW 97304
Fir Grove Ln N 97303
Fir Knoll Ln NE 97317
Fir Rest Way NE 97301
Fir Tree Dr SE 97317
Fircrest Ct & St 97306
Fire Fox St NW 97304
Firefly Ct NW 97304
Firestone Ave SE 97306
Firth Ave S 97302
Firview Pl N 97303
Fisher Ct & Rd 97305
Fitzpatrick Ave SE 97306
Flag Stone Ct NE 97303
Flagstaff Ct SE 97302
Flairstone Ct & Dr 97306
Flat Rock Ct NW 97304
Flicker Dr SE 97306
Flint Ct S 97306
Flint Ridge St SE 97306
Flintlock Ct & Dr 97305
Florence Ave NE 97301
Florgon St NE 97303
Flower Ave NE 97301
Flying Eagle Cir S 97306
Flying Eagle St NW 97304
Flying Squirrel Way NW 97304
Fontana Ct & St 97317
Foothill Ct NE 97303
Ford St SE
400-999 97301
1100-1799 97302
Forest Ln NE 97303
Forest Ln S 97306
Forest Glen Ct SE 97306
Forest Hills Way NW 97304
Forrest Gump Ln SE 97317
Forsythe Dr SE 97302
Fort Hill Ave NW 97304
Fort Rock Ave & Ct 97306
Fountain Ct N 97303
Fountain Valley Way NE 97301
Fountainhead St SE 97306
Four H Rd NW 97304
Four Point St NE 97301
Four Seasons Ct NE 97305
Four Winds Dr N 97303
Fox Ct & Ln 97306
Fox Hollow Dr SE 97317
Foxglove St SE 97306
Foxhaven Ct & Dr 97306
Foxtail Ct NW 97304
Fran St SE 97306
Franklin St NW 97304
Frantz Ct S 97306
Franzen St NE 97301
Fraser Ln SE 97302
Fred Way NE 97305
Fredrick St NE 97301
Fredrickson Ln SE 97306
Freedom Loop SE 97302
Freeman Ct NE 97303
Freeway Ct NE 97301
Friar Ct SE 97302
Friendship Ave SE 97302
Frisco Ct SE 97306
Front St NE 97301
Frontage Rd NW 97304
Frontier Dr NW 97304
Fruitland Rd NE 97317
Fuhrer Ct & St 97305
Fuller Ln SE 97306
Fultz Ave NE 97301
Fussy Duck Ln NE 97301
Future Dr & Rd 97305
Gable Ct NE 97303
Gabriela Ct NE 97301
Gadwall Ave SE 97306
Gaffin Rd SE 97317

Gaines St NE 97301
Gale St SE 97317
Galloway St S 97302
Galven Pl NE 97305
Gander Way N 97303
Ganon St SE 97317
Garden Ct NE 97303
Garden Ct SE 97317
Garden Creek Ln SE 97317
Gardenia Dr N 97303
Gardner Rd SE 97302
Garfield St NE 97301
Garland Ct & Way 97303
Garlock St S 97302
Garnet St NE 97301
Garwood Way N 97303
Gary St NE 97303
Gath Rd SE 97317
Gearhart Ave NW 97304
Geartz Ln SE 97317
Gehlar Ave & Rd 97304
Gem Pl NE 97301
Gemma St NW 97304
Genesis Ct & St 97306
Geneva Ave NE 97301
Genie Ct & St 97306
Geoff St S 97306
George Ct & St 97304
Georgia Ave SE 97302
Geranium Ave & Loop 97305
Gerleon St SE 97302
Gerth Ave NW 97304
Gibson Rd NW 97304
Gibsonwoods Ct NW 97304
Gifford St SE 97317
Gilbert St S 97302
Giles Way NE 97303
Gill St NE 97305
Gilmer St NW 97304
Ginger Ave SE 97306
Ginwood Ct SE 97306
Glacier Ct SE 97302
Glacier View St SE 97317
Gladmar St SE 97302
Gladys St NE 97305
Glazemeadow St NE 97303
Glen Creek Rd NW 97304
Glen Echo Ct NW 97304
Glen Eden Ct NW 97304
Glenada Ln SE 97317
Glenallen Ct NE 97305
Glencoe St NE 97301
Glendale Ave NE
3000-3399 97301
4000-4899 97305
Glendora Ave SE 97306
Glenview Way NW 97304
Glenwood Dr & Loop 97317
Glodcrest Ave NW 97304
Glory Ct NE 97305
Glory Ridge Ct & St 97304
Glynbrook St N 97303
Glyneagle Dr SE 97306
Gobert Ave NE 97303
Gold Dust St NE 97305
Goldcrest Ave NW 97304
Golden Ln N 97303
Golden Eagle Ct & St 97304
Goldenrod Ave NE 97305
Goldstone Ct NE 97305
Golf Course Rd S 97302
Goodall St SE 97302
Goodin Pl 97302
Gordon St SE 97317
Graber Ave NE 97305
Grace Ave NE 97305
Gracie Ln N 97303
Granada Way S 97302
Grand Fir Ln S 97302
Grand View Pl NW 97304
Grandon Ln S 97302
Grandover Ave SE 97306
Granite Ct SE 97306
Grant St NE 97301
Grasshopper Ln SE 97317
Grassland Ct NE 97305

Gray Oak Ln S 97302
Grayce Ct SE 97317
Grayhawk Ct NW 97304
Grear St NE 97301
Great Oaks Ln SE 97317
Great Plains Dr NE 97305
Green Ridge Ct S 97306
Greenacre Dr NW 97304
Greenbriar St NE 97301
Greenbrook Ct NE 97305
Greencrest St NE 97301
Greenfield Ln NE 97305
Greenlea Way SE 97317
Greenstone Ct SE 97306
Greentree Ct & Dr 97305
Greenway Dr NE 97301
Greenwood Dr NE 97303
Gregory Ct & Ln 97302
Gretchen Ln SE 97306
Greyback Ct NW 97304
Greymar St NE 97305
Grice Hill Ct & Dr 97304
Griswold Ave NE 97303
Grizzle Ct NE 97303
Grouse Dr SE 97317
Grove St NE 97301
Guava Ct NE 97305
Gulfport St NE 97305
Gwendolyn Loop NE 97301
Gwinn Way SE 97317
Gypsy Ln SE 97317
Ha Mar Ave NE 97301
Haas Ln SE 97302
Hackney Ct SE 97317
Hadley St NE 97301
Hager St SE 97317
Hagers Grove Rd SE 97317
Haley St NE 97305
Halifax Sq SE 97302
Hall St NE 97301
Hallelujah Dr NE 97305
Hallelujah St NW 97304
Hallet Ct NW 97304
Halls Ferry Rd S 97302
Hamlet Ct S 97302
Hammel St NE 97301
Hampden Ln NE
300-1400 97317
1402-1698 97317
1700-1999 97305
Hancock Ave NE 97305
Hanover Ct S 97302
Hansen Ave S 97302
Happy Dr NE 97305
Happy Valley Way SE 97317
Hapuna Ave SE 97306
Harbour Ln NE 97303
Harbourtown Ct SE 97306
Harcourt Ave NE 97303
Hardin Ave NW 97304
Harding Ave & Ct 97304
Hari Ln NE 97305
Harlan Dr NE 97305
Harlandale Ave SE 97306
Harley Way SE 97317
Harmony Dr NE 97303
Harney St S 97302
Harold Dr NE 97305
Harper Ln SE 97317
Harpole St SE 97317
Harris St SE 97302
Harrison St NE 97301
Harritt Dr NW 97304
Hart Dr N 97303
Harvard Ct SE 97302
Harvest Dr NE 97303
Harvestview Ln S 97306
Harvey St SE 97302
Hasbrook Ave NE 97303
Hassell Ct NE 97303
Hastings St SE 97317
Hawaii St SE 97317
Hawk Ct NW 97304
Hawk Hill St SE 97306
Hawksview Ave SE 97306
Hawthorne Ave & Ct 97301

Hay Ln SE 97317
Hayden St NE 97301
Hayesville Ct, Dr & Pl 97305
Hayward St S 97306
Hazel Ave NE 97301
Hazelbrook Dr N 97303
Hazelgreen Rd NE 97305
Hazelgrove St NE 97305
Hazelnut Ln NE 97317
Hazeltine Ave SE 97306
Hearth Ct & St 97305
Hearthside Ct NW 97304
Heath St S 97302
Heather Ln SE 97302
Heather Stone Ct NE 97303
Heatherwood Ave NE 97303
Heathwood St NE 97305
Heavens Way S 97302
Hebo Ct NW 97304
Heckart Ln SE 97306
Helen Ave SE 97302
Helm St SE 97301
Helton Way SE 97317
Hemlock Ct & St 97304
Hennerth Rd NE 97305
Hennessy Ln NE 97303
Henning Way N 97303
Heritage Hill Rd SE 97317
Hermitage Way S 97302
Hermosa Ct NE 97305
Heron St NE 97305
Herrin Ct & Rd 97305
Hertel Dr S 97302
Hickory St NE 97301
Hickory Hill Dr SE 97306
Hidden Creek Dr &
Loop 97303
Hidden Hills Ln S 97306
Hidden Valley Dr NW 97304
Hidden View Ln NE 97305
Hideaway Ln SE 97317
High St NE 97301
High St SE
100-799 97301
801-1497 97302
1499-2999 97302
High Ridge Ct S 97302
Highland Ave NE 97301
Highlight Ct S 97302
Highway Ave NE 97301
Hilda St SE 97317
Hile Ln NE 97301
Hilfiker Ln SE 97302
Hill Villa Ave & Ct 97306
Hillcrest Ct & Dr 97304
Hillendale Dr SE 97302
Hillrose St SE 97302
W Hills Way NW 97304
Hills Creek Ct N 97303
Hillside Ln SE 97302
Hilltop Dr NW 97304
Hillview Dr SE 97302
Hillwood Ct S 97302
Hines St SE 97302
History Ct S 97302
Hoffman Rd NE
700-1599 97301
1800-2099 97305
Hogan Dr N 97303
Hoiland Ln S 97306
Holder Ln SE 97306
Holiday Ct & Dr 97302
Holly Ct NE 97303
Holly St NW 97304
Holly Berry Ln SE 97317
Hollyhock Pl N 97303
Hollyridge Loop NE 97305
Hollywood Dr NE 97305
Holmes Ct SE 97302
Holt Loop NE 97305
Homer Rd NE 97305
Homestead Ct NE 97303
Homestead Rd S 97302
Homewood Ct N 97303
Honestus Dr SE 97317
Honeysuckle St N 97303

Honeysuckle Way NE 97301
Honeywood Ct NE 97303
Hoo Doo Ct & Dr 97304
Hood St NE 97301
Hoover Ave NW 97304
Hope Ave NE 97305
Hope Ave NW 97304
Hope Chapel Ln SE 97306
Hopewell Rd NW 97304
Hopkins Ct NE 97303
Horizon Ct NE 97303
Horizon Ridge Ct & Dr 97303
Horizon View St SE 97306
Hornbeam St NE 97305
Hornet Ct & Dr 97303
Horse Clover Dr NW 97304
Horseback Ct NE 97301
Horseclover Dr NW 97304
Horseshoe Ct SE 97317
Hosanna Ct NW 97304
Hovenden Ct SE 97302
Howard St SE 97302
Howell Prairie Rd NE
100-1699 97317
2100-11199 97305
Howell Prairie Rd SE 97317
Howser Ln SE 97317
Hoyt St S & SE 97302
Hrubetz Rd SE 97302
Huckleberry Ct S 97302
Hudson Ave NE 97301
Huff Ave NE 97303
Hulsey Ave & Ct 97302
Hummingbird St NE 97301
Hunt St NE 97301
Hunter Ave N 97303
Huntington Cir SE 97306
Huron Ct SE 97302
Hyacinth St NE 97301
Hyde Ct & St 97301
Hylo Rd SE 97306
Hyson Ct NE 97303
Ian Ave NW 97304
Iberis St NE 97305
Ibex St NE 97305
Ibis Ct & St 97305
Ibsen St SE 97302
Icabod Ct & St 97305
Icel Ct NE 97301
Idaho Ave NE 97305
Idanha Ct SE 97302
Idell Ct SE 97302
Idylwood Dr SE 97302
Iler St S 97302
Illahe Heights Dr & Rd 97302
Illahe Hill Rd S 97302
Illinois Ave & Ct 97301
Imperial Dr NE 97301
Independence Dr SE 97302
Independence Rd NW 97304
Indian Ct SE 97317
Indian Earth Ave & Ct 97305
Indian Hills Ct SE 97302
Indian School Rd NE 97305
Indian Trails Ln SE 97317
Indian Wells Loop S 97302
Indiana Ave & Ct 97302
Indigo Ct & St 97305
Industrial Way NE 97301
Ingram Ln NW 97304
Inland Dr S 97302
Inland Shores Way N 97303
Innsbrook Ct SE 97302
Insignia St SE 97306
Inspiration Ln SE 97317
Integra Ave SE 97306
Interstate Pl NE 97303
Inverness Ct & Dr 97306
Inwood Ln S 97306
Irene Ct S 97302
Iris Ln NW 97304
Irish Ct NW 97304
Ironwood Dr SE 97306
Irwin Ct N 97303
Island View Dr NE 97303
Islander Ave NW 97304

Iva Ln NE 97317
Ivory Ct & Way 97305
Ivy St NE 97305
Ivy Way NE
700-1399 97303
3700-3899 97305
J David St SE 97306
Jacinda Ln S 97306
Jack St N 97303
Jackpine St NE 97305
Jackson Hill Rd SE 97306
Jackson Valley Ln SE 97306
Jackwood Ct & St 97306
Jacobe St NE 97303
Jacobson St N 97303
Jade St NE 97305
Jaime Ln SE 97317
Jake Ln SE 97317
Jakewood Ct NE 97303
James St NE 97303
Jamestown St SE 97302
Jamison Dr SE 97306
Jan Ree Ct & Dr 97305
Jana Ave S 97302
Jane Dr NE 97301
Janelle Ct SE 97317
Janet Ave & Ct 97303
Jani Ct NE 97303
Janice Ave NE 97305
Japonica St NE 97305
Jasmine Ct NE 97305
Jason St NE 97301
Jaspen Ct N 97303
Jasper Way NW 97304
Jay Ct NW 97304
Jaymar Dr NE 97303
Jays Dr NE 97303
Jean Ct & St 97305
Jean Marie Ln SE 97306
Jefferson St NE 97301
Jeffrey Ct N 97303
Jelden St NE 97301
Jenah Ct & St 97317
Jenniches Ln SE 97317
Jennifer Ave, Ct & St 97302
Jenny Ct S 97306
Jensen St NE 97301
Jentif Ct NE 97303
Jerdon Ct N 97303
Jericho Ct SE 97306
Jerris Ave SE 97302
Jerusalem Hill Rd NW 97304
Jessica Marie Ct NE 97303
Jessie Way NE 97305
Jesslyn Ct SE 97302
Jester Ct NE 97301
Jetto Ln NE 97303
Jev Ct NW 97304
Jewel St NW 97304
Jimmy Ct NE 97301
Joan Dr N 97303
Joanie Rose Ln NE 97305
Jodelle Ct N 97303
Joel Ct SE 97317
Johan Ct NW 97304
John St S 97302
John Muir Cir SE 97302
Johnisee Ct NE 97305
Johns Pl SE 97317
Johnson St NE 97301
Joien Ct SE 97302
Jolin Way NE 97317
Jonah Ave SE 97306
Jonathan Ct NE 97303
Jones Rd SE
4300-4999 97302
5000-5299 97306
Jonmart Ave SE 97306
Joplin Ct & St 97302
Jordan Dr S 97302
Jordan St SE 97317
Jorgenson Ln SE 97317
Jorie Ln NE 97303
Jory Hill Rd S 97306
Joryville Ln S 97306
Joseph Ct SE 97302

Joseph St S 97302
Joseph St SE
500-699 97302
5300-6999 97317
Joshua Ave NE 97305
Joy Haven Ln SE 97317
Joyce St NE 97303
Jubil Ln SE 97317
Jubilee Ln NE 97305
Judson St S & SE 97302
Judy Ave NE 97305
Juedes Ave N 97303
Julia Ann Ct NE 97303
Juliana Loop SE 97317
Julie St N 97303
Juliet Ct S 97302
Juliet Way S 97306
June Ave NE 97305
June Reid Pl NE 97303
Juneau Ct, Dr & St 97302
Juneva Pl SE 97317
Juniper Ct N 97303
Juniper St N 97303
Juniper St NE 97305
Juntura Ct S 97302
Juntura Ct SE 97302
Juntura St SE 97302
Juntura Way SE
500-699 97302
5500-5799 97317
Jurand Ln NE 97305
Justice St S 97306
Justice St SE 97302
Justice Way S 97302
Justice Way Ct S 97302
Kacey Cir NE 97305
Kafir Dr NE 97303
Kailua St SE 97317
Kalakala Cir S 97306
Kale St NE 97305
Kaley Ave NW 97304
Kali St SE 97306
Kalisa Ln SE 97306
Kalmia Dr NE 97303
Kaloken Ct S 97306
Kamela Dr S 97306
Kamet Ct NE 97303
Kampstra St SE 97302
Kansas Ave NE 97301
Kanuku Ct & St 97306
Kanz Ct NE 97301
Kare Bear Ln NE 97317
Karen Ave S 97302
Karen Way NW 97304
Kari Dawn Ave SE 97306
Karm Ln NE 97303
Karma Ct S 97306
Kashmir Ct SE 97306
Kashmir Dr S 97306
Kashmir St SE 97306
Kashmir Way SE 97317
Kate Ln NE 97303
Katey Ct NE 97301
Katherine St NE 97303
Kathleen Ave NE 97301
Kathy Ct, St & Way 97306
Katie Ave NE 97303
Katrina Ct NE 97305
Katy Ln S 97306
Katybug Ct SE 97306
Kauai St SE 97317
Kaufman Loop SE 97306
Kay St NE 97301
Kay Lynn Way NE 97301
Kayak Way NE 97303
Kayla Shae Loop & St 97303
Kearney St S & SE 97302
Keen Ave & Ct 97301
Keiko Ct NE 97305
Keizer Ct NE 97303
Keizer Ln NE 97301
Keizer Rd NE 97303
Keizer Station Blvd
NE 97303
Kellogg Way SE 97317
Kelly St NE 97303

Kelsey Way NE 97301
Kenard Ct & St 97304
Kendell Ave & Ct 97302
Kennedy Cir NE 97303
Kens Way S 97306
Kensington Ct NE 97303
Kent St NW 97304
Kenwood St NE 97301
Kephart Ct NE 97303
Kermit Ct NE 97305
Kersey Way NE 97303
Kerstin Way NE 97303
Kessler Dr SE 97306
Kestrel St N & NE 97303
Ketchikan Ave NE 97305
Kettle Ct SE 97301
Kevin Ct & Way 97306
Kewanna Ct NE 97305
Keystone Loop NE 97303
Khartoum St SE 97306
Khyber Ave & Ct 97306
Kiger Way SE 97317
Killdeer St NE 97305
Kimberly Ct NE 97303
Kimeroff Ln SE 97306
Kimeron St SE 97306
King Ct NE 97301
King St S 97302
King Arthurs Ct SE 97302
Kingbird Ct SE 97317
Kingdom Way NE 97301
Kinglet Way NE 97303
Kingston Ct & Dr 97305
Kingwood Ave & Dr 97304
Kinsington St SE 97302
Kinslo Ct, Ln & St 97317
Kinzua Ct S 97306
Kipling Ct SE 97302
Kirby Ave NE 97303
Kirkwood Rd NW 97304
Kite Ct N 97303
Kitsap Ct & St 97304
Klamath Ct & St 97306
Klarr Ct NW 97304
Klicitat Dr NE 97303
Kloshe Ct S 97306
Knapp Pl NE 97301
Knights Ct NE 97301
Knoll Ct S 97302
Knox Ave NE 97301
Koala St N 97303
Koda St SE 97306
Kodiak Ct NE 97305
Kolb Ln NE 97301
Koln Ln NE 97301
Kona Ct SE 97317
Konaway Loop S 97306
Koosaw Ln S 97306
Kotzy Ave S 97302
Koufax Ln NE 97303
Kristin Ct NE 97305
Krystie Ct NE 97303
Kuebler Rd S 97302
Kuenzi Hill Ln S 97317
Kumler St SE 97302
Kurt Dr NW 97304
Kurth St S 97302
Kwonesum Ct S 97306
Kyle Ln SE 97317
La Branch St SE 97317
La Costa Loop S 97302
La Cresta Ct & Dr 97306
La Jolla Ct & Dr 97304
La Palms Ln NE 97305
La Tosca Ct NW 97304
La Vista Way SE 97317
Labish Center Rd NE 97305
Labish Garden Rd NE 97305
Lacey Ct N 97303
Lachs Ct S 97302
Ladd Ave NE 97301
Lady Bug Ct NE 97301
Lafayette Hwy NW 97304
Laguna Dr NE 97303
Lahaina Ln NE 97317
Lake Dr SE 97306

Lake Labish Rd NE 97305
Lake Vanessa Cir NW 97304
Lakefair Cir & Pl 97303
Lakepoint Pl N 97303
Lakeport St N 97303
Lakeshore Ct N 97303
Lakeside Dr NE 97305
Lakeview Ct, Dr & Pl 97304
Lakota Ln S 97306
Lamberson St NE 97301
Lambert Ct NW 97304
Lambert Ln SE 97317
Lambert St NW 97304
Lamp Ln SE 97317
Lamplighter Cir SE 97302
Lana Ave NE
1700-1900 97301
1902-2098 97301
1905-1905 97303
2001-2099 97301
Lanai St SE 97317
Lancaster Dr NE
100-1681 97301
1683-1685 97301
1700-4899 97305
Lancaster Dr SE 97317
Lance Ct NE 97305
Lancers Ct NE 97303
Landaggard Dr NW 97304
Landau St SE 97306
Landon St SE 97306
Lands End Ln NE 97305
Lane Pl S 97302
Langley St SE 97317
Lansdowne Ct NE 97305
Lansford Dr SE 97302
Lansing Ave NE 97301
Lantana Ave SE 97306
Lantz St SE 97302
Larch Loop & St 97305
Larchwood St NE 97303
Lardon Rd NE 97305
Lariat Ct NE 97305
Lark Ct & Dr 97301
Larkspur Ln NW 97304
Larmer Ave NE 97301
Larry Ave N 97303
Larson Ave SE 97317
Larussa Ct NE 97301
Latona Ct & Dr 97303
Latosca Ct NW 97304
Lauderback St NE 97303
Laura Ln NE 97305
Laurel Ave NE 97301
Laurelridge Loop & St 97303
Laurelwood Ct NW 97304
Laurens Ct SE 97302
Laurine Ct & St 97301
Lava Ct SE 97306
Lavona Dr NW 97304
Lavonne Ave SE 97306
Lawless St NE 97303
Lawnridge St N 97303
Lawnview St NE 97303
Lawrence St SE 97302
Lawson St NE 97305
Lazy Creek Ct & Dr 97303
Leafwood Ave NE 97305
Leah St NE 97305
Lee St SE
1100-1198 97302
1200-1859 97302
1860-1898 97301
1900-2699 97301
Lee Ann Ct NW 97304
Leeward Ct N 97303
Leewood Ave NE 97303
Leffelle St S & SE 97302
Lefor Dr NW 97304
Legacy St SE 97306
Lemon St NE 97305
Lemongrass Loop SE 97306
Lent Ct NE 97303
Leo St NE 97303
Leona Ln S 97302
Leonard Pl NE 97303
Leonardo Ct S 97306
Leprichaun Ct NE 97303
Leslie St SE 97301
Letteken Way NE 97305
Levi St NW 97304
Lewis St SE 97302
Lexie Ct NE 97303
Lexington Cir SE 97306
Liberal Ave NE 97305
Liberty Cir S 97306
Liberty Rd S
2901-3097 97302
3099-4799 97302
4800-10399 97306
Liberty St NE 97301
Liberty St SE
100-799 97301
800-1799 97302
Lidbeck Ct SE 97302
Lilac Ln NE 97305
Lillian Ct & St 97306
Lilligard Ln S 97302
Lilly Ave SE 97302
Lilly Ct NE 97301
Limelight Ave & Ct 97304
Limestone Ave SE 97306
Lincoln Rd NW 97304
Lincoln St S 97302
Lincoln St SE 97302
Lind Ln SE 97317
Linda Ave NE 97303
Linda Ct SE 97306
Linday St SE 97306
Linden Ln S 97302
Linfield Ct NE 97305
Link Ct S 97302
Linn Haven Dr SE 97306
Linnet St NE 97305
Linus Ct NE 97301
Linwood St NW 97304
Lipscomb St SE 97317
Lisa Ct NE 97303
Lisa St NE 97305
Litchfield Pl SE 97317
Little Ln SE 97317
Little Haven Ln S 97302
Little John Loop NW 97304
Little Springs Ln S 97302
Littler Dr N 97303
Livingston St NE 97301
Lloyd Ct SE 97317
Loch Ct N 97303
Lockhart Dr NW 97304
Lockhaven Dr N & NE 97303
Lockmere Ave S 97302
Locksley Ave SE 97306
Lockwood Ln S 97302
Locust St NE 97301
Loess Ln SE 97317
Lofty Loop SE 97317
Log Dr NE 97305
Logan Ct NE 97305
Lois Ct SE 97317
Lolo Pass Way NE 97305
Lombardy Ln S 97306
Lompoc Ct S 97306
Lone Crest St SE 97306
Lone Fir Ave & Ct 97306
Lone Oak Rd SE
3800-4950 97302
4952-4998 97302
5000-6599 97306
Lone Star Rd NW 97304
Lone Tree Ct NE 97305
Lonebrook Ct SE 97302
Long Creek Ct N 97303
Longacres Ave NE 97301
Longsome Ln NE 97305
Longview Way NW 97304
Lopez Ct N 97303
Lor Ln NE 97303
Lorain Ct SE 97302
Lords Ct NE 97301
Lori Ave SE 97302
Lorian Ln SE 97302
Lorida Ave S 97302
Loring Dr NW 97304
Lost Ln N 97303
Lost Creek Ct N 97303
Lottie Ln NW 97304
Loucks Ct NE 97301
Lowell Ave NE 97303
Lowell Ct NW 97304
Lowen St NW 97304
Lower Ben Lomond Dr
SE 97302
Lower Breckenridge Loop
NW 97304
Lower Lavista Ct NW 97304
Lucille Ave & Ct 97302
Lucinda Ave NE 97303
Lucy Ln S 97306
Luke Ct NW 97304
Lupin Ln NW 97304
Luradel Ave S 97302
Luree Ct NE 97305
Luther St S 97302
Lyman Ln SE 97302
Lynda Ct & Ln 97304
Lynette Ct NE 97305
Lynn St NE 97301
Lynx Ln SE 97306
Mabel Ave NE 97301
Mac St SE 97306
Macaw St NW 97304
Macinness Ln NE 97317
Macleay Rd SE 97317
Macy Ct NE 97301
Madal Ct NE 97301
Madalyn Ct NE 97303
Maddy Ave NE 97303
Madelyn Ave SE 97306
Mader St SE 97302
Madison St NE 97301
Madras St SE
1000-2099 97306
7600-7799 97317
Madrona Ave, Ct & Loop
S & SE 97302
Maebelle Ln NE 97303
Maggie Ln SE 97306
Magness Rd NW 97304
Magnolia Ct NW 97304
Mahalo Ct & Dr 97317
Mahaya Ct SE 97317
Mahogany Ct NE 97301
Mahonia Way SE 97306
Mahrt Ave & Ln 97317
Maine Ave NE 97303
Mainline Dr NE 97301
Majestic View Ave &
Ct 97306
Mall Ct NE 97305
Mallard St SE 97306
Mallard View Ln SE 97317
Mallory Ln NE 97303
Manbrin Dr N & NE 97303
Mandarin St & Way 97303
Mandy Ave & Ct 97302
Mango Ave SE 97317
Manning Ct & Dr 97305
Manor Dr NE 97301
Manorview Cir & Ln 97304
Manzanita St & Way 97303
Maple Ave NE 97301
Maple Glen Ln S 97302
Maple Grove Ct SE 97317
Maple Hill Dr NW 97304
Maple Tree Ln SE 97317
Mapleleaf Ct NW 97304
Maplewood Ct & Dr 97306
Marble Ct SE 97306
Marcey Ct NE 97305
March Ave NE 97301
Marcia Dr NE 97301
Marcus Ct NE 97305
Margarett St NW 97304
Marguerite St NE 97305
Maria Ave NE 97305
Marietta St SE
100-3199 97302
3200-3499 97317
Marigold St NE 97303
Marilyn St SE 97302
Marine Dr NW 97304
Mariner Way NE 97301
Marino Dr N 97303
Marion St NE 97301
Marionberry Way NE 97305
Mark Ct SE 97317
Market St NE 97301
Markham St SE 97317
Marks Dr NE 97303
Marley Ln S 97306
Marlin Ct SE 97302
Marmot Ct NE 97305
Marquette Ln S 97306
Marshall Dr SE 97302
Marstone Ct SE 97306
Martin Ct S 97306
Martinsson Ln S 97302
Marvin Ct NW 97304
Mary Ave SE 97302
Mason St NE 97303
Massey Ln SE 97317
Matt Pl NE 97303
Matthew Ct NE 97305
Matthews Loop & St 97302
Maui Ct NE 97301
Maverick Ln SE 97317
Max Ct N 97303
May St NE 97303
Mayfield Pl N 97303
Mayflower Ct SE 97306
Mayfly Ave NW 97304
Maywood Dr SE 97302
Mcahren Ln S 97306
Mccammon Ln SE 97317
Mcclure St N 97303
Mccoy Ave NE 97301
Mcdonald St NE 97301
Mcgee Ct NE 97303
Mcgilchrist St S & SE 97302
Mcintosh Ct N 97303
Mckay Dr S 97302
Mckenzie Ct NE 97305
Mckenzie Pass Way
NE 97305
Mckinley Ln NW 97304
Mckinley St SE 97302
Mcleod Ln NE 97303
Mcmaster Ct NE 97305
Mcnary Ave NW 97304
Mcnary Estates Dr N 97303
Mcnary Heights Dr N 97303
Meadow Park Loop
NE 97305
Meadowbrook Ct NE 97303
Meadowglen St NE 97303
Meadowlark Dr NE 97303
Meadowlawn Dr &
Loop 97317
Meadowridge St NE 97303
W Meadows Dr NW 97304
Meadowwood St NE 97303
Medical Center Dr NE 97301
Medina Ln SE 97317
Megan Lee Ln N 97303
Mehama Loop & St 97305
Melandy Ln NE 97317
Melas Way SE 97306
Melba Ln SE 97317
Melinda Ct S 97306
Melissa St SE 97306
Melody Ln SE 97302
Melow Rd NE 97317
Melrose Ct N 97303
Mendocino Dr NE 97305
Menlo Dr N 97303
Merced Ct SE 97306
Merdel Ave S 97302
Meriweather Ct & St 97306
Merlin Ct NW 97304
Merlot Ave NE 97303
Merrill Ln 97304
Merrimac Ct NE 97305
Merritt St S 97302
Mesa St S 97302
Metolius Ave & Ct 97306
Mica View Ct SE 97302
Micah Ct SE 97306
Michael Ct & Dr 97305
Michel St NE 97305
Michelle Way SE 97317
Michigan City Ln & Rd 97304
Middle Grove Dr NE 97305
Middlecrest Ct S 97306
Midland Ct NE 97305
Midway Ave NE 97301
Mikkelobe Dr & Pl 97304
Milano Ave S 97306
Mildred Ct & Ln 97306
Militia Way SE 97301
Milkey Way NE 97305
Mill St SE
400-498 97301
410-410 97308
701-797 97301
799-2299 97301
Miller St S & SE 97302
Milton St NE 97305
Mimosa St S 97302
Miners Way SE 97306
Mink Ct NE 97305
Mink Hollow St SE 97306
Minno Ln NE 97305
Mirage St N 97303
Miranda Ave SE 97306
Mirasol Ave SE 97306
Mission St S & SE 97302
Mission Hills St SE 97306
Missouri Ave S 97302
Mistletoe Loop N 97303
Mistwood Dr NE 97303
Misty Pl NW 97304
Misty Hill Ln SE 97306
Misty Pine Ln S 97302
Mistymorning Ave SE 97306
Mitchell St NE 97301
Mitzur St S 97302
Mize Rd SE 97302
Mjb Pl SE 97317
Mock Orange Ct S 97302
Mockingbird Dr S 97302
Modesto Ct S 97306
Modoc Dr NE 97303
Mogul St NW 97304
Mohawk Ct S 97306
Molokai St SE 97317
Monarch Ct & Dr 97301
Monarchy Dr NE 97301
Moneda Ave & Ct 97303
Monroe Ave & Ct 97301
Montaigne Ln S 97302
Montana Ln SE 97317
Montera Ct SE 97302
Monterey Ct & Dr 97306
Montevallo St SE 97306
Montrose Ave NW 97304
Moonbeam Ct NW 97304
Moondancer Ln SE 97317
Moonflower St NE 97301
Moonlight Ave SE 97302
Moonpenny Ct NE 97305
Moonstone Loop SE 97306
Moonwood Ct SE 97306
Moore Rd S 97306
Mooreland Ave & Ct 97305
Moores Way NW 97304
Mooseberry Ct & St 97306
Morgan Ave NE 97301
Morley Ln S 97306
Morning Dove Ct NW 97304
Morningside Ct & Dr 97302
Morningstar Pl NW 97304
Morrow Ct NW 97304
Mosier St SE 97317
Mosswood Ct S 97306
Mote Ln SE 97306
Motor Ct NE 97301
Mount Kuebler Dr S 97302
Mount Laurel Way S 97302
Mountain Crest Way S 97302
Mountain View Dr S 97302
Mountain Vista Ave
SE 97306
Mousebird Ave NW 97304
Moyer Ln NW 97304
Mozell Ln NE 97303
Mt Hood Ln SE 97317
Mt Jeff Ln SE 97317
Mud Puppy Ln SE 97317
Muirfield Ave & Ct 97306
Mulberry Dr S 97302
Mule Deer Ct, Pl & St 97304
Mulligan Ct SE 97306
Mullusk Ave NW 97304
Mulvehill Ct N 97303
Muncie St NE 97305
Munkers Ct & St 97317
Murdock Ct NE 97305
Murhammer Ln S 97302
Murlark Ave NW 97304
Murphy Ave NE 97303
Murray St SE 97306
Muscovy Ln SE 97317
Musgrave Ave NW 97304
Music St SE 97302
Musket Ct NE 97305
Mustang Ct SE 97317
Myers St S & SE 97302
Mykala St NE 97303
Myrla Ct S 97302
Myrtle Ave NE 97301
Mystical Ln SE 97317
Nadine Dr SE 97302
Nalani Ct SE 97302
Nandale Dr NE 97305
Nandina Ct NE 97303
Nando St NE 97305
E & W Nanitch Cir 97306
Naples St N 97303
Narcissus Ct NW 97304
Natalie Ave S 97306
Nathan St SE 97317
National Ct SE 97306
Natures View Ct NW 97304
Nautilus Ave NW 97304
Navaho Ct SE 97306
Neahkahnie St SE 97306
Nebraska Ave & Ct 97301
Neef Ave SE 97302
Neelon Dr S 97302
Nehalem St S 97306
Nelson Pl SE 97306
Neota St NE 97301
Neptune Ct SE 97317
Nesting Pl SE 97317
Nestor Ln NE 97305
Nestucca Ct S 97306
Nevada St NE 97305
New Carissa Ln NE 97305
New Haven Dr NE 97317
New Terrace Ct & Dr
NE 97303
Newberg Dr N 97303
Newberry St S 97306
N & S Newcastle Cir 97305
Newport Rd SE 97306
Newton Ct N 97303
Newtown Ave SE 97302
Niagra St N 97303
Nicholas Ct NE 97305
Nichols Heights Way
SE 97306
Nicklaus Loop N 97303
Nicks Ct NE 97305
Nicole Ct SE 97306
Nightcap St SE 97306
Nighthawk Ct NE 97305
Nightingale Ct NE 97303
Nightlight Ln SE 97317
Niles Ave NE 97305
Nimbus Pl NW 97304
Nina Ave SE 97302
E & W Nob Hill St 97302
Noble Fir Ln S 97306
Nocturne Ct SE 97306
Nohlgren St S 97302
Nola Ave SE 97302
Nolan Ln NE 97305
Nomad Ct SE 97306
Nomore St N 97303
Nona Ave NW 97304
Noon Ave NE 97303
Nordal Ln S 97306
Nordic Ct N 97303
Noren Ave NE 97303
Norma Ave & Ct 97306
Norman Ave NE 97301
Normandy Ave S 97302
Norris Ln S 97302
Northern Heights Loop
NE 97303
Northgate Ave NE 97301
Northmont Ln NE 97303
Northridge Ct N 97303
Northrup Ct NE 97303
Northshire Ct NE 97303
Northside Dr NE 97303
Northstar Ct NE 97305
Northtree Ct & Dr 97303
Northview Dr NE 97303
Northwind Ct N 97303
Northwood Dr NE 97317
Norway St NE 97301
Norwood St SE 97302
Nottingham Dr NE 97303
Nougat Ct SE 97306
Novak Ct SE 97306
Novare Ct SE 97306
Nut Tree Dr NW 97304
Nutmeg St NE 97305
O Connor Ct SE 97317
Oahu Ave SE 97317
Oak Dr SE 97306
Oak Rd NW 97304
Oak St SE 97301
Oak Way NE 97301
Oak Dell Ln SE 97317
S Oak Grove Rd 97304
Oak Heights Ct SE 97306
Oak Hollow Ln SE 97302
Oak Knoll Rd NW 97304
Oak Park Ct & Dr 97305
Oakcrest Dr NW 97304
Oakhill Ave SE 97302
Oakland Loop SE 97317
Oakleaf Ct NE 97305
Oakman St S 97302
Oakmont Ct SE 97317
Oakridge Ct SE 97306
Oakstone Dr SE 97306
Oakwood St NE 97303
Oasis Ct SE 97306
Obrien Ave S 97306
Obsidian Ct SE 97306
Ocean Ave NE 97301
Ochoco Ct SE 97317
Oda Ln SE 97317
Odessa Ln NE 97301
Offenbach Ct NE 97303
Ogle St SE 97317
Ohmart Ave SE 97302
Ojai Ct & Dr 97304
Old Farm Ave NW 97304
Old Liberty Rd S 97306
Old Orchard Way SE 97317
Old Sage Ln NE 97317
Olin Ct NE 97303
Olive St NE 97301
Olivia Ct SE 97302
Ollie Ln SE 97317
Olney St SE 97317
Olympia Ave & Ct 97304
Olympic Ave SE 97306
Oneil Rd NE 97303
Onyx St NW 97304
Opaque Ave NW 97304
Open Range Ln SE 97317
Oppek St NE 97303
Orchard Ct & St 97303
Orchard Heights Ct, Pl &
Rd 97304
Orchardview Ave NW 97304
Oregon Ave NE 97301

Oregon Trail Ct NE 97305
Orendale St NE 97301
Oriole Ct NE 97305
Orlando Ln NE 97303
Orville Rd S 97306
Osage Dr NW 97304
Osborn Ave NE 97301
Oscar Ln SE 97317
Osprey Ave & Ct 97306
Otelagh Ct S 97306
Otter Way N 97303
Otter Run Ct NE 97305
Overlook Ave NW 97304
Overview Ct NW 97304
Owens St S & SE 97302
Owl Dr SE 97306
Owyhee Ct SE 97302
Oxen Ct SE 97317
Oxford St SE 97302
Pacific Ct NE 97301
Pacifica Way NE 97305
Pacwood Ct SE 97306
Padick Ln SE 97317
Page Ct & St 97301
Paintbrush Ct NE 97305
Palace Dr NE 97301
Pali Dr NW 97304
Palisades Dr SE 97302
Palm Ct SE 97317
Palma Ln SE 97317
Palmer Dr N 97303
Palomino Ct SE 97317
Pam Ave SE 97302
Panorama Ct SE 97302
Pansy Way NE 97301
Panther Ct NE 97303
Par Three St S 97302
Paradise Ct NW 97304
Paragon Ct NW 97304
Paramount Ln SE 97317
Park Ave NE 97301
E Park Ave NE 97301
Park Ct SE 97306
W Park Ct NW 97304
W Park St NW 97304
Park Terrace Dr NE 97303
Parker Ct S 97306
Parklawn Ct NE 97303
Parkmeadow Dr & Loop 97303
Parkplace Ct & Dr 97303
Parkridge St NE 97303
Parkshadow Ct NE 97303
Parkside Ct NE 97303
Parktree Ln NE 97303
Parkview Ct NE 97303
Parkway Dr NE 97305
Parkway Dr NW 97304
Partridge Ln NE 97303
Pastureland Ln NE 97317
Patricia Ct & St 97305
Patrick Ln NE 97303
Patriot Ct SE 97302
Patterson St NW 97304
Patty Ave NE 97303
Paul Ct NE 97305
Paula Ct NE 97305
Paulanna Ln SE 97317
Paulette St NE 97303
Pauline Ave SE 97302
Pawnee Cir SE 97306
Peace St SE 97302
Peaceful Ln SE 97306
Peachtree St NE 97305
Peachwood Ct SE 97306
Peakaview Way SE 97317
Pear Grove Ct NW 97304
Pear Tree Ct NW 97304
Pear Tree Ln SE 97317
Pearl St NE 97301
Pearl Springs Ln S 97306
Pebble Ln S 97306
Pebbles Ln SE 97317
Pecan Ct NW 97304
Peck Ave SE 97302
Pelican Ct NW 97304
Pelton Ct SE 97306
Pembrook St SE 97302
Pence Loop SE 97302
Pender Ct N 97303
Penn Ln SE 97317
Pennsylvania Ave SE 97317
Penny Dr S 97302
Penticton Cir NE 97305
Pepper Ln NE 97301
Pepper Tree Ct SE 97306
Peppermint Ln NE 97301
Percheron Ct SE 97317
Periwinkle Dr SE 97317
Perkins St NE
2000-3699 97303
3700-7499 97305
Perry St NE 97303
Pesola Ln SE 97317
Peters Pl SE 97306
Peterson St SE 97306
Petty Grove Ct NE 97303
Pettyjohn Rd S 97302
Peyton St N 97303
Phantom Creek Ln S 97302
Pheasant Ave SE 97302
Phillip Ln SE 97317
Phipps Cir & Ln 97305
Phoenix Ave SE 97306
Phyllis St NE 97305
Piedmont Ave NW 97304
Pierce Ct & Dr 97303
Pigeon Hollow Rd S 97302
Pike Ct S 97306
Pikes Pass Ct & St 97306
Pilgrim St SE 97302
Pine St NE 97301
Pinehurst Ave & Ln 97303
Pineview St NE 97303
Pintail Ave & Ct 97306
Pinto Ct SE 97317
Pioneer Dr SE 97302
Pipebend Pl NE 97301
Pippin St NE 97305
Plant Ln SE 97317
Plateau St NE 97305
Player Dr N 97303
Plaza St NW 97304
Plaza Del Rey NE 97303
Pleasant Ct NE 97303
Pleasant Hill Ln S 97302
Pleasant View Dr NE
3500-3599 97301
3600-3999 97303
Plow Ct NE 97305
Plum Tree Ct NE 97303
Plymouth Dr NE 97303
Poinsettia St NE 97305
Polaris St NE 97305
Pollyanne Ave SE 97306
Polo Ct SE 97317
Pomona Ct S 97306
Pond Ln S 97306
Ponderosa Dr S 97302
Popcorn Ct & St 97304
Poplar Ct SE 97306
Poppy Hills St SE 97306
Port Stewart Ct SE 97306
Porter Ln NW 97304
Portland Rd NE
2500-4299 97301
4500-11299 97305
Potts Dr NE 97303
Powder Creek Ct N 97303
Powderhorn Ct SE 97317
Prairie St NE 97303
Prairie Clover Ave NE 97303
Prairie Grass Ave NE 97303
Prairie Star Ct NE 97305
Pratum Ave NE 97305
Pressler Ct S 97306
Prestige Ct NE 97303
Prestwick Ct S 97302
Pries Dr NE 97303
Primrose St NW 97304
Prince Ct NE 97305
Princess Ct NE 97305
Princess Ln NE 97301
Pringle Rd SE 97302
Pringle Creek Ct SE 97302
Prominent Ct S 97302
Promontory Pl SE 97302
Prospect Pl S 97302
Prospect Ridge Rd S 97306
Providence Pl N 97303
Ptarmigan Ct & St 97304
Pudding Creek Dr & Ln 97317
Pueblo Ave NE 97305
Pullman Ave & Ct 97302
Pummel Ct SE 97317
Purisima Ct NE 97305
Quail St NE 97305
Quail Hollow St SE 97306
Quail Run Ln S 97306
Quartz St NE 97303
Queen Ct NE 97301
Queens Ave NE 97303
Quiet Way SE 97306
Quin Way Ave SE 97317
Quinaby Rd NE
2500-3999 97303
4000-4599 97305
Quinaby Acres Ln NE 97303
Quinaby Meadows Ln NE 97303
Quinalt St SE 97306
Quince St NE 97305
Raccoon Ave & Ct 97305
Rachel Ln NE 97301
Radell Dr SE 97317
Radiance Ave SE 97306
Radiant Dr NE 97303
Radio Ct NW 97304
Rafael Ct & St 97303
Raffon Ct & Dr 97317
Ragweed Ct NE 97301
Railroad Ave SE 97317
Rainbow Dr SE 97306
Rainbow Hills Ln SE 97306
Rainbow Valley Ln SE 97306
Rainier Dr SE 97306
Rainmaker Ct NW 97304
Rainsong Dr NW 97304
Raintree Ct NE 97305
Rambeau Ln SE 97317
Rambler Dr NE 97305
Ramp St NE 97305
Ramsgate Sq S 97302
Ranay Dr SE 97317
Randel Ct SE 97302
Randi Ln NE 97305
Ranier Loop NW 97304
Ratcliff Dr & Ln 97302
Raven Ave SE 97306
Ravena Dr N 97303
Ravenwood Ct NE 97305
Ravine Ave & Ct 97305
Rawhide Ct NE 97305
Rawlins Ave NE 97301
Raynor St SE 97302
Rayona St SE 97317
Raywanda Ct NE 97301
Reading Ct SE 97302
Reagan Ave NW 97304
Rebecca Ct & St 97305
Red Cherry Ct SE 97317
Red Cloud Ct SE 97317
Red Fox Ln SE 97306
Red Leaf Dr S 97306
Red Oak Dr S 97302
Redfir Ct NW 97304
Redhill Dr SE 97302
Redinger Ct S 97302
Redstone Ave SE 97306
Redwing Ct NW 97304
Redwood St NW 97304
Ree Del Ct NE 97301
Reed Ct SE 97306
Reed Ln SE 97306
Reed Rd SE 97302
Reedy Dr NE 97301
Rees Hill Rd SE 97306
Reflection Way S 97302
Regal Dr NE 97301
Regan Ct SE 97306
Regina Ct NE 97305
Reimann St NE 97305
Reindeer Ave NW 97304
Remington Pl NE 97305
Renee Ave & Ct 97304
Restmore Ct N 97303
Revere Ct S 97302
Rex St S 97302
Rhine View Pl SE 97317
Rhinestone Ct SE 97306
Rhododendron St SE 97317
Rialto Ave S 97306
Rich Dr NE 97305
Richard St NE 97305
Richland Ave NE 97305
Richmond Ave SE 97301
Rickey St SE 97317
Rickman Rd NE 97303
Ricks Ln NE 97305
Ridge Dr NE
4200-5099 97301
5400-5699 97303
E Ridge St S 97306
Ridgecrest Dr N 97303
Ridgemont Dr N 97303
Ridgepoint St NE 97303
Ridgetop Dr NE 97303
Ridgeview Ct & Dr 97303
Ridgewood Ln SE 97302
Riesling Way SE 97306
Riggs St NW 97304
Riley Ct SE 97306
Rim Rock Ct NE 97303
Ring Ln & St 97303
Rio Vista Way S 97302
Rippling Brook Dr SE 97317
Rising St SE 97302
Rising Iris Ln SE 97317
Riting Ct SE 97302
Ritter Ln SE 97317
River Rd N 97303
River Rd NE 97303
River Rd S
1900-6399 97302
6400-7699 97306
River St NE 97301
River Bend Rd NW 97304
River Heights Ln S 97306
River Rock Dr NE 97303
River Springs Dr S 97306
River Valley Dr NW 97304
Rivercrest Dr N 97303
Riverdale Rd S 97302
Riverglen Dr N 97303
Rivergrove Ct N 97303
Riverhaven Dr S 97302
Riverside Dr & Rd 97306
Riverton St NE 97305
Riverview Dr NW 97304
Riverwood Ct & Dr 97303
Riviera Dr NE 97303
Roanoke Dr NE 97305
Robert Ave NE 97301
Roberta Ave S 97302
Roberts Ridge Rd S 97302
Robin Hood St SE 97306
Robindale Dr N 97303
Robins Ln SE
2000-2647 97306
2648-2899 97317
Rochester St NE 97305
Rock Creek Ct & Dr 97306
Rock Crystal Ln NE 97303
Rock Ledge Ct & Dr 97303
Rockdale St NE 97305
Rocking Horse Rd SE 97317
Rockingham Ct NE 97301
Rockland Dr NW 97304
Rockwood St SE 97306
Rockwood Park Ct & Dr 97305
Rocky Way SE 97306
Rocky Ridge Ave SE 97306
Rodan Ave SE 97306
Rodeo Dr NE 97305
Rodgers Creek Ln SE 97306
Rodney Ln SE 97317
Roger Ln SE 97302
Rogers Ln NW 97304
Rogets Ct NE 97301
Roggy Ct SE 97317
Rogue Ave S 97302
Rolletti Dr SE 97306
Rollin Ave NW 97304
Rolling Hills Ave SE 97306
Ronald Ave SE 97306
Ronelle St S 97306
Roosevelt Loop NW 97304
Roosevelt St NE 97301
Roosevelt St NW 97304
Rose St NE 97301
Rose Blossom Ct NW 97304
Rose Park Ln NE 97303
Rosebowl Ln SE 97317
Rosebrook Ct SE 97306
Rosedale Ln S 97306
Roselawn Dr NE 97305
Roselle Way SE 97302
Rosemary Ln SE 97302
Rosemeadow Ln NE 97317
Rosemont Ave NW 97304
Rosetta Ln SE 97317
Roseway Ct SE 97302
Rosewood Dr NW 97304
Rosey View Ln & St 97302
Ross Ct SE 97306
Round Table Ave SE 97306
Round Tree Ave NW 97304
Roush Ct SE 97317
Rowan Ave N 97303
Royal St NE 97301
Royal Crown Ave NW 97304
Royal Oak Ct NE 97301
Royalann Ct NW 97304
Royalty Cir & Dr 97301
Royer Rd S 97306
Royvonne Ave SE 97302
Rozilla Ct NE 97303
Ruby Ct NE 97305
Ruge St NW 97304
Ruggles Ave S 97306
Rulers Ct NE 97301
Rumsey Ct & Rd 97304
Rupp Ave NE 97303
Rural Ave S & SE 97302
Rushmore Ave N 97303
Russell St NE 97301
Russett Dr N 97303
Rustique Rd SE 97317
Ruxton Way S 97302
Ryan Dr SE 97301
Rye Ln NW 97304
Sabra Ln NE 97301
Sacramento Ct NE 97305
Saddle Club St SE 97317
Saddle Horn Ct SE 97317
Sage Ave SE 97306
Sagebrush St NE 97303
Saghalie Dr S 97306
Saginaw St S 97302
Sagrada Cir & St 97303
Sahalee Ct & Dr 97306
Saint Andrews Loop S 97302
Saint Croix Way NE 97303
Salal St SE 97306
Salem Dallas Hwy NW 97304
Salem Heights Ave S & SE 97302
Salem Industrial Dr NE 97301
Salem View Dr SE 97317
Salinas Ct S 97306
Salishan St SE 97302
Salmon St N 97303
Salmon River St NW 97304
Samanna Ave NW 97304
Samantha Ave & Ct 97305
Samaritan Ln SE 97306
Samm Ln SE 97317
San Antonio Ct NE 97305
San Carlos Ct NE 97305
San Clemente Ln NE 97305
San Diego Dr NE 97305
San Francisco Ct & Dr 97305
San Gabriel Ct NE 97305
San Juan Ct NE 97305
San Miguel Ct NE 97305
San Rafael Ct NE 97305
Sand Piper Ave & Ct 97301
Sandal Ct NE 97305
Sandalwood Ln NW 97304
Sandpine Loop NE 97303
Sandra Ave N 97303
Sandringham Dr NE 97305
Sandstone Ct S 97306
Sandwedge Ct NE 97303
Sandy Dr N 97303
Sandys Ln SE 97317
Sanrodee Dr SE 97317
Santiam St NE 97305
Santiam Pass Way NE 97305
Santiam Springs Ct SE 97317
Sapphire Ct NE 97305
Saragosa Way NE 97303
Sarah Ln S 97306
Sarah Jean Ct NE 97303
Saramae Ln NE 97303
Saratoga Dr NE 97305
Sasha Way NE 97305
Sassy Ln SE 97317
Satara Ave & Ct 97304
Satter Dr & Pl 97305
Saturn Ct SE 97317
Saunders Ln SE 97306
Saundra Lee Way NE 97303
Saunter Loop NE 97305
Savage Rd NE 97301
Sawgrass St SE 97306
Sawmill Rd S 97302
Saxon Dr S 97302
Scenic Heights Dr SE 97306
Scenic View Dr SE 97302
Scepter Ct & Way 97301
Schaefer Ct NE 97305
Schafer Rd NE 97305
Schanins St NE 97317
Schick Pl SE 97306
Schoolhouse Ct NW 97304
Schurman Dr S 97302
Scism Way NE 97305
Scooter Ln NE 97301
Scotch Ave SE 97306
Scott Ave NE 97305
Scott Pl NE 97303
Scottish Highland Ln SE 97317
Scotto Way S 97302
Sea Gale Way N 97303
Seaton Ln NE 97305
Seattle Slew Dr SE 97317
Sedona Ave NE 97301
Seeger Ct & Ln 97306
Selby Ct NE 97305
Selway St NE 97305
Senate St NW 97304
Seneca Ave SE 97302
Sequoia St NE 97305
Serena Way SE 97317
Serendipity St SE 97317
Serenity Dr SE 97317
Sereno Ct S 97306
Serge Ln NE 97301
Serline Way SE 97317
Serra Ct NE 97305
Sesame Ln & St 97305
Settlers Ct & Dr 97305
Settlers Spring Dr NW 97304
Shade St NE 97301
Shade Tree Ln NE 97301
Shadow Ln SE 97317
Shadowwood Ct, Loop & St 97303
Shady Ct, Ln & Pl 97303
Shady Oak Way S 97302
Shale St S 97302
Shamrock Dr SE 97302
Shangri La Ave NE 97303
Shaniko Ct & Way 97302
Shannon Ave SE 97306
Shannon Ct NE 97303
Sharon Loop SE 97306
Shasta St SE 97306
Shaw St NW 97304
Shawn Ct NE 97305
Shawnee Dr & Ln 97317
Shelby Ln NE 97303
Shelley St NE 97301
Shellyanne Way NE 97305
Shelton St SE 97301
Shenandoah Dr SE 97317
Shepherd Ct N 97303
Sherry Ct NE 97301
Sherwood Ct S 97302
Shetland Ct SE 97317
Shiloh Ct & St 97306
Shipman Ln SE 97317
Shipping St NE 97301
Shipps Pl NE 97305
Shire Ct SE 97317
Shirley Ct & Ln 97303
Shore Pointe Pl N 97303
Shoreline Dr & Loop 97303
Shores St NE 97301
Shoreview Ln N 97303
Short St SE 97302
Shoshone Ct SE 97317
Shropshire Ave S 97302
Shultz Way SE 97317
Shyrina Ct N 97303
Siddall St NE 97305
Sidney Rd S 97306
Sieberg St NE 97303
Sienna Dr NE 97301
Sierra Dr SE 97306
Siesta Ct NE 97305
Silas Ct NW 97304
Silby Ln NE 97301
Silva Ave NW 97304
Silver Loop NE 97305
Silver Hills Cir SE 97306
Silvercedar Pl NE 97305
Silverpark Pl NE 97305
Silverstone Ct & Dr 97305
Silverton Rd NE
1300-3499 97301
3500-8199 97305
Simmons St NW 97304
Simon St N 97303
Simpson St SE 97301
Singlestrand Ave SE 97302
Sir Lancelot Ct NE 97303
Siskyou Ave SE 97317
Sisters Ct & Way 97304
Sitka Deer Ct NW 97304
Sizemore Dr NE 97305
Skopil Ave S 97302
Sky Ln SE 97317
Sky Ter SE 97306
Skydancer Ln SE 97317
Skyflower Ave NE 97301
Skyler Pl NE 97305
Skyline Ct, Rd & Way 97306
Skyline Village Loop S 97306
Skyway Ct & St 97302
Smintres St SE 97306
Smith Rd SE 97317
Smith St NE 97301
Smith Rock St SE 97306
Smoketree Dr SE 97306
Smokey Way NE 97305
Snead Dr N 97303
Snoopy Ct & Ln 97301
Snow Ball Ave SE 97306
Snow Peak Way SE 97306
Snow White Way SE 97302
Snowberry St NE 97305
Snowbird Ct & Dr 97304
Snowflake St SE 97306
Soapstone Ave SE 97306

Solitude Ln S 97302
Somerset Ct & Dr 97305
Sonata Ln N 97303
Song Sparrow St NE 97301
Songbird Ct SE 97306
Sonora Way S 97302
Sonya Dr SE 97317
Sophia St NE 97303
Sorenson Ct NE 97301
Sorrel Ct SE 97317
South St NE 97301
Southampton Ct & Dr 97302
Southbend Dr SE 97306
Southridge Pl S 97302
Southstar Ct NE 97305
Southwood Ct SE 97306
Sparky Ln NE 97317
Sparrow Ct & Dr 97301
Sparta Loop SE 97306
Spears Ave SE 97302
Spelbrink Ln SE 97317
Spencer Pl SE 97317
Sphinx Ct NE 97301
Spicetree Ln SE 97306
Spirit Way NE 97303
Spooner Ct S 97302
Sprice Ct SE 97306
Spring St S 97302
Spring Hollow Ln S 97302
Spring Leaf Ct N 97303
Spring Valley Ln & Rd 97304
Springcrest Ct & Dr 97306
Springdale Ct SE 97317
Springer Ave SE 97302
Springfield Ct N 97303
Springridge Dr N 97303
Springtime Ct NE 97303
Springwood Ave SE 97306
Spruce St NE 97301
Spyglass Ct SE 97306
Squire Ct NE 97301
Squirrel Hill Rd SE 97306
St Charles Pl & St 97303
St Helens St NW 97304
Stacy Pl NE 97305
Stafford Ln NE 97301
Stagecoach Way SE 97302
Stageline Ln SE 97317
Stair Way NE 97305
Standish Ct SE 97302
Stanley Ln S 97302
Stardancer Ln SE 97317
Stardust Ln SE 97317
Starflower Ct S 97302
Stark St N 97303
Starlight Dr NW 97304
Starr Ct NE 97301
Starview Ln S 97302
State St
200-4900 97301
4902-4998 97301
5000-12399 97317
12700-12799 97317
State Of Or 97301
Statesman St NE 97301
Stauber Ln SE 97317
Steamboat Ln NE 97303
Steele Ln SE 97317
Steelhead Ln NE 97305
Steens Ct NW 97304
Stefon Ct SE
2000-2099 97302
5500-5599 97306
Stellers Eagle St NW 97304
Stephens St NE 97305
Stephi Ln NE 97303
Steven Ave & Ct 97303
Stevie Ln NE 97317
Stewart St NE 97301
Stickles Ct NE 97303
Stilson Ln S 97306
Stinnett Ln NE 97303
Stockton Ave S 97306
Stone Hedge Ct & Dr 97303
Stone Mason Ln NE 97303
Stonebridge Ave NE 97303
Stonecrest Dr S 97306
Stonefield Pl N 97303
Stonehaven Dr SE 97302
Stonehill Ave S 97306
Stoneway Ct, Dr &
Ter 97304
Stortz Ave NE
2000-3199 97301
3500-4199 97305
Storybook Ln NW 97304
Strand Ave SE 97301
Stratford Dr NE 97305
Stratus Ct S 97302
Straw Dr N 97303
Strawberry Ct NE 97305
Stroll Ct NE 97305
Strong Rd SE 97302
Stubb St SE 97306
Studio Ct NE 97305
Sturgess Ln SE 97317
Suffolk Ln & Rd 97303
Sugar Ln NE 97305
Sugar Plum Ave & St 97306
Sugarpine Ct SE 97306
Sullenger Ln NE 97303
Sullivan Ct NW 97304
Sumac Dr S 97302
Summer St NE 97301
Summer St SE 97302
Summer Breeze Dr N 97303
Summer Leaf Ct N 97303
Summer Wind Ct NE 97305
Summercrest Ct & Dr 97306
Summerfield Dr SE 97306
Summerlake St SE 97306
Summerside St SE 97306
Summit Ave NW 97304
Summit View Ave SE 97306
Sun Ct SE 97306
Sun Valley Ct NW 97304
Sunbeam Ct SE 97302
Sunburst Ter NW 97304
Suncrest Ave & Ct 97304
Sundance Pl & St 97304
Sundown Ct NE 97305
Sunflower Way NE 97305
Sunland St SE 97302
Sunmeadow Ct NE 97305
Sunmist Ct SE 97306
Sunnybrook Ln SE 97317
Sunnyside Rd SE
1500-1599 97306
4300-4999 97305
5000-9999 97306
Sunnyview Rd NE
1000-1051 97301
1050-1050 97303
1052-3398 97301
1053-3399 97301
3500-9199 97305
9300-12499 97317
Sunray Ave S 97302
Sunridge Dr S 97302
Sunrise Ave S 97302
Sunrise Cir NW 97304
Sunset Ave N 97303
Sunset Rdg S 97302
Sunset View Ln S 97302
Sunstone St SE 97306
Suntree Ct & Dr 97302
Sunwood Ct & Dr 97304
Superior St S & SE 97302
Supreme Ct SE 97302
Sure Fire Way SE 97317
Surf Ct NE 97305
Surfwood Dr NE 97305
Susan Ct NE 97303
Sussex Ave SE 97306
Suzanne Lea St SE 97302
Swallow Ct & Dr 97301
Swallow Tail St SE 97306
Sweet Ln S 97302
Sweetwater Ln SE 97317
Swegle Rd NE
4500-4999 97301
5000-5499 97317
Swindoll Pl NE 97305
Swingwood Ct & Dr 97303
Sycamore Ct N 97303
Sycan Ct SE 97306
Sylvan Ave SE 97302
Sylvia Ct & St 97317
Tacoma St NE 97305
Taft St NE 97301
Taggart Dr NW 97304
Tahoe Ave SE 97306
Takelma Ct NE 97303
Talana Ct NW 97304
Talawa Ct NE 97303
Talis Ct S 97306
Talisman Ave & Ct 97302
Tall Maple Ln NE 97305
Tallan Ln S 97306
Talloc Ave SE 97306
Tamara Ave & Ct 97306
Tamarack St NE 97301
Tan Way SE 97317
Tanager Ave NW 97304
Tandem Ave NE 97301
Tangent Way SE 97317
Tanglewood Ct & Way 97317
Tango St NE 97305
Tanner Way NE 97317
Tannet Ave NW 97304
Tanoak Ave SE 97306
Tara Way SE 97317
Tariff Ct SE 97306
Tate Ave N 97303
Taurus Loop NE 97303
Taybin Rd NW 97304
Taylor St NE 97301
Tayside St S 97302
Teak Ct SE 97306
Teakwood Ave NW 97304
Teal Dr SE 97306
Tecumseh St NE 97303
Teddy Bear Ln SE 97317
Templar Way NE 97305
Tepper Ln NE 97303
Tepper Park Way NE 97303
Teral Ct SE 97317
Terrace Dr NW 97304
Terraza Ct NE 97301
Terry Ct SE 97317
Terrylee Ct SE 97306
Tess Ave NE 97301
Teton Ct SE 97317
Teviot Pl NW 97304
Texas Ave NE 97305
Textrum Ct & St 97302
Thelma Ln NE 97301
Thomas Ln NE 97301
Thompson Ave NE 97301
Thor Ct NE 97305
Thoreau Ave SE 97302
Thorman Ave NE 97303
Thorndale Rd NE 97301
Thrush Ct SE 97306
Thrush Dr NE 97301
Thunder Pl NW 97304
Tiburon Ct SE 97302
Tide Ct NE 97305
Tie St NE 97305
Tierra Ct NE 97301
Tierra Dr NE
500-1699 97301
3000-3499 97305
Tiffany Pl NE 97303
Tillikam Ct S 97306
Tillman Ave SE 97302
Timber Ct S 97302
Timber Ridge Dr SE 97317
Timber View St NW 97304
Timberline Ln SE 97306
Timbet Dr SE 97317
Timothy Dr NW 97304
Timothy Ln NE 97303
Tiny Ct NE 97303
Titan Dr NW 97304
Todd Ct N 97303
Toledo Ave NE 97305
Tomahawk Way NE 97303
Tompkins Ln SE 97317
Toms Way SE 97317
Toni Ave N 97303
Top Knot Ln NE 97317
Topaz St NE 97305
Torrance St S 97306
Torrey Pines Dr S 97302
Toucan St NW 97304
Tournament Ave SE 97306
Tower Dr NW 97304
Towers Ct NE 97301
Towhee Ct S 97302
Townsend Way SE 97301
Tracy St NE 97303
Trade St SE 97301
Trade Wind Ave N 97303
Tragen Ct SE 97302
Trail Ave NE 97303
Trail Creek Ln SE 97317
Trailblazer Pl SE 97317
Trails End Ct SE 97317
Tranquility Ct SE 97317
Trapper Dr NE 97305
Travis Ct NE 97301
Trebber St NE 97303
Tree Ln NE 97305
Treemont Ct S 97302
Treeside Ct & Dr 97305
Treewood Ln SE 97317
Trent Ave N 97303
Trevino Ct N 97303
Triad Ct SE 97306
Triangle Dr SE 97302
Trillion St NW 97304
Trillium Ln SE 97306
Trilogy St SE 97306
Trinity St NE 97305
Triple Tree Cir N 97303
Tripp St SE 97302
Tristen Ln NE 97305
Triton Ct NW 97304
Troth Ct SE 97302
Trout Ct SE 97317
Troy St NE 97303
Truckman Way NE 97303
Trudy Ln NE 97303
Truman Rd NE 97301
Trust Ln SE 97306
Tryon St NE 97301
Tuition Way S 97306
Tulare Ave S 97302
Tulip Ln NW 97304
Tullimoor St SE 97306
Tullimour St SE 97306
Tumalo Dr SE 97317
Tumbleweed Cir NE 97305
Tunbridge Wells St SE 97302
Turnage St NW 97304
Turner Rd SE
1900-3899 97302
4000-6499 97317
Turquoise Ave SE 97317
Turtle Bay Ct SE 97306
Turtle Bug Ln NE 97301
Tuscana Ave S 97306
Twilight Ct SE 97317
Twin Ln SE 97317
Twin Fir Ln S 97306
Twin Oak Pl NW 97304
Twinberry Ave SE 97306
Twinwood Ct NW 97304
Tyler Ct NW 97304
Tyler Ln NE 97303
Tynel Ct NE 97303
Tyrone Ln SE 97317
Udder Way NE 97305
Ulali Dr NE 97303
Ullman Ave NW 97304
Umatilla St NE 97305
Umpqua St NE 97305
Unger St S 97302
Union St NE 97301
University St SE
601-799 97301
2000-2199 97302
Upper Autumn St NW 97304
Upper Ben Lomond Dr
SE 97302
Upper Breckenridge Loop
NW 97304
Upper Lavista Ct NW 97304
Urban Ln NW 97304
Utah Ave NE 97305
Val Vista Ave NE 97305
Valderama Ave SE 97306
Vale Ct SE 97306
Vallejo St NE 97301
Valley St NW 97304
Valley Creek Rd NW 97304
Valley High St S 97302
Valley View Dr NW 97304
Valleywood Dr & Loop 97306
Valpak Rd NE 97301
Van Buren Dr NW 97304
Van Kleeck Ct & Pl 97304
Vasend Ct NE 97305
Vaughn Ave NE 97305
Veall Ln NW 97304
Venice St SE 97306
Ventura Loop & St 97303
Venus Ct SE 97317
Veranda Ct N 97303
Verda Ct & Ln 97303
Vernon Loop & St 97305
Verona St S 97306
Veronica Ln SE 97317
Veterans Pl SE 97317
Vibbert St S 97302
Vick Ave NW 97304
Vickery Dr NW 97304
Vicky Way NE 97305
Victoria Dr NE 97301
W View Ct NE 97317
View Dr NW 97304
View Dr S 97302
S View Pl S 97302
Viewcrest Rd S 97302
Viking Ln SE 97317
Village Pl NE 97303
Village Center Dr SE 97302
Village East Way SE 97317
Vinca St SE 97317
Vine St SE 97302
Vineyard View Way S 97306
Vintage Ave SE 97306
Vinyard Ave NE 97301
Virginia St NE 97301
Vision St NW 97304
W Vista Ave SE 97302
Vitae Springs Ln & Rd 97306
Volcano St SE 97306
Vosburg St NW 97304
Wabash Dr NE 97305
Waconda Rd NE
4000-4899 97303
4900-9699 97305
Wade Ln NE 97303
Wadsworth Ln SE 97317
Wagner Ct SE 97317
Wagon Rim Ct SE 97317
Wagon Road Ct & Dr 97317
Wagon Trail Ct SE 97317
Wagon Wheel Dr SE 97317
Wagtail Ct NW 97304
Wahl Ln S 97306
Waikiki St SE 97317
Wakefield Ct NW 97304
Waldo Ave SE 97302
Waldo Hills Dr SE 97317
Walina Ct SE 97317
Walker Rd NE
1000-1199 97301
1600-2899 97305
Walker St NE 97301
Walking Horse Way
SE 97317
Wallace Rd NW 97304
Wallace Hills Ct NW 97304
Waller St SE 97302
Wallowa Ave NW 97304
Waln Creek Ct & Dr 97306
Walnut Ave NE 97301
Walnut Pl NW 97304
Walnwood Ct SE 97306
Walter Ln NE 97305
Waltman Ct NE 97303
Wander Way SE 97301
Wapato St NE 97305
Wapiti Ave NW 97304
Warbler Ct & Dr 97317
Ward Ct, Dr & Pl 97305
Wardell Ln S 97302
Warner Dr SE 97317
Warner St NE 97301
Warren St S 97302
Warrington St SE 97302
Wasco Ct NE 97305
Washington St S &
SE 97302
Water St NE 97301
Waterford Way N 97303
Watergate Ct S 97302
Waterloo St NE 97303
Watson Ave NE
3000-3400 97301
3402-3498 97301
3600-4199 97305
Waymire St NW 97304
Wayne Dr N 97303
Waypark Dr NE 97305
Wayside Ter NE 97301
Wb Post Dr NE 97305
Weatherford Ct NW 97304
Weathers St NE 97301
Webb Ave NE 97305
Webber St SE 97302
Webster Ct & Dr 97302
Wedgewood Ct NE 97301
Weeks Dr N & NE 97303
Weigart Ct NE 97305
Welcome Ct & Way 97302
Wellington Ct NE 97305
Welsh St SE 97317
Welty Ave SE 97302
Wembley Ave & Ct 97304
Wendy St NE 97305
Werner Ave NE 97301
Wesley Ln NE 97301
West Way NW 97304
Westbrook Dr NW 97304
Westchester Ct NW 97304
Western Heights Ct &
Loop 97304
Westfarthing Way NW 97304
Westhaven Ave NW 97304
Westlake Loop N 97303
Westlawn Ct SE 97317
Westminster Ave & Ct 97304
Weston Ct NE 97301
Westport Ct & St 97304
Westridge Ct N 97303
Westridge Pl S 97302
Westwind Ave NW 97304
Westwood Dr NW 97304
Wheat Ave & Ct 97305
Wheatland Loop N 97303
Wheatland Rd N 97303
Wheatland Rd NW 97304
Wheeler Ave & Ct 97305
Whetstone Ct NW 97304
Whimsey Way SE 97317
Whipplewood Ave SE 97306
Whippoorwill Ct NW 97304
Whisper Ln NE 97303
Whisper Creek Loop
NE 97303
Whispering Way SE 97317
Whispering Pines Loop
SE 97317
Whistle Ct NE 97301
Whitcomb Ct & Dr 97304
White Cloud Ct & Dr 97317
White Horse Ct NW 97304
White Oak Ct NE 97305
Whitesell Ct NE 97301
Whitetail Deer St NW 97304
Whitewater St NE 97305
Whitman Cir NE 97305
Whitney Dr NW 97304
Wickshire Ave & Ct 97302
Wiessner Dr NE 97303
Wigeon St SE 97306
Wiggles Ct NE 97301
Wilark Dr NW 97304
Wilbur St SE 97302
Wild Rose Ln SE 97317
Wild Rose Way S 97306
Wildberry Ln SE 97306
Wildcherry Ct & Dr 97317
Wildflower St NE 97301
Wildlife Ln SE 97317
Wildridge Ave SE 97302
Wildwind Dr SE 97302
Wildwood Ct NW 97304
Wildwood Dr SE 97306
Wildwood Pl NE 97303
Wiley Ln SE 97317
Willa Ln SE 97302
Willamette Dr N 97303
Willapa Ct & St 97303
Williams Ave NE 97301
Willie Way NW 97304
Willow Ct SE 97302
Willow St NE 97301
Willow Creek Dr NW 97304
Willow Lake Rd N 97303
Willow Leaf Ct & St 97303
Wilma Ct NE 97305
Wilmington Ave NW 97304
Wilshire Dr N 97303
Wilson St S & SE 97302
Wilton Ave NE 97305
Wiltsey Ct SE 97306
Wiltsey Loop SE 97317
Wiltsey Rd SE 97306
Wiltsey St SE 97317
Wimbledon Ct NW 97304
Winchester St NW 97304
Wind Meadows Way
NE 97301
Wind Park St NE 97301
Wind Spring Way NE 97301
Wind Stone Way NE 97301
Windemere Dr NW 97304
Windflower Ct NE 97305
Windgate St S 97302
Winding Ct & Way 97302
Windmill Ct S 97306
Windsong Ct NW 97304
Windsor Ave & Way 97301
Windsor Island Rd N 97303
Windyridge Dr SE 97317
Winema Pl NE 97305
Wing Tip Ave NW 97304
Winners Ct NW 97304
Winola Ave S 97302
Winona Ct NE 97301
Winslow Ct & Way 97304
Winter St NE 97301
Winter St SE
200-799 97301
1500-1598 97302
1600-2999 97302
Winter Leaf Ct N 97303
Wintercreek Way SE 97306
Wintergreen Ave NW 97304
Wipwood Dr SE 97306
Wisdom Ave NE 97303
Wishing Ln SE 97317
Wisper Ln SE 97317
Wisteria Ct NW 97304
Witten St SE 97317
Wittenberg Ln NE 97303
Witter Ln NE 97305
Witzel Rd SE 97317
Wolf St N 97303
Wolverine St NE 97305
Woodacre Dr SE 97302
Woodard Ave SE 97317
Woodbridge Ct SE 97302
Woodcrest Ct N 97303
Wooddale Ave NE 97301
Woodgrove Ct N 97303
Woodhaven Ct & St 97304

Woodhill St NW 97304
Woodland Dr NW 97304
Woodland Hills Way S 97306
Woodlawn Ct & Dr 97303
Woodleaf St NE 97305
Woodmansee Ct SE 97302
Woodmill Dr SE 97306
Woodrow St NE 97301
Woodscape Ct & Dr 97306
Woodside Ct & Dr 97306
Woodstock Cir NW 97304
Woodview Ct SE 97306
Woodward Ct & St 97303
Woodwind Ct N 97303
Wormwood Ct & St 97306
Wotherspoon Dr NE 97303
Wren Ct NE 97301
Writers Way S 97302
Wyant Ave & Ct 97305
Wyatt Ct NE 97301
Wyoming Ave & Cir 97305
Yakima Ct NW 97304
Yankee Way SE 97317
Yellowbird Ln NE 97301
Yellowstone Ct NE 97305
Yew St SE 97302
York Ave NE 97305
Yorkshire Ct SE 97317
Yosemite Ct NE 97305
Young Ln S 97306
Yukon Ct NE 97305
Yvonne Ct & St 97306
Zachris Ct NE 97303
Zee Ln NE 97303
Zena Rd NW 97304
Zieber Ln NW 97304
Zielinski Ln NE 97305
Zinfandel St NE 97303
Zosel Ave S 97306

NUMBERED STREETS

1st Ct N 97303
1st Pl SE 97302
2nd Ave N 97303
2nd Ave SE
4700-4799 97302
5100-5199 97306
2nd Pl SE 97302
2nd St NW 97304
2nd Way SE 97302
3rd Ave N 97303
3rd Ave SE 97302
3rd St NW 97304
4 J Ln SE 97317
4th Ave N 97303
4th Ave S 97302
4th Pl N 97303
4th St NE 97301
5th Ave N 97303
5th Pl NE 97303
5th St NE 97301
6th Ave NE 97303
6th Ave S 97302
6th St NW 97304
7th Ave NE 97303
7th Ave SE
4600-4999 97302
5200-5599 97306
7th Ct S 97302
7th Pl NE 97303
7th St NW 97304
8th Ave NE 97303
4800-4899 97302
5400-5599 97306
8th Ct NE 97303
8th St NW 97304
9th Ave N 97303
9th Ct NE 97303
9th Ct SE
2600-4099 97302
5200-5399 97306
9th St NW 97304
10th Ave NE 97303
10th Ct SE 97302
10th Pl N 97303
10th Pl S 97306
10th St SE 97306
11th Ave NE 97303
11th Ave SE 97302
12th Ave N 97303
12th Ave NE 97303
12th Ave S 97302
12th Ct SE 97302
12th Pl S 97302
12th Pl SE 97302
12th St NE 97301
12th St SE
200-498 97301
500-699 97301
701-799 97301
800-4399 97302
12th St Cut Off SE 97302
13th Ave N 97303
13th Ave NE 97303
13th Ave SE
3600-3799 97302
6101-6197 97306
6199-6599 97306
13th Pl SE 97302
13th St NE 97301
13th St SE
100-598 97301
701-799 97301
900-3599 97302
14th Ave NE 97303
14th Ave NW 97304
14th Ave SE 97306
14th Ct S 97302
14th Pl S
4500-4599 97302
4800-5399 97306
14th St NE 97301
14th St SE
100-400 97301
800-1400 97302
15th Ave N 97303
15th Ave NW 97304
15th Ct NE 97303
15th Ct S 97302
15th St NE 97301
15th St SE
100-600 97301
602-698 97301
800-1399 97302
16th Ct NE 97303
16th Ct S 97302
16th St NE 97301
16th St SE
200-599 97301
800-1999 97302
17th Ave NE 97303
17th Ave S 97302
17th Ct S 97302
17th St NE 97301
17th St SE
100-198 97301
200-599 97301
901-997 97302
999-1199 97302
18th Ave NE 97303
18th Ct NE 97303
18th Pl S 97302
18th St NE 97301
18th St SE
100-799 97301
1001-1097 97302
1099-1199 97302
19th Ct S 97302
19th Pl NE 97303
19th Pl NW 97304
19th St NE 97301
19th St SE
100-799 97301
2500-2698 97302
2700-2999 97302
20th Ave S
4700-4899 97302
7400-7599 97306
20th Ave SE 97306
20th Ct S 97302
20th St NE 97301
20th St SE
200-999 97301
1100-1599 97302
21st Ave S 97302
21st Pl NW 97304
21st St NE 97301
21st St SE 97301
22nd Ave N 97303
22nd Ave NE 97301
22nd Ave NW 97304
22nd St NE 97301
22nd St SE
200-1100 97301
1102-1110 97301
1111-3199 97302
23rd Ct NW 97304
23rd St NE 97301
23rd St SE
100-1100 97301
1102-1198 97301
1200-1899 97302
24th Pl & St 97301
25th Ave NE 97301
25th St NE 97301
25th St SE
100-1099 97301
1050-1050 97309
1101-1199 97301
1400-3599 97302
27th Ave SE
3900-4799 97302
4800-4899 97306
27th Ct SE 97302
27th Pl NW 97304
29th Ct & Pl 97304
30th Ave NE 97301
30th Ct NW 97304
30th Dr NE 97301
30th Pl NE 97301
30th Pl NW 97304
30th Way NE 97301
31st Ave NE 97301
31st Ave SE 97317
31st Ct NW 97304
32nd Ave NE 97301
32nd Ave NW 97304
32nd Ave SE 97317
32nd Ct NW 97304
32nd Pl NE 97301
34th Ave NE 97301
34th Ave NW 97304
35th Ave NE 97303
35th Ave NW 97304
35th Pl NE 97305
36th Ave NE 97301
36th Ave NW 97304
36th Ave SE 97317
37th Ave NE
100-198 97301
200-1099 97301
4500-4699 97305
37th Ave NW 97304
37th Ave SE 97317
37th Pl NE 97301
37th Pl NW 97304
38th Ave NE
1000-1299 97301
4500-4799 97305
38th Ave NW 97304
38th Pl NE 97305
39th Ave NE
1000-1399 97301
3900-4699 97305
40th Ave NW 97304
40th Ct NE 97305
40th Pl NE 97301
40th Pl SE 97317
41st Ave NE 97305
41st Ave SE 97317
41st Pl NE 97301
41st Way NE 97301
42nd Ave NE 97305
42nd Ave SE 97317
42nd Pl NE 97305
42nd Pl NW 97304
43rd Ave, Ct, Pl & Way
NE 97305
44th Ave NE
100-299 97301
5600-5699 97305
44th Ave SE 97317
44th Ct NE 97305
44th Pl NE 97301
45th Ave NE
100-1699 97301
1700-4500 97305
4502-4598 97305
10100-10599 97303
45th Ave SE 97317
45th Ct NE 97301
45th Pl NE
400-699 97301
7700-7799 97305
45th Pl SE 97317
46th Ave NE
500-578 97301
580-598 97301
3800-3898 97305
3900-4699 97305
46th Ave SE 97317
46th Ct SE 97317
46th Pl SE 97317
47th Ave NE
100-199 97301
2200-4699 97305
47th Ave SE 97317
47th Ct NE 97305
47th Ct SE 97317
47th Pl SE 97317
48th Ave NE 97305
48th Ct SE 97317
49th Ave NE 97305
49th Ave SE 97317
50th Ave NE 97305
50th Ave NW 97304
52nd Ave NE 97305
52nd Ave NW 97304
53rd Ave NW 97304
53rd Pl NE 97317
54th Ave NE 97305
54th Ct SE 97317
55th Ave NE 97305
55th Ave NW 97304
55th Ct SE 97317
56th Ct SE 97317
57th Ave NE 97305
57th Ct SE 97317
59th Ave NE
1000-1198 97317
8600-9499 97305
59th Ave SE 97317
59th Ct SE 97317
60th Ave NE
900-998 97317
4100-4799 97305
60th Ct SE 97317
62nd Ave NE 97305
62nd Ave SE 97317
62nd Ct NE 97317
63rd Ave NE
300-1699 97317
1700-2099 97305
64th Ave SE 97317
64th Ln SE 97317
64th Pl NE 97305
65th Ave NE 97305
65th Ave SE 97317
66th Ave NE 97305
67th Ave NE 97305
69th Ave NE 97317
70th Ave SE 97317
71st Ave NE 97305
71st Ave SE 97317
72nd Ave NE 97305
72nd Ave SE 97317
74th Ave NE 97305
74th Ave SE 97317
75th Ave NE 97305
75th Ave SE 97317
75th Pl SE 97317
76th Ave NE 97305
76th Ave SE 97317
77th Ave SE 97317
78th NE & SE 97317
80th Ave NE 97305
81st Ave NE 97305
81st Ave SE 97317
82nd Ave NE 97305
82nd Ave SE 97317
83rd Ave & St 97317
84th Ave & Pl 97317
86th Ave NE 97305
88th Ave NE 97305
93rd Ave SE 97317
95th Ave NE 97317
105th Ave NE 97317
117th Ave NE 97317
119th Ave SE 97317

SPRINGFIELD OR

General Delivery 97477

POST OFFICE BOXES MAIN OFFICE STATIONS AND BRANCHES

Box No.s
AA - AA 97477
CC - CC 97477
DD - DD 97477
EE - EE 97477
FF - FF 97477
GG - GG 97477
HH - HH 97477
D - X 97477
1 - 1878 97477
7000 - 77003 97475

NAMED STREETS

A St
100-100 97477
102-2599 97477
4000-7499 97478
S A St
101-701 97477
703-2100 97477
2102-2158 97477
3500-8199 97478
W A St 97477
Aaron Ln 97478
Alcona St 97478
Alden Ln 97478
Alder Branch Rd 97478
Aldridge Pl 97478
Alexis Ave 97478
Allen Ave 97477
Ambleside Dr 97477
Anderson Ln 97477
Ann Ct 97477
S Ash St 97477
Aspen St 97477
Aster St
1800-1899 97477
3200-7099 97478
B St
100-1599 97477
3200-7499 97478
S B St 97477
W B St 97477
Baldy View Ln 97477
Beaver St 97478
Beltline Rd 97477
Beverly St 97477
Billings Rd 97478
Black Canyon Rd 97478
Blackstone Ct & St 97477
Bluebelle Ct & Way 97478
Boiler Creek Rd 97478
Bonnie Ln 97477
Booth Kelly Rd 97478
Boscage Ln 97477
Bowen Dr 97478
Bradley Way 97477
Brand S Rd 97478
Brandy Way 97477
Bridge St 97478
Broadway St 97477
Brookdale Ave 97477
Bryant Ln 97478
Buck Point Way 97478
Burlington Ave 97477
C St
100-2799 97477
3400-7199 97478
S C St
224-224 97477
226-245 97477
247-399 97477
7900-8199 97478
W C St 97477
Cambridge St 97477
Camellia Ct & St 97478
Camp Creek Rd 97478
Canal St 97477
Canterbury St 97477
Cardinal Way 97477
Carriage Pl 97477
Carter Ln 97477
Cascade Dr 97478
Castle Dr 97477
E Cedar Flat Rd 97478
Centennial Blvd
100-532 97477
534-2699 97477
2701-2799 97477
2900-2999 97478
W Centennial Blvd 97477
Central Blvd 97477
Chapman Ln 97478
Charley Ln 97478
Chateau Pl 97477
Cheek St 97477
Cherokee Dr 97478
Chita Loop 97478
Cinder St 97478
City View Blvd 97477
Clear Vue Ln 97477
Clearwater Ln 97478
Clemens Rd 97478
N & S Cloverleaf Loop 97477
Cole Way 97478
Collier Dr 97478
Collins Ln 97478
Colonial Dr 97477
Commercial Ave 97478
Conley Rd 97478
Corral Ct & Dr 97477
Cottonwood Ave 97477
Cress Creek Rd 97478
Crest Ln 97477
Crosby Ave 97477
Custom Way 97477
Cynthia Ct 97478
Cypress Ct 97477
D Ct 97478
D Pl 97478
D St
1-211 97477
213-2799 97477
4900-7099 97478
S D St 97477
W D St 97477
Daisy St 97478
Daphne St 97477
Darlene Ave 97477
Deadmond Ferry Rd 97477
Debra Dr 97477
Deerhorn Rd 97478
Delrose Ave, Ct & Dr 97477
Depue St 97477
Diamond St 97477
Dixie Dr 97478
Dogwood St 97478
Don St 97477
Dondea St 97478
Donna Ln & Rd 97478
Donnelly Dr 97477
Dornoch St 97477
Dorris St 97477
Dotie Dr 97477
Douglas Dr 97478
Dowdy Ln 97477
Dubens Ln 97477
Duke St 97478
Dumas Dr 97477
E Ct 97478
S E Ct 97478
E St
2-198 97477
200-2799 97477
3300-3552 97478
3554-7199 97478
S E St
230-234 97477
236-237 97477
239-399 97477
3501-3503 97478
3505-7099 97478
W E St 97477
Easton Ln 97478
Easy Ln 97478
Edgehill Rd 97478
Edgemont Way 97477
Edie Dr 97477
El Bonita Pl 97477
El Toro Ct 97477
Elderberry Loop & St 97478
Ellington Dr 97478
Elliot Ln 97478
Emerald Way 97478
Erma Ct 97477
Ermi Bee Rd 97478
Estate Ct 97477
Ethan Ct 97477
Ewing Rd 97478
F Pl 97478
F St
100-198 97477
200-2699 97477
5100-7099 97478
S F St
317-2229 97477
3800-4099 97478
W F St 97477
Fairhaven Dr 97477
W Fairview Dr 97477
Fairway Pl 97477
Falcon Dr 97477
Fallin Ln 97478
Farkas Ln 97478
Fawn Way 97478
S Fern Way 97478
Fernhill Ct & Loop 97478
Fiesta Dr 97477
Filbert Ln 97477
Filbert Meadows Way 97478
Fireside Ct 97477
Firth Ave 97477
Flamingo Ave 97477
Flowerdale Dr 97478
Forest Ridge Rd 97478
Forsythia Dr & St 97478
Fuchsia St 97477
G St
155-297 97477
299-2799 97477
4800-7199 97478
S G St 97477
W G St 97477
E Game Farm Rd 97477
Garden Ave 97478
Garson Ln 97477
Gateway Loop 97477
Gateway St
2501-2697 97477
2699-3033 97477
3035-3599 97477
3100-3150 97475
3180-3698 97477
Gem Ave 97478
Gemstone Way 97478
Glacier Dr & St 97478
Glacier View Dr 97478
Goats Rd 97478
Grand Vista Dr 97477

Street	ZIP
Grandview Dr	97478
Granite Pl	97477
Graves Ln	97478
Graystone Loop	97478
Greenbriar St	97477
Greenvale Dr	97477
Grouse St	97477
Grovedale Dr	97477
W H St	97477
H F Williams Rd	97478
Hailey Ct	97478
Hamilton St	97477
Harbor Dr	97477
Harlow Rd	97477
Harmon Ln	97478
Hartman Ln	97478
Harvest Ln	97477
Hayden Bridge Pl, Rd & Way	97477
Hazelnut Ln	97478
Heather Dr	97478
Hendricks Park Rd	97478
Heritage Ln	97478
High Ranch Dr	97478
Highbanks Rd	97478
Hill Rd	97478
Hills Creek Rd	97478
Holden Ct	97478
Holden Creek Ln	97478
Holly St	97478
Homestead Rd	97478
Hosanna Ln	97477
Hutton St	97477
I St	
700-1498	97477
1500-2799	97477
5300-5399	97478
W I St	97477
Ilex Ct	97478
Indian Ford Rd	97478
Industrial Ave	97478
Inland Way	97477
International Ct & Way	97477
Island Ct & St	97477
Ivy St	97478
J St	
100-2799	97477
5400-5499	97478
W J St	97477
J Mechling Rd	97478
Jacob Ln	97478
Jade Ave	97478
Jannette Ct	97477
Janus Ct & St	97477
Jasper Rd	97478
Jessica Dr & Ln	97478
Jones Acres Rd	97478
Jules Pl	97478
June Ln	97478
Juniper Ln	97477
W K St	97477
Kalmia Ln & St	97478
Kathleen Ct	97477
Kathryn Ave	97478
Keeney St	97478
Keller Ln	97478
Kellogg Rd	97477
Kelly Blvd	97477
Kenray Loop	97477
Keola Ct & Ln	97478
Kickbusch Ln	97478
Kiev St	97477
King Henrys Ct	97477
Kintzley Ave	97478
Kirk Ave	97477
Kremont Ave	97477
Kruse Way	97477
W L St	97477
La Lone Rd	97478
Laksonen Loop	97478
Laralee St	97477
Latta Rd	97478
Laura St	97477
Laurel Ave	97478
Lawnridge Ave	97477
Leavitt Ln	97478
Leota St	97478
Level Ln	97477
Lilac Ln	97478
Linda Ln	97478
Lindale Dr	97477
Linden Ave	97477
Lisa Ct	97478
Little Deerhorn Ln	97478
Loch Dr	97477
Lochaven Ave	97477
Locust St	97477
Lodgepole Ct	97477
Lomond Ave	97477
Long Ridge Dr	97478
Lorie Ct	97477
Lorne Loop	97478
Lupe Ln	97478
M St	97477
M J Chase Rd	97478
Madrone St	97478
Mahogany Ln	97478
Maia Loop	97477
Main St	
100-2799	97477
2800-7306	97478
7308-7498	97477
Mallard Ave	97477
Manor Dr	97477
Mansfield St	97477
Maple Ln	97478
Maple Island Farm Rd	97477
Maranatha Ln	97478
Marcola Rd	
1900-3999	97477
88700-92099	97478
Marilyn Ct	97477
Market St	97477
Marpar Ln	97478
Martin Luther King Jr Pkwy	97477
Mccauley Ridge Dr	97478
Mccumber Ln	97478
Mcdonald Ct	97477
Mcgowen Creek Rd	97478
Mcgowen View Ln	97478
Mckenzie Hwy	97478
Mckenzie Acres Dr	97478
Mckenzie Crest Dr	97477
Mckenzie View Dr	97478
Mcpherson Pl	97477
Mctavish Ct	97477
Meadow Glen Dr	97478
Mellowood Ct	97477
Menlo Loop	97477
Merryhill Ct	97477
Mica St	97478
S Mill St	97477
Miller Ave	97478
Millican Rd	97478
Mineral Way	97478
Mint Meadow Way	97478
Missy Ln	97478
Mitten Ln	97478
Modoc St	97477
Mohawk Blvd	97477
Montclaire Ln & Way	97478
Montebello Ave	97477
Montview Way	97477
Moses Pass	97478
Moss Rd	97478
Mountaingate Dr	97478
Mt Vernon Rd	97478
Mt Vernon Cemetary Rd	97478
W N Ct & St	97477
Nadeau Rd	97478
Nancy Ave	97477
Natures Garden St	97478
Nebo Dr	97478
Neptune Ave	97477
Nicholas Dr	97477
Night Hawk Ln	97477
North St	97478
Northridge Ave	97477
Nova St	97477
Oak Meadows Pl	97477
Oak Point Rd	97478
Oakdale Ave	97477
Oakshire Dr	97478
Obsidian Ave	97478
E Of Eden Rd	97478
Oksanna St	97477
Old Mohawk Rd	97478
Old Orchard Ln	97477
Olympic St	
500-2799	97477
2800-3800	97478
3802-4198	97478
W Olympic St	97477
Opaca Ct	97478
Orchid Ln	97478
Oregon Ave	97478
Oriole St	97477
Osage St	97478
Osprey Dr	97477
Otto St	97477
Pacific Ave	97477
Page Ln	97478
Panorama Rd	97478
Park St	97477
Parker Ln & St	97477
Parsons Creek Rd	97478
Partridge Ln	97478
Partridge Way	97477
Pebble Ct	97478
Peel Ln	97478
Pentilla Rd	97478
Peridot Way	97478
Periwinkle Rd	97478
Perry St	97477
Pheasant Blvd	97477
Pico St	97478
Piedmont St	97477
Pierce Pkwy	97477
Pine St	97477
Pinedale Ave	97477
Pinyon St	97478
Pioch Ln	97478
Pioneer Pkwy E & W	97477
Pleasant St	97477
Poltava St	97477
Ponderosa Ct	97477
Postal Way	97477
Potter Ln	97478
Potter Creek Ln	97478
Prasad Ct	97477
Prescott Ln	97477
Pumice Pl & St	97478
W Q St	97477
Quarry Rd	97477
Quartz Ave	97478
W Quinalt St	97477
R St	97477
R R Baker Rd	97478
Rainbow Dr & Loop	97477
Raintree Way	97477
Raleighwood Ave	97477
Rambling Dr	97477
Ranch Dr	97477
Ranch Corral Dr	97477
Ranneran St	97478
Rayner Ave	97477
S Redwood Dr	97478
Regal Ln	97478
Rhododendron St	97477
Richland St	97478
Ridge Ct	97478
Ridgecrest Dr	97478
River Heights Dr	97477
River Hills Dr	97477
River Knoll Way	97477
Riverbend Dr	97477
Riverview Blvd	97477
Riviera Ct	97477
Robby Ln	97478
Rocky Rd	97478
Rodney Ct	97477
Roland Way	97477
Rose Blossom Dr	97477
Ross Ln	97478
Rowan Ave	97477
Royal Caribbean Way	97477
Royaldel Ln	97477
Ruby Ln	97478
Running Springs Dr	97478
S St	97477
Saunders Rd	97478
Scott Rd	97477
Scotts Glen Dr	97477
Sequoia Ave & Ct	97477
Seward Ave	97477
Shadows Dr	97478
Shady Loop	97477
Shady Creek Dr	97478
Shadylane Dr	97477
Shaleans St	97477
Shasta Blvd	97477
Shelley St	97477
Shenandoah Ln & Loop	97478
Sherra Ln	97478
Short St	97477
Simeon Dr	97478
Sky High Dr	97478
Smith Loop & Way	97478
Southway Loop	97478
Spicer Ln	97478
Sports Way	97477
Springdale Ave	97477
Stellar Way	97478
Stephens Rd	97478
Storment Ln	97478
Sue Ann Ct	97477
Summit Blvd	97477
Sunderman Rd	97478
Sunset Dr	97477
Swan Ct	97477
Swank Ct	97477
Swearingen Rd	97478
T St	97477
Tamarack St	97477
Tamora Dr	97478
Thienes Ln	97478
Thurston Rd	97478
Tiki Ln	97478
Tinamou Ln	97477
Tonga Ln	97478
Tovey Dr	97478
Tree Farm Rd	97478
Trestle Dr	97478
Twin Firs Rd	97478
U St	97477
Union Ave	97477
Union Ter	97478
Upland St	97478
Upper Camp Creek Rd	97478
V St	97477
Valentine Ct	97477
Valley Meadows Ct	97477
Valley View St	97477
Vera Dr	97477
Viewmont Ave	97477
Villa Way	97477
Virginia Ave	97478
Vitus Ln	97477
W St	97477
Wallace Ln	97477
Wallace Creek Rd	97478
Walnut Pl & Rd	97477
Walnut Ridge Dr	97477
Walterville Ln & Loop	97478
Water St	97477
Watermark Ct & Dr	97477
Wayside Ln & Loop	97477
Weaver Rd	97478
Wemberly Way	97477
Whitewater Dr	97478
Whitsell Ln	97478
Whitworth Ln	97477
Willacade Ct	97477
Wimbledon Pl	97477
Windsor Ct	97477
Winslow Ave	97477
Winston Pl	97477
Woodcrest Dr	97477
Woodlane Dr	97477
Worth Rd	97478
Yenta Ave	97477
Yolanda Ave	97477
York Ln	97478

NUMBERED STREETS

Street	ZIP
1st Pl & St	97477
S 2nd	97477
S 3rd Pl & St	97477
S 4th	97477
S 5th	97477
S 6th	97477
7th St	97477
8th St	97477
S 9th	97477
10th St	97477
S 11th Pl & St	97477
12th St	97477
13th St	97477
S 14th Pl & St	97477
S 15th	97477
S 16th	97477
S 17th Pl & St	97477
S 18th	97477
S 19th	97477
20th St	97477
S 21st	97477
S 22nd	97477
23rd St	97477
24th St	97477
25th Pl & St	97477
S 26th Pl & St	97477
27th St	97477
S 28th	97477
30th St	97478
S 31st Pl	97478
31st St	
1100-1499	97478
2000-2799	97477
S 32nd Pl	97478
32nd St	
200-298	97478
300-1699	97478
2200-2799	97477
S 32nd St	97478
33rd St	
100-1499	97478
2252-2252	97477
34th Ct	97477
S 34th Pl	97478
34th St	
300-410	97478
412-1499	97478
2400-2599	97477
S 34th St	97478
35th Ct	97478
35th Pl	97477
35th St	
100-150	97478
152-1300	97478
1302-1498	97478
2279-2579	97477
2581-2599	97477
S 35th St	97478
36th Ct	97477
36th St	97478
37th Pl	97477
S 37th Pl	97478
37th St	
100-1299	97478
2100-2599	97477
S 37th St	97478
38th Pl	97478
38th St	
101-123	97478
125-1299	97478
2400-2599	97477
S 38th St	97478
39th Pl & St	97478
40th Ct, Pl & St	97478
41st Ct, Pl & St	97478
S 42nd Pl	97478
42nd St	
100-198	97478
200-802	97478
804-898	97478
1500-1899	97477
S 42nd St	97478
S 43rd Pl & St	97478
44th Pl & St	97478
45th Pl & St	97478
S 46th St	97478
47th Pl & St	97478
48th Pl & St	97478
S 49th Loop, Pl & St	97478
S 50th Pl	97478
51st Pl & St	97478
S 52nd Pl & St	97478
S 53rd Pl & St	97478
S 54th Pl & St	97478
S 55th Pl & St	97478
S 56th Pl & St	97478
57th Pl & St	97478
58th Pl & St	97478
S 59th St	97478
S 60th Pl & St	97478
S 61st	97478
62nd Pl & St	97478
S 63rd	97478
64th Pl & St	97478
65th Pl & St	97478
66th Pl & St	97478
67th Ct, Pl & St	97478
68th Ct, Pl & St	97478
S 69th Pl & St	97478
70th Pl & St	97478
S 71st Pl & St	97478
S 72nd Pl & St	97478
S 73rd Pl & St	97478
74th Pl & St	97478
75th St	97478
S 79th St	97478

Pennsylvania

People QuickFacts	Pennsylvania	USA
Population, 2013 estimate	12,773,801	316,128,839
Population, 2010 (April 1) estimates base	12,702,379	308,747,716
Population, percent change, April 1, 2010 to July 1, 2013	0.6%	2.4%
Population, 2010	12,702,379	308,745,538
Persons under 5 years, percent, 2013	5.6%	6.3%
Persons under 18 years, percent, 2013	21.3%	23.3%
Persons 65 years and over, percent, 2013	16.4%	14.1%
Female persons, percent, 2013	51.1%	50.8%
White alone, percent, 2013 (a)	83.2%	77.7%
Black or African American alone, percent, 2013 (a)	11.5%	13.2%
American Indian and Alaska Native alone, percent, 2013 (a)	0.3%	1.2%
Asian alone, percent, 2013 (a)	3.1%	5.3%
Native Hawaiian and Other Pacific Islander alone, percent, 2013 (a)	0.1%	0.2%
Two or More Races, percent, 2013	1.8%	2.4%
Hispanic or Latino, percent, 2013 (b)	6.3%	17.1%
White alone, not Hispanic or Latino, percent, 2013	78.4%	62.6%
Living in same house 1 year & over, percent, 2008-2012	87.8%	84.8%
Foreign born persons, percent, 2008-2012	5.8%	12.9%
Language other than English spoken at home, pct age 5+, 2008-2012	10.2%	20.5%
High school graduate or higher, percent of persons age 25+, 2008-2012	88.3%	85.7%
Bachelor's degree or higher, percent of persons age 25+, 2008-2012	27.0%	28.5%
Veterans, 2008-2012	981,865	21,853,912
Mean travel time to work (minutes), workers age 16+, 2008-2012	25.8	25.4
Housing units, 2013	5,565,157	132,802,859
Homeownership rate, 2008-2012	70.1%	65.5%
Housing units in multi-unit structures, percent, 2008-2012	20.6%	25.9%
Median value of owner-occupied housing units, 2008-2012	$164,900	$181,400
Households, 2008-2012	4,959,633	115,226,802
Persons per household, 2008-2012	2.47	2.61
Per capita money income in past 12 months (2012 dollars), 2008-2012	$28,190	$28,051
Median household income, 2008-2012	$52,267	$53,046
Persons below poverty level, percent, 2008-2012	13.1%	14.9%

Business QuickFacts	Pennsylvania	USA
Private nonfarm establishments, 2012	296,872	7,431,808
Private nonfarm employment, 2012	5,169,196	115,938,468
Private nonfarm employment, percent change, 2011-2012	1.8%	2.2%
Nonemployer establishments, 2012	774,209	22,735,915
Total number of firms, 2007	981,501	27,092,908
Black-owned firms, percent, 2007	4.6%	7.1%
American Indian- and Alaska Native-owned firms, percent, 2007	0.3%	0.9%
Asian-owned firms, percent, 2007	3.2%	5.7%
Native Hawaiian and Other Pacific Islander-owned firms, percent, 2007	0.0%	0.1%
Hispanic-owned firms, percent, 2007	2.3%	8.3%
Women-owned firms, percent, 2007	27.0%	28.8%
Manufacturers shipments, 2007 ($1000)	234,840,418	5,319,456,312
Merchant wholesaler sales, 2007 ($1000)	142,859,202	4,174,286,516
Retail sales, 2007 ($1000)	166,842,778	3,917,663,456
Retail sales per capita, 2007	$13,323	$12,990
Accommodation and food services sales, 2007 ($1000)	19,625,449	613,795,732
Building permits, 2012	18,796	829,658

Geography QuickFacts	Pennsylvania	USA
Land area in square miles, 2010	44,742.70	3,531,905.43
Persons per square mile, 2010	283.9	87.4
FIPS Code	42	

(a) Includes persons reporting only one race.
(b) Hispanics may be of any race, so also are included in applicable race categories.
FN: Footnote on this item for this area in place of data
NA: Not available
D: Suppressed to avoid disclosure of confidential information
X: Not applicable
S: Suppressed; does not meet publication standards
Z: Value greater than zero but less than half unit of measure shown
F: Fewer than 100 firms
Source: US Census Bureau State & County QuickFacts

Pennsylvania

3 DIGIT ZIP CODE MAP

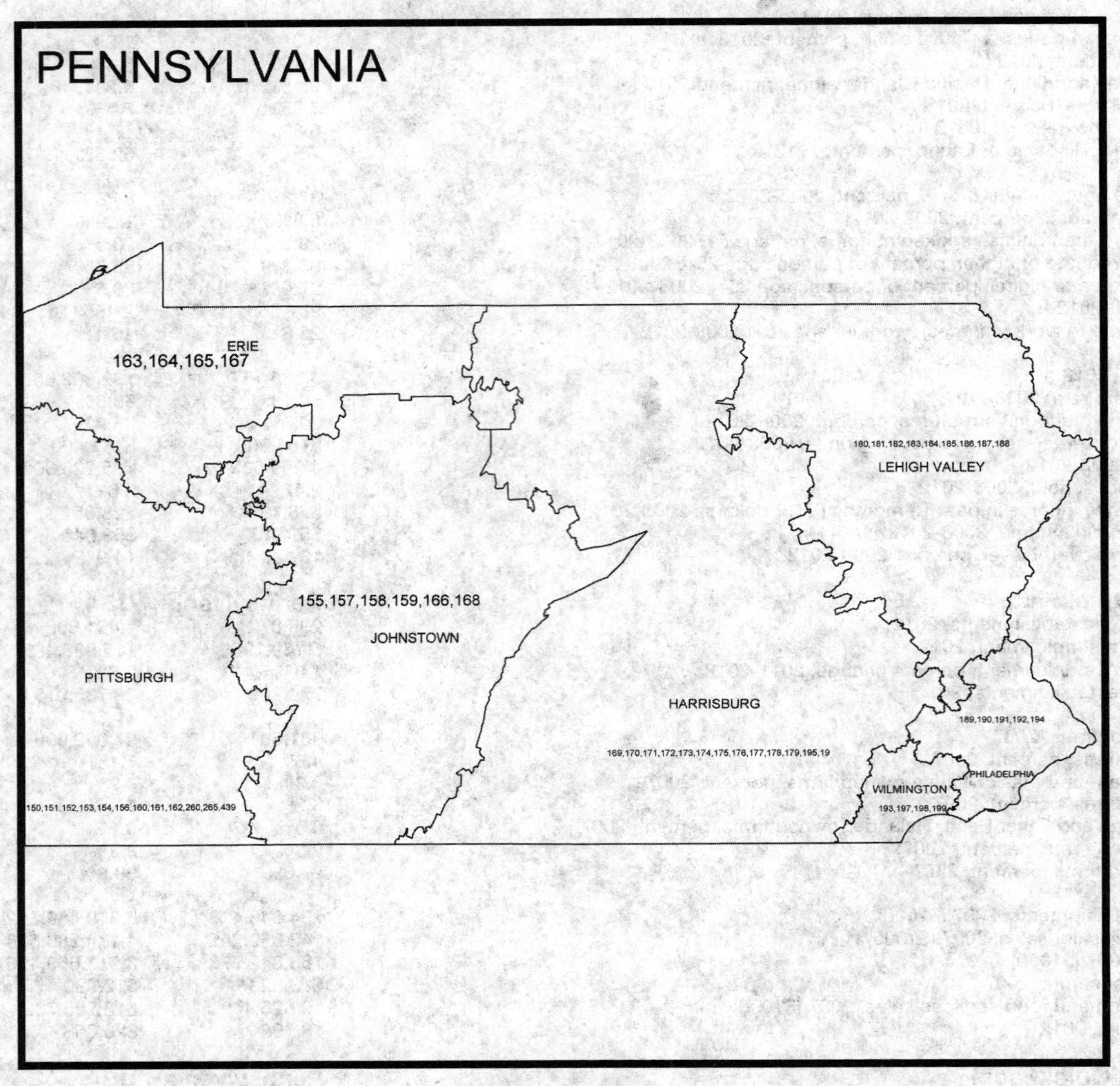

Pennsylvania

(Abbreviation: PA)

Post Office, County — ZIP Code

Places with more than one ZIP code are listed in capital letters, See pages indicated.

Aaronsburg, Centre 16820
Abbottstown, Adams 17301
Abington, Montgomery 19001
Ackermanville, Northampton 18010
Acme, Westmoreland 15610
Acosta, Somerset 15520
Adah, Fayette 15410
Adamsburg, Westmoreland 15611
Adamstown, Lancaster 19501
Adamsville, Crawford 16110
Addison, Somerset 15411
Adrian, Armstrong 16210
Airville, York 17302
Akron, Lancaster 17501
Alba, Bradford 16910
Albion, Erie 16401
Albrightsville, Carbon 18210
Alburtis, Lehigh 18011
Aldan, Delaware 19018
Aleppo, Greene 15310
Alexandria, Huntingdon 16611
Aliquippa, Beaver 15001
Allegheny, Allegheny 15212
Allenport, Washington 15412
Allensville, Mifflin 17002
ALLENTOWN, Lehigh
(See Page 3188)
Allenwood, Union 17810
Allison, Fayette 15413
Allison Park, Allegheny 15101
Allport, Clearfield 16821
ALTOONA, Blair
(See Page 3190)
Alum Bank, Bedford 15521
Alverda, Indiana 15710
Alverton, Westmoreland 15612
Amberson, Franklin 17210
Ambler, Montgomery 19002
Ambridge, Beaver 15003
Amity, Washington 15311
Analomink, Monroe 18320
Andalusia, Bucks 19020
Andreas, Schuylkill 18211
Anita, Jefferson 15711
Annandale
(See Boyers)
Annville, Lebanon 17003
Antes Fort, Lycoming 17720
Apollo, Westmoreland 15613
Aquashicola, Carbon 18012
Arcadia, Indiana 15712
Archbald, Lackawanna 18403
Ardara, Westmoreland 15615
Ardmore, Montgomery 19003
Arendtsville, Adams 17303
Aristes, Columbia 17920
Armagh, Indiana 15920
Armbrust, Westmoreland 15616
Armstrong, Lycoming 17702
Arnold, Westmoreland 15068
Arnot, Tioga 16911
Arona, Westmoreland 15617
Arsenal, Allegheny 15201
Artemas, Bedford 17211
Ashfield, Carbon 18212
Ashland, Schuylkill 17921
Ashley, Luzerne 18706
Ashville, Cambria 16613
Aspers, Adams 17304
Aspinwall, Allegheny 15215
Aston, Delaware 19014
Atglen, Chester 19310
Athens, Bradford 18810
Atlantic, Crawford 16111
Atlasburg, Washington 15004
Auburn, Schuylkill 17922
Audubon, Montgomery 19403
Audubon, Montgomery 19407
Aultman, Indiana 15713
Austin, Potter 16720
Avalon, Allegheny 15202
Avella, Washington 15312
Avis, Clinton 17721
Avoca, Luzerne 18641
Avondale, Chester 19311
Avonmore, Westmoreland 15618
Baden, Beaver 15005
Bainbridge, Lancaster 17502
Bairdford, Allegheny 15006
Bakers Summit, Blair 16673
Bakerstown, Allegheny 15007
Bala Cynwyd, Montgomery 19004
Bally, Berks 19503
Bangor, Northampton 18010
Barking, Westmoreland 15068
Barnesboro, Cambria 15714
Barnesville, Schuylkill 18214
Barree, Huntingdon 16611
Bart, Lancaster 17503
Barto, Berks 19504
Bartonsville, Monroe 18321
Bastress, Lycoming 17702
Bath, Northampton 18014
Bausman, Lancaster 17504
Beach Haven, Luzerne 18601
Beach Lake, Wayne 18405
Beallsville, Washington 15313
Bear Creek, Luzerne 18602
Bear Creek Township, Luzerne 18702
Bear Lake, Warren 16402
Beaver, Beaver 15009
Beaver Falls, Beaver 15010
Beaver Meadows, Carbon 18216
Beaver Springs, Snyder 17812
Beaverdale, Cambria 15921
Beavertown, Snyder 17813
Beccaria, Clearfield 16616
Bechtelsville, Berks 19505
Bedford, Bedford 15522
Bedminster, Bucks 18910
Beech Creek, Clinton 16822
Belle Vernon, Fayette 15012
Belle Vrn Br, Fayette 15012
Bellefonte, Centre 16823
Belleville, Mifflin 17004
Bellevue, Allegheny 15202
Bellvue, Allegheny 15202
Bellwood, Blair 16617
Belmont Hills, Montgomery 19004
Belsano, Cambria 15922
Ben Avon, Allegheny 15202
Bendersville, Adams 17306
Benezett, Elk 15821
Benezette, Elk 15821
Bensalem, Bucks 19020
Bensalem, Bucks 19021
Bentleyville, Washington 15314
Benton, Columbia 17814
Berlin, Somerset 15530
Bernville, Berks 19506
Berrysburg, Dauphin 17005
Berwick, Columbia 18603
Berwyn, Chester 19312
Bessemer, Lawrence 16112
Bethany, Wayne 18431
Bethel, Berks 19507
Bethel Park, Allegheny 15102
BETHLEHEM, Northampton
(See Page 3192)
Beyer, Indiana 16211
Big Cove Tannery, Fulton 17212
Big Run, Jefferson 15715
Bigler, Clearfield 16825
Biglerville, Adams 17307
Birchrunville, Chester 19421
Bird In Hand, Lancaster 17505
Birdsboro, Berks 19508
Birmingham, Blair 16686
Black Horse, Montgomery 19401
Black Lick, Indiana 15716
Blain, Perry 17006
Blairs Mills, Huntingdon 17213
Blairsville, Indiana 15717
Blakely, Lackawanna 18447
Blakeslee, Monroe 18610
Blanchard, Centre 16826
Blandburg, Cambria 16619
Blandon, Berks 19510
Blawnox, Allegheny 15238
Bloomfield, Allegheny 15224
Blooming Glen, Bucks 18911
Blooming Grove, Pike 18428
Bloomsburg, Columbia 17815
Blossburg, Tioga 16912
Blue Ball, Lancaster 17506
Blue Bell, Montgomery 19422
Blue Ridge Summit, Franklin 17214
Boalsburg, Centre 16827
Bobtown, Greene 15315
Boiling Springs, Cumberland 17007
Bolivar, Westmoreland 15923
Boothwyn, Delaware 19060
Boston, Allegheny 15135
Boswell, Somerset 15531
Bovard, Westmoreland 15619
Bowers, Berks 19511
Bowmansdale, Cumberland 17055
Bowmanstown, Carbon 18030
Bowmansville, Lancaster 17507
Boyers, Butler 16020
Boyertown, Berks 19512
Boynton, Somerset 15532
Brackenridge, Allegheny 15014
Brackney, Susquehanna 18812
Braddock, Allegheny 15104
Bradenville, Westmoreland 15620
Bradford, Mckean 16701
Bradfordwoods, Allegheny 15015
Branchdale, Schuylkill 17923
Branchton, Butler 16021
Brandamore, Chester 19316
Brandy Camp, Elk 15822
Brave, Greene 15316
Breezewood, Bedford 15533
Breinigsville, Lehigh 18031
Brentwood, Allegheny 15227
Bressler, Dauphin 17113
Bridgeport, Montgomery 19405
Bridgeville, Allegheny 15017
Brier Hill, Fayette 15415
Brisbin, Clearfield 16620
Bristol, Bucks 19007
Broad Top, Huntingdon 16621
Brockport, Elk 15823
Brockton, Schuylkill 17925
Brockway, Jefferson 15824
Brodbecks, York 17329
Brodheadsville, Monroe 18322
Brogue, York 17309
Brookhaven, Delaware 19015
Brookline, Allegheny 15226
Brooklyn, Susquehanna 18813
Brookville, Jefferson 15825
Broomall, Delaware 19008
Browndale, Susquehanna 18421
Brownfield, Fayette 15416
Brownstown, Lancaster 17508
Brownsville, Fayette 15417
Bruin, Butler 16022
Brush Valley, Indiana 15720
Bryn Athyn, Montgomery 19009
Bryn Mawr, Delaware 19010
Buck Hill Falls, Monroe 18323
Buckingham, Bucks 18912
Buena Vista, Allegheny 15018
Buffalo Mills, Bedford 15534
Bulger, Washington 15019
Bunola, Allegheny 15020
Burgettstown, Washington 15021
Burlington, Bradford 18814
Burlington Township, Bradford 18848
Burnham, Mifflin 17009
Burnside, Clearfield 15721
Burnt Cabins, Fulton 17215
Bushkill, Pike 18324
Bushkill, Pike 18371
BUTLER, Butler
(See Page 3195)
Butztown, Northampton 18017
Byrnedale, Elk 15827
Bywood, Delaware 19082
Cabot, Butler 16023
Cadogan, Armstrong 16212
Cairnbrook, Somerset 15924
California, Washington 15419
Callensburg, Clarion 16213
Callery, Butler 16024
Calumet, Westmoreland 15621
Calvin, Huntingdon 16622
Cambra, Luzerne 18611
Cambridge Springs, Crawford 16403
Cammal, Lycoming 17723
CAMP HILL, Cumberland
(See Page 3197)
Campbelltown, Lebanon 17010
Camptown, Bradford 18815
Canadensis, Monroe 18325
Canonsburg, Washington 15317
Canton, Bradford 17724
Carbondale, Lackawanna 18407
Cardale, Fayette 15420
CARLISLE, Cumberland
(See Page 3198)
Carlisle Barracks, Cumberland 17013
Carlton, Mercer 16311
Carmichaels, Greene 15320
Carnegie, Allegheny 15106
Carroll Park, Montgomery 19096
Carrolltown, Cambria 15722
Carson, Allegheny 15203
Carversville, Bucks 18913
Cashtown, Adams 17310
Cassandra, Cambria 15925
Cassville, Huntingdon 16623
Castanea, Clinton 17726
Castle Shannon, Allegheny 15234
Catasauqua, Lehigh 18032
Catawissa, Columbia 17820
Cecil, Washington 15321
Cedar Run, Lycoming 17727
Cedarhurst, Allegheny 15243
Cedars, Montgomery 19423
Center Square, Montgomery 19422
Center Valley, Lehigh 18034
Centerport, Berks 19516
Centerville, Crawford 16404
Central City, Somerset 15926
Centralia, Schuylkill 17921
Centre Hall, Centre 16828
Chadds Ford, Delaware 19317
Chalfont, Bucks 18914
Chalk Hill, Fayette 15421
CHAMBERSBURG, Franklin
(See Page 3200)
Chambersville, Indiana 15723
Champion, Westmoreland 15622
Chandlers Valley, Warren 16312
Charleroi, Washington 15022
Chatham, Chester 19318
Chatham, Chester 19390
Cheltenham, Montgomery 19012
Cherry Tree, Indiana 15724
Cherryville, Northampton 18035
Chest Springs, Cambria 16624
CHESTER, Delaware
(See Page 3201)
Chester Heights, Delaware 19017
Chester Springs, Chester 19425
Chester Township, Delaware 19013
Chesterbrook, Delaware 19087
Chestnut Ridge, Fayette 15422
Cheswick, Allegheny 15024
Cheyney, Delaware 19319
Chicora, Butler 16025
Childs, Lackawanna 18407
Chinchilla, Lackawanna 18410
Christiana, Lancaster 17509
Churchville, Bucks 18966
City Of Wilkes Barre, Luzerne 18702
Clairton, Allegheny 15025
Clarence, Centre 16829
Clarendon, Warren 16313
Claridge, Westmoreland 15623
Clarington, Forest 15828
Clarion, Clarion 16214
Clark, Mercer 16113
Clarks Green, Lackawanna 18411
Clarks Mills, Mercer 16114
Clarks Summit, Lackawanna 18411
Clarksburg, Indiana 15725
Clarksville, Greene 15322
Claysburg, Blair 16625
Claysville, Washington 15323
Clearfield, Clearfield 16830
Clearville, Bedford 15535
Cleona, Lebanon 17042
Clifford, Susquehanna 18413
Clifford Township, Lackawanna 18407
Clifton, Wayne 18424
Clifton Heights, Delaware 19018
Clifton Township, Wayne 18424
Climax, Clarion 16242
Clinton, Beaver 15026
Clintonville, Venango 16372
Clune, Indiana 15727
Clymer, Indiana 15728
Coal Center, Washington 15423
Coal Township, Northumberland 17866
Coaldale, Schuylkill 18218
Coalport, Clearfield 16627
Coatesville, Chester 19320
Cobbs Lake Preserve, Wayne 18436
Coburn, Centre 16832
Cochranton, Crawford 16314
Cochranville, Chester 19330
Cocolamus, Juniata 17014
Codorus, York 17311
Cogan Station, Lycoming 17728
Cokeburg, Washington 15324
Colebrook, Lebanon 17042
College Hill, Northampton 18042
Collegeville, Montgomery 19426
Collegeville, Montgomery 19473
Collingdale, Delaware 19023
Collomsville, Lycoming 17702
Colmar, Montgomery 18915
Columbia, Lancaster 17512
Columbia Cross Roads, Bradford 16914
Columbus, Warren 16405
Colver, Cambria 15927
Commodore, Indiana 15729
Concord, Franklin 17217
Concordville, Delaware 19331
Conemaugh, Cambria 15909
Conestoga, Lancaster 17516
Confluence, Somerset 15424
Conneaut Lake, Crawford 16316
Conneautville, Crawford 16406
Connellsville, Fayette 15425
Connoquenessing, Butler 16027
Conshohocken, Montgomery 19428
Conway, Beaver 15027
Conyngham, Luzerne 18219
Cooksburg, Forest 16217
Coolbaugh Township, Monroe 18466
Coolspring, Jefferson 15730
Coopersburg, Lehigh 18036
Cooperstown, Venango 16317
Coplay, Lehigh 18037
Coral, Indiana 15731
Coraopolis, Allegheny 15108
Corliss, Allegheny 15204
Cornwall, Lebanon 17016
Cornwall Borough, Lebanon 17042
Cornwells Heights, Bucks 19020
Corry, Erie 16407
Corsica, Jefferson 15829
Coudersport, Potter 16915
Coulters, Allegheny 15028
Coupon, Cambria 16629
Courtdale, Luzerne 18704
Covington, Tioga 16917
Covington Township, Wayne 18424
Cowanesque, Tioga 16950
Cowansville, Armstrong 16218
Crabtree, Westmoreland 15624
Crafton, Allegheny 15205
Craigsville, Armstrong 16262
Craley, York 17312
Cranberry, Venango 16319
Cranberry Township, Butler 16066
Cranesville, Erie 16410
Creamery, Montgomery 19430
Creekside, Indiana 15732
Creighton, Allegheny 15030
Crescent, Allegheny 15046
Cresco, Monroe 18326
Cresson, Cambria 16630
Cressona, Schuylkill 17929
Crosby, Mckean 16724
Cross Fork, Potter 17729
Crossingville, Erie 16412
Crown, Clarion 16220
Croydon, Bucks 19021
Crucible, Greene 15325
Crum Lynne, Delaware 19022
Crystal Spring, Fulton 15536
Cuddy, Allegheny 15031
Cumbola, Schuylkill 17930
Curllsville, Clarion 16221
Curryville, Blair 16631
Curtisville, Allegheny 15032
Curwensville, Clearfield 16833
Custer City, Mckean 16725
Cyclone, Mckean 16726
Dagus Mines, Elk 15831
Daisytown, Washington 15427
Dallas, Luzerne 18612
Dallastown, York 17313
Dalmatia, Northumberland 17017
Dalton, Lackawanna 18414
Damascus, Wayne 18415
Danboro, Bucks 18916
Danielsville, Northampton 18038
Danville, Montour 17821
Darby, Delaware 19023
Darlington, Beaver 16115
Darragh, Westmoreland 15625
Dauberville, Berks 19533
Dauphin, Dauphin 17018
Davidsville, Somerset 15928
Davistown, Greene 15349
Dawson, Fayette 15428
Dayton, Armstrong 16222
De Lancey, Jefferson 15733
De Young, Elk 16728
Defiance, Bedford 16633
Delano, Schuylkill 18220
Delaware Water Gap, Monroe 18327
Delmont, Westmoreland 15626
Delphi, Montgomery 19473
Delta, York 17314
Denbo, Washington 15429
Denver, Lancaster 17517
Derrick City, Mckean 16727
Derry, Westmoreland 15627
Devault, Chester 19432
Devon, Chester 19333
Dewart, Northumberland 17730
Dickerson Run, Fayette 15430
Dickson City, Lackawanna 18519
Dickson Cty, Lackawanna 18447
Dilliner, Greene 15327
Dillsburg, York 17019
Dilltown, Indiana 15929
Dimock, Susquehanna 18816
Dingmans Ferry, Pike 18328
Distant, Armstrong 16223
Dixonville, Indiana 15734
Donaldson, Schuylkill 17981

Donegal, Westmoreland 15628
Donora, Washington 15033
Dornsife, Northumberland 17823
Douglassville, Berks 19518
Dover, York 17315
Downingtown, Chester 19335
Downingtown, Chester 19372
Doylesburg, Franklin 17219
DOYLESTOWN, Bucks
(See Page 3202)
Dravosburg, Allegheny 15034
Dresher, Montgomery 19025
Drexel Hill, Delaware 19026
Drifting, Clearfield 16834
Drifton, Luzerne 18221
Driftwood, Cameron 15832
Drumore, Lancaster 17518
Drums, Luzerne 18222
Dry Run, Franklin 17220
Du Bois, Clearfield 15801
Dublin, Bucks 18917
Dubois, Clearfield 15801
Duboistown, Lycoming 17702
Dudley, Huntingdon 16634
Duke Center, Mckean 16729
Dunbar, Fayette 15431
Duncannon, Perry 17020
Duncansville, Blair 16635
Dunlevy, Washington 15432
Dunlo, Cambria 15930
Dunmore
(See Scranton)
Dupont, Luzerne 18641
Duquesne, Allegheny 15110
Durham, Bucks 18039
Duryea, Luzerne 18642
Dushore, Sullivan 18614
Dysart, Cambria 16636
Eagle, Chester 19480
Eagles Mere, Sullivan 17731
Eagleville, Montgomery 19403
Eagleville, Montgomery 19408
Earlington, Montgomery 18918
Earlville, Berks 19518
Earlville, Berks 19519
East Bangor, Northampton 18013
East Berlin, Adams 17316
East Brady, Clarion 16028
East Butler, Butler 16029
East Earl, Lancaster 17519
East Fallowfield Township,
Chester 19320
East Freedom, Blair 16637
East Greenville,
Montgomery 18041
East Hickory, Forest 16321
East Lancaster, Lancaster 17605
East Lansdowne, Delaware ... 19050
East Liberty, Allegheny 15206
East Mc Keesport,
Allegheny 15035
East Millsboro, Fayette 15433
East Norriton
(See Norristown)
East Pennsboro,
Cumberland 17025
East Petersburg, Lancaster ... 17520
East Pittsburgh, Allegheny 15112
East Prospect, York 17317
East Smethport, Mckean 16730
East Smithfield, Bradford 18817
East Springfield, Erie 16411
EAST STROUDSBURG,
Monroe
(See Page 3203)
East Texas, Lehigh 18046
East Vandergrift,
Westmoreland 15629
East Waterford, Juniata 17021
East York, York 17402
EASTON, Northampton
(See Page 3206)
Eau Claire, Butler 16030
Ebensburg, Cambria 15931
Ebervale, Luzerne 18223
Eddington, Bucks 19020

Eddystone, Delaware 19013
Edgely, Bucks 19007
Edgemont, Delaware 19028
Edgeworth, Allegheny 15143
Edinboro, Erie 16412
Edinburg, Lawrence 16116
Edmon, Westmoreland 15618
Edwardsville, Luzerne 18704
Effort, Monroe 18330
Eighty Four, Washington 15330
Elco, Washington 15434
Eldersville, Washington 15021
Elderton, Armstrong 15736
Eldred, Mckean 16731
Elgin, Erie 16413
Elizabeth, Allegheny 15037
Elizabethtown, Lancaster 17022
Elizabethville, Dauphin 17023
Elkins Park, Montgomery 19027
Elkland, Tioga 16920
Elliottsburg, Perry 17024
Ellport, Lawrence 16117
Ellsworth, Washington 15331
Ellwood City, Lawrence 16117
Elm, Lancaster 17521
Elmhurst, Lackawanna 18416
Elmhurst Township,
Lackawanna 18444
Elmora, Cambria 15737
Elrama, Washington 15038
Elton, Cambria 15934
Elverson, Chester 19520
Elwyn, Delaware 19063
Elysburg, Northumberland 17824
Emeigh, Cambria 15738
Emerald, Lehigh 18080
Emigsville, York 17318
Emlenton, Venango 16373
Emmaus, Lehigh 18049
Emporium, Cameron 15834
Emsworth, Allegheny 15202
Endeavor, Forest 16321
Endeavor, Forest 16322
Enola, Cumberland 17025
Enon Valley, Lawrence 16120
Entriken, Huntingdon 16638
Ephrata, Lancaster 17522
Equinunk, Wayne 18417
Erdenheim, Montgomery 19038
ERIE, Erie
(See Page 3208)
Ernest, Indiana 15739
Erwinna, Bucks 18920
Espyville, Crawford 16424
Essington, Delaware 19029
Etna, Allegheny 15223
Etters, York 17319
Evans City, Butler 16033
Evansville, Berks 19522
Everett, Bedford 15537
Everson, Fayette 15631
Excelsior, Northumberland 17866
Exeter, Luzerne 18643
Export, Westmoreland 15632
Exton, Chester 19341
Exton, Chester 19353
Eynon, Lackawanna 18403
Factoryville, Wyoming 18419
Fair Oaks, Beaver 15003
Fairbank, Fayette 15435
Fairchance, Fayette 15436
Fairfield, Adams 17320
Fairhope, Somerset 15538
Fairless Hills, Bucks 19030
Fairmount City, Clarion 16224
Fairview, Erie 16415
Fairview Village,
Montgomery 19409
Fallentimber, Cambria 16639
Falls, Wyoming 18615
Falls Creek, Jefferson 15840
Fallsington, Bucks 19054
Fannettsburg, Franklin 17221
Farmington, Fayette 15437
Farrandsville, Clinton 17745
Farrell, Mercer 16121

Fawn Grove, York 17321
Fayette City, Fayette 15438
Fayetteville, Franklin 17222
Feasterville Trevose, Bucks .. 19053
Felton, York 17322
Fenelton, Butler 16034
Fern Glen, Schuylkill 18241
Ferndale, Bucks 18921
Finleyville, Washington 15332
Fisher, Clarion 16225
Fishertown, Bedford 15539
Fleetville, Lackawanna 18420
Fleetwood, Berks 19522
Fleming, Centre 16835
Flemington, Clinton 17745
Flicksville, Northampton 18050
Flinton, Cambria 16640
Floreffe, Allegheny 15025
Florin, Lancaster 17552
Flourtown, Montgomery 19031
Fogelsville, Lehigh 18051
Folcroft, Delaware 19032
Folsom, Delaware 19033
Fombell, Beaver 16123
Forbes Road, Westmoreland .. 15633
Force, Elk 15841
Ford City, Armstrong 16226
Ford Cliff, Armstrong 16228
Forest City, Susquehanna 18421
Forest Grove, Bucks 18922
Forestville, Butler 16035
Forks Township,
Northampton 18040
Forkston Township, Sullivan . 18614
Forksville, Sullivan 18616
Fort Hill, Somerset 15540
Fort Littleton, Fulton 17223
Fort Loudon, Franklin 17224
Fort Washington,
Montgomery 19034
Forty Fort, Luzerne 18704
Fountain Hill, Northampton 18015
Fountainville, Bucks 18923
Foxburg, Clarion 16036
Foxcroft Square,
Montgomery 19046
Frackville, Schuylkill 17931
Franconia, Montgomery 18924
Franklin, Venango 16323
Franklin Center, Chester 19341
Franklintown, York 17323
Frazer, Chester 19355
Frederick, Montgomery 19435
Fredericksburg, Lebanon 17026
Fredericktown, Washington 15333
Fredonia, Mercer 16124
Freeburg, Snyder 17827
Freedom, Beaver 15042
Freeland, Luzerne 18224
Freemansburg, Northampton ... 18017
Freeport, Armstrong 16229
Frenchville, Clearfield 16836
Friedens, Somerset 15541
Friedensburg, Schuylkill 17933
Friendsville, Susquehanna 18818
Frostburg, Jefferson 15767
Fruitville, Montgomery 19473
Fryburg, Clarion 16326
Furlong, Bucks 18925
Gaines, Tioga 16921
Galeton, Potter 16922
Galilee, Wayne 18415
Gallitzin, Cambria 16641
Ganister, Blair 16693
Gans, Fayette 15439
Gap, Lancaster 17527
Garards Fort, Greene 15334
Garden City, Delaware 19063
Gardners, Adams 17324
Garland, Warren 16416
Garnet Valley, Delaware 19060
Garnet Valley, Delaware 19061
Garrett, Somerset 15542
Gastonville, Washington 15336
Geigertown, Berks 19523

GENESEE, Potter
(See Page 3211)
George School, Bucks 18940
Georgetown, Beaver 15043
Germansville, Lehigh 18053
Gettysburg, Adams 17325
Gibbon Glade, Fayette 15440
Gibson, Susquehanna 18820
Gibsonia, Allegheny 15044
Gifford, Mckean 16732
Gilbert, Monroe 18331
Gilberton, Schuylkill 17934
Gilbertsville, Montgomery 19525
Gillett, Bradford 16925
Ginter, Clearfield 16651
Gipsy, Indiana 15741
Girard, Erie 16417
Girardville, Schuylkill 17935
Gladwyne, Montgomery 19035
Glasgow, Cambria 16644
Glassport, Allegheny 15045
Glen Campbell, Indiana 15742
Glen Hope, Clearfield 16645
Glen Lyon, Luzerne 18617
Glen Mills, Delaware 19342
Glen Richey, Clearfield 16837
Glen Riddle, Delaware 19037
Glen Riddle Lima, Delaware .. 19037
Glen Rock, York 17327
Glencoe, Somerset 15538
Glendon, Northampton 18042
Glenmoore, Chester 19343
Glenolden, Delaware 19036
Glenshaw, Allegheny 15116
Glenside, Montgomery 19038
Glenville, York 17329
Glenwillard, Allegheny 15046
Good Spring, Schuylkill 17981
Goodville, Lancaster 17528
Gordon, Schuylkill 17936
Gordonville, Lancaster 17529
Gouldsboro, Wayne 18424
Gowen City, Northumberland . 17872
Graceton, Indiana 15748
Gradyville, Delaware 19039
Grampian, Clearfield 16838
Grand Valley, Warren 16420
Grantham, Cumberland 17027
Grantville, Dauphin 17028
Granville, Mifflin 17029
Granville Summit, Bradford 16926
Grapeville, Westmoreland 15634
Grassflat, Clearfield 16839
Gratz, Dauphin 17030
Gray, Somerset 15544
Graysville, Greene 15337
Great Bend, Susquehanna 18821
Greeley, Pike 18425
Green Lane, Montgomery 18054
Green Park, Perry 17024
Greencastle, Franklin 17225
Greenfield Township,
Lackawanna 18407
Greenock, Allegheny 15047
Greensboro, Greene 15338
Greensburg, Westmoreland ... 15601
Greenstone, Adams 17320
Greentown, Pike 18426
Greentree, Allegheny 15242
Greenville, Mercer 16125
Grindstone, Fayette 15442
Grove City, Mercer 16127
Grover, Bradford 17735
Guilford Township, Franklin .. 17202
Gulph Mills, Montgomery 19428
Guys Mills, Crawford 16327
Gwynedd, Montgomery 19436
Gwynedd, Montgomery 19454
Gwynedd Valley,
Montgomery 19437
Hadley, Mercer 16130
Halifax, Dauphin 17032
Hallam, York 17406
Hallstead, Susquehanna 18822
Hallton, Jefferson 15860
Hamburg, Berks 19526

Hamilton, Jefferson 15744
Hamlin, Wayne 18427
Hampden Township,
Cumberland 17050
Hannastown, Westmoreland .. 15635
Hanover, York 17331
Hanover Township, Luzerne .. 18706
Harborcreek, Erie 16421
Harding, Luzerne 18643
Harford, Susquehanna 18823
Harleigh, Luzerne 18225
Harleysville, Montgomery 19438
Harmonsburg, Crawford 16422
Harmony, Butler 16037
HARRISBURG, Dauphin
(See Page 3212)
Harrison City, Westmoreland . 15636
Harrison Valley, Potter 16927
Harrisonville, Fulton 17228
Harrisville, Butler 16038
Hartleton, Union 17829
Hartstown, Crawford 16131
Hartsville, Bucks 18974
Harveys Lake, Luzerne 18618
Harwick, Allegheny 15049
Hastings, Cambria 16646
Hatboro, Montgomery 19040
Hatfield, Montgomery 19440
Haverford, Montgomery 19041
Havertown, Delaware 19083
Hawk Run, Clearfield 16840
Hawley, Pike 18428
Hawley, Wayne 18438
Hawthorn, Clarion 16230
Hazel Hurst, Mckean 16733
Hazelwood, Allegheny 15207
Hazen, Jefferson 15825
Hazle Township
(See Hazleton)
HAZLETON, Luzerne
(See Page 3216)
Hegins, Schuylkill 17938
Heidelberg, Allegheny 15106
Heilwood, Indiana 15745
Helfenstein, Schuylkill 17921
Hellam, York 17406
Hellertown, Northampton 18055
Hendersonville, Washington .. 15339
Henryville, Monroe 18332
Hereford, Berks 18056
Herman, Butler 16039
Herminie, Westmoreland 15637
Hermitage, Mercer 16148
Herndon, Northumberland 17830
Herrick Center,
Susquehanna 18430
Hershey, Dauphin 17033
Hesston, Huntingdon 16647
Hibbs, Fayette 15443
Hickory, Washington 15340
Hidden Valley, Somerset 15502
Highland Park, Delaware 19082
Highspire, Dauphin 17034
Hilldale
(See Wilkes Barre)
Hiller, Fayette 15444
Hilliards, Butler 16040
Hillsdale, Indiana 15746
Hillsgrove, Sullivan 18619
Hillsville, Lawrence 16132
Hilltown, Bucks 18927
Hokendauqua, Lehigh 18052
Holbrook, Greene 15341
Holicong, Bucks 18928
Holland, Bucks 18966
Hollidaysburg, Blair 16648
Hollsopple, Somerset 15935
Hollywood, Montgomery 19046
Holmes, Delaware 19043
Holtwood, Lancaster 17532
Home, Indiana 15747
Homer City, Indiana 15748
Homestead, Allegheny 15120
Homewood, Allegheny 15208
Honesdale, Wayne 18431
Honey Brook, Chester 19344

Honey Grove, Juniata 17035
Hookstown, Beaver 15050
Hooversville, Somerset 15936
Hop Bottom, Susquehanna ... 18824
Hopeland, Lancaster 17533
Hopewell, Bedford 16650
Hopwood, Fayette 15445
Horsham, Montgomery 19044
Hostetter, Westmoreland 15638
Houston, Washington 15342
Houtzdale, Clearfield 16651
Howard, Centre 16841
Hublersburg, Centre 16823
Hudson
(See Wilkes Barre)
Huey, Clarion 16248
Hughestown, Luzerne 18640
Hughesville, Lycoming 17737
Hulmeville, Bucks 19047
Hummels Wharf, Snyder 17831
Hummelstown, Dauphin 17036
Hunker, Westmoreland 15639
Hunlock Creek, Luzerne 18621
Hunlock Township, Luzerne .. 18621
Huntingdon, Huntingdon 16652
Huntingdon Valley,
Montgomery 19006
Huntington Mills, Luzerne 18622
Hustontown, Fulton 17229
Hutchinson, Westmoreland 15640
Hyde, Clearfield 16843
Hyde Park, Westmoreland 15641
Hydetown, Crawford 16328
Hyndman, Bedford 15545
Ickesburg, Perry 17037
Idaville, Adams 17337
Imler, Bedford 16655
Immaculata, Chester 19345
Imperial, Allegheny 15126
Indian Head, Fayette 15446
Indian Valley, Montgomery 18969
Indiana, Indiana 15701
Indianola, Allegheny 15051
Industry, Beaver 15052
Ingomar, Allegheny 15127
Inkerman, Luzerne 18640
Intercourse, Lancaster 17534
Irvine, Warren 16329
Irvona, Clearfield 16656
Irwin, Westmoreland 15642
Isabella, Fayette 15447
Ivyland, Bucks 18974
Jackson, Susquehanna 18825
Jackson Center, Mercer 16133
Jackson Township, Luzerne .. 18708
Jacobs Creek,
Westmoreland 15448
Jacobus, York 17407
James City, Elk 16734
James Creek, Huntingdon 16657
Jamestown, Mercer 16134
Jamison, Bucks 18929
Jeannette, Westmoreland 15644
Jefferson, Greene 15344
Jefferson Hills, Allegheny 15025
Jefferson Township, Wayne .. 18436
Jeffersonville, Montgomery 19403
Jenkins Township, Luzerne ... 18640
Jenkintown, Montgomery 19046
Jenners, Somerset 15546
Jennerstown, Somerset 15547
Jermyn, Lackawanna 18433
Jerome, Somerset 15937
Jersey Mills, Lycoming 17739
Jersey Shore, Lycoming 17723
Jersey Shore, Lycoming 17727
Jessup, Lackawanna 18434
Jim Thorpe, Carbon 18229
Joffre, Washington 15053
Johnsonburg, Elk 15845
JOHNSTOWN, Cambria
(See Page 3218)
Joliett, Schuylkill 17981
Jones Mills, Westmoreland 15646
Jonestown, Lebanon 17038
Josephine, Indiana 15750

Julian, Centre 16844
Juneau, Jefferson 15767
Junedale, Carbon 18230
Kane, Mckean 16735
Kantner, Somerset 15548
Karns City, Butler 16041
Karthaus, Clearfield 16845
Kaska, Schuylkill 17959
Keisterville, Fayette 15449
Kelayres, Schuylkill 18231
Kelton, Chester 19346
Kemblesville, Chester 19347
Kempton, Berks 19529
Kennerdell, Venango 16374
Kennett Square, Chester 19348
Kent, Indiana 15752
Kersey, Elk 15846
Kilbuck, Allegheny 15233
Kimberton, Chester 19442
King Of Prussia, Montgomery 19406
Kingsley, Susquehanna 18826
Kingston, Luzerne 18704
Kintnersville, Bucks 18930
Kinzers, Lancaster 17535
Kirklyn, Delaware 19082
Kirkwood, Lancaster 17536
Kittanning, Armstrong 16201
Kleinfeltersville, Lebanon 17039
Klingerstown, Schuylkill 17941
Knox, Clarion 16232
Knox Dale, Jefferson 15847
Knoxville, Tioga 16928
Koppel, Beaver 16136
Korn Krest, Luzerne 18702
Kossuth, Clarion 16331
Kreamer, Snyder 17833
Kresgeville, Monroe 18333
Kulpmont, Northumberland 17834
Kulpsville, Montgomery 19443
Kunkletown, Monroe 18058
Kutztown, Berks 19530
Kylertown, Clearfield 16847
La Belle, Fayette 15450
La Jose, Clearfield 15753
La Plume, Lackawanna 18440
Laceyville, Wyoming 18623
Lackawaxen, Pike 18435
Lafayette Hill, Montgomery 19444
Lahaska, Bucks 18931
Lairdsville, Lycoming 17742
Lake Ariel, Wayne 18436
Lake City, Erie 16423
Lake Como, Wayne 18437
Lake Harmony, Carbon 18624
Lake Lynn, Fayette 15439
Lake Lynn, Fayette 15451
Lake Winola, Wyoming 18625
Lakeview Township, Pike 18328
Lakeville, Wayne 18438
Lakewood, Wayne 18439
Lamar, Clinton 16848
Lamartine, Clarion 16375
Lamberton, Fayette 15458
Lamott, Montgomery 19027
Lampeter, Lancaster 17537
LANCASTER, Lancaster (See Page 3221)
Landenberg, Chester 19350
Landingville, Schuylkill 17972
Landisburg, Perry 17040
Landisville, Lancaster 17538
Lanesboro, Susquehanna 18827
Langeloth, Washington 15054
Langhorne, Bucks 19047
Langhorne, Bucks 19053
Lansdale, Montgomery 19446
Lansdowne, Delaware 19050
Lanse, Clearfield 16849
Lansford, Carbon 18232
Laporte, Sullivan 18626
Large, Allegheny 15025
Larimer, Westmoreland 15647
Larksville, Luzerne 18651
Latrobe, Westmoreland 15650
Lattimer Mines, Luzerne 18234
Laughlintown, Westmoreland 15655
Laurel Run, Luzerne 18706
Laureldale, Berks 19605
Laurelton, Union 17835
Laurys Station, Lehigh 18059
Lavelle, Schuylkill 17943
Laverock, Montgomery 19038
Lawn, Lebanon 17041
Lawrence, Washington 15055
Lawrenceville, Tioga 16929
Lawton, Susquehanna 18828
Layton, Fayette 15473
Le Raysville, Bradford 18829
LEBANON, Lebanon (See Page 3224)
Leck Kill, Northumberland 17836
Leckrone, Fayette 15454
Lecontes Mills, Clearfield 16850
Lederach, Montgomery 19450
Leechburg, Armstrong 15656
Leeper, Clarion 16233
Leesport, Berks 19533
Leetsdale, Allegheny 15056
LEHIGH VALLEY, Northampton (See Page 3226)
Lehighton, Carbon 18235
Lehighton Borough, Carbon 18235
Lehman, Monroe 18301
Leisenring, Fayette 15455
Lemasters, Franklin 17231
Lemont, Centre 16851
Lemont Frnce, Fayette 15456
Lemont Furnace, Fayette 15456
Lemoyne, Cumberland 17043
Lenhartsville, Berks 19534
Lenni, Delaware 19052
Lenoxville, Susquehanna 18441
Leola, Lancaster 17540
Leroy, Bradford 17724
Lester, Delaware 19029
LEVITTOWN, Bucks (See Page 3226)
Lewis Run, Mckean 16738
Lewisberry, York 17339
Lewisburg, Union 17837
Lewisburg, Union 17886
Lewistown, Mifflin 17044
Lewisville, Chester 19351
Liberty, Tioga 16930
Library, Allegheny 15129
Lickingville, Clarion 16332
Lightstreet, Columbia 17839
Ligonier, Westmoreland 15658
Lilly, Cambria 15938
Lima, Delaware 19037
Limekiln, Berks 19535
Limeport, Lehigh 18060
Limerick, Montgomery 19468
Limestone, Clarion 16234
Lincoln University, Chester 19352
Linden, Lycoming 17744
Line Lexington, Bucks 18932
Linesville, Crawford 16424
Linfield, Montgomery 19468
Linglestown, Dauphin 17112
Linwood, Delaware 19061
Lionville, Chester 19353
Listie, Somerset 15549
Listonburg, Somerset 15424
Lititz, Lancaster 17543
Little Marsh, Tioga 16950
Little Meadows, Susquehanna 18830
Littlestown, Adams 17340
Liverpool, Perry 17045
Llewellyn, Schuylkill 17944
Lock Haven, Clinton 17745
Locust Gap, Northumberland 17840
Locustdale, Schuylkill 17945
Loganton, Clinton 17747
Loganville, York 17342
Long Pond, Monroe 18334
Lopez, Sullivan 18628
Lords Valley, Pike 18428
Loretto, Cambria 15940
Lost Creek, Schuylkill 17946
Lowber, Westmoreland 15660
Lower Burrell, Westmoreland 15068
Lower Gwynedd, Montgomery 19002
Lower Merion, Delaware 19083
Lower Paxton (See Harrisburg)
Lower Salford, Montgomery 19438
Lower Shaft, Schuylkill 17976
Loyalhanna, Westmoreland 15661
Loysburg, Bedford 16659
Loysville, Perry 17047
Lucernemines, Indiana 15754
Lucinda, Clarion 16235
Ludlow, Mckean 16333
Lumberville, Bucks 18933
Lundys Lane, Erie 16401
Lurgan, Franklin 17232
Luthersburg, Clearfield 15848
Luxor, Westmoreland 15662
Luzerne, Luzerne 18709
Lykens, Dauphin 17048
Lyndell, Chester 19354
Lyndora, Butler 16045
Lyon Station, Berks 19536
Macarthur, Beaver 15001
Mackeyville, Clinton 17750
Macungie, Lehigh 18062
Madera, Clearfield 16661
Madison, Westmoreland 15663
Madison Township, Lackawanna 18444
Madisonburg, Centre 16852
Mahaffey, Clearfield 15757
Mahanoy City, Schuylkill 17948
Mahanoy Plane, Schuylkill 17949
Mainesburg, Tioga 16932
Mainland, Montgomery 19451
Malvern, Chester 19355
Mammoth, Westmoreland 15664
Manayunk, Philadelphia 19127
Manchester, York 17345
Manheim, Lancaster 17545
Manns Choice, Bedford 15550
Manor, Westmoreland 15665
Manorville, Armstrong 16238
Mansfield, Tioga 16933
Maple Glen, Montgomery 19002
Mapleton Depot, Huntingdon 17052
Mar Lin, Schuylkill 17951
Marble, Clarion 16334
Marchand, Indiana 15758
Marcus Hook, Delaware 19060
Marcus Hook, Delaware 19061
Marianna, Washington 15345
Marienville, Forest 16239
Marietta, Lancaster 17547
Marion, Franklin 17235
Marion Center, Indiana 15759
Marion Heights, Northumberland 17832
Markleton, Somerset 15551
Markleysburg, Fayette 15459
Mars, Butler 16046
Marshalls Creek, Monroe 18335
Marsteller, Cambria 15760
Martin, Fayette 15460
Martindale, Lancaster 17549
Martins Creek, Northampton 18063
Martinsburg, Blair 16662
Marwood, Butler 16023
Mary D, Schuylkill 17952
Marysville, Perry 17053
Masontown, Fayette 15461
Matamoras, Pike 18336
Mather, Greene 15346
Mattawana, Mifflin 17054
Maxatawny, Berks 19538
Mayfield, Lackawanna 18433
Mayport, Clarion 16240
Maytown, Lancaster 17550
Mc Alisterville, Juniata 17049
Mc Clellandtown, Fayette 15458
Mc Clure, Mifflin 17841
Mc Connellsburg, Fulton 17233
Mc Connellstown, Huntingdon 16660
Mc Donald, Washington 15057
Mc Elhattan, Clinton 17748
Mc Ewensville, Northumberland 17749
Mc Grann, Armstrong 16236
Mc Intyre, Indiana 15756
Mc Kean, Erie 16426
Mc Kees Rocks, Allegheny 15136
Mc Knight, Allegheny 15237
Mc Knightstown, Adams 17343
Mc Murray, Washington 15317
Mc Sherrystown, Adams 17344
Mc Veytown, Mifflin 17051
Mcadoo, Schuylkill 18237
Mcgees Mills, Clearfield 15757
Mckean, Erie 16426
MCKEESPORT, Allegheny (See Page 3227)
Mcknight, Allegheny 15237
Mcmurray, Washington 15317
Meadow Lands, Washington 15347
Meadowbrook, Montgomery 19046
Meadville, Crawford 16335
MECHANICSBURG, Cumberland (See Page 3228)
Mechanicsville, Bucks 18934
MEDIA, Delaware (See Page 3230)
Mehoopany, Wyoming 18629
Mehoopany Twp, Wyoming 18657
Melcroft, Fayette 15462
Melrose, Montgomery 19027
Melrose Park, Montgomery 19027
Mendenhall, Chester 19357
Menges Mills, York 17362
Mentcle, Indiana 15761
Mercer, Mercer 16137
Mercersburg, Franklin 17236
Meridian, Butler 16001
Merion Station, Montgomery 19066
Merrittstown, Fayette 15463
Mertztown, Berks 19539
Meshoppen, Wyoming 18630
Messiah College, Cumberland 17027
Mexico, Juniata 17056
Meyersdale, Somerset 15552
Middle City East, Philadelphia 19102
Middle City West, Philadelphia 19103
Middle Creek (See Beaver Springs)
Middleburg, Snyder 17842
Middlebury Center, Tioga 16935
Middleport, Schuylkill 17953
Middletown, Dauphin 17057
Midland, Beaver 15059
Midway, Washington 15060
Mifflin, Juniata 17058
Mifflinburg, Union 17844
Mifflintown, Juniata 17059
Mifflinville, Columbia 18631
Milan, Bradford 18831
Milanville, Wayne 18443
Mildred, Sullivan 18632
Milesburg, Centre 16853
Milford, Pike 18337
Milford Square, Bucks 18935
Mill Creek, Huntingdon 17060
Mill Hall, Clinton 17751
Mill Run, Fayette 15464
Mill Village, Erie 16427
Millbourne, Delaware 19082
Millersburg, Dauphin 17061
Millerstown, Perry 17062
Millersville, Lancaster 17551
Millerton, Tioga 16936
Millheim, Centre 16854
Millmont, Union 17845
Millrift, Pike 18340
Mills, Potter 16937
Millsboro, Washington 15348
Millvale, Allegheny 15209
Millville, Columbia 17846
Milmont Park, Delaware 19033
Milnesville, Luzerne 18239
Milroy, Mifflin 17063
Milton, Northumberland 17847
Mineral Point, Cambria 15942
Mineral Springs, Clearfield 16855
Miners Mill, Luzerne 18705
Minersville, Schuylkill 17954
Mingoville, Centre 16856
Minisink Hills, Monroe 18341
Miquon, Montgomery 19444
Mocanaqua, Luzerne 18655
Modena, Chester 19358
Mohnton, Berks 19540
Mohrsville, Berks 19541
Monaca, Beaver 15061
Monessen, Westmoreland 15062
Monocacy Station, Berks 19542
Monongahela, Washington 15063
Monroe Township, Snyder 17870
Monroe Township, Snyder 17870
Monroeton, Bradford 18832
Monroeville, Allegheny 15140
Monroeville, Allegheny 15146
Mont Alto, Franklin 17237
Mont Clare, Montgomery 19453
Montandon, Northumberland 17850
Montgomery, Lycoming 17752
Montgomeryville, Montgomery 18936
Montour, Allegheny 15244
Montoursville, Lycoming 17754
Montrose, Susquehanna 18801
Moon Township, Allegheny 15108
Moon Twp, Allegheny 15108
Moosic, Lackawanna 18507
Morann, Clearfield 16663
Morea, Schuylkill 17948
Morgan, Allegheny 15064
Morgantown, Berks 19543
Morris, Tioga 16938
Morris Run, Tioga 16939
Morrisdale, Clearfield 16858
Morrisville, Bucks 19067
Morton, Delaware 19070
Moscow, Lackawanna 18444
Moshannon, Centre 16859
Mount Aetna, Berks 19544
Mount Bethel, Northampton 18343
Mount Braddock, Fayette 15465
Mount Carmel, Northumberland 17851
Mount Cobb, Wayne 18436
Mount Gretna, Lebanon 17064
Mount Holly Springs, Cumberland 17065
Mount Jewett, Mckean 16740
Mount Joy, Lancaster 17552
Mount Morris, Greene 15349
Mount Oliver, Allegheny 15210
Mount Penn, Berks 19606
Mount Pleasant, Westmoreland 15666
Mount Pleasant Mills, Snyder 17853
Mount Pocono, Monroe 18344
Mount Union, Huntingdon 17066
Mount Union, Huntingdon 17260
Mount Washington, Allegheny 15211
Mount Wolf, York 17347
Mountain Top, Luzerne 18707
Mountainhome, Monroe 18342
Mountville, Lancaster 17554
Moylan, Delaware 19065
Mt Lebanon, Allegheny 15228
Mt Morris, Greene 15349
Mt Oliver, Allegheny 15210
Mt Pleasant Mills, Snyder 17853
Muhlenberg Township, Berks 19605
Muir, Schuylkill 17957
Muncy, Lycoming 17756
Muncy Valley, Sullivan 17758
Munhall, Allegheny 15120
Munson, Clearfield 16860
Murrysville, Westmoreland 15632
Murrysville, Westmoreland 15668
Muse, Washington 15350
Myerstown, Lebanon 17067
N Bell Vernon, Fayette 15012
N Belle Vernon, Fayette 15012
Nanticoke, Luzerne 18634
Nanty Glo, Cambria 15943
Narberth, Montgomery 19072
Narvon, Lancaster 17555
Natrona Heights, Allegheny 15065
Nazareth, Northampton 18064
Needmore, Fulton 17238
Neelyton, Huntingdon 17239
Neffs, Lehigh 18065
Neffsville, Lancaster 17601
Neiffer, Montgomery 19473
Nelson, Tioga 16940
Nemacolin, Greene 15351
Nescopeck, Luzerne 18635
Neshannock, Lawrence 16105
Nesquehoning, Carbon 18240
New Albany, Bradford 18833
New Alexandria, Westmoreland 15670
New Baltimore, Somerset 15553
New Bedford, Lawrence 16140
New Berlin, Union 17855
New Berlinville, Berks 19545
New Bethlehem, Clarion 16242
New Bloomfield, Perry 17068
New Boston, Schuylkill 17948
New Brighton, Beaver 15066
New Britain, Bucks 18901
New Buffalo, Perry 17069
NEW CASTLE, Lawrence (See Page 3231)
New Columbia, Union 17856
New Columbia, Union 17886
New Cumberland, Cumberland 17070
New Derry, Westmoreland 15671
New Eagle, Washington 15067
New Enterprise, Bedford 16664
New Florence, Westmoreland 15944
New Freedom, York 17349
New Freeport, Greene 15352
New Galilee, Beaver 16141
New Geneva, Fayette 15467
New Germantown, Perry 17071
New Holland, Lancaster 17557
New Hope, Bucks 18938
New Kensington, Westmoreland 15068
New Kingstown, Cumberland 17072
New London, Chester 19360
New London Township, Chester 19352
New Milford, Susquehanna 18834
New Millport, Clearfield 16861
New Oxford, Adams 17350
New Paris, Bedford 15554
New Park, York 17352
New Philadelphia, Schuylkill 17959
New Providence, Lancaster 17560
New Ringgold, Schuylkill 17960
New Salem, Fayette 15468
New Salem Borough, York 17408
New Stanton, Westmoreland 15672
New Tripoli, Lehigh 18066
New Wilmington, Lawrence 16142
Newburg, Cumberland 17240
Newell, Fayette 15466
Newfoundland, Wayne 18445
Newlondon Twp, Chester 19352
Newmanstown, Lebanon 17073
Newport, Perry 17074
Newportville, Bucks 19056
Newry, Blair 16665
Newton Hamilton, Mifflin 17075
Newtown, Bucks 18940

Newtown Square, Delaware 19073
Newville, Cumberland 17241
Nicholson, Susquehanna 18441
Nicholson, Wyoming 18446
Nicktown, Cambria 15762
Ninepoints, Lancaster 17509
Nineveh, Greene 15353
Nisbet, Lycoming 17702
No Huntingdon, Westmoreland 15642
Noblestown, Allegheny 15071
Normalville, Fayette 15469
NORRISTOWN, Montgomery (See Page 3233)
North Abington Township, Lackawanna 18414
North Apollo, Armstrong 15673
North Belle Vernon, Fayette 15012
North Bend, Clinton 17760
North Bingham (See Genesee)
North Charleroi, Washington 15022
North East, Erie 16428
North Huntingdon, Westmoreland 15642
North Irwin, Westmoreland 15642
North Leechburg, Armstrong 15656
North Penn, Montgomery 19440
North Scranton, Lackawanna 18508
North Springfield, Erie 16430
North Versailles, Allegheny 15137
North Wales, Montgomery 19436
North Warren, Warren 16365
North Washington, Butler 16048
Northampton, Northampton 18067
Northern Cambria, Cambria 15714
Northpoint, Indiana 15763
Northumberland, Northumberland 17857
Norvelt, Westmoreland 15674
Norwood, Delaware 19074
Nottingham, Chester 19362
Noxen, Wyoming 18636
Nu Mine, Armstrong 16244
Nuangola, Luzerne 18707
Numidia, Columbia 17858
Nuremberg, Schuylkill 18241
Oak Ridge, Armstrong 16245
Oakdale, Allegheny 15071
Oakford, Bucks 19053
Oakland, Allegheny 15213
Oakland Mills, Juniata 17076
Oakmont, Allegheny 15139
Oaks, Montgomery 19456
Oberlin, Dauphin 17113
Observatory, Allegheny 15214
Ogden, Delaware 19061
Ogontz Campus, Montgomery 19001
Ohiopyle, Fayette 15470
Oil City, Venango 16301
Olanta, Clearfield 16863
Old Forge, Lackawanna 18518
Old Zionsville, Lehigh 18068
Oley, Berks 19547
Oliveburg, Jefferson 15764
Oliver, Fayette 15472
Olyphant, Lackawanna 18447
Oneida, Schuylkill 18242
Ono, Lebanon 17077
Ontelaunee, Berks 19605
Orangeville, Columbia 17859
Orbisonia, Huntingdon 17243
Orefield, Lehigh 18069
Oreland, Montgomery 19075
Ormsby, Mckean 16726
Orrstown, Franklin 17244
Orrtanna, Adams 17353
Orson, Wayne 18449
Orviston, Centre 16864
Orwigsburg, Schuylkill 17961
Osceola, Tioga 16942
Osceola Mills, Clearfield 16666
Osterburg, Bedford 16667
Oswayo, Potter 16915
Ottsville, Bucks 18942
Overbrook Hills, Philadelphia 19151
Oxford, Chester 19363
Palm, Montgomery 18070
Palmer (See Easton)
Palmer Township, Northampton 18045
Palmerton, Carbon 18071
Palmyra, Lebanon 17078
Paoli, Chester 19301
Paradise, Lancaster 17562
Paradise Valley, Monroe 18326
Pardeesville, Luzerne 18202
Paris, Washington 15021
Park, Westmoreland 15690
Parker, Armstrong 16049
Parker Ford, Chester 19457
Parkesburg, Chester 19365
Parkhill, Cambria 15945
Parnassus, Westmoreland 15068
Parryville, Carbon 18244
Parsons, Luzerne 18705
Patterson Heights, Beaver 15010
Patton, Cambria 16668
Paupack, Pike 18451
Paxinos, Northumberland 17860
Paxtang, Dauphin 17111
Paxtonia, Dauphin 17112
Paxtonville, Snyder 17861
Peach Bottom, Lancaster 17563
Peach Glen, Adams 17375
Peckville, Lackawanna 18452
Pen Argyl, Northampton 18072
Penbrook (See Harrisburg)
Penfield, Clearfield 15849
Penllyn, Montgomery 19422
Penn, Westmoreland 15675
Penn Hills, Allegheny 15235
Penn Run, Indiana 15765
Penn State University, Centre 16802
Penn Valley, Montgomery 19072
Penn Wynne, Montgomery 19096
Penndel, Bucks 19047
Penns Creek, Snyder 17862
Penns Park, Bucks 18943
Pennsburg, Montgomery 18073
Pennsdale, Lycoming 17756
Pennsylvania Furnace, Centre 16865
Penryn, Lancaster 17564
Pequea, Lancaster 17565
Perkasie, Bucks 18944
Perkiomenville, Montgomery 18074
Perryopolis, Fayette 15473
Petersburg, Huntingdon 16669
Petrolia, Butler 16050
Pgh Int Arprt, Allegheny 15231
Phila (See Philadelphia)
PHILADELPHIA, Philadelphia (See Page 3235)
Philipsburg, Centre 16866
Phoenixville, Montgomery 19453
Phoenixville, Chester 19460
Picture Rocks, Lycoming 17762
Pilgrim Gardens, Delaware 19026
Pillow, Dauphin 17080
Pine Bank, Greene 15352
Pine Forge, Berks 19548
Pine Grove, Schuylkill 17963
Pine Grove Mills, Centre 16868
Pineville, Bucks 18946
Pipersville, Bucks 18947
Pitcairn, Allegheny 15140
Pitman, Schuylkill 17964
PITTSBURGH, Allegheny (See Page 3248)
Pittsfield, Warren 16340
PITTSTON, Luzerne (See Page 3267)
Pittston Township, Luzerne 18640
Plainfield, Cumberland 17081
Plains (See Wilkes Barre)
Plains Township (See Wilkes Barre)
Pleasant Gap, Centre 16823
Pleasant Hall, Franklin 17246
Pleasant Hills, Allegheny 15236
Pleasant Mount, Wayne 18453
Pleasant Unity, Westmoreland 15676
Pleasantville, Venango 16341
Plum, Allegheny 15239
Plumsteadville, Bucks 18949
Plumville, Indiana 16246
Plymouth, Luzerne 18651
Plymouth Meeting, Montgomery 19462
Pocono Lake, Monroe 18347
Pocono Lake, Monroe 18348
Pocono Lake Preserve, Monroe 18348
Pocono Manor, Monroe 18349
Pocono Pines, Monroe 18350
Pocono Summit, Monroe 18346
Pocopson, Chester 19366
Point Marion, Fayette 15474
Point Pleasant, Bucks 18950
Polk, Venango 16342
Pomeroy, Chester 19367
Port Allegany, Mckean 16743
Port Carbon, Schuylkill 17965
Port Clinton, Schuylkill 19549
Port Griffith, Luzerne 18640
Port Matilda, Centre 16870
Port Royal, Juniata 17082
Port Trevorton, Snyder 17864
Portage, Cambria 15946
Porters Sideling, York 17354
Portersville, Butler 16051
Portland, Northampton 18351
Portland Mills, Elk 15853
Pottersdale, Clearfield 16871
Potts Grove, Northumberland 17865
POTTSTOWN, Montgomery (See Page 3269)
Pottsville, Schuylkill 17901
Poyntelle, Wayne 18454
Presto, Allegheny 15142
Preston Park, Wayne 18455
Pricedale, Westmoreland 15072
Primos, Delaware 19018
Primos Secane, Delaware 19018
Pringle, Luzerne 18704
Prompton, Wayne 18456
Prospect, Butler 16052
Prospect Park, Delaware 19076
Prosperity, Washington 15329
Pulaski, Lawrence 16143
Punxsutawney, Jefferson 15767
Puritan, Cambria 15946
Quakake, Schuylkill 18245
Quakertown, Bucks 18951
Quarryville, Lancaster 17566
Quecreek, Somerset 15555
Queen, Bedford 16670
Quentin, Lebanon 17083
Quincy, Franklin 17247
Racine, Beaver 15010
Radnor, Delaware 19008
Railroad, York 17355
Ralston, Lycoming 17763
Ramey, Clearfield 16671
Rankin, Allegheny 15104
Ranshaw, Northumberland 17866
Ransom, Lackawanna 18653
Ravine, Schuylkill 17966
Rea, Washington 15312
READING, Berks (See Page 3270)
Reading Station, Berks 19606
Reamstown, Lancaster 17567
Rebersburg, Centre 16872
Rebuck, Northumberland 17867
Rector, Westmoreland 15677
Red Hill, Montgomery 18073
Red Hill, Montgomery 18076
Red Lion, York 17356
Reeders, Monroe 18352
Reedsville, Mifflin 17084
Refton, Lancaster 17568
Rehrersburg, Berks 19550
Reinholds, Lancaster 17569
Renfrew, Butler 16053
Reno, Venango 16343
Renovo, Clinton 17764
Republic, Fayette 15475
Revere, Bucks 18953
Revloc, Cambria 15948
Rew, Mckean 16744
Rexmont, Lebanon 17085
Reynoldsville, Jefferson 15851
Rheems, Lancaster 17570
Rices Landing, Greene 15357
Riceville, Crawford 16432
Richboro, Bucks 18954
Richeyville, Washington 15358
Richfield, Juniata 17086
Richland, Lebanon 17087
Richlandtown, Bucks 18955
Richmondale, Susquehanna 18421
Riddlesburg, Bedford 16672
Ridgway, Elk 15853
Ridley, Delaware 19070
Ridley Park, Delaware 19078
Riegelsville, Bucks 18077
Rillton, Westmoreland 15678
Rimersburg, Clarion 16248
Ringgold, Jefferson 15770
Ringtown, Schuylkill 17967
Riverside, Northumberland 17868
Rixford, Mckean 16745
Roaring Branch, Tioga 17765
Roaring Brook Twp, Wayne 18436
Roaring Spring, Blair 16673
Robertsdale, Huntingdon 16674
Robesonia, Berks 19551
Robinson, Indiana 15949
Rochester, Beaver 15074
Rochester Mills, Indiana 15771
Rock Glen, Luzerne 18246
Rockhill Furnace, Huntingdon 17249
Rockledge, Montgomery 19046
Rockton, Clearfield 15856
Rockwood, Somerset 15557
Rogersville, Greene 15359
Rohrerstown, Lancaster 17603
Romansville, Chester 19320
Rome, Bradford 18837
Ronco, Fayette 15476
Ronks, Lancaster 17572
Roscoe, Washington 15477
Rose Valley, Delaware 19063
Roseto, Northampton 18013
Roslyn, Montgomery 19001
Rossiter, Indiana 15772
Rossville, York 17358
Roulette, Potter 16746
Rouseville, Venango 16344
Rouzerville, Franklin 17250
Rowland, Pike 18457
Roxbury, Franklin 17251
Royersford, Montgomery 19468
Ruffs Dale, Westmoreland 15679
Rural Ridge, Allegheny 15075
Rural Valley, Armstrong 16249
Ruscombmanor Twp, Berks 19522
Rushland, Bucks 18956
Rushville, Susquehanna 18828
Russell, Warren 16345
Russellton, Allegheny 15076
Rutledge, Delaware 19070
Rydal, Montgomery 19046
S Abington Twp, Lackawanna 18411
S Connellsvl, Fayette 15425
S Williamspor, Lycoming 17702
S Williamsport, Lycoming 17702
Sabinsville, Tioga 16943
Sacramento, Schuylkill 17968
Sadsburyville, Chester 19369
Saegertown, Crawford 16433
Sagamore, Armstrong 16250
Saint Benedict, Cambria 15773
Saint Boniface, Cambria 16675
Saint Clair, Schuylkill 17970
Saint Clairsville, Bedford 16667
Saint Davids, Delaware 19087
Saint Johns, Luzerne 18247
Saint Marys, Elk 15857
Saint Michael, Cambria 15951
Saint Peters, Chester 19470
Saint Petersburg, Clarion 16054
Saint Thomas, Franklin 17252
Salford, Montgomery 18957
Salfordville, Montgomery 18958
Salina, Westmoreland 15680
Salisbury, Somerset 15558
Salix, Cambria 15952
Salladasburg, Lycoming 17740
Salona, Clinton 17767
Saltillo, Huntingdon 17253
Saltsburg, Indiana 15681
Salunga, Lancaster 17538
Sanatoga, Montgomery 19464
Sandy Lake, Mercer 16145
Sandy Ridge, Centre 16677
Sarver, Butler 16055
Sassamansville, Montgomery 19472
Saxonburg, Butler 16056
Saxton, Bedford 16678
Saylorsburg, Monroe 18353
Sayre, Bradford 18840
Scenery Hill, Washington 15360
Schaefferstown, Lebanon 17088
Schellsburg, Bedford 15559
Schenley, Armstrong 15682
Schnecksville, Lehigh 18078
Schuylkill Haven, Schuylkill 17972
Schwenksville, Montgomery 19473
Sciota, Monroe 18354
Scotland, Franklin 17254
Scotrun, Monroe 18355
Scott Township, Lackawanna 18411
Scott Township, Lackawanna 18411
Scottdale, Westmoreland 15683
SCRANTON, Lackawanna (See Page 3275)
Seanor, Somerset 15953
Secane, Delaware 19018
Selinsgrove, Snyder 17870
Sellersville, Bucks 18960
Seltzer, Schuylkill 17974
Seminole, Armstrong 16253
Seneca, Venango 16346
Seven Fields, Butler 16046
Seven Valleys, York 17360
Seward, Westmoreland 15954
Sewickley, Allegheny 15143
Shade Gap, Huntingdon 17255
Shady Grove, Franklin 17256
Shadyside, Allegheny 15232
Shamokin, Northumberland 17872
Shamokin Dam, Snyder 17876
Shanksville, Somerset 15560
Sharon, Mercer 16146
Sharon, Mercer 16148
Sharon Hill, Delaware 19079
Sharpsburg, Allegheny 15215
Sharpsville, Mercer 16150
Shartlesville, Berks 19554
Shavertown, Luzerne 18708
Shawanese, Luzerne 18654
Shawnee, Monroe 18356
Shawnee On Delaware, Monroe 18356
Shawville, Clearfield 16873
Sheakleyville, Mercer 16151
Sheffield, Warren 16347
Shelocta, Indiana 15774
Shenandoah, Schuylkill 17976
Shenango, Mercer 16125
Sheppton, Schuylkill 18248
Shermans Dale, Perry 17090
Shickshinny, Luzerne 18655
Shillington, Berks 19607
Shinglehouse, Potter 16748
Shippensburg, Cumberland 17257
Shippenville, Clarion 16254
Shippingport, Beaver 15077
Shiremanstown, Cumberland 17011
Shirleysburg, Huntingdon 17260
Shoemakersville, Berks 19555
Shohola, Pike 18458
Shrewsbury, York 17361
Shunk, Sullivan 17768
Sidman, Cambria 15955
Sigel, Jefferson 15860
Silver Spring, Lancaster 17575
Silver Spring Township, Cumberland 17050
Silverdale, Bucks 18962
Simpson, Lackawanna 18407
Sinking Spring, Berks 19608
Sinnamahoning, Cameron 15861
Sipesville, Somerset 15561
Six Mile Run, Bedford 16679
Skippack, Montgomery 19474
Skytop, Monroe 18357
Slate Run, Lycoming 17769
Slatedale, Lehigh 18079
Slatington, Lehigh 18080
Slickville, Westmoreland 15684
Sligo, Clarion 16255
Slippery Rock, Butler 16057
Slovan, Washington 15078
Smethport, Mckean 16749
Smicksburg, Indiana 16256
Smithfield, Fayette 15478
Smithmill, Clearfield 16680
Smithton, Westmoreland 15479
Smock, Fayette 15480
Smokerun, Clearfield 16681
Smoketown, Lancaster 17576
Snow Shoe, Centre 16874
Snydersburg, Clarion 16257
Snydertown, Bradford 16910
Snydertown, Northumberland 17877
Solebury, Bucks 18963
Somerset, Somerset 15501
Sonestown, Sullivan 17758
Soudersburg, Lancaster 17572
Souderton, Montgomery 18964
South Abington Township, Lackawanna 18411
South Canaan, Wayne 18459
South Fork, Cambria 15956
South Gibson, Susquehanna 18842
South Heidelberg Twp, Berks 19608
South Heights, Beaver 15081
South Hills, Allegheny 15216
South Montrose, Susquehanna 18843
South Mountain, Franklin 17261
South Park, Allegheny 15129
South Sterling, Wayne 18445
South Waverly, Bradford 18840
South Williamsport, Lycoming 17702
Southampton, Bucks 18954
Southampton, Bucks 18966
SOUTHEASTERN, Chester (See Page 3277)
Southview, Washington 15361
Southwest, Westmoreland 15685
Spangler, Cambria 15775
Spartansburg, Crawford 16434
Spinnerstown, Bucks 18968
Spraggs, Greene 15362
Sprankle Mills, Jefferson 15776
Spring Brook Township, Lackawanna 18444
Spring Church, Armstrong 15686
Spring City, Chester 19475
Spring Creek, Warren 16436
Spring Glen, Schuylkill 17978
Spring Grove, York 17354
Spring Grove, York 17362
Spring House, Montgomery 19436

Spring House, Montgomery 19477
Spring Mills, Centre 16875
Spring Mount, Montgomery 19478
Spring Run, Franklin 17262
Springboro, Crawford 16435
Springdale, Allegheny 15144
Springettsbury Township, York 17402
Springfield, Delaware 19064
Springs, Somerset 15562
Springtown, Bucks 18081
Springville, Susquehanna 18844
Sproul, Blair 16682
Spruce Creek, Huntingdon 16683
Squirrel Hill, Allegheny 15217
St Clairsville, Bedford 16667
St Davids, Delaware 19087
Stahlstown, Westmoreland 15687
Star Junction, Fayette 15482
Starford, Indiana 15777
Starlight, Wayne 18461
Starrucca, Wayne 18462
STATE COLLEGE, Centre (See Page 3277)
State Line, Franklin 17263
Steelton, Dauphin 17113
Steelville, Chester 19310
Sterling, Wayne 18463
Stevens, Lancaster 17578
Stevensville, Bradford 18845
Stewartstown, York 17363
Stillwater, Columbia 17878
Stockdale, Washington 15483
Stockertown, Northampton 18083
Stockertown Township, Northampton 18040
Stoneboro, Mercer 16153
Stony Run, Berks 19529
Stouchsburg, Berks 19567
Stowe, Montgomery 19464
Stoystown, Somerset 15563
Strabane, Washington 15363
Strafford, Delaware 19087
Strasburg, Lancaster 17579
Strattanville, Clarion 16258
Strausstown, Berks 19559
Strongstown, Indiana 15957
Stroudsburg, Monroe 18360
Stump Creek, Jefferson 15863
Sturgeon, Allegheny 15082
Sugar Grove, Warren 16350
Sugar Notch, Luzerne 18706
Sugar Run, Bradford 18846
Sugarloaf, Luzerne 18249
Summerdale, Cumberland 17093
Summerhill, Cambria 15958
Summerville, Jefferson 15864
Summit Hill, Carbon 18250
Summit Station, Schuylkill 17979
Sumneytown, Montgomery 18084
Sunbury, Northumberland 17801
Suplee, Chester 19371
Susquehanna, Susquehanna 18847
Sutersville, Westmoreland 15083
Swarthmore, Delaware 19081
Swatara, Dauphin 17111
Swatara Township, Lebanon 17046
Sweet Valley, Luzerne 18656
Swengel, Union 17880
Swiftwater, Monroe 18370
Swissvale, Allegheny 15218
Swoyersville, Luzerne 18704
Sybertsville, Luzerne 18251
Sycamore, Greene 15364
Sykesville, Jefferson 15865
Sylvan Dell, Lycoming 17702
Sylvania, Bradford 16945
Tafton, Pike 18464
Talmage, Lancaster 17580
Tamaqua, Schuylkill 18252
Tamiment, Pike 18371
Tannersville, Monroe 18372
Tarentum, Allegheny 15084
Tarrs, Westmoreland 15688
Tatamy, Northampton 18085
Tatamy Borough, Northampton 18045
Taylor, Lackawanna 18517
Taylorstown, Washington 15365
Telford, Montgomery 18964
Telford, Montgomery 18969
Temple, Berks 19560
Templeton, Armstrong 16259
Terre Hill, Lancaster 17581
Thomasville, York 17364
Thompson, Susquehanna 18465
Thompsontown, Juniata 17094
Thorndale, Chester 19372
Thornhurst, Wayne 18424
Thornton, Delaware 19373
Three Springs, Huntingdon 17264
Throop, Lackawanna 18512
Tidioute, Warren 16351
Timblin, Jefferson 15778
Tioga, Tioga 16946
Tiona, Warren 16352
Tionesta, Forest 16353
Tipton, Blair 16684
Tire Hill, Somerset 15959
Titusville, Crawford 16354
Tobyhanna, Monroe 18466
Todd, Huntingdon 16685
Topton, Berks 19562
Torrance, Westmoreland 15779
Toughkenamon, Chester 19374
Towanda, Bradford 18848
Tower City, Schuylkill 17980
Townville, Crawford 16360
Trafford, Westmoreland 15085
Trainer, Delaware 19061
Transfer, Mercer 16154
Trappe, Montgomery 19426
Tredyffrin, Chester 19312
Treichlers, Northampton 18086
Tremont, Schuylkill 17981
Tresckow, Carbon 18254
Trevorton, Northumberland 17881
Trevose, Bucks 19053
Trexlertown, Lehigh 18087
Trooper, Montgomery 19403
Trout Run, Lycoming 17771
Troutville, Clearfield 15866
Troxelville, Snyder 17882
Troy, Bradford 16947
Trucksville, Luzerne 18708
Trumbauersville, Bucks 18970
Tullytown, Bucks 19007
Tunkhannock, Wyoming 18657
Turbotville, Northumberland 17772
Turkey City, Clarion 16058
Turtle Creek, Allegheny 15145
Turtlepoint, Mckean 16750
Tuscarora, Schuylkill 17982
Twin Rocks, Cambria 15960
Tyler Hill, Wayne 18469
Tylersburg, Clarion 16361
Tylersport, Montgomery 18971
Tylersville, Clinton 17747
Tyrone, Blair 16686
Uledi, Fayette 15484
Ulster, Bradford 18850
Ulysses, Potter 16948
Union City, Erie 16438
Union Dale, Susquehanna 18470
Uniontown, Fayette 15401
Unionville, Chester 19375
United, Westmoreland 15689
Unity House, Pike 18373
Unityville, Lycoming 17774
University Park, Centre 16802
Upland, Delaware 19015
Upper Black Eddy, Bucks 18972
Upper Chichester, Delaware 19013
Upper Chichester, Delaware 19013
Upper Darby, Delaware 19082
Upper Gwynedd, Montgomery 19446
Upper Holland, Bucks 19047
Upper Makefield, Bucks 18940
Upper Saint Clair, Allegheny 15241
Upper St Clair, Allegheny 15241
Upperstrasburg, Franklin 17265
Uppr Moreland, Montgomery 19040
Ursina, Somerset 15424
Ursina, Somerset 15485
Utica, Venango 16362
Uwchland, Chester 19480
Valencia, Butler 16059
Valier, Jefferson 15780
VALLEY FORGE, Chester (See Page 3278)
Valley Township, Chester 19320
Valley View, Schuylkill 17983
Van Meter, Westmoreland 15479
Van Voorhis, Washington 15366
Vanderbilt, Fayette 15486
Vandergrift, Westmoreland 15690
Vandling, Susquehanna 18421
Vanport, Beaver 15009
Venango, Crawford 16440
Venetia, Washington 15367
Venus, Venango 16364
Verona, Allegheny 15147
Vestaburg, Washington 15368
Vicksburg, Union 17883
Villa Maria, Lawrence 16155
Villanova, Delaware 19085
Vintondale, Cambria 15961
Virginville, Berks 19564
Volant, Lawrence 16156
Vowinckel, Clarion 16260
W Cnshohocken, Montgomery 19428
W Hazleton, Luzerne 18202
Wabash, Allegheny 15220
Wagontown, Chester 19376
Wall, Allegheny 15148
Wallaceton, Clearfield 16876
Wallingford, Delaware 19086
Walnut Bottom, Cumberland 17266
Walnutport, Northampton 18088
Walston, Jefferson 15781
Waltersburg, Fayette 15488
Wampum, Lawrence 16157
Wapwallopen, Luzerne 18660
Warfordsburg, Fulton 17267
Warminster, Bucks 18974
Warren, Warren 16365
Warren Center, Bradford 18851
WARRENDALE, Allegheny (See Page 3278)
Warrington, Bucks 18976
Warrior Run, Luzerne 18706
Warriors Mark, Huntingdon 16877
Warwick, Bucks 18974
Washington, Washington 15301
Washington Boro, Lancaster 17582
Washington Crossing, Bucks 18977
Washington Xing, Bucks 18977
Washingtonville, Montour 17884
Waterfall, Fulton 16689
Waterford, Erie 16441
Waterman, Indiana 15748
Waterville, Lycoming 17776
Watsontown, Northumberland 17777
Wattsburg, Erie 16442
Waverly, Lackawanna 18471
Waymart, Wayne 18472
Wayne, Delaware 19080
Waynesboro, Franklin 17268
Waynesburg, Greene 15370
Weatherly, Carbon 18255
Webster, Westmoreland 15087
Weedville, Elk 15868
Weikert, Union 17885
Weissport, Carbon 18235
Wellersburg, Somerset 15564
Wells Tannery, Fulton 16691
Wellsboro, Tioga 16901
Wellsville, York 17365
Wendel, Westmoreland 15691
Wernersville, Berks 19565
Wescosville, Lehigh 18106
West Abington Township, Lackawanna 18414
West Alexander, Washington 15376
West Aliquippa, Beaver 15001
West Bradford, Chester 19320
West Brandywine, Chester 19320
West Brandywine, Chester 19320
West Bridgewater, Beaver 15009
West Bristol, Bucks 19007
West Burlington Township, Bradford 16947
WEST CHESTER, Chester (See Page 3278)
West Decatur, Clearfield 16878
West Easton, Northampton 18042
West Elizabeth, Allegheny 15088
West Finley, Washington 15377
West Grove, Chester 19390
West Hanover, Dauphin 17112
West Hazleton, Luzerne 18202
West Hickory, Forest 16370
West Homestead, Allegheny 15120
West Lawn, Berks 19609
West Lebanon, Indiana 15783
West Leechburg, Armstrong 15656
West Leisenring, Fayette 15489
West Manchester Twp, York 17408
West Middlesex, Mercer 16159
West Middletown, Washington 15379
WEST MIFFLIN, Allegheny (See Page 3281)
West Milton, Union 17886
West Newton, Westmoreland 15089
West Pennsboro, Cumberland 17015
West Pittsburg, Lawrence 16160
West Pittston, Luzerne 18643
West Point, Montgomery 19486
West Reading, Berks 19611
West Salisbury, Somerset 15565
West Springfield, Erie 16443
West Sunbury, Butler 16061
West View, Allegheny 15229
West Willow, Lancaster 17583
West Wyoming, Luzerne 18644
West York, York 17404
Westfield, Potter 16927
Westfield, Tioga 16950
Westford, Mercer 16134
Westland, Washington 15378
Westline, Mckean 16740
Westmoreland City, Westmoreland 15692
Weston, Luzerne 18256
Westover, Clearfield 16692
Westport, Clinton 17778
Westtown, Chester 19395
Wexford, Allegheny 15090
Wheatlandyork, Mercer 16161
White, Fayette 15490
White Deer, Union 17887
White Haven, Luzerne 18661
White Mills, Wayne 18473
White Oak, Allegheny 15131
Whitehall, Lehigh 18052
Whitney, Westmoreland 15693
Whitsett, Fayette 15473
Wickhaven, Fayette 15492
Wiconisco, Dauphin 17097
Widnoon, Armstrong 16261
Wilburton, Columbia 17888
Wilcox, Elk 15870
Wildwood, Allegheny 15091
WILKES BARRE, Luzerne (See Page 3281)
Wilkes Barre Township (See Wilkes Barre)
Wilkinsburg, Allegheny 15221
William Penn Annex East, Philadelphia 19106
William Penn Annex West, Philadelphia 19107
Williams Township, Northampton 18042
Williamsburg, Blair 16693
WILLIAMSPORT, Lycoming (See Page 3284)
Williamstown, Dauphin 17098
Willow Grove, Montgomery 19090
Willow Hill, Franklin 17271
Willow Street, Lancaster 17584
Wilmerding, Allegheny 15148
Wilmore, Cambria 15962
Wilmot Township, Sullivan 18614
Wilpen, Westmoreland 15658
Winburne, Clearfield 16879
Wind Gap, Northampton 18091
Wind Ridge, Greene 15380
Windber, Somerset 15963
Windsor, York 17366
Winfield, Union 17889
Wingate, Centre 16823
Witmer, Lancaster 17585
Womelsdorf, Berks 19567
Wood, Bedford 16694
Woodbury, Bedford 16695
Woodland, Clearfield 16881
Woodlyn, Delaware 19094
Woodward, Centre 16882
Woolrich, Clinton 17779
Worcester, Montgomery 19490
Wormleysburg, Cumberland 17043
Worthington, Armstrong 16262
Worthville, Jefferson 15784
Woxall, Montgomery 18979
Wrightsville, York 17368
Wyalusing, Bradford 18853
Wyano, Westmoreland 15695
Wycombe, Bucks 18980
Wyncote, Montgomery 19095
Wyndmoor, Montgomery 19038
Wynnewood, Montgomery 19096
Wyoming, Luzerne 18644
Wyomissing, Berks 19610
Wysox, Bradford 18854
Yardley, Bucks 19067
Yatesboro, Armstrong 16263
Yatesville, Luzerne 18640
Yeadon, Delaware 19050
Yeagertown, Mifflin 17099
Yoe, York 17313
YORK, York (See Page 3285)
York Haven, York 17370
York New Salem, York 17371
York Springs, Adams 17372
Yorkana, York 17406
Youngstown, Westmoreland 15696
Youngsville, Warren 16371
Youngwood, Westmoreland 15697
Yukon, Westmoreland 15698
Zelienople, Butler 16063
Zerbe, Schuylkill 17981
Zieglersville, Montgomery 19492
Zieglerville, Montgomery 19492
Zion Grove, Schuylkill 17985
Zionhill, Bucks 18981
Zionsville, Lehigh 18092
Zullinger, Franklin 17272

ALLENTOWN PA

General Delivery 18105

POST OFFICE BOXES MAIN OFFICE STATIONS AND BRANCHES

Box No.s
9A - 9B 18105
B - O 18105
328A - 328A 18105
1260C - 1260C 18105
1910C - 1910C 18105
FC - FC 18105
1 - 1999 18105
3001 - 3880 18106
4000 - 9422 18105
90001 - 92005 18109

RURAL ROUTES

01, 03, 08, 11, 13, 17, 22 18104
05, 09, 12, 14, 16, 19, 21 18106

NAMED STREETS

Aberdeen Cir 18104
Abigail Ln 18104
Acorn Ave 18103
Adams Is 18109
Adams Ln 18109
E Adams St 18103
N Adams St 18104
S Adams St 18104
W Adams St 18103
Agnes Dr 18103
Aiden Dr 18104
Airport Rd 18109
Airport Center Dr 18109
S Albert St
  1-99 18109
  900-2499 18103
  2501-2599 18103
N Albright Ave 18104
Alex Ct 18103
Alexander Dr 18104
Algonquin Trl 18104
S Alice St 18103
Allen Ave 18103
Allen St 18104
E Allen St 18109
W Allen St
  1-1699 18102
  1700-2999 18104
Allenbrook Dr 18103
Allentown Dr 18109
Allison Ln 18104
W Allorner St 18104
Alma Dr 18103
Alton Ave & St 18103
Amanda St 18102
Ambassador Dr 18106
American Pkwy 18101
American Pkwy NE 18109
Americus Ave & Dr 18103
Amherst Rd 18104
Andrea Dr
  2600-2899 18103
  5200-5499 18106
Andrew St 18102
Androsky Rd 18104
Angus Pl 18104
Anjou Rd 18104
S Ann St 18109
Antler Ct 18104
Apache Ct 18104
Appel St 18103
Arcadia Ave 18103
Arch St SW 18103
N Arch St 18104
S Arch St 18103
S Armour Ct & St 18103
Ascot Cir 18103
Ashley Ln 18103
Aspen Ct & Dr 18104
Aster Ct & St 18104
S Aubrey St
  101-397 18109
  399-699 18109
  1900-2399 18103
Auburn St 18103
Auden Ln 18104
S Austin St 18109
Avon Rd 18104
Azalea Rd 18103
Baker Dr 18103
Baldwin Ct 18103
Balsam St 18104
Barber St 18103
Barn Swallow Ln 18104
E & W Barner St 18103
Barnes Ln 18103
Barness Dr 18109
Barnsdale Rd 18103
Barnside Ct & Rd 18103
Barrington Dr 18104
Barrington Ln 18103
Basin St 18103
Bastian Ln 18104
Bayard St 18104
Beacon Rd 18103
Becker St 18106
Bedford Ct 18104
Beechwood Ln 18103
Belford Rd 18103
Bell Ave 18103
Bellair Ct & Dr 18103
Bellevue St 18102
Bellflower Way 18104
Belmont Ave 18103
Belmont Cir 18106
Belmont St 18104
Benner Rd 18104
Benton St 18103
Berger St 18103
N & S Berks St 18104
Bert Ln 18104
Beth Ln 18103
Beverly Dr
  400-699 18104
  900-999 18103
Bevin Dr 18103
Birch Ave 18103
Birchwood Dr & Rd 18103
Birdie St 18106
Bishop Rd 18103
Black Gum Dr 18103
Blaise Ct 18104
N & S Blank St 18102
Blue Barn Rd 18104
Blue Bird Ln 18104
Blue Heron Dr 18103
Blue Sage Dr 18104
Bobalew Trl 18103
Bogie Ave 18106
Box Elder Rd 18103
N Boyer St 18102
Bradford Ln 18104
N Bradford St 18109
S Bradford St
  1-599 18109
  1000-2499 18103
Brandywine Rd 18104
Brassie St 18106
Brentwood Ct 18104
Brewster Ct 18104
Briarcliff Rd 18104
Briarcliff Ter 18103
Briarwood Ct 18104
Briarwood Ln 18103
N Brick St 18102
S Brick St 18103
Brickyard Rd 18104
Bridge St 18102
Bridgets Way 18103
Bridle Path Rd 18103
N Broad St
  100-1599 18104
  700-798 18106
  800-899 18106
Broadway 18104
  4900-7699 18106
Broder St SW 18103
Brook Ave 18103
N Brook St 18109
S Brook St 18109
E & W Brookdale St 18103
Brookhaven Dr E & W 18103
N Brookside Rd 18106
Broome St 18102
Brown St 18104
W Brush St 18102
N Bryan St
  101-199 18101
  201-297 18102
  299-399 18102
  401-699 18102
Bryant St 18104
Buchman St 18104
Buck Trail Rd 18104
Buckingham Dr 18103
Bulldog Dr 18104
Bulwer St 18104
Burrell Blvd 18104
Business Park Ln 18109
Buttonwood St 18103
Butz Ln 18103
Byfield St 18103
Byrd Ave 18103
Cambridge Cir 18104
E Cambridge St 18109
Camelot Dr 18103
Cameo Dr 18104
Capital St 18103
S Carbon St 18103
Cardinal Ct 18104
E Carey St 18109
W Carey St 18102
S Carl St 18109
Carldon St 18103
N Carlisle St 18109
S Carlisle St
  1-600 18109
  602-698 18109
  1000-1012 18103
  1014-1123 18103
  1125-1199 18103
Carole Ln 18104
Caroline Rd 18103
W Carrott St 18102
Cartier Dr 18104
Cascade Dr 18109
Castle Ct 18103
Catalina Ave 18103
Catasauqua Ave 18102
Catasauqua Rd 18109
Cathedral Ln 18104
Catherine Ave 18103
Cedar Ln 18103
E Cedar St 18109
W Cedar St
  201-297 18102
  299-1699 18102
  1700-3299 18104
Cedar Creek Blvd 18104
N Cedar Crest Blvd 18104
S Cedar Crest Blvd
  40-108 18104
  110-112 18104
  114-214 18104
  301-397 18104
  399-2500 18103
  2502-2698 18103
Cedar Hill Dr 18109
S Cedarbrook Rd
  1-97 18104
  99-399 18104
  4400-4498 18103
  4500-4599 18103
Cedarwood Rd 18104
Celandine Dr 18104
Celia Dr 18106
Center Pl 18103
Center St 18104
Cetronia Rd
  200-498 18104
  500-599 18104
  4900-7699 18106
Chalmette Rd 18104
Chapel Ave 18103
Chapmans Rd
  4700-5800 18104
  5802-5998 18104
  6300-6599 18106
Charles Dr & St 18104
Chatter Way 18103
Chelsea Ln 18104
Chester St 18103
Chestertown Rd 18104
Chestnut Dr 18104
Chestnut St
  101-131 18101
  133-299 18101
  400-499 18102
  500-599 18101
  701-797 18102
  799-1199 18102
Chew St
  100-1638 18102
  1640-1698 18102
  1700-4200 18104
  4202-4298 18104
E Chew St 18109
W Chew St 18104
Chippewa Dr 18104
Chris Ln 18103
Church Rd
  1500-1638 18103
  1639-1639 18104
  1640-1798 18103
  1701-1799 18103
  1801-1897 18104
  1899-2099 18104
N Church St
  100-199 18101
  200-499 18102
S Church St 18103
Churchill Ln 18106
E Clair St 18109
Clarence Ave 18109
Clay St 18102
E Clay St 18109
Clear Way 18103
Clearview Cir 18103
Clearwood Dr 18103
Cleveland St 18103
Clifford St
  600-699 18103
  1801-1899 18104
Club Ave 18109
Club Dr 18103
Club House Ln 18106
Cobbler Ln 18104
Coffeetown Rd 18104
Cold Spring Rd 18103
E Coleman St 18103
College Dr
  1-599 18104
  601-2899 18104
  700-798 18103
  2800-2898 18104
College Ln 18103
N College St 18102
S College St 18104
College Heights Blvd 18104
Colonial Ct 18104
Colonial Rd 18109
Colorado St 18103
E Columbia St 18109
W Columbia St 18104
Concord Ave 18103
E Congress St 18109
W Congress St
  1300-1699 18102
  1700-3799 18104
Constitution Dr 18103
Coolidge St 18104
Coplay Creek Rd 18104
S Corn St 18103
Cornell Rd 18104
Cornerstone Rd 18106
Coronado St 18103
Cottonwood Cir 18104
Cottonwood Ct 18103
Cottonwood St 18104
Country Ln 18104
Country Club Rd
  1200-1699 18106
  2600-3632 18103
  3634-3642 18103
E Court St 18109
W Court St
  101-297 18101
  299-1199 18101
  1201-1397 18102
  1399-1699 18102
Courtney Pl 18104
Covelle Rd 18104
Covenant Ct 18106
Coventry Cir 18103
Coventry Rd 18104
Covered Bridge Ln & Xing 18104
Crackersport Rd 18104
E Crairedg St 18109
Creek Rd 18104
Cressman Dr 18104
Crest Ave & Ln 18104
Crest View Dr 18103
Crocus Ln 18103
W Croneren St 18102
Crownwood St 18103
E & W Cumberland St 18103
Custer St 18104
Cypress Ave 18103
Cypress St 18106
Dale St 18102
Dale Trl 18104
Daniel St 18104
Daniels Dr 18106
Danweber Way 18104
Dartmouth Rd 18104
N Dauphin St 18109
S Dauphin St
  1-299 18109
  301-399 18109
  1105-1109 18103
  1111-2499 18103
Dawes St 18104
Dayspring Dr 18106
Debbie Ln 18103
Deerfield Dr 18104
S Delaware Ave & St 18103
Dell St 18103
N & S Delp St 18109
E Dent St 18109
Devon Cir 18104
Devonshire Rd 18103
Dewalt St 18103
Diamond Ave 18103
Diane Blvd 18109
Diehl Ct 18104
Divot Dr 18106
Dixon St 18103
Doe Trail Rd 18104
Dogwood Ln 18103
Dogwood Trl
  3800-3899 18103
  5100-5199 18104
Dominic Dr 18103
Donald St 18103
Donna Dr 18104
Donna Jo Way 18109
Doris Dr 18106
Dorney Ave 18103
Dorney Park Rd 18104
Dorothy Way 18109
Dorset Ct & Rd 18104
Douglas Rd 18103
Dove Ter 18106
Downyflake Ln 18103
Driftwood Ln 18103
Driver Pl 18106
Duffield Ct 18103
Dulles Rd 18103
Duxbury Ct 18104
Dylan Dr 18104
Eagle St 18106
Earls Ct 18103
Early St 18102
S East St 18103
E Eaton St 18103
Eck Rd 18104
Edgemont Dr 18103
Edgewood Ridge Ct 18106
Edinburgh Rd 18104
Edison St 18101
E Edison St 18109
Edward Ave 18103
S Edward St
  100-199 18104
  800-999 18103
Egge St 18102
Ehret Ln 18103
Eisenhower Ave 18103
Elbow Ln 18103
S Elizabeth St 18103
Elliger St 18102
N Ellsworth St 18109
S Ellsworth St
  1-599 18109
  1100-1298 18103
  1300-2300 18103
  2302-2310 18103
Elm Ct
  300-2799 18104
  2800-2999 18103
Elm Dr 18103
Elm Rd 18104
E Elm St 18109
W Elm St
  1600-1699 18102
  1700-2098 18104
  2100-2699 18104
E & W Emaus Ave 18103
Emerson Ln 18104
Emerson St
  100-599 18104
  900-999 18103
N Emery St 18102
E Emmaus Ave 18103
Emmett St 18102
W Erie St 18103
Erney St 18103
Essex Rd 18103
Estate Dr 18103
W Ethel St 18103
Eton Rd 18104
Euclid St
  500-599 18103
  2400-2499 18104
Eugene St 18103
Evangate Dr 18104
Evans St 18103
Evening Star Ter 18104
Evergreen Rd 18104
Exeter Cir & Rd 18103
N Fair St 18102
S Fair St 18103
Fairbanks St 18103
Fairfax St 18103
Fairfield Dr N 18103
E Fairmont St 18109
W Fairmont St
  1400-1699 18102
  1700-3099 18104
S Fairview Rd 18103
E Fairview St 18109
W Fairview St
  460A-460D 18102
  400-1500 18102
  1502-1598 18102
  1800-2799 18104
  2800-2999 18103
  3200-3499 18104
  3501-3599 18104
Fairway Ln 18106
Faith Cir 18106
Fallow Dr 18104
Farm Dr 18104
Farm Bureau Rd 18106
Farmington Cir 18104
Fashion Dr 18109
S Fawn St 18103
Fawn Trail Rd 18104
Fayette St 18103
E & W Federal St 18103
N Fenwick St 18109
Fern Ln 18103
Fern St 18102
N Fern St 18102
Fernor St 18103
Fetters Ln 18106
Fieldstone St 18106
N Filbert St
  1-599 18109
  1600-1899 18104
S Filbert St
  1-99 18109
  1001-1101 18103
  1103-2499 18103
S Filmore St 18103
Fir Rd 18104
S Firr St 18103
Fish Hatchery Rd 18103
Flexer Ave & Ct 18103
Focht Ave 18104
E Ford St 18109
Forest Dr
  700-1099 18103
  1400-1499 18104
Forest Ln 18103
Forest Knoll Ct 18106
Forsythia Ln 18104
Foundry St 18102
N Fountain St 18102
S Fountain St
  100-199 18102
  1000-2499 18103
  1316-1-1316-2 18103
  1318-1-1318-2 18103
  1320-1-1320-2 18103
  1322-1-1322-2 18103
  1324-1-1324-2 18103
  1326-1-1326-2 18103
  1328-1-1328-2 18103
  1330-1-1330-2 18103
Fox Meadow Dr 18104
Fox Run Dr 18103
Francis St 18103
Frankenfield St 18104
N & S Franklin St 18102
Frederick St 18104
Fretz Ave 18103
N Front St 18102
S Front St 18103
Fugazzotto Dr 18104
Fullerton Ave 18102
N & S Fulton St 18102
Furnace St 18102
W Gage St 18102
Gail Ave 18103
Ganz Ln 18103
Garden Ave 18103
Gaskill St 18103
Genesee St 18103
George St 18102
N Gilmore St 18109
S Gilmore St
  100-199 18109
  1000-1198 18103
  1200-2099 18103
Girard Ave 18104
Glacier Ct 18104
Glenlivet Dr 18106
Glenwood St SW 18103
N Glenwood St 18104
S Glenwood St
  1-599 18104
  601-699 18104
  700-899 18103
Glick Ave 18103
N Godfrey St 18109
Golf Course Rd 18104
E Gordon St 18109
W Gordon St
  100-1599 18102
  2100-3000 18104

3002-3098 18104
Grace St 18103
N Graham St 18109
Grammes Rd
1-99 18103
600-699 18104
1800-1899 18103
4700-4899 18104
Grandview Ave 18104
Grange Rd 18106
Grant St 18102
Grant Way 18106
Grape St 18104
N Grape St 18109
E Green St 18109
W Green St
100-1199 18102
1201-1499 18102
1701-1797 18104
1799-2099 18104
Green Acres Dr 18103
Green Tree Ln 18104
Greenawalds Ave 18104
Greenbriar Ln 18103
Greenleaf Cir 18103
E Greenleaf St 18109
W Greenleaf St
300-1699 18102
1700-3199 18104
Greens Dr 18106
Greenwood Rd & St 18103
Greystone St 18106
Grove Rd 18109
Grove St 18104
Guth Rd 18104
Haasadahl Rd 18106
Haines Mill Rd 18104
N Hall St 18102
S Hall St
100-199 18101
700-2100 18103
2102-2398 18103
N Halstead St 18109
S Halstead St
1-199 18109
1200-2000 18103
2002-2098 18103
Hamilton Blvd
2601-2697 18104
2699-2899 18104
2900-4800 18103
4801-4911 18106
4912-6800 18106
6802-6898 18106
7201-7203 18195
Hamilton St
101-441 18101
442-1198 18101
442-442 18105
443-1199 18101
1200-1699 18102
1700-3299 18104
E Hamilton St 18109
Hamilton Boulevard
Byp 18103
Hampshire Ct 18104
Hampstead Rd 18103
Hampton Ct 18103
Hampton Rd 18104
Hangar Pl 18109
Hanover Ave 18109
Hanover Dr 18106
Hardner Dr 18103
Harold Ave 18104
Harriet Ave 18103
Harrison St 18103
Harvest Way 18104
Hausman Ave 18103
Hausman Rd 18104
Hawthorn Rd 18103
Hawthorne Cir 18104
Hayden Cir 18109
S Hays St 18103
N Hazel St 18102
S Hazel St 18101
Heather Ct 18104
N & S Hedgerow Dr 18103
Hedgewood Dr 18106
Helen Ave, Dr & St 18104
Hemlock Ct 18106
Hemlock Rd 18104
Hemlock St 18106
Herbert Dr 18104
Herbert St 18103
S Herelian St 18103
Herman Ln 18104
Hess Cir 18103
Hickory Cir 18103
Hickory Ln
300-398 18102
800-898 18106
900-2600 18106
2602-7098 18106
E Hickory St 18109
W Hickory St
700-899 18101
1200-1299 18102
1301-1399 18102
Hidden Valley Rd 18103
High Saddle Ln 18104
Highland Ct 18103
E Highland St 18109
W Highland St
1200-1699 18102
1700-3899 18104
Highpoint Dr 18103
Hill Dr
900-1099 18103
5800-5899 18104
W Hill St 18102
Hillcrest Ave 18103
Hillside Ln 18104
Hillside Rd 18103
Hilltop Rd 18106
S Hillview Dr & Rd 18103
Hoe St 18103
Holiday Dr 18104
Hollow Ct 18104
Holly Rd 18106
Honeysuckle Ln & Rd 18103
Honochick Dr 18104
Hoover Ave 18109
Hope Ln 18106
Hopewell Dr 18104
Horadeli Rd 18106
S Howard Ct 18103
N Howard St
2-98 18101
200-699 18102
S Howard St
1-100 18102
102-198 18102
1000-2399 18103
2401-2599 18103
E Howe St 18109
W Howe St
1300-1398 18102
1801-1899 18104
Huckleberry Rd 18104
Huron St 18103
S Idaho St 18103
Illingsworth St 18103
Imperial Dr
1-99 18109
3000-3099 18103
Imperial Way
7601-7699 18106
7660-7660 18195
Independence Ct 18104
Indigo Way 18104
Industrial Blvd 18106
N Ingram St 18109
S Inn St 18109
Innovation Way 18109
Irma Dr 18109
Iron Bridge Rd 18104
Iron Pigs Way 18109
Ironwood Ln 18103
Iroquois Trl 18104
N Irving St 18109
Ithaca St 18103
Ives St 18109
Ivy Ln 18106
N Ivy St 18102
S Ivy St 18103
Jabber Ln 18104
Jackson St 18102
Jade Ln 18104
Jaime Cir 18106
James Dr 18104
James St 18102
Jamestown Ct 18104
N Jane St 18109
S Jane St 18109
W Jane St 18104
N Jasper St 18109
Jay St 18109
Jeanette Cir 18104
Jefferson Ave 18103
N Jefferson St 18102
S Jefferson St
1-299 18102
700-1499 18103
1501-1599 18103
Jennie Ave 18104
N & S Jerome St 18109
Jervin Dr 18104
Joanne Marie Way 18109
E & W Johnston St 18103
Jolan Dr 18109
Jonagold Rd 18104
E Jonathan St 18109
W Jonathan St
1500-1599 18102
1700-1899 18104
N Jordan Dr & St 18102
Joseph Cir 18104
Joyce Cir 18106
E & W Juniata St 18103
Jute St 18103
N Jute St 18102
S Jute St 18103
Kaitlyn Rd 18103
Kart Dr 18106
Kathleen Ave 18103
Kay Dr 18106
N Kearney St 18109
E Keats St 18109
W Keats St 18104
Keck St 18103
Keebler Way 18106
Kemmerer Ln 18104
Kenneth Dr 18104
Keystone Ave & Rd 18103
Kilmer Ave 18104
Kingsbridge Ln 18103
Kingston Pl 18104
N Kiowa St 18109
Klein St 18103
Knauss Cir 18103
Knight St 18104
Kohler Dr 18103
Kraft Dr 18104
Kressler Rd 18103
Kris Dr 18104
Kristin Ln 18104
Krocks Ct 18106
Krocks Rd
1-299 18104
500-655 18106
N Krocks Rd 18106
S Krocks Rd 18106
Kurt Dr 18104
Kurtz St 18102
N Lacrosse St 18109
Ladybug Ln 18104
N & S Lafayette St 18104
Lamb Ter 18106
Lancaster Ave 18103
Lanze Ln 18103
Lapp Rd 18104
Larkspur Dr 18103
Latta St 18104
N Law St
1-97 18101
99-199 18101
200-699 18102
S Law St
1-29 18101
1900-2699 18103
Lawfer Ave 18104
Lawrence Ct 18102
Lawrence Way 18104
N & S Leh St 18104
Lehigh Ave 18103
Lehigh Ct 18106
Lehigh Pkwy E 18103
Lehigh Pkwy N 18103
Lehigh Pkwy S 18103
Lehigh St
200-399 18102
400-3499 18103
Leicester Pl 18104
Lenape Trl 18104
W Leslie St 18103
N & S Levan St 18102
Levans Rd 18104
N Lewis St 18102
S Lewis St 18103
E & W Lexington St 18103
Liberator Ave 18103
Liberty Ln 18106
Liberty St 18104
E Liberty St 18109
W Liberty St
1-1699 18102
1719-1997 18104
1999-3199 18104
Lichtenwalner Ave 18103
Lilac Dr 18104
Lilac Rd 18103
Lime Kiln Rd 18104
N Limestone St 18102
Lincoln Ave 18103
Lincoln Dr 18103
Lincoln St 18102
Linda Ln 18103
Lindberg Ave 18103
Linden Ct 18103
E Linden St 18109
W Linden St
100-116 18101
118-299 18101
301-333 18101
335-397 18102
399-498 18102
500-999 18101
1000-1599 18102
1601-1699 18102
1700-1798 18104
1800-4099 18104
4101-4199 18104
Linden Hollow Ln 18104
Lisa Ct 18104
Lisa Ln
2400-2499 18104
4300-4699 18103
Little Cedar Ct 18104
Little John Ln 18103
E Livingston St 18109
W Livingston St
1200-1699 18102
1700-3099 18104
Lloyd St 18109
Lochhaven Ct & St 18106
Lois Ln 18104
Lone Ln 18104
Lone Pond Ln 18104
E & W Long St 18103
Longfellow St 18104
Loring Dr 18104
Lorraine Cir 18104
Louise Ct & Ln 18103
Lova Ln 18103
Lowell St 18104
Lower Macungie Rd 18106
Loxley Ln 18103
N Lumber St
1-99 18101
101-297 18102
299-999 18102
S Lumber St
1-199 18101
800-2599 18103
Lynnfield Ln 18104
Lynnwood Dr 18109
Lynnwood Rd 18103
E Lynnwood St 18103
W Lynnwood St 18103
Mack Blvd 18103
N Madison St 18102
S Madison St
1-299 18102
301-399 18102
1000-1099 18103
N Main St 18104
S Main St 18103
Manchester Rd 18104
Manor Dr
1000-1099 18103
4201-4299 18104
Maple Cir 18104
Maple St 18104
E Maple St 18109
W Maple St
400-498 18102
500-999 18101
1000-1299 18102
1301-1399 18102
Maplewood Cir & Ln 18103
Maranatha Way 18106
Marcon Blvd 18109
Margaret Cir & St 18103
Maria Ln 18104
Market St
300-499 18103
2200-2499 18104
E Marks St 18109
Marlow St 18103
Marshall St SW 18103
N Marshall St 18104
S Marshall St 18103
Martin St 18103
Martin Luther King Jr Dr
401-1197 18102
1199-1599 18102
1900-2000 18104
2002-2098 18104
Mary St 18102
Mary Ann Way 18109
Maryland Ave 18103
Mashie Dr 18106
Mauch Chunk Rd
1500-3898 18104
1501-1515 18102
1725-3899 18104
Maulfair Dr & Pl 18103
Maumee Ave 18103
Max St 18103
N Maxwell St 18109
Meadow Ln 18104
N Meadow St 18102
S Meadow St 18103
Meadowbrook Cir N 18103
Mechanicsville Rd 18104
Medical Center Cir 18106
Memorial Rd
5500-6199 18104
6300-6529 18106
6531-6599 18106
Menges Ave 18103
Mercer St 18102
Merry Ln 18103
Mertz Dr & Ln 18104
Middlesex Rd 18103
Midland Rd 18104
Milkweed Dr 18104
Mill Rd 18106
Mill St 18103
Millcreek Rd 18106
Miller St 18103
S Miller St 18104
Minesite Rd 18103
Minnich Rd 18104
Minnie Ln 18104
Mitchell Ave 18103
Mocking Bird Ct 18103
Mohawk St 18103
N Mohr St 18102
Molinaro Dr 18104
Monroe St 18102
E & W Montgomery St 18103
Moravian Ave 18103
Morning Side Ave 18103
Morning Star Dr 18106
Morris Ct 18106
N Morris St 18102
Mosser Dr 18103
Mosser St 18103
E Mosser St 18109
W Mosser St 18104
E & W Mountain Ln &
Rd 18103
Mountain Park Rd 18103
Mountain Top Ln 18103
Mountain View Ct 18106
N Muhlenberg St 18104
S Muhlenberg St
1-699 18104
700-799 18103
Mulberry St 18102
Murray Dr 18104
Muth Cir 18104
Mylinda Ln 18104
N Nagle St
2-98 18101
100-298 18102
300-799 18102
S Nagle St 18101
Nassau Ct 18104
Natalie Dr 18104
N Nelson St 18109
Neva St 18104
Nevada St 18103
New St 18106
N New St 18102
New York Ave 18103
Newgate Dr 18103
Newton St 18102
Niblick Pl 18106
Nicole Cir 18103
Nittany Ct 18104
Nonnemacher Ln 18103
E & W Normandy St 18103
North Ln 18106
North St 18102
Nottingham Rd 18103
Oak Ln 18104
Oak St 18102
Oaklea Ln 18103
Oakleigh Rd 18104
Oakview Dr 18104
Oakwood Trl 18103
Old Sentry Rd 18104
Oldstone Rd 18103
Olin Way 18106
Olivia Cir 18103
Oplinger Rd 18106
Orchard Ave 18104
Orefield Rd 18104
N Oswego St 18109
N Ott St 18104
S Ott St
1-599 18104
800-999 18103
Overhill Rd 18103
Overlook Ct 18106
Oxford Cir S 18104
Oxford Dr 18103
Pa Route 309 18104
Page St
600-698 18102
1601-1699 18102
4000-4199 18104
Palomino Dr 18106
E & W Paoli St 18103
Par Cswy 18106
Park Ave 18103
Park Blvd 18104
Park Dr 18103
Park Pl 18104
Park St 18102
Park Vista Ter 18104
Parkland Dr 18104
Parkside Ct 18104
Parkview Ave 18104
Parkview Ln 18103
Parkway Blvd & Rd 18104
Parkwood Dr 18103
Pat Ct 18103
Patricia Dr 18103
Patterson Ct 18106
Pavlochik Dr 18103
Pawnee Ct 18104
Paxford Rd 18103
Peach St 18102
Peachtree Rd 18104
Pearl Ave & St 18103
Pembroke Ct 18103
Penn Cir 18102
Penn Dr 18106
N Penn St 18102
S Penn St 18102
Penn Xing 18104
Pennbrook Way 18104
Pennfield Ct 18104
Pennsylvania Ave 18109
E Pennsylvania St 18109
W Pennsylvania St
1300-1398 18102
1400-1699 18102
1700-3799 18104
Pennycress Rd 18104
N Perry St 18102
Pheasant Ct
3500-3599 18104
4000-4199 18103
Pheasant Hill Dr 18104
Piccadilly Cir 18103
N Piedmont St 18109
S Pike Ave 18103
E Pine St 18109
W Pine St 18102
Pine Grove Cir 18106
Pine Meadows Cir &
Ln 18104
Pinehurst Ct 18109
Pinnacle Dr 18103
Pinto Pl 18106
Pinyon Ln 18103
Pioneer St 18102
Pirma Ave 18104
Pittston St 18103
Platt Ct 18104
Plaza Ln 18104
Pleasant Ave 18103
N Plum St 18102
Plymouth St 18109
Polk St 18109
Pond Rd 18104
Ponds Edge Ln 18104
Pope Rd 18104
Poplar Ln 18103
N Poplar St
1-99 18101
100-699 18102
S Poplar St
1-99 18102
101-199 18102
701-797 18103
799-2399 18103
Portland Ct 18106
Post Rd 18106
Postal Rd 18109
Potomac St 18103
Pratt St 18102
Primrose Dr & Ln 18104
Princeton Ct 18104
Priscilla St 18103
Promise Ln 18106
Prophets Way 18106
Prospect Ave 18103
Pump Pl 18102
Putter Dr 18106
Quail Dr 18104
N Quebec St 18109
Quince Rd 18106
Quincy St 18109
Rabenold Ln 18104
E Race St 18109
S Race St 18103
N Railroad St 18102
Rainbow Ct 18106

N Ralph St 18102
Ramapo Trl 18104
Randolph St 18109
Ravenswood Rd 18103
Raymond Way 18104
Reading Rd
  2000-2845 18104
  2846-2998 18103
  2847-2899 18104
Red Clover Ln 18104
Red Maple Ln 18104
Redwood Cir 18103
Redwood Ct 18104
Redwood Ln 18103
Reed St 18109
N Refwal St 18102
Regent Ct 18103
Reid Ln 18104
Reilly Rd 18104
Reppert Ln 18106
Reservoir St 18103
Rhonda Ln 18103
Richard Dr 18104
Ridge Ave
  100-124 18101
  126-198 18101
  200-1199 18102
Ridgeview Dr 18104
Riga Cir 18104
Ritter Ln & Rd 18104
River Dr 18109
River Rd
  800-950 18109
  4000-4199 18104
Riverbend Cir & Rd 18103
Robert Dr 18104
Robin Ln 18106
Robin Rd 18104
Robin Hood Dr 18103
Roble Rd 18109
Rochelle Dr 18104
E & W Rock Rd 18103
Ronca Blvd 18109
Roosevelt St 18104
Rosewood Ln 18103
Roth Ave
  1200-1599 18102
  1700-1899 18104
Round Top Cir 18104
N & S Route 100 18106
Roxford Rd 18103
Roy St SW 18103
Royal Fern 18104
Ruppsville Rd 18106
N & S Rush St 18102
Russell St
  1000-1400 18102
  1402-1598 18102
  2500-2899 18104
Russett Rd 18104
Ruth St 18104
Ryan Dr 18103
Rye St 18103
Sabrina Cir 18104
Sage St 18103
Saint Basil St 18104
N & S Saint Cloud St & Ter 18104
N & S Saint Elmo St 18104
N & S Saint George St 18104
Saint John St 18103
N & S Saint Lucas St 18104
Saint Michael St 18103
Salisbury Dr & Rd 18103
Salisbury Hills Dr 18103
Sandtrap Ln 18106
Saratoga Ct 18104
Sassafrass Ln 18103
W Saucon Ave & St 18103
Saul St 18109
Savercool St 18103
Sawgrass Dr 18104
Saxon St 18103
N & S Scenic St 18104
N & S Schaeffer St 18104
Schaller Dr 18104
Schallers Ln 18103
Schantz Rd
  200-218 18104
  220-6699 18104
  6700-7699 18106
Scherer Rd 18104
Scherersville Rd 18104
Schoenersville Rd 18109
Scott St 18102
Seneca Trl 18104
Sequoia Ct & Trl 18104
Sesqui St 18103
Shaler St 18103
Shankweiler Rd 18104
Shelburne Ct 18104
Shell St 18109
Shenandoah Ct 18104
Shepherd Hills Ave 18106
Sherman St 18109
Sherwood Cir 18103
Sherwood Ct 18109
Sherwood Rd 18103
Sherwood St 18109
Shetland Ct 18106
Shiloh Ct 18104
Shiloh Rd 18106
Short Hill Dr & Ln 18104
Shrewsbury Rd 18104
Shuler St 18103
Sidney St 18103
N Silk St 18102
Skyline Dr 18103
Snapdragon Way 18104
Snowdrift Rd 18106
Snowy Orchid Ln 18104
South Dr 18103
E South St 18109
W South St
  1501-1699 18102
  1701-2297 18104
  2299-2699 18104
  2700-2899 18103
  2901-2999 18103
Spring Ln 18103
Spring Garden St 18102
Spring Wood Ct & Dr 18104
Springhouse Ct & Rd 18104
Springside Ct 18104
Spruce Rd 18106
Spruce St
  1-99 18101
  200-234 18102
  236-699 18102
Stallion Dr 18106
Stanley Ave 18103
W Stanley St 18104
Star Rd 18106
Steelstone Rd 18109
Steeplechase Ln 18106
N Sterling St 18104
Sterner Ln 18103
Stonecroft Ln 18106
Stonegate Ct & Dr 18106
Stoneridge Rd 18104
Stoney Brook Ct 18104
Stratford Ct 18103
Strohl Rd 18104
Sturbridge Pl 18104
Sugarberry Dr 18104
Summit Ct 18103
Sumner Ave & Ct 18102
Suncrest Dr 18104
Sundew Ct 18104
Sunrise Ave 18103
Sunrise Dr 18104
Sunrise Ridge Dr 18106
Sunset Ave 18103
Sunshine Rd 18103
Surrey Ct 18104
Surrey Dr 18103
E Susquehanna St 18103
W Susquehanna St 18103
Susquehanna Trl 18104
Sussex Rd 18103
Suzanne Way 18109
Sweetbriar Ct 18103
Sycamore St 18104
E Sycamore St 18109
W Sycamore St 18102
Sylvia Ln 18104
Tacoma Ct & St 18109
Taft Ave 18103
Taft St 18109
Tamarack Dr 18104
Tanglewood Ln Ln 18106
Tee Ct 18106
Tennyson Dr 18104
Terra Dr 18104
Terrace Cir 18103
E Texas Blvd
  2101-2199 18104
  2400-2899 18103
E Texas Rd
  3900-4699 18103
  4700-5199 18106
The Strand 18103
Tilghman St
  5200-6099 18104
  6300-7699 18106
E Tilghman St 18109
W Tilghman St
  1-1699 18102
  1700-5199 18104
Timber Trl 18106
Timberidge Ln 18106
E & W Tioga St 18103
Township Line Rd 18106
Trapps Ln 18103
Traylor Dr 18103
Treeline Cir & Dr 18103
E Tremont St 18109
W Tremont St
  1200-1699 18102
  1700-3099 18104
Trexler Blvd 18104
Trexlertown Rd 18106
Trout Dr 18103
Trout Creek Ln 18103
Troxell Ct & St 18109
Trump St 18109
Truth Pl 18106
Tulip Dr 18104
Tupelo Ct 18104
Tupelo Rd 18104
Tupelo St 18103
E Turner St 18109
W Turner St
  100-199 18102
  200-218 18101
  220-298 18101
  301-397 18102
  399-1699 18102
  1701-1797 18104
  1799-4099 18104
Tweed Ave 18103
Ueberroth Ave 18103
Uhl St 18109
Ulana Ln 18104
Ulster Rd & St 18109
Union Blvd 18109
E Union St 18109
W Union St
  100-198 18102
  200-411 18101
  413-499 18102
  500-799 18101
  1001-1097 18102
  1099-1699 18102
  1700-1798 18104
  1800-3599 18104
Utica St 18102
Vale View Dr 18103
Valley Dr 18104
Valley Forge Rd 18104
Valley View Dr 18103
N Van Buren St 18109
Van Vetchen Ave 18103
Vermont Ave 18103
Victoria Cir 18103
Victoria Dr 18109
Victoria Ln 18104
Village Round 18106
Vine St 18103
Virginia St 18103
Voortman Ave 18103
Vultee St 18103
W Wabash St 18103
N Wahneta St 18109
Walbert Ave 18104
Waldheim Park 18103
Walker Way 18106
Wall St 18109
E Wallis St 18103
Walnut Ln 18102
E Walnut St 18109
W Walnut St
  100-499 18102
  500-799 18101
  800-820 18102
  822-1600 18102
  1602-1698 18102
  1700-1798 18104
  1800-4299 18104
Warba Dr 18104
Ward St 18103
Warren St 18102
Warwick Pl 18104
Washington Ave 18103
E Washington St 18109
W Washington St
  300-1599 18102
  1601-1699 18102
  1701-1797 18104
  1799-3999 18104
Water Lilly Ct 18104
E Wayne Ave 18103
W Wayne St 18102
Weaversville Rd 18109
Webster Ave 18103
Webster St 18102
Wedge Ln 18106
Wedgewood Rd 18104
Wehr Ave 18104
Wehr Mill Rd 18104
Weida Ln 18103
Weiss Ct 18103
Wellington Ter 18103
Wells Ct 18103
Wenner St 18103
Werley Rd 18104
Werleys Ln 18103
N & S West St 18102
Westley Pl 18104
Westminster St 18109
Westview Dr 18104
Wethersfield Dr 18104
Wetzel St 18106
Wharf St 18104
Whispering Woods Cir 18106
White Oak Rd 18104
Whitehall Ave 18104
W Whitehall St
  300-1699 18102
  1700-3099 18104
Whitetail Ct 18104
N Whitman St 18104
Whittier Dr 18103
Wild Mint Ln 18104
Wildflower Dr 18104
William Ave 18106
William Ct 18104
N Williams St 18102
Willow Cir 18102
Willow St
  449-457 18102
  3000-3099 18104
W Willow St 18102
Willowbrook Rd 18109
Winchester Rd
  3200-3398 18104
  3400-3500 18104
  3502-4298 18104
  3541-3541 18195
  3701-4299 18104
Windermere Ave & Ct 18104
Windsor Dr
  4100-4299 18104
  7100-7198 18106
  7200-7300 18106
  7302-7424 18106
  7535-7535 18195
  7540-7540 18195
Windy Hill Rd 18103
Winterberry Pl 18104
E Winton St 18109
Wisdom Pl 18106
Wolf Dr 18104
Wood Ln
  2300-2399 18103
  5600-5699 18106
N Wood St 18101
S Wood St 18103
Woodbrush Way 18104
Woodcrest Cir 18103
Woodhaven Dr 18103
Woodland Dr 18103
E Woodlawn St 18109
W Woodlawn St
  1400-1699 18102
  1700-3099 18104
Woods Hollow Ln 18103
Woodside Ct 18103
S Woodward St 18103
Wordsworth St 18104
Wyndham Dr 18104
E & W Wyoming St 18103
Yale Ct 18104
Yeker Farms Ln 18103
Yolanda Ct 18104
Yorkshire Cir & Rd 18103
Zieglers Ct 18102
Zoar Ave 18103

NUMBERED STREETS

1st Ave 18106
N 2nd St
  1-21 18101
  23-199 18101
  200-799 18102
S 2nd St
  1-1 18101
  100-199 18102
  900-1498 18103
  1500-2499 18103
N 3rd St
  23-199 18101
  201-297 18102
  299-599 18102
S 3rd St
  100-299 18102
  1200-2499 18103
3rd And Walnut St 18102
N 4th St 18102
S 4th St
  1-199 18102
  801-897 18103
N 5th St
  1-31 18101
  100-999 18102
S 5th St
  205A-205D 18102
  2-30 18101
  32-199 18101
  201-299 18102
  600-2699 18103
N 6th St
  1-199 18101
  200-1099 18102
S 6th St
  1-199 18101
  600-2599 18103
N 7th St
  1-199 18101
  200-999 18102
S 7th St
  1-170 18101
  172-198 18101
  800-1299 18103
N 8th St
  1-199 18101
  200-900 18102
  902-998 18102
S 8th St
  1-199 18101
  700-1399 18103
  1401-2399 18103
N 9th St
  2-8 18101
  10-99 18101
  100-999 18102
S 9th St
  1-23 18102
  25-199 18102
  901-997 18103
  999-2399 18103
N 10th St
  1-99 18101
  100-825 18102
S 10th St
  1-199 18102
  600-2500 18103
N 11th St
  1-99 18101
  100-899 18102
S 11th St
  1-199 18102
  700-2399 18103
N 12th St
  1-99 18101
  100-1099 18102
S 12th St
  1-199 18102
  800-2399 18103
N & S 13th 18102
N 14th St 18102
S 14th St
  1-300 18102
  900-999 18103
N & S 15th 18102
N 16th St
  2-198 18102
  1600-1699 18104
S 16th St 18102
17th St SW 18103
N 17th St 18104
S 17th St 18104
N & S 18th 18104
N & S 19th 18104
N 20th St 18104
N & S 21st 18104
N & S 22nd 18104
N & S 23rd 18104
N 24th St 18104
S 24th St
  1-600 18104
  602-698 18104
  700-1299 18103
  1301-1399 18103
N 25th St 18104
  1-699 18104
  700-899 18103
26th St SW 18103
N 26th St 18104
S 26th St 18104
27th St SW 18103
N 27th St 18104
28th St SW 18103
N 28th St 18104
29th St SW 18103
N 29th St 18104
30th St SW 18103
N 30th St 18104
31st St SW 18103
N 31st St 18104
32nd St SW 18103
N 32nd St 18104
33rd St SW 18103
N 33rd St 18104
S 33rd St 18104
N & S 34th 18104
N & S 35th 18104
36th Ct & St 18104
37th Ct & St 18104
N & S 38th 18104
N & S 39th 18104
N & S 40th 18104
N & S 41st 18104
N & S 42nd 18104

ALTOONA PA

General Delivery 16603

POST OFFICE BOXES MAIN OFFICE STATIONS AND BRANCHES

Box No.s
1 - 3298 16603
10000 - 10000 16601
20000 - 20000 16602

RURAL ROUTES

01, 02, 03, 04, 05, 06, 07 16601

NAMED STREETS

Aberdeen St 16602
Adams Ave 16602
Albert Dr 16602
Albright Dr 16602
Aldrich Ave 16602
Alison Ln 16601
Allegheny Ave & St 16601
Alpaca Ln 16601
Alpine Dr 16602
Alpine Ln 16601
E Alta Ave 16601
Alta Vista Dr 16601
Alto Reste Park 16601
E Altoona Ave 16602
Amelia Ave 16601
Andrew Rd 16602
Angus Ln 16601
Annapolis Dr 16602
Antis Rd 16601
Antrim Ln 16601
Apple Ln 16601
Arden St 16602
Arlaryd St 16602
Art Ln 16601
Asbury Ln 16601
Ash St 16602
Ashwood Dr 16601
E Atlantic Ave 16602
Aurora Ln 16601
Autumn Ln 16601
Avalon Rd 16601
Avondale Ave 16601
Baker Blvd 16602
Baker Ct 16602
Baker Dr 16601
Baker Ln 16601
E Baltzell Ave 16602
Barn Oak Ln 16601
Barry Ct 16601
Bartley Ln 16601
Baylor Ln 16602
Baynton Ave 16602
Beacon St 16601
Beale Ave 16601
Bear Hollow Ln 16601
Beaumont Dr 16602
Beck Ln 16602
Beckers Ln 16601
S Beckman Dr 16602
E Beech Ave & Ct 16601
Beech Street Lakemont 16602
Beechwood Dr 16601
E Bell Ave 16602
Bellmeade Dr 16602
Bellview St 16602
Bellwood Ave 16602
Bellwood Rd 16601
Bennetti Dr 16602
Bernard Ln 16601
Beverly Blvd & Dr 16601
Birch Tree Ln 16601
Blackberry Ln 16601
Blackhawk Ln 16601

Street	ZIP
Blackie Ln & Rd	16601
Blain Ave	16602
E Blair Ave	16602
Bloom Rd	16601
Blue Spruce Ln	16601
Bonfire Ln	16601
Boone Ln	16601
Bowling Ln	16601
Boxcar Ln	16601
Boyce Ave	16602
Boyles Ln	16601
Bramble Ln	16601
N Branch Ave	16601
Brandt Ln	16601
Bream Rd	16601
Breezy Country Ln	16601
Briar Cliff Rd	16601
Brickley Rd	16601
Bridge St	16601
Briggs Dr	16601
Broad Ave	16601
Broadway	16601
Brook Run Dr	16601
Brookside Dr	16601
Brookwood Dr	16601
Browning Ave	16602
Brubaker Ln	16601
Brush Mountain Rd	16601
Brush Oaks Dr	16602
Bryant Ave	16602
Bucknell Ln	16602
Bucknell Lane Ext	16602
Bud Cir	16602
Buechele Dr	16601
Burgoon Rd	16602
Burns Ave & Dr	16601
Buschle Ln	16601
Busy Bee Ln	16601
Byron Ave	16602
Calder St	16602
California Ave	
5600-5920	16602
5921-5935	16601
5922-5936	16602
5937-6099	16601
California Dr	16602
Campbell Ave	16602
Campus View Dr	16601
Canterberry Dr	16602
S Carl Ave & St	16602
Carlee Ln	16601
S Carlisle Ln	16602
Carlow Ln	16601
E Caroline Ave	16602
Cashman Rd	16601
Castle Farms Rd	16601
Castleberry Ln	16601
Cathedral Sq	16601
S Catherine St	16602
Cayuga Ave & Cir	16602
Cedar St	16602
Celebration Dr	16602
Celestial Way	16601
Celtic Ln	16601
Chapel Dr	16602
Charles Pl	16602
Charlotte Dr	16601
Chartiers St	16601
Cherry Ave	16601
E Cherry Ave	16601
Cherry St	16602
Cherrywood Dr	16601
Chester Ln	16601
Chestnut Ave	16601
Chief Logan Cir	16602
Circle Ave	16602
City View St	16601
Clair St	16601
Clairmont Dr	16601
Clapper Rd	16601
Clarion Ln	16602
Claybrooke Dr	16602
E Clemson Rd	16602
Cleveland Ave	16602
Clover Ln	16601
Cogan Rd	16601
Colclesser Ave	16601
Coleman Ln	16601
Coleridge Ave	16602
S Colgate Ln	16602
College Heights Dr	16601
College Park Dr	16601
Colonel Drake Hwy	16601
Colorado Dr	16602
Columbia Dr	16602
Concord Ln	16601
Conrail Access Rd	16601
Convention Center Dr	16602
Cooney Ln	16601
Copp Ln	16601
Coral Dr	16601
Cornell Ln	16602
Cortland Ave	16601
Cottonwood Dr	16601
Court Ln	16601
Cowboy Ln	16601
Cox Ln	16601
Craft Ln	16601
E Crawford Ave	16602
Creamer Ln	16601
Creekside Dr	16601
Crescent Rd	16602
Cricket Club Ln	16601
Cross Creek Dr & Ln	16601
Crosswinds Ct	16602
Cunningham Ln	16601
S Curve Rd	16601
Daily St	16601
Dakota Ln	16602
Dale Cir	16601
S Dartmouth Ln	
100-299	16601
400-699	16602
Davis Rd	16601
Deb Ln	16602
Deb Lane Ext	16602
Decker Court Ln	16601
Deerfield Ln	16601
Delgrosso Dr	16601
Delray Ln	16601
Denby Ln	16601
Detrich Dr	16601
Dewberry Ln	16601
Dewey St	16602
Dibert Ln	16601
Dick Ln	16601
Dickinson Rd	16602
Diebold Dr	16601
Dixie Ln	16602
Dogpatch Ln	16601
Dons Dr	16601
Dorminy Ln	16601
Dove Ave	16602
Drexel Ln	16602
Duff Dr	16602
Duke Rd	16602
Dunkle Ln	16601
Duquesne Ln	16602
Dysart Ave	16602
Eagle Ln	16601
Earnhardt Dr	16601
East St	16602
Eberhardt Ln	16601
Eckels Ln	16601
Edgewood Dr	16602
Edinboro Dr	16602
Edison Ave	16601
Eisenhower Ave	16601
Eldon Ave	16602
Eldorado Ave	16601
Electric Ave	16601
Elizabeth Rd	16602
Ellenberger Dr	
7000-7039	16602
7041-7099	16601
Elm St	
101-297	16602
299-499	16602
2700-2999	16601
Elm Spring Dr	16602
Elwood Ln	16601
Emerson Ave	16602
Ensbrenner Dr	16601
Enterprise Campus Dr	16601
Equestrian Ln	16602
Erin Dr	16602
Eveningtide Ave	16602
Evergreen Ct	16602
Ewing Dr	16601
Eyers Ln	16601
Fairground Rd	16601
E Fairview Ave	16601
Fairway Dr	16602
Falling Leaf Ln	16601
Falon Ln	16602
Fay Ln	16601
Feather Ln	16601
Ferguson Dr	16601
Ferncliff Rd	16601
Filmore Ave	16602
Finch Dr	16601
Findley Ave	16601
Firehouse Rd	16601
Flagstone Ave	16602
Flamingo Dr	16602
Fleig Ln	16601
Focht St	16602
Forbes Ln	16601
Fordham Cir	16602
Forest Hill Dr	16601
Forgas Ln	16601
Forge Rd	16601
Forrest St	16602
Forshey Ln & St	16601
Forsht Ln	16601
Fort Roberdeau Ave	16602
Fort Roberdeau Rd	16601
Foust Dr	16601
Fowler Ln	16601
Foxglove Rd	16601
Franco Ln	16601
Franklin Cir & Dr	16601
Frankstown Rd	
100-699	16602
700-1048	16601
Frederick Rd	16602
Frito Ln	16601
Front St	16602
Frost Ave	16602
Furnace Ave	16602
Gage Ave	16602
Game Land Rd	16601
Garden St	16602
Gazebo Ln	16601
Geneva Ln	16602
George Ave	16602
Georgetown Ln	16602
Gesser Ave	16602
Gibbs Rd	16601
Gill Ln	16601
Glenwood Dr	16601
Golf Course Rd	16601
Golfview Dr	16601
Gonzaga Ln	16602
Good Shepherd Rd	16601
Goods Ln	
5500-5598	16602
5501-5597	16601
5599-5699	16601
Goods View Ln	16601
Gospel Hollow Ln	16601
Grace Rd	16602
Graham Dr	16601
Granada Way	16601
Grand Prix Dr	16601
Grandview Ave & Rd	16601
E Granite Ave	16601
E Grant Ave & St	16602
Grapevine Ln	16601
Grassmyer Ln	16601
Greeley St	16601
Green Ave	16601
Green Thumb Ave	16601
Greenway Dr	16601
Greenwood Rd	16602
Grimminger Ln	16601
Grove City Ln	16602
Gwin Rd	16601
S Hagerty St	16602
Halbritter Dr	16601
Halleck Pl	16602
Hamer Dr	16601
E Hamilton Ln	16602
Hamilton St	16601
Hammer Dr	16601
Hanover Ln	16602
Hardy Ln	16601
Harmony Dr	16601
Harris Ln	16601
Harrison Ave	16602
Hartwood Ln	16601
Hartzell Ave	16602
Harvard Ln	16602
Hawk Eye Ln	16602
Hawthorne Dr	16602
Haymaker Ln	16601
Heather Ave	16602
Hedberg Ln	16601
Hegarty Rd	16601
Heidaway Ln	16601
Hemlock St	16602
Hen House Ln	16601
Hench Cir	16602
Heritage Ln	16601
Herron Ln	16601
Hidden Ln	16601
Hiergeist Ln	16601
Highland Ave	16602
Highland Pl	16601
Highland Ter	16602
Highland Park Ave	16602
Hileman St	16602
Hill St	16601
Hillside Ave & Dr	16601
Hilltop Cir & Dr	16601
Hobbit Hollow Rd	16601
Hodge Ln	16601
Hoffman Ln	16601
Holbrook Ln	16601
Holly Rdg	16601
E & W Holmes Ave	16602
Homan Ln	16601
Homers Gap Rd	16601
Homestead Ln	16601
Homewood Dr	16601
Honey Suckle Ln	16601
Hope Ln	16601
Hopewell Dr	16602
Horner Dr	16601
Hornung Dr	16601
Horseshoe Dr	16601
E Howard Ave	16601
Howard Avenue	
Lakemont	16602
E Hudson Ave	16602
Hughes Dr	16601
Husick Ln	16601
Illinois Dr	16602
Imler St	16602
Indian Pl	16602
Indiana Dr	16602
Industrial Ave	16601
Industrial Park Dr	16602
Ingham Dr	16601
Irish Eyes Ln	16601
Irwin Dr & Ln	16601
Iup Ln	16602
Ivan Ln	16602
Ivy Pl	16602
Ivyside Dr & Park	16601
Ivyside Estates Ln	16601
Jackson Ave	16602
Jackson Ln	16601
Jade Ave	
600-933	16602
934-981	16601
S Jaggard St	16602
Jaguar Ave	16602
James Rd	16602
Jasmine Ave	16602
Jayne Ln	16601
Jefferson Ave	16602
Jefferson St	16601
Joffre Ave	16601
S John St	16602
John Deere Rd	16601
Jones Ln	16601
Jones Farm Ln	16601
Jordan Ln	16601
Jospen Ct	16602
Juniata Ln & St	16602
Juniata Gap Rd	16601
Juniata Springs Dr	16601
Katherine Rd	16602
Keisha Ln	16601
Kennedy Dr	16601
Kenneth Rd	16602
Kentucky Ave	16602
Kerbaugh Rd	16601
Kerlin Ln	16601
Kerr Dr	16601
Kettle Rd	16601
Kettle St	
400-499	16602
1000-1002	16601
1004-2399	16601
S Kettle St	
100-999	16602
1000-1000	16601
1001-1001	16602
1002-1039	16601
Kettle Nursery Rd	16601
Keystone St	16602
Kiesel Ave	16601
Kings Hwy	16602
Kissell Ave	16601
Knob Ln	16601
Koeck Dr	16601
Kristel Ln	16601
Kurtz Dr	16601
Lafayette Ln	16602
Lake Ave	16602
Lakemont Park Blvd	16602
Lakeside Dr	16601
Landis St	16602
Largent Dr	16601
Lark Ave	16602
Lasalle Ln	16602
Laughlin Cir	16602
Laurel Dr & Ln	16601
Laurie Ln	16601
Lawn Ln	16601
Lear Rd	16601
Lecrone Rd	16601
E Lee Ave	16601
Lefevre Ln	16601
Lehigh Ln	16602
Leslie Ave	16602
Lewis Dr	16601
Lexington Ave	16601
Liberty St	16602
Limestone St	16601
Linbrook Ln	16601
E Lincoln Ave	16601
Lincoln Mnr	16602
Linda Ct	16602
Linwood Rd	16602
Little Dr	16601
Lloyd St	
100-599	16602
1400-2699	16601
S Lloyd St	16602
Llyswen Ct	16602
Lock Haven Ln	16602
Locust St	16602
Lodge Ln	16601
Log Cabin Ct	16602
Logan Ave	16602
E Logan Ave	16602
Logan Blvd	16602
N Logan Blvd	16602
S Logan Blvd	16602
Logan Pl	16602
E Logan St	16601
Logan Valley Mall	16602
Loganbell Ln	16601
Logandale Dr	16601
Longfellow Ave	16602
Longs Ln	16601
Longview Dr	16601
Loose Ln	16601
Lotz Ave	16602
Lowell Ave	16602
Lower Riggles Gap Rd	16601
Lower Skelp Rd	16601
Luke Ln	16601
Lycoming Ln	16602
Lyndale Rd	16602
Lynne Dr	16601
Lynwood Dr	16602
Madison Ave	16602
Magill Dr	16601
S Main St	16602
Maine Dr	16602
Mansion Blvd	16602
E Maple Ave, Ct & St	16601
Maplewood Dr	16601
Marble St	16601
Margaret Ave	16601
Margaret Rd	16602
Marie Ln	16601
Marjorie Rd	16601
Martin Ln	16601
Mary Ln	16601
Maryland Ave	16602
Mauk Dr	16601
Mc Connell Ln	16601
Mccloskey Ln	16601
Mccutcheon Rd	16601
Mcgough Ln	16601
Mcmahon Rd	16602
Mcmullen Rd	16601
Meade Ln	16602
Meadow St	16602
Meadowlark Ave	16602
Mennonite Rd	16601
Mercer Ln	16602
Mercyhurst Ln	16602
Meyers Ln	16601
Michelle Dr	16602
Michigan Dr	16602
Mill Run Rd	16601
Miller Ln & Rd	16601
Millville Rd	16601
Milton Ave	16602
Missley Aly	16601
Misty Brook Ln	16601
Mitchell Ln	16601
Mobile Ln	16601
Mocking Bird Ln	16601
Monroe Ave	16602
Monte Dr	16602
Monte Carlo Dr	16601
Montler Ln	16601
Montrose Ave	16602
Morningside Ave	16602
Moser Rd	16601
Mosser St	16602
Mosside Cir	16601
Mountain Ave	16602
Mountain View Dr	16601
Moyer Ln	16601
Moyer Farm Rd	16601
Mulberry Ln	16601
Neal Ave	16602
Nearhoof Dr	16601
Nebgen Ln	16601
Nelson Rd	16601
Nittany Ln	16601
Noonan Dr	16601
North St	16602
Norway Ave	16602
Notre Dame Rd	16602
Novack Rd	16601
Oak Ave	16601
Oak Ln	
900-999	16601
3401-3599	16602
Oak St	16601
S Oak St	16602
Oak Crescent Ln	16601
Oak Hill Ter	16601
Oak Knoll Dr	16601
Oakwood Dr	16601
Ohio Ave & Dr	16602
Old 6th Avenue Rd	16601
Old Mill Run Rd	16601
Old Route 220 N	16601
Olde Dominion Dr	16602
Oliver St	16602
Olmes St	16602
Oneida Ave	16602
Orangewood Dr	16601
Orchard Ave	
200-399	16602
400-499	16601
Ore Hill Rd	16602
Orpwood Ln	16601
Osgood Dr	
1300-1399	16601
1500-1799	16602
Overland Pass	16602
Overlook Pl	16602
Oxford Rd	16602
Pace Ln	16602
Palm Spring Ln	16601
Palmetto Ln	16602
Paradise Ln	16601
Park Ave	16602
E Park Ave	16601
Park Blvd	16601
Park Dr	16602
S Park Dr	16601
Park Pl	16601
Park Forest Ln	16601
Park Hills Plz	16602
Parkside Dr	16601
Parkview Ln	16601
Parkway Dr	16602
Parrish St	16602
Parshall Ln	16602
Partridge Dr	16601
Patterson Dr	16601
Peachwood Dr	16601
Pearl St	16602
Pearwood Dr	16601
Pease Dr	16601
Pebble Ln	16601
Pecan Ave	16601
E Penn Ave	16601
Penn Circle Dr	16602
Penn State Dr	16602
Penn Wood Dr	16602
Pennbrook St	16601
Pennsylvania St	16602
Pennway Ave	16601
Penny Ln	16601
Perry Ln	16601
Peters Dr	16601
Philip Ln	16602
Phoenix Ln	16601
Pierce Ave	16602
Pierce St	16601
Pine Ave	16601
E Pine Ave	16601
Pine Dr	16601
N Pine St	16602
S Pine St	16602
Pine Manor Ln	16602
Pinecroft Ave	16601
Pinewood Dr	16602
Pink Pig Ln	16601
Pioneer Ln	16601
Piper Ln	16601
Pistol Club Rd	16601
Pitt Rd	16602
Plank Rd	16601
E Plank Rd	16602
W Plank Rd	16602
Plateau St	16602
Pleasant Valley Ave	16602
Pleasant Valley Blvd	16602
E Pleasant Valley Blvd	
1876A-1876B	16602
100-2099	16602
2100-4099	16601
Pleasant View Ave	16602
Poe Pl	16602
Poland Ave	16601
Polk Ave	16602
Ponderosa Dr	16601
Pope Ave	16602

Porta Rd 16601
Pottsgrove Rd 16602
Preston Ln 16601
Priddy Dr 16601
Primrose Ln 16601
Princeton Rd 16602
Priority St 16602
Prospect Ln 16601
Purdue Dr 16602
Quad St 16601
Quail Ave 16602
Quartz Ln 16601
Queens Way 16601
Race St 16601
Rainbow Dr 16601
Rattler Rdg 16601
Raven Rocks Ln 16601
Rebecca St 16602
Red Oak Leaf Ln 16601
Redrockhill Dr 16601
Redtail Ln 16601
Reeds Ln 16601
Reid St 16602
Reighard Ln 16601
Reiling Ln 16601
Reimer St
200-225 16602
400-413 16601
Remington Ln 16601
Reo Ln 16601
Rhett Ln 16602
Rhode Island Ave 16601
Rhodes Ln 16601
Rice Rd 16602
Ricotta Ln 16601
Riddle Ln 16601
Rider Farm Rd 16601
Ridge Ave 16602
Rifle Dr 16601
Riggin Ln 16601
Riggles Gap Rd 16601
Riggles Gap Sportsmen Rd 16601
Rita Ln 16601
Ritts Rd 16601
Ritz Rd 16601
Robert Morris Ln 16602
Robin Ave 16602
Rosehill Dr 16602
Rosehill Drive Ext 16602
Roselawn Ave 16602
Rosewood Dr 16601
Roswell St 16602
Roundhouse Rd 16601
Route 764 16601
Roy Ln 16602
Ruby Ln 16601
Rudolph Ln 16602
Ruskin Dr 16602
Russell Dr 16601
Rustic Hollow Ln 16601
Rutgers Ln 16602
Ruths Ln 16601
Sabbath Rest Rd 16601
Sagemore Ln 16601
Saint Francis Ln 16602
Saleen Dr 16601
Sandbank Rd 16601
Sandy Run Rd 16601
Sap Ln 16601
Sarah Dr 16601
Saylor Ln 16601
Scarlet Ln 16602
Scenic Rd 16601
Schoolhouse Ave 16602
Scott Ave 16602
Seaway Ave 16601
Sellers Dr 16601
Seneca Ave 16602
Serenity Ln 16601
Sesame St 16602
Shady Rd 16601
Shand Ave
600-698 16602
700-1016 16602
1017-1099 16601
Shannon Rd 16601
Sharer Ln 16601
Sharon Ave 16602
Sharp Ave 16601
Sharrar Dr 16602
Shawnee Ave 16602
Shelley Ave 16602
Sheraton Dr 16601
Sheridan St 16602
Sherwood Rd 16602
Short Dr 16601
Shroeder St 16601
Sickles Corner Back Rd 16601
Side Mountain Rd 16601
Sierra Dr 16601
Sipes 16601
Skelp Mountain Rd 16601
Skidmore Ln 16602
Solar Ln 16602
Sophrira Ln 16602
Soriano Dr 16601
South St 16602
E & W Southey Ave 16602
Southwood Rd 16601
Spook Hollow Rd 16601
Sprankle Ave 16602
Spring Ave 16601
Spring Run Dr 16601
Spruce Ave 16601
E Spruce Ct 16601
Spruce St 16602
Stadium Dr 16601
Stagecoach Rd 16601
Stanford Ln 16602
Steinbeiser Dr 16601
Stephenson Pl 16601
Sterling St 16602
Sterling Acres Rd 16601
Stevens Hill Rd 16601
Stewart St 16602
Stillwood St 16601
Stitt Ln 16601
Stoney Pt & St 16601
Stroehman Dr 16601
Stump Ranch Ln 16601
Sugar Run Rd 16601
Sunny Crest Ln 16601
Sunny Mead Ln 16601
Sunrise Ct 16601
Sunset Dr 16601
Swanger Dr 16601
Swartz Rd 16601
N Sycamore St 16602
Tahoe St 16601
Talbot Ln 16601
Tara Ln 16602
Taylor Ave 16602
E & S Temple Ln 16602
Tennyson Ave 16602
Terra Ln 16601
N & S Terrace Dr 16602
Thunderbird Dr 16601
Timberline Dr 16601
Timberline Drive Ext 16601
Tomahawk Ln 16601
Triangle St 16601
Trickey Ln 16601
Trinity Ln 16601
Tulane Ln 16602
Turkey Dr 16601
Tuscarora Ln 16601
Twilight Dr 16601
Tyler Ave 16602
Ucla Ln 16602
Union Ave
1-19 16602
21-399 16602
1800-2299 16601
2300-3099 16602
Unity Ln 16601
University Dr 16602
Utah Rd 16602
Valley Ave 16601
Valley View Blvd 16602
Van Buren Ave 16602
Vargo Ln 16601
Vaughn Farm Ln 16601
Ventre Rd 16602
Veterans Memorial Hwy 16601
Vicars Ln 16601
Victoria Ct 16601
Vine Ln 16601
Wachter Dr 16601
Waites Ln 16601
E Walnut Ave 16601
Walters Ln 16601
E Walton Ave 16602
Ward Ave 16602
Ward Trucking Dr 16602
Washington Ave 16601
Water St 16601
Waterloo Rd 16601
Wayne Ave 16602
Weaver St 16601
Webster St 16602
Wehnwood Rd 16601
Wenrich Rd 16601
Wertz Ave 16601
Wesley Ln 16602
West Ave 16602
Western Ln 16601
Westlawn Ln 16601
Westley Ave 16602
Westpoint Cir 16602
Westwood Park Rd 16601
Wharton Ave 16602
White Fox Rd 16601
E & W Whittier Ave 16602
Wicker St 16601
Wilderness Ln 16601
Will Ln 16602
Williams Ln 16601
E Willow Ave & Dr 16601
Wilson St 16602
Wilt Ln 16601
Windbrook Ln & St 16601
Winding Knoll Rd 16601
Windrose Ave 16602
Windsor Dr 16601
Winshire Ln 16601
Winston Dr 16601
Winterberry St 16602
Wise Ln 16601
Wolfe Ln 16601
Woodland Ave 16601
Woodland Rd 16602
Woods Ln 16601
Woomer Rd 16601
E Wopsononock Ave 16601
Wordsworth Ave 16602
Wren Ave 16602
Wyngate Ln 16601
Yale Ln 16602
Yoders Dr 16601
Young St 16601
Youngstone Ln 16601
S Zajac Dr 16602

NUMBERED STREETS

1st Ave 16602
E 1st Ave 16602
1st St
100-599 16602
1200-3099 16601
S 1st St 16602
2nd Ave 16602
E 2nd Ave 16602
2nd St
100-699 16602
1200-2999 16601
N 2nd St 16601
S 2nd St 16602
3rd Ave 16602
E 3rd Ave 16602
N 3rd Ave 16601
3rd St
100-799 16602
1200-3199 16601
N 3rd St 16601
S 3rd St 16602
4th Ave 16602
E 4th Ave 16602
N 4th Ave 16601
4th St
100-198 16602
200-999 16602
1200-3199 16601
N 4th St 16601
S 4th St 16602
4th Street Lakemont 16602
5th Ave 16602
E 5th Ave 16602
N 5th Ave 16601
5th St
101-197 16602
199-799 16602
1500-2899 16601
N 5th St 16601
S 5th St 16602
6th Ave 16602
6153-6199 16601
6154-6198 16602
E 6th Ave 16602
N 6th Ave 16601
6th St
100-799 16602
1800-1899 16601
N 6th St 16601
S 6th St 16602
6th Street Lakemont 16602
7th Ave 16602
N 7th Ave 16601
W 7th Ave 16601
7th St
100-799 16602
1200-1999 16601
N 7th St 16601
S 7th St 16602
7th Street Lakemont 16602
8th Ave 16602
N 8th Ave 16601
W 8th Ave 16601
8th St
100-700 16602
702-898 16602
1200-1999 16601
N 8th St 16601
S 8th St 16602
9th Ave 16602
N 9th Ave 16601
W 9th Ave 16601
9th St
100-899 16602
1100-2999 16601
N 9th St 16601
S 9th St 16602
10th Ave 16601
N 10th Ave 16601
S 10th Ave 16601
W 10th Ave 16601
10th St
100-799 16602
1100-2799 16601
N 10th St 16601
S 10th St 16602
11th Ave 16601
N 11th Ave 16601
W 11th Ave 16601
11th St
300-800 16602
802-898 16602
1000-2999 16601
E 11th St 16601
N 11th St 16601
12th Ave 16601
N 12th Ave 16601
W 12th Ave 16601
12th St
100-198 16602
200-899 16602
1000-2599 16601
N 12th St 16601
S 12th St 16602
13th Ave 16601
N 13th Ave 16601
W 13th Ave 16601
13th St
101-197 16602
199-899 16602
1000-2999 16601
N 13th St 16601
S 13th St 16602
14th Ave 16601
N 14th Ave 16601
W 14th Ave 16601
14th St
100-899 16602
1000-3099 16601
N 14th St 16601
S 14th St 16602
15th Ave 16601
N 15th Ave 16601
W 15th Ave 16601
15th St
100-799 16602
1000-2999 16601
N 15th St 16601
S 15th St 16602
16th Ave 16601
N 16th Ave 16601
16th St
100-399 16602
1000-3199 16601
N 16th St 16601
S 16th St 16602
17th Ave 16601
N 17th Ave 16601
17th St
100-819 16602
820-2999 16601
N 17th St 16601
18th Ave 16601
N 18th Ave 16601
18th St
100-799 16602
1000-1098 16601
1100-3099 16601
N 18th St 16601
19th Ave 16601
N 19th Ave 16601
19th St
100-799 16602
820-3199 16601
N 19th St 16601
S 19th St 16602
20th Ave 16601
N 20th Ave 16601
20th St
100-799 16602
820-2499 16601
N 20th St 16601
S 20th St 16602
21st Ave 16601
E 21st Ave 16601
21st St
100-819 16602
1000-2199 16601
22nd Ave 16601
E 22nd Ave 16601
22nd St
100-819 16602
840-1699 16601
S 22nd St 16602
23rd Ave 16601
E 23rd Ave 16601
23rd St
300-819 16602
820-2899 16601
24th Ave 16601
E 24th Ave 16601
24th St
100-819 16602
820-1799 16601
S 24th St 16602
25th Ave 16601
E 25th Ave 16601
25th St
100-700 16602
702-798 16602
820-1699 16601
S 25th St 16602
26th Ave 16601
E 26th Ave 16601
26th St
400-699 16602
820-1599 16601
S 26th St 16602
27th Ave 16601
E 27th Ave 16601
27th St
300-819 16602
820-999 16601
S 27th St 16602
28th Ave 16601
28th St
300-819 16602
820-999 16601
29th Ave 16601
29th St
200-799 16602
820-999 16601
30th Ave 16601
30th St
100-599 16602
860-999 16601
31st Ave 16601
31st St
101-397 16602
399-819 16602
820-858 16601
860-999 16601
32nd Ave 16601
32nd St
500-598 16602
800-999 16601
33rd St 16601
35th St 16602
940-1099 16601
36th St 16601
37th St 16602
840-999 16601
38th St
200-599 16602
840-899 16601
39th St
200-820 16602
821-3999 16601
40th St
100-599 16602
840-999 16601
41st St
100-599 16602
840-899 16601
42nd St 16601
43rd St 16602
44th St 16602
45th St 16602
48th St 16601
49th St 16602
1200-1399 16601
50th St 16602
1000-1099 16601
51st St
200-599 16602
1100-1299 16601
52nd St 16602
53rd St 16602
1100-1199 16601
54th St
200-599 16602
800-1199 16601
55th St
200-599 16602
800-999 16601
56th St
200-599 16602
800-899 16601
57th St 16602
58th St 16602
700-1599 16601
59th St
100-699 16602
1100-1299 16601
60th St
100-399 16602
1100-1199 16601
61st St 16601
62nd St 16601
65th St 16601
14 1/2 St 16601
18 1/2 St 16601

BETHLEHEM PA

General Delivery 18016

POST OFFICE BOXES MAIN OFFICE STATIONS AND BRANCHES

Box No.s
1 - 1998 18016
3001 - 3534 18017
4001 - 4714 18018
5001 - 5538 18015

NAMED STREETS

Aaron St 18015
Abbe Ct 18017
Abbey Ct 18020
Abington Rd 18018
Acker Ave 18015
Adams Ave & St 18015
Adler Pl 18017
Airport Rd 18017
Alaree St 18015
Alaska St 18015
Alder Ln 18015
Alder Rd 18020
Alexander Rd 18017
Alfred Dr 18017
Alice Dr 18015
Allegheny Ln 18017
Allegiance Dr 18017
Allen Cir 18017
Allen Dr 18017
Allen St 18020
Allen Way 18017
Allwood Dr 18018
Altonah Rd 18017
Alyssa Pl 18017
Ambassador Dr 18017
American Way 18017
Amherst Ct
1400-1599 18015
3701-3799 18020
Amherst Dr 18015
Amherst Rd 18018
Amplex St 18015
Andover Rd 18018
Andrea Cir 18017
Angela Dr 18017
Angelo Dr 18017
Anthony Ct 18020
Anthony Dr 18020
Anthony Rd 18017
Apache Ln 18017
Apollo Dr 18017
Apple St 18015
Apple Tree Ln E 18015
Applebutter Rd 18015
Apples Church Rd 18015
Applewood Ct & Dr 18020
Arcadia St 18018
Arch St 18018
Arden Ln 18015
Argus Ct & St 18015
Aripine Ave 18018
Arlington St 18017
Armstrong Rd 18017
Artemis Cir 18017
Asa Dr 18015
Ash St 18015
Ashley Ln 18017
Ashton Dr 18017
Aspen Ct 18020
Aster Rd 18018
Athena Dr 18017
Atlantic St 18015
Atlss Dr 18015

Auburn St 18015
Aurora St 18018
Autumn Ridge Rd 18017
Avenue A 18017
Avenue B 18017
Avenue C 18017
Avenue Du Vlg 18015
Avon Rd 18017
Bach Ct 18017
Bachman Dr 18020
Baglyos Cir 18020
Banner Dr 18017
Barbara St 18017
Barbary St 18017
Barclay Ct 18015
Barclay Dr 18017
Bard St 18017
Barlow Pl 18020
Barner Ct 18015
Barnsdale Rd 18017
Barrett Dr 18017
Barrington Rd 18018
Barry Dr 18017
Barrymore Ln 18017
Bastian St 18015
Bates Ave 18017
Bath Pike 18017
Bathgate Rd
1700-1798 18017
1900-1999 18018
Bayard St 18017
Bayberry Ln 18018
Beacon Ave 18017
Beasholi Ave 18018
Beaufort Dr 18017
Bedford Dr 18020
Beech St
400-408 18018
410-431 18018
433-499 18018
1600-1699 18015
Beechwood Ct 18015
Beeline Dr 18015
Belaire Rd 18017
Bella Vista Dr 18017
Belmont St 18017
N & S Benner Ave 18015
Benton Ct 18015
Bergen Cir 18017
N Bergen St 18015
S Bergen St 18015
Best Pl 18017
Bethlehem Dr 18017
Bethlehem Plz 18018
Bethlehem Fields Way 18015
Betsy Ross Cir 18017
Beverly Ave 18018
Biafore Ave 18017
Bierys Bridge Rd 18017
Bigal Ct 18020
Bingen Rd 18015
Biondo Ct 18017
Birch Dr 18020
Birch Knoll Ln 18015
Birchwood Dr 18017
Birkel Ave 18015
Birmingham Sq 18017
N & S Bishopthorpe St 18015
Black River Rd 18015
Blair Rd 18017
Blake Ct & St 18017
Blossom Cir 18017
Blossom Ln
1900-1999 18015
2000-2199 18018
Blue Ridge Dr 18020
Bluestone Dr 18017
Bonnie Ave 18017
Bonnie Dr 18018
Borda Ln 18020
Boswell Ct 18020
Boulevard Grand Cru 18015
Bowler Ct 18020
Boyd St 18017
Brad Ln 18015
Brader St 18020
Bradford St 18018
Bradley St 18015
Brandeis Ave 18020
Brandford Ct 18020
Brandon Rd 18017
Brandywine Dr 18020
Brentwood Ave 18017
Brian Jones Way 18015
Briarclift Dr 18017
Briarstone Rd 18017
Briarwood Cir 18015
Briarwood Dr 18020
Briarwood Ln 18020
Briarwood Pl 18017
Bridge Ln
1900-1999 18015
2800-3099 18020
Bridge St 18018
Bridle Path Pl & Rd 18017
Bright Ln 18015
Brighton St 18015
E & W Broad St 18018
Broadhead Ct 18015
Broadway 18015
Brodhead Ave 18015
Brodhead Rd
100-278 18017
280-298 18017
2200-3699 18020
Brook Ln 18015
Brookside Dr 18018
Brown St 18017
Browning Ln 18017
Bruce Ln 18020
Brumar Dr 18017
Brunswick Ct 18015
Buchanan St 18015
Buck Ave 18015
Buckingham Dr 18017
Bucknell Cir, Ct & Dr 18015
Budd Ave 18018
Burgess Pl 18017
Burtis Rd 18017
Butztown Rd
100-300 18020
302-398 18020
1100-2200 18017
2202-2698 18017
Callone Ave 18017
Calypso Ave 18018
Camac Ave 18015
Cambria St 18017
Cambridge Ave 18018
Cambridge Ct 18015
Camelot Dr 18017
Campbell Dr 18020
Campbell St 18017
Campus Sq 18015
Canning St 18015
Cannon Ave 18015
Canterbury Ct & Rd 18020
Cardinal Dr 18015
Carlisle St 18017
Carls Ln 18015
Carlton Ave 18015
Carmen St 18015
Carol Ave 18018
Carol Ann Way 18015
Carriage Knoll Dr 18015
Carter Rd 18020
Carver Dr 18017
Catasauqua Rd
1420A-1420G 18017
Cawley Ave 18020
Cayuga St 18017
Cedar Ln 18015
Cedar St 18017
Cemetery Ln 18015
Centennial Dr
1-99 18015
2600-2699 18017
Center St
301-397 18018
399-1599 18018
1600-3199 18017
3201-3299 18017
Central Blvd 18018
Central Park Ave 18018
Chalfonte Ave 18020
Chapel Ln 18015
Charles St 18020
Chaucer Ln 18017
Chauncey St 18020
Chelsea Ave 18018
Chelsea Ct 18020
Chelsea Dr 18020
Chenango Dr 18017
Chenault Dr 18017
Cherokee St 18015
Cherry Ave 18017
Cherry Ln 18015
Cherry St 18020
Cherry Blossom Ct N & S 18020
Cherrywood Ct 18020
Cheryl Dr 18017
Chester Ave 18020
Chester Rd 18017
Chester St 18017
Chesterfield Ln 18017
Chestnut St 18017
Chippendale Cir 18017
Christian St 18015
Christian Spring Rd 18020
Christine Ct 18017
Christine St
1400-1499 18015
2800-3199 18020
Church Ln 18015
Church Rd 18015
Church St
12-98 18017
1300-1400 18015
1402-1498 18015
E Church St 18018
W Church St 18015
Ciara Dr 18017
Circle Dr 18020
City Line Rd 18017
Claire St 18017
Clauser Dr 18015
Clay St 18018
Clearfield Ave 18015
Clearfield St 18017
Clearview Ln 18017
Clermont St 18017
Cleveland St 18017
N & S Clewell St 18015
Clifton Ave
1400-1499 18018
2900-3399 18020
Clos Renoir 18015
Clos St Vincent 18015
Clover Ave 18018
Cloverdale Rd 18018
Cloverleaf St 18017
Club Ave 18018
Clubhouse Dr 18020
Coal Yard Rd 18015
Cobblestone Ln 18020
Coke Works Rd 18015
Coleman St 18020
Colesville Rd 18015
Colgate Ct 18020
Colgate Dr 18015
Collingswood Dr 18018
Collins Ave 18015
Colonial Ct 18020
Colony Dr 18017
Columbia Ct 18020
Columbia St 18015
Columbine Ave 18018
Comfort Cir 18017
N & S Commerce Way 18017
Commerce Center Blvd 18015
Commonwealth Dr 18020
Concord Ave 18017
Concord Ln 18015
Conestoga St 18018
Congress Way 18017
Connolly Ave 18015
Constitution Dr 18017
Constitution Rd 18015
Copenhagen Sq 18017
Coppee Dr 18015
Cornell Rd 18020
Cornwall Rd 18017
Corona St 18018
Cortez St 18015
Cortland Ln 18015
Cortland St 18018
Cottage Ave 18018
Cottage Dr 18020
Cottage Ln 18020
Country Ln 18017
Country Pl 18018
Country Rd 18015
Country Top Ct & Trl 18020
Courtney St 18017
Cove Ct 18017
Coventry Ct 18015
Covington Ave & Pl 18017
Craig Ave 18018
Crawford Dr & St 18017
Creek Rd 18015
Creek View Rd 18015
Crest Ave 18015
Crest Park Ct 18015
Crestline Ave 18015
Crestwood Dr 18020
Crestwood Rd 18018
Crofton Dr 18017
Cross Ln 18015
Cross Creek Ct & Rd 18017
Crystal Dr 18020
Cumberland St 18017
Cypress Ct 18020
Cypress Ln 18020
Cypress Rd 18018
Dakotah St 18015
Dale Ln 18018
Dalehurst Dr 18018
Daly Ave 18015
Darien Rd 18020
Darrel Ct 18020
Dartford Rd 18015
Dartmouth Dr
1301-1397 18017
1399-1599 18017
3400-3999 18020
Davann Dr 18017
Davis St 18015
Dearborn St 18015
Debrecen Sq 18017
Decatur St 18017
Dech St 18018
Declaration Dr 18017
Deer Run Rd 18015
Delaware Ave 18015
Delaware Rd 18017
Dellwood St 18018
Delong Ave 18020
Delwin Ct 18020
Dennis Ct 18020
Dennis Ln 18015
Dennis St 18020
Derby Ln 18020
Deschler St 18015
Devonshire Dr 18017
Devonshire Rd 18020
Dewalt St 18020
Dewberry Ave 18017
Dickinson Ln 18015
Diehl Ave 18015
Dixon Ct 18015
Dodson St 18015
Dogwood Ln 18018
Dogwood Rd 18017
Dolores Ln
200-266 18020
268-298 18020
4500-4599 18017
Donegal Dr 18020
Dorothy Ave 18015
Douglas Ct 18015
Douglas Dr 18020
Dove Dr 18017
Dover Ln 18017
Dravo Dr 18015
Drift Ct 18020
Driftwood Pl 18020
Drighton Ct 18020
Drury Ln 18018
Dublin Ct 18020
Duh Dr 18015
Dundee Ct & Rd 18020
Dusseldorf Sq 18017
East Blvd 18017
Easthill Dr 18017
Eastman Ave 18018
Easton Ave
1300-1328 18018
1330-1499 18018
1500-3099 18017
3101-3199 18017
3200-4599 18020
Easton Rd 18015
N Easton Rd 18015
Eastwood Dr 18018
Eastwood Rd 18017
Eaton Ave 18018
Ebner Ct 18020
Echo Cir 18018
Eden Ln 18018
Edge St 18017
Edgeboro Blvd 18017
Edgehill Rd 18017
Edgewood Ave 18017
Edna Terrace Ave 18020
Edward St 18015
Eileen Ct 18020
Eisenhower Dr 18020
Elayne St 18017
Elder St 18020
Elinor St 18015
E & W Elizabeth Ave 18018
Elliott Ave 18018
Elm St
1-99 18017
500-698 18018
700-1499 18018
1500-1500 18017
1501-1501 18018
1502-1899 18017
Elmhurst Ave 18017
Elmira Dr 18017
Emerson Cir 18017
Emery St 18015
Empire Ct 18020
Emrick Blvd 18020
Englewood St 18017
Erny Ave 18015
Essex Ct
1000-1099 18017
1400-1499 18015
E & W Ettwein St 18018
Euclid Ave
800-899 18015
901-999 18015
1701-1759 18018
1761-1799 18018
Evans St 18015
Evergreen Dr
1200-1399 18015
3900-4099 18020
Evergreen Pl 18017
Exeter Ct 18017
Fairfax Ct & Rd 18020
Fairland Ave 18018
Fairlee Ct 18020
Fairmount St 18017
Fairview St
2700-3299 18020
3500-3598 18017
3600-3799 18017
E Fairview St 18018
W Fairview St 18018
Fairway Rd 18020
Falcon Ct & Dr 18017
Falmer Dr 18020
Farm Ln 18018
Farm View Ct 18020
Farmersville Rd 18020
Federal Dr 18017
Ferncroft Ln 18020
Fernway Ave 18018
Fernwood St 18018
Field Dr 18020
Fieldstone Dr 18015
Fieldview Ln 18015
Filbert St 18018
Fillmore St 18015
Finady Ave 18015
Finches Garden Rd 18015
Fiot Ave & St 18015
Fire Ln 18015
Fireside Dr 18018
Flagstone Dr 18017
Flammer St 18020
Fleming St 18017
Fleur Ln 18018
Flora Ln 18020
Florence Ave 18018
Flower Dr 18017
Focht Ave 18015
Foothill Rd 18015
Forge Run 18015
Fornance Rd 18020
Forrest Ave 18017
Forrest St 18015
Forrest Hill Dr 18015
Fortuna St 18015
Founders Ct 18020
Founders Way 18015
Fox Dr 18017
Fox Ln 18015
Fox Chase Dr 18020
Foxview Dr 18017
Francis St 18015
Frank St 18020
E & W Frankford St 18018
Franklin Aly 18018
Franklin Ct
100-199 18020
1400-1499 18015
Franklin Ln 18015
Franklin St 18018
Frederick St 18015
Freedom Ct 18020
Freeman St 18020
Freemansburg Ave & Rd 18020
Friebley Ave 18015
Friedensville Rd 18015
Fritch Dr 18020
Fritz Ave 18015
Fritz Dr 18017
Fulmer St 18018
Gable Dr 18020
Gail Ln 18017
Galway Dr 18020
Garden Ct 18017
Garfield St 18017
Garrett Cir & Rd 18017
E & W Garrison St 18018
Gary St 18018
Gaspar Ave 18017
Gateway Dr 18017
Gatewood Ln 18018
Geissinger St 18018
General Dr 18017
Georgetown Rd 18020
Georgia Ave 18017
Geraldine St 18017
Gilly Ave 18015
Ginger Ln 18020
Girard Ave 18015
Glassboro Pl 18020
Glen View Dr 18015
Glendale Ave 18018
Glendon Rd 18017
Glenmere St 18017
Glenwood Ct 18015
Glenwood Dr 18015
Glenwood St 18017
Glerlea St 18020
Gloria Ln 18017
Glory Way 18017
Gloucester Dr & Pl 18020
Goepp Cir 18018
E Goepp St
1-799 18018
901-999 18017
W Goepp St 18018
Goodman Dr 18015
Gordon Ct 18017
Gordon St 18020
Gottwald Dr 18015
Grace Ave 18017
Gradwohl St 18020
Graham Pl & St 18015
Gramercy Pl 18020
Grandview Blvd 18018
Granite Cir & Dr 18017
Grant St 18015
Green Ln 18017
Green St
1-299 18017
1900-1998 18018
2001-2099 18018
Green Acres Dr 18015
Green Meadow Cir & Dr 18017
Green Pond Rd 18020
Greenbriar Dr 18017
Greencrest Dr 18017
Greene Ct 18015
Greenfield Rd 18017
Greenhouse Dr 18017
Greenleaf Ct, Dr & St 18017
Greenview Dr 18018
E & W Greenwich St 18018
Greenwood Ave 18017
Greenwood Ct
1300-1399 18015
1401-1499 18015
4200-4299 18020
Greenwood Dr
1200-1299 18017
3800-4199 18020
W Greenwood Dr 18020
Greiner St 18020
Grenadier Blvd 18018
Gresham St 18017
Grouse Dr 18017
Grove Rd 18018
Guetter St 18018
Gwenmawr Rd 18017
Hader Ln 18015
Hafler Rd 18015
N & S Halbea St 18017
Hale Ave 18017
Haller Ave 18020
Hamilton Ave
100-799 18017
1700-1799 18015
Hampshire Dr & Rd 18017
Hampton Rd 18020
Hannahs Ln 18020
Hanover St
300-600 18018
602-698 18018
4000-6999 18017
Hanoverville Rd
4400-4999 18020
5000-6399 18017
Harmor Cir & Ln 18017
Harper Ct 18020
Harriet Ln 18017
Harrison Ave 18015
Hart St 18017
Hartman Rd 18020
Harvard Ave 18015
Harvard Pl 18020
Harvey Rd 18020
Hastings Rd 18017
Hawthorne Rd
621-697 18018
699-899 18018
1700-1799 18015
Hay Ave 18020
Hayes St 18015
Hazlewood Ln 18018

Heckewelder Pl 18018
Hecktown Rd 18020
Helen St 18017
Hellener St 18015
Hellertown Rd 18015
Helsinki Sq 18017
Hemlock Pl 18017
Henderson Pl & St 18017
Herbert Dr 18018
Hercules Dr 18017
Hertzog Ave 18015
Hess St 18015
Hickory St 18017
Hickory Hill Rd 18015
Hidden Hill Dr 18017
High St 18018
High Point Blvd & Dr 18017
High Ridge Rd 18015
Highbridge Ct 18020
Highfield Cir & Dr 18020
Highland Ave
1-49 18017
51-99 18017
600-1299 18018
1900-2399 18020
2401-2599 18020
Highland Ct 18015
Highland Dr 18015
Hill Rd & St 18015
Hillcrest Ave
300-399 18020
1600-1699 18015
Hillcrest Rd 18018
Hillmond St
2-42 18018
44-99 18018
201-299 18017
Hillside Ave & Dr 18015
Hilltop Cir 18020
Hilltop Pl 18020
Hilltop Rd 18015
Hilltop Ter 18018
Hilly Rd 18017
Hilton St 18017
Hobart St 18015
Hoch St 18015
N & S Hoffert St 18015
Holland Ave 18017
Holly Ct 18020
Holly Pl 18018
Homestead Ave 18018
Honeysuckle Rd 18015
Honor Dr 18017
Hopewell Cir & Rd 18017
Hottle Ave 18018
Howard St 18017
Hummingbird Ln 18020
Huntington St 18017
Hurley Ct 18020
Illes Ln 18015
Illicks Mill Rd 18017
Independence Ct 18020
Industrial Dr 18017
Irene St 18017
Iris Pl 18018
Irlyn Rd 18015
Iron St 18018
Ironstone Ct & Rd 18020
Itaska St 18015
Ivan St 18020
Ivanhoe Rd 18017
Ivy Ct 18015
Ivywood Ave 18015
Jackson St
1-99 18017
400-799 18015
Jacksonville Rd 18017
Jaclyn Ln 18017
Jadden Ct 18015
Jaindl Blvd 18017
Jamann Ct 18017
James St
1400-1498 18015
2500-2598 18020
Janet Ln 18017
Janmar Ct 18017

Jasmine Dr 18020
Jean Ln 18015
Jeanette Dr 18020
Jeannie Dr 18017
Jefferson Ave
1500-1799 18017
4200-4399 18015
Jefferson Pl 18020
Jefferson St 18020
Jendy Ln 18017
Jenna Ct 18020
Jennings Pl & St 18017
Jerome St 18018
Jeter Ave 18015
Jill St 18017
Jischke St 18015
Jodi Ct 18020
John St 18015
Johnston Ave 18015
Johnston Dr
1419A-1419D 18017
1423A-1423D 18017
1427A-1427D 18017
1431A-1431D 18017
1435A-1435D 18017
1438A-1438D 18017
1439A-1439D 18017
1440A-1440D 18017
1443A-1443D 18017
1447A-1447D 18017
1450A-1450D 18017
1451A-1451D 18017
1452A-1452D 18017
1461A-1461D 18017
1465A-1465D 18017
1467A-1467D 18017
1508A-1508D 18017
1510A-1510D 18017
1515A-1515D 18017
1519A-1519D 18017
1520A-1520D 18017
1522A-1522D 18017
200-2099 18017
2100-2198 18020
Jonathan Ln 18015
Jones St 18018
Judith St 18020
Julia Ct 18017
Julick Dr 18020
Juniata St 18017
Juniper Dr & Ln 18020
Kadel Dr 18018
Karen Dr 18017
Karoly St 18017
Kathi Dr 18017
Kaywin Ave 18018
Keen St 18015
Kelchner Rd 18018
Kelchner St 18020
Kemmerer St 18017
Kenchen St 18017
Kendall Ct 18020
Kenilworth Ct 18018
Kenmore Ave 18018
Kennedy Ct 18020
Kenny Dr 18018
Kenrick Dr 18020
Kensington Rd 18018
Kenwick Cir & Dr 18017
Kenwood Dr 18017
Kerchner Dr 18017
Kern St 18015
Kevin Dr
300-599 18017
1600-1699 18015
Keystone Ave 18018
Keystone Dr 18020
Keystone St 18020
Kieffer St 18015
Killarney Dr 18020
Kim St 18017
Kimberly Ct 18020
Kimberly Rd 18018
Kingsley Dr 18018
Kipling Pl 18017
Kipton Ct 18020
Kirkland Village Cir 18017

Kistler Ave 18015
Klein Ct & St 18020
Kline St 18015
Knollwood Rd 18015
Koehler Dr 18015
Kossuth St 18017
Lafayette Ave 18017
Lafayette Dr 18020
Laible St 18015
Lamb St 18015
Landis Mill Rd 18015
Lane Ave 18017
E & W Langhorne Ave & Dr 18017
Lansdale Ave 18017
Lark Dr 18017
Laubach Ln 18020
Laufer St 18015
Laurel Ct 18020
Laurel Dr 18017
E Laurel St 18018
W Laurel St 18018
Laury St 18015
Lavan St 18015
Lawrence Dr & St 18015
Lebanon St 18017
Lechauwecki Ave 18015
Lehigh St 18020
E Lehigh St 18018
W Lehigh St 18018
Leibert St 18018
Lenaire Rd 18020
Lenox Ave 18018
Lenox Dr 18017
Levering Pl 18017
Lewis Ave
3200-3399 18020
4200-4299 18015
Lewis St 18017
Lexington Ave 18017
Liberty Blvd 18017
Liberty Ct 18017
Liberty St 18018
Library Dr 18015
Lilac Dr 18017
Lime St 18020
Limerick Sq 18017
Limestone Cir 18017
Lincoln Ct & St 18017
Lindberg St 18020
Linden St
400-1499 18018
1500-1917 18017
1919-3599 18017
1928-1928 18020
2000-3412 18017
3414-3414 18020
3464-3534 18017
3550-3710 18020
3712-3927 18020
3929-3935 18020
Linden Oaks Ln 18015
Line Ct 18017
Linwood St 18017
Lisa Dr 18020
Lisa Ln 18015
Livingston St 18017
Lock House Rd 18017
Locksley Dr 18018
E & W Locust St 18018
Lois Ln 18018
Long Ct 18020
Long Dr 18020
Long St
400-599 18018
601-799 18018
900-998 18015
901-999 18015
Longfellow Pl 18017
Longwood Dr 18020
Lorain Ave 18018
Loraine Ln 18017
Lord Byron Dr 18017
Lowell Pl 18020
Lower Sayre Park Rd 18015
Loyal Dr 18017

Lucas Dr 18017
Ludwig Ln 18017
Luna St 18018
Luther St 18018
Luzerne St 18017
Lynfield Ct & Dr 18015
N & S Lynn Ave & St 18015
Lynnhurst Cir, Dr & Pl 18017
Lyons St 18018
E & W Macada Rd 18017
Madison Ave
1300-1499 18018
1500-2799 18017
4200-4299 18015
Madison Dr 18020
Madison St 18017
Magnolia Ct 18020
Mahopac Dr 18017
Main St
1-699 18017
418-434 18018
436-1828 18018
701-827 18017
1829-2999 18017
Majestic Overlook Dr 18015
Major St 18017
Manchester Rd 18018
Manor Dr 18015
Manor Rd 18020
Mansfield Ct 18017
Maple Ave 18015
Maple St
400-1499 18018
1500-1999 18017
Maplewood Ave 18020
Marble Cir & Dr 18017
Marchant Dr 18017
Margate Rd 18020
Maria Dr 18020
Maria Ln 18017
Marick Cir 18015
Marion St 18017
Mark Twain Cir 18017
Market St
1-199 18017
3300-3399 18020
E Market St
1-499 18018
501-599 18018
900-1999 18017
2001-2099 18017
W Market St 18018
Markham Dr 18017
Mars Ct 18017
Marshall St 18017
Martel St 18015
Martin Ct 18018
Martin Tower 18018
Martins Ln 18018
Marvine St 18017
Mary St 18017
Maryann Ln 18017
Masslich St 18018
Mathews Ave 18015
Matts Dr 18017
Mauch Chunk Rd 18018
E Mayfield Cir 18020
Mccloskey Ave 18015
Mckinley Ave 18015
Mckinley St 18017
Meade St 18015
Meadow Cir 18017
Meadow Ln 18020
Meadow Lark Way 18015
Meadow Ridge Ct 18015
Meadow View Dr 18020
Meadows Rd 18015
Mechanic St 18015
Media St 18017
Melanie Ct 18020
Melina Ct 18017
Melrose Ave 18017
N Melrose Ave 18015
S Melrose Ave 18015
Melrose Ct 18020
Memorial Ave 18017

Memorial Dr E 18015
Memorial Dr W 18015
Mercury St 18018
Merriman Ct 18017
Merrivale Rd 18017
Merryweather Dr 18015
Mertwood St 18015
Meyer Ct & Rd 18020
Mica Cir 18017
Michael St 18017
Michigan Ct 18020
Middle Rd 18017
Middletown Rd 18020
Mikron Rd 18020
Mildred Ln 18015
Mill St 18020
Millard St
1400-1498 18018
1600-1899 18017
Miller Cir N 18020
Miller St
700-799 18018
801-899 18018
3600-3799 18020
Millstone Dr 18020
Milton St 18018
Minsi Trail St 18018
Mission Rd 18017
Mixsell Ave 18015
Mockingbird Hill Rd 18015
Moffitt Ave 18018
Mohawk Dr 18017
Mohican St 18015
Monocacy Dr 18017
Monocacy St 18018
Monocacy Creek Rd 18017
Monroe St
710A-710C 18017
1-1099 18017
300-398 18015
1700-3398 18020
Montauk Ln 18017
Montclair Ave 18015
Montgomery St 18017
Montrose Ave 18018
Moravia St 18015
Moravian Ct 18020
Moreland Ave 18017
Morningstar Ln 18018
Mortimer St 18015
E & W Morton St 18015
Mosselle Ave 18020
Motel Dr 18018
Mount Airy Ave 18018
Mountain Dr N 18015
Mountain View Dr 18015
Mountainview Cir 18017
Muhlenberg Ct 18017
Mulberry Dr 18017
Munsee Ln 18017
Muschlitz St 18015
Myriah Ct 18020
Nace Ave 18015
Nala Dr 18017
Nantucket Cir 18015
Nazareth Pike 18020
Nemeth Dr 18015
New St 18017
N New St 18018
S New St 18015
New World Ct 18020
Newburg Rd 18020
Nicholas St 18017
Nicholson Ct & Rd 18020
Nicole Ln 18017
Nijaro Rd 18020
Nolf St 18018
Norfolk Dr 18020
Norma Ln 18017
North Blvd 18017
North Cir 18018
North Ct 18017
North Dr 18015
E North St
1-650 18018
652-764 18018
801-825 18017
827-899 18017
W North St 18018
Northampton Ave 18015
Northampton St 18020
Northgate Dr 18017
Norton St 18020
Norway Pl 18015
Norwood St 18015
Notre Dame Ct 18020
Nottingham Ct & Rd 18017
N & S Oak St 18017
E Oakhurst Dr 18015
Oakland Rd
2800-2898 18017
2900-2999 18017
3000-4199 18020
Oakland St 18017
Oakland Square Dr 18020
Oakside Cir & Dr 18017
Oakwood Ct 18015
Oakwood Dr 18017
Oberly St 18015
Obriens Ct 18015
Ohley Ct 18020
Old Bethlehem Pike 18015
Old Farmersville Rd 18020
Old Mill Rd 18015
Old Nazareth Pike 18020
Old Philadelphia Pike 18015
Old York Rd 18018
Olde Glory Ln 18017
Oliver Ave & Ct 18020
Olivia Ct 18017
Ontario Ln 18017
Ontario St 18015
Opus Way 18020
Orchard Ln
500-1500 18017
1502-1798 18017
3400-4098 18020
4100-4199 18020
Orchard St 18018
Orion St 18018
Orth St 18020
Osage Ln 18017
Osborne Ct 18015
Ostrum St 18015
Oswego Dr 18017
Overlook Dr 18017
Oxford Dr 18017
E & W Packer Ave 18015
Park Ave 18020
Park Pl
500-599 18018
3400-3499 18017
4100-4199 18020
Park Rd 18020
Parkhill St 18015
Parkview Ct 18018
Parson St 18017
Patriots Dr 18017
Patterson Dr 18017
Paul Ave 18018
Paupack Cir & Ln 18017
Pawnee St 18015
Peach Tree Ln 18015
Peacock Dr 18020
Pelham Rd 18018
Pembroke Pl 18020
Pembroke Rd
401-497 18018
499-899 18018
900-1198 18017
1200-1399 18017
1401-1599 18017
Penn St 18018
Penn State Ct 18020
Pennsylvania Ave 18018
Penstock Ct 18015
Perry St 18015
Pheasant Ct 18015
Pheasant Ln 18020
Pheasant Rd 18017
Pheasant Run Ct 18020
Phillip St 18015

Pickwick Pl 18020
Pierce St 18015
Pike St 18018
Pine St 18018
Pine Top Cir, Dr, Pl & Trl 18017
Pinehurst Rd 18018
Pinel Ln 18020
Pioneer Rd 18017
Place Rd 18017
Pleasant Dr 18015
Pleasant View Rd 18015
Plymouth St 18015
W Point Dr 18015
Polk St 18015
Pond Cir 18020
Pond View Ct 18020
Poplar St 18017
Portage Rd 18020
Post Dr 18017
Powder Mill Cir & Rd 18017
Preakness Pl 18020
Prescott Rd 18020
Presidential Blvd 18017
Presidential Dr 18020
Presidents Dr 18017
Primrose Ct 18020
Primrose Ln 18018
Princeton Ave 18015
Princeton Dr 18017
Princeton Pl 18020
Priscilla Ln 18018
Prospect Ave 18018
Public Rd 18015
Puggy Ln 18015
Pulaski St 18018
Quad Dr 18015
Quail Ct 18015
Quail Creek Rd 18017
Quaker Dr 18020
Quarry Dr 18020
Quarter Mile Rd 18015
Quincy Ave 18015
Quincy Ln 18017
Rabold Cir S 18020
Rachel Dr 18020
Radclyffe St 18017
Rader Ave 18015
E & W Raders Ln 18015
Railroad St 18015
Rainbow Dr 18017
Ralston Rd 18018
Rambeau Rd 18020
Ramblewood Ln 18017
Rambling Rose Ct 18015
Randolf Rd 18017
E & W Raspberry St 18018
Rauch St 18018
Ravena St 18015
Ravenwood Dr 18018
Raymond Ave 18018
Reading Dr 18015
Red Hawk Way 18015
Red Lawn Dr 18017
Red Oak Cir & Ln 18017
Redfern Ln 18017
Redwood Ct & Dr 18020
Reeve Dr 18020
Regal Rd 18020
Regency Ct 18020
Reilly Ln 18015
Remaley St 18017
Renwick St 18017
Republic Way 18017
Research Dr 18015
Resolution Dr 18017
Rexford Dr 18020
Richard Ave 18018
Richmond Ave 18018
Ridge St 18015
Ridge View Ct 18020
Ridgelawn Ave 18018
Ridon Ct 18020
Riegel St
500-598 18018
2500-2799 18020

Rim Rd 18020
Ringhoffer Rd 18015
Rink St 18015
Ritter Ave 18020
Ritter St
1700-1799 18015
1900-1998 18018
River Dr 18015
River St
1-199 18015
100-198 18018
Riverside Dr 18015
Riverwoods Way 18018
Roberts Ave 18015
Robin Ct 18015
Robin Way 18018
E Rock Rd 18015
Rockhill Cir 18017
Rockingham Dr 18018
Rockland St 18017
Rodgers St 18017
Rohn Ln 18020
Ronca St 18015
Roosevelt Ave 18015
Roosevelt Dr 18020
Roosevelt St
300-430 18017
432-498 18017
2700-3199 18020
Rose Ave 18018
Rosebay Ct E & W 18020
Rosedale Ln 18017
Roselawn Dr 18017
E & W Rosemont Dr 18018
Rosewood Dr 18017
Ross Rd 18020
Roth St 18017
Rotterdam Sq 18017
Round St 18018
Route 378 18015
Route 512 18017
Rovaldi Ave 18015
Rowe Ln 18015
Royal Ln 18017
Ruby Ct 18020
Ruch Rd 18017
Rudolph Dr 18018
Rumson Ct 18015
Russell Ave 18015
Rutgers Dr 18020
Ruth Rd 18020
Rutland Rd 18020
Ryan St 18015
Rye Ct 18020
Saddle Dr 18020
Saddlebrook Ln 18017
Saint Lukes Pl 18015
Salinka Sq 18017
Sanbrook Ct & Dr 18015
Sandra St 18020
Sands Blvd 18015
Santee Dr 18017
Santee Rd
2701-2797 18020
2799-3300 18020
3302-3466 18020
3401-3499 18017
Santee Mill Rd 18017
Sapphire Ln 18020
Sarah Beth Ln 18020
Sassafras St 18015
Saucon Ave & Ln 18015
Saucon Dale Cir 18015
Saucon Meadow Ct 18015
Saucon Valley Rd 18015
Saucon View Dr 18015
Savercool Ave 18015
Sayre Dr 18015
Schaffer St 18018
Schelden Cir 18017
Scherman Blvd 18020
Schlegel Ave 18020
Schoenersville Rd
1805A-1805D 18018
Scholl Ave 18015
School Ct 18017
School St
600-899 18018
801-949 18015
900-950 18015
901-919 18018
951-952 18015
953-999 18015
954-998 18015
1000-1098 18018
Schwab Ave 18015
Schweitzer Ave 18020
Scott St 18015
Scottie Ln 18015
Sculac Rd 18020
Searfoss St 18020
Seidersville Rd 18015
Seip Rd 18017
Selfridge St 18015
Seminole St 18015
Senate Dr 18017
Seneca St 18015
Sequoia Rd 18020
Service Dr 18015
Sesame St 18015
Shakespeare Rd 18017
Shannon Ave 18020
Sharon Ct 18020
Shawnee Dr 18017
Shawnee St 18015
Sheets St 18015
Shelbourne Dr 18018
Shelley Ln 18017
Shelton Ave 18020
Sherbrooke Dr 18015
Sheridan Cir 18017
Shields St 18015
Shileagh Ct 18020
Shimer Ave 18018
Shimersville Rd 18015
Shipman St 18018
Shows Rd 18017
Siegfried St 18017
Silk Mill St 18018
Silvex Rd 18015
Sioux St 18015
Skibo Rd 18015
Skyline Dr
2100-2299 18015
3500-3599 18020
Smiley Ave 18015
Smith Dr 18017
Smolt Cir 18018
Snowdrift Rd 18017
Snyder Ave 18015
Snyder St 18017
Somerset St 18017
Sondor Pl 18020
Sonoma Dr 18015
Sour Apple Ln 18015
South Blvd & Ct 18017
Southgate Cir 18020
Southland Dr 18017
Spear St 18020
Spiegel St 18015
Spillman Dr 18015
Spring Ct 18017
Spring St 18018
Spring Garden St 18017
Spring Valley Rd 18015
Springfield Dr 18018
Springwood Rd 18015
Spruce Ct 18020
Spruce St 18017
E Spruce St 18018
W Spruce St 18018
Stafford Ave 18020
Stafford St 18015
Stafore Dr 18017
Stanbridge Ct 18020
Stanford Rd 18018
Stanhope St 18017
Stanley Ave 18015
Star Ct 18017
Stark Rd 18017
Starview Ln 18020
State St 18015
Station Ave 18015
Statten Ave 18017
Steel Ave 18015
Stefko Blvd 18017
Stehr St
1400-1499 18018
1500-1599 18017
Stenton Dr 18017
Stephanie Dr 18020
Stephen Crane Ln 18017
Sterners Way 18017
Steuben Rd 18020
Steven St 18020
Stoke Park Rd 18017
Stone Stack Dr 18015
Stonehenge Rd 18018
Stonehill Way 18015
Stonehouse Ct 18017
Stonehurst Ct 18015
Stoneman St 18015
Stonepark Dr 18017
Stonesthrow Rd 18015
Stonewood Dr 18017
Stonington Rd 18018
Stratford St 18018
Strauss Ave 18015
Sturbridge Dr 18020
Sugar Maple Ct 18017
Sugar Maple Ln 18020
Sullivan St 18015
Summer Ave 18015
Summer Ln 18017
Summit Ct 18020
Summit St 18015
Suncrest Ln 18020
Sunderland Dr 18015
Sunrise Ln 18015
Sunset Dr 18020
Sunset Ln 18015
Sunset Pl 18017
Sunset View Cir & Dr 18017
Surrey Rd 18015
Susan Dr 18017
Sutton Pl 18020
Sycamore Ave 18017
Sycamore Rd 18015
Sycamore St 18017
Sydna St 18017
Tamarack Trl 18020
Tamarind Dr 18020
E & W Taurus St 18018
Taylor Dr & St 18015
Technology Dr 18015
Temple Ct 18020
Tennis Ct 18015
Terrace Ave 18018
Thomas Ct 18020
Thomas St 18015
Thompson Ave 18017
Timber Ln 18020
Timothy Ave 18020
Timothy Dr 18017
Timothy Ln 18020
Tioga Ave 18018
Tioga Dr 18017
Tolstoy St 18017
Tombler St 18015
Toni Ln 18017
Towanda Dr 18017
Township Line Rd
200-300 18017
302-598 18017
3600-4099 18020
4900-5099 18017
Tracey Ln 18017
Tracy Ln 18020
Trembley Dr 18015
Trent Ct 18020
Trone St 18015
Trotter Ln 18015
Troy Ct 18020
Truman Ln 18020
Trythall St 18020
Tudor Ct 18020
Tulip Ln 18015
Turner St
500-600 18018
602-698 18018
3400-4199 18020
Tuskegee Dr 18020
Tyler Way 18017
Uelen Ct 18018
Uncas St 18015
E Union Blvd 18018
W Union Blvd 18018
Union Ct 18017
E Union St 18017
Union Station Plz 18015
E & W University Ave & Dr 18015
Upper Sayre Park Rd 18015
Valencia Sq 18017
Valerie Ln 18015
Valley Park & Rd S 18018
Valley Center Pkwy 18017
Valley View Rd 18020
Valor Dr 18017
Van Buren St 18015
Vassar Ave 18017
Venice Sq 18017
Vera Cir 18017
Vernon St 18015
Versailles Sq 18017
Victory Way 18017
Village Dr 18018
Village Ln 18015
Villanova Ct 18020
Vine St 18015
Virginia Ave 18015
Virginia Dr 18017
Vista Dr 18018
Wafford Ln 18017
Wagner Dr 18020
Waldheim Rd 18015
Walker Pl 18017
E Wall St 18018
Walnut St
100-199 18017
3200-3899 18020
E Walnut St 18018
W Walnut St 18018
Walt Whitman Ln 18017
Walter Rd 18020
Walter St 18015
Walters St 18017
Walton St 18018
Warren Sq 18015
Warren St
1-99 18015
1800-1899 18020
Warwick St 18018
Washburn Ln 18015
E Washington Ave
2-28 18018
30-399 18018
400-899 18017
W Washington Ave 18018
Washington Ln 18015
Washington St
2-98 18017
100-199 18017
201-599 18017
700-798 18017
2700-4171 18020
4173-4199 18020
Watkins St 18017
Wayne St 18020
Weaversville Rd 18017
Webster St 18015
Wedgewood Rd 18017
Wegmans Dr 18017
Weil St
700-899 18015
1601-1799 18018
Wellesley Rd 18017
Wellington Dr 18020
Wellington Rd 18017
Wellington Court 2 18020
Wendel Ct 18020
Wendy Ln 18017
Werner Cir 18018
Wesley St 18018
West Blvd 18017
West St 18018
Westbury Cir & Dr 18017
Westfield Ter 18017
Westgate Cir & Dr 18017
Westminster Rd 18017
Westmont St 18015
Weston Pl 18018
Westwood Dr 18018
Weyhill Cir & Dr 18015
Weyhill Crescent Dr 18015
Weyhill Farm Rd 18015
Wharton Ln 18017
Wheaton Dr 18017
Wheatsheaf Ln 18017
White Acre Dr N 18015
White Birch Ln 18017
White Oak Cir 18017
Whitebriar Dr 18020
Whitehall Ave 18020
Whitewood Rd 18017
Wildberry Rd 18015
Wiley St 18015
Wilhelm Rd 18015
William St 18015
Williams Ave 18020
Williams Dr 18015
Willow Ct 18020
Willow Park Rd 18020
Willowbrook Ct & Dr 18015
Wilshire Ct 18018
Wilson Ave
1700-1798 18018
1800-1899 18018
3100-3899 18020
3901-4299 18020
Wimmer Rd
3201-3299 18020
6900-7899 18015
Win Dr 18017
Winding Way
300-399 18020
2800-2899 18017
Windsor Cir, Pl & Rd 18017
Windswept Dr 18020
Winside Dr 18017
Winston Cir & Rd 18017
Winters Ave 18018
Winthrop Ave 18017
Wistar St 18015
Withee Ct 18020
Wood St
500-698 18018
700-1299 18018
1400-1499 18017
Woodbine St 18017
Woodbridge Cir 18017
Woodbury Rd 18017
Woodcrest Ave 18017
Woodfield Dr 18015
Woodland Cir 18017
Woodland Dr 18015
Woodlark Cir 18017
Woodlawn Ave 18018
Woodlawn Dr 18020
Woodmere Dr 18017
Woodmont Dr 18018
Woodside Rd 18017
Woodstock Dr 18017
Worthington Ave 18017
Wright St 18015
Wyandotte St 18015
Wydnor Ln 18015
Wyndham Ter 18015
Wynnewood Dr 18017
Yale Ave 18015
Yale Ct 18020
Yeates St 18017
Yob Ln 18015
Yorkshire Dr & Rd 18017
Yost Ave 18015
Yuhas Ln 18015

NUMBERED STREETS

1st Ave 18018
1st St 18020
E 1st St 18015
1st Ter 18015
2nd Ave 18018
2nd St 18020
E 2nd St 18015
W 2nd St 18015
3rd Ave 18018
3rd St 18020
E 3rd St 18015
W 3rd St 18015
4th Ave 18018
4th St 18020
E 4th St 18015
W 4th St 18015
5th Ave 18018
5th St 18020
E 5th St 18015
6th Ave 18018
6th St 18020
E 6th St 18015
7th Ave 18018
7th St 18020
E 7th St 18015
8th Ave 18018
8th St 18020
E 8th St 18015
W 8th St 18015
9th Ave 18018
9th St 18020
E 9th St 18015
W 9th St 18015
10th Ave 18018
10th St 18020
E 10th St 18015
11th Ave 18018
11th St 18020
12th Ave 18018
12th St 18020
13th Ave 18018
13th St 18020
14th Ave 18018
14th St 18020
15th Ave 18018
15th St 18020
16th Ave 18018

BUTLER PA

General Delivery 16001

POST OFFICE BOXES MAIN OFFICE STATIONS AND BRANCHES

Box No.s
All PO Boxes 16003

NAMED STREETS

Abiline Ln 16001
Ableview Dr 16001
Abner Dr 16001
Acre Ave 16001
Acton Ln 16001
Adobe Way 16002
Adrian Ln 16001
Adventure Ln 16001
E Airport Rd 16002
Alameda Plz & Rd 16001
Alameda Park Rd 16001
Albert Ln 16001
Alexi Ln 16001
Alhambra Dr 16001
Allen Ln 16001
Alpine Ln 16001
Alyssum Dr 16001
Amberwood Ln 16002
Ambler Dr 16001
American Ave 16001
Amherst Dr 16001
Amy Ave & Ln 16001
Anderson Rd 16002
Andrews Trce 16001
Ann Arbor Ln 16001
Apple Ln 16001
Applewood Dr 16001
Apricot Ln 16002
Arabian Cir 16001
Arbutus Ln 16001
Arden Ln 16001
Ardenlee Ln 16002
Arlington Ave 16001
Armstrong Ave & Pl 16001
Art Crest Dr 16001
Art Lin Dr 16001
Arthur Dr 16001
Artlee Ave 16001
Asbury Ln 16002
Ash Ln 16002
Ash St 16001
Ashland Ave 16001
Ashmont Dr 16002
Aspen Rd 16001
Aubrey Dr 16001
August Ln 16001
Autumn Dr 16001
Autumn Hill Ln 16002
Avena St 16001
Avon Dr 16001
Ayers Ave 16001
Ayleshire Rd 16001
Azelea Ln 16002
Balboa Ct 16001
Bantam Ave 16001
Barleyfield Ln 16002
Barnes Ridge Ln 16001
Barracks Rd 16001
Barrickman Dr 16001
Barron Ln 16001
Bartley Ave 16001
Barton Ave 16001
Bauer Ln 16001
Baum Ln 16001
Baumgart Ln 16001
Baxter Ln 16001
Bay St 16002
Bay Leaf Ln 16002
Bay Street Ext 16002
Bay Tree Ln 16002
Beachem Ln 16001
Beacon Ln 16001
Bean St 16001
Beaver Dam Rd 16001
Beblo Ln 16002
Beck Rd
100-199 16001
3200-3599 16002
Becker Rd 16002
Beckert Ave 16001
Bedford Ct 16001
Beech Rd 16001
Beechwood Blvd 16001
Beilstein Ln 16002
Bellefield Dr 16001
Belleshire Dr 16001
Belmont Rd 16001
Benbrook Rd 16001
Benbrooke Pl 16001
Bennett Dr 16001
Benninger Ln 16002
Bent Creek Ln 16002
Berrywood Ln 16002
Betty Ln 16002
Beulah Rd 16001
Beverly Rd & Way 16001
Binsey Rd 16002
E & W Birch St 16001
Birchwood Dr 16001
Birds Ln 16002
Bish Rd 16002
Blackberry Hill Ln 16002
Blackshire Rd 16001
Blackthorn Dr 16002
Blain Ln 16001
Blair Dr 16001
Blakely Rd 16002
Blazing Star Dr 16002

- Blossom Dr 16001
- Bluegrass Dr 16001
- N & S Bluff St 16001
- Bocce Dr 16001
- Boff Ln 16002
- Bon Aire Dr & Plz 16001
- Bonnie Dr 16002
- Bonniebrook Rd 16002
- Bortmas Aly 16001
- Boulder Ln 16002
- E & N Boundary St 16001
- E & W Boyd Ave & Dr 16001
- Boydstown Rd 16001
- Bp Ln 16001
- Bradmoor Ln 16001
- E & W Brady St 16001
- Braethorn Dr 16001
- Bramble Ave 16001
- E Brandon Rd 16001
- Brannon Ln 16001
- Bredin St 16001
- Breese Ln 16001
- N & S Breezewood Dr 16001
- E & W Brewster Rd 16001
- Bricker Ave 16002
- Bridle Path Dr 16001
- Brier Hill Ln 16002
- Brinker Rd 16002
- Britt Ln 16002
- Broad St 16001
- Brook Ct 16001
- Brooksedge Dr 16001
- Brookstone Ct 16001
- Brown Ave 16001
- Brown Rd
  - 5100-5200 16001
  - 5202-5298 16001
  - 6101-6107 16002
  - 6109-6199 16002
- Brownsdale Rd 16002
- Brugh Ave 16001
- Bryson Rd 16001
- Bullcreek Rd 16002
- Bunchberry Ln 16002
- Burtner Rd 16002
- Butler Cmns 16001
- Butler Mall 16001
- Butler Rd 16001
- E Butler Rd 16002
- Butler Xing 16001
- Buttercup Rd 16001
- Caldwell Dr 16002
- Camelot Dr 16001
- Campbell Ave, Dr & St 16001
- Campbells Ln 16001
- Campus Ln 16001
- Candleford Ct 16001
- Candy Tuft Ln 16002
- Cantrell St 16001
- Cara Ln 16001
- Caravan Ln 16001
- Carbon St 16001
- Carbon Center Rd 16002
- Carissa Ln 16002
- Carl Ave 16001
- Carnegie St 16001
- Carrington Ave 16001
- Carroll Ave 16001
- Cashdollar Ln 16001
- Caterado Rd 16001
- Causer Ln 16001
- Cayman Dr 16002
- Cayuga Dr 16001
- Cdc Dr 16001
- Cecelia St 16001
- N Cedar Rd, Rdg & St 16001
- Cendell Ln 16001
- Center Ave & St 16001
- Central Dr 16001
- Charlemagne Dr 16002
- Charles Dr & St 16001
- Charlon St 16001
- Chase St 16001
- Chateau Ln 16001
- Cheers Ln 16002
- Cherokee Dr 16001
- Cherry St 16001
- N & S Chestnut Dr & St 16001
- Chestnut Ridge Rd 16001
- Chet Ln 16001
- Chevy Ln 16002
- Cheyenne Dr 16001
- Chick Ln 16002
- Chicora Rd 16001
- Chrie Ln 16001
- Chris Bel Dr 16002
- E & W Christie Ave 16001
- W Christie Avenue Ext 16001
- Church Rd 16002
- N Church St 16001
- S Church St 16001
- City View Hts 16001
- Clark Ave 16002
- Clayton Ave 16001
- Claytonia Rd 16001
- Clearview Cir & Mdws 16001
- Cleveland St 16001
- N & S Cliff St 16001
- Clinton Ave 16001
- Cloverleaf Ln 16001
- Clyde Ln 16001
- Coal St 16001
- Colleen St 16001
- College Dr 16002
- College St 16001
- Collins Ln 16002
- Colonial Ave 16001
- Columbia St 16001
- Comfort Ln 16001
- Concordia Way 16001
- Connemara Ln 16001
- Conrad Ln 16002
- Corks Ln 16001
- Cornell Dr 16001
- Cortland Ln 16001
- Cottage Ave & Ln 16001
- Cottage Hill Ave 16001
- Cottonwood Dr 16001
- Country Club Hts 16002
- Country Club Rd
  - 100-399 16002
  - 7100-7399 16001
- Country Lane Rd 16001
- Countryside Ln 16002
- Court Side Ln 16001
- Cove Dr 16002
- Coventry Dr 16001
- Coverdale Rd 16001
- Covewood Dr 16001
- Covington Dr 16001
- Cozy St 16001
- Crabapple Dr 16001
- Creek Rd 16002
- Creek Shore Ln 16002
- Cresthaven Dr 16002
- Crestmont Dr 16002
- Crestview Dr 16001
- Crevar Dr 16001
- Crider Ln 16002
- Crisswell Rd 16002
- Crocus Ln 16002
- Cross St 16001
- Crossland Rd 16002
- Crosthwaite Dr 16002
- E & W Cruikshank Rd 16002
- Crystal Ave 16001
- Cubbage Ln 16001
- E & W Cunningham St 16001
- Cups St 16001
- Cypress St 16001
- Dairy Ln 16001
- Dakota Dr 16001
- Dale Ln 16001
- Dallyson Ln 16002
- Dalmagro Rd 16002
- Dana Ln 16001
- Daum Ln 16001
- Davero Mnr 16001
- David Dr 16001
- Davis Rd
  - 100-199 16002
  - 1100-1199 16001
  - 2100-2199 16002
- Deahl Creek Ln 16002
- Decatur Dr 16002
- Dee Ln 16001
- Deer Run Dr 16001
- Deer Trail Ln 16002
- Deerhurst Ln 16002
- Delason Ave 16001
- Delaware Dr 16001
- Delta Way 16001
- Delwood Rd 16001
- Demi Ln 16001
- Dershimer Dr 16001
- Deshon Ct & Mnr 16001
- Dewey Ave & Ln 16001
- E & W Diamond St 16001
- Dick Rd 16001
- Dietrich Ln 16001
- Dinnerbell Rd 16002
- Dittmer Rd 16002
- Divet St 16001
- Doctor Pepper Ave 16001
- Dodds Rd 16002
- Dogwood Ct & Dr 16001
- Dolphin Dr 16002
- Domestic Ln 16001
- Donaghy Ave 16001
- Doral Dr 16001
- Dorenkamp Ln 16001
- Downham Dr 16002
- Draper Ave 16001
- Dreher Rd 16002
- Dubarry Ln 16002
- Dubbs Ln 16001
- Dubois St 16001
- N & S Duffy Rd 16001
- Dumbaugh St 16001
- Duncan Dr 16001
- Dusty Ln 16002
- Dutch Ln 16001
- Dutchtown Rd & Vlg 16002
- Eagle Mill Rd 16001
- Eagle Ridge Ln 16001
- East Dr
  - 1200-1299 16002
  - 4200-4299 16001
- Eastbrook Ln 16002
- Eastview Dr 16001
- Eastwood Dr 16001
- Easy St 16001
- Eau Claire St 16001
- N & S Eberhart Rd 16001
- Echo Dr 16001
- Edgewood Rd 16001
- Eds Ln 16001
- Edwards Ave 16001
- Eiffler Ln 16002
- Elderwood Ln 16002
- Election House Rd 16001
- Elfin Ave 16001
- Elgie Dr 16001
- Elise Dr 16001
- Elizabeth Dr & St 16001
- Ellington Dr 16001
- Elliott Dr & Rd 16001
- N Elm Ct & St 16001
- Elmwood Ln 16001
- Elsie Dr 16001
- Emrick Ln 16001
- England St 16001
- Entwood Ln 16002
- Equine Ln 16001
- Erdley Ln 16001
- Espy Ln 16001
- Estate Ln 16001
- Etna St 16001
- Etzel Ln 16002
- Euclid Ave & Rd 16001
- Euclid School Rd 16001
- Evans Rd 16001
- Evans City Rd 16001
- Everest Ln 16002
- Ewing Ln 16001
- Eyth Rd 16002
- Eyth St 16001
- Fairfield Ln 16001
- Fairground Hill Rd 16001
- Fairlane Dr 16001
- Fairlawn Dr 16001
- Fairview Ave 16001
- Fairway Dr 16001
- Fairway Ln 16002
- Faith Way 16001
- Fallecker Rd 16002
- Family Ln 16002
- Fared Dr 16001
- Farmington Dr 16001
- Federal St 16001
- Fennell Dr 16002
- Ferguson Ave 16001
- Fern Ln 16001
- Ferndale Ln 16002
- Fernwood Dr 16001
- Ferraro Ln 16002
- Fiechuk Ln 16001
- Filbert Rd 16001
- Filer Ln 16001
- Fincher Ln 16001
- Firbank Dr 16002
- Fisher Rd 16002
- Flick Ln 16001
- Folk Ln 16001
- Fontana St 16001
- Forcht St 16001
- Forest Dr 16002
- Forest Hts
  - A11-A34 16001
  - B11-B34 16001
  - C11-C34 16001
  - D11-D34 16001
  - E11-E34 16001
  - F11-F34 16001
  - G11-G35 16001
  - H11-H35 16001
  - I11-I35 16001
  - J11-J35 16001
  - K11-K35 16001
  - 100-199 16001
- Forest Mere Cir 16002
- Forrest Trl 16002
- Forresta Dr 16002
- Foster Dr 16001
- Foster Ln 16002
- Fox Hollow Dr 16001
- Foxcroft Dr 16001
- Foxshire Dr 16001
- Franklin St 16001
- Franklin Oaks Dr 16001
- Franks Towne Ln 16002
- Frazier Rd 16002
- Freedom Rd 16001
- Freemont Ave 16001
- Freeport Rd 16002
- Frontier Ln 16002
- Fry Ln 16002
- E & W Fulton St 16001
- Game Reserve Rd 16002
- Gameland Rd 16002
- Garden Ave 16001
- Garden Grove Dr 16002
- Garfield Ave 16001
- Garland Ln 16002
- Geibel Rd 16002
- Georgian Dr 16002
- Germaine Rd 16001
- Gibson St 16001
- Gilbert Ave 16001
- Ginger Ln 16002
- Glendale Ave 16001
- Glenn Ave 16001
- Glenwood Way 16001
- Gold Rd 16001
- Golden Ln 16001
- Goldwood Ave 16001
- Graceann Ln 16001
- Graham Rd 16001
- Grandview Ave, Blvd & Ln 16001
- Grant Ave 16002
- Grant St 16001
- Grant Avenue Ext 16001
- Grayrigg Dr 16002
- Grayvine Ln 16001
- Great Belt Rd 16002
- Greater Butler Mart 16001
- Green Acres Ct 16002
- Green Manor Dr 16002
- Greenery Ln 16002
- Greenhill Dr 16001
- Greenview Dr 16001
- Greenview Ln 16002
- Greenwood Dr 16001
- Gregden Rd 16001
- Greilich Ln 16002
- Greystone Ln 16002
- Grohman Rd 16002
- Grossman Dr 16001
- Grosvenor Ave 16001
- Grove Ave 16001
- Grundman Dr 16001
- Gustav Ln 16001
- Gusty Dr 16001
- Haley St 16001
- Halifax Ln 16002
- Hall Rd 16001
- Halland Ter 16001
- Hallet St 16001
- Hallstein St 16001
- Hamilton Rd 16002
- Hampton Ct 16002
- Hannastown Rd 16002
- Hansen Ave 16001
- Harley Ln 16001
- Harper Ave 16001
- Harris Rd 16002
- Harrison Ave 16001
- Hartel Ln 16002
- Harvest Ln 16002
- Hathaway Dr 16001
- Havenhill Dr 16001
- Haverford Dr 16001
- Hawksview Ln 16002
- Hawthorne Ln 16002
- Hayden Ln 16002
- Hayes Ave 16001
- Haylees Ln 16002
- Hays Ln 16001
- Hazel Ave 16001
- Hazlett Ave 16001
- Headland Rd 16002
- Heartland Dr 16001
- Heather Dr 16001
- Heim Ave 16001
- Heineman St 16001
- Heinz Rd 16001
- Heist Rd 16002
- Heller Rd 16002
- Helt Ln 16001
- Hemlock Dr 16001
- Hempfling St 16001
- Henley Dr 16001
- Henricks Rd 16001
- Heritage Ln 16001
- Herman Rd 16002
- Hermitage Rd 16001
- Hesidenz Rd 16002
- Hettie Way 16001
- Hewitt Ln 16001
- Hickey Ln 16002
- Hickory St 16001
- High St 16001
- W High Meadow Dr 16002
- Highfield Rd 16001
- Highland Ave 16001
- Highland Dr 16002
- Highland Rd 16001
- Hillside Terrace Ln 16002
- Hilltop Ave & Dr 16001
- Hillvue Dr & Ln 16001
- Hinchberger Rd 16002
- Hindman Ln & Rd 16001
- Hoch Rd 16002
- Holcomb Ave 16001
- Holland Dr 16002
- Hollow Ln 16001
- Hollywood Dr 16001
- Holt Ln 16001
- Holyoke Rd 16001
- S Home Ave 16001
- Homewood Dr 16001
- Hoon Rd 16001
- Hopewell Ave 16001
- Hospital Way 16001
- Hoss Ln 16001
- Howard St 16001
- Huckleberry Ln 16002
- Hummingbird Ln 16002
- Hunt Rd 16001
- Hunter Ln 16002
- Hunter Ridge Rd 16001
- Huselton Dr 16002
- Hyvue Ln 16002
- Idris Ln 16001
- Ietto Dr 16001
- Ifft Ln 16001
- Independence Ln 16001
- Integra Ln 16002
- Irene Dr 16001
- Iroquois Dr 16001
- Isabella St 16001
- Island Dr 16002
- Isle Rd 16001
- J L C Ln 16002
- N & S Jackson St 16001
- Jacobs Ln 16001
- Jamisonville Rd 16001
- Jan Dr 16001
- Jarrett Ave 16001
- Jason Dr 16002
- Jeanette Ln 16002
- W Jefferson Rd 16002
- E Jefferson St 16001
- W Jefferson St 16001
- Jenelle Dr 16001
- Jenny Dr 16001
- Jersey Dr & Ln 16001
- Jill Dr 16001
- Jodi Ln 16002
- John Deere Ln 16001
- Johnson Dr 16001
- Jones Rd 16002
- Joseph Ln 16001
- Joy Ln 16001
- Judson Ave 16001
- Just A Ln 16002
- K Ln 16002
- K And L Ln 16001
- Kaiser Rd 16002
- Karla Dr 16001
- Karnes Rd 16002
- Kaufman Dr 16001
- Keck Rd 16002
- Keel Ln 16002
- Kelly Rd 16001
- Kemar Dr 16002
- Kemper Rd 16002
- Kenbar Ln 16001
- Kennedy Dr 16001
- Kennedy Ln 16002
- Kenyon Ln 16002
- Kerry Dr 16001
- Kildoo Rd 16001
- Kiley Ln 16002
- Kilgallen Rd 16002
- Kilroy Ln 16002
- Kinzua Ln 16001
- Kittanning St
  - 100-198 16001
  - 200-299 16002
- Knotingham Ln 16001
- Knox Ave 16001
- Kobert Ln 16002
- Kohler Avenue Ext 16001
- Kozik Ln 16002
- Kramer Ln 16002
- Krenitsky Ln 16001
- Kresh Ln 16001
- Kriess Rd 16001
- Kriley Grv & Ln 16002
- Kummer Ln 16001
- L Dr 16001
- La Ray Dr 16001
- La Vista Ln 16001
- Lake Mnr 16002
- Lake Rd 16001
- Lake Vue Dr 16002
- Lakeshore Dr 16001
- Lakeview Dr 16001
- Lakewood Dr 16001
- Lamont Ln 16002
- Landon Ln 16001
- Larchwood Dr 16002
- Lariando Rd 16002
- Larkspur Cir 16002
- Laurel Oak Ln 16001
- Lawrence Ave 16001
- Lawton Ave 16001
- Layton Dr & Rd 16001
- Lazalea Dr 16001
- Le Donne Ln 16001
- Lea Dr 16001
- Lees Way 16002
- Leeward Dr 16001
- Legion Memorial Dr 16001
- Leja Ln 16002
- Lemont Dr 16001
- Lena Ln 16002
- Leo St 16001
- Leroy Ln 16002
- Lesney Ln 16001
- Lessner Ln 16001
- Levi Ln 16002
- Liberty St 16001
- Limberg St 16001
- Lincoln Ave 16001
- Linden Ave 16001
- Lindsay Ln 16002
- Linhurst Ave 16001
- S Links Ave 16001
- Linsdale Dr 16001
- Linwood Dr 16001
- Lions Rd 16001
- Lite Ln 16001
- Litman Rd 16001
- Litman Grove Ln 16001
- Little Stone Ln 16002
- E & W Locust St 16001
- Lokhaiser Ln 16001
- Longview Dr 16001
- Lorenz St 16001
- Loring St 16001
- Lumar Vlg 16001
- Lyn Dale Dr 16001
- Lynn Mar Ln 16002
- Lynne Ln 16001
- Lyon Ave 16001
- Mackey Ave 16001
- Macklin Ln 16001
- Madison Ave 16001
- N & S Magnolia Dr 16001
- Maharg St 16001
- Mahood Rd 16001
- N Main St 16001
- S Main St
  - 100-346 16001
  - 345-345 16003
  - 347-1399 16001
  - 348-1398 16001
- N Main Street Ext 16001
- Majestic View Dr 16001
- Malwood Dr 16001
- Manor Ct & Dr 16001
- Manor Hill Dr 16001
- Mansion Ln 16002
- N Maple Ave & Dr 16001
- Maple Grove Dr 16001
- Maplewood Dr 16001
- Mar Vel Dr 16001
- Marbury Ave 16001
- Margate Dr & Ln 16001
- Marion Dr 16001
- Markirk Ln 16001
- Marquis Ln 16002
- Marra Ln 16002
- Martin Ln 16002
- Martsoff Ln 16001
- Marvin St 16001

Mary Beth Dr 16001
Marybelle Ln 16001
Maryland Ave 16001
Maser Rd 16001
Maui Dr 16002
Mayfield Ave 16001
Mcbride Hill Rd 16002
Mccalip Farm Ln 16002
Mccall Rd 16001
Mccandless Ave, Pl & Rd 16001
Mcclain Ave 16001
Mcclellan Dr 16001
Mcclung Blvd 16001
Mcconnell Dr 16001
Mccune Dr 16001
Mcdonnell Ln 16002
Mcfadden Rd 16001
Mcgeary St 16001
Mcgrady Hollow Rd 16002
Mcgregor Rd 16001
Mcguire Ave 16001
Mckain Ln 16001
N & S Mckean St 16001
Mckinley Ave 16001
Mcknight Ln 16001
E & W Mcquistion Rd 16001
Meadow Ct 16001
Meadow Brook Ln 16001
Meadow Valley Dr 16001
Meadow View Ln 16001
Meadow Village Dr 16001
Mechling Dr & Ln 16001
Melanie Ln 16002
Mellon St 16001
Melody Ln 16002
Mens Club Ln 16002
Mercedes Bnd 16001
Mercer Rd & St 16001
Meridian Rd 16001
Merritt Dr 16001
Merry Ln 16001
E & W Metzger Ave 16001
Miami Dr 16002
Michael Ave 16001
Middle Trl 16002
Midway Ln 16001
Miles Ln 16001
Milheim Dr 16001
Mill St 16001
Miller Ave, Dr & St 16001
Minich Rd 16001
Minson Ln 16001
Minteer Rd 16001
Mintwood Ln 16002
Mitchell Ave 16001
Mitchell Hill Rd 16002
Mockingbird Dr 16001
Mohawk Dr 16001
Molakai St 16002
Monaco St 16002
Monroe Rd 16002
N Monroe St 16001
S Monroe St 16001
Mont Rd 16001
Moore Rd
  100-199 16001
  2501-2599 16002
Moraine Pointe Plz 16001
Moran Rd 16002
Morgan Ln 16001
Morgan Rd 16002
Morningside Dr 16002
Morter Ln 16001
Morton Ave 16001
Motor Pool Way 16001
Mount View Ln 16001
Mountain Laurel Dr 16002
Mountain View Ln 16001
Muddy Creek Dr 16001
Mulberry Dr 16001
Muldoon Rd 16001
E & W Muntz Ave 16001
Muranko Ln 16002
Murin Ln 16002
Murphy Ln 16001
Mushrush Rd 16002
Nacam Ln 16002
Nazarene Cir & Ln 16001
Neely Ln 16001
Negley Ave 16001
Neigh Ln 16002
New St 16001
New Castle Rd & St 16001
Newhaven Ln 16001
Nickel Ln 16001
Nixon Ave 16001
Noah Ln 16001
North Dr
  100-300 16001
  302-4198 16001
  1201-1299 16002
  4101-4199 16001
North Rd 16001
E North St 16001
W North St 16001
North Trl 16002
Northridge Ln 16001
Now Here Ln 16001
Nulph Ln 16001
Nursery Ln 16002
Oak St 16001
Oak Crest Ln 16002
Oak Forest Ln 16001
Oak Hills Hts & Mnr 16002
Oak Leaf Ln 16001
Oak Ridge Dr 16002
Oakdale Rd 16001
Oakhurst Dr 16002
Oakland Ave & Ln 16001
Oakridge Dr 16001
Oakvale Blvd 16001
Oakwood Dr 16002
Oberlin Dr 16001
October Dr 16002
Ojibwa Dr 16001
Old East Butler Rd 16002
Old Eberhart Rd 16001
Old Frazier Mill Ln 16002
Old Harvest Ln 16002
Old Plank Rd
  1-99 16001
  100-6499 16002
Old Route 422 E 16002
W Old Route 422 16001
Old Route 8 N 16002
Olive St 16001
Oliver Dr 16002
Oliverio Ln 16001
Oneida Valley Rd 16001
Orchard Ave 16001
Orchard Dr 16001
Orchard Dr E 16001
Orchard Ln
  100-299 16001
  6100-6199 16002
N Osche Rd 16002
Otterson Ln 16001
Outlaw Ln 16001
Overlook Rd 16001
Oxcart Ln 16001
Pagenhardt Ln 16001
Pal Mar Dr 16001
Palamino Cir 16001
Palm Dr 16001
Palmer Rd 16001
Paradise Ln 16002
Park Mnr 16001
Park Crest Ln 16001
Partell St 16001
Patricia Ln 16001
Patriot Ln 16001
Patten Ln 16001
E Patterson Ave 16001
W Patterson Ave 16001
Patterson Rd 16002
Pauls Ln 16001
Peach St 16001
Pearl St 16001
Pembrooke Ln 16002
Penn Dr 16002
E Penn St 16001
W Penn St 16001
Pennfield Ln 16002
Pepperland Blvd 16001
Percent Ln 16001
Percil Dr 16001
Perdew Ln 16001
Peters Ln 16001
Pfister Ln 16001
Pflugh Rd 16001
Pheasant Ridge Dr 16001
Phil Mar Dr 16002
Pier Dr 16002
Pillow St 16001
Pine Dr
  100-199 16001
  200-499 16002
Pine St 16001
W Pine St 16001
N Pine Aire Dr 16001
Pine Line Ln 16002
Pine Needles Ln 16002
Pine Ridge Ln 16002
Pine Tract Rd 16001
Pinecrest Ct 16001
E & W Pinehurst Dr & Rd 16001
Pinewood Dr & Ln 16001
Piper Ln 16001
Pittsburgh Rd
  448-1A-448-1A 16002
  1-249 16001
  250-999 16002
Pittsburgh Pike Rd 16001
Pleasantview Ave 16001
Plum St 16001
Point Plz 16001
Polk St 16001
Pollard Ave 16001
Port O Call Blvd 16002
Portman Rd 16002
Powell Rd 16002
Preston Dr 16001
Primrose Cir 16002
Protzman Mnr & Rd 16002
Providence Dr 16001
Puff Ln 16001
Pullam Park Pl 16001
Pullman Sq 16001
Purvis Rd 16001
E & W Quarry St 16001
Queen Junction Rd 16001
Queens Court Ln 16001
Race St 16001
Ragan Rd 16001
Rail Ln 16002
Raisley Ln 16001
Rancindin Rd 16002
Randy Dr 16002
Rattigan St 16001
Ravenhurst Ln 16001
Reamer Rd 16002
Reay Ln 16002
Red Dog Rd 16001
Red Oak Dr & Ln 16001
Red Rose St 16001
Redwood Ln 16002
Reed Ln
  100-199 16002
  500-599 16001
Reeder St 16001
Reich Ave 16001
Rembrandt Dr 16002
Remil Dr 16001
Renaissance Dr 16001
Rennick Rd 16002
Reo St 16001
Rider Church Rd 16001
N Ridge Ave, Dr & Rd 16001
Ridgemont Dr 16001
Rieger Rd 16001
Rimp Rd 16002
Ringneck Ln 16002
Ritenour Ln 16001
Ritter Dr & St 16001
Rittswood Dr 16001
Rivers Ln 16002
Roads End Ln 16001
Roberta St 16001
Robinson Run Rd 16002
Rockaway Ave 16001
Rockdale Rd 16002
E & W Rockenstein Ave 16001
Rodgers Ln 16002
Roe Ave & Rd 16001
Rolling Valley Ln 16001
Rollingstone Ln 16002
Roosevelt Blvd 16001
Root Ave 16001
Roper Ln 16001
Rothen Ave 16001
Route 422 E 16002
Royal Oak Dr 16002
Rural Dr 16001
Rushford Ln 16002
Rustic Ridge Ln 16002
Rustique Ln 16002
Saddle Brook Cir 16001
Saeler Ln 16002
Saint Andrews Dr 16001
Saint Joe Rd 16002
Saint Marys St 16001
Saint Paul St 16001
Saint Wendelin Rd 16002
Sampson Ln 16002
Santa Rita Ln 16001
Sarra Ln 16001
Sarvey Ln 16001
Sassafrass Ln 16002
Sawmill Ln 16001
Sawmill Run Rd 16001
Saxonburg Rd 16002
Scaife Ln 16001
Schaffner Ln & Rd 16001
Schenck Ln 16001
Schiebel Rd 16002
Schnur Rd 16002
School St 16001
Schramm Ln 16002
Schultz Ln 16002
Schweppe St 16001
Seminole Trl 16001
Seneca Dr 16001
September Dr 16002
Serene Ln 16002
Shacklee Dr 16002
S Shady Ave & Dr 16001
Shady Tree Ln 16001
Shagalorry Ln 16002
Shanahan Rd 16001
Shanor Hts 16001
Sharon Dr 16001
Shawnee Dr 16001
Shearer Rd 16001
Sheetz Dr 16002
Sheldon Rd 16002
Shepperd Dr 16002
Sherman Ave & Ln 16001
Shockey Ln 16001
Shook Ln 16001
Shore St 16001
Short St 16001
Shottery Dr 16001
Shrader Ln 16002
Shroyer Mill Rd 16001
Silver Ln 16001
Silverton Dr 16001
Simon Dr 16002
Skyline Ln 16001
Slagle Ave 16001
Smith Rd 16002
Snyder Ave 16001
Snyder Ln 16002
South Dr 16001
South St 16001
South Trl 16002
Space Ln 16001
Spang Ave 16001
Spanish Dr 16002
Sparks Ave 16001
Spear Ave 16001
Spillway Ln 16001
Spooner Dr 16002
Spring St 16001
Spring Ridge Dr 16001
Spring Run Rd 16001
Springhouse Dr 16001
Spruce St 16001
Stacey Ln 16002
Stage Coach Ln 16002
Staley Ave 16001
Stamm Ln 16001
Standard Ave 16001
Stanley Ave 16001
Star Grille Rd 16002
Starcher Ln 16001
State St 16001
Steelton Ave 16001
Steiger Ln 16001
Stein Rd 16001
Steppland Rd 16002
Sterling Ave 16001
Stewart Dr 16002
Stewart St 16001
Stirling Dr & Vlg 16001
Stone Ln & St 16001
Stone Cliff Ln 16001
Stonecrest Dr 16001
Stonegate Ln 16001
Stoneridge Blvd 16001
Stoney Hill Ln 16002
Stoney Run Rd 16001
Stratford Dr 16002
Stutz Rd 16002
Sugar Creek Dr 16002
Sullivan Rd & St 16001
Summer St 16001
Summit Rd & St 16001
Summit Park Ln 16002
Sumner Ave 16001
Sun Ridge Ct 16001
Sunburst Ct 16001
W Sunbury Est & Rd 16001
Sunbury Fields Ln 16001
Sundale St 16001
Sunflower Rd 16001
Sunnyview Cir 16001
Sunrise Cir & Vlg 16001
Sunrise Cove Ln 16001
Sunset Dr 16001
Surf Dr 16002
Surrey Ln 16001
Sutton Ln 16001
Swamp Run Rd 16001
Swan St 16001
Tabacchi Ln 16002
Tacoma Ave 16001
Taft St 16001
Taylor St 16001
Teakwood Rd 16001
Technology Dr 16001
Terraza Ln 16001
Thoma Ln 16002
Thomas Ave 16001
Thompson Rd 16001
Thorn Dr 16001
Thorn Apple Dr 16001
Thorn Run Rd 16001
Thornbrook Dr 16002
Thorncrest Dr 16002
Thornley Dr 16001
Thornwood Dr 16001
Three Degree Rd
  100-197 16001
  199-1299 16002
Tiffany Ln 16001
Timberland Ln 16001
Timberline Ln 16001
Timblin Rd 16001
Timothy Ln 16001
Tom Len Ln 16002
Toms Ln 16001
Tower Ln 16001
Tower View Dr 16002
Township Ln 16002
Township Line Rd 16002
Tracy Ln 16001
Trailwood Ln 16001
Tranquil Ave & Ln 16002
Treeline Ln 16002
Tricia Ln 16001
Trieste St 16002
Trillium Cir 16002
Trinidad St 16002
Trinity Ln 16002
Troll Creek Ln 16001
Trottingwood Cir 16001
Tuck Ln 16001
Tudor Dr 16001
Turrano Ln 16002
Twin Ln 16002
Twin Lakes Ln 16002
Twisted Ln 16001
Unionville Rd 16001
Uram Dr 16001
Valencia St 16002
Valley St 16001
Valley View Dr 16002
Valley Vista Ln 16001
Valleyview Ln 16001
Van Mar Dr 16001
Vanderzee Ln 16002
Vanessa Dr 16001
Verndale Dr 16002
Vernon Ln 16001
Vero St 16001
Vets Club Rd 16001
Vics Ln 16001
Victor Rd 16001
Victoria Ln 16001
Victoria Mnr 16002
Villa Dr 16001
Village Dr 16001
Virginia Ave & Ln 16001
Vista Dr 16001
Vogel Rd 16002
Vogeley Way 16001
Vogleyville Rd 16002
Volkswood Dr 16001
Wacomor St 16001
Wagner Ave 16001
Waikiki St 16002
Walker Ave & Dr 16001
Wallula Ave 16001
Walney Dr 16002
E & W Walnut St 16001
Walter St 16001
Walton Ave 16001
N & S Washington St 16001
Water Tower Ln 16001
Watterson Ln 16001
E & W Wayne St 16001
Webb Rd 16001
Weckerly Rd 16002
Weir Ave 16001
Weitzel Rd 16002
Welter Rd 16002
Wendells Ln 16002
Wesley Ln 16002
West Dr & Rd 16002
Westbrook Dr 16001
Westview Dr 16001
Westward Ln 16001
Westwood Mnr 16001
Whippo Ave 16001
Whipporwill Rd 16001
White Ave 16001
White Oak Dr 16001
Whitestown Rd & Vlg 16001
Whitetail Ln 16001
Whitmire Ave 16001
Wick St 16001
Wigton Ln 16001
Wilbert Ln 16001
Wildwood Dr 16002
Wilkens Ave 16001
Wilkes Ave 16001
Willard Ave 16001
William Flynn Hwy 16001
Williams Rd 16001
Willow Dr 16002
Willow Run Dr 16001
Willow Wood Dr 16001
Wilmoote Dr 16001
Wilson Ave 16001
Wilson Way 16002
Wiltshire Ave 16001
Windmill Rd 16002
Windsor Dr 16002
Windy Dr 16001
Windy Knoll Ln 16002
Wintergreen Dr 16001
Winters Rd 16002
Winterwood Dr 16001
Wise Rd 16002
Wisr Way 16001
Wood St 16001
Wood Glen Ln 16001
Wood Hawk Ln 16001
Woodbine Ln 16001
Woodbury Dr 16001
Woodcrest Rd 16002
Woodland Ave 16001
Woodland Rd 16002
S Woodlawn Rd 16001
Woodoak Ln 16002
Woodridge Rd 16001
Woody Dr 16001
Wrbas Ln 16002
Wren St 16001
Wycliffe Way 16001
Wyle Ave 16001
Wymer Ln 16001
Wyncrest Dr 16001
Wynnewood Dr 16002
Wyoma Ave 16001
Youkers Rd 16001
Young Ave 16001
Zang Ln 16002
Zeigler Ave 16001
Zenith Rd 16001
Zetta Ln 16002
Zillweger Ln 16002

NUMBERED STREETS

All Street Addresses 16001

CAMP HILL PA

General Delivery 17011

POST OFFICE BOXES MAIN OFFICE STATIONS AND BRANCHES

Box No.s
1 - 1610 17001
3001 - 4534 17011
8300 - 8910 17001

NAMED STREETS

Abbey Ln 17011
Accent Cir 17011
Alinda Cir 17011
Allen Ct & Rd 17011
Allendale Way 17011
Amherst Dr 17011
Appleton St 17011
Appletree Rd 17011
April Dr 17011
Arlington Rd & St 17011
Arnold St 17011
Ashford Way 17011
Athol St 17011
Beaver Rd 17011
Bedford Dr 17011
Beechcliff Rd 17011
Belaire Dr 17011
Bellmore Rd 17011
Bellows Dr 17011
Benton Rd 17011
Beverly Rd 17011
Birch Ct 17011
Bishop Pl 17011

Blacklatch Ln 17011
Blackmore Ct 17011
Blacksmith Rd 17011
Boxwood Ln 17011
Bramar Rd 17011
Brandy Cir 17011
Brentwater Rd 17011
Brentwood Rd 17011
Briar Ln 17011
Briarwood Ct & Ln 17011
Bridle Ln 17011
Brier Rd 17011
Brighton Ln 17011
Brook Rd 17011
Bryce Rd 17011
Burd Dr 17011
Camp Hill Byp
1100-1398 17011
1601-1699 17011
1675-1675 17001
Campbell Pl 17011
Candle Light Dr 17011
Candlewyck Rd 17011
Capital City Mall Dr 17011
Carleton Ct 17011
Carlisle Pike & Rd 17011
Carriage House Dr 17011
Cedar Ave 17011
Cedar Cliff Dr 17011
Cedar Run Dr 17011
Cedar Run Drive Ext ... 17011
Cedarhurst Ln 17011
Center Dr & St 17011
Central Ave & Blvd 17011
Charisma Dr 17011
Chatham Dr & Rd 17011
Chelton Cir 17011
Cherish Dr 17011
Cherokee Ave 17011
Chesterbrook Ct 17011
E Chestnut Ave, Cir & St 17011
Church St 17011
Circle Dr & Pl 17011
Citadel Dr 17011
Clarendon St 17011
E, N, S & W Clearview Dr 17011
Clemson Dr 17011
Clifton Rd 17011
Clover Rd 17011
Coach Ln 17011
Colgate Dr 17011
Colony Rd W 17011
Columbia Ave & Dr 17011
Commercial Dr 17011
Conestoga Rd 17011
Conodoguinet Ave & Dr 17011
Conway Heath 17011
Cooper Cir 17011
Copper Kettle Rd 17011
Cornell Dr & Rd 17011
Corporate Center Dr ... 17011
Country Club Pl & Rd .. 17011
Countryside Ct, Ln & Pl 17011
E & W Courtland Ave, Rd & St 17011
Coventry Close 17011
Creek Rd 17011
Creekside Ln 17011
Creekwood Dr 17011
Creston Rd 17011
Crestview Ct 17011
E & W Crestwood Dr ... 17011
Cricket Ln 17011
Criswell Pl 17011
Cumberland Blvd, Dr & Rd 17011
Cushing Grn 17011
Cypress Pl 17011
Dartmouth St 17011
David Dr 17011
Deanhurst Ave 17011
Deerfield Rd 17011
Derby Ave 17011
Deubler Rd 17011
Devon Rd 17011
Diane Cir 17011
Dickinson Ave 17011
Dighton St 17011
Dogwood Ct 17011
Dulles Dr E & W 17011
Eastgate Dr 17011
S Eberly Ave 17011
Echo Dr 17011
Edgar Ln 17011
Ellen Rd 17011
Elmhurst Rd 17011
Elmwood Ct 17011
Enfield St 17011
Entry Ln 17011
Equus Dr 17011
Erford Rd 17011
Essex Rd 17011
Europeana Cir 17011
Fairview Dr & Rd 17011
Fairway Dr 17011
Fallowfield Rd 17011
Fargreen Rd 17011
Farm House Ln 17011
Fashion Cir 17011
Faulkner St 17011
Fernwood Ave 17011
Fieldstone Rd 17011
Fineview Rd 17011
Fireside Dr 17011
Forest Dr 17011
Forge Rd 17011
W Foxcroft Dr 17011
Freight St 17011
Front St 17011
Furlong Ln 17011
Futurity Dr 17011
Gale Cir & Rd 17011
Garrett Ln 17011
Gettysburg Rd 17011
Glendale Dr 17011
Glenn Rd 17011
Glenside Ln 17011
E & W Glenwood Ave, Dr & Rd 17011
Golfview Rd 17011
Grandview Ave 17011
Grant Dr 17011
Graystone Manor Dr 17011
E & W Green Cir & St . 17011
Green Lane Dr 17011
Grinnel Dr 17011
Hampden Ave 17011
Harmony Ln 17011
Harness Ln 17011
Hartzdale Dr 17011
Harvard Ave & Pl 17011
Hawthorne Dr 17011
Hearth Rd 17011
Hearthstone Rd 17011
Heidi Ter 17011
Hickory Pl 17011
N High St 17011
Highland Cir & Dr 17011
Hillcrest Ct & Rd 17011
Hillside Cir & Dr 17011
Hilltop Ct 17011
Holly Dr 17011
Hollywood Cir 17011
Homestead Ln 17011
Hood Ln 17011
House Ave 17011
Hummel Ave 17011
Hunter Ln 17011
Industrial Park Rd 17011
Joyce Rd 17011
June Dr 17011
Juniper Dr 17011
Karen Ct 17011
Kelton Rd 17011
Kensington Dr 17011
Kent Dr, Rd & St 17011
Kevin Ct 17011
Kingsley Rd 17011
Kohler Pl 17011
Kranzel Dr 17011
Lamp Post Ln 17011
Landau Ct 17011
Lantern Ln 17011
E & W Lauer Ln 17011
Laurel Ave & Ln 17011
Lebanon Ave 17011
Lenker Dr 17011
Lenox St 17011
Letchworth Dr & Rd 17011
Limestone Dr 17011
Lincoln Dr & St 17011
Linda Ln 17011
Linden Ct & Dr 17011
Linewood Dr 17011
Lisburn Rd 17011
Little Run Rd 17011
N & S Locust Rd & St . 17011
Logan Ct & St 17011
Lower Allen Dr 17011
Lowther Rd 17011
Lynnwood Ct 17011
E & W Main St 17011
Mallard Ln & Rd 17011
Manchester Rd 17011
Mandy Ct & Ln 17011
Manor Dr & Rd 17011
W Maple Ave & Rd 17011
March Dr 17011
Margo Rd 17011
Marina Dr 17011
S Market St 17011
Marlin Rdg 17011
Marshall Dr 17011
Martingale Dr 17011
Massachusetts Ave 17011
Matthew Rd 17011
May Dr 17011
Mayfair Ct 17011
Mayfred Ln 17011
Meadow Dr & Ln 17011
Merion Rd 17011
Middle Ln 17011
Milltown Rd 17011
Morningside Dr 17011
Motter Ln 17011
Myrtle Ave 17011
Nailor Dr 17011
Neponsit Ln 17011
New York Ave 17011
Norman Rd 17011
Northgate Dr 17011
Nottingham Rd 17011
November Dr 17011
Oak Ave & Dr 17011
Oakwood Cir & Ct 17011
October Dr 17011
Old Farm Rd 17011
Old Federal Rd 17011
Old Ford Dr 17011
Old Mill Dr 17011
Old Orchard Cir & Ln ... 17011
Old Pioneer Rd 17011
Olmsted Way E & W 17011
Oneida Rd 17011
Orchard Ave & Rd 17011
Orrs Bridge Rd 17011
Oxbow Dr 17011
Oyster Mill Rd 17011
Packard Ln 17011
Paddock Ln 17011
Page St 17011
Palmer Dr 17011
Park Cir, Ln, Pl & St ... 17011
Parkside Rd 17011
Parkview Ct 17011
Parrish Aly 17011
Pelham Rd 17011
Penn Ayr Rd 17011
Pennsylvania Ave 17011
Pine St 17011
Pinewood Dr 17011
Plainview Rd 17011
Poplar Church Rd 17011
Porsha Ter 17011
Primrose Ave 17011
Princeton Ave 17011
Prowell Dr 17011
Putter Ln 17011
Queen Anne Ct 17011
Railroad Ave 17011
Rana Villa Ave 17011
Rathton Rd 17011
E & W Red Gold Cir ... 17011
Redwood Ct & Pl 17011
Reeser Rd 17011
Regent St 17011
Richland Ln 17011
Riddle Rd 17011
Ridge Rd 17011
Ridgewood Dr 17011
Rockaway Dr 17011
Rodney Ln 17011
Rosemont Ave 17011
Round Hill Rd 17011
Royal Oak Cir & Rd 17011
Runson Rd 17011
Rupley Rd 17011
Rupp Ave 17011
Russell Rd 17011
Rutland St 17011
N & S Saint Johns Dr & Rd 17011
N Saint Johns Church Rd 17011
Santa Maria Ave 17011
Saratoga Pl 17011
Scarsdale Dr 17011
Schuykill Ave 17011
Selwick Rd 17011
Senate Ave 17011
Seneca Ave 17011
September Dr 17011
Shady Rd 17011
Shetter Ln 17011
W Shore Dr 17011
Shoreham Rd 17011
Simpson Ferry Rd 17011
Skyview Dr 17011
Slate Hill Rd 17011
Society Hill Dr 17011
Somerset Dr 17011
Spangler Rd 17011
Spangler Mill Rd 17011
Spartan Cir 17011
Spring House Rd 17011
Sprint Ln 17011
S Spruce Cir & St 17011
Stailey Cir 17011
State Rd & St 17011
Stephen Rd & Ter 17011
Sterling St 17011
Stone Spring Ln 17011
N & S Stoner Ave 17011
Strafford Rd 17011
Strawberry Aly 17011
Summit Ave 17011
Sunfire Ave 17011
Sunset Dr & Way 17011
Surrey Ct 17011
Susan Rd 17011
Sussex Cir & Rd 17011
Sycamore Cir 17011
Tall Tree Dr 17011
Tanwood Ct 17011
Terminal Rd 17011
Thomas Rd 17011
Trindle Rd 17011
Tuscany Ct 17011
Utley Dr 17011
Valley Rd 17011
Victoria Way 17011
Village Rd 17011
E & W Vine Cir & St 17011
Vista Cir & Dr 17011
E Walnut Cir, Ln & St .. 17011
Warwick Rd 17011
Waterford 17011
Wayne Cir & Rd 17011
Well Dr 17011
Wentworth Dr 17011
West Ave & Cir 17011
Westbury Ct 17011
Westerly Rd 17011
Westminster Blvd 17011
William Penn Dr 17011
Willow Ave & Rd 17011
Winchester Dr 17011
Winding Way 17011
Windsor Way 17011
Windswept Way 17011
Winfield Dr 17011
Woburn Ct 17011
Woburn Abbey Ave 17011
Wood St 17011
Woodcrest Ln 17011
Woodmere Dr 17011
Wyndham Rd 17011
Wynnewood Rd 17011
Yale Ave 17011
Yellow Breeches Dr 17011
Yetter Ct 17011
Yverdon Dr 17011
Zimmerman Dr 17011

NUMBERED STREETS

All Street Addresses 17011

CARLISLE PA

General Delivery 17013

POST OFFICE BOXES MAIN OFFICE STATIONS AND BRANCHES

Box No.s
All PO Boxes 17013

NAMED STREETS

A St
2-98 17013
2-100 17015
100-499 17013
102-113 17015
Abbey Ct 17015
Abrams Ave 17013
Acorn Rd 17015
Acre Dr 17013
Adams Rd 17015
Adele Ave 17015
Aeronca St 17013
Airport Dr 17013
Aldenwood Dr 17015
Alexander Ave 17013
Alexander Spring Rd 17015
Alexandra Ct 17015
Allegheny Ln 17013
Allen Rd
100-198 17013
200-399 17013
400-799 17015
Allen St 17013
Alliance Dr 17013
Alpine Dr 17015
Alters Rd 17015
Amara Ln 17015
Amherst Ln 17015
Amy Dr 17013
Andrew Ct 17015
Annendale Dr 17015
Appalachian Ave 17013
Appalachian Dr 17015
Appaloosa Way 17015
Appian Dr 17015
Apple Aly 17015
Arch St 17013
Arlington Dr 17015
Armstrong Rd 17013
Army Heritage Dr 17013
Asbury Ln 17015
Ascot Ln 17013
Ash Ave 17013
Ashburn Dr 17013
Ashland Ave 17013
Ashton St 17015
Aspen Ln 17015
Augusta Pl 17013
Autumn Dr 17015
Avon Dr 17013
B St
1-499 17013
113-115 17015
501-599 17013
Back St 17015
Bahama Cir 17015
Baird Ct 17013
Baker Dr 17015
Bald Eagle Blvd 17013
E & W Baltimore St 17013
Barley Field Cir 17015
Barnitz Rd 17015
Barnstable Rd 17015
Basin Hill Blvd 17013
Bayberry Rd 17013
Bayley St 17013
Beagle Club Rd 17013
Bears Rd 17015
Bears School Ln 17015
N & S Bedford St 17013
Beech St 17013
Beechcliff Dr 17015
Beecher Dr 17015
Bella Ln 17015
Bellair Park Rd 17013
Bellaire Ave 17013
Belle Dr 17015
Bellows Dr 17015
Bellwood Ct 17013
Belvedere St 17013
Bentley Pl 17013
Berkshire Dr 17015
Bernheisel Bridge Rd ... 17015
Beverly Ct 17015
Bicentennial Dr 17013
Biddle Dr 17013
Biddle Rd 17015
Birch Ln & Rd 17015
Blair Ct 17015
Bloserville Rd 17015
Bluebird Dr 17013
Bobcat Rd 17015
Bolton Ave 17013
Bonnybrook Rd
1-199 17013
200-399 17015
Bosler Dr & Pl 17013
Boxwood Ln 17015
Boyer Rd 17015
Bradford Pl 17015
Bradi Dr 17015
Bradley Dr 17013
N Brallare Pl N 17015
Bream Rd 17015
Bretz Ave 17013
Brian Dr 17015
Briar Oak Ln 17015
Briar Patch Dr 17015
Briarly Dr 17015
Briarwood Ln 17015
Brighton Dr 17015
Brittney Dr 17013
Brook Dr 17015
Brook Side Dr 17013
Brookwood Ave 17015
Brookwood Dr 17015
Browning Ln 17015
Bryn Mawr Rd 17013
Buchannon Dr 17013
Buck Dr 17015
Buckeye Ln 17013
Buckingham Pl 17013
Buckthorn Dr 17015
Bullock Cir 17015
Burgners Rd 17015
Burgners Mill Rd 17015
Burnt House Rd 17015
Burr Ave 17013
Butler Ct & Rd 17013
Buttonwood Ln 17015
Byers Rd 17015
C St 17013
Cactus Hill Rd 17013
Cambridge Ct 17013
Camelot Dr 17013
Campground Rd 17015
Canary Dr 17013
Candlelite Dr 17013
Cardinal Dr 17015
Carlisle Pike 17015
Carlisle Barracks 17013
Carlisle Springs Rd 17013
Carlton Ave 17013
Carlton Lace Cir 17015
Carlwynne Mnr 17013
Carolina Way 17015
Carriage Ln 17015
Carter Pl 17013
Cavalry Rd & St 17013
Cave Hill Dr 17013
Cedar Ave 17013
Cedar Ct E 17015
Cedar Ct W 17015
Cedar Ln 17015
Cedar Rd 17015
Cedar St 17013
Cedar Vw 17013
Cedar Ridge Dr 17015
Cemetery Ave 17013
Center St 17013
Cessna St 17013
Channel Dr 17013
E & W Chapel Ave 17013
Charles St 17013
Charley Ct 17015
Chatham Dr 17013
Chelsea Ln 17015
Cheltenham Ln 17015
Cherry Ct 17013
Cherry Ln 17015
Cherry St 17013
Cherry Blossom Ct 17013
Chester St 17013
Chestnut Ave 17013
Chestnut Dr 17015
Chickamauga Dr 17013
Choate Way 17015
W Church Ave 17013
Church Ln 17015
Church Rd 17015
Church St 17015
Cinda Ln 17015
Circle Dr 17015
Circle Rd 17013
Clara Rd 17013
Claremont Rd
800-1099 17013
1100-1285 17015
Clarindon Pl 17013
Clay Rd 17015
Clay St 17013
Clearview Ave 17013
Clearview Dr 17013
Clearview Pl 17013
Clearwater Dr 17013
Clemson Dr 17013
Clifton Ter 17015
Clinton Ave 17013
Clover Ln 17015
Clubhouse Rd 17015
Cobblestone Dr 17015
Codorus Creek Ct 17013
Cold Springs Rd 17015
N & S College St 17013
Comman Rd 17013
Commerce Ave 17015
Conifer Ridge Dr 17015
Conodoguinet Ave 17015
Conrad Rd 17015
Conway St 17013
Cooper Cir 17015
Copper Cir 17015
Coral Dr 17013

Cornman Dr 17015
Cornman Rd 17013
Cottonwood Ct 17013
Country Rd 17013
Country Club Rd 17015
Country Side Dr 17013
Court Ln 17013
Court House Ave & Sq 17013
Courtyard Dr 17013
Coventry Dr 17015
Coyote Ln 17013
Crabapple Way 17015
Craig Ln & Rd 17013
Crain Dr 17013
Crandle Dr 17015
Cranes Gap Rd 17013
N Creek Ave 17013
Creek Rd
 1-699 17013
 700-1499 17015
 1501-1599 17015
Creekside Dr & Ln 17015
Creekview Dr 17015
Crest Vw 17013
Croghan Dr 17013
Crossroad School Rd 17015
Crown Vw 17013
Crystal Ln 17015
Cumberland Dr 17013
Curtis Dr 17013
Cypress Ln 17015
D St 17013
Dale Pl 17013
Dannah Dr 17015
Darr Ave 17015
David Glenn Dr 17015
Davis Rd 17013
Dawn Dr 17013
Daytona Blvd 17015
Deer Ln 17015
Deer Ridge Ln 17015
Deerfield Ln 17015
Demi Ct 17015
Derbyshire Dr 17015
Devonshire Dr 17013
Diane Ct 17015
Dickinson Ave & Dr 17013
Dickinson College 17013
N Dickinson School Rd 17015
Diehl Dr 17015
Distribution Dr 17013
Doe Dr 17015
Dogwood Ct
 1-5 17015
 400-402 17013
 404-499 17013
Dogwood Ln 17015
Donegal Dr 17013
Dorwood Dr 17013
Douglas Ct & Dr 17013
Downing St 17013
Dranoel Dr 17015
Drayer Ct 17013
Dunbar Rd 17013
Dunwoody Dr 17015
Dyarman Rd
 300-399 17013
 400-599 17015
E St 17013
N & S East St 17013
Eastgate Dr 17015
Eastwick Ct & Ln 17015
Eastwood Dr 17015
Easy Rd
 2-98 17013
 100-399 17013
 400-1299 17015
Echo Rd 17015
Ege Dr 17015
Eisenhower Dr 17013
Eldon Ln 17015
Elicker Rd 17015
Elk Dr 17015
Elm Dr & St 17013

Elton Dr 17015
Emerald Cir 17015
Emerson Dr 17015
Encks Mill Rd 17015
Engineer Ave 17013
Enola Rd
 300-2699 17013
 2700-3599 17015
E & W Eppley Dr 17015
Erin Pl 17015
Essex Dr 17015
Esther Dr 17013
Evandale Ct 17015
Evergreen Ln 17015
F St 17013
Factory St 17013
Fairfield St 17013
Fairground Ave 17013
Fairview Dr 17013
Fairview Rd 17013
Fairview St 17015
Fairway Dr 17015
Faith Cir 17013
Falcon Dr 17013
Farm Ln 17015
Farmhouse Ln 17013
Farview Ave 17013
Fawn Dr 17015
Fenwick Dr 17015
Fern Ave 17013
Fieldstone Dr 17015
Flagstone Dr 17015
Fleetwood Dr 17013
Fletcher Rd 17013
Flower Rd 17013
Forbes Ave & Rd 17013
Forest Ct 17013
Forest Ln 17015
Forge Rd
 600-1099 17015
 1100-1198 17015
 1200-1300 17015
 1302-1398 17013
Forgedale Dr 17015
Four Wheel Dr 17015
Fox Hollow Ln 17015
Foxanna Dr 17015
Foxcrest Dr 17013
Franklin St 17013
Frederick Ave 17013
Fry Loop Ave 17015
Frytown Rd 17015
Fuller Way 17015
G St 17013
Gap Vw 17013
Garden Dr & Pkwy 17013
Garfield Dr 17015
E Garland Ct & Dr 17015
Garrison Ln 17013
Gasoline Aly 17013
George Ave 17013
Georgetown Cir 17013
Giant Ln 17013
Gibner Rd 17013
Gibson St 17013
Gladwyn Dr 17015
Glendale Ct & St 17013
Glenn Vw 17013
Glenn View Ct 17013
Glenridge Dr 17015
Gobin Dr 17013
Goldenrod Dr 17015
Golf Ct 17015
Goodyear Rd 17015
Gordon Dr 17013
Graham St 17013
Grahams Woods Rd 17015
Grandview Ct 17013
Grant Ct 17013
Greason Rd 17013
Green Acre Ln 17015
Green Ridge Rd 17015
Greenfield Dr 17015
Greenmeadows Dr 17013
Greenview Dr 17015
Greenwich Dr 17015

Grey Goose Cir 17015
Greystone Rd 17013
Grove Rd 17015
Guardhouse Ln 17013
H St 17013
Hamilton Ct & St 17013
Hampton Ct 17013
N & S Hanover Mnr & St 17013
Har-John Dr 17015
E & W Harmon Dr 17015
Harmony Hall Dr 17015
Harriet St 17013
Harrisburg Pike
 800-898 17013
 900-1299 17013
 1400-1498 17015
 1500-1999 17015
 2001-2099 17015
Harvest Dr 17013
Hathaway Dr 17015
Hawthorn Ct 17015
Hawthorne Rd 17015
Heather Dr 17013
Hedge Row Ln 17015
Heisers Ln 17015
Heishman Gdns 17013
Helena Ln 17015
Hemlock Ave 17013
Hendel Loop 17015
Henderson St 17013
Heritage Ct 17015
Heron Way 17015
Hickory Rd 17015
Hickorytown Rd 17015
Hidden Meadows Dr 17015
Hidden Noll Rd 17015
E & W High St 17013
Highland Ave & Ct 17013
Hill Dr 17013
Hill Pl 17015
Hill Rd 17015
Hillcrest Dr 17015
E Hillcrest Dr 17013
W Hillcrest Dr 17013
Hillside Dr 17013
Hilltop Cir & Dr 17015
Hillview Dr 17015
Hilton Head Ave 17015
Hollenbaugh Rd 17015
Hollowbrook Dr 17013
Holly Pike
 1200-1399 17013
 1400-1999 17015
Hoover Rd 17015
Hope Ter 17013
Horners Rd 17015
Horseshoe Rd 17015
Hosfeld Rd 17015
Houser Ln 17013
Hoy Rd 17013
Hummingbird Ln 17015
E & W Hunter Rd 17015
E & W I St 17013
Imperial Ct 17013
Independence Dr 17015
Industrial Dr 17015
Irene Ct 17013
Ironbridge Rd 17015
Ironstone Dr 17015
Irvine Row 17013
Ivy Ter 17013
James Ct 17015
James Rd 17015
Jane Ln 17013
Jefferson Dr 17015
Jenni Ln 17013
Jennifer Ct 17015
Jessica Dr 17013
Jim Thorpe Rd 17013
Jody Ln 17013
John Dr 17015
Juniper St 17013
K St 17013
Karen Dr 17013
Kaseeta Dr 17015

Katie Ln 17015
Kelly Dr 17015
Ken Lin Dr 17015
Kengrey Dr 17015
Kennsington Ct 17013
Kenwood Ave & Dr 17013
Kerrs Ave 17013
Kerrs Rd 17015
Kerrsville Rd 17015
Keswick Ln 17015
Key Largo Dr 17015
Key West Blvd 17015
Kimberly Ln 17015
Kiner Blvd 17015
King Dr 17015
Kings Gap Rd 17015
Kingsbridge Cir 17013
Kingswood Ter 17013
Kitszell Dr 17015
Kost Rd 17015
Kuhn Dr 17015
Kutz Rd 17015
Ladnor Ln 17015
Lakeview Dr 17013
Lamplite Dr 17013
Laurel Dr 17015
Lawrence Ln 17015
Lebo Rd 17015
Lee Ct 17013
Lehman Dr 17013
Leida Dr 17013
Lennon Ln 17015
Lerew Rd 17015
Lesli Ln 17015
Letort Dr & Ln 17015
Letort Spring Rd 17013
Liam Ln 17015
E Liberty Ave 17013
Liberty Ct 17015
Liggett Rd 17013
Limekiln Rd 17015
Limestone Rd 17015
Lincoln Ave & St 17013
E & W Linden Ct & Dr 17015
Lindsay Ln 17015
Lindsey Rd 17013
Linn Dr 17015
Linnview Ln 17013
W Lisburn Rd 17015
Little Rd 17015
E Locust Ave 17013
W Locust Ave 17013
Locust Holw 17015
Locust Ln 17015
Locust Way 17015
Logistics Dr 17013
Long Vw 17015
Longs Gap Rd 17013
Longsdorf Way 17015
Longstreet Dr 17013
Louis Pkwy 17015
E & W Louther St 17013
Lovell Ave 17015
Lucinda St 17015
Luke Ln 17013
Macarthur Dr 17013
Madison Cir 17015
Magaw Ave 17015
Magnolia Ln 17015
E & W Main St 17015
Majestic Ridge Rd 17013
Makenzee Ct & Dr 17015
Malibu Blvd 17015
Manada Creek Cir 17013
Maple Ave 17013
Maple Ln 17015
Maple St 17013
Maplewood Dr 17013
Mara Cir 17013
Marbeth Ave 17013
Marcella Way 17015
Mare Rd 17015
Marilyn Dr 17013
Marion Ave 17013
Mark Cir 17013
Markris Ct 17015

Marsh Dr 17015
Marshall Dr, Rd & Rdg 17013
Martin Rd 17015
Mary Ln 17013
Matthew Ct 17015
Mayapple Dr 17015
Mayfield Ct 17013
Mcallister Church Rd 17015
Mcbride Ave 17013
Mcclures Gap Rd
 1-1199 17013
 1200-1999 17015
Mccoy Ln 17015
Mcknight St 17013
Meade Dr 17013
Meadow Blvd 17013
Meadow Dr 17015
Meadowbrook Rd 17015
Meadowlark Ln 17015
Meadowview Ln 17013
Meals Dr 17015
Media Rd 17013
Meeting House Rd 17013
Meeting House Spring Rd 17013
Mel Ron Ct 17015
Melissa Ct 17015
Melody Ln 17013
Merrihill Dr 17015
W Middlesex Dr 17013
N Middlesex Rd 17013
S Middlesex Rd 17015
N Middleton Ave & Rd 17013
Midway Dr 17015
Mill Rd 17013
Mill Race Ct & Rd 17015
Milwick Rd 17015
Mimosa Ln 17015
Minich Dr 17015
Monarch Dr 17015
Montsera Rd 17015
Moongale Dr 17015
Moore Cir 17015
Mooredale Rd 17015
Mooreland Ave 17013
Morgan Dr 17015
Morrison Way 17015
Mount Rock Rd 17015
Mount Zion Rd 17015
Mountain Rd 17015
Mountainview Dr 17013
E Mulberry Ave 17013
W Mulberry Hill Rd 17013
Myers Rd 17015
Nelson Dr 17015
Nesbit Dr 17013
Netherby Ln 17015
Newville Rd
 801-897 17013
 899-1399 17013
 1400-2299 17015
 1400-1-1400-7 17015
Nicolas Dr 17015
Noble Ave & Blvd 17015
Norestre Rd 17013
E & W North St 17013
Northfield Dr 17015
Northview Dr 17013
Oak St 17013
Oak Lane Dr 17015
Oak Park Ave 17015
Oak Ridge Rd 17015
Oakhill Rd 17015
E & W Oakwood Dr & Pl 17015
Old Coach Ln 17013
Old Gap Rd 17013
Old Longs Gap Rd 17013
Old Mill Rd 17015
N Old Stonehouse Rd S 17015
E & W Old York Rd 17015
Olson Dr 17013
Opossum Lake Rd 17015
N & S Orange St 17013

Orchard Ave 17015
Oriole Dr 17013
Otto Ave 17013
Over Vw 17013
Overfield Dr 17015
Padre Dr 17015
Palm Beach Ave 17015
Paradise Dr 17015
Park Dr 17015
E Park St 17013
W Park St 17013
Parker St 17013
Parker Spring Ave 17013
Parkview Dr 17013
Parkway Dr 17013
Partridge Cir 17013
Patton Dr & Rd 17015
Paul Ct 17015
Peach Ln 17015
Peacock Dr 17015
Pearl Dr 17013
Pearl Ln 17015
Peiper Ct 17015
Pelham Ct 17013
E & W Penn St 17013
Pennsylvania Ave 17013
Pennway Cir & Dr 17015
Penny Ln 17013
Penrose Pl 17013
Pershing Rd 17013
Petersburg Rd
 100-299 17013
 300-999 17015
Peyton Dr 17015
Pheasant Dr N 17013
Pheasant Dr S 17013
Pheasant Ln 17015
Pin Oak Dr & Ln 17015
Pine Ln 17015
Pine Rd 17015
Pine St 17013
Pine Creek Dr 17013
Pine Hill Dr & Rd 17013
Pine Lake Dr 17015
Pinedale Rd 17015
N & S Pitt St 17013
Pleasant Hall Rd 17013
E & W Pomfret St 17013
Ponderosa Rd 17015
Porter Ave 17013
Potato Rd 17015
Pratt Ave 17013
Prickly Pear Dr 17013
Primrose Ln 17015
Princeton Dr 17013
Prospect Rd 17015
Public Safety Dr 17013
Pumphouse Rd 17015
Quail Dr 17013
Rachel Dr 17013
Rapuano Way 17015
Rasp Dr 17013
Rebecca St 17013
Redwood Dr 17013
Redwood Ln 17015
Redwood Hills Cir 17015
Regal Vw 17013
Regency Woods N 17015
Regent Ct 17013
Rellim St 17015
Reservoir Dr 17013
Rex Dr 17015
Rich Valley Rd 17015
Richland Rd 17015
Richmond Run 17015
Ridge Ave 17013
Ridge Dr 17015
Ridge Rd 17015
E Ridge St 17013
W Ridge St 17013
Ridge Hill Rd 17015
Ridgeview Dr 17013
Ridgeway Dr 17015
Ridley Ln 17015
Ritner Hwy
 1000-1999 17013
 2000-3099 17015
Roadway Dr 17015
Roaring Creek Ct 17013
Robbins Ln 17013
Robert Ln 17013
Robin Dr 17015
Rockey Ln 17015
Rockledge Ct 17015
Rockledge Dr
 900-999 17013
 1000-1799 17015
Rockwell Ct 17015
Rolling Dr 17013
Rosewood Ct 17013
Royal Dr 17015
Royal American Cir 17013
Royer Rd 17013
Run Rd 17015
Rush Dr 17013
Russell Rd 17015
Sable Dr 17013
Sadler Ct & Dr 17013
Sandy Bottom Rd 17015
Santa Monica Ave 17015
Sarah Ln 17015
Sarasota Cir 17015
Saria Ln 17015
Sassafras Ln 17015
E & W Scenic Dr 17015
Schimmel Way 17015
Schneider Dr 17015
School Ave 17013
Schoolfield Dr 17013
Seaton Ct 17015
Sebastian Way 17015
Seneca Cir 17015
Sentinel Dr 17015
Shady Ln
 1-97 17013
 99-200 17013
 202-298 17013
 300-399 17015
Shagbark Ln 17015
Shank Rd 17015
Shannon Ln 17013
Shatto Dr 17013
Shea Ct 17015
Sheaffer Dr 17015
Sheaffer Rd 17013
S Shearer Dr 17013
Shellbark Ct 17015
Sheraton Dr 17013
Sherman Ave 17013
Sherwood Dr
 1-499 17015
 600-1299 17013
Shirley Ave 17013
Short Rd 17015
Shover Dr 17013
Shughart Cir 17015
Shughart Rd 17015
Shuman Dr 17015
Silkwood Ln 17015
Sipe Rd 17015
Skyline Vw 17013
E & W Slate Hill Rd 17013
Soldiers Dr 17013
E & W South St 17013
Sovereign Dr 17015
Spring Rd 17013
Spring Farm Cir 17015
Spring Garden Est 17015
N Spring Garden St 17013
S Spring Garden St
 8-799 17013
 900-1199 17015
Spring View St 17013
Springview Rd 17015
E Springville Rd 17015
Sprint Dr 17015
Spruce Ave 17013
Spruce Dr 17015
Spruce Ln 17015
Spruce St 17013
Spur Rd 17013
Stallion Rd 17015

Stambaugh Ln 17015
Stanwix Cir 17013
State Ave 17013
Sterretts Gap Ave 17013
Stewart Dr 17013
Stine Ave 17013
Stone Church Rd 17015
Stonehedge Dr & Way 17015
Stonehouse Rd 17015
Stoney Knoll Ln 17015
Stony Creek Ct 17013
Stought Rd 17015
Stover Dr 17015
Stratford Dr 17013
Strawberry Dr & Ln 17013
Strayer Dr 17013
Stuart Rd 17015
Sulphur Spring Rd 17013
Summerfield Dr 17015
Summit Dr & Vw 17013
Sumner Rd 17013
W Suncrest Dr 17013
Sundance Ln 17013
Sunnyside Dr 17015
Sunset Dr 17013
Susan Ln 17013
Sussex Dr 17013
Sutton Dr 17013
Taunton Dr 17013
Taylor Ave 17013
Teaberry Dr 17015
Teagan Ct 17015
Terrace Ave & Vw 17013
Terri Dr 17015
Thomas Dr 17013
Thompson Ln 17015
Thorncrest Dr 17015
Thornhill Ct 17015
Thornwood Ln 17013
N & S Thrush Dr 17015
Tiday Ct 17015
Tiffany Dr 17015
Tioga Ln 17015
Tiptop Cir 17015
Todd Cir & Rd 17013
Topview Dr 17015
Touchstone Dr 17015
Tower Cir 17015
Trayer Ln 17013
Tree Vw 17013
Trindle Rd
900-1299 17013
1401-1699 17015
1701-1799 17015
W Trindle Rd
1300-1799 17015
1800-2199 17013
True Temper 17015
Tunbridge Ln 17015
Tuscarora Trl 17013
Tussey Trl 17013
Tyler Ct 17015
Union Hall Rd 17013
Valley Dr & St 17013
Valley View Dr 17013
Vasilios Dr 17015
Venice Ave 17015
Veterans Way 17013
Viewmore Dr 17015
Village Dr 17015
Vine Dr 17015
Virginia Ave 17013
Virginia Beach Ave 17015
Waggoners Gap Rd
701-797 17013
799-2400 17013
2402-2498 17013
2501-2797 17015
2799-3699 17015
3701-3799 17015
Wagner Dr & St 17013
Waidner Way 17013
Walnut Ln
1-399 17015
800-899 17013
901-999 17013
Walnut St 17013
Walnut Bottom Rd
200-800 17013
802-898 17013
900-2699 17015
Walton Ave 17013
Walton Dr 17015
Washington Ln 17013
Waterloo Rd 17015
Waterside Dr 17015
Watson Dr 17015
Watts Ln 17013
Waverly Ln 17015
Wayne Ave 17013
Webster Dr 17015
Webster St 17013
Wedgewood Dr 17015
Wellington Ct & Dr 17013
Wertz Run Rd 17013
Wertzville Rd
7100-7699 17015
7700-7899 17013
Wesley Dr 17015
N & S West St & Vw 17013
Westlake Dr 17015
Westminster Ct & Dr 17013
Westpoint Dr 17013
Wexford Ct 17015
Wheatfield Dr 17015
Whispering Pines Ln 17015
White Birch Ln 17013
White Deer Way 17013
White Oak Dr 17015
Whitetail Dr 17015
Whittley Ct 17015
Wilbert Dr 17013
Wild Rose Cir 17015
Wildflower Dr 17015
Wildwood Rd 17015
William Dr 17013
Willow Ln 17015
Willow Rd 17013
E Willow St 17013
W Willow St 17013
Willow Grove Rd
1-499 17013
500-899 17015
Willow Lake Dr 17015
Willow View Dr 17015
Wilson St 17013
Wiltshire East St 17015
Wiltshire West St 17015
Winchester Gdns 17013
Windcroft Ct 17015
Winding Ln 17013
Windsor Ct 17013
Wolf Bridge Rd 17013
Wood Ave & Ln 17013
Woodcrest Dr 17015
Woodland Ave 17013
Woodlawn Ln 17015
Woodward Dr 17013
Wright Ave 17013
Wyndham Dr 17013
Wynnwood Ave 17013
E & W Yellowbreeches Rd 17015
York Rd
2-98 17013
100-399 17013
400-498 17015
500-1699 17015
Yorkshire Dr 17013
Yorwick Rd 17013
Young Dr 17015
Zimmerman Rd 17015
Zion Rd 17015

NUMBERED STREETS

All Street Addresses 17013

CHAMBERSBURG PA

General Delivery 17201

POST OFFICE BOXES MAIN OFFICE STATIONS AND BRANCHES

Box No.s
All PO Boxes 17201

NAMED STREETS

Abishire Way 17201
Acorn Cir 17202
Adams Dr 17201
Adin Ln 17202
Adrienne Ln 17202
Advantage Ave 17201
Airport Rd 17201
Alandale Dr 17202
Alexander Ave 17201
Alleman Rd 17202
Allen Dr 17202
Alligator Reef Ave 17202
Amethyst Dr 17202
Amsley Dr 17202
Angle Rd 17202
Anthony Hwy 17202
Apple Way 17202
Apple Blossom Way 17201
Applecross Ave 17202
Appleyard Dr 17202
Arbor Rdg 17201
Arbutus Dr 17202
Archer Dr 17201
Armory Dr 17202
Ashley Dr 17201
Aspen Ln 17202
Atherton Ave 17202
Aubrey Dr 17202
Audubon Ct 17202
Austin Ave 17202
Baltusrol Dr 17202
Banbury Ln 17202
Bard Dr 17202
Barnegat Light Dr 17202
Barnes Rd 17202
Bassett Dr 17201
Bayberry Dr 17201
Beacon Ct 17201
Beamer Ln 17202
Beddington Blvd 17201
Beechwood Ct & Ln 17201
Belair Dr 17202
Bell Ave 17202
Bellhurst Dr 17202
Bellows Ct 17202
Belmont Way 17202
Bender Ave 17201
Benedict Dr 17201
Bengate Rd 17202
Benjamin Dr 17201
Big Dipper Ln 17202
Bikle Rd 17202
Birch St 17201
Birchway Dr 17202
Bishop Ave 17201
Black Ave 17201
Black Gap Rd 17202
Blakewood Dr 17201
Blanchard Ave 17201
Bloom Ave 17201
Blueberry Ln 17202
Bodie Island Dr 17202
Bony Ln 17202
Boundary Rd 17202
Bowman Rd 17202
Bowman St 17201
Boxwood Ct 17202
Boyer Rd 17202
Boyer Mill Rd 17202
Bracken Dr 17201
Bradbury Ct 17202
Braemar Ct & Dr 17202
Bramble Ct 17201
Brandon Dr 17201
Brechbill Rd 17202
Brechbill Loop Rd 17202
Briar Ln 17202
Bricker Rd 17202
Bridle Hill Ct 17202
Brim Blvd 17201
Broad St 17201
Brookline Ct 17201
Brookmeadow Ln 17201
Brookview Ave
100-199 17201
201-299 17202
Brookwood Dr 17201
Browns Mill Rd 17202
Brumbaugh Ave 17201
Buchannan St 17201
Buckingham Dr 17201
Bunker Ct 17202
Burdock Ct 17202
Burkett Rd 17202
W Burkhart Ave 17201
Burkholder Rd 17202
Buttercup Dr 17202
Butternut Ln 17201
Byers Ave 17201
Byers Rd 17202
Cambridge Ct & Ln 17201
Camelot Dr 17202
Camp Robin Hood Rd 17202
Candice Ln 17201
Candlestick Ct 17201
Canterbury Dr 17201
Carbaugh Ave 17201
Carbaugh Dr
1-299 17202
600-663 17201
Carey Dr 17202
Carlton Ave 17201
Carmack Dr 17202
Carnelian Dr 17202
Carnoustie Dr 17202
Carolina Ct 17201
Carrera Dr 17202
Castleton Dr 17202
E & W Catherine St 17201
Cayenne Ct 17202
Cedar St 17201
Center Dr 17202
Center St 17201
S Central Ave 17201
Chamberlayne Dr 17202
Chambers St 17201
Chambersburg Mall 17202
Chancellor Dr 17202
Channing Dr 17201
Chapman Ct 17202
Charleston Dr 17202
Cherry Ave 17202
Cherry Lane Dr 17202
Church Ln, Rd & St 17202
Cider Press Rd 17202
Cinder St 17202
Circle Dr 17202
Clay Hill Rd 17202
Cleveland Ave 17201
Clinton Ave 17201
Clover Cir 17201
Clover Rd 17202
Coble Rd 17202
Coffey Ave 17201
N & S Coldbrook Ave 17201
College Ave 17201
College Rd 17202
Colonial Dr 17202
Colorado St 17202
E & W Commerce St 17201
Community Center Rd 17202
Conner Ave 17201
Conner Dr 17202
Constellation Dr 17202
Constitution Dr 17201
Coontown Rd 17202
Cornerstone Ct 17201
Cornertown Rd 17201
Cornwall Rd 17202
Cosell Dr 17201
Country Rd 17202
Country View Dr 17202
Courtney Dr 17201
Cove Dr 17202
Cranberry Dr 17202
Creekside Dr 17202
Cresson Dr 17202
Crestwood Dr 17202
Criders Church Rd 17202
Crottlestown Rd 17202
Cumberland Ave 17201
Cumberland Hwy 17202
Cypress Ln 17202
Cypress St 17201
Dairy Rd 17202
Dartmouth Green Ct 17201
Dawn Ln 17202
Deborah Ct 17201
Debrina Ct 17201
Delano Dr 17201
Derbyshire St 17201
Development Ave 17201
Devon Ct & Dr 17201
Dewberry Ct 17201
Dickeys Dr 17202
Diopside Dr 17202
Dixie Ave 17202
Doron Dr 17202
Dorset Ct 17201
Downey Dr 17202
Downing Ct 17201
Duffield Rd 17202
Duncan Ave 17201
Durham Dr 17202
Dwarf Rd 17202
Eagle Dr 17202
Eastland Dr 17202
Eberly Ct 17202
Echo Dr 17202
Echo Springs Rd 17202
Eden Dr 17202
Edenville Rd 17202
Edenville Cheesetown Rd 17202
Edgar Ave 17201
Edgelea Dr 17201
Edgewater Dr 17202
Edgewood Cir & Rd 17202
Edith Dr 17202
N & S Edwards Ave 17202
Eisenhower Dr 17201
Elder St 17201
Elevator St 17202
Elizabeth Ct & Dr 17202
Elm Ave 17201
Elrock Dr 17201
Elser Dr 17202
Emerald Dr 17202
Epic Dr 17201
Equestrian Dr 17202
Esther Dr 17202
Eton Ct 17201
Etter Rd 17202
Eucalyptus Ct 17202
Eugene Dr 17202
Excel Ave 17201
Fairground Ave 17201
Fairview Ave 17202
Falcon Ln 17202
Falling Spring Rd 17202
Farm Ln 17202
Farm Credit Dr 17202
Farmington Rd 17202
Farthell Rd 17201
Feaster Rd 17202
N & S Federal St 17201
Fern Ln 17202
Fersfield Rd 17202
Fetterhoff Chapel Rd 17202
Fiddlers Rd 17202
Field Cir 17202
Fillmore Dr 17201
Fisher Rd 17202
Floral Ave 17201
Fluorite Dr 17202
Foltz Ave 17201
Forest Ln & Rd 17202
Fort Mccord Rd 17202
Fox Den Dr 17202
Fox Hill Dr 17202
Fox Meadow Rd 17202
Frank Rd 17202
Franklin Rd 17202
N Franklin St 17201
S Franklin St 17201
Franklin Farm Ln 17202
Franklin Square Dr 17201
Frecon Rd 17202
Frederick Mill Rd 17202
Frey Rd 17202
Friendship Village Rd 17202
Fritz Way 17201
Front St 17202
Funk Rd 17201
Gabler Rd 17201
Gabrielle Ln 17202
Galaxy Dr 17202
Galitzin Dr 17202
Garber Rd 17202
Garber St 17201
E Garfield St 17201
Garman Dr 17202
Garver Ln 17202
Gary Way 17202
Gateway Ave 17201
Gayman Rd 17202
George St 17201
Georgia Ave 17201
Geyer Cir & Dr 17201
E Gilbert Ave 17201
Gilbert Rd 17202
Ginkgo Ct 17201
Glen St 17201
Glen Abbey Dr 17202
Glen Eagles Dr 17202
Glen Elen Dr 17202
Glendale Dr 17202
Gloss Rd 17202
Gomer Rd 17202
Governors Ct 17201
Grand Ave 17201
Grand Point Rd 17202
Grandview Ave & Xing 17201
Grant St 17201
Grapevine Rd 17202
Green Way 17202
Green Corner Rd 17202
Green Meadow Ln 17201
Greenbriar Cir 17202
Greene St 17201
Greene Meadow Dr 17202
Greenfield Ct & Dr 17202
Greenlea Way 17202
Greenleaf Rd 17202
Greenside Ct 17202
Greenvillage Rd 17202
Gregway Dr 17202
Greystone Cir 17201
Grimsby Ct 17201
Grindstone Hill Rd 17202
Gsell Dr 17202
Guilford Ave 17201
Guilford Dr 17202
Guilford Sta 17202
Guilford Spring Rd 17202
Guitner Rd 17202
N & S Hackberry Dr 17201
Hade Rd 17202
Hades Church Rd 17202
Hamilton Ave 17202
Hamilton Dr 17202
Hamilton Rd 17201
Hamilton Hills Dr 17202
Hammond Dr 17201
Hampton Dr 17202
Harbo Rd 17202
N & S Harrison Ave & Dr 17201
Harshman Rd 17202
Hartzok Rd 17202
Harvest Ln 17202
Haulman Rd 17202
Hawthorne Ln 17202
Hazel St 17201
Hearthside Dr 17202
Heather Dr 17202
Hedgerow Dr 17202
Heidi Cir 17202
Heintzelman Ave 17201
Helman Rd 17202
Hemlock Cir 17201
Henry Ln & Rd 17202
Heritage Rd 17202
Hickory Ct & Ln 17202
Hidden Way 17202
High Ave 17201
High St
200-599 17201
601-697 17202
699-899 17202
Highfield Ct 17202
Highfield Ln N 17201
Highfield Ln S 17201
Highland Ave 17201
Highland Cir 17202
Highland Dr 17202
Highland Rd 17202
Hillcrest Ave & Dr 17202
Hillen Ln 17202
Hillendale Rd 17202
Hillside Dr 17202
Hilltop Dr 17202
Hoke Dr 17202
Holly Dr & Ln 17202
Hollywell Ave 17201
Honey Rock Ct & Rd 17202
Hood St 17201
Hoover Dr 17202
Horst Ave 17201
Horst Ln 17202
Horst Rd 17202
Hospitality Dr 17202
Howard St 17201
Hudson Ave 17201
Hultzapple Dr 17201
Hunters Ln 17202
Hunters Chase 17202
Independence Dr 17201
Industrial Dr 17201
Ingram Dr 17202
Innovation Way 17201
Interchange Dr 17202
Inverness Ct 17202
Iron Bridge Rd 17202
E & W Irva Dr 17201
Ivan Rd 17202
Jack Rd 17202
Jacks Mill Rd 17202
Jackson Dr 17201
Jade Dr 17202
Jameslee Dr 17202
Jed Ct 17202
Jefferson Dr 17201
Jeffries Ct 17202
Jenny Ln 17202
Johnson Dr 17201
Johnson Rd 17202
Juniper Rd 17202
Justine Dr 17201
Kaiser Ln 17202
Karvois Ct 17202
Kauffman Rd & St E 17202
Keefer Rd 17201
Kel High Dr 17201
Kennebec Dr 17201
Kennedy Ct 17202
Kennedy Dr 17201
Kennedy St
1-15 17201
17-21 17201
23-99 17201
106-106 17202
116-122 17201
123-125 17202
126-142 17202

128-128 17202
131-133 17201
135-176 17201
144-146 17202
148-162 17202
177-177 17202
178-198 17201
179-183 17201
185-199 17202
201-209 17201
252-254 17202
256-257 17202
Kennedy Street Ext 17202
Kenny Hill Dr 17201
Kensington Dr 17201
Kenwood Rd 17201
Keystone Ave 17202
King Dr 17202
E King St 17201
W King St 17201
Kittatinny Dr 17202
Kohler Rd 17202
Kolpark Dr 17202
Kraiss Ave 17201
Kriner Rd 17202
Kunkle Dr 17202
Kyle Ave 17201
Lacebark Cir 17201
Lakeshore Dr 17202
Lakewood Ct 17201
Landfill Rd 17202
Landmark Ct 17201
Lantern Ln 17201
Larch Ave 17201
Larkspur Ln 17202
Laurel Ave 17201
Laurelton Ct 17201
Laurich Dr 17202
Lawyers Rd 17201
Lea Dr 17202
Leafmore Rd 17202
Ledge Dr 17202
Lee St 17201
Leedy Dr & Way 17202
Lehman Dr & Rd 17202
Leidig Dr 17201
Leisure Dr 17202
Lesher Rd 17202
Letterkenny Rd W 17201
Letterkenny Army
Depot 17201
Levi Ln 17201
Liberty Dr 17202
E Liberty St 17201
W Liberty St 17201
Lighthouse Rd 17202
Lime Kiln Rd 17202
Limekiln Dr 17201
Limestone Dr 17202
Lin Mar Dr 17202
Lincoln Rd 17201
Lincoln St 17202
Lincoln Way E
100-154 17201
156-1199 17201
1200-1218 17202
1220-2200 17201
2202-2298 17202
Lincoln Way W
19-37 17201
39-700 17201
702-708 17201
800-4199 17202
Linden Ave 17201
Linden Rd 17202
Lindia Dr 17202
Lindman Dr 17202
Linoak Rd 17202
Linwood Dr 17202
Lisbon Dr 17202
Little Mountain Ter 17202
Liverpool Ct 17201
Lockaber Ave 17202
Locust Ln & St 17202
Long Ln 17201
Loop Rd 17202
Lorford Dr 17202
Lorraine Ln 17202
Lortz Ave 17201
Loudon Rd 17202
W Loudon St 17201
Lucey Ln 17202
E & W Ludwig Ave 17201
Luther Dr 17202
Macintosh Way 17201
Madison Ave 17202
Magnolia Ct 17202
Mahantango Dr 17202
N & S Main St 17201
Majestic Ct & Dr 17202
Malibu Dr 17202
Mallard Dr E & W 17202
Manor Ln 17202
Maraposa Dr 17202
Marcella Dr 17201
Maribeth Dr 17202
Marilyn Ct 17202
Marion Rd 17202
Marion Main St 17202
Mark Dr 17201
Martin Ave 17201
Martina Dr 17201
Marvern Dr E & W 17202
Marvic Dr 17202
Maryland Ave 17201
Matthew Dr 17201
May Mar Dr 17201
Maylinn Dr 17202
Mccleary Dr 17201
Mcdermott St 17202
Mcilvaine Ln 17202
Mckenrick Dr 17201
Mckenzie Rd 17202
E Mckinley St
100-1199 17201
1200-1299 17202
Meadow Dr 17201
Meadow Ln 17202
Meadow Green Ln 17202
Meadowbrook Ln 17201
Meadowcreek Dr N &
S 17202
Meadowview Cir 17202
Memory Ln 17201
Menno Vlg 17201
Menno Haven Dr 17201
Mentzer Ave 17201
Merriweather Dr 17201
Mickey Inn Ln & Rd 17202
Middle Dr 17202
Middle St 17201
Midland Dr 17202
Milestone Ct 17201
Milhouse Ave 17202
Mill Rd 17201
Millennium Dr 17202
Miller Rd 17202
Miller St 17201
Minnich Rd 17201
Miracle Ln 17202
Miramar Dr 17202
Molly Pitcher Hwy 17202
Mondor Dr 17202
Monroe Dr 17201
Mont Alto Rd 17202
Montgomery Ave 17201
Monticello Ct 17202
Moosic Dr 17202
Morrow Pl 17201
Mount Moriah St 17201
Mount Olivet Rd 17202
Mountain Dr & Rd 17202
Mountain Brook Rd 17202
Mountain View Dr 17202
Mower Rd 17202
Muirfield Dr 17202
Murray Rd 17202
Murtha Dr 17202
Nelson St
235-237 17202
239-241 17202
243-243 17202
400-999 17201
1001-1099 17201
New Ln 17202
New Franklin Rd 17202
New York Ave 17201
Newcomer Rd 17202
Nighthawk Ln 17202
Nittany Dr 17202
Nitterhouse Dr 17201
Nolts Rd 17202
Norland Ave 17201
Norman Dr 17202
North Ave & St 17201
Northfield Dr 17201
Northgate Commons
Rd 17201
Nottingham Dr 17201
Nyesville Rd 17202
Oak St 17201
Oakwood Ct 17201
Obsidian Dr 17202
Ocracoke Island Ct 17202
Ohio Ave 17201
Old Kiln Dr 17202
Olde Pine Dr 17202
Olde Scotland Rd 17202
Olde Walker Rd 17202
Onyx Dr 17202
Opal Dr 17202
Opportunity Ave 17201
Orchard Ave 17202
Orchard Ct 17201
Orchard Dr 17201
Orchard Rd 17202
Orion Dr 17202
Overcash Ave 17201
Overcash Rd 17202
Overhill Dr 17202
Overlea Ct 17201
Oxford Ct 17201
Oyler Dr 17201
Pa Harry Dr 17202
Palm Springs Dr 17202
Pampas Cir 17202
Paper Mill Rd
500-699 17201
800-1199 17202
Park Ave 17201
Park Cir 17202
Park Cir W 17202
Park Terrace Dr 17202
Park View Dr 17201
Parker Dr 17202
Parks Dr 17202
Parkside Ct 17201
Parkwood Dr 17201
S Patrol Rd 17201
Paul Ave 17201
Paul Mar Dr 17202
Paxton Ct 17202
Peach Dr 17201
Peachtree Ln 17202
Peckman Dr 17202
N & S Penn Hall Dr 17201
Penn Wood Ct 17201
Penncraft Ave 17201
Pennsylvania Ave 17201
Percy Ave 17201
Pheasant Cir 17202
Philadelphia Ave
251-3000 17201
3002-3298 17201
3801-3997 17202
3999-5799 17202
Phoenix Dr 17201
Pin Oak Dr 17201
Pine Ct 17201
Pine Ln 17202
Pine St 17201
Pine Stump Rd 17202
Piper Ave 17201
Plasterer Ave 17201
Pleasant St 17201
Pleasantview Dr 17202
Poe Rd 17202
E Point Ave 17201
Ponds Turn Rd 17202
Poplar Ave 17201
Portico Rd 17202
Portrait Way 17202
Potato Roll Ln 17202
Powell Dr 17201
Prairie Dr 17202
Progress Rd 17201
Quarry Rd 17202
E & W Queen St 17201
Quigley Dr 17202
Quilters Ct 17202
S Ragged Edge Rd 17202
Railroad Rd & St 17202
Raleigh Ave 17202
Ramsey Ave 17201
Raven Dr 17202
Raymond Dr 17202
Reagan Dr 17202
Redwood St 17201
Reservoir St 17201
Rice Rd 17202
Richard Ave 17201
Richardson Dr 17202
Ricklyn Dr 17202
Riddle Rd 17201
Rife St 17201
Rock Rd 17202
Rock Hill Rd 17202
Rockview Ave 17202
Rocky Spring Rd 17201
Roland Ave 17201
Rolling Ct, Ln & Rd 17202
Romance Ln 17202
Roosevelt Dr 17201
Roosevelt Arms Ct 17201
Rose St 17201
Rose Ann Dr 17201
Rosehill Ct 17202
Rosewood Ct 17201
Rotz Rd 17202
Rowe Run Rd 17202
Roy Pitz Ave 17201
Ruby Dr 17202
Rumler Rd 17202
Ruritan Dr 17202
Rustic Hill Dr 17201
Saint Andrews Dr 17202
Saint Johns Dr 17202
Saint Paul Rd 17202
Saint Pauls Dr 17201
Saint Thomas Edenville
Rd 17202
Saint Thomas Williamson
Rd 17202
Salem Rd 17201
Samerica Dr 17202
Sanders Cir 17202
Sandhurst Dr 17202
Sandoeshire Ln 17201
Sandy Cir 17202
Sanibel Ln 17201
Sarah Pl 17202
Sardonyx Dr 17202
Scotland Ave 17201
Scotland Rd
11-2197 17201
2199-2599 17201
2801-3097 17201
3099-3658 17202
3680-3682 17201
3700-3798 17202
Scotland Main St 17202
Scott Rd 17202
Sequoia Ct 17201
Shadow Ln 17202
Shadyside Dr 17202
Shar Pei Dr 17202
Shatzer Rd 17201
Shatzer St 17202
Shatzer Orchard Rd 17202
Sheffield Dr 17201
Sheffler Dr 17201
Sheller Ave 17201
Sheller Rd 17202
Sherry Dr 17202
Sherwood Dr 17202
Shields Rd 17202
Shinnecock Dr 17202
Shively Rd 17202
Short Cut Rd 17201
Siloam Rd 17201
Skelly Rd 17201
Skye Ave 17202
Sleichter Ln 17202
Slothour Rd 17202
Smith Rd 17202
Snider Rd 17202
Snowcreek Rd 17202
Social Island Cir & Rd 17202
Sollenberger Dr & Rd 17202
Somerset Rd 17202
E & W South St 17201
Southgate Mall 17201
Spanish Moss Ln 17202
Spring Ln 17201
Spring Rd 17202
Spring St 17201
Spring Side Ct & Dr 17202
Spring Valley Rd 17202
Springfield Dr 17202
Springview Cir & Dr 17202
St Joseph Ln 17202
St Pauls Dr 17201
Stamford Dr 17202
Stanley Ave
300-398 17201
400-1200 17201
1202-1224 17201
1226-1298 17202
1300-1400 17202
1402-1498 17202
Stanley Ct 17201
Starr Ave 17202
State St 17202
Statler Rd 17202
Sterling Bridge Rd 17202
Stevens Ct 17202
Stitley Rd 17202
Stone Quarry Rd 17202
Stonegate Cir & Ct 17201
Stonybridge Dr 17202
Stouffer Ave 17201
Streamside Dr 17202
Strite Rd 17202
Strock Dr 17202
E & W Strohm Dr 17202
Stullfield Rd 17202
Stump Ln 17202
Suburban Dr 17202
Sue Linn Dr 17201
Sugar Bush Ln 17202
Summer St 17201
Summer Breeze Ln 17202
Sunbrook Dr 17201
Sundown Dr 17202
Sunny Ln 17202
Sunny Side Dr 17202
Sunset Ave, Blvd, Ct,
Ln & Pike E & W 17202
Superior Ave 17201
Surrey Ct & Dr 17202
Sutherland Ct 17202
Swamp Fox Rd 17202
Swope Rd 17202
Sycamore Grove Rd 17202
Talhelm Rd 17202
Tallow Hill Rd 17202
Tanglewood Ln 17202
Tanya Dr 17202
Tattoo Dr 17202
Technology Ave 17201
Terrilynn Dr 17202
Texas Ave 17201
Theodore Dr 17202
Thistledown Dr 17202
Thompson Ln 17202
Tobin Dr 17201
Tolbert Ave 17201
Topaz Dr 17202
Tower Rd 17202
Tristan Trl 17202
Troon Dr 17202
Tucker Dr 17201
Turnberry Dr 17202
Tussey Dr 17202
Twin Dr 17202
Twin Bridge Rd 17202
Twin Oak Turn 17202
Tyler Dr 17201
S Uninert Trl S 17202
Valley Pine Ct 17202
Valley View Dr 17202
Vaughn Dr 17202
Vernon Dr 17202
Village Sq 17201
E & W Vine St 17201
Vinell Ln 17202
Wagner Rd 17202
Walker Rd
115-431 17201
433-440 17201
600-1799 17202
Wallace Ave 17201
Warm Spring Rd 17202
Warwick Ct & Dr 17201
E & W Washington St 17201
S Water St 17201
Wayne Ave
201-297 17201
299-1099 17201
1101-1115 17202
1117-1199 17202
Wayne Rd 17202
Weaver Ave 17201
Weber Rd 17202
Wellslee Dr 17201
Wenger Ln 17201
Wenger Rd 17202
Wenger Way 17202
Wennington Dr 17201
Westgate Dr 17201
Westover Way 17202
Whinstone Way 17202
White Church Rd 17202
White Pine Dr 17202
White Rock Rd 17202
Whitley Dr 17201
Wibymarch Dr 17202
Wiles Rd 17202
Wilhelm Dr 17202
Wilkson Ln 17202
William Penn Dr 17201
Williamsburg Cir 17202
Willow St 17202
Willowbrook Ct & Dr 17202
Wills Dr 17202
Wilson Ave 17201
Wind Flower Rd 17202
Winterberry Dr 17202
Wisteria Dr 17202
Wolf Ave 17201
Wood Duck Dr E & W 17202
Woodbriar Dr 17202
Woodland Dr & Way 17202
Woodlawn Cir & Dr 17201
Woodstock Rd
400-498 17201
500-599 17201
1800-3799 17202
Woodvale Dr 17201
Wren Ct 17202
Yorktowne Dr 17202
Zircon Dr 17202

NUMBERED STREETS

2nd Ave 17202
2nd St 17202
N 2nd St 17201
S 2nd St 17201
3rd Ave 17202
3rd St 17202
N 3rd St 17201
S 3rd St 17201
4th Ave 17202
N 4th St 17201
S 4th St 17201
S 5th Ave & St 17201
N & S 6th 17201
N & S 7th 17201
S 8th St 17201

CHESTER PA

General Delivery 19013

POST OFFICE BOXES MAIN OFFICE STATIONS AND BRANCHES

Box No.s
All PO Boxes 19016

NAMED STREETS

Aarons Way 19013
Abbott St 19013
Andrews Ct 19014
Applewood Ct 19014
Arbor Cir & Dr 19013
Attucks Ter 19013
Atwell St 19013
Avenue Of The States 19013
Baker Pl & St 19013
Baldwin St 19013
Barclay St 19013
E Beacon Light Ln 19013
Bender Dr 19014
Bernard St 19014
Bethel Ave 19014
Bethel Rd 19013
Beverly Ln 19013
Bickley Pl 19013
Bing Pl 19013
Blakley St 19013
Bobby May Dr 19013
Booker Ave 19014
Booth St 19013
Boxwood Dr 19014
Boyle St 19013
Bradley St 19013
Broadway Ave 19014
Broomall St 19013
Brown St 19013
Buffington Rd 19014
Bunting St 19013
Burdett Dr 19014
Butler St 19013
Byram St 19013
Caldwell St 19013
W Carlas Ln 19013
Carole Dr 19014
Carriage Cir 19014
Carter Ave & Ln 19013
Carver Pl 19013
Cedarcrest Ln 19014
Cella Dr 19014
Central Ave 19013
Chatham Cir 19014
Chelsea Rd 19014
Cherry St 19013
Cherry Tree Rd 19014
Cherrywood Cir 19014
Chester Pike 19022
Chestnut St 19013
Chichester Ave 19014
Church St 19013
Clayton St 19013
Clover Ln 19013
Columbia Ave 19013
Commission St 19013
Concord Ave & Rd 19013
Congress St 19013
Copeland Pl 19013
Cotton Ln 19014
Cotton St 19013
Crosby Sq & St 19013
Culhane St 19013
Curran St 19013

Curry St 19013
Dana Ct 19014
Delaware Ave 19013
Desmond Pl 19013
Dock St 19013
Dogwood Cir 19014
Dorian Dr 19013
Douglas Ave 19014
Dupont St 19013
Dutton St 19014
Ebright Ave 19013
Edgmont Ave 19013
Edwards St 19013
Elizabeth St 19013
Elk St 19013
E & W Elkinton Ave 19013
Ellsworth St 19013
Elsinore Pl 19013
Emerald St 19013
Engle St 19013
Esrey St 19013
Evergreen Ln 19014
Excelsior Dr 19014
Eyre Dr 19013
Felton St 19013
Florence Dr 19013
Flower St 19013
Forwood St 19013
Fourth St 19013
Frank Young Ave 19013
Franklin St 19013
W Front St 19013
Fulton St 19013
Garfield Ave 19014
Gingko Ln 19013
Glen Ter 19013
Grace St 19013
Gray St 19013
Green St 19013
Hancock St 19013
Harrahs Blvd 19013
Harris St 19013
Harwick St 19013
Hawthorne Ln 19014
Hayes St 19013
Heather Ln 19014
Hidden Valley Rd 19014
Highland Ave 19013
Hinkson St 19013
Holland Ter 19013
Honan St 19013
Houston St 19013
Howard St 19013
Huber St 19013
Hughes St 19013
Hunt Ter 19013
Hyatt St 19013
Iowa St 19013
Irvington Pl 19013
Ivy St 19013
Jackson Ave 19014
Jefferson St 19014
Jeffrey St 19013
John St 19013
Johnson St 19013
Kane St 19013
Kates Gln 19014
Kathleen Dr 19014
Kerlin St 19013
Keystone Rd
100-199 19014
101-197 19013
199-1299 19013
1301-1499 19013
Knight Pl 19013
Kristen Way 19014
Lamokin St 19013
Lehman St 19013
Lewis St 19013
Lily Ave 19013
Lincoln St & Ter 19013
Lindsay St 19013
Litwa Ln 19014
Lloyd St 19013
Locke Ter 19013
Locksley St 19013
Logan Way 19013
Longbotham Dr 19014
Louis James Ct 19014
Lytle Ter 19013
M L King Pedestrian Way 19013
Macadam St 19013
Macdade Blvd 19013
Madison St 19013
Market St 19014
Marten Ave 19014
Martin Ln 19013
Mary Dr 19014
Mary St 19013
Mccaffrey Pl 19013
Mccarey St 19013
Mcdonald St 19013
Mcdowell Ave 19013
Mcilvain St 19013
Mcmanus Ct 19013
Meade St 19013
Meadow Ln 19013
Medical Center Blvd 19013
Meetinghouse Rd 19014
Melrose Ave 19013
Mill St 19013
Minor St 19013
Modesto Cir 19013
Monticello Ave 19014
Morris St 19013
Morton Ave 19013
Moser St 19014
Mosley Ct 19013
E & W Mowry St 19013
Moya St 19013
Murray Pl 19013
Nate Ellis Dr 19013
Nicholas Ct 19014
Nichols Ter 19013
Nolan St 19013
Nooker St 19013
Norris St 19013
North St 19013
Nugent Pl 19013
Orchard Way 19014
Oxford Pl 19014
Palmer St 19013
Parker St 19013
E & W Parkway Ave 19013
Patrick St 19013
Patterson St 19013
Pearl Pl 19013
Penn St 19013
Pennell St 19013
Peoples St 19013
Perkins St 19013
Peterson St 19013
Phillips Pl 19013
Pine Ln 19013
Potter St 19013
Price St 19013
Providence Ave 19013
Prunus Cir 19013
Pulaski Dr 19013
Purdy St 19013
Pursley Pl 19013
Pusey St 19013
Quillen Ln 19014
Reading Dr 19013
Reaney St 19013
Remington St 19013
Renshaw Rd 19013
Richardson Ter 19013
Ridley Ave 19013
S Riveria Ln 19014
Rodgers Ave 19014
Rose St 19013
Rothwell Ter 19013
Ruby St 19013
Rural Ave & Cir 19013
Ruth Ave 19014
Ruth L Bennett Pl 19013
Sandeland St 19013
Seaport Dr 19013
Seigel St 19013
Shannon St 19013
Shaw Ter 19013
Sidell Pl 19013
Smith St 19013
Smithers St 19013
Somerset Ln 19014
Sommers Ln 19014
Springton Cir 19014
Sproul St 19013
Spruce St 19013
Stadium Dr 19013
Stanley Ct 19014
Stewart St 19013
Story Rd 19014
Stoval Pl 19013
Sun Dr 19013
Sunnyside Ave 19013
Swarts St 19013
Tansey Dr 19014
Taylor Ter 19013
Taylors Pl 19013
Terrill St 19013
Thomas Ave 19014
Thomas St 19013
Thurlow St 19013
Tilghman St 19013
Tilia Cir 19013
Tolston St 19013
Townsend St 19013
Township Line Rd 19013
Trainer St 19013
Ulrich St 19013
W Union St 19013
University Pl 19013
Upland Ave & St 19013
Valentine Ter 19013
Vauclain St 19013
Villa Dr 19013
Walnut St 19013
Ward St 19013
Washington Ave
1-200 19014
202-298 19014
1400-1699 19013
Weir Rd 19014
Welsh St 19013
Wetherill St 19013
Wheatley Pl 19013
White St 19013
Whittington Pl 19013
Willers Rd 19014
Williams Ave 19014
E Williams Cir 19013
N Williams Cir 19013
S Williams Cir 19013
Willison St 19013
Wilson St 19013
Wolverson Ave 19014
Woodgate Ln 19014
Woodrow St 19013
Wooten Ln 19014
Worrell St 19013
Wright Ter 19013
Yarnall St 19013

NUMBERED STREETS

All Street Addresses 19013

DOYLESTOWN PA

General Delivery 18901

POST OFFICE BOXES MAIN OFFICE STATIONS AND BRANCHES

Box No.s
All PO Boxes 18901

NAMED STREETS

Aarons Ave 18901
Abbey Cir 18901
Abraham Freed Rd 18902
Addison Ct 18901
Airport Blvd 18902
Alder Dr 18902
Algonquin Rd 18901
Almond Cluster 18901
Almshouse Rd 18901
Aly Dr 18902
Alyssa Ln 18901
Amberton Ct & Way 18902
Amherst Dr 18901
Anderson Rd 18902
Angus Cir 18902
Ann Davis Dr 18902
Anne Ln 18902
Antler Dr 18902
Anvil Pl 18902
Appian Way 18901
April Ln 18902
Aquetong Rd 18902
Arbor Ln 18902
Arbor Hill Ct 18902
Arbor Lea Cir 18901
Ash Rd 18902
Ash Way 18901
Ash Mill Rd 18902
E & W Ashland St 18901
Ashton Ct 18902
Aspen Way 18901
Aster Ct 18901
Atkinson Dr 18901
Aurora Ct 18901
Autumn Leaf Dr 18901
Avalon Ct 18901
Avenue A 18901
Bailey Ct E 18902
Barner Rd 18901
Barness Ct 18902
Barrett Dr 18901
Barrie Cir 18901
Beacon Hill Ct 18902
Bedford Ave 18901
Bedford Dr 18902
Beech Ln 18902
Beech Cluster 18901
Beek St 18901
Bella Cir 18901
Bellows Pl 18902
Belmont Ave, Ct & Sq 18901
Bennett Dr 18901
Bergstrom Rd 18902
Berkeley Ct 18901
Berkshire Rd 18902
Berry Ln 18902
Beulah Rd 18901
Biddeford Cir 18902
Binny Rd 18902
Birch Rd 18901
Birchwood Dr 18901
Birdie Ln 18901
Birdsong Way 18901
Bishop Cir 18902
Bishops Gate Ln 18901
Bittersweet Dr 18901
Bittersweet Ln 18902
Blackfriars Cir 18901
Blakemore Ct 18901
Blenheim Dr 18902
Blue Ridge Dr 18902
Blythewood Rd 18901
Bogarts Tavern Rd 18902
Bogey Cir 18901
Bomaca Dr 18901
Boxwood Cir 18902
Braddock Ct 18902
Bradley Ct 18902
Branches Ln 18902
E & W Brandon Way 18902
Brayson Ln 18902
Brendon Knls 18902
Brentwood Dr 18902
Briar Cir 18902
Briarwood Ct 18901
Bridge St 18901
Bridgepoint Ct 18901
Bridle Ct 18902
Brinker Dr 18901
Bristol Rd 18901
Britain Dr 18901
Brittany Cir 18901
N & S Broad St 18901
Broadale Ct & Rd 18901
Brook Dr 18901
Brookdale Dr 18901
Brookside Ct 18902
Buck Run Dr 18901
Buck Run Rd 18902
Buckingham Dr 18902
Bunker St 18901
Bunker Hollow Rd 18901
Burke Cir 18901
Burnt House Hill Rd 18902
E & W Butler Ave 18901
Buttonwood Dr 18902
Buttonwood Ln 18901
Byron Ct & Dr 18902
Caddy Dr 18901
Calais Cir 18902
Callowhill Rd 18901
Cambridge Cir 18902
Campbell Ave 18901
Canterbury Rd 18902
Captain Molly Cir 18902
Carousel Cir 18901
Carriage Dr 18901
Carversville Rd 18902
Catherine Ave 18901
Cavallo Way 18901
Cayuga Cir 18901
Cedar Dr & Ln 18901
Cedar Crest Ct 18901
Cedar Woods Cir & Dr 18901
Center St 18901
Cephas Child Rd 18902
N & S Chapman Ave & Rd 18901
Charing Cross Rd 18901
Charter Cir 18901
Charter Club Dr 18902
Charter Oak Ct 18901
Cheese Factory Rd 18901
Cherokee Rd 18901
Cherry Ln 18901
Cheshire Rd 18902
Chestnut Dr 18902
Chestnut Cluster 18901
Chestnut Valley Dr 18901
Christopher Ln 18901
Christopher Day Rd 18902
N & S Chubb Dr 18901
Church Rd 18902
N Church St 18901
S Church St 18901
Church School Rd 18902
Cinnamon Ct 18902
Claremont Dr 18901
Clay Rd 18902
Clearwater Ct 18902
Clemens Rd 18901
Clermont Ct 18902
N & S Clinton St 18901
Clover Ln 18902
Cobblestone Ct 18902
Cobblestone Way 18901
Cold Spring Creamery Rd 18902
Coldbrook Cir 18902
Coles Dr 18901
Colonial Heritage Park 18901
Colts Ct 18902
Comley Cir 18902
Commons Way 18901
Concord Rd 18902
Constitution Ave 18901
Cookes Ln 18902
Cornerstone Ct 18901
Corrigan Rd 18902
Cottage St 18901
Cottageville Ln 18902
Cottonwood Ct 18901
Country Brook Dr 18901
Country Club Dr & Ln 18901
Country View Dr 18902
Countryside Dr 18902
E & W Court St 18901
Covenant Ct 18902
Covered Bridge Ln 18901
Covington Ln 18902
Cranberry Rd 18902
Creek Dr & Rd 18901
Crestland Ter 18901
Crestview Way 18902
Crosskeys Dr 18902
Crosspoint Dr 18902
Curly Hill Rd 18902
Danielle Dr 18902
Dartmouth Dr 18901
Davis Dr 18902
Davis Rd 18901
Daystar Dr 18902
Deborah Ct 18902
Decatur St 18901
Deep Creek Way 18902
Deep Glen Way 18902
Deer Path Rd 18901
N & S Deer Run Rd 18902
Deerfield Ln 18901
Dell Dr 18901
Dell Haven Dr 18901
Derby Ln 18902
Devon Ln 18901
Dewees Rd 18902
Diane Way 18902
Dickinson Ct & Way 18902
Dillon Rd 18902
Dogwood Ln
3902A-3902A 18902
1-99 18901
3600-3903 18902
3905-3927 18902
Dogwood Cluster 18901
Donaldson St 18901
Dorothy Ave 18901
Dorset Ct 18901
Doyle St 18901
Duane Rd 18901
Durham Rd 18902
Eagle Ln 18901
East Rd & St 18901
Easthill Dr 18901
N Easton Rd 18902
S Easton Rd 18901
Eastwoods Cir 18901
Edgewood Rd 18902
Edison Ln & Rd 18901
Edison Furlong Rd 18901
Elfman Dr 18901
Eljan Dr 18901
Ellen Pl 18902
Elm Ter 18901
Emily Dr 18902
Enders Way 18902
Ephross Cir 18902
Erica Dr 18902
Essex Dr 18902
Estates Dr 18902
Esther Reed Dr 18902
Euonymous Cluster 18901
Evergreen Dr 18901
Everview Dr 18902
Fairfield Ln 18901
Farm Ln 18901
Fawn Ct 18902
Fell Rd 18902
Ferguson Dr 18902
Ferris Ln 18901
Ferry Rd
1-1 18901
8-1699 18901
3601-3897 18902
3899-6499 18902
Fiaba Ct 18901
Fieldstone Dr 18902
Flint Cir 18901
Fonthill Dr 18901
Foothill Dr 18902
Forest Dr
1-99 18901
3801-3823 18902
3825-3999 18902
Forge Pl 18902
E Fox Chase Cir 18902
W Fox Chase Cir 18902
Fox Chase Ln 18901
Fox Hill Rd 18901
Fox Hound Dr 18901
Fox Valley Dr 18902
Foxcroft Dr 18901
Foxglove Ct 18901
Foxglove Dr 18902
Francis Meyers Rd 18901
N & S Franklin St 18901
French Dr 18902
Friendly Ln 18901
Fringe Tree Ct 18901
Frost Ln 18902
Frosterly Dr 18901
Furlong Rd 18902
Furnace Pl 18902
Gail Cir 18902
Gannet Ln 18902
Garden Aly & Path 18901
Gatehouse Cir & Ln 18901
Gayman Rd 18902
Gibson Ln 18902
Glen Dr
1-199 18901
3801-3847 18902
3849-3999 18902
Gloucester Dr 18902
Goldeneye Ct 18901
Golf View Rd 18901
Gordon Rd 18902
Grandview Ln 18902
Granite Cir 18901
Grape Bay 18902
Grayce Ln 18902
Green St 18901
Green Heather Ct 18902
Green View Ln 18901
Greentree Dr 18901
Gregory Dr 18902
Greystone Dr 18902
Grundy Way 18902
Hagan Ct 18902
N & S Hamilton St 18901
Hampton Ct 18901
Hampton Dr 18902
Hancock Ln 18902
Hansell Rd 18902
Happ Dr 18901
Haring Rd 18902
Harmony Ct E 18902
Harrington Ct 18902
Harrison Rd 18902
Hart Ave 18901
Harvey Ave 18901
Hastings Ct 18901
Haverhill Ln 18902
Hawk Cir
1-99 18901
4200-4399 18902
Hayfield Ct 18901
Haywick Dr 18902
Hearth Pl 18902
Heather Ln 18902
Heckler Hollow Ct 18901
Hedgerow Ln 18901
Henley Ct 18901
Herbst Dr 18902
Heritage Ln 18901
Hibiscus Ct 18901
Hickory Dr & Ln 18901
Hickory Hollow Ln 18902
Hidden Ln 18901
Hidden Den Cir 18901
Hidden Valley Dr 18902
High Ridge Cir 18902
Hillcrest Cir & Dr 18901
Hillendale Dr 18901
Hillside Ave 18901
Hillside Cir 18902

Hillside Ln 18901
Hilltop Cir 18902
Hogan Ct 18901
Holicong Rd 18902
Holly Way 18902
Holly Cluster 18901
Homestead Dr 18901
Honey Hollow Rd 18902
Honeysuckle Ln 18902
Horseshoe Way 18901
Houk Rd 18901
Howley Ln 18901
Hudson Ct 18901
Hunt Dr 18902
Hunt Field Dr 18902
Hunter Ln 18901
Hunters Pl 18902
Hyde Park 18902
Independence Way 18901
Indian Ridge Rd 18902
Indian Springs Rd 18902
Industrial Dr 18901
Iron Way 18902
Iron Hill Rd 18901
Iroquois Ave 18901
Jackson St 18901
Jacob Stout Rd 18902
Jasmine Cluster 18901
Jefferson St 18901
Jennifer Ct 18902
Jenny Rd 18902
Jester Ln 18902
John Dyer Way 18902
Johns Way 18902
Joshua Ln 18902
Julie Ct 18902
Julie Ln 18901
June Meadow Dr 18902
Juniper Dr 18901
Katsura Cluster 18901
Kavan Ct 18902
Keeley Ave 18901
Kent Dr 18902
Kershaw Ave 18901
King Rd 18901
King Fisher Ln 18902
Kings Rd 18902
Kings Cross Cir 18901
Kirkbride Ln 18901
Klein Ct 18901
Knights Way 18902
Knolls Bend Ct 18902
Kreutz Ave 18901
Lace Leaf Dr 18902
Lacey Ave 18901
Lafayette St 18901
Lakeview Cir 18902
Lamp Post Rd 18901
Lancaster Dr 18902
Landis Greene Dr 18902
S Landis Mill Rd 18901
Landisville Rd 18902
Lantern Dr 18901
Larch Cir 18901
Larch Cluster 18901
Latham Ct 18901
Layle Ln 18901
Leapson Ln 18901
Lenape Dr & Ln 18901
Leslie Dr 18902
Lexington Dr 18902
Liberty Pl 18901
Lily Dr 18902
Limekiln Rd 18901
Lincoln Ave 18901
Linden Ave 18901
Liz Cir 18902
Logan St 18901
Logus Ln 18902
W Long Ln 18902
Longfellow Ct 18902
Longview Ln 18902
Longwood Cir 18901
Louise Saint Claire Dr 18902
Lovering Dr 18902
Lower State Rd 18901

Lucy Dr 18902
Luke Dr 18902
Lynbrook Ln 18901
Lynn Cir 18902
Lyon Cir 18902
Magnolia Ct 18901
Magnolia Cluster 18901
Mahogany Ct 18901
N & S Main St 18901
N & S Mallard Ln 18902
Manion Way 18902
Maple Ave, Ct & Ln 18901
Maple Leaf Ln 18901
Marie Cir 18902
Marlene Rd 18902
Mary St 18901
Masters Manor Rd 18901
Mathews Ave 18901
Matisse Ct 18902
Mcconnell St 18901
Mcginnis Ct 18902
Mckinstry Dr 18901
Mclaughlin Dr 18901
Mcneil Rd 18902
Mead Dr 18902
Meadow Ln 18901
Meadow View Dr 18902
Mechanics St 18901
Mechanicsville Rd 18902
Meetinghouse Rd 18901
Melissa Ct 18902
Memorial Dr 18901
Mercer Ave 18901
Mercer Gate Dr 18901
Mia Ln 18901
Michener Rd 18902
Miladies Ln 18902
Mill Rd 18902
Miller Ave 18901
Millhurst Ln 18902
Milords Ln 18902
Miriam Dr 18902
Mohawk Ave 18901
Mohegan St 18901
Monet Cir 18902
Morgan Hill Dr 18901
Morlen Rd 18902
Morrison Way 18902
Murray Dr 18901
Myers Dr 18901
Mystic View Ln 18901
Nancy Ward Cir 18902
Nanlyn Farm Cir 18902
Neshaminy Dell Dr 18901
New Rd 18901
New Britain Rd 18901
New Galena Rd 18901
Newbolt Ct 18902
Nicklaus Dr 18901
Norfolk Ln 18902
Normandy Ct 18902
North St 18901
Northview Ln 18902
Northwoods Ln 18902
Nottingham Way 18902
Oak Dr 18901
Oak Crest Dr 18902
Oak Leaf Ln 18901
E & W Oakland Ave 18901
E & W Oakview Ct 18902
Old Colonial Dr 18901
Old Dublin Pike 18901
Old Easton Rd 18902
Old Ironhill Rd 18901
Old Limekiln Rd 18901
Old New Rd 18901
Old Oak Rd 18902
Old Pebble Hill Rd 18901
Old York Rd 18902
Oneida Ln 18901
Orchard Ln 18901
Overholt Dr 18902
Overlook Cir 18902
Pagoda Cluster 18901
Paine St 18901
Paist Rd 18902

Paprika Rd 18902
Par Dr 18901
Park Dr 18901
Paunncussing Creek Rd 18902
Pawnee Rd 18901
Pear Dr 18902
Pearl Dr 18901
Pebble Hill Rd 18901
Pebble Valley Dr 18901
Pebble View Ln 18901
Pebble Woods Dr N 18901
Pelham Pl 18902
Penn St 18901
Pheasant Ln 18902
Pheasant Rd 18902
Pheasant Run Dr 18901
Philena Ave 18901
Phillips Cir 18902
Philmont Dr 18902
Piccadilly Cir 18901
Pickwick Dr 18901
Pierce Ln 18902
Pin Oak Dr 18902
N & S Pine Cir & St 18901
Pine Mill Cir 18902
Pine Run Rd 18901
Pine Valley Rd 18901
Pine View Dr 18901
Pine Wood Dr 18901
Pinevale Rd 18901
Player Ln 18901
Plumcrest Ln 18902
Plumridge Rd 18902
Point Pleasant Pike 18902
Pointers Pl 18902
Poplar Ln
 1-22 18902
 23-37 18901
 24-38 18902
 39-46 18901
 48-50 18901
Portsmouth Ct 18901
Preston Way 18902
Princeton Cir 18902
Printers Aly 18901
Private Rd 18902
Progress Dr 18901
Progress Meadow Dr 18902
Providence Ave 18901
Pueblo Rd 18901
Putters Pl 18901
Quail Dr
 1-199 18901
 5600-5699 18902
Quarry Rd 18901
Queensbury Pl 18901
Quince Cluster 18901
Radcliff Dr 18901
Raintree Ct 18902
Rebecca Fell Dr 18902
Red Gate Dr 18902
Redbud Cir 18902
Redeux Ct 18902
Redfield Rd 18902
Redwood Ct 18902
Redwood Cluster 18901
Regina Pl 18902
Rickert Rd 18901
Ridgetop Rd 18902
Ridgeview Dr 18902
Ridgeview Ln 18901
Ridings Ln 18902
Rinker Cir 18902
River Birch Dr 18902
Robyn Ln 18901
Rohr Dr 18901
Roseberry Dr 18902
Rosewood Dr 18902
Route 202 18902
Ruckman Way 18902
Ruth Ln 18901
Sablewood Dr 18902
Saddleview Ln 18902
Sagamore Ct 18902
Sagewood Ct 18902

Saint George Cir 18902
Salem St 18902
Salome Rd 18902
S Sand Rd 18901
Sand Sam Cir 18901
Sanderling Rd 18902
Sandy Knoll Cir & Dr 18901
W Sandy Ridge Dr & Rd 18901
Sandywood Dr 18901
Sarahs Ln 18902
Sauerman Rd 18901
Sawmill Rd 18902
Scarlet Oak Dr 18901
Scenic View Cir 18902
School Hill Dr 18901
Scott Ln 18902
Scott Rd 18901
Scout Way 18901
Secondwoods Rd 18902
Selner Ln 18901
Seneca Ct 18902
Seneca Dr 18901
Settlers Dr 18901
Shadbush Cluster 18901
Shady Grove Cir 18901
N & S Shady Retreat Rd 18901
Shady Springs Dr 18901
Shedden Cir 18902
Sheffield Dr 18902
Sheridan Rd 18901
Sherwood Ln
 1-99 18901
 3800-3999 18902
Shetland Dr 18902
Shewell Ave 18901
Short Rd 18901
Signature Dr 18902
Silo Hill Rd 18902
Simpson Cir 18902
Sioux Rd 18901
Sir Andrew Cir 18902
Skyron Dr 18902
Smoke Rd 18902
Snake Hill Rd 18902
Southview Ln 18901
Southwind Dr 18901
Southwoods Ln 18901
Spangler Ct 18902
Spring Lake Dr 18901
Spring Meadow Ln 18901
Spring Valley Rd
 600-882 18901
 884-898 18901
 3700-4099 18902
Springs Dr 18901
Spruce Dr 18902
Spruce St 18901
Squirrel Rd 18901
Stable Ct 18902
Stacey Dr 18901
Stags Leap Cir 18901
E & W State St 18901
Steeplechase Dr 18901
Sterling Crest Ct 18901
Stillwater Cir 18902
Stirrup Dr 18902
Stoke Pl 18902
Stony Ln 18902
Stover Trl 18902
Stovers Mill Rd 18902
Street Rd 18902
Stringer Dr 18901
Strouse Ln 18902
Stryker Ave 18901
Stump Rd 18902
Sugar Hill Ct 18902
Summer Meadow Dr 18902
Summerhill Dr 18902
Sundance Ct 18902
Sunflower Dr 18902
Sunnybrook Dr 18901
Sunnyside Dr 18902
Sunrise Dr 18901
Sunset View Dr 18901

Sussex Ter 18902
Sutton Pl 18902
Swamp Rd
 500-600 18901
 602-698 18901
 2700-3199 18902
E Swamp Rd
 1-300 18901
 302-450 18901
 3500-4199 18902
W Swamp Rd
 2-598 18901
 301-305 18902
 501-599 18901
 4200-4499 18902
 4700-4999 18901
Swetland Dr 18902
Sycamore Way 18901
Taifer Ave 18901
Tall Oak Ct 18902
Tally Ho Way 18901
N & S Tamenend Ave 18901
Taylor Ave 18901
Taylor Ln 18902
Teal Dr 18901
Tersher Dr 18902
Terwood Dr 18902
Tether Way 18901
Theodore Way 18901
Thisal Ln 18902
Timothy Dr 18901
Tower Hill Rd 18901
Town Ctr 18901
Townview Dr 18901
Tracy Dr 18901
Trafalgar Rd 18901
Trail Way E & W 18902
Trellis Path 18901
Tremont Ave 18901
Trophy Ln 18901
Tupelo Cluster 18901
Turk Rd 18901
Twin Oaks Dr 18901
Twin Silo Rd 18902
Twinbrook Cir 18902
Union St 18901
Upper State Rd 18901
Ursulas Way 18902
Ute Rd 18901
Vale View Dr 18901
Valley Cir 18901
Valley Green Dr 18901
Valley Park Rd 18902
Valley Stream Dr 18902
Valley View Dr 18902
Versailles Cir 18901
Veterans Ln 18901
Viburnum Cluster 18901
Victoria Ct 18901
Village Ln 18902
Vine St 18901
Wagon Wheel Ln 18901
Walden Way 18902
Walnut Ln 18901
Walton Ave 18901
Warden Rd 18901
Washington Sq & St 18901
Watercrest Dr 18901
Watson Dr 18902
Weldon Dr 18901
Wellington Rd 18902
Wells Rd 18901
Wellsford Ln 18902
N & S West St 18901
Westbury Ct 18901
Westminster Ln 18902
Weyhill Ln 18902
White Tail Ct 18902
Whitehall Dr 18901
Wilkshire Rd 18901
William Daves Rd 18902
Willow Wood Dr 18901
Willowbrook Dr 18901
Winchester Dr 18902
Windey Way Ln 18901
Windover Ln 18901

Windridge Dr 18902
Windrose Cir 18901
Windsong Dr 18901
Windsor Way 18901
Windtree Dr 18902
Windy Run Rd 18901
Winfield Pl 18902
Winterberry Dr 18902
Winterson Ct 18902
Wismer Rd 18902
Wood St 18901
Woodard Ct 18901
Woodbridge Dr 18901
Woodcrest Ln 18901
Woodfield Cir 18902
Woodland Dr 18901
Woods End Dr 18902
Woodspring Cir 18901
Woodstone Dr 18901
Woodview Dr 18901
Woodward Dr 18902
Worthington Rd 18902
N Worthington Rd 18902
Worthington St 18901
Yellowwood Cluster 18901
York Dr & Rd 18902
Yorkshire Rd 18902

EAST STROUDSBURG PA

General Delivery 18301

POST OFFICE BOXES MAIN OFFICE STATIONS AND BRANCHES

Box No.s
All PO Boxes 18301

RURAL ROUTES

02, 03, 05, 07, 15, 21, 22 18301
01, 04, 06, 08, 13, 18, 20, 21 18302

NAMED STREETS

Abbey Ln 18302
Abbington Dr 18302
Abeel Cir & Rd 18301
Academy Dr 18301
Access Rd 18302
Ace Ln 18301
Ace Mountain Rd 18302
Acer Ct 18302
Acorn Cir, Ct & Ln 18302
Acres Rd 18301
Adam Labar Rd 18302
Adams Dr 18302
Adams St 18301
Adventure Dr 18302
Airport Rd 18301
Airstrip Rd 18301
Albert Ln 18301
Alder Rd 18302
Alexander Ct 18302
Allegheny Ln 18302
Allen Rd 18302
Alpine Dr 18302
Althea Ln 18301
Alwen Ave 18301
Amber Ct 18302
Amber Ln 18301
Amelia Ln 18301
American Way 18301
Analomink Rd & St 18301
Angus Dr 18301
Anna Mae Rd 18301
Antler Point Way 18302

Apache Dr 18302
Arapahoe Dr 18302
Arbor Rd 18301
Arbutus Ln 18302
Archers Mark 18301
Arctic Dr 18302
Armitage Rd 18301
Arnold Dr 18302
Arrowhead Ln 18302
Arrowhead Rd 18301
Arrowwood Dr 18302
Arthur Ave 18301
Artist Trail Ln 18301
Ash Ln 18301
Ash Rd 18302
Ash Ter 18301
Ashburn Dr 18301
Ashwood Ln 18301
Aspen Cir, Cmn & Ln 18302
Aster Rd 18302
Astilbe Way 18301
Auburn Way 18302
Autumn Ct 18302
Autumn Ln 18301
Avalon Way 18301
Ave De Guy 18302
Avon Ct 18301
Azalea Dr 18301
Azalea Way 18302
Azure Ct 18301
Bald Eagle Dr 18301
Bamboo Ln 18301
Barn Rd 18301
Barn Owl Way 18301
Barnum St 18301
Barren Rd 18302
Barron Ct 18302
Basswood Ln 18302
Bay Laurel Way 18302
Bayberry Ct 18301
Baywatch Rd 18302
Beacon Hill Rd 18301
Beanpole Rd 18302
Bear Rd 18302
Bear Swamp Rd 18302
Beaver Dr 18301
Beaver Ln
 101-105 18301
 126-128 18301
 2100-2199 18302
Beech Ln 18302
Beech Pl 18301
Beechwood Ln 18301
Begonia Rd 18302
Behrens Ln 18301
Belaire Dr 18301
Benson Ct 18302
Bernardine Rd 18302
Berry Ln 18302
Berwick Heights Rd 18301
Berwood Ter 18301
Besecker Dr 18302
Big Bear Dr & Rd 18302
Big Buck Ln 18302
Big Pine Ln 18301
Big Pines Ln 18301
Big Ridge Dr & Ests 18302
Big Winona Rd 18302
Binnekill Ln 18301
Birch Dr 18301
Birch Ln
 100-199 18301
 400-499 18302
Birch Rd 18302
Birch St 18301
Birch Acres 18301
Birch Tree Ct 18301
Birchwood Dr 18302
Birchwood Rd 18301
Black Bear Dr 18301
Black Cherry Ln 18301
Black Forest Ln 18302
Black Walnut Ln 18301
Blackberry Ter 18301
Blair Ct 18301
Blossom Ct 18301

Blue Beech Dr 18301
Blue Bird Ln 18301
Blue Bird Way 18302
Blue Jay Ln 18301
Blue Mountain Lk & Xing 18301
Blue Mountain Lake Dr 18301
Blue Spruce Ln 18301
Bluebell Dr 18301
Bluestone Ln 18301
Blushingwood Grv 18301
Bobcat Trl 18302
Bobwhite Ln 18301
Bobwhite Trl 18302
Bog Rd 18301
Bonnie Dr 18301
Borough St 18301
Boulder Ln 18302
Bowie Ln 18302
Bowwood Ct 18301
Box Car Ln 18301
Boyer Ln 18301
Boyer Rd 18302
Braeside Ave 18301
Brahms Ct 18301
Branch Ln 18301
Branch Brook Dr 18301
Branchwood Ct 18302
Brentwood Dr 18301
Brewster Way 18301
Briarleigh Dr 18301
Briarwood Rd 18302
Brick Ter 18301
Bridge Port Ln 18302
Bridge Side Dr 18302
Brinleigh Dr 18301
Bristol Cir E & W 18302
E & W Broad St 18301
Brodhead Ave 18301
Brook Hollow Rd 18302
Brook Song Way 18301
Brookfield Ln 18301
Brookside Ave 18301
Brookside Trailer Park 18301
E Brown St 18301
Brown Bear Ct 18302
Brownell Rd Dr 18301
Browning Rd 18301
Brush Dr 18302
Brushy Mountain Rd
1-1099 18301
1500-1799 18302
3000-4998 18301
5000-5099 18301
Buck Rd 18302
Buck Horn Dr 18302
Buck Valley Cir & Dr 18301
Buckhorn Dr 18302
Bull Pine Rd 18301
Bulldog Hl 18301
Bunny Trl 18302
Bunsen Ct 18302
Burch Ln 18301
Burgoon Rd 18301
Burnside Ter 18301
Burntwood Dr 18301
Buroojy Ct 18302
Burson St 18301
Bush Dr 18301
Business Dr 18302
Buttermilk Falls Rd 18301
Buttermilk Heights Dr 18301
Buttonwood Ct 18301
Cabanna Ln 18301
Cabinsglade Ct 18301
Calvary Ct 18302
Camp Rd 18302
Camp Fire Ct 18302
Campanile Ct & Dr 18301
Campground Rd 18301
Canal Rd 18302
Candlewood Dr 18301
Cannon Ln 18302
Canterbury Cir
100-199 18301
3400-3499 18302
Canterbury Ct 18301
Canterbury Dr 18301
Canterbury Main 18301
Canyon Dr 18301
Cardinal Dr 18301
Cardinal Ln 18302
Carillon Dr 18301
Carly Ct 18301
Carnation Rd 18302
Carol Rd 18302
Carpenter Ct 18302
Carriage Ln 18301
Caryl K Ln 18302
Casa Ln 18302
Casper Rd 18302
Castle Dr 18302
Castle Rock Acres 18302
Castor Rd 18302
Catalpa Ln 18302
Cathleen Dr 18302
Catnip Dr 18301
Cattail Ln 18301
Cedar Ct 18302
Cedar Grv 18301
Cedar Ln
100-199 18302
500-599 18301
Cedar Way 18302
Cedar Crest Ct 18301
Center Ct 18302
Center Rd 18301
Center St 18301
Center Valley Ct 18302
Century Dr 18302
Cerise Way 18302
Chalet Ct 18301
Chamberlain Dr 18302
Champion Way 18302
Chancellor Rd 18302
Chapman Rd 18301
Chariton Dr 18301
Charley Dr 18302
Charlotte Ln & Way 18302
Chateau Dr 18302
Chelsea Ct 18301
Cherokee Rd 18302
Cherry Ln 18302
Cherry Lane Rd 18301
Cherry Lane Church Rd 18301
Chestnut Ln 18302
Chestnut Rd 18302
Chestnut St 18301
Chickadee Ct 18301
Chickadee Way 18302
Chinook Ln 18302
Chip Ct 18302
Chipmunk Ln 18302
Chipperfield Dr 18301
Chris Ali State Pl 18302
Chrisjan Dr 18301
Chucks Rd 18302
Churchill Ln 18301
Cindy Ct & Ln 18301
Circle Ct 18302
Circle Dr 18301
Circle H Rd 18302
Clark Rd 18301
Clarke Pl 18302
Clearspring Ct 18302
Clearview Dr 18302
Clemens Cir 18301
Clicko Ln 18301
Cliff Ct 18302
Cliffside Dr 18302
Cliffview Ln 18302
Clover Ln 18301
Club House Ct 18302
Clubhouse Dr 18302
Cobble Ln 18301
Coco Ln 18302
Cold Spring Rd 18302
Cold Springs Rd 18302
Colgate Ln 18301
College Cir 18301
Colonial Dr 18302
Columbia Blvd 18302
Columbia Dr 18301
Comanche Dr 18302
Commons Ct 18301
Cone Rd 18302
Coolbaugh Rd 18302
Cooper Rd 18301
Copper Rd 18302
Corn Oak Ln 18301
Cornerstone Way 18301
Corral Ct 18302
Corvair Ln 18301
Cottage Ln 18302
Cottontail Ln
300-499 18301
5800-7499 18302
Council Rd 18302
Country Creek Ln 18302
Country Woods 18302
County Bridge Rd 18301
N & S Courtland St 18301
Courtney Dr 18302
Courtright Ln
901-999 18301
1000-1199 18302
Coyote Ct 18302
Crabapple Ln
100-199 18301
216-282 18302
Craigs Meadow Rd
100-499 18301
500-502 18302
504-522 18302
524-534 18302
550-699 18301
Cranberry Rd 18301
Cranberry Heights Dr 18301
Creek Dr 18301
Creek Rd 18302
Creek Run 18302
Creek Cabin Ln 18302
Creenti Rd 18302
Crest Cir & Dr 18301
Crestmont Rd 18301
Crestwood Dr 18301
Cricket Dr 18301
Crocus Dr & Way 18301
Cromwell Cir 18302
Crosswood Dr 18302
Crowe Rd 18301
Crown Point Dr 18302
Crown Pointe Ct S 18302
Crystal St 18301
Cub Ln 18302
Curve View Ct 18302
Custard Dr 18302
Cypress Ct 18301
Cypress Dr 18302
Daffodil Dr 18301
Daffodil Rd 18302
Dalmar Pl 18302
Dancing Ridge Rd 18301
Dannas Ct 18302
Dansbury Ter 18301
Davis Dr 18302
Dawn Ave & Ln 18302
Day St 18301
Days Cir 18302
Deborah Dr 18301
Deer Dr N 18302
Deer Dr S 18302
Deer Ln 18301
Deer Path 18302
Deer Path Dr 18302
Deer Track Dr & Ln 18302
Deerfield Dr 18301
Del Sol Dr 18301
Delaware Ave 18301
Delia Ter 18301
Delilah Rd 18302
Delwood Ct 18301
Denise Ln 18302
Dennis Ct 18301
Dependent Dr 18302
Derrig Dr 18301
Dewitt Ln 18302
Diane Ct 18301
Dimmick Ln 18301
District Ln 18302
Dogwood Ct 18302
Dogwood St 18301
Dogwood Ter 18301
Dominicks Way 18302
Doral Ct 18302
Dornick Rd 18302
Dougherty Dr 18302
Dove Ct 18302
Dove Ln 18301
Drake St 18301
Dry Pond Dr 18302
Dunmer Ct 18301
Eagle Dr 18302
Eagle Valley Ln & Mall 18301
Eagle Valley Senior Apts 18301
Eagles Glen Plz 18301
Eagles Glenn Mall 18301
Eaglesmere Cir 18301
Earl Run 18301
Eastridge Ln 18302
Eastshore Dr 18301
Echo Valley Way 18302
Echo Valley Cottages 18302
Eddy Ln 18301
Edelweiss Rd 18302
Edgeview Dr 18301
Edward Smith Blvd 18302
Egret Way 18302
Eilenberger Rd 18301
Elderberry Ct 18301
Elderberry Ln 18302
Eli St 18301
Elizabeth St 18301
Elk St 18301
Ellies Ln 18301
Elm Rd 18302
Elm St 18301
Elm Tree Ct 18301
Elmhurst Rd 18302
Elmwood Dr 18301
Emerald Ct 18301
Emerald Dr 18302
Emerald Lake Dr 18302
Emerson Rd 18301
Empty Ln 18302
Epic Ct 18302
Escoll Dr 18301
Estate Dr
2-98 18301
100-199 18301
200-399 18302
Evening Shade Ln 18302
Evergreen Ct 18302
Evergreen Dr 18302
Evergreen Est 18301
Evergreen Ests 18302
Evergreen Ln 18302
Everitt Imbt Rd 18301
Exchange St 18301
Exeter Ter 18302
Fairfax Ter 18302
Fairview St 18301
Fairway Dr & Ln 18302
Fairway Villas Blvd 18302
Falcon Crst 18302
Falling View Ct 18302
Faratol Rd 18302
Farm St 18301
Farmer Bush Rd 18301
Farmers Ridge Rd 18301
Farmhouse Cv 18301
Farview Dr 18302
Fawn Rd 18301
Fawn Acres 18301
Fazio Way 18302
Fenical Ln 18302
Fern Ln 18302
Fernwood Dr 18301
Fernwood Ln 18302
Ferry Ln 18302
Fields Rd 18302
Fieldstone Ln 18301
Fig Ct 18302
Fillmore St 18301
Fir Rd 18302
Fire House Ln 18301
Firefly Ct 18301
Firestone Ln 18302
Fish Ct 18302
Fish Ln 18301
Fish Hill Rd 18301
Five Star Ln 18301
Flag Ln 18302
Flagstone Ln 18302
Flicker Rd 18302
Floral Ln 18301
Flory Rd 18301
Fly Line Dr 18302
Foliage Way 18302
Foot Hl E & W 18301
Footprint Rd 18302
E Foralto Rdg 18301
Forest Dr, Ln & Run 18302
Forest Lake Dr 18302
Forge Rd 18301
Fox Ln 18302
Fox Chapel Dr 18301
Fox Glen Apts 18302
Fox Run Ln 18302
Foxdale Ter 18301
Foxmoor Dr & Vlg 18302
Foxtail Dr 18301
Frailey Ln 18301
Franklin Ct 18302
Franklin Hill Ct, Ln & Rd 18301
Freda Ln 18301
Frederick Rd 18301
Freedom Ln 18301
Freedom Rd 18302
Fringe Dr 18302
Fritz Ln 18302
Frog Pond Ln 18301
Frontier Rd 18302
Fruchey Rd 18302
Frutchey Dr 18302
Fulton St 18301
Gabriel Dr & Est 18301
Gabrielle Ln 18301
Gallahad Pass 18302
Gander Rd 18302
Gap View Dr 18301
Gapview Dr 18301
Gapview Heights Rd 18301
Garden Ct 18301
Garden Ln 18302
Garden Ter 18301
Garfield Ln 18301
Garnet Ln 18301
Garris Pl 18302
Gay St 18301
Georganna Dr 18302
Georgellen Ave 18301
Georgianna Dr 18302
Geranium Dr 18301
Geranium Rd 18302
Gilliland Dr 18301
Ginger Ln 18301
Gingerbread Ln 18302
Glacier Dr 18302
Glacier Ridge Rd 18302
Glade Ter 18301
Glen Oak Dr & Frst 18301
Glenoak Dr 18301
Glenview Ct 18302
Glenwood Dr 18301
Gold Ln 18302
Gold St 18301
Golf Dr 18302
Golf Rules Ct 18302
Gorden Ridge Dr 18302
Goshawk Trl 18302
Grace St 18301
Grain Ln 18301
Grand St 18301
Grandview St 18301
Granite Rd 18302
Grasshopper Trl 18302
Gravel Ridge Est 18302
Gravel Ridge Rd
1-99 18302
2-98 18301
Great Bear Way 18302
Great Bear Way Rd 18302
Great Buck Dr 18301
Great Lodge Way 18302
Great Oak Dr 18301
N & S Green St 18301
Green Meadow Dr 18302
Green Meadow Ln 18301
Green Mountain Dr
100-199 18302
2100-2199 18301
Green Mountain Est 18302
Greenbriar Dr 18301
Greentree Dr 18301
Grey Cliff Dr 18302
Grey Fox Rd 18302
Grinrod Ct 18302
Grizzly Ln 18301
Grouse Ct 18301
Grouse Ln 18301
Grouse Rd 18302
Grouse Trl 18302
Grove St 18301
Gwendolyn St 18301
Halfmoon Ln 18302
Hallet Rd & St 18301
Hallowood Dr 18302
Hallowood Acres 18302
Hamlet Ct 18302
Hammons Ln 18301
Hannah Ct 18301
Hannan Ln 18302
Hannick Ct 18302
Harding Ct 18301
Harmony Dr 18301
Harris St 18301
Hartman Ln 18301
Haven Lk 18301
Havenwood Dr 18302
Hawk Nest Ct 18302
Hawks Nest Rd 18302
Hawthorn Hall 18301
Hawthorne Village Ct 18302
Hayfield Rd 18301
Hazen St 18301
Heath Ln 18301
Heather Cir & Ln 18301
Heavens Gate Dr 18302
Heights Dr 18302
Hemlock Ln & Way 18302
Hemlock Hall 18301
Henry St 18301
Heron Point Rd 18302
Heron Woods Rd 18302
Hiawatha Rd 18302
Hickory Dr 18301
Hickory Ln 18301
Hidden Lake Dr & Rd 18302
Hidden Valley Dr
101-107 18301
109-111 18301
113-199 18301
2201-2299 18302
Hideaway Ln
100-199 18301
200-298 18302
High Meadow Dr 18302
High Point Ct 18301
Highland Dr 18302
Highland Rd 18301
Highland Ter 18301
Highlawn Dr 18302
Hikers Dr 18302
Hikers Hill Ln 18301
Hilda Ct 18301
Hill Rd 18302
Hill St 18301
Hillbrow Ct N & S 18302
Hillock Ct 18302
Hillside Ct & Dr 18301
Hilltop Cir
1-99 18302
5100-5399 18301
Hiro Ln 18301
Hoffman St 18301
Hollow Dr 18301
Hollow Rd
2-98 18302
100-300 18302
302-400 18302
500-899 18301
Holly Cir 18301
Holly Ln 18301
Holly Rd 18302
Holstein Rd 18301
Homestead Ln 18302
Honeycomb Ln 18302
Honeysuckle Dr 18302
Horizon Dr 18302
Horning Rd 18302
Horseshoe Cir 18302
Horseshoe Dr 18301
Hosta Ln 18301
Howard Dr 18302
Howeytown Rd
1-1299 18302
2-98 18301
1200-1298 18302
Huck Ln 18302
Huckleberry Dr 18302
Huffman Hill Rd 18302
Hull Rd 18302
Hunters Woods Dr 18301
Huntington Dr 18302
Hutson Hl 18302
Hyacinth Rd 18302
Hyland Dr 18301
Imperial Dr 18302
Independence Rd 18301
Indian Dr & Way 18302
Interstate 80 W 18301
Inverness Dr 18302
Iris Rd 18302
Island Rd 18302
Ithaca Ct 18301
Jackson Dr & Rd 18302
Jacob Ott Rd 18301
Jade Ave 18301
Jakes Rd 18302
James Ct 18301
James Rd 18302
Janet St 18301
Jasper Ln 18301
Java Hl 18302
Jay St 18301
Jays Way 18302
Jefferson Ave & Dr 18301
Jen St 18301
Jennifer Dr 18301
Jennifer Ln 18302
Jennis Ln 18301
Jersey Ln 18301
Joel St 18301
Jonathan Ct 18302
Jones Ln 18302
Jonquil Rd 18302
Joseph Ln 18301
Josephine Ct 18302
Julian Ter 18301
June Rd 18302
Juneberry Rd E & W 18302
Juniper Ct & Ln 18301
Kahkout Mtn 18302
Kahkout Mountain Cir 18302
Kansa Rd 18302
Karyleigh Ct 18301
Kasak 18302
Katie Ln 18301
Katydid Ln 18302
Keitha Ln 18302
Keller Dr 18301
Kennedy Ct 18301
Kenneth Ct 18302
Kensington Dr 18301
Kenwood Ter 18301
Keystone Rd 18302

Keystone Farm Ct 18302
Kimball Ct 18302
Kimberleigh Ct 18301
King St 18301
Kingbird Ln 18301
Kingbird Trl 18302
Kings Pond Rd 18301
Kinsley Ln 18301
S Kistler Plz & St 18301
Kiwanis St 18301
Kline Ct 18302
Knight Ct 18302
Knob Hill Cir 18302
Knoll Dr 18302
Koritia Rd 18302
Kulick Dr 18302
Labar Ln 18301
Lace Dr 18302
Lackawanna Ave 18301
Lady Bug Ln 18301
Lagoon Cir 18302
Lake Dr
  305-347 18302
  349-899 18302
  901-1299 18302
  5115-5147 18301
  5149-5158 18301
  5160-5160 18301
Lake Ln 18301
Lake Of The Pnes 18302
Lake Of The Pines Blvd N & S 18302
Lake Valhalla 18301
Lake View Ln 18302
Lakeshore Dr E & W 18302
Lakeside Dr
  1-3 18302
  5-25 18302
  27-99 18302
  400-549 18301
  551-569 18301
  604-604 18302
  606-607 18302
  609-615 18302
  619-619 18301
  621-638 18301
  640-642 18301
Lakeside Manor Apts 18301
Lakeview Ln 18302
Lakewood Ct 18301
Lakota Rd 18302
Landing Ln 18301
Landmark Ctr 18301
Lane St 18301
Lansdale Dr 18301
Laurel Dr 18301
Laurel Ln 18301
Laurel Rd 18302
Laurel Hall 18301
Laurel Lake Rd 18301
Laurel Ridge Dr & Rd 18302
Lavender Ln 18301
Leaf Ct 18302
Leander Rd 18302
Leap Frog Ln 18302
Learn Ln 18301
Leas Run 18302
Ledgewood Ct 18302
Ledgewood Dr 18301
Lee Rd 18302
Lees Ln 18301
Lees Run Cir 18302
Legacy Way 18302
Legends Ct 18302
Leisure Lands Rd 18302
Leland Ter 18301
Lenape Ct 18302
Lenape Dr 18302
Lenape Rd 18302
Lenape St 18301
Lenape Hall 18301
Lenox Ave 18301
Liberty Ct
  400-499 18301
  600-610 18302
Liberty Sq 18302

Lilac Dr & Way 18301
Lilium Ln 18301
Lily Rd 18302
Lincoln Ave 18301
Lincoln Ln 18301
Lincoln Rd 18302
Linda Ln & St 18301
Linden Ln
  1-99 18301
  2200-2220 18302
  2222-2298 18302
Linden Hall 18301
Lions St 18301
Little Bear Ln 18302
Little Creek Ln 18301
Little Doe Ln 18301
Lock Ln 18301
Locust Ct 18302
Locust Dr 18301
Lois Ln 18302
Lombardy Ln 18301
Longdon Ct 18301
Longfellow Rd 18301
Longshore Cir 18302
Lorne Dr 18301
Lost Ln 18301
Lost Lantern Ln 18301
Lovena Ct 18301
Lower Lakeview Dr 18302
Lower Pmhe North Dr 18302
Lower Pmhe South Dr 18302
Lower Ridge View Cir 18302
Lumberjack Dr 18302
Lunar Ln 18301
Lunn Rd 18302
Lynn Rd 18302
Lynnwood Dr 18302
Lynwood Acres 18302
Mac Ln 18301
Mackenzie Dr 18302
Macy Way 18302
Madison St 18301
Magnolia Cir 18301
Magnolia Dr 18302
Magnolia Ln 18301
Mahlon Dr 18301
Main Rd 18301
Majestic Ct 18302
Mallard Way 18302
Maloney Ln 18301
Mandy Ridge Dr 18302
Manor Dr 18301
Manzanedo Lk & Rd 18302
Manzanedo Lake Rd 18302
Map Ln 18302
Maple Ave 18301
Maple Ln 18302
Maple Loop 18301
Maplewood Ct & Dr 18302
Marcel Ct 18301
Marco Way 18302
S Marguerite St 18301
Marjorie Ct 18302
Marsh Ct 18302
Marsh Dr 18301
Marshalls Creek Rd 18302
Mary St 18301
Masons Dr & Ln 18302
May Ln 18302
Mayfield Ct 18301
Mayflower Ln 18301
Mccole Rd 18302
Mcdonald St 18301
Mcewan Blvd 18302
Mckinley Ave & Way 18301
Meadow Ct 18301
Meadow Lk 18302
Meadow Ln 18302
Meadow View Ct 18302
Meadowlark Ln 18301
Meadowlark Way 18302
Meadowsage Ct 18301
Meander Way 18302
Melody Ct & Ln 18301
Melrose Ter 18301
Melvin Ln 18302

Mercedes Ct 18301
Merlot Ln 18302
Merten St 18301
Mesa Dr 18301
Metzgar Ln & Rd 18301
Meyers St 18301
Michaels Rd 18302
Midwood Dr 18301
Milestone Dr 18302
Milford Rd
  748A-748D 18301
Mill Creek Rd 18301
Millertown Rd 18302
Milly Ln 18302
Mimosa Rd 18302
Minsi Rd 18302
Minsi Hall 18301
Misty Rdg 18302
Misty Creek Ln 18301
Mockingbird Way 18301
Mockingbird Hill Rd 18301
Mohawk Dr 18302
Mohican Rd 18302
Monroe St 18301
Monroe Heights Rd 18301
Monroe Lake Shrs 18302
Monterey Rd 18302
Morgan Way 18302
Morning Side Ter 18302
Morningside Ter 18302
Morris Rd 18302
Moschella Ct 18302
Mosiers Knob Rd 18301
Moss Ln 18301
Mountain Ct & Mnr 18302
Mountain Laurel Dr
  1-99 18302
  3200-3399 18301
  12400-12499 18302
Mountain Peak Rd 18302
Mountain Top Rd 18302
Mountain View Cir 18302
Mountain View Ct 18301
Mountain View Pl 18302
Mountainview Dr & Rd 18301
Mt Nebo Rd
  1-5 18302
  2-14 18301
  16-661 18301
  663-699 18301
Mt Tom Rd 18301
Muirfield Way 18302
Mulberry Ct 18301
Mulberry Ln 18302
Municipal Dr 18302
Murphy Cir 18302
Murray Hill Rd 18302
Music Center Dr 18301
Naomi Ln 18301
Nature Trail Ln 18302
Nature View Rd 18301
Navaho Rd 18302
Navajo Ct & Rd 18302
Nebo Ln 18301
New Jersey Dr 18302
Newton Run Dr 18302
Nightshade Ct 18302
Nipper Rd 18302
Noble Ln 18301
Normal St 18301
Norman Ct & Dr 18302
North Ln 18301
Northpark Dr & Est 18302
Northslope Ii Rd 18302
Norwood Dr 18301
Nota Rd 18302
Nottingham Way 18302
O Donovan Dr 18301
Oak Ct 18302
Oak St 18301
Oak Field Ter 18302
Oak Grove Rd 18302
Oak Leaf Ln 18301
Oakgrove Dr 18302
Oakland Ave & Ter 18301
Oakridge Est 18302

Oakwood Ct 18302
Old Barn Ln 18301
Old Farm Rd 18302
Old Independence Ln & Rd 18301
Old Mill Rd 18301
Old Oak St 18301
Old Orchard Dr 18302
Oneida Dr 18302
Onyx Ln 18301
Opal Way 18302
Orange Ln 18302
Orchard Rd
  100-109 18302
  111-199 18302
  190-198 18301
  200-299 18301
Orchard St 18301
Oriole Way 18302
Osadtsa Ln 18301
Osprey Ct 18301
Osprey Way 18302
Otter Ln 18301
Otter Lake Rd 18302
Our Way 18301
Outlook Ct 18302
Outside Ln 18302
Overlook Ct 18302
Overlook Dr 18301
Overlook Ln 18302
Owl Trl 18302
Panda Ln 18302
Paper Ln 18302
Papillion Ct 18301
Papoose Dr 18302
Paradise Trl 18301
Pardees Loop 18302
Parish Park 18301
Park Dr 18302
Park Ln 18301
Park St 18301
Parker Ln 18302
Parkinsons Rd 18301
Parliament Dr 18302
Parsley Rd 18302
Pasquin Dr 18301
Pastel Ln 18302
Pasture Ln 18301
Payton Pl & Rd 18302
Peace Fall Rd 18302
Peace Falls Rd 18302
Pearl St 18301
Pebble Ln 18302
Pebble Beach Ct 18302
Peggy Rd 18302
Penn Est & St 18301
Pennsylvania Ave 18302
Penny Ln 18302
Pepper Rd 18302
Perry St 18301
Pheasant Run 18302
Pierce Ln 18301
Pin Oak Ln 18302
Pin Oak Ter 18301
Pine Ct & Dr 18302
Pine Creek Ests 18302
Pine Grove Dr 18301
Pine Hill Ct & Rd 18302
Pine Ridge Rd 18301
Pine Ridge Rd N 18302
Pine Ridge Rd S 18302
Pine Tree Dr 18302
Pine Valley Way 18302
Pine View Ln 18302
Pinebrook Rd 18301
Pinecrest Dr & St 18301
Pines Way 18301
Pinewood Dr N & S 18302
Pipe Line Ln 18301
Pitch Pine Rd 18302
Place Ln 18301
Plasencia Est & Way 18302
Plasencias Way 18302
Plateau Dr 18301
Players Ct 18302
Plaza Ct 18301

Pleasant Ridge Rd 18302
Pocahontas Rd 18301
Poco Ln 18301
Pocohontas Dr 18302
Pocohontas Rd 18301
Pocono Dr & Hts 18302
Pocono Forested Dr 18302
Pocono Forested Acres 18302
Pocono Forested Lands 18302
Pocono Lutheran Vlg 18301
Pocono Mobile Homes Est 18302
Polar Ct 18302
Polaris Ct 18302
Pond Ln 18302
Ponderosa Ln 18302
Pondview Ln 18302
Pony Trail Way 18302
Poole Rd 18301
Poplar Dr 18302
Poplar Ln 18301
Poplar Pl N 18302
Poplar Pl S 18302
Poplar Bridge Ct & Est 18302
Portuguese Ln 18302
Possum Trl 18302
Post Office Rd 18301
Pow Wow Trl 18301
Prairie Ln 18302
Praline Ln 18301
Prices Lndg 18301
Prices Landing Rd 18301
Primrose Dr & Ln 18302
Progress St 18301
Promise Hill Dr 18302
Prospect Dr, Hls & St 18301
Puddle Ct 18302
Pugh Ln 18301
Quail Ln 18301
Questing Rd 18302
Quill Rd 18302
R Own Rd 18302
Rabbit Ln 18302
Rabbit Foot Rd 18301
Race St 18301
Racoon Ln 18302
Rainbow Aly 18301
Rake St 18301
Ralston Ct 18302
Ranch Ln 18302
Randall St 18301
Range Dr 18302
Rangoon Ln 18302
Ransberry Ave 18301
Raspberry Ln 18302
Raven Dr 18302
Ravine Ln & Rd 18302
Reagan Dr 18301
Red Bud Ter 18301
Red Fox Ct 18302
Red Fox Rd 18301
Red Fox Trl 18302
Red Oak Ln 18301
Red Squirrel Ct 18302
Red Tail Ct 18301
Red Wing Ln 18301
Redwood Ln 18301
Rehm Ln 18301
Remington Ct 18302
Remington Rd 18301
Reservoir Rd 18302
Reservoir Ridge Rd 18302
Resica Falls Rd 18302
Resort Ln 18301
Reston Dr 18301
Reunion Rdg 18302
Rhapsody Run 18301
Ridge Ln, Rd & Xing 18302
Ridge Farm Rd 18301
Ridge View Cir & Rd 18302
Ridgeway St 18301
Ridgewood Dr 18301
Rim Rd 18302

Rising Meadow Way 18302
River Rd
  2-98 18302
  101-197 18301
  199-500 18301
  502-898 18301
River St 18301
Riverbend Ter 18301
Riverstone Gate 18301
Roaring Brook Rd 18302
Robin Ln
  100-199 18302
  201-299 18301
Robinwood Ter 18301
Rock Rd 18302
Rocky Rd 18301
Rocky Rdg 18302
Rocky Ridge Rd 18302
Roller St 18301
Rolling Hill Way 18302
Rolling Hills Dr 18302
Roosevelt Rd & St 18301
Rosado Ct 18302
Rose Ln 18301
Rose Marie Ln 18302
Rosewood Ln 18301
Rosewood Rd E 18302
Rosewood Rd W 18302
Rosewood Ter 18301
Route 447 18302
Rue De John 18302
Runnymede Dr 18301
Russell Ridge Rd 18302
Rustic Dr 18302
Ruth St 18301
Saddle Way 18302
Sadie Ln 18301
Sage Ln 18301
Salvation Army Dr 18301
Sambo Rd 18301
Sanctuary Dr 18302
Sand Hill Rd 18302
Sanders Ct 18302
Sandlewood Dr 18301
Sandra Ct 18302
Santosha Ln 18301
Sarah Ct 18301
Sarah Ln 18302
Sarah Way 18301
Sassafrass Dr 18302
Savage Trl 18301
Saw Ct N & S 18302
Saw Mill Ct
  1-99 18302
  2-98 18301
Sawmill Ct 18301
Scenery Ct 18302
Scenic Dr 18302
Scheller Rd 18302
Schoolhouse Rd 18302
Schoonover Ln 18301
Schubert Rd 18301
Scoter Dr 18301
Scout Cir 18302
Scout Trl 18301
Sebring Dr 18301
Secor Ave 18301
Sellersville Dr 18302
Seneca Rd 18302
September Cir 18301
Sequoia Dr 18302
Seven Bridge Rd 18301
Sewer Plant Ln 18301
Shadowbrook Cottages 18301
Shady Ln 18302
Shady Hill Rd 18302
Shady Oaks Ln 18301
Shady Tree Dr 18301
Shale Ridge Dr 18302
Shawnee Dr & Vly 18302
Shawnee Hall 18301
Shawnee Valley Dr 18302
Sheriff Ln 18302
Shire Ln 18301
Shirley Ct 18301

Shirley Futch Plz 18301
Short Hill Rd 18301
Sidorick Ln 18302
Sierra Trl 18302
Sierra Trails Dr 18302
Sioux Dr 18302
Ski Lodge Cir 18302
Sky Hawk Trl 18302
Sky Pine Way 18301
Sky View Cir, Dr & Ln 18302
Skycloud Dr 18302
Skyline Dr 18301
Skyview Ln 18302
Sleepy Hollow Ests & Ln 18302
Slope Rd 18302
Smith Ln 18302
Smith St 18301
S Smith St 18301
Smithfield Ct & Vlg 18301
Smithfield Trailer Ct 18301
Smoke Ridge Dr 18302
Snapdragon Pt 18301
Snow Shoe Trl 18302
Somerset Dr 18301
Song Ln 18301
Sopher St 18301
Southridge Dr 18302
Southshore Mdws 18301
Southwood Ln 18302
Spa Ct 18302
Spangenburg Ave 18301
Sparrow Ct 18302
Sparrow Ln 18301
Spicebush Dr 18301
Spicewood Ln 18302
Split Rd 18302
Sports Camp Rd 18302
Spring Ln & St 18301
Spring Brook Rd 18302
Spring Hill Ln 18301
Spring Hill Farm Ct & Ln 18302
Spring House Ln 18301
Spring Lake Dr 18301
Springmeadow Blvd 18302
Spruce Ln
  1-111 18302
  100-110 18301
  112-199 18301
  5300-5399 18302
Spruce St 18301
Spyglass Ct 18302
Squirrel Hill Dr 18302
Stable Ln 18301
Stallion Ct 18302
Starlight Dr 18302
Starview Dr 18301
State St 18301
Stemple St 18301
Sterling Dr 18301
Stites Mt Rd 18301
Stokes Ave 18301
Stokes Mill Rd 18301
Stone Gate Dr 18301
Stone Wall Ct 18302
Stonehenge Dr 18301
Stoneleigh Dr 18301
Stones Throw 18301
Stoney Brook Dr
  2-18 18302
  20-98 18301
Stoney Ledge Dr 18302
Stony Brook Dr 18302
Stony Creek Rd 18302
Stony Hollow Cir & Dr 18302
Stony Ledge Dr 18302
Stratton Dr 18302
Stream Ln 18301
Streamside Ave 18301
Stroud Ln 18302
Sugar Cone Ln 18301
Sugar Maple Ln 18302
Sugar Works Dr 18302
Summerton Cir 18301
Summit Dr 18302

Street	ZIP
Summit Ter	18301
Sumner Dr	18302
Sunbright Ter	18301
Sunbury Dr	18301
Sundance Rd	18302
Sundew Dr	18301
Sunhaven Ct	18302
Sunny Brook Ct	18302
Sunrise Ct	18302
Sunrise Dr	18301
Sunset Dr	18301
Sunset Rd	18302
Sunset Ter	18301
Sunshine Ln	18301
Supreme Ct	18302
Surf Cir	18302
Susan Cir	18301
Swan Ct	18302
Swartz Ln	18301
Sweet Water Ln	18302
Sweetwater Ln	18301
Sycamore Dr	18301
Sycamore Ln	
500-599	18302
3136-4098	18301
4100-4136	18301
Sylvan Ln	18301
Symphony Cir	18301
Tadeka Pl	18301
Talberts Ct	18302
Talisman Dr	18302
Tall Timber Cir	18302
Tamaqua Dr & Rd	18302
Tamarack Ct	18302
Tan Dr	18302
Tanager Ln	18302
Tara Dr	18301
Taylor Dr & St	18301
Teaberry Ln	18301
Teak Ln	18301
Tee Dr	18302
Tego Lake Rd	18302
Terra Green Dr	18301
Terrace Dr	18301
Terrapin Trl	18302
Terry St	18302
Thomas Pt	18301
Thorin Way	18302
Thornberry Ct	18302
Thornley Rd	18301
Tiger Ct	18302
Tiger Ln	18301
Timber Dr	18302
Timber Mtn	18302
Timber Rdg	18301
Timber Mountain Dr	
100-125	18302
126-199	18301
1500-1598	18302
Timber Ridge Rd	18301
Timbercrest Ln	18302
Timberline Dr	18301
Timothy Lake Rd	18302
Tinney Ln	18301
Tioga Rd	18302
Toby Ct	18301
Tom Ln	18301
Tom X Rd	
1-100	18302
101-199	18301
102-198	18302
201-299	18301
Toms Way	18301
Tournament Ct	18302
Tower Dr	18302
Townsend Cir	18301
Trader Rd	18302
Trafalgar Ave	18302
Travis Dr	18302
Tree Ln	18301
Tree House Ct	18302
Tree Line Dr	18301
Trellis Way	18301
Trilland Ter	18301
Trillium Ter	18301
Trophy Dr	18302
Truman Rd	18301
Tucker Ln	18301
Tulip Ln	
100-199	18301
3113-3299	18302
3400-3499	18301
Tumble Ct	18302
Tupelo Ln	18302
Turkey Foot Trl	18302
Turkey Ridge Rd	18302
Turmac Ct	18302
Turnberry Vlg	18302
Turr Ln	18301
Twig Ct	18302
Twin Falls Rd	18301
Tyler Dr	18301
Underwood Rd E & W	18302
University Apts	18301
Upper Lakeview Dr	18301
Upper Pmhe North Dr	18302
Upper Pmhe South Dr	18302
Upper Ridge View Dr	18302
Utopia Ln	18302
Valhalla Dr	18301
Valhalla View Dr N	18301
Valley Dr	18302
Valley Ter	18301
Van Gordon St	18301
Vanvliet Rd	18301
Venue Rd E & W	18302
Victoria Way	18302
Victoria Heights Rd	18301
View Cir & Ct	18302
Village Ctr	18301
Vine St	18301
Vista Cir	18302
Vna Rd	18301
Wagon Trail Rd	18302
Wales Ct	18301
Walker Dr	18302
Walker Run	18301
Walnut Dr	18302
Walnut St	18301
Walnut Grove Rd	18301
Waltz St	18301
Wapita Dr & Rd	18302
Warehouse Dr	18302
Warren Ct & St	18301
Washington St & Xing	18302
Water Tower Cir	18301
Watershed Way	18302
Waverly Dr	18302
Way Ln	18301
Wayne Ave	18301
Wedge Ct	18302
Weiss Farm Rd	18301
Wellington Dr	18302
Wellsleigh Ct	18301
Wendell Rd	18301
Westlake Dr	18302
Westminster Dr	18302
Westridge Ct	18302
Whipporwill Ln	18302
Whispering Hills Dr & Est	18301
Whispering Pines Ct	18302
White Birch Cir	18302
White Birch Dr	18302
White Birch Ln	18302
White Birch St	18301
White Blossom Ln	18301
White Dove Dr	18302
White Heron Lk	18302
White Heron Lake Dr	18302
White Oak Dr W	18301
White Oaks Manor Dr	18301
White Pine Ter & Trl	18301
Wicks Ln	18301
Wigwam Park Rd	18301
Wilbur Bloom Blvd	18302
Wild Cherry Ln & Rd	18301
Wilderness Acres	18302
Wildwood Ct	18301
William St	18301
Williams Dr	18302
Williamson Dr	18301
Willow Run & St	18301
Willow Pond Ct & Dr	18301
Willowicke Ter	18301
Wilson Ave	18301
Wilson Ln	18302
Winchester Dr	18301
Winchester Way	18302
Windfall Cottage Ln	18302
Winding Brook Rd	18301
Winona Lks	18302
Winona Ter	18301
Winona Falls Rd E	18302
Wintergreen Cir	18301
Wintergreen Rd	18302
Wisteria Ct	18301
Witness Tree Cir & Ct	18301
Wolbert Farm Rd	18301
Wood Ln & Rd W	18302
Wood Hill Ln	18301
Woodacres Dr	18301
Woodale Rd	18302
Woodbine Ln	18301
Woodchip Ln	18301
Woodchuck Ct	18301
Woodchuck Ln	
1-99	18301
2100-2199	18302
6100-6199	18301
Woodcrest Dr	18302
Woodcrest Ln	18301
Wooddale Cir	18301
Wooddale Rd	
100-110	18301
112-112	18302
116-134	18301
201-299	18301
300-1299	18302
Woodhaven Ter	18302
Woodland Dr	18301
Woodland Trl	18302
Woodland Xing	18302
Woodland Lake Dr	18302
Woodlands Dr	18302
Woods Rd	18301
Woods Rd E	18302
Woods Rd W	18302
Woods Edge Dr	18302
Woodside Dr	18301
Woodwind Ct	18301
Woomera Ln	18302
Wrangler Rd	18302
Wysteria Ln	18302
Xander Loop	18301
Yale Ct	18302
Yellow Ln	18302
Yellow Leaf Ct	18302
Youngwood Cir & Dr	18301
Yukon Dr	18302
Zephyr Rd	18302
Zinc Ln	18302

NUMBERED STREETS

Street	ZIP
All Street Addresses	18301

EASTON PA

General Delivery	18042

POST OFFICE BOXES MAIN OFFICE STATIONS AND BRANCHES

Box No.s	ZIP
A - L	18044
1 - 2130	18044
3001 - 4736	18043
3170 - 3170	18044

RURAL ROUTES

Route	ZIP
07	18040

NAMED STREETS

Street	ZIP
Aarons Pl	18040
Abbey Rd	18040
Aberdeen Dr	18045
Acorn Dr	18040
Acworth Pl	18045
Adams St	18040
Adamson St	18042
Adrian Dr	18040
Agnes St	18045
Aicher Dr	18045
Albie Ln	18042
Alder St	18042
Alex Rd	18040
Alexus Ct	18045
Allen St	18045
Alpine Dr	18045
Alton Dr	18045
American General Dr	18040
Andrew Dr	18040
Ann St	18042
Ann Marie St	18045
Anthony Ct	18045
Appian Way	18040
S Apple St	18042
Apple Blossom Rd	18040
Apple Hill Dr	18040
Applewood Dr	18045
Arch St	18045
Ariel Ct	18040
Arlington St	18045
Arndt Rd	18040
Arrowwood Dr	18040
Ashlee Ct	18045
Aspen Ct	18040
Aspen St	18042
Auburn Ave	18045
Auburn Dr	18042
Audubon St	18045
Augusta Ter	18042
Austin Dr	18040
Avon St	18045
Avona Ave	18042
Ayers Rd	18040
Babbling Brook Rd	18045
Bachman Ln	18042
Baden Ct	18045
Balata St	18042
Baldwin Dr	18045
Bangor Rd	18040
N & S Bank St	18042
Barberry Ln	18045
Barnyard Vw	18040
Barron Hill Rd	18042
Barry Ct	18040
Baurkot Dr	18045
Bayard St	18045
Beacon St	18045
Beaujolais Pl	18045
Beaver Ln	18045
Bedford Dr	18045
Belcourt Rd	18040
Belmont St	18042
Ben Jon Rd	18040
Bennett Ct	18042
Bennington Ct	18040
Berger Rd	18042
Berhel Rd	18040
Berkley St	18045
Berks St	18045
E & W Berwick St	18042
Bethman Rd	18045
Bethpage Ter	18042
Betty Ln	18040
Bianco Pl	18045
Biddle Ln	18040
Biltmore Ave	18040
Binney Ct	18040
Birch St	
300-399	18040
2100-2499	18042
E Bird St	18042
Birkland Pl	18045
Black Hill Rd	18040
Blair St	18045
Blenheim Dr	18045
Blossom Hill Rd	18040
Blue Spruce Ln	18040
Blush Ct & Dr	18045
Boileau Ave	18042
Bonnie Cir	18040
Bonnie Ln	18045
Bougher Hill Rd	18042
Bourdon Ter	18042
Braden Blvd & St E	18040
Brandywine Ct	18040
Brant Ln	18040
Brendan Rd	18045
Brenton Ct	18040
Brentwood Ave	18045
Briarwood Ln	18040
Bridgette Ct	18045
Bridlepath Rd	18045
Brinker Ln	18040
Broad St	18045
Broadway Rd	18040
Brodhead St	18042
Brook Ln	18040
Brookwood Ln	18045
Brotzman Dr	18042
Browns Dr	18042
Bruen Ln	18040
Brynwood Dr	18045
Bunker Hill Ct	18040
Burgundy Ln	18040
E & W Burke St	18042
E Burr St	18042
Burrows St	18042
Bushkill Dr	
108A-108A	18040
101-105	18042
107-1276	18042
1278-1498	18042
1301-1797	18040
1799-2899	18040
2901-3499	18040
3801-3899	18045
Bushkill St	
100-102	18042
104-106	18045
126-1698	18042
163-333	18045
601-1599	18042
2700-2799	18045
Bushkill Park Dr	18040
Butler St	18042
Buttermilk Rd	18042
Butternut Ln	18045
Buttonwood St	18042
Cabernet Pl	18045
Camden St	18045
Camelia Ave	18040
Camelot Dr	18045
Campus Ln	18042
W Canal Park, Rd & St	18042
W Canal And Mauch Chunk St	18042
Canterbury Ct	18040
Canterbury Ln	18045
Capp Rd	18040
Cara Ct	18045
Carbon St	18045
Cardinal Dr	18045
Carolyn St	18045
Carousel Ln	18045
Carrington Cir	18045
Carter Rd	18045
Cattell St	18042
Cedar St	18045
Cedar Park Blvd	18042
Cedarville Rd	18042
Center St	
110-114	18042
116-214	18042
121-121	18040
123-203	18042
300-399	18040
523-997	18042
999-1000	18042
1002-1098	18042
E Center St	18040
Central Dr	18045
Centre Sq & St	18042
Chain Dam Rd	18045
Chardonnay Dr	18045
Charles Ct	18045
Charles St	
100-699	18042
4300-4999	18045
Charlotte Ave	18045
Chateau Ln	18042
Chateau Pl	18045
Chelsea St	18045
Cherry Ave	18040
N Cherry St	18042
S Cherry St	18042
Chestnut Ln	
700-899	18045
2400-2799	18040
Chestnut Ter	18042
Chestnut Commons Ct	18040
Chestnut Ridge Cir	18042
Chetwin Ter	18045
Chianti Pl	18045
Chidsey St	18042
Chief Tatamy Ln	18040
Chief Tatamy St	18045
Chipman Rd	18045
Chipmonk Ln	18040
Church Ln	18040
Church Rd	18045
Church St	18042
Cibby St	18045
Cider Press Rd	18042
Circle Dr	18045
Clairmont Ave	18045
Clarendon Dr	18040
Clark Pl	18040
Clayton St	18045
Clearview St	18045
Clinton Pl & Ter	18042
Clover Ct	18040
Clover Dr	18045
Clover Hollow Rd	18045
Clubhouse Dr	18042
Coal St	18042
Cobblestone Dr	18045
Coffeetown Rd	18042
Cog Cir	18045
Coleman St	18042
College Ave	18042
Colmar Ave	18045
Colonial Ct	18045
Colonna Dr	18042
Columbia St	18045
Commerce Ln	18045
Commerce Park Dr	18045
Community Dr	18045
Concord Cir	18045
Concord Ct	18040
Concord Dr	18045
Connard Dr	18042
Conroy Pl	18040
Conway Ct	18045
E & W Cooper St	18042
Corn Crib Ct	18040
Cornwallis Dr	18040
Corporate Dr	18045
Corriere Dr & Rd	18045
Cory Ter	18040
Cosenza Ct	18040
Cottage St	18040
Country Club Rd	18045
Country Side Ct	18045
County Line Rd E	18042
Courtney Ct	18045
Craigie St	18045
Cramers Ln	18045
Creek Ct	18040
Creek Ln	18045
Creek View Ct	18045
Crescent Dr	18045
Crescent St	18042
Cresmont Ave	18045
Crest Blvd	18045
Crestview Ave	18045
Crossing Ct	18045
Crosswinds Dr	18045
Crown Dr	18040
Crown Plz	18045
Crown View Dr	18040
Cypress Ln	18040
Dakota Dr	18045
Dalton St	18045
Danberry Dr	18045
Danforth Rd	18045
Danser Hill Rd	18040
Dartmoor Dr	18040
Davis St	18042
Dayton Dr	18040
Dearborn St	18045
Debbie Ln	18045
Deemer Rd	18042
Deena Dr	18040
Deendary St	18045
Deer Path Rd	18040
N Delaware Dr	
1-800	18042
802-898	18042
900-1598	18040
1600-4400	18040
4402-4498	18040
S Delaware Dr	
5804AA-5804AA	18040
5498A-5498B	18040
4760A-4760B	18040
5737A-5737C	18040
1-2800	18042
2802-3200	18042
4400-5899	18040
Demaria Dr	18040
Derhammer St	18040
Destiny Ln	18040
Devils Cave Trl	18040
Devon Dr	18045
Devonshire Dr	18045
Dewalt Dr	18040
Diamond St	18042
Diane Ln	18045
Diehl Rd	18042
Division St	18045
Dogwood Ln & Ter	18040
Donald St	18045
Douthenc Rd	18040
Driftwood Dr	18040
Dryland Way	18045
Duke Ct	18045
Dunkle St	18045
Durham Rd	18042
Dusty Rd	18045
Eagles Creek Ct	18042
Ealer Ave	18042
Early St	18042
East Ln	18045
East St	18042
Easton Nazareth Hwy	18045
Eastview Ter	18045
Echo Trl	18040
Echo Ridge Ln	18042
Edamy St	18045
Eden Ter	18042
Edgemore Ave	18045
Edgewood Ave	18045
Edie Ln	18045
Edinburgh Dr	18045
Edswood Ter	18042
Edward St	18042
Eichlin Rd	18045
S Elder St	18042
Eldridge Ave	18045
E & W Elizabeth Ave	18040
Elm St	18042
Elwood St	18045
Embur Ter	18045
Emerick Ter	18045
Epler Dr	18040
Erie St	18045
Esquire Ct & Dr	18045
Eugene St	18045
E Fairfield Ave	18040
W Fairfield Ave	18040
Fairfield Ct	18045

Fairview Ave 18042
Fairway Dr
800-998 18040
1000-1099 18040
4400-4499 18045
Faith Ave 18040
Falk St 18040
Fallen Oak Dr 18040
Falwood Dr 18040
Farmersville Ct & Rd 18045
Farmhouse Ct N & S 18045
Farmstead Rd 18040
Farmview Rd 18040
Farragut St 18040
Farrcroft Dr 18040
Fayette Ct 18045
Fehr St 18045
Fern Ct 18045
Fernwood Dr 18040
Ferry St
200-2298 18042
201-2299 18042
201-201 18044
Fieldstone Dr 18045
Fieldstone Trl 18040
Filbar St 18045
Filbert St 18042
Firethorne Dr 18045
Firmstone St 18042
Fischer Rd 18045
Flafair Dr 18042
Flagler St 18042
Flecks Ln 18045
Fleetwood Dr & St 18045
Florentine Dr 18040
Florian St 18045
Folk St 18042
Forest St 18042
Forest Line Rd 18045
N & S Fork Dr 18040
Forks Ave 18040
Forks St 18045
Forks Church Rd 18040
Forrest Stand Dr 18042
Fort Lee Ct 18040
Fox Cir 18042
Fox Rdg 18040
Fox Run 18042
Fox Hill Rd 18045
Fox Hollow Ln 18040
Fox Run Rd 18040
Foxwood Cir 18040
Franklin St 18042
Fraser Dr 18040
Frederick St 18042
Freds Ct 18042
Freedom Ct 18040
Freedom Ter 18045
Freemansburg Ave
1800-2499 18042
2500-5299 18045
Friendenstahl Ave 18040
Friendly Tavern Ln 18040
Fringe Ln 18040
Front St
1-99 18042
300-2499 18042
5100-6199 18040
Frost Hollow Rd 18040
Frutchey Hill Rd 18040
Frya Run 18042
Gaffney Hill Rd 18042
Gall Rd 18040
Garden Ct 18040
Garr Rd 18040
Gates St 18040
Gateway Ter 18045
George Ct 18045
George St
915-O-915-O 18042
901A-921A 18042
901B-921B 18042
901C-921C 18042
901D-921D 18042
901E-921E 18042
901F-921F 18042
1001-1197 18040
1199-1399 18040
Georgian Ln 18045
Gerspach Ct 18042
Gila Dr 18040
Gillian Ln 18040
Glasgow Way 18045
Glen Ave 18045
Glendon Ave 18042
Glendon Hill Rd 18042
Glenfield Ct 18045
Glenmoor Cir & Ct 18045
Glover Rd 18040
Gold Rose Ln 18045
Gordon Dr 18045
Gorham Rd 18045
Gradwohl Switch Rd 18045
Grand View Rd 18042
Grandview Dr 18045
E & W Grant St 18042
Green Ct 18040
N Green St 18042
Green Trl 18040
Green Pond Rd 18045
Greenhill Ave 18045
Greening Dr 18045
Greenleaf St 18040
Greenway St 18040
N Greenwood Ave 18045
S Greenwood Ave
100-649 18045
650-650 18043
651-1099 18045
700-998 18045
Grigio Pl 18045
Grist Mill Ln 18045
Grouse Ct 18040
Grove St 18045
Gruver Ave 18045
Guyton St 18045
Hackett Ave 18045
Hackettview Ave 18045
Hamilton St 18042
Harding Ct 18045
Harriv St 18045
Hart St 18042
Hartley Ave 18045
Harvest Dr S & W 18040
Haupt St 18045
Hawthorn Dr 18045
Hawthorne Ct 18045
Hay St 18042
Hay Ter
1800-2099 18042
2701-2897 18045
2899-2999 18045
Haymont St 18045
Hazelton Ct 18042
Heather Ln 18040
Hecktown Rd 18045
Hedgerow Ct & Dr 18040
Helen Ct 18042
Hennaberry Ln 18040
Henry St 18045
Heritage Ln 18045
Hermitage Ave 18045
Hexenkopf Rd 18042
Hickory Dr 18040
Hickory Ln 18045
Hidden Meadow Dr 18042
High St
1-219 18042
123-127 18042
200-512 18042
205-205 18045
217-699 18042
532-532 18045
730-740 18042
High Point Ct 18045
High Point Ln 18042
Highfield Dr 18042
Highland Ct & Dr 18045
Highland View Ct 18042
Highlands Blvd & Cir 18042
Hill Rd 18040
Hillcrest Dr 18045
Hills Dr 18045
Hillside Ave
100-199 18040
900-2499 18042
Hillside Ct N 18045
Hillside Ct S 18045
Hilltop Cir 18045
Hillview Ave 18045
Hilton St 18042
Hobson St 18045
Hodle Ave 18045
Hoffman Ter 18042
Hollo Rd 18045
Hollow View Dr 18040
Holly Ct 18040
Holly St 18042
Holt St 18042
Homestead Dr 18040
E Homestead Ln 18042
W Homestead Ln 18042
Hoops Ln 18040
Hope Rd 18045
Hope St 18040
Hope Ridge Dr 18045
Hopkins Ln 18040
Horseshoe Dr 18040
Howard Ln 18045
Howe St 18040
Howell Rd 18040
Howie Pl 18045
Hoyt St 18042
Hugh Moore Park Rd 18042
Hunter Ct 18045
Hunter Rd 18040
Hunter St 18045
Huntington Ln 18040
Ian St 18040
Illinois St 18045
Indian Trl 18040
Indiana St 18045
Industrial Blvd 18040
Industrial Dr 18042
Industrial Dr N 18042
Inverness Cir 18042
Inverness Ln 18045
Iron Ln 18040
Iron St 18042
Ironwood Dr 18040
Iroquois Dr 18040
Island Ct 18042
Island Park Rd 18042
Ivy Ct & Ln 18045
Jackson St 18042
James Ct 18042
James Pl 18045
James St 18042
Jamie Ct 18040
Jeanette St 18042
Jeannette Ln 18040
Jefferson St 18042
Jeffrey Ln 18045
Jeffrey St 18042
Jenkins Dr 18040
Jenna Ln 18045
Jeremy Ct 18045
Jewel St 18045
Joan St 18042
John St 18045
Johnson St 18040
Jonathan Dr 18045
Jones Blvd 18045
Jones Houston Way 18042
Jordans Ct 18045
Joseph Dr 18045
Jubilee Dr 18040
Juniper Ave 18045
S Kathryn St 18045
Katie Ct 18040
Kaywood Dr 18045
Keane St 18045
Kelso Rdg 18045
Kendon Dr 18045
Kent Ln 18045
Kesslersville Rd 18040
Keystone Ave 18042
Kiefer St 18042
Kinderwood Dr 18042
King Ave 18045
Kings Ave 18045
Kingston Rd 18045
Kingsview Ave 18045
Kingwood St 18045
Kirkland Rd 18040
Klein Rd 18040
E & W Kleinhans St 18042
Knollcroft St 18045
Knollwood Dr 18042
Knollwood Way 18040
Knowlton St 18045
Knox Ave
800-900 18042
902-998 18042
1000-1200 18040
1202-1498 18040
Kressman Rd 18042
Kuebler Rd 18040
Kunkle Dr 18045
Kykuit Pl 18040
Lachenour Ave 18042
E & W Lafayette St 18042
Lambert Ct 18040
Lantern Pl E & W 18045
Larkspur Ln 18045
Larry Holmes Dr 18042
N Law St 18042
Lawnherst Ave & Ct 18045
Lee Ln 18040
Leeman St 18045
Lefevre Rd 18040
Lehigh Dr 18042
Lehigh Rd 18040
Lehigh St 18042
Lehns Ct 18042
Leigh Dr 18040
Lenape Way 18040
Lennox St 18042
Lerch St 18045
Lewis Cir & St 18045
Lexington Ct 18040
Liberty St
300-398 18042
301-1297 18042
1299-2199 18042
2500-2999 18045
Liberty Ter 18040
Lieb Rd 18040
Lieberman Ter 18045
E & W Lincoln Ave & St 18042
Lindenwood Ln 18040
Line St 18042
N & S Locust St 18042
Logan Dr 18045
Lois Ln 18045
Lone Cedar Dr 18040
Long Rd & Way 18040
Longhill Dr 18045
Loomis St 18045
Lord Ct 18045
Lorton Dr 18040
Louis St 18042
Low St 18042
Lower Way 18040
Lower Mud Run Rd 18040
Lower Saucon Rd 18042
Lower Way Rd 18045
Ludlow St 18045
Lynn St 18042
Lynwood Ave 18045
E & W Madison St 18042
Magnolia Dr 18045
Main St
11-17 18040
19-41 18040
43-87 18040
54-98 18042
73-99 18042
100-100 18042
100-299 18042
102-199 18040
200-710 18045
200-200 18040
408-550 18045
600-713 18040
715-799 18040
3300-3399 18045
Maple Ave 18040
Maple Ln 18045
S Maple St 18042
W Maple St 18042
Maplecroft Ave 18045
Marble Pl 18040
Marc Ln 18045
March St 18042
Margaret Ct 18040
Margarete Ter 18042
Marigold Dr 18040
Mariska Ln 18045
Markle Hall 18042
Marquis St 18042
Marruth Ave 18040
Marwood Ln 18045
Mary St 18045
Marywood Ln 18042
Masters Way 18042
Mattes Ln 18042
Mauch Chunk St 18042
Maxwell Dr 18040
Maywood St 18045
Mccartney St 18042
Mcfadden Rd 18045
Mcintosh Dr 18045
Mckeen St 18042
Meadow Ave 18045
Meadow Lane Dr 18040
Meco Rd E 18040
Melanie Ln 18045
Melchor Dr 18042
Melissa Dr 18045
Mercer Way 18040
Merion Ave 18045
Merion Ln 18042
Merlot Dr 18045
Meyer Ln 18045
Michael Koury Pl 18042
Middle Ct 18045
Middle Pl 18045
Middle Way 18040
Midland Dr 18045
Mikol Ln 18045
Milano Dr 18040
Mile Rd 18042
Milford Ct & St 18045
Mill St 18042
Mill Race Dr 18045
Millbrook Ct 18045
Miller St 18042
E & W Milton St 18042
Mine Lane Rd 18045
Mitman Rd 18042
Mixsell St 18042
Mohawk Ln 18040
Mohican Dr 18040
Monmouth Ct 18040
E & W Monroe St 18042
Moor Dr 18045
Moore St 18042
Moravian Ave 18045
Morgan Dr 18040
Morgan Hill Rd 18042
Morningside Dr 18045
Morris St 18045
Morrison Ave 18042
Mort Dr 18040
Morvale Rd 18042
Moss Ct 18045
Mount Jefferson St 18042
Mountain Top Dr 18045
Mountain View Ave 18045
Movie Ct 18045
Moyers Ln 18042
Muirfield Way 18042
N & S Mulberry St 18042
Murray Dr 18042
Myrtle Ave 18040
Napa Dr 18040
Nazareth Rd 18045
Nelson Ave 18040
E & W Nesquehoning St 18042
Nevin Ter 18042
New Hampshire Ave 18045
Newburg Rd 18045
Newlins Rd E & W 18040
Newlins Mill Rd 18045
Newton St 18045
Nicholas Ct & St 18045
Nicole Pl 18045
Nightingale Dr 18045
North St 18045
Northampton St
100-2299 18042
2400-2401 18045
2402-2498 18042
2403-3099 18045
2500-2998 18045
Northgate Blvd 18045
Northview Ave 18045
Northwood Ave 18045
Norton Ave 18045
Norwood Ave 18045
Nottingham Ln 18045
N & S Nulton Ave 18045
Oak Dr 18042
Oak Ln 18045
N Oak St 18042
Oak Hill Ct 18042
Oak Tree Ln 18040
Oakdale Ave 18045
Oakmont Ct 18042
Oakwood St 18045
Ohio St 18045
Old Carriage Dr 18045
Old Course Ln 18045
Old Easton Rd 18040
Old Mill Ln & Rd 18040
Old Nazareth Rd 18045
Old Orchard Dr 18045
Old River Rd 18040
Old Well Rd 18042
Olde Penn Dr 18045
Olympic Way 18042
Orchard Rd 18040
Orchard St 18042
Orchid Ct 18045
Oregon St 18045
Orvieto Ct 18040
Overlook Cir 18045
Owls Nest Rd 18040
Oxford Dr 18045
Packer St 18042
Padula Rd 18040
Palmer St 18042
Palmer Park Mall 18045
Palmetto Dr 18045
Pardee St 18042
Park Ave 18045
Park Pl 18042
Park Rd 18040
Park Ridge Dr 18040
Parker Ave 18042
Parkridge Ave 18045
Parsons St 18042
Pastor Fred Davis St 18042
Patriot Ln 18040
Patriots Ln 18040
Patterson Walk 18040
Paul St 18045
Paul Eaton Rd 18040
Paulynne Ln 18040
Paxinosa Ave 18042
Paxinosa Rd E 18040
Paxinosa Rd W 18040
S Peach St 18042
Peach Tree Trl 18040
Pearl St 18042
Peggy St 18045
Pemberton Pl 18040
Penacook Dr 18045
Penns Grant Dr 18045
Penns Ridge Blvd 18040
Pennsylvania Ave 18042
Pennsylvania St 18045
Penny Ln 18040
Periwinkle Pl 18040
Pheasant Ct 18040
Philadelphia Rd 18042
Phillips St 18042
Piedmont Ln 18040
E & W Pierce St 18042
Pike St 18045
Pin Oak Ln 18040
Pine Ln 18042
Pine St 18042
Pine Trl 18040
Pine Grove Dr 18045
Pine Valley Ter 18042
Pinehurst Ln 18042
Pink Rose Ln 18045
Plymouth Dr 18045
Pond Dr 18040
Porter St 18042
Preston Dr 18040
Prestwick Dr 18042
Prima Dr 18045
Primrose Path 18040
Prince St 18045
Princeton Ct 18040
Prologis Pkwy 18045
Prospect Ave 18042
Quad Dr 18042
Quail Ct 18040
Quaker Ridge Ter 18042
Queen Ave & St 18045
Quincy Ave 18045
Radcliffe St 18045
Ramblewood Dr 18040
Ranee St 18045
S Raspberry St 18042
Rau Ln 18045
Raub St 18042
Raubsville Rd 18042
Raynessa Ct 18045
Red Barn Dr 18040
Red Fox Ln 18040
Red Maple Ln 18040
Red Rose Ln 18045
Reeder St 18042
Reese St 18042
Rensselaer Ave 18040
Reston Dr 18040
Reveres Way 18040
Reynolds St 18042
Rhine Ct, Dr & Pl 18045
Richmond Rd 18040
N Ridge Ct 18045
Ridge Rd
2-11 18045
13-25 18045
64-199 18042
Ridge St 18042
Ridge Trl 18040
Ridgeline Ln 18045
Ridgewood Rd 18045
Riesling Dr 18045
Rinaldi Ln 18040
Rismiller Ln 18042
Riverside Cir 18045
N Riverside Dr 18042
Riverview Cir 18045
Riverview Dr 18042
Riverview Pl 18040
Robin Rd 18045
Rock Rd & St 18042
Rocky Ln 18045
S Rose Ct & St 18042
Rosecliff Dr 18040
Rosemont Ct 18045
S Rosewood Ct & St 18042
Roy Ct & Ln 18040
Royal Manor Rd 18042
Ruben Ct 18045
Russet Dr 18045
Saddle Ln 18045
Saint John St 18042
E & W Saint Joseph St 18042
San Simeon Pl 18040
Sandts Ct 18042
Sandy Ln 18045

Saratoga Ct 18040
Sassafras St 18042
Saylors Ln 18042
Scenic View Dr 18040
Schaffer St 18045
Schaffers Ct 18042
School House Ln 18042
Schuler Ln 18042
Schuyler Dr 18040
Scott St 18042
Scotty Dr 18045
Seip Ave 18045
Seitz St 18042
Seneca Ln 18040
Shadowstone Dr 18040
Shawnee Ave & Dr 18042
Sheffield Dr 18040
Shelley St 18045
Sheridan Dr 18045
Sheriff Dr 18040
Sherwood Dr 18040
Sherwood Rd 18045
Shirley St 18042
Short Rd 18040
Shrine Ave 18045
Silo Dr 18040
N & S Sitgreaves St 18042
Sky Line Dr 18042
Smith Ave 18042
Snyder St 18042
Sofet Ln 18042
Somerset Ln 18045
Somerset Ter 18042
Sonoma Ln 18040
Southmont Way 18045
Southwood Dr 18045
Spengler Ave 18040
Spring Ln 18040
Spring Rd 18040
Spring St 18042
Spring Garden St
100-1900 18042
1902-2198 18042
2600-2624 18045
2626-2799 18045
Spring Hill Rd 18042
Spring Valley Rd 18042
Spring Water Ct 18042
Springfield Rd 18042
Springfield Way 18045
Spruce St 18042
Stafford Dr 18040
Stage Coach Dr 18042
Stanley St 18042
Stanton Ct 18042
Starlight Dr 18045
Steele Ln 18040
Steely Hill Rd 18042
Steeplechase Dr 18040
Stephanie Dr 18045
Stephens St 18045
Sterlingworth Ter 18042
Steuben Ln 18040
Stewart Ct & St 18042
Stocker Mill Rd 18045
Stonebridge Ln 18040
Stonecreek Ct 18045
Stonecroft Dr 18045
Stones Crossing Rd 18045
Stonewall Ter 18042
Stoudts Ln 18042
Stouts School Rd 18042
Stouts Valley Rd 18042
Stump Rd 18040
Sturbridge Ave 18045
Sullivan Rd 18042
Sullivan Trl
700-710 18042
900-5699 18040
Summit Ave 18045
Summit Dr 18042
Sunflower Dr 18040
Sunnyside Rd 18042
Sunrise Dr 18040
Surrey Dr 18045
Susan Cir 18040
Sutton Pl & Rd 18045
Swanson St 18045
Sycamore Ave 18040
Sycamore Dr 18045
Sycamore St 18042
Tamarack Ct 18040
Tamarack Path 18045
Tamlynn Ct & Ln 18045
Tammy Ln 18042
Tanglewood Rd 18042
Tatamy Rd 18045
Taylor Ave 18042
Terri Ln 18040
Terry St 18042
Texas Rd 18042
Thomas Dr 18040
Thomas Bright Ave 18042
Thornwood Vw N 18040
Tiffany Dr 18045
Timber Ridge Dr 18045
Timberlane Dr 18045
Timothy Trl N & S 18040
Toboggan Trl 18040
Toursdale Dr 18045
Town Center Blvd 18040
Towpath Cir E & W 18045
Trails End Ct 18040
Treeline Dr 18040
Trisha St 18045
Troon Ct 18042
Tulip Ct 18045
Tumble Creek Rd 18042
Tuscany Dr 18040
Uhler Rd 18040
N & S Union St 18042
Upper Way 18040
Upper Mud Run Rd 18040
Upper Shawnee Ave
100-300 18042
302-534 18040
536-536 18042
538-598 18040
Upper Way Rd 18045
Upstream Farm Rd 18040
Val Vista Dr 18045
Valley Ave 18042
Valley View Rd 18042
Van Buren Rd 18045
Vaughn St 18045
Veile St 18042
Venetian Dr 18040
Veneto Ct 18040
Vera Cir 18045
Vera Dr 18040
Vermont Dr & St 18045
Victor St 18042
Victoria Ct & Ln 18045
Village At Stones
Crossing Rd 18045
Vine St 18042
Vintage Dr 18045
Virginia St 18045
Vista Ct 18040
Vista Dr
1-99 18040
101-125 18042
105-299 18040
127-304 18042
305-315 18040
306-698 18042
323-699 18040
Wagener Ln 18040
Wagner Dr 18045
Wagon Wheel Dr 18040
Walnut Ln 18040
Walnut St 18042
Walter Ave 18045
Waltman Loop Ln 18045
N & S Warren St 18042
Warrior Ln 18042
Washington Blvd 18042
Washington Ct 18042
Washington St
400-1599 18042
2600-2999 18045
Water Wheel Ln 18045
Waterford Ter 18042
N & S Watson St 18045
Waverly Ave 18040
E Wayne Ave 18042
W Wayne Ave 18042
Wayne St 18045
Wedgewood Dr 18045
Weiss Ave 18042
Wellco Rd 18045
Weller Pl 18045
Wentworth Pl 18045
West Ct 18045
West Ln 18045
N West St 18042
S West St 18042
Westfield Dr 18042
Westgate Ave 18045
Westgate Dr 18040
Westwind Dr 18040
Westwood Dr 18045
Weygadt Dr 18042
White Rose Ln 18045
Whitehall Ave 18045
Whitemarsh Dr 18040
Whitney Ave 18045
Wilbur St 18042
Wilden Dr 18045
E & W Wilkes Barre
St 18042
William Penn Hwy 18045
Williams St 18042
Williamson St 18045
Willow Dr
1-199 18045
1400-1899 18040
Willow St 18042
Wilmore St 18045
Winchester Dr & St 18040
Winding Way 18045
Windrift Ct 18045
Windsor St 18045
Windwood Hl 18045
Winfield Ct & Ter 18045
Winona St 18040
Winter Ln 18040
Winter St 18042
Winterthur Way 18040
Wirebach St 18042
Wisteria Dr & Pl 18045
Wolf Ave 18042
S Wood Ave 18042
Woodland Rd 18042
Woodlawn Ave 18045
Woodmont Cir 18045
Woodridge Ter 18045
Woodrun Ct 18042
Woodshire Dr 18042
Woodside Dr
1-99 18042
100-199 18045
Wottring Mill Rd 18042
N Wright St 18042
Wynnwood Ln E & N 18040
Yellow Rose Ln 18045
York Pl 18045
W Young St 18042
Youngs Hill Rd 18040
Zinfandel Ct E & W 18045
Zucksville Rd 18040

NUMBERED STREETS

1st Ter 18042
N & S 2nd St & Ter 18042
N & S 2nd St & Ter 18042
N & S 3rd St & Ter 18042
N & S 3rd St & Ter 18042
N & S 4th 18042
N & S 4th 18042
5th St 18042
6th St 18042
7th St 18042
N 7th St
1-127 18042
107-107 18045
129-245 18042
142-196 18045
200-216 18042
267-288 18045
300-398 18042
400-499 18042
S 7th St 18042
N 8th St
1-120 18042
122-498 18042
127-199 18045
201-499 18042
S 8th St
1-99 18042
101-199 18042
126-126 18045
132-198 18042
9th St 18042
10th St 18042
N & S 11th 18042
N & S 12th 18042
N & S 13th 18042
N & S 14th 18042
N & S 15th 18042
N & S 16th 18042
N & S 17th 18042
N & S 18th 18042
N & S 19th 18042
N & S 20th 18042
N & S 21st 18042
S 22nd St 18042
S 23rd St 18042
S 24th St 18042
S 25th St
300-2098 18042
301-1499 18045
S 26th St 18045
S 27th St 18045

ERIE PA

General Delivery 16501

POST OFFICE BOXES MAIN OFFICE STATIONS AND BRANCHES

Box No.s
1 - 1440 16512
339 - 339 16514
1501 - 2006 16512
1699 - 1699 16514
2027 - 2094 16512
3001 - 3960 16508
4000 - 6630 16512
8001 - 9898 16505
9901 - 9901 16565
9998 - 9998 16507
10000 - 13801 16514

NAMED STREETS

Aaron Rd 16511
Abbey Ln 16502
Aberdeen Ave 16506
Abington Way 16506
Academy Ave 16509
Adams St 16505
Adelaide Dr 16510
Adiutori Dr 16505
Adrienne Ct 16506
Afton Dr 16509
Ahoy Dr 16505
Alan Dr 16510
Albermarle Ave 16509
Alden Ln 16505
Alexandra Dr 16506
Algeria Rd 16505
Aline Dr 16509
Alison Ave 16506
Allegheny Rd
3200-3799 16508
3800-4599 16509
Almon Ave 16509
Alpine Dr 16506
Alvin St 16510
Amber Ct 16502
Amberwood Ln 16505
Amherst Rd 16506
Amidon Ave 16510
Amy Ave 16504
Anderson Dr 16509
Andover Ln 16509
Andrea Ct 16506
Andrews Park Blvd 16511
Angel Ct 16506
Angle St 16506
Anna Ct 16504
Anne Marie Dr 16506
Annendale Dr 16506
Antietam Dr 16510
Antoinette Ct 16506
Appaloosa Ct 16506
Apple Grove Ln 16506
Appleberry Dr 16510
Applejack Dr 16509
Appleman Rd 16509
Appletree Ln 16509
Applewood Ln 16509
Arborwood Ln 16505
Arbuckle Rd 16509
Arcadia Ave 16506
Arden Rd 16504
Ardmore Ave 16505
Ardsley Dr 16506
Argy Pl 16510
Argyle Ave 16505
Aris Dr 16505
E Arlington Rd
1-199 16509
1000-1299 16504
W Arlington Rd 16509
Arneman Ct 16511
Asbury Rd
1100-1999 16505
2200-4899 16506
Ash St
200-599 16507
600-2599 16503
2600-3799 16504
Asheboro Dr 16510
Ashwood Ln 16509
Aspen Dr 16506
Athens St 16510
Atkins St 16503
Atlantic Ave 16506
Auburn St 16508
Autumnwood Trl 16506
Avellino Dr 16510
Aveniel Ct 16506
Averlon Ave 16509
Avon Dr 16509
Azalea Cir 16506
Backus Rd 16510
Bacon St 16511
Baer Dr 16505
Baer Beach Rd 16505
Bailey Ave 16510
Baker Ave 16511
Balboa Ave 16509
Bancroft Ave 16509
Bank Dr 16505
Barber Pl 16507
Bargain Rd 16509
Basin Cir 16509
Basswood Dr 16506
Baur Ln 16502
E Bay Dr 16507
Bay Mist Dr 16505
Bayberry St 16509
E & W Bayfront Pkwy 16507
Bayview Ave 16505
Baywood Dr 16509
Beach Haven Ln 16505
Beachgrove Dr 16505
Beacon Hill Dr & Ln 16509
Bear Creek Ln 16509
Beaumont Ave 16505
Beaver Dr 16509
Beech Ave 16508
Beech Tree Ln 16510
Beechwood Ln 16511
Bell St 16511
Bellaire Dr 16506
Belle Village Dr E 16509
Bellefield Dr 16509
Belleview Dr 16504
Belmont Ave 16509
Bement St 16506
Bendelow Dr 16505
Benjamin Rd 16509
Bennett Rd 16510
Berkeley Rd 16506
Berkshire Ln 16509
Bernwood Dr 16510
Berry St 16509
Berst Ave 16502
Beverly Dr 16505
Biebel Ave 16509
Birch Ct 16503
N Birch Run 16506
S Birch Run 16506
Birchwood Ln 16505
Bird Dr 16510
Birwood Dr 16511
Bison Ct 16509
Blackmoor Dr 16510
Blackstone Dr 16505
Bladen Rd 16509
Bliley Rd 16510
W Bloomfield Pkwy 16509
Blossom Ter 16506
Blue Ridge Dr 16509
Blueberry Dr 16510
Bluff Rd 16508
E & W Boardwalk Pl 16506
Bogey Way 16505
Bolivar St 16508
Bon View Dr 16506
Bonaventure Dr 16505
Bondy Dr 16509
Bonica Cir 16506
Bonnie Brae 16511
Border Dr 16506
Boston Store Pl 16501
Bowman Ct 16505
Boyer Rd 16511
Bradford Ave 16506
Bramblewood Ln 16505
Branch St 16509
Brandes St
600-2599 16503
2600-4799 16504
Braund Rd 16509
Breezeway Dr 16506
Breezewood Ln 16506
Brent Ave 16509
Brentwood Ct 16506
Brewer Ave 16510
Brewster Ln 16505
Brewster St 16503
Briar Dr 16506
Bridgewood Dr 16509
Briercrest Dr 16509
Brierwood Dr 16510
Briggs Ave 16504
Brighton Ave 16509
Broad St 16503
Broadlawn Dr 16506
Brookhollow Ct 16506
Brooklyn Ave 16510
Brooks St 16506
Brooks Bay Dr 16505
Brooksboro Dr 16510
Brookside Dr 16505
Brookwood Dr 16509
Brookwood Village Dr 16509
Brown Ave 16502
Browning Cir 16505
Bryant St 16509
Buckthorn Dr 16506
Budd Dr 16506
Buffalo Rd
1808A-1808Z 16510
Bundy Dr 16509
Bunny Ln 16509
Burgundy Dr 16506
Burkhart Ave 16511
Burns Ave 16504
Burton Ave 16504
Butt St 16506
Cabernet Ct 16506
Cabot Ave 16511
Calico Dr 16506
California Dr 16505
Cambridge Rd 16511
Cameo Way 16506
Cameron Rd 16510
Campbell Ave 16505
Camphausen Ave
1200-1299 16511
1800-2599 16510
Candlewood Ln 16505
Candy Ln 16505
Canterbury Dr 16506
Canton Ave 16508
Cardinal Dr 16509
Carey Farms Rd 16511
Carla Way 16509
Carleton Ct 16506
Carney Ave 16510
Caroline Dr 16509
Carriage Hill Dr 16509
Carrie St 16511
Carter Ave 16506
Carters Beach Rd 16511
Carver Ave 16511
Cascade St
200-599 16507
600-2599 16502
2600-3799 16508
Castle Dr 16510
Castlewood Ct 16509
Catawba Dr 16506
Cathedral Dr 16506
Caton St 16506
Caughey Rd 16506
Cavaliero St 16511
Cedar St 16503
Cedar Ridge Dr 16509
Cedarwood Ct 16506
Cedarwood Ln 16509
Center St 16510
Central Dr 16505
Central Belle Village
Dr 16509
Chablis Dr 16506
Chadwick Rd 16510
Chapel Hill Dr 16506
Chapin St 16508
Charles St 16509
Charleston Ave 16509
Charlotte St 16508
Chatam Dr 16510
Chautauqua Blvd 16511
Chelsea Ave 16505
Chelsie Dr 16509
Cherokee Dr 16505
Cherry St
200-599 16507
600-999 16502
1000-1299 16501
1400-2100 16502
2102-2598 16502
2600-3799 16508
3800-4999 16509
Cherry Blossom Dr 16510
Cherry Hill Blvd 16509
Cherry Street Ext 16509
Cherryboro Dr 16510
Cherrywood Ln 16509
Cheryl Ct 16506
Chestnut St
100-198 16507
200-599 16507
600-999 16502
1000-1399 16501
1400-2199 16502
2201-2599 16502
2600-3199 16508
Chestnut Hill Dr 16509

Chilton Ct & Ln 16505
Chipmunk Dr 16509
Chitanne Dr 16505
Church St 16509
Cider Mill Rd 16509
Cindy Ln 16506
Circle Ct 16510
Clarinda Dr 16505
Clark Rd 16510
Clark Road Ext 16510
Clayton Ave 16509
Clearview Dr 16505
Cliff Dr 16511
Clifford Dr 16505
Clifton Dr 16505
Clinton St 16509
Clover Hill Dr 16509
Cloveridge Dr 16509
Club House Dr 16509
Clyde St 16509
Cobblestone Dr 16509
Cochran St 16508
Cold Spring Dr 16508
Cole Dr 16505
Coleridge Dr 16506
Colleen Dr 16505
Colonial Ave 16506
N Colonial Pkwy 16509
S Colonial Pkwy 16509
Colony Dr 16505
Colorado Dr 16505
Colt Ln 16506
Colt Rd 16510
Columbia Cir 16505
Columbus Dr 16506
Commercial St 16503
Commodore Dr 16505
Compass Dr 16505
Concord Rd 16506
Concordia Dr 16506
Connecticut Dr 16505
Conrad Rd 16510
Contessa Ln 16506
Conti Dr 16505
Conway St 16509
Cook Ave 16510
Cooper Rd 16510
Copper Dr 16509
Corvette Dr 16510
Cottage Ave 16503
Cottonwood Dr 16506
Country Ln 16506
Countryside Dr 16511
Court Ave 16506
Courtland Dr 16509
Courtney Dr 16506
Coventry Dr 16506
Covert Cir 16509
Covington Valley Dr 16509
Cowells Beach Rd 16511
Crabapple Dr 16509
Craig St 16508
Cranberry St
400-599 16507
600-1199 16502
1200-1399 16501
1600-2599 16502
Cranch Ave 16511
Crandall Ave 16502
Cray Rd 16509
Creek Ln 16511
Crescent Dr
300-499 16505
2400-2799 16506
Crest Dr 16509
Crestmont Ave 16508
Crestview Dr 16509
Crestwood Dr 16510
Cricket St 16510
Cristina Ct & Dr 16506
Crosley Rd 16511
Crosswinds Dr 16506
Crotty Dr 16511
Crotty Drive Ext 16511
Crowell St 16509
Crystal Dr 16505
Crystal Point Dr 16505
Culpepper Dr 16506
Cumberland Rd 16510
Cunningham Dr 16511
Curtis Rd 16509
Custer Dr 16505
Cypress St 16504
Dale Dr 16511
Daniels St 16510
Darcie Dr 16506
Dauphin Pkwy 16506
Davenport Ave 16509
David Rd 16510
Davis Ave 16509
Davison Ave 16504
Dawson Rd 16510
Debra Dr 16506
Dee Jay Ave 16510
Deepwood Ln 16505
Deer Dr 16509
Deer Run Trl 16509
Deerfield Dr 16509
Delaware Ave 16505
Delmar Dr 16506
Delphos Dr 16509
Dentonboro Ct 16510
Depot Rd 16510
Depot Road Ext 16510
Devoe Ave 16508
Devon Ln 16509
Dexter Ave 16504
Dias St 16510
Dickens Ct 16505
Dinicola Dr 16510
Dion Ct 16506
Division St 16503
Dixson Dr 16509
E Dobbins Lndg 16507
W Dobbins Lndg 16507
Dobbins Rd 16511
Dodi Ct 16509
Dogleg Trl 16510
Dogwood Dr 16509
Dolphin Way 16509
Dominic Dr 16506
Dominion Dr 16510
Don Dr 16510
Donahue Rd 16506
Donald St 16511
Donation Rd 16509
Donlin Rd 16510
Donna Dr 16509
Dorchester Dr 16509
Doris Dr 16509
S Dougan Rd 16510
Douglas Dr 16505
Douglas Pkwy 16509
Douglas Rd 16510
Downhill Dr 16505
Downing Ave
600-1699 16511
2000-2799 16510
Downing Ct 16502
Downs Dr 16509
Drake Dr 16505
Draper Pl 16511
Drexel Dr 16506
Driftwood Dr 16511
Dudley St 16509
Dumar Rd 16509
Duncan Rd 16505
Dundee Rd 16509
Dunford Way 16509
Dunn Blvd 16507
Dunn Valley Rd 16509
Dynes Ave 16510
Eagle Point Blvd 16511
N Eaglewood Dr 16511
Earl Dr 16509
East Ave
100-599 16507
600-2599 16503
2600-4099 16504
East Dr 16511
East Rd 16509
Eastern Ave 16510
Eastlawn Pkwy 16510
Eastwind Cir & Ln 16506
Ebco Dr 16506
Ebersole Dr 16511
Echo Ln 16506
Edgebrook Way 16506
Edgemont Pkwy 16505
Edgevale Dr 16509
Edgewater Cir 16509
Edgewood Dr 16509
Edinboro Rd 16509
Edison Ave 16510
Edward St 16505
Eiji Oue Pl 16501
Eisenhower Rd 16510
El Corto Way 16506
Elderwood Ln 16505
Eldred St 16511
Eliot Rd 16508
Elizabeth Ln 16505
Elk Dr 16509
Ellenboro Ct 16510
Eller Ln 16509
Ellington Dr 16506
Ellsworth Ave
2600-3799 16508
3800-4599 16509
Elm Ct 16503
Elm St
2000-2199 16503
2600-2799 16504
Elmwood Ave
2600-3799 16508
3800-4499 16509
Elsie St 16511
Ely Ln 16505
Emerick Ct 16506
Emerson Ave
2100-2499 16502
2600-3599 16508
Emery Dr 16509
Emmaline Dr 16509
Emmet Dr 16511
Emmett Dr 16511
Enfield Ln 16509
English Ave 16510
Ennis Dr 16509
Equestrian Dr 16506
Eragas Dr 16511
Erica Dr 16509
W Erie Plz 16505
Erie St 16508
Essex Ave 16504
Estate Ct & Dr 16509
Euclid Ave 16511
Euclid Blvd 16510
Evans Rd 16509
Evanston Ave 16506
Everett Dr 16510
Evergreen Dr 16505
Exeter Rd 16509
Fair Ave 16511
Fairfax Ave 16505
Fairfield Ave 16509
Fairlawn St 16509
Fairmont Pkwy
1400-1499 16503
1500-2699 16510
Fairway Dr 16505
Falmouth Rd 16506
Fargo St 16510
Farrel Rd 16505
Fay St 16511
Fayland Dr 16509
Feasler St 16506
Feidler Dr 16506
Ferncliff Bch 16505
Fernwood Ln 16505
Ferrick Dr 16509
Field St 16511
Fieldcrest Dr 16505
Fieldstone Ct 16509
Fieldstone Dr 16509
Fieldstone Way 16505
Filley Rd 16510
Filmore Ave
800-1899 16505
2000-2599 16506
Firman Rd 16510
Fischer Dr 16511
Fisher Ct 16505
Fleetwood Dr 16510
Florence Ave 16504
Florida Ave 16504
Flower Rd 16509
Footemill Rd 16509
Forbes St 16510
Ford Ave 16505
Forest Dr 16505
Forest Gln 16506
Forest Run 16509
Forest Xing 16506
Fossilwood Ct 16506
Fountain Way 16506
Fountaine Ct 16506
Four Seasons Trl 16506
Fox Hollow Ln 16511
Foxboro Ct 16510
Foxglove Ln 16505
Foxhill Dr 16510
Foxwood Dr 16510
Francis St 16510
Frank Ave 16509
Franklin Ave
600-1099 16511
1700-2099 16510
Frazier St 16510
Frederick Dr 16510
Freeman Rd 16510
Fremont St 16510
French St
200-499 16507
500-1799 16501
1800-2599 16503
2600-4299 16504
E & W Front St 16507
Frontenac Dr 16511
Frontier Dr 16505
Fruit St 16504
Fryling Rd 16510
Fulda Dr 16505
Fulton St 16503
Gable Ct 16506
Ganzer Ln 16506
Garden Ave 16508
Gardner Dr 16509
Garland St 16506
Garloch Dr 16505
Garries Rd 16506
Gaskell Ave 16503
Gatesmill Dr 16510
Gay Rd 16510
Geist Rd 16502
Gem Ct 16504
Genesee Ave 16510
Genevieve Ave 16509
Georgetown Dr 16509
Georgian Ct 16506
German St
100-599 16507
600-2599 16503
2600-3299 16504
Gerry Ave 16508
Gilson St 16503
Glacier Dr 16510
Glade Dr 16509
Gladstone Ct 16511
Glen Crest Dr 16509
Glen Eagles Dr 16509
Glencoe Rd 16509
Glendale Ave 16510
Glenhaven Ln 16509
Glenmar Dr 16509
Glenridge Rd 16509
Glenruadh Ave 16505
Glenside Ave 16508
Glenview Dr 16509
Glenwood Blvd 16509
Glenwood Park Ave
2600-3799 16508
4600-5799 16509
Gloth Ave 16504
Gold Ave 16509
Gold Flower St 16509
Golden Dr 16509
Goldsboro Dr 16510
Golf Club Rd 16509
Gonda Dr 16509
Goodrich St 16508
Gordon Ln 16509
E Gore Rd
1-999 16509
1000-1499 16504
1900-2599 16510
W Gore Rd 16509
Gorman Dr 16505
Grace St 16505
Graham Dr 16509
Granada Dr 16509
Grand Harbour Dr 16505
E Grandview Blvd
300-1499 16504
1500-2599 16510
W Grandview Blvd
200-399 16508
400-2199 16509
2200-2799 16506
Granite Ct 16505
Grannery Dr 16510
Grant Ave 16505
Gray Ave 16510
Greeley Ave 16506
Green View Dr 16509
Greenacre Dr 16506
Greenbriar Dr 16510
Greencrest Dr 16506
Greenfield Dr 16509
Greengarden Blvd 16508
Greengarden Rd
900-1799 16501
1800-2599 16502
3800-4699 16509
Greenhill Dr 16506
Greenhurst Dr 16509
Greenlawn Ave 16510
Greentree Dr 16509
Greenway Dr 16506
Greenwood St 16509
Gridley Ave 16508
Griffin Ave 16511
Grimm Dr 16501
Griswold Plz 16501
Grove Dr 16505
Groveland Ave 16510
Grubb Rd 16506
Guetner Ave 16505
Guilford Dr 16506
Gullane Dr 16506
Gunnison Rd 16509
Haas Ave 16505
Haft Rd 16510
Haibach Dr 16509
Halley St 16511
Hamilton Rd 16510
Hamlet Ave 16506
Hammocks Dr 16506
Hamot Rd 16509
Hampshire Rd 16506
Hampton Rd
2000-2599 16502
2600-3199 16508
Hannon Rd 16510
Harbor Rd 16511
Harbor Ridge Trl 16510
Harborgreene Rd 16510
Harborview Dr 16508
Harbour Dr 16505
Harding Dr 16509
Hardscrabble Blvd 16505
Hare Way 16510
Harmony Dr 16505
Harold Rd 16509
Harper Dr 16505
Harrison St 16510
Hartley Ln 16505
Hartman Rd 16510
Hartt Rd 16505
Harvard Rd
2600-3799 16508
3800-4499 16509
Harvest Bnd 16506
Harvest Moon Dr 16509
Harvey Ave 16511
Hassell Ln 16509
Hastings Rd 16506
Haven St 16509
Hawick Rd 16509
Hawthorne Dr 16509
Haybarger Ave 16502
Hayes St 16504
Hayfield Cir 16509
Hazard Ct 16510
Hazel St 16508
Head Dr 16506
E Heandong St 16503
Hearthstone Ln 16505
Heibel Rd 16510
Heidt Ave 16509
Helen St 16505
Helena Dr 16510
Hemingway Dr 16505
Hemlock Dr 16506
Henderson Rd 16509
Henry St 16509
Hereford Rd 16510
Heritage Dr 16509
Herman Dr 16509
Herrelar St 16507
Hershey Rd
1900-2799 16509
2800-4099 16506
Hess Ave
1-599 16507
600-1199 16503
Hessinger Dr 16509
Hewitt Rd 16509
Hialeah Ct 16506
Hickory Ln 16509
Hickory St 16502
Hidden Ln 16506
Hidden Springs Dr 16506
High St 16509
Highland Rd 16506
Highline Blvd 16509
Highview Blvd 16509
Hilborn Ave 16505
Hill Rd 16508
S Hill Rd 16509
Hillborn Rd 16509
Hillcrest Ave 16509
Hillhaven Dr 16509
Hillock Dr 16509
Hillsdale Ave 16509
Hilltop Rd 16509
Hillwood Dr 16509
Holbrook Ave 16511
Holiday Dr 16506
Holland St
1-499 16507
501-599 16507
600-1099 16501
1100-2599 16503
2600-3799 16504
Holly Dr 16510
Holly Rue 16506
Holly Park Dr 16509
Holly Vista Dr 16509
Hollydale Dr 16509
Holman Dr 16509
Holmes St 16504
Home Rd 16509
Homeland Blvd 16509
Homer Ave 16506
Homestead Dr 16506
Honey Ln 16509
Honeysuckle Dr 16509
Honeywood Ln 16505
Hoover St 16504
Hope Dr 16510
Horseshoe Dr 16510
Horstman Ct 16504
Horton St 16508
Howe Ave 16511
Hoyt St 16510
Hrinda Dr 16506
Hudson Rd 16508
Hull Dr 16509
Hummingbird Ct 16509
Hunter Willis Rd 16509
Hunters Creek Rd 16509
Hunters Ridge Dr 16510
Huntington Dr 16505
Huron St 16502
Idaho Ave 16505
Idlewood Dr 16510
Idyllbrook Ct & Ln 16506
Idyllbrook Village Ct & Dr 16506
Illinois Ave 16505
Imperial Dr 16506
Indian Dr 16511
Indiana Dr 16505
Industrial Dr 16505
Interchange Rd
1900-2059 16509
2060-2098 16565
2061-2099 16509
Interstate Dr 16509
Intrepid Dr 16509
Irene Dr 16510
Ironwood Ln 16505
Iroquois Ave 16511
Irvine Dr 16511
Irwin Dr 16505
Ivy Ln 16506
Jackson Ave 16504
Jackson Pl 16510
James Ave 16506
James St 16509
Jamestown Dr 16506
Jane Ln 16510
Japan St 16502
N & S Jarrod Ct 16506
Jasmine Dr 16509
Jason Dr 16506
Jefferson Ave 16509
Jodie Ln 16509
Joel Ave 16509
E & W Johnson Rd 16509
Joliette Ave 16511
Jonathan Dr 16509
Jones Ln 16505
Jones Rd 16510
Jordan Rd 16510
Joseph Dr 16506
Joshua Dr 16511
Julie Ct & Dr 16506
Julie Ann Ln 16509
June St 16510
Juniper St 16509
Kahkwa Blvd 16505
Kahkwa Club Rd 16506
Kahn Dr 16509
Kane Hill Rd 16510
Kates Way 16509
Kay Gie Way 16510
Kaylin Ct 16506
Keats Ave 16508
Kellogg St 16508
Kelso Dr 16505
W Kenchint St 16508
Kerry Ln 16505
Keystone Dr 16509
Kilpatrick Ave 16503
Kimberly Dr 16509
King Rd 16509
King Arthur Dr 16506
Kingston Ct 16506
Kirsch Rd 16510
E Kmart Plaza Dr 16510
Knipper Ave 16510
Knoll Ave 16510
Knowledge Pkwy 16510
Knoyle Rd 16510
Koala Dr 16510
Koehler Rd 16510
Kosiorek Dr 16509
Kozlowski Dr 16506
Kraus Dr 16511

Kristie Dr 16506
Kruger Ave 16509
Kuhl Rd 16510
Kuntz Rd 16509
La Rae Dr 16506
La Salle Ave 16511
Lacey Dr 16510
Lafayette Rd 16506
Laird Ave 16505
Lake Ave 16511
E Lake Rd
1000-1499 16507
1500-8899 16511
8899 1/2-8899 3/4 16511
W Lake Rd 16505
Lake Cliff Dr 16511
Lake Forest Dr 16511
Lake Front Dr 16505
Lake Haven Ct 16511
Lake Lure Dr 16505
Lake Pleasant Rd
3800-4999 16504
5000-9899 16509
Lake Shore Dr 16505
Lakeside Dr 16511
E Lakeview Blvd 16504
W Lakeview Blvd 16508
Lakeview Dr 16506
Lancaster Rd 16506
Langdon Rd 16509
Langmore Ln 16505
Lansing Way 16506
E Lantrend St 16504
Larchmont Dr 16509
Latempia Dr 16505
Laurel Dr 16509
Laurelwood Ct 16506
Laurie Ln 16509
Lawndale Dr 16506
Lawrence Pkwy 16511
Lawrence Pier 16507
Leary Rd 16511
Lecom Pl 16505
Ledgewood Ct 16511
Ledwick Dr 16511
Lee Ave 16511
Leemar Ct 16505
Legion Rd
2700-2706 16506
2707-2709 16515
2708-3198 16506
2711-3199 16506
2711-2711 16505
Lehigh St 16509
Lena Ct 16506
Leo Ave 16510
Leprechaun Ln 16510
Lester Ln 16506
Lexington St 16509
Liberty St
100-599 16507
600-2599 16502
2600-3799 16508
3800-4199 16509
Lighthouse St 16507
Lilac Ct 16506
Lincoln Ave 16505
Lindberg Ave 16509
Linden Ave 16505
Lindenfield Dr 16505
Lindsay Ct 16509
Link St 16509
Linoff Ln 16510
Linwood Ave 16510
Little Creek Rd 16509
Lochiel Ave 16505
Locust St 16508
Logan Dr 16506
Lone Pine Ct 16505
Long Point Dr 16505
Longacre Ave 16509
Longfellow Dr 16509
Longview Ave 16510
Longwood Dr 16505
Lookout Dr 16507
Lorna Ln 16506

Lorwood Dr 16510
Louise St 16510
Love Rd 16506
Loveland Ave 16506
Lovell Pl 16503
Lowell Ave
600-1699 16505
2000-2599 16506
Lowry Rd 16511
Lucille Dr 16510
Lucky Ln 16509
Luna Ln 16506
Lunger Rd 16510
Luxury Dr 16510
Lyme Ct 16505
Lymehurst Dr 16509
Lynn St 16503
Madeira Dr 16506
Madison Ave 16505
Magnolia Ct 16510
Magnolia Dr 16504
Magnolia Blossom Dr 16510
Maiden Ln 16504
Main St 16511
Malerree Rd 16509
Manchester Rd
1200-2199 16505
2200-2599 16506
Manistee Ave 16511
N & S Manor Dr 16505
Maple St 16508
Maple Grove Dr 16510
Maple Hill Dr 16509
Maple Leaf Dr 16508
Maplehurst Dr 16509
Maplenut Ln 16510
Maplewood Ct 16506
Maplewood Dr 16510
Marcella Dr 16506
Marchmont Dr 16509
Marcia Ln 16506
Margo Ct 16505
Maria Dr 16506
Marianna Ave 16509
Marion St 16510
Mark Rd 16509
Market St 16510
Markwood Dr 16510
Marmon Dr 16509
Marne Rd 16511
Marsh St 16508
Marshall Dr 16505
Martin Rd 16509
Martinwood Dr 16509
Marvin Ave 16504
Mary Jos Way 16509
Maryland Ave 16505
Massing Ct 16505
Matthew Ct 16504
Maxwell Ave 16504
Mayfair Ct 16505
Mayflower Dr 16506
Mccain Ave 16510
Mccarter Ave 16503
Mcclelland Ave 16510
Mcconnell Ave 16505
Mccreary Rd 16506
Mckee Rd 16506
Mckinley Ave 16503
Mclaughlin Dr 16506
Mcmillen Dr 16505
Meade Ave 16509
Meadow Dr 16506
Meadowbrook Dr 16510
Meadowland Cir 16509
Meadowrue Ln 16505
Meadowview Dr 16509
Mediterranean Pl 16506
Megan Ct 16509
Melrose Ave
2600-3799 16508
3800-4499 16509
Melvin Rd 16509
Merenney Rd 16510
Meridian Dr 16509
Merilee Dr 16506

Merle Ave 16509
Merline Ave 16509
Merwin Ln 16510
E Metcalf St 16504
W Metcalf St 16508
Metz St 16508
Micah Dr 16511
Michele Ct 16504
Michigan Blvd 16505
Middle Dr 16505
Midland Dr 16506
Mill St 16509
Millcreek Mall, Plz & Sq 16565
Millcrest Rd 16509
Miller Ave 16509
Millfair Rd
1500-2099 16505
2200-2498 16506
2500-4219 16506
Mindi Ct 16510
Mineo Dr 16509
Mingo Ave 16510
Mink Dr 16509
Mintwood Ct 16506
Mission Dr 16509
Mitchell St 16509
Mobile Ave 16502
Mohawk Dr 16505
Monarch Cir 16509
Monoca Dr 16505
Monroe Ave 16504
Montmarc Blvd 16504
Montpelier Ave 16505
Montrose Ave 16505
Montroyale Dr 16504
Moonlite Dr 16509
Moorehead St 16508
Moose Dr 16509
Moraine Dr 16509
Morehouse Rd 16509
Morning Glory Ct 16509
Morning Sun Ct 16506
Morningside Dr 16506
Morrison Dr 16505
Morse St 16511
Mountain Laurel Dr 16510
Mulligan Ct 16510
Murial Dr 16506
Myrtle St
100-599 16507
600-999 16502
1000-1399 16501
1500-2599 16502
2600-4099 16508
Mystic Rdg 16506
Nagle Rd
400-1299 16511
1800-1808 16510
1810-3299 16510
Nancy Ave 16510
Napier Ave 16511
Naples Ave 16509
Natalie Ct 16506
Nathan Cir 16509
Neptune Dr 16506
Nevada Dr 16505
New St 16504
Newman St 16507
Newton Ave 16511
Niagara Pl 16511
Niagara Pier 16507
Niagara Point Dr 16507
Nicholson St 16509
Nickel Dr 16509
Niemeyer Rd 16509
Nina Dr 16506
Nobel Ave 16511
Norcross Rd 16510
Norman Way 16508
Normandy Rue 16506
Norris Dr 16509
North St 16510
Northcrest Dr 16509
Northgate Dr 16505
Northview Dr 16511

Northwood Ln 16509
Oak Tree Ct 16511
Oakbark Ct 16506
Oakdale Pkwy 16505
Oakhill Rd 16506
Oakland St 16509
Oakley Dr 16506
Oakmont Ave 16505
E, N, S & W Oakridge Cir & Ct 16509
Oakwood St 16508
Ohio St 16505
Old French Rd
2800-4599 16504
4600-8999 16509
Old Mill Rd 16505
Old Oliver Rd 16509
Old Orchard Dr 16506
Old Perry Hwy 16509
Old Sterrettania Rd 16506
Old Waterford Rd 16509
Old Wattsburg Rd 16510
Old Zuck Rd 16506
Olde Farm Ln 16505
Oliver Rd 16509
Oneida St 16511
Oraindow Ave 16511
Orchard St 16508
Ore Dock Rd 16507
Oregon Ave 16505
Oriole Dr 16509
Ottawa Dr 16505
Otto St 16510
Overlook Dr 16505
Oxer Rd 16505
Oxford St 16505
Pacific Ave 16506
Pagan Rd 16509
Page St 16510
Palermo Cir & Dr 16506
Palomino Ct 16506
Pandora Dr 16505
Parade Blvd 16504
Parade St
100-599 16507
600-2599 16503
2600-3799 16504
Paragon Dr 16510
Park Ave E 16502
Park Ave N 16502
Park Ave S 16502
E Park Ln 16506
N Park Ln 16506
S Park Ln 16506
W Park Ln 16506
N Park Row 16501
S Park Row 16501
Park Harbor Dr 16511
Parker Ave 16510
Parkside Ave 16508
Parkside Dr 16511
Parkview Dr
100-199 16509
4100-4199 16506
Parkway Dr 16511
Parkwood Dr 16510
Parson Rd 16509
Partridge Dr 16509
Pasadena Dr 16505
Patio Dr 16506
Patlin Ct 16505
Patterson Ave 16508
Patton St 16509
Payne Ave 16503
Peach St
100-499 16507
500-1899 16501
1900-2599 16502
2600-3799 16508
3800-5623 16509
5624-5638 16565
5625-8899 16509
5642-5798 16509
5800-5802 16565
5804-8898 16509
Peach Grove Dr 16509

Peachtree Blvd 16509
Pear St 16510
Pearce Park 16502
Pearl Ave 16510
Pebble Dr 16508
Pebblestone Ct 16506
Peck Rd 16510
Pelham Rd 16511
Penelec Park Dr 16509
Peninsula Dr
1-1899 16505
2000-2599 16506
Pennbriar Dr 16509
Pennsylvania Ave
100-599 16507
600-2599 16503
2600-4199 16504
Pepper Ct 16505
Pepper Tree Dr 16510
Pepperwood Cir 16506
Perennial Way 16510
Perinella Dr 16505
Perkins St 16509
Perry Hwy 16509
Perry St
500-599 16507
600-2599 16503
2600-4399 16504
Pershing Ave 16509
Persimmon Dr 16509
Phyllis Dr 16510
Pier B Dr 16511
Pierpont Ave 16509
Pilgrim Dr 16509
Pin Oak Dr 16504
Pine Ave 16504
Pine Leaf Dr 16510
Pine Tree Ter 16506
Pinebark Ct 16506
Pinecrest Dr 16509
Pinegrove Way 16509
Pinehurst Dr 16509
Pinelawn Dr 16506
Pinesdale Ave 16510
Pineview Ct 16506
Pinewood Ln 16509
Pinnacle Ct 16506
Pinta Dr 16506
Pittsburgh Ave
200-1799 16505
1800-2599 16502
2700-3799 16508
4600-4999 16509
Plantation Ct 16505
Platinum Dr 16509
Plaza Dr 16506
Pleasant Valley Dr 16506
Pleasantview Ave 16509
Pleria Dr 16506
Plum Rd 16510
Plum St
100-599 16507
600-2599 16502
2600-3799 16508
Plymouth St 16505
Polito Dr 16505
Polk St 16503
Pond View Dr 16506
Ponderosa Dr 16509
Pontiac St 16511
Poplar St
100-599 16507
600-999 16502
1100-1199 16501
1300-2599 16502
2600-3799 16508
Port Access Rd 16507
Post Ave 16508
Potomac Ave 16505
Powell Ave
100-2099 16505
2100-2599 16506
Presque Isle Blvd 16505
Presta Ct 16506
Preston Ave 16511
Prestwick Dr 16506

W Prierso St 16502
Priestley Ave 16511
Prindle Rd 16510
Priscilla Dr 16506
Proctor Ave 16509
Prospect Ave 16510
Protane Blvd 16506
Providence Way 16509
Putnam Dr 16511
Queen St 16507
Quirk Dr 16509
Race Ave 16509
Rachel Ct 16509
Randolph Rd 16505
Rankine Ave 16511
Raspberry St
300-599 16507
600-2599 16502
2600-3799 16508
3800-4099 16509
Ravenwood Ln 16505
E Ravine Dr 16505
Ray St 16511
Raymond Ct 16505
Red Pine Ln 16506
Reed St
300-599 16507
600-2599 16503
2600-3799 16504
Reese Rd 16510
Regent St 16506
Regis Dr 16510
Reichert Rd 16509
Reilly Rd 16510
Rena Dr 16510
Rescue Ln 16510
Rice Ave 16510
Rice Ct 16505
Richard Dr 16509
Richmond St 16509
Ridge Blvd 16506
Ridge Pkwy 16510
W Ridge Rd 16506
Ridgedale Dr 16506
Ridgeview Dr 16505
Ridgewood Dr 16506
Rilling Ave 16509
Rinderle Dr 16509
Ripley Dr 16510
Rita Dr 16509
Riverside Dr 16510
Roberts Rd 16510
Robin Dr
2000-2199 16505
8600-8799 16509
Robinhood Ln 16509
Robison Rd E & W 16509
Rockledge Dr 16511
Roland Rd 16510
Rollahome Dr 16506
Roma Dr 16510
Rome Ct & Dr 16509
Rondeau Dr 16505
Rose Ave 16510
Rosebay St 16509
Rosedale Ave 16503
Rosemont Ave 16505
Rosewood Ln 16509
Roslindale Ave 16509
Roslyn Ave 16505
Ross St 16507
Rotunda Dr 16509
Route 8 16509
Roxanna Dr 16510
Roxbury Pl & Rd 16506
Royal Ave 16509
Rudolph Ave
1800-2599 16502
2600-3199 16508
Rumsey Ave 16511
Rustic Ln 16506
Ruth Ave 16509
Saddlehorn Dr 16506
Saga St 16510
Saint Andrew Dr 16509
Saint Ann Dr 16509

Saint Clair Ave 16505
Saint Mary Dr 16509
Saltsman Rd 16510
Saltsman Road Ext 16510
Samick Dr 16509
Sampson Rd 16509
Sandalwood Ct & Dr 16506
Sandstone Ct 16505
Sandy Trl 16510
Sanford Pl 16511
Santa Maria Dr 16506
Sara Ct 16504
Sassafras St
100-599 16507
600-1399 16501
1500-2599 16502
2600-4299 16508
Sassafras Pier 16507
Saybrook Pl 16505
Scarboro Rd 16506
Scarlett Cir 16506
Schaaf Pl 16503
Schaal Ave 16510
Schaper Ave
1900-2499 16502
2700-4199 16508
4200-4523 16509
4525-4599 16509
Schley St 16508
Schlindwein Dr 16509
School Rd 16505
Schrimper Rd 16510
Schultz Rd 16509
Schwab Rd 16510
Schwartz Dr 16509
Scoralls Mall 16565
Scott St 16508
Selden Rd 16505
Selinger Ave 16505
Seminole Dr 16505
Seneca St 16511
Shades Beach Rd 16511
Shady Ave & Dr 16509
Shady Hollow Dr 16506
Shadybrook Dr 16506
Shadyside Dr 16505
Shamrock Ct 16510
Shannon Rd 16510
Sharpe Ave 16510
Shawnee Dr 16505
N Shelby Dr 16509
Sheldon Dr 16509
Shellbark Ct 16506
Shenk Ave 16505
Shenley Dr 16505
Shepard Dr 16509
Sheridan Ave 16509
Sherwood Dr 16506
N Shore Dr 16511
S Shore Dr 16505
Shorehaven Dr 16505
Short St 16507
Shunpike Rd 16508
Side Wood Dr 16505
Sierra Dr 16506
Sigsbee St 16508
Sill Ave 16505
Silliman Ave 16511
Silo Ct 16509
Silver Dr 16509
Silver Maple Cir 16509
Silverwood Ln 16505
Sir Andred Dr 16506
Sir Hue Dr 16506
Sir Kay Dr 16506
Sir Lancelot Dr 16506
Skellie Ave 16510
Sky Dr 16510
Skyline Dr 16509
Smithson Ave 16511
Snowbury St 16509
Snug Harbor Ct 16505
Sobieski St 16507
Society Ct 16509
Sodhaven Dr 16509
Solar Dr 16506

Sommerheim Dr 16505
South St 16510
E South Shore Dr 16511
Southern Cir & Dr 16506
Southgate Dr 16509
Southland Dr 16509
Southview Dr 16509
Southwest Cir 16506
Southwind Ln 16506
Sparkhill Ave 16511
Sparton Dr 16510
Spiral Ct 16510
Spires Dr 16509
Spring Lake Dr 16505
Spring Valley Dr 16509
Springland Ter 16506
Springview Dr 16509
Spruce Dr 16506
Sprucewood Ln 16509
Squirrel Dr 16509
Stafford Ave 16508
Stanley Ave 16504
Stanton St 16510
Starflower Dr 16509
State St
1-399 16507
400-1400 16501
1401-1999 16501
1401-1401 16512
1402-1998 16501
2100-2599 16503
2600-4299 16508
4300-4699 16509
1911-1919-1911-1919 16501
Station Rd 16510
Steger Rd 16510
Steimer Rd 16510
Stellar Dr 16506
Sterling Ave 16510
Sterrettania Rd 16506
Stewart Dr 16510
Stillwater Cir 16506
Stirrup Dr 16506
Stockbridge Dr 16505
Stone Dr 16509
Stone Creek Dr 16506
Stonebridge Dr 16506
Stonegate Dr 16505
Stoney Trace Ln 16510
Stoneybrook Dr 16510
Stough Ave 16508
Stoughton Rd 16506
Strathmore Ave 16505
Streamwood Dr 16506
Strong Dr 16505
Stuart Way 16509
Sturbridge Dr 16509
Suburban Ln 16506
Summer St 16509
Summerland Trl 16506
Summerville Rd 16510
Summit St 16508
Sumner Dr 16505
Sun Ct 16509
Sun Valley Ct 16509
Sunlight Dr 16509
Sunnycrest Dr 16506
Sunnydale Blvd 16509
Sunnylane Dr 16505
Sunrise Lakes Dr 16509
Sunset Blvd 16504
Superior Ave 16505
Susan St 16510
Suzanne Dr 16510
Swan Lake Ln 16506
Swanville Rd 16506
Sybil Dr 16505
Sycamore Dr 16505
Tacoma Rd 16511
Taggert St 16510
Taki Dr 16505
Talley Rd 16509
Talmadge Rd 16509
Tamarack Dr 16506
Tampa Blvd 16509
Tanager Dr 16506
Tanglewood Dr 16510
Tarra St 16510
Tate Rd 16509
Taylor Ave 16511
Taylor Ridge Ct 16505
Teakwood Ct 16506
Tennyson Ct 16509
Teri Ave 16510
Terrace Dr 16505
Thelma Dr 16510
Thompson St 16510
Thoroughbred Loop 16506
Timber Ln 16506
Timber Ridge Dr 16509
Timbercreek Dr 16509
Timbercrest Ct 16506
Timberline Dr 16506
Timberwood Ln 16509
Tomart Dr 16509
Tonquin St 16506
Top Rd 16505
Tory Dr 16509
Tower Ln 16505
Townhall Rd W 16509
Townsend Dr 16505
N & S Tracy Dr 16505
Tramarlac Ln 16505
Trask Ave 16508
Tree Haven Ct 16506
Treetop Dr 16509
Tremont Pkwy 16509
Trimble Stone 16506
Trinity Dr 16505
Troon Ave 16506
Tulane Ave 16506
Tulip Tree Dr 16506
Turnpike St 16501
Tuttle Ave 16504
Twilight Dr 16505
Tyndall Ave 16511
Union Ave 16510
Upland Dr 16509
Usonia Ave 16509
Valencia Ct 16506
Valley View Cir 16509
Vallindi St 16501
Van Buren Ave 16504
Vandalia Ave 16511
Vanessa Ln 16506
Vanintan Rd 16515
Vassar Dr 16506
Veit Dr 16509
Venice Dr 16506
Ventoura Dr 16510
Vermont Ave 16505
Vernon Dr 16505
Veshecco Dr 16501
Vicki Ct 16509
Victoria Way 16509
Victory Dr 16510
Village St 16506
Village Common Dr 16506
Vine St 16503
Vineyard Dr 16506
Virginia Ave 16505
Vista Dr 16506
Volkman Rd 16506
Voyageur Dr 16505
Vulcan Dr 16505
Wabash Ave 16509
Wager Rd 16509
Wagner Ave 16510
Wagner Rd 16509
Walbridge Rd 16511
Wales Rd 16510
Walker Blvd 16509
Wallace St
100-599 16507
600-2599 16503
2600-3799 16504
Walnut Rdg 16506
Walnut St
100-599 16507
600-999 16502
1100-1299 16501
1400-1899 16502
2900-3199 16508
Walten Pt 16511
Walten Creek Dr 16511
Walten Woods Dr 16511
Wana Dr 16505
Warfel Ave
2000-2399 16503
2500-2699 16510
Warsaw Ave 16504
Washington Ave
2400-2499 16502
2600-3799 16508
3800-6799 16509
Washington Pl
300-399 16505
600-2399 16502
Water St 16510
Water View Ln 16509
Waterhouse Dr 16510
Watson Rd 16505
Wattsburg Rd
4600-5099 16504
5100-10879 16509
Wattsburg Road Ext 16509
Wave Dr 16505
Wayne St
1-599 16507
600-2599 16503
2600-4599 16504
N & S Wayside Dr 16505
Weatherwood Trl 16506
Weber Ln 16509
Webster Dr 16505
Wedgewood Dr 16505
Weiss Ct 16505
Wellington Rd 16506
Weschler Ave 16502
Wesley Ave 16510
West St 16509
Westbury Rdg 16506
Westbury Farms Dr 16506
Western Ln 16505
Westgate Dr 16509
Westline St 16506
Westminster Blvd 16506
Westwind Ln 16506
Westwood Dr 16505
Westwood Estates Dr 16506
White Birch Ln 16509
White Oak Cir 16506
White Pine Dr 16506
Whitehouse Dr 16505
Whitley Ave 16503
Whitney Way 16511
Wild Cherry Ln 16509
Wildberry Ln 16505
Wildflower Ct 16509
Wildman Rd 16510
Wildwood Way 16511
Wilkins Rd 16505
Williams Rd 16510
Willis St 16506
Willow Gln 16509
Willow Rd 16505
Willow St 16510
Willowood Dr 16506
Wilshire Rd 16509
Wilson St 16507
Wiltsie Rd 16510
Winchester Rd 16506
Windcrest Dr 16510
Windsor Dr 16506
Windsor Beach Ct 16511
Windward Dr 16505
Winesap Dr 16509
Winners Cir 16506
Winslow Dr 16509
Winterberry Ln 16510
Wintergreen Dr 16510
Winthrop Dr 16506
Wolf Rd 16505
Wolf Point Dr 16505
Wolf Run Ct & Dr 16505
Wolf Run Village Ln 16505
Wolverine Ave 16511
Wood Ln 16511
Wood St 16509
Wood Hills Dr 16510
Woodbine Ter 16504
Woodbriar Ln 16505
Woodbridge Ct 16509
Woodbrook Lndg 16506
Woodbury Dr 16510
Woodcrest Ct 16506
Woodhaven Dr 16506
Woodland Dr 16505
Woodland Hills Cir 16509
Woodlawn Ave 16510
Woodrose Ln 16510
Woodrow St 16502
N Woods Dr 16511
Woodsdale Ave 16510
Woodside Dr 16505
Woodview Dr 16506
Woodward Dr 16509
Wynburne Ave 16509
Wyndemere Dr 16505
Wyndham Ct 16505
Wyngate Rd 16505
Wyoming Ave 16505
Yale Dr 16510
Yoder Dr 16506
Young Rd 16509
Zachary Dr 16510
Zaunegger St 16509
Zemville Dr 16509
Zenith Dr 16510
Zephyr Ave 16505
Zimmerly Rd
1700-2199 16509
2200-4099 16506
Zimmerman Rd 16510
Zoar Ave 16509
Zuck Rd
2600-5599 16506
6200-6999 16509
Zwilling Rd E & W 16509

NUMBERED STREETS

E 1st St 16507
E 2nd St
1-1099 16507
1800-2199 16511
W 2nd St 16507
E & W 3rd 16507
E 4th St
1-1199 16507
1800-2199 16511
W 4th St
1-1199 16507
1400-2599 16505
E & W 5th 16507
E 6th St
101-199 16501
200-999 16507
1800-1899 16511
W 6th St
100-108 16501
110-199 16501
200-1299 16507
1300-3099 16505
E 7th St
1-199 16501
200-1499 16503
1800-2199 16511
W 7th St
1-299 16501
300-1299 16502
E 8th St
1-199 16501
200-1499 16503
1800-1999 16511
W 8th St
1-299 16501
300-1439 16502
1441-1499 16502
1500-2899 16505
E 9th St
1-99 16501
200-1499 16503
W 9th St
1-299 16501
300-1399 16502
1600-2599 16505
E 10th St 16511
E 10th St 16511
E 10th St 16511
1-199 16501
200-1499 16503
1500-2199 16511
W 10th St
1-299 16501
300-1499 16502
2500-4199 16505
E 11th St
2046A-2046Z 16511
1-199 16501
200-1399 16503
2000-2099 16511
W 11th St
1-799 16501
800-1499 16502
1600-4399 16505
E 12th St
1-199 16501
200-1499 16503
1500-2199 16511
W 12th St
1-1599 16501
1600-4699 16505
E 13th St
1-99 16501
100-799 16503
W 13th St
1-199 16501
1600-3599 16505
E 14th St
1-99 16501
100-799 16503
W 14th St
1-199 16501
700-899 16502
1671-4199 16505
E 15th St 16503
600-699 16502
1600-4199 16505
E 16th St
1-99 16501
100-599 16503
1900-2299 16510
W 16th St
200-1399 16502
1600-3999 16505
4001-4099 16505
E 17th St
1-99 16501
100-499 16503
1900-2299 16510
W 17th St
200-1299 16502
2600-3599 16505
E 18th St
1-99 16501
100-1499 16503
1500-2299 16510
W 18th St
1-199 16501
200-1399 16502
2700-2799 16505
E 19th St
100-1499 16503
1500-2299 16510
W 19th St 16502
E 20th St
100-1499 16503
1500-2299 16510
W 20th St
100-2099 16502
2500-2699 16506
3800-4099 16505
E 21st St 16503
1-2199 16502
2300-2899 16506
E 22nd St 16503
100-2199 16502
2500-3599 16506
E 23rd St 16503
100-2199 16502
2200-4999 16506
E 24th St 16503
1-2099 16502
2500-3299 16506
E 25th St 16503
100-2099 16502
2500-3299 16506
E 26th St
1-1299 16504
1500-2699 16510
W 26th St
1-2199 16508
2400-3799 16506
E 27th St
200-1299 16504
1600-2999 16510
W 27th St
800-2099 16508
3600-3799 16506
E 28th St
100-1499 16504
1700-2999 16510
W 28th St
400-1599 16508
4000-4499 16506
E 29th St
1-1499 16504
2600-2999 16510
W 29th St
1-2199 16508
2200-2499 16506
E 30th St
1-1499 16504
1500-2999 16510
W 30th St
1-2099 16508
2600-4199 16506
E 31st St
1-1499 16504
1500-2999 16510
W 31st St
1-1799 16508
2600-2999 16506
E 32nd St
1-1499 16504
2400-2999 16510
W 32nd St
1-2199 16508
2200-4299 16506
E 33rd St
1-1499 16504
1800-3099 16510
W 33rd St
1-2199 16508
2700-3599 16506
E 34th St
1-1499 16504
1800-2799 16510
W 34th St
1-2199 16508
2300-3599 16506
E 35th St
1-1499 16504
1500-2799 16510
W 35th St
1-2199 16508
2500-2899 16506
E 36th St
1-1499 16504
1901-1997 16510
1999-2799 16510
W 36th St
1-2199 16508
2200-2499 16506
E 37th St
1-1499 16504
1600-2699 16510
W 37th St
1-2139 16508
2141-2199 16508
2300-2699 16506
E 38th St
1-1499 16504
1500-2105 16510
2106-2108 16515
2107-3099 16510
2108-2108 16514
2110-3098 16510
W 38th St
1-2199 16508
2200-5599 16506
E 39th St
200-1199 16504
2500-2599 16510
W 39th St
1-399 16508
600-1799 16509
3200-3399 16506
E 40th St
700-1499 16504
1500-2599 16510
W 40th St
180-198 16508
200-399 16508
600-1799 16509
3100-3499 16506
E 41st St
1-1499 16504
1700-2799 16510
W 41st St
1-399 16508
1100-1799 16509
3100-3499 16506
E 42nd St
100-1299 16504
1500-2799 16510
W 42nd St
1-299 16508
1300-1799 16509
2900-3599 16506
E 43rd St
2324A-2324Z 16510
2340A-2340Z 16510
600-1099 16504
1700-2799 16510
W 43rd St
1300-1599 16509
3200-3599 16506
E 44th St
800-899 16504
2300-2799 16510
W 44th St 16509
W 45th St 16509
W 50th St
600-1899 16509
2200-2399 16506
W 51st St 16509
W 52nd St 16509
W 53rd St 16509
3000-3199 16506
W 54th St 16509
W 55th St 16509
W 56th St 16509
W 57th St 16509
W 59th St 16509

GENESEE PA

General Delivery 16923

POST OFFICE BOXES MAIN OFFICE STATIONS AND BRANCHES

Box No.s
All PO Boxes 16923

NAMED STREETS

Academy St 16923
Andrew Settlement Rd 16923
Bacon Rd 16923
Bailey Corners Rd 16923
Ben Green Rd 16923
N & W Bingham Rd 16923
Bingham Center Rd
1-1699 16923
1800-2399 16941
Blair Rd 16923
Brizzee Hollow Rd 16923

N Brookland Rd ... 16923
Butter Creek Rd ... 16923
Cemetary Rd ... 16923
Church St ... 16923
Cobb Hill Rd ... 16923
Collins Hill Rd ... 16923
Commercial St ... 16923
Cooney Rd ... 16923
Cooper Rd ... 16923
Corcoran Rd ... 16923
Dogtown Rd ... 16923
Easton Rd ... 16923
Eleven Mile Rd ... 16923
Ellisburg Rd ... 16923
Estes Rd ... 16923
Flat Jack Rd ... 16923
French Rooney Rd ... 16923
G Crippen Rd ... 16923
Gazdag Rd ... 16923
N Genesee St ... 16923
Genesee Mills Rd
600-2399 ... 16923
2100-2799 ... 16941
Glenhaven Ln ... 16923
Gold Rd ... 16923
Grover Hollow Rd ... 16923
Haskell Rd ... 16923
Hemlock Hollow Rd ... 16923
Hickox Rd ... 16923
Hickox Ulysses Rd ... 16923
Hillcrest Rd ... 16923
Junction Rd ... 16923
Kidney Rd ... 16923
Kinney Rd ... 16923
Leadville Hollow Ln ... 16923
Low Rd ... 16923
Main St ... 16923
Mcginnis Rd ... 16923
Mchale Rd ... 16923
Millstead Dr ... 16923
Morley Rd ... 16923
Mountain View Rd ... 16923
Odonnell Rd ... 16923
Outback Ln ... 16923
Peet Brook Rd ... 16923
Pierce Hill Rd ... 16923
Plearra Rd ... 16941
Pratt Dr ... 16923
Pump Station Rd ... 16923
Raghill Rd ... 16923
Rapley Rd ... 16923
Reynoldstown Rd ... 16923
Ridge Rd ... 16923
River Rd ... 16923
Rocco Dr ... 16923
Rooks Rd ... 16923
Rose Lake Ln & Rd ... 16923
School St ... 16923
School House Rd ... 16923
Scoville Hill Rd ... 16923
Shongo St ... 16923
Silver Fox Ln ... 16923
Simmon Hollow Rd ... 16923
Slingerland Rd ... 16923
Smoker Rd ... 16923
State Route 449 N ... 16923
State Route 49 W ... 16923
Teeter Rd ... 16923
Weaver Rd ... 16923
Webster Rd ... 16923
Whitney Hill Rd ... 16923
Wiles Rd ... 16923
Windfall Rd ... 16923
Wintergreen Rd ... 16923

HARRISBURG PA

General Delivery ... 17105

POST OFFICE BOXES MAIN OFFICE STATIONS AND BRANCHES

Box No.s
1 - 1298 ... 17108
1 - 3 ... 17129
1301 - 3899 ... 17105
4001 - 4999 ... 17111
5001 - 5980 ... 17110
6001 - 6997 ... 17112
7246 - 7651 ... 17113
8001 - 8945 ... 17105
9002 - 9500 ... 17108
10032 - 10778 ... 17105
11401 - 12112 ... 17108
13001 - 13240 ... 17110
15001 - 15758 ... 17105
60001 - 81240 ... 17106
90005 - 90235 ... 17109
126101 - 126754 ... 17112

NAMED STREETS

A Ln ... 17111
A V Acri Rd ... 17112
Abbey Ln ... 17112
Abbington Dr ... 17109
Aberdeen Ct & Dr ... 17111
Academy Dr ... 17112
Acorn Dr ... 17111
Acri Dr ... 17111
Adams Ave ... 17112
Adams St ... 17113
Adrian St ... 17104
Agate St ... 17110
Agnes St ... 17104
Ailanthus Ln ... 17110
Akron Dr ... 17109
Albany Rd ... 17112
Albright Rd ... 17110
Alden Dr ... 17112
Alden St ... 17109
Alessandro Blvd ... 17110
Alexis Dr ... 17110
Alfano Dr ... 17112
Allegheny Dr ... 17112
Allen Hall ... 17104
Allentown Blvd ... 17112
Alleo Ln ... 17111
Allison St ... 17104
Almari Ln ... 17111
Alpine St ... 17112
Alricks St ... 17110
Altavista Ave
400-699 ... 17109
800-999 ... 17111
Althea Ave ... 17112
Alva Dr ... 17112
Amanda Dr ... 17112
Amber Ln
1100-1299 ... 17111
1300-1399 ... 17112
Ambrosia Cir ... 17110
Amesbury Ln ... 17112
Amherst Dr ... 17109
Amity Rd ... 17111
Amy Dr ... 17112
Anaheim Ct ... 17112
Andrea Ave ... 17109
Angenese St ... 17110
Angle Ave
1-99 ... 17103
300-399 ... 17113
Ann St ... 17111
Anthony Dr ... 17111
Antoine St ... 17110
Anton St ... 17113
Apollo Ave ... 17110
Appalachian Trl E & W ... 17112
Appleby Ct & Rd ... 17112
Appletree Rd ... 17110
Apricot St ... 17103
Arbys Rd ... 17109
Arcadia St ... 17112
Ardin Dr ... 17111
Argyle St ... 17104
Arklow Dr ... 17111
N & S Arlene St ... 17112
N & S Arlington Ave ... 17109
Arminda St ... 17109
Arney Rd ... 17111
Arnold Ave & Dr ... 17112
Arrow Rd ... 17109
Arsenal Blvd ... 17103
Arthur Dr ... 17110
Ash St ... 17109
Ashbury Dr ... 17112
Ashdon Dr ... 17112
Ashwood Way ... 17109
Aspen Dr ... 17109
Aspen Way ... 17110
Aster Dr ... 17112
Aston Ct ... 17111
Athena Ave ... 17110
Atlas St ... 17110
Atmore St ... 17112
Atticks Ln ... 17111
Audubon Dr ... 17111
Augusta Dr ... 17112
Autumn Dr ... 17111
Autumn Chase ... 17110
Autumn View Dr ... 17112
Autumn Wood Dr ... 17112
Avalon Ct ... 17111
Avila Rd ... 17109
Avis Ln ... 17112
Avon Dr ... 17112
Avondale Ter ... 17112
Aynlee Way ... 17112
Azalea Dr ... 17110
E Azalea Dr ... 17110
Azalea Trl ... 17112
B Ln ... 17111
Baikel Ct ... 17112
Bailey St
1228A-1228F ... 17103
101-297 ... 17113
299-399 ... 17113
401-499 ... 17113
1100-1399 ... 17103
Baker St ... 17103
Baldwin Ln ... 17110
Balm St ... 17103
Balthaser St ... 17112
Bamberger Rd ... 17110
Banbridge Dr ... 17112
Banks St ... 17103
Barbara Dr ... 17111
Barbara Ln
2-98 ... 17112
100-199 ... 17112
200-299 ... 17111
Barbara St ... 17101
Barkley Ln ... 17104
Barley Corn Sq ... 17112
Barnett Cir ... 17112
Barnsley Dr ... 17111
Barnwood Pl ... 17112
Bartine St ... 17102
Bartlett Rd ... 17110
Baseshore Dr ... 17112
Basin St ... 17102
Bass Lake Dr ... 17111
Batesfield Rd ... 17109
Baumgardner Dr ... 17112
E & W Bayberry Dr ... 17112
Baywood Dr ... 17111
Beacon Dr ... 17112
Beale St ... 17113
Beaucrest St ... 17111
Beaufort St ... 17111
Beaufort Farms Rd ... 17110
Beaufort Hills Rd ... 17110
Beaufort Hunt Dr ... 17110
Beaver Rd ... 17112
Beaver Creek Rd ... 17112
Beaver Spring Rd ... 17111
Beck Cir ... 17111
Bedford St ... 17111
Beech Dr & St ... 17110
Beech Tree Dr ... 17111
Beechwood Ln & Rd ... 17112
Belair Rd ... 17109
Bell Rd ... 17111
Bellevue Rd ... 17104
Belmont Dr ... 17112
Belvedere Rd ... 17109
Bennington Dr ... 17112
Benton Ct ... 17112
Benton St ... 17104
Bergner St ... 17110
Berkley Dr ... 17112
Berkley St ... 17109
Berkshire Ln ... 17111
Berkstone Cir & Dr ... 17112
Berry Dr & Ln ... 17112
Berryhill Rd ... 17109
Berryhill St ... 17104
Bertha Dr ... 17113
Berwyn Dr ... 17112
Bessemer St ... 17113
Bethel Dr ... 17111
Bethlynn Dr ... 17112
Beverly Dr ... 17109
Bigelow Ct & Dr ... 17103
Birch St ... 17109
Birch Knoll Dr ... 17111
Birchwood Cir ... 17110
Birchwood Dr ... 17109
Birchwood Rd ... 17112
Birmingham Pl ... 17111
Bishop Ave ... 17113
Blachamb St ... 17109
Black Bear Ln ... 17112
Blackberry Ln ... 17112
Blackberry St ... 17113
Blackheath Ln ... 17109
Blacksmith Ln ... 17112
Blakeslee Ave ... 17111
Blanchester Rd ... 17112
Blarney Dr ... 17112
Blue Bell Ave ... 17112
Blue Bird Ave ... 17112
Blue Eagle Ave ... 17112
Blue Flag Ave ... 17112
Blue Grass Ave ... 17112
Blue Hen Ct ... 17112
Blue Jay Rd ... 17111
Blue Mountain Pkwy ... 17112
N & S Blue Ribbon Ave ... 17112
Blue Ridge Ave ... 17112
Blue Ridge Cir ... 17110
Blue Ridge Rd ... 17110
Blue Stone Ave ... 17112
Blue Valley Ave ... 17112
Blueberry Ln ... 17111
Boas St
217A-217F ... 17102
100-500 ... 17102
502-698 ... 17102
1500-3199 ... 17103
Bobali Dr ... 17104
Bogar Ave ... 17110
Bollinger Rd ... 17109
Bolton Dr ... 17112
Bolton Notch Pl ... 17110
Bombaugh St ... 17103
Bonita Ct ... 17110
Bonnybrook Rd ... 17109
Bonnymead Ave & Cir ... 17111
Bonnyview Rd ... 17109
Bonnywick Dr ... 17111
Booser Ave ... 17103
Bordeaux Ct ... 17112
Boundbrook Rd ... 17109
Bower Ln ... 17112
Bowling Rd ... 17112
Boyd St ... 17102
Boyer St ... 17113
Bradford Blvd & Rd ... 17112
Bradley Ct ... 17112
Bradley Dr ... 17110
Brady St ... 17103
Braeburn Ln ... 17110
Braewood Dr ... 17111
Brandywine Ct, Dr & Rd ... 17110
Breckenridge Dr ... 17112
Brei Cir ... 17112
Bretney Dr ... 17112
Bretz Dr ... 17112
Brian Dr ... 17110
Briar Dr ... 17111
Briar Cliff Rd ... 17104
Briarsdale Rd ... 17109
Briarwood Ct ... 17110
Bridle Ct ... 17111
Bridle Ln ... 17112
Briggs St
200-270 ... 17102
272-298 ... 17102
1500-2099 ... 17103
Brighton Ct ... 17112
Brighton St ... 17113
Brindle Dr ... 17110
Brisban St ... 17111
Bristol Dr ... 17109
Britannia Ct ... 17112
Brittan Rd ... 17111
Brittany Blvd ... 17109
Broadway St ... 17111
Brook Ln ... 17111
Brook St
300-399 ... 17104
600-699 ... 17110
Brookdale Dr ... 17111
Brookdale Rd ... 17112
Brookes Ln ... 17110
Brookfield Rd ... 17109
Brookridge Ct ... 17112
Brookridge Ter ... 17109
Brookside Dr ... 17109
Brooksvale Ct ... 17110
Brookwood St
1801-1845 ... 17104
1847-2599 ... 17104
2600-3199 ... 17111
Brookwood Ter ... 17110
Brown St ... 17109
Brushfield Ct ... 17109
Brynfield Way ... 17112
Brytton Ln ... 17110
Buck Run Ln ... 17110
Buckingham Ave & Rd ... 17111
Buckley Dr ... 17112
Bucks St ... 17111
Buckthorn St ... 17104
Buick Ave ... 17109
Bur Ct ... 17112
Burchfield St ... 17104
Burgundy Rd ... 17112
Burlington Dr ... 17112
Burton Ln ... 17110
Butler St ... 17103
Buttermilk Ct ... 17111
Buttonwood Cir ... 17110
Buttonwood Dr ... 17109
Buttonwood Pl ... 17109
Buxton Ct & Rd ... 17110
Byron Ave ... 17109
C Ln ... 17111
Calder St
100-599 ... 17102
1400-1499 ... 17103
Caledonia St ... 17104
California Ave ... 17109
Calvary Rd ... 17112
Calvert St ... 17109
Cambria Ave ... 17111
Cambridge St ... 17109
Camden Ct & Dr ... 17112
Camelot Dr ... 17110
Cameron St ... 17113
N Cameron St
2-24 ... 17101
26-149 ... 17101
151-999 ... 17101
1000-1098 ... 17103
1100-2000 ... 17103
2002-2098 ... 17103
2300-2306 ... 17110
2308-2398 ... 17110
S Cameron St
1459A-1459B ... 17104
8-72 ... 17101
74-499 ... 17101
501-597 ... 17104
599-1799 ... 17104
Cameron Ter ... 17104
Camp St ... 17110
Camp Reiley Rd ... 17112
Campbell Ct ... 17112
Canby St
2300-3099 ... 17103
3400-3599 ... 17109
Candlestick Dr ... 17112
Candlewood Dr ... 17112
Canter Ct ... 17111
Canterbury Rd ... 17109
Canton St ... 17113
Canyon Rd ... 17111
Capital Dr
1-99 ... 17110
7201-7299 ... 17111
Capital St ... 17102
Carbon Ave ... 17111
Cardiff St ... 17109
Cardigan Ct ... 17112
Cardinal Ct & Dr ... 17111
Care St ... 17109
Carey St ... 17103
N Carl St ... 17112
Carlisle St
200-298 ... 17113
301-301 ... 17104
303-399 ... 17104
Carlson Rd ... 17112
Carlton Ave ... 17111
Carmen Ct ... 17112
Carnation St ... 17103
Carol Dr ... 17110
N & S Carolina Ct & Dr ... 17112
Carolyn St ... 17112
Carrington Ct ... 17112
Carrollton Dr ... 17112
Carter Dr ... 17109
Cassel Ave ... 17112
Catalina Ln ... 17109
Catherine Dr
7100-7299 ... 17112
7600-7699 ... 17111
Catherine St
200-298 ... 17113
300-399 ... 17113
401-499 ... 17113
1400-1699 ... 17104
2500-2899 ... 17109
5700-6399 ... 17112
Cattail Dr ... 17111
Caughey Dr ... 17110
Cedar Ln ... 17112
Cedar Rd ... 17110
Cedar Ridge Ln ... 17112
Center Ct ... 17111
Center St ... 17113
Centerfield Dr ... 17112
Centerfield Rd ... 17109
Central Ave ... 17112
Central Ter ... 17111
Chadwick Ct ... 17110
Chambers St ... 17113
Chambers Hill Rd ... 17111
Championship Way ... 17101
Chapel St ... 17112
Charcoal Rd ... 17112
Charles Dr ... 17112
Charles St
200-298 ... 17102
3100-3199 ... 17103
Charlton Rd ... 17112
Chartwood Dr ... 17111
Chatham Ct ... 17111
Chatham Dr ... 17111
Chatham Way ... 17110
Chatham Glenn Way N ... 17111
Chaucer Dr ... 17111
Chelsea Ln ... 17109
Chelton Ave ... 17112
Cheraliz Rd ... 17112
Cherrington Dr ... 17110
Cherrington Ln ... 17111
Cherry Rd ... 17110
Cherry Hill Rd ... 17111
Chervil Ct ... 17112
Cheryl Dr ... 17109
Chesterfield Ct ... 17112
Chestnut Ave ... 17112
Chestnut St
1-99 ... 17113
100-198 ... 17101
200-399 ... 17101
1000-1099 ... 17113
1200-2499 ... 17104
3900-3999 ... 17109
N Chestnut St ... 17109
Chestnut Ridge Ln ... 17112
Chevy Chase Dr ... 17110
Chiara Dr ... 17112
Chloe Ct ... 17110
Christian St
300-398 ... 17113
1100-1299 ... 17104
Christians Dr ... 17112
Christopher Pl ... 17110
Church Ln ... 17112
Church St
600-698 ... 17101
900-1098 ... 17113
Churchill Rd ... 17111
Cider Press Rd ... 17111
Circle Dr ... 17112
E Circle Dr ... 17111
N Circle Dr ... 17110
S Circle Dr ... 17110
W Circle Dr ... 17110
Clarendon St ... 17109
Clark St ... 17110
Clayton Ave ... 17109
Clearfield St ... 17111
Clearview Ave ... 17111
Clermont Dr ... 17112
Clifdon Ct ... 17111
Cliff Rd ... 17112
Clinton Rd ... 17109
Clinton St ... 17102
Clover Ct ... 17111
Clover Ln ... 17113
N Clover Ln ... 17112
S Clover Ln ... 17112
Clover Rd ... 17112
Clover Lee Blvd ... 17112
Cloverdale Rd ... 17112
Cloverfield Rd ... 17109
Cloverly Rd & Ter ... 17104
Club Dr ... 17110
Clubhouse Ct, Dr & Pl ... 17111
Cobble Stone Cir & Dr ... 17112
Cockley Rd ... 17111
Colchester Ave ... 17111
Coles Dr ... 17109
Colleen Dr ... 17109
Collier Way ... 17111
Collingswood Dr ... 17109
Collington Ct ... 17112
Colonial Rd
100-298 ... 17109
300-499 ... 17109
500-898 ... 17112
900-2799 ... 17112
3500-3899 ... 17109
Colonial Club Dr ... 17112
Colonial Park Mall ... 17109
Colorado Ave ... 17109
Columbia Ave ... 17109
Columbia St ... 17113
Colwyn Dr ... 17109
Commerce Dr ... 17110
Commons Dr ... 17112
Community Dr ... 17103
Compass St ... 17104
Compton Dr ... 17112
Concert Dr ... 17103
Concord Cir ... 17110
Concord St ... 17109
Conestoga St ... 17113
Connecticut Dr ... 17112
Conoy St ... 17104

Constitution Ave 17109
Continental Dr
2000-2300 17110
2302-2498 17110
4000-4399 17112
Conway Rd 17111
Copperfield Dr 17112
Copperstone Rd 17111
Cordial Ln 17111
Corey Rd 17109
Coriander Way 17112
Cornell Ct 17111
Cornell Rd 17112
Corporate Cir 17110
Cortland Rd 17110
Cotswold Dr 17110
Cottage Dr 17112
Cottagehill Ln 17113
Cotton Dr 17112
Count St 17109
Country Club Rd 17110
Country Hill Dr 17111
Country Lake Dr 17111
Country View Dr 17112
Countryside Dr 17110
Countryside Ln 17112
N Court St 17101
S Court St 17104
Cove Rd 17109
Coventry Rd 17109
Covey Ct 17110
Cowden St 17102
Cranberry Cir 17110
Credit Union Pl 17110
Creek Dr 17112
Creek Bed Dr 17110
Creek Bottom Dr 17112
Creek Crossing Dr 17111
Creek Run Rd 17111
Creekwood Dr 17109
Crescent St 17104
Crest Rd 17109
Crestmont Dr 17112
Crestview Rd 17112
Crestwood Dr 17109
Cricket Ln 17112
Crispen Villa Rd 17112
Crooked St 17104
Crooked Hill Rd
1300-1400 17110
1402-4698 17110
1425-1425 17106
1425-1425 17105
1601-4699 17110
Crosby St 17112
Crown Ave 17109
Croyden Rd 17104
Crums Ln 17112
Crums Mill Rd
1300-1399 17112
1400-2299 17110
4000-4198 17112
4200-4299 17112
Crusader Way 17111
Cumberland Ave 17110
Cumberland Ct 17102
Cumberland Rd
1100B-1116B 17103
1100D-1120D 17103
1200E-1218E 17103
1200F-1216F 17103
1200G-1216G 17103
1200H-1220H 17103
1101B-1117B 17103
1101C-1117C 17103
1101D-1121D 17103
1201E-1219E 17103
1201F-1217F 17103
1201G-1217G 17103
1201H-1221H 17103
1100A-1116A 17103
1100C-1106C 17103
1101A-1117A 17103
1109-1109 17103
Cumberland St
100-299 17102
900-1298 17103
1300-1499 17103
1501-1799 17103
4400-4798 17111
4800-5000 17111
5002-5098 17111
Cumbler St 17113
Curtin St 17110
Curvin Dr 17112
Cushing Pl 17109
Custan Dr 17110
Custer Dr & Ter 17110
Cypress Dr 17110
Cypress Rd 17112
Cypress St 17113
D Ave 17113
D Ln 17111
Dairy Ct 17111
Daisy St 17104
Dana Dr 17109
Danbury Rd 17109
Daniel Dr 17112
Danner Rd 17112
Darby Pl & Rd 17109
Darlington Ave 17111
Darlington Dr 17112
Daron Aly 17113
Dartmouth St 17109
Dauphin St 17102
Davids Rd 17111
Davis St 17109
Dawn Mar St 17111
Day Star Dr 17111
Daybreak Cir 17110
Dayhill Rd 17109
Dayton Rd 17113
Deaven Rd
100-199 17112
201-299 17112
301-303 17111
305-399 17111
Deckert Rd 17109
Deer Forest Rd 17111
Deer Path Rd 17110
Deer Run Ct 17112
Deerfield Dr 17112
Deimler Ln 17111
Delano Blvd 17111
Delaware St 17102
Delmont Ave 17111
Delmont Ct 17112
Dennis Cir 17111
Derby Ct 17112
Derbyshire Rd 17112
Derrick Dr 17112
Derry St
1100-2399 17104
2400-8000 17111
8002-8198 17111
Devon Dr 17112
Devonshire Rd
4300-5099 17109
5101-5397 17112
5399-6099 17112
Devonshire Heights Rd
5601-5687 17112
5689-6299 17112
6400-7399 17111
S Dewberry St
2-98 17101
201-299 17104
Dewey Dr 17112
Dewey St 17113
Dewitt Ave 17109
Diaiuto Dr 17111
Diamond Ct 17111
Diana Dr 17110
Dianne Dr 17111
Dietz Ln 17112
Disbrow St 17103
Division St 17110
Dodson Ct 17110
Doehne Rd 17110
Dogwood Ave 17110
Dogwood Dr
1500-1599 17110
6200-6299 17112
Dogwood Rd 17110
Donald Dr 17111
Donlar St 17112
Donna Jane Ct 17109
Dora Cir & Dr 17110
Doral Dr 17112
Dorchester Rd 17112
Doris Ct & Dr 17112
Doris View Dr 17112
Dorset Way 17111
Douglas St 17103
Dove Dr 17112
Dover Rd 17112
Dowhower Rd 17111
Downington Ct 17112
Dps 3m Record 17103
Drake Dr 17112
Drexel Rd 17109
Driftstone Dr 17110
Driftwood Ave 17112
Driftwood Dr 17111
Drummond St 17104
Dublin Rd 17111
Duke St
2400-2499 17104
2500-3299 17111
4700-4799 17109
Dunkle St
500-599 17104
601-643 17104
645-697 17113
699-899 17113
Dunley Ct 17112
Dunmore Dr 17112
Durham Rd 17110
Dwight Ave 17112
E Ave 17113
E Ln 17111
Eaglecrest Ct 17109
Earl Ave 17109
Earl Ct 17112
Earl Dr 17112
Earl View Dr 17112
Earle St 17109
Eastbrook Rd 17109
Eastern Dr 17111
Eastfield Rd 17112
Eastman Dr 17109
Eastwood Dr 17109
Easy St 17109
Echoglen Rd 17109
Eddington Ave 17111
Edgemont Rd 17109
Edgewood Rd 17104
Edsel St 17109
Edward St 17110
Edwin St 17110
Egret Dr 17112
Eisenhower Blvd 17111
Elaine Ave 17112
Elaran Dr 17112
Elba Ln 17109
Elbridge Rd 17112
Elder Rd 17111
Elder St
700-799 17104
821-899 17111
Elderberry Ln 17112
Elizabeth Ct 17112
Elizabeth St
400-499 17109
2200-2299 17110
Elk St 17111
Ella Cir 17112
Ellerslie St 17104
Ellis Dr 17110
Ellsworth St 17103
Elm Ave 17112
Elm Cir 17111
Elm St
2428A-2428B 17103
100-798 17113
200-298 17113
500-599 17112
800-899 17113
1600-3099 17103
3100-3299 17109
Elmer Ave 17112
Elmerton Ave
900-902 17110
904-2499 17110
3400-4299 17109
Elmwood Dr
100-199 17109
3200-3799 17110
Elwill Dr 17112
Embassy Dr 17109
Embers Ln 17109
Emerald Ct 17104
Emerald Ln 17112
Emerald St 17110
Emily Dr 17112
N & S Emma Ave 17112
Englewood Ave 17109
Enterline Rd 17110
Eric Dr
1-99 17111
1000-1199 17110
Erie Rd 17111
Eshenaur Dr 17112
Essex Rd 17111
Essex St 17113
Estherton St 17110
Ethan Ct 17112
Ethel St 17109
Etta Rd 17111
Euclid St 17111
Evans Ave 17109
Evelyn St 17111
Eveningstar St 17112
Evergreen Ln 17112
Evergreen Rd 17109
Evergreen St 17104
Executive Park Dr 17111
Fair St 17104
Fairchild Rd 17110
Fairfax Dr 17111
Fairfax Vlg 17112
Fairfield St 17109
Fairlane Ct 17112
Fairmont Dr
1100-1299 17112
1400-1499 17109
Fairview Dr 17112
N & S Fairville Ave 17112
Fairway Ln 17112
Faith Cir 17112
Fanning Way 17111
Fargreen Rd 17110
Farmcrest Ln 17111
Farmdale Ave & Rd 17112
Farmers Ln 17111
Farmhouse Ln 17111
Farmington Rd 17112
Fawn Ct 17110
Fawn Dr 17112
Fawn Rdg N 17110
Fawn Sq 17112
Fawn Ridge Rd 17111
Feeser Rd 17109
Felton St 17113
Felty Dr 17111
Fenton Ave 17109
Fenway Dr 17112
Fenwick Dr 17110
Fenwick Pl 17111
Fern Dr, Rd & St 17112
Fernando Dr 17111
Fernwood Ave 17112
Ferree St 17109
Fillmore St 17104
Finch Dr 17110
Finch Ln 17111
Fir St 17103
Firehouse Ln 17111
Fireside Cir 17109
Fishburn St 17109
Fishing Creek Valley
Rd 17112
Flank Dr 17112
Fleetwood Dr 17109
Florence Dr 17112
Florence St 17110
Flume Cir 17110
Follins Ct 17112
Ford Ave 17109
Fordham Ave 17111
Forest Ln 17112
Forest St 17104
Forest Hills Dr 17112
Forest Oak Ln 17110
Forney St 17103
Forney Way 17112
Forrest Rd 17112
Forrest St 17110
Forrestal Cir 17112
Forster St
100-200 17102
202-426 17102
1600-2399 17103
2401-2499 17103
Fort Hunter Rd 17110
Fort Patton Dr 17112
Fort Stewart Dr 17112
Fox Ln 17112
Fox St
1-499 17109
5800-5999 17112
Fox Chase Dr 17111
Fox Hill Rd 17112
Fox Hollow Dr 17113
Fox Hollow Rd 17112
Fox Hunt Ln 17110
Fox Mill Rd 17112
Fox Ridge Ct 17102
Foxchase Cir 17111
Frances Dr 17109
Francis St 17113
Francis L Cadden
Pkwy 17111
Franklin Ave 17109
Franklin Dr 17112
Franklin St
108-118 17113
800-898 17103
901-999 17103
4400-4498 17111
4500-5099 17111
S Franklin St 17109
W Franklin St 17113
Freedom St 17112
Fresno Dr 17112
Friar Rd
101-199 17112
6101-6129 17111
6131-6199 17111
Friendship Rd 17111
Fritchey St 17109
Frog Hollow Rd 17112
N Front St
1-9 17113
11-842 17113
17-301 17101
303-615 17101
617-703 17101
801-2037 17102
844-898 17113
2101-5197 17110
5199-5399 17110
S Front St
51A-51D 17113
2447A-2447D 17113
1-2799 17113
25-111 17101
200-299 17104
301-1199 17104
Front And Market St 17101
Fulcroft Ave 17111
Fulton St
1300-1398 17102
1400-2099 17102
6100-6199 17111
Furnace Rd 17112
Gale Dr 17110
N Galen Rd 17110
Gales Ferry Ct 17110
Galion St 17111
Gallo Way 17112
Gallop Rd 17111
Galloway Ln 17111
Gander Ct 17112
Gannett St 17112
Garalyn Rd 17110
Garden Cir 17109
Garden Dr 17111
Garden Ln 17109
Garrison Ave 17110
Gateway Ct & Dr 17110
Gaynor Ln 17111
Geary St 17110
Geiger St 17102
Geisel Rd 17112
Geisel Highpoint Cir 17112
Gensemer Ln 17111
George St 17109
Georgia Ct 17112
Georgian Pl 17111
Gerald Dr 17112
Geraldine Dr 17112
Gibbel Rd 17112
Gibson Blvd
600-799 17104
901-999 17113
Gibson St
101-499 17104
200-298 17113
400-498 17113
Gilberg Ln 17112
Gillingham Ln 17111
Ginko Dr 17110
Girard St 17104
Glen St 17112
Glenbrook Dr 17110
N & S Glendale Ln 17112
Glendell Rd 17112
Glendore Dr 17112
Glenn Ave 17112
Glenn Ct 17111
Glenn Dr 17111
Glenside Dr 17109
Glenview Ave 17112
Glenwood Ave 17112
Gloucester St 17109
Goldcrest Pl 17111
Golden Rod Dr 17112
Golf Dr 17110
Good St 17113
Goodwill Dr 17101
Goose Valley Rd
2200-2299 17110
4300-4398 17112
4400-4499 17112
4501-4631 17112
Gordon Dr 17112
Gorse Dr 17110
Grace Rd 17110
Gracie Dr 17112
Graham St 17110
Grand St 17102
Grandview Dr 17110
Grandview Rd 17111
Grant Ct 17112
Graybill Dr 17112
Grayson Rd 17111
Great Oak Ln 17110
Green Ct 17110
Green St
700-2099 17102
2100-4099 17110
Green Hall 17104
Green Hill Rd
3400-7299 17111
7400-7999 17112
Green Tree Rd 17112
Greenawalt Ln 17110
Greenbriar Ter 17109
Greenfield Ln 17112
Greenhill Ln 17112
Greening Ln 17110
Greenridge Ln 17112
Greenwood Blvd 17109
Greenwood Ct 17109
Greenwood Rd 17112
Greenwood St
1901-1911 17104
1913-2299 17104
2500-3299 17111
Greggs Rd 17110
Gregs Dr 17111
Greystone Dr 17112
Griffin Ln 17110
Griffin St 17112
Grindstone Ln 17110
Grist Mill Cir 17112
Grouse Dr
100-199 17110
5400-5599 17111
Grove Ave 17112
Grove Rd 17111
Guineveres Dr 17110
Hacc Dr 17110
Haddam Neck Ct 17110
Hadley Way 17111
Haehnlen St 17104
Hagy Way 17110
Hale Ave 17104
Hall Mnr 17104
Hallman Ln 17112
Hamilton Cir 17111
Hamilton Dr 17109
Hamilton St 17102
Hamlin Ln 17110
Hammaker Dr 17110
Hampshire Rd 17112
Hampton Ct 17112
Hampton Court Rd 17112
Hampton Hill Ct 17111
Haney Dr 17109
Hanna St 17104
Hanover Ln 17112
Hanover Rd 17112
Hanover St 17104
Hanover View Cir 17112
Hanoverdale Dr 17112
Hanshue St 17113
Harcourt Dr 17110
Harding Ave 17112
Harford Ave 17111
Harman Dr 17112
Harmony Ln 17112
Harper Dr 17112
Harris St 17102
Harris Ter 17104
N & S Harrisburg St 17113
Harrise Cir & Dr 17112
Harrogate Dr 17111
Harvard Ct 17111
Harvest Dr 17111
Harvest Field Ln 17111
Harwich Rd 17109
Harwood Dr 17111
Hastings Dr 17109
Haven Croft Rd 17110
Haverford Rd 17109
Hawthorn Dr 17111
Hazel St 17112
Heagy St 17104
Heather Ct 17112
Heather Dr 17112
Heather Pl 17104
Heatherfield Way 17112
Heathrow Ct 17109
Hedgerow Ln 17111
Heister Rd 17110
Helen Ave 17112
Hemlock Ct
1-9 17109
1300-1499 17112
Hemlock Dr 17110
S Hemlock Dr 17110
Hemlock Rd 17112
Hereford St 17109
Herr St
101-105 17102
107-499 17102
800-998 17103
1000-2900 17103
2902-3098 17103
Hersha Dr 17102
N & S Hershey Rd 17112
Hetrick Dr 17109

Hetrick Ln 17112
Hetrick St 17104
Hickory Ln
1001-1099 17111
6700-6799 17112
Hickory St 17113
Hickory Hill Rd & Ter 17109
Hickory Hollow Rd 17112
Hidden Knoll Rd 17112
Hidden Lake Dr 17111
Hidden Valley Ln 17112
Hiddenwood Dr 17110
High St
390A-390D 17113
300-1199 17113
3500-3899 17109
High Pointe Blvd 17111
High Pointe Dr 17110
Highland Ave 17109
Highland Cir
2200-2299 17110
2400-2499 17112
Highland Ct 17110
Highland St
1-97 17113
99-100 17113
101-199 17111
102-198 17113
388-398 17113
400-1399 17113
1600-5000 17111
5002-5098 17111
N & S Highlands Cir, Ct & Dr 17111
Highspire Rd 17111
Hillcrest Ave 17112
Hillcrest Rd 17109
Hillcrest St 17109
Hillsborough Ct 17111
Hillsdale Rd 17112
Hillside Ave 17112
Hillside Ct 17110
Hillside Rd
100-399 17104
4600-4799 17109
7000-7100 17112
7102-7198 17112
Hillside St 17109
Hillside Vlg 17103
Hilltop Dr 17111
Hilltop Rd
600-799 17112
4900-4999 17111
Hillymede Cir & Rd 17111
Hilton Ct 17112
Hinkle St 17112
Hivner Rd 17111
Hocker Dr 17111
Hocker St 17112
Hoerner St 17103
N Hoernerstown Rd 17111
Hoffer St
301-399 17113
2300-3199 17103
Hoffman Dr 17111
Hoffman St 17110
Holbrook St 17109
Holland Dr 17111
Hollow Dr 17112
Holly Cir 17110
Holly Dr 17110
Holly St 17104
Holly Hills Dr 17110
Holly Ridge Ln 17112
Hollywood Dr 17109
Holstein Rd 17112
Homestead Ave 17112
Honey St 17104
N & S Houcks Rd 17109
Houston Ave 17103
Howard St 17104
Huckleberry Ln 17112
Hudson St 17104
Hummel St 17104
Hummingbird Ln 17112
Humphrey Ct 17109

Hunt Cir 17112
Hunter Ln 17112
Hunter St 17104
Hunters Ridge Dr 17110
Hunters Run Rd 17111
Huntingdon Cir & St 17111
Huntley Dr 17112
Huntsdale Ct 17110
Huntshire Cir 17112
N Huntsmen Dr 17111
Hurlock St 17110
Huron Dr 17111
Industrial Rd 17110
Interstate Dr 17110
Ione St 17104
Ionoff Rd 17110
Irene Dr 17112
Ironwood Dr 17112
Ironwood Ln 17110
Iroquois Ct 17109
Iru Ln 17112
Ivey Ln 17104
Ivy Ln 17111
J K Dr 17112
J L Moyer Ct 17112
Jacobs Ave 17112
James Dr 17112
James St
400-498 17113
900-998 17102
1301-1399 17102
Jamestown Ct 17111
Janelle Dr 17112
Janet Dr 17112
Jay Dr 17112
Jaycee Ave 17112
Jefferson St
1-197 17113
199-299 17113
2100-2999 17110
6500-7399 17111
Jeffrey Cir 17112
Jennifer Dr 17112
Jericho Dr 17110
Jerome Blvd & Cir 17112
Jessamine Ave 17113
Jessamy Ct 17112
Joanna St 17112
Jodi Ct 17111
John Cir 17112
N & S Johnson St 17112
Jonagold Dr 17110
Jonathan Ln 17110
Jones St 17113
Jonestown Rd
5106A-5106I 17112
Jordan Dr 17111
Joya Cir 17112
Joyce Rd 17112
Jplwick Dr 17111
Judith Dr 17112
Judy Ln 17112
Julia St 17103
Kaby St 17110
Kalla Dr 17109
Karen Dr 17109
Katie Ct 17109
Kay St 17109
Kaylor Dr 17111
Keamy Ave 17111
Keckler Rd 17111
Kelker St
101-165 17113
179-203 17113
200-245 17102
205-207 17113
209-209 17113
246-298 17113
247-699 17102
300-422 17113
330-698 17102
424-518 17113
520-598 17113
Keller Ave 17112
Kelley Rd 17113
Kelsey Ct 17112

Kelso St 17111
Kempton Ave 17111
Kendale Dr 17111
Kennedy Dr 17112
Kennedy Ln 17113
Kennel Dr 17112
Kensington St 17104
Kensington Way 17112
Kent Dr 17111
Kent Ln 17104
Kenton Ln 17110
Kentucky Dr 17112
Kenwood Ave 17112
Keystone Dr & Rd 17112
Killington Dr 17112
Kilroy Cir 17111
Kimbers Rd 17112
King Ave 17109
King St 17113
King Arthurs Ct 17110
King George Dr 17109
King Russ Rd 17109
Kings Mill Ct 17110
Kingsley Dr 17110
Kingston Rd 17112
Kingswood Ct & Dr 17112
Kirkwood Rd 17110
Kittatinny St 17104
Kiwanis Rd 17112
Kline Vlg 17104
Knacklyn Farms Ct 17111
Knapp Dr 17111
Knight Dr & Rd 17111
Knisley St 17112
Knollcrest Rd 17112
Knollwood Dr 17109
Knox St 17104
Koch Ln 17112
Kohn Rd 17110
Koons Park Rd 17112
Kota Ave 17110
Kramer St 17109
Kristen Ct 17111
Kristy Ln 17111
Kury Rd 17112
Lab Ln 17110
Laboure Dr 17111
Lafayette St 17109
Lake Dr 17112
Lakepoint Dr 17111
Lakeside Ave 17112
Lakeside Dr 17110
Lakeview Ct 17110
N Lakeview Dr 17110
S Lakeview Dr 17110
Lakeview Rd 17112
Lakewood Dr
300-599 17112
900-1099 17109
Lancaster Ave 17112
Lancaster St
201-397 17113
399-400 17113
402-498 17113
4301-4397 17111
4399-5699 17111
Lancer Ct, Dr & St 17109
Laporte St 17112
Laraby Dr 17110
Larch Cir 17112
Larch Dr 17109
Larch St 17113
Lark Dr 17111
Larkin Ave 17112
Larry Dr 17109
Larry Ln 17112
Larue St 17112
Latsha Dr 17110
Latshmere Dr 17109
Laura Ln 17110
Laurel Dr 17110
Laurel Ln 17109
Laurel Rd 17112
Laurel St
1-99 17109
5800-5899 17112

Laurel Den Cir 17110
Laurel Glen Ct & Dr 17110
Laurel Point Cir 17110
Laurel Ridge Dr 17110
Laurelwood Dr 17110
Lavalle Ln 17111
Lavenda Ct 17111
Lawntara St 17111
Lawrence Ct 17112
Lawrence Dr
200-299 17112
500-510 17109
512-599 17109
Lawton St 17102
Lebanon St 17113
Leeds Ct 17112
Lehigh Ave 17111
Lemar Ave 17112
Lenker Pl & Rd 17111
Lenox St 17104
Lentz Dr 17112
Leo Dr 17111
Leon Ave 17111
Leonard Dr & Ln 17111
Lescure Ave & Dr 17109
Lesentier Ln 17112
Lester Ct 17112
Lester Rd 17113
Levan St 17109
Lewis Rd 17111
Lewis St 17110
Lexington Ct 17112
Lexington St
2500-2598 17110
2600-2799 17110
3800-4499 17109
Liberty Ct 17111
Liberty St
200-298 17101
1300-1600 17103
1602-1698 17103
Lilac Ln 17111
Lilac St 17110
Lincoln Ave
1-332 17111
1300-1399 17112
Lincoln Cir 17103
Lincoln Pl 17112
Lincoln St
100-212 17112
101-117 17113
119-599 17113
214-216 17112
600-699 17113
701-899 17113
Linda Ln 17111
Linden Pkwy 17110
Linden St 17109
N Linden St 17103
Lindenwood Ln 17113
Lindle Rd 17111
Linglestown Rd
101-127 17110
129-3999 17110
4000-4000 17112
4002-7999 17112
Linn St
1-399 17109
400-699 17103
Liptak Dr 17112
Lisa Dr
600-699 17111
4100-4199 17112
Litchfield Rd 17112
Little St 17109
Little Run Rd 17110
Livingston St 17113
Liz Ln 17111
Lloyd Rd 17109
N & S Lockwillow Ave 17112
Lockwood Ct 17112
Locust Ln 17109
Locust St
2-26 17113
28-399 17113
30-99 17113
100-100 17101

102-214 17101
216-216 17101
3000-3099 17109
5500-5518 17112
5520-6299 17112
6500-6598 17111
Locust Grove Ct 17109
Logan St
1601-1697 17102
1699-2099 17102
2101-2197 17110
2199-2499 17110
London Ct 17112
Londonderry Rd 17109
Lone Pine Ct 17113
Long Dr 17112
Long St 17103
Longview Dr 17111
Longview Rd 17112
Loop Ct & Dr 17112
Lopax Rd 17112
Lori Dr 17112
Lori Ln 17110
Lowell St 17104
Luce St 17104
Lucknow Rd 17110
Ludwig St 17103
Luther Pl 17111
Luther Rd 17111
Luther St 17112
Lyters Ln 17111
M St 17112
M W Smith Homes 17103
Macarthur Dr
800-899 17111
6101-6199 17112
Maclay St
201-231 17110
233-699 17110
901-1099 17103
N & S Madison St 17109
Magnolia Dr
5-5 17110
2301-2347 17104
2349-2499 17104
Magnolia Ter 17110
Maiden Creek Dr 17111
Maidstone Rd 17111
Main St
1062A-1062B 17113
400-1399 17113
7300-7399 17112
Mall Rd 17111
Malvern Cir 17112
Manada Ct 17112
Manada St 17104
Manada Bottom Rd 17112
Manada Creek Dr 17112
Manada Glen Ln 17112
Manada View Dr 17112
Manayunk Rd 17109
Mance Dr 17112
Manchester Blvd 17112
Mandarin Ct 17110
Manor Ct 17113
Manor Dr
900-999 17113
3800-3899 17110
7300-7999 17112
Manor St 17110
Manor Ter 17111
Manor Hill Cir 17111
Maple Dr 17111
Maple Ln 17110
Maple Rd 17109
Maple St 17109
Maple Shade Dr 17110
Mapleton Blvd & Dr 17112
Maplewood Dr 17109
Maplewood Rd 17112
Marblehead St 17109
Marcel Dr 17109
Marene Dr 17109
Margaret Ave 17112
Margaret Ln 17110
Margarets Dr 17110

Margate Rd 17111
Maria Dr 17109
Marion Dr 17112
Marion St 17102
Marion View Dr 17112
Mark Ave 17110
Market Pl 17110
Market St
100-500 17101
502-1098 17101
813-813 17105
815-1099 17101
1100-2599 17103
Market Street Rd
2800-2999 17103
3000-3099 17109
Markle Dr 17111
Marlborough Ave 17111
Marmore Dr 17112
Mars Ave 17112
Mars St 17113
Marshall St 17113
Marshfield Rd 17109
Martin Ln 17111
Martina Dr 17110
Mary St 17104
Maryland Ct 17112
Massachusetts Ct 17112
Matthew Rd 17109
Mauretania Ave 17109
May St 17103
Mayfair Dr 17112
Mayfield St 17109
Mayflower St 17104
Mcclean Rd 17112
Mccleaster St 17104
Mccord St 17113
Mccormick Ln 17111
Mcilhenny Ave 17112
Mcintosh Rd 17112
Meade Ct 17112
Meadow Ln
1-99 17113
200-298 17112
201-203 17104
201-203 17112
205-299 17112
301-399 17104
1201-1299 17113
3100-3299 17109
N Meadow Ln 17112
Meadow Run Pl 17112
Meadowbrook Dr 17112
Meadowcrest Rd 17112
Meadowlark Pl 17104
Meadowlark Way 17110
Meadowview Ct & Dr 17111
Megoulas Blvd 17109
Mehaffie Ln 17112
Melaradi St 17103
Melbourne Dr 17112
Mell Dr 17111
Melrose St 17104
Mels Ln 17112
Memory Ln 17111
Mercedes Ct 17112
Mercer St 17104
Mercury Ct & Rd 17109
Merivale Ct 17112
Merle Ave 17112
Merrimac Ave 17109
Michigan Dr 17111
Middle Ave 17109
Midland Rd 17104
Mifflin Ave 17111
N Mill Rd 17112
Mill Plain Ct 17110
Mill Pond Cir 17110
Mill Race Rd 17112
Miller Ln 17110
Miller Rd 17109
Miller St 17103
Millwood Dr 17110
Milroy Rd 17111
Milton Dr 17112
Mimosa St 17112

Mindy Dr 17112
Minglewood Rd 17112
Minute Rd 17112
Missent 17103
Missequenced 17103
Missort 17103
Mitchell Rd 17110
Mobile Rd 17109
Mockingbird Rd 17112
Mohn St 17113
Moline Ln 17111
Mollie Dr 17112
Moltke St
1900-2099 17102
2100-2199 17110
Monroe St
400-1099 17113
1301-1399 17103
7900-7999 17112
Montclair Ct 17112
Montfort Dr 17110
Monticello Ln 17112
Montour St 17111
Montrose St 17110
Moore St 17110
Morning Mist Dr 17111
Morningside Way 17113
Morningstar Ave 17112
Morris Dr 17110
Morton Dr 17109
Motter St 17103
Mount Pleasant Ave 17104
Mount Vernon Cir 17110
Mountain Rd 17112
Mountain Laurel Cir 17110
Mountain Ridge Dr 17110
Mountain Ridge Ln 17112
Mountain Rise Dr 17110
Mountain Top Rd 17112
Mountain View Rd 17110
Mountain View St 17112
Moyer Ln & Rd 17112
Muench St 17102
Mulberry St
200-398 17113
201-1147 17104
1149-2099 17104
Mumma Rd 17112
Mushroom Hill Rd 17111
Myers St 17102
Myrtle Ct & Dr 17112
Nagle Ct 17112
Nagle St 17104
Nancy Dr 17109
Nantucket Rd 17112
Nassau Rd 17112
Nationwide Dr 17110
Naudain St 17104
Nectarine St 17104
Needlewood Dr 17112
Nelley Ct 17113
Nesbit Dr 17112
Nestside Ct 17110
Nevada Ave 17109
New Dawn Dr 17110
New Hampshire Dr 17112
New Jersey Ave & Ct 17112
New Oxford Rd 17112
New Providence Dr 17111
New York Ct 17112
Newside Rd 17111
Newtown Dr 17110
Nicolas Ct 17110
Nittany Ln 17109
Noble Ln 17112
Noll Rd 17112
Nora Dr 17111
Norfolk Pl 17111
North Dr 17110
North Rd 17109
North St
101-197 17101
199-299 17101
500-542 17113
544-611 17113
1500-2099 17103

Northampton Ct 17111
Northfield Rd 17104
Northridge Dr 17112
Northstar Dr 17112
Northview Ln
1300-1399 17112
2100-2299 17110
Northway Rd 17109
Northwood Dr 17109
Northwood Rd 17110
Northwoods Park Dr 17110
Norton Rd 17113
Norwalk Dr 17112
Norwall St 17109
Norwich Ct 17112
Norwood St 17104
Nottingham Pl & Way 17109
Novak Rd 17112
Nyes Rd 17111
N Nyes Rd 17112
Oak Ave 17112
Oak Cir 17111
Oak St
1-119 17109
120-122 17111
121-399 17109
200-398 17109
600-698 17110
N Oak Grove Rd 17112
S Oak Grove Rd
100-310 17112
312-398 17112
401-497 17111
499-600 17111
602-698 17111
Oak Knoll Dr 17111
Oak Leaf Ln 17111
Oak Park Cir & Rd 17109
Oak Ridge Dr 17111
Oak Ridge Rd 17112
Oak View Dr 17112
Oakdale St 17111
Oakhurst Blvd 17110
Oaklea Rd 17110
Oakleigh Ave 17111
Oakley Ct 17111
Oakmont Rd 17109
Oakwood Dr 17110
Oakwood Ln 17110
Oakwood Rd 17104
Ober St 17113
Oberlin Rd 17111
Oberlin St 17113
Ohio Ave 17109
Old Colonial Rd 17112
Old Crooked Hill Rd 17110
Old Farm Ln 17112
Old Federal Rd 17110
Old Field Rd 17112
Old Forge Ct 17111
Old Locust Ln 17109
Old Orchard Rd 17109
Old Pond Rd 17112
Old Post Rd 17110
Old Township Rd 17111
Old Union Deposit Rd 17111
Olde Mill Rd 17112
Olde Salem Rd 17112
Oliver Dr 17109
Oliver Ln 17111
Oliver St 17102
Omar Ct 17112
Oneida Dr 17111
Ontario Dr 17111
Orange St
900-1099 17113
2300-2398 17110
Orchard Dr 17113
Orchard St 17109
Orchard Hill Rd 17110
Oriole Ct & Dr 17111
Orlando St 17111
Outerbridge Xing 17112
Over Dr 17109
Overbrook Rd 17109
Oxford Ave 17109
Oxford Rd 17109
Oxford St 17110
Oyler Rd 17104
P St 17113
Pa Dept Of Revenue 17129
Page Rd 17111
Painted Sky Dr 17111
Pajabon Dr 17111
Palm St 17112
Palmer Dr 17112
Pamela Rd 17112
Park Ave 17113
E Park Cir 17111
Park Dr
2400-2499 17110
8100-8199 17111
E Park Dr 17111
Park Ln 17112
Park Rd 17111
Park St
1-499 17109
1600-1999 17103
Park Ter 17111
Park Hill Ln 17104
Park View Dr 17110
Parkside Ln 17110
Parkview Ln 17111
Parkway E 17112
Parkway W 17112
Parkway Blvd 17103
Parkway Dr 17103
Parkway Rd
200-599 17110
1701-1799 17103
N & S Parrish St 17103
Parson Dr 17111
Partridge Ct 17111
Patterson Cir & Dr 17112
Patton Rd 17112
Paul Dr 17109
N & S Paxtang Ave 17111
Paxton Dr 17110
Paxton St
100-154 17104
156-1999 17104
601-799 17113
2000-5599 17111
5601-8099 17111
Paxton Church Rd 17110
Peace Ln 17112
Peach St 17112
Peach Tree St 17111
Pearl St 17109
Peastrai 17129
Pebble Ct 17110
Pebble Brook Ln 17110
Peffer St 17102
Peiffers Ln
700-898 17109
900-1099 17109
1300-1499 17113
Pelham Rd 17110
Penbrook Ave
2400-2498 17103
2500-3099 17103
3100-3299 17109
Pendale Rd 17111
Penhar Rd 17111
Penn St
41-199 17113
401-597 17113
599-700 17113
702-798 17113
800-899 17102
901-919 17113
901-919 17102
902-902 17113
904-906 17102
910-910 17113
912-928 17102
1000-1099 17113
1100-2099 17102
2100-2452 17110
2454-2498 17110
Pennsylvania Ave
900-999 17112
1000-1099 17111
1100-1298 17112
1301-1399 17112
Pennwood Rd 17110
Penrose St 17109
Peterborough Rd 17109
Pheasant Rd 17112
Pheasant Hill Rd 17110
Phillip Ct 17112
Piccadilly Ct 17112
Picnic Cir 17112
Pike St 17111
Piketown Rd 17112
Pin Oak Dr 17112
Pine Dr 17103
Pine Rd 17112
Pine St
1-899 17113
100-225 17101
227-227 17101
3400-3599 17109
5500-6399 17112
Pine Hill Rd 17111
Pine Hollow Ct & Rd 17109
Pine Knoll Dr 17111
Pine Needles Dr 17112
Pine Ridge Dr 17111
Pine Ridge Rd 17110
Pine Tree Ave 17112
Pinecrest Dr
200-299 17110
700-799 17112
Pinedale Ct 17111
Pinewood Ct 17112
Piney Hill Ln 17112
Plainview Dr 17112
Plainview Rd 17111
Platt St 17104
Pleasant Ave 17113
Pleasant Rd 17111
Pleasant Hill Rd 17112
Plowman Rdg 17112
Plymouth St 17109
Pond Ave 17109
Pond Rd 17111
Pond Meadow Ct 17110
Pond Ridge Dr 17111
Pond View Ct 17110
Pool Dr 17109
Poplar St
301-399 17113
401-499 17113
3600-3699 17109
5500-5599 17112
Port View Dr 17111
Porter Ln 17111
Potato Valley Rd 17112
Potteiger Ave 17112
Powers Ave 17109
Prince St
2-46 17109
48-699 17109
700-799 17102
3000-3199 17111
3201-3299 17111
Princess Ave 17109
Princess Dr 17113
Princeton Rd 17111
Pritchard Ct 17111
N Progress Ave
1-599 17109
601-1299 17109
2000-2698 17110
2700-4664 17110
4666-4698 17110
S Progress Ave
2-48 17109
50-599 17109
800-1099 17111
Prospect Dr 17111
Prosperous Dr 17112
Putnam St 17104
Q St 17113
Quail Hollow Rd 17112
Quail Ridge Ct 17111
Quality Cir 17112
Quarry Dr 17110
Quarry Rd 17111
Queen St
600-798 17113
800-999 17113
4700-4999 17109
Queens Dr 17110
Quentin Rd 17111
Quiggley Cir 17112
Quince St 17111
R St 17113
Rabbit Ln 17112
Rabuck Dr 17112
Race St 17104
Radcliffe Dr 17109
Radle Rd 17112
Radnor Dr 17112
Radnor St 17110
Rainbow Rd 17113
Rambo Ln 17110
Randolph Ct 17111
Randolph St 17104
Ranger Rd 17112
Raspberry Ln 17112
Rathlin Ct 17112
Rauch St
3900-3999 17109
7600-7699 17112
Rawleigh St 17109
Ray View Dr 17112
Reading St
1-499 17113
800-899 17104
Red Rd 17110
Red Fox Ln 17112
Red Pine Rd 17112
Red Top Rd 17111
Redbud Ct 17110
Redstone Dr 17112
Redwood St 17109
Reel St 17110
Reese St 17104
Regency Cir 17110
Regent Dr & Rd 17112
Regina St 17103
Rehrer Ln 17112
Reichert Rd 17110
Reily Rd 17103
Reily St 17102
Reist Ct 17110
Reservoir Rd 17113
Reservoir St 17103
Resort Dr 17112
Restview Dr 17112
Revenue Pl 17129
Revere St
1400-1799 17104
2901-2999 17111
S Revere St 17109
Revere Hall 17104
Reynders St 17113
Reynolds Ln 17111
Rhode Island Ct 17112
Richland Ave 17109
Richmond Ct 17111
Ricker St 17109
Rider Ln 17112
Ridge Ave 17111
Ridge Dr 17109
Ridge Rd 17112
Ridge St 17113
Ridgeview Dr 17112
Ridgeview Ln 17110
Ridgeview Rd 17112
Ridgeway Rd 17109
Riegle Rd 17112
Ring Neck Dr 17112
Ritter Rd 17109
N River Aly 17113
S River Aly 17113
River Rd 17110
River St 17102
N River St
2-98 17101
101-199 17101
3100-3199 17110
S River St
1-29 17101
300-399 17104
Riverside Ct 17112
Riverside Dr 17101
Riverview St 17113
Rivington Ter 17103
Robert Rd 17112
Roberts Valley Rd 17110
Robin Rd
2200-2399 17112
7700-7899 17111
Rock Fall Rd 17110
Rock Ledge Dr 17110
Rockford Dr 17112
Rockland Dr 17112
Rodgers Ave 17112
Rodkey Rd 17110
Roller Dr 17113
Rolleston St 17104
Rolling Glen Dr 17109
Roman Knoll Ct 17109
Rome Ter 17110
Roosevelt St 17111
Rose St 17102
Rose Hill Rd 17110
Rosewall Ct 17112
Rosewood Dr 17109
Rosewood Ln 17111
Ross St 17110
Roth St 17113
Rothford Ln 17112
Round Hill Rd 17110
Rowe Dr & Ln 17112
Roxbury Dr 17112
Royal Ave 17109
Royal Ct 17109
Royal Ter 17103
Royal Oak Dr 17112
Royal Terrace Dr 17112
Rudy Rd 17104
Rumson Dr 17104
Rupp Hill Rd 17111
Russell Dr 17112
Rustic Dr 17109
Ruth Ann St 17109
Rutherford Rd 17109
Rutherford St 17111
Rutland Dr 17111
Ryan Dr 17112
Ryecroft Dr 17111
S St 17113
Saddle Ln 17111
Saddle Ridge Ct & Dr 17110
Saddlebrook Dr 17112
Saint Andrews Way 17112
Saint Clair Ct 17110
Saint George Dr 17112
Saint Marys Dr 17113
Saint Thomas Blvd 17112
Salem Rd
600-699 17111
3601-3609 17109
3611-3699 17109
Samantha Ct 17112
Samoset Dr 17109
Sandra Ave 17109
Sandy Ln 17112
Sandy Hollow Rd 17112
Sandy View Ln 17112
Sanibel Dr 17111
Santa Claus St 17109
Santanna Dr 17109
Santo Cir 17112
Saphire Dr 17111
Saradana Rd 17112
Sarah St 17112
N Sarayo Cir 17110
Sarhelm Rd 17112
Sarkuni Ave 17110
Sassafras St 17102
Sauers Rd 17110
Saul Aly 17110
Sawgrass Ct 17111
Sawmill Rd 17112
Saybrook Ct & Ln 17110
Sayford St 17102
Scarsborough Dr 17112
Scenery Dr & Pl 17109
Scenic Ct 17111
N Scenic Rd 17109
S Scenic Rd 17109
Schaffner Dr 17112
Schefield Cir 17112
Schills Ln 17112
Schoolhouse Ln 17109
Schuyler Hall 17104
Schuylkill St 17110
Scott Dr 17112
Scott Meadow Ct 17110
Seashamb Rd 17112
Seemore Dr 17111
Seibert Ave 17112
Seneca St 17110
Sequoia Dr 17109
Serenity Way 17112
Severna Pl 17111
Shady Dr 17111
Shady Ln 17112
Shakespeare St 17113
Shamokin St 17110
Shannon Dr & Rd 17112
Shanois St 17104
Sharon St 17111
Shasta Dr 17111
Shatto Dr 17111
Shawn Dr 17112
Shawnee Dr 17112
Shea Ln 17112
Sheffield Ct 17112
Sheffield Ln 17110
Shelahamer Rd 17112
Shell St 17109
Shelling Dr 17112
Shellis St 17104
Sherbourne Ct 17112
Sherman Ave 17103
Sherman St 17112
Sherwin Ct 17112
Sherwood St 17111
Shield St 17109
Shoop St 17103
Shope Pl 17109
Shope St 17113
Short St
1-299 17109
300-329 17112
319-399 17113
1200-1299 17113
Showers St 17104
Shrub St 17103
Shutt Mill Rd 17110
Siegfried St 17113
Silver Lake Dr 17112
Silver Leaf Rdg 17110
Silver Maple Dr 17112
Simpson Rd 17111
Simsbury Dr 17111
Sir Lancelot Dr 17110
Sir Thomas Ct 17109
Skyline Dr 17112
Skyview Cir 17110
Slate Ridge Rd 17112
Sleepy Hollow Rd 17112
Slepian St 17112
Smith St 17109
Smithfield St 17112
Smokehouse Ln 17110
Snavely Ct 17111
Snell Dr 17109
Snyder Dr 17112
Society Park Ct 17109
Somerset St 17111
South Rd 17109
South St 17101
Southfield Ct 17111
Southfield Rd 17104
Southridge Ter 17111
Sparton Rd 17109
Spencer St 17104
Spring St
1-99 17103
2-98 17113
100-200 17113
202-1098 17113
3200-3399 17109
Spring Creek Rd 17111
Spring Knoll Ct & Dr 17111
Spring Valley Rd 17109
Springfield St 17112
Springford Dr & Ter 17111
Springhouse Ct 17111
Springhouse Ln 17112
Springhouse Rd 17111
Springlake Rd 17112
Springtide Dr 17111
Springtop Dr 17111
Spruce Dr
1000-1099 17110
2300-2399 17112
8100-8199 17111
Spruce Ln 17112
Spruce St
100-2798 17109
201-297 17113
299-600 17113
602-698 17113
2800-2999 17109
Squire Rd 17111
Stable Ct 17111
Stacey Dr E 17111
Stafford Ave 17111
Stanley Dr 17103
State Dr 17112
State St
2-298 17113
100-300 17101
300-499 17113
302-1198 17101
1300-2499 17103
State Farm Dr 17110
Station Rd 17101
Staunton Ln 17112
Steck Ct 17111
Steeple Chase Ln 17112
Stein Ln 17112
Stephen Dr 17111
Sterling Rd 17112
Stevenson Ave 17112
Stikle St 17113
Stillwell Ct 17112
Stirrup Ct 17111
Stirrup Ln 17112
Stockton Ct 17111
Stone Ridge Cir 17112
Stoneleigh Ct 17112
Stoneybrook Dr 17111
Storeys Ct 17109
Stradford Dr 17112
Straw Hollow Rd 17112
Strawberry Sq 17101
Stricker Rd 17111
Strites Rd 17111
Stuart Pl 17109
Sturbridge Dr 17110
Sue Ann Dr 17112
Suffolk Rd 17112
Summers St 17113
Summerwood Dr 17111
Summit Ave 17111
Summit St 17113
N Summit St 17103
S Summit St 17104
Summit Pointe Dr 17111
Sumner Dr 17109
Sun Dr 17109
Sunday Dr 17111
Sunny Dr 17112
Sunny Hill Ln 17111
Sunnycrest Dr 17109
Sunnyside Ave 17109
Sunrise Cir 17111
Sunset Ave 17112
Sunset Dr
3800-3899 17111
4900-7899 17112
Superior Dr 17111
Surrey Rd 17109

Susan Rd & Way 17109
Susquehanna St
700-2020 17102
2022-2098 17102
2100-2399 17110
2401-3199 17110
Sussex Dr 17109
Sutton Dr 17112
Swan St 17111
Swatara Dr
906-999 17111
4000-4100 17113
4102-4198 17113
Swatara St
200-499 17113
501-599 17113
1200-2499 17104
Sweetbriar Dr 17111
Sweetbrier Dr & Ter 17111
Sycamore Ct 17109
Sycamore Dr
300-699 17110
2100-2199 17112
Sycamore St
900-1899 17104
2201-2497 17111
2499-3200 17111
3202-3298 17111
Sylvan Pl 17109
Sylvan Ter 17104
Sylvan Ridge Rd 17113
T St 17113
Talbott Ln 17110
Tall Pine Dr 17110
Tamar Dr 17111
Tamarack Sq 17112
Tanager Dr 17111
Tanza Ct 17112
Tarryton Rd 17109
Taunton Rd 17111
Taylor Blvd 17103
Teal Dr 17111
Technology Park 17110
Tecport Dr 17111
Tee Rd 17112
Tennessee Ct 17112
Terrace Ave 17113
Terrace Ct 17111
Terrace Dr 17110
Terrace Pl 17110
Terrace Way 17111
Terrann Dr 17112
Terrill Rd 17109
Terry Dr 17113
Terry Ln 17112
Terry Davis Ct 17111
Thea Dr 17110
Thetford Ct 17111
Thicket Ln 17110
Thomas St
1-99 17103
100-199 17112
2500-2599 17103
Thompson St 17104
Thornton Rd 17109
Thornwood Rd
1-99 17112
200-298 17104
Three Rivers Dr 17112
Thrush Ct 17111
Tiffany Ln 17112
E & W Tilden Rd 17112
N Timber Ct 17110
S Timber Ct 17110
Timber Ln 17112
Timber Line Ct 17112
N & S Timber Ridge Dr 17110
Timber Trail Ln 17112
Timber View Dr 17110
Timothy Rd 17112
Tipton Rd 17111
Tiverton Ln 17112
Toftree Dr 17112
Toms Rd 17112
Topview Dr 17112

Tracey Ln 17110
Tracy Cir 17112
Tree Farm Ln 17112
Trent Rd 17109
Trent St 17112
Trewick St 17113
Trinity Rd 17109
Trudy Rd 17109
Tucker St 17112
Tudor Dr 17109
Tupelo St 17110
Turkey Trot Rd 17112
Turner St 17110
Tuscarora St
1-199 17104
4700-4799 17110
Twilight Dr 17111
Twin Lakes Dr 17111
Twinn Ave 17109
Tyler Dr 17112
Umberger Rd & St 17112
Union St
100-299 17102
300-399 17113
3000-3099 17109
Union Deposit Rd
3880-A-3880-A 17109
3100-4099 17109
4200-6699 17111
Ups Dr 17104
Upton Dr 17110
Utah Ave 17109
Valley Dr 17112
W Valley Ln 17112
Valley Rd
200-2499 17104
2800-2899 17110
4000-4299 17112
Valleyview Ave & Rd 17112
Van St 17112
Vartan Ct & Way 17110
Vaughn St 17110
Venus Ave 17112
Vera St 17112
Verbeke St
100-198 17102
200-400 17102
402-498 17102
1300-1799 17103
Vermont Ct 17112
Vernon Ave 17109
Vernon St 17104
Verona Dr 17110
Versailles Dr 17112
Vesta Dr 17112
Vesta Ln 17110
Veterans Ln 17112
Via Firenze 17112
Via Toscana 17112
Victoria Ave 17109
N Victoria Way 17112
S Victoria Way 17112
View Crest Dr 17112
Village Rd & Way 17112
Village Glen Dr 17112
Vine St 17104
Vineyard Ave 17103
Vineyard Rd 17104
Vintage Ct 17109
Virginia Ave 17109
Vista Ter 17111
Vista View Ln 17112
Wading Spring Ln 17110
Wagon Wheel Ct 17109
Wakefield Rd 17109
Walden Rd 17112
Waldo St 17110
Walker Mill Rd 17110
Wallace St 17102
Walls St 17112
Walnut 17108
Walnut Ave 17112
Walnut Rd 17113
Walnut St
1216A-1216F 17103
3105A-3105F 17109

18-330 17113
101-101 17101
103-638 17101
332-398 17113
640-998 17101
1196-1198 17103
1200-3099 17103
3100-3100 17109
3102-4199 17109
5500-5599 17112
Walnut Run Ct 17112
Walters St 17113
Wanda Ln 17109
Wandering Way 17110
Warren Ave 17112
Washington Ave 17109
Washington St
100-199 17104
101-103 17113
Watson St
100-199 17113
2801-2899 17111
Waverly Rd 17109
Waverly Woods Dr 17110
Wayne Ave 17109
Wayne Dr 17112
Wayne St
1300-1498 17104
1500-1799 17104
2900-3299 17111
Wayne Hall 17104
Webner Rd 17111
Wedgewood Rd 17109
Welarall Rd 17110
Wellington Rd 17109
Wells Dr 17112
Wendy Dr 17112
Wenrich St 17112
Wert Pl 17104
Wesley Dr 17112
West Ave 17109
West Dr 17111
Westchester Dr 17112
Westerly Ct 17111
Westfield Rd 17112
Westford Cir 17112
Westminster Rd 17109
Wexford Ct 17112
Wheatfield Dr 17112
Wheaton Pl 17112
Whisper Wood Ln 17112
White Birch Ln 17112
White Haven Rd 17111
White Pine Dr & Rd 17112
Whitehall Dr 17110
Whitehall St 17103
Whitley Dr 17111
Wicklow Dr 17112
Wiconisco St 17110
Wil-Lo Farm Ln 17111
Wild Lilac Ct 17110
Wild Strawberry Ln 17111
Wildwood Way 17110
Wildwood Park Dr 17110
Wilhelm Rd 17111
William Ave 17109
Williams St
300-399 17113
1300-1499 17102
3900-3998 17109
Williams View Dr 17112
Williamsburg Dr 17109
Willoughby Rd 17111
Willow Ct 17110
Willow Ln 17110
Willow Rd 17109
Willow St 17101
Willow Spring Rd 17111
Wilshire Rd 17112
Wilson Ct 17112
Wilson Pkwy 17104
Wilton St 17109
Wimbledon Dr 17112
Winand Dr 17109
Windcrest Rd 17112
Winding Ln 17111

Winding Way 17109
Windmere Pl & Rd 17111
Windsor Rd 17112
Windsor Locks Pl 17110
Winfield St 17109
Wingfield Ct 17112
Winsford Rd 17109
Winston Rd 17112
Wintertide Dr 17111
Winthrop Dr 17112
Winwood Ct 17111
Wister St 17104
Wisteria Ln 17112
Withers Ct 17111
Witmer Dr 17111
Wood St
1-899 17109
800-898 17113
900-999 17113
1700-1999 17102
2001-2099 17102
Wood Creek Ct 17110
Woodbine St
200-627 17110
240-242 17113
629-699 17110
Woodcrest Cir 17112
Woodcrest Dr 17110
Woodcrest Ln 17112
Woodcrest Rd 17112
Wooded Pond Dr 17111
Woodland Rd 17112
Woodland View Ct 17110
Woodlawn Dr 17109
Woodlawn St
2201-2297 17104
2299-2399 17104
2500-2799 17111
Woodley Dr 17109
Woodlyn Ct 17111
Woodridge Dr 17110
Woodrow Ave 17112
Woodruff Way 17112
Woodside Ave 17112
Woodsman Dr 17111
Woodthrush Ct 17110
Woodvale Rd 17109
Woodview Dr 17112
Woodview St 17113
Woodward Dr 17111
Worcester Ave 17111
Wrigley Ln 17112
Wyatt Rd 17104
Wyeth St 17102
Wyndham Ct & Way 17109
Wynnewood Rd 17109
Wyoming Ave 17109
Yale St
200-299 17104
400-899 17111
Yankee Ln 17112
Yellowstone Dr 17112
Yew Pl 17104
York Ln 17110
York St
1901-1999 17103
4100-4499 17111
4501-4699 17111
Yorkshire Dr 17111
Zarker St 17104

NUMBERED STREETS

2nd Ave 17113
2nd St 17113
N 2nd St
458A-458C 17113
1-621 17101
30-30 17113
623-623 17101
700-1923 17102
828-840 17113
1925-2099 17102
2100-4099 17110
S 2nd St
158A-158B 17113
2-14 17101
12-2799 17113
16-101 17101
218-406 17104
3rd Aly 17113
3rd Ave 17113
S 3rd Ave 17113
3rd St 17113
N 3rd St
1-17 17101
4-10 17113
30-620 17101
700-898 17102
708-710 17113
900-2099 17102
2100-4399 17110
S 3rd St
1-36 17101
1-2900 17113
38-198 17101
200-206 17104
2902-2998 17113
4th Ave 17113
N 4th St
25A-25B 17101
1-26 17113
14-17 17101
19-25 17101
28-38 17113
1300-2099 17102
2100-3799 17110
S 4th St
40A-40C 17113
1-2699 17113
15-21 17101
23-25 17101
5th Ave 17113
N 5th St
5-7 17101
1500-1904 17102
1906-2098 17102
2100-3299 17110
S 5th St 17113
6th Ave 17113
N 6th St
900-2099 17102
2100-4499 17110
S 6th St 17113
N 7th St
901-997 17102
999-1619 17102
1621-2013 17102
2101-2135 17110
2137-3199 17110
S 7th St 17113
N 10th St
100-199 17101
1101-1199 17103
S 10th St
1-99 17101
801-1099 17104
N 12th St
1-99 17103
600-698 17101
1000-1598 17103
S 12th St 17104
N 13th St 17103
S 13th St 17104
N 14th St 17103
S 14th St 17104
N 15th St 17103
S 15th St 17104
N 16th St 17103
S 16th St 17104
N 17th St 17103
S 17th St 17104
N 18th St 17103
S 18th St 17104
N 19th St 17103
S 19th St 17104
N 20th St 17103
S 20th St 17104
N 21st St
800-998 17103
1100-1599 17109
S 21st St 17104
N 22nd St
1000-1098 17103
1100-1310 17109
S 22nd St 17104
N 23rd St 17103
S 23rd St 17104
N 24th St
1-99 17103
101-199 17103
1300-1799 17109
S 24th St
1-7 17103
9-53 17103
55-99 17103
500-799 17104
N 25th St
1-97 17103
99-199 17103
1300-1699 17109
S 25th St
2-98 17103
101-297 17104
299-699 17104
700-799 17111
N 26th St
100-198 17103
1300-1999 17109
S 26th St
401-497 17103
499-500 17103
502-598 17103
600-799 17111
801-899 17111
N 27th St
1-99 17103
101-199 17103
1300-1899 17109
S 27th St
1-599 17103
600-899 17111
N 28th St
1-99 17103
100-699 17109
S 28th St
651A-651D 17111
1-660 17103
662-698 17103
700-1292 17111
700-702 17103
1294-1298 17111
N 29th St 17109
S 29th St
1-320 17103
321-323 17104
322-324 17103
325-399 17104
400-499 17103
501-503 17104
510-510 17103
528-560 17104
600-1100 17111
N 30th St 17111
100-106 17109
101-107 17111
108-208 17109
209-299 17111
300-599 17109
302-302 17111
304-309 17111
S 30th St 17103
N 31st St
1-5 17109
4-299 17111
300-300 17111
301-399 17109
S 31st St
2-398 17109
15-31 17111
97-399 17109
500-599 17103
601-699 17103
800-898 17111
N 32nd St
1-9 17111
11-130 17111
132-198 17111
200-200 17111
200-207 17109
207-299 17111
209-399 17109
419-421 17111
S 32nd St 17109
S 33rd St 17111
N 34th St 17109
N 36th St 17109
N 38th St 17109
S 38th St 17111
N & S 39th 17109
S 40th St 17111
S 41st St 17111
S 42nd St 17111
S 43rd St 17111
N 44th St 17111
N & S 45th 17111
N & S 46th 17111
N & S 47th 17111
N & S 48th 17111
N 49th St 17111
N 50th St 17111
S 59th St 17111
S 60th St 17111
N & S 61st 17111
N 62nd St 17111
N & S 63rd 17111
N 64th St 17111
N 65th St 17111
N 66th St 17111
N 67th St 17111
N 68th St 17111
N 69th St 17111
N 70th St 17111
N 71st St 17111
N 72nd St 17111
N 73rd St 17111
S 80th St 17111
S 82nd St 17111
S 30 1/2 St 17103

HAZLETON PA

General Delivery 18201

POST OFFICE BOXES MAIN OFFICE STATIONS AND BRANCHES

Box No.s
All PO Boxes 18201

RURAL ROUTES

05 18201
01, 02, 03, 04 18202

NAMED STREETS

A Court St 18201
W Acacia St 18201
Acorn St 18202
Adams Ave 18202
Adobe Way 18202
Airport Rd 18202
Alder Way 18202
Alexander Dr 18202
Algonquin Dr 18202
Allegheny Dr 18202
Allen Dr 18201
Allen St
200-508 18202
509-527 18202
510-528 18202
529-999 18202
829-829 18201
Alliance Dr 18202
Alter St
500-1012 18201
1013-1099 18202
Amity Ln 18201
Anchor St 18202

Andrews Ct 18201
Angelo Dr 18202
Anthony Pl 18202
Anthracite St 18202
Appian Way 18202
Arapaho Cir & Ln 18202
E Arbutus St 18201
Arrowhead Dr 18202
Arthur St 18201
E Arthur Gardner Pkwy 18201
Ash Ct 18202
Ashmore Rd 18201
Aspen Ct 18202
W Aspen St 18201
Aspen Way 18202
Autumn Ln 18202
Banyon Cir 18202
Barletta Rd 18202
Bator St 18202
Beaver Brook Rd 18201
Bee Aly & St 18202
Beech Ct 18202
E Beech St 18201
W Beech St 18201
N & S Bennett Ct 18201
Bent Pine Rd & Trl 18202
Bernard Blvd 18202
Berner Ave 18201
Beryllium Rd 18201
Birch Ct 18202
Birch Rd 18202
E Birch St 18201
W Birch St 18201
Birch Knoll Dr 18201
Birk Dale Ct 18202
Blackhawk Blvd 18202
Blue Mountain Dr N & S 18202
Bonn Ct 18201
Book Ct 18201
Boone Ct 18201
Boot Ln 18202
Boundary St 18202
Bow St 18202
Bowmans Mill Rd 18202
Branch Ct
530-588 18201
590-805 18201
807-843 18201
870-999 18202
E Branch St 18202
W Branch St 18202
Breaker St 18202
Bridle Ct 18202
E Broad St
1-1799 18201
1-241 18202
243-399 18202
N Broad St 18202
S Broad St 18202
W Broad St
1-41 18202
1-3 18201
5-799 18201
43-43 18202
Business Exchange 18201
Butler Dr 18201
N & S Butler Terrace Dr 18202
Butte Rd 18202
Buttonbush Ln 18202
E & W Buttonwood St 18201
Cactus Ct 18202
Caddo Dr 18202
Cafe Ct 18201
Calbeth Cir 18202
Calmut Cir 18202
Campbell St 18201
Can Do Expy 18202
Candlewood Cir 18201
Canoga Dr 18202
Carleton Ave 18201
Carnival St 18202
Carson St
500-1024 18201
1025-1099 18202
Cayuga Cir 18202
Cedar Cir 18202
N Cedar St 18201
S Cedar St 18201
Center St 18202
Center City Medical Complex 18201
E & W Chapel St 18201
Charles St 18202
Charlotte Ln 18202
Cherry Blossom Dr 18202
E & W Chestnut St 18201
Chestnut Hill Dr 18202
Cheyenne Dr 18202
Cheyney Dr 18202
Chinook Dr 18202
Chrismark Rd 18201
Christine Rd 18202
Christopher Rd 18201
Chupailo St 18202
Church St 18201
N Church St
7-37 18201
39-1016 18201
1017-1017 18202
1018-1018 18201
1019-1600 18202
1602-1698 18202
S Church St 18201
W Church St 18201
Cindy St 18202
Cinnamon Oak Dr 18202
Circle Dr 18201
Clark St 18202
E & W Clay Ave 18202
Cleveland St 18201
Clinton Ct 18201
Clouds Blvd 18201
Club Forty Rd 18201
Clubhouse Cir 18202
Coach Rd 18201
Coal St 18201
Colony Dr 18202
Columbus Ave 18202
Columbus Ct 18201
Columbus Pl 18201
N & S Conahan Dr 18201
Conlin Dr 18202
Conyngham Dr 18202
Corn Silk Ave 18202
Corr Ct 18201
Corral Rd 18202
Costello Rd 18202
Council Crest Ln 18202
Country Club Dr 18202
Coxe St 18201
E Cranberry Ave
1-199 18202
100-198 18201
200-1399 18201
W Cranberry Ave 18202
Cranberry Rd 18202
Crest Rd 18202
Crista Ln 18202
Crooked Stick Ln 18202
Cross St 18202
Cross Road Ln 18202
Crystal Rdg 18202
Crystal Ridge Ct & Rd 18202
Cypress Point Rd 18202
Dakota Dr 18202
David Rd 18201
Deer Path Rd 18202
Deer Run Rd 18202
Dela St 18202
Delaware Dr W 18202
Dessen Dr 18202
Dewey Ct 18201
E Diamond Ave 18201
W Diamond Ave
1-999 18201
1-7 18202
Diana Ln 18202
Dietrich Ave 18201
Dina Ave 18201
Dons Ave 18201
Driftwood Cir 18202
Dudeck Rd 18202
East Ct 18201
East Rd 18202
East St 18201
Ebervale Rd 18202
El Camino Rd 18201
Elm Ct 18202
Elm Rd 18202
E Elm St 18201
W Elm St 18201
Emerald Ct
500-1013 18201
1014-1199 18202
1060-1099 18202
W Emerald Ct 18201
Estate Blvd 18201
Evans St 18201
Evergreen Dr 18202
Express Ct 18202
Fairlawn Blvd 18202
N & W Fairways Cir 18202
Faith Dr 18202
Fall Ct 18201
Falling Leaves Ln 18201
Father Angelo Dr 18202
Fawn Dr 18202
Fern Ct 18202
W Fern St 18201
Fernwood Cir 18202
Ferrara Ave
1-99 18202
101-101 18202
102-102 18201
103-499 18202
104-121 18201
123-123 18201
Fetchko Dr 18202
S Filmore Ct 18201
Fir Ct 18202
Firehouse Ct 18202
Fireside Dr 18202
Fishers Hl 18202
Fluri Rd 18202
Forest Ln & Rd 18202
Forest Hill Rd 18202
Forest Hills Dr 18201
Forest Hills Acres 18201
Four Seasons Ct & Dr 18201
Four Seasons Trailer Ct 18201
Fox Manor Rd 18202
Francis St 18202
Franklin St 18201
Freedom Cir & St 18202
Freemont Ct 18201
Front St 18202
N Fulton Ct 18201
S Fulton Ct 18201
Fulton St 18202
Gabriele St 18202
Garfield St 18201
Garibaldi Ct 18201
Garrison Rd 18202
George Dr 18202
Getz Dr 18201
Glen Abbey Rd 18202
Glenn Eagles Dr 18202
Golfwood Dr 18202
Goshen Ave 18202
Granite Ct 18202
Grant St
500-1020 18201
1021-1023 18202
1022-1024 18201
1025-1099 18202
Grape Vine Ln 18202
Green St 18201
E Green St
1-308 18202
13-21 18201
23-227 18201
229-239 18201
310-320 18202
W Green St
2-130 18201
97-97 18202
99-541 18202
132-599 18201
543-543 18202
600-826 18202
601-629 18201
828-840 18202
Green Forest Rd 18202
Green Mountain Rd 18202
Greenbriar Ln 18202
Grey Birch Ct 18202
Gulas Dr 18201
H N B Professional Bldg 18201
Hagelgans St 18202
N Hall Rd 18202
Hanover Ct
541-999 18201
1001-1019 18201
1026-1028 18202
1057-1059 18202
1061-1099 18202
Hansel St 18201
Harding St 18201
Harleigh Blvd 18202
Harleigh Terrace Ave 18202
Harmony Dr 18201
Harrison St 18201
S Harvey St 18202
Harwood Rd 18202
E Hawthorne St 18201
Hayes St
500-720 18201
721-899 18201
722-998 18201
1001-1099 18202
Hazle St 18202
S Hazle St 18201
S Hazle Brook Rd 18201
Hazle Township Blvd 18202
Hazleton Apts 18202
Hazleton Medical Arts 18201
Hazleton Professional Plz 18202
Hazlewood Dr 18202
Hazlewood Apts 18202
Hemlock St 18202
E Hemlock St 18201
W Hemlock St 18201
Heritage Cir 18202
Hess Rd 18202
E Hickory St 18201
Hill St 18201
Hillcrest Dr 18202
Hillside Dr 18202
Hilltop Dr & Rd 18201
Hollars Hl 18202
E & W Holly St 18201
Holly Lynn Dr 18202
Hollylynn Cir 18202
E, S & W Hollywood Blvd & Crst N 18202
Hope St 18201
Horn St 18202
Horseshoe Dr 18202
Humboldt St 18202
S Hunter Hwy 18202
Hunter Rd 18201
N & S Huron Cir 18202
Inca Dr 18202
Indigo Cir 18202
N & S Iroquois Cir & Dr 18202
Irving St 18202
Jacaranda Cir 18202
Jackson Ave 18202
N James St
1-1020 18201
1021-1023 18202
1022-1024 18201
1025-1099 18202
Jan Ct 18202
N & S Janhanna Cir 18202
Jason Rd 18201
Jaycee Dr 18202
Jeansville Rd 18201
Jeansville Peak Rd 18201
E & W Jefferson Ave 18202
Johns Ave 18201
Johns St 18202
N Johns St 18202
S Johns St 18202
Jumano Dr 18202
E & W Juniper St 18201
Kendall Cir 18202
Kenoza Dr 18202
Kickapoo Dr 18202
Kiefer Ave 18201
Kiowa Dr 18202
Kirk St 18202
Kit Dr 18201
Kiwanis Blvd 18202
La Mesa Dr 18202
Lacona Dr 18202
Lafayette Ct
500-1012 18201
1013-1056 18202
1057-1099 18202
1058-1098 18202
Lahm Ave 18201
Lahn St 18202
Lake Valley Dr 18202
Landmesser Ave 18202
Lattimer Rd 18202
Laurel Hl 18201
Laurel Mall 18202
N Laurel St
1-1024 18201
1025-1099 18202
S Laurel St 18201
Laurel Mall Rd 18202
N Lee Ct
1-59 18201
61-899 18201
1600-1699 18202
S Lee Ct 18201
Left Ln 18202
Lehigh St 18201
Lehigh Valley Dr 18202
Lenape Ln 18202
Liberty Ave 18202
Liberty Cir 18202
Liberty Ct
500-861 18201
862-862 18202
863-863 18201
864-921 18202
923-999 18202
Lincalis St 18202
N Lincoln St 18201
Linda Ln 18201
Lions Dr 18202
Locust Cir 18202
N Locust St
1-1012 18201
1013-1019 18202
1014-1020 18201
1021-1099 18202
S Locust St 18201
Loop Ln 18202
Louis Schiavo Dr 18202
Lower St 18202
E Lower St 18201
W Lower St 18201
Luzerne St 18201
Lynn Ct 18202
Lyon Ct 18201
E & W Madison Ave 18202
E & W Magnolia St 18201
Mahopac Dr 18202
N Main Ct 18201
Main St
85-99 18202
101-117 18201
119-147 18201
149-149 18202
150-154 18202
155-155 18201
156-160 18202
157-167 18202
162-164 18201
166-170 18202
179-200 18201
202-350 18201
203-205 18202
209-399 18201
600-700 18202
702-1002 18201
E Main St 18201
N Main St 18201
S Main St 18201
W Main St 18201
Make It Work Rd 18201
Manayunk Ave 18202
N Manhattan Ct
2-118 18201
120-1008 18201
1010-1038 18202
1040-1041 18202
1043-1099 18202
S Manhattan Ct 18201
N Manhatten Ct 18201
Manor St 18202
Maple Cir 18202
Maple St
17-99 18201
800-899 18202
E Maple St
9-105 18202
13-31 18201
33-229 18201
107-132 18202
134-238 18202
231-299 18201
W Maple St 18201
Maplewood Blvd & Dr 18202
Mark Rd 18201
Masters Ln 18202
Maverick Way 18202
Mckinley St
500-861 18201
862-862 18202
863-863 18201
864-999 18202
Mcnair St
700-859 18201
860-999 18202
Meade Ct
501-599 18201
601-1020 18201
1021-1099 18202
Melrose St 18202
Merion Dr 18202
Mid Ct 18202
Mike Ct 18201
Mill St 18201
Mine St 18202
E Mine St 18201
W Mine St 18201
Mohican Ct 18202
Moisey Dr 18202
Monges St 18201
E & W Monroe Ave 18202
Monument Dr 18202
Moonlit Hollow Ln 18201
Morris Ln 18201
Morrison Cir 18201
E & W Mount Laurel Dr 18201
Mountain View Dr 18201
Mt Pleasant Ln 18202
Mt Top Ct 18202
Muir Ave 18201
Muirfield Ln 18202
Muskegon Cir 18202
Navaho Dr 18202
New St 18202
New Cranberry Rd & St 18202
Newberry Cir 18202
Newport Dr 18201
Nicole Ln 18202
E & W Noble St 18201
North St 18202
Oak Ct 18202
Oak Dr 18202
E Oak St
1-100 18201
1-299 18202
102-198 18201
W Oak St 18201
Oak Ridge Rd 18202
Oakland St 18202
Oakmont Dr 18202
Oakmont Acres 18202
Oakridge Rd 18202
Old St 18202
Old Airport Rd 18202
Old Cranberry Rd & St 18202
Old Post Ct 18202
Old Route 93 18202
Old St Humboldt 18202
Olive Cir 18202
Olympic Ln 18202
Owego Dr 18202
Oyster Bay Ct 18202
Palance Ave 18202
Pansy Ln 18202
Pardee St 18201
Pardeesville Rd 18202
N Park Cir, Dr, Pl & St 18202
Parkview Rd 18202
Parkwood St
900-1010 18201
1011-1099 18202
Patch Rd 18202
Patriot Cir 18202
Pawnee Ave 18202
Peace St
500-1021 18201
1022-1024 18202
1023-1025 18201
1026-1069 18202
1070-1098 18202
1071-1099 18202
Pebble Beach Dr 18202
Pecora Blvd 18202
Pence Dr 18202
Penn Ct
500-924 18201
926-1012 18201
1013-1069 18202
1014-1068 18202
1070-1099 18202
Penn St 18202
Penn State Campus 18202
Pentralm St 18202
Perry Ct
561-1024 18201
1025-1099 18202
Pilot Pt 18202
Pine Ct E 18202
Pine Ct W
2-98 18202
1000-1099 18202
N Pine St 18201
S Pine St 18201
N & S Pine Tree Rd 18201
Pine Valley Ln 18202
Pinecrest Rd 18202
Pinehurst Dr 18202
Pinewood Cir 18202
E & W Players Way 18202
Playground Ct 18202
Point Of Woods 18202
Poolside Dr 18202
N & S Poplar St 18201
Poppy Hills Rd 18202
Post Cir 18201
Powell Dr 18201
Ppl Sub Rd 18202
Providence Rd 18202
Pump St 18202
Putnam St 18202
Quality Rd 18202
Quapaw Dr 18202
Quincy St 18202
Railroad St 18201
Randon Ln 18201
Red Oak Ct 18202
Renaissance Ctr 18201
N & S Ridge Ave, Ct & Rd N & S 18202
Roberts Ave 18201

Rock Ln 18202
Rocky Rd 18201
Roosevelt St
1-99 18202
600-816 18201
818-860 18201
857-859 18202
861-999 18202
Rose St 18202
Rosewood Cir 18202
Rotary Dr 18202
Route 924 18202
Royal Aberdeen Dr 18202
Saint Angela Dr 18202
Saint Anns Dr & Rd 18202
Saint Charles Dr 18201
Saint Charles Pl 18202
Saint James Dr 18202
Saint John Dr 18202
Saint Joseph Dr 18202
Saint Matthews Dr 18202
Saint Theresa Dr 18202
Samantha Ln 18202
Samuels Ave 18201
Scamper St 18202
Schan St 18202
School St 18202
W Scornew St 18201
Scotch Hill Dr & Rd 18202
Scotch Pine Dr 18202
Scott Ct 18201
Segal Ct 18201
Seminole Cir 18202
Seneca Cir 18202
Sesame St 18202
Seybert St
521-1020 18201
1021-1099 18202
Shaft Rd 18201
Sharon Dr 18201
Shawnee Cir 18202
Shenango Dr 18202
Sherman Ct 18202
N Sherman Ct
61-119 18201
121-984 18201
986-1004 18201
1001-1099 18202
1050-3098 18202
3100-3199 18202
S Sherman Ct 18201
Shinnecock Hills Ln 18202
Shipper St 18202
Short St 18202
Silver Cloud Ln 18202
Simmons Dr 18202
Sissock Dr 18201
Ski Ct 18202
Skuba Ln 18202
Skyline Dr 18202
Southern Hills Ct 18202
Southgate Office Complex 18201
Spice Bush Dr 18202
W Spring Ct & St 18201
Spring Hill Dr 18201
Spruce Ct 18202
E Spruce St
7-23 18202
25-319 18202
33-237 18201
320-322 18201
321-325 18202
W Spruce St 18201
Spur Ln 18202
Stacie Dr 18201
Stankevich St 18202
Star Mor Ln 18202
State Ct
600-699 18201
800-898 18202
900-999 18202
State Route 93 18202
State Route 940 18202
Station Cir 18202
Steelers Dr 18201
Stockton 7 Rd 18201
Stockton Mountain Rd 18201
Stoney Creek Rd 18202
Strawberry Ln 18202
Strip Mall Ln 18202
W Sugarloaf Ln 18202
Summer Ct 18201
Summit Rd 18202
Sun Ct 18202
Sunburst Dr 18202
Sunflower Ct 18202
Sunset Dr 18201
Susquehanna Blvd & Dr 18202
Taft St 18201
Tamaqua St 18201
Tamarack St 18202
E Tamarack St 18201
W Tamarack St 18201
Taylor Ct 18201
Terrace Ave 18202
Terrace Blvd 18201
Thirwell Ave 18201
Thomas Ln 18202
Thompson St 18201
Three Winds Way 18202
Tim Dr 18201
Tioga Dr 18202
Top Of The 80s Rd 18202
Torrey Pines Dr 18202
Tournament Way 18202
Transportation Dr 18201
Troon Rd 18202
Turnberry Ct & Ln 18202
Tuscarora Dr W 18202
Twin Oaks Rd 18202
Unami Cir 18202
Unico Dr 18202
University Dr 18202
Upper St 18202
Vall St 18202
Valley View Dr 18202
Valmont Pkwy 18202
Valmont Industrial Park 18202
Valmont Trailer Ct 18202
Vell St 18202
Venisa Dr 18202
Veterans Rd 18202
Village St 18202
Vincent St 18202
N Vine St
2-18 18201
20-1015 18201
1016-1022 18202
1017-1023 18201
1024-1100 18202
1102-1198 18202
1200-3199 18202
S Vine St 18201
Virginia Cir 18201
Walden Ct & Dr 18202
E & W Walnut St 18201
Wampum Cir 18202
Wanaki Cir 18202
N & S Warren St 18202
Washington Ave & St 18202
Wasko Ct 18202
Wayne Ave & St 18202
Webster Ave 18202
Wedgewood Rd 18202
Weis Ln 18202
West Rd 18202
Westgate Dr 18202
White Birch Rd 18202
Wichita Ln 18202
Wilbur Ct
500-1019 18201
1021-1099 18202
N Wilson Dr & St 18201
Winds Way 18202
Winged Foot Dr 18202
Winters Ave 18202
Wood Dr 18201
Woodbine St 18202
Woodcrest Blvd 18202
Woodlawn Dr 18202
S Woodward Ct 18201
N & S Wyoming St 18201
Yanac St 18202
York Ct 18201
Yorktown Dr 18201

NUMBERED STREETS

E & W 1st 18201
E & W 2nd 18201
E & W 3rd 18201
E & W 3rd 18202
E & W 4th 18201
E & W 4th 18202
E & W 5th 18201
E & W 5th 18202
E 6th St 18201
N 6th St 18202
W 6th St 18201
E & W 7th 18201
E & W 8th 18201
E & W 9th 18201
E & W 10th 18201
E & W 11th 18201
E & W 12th 18201
E & W 13th 18201
E & W 14th 18201
E & W 15th 18201
W 16th St 18201
E 17th St 18201
W 17th St
1-899 18201
900-934 18202
901-1099 18202
936-1030 18202
1032-1198 18202
W 18th St 18201
W 19th St
1-899 18201
900-998 18202
901-997 18202
999-1099 18202
E 20th St 18201
W 20th St
1-855 18201
856-898 18202
857-877 18201
879-885 18202
887-1099 18202
900-1999 18202
1101-1109 18202
E 21st St 18201
W 21st St
1-899 18201
900-946 18202
E 22nd St 18202
W 22nd St 18202
E 23rd St 18202
W 24th St 18202
W 27th St 18202
W 28th St 18202
W 30th St 18202
W 31st St 18202
E 32nd St 18202
W 32nd St 18202
E 34th St 18202
E & W 36th 18202
E & W 37th 18202

JOHNSTOWN PA

General Delivery 15907

POST OFFICE BOXES MAIN OFFICE STATIONS AND BRANCHES

Box No.s
1 - 1889 15907
5001 - 5720 15904
6000 - 9750 15907

NAMED STREETS

Academic Ave 15904
Academy St 15906
Adams Ave 15909
Adams St 15901
Adda Ln 15905
Admiral Peary Hwy 15909
Agnes Ave 15905
Airport Rd
100-199 15902
200-599 15904
Akers St 15905
Albany St 15906
Albert Ave 15906
Alberta Ave 15905
Albright Ave 15905
Aldan Rd 15909
Alexander St 15906
Alfa Ave 15909
Alfred St 15904
Algonquin St 15904
Alicia Ln 15905
Allbaugh Park Rd 15909
Allenbill Dr 15904
Alliene Ave 15904
Allison Dr 15904
Alma Ave 15902
Almira St 15905
Alois St 15904
Alpha Dr 15904
Alvin St 15904
Alwine St 15904
Amc Ln 15902
American St 15905
Ames Ct 15905
Amherst Rd 15905
Amos Ln 15909
Anderson Dr 15909
Anderson Ln 15905
Andrew Dr 15905
Angeline Ave 15902
Angle Ln 15905
Angler Pl 15906
Ann St 15905
Annette St 15904
Annie St 15902
Anthony St 15906
Antonazzo Ln 15902
Antonia St 15905
April Ln 15906
Arbutus Ave & Vlg 15904
Arch St 15905
Arlington St 15905
Arnold St 15906
Arrowhead Ct 15905
Arthur Dr 15909
Arthur St 15902
Arvilla St 15904
Ash St 15902
Ashcraft Ln 15906
Ashlyn Dr 15904
Aspen Way 15906
Aspen Woods Ln 15904
Asphalt Rd 15906
Atlantic St 15904
Atlee St 15905
Austin St 15905
Autumn Dr 15904
Avalon Ave 15906
Aviation Dr 15902
Avis Ave 15905
Azurite Ln 15902
B St 15906
Baffin Dr 15904
Baiker St 15902
Bailing St 15909
Baker St 15906
Bakers Acres Ln 15905
Bald Eagle St 15909
Baldwin Aly 15902
Ballow Ln 15909
Balsam St 15909
Bansky Ave 15909
Bantel St 15905
Banyan Dr 15904
Barbera Dr 15904
Barbush St 15906
Barclay St 15901
Barn Swallow Ln 15905
Barnett St 15905
Barnhart St 15905
Barron Ave 15906
Barry James Pl 15904
Bartlett St 15909
Bass Ave 15904
Basset Ln 15906
Bates Dr 15905
Batzel Rd 15906
Baumer St 15902
Baun Ln 15905
Bay St 15902
Bayush St 15902
Baywood St 15901
Beacon St 15905
Bear St 15906
Beatrice Ave 15906
Beatty Ave 15906
Beaver Ct 15905
Beckley Ave 15902
Bedford St
200-399 15901
500-1899 15902
1900-3099 15904
Beech Ave 15901
Beech Hill Rd 15904
Beechspring St 15904
Beechwood St 15904
Beiter Dr 15909
Bel Air Dr 15904
Bella Vista Dr 15904
Bellevue St 15905
Belmont St 15904
Belton St 15904
Benchmark Ln 15905
Benedict St 15906
Benshoff St 15906
Benshoff Hill Rd
473-497 15906
499-1699 15906
1701-1935 15906
2000-3249 15909
3251-3253 15909
Bentwood Ave 15904
Berg St 15902
Berkebile St 15902
Berkey Dr 15904
Berkley Rd 15905
Berks Dr 15905
Berkshire Dr 15904
Bernard St 15904
Bertmin St 15904
Berwick Rd 15904
Beta Dr 15904
Bethel St 15906
Betheny Dr 15904
Bheam Ave 15906
Biffs Aly 15906
Big Rock Ln 15906
Billow Park Ln 15906
Binder Ln 15909
Birch Ave 15906
Birch St 15909
Birtle Rd 15904
Bishop St 15902
Black Bear Trl 15904
Blackberry St 15906
Blackburn Rd 15909
Blackner Rd 15905
Blaine St 15906
Blair St 15905
Blawn St 15906
Blenck St 15904
Blenny Pl 15906
Bliss St 15905
Bloom St 15902
Bloomfield St 15904
Blossom St 15905
Blough Rd 15905
Blough St 15902
Blue Diamond St 15902
Blue Dolphin Rd 15909
Bluff St 15905
Bob St 15904
Bobwhite St 15904
Bockel Cir 15905
Boise St 15904
Bole St 15906
Boltz St 15902
Bon Air St 15909
Bond St 15902
Bonita St 15904
Border Ln 15906
Bossler St 15902
Boston St 15905
Boulder Dr 15905
Bowser Ln 15905
Boxler Dr 15904
Boyd Ave 15905
Boyer St 15906
Bracken St 15909
Braddock St 15905
Bradley Ln 15904
Brallier Pl 15906
Brandle St 15904
Brazil Ln 15909
Breck Ln 15904
Breezewood Dr 15905
Brehm Ave 15906
Brendel St 15906
Brenlin St 15904
Brenton Dr 15909
Bretton Rd 15905
Briarwood Dr 15904
Bridge St
1-199 15902
1001-1399 15909
Brier Ave 15902
Briggs Ave 15909
Broad St 15906
Broadwing St 15909
Bronx St 15905
Brook Ln 15904
Brookside Way 15904
Brothers Ln 15905
Brotz Pl 15901
Bruce St 15902
Bruin St 15909
Brumbaugh St 15904
Brush Ave 15906
Bryan St 15902
Buchan Rd 15906
Buchanan Ave 15904
Buck Ave 15902
Bucknell Ave 15905
Bud Ln 15909
Budfield St 15904
Bunker St 15902
Buriak Rd 15909
Burk Ave 15904
Burkhard St 15906
Burley St 15906
Bushwack Rd 15904
Butler Ave 15906
C St 15906
Caitlyn Dr 15904
Caldwell St 15904
Calhoun St 15906
Calvin Dr 15905
Cambria Pl 15906
Cambria St 15909
Cambridge Rd 15905
Camden Ave 15904
Camelot Ct 15904
Campbell Ave 15902
Campus Dr 15905
Campus Commons Ln 15904
Candler Ln 15909
Canfield Ave 15904
Cannon St 15905
Canterbury Way 15904
Capital Ave 15905
Cardiff St 15906
Cardinal Ln 15905
Carlisle St 15905
Carmel St
100-199 15902
200-899 15904
Carnation St 15902
Carnegie Ave 15905
Caroline St 15906
Carrier St 15905
Carroll Dr 15905
Carwyn Dr 15904
Case Ave 15905
Castle St 15906
Catalina Dr 15904
Catherine St
100-199 15901
1100-1199 15905
Catskill Ln 15904
Cauffiel Ln 15905
Cedar St 15902
Celeste Dr 15905
Cemetery Dr 15904
Center Pl 15906
Central Ave 15902
Cernic Rd 15906
Champagne Ave 15905
Chancellor St 15904
Chandler Ave 15906
Chapel Ln 15909
Chapin St 15901
Charles St 15902
Chaser St 15909
Cheney St 15905
Cheney Oak Dr 15905
Cherokee St 15904
Cherry Ln 15904
Cherry Crest Dr 15906
Chester St 15906
Chestnut St
424R-424R 15909
100-999 15906
401-423 15909
425-531 15909
533-599 15909
Cheswick Dr 15904
Chickaree Hill Rd 15909
Chime Rd 15906
Chippewa Rd 15904
Chris Dr 15909
Christine Ct 15905
Christopher St 15905
Christy Dr 15904
Chrysler Ave 15904
Chuk Ln 15909
Church Ave 15901
Church Dr 15909
Churchill St 15904
Cindy St 15904
Cinema Dr 15905
Clair Ave 15902
Clapboard Run Rd 15904
Clarence St 15905
Clarion St 15905
E & W Clarissa Ln 15909
Clark St 15902
Clay St 15905
Claythorne Dr 15904
Clayton Dr 15904
Clear Spring Ln 15904
S Clearfield St 15905
Clearview Ct 15905
Clearwater St 15904
Cleo Ln 15902
Clermont St 15904
Cleveland St 15902
Cliff St 15902
Clifford St 15906
Clinton St 15901
Clover St 15902
Club Dr 15905
Coal St 15901
Coconut Pl 15901
Coldren St 15904
Coleman Ave 15902
Colgate Ave 15905
Colleen St 15906
College Park Plz 15904
Collegiate Dr 15904
Collier St 15902
Collins St 15901
Colonial St 15905

Colonial Ridge Rd 15904
Columbia St 15905
Comet Ct 15905
Commerce Ct 15904
Community College Way 15904
Concord St 15902
Confer Ave 15905
Congress Ave 15905
Connelly Ave 15906
Conrad St 15905
Constable Ave 15904
Conway Ct 15901
Cook St 15906
Cookietown Rd 15905
Coon Ridge Rd 15905
Cooper Ave 15906
Coral Ave 15904
Cord St 15906
Corinne Ave 15906
Cornell Pl 15905
Corning St 15905
Corrigan Dr 15904
Cottage Pl 15901
Coty Ln 15909
Coulter Aly 15909
Country Ln 15904
Country Club Rd 15905
Country Side Ln 15904
Court Dr 15905
Courter Ave 15909
Cove St 15906
Coventry Ct 15905
Cover St 15902
Covered Bridge Rd 15905
Covington Dr 15904
Cox St 15905
Coyote St 15909
Crabtree Ln 15905
Cramer Pike 15906
Crane St 15909
Crawford Ln 15904
Creek Ln 15905
Creek View Ln 15906
Creekside Dr 15909
Cresswood St 15901
Crest Ave 15902
Crestview Dr 15904
Cronin Pl 15901
Crouse Ave 15901
Croyle St 15905
Crystal St 15906
Ctc Dr 15904
Cub St 15906
Culin St 15905
Cullis Ln 15909
Cummins St 15902
Cunard Ln 15904
Curtis Dr 15904
Cushon St 15902
Custom Ln 15909
Cypress Ave 15902
D St 15906
D Street Ext 15906
Dahlia St 15905
Daisy St 15905
Dakota Pl 15902
Dakota St 15904
Dalton Run Rd 15905
Damian Dr 15905
Danchare St 15909
Daniel St 15906
Danner St 15904
Darlene St 15904
Darlington Dr 15904
Darr St 15904
Dartmouth Ave 15905
David St 15902
Davis St 15906
Dawn Ln 15905
Debra Ln 15905
Debran Ln 15905
Decker Ave 15906
Deer Run Ct 15904
Deerfield Ln 15905
Delaware Ave 15906
Dell St 15905
Delta Dr 15904
Demuth St 15904
Denali Ln 15905
Denton St 15902
Derby St 15905
Derrick Ln 15905
Derubis Ln 15909
Devlin St 15901
Devon Dr 15904
Dewey St 15902
Diamond Blvd 15905
Diana Ave 15906
Dibert St 15901
Dickert St 15906
Dickinson St 15905
Dill Ln 15905
Dishong Mountain Rd 15906
Dithridge Dr 15905
Dobson Dr 15904
Doe Run 15905
Doel Rd 15905
Dogwood Way 15905
Dolphin St 15904
Domo Ave 15906
Donald Ln 15904
Donato Ct 15905
Donjay St 15909
Donna Dr 15905
Donruth Ln 15909
Doreen St 15904
Dormar Pl 15905
Dormer St 15909
Dorothy Ave 15906
Dowling Rd 15904
Dravis St 15904
Drew St 15906
Drexel Ave 15905
Drury Ln 15905
Dry Run St 15909
Drzal St 15902
Duchess Ln 15904
Duke Pl 15901
Duncan Pl & Way 15905
Dundee Ln 15905
Dupont St 15902
Durant St 15906
Dutch Ln 15902
Duwell St 15906
Dwight Dr 15904
Dynamo St 15909
Eagle Dr 15909
Earl St 15906
East Ave 15905
Ebensburg Rd 15901
Echo Rd 15909
Eckel St 15906
Eda Ln 15909
Edge Ave 15909
Edgehill Dr 15905
Edgewood Ave 15906
Edith Ave 15906
Edmonds Pl 15905
Edson Ave 15905
Edward Hls & St 15905
Eifler Ln 15905
Eisaman Rd 15905
Eisenhower Blvd
100-399 15905
400-1500 15904
1502-1598 15904
Elbert St 15904
Elder St 15902
Electra Dr 15904
Elgin Dr 15904
Elim St 15905
Elizabeth Ct 15905
Elknud Ln 15905
Ellsmere Dr 15904
Ellsworth St 15905
Elm Dr 15905
Elmar St 15904
Elsie Dr 15904
Elton Rd 15904
Ember St 15909
Emerald St 15902
Emilio St 15904
Emmel Ln 15909
Emmett Dr 15905
Emory Ave 15905
Engbert Rd
100-165 15902
166-298 15904
300-399 15904
Englewood St 15901
Enterprise Ln 15902
Enterprise St 15906
Entrance Dr 15905
Erickson Dr 15904
Erie St 15905
Erin Rd 15905
Erma St 15904
Esterville Rd 15905
Esther St 15906
Esty St 15905
Euclid Ave 15904
Eugene St 15904
Eureka Ln 15902
Evans St 15905
Evelyn Ln 15904
Evergreen St 15904
Everhart St 15901
Faight Ct 15909
Fair Ave 15904
Fair Oaks Dr 15905
Fairfield Ave 15906
Fairlane Ct 15906
Faith Ln 15905
Falcon Dr 15905
Falls Run Rd 15904
Family Ln 15905
Fan Ct 15906
Farm Ln 15905
Farragut St 15905
Farrell Ave 15906
Fawn Ln 15904
Fayette St 15905
Federal St 15905
Feeder St 15901
Felix Rd 15906
Fender Ln 15905
Fenn Aly 15901
Ferg St 15902
Ferndale Ave 15905
Fernwood Dr & Pl 15905
Ferry St 15904
Fieldstone Ave 15904
Fifty Acre Rd 15904
Figg Ave 15901
Figg St 15906
Fillmore Ave 15906
Fillmore St 15905
Final Approach Ln 15904
Finch St 15905
Fingerhoot St 15902
Fiocca Dr 15904
N Fir Dr 15905
Fir St 15909
Fisher Ln 15905
Fisk Ave 15905
Flag Ave 15902
Flax Ave 15905
Fleetwood St 15901
Fleming Ave 15905
Flinn St 15905
Flintlock St 15909
Flora St 15906
Florida Ave
1100-1959 15902
1960-2099 15904
Floyd St 15905
Forbes Ct 15905
Ford St 15906
Fordhook Ave 15904
Forest Ave 15902
Forest Edge Dr 15905
Fortune Ln 15905
Foster St 15902
Foust Ave 15902
Foust Dr 15904
Fox Run 15904
Fox Run Rd 15904
Frances St 15904
Franco Ave 15905
Frank St 15906
Franklin St
1288RR-1290RR 15905
1-99 15909
100-106 15901
108-112 15901
111-113 15907
114-848 15901
115-849 15901
850-2432 15905
2434-2436 15905
Frankstown Rd 15902
Frazier St 15906
Frederick St 15902
Freedom Ave 15904
Freeman Dr 15904
Freidhoff Ln 15902
Frick Ave 15902
Frieda Ave 15902
Fritz St 15905
Froan St 15906
Fronheiser St 15902
Frosty Ln 15905
Fuge Ln 15905
Fulmer Rd 15904
Fulton St 15901
Furnari Ave 15905
Fye St 15904
G St 15906
Gable St 15906
Gail St 15902
Galena Ln 15904
Galleria Dr 15904
Galleria Dr Ext 15904
Gamma Dr 15904
Gap Ave 15904
Gapvax Ln 15904
Gardner St 15905
Garfield St 15906
Garland Ave 15905
Garman Dr 15909
Garnet St 15909
Garrison Rd 15909
Garvey Pl 15906
Gaston Dr 15904
Gates St 15906
Gauntner St 15902
Gautier St 15901
Gayview Ter 15905
Gazebo Park 15901
Geis St 15904
Gemini Dr 15904
George St 15905
Georgian Pl 15905
Gerald Ct 15902
Gerber St 15902
Gerry Ln 15904
Gertrude Ct 15905
Getta Way 15909
Gibby Ln 15904
Gilbert St 15906
Girard St 15905
Glacken Ave 15909
Glass Rd 15902
Glenn St 15906
Glenwood Ave 15905
Glessner Rd 15905
Golde St 15902
Goldfinch Ln 15909
Golias Ct 15905
Goller Dr 15902
Good St 15905
Goodman Ln 15905
Gothal Dr 15902
Goucher St 15905
Goughnour St 15909
Gould Ave 15904
Govier Ln 15905
Grace Ave 15902
Graham St 15906
Grambling St 15904
Granger Dr 15905
Grape Ave 15906
Grass Ave 15906
Grata Ln 15906
Gray Ave 15901
Graybill Pl 15906
Grayson Ave 15904
Graystone Ln 15905
Graywood St 15901
Grazier St 15905
Green Valley St 15902
Greene St 15905
Greenhouse Rd 15905
Greenich St 15902
Greentree Ln 15905
Greenwich Rd 15904
Greeve St 15909
Gregg Ave 15906
Gregory Rd 15905
Griffith Ave 15909
Grove Ave 15902
Guard St 15906
Gurth Ln 15905
Gusty Ct 15905
H St 15906
Habicht St 15906
Hagen St 15906
Hahn Pl 15901
Haldon Dr 15905
Halite Pl 15901
Hall St 15906
Hamalin Dr 15905
Hamel Ln 15905
Hammer Ave 15905
Hancock St 15904
Hannah Ave 15909
Harding St 15905
Harlan Ave 15905
Harmony Dr 15909
Harold Ave 15906
Harrison St 15906
Harry Pl 15902
Harshberger Rd 15905
Harteis Ln 15905
Harteis Rd 15904
Harwood St 15901
Hastings St 15904
Hatch Ln 15902
Hatch Hollow Rd 15904
Hattie Ave 15906
Havana St 15904
Haverford St 15905
Hawkins St 15902
Hawthorne St 15904
Hay Ave
100-198 15905
200-299 15902
Hayden Dr 15905
Haynes St 15901
Hazel St 15909
Headrick Aly 15909
Headricks Rd 15909
Healy Ln 15905
Hearthside Rd 15906
Heather Ln 15904
Heeney Ave 15904
Heidelberg Ln 15905
Heinlein Ln 15904
Heinrich St 15904
Heinz Ct 15904
Held Ln 15902
Helen St 15905
Helsel Rd 15904
Hemlock St 15906
Henry St 15905
Hereford Ln 15905
Heritage St 15909
Herman Ln 15909
Hester St 15905
Hickory St 15902
Hidden Valley Dr 15905
Highfield St 15904
Highland Ave 15902
Highland Park Rd 15904
Hildebrand St 15909
Hill Aly 15901
Hill Dr 15909
Hillcrest Ct 15905
Hillholm St 15905
Hillside Ct 15902
Hillside Trl 15905
Hillson St 15905
Hillview St 15905
Hinkston Run Rd
101-199 15906
829-835 15909
Hipp St 15902
Hofecker Ln 15905
Hoffman Ave 15906
Hoffman Dr 15904
Holbay Dr 15906
Holly St 15902
Home St 15906
Homestead Ave 15902
Honan Ave 15906
Hood Ave 15905
Hoover Ave 15904
Hope St 15902
Hopp Ave 15905
Hopwood St 15902
Horner St 15902
Hornet Ave 15902
Hornick St 15904
Horrocks St 15901
Hostetler Rd 15904
W Howard St 15906
Hoyt St 15904
Hudson St 15901
Hughes Pl 15906
Hull Ave 15906
Hummel St 15902
Hunsinger Rd 15904
Hunt Rd 15909
Hunt St 15905
Hurton St 15902
Hystone Ave 15905
I St 15906
Ihmsen Ave 15901
Indiana St 15905
Industrial Park Rd 15904
Inez St 15904
Iolite Ave 15901
Irene St 15905
Iron St 15906
Iroquois St 15904
Irving St 15905
Irwin Ln 15909
Ivy Rd 15905
J St
1-199 15906
400-499 15905
Jackson St
1-199 15909
111-121 15901
126-134 15901
E Jackson St 15909
Jacob St 15902
Jacob Albright Dr 15904
Jacoby St 15902
Jacqueline Dr 15904
Jade St 15906
Jaffa Dr 15905
James St 15902
Janet St 15905
Janie St 15902
Jari Dr 15904
Jason Dr 15904
Jasper Aly 15901
Jaycee Dr 15904
Jean Ave 15906
Jefferson St 15905
Jeffrey Dr 15905
Jennie Ln 15904
Jesse Ln 15909
Jessell Dr 15904
Jim Edwards Dr 15904
Jimdot Ln 15905
Johns St 15901
Johnson St 15902
Jordan Dr 15904
Joseph Ave 15902
Joy Ave 15902
Jude Dr 15909
Judith Dr 15905
Judy St 15905
Julia Dr 15905
Juliana Ln 15904
Julz Dr 15904
Juniper St 15905
K St 15906
Karen Way 15904
Kartes St 15906
Kasic Ave 15909
Kathleen Ave 15905
Kathy Ct 15905
Kathy Dr 15904
Keafer Rd 15905
Keafer Hill Rd 15905
Kegg Ave 15904
Keiper Ln 15909
Kemmer St 15905
Kemp Ln 15904
Kenesaw Ln 15905
Kennard St 15906
Kennedy Ave 15901
Kenneth Ave 15904
Kenruth Ave 15905
Kensington Dr 15905
Kenwood Ave 15909
Kepple Rd 15909
Keppler Dr 15905
Kerr Dr 15904
Kerry Ct 15905
Kiawa St 15904
Killian Ave 15909
Killian St 15906
Killiwhat St 15902
Kimberly Dr 15904
Kinamrok St 15904
King St 15905
Kingston Pl 15901
Kinzey St 15904
Kissell Ln 15909
Kleban Dr 15904
Kleinmans Rd 15905
Kline Ave 15909
Knauer Ln 15909
Knox St 15906
Koch Ave 15902
Kohan St 15906
Kohler St 15902
Kordell Ln 15905
Kraft St 15905
Krider St 15905
Kring St
8-98 15904
100-499 15904
1901-2097 15905
2099-2300 15905
2302-2726 15905
Krise Pl 15905
Krissay St 15904
Kunkle St 15906
Kurtz St 15902
L St 15906
Labraddor Ln 15906
Labrador Ln 15905
Lafree St 15904
Lager Ln 15906
Lake St 15906
Lakeshore Dr 15905
Lakewood Ave 15904
Lamberd Ave 15904
Lancer Ct 15906
Langhorne Ave 15905
Laporta Ln 15904
Lark Dr 15905
Laura St 15906
Laurel Ave 15906
Laurel Way 15905
Laurel Ridge Rd 15909
Laurelview Dr 15905
Lauren Ln 15905
Lauretta Ln 15904
Laurlis Ln 15904
Lawrence St 15904
Layton Ln 15904
Lazo Grv 15909
Lazos Grove Rd 15909
Leaf St 15904
Ledwich Ln 15904

Leffler Dr 15904
Legend Ave 15905
Lego Ave 15909
Lehigh St 15905
Lehman Pl 15902
Leidy Ln 15909
Leila St 15905
Leisure Ave 15904
Lemon St 15902
Lenhart St 15901
Lennox Aly 15905
Lenore St 15904
Leon St 15905
Leonard St 15902
Leroy St 15906
Leslie Dr 15905
Leslie St 15906
Leventry Rd 15904
Levergood St 15901
Levi Ln 15905
Lexington Ave 15902
Liberty Ave 15905
Lichtenfels Rd 15905
Liffey Ln 15904
Ligonier Pike 15905
Lillie Dr 15904
Lina St 15902
Lincoln St 15901
Linda Dr & St 15905
Lindberg Ave 15905
Linden Ave 15902
Linden St 15909
Lindsey Pl 15905
Linkville Rd 15906
Lintner Ave 15902
Linton St 15905
Linwood Ave 15902
Lion St 15904
Littlejohn Ln 15905
Lloyd Ct 15906
Locher Rd 15904
Locust St
2-18 15909
20-425 15909
233-241 15901
243-799 15901
1001-1097 15909
1099-1200 15909
1202-1398 15909
Logan St 15905
Lohr Pl 15902
Long St 15902
Longview Ln 15905
Lorain St 15905
Louis St 15902
Louisa Pl 15905
Lovejoy Ln 15904
Low St 15906
Lower Newtown Rd 15904
Lowman St 15901
Lucas Pl 15901
Lucetta St 15905
Ludwig St 15904
Lulay St 15904
Luna Ln 15904
Lundy Ln 15904
Lunen St 15902
Luray Ave 15904
Luther Rd 15904
Luzerne St 15905
Luzerne Street Ext 15905
Luzon Ave 15902
Lydia Ave 15904
Lyle Ct 15905
Lyman Ln 15909
Lyndy St 15904
Lynn St 15906
Lyter Dr 15905
M St 15906
Mabel St 15905
Mack Ave 15906
Macridge Ave 15904
Madison Ave 15909
Magdalene Way 15905
Mage Ln 15906
Maggie Ln 15905
Main St
1-23 15909
25-417 15909
100-799 15901
419-509 15909
1000-1299 15909
Maken Dr 15904
Malachite Dr 15902
Malbranc Rd 15905
Malloy Pl 15901
Maple Ave 15901
Maple Gates Ln 15906
Maple Leaf St 15909
Maplebrook Ln 15905
Maplewood Dr 15904
Marble Aly 15909
Marbury Ave 15906
Mardis Ave 15906
Margaret Ave 15905
Margaret Ln 15909
Marhefka Dr 15909
Marietta Dr 15904
Marilyn Way 15904
Marion Pl 15901
Mark Ln 15905
Market St 15901
Markley Ct 15902
Marlene St 15902
Marlin St 15905
Mars St 15905
Marsh Ave 15902
Marshall Ave 15905
Martha Ln 15905
Martin Rd 15904
Martina Ln 15909
Mary Ct 15902
Mary Dr 15905
Mary Ann Ct 15906
Mary Grace Ln 15901
Maryland Ave 15906
Masoryax Ln 15906
Matley Ct 15906
Matthew St 15901
Maxwell Ave 15904
May St 15902
Mayer Ave 15905
Mayluth Rd 15904
Maywood St 15909
Mcarthur St 15904
Mccabe St 15901
Mccaffrey Ln 15905
Mccauley Ave 15906
Mcclain St 15905
Mccleester Ln 15906
Mccord Ave 15902
Mccort Pl 15904
Mccreary St 15906
Mcgregor Ln 15904
Mckee Ave 15906
Mckeever St 15906
Mckinley Ave 15905
Mcmillen St 15902
Mcminn St 15904
Meade St 15901
Meadow Dr 15905
Mechanics Rd 15909
Melander St 15905
Melanie Dr 15904
Meldende St 15906
Mellon Ct 15905
Mellott Dr 15905
Melvin St 15904
Menoher Blvd
200-850 15901
851-997 15905
999-4199 15905
Mercedas St 15904
Merchant St 15904
Mercury Ave 15906
Meridian Ave 15906
Merritt St 15906
Mervine Ln 15902
Messenger St 15902
Metzler St 15904
Meyer Ave 15906
Miami St 15905
Michele Dr 15904
Michigan Ave 15905
Midway Dr 15905
Mifflin St 15905
Mildred Ave 15902
Mile Hill Rd 15909
Miles St 15902
Milford St 15905
Millard Ave 15906
Millcreek Holw 15905
Millcreek Rd
400-799 15901
800-899 15905
Miller Ave 15902
Milling Dr 15906
Mills St 15904
Milo Ln 15904
Milton St 15905
Minno Dr 15905
Mitchell Ct 15905
Mitnik Ave 15909
Mizel Ln 15902
Mockingbird Ln 15909
Mohawk Dr 15905
Montag St 15902
Montour St 15905
Moonlit Dr 15904
Moonshine Hollow Rd 15905
Moore St 15901
Morgan Pl 15901
Morrell Pl 15901
Morris St 15904
Moschgat Ave 15902
Moshannon Dr 15909
Mosholder St 15905
Moss Ln 15904
Mossy Ln 15905
Mount Airy Dr 15904
Mount View Dr 15905
Mountain Rd 15906
Mountain Laurel Ln 15905
Mowery Ave 15905
Muel Dr 15906
Mulberry St 15905
Muncie St 15905
Murdock St 15902
Murphy Dr 15905
Murton Ave 15902
Mushroom St 15905
Mya Dr 15904
Myrtle Pl 15905
Mystic Ct 15906
Nadona Ave & St 15904
Nancy Lynn Dr 15902
Napoleon Pl & St 15901
Nash St 15906
Natalie St 15906
Nathaniel St 15902
Naugle Dr 15904
Navin Aly 15901
Naylor Rd 15906
Nedrich Ln 15909
Nees Ave 15904
Neil St 15904
Nellik Ln 15909
Nevin St 15904
New St 15901
Newbaker Dr 15904
Niagara St 15909
Nice Ave 15905
Nimby Ln 15909
Nitch Ln 15905
Noahs Ark Ln 15904
Noble Rd 15905
Noradera St 15904
North St 15906
Northfork Rd 15905
Northwood Ave 15905
Norton Rd 15906
Norwood Gdns 15905
Norwood St 15904
Nutmeg Ct 15909
Oak St
1-413 15909
306-318 15902
320-999 15902
415-425 15909
Oak Eden Dr 15904
Oakbrook Ln 15904
Oakhurst Homes 15906
Oakland Ave 15902
E & W Oakmont Blvd 15904
Oakridge Dr 15904
Ober St 15902
Oberlin St 15905
Ocala Ave 15902
Oconnor St 15905
Odax St 15902
Ofsanko Ln 15902
Ogle St 15905
Ohio St 15902
Old Airport Rd 15904
Old Colony Dr 15904
Old Country Rd 15905
Old Delta Ln 15905
Old Farm Ln 15904
Old Hickory Ln 15905
Old Keafer St 15905
Old Krings Rd 15904
Old Orchard Way 15905
Old Peterson Dr 15905
Old Rocky Rd 15905
Old Scalp Ave 15904
Old Soap Hollow Rd 15905
Old Somerset Pike 15905
Old State Hwy 15905
Old Tire Hill Rd 15905
Old Walsall Rd 15904
Olds Ave 15906
Olim St 15904
Olive St 15905
Oliver Ave 15909
Olympic Ln 15904
Omar Dr 15905
Omega Dr 15904
Orange Ave 15906
Orchard St 15905
Orlando St 15905
W Osborne St 15905
Osprey Pl 15901
Ottawa St 15904
Otterbein Ln 15904
Otto Ct 15905
Owen Dr 15904
Owens Rd 15905
Packer St 15904
Palliser St 15905
Palm Ave 15905
Palmer Ave 15906
Pamela Ln 15905
Panarama Dr 15906
Pansy St 15905
Paradise Rd 15909
Park Ave 15902
Parker Rd 15904
Parkhill Dr 15909
Parkside Dr 15904
Parkview Dr 15905
Parsons St 15902
Partridge Ct 15904
Pasquerilla Plz 15901
Pasture Ln 15909
Patrick Dr 15904
Patton Ter 15909
Paul St 15905
Pauline St 15904
Paulsen St 15906
Paulton St 15905
Pawnee Rd 15904
Peach Ave 15906
Pebbley St 15905
Peden Ln 15905
Peelor St 15901
Peggy Ln 15904
Pender Rd 15905
Penmar Ln 15904
Penn Ave 15905
Pennsylvania Ave 15906
Pennwoods Rd 15905
Pennzoil Dr 15909
Penrod St 15902
Penrose St 15906
Pershing St
1800-1899 15902
1900-1999 15904
Peter St 15901
Peterson Dr 15905
Phillips St 15904
Phoebe Ct 15901
Pickering Way 15905
Picklo St 15906
Pickworth St 15902
Pierce St 15906
Pike Aly 15902
Pike Rd 15909
Pilgrim Ct 15905
Pine Dr 15905
Pine St
177-197 15902
199-899 15902
1000-1004 15909
1006-1199 15909
Pinecrest Blvd & Way 15905
Pinegrove Ln 15905
Piney Pl 15906
Pitt Ave 15905
Plainfield Ave 15905
Platt Dr 15904
Playground Dr 15904
Plaza Dr 15905
Pleadone St 15905
Pleasant Dr 15904
Pleasant View Dr 15905
Plitt Ct 15905
Plum St 15901
Plymouth Ave 15906
Pocahontas Dr 15905
Podlucky St 15902
Poehners Greenhouse Rd 15905
Polaris Dr 15909
Pomona Dr 15905
Pond Rd 15906
Poplar St 15902
Porpoise Pl 15906
Porter St 15902
Power St 15906
Price St 15902
Princeton Ave 15905
Prospect St 15901
Prosser St 15901
Prosser Hollow Rd 15906
Providence Dr 15904
Pudliner Ln 15909
Pulaski Ln 15906
Purse Ave 15902
Quail Ave 15902
Quaker Ave 15905
Rachel St 15904
Radcon St 15904
Radian Dr 15904
Railroad St
200-398 15909
601-629 15901
631-1000 15901
1002-1098 15901
Rainbow Dr 15904
Ralph Ln 15909
Ralph St 15904
Rambo St 15905
Ramsey Ln 15909
Ranch Rd 15909
Random Way 15904
Randy Ln 15904
Ravine Ave 15905
Raymond Dr 15909
Rean St 15904
Rebecca Dr 15902
N & S Red Dr 15905
Red Oak Ln 15909
Redstar Ct 15901
Redwood Ave 15905
Reed Ct 15902
Reeder Ave 15905
Regal Dr 15904
Remington Dr 15902
Rena St 15904
Reservoir Dr 15909
Resty Ct 15905
Revere St 15904
Richard Ct 15905
Richland St 15904
Riders Rd 15906
Ridge Ave 15901
Ridge St 15905
Ridgeview Ln 15909
Ridgeway Dr 15904
Riffith St 15902
Rigo Ln 15905
Riley Pl 15901
Rimrock St 15909
Ringling Ave 15902
Ripple Ave 15906
Risher Bridge Rd 15905
Rita St 15905
Ritter Rd 15904
River Ave 15909
Riverside Ave 15905
Robb Ave 15901
Robert Ln 15904
Roberts Rd 15904
Robin St 15905
Robinson Ave 15905
Rock Ave 15902
Rockwell Ave 15905
Rockwood Ln 15905
Rocky Rd
100-199 15909
1000-1099 15905
Rodgers Ave 15902
Rolling Hills Rd 15905
Ronald St 15902
Roosevelt Blvd 15906
Rosa Ln 15905
Rose Aly 15906
Rose St 15905
Rose Branch St 15909
Rosedale St 15906
Rosefield St 15904
Rosemary Ln 15905
Rosemont Ave 15905
Rosenbaum St 15909
Rosewood St 15904
Ross Ln 15909
Ross St 15905
Roxbury Ave 15905
Royal Ave 15905
Ruby St 15902
Rudolph St 15904
Rudy Dr 15905
Russell Ave 15902
Rustic Ave 15904
Ruth Pl 15905
Rutledge St 15905
Sadie St 15906
Saint Clair Rd 15905
Saint Petkas Ln 15906
Saintz St 15906
Saipan Ave 15902
Sally Rd 15906
Salmon Ave 15904
Sam St 15902
Samuel St 15906
Sanbor Ave 15905
Sandak Ct 15906
Sandstone Ln 15906
Sandy Dr 15905
Sann St 15904
Sanrue Dr 15904
Santichen Aly 15906
Sara Ln 15904
Sarah Pl 15901
Saratoga St 15902
Saucon Way 15905
Sauers Ave 15906
Saybrook Pl 15906
Saylor St 15905
Saylor School Rd 15905
Scalp Ave 15904
Scenic Ln & Way 15905
Sceptor Ave 15909
Scheidinger St 15906
Schneider St 15906
School Pl 15901
School St 15905
Schoolhouse Rd 15904
Schrader Ave 15902
Scott Ave 15902
Seese Dr 15904
Seibert St 15902
Sell St 15905
Seminole St 15904
Seneca St 15904
Shadow Ln 15904
Shady Ln 15905
Shady Oak Dr 15905
Shaffer Rd & St 15905
Shaker St 15906
Shamrock St 15909
Shannon Way 15905
Sharkey Rd 15909
Shaw Ave 15904
Shawnee Rd 15904
Shearer St 15906
Shekomeko Ln 15905
Shelburne Pl 15905
Shelby St 15906
Shenandoah St 15909
Shenkelview Dr 15905
Shepard St 15909
Sheridan St 15906
Sherman St 15901
Sherwood Dr 15905
Shiloh Ave 15902
Shomo St 15902
Short St 15901
Shroyer Rd 15905
Silver Birch Ln 15905
Simchock Ln 15905
Simko Ln 15905
Simmons Ln 15909
Singer St 15901
Singer Hill Rd 15902
Sioux St 15904
Skee Way 15904
Skelly St 15905
Skyline Dr 15902
Slagle St 15902
Slater St 15905
Slick Ave 15902
Smith Ave 15909
Smith Pl 15901
Smithfield St 15905
Smokie Ln 15905
Snably Ave 15909
Snyder Rd 15909
Soap Hollow Rd 15905
Solomon St 15902
Solomon Homes 15902
Solomon Run Rd 15904
Somerset Pike 15905
Somerset St 15901
Songbird Ln 15904
Sons Of Italy Rd 15905
South St 15901
Southmont Blvd 15905
Southview Ave 15905
Sozel Dr 15909
Space St 15902
Spear Ave 15905
Spindle St 15909
Spory St 15905
Spridall St 15902
Spring St 15906
Spruce Dr 15905
Spruce St 15909
Stackhouse St 15906
Stanford Ave 15905
Stanley Dr 15904
Stans Ln 15909
Stardust Dr 15904
Starr St 15906
Starvis Ln 15905
State St 15905
Station St 15905
Statler Pl 15902
Steel St 15901
Steeple Ln 15909
Stenger St 15904
Stephens St 15905

Stombaugh Ave 15906
Stone St 15906
Stone Hollow Rd 15905
Stonehedge Ct 15904
Stoner Ln 15902
Stoney Ln 15905
Stonybrook Ln 15904
Stonycreek St 15901
Storey Ave 15906
Stormer Pl 15901
Stow Ln 15905
Strauss Ave 15901
Strayer St 15906
Stuart St 15906
Studebaker Ct 15906
Stutzman St 15906
Stuver Dr 15905
Suie St 15904
Summit Ave 15905
Sunapee Dr 15904
Sunberry St 15904
Sunday St 15902
Sunnehanna Dr 15905
Sunny Ct 15905
Sunray Dr 15905
Sunrise Dr 15905
Sunset Ave 15905
Sunshine Ave 15905
Suppes Ave
1-199 15905
200-299 15902
Susan Dr 15905
Susanna Ct 15905
Susquehanna St 15905
Suter St 15905
Swan Dr 15909
Swank St 15905
Sylvan Dr 15902
Sylvia St 15904
Taft St 15906
Tall Timber Dr 15904
Tamarack Ln 15905
Tammie Ct 15905
Tampa Ave 15902
Tanase Ct 15901
Tank Dr 15904
Tanner St 15906
Tara Dr 15905
Taylor Ave 15906
Teaberry Ln 15904
Teak St 15902
Tech Park Dr 15901
Teeter Rd 15906
Tener St 15904
Tennessee Ave 15906
Terlyn Dr 15904
Terrace Dr 15904
Terry St 15902
Theatre Dr 15904
Thelma St 15902
Theo Ct 15905
Theodore St 15905
Theresa Pl 15901
Thermal Ave 15905
Thistle Pl 15905
Thoburn St 15905
Thomas Ave 15901
Thomas Ln 15909
Thora St 15904
Thorne St 15909
Thornton St 15904
Thrasher St 15909
Thunderbird Dr 15905
Ticonderoga Ln 15902
Tiffany St 15905
Tillman Ave 15905
Timothy St 15904
Timson St 15905
Tioga St 15905
Tire Hill Rd 15905
Tollgate Rd 15906
Toms Cir 15905
Town Centre Dr 15904
Township Shed Rd 15904
Traverse St 15905
Treasure Ln 15905
Trees Dr 15905
Tremont Rd 15906
Trent St 15901
Tripoli St 15902
Trojan Ln 15906
Trout St 15909
Troy St 15906
Truman Blvd 15902
Tunnel Ave 15905
Turbo Dr 15904
Twin Dr 15909
Tyke Rd 15909
Tyler Ct 15904
Union St 15901
Universal Dr 15904
Upper Newtown Rd 15904
Valley Pike 15905
Valley Run Rd 15904
Van Buren St 15909
Vance St 15905
Varner Ln 15909
Vaughn St 15906
Vella Ln 15904
Venango St 15905
Venture St 15909
Venus Ave 15905
Vesta Ln 15905
Veta Ln 15905
Vickroy Ave 15905
Victor St 15902
View St 15902
Viewmont Ave 15905
Viewtop St 15909
Village St 15902
Vine St 15901
Vineyard St 15906
Violet St 15905
Virginia Ave 15906
Vivian Dr 15904
Vo Tech Dr 15904
Vogel St 15902
Von Lunen Rd 15902
Waldo Ln 15906
Wales Ave 15904
Walker Ave 15906
Wall St 15906
Wallace St 15904
Walnut St 15901
Walters Ave 15904
Walton St 15905
Walts Ln 15906
Warbler St 15906
Warranso St 15901
Warren St 15905
Warrior St 15909
Washington St
101-197 15901
199-500 15901
502-598 15901
1100-1199 15905
Washko Ln 15904
Wassail Ave 15909
Water Rock Rd 15909
Waterfall Dr 15906
Watson St 15905
Wayne St 15905
Weaver Ct 15905
Weaver Rd 15904
Weber Rd 15905
Webster Ave 15905
Wedgewood Dr 15904
Weeping Willow Ln 15906
Weimer St 15904
Wellington Way 15904
Welsh Valley Dr 15905
Wertz Rd 15902
Wesley Dr 15904
Wess St 15902
West St 15905
Western Ave 15904
Westgate Dr 15905
Westinghouse Ave 15905
Westridge Rd 15904
Westview Ctr 15901
Westview Dr 15905
Wheat St 15902
Wheatland Ave 15909
Whispering Pines Ln 15905
N & S White Dr 15905
White Oak Ln 15904
Whitetail Dr 15902
Whitetail Rd 15909
Whysong Ln 15906
Widman St 15902
Wild Hemlock Ln 15905
Wildcat Rd 15906
Wildwood Ave 15904
Wiley St 15905
Willett Dr 15905
William Penn Ave
2-98 15901
100-499 15901
545-597 15906
599-1561 15905
1563-1563 15906
1571-3787 15909
Williams St 15904
Willis St 15906
Willow St 15901
Willow Pond Ln 15902
Willys St 15906
Wilshire Blvd 15905
Wilson St 15906
Winchester Dr 15905
Windan Ln 15905
Windsor Dr 15904
Wineland St 15904
Winter St 15902
Winton St 15905
Wissinger Hollow Rd 15904
Wonder St 15905
Wood St 15902
Woodcrest Dr 15905
Woodhaven Ln 15905
Woodland Ave 15902
Woodmont Rd 15905
Woodruff St 15905
Woodside Ave 15904
Woodvale Ave 15901
Work Dr 15904
Worth St 15905
Wos St 15906
Wren St 15905
Wyatt Ave 15909
Wyndemere Dr 15904
Wyndhaven Ct 15904
Wynn St 15906
Wyoming St 15905
Yale Ave 15905
Yeoman St 15906
Yingling Rd 15909
Yoder St 15901
Yost Ln 15904
Young St
300-399 15904
1901-1997 15902
1999-2099 15902
Younkers St 15902
Zallar St 15902
Zane Ln 15909
Zucco Ln 15905
Zurenda Ln 15909

NUMBERED STREETS

1st St 15909
2nd Ave 15906
2nd St 15909
3rd Ave 15906
3rd St 15909
4th Ave 15906
4th St 15909
5th Ave 15906
5th St 15909
6th Ave 15906
7th Ave 15906
8th Ave 15906
9th Ave 15906

LANCASTER PA

General Delivery 17604
General Delivery 17608

POST OFFICE BOXES MAIN OFFICE STATIONS AND BRANCHES

Box No.s
1 - 2956 17608
3001 - 4992 17604
5001 - 5555 17606
6001 - 6480 17607
7001 - 9120 17604
9998 - 9998 17611
10001 - 12425 17605
83080 - 83888 17608

NAMED STREETS

Aaron Ln 17601
Abbas Ave 17602
Abbeyville Rd 17603
Abe Ave 17601
Aberley Ln 17601
Abilene Ln 17603
Abington Ct 17603
Abraso St 17601
Acer Pl 17601
Acorn Blvd 17602
Addison Pl 17601
Alans Grn 17602
Albern Blvd 17601
Albright Ave 17603
Alden Dr 17601
Alderwood Way 17601
Aldred Cir 17601
Alfa Dr 17601
Allan Dr 17603
Almanac Ave 17602
Alston Ct 17601
Altheas Way 17603
Amanda Cir 17602
Ambassador Cir 17603
Amberly St 17601
American Ave 17602
Amesbury Rd 17601
Amity Dr 17601
Amsterdam Rd 17603
Amy Ln 17601
E Andrew St 17602
W Andrew St 17603
Angelica Dr 17601
N & S Ann St 17602
Anne Ave 17601
Apollo Dr 17601
Apostle Way 17603
Apple Ln & Rd 17601
Apple Blossom Dr 17602
Aquilla Dr 17601
Arbor Rd 17601
Arcadia Rd 17601
N & S Arch St 17603
Archers Gln 17601
Armel Dr 17603
Armstrong Ln 17603
Arrowwood Ct 17603
Ashbourne Ave 17601
Ashford Dr 17601
Ashland Dr 17601
Ashley Ct 17601
Aspen Ct 17603
Atkins Ave 17603
Atlantic Ave 17602
Aylesbury Dr 17601
Ayres Ct 17602
Bachman Rd 17602
Bald Eagle Ct 17601
Baldwin Dr 17602
Bank Barn Ln 17602
Banner Dr 17601
Bantam Ln 17601
Banyan Rd 17601
Banyan Circle Dr 17603
Barberry Dr 17601
Barclay Dr 17601
Barley Ave 17602
Baron Dr 17603
Barr Blvd 17603
Barrcrest Ln 17603
Barre Dr 17601
Barrholly Dr 17603
Barrister Pl 17601
Barrwick Ln 17603
Barton Dr 17603
Bassett Dr 17601
Basswood Dr 17602
Baumgardner Rd 17603
N Bausman Dr 17603
Bay St 17603
Bayberry Dr 17603
Beacon Hill Rd 17601
Beaconfield Ln 17601
Bean Blossom Dr 17603
Bean Hill Rd 17603
Beaver St 17603
Beaver Valley Pike 17602
Beech Ln 17601
Beechwood Rd 17601
Belair Dr 17601
Belle Meade Dr 17601
Belle Valley Rd 17603
Bellecrest Rd 17601
Bellevue Ct 17603
Belmont Ave 17601
Belmont St 17602
Bender Rd 17603
Bender Mill Rd 17603
Benedict Rd 17603
Benmar Dr 17603
Bennett Ave 17601
Bent Pine Ct N & S 17603
Bent Tree Dr 17603
Bentley Ln & Smt 17603
Bentley Ridge Blvd 17602
Berkshire Rd 17603
Bermuda Rd 17603
Bethany Ct 17601
Bethel Dr 17601
Betz Farm Dr 17603
Beverly Dr 17601
Big Bend Rd 17603
Billview Dr 17601
Biltmore Ave 17601
Birch Ct 17603
Birchpoint Pl 17601
Birchwood Rd 17603
Biscayne Rd 17601
Black Oak Dr 17602
Blacksmith Way 17601
Blaikley Cir 17601
Bloomingdale Ave 17601
Blossom Hill Dr 17601
Blossom Valley Rd 17601
Blue Grass Rd 17601
Blue Jay Dr 17601
Blue Ridge Dr 17603
Blue Rock Rd 17603
Blueberry Cir 17602
Bluff View Dr 17601
Bob White Ln 17601
Bonnie Dr 17601
Book Rd 17602
Booth Ave 17602
Boundary St 17601
Bowman Rd
199A-199A 17602
1-199 17602
2900-3200 17601
3202-3298 17601
Boxwood Ln 17602
Boyce Ave 17601
Bracken Dr 17601
Brandon Ct 17603
Brandywine Rd 17603
Braxton Dr 17602
Breckenridge Way 17601
Breda Dr 17603
Breeze Way 17602
Breezewood Dr 17601
Brenneman Rd 17603
Brewster Dr 17603
Briarwood Blvd 17601
Bridge Rd 17602
Bridle Cir 17603
Bridle Wreath Ln 17601
Bridlewood Ct N & S 17603
N & S Broad St 17602
Broad Lawn Cir 17603
Broadstone St 17603
Brockton Rd 17601
Brook Ter 17603
Brook Farms Rd 17601
Brookfield Rd 17601
Brookhaven Dr 17601
Brookline Rd 17603
Brookshire Dr 17601
Brookside Dr 17601
Browning Rd 17602
Brubaker Run Rd 17603
Brunswick Mall 17602
Bryan Dr 17601
Buch Ave 17601
Buchanan Ave 17603
Buchers Ml 17601
Buchmiller Park Dr 17602
Bucknell Ave 17603
Buckthorn Dr 17601
Buckwalter Rd 17602
Burlington Dr 17601
Burnham Ct 17601
Burrowes Ave 17602
Butler Ave 17601
Butter Rd 17601
Buttercup Rd 17602
Butterfield Rd 17601
Buttonwood Dr 17601
Buttonwood Ln 17603
Cadwell Ln 17601
Calvary Dr 17601
Calvert Ln 17603
Cambridge Vlg 17602
Camden Ct 17602
Camellia Pl 17601
Cameron Ave 17601
Campbell Ave 17603
Candlewyck Rd 17601
Canterbury Turn 17601
Capri Rd 17603
Cardinal Ct 17603
Cardinal Rd 17601
Carerra Dr 17601
Carlton Dr & Pl 17601
Caroline St 17603
Carriage Dr 17601
Carrie Ct 17601
Carroll Ln 17601
Carter Moir Dr 17601
Catherine St 17603
Cedar Ct 17603
Cedar Ln 17601
Cedar Rd 17601
Cedar Acres Dr 17602
Cedarhurst Cir 17603
Center Ave 17601
Center Dr 17601
Center Rd 17603
Centerville Rd
1-97 17603
99-261 17603
263-299 17603
300-1100 17601
1102-1198 17601
S Centerville Rd 17603
Central Plz 17602
Central Manor Rd 17603
Chadwick Cir 17603
Chambers St 17603
Chapel Rd 17603
Chapel Forge Ct & Dr 17601
Charles Rd 17603
Charlestown Rd 17603
N Charlotte St 17603
Charmayne Ave 17603
Charter Ln 17601
Chase Dr 17601
Chateau Hl 17602
Chelsea Dr 17601
Chelsea Loop 17602
N Cherry St 17602
Chesapeake St 17602
Chesley Dr 17603
Chester St 17602
E Chestnut St 17602
W Chestnut St
1-699 17603
48-50-48-50 17603
48-50-48-50 17608
Chestnut Ridge Dr 17601
Chestnut Valley Dr 17601
Chestnut View Dr 17603
Cheves Pl 17603
Chiswell Pl 17601
Chowning Pl 17601
N & S Christian St 17602
Christine Ln 17601
Chryst Cir 17601
Chukar Ct 17602
Church Rd 17603
Church St
1-599 17602
2000-2098 17603
2100-2299 17603
217-219-217-219 17602
Cindy Ln 17602
Circle Ave 17602
Circle Rd 17601
City Mill Rd 17602
Clarendon Dr 17603
Clark St 17602
E Clay St 17602
W Clay St 17603
Clayton Ave 17602
Clayton Rd 17603
Clearfield Ct E & W 17603
Clearview Ave 17601
Clearview Rd 17602
Clemens Cir & Rd 17602
Clermont Ave 17602
Cliff Ave 17602
Cloister Dr 17601
Clover Ave 17602
Clover Ct 17601
Clover Heights Rd 17602
Clover Hill Rd 17603
Coach Light Ln 17601
Cobblestone Ln 17601
Cochran Dr 17601
Colchester Dr 17603
Cold Stream Dr 17603
Colebrook Rd 17601
Colgate Ave 17603
Colleens Way 17601
College Ave 17603
Colonial Rd 17603
Colonial Crest Dr 17601
Colonial Manor Dr 17603
Colonial Village Ln 17601
Colony Cir 17601
Columbia Ave 17603
Commerce Dr & Park
E 17601
Community Way 17603
Conard Rd 17602
Concord Pl 17601
N Concord St 17603
Conestoga Ave 17602
Conestoga Blvd 17602
Conestoga Dr 17602
N Conestoga Dr 17602
Conestoga Rd 17602
Conestoga St 17603
Conestoga Woods Rd 17602
Conewago Ln 17601
Conley Ln 17603
Continental Dr 17601
Cool Creek Way 17602
Coopers Ct 17601
Copley Dr 17601
Copperfield Dr 17601
N Coral St 17603

Coreopsis Dr 17602
N & S Cornell Ave 17603
Cornerstone Dr 17603
Coronet Ave 17601
Corporate Blvd 17601
Corry Ave 17601
Corvair Rd 17601
Cotswold Ct 17601
Cottage Ave 17602
Cottontail Ct 17603
Cottonwood Ct 17601
Country Club Dr 17601
Country Meadows Dr 17602
Country Place Dr 17601
Countryside Dr 17601
Coventry Rd 17601
Covered Bridge Dr 17602
Covington Pl 17601
Cranberry Cir 17602
Creek Hill Rd 17601
Creek View Dr 17602
Creekside Dr 17602
Creekwood Dr 17602
Crescent Ave 17601
Crest Ave 17602
Crest Ln 17601
Crestmont Ave 17602
Crestwood Dr 17602
Cricket Grn 17602
Cricklewood Ct 17603
Crofft Dr 17601
Crooked Oak Dr 17601
Croquet Ln 17601
Crosscreek Ln 17602
Crossfield Dr 17603
Crosswick Ln 17601
Crown Ave 17601
Crystal Ln 17601
Crystal St 17603
Cutler Cir 17601
Cypress Dr 17602
Dahlia Rd 17602
Dairy Rd 17601
Daisy Ln 17602
Dale Dr 17601
Danbury Dr 17601
Danesfiled Ln 17601
Dante Blvd 17603
Darby Ln 17601
Darlington Ct 17601
Dartmouth Dr 17603
Dauphin St 17602
Davis Dr 17603
Davis St 17602
Dawn View Dr 17601
Dawnfield Ct 17603
De Witt Dr 17601
Debbie Dr 17601
Debra Ln 17602
Deep Hollow Ln 17603
Deer Ln 17601
Deer Ford Dr 17601
Deerfield Dr 17602
Deerfield Rd 17603
Delancy Pl 17601
Dell Ln 17603
Della Rd 17602
E Delp Rd 17601
Den Mil Dr 17601
Derby Ln 17603
Derbyshire Rd 17601
Descartes Dr 17603
Devon Dr 17603
Devonshire Rd 17601
Dewberry Ln 17601
Dickens Dr 17603
Dickinson Ave 17603
Dillerville Rd
1000-1039 17603
1041-1099 17603
1100-1199 17601
Divot Ct 17602
Doe Run Ln 17603
Dogwood Ct 17603
Dogwood Ln 17602
Dohner Dr 17602
Dolly Dr 17601
Donerville Rd 17603
Donna Ave 17603
Doris Dr 17602
Dorsea Rd 17601
Douglas Dr 17602
Dovefield Dr 17603
Doveland Ct 17602
Drake Ln 17601
Drexel Ave 17602
Driver Ave 17602
Druid Hill Dr 17601
Drummers Ln 17603
Duff Ave 17601
Duke St 17601
N Duke St 17602
S Duke St 17602
Duncan St 17602
Dunharrow Dr 17601
Dunmore Dr 17602
Duo Dr 17603
Dustin Dr 17601
Dutch Gold Dr 17601
Dylan Ln 17603
Eagle Dr 17602
Eagles Vw 17601
Eagles Nest Ct 17601
Eaglet Cir 17601
Earl Ave 17603
N & S Eastland Dr 17602
Eastman Ave 17603
Echo Valley Ln 17601
Eckman Rd
1-149 17602
150-399 17603
N Eden Rd 17601
Edenwald Ln 17601
Edgehill Dr 17603
Edgemere Dr 17601
Edgemoor Ct 17601
Edgewood Ave 17603
Edinburgh Dr 17601
Edington Pl 17603
Eisenhower Blvd 17603
Elder Ct 17603
Elderberry Pl 17601
Eliot St 17603
Elizabeth Ave 17601
Elizabeth Dr 17601
Elizabeth St 17603
Ellendale Ave & Dr 17602
Ellsworth Rd 17601
Elm Ave, Ct & St 17603
Elmae Dr 17601
Elmshire Dr 17603
Elmwood Rd 17602
Elmwood Ter 17601
Elwood Ave 17603
Embassy Dr 17603
Emerald Dr 17603
Emerson Ct 17602
Empire Cir 17601
E End Ave 17602
Enfield Dr 17601
English Rose Ct 17602
Enterprise Way 17601
Erick Rd 17601
Erin Ct 17601
Esbenshade Dr & Rd 17601
Eshelman Rd 17601
Eshelman Mill Rd 17602
Essex Pl 17601
Estelle Dr 17603
Esther Dr 17601
Euclid Ave 17603
Euclid Dr 17601
Evergreen Dr 17601
Exhibit Farm Rd 17602
Fairfax Dr 17603
Fairview Ave 17603
W Fairway Dr 17603
Faith Dr 17601
Falcon Ct 17603
Fallon Dr 17601
Fallwood Ln 17601
Fannie Ave 17602
Farm Ln 17603
Farm House Rd 17602
Farmingdale Rd
700-799 17603
800-1199 17601
Farmington Ln 17601
Farmstead Dr 17603
E Farnum St 17602
W Farnum St 17603
Faulkner Dr 17601
Fawn Meadow Ct &
Xing 17603
Fawnwood Dr 17601
Federal Way 17601
Fellowship Dr 17601
Felsinger Dr 17603
Fenton Ave 17601
Feree Cir 17601
Fern Ln 17601
Fernbrook Cir 17601
Fiddlers Grn 17602
Fiddlers Green Rd 17601
Fiddlewood Dr 17602
N Field Dr 17603
Fieldbridge Ct 17603
Fieldcrest Rd 17601
Fieldgate Dr 17603
Fieldstead Ln 17603
Fieldstone Ct 17603
E & W Filbert St 17603
Finch Ct 17603
Fir Ct 17603
Flagstone Ct 17603
Fleetwood Dr 17601
Fleming Pl 17601
Flory Mill Rd 17601
Foal Ct 17602
Fondersmith Dr 17601
Forest Rd 17601
Forrey Rd 17603
Forry Rd 17601
Fountain Ave 17601
Fox Hollow Dr & Ln 17602
Fox Run Ct 17603
Foxcroft Dr 17601
Foxglove Pl 17601
Foxshire Dr 17601
Frances Ave
100-299 17602
1000-1199 17601
Franklin Cir 17601
N Franklin St 17602
S Franklin St 17602
E Frederick St 17602
W Frederick St 17603
Freedom Rd 17601
Fremont St 17603
Fresh Meadow Dr 17603
Friends Ln 17603
Friendship Ave 17601
Fritz Ln 17602
Frockers Rd 17602
Frost Ln 17601
Fruitville Pike 17601
E Fulton St 17602
W Fulton St 17603
Gable Park Rd 17603
Gail Pl 17601
Gamber Ln 17603
Garden Ct 17602
Garden City Dr 17602
Garden Hill Ln 17603
Garden Park Cir 17601
Gardenia Pl 17601
Garfield Ave 17601
Garland Cir 17602
Garnet Ave 17603
Gary Dr 17602
Gehman Ln 17602
Geist Rd 17601
Gemstone Dr 17601
Gentlemens Way 17603
Gentry Dr 17603
George St 17603
Georgetown Dr 17601
Geraldson Dr 17601
Getz Way 17601
Gibney Rd 17602
Gilbert Ave 17601
Ginko Ct 17603
Girard Ave 17603
Glebe Ln 17602
Glen Moore Cir 17601
Glen Oaks Dr 17603
Glen Ridge Dr 17601
Glenbrook Ave & Ct 17603
Glendale Dr 17602
Glendower Dr 17601
Glengreen Dr 17601
Glenn Rd 17601
Glenwood Ave 17602
Gloucester St 17601
Glover Dr 17601
Golden Eagle Way 17601
Goldenfield Dr 17603
Goldenrod Ct 17603
Golf Rd 17602
Gondola Dr 17601
Good Dr
2-98 17603
100-202 17603
204-314 17603
675-687 17601
689-695 17601
Gordon Rd 17603
Grace Ridge Dr 17601
Grafton Cir 17603
Gralan Dr 17601
Grande Oak Pl 17601
Grandview Ave 17603
Grandview Blvd 17601
Granite Run Dr 17601
E Grant St 17602
W Grant St 17603
Grassy Way 17601
Great Lawn Cir 17602
Green St 17602
Green Ter 17601
Green Hill Dr 17603
Green Spring Cir 17603
Greenbriar Cir 17603
Greenbriar Dr 17601
Greenfield Rd
10A-10E 17602
1-99 17602
100-600 17601
602-898 17601
555-575-555-575 17601
Greenhedge Dr 17603
Greenland Dr 17602
Greenridge Dr 17601
Greentree Dr 17601
Greenview Dr 17601
Greenwood Ave 17603
Greyfield Dr 17603
Greythorne Rd 17603
Gridley Rd 17602
Gridley St 17601
Groff Ave 17603
Grofftown Rd 17602
Grouse Dr 17603
Grove St 17602
Gypsy Hill Rd 17602
Habecker Church Rd 17603
Hager Aly & St 17603
Hamilton Rd 17603
Hamilton St 17602
Hamilton Park Dr 17603
Hammock Way 17601
Hampshire Ave 17601
Hampton Ln 17601
Hancock Dr 17601
Hand Ave 17602
Hannington Dr 17601
Hansom Dr 17603
Harclay Pl 17601
Hardy Ct 17602
Harmony Hill Dr 17601
Haroldson Ave 17601
Harper Ave 17601
Harriet Ave 17601
Harrington Dr 17601
Harrisburg Ave 17603
Harrisburg Pike
1342-1399 17601
1400-1400 17604
1401-2799 17601
1402-2898 17601
Harrison St 17602
Harrogate Rd 17601
Harrow Ln 17602
Hartford Grn 17601
Hartman Bridge Rd 17602
Hartman Station Rd 17601
Hartwell Ct 17601
Harvard Ave 17603
Harvest Rd 17602
Harvey Ave 17602
Haskell Dr 17601
Hathaway Rd 17602
Hathaway St 17601
Haverhill Rd 17601
Hawley Dr 17603
Hawthorne Cir 17602
Hawthorne Dr 17603
Hayes Ave 17602
Hazel St 17603
Hazelwood Rd 17601
Hearthside Ln 17601
Hearthstone Rd 17603
Heather Ln 17603
Heatherstone Way 17601
Heatherton Dr 17601
Hebrank St 17603
Hedera Pl 17601
Hedgerow Ln 17601
Hedgewick Dr 17603
Hedgewood Ct 17603
Helen Ave 17601
Helena Rd 17603
Hemlock Dr 17602
Hemlock Rd 17603
Hempfield Dr 17601
Hempland Rd 17601
Hempstead Rd 17601
Henbird Ln 17601
Henrietta Ave 17602
Henry Ct 17601
Hensel Ave 17602
Heritage Ave 17603
Heritage Rd 17602
Hermosa Ave 17601
Herr Ave 17602
Hershey Ave & Ln 17603
Hess Blvd 17601
Hickory Dr 17602
Hidden Grn 17602
Hidden Ln 17603
Hiemenz Rd 17601
High St 17603
Highland Ave 17603
Highland Dr 17602
Highland View Dr 17601
Highmeadow Ct 17601
Highview Dr 17602
Hill St 17602
Hillaire Rd 17601
Hillard Fld 17603
Hillcrest Ave 17601
Hillcrest Rd 17603
Hillside Ave 17603
Hillside Ct 17602
Hillside Dr 17603
Hillside Ln 17601
Hilltop Approach 17601
Hilton Dr 17603
Hitching Post Ln 17602
Hobson Rd 17602
Hoffman Ter 17603
Holbein Dr 17601
Holbrook Ave 17601
Hollinger Rd 17602
Holly Cir 17602
Holly Dr 17603
Holly Ln 17602
Holly Ann Cir 17603
Hollytree Ct 17601
Hollywood Dr 17601
Homeland Dr 17601
Homestead Dr 17602
Homestead Ln 17603
Homestead Rd 17603
Honey Locust Sq 17602
Honeysuckle Ln 17603
Hoover Rd 17603
Horizon Dr 17601
Hornig Rd 17601
Horseshoe Dr 17601
Horseshoe Rd
1800-1898 17602
1900-2099 17602
2100-2599 17601
Hospitality Dr 17601
Hostetter Ln 17602
Houser Rd 17602
Housman Pl 17601
Howard Ave 17602
Hudson Rd 17601
Huffman Pl 17601
Hull Ct 17603
Hunsicker Rd 17601
Hunt Club Ln 17601
Hunter Dr 17601
Hunters Path 17601
Huntington Pl 17601
Huntingwood Dr 17602
Huntsman Ln 17602
Hyde Park Dr 17601
Hydrant Dr 17601
Ice Ave 17602
Imperial Dr 17601
Independence Ct 17601
Indian Springs Dr 17601
Industrial Cir 17601
Industry Dr 17603
Iris Dr 17602
Ironstone Ridge Rd 17603
Irwin Ave 17603
Ivy Dr & Ter 17601
Ivywood Ct 17603
Jackson Dr & St 17603
Jacobs Crk 17601
Jade Ave 17601
Jamaica Rd 17602
E James St 17602
W James St 17603
Jamestown Ct 17602
Janet Ave 17601
Jarvis Rd 17601
Jasmine Ln 17601
E, N & S Jefferson Ct &
St 17602
Jemfield Ct 17603
Jennings Dr 17603
Jimanna Rd 17602
John St 17602
John Adams Dr 17601
John Hoff Pl 17602
Joseph Rd 17603
Judie Ln 17603
Juliette Ave 17601
Juniata Ave & St 17602
Juniper Ct 17603
Juniper Dr 17602
Karen Cir 17602
Katherines Way 17602
Kathryn Ct 17603
Katie Ln 17602
Kay Dr 17603
Kayo Ave 17601
Keller Ave 17601
Kelley Dr 17601
Kendale Pl 17601
Kennedy St 17602
Kenneth Dr 17601
Kensington Rd & Ter 17603
Kent Ct & Rd 17603
Kenton Rd 17601
Kentshire Dr 17603
Kentwood Dr 17601
Keper Ave 17603
Kestrel Ct 17603
Keystone Dr 17603
Kilgannon Ln 17603
Kimberly Ct 17602
Kimberly Rd 17603
Kincaid Ave 17601
E King St 17602
W King St 17603
Kings Ln 17601
Kings Arms Ln 17602
Kingsway Dr 17601
Kissel Hill Rd 17601
Kloss Dr 17603
Knight Ln 17602
Knights Ln 17601
Knollwood Dr 17601
Kolb Dr 17601
Koser Rd 17601
Kreider Ave 17601
Kreps Rd 17603
Kress Cir 17602
Krista Ct 17601
Krystle Dr 17602
Kurtz Ml 17601
La Salle Ave 17601
Ladderback Dr 17601
Lafayette St 17603
Lake St 17603
Lakeview Dr 17601
Lambeth Rd 17601
Lampeter Rd 17602
Lamplight Cir 17601
Lamppost Ln 17602
Lancaster Ave 17603
Landis Ave
1-99 17602
800-999 17603
Landis Dr 17602
Landis Valley Rd 17601
Landmark Cir 17603
Landon Way 17601
Langford Cir 17601
Langley Sq 17603
Lantern Ln 17602
Larchmont Ln 17601
Lark Ln 17603
Larkspur Loop 17602
Laurel Ln 17601
Laurel St 17603
Laurel Oak Ln 17602
Lausch Ln 17601
Lawrence Blvd 17601
Leabrook Rd 17601
Leaman Rd
1-199 17603
2200-2399 17602
Lee Ave 17603
Leeds Ct 17602
Lefever Ave 17603
Lehigh Ave 17602
Lehman Ave 17602
Lehn Dr 17601
E Lemon St 17602
W Lemon St 17603
Leona Ave 17601
Lepore Dr 17602
Levingston Cir 17601
Lewiston Cir 17601
Lexington Rd 17603
E Liberty St 17602
W Liberty St 17603
Lichfield Ln 17601
Lightfoot Dr 17602
Lilac Dr 17602
N & S Lime St 17602
Lime Valley Rd 17602
Lincoln Ave 17603
Lincoln Hwy E 17602
Linda Ave 17602
Linden Ave 17601
Lindsay Ln 17601
Linwood Ave 17603
Lititz Ave 17602
Lititz Pike 17601
Little Hl 17602
Little Brook Rd 17603
Little Creek Rd 17601
Livingston Ln 17603
Locust St 17602

Street	ZIP
Locust Point Ln	17603
Lois Ln	17601
London Dr	17601
Long Ln	17603
Long Farm Ln	17601
Long Lane Acres W	17603
Long Rifle Rd	17602
Longfellow Dr	17602
Longiron Dr	17601
Longmeadow Rd	17601
Longview Dr	17601
Longwood Ct E & W	17603
Loop Rd	17601
Lotus Cir	17602
Louise Ave	17601
Louxmont Dr	17603
Lower Grn	17602
Lucilla Ct	17603
Ludwell Dr	17601
Lupine Cir	17602
Lyndana Dr	17601
Lyndell Dr	17601
Lyndon Ave	17602
Lynn Ave	17601
Lynndale Rd	17603
Mabel Ave	17602
Mackin Ave	17602
Madge Dr	17603
E Madison St	17602
W Madison St	17603
Magnolia Dr	17602
Mahogany Dr	17602
Malibou Dr	17603
Mallard Dr	17601
Malory St	17603
Manchester Ln	17601
Manheim Ave	17603
Manheim Pike	17601
Manor Blvd & St	17603
Manor House Ln	17603
Manor Ridge Dr	17603
Maple Ave	
300-399	17602
901-997	17603
999-1399	17603
Maple Ln	17601
Maplecrest Ter	17601
Maplewood Ave	17601
Marble Dr	17601
Marcia Ln	17601
Marietta Ave	
600-2399	17603
2400-3699	17601
Marion Ct	17602
E Marion St	17602
W Marion St	17603
Marjory Ter	17603
Mark Ave	17602
N Market St	17603
Marshall Ave	17601
N Marshall St	17602
S Marshall St	17602
Martha Ave	17601
Marticville Rd	17603
N & S Mary St	17603
Mason Ct	17602
Maxson Rd	17601
Mayer Ave	17603
Mayfair Dr	17603
Mayflower Cir	17603
E Mcgovern Ave	
1-99	17602
2-4	17603
10-32	17602
Mcgovernville Rd	17601
Mcgrann Blvd	17601
Meadia Ave	17602
Meadow Ln	17601
Meadow Hill Dr	17601
Meadow Ridge Dr	17601
Meadow Spring Rd	17601
Meadowbrook Rd	17603
Meadowcreek Ln	17603
Meadowcroft Dr	17603
Meadowview Ave	17602
Meetinghouse Ln	17601
Melody Ln	17601
Melrose Ln	17601
Mennonite School Rd	17602
Mentzer Rd	17602
Mercers Ml	17601
Merchants Sq	17601
Mews Blvd	17603
Michele Lynn Dr	17602
Michelle Dr	17603
Michener Dr	17601
Michigan Ave	17602
Middle Grn	17602
Middle St	17601
Middlefield Ln	17603
Middlegreen Ct	17601
Midway Ave	17601
Midway Farms Ln	17602
E Mifflin St	17602
W Mifflin St	17603
Milford Dr	17602
Mill Ave & St	17603
Mill Mar Rd	17601
Mill Pond Dr	17603
Mill Ridge Ct	17601
Millcreek Rd	17602
Millcross Rd	17601
Millers Run Ln	17601
Millersville Pike & Rd	17603
Millport Rd	17602
Millrace Dr	17603
Millstream Rd	17602
Millwood Rd	
100-249	17602
250-299	17603
Milton Rd	17602
Mimosa Ln	17601
Mission Rd	17601
Misty Dr	17603
Mitric Ln	17601
Mohawk Dr	17601
Mondale Rd	17601
Mondamin Farm Rd	17601
Monticello Ln	17603
Montrose Ave	17603
Moorgate Rd	17601
Morelle Pl	17601
Morgan Dr	17601
Morningside Dr	17602
Mount Sidney Rd	17602
N & S Mulberry St	17603
Municipal Dr	17601
Murry Hill Cir & Dr	17601
Musser Ave	17602
Myers Xing	17602
Myrtlewood Ct	17603
Nancy Ln	17601
Nanticoke Rd	17601
Nassau Rd	17602
Natures Way	17602
Nectar Ter	17602
Neff Rd	17601
Nettie Ln	17603
Nevin Cir & St	17603
E New St	17602
W New St	17603
New Danville Pike	17603
New Dauphin St	17602
New Dorwart St	17603
New Garden Ave	17603
New Green St	17602
New Holland Ave	
798A-798E	17602
201-297	17602
299-807	17602
809-809	17602
810-1099	17601
1101-1199	17601
New Holland Pike	17601
Newport Dr	17602
Newswanger Rd	17603
Newton Rd	17603
Niblick Ave	17602
Nicholas Rd	17603
Nicholson Square Dr	17601
Nissley Rd	17601
Noll Dr	17603
Nolt Rd	17601
Norcross Rd	17603
Nordick Dr	17602
Norlam Dr	17601
Norlawn Cir	17601
Norman Rd	17601
North St	17602
Northbrook Dr	17601
Northgate Ln	17601
Northlawn Ct & Dr	17603
Northview Dr	17601
Norwick Rd	17601
Nottingham Ave	17601
Nursery Ln	17603
O Henry Cir & Pl	17601
Oak Ave	17601
Oak Dr	17601
Oak Ln	
1-99	17603
1600-1698	17601
Oak Grove Dr	17601
Oak Leaf Ln	17602
Oak Ridge Dr	17603
Oak Thorne Ln	17602
Oak View Rd	17602
Oakfield Ct E & W	17603
Oakglen Ct	17601
Oakmont Dr	17601
Oakwood Ln	17603
Ocean Ave	17603
Ohio Ave	17602
Old Blue Rock Rd	17603
Old Delp Rd	17601
Old Dorwart St	17603
Old Eagle Rd	17601
Old Farm Ln	17602
Old Manheim Pike	17601
Old Orchard Rd	17601
Old Philadelphia Pike	17602
Old Tree Dr	17603
Old Trinity Pl	17602
Olde Forge Xing	17601
Olde Hickory Rd	17601
Olde Homestead Ln	
1801-1809	17601
1811-1814	17601
1813-1813	17605
1815-1919	17601
1816-1820	17601
Olde Saybrook Rd	17601
Oldham Ct	17602
Olive St	17602
Oliver Dr	17601
E Orange St	17602
W Orange St	17603
Orchard Dr	17601
Orchard Ln	17603
Orchard Rd	17601
Orchard St	17601
Oregon Blvd & Pike	17601
Oreville Rd	17601
Oriole Ct	17603
Overhill Dr	17602
Overland Ln	17601
Overlook Ave	17601
Oxford Dr	17601
Oxford Rd	17601
Oxford Vlg	17602
Pacific Ave	17603
Paddington Dr	17601
Paddock Ln	17603
Palm St	17602
Palomino Dr	17601
Paramount Ave	17602
Park Ave	17602
Park Ln	17603
Park Plz	17601
Park Rd	17601
Park Circle Dr	17603
Park City Ctr	17601
Park Hill Rd	17603
Parker Dr	17601
Parklawn Ct	17601
Parkside Ave	17602
Parkside Ln	17601
Parkview Ln	17602
Parkwood Dr	17603
Parkwynne Rd	17601
Partridge Ln	17601
Parvin Rd	17601
Passey Ln	17603
Patriot Dr	17601
Peach Ln	17601
Peacock Dr	17601
S Pearl St	17603
Pebble Run	17602
Pebblebrook Dr	17601
Pebbleside Ln	17602
Penn Ave	17602
Penn Sq	
1-1	17602
28-28	17603
Penn Grant Rd	17602
W Penn Grant Rd	17603
Pennshire Dr	17603
Pennsylvania Ave	17602
Pennwick Rd	17601
Pennwood Cir & Rd	17601
Penrose Ave	17603
Pentail Dr	17601
Peony Rd	17602
Pequea Ln	17602
Perry Ave	17603
Pershing Ave	17602
Persimmon Dr	17601
Perthshire Dr	17603
Petersburg Rd	17601
Pheasant Dr	17601
Pheasant Ridge Cir	17603
Philmont Dr	17601
Pickering Trl	17601
Picket Dr	17601
Pickford Dr	17603
N Pier Dr	17603
Pike Ln	17603
Pilgrim Dr	17603
Pin Oak Dr	17601
Pin Oak Pl	17602
Pine Dr	17601
N Pine St	17603
Pine Bridge Ln	17603
Pinehurst Ave	17601
Pinetree Way	17601
Pinewood Rd	17601
Pinewyn Cir	17601
Pinnacle Point Dr	17601
Pioneer Rd	17602
Pitney Rd	
1-142	17602
144-198	17601
200-299	17601
301-399	17601
Pitt Ct	17602
Plainfield Ct	17603
Plane Tree Dr	17603
Plaza Blvd	17601
Pleasant Dr	17602
Pleasant Pl	17601
Pleasant Pt	17602
Pleasant St	17602
Pleasure Rd	17601
N Plum St	
1-999	17602
1000-1300	17601
1302-1398	17601
S Plum St	17602
Plumeria Pl	17602
Plymouth Ave	17602
Plymouth Rd	17603
Poe Dr	17603
N Pointe Blvd	17601
Ponderosa Dr	17601
Pool Frg	17601
Poplar St	17603
Porter Way	17601
Post Oak Rd	17603
Powell Dr	17601
Prangley Ave	17603
Prellor Dr	17601
Prentis Pl	17601
Prescot St	17601
N & S President Ave	17603
Prestige Ln	17603
Preston Rd	17601
Primrose Ave	17601
N & S Prince St	17603
Prince George Dr	17601
Princess Ave	17601
Princess Anne Dr	17601
Princeton Ave	17603
Prospect St	17603
Pullman Rd	17601
Pulte Rd	17601
Putnam Dr	17602
Putter Ave	17602
Pyrus Pl	17601
Quail Dr	17601
Quaker Hills Rd	17603
Quarry Ln	17603
Queen Ln	17601
N Queen St	17603
S Queen St	17603
Queen Annes Ct	17601
Rabbit Hill Ln	17603
Race Ave	17603
Rachael Dr	17601
Raleigh Dr	17601
Ramsgate Ln	17603
Ranck Ave	17602
Ranck Mill Rd	17602
Randall Ct	17602
Randy Rd	17601
Raven Ct	17603
Raymee Dr	17601
Raymond Dr	17601
Red Leaf Ln	17602
Red Maple Rd	17602
Red Oak Rd	17602
Red Rose Ct	17601
Redwood Dr	
1-499	17603
600-618	17602
Reedy Ln	17602
Reese Ave	17602
Regal Aly	17601
Regent Dr	17601
Reiker Ave	17603
Rembrandt Dr	17603
Reo Ave	17603
Resch Ln	17602
N & S Reservoir St	17602
Revere Rd	17601
Reynolds Ave	17602
Rhoda Dr	17601
Rice Rd	17603
Richardson Dr	17603
Richland Dr	17601
Richmond Dr	17601
Richmond Rd	17603
Rider Ave	17603
Ridge Dr & Rd	17603
Ridgedale Dr	17601
Ridgefield Dr	17602
Ridgeview Ave	17603
Ridgewood Rd	17603
Ridings Way	17601
Ringneck Ln	17601
Risser Ln	17601
Rittenhouse Ct	17601
River Dr	17603
River Bend Park	17602
Riverside Ave	17602
Robert Rd	17601
Robin Rd	17601
Robindale Ave	17601
Rock St	17602
Rock Ledge Ct	17603
Rockford Ln	17601
Rockford Rd	17602
Rockland St	17602
Rocklawn Ln	17601
Rockvale Rd	17602
Rodney St	17603
Roesser Dr	17601
Rohrer Ave	17601
Rohrer Rd	17603
Rohrerstown Rd	
---	17603
1-712	17603
714-798	17603
800-1899	17601
Rolridge Ave	17603
Romarin Pl	17601
Roosevelt Blvd	17601
Rose Ave	17601
Rose Dr	17602
Rosedale Ave	17603
Roselawn Ave	17603
Roselle Ave	17603
Rosemont Ave	17601
E & W Roseville Rd	17601
Rosewood Dr	17603
Roslyn Ave	17602
E Ross St	17602
W Ross St	17603
Round Hill Ln	17603
Roundtop Dr	17601
Royal Rd	17603
Royal View Dr	17601
Royer Dr	17601
Rozet Ave	17602
Rubia Pl	17601
Ruby St	17603
Rumford Ct	17602
Running Pump Rd	
1-400	17603
402-438	17603
440-500	17601
502-698	17601
Ruth Ridge Dr	17601
Rutledge Ave	17601
Saddle Dr	17601
Saddleback Dr	17603
Saddleford Ct N & S	17603
Saddleridge Rd	17601
Saffin Cir	17601
Sage Dr	17602
Saint Georges Dr	17603
Saint Joseph St	17603
Saint Paul Cir	17603
Saint Phillips Dr	17603
Saint Regis Ln	17603
Saint Thomas Rd	17601
Salem Dr	17601
Salisbury Ct	17601
Salvatore Ct	17603
Sammar Rd	17601
Samuel Rd	17601
Sandalwood Path	17601
Sandstone Dr	17601
Santa Barbara Dr	17601
Sarah Ln	17602
Saratoga Rd	17603
Savo Ave	17601
Scarsdale Cir	17603
Scenic Dr	17603
N & S School Ln	17603
School House Rd	17603
Schuylkill St	17602
Scotland Ct	17601
Second Lock Rd	17603
Seitz Dr	17601
Seltzer Ct	17601
September Dr	17603
Serene Way	17602
Service Rd	17601
Settlement Cir	17601
Settlers Bnd	17601
Seymour St	17603
Shaaron Dr	17601
Shade Tree Dr	17603
Shadowstone Dr	17603
Shannon Dr	17603
Shaub Rd	17601
Sheaffer Rd	17602
Shearers Dr	17601
Shelley Rd	17602
Sherman St	17602
Sherreem Rd	17601
Sherry Ln	17601
Sherwal Ave	17601
Sherwood Ln	17603
Shetland Dr	17601
N & S Shippen St	17602
Short Ln	17603
Shreiner Ave	17603
Shreiner Rd	17601
Shultz Rd	17603
E Side Dr	17601
Signal Hill Ln	17601
Silver Birch Dr	17602
Silver Spring Plz & Rd	17601
Silver Wind Ct N & S	17603
Single Tree Ln	17602
Skyline Dr	17601
Skywalk Ln	17601
Somerset Rd	17601
Southbrook Dr	17603
Southeast Ave	17602
Southgate Dr	17602
Southlawn Dr	17603
Southport Dr	17603
Southridge Dr	17602
Southrun Dr	17602
Southwick Dr	17601
Speedwell Rd	17601
Spencer Ave	17603
Spiraea Pl	17601
Split Rock Rd	17601
Spottswood Dr	17601
Sprecher Rd	17603
Spring Ave	17602
Spring Dell Rd	17601
Spring Grove Ave	17603
Spring Haven Dr	17601
Spring Ridge Ct	17601
Spring Ridge Ln	17603
Spring Valley Rd	17601
Spring Walk Ct	17601
Springbrook Ct	17603
Springfield Ct	17603
Springhouse Rd	17603
Springlawn Dr	17601
Springside Dr	17603
Springton Way	17601
Spruce St	17603
Stable Dr	17603
Stagecoach Ln	17601
Standardbred Dr	17603
Stanley K Tanger Blvd	17602
Starlite Dr	17602
State Rd	17601
State St	17603
Stayman Dr	17602
Steel Way	17601
Steelton Rd	17601
Steepbank Rd	17602
Steeplechase Dr	17601
Stehman Rd	17603
Steinman Ct & Dr	17603
Sterling Pl	
100-1199	17603
1900-1999	17601
Stevens Ave	17602
Stevens St	17603
Stillwater Rd	17601
Stillwell Dr	17601
Stockbridge Cir	17603
Stockdale Dr	17601
Stone Creek Rd	17603
Stone Heath Dr	17601
Stone Mill Rd	17603
Stonebridge Dr	17601
Stonecrest Dr	17601
Stonegate Xing	17601
Stonemanor Dr	17603
Stonewyck Dr	17603
Stoney Ln	17603
Stony Battery Rd	17601
Stonyridge Dr	17601
Strasburg Pike	17602
Stratford Rd	17603
Stratford Vlg	17602
Strawberry Ln	17602
E Strawberry St	17602
W Strawberry St	17603
Stumpf Hill Dr	17601
Stumptown Rd	17602
Sturbridge Dr	17601
Sue Ann Dr	17602

Summer Ct 17602
Summers Dr 17601
Summit Dr 17601
Summitville Ct 17603
Suncrest Rd 17601
Sundra Ave 17602
Sunglo Rd 17601
Sunlite Cir 17602
Sunningdale Ct N & S 17603
Sunrise Ave 17601
Sunset Ave, Dr & Pl 17601
Sunvalley Rd 17603
Sunwood Ln 17601
Supervisors Rd 17603
Surrey Dr 17601
Susan Ave 17602
Susquaw Pl 17601
Susquehanna St 17602
Sutherland Rd 17603
Sutton Pl 17601
Swarr Run Rd 17601
Sweetbriar Way 17601
Sycamore Ave 17601
Sycamore Dr 17602
Sylvan Rd 17601
Talbot Cir 17603
Tallgrass Path 17602
Tanglewood Ln 17601
Tarpley Dr 17601
Tartan Ct 17601
Taylor Dr 17601
Teal Ter 17601
Teddy Ave 17601
Temple Ave 17603
Tenby Way 17601
Tennyson Dr 17602
Terrace Dr 17601
Terrapin Ct 17603
Terry Ln 17603
The Pkwy 17602
Thicket Ln 17602
Thistle Dr 17601
Thistle Grn 17602
Thomas Ave 17603
Thomas Rd 17602
Thornapple Dr 17601
Thoroughbred Ln 17601
Thrush Ct N & S 17603
Thunder Ln 17602
Thunderbird Ln 17601
Tiercel Ln 17603
Timber Point Ln 17603
Timothy Dr 17603
Timothy Ln 17602
Todd Ln 17601
Toll Gate Sta 17601
Tom Paine Dr 17603
Tompkins Ln 17601
Topaz Dr 17603
Topland Dr 17601
Townhouse Ln 17603
Townsend Ct 17603
Tracy Rd 17601
Tracy Berg Rd 17603
Trading Post Ln 17602
Trails End Ct N & S 17603
Travelo Dr 17603
Travis Ln 17601
S Tree Ln 17603
Treetops Ct & Dr 17601
Trena Ave 17601
Tulane Ter 17603
Tulip Dr 17602
Turnbridge Dr 17603
Tusitala Dr 17601
Twain St 17603
Twin Oaks Holw 17601
Union St 17603
Upper Grn 17602
Urban Dr 17603
Ursinus Ave 17603
Valette Dr 17602
Valley Dr 17603
Valley Rd
1-999 17601
1101-1197 17603
1199-1599 17603
Valley Forge Rd 17603
Valley View Dr 17601
Valleybrook Dr 17601
Veranda Way 17601
Verdant Grv 17601
Vermont Ave 17603
Veumont Dr 17601
Vickery Ln 17601
Victoria Ln 17603
S View Dr 17602
W View Dr 17603
S View Rd 17602
Villa Ct 17603
Villa Rd 17601
Village Cir 17603
Village Dr 17601
Village Rd 17602
Village Green Ln 17603
Vinca Pl 17601
E Vine St 17602
W Vine St 17603
Virginia Ave 17603
Vista Rd 17601
Voltaire Blvd 17603
Wabank Rd & St 17603
Wagon Rd 17602
Walfield Dr 17601
Wallingford Rd 17601
Walnut Ln 17603
E Walnut St 17602
W Walnut St 17603
Walter Ave 17602
Wanda Cir 17602
Warren Way 17601
Washington Ave & St 17602
N & S Water St 17603
Water Leaf Rd 17603
Water Valley Rd 17603
Waterford Ct 17603
Waterford Dr 17601
Waterfront Dr 17602
Waterfront Estates Dr 17602
Waters Edge 17602
Watson Ave 17603
Waverly Ave 17601
Waypoint Dr 17603
Weatherfield Pl 17603
Weaver Rd
2-98 17603
100-399 17603
2700-2999 17601
Weaver Way 17603
Wellington Rd 17603
Welsh Dr 17601
Wendover Way 17603
N West End Ave
1-399 17603
1401-1499 17601
S West End Ave 17603
Westbrook Dr 17603
Westcott Dr 17603
Westminster Dr 17601
Westmore Way 17603
Weston Rd 17603
Westover Dr 17601
Westwood Dr 17601
Wetherburn Dr 17601
Wexford Dr 17601
Wheatland Ave 17603
Wheatland Park Ln 17602
Wheatland School Rd 17602
Wheaton Dr 17603
Whipporwill Dr 17603
White Chapel Rd 17603
White Gate Ln 17601
White Oak Dr 17601
White Tail Ct 17603
White Tail Path 17602
White Water Rd 17603
Whitefield Ln 17602
Whitemarsh Dr 17601
Whitman Dr 17601
Whitney Rd 17603
Whittier Ln 17602
Wickersham Ln 17603
Wicklawn Dr 17603
Wicklyn Rd 17601
Wiker Ave 17602
Wildbriar Ct N & S 17603
Wilderness Rd 17603
Wildflower Ln 17603
Wilkes Rd 17601
William Ln 17602
William Flynn Cir 17601
William Penn Way 17601
Williamsburg Rd 17603
Willis Ln 17602
Willow Ln & Rd 17601
Willow Glen Dr 17602
Willow Hill Dr 17602
Willow Street Pike 17602
Willow Valley Dr & Sq 17602
S Willowdale Dr 17602
Wilson Ave & Dr 17603
Wimbledon Ln 17601
Winchester Dr 17601
Winding Way 17602
Winding Hill Dr 17601
Windon Ave 17603
Windover Turn 17601
Windrow Dr 17602
Windsong Ln 17602
Windsor Ave 17601
Windy Hill Rd 17602
Winthrop Dr 17603
Wise Ave 17603
Witmer Rd 17602
Wohlsen Way 17603
Wolgemuth Dr 17602
N Wood Rd 17602
Wood St 17603
Wood Lot Ln 17601
Wood Summit Way 17601
Woodbine Blvd 17603
Woodcrest Dr 17602
Woodfield Xing 17602
Woodland Ave 17602
Woodlyn Ct 17602
Woodlyn Farm Way 17601
Woodridge Blvd 17601
Woods Ave 17603
Woodside Rd 17601
Woodview Dr 17601
Woodward St 17602
Woodwick Rd 17601
Woodworth Dr 17601
Wren Way 17601
Wyncroft Ln & Ter 17603
Wyndham Way 17601
Wynfield Dr 17601
Wynnewood Dr 17601
Wythe Cir 17601
N & S Yale Ave 17603
Yardley Grn 17603
Ye Olde Mill Rd 17601
Yellow Goose Rd 17601
York Ct 17602
Yorkshire Dr 17603
Yorktown Rd 17603
Zarker Rd 17601
Zook Ave 17602
Zooks Ln 17601

NUMBERED STREETS

All Street Addresses 17603

LEBANON PA

General Delivery 17042

POST OFFICE BOXES MAIN OFFICE STATIONS AND BRANCHES

Box No.s
All PO Boxes 17042

RURAL ROUTES

09 17042

NAMED STREETS

Abbey St 17042
Academy Dr 17046
Acorn Cir, Ct, Dr & Ln 17042
Adam Dr 17042
Agnes St 17042
Alden Ln & Way 17042
Allegheny Ave 17042
Allwein Dr 17042
Alpha Ave 17046
Amelia St 17046
Ann Ln 17042
Anne Ave 17042
Anthracite Rd 17042
Apple Ln 17046
Applewood Ct 17046
Arborvitae St 17042
Arch St 17042
Arnold Ct 17042
Arnold Ln 17046
Arnold St 17046
E Arnold St 17046
Ash Ct & Ln 17042
Ashford Dr 17042
Ashton Dr 17046
Aspen Ave 17042
Aspen Ln 17042
Aspen Way 17046
Aubrey Ave 17042
Auburn Dr 17042
Autumn Ct 17042
Baldwin St 17046
Balsam Cir 17042
Band St 17042
Barbara Ann Dr 17046
Barberry Ln 17042
Batdorf Dr 17042
Bauer Dr 17046
Bayberry Ct 17042
Beagle Rd 17046
Beaumont St 17046
Beckleys Cor 17042
Beech Dr 17042
E Beech St 17046
Beechwood Ave 17042
Behney Rd 17042
Behney St 17046
E Behney St 17046
Belmont St 17046
Bender Ln 17042
Bentley Ct 17042
Berbec Ave 17042
Berry Dr 17046
Berwyn Park 17042
Beta Ave 17046
Birch Ln 17046
Birch Rd 17042
Birch St 17046
E Birch St 17046
Bittner Blvd 17046
Black Ln 17042
Black Oak Rd 17046
Blackberry Ln 17046
Blair St 17046
Blue Jay Way 17042
Blueberry Ln 17046
Boat Ct 17046
Boger St 17042
Bollman St 17042
Boltz Ln 17046
Bowman St 17046
Boxwood Dr 17042
Boyd St 17042
Boyer Rd 17046
Bradford Cir 17042
Brandthaven Dr 17046
Brandywine Dr 17042
Brandywine St 17046
Brendle Ln 17046
Briar Rd 17042
Briar Edge Ct 17046
Briarwood Ct 17042
Brick Plant Ln 17042
Bricker Ln 17046
E Broad St 17046
S Broad St 17042
Broadway 17042
Brock Dr 17046
Brook Dr 17046
E & W Brookfield Dr 17046
Brookside Ln 17042
Brookside Apartments 17046
Brown Ave 17042
Bucher Ln 17042
Buck Run 17046
Burd Coleman Rd 17042
Butler Rd 17042
Buttonwood St 17046
Cable Ln 17042
Calico Ct 17046
Cambridge Dr 17042
E Canal St 17046
Canton St 17042
Cappa Ave 17046
Carlton Ct & Dr 17042
Carol Ann Dr 17046
Cart Way 17042
Cassadee Ct 17042
Cat Tail Ct 17042
Cathedral St 17046
Catherine Ct 17042
Cedar Ct 17042
Cedar Ln 17046
Cedar St 17042
Cedar Crest Dr 17046
Cedar Run Rd 17046
Cedarview Dr 17042
Center St 17042
E Center St 17046
N Center St 17042
S Center St
101-197 17042
199-299 17042
401-499 17046
W Center St 17046
Challenge Dr 17042
N Chapel St 17046
Charles St 17042
Charlotte St 17046
Chase Dr 17046
Cherry Ave 17042
Cherry Ln 17046
Cherry St 17046
E Cherry St 17046
N Cherry St 17046
S Cherry St 17042
Chestnut St 17042
E Chestnut St 17046
N Chestnut St 17046
W Chestnut St 17042
Chicory Dr 17042
Chris Ln 17042
N & S Christian St 17042
Christine Dr 17046
Church Rd 17042
Church St 17046
E Church St 17046
Cider Ln 17046
Clays Xing 17042
Clearview Dr & Ln 17042
Cleona Blvd 17042
Cloister St 17042
Clover Dr 17042
Clover Pl 17042
Clover St 17046
Cloverfield Dr 17046
Club Ter 17042
Cobblestone Dr 17042
Colebrook Rd 17042
Coleman Cir 17046
Colonial Cir 17046
Colonial Dr 17042
Colony Ct 17042
Conewago Hls 17042
Copenhaver Ln 17042
Copper Ln 17042
Cornerstone Ln 17042
Cornwall Rd 17042
Cornwall Hills Dr 17042
Cottonwood Dr 17042
Country Club View Dr 17042
Country View Dr 17042
Cranberry Ct 17046
Creek Dr 17042
Creek Run Ln 17042
Creekside Dr 17042
Crest Rd 17042
Creston Dr 17046
W Crestview Dr 17042
Crimson Ct 17042
Crooked Ln 17042
Cross Creek Ct 17042
Crosswind Way 17042
Crowell St 17046
Culvert St 17042
Cumberland St 17042
Cut Off Rd 17042
Cypress Ln 17046
N & S Cyrus St 17042
Daffodil Dr 17042
Dairy Rd 17042
Daniel Ave 17042
Daniels St 17042
David Dr 17046
Davis Ln 17042
Dawson St 17042
Dead End Rd 17046
Deer Dr 17046
Dewey Ave 17046
Diamond Dr 17042
Dock Dr 17046
Dodge St 17046
Dogwood Dr & Ln 17042
Dohner St 17042
Donmoyer St 17046
Doris Dr 17046
Douglas Fir Cv & Dr 17042
Duke St 17042
Duquesne Dr 17042
Eagle Ave 17046
East St 17042
Eastfield Dr 17042
Ebenezer Rd 17046
Edgewood Dr 17046
Edna St 17046
Edward Ave 17042
Ehrhorn St 17046
Elder St 17042
Elderberry Ln 17046
Elias Ave 17046
Elizabeth Ave 17042
Elizabeth St
300-398 17042
600-699 17046
900-999 17042
Elizabethtown Rd 17042
Elk Dr 17046
Elm Dr 17046
Elm St 17042
E Elm St 17042
W Elm St 17042
Emma Rd 17046
Emma St 17042
Endress Rd 17042
English Dr 17042
Enterprise Ct 17042
Erinn Ln 17042
Esther Dr 17042
Eve Ave 17046
Evelyn Dr 17042
E Evergreen Rd 17042
Fairview Cir, Dr & Ln 17042
Fairway Cir 17042
Falcon Cir 17042
Farmers Dr 17046
Farmstead Cir 17042
Fawnwood Dr 17046
Federal St 17042
Fern Cir 17042
Fieldcrest Rd 17042
Finch Dr 17042
Fisher Ln 17042
Flinchbaugh Ln 17046
Flintville Rd 17042
Florence St 17042
Folmer St 17042
Fonderwhite Rd 17042
Fontana Ave & Rd 17042
Forest St 17046
Forney Ln & Rd 17042
Forneydale Rd 17046
Fox Rd 17042
Fox Ridge Ln 17042
Fox Run Rd 17042
Foxchase Ln 17042
Frances Ann Dr 17046
Franklin Ave 17042
Freeman Dr 17042
Freeman St 17046
Freeport Rd 17046
Furnace Ct & St 17042
N Gannon St 17046
S Gannon St 17042
Garden Ave 17046
Garfield Ave 17046
Garfield St 17046
N Garfield St 17042
S Garfield St 17042
Gary Ave 17046
Gary St 17042
George St 17042
Gerdes Cir 17042
Gibble Ave 17046
Gibble Rd 17042
Glenn Lebanon Dr 17046
Glenwood Ln 17042
Glenwood St 17046
Gold Ln 17042
Golf Rd 17046
Grace Ave 17046
Granite St 17042
Grant Ave 17046
Grant Cir 17042
Grant St 17046
E Grant St 17042
N Grant St 17042
S Grant St 17042
Great Hall Dr 17042
Greble Rd 17046
Green Ln 17042
Green St 17046
Green Acres Trailer Ct 17046
Green Woods Ln 17046
Greenfield Dr 17042
Greentree Vlg 17042
Greenview Cir & Ln 17042
Greenwood Dr 17046
Greiner St 17042
Greth St 17042
Greystone Dr & Xing 17042
Groy Ave 17046
Grubb Ave 17046
Grumbine Ln 17042
E Guilford St 17046
Hain Ave 17046
Halteman Ln 17046
Hanford Dr 17046
N Hanover St 17046
S Hanover St 17042
Harding Ln 17042
Harding St 17046
Harmony Hl 17046
N & S Harris St 17042
Harrison St 17046
Hartman Ln 17042
Harvest Dr 17046
Harvey John Ave 17042
Hathaway Park 17042
Hauck St 17042
Hazel Ct & St 17042
Heagy Dr 17046
Heart Ln 17046
Hearthside Ln 17042
Hearthstone Ln 17042
Heffelfinger Rd 17046
Heilmandale Rd 17046
Helen Dr 17042
Hemlock Ct 17042

Hemlock Ln
2-98 17046
500-599 17042
Henry Houck Ln 17042
Herb Hill Ln 17046
Heritage Ave 17046
Heritage Ln 17042
E Herman Ave 17042
Hernley Ln 17046
Herr St 17042
Hess Dr 17046
Hickory Blvd 17042
Hickory Dr 17042
Hickory St 17046
E High St 17042
Highland Glen St 17042
Hill St 17046
Hill Church Rd 17046
Hillcrest Rd 17042
Hillside Dr 17046
Hillside St 17042
Hockley Ave 17042
Hoffer St 17042
Hoffman St 17046
Hoke Ave 17042
Holly Ln 17042
Homestead Dr 17046
Hoover Dr 17046
Horizon Blvd 17046
Hornet St 17046
Horse Ln 17046
Horseshoe Cir & Pike 17042
Horseshoe Trail Dr 17042
Horst Ave 17042
E Horst Ave 17042
Horst Dr 17046
E Horst Dr 17046
Huckleberry Ln 17046
Hunter Ct 17042
Hunter Ln 17046
Hunters Chase Ln 17046
Iona Rd 17042
Iron Valley Dr 17042
Ironmaster Rd 17042
Isabel Dr 17042
Jackson Blvd & Rd 17042
Janet Ave 17046
Janlan Rd 17042
Jay St 17046
Jayann Dr 17042
Jaydell Dr 17042
Jeffsu Ln 17042
Jessica Dr 17046
Jill Ann Dr 17042
Jimmys Ln 17046
Jody Ave 17046
Joel Dr 17046
Joffre St 17046
Johns Ave 17042
Jones St 17046
Jonestown Rd 17046
Joseph Ave 17042
Josephine Ann Dr 17046
Joyce St 17046
Julia Ln 17042
Juliada Dr 17042
Juniper St 17042
Justa Ln 17046
Karinch St 17042
Katherine Ave 17042
Kathleen St 17046
Kathy Ct 17042
Kathy Dr 17046
Keeler Pkwy 17042
S Keener Ln 17042
Keeney Rd 17042
Keller Dr 17042
Kenbrook Rd 17046
Kercher Ave 17046
Keystone Dr 17042
Kimmerlings Rd 17046
Kiner Ave 17042
E King St 17042
Kings Dr 17046
Klein Ave 17042
Kline St 17042

E Kline St 17046
Klinger Ln 17042
Kochenderfer Rd 17046
Kreider St 17042
Kreiser St 17042
Kreitzer Ln 17046
Krim Ct 17042
Lackawanna Dr 17042
Lafayette St 17042
Lake Dr
2-698 17042
700-799 17042
801-899 17042
1800-1899 17046
Lakeview Cir 17042
S Lancaster St
300-499 17046
500-599 17042
Lantern Dr 17046
Larch Cir 17042
Larch Ln 17046
Larkspur Ln 17042
Laurel Ln
1-199 17046
300-399 17042
Laurel St 17046
S Laurel St 17042
Laurelwood Dr 17042
Leah Dr 17046
Lebanon Ave 17042
N Lebanon St 17042
S Lebanon St 17042
Lebanon Vlg 17046
Lebanon Valley Ct 17046
Lebanon Valley Mall 17042
Lebanon Valley Pkwy 17042
E Lehman St 17046
Leinbaugh Ave 17042
Lemke Ln 17046
Lentz Dr 17042
Leslie Ave 17042
W Liberty Aly 17042
N Liberty St 17046
S Liberty St 17042
Light Ave & St 17046
Lights Rd 17046
Lights Church Rd 17046
Lilac Aly & Ln 17042
N Lincoln Ave 17046
S Lincoln Ave 17042
Lincoln St 17046
N Lincoln St 17042
S Lincoln St 17042
Linda Dr & Ln 17046
Linden Rd 17042
Linden St
500-898 17042
900-999 17042
1000-1024 17046
1026-1098 17046
Little Pond Ln 17042
Lochwood Dr 17046
Lock Ln 17046
E & W Locust Ln & St 17042
Long Ln & Rd 17046
Loretta Dr 17046
Lori Ann Ct 17042
Louser Rd 17042
Lovers Ln 17046
Lynch Dr 17042
M T C Ln 17042
Madison Ave 17046
Mae Ave 17046
Magnetite Ln 17042
Magnolia Ln 17042
E & W Main St 17042
Mallard Ln 17046
Manor Dr 17042
Mantriew St 17046
Maple Dr 17042
Maple Ln
100-199 17042
800-999 17046
Maple St
1-123 17046
120-124 17042

125-1199 17046
126-1198 17046
E Maple St
1-1099 17046
1-599 17042
W Maple St
1-199 17042
1-2199 17046
Marcon Dr 17046
Margaret Ave 17042
Margin Rd 17042
Maria Cir 17042
Marion Dr 17042
Marquette Ln 17042
Martin Dr 17046
Martin St 17046
Marvin Ave 17042
Mary St 17046
Mccurdy Ln 17042
N & S Mckinley Ave 17046
Meadow Dr & Ln 17042
Meadowbrook Ln 17046
Meadowfield Dr 17046
Meadowood Cir 17042
Meadowview Dr & Ln 17042
Mechanic St 17046
Meily St 17046
Melody Ln 17046
Metro Dr 17042
E Mifflin St 17046
Mill Rd 17046
Mill St 17042
N Mill St
1-399 17042
700-1099 17046
S Mill St 17046
Mill Link 17042
Millbridge Dr 17042
Miller Ln 17042
Miller St
401-497 17046
499-999 17046
1200-1599 17042
Millview Ct 17042
N Mine Rd 17042
Mishs Mill Rd 17046
N Monroe Ave & St 17046
Monticello Dr 17042
Monument St 17046
Moore Rd 17046
Moravian St 17042
Morgan Dr 17042
Moritz Dr 17046
Morningside Ave 17042
Morrissey Dr 17046
Mount Gretna Rd 17042
Mount Lebanon Dr 17046
Mount Pleasant Rd 17042
Mount Wilson Rd 17042
Mount Zion Rd 17046
Mountain Ln 17042
Mountville Dr 17042
Mulberry Ln 17046
Mulenberg Dr 17042
Mull Ln 17046
Mumma St 17042
Murray St 17046
Nancy Ln 17046
Nancy Lee Ave 17042
Narrows Dr 17046
Natalie Ln 17042
New St 17046
New Bunkerhill St 17046
Noble St 17042
Nolt Ln 17046
Norfolk Ln 17042
Norman Dr 17042
Norman Keller Dr 17042
Northcrest Acres 17046
Northfield Dr 17042
Northgate Dr 17042
Northwest Dr 17042
Northwood Ct & Dr 17042
Norway Ln 17042
Nottingham Way 17042
Nowlen St 17042

Oak Ln
41-99 17042
800-999 17046
Oak St
1-1 17042
3-6 17046
7-7 17042
7-7 17046
8-24 17046
9-9 17046
300-498 17046
500-4199 17042
Oak Knoll Cir 17042
Oak View Ct 17042
Oaklyn Rd 17042
Oakridge Ct 17046
Obie Rd 17042
Old Canal St 17046
E Old Cumberland St 17042
Old Ebenezer Rd 17046
Old Furnace Rd 17042
Old Hickory Ln 17046
Old Jonestown Rd 17046
Old Mine Rd 17042
Old Mount Gretna Rd 17042
Olde Meadow Ln 17042
On The Grn 17042
Orange Ln 17046
Orange St 17042
Orchard Ave 17046
Osceola St 17042
Overlook Dr 17042
Oxford Dr 17042
Paddle Pl 17046
Palm Ave & Ln 17042
Palmer St 17042
Pamela Ln 17042
Paradise Ln 17046
Park Ave, Dr & St 17042
Parkside Dr 17042
Parkway Dr 17046
Parkwood Ct 17042
Parr St 17046
N Partridge St 17046
S Partridge St 17042
Patmar Dr 17046
Patricia Dr 17042
Peace Ln 17042
N Peach St 17046
E & W Penn Ave & St 17042
Pennsylvania Ave 17046
E Pennsylvania Ave 17042
N Pennsylvania Ave 17046
Pennwood Rd 17042
Penny Ln 17046
Percy Ln 17042
Perry St 17046
Pershing Ave 17042
E Pershing Ave 17042
Pershing St 17046
Pesta Ln 17046
Pheasant Dr 17046
S Pheasant St 17042
Pier Pl 17046
Piergallini Ln 17046
Pine Aly 17042
Pine Ave 17042
Pine Ln 17042
Pine St
100-199 17042
600-1099 17042
1900-1999 17042
E Pine St 17042
W Pine St 17046
S Pine Grove St 17046
Pine Meadow Rd 17046
Plaza Apartments 17042
Pleasant View Dr 17046
Plum Ln 17042
N Plum St 17046
S Plum St 17042
Pondside Ln 17042
Poplar Ln 17046
Poplar St
1-7 17042
9-649 17042

650-699 17046
700-2099 17042
E Poplar St 17042
N Poplar St 17046
Poralend St 17046
Prescott Dr 17046
Prescott Rd 17042
Primrose Ct & Ln 17046
Princeton Ave & Pl 17042
Progress Ave 17042
Prune Aly 17042
N Prune St 17046
Quail Ln 17042
Quarry Rd 17046
Quentin Rd 17042
N Quince St 17046
S Quince St 17042
Quittapahilla Dr 17042
Race St 17042
Railroad St 17042
Ramblewood Ln 17042
S Ramona Rd 17042
Ranch Ave 17042
Raspberry Ln 17046
Raven Ln 17042
Rebecca Ln 17046
Reber St 17042
Redwood Ln 17046
Reinoehl St 17046
Reist Rd 17042
Renova Ave 17046
Rex Ave & St 17042
Rexmont Rd 17042
Richard Ave 17042
Richard Dr 17046
Richfield Dr 17042
Riders Way 17042
Ridge Ave 17042
Ridge Rd 17046
Ridgeview Rd 17042
Rill Dr 17042
Rita Ln 17042
Ritter Way 17042
Robin Rd 17042
Rocherty Rd 17042
Rockledge Dr 17046
Rolling Meadow Rd 17046
Rosemont Ave 17042
Rossi Rd 17046
Roundtop Dr 17042
Roush Ln 17042
Royal Rd 17042
Royer Ln 17042
Russell Dr 17042
Russell Rd 17046
Rutherford Cir 17042
Saam Ln 17046
Saint Francis Dr 17042
Saint Jacobs Dr 17046
Sallyann Dr 17046
Sand St 17042
Sandhill Rd 17046
Sandra Dr 17042
E Sarah St 17046
Sassafras Dr 17042
Schaeffer Rd 17042
Schneider Dr 17042
Schone Ln 17042
School Ln 17042
E Scull St 17046
Sebastian Ln 17046
Shadow Creek Dr 17042
Shellie St 17046
Sherri Dr 17046
Shirksville Rd 17046
Shirley Dr 17042
Sholly Ave 17046
Shore Landing Dr 17046
Short Rd
101-199 17046
500-799 17042
Short St 17042
Silver Ln 17042
Sioux Ave 17042
Skyline Dr 17046
Smaltz St 17046

Smith Ave 17042
Smiths Ln 17046
Smokehouse Ct 17046
Snitz Rd 17042
Snow Dr 17046
Solar Dr 17046
Soliday Ct 17046
Southfield Rd 17042
Southgate Dr 17042
Spangler Rd 17042
E Spring Aly 17042
Spring St 17046
Spring St E
300-310 17042
1-99 17046
401-499 17042
Spring Creek Ln 17046
Spring Hill Ln 17042
Spruce Ln 17046
Spruce St
101-107 17042
400-1399 17046
Spruce Park
Apartments 17046
Stanford Dr 17042
Starner Rd 17042
State Dr 17042
State Route 117 17042
State Route 343 17046
State Route 72 N 17046
Steckbeck St 17046
Steele St 17046
Steitz St 17042
Stevens Ln 17042
Stone Hedge Ct & Dr 17042
Stonebridge Dr 17042
Stoneleigh Dr 17042
Store Ln 17042
Stover St 17046
Stracks Dam Rd 17046
Strathford Dr 17042
Stuart St 17046
Sue Cir 17042
Summit Ct & St 17042
Sun Dr 17046
Sunrise Ct 17046
Sunrise Dr 17046
Sunset Ln 17046
Suzanne Dr 17046
Suzy St 17046
Swatara Rd 17046
Sweetbriar Ln 17046
Sycamore Ln 17046
Sycamore Hill Ct 17042
Sylvan Ln 17042
Tabor St 17042
Tanglewood Ct 17042
Tavern Ln 17042
Taylor St
300-399 17042
2400-2499 17046
Temple Ave 17042
Terry Ln 17042
Theatre Dr 17046
Thompson Ave 17046
Thornton Ln 17042
Thru St 17042
Tice Ln 17042
Tiffany Ln 17046
Timber Blvd, Cv, Ln &
Rd 17042
Timberbridge Rd 17042
Timothy Ave 17042
Tiverton Ct 17042
Tow Path Way 17046
Troon Way 17042
Troy Ave 17046
Tuck Ct & St 17042
Tudor Ln 17042
Tulip Tree Dr 17042
Tunnel Hill Rd 17046
Twigg Ave 17046
E Union Aly 17042
W Union Aly 17042
Union Rd 17046
Union St 17042

Union Canal Dr 17046
Valley Rd 17042
Valley View Dr & Pl 17042
Van Buren St 17046
Varney Aly 17042
Victor St 17042
Victoria St 17046
Villa Dr 17042
Village Ct & Dr 17042
E Vine St 17042
Walden Rd 17042
Walker St 17042
Walnut Ln 17042
Walnut St
1-2599 17042
2-22 17046
5-15 17046
24-2598 17042
Walnut St W
15-17 17046
E Walnut St 17042
W Walnut St
2-8 17042
Walnut Crest Dr 17046
Walnut Mill Ln 17042
E Walton St 17042
Wampler Ln
1-99 17046
1000-1099 17042
Warren Dr 17042
Washington Ave 17046
Washington St 17042
N Washington St
1-199 17042
400-499 17046
S Washington St 17042
Water St
1-99 17042
700-798 17046
800-2199 17046
Water Edge Ct 17046
Waterford Way 17042
Waterside Cir 17042
Watson St 17046
Weaber Ln 17042
Weaver Ln 17046
Weavertown Rd 17046
N Weber St 17046
Wedgewood Dr 17042
E Weidman St 17046
Weiss Ave 17042
Wenger St 17042
Werni Dr 17042
Weymouth Dr 17042
Wheatfield Ln 17042
Wheatland Cir 17042
Wheatstone Ln 17042
S White Oak Cir & St 17042
Whitman Rd 17042
Whitney Way 17042
Wildflower Cir 17046
Wilhelm Ave 17042
Wilkin St 17042
Willow Ave 17042
Willow Ln 17046
Willow St
200-298 17046
300-1499 17046
1501-1599 17046
1600-1699 17042
Wilshire Dr 17042
S Wilson St 17042
Winchester Cir 17046
Wintermere Rd 17042
Woodbine St 17046
Woodland Cir, Est &
St 17042
Woodlawn Dr 17042
Woodlea Ave 17046
Woodridge Ct 17046
Woodward St 17046
Worden St 17046
Worth St 17042
Wren Dr 17042
Wunderlichs Ln 17046
Wynnwood Dr 17046

York St 17042
Zartman Ln 17046
Zimmerman Ln 17042
Zinns Mill Rd 17042

NUMBERED STREETS

N 1st Ave 17046
S 1st Ave 17042
N 1st St 17046
S 1st St 17042
N 2nd Ave 17046
S 2nd Ave 17042
N 2nd St 17046
S 2nd St 17042
N 3rd Ave 17046
S 3rd Ave 17042
N 3rd St 17046
S 3rd St 17042
N 4th Ave 17046
S 4th Ave 17042
N 4th St 17046
S 4th St 17042
N 5th Ave 17046
S 5th Ave 17042
N 5th St 17046
S 5th St 17042
N 6th Ave 17046
S 6th Ave 17042
N 6th St 17046
S 6th St 17042
N 7th Ave 17046
N 7th St 17046
S 7th St 17042
N 8th Ave 17046
N 8th St 17046
S 8th St 17042
N 9th Ave 17046
N 9th St 17046
S 9th St 17042
N 10th Ave 17046
N 10th St 17046
S 10th St 17042
N 11th Ave 17046
N 11th St 17046
S 11th St 17042
N 12th St 17046
S 12th St 17042
S 13th Ave 17042
N 13th St 17046
S 13th St 17042
S 14th Ave 17042
N 14th St 17046
S 14th St 17042
N 15th Ave 17046
S 15th St 17042
N 16th St
1-299 17042
300-498 17046
S 16th St 17042
S 17th St 17042
N 18th St 17046
S 18th St 17042
N 19th Ave 17046
N 19th St 17046
S 19th St 17042
N 20th St 17046
S 20th St 17042
N 21st Ave 17046
N 21st St 17046
S 21st St 17042
N 22nd St 17046
S 22nd St 17042
N 23rd St 17046
S 23rd St 17042
N 24th St 17046
N 25th St
1-199 17042
400-799 17046
N 31st St 17046
N 32nd St 17046
N 33rd St 17046

LEHIGH VALLEY PA

General Delivery 18002

POST OFFICE BOXES MAIN OFFICE STATIONS AND BRANCHES

Box No.s
All PO Boxes 18002

NAMED STREETS

All Street Addresses 18002

LEVITTOWN PA

General Delivery 19055

POST OFFICE BOXES MAIN OFFICE STATIONS AND BRANCHES

Box No.s
All PO Boxes 19058

NAMED STREETS

A Ave 19056
Access Ln 19055
Ailanthus Ln 19055
Airacobra St 19057
Airport Rd 19057
Alder Ln 19055
Almond Ln 19055
Ambling Ln 19055
Amelia Dr 19054
Amesbury Rd 19054
Apple St 19057
Appletree Dr 19055
Apricot Ln 19055
April Ln 19055
Arbor Ln 19055
Arch Ln 19055
Aspen Ln 19055
Aster Ln 19055
Autumn Ln 19055
Azalea Ln 19055
B Ave 19056
Bald Cypress Ln 19054
Balsam Rd 19057
Barberry Ln 19054
Basswood Rd 19057
Beaver Dam Rd 19057
Beechtree Rd 19057
Begonia Ln 19054
Bentwood Ln 19054
Birch Dr 19054
Bittersweet Rd 19057
Black Pine Ln 19054
Black Walnut Rd 19057
Bloomsdale Rd 19057
Blue Lake Rd 19057
Blue Ridge Dr & Way 19057
Blue Ridge Turn 19057
Blue Spruce Ln 19054
Border Rock Rd 19057
Boston Ivy Rd 19057
Boulder Ln 19054
Briaroot Ln 19054
Bristol Pike 19057
Bristol Emilie Rd 19057
Bristol Oxford Valley Rd 19057
Broadleaf Rd 19057
Brown Bark Rd 19057
Burning Bush Ln 19054
Butterfly Ln 19054
Butternut Rd 19057
Buttonwood Ln 19054
Bypass Ln 19054
C Ave 19056
Cable Rd 19057
Cactus Rd 19057
Calicobush Rd 19057
Camellia Rd 19057
Cameo Pl & Rd 19057
Canal Rd 19057
Canary Rd 19057
Candle Rd 19057
Candytuft Rd 19057
Canna Rd 19057
Canoebirch Rd 19057
Canyon Rd 19057
Cardinal Rd 19057
Catalpa Ln 19055
Catherine Ct 19057
Centre St 19057
Chamberlain Way 19054
Cherry Ln 19055
Chestnut Ln 19055
Cinder Ln 19057
Cinnamon Rd 19057
Circle Rd 19057
Cleft Rock Rd 19057
Cliff Rd 19057
Cloister Rd 19057
Clover Ln 19055
Cobalt Cross Rd 19057
Cobalt Ridge Dr E 19057
Colette Ct 19057
Conifer Rd 19057
Copper Beech Ln 19055
Coral Ln 19055
Coral Rock Rd 19057
Cornflower Ln 19055
Cosmos Rd 19057
Cotton Rd 19057
County Way 19055
Crabtree Dr 19055
Cranberry Ln 19055
Crescent Ln 19055
Crestwood Rd 19057
Crimson King Ln 19055
Crosswood Ln 19055
Crown Rd 19057
Crystal Pl & Rd 19057
Curry Hill Rd 19057
Curtis Ave 19057
Cypress Ln 19055
Daffodil Ln 19055
Dahlia Ln 19055
Dark Leaf Ln 19055
Dawn Rd 19056
Deep Dale Dr E & W 19056
Deepgreen Ln 19055
Devon Way 19057
Dewberry Ln 19055
Disk Ln 19055
Dogwood Dr 19055
Dogwood Turn 19055
Dolphin Rd 19056
Downhill Rd 19056
E Ave 19056
East Ln 19054
Eastend Ave 19056
Easter Ln 19054
Echo Ln 19054
Edgely Rd 19057
Edgewood Ln 19054
Elderberry Dr 19054
Elizabeth Ln 19057
Elkins Ave 19057
Ellerdale Rd 19054
Elm Ln 19054
Elves Ln 19054
Ember Ln 19054
Emerald Ln 19054
Eventide Ln & Pl 19054
Evergreen Ln 19054
Everturn Ln 19054
Falcon Rd 19056
Fallenrock Rd 19056
Falls Tullytown Rd 19054
Farmbrook Dr 19055
Favored Ln 19055
Fawn Ln 19055
Fern Ln 19055
Field Ln 19055
Fieldstone Rd 19056
Firebush Rd 19056
Fireside Ln 19055
First St 19054
Firtree Rd 19056
Flagstone Pl 19056
Flamehill Rd 19056
Flamingo Rd 19056
Fleetwing Dr 19057
Flower Ln 19055
Forest Ln 19055
Forsythia Dr & Way E, N & S 19056
Fortune Ln 19055
Fountain Rd 19056
Four Leaf Rd 19056
Foxglove Rd 19056
Franklin St 19054
Freedom Ln 19055
Friendly Ln 19055
Frosty Hollow Rd 19056
Fruitree Rd 19056
Full Turn Rd 19056
Gable Hill Rd 19057
Gamewood Rd 19057
Gaping Rock Rd 19057
Garden Ln 19055
Gardenia Rd 19057
Gate Ln 19055
Gatewood Rd 19057
Gentle Rd 19057
Geranium Rd 19057
Gingerbush Rd 19057
Glen Rd 19057
Glenwood Ln 19055
Goldengate Rd 19057
Goldenridge Dr 19057
Good Ln 19055
Goodrock Rd 19057
Goodturn Rd 19057
Gooseneck Rd 19057
Graceful Ln 19055
Grand Pine Rd 19057
Granite Rd 19057
Grapevine Rd 19057
Grasspond Rd 19057
Graystone Ln 19055
Great Oak Rd 19057
Green Ln 19057
Green Lynne Dr 19057
Greenbrier Rd 19057
Greenbrook Dr 19055
Gridiron Rd 19057
Grieb Ave
1-99 19057
1600-1899 19055
Grove Ln 19055
Groveland Ave 19056
Gun Rd 19057
Haines Rd
1400-1499 19057
1500-1598 19055
1600-2700 19055
2702-2798 19055
7501-7527 19057
7529-7599 19057
Hale Rd 19056
Halfturn Rd 19056
Hamlet Rd 19056
Handy Rd 19056
Hanford St 19057
Harbor Rd 19056
Hardy Rd 19056
Hardy St 19057
Harmer St 19057
Harmony Rd 19056
Harp Rd 19056
Harrow Rd 19056
Hartel Ave 19057
Harvest Rd 19056
Haven Rd 19056
Hawk Rd 19056
Hawthorne Ln 19055
Hay Rd 19056
Headley Ave 19057
Headley Ct 19057
Headley Ln 19054
Headley Pl 19054
Hearth Rd 19056
Heartwood Rd 19056
Heartwood Turn 19056
Heather Ln 19055
Hedge Rd 19056
Hemlock Rd 19056
Hibbs Ln 19057
Hickory Ln 19055
Hidden Rd 19056
High Rd 19056
Highland Park Dr, Pl & Way 19056
Hillside Ave 19056
Hillside Ln 19054
Hillside Rd 19056
Hilltop Rd 19056
Hoe Rd 19056
Hollow Rd 19056
Holly Dr 19055
Hollyhock Ln 19055
Homestead Rd 19056
Honey Locust Rd 19056
Honeysuckle Ln 19055
Hook Rd 19056
Hope Rd 19056
Horn Rd 19056
Horseshoe Ln 19055
Host Rd 19056
Huckleberry Ln 19055
Hunt Rd 19056
Hyacinth Rd 19056
Hybrid Rd 19056
Hydrangea Rd 19056
Ice Pond Rd 19057
Idlewild Pass & Rd 19057
Idolstone Rd 19057
Inbrook Rd 19057
Incurve Rd 19057
Indian Creek Dr, Pass, Pl & Way 19057
Indian Creek Entry 19057
Indian Creek Turn 19057
Indian Park Rd 19057
Indian Park Turn 19057
Indian Red Rd 19057
Indigo Rd 19057
Indigo Turn 19057
Inkberry Rd 19057
Inland Rd 19057
Inlet Rd 19057
Inwood Rd 19057
Iris Rd 19057
Ironwood Rd 19057
Iroquois Rd 19057
Island Rd 19057
Islet Rd 19057
Ivory Rock Rd 19057
Ivy Hill Rd 19057
Jade Ln 19055
Jadewood Rd 19056
James St 19057
Jasmine Rd 19056
Jennifer Ct 19057
Jensen Dr 19054
Jester Ln 19055
Jewel Ln 19055
Joan Ct 19057
Jolly Ln 19055
Jollybrook Rd 19056
Jonquil Ln 19055
Joseph Pl 19057
Joy Ln 19055
Juanita Ct 19057
Jump Hill Rd 19056
June Rd 19056
Junewood Dr 19055
Juniper Dr 19056
Kentucky Ln 19055
Kenwood Dr & Xing 19055
Kernel Ln 19055
Keystone Ln 19055
Kindle Ln 19055
Kingapple Ln 19055
Kingwood Ln & Pl 19055
Kraft Ln 19055
Lacrosse St 19054
Lakeside Dr 19054
Larkspur Rd 19056
Laurel Ln 19054
Lauren Ct 19057
Lavender Ln 19054
Learning Ln 19054
Leisure Ln 19054
Levittown Ctr 19055
Levittown Pkwy
2-152 19054
143-175 19055
177-181 19055
183-189 19055
186-198 19054
200-299 19054
300-398 19055
301-599 19054
3800-3898 19054
Liberator St 19057
Library Way 19055
Lilac Ln 19054
Limewood Rd 19056
Lincoln Hwy 19056
Linden Ln 19054
Little Ln 19054
Locust Ln 19054
Long Loop Rd 19056
Lower Rd 19056
Lower Morrisville Rd 19054
Lower Orchard Dr 19056
Lower Orchard Turn 19056
Lynn Ave 19054
Macintosh Rd 19056
Magnolia Dr 19054
Magnolia Park Ln 19054
Main St 19054
Mallow Ln 19054
Manning Blvd 19057
Maple Ln 19054
Maplewood Dr 19056
Margin Rd 19056
Margin Turn 19056
Marigold Cir 19054
Marion Ave & Ct 19055
Maroon Rd 19056
Martha Cir & Dr 19054
Mary Ln 19057
Mayflower Rd 19056
Mcpherson St 19057
Meadow Ln 19054
Meetinghouse Sq 19054
Merry Turn Rd 19056
Micahill Rd 19056
Michael Pl 19057
Michele Ct 19057
Middle Rd 19056
Midwood Ln 19054
Mill Dr & Pl 19056
Mill Bend Rd 19056
Mill Creek Pkwy
7901-7999 19055
8000-8099 19054
Mill Creek Rd
1-7099 19057
7101-7101 19057
9000-9080 19054
Mimosa Ln 19054
Mintleaf Rd 19056
Mistletoe Ln 19054
Misty Pine Rd 19056
Mitchell Rd 19057
Mockorange Ln 19054
Moon Dr 19054
Morning Glory Ln 19054
Mountain Ln 19054
Mulberry Ln 19054
Mustang St 19057
Myrtle Ln 19054
Nancia Dr 19054
Naomi Ct 19057
Naples St 19056
Narcissus Ln 19054
Nasturtium Ln 19054
Natalie Ct 19057
Nature Ln 19054
Nearwood Ln 19054
Nebraska Ave 19056
Nectar Ln 19054
Needlepine Ln 19054
Nelson St 19056
Neptune Ln 19054
Nestingrock Ln 19054
Nettletree Ln 19054
New Falls Rd
2100-5400 19056
5402-6098 19056
6500-6898 19057
6900-7099 19057
7100-7199 19055
7200-7998 19055
7200-7200 19058
7201-7901 19055
8500-9200 19054
9202-9398 19054
New Pond Ln 19054
New School Ln 19054
Newberry Ln 19054
Newman St 19056
Newportville Rd 19056
Nice St 19056
Nichol Ave & St 19056
Nickelhill Ln 19054
Nightingale Ln 19054
Noah Ave 19056
Noblewood Ln 19054
Norman Ave 19055
Northcourt Ln 19054
Northpark Dr & Way 19054
Northturn Ln 19054
Nottingham Ct & Dr 19054
Nursery Ave 19057
Nutmeg Ln 19054
Oakland Ave 19056
Oaktree Dr 19055
Old Brook Rd 19057
Old Locust Ave 19054
Old Pond Rd 19057
Old Spruce Ln 19055
Openwood Ln 19055
Orangewood Dr 19057
Orchard Dr 19054
Orchard Ln 19055
Orchid Ln 19055
Outlook Ln 19055
Oval Turn Ln 19055
Overbrook Ln 19055
N Oxford Valley Rd 19056
Palm Ln 19054
Pamela Ct 19057
Park Ln 19054
Parkside Cir 19056
Patricia Ln 19057
Patrician St 19057
Patterson Ave 19057
Peachtree Ln 19054
Peartree Ln 19054
Pebble Ln 19054
Penn Ave 19057
Penn Ln 19054
Penn Valley Rd 19054
Pensive Ln 19054
Peony Rd 19056
Peppermint Rd 19056
Petunia Rd 19056
Pine Ave 19056
Pine Needle Rd 19056
Pinewood Dr 19054
Pleasant Ln 19054
Plumbridge Dr, Pass & Way 19056
Plumtree Pl & Rd 19056
Plumtree Turn 19056
Pond Ln 19054
Poplar Ln 19054
Post Ln 19054
Primrose Ln 19054
Prunewood Rd 19056

Pumpkin Hill Rd 19056
Quail Rd 19057
Quaint Rd 19057
Quaker Hill Rd 19057
Quaker Hill Turn 19057
Quakeroak Rd 19057
Quarry Rd 19057
Quarter Turn East Rd .. 19057
Quarter Turn West Rd .. 19057
Quartz Rd 19057
Quay Rd 19057
Queen Anne Rd 19057
Queen Lily Rd 19057
Queens Bridge Rd 19057
Quest Rd 19057
Quickset Rd 19057
Quiet Rd 19057
Quill Rd 19057
Quincy Dr 19057
Rain Lily Rd 19056
Rainbow Ln 19055
Rambler Ln 19055
Randall Ave 19057
Ravine Ln 19055
Red Berry Rd 19056
Red Cedar Dr 19055
Red Maple Ln 19055
Red Ridge Rd 19056
Red Rose Dr & Way 19056
Redbrook Ln 19055
Reedman Ave 19057
Return Ln 19055
Ridge Ln 19055
Ring Ln 19055
River Ln 19055
Roberts Ave 19057
Robin Hill Ln 19055
Robin Hood Dr 19054
Rockwood Rd 19056
Rocky Pool Ln 19055
Rolling Ln 19055
Rose Ct 19056
Rose Apple Rd 19056
Rose Arbor Ln 19055
Round Hill Rd 19056
Roundabout Ln 19055
Roundwood Ln 19055
Roving Rd 19056
Ruby Ln 19055
Rue Ct 19057
Runway Dr 19057
Russett Ln 19055
Rust Hill Rd 19056
Rustleaf Ln 19055
Saddlebrook Dr 19057
Scarlet Oak Rd 19056
Schoolhouse Ln 19055
Seckelpear Rd 19056
Second St 19054
Serpentine Ln 19055
Shadetree Ln 19055
Shadywood Rd 19056
Shellflower Rd 19056
Shelter Ln 19055
Shepherd Ln 19055
Sherwood Dr 19054
Short Ln 19055
Silver Birch Ln 19055
Silverbell Rd 19056
Silverspruce Rd 19056
Silvi Ave 19057
Smoketree Rd 19056
Snowball Dr 19056
South Ln 19055
Spicebush Rd 19056
Spindletree Rd 19056
Spinythorn Rd 19056
Spiral Ln 19055
Spring Ln 19055
Spring Valley Rd 19056
Starlight Ln 19055
Steeplebush Rd 19056
Stewart Ave 19057
Stonybrook Dr 19055
Strawberry Ln 19055
Stream Ln 19055
Sugarmaple Ln 19055
Sugarplum Rd 19056
Summer Ln 19055
Sunflower Rd 19056
Sunset Ave 19056
Sunset Ln 19055
Swan Ln 19055
Sweetbriar Ln 19055
Sweetgum Rd 19056
Sycamore Rd 19056
Sycamore Ridge Dr 19056
Tall Pine Ln 19054
Tamarack Ln 19054
Tanglewood Ln 19054
Tapered Oak Ln 19054
Tawny Rd 19056
Taylor Dr 19054
Teaberry Ln 19054
Tearose Ln 19054
Tempo Rd 19056
Terrace Rd 19056
Thaliabush Ln 19054
Thimbleberry Ln 19054
Thinbark Ln 19054
Thistle Rd 19056
Thomas Pl 19057
Thornridge Dr, Pl &
Way 19054
Thornyapple Ln 19054
Tiger Lily Ln 19054
Timber Ln 19054
Timothy Ln 19054
Tinder Rd 19056
Tinsel Rd 19056
Top Rd 19056
Top Hill Ln 19054
Towns Rd 19056
Towpath Rd 19056
Trail Rd 19056
Tree Ln 19054
Trellis Rd 19056
E Trenton Ave 19054
Trenton Rd
1000-1099 19054
1700-2098 19056
2100-2799 19056
Trim Rd 19056
Tulip Ln 19054
Tulip Tree Rd 19056
Turf Rd 19056
Turn Hill Ln 19054
Turnabout Ln 19054
Tweed Rd 19056
Twig Ln 19054
Twin Leaf Ln 19054
Twin Oak Dr & Way 19056
Twisting Ln 19054
W Tyburn Rd 19054
Umber Rd 19056
Underwood Rd 19056
Unity Turn 19056
Uphill Rd 19056
Upland Rd 19056
Upper Orchard Dr, Pass
& Way 19056
Valentine Ln 19054
Valley Rd 19057
Valor Ln 19054
Vase Ln 19054
Velvet Ln 19054
Venture Ln 19054
Verdant Rd 19057
Vermillion Dr, Ln, Pl &
Way 19054
Vermont Ln 19054
Vermont Turn 19054
Vestry Ln 19054
Veterans Hwy 19056
Viaduct Ln 19054
Viburnum Ln 19054
Vicar Ln 19054
Victoria Ln 19054
Viewpoint Ln 19054
Viking Ln 19054
Village Ln & Pass 19054
Village Turn 19054
Vine Ln 19054
Vineyard Rd 19057
Violet Rd 19057
Violetwood Dr 19057
Virga Ave 19054
Vista Rd 19057
Vitaloak Ln 19054
Vividleaf Ln 19054
Vulcan Rd 19057
Walnut Ln 19054
Ward Ln 19057
Water Oak Rd 19057
White Spruce Ln 19054
Whitewood Dr 19057
Wildflower Rd 19057
Wildrose Ln 19054
Williams Ave 19057
Williamson Ave 19054
Willow Dr 19054
Winding Rd 19057
Wisteria Ln 19054
Woerner Ave 19057
Wood Ln 19054
Woodbine Rd 19057
Woodbourne Rd
201-299 19056
900-1900 19057
1902-4222 19057
Woodside Ave 19057
Yardley Ave 19054
Yellowood Dr 19057
Young Birch Rd 19057

MCKEESPORT PA

General Delivery 15134

POST OFFICE BOXES MAIN OFFICE STATIONS AND BRANCHES

Box No.s
A - D 15134
1 - 606 15134
1 - 121 15135
691 - 9998 15134

NAMED STREETS

A St 15133
Abraham St 15132
Albion St 15132
S Allegheny Dr 15133
Allen Way 15131
Allison St 15132
Alquin St 15133
Amherst St 15131
Anderson St 15132
Andrew Dr 15131
Ann St 15132
Anthony Dr 15131
Antonelli Dr 15135
Apple Way 15132
Aqua Ct 15135
Arboretum Dr 15132
Arch St 15132
Archer St 15132
Archies Way 15133
Arctic St 15132
Arlington St
500-799 15132
800-998 15133
1000-1099 15133
Arnold Dr 15132
Arthur St 15131
Ashland St 15133
Atcheson St 15132
Atlantic Ave 15132
Auberle St 15132
Auburn St 15132
B St 15133
Bailey Ave 15132
Baldwin St 15132
Balmer Dr 15133
Bank St 15132
Banker St 15132
Barkley Rd 15133
Barnsdale St 15132
Bartwood St 15132
Bassi Dr 15132
Bayne St 15132
Bea Mar Dr 15135
Beacon St 15132
Beadondo St 15135
Beale St 15132
Beaver St 15132
Beckman Dr 15132
Beech St 15132
Bellaire Dr 15133
Bellefonte St 15132
Belleview St 15132
Bennett St 15132
Bernard Dr 15131
Beverly Rd 15133
Birch St 15132
Bluff St 15132
Bonita Ct 15131
Boston Hollow Rd 15135
Botkin Pl 15135
Bouquet St 15132
Bowman Ave 15132
Boyd St 15132
Boyle St 15132
Braemont Pl 15135
Brandywine Pl 15135
Briarhill Ct 15131
Briarwood Dr 15135
Bridge St 15132
Bridgeview St 15131
Brinkman Ln 15135
Brisbane Aly 15132
Brom St 15132
Brownlee St 15132
Brushton St 15133
Bunker Hill Rd 15135
Burbank St 15133
Burbridge St 15133
Burning Tree Ct & Dr ... 15135
Butler St 15132
Byron St 15132
C St 15133
California Ave 15131
Calvin St 15132
Camp St 15132
Canterbury Ln 15135
Capitol St 15131
Carmella Dr 15131
Carnegie St 15132
Carolina Way 15131
Carson St 15132
Cascade Dr 15135
Centennial St 15132
Center St
1-1099 15132
1100-2499 15131
Center Street Ext 15131
Chauncey Cir 15132
Cherry Ln & St 15132
Chesapeake St 15131
Chesney St 15135
Chester St 15132
Chestnut St 15132
Chicagoion St 15135
Circle Dr 15131
Clark St 15131
Clay St 15132
Clearview St 15131
Cleveland St 15132
Cliff St 15132
Clinton St 15131
Clyde Dr 15131
Clydesdale St 15135
Coal Aly 15133
Colfax St 15132
Collins St 15132
Colonial Dr 15135
Colonial Manor Rd 15131
Columbia St 15132
Complex Dr 15135
Concord Dr 15135
Congress St 15131
Constitution Blvd 15135
Converse St 15132
Cook Rd 15131
Cool Springs Rd 15131
Cornell St 15132
Cornwallis Dr 15135
Coronado Dr 15133
Coulter Rd 15131
Country Club Dr 15135
Coursin St 15132
Craig St 15132
Crawford Vlg 15132
Cronemeyer St 15132
Crossland St 15133
Crown Plz 15132
Cypress Dr 15131
D St 15133
Dale St 15132
Dalewood St 15135
Dalton St 15132
Daren Ct 15131
Daugherty Ln 15133
Dawson St 15132
Day St 15132
Dearborn Dr 15131
Deaton Ln 15131
Deer Ln 15133
Delaware Ave 15131
Delaware St
800-1299 15131
2600-2799 15132
Delrose Dr 15133
Demmler Rd 15132
Demmler St 15131
Dersam St 15133
Desota St 15132
Devonwood Dr 15135
Dewees St 15132
Diehl Dr 15132
Dinsmore St 15132
Dome St 15131
Donner St 15135
Douglas St 15132
Douglas Way 15133
Downey St 15132
Drake St 15132
Drumlin Ln 15135
Dry St 15132
Duncan Station Rd 15135
Dunn St 15132
Duquesne Ave 15132
E St 15133
Easler St 15132
East St 15132
Eaton St 15132
Eden Park Blvd 15132
Edmundson St 15133
Educational Dr 15131
Edward Dr 15132
Edwin St 15132
Eisenhower Dr 15131
Elenick Ct 15131
Elizabeth St
800-999 15133
3800-3999 15132
Elm St
200-499 15132
700-2499 15133
4600-5299 15132
Elmwood St 15133
Emerson St 15135
Enterprise St 15132
Erie St 15132
Euclid St 15132
Evans Ave 15132
Everglade Dr 15135
Express Aly 15132
F St 15133
Fairmont St 15132
Fairview St
600-799 15132
3200-3299 15131
Fawcett Ave
500-1099 15132
1100-2299 15131
Fayette St 15132
Federal St 15132
Ferintri St 15131
Fern Aly 15132
Fey Rd 15135
Flagler St 15132
Ford St 15132
Forest St 15132
Foster Rd 15131
Franklin St
700-1099 15132
1100-1299 15131
Frederick Dr 15135
Freeland St 15132
Freemont St 15132
Friendship Dr 15135
Fritchie St 15133
Front St 15133
Garbett St 15132
Garden St 15131
Gardner St 15132
Gas St 15132
George St 15131
George Young Dr 15132
Georgetown Pl 15135
Glass St 15131
Gleason St 15132
Gleditsch Aly 15132
Glendale St 15133
Glenn Ave 15133
Glenshire Ln 15132
Golfview Dr 15135
Gordon St 15132
Grandview Ave 15132
N Grandview Ave 15132
Grandview Dr 15133
Grant St 15132
Gray St 15133
Greenock Buena Vista
Rd 15135
Greenwood St 15132
Gross St 15132
Grove St 15133
Grover St 15132
Gumbert St 15133
H St 15133
Haberlin St 15132
Halkett St 15135
Halsey Dr 15132
Hamilton St 15132
Hamilton Xing 15133
Hankins Dr 15135
Harley Dr 15131
Harmony St 15133
Harper St 15135
Harphen St 15132
Harris St 15131
Harrison St & Vlg 15132
Hart St 15135
Hartman St 15133
Haslage St 15133
Havilla St 15132
Hayes St 15133
Hazel St 15132
Heather Ln 15133
Heatherlynn Ct 15131
Hemlock Dr 15131
Henderson Rd 15131
Henry St 15132
Hershey Dr 15132
Hickory Aly 15132
Hicks St 15132
High Dr 15131
High St 15132
Highland Ave
900-1099 15133
2100-3099 15133
Highland Avenue Ext 15132
Hill St
1600-1899 15131
2600-3199 15132
Hillview St 15132
Holsing St 15135
Hopkins St 15132
Horizon Dr 15131
Horseshoe Dr 15131
Hospital Way 15132
Howe Dr 15132
Huber St 15133
Huey St 15132
Hunter St 15133
I St 15133
Idaho St 15132
Indiana Ave 15132
Industry Blvd 15132
Inglewood Dr 15131
Irene Aly 15132
Irwin St 15132
Ivy St 15132
Jacks Run Rd 15131
James St 15132
Jefferson St 15132
Jeffrey Dr 15133
Jenny Lind St 15132
Jerry Ln 15131
Jersey St
800-899 15133
2900-3199 15132
Johnson St 15133
June Dr 15133
Juniata St 15132
Juniper St 15132
Kaler St 15133
Kansas Ave 15131
Kansas St 15132
Keddie Rd 15135
Kelly St 15131
Kent St 15132
King St 15132
Koch Ln 15135
Kollar Dr 15133
Kountz Aly 15132
Lafayette St 15132
Lamont St 15132
Larch St 15132
Larchfield Dr 15135
Laredo St 15133
Larkin St 15132
Latrobe St 15133
Lauck St 15133
Laurel Ln 15131
Laurel St 15132
Lawndale St 15132
Lawnview Dr 15135
Lawrence Ave 15132
Lebanon Dr 15135
Lee Ct 15135
Lee St 15132
Leech St 15132
Lemon St 15132
Leonard St 15131
Lewis St 15131
Lexington Dr 15135
Lexington St 15132
Liberty Way 15133
Library St 15132
Lilly Aly 15132
Lime St 15132
Lincoln St 15132
Lincoln Way
500-1099 15132
1100-2899 15131
Lindalan Dr 15135
Lindberg Dr 15132
Linden St 15132
Linwood St 15132
Litman Ln 15131
Locust St 15132
Lodge St 15135
Long Run Rd
300-1099 15132
1100-1299 15131
Longvue Dr 15131
Lower Heckman Rd 15131
Luray St 15132
Lynn Aly 15132
Lysle Ave 15133
Lysle Blvd 15132
Madison St 15132

Main St
200-3999 15132
2600-2699 15131
Manning Ave 15132
Manor Ave & St 15132
Maple Dr 15131
Maple St 15132
Maplewood St 15132
Marcella Dr 15133
Marietta Dr 15131
Marion Way 15132
Market St 15132
Maroon Ln 15131
Marshall Dr 15132
Martin St 15132
Mason Rd 15131
May St 15132
Mayfair St 15132
Mcarthur Dr 15132
Mccarrell St 15132
Mccleary St 15132
Mcclelland Dr 15133
Mcclintock Rd 15131
Mcclure Dr 15133
Mcclure Ln 15131
Mccully St 15131
Mcintosh Dr 15132
Mckee Rd 15131
Mckinley St 15132
Mclean Dr 15133
Meade St 15135
Meadow St 15132
Meashins St 15133
Melvina St 15132
Memory Ln 15133
Mercantile St 15132
Merritt St 15132
Messinger Ln 15131
Middle Dr 15131
Middlesex Rd 15135
Midway Dr 15131
Milburn St 15132
Miller St 15132
Miller Ridge Rd 15133
Mohawk Dr 15135
Mohawk St 15132
Monaca Dr 15133
Monongahela Blvd
1100-1500 15131
2000-2299 15132
Monroe Ave 15133
Monterey St 15132
Morlock St 15132
Morton Ave 15133
Mound St 15132
Mount Vernon Dr 15135
Mulberry Aly 15132
Muse Ln 15131
Myer Ave 15133
Myer Blvd 15132
Myers Ln 15131
Narragansett Dr 15135
Navy St 15131
Neal Dr 15135
Nelson St 15131
Nessley St 15132
Nevada St 15133
New Jersey St 15131
New York Ave 15133
Nimitz Dr 15132
North Ln 15132
Norwood St 15133
Oak St 15132
Oakland Ave 15133
Oakland Dr 15133
Oakland St 15132
Oakview Dr & St 15131
Oakwood St 15132
Oard St 15132
Oberdick Dr 15135
Odair St 15132
Ohio Ave 15131
Ohio St 15132
Old Hills Rd 15135
Old Orchard Dr 15135
Olive St 15132

Oliver Aly 15132
Oliver Dr 15131
Olympia St 15132
Olympia Park Plz 15132
Oneil Blvd
600-3899 15132
2300-2899 15131
Orange St 15132
Orchard Dr 15133
Orchard St 15132
Oriole St 15132
Orofino St 15132
Osborne St 15131
Osceola Dr 15131
Outlook Dr 15135
Overlook Dr 15133
Owens Aly 15132
Owens Ave 15133
Oxford Dr 15132
Pacific St 15132
Packer St 15132
Palm St 15132
Palmer St 15132
Palmgreen St 15132
Park Ln 15132
Park Rd 15132
Park St 15132
Park Way
100-228 15131
215-399 15132
230-298 15131
Park Manor Dr 15132
Parker Dr 15135
Pasadena Dr 15133
Patterson St 15132
Peebles Ln 15132
Pendelac St 15132
Penhurst Ext & St 15135
Penn Way 15132
Penn Crest Dr 15131
Pennsylvania Ave 15131
Penny St 15132
Penrod St 15135
Penrod Street Ext 15135
Perry St 15132
Peterson St 15132
Petty St 15132
Pike St 15133
Pin Oak Dr 15132
Pine St
200-312 15132
314-498 15132
345-399 15133
401-499 15132
600-699 15133
Pinecrest Dr 15135
Pirl St 15132
Pitt St 15135
Pleasant Ave 15133
Pleasant Dr 15131
Poinsettia Dr 15131
Point St 15132
Pond Way 15131
Port Vue Ave 15133
Porter St 15132
Portsmouth Dr 15133
Powderly St 15132
Powers St 15132
Prescott St 15131
Pride St 15133
Public Rd 15131
Quay St 15131
Queen St 15132
Rack St 15135
Railroad St 15132
Rankin Rd 15131
Rankin St 15133
Ravine St 15132
Reba St 15132
Rebecca St
200-699 15132
800-999 15133
Reed St 15132
Reiman St 15131
Renzie Park 15132
Renzie Rd 15135

Reynolds St 15132
Ridge Rd 15135
Ridge St
200-299 15133
500-1399 15132
Ringgold St 15132
Ripple Rd 15132
Rison Aly 15132
River Rd 15132
River Ridge Rd 15133
Riverview Dr 15131
Riverview St 15132
Roberts St 15133
Rockwood St 15132
Rogena St 15132
Romine Ave
100-799 15132
800-1999 15133
Rooney St 15131
Rose St 15132
Roslyn St 15135
Ross St 15132
Royal Oak Dr 15131
Saint Andrews Cir 15135
Saint David Dr 15135
Salem St 15135
Sally St 15131
San Jose Dr 15133
San Juan Dr 15133
Sand Aly 15132
Santa Monica Dr 15133
Sarah St 15132
Saratoga Dr 15135
Sceneridge Rd 15133
School Aly 15132
Schweitzer Rd 15135
Scott St 15132
Seabury St 15132
Senate St 15131
Seneca Ct 15135
Shady St 15132
Sharp Rd 15131
Shaw Ave 15132
Sherbine Way 15131
Shields St 15133
Short St 15132
Silver Ln 15131
Sinclair St 15132
Skelly St 15131
Smith St 15133
Smithfield St 15135
Soles St 15132
Sommerset St 15135
Southern St 15133
Spring St 15132
Spruce St 15132
Staisey St 15131
State St 15131
Steele St 15132
Stegman Ave 15133
Sterling St 15132
Stewart St 15132
Stewartsville Hollow
Rd 15131
Stockholm St 15132
Stonehaven Ln 15131
Stoner St 15135
Strawberry St 15132
Sumac St 15132
Summitt St
500-1099 15132
1100-1699 15131
Sunset Dr 15131
Sunset Ln 15133
Surrey Ln 15135
Swallow Hill Rd 15135
Sylvan St 15132
Sylvester Way 15133
Tacoma Ave 15133
Tangleview Dr 15131
Terrace Dr 15135
Terrapin Dr 15133
Terrytown Dr 15135
Thomas Dr 15131
Thompson St 15133
Thunderbird Dr 15135

Tomco Ln 15131
Transit Dr 15135
Trenton Pl 15135
Trimble Ave 15133
Tube Works Aly 15132
Tulip Dr 15132
Turkeyfoot Rd 15135
Turner St 15131
Union Ave 15132
University Dr
--- 15132
1-400 15131
100-199 15132
201-4001 15132
402-4098 15131
Upston St 15133
Valley St 15133
Valley Ridge Rd 15133
Valley View Dr 15131
Van Kirk Aly 15132
Vermont Ave 15131
Vernor Aly 15132
Versailles Ave 15132
Victoria Dr 15131
Victory St 15135
Vine St
800-899 15133
4500-4899 15132
Virginia Dr 15133
Virginia St 15135
Wabash St 15132
Wainwright Dr 15132
Walker St 15132
Walnut St
409-497 15132
499-845 15132
847-5399 15132
850-850 15134
854-5398 15132
Walter St 15135
Washington Blvd 15133
Washington St 15132
Water St 15132
Waymouth Dr 15133
Wayne St 15132
Weldon St 15133
Wesley St 15132
Wexford St 15135
Whigham St 15132
White St 15132
White Oak Dr 15131
White Tail Ln 15131
Wide Dr 15135
Will St 15132
Willard St 15131
Williams St 15132
Willis St 15135
Willow St 15132
Wilson St 15132
Windsor St 15132
Woodbine St 15132
Woodland Dr 15133
Woodland St 15132
Woodrow St 15133
Woodward St 15132
Worthington St 15132
Wunderly Dr 15133
Yankee Ct 15133
Yates St 15135
Yester Sq 15132
York St
1200-1299 15131
3000-3899 15132
Yorktown Pl 15135
Yough St
1-99 15135
500-599 15132
601-699 15132
Youghiogheny Dr 15135
Zimmer Ln 15135

NUMBERED STREETS

All Street Addresses 15132

MECHANICSBURG PA

General Delivery 17055

POST OFFICE BOXES MAIN OFFICE STATIONS AND BRANCHES

Box No.s
1 - 3701 17055
7069 - 7069 17050

NAMED STREETS

Abington Way 17050
Acorn Ct 17055
Acri Rd 17050
Ada Dr 17050
Adam Ln 17050
Addison Dr 17050
Adeline Dr 17050
Airport Dr 17050
Alberta Ave 17050
Albright Dr 17055
Alder St 17055
Aldersgate Cir 17050
Alexandria Ct 17050
Alison Ave 17055
Allegheny Dr 17055
Allegiance Dr 17050
E & W Allen St 17055
Allen Glen Dr 17055
Allen Grange Ct 17055
Allendale Rd
101-199 17050
200-1299 17055
Allenview Dr 17055
Alma Ln 17055
Amanda Ct 17050
Amelias Path E & W 17050
Amherst Ct 17050
Amity Ln 17050
Andersontown Rd 17055
Andes Dr 17055
Antelope Ct 17050
Anthony Dr 17050
Antietam Ct 17050
Antilles Ct 17050
Antrim Dr 17050
Apache Dr 17050
Apache Trl 17055
Appalachian Ave 17055
Appaloosa Dr 17050
Apple Cir & Dr 17055
Appletree Ln 17055
Appomattox Ct 17050
Arbor Ct 17055
N & S Arch St 17055
Arcona Rd 17055
Argali Ln 17055
Ariel Ct 17055
Armitage Way 17050
Artcraft Dr 17050
Arthur Ave 17050
Asbury Dr 17055
Ascott Way 17055
Ash Dr 17050
Ashburg Dr 17050
Ashburn Way 17055
Aspen Ave & Dr 17055
Atland Dr 17055
Auburn Dr 17050
Audubon Rd 17055
Augusta Dr 17050
Autumnwood Dr 17055
Avery Way 17050
Baden Powell Ln 17050
Baish Rd 17055
Baker Dr 17055
Baldwin Ct & St 17055
Balfour Dr 17050
Bali Hai Rd 17050
Balmoral Ct 17050
Barbara Dr 17050

Barbara Ln 17055
Bare Rd 17050
Barnstaple Rd 17050
Baron Ct 17050
Barry Ct 17050
Basehore Rd 17050
Battersea Pkwy 17050
Bauman Ct 17055
Bay St 17050
Bayberry Ct & Dr 17050
Baythorne Dr 17050
Beacon Cir 17055
Bearcreek Dr 17050
Beard Rd 17050
Beaver Dr 17050
Bedford Ct 17050
Beech Run Ln 17050
Beechwood Dr 17055
Beilman Ct 17055
Bella Vista Dr 17050
Belmont St 17055
Beltsville Dr 17050
Belvedere Dr 17055
Bencru Ave 17055
Bennington Rd 17050
Bent Creek Blvd 17050
Bentley Rd 17050
Bentzel Dr 17050
Berkeley Dr 17050
Berkshire Ln 17050
Berkshire Rd 17055
Bethany Dr 17055
Bethpage Dr 17050
Beverly Ln 17050
Bianca Ct 17050
Big Horn Ave 17055
Billet Dr 17055
Billingsgate 17050
Birch St 17050
Birchwood Ln 17055
Bishop Rd 17055
Bittersweet Ln 17050
Black Pine Dr 17050
Blackfriars Way 17050
Blue Mountain Vis 17050
Bluebell Dr 17050
Boiling Springs Rd 17055
Bonny Ln 17055
Bonnyrigg Ct 17050
Boston Ct 17050
Bourbon Red Dr 17050
Boxwood Ct 17050
Boxwood Ln 17055
Brackbill Blvd 17050
Bracken Ct 17050
Brad St 17055
Bradford Ct & Dr 17055
Braeburn Dr 17055
Brandt Rd 17055
Brandton Rd 17055
Brandy Ln
300-499 17055
6300-6599 17050
Brandywine Dr & Way 17050
Braxton Ter 17050
Breezewood Ct 17050
Breezewood Dr 17055
Brenneman Cir 17050
Brenneman Dr 17055
Brian Ct & Rd 17050
Briargate Rd 17050
Briarwood Ct 17050
Bridgeport Dr 17050
Brigantine Ct 17050
Brighton Pl 17055
Brindle Rd 17055
S Broad Cir & St 17055
Broad Wing Ct 17050
Broadmoor Dr 17055
Broadwell Ln 17055
Brom Ct 17050
Brook Cir 17050
Brook Meadow Dr 17050
Brookridge Dr 17050
Brookview Ct 17050
Brookwood Dr 17055

Brunswick Ave 17055
Bryant St 17050
Buckingham Ave 17055
Bull Run Ct 17050
Bumble Bee Hollow
Rd 17055
Burns Rd 17055
Burwick Dr 17050
Butternut Ln 17050
Buttonwood Ct 17050
Byers Ave 17055
Cabot Aly 17050
Cain Aly 17050
Calvert Dr 17050
Cambridge Blvd 17050
Cambridge Dr 17055
Candlelight Dr 17055
Cannon Dr 17050
Canterbury Ct 17050
Canterbury Dr 17055
Canyon Crk 17055
Cardamon Dr 17050
Carlisle Pike 17050
Carmella Dr 17050
Carothers Cir 17050
Carriage Ln 17050
Carrington Ct E & W 17050
Cascade Rd 17055
Cedar Ave 17055
Cedar Rd
1-99 17055
900-999 17050
Cedar St 17055
Cedar Heights Dr 17055
Cedar Ridge Ln 17055
Central St 17055
Century Dr 17055
Chantilly Ct 17050
Charing Cross 17050
Charles Ave 17055
Charles Cir 17055
Charles Rd 17050
Charles St 17055
Charlton Way 17050
Chelmsford Dr 17050
Chelsea Way 17050
Chelsen Cross 17050
Cherokee Dr 17050
Cherry Cir 17055
Cherry Tree Ct 17055
Cheryl Ave 17055
Cherylbrook Dr 17050
Chesterfield Ln 17050
S Chestnut St 17055
Chestnut Ridge Dr 17055
Chick A Dee Dr 17050
Chickory Cir 17050
Chiltern Way 17055
Chippenham Rd 17050
Chloe Ln 17050
Choco Chase 17055
Christian Ct 17050
W Church Rd 17055
Cicada Dr 17050
Cider Hill Dr 17055
Cider Press Rd 17055
Circle Dr 17055
Circle Ln 17050
Clairburn Dr 17050
Clark St 17055
Claverton Rd 17050
Cloud Ct 17050
Cloudless Sky Dr 17050
Clouser Rd 17055
Clouser Road Spur 17055
Clover Dr 17055
Clover Ln 17050
Club House Dr 17050
Cobbler Ct 17050
Cobblestone Dr 17055
Cockleys Dr 17050
Cocklin Ct & St 17055
Coffmans Point Dr 17050
College Ave 17055
Collier Dr 17055
Collingdale Cir 17050

Colonial Ct 17050
Colonial Dr
200-299 17050
4900-4999 17055
Colonial View Rd 17055
Commerce Dr 17050
Community Ctr 17050
Cona Rd 17055
Concord Rd 17050
Conestoga Ln 17050
Congress Dr 17050
Conifer Ln 17050
Conley Dr 17055
Connell St 17055
Connie Dr 17050
Constitutional Ct 17050
Contemdra Dr 17055
Conway Dr 17055
E & W Coover St 17055
Cope Dr 17055
Copper Creek Dr 17050
Cortland Aly 17050
Cottage Ct 17050
Cottage Brook Ln 17055
Country Dr 17055
Cove Ct 17050
Coventry Ct & Dr 17055
Creek Rd
1-99 17050
1100-1299 17055
Creek Bank Dr 17050
Creek View Ln 17055
Creek View Ter 17050
Creekbend Dr 17050
Creekview Rd 17050
Cressman Cir 17055
Crimson Ct 17050
Crofton Ct 17050
Croghans Ln 17050
Cromwell Ct 17050
Crooked Stick Dr 17050
Cross Aly 17050
Cross Creek Dr 17050
Crossgate Dr 17050
Crosswick Cir 17050
Crystal Creek Dr 17050
Cumberland Dr 17050
Cumberland Pkwy 17055
Cumberland Estates
Dr 17050
Cumberland Pointe Cir 17055
Cypress Ct 17055
Cypress Point Ct 17050
Cyprus Ln 17050
Daisy Dr 17050
Dalkeith Dr 17050
Danbury Dr 17050
Dapp Ln 17050
Darla Rd 17055
Dartmoor Dr 17050
Dartmouth Ct 17055
Dauphin Rd 17050
David Dr 17050
Debra Rd 17050
Deerburn Ct 17050
S Deerfield Ave & Rd 17050
Deerview Dr 17055
Deitch Ln 17050
Delancey Ct 17055
Delbrook Ct & Rd 17050
Delta Dr 17055
Delwood Dr 17050
Derbyshire Ave 17055
Detroit Ave 17050
Devereux Ln 17050
Devonshire Sq 17050
Dewalt Dr 17050
Dewberry Ct 17055
Diehl Rd 17055
Dishley Dr 17055
Dogwood Ct & Dr 17055
Donald St 17050
Dorset Dr 17050
Dover Ct 17055
Downing Pl 17050
Drayton Ct 17055
Drury Ln 17050
Dry Powder Cir 17050
Dubs Cir 17050
Dunbar Dr 17050
Dunkleburger Dr 17055
Dunlin Ct 17050
Duntanso Dr 17050
Dwayne Ave 17050
E St 17050
Eagle Ct 17050
East Dr 17050
Easterly Dr 17050
Easy St 17050
Eberly Dr 17050
Edgeware Rd 17050
Edgewood Dr & Ln 17055
Edson Dr 17050
Edward Dr 17050
Egret Ct 17050
Eldindean Ter 17050
Elgin Cir 17055
Eliza Way 17050
Elk Ct 17050
Ellesmere Ln 17055
Ellington Rd 17050
Ellis Aly 17050
Elm St 17050
E & W Elmwood Ave 17055
Elstar Ln 17055
Emil Ridge Dr 17050
Emily Dr 17055
Emlyn Ln 17055
Empire Cir 17055
Empress Dr 17055
English Dr 17055
Eppley Rd 17055
Erbs Bridge Rd 17050
Eric Dr 17055
Eton Pl 17055
Evelyn Ave 17055
Evergreen Ln 17050
Ewe Rd 17050
E & W Factory St 17055
Fairfield Ln 17050
Fairfield St
800-899 17055
1100-1199 17050
Fairmont Dr 17055
Fairway Dr 17055
Falcon Ct 17055
Falkstone Dr 17050
Fawns Leap Way 17050
Federal Dr 17050
Fenwick Ave 17055
Fertenbaugh Ln 17055
Fetrow Dr 17050
Field Stone Dr 17050
Fieldcrest Dr 17050
N & S Filbert St 17055
Firethorn Ln 17055
Fisher Rd 17055
Flamingo Dr 17055
Fleetwood Ave 17050
Fleming Dr 17055
Flintlock Ridge Rd 17055
Florence Ave 17055
Florence Cir 17050
Floribunda Ln 17055
Flowers Dr 17050
Folsom Aly 17050
Ford Farm Rd 17055
Forest Dr 17055
Forest Oaks Ct 17050
Forrest Dr 17055
Founders Way 17050
Fowlers Hollow Dr 17055
Fox Dr 17050
Fox Hollow Cir & Rd 17055
Foxchase Way 17050
Foxfield Ct 17050
Foxfire Cir & Dr 17055
Foxtail Ct 17050
Foxwood Blvd 17050
Fragrant Pear Dr 17050
Francis Dr 17050
Franklin Ave & Sq 17050
N & S Frederick St 17055
Freedom Rd 17055
Freedom St 17050
Friar Ct 17050
Frost Rd 17050
Fry Dr 17050
Gale St 17055
Galleon Dr 17050
Garden Dr 17055
Gateway Dr 17050
General Dr 17050
General Couch Cir 17050
General Jenkins Dr 17050
General Knipe Dr 17050
Geneva Dr 17055
Genevieve Dr 17055
S George Cir & St 17055
Georgetown Rd 17050
Gettysburg Pike & Rd 17055
Ginger Dr 17050
Ginkgo Grv 17055
Gladstone Ct 17055
Glen Ct 17055
Glendale Dr
1-26 17055
27-199 17050
Gleneagles Dr 17050
Glenfield Dr 17050
Glenfinnan Pl 17055
Glenn St 17055
Glenwood St 17050
Glime Dr 17055
Gloucester St 17050
Golden Ct 17055
Golfview Dr 17050
Good Hope Rd 17050
Governors Dr 17050
Granada Ln 17055
Grandia Flora Dr 17055
Grandon Ct & Way 17050
Grandview Ave & Ct 17055
Grange Ave 17055
W Grantham Rd 17055
Gray Dr & Pl 17055
E & W Green Ln & St 17055
Green Acres St 17055
Green Hill Rd 17050
Green Ridge Rd 17050
Greenbriar Dr & Way 17050
Greenfield Dr 17055
Greenspring Dr 17050
Greenway Dr 17055
Greenwich Dr 17050
Gregor Ct 17050
Gross Dr 17050
Grouse Ct 17050
Gull Ct 17050
Gunpowder Rd 17050
Gunstock Ln 17050
Gustin Dr 17050
Gutshall Ln 17055
Hamilton Ave & Cir 17055
Hamlet Cir 17050
Hampden Park Dr 17050
Hann Way 17050
Haralson Dr 17055
Harpers Ferry Way 17050
Harrison St 17050
Hart Xing 17055
Harvest Dr & Ln 17055
Hastings Dr 17050
Hauck Rd 17055
Havenwood Ct 17050
Hawk Ct 17050
Hawthorne Ave 17055
Haydon Ct 17050
Haymarket Way 17050
Haywood Dr 17050
Hazel Cir 17050
Hazelwood Ct & Path 17050
Hearthstone Ct 17050
Heinz St 17055
Heisey Rd 17055
Helen Ave 17055
Hellam Dr 17055
Hemlock Cir, Ct, Dr &
Rd 17055
Hempt Dr & Rd 17050
Henry St 17055
Heritage Ct 17050
Herman Dr 17055
Heron Ct 17050
Hertzler Rd 17055
Hickory Ln 17055
Hidden Meadow Dr 17050
High Holw 17050
High St 17055
N High St 17055
S High St 17055
High Meadows Ln 17055
High Ridge Trl 17050
Highfield Ct 17055
Highland Ct 17050
Highland Dr 17055
Highlander Way 17050
Hilda Ct 17050
Hill Blvd 17055
N Hill Dr 17050
Hill Ln 17050
W Hill Rd 17050
Hillcrest Dr
1-6 17050
2-8 17055
10-99 17055
Hillside Dr 17055
Hillside Ln 17050
Hillside Rd 17050
Hilltop Cir 17055
Hogestown Rd 17050
Hoke Farm Way 17050
Holly Dr 17055
Holly Ln 17050
Honeysuckle Dr 17050
Honor Dr 17050
Hopi Dr 17050
Horsham Dr 17050
Houston Dr 17050
Humer Dr 17050
Hummingbird Dr 17050
Hunt Pl 17050
Hunter Dr 17050
Hunters Ridge Dr 17050
Huron Dr 17050
I St 17050
Ichabod Ct 17050
Inared Ct 17055
Independence Ave 17055
Independence Ct 17050
Independence Way 17050
Indian Ln 17055
Indian Creek Dr 17050
Indian Peg Rd 17055
Inverness Dr 17050
Iris Ln 17050
Irongate Ct 17050
Iroquois Way 17050
Jacob Ln 17050
Jaguar Dr 17050
James Ln & St 17055
James Madison Dr 17050
Jamestown Sq 17050
Jarod Ct 17050
Jeffrey Dr & Rd 17050
Jenna Ct 17055
Jennifer Cir 17050
Jerusalem Rd 17050
Joel Dr 17050
John King Ln 17050
John Mar Ct 17055
Johns Dr 17050
Jonagold Cir 17055
Jonathan Ct 17055
Joseph Junkin Ln 17050
Joshua Rd 17050
Julie Ct 17055
July Breeze Dr 17050
Juniper Dr 17055
Kacey Ct 17055
Katrina Ct 17050
Kay Rd 17050
Keefer Way 17055
Keener Dr 17050
Keith Rd 17050
E & W Keller St 17055
Kendall Dr 17055
Kensington Sq 17050
Kent Dr
400-499 17055
700-3699 17050
Kentwood Dr 17050
Kerry Ct 17050
Keswick Ct 17055
Keswick Dr 17050
Kevin Rd 17050
Keystone Dr 17050
Kim Acres Dr 17055
King Arthur Dr 17050
Kings Cir 17055
Kings Arms 17050
Kingswood Dr 17055
Kirk Ct 17050
Kittatinny Dr 17050
Knepper Dr 17055
Konhaus Rd 17050
Kower Ct 17055
Kunkle Ln 17050
Kushner Aly 17050
Kylock Rd 17055
Lafayete Ct 17050
Lake Dr 17055
Lambs Gap Rd 17050
Lamont Ave 17055
Lancaster Blvd 17055
Lancelot Ave 17055
Landau Way 17050
Lantzy Rd 17055
Larch Loop 17055
Latchgate Ln 17050
Laurel Dr 17055
Laurel Ln 17050
Laurel St 17055
Lavina Dr 17055
Lavynndon Ln 17055
Lawncrest Dr 17050
Lee Anne Ln 17050
Leib Rd 17055
Leidig Dr 17055
Lena Dr 17055
Lenker St 17050
Lenox Ct 17050
Leona St 17050
N & S Lewisberry Rd 17055
Lexington Ave 17055
Lexington Dr 17050
Leyland Dr 17050
Leyton Way 17055
Liberty Ct 17050
Liberty Cv 17055
Liberty Dr 17055
Lighthouse Dr 17050
Lilac Dr 17050
Lilly Ln 17050
Limestone Dr 17050
Linda Dr
1-199 17050
200-299 17055
Linden Ave 17055
Linden St 17050
Lindham Ct 17055
Line Rd 17050
Lisburn Rd 17055
Lismore Pl 17050
Liz Burns Pl 17055
Lobach Dr 17055
Locust Cir 17050
Locust Ln
500-699 17055
6000-6399 17050
N Locust Ln 17050
S Locust Ln 17050
E Locust St 17055
W Locust St 17055
N Locust Point Rd 17050
S Locust Point Rd 17055
Lodge Rd 17055
Lois Ln 17050
Long Ln 17050
Longmeadow St 17055
Longview Dr 17050
Longwood Dr 17050
Lonk Ln 17055
Lookout Dr 17050
N Loop Rd 17055
Lori Cir 17050
Loring Ln 17055
Louisa Ln 17050
Louise Dr 17055
Loyal Dr 17050
Lucie St 17050
Lucinda Ln 17055
Ludgate Cir 17050
Lutztown Rd 17055
Lynchburg Ct 17055
Lynnbrook Way 17055
Lynndale Ct 17050
Macoun Dr 17055
Madder Dr 17050
Madison Rd 17050
Magnolia Ct 17055
Main St 17055
Mallard Ct & Way 17055
Manassas Ct 17050
Manor Dr
1-99 17055
300-399 17050
1205-4497 17055
4499-4599 17055
Maple Ave 17055
Maple Dr 17050
Maple Ln 17055
Maple Mall 17055
Maple Leaf Ct 17055
E & W Maplewood
Ave 17055
Marble St 17050
E Marble St 17055
W Marble St 17055
Margaret Ct & Dr 17050
N & S Market St 17055
Market Plaza Way 17055
Marla Dr 17055
Marlton Rd 17055
Martin Dr 17055
Mary Ave 17055
Matter Dr 17050
Maybelle Ct 17050
Mayberry Ln 17050
Mayfield Rd 17055
Maywood Ct 17050
Mccormick Dr & Rd 17055
Mcdonald Dr 17050
Mcintosh Dr 17055
E, N, S & W Meadow Dr,
Ln & Trl 17055
Meadow Creek Ln 17050
Meadow Croft Cir 17055
Meadow View Ct 17050
Meadowbrook Dr 17050
Meggan Ln 17050
Melbourne Ln 17055
Melwood Ln 17050
Memory Ln 17050
Mendenhall Dr 17050
Mercury Dr 17050
Meridian Cmns, Ln &
Way 17055
Merino Ln 17055
Merlerle Dr 17055
Merrimac Ave 17055
Merrimack Ct 17050
Messiah Cir 17055
Midland Rd 17055
Mill Rd
1-1000 17050
1002-1098 17050
2100-2198 17055
2200-2799 17055
Millbank Dr 17050
Miller Ave & Blvd 17055
Millers Rd 17055
Millfording Rd 17050
Mimosa Dr 17055
Minnich Rd 17055
Mitchell Dr 17050
Mockingbird Dr 17050
Monarch Ln 17050
Monroe St 17055
Montego Ct 17050
Monterey Dr 17050
Montrose Cir 17050
Moores Mountain Rd 17055
Moorgate 17050
Morefield Way 17050
Moreland Ct 17055
Morning Star Ct 17055
Mount Allen Dr 17055
Mountain Pine Dr 17050
Mountain View Dr &
Rd 17050
Muirfield Pl 17050
Mulberry Dr 17050
Mumma Ave 17055
Musket Ln 17050
Muskrat Lndg 17050
Myrtle Dr 17055
Nabal Rd 17055
Nanroc Dr 17055
Nantucket Dr 17050
Naragansett Dr 17050
Newbold Ln 17050
Newgate Cir 17050
Newtown Cir 17050
Nicholson Ct 17050
Nita Ct 17050
Nittany Dr 17055
Nixon Dr 17055
Nook Aly 17050
Norfolk Ct 17055
Norland St 17055
North Dr & Rd 17050
Northern Spy Dr 17055
Northfield Way 17050
Northview Dr 17050
Northwatch Ln 17050
Northwood Cir 17050
S Norway St 17055
Nottingham Dr 17050
Nursery Dr N & S 17050
Oak Ln 17050
Oak Oval 17055
Oak Grove Ct 17055
Oakmont Grn 17050
Oakwood Ave 17055
Old Farm Ln 17050
Old Grove Rd 17055
Old Hollow Rd 17055
Old Schoolhouse Ln 17055
Old Silver Spring Rd 17055
Old Silver Springs Rd 17050
Old Stone House Rd
S 17055
Old Willow Mill Rd 17050
Olde Oak Ct 17050
Orchard Blvd, Ln & St 17055
Oriole Dr 17050
Orrs Bridge Rd 17050
Osage Way 17050
Osborne Ct 17050
Osprey Cir 17050
Otterbein Dr 17055
Otto Dr 17055
Ovis Dr 17055
Owl Ct 17050
Oxford Cir & Dr 17055
Oyster Bay Dr 17050
Pamay Dr 17050
Pamela Dr & Pl 17050
Pamelas Ln 17050
Panza Dr 17050
Park Ave 17055
Park Cir 17055
Park Pl 17055
Park Rd 17050
Park Hills Dr 17055
Park Ridge Dr 17055
Partridge Ct 17050
Patricia Ct 17055
Patriot Dr 17050
Patton Rd 17055

Paul Cir 17055
Pawnee Dr 17050
Peace Dr 17055
Peachtree Dr 17055
Pebble Ct 17050
Pebble Beach Ct 17050
Peffer Rd 17055
Pennington Dr 17055
Penns Run Rd 17050
Penns Way Rd 17050
Pennsboro Dr 17050
Peregrine Way 17050
Peters Dr 17050
Petersburg Ct 17050
Pheasant Ct 17055
Pheasant Dr 17055
Pheasant St 17050
Pheasant Hollow Rd 17050
Phico Dr 17050
Pickering Ln 17050
Piedmont Ct 17050
Pima Cir 17055
Pin Oak Ct 17050
Pin Oak Dr 17055
Pine Hill Ave 17050
Pine Tree Dr 17055
Pinehurst Way 17050
Pipher Ln 17050
Pleasant Grove Rd 17050
Pleasant View Dr 17050
Pocono Dr 17055
Poplar Dr 17050
Poppy Cir 17050
Porter Aly 17050
E & W Portland St 17055
E, N, S & W Powderhorn Rd 17050
Presbyterian Dr 17050
Presidents Dr 17050
Primrose Ln 17050
Princeton Rd 17050
Putnam Way 17050
Quail Ct 17050
Quail Hollow Dr 17055
Quiet Pond Ct 17050
N Race St 17055
N Railroad Ave 17055
Raintree Ln 17050
Raptor Ct 17050
Raspberry Dr 17050
Raudabaugh Rd 17050
Raven Ct 17050
Raven Hill Rd 17055
Ravenwood Rd 17055
Rebert Dr 17055
Red Fox Ln 17050
Red Spruce Ln 17050
Redbud Dr 17050
Redstone Ct 17050
Redwood Rd 17055
Republic Way 17050
Reservoir Rd 17055
Revere Dr 17050
Reynolds St 17055
Rhoda Blvd 17055
Rich Valley Rd 17050
Richard Ln 17055
Richard Rd 17050
Ricketts Rd 17050
Ricky Rd 17055
Riders Ln 17055
Ridge Dr 17055
Ridge Hill Rd 17050
Ridgeland Blvd 17050
Ridgeway Dr 17050
Ridgewood Dr 17050
Rife Dr 17050
Rittenhouse Sq 17050
Ritter Rd 17055
Rivendale Blvd & Ct 17050
Riverstix Ln 17050
Robert Dr 17050
Robert St 17055
Robin Ct 17055
Rockledge Dr 17050
Rocky Rd 17055
Rolling Hills Dr 17055
Rolo Ct 17055
Ronald Rd 17050
Rosebriar Rd 17055
E, N, S & W Rosegarden Blvd 17055
Rossmoyne Rd 17055
Roth Ln 17050
Roth Farm Village Cir 17050
Round Ridge Rd 17055
Roundtop Ct 17050
Roxbury Ct 17055
Royal Dr 17055
Royal Palm Dr 17050
Rumford Way 17050
Rupp Ave 17055
Rusty Dr 17050
Rutledge Aly 17050
Rycroft Dr 17050
Rye Cir 17055
Ryegate Rd 17055
Ryland Dr 17050
Sabre St 17050
Saffron Dr 17050
Saint Andrews Ct 17050
Saint James Cir 17055
Saint James Ct 17050
Saint Marks Rd 17050
Salem Church Rd 17050
Salem Park Cir 17050
Salmon Rd 17050
Sample Bridge Rd 17050
San Juan Dr 17055
Sand Pine Ct 17050
Sanddollar Dr 17055
Sanderson Dr 17055
Sandpiper Ct 17050
Sapling Ct 17055
Sarah Ct 17050
Sassafras Ln 17055
Sassafrass Ct 17055
Saw Mill Rd 17055
Sawgrass Ln 17050
Sawyer Ln 17050
Scenery Dr 17050
Scenic Dr 17055
E & W Schoolside Dr 17055
Scottish Ct 17050
Sears Run Dr 17050
Seedling Ct 17055
Seltzer Ct 17050
Seneca Dr 17050
Settlers Dr 17050
Shadow Oak Dr 17050
Shady Lane Dr 17050
Sharberry Ln 17050
Sharon Ave 17055
Shasta Way 17050
Shaw St 17050
Sheely Ln
300-499 17050
800-999 17055
Sheepford Rd 17055
Sheffield Ave 17055
Shenandoah Ct 17050
Shepherdstown Rd 17055
Sheridan Ct 17050
Sherwood Dr 17050
Shetland Ct 17050
Shiloh Ct 17055
Shingus Cir 17055
Shiremont Dr 17050
Shoemaker Ln 17050
Shoff Ct 17055
Sholly Dr 17050
Shuler St 17055
E Siddonsburg Rd 17055
Signal Hill Dr 17050
Silver Dr 17050
Silver Brook Dr 17050
Silver Creek Dr 17050
Silver Crown Dr 17050
Silver Fox Dr 17055
Silver Pine Cir 17050
Silver Spring Rd 17050
Simmons Rd 17055
E & W Simpson St 17055
Simpson Ferry Rd 17050
Sinclair Rd 17055
Sioux Dr 17050
Skyline Dr 17050
Skyport Rd 17055
Skyview Ct 17050
Slate Hill Rd 17055
Sleepy Hollow Dr 17055
Sleepy Hollow Ln 17050
Slover Rd 17055
Smiley Dr 17050
Smith Dr 17050
Sna Ln 17055
Somerset Dr 17055
Sommerton Dr 17050
Sorbie Ln 17050
Souder Ct 17050
South Rd 17050
Southpoint Dr 17055
Southridge Dr 17055
Southview Dr 17050
Southwatch Ln 17050
Spartan Dr 17055
Speedway Dr 17055
Spigold Ct 17055
Sporting Green Dr 17050
N & S Sporting Hill Rd 17050
Spring Cir 17055
Spring Brook Ln 17050
Spring Rock Ct 17055
Spring Run Dr 17055
Spring Valley Ln 17055
Spring View Ct 17050
Springdale Ct & Way 17050
Springwillow Dr 17055
Spruce Ct 17055
Spyglass Ln 17050
Stable Ln 17050
Stallion St 17050
Standlake Way 17055
Stanford Ct 17050
State Rd 17050
Station Dr 17050
Stephens Xing 17050
Sterling Pkwy 17050
Sterling Glen Way 17050
Stockwood St 17050
Stone Barn Rd 17050
Stone Run Dr 17050
Stonecrest Ln 17050
Stonehedge Ln 17050
Stoner Dr & Rd 17055
Stoner Drive Ext 17055
Stratford Ln 17050
Strathmore Dr 17050
E & W Strawberry Ave 17055
Strock Dr 17055
Stroup Cir 17050
Stuart Dr 17055
Stumpstown Rd 17055
Sugar Maple Way 17050
Sugar Shack Ln 17050
Sullivan St 17050
Summer Ln 17050
Summerfield Dr 17055
Summit Dr 17050
Summit Way 17050
Sunhaven Cir 17050
Sunset Cir 17050
Sunset Ct 17055
Sunset Dr 17050
Sunset Creek Ln 17050
Surrey Ln 17050
Susan Ln 17055
Sutherland Way 17050
Swan Dr 17050
Swindon Ln 17050
Sycamore Ct 17055
Sycamore Dr 17050
Tall Oak Dr 17050
Tamanini Way 17055
Tamar Rd 17050
Tanglewood Dr 17050
Tavern House Hl 17050
Tavistock Rd 17050
Tavy Ct 17050
Teal Rd 17050
Technology Pkwy 17050
Terrace Rd 17050
Texaco Rd 17050
Thistle Dr 17050
Thomas Dr 17050
Thompson Ln 17055
Thorncroft Dr 17050
Thornton Dr 17055
Thrush Ct 17050
Thyme Ct 17050
Timber Rd 17050
Timber Brook Dr 17050
Timber Chase Dr 17050
Timber View Dr 17050
Tiverton Rd 17050
Torrey Pines Dr 17050
Trayer Ln 17050
E Trindle Rd 17050
W Trindle Rd 17055
Trudy Cir 17050
Truffle Glen Rd 17050
Tunberry Ct 17050
Tunbridge Ln 17050
Turmeric Dr 17050
Turtle Ln 17050
Tussey Ct 17050
Upland St 17055
W Valley Rd & St 17055
Valley View Ave 17055
Valley View Dr 17050
Valleybrook Dr 17050
Valor Dr 17050
Vicki Ct 17050
Vicksburg Ct 17050
Victor Ln 17050
Victoria Dr 17055
Village Ct & Rd 17050
Violet Cir 17050
Virginia Ct & Rd 17050
Vista Dr 17055
Wagner Dr 17050
Wakefield Ave 17055
Walden Way 17050
Wall St 17050
Wallingford Way 17050
Walnut Ln 17050
N Walnut St 17055
S Walnut St 17055
Walnut Way 17055
Wansford Rd 17050
Ward Ln 17055
Warleigh Way 17050
Warm Sunday Way 17050
Warren Way 17050
Warrington Ave 17055
Warwick Cir 17050
N & S Washington St 17055
N & S Waterford Dr & Way 17050
Waterleaf Ct 17050
Wayne Dr 17055
Wedgewood Way 17050
Well St 17050
Wellgate Ln 17055
Wertz Ave 17055
Wertzville Rd 17050
Wesley Dr 17055
Westfield Ct 17050
Westfields Dr 17050
Westhafer Ct 17055
Westland Ct 17055
Westover Dr 17050
Westport Dr 17055
Westview Dr 17055
Weymouth Dr 17050
N & S Wharf Rd 17055
Wheatland Dr 17050
White Birch Ave, Cir & Ln 17050
White Dawn Ln 17055
White Oak Blvd 17050
Whitefield Dr 17055
Whitehill Dr 17050
Whitlock Ln 17055
Widders Dr 17055
Wild Rose Ln 17050
Willcliff Dr 17050
William Dr 17050
William Way 17055
Williams Grove Rd 17055
Williamsburg Way 17050
E Willow Ter 17050
W Willow Ter 17050
Willow Way 17055
Willow Bend Rd 17055
Willow Mill Park Rd 17050
Willshire Dr 17050
Wilson Ln 17055
Winchester Ct 17055
Winding Creek Blvd 17050
E & W Winding Hill Dr & Rd 17055
Windrush Ln 17055
Windsor Blvd 17055
Windsor Pl 17055
Windsor Rd 17050
Wineberry Dr 17055
Wingate Dr 17050
Wingert Dr 17055
Winston Dr 17055
Wintergreen Dr 17050
Winterhaven Dr 17055
Winthrop Ave 17050
Wister Cir 17055
Woodbine St 17055
Woodbox Ln 17055
Woodbury Cir 17050
Woodcreek Dr 17055
Woodcrest Dr 17050
E & W Woodland Dr & St 17055
Woodley Dr 17050
Woods Dr 17050
Woods Way 17055
Woodside Dr 17055
Woodstock Ct 17050
Woodward Dr 17050
Wooley Hollow Ct 17055
Wren Ct 17050
Wyncote Ct 17055
York Cir
1-99 17050
600-699 17055
York Rd 17055
N York Rd 17055
N York St 17055
S York St 17055
Yorkshire Dr 17055
Yorktowne Rd 17050
Yorkview Dr 17055
Zenu Rd 17055

NUMBERED STREETS

All Street Addresses 17055

MEDIA PA

General Delivery 19063

POST OFFICE BOXES MAIN OFFICE STATIONS AND BRANCHES

Box No.s
A - F 19063
1 - 572 19063
1 - 300 19065
601 - 4315 19063
9998 - 9998 19065

NAMED STREETS

Abel Pl 19063
Ahrens Ln 19063
Allen Ln & St 19063
Allyssa Dr 19063
Amanda Dr 19063
Amber St 19063
Anderson Ave & St 19063
Andrew Cir 19063
Anvil Ln 19063
Apple Ave 19063
Applebough Ln 19063
Appletree Dr 19063
Arbor Cir & Ln 19063
Arlington 19063
Arrowhead Trl 19063
Astor Sq 19063
Autumn Ln 19063
Azalea Ln 19063
E & W Baker St 19063
E & W Baltimore Ave & Pike 19063
Bancroft Rd 19063
Barren Rd 19063
Beatty Rd 19063
Beechwood Ave & Rd 19063
Bent Rd 19063
Berry Ln 19063
Birnam Wood Ln 19063
E & W Bishop Hollow Rd 19063
Bittersweet Way 19063
Black Bass Ln E & W 19063
Black Hawk Ct 19063
Blackhorse Ln 19063
Blacksmith Ln 19063
Bobbin Mill Rd 19063
Bonnie Ln 19063
Bortondale Rd 19063
Bowater Ct 19063
Bowers Ln 19063
Boxwood Ct 19063
Brakel Ln 19063
Brandywine Dr 19063
Braves Trail Ln 19063
Briar Ln 19063
Briarcrest Dr 19086
Briarwood Ln 19063
Bridle Ln 19063
Bridlebrook Ln 19063
Brinton Ave 19063
Brooke St 19063
Brookview Ln 19086
N Broomall St 19063
N & S Bryn Mawr Pl 19063
Burnt Church Ct 19063
Buttonwood Way 19063
Cabot Ct 19063
Calabrese Dr 19063
Camby Chase Rd 19063
Cape Cod Dr 19063
Carlton Pl 19063
Carnoustie Way 19063
Carriage Dr 19063
Catch Penny Ln 19063
Cedar Ct 19063
Cedar Grove Rd 19063
Cedar Hill Ln 19063
Cedar Hollow Dr 19086
Cedar Meadow Ln 19063
Centennial Ave 19063
Chapel Hill Rd 19063
Chatham Pl 19063
Cherry St 19063
Cherrywood Ln 19063
Chesley Dr 19063
Chestnut Ave & Ln 19063
Chipmunk Ln 19063
Christine Ln 19063
Church Rd & St 19063
Citation Ln 19063
Citron St 19063
Claudia Cir 19063
Clearwater Dr 19063
Clover Cir 19063
Coldspring Ln 19063
Collins Ave 19063
Colt Rd 19063
Consort Hl 19063
N & S Constance Dr 19063
Cook Ave 19063
Cool Valley Ln 19063
Copes Ln 19063
Country Village Way 19063
Courtney Ln 19063
Cove Ln 19063
Coventry Ln 19063
Crestview Cir 19063
Cricket Ln 19063
Crum Creek Rd 19063
E & W Daffodill Ln 19063
Dale Rd 19063
Dam View Rd 19063
Daria Rose Ct 19063
Darlington Rd 19063
Dartmouth Cir 19063
Dash Ave 19063
Dauphin Dr 19063
David Dr 19063
Davis Dr 19063
Dayton Cir 19063
Deer Run 19063
Deer Path Rd 19063
E & W Deerfield Dr 19063
Devon Ln 19063
Diemer Dr 19063
Dobson Ct 19063
Dog Kennel Rd 19063
Dogwood Rd 19063
Dora Dr 19063
Douglas Ln 19063
Down St 19063
Drake Dr 19063
Dundee Mews 19063
Dunns Cove Rd 19063
Dyanna Ln 19063
Eastwood Rd 19063
Ebie Cir 19063
N & S Edgemont St 19063
Edgewold Ln 19063
W Eighth St 19063
Elizabeth Dr 19063
Elm Ave 19063
Elwyn Ave & Rd 19063
Emerald Ln & St 19063
Eric Ln 19063
Evans Rd 19063
Evergreen Ave 19063
Fairfax Vlg 19063
Fairview Ave 19063
Farmhouse Ln 19063
Farnum Rd 19063
Fawn Hill Ln 19063
Feather Hill Ln 19063
N & S Feathering Ln 19063
E & W Fifth Ave & St 19063
First Ave 19063
Forest Lake Dr 19063
Forest View Rd 19086
E Forge Rd 19063
Forrest Ave 19063
E & W Fourth Ave & St 19063
Fox Rd 19063
Fox Lair Vlg 19063
Foxcatcher Ln 19063
Foxchase Ln 19063
Foxcroft Ln 19063
Foxdale Rd 19063
Foxwood Ln 19063
E & W Franklin St 19063
E & W Front St 19063
Gallant Fox Dr 19063
Garfield Rd 19063
Gayley St 19063
Geist View Cir 19063
General Steuben Dr 19063
General Washington Dr 19063
General Wayne Dr 19063
Gilbert St 19063
E & W Glen Cir 19063
Glen Riddle Rd 19063
Glenwood Ave & Cir 19063
Gordon Dr 19063
Grandview Rd 19063

Granite Dr 19063
Great Oak Dr 19063
Greenhill Rd 19063
Grubb St 19063
Guernsey Ln 19063
Halcyon Dr 19063
Haldeman St 19063
Hampton 19063
Hare St 19063
Hargrave Ln 19063
Harvard Dr 19063
Heathdale Ln 19063
Heather Ln 19063
Heather Knoll Ln 19063
Heatherwood Dr 19063
N & S Heilbron Dr 19063
Hemlock Rd 19063
Hermitage Ln 19063
Hidden Acres Ln 19063
Hidden Hills Rd 19063
Hidden Valley Rd 19063
Hidden Villa Dr 19063
High Meadow Dr 19063
Highland Ave & Dr 19063
Highpoint Dr 19063
Highview Ln 19063
Hillcrest Ct 19063
Hillendale Rd 19063
Hilltop Rd
1-11 19063
1-99 19086
Horseshoe Dr 19063
Howarth Ave & Rd 19063
Hunt Club Ln 19063
Hunter St 19063
Hunting Hills Ln 19063
Idlewild Cir & Ln 19063
Indian Ln 19063
Indian Spring Rd 19063
Indian Springs Dr 19063
Iris Ln 19063
N & S Jackson St 19063
Jacques Ln 19063
Jamestown 19063
E & W Jasper St 19063
E & W Jefferson St 19063
Jessica Way 19063
Jonathan Morris Cir 19063
Josephs Way 19063
Judith Ln 19063
Karen Ln 19063
Kelly Ln 19063
Kenmore Ln 19063
Kevin Ln 19063
Kimberwick Rd 19063
Kincaid Ct 19063
Kingston Rd 19063
Kirk Ln 19063
E & W Knowlton Rd 19063
Lafayette Cir 19063
Lake Ave & Dr 19063
Lakeside Ln 19063
Lakeview Dr 19063
Lakewood Dr 19063
Langstoon Ln 19063
Lantern Ln 19063
Latches Ln 19063
Laurel Ln 19063
Leedom Dr 19063
Leiper St 19063
N & S Lemon St 19063
Lenni Rd 19063
Letitia Ln 19063
Levis Ave 19063
Lexington 19063
Lilac Way 19063
Lima School Ct 19063
E & W Lincoln St 19063
Linda Ln 19063
Linden Ln 19063
Linville Rd 19063
Little Ln 19063
Locust Ln
1-199 19063
1-99 19086
Logtown Rd 19063

Longfellow Ln 19063
N & S Longpoint Ln 19063
N Longview Cir 19063
Luckie Ln 19063
Lungren Rd 19063
Man O War Dr 19063
Manchester Ave & Rd 19063
Mancil Rd 19063
N & S Manor Dr 19063
Mansion Dr 19063
Maple Ave 19063
Marcella Ln 19063
Markham St 19063
Martingale Rd 19063
Martins Ln & Run 19063
Mattrissa Rdg 19063
Meadowbrook Ln 19063
Meadowburn Ln 19063
Meadowcroft Ln 19063
Meadowglen Ln 19063
Meadowhurst Ln 19063
Meadowpark Ln 19063
Meadowvale Ln 19063
Meadowwood Ln 19063
Media Line Rd 19063
Media Station Rd 19063
Meetinghouse Ln 19063
Meghan Cir 19063
Meredith Dr 19063
Michele Dr 19063
N Middletown Rd 19063
Mill Brook Ln 19063
Moccasin Trl 19063
N & S Monroe St 19063
Monticello 19063
Moore Cir & Dr 19063
Morgan Ln 19063
Mount Alverno Rd 19063
Moyers Ln 19063
Moylan Ave 19063
Mulberry Ln 19063
Mystic Ln 19063
Nelson Dr 19063
New Darlington Rd 19063
S New Middletown Rd 19063
Newtown Street Rd 19063
Nicole Dr 19063
Northbrook Dr 19063
Northgate Vlg 19063
Oak Ave & Ln 19063
Oak Crest Ln 19063
Oak Valley Rd 19063
Oakbridge Ter 19063
Oakland Ave 19063
Oakmont Pl 19063
Oakview Dr 19063
Ogden Ct 19063
E Old Baltimore Pike 19063
Old Forge Rd 19063
N & S Old Middletown Rd 19063
Old Mill Dr & Ln 19063
Old Orchard Rd 19063
Old Pennell Rd 19063
Old Quarry Ct 19063
Old State Rd 19063
Olde Farm Rd 19063
Olde House Ln 19063
N & S Olive St 19063
N & S Orange St 19063
Orchard Ave 19063
Orchard Ln 19086
Oriole Ave 19063
Osage Ln 19063
N & S Overhill Cir & Rd 19063
Overlook Cir & Dr 19063
Paddock Ln 19063
Painter Rd & St 19063
Palmers Ln 19063
Palmers Mill Rd 19063
Park Ave, Dr & Pl 19063
Parkmount Rd 19063
Parkridge Dr 19063
Parks Edge Ln 19063
Parkview Cir 19063

Patricia Pl 19063
Paxon Pl 19063
Paxon Hollow Rd 19063
Pearl St 19063
Pembroke Dr 19063
Penn Way 19063
Penn Charter Dr 19063
Penn Valley Rd 19063
Pennell Rd 19063
Pennock Pl 19063
Pennsford Ln 19063
Pennsgrove Ct 19063
Pickering Ln 19063
Pin Oak Dr 19063
Pine Ridge Rd 19063
Pine Tree Dr 19063
Pinebrook Dr 19063
Pineview Dr 19063
N & S Plum St 19063
Porter Ln 19086
W Possum Hollow Rd 19086
Post House Rd 19063
Potter Ct 19063
Powderhorn Ln 19063
Preston Rd 19063
Prices Ln 19063
Prince Edward Ln 19063
Prince Eugene Ln 19063
N & S Providence Rd 19063
Quaint Rd 19063
Quiet Hollow Rd 19063
Rabbit Run Rd 19086
Raccoon Pl 19063
Rachel Dr 19063
Radnor St 19063
Rampart E & W 19063
Ravenscliff Dr 19063
Red Fox Pl 19063
Reservation Trl 19063
Rhoads Ln 19063
Riddlewood Dr 19063
N & W Ridge Ave, Ln & Rd 19063
Ridgewood Rd 19063
N & S Ridley Creek Dr & Rd 19063
Roberts Rd 19063
Robin Rd 19063
Robin Hill Rd 19063
Rockhouse Ln 19063
Ronaldson St 19063
Rose Hill Rd 19063
E & W Rose Tree Rd & Vlg 19063
Rose Valley Rd 19063
W Rose Valley Rd 19086
Rosemary Cir & Ln 19063
Roylencroft Ln 19063
Rushley Way 19063
Ruskin Ln 19063
Sackville Ln 19086
Saddlebrook Cir 19063
Saint Andrews Dr 19063
Sandy Bank Rd 19063
Saul Ln 19063
School Ln 19063
E & W Second Ave & St 19063
Secretariat Cir 19063
W Seventh Ave & St 19063
Shadeland Ave 19063
Shady Hill Rd 19063
Sharpless Ln 19063
Shasta Ln 19063
E & W Sixth Ave & St 19063
Smedley Ave 19063
Soldier Song Ln 19063
South Ave 19063
Spring Run & St 19063
Spring Hollow Ln 19063
Spring Hunt Ln 19063
E & W Spring Oak Cir 19063
Spring Valley Rd 19063
Springhouse Ln 19063
Springlawn Dr 19063
Springton Lake Rd 19063

Springton Mews Cir 19063
Squirrel Ln 19063
Stable Ln 19063
E & W State Rd & St 19063
Station Rd 19063
Steeplechase Dr 19063
Stoneridge Ln 19063
Strawberry Ln 19063
Summer St 19063
Summit Ct & Rd 19063
Surrey Ln & Rd 19063
Sycamore Ct & Rd 19063
Sycamore Mills Rd 19063
Talbot Ct 19063
Tamiters Rd 19063
Tanglewood Dr 19086
Taylor St 19063
E & W Third Ave & St 19063
Thistle Ln 19063
Thornpath Ln 19063
Timber Jump Ln 19063
Timber Lake Dr 19063
Todmorden Dr & Ln 19086
Toft Woods Way 19063
Tower Rd 19063
Townsend Ter 19063
Travelo Ln 19063
Traymore Ln 19063
Trout Run Dr & Mews 19063
Truepenny Rd 19063
Tulip Ln 19086
Turner Ln & Rd 19063
Twyckenham Rd 19063
Valley Pl & Rd 19063
Valley View Rd 19063
Valleybrook Rd 19063
Van Leer Ave 19063
Vernon Ln & St 19063
Veterans Sq 19063
Victoria Sq 19063
Villa Plz 19063
Vineyard Ln 19063
Wallingford Ave 19063
Walnut Hill Blvd 19063
Walter Dr 19063
War Admiral Ln 19063
War Trophy Ln 19063
Warbel Ln 19063
Washington Ave 19063
Water Mill Ln 19063
Waters Edge 19063
Wawa Rd 19063
Wedgewood Ln 19063
Wellington Dr 19063
Wells Fleet Way 19063
West St 19063
Westbriar Dr 19063
Westend Ave 19063
Whirlaway Rd 19063
Whispering Brook Way 19063
White Pine Ln 19063
White Sands Dr 19063
White Tail Ln 19063
Wildflower Ln 19063
Wildwood Ave 19063
Williamsburg 19063
Williamson Cir 19063
Willowbrook Ct & Ln 19063
Willowgate Ln 19063
Wilton Woods Ln 19063
Winding Ln 19063
Winter St 19063
Wisteria Ln 19063
Woodbriar Dr 19063
Woodcliffe Ave 19063
Woodcrest Ln & Rd 19063
Wooded Ln 19063
Wooded Way Dr 19063
Woodhill Ln 19063
Woodland Ave 19063
Woodlark Ln 19063
Woodridge Ln 19063
Woodview Ln 19063
Woodward Rd 19063
Worthington Ln 19063
Wrights Ln 19063

Wychwood Ln 19086
Wyncroft Dr 19063
Wynmoor Rd 19063
Yarmouth Ln 19063
Yearsley Mill Rd 19063
Youth Way 19063

NEW CASTLE PA

General Delivery 16108

POST OFFICE BOXES MAIN OFFICE STATIONS AND BRANCHES

Box No.s
630A - 630A 16103
1 - 1019 16103
1 - 1 16107
1101 - 1848 16103
5001 - 5552 16105
7001 - 9360 16107

RURAL ROUTES

03 16105

NAMED STREETS

Abbey Ln 16101
Abbey Rd 16105
Acorn Dr & St 16101
Acre Rd 16101
Adams Ln 16105
Adams St 16101
Addis St 16101
Adella St 16102
Agnew St 16101
Aiken Rd 16101
Alan Way 16101
Albert St 16105
Albert Street Ext 16105
Alborn Ave & Rd 16101
Aleyna Ln 16105
Algoma Ln 16105
Allegheny Ave 16101
Allen St 16101
Allison Memorial Hwy 16101
Almi Dr 16102
Almira Ave 16101
Altman Rd 16101
Alveretta Blvd 16101
Alyssa Dr 16105
Ambrose Ln 16101
Amhurst Ave 16101
N And N Ln 16105
Andrew St 16101
Andrews Trce 16102
Angela Ln 16101
Ann St 16101
Anne Dr 16105
Annette Dr 16101
Anoka Dr 16105
Antigua Dr 16105
N & S Apple Way 16101
Applegate Way 16101
N & S Arbor Dr & Ter 16101
Arch St 16102
Arlington Ave 16101
Armstrong Dr 16101
Arrowhead Ct 16105
Arthur St 16102
Ashberry Ln 16105
N & S Ashland Ave 16102
Aspen Ln 16101
Assid Ln 16101
Atkinson St 16101
S Atlantic Ave 16101
Atlas Rd 16101
Auction Ln 16101
Audia Dr 16101
Audley Ave 16105

Avalon Dr 16101
Avon St 16101
Baker Dr 16101
Baldwin Rd 16101
E & W Balph Ave 16102
Banberry Ln 16105
Barbour Pl 16101
Barbra Ln 16101
Barker Ave 16101
Barkett Ave 16101
Barns Ln 16101
Bartram Ave 16101
Basilone Dr 16101
Battery B St 16102
Beatrice St 16101
Beatty Ave 16101
N Beaver St
100-1199 16101
1400-2999 16105
S Beaver St
1-99 16101
1600-2499 16102
Becker St 16101
Beckford St 16101
Beech St 16101
Beechwood Way 16105
Bell Ave 16101
Bellaire Dr 16105
Bellview Ave 16101
Belmont St 16101
Benjamin Franklin Pkwy 16101
Berger Pl & St 16101
Berwyn St 16101
Bessell Rd 16101
Bessemer Mount Jackson Rd 16102
Bettery St 16102
Bialowas Ln 16101
Big Run Rd & St 16101
Big Run Creek Rd 16101
Bill Dr 16101
Bintrim Ln 16101
Bintrim Farm Ln 16101
Birchcrest Dr 16101
Birdhouse Ln 16101
Birt Ave 16101
Bishop Ln 16105
Blackberry Ln 16101
Blackstone Dr 16105
Blackstone Drive Ext 16105
Blaine St
400-1199 16101
1400-1599 16105
Blair Dr 16105
Blanchard St 16102
Blaze Ln 16102
Bleakley Ave 16101
Blews Way 16105
Blind Ln 16101
Blossom Ln 16105
Blue Heron Dr 16105
Blue Sky Dr 16105
Bluff St 16101
Blunston Ave 16101
Boak Rd 16101
Bodziach Rd 16101
Bon Aire Ave 16105
Bonzo St 16101
Book Ln 16101
Booker Dr 16101
Boroline St 16101
Boston Ave 16101
Botham St 16101
Boughter Dr 16101
N Boulevard Ext 16102
Bowden Rd 16105
Boyd Ave 16101
Boyd School Rd 16101
Boyer Ln 16105
Boyles Ave 16101
Bradner Ave 16101
Brandy Way 16105
Bratz Ln 16101
Brentwood Ave & St 16101
Brest Rd 16105

Brewster Rd 16102
Briar Ln 16101
Briar Hill Rd 16105
Brigadoon Ln 16101
Bright Ln 16102
Brinton St 16101
Bristol Ln 16105
Broodway Ave 16101
Brook Dr 16105
Brook Valley Dr 16105
Brooklyn Ave 16101
Brookshire Dr 16101
Brown St 16101
Brownhome Rd 16101
Bryan Ave & St 16102
Bryn Mawr Ave 16101
Bryson Mill Rd 16102
Buena Vista Way 16105
Burke St 16101
Burns St 16101
Butler Ave 16101
Buttermore Dr 16102
Butz St 16101
E Byers Ave 16102
W Byers Ave
1-99 16102
100-299 16101
Cabernet Dr 16105
Cadet St 16101
Calabrese Rd 16101
Caldwell Ave 16102
Caldy Ln 16101
Calvert Ln 16101
Cambridge St 16105
Cambridge Way 16101
Camden Ave 16101
Cameron Ave 16101
Cameron Rd
500-799 16101
901-999 16105
Camp Eastbrook Dr 16105
Canterberry Dr 16105
Canyon St 16101
Carbone Dr 16101
Cardinal Ln 16105
Carl St 16101
Carlisle St
700-899 16101
1400-2799 16105
Carlsbad Pl 16101
Carmela Dr 16105
Carol Dr 16105
Carr St 16101
Carson St 16101
Cascade Blvd 16101
N Cascade St 16101
S Cascade St
100-434 16101
435-435 16108
436-1230 16101
437-1299 16101
Cascade Galleria 16101
S Cascade Rear St 16101
Cass St 16101
Castle Ave 16102
Castle St 16101
Catalina Dr 16105
Cathcart Dr 16105
Cayuga Dr & St 16102
Cecil Ave 16101
N & S Cedar St 16102
Cemetery Ln 16105
Centennial Ln & St 16101
E & W Center St & Way 16101
Center Church Rd 16101
Chapel Ln 16102
Chapin Ln & Rd 16105
Chardonnay St 16105
Charles Dr 16101
Charles St 16102
Charlotte Ln 16101
E Chartes St 16102
W Chartes St
1-199 16102
200-299 16101

Street	ZIP
E & W Cherry St	16102
Cherry Hill Ct	16105
E Cherry Street Ext	16102
Cherry Tree Ln	16101
Chestnut St	16101
Chill Dr	16105
Chippewa Dr	16105
Church Aly	16101
Church Ln	16105
Church Rd	16101
Ciara Dr	16105
Cindy Dr	16101
Circle Dr	16101
City Line St	16101
Clair Dr	16101
Clarence Ave	16101
Clark St	16102
Clarksen Dr	16101
Classic Ln	16105
Clayton Cir	16101
E Clayton St	16102
W Clayton St	16102
Clearview Ave	16101
Cleland Mill Rd	16102
E & W Clen Moore Blvd	16105
Cleveland Ave	16101
Cliff St	16101
Cline St	16101
Clover Ln	16105
Cloverdell Dr	16101
Club Dr	16105
Coates Ave	16101
Cobb Dr	16101
Cochran Dr	16105
N Cochran Way	16101
S Cochran Way	16101
Coconut Dr	16105
Cody Ln	16102
Cole Rd	16101
Colonial Dr	16105
Columbiana Rd	16102
Columbus Dr	16101
N Columbus Interbelt	16101
Comanche Trl	16102
Commerce Ave	16101
Concord St	16105
Conestoga Dr	16105
Confederate Ln	16101
N Conkle Ave	16101
Connor Ave	16101
Conrad St	16101
Continental Ln	16101
Coolidge St	16101
Copper Rd	16101
Cornell Ave	16101
Coronado Dr	16105
Cottage Grv	16105
Cottage Ln	16101
Cottage St	16101
Country Ln	16101
Country Club Dr	16105
County Line Rd	16101
Countyline Rd & St	16101
Court St	16101
Cover Rd	16105
Covert Rd	
100-499	16102
500-506	16101
501-863	16102
508-862	16102
1001-1099	16101
1200-1298	16101
Covington Dr	16105
Cow Path Ln	16101
Craig St	16101
Cranbrook St	16101
N & S Crawford Ave & Ter	16101
Crescent Ave	16101
Crest Ave	16102
Creston Ave	16101
Crestwood Dr	16101
Crimson Cir	16105
Croach Blvd	16101
Crocker Ln	16105
N & S Croton Ave	16101
Crowe St	16101
Cuba St	16101
Culbertson Pl	16101
Cumberland Ave	16101
Cunningham Ave	16101
Cunningham Ln	16105
Currie Ln	16101
Cutoff Rd	16105
Dagres Ln	16101
Dale Ave	16101
Darlington Ave	16102
Davies Ave	16101
Dean Dr & Rd	16101
Decker Dr	16105
Declaration Ln	16101
Decorath Ln	16101
Deer Run	16105
Delaware Ave	16105
Dematteo Ln	16101
Denny Dr	16101
Denver Ave	16101
Denvue Dr	16101
Deshon Rd	16101
Devils Backbone Rd	16102
Devils Elbow Rd	16101
Devin Dr	16101
Dewey Ave	16101
Diana Dr	16101
Dickson St	16101
Dillworth Ave	16101
Division St	16101
Dogwood Dr	16101
Dollard Ln	16102
Dominick Dr	16101
Donald Rd	16102
Donley Dr	16101
Doris St	16101
Double J Ln	16101
Dougherty Rd	16101
Douglas Dr	16101
Drespling Ln	16101
Duquesne St	16101
Dushane St	16101
Dwight Dr	16102
Dylan Dr	16101
Earnhardt Ln	16101
East St	16101
Eastbrook Rd	
1211-2199	16101
2200-2521	16105
Eastbrook St	16101
Eastbrook Harlansburg Rd	
100-201	16105
202-298	16101
300-1799	16101
Eastbrook Neshannock Falls Rd	16105
Eastbrook Volant Rd	16105
Eddy St	16101
E Edgewood Ave	16105
Edgewood Acres	16105
Edinburg Rd	16102
E & W Edison Ave	16101
Edwin Dr	16101
Elbon St	16101
Elder St	16101
Eldogor Ln	16105
Eleanor Dr	16105
Electric St	16101
E & W Elizabeth St	16105
Ellsworth Way	16101
Ellwood Rd	16101
Elm Dr	16105
Elm St	16101
Elmwood St	16101
Emerson Ave	16101
Emery St	16101
Enclave Dr	16105
Energy Dr	16101
Engine House Way	16101
E & W Englewood Ave	16105
English Ave	16101
English Hollow Rd	16101
Epworth St	16101
Erie Ave	16101
Erie St	16102
Etna St	16101
E & W Euclid Ave	16105
Evergreen Ave	16105
Faddis Ave	16105
E & W Fairfield Ave	16105
Fairgreen Ave	16105
Fairground Rd	16101
Fairhill Dr	16105
E & W Fairmont Ave	16105
Fairview Ave	16101
Fairway Dr	16105
Fairway Shenango Dr	16101
Falcon St	16101
Falls Ave	16105
E Falls St	16101
W Falls St	16101
Farm Ln	16101
Fast Ln	16102
Fawn Ln	16105
Federal St	16101
Feil Ln	16101
Fern St	16101
Fernwood Ln	16105
Fields Dr	16101
Fieldsrun Rd	16105
Fife St	16101
Finch St	16101
Firehall Rd	16101
Fireside Dr	16105
Fisher Dr	16105
Fleming Way	16101
Florence Ave	
201-205	16102
206-599	16101
Florine Ln	16101
Forbes Rd	16101
Fording Rd	
101-197	16101
199-799	16101
2000-2199	16105
Forest Ave	16101
Forney Ln	16105
Forrest Rd	16105
Forrest St	16101
Forrest Road Ext	16105
Fowler Ln	16101
Fox Rd	16101
Francis Pl & St	16101
Frank Ave & Way	16101
Frank Farone Dr	16101
Franklin Ave	16101
Frazier Dr	16105
Frazier Lake Dr	16105
Fredericks Ln	16101
Frenz Dr	16101
Frew Mill Rd	16101
Fridays Hill Rd	16101
Friendship St	16101
N & S Front St	16101
Fruitland Dr	16105
Fulkerson Ln	16105
Fulkerson St	16101
Fullerton Rd	16102
E & W Fulton St	16102
Furnace St	16101
Galbreath St	16101
Gale St	16101
Gallaher Ln	16101
Game Farm Rd	16101
Gardner Ave & Ln	16101
Gardner Center Rd	16101
Gardner Stop Rd	16101
E & W Garfield Ave	16105
N Gate Industrial Park	16105
Gaylord Ln	16101
Gencedge Rd	16105
George Dr & St	16101
George Washington Rd	16101
Germanski Ln	16102
Gibson Ave & St	16101
Gilmore Rd & St	16102
Glass Rd & St	16101
Glen Rd	16105
Glenda Dr	16101
Glendale Ave	16105
Glenn Ave	16101
Glover Rd	16105
Good Ave	16102
Graceland Rd	16105
Graham Ave	16101
Grandview Ave	16101
Grange Hall Rd	16101
Grant St	16102
E Grant St	16101
W Grant St	16101
Grasshopper Ln	16101
Gray Hill Ln	16105
Graziani Dr	16101
Green St	16101
Green Acres Ln	16101
Green Leaf Ct	16105
Green Ridge Rd	16105
Green Street Ext	16101
Greenfield Rd	16105
Greentree Cir	16105
N & S Greenwood Ave	16101
Gregor Ln	16101
Grenway Rd	16105
Gretchen Ave	16101
Griffith Dr	16105
Grigsby St	16101
Grimes St	16101
Grove Ave & St	16101
Guadalcanal Rd	16105
Halco Dr	16101
Hale St	16101
Hall St	16102
Hamilton St	16101
Hanna Ln	16105
Hanna St	16102
E & W Harbor Rd & St	16101
Harbor Edinburg Rd	16101
Harding St	16101
Harlansburg Rd	16101
Harman Ln	16102
Harmony Baptist Rd	16101
Harrison St	16101
Hart St	16101
Hartman St	16101
Hartzell Rd	16105
Harvest Ln	16105
Harvey St	16101
Haus Ave	16101
Haus Avenue Ext	16101
Haven Point Dr	16105
Hawthorne Rd & St	16101
Hayes Ln	16105
Hazel St	16101
E & W Hazelcroft Ave	16105
Hazen St	16101
Hearthstone Dr	16105
Heather Glen Ests	16105
Heckathorne Rd	16101
Hemlock St	16101
Hennon Ln	16101
Henry Rd	16101
Herrick St	16101
Hettenbaugh Xing	16101
Hichiney St	16101
Hickory Dr	16101
Hickory View Dr	16102
Hidden Brooke Ct	16105
Hidden Lake Dr	16101
Hideaway Ln	16101
High St	16101
High Meadow Dr	16101
Highland Ave	
300-999	16101
1000-2701	16105
2703-2703	16105
Highland View Rd	16101
Highview Dr	16101
Hill Ave	16101
E & W Hillcrest Ave	16105
Hillcrest Acres	16102
Hillside Way	16101
Hobart St	16102
Hoffmaster Rd	16102
Hollow Rd	16101
Holly Ln	16105
E & W Home St	16101
Home Rear St	16101
Homestead St	16101
Honey Bee Ln	16105
Honeybee Ln	16105
Hoover Ave	16102
Hoover Rd	16101
Houk Rd	16101
Howard Dr	
100-199	16101
3000-4499	16102
Howard Way	16101
Huckleberry Ln	16101
Hudson Ln	16105
Huey St	16101
Hunt Rd	16101
Hunter Ln	16101
Hunters Woods Blvd E	16105
Huron Ave	16101
Husky Ln	16105
Hutchinson St	16101
Hutchison Ln	16105
Ida Ln	16101
Independence Ln	16101
Industrial St	16102
Iraquois Dr	16105
Isabelle Ave	16101
Ivy Dr	16105
Ivywood Ln	16105
Jackson Ave	16101
James Cir	16102
Janeway Dr	16105
Janiels Ln	16101
Jay Dr	16101
N Jefferson St	16101
S Jefferson St	
1-1399	16101
1400-2499	16102
S Jefferson Rear St	16101
N Jefferson Street Ext	16105
Jennie Ln	16101
Jenny Ln	16101
Joes Ln	16101
John St	16101
Johns Ln	
100-199	16102
1100-1299	16101
Johnson St	16101
Jones Ln & St	16101
Joyce Ln	16102
Judah Ln	16101
Junior High St	16101
Justice Ln	16105
Justin Ln	16101
Kahl St	16102
Kalchris Ln	16101
Kaldy Dr	16101
Karen Dr	16101
Karon Dr	16101
Kasevic Ln	16101
Kate Houk Rd	16101
Katherine St	16105
Kathleen Dr	16105
Katie Ext	16101
Kaufman Rd	16101
Kelso Ave	16101
W Kenneth Ave	16105
Kerr Rd & St	16101
Keystone Dr	16105
Kildoo Rd	16102
Kimberly Ln	16101
King Ave	16101
Kings Chapel Rd	16105
Kingswood Rd	16105
Kittery Ridge Dr	16101
Knoll Dr	16102
Knox Ave	16101
Kosciuszko Way	16101
Kozal Rd	16101
Kristen Ln	16101
Kurtz Ln	16102
Kyle Rd	16102
Laclair Dr	16101
Lacock St	16102
N & S Lafayette St	16102
Lake Dr	16105
Lake Rd	16102
Lakeside Dr	16105
Lakeview Ave	16101
Lakewood Rd	16101
Lakewood Gardens Rd	16105
Lakewood Neshannock Falls Rd	16105
Lanewood Dr	16105
Lathrop St	16101
Lattavo Dr	16105
Lattimer Ln	16105
E & W Laurel Ave, Blvd & Pl	16101
Laurelwood Dr	16101
Lawnview Ave	16105
E Lawrence St	16101
E Leasure Ave	
1-99	16105
100-399	16101
400-599	16105
W Leasure Ave	16105
Leasure Dr	16101
Leasure Ave Ext	16105
Leasure Valley Dr	16101
Leawood Dr	16105
N & S Lee Ave	16101
Leeper Dr	16102
Lemack Ln	16101
Leon Dr	16101
Levine Way	16101
Lexington Dr	16105
N Liberty St	
1-1164	16102
1165-1169	16101
1166-1168	16102
S Liberty St	16102
Lightner Pl	16105
Lilac Rd	16105
E & W Lincoln Ave	16101
Linda Dr	16101
Linden St	16101
Lindsey Ln & Rd	16105
Line Rd	16105
Links Dr	16101
Locke Dr	16101
Lockhart Dr	16101
Locust Ln	16105
Locust St	16101
Logan Rd	16102
Logan St	
500-699	16101
900-1099	16105
E & W Long Ave	16101
Long Branch Dr	16105
Loraine Ave	16101
Louis Ln	16105
Lower Cunningham Ave	16101
Lower Idlewild Dr	16101
Lowland Dr	16105
Luanne Dr	16105
Lucas Ln	16101
Lucymont Dr	16102
Ludwig Rd	16105
E & W Lutton St	16101
Lydia Ln	16105
Lyndal St	16101
Lynn St	16101
Mabel St	16101
E & W Madison Ave	16102
Madonna Dr	16101
Magee St	16101
Maggie Ln	16101
Mahoning Ave	16102
E Main St	16101
E Maitland Ln	
1-1199	16105
1200-1399	16101
W Maitland Ln	16105
Maitland St	16101
Manor Ave	16105
Mapeat Ln	16101
Maple Dr	16105
S Maple Dr	16101
Maple Ln	16101
Maple St	16101
E Maple St	16102
W Maple St	16102
Margaret St	16101
Marie Ave	16101
Marie Dr	16105
Marilyn Dr	16105
Marion Ave	16105
Marion Ct	16101
Market Way	16101
Marlboro St	16101
Marshall Ave, Pl & St	16101
Martha St	16101
Martha Street Ext	16101
Martin Rd & St	16101
Maryland Ave	16101
Mathews Way	16101
Matilda Ave	16101
Mayberry Ln	16105
Mazur Ln	16101
Mcbride Acres	16102
Mccarty Ln	16105
Mccaslin Rd	16101
Mcclain Ave	16101
Mcclain Ln	16105
Mccleary Ave	16101
Mcclelland Ave	16101
Mcclelland Rd	16102
Mccombs Cir	16101
Mccormick Ln	16101
Mccoy Ln	16105
Mccracken Dr & Ln	16101
Mccreary Dr	16105
Mcelwain Ln	16101
Mcgary Rd	16105
Mcgrath Ave	16101
Mcguffey Blvd	16101
Mckee Xing	16105
Mckee Fording Rd	16105
Mckim Rd	16102
Mckinley Ln	16102
Mcmurray Ln	16102
Mcquiston Dr	16105
Meadow Ave	16101
Meadow Dr	16101
N Meadow Dr	16101
Meadow Ln	16105
Meadowbrook Dr	16105
Meadowcroft Dr	16101
Meadowview Blvd	16105
Mechanic St	16101
Medure Ln	16101
Meegan Ave	16101
Melody Ln	16101
Melody Lane Ext	16101
Melrose Ave	16101
Melvin Dr	16105
Memorial Dr	16102
Memory Ln	16101
Mercer Rd	16105
N Mercer St	
1-1099	16101
1200-2999	16105
S Mercer St	16101
N Mercer Street Ext	16105
Meriline Ave	16101
Merle Ln	16101
Merritt Rd	16105
E & W Meyer Ave	16105
Michael Dr	16105
Michael Ln	16101
Michigan St	16102
Midfield Ln	16105
Midway Is	16105
Midway Rd	16101
N Mill St	16101
S Mill St	16101
W Mill St	16102
Mill Bridge Rd	16101
Miller Ave	16101
Miller Rd	16101
W Miller St	16102
Milligan Rd	16101

Million Dr 16102
Mills Way 16101
Milton St 16101
Miro Ln 16102
Misco Ln 16101
Mission Meade Dr & Ext 16105
Mitchell Rd 16105
Mitchell St 16101
Mitcheltree Ln 16101
Mocasin Trl 16105
W Moffatt Rd 16101
Mohawk Dr 16105
Mohawk School Rd 16102
Monroe St 16101
Monsour Dr 16101
Montgomery Ave 16102
Montgomery Ln 16101
E Moody Ave
  1-307 16101
  308-322 16105
  309-323 16101
  324-599 16105
W Moody Ave 16101
Mooney Dr 16105
Moore Ave 16101
Moorehead Ave 16102
Moravia St 16101
Moravia Street Ext 16101
E Morehead Ave 16102
Morningstar Ln 16105
Morris St 16102
Morton St 16101
Mosser Dr 16101
Motor St 16101
Mount Air Rd 16102
Mount Herman Church Rd 16101
Mount Hope Rd 16101
Mount Jackson Rd 16102
Mount Pleasant St 16101
Mountain View Rd 16101
Moyer Rd 16101
Muddy Creek Rd 16101
N & S Mulberry St 16101
Municipal Dr 16101
Mustang Ave 16102
Muzzy Dr 16101
Myers Ln 16102
Nadine Dr 16101
Nashua Rd 16105
National St 16101
Neal St 16101
Nearwood Dr 16101
Nemo St 16101
Nesbit St 16102
Nesbitt Rd 16105
Neshannock Ave 16101
Neshannock Blvd
  400-899 16101
  1300-1799 16105
Neshannock Avenue Ext 16101
Neshannock Heights Rd 16105
Neshannock Trails Dr 16105
New Butler Rd 16101
Newell Ave 16102
Newman Rd 16101
Noble House Ln 16105
Norco Rd 16101
Norman Ln 16101
North Blvd 16102
E North St 16101
W North St 16101
Northgate Cir 16105
E Northview Ave 16105
S Northview Ave 16102
W Northview Ave 16105
Norwood Ave 16105
Nutt St 16101
Oak St 16101
Oak Grove Ln 16101
Oak Park Ln 16101
Oak Ridge Ln 16105
Oak Tree Dr 16105
Oakland Ave 16101
Oakwood Ave 16101
E Oakwood Way 16105
W Oakwood Way 16105
Obrien Ave 16101
Okinawa Dr 16105
Old Butler Rd 16101
Old Coal Rd 16101
Old Colony Dr 16105
Old Hickory Rd 16102
Old Long Ave 16101
Old Mercer Rd 16105
Old Pittsburgh Rd 16101
Old Plank Rd 16105
Old Princeton Rd 16101
Old Pulaski Rd 16105
Old Route 108 16101
Old Route 19 16101
Old Route 422 Ext 16101
Old State Rd 16101
Old Youngstown Rd 16101
Oliver Dr 16102
Oneida St 16102
Onondaga St 16102
Orange St 16101
Orchard St
  1-199 16102
  600-698 16101
  700-799 16101
Orchard Way 16105
Orchard Park Dr 16105
Orchardale Dr 16101
Orlando Ave 16105
Osage St 16101
Oticon Dr 16105
Our Way 16101
Overhill Dr 16105
Oxford Dr 16105
Paden Rd 16102
Painter Dr 16105
Parady Ave 16102
Park Ave 16101
W Park Ave 16101
Park Ln 16105
Park Rd 16101
S & W Parkside Dr 16105
W Parkway St 16101
Parkwood Ct 16101
Patterson Rd & St 16101
Patton Rd 16105
Paul St 16101
Pauline Dr 16102
Pauls Hill Ln 16105
Peach St 16101
Pearl Dr
  2701-2799 16101
  3100-3199 16105
E Pearl St 16101
W Pearl St 16101
Pearlwood St 16101
Pearson St 16101
Pearson Mill Rd 16101
Pearson Park Dr 16105
Pencente Rd 16102
Penn Blvd 16101
Penn St 16102
Pennsylvania Ave 16101
Penny Ln
  101-197 16101
  199-299 16101
  3200-3299 16105
Perry Hwy 16101
Pharr Cir 16101
Phelps Way 16101
Phillips Dr, Ln, Pl & St 16101
Phillips School Rd 16105
Piela Ct 16105
Pike Ave 16102
Pin Oak Dr 16101
Pine Dr, Ln & St 16101
Pinehurst Dr 16105
Pitts Pt 16102
Pitts Point Ln & St 16102
W Pittsburg Rd 16101
Plank Rd 16105
Pleasantview Dr 16101
Plum St 16101
Point Dr & Pl 16105
E Poland Rd 16102
Pollock Ave 16101
Poplar St 16102
Porter St 16101
Power St 16102
Presnar Dr 16105
Princeton Ave & Rd 16101
Princeton Station Rd 16101
Proch Dr & Ln 16101
Produce St 16101
Progessive Ln 16105
Progress Ave 16101
Prospect St 16102
Pulaski Rd
  1600-4091 16105
  4100-4199 16101
  4201-4299 16101
Pusnik Ln 16102
Quarry Rd 16101
Quay St 16101
Quest St 16101
Rabbit Ave 16102
Randall Dr 16105
Randolph St 16101
E & W Ranney Ave 16102
Rapson Ave 16101
Raptor Cir 16105
N & S Ray St 16101
Raymond St 16105
Rear Mabel St 16101
Rebecca St 16101
Reed Ave 16101
Reed Rd 16102
Reiber Ln 16105
Reis St 16101
Reno Ln 16101
E & W Reynolds Dr & St 16101
Rhodes Ln & Pl 16101
Rich Dr 16101
Richie Ln 16105
Richlieu Ave 16101
Richview Dr 16101
Ridge Ave & St 16101
Ridgelawn Ave 16105
Ridgewood Ct 16101
Ridgewood Way 16105
Riesling St 16105
Rife Dr 16101
Rigby St 16101
Rigotti Dr 16101
River Rd 16102
Riverpark Dr 16101
Riverside Ln 16105
Riverview Ave 16101
Roberts Ln 16105
Robinson Ln 16101
Robinson Rd 16105
Robinson St 16101
Robinwood St 16101
Rock Springs Rd 16101
Rockwell Dr 16102
Rocky Rd
  125-299 16105
  2200-2299 16101
Rodgers Ln 16101
Rogers Rd 16105
Rolling Acres Ln 16101
Ron Dr 16101
Roosevelt St 16101
Rose Ave 16101
Rose Hill Dr 16105
Rose Point Rd 16101
Rose Point Harlansburg Rd 16101
Rose Stop Rd 16101
Rosedale Ave 16105
Rosewood Dr 16105
Ross Dr 16102
N & S Round St 16101
Route 18 S 16105
Roy Dr 16101
Rundle Rd 16102
Rung Ln 16105
Rutgers Dr 16105
Ruth Ave & St 16101
Ryan Ave 16101
Sagers Automotive Ln 16101
Saint Charles Pl 16101
Sally Dr 16101
Sampson St 16101
Samuel Dr 16101
Sankey Ln 16105
Sankey St 16101
Saratoga Cir 16105
Savannah Rd 16101
Savannah Gardner Rd 16101
Schenley Ave 16101
Schley St 16101
School St 16101
Schooley Ln 16101
Schwarz Ln 16105
Sciota St 16101
S Scotland Ln 16101
Scott Dr 16105
N Scott St 16101
S Scott St 16101
Senaca Way 16102
Seneca Ct 16105
Seneca Way 16102
Sequoia Dr 16105
Servedio Dr & Rd 16101
Service St 16101
Seton Dr 16105
Shady Ln 16105
Shady Grove Ln 16105
Shadylane Dr 16105
Shadyside St 16101
Shaffer Rd 16101
Shannon Ave 16102
Shannon Dr 16105
E & W Sharp St 16102
Shaw Rd & St 16101
Sheets St 16101
Shefflers Way 16101
Shenango Rd 16105
Shenango St 16105
N Shenango St 16101
Shenango Park Dr 16101
Shenango Stop Rd 16101
Shepherd Ln 16101
E & W Sheridan Ave 16105
Sherwood Dr 16101
Shiderly Dr 16105
Shiderly Ln 16102
Shingledecker Dr 16101
Shira St 16101
Shirley Ln 16102
Short St 16102
Skyview Dr 16102
Slate St 16101
Smalls Ferry Rd 16102
Smith Ln 16105
Smith Rd 16105
Smith St 16101
Smithfield St 16101
Soils Dr 16101
Sophia Dr 16105
South Blvd 16102
South St 16102
E South St 16101
Southbrook Dr 16105
Southview Ave 16101
Spartan Dr 16101
Spicher Ave 16105
Spiker Ln 16105
Spring St 16101
Spring Garden Ave & Rd 16105
Spring Hill Ln 16101
Spring Lake Dr 16101
Spring Valley Ln 16105
Springfield Dr 16105
Spruce St 16101
Stanton Ave 16101
Star Dr 16105
State Rd
  1001-1297 16101
  1299-2999 16101
  3000-3467 16105
  3469-3497 16101
  3499-3999 16101
W State St 16101
State Route 18
  117-117 16105
State Route 18
  4324-5399 16102
State Route 956
  408-408 16101
  2862-3599 16105
Station Rd 16101
Stavich Bike Trl E & W 16101
Steinbrink Pl 16101
Stephen Dr 16105
Stewart Ave & Pl 16101
Stickle Rd 16101
Stone Bridge Ln 16105
Stoner Dr 16101
Sugarberry Ln 16105
Summerlin Dr 16101
Summit St
  100-199 16102
  1000-1200 16101
  1202-4098 16101
Summit View Dr 16105
Sumner Ave 16105
Sunny Ave 16101
Sunny Ln 16105
Sunny Avenue Ext 16101
Sunnybrook Dr 16105
Sunnyside Rd 16102
Sunrise Dr
  900-998 16101
  1100-2499 16105
E Sunset Dr 16105
Sunset Valley Rd 16105
Sunview Dr 16105
Sunwood Dr 16105
Superior St 16101
Swamp Rd 16101
E & W Swansea St 16102
Sycamore St 16101
Syling St 16101
Sylvan Heights Dr 16101
Sylvane Dr 16105
Tall And Short Way 16101
Tall Maples Dr 16101
Tall Trees Ct 16105
Tamarac Dr 16105
Tanglewood Dr 16105
Taylor Dr 16101
Taylor Rd 16105
Taylor St 16101
Tebay Ln 16105
E & W Tempalena Ave 16102
Temple Ave 16101
E & W Terrace Ave & Dr 16102
Terrace North Ln 16105
Thomas Rd 16101
Thornhill Dr 16101
Thorpe St 16101
Timber Ln
  100-199 16101
  2000-2299 16105
Timberland Trl 16102
Toby Ln 16101
Tomahawk Trl 16102
Tony St 16101
Towne Mall 16101
Tradewinds Dr 16102
Trail 1 16105
Trail 2 16105
Trail 3 16105
Trail 4 16105
Tremont St 16102
E & W Treser Ave 16102
Trillium Ln 16105
Tucker Way 16101
Tulagi Way 16105
Tuscarora Dr 16105
Twin Oaks Dr 16101
Uber St 16101
Ubry Ln 16101
Under Par 16105
Underwood St 16101
Union St 16101
Upland Dr 16105
Upper Idlewild Dr 16101
Us 422 16101
Valhalla Dr 16105
Valley Rd 16105
Valley St 16101
Vance Rd 16102
Veronica Rd 16101
Victoria Dr 16105
Village Ln 16101
N & S Vine St 16101
Vineyard Ln 16105
Virginia Ave 16105
Vivienne Ln 16105
Vogan St 16101
E & W Wabash Ave 16102
Waldo St 16101
E Wallace Ave 16101
W Wallace Ave 16101
Wallace Cir 16101
Wallace Dr 16105
Wallace Rd 16102
Walls St 16101
N & S Walnut Dr & St 16101
Walnut Run Ln 16101
Walter St 16101
Walters Ln 16101
Wampum Rd 16102
Warner Aly 16101
Warren Ave & Dr 16101
Warrior Trl 16102
E & W Washington St 16101
N & S Wayne St 16102
Wear Dr 16102
Weaver St 16101
Weingart Ln 16105
Weinschenk Rd 16101
Wellman Ln 16101
Wellsley Ave 16105
Werner Rd 16102
West Ave 16101
Westfield Memorial Dr 16102
Westgate Dr 16101
Westview Rd 16101
Whippo St 16101
Whispering Trl 16105
White St 16101
Whitehill Dr 16105
Whitetail Dr 16101
Whitney Dr 16105
Wick Ave 16101
Wilbur Rd 16101
Wild Cherry Rd 16105
Wild Grape Rd 16105
Wilder St 16102
Wildlife Dr 16101
Wildwood Ave 16105
Wiley Ln 16101
Willard Ave 16101
Williams Dr & St 16101
Willis Dr 16101
Willow Dr 16102
Willow Way Dr 16101
Willowbrook Rd 16101
Willowhurst Cir 16101
Wilmington Ave
  600-1199 16101
  1200-1406 16105
Wilmington Rd 16105
Wilson Ave
  100-115 16102
  1400-2099 16101
  5100-5199 16102
Wilson Dr 16101
Wilson Rd 16101
Wilson Mill Rd 16105
Wilson Rear Ave 16101
Windemere Dr 16105
Windsor Rdg 16105
Winslow Ave 16101
E Winter Ave
  100-399 16101
  400-599 16105
W Winter Ave 16101
Winter Rd 16101
Wolfe St 16101
Wood St
  100-199 16102
  3900-3999 16101
Woodcrest Dr 16102
Woodland Ave 16101
Woodland Dr 16105
Woodland Hills Dr 16101
Woodmere Dr 16101
Woodmere Drive Ext 16101
Woodrow St 16101
Woods St 16101
Woodview Dr 16101
Wooley Ave 16101
Workman Rd 16101
Worthington Ave 16105
Yoho Aly 16101
Young Rd & St 16101
Youngwood Dr 16101
Zinfandel Ln 16105

NUMBERED STREETS

All Street Addresses 16102

NORRISTOWN PA

General Delivery 19401

POST OFFICE BOXES MAIN OFFICE STATIONS AND BRANCHES

Box No.s
All PO Boxes 19404

NAMED STREETS

Abbott Ct 19403
Acorn Way 19403
E & W Adair Dr 19403
Adams Ave
  1-99 19401
  800-998 19403
  1000-1199 19403
E Airy St
  1-29 19401
  28-28 19404
  31-899 19401
  40-698 19401
W Airy St 19401
Alan Rd 19401
Alden Rd 19403
Alexander Dr 19403
Alexandra Dr 19403
Amber Cir 19401
Amelia St 19403
Amy Dr 19403
Anders Pl 19403
Ann St 19401
Apple Valley Ln 19403
Appledale Rd 19403
Applewood Dr 19403
Arbour Ct 19403
Arch Rd & St 19401
Archer Ct 19403
Ardin Dr 19403
Artmar Rd 19403
Ashley Cir 19403
Ashwood Ln 19403
Astor St 19401
Auburn Dr 19403
Audubon Dr & Rd 19403
Audubon Village Dr
  2800-2899 19403
  2838-2838 19407
Avon Rd 19403
Avondale Rd 19403
Baker Dr 19403
Baldeagle Cir 19403

Street	ZIP
Baldwin Ave	19403
Barbadoes St	19401
Barbara Dr	19403
Barley Sheaf Ct & Dr	19403
Barnwood Cir	19403
N & S Barry Ave	19403
E & W Basin St	19401
Bassett Ln	19403
Bayless Pl	19403
Bayton Rd	19403
Bean Rd	19403
Beaver Hollow Rd	19403
Beech Dr	19403
W Beech St	19401
Beechwood Rd	19401
Belair Cir	19401
Belmont Ave	19403
Berkley Rd	19403
Berks Rd	19403
Bettie Ln	19403
Betzwood Dr	19403
Beyer Ln	19403
Birch Dr	19401
Birchwood Cir & Dr	19401
Bishop Dr	19403
Bittersweet Ct	19403
Black Bird Cir	19403
Black Hawk Cir	19403
Blackberry Aly & Pl	19401
Blackswift Rd	19403
Blue Bird Cir	19403
Blue Meadow Dr	19403
Blue Teel Cir	19403
Borton Rd	19403
Boulevard Of The Generals	19403
Boyer Blvd	19401
Bradbury Dr	19401
Brambling Ln	19403
Brandon Rd	19403
Brandywine Dr	19403
Brant Rd	19403
Bratton Dr	19403
Breckenridge Blvd	19403
Brenda Ln	19403
Briar Ln	19401
Briar Hill Rd	19403
Bridle Path Rd	19403
Brimfield Rd	19403
Brindle Ct	19403
Bringhurst Pl	19401
Bristol Ave	19401
Bristol Ct	19403
Broadview Ln	19403
Broadwing Ct	19403
Brookside Rd	
200-243	19401
212-218	19403
245-249	19401
E & W Brown St	19401
Browning Ct	19403
Brownstone Dr	19401
Bryans Rd	19401
Buchannon Ave	19401
Buckwalter Rd	19403
Buggywhip Cir	19403
Bunting Cir & Rd	19403
Burnside Ave	19403
Butcher Dr	19403
Butchers Ln	19401
Butler Ave	19403
Buttonwood St	19401
Byrd Dr	19403
Calamia Dr	19401
Caln Cir	19401
Campus Ln	19403
Candy Ln	19403
Canterbury Rd	19403
Capitol Cir & Rd	19403
Caralea Dr	19403
Cardin Pl	19403
Cardinal Cir & Rd	19403
Carey Ln	19403
Carmen Dr	19401
Carol Ln	19401
Caroline Dr	19401
Carousel Cir	19403
Carriage Ln	19401
Carson Dr	19403
Caspian Ln	19403
Casselberry Dr	19403
Catfish Ln	19403
Cathedral Ln	19403
Cedar Ct & Ln	19401
Cedar Grove Ln	19403
Central Ave	19401
Centre Ave	19403
Chadwick Cir	19403
Chain St	19401
Chaise Ln	19403
Champagne Cir	19403
Chancelor Ct	19403
Chariot Ln	19403
Chaucer Ct	19403
Cherry St	19401
Chestnut Ave	19403
E Chestnut Ave	19403
E Chestnut St	19401
W Chestnut St	19401
Christopher Ln	19403
Church Rd	19403
Church St	19401
Cirak Ave	19403
Circle Dr	19403
Clara St	19403
Clark Hill Dr	19403
Clearfield Ave	19403
Clearview Ave	19403
Clemens Cir	19403
Clinton Rd	19403
Clydesdale Cir	19403
Clyston Cir & Rd	19403
Coach Ln	19403
Cobblestone Cir	19403
Coles Blvd	19401
Colleen Ct	19401
Colonial Ave	19403
Colonial Cir	19401
Colonial Ct	19403
Colonial Dr	19401
Colony Dr	19403
Concord Cir	19403
Condor Cir & Dr	19403
Condor Ridge Ct	19403
Conestoga Ln & Way	19403
Congress Rd	19403
Connor St	19401
Constitution Ave	19403
Cooke Ln	19401
Coolidge Blvd	19401
Cooper Cir	19403
Coppermine Rd	19403
Corson St	19401
Cottage Ln	19401
Country Cir	19403
Countryside Ln	19403
Craftsman Rd	19403
Cranberry Dr	19403
Crawford Dr & Rd	19403
Cresswell Dr	19403
Crest Ter	19403
Cricket Ter	19403
Crimson Dr	19401
E & W Crossing Cir	19403
Crystal Ln	19403
Culp Rd	19403
Dairy Ln	19403
Dana Dr	19403
Darland Rd	19403
Dartmouth Dr	19401
David Ln	19403
Davis Dr	19403
Deacon Dr	19403
Deer Run	19403
Deerfield Dr & Rd	19403
Defford Cir, Pl & Rd	19403
Dekalb Blvd, Pike & St	19401
Dell Rd	19403
Delta Ln	19403
Denise Ct & Rd	19403
Dermond Rd	19403
Devon Dr	19403
Diane Cir	19403
Dickens Ct	19403
Discovery Ct	19401
Dobbs Ct	19403
Dogwood Ln	19401
Donna Dr	19403
Doris Ln	19403
Dorp Cir & Ln	19401
Dragon Cir	19403
Driftwood Dr	19403
Dunkirk Ct	19403
Dutch Dr	19403
Eagle Dr	19403
Eagle Stream Dr	19403
Eagleville Rd	19403
Egypt Rd	19403
Eisenhower Ave & Rd	19403
Elizabeth Dr	19403
Elm Ave	19403
E Elm St	19401
W Elm St	19401
Elysia Ln	19403
Embassy Cir	19403
Equestrian Way	19403
Essex Ct	19403
Ethel Ave	19403
Eva Ct	19401
Evan Dr	19403
Evans Rd	19403
Evelyn Dr	19403
Evergreen Rd	
1-99	19403
500-599	19401
Fair View Ln	19403
Fairbanks Ave	19401
Faircourt Ave	19401
Fairway Ln	19403
Faith Dr	19403
Falcon Rd	19403
Farm Cir	19403
Farmhouse Dr	19403
Farview Ave	19403
Farview Rd	19401
Featherbed Ln	19403
Felton Rd	19401
Ferry Ave	19401
Fieldcrest Ave & Way	19403
Fillmore Rd	19403
Flannery Dr	19403
Ford St	19401
Forge Ave & Way	19403
E & W Fornance St	19401
S Forrest Ave	19401
Foster Ave	19403
Foundry Rd	19403
Francis Ave	19401
Franklin Dr	19403
Franklin St	19401
E & W Freedley St	19401
Galbraith Ave	19403
Gary Ln	19401
General Armistead Ave	19403
General Washington Ave	19403
Generals Dr	19403
George St	19401
E Germantown Pike	19401
W Germantown Pike	
102B-102C	19401
104A-104B	19401
110A-110B	19401
142A-142B	19401
106A-106B	19401
1-299	19401
300-3299	19403
Glade Dr	19403
Glen Ln	19403
Glen Valley Dr	19401
Glenn Oak Rd	19403
Glenwood Ave	19403
Godspeed Ct	19401
Goldfinch Cir	19403
Golf Cart Dr	19403
Goshawk Cir	19403
Grandview Ave	19403
Grant Ct	19403
Green St	19401
Green Briar Dr	19403
Green Ridge Dr	19403
Green Valley Rd	19401
Greenhill Ln	19401
Greentree Ln	19403
Griffith Rd	19403
Haines Rd	19401
Hamilton St	19401
Hampton Ct	19403
Hancock Ave	19401
Hannah Ave	19401
Hanover Ln	19401
Harding Blvd	19401
Harrier Dr	19403
Harrison Ct & Rd	19403
Harrow Cir	19403
Harry Rd	19403
W Hartranft Ave & Blvd	19401
Harvest Cir	19403
Haws Ave	19401
E Hayes Rd	19403
Hazelton Ave	19401
Heather Ln	19401
Heatherwood Dr	19403
Heatherwood Hills Rd	19403
Hemlock Dr	19401
Hemlock Rd	19403
Henry Rd	19403
Heritage Dr	19403
Heston Ave	19403
Hickory Hill Rd	19403
High St	19401
Highgate Rd	19403
N Highland Ave	19403
Highley Rd	19403
Highview Dr	19403
Hillcrest Ave	19401
Hillendale Dr	19403
N Hills Dr	19401
N Hillside Ave, Cir, Dr & Ln	19403
Hilltop Ave	19401
Hollow Rd	19403
Holloway Rd	19403
Hollywood Ave	19403
Hoover Ave	19403
Horseshoe Rd	19403
Hurst Aly	19401
Independence Rd	19403
E & W Indian Ln	19403
Industry Ln	19403
Irenic Ct	19403
Iris Dr	19403
Ivy Cir	19403
Jackson St	19401
Jacoby St	19401
James Cir	19403
James St	19401
W James St	
900-1399	19401
1400-1899	19403
Jamestown Cir	19403
Janeway Dr	19401
Jasper Ct	19403
Jefferson Ave	
1-20	19401
10-99	19403
100-898	19403
900-941	19403
943-975	19403
Jefferson Ct	19401
Jefferson St	19401
Jefferson Crossing Blvd	19401
Jennifer Dr	19401
Jennifer Ln	19401
Jode Rd	19403
E & W Johnson Hwy	19401
Joseph Dr	19401
Joseph St	19403
Juniata Rd	19403
Juniper St	19401
Keenwood Rd	19403
Kelly Dr	
800-899	19403
5103-7524	19401
Kendrick Ln	19401
Kennedy Ct & Rd	19403
Kestral Cir	19403
Keswick Way	19403
Killington Ct	19403
Kimberly Dr	19401
Kinglet Dr	19403
Knoeller Rd	19403
Knottywood Knls	19403
Knox St	19401
Koegel Ln	19403
Kohn St	19401
Kramer Dr	19403
Kriebel Mill Rd	19403
Kristin Ct	19401
Lafayette Dr	19403
Lafayette Rd	19401
E Lafayette St	19401
W Lafayette St	19401
Landis Rd	19403
Lantern Ln	19403
Lark Ln	19403
Larkin Ln	19403
Lauman Ave	19403
Laura Ln	19401
Laurel Ln	19403
Lawn Ave	19403
Lawnton Rd	19401
Lawrence Rd	19403
Lee Rd	19403
Lena Ln	19403
Leon Ave	19403
Lewis Ln	19403
Lexington Ct & Ln	19403
Liberty Ave & Ct	19403
Lincoln Ave	19401
Lincoln Ter	19403
Linda Ln	19401
Linnet Rd	19403
Linwood Ave	19401
Lisa Rd	19403
Lloyd Ln	19403
Locust St	19401
E & W Logan St	19401
Long Meadow Rd	19403
Longacre Rd	19403
Longspur Rd	19403
Lynn Dr	19403
Madison Ave	19403
Magnolia Ln	19403
E Main St	19401
W Main St	
1-1399	19401
1400-3076	19403
3078-3098	19403
Mallard Cir	19403
Manchester Rd	19403
Mann Rd	19403
Maple Aly	19401
Maplewood Mews	19403
March Aly	19401
Marcia Ln	19403
Marielle Ln	19401
Marilyn Ave	19403
Marion Ave	19403
Mark Ln	19403
Markle Rd	19403
Markley St	19401
Marna Ct	19403
Marsha Rd	19403
E Marshall St	19401
W Marshall St	
1-1299	19401
1301-1399	19401
1400-1410	19403
1412-1999	19403
2001-2099	19403
Martha Ln	19403
Mary Bell Rd	19403
Matlack Dr	19403
Mckinley Ave	19401
Meadow Ln	19403
Meadowbrook Rd	19401
Meadowlark Rd	19403
Megann Ct	19401
Merion Way	19403
Merlin Cir	19403
Merri Claude Dr	19401
Merwin Dr	19403
Methacton Ave	19403
Miami Ave & Rd	19403
Michael Ln	19403
Michele Dr	19403
Middle School Dr	19403
Middleton Pl	19403
N & S Midland Ave	19403
Mill Rd	
1-199	19401
2000-3299	19403
Mill St	19401
Mill Grove Dr	19403
Minor St	19401
Minutemen Ln	19403
Mockingbird Ln	19403
Mohill Dr	19403
Monroe Blvd	19403
Montgomery Ave	
1-308	19401
310-398	19401
1000-1099	19403
N Montgomery Ave	19403
S Montgomery Ave	19403
Montgomery Plz	19401
E Moore St	19401
E & W Mount Kirk Ave	19403
Mourning Dove Rd	19403
Mustang Way	19403
Mystic Ln	19403
Nancy Dr	19403
Nassau Pl	19401
Natalie Ln	19401
Nester Dr	19403
New St	
1-99	19403
200-298	19401
New Hope St	19401
Nicole Dr	19403
Nighthawk Cir	19403
Noble St	19401
Norma Ln	19401
Norrington Dr	19403
Norris St	19401
Norris City Ave	19401
Norris Hall Ln	19403
Norriton Dr	19403
Northhampton Rd	19403
Northridge Dr	19403
Northview Blvd	19401
Norwood Ln	19401
Nottingham Rd	19403
E & W Oak Dr & St	19401
Oak Tree Rd	19401
Oakdale Ave	19403
Oakland Dr	19403
Oaklyn Ave	19403
Oakridge Cir	19403
Oakwood Ave	19401
Old Arch Rd	19401
Old Forge Way	19403
Old Orchard Rd	19403
Orchard Ln	
14-30	19403
32-99	19403
200-299	19401
W Orchard Ln	19403
Oriole Ct	19403
Osprey Dr	19403
Overhill Dr	19403
Overhill Rd	19401
Overlook Dr	19403
Owl Rd	19403
Oxford Cir & Ct	19403
Pacer Ln	19401
Paddock Cir	19403
Palmer Dr	19403
N & S Park Ave, Dr & Ln	19403
Parklane Dr	19403
N & S Parkview Dr	19403
Patricia Cir	19401
Patriot Ln	19403
Patriots Ln	19403
Patterson Ave	19401
Pawlings Rd	19403
Peachtree Ln	19403
Peacock Dr	19403
Pearl St	19401
Pembrooke Rd	19403
Penfield Ave	19403
E & W Penn St	19401
Penn Crossing Dr	19401
Penn Square Rd	19401
Penn View Ln	19403
Pennburn Rd	19403
Percy Ct	19401
Peregrine Cir	19403
Pheasant Ln & Rd	19403
Pheasant Run Rd	19403
Pierce Rd	19403
Pimlico Dr	19403
Pine Ct	19401
Pine St	
1000-1099	19403
1200-1899	19401
Pinecrest Rd	19403
Pinetown Rd	19403
Pinetree Dr	19403
Pintail Dr	19403
Plowshare Rd	19403
Plumlyn Ave	19403
Plymouth Blvd	19401
Polk Rd	19403
Pondview Dr	19403
E & W Poplar St	19401
Port Indian Rd	19403
Potshop Ln & Rd	19403
Potts Ave	19403
Powell St	19401
Prelate Cir	19403
Prescott Cir	19403
Prince Dr	19403
N Prospect Ave	19403
Providence Rd	19403
Quarry Hall Rd	19403
Rafter Rd	19403
Rahway Ave	19401
Rapp Aly	19401
Raptor Dr	19403
Reagan Ct	19403
Redtail Rd	19403
Redwing Ln	19403
Redwood Ln	19401
Regatta Cir	19401
Regency Dr	19403
Reid Dr	19403
Reiner Rd	19403
Republic Ave	19403
Rich Aly	19401
Richfield Ave	19403
Ridge Pike	
3055A-3055C	19403
3100-3399	19403
3200-3200	19408
Ringneck Rd	19403
Rittenhouse Blvd & Rd	19403
River Brook Cir	19403
Riversedge Dr	19403
Riverview Rd	19403
Roanoke Cir	19403
E & W Roberts Aly, Cir & St	19401
Robin Ln	19401
Rockwood Dr	19401
Rogers Rd	19403
Roland Dr	19401
Romano Ct	19401
Roosevelt Ave	19401
Rosa Ln	19403
Rose Ave	19403
Rosedale Ct	19401
Rosemont Ave	19401
Russwood Dr	19401
Saint Davids Ln	19403

Saint Vincent St 19403
Salem Dr 19403
Sand Trap Ct 19403
Sandalwood Ln 19403
Sanderling Cir 19403
Sandown Rd 19403
Sandpiper Rd 19403
Sandra Ln 19403
Sandy St 19401
Sandy Hill Rd 19401
Sarah Ave 19403
Saratoga Ln 19403
Sardaro Ln 19401
Saw Mill Ct 19401
Sawmill Run 19401
Scenic Rd 19403
Schara Ln 19403
School Ln 19403
Schultz Rd 19403
Schuylkill Ave 19401
N Schuylkill Ave 19403
S Schuylkill Ave 19403
Selma St 19401
Senator Rd 19403
Sentinel Rdg 19403
Sentry Ct 19401
Sentry Ln 19403
Serenity Ct 19401
Shamokin Ave 19401
Shannondell Blvd, Dr & Rd 19403
Sharon Ln 19403
Shearwater Dr 19403
Shepherd Ln 19403
Sheridan Ln 19403
Sherry Ln 19403
Shire Dr 19403
Shirlene Rd 19403
Shirley Ln 19403
Sienna Dr 19401
Singer Ln 19403
Single Tree Ln 19403
Skippack Pike 19403
Sky Dr 19403
Skyline Cir & Dr 19403
Smith St 19401
Snowflake Cir 19403
Soni Dr 19403
Sparrow Rd 19403
Spera Ln 19403
Splitrail Cir 19403
Spring Cir 19403
Spring Hill Rd 19403
Spring House Ln 19403
Springview Rd 19401
E & W Spruce St 19401
Stable Rd 19403
Stanbridge Rd & St 19401
Statesman Rd 19403
Sterigere St
700-1399 19401
1400-1798 19403
1800-2099 19403
W Sterigere St 19401
Steven St 19403
Stinson Ln 19403
Stone Ridge Dr 19403
Stoney Creek Rd 19401
Stony Way 19403
Stonybrook Dr 19403
Stuart Dr 19401
Summit Ave 19403
Summit St 19401
Sunnyside Ave 19403
W Sunset Ave 19403
Surrey Ln 19403
Susan Ln 19403
Susan Constant Ct 19401
Swan Cir 19403
Swede Rd & St 19401
Swift St 19401
Sycamore Cir 19403
Sycamore Ln 19401
Taft Rd 19403
Tanglewood Ct & Ln 19403
Teakwood Ct 19401

Teakwood Ter 19403
Teardrop Cir 19401
Tennyson Ct 19403
Terrace Dr 19401
Theresa St 19403
Thomas Cir & St 19401
Thomas Barone St 19401
Thornwood Ter 19403
Thrush Ln 19403
Timothy Trl 19403
Toll Gate Dr 19403
Tomstock Cir & Rd 19403
Township Line Rd 19403
E Township Line Rd 19401
W Township Line Rd
2-98 19401
101-597 19403
599-699 19403
701-2799 19403
Treetop Ln 19403
Tremont Ave 19401
Trent Ln 19401
Trolley Ln 19403
N & S Trooper Rd 19403
Trout Ln 19403
Truman Ct & Rd 19403
Tyler St 19401
Union St 19403
Upper Farm Rd 19403
Valley Ln 19403
Valley Forge Rd 19403
Valley View Cir & Rd 19401
Van Buren Ave 19403
Varnum Rd 19403
Vienna Ave 19403
Village Green Ln 19403
Vincent Way 19401
Violet St 19401
Virginia Ln 19403
Wagon Wheel Rd 19403
N & S Wakefield Rd 19403
N Wales Rd 19403
Walker Ln 19403
Waller Way 19403
Walnut St 19401
Wanda Ln 19403
W Warren St 19401
Warsaw Ave 19401
Washington Ave 19401
Washington Blvd 19403
Washington Dr 19403
E Washington St 19401
W Washington St 19401
Water St 19401
Water Street Rd 19403
Waterview Dr 19403
Wayfield Dr 19403
Wayne Ave
12-30 19403
32-34 19403
101-122 19403
111-113 19401
115-134 19403
136-136 19401
Wayne Dr 19403
Weber Ln 19403
Wedgewood Way 19403
Wellington Rd 19403
Wendover Dr 19403
Westover Club Dr 19403
Wheatsheaf Ln 19403
Whippoorwill Rd 19403
Whitehall Rd 19403
Whitley Dr 19403
William Ct 19401
William Penn Dr 19403
Williams Way 19403
Willow Ave 19403
Willow St 19401
Willowbrook Dr 19403
Wilson Blvd 19403
Windmill Cir 19403
Windsor Dr 19403
Windswept Ln 19403
Windy Hill Rd 19403
Winterfall Ave 19403

E & W Wood St 19401
Wooded Pl 19403
Woodland Ave & Ln 19403
Woodlawn Rd 19401
Woodlyn Ave
1-199 19403
500-599 19401
2900-3099 19403
Woodsedge Rd 19403
Woodstream Dr 19403
Wren Rd 19403
Yerkes Aly 19401
Yorktown N & S 19403
Zummo Way 19401

NUMBERED STREETS

1st St 19403
2nd St
1900-2098 19401
2800-2999 19403
3rd St
1900-2098 19401
2800-2999 19403
4th St
2200-2298 19401
2900-2999 19403
5th St 19403
6th St 19403
7th St 19403

PHILADELPHIA PA

General Delivery 19104

POST OFFICE BOXES MAIN OFFICE STATIONS AND BRANCHES

Box No.s
1 - 6 19115
1 - 1996 19105
1212 - 1212 19146
2000 - 2399 19103
2021 - 2099 19122
2401 - 2590 19147
2601 - 2676 19130
2701 - 2800 19120
2803 - 2898 19122
2901 - 2990 19141
3200 - 3310 19130
3400 - 3599 19122
3601 - 3799 19125
3801 - 3999 19146
4001 - 4096 19118
4101 - 4296 19144
4301 - 4400 19118
4401 - 4499 19140
4501 - 4598 19131
4601 - 4699 19127
4700 - 4799 19134
4800 - 4897 19124
4901 - 4999 19119
5000 - 5099 19111
5100 - 5290 19141
5301 - 5398 19142
5400 - 5596 19143
5600 - 5696 19129
5701 - 5800 19120
5801 - 5899 19128
5901 - 5999 19137
6001 - 6099 19114
6100 - 6199 19115
6200 - 6299 19136
6301 - 6399 19139
6401 - 6499 19145
6501 - 6599 19138
6601 - 6698 19149
6701 - 6995 19132
7000 - 7099 19149
7100 - 7198 19101
7217 - 8796 19176

8900 - 8999 19135
9101 - 9499 19139
9500 - 9591 19124
9601 - 9672 19131
9700 - 9899 19140
9737 - 9737 19101
9901 - 9994 19118
10000 - 10000 19101
11000 - 11097 19141
11100 - 11299 19136
11301 - 11349 19137
11400 - 11494 19111
11501 - 11695 19116
11700 - 11799 19101
11786 - 11786 19176
11800 - 11898 19128
11900 - 11999 19145
12010 - 12060 19105
12201 - 12298 19144
12301 - 12380 19119
12400 - 12599 19151
12601 - 12699 19129
12701 - 12798 19134
12800 - 12999 19176
13000 - 13998 19101
13069 - 13951 19176
14000 - 14089 19122
14100 - 14299 19138
14301 - 14599 19115
14601 - 14850 19134
14901 - 14992 19149
15001 - 15196 19130
15200 - 15299 19125
15300 - 15398 19111
15400 - 15498 19149
15501 - 15619 19131
15700 - 15999 19103
16000 - 16396 19114
16401 - 16598 19122
16601 - 16750 19139
16801 - 16999 19142
17001 - 17599 19105
17600 - 17819 19135
18001 - 18099 19147
18100 - 18196 19116
18301 - 18500 19120
18500 - 18590 19129
18600 - 18789 19132
18801 - 18999 19119
19001 - 19099 19138
19101 - 19440 19143
19500 - 19699 19124
19701 - 19996 19143
20000 - 20188 19145
20205 - 20437 19137
20500 - 20799 19138
20800 - 20999 19141
21001 - 21296 19114
21301 - 21499 19141
21501 - 21603 19131
21701 - 21841 19146
21900 - 21999 19124
22000 - 22240 19136
22301 - 22720 19110
23000 - 23299 19124
23401 - 24000 19143
24001 - 24199 19139
24201 - 24599 19120
24600 - 24799 19111
24801 - 24869 19130
24900 - 24930 19120
25001 - 25195 19147
25200 - 25327 19119
25400 - 25598 19140
25601 - 25799 19144
25801 - 26100 19128
26201 - 26699 19141
26701 - 26976 19134
27001 - 27786 19118
28001 - 28221 19131
28301 - 28599 19149
28600 - 29050 19151
29101 - 29178 19127
29200 - 29499 19125
29500 - 29699 19144
29701 - 29938 19119

30000 - 30639 19103
30700 - 30980 19104
31001 - 31760 19147
31801 - 31999 19104
32001 - 32420 19146
33001 - 33903 19142
34001 - 34987 19101
35001 - 35234 19128
36601 - 36880 19107
37000 - 37021 19122
37101 - 37560 19148
37600 - 38051 19101
38001 - 38400 19140
38501 - 38940 19104
39000 - 39599 19136
39701 - 40534 19106
40601 - 40936 19107
41001 - 41178 19127
41400 - 42999 19101
41582 - 42940 19176
43001 - 43429 19129
43501 - 43799 19106
44001 - 44620 19144
45001 - 45392 19124
45501 - 45934 19149
46001 - 47875 19160
48001 - 48504 19144
49001 - 49199 19141
50000 - 50994 19132
51001 - 52997 19115
53000 - 54360 19105
54401 - 55380 19148
55401 - 55958 19127
56001 - 56340 19130
56500 - 57999 19111
58001 - 60257 19102
60401 - 60602 19145
60600 - 60999 19133
63001 - 63460 19114
63501 - 63997 19147
65001 - 65782 19155
70101 - 71410 19176
90101 - 90999 19190
91000 - 91000 19019
91619 - 916535 19101

NAMED STREETS

A St
2500-2599 19125
2700-2898 19134
2900-3699 19134
4501-4597 19120
4599-6099 19120
Abbottsford Ave 19129
E Abbottsford Ave 19144
W Abbottsford Ave 19144
Abby Rd 19154
Aberdale Rd 19136
N Aberdeen St 19131
Abigail St 19125
E & W Abington Ave 19118
Academy Cir 19146
Academy Pl 19154
Academy Rd
3500-3642 19154
3644-3799 19154
9100-9998 19114
9101-9115 19136
9125-10501 19114
10801-11097 19154
11099-12499 19154
Ace Way 19114
Acker St 19126
Acorn St 19128
Adams Ave
400-699 19120
700-4651 19124
4653-4691 19124
Addison St
500-1300 19147
1302-1398 19147
1500-1598 19146
1602-2100 19146
2102-2198 19146
5200-6299 19143

Admiral Peary Way 19112
Admirals Way 19146
Adrian Way 19139
Afton St
900-1999 19111
2100-2332 19152
2334-2398 19152
Agate St
2600-2699 19125
2800-3399 19134
3399 1/2-3399 1/2 19134
Agusta St
5900-6099 19149
8500-8699 19152
S Aikens St 19142
Ainslie St 19129
E Airdrie St 19124
W Airdrie St 19140
N Airedar St 19122
Akron St
5000-5499 19124
5800-7199 19149
N Alantrid St 19132
E Albanus St 19120
W Albanus St
100-399 19120
1300-1899 19141
Albemarle Ln
10200-10299 19114
10700-10799 19154
E Albert St 19125
W Albert St 19132
Alberta Dr, Pl & Ter 19154
Albion St 19136
Albright St 19134
Alburger Ave 19115
Alcott St
400-699 19120
1033-1599 19149
E Alcott St 19135
Alden Ave 19127
N Alden St
200-299 19139
1200-1599 19131
S Alden St
100-299 19139
700-2599 19143
Alder Pl 19123
N Alder St
2000-2098 19122
2500-2599 19133
S Alder St
200-298 19107
400-1399 19147
1800-2899 19148
Aldine St
1300-1499 19111
3300-4599 19136
Alexandria Ln 19116
Alexis Ln 19115
Alfred St
3900-3999 19140
5300-5399 19144
Algard St 19135
Algon Ave
5901-5999 19149
6000-7999 19111
8000-8499 19152
8501-8699 19152
Alicia St
8300-8599 19111
8600-9999 19115
E Allegheny Ave 19134
W Allegheny Ave
171A-171B 19140
100-160 19133
161-169 19140
162-1298 19133
173-1299 19133
1300-3599 19132
2233-33-2233-43 19132
Allen Ct 19112
E Allen St
100-399 19125
401-499 19125
3400-3500 19134
3502-3640 19134

4401-4499 19137
W Allen St 19123
Allengrove St
500-699 19120
900-1649 19124
E Allens Ln
300-699 19119
900-999 19150
W Allens Ln 19119
Allens Pl 19119
N Allison St
100-199 19139
500-1799 19131
S Allison St 19143
Allman St 19142
Alma St
5900-6199 19149
7400-7599 19111
8300-8398 19152
Almatt Dr, Pl & Ter 19115
Almond St
800-2699 19125
2700-3699 19134
4200-4298 19137
4300-4799 19137
4801-4899 19137
Alnus Pl & St 19116
Alpena Rd 19115
Alresford St 19137
Alter St
100-900 19147
902-1398 19147
1500-1698 19146
1700-2599 19146
5800-5899 19143
Alton Pl & St 19115
Ambassador Pl & St 19115
Amber St
2000-2699 19125
2745-2747 19134
2749-3599 19134
3601-3699 19134
Ambridge Pl 19114
Ambrose St 19144
N American St
2-98 19106
400-498 19123
500-1199 19123
1200-2161 19122
2163-2199 19122
2200-3099 19133
3200-4499 19140
5200-6099 19120
6500-6699 19126
S American St
300-399 19106
600-1326 19147
1328-1398 19147
2301-2397 19148
2399-2599 19148
Amherst Pl 19136
Amity Rd 19154
Anchor St
500-699 19120
800-2199 19124
Ancona Rd 19154
Andale St 19149
Anderson St
5601-5697 19138
5699-6399 19138
6460-6648 19119
6650-7599 19119
8000-8599 19118
Andorra Rd 19118
Andover Rd 19114
Andrea Rd 19154
Andrews Ave 19138
Angelo Pl 19153
Angora Ter 19143
Angus Pl & Rd 19114
Anita Dr 19111
E Ann St 19134
Anna Dr 19116
Annapolis Rd 19114
Annin St
600-1399 19147
1600-2799 19146

E Annsbury St
600-699 19120
726-798 19124
W Annsbury St 19140
Apalogen Rd 19129
Apollo Pl 19153
Apostolic Sq 19146
Appian Way 19139
Apple St 19127
Apple Blossom Dr & Way 19111
Applehouse Rd 19114
Appletree Ct 19106
Appletree St
777-777 19106
1000-1099 19107
2000-2199 19103
5600-5699 19139
W Apsley St 19144
Aramingo Ave
801-2197 19125
2199-2599 19125
2601-2699 19125
2700-2798 19134
2800-3699 19134
3700-3999 19137
4000-4198 19124
4200-4599 19124
Arbor St
3000-3199 19134
3201-3499 19134
5100-5699 19120
Arbutus St 19119
Arcadia St
2500-2599 19125
3900-3999 19124
Arch St
100-799 19106
800-898 19107
900-1200 19107
1202-1324 19107
1401-1599 19102
1600-1628 19103
1630-2299 19103
2901-3297 19104
3299-3399 19104
4900-5937 19139
5939-6299 19139
Archer St 19140
S Arcola St 19153
S Ardell St 19153
Ardleigh St
5500-6399 19138
6400-6458 19119
6460-7499 19119
7600-8500 19118
8502-8598 19118
Arendell Ave 19114
Argus Rd 19150
Argyle St
3300-3399 19134
6100-6499 19111
E Arizona St 19125
W Arizona St
900-1099 19133
2500-3299 19132
Arlan St 19136
Arlington St
1700-3299 19121
5200-5699 19131
E Armat St 19144
E Armstrong St 19144
Arnold St
500-999 19111
1700-1840 19152
1842-1898 19152
3300-3399 19129
Arrivals Rd 19153
Arrott St 19124
Arthur St
500-699 19111
1700-2399 19152
3400-3599 19136
Artwood Dr 19115
Asbury Ter 19126
Ascot Pl 19116
Ash St 19137

Ashburner St 19136
E Ashdale St 19120
W Ashdale St
100-198 19120
200-599 19120
1800-1899 19141
Ashfield Ln 19114
S Ashford St 19153
Ashland Ave 19143
Ashland St 19124
Ashley St
1800-1899 19126
1900-1999 19138
E & W Ashmead Pl & St N & S 19144
Ashton Rd
8700-9099 19136
9125-9197 19114
9199-9700 19114
9702-9898 19114
Ashurst Rd 19151
Ashville St 19136
Ashwood Ave 19154
Aspen St
2201-2297 19130
2299-2599 19130
2601-2699 19130
3501-3597 19104
3599-4400 19104
4402-4498 19104
4500-4798 19139
4800-5099 19139
5101-5199 19139
Aspen Way 19139
Aster Ct 19136
Aster Rd 19154
E Atlantic St 19134
W Atlantic St 19140
Atmore Rd 19154
Atwood Rd 19151
Aubrey Ave 19114
E Auburn St 19134
W Auburn St
900-999 19133
1300-1399 19132
Audubon Ave, Pl, Plz & Ter 19116
August St 19137
Aurania St 19128
Auth St 19124
Authority Ter 19129
Autumn Rd 19115
Autumn Hill Dr 19115
Autumn River Run 19128
Avalon Pl & St 19114
Avenue Of The Arts 19102
Avenue Of The Republic Ave 19131
Avner St 19114
Avon Pl, Rd, St & Ter 19116
N Avondale St 19139
S Avondale St 19142
Avonhoe Rd 19138
Awbury Rd 19138
Axe Factory Rd 19152
Aylwyn Dr N & S 19145
Ayrdale Cres, Pl & Rd 19128
Azalea Dr 19136
B St
2600-2699 19125
2723-2797 19134
2799-3599 19134
3601-3699 19134
4700-5999 19120
Bach Pl 19102
N Bailey St
800-899 19130
1500-1899 19121
2800-3099 19132
3200-3399 19129
S Bailey St
1500-1599 19146
1600-1699 19145
Bailey Ter 19145
Bainbridge St
100-1399 19147
1400-1410 19146
1412-2299 19146
2301-2799 19146
Baker St 19127
Bakers Ln 19140
Baldwin St
100-299 19127
7801-7997 19150
7999-8099 19150
Balfour St 19134
Balston Rd 19154
Baltimore Ave
3901-4001 19104
4003-4499 19104
4500-6099 19143
Baltz St 19121
Balwynne Park Rd 19131
N Bambrey St
800-999 19130
1700-2099 19121
2800-3199 19132
3200-3299 19129
S Bambrey St 19146
Bambrey Ter 19145
N Bancroft Ct 19132
S Bancroft Ct 19146
N Bancroft St
2200-3199 19132
4400-4499 19140
S Bancroft St
700-1599 19146
1600-2653 19145
2655-2699 19145
Bandon Dr 19154
Banes St
9300-9699 19115
11600-11700 19116
11702-11798 19116
S Bank St 19106
N Bantinte St 19121
Barbara St 19145
Barbary Pl & Rd 19154
Barcalow Ave 19116
Barclay St 19129
N Barelach St 19123
Baring St 19104
Barlow St & Ter 19116
Barnard St 19149
Barner Dr 19114
Barnes St
501-597 19128
599-699 19128
7821-7999 19111
Barnett St
1300-1399 19111
3100-3199 19149
4000-4098 19135
4100-4299 19135
Barney Ct 19112
Barracks Ave 19112
E Barringer St
1100-1399 19119
1400-1699 19150
Barry Rd 19114
Bartlett Pl & St 19115
Barton St 19135
Bartram Ave 19153
Bartram Dr 19143
Basile Rd 19154
Basilica Cir 19128
Basin Bridge Rd 19112
Bass St 19119
Bastian Ter 19145
Bath St 19137
Battersby St
6300-6326 19149
6328-6330 19149
6332-7298 19149
7400-7526 19152
7528-7599 19150
Bayard St 19150
Baynton St 19144
N Beach St
500-698 19123
700-799 19123
1325-1799 19125
Beacon Rd 19115
Beaumont Ave 19143

Beck St 19147
N Beechwood St
100-198 19103
800-899 19130
2300-2399 19132
5700-6599 19138
S Beechwood St
100-199 19103
1900-2299 19145
Belden St
5900-6199 19149
7300-7499 19111
Belfield Ave
1300-1420 19140
1422-1520 19140
1521-1525 19141
1527-1799 19141
1801-1899 19141
5100-6200 19144
6202-6298 19144
6400-6427 19119
6429-6599 19119
Belfry Dr 19128
Belgrade St
200-2699 19125
2701-2797 19134
2799-3661 19134
3663-3687 19134
4301-4397 19137
4399-4599 19137
4601-4799 19137
Belgreen Pl, Rd & Ter 19154
Bellaire Pl & Rd 19154
Bellevue St 19140
S Bellford St 19153
Bellmore Ave 19134
Bells Ct 19106
Bells Mill Rd 19128
E Bells Mill Rd 19118
W Bells Mill Rd 19118
Belmar St 19142
Belmar Ter 19143
Belmont Ave
800-1399 19104
1401-1599 19104
2101-2197 19131
2199-2800 19131
2802-2898 19131
Belmont Mansion Dr 19131
E Benezet St 19118
Benjamin Ct 19114
Benjamin Franklin Pkwy
3-3 19102
1601-1697 19103
1699-1800 19103
1802-1998 19103
2001-2099 19130
2200-2698 19130
Benner St
200-619 19111
621-699 19111
1400-2999 19149
4000-4999 19135
Bennett Rd 19116
Bennington St
3800-4399 19124
5900-5999 19120
Benson St
400-999 19111
1600-2499 19152
4000-4599 19136
4601-4699 19136
Benton St 19152
E Bentrive St 19125
S Berbro St 19153
Berdan St 19119
Berea St 19114
Bergen Pl 19111
Bergen St
501-697 19111
699-999 19111
1700-2099 19152
4600-4698 19136
Bergen Ter 19111
Berges St 19125
Berkeley Dr 19129
W Berkley St 19144

E Berks St 19125
W Berks St
100-158 19122
160-1332 19122
1334-1398 19122
1701-1797 19121
1799-3299 19121
5200-5699 19131
Berkshire St
1900-1999 19124
2701-2799 19137
Bermuda St
4101-4297 19124
4299-4599 19124
4600-4698 19137
Bernita Dr 19116
Berwyn Pl & St 19115
Beth Dr 19115
Bethlehem Pike 19118
Betsy Ross Pl 19122
Betts St 19124
Beulah Pl 19123
S Beulah St
900-1398 19147
1400-1599 19147
1600-2899 19148
Beverly Dr 19116
Beverly Rd 19138
Beyer Ave 19115
S Bialy St 19153
Bickley St 19115
Biddle Ave & Rd 19112
Biggans Pl 19154
Bigler St
700-1398 19148
1601-1697 19145
1699-1800 19145
1802-1898 19145
Bigler Ter 19145
Bingham St
1000-1199 19115
4700-5999 19120
6000-8099 19111
Birch Rd 19154
E Birch St 19134
W Birch St 19133
Birwood St 19115
Biscayne Dr & Pl 19154
Bittern Pl 19142
Black Lake Pl 19154
Blackwell Pl 19147
Blackwood Dr 19145
Bladens Ct 19106
Blaine St 19140
Blair St 19125
Blakemore St
5500-5699 19138
6600-6700 19119
6702-6798 19119
Blakeslee Ct & Dr 19116
Blakiston St 19136
Blavis St 19140
Bleigh Ave
800-1911 19111
1913-1999 19111
2000-2099 19152
2101-2535 19152
3300-5299 19136
Bloomdale Rd 19115
Bloomfield Ave & Pl 19115
Bloyd St 19138
Blue Grass Rd
8800-8999 19152
9100-9899 19114
9901-9999 19114
Bluebell Ct 19116
Boathouse Row 19130
Bobolink Pl 19142
N Bodine St
500-1199 19123
1500-2100 19122
2102-2198 19122
2300-2599 19133
3400-4400 19140
4402-4598 19140
S Bodine St
1-99 19106
900-1199 19147
Boise Pl 19145
Bolton St & Way 19121
Bonaffon St 19142
Bonaparte Ct 19107
Bonitz St 19140
Bonner St 19115
Bonnie Gellman Ct 19114
N Bonsall St
1700-1799 19121
2700-3099 19132
S Bonsall St
100-299 19103
901-1197 19146
1199-1299 19146
1900-2399 19145
Bonsall Ter 19145
Boone St
4001-4045 19127
4047-4057 19127
4059-4099 19127
4201-4297 19128
4299-4569 19128
4571-4599 19128
Borbeck Ave
200-1999 19111
2100-2399 19152
Boreal Pl 19153
W Boston Ave 19133
W Boston Pl 19133
E Boston St 19125
W Boston St 19132
Botanic Ave 19143
Bott St 19140
Boudinot St
2700-3299 19134
4600-5099 19120
N Bouvier St
1400-1899 19121
2200-2699 19132
3300-4599 19140
4800-6299 19141
6500-7399 19126
S Bouvier St
301-399 19103
1000-1599 19146
1900-2699 19145
Bowler St 19115
Bowman St
3300-3599 19129
5100-5198 19131
Boyer St
5500-5709 19138
5711-6199 19138
6400-7599 19119
Braddock St
2600-2699 19125
2800-2998 19134
3000-3599 19134
Bradford Aly 19147
Bradford St
6801-7197 19149
7199-7299 19149
7601-7697 19152
7699-7999 19152
8001-8199 19152
8800-8899 19115
Bradford Ter 19149
Bradistr St 19127
Brandon Pl & Rd 19154
Brandywine St
701-997 19123
999-1199 19123
1201-1399 19123
1500-2299 19130
3100-3999 19104
4001-4199 19104
Brant Pl 19153
N Bread St 19106
Brentwood Rd 19151
Brewerytown Ct 19121
Brewster Ave 19153
Briar Rd 19138
Bridge St
800-2199 19124
2200-2999 19137
Bridget St 19144

Bridle Rd
8000-8599 19111
8600-9999 19115
10000-10199 19116
Brier St 19152
Brierdale Rd 19128
Briggs St 19124
Brighton Pl 19149
Brighton St
600-1499 19111
2100-3499 19149
Brill St
600-699 19120
800-2099 19124
2200-2799 19137
2801-2899 19137
E & W Bringhurst St 19144
Brinley Ct 19146
E Brinton St
500-599 19144
600-699 19138
E Bristol St
1300-1398 19124
1400-1500 19124
1502-1698 19124
2800-2898 19137
W Bristol St 19140
Bristow Pl 19123
N Broad St
1-399 19107
100-298 19102
400-998 19130
401-401 19108
425-999 19123
1200-2198 19121
1201-2199 19122
2200-3199 19132
3200-4699 19140
4700-6337 19141
6339-6399 19141
6344-6398 19126
6400-7299 19126
S Broad St
1-121 19107
100-100 19110
123-135 19109
140-398 19102
201-319 19107
323-323 19102
333-337 19107
400-1598 19146
401-1217 19147
1221-1221 19146
1231-1599 19147
1600-3398 19145
1601-3901 19148
4300-4398 19112
4400-5199 19112
Brocklehurst St 19152
Brockton Rd 19151
Brookdale Rd 19114
Brookhaven Rd 19151
N Brooklyn St 19104
Brookshire Crk, Ct, Dr, Ln, Pl, Plz, Ter & Way 19116
Brookview Rd 19154
Broomall St 19143
Broughton St 19112
Brous Ave
6200-7299 19149
7300-9099 19152
Brown Pl 19123
Brown St
1-97 19123
99-1399 19123
1413-1497 19130
1499-2799 19130
2801-2813 19130
3600-3798 19104
3800-4399 19104
4401-4499 19104
4500-5199 19139
Brunner St 19140
Brunswick Ave & Pl 19153
Brush Rd 19138
Bryan St 19119
Bryn Mawr Ave 19131

Buck Ln 19145
Buckingham Pl 19104
Buckius St
1800-1898 19124
1900-2099 19124
2301-2629 19137
2631-2799 19137
Buckley Dr, Pl & Ter 19115
N Bucknell St
700-899 19130
1800-1899 19121
S Bucknell St
1200-1299 19146
2000-2299 19145
2301-2399 19145
Bucknell Ter 19145
Bucknell Way 19121
N Budd St 19104
Buist Ave
6000-7099 19142
7101-7299 19142
7300-8300 19153
8302-8398 19153
Bunting Pl 19153
Burbank Rd 19115
Burbridge St 19144
Burgess St 19116
Burholme Ave 19111
Burke Dr N & S 19145
Burnham Rd 19119
Burnside St
100-198 19127
300-398 19128
Burton St 19124
N Busti St 19104
Bustleton Ave
5300-5398 19124
5800-7299 19149
7300-7310 19152
7312-8700 19152
9100-9100 19115
9102-9999 19115
10000-10098 19116
10100-15599 19116
Buthored St 19129
Butler Ave 19107
E Butler St 19137
W Butler St 19140
Buttonwood Pl 19128
Buttonwood St
900-998 19123
1000-1399 19123
1801-1899 19130
Buxmont St 19116
Byberry Rd
100-2199 19116
3000-4399 19154
Byrne Rd 19154
C St
2700-3154 19134
3156-3498 19134
4600-5299 19120
Cabell Rd 19154
Cabot Pl 19121
E Cabot St 19125
W Cabot St 19121
Cadillac Ln 19128
N Cadwallader St 19122
Caesar Pl 19153
Caledonia St 19128
Calera Rd
10100-10198 19114
10200-10299 19114
10800-11099 19154
Callowhill St
1-1399 19123
1400-1698 19130
1700-1999 19130
5900-5998 19151
6000-6599 19151
6601-6799 19151
Calpine Rd 19154
Calumet St 19129
Calvert St
201-263 19120
265-299 19120
6300-7299 19149
7501-7797 19152
7799-8999 19152
N Camac St
200-299 19107
800-899 19123
2100-2199 19122
2200-3199 19133
3500-4699 19140
4700-6399 19141
6400-6599 19126
S Camac St
200-399 19107
400-408 19147
410-1599 19147
1600-2899 19148
Camas Dr 19115
E Cambria St 19134
W Cambria St
100-154 19133
156-1299 19133
1300-1322 19132
1324-2311 19132
2313-2899 19132
Cambridge Ct 19123
Cambridge Mall 19123
Cambridge St
306-998 19123
1000-1200 19123
1202-1398 19123
1400-3099 19130
3800-4149 19104
4151-4199 19104
5500-5698 19131
5700-5799 19131
9200-9399 19114
Cameron St 19130
Campus Ln 19114
Canal St 19123
Canby Dr 19154
N & S Canterbury Rd 19114
Canton St 19127
Cantrell St
300-1199 19148
1601-2197 19145
2199-2899 19145
Cantrell Ter 19145
Capital View Dr 19129
N Capitol St 19130
S Capitol St 19146
Capri Ct & Dr 19145
Captains Way 19146
Cardella Pl 19116
E Cardeza St
1200-1399 19119
1400-1699 19150
Cardiff St 19149
Cardin Rd 19128
Cardinal Ave 19131
Carey Pl 19154
Carey Plz 19154
Carey Rd 19154
E Carey St 19124
W Carey St 19140
Carey Ter 19154
Cargill Ln 19115
Cargo City 19153
N Carlisle St
800-999 19130
1200-1298 19121
1300-2199 19121
2200-3199 19132
3200-4599 19140
4700-4798 19141
4800-5399 19141
6700-6899 19126
S Carlisle St
400-1599 19146
1600-3099 19145
Carlton St
1200-1298 19107
1401-1499 19102
1801-1899 19103
6400-6499 19139
Carnation St 19144
Carnwath St 19152
Caroline Rd 19154
Carpenter Ln 19119
Carpenter St
100-118 19147
120-1300 19147
1302-1398 19147
1500-2599 19146
5600-6299 19143
Carriage Ln 19104
S Carroll St 19142
Carson St
101-127 19127
129-299 19127
300-399 19128
Carswell Ter 19144
Carter Rd 19116
Carteret Dr 19114
Carver St 19124
E Carver St 19120
Carwithan St
1800-1899 19152
4400-4598 19136
Caryl Ln 19118
N Cashitt St 19130
Casimir St 19137
Caskey St 19140
Cassin Pl N & S 19145
Castle Ave
1300-1336 19148
1338-1398 19148
1400-1498 19145
Castor Ave
1900-1998 19134
2000-3100 19134
3102-3198 19134
3701-3797 19124
3799-5299 19124
5301-5399 19124
5800-7299 19149
7300-8599 19152
Cates Way 19115
Catharine St
2-98 19147
100-1324 19147
1326-1398 19147
1400-1412 19146
1414-2699 19146
4901-4997 19143
4999-6299 19143
E Cathedral Cir & Rd 19128
E Cayuga St
603-699 19120
800-1299 19124
1301-1599 19124
W Cayuga St 19140
N Cecil St 19139
S Cecil St
1-299 19139
700-2199 19143
Cecil B Moore Ave
100-1399 19122
1401-1401 19121
1403-3299 19121
Cedar Ave 19143
Cedar St
1800-2645 19125
2647-2699 19125
2800-3299 19134
3301-3599 19134
Cedar Grove Dr 19131
Cedar Park Ave 19138
Cedarbrook Ave 19150
Cedarhurst St 19143
Cemetery Ave 19142
Centaur Pl 19153
Centennial Sq E 19116
Central Ave 19111
N Chadwick St
2200-3199 19132
4400-4499 19140
S Chadwick St
300-313 19103
315-399 19103
700-1599 19146
1600-2655 19145
2657-2699 19145
Chalfont Dr & Pl 19154
Chalmers Ave 19132
Chamounix Dr 19131
Champlost Ave 19138
E Champlost St 19120
W Champlost St
1-500 19120
502-799 19120
900-1899 19141
Chancellor St
1200-1298 19107
1300-1399 19107
1400-1499 19102
1600-2110 19103
2112-2198 19103
4001-4099 19104
4900-6199 19139
Chandler St
300-1999 19111
2100-2199 19152
Chapel Rd 19115
Chapelcroft St 19115
Charette Rd 19115
Charles St
4900-5499 19124
5701-6097 19135
6099-7299 19135
7901-7999 19136
Charles Ter 19124
Charlton St 19119
Charter Rd 19154
Charteris Rd 19154
Chase Rd 19152
Chatham St 19134
Chaucer St 19145
Chelfield St 19136
Chelsea Pl 19114
Chelten Ave 19120
E Chelten Ave
1-799 19144
800-2199 19138
W Chelten Ave
1-516 19144
517-597 19126
518-598 19144
599-1800 19126
1802-1898 19126
E Cheltenham Ave
100-298 19120
300-699 19120
1000-4824 19124
4826-4998 19124
W Cheltenham Ave
2-198 19120
200-1898 19126
1900-2298 19138
2201-2297 19150
2299-3000 19150
3002-3498 19150
Chelwynde Ave
6200-6999 19142
7300-8399 19153
Chelwynde Pl 19153
Cherion Pl 19153
Cherokee St
6300-6350 19144
6352-6399 19144
6400-7099 19119
7101-7117 19119
7600-7800 19118
7802-8198 19118
Cherry St
200-399 19106
801-897 19107
899-1099 19107
1400-1599 19102
1601-1699 19102
1700-1798 19103
1800-2299 19103
2301-2399 19103
3210-3210 19104
3301-3399 19104
5501-5597 19139
5599-5799 19139
Cherry Blossom Way 19111
Chesapeake Pl 19122
Chester Ave
4100-4299 19104
4500-5999 19143
6000-7000 19142
7002-7098 19142
Chesterfield Rd 19114
Chestnut Ln 19115
Chestnut St
100-799 19106
800-1399 19107
1400-1498 19102
1500-1599 19102
1600-1600 19103
1602-2400 19103
2402-2498 19103
2900-2998 19104
3000-3098 19104
3000-3000 19101
3100-4499 19104
4500-6299 19139
E & W Chestnut Hill Ave 19118
Cheswick Rd 19128
Chesworth Rd 19115
Chew Ave
5300-6399 19138
6401-6457 19119
6459-7199 19119
E Chew Ave 19120
W Chew Ave
100-600 19120
602-698 19120
2100-2199 19138
W Chew St 19141
Chilton Rd 19154
S Chincom St 19145
Chineric Dr 19113
Chippendale St 19136
Chippewa Rd 19128
Christian St
1-97 19147
99-1299 19147
1301-1399 19147
1400-2700 19146
2702-2798 19146
5400-6299 19143
Christina Pl 19139
Christopher Dr 19115
Church Ln
800-911 19138
913-999 19138
1500-1999 19141
2000-2199 19138
E Church Ln 19144
Church Rd
5200-5299 19131
6300-6499 19151
Church St
100-299 19106
1300-2408 19124
2410-2548 19124
Churchill Ln 19114
Cinnaminson St 19128
Cinnamon Dr 19128
Citizens Bank Way 19148
City Ave
3900-4000 19131
4002-6198 19131
6300-7998 19151
Civic Center Blvd 19104
Claire Rd 19128
E & W Clapier St 19144
E Claremont Rd 19120
Clarence St 19134
Clarenden Rd 19114
Claridge St
3900-5399 19124
5401-5499 19124
6600-7599 19111
N Clarion St
200-299 19107
2400-2499 19132
S Clarion St
600-1599 19147
1600-2599 19148
N Clarissa St 19140
Clark Pl 19116
Clark St
9300-9899 19115
10100-10699 19116
E Clarkson Ave 19120
W Clarkson Ave
100-199 19120
201-399 19120
2100-2199 19144
2201-5299 19144
Clay St 19130
S Claymont St 19153
Clayton St 19152
E Clearfield St 19134
W Clearfield St
101-103 19133
105-1000 19133
1002-1098 19133
1300-3599 19132
Clearview St
1400-1599 19141
6200-6299 19138
6400-7099 19119
E Clementine St 19134
W Clementine St 19132
N Cleveland St
2000-2099 19121
2200-2599 19132
4400-4499 19140
S Cleveland St
700-1599 19146
1700-2999 19145
S Cliancom St 19147
Cliff Rd 19128
Cliffe Dr 19154
Clifford Ln 19116
Clifford St 19121
Clifford Ter 19151
Cliffwood Rd 19115
N Clifton St 19107
S Clifton St
201-299 19107
600-1199 19147
Clinton St 19107
E Cliveden St
1-97 19119
99-1399 19119
1400-1699 19150
W Cliveden St
100-1099 19119
2001-2003 19150
Cloister Cir 19128
Cloud Ct & St 19124
Clover St 19107
Cloverly Rd
9001-9099 19136
9300-9399 19114
Clyde Ln 19128
Clymer St
500-799 19147
801-1299 19147
1400-1998 19146
2000-2199 19146
Cobbs Creek Pkwy
601-697 19143
699-1199 19143
1201-1699 19143
1700-1998 19142
2000-2099 19142
2101-2199 19142
5800-6099 19143
6101-6299 19143
6400-6898 19142
6900-6999 19142
Colebrook Rd 19115
Colfax St 19136
Colgate St
5700-5898 19120
5900-5999 19120
6000-6099 19111
6101-6199 19111
Colima Rd 19115
N College Ave 19121
S College Ave 19121
W College Ave
900-998 19130
1200-1204 19121
1206-1299 19121
College Hall 19104
Colli Dr 19145
Collins St
2300-2699 19125
3000-3499 19134
E Collom St 19144
Colman Pl, Rd & Ter 19154
E Colona St 19125
W Colona St
1000-1098 19133
1101-1199 19133
3000-3099 19132
Colonial St 19138
E Colonial St 19120
W Colonial St 19126
Colony Dr 19152
N Colorado St
2200-2699 19132
4400-4599 19140
S Colorado St
700-1599 19146
2000-3099 19145
E Columbia Ave 19125
W Columbia Ave
5100-5399 19131
5900-6399 19151
N Columbus Blvd
1-97 19106
99-299 19106
301-399 19106
400-500 19123
502-698 19123
S Columbus Blvd
201-401 19106
501-697 19147
699-1599 19147
1600-3499 19148
3501-3501 19148
Colwyn St 19140
Comly Pl 19154
Comly Rd 19154
Comly St 19135
E Comly St
100-198 19120
200-499 19120
501-699 19120
1000-1698 19149
1001-1099 19111
1401-1701 19149
S Commerce Dr 19131
Commerce St
1300-1398 19107
5700-5799 19139
Commerce Way 19154
E Commissioner St 19134
W Commissioner St 19132
Commodore Ct 19146
Conard St 19111
Conarroe St
101-121 19127
123-199 19127
300-499 19128
501-599 19128
Concord St 19144
S Concourse Dr 19131
N Conestoga St
1-199 19139
600-1599 19131
1601-1699 19131
S Conestoga St
1-99 19139
500-1899 19143
Conestoga Ter 19143
Conestoga Way 19139
Conklin St 19124
Conlyn St
1400-1999 19141
2000-2199 19138
Conrad St 19129
Conshohocken Ave 19131
Constance Rd 19114
Constitution Ave 19112
Convent Ave
8901-8997 19136
8999-9071 19136
9073-9083 19136
9100-9198 19114
9200-9699 19114
Convent Ln 19114
N Convent Ln 19114
S Convent Ln 19114

Convent Pl 19114
Convention Ave 19104
Conwell Ave 19115
Cooper St 19137
Copley Rd 19144
Corainda Rd 19114
Coral St
2000-2699 19125
2700-3499 19134
3700-3998 19124
Corestates Complex 19148
Corinthian Ave 19130
N Corlies St
1400-2199 19121
2400-2699 19132
S Corlies St
1300-1599 19146
1600-1899 19145
Cormorant Pl 19142
Cornelia Pl 19118
Cornelius St
6600-7299 19138
8000-8099 19150
E Cornwall St 19134
W Cornwall St 19140
Corry Pl & Rd 19154
E Cosgrove St 19144
Cosmos Ct 19136
Cottage St
4900-5199 19124
5201-5399 19124
5700-7299 19135
7300-8899 19136
9200-9399 19114
Cottman Ave
2301A-2301B 19149
301-697 19111
699-1999 19111
2000-3599 19149
4000-5199 19135
Cotton St
1-180 19127
182-184 19127
200-399 19128
E Coulter St 19144
W Coulter St
1-500 19144
502-598 19144
3000-3499 19129
Country Club Blvd 19115
E Country Club Rd 19131
W Country Club Rd 19131
Country Lane Dr & Way 19115
County Line Rd 19116
E Courtland St 19120
W Courtland St 19140
Covered Bridge Path 19115
Covert Rd 19154
Covington Rd 19120
Cowden St
9500-9899 19115
10600-10699 19116
Crabtree St 19136
Crafton St 19149
Craig St 19136
Crane St 19153
Cranston Rd 19131
Cratin Pl 19153
Crawford St 19129
Cread Ct 19145
Crease Ln 19128
Crease St 19125
Crefeld St 19118
N Creighton St
200-299 19139
500-1799 19131
Crescent Dr 19112
Crescentville Rd 19120
Cresco Ave 19136
Cresheim Rd
6700-7399 19119
7401-7499 19119
7701-7797 19118
7799-7899 19118
Cresson St
3201-3397 19129
3399-3500 19129
3502-3598 19129
3600-3698 19127
3700-4499 19127
Crest Park Rd 19119
Crestmont Ave
9900-9999 19114
10700-10899 19154
Creston St
1400-1699 19149
4000-4099 19135
Crestview Rd 19128
Creswell St 19129
Creswood Rd 19115
Crispin Dr 19136
Crispin St
7301-7997 19136
7999-8099 19136
8101-8299 19136
9100-9399 19114
Crittenden St
5700-6399 19138
6700-7500 19119
7502-7598 19119
7601-7697 19118
7699-8399 19118
Croatan Pl 19145
Cromwell Rd 19114
Crosby Rd & St 19112
N Croskey St
100-199 19103
700-799 19130
1700-2011 19121
2013-2099 19121
2301-2697 19132
2699-3199 19132
S Croskey St
400-499 19146
1900-2399 19145
Croskey Ter 19145
Croskey Way 19121
Cross St
300-1199 19147
2100-2399 19146
Crossland Rd 19154
Crowell St 19129
E Crown Ave 19114
W Crown Ave 19114
Crown Way 19154
Crowson St
5500-5699 19144
6600-6699 19119
6701-6799 19119
Croyden St 19137
Crystal St
3400-3499 19134
5900-5999 19120
Culp St 19128
E Cumberland St 19125
W Cumberland St
101-117 19133
119-1099 19133
1101-1299 19133
1300-3399 19132
Curie Blvd 19104
Curlew Pl 19142
Curtin St & Ter 19145
Custer St 19134
Custis Pl 19122
Cuthbert St
100-199 19106
201-299 19106
901-999 19107
Cutler St 19126
Cypress St
300-532 19106
534-598 19106
900-1298 19107
1300-1343 19107
1345-1399 19107
1601-1997 19103
1999-2199 19103
D St
2800-3699 19134
3700-3999 19124
4500-5299 19120
N Daggett St
200-299 19139
400-499 19151
S Daggett St 19142
Dahlia Dr 19116
E Dakota St 19125
W Dakota St
900-1099 19133
2500-3199 19132
3201-3299 19132
5100-5199 19131
Dale Ct 19112
Dale Rd 19115
Daleadwa Ave 19150
Dalkeith St 19140
Dallas Rd
1700-1899 19126
1900-1998 19138
Dalton St 19111
Daly St
100-1299 19148
1800-1899 19145
Daly Ter 19145
Damar Dr 19116
Dana Ave 19116
Danbury St 19152
Daner Ln 19114
Danforth St 19152
Daniel St 19144
Danley Rd 19154
Daphne Rd 19131
Darby Ct 19145
N Darien St
901-999 19123
1500-1898 19122
1900-2199 19122
2600-3199 19133
3600-4399 19140
S Darien St
201-299 19107
500-698 19147
700-1499 19147
2000-2899 19148
N Darien Way 19123
Darlington Rd 19115
Darnell Rd 19154
Darrah St 19124
Dartmouth Pl 19136
W Dauphin Dr 19132
E Dauphin St 19125
W Dauphin St
100-106 19133
108-1299 19133
1301-1411 19132
1413-3299 19132
5100-5198 19131
Davidson Rd 19118
Davinci Dr 19145
Davis Ave 19112
Davis St 19127
Dawson St
100-199 19127
200-399 19128
Day St 19125
Deacon St 19129
Deal St 19124
N Dearborn St 19139
Dearnley St 19128
Decatur Rd 19154
Decatur St 19136
Dedaker Dr 19116
Dedaker St
9600-9799 19115
10200-10299 19116
Deer Ln 19136
Deer Run Pl & Rd 19154
Deerpath Ln 19154
Defense Ter 19129
N Dekalb St 19104
Delaire Landing Rd 19114
Delancey Pl 19103
Delancey St
100-198 19106
200-799 19106
1500-1599 19102
1700-2420 19103
2422-2498 19103
3900-3998 19104
4001-4099 19104
5100-6299 19143
Delaware Ave 19112
N Delaware Ave
600-898 19123
900-999 19123
1000-1799 19125
3200-3499 19134
3501-3699 19134
3801-3897 19137
3899-4099 19137
4101-4399 19137
6100-7199 19135
8900-9198 19136
9200-9398 19114
N Delhi St
2200-2499 19133
3700-3999 19140
S Delhi St
200-210 19107
212-299 19107
600-999 19147
1001-1199 19147
Delia Ln 19115
Dell St 19140
Delmar St 19128
Delphi Pl 19153
Delphine St 19120
Delray St 19116
Denfield Pl 19145
Denise Dr 19116
Denman Rd 19154
Dennie St 19140
Densmore Rd & St 19116
Depue Ave & Pl 19116
Derry Pl, Rd & Ter 19154
Devereaux Ave
101-197 19111
199-1399 19111
1400-2999 19149
3001-3099 19149
Devereaux St 19135
Devitt Pl 19142
Devon Pl 19138
Devon St
5500-5699 19138
7100-7128 19119
7130-7499 19119
7501-7599 19119
7700-8199 19118
Dewees St
8800-8999 19152
9101-9197 19114
9199-9249 19114
9251-9251 19114
N Dewey St 19139
S Dewey St
1-99 19139
2500-2999 19142
Dexter St 19128
Diamond St
100-182 19122
184-1199 19122
1201-1299 19122
5001-5097 19131
5099-5699 19131
W Diamond St 19121
Dickens Ave
5800-5899 19143
6200-6298 19142
6300-6499 19142
7601-7699 19153
Dickens Pl 19153
Dickinson St
100-1332 19147
1334-1398 19147
1401-1403 19146
1405-3399 19146
Dicks Ave
6201-6297 19142
6299-7099 19142
7100-7298 19153
7300-7699 19153
Dicks Pl 19153
Dillman St 19140
Dimarco Dr 19154
Diplomat Dr 19113
Diplomat Pl 19115
Discher St 19124
Disston St
501-697 19111
699-1499 19111
2000-3499 19149
4000-4920 19135
4922-4998 19135
Ditman St
4500-5300 19124
5302-5398 19124
5722-5798 19135
5800-7299 19135
7301-7697 19136
7699-8899 19136
9200-9699 19114
S Divinity St 19143
Division St 19129
Dobson Row & St 19129
Dock St 19106
Dogwood Ln 19115
Domino Ln 19128
Donaldson St 19114
Donath St 19140
Dondill Pl 19122
Dora Dr 19154
Dorcas St
6400-7999 19111
8000-8399 19152
Dorcas Ter 19111
Dorchester Rd 19154
Dorel St
6400-6799 19142
7100-7199 19153
Dorothy Dr 19116
S Dorrance St
700-1599 19146
1700-2100 19145
2102-2198 19145
E Dorset St
200-698 19119
700-899 19119
900-1199 19150
Dothan Plz & Ter 19153
N Douglas St
500-599 19104
2400-2699 19132
S Douglas St 19145
Dounton St 19140
N Dover St
1200-2199 19121
2400-2799 19132
3200-3299 19129
S Dover St
1200-1599 19146
1601-1697 19145
1699-1899 19145
Dowitcher Pl 19142
Downing Pl 19114
Downs Pl 19116
Dows Rd 19154
Drake Dr 19154
Draper St 19136
Dreer St 19125
Drexel Rd
5200-6099 19131
6300-7499 19151
Driftwood Dr 19129
Druim Moir Ln 19118
Drummond Rd
10300-10399 19154
10380-10380 19114
10400-10598 19154
10401-10599 19154
Drumore Dr & Pl 19154
Drury St 19107
Dudley St
100-999 19148
1800-2799 19145
Duffield St
4600-5300 19124
5302-5398 19124
6000-6098 19135
Duffy Ln 19154
Dumont Pl & Rd 19116
Duncan St 19124
E Duncannon Ave 19120
W Duncannon Ave
100-700 19120
702-798 19120
900-1599 19141
Dungan Rd
7100-7999 19111
9500-9598 19115
9600-9999 19115
Dungan St 19124
Dunks Ferry Pl & Rd 19154
Dunlap St 19131
Dunmore Rd 19115
E Dunton St 19123
Dupont Ave 19112
Dupont Pl 19128
Dupont St
100-239 19127
240-699 19128
W Durand St 19119
E Durard St
200-299 19119
900-999 19150
Durfor St
100-1299 19148
1900-2000 19145
2002-2498 19145
E Durham St
1-699 19119
900-1300 19150
1302-1698 19150
W Durham St 19119
Dutton Rd 19154
E Duval St
1-199 19144
201-299 19144
1200-1699 19138
W Duval St 19144
Dyre St 19124
E St 19134
Eadom St 19137
Earl Ct & St 19125
E Earlham St 19144
W Earlham St 19129
W Earlham Ter 19144
Earp St
201-297 19147
299-899 19147
1800-2098 19146
2100-3699 19146
East St
119-125 19127
127-182 19127
200-299 19128
Eastburn Ave 19138
Easton Rd 19150
Eastview St 19152
Eastwick Ave
5600-5799 19143
6100-6498 19142
6500-6599 19142
8000-8099 19153
8101-8599 19153
Eastwick Ter 19143
Eastwood St
6300-7299 19149
7900-7998 19152
Easy St 19111
Eddington St 19137
Eden St 19114
Eden Hall Ln 19114
Edgely Rd 19131
Edgemont St
2500-2699 19125
2700-3699 19134
3801-4097 19137
4099-4719 19137
4721-4799 19137
Edgemore Rd 19151
N Edgewood St
1-399 19139
400-1799 19151
S Edgewood St
200-299 19139
1200-1299 19143
1700-2599 19142
Edgley St
900-999 19122
1600-2999 19121
Edison Ave 19116
Edmund St
4600-4799 19124
6000-7299 19135
7301-7397 19136
7399-7499 19136
7501-7699 19136
9200-9298 19114
9300-9399 19114
Edward St 19123
Edwin Walk 19130
Egret Pl 19142
Elaine St 19150
Elberon Ave 19111
Elbow Ln 19119
Elbridge St
201-1097 19111
1099-1399 19111
1400-2999 19149
4100-4299 19135
E Eleanor St 19120
W Eleanor St
500-599 19120
1300-1899 19141
Elfreths Aly 19106
Elgin St 19111
Elizabeth St 19124
E Elkhart St 19134
W Elkhart St
200-299 19133
2400-2415 19132
2417-2499 19132
Elkins Ave
500-699 19120
2100-2199 19144
Ella St
2900-3599 19134
4600-5999 19120
Elleastr Ave 19138
Ellet Ln 19119
E Ellet St
200-299 19119
900-1099 19150
W Ellet St 19119
Ellicott Rd 19154
Ellie Dr 19114
Ellington Rd 19131
Elliott St 19143
Elliston Cir 19114
S Ellonere St 19142
Ellsworth St
100-1399 19147
1400-2700 19146
2702-2998 19146
5800-6299 19143
Elmhurst St
5900-5999 19149
6300-6399 19111
Elmhurst Ter 19111
Elmore Pl, Rd & Ter 19154
Elmwood Ave
5501-5597 19143
5599-5999 19143
6000-7315 19142
7317-7343 19142
7345-7397 19153
7399-7699 19153
Elnora Rd 19154
Elser St 19140
Elsinore St
3800-4399 19124
5900-5999 19120
Elston St
1700-1899 19126
1900-1999 19138
E Elwood St 19144
Emeadont St 19128
Emerald St
2200-2699 19125
2700-3699 19134
Emerick St 19125
Emerson St
500-999 19111
1600-2399 19152

4600-4699 19136
Emery St
2500-2698 19125
3100-3200 19134
3202-3298 19134
4600-4699 19137
Emily St
100-1299 19148
1500-2699 19145
Emlen St 19119
Emmons St 19112
W End Dr 19151
Endicott St 19116
Enfield Ave 19136
Englewood St
1100-1499 19111
3100-3599 19149
Enola St 19111
Enterprise Ave 19153
Envoy Ave 19153
Epiphany Pl 19128
Erdrick St
5100-5499 19124
5700-7299 19135
7900-7998 19136
8000-8199 19136
Erica Pl, St & Ter 19116
E Erie Ave
100-298 19134
300-899 19134
901-949 19134
1000-1599 19124
1601-1699 19124
W Erie Ave 19140
Ernest St 19147
Ernest Way 19111
Ernie Davis Cir 19154
Ernst St 19145
Erringer Pl 19144
Erwin St 19116
Escort St 19153
Essex Ln 19114
Essington Ave 19153
Estaugh St 19140
Este Ave 19153
Etta St 19114
N Etting St
1200-2099 19121
3200-3299 19129
S Etting St
1400-1599 19146
1600-2099 19145
Etting Ter 19145
Euclid Ave 19121
Euclid St 19131
Eva St 19128
Evans St
9200-9799 19115
10600-10698 19116
Evarts St 19152
Eveline St 19129
Everett St 19149
Evergreen Ave 19128
E Evergreen Ave 19118
W Evergreen Ave 19118
Evergreen Pl 19118
Evergreen Way 19115
Executive Ave 19153
Exeter Rd 19114
E Eyre St 19125
W Eyre St 19121
F St
3001-3097 19134
3099-3599 19134
5000-5200 19124
5202-5298 19124
Factory St 19124
Fairdale Rd 19154
Fairfield St
3000-3098 19136
3100-3199 19136
7600-8999 19152
Fairgreen Ln 19114
N Fairhill St
2100-2199 19122
2200-2999 19133
3200-4500 19140
4502-4698 19140
4800-6199 19120
6200-6699 19126
S Fairhill St
900-1399 19147
2200-2899 19148
Fairmount Ave
1-97 19123
99-1300 19123
1302-1398 19123
1400-2399 19130
2401-2499 19130
3300-3398 19104
3400-4499 19104
4501-4597 19139
4599-4999 19139
Fairmount Park
--- 19121
3-3 19132
3300-3324 19132
Fairthorne Ave 19128
Fairview St 19136
Fairway Ter 19128
N Fallon St
801-879 19139
881-899 19139
900-999 19131
S Fallon St
1-99 19139
1400-1499 19143
E Falls Cir & Ln 19129
Fanshawe St
300-1499 19111
2100-3299 19149
Faraday St 19116
E Fariston Dr 19120
Farmdale Rd 19154
Farnsworth St
6201-6297 19149
6299-6399 19149
7800-8199 19152
Farragut Ct 19112
S Farragut St
1-299 19139
900-1099 19143
Farrell Ct 19154
Farrington Rd 19151
N Farson St
1-899 19139
900-1298 19131
1300-1399 19131
Farthess St 19107
Farwell Rd 19154
Faunce St
500-1999 19111
2000-2400 19152
2402-2598 19152
N Fawn St 19133
S Fawn St
300-327 19107
700-798 19147
Fayette St
7400-7499 19138
7500-8699 19150
Federal St
100-1316 19147
1318-1398 19147
1400-2799 19146
Fedor Pl & Rd 19154
N Felton St
1-399 19139
400-1799 19151
S Felton St
200-299 19139
600-699 19143
2200-2999 19142
Fenn Dr 19154
Fenwick Pl & Rd 19115
Ferierso St 19124
Fern St 19120
Ferndale St
7700-8522 19111
8600-9999 19115
10000-12099 19116
Fernhill Rd 19144
Fernon St
100-1099 19148
1700-2399 19145
Fernwood St 19143
Filbert St
701-799 19106
801-997 19107
999-1199 19107
1201-1317 19107
3601-3997 19104
3999-4029 19104
4031-4299 19104
5200-5832 19139
5834-5998 19139
Filbert And Market St 19107
Fillmore Pl 19124
Fillmore St
900-1899 19124
2600-2699 19137
7601-7999 19111
Fillmore Ter 19124
Finch Pl 19142
E Firth St 19125
W Firth St
800-1299 19133
1500-3399 19132
E Fisher Ave 19120
W Fisher Ave
100-799 19120
800-1299 19141
1301-1499 19141
W Fisher Ln 19141
E Fishers Ln 19124
Fisk Ave 19129
Fitler St 19114
Fitlers Walk 19103
Fitzgerald St
100-1299 19148
1900-2499 19145
Fitzwater St
100-1399 19147
1401-1419 19146
1421-2399 19146
Flagship Ave 19112
Flagstaff Pl & Rd 19115
Flamingo St 19128
Flanders Rd 19151
Flarangt St 19116
Flat Rock Rd 19127
Fleming St 19128
E Fletcher St 19125
W Fletcher St 19132
E Flora St 19125
W Flora St
901-1299 19122
1400-2999 19121
Florence Ave 19143
Florist St 19106
Foggia Dr 19145
Folsom Ct 19139
Folsom St
1700-2598 19130
2600-2799 19130
3800-3999 19104
4600-5098 19139
5100-5199 19139
Fontain St 19121
Ford Rd 19131
Fordham Rd 19114
Forest Hills Ave 19116
Forrest Ave
6800-7499 19138
7500-8699 19150
Forrestal St 19145
W Fort Mifflin Rd 19153
Foster St 19116
Foulkrod Pl 19124
Foulkrod St
600-699 19120
700-798 19124
800-1899 19124
Fountain St
101-113 19127
115-171 19127
173-179 19127
194-248 19128
250-250 19127
251-251 19128
253-699 19128
Fowler St
4700-4729 19127
4731-4799 19127
6900-7599 19128
Fox St
2800-2940 19129
3000-3199 19132
3200-3399 19129
3401-3699 19129
Fox Chase Rd 19152
Fox Run Ln 19111
Foxglove Ln 19116
Foxhill Rd 19120
Foxx Ln 19144
Fraley St
2000-2199 19124
2200-2299 19137
Francis St 19130
Frankford Ave
901-997 19125
999-2699 19125
2700-3699 19134
3700-5299 19124
5301-5399 19124
5700-7299 19135
7300-8999 19136
9001-9097 19114
9099-10000 19114
10002-10004 19114
Franklin Pl 19123
N Franklin St
700-899 19123
901-911 19123
1200-2199 19122
2200-3199 19133
3700-4499 19140
4800-6199 19120
6800-6899 19126
S Franklin St
1100-1122 19147
1124-1599 19147
1600-2899 19148
2901-2999 19148
Franklin Mills Blvd & Cir 19154
Franklin Town Blvd 19103
N Frazier St
1-100 19139
102-198 19139
600-1599 19131
S Frazier St
200-299 19139
300-2499 19143
Frederick St 19129
Freeland Ave 19128
French St
900-999 19122
1600-3199 19121
Friar Pl & Rd 19154
Friel Pl 19116
Friendship St
300-1499 19111
2100-3499 19149
4741-4797 19135
4799-5099 19135
N Front St
2-298 19106
300-350 19106
352-358 19106
400-1199 19123
1200-2199 19122
2200-3199 19133
3200-4399 19140
4350-4350 19160
4400-4698 19140
4401-4699 19140
4700-6299 19120
6301-6499 19120
S Front St
2-338 19106
400-698 19147
700-1500 19147
1502-1598 19147
1600-2098 19148
2100-3599 19148
Frontenac St
5601-5699 19124
5900-6099 19149
6101-6199 19149
6200-6898 19111
6900-7999 19111
8000-8038 19152
8040-8799 19152
Frost St 19136
Fuller St
300-1299 19111
1700-2400 19152
2402-2898 19152
3200-3299 19136
3301-3399 19136
Fulmer St 19115
Fulton St 19147
Funston St 19139
Furley St
200-299 19120
2100-2199 19138
G St
3100-3118 19134
3120-3651 19134
3653-3699 19134
3900-4299 19124
4301-4399 19124
4400-4699 19120
Gainor Rd 19131
Galahad Rd 19116
Galdi Ln 19154
E & W Gale St 19120
S Galloway Pl 19147
N Galloway St 19123
S Galloway St 19148
Gamble Ct 19112
Gannet Pl 19153
Gantry Rd 19115
Garden St 19137
Gardenia Ln 19115
Gardenia St 19144
Gardner St 19116
E & W Garfield St 19144
Garland St
601-699 19120
700-766 19124
768-768 19124
Garman St
6400-6999 19142
7300-7399 19153
N Garnet St
2300-2899 19132
6301-6399 19141
S Garnet St
1300-1599 19146
2000-2599 19145
E Garrett St 19119
Garth Rd 19116
Garvey Dr 19114
Gaskill St 19147
Gaston Ln 19116
Gate Ln 19119
Gate House Ln 19118
Gates St
101-197 19127
199-241 19127
243-243 19127
300-699 19128
Gateway Dr 19145
Gaul St
600-2541 19125
2701-2797 19134
2799-3599 19134
3601-3657 19134
4501-4535 19137
Gay St
106-120 19127
122-179 19127
181-187 19127
182-198 19128
200-299 19128
Geary St
1300-1398 19148
1800-1998 19145
Geary Ter 19145
Geiger Rd 19115
Gelena Rd 19152
Gendont St 19149
Genesee Dr & Pl 19154
Geneva Ave 19120
Genoa Dr 19145
George Pl 19123
E George St 19125
W George St
200-499 19123
1901-2697 19130
2699-2799 19130
Georges Ln 19131
Georgian Rd 19138
Gerhard St 19128
Germania St 19114
Germantown Ave
4428B-4460B 19140
1001-1047 19123
1049-1199 19123
1200-2199 19122
2200-3099 19133
3101-3199 19133
3200-4450 19140
4452-4460 19140
4500-4526 19144
4528-6399 19144
6400-6400 19119
6401-6401 19144
6402-7611 19119
7613-7619 19119
7620-9702 19118
9704-9898 19118
Gerritt St
200-1299 19147
1800-2999 19146
Gerry St 19138
Gesner St 19142
Gettysburg Ave 19128
Gibbs Pl 19153
Gibson Dr 19143
Gibson Pl 19153
Gifford St 19116
Gilbert St
7400-7499 19138
7500-8699 19150
Gilham St
200-1499 19111
2800-3299 19149
4000-4199 19135
Gillespie St
5200-5298 19124
5300-5399 19124
6100-7299 19135
8600-8799 19136
9200-9399 19114
Gillingham St
1300-1398 19124
1400-2199 19124
2500-2899 19137
Gina Dr 19115
Ginger Ln 19128
Ginnodo St 19130
E Girard Ave 19125
W Girard Ave
1-800 19123
801-899 19122
802-1398 19123
901-1399 19123
1400-3099 19130
3101-3299 19130
3400-3998 19104
4000-4300 19104
4302-4498 19104
4501-4597 19131
4599-5800 19131
5802-5898 19131
5900-6599 19151
6601-6699 19151
Gladstone St
100-399 19148
1800-1899 19145
Glen Campbell Rd 19128
Glen Echo Rd 19119
Glenbrook Pl 19114
Glencoe St 19111
Glendale Ave
1700-1798 19111
1800-1999 19111
2000-2098 19152
2100-2200 19152
2202-2298 19152
Glendale St 19124
Glenfield Rd 19154
Glengarry Rd 19118
Glenhope Rd 19115
Glenifer St 19141
Glenloch Pl 19136
Glenloch St
5000-5198 19124
5200-5399 19124
6100-7299 19135
8400-8598 19136
8600-8768 19136
9200-9599 19114
Glenmore Ave
4801-5297 19143
5299-5399 19143
6100-6500 19142
6502-6598 19142
7401-7499 19153
Glenn St
800-1199 19115
3500-3799 19114
Glenroy Rd 19128
Glenview St
501-597 19111
599-1499 19111
2000-3399 19149
4100-4299 19135
E Glenwood Ave
1800-1999 19134
2000-2099 19124
W Glenwood Ave
101-179 19140
181-700 19140
702-798 19140
900-998 19133
1000-1199 19133
1201-1299 19133
1300-2199 19132
2201-2209 19132
2300-2398 19121
2400-3100 19121
3102-3198 19121
Glenwood Dr 19121
Global Rd 19115
Gloucester Ln 19114
Godfrey Ave 19138
E Godfrey Ave
101-297 19120
299-699 19120
700-798 19124
800-999 19124
W Godfrey Ave
2-88 19120
90-399 19120
401-499 19120
501-517 19126
519-700 19126
702-798 19126
900-998 19141
1000-1999 19141
2000-2199 19138
Golf Rd 19131
Gollaral St 19137
Good St 19119
Goodford Rd 19154
Goodman St 19140
Goodnaw St 19115
E Gordon St 19125
W Gordon St 19132
Gorgas Ln 19128
E Gorgas Ln
1-699 19119
900-1100 19150
1102-1312 19150
W Gorgas Ln 19119
Gorman St 19116
Gorsten St 19119
S Gould St 19142
Governors Ct 19146
E Gowen Ave
1-499 19119
900-1399 19150
1401-1699 19150
W Gowen Ave 19119
Grace Ln 19115

Graduate Plz 19146
Graham St 19131
Grakyn Ln 19128
W Grange Ave
  100-499 19120
  501-707 19120
  1100-1298 19141
  1300-1799 19141
  1801-1899 19141
  2100-2199 19138
Granite St
  800-2142 19124
  2144-2198 19124
  2200-2299 19137
Gransback St
  2900-3399 19134
  4800-5099 19120
Grant Ave
  947-997 19115
  999-2199 19115
  2201-2299 19115
  2401-2497 19114
  2499-5100 19114
  5102-5198 19114
Granville Rd 19128
Grape St
  100-179 19127
  181-183 19127
  212-214 19128
  216-299 19128
N Gratz St
  1400-2199 19121
  2200-2799 19132
  3300-4599 19140
  5000-6098 19141
  6100-6399 19141
  6500-6899 19126
E & W Gravers Ln 19118
E Gray St 19144
Grays Ave
  4900-5799 19143
  6100-7299 19142
Grays Ferry Ave
  1400-1430 19143
  1432-1498 19143
  2201-2297 19146
  2299-3699 19146
Grayton Pl 19154
Grebe Pl 19142
Greeby St
  1200-1499 19111
  4000-4299 19135
Green Ln
  100-212 19127
  213-217 19128
  214-218 19127
  219-699 19128
  1400-1498 19141
Green St
  201-297 19123
  299-1219 19123
  1221-1223 19123
  1400-1498 19130
  1500-2399 19130
  4000-4099 19104
Green Tree Rd 19118
Green Valley Dr 19128
Greenacres Rd 19154
Greendale Rd 19154
Greene St
  4100-4199 19140
  4421-4497 19144
  4499-6399 19144
  6400-7299 19119
Greenhill Ln 19128
Greenhill Rd 19151
Greenland Dr 19131
Greenmount Rd 19154
Greenough St 19127
Greenway Ave
  4800-5999 19143
  6000-7299 19142
Greenway Pl 19142
Greenwich St
  100-1199 19147
  2200-2399 19146
Greenwood Ave 19150
Gregg St
  1101-1103 19115
  1105-2199 19115
  2400-2498 19114
Greiner Pl & Rd 19116
N Grelarel St 19133
Greycourt Rd 19115
S Greylock St 19143
Greymont St 19116
Griffith St
  800-1999 19111
  2000-2399 19152
Griscom St 19124
Grosbeak Pl 19142
N Gross St
  101-197 19139
  199-399 19139
  400-599 19151
S Gross St 19142
S Grove St 19146
Grovers Ave
  6700-6800 19142
  6802-6998 19142
  8000-8098 19153
  8100-8200 19153
  8202-8298 19153
Guardian Dr 19104
Guilford Pl 19122
Guilford St
  1700-1799 19111
  2801-2807 19152
  2809-3199 19152
  3200-3399 19136
Gurley Rd 19154
W Gurney St 19133
Guyer Ave
  6300-6899 19142
  7100-7299 19153
Gypsy Ln 19129
H St
  3200-3499 19134
  4000-4198 19124
  4200-4500 19124
  4502-4698 19124
Haddington Ln 19151
Haddington St 19131
Hadfield St 19143
E Hagert St 19125
W Hagert St 19132
Hagner St 19128
Hagys Mill Rd 19128
Haines St
  100-199 19127
  1301-1497 19126
  1499-1600 19126
  1602-1698 19126
E Haines St
  1-799 19144
  800-2199 19138
W Haines St 19144
Haldeman Ave
  9800-9999 19115
  10100-10799 19116
Hale St
  1200-1399 19111
  2900-3099 19149
  4500-4599 19135
Hall Pl & St 19147
Halsey Pl 19145
Halstead St
  7800-7820 19111
  7822-8311 19111
  8313-8315 19111
  10600-11899 19116
Hamilton Cir 19130
Hamilton St
  901-997 19123
  999-1299 19123
  1301-1399 19123
  1501-1897 19130
  1899-2002 19130
  2004-2098 19130
  3101-3197 19104
  3199-3899 19104
Hamilton Walk 19104
Hammond Ave 19120
E & W Hampton Rd 19118
N Hancock St 19140
Hanford St 19149
W Hansberry St 19144
Hansen Sq 19147
S Hanson St
  200-299 19139
  300-1198 19143
  1200-1599 19143
Harbison Ave
  5201-5297 19124
  5299-5599 19124
  5700-5722 19135
  5724-6199 19135
  6200-6799 19149
Hardy Rd 19115
Hargrave St
  2800-2899 19136
  8700-8722 19152
  8724-8899 19152
Harlan St
  400-499 19122
  1800-2599 19121
  5100-5499 19131
  6500-6598 19151
Harley Ave
  5300-5398 19143
  6101-6197 19142
  6199-6299 19142
  8101-8199 19153
Harley Dr 19143
Harley Pl 19153
Harley St 19142
Harley Ter 19143
Harmer St 19131
Harmon Rd 19128
S Harmony St 19146
Harner St 19128
E Harold St 19125
W Harold St
  600-1198 19133
  1200-1299 19133
  2200-3399 19132
Harper St 19130
W Harper St 19123
Harrison St 19124
Harrow Rd 19154
S Harshaw St 19146
Hart Ln 19134
Hartel Ave
  200-1999 19111
  2000-2400 19152
  2402-2498 19152
  3300-4799 19136
  7601-7697 19152
  7699-7799 19152
Hartranft St 19145
Hartville St 19134
E & W Hartwell Ln 19118
Harvard Pl 19136
W Harvey St 19144
Harveys Ct 19146
Hasbrook Ave
  5712-5998 19120
  6000-6198 19111
  6200-7841 19111
  7843-7899 19111
Haven Pl 19152
Haverford Ave
  3100-4499 19104
  4500-5561 19139
  5563-5599 19139
  5600-5899 19131
  5900-7599 19151
Hawley Rd 19154
Haworth St
  1000-2199 19124
  2201-2597 19137
  2599-2700 19137
  2702-2798 19137
Hawthorne St
  4500-5499 19124
  6100-6199 19135
  6401-6499 19149
Hayden St 19115
Haywood St 19129
Hazel Ave 19143
Hazelhurst St
  5300-5399 19131
  6000-6099 19151
Hazell Ln 19116
Hazelwood Dr 19150
E Hazzard St 19125
W Hazzard St
  200-1299 19133
  1500-1599 19132
Headhouse Ct 19147
Heather St 19116
Hedge St 19124
Hedgerow Ln 19115
Hedley St 19137
Heflin Rd 19154
Hegerman St
  5601-5699 19124
  5700-5798 19135
  5800-7299 19135
  8300-8599 19136
  9200-9400 19114
  9402-10098 19114
Hegerman Ter 19114
Heiskell St 19144
Helen St 19134
Helene Pl 19116
Hellerman St
  300-1399 19111
  1400-3299 19149
  4000-4700 19135
  4702-4816 19135
Helmer Dr 19154
N Hemberger St 19132
S Hemberger St 19145
Hemberger Ter 19145
Hemberger Way 19121
Hemlock Dr, Pl & St 19116
Hendren St 19128
Hendrix Pl, St & Ter 19116
Henley St
  5100-5198 19144
  6900-6999 19119
Hennig St 19111
Henry Ave
  3101-3111 19129
  3113-3999 19129
  4201-4299 19144
  5458-5814 19128
  5816-8546 19128
  8548-8698 19128
Henslow Pl 19153
Herbert Ct & St 19124
N & S Hereford Ln 19114
Herkness St 19124
E Herman St 19144
Hermes Pl 19153
Hermit Ln 19128
E Hermit Ln 19128
W Hermit Ln 19144
Hermit St
  100-199 19127
  201-297 19128
  299-699 19128
Hermit Ter 19128
Hermitage St
  337A-337C 19128
  100-299 19127
  300-699 19128
Herschel Pl & Rd 19116
Hess St 19136
Heston St 19131
E Hewson St 19125
W Hewson St 19122
Heyward St 19119
Hickory Dr 19136
Hickory Hill Rd 19154
N Hicks St
  2700-2999 19132
  4200-4599 19140
S Hicks St
  300-399 19102
  700-1599 19146
  1600-2699 19145
Higbee St
  200-299 19111
  1400-1499 19149
  4000-4799 19135
Higbee Ter 19111
High St 19127
E High St 19144
E & W Highland Ave 19118
Hill Rd 19128
E, N, S & W Hill Creek Cir, Ct, Dr, Mall, Park, Pl & Ter 19120
Hillcrest Ave 19118
Hilltop Rd 19118
Hilspach St 19115
E Hilton St 19134
W Hilton St
  1100-1198 19140
  1200-1999 19140
  2400-3299 19129
Hiola Rd 19128
N Hirst St
  1-99 19139
  1400-1499 19151
S Hirst St 19139
N Hobart St
  1-299 19139
  400-2299 19131
S Hobson St 19142
Hoff St
  9300-9899 19115
  10301-10399 19116
Hoffman Ave 19143
Hoffman Dr 19145
Hoffman Pl 19123
Hoffman St
  100-999 19148
  1800-1999 19145
Hoffnagle Pl 19111
Hoffnagle St
  300-999 19111
  1600-2399 19152
  2401-2499 19152
Hog Island Rd 19153
S Holbrook St
  2500-2598 19142
  2600-2738 19142
  2740-2798 19153
Holden St 19104
Hollingsworth St 19125
Hollins Rd 19154
Hollis St
  6600-6700 19138
  6702-6798 19138
  8000-8099 19150
Holly Mall 19104
Holly Rd 19154
N Holly St 19104
N Hollywood St
  1200-1999 19121
  2400-2799 19132
S Hollywood St
  1300-1599 19146
  1700-2099 19145
Holme Ave
  2600-2876 19152
  2878-2898 19152
  2900-3094 19136
  3096-3098 19136
  3201-3399 19114
Holme Dr 19136
Holmesburg Ave 19136
Holstein Ave 19153
Holyoke Rd 19114
Homer St
  2100-2199 19138
  6200-6399 19144
Homestead St
  2100-2198 19145
  5000-5099 19135
Homestead Ter 19145
Honeysuckle Ln 19116
Hoopes St 19139
N Hope St
  1000-1199 19123
  1200-2199 19122
  2200-3099 19133
  3101-3199 19133
  3200-3499 19140
  3501-3599 19140
  4800-6299 19120
Hopkins Ct 19112
Horatio Rd 19114
Hornig Rd 19116
Horrocks St
  4300-5399 19124
  5401-5499 19124
  5830-5898 19149
  5900-7255 19149
  7257-7299 19149
  7501-7897 19152
  7899-8099 19152
Horticultural Dr 19131
N Horton St
  200-399 19139
  400-499 19151
E Hortter Pl 19119
E Hortter St
  1-899 19119
  900-1199 19150
W Hortter St 19119
Houghton Pl & St 19128
Hoven Rd 19115
N Howard St
  1100-1109 19123
  1111-1199 19123
  1200-2099 19122
  2101-2199 19122
  2200-3100 19133
  3102-3106 19133
  3201-3297 19140
  3299-4599 19140
  4800-6299 19120
S Howard St
  601-797 19147
  799-1400 19147
  1402-1498 19147
  2100-2699 19148
Howard Ter 19119
Howard Arthur Dr 19116
E Howell St
  200-499 19120
  900-1699 19149
  4100-4899 19135
Hower Ln 19115
Howland St 19124
Hoyt Ter 19145
Hull Ct 19112
Hulseman St & Ter 19145
Humming Bird Pl 19153
Hunter St 19131
E Hunting Park Ave 19124
W Hunting Park Ave
  101-297 19140
  299-2300 19140
  2302-2398 19140
  2400-2598 19129
  2600-2999 19129
  3000-3098 19132
  3100-3399 19132
  3401-3499 19132
E Huntingdon St 19125
W Huntingdon St
  101-105 19133
  107-1299 19133
  1500-1598 19132
  1600-3499 19132
Hurley St
  2900-3499 19134
  4400-4699 19120
Huron Ln 19119
Huron St 19118
N Hutchinson Pl
  800-800 19123
  802-899 19123
  1300-1399 19122
N Hutchinson St
  900-999 19123
  2500-3199 19133
  3439-3599 19140
  4700-6000 19141
  6002-6098 19141
S Hutchinson St
  200-299 19107
  401-413 19147
  415-899 19147
  2000-2899 19148
N Hutton St 19104
I St
  3300-3699 19134
  3801-3897 19124
  3899-4400 19124
  4402-4498 19124
Ibis Pl 19142
Idell St 19119
Imogene St 19124
Ina Dr 19116
S Indelde St 19146
Independence Ave 19126
Independence Ct 19147
N Independence Mall E 19106
N Independence Mall W 19106
S Independence Mall E 19106
S Independence Mall W 19106
Independence St 19138
Indian Queen Ln 19129
E Indiana Ave 19134
W Indiana Ave
  177-1199 19133
  1401-1597 19132
  1599-3499 19132
Industrial Hwy 19113
Ingersoll St 19121
Internal Revenue Service 19154
International Plz 19113
Intrepid Ave 19112
Inverness Ln 19128
Inwood Ln 19154
Ionic St 19103
Iris Ln 19116
Irving St
  900-1098 19107
  1301-1399 19107
  3900-3938 19104
  3940-4099 19104
  5000-6199 19139
S Iseminger St
  300-399 19107
  400-1599 19147
  1600-2899 19148
Island Ave
  2200-2398 19142
  2400-2498 19153
  2500-4999 19153
Island Rd 19142
N Ithan St
  1-99 19139
  1400-1499 19131
S Ithan St
  200-299 19139
  700-2399 19143
Ivins Rd 19128
Ivy Hill Rd 19150
J St
  3401-3407 19134
  3409-3499 19134
  3800-4399 19124
Jackson Pl 19124
Jackson St
  2-98 19148
  100-1300 19148
  1302-1398 19148
  1400-2900 19145
  2902-3798 19145
  5000-5600 19124
  5602-5698 19124
  5800-7299 19135
  7300-7698 19136
  7700-8800 19136
  8802-8898 19136
  9200-9399 19114
Jacob St 19128
James St
  4600-5200 19137
  5202-5412 19137
  5500-7098 19135
  7100-7199 19135
  7300-7399 19136
  9200-9587 19114
  9589-9699 19114

Jamestown St
2-98 ... 19127
100-156 ... 19127
200-699 ... 19128
Jamison Ave
9200-9399 ... 19115
10100-10198 ... 19116
10200-10300 ... 19116
10302-10800 ... 19116
Jane St ... 19138
Janice St ... 19114
Jannette St ... 19128
Janney St
2600-2699 ... 19125
2901-2997 ... 19134
2999-3699 ... 19134
Jarden Ter ... 19145
Jason Pl ... 19153
Jasper St
2301-2397 ... 19125
2399-2699 ... 19125
2700-3699 ... 19134
3700-3843 ... 19124
3845-3899 ... 19124
Jay Pl ... 19153
Jeanes Pl ... 19116
Jeanes St
301-397 ... 19116
399-499 ... 19116
8000-8599 ... 19111
9700-9999 ... 19115
10000-11899 ... 19116
N Jefferson Ln ... 19122
E Jefferson St ... 19125
W Jefferson St
100-1300 ... 19122
1302-1398 ... 19122
1401-1497 ... 19121
1499-3199 ... 19121
4700-5098 ... 19131
5100-5799 ... 19131
5900-6599 ... 19151
Jenks St ... 19137
Jennifer Rd ... 19116
Jennifer Ter ... 19115
Jenny Pl ... 19136
Jericho Rd ... 19124
Jerome St ... 19140
Jessup Pl ... 19123
N Jessup St ... 19133
S Jessup St
205-209 ... 19107
211-299 ... 19107
400-799 ... 19147
801-999 ... 19147
1600-2699 ... 19148
Joey Dr ... 19136
John St ... 19124
John F Kennedy Blvd
1400-1498 ... 19107
1401-1497 ... 19102
1499-1521 ... 19102
1523-1599 ... 19102
1600-1999 ... 19103
E Johnson St
2-98 ... 19144
100-300 ... 19144
302-598 ... 19144
600-898 ... 19138
900-1699 ... 19138
W Johnson St ... 19144
Johnston St
504-598 ... 19148
600-1230 ... 19148
1232-1298 ... 19148
1700-1999 ... 19145
Jonathan Pl ... 19115
Jones Ct ... 19112
Joseph Kelly Ter ... 19154
Josephine St ... 19124
Joyce St ... 19134
N Judson St
500-899 ... 19130
1700-2099 ... 19121
2700-3199 ... 19132
3400-3599 ... 19140
Judson Way ... 19121
N & S June Ct & St ... 19139
E Juniata St ... 19137
W Juniata St ... 19140
N Juniper St ... 19107
S Juniper St
101-197 ... 19107
199-399 ... 19107
400-402 ... 19147
404-1599 ... 19147
1600-3299 ... 19148
K St
3500-3699 ... 19134
3701-3797 ... 19124
3799-4399 ... 19124
Kallaste Dr ... 19116
Kalos St ... 19128
Kane Rd ... 19154
Karen St ... 19114
Kater St
300-1399 ... 19147
1400-1498 ... 19146
1500-2299 ... 19146
Kauffman St ... 19147
Kayford Cir ... 19114
Keely Ct, Pl & St ... 19128
Keiffer St ... 19128
Keim St ... 19134
Kelanins St ... 19119
Kelly Dr ... 19129
Kelvin Ave ... 19116
Kemble Ave
5700-5899 ... 19141
5900-5999 ... 19138
Kendrick Pl ... 19111
Kendrick St
500-798 ... 19111
800-999 ... 19111
1700-1899 ... 19152
4001-4397 ... 19136
4399-4699 ... 19136
Kenilworth Ave
200-299 ... 19120
700-799 ... 19126
Kenilworth St
100-900 ... 19147
902-1298 ... 19147
1400-1498 ... 19146
Kenmore Rd ... 19151
Kennedy Ct ... 19124
Kennedy St
1300-2199 ... 19124
2200-2299 ... 19137
Kenny Rd ... 19154
Kensington Ave
2400-2699 ... 19125
2700-3699 ... 19134
3700-4200 ... 19124
4202-4298 ... 19124
Kent Ln ... 19115
Kentwood St ... 19116
Kenwyn St ... 19124
Kerbaugh St ... 19140
Kern St ... 19125
Kerper St ... 19111
Kershaw St
4900-5399 ... 19131
6000-6099 ... 19151
S Keswick Cir ... 19114
S Keswick Plz ... 19114
E Keswick Rd
10200-10299 ... 19114
10700-10748 ... 19154
10750-11099 ... 19154
S Keswick Rd ... 19114
W Keswick Rd ... 19114
S Keswick Ter ... 19114
Kevin Ct ... 19116
Keyser St ... 19144
Keystone St
5700-5798 ... 19135
5800-7299 ... 19135
7300-7399 ... 19136
9200-9399 ... 19114
Kilburn Rd ... 19114
Kimball St
600-999 ... 19147
1001-1299 ... 19147
1900-2599 ... 19146
Kimberly Dr ... 19151
Kindred St ... 19149
W King St ... 19144
King Arthur Rd ... 19116
Kingfield Rd ... 19115
Kinglet Pl ... 19153
Kings Pl ... 19122
Kings Oak Ln ... 19115
Kingsessing Ave
4500-5999 ... 19143
6000-6999 ... 19142
Kingsley St
100-199 ... 19127
300-699 ... 19128
W Kingsley St ... 19144
Kingston St ... 19134
Kinsdale St ... 19126
Kinsey St ... 19124
Kip St ... 19134
Kipling Ln & Pl ... 19154
Kirby Dr ... 19154
Kirkbride St ... 19137
Kirkwood Rd ... 19114
Kirwyn Pl N & S ... 19145
Kismet Rd ... 19115
Kitchens Ln ... 19119
Kitty Hawk Ave ... 19112
Knights Pl ... 19154
Knights Rd
10500-10800 ... 19114
10801-10857 ... 19154
10859-12700 ... 19154
12702-12798 ... 19154
Knights Ter ... 19154
Knorr Ct ... 19135
Knorr St
400-1499 ... 19111
2001-2097 ... 19149
2099-3399 ... 19149
4101-4413 ... 19135
4415-5028 ... 19135
5030-5098 ... 19135
Knox St ... 19144
Kohl St ... 19115
Konrad Pl ... 19116
Kovats Dr ... 19116
Krail St ... 19129
Krams Ave
100-239 ... 19127
241-241 ... 19127
242-499 ... 19128
Kraydor St ... 19136
Krewstown Rd ... 19115
Kubach Rd ... 19116
Kyle Rd ... 19154
L St
3600-3698 ... 19134
3700-4399 ... 19124
Lackland Dr, Pl & Ter ... 19114
Lafayette Pl ... 19122
Lafayette St ... 19129
Laird St ... 19139
Lakeside Ave ... 19126
Lamar Pl ... 19154
N Lambert St
100-199 ... 19103
1400-2199 ... 19121
2200-3399 ... 19132
5700-6599 ... 19138
S Lambert St
1300-1599 ... 19146
1900-2599 ... 19145
Lancaster Ave
3201-3397 ... 19104
3399-4499 ... 19104
4500-5899 ... 19131
5901-5997 ... 19151
5999-6399 ... 19151
Lancelot Pl ... 19154
Landis St ... 19124
Lanett Rd ... 19154
Langdon St
4800-5599 ... 19124
5900-5999 ... 19149
6201-6297 ... 19111
6299-7999 ... 19111
8000-8400 ... 19152
8402-8498 ... 19152
Langley Ave ... 19112
Lanier Ct ... 19145
Lankenau Ave & Rd ... 19131
Lansdowne Ave
5300-5899 ... 19131
5900-6900 ... 19151
6902-7798 ... 19151
Lansford St ... 19114
Lansing St
900-1999 ... 19111
2000-2299 ... 19152
3300-4799 ... 19136
Lantern Ln ... 19128
Lantern Sq ... 19107
Lanvale Pl ... 19145
Lapsley Way ... 19139
Lapwing Pl ... 19153
Laramie Pl & Rd ... 19115
Larchwood Ave
4300-4499 ... 19104
4500-6299 ... 19143
Lardner St
200-299 ... 19111
301-457 ... 19111
1400-2999 ... 19149
4525-4599 ... 19135
Lardner Ter ... 19111
Lare St ... 19128
Large St
4600-5400 ... 19124
5402-5498 ... 19124
5500-5998 ... 19149
6000-7299 ... 19149
7400-7698 ... 19152
7700-8200 ... 19152
8202-8498 ... 19152
Lark Pl ... 19153
Larkspur Pl & St ... 19116
S Larry St ... 19142
Larue St
2000-2199 ... 19124
2200-2299 ... 19137
Latimer St
900-999 ... 19107
1001-1199 ... 19107
1500-1598 ... 19102
1600-2099 ... 19103
2101-2299 ... 19103
Latona St
700-1299 ... 19147
1301-1399 ... 19147
1501-1597 ... 19146
1599-3299 ... 19146
5900-6099 ... 19143
Laughlin Ln ... 19118
Laura Ln ... 19116
E & W Laurel St ... 19123
Laurens St ... 19144
Laurie Ln ... 19115
Lauriston St ... 19128
Laveer St
200-299 ... 19120
1900-1999 ... 19141
2000-2098 ... 19138
2100-2199 ... 19138
Lavender Pl ... 19154
Lavender St ... 19114
Lawler Pl, St & Ter ... 19116
Lawn St ... 19128
Lawnbrook Rd ... 19154
Lawndale Ave ... 19111
Lawndale St
3800-4399 ... 19124
5900-5999 ... 19120
Lawnside Rd ... 19154
Lawnton Ave
6300-6399 ... 19141
6400-6999 ... 19126
Lawnton St ... 19128
Lawrence Ct ... 19106
N Lawrence St
200-399 ... 19106
500-1099 ... 19123
1200-1298 ... 19122
1300-2099 ... 19122
2200-3099 ... 19133
3300-4500 ... 19140
4502-4598 ... 19140
4700-6299 ... 19120
6600-6799 ... 19126
S Lawrence St
800-1298 ... 19147
1300-1399 ... 19147
1600-3699 ... 19148
Layton Rd ... 19115
League Pl ... 19147
League St
100-999 ... 19147
1901-2299 ... 19146
League Island Blvd ... 19112
Lebanon Ave
5100-5800 ... 19131
5802-5898 ... 19131
6100-6799 ... 19151
N Lee St
1100-1199 ... 19123
2400-2599 ... 19125
2800-3599 ... 19134
4500-4599 ... 19120
S Lee St ... 19148
Leeds St ... 19151
Lefevre St ... 19137
Legion Pl ... 19154
Legion St
9400-9698 ... 19114
9700-9800 ... 19114
9802-9898 ... 19114
12000-12099 ... 19154
E Lehigh Ave ... 19125
W Lehigh Ave
100-1299 ... 19133
1300-3499 ... 19132
3501-3501 ... 19132
Lehman Ln ... 19144
Leidy Ave ... 19104
Leiper St ... 19124
N Leithgow St
800-1099 ... 19123
1200-2035 ... 19122
2037-2199 ... 19122
2200-3099 ... 19133
4800-5999 ... 19120
S Leithgow St
200-298 ... 19106
500-899 ... 19147
901-1399 ... 19147
Leland St ... 19130
Lemon St ... 19123
Lemonte St ... 19128
Lena St ... 19144
Lenape Rd ... 19131
Lenola St ... 19136
Lenox Ave ... 19140
Lensen St
6100-6199 ... 19144
6400-6499 ... 19119
Leon St
7700-7898 ... 19136
7900-8299 ... 19136
9200-9599 ... 19114
9601-9699 ... 19114
Leonard St
5700-7299 ... 19149
7600-8999 ... 19152
Leopard St
1100-1199 ... 19123
1200-1299 ... 19125
Leroy St ... 19128
Lesher St ... 19124
Lester Pl & Rd ... 19154
S Letitia St ... 19106
E Letterly St ... 19125
W Letterly St ... 19132
Levering St
100-112 ... 19127
114-189 ... 19127
191-199 ... 19127
200-299 ... 19128
Leverington Ave
1-276 ... 19127
278-284 ... 19127
286-298 ... 19128
300-699 ... 19128
Levick St
200-1399 ... 19111
1400-3199 ... 19149
4000-4098 ... 19135
4100-5000 ... 19135
5002-5198 ... 19135
Lewin Pl ... 19136
Lewis St
1600-1699 ... 19124
13001-13007 ... 19116
13009-13099 ... 19116
13101-13199 ... 19116
N Lex St ... 19104
Lexington Ave ... 19152
Leyte Pl ... 19145
Liacouras Walk ... 19122
Liberty Ln ... 19116
Lidia Pl ... 19142
Lilac Ln ... 19136
Lima St ... 19120
Limekiln Pike
6001-6097 ... 19141
6099-6299 ... 19141
6300-7499 ... 19138
7500-7899 ... 19150
7901-7999 ... 19150
Lincoln Dr
200-299 ... 19144
6500-7299 ... 19119
7600-7698 ... 19118
7700-8100 ... 19118
8102-8198 ... 19118
Lincoln Financial Field
Way ... 19148
Linda Pl ... 19111
Lindbergh Blvd
7500A-7500A ... 19153
5300-5899 ... 19143
5901-5999 ... 19143
6000-6999 ... 19142
7000-7399 ... 19153
7401-8699 ... 19153
7500-7598 ... 19176
7650-8698 ... 19153
Linden Ave ... 19114
Linden Pl ... 19144
Linden Ter ... 19144
Lindenhurst St ... 19116
N Lindenwood St
1-199 ... 19139
1600-1799 ... 19131
S Lindenwood St ... 19143
Lindley Ave
200-711 ... 19120
713-799 ... 19120
801-897 ... 19141
899-1600 ... 19141
1602-1898 ... 19141
Lindsay St ... 19116
Linmore Ave
4500-5599 ... 19143
6301-6497 ... 19142
6499-6899 ... 19142
6901-6999 ... 19142
Linn St ... 19147
Linton St ... 19120
E Lippincott St ... 19134
W Lippincott St
100-299 ... 19133
1300-3499 ... 19132
Lister St ... 19152
Litchfield St ... 19143
Little Sigel St ... 19148
Livezey Ln
700-799 ... 19128
1000-1100 ... 19119
1102-1198 ... 19119
Livezey St
300-599 ... 19128
3300-3398 ... 19154
Livingston St
401-797 ... 19125
799-2699 ... 19125
2700-3699 ... 19134
4400-4499 ... 19137
4498 1/2-4498 1/2 ... 19137
Lloyd Ct ... 19142
S Lloyd St
2100-2198 ... 19142
2200-2599 ... 19142
2600-2699 ... 19153
Lochwood Rd ... 19115
Lock St ... 19127
Lockart Ct, Ln, Pl, Plz,
Rd & Ter ... 19116
E Locust Ave
400-799 ... 19144
800-999 ... 19138
Locust St
200-278 ... 19106
280-799 ... 19106
800-1325 ... 19107
1327-1399 ... 19107
1401-1531 ... 19102
1533-1601 ... 19102
1600-1600 ... 19103
1602-2401 ... 19103
2403-2429 ... 19103
4000-4000 ... 19104
4002-4499 ... 19104
4500-6199 ... 19139
Locust Walk ... 19104
Lodge Rd ... 19128
Lofty St ... 19128
Logan Ct ... 19103
Logan Sq ... 19103
Logan St ... 19141
E Logan St ... 19144
W Logan St ... 19144
Lombard St
100-1399 ... 19147
1400-2599 ... 19146
2601-2699 ... 19146
Lomond Ln ... 19128
London Rd ... 19116
Loney St
200-1999 ... 19111
2000-2400 ... 19152
2402-2798 ... 19152
Longford St ... 19136
Longmead Ln ... 19115
Longshore Ave
201-297 ... 19111
299-1499 ... 19111
1500-3399 ... 19149
3401-3401 ... 19149
4100-5026 ... 19135
5028-5098 ... 19135
Longspur Pl ... 19153
Loretto Ave
7525A-7525B ... 19111
5001-5597 ... 19124
5599-5799 ... 19124
5850-5898 ... 19149
5900-6199 ... 19149
6208-6398 ... 19111
6400-7999 ... 19111
8016-8298 ... 19152
8301-8499 ... 19152
Loring St ... 19136
Lorna Dr ... 19111
Lorraine St ... 19116
Lorry Pl ... 19114
Lothian Pl ... 19128
Lott St ... 19115
Lotus Rd ... 19151
E Louden St ... 19120
W Louden St
100-599 ... 19120
1001-1097 ... 19141
1099-1699 ... 19141
Louis Ct ... 19114
Louise Rd ... 19138
Lovatt Ter ... 19111
Lowber Ave ... 19150
Lowber St ... 19138
N Lowber St ... 19104
Loxley Ct ... 19106
Luce Ct ... 19112
Ludlow St
901-999 ... 19107
1100-1298 ... 19107
1800-2098 ... 19103

3800-3898 19104
3900-4499 19104
4501-4997 19139
4999-6299 19139
Lukens St 19116
E Luray St 19120
W Luray St 19140
Luther Pl 19153
E Luzerne St
101-197 19124
199-1599 19124
1601-1699 19124
2700-2799 19137
W Luzerne St 19140
Lyceum Ave 19128
E Lycoming St 19124
W Lycoming St 19140
Lykens Ln 19128
Lyman Dr 19114
Lynford St 19149
Lynnebrook Ln 19118
Lynnewood Rd 19150
Lyons Ave & Pl 19153
M St 19124
Macalester St 19124
Macdonough Ct 19112
Macon St 19152
Madison Ave 19153
Madison Pl 19153
Madison Sq 19146
E Madison St 19134
W Madison St 19140
Magdalena St 19128
Magee Ave
300-1499 19111
1500-2098 19149
2100-3299 19149
4000-4999 19135
Magnolia Pl 19115
Magnolia St
501-5297 19144
5299-6399 19144
6401-6497 19119
6499-6599 19119
Maiden Ln 19145
Maiden St 19127
Main St 19127
Malcolm St 19143
Mallard Pl 19153
Mallory St 19127
Malta St
3300-3599 19134
4200-4499 19124
5900-5999 19120
Malvern Ave
5700-5999 19131
6301-6397 19151
6399-7499 19151
7501-7699 19151
Manatawna Ave 19128
Manayunk Ave 19128
Manchester Ave 19152
Mandela Way 19139
W Manheim St 19144
Manning St
700-798 19106
900-1114 19107
1116-1298 19107
1700-1918 19103
1920-2499 19103
5901-5999 19139
Manning Walk 19106
Manor St 19128
Mansfield Ave
7200-7299 19138
8000-8519 19150
8521-8699 19150
Mansion St 19127
Manti St 19128
Manton St
100-799 19147
1500-2699 19146
Mantua Ave 19104
Maple Ave 19116
Maple Ln 19124
Maplewood Ave & Mall 19144
Marcella St 19124
Marchman Rd 19115
Marcy Pl 19115
Margaret Pl 19124
Margaret St
1600-2199 19124
2200-2316 19137
2318-2344 19137
Marigold Ln 19116
Marigold Pl 19136
Mario Lanza Blvd 19153
Marion Ln 19119
Marion St 19144
Maris St 19128
Marita St 19116
Mark Pl 19115
Market Sq 19144
Market St
100-799 19106
800-899 19107
900-900 19105
900-1398 19107
901-1399 19107
1500-1512 19102
1514-1521 19102
1523-1525 19102
1600-2400 19103
2402-2498 19103
2955-2967 19104
2969-4400 19104
4402-4498 19104
4500-6299 19139
3711-37-3711-37 19104
Markland St 19124
Markle St
101-157 19127
159-171 19127
173-177 19127
179-183 19128
185-699 19128
N Markoe St
701-797 19139
799-899 19139
900-999 19131
S Markoe St 19143
Marlborough St 19125
Marley Rd 19124
Marlowe St 19124
Marlton Ave 19104
Marlyn Rd 19151
Marple Dr 19115
Marple St 19136
Mars Pl 19153
Marsden St
5300-5398 19124
5400-5499 19124
6100-7299 19135
7900-8799 19136
9200-9399 19114
Marshall Ct 19123
Marshall St 19114
N Marshall St
600-1099 19123
1200-1298 19122
1300-2199 19122
2200-2298 19133
2300-3030 19133
3032-3040 19133
3200-4499 19140
4701-4797 19120
4799-6199 19120
S Marshall St
700-1599 19147
2300-2899 19148
Marstan Rd 19118
Marston Ct 19121
N Marston St
1300-2199 19121
2400-3199 19132
3200-3299 19129
3301-3399 19129
S Marston St
1400-1599 19146
1600-1699 19145
Marston Ter 19145
Martha St
2000-2699 19125
2701-2753 19134
2755-3100 19134
3102-3198 19134
Martin St 19128
S Martin St 19146
Martin Luther King Dr 19104
Martindale St 19136
Martins Mill Rd 19111
N Marvine St
700-999 19123
2001-2097 19122
2099-2199 19122
2700-3099 19133
3500-4699 19140
4700-6099 19141
S Marvine St
700-799 19147
2700-2899 19148
Marwood Rd E 19120
N Mascher St
3226A-3226F 19140
Masland St 19115
S Massey St 19142
Master St
4900-4998 19131
5000-5899 19131
5900-5998 19151
6000-6200 19151
6202-6298 19151
W Master St
100-1299 19122
1400-3199 19121
Mather St 19115
Matthews St
5500-5699 19138
6400-6499 19119
Matthias St 19128
Maureen Dr 19154
Maxwell Pl 19152
Maxwell St
2500-2699 19152
2700-2899 19136
May Ct 19139
N May Pl 19139
N May St 19139
S May St 19143
Mayfair St
600-699 19120
700-799 19124
E Mayfield St 19134
W Mayfield St
200-699 19133
1400-2499 19132
Mayland St 19138
E Mayland St
100-599 19144
1500-1999 19138
Maywood St 19124
Mccallum St
5900-6399 19144
6600-7399 19119
7501-7509 19118
7511-7799 19118
Mccarthy Cir 19154
Mcclellan St
100-1399 19148
1700-2399 19145
Mcferran St 19140
Mckean Ave 19144
Mckean St
100-1399 19148
1400-1498 19145
1500-2800 19145
2802-2998 19145
Mckinley St
501-527 19111
529-1399 19111
1400-3099 19149
4400-4699 19135
Mcmahon St 19144
Mcmenamy St 19136
Mcmichael St 19129
Mcnulty Rd 19154
E Mcpherson St
1-99 19119
900-1699 19150
E & W Meade St 19118
Meadow Ln 19154
Meadow St 19124
Meadow Lark Pl 19153
Meadowbrook Ave 19118
Meadowbrook Dr 19111
Meanchea St 19139
Mebus St 19124
E Mechanic St 19144
Mechanicsville Pl & Rd 19154
Medary Ave
600-799 19126
1000-1999 19141
2000-2199 19138
W Medary Ave 19120
Medford Pl & Rd 19154
Media St
5100-5298 19131
5300-5799 19131
5801-5899 19131
5927-5997 19151
5999-6600 19151
6602-6798 19151
Medina St 19147
Medrick Pl 19153
Medway Rd 19115
E Meehan Ave 19119
Meetinghouse Rd
2701-2797 19114
3000-3098 19154
Megargee St
1700-1899 19152
4300-4399 19136
4401-4699 19136
Melite Pl 19115
Melon St
1100-1398 19123
1401-1497 19130
1499-1600 19130
1602-1798 19130
3300-3598 19104
3600-3999 19104
4701-4799 19139
Melon Ter 19123
Melrose St
4301-4497 19124
4499-4599 19124
4600-4799 19137
7300-7344 19136
7346-7399 19136
9200-9399 19114
Melvale St
100-198 19125
3101-3397 19134
3399-3499 19134
4700-4798 19137
S Melville St
200-299 19139
500-1399 19143
Melvin St 19131
Memorial Ave 19104
Memphis St
400-2699 19125
2800-3292 19134
3294-3398 19134
E Mentor St 19120
W Mentor St
200-499 19120
1300-1598 19141
1600-1699 19141
Mercer St
200-2699 19125
2700-3600 19134
3602-3698 19134
4500-4799 19137
Mercury Pl 19153
Mercy St
100-1299 19148
2000-2099 19145
Meredith St
2400-2599 19130
4601-4699 19139
Merganser Pl 19153
Meridian St 19136
Merion Ave 19131
Merlin Pl & Rd 19116
E & W Mermaid Ln 19118
Merribrook Ln 19151
Merrick Rd 19129
Merrick St 19128
Mershon St 19149
Messina Way 19145
Meyer Pl 19114
Michael Rd 19152
Michelle Dr 19116
Michener Ave 19150
Michener St 19115
Midas Pl 19153
Middleton St 19138
Midland Ave 19136
Midvale Ave 19129
W Midvale Ave 19144
Mifflin St
1-97 19148
99-1399 19148
1500-3199 19145
S Milan St 19153
Milano Dr 19145
S Mildred St
700-1299 19147
1301-1499 19147
2000-2899 19148
Milford St 19116
Mill St 19136
Millbrook Pl & Rd 19154
Miller St
400-2699 19125
2800-3699 19134
4300-4498 19137
4500-4599 19137
Millett St 19136
N Millick St 19139
S Millick St
1-299 19139
1200-1299 19143
2400-2599 19142
Millman Pl & St 19118
Millwood Rd 19115
W Milne St 19144
Milnor St
4300-4599 19124
4600-4699 19137
7000-7098 19135
7100-7299 19135
7300-7399 19136
9200-9699 19114
Milton St
6300-6399 19138
6400-6899 19119
W Mimi Cir 19131
Minden Rd 19154
Minerva St 19128
S Minesti St 19148
Mingo Ave 19153
Mintines St 19144
Miriam Rd 19124
Mitchell St 19128
Modena Dr, Pl & Ter 19154
Mohican St 19138
N Mole St
100-199 19102
2201-2397 19132
2399-2499 19132
2501-2599 19132
4500-4599 19140
S Mole St
700-1599 19146
1600-2799 19145
Mollbore Ter 19148
Monastery Ave 19128
E Monmouth St 19134
W Monmouth St 19133
Monroe St 19147
Montague St
5400-5499 19124
6000-7299 19135
8000-8099 19136
E Montana St 19119
E Montgomery Ave 19125
W Montgomery Ave
100-1399 19122
1500-1598 19121
1600-3299 19121
5200-5499 19131
6300-6398 19151
Montgomery Dr 19131
Montour St
2000-2098 19115
5100-5299 19124
6340-6360 19111
6362-7599 19111
9800-9999 19115
Montrose St
200-1299 19147
1400-2599 19146
5600-5899 19143
Montrose Way 19147
Monument Rd 19131
Monument St 19121
Moore St
1-97 19148
99-1399 19148
1400-3600 19145
3602-3698 19145
Moravian St 19103
Moredun Pl & Rd 19115
Morefield Pl & Rd 19115
E & W Moreland Ave & Cir 19118
Morning Glory Rd 19154
Moro St 19136
Morrell Ave 19114
Morrell Cir 19114
Morrell St 19115
Morris Ct 19112
Morris St
100-1399 19148
1400-3200 19145
3202-3898 19145
4401-4597 19144
4599-5899 19144
5901-6199 19144
E Morris St 19148
Morris Park Rd 19151
Morse St
501-521 19122
523-599 19122
1900-1999 19121
2001-3221 19121
5316-5328 19131
5330-5499 19131
Morton St
5500-6371 19144
6373-6399 19144
6400-6499 19119
N Moss St 19139
E Mount Airy Ave
1-699 19119
900-1299 19150
1301-1699 19150
W Mount Airy Ave 19119
Mount Airy Pl 19119
Mount Airy Ter 19119
E Mount Pleasant Ave
1-616 19119
618-698 19119
900-1699 19150
W Mount Pleasant Ave 19119
Mount Pleasant Dr 19121
N Mount Pleasant Pl 19119
N Mount Pleasant Rd 19119
S Mount Pleasant Rd 19119
Mount Vernon St
900-1299 19123
1301-1335 19123
1400-1598 19130
1600-2299 19130
3100-3198 19104
3200-3999 19104
Mountain Dr 19145
Mountain St
101-197 19148
199-1099 19148
1800-2399 19145
Mouthess St 19135
Mower St
1800-2799 19152
6800-7099 19119
E Moyamensing Ave
901-1599 19147
1601-1697 19148
1699-2099 19148
W Moyamensing Ave
500-598 19148
600-1399 19148
1401-1497 19145
1499-2100 19145
2102-2198 19145
Moyer St 19125
Moylan St 19144
S Muhlfeld St
2600-2699 19142
2700-2799 19153
Mulberry St
4500-5499 19124
6100-6299 19135
Mullan Ct 19112
Murdoch Rd 19150
E Murdoch Rd 19119
Murray St 19115
Murty Ln 19116
Musgrave St
5501-5697 19144
5699-6336 19144
6338-6398 19144
6400-6899 19119
Mustin St 19112
Mutter St 19140
N Mutter St
1800-1999 19122
2200-2999 19133
Myers Cir 19115
Myrtle Pl 19123
Myrtle St
400-499 19123
2200-2299 19130
N Myrtlewood St
800-899 19130
1200-1999 19121
2300-2699 19132
S Myrtlewood St 19146
Nadina Pl 19142
Nandina Ct, Ln, Pl, Plz, St, Ter & Way 19116
Nanton Dr, Pl & Ter 19154
Naomi St 19128
W Naomi St 19144
N Napa St
401-499 19104
1900-1999 19121
2400-3199 19132
S Napa St
1200-1599 19146
1600-1899 19145
Napfle Ave 19111
Napfle St 19152
Napier St 19116
Naples St 19124
Napoli Way 19145
Narcissus Rd 19154
Narragansett St 19138
E Narragansett St 19144
Narvon St 19136
Nassau Rd
5700-5799 19131
5900-6199 19151
Nassau St 19121
Nathaniel Dr 19116
National St 19135
N Natrona St
500-599 19104
1500-2199 19121
2200-3199 19132
S Natrona St 19145
Nature Rd 19154
Naudain St
100-199 19147
1401-1497 19146
1499-2699 19146
Nauldo Rd 19154
Nautilus Rd 19154
Navajo St 19118
Nectarine St
1300-1398 19123
1900-1998 19130
3900-3999 19104
Nedla Rd 19154

Nedro Ave ... 19141
W Nedro Ave
1-799 ... 19120
2003-2137 ... 19138
2139-2199 ... 19138
Nehemiah Way ... 19139
Neil Rd ... 19115
Neilson St ... 19124
Nelson St ... 19138
Neptune Ct & Rd ... 19154
Nesper St ... 19152
Nester Pl & St ... 19115
Nestling Rd ... 19154
Nestor Rd ... 19154
Netherfield Rd ... 19129
Nevada St ... 19131
W Nevada St
1000-1199 ... 19133
2500-3099 ... 19132
New Pl ... 19139
New St ... 19106
New Hope St ... 19145
New Market Sq ... 19147
New Market St ... 19123
New Queen St ... 19129
New State Rd ... 19135
Newberry Rd ... 19154
Newcomb St ... 19140
Newhall St
4100-4199 ... 19140
4600-5399 ... 19144
N Newkirk St
800-899 ... 19130
1200-2199 ... 19121
2400-2899 ... 19132
3200-3299 ... 19129
S Newkirk St
1200-1599 ... 19146
1600-2099 ... 19145
2101-2599 ... 19145
Newland St ... 19128
Newport Pl ... 19122
Newton St ... 19118
Newtown Ave
5500-5798 ... 19120
5800-5999 ... 19120
6000-6298 ... 19111
6300-6599 ... 19111
Nice St ... 19140
Nicholas Ct ... 19112
Nicholas St ... 19121
Nicklaus Dr ... 19115
Nightingale Rd ... 19154
W Nippon St ... 19119
Nittany Ln ... 19128
Nixon St ... 19128
Noble St
900-999 ... 19123
1001-1399 ... 19123
6101-6199 ... 19151
Nolan St ... 19138
Norcom Ct & Rd ... 19154
Norcross Ln ... 19114
Norfolk St ... 19143
Norman Ln ... 19118
Normandy Dr ... 19154
Norris Ct ... 19121
Norris Dr ... 19121
E Norris St ... 19125
W Norris St
100-1399 ... 19122
1400-1418 ... 19121
1420-3299 ... 19121
North St
1100-1198 ... 19123
1500-1999 ... 19130
2001-2099 ... 19130
North Ter ... 19123
Northeast Ave
9500-9999 ... 19115
10000-10300 ... 19116
10302-11498 ... 19116
Northview Rd ... 19152
Northwestern Ave ... 19128
E Northwestern Ave ... 19118
W Northwestern Ave ... 19118
Northwood St ... 19124
Norvelt Dr ... 19115
Norwalk Rd ... 19115
Norwich Dr ... 19153
Norwood Ave ... 19118
N Norwood St ... 19138
S Norwood St ... 19145
Nottingham Ln ... 19114
Novacare Way ... 19145
O St ... 19124
O Neil St ... 19123
Oak Dr ... 19136
Oak Rd ... 19118
Oak Lane Ave & Rd ... 19126
E Oakdale St ... 19125
W Oakdale St
1000-1098 ... 19133
1100-1299 ... 19133
1500-2899 ... 19132
2901-3099 ... 19132
Oakfield Ln ... 19115
Oakford St ... 19146
Oakhill Rd ... 19154
Oakland St
4400-5499 ... 19124
5800-7260 ... 19149
7262-7298 ... 19149
Oakley St ... 19111
Oakmont St
900-1899 ... 19111
2000-2399 ... 19152
3300-4799 ... 19136
Obrien Ct ... 19112
Ogden Pl ... 19123
Ogden St
1000-1399 ... 19123
1500-2999 ... 19130
3900-4235 ... 19104
4237-4399 ... 19104
4500-5399 ... 19139
Ogle St ... 19127
Ogontz Ave
5000-5498 ... 19141
5500-6399 ... 19141
6400-6799 ... 19126
6800-7499 ... 19138
7500-8099 ... 19150
8101-8199 ... 19150
Old 2nd St ... 19120
Old Ashton Rd ... 19152
Old Bridge Rd ... 19129
Old Bustleton Ave ... 19115
Old Farm Rd ... 19115
Old Lindbergh Blvd ... 19153
Old Line Rd ... 19128
Old Newtown Rd ... 19115
Old York Rd
3301-3397 ... 19140
3399-4699 ... 19140
4700-6399 ... 19141
6401-6597 ... 19126
6599-7200 ... 19126
7202-7298 ... 19126
Olive Pl ... 19123
Olive St
101-397 ... 19123
399-499 ... 19123
1600-2499 ... 19130
2501-2599 ... 19130
3600-4299 ... 19104
4800-4999 ... 19139
E Olney Ave ... 19120
W Olney Ave
100-899 ... 19120
900-1999 ... 19141
2100-2198 ... 19144
Olympia Pl ... 19145
Olympus Pl ... 19153
E Ontario St ... 19134
W Ontario St ... 19140
N Opal St
800-899 ... 19130
2300-2899 ... 19132
5900-6000 ... 19141
6002-6398 ... 19141
6600-6699 ... 19138
S Opal St
1300-1599 ... 19146
2000-2499 ... 19145
Orange St ... 19125
Orchard Ln ... 19154
Orchard St ... 19124
E Oregon Ave ... 19148
W Oregon Ave
100-108 ... 19148
110-1229 ... 19148
1231-1399 ... 19148
1400-2400 ... 19145
2402-2498 ... 19145
N Orianna St
101-199 ... 19106
500-1199 ... 19123
1210-1298 ... 19122
1300-2199 ... 19122
2200-3099 ... 19133
3400-4499 ... 19140
S Orianna St
600-1499 ... 19147
1700-1899 ... 19148
Oriole St ... 19128
Orion Rd ... 19154
N Orkney St
700-1099 ... 19123
1400-2102 ... 19122
2104-2198 ... 19122
2200-3099 ... 19133
3300-3399 ... 19140
S Orkney St ... 19148
Orland St ... 19126
E Orleans St ... 19134
W Orleans St ... 19133
Ormes St
2800-3499 ... 19134
4900-5699 ... 19120
Ormond St ... 19124
Orpheus Pl ... 19153
Orthodox St
900-2199 ... 19124
2200-3199 ... 19137
3201-3299 ... 19137
Orwell Rd ... 19119
Osage Ave
4200-4499 ... 19104
4500-6299 ... 19143
Osborn St ... 19128
Osceola St ... 19144
Osmond St ... 19129
Otter St ... 19104
Outlook Ave ... 19114
Overbrook Ave
4400-6099 ... 19131
6300-7599 ... 19151
7601-7799 ... 19151
Overhill Ave ... 19116
Overington St
1100-1599 ... 19124
2800-2899 ... 19137
Overlook Rd ... 19128
Oxford Ave
6010A-6010B ... 19149
4700-5499 ... 19124
5700-5999 ... 19149
6000-6098 ... 19111
6001-6061 ... 19149
6100-8099 ... 19111
8101-8199 ... 19111
E Oxford St ... 19125
W Oxford St
100-1299 ... 19122
1402-1414 ... 19121
1416-3299 ... 19121
5200-5600 ... 19131
5602-5798 ... 19131
5900-6199 ... 19151
E Pacific St ... 19134
W Pacific St ... 19140
Packer Ave
2-298 ... 19148
300-700 ... 19148
702-998 ... 19148
1500-1899 ... 19145
Packer Ter ... 19145
Page St ... 19121
Palairet Rd ... 19128
Palermo Dr ... 19145
N Palethorp St
1200-2199 ... 19122
2200-2999 ... 19133
3001-3199 ... 19133
3300-3600 ... 19140
3602-4698 ... 19140
4800-6299 ... 19120
Palisades Dr ... 19129
N Pallas St ... 19104
N Palm St ... 19104
Palmer Dr ... 19115
E Palmer St ... 19125
W Palmer St ... 19122
Palmetto St
3400-3599 ... 19134
3800-4399 ... 19124
5900-5999 ... 19120
6000-8099 ... 19111
Panama Mall ... 19103
Panama St
600-698 ... 19106
1200-1208 ... 19107
1210-1299 ... 19107
1700-2520 ... 19103
2522-2598 ... 19103
Pandrail Pl ... 19116
Paoli Ave ... 19128
Par Dr ... 19115
N Park Ave
800-899 ... 19123
1600-1698 ... 19122
2200-3199 ... 19132
3200-4299 ... 19140
5501-5697 ... 19141
5699-6399 ... 19141
6400-6599 ... 19126
S Park Ave ... 19147
W Park Ln ... 19144
Park Pl ... 19136
Park Ter ... 19128
Park Line Dr ... 19119
Parkdale Rd ... 19154
Parker Ave ... 19128
Parkhollow Ln ... 19111
Parkside Ave
4000-4100 ... 19104
4102-4398 ... 19104
4301-4697 ... 19131
4699-5200 ... 19131
5202-5298 ... 19131
4801-4999 ... 19131
Parkview Ave ... 19119
Parkview Rd ... 19154
Parkwood Ln ... 19128
Parkwyn Rd ... 19131
Parlin Pl, St & Ter ... 19116
Parma Rd ... 19131
Parnell Pl ... 19144
Parrish St
500-1399 ... 19123
1400-2799 ... 19130
2801-2899 ... 19130
3800-3898 ... 19104
3900-4499 ... 19104
4501-4597 ... 19139
4599-5399 ... 19139
Paschall Ave
4600-5599 ... 19143
5601-5699 ... 19143
6200-6298 ... 19142
6300-7299 ... 19142
Passmore St
200-1399 ... 19111
2900-2957 ... 19149
2959-2999 ... 19149
4001-4097 ... 19135
4099-4299 ... 19135
Passyunk Ave
6000-6599 ... 19153
7000-7399 ... 19142
E Passyunk Ave
601-697 ... 19147
699-1599 ... 19147
1600-1999 ... 19148
1352-56-1352-56 ... 19147
W Passyunk Ave ... 19145
E Pastorius St
1-199 ... 19144
1500-1899 ... 19138
W Pastorius St ... 19144
Pathestr Ave ... 19153
Patrician Dr ... 19154
Patrick Henry Pl ... 19122
Patrol Rd ... 19112
Pattison Ave
1-800 ... 19148
802-1098 ... 19148
1700-2000 ... 19145
2002-2098 ... 19145
Pattison Ter ... 19145
N Patton St
1600-1898 ... 19121
1900-1999 ... 19121
2400-3199 ... 19132
S Patton St ... 19146
Paul St ... 19124
Pawling St ... 19128
Pawnee Ave ... 19112
N Paxon St
1-299 ... 19139
500-1799 ... 19131
S Paxon St ... 19143
N Peach St
1-299 ... 19139
600-1799 ... 19131
S Peach St
100-199 ... 19139
1100-1299 ... 19143
Peach Ter ... 19143
Peach Tree Ln ... 19111
Pear St ... 19124
Pearce St
4200-4599 ... 19124
4601-4699 ... 19137
Pearl St
3200-3699 ... 19104
3701-3899 ... 19104
5400-5498 ... 19139
5500-6499 ... 19139
Pearson Ave ... 19114
Pearson St ... 19115
Pecan Dr ... 19115
Pechin St ... 19128
Pedley Rd ... 19128
Pedrick Rd ... 19154
Pelham Rd ... 19119
Pelle Cir ... 19154
Peltz St ... 19146
Pemberton St
100-799 ... 19147
1400-2399 ... 19146
5500-5899 ... 19143
Pembrook Rd ... 19128
Penfield St
1800-1899 ... 19126
1900-1999 ... 19138
Penn Blvd ... 19144
Penn Ctr ... 19102
Penn Sq E
1-2 ... 19107
100-100 ... 19107
S Penn Sq
1-3 ... 19107
1400-1498 ... 19102
Penn St
4200-5300 ... 19124
5302-5334 ... 19124
5800-5999 ... 19149
E Penn St ... 19144
N Penn St ... 19123
W Penn St
16-22 ... 19144
24-499 ... 19144
3100-3499 ... 19129
Pennhurst St
3500-3599 ... 19134
4500-4699 ... 19124
Pennington Rd ... 19151
N Pennock St
700-899 ... 19130
1201-1299 ... 19121
3100-3199 ... 19132
Penns Ct ... 19144
Penns Lndg S ... 19147
Pennsgrove St
3800-4399 ... 19104
5200-5427 ... 19131
5429-5499 ... 19131
Pennsylvania Ave ... 19130
Pennway St
4900-5299 ... 19124
7101-7299 ... 19111
7400-7412 ... 19111
Pennwood Rd ... 19151
Penny Ln ... 19111
Pennypack St ... 19136
Penrose Ave
2000-3411 ... 19145
3413-3499 ... 19145
7800-8000 ... 19153
8002-8098 ... 19153
Penrose Dr ... 19145
Penrose Ferry Rd
3100-3298 ... 19145
3300-3399 ... 19145
7400-7416 ... 19153
7418-7998 ... 19153
Pensdale St
100-103 ... 19127
105-199 ... 19127
200-419 ... 19128
421-499 ... 19128
Pentridge St ... 19143
Pepper Ter ... 19145
Perch Ln ... 19136
Percy Pl ... 19123
N Percy St
400-998 ... 19123
1300-2098 ... 19122
2100-2199 ... 19122
3000-3199 ... 19133
3600-3999 ... 19140
S Percy St
600-1399 ... 19147
1401-1499 ... 19147
2000-2699 ... 19148
Peregrine Pl ... 19153
Perkiomen St ... 19130
Perot St ... 19130
Perrin Rd ... 19154
Perry Ct ... 19112
Perth Pl ... 19123
N Perth St ... 19122
S Perth St ... 19147
Peters St ... 19147
Peyton St ... 19116
Pheasant Dr ... 19136
Pheasant Hill Dr ... 19115
E Phil Ellena St
1-97 ... 19119
99-899 ... 19119
900-1199 ... 19150
W Phil Ellena St ... 19119
Phila Intl Airport ... 19153
Phila Naval Base ... 19112
Phila Naval Business
Ctr ... 19112
Phila Naval Shipyard ... 19112
Philcrest Rd ... 19154
Philip Pl ... 19106
N Philip St
601-699 ... 19123
1400-2199 ... 19122
2201-2397 ... 19133
2399-3099 ... 19133
3200-3599 ... 19140
3601-4499 ... 19140
5800-6099 ... 19120
S Philip St
300-399 ... 19106
501-697 ... 19147
699-1499 ... 19147
1701-1997 ... 19148
1999-2599 ... 19148
Phillips Ter ... 19153
Philmont Ave, Pl &
Ter ... 19116
Phoebe Pl ... 19153
Pickering St ... 19150
Pickwick St ... 19134
Pier ... 19106
Pierce Dr ... 19145
Pierce St
100-1299 ... 19148
1700-2400 ... 19145
2402-2798 ... 19145
Piermont St ... 19116
N Piers ... 19123
Pietro Way ... 19145
Pigs Aly ... 19130
E Pike St ... 19124
W Pike St ... 19140
Pilgrim Ln ... 19114
Pilling St ... 19124
Pine Pl W ... 19115
Pine Rd
1620-1620 ... 19115
8000-8008 ... 19111
8010-8499 ... 19111
8501-8699 ... 19111
8970-8998 ... 19115
9000-9699 ... 19115
9701-9701 ... 19115
Pine St
99-799 ... 19106
800-898 ... 19107
900-1338 ... 19107
1340-1398 ... 19107
1400-1599 ... 19102
1600-2699 ... 19103
3900-4431 ... 19104
4433-4499 ... 19104
4500-6299 ... 19143
Pine Hill Ave ... 19115
Pine Valley Blvd ... 19111
Pinewood Pl & Rd ... 19116
Pitt Pl ... 19114
Pittville Ave ... 19126
Placid St
1600-1899 ... 19152
4000-4098 ... 19136
Plainfield St ... 19150
Plane Rd ... 19115
Player Dr ... 19115
N, S & E Pleasant Pl &
St ... 19119
N Plenw St ... 19120
Plover St ... 19153
Plum St
1700-2033 ... 19124
2035-2099 ... 19124
2700-2899 ... 19137
Plymouth St
1700-1899 ... 19126
1900-1999 ... 19138
Pocasset Rd ... 19115
Pocono St ... 19118
Point Breeze Ave
1200-1500 ... 19146
1502-1598 ... 19146
1600-2099 ... 19145
2101-2299 ... 19145
Pollard St ... 19123
Pollock St & Ter ... 19145
E & W Pomona St ... 19144
Pompey Pl ... 19153
Pontiac Ave ... 19153
Poplar Ct ... 19131
Poplar St
1-97 ... 19123
99-1399 ... 19123
1420-3099 ... 19130
3800-4199 ... 19104
5300-5498 ... 19131
5500-5799 ... 19131
Poppy Dr ... 19136
Poquessing Ave ... 19116
Poquessing Creek Dr &
Ln ... 19116
Port Royal Ave ... 19128
Porter Ave ... 19112
E Porter St ... 19148
W Porter St
100-1399 ... 19148
1400-2800 ... 19145
2802-2898 ... 19145
Portico St ... 19144

Portis Rd 19115
Potter St
2500-2699 19125
3000-3399 19134
4001-4297 19124
4299-4399 19124
Potterton Hts 19144
Potts St 19123
Powelton Ave 19104
Powers St 19129
Pratt St
700-798 19124
800-2189 19124
2191-2199 19124
2200-2899 19137
Preble Ave 19112
Prelate Cir 19128
President St
1900-2099 19115
2101-2199 19115
3500-3799 19114
9900-9999 19115
Presidential Blvd 19131
N Preston St 19104
E Price St
1-799 19144
800-1399 19138
W Price St 19144
Priestly St 19116
Prima Ct 19145
Primrose Rd 19114
Prince Cir 19114
Princeton Ave
300-1499 19111
1901-2097 19149
2099-3499 19149
4000-4098 19135
4100-5199 19135
Priscilla St
3900-3999 19140
5300-5399 19144
Priventr St 19136
Proctor Pl & Rd 19116
Prospect Ave 19118
Provident Rd 19150
Pulaski Ave
3700-3900 19140
3902-4098 19140
4501-4597 19144
4599-5999 19144
Purdy St 19140
Puritan Rd 19114
Quarry St
100-198 19106
200-299 19106
5500-5598 19139
E Queen Ln 19144
W Queen Ln
2-16 19144
18-599 19144
2801-2897 19129
2899-3499 19129
Queen St 19147
Queens Ct 19147
Queens Pl 19122
Quentin St 19128
S Quince St
200-206 19107
208-399 19107
400-413 19147
415-499 19147
Quincy St 19119
Race St
100-214 19106
216-600 19106
602-700 19106
900-1399 19107
1400-1498 19102
1500-1599 19102
1700-2299 19103
2301-2399 19103
3200-3599 19104
5000-6399 19139
6401-6599 19139
Rachael St 19115
Radburn Rd 19115
Rainey Ct 19103
Rambler Rd 19154
Rambo Ter 19145
Ramer Rd 19154
Ramona Ave
700-798 19120
800-4698 19124
4700-4738 19124
4740-4798 19124
N Ramsey St 19139
Rand St 19134
Randolph Ct 19147
N Randolph St
301-399 19106
900-1099 19123
1200-2199 19122
3200-3799 19140
S Randolph St
501-1116 19147
1118-1198 19147
2700-2899 19148
2901-2999 19148
Ranier Rd 19154
Ranstead St
400-498 19106
601-699 19106
1501-1599 19102
1700-1798 19103
1800-2099 19103
2101-2399 19103
4201-4299 19104
5100-5199 19139
Raritan Rd 19112
Raven Pl 19153
Rawle St
2800-3299 19149
4700-4999 19135
Rayland Rd 19154
E Raymond St 19120
W Raymond St 19140
Reach St
3100-3499 19134
4600-5999 19120
6000-6199 19111
Rebecca Dr 19116
Rector St
1-147 19127
149-199 19127
200-699 19128
Recycling Center Drive
Way 19131
Red Lion Rd
1-67 19115
69-1100 19115
1102-2198 19115
1901-1901 19116
2001-2199 19115
2600-2698 19114
2700-3900 19114
3902-3998 19114
Redd Rambler Dr, Pl &
Ter 19115
N Redfield St
1-399 19139
400-1799 19151
2101-2199 19131
S Redfield St
1-199 19139
500-2099 19143
Redner St & Way 19121
Redwing Pl 19153
Reed St
1-1339 19147
1341-1399 19147
1400-3699 19146
Reed Bird Pl 19142
Reedland St
5700-5799 19143
6100-7099 19142
N Reese St
1801-2097 19122
2099-2199 19122
2200-2999 19133
3001-3099 19133
3200-4524 19140
S Reese St
501-997 19147
999-1399 19147
2200-2599 19148
Regatta Dr 19146
Regent Sq 19104
Regent St
4500-5599 19143
6000-6899 19142
W Reger St 19144
Regina St 19116
Reilly Rd 19115
Reinhard St
4700-4798 19143
4800-5399 19143
6000-6199 19142
Remsen Rd 19115
Rennard Cir, Pl, St &
Ter 19116
Reno Pl 19123
Reno St
301-599 19123
800-898 19123
2700-2799 19130
3800-4399 19104
4900-5199 19139
Renovo St 19138
Renz St 19128
S & W Reserve Dr 19145
Reservoir Dr 19121
Retta Ave 19128
Revere St
6200-7299 19149
7300-9199 19152
Rex Ave 19118
Rexford St 19131
Reynolds St 19137
Rhawn St
400-1999 19111
2000-2899 19152
3201-3297 19136
3299-4900 19136
4902-4998 19136
Rhett Rd 19154
Rhoads St 19151
Richard St 19152
Richmond St
100-2299 19125
2801-2897 19134
2899-3699 19134
3700-4900 19137
4902-5098 19137
Richton Rd 19154
Richwood Rd 19116
Ridarale St 19118
N Ridelins St 19126
Ridge Ave
900-999 19107
1000-1399 19123
1401-1814 19130
1815-1827 19121
1816-1828 19130
1829-3199 19121
3200-3899 19132
3901-3999 19132
4000-4006 19129
4008-4899 19129
4900-9099 19128
9101-9199 19128
Ridge Dr 19121
Ridge Pike 19128
Ridgefield Rd 19154
Ridgerun Ln 19111
Ridgeway Pl 19116
Ridgeway Plz 19116
Ridgeway St
200-399 19116
7900-8599 19111
11100-11199 19116
Ridgeway Ter 19116
Ridgewood St 19143
Ridley St 19138
Righter St 19128
N Ringgold St
700-899 19130
1200-1961 19121
1963-1999 19121
2700-3099 19132
S Ringgold St
1200-1599 19146
1600-1899 19145
Ripka St
305A-305G 19128
Ripley St
700-1999 19111
2000-2399 19152
Rising Sun Ave
400-1399 19140
1401-4699 19140
3900-3998 19120
4200-4626 19140
4700-5999 19120
6000-8599 19111
8800-9538 19115
9540-9598 19115
Rising Sun Pl 19115
Ritchie St 19127
W Ritner St
1-1300 19148
1302-1398 19148
1400-2499 19145
2501-2599 19145
Rittenhouse Sq 19103
W Rittenhouse Sq 19103
E Rittenhouse St
1-799 19144
800-2099 19138
W Rittenhouse St 19144
Ritter St 19125
W River Dr 19131
River Rd 19128
Riverhouse Rd 19114
Riverside Dr 19154
Riverview Dr 19104
Riverview Ln 19129
Roanoke St 19118
Robat St 19120
Robbins Ave
1400-3199 19149
4000-5200 19135
5202-5298 19135
Robbins St 19111
Roberts Ave
1900-1998 19140
2601-2697 19129
2699-2999 19129
W Roberts Ave 19144
Robina Pl, St & Ter 19116
N Robinson St
1-399 19139
400-1799 19151
S Robinson St
1-99 19139
2500-2999 19142
Rochelle Ave 19128
Rock St 19128
E Rockland St 19120
W Rockland St
1-99 19144
100-799 19120
900-998 19141
1000-1900 19141
1902-1950 19141
Rockwell Ave 19111
Rodman St
500-698 19147
700-1399 19147
1400-2099 19146
2101-2199 19146
5200-5899 19143
Rodney St
6800-6999 19138
8000-8399 19150
Rogers Ct 19112
Roma Dr 19145
Romain St 19124
Ronnald Dr 19154
Ronnie Cir & Ln 19128
Roosevelt Blvd
3900-5300 19124
5302-5498 19124
5800-7299 19149
7301-7397 19152
7399-8499 19152
8501-8999 19152
8800-9998 19115
9101-9899 19114
10000-11598 19116
10101-11499 19154
11501-11599 19154
11600-11698 19116
11601-12099 19154
11602-11652 19154
11700-13598 19116
9173-75-9173-75 19114
E Roosevelt Blvd 19120
W Roosevelt Blvd
100-599 19120
600-698 19140
700-1499 19140
Rorer St
2900-3399 19134
3401-3499 19134
4700-5299 19120
Rosalie St
500-699 19120
1000-1599 19149
2000-4899 19135
Rose Ln 19136
Rose Petal Dr & Way 19111
Roseberry St
100-399 19148
1801-1899 19145
Rosehill St
2800-3000 19134
3002-3498 19134
4600-5699 19120
Rosella Pl & St 19153
Roselyn St
1-499 19120
1500-1899 19141
Rosemar St 19120
Rosemary Ln 19119
N Rosewood St 19132
S Rosewood St
700-799 19146
1600-2699 19145
Ross St
6000-6399 19144
6400-6649 19119
6651-6655 19119
E Roumfort Rd
1-599 19119
900-1699 19150
Rouse Blvd 19112
Rowan St 19140
Rowena Dr 19114
Rowland Ave
6700-6799 19149
7300-7998 19136
8000-8199 19136
8201-8299 19136
Roxborough Ave
100-166 19127
168-198 19127
200-699 19128
Roy St 19140
Royal St 19144
Ruan St 19124
Rubicam St
200-299 19120
4900-5299 19144
Rubin Ln 19116
N Ruby St
1-299 19139
1700-1799 19131
S Ruby St
1-199 19139
1100-1799 19143
Ruby Ter 19143
Rudy Robinson Way 19139
Ruffner St 19140
Rugby St
7300-7499 19138
7500-8699 19150
Rupert St 19149
Rural Ln 19119
E Ruscomb St
100-698 19120
700-798 19124
W Ruscomb St
100-600 19120
602-698 19120
1001-1007 19141
1009-1900 19141
1902-1998 19141
E Rush St 19134
W Rush St
601-1197 19133
1199-1299 19133
1300-1499 19132
Ruskin Rd 19151
E Russell St 19134
W Russell St 19140
Ruth St 19134
Ruth Way 19114
Rutland St
4700-5398 19124
5400-5499 19124
6600-7299 19149
Rutledge St 19134
Ryan Ave
2600-2998 19152
3000-3100 19152
3102-3198 19152
3200-3599 19136
Ryers Ave 19111
Ryerson Pl & Rd 19114
Saber St 19140
Sackett St
6300-6398 19149
6400-6599 19149
7300-7319 19152
7321-7399 19152
Sagamore Rd 19128
Sage Ln 19128
Saint Albans St
700-798 19147
2000-2399 19146
Saint Andrews Rd 19118
N Saint Bernard St
1-99 19139
900-1299 19131
1301-2399 19131
S Saint Bernard St
200-299 19139
300-1299 19143
Saint Christopher Dr 19148
Saint Christopher Ln 19116
Saint Davids St 19127
Saint Denis Dr 19114
Saint Georges Rd 19119
Saint James Ct 19106
Saint James Pl 19106
Saint James St
1200-1299 19107
2001-2097 19103
2099-2299 19103
Saint John Neumann Pl
& Way 19123
Saint Josephs Way 19106
Saint Luke St 19140
Saint Malachys Way 19139
Saint Marks Sq 19104
Saint Martins Ln 19118
Saint Michael Dr 19148
Saint Pauls St 19140
Saint Peters Way 19106
Saint Thomas Dr 19116
Saint Vincent St
300-1499 19111
2100-2820 19149
2822-3499 19149
E Salaignac St 19128
W Salaignac St
100-150 19127
151-399 19128
Salem St 19124
Salerno Way 19145
N Salford St
1-399 19139
400-499 19151
2200-2299 19131
S Salford St
1-199 19139
500-2099 19143
Salina Pl & Rd 19154
Salmon St
401-2497 19125
2499-2699 19125
2700-3699 19134
4200-4238 19137
4240-4799 19137
4801-4999 19137
Salter St 19147
San Vincenzo Dr 19145
Sandanne Rd 19115
Sanderling Pl 19153
Sandmeyer Ln 19116
Sandpiper Pl 19153
Sandy Rd 19115
Sandyford Rd 19152
Sanford St 19116
E Sanger St
300-699 19120
800-2199 19124
Sanibel St 19116
Sansom St
601-697 19106
699-799 19106
800-1399 19107
1415-1417 19102
1419-1599 19102
1600-2399 19103
3400-4499 19104
4500-6299 19139
Sansom Walk 19106
Sarah St 19125
N Saratoga Pl 19122
Sartain Pl 19123
N Sartain St 19133
S Sartain St
200-221 19107
223-225 19107
501-599 19147
730-798 19147
1800-2699 19148
Saturn Pl 19153
Saul St
4900-5499 19124
5800-7299 19149
N Saunders Ave 19104
Saxon Pl 19114
Saxton Rd 19114
Saybrook Ave
7222A-7222B 19142
4800-5599 19143
6300-7299 19142
Scattergood St 19124
S Schell St
201-299 19107
700-999 19147
E Schiller St 19134
W Schiller St 19140
Schley St 19145
E School House Ln 19144
W School House Ln
1-97 19144
99-3100 19144
3102-3298 19144
3301-3397 19129
3399-3699 19129
3701-3799 19129
421-1-421-1 19144
Schuyler St
3701-3799 19140
4901-4997 19144
4999-5299 19144
Schuylkill Ave
600-1499 19146
1600-1700 19145
Schuylkill Falls Ln 19129
Scotchbrook Dr 19115
Scotforth Rd 19119
Scotia Rd 19128
Scott Way 19113
Scotts Ln 19129
Sears St
100-298 19147
300-899 19147
2100-3699 19146
Seashalm St 19134
Sebring Rd 19152
Secane Dr & Pl 19154
E Sedgley Ave
1100-1198 19134
1200-1399 19134
1800-1999 19124

W Sedgley Ave
201-275 19140
277-999 19140
1000-1198 19133
1001-1099 19140
1201-1299 19133
1300-2599 19132
2601-2797 19121
2799-3099 19121
W Sedgley Dr 19130
E Sedgwick St
1-699 19119
900-1099 19150
1101-1399 19150
W Sedgwick St 19119
Seffert St 19128
Sellers St
1300-1699 19124
2800-2899 19137
Selma St 19116
Selmer Pl, Plz, Rd & Ter 19116
E Seltzer St 19134
W Seltzer St
900-1299 19133
1300-2799 19132
Seminole St 19118
Sentner St 19120
Sepviva St
400-1698 19125
1700-2699 19125
3501-3597 19134
3599-3699 19134
3700-3799 19137
3801-3899 19137
4100-4598 19124
Sequoia Rd 19128
E Sergeant St 19125
W Sergeant St
200-1299 19133
1500-3399 19132
Serota Dr 19116
Serota Pl 19115
Service Dr 19104
Seville St
100-199 19127
400-699 19128
Sewell Rd 19116
Seybert Mall 19122
W Seybert St 19121
E & W Seymour St 19144
Shackamaxon St 19125
Shalkop St 19128
Shallcross St 19124
Shamokin St 19130
Shancedg Ave 19112
Sharon Ln 19115
Sharp St 19127
E Sharpnack St
1-899 19119
900-1174 19150
1176-1416 19150
W Sharpnack St 19119
Sharswood St
1900-2599 19121
5400-5499 19131
Shaw St 19128
Shawmont Ave 19128
Shawnee St 19118
Shearwater Pl 19153
E Shedaker St 19144
N Shedwick St
100-598 19104
600-799 19104
3000-3199 19104
Sheffield St 19136
Shelbourne St
3201-3497 19134
3499-3599 19134
4500-4699 19124
6101-6197 19111
6199-7399 19111
Sheldon St
4600-4799 19127
4925-5199 19144
E Sheldon St 19120
W Sheldon St 19120
Sheldrake Pl 19153
Shelly Ln 19115
Shelly Rd 19152
Shelmire Ave
501-897 19111
899-1999 19111
2000-2599 19152
3300-4799 19136
N Sheridan St
1800-1899 19122
3100-3199 19133
S Sheridan St
700-1000 19147
1002-1298 19147
2400-2899 19148
Sherman St
6300-6399 19144
6700-6798 19119
6800-7299 19119
Sherrie Rd 19115
Sherwood Rd
4400-4499 19131
4501-4599 19131
6300-7600 19151
7602-7698 19151
S Shields St 19142
Shipley Pl & Rd 19152
Shirley St 19130
Shisler St
5900-6199 19149
7300-7499 19111
Shoppers Ln 19150
W Shunk St
1-1399 19148
1400-2200 19145
2202-2298 19145
Shurs Ln
1-168 19127
170-172 19127
200-499 19128
N Sickels St
100-499 19139
600-699 19131
S Sickels St 19139
Sickle Way 19139
Siena Ct 19145
Sigel St
100-1399 19148
1700-2299 19145
E Silver St 19134
W Silver St
900-1199 19133
1201-1299 19133
1301-1325 19132
1327-2799 19132
Silverwood St
4201-4329 19127
4331-4599 19127
4600-6999 19128
7001-7599 19128
Simms St 19116
Simon St
2000-2199 19124
2200-2299 19137
Simpson Ct 19112
N Simpson St
200-399 19139
400-599 19151
S Simpson St 19142
N Sloan St 19104
E Slocum St
1-499 19119
900-1199 19150
Smedley St 19121
N Smedley St
2300-2399 19132
3300-4599 19140
4900-6299 19141
6400-6799 19126
S Smedley St
300-399 19103
700-799 19146
2700-3299 19145
Smick St 19127
Smith Walk 19104
Smithfield Ave 19116
Smylie Rd 19124
Snyder Ave
1-7 19148
9-1299 19148
1301-1337 19148
1400-2899 19145
2901-2999 19145
Solly Ave
301-397 19111
399-1199 19111
1500-2799 19152
2801-2899 19152
3301-3397 19136
3399-4699 19136
Solly Pl 19111
E Somerset St 19134
W Somerset St
101-153 19133
155-1299 19133
1300-2799 19132
2801-2899 19132
Somerton Ave 19116
E Somerville Ave 19120
W Somerville Ave
200-599 19120
1100-1300 19141
1302-1498 19141
Sommers Rd 19138
Sorrento Ct 19145
Sorrento Rd 19131
Souder St 19149
South St
100-110 19147
112-1336 19147
1338-1360 19147
1400-2799 19146
3000-3260 19104
W Southampton Ave 19118
Southampton Rd
500-2699 19116
2700-2999 19154
N Spangler St
2500-3199 19132
3200-3299 19129
Sparks St 19120
W Sparks St 19141
W Spencer St
1-499 19120
501-515 19120
900-1999 19141
2000-2199 19138
Sperry St 19152
Spicebush Ln 19115
Sprague St
5500-6399 19138
6400-7499 19119
Spring Ln 19128
Spring St
901-905 19107
907-1299 19107
2100-2198 19103
5400-6099 19139
Spring Garden St
1-1399 19123
1400-1498 19130
1500-2199 19130
2201-2299 19130
3100-4099 19104
4101-4199 19104
Springbank St 19119
E & W Springer St 19119
Springfield Ave
4500-5999 19143
6000-6099 19142
E Springfield Ave 19118
S Springfield Ave 19142
W Springfield Ave 19118
Springhouse Rd 19114
Springview Rd 19115
Spruce St
100-799 19106
800-1399 19107
1401-1497 19102
1499-1599 19102
1600-2499 19103
3301-3397 19104
3399-4499 19104
4500-6299 19139
E Stafford St
100-699 19144
800-1299 19138
W Stafford St 19144
Stamford St
2800-2899 19152
3001-3097 19136
3099-3199 19136
Stamper St 19147
Stamper Blackwell Walk 19147
N Stanley St
1900-2199 19121
2400-2699 19132
S Stanley St 19146
Stanton St 19129
Stanwood Ct 19136
Stanwood St
300-1299 19111
1600-2499 19152
2501-2799 19152
3000-3699 19136
3701-4199 19136
Stardust Ln 19136
State Rd
5001-6397 19135
6399-7299 19135
7300-9100 19136
9102-9198 19136
9200-9700 19114
9702-9798 19114
N State St 19104
States Dr 19131
Station Ln 19118
Station St 19127
Staub St 19140
Stearly St 19111
Steeple Dr 19128
Steinber St 19124
E Stella St 19134
W Stella St
100-1099 19133
2000-2199 19132
Stella Maris St 19148
Stelwood Dr 19115
Stenton Ave
1400-1600 19141
1602-1898 19141
1901-1997 19138
1999-2199 19138
2201-2299 19138
4501-4597 19144
4599-5199 19144
5801-6097 19138
6099-6399 19138
6400-7298 19150
6401-7199 19138
7300-7499 19150
7501-8599 19150
7600-9498 19118
Sterling St 19138
E Sterner St 19134
W Sterner St
900-999 19133
2500-2799 19132
S Stetler St 19142
Stevens Dr 19113
Stevens Rd 19116
Stevens St
200-399 19111
1400-2899 19149
Stevens Ter 19111
Stevenson Ln 19114
Stewart Pl 19116
Stewart St
2100-2500 19121
2502-2598 19121
5600-5799 19131
Stewarts Way 19154
E Stiles St
4300-4599 19124
4600-4699 19137
W Stiles St
200-300 19122
302-1198 19122
1400-3099 19121
4100-4198 19104
4200-4299 19104
4900-5399 19131
6200-6299 19151
6301-6599 19151
N Stillman St
800-899 19130
1500-2099 19121
2800-3199 19132
3200-3299 19129
S Stillman St 19146
Stirling St
1200-1399 19111
1400-3199 19149
4000-4299 19135
Stocker St 19145
Stockton Ct 19112
Stockton Rd 19138
Stokes St 19144
Stokley St
3001-3297 19129
3299-3300 19129
3302-3698 19129
3303-3399 19140
3601-3899 19129
Stoney Ln 19115
Stouton St 19134
Strahle Pl 19111
Strahle St
400-1199 19111
1600-2300 19152
2302-2398 19152
4400-4799 19136
Strahle Ter 19111
Stratford Dr 19115
S Strawberry St 19106
Strawberry Mansion Dr 19132
Suffolk Ave & Pl 19153
Sulis St 19141
W Sulis St 19120
Sumac St 19128
Summer Pl 19139
Summer St
1200-1299 19107
2200-2298 19103
3200-3299 19104
5000-6399 19139
Summerdale Ave
4800-4800 19124
4802-5092 19124
5094-5698 19124
5901-6099 19149
6200-6798 19111
6800-7999 19111
8000-8098 19152
8100-8599 19152
Summit Ave 19128
Summit Pl 19128
Summit St 19118
Sunflower Dr 19116
Sunnyside Ave 19129
Sunrise Ln 19118
Sunset Ave 19128
E Sunset Ave 19118
W Sunset Ave 19118
Surgeon Generals Ct 19146
Surrey Rd 19115
Susan Rd 19115
Susan Ter 19116
E Susquehanna Ave 19125
W Susquehanna Ave
100-1399 19122
1400-1428 19121
1430-3298 19121
1501-1599 19132
1601-3299 19121
Susquehanna Rd 19111
Sussex Ln 19114
Swain St 19130
Swain Walk 19104
N Swanson St 19134
S Swanson St
800-998 19147
1801-1997 19148
1999-2299 19148
2301-2599 19148
Sweet Briar Pl & Rd 19154
Sweetbriar Dr 19131
Sycamore Dr 19136
Sycamore Ln 19128
Sycamore St 19120
N Sydenham St
600-699 19130
1400-1799 19121
2200-3099 19132
3200-4694 19140
4696-4698 19140
4800-5699 19141
6400-6899 19126
S Sydenham St
200-299 19102
400-1098 19146
1100-1199 19146
2800-3299 19145
E Sydney St
200-299 19119
900-1299 19150
S Sylmar St 19142
E & W Sylvania St 19144
Sylvester St
5200-5499 19124
5801-6297 19149
6299-6999 19149
Sylvia Ln 19115
Tabor Ave
5300-5622 19120
5624-5998 19120
5801-5997 19111
5999-8300 19111
8302-8398 19111
Tabor Ln 19111
Tabor Pl 19111
Tabor Plz 19111
Tabor Rd 19120
E Tabor Rd 19120
W Tabor Rd
100-799 19120
801-801 19120
850-898 19141
900-1201 19141
1203-1399 19141
Tabor Ter 19111
Tackawanna Pl 19124
Tackawanna St
4200-4216 19124
4218-5499 19124
5700-6699 19135
Tacoma St
4100-4198 19140
5000-5099 19144
5101-5499 19144
Tacony St
4201-4297 19124
4299-4599 19124
4600-5099 19137
5101-5399 19137
5600-5698 19135
5700-5799 19135
5801-6399 19135
Taggert St 19125
Tambearn Rd 19154
Tampa St
3201-3397 19134
3399-3499 19134
4500-4799 19120
Tanager Pl 19153
Taney Ct 19121
N Taney St
700-999 19130
1200-1899 19121
2800-3099 19132
S Taney St
400-1599 19146
1600-1699 19145
Taney Ter 19145
Tara Rd 19154
Tasker St
100-1399 19148
1400-3199 19145
3201-3399 19145
Tate Pl 19142
Taunton St 19152
N Taylor St
700-899 19130
1200-1942 19121
1944-1998 19121
2700-3199 19132
S Taylor St
1201-1297 19146
1299-1599 19146
1601-1697 19145
1699-1899 19145
Taylor Ter 19145
Teal Ave 19136
Teesdale St
1700-1799 19111
2900-3199 19152
3200-4599 19136
Telfair Rd 19154
Telford Rd 19154
Telner St 19118
Temple Rd 19150
Templeton Dr 19154
Tennis Ave 19120
Terleare St 19104
Terminal Ave 19148
Terrace St 19128
Terry St 19136
Teton Rd 19154
E Thayer St 19134
W Thayer St 19140
The Oak Rd 19129
E Thelma St 19120
W Thelma St 19140
Theodore St
5800-5899 19143
6000-6298 19142
6300-7199 19142
7201-7299 19142
7300-7399 19153
Theresa Dr 19116
Tholisti Rd 19115
Thomas Ave 19143
Thomas Rd 19118
Thomas Mill Ter 19128
E Thompson St
200-2699 19125
2700-3699 19134
3700-4734 19137
4736-4898 19137
W Thompson St
1-11 19125
13-22 19125
100-1299 19122
1401-1497 19121
1499-3164 19121
3166-3198 19121
4200-4398 19104
4900-5599 19131
5601-5899 19131
5900-6099 19151
6101-6199 19151
Thornbrook Pl 19114
Thorndike Rd 19115
Thornton Rd 19154
Thornwood Pl 19154
Thouron Ave
7301-7397 19138
7399-7499 19138
7500-8699 19150
Thyme Ln 19128
Tibben St 19128
Tiber St 19140
Tilden St 19129
Tilghman St 19122
Tilton St
2500-2699 19125
2700-3499 19134
4600-4699 19137
Timber Ln 19129
Tinicum Ave & Blvd 19153
Tinicum Island Rd
1-1 19113
1000-1000 19153
1002-1098 19113
2000-2050 19153
E Tioga St 19134
W Tioga St 19140
Tiona St 19128
Titan Pl 19153
Titan St
107-1299 19147

1301-1399 19147
1600-3099 19146
Tohopeka Ln 19118
Tolbut St
1800-2799 19152
2800-4699 19136
4701-4799 19136
8500-8599 19152
Tomlinson Ct, Pl, Plz, Rd
& Ter 19116
E Toronto St 19134
W Toronto St 19132
Torresdale Ave
1800-5599 19124
5700-7299 19135
7300-8899 19136
8901-9199 19136
9200-9699 19114
Torrey Rd 19154
Towanda St 19118
Tower St 19127
Townsend Rd 19154
Townsend St 19125
Tracey St 19115
Treaty Rd 19114
Tree St
100-1299 19148
1800-1899 19145
Tree Ter 19145
Tremont St
2625A-2625B 19152
1901-2097 19115
2099-2399 19115
2401-2499 19115
2600-2699 19152
2700-3099 19136
Trenton Ave
2000-2599 19125
2601-2699 19125
4600-4698 19124
Trevett Ct 19112
Trevi Ct 19145
Trevose Rd 19116
Trichans St 19111
Trieste Way 19145
Trina Dr 19116
Trinity Pl 19143
Trinity St
5400-5999 19143
6000-6799 19142
Trotter St 19111
Trout Rd 19115
Truxton Ct 19112
Tryon Ct & St 19146
E Tucker St 19125
W Tucker St
1200-1299 19133
1501-1599 19132
Tudor St
1300-1499 19111
3300-4599 19136
Tulip St
1700-2699 19125
2700-2800 19134
2802-3623 19134
3625-3699 19134
5000-5699 19124
5700-7299 19135
7300-7399 19136
9300-9499 19114
9501-9599 19114
Tulpehocken St 19138
E Tulpehocken St
1-599 19144
801-1297 19138
1299-2099 19138
W Tulpehocken St 19144
Turner St
100-498 19122
500-600 19122
602-998 19122
1901-1997 19121
1999-3299 19121
5300-5399 19131
5900-5999 19151
Turnstone Pl 19153
Turton Dr 19115
Tuscany Dr 19145
E Tusculum St 19134
W Tusculum St
100-155 19133
600-699 19140
Tustin St
900-998 19111
1600-1999 19152
Twist Rd 19115
Tyler Ct 19111
Tyrone Rd 19154
Tyson Ave
300-1499 19111
1501-1997 19149
1999-3499 19149
4000-4999 19135
N Uber St
700-899 19130
1500-2199 19121
2200-2299 19132
3300-4599 19140
4900-5699 19141
6500-7199 19138
S Uber St
400-499 19146
3100-3199 19145
S Ulena St 19153
Ulmer St 19128
Umbria St
4600-4899 19127
4900-5399 19128
Union Ct 19147
N Union St 19104
Unity St 19124
University Ave &
Mews 19104
Unruh Ave
300-1499 19111
2100-3299 19149
4000-5299 19135
Upland St
4700-5599 19143
6000-7199 19142
Upland Way 19131
E Upsal St
1-899 19119
900-1600 19150
1602-1698 19150
W Upsal St 19119
Utah St 19144
Vader Rd 19154
Vale Ln 19114
Valetta St 19124
Valley Ave 19128
Valley Pl 19124
Valley St 19124
Valley Forge Pl 19122
Valley Green Ct 19128
Valley View Rd 19118
Van Horn St 19123
Van Kirk St
200-600 19120
602-698 19120
1000-1599 19149
1601-1899 19149
4100-4927 19135
4929-4999 19135
N Van Pelt St
100-199 19103
1800-2199 19121
2200-2952 19132
2954-2998 19132
S Van Pelt St
1-97 19103
99-299 19103
400-499 19146
Vandike St
1600-1698 19124
5700-7299 19135
7901-7999 19136
9200-9399 19114
Vare Ave 19145
Vassar St 19128
Vaux St 19129
E Venango St 19134
W Venango St 19140
Venus Pl 19153
Verbena Ave 19126
Verda Dr 19154
Vermeer Pl 19153
E Vernon Rd
300-899 19119
900-1500 19150
1502-1598 19150
Verona Dr 19145
Veronica Ln 19116
Verree Rd
7500-8599 19111
8600-8698 19115
8700-9999 19115
10000-10098 19116
10100-10186 19116
10188-10198 19116
Vestry Cir 19128
Vicaris St 19128
Vici St 19124
Victoria St 19140
E Victoria St 19134
Village Ln 19154
Vine St
100-198 19106
200-499 19106
501-599 19106
901-1097 19107
1099-1399 19107
1401-1497 19102
1499-1601 19102
1601-1999 19103
1603-1699 19102
5200-5298 19139
5300-6599 19139
Vineyard St 19130
Vinton Rd 19154
Viola St
4100-4299 19104
5100-5183 19131
5185-5199 19131
Violet Dr 19154
Virginian Rd 19141
Vista St
1300-1799 19111
2000-3099 19152
3300-4799 19136
N Vodges St
100-299 19139
500-1499 19131
S Vodges St 19143
Voight Rd 19128
Voits Ln 19115
Vollmer St 19148
Wade St 19144
Wadsworth Ave 19119
E Wadsworth Ave 19150
Wagner Ave 19141
Wakefield St 19144
Wakeling St
900-2099 19124
2101-2199 19124
2201-2299 19137
Waldemire Dr & Pl 19154
N Walencom St 19131
Wales Pl 19116
Walker St
5100-5499 19124
5700-7299 19135
7701-7997 19136
7999-8399 19136
8401-8499 19136
9200-9399 19114
Wallace Pl 19139
Wallace St
401-697 19123
699-1300 19123
1302-1310 19123
1401-1497 19130
1499-2399 19130
3200-4399 19104
Walley Ave 19115
Wallingford Ct 19112
Waln St 19124
Walnut Ln
500-700 19128
702-898 19128
7201-7297 19138
7299-7599 19138
E Walnut Ln
1-599 19144
1500-2099 19138
2101-2199 19138
W Walnut Ln 19144
Walnut St
101-197 19106
199-799 19106
800-1399 19107
1401-1411 19102
1413-1531 19102
1533-1601 19102
1600-1600 19103
1602-2499 19103
3000-4499 19104
4500-6299 19139
Walnut Hill St 19152
Walnut Park Dr 19120
Walter St 19111
Walton Ave 19143
N Wanamaker St
100-299 19139
400-2299 19131
S Wanamaker St 19143
Waradera St 19106
Warden Dr 19129
Warfield Pl 19114
S Warfield St
1300-1599 19146
1600-1698 19145
Waring St 19116
N Warnock St
700-899 19123
1400-1999 19122
2500-3099 19133
3500-3600 19140
3602-3698 19140
4700-6199 19141
S Warnock St
200-299 19107
700-1399 19147
1900-2899 19148
Warren St
3601-3697 19104
3699-4199 19104
5000-5399 19131
Warrington Ave 19143
Wartman St 19128
Warwick St 19116
Washington Ave
1-97 19147
99-1399 19147
1500-2699 19146
5601-5797 19143
5799-6299 19143
E Washington Ln
1-599 19144
800-2299 19138
W Washington Ln 19144
S Washington Sq 19106
W Washington Sq 19106
N Water St
300-398 19106
400-499 19123
2500-2599 19125
2800-3599 19134
5300-6099 19120
S Water St
901-1599 19147
1701-2499 19148
Water Works Dr 19130
Waterloo St
1700-2099 19122
3300-3399 19140
N Waterloo St 19133
Waterman Ave 19118
Waterview Ln 19154
Watkins St
100-1199 19148
1700-2399 19145
Watson St 19111
N Watts St
101-299 19107
600-999 19123
2800-2899 19132
3500-3599 19140
S Watts St
301-399 19107
401-697 19147
699-800 19147
802-1150 19147
1801-2397 19148
2399-2699 19148
Waverly St
600-898 19147
900-1200 19147
1202-1398 19147
1500-2599 19146
Waverly Walk 19147
Waxwing Pl 19142
Wayne Ave
4100-4198 19140
4200-4423 19140
4425-4497 19144
4499-6399 19144
6400-7299 19119
Wayside Rd 19116
Weatham St 19119
Weaver St
71-199 19119
1300-1499 19150
Webb St
2500-2699 19125
2700-2800 19134
2802-3298 19134
Webster St
1100-1198 19147
1200-1399 19147
1500-1598 19146
1600-2699 19146
5100-6299 19143
Weccacoe Ave 19148
Weightman St 19129
Weikel St 19134
E Wellens Ave 19120
W Wellens Ave
100-799 19120
800-899 19141
Wellesley Rd 19119
Wellington St
1100-1499 19111
3000-3098 19149
3100-3599 19149
4100-4698 19135
4700-5099 19135
Wells St
1300-1399 19111
4000-4099 19135
Welsh Ct
2300-2399 19112
4200-4299 19136
Welsh Rd
2998A-2998A 19152
2999A-2999B 19152
1-2135 19115
2137-2199 19115
2301-2611 19114
2500-2698 19152
2700-2996 19152
2998-2998 19152
3001-4200 19136
4202-4298 19136
Welton St 19116
Wendle Ct 19123
N Wendle St 19133
Wendover St
100-198 19127
200-300 19128
302-698 19128
E Wensley St 19134
W Wensley St 19140
Wentworth Rd 19131
Wentz St 19120
Wesleyan Rd
9000-9099 19136
9200-9299 19114
Wessex Ln 19114
Westbourne Pl 19114
Westbury Dr 19151
Westford Rd 19120
Westhampton Dr 19154
Westminster Ave
4024-4098 19104
4100-4399 19104
4500-5599 19131
5601-5699 19131
Westmont St
600-699 19122
2900-3199 19121
E Westmoreland St 19134
W Westmoreland St
180A-180B 19140
114-198 19140
200-2399 19140
2400-2400 19129
2402-3499 19129
Weston St 19136
Westview St 19119
Wexford Pl 19116
Weymouth St
3100-3199 19134
3201-3499 19134
4500-4598 19120
4600-5999 19120
Wharton St
101-105 19147
107-1399 19147
1400-3699 19146
5900-5999 19143
6001-6099 19143
Wheatsheaf Ln
2000-2099 19124
2100-2700 19137
2702-2798 19137
Wheeler St
5500-5799 19143
6100-7099 19142
7300-7699 19153
Wheelpump Ln 19118
Whinche St 19152
Whitaker Ave
3801-3997 19124
3999-4399 19124
4400-4799 19120
4800-5599 19124
7100-7298 19111
7300-7899 19111
Whitby Ave 19143
Whitehall Ln 19114
Whitemarsh Ave 19118
Whiting Pl & Rd 19154
Whitney St 19116
Wick Rd 19115
Wickes Ct 19112
Wickley Rd 19154
Widener Pl
1400-1899 19141
2000-2099 19138
Widener St 19120
Wiehle St 19129
Wigard Ave 19128
Wilbrock St 19136
Wilbur St 19116
Wilcox St 19130
Wilde St 19127
Wilder St
101-197 19147
199-1299 19147
1800-2999 19146
E Wildey St
1-47 19123
101-147 19125
149-513 19125
515-699 19125
W Wildey St 19123
Wildflower Way 19116
E Willard St 19134
W Willard St
501-1897 19140
1899-1999 19140
2501-2739 19129
3200-3298 19129
William Pl 19142
E William St 19134
W William St
1201-1299 19133
1300-1399 19132
Williams Ave 19150
Willig Ave 19125
Willings Aly 19106
Willings Alley Mews 19106
N Willington St 19121
Willits Rd
2601-3299 19114
2700-2736 19152
2738-3398 19136
Willow St
200-300 19123
302-598 19123
3900-3999 19104
E & W Willow Grove
Ave 19118
Willows Ave 19143
Wilmot St
1800-2099 19124
2600-2798 19137
2800-2899 19137
Wilson St 19136
E Wilt St 19125
W Wilt St
101-597 19122
599-699 19122
1800-2000 19121
2002-3198 19121
N Wilton St
100-499 19139
600-1799 19131
S Wilton St 19143
Winchester Ave
1801-2299 19115
2500-2699 19152
2701-2799 19152
2801-3199 19136
8801-8899 19115
Winding Dr 19131
Windish St 19152
Windrim Ave
1000-1799 19141
1800-1999 19140
Windsor Ave 19143
Windsor St 19142
Wingate St 19136
Wingohocking Hts 19144
E Wingohocking St
100-598 19120
1500-4499 19124
W Wingohocking St
100-170 19140
172-1822 19140
1824-1920 19140
2000-2099 19144
Wingohocking Ter 19144
Wingtip Rd 19115
Winona St 19129
W Winona St 19144
Winston Rd 19118
Winter Pl 19139
Winter St
900-1098 19107
2100-2198 19103
3200-3299 19104
Winters Ct 19107
Winthrop St 19136
Winton St
300-1099 19148
1101-1199 19148
2200-2899 19145
Winton Ter 19145
N Wiota St 19104
Wises Mill Rd 19128
E Wishart St 19134
W Wishart St
100-299 19133
1300-2999 19132
Wissahickon Ave
1-6 19119
3901-4197 19129
4199-4399 19129
4601-4697 19144
4699-6300 19144
6302-6398 19144
6400-7299 19119
8500-8899 19128
Wissahickon Ln 19119
Wissinoming St
7100-7298 19135
7300-7399 19136

9200-9699 ... 19114
Wistaria St ... 19115
Wister Ave ... 19138
Wister St ... 19138
E Wister St ... 19144
Witler St ... 19115
Witte St ... 19134
Woburn Pl ... 19114
Wolcott Dr ... 19118
Wolf St
5-13 ... 19148
15-1399 ... 19148
1400-2799 ... 19145
E Wolf St ... 19148
Womrath St ... 19124
Wood St
200-498 ... 19106
900-1299 ... 19107
1301-1399 ... 19107
1401-1499 ... 19102
1601-1699 ... 19103
Wood Pipe Ln ... 19129
Woodale Rd ... 19118
Woodbine Ave
5000-5999 ... 19131
6001-6099 ... 19131
6200-7600 ... 19151
7602-7798 ... 19151
Woodbridge Rd ... 19114
Woodbrook Ln
400-599 ... 19119
900-1699 ... 19150
Woodcrest Ave
4900-5899 ... 19131
5901-6099 ... 19131
6400-7699 ... 19151
Wooden Bridge Rd ... 19136
Woodenbridge Rd ... 19114
Woodfern Rd ... 19115
Woodhaven Pl ... 19116
Woodhaven Plz ... 19116
Woodhaven Rd
382-398 ... 19116
400-1999 ... 19116
2001-2099 ... 19116
2800-2898 ... 19154
2900-4299 ... 19154
4301-4599 ... 19154
Woodhaven Ter ... 19116
Woodland Ave
3900-3998 ... 19104
4000-4200 ... 19104
4202-4398 ... 19104
4500-5999 ... 19143
6000-7299 ... 19142
7301-7399 ... 19142
Woodland Ter ... 19104
Woodland Walk ... 19104
E Woodlawn Ave ... 19138
E Woodlawn St ... 19144
W Woodlawn St ... 19144
N Woodstock St
100-198 ... 19103
800-899 ... 19130
1501-1697 ... 19121
1699-2199 ... 19121
2200-3099 ... 19132
3200-3299 ... 19140
5700-6799 ... 19138
S Woodstock St
1500-1599 ... 19146
1900-2499 ... 19145
Woodward St
2301-2399 ... 19115
2600-2699 ... 19152
Woolston Ave
6700-7299 ... 19138
7301-7499 ... 19138
7501-7697 ... 19150
7699-8399 ... 19150
Workmans Pl ... 19147
Worrell Ct & St ... 19124
Worth St ... 19124
Worthington Rd ... 19116
Wright St
130-152 ... 19127
154-199 ... 19127
300-399 ... 19128
Wyalusing Ave
3800-4399 ... 19104
4500-5098 ... 19131
5100-5799 ... 19131
Wylie St ... 19130
Wyncote Ave ... 19138
Wyndale Ave
4900-5799 ... 19131
7600-7699 ... 19151
Wyndmoor St ... 19118
Wyndom Rd ... 19154
W Wyneva St ... 19144
Wynmill Pl, Rd & Ter ... 19115
Wynnefield Ave ... 19131
Wynnewood Rd ... 19151
Wynsam St ... 19138
E Wyoming Ave
100-651 ... 19120
653-723 ... 19120
725-1399 ... 19124
W Wyoming Ave ... 19140
Yale Pl ... 19136
Yelland St ... 19140
Yerkes St
1200-1399 ... 19119
1400-1699 ... 19150
N Yewdall St
1-199 ... 19139
600-699 ... 19131
S Yewdall St
1-99 ... 19139
500-1899 ... 19143
Yewdall Ter ... 19143
Yocum St
4800-5899 ... 19143
6000-7299 ... 19142
York Ave ... 19106
E York St ... 19125
W York St
106-106 ... 19133
108-1100 ... 19133
1102-1298 ... 19133
1300-1324 ... 19132
1326-3299 ... 19132
3301-3399 ... 19132
W Zeralda St ... 19144

NUMBERED STREETS

N 2nd St
3-35 ... 19106
400-498 ... 19123
1200-2199 ... 19122
2200-3199 ... 19133
3200-4299 ... 19140
4700-6099 ... 19120
6500-6699 ... 19126
11-15-11-15 ... 19106
S 2nd St
1-399 ... 19106
400-1599 ... 19147
1600-2699 ... 19148
N 3rd St
1-3 ... 19106
401-441 ... 19123
1200-2199 ... 19122
2200-3099 ... 19133
3200-4699 ... 19140
4701-4897 ... 19120
6500-6799 ... 19126
S 3rd St
1-399 ... 19106
400-1400 ... 19147
1900-3600 ... 19148
N 4th St
1-199 ... 19106
400-1155 ... 19123
1200-2199 ... 19122
2200-3099 ... 19133
3300-4298 ... 19140
4700-6299 ... 19120
6500-6799 ... 19126
S 4th St
1-399 ... 19106
500-1599 ... 19147
1600-1698 ... 19148
N 4th Rear St ... 19106
N 5th St
40-398 ... 19106
400-1099 ... 19123
1200-2199 ... 19122
2200-3199 ... 19133
3200-4699 ... 19140
4700-6299 ... 19120
6300-6498 ... 19126
S 5th St
100-399 ... 19106
400-498 ... 19147
1600-2599 ... 19148
N 6th St
2-98 ... 19106
400-598 ... 19123
1200-2131 ... 19122
2200-3002 ... 19133
3200-4499 ... 19140
4700-4798 ... 19120
6200-6799 ... 19126
S 6th St
200-399 ... 19106
400-416 ... 19147
1600-2699 ... 19148
N 7th St
1-97 ... 19106
400-999 ... 19123
1200-2171 ... 19122
2200-3199 ... 19133
3200-4507 ... 19140
4700-6199 ... 19120
6200-6899 ... 19126
S 7th St
1-399 ... 19106
400-524 ... 19147
1600-3399 ... 19148
N 8th St ... 19107
3-299 ... 19106
400-999 ... 19123
1200-1298 ... 19122
2200-3199 ... 19133
3400-3498 ... 19140
4700-6199 ... 19120
6200-6799 ... 19126
S 8th St
3-399 ... 19106
100-298 ... 19107
401-497 ... 19147
1600-2899 ... 19148
N 9th St
1-45 ... 19107
400-899 ... 19123
1200-1498 ... 19122
2200-3199 ... 19133
3300-4599 ... 19140
4700-5299 ... 19141
6500-6899 ... 19126
S 9th St
1-97 ... 19107
400-1599 ... 19147
1600-2899 ... 19148
N 10th St
2-98 ... 19107
401-445 ... 19123
1200-2199 ... 19122
2200-3099 ... 19133
3200-4501 ... 19140
4508-4698 ... 19141
6400-6899 ... 19126
S 10th St
1-320 ... 19107
400-1599 ... 19147
1600-2899 ... 19148
N 11th St
49-97 ... 19107
99-399 ... 19107
401-497 ... 19123
499-999 ... 19123
1200-1298 ... 19122
1300-2100 ... 19122
2102-2198 ... 19122
2200-3099 ... 19133
3200-3700 ... 19140
3702-4698 ... 19140
4501-4697 ... 19141
4699-6399 ... 19141
6400-6899 ... 19126
8-12 ... 19107
14-325 ... 19107
327-329 ... 19107
401-407 ... 19147
409-1599 ... 19147
1600-2900 ... 19148
2902-2998 ... 19148
4901-5097 ... 19112
5099-5199 ... 19112
N 12th St
1-45 ... 19107
400-947 ... 19123
1201-1231 ... 19122
2200-3199 ... 19133
4000-4699 ... 19140
4700-6399 ... 19141
6400-7099 ... 19126
S 12th St
1-97 ... 19107
400-1599 ... 19147
1600-2899 ... 19148
4800-4898 ... 19112
13th St ... 19132
29-197 ... 19107
199-399 ... 19107
401-413 ... 19123
415-999 ... 19123
1201-1497 ... 19122
1499-2199 ... 19122
2200-3199 ... 19133
3200-3210 ... 19140
3212-4699 ... 19140
4700-6399 ... 19141
6400-6800 ... 19126
6802-6898 ... 19126
1-97 ... 19107
99-335 ... 19107
337-399 ... 19107
400-1599 ... 19147
1600-3200 ... 19148
3202-3298 ... 19148
4700-4798 ... 19112
4800-4999 ... 19112
5001-5199 ... 19112
N 15th St
101-399 ... 19102
500-538 ... 19130
1201-1219 ... 19121
2200-2212 ... 19132
3200-4699 ... 19140
4700-6299 ... 19141
6400-6899 ... 19126
S 15th St
30-98 ... 19102
400-1599 ... 19146
1600-3099 ... 19145
4900-4998 ... 19112
N 16th St
110-314 ... 19102
500-552 ... 19130
1200-2100 ... 19121
2200-3199 ... 19132
3200-4599 ... 19140
4701-4797 ... 19141
6400-6899 ... 19126
S 16th St
1-399 ... 19102
400-1592 ... 19146
1599-1599 ... 19112
1600-1608 ... 19145
4701-4897 ... 19112
N 17th St
24-198 ... 19103
400-538 ... 19130
1201-1303 ... 19121
2200-3199 ... 19132
3200-4599 ... 19140
4900-6299 ... 19141
6401-6497 ... 19126
S 17th St
30-34 ... 19103
400-1599 ... 19146
1600-3299 ... 19145
5000-5199 ... 19112
N 18th St
100-224 ... 19103
500-999 ... 19130
1214-1298 ... 19121
2200-2902 ... 19132
3300-4699 ... 19140
4700-6399 ... 19141
6401-6497 ... 19126
S 18th St
2-26 ... 19103
400-406 ... 19146
1600-3299 ... 19145
5101-5199 ... 19112
N 19th St
311-399 ... 19103
400-498 ... 19130
1201-1245 ... 19121
2200-2900 ... 19132
3238-3298 ... 19140
4900-5598 ... 19141
6800-7399 ... 19126
S 19th St
2-20 ... 19103
400-1599 ... 19146
1600-3199 ... 19145
4901-5199 ... 19112
N 20th St
100-200 ... 19103
400-999 ... 19130
1400-2199 ... 19121
2200-3100 ... 19132
3201-3225 ... 19140
4900-5099 ... 19144
5700-7500 ... 19138
S 20th St
1-299 ... 19103
400-1599 ... 19146
1600-3400 ... 19145
N 21st St
100-200 ... 19103
401-497 ... 19130
1301-1333 ... 19121
2200-3099 ... 19132
3200-3699 ... 19140
5701-5897 ... 19138
S 21st St
1-17 ... 19103
400-1599 ... 19146
1600-2499 ... 19145
N 22nd St
1-97 ... 19103
500-899 ... 19130
1300-2199 ... 19121
2200-3199 ... 19132
3224-3230 ... 19140
S 22nd St
1-399 ... 19103
400-1599 ... 19146
1600-2599 ... 19145
N 23rd St
2-98 ... 19103
500-899 ... 19130
1200-2299 ... 19121
2400-3099 ... 19132
3400-3498 ... 19140
S 23rd St
1-399 ... 19103
400-1499 ... 19146
1601-1605 ... 19145
S 23rd Ter ... 19145
N 24th St
600-899 ... 19130
1200-2199 ... 19121
2300-3199 ... 19132
3500-3599 ... 19140
S 24th St
101-197 ... 19103
400-1599 ... 19146
1600-2599 ... 19145
N 25th St
700-899 ... 19130
1200-2099 ... 19121
2300-3199 ... 19132
3200-3299 ... 19129
S 25th St
201-399 ... 19103
400-1399 ... 19146
1601-1697 ... 19145
N 26th St
701-751 ... 19130
1200-1833 ... 19121
2200-3031 ... 19132
3200-3299 ... 19129
S 26th St
301-399 ... 19103
400-1599 ... 19146
1600-3700 ... 19145
4000-4398 ... 19112
N 27th St
700-999 ... 19130
1201-1209 ... 19121
2201-2297 ... 19132
3200-3299 ... 19129
S 27th St
500-1599 ... 19146
1600-2099 ... 19145
N 28th St
800-927 ... 19130
1200-2199 ... 19121
2200-3199 ... 19132
S 28th St
1201-1233 ... 19146
1235-1599 ... 19146
1600-2599 ... 19145
N 29th St
800-999 ... 19130
1200-2199 ... 19121
2200-3199 ... 19132
3201-3299 ... 19129
S 29th St
1200-1599 ... 19146
1601-1697 ... 19145
1699-2099 ... 19145
N 30th St
800-999 ... 19130
1200-2199 ... 19121
2200-3199 ... 19132
S 30th St
2-98 ... 19104
100-131 ... 19104
133-199 ... 19104
1300-1599 ... 19146
1600-1999 ... 19145
N 31st St
400-498 ... 19104
500-599 ... 19104
1200-2137 ... 19121
2139-2199 ... 19121
2200-2700 ... 19132
2702-3198 ... 19132
S 31st St
100-199 ... 19104
1100-1599 ... 19146
1600-1899 ... 19145
N 32nd St
1-219 ... 19104
1301-1397 ... 19121
2200-2298 ... 19132
S 32nd St
200-249 ... 19104
1201-1297 ... 19146
1601-1697 ... 19145
N 33rd St
101-213 ... 19104
1500-2199 ... 19121
2201-2397 ... 19132
3200-3299 ... 19129
S 33rd St
2-198 ... 19104
1200-1599 ... 19146
N 34th St
1-699 ... 19104
2500-3199 ... 19132
3200-3299 ... 19129
S 34th St
1-97 ... 19104
99-339 ... 19104
341-401 ... 19104
1101-1197 ... 19146
1199-1399 ... 19146
1800-1899 ... 19145
N 35th St
100-699 ... 19104
3000-3199 ... 19132
S 35th St ... 19146
N 36th St ... 19104
S 36th St
1-300 ... 19104
1200-1399 ... 19146
N 37th St ... 19104
100-298 ... 19104
1300-1399 ... 19146
N & S 38th ... 19104
N & S 39th ... 19104
N & S 40th ... 19104
N & S 41st ... 19104
N & S 42nd ... 19104
N & S 43rd ... 19104
N & S 44th ... 19104
N 45th St
700-1099 ... 19104
2700-2799 ... 19131
S 45th St ... 19104
N 46th St
36-42 ... 19139
900-2799 ... 19131
S 46th St
2-98 ... 19139
100-299 ... 19139
300-1399 ... 19143
N 47th St
701-797 ... 19139
799-885 ... 19139
887-899 ... 19139
901-2697 ... 19131
2699-2899 ... 19131
S 47th St
201-299 ... 19139
300-1499 ... 19143
1501-1599 ... 19143
N 48th St
1-597 ... 19139
599-899 ... 19139
900-1000 ... 19131
1002-1098 ... 19131
S 48th St
2-98 ... 19139
100-237 ... 19139
239-299 ... 19139
300-1599 ... 19143
N 49th St
100-899 ... 19139
1301-1697 ... 19131
1699-2100 ... 19131
2102-2198 ... 19131
S 49th St
120A-120B ... 19139
2-126 ... 19139
128-299 ... 19139
300-1699 ... 19143
N 50th St ... 19139
900-2499 ... 19131
S 50th St
1-231 ... 19139
233-299 ... 19139
300-1599 ... 19143
N 51st St
1-199 ... 19139
201-899 ... 19139
900-1198 ... 19131
1200-2499 ... 19131
S 51st St
1-299 ... 19139
300-1500 ... 19143
1502-1698 ... 19143
N 52nd St
1-459 ... 19139
461-499 ... 19139
500-2499 ... 19131
S 52nd St
1-299 ... 19139
300-1699 ... 19143
N 53rd St
1-499 ... 19139
500-598 ... 19131
600-2499 ... 19131
S 53rd St
1-299 ... 19139
541-733 ... 19143
735-1799 ... 19143
S 54th Dr ... 19143
N 54th St
1-499 ... 19139
500-2499 ... 19131

Street	ZIP
S 54th St	
1-299	19139
400-498	19143
500-2499	19143
S 55th Dr	19143
N 55th St	
100-499	19139
500-1799	19131
S 55th St	
121A-121B	19139
1-299	19139
300-1899	19143
55th Ter	19143
N 56th St	
1-334	19139
336-398	19139
500-2499	19131
S 56th St	
1-299	19139
300-3099	19143
3101-3199	19143
N 57th St	
1-230	19139
232-398	19139
401-497	19131
499-2299	19131
2301-2499	19131
S 57th St	
2-130	19139
132-299	19139
400-2799	19143
N 58th St	
1-299	19139
400-498	19131
500-2399	19131
S 58th St	
2-26	19139
28-299	19139
300-2700	19143
2702-2798	19143
N 59th St	
1-300	19139
302-398	19139
400-1823	19151
1825-1899	19151
2000-2499	19131
S 59th St	
1-299	19139
300-2537	19143
2539-2599	19143
N 60th St	
1-399	19139
400-1799	19151
1801-1999	19151
S 60th St	
1-299	19139
300-1200	19143
1202-1298	19143
1601-1697	19142
1699-2699	19142
N 61st St	
1-399	19139
400-2099	19151
S 61st St	
1-299	19139
400-699	19143
701-1299	19143
2000-2098	19142
2100-2999	19142
3000-3599	19153
N 62nd St	
1-399	19139
400-2199	19151
S 62nd St	
1-299	19139
300-741	19143
2000-2198	19142
2200-2999	19142
N 63rd St	
1-97	19139
99-399	19139
400-2199	19151
S 63rd St	
1-197	19139
199-299	19139
301-727	19143
2100-2699	19142
2701-2799	19142
3001-3299	19153
64th Ave	19126
E 64th Ave	19120
N 64th St	
200-315	19139
317-399	19139
400-1100	19151
1102-1298	19151
S 64th St	19142
65th Ave	
200-1600	19126
1602-1798	19126
1900-2199	19138
E 65th Ave	19120
W 65th Ave	19120
N 65th St	
200-399	19139
400-1299	19151
S 65th St	19142
66th Ave	
200-1599	19126
1601-1615	19126
2000-2199	19138
N 66th St	19151
S 66th St	19142
67th Ave	
200-1899	19126
1901-2099	19138
N 67th St	19151
S 67th St	
1800-1998	19142
2000-2699	19142
2701-2999	19142
3201-3297	19153
3299-3400	19153
68th Ave	
1200-1899	19126
1900-2099	19138
N 68th St	19151
S 68th St	19142
69th Ave	
800-1499	19126
1900-1999	19138
N 69th St	19151
S 69th St	19142
70th Ave	19126
S 70th St	
1900-3099	19142
3100-3298	19153
71st Ave	
1300-1499	19126
1901-1947	19138
1949-1999	19138
N 71st St	19151
S 71st St	
2000-2525	19142
2527-2699	19142
2701-2799	19153
72nd Ave	
1300-1899	19126
1901-1997	19138
1999-2199	19138
N 72nd St	19151
S 72nd St	
2100-2542	19142
2544-2598	19142
2600-2998	19153
3000-3099	19153
73rd Ave	
1800-1899	19126
1900-1999	19138
S 73rd St	
2401-2497	19142
2499-2599	19142
2600-2800	19153
2802-2898	19153
74th Ave	19138
S 74th St	19153
75th Ave	19138
N 75th St	19151
S 75th St	19153
76th Ave	19150
N 76th St	19151
S 76th St	19153
77th Ave	19150
N 77th St	19151
S 77th St	19153
78th Ave	19150
S 78th St	19153
79th Ave	19150
80th Ave	19150
S 80th St	19153
S 81st St	19153
S 82nd St	19153
S 83rd St	19153
S 84th St	19153
S 86th St	19153

PITTSBURGH PA

Street	ZIP
General Delivery	15232
General Delivery	15233

POST OFFICE BOXES MAIN OFFICE STATIONS AND BRANCHES

Box No.s	ZIP
CARING - CARING	15230
THANKS - THANKS	15230
PENS - PENS	15230
WALK - WALK	15230
WARM - WARM	15230
1 - 3999	15230
1 - 4	15205
1 - 20	15236
1 - 4	15227
2 - 2	15218
4 - 4	15243
5 - 6	15242
4001 - 4098	15201
4100 - 4224	15202
4225 - 4299	15203
4401 - 4598	15205
4600 - 5569	15206
5001 - 5008	15235
5575 - 5674	15207
5675 - 5799	15208
5800 - 5899	15209
5901 - 5998	15210
6001 - 6088	15211
6101 - 7100	15212
7101 - 7598	15213
7701 - 7899	15215
7901 - 8092	15216
8101 - 8250	15217
8251 - 8440	15218
8451 - 8583	15220
8600 - 8997	15221
9000 - 9280	15224
9501 - 9590	15223
9601 - 9699	15226
9700 - 9799	15229
9998 - 9998	15244
10001 - 10060	15236
10101 - 10294	15232
10300 - 10499	15234
10500 - 10695	15235
10700 - 10799	15203
10801 - 10999	15236
11000 - 11196	15237
11201 - 11596	15238
12000 - 12059	15240
12101 - 12499	15231
12500 - 12994	15241
13001 - 13665	15243
14001 - 14496	15239
14500 - 14958	15234
15000 - 15499	15237
15501 - 15958	15244
16000 - 16535	15242
17001 - 17999	15235
18000 - 18919	15236
19001 - 19819	15213
22001 - 23720	15222
24000 - 24205	15206
24501 - 24600	15234
25301 - 25521	15220
27010 - 27298	15235
38001 - 38812	15238
40101 - 40400	15201
41000 - 41168	15202
42250 - 42461	15203
44001 - 44472	15205
53001 - 53180	15219
54001 - 54294	15244
55001 - 55446	15207
56750 - 57380	15208
58001 - 58194	15209
59001 - 59500	15210
60001 - 60150	15211
61001 - 61090	15212
62001 - 62490	15241
64000 - 64000	15264
71001 - 71499	15213
77000 - 77197	15215
79001 - 79420	15216
81001 - 81980	15217
82501 - 82670	15218
86001 - 86364	15221
90001 - 90363	15224
95000 - 95284	15223
96000 - 96160	15226
97000 - 97295	15229
97701 - 98190	15227
99181 - 100278	15233
101000 - 101857	15237
106000 - 106100	15230
110001 - 110316	15232
111201 - 111598	15238
112501 - 113860	15241
114001 - 114100	15239
340777 - 340777	15230
534001 - 543005	15253
640007 - 646115	15264
740766 - 747501	15274

RURAL ROUTES

Route	ZIP
05, 06	15205

NAMED STREETS

Street	ZIP
A St	
100-199	15235
1800-1998	15212
Aachen Pl	15237
Aaron St	15234
Abard Dr	15237
Abbey Ln	15236
Abbeyville Rd	15228
Abbott Dr	15227
Abbott St	15221
Abby Rose Ct	15237
Abdell St	15233
Abel St	
400-599	15227
2100-2199	15210
Aberdeen Dr	
100-199	15237
200-343	15239
345-399	15239
Abers Creek Rd	15239
Aberyl Dr	15237
Abington Dr	15216
Abner Ave	15210
Abstract Ave	15226
Acacia Ln	15212
Acacia Building	15220
Academy Ave	15228
Academy Pl	15243
Academy Way	15222
Acorn St	15207
Acre Woods	15237
Adam Dr	15216
Adam St	15235
Adams Ave	15243
Adams Dr	15241
Adams St	
200-299	15221
500-599	15237
1200-1499	15233
Adara St	15210
Addison St	15219
Adelaide St	15219
Adele Ct	15229
Adele Rd	15237
Adele St	15223
Adeline Ave	15228
Adelphia St	15206
Adena St	15204
Adger St	15205
Admiral St	15212
Admiral Dewey Ave	15205
Adna St	15214
Adobe Dr	15236
Adolph St	15220
Adon St	15204
Adrian Ave	15229
Advent St	15220
Aetna Dr	15241
Afton St	15205
Agnes Rd	15227
Agnes St	15218
E Agnew Ave	15210
Agnew Rd	15227
Ahlers Way	15212
Aidan Ct	15226
Aidyl Ave	15226
N Aiken Ave	15206
S Aiken Ave	
100-299	15206
300-999	15232
N Aiken Ct	15224
Aiken Pl	15232
Ainsworth St	15220
Airport Blvd	15231
Aisbett Way	15224
Ajax St	15213
Akehurst Rd	15220
Akron Ave	15216
Alabama Ave	15216
Alamo Dr	15241
Alan St	15227
Albany St	15220
Albemarle Ave	15217
Albemarle Dr	15237
Albern Ave	15216
Albert St	15211
Albertise Way	15208
Albion St	15208
Album St	15206
Alcan Dr	15239
Alcoma Blvd & Dr	15235
Alcon St	15220
Alcor St	15212
Alden Dr	15220
Alden Rd	15216
Aldenford Dr	15237
Alder Dr	15202
Alder St	
5800-5999	15232
6100-6299	15206
Alder Way	15232
Alderson St	15217
Aldred Ln	15227
Aleta St	15215
Alex Ln	15205
Alexander Pl	15243
Alexander St	15220
Alexis St	15207
Alfred St	
1-99	15228
101-299	15228
2000-2099	15212
Alger St	15207
Algoma Dr	15236
Algonquin Dr	15205
Algonquin Rd	15241
Alhambra Way	15224
Ali St	15215
Alice Pl	15234
Alice St	
1-99	15205
200-499	15210
900-999	15220
Aljo Dr	15241
Allearri Ave	15227
Allegheny Ave	
1-1	15212
100-220	15202
200-218	15202
208-218	15239
221-221	15239
222-298	15202
225-249	15202
300-322	15239
324-498	15239
331-333	15212
401-499	15239
700-1599	15233
1601-1699	15233
Allegheny Cmns W	15212
Allegheny Ctr	15212
Allegheny Sq	15212
Allegheny Ter	15207
Allegheny Center Mall	15212
Allemac Ave	15229
Allen Dr	15214
Allen Hl	15260
Allen St	15210
Allenberry Cir	15234
Allenberry Dr	15237
Allenby Ave	15218
Allenclair Cir	15241
Allendale Cir	15204
Allendale Pl	15228
Allendale St	15204
Allender Ave	15220
Allendorf St	15204
Allequippa St	
1-2600	15213
2602-3498	15213
4100-4199	15219
Alleyne Dr	15215
Allied Way	15201
Allison Ave	15202
Allison Dr	
100-199	15238
1500-2099	15241
Alluvian St	15207
Alma Dr	15238
Alma St	15223
Almanack Ct	15237
Almar Dr & Pl	15237
Almeda St	15207
Almond Way	15201
Almont Ave & St	15210
Almora St	15227
Aloe St	15224
Aloha Dr	15239
Alpark Ave	15216
Alpena St	15213
Alpha Dr W	15238
Alpine Ave	15212
Alpine Blvd	15221
Alpine Cir	15215
Alplaus St	15210
Alries St	15210
Alroy Way	15212
Alsace St	15208
Alsop Rd	15215
Alstead St	15234
Altadena Dr	15228
Altaview Ave	15226
Alter Dr	15239
Althea Dr	15235
Althea St	15210
Altmar St	15226
Altmeyer Aly	15215
Alton Ave	15216
Altoona Pl	
1-299	15228
300-399	15243
500-599	15228
Alturia St	15216
Alumni Hl	15260
Alverado Ave	15216
Alwyn St	15226
Amabell St	15211
E Amanda Ave	15210
Amaryllis Dr	15237
Ambard Ave	15202
Amber St	15206
Amberson Ave & Pl	15232
Ambleside Dr	15237
Amboy St	15224
American St	15207
Ames St	15214
Amesbury Dr	15241
Amethyst St	15202
Amherst Ave	15229
Amherst St	15220
Amman St	15226
Amos Hl	15260
Amos Way	15214
Ampere St	
1-2599	15212
5000-5099	15207
Amsterdam St	
4600-4699	15201
4800-4899	15206
Amy Dr	15205
Anaheim St	15219
Anawanda Ave	15228
Anchor Dr	15238
Andersen Dr	15220
Anderson Ave	15239
Anderson Ln	15239
Anderson Rd	
1000-1699	15209
9400-9699	15237
Anderson St	15212
Andover Ter	15213
Andrade St	15227
Andrea Ct	15237
Andrea Dr	15234
Andrew Dr	15275
Andrews Ave & Dr	15221
Ange Dr	15235
Angela Dr	15221
Angelo Dr	15236
Angelo Ln	15221
Angena Dr	15205
Angle Aly	15223
Angle St	15220
Anglon Way	15216
Anita Ave	15217
Ann St	
1-99	15223
2-2	15215
14-98	15223
Ann Arbor Ave	15229
Annapolis Ave	15216
Annex	15260
Annex Ave	15216
Ansley St	15206
Ansonia Pl	15210
Antenor Ave	15210
Anthon Dr	15235
Anthony St	15210
Antico Pl	15235
Antietam St	15206
Antrim Ct	15237
Antrim St	15212
Apache Rd	15241
Apdale St	15207
Apollo St	15213
Appennine Rd	15239
Appian Way	15210
Apple Ave	
300-399	15239
6300-7199	15206
Apple Ln	15238
Appletree Dr	15241
April Ln	15236
Aqua Dr	15238
Arabella St	15210
Arapahoe Rd	15241
Arbor Ct	15238
Arbor Dr	
100-199	15237
1000-1054	15220
1056-2699	15220
Arbor Ln	15236
Arbor St	15206
Arcadia Dr	15237
Arcadia Park Dr	15239
Arcata St	15227
Arcena St	15219
Arch Ave	
100-199	15202

900-1099 15234
Arch St 15212
Archer St 15235
Arcola Way 15212
Ardary St 15206
Ardelle Dr 15236
Arden Ln 15243
Arden Rd 15216
Ardmore Blvd 15221
Ardmore St 15218
Ardmore Manor Dr 15221
Ardsley St 15226
Arendell St 15214
Argonne Ave 15223
Argow Dr 15239
Arion St 15211
Ariston St 15210
Arizona Ave 15225
Arkansas Ave 15216
Arla Dr 15220
Arlington Ave
100-398 15203
400-1199 15203
1200-3299 15210
Arlington Ct 15223
Arlington Dr 15239
Arlington Park 15234
Arlington Rd 15235
Arlington St 15209
Arlor Dr 15214
Armandale St 15212
Armitage Way 15206
Armour Blvd 15205
Armstrong Way 15206
Arndt Rd 15237
Arnold St
1-7 15205
9-51 15205
53-1199 15205
1200-1475 15220
1476-1498 15205
1500-1799 15205
Arnold Acres Dr 15205
Arrowood Dr 15243
Arsenal Pl 15201
Art Rooney Ave 15212
Arthur St
2-98 15218
500-699 15219
Artvue Dr 15243
Asbury Pl 15217
Ascot Pl 15237
Ash Dr 15209
Ashbury Ln 15237
Ashdale St 15210
Ashford Ave 15229
Ashford Ct 15237
Ashland Ave 15228
Ashland Dr 15239
Ashlawn Dr 15241
Ashley Cir 15241
Ashley Ct 15221
Ashley St 15206
Ashlyn St 15204
Ashtola St 15204
Ashton Ct 15202
Ashton St 15207
Ashwood Cir 15241
Ashwood Ct 15237
Asia Way 15224
Aspen Dr 15239
Aspen St 15224
Aspin Ct 15215
Aster Cir 15241
Aster St 15235
Asteroid Way 15210
Astronaut Cir 15241
Ater Way 15201
Athena St 15210
Athens St 15221
Atkins St 15212
Atkinson Pl 15235
Atlanta Dr 15228
Atlanta Pl 15228
Atlanta St 15212
Atlantic Ave
1-99 15202
100-199 15237
400-799 15221
N Atlantic Ave 15224
S Atlantic Ave 15224
Atlas St 15235
Atmore St 15212
Attica St 15220
Atwell St 15206
Atwood St 15213
Auburn St
100-112 15206
114-198 15206
115-117 15235
119-199 15206
200-239 15235
201-201 15206
203-231 15206
233-299 15206
241-299 15235
300-399 15235
6200-6298 15206
Audbert Dr 15236
Audrey Dr 15236
Audubon Ave 15228
Augusta Ave 15235
Augusta Dr 15237
Augusta St 15211
Augusta Way 15236
Augustine St 15207
Aurelia St 15206
Aurelius St 15218
Aurora Dr
1000-1098 15236
1100-1199 15236
2201-2299 15237
Austin Ave 15243
Austin St 15235
Auto Way 15206
Autumn Path Ln 15238
Autumn Wood Ct 15239
Autumnwood Dr 15216
Avacoll Dr 15220
Avalon St 15219
Avenue E 15221
Avenue A 15221
Avenue B 15221
Avenue D 15221
Avenue F 15221
Avenue G 15221
Avenue K 15221
Avenue L 15221
Avery St 15212
Avila Ct 15237
Avon Ct 15237
Avon Dr
1-99 15202
300-499 15228
Avon Pl 15221
Avondale Pl 15206
Avondale St 15237
Avonworth Heights Dr 15237
Ayers St 15213
Aylesboro Ave & Ln 15217
Azalea Dr
5000-5199 15236
11000-11499 15235
Azalia St 15220
Aztec Way 15211
Azul St 15210
B St
100-198 15235
1800-1898 15212
1900-1999 15212
Babcock Blvd
1300-2199 15209
2200-9000 15237
9002-9358 15237
Badali St 15215
Bader St
100-199 15215
1800-1999 15212
Bahama Dr 15239
Bailey Ave 15211
Bainton St 15212
Bajo St 15210
Baker Dr
100-158 15236
101-147 15237
149-185 15237
160-162 15236
186-198 15237
187-199 15237
200-231 15237
233-299 15237
Baker St 15206
Bakery Square Blvd 15206
Balboa St 15213
Balconade Dr 15236
Baldauf St 15203
Baldwick Rd 15205
Baldwin Dr 15227
Baldwin Rd
201-297 15207
299-326 15207
328-362 15207
333-339 15205
353-369 15207
382-392 15205
394-400 15205
401-405 15207
402-406 15205
407-409 15207
410-412 15205
414-443 15205
444-448 15207
445-639 15205
466-498 15205
500-638 15207
640-699 15207
700-706 15205
701-707 15207
708-718 15205
715-729 15207
720-732 15205
731-1099 15207
Baldwin St 15234
Baldwin Manor Rd 15227
Bale Dr 15235
Balfour St 15220
Balkan Dr 15239
Ballard Way 15206
Ballinger St 15210
Balmoral Dr 15237
N & S Balph Ave 15202
Balsam St 15202
Baltic Way 15210
Baltimore St 15207
Balver St 15205
Banbury Ln
1-99 15202
100-299 15220
Bancroft St 15201
Bandera St 15201
Banfield St 15235
Bangor St 15211
Banks St 15215
Banksville Ave 15216
Banksville Pl 15220
Banksville Rd 15216
Banner Way 15201
Banyon Dr 15235
Baptist Rd
4600-4999 15227
5000-6099 15236
Bar Harbor Dr 15239
Barbadoes Ave 15226
Barbara Dr 15227
Barbara Way 15205
Barberry St 15207
Barbour Dr 15209
Barckhoff St 15235
Barclay Ave 15221
Baredari St 15203
Bark St 15214
E & W Barkhurst Dr 15237
E & W Barlind Dr 15227
Barnes St 15221
Barnesdale St 15217
Barnett St 15239
Barnett Way 15219
Barnwood Ln 15237
Barone Dr 15227
Barr Ave
1-99 15202
101-1297 15205
1299-1799 15205
Barrington Dr 15209
Barron Way 15221
Barry Dr 15237
Barry St 15203
Bart Dr 15235
Barth Ave 15228
Barthwood St 15227
Bartlett St 15217
Bartley Rd 15241
Bartola St 15243
Bartold St 15212
Barton Dr
1-99 15221
9200-9299 15237
Bartow St 15205
Bartsch Ln 15209
Bascom Ave
1-499 15214
500-699 15212
Basil Way 15211
Basin St 15212
Bassler St 15210
Batavia Rd & St 15221
Bateman St 15209
Bates St 15213
Bauerlein St 15209
Baum Blvd
4600-5099 15213
5100-5299 15224
5301-5399 15224
5400-5599 15232
5600-5999 15206
Baum Rd 15239
Bauman Ave 15227
Baumer St 15209
Baun Rd 15212
Bausman St 15210
Baxter St 15208
Bayard Ct 15237
Bayard Pl 15213
Bayard Rd 15213
Bayard St
4400-5099 15213
5100-5199 15232
Bayberry Dr 15237
Bayer Rd 15205
Bayers Ln 15235
Bayne Ave 15202
Bayonne Ave 15216
Bayridge Ave 15226
Baytree St 15214
Baywood Ave 15228
Baywood St 15206
Bazore St 15216
Beacon Rd 15205
Beacon St 15217
Beacon Way 15241
Beacon Hill Dr 15221
Beaconhill Ave 15216
Beaconview Rd 15237
Beadling Rd 15228
Beall Dr 15236
Beam Dr 15236
Beam Way 15211
Bear Run Dr 15237
Beardsley Ln 15217
Beatty St 15221
N Beatty St 15206
S Beatty St 15206
Beaufort Ave & Ct 15226
Beaumont Ln 15217
Beaver Ave
100-199 15202
800-2199 15233
2201-2399 15233
Beaver Dr 15221
Beaver Rd 15202
Becker Dr 15237
E Beckert Ave 15212
W Beckert Ave 15212
Beckert St 15209
Beckfield St 15212
Beckham St 15212
Becks Run Rd 15210
Becky Dr 15236
Bedford Ave 15219
Bedford Sq 15203
S Bee St 15220
Beech Ave
1-399 15202
800-1099 15233
Beech Ct
500-599 15237
700-799 15238
Beech Rd 15239
Beech St
100-399 15218
1900-2099 15221
3406-3406 15212
7800-7899 15237
Beecham Dr 15205
Beechdale St 15227
Beecher St 15208
Beechford Rd 15235
Beechland St 15207
Beechmont Ave 15229
Beechmont Rd 15206
Beechnut Dr 15205
Beechview Ave 15216
Beechwood Blvd
1000-1299 15206
1300-4099 15217
4101-4199 15207
Beechwood Ct 15206
Beechwood Ln 15206
Beedle Circle Dr 15236
Beehner Rd 15217
Beelen St 15213
Beeler St 15217
Beelermont Pl 15217
Beggs St 15207
Begonia Ave 15235
Behan St 15233
Behrens St 15205
Behring St 15203
Beisner Ave 15227
Bel Air Dr 15227
Belasco Ave 15216
Beldale St 15233
Belgreen Pl 15213
Belham St 15216
Belhurst Ave 15204
Belinda St 15219
Bell Ave 15205
Bell Dr 15229
Bellaire Ave & Pl 15226
Bellamy Pl 15210
Bellanca Ave 15227
Bellbrook St 15226
Bellcrest Pl & Rd 15237
Belle Isle Ave 15226
Belle Riviere Ct 15202
Belleau Dr 15212
Belleau St 15214
E & W Bellecrest Ave 15227
N Bellefield Ave 15213
S Bellefield Ave 15213
Bellefield Hl 15260
Bellefonte St 15232
Bellerock Pl & St 15217
Belleville St 15234
Bellevue Ave 15229
E Bellevue Ave 15202
Bellevue Dr 15235
Bellevue Rd 15229
Bellevue Ter 15202
Bellingham Ave 15216
Bellmonte Rd 15237
Bellpark Dr 15229
Bellwood Ct 15237
Bellwood Dr
100-899 15229
2300-2499 15237
Belmar Dr 15223
Belmar Pl 15218
Belmar St 15208
Belmont Ln 15236
Belmont St
600-699 15233
900-1299 15221
Belonda St 15211
Belplain St 15227
Belrose Ave 15216
Beltram Ave 15226
Beltzhoover Ave 15210
Belva St 15202
Belvidere St 15205
Ben Avon Heights Rd
1-99 15202
100-199 15237
Ben Franklin Dr 15237
Ben Hur St 15208
Ben Til Dr 15236
Bench Dr 15236
Bending Oak Ln 15238
Bendview Dr 15221
Benner Way 15218
Bennett Pl 15208
Bennett St
6900-7899 15208
7900-8299 15221
Bennington Ave 15217
Bennington Woods Dr 15237
Benson Aly 15215
Benson Circle Dr 15227
Bensonia Ave 15216
Bentley Dr
100-199 15238
2000-2199 15219
2200-2298 15213
Benton Ave & Pl 15212
Bepler Ave 15229
Berdella St 15220
Berg Dr 15238
Berg Pl 15210
Berg St
200-299 15235
2300-2800 15203
2802-2898 15203
Bergen Pl 15220
Bergman St 15204
Berkeley Rd 15237
Berkeley Meadows Ct 15237
Berkley Ave 15221
Berkshire Ave 15226
Berkshire Dr
600-699 15215
2300-2499 15241
Berkwood Dr 15243
Berlin Rd 15221
Berlin Way 15201
Bernadette Dr 15236
Bernard St 15234
Bernardi Dr 15214
Bernd St 15210
Berner St 15215
Bernice St 15237
Berringer Pl 15202
Berry St
1-100 15205
102-114 15205
900-1499 15204
Bertha St 15211
Berwick Ct 15237
Berwick Dr 15215
Berwick St 15207
Berwin Ave 15226
Berwyn Rd 15237
Beryl Dr 15227
Bessemer St 15201
Bessica St & Ter 15221
Bessie Ave 15212
Best Dr 15202
Beta Dr 15238
Bethany Dr
1-99 15215
800-899 15243
Bethel Church Rd 15241
Bethesda St 15227
Bethoven St
3300-3499 15219
3500-3699 15213
Betty Jane Ct 15235
Betty Rae Dr 15236
Beulah Ln 15235
Beulah Rd 15235
Beulah St 15209
Bevan Rd 15227
Beverly Pl 15206
Beverly Rd
100-499 15216
600-699 15243
Bevington Rd 15221
Beyrleye Ave 15223
Bickar St 15227
Biddeford Rd 15202
Biddle Ave 15221
Bidwell St 15233
Big Horn Rd 15239
Bigbee St 15211
Bigelow Blvd
1000-1099 15260
3000-3399 15219
3401-3697 15213
3699-4499 15213
Bigelow Sq 15219
Bigelow St 15207
Bigger St 15210
Biggert Mnr 15205
Biggs Ave 15214
Bigham St 15211
Billings Dr 15241
Billy Dr 15235
Bilmar Dr 15205
Biltmore Ave 15216
Biltmore Ln 15217
Bingay Dr 15237
Bingham Dr 15241
Bingham St 15203
Birch Ave
100-118 15209
129-137 15237
188-194 15228
195-197 15237
196-298 15228
199-399 15228
200-299 15237
300-304 15237
301-315 15237
306-314 15228
320-322 15237
334-398 15228
Birch Ct 15237
Birch St 15238
Birch Way 15202
Birchwood Ave 15217
Bird Park Dr 15228
Birkhoff St 15212
Birmingham Ave 15210
N Birmingham Ave 15202
S Birmingham Ave 15202
Biro Dr 15227
Birtley Ave 15226
Biscayne Dr 15210
Biscayne Rd 15239
Biscayne Ter 15212
Bishop Dr 15237
Bishop St 15206
Bismark St
1-99 15209
3400-3499 15213
Bittner St 15223
Black St
100-199 15209
5400-5899 15206
Black Forest Dr 15235
Black Hills Rd 15239
Black Oak Dr
1-99 15235
100-112 15220
114-299 15220
1600-1699 15237
Blackadore Ave
1-99 15235
900-1299 15221
1300-1599 15235
Blackberry Way 15201
Blackhawk St 15218
Blackheath Dr 15205
Blackmore St 15217

Street	ZIP
Blackridge Ave & Rd	15235
Blackstone St	15207
Blaine St	15226
Blair Pl	15239
Blair St	15207
Blairmont Dr	15241
Blanche Ave	15212
Blanford Ct	15206
Blanton St	15207
Blaranso St	15204
Blaw Ave	15238
Blenheim Ct	15208
Blessing St	15213
Bliss Dr	15236
Bloomer Way	15219
Blossom Dr	15236
Blossom Rd	15236
Blossom Way	15212
Blossom Hill Rd	15234
Blue Jay Dr	15243
Blue Ridge Dr	15205
Blue Ridge Rd	15239
Blue Spruce Cir	15243
Bluebelle St	15214
Bluff St	
800-899	15219
5000-5199	15236
Bluffland St	15207
Blvd Of The Allies	
2-399	15222
Blvd Of The Allies	
400-1899	15219
1901-2099	15219
2800-3799	15213
Bly St	15212
Bockstoce Ave	15234
Bodkin St	15226
Boggs Ave	
1-899	15211
2000-2099	15221
Boggston Ave	15210
Bohem St	15213
Bolton St	15207
Bon Air Ave	15210
Bon Air Rd	15235
Bonaventure Way	15212
Bond Ave	15237
Bond St	
1-99	15220
2200-2299	15237
Bonel Ct	15227
Boni Dr	15236
Bonifay St	15210
Bonita Ter	15212
Bonnett Dr	15237
Bonvue Dr	15243
Bonvue St	15214
Book Ctr	15260
Bookbinders Cir	15212
Bookman Ave	15227
Borland Rd	15243
Borland St	15206
Borough St	15212
Borough Park Dr	15236
Bossart St	15206
Boston St	15212
Bostwick Dr	15229
Bostwick St	15204
Bothwell St	15214
Bottomfield St	15223
Boulder Dr	15239
Boulevard Dr	15217
Boundary St	
524R-524R	15213
1-83	15213
94-98	15207
100-199	15207
400-525	15213
3800-3898	15207
S Bouquet St	15213
Bour St	15227
Boustead St	15216
Bower St	15206
Bower Hill Rd	
1-599	15228
600-1468	15243
1469-1469	15241
1470-1474	15243
1471-1507	15243
1476-1480	15241
1500-1512	15243
1509-1509	15241
1511-1579	15243
1520-1520	15241
1530-1998	15243
1581-1581	15241
1583-1599	15243
1601-1601	15241
1603-1999	15243
2100-2199	15241
Bowery Way	15201
Bowstone Rd	15235
Boxfield Rd	15241
Boyce Rd	
600-658	15205
660-661	15205
1000-1200	15241
1202-1660	15241
Boyce Park Dr	15239
Boyce Plaza Rd	15241
Boyd Ave	15238
Boyer St	15214
Boyle St	15212
Brabec St	15212
Bracey Ct & Dr	15221
Bracken Ave	15227
Bracken Pl	15239
Brackenridge St	15219
Brackenridge Hall	15260
Bradberry Dr	15215
N Braddock Ave	15208
S Braddock Ave	
100-999	15221
1000-2699	15218
Braddock Rd	15221
Braddsley Dr	15235
Braden Ct	15229
Bradford Ave	15205
Bradish St	15203
Bradley Ct	15228
Braeburn Pl	15232
Brafferton Dr	15228
Brahm St	15212
Braid Way	15234
Brainard St	15227
Brallier Ct	15236
Bramble Ln	15237
Branch St	15215
Branchport St	15233
Brandon Ct	15237
Brandon Rd	15212
Brandon Way	15210
Brandt St	15237
Brandt School Rd	15237
Branning Rd	15235
Brant Ave	15237
Brant Dr	15236
Brashear St	15221
Braun St	15223
Braunlich Dr	15237
Bray St	15209
Brazil St	15227
Breading Ave	15202
Brednick St	15227
Breed St	15203
Breesport St	15224
Breeze Way	15210
Breezewood Dr	15237
Breining St	
1300-1599	15226
1600-1699	15234
Breker St	15212
Bremen Ave	15227
Brenford Ave	15205
Brenham St	15213
Brent St	15210
W Brentridge Ave	15227
Brentshire Vlg	15227
Brentview Dr	15236
Brentwood Ave	15227
Brentwood Rd	15236
Brereton St	15219
Brethauer Ave	15214
Brett St	15205
Bretton Way	15237
Brevard Ave	15227
Briar Way	15218
Briar Cliff Rd	
1-99	15202
500-599	15221
Briar Meadows Dr	15216
Briarleaf Dr	15205
Briarwood Ave	15228
Briarwood Dr	
100-299	15235
1600-1699	15237
Briarwood Ln	15239
Bricelyn St	15221
Brickley Dr	15227
Bridge St	
1-99	15223
100-198	15228
101-103	15209
105-299	15228
200-200	15223
210-298	15228
Bridgely St	15204
Bridgewater Dr	15216
Brierly Ln	15236
Briggs St	15234
Brighton Pl	15212
Brighton Rd	
100-198	15202
200-299	15202
701-1197	15233
1199-1399	15233
1400-4100	15212
4102-4198	15212
6500-7600	15202
7602-7698	15202
Brighton Woods Rd	15212
Brightridge St	15214
E & W Brightview Ave	15227
Brightwood Ave	15229
Brightwood Trl	15237
Brilliant Ave	15215
Brim Way	15212
Brintell St	15201
Brinton Rd	15221
Brinton Manor Dr	15221
Brinwood Ave	15227
Briscoe St	15204
Bristol Sq	15238
Bristol St	15207
Bristriv Rd	15238
Brittany Ct & Pl	15237
Broad St	
4800-5399	15224
5400-5406	15236
5400-5498	15206
5401-5497	15206
5499-6399	15206
Broad Hill Dr	15237
Broadcrest Dr	15235
Broadhead Ave	15205
Broadhead St	15206
Broadhead Fording Rd	15205
Broadlawn Dr	
2400-2499	15241
8000-8066	15237
8068-8098	15237
Broadlea Dr	15236
Broadmeadow Dr	15237
Broadmoor Ave	15228
Broadway Ave	
1500-2899	15216
2900-3299	15234
Broadway Dr	15236
Broglie Dr	15236
Bronx Ave	15229
Brook St	15210
Brookdale Dr	
400-498	15215
500-599	15215
3300-3499	15241
Brookfield Rd	15243
Brookhaven Ln	15241
Brooklawn Dr	15227
Brookline Blvd	15226
Brookmeade Dr	15237
Brookshire Dr	15237
Brookside Ave	15216
Brookside Blvd	15241
Brookside Dr	
101-297	15205
299-399	15205
700-703	15239
1000-1099	15205
Brookview Ln	15237
Brosville St	15203
Broughton Rd	15236
Broughton St	15213
Brown St	15209
Brown Way	15224
Brownell St	15232
Browning Rd	15206
Browns Ln	15237
Browns Hill Rd	15217
Brownshill Rd	15238
Brownsville Rd	
100-2599	15210
2600-4233	15227
4235-4299	15227
4300-6599	15236
6601-6699	15236
Bruce Hl	15260
Bruce St	15201
Bruce Way	15218
E & W Bruceton Rd	15236
Brucewood Dr	15228
Brule St	15214
Brunner Ct	15214
Brunner Dr	15237
Brunot Ave	15204
Brushcliff Rd	15221
Brushglen Ln	15236
Brushton Ave	
1-399	15221
400-1399	15208
1400-7399	15235
Brushy Ridge Ct	15239
N Bryant Ave	15202
S Bryant Ave	15202
Bryant Ct	15206
Bryant Dr	15235
Bryant St	15206
Bryn Ct	15237
Bryn Mawr Ct E	15221
Bryn Mawr Ct W	15221
Bryn Mawr Rd	
1-99	15221
600-4299	15219
Bryson Ave	15202
Buchanan Pl	15228
Buchannon Rd	15235
Buckeye Way	15223
Buckhill Rd	15237
Buckingham Dr	15237
Buckingham Pl	15215
Buckingham Rd	15215
Bucknell St	15208
Bucyrus St	15220
Buehner Dr	15237
Buena Vista St	
1100-1799	15212
1800-1898	15214
1801-1805	15212
1900-1999	15214
2300-2699	15218
Buente St	15212
Buffalo St	15213
Buffington Ave	15210
Bunkerhill St	15206
Bunny Way	15237
Bunts Dr	15236
Burchfield Ave	15217
Burdine St	15227
Burdock Way	15212
Burgess St	15227
E Burgess St	15214
W Burgess St	15214
Burham St	15203
Burketon Ln	15217
Burkhart Ave	15229
Burlington Rd	15221
Burnaby Dr	15235
Burns St	15221
Burnside Ave	15202
Burr St	15210
Burrows St	15213
Burton Dr	15235
Burton St	15218
Burwick Ct	15238
Business Center Dr	15205
Butler St	
3-131	15209
133-135	15209
181-185	15223
187-999	15223
3400-6399	15201
6600-7399	15206
Butterfield St	15223
Butterfield Way	15212
Buttermilk Hollow Rd	15207
Butternut Ct	15238
Buttonwood St	15220
Bygate Cir	15220
Byrd Ave	15209
Byrlee Dr	15237
Byrnwick Dr	15243
Byron Rd	15237
Cabin Ln	15238
Cabin St	15212
Cabinet St	15224
Cabinet Way	15201
Cable Ave	15238
Cable Pl	15213
Cabot Way	15203
Cabrini Dr	15220
Cactus Dr	15236
Cadberry Ct	15241
Cadbury Dr	15235
Cadet Ave	15226
Caesar Way	15203
Cagwin Ave	15216
Cain Way	15235
Cairo St	15211
Cake Way	15212
Calais Dr	15237
Calderwood Ave	15202
Caldonia Way	15204
Caldwell Ave	15235
Calera St	15207
Calgon Carbon Dr	15205
Calhoun Ave	15210
California Ave	
1-799	15202
800-900	15212
800-900	15202
801-999	15202
902-998	15212
902-998	15202
1000-1000	15212
1001-1001	15290
1001-1001	15233
1003-1011	15202
1013-1015	15202
1017-1099	15202
1200-2198	15212
2200-4099	15212
Calistoga Pl & St	15221
Calle St	15210
Callender Rd	15237
Callery St	15206
Callio St	15210
Callowhill St	15206
Calmont Dr	15235
Calumet St	15218
Calvert Ave	15227
Calvin St	
4200-4299	15201
10000-10099	15235
Calway St	15208
Camarta Dr	15227
Camberwell Dr	15238
Cambria Ct	15206
Cambria Point St	15209
Cambridge Rd	15202
Cambridge St	15213
Cambronne St	15212
Camden Ct	15237
Camden Dr	15215
Camden St	15220
Camelia St	15201
Camelot Ct	
1-99	15235
400-499	15220
Camelot Dr	
100-299	15237
300-306	15237
301-999	15237
304-398	15220
400-998	15237
Cameo Way	15212
Camera Dr	15235
Cameron Dr	15235
Camfield St	15210
Camp St	15219
Camp Horne Rd	
2-98	15202
100-399	15202
400-1199	15237
Campania St	15206
Campbell Dr	
100-198	15238
5200-5299	15236
Campbell St	15221
Campbells Run Rd	
500-599	15238
4100-5599	15205
5601-6099	15205
Campo Way	15210
Campus St	15212
Canal St	15234
N Canal St	15215
S Canal St	
800-899	15212
1301-1497	15215
1499-1899	15215
Canaveral Dr	15235
Canbet Dr	15234
Canby Dr	15209
Candace St	15216
Candleway Dr	15237
Candlewood Dr	15241
Cannon St	
1-99	15205
7700-7799	15218
Canoe Way	15224
Canopolis St	15204
Canterbury Dr	15238
Canterbury Ln	15232
Canterbury Rd	15202
Canton Ave	15216
Canvasback Rd	15238
Cape Cod Dr	15239
Cape May Ave	15216
Caperton St	15210
Capital Ave	15226
Capitol Dr	15236
Capri Ct	15239
Cara Lin Dr	15221
Caramel Way	15219
Card Ln	15208
Cardiff Rd	15237
Cardinal Cir	15237
Cardinal Dr	15243
Carey Way	15203
Cargill St	15219
Cargo Rd	15231
Cargo Bldg	15231
Carillo St	15260
Carl St	
100-199	15223
400-499	15210
Carla Dr	15238
Carleton Dr	15243
Carlisle Ave	15229
Carlisle Dr	15223
Carlsbad Rd	15239
Carlton St	
300-399	15235
4600-4699	15201
Carlyn Dr	15236
Carmel Ct	15221
Carmelita Dr	15241
Carmell Dr	15241
Carmella Dr	15227
Carmen Dr	15236
Carnahan Rd	
2-98	15220
900-1200	15216
1202-1232	15216
1250-1298	15220
1300-1499	15220
Carnation Ave	15229
Carnegie Dr	15243
Carnegie Pl	15208
Carnegie St	15201
Carnival Dr	15239
Carnival Way	15210
Carol Cir	15227
Carol Ln	15209
Carol Pl	15220
Caroline Dr	15234
Carolyn Ave	15202
Carolyn Dr	15236
Carpenter Dr	15239
Carpenter Ln	15212
Carpenter Way	15212
Carriage Blvd	15239
Carriage Cir	15205
Carriage Ct	15238
Carriage Dr	
100-199	15239
100-199	15237
4700-4799	15236
Carriage Ln	
100-299	15241
7500-7599	15221
Carriage Rd	15220
Carrick Ave	15210
Carrie St	15212
Carrington St	15212
Carroll St	15224
Carron St	15206
Carson Ave	15202
Carson St	15210
E Carson St	
2-70	15219
72-399	15219
401-797	15203
799-3499	15203
4901-4999	15207
W Carson St	
1-1999	15219
2401-3499	15204
Carver St	15206
Caryl Dr	
101-197	15236
199-499	15236
500-699	15235
Casa Dr	15241
Casa Grande Dr	15237
Cascade Rd	15221
Casement St	15212
Casino Dr	15212
Casper Ave	15229
Cassatt St	15219
Cassina Way	15208
Cassius St	15235
Caste Dr & Vlg	15236
Castle Ave	15210
Castle Dr	15235
Castle Rd	15234
Castle Shannon Blvd	
1-299	15228
300-1199	15234
Castlegate Ave	15226
Castlegate Rd	15221
Castleman St	15232
Castleview Dr	15227
Castleview Rd	15234
Castone Ln	15237
Catalina Dr	
100-199	15239
300-399	15241
Catalpa Pl	15228
Catalpa Ridge Rd	15238
Cathedral St	15210
Cathedral Of Learning	15260
Cathell Rd	
542-1198	15236

1200-1448 15236
1450-1798 15236
1451-1451 15227
1453-1799 15236
Catherine St
1-1 15209
2-6 15223
3-19 15209
8-39 15223
41-99 15223
Cato St 15213
Catoma St 15212
Caton St 15217
Catskill Ave 15227
Catskill Dr 15239
Caughey Ave 15202
Cavan Dr 15236
Cavendish Pl 15220
Cayuga Dr 15239
Cecil Pl 15222
Cecil St 15215
Cecilia Dr 15227
Cedar Ave
1-99 15202
101-119 15202
112-112 15221
114-118 15202
122-122 15221
124-126 15221
128-128 15221
300-1098 15212
Cedar Blvd 15228
Cedar Dr 15237
Cedar Ln 15237
Cedar St
1-69 15223
200-298 15236
301-399 15236
Cedar Ridge Dr 15205
Cedarbrook Dr 15220
Cedarcove St 15227
Cedarhurst St 15210
Cedarville St 15224
Cedarvue Dr 15241
Cedarwood Dr
100-599 15214
700-999 15235
Cedric Ave 15226
Cedricton St 15210
Celadine St 15201
Celeron Ave 15216
Celeron St 15221
Celia Pl 15224
Celina Pl 15204
Celmar St 15237
Celtic St 15210
Cemetery Ave 15214
Cemetery Ln
100-227 15237
229-299 15237
274-298 15238
Cencenco Dr 15236
Cenceno Dr 15236
Center Ave
1-37 15229
2-6 15229
4-1199 15215
15-15 15202
17-274 15202
20-198 15202
39-1120 15229
100-198 15238
200-805 15238
200-668 15202
276-298 15202
307-323 15229
325-399 15229
670-698 15202
701-805 15238
703-709 15202
711-899 15202
807-943 15238
930-998 15238
1000-1356 15229
1122-1144 15229
1358-1720 15229
1722-1736 15229
7500-7599 15218
Center Rd 15239
Center St
11-29 15205
51-51 15223
97-1599 15221
100-106 15209
101-707 15221
114-122 15239
124-208 15239
200-298 15239
210-240 15239
300-1598 15221
709-907 15221
2600-2800 15205
2802-2902 15205
2901-2911 15227
2913-2999 15227
3010-3010 15205
3015-3115 15205
Center Hill Rd 15239
Center New Texas Rd 15239
Center Oak Dr 15237
Centeridge Ave 15237
Central Ave
2-182 15238
184-499 15238
501-599 15238
3100-3299 15212
Central Sq 15228
Central St 15235
Central Way 15228
Centralia St 15204
Centre Ave
701-733 15215
701-701 15219
735-999 15215
1000-3118 15219
3120-3198 15219
4101-4197 15213
4199-5099 15213
5100-5116 15232
5117-5119 15213
5118-5598 15232
5201-5599 15232
5700-6500 15206
6502-6598 15206
Centurion Dr 15221
Century Ave 15207
Ceres Way 15210
Cerise St 15214
Cessna Way 15201
Chadwick St 15235
Chalet Dr 15221
Chalfant St 15221
Chalfont St 15210
Chalfonte Ave 15229
Challen Dr 15236
Chalmers Pl 15243
Chalmers St 15218
Chambord Dr 15209
Champa St 15235
Chance Way 15207
Chandler Pl 15212
Chaney Ct 15206
Chanticleer Dr 15235
Chapel Ct 15237
Chapel Dr 15237
Chapel Pl 15235
Chapel Way 15233
Chapel Crest Ter 15238
Chapel Harbor Dr 15238
Chapel Hill Dr 15238
Chapel Hill Rd 15235
Chapel Knoll Dr 15238
Chapel Oak Rd 15238
W Chapel Ridge Ct, Pl &
Rd 15238
Chapelwood Dr 15241
Chapin St 15214
Chaplain Way 15207
Chapman St
14-37 15205
1800-2099 15215
Chapparal Dr 15239
Chappel Ave 15216
Charcot St 15210
Charlemagne Cir 15237
Charlemma Ct & Dr 15214
Charles St
5-5 15202
10-11 15210
15-15 15202
40-54 15209
100-120 15238
104-498 15210
105-109 15210
111-142 15210
122-200 15238
144-250 15210
175-179 15237
209-499 15210
N Charles St
1800-1999 15212
2000-2999 15214
Charleston Ave 15218
Charleston Dr 15235
Charley Dr 15209
Charlotte Dr 15236
Charlotte St 15201
Charlton St 15205
Charm Ave 15226
Charnwood Dr 15235
Charterwood Dr 15237
Chartiers Ave
2-98 15205
100-292 15205
294-298 15205
700-1399 15220
1401-1499 15220
1500-3999 15204
Chartiers Pl 15205
Chartwell Dr 15241
Chateau Ct 15239
Chateau St 15233
Chatham Ctr 15219
Chatham Ln 15238
Chatham Sq 15219
Chatham Park Dr
100-900 15220
902-958 15220
960-1299 15216
Chatsworth Ave 15202
Chatsworth St 15207
Chaucer Dr 15235
Chaucer St
6900-7100 15208
7102-7140 15208
7142-7148 15206
Chauncey Dr & St 15219
Chautauqua Ct & St 15214
Chauvet Dr 15275
Chavelle Ct 15239
Chellis St 15212
Chelsea Ave 15221
Chelsea Ct
400-499 15241
1600-1699 15237
Chelton Ave 15226
Chemistry Building 15260
Cherokee Dr 15205
Cherokee Pl 15228
Cherokee Rd 15241
Cherokee St 15219
Cherrington Dr 15237
Cherry Ct 15237
Cherry St
1-199 15223
800-999 15205
Cherry Way 15219
Cherry Valley Rd 15221
Cherrydale Ct 15237
Cherrydell Dr 15220
Cherryfield St 15214
E & W Cherryhill St 15210
Cherryland St 15214
Cherryvale Dr 15236
Cherrywood Dr 15214
Cheryl Dr 15237
Cheryl Ln 15236
Chesapeake Ave 15237
Chesboro St 15212
Chesna Dr 15234
Chess St
500-599 15205
600-699 15211
Chessland Pl & St 15205
Chester Ave
200-699 15214
800-999 15202
Chesterfield Rd 15213
Chestnut St
8-10 15221
10-16 15202
25-27 15221
59-61 15229
200-399 15218
400-900 15212
900-922 15234
902-924 15212
915-925 15212
923-999 15234
924-998 15234
1000-1099 15212
1101-1199 15212
5300-5499 15236
N Chestnut St 15202
S Chestnut St 15202
Chestnut Ridge Dr 15205
Cheston St 15227
Chetopa St 15204
Cheyenne Dr 15205
Cheyenne St 15218
Chicago St 15214
Chickasaw Ave 15237
Chidell St 15212
Child Dr 15236
Childrens Way 15212
Childrens Hospital Dr 15224
Childs St 15213
China St 15220
Chincend Ave 15225
Chislett St 15206
Choate Way 15224
Chocolate Sq 15201
Chris Ct 15239
Chris Ln 15209
Christler St 15223
Christopher Cir 15205
Christopher St 15201
Christy St 15204
Church Ave
100-199 15210
200-200 15202
205-235 15202
247-247 15210
249-399 15210
6500-7599 15202
Church Ln 15238
Church Pl 15216
Church Rd
100-199 15209
200-299 15241
Church St
69-69 15223
200-399 15215
6900-7499 15218
Church Hill Rd 15205
Churchill Ave 15235
Churchill Rd
2-40 15235
5-41 15235
5-5 15205
42-400 15235
100-100 15235
100-100 15205
402-2598 15235
Churchland St 15206
Churchview Ave 15227
Churchview Avenue
Ext 15236
Chute Way 15214
Cimarron Dr 15235
Cinema Dr 15203
Circle Ave 15207
Circle Dr
100-100 15237
102-128 15237
130-198 15237
141-145 15228
500-600 15221
601-799 15241
602-1298 15221
1201-1299 15221
3000-3399 15227
Circuit Ln 15221
Citadel St 15204
Citizens Way 15202
Citron Way 15212
City View Ave 15202
Claim St 15212
Clair Ave 15235
Clair Dr 15241
Clairhaven St 15205
Clairmont Ave 15229
Clairmont Dr 15241
Clairton Blvd 15236
Clairtonica St 15205
Clapp Hl 15260
Clara St
100-299 15209
1200-1399 15234
Clare Ave 15209
Clare Dr 15237
Clarence St 15211
Clarendon Pl 15206
Clarendon St 15238
Clarette Rd 15237
Claridge Pl 15208
Clarinda St 15211
Clarion Ave 15202
Clarion St 15207
Clarissa St 15219
Clark St
100-198 15223
1300-1899 15221
Clarkton St 15204
Clarwin Ave 15229
Claus Ave 15227
Clawson St 15208
Clay Dr 15235
Clay St 15215
Claybourne St 15232
Clayton Ave 15214
Clearfield Pl & St 15204
Clearview Ave
1-9 15205
11-101 15205
101-277 15205
103-1325 15205
150-198 15229
157-195 15229
219-221 15202
700-898 15205
Clearview Dr
1-99 15205
1700-1799 15241
Clearview Rd 15202
Clearvue Rd 15237
Clelia Dr 15236
Clematis Blvd 15235
Clement Way
3800-3899 15201
3900-3999 15224
Clements Rd 15239
Clemesha Ave 15226
Clemson Dr 15243
Clermont Ave 15227
Cleveland Ave
101-131 15202
133-199 15202
152-154 15214
200-398 15202
203-225 15202
205-205 15214
211-227 15214
301-399 15202
Cliff Ave 15202
Cliff St 15219
Cliffmine Rd 15275
Clifford Ave 15238
Clifford Dr 15220
Clifford St 15206
Cliffside Mnr 15202
Cliffview Rd 15212
Cliffwood Trl 15235
Clifton Ave
100-199 15238
200-299 15215
Clifton Blvd 15210
Climax St 15210
Clinton Dr 15235
Clinton Pl 15202
Clinton St 15203
Clinton Way 15210
Clippert St 15226
Clive St 15202
Clokey Ave 15228
Clovelly Rd 15202
Clover Dr 15236
Clover St
100-399 15210
1200-1398 15203
1401-1499 15203
Clover Circle Ct 15227
Clover Hill Dr 15237
Cloverdale St 15210
Cloverfield Dr 15227
Cloverlea St 15227
Cloverview Cir 15239
Club Dr E & W 15236
Club House Ln 15237
Clubvue Dr 15236
Clyde St 15213
Coal St
100-199 15235
300-1799 15221
Coal Hollow Rd 15235
Coast Ave 15216
Cobalt Way 15201
Cobb Ave 15205
Cobbler Cir 15212
Cobblestone Dr
100-101 15239
102-102 15237
103-123 15239
104-118 15239
120-120 15239
120-120 15237
122-122 15237
124-299 15237
Cobden St 15203
Cochise Dr 15241
Cochran Rd
100-499 15228
1000-1599 15243
1600-1698 15220
1700-1999 15220
2001-2099 15220
Cochrans Mill Rd 15236
Cohassett St 15211
Cohutta St 15212
Cola St 15203
Colbert Ln 15215
Colby St & Ter 15214
Cold Spring Dr 15237
Colebrook Ave 15216
Coleen Dr 15236
Coleman St 15207
Coleman Way 15223
Colerain St 15210
Coleridge Pl & St 15201
Colescott St 15205
Colewood Dr 15236
Colfax St 15212
College Ave
100-199 15239
600-999 15232
Collier St 15208
Collingwood St 15218
Collins Ave 15206
Collins Dr 15235
Collins Rd
1500-2299 15221
2300-2599 15235
Collinwood Dr 15215
Colmar St 15213
Cologne St
1-99 15203
100-199 15210
1323-1323 15203
Colonial Dr 15216
Colonial Pl 15232
Colonial Park Dr 15227
Colonial Village Dr 15235
Colony Cir 15243
Colony Ct
200-299 15205
2200-2399 15237
Colony Sq 15239
Colony Oaks Dr 15209
Colorado Way 15212
Colquitt Dr 15238
Colson Dr 15236
Coltart Ave 15213
Colton St 15209
Columbia Ave
1-1 15223
2-252 15229
2-6 15223
5-126 15229
182-182 15235
187-217 15235
206-258 15235
221-221 15229
223-257 15235
300-315 15229
316-318 15235
317-499 15229
322-498 15229
1001-1099 15234
1900-2599 15218
2700-2799 15221
7501-7599 15235
Columbia Dr
100-299 15236
3300-3399 15234
Columbia Pl 15212
Columbia St 15205
Columbo St
4800-5353 15224
5355-5399 15224
5400-5599 15206
Columbus Ave 15233
Colvin Ct 15236
Colwell St 15219
Colwyn Dr 15237
Comanche Rd 15241
Comer St 15207
Comet Way 15232
Commerce Dr
1-6 15239
8-20 15239
100-2000 15275
Commerce St
500-599 15215
5871-5877 15206
W Commerce Way 15206
Commercial Ave 15215
Commercial St 15218
E, N, S & W
Commons 15212
Commonwealth Pl 15222
Community Ct 15205
Community Park Dr 15234
Complete St 15212
Compromise St 15212
Compton St 15216
Comstock Way 15220
Concord Rd 15221
Concord St 15212
Concordia St 15210
Concourse D 15231
Conemaugh St 15221
Conestoga Rd 15235
Conestoga St 15204
Conewanta Rd 15241
Congalton Rd 15237
Congress Dr 15236
Congress St 15219
Conneaut Dr 15239
Connecticut Ave 15216
Connecting Rd 15228
Connie Dr 15214
Conniston Ave 15210
Connolly Ave 15236
Connor Rd
700-798 15228
900-1067 15234
1069-1099 15234

Connor St 15207
Conover Rd 15208
Conrad Dr
100-199 15238
200-299 15227
300-399 15238
Conroy Dr 15205
Conson Rd 15227
Constance St 15212
Constitution Dr 15236
Continental St 15206
Convent Ave 15209
Converse Dr 15236
Converse St 15204
Conway St 15210
Cook Ave 15236
Cook School Rd 15241
Cooke Dr & Ln 15234
Coolidge Ave 15228
Cooper Ave 15212
Cooper Run Ct 15237
Copeland St 15232
Copperfield Ave 15210
Cora St 15208
Corace Dr 15243
Coral Dr
1-99 15238
200-299 15241
12800-12899 15235
Coral St
5000-5098 15224
5100-5300 15224
5302-5398 15224
5400-5549 15206
5551-5599 15206
Corbett Ct 15237
Corbett Dr 15234
Cord St 15235
Corday Way 15224
Cordell Pl 15210
Cordova Rd 15206
Corey St 15218
Corfu St 15220
Corliss St 15220
Cornell Ave 15229
Cornell Pl 15228
Cornell Rd 15205
Cornell St 15212
Cornell Avenue Ext 15229
Cornwall Dr 15238
Cornwall St 15224
Corona St 15212
Corporate Dr 15237
Corteland Dr 15241
Cortina Way 15234
Cosentino Dr 15217
Cosenza Ct 15235
Cosmos St 15207
Costa Ln 15237
Costco Dr 15205
Cottage Pl 15212
Cottage St 15225
Cotton Ln 15237
Cotton Way 15201
Couch Farm Rd 15243
Coulter St 15205
Country Ln 15229
Country Club Dr
--- 15205
1-57 15241
59-95 15241
97-99 15241
98-98 15205
100-199 15235
200-499 15205
501-601 15205
600-688 15228
690-999 15228
1600-1699 15237
2200-2200 15205
2201-2227 15241
2210-2230 15205
2228-2298 15241
2229-2299 15241
2300-2799 15205
4400-4499 15236
4501-4799 15236
Country Club Ln 15215
Country View Ct 15205
Court Pl 15219
Courtland St 15207
Courtney St & Way 15202
Courtney Mill Rd
100-169 15229
170-199 15202
Courtright St 15212
Cove Pl 15207
Covel Way 15219
Coventry Ln 15228
Coventry Rd 15213
Coverdale St 15220
Covert St 15210
Covington St 15219
Covode Pl & St 15217
Cowan St 15211
Cowley St 15212
Cox Ave & Pl 15207
Coyne Ter 15207
Crab Hollow Rd 15235
Craft Ave
1-99 15223
100-298 15213
300-399 15213
Craft Pl 15213
Craft St 15221
Craftmont Ave 15205
E & W Crafton Ave, Blvd
& Sq 15205
Crafton Ingram Shp
Ctr 15205
Craig Ct 15228
Craig Hl 15260
N Craig St 15213
S Craig St
200-208 15260
201-209 15213
211-499 15213
Craig Way 15205
Craighead St 15211
Craigview Dr 15243
Crailo Ave 15210
Cramden Rd 15241
Crane Ave
200-899 15216
1100-1599 15220
Crawford Ave 15202
Crawford Hl 15260
Crawford Ln 15238
Crawford Rd 15237
Crawford St 15219
Cready Hill Rd 15236
Creedmoor Ave & Pl 15226
Creekedge Dr 15235
Creekside Ln 15237
Creighton Ave 15205
Cremona Dr 15241
Crennell Ave 15205
Creole Cir 15241
Creole Dr 15239
Crescent Dr
2-98 15228
100-199 15228
300-399 15238
Crescent Pl 15217
Crescent St 15223
Crescent Gardens Dr 15235
Crescent Hills Rd 15235
Cresson Ave 15229
Cresson St 15221
Cresswell St 15210
Crest Dr 15215
Crest Rd 15237
Cresthaven Dr 15239
Cresthaven Ln 15237
Crestline Ct 15221
Crestline Dr
100-199 15237
500-599 15234
Crestline Pl 15221
Crestline St 15221
Crestmont Dr 15220
Crestmont Rd 15237
Crestnol Dr 15237
Crestvale Rd 15237
Crestview Dr
116-122 15236
124-299 15236
300-399 15209
400-599 15239
1500-1599 15237
Crestview Rd
100-228 15235
230-298 15235
2200-2399 15216
Crestvue Manor Dr 15228
Crestwood Dr
100-102 15209
101-105 15237
104-122 15209
107-113 15237
124-140 15209
Crete Way 15221
Crider Hill Rd 15237
Criders Ln 15237
Crimson Dr 15237
Criss St 15204
Crocus Ave 15235
Croesus Way 15219
Croft St 15212
Crofton Dr 15238
Crombie St 15217
Cromwell Dr 15237
Cromwell St 15221
Cronemeyer St 15212
Crosby Ave 15216
Cross St
1-9 15205
2-8 15214
2-6 15209
11-15 15205
34-39 15221
41-45 15221
900-999 15209
5600-5699 15236
Cross Creek Ct 15237
Crossman St 15203
Crosswinds Dr 15220
Crotzer Ave 15205
Crucible St
106-108 15220
110-1399 15220
1400-1599 15205
1601-1699 15205
Crysler St 15226
Crystal Dr 15228
Cullen St 15224
Culloden Way 15232
Cumberland Rd 15237
Cumberland St 15205
Cummings Rd 15231
Cunliffe Way 15203
Curranhill Ave 15216
Curry Rd 15236
Curry Hollow Rd 15236
Curtin Ave 15210
Curtis St
100-299 15235
600-698 15211
Curtis St W 15235
Cushing St 15235
Cushman St 15211
Cust St 15207
Custer Ave
2400-2499 15210
2600-3099 15227
Cuthbert St 15211
Cutler St 15214
Cynthia Dr 15227
Cynthia Ln 15241
Cypress Dr 15241
Cypress St
4700-5148 15224
5150-5198 15224
7900-7999 15237
Cypress Way 15228
Cypress Hill Dr 15235
Cyrano Ave 15214
Cyril Dr 15239
D St 15209
Daffodil Ln 15237
Dagmar Ave 15216
Dahlem Way 15206
Dailey Rd 15227
Daisy St 15214
Dakota Ave 15202
Dakota St
1-99 15205
4201-4399 15213
Dale Dr 15220
Dale St 15205
Daleland Ave 15220
Dalemount St 15216
Daleran Dr 15237
Dalewood St 15227
Dalgate Pl 15218
N Dallas Ave 15208
S Dallas Ave
1-99 15217
101-115 15208
117-599 15208
600-1498 15217
1500-1699 15217
Dallett Rd 15227
Dalton Ave 15214
Dalton Dr 15237
Dalzell Ave 15202
Dalzell Pl 15217
Damas St 15212
Dan Dr 15216
Danbury St 15214
Daniels St 15210
Danley St 15220
Danube Dr 15209
Danube St 15219
Danvers Ave 15205
Dargan St 15224
Darkerad St 15219
Darlan Hill Dr 15239
Darlene Dr 15237
Darlington Ct 15217
Darlington Ln 15229
Darlington Rd 15217
Darragh St 15213
Darrell Dr
400-499 15235
9200-9299 15237
Darsie St 15224
Dartmore St 15210
Dartmouth Ave 15229
Dartmouth Rd 15205
Daschbach Dr 15236
Dashwood Dr 15235
Datura Dr 15235
Daub Way 15227
Daube Dr 15236
Dauntless Dr 15235
Dauphin Ave 15227
Davenport St & Way 15219
David Dr 15237
David St 15209
David Lawrence Hl 15260
Davidson Rd 15239
Davis Ave
100-199 15202
200-300 15223
301-599 15209
801-897 15212
899-1899 15212
Davis Blvd 15275
Davis Row 15212
Davis St 15209
Davison St 15201
Davonshire Dr 15238
Dawes St 15210
Dawn Ave 15226
Dawson Ave 15202
Dawson Ct 15213
Dawson St 15213
Day Way 15212
Daytona St 15210
De Angelo Dr 15209
De Arment Pkwy 15241
De Haviland Dr 15239
De Ruad St 15219
De Victor Pl 15206
De Witt St 15211
Dean St 15206
Dearborn St 15224
Deary St 15206
Debbie Dr 15227
Deborah Jane Dr 15239
Debra Dr 15236
Decatur Ave 15221
Decatur St 15233
Decker Ln 15237
Deely St 15217
Deemer Dr 15234
Deepwood Dr 15241
Deer Dr 15235
Deer Ln 15202
Deer Rd 15237
Deer Meadow Dr 15241
Deer Spring Ln 15238
Deerbrooke Ln 15238
Deerfield Dr 15235
Deervue Dr 15227
Deerwood Dr 15235
Defoe St 15214
Dehaven St 15212
Deimling Rd 15229
Del Rio Dr 15236
Delafield Rd
100-1099 15215
1010-1020 15240
Delaney Dr 15235
Delano Dr 15236
Delaware Ave
800-1099 15221
1900-2599 15218
Delaware St 15214
Delco Rd 15227
Delehanty St 15207
Delevan St 15217
Delford St 15207
Delgar St 15214
Dell Ave 15216
Dell Ln 15237
Dellaglen Ave 15207
Dellrose St 15210
Delma Dr 15236
Delmar Way 15218
Delmont Ave 15210
Delp St 15202
Delray St 15222
Delta Dr 15238
Delwar Rd 15236
Delwood Ave 15216
Demmer Ave 15221
Demmler Ct & Dr 15237
Dengler St 15210
Denise St 15210
Denisonview St 15205
Denlin St 15216
Denmarsh St 15207
Dennis Dr 15239
Denniston Ave 15218
Denniston St
100-118 15206
120-499 15206
1200-1799 15217
Denny Est 15238
Denny St 15201
Denny Park Dr 15214
Denver St 15213
Dersam St 15235
Derwent Dr 15237
Desdemona St 15217
Desoto St
1-99 15205
100-199 15213
200-298 15205
Devereaux Ln 15232
Devilliers St 15219
Devlin St 15210
Devon Ln 15202
Devon Rd 15213
Devonshire Rd & St 15213
Devonwood Dr 15241
Dewalt Ave 15227
Dewalt Dr 15234
Dewey Ave
300-399 15218
3900-3999 15214
Dewey St
1-186 15223
100-106 15218
100-139 15223
108-199 15218
188-188 15223
200-299 15218
Dewey Avenue Ext 15223
Dexter St 15220
Di Marchi Dr 15236
Diablo Dr 15241
Diamond St 15219
Diana Pl 15212
Diann Dr 15236
Diaz Way 15219
Dick St 15206
Dickens St
800-899 15204
1200-1399 15220
Dickey St 15209
Dickson Ave 15202
Dickson St
1200-1499 15212
7500-7599 15218
Diehl Ave 15210
Dietrich Rd 15238
Diller Ave & Pl 15207
Dillon Dr 15243
Dilworth St 15211
Dimling Way 15213
Dinell Dr 15221
Dinsmore Ave 15205
Dinwiddie St 15219
Diploma St 15212
Dippen Ave 15226
N & S Dithridge St 15213
Ditzler St 15204
Diulus Way 15213
Divine Dr 15236
Divinity St 15214
Division Ave
200-500 15202
501-503 15229
502-698 15202
511-699 15202
Division St
1-99 15205
151-199 15215
Dixie Dr 15235
Dixon Ave 15216
Dixon Dr 15209
Doak St 15235
Dobson St 15219
Dodds St 15216
Dodge Way 15206
Doe Ct 15235
Doe Ter 15212
Doerr St 15233
Doerrville St 15207
Dogwood Ct 15237
Dogwood Dr 15235
Dogwood Hts 15239
Dogwood Ln
100-113 15238
100-104 15237
106-106 15237
Doll Way 15212
Dollman Rd 15235
Dolores Dr
100-199 15223
4900-5199 15227
Dolphin St 15207
Dombey Dr 15237
Dominion Ct, Dr & Hts 15241
Donahue Dr 15236
Donald Ave 15209
Donald Rd 15235
Donaldson Dr 15226
Donati Rd 15241
Donmor Dr 15237
Donna Dr 15237
Donna St 15224
Donora St 15212
Donson Way 15201
Doral Cir, Ct & Dr 15237
Doray Dr 15237
Dorchester Ave 15226
Dorchester Dr 15241
Dorf Dr 15209
Doris Dr
200-299 15236
600-799 15243
Dormar Ct & Dr 15237
Dormont Ave & Sq 15216
Dornbush St 15221
Dornestic St 15214
Dorothy Dr 15235
Dorothy Pl 15206
Dorsch St 15212
Dorset St 15213
Dorseyville Rd
100-460 15215
461-999 15238
Doubletree Dr 15205
Douglas Dr
100-199 15215
900-999 15239
1700-1799 15221
Douglas St 15217
Douglas Fir Dr 15239
Doulton Rd 15229
Dounreay Pl 15237
Dounton Way 15233
Dover Dr 15238
Doverdell Dr 15236
Dowling Ave 15221
Dowling Dr 15215
Dowling St 15210
Downing Dr 15238
Downing St 15219
Downlook St 15201
Doyle Rd 15227
Doyle St 15221
Drake Rd 15241
Dravo St 15209
Dravo Way 15206
Dravo Street Ext 15209
Drebert Ave 15227
Drennen Rd 15239
Dresden Way 15201
Drexel Ln 15214
Drexel Rd 15212
Driftwood Dr
600-699 15238
1100-1299 15243
Drive St 15201
Drood Ln 15237
Drovers Way 15212
Drum St 15214
Drv Dr 15221
Drycove St 15210
Dryden Way 15224
Duane Dr N 15239
Duane Dr S 15239
N Duane St 15205
Duart St 15210
Dubois St 15204
Duchess Ln 15236
Dudley Ct 15206
Duff Rd 15235
Duff St 15219
Duffield Ave 15235
Duffield St 15206
Duffland St 15210
Duluth St 15234
Dunbar Ave 15202
Dunbar Dr 15235
Duncan Ave
1-99 15205
100-1500 15237
1502-8798 15237
Duncan Dr 15237
Duncan Ln 15236
Duncan St 15201
Dundalk Dr 15235
Dundee Ct 15239
Dunfermline St 15208
Dunkeld Way 15201
Dunkirk St 15206
Dunlap St 15214
Dunloe St 15212

Dunluce Dr 15227
Dunmore St 15206
Dunmoyle Ave & Pl 15217
Dunn Dr 15227
Dunseith St 15213
Dunster St 15226
Dupont Cir 15243
Duquesne Ave 15218
Duquesne Dr 15243
Durango Way 15208
Durbin St 15205
Durham Ave 15216
Dutch Ln 15236
Dwight Ave 15216
Dyke St 15207
E St 15209
Eads St 15210
Eagle Trail Dr 15235
Eaglewood Ct 15237
Eakin Ave 15214
Earl St 15204
Earlford Dr 15227
Earlham St 15205
Earlsdale Rd 15234
Earlsmere Ave 15216
Earlswood Ave 15228
Earlton St 15210
Earlwood Rd 15235
Easley Rd 15237
East Ln 15212
East Rd
100-199 15209
9700-9799 15237
East St
701-797 15212
799-999 15212
1001-1099 15212
1100-1199 15221
1500-2299 15212
3414-3698 15214
3700-3899 15214
Eastchester St 15206
Eastern Ave 15215
Eastgate Dr 15235
Eastgate Rd 15231
Eastmont Ave 15216
Easton Dr 15238
Eastview St 15208
Eastvue Dr 15239
Eastwood Rd 15235
Eathan Ave 15226
Eaton Ct 15237
Ebdy St 15217
Ebel St 15206
Eben St 15226
Eberhardt St 15212
Eccles St 15210
Echo Glen Dr 15236
Ecker Way 15221
Eckert St 15212
Eckstein Pl 15213
Eddington St 15207
Eden Way 15201
Edenburg Dr 15239
Edenvale St 15212
Edgar St
2300-2499 15210
2500-2699 15227
Edge Rd 15227
Edgebrook Ave 15226
Edgecliff Ave 15223
Edgehill Ave 15216
Edgemont St
400-499 15211
600-699 15210
Edgemoor Ln 15238
Edgeridge Dr 15234
Edgerton Ave
6700-7199 15208
7600-7799 15221
Edgerton Pl 15208
Edgewood Ave
101-599 15218
700-799 15215
800-898 15234
900-999 15234
1001-1099 15234
7600-7998 15218
Edgewood Dr
100-199 15237
2400-2599 15241
Edgewood Rd
1-99 15215
200-699 15221
Edies Way 15229
Edinburg Dr 15235
Edison St 15212
Edith Ave
1-99 15221
1100-1199 15236
Edith Pl 15213
Edith St 15211
Edlam Way 15224
Edmond St 15224
Edmore St 15204
Edna St
1301-1399 15234
1600-1799 15219
Edward Ave 15216
Edward Dr 15227
Edward Ln 15205
Edwards Dr 15209
Edwards Way 15203
Edwood Ct & Rd 15237
Eggers St 15212
Eichenlaub Rd 15237
Eicher Rd 15237
Eighmy Rd 15239
Eileen Dr
100-156 15214
101-101 15227
103-158 15227
158-158 15214
160-198 15227
161-199 15227
Eiler Ave 15210
Eisenhower Dr 15228
El Ct 15208
El Paso St 15206
El Rancho Dr 15220
Elaine Dr
400-699 15236
8200-8399 15237
Elatan Dr 15243
Elba St 15219
Elbe Dr 15209
Elberton St 15204
Elbon St 15220
Elbow St 15212
Elderslee Rd 15227
Eldora Pl 15210
Eldridge St 15217
Eleanor St
1-1000 15203
1002-1398 15203
1400-1699 15210
8200-8299 15237
Electric St 15207
Elena Ct 15201
Elf St 15220
Elfort Dr 15235
Elgin St 15206
Elias Dr 15235
Elicker Rd 15239
Eliska St 15204
Elizabeth Ave 15202
Elizabeth Blvd 15221
Elizabeth Dr 15235
Elizabeth Ln 15237
Elizabeth Rd 15237
Elizabeth St
6A-6A 15209
1-48 15210
1-499 15223
2-4 15209
6-7 15209
8-34 15209
9-67 15209
36-36 15223
38-38 15209
39-40 15210
42-42 15210
46-98 15209
100-209 15209
210-210 15210
211-399 15209
212-398 15209
509-509 15210
800-1099 15221
3800-3899 15227
E Elizabeth St 15207
W Elizabeth St 15207
Elk Rd 15235
Elkland St 15214
Elkton St 15220
Ella St
200-399 15224
403-405 15224
406-412 15221
407-443 15224
414-499 15221
445-445 15224
500-699 15221
700-899 15243
1300-1398 15223
Ellen Dr 15227
Ellendell St 15210
Ellers St 15213
Ellesmere Ave 15218
Elliot Ln 15229
Elliott St 15220
Ellis St
1-99 15207
2600-2799 15214
Ellopia St 15204
Ellsworth Ave
4700-4999 15213
5100-5930 15232
5931-5939 15206
5932-5938 15232
6100-6198 15206
Ellsworth Pl 15232
Ellsworth Ter 15213
Ellwood Dr 15209
Ellwood Avenue Ext 15239
Ellzey St 15214
Elm Ave 15234
Elm Ct 15237
Elm Dr 15238
Elm Ln 15223
Elm Rd
100-100 15237
101-149 15237
103-105 15239
106-110 15237
107-299 15239
116-116 15239
120-150 15237
200-298 15239
Elm St
100-199 15218
200-200 15218
200-203 15225
202-299 15218
1300-1599 15221
7800-7999 15237
Elm Spring Rd 15243
Elma St 15227
Elmbank St 15226
Elmbrook Ln 15243
Elmdale Rd 15205
Elmer St
1-199 15214
400-499 15218
5400-5899 15232
Elmer L Williams Sq 15206
Elmhill Rd 15221
Elmhurst Ave 15212
Elmhurst Rd
1-99 15220
901-997 15215
999-1099 15215
E Elmhurst Rd 15220
Elmont St 15205
Elmore Rd 15221
Elmore Sq 15219
Elmore St 15219
Elmspring Ct 15220
Elmwood Dr 15227
Elmwood Rd 15209
Elmwood St 15205
Eloise St 15212
Elrod Way 15206
Elrond Dr 15235
Elrose Dr 15237
Elroy Ave 15227
Elsdon St 15214
Elsie St
200-299 15225
2100-2699 15210
Elsinburg Way 15210
Elter Ct 15209
Elton St 15227
Elvia Way 15221
Elwell St 15207
Elwood Ave 15235
Elwood Dr 15235
Elwood St 15232
Elwyn Ave 15234
Ely St 15226
Elysian St 15206
Emahlea St 15207
Emanuel St 15212
Emblem Dr S 15236
N Emblem Dr 15227
Emearist Rd 15239
Emerald Dr 15237
Emerald St 15210
Emerson Ave
1-99 15205
100-499 15215
Emerson Rd 15209
Emerson St
200-699 15206
9600-9699 15235
Emery Dr 15227
Emily Dr 15215
N Emily St 15205
S Emily St 15205
Emlin Way 15212
Emma Dr 15223
Emma St
1-99 15212
300-399 15243
Emma Jo Dr 15236
Emporia St 15204
Emrose Dr 15235
E End Ave
100-1099 15221
1100-1299 15218
E End Ext 15218
Enfield St 15213
Engelwood Dr 15241
Enger Ave 15214
Englewood Dr 15237
English Ln 15217
Engstler St 15210
Ennerdale Ln 15237
Ennis St 15211
Enoch St 15219
Enon Way 15203
Enright Ct & Pl 15206
Ensign Ave 15226
Enterprise Dr 15275
Enterprise St 15206
E Entry Dr 15216
Epsilon Dr 15238
Erdner Ave 15202
Erhardt Dr 15235
Erin Ct 15237
Erin St
1-299 15219
300-398 15209
301-599 15219
500-598 15219
Ernie St 15220
Esmond Ct 15206
Esplen Way 15204
Espy Ave 15216
Essen St 15214
Essex Ct
600-699 15238
5000-5099 15237
Estella Ave
1-199 15211
200-899 15210
Esther St 15227
Ethelthorpe Rd 15237
Etna Ave 15215
Etna Dr 15237
Etola St 15212
Eton Dr 15215
Eton Rd
1-99 15241
200-299 15205
Ettwein St 15217
N Euclid Ave
1-199 15202
300-1499 15206
S Euclid Ave
1-151 15202
153-179 15202
180-299 15206
N Euclid St 15206
Eugene Ave 15202
Eugene Way 15210
Euler Way 15213
Eureka St
1-499 15211
600-999 15210
Eutaw St 15211
Eva St 15206
Evaline St 15235
N Evaline St 15224
S Evaline St 15224
Evan Dr 15204
Evandale Dr 15220
Evandale Rd 15212
Evans Ave 15205
Evans St 15218
Evanston St 15204
Eve Dr 15216
Evelyn Rd 15227
Everett St 15221
Everglade Dr 15235
Evergreen Ave 15209
Evergreen Dr 15235
Evergreen Rd
100-199 15238
2200-2206 15237
2201-2205 15209
2207-2211 15209
2213-2249 15209
2251-2251 15237
2253-3499 15237
3800-4499 15214
Evergreen Heights Dr 15229
Evernia Dr 15235
Evers Dr 15206
Everton St 15206
Ewart Dr 15219
Ewing Ave 15205
Ewing Cir 15241
Ewing Rd 15205
Ewing St
700-799 15236
800-899 15221
Excelsior St 15210
Exeter St 15217
Eymard St 15221
F St 15209
Faber St & Ter 15214
Fabyan St 15212
Fadette St 15204
Fahnestock Ave 15221
Fahnestock Rd 15215
Fair Ave 15226
Fair Acres Ave 15216
Fair Oaks Dr 15238
Fair Oaks St 15217
Fairbanks Ave 15214
Fairdale Ct 15237
Fairdale St
100-102 15237
104-198 15237
800-1299 15204
Fairfax Rd 15221
Fairfield Ct 15201
Fairfield Rd 15237
Fairfield St 15201
Fairgreen Dr 15241
Fairgrove Dr 15238
Fairhaven Dr 15215
Fairhope St 15210
Fairland St 15210
Fairlawn Dr 15237
Fairlawn St 15221
Fairlee St 15212
Fairley Rd 15237
Fairmont St 15221
N Fairmount St 15206
S Fairmount St
100-299 15206
300-499 15232
Fairstead Ln 15217
Fairston St 15204
Fairview Ave
1-99 15229
100-714 15220
101-101 15238
105-619 15220
1000-1098 15238
1101-1199 15238
Fairview Ave E 15237
Fairview Ave W 15237
Fairview Rd
1-99 15221
200-999 15238
Fairview Manor St 15238
Fairway Cir
100-199 15241
2400-2499 15237
Fairway Dr 15227
Fairway Ln 15238
Fairwood St 15205
Fairywood St 15205
Faith Dr 15236
Falck Ave 15212
Falconhurst Dr N 15238
Falkirk Dr 15235
Fall Way 15212
Fall Run Rd 15221
Fallania St 15212
Fallow Ave 15226
Fallowfield Ave 15216
Falls Village Rd 15239
Fannell St 15224
Fareham Ct 15206
Fargo Way 15221
Farkas Pl 15218
Farley Way 15201
Farm Ln 15236
Farm House Rd 15206
Farmington Ct 15237
Farmington Rd 15215
Farndale Rd 15238
Farnsworth St 15207
Faronia St 15204
Farragut Ave 15202
Farragut St
--- 15209
500-699 15209
800-1299 15206
Farris St 15214
Fassinger Ln 15237
Faulkner St 15204
Faulsey Way 15233
Faust St 15204
Fawn Ct 15239
Fawn Meadow Ct 15238
Fedele Ln 15239
Federal Dr 15235
Federal St 15212
Federal Street Ext 15214
Feilbach St 15209
Felicia Way 15208
Felicity Dr 15237
Felix Dr 15236
Felmeth St 15210
Fennimore St 15206
Fenway Rd 15209
Fenwick Dr
100-101 15235
102-109 15237
110-112 15235
114-136 15235
138-198 15235
Ferdinand Way 15208
Ferguson Pl 15223
Fern Cir & St 15224
Ferncliffe Ave 15226
Ferndale St 15221
Fernhill Ave 15226
Fernland St 15234
Fernleaf Ave 15202
Fernleaf St 15210
Fernridge Dr 15241
Fernwald Rd 15217
Fernwood Ave 15228
Ferraro Dr 15235
Ferree St 15217
Ferris Ct 15208
Festus Way 15219
Fetzer St 15211
Fiat St 15210
Fidelity Dr 15236
Field Club Ct 15237
Field Club Dr 15237
Field Club Rd 15238
Field Club Ridge Rd 15238
Fieldbrook Dr 15228
Fieldcrest Dr
100-299 15221
500-599 15209
5000-5399 15236
5401-5499 15236
Fieldgate Dr 15241
Fielding Dr 15235
Fielding Way 15208
Fieldmont Dr 15241
Fieldstone Ct 15239
Fieldstone Dr 15220
Fieldvue Ln 15215
Fiesta Dr 15239
Fife Dr 15241
Filbert St 15232
Filmore Rd 15221
Filmore St 15213
Filson St 15212
Finance St 15208
Findley Dr 15221
Fineview Dr 15235
Fingal St 15211
Finland St 15219
Finley Rd 15239
Finley St 15206
Firston Cir 15241
Firth St 15212
Firwood Dr
1-299 15239
900-1399 15243
Fischer Ave 15223
Fisher St 15210
Fisk Ave 15202
Fisk St
200-399 15201
400-442 15224
444-598 15224
Fitler St 15210
Fitzgerald St 15213
Fitzhugh Way 15226
Five Acres Dr 15238
Flaccus Rd 15202
Flack St 15210
Flagstaff Dr 15237
Flamingo Ave 15235
Flamingo Dr 15236
Flavian St 15219
Fleck St 15212
Fleet St 15220
Fleiner St 15212
Fleming Ave 15212
Fleming St 15218
Flemington St 15217
Fletcher Way 15208
Fleury Way 15208
Flint Ridge Rd 15243
Flora Rd 15227
Flora St 15212
Florence Ave
1-899 15202
7300-7314 15218
7316-7398 15218
Florence Dr 15220
Florence Pl 15228

N Florence Rd 15237
Florida Ave
600-999 15228
1500-1599 15221
9200-9299 15235
Florien St 15204
Flotilla Way 15221
Flowers Ave
100-507 15207
509-599 15207
800-899 15236
Foliage St 15221
Folkstone Dr 15243
Fontana Dr 15241
Fontella St 15233
Forbes Ave
100-399 15222
400-2299 15219
2600-3098 15213
3100-3799 15213
3800-3898 15213
3801-3999 15213
3802-3898 15260
3900-3999 15260
4400-5099 15213
5101-5199 15213
5200-6600 15217
6602-6698 15217
7600-7799 15221
Forbes Rd 15235
Forbes Ter 15217
Forbes Quadrangle 15260
Forbes Res Hl 15260
Forbes Tower 15260
Ford Ave 15235
Ford St 15205
Fordham Ave
1-99 15229
500-1099 15226
Fordyce St 15210
Foreland St 15212
Foreside Pl 15219
Forest Ave
2-44 15202
46-794 15202
795-806 15209
808-814 15209
898-899 15202
900-904 15209
900-920 15202
901-1099 15202
906-920 15209
922-998 15202
1100-1199 15236
8300-8599 15237
E Forest Ave 15202
Forest Dr
2-48 15220
50-54 15220
56-90 15220
100-199 15238
300-328 15220
341-341 15235
343-2499 15235
Forest St 15209
Forest Way 15208
Forest Brook Dr 15241
Forest Estates Dr 15241
Forest Glen Dr
1-99 15228
100-199 15221
Forest Glen Rd 15217
Forest Highlands Dr 15238
Forest Hills Plz & Rd 15221
Forest Ridge Dr
100-899 15221
1600-1630 15237
1632-1698 15237
Forestview Dr 15234
Forestwood Dr 15237
Forisou St 15201
S Fork Dr 15229
Formosa Way 15208
Fornof Ln 15212
Fornoff St 15209
Forrester St 15207
Forsaith St 15223
Forsythe Rd 15220
Forsythe St 15212
Fort Couch Rd 15241
Fort Duquesne Blvd 15222
Fort Pitt Blvd
101-399 15222
401-445 15219
Fortuna Ave 15226
Forward Ave 15217
Foster Ave 15205
Foster Sq 15212
Foster St 15201
Foster Way 15201
Foundry St 15215
Fountain St
2-14 15205
5-99 15205
16-16 15212
22-170 15205
67-103 15212
101-130 15205
105-127 15212
132-136 15205
300-398 15238
400-699 15238
3701-3799 15234
Four Mile Run Rd 15207
Four Winds Rd 15214
Fox Dr 15237
Fox Rd
400-499 15239
501-509 15237
511-9700 15237
9702-9898 15237
Fox Way 15203
Fox Chapel Rd 15238
Fox Chase Ln 15241
Fox Hollow Dr 15237
Fox Hunt Rd
300-399 15238
8800-9199 15237
Fox Pointe Dr & Pl 15238
Fox Ridge Rd 15237
Fox Ridge Farms Dr 15215
Fox Run Cir 15241
Foxburg Dr 15205
Foxcroft Rd 15220
Foxhurst Dr & Rd 15238
Foxland Dr 15243
Foxtail Dr 15239
Foxtop Dr 15238
Foxwood Ct 15220
Foxwood Dr 15238
Foxwood Ln 15220
Fram St 15208
Frame Dr 15239
Frampton Ave 15210
Francis Ave 15218
E Francis Ave 15227
W Francis Ave 15227
Francis Ct 15219
Francis Rd
100-599 15239
1000-1099 15234
Francis St 15219
Francisco St 15204
Frank St
1-11 15209
700-899 15227
3800-3898 15234
3900-3999 15234
4101-4197 15217
4199-4300 15217
4301-4327 15227
4302-4308 15217
4329-4377 15227
4379-4399 15227
Frankella Ave 15221
Frankfort Ave 15229
Franklin Ave
100-199 15209
200-1499 15221
Franklin Ct 15203
Franklin Dr
100-238 15241
240-2709 15241
2711-2799 15241
3200-3399 15235
Franklin Rd 15214
Franklin St
1-3 15223
2-2 15209
2-2 15223
4-11 15209
N Franklin St 15233
Franklin Way 15205
Franklin Run Ct 15237
Frankstown Ave
6400-6698 15206
6700-7899 15208
7900-8399 15221
Frankstown Rd 15235
Frankwood Rd 15235
Frayne St 15207
Frazier Dr 15235
Frazier St 15213
Freda St 15235
Fredanna St 15207
Fredell St 15210
Frederick Ct 15227
Frederick Dr 15241
Frederick St
1-99 15209
101-105 15209
107-139 15210
107-127 15209
140-210 15210
2700-3199 15212
3800-3899 15227
3865-3899 15227
3901-3939 15227
3915-3919 15234
3921-3931 15234
3933-3941 15234
3941-3955 15227
Fredericka Dr 15236
Fredonia St 15220
Freedmore St 15212
Freedom Ave 15226
Freeland St 15210
Freeport Rd
1-99 15215
2-98 15215
100-164 15238
100-305 15215
121-697 15238
166-814 15238
307-353 15215
405-701 15215
699-702 15238
704-798 15238
815-815 15215
816-2998 15238
817-2999 15238
Freeport St 15223
N Fremont Ave 15202
S Fremont Ave 15202
Fremont Pl 15216
Fremont St
100-199 15210
501-597 15209
599-699 15209
French St 15222
Frew St 15213
Frey Rd 15235
Freyburg St 15203
Frich Dr 15227
Frick Ln 15217
Frick Rd 15238
Frick Fine Arts 15260
Friday Rd 15209
Friendship Ave
4500-5399 15224
5400-5499 15232
5600-5799 15206
Friendship Cir 15241
Fritz St 15203
Froman St 15212
Front St
400-498 15237
1700-1898 15215
Front River Rd 15225
Frontenac St 15204
Frontier St 15212
Fruithurst Dr 15228
Frustum St 15204
Fulton Pl 15210
Fulton St 15233
Funston Ave 15235
Furley St 15220
Fusion St 15204
Gable St 15210
Gadshill Pl 15237
Gail Dr 15237
Gailey Ave 15214
Galaxy Cir 15241
Galbraith St 15227
Gales Dr 15236
Gallion Ave 15226
Gallupe Dr 15226
Galveston Ave 15233
Gamble Ave 15212
Gamma Dr 15238
Gandy St 15214
Ganges Way 15207
Gangwish St 15224
Ganlet Dr 15227
Ganster St 15223
Garden Aly 15223
Garden Dr 15236
E Garden Rd 15227
W Garden Rd 15227
Garden Ter 15221
Garden Way 15201
Garden Glen Ln 15238
Gardenia Dr 15235
Gardenview Dr 15212
Gardenview Rd 15236
Gardenville Rd 15236
Gardner Pl 15237
Gardner St
1-99 15223
1300-1398 15212
1400-1499 15212
1501-1599 15212
Gardner Steel Conf Ctr 15260
Garetta St 15217
Garfield Ave
700-1099 15221
1500-1699 15212
Garland Dr 15235
Garland St 15218
Garlow Blvd 15239
Garlow Dr 15235
Garner Ct 15213
Garnet Way 15224
Garnier St 15215
Garrick Dr 15235
Garvin St 15214
Garwood Way 15201
Gary Ct 15237
Gary Dr 15227
Gaskell St 15211
Gass Ave 15212
Gass Rd 15229
Gate Lodge Way 15207
Gatewood Dr 15217
Gay Ln 15202
Gaylord Ave 15216
Gaymor Dr 15214
Gaywood Cir 15241
Gaywood Dr 15235
Gazzam St 15213
Gearing Ave 15210
Gebhart St 15212
Geisler Dr 15221
Gelston St 15220
Gem Way 15224
Gena Ct 15209
Gencenc Dr 15243
Gene Dr
100-199 15237
1400-1499 15234
E & W General Robinson St 15212
Genesee Rd 15241
E & W Genessee Ave 15223
Geneva St
1-99 15223
4000-4399 15201
Gensler Rd 15236
Gentry Way 15212
George Ln 15235
Georgekay Rd 15207
Georgetown Ave 15229
Georgetown Pl 15235
Georgette St 15234
Georgia Ave 15210
Georgia Dr 15209
Georgian Pl 15215
Geranium St 15214
Gerard Dr 15209
Gerber Ave 15212
Gerber Ter 15229
German Sq 15203
Gerrie Dr 15241
Gerritt St 15208
Gerry Dr 15236
Gershon St 15235
Gertrude St 15207
Gerwig St 15209
Gettie St 15201
Gettysburg St 15206
Geyer Ave 15212
Geyer Rd
800-849 15212
869-877 15209
879-1099 15209
1101-1199 15209
Geyer Road Ext
800-849 15212
850-899 15209
Geyser Rd 15205
Giant Oaks Dr 15241
Gibb St 15202
Gibralter Dr 15239
Gibson Ln
100-299 15225
901-999 15236
Gibson St
1-99 15202
900-999 15220
10100-10199 15235
Giddings St 15207
Gien Dr 15209
Giese Dr 15227
Giffin Ave 15210
Gifford St 15212
Gilboa Way 15227
Gilchrest Dr 15235
Gilda Ave 15217
Gildenfenny St 15215
Gilford Ct 15206
Gilkeson Rd 15228
Gilleland Ct & Ln 15237
Gillespie Way 15221
Gilliland Pl 15202
Gilmore Ave & Dr 15235
Girard Rd 15227
Girard St 15202
Gist St 15219
Gittens St 15212
Glade St 15210
Gladefield St 15206
Gladstone Rd 15217
Gladstone St 15207
Gladys Ave 15216
Glaids Dr 15243
Glarius St 15202
Glaser Ave 15202
Glasgow Rd 15221
Glasgow St 15204
Glass Rd 15205
Glass Run Rd
200-299 15207
501-507 15236
509-699 15236
800-811 15227
812-816 15236
813-817 15227
818-1299 15236
Glearler St 15218
Glen Ln 15237
Glen Allen Dr 15236
Glen Arden Dr 15208
Glen Brook Dr 15215
Glen Caladh St 15207
Glen Da Lough Ct 15237
Glen David Dr 15238
Glen Elm Dr 15236
Glen Haven Ln 15238
Glen Lytle Rd 15217
Glen Manor Rd 15237
Glen Ridge Ln 15243
Glen Robin Dr 15236
Glenarm Ave 15226
Glenbrook Dr
1-99 15235
200-299 15237
Glenburn Dr 15236
Glenbury St 15234
Glencairn Cir 15241
Glenchester Dr 15237
Glencoe Ave
71-953 15220
955-1200 15220
1201-1217 15205
1202-1210 15220
1219-1399 15205
1401-1599 15205
Glendale Ave 15227
Glendale Dr 15241
Glendale Rd 15235
Glendon Ave 15205
Glenellen Dr 15237
Glenfield Dr 15235
Glengarry Ct 15239
Glengary Dr 15215
Glenhurst Rd 15207
Glenmawr St 15204
Glenmore Ave
1-199 15229
2700-2999 15216
Glenn Ave
100-199 15215
700-1499 15221
Glenn St
1-99 15202
100-150 15205
152-199 15205
Glennvue Dr 15205
Glenover Pl 15215
Glenroy St 15210
Glenshannon Dr 15234
Glenside St 15214
Glenview Pl 15206
Glenvue Dr 15237
Glenwood Ave
2-6 15207
111-127 15209
129-150 15209
200-5499 15207
Glenwood Dr 15209
Glenwood Pl 15209
Glenwood Rd 15241
Glo Min Dr 15241
Gloria St 15237
Gloster St 15207
Gloucester Dr 15241
Glowood Dr 15227
Godec Dr 15236
Goe Ave 15212
Goehring St 15212
Goettel St 15227
Goettman St 15212
Gold Way 15213
Goldbach St 15210
Golden Eye Ln 15238
Golden Mile Hwy 15239
Golden Oaks Ln 15237
Goldenbrook Ln 15237
Goldsmith Rd 15237
Goldstrom Ave 15216
Golf Dr 15229
Golfview Dr 15241
Golliste Ave 15232
Good Ln 15237
Goodman St 15218
Goodwin St 15209
Gopher St 15206
Gordon Dr 15205
Gordon St 15218
Gorgas St 15210
Gorman Way 15213
Goshen St 15214
Goucher Dr 15236
Gould Ave 15214
Grace Dr 15237
Grace St
2-98 15205
303-699 15211
311-317 15211
312-314 15236
316-491 15236
319-473 15211
378-396 15236
493-499 15236
500-698 15211
5201-5299 15236
Grace Del Ln 15237
Graeme St 15222
Graeser Ave 15241
Graff Ave 15218
Grafton St 15206
Graham Blvd
800-899 15221
1000-3099 15235
Graham Pl 15232
Graham Rd 15237
N Graham St 15206
S Graham St
100-299 15206
300-599 15232
Graham Boulevard Ext 15235
Graib St 15212
Grall Ave 15209
Gramac Ln 15235
Grand Ave
400-498 15225
700-807 15221
809-809 15221
819-827 15212
829-950 15212
951-951 15221
952-1198 15212
1001-1199 15212
2800-7699 15225
Grandin Ave 15216
Grandview Ave
1-5 15211
6-8 15223
10-10 15214
12-28 15223
21-61 15214
111-137 15211
169-181 15223
200-298 15202
201-219 15211
221-221 15202
223-497 15211
499-607 15211
609-609 15211
614-621 15202
620-636 15211
623-733 15202
646-656 15202
700-798 15211
800-912 15211
914-918 15211
982-984 15237
986-999 15237
1000-1037 15237
1000-1799 15211
1039-1099 15237
2500-2699 15235
2700-2799 15226
9900-10099 15235
N Grandview Ave 15205
S Grandview Ave 15205
Grandview Dr N 15215
Grandview Dr S 15215
Grandview Rd 15237
Granger St 15207
Grant Ave
4-4 15202
6-16 15202
14-56 15223
15-117 15223

18-238 15202
58-109 15223
101-121 15209
110-110 15237
111-161 15223
112-112 15223
114-114 15209
116-118 15223
119-190 15223
123-127 15237
123-226 15209
129-241 15237
240-240 15202
251-255 15202
300-599 15209
Grant St
200-298 15219
300-707 15219
709-717 15219
2203-2223 15218
2225-2227 15218
2229-2299 15218
3601-3697 15234
3699-3799 15234
Granville St 15219
Grape St 15210
Graper St 15227
Grapevine St 15206
Graphic St 15217
Grasmere St 15205
Grassmere Ave 15216
Gray St 15211
Graydon Dr 15209
Grayhurst Dr 15235
Graymore Ave 15216
Graymore Rd 15221
Grayson Ave 15227
Great Oak Dr 15220
Great Smokey Dr 15239
Greeley Ave 15223
Greeley St 15203
Green Ct 15234
Green Dr 15236
Green St 15221
Green Commons Dr 15243
Green Glen Dr 15227
Green Haven Ct 15239
Green Leaf Ln 15238
Green Meadow Ct 15239
Green Oak Ln 15220
Green Valley Dr 15235
Green Valley Rd 15237
Green View Ct 15237
Green Vista Dr 15237
Greenboro Ln 15220
Greenbriar Dr 15220
Greenbriar Way 15232
Greenbush St 15211
Greencrest Dr 15226
Greendale Ave 15218
Greendale Dr 15239
Greenfield Ave
100-700 15207
701-759 15217
702-760 15207
761-1199 15217
Greenhill Rd
1-97 15237
99-199 15237
700-1299 15209
Greenhill Road Ext 15209
Greenhurst Dr 15243
Greenlawn Dr
1-99 15220
1002-1002 15216
1004-1022 15216
1024-1026 15216
1027-1027 15220
1029-1199 15220
Greenleaf St 15211
Greenlee Rd 15227
Greenmount Ave 15216
Greenough Ave 15202
Greenridge Dr 15236
Greenridge Ln 15220
Greenridge Rd 15234
Greensburg Pike 15221
Greenside Ave 15220
Greentree Rd 15220
Greenvalley Ct & Dr 15220
Greenway Dr
1-99 15204
300-323 15235
324-390 15235
325-405 15235
390-390 15204
471-799 15204
801-830 15204
832-1370 15204
Greenwood Ave
2-8 15205
10-99 15205
100-299 15202
Greenwood Dr 15236
Greenwood Rd
1-99 15221
100-199 15238
Greenwood St
400-451 15209
453-499 15209
6600-6999 15206
Greer St 15217
Greeves Way 15212
Gregory St 15203
Greismere St 15223
Grenada St 15212
Grey Mill Dr 15241
Greyfriar Dr 15215
Greylock Dr 15235
Greystone Dr
1200-1399 15241
1400-1499 15206
Griffin St 15211
Griffith St 15209
Griffiths St 15213
Grimes Ave 15210
Grizella St 15214
Grogan St 15210
Grosick Rd 15237
Gross St 15224
Grotto St 15206
Grouse Dr 15243
Grove Ave
1-99 15202
100-299 15229
Grove Pl
1-99 15236
2000-2099 15219
Grove Rd
1100-1363 15234
1365-1399 15234
1400-5399 15236
Grove St
100-299 15215
400-499 15219
Grove Crest Dr 15239
Groveland St 15234
Grovemount Rd 15220
Grover Ave 15223
Groveton St 15234
Guarino Rd 15217
Guckert Way 15212
Guenevere Dr 15237
Gulf Lab Rd 15238
Guthrie St 15221
Guy St 15217
Guyasuta Ln & Rd 15215
Guyland St 15205
Guylyn Dr 15235
Guys Run Rd 15238
Gypsy Ln 15228
Haas St 15204
Haberman Ave
1-45 15211
47-169 15211
171-699 15210
Haberstich Ln 15238
Hacienda Dr
2400-2499 15241
5300-5599 15236
Hackstown St 15203
Haddon Way 15226
Hafner Ave 15223
Hagy Pl 15232
Hahn Rd 15209
Hailman St 15206
Halchess St 15207
Haldane St
1-199 15205
4000-4399 15207
Hale St 15208
Halket Pl & St 15213
Hall Ave 15205
Hall Dr 15235
Hall St
1-99 15205
1000-1199 15212
Hallam St 15221
Haller St 15212
Hallett Pl 15202
Hallett St 15219
Halliford Dr 15235
Halliwell Dr 15239
Hallmark Dr 15235
Hallock St 15211
Hallowell St 15210
Hallsborough Dr 15238
Halsey Ave 15221
Halsey Ct 15228
Halsey Pl 15212
Halverson Rd 15231
Hamburg St 15220
Hamilton Ave
1000-1099 15202
6400-6699 15206
6700-6852 15208
6853-6853 15206
6854-7998 15208
6855-7999 15208
Hamilton Dr 15235
Hamilton Rd
500-600 15205
602-698 15205
1200-1599 15234
4101-4497 15236
4499-4799 15236
4801-5699 15236
Hamilton Drive Ext 15235
Hamlet Ct 15227
Hamlet Pl 15213
Hamlin St 15233
Hammond St 15204
Hampshire Ave 15216
Hampshire Ct 15237
Hampstead Dr 15235
Hampton Ave
400-699 15221
3101-3199 15234
Hampton Rd 15215
Hampton St
2000-2299 15218
5400-6399 15206
Hancock St
300-499 15219
500-898 15213
Hancock Camp Rd 15238
Handler St 15203
Hangar Rd 15231
Hanover St
1-99 15210
1800-1999 15218
Hansel St 15235
Hansen St 15209
Hanway St 15229
Harbeth Dr 15237
Harbison Ave 15212
Harbison Pl 15212
E Harbison Rd 15205
W Harbison Rd 15205
Harbison St 15212
Harbor St 15212
Harborview Dr 15239
Harcor Dr 15226
Harcum Way 15203
Harden Dr 15229
Hardie Way 15213
Harding Rd
100-106 15235
101-125 15215
110-122 15229
115-199 15229
124-124 15215
126-198 15229
9401-9497 15237
9499-9699 15237
Harding St 15219
Harding Way 15215
Hardwood Rd 15235
Hardy Dr 15241
Hardy St 15205
Hargrove St 15226
Harker St 15220
Harlan Ave 15214
Harlem St 15207
N & S Harleston Dr 15237
Harlow Dr 15204
Harlow Pl 15204
Harlow St
100-199 15218
1501-1535 15204
1537-1699 15204
Harmain Rd 15235
Harmar St 15219
Harmening Ave 15227
Harmony Dr, Pkwy & Rd 15237
Harold Pl & St 15237
Harpen Rd 15214
Harper Dr 15237
Harper Rd 15231
Harpster St 15212
Harriet St 15232
Harriett St 15224
Harris Ave 15205
Harrisburg St 15204
Harrison Ave
100-399 15202
801-897 15221
899-900 15221
902-998 15221
7100-7199 15218
N Harrison Ave 15202
S Harrison Ave 15202
Harrison St
1-99 15205
500-599 15237
1000-1099 15234
4800-5699 15201
Harrogate Rd 15241
Harrow Rd
200-299 15238
2300-2399 15241
Harry St 15213
Hart Dr 15235
Hart St 15221
Harter Cir 15236
Hartford St 15203
Hartl Ln 15227
Hartle Ln 15228
Hartle St 15209
Hartman St 15212
Hartmans Ln 15206
Hartranft St 15226
Harts Run Rd 15238
Hartwell St 15205
Hartwood Dr 15208
Hartwood Trl 15238
Hartwood Acres 15238
Harvard Ave
1-199 15229
1700-1799 15218
Harvard Cir 15212
Harvard Dr 15235
Harvard Rd 15205
Harvard Sq 15206
Harvat St 15239
Harvest Hill Dr 15239
Harvest Manor Dr 15237
Harvester Cir 15241
Harveys Ln 15237
Harwick Dr 15235
Harwood St 15211
Haslage Ave 15212
Hasley Ln 15217
Hassler St 15220
Hastie Rd 15234
Hastings St
100-799 15206
800-999 15217
Hastings Mill Rd 15241
Hatfield St 15201
Hathaway Ct 15235
Hathaway Ln 15241
Hatteras St 15212
Hauck Dr 15235
Hauden Dr 15205
Haug St 15212
Haugh Dr 15237
Havana Dr 15239
Havelock Ave 15234
Havelock Way 15211
Haven St 15204
Haverford Cir 15228
Haverford Rd 15238
Haverhill Rd 15228
Haverhill St
500-599 15221
600-614 15208
601-699 15221
616-618 15221
620-620 15208
622-626 15221
628-628 15208
630-698 15221
Hawkins Ave 15214
Hawley Ave 15202
N & S Hawthorn Ct 15237
Hawthorne Ave
1-91 15205
93-99 15205
101-101 15205
103-105 15229
103-115 15205
107-155 15229
157-159 15229
200-298 15229
2200-2399 15218
Hawthorne Ct
100-199 15201
200-299 15221
351-386 15237
Hawthorne Dr 15235
Hawthorne Rd
1-20 15221
22-22 15221
96-116 15209
100-110 15221
100-109 15238
111-111 15238
118-499 15209
N Hawthorne Rd 15209
Hawthorne St
100-299 15218
1300-1699 15201
Hay St 15221
Hays Ave 15210
Hays Rd 15241
Hays St
1-30 15209
32-198 15209
1649-1697 15218
1699-1799 15218
5400-5899 15206
Hayson Ave
2000-2236 15216
2238-2298 15216
2247-2297 15220
2299-2599 15220
Hazel Dr 15228
Hazel Pl 15221
Hazel Rd 15235
Hazel St 15236
Hazeldell St 15210
Hazelhurst Ave 15227
Hazeltine Way 15218
Hazelton St 15214
Hazelwood Ave
100-128 15207
130-162 15207
164-650 15207
195-299 15202
200-258 15207
202-278 15202
301-649 15207
651-899 15217
901-999 15217
Hazlett Rd 15237
Hazlett St 15214
Headenso St 15220
Heanint St 15210
Heart Ct 15208
Hearthstone Dr 15235
Heartwood Dr 15241
Heasley Rd 15223
Heather Ct 15239
Heather Dr 15209
Heather Ln 15205
Heather Pl 15237
Heathergate Dr 15238
Heathmore St 15227
Heber St 15210
Heberton St 15206
Hebron Dr 15235
Heckelman St 15212
Heckler Dr 15220
Hedge St 15206
Heidcrest Dr 15237
Heights Dr 15209
Heinen Way 15236
Heinz St 15212
Heinz Ter 15215
Heinz Chapel 15260
Heldman St 15219
Helen Dr 15216
Helen Way 15210
Heltzell Dr 15235
Hemans St 15219
Hemingway Ln 15215
Hemingway St 15213
Hemlock Ct 15237
Hemlock St
1-7 15228
9-13 15228
15-99 15228
16-16 15212
20-120 15228
101-497 15212
110-124 15212
499-599 15212
600-799 15202
7600-7999 15237
Hemphill St 15214
Hempstead Ave 15229
Hempstead Ln 15241
Hempstead Rd 15217
Henderson Rd 15237
Henderson St
1-99 15212
100-112 15235
122-130 15212
132-299 15212
Hendon Ct 15206
Henger St 15210
Henley Dr 15235
Hennig Dr 15236
Henrietta St 15218
Henry St 15213
Herbert Way 15207
Herbst Dr 15209
Heritage Dr
300-399 15235
1600-1699 15237
Herman Dr 15239
Herman St
1-99 15223
1300-1399 15212
Hermitage St 15208
Herndon St 15220
Herr St
3-3 15221
61-85 15209
1100-1199 15221
Herrod St 15220
Herron Ave
1-99 15202
500-1299 15219
Herschel St 15220
Hershey Rd 15235
Hervey St 15210
Hespen St 15212
Hestor Dr 15220
Hetherton Dr 15237
Hethlon St 15220
Heths Ave 15206
Hetzel St 15212
Hewitt St
2-98 15205
3900-3999 15214
Hi Tor Dr 15236
Hialeah Dr 15239
Hiawatha St 15212
Hibiscus Dr 15235
Hickent St 15215
Hickentr St
3400-3498 15210
3400-3498 15215
Hickory Ct 15238
Hickory St 15223
Hickory Hill Rd 15238
Hidden Fls & Rdg 15238
Hidden Meadow Ln 15238
Hidden Spring Ln 15238
Hidden Timber Dr
1400-1499 15220
2300-2399 15241
Hidden Valley Ct 15237
Hidden Valley Dr 15237
Hidden Valley Rd 15241
Hieber Rd 15229
Higgins St 15223
High St
1-1 15205
2-4 15223
6-199 15223
110-111 15237
600-799 15215
801-915 15215
955-997 15212
999-1899 15212
8200-8299 15237
High Knoll Dr 15241
High Oak Ct 15241
High Oak Dr 15220
High Oak Pl 15220
High Park Pl 15206
High Sierra Cir 15241
Highgate Rd 15241
Highgrove Rd 15236
Highland Ave
1-13 15212
11-37 15223
18-38 15205
39-39 15223
60-60 15223
80-81 15205
98-98 15229
100-499 15229
700-999 15215
2000-2098 15212
2100-2199 15212
7600-7699 15218
N Highland Ave 15206
S Highland Ave 15206
Highland Ct 15206
Highland Dr
1-99 15202
7000-7168 15206
7170-7176 15206
7178-7198 15206
S Highland Mall 15206
Highland Pl 15202
Highland Rd
100-100 15238
105-197 15238
111-203 15235
120-498 15235
199-216 15238
205-252 15235
205-217 15238
218-218 15238
254-298 15235
301-499 15235
8601-8847 15237
8849-9699 15237
N Highland Rd
1600-1610 15228
1630-1698 15241
1700-1799 15241

Highland Ter 15215
Highland Pines Ct & Dr 15237
Highland View St 15235
Highland Villa Rd 15234
Highlander Dr 15238
Highman St 15205
Highmeadow Rd 15215
Highmont Rd 15232
Highpoint Dr 15235
Highpointe Cir & Dr 15220
Highridge Cir 15234
Highridge Dr 15226
Highridge St 15214
Hightower Blvd 15205
Highview Ave
1-99 15238
101-111 15238
110-110 15229
110-130 15238
115-117 15229
119-133 15229
121-121 15238
128-128 15229
135-143 15229
161-197 15238
199-299 15238
Highview Dr 15241
Highview Rd
400-499 15228
500-999 15234
Highview St
300-399 15237
800-999 15206
Highvue Rd 15228
Highwood St 15212
Hiland Ave 15202
Hiland Valley Dr 15229
Hilands Ave 15202
Hilands Pl 15237
Hilda St 15235
Hilf St 15228
Hilglor Dr 15209
Hilke St 15202
Hill Ave 15221
Hill Rd 15206
Hill St
1-99 15215
100-198 15223
700-780 15226
782-794 15226
796-798 15226
799-800 15209
802-898 15209
2300-2599 15235
Hill Building 15260
Hillaire Dr 15243
Hillburn St 15207
Hillcrest Ave
300-399 15237
1100-1199 15220
Hillcrest Cir 15237
Hillcrest Dr
1-20 15202
79-97 15237
99-199 15237
Hillcrest Pl 15216
Hillcrest Rd
1-99 15221
100-299 15238
9000-9099 15237
Hillcrest St
5100-5363 15224
5365-5365 15224
5400-5499 15206
Hilldale Dr 15236
Hillendale Rd 15237
Hillgate Pl 15220
Hillgrove Ave 15216
Hilliard Dr 15212
Hilliard Rd 15237
Hilliards St 15206
Hillman St 15227
Hillman Library 15260
Hillock Ln 15236
E Hills Dr 15221
S Hills Vlg 15241
Hillsboro St 15204
Hillsdale Ave 15216
Hillsdale St 15234
Hillside Dr
200-299 15219
600-699 15235
Hillson Ave 15227
Hillsview Rd 15205
Hillsview Ter 15220
Hillview St 15234
Hillvue Ln 15237
Hillwood Rd 15209
Hilpert St 15227
Hilton Dr 15209
Hilton St 15220
Himber St 15209
Himmer Way 15225
Hinkel Rd 15229
Hiram St 15209
Hiscott Dr 15241
Hivue Ln 15237
Hiwood Dr 15234
Hobart St 15217
Hobbs St 15212
Hobson Ave 15226
Hochberg Rd 15235
Hochberg Road Ext 15235
Hodge St 15213
Hodgkiss St 15212
Hodgson Ave 15205
Hodil Ter 15238
Hoff St 15212
Hoffman Blvd 15209
Hoffman Rd
200-499 15212
900-1099 15209
Hoffman St 15233
Hohman Ln 15237
Holbrook St 15212
Holcomb Ave 15226
Holden St 15232
Holdsworth Dr 15236
Holiday Dr
1-99 15220
300-399 15237
400-1099 15220
5200-5399 15236
5401-5401 15236
Holiday Park Dr 15239
Hollace St 15219
Holland Ave 15221
Holland Dr 15238
Holland Hl 15260
Holland Rd 15235
Hollenden Pl 15217
Hollow Haven Dr 15236
Hollow Tree Dr 15241
Holly Dr 15235
Holly Ln 15216
Holly Way 15201
Holly Hill Dr 15237
Holly Lynne Dr 15236
Hollycrest Dr 15228
Hollydale Cir & Dr 15241
Hollyford Pl 15216
Hollyrood Rd 15227
Hollywood Dr 15235
Hollywood St 15205
Holmes Pl 15213
Holmes St
500-699 15221
5100-5399 15201
Holt St 15203
Holyoke St 15214
Holyrood Rd 15213
Holzer St 15210
Home Ave
1-99 15205
3000-3299 15234
N Home Ave 15202
S Home Ave 15202
Home Dr
100-199 15223
400-499 15275
Home St 15201
Homehurst Ave 15234
Homekort Ave 15229
Homeland St 15207
Homer Ave 15237
Homer Dr 15235
Homer Pl 15223
Homer St 15212
Homestead St 15218
E Homestead St 15212
W Homestead St 15212
N Homewood Ave 15208
S Homewood Ave 15208
Homewood Dr 15235
Hood St 15214
Hoodridge Dr
1-199 15228
200-500 15234
502-598 15234
Hoodridge Ln 15228
Hooker St 15206
Hoosac St 15207
Hoover Rd 15235
Hoover St 15204
Hope St 15220
Hope Way 15218
Hopeland St
10-2298 15210
2300-2399 15210
2401-2405 15210
2455-2459 15227
Hopkins St 15233
Horizon Dr
100-199 15237
700-799 15231
Horizon View Dr 15235
Horn St 15210
Hornaday Rd 15210
Horne St 15204
Horner St 15211
Horning Ave 15227
Horning Rd 15236
Horsman Dr 15228
Horton St 15219
Hot Metal St 15203
Hough Dr 15236
Houston Rd 15237
Houston St
1-199 15223
2700-2899 15212
2901-2997 15212
6000-6099 15206
N Howard Ave 15202
S Howard Ave 15202
Howard Dr 15241
Howard St
1-100 15209
101-127 15209
115-117 15235
119-167 15235
129-133 15209
135-143 15209
171-173 15235
175-299 15235
1901-1999 15212
Howden St 15202
Howe St
5400-5999 15232
6000-6499 15206
Howley St
3500-3899 15201
3900-4199 15224
4201-4499 15224
Hubbard Pl & St 15212
Hubbs Ln 15236
Hubert St 15225
Hudderford Rd 15237
Hudson St 15218
Huebner Dr 15237
Hugel Dr 15209
Hughes St 15205
Hulem Way 15221
Humber Way 15219
Humbolt St 15238
Humes Farm Ln 15238
Hunnell St 15212
Hunt Rd
200-300 15215
302-348 15215
350-399 15238
Hunt St 15204
Hunt Club Ln 15215
Hunter Dr 15237
Hunter St 15221
Hunters Path Ln 15241
Huntingdon Dr 15235
Huntington Ave 15202
Huntington Dr 15241
Huntress St 15206
Hurl Dr & Ln 15236
Huron Ave 15237
Huron St 15203
Hurston Way 15227
E & W Hutchinson Ave 15218
Huxley St 15204
Hyatt St 15206
Hybla St 15212
Hycroft Dr 15241
Hyde St 15205
Hydin Rd 15217
Hyena Way 15212
Hyman Pl 15213
Iben St 15227
Iberia St 15211
Ibis Way 15210
Ibsen St 15217
Ida Ln 15209
Idaho Ave 15225
Idaline St 15224
Idaway Dr 15237
Idlewild St 15208
Idlewood Rd
100-699 15235
1200-2699 15205
2701-2999 15205
Ilex Dr 15237
Ilion St 15207
Illinois Ave
501-597 15221
599-699 15221
701-999 15221
922-930 15216
934-994 15221
1100-1399 15216
Imogene Rd 15217
Impala Dr 15239
Imperial Ct 15215
Imperial Dr 15236
Imperial St 15217
Independence St 15220
Indian Dr 15238
Indian Hill Rd 15238
Indiana Ave 15221
Indiana Way 15206
Indianola Rd 15238
Indisont Ave 15221
Indus St 15207
Industry Dr 15275
Industry Ln 15275
Industry St 15210
Ingalls Way 15224
Ingham St 15212
Inglefield Dr 15236
Inglenook Pl 15208
Inglewood Dr 15228
Inglewood Ln 15237
Ingliss St 15212
W Ingomar Rd 15237
Ingomar St 15216
Ingomar Ter 15237
Ingomar Heights Rd 15237
Ingram Ave 15205
Ingress Way 15203
Institute St 15210
Integrity Dr 15235
Interboro Ave 15207
Inverness Ave 15217
Inverness Dr 15237
Invicta Dr 15235
Inwood Rd 15237
Inwood St 15208
Iona St 15212
Iowa St 15219
Ipswich Ct 15206
Ireland Way 15212
Irene Ave 15223
Irene Ln 15236
Iris Dr 15235
Iron City Dr 15205
Iroquois Ave 15237
Iroquois Dr
9-21 15228
23-88 15228
27-53 15205
90-198 15228
400-1499 15205
Iroquois Rd 15241
Irvine St
1-4651 15207
4653-4799 15207
7400-7432 15218
7434-7498 15218
Irwin Ave
100-299 15202
1801-1897 15212
1899-1999 15212
2000-2298 15214
2300-2599 15214
S Irwin Ave 15237
Irwin Dr 15236
Irwin Ln 15212
Isabella St
1-99 15223
2-98 15212
100-299 15212
Isis Way 15213
Island Ave
1101-1197 15212
1199-1399 15212
1700-1899 15233
Isolda Dr 15209
Isoline St 15204
Itin St 15212
Ivanhoe Rd 15241
Ives Way 15212
Ivondale St 15207
Ivory Ave 15214
Ivy Ln 15236
Ivy Rd 15229
Ivy St
100-199 15218
500-999 15232
Ivy Rose Ln 15238
Ivyglen St & Way 15227
Ivyland Dr 15235
Izora St 15214
Jachindo Ave 15226
Jackman Ave 15202
Jacks Run Rd
100-299 15214
300-599 15202
Jackson Ave 15237
N Jackson Ave 15202
S Jackson Ave 15202
Jackson Cir 15229
Jackson Rd 15239
Jackson St
101-199 15237
200-499 15221
500-599 15237
701-799 15238
1100-1199 15221
5400-6799 15206
Jacksonia St 15212
Jacob Dr 15235
Jacob St
10-100 15234
102-199 15234
300-399 15210
1800-2099 15226
2101-2199 15226
2186-2198 15234
2200-2299 15234
Jacobson Dr 15227
Jamaica Ave 15229
Jamal Pl 15213
James Dr
2100-2199 15212
2342-2399 15237
James Pl 15228
James St
1-99 15223
700-899 15212
900-922 15221
901-925 15212
902-924 15212
925-941 15221
1000-1099 15234
1101-1199 15221
1104-1112 15212
1120-1120 15221
1200-1498 15212
James Henry Jr Pl 15213
James Ross Pl 15215
Jamesborough Dr 15238
Jameson Dr
2800-3099 15226
3300-3399 15227
Jamestown Ct 15216
Jamestown Dr 15216
Jamestown Pl 15235
Jancey St 15206
Jane Ave 15209
Jane St
700-899 15239
1100-1199 15221
1700-2900 15203
2902-3398 15203
5500-5599 15225
Janero Way 15206
Janet Dr
1700-1799 15234
5600-5799 15236
Janewood Way 15220
Janice Dr 15235
Janie Dr 15227
Janthia Dr 15220
Japonica Way 15232
Jarvis Ct 15237
Jasmine Ct 15237
Jasper St 15211
Java Way 15206
Jawett St 15212
Jay St 15212
Jaycee Dr 15243
Jayson Ave 15228
Jean Dr 15236
Jean St 15204
Jeanette St
2-98 15211
101-199 15211
500-599 15221
Jeffers St 15204
Jefferson Ave
200-499 15202
900-1099 15209
Jefferson Ct 15243
Jefferson Dr
100-499 15228
700-999 15229
Jefferson Rd 15235
Jefferson St
9-19 15209
35-37 15221
39-52 15221
54-58 15221
500-599 15237
E Jefferson St 15212
W Jefferson St 15212
Jefferson Heights Rd 15235
Jeffrey Ln 15238
Jenkins Dr 15241
Jenkins St 15205
Jenkinson Dr 15237
Jenne Dr 15236
Jennie St 15211
Jennings Ct 15206
Jenny Lynn Ct 15239
Jeremias St 15218
Jericho Way 15220
Jerome St 15220
Jessica Dr 15237
Jessie St 15216
Jewel Dr 15236
Jhf Dr 15217
Jill Dr
100-299 15236
893-897 15227
899-999 15227
Jillson St 15226
Joan Dr
100-199 15209
11500-12199 15235
Joanne St 15215
Joe Hammer Sq 15213
Joel St 15205
John St
2-98 15205
7-11 15209
23-25 15205
100-104 15237
105-199 15210
200-399 15227
500-599 15212
John Smith Ln 15238
Johnanna Dr 15237
Johnson St 15209
Johnston Ave 15207
Johnston Rd
1-99 15241
100-114 15241
101-357 15241
112-114 15235
116-350 15235
116-346 15241
170-208 15235
210-210 15241
212-236 15235
238-238 15241
240-252 15235
254-254 15241
256-256 15235
260-346 15241
348-416 15241
352-448 15235
354-354 15235
401-423 15235
425-425 15241
427-445 15235
Johnston St
9-9 15205
11-19 15205
21-25 15205
100-199 15209
Joliet Way 15224
Jonathan Ct & Pl 15208
Joncaire St 15213
Jones Ave 15221
Jones Ln 15237
Jones St 15223
Jones Way 15220
Jonquil Pl 15228
Jonquil St 15210
Jordan Ave
2-198 15215
2600-2799 15235
Jordan Ln 15209
Jordan Way 15224
Joseph St
2-18 15209
25-37 15206
85-93 15227
95-1099 15227
6200-6399 15206
Josephine St
1-99 15205
400-499 15202
1900-2598 15203
2600-3199 15203
3201-3299 15203
Josephs Ln 15237
Josh Gibson Pl 15214
Joshua St 15206
N Joslyn Dr 15235
S Joslyn Dr 15235
Joslyn St 15204
Journal St 15220
Joyce Dr 15212
Joyce Ter 15207
Jucunda St 15210
Jude Dr 15237
Judicial St 15211
Judith Dr 15236
Judy Ann Pl 15237

Julian Dr 15235
Julie Dr 15227
Juliet St 15213
Julius St 15206
Jumonville St 15219
June Dr
 200-399 15236
 1601-1799 15209
Juneann Dr 15236
Juniata Ct 15208
Juniata Pl 15208
Juniata St
 1200-1499 15233
 7700-7799 15218
Junilla St 15219
Junior Dr 15227
Juniper St 15224
Junius St 15220
Juno St 15213
Justine Dr 15239
Justine St 15204
Kaelin Dr 15239
Kaercher St 15207
Kaiser Ave 15212
Kalida Dr 15206
Kalkirk Dr 15238
Kaloramo Way 15212
Kambach St 15211
Kamin St 15217
Kane Blvd 15243
Kane Ln 15202
Kane Rd 15239
Kaplan Ave 15227
Kappa Dr 15238
Karen Dr
 1-99 15237
 200-299 15209
 301-897 15209
 2000-2099 15237
Karl St 15221
Karwich St 15212
Katherine St 15214
Kathleen Dr 15227
Kathleen St 15211
Kathy Dr 15204
Kathy Lynn Dr 15239
Katz St 15235
Kaufman Ave 15227
Kay Dr
 1-199 15223
 100-113 15223
 101-110 15236
 300-399 15236
Kaylor Rd 15237
Kearney Way 15219
Kearns Ave
 100-198 15220
 200-600 15220
 602-1056 15220
 1800-1898 15205
 1900-2099 15205
Kearns Pl 15205
Kearsarge St 15211
Keating Ave 15229
Keck Dr 15238
Kedron St 15208
Kedzie St 15204
Keefe St 15207
Keefer Dr 15235
Keenan Dr 15236
Keeport Dr 15236
Keever Ave 15205
Keibs Way 15203
Keifer Dr 15241
Keiners Ln 15205
Keith Dr 15239
Keleket Dr 15235
Keller Way 15201
Kellingwood Dr 15238
Kelly Ave 15221
Kelly St
 6600-6699 15206
 6700-7899 15208
Kelso Rd 15243
Kelton Ave 15216
Kelvin St 15204
Kemper St 15217
Kenberma Ave 15216
Kencenes Ave 15216
Kendall Ave 15202
Kendall St 15201
Kendon Dr E & W 15221
Kenforest Dr 15216
Kenilworth Dr 15228
Kenilworth St 15226
Kenmont Ave
 100-399 15216
 400-599 15228
Kenmore Ave 15221
Kenn St 15214
Kennebec Rd 15241
Kennebec St 15217
E Kennedy Ave 15214
Kenneth Dr 15223
Kennett Sq 15213
Kenney Way 15219
Kenova St 15211
Kensington Ct 15238
Kensington Dr 15237
Kensington St 15221
Kent Ct
 100-154 15241
 300-399 15237
Kent Dr 15241
Kent Rd
 1-99 15202
 1800-1899 15241
Kent Way 15201
Kentmoor Dr 15220
Kentucky Ave
 5400-5999 15232
 6000-6499 15206
Kentzel Rd 15237
E Kenwood Ave 15214
Kenyon Ave 15229
Kenyon Ct 15229
Kenyon Rd 15205
Kenzie Dr 15205
Kenzig Ave 15212
Kerr St 15220
Kerrwood Dr 15215
Kerry Hill Dr 15234
Kersten Ln 15235
Kessler St 15210
Kestner Ave 15227
Keswick Ave 15202
Kewanna Ave 15234
Key Ave 15216
Key Dr 15235
Key West Dr 15239
Keystone St
 500-599 15215
 5100-5699 15201
Kilbourne St 15207
Kilbuck St 15202
Kilkenbeck St 15212
Killarney Dr 15234
Kilmer St 15221
Kilmeyer Dr 15239
Kiltie Dr 15235
Kilvington Dr 15235
Kimbol St 15210
Kincaid St
 4700-5399 15224
 5400-5499 15206
Kincollo Ave 15202
Kind Dr 15237
King Ave
 100-299 15229
 1000-1399 15206
King Albert Dr 15237
King Charles Dr 15237
King David Dr 15237
King Edward Dr 15237
King George Ct 15237
King Henry Dr 15237
King James Dr 15237
King John Dr 15237
King William Dr 15237
Kinglake St 15207
Kingridge Cir & Rd 15237
Kings Hwy 15205
Kings Ln 15241
Kings Rd 15221
Kingsberry Cir 15234
Kingsberry Ct 15237
Kingsboro St 15211
Kingsdale Rd 15221
Kingsford Dr 15202
Kingsland Ave 15205
Kingsland Dr 15202
Kingsley Ave 15227
Kingston Ave 15205
Kingston Dr 15235
Kingwood St 15234
Kinkura Dr 15212
Kinley Ave 15207
Kinmount St 15205
Kinross Ln 15237
Kinsdale Dr 15237
Kinsman Rd 15217
Kinvara Ct & Dr 15237
Kinzua Rd 15239
Kipling Rd
 100-199 15237
 5400-5499 15217
Kiralfy Ave 15216
Kirk Ave
 101-179 15227
 181-699 15227
 198-198 15238
 200-2714 15227
Kirkbride St 15212
Kirkpatrick St 15219
Kirkwall Dr 15215
Kirkwood Dr 15215
Kirkwood St 15206
Kirsopp Ave 15220
Kirtland St 15208
Kish Way 15217
Kisow Dr 15205
Kittanning Pike 15215
Kittanning St
 1-199 15223
 200-400 15215
 402-498 15215
Klamath Dr 15205
Kleber St 15212
Klein Pl 15226
Klementina Dr 15212
Klemont Ave 15202
Klir Rd 15209
Klopfer St 15209
Knapp St 15212
Knickerbocker Dr 15235
Knoedler Rd 15236
Knoll St 15212
Knollview Dr 15239
Knollwood Ct 15239
Knollwood Dr 15215
Knott St 15233
Knowlson Ave 15226
Knox Ave 15210
Kocher Dr 15239
Koeffler Dr 15236
Koegler Ave 15227
Koehler St
 100-114 15223
 106-110 15210
 112-136 15210
 138-140 15210
Koerner Ave 15214
Kohen St 15234
Kohlman Dr 15214
Kohlmeyers Ln 15211
Kohne St 15210
Konzier Dr 15237
Koomatuck Dr 15239
Kooser Dr 15239
Korb Way 15227
Korhnak Ln 15221
Kosciusko Way 15203
Kramer Way 15211
Krepp Ct 15237
Kress Dr 15239
Kreston Pl 15205
Kriss Dr 15223
Krist Glen Dr 15218
Kroll Dr 15233
Krupp St 15204
Kuhlview Dr 15237
Kuhn St 15211
Kunkle Way 15212
Kurt Dr 15243
La Costa Ct 15237
La Moine St 15226
La Place St 15219
La Salle Ave 15216
La Schall St 15208
Labelle St
 1-99 15221
 101-111 15211
 113-399 15211
 1100-1399 15221
Lacebark Ct 15239
Lacey Way 15206
Lachman Way 15227
Laclair St 15218
Laclede St 15211
E Lacock St 15212
Lacona St 15210
Lacrosse St 15218
Ladley St 15209
Ladoga St 15204
Ladora Ln 15234
Ladora Way 15207
Ladson St 15206
Lafayette Ave 15214
Lafayette Rd 15221
Lafayette St 15218
Lafferty Ave 15210
Lafferty Dr 15227
Lager St 15212
Laird St 15212
Lake St 15233
Lakemont Dr 15243
Lakeside Rd 15238
Laketon Rd
 1300-2499 15221
 2500-3699 15235
Lakewood Ave
 1-299 15229
 1000-1399 15220
 1401-1499 15220
Lamar Ave 15221
Lamar Rd 15241
Lamar St 15214
Lamarido St 15226
Lambeth Dr 15241
Lamesa St 15223
Lamont Pl 15232
Lamont St 15212
Lamplighter Cir 15212
Lamplite Ln 15237
Lamson Cir 15241
Lanark St 15214
Lancaster Ave
 100-199 15228
 1001-1097 15218
 1099-1399 15218
Lancelot Dr 15237
Lancers Way 15237
Lancewood Dr 15235
Lander St 15220
Landings Dr 15238
Landis St 15204
Landleiss Pl 15219
Landmarks Sq 15212
Landon Knl 15238
Landon Gate Gdn 15238
Landview Rd 15217
Lane Way
 1-99 15212
 600-699 15227
Lanford Dr 15235
N Lang Ave
 100-1605 15208
 1606-1699 15206
S Lang Ave 15208
Lang Ct 15208
Langfitt St 15212
Langhorn St 15207
Langley Ave 15214
Langley Hl 15260
Langport Dr 15241
Langtry St 15212
Lanmore Ave 15227
Lanpark St 15204
Lansdale Ct 15237
Lansdale Pl 15228
Lansing Ave 15229
Lantern Hill Dr 15236
Lantern Hill Drive Ext 15236
Lapish Rd 15212
Laporte St 15206
Lappe Ln 15212
Larch Ln 15234
Larchdale Dr 15243
Larchmont Rd 15243
Lareda St 15212
Laredo Dr 15241
Larimer Ave & Pl 15206
Larkins Way 15203
Larose St 15226
Larraine Dr 15205
Larsen Dr 15243
Larthela Dr 15237
Las Vegas Dr 15239
Latana St 15206
Latham St 15206
Latimer St 15214
Latonia Ave 15216
Latourelle Ln 15215
Lattidome Dr 15241
Lauch Way 15210
Lauder St 15207
Laughlin Ave 15210
Laurel Ave 15202
Laurel Ct 15202
Laurel Dr
 200-399 15236
 1300-1499 15235
Laurel St
 300-399 15218
 700-799 15238
 901-973 15234
 975-999 15234
Laurel Vlg 15202
Laurelwood Dr 15237
Lauria Way 15211
Laurie Dr 15235
Lautner St 15212
Lavender Heights Ct 15235
Lavern St 15235
Laverne St 15210
Laveton St 15227
Lavina Ave 15216
Law Building 15260
Lawn St 15213
Lawncroft Ave 15228
Lawndale St 15221
Lawnview Ave 15227
Lawnwood Ave 15227
Lawrence Ave 15238
Lawrence St
 1-99 15209
 4500-4599 15201
Lawson Ave 15205
Lawson St 15219
Lawton Ave 15214
Lawton St 15235
Laxton St 15206
Layton Ave 15216
Le Grogan Dr 15237
Le Roi Rd 15208
Lea St 15223
Leafy Ln 15243
Leander St 15219
Lear Dr 15235
Learning Res Devel Ctr 15260
Leaside Dr 15207
Leavitt St 15226
Lebanon Ave
 200-799 15228
 900-999 15234
Lebanon Rd 15207
Lebanon Church Rd 15236
Lebanon Hills Dr 15228
Lebeau Pike 15221
Leblanc St 15218
Lechner Ln 15227
Lecky Ave 15212
Lederer Ave 15209
Ledgedale St 15205
Ledlie St 15219
Leduc Way 15212
Lee Ave
 1-99 15221
 118-122 15237
 124-499 15237
Lee Dr 15235
Lee Rd 15237
Lee St 15212
Lee Ann Ct 15239
Lee Avenue Ext 15237
Leech Rd 15236
Leech St 15201
Leech Farm Rd 15206
Leechburg Rd
 1700-2599 15235
 2600-3499 15239
 3501-3599 15239
Leendia Ave 15209
Legion Way 15214
Legrande Dr 15221
Lehigh Ave
 1-99 15229
 200-246 15232
 209-236 15218
 248-248 15232
 300-384 15232
 386-398 15232
Lehigh Rd 15205
Lehigh St 15218
Lehr Ave 15223
Lehrman Way 15203
Leister St 15212
Leith Way 15217
Leland Dr 15236
Leland St 15214
Lelia St 15211
Lemington Ave
 6900-7299 15206
 7300-7399 15235
E Lemington Ave 15235
Lemoyne Ave 15228
Lennox Dr 15235
Lenora Dr 15237
Lenora St 15206
Lenox Ave 15221
Lenox Dr 15238
Lenox Oval 15237
Leola Ave 15227
Leolyn St 15210
Leon Rd 15220
Leona Dr 15227
Leonard St
 101-199 15223
 4900-4999 15213
Leroy St 15239
Leslie St 15205
Lesnett Rd 15241
Lessing St 15220
Leticoe St 15203
Letort St 15212
Letsche St
 1-99 15214
 1700-1899 15212
 1900-2199 15214
Lettie Hill St 15216
Lewin Ln 15235
Lewis Ct 15236
Lewis Dr 15235
Lewis St
 1-25 15223
 300-898 15238
 900-999 15238
 1201-1299 15220
Lexington Ave 15215
S Lexington Ave 15208
Lexington Ct 15223
Lexington Pl 15208
N Lexington St 15208
Ley St 15212
Leydon St 15201
Lib Info Science Bldg 15260
Liberto Rd 15235
Liberty Ave
 300-2899 15222
 2900-2998 15201
 3000-3899 15201
 3900-5183 15224
 5182-5182 15232
 5184-5398 15224
 5185-5299 15224
W Liberty Ave
 1100-2599 15226
 2600-3299 15216
 3301-3399 15216
E Liberty Blvd 15206
Library Anx 15260
Library Rd 15234
Lieb Way 15212
Liedertafel Way 15212
Lighthill St 15233
Lighthouse Pt 15221
Ligonier St 15201
Lila St 15235
Lilac Ave 15229
Lilac St 15217
Lillian Rd 15237
Lillian St 15210
Lilly Ln 15221
Lilmont Dr 15218
Lily Ave 15229
Lima Way
 3000-3099 15216
 4800-4898 15224
Lime St 15220
Lime Hollow Rd 15235
Lime Oak Dr 15235
Limecrest Rd 15221
Limestone Ct 15239
Lincoln Ave
 1-16 15205
 18-20 15205
 18-98 15205
 22-61 15205
 25-621 15202
 63-99 15205
 75-121 15237
 100-120 15202
 107-109 15218
 111-299 15218
 111-524 15209
 123-538 15237
 153-691 15202
 201-401 15206
 328-330 15206
 400-400 15237
 403-827 15206
 440-798 15202
 526-614 15209
 623-661 15202
 799-824 15215
 825-829 15206
 826-826 15215
 829-915 15206
 900-914 15206
 905-913 15215
 915-916 15215
 920-998 15206
 1000-1799 15206
 1862-1898 15235
N Lincoln Ave 15233
Lincoln Blvd 15237
Lincoln Dr 15241
Lincoln Rd 15235
Lincoln St
 1-99 15223
 200-298 15205
 1800-1899 15202
Lincoln Avenue Ext 15235
Lincoln Club Dr 15237
Linda Dr
 601-611 15226
 613-899 15226
 4900-4999 15236
Linda Ln 15243
Lindberg Ave
 1100-1200 15207
 1202-1298 15207

10300-10599 15235
10601-10699 15235
Lindbergh Ave 15223
Lindell St 15212
Linden Ave
100-199 15218
200-201 15215
203-399 15215
210-298 15238
300-398 15215
3600-3698 15234
3700-3799 15234
N Linden Ave 15208
S Linden Ave 15208
Linden Ct 15237
Linden Ln 15208
Linden Pl 15212
Linden Way 15202
Lindendale Dr
900-1200 15243
1201-1201 15228
1202-1202 15243
1203-1299 15228
Lindenwood Ave 15228
Lindenwood Dr
100-299 15209
800-999 15234
2500-2699 15241
Lindisfarne Dr 15237
Lindley Ln 15237
Lindsay Rd
2000-2199 15221
9700-9799 15237
Lindsey Ln 15239
Line St 15210
Lingrove Pl 15208
Linhart Ln 15236
Linhart St 15220
Linial Ave 15226
Link Ave 15237
Linnie Lou Dr 15234
Linnview Ave 15210
Linoleum Way 15219
Linshaw Ave 15205
Linton St 15219
Lintred St 15206
Linwood Ave 15214
N Linwood Ave 15205
S Linwood Ave 15205
Linwood Dr 15215
Linwood Rd 15229
Lipp Ave 15229
Lippert St 15209
Lisbon St 15213
List St 15212
Litchfield St 15204
Litchfield Towers A 15260
Litchfield Towers B 15260
Litchfield Towers C 15260
Lithgow Ave 15214
Little Ln 15215
Little Meadow Rd 15241
Little Pine Creek Rd 15223
E & W Littlewood St 15223
Liverpool St 15233
Living Pl 15206
Livingston Ave & Mnr 15238
Llewellyn Pl 15206
Lloyd Ave 15218
Lloyd St 15208
Locarna Way 15201
Locharron Ct 15239
Lochinvar Dr 15237
Lochlin Dr 15243
Lock Way E & W 15206
Lockhart Ln 15209
Lockhart St 15212
Lockridge Rd 15234
Locksley Dr 15235
Locust Ave
902-998 15234
1100-1199 15236
Locust Ct 15237
Locust Dr
7-21 15238
100-107 15237
109-113 15237
2600-2899 15241
Locust Ln
1-31 15241
33-37 15241
50-50 15238
52-55 15238
100-599 15241
800-899 15238
1000-1099 15243
Locust Rd 15237
Locust St
3-19 15223
8-8 15205
13-101 15202
21-119 15223
35-51 15209
53-55 15209
65-81 15223
101-137 15202
103-143 15202
108-108 15210
110-233 15210
121-123 15223
139-190 15202
192-196 15202
201-205 15229
201-207 15202
209-227 15202
214-222 15202
224-234 15202
244-250 15229
300-599 15218
1000-1899 15219
2000-2199 15218
3000-3099 15221
Locust Ridge Dr 15209
Lodge St 15227
Lodi Way 15201
Loeffler Building 15260
Lofink St 15212
Logan Dr 15229
Logan St 15209
Logans Ferry Rd 15239
Logue St 15220
Lohengrin Dr 15209
Loire Valley Dr 15209
Lois Dr 15236
Loleta Way 15210
Loma Dr 15234
Lombard St 15219
Lombardi Dr 15236
Lombardy Dr 15237
Lomond Dr 15235
London Towne Dr 15226
Londonderry Dr 15234
Lone Oak Dr 15209
Lonergan Way 15216
Long Dr 15241
Long Rd 15235
Long St 15209
Long Meadow Dr 15238
Long Shadow Ct 15238
Longbow Dr 15235
Longfellow Ct 15218
Longfellow Rd 15215
Longmore Ave
1-99 15202
100-1660 15216
Longmount Dr 15214
Longridge Dr 15243
Longuevue Dr 15228
Longvue Dr 15237
Longwood Dr 15227
Lonsdale St 15212
Lookout Ln 15238
Lookout St 15212
Loop St 15215
Lopella St 15212
Loraine St 15212
Loredge Dr 15214
Lorenz Ave 15220
Loretta Dr 15235
Loretta St 15217
Loretto Rd 15217
Lori Ann Way 15209
Loridge Dr 15209
Lorigan St 15224
Lorish Rd 15205
Lorlei Ln 15229
Lorlita Ln 15241
Lorna Way 15210
Lorraine Dr 15227
Lorraine Rd 15221
Los Angeles Ave 15216
Losca Way 15221
Lothrop St 15213
Lott Rd 15235
Lotus Way 15201
Louann St 15223
Lougean Ave 15207
Lougeay Rd 15235
Louisa Ct 15227
Louisa St
700-899 15210
3400-3699 15213
3700-3899 15227
Louise Rd & St 15237
Louisiana Ave 15216
Louisville Pl 15237
Louthel 15260
Love Pl & St 15218
Lovelace St 15220
Lovingston Dr 15216
Lovitt Way 15212
Lowe St 15220
Lowell St 15206
Lowen St 15211
Lowenhill Ave 15216
Lower Rd 15215
Lower Arrowhead Rd 15237
Lowgar Dr 15239
Lowland Dr 15214
Lowrie St 15212
Lowries Run Rd 15237
Lowry St 15202
Loyal Way 15210
Lucerne Ave 15214
Lucia Rd 15221
Lucille Dr
100-199 15235
1501-1511 15234
1513-1699 15234
Lucille St 15218
Lucina Ave 15210
Lucy Dr 15236
Ludwick St 15217
Luella St 15212
Lundy St 15204
Lupine Dr 15209
Lupton St 15211
Luray Dr 15239
Luray St 15214
Luster St 15217
Luther St 15210
Luty Ave 15212
Lutz Ave 15210
Lutz Hollow Rd 15207
Luzzo Ct 15206
Lydia St 15207
Lyman St 15221
Lynch St 15205
Lyndell Ct & St 15234
Lyndhurst Ave 15216
Lyndhurst Dr 15206
W Lyndhurst Dr 15206
Lyndhurst Grn 15206
Lynette Pl 15237
Lynfield Dr 15202
Lynhurst Dr 15237
Lynmar Rd 15209
Lynn Dr 15236
Lynn Way 15208
Lynn Haven Dr 15228
Lynn Haven Rd 15217
Lynnbrook Ave 15226
Lynnwood Dr 15235
Lynton Ln 15202
Lyon St 15219
Lyons St
1-99 15205
100-200 15209
202-298 15209
Lyric St 15206
Lysle St 15212
Lytle St 15207
Lytle Way 15221
Lytton Ave 15213
Lyzell St 15214
Maberly St 15205
Mabrick Ave 15228
Macarthur Dr 15228
Macassar Dr 15236
Macbeth Dr 15235
Macek Dr 15227
Macfarlane Dr 15235
Mackenzie Ln 15229
Mackey St 15213
Mackin Ave 15205
Mackinaw Ave 15216
Macon Ave 15218
Madeline St 15210
Madiera St 15221
Madison Ave
300-398 15243
500-699 15202
800-1098 15212
1100-1599 15212
E Madison Cir 15229
W Madison Cir 15229
Madison Pl 15237
Madison St 15237
Madonna St 15221
Maeburn Rd 15217
Magdalena St 15203
Magee St 15219
Magellan Dr 15237
Maginn St 15214
Magnet St 15214
Magnolia Ave 15229
Magnolia Dr 15234
Magnolia Pl 15228
Magnolia St 15212
Magnus St 15205
Mahon St 15219
Mahoning Dr 15235
Mahopac St 15205
Main Blvd 15237
Main St
101-119 15215
201-205 15201
207-399 15201
600-2238 15215
2100-2350 15235
2100-2312 15215
2239-2300 15235
2301-2301 15215
2302-2898 15235
2315-2321 15235
2323-2323 15215
2325-2899 15235
4100-4399 15224
N Main St 15215
S Main St
101-101 15215
106-108 15215
110-110 15220
112-114 15220
116-198 15220
201-407 15215
203-397 15220
300-301 15215
303-313 15215
310-312 15220
316-316 15215
317-446 15220
399-427 15220
409-411 15215
413-413 15215
448-698 15220
501-511 15215
515-699 15220
Main Entrance Dr 15228
Maine St 15221
Mainsgate St 15205
Mairdale St
1-199 15214
500-599 15212
Maize Dr 15236
Malabar Dr 15239
Malcolm Ave 15212
Malden St 15212
Malibran Dr 15237
Maline St 15214
Mallard Dr 15238
Mallissee Rd 15239
Malone St 15239
Malor Dr 15227
Malvern Ave
100-199 15237
1200-1399 15217
Malvern Rd 15202
Manchester Cir 15237
Mandlin Way 15212
Mandrake Dr 15209
Manetta Pl 15206
Manhassett Rd 15227
Manhattan Ave 15223
Manhattan St 15233
E Manilla Ave 15220
W Manilla Ave 15220
Manilla St
15-799 15219
20-22 15235
34-798 15219
7500-7599 15235
Manion Way 15201
Manistee St 15206
Manley St 15205
Mannheim St 15212
Manning St 15206
Manor Ave 15218
Manor Ct 15241
Manor Dr
200-299 15236
1200-1399 15241
W Manor Dr 15238
Manor Ln 15238
Manor Pl 15243
Manor Rd 15237
Manor St
2-98 15205
1000-1098 15203
Manor Way 15241
Manordale Rd 15241
Manorview Dr 15227
Manorview Rd 15220
Mansfield Ave
300-308 15220
310-399 15220
401-497 15205
499-799 15205
Mansion Ave 15209
Mansion Pl 15218
Mansion St 15207
Manton Way 15210
Manuel St 15214
Manville Dr 15237
Maolis Way 15233
Maple Ave
51-100 15202
101-115 15218
102-112 15202
117-131 15218
133-299 15218
140-198 15202
200-304 15218
200-250 15202
300-310 15218
306-362 15218
311-312 15215
320-326 15218
328-390 15218
364-454 15218
400-400 15215
402-412 15215
414-416 15215
415-455 15218
701-799 15238
900-999 15234
1000-1299 15221
2300-2699 15214
130 1/2-130 1/2 15218
Maple Ct 15237
Maple Dr
1400-1499 15227
3200-3399 15237
Maple Ln
1-49 15202
200-299 15225
2501-2599 15241
Maple Rd 15239
Maple St
7900-7999 15237
9000-9199 15239
Maple Ter 15211
Maple Way 15238
Maple Heights Ct &
Rd 15232
Maple Lo Dr 15235
Maplehill Ave 15234
Maplene Ave 15234
Mapleton Ave 15228
Maplevale Dr 15236
Mapleview Dr 15220
Maplewood Ave
1-99 15205
1600-1899 15221
Maplewood Ct 15237
Maplewood Dr
300-399 15243
800-999 15234
1200-1299 15243
Maplewood Rd
47-47 15209
49-50 15209
52-70 15209
96-299 15214
Maplewood St 15223
Marathon Dr 15235
Marathon St 15212
Marberry Dr 15215
Marbury Rd 15221
Marc Dr 15236
Marchand St 15206
Marchmont St 15205
Marcus Way 15210
Mardi Gras Dr 15239
Marena St 15220
Marengo St 15210
Margaret St
1-99 15238
100-799 15210
1000-1999 15209
2100-2399 15235
3200-3499 15227
Margaret Morrison St 15213
Margaretta Ave
1-99 15202
900-999 15234
Margaretta St
100-199 15229
5500-5599 15206
Margarite Dr 15216
Margate Rd 15221
Marge Dr 15234
N & S Margery Dr 15238
Margray St 15207
Marhoefer Dr 15236
Mariah Dr 15239
Marie Ave
1-7 15223
1-3 15202
5-25 15202
9-9 15223
27-211 15202
100-198 15202
103-221 15209
200-200 15209
208-210 15202
218-224 15209
300-599 15202
Marie Dr 15237
Marie St 15221
Marietta Pl 15228
Marietta St 15206
Marilynn Dr 15236
Marilynn Rd 15235
Marin Ct 15239
Mariner Ct 15238
Mario Lemieux Pl 15219
Marion Ave 15221
Marion Dr
1-99 15229
1400-1499 15236
Marion St
1-1 15219
3-9 15205
4-8 15219
10-14 15219
16-18 15219
21-21 15205
23-42 15205
44-44 15205
51-97 15219
99-499 15219
Maripoe St 15213
Marisa Ct 15239
Marjorie Dr 15223
Mark Ln 15236
Market Sq & St 15222
Markham Dr 15228
Marland St 15210
Marlane Dr 15227
Marlboro Ave 15221
Marlboro Rd 15238
Marlborough Rd 15217
Marlin Dr
300-399 15216
400-499 15228
Marlin Dr E 15216
Marlin Dr W 15216
Marloff Pl 15226
Marlow St 15220
Marmaduke St 15212
Marmion Dr 15237
Marne Way 15211
Maromas St 15217
Marose Dr 15235
Marquette Rd 15229
Marquis Dr 15237
Marquis Way 15212
Marsden St 15207
Marshall Ave
100-899 15214
1100-1499 15212
E Marshall Ave 15214
Marshall Cir 15236
Marshall Dr
100-148 15228
101-101 15228
101-105 15215
103-103 15235
104-128 15215
105-138 15235
105-105 15228
107-109 15215
109-113 15228
117-117 15215
117-117 15228
121-121 15215
121-121 15228
123-125 15215
125-125 15228
127-129 15215
133-149 15228
140-146 15235
150-198 15235
200-399 15235
Marshall Rd 15214
Marshfield Dr 15241
Marsonia St 15214
Marta Dr 15236
Martera Pl 15205
Martha Ave
100-299 15209
1000-1099 15228
Martha St
1-99 15223
1200-1399 15234
1700-6699 15206
Martha Way 15239
Martin Ave 15216
Martin Rd 15237
Martindale St 15212
Martinique Dr 15235
Martsolf Ave 15229
Maruth Dr 15237
Marvelwood Pl 15215
Marvin Ave 15209
Marvista St 15212

- Marwood Ave 15221
- Marwood Dr 15241
- Mary Ave 15209
- Mary Dr 15212
- Mary Pl 15234
- Mary St
  - 1-99 15215
  - 100-149 15214
  - 207-299 15215
  - 280-298 15227
  - 300-499 15227
  - 500-699 15209
  - 1700-3236 15203
  - 3238-3298 15203
  - 9100-9299 15237
- Mary Ann Dr 15227
- Mary Ann St 15203
- Mary Lue Dr 15223
- Mary Vue Dr 15237
- Maryal Dr 15236
- Marycrest Dr 15235
- Maryland Ave
  - 1-299 15209
  - 504-511 15232
  - 513-515 15232
  - 551-551 15202
  - 553-556 15202
  - 558-564 15202
  - 600-650 15202
  - 621-623 15232
  - 625-999 15232
  - 636-648 15232
  - 653-665 15232
  - 655-673 15202
- Maryland Dr 15241
- Marylea Ave 15227
- Marymont Dr
  - 1-99 15235
  - 9200-9599 15237
- Marys Ave 15215
- Marys Ln 15237
- Marzolf Rd 15209
- Marzolf Road Ext
  - 100-199 15209
  - 200-799 15223
- Mason Rd 15235
- Masonic Way 15237
- Massachusetts Ave 15212
- Mastreli St 15211
- Mathews Ave 15210
- Mathias St 15212
- Mathilda St
  - 2-198 15209
  - 200-1199 15209
  - 4101-4199 15234
- N Mathilda St 15224
- S Mathilda St 15224
- Matson St 15214
- Mattern Ave 15216
- Matthews Way 15206
- Mattier Dr 15238
- Mattys Dr 15212
- Mauch St 15212
- Maurers Ln 15215
- Maurice Ct 15235
- Mause Ave 15216
- Maxwell Dr 15236
- Maxwell St 15205
- Maxwell Way 15206
- May St
  - 2200-2399 15235
  - 2900-3299 15234
- Maydell St 15216
- Mayer Dr 15237
- Mayfair Dr 15228
- Mayfair St 15204
- Mayfield Ave 15214
- Mayflower Dr
  - 100-199 15238
  - 3100-3299 15227
- Mayflower Pl 15225
- Mayflower St 15206
- Maynard St 15217
- Maytide St 15227
- Mayview Rd 15241
- Mayville Ave 15226
- Maywood St 15214
- Mazer St 15214
- Mazette Pl & Rd 15205
- Mcadams Ln 15237
- Mcalister Dr 15235
- Mcanulty Rd 15236
- Mcardle Roadway 15203
- Mcauliffe Ln 15237
- Mcbride St 15207
- Mccabe St 15201
- Mccague St 15218
- Mccandless Ave 15201
- Mccann Pl 15216
- Mccartney St 15220
- Mccaslin St
  - 701-799 15217
  - 801-4399 15217
  - 4400-4499 15207
- Mccaw Dr 15204
- Mcclaren St 15219
- Mcclellan Dr 15236
- Mcclelland Dr 15238
- Mcclintock Ave 15214
- Mcclure Ave
  - 3100-3999 15212
  - 6900-7499 15218
- Mccomb Ln 15239
- Mccombs St 15208
- Mcconnells Mill Ln 15228
- Mccook St 15212
- Mccord St 15203
- Mccormick Hl 15260
- Mccormick Ln 15226
- Mccormick Rd 15205
- Mccrady Rd 15235
- Mccrea Rd 15235
- Mccullough St 15212
- Mccully Dr 15235
- Mccully Rd 15234
- Mccully St
  - 200-599 15216
  - 600-699 15243
- Mccurdy Dr 15235
- Mccurdy Pl 15202
- Mccutcheon Ave 15237
- Mccutcheon Ln 15235
- Mcdonald Ave 15223
- Mcdonald St 15206
- Mcdowell St 15212
- Mcelheny Rd 15209
- Mcelhinny Ave 15207
- Mcfarland Rd 15216
- Mcfarland St 15212
- Mcfarren St 15217
- Mcholme Dr 15275
- Mcilrath Dr 15229
- E Mcintyre Ave 15214
- W Mcintyre Ave 15214
- Mcintyre Pl 15214
- Mcintyre Rd 15237
- Mcintyre Square Dr 15237
- Mcjunkin Rd 15239
- Mckay St 15218
- Mckean St 15219
- Mckee Dr 15236
- Mckee Pl 15213
- Mckee St 15221
- Mckelvey Ave 15218
- Mckelvey Rd 15221
- Mckenna Ave 15205
- Mckenzie Dr 15235
- Mckim Dr 15239
- Mckim St 15218
- Mckinley Ave
  - 100-199 15223
  - 200-244 15202
  - 205-295 15202
  - 225-225 15221
  - 271-271 15221
  - 274-286 15221
  - 300-399 15202
  - 900-999 15238
- Mckinley St
  - 1-99 15202
  - 200-399 15210
- Mckinley Ter 15202
- Mckinney Ln 15220
- Mcknight Cir 15237
- Mcknight Rd
  - 4200-4499 15214
  - 4500-9806 15237
  - 9808-9898 15237
- Mcknight St 15220
- Mcknight East Dr 15237
- Mcknight Park Dr 15237
- Mclain St 15210
- Mclaughlin Run Rd 15241
- Mclean Pl 15217
- Mcmanus St 15210
- Mcmichael Rd 15205
- Mcmillan Rd
  - 300-399 15205
  - 1600-1999 15241
  - 3000-3099 15205
- Mcmonagle Ave
  - 1-299 15220
  - 2200-2499 15216
- Mcmunn Ave 15205
- Mcmurray Rd 15241
- Mcnair St 15221
- Mcnary Blvd
  - 1600-2299 15221
  - 2300-2399 15235
- Mcnary Way 15212
- Mcnaugher St 15214
- Mcneil Pl 15219
- Mcneilly Ave 15216
- Mcneilly Rd 15226
- Mcpherson Blvd 15208
- Mcroberts Rd 15234
- Meade Ave 15202
- Meade Pl 15208
- Meade St
  - 100-198 15209
  - 200-299 15209
  - 300-399 15221
  - 6800-7300 15208
  - 7302-7598 15208
  - 7600-7699 15221
- Meadow Ave 15235
- N Meadow Ave 15235
- Meadow Ct 15229
- Meadow Dr 15235
- Meadow Ln 15220
- Meadow Rd 15237
- Meadow St
  - 1-99 15206
  - 102-116 15202
  - 103-275 15202
  - 115-121 15206
  - 123-6499 15206
  - 277-284 15202
  - 286-328 15202
  - 5200-5299 15236
  - 5900-6699 15206
- Meadow Crest Dr 15237
- Meadow Heights Dr 15215
- Meadow Park Dr 15236
- Meadow Park Ln 15215
- Meadow Springs Farm Ln 15238
- Meadow View Ct 15239
- Meadow Wood Dr 15239
- Meadowbrook Blvd 15227
- Meadowcrest Dr 15241
- Meadowcrest Rd 15236
- N Meadowcroft Ave 15216
- S Meadowcroft Ave 15228
- Meadowdell Dr 15227
- Meadowgreen Dr 15236
- Meadowlark Dr 15243
- Meadowmont Dr 15241
- Meadowood Ct, Dr & Ln 15215
- Meadowvue Dr 15227
- Meadville St 15214
- Means Ave 15202
- Mechanic St 15218
- Medhurst St 15216
- Meier Ln 15223
- Meinert St 15209
- Meirsch St 15212
- Melba Pl 15213
- Melbourne St 15217
- Melia Dr 15234
- Mella St 15212
- Mellon St & Ter 15206
- Mellon Park Ct 15232
- Mellott Rd 15227
- Mellow Ln 15238
- Melrose Pl 15241
- Melrose St
  - 66-799 15214
  - 801-899 15214
  - 7500-7599 15218
- Melvin Ct 15235
- Melvin Dr 15236
- Melvin St 15217
- Melvina St
  - 1-1999 15212
  - 2-98 15227
  - 1900-1998 15212
- Melwood Ave
  - 200-699 15213
  - 3300-3499 15219
  - 3500-3899 15213
  - 8301-8397 15237
  - 8399-8499 15237
- Memorial Dr
  - 5-7 15202
  - 1601-1699 15216
  - 8800-8898 15237
- Memory Ln 15219
- Menges St 15204
- Menlo St 15214
- Mercedes Dr 15236
- Mercer St 15219
- Merchant Ln 15205
- Mercia Dr 15237
- Mercy St 15214
- Mere St 15207
- Meredith St 15210
- Merganser Dr 15238
- Meridan St 15211
- Meridian Dr 15228
- Merion Dr 15228
- Merle St 15204
- Merlin Dr 15237
- Mero Way 15212
- Merrick Ave 15226
- Merrie Woode Dr 15235
- Merrimac St 15211
- Merriman Ct, Mews & Way 15203
- Merritt Ave 15227
- Merritt Ln 15236
- Merryfield St 15204
- Merryoak Ln 15241
- Merton Rd 15202
- Mervin Ave 15216
- Mervis Hl 15260
- Merwood Dr 15214
- Merwyn Ave 15204
- Mesa Cir 15241
- Mesa Rd 15218
- Meta St 15211
- Meteor Cir 15241
- Methyl St 15216
- Metropolitan St 15233
- Mexico St 15212
- Meyeridge Rd 15209
- E Meyers Ave 15210
- W Meyers Ave 15210
- Meyers St 15235
- Meyran Ave 15213
- Miami Ave 15228
- Michael Dr 15227
- Michigan Ave 15218
- Michigan Rd 15235
- Michigan St 15210
- Middle Rd
  - 800-899 15234
  - 900-999 15223
- Middle St
  - 1-99 15205
  - 400-599 15227
  - 600-1299 15212
  - 1300-2099 15215
- Middle Way 15210
- Middleboro Rd 15234
- Middletown Rd
  - 1000-2498 15205
  - 2500-2799 15205
  - 2800-3799 15204
- Midland St
  - 500-799 15221
  - 2800-2899 15226
- Midtown Sq 15219
- Midway Dr 15215
- Midway Rd 15216
- Midwood Ave 15210
- Mifflin Ave
  - 500-1099 15221
  - 1100-1200 15218
  - 1202-1298 15218
- Mifflin Rd 15207
- Mifflinridge Rd 15207
- Milan Ave 15226
- Milbert Dr & Ln 15237
- Milbeth Dr 15228
- Mildred St
  - 1-5 15223
  - 7-7 15223
  - 9-24 15223
  - 10-12 15205
  - 14-25 15205
- Miles Ave
  - 1-99 15205
  - 2700-2799 15216
- Milgate St 15224
- Mill St 15221
- Mill Grove Rd 15241
- Millbridge St 15210
- Miller Ln 15237
- Miller Rd
  - 101-119 15237
  - 108-124 15239
  - 121-123 15239
  - 124-134 15237
  - 133-133 15237
  - 137-145 15239
- Miller St
  - 1-499 15219
  - 6-10 15202
  - 18-498 15219
  - 1500-4099 15221
- Miller Valley Cir 15220
- Millerdale St 15201
- Millers Ln 15239
- Millerton Ave 15212
- Millet Ln 15236
- Milligan Ave & Way 15218
- Milliken Ave 15235
- Millington Rd 15217
- Millstone Dr & Ln 15238
- N Millvale Ave 15224
- S Millvale Ave
  - 200-699 15224
  - 700-999 15213
- Millview Dr 15238
- Milnor St 15205
- Milroy St 15214
- Miltenberger St 15219
- Milton Rd 15234
- Milton St
  - 100-199 15202
  - 829-897 15218
  - 899-1399 15218
- Milwaukee St 15219
- Mimosa Way 15212
- Mina St 15212
- Mindora St 15211
- Mineola Ave 15229
- Mineral Way 15201
- Mineral Industries Bld 15260
- Minerva St 15224
- Mingo St 15206
- Minnesota St
  - 1-699 15207
  - 4200-4299 15217
- Minnie St 15212
- Minnock Dr 15237
- Minnotte Sq 15220
- Minooka St 15210
- Minott St 15212
- Minsinger St 15211
- Minton St 15204
- Mintwood St
  - 3600-3899 15201
  - 3900-4099 15224
- Mira Ave 15227
- Miranda Rd 15241
- Miriam St 15218
- Mirror St 15217
- Mission Dr 15228
- Mission Ln 15238
- Mission St 15203
- Missionary Dr 15236
- Mississippi Ave 15216
- Missouri St 15206
- Mitchell Dr 15241
- Mitchell St 15212
- Mitre Way 15224
- Moale St 15212
- Mobay Rd 15205
- Mobile Dr 15223
- Mobile St 15207
- Modena Way 15227
- Modoc Way 15201
- Moffett St 15243
- Moga St 15206
- Mohawk Dr 15228
- Mohawk Rd 15241
- Mohawk St 15213
- Mohawk Trail Dr 15235
- Mohican Ave 15237
- Mohican Dr 15228
- Mohler St
  - 1-50 15208
  - 51-99 15235
  - 800-1199 15208
  - 1201-1299 15208
- Mohrbach St 15207
- Monaca Pl 15219
- Monastery Ave, Pl & St 15203
- Moneta St 15212
- Monica Dr 15239
- Monitor Ave 15202
- Monitor St 15217
- Monongahela Ave 15218
- Monongahela St 15207
- Monroe Ave 15202
- E Monroe Cir 15229
- W Monroe Cir 15229
- Monroe Ct 15243
- Monroe Dr 15229
- Monroe St
  - 500-599 15237
  - 1600-2099 15218
  - 3301-3397 15213
  - 3399-3400 15213
  - 3402-3498 15213
- Montague St 15219
- Montana Ave 15221
- Montana St
  - 1-3 15205
  - 5-5 15205
  - 14-16 15214
  - 18-299 15214
- Montclair Ave
  - 1-123 15229
  - 125-127 15229
  - 130-174 15237
  - 176-212 15237
  - 198-200 15229
  - 201-205 15229
  - 202-212 15229
  - 205-205 15237
  - 207-213 15229
  - 215-217 15229
  - 219-227 15229
  - 224-224 15237
  - 226-238 15229
  - 231-231 15237
  - 235-299 15229
- Montclair Dr 15241
- Montclair St 15217
- Monte Carlo Dr 15239
- Monteiro St 15217
- Monterey Dr
  - 1-99 15235
  - 2500-2699 15241
- Monterey St 15212
- Monterey Ter 15212
- Montezuma St 15206
- Montgomery Ave & Pl 15212
- Monticello Pl & St 15208
- Montier St 15221
- Montooth St 15210
- Montour Ct 15239
- Montour Way 15219
- Montpelier Ave 15216
- Montrose Ave 15238
- Montrose Ter 15202
- Montview Pl 15221
- Montview St 15214
- Montville St 15214
- Moon Ridge Dr 15241
- Moon Run Ave 15205
- Mooney Rd 15207
- Moore Ave 15210
- Mooreridge Dr 15227
- Moorhead Pl 15232
- Mooseheart St 15221
- Moraine Rd 15239
- Morange Rd 15205
- Moravian Way 15212
- Moredale St 15210
- Morefield St 15214
- Moreland Dr 15243
- Moreland Rd 15237
- Morelli Dr 15237
- Morelock St 15223
- Moresby St 15227
- Morewood Aly & Ave 15213
- Morgan Ave 15223
- Morgan St 15219
- Morley St 15204
- Morlow Dr 15235
- Morningrise Dr 15236
- Morningside Ave 15206
- Morrell St 15212
- Morris St
  - 400-499 15218
  - 1900-1999 15214
- Morrisey St 15214
- Morrison Dr 15216
- Morrison St 15212
- Morrow Dr 15235
- Morrow Rd 15241
- Morrow St 15221
- Morrowfield Ave 15217
- Morse Way 15207
- Morton Ln 15226
- Morton Rd 15241
- Morton St
  - 2-98 15205
  - 118-298 15234
  - 300-2499 15234
- Mosgrove St 15210
- Moss Ct 15237
- Mossfield Ct & St 15224
- Motor St 15204
- Moultrie St 15219
- Mount Airy Ave 15205
- Mount Allister Rd 15214
- Mount Carmel Rd 15235
- Mount Hood Dr 15239
- Mount Hope Rd 15212
- Mount Hope St 15223
- Mount Ivy Ln 15209
- Mount Joseph St 15210
- Mount Lebanon Blvd
  - 1-199 15228
  - 200-499 15234
- Mount Nebo Rd 15237
- Mount Nebo Pointe Rd 15237
- Mount Oliver St 15210
- Mount Pisgah Rd 15205
- Mount Pleasant Rd 15214
- Mount Royal Blvd 15223
- Mount Royal Ct 15223
- Mount Royal Rd 15217
- Mount Troy Rd
  - 1900-3999 15212
  - 4000-4299 15214
- Mount Troy Road Ext 15214
- Mount Vernon Ave 15229

Mount Vernon Dr 15223
Mount Vernon St 15208
Mountain St 15210
Mountford Ave 15214
Mower Dr 15239
Mowry Dr 15236
Moye Pl 15210
Moyer St 15204
Moynelle Dr 15243
Mueller Ave 15205
Muirfield Ct 15239
Mulberry Ct 15227
Mulberry Ln
1-99 15238
100-199 15235
Mulberry St
1-99 15215
600-1199 15221
Mulberry Way
2500-2899 15222
2900-3799 15201
Muldowney Ave 15207
Mulford St 15208
Mulhatton St 15217
Mulkerin Dr 15214
Mullins St 15212
Mullooly St 15227
Munhall Rd 15217
Municipal St 15204
Munsey Ave 15227
Murdoch Rd 15217
Murdstone Rd 15241
Muriel St 15203
Murray Ave 15217
Murray Ct 15239
Murray St 15215
Murrayhill Ave & Pl 15217
Murrays Ln 15234
N & S Murtland St 15208
Musgrave St 15207
Music Building 15260
Muskego Way 15211
Mustang Rd 15231
Muti Way 15208
Mutschler Way 15210
Mutual St 15204
Myler St 15212
Myrna Dr 15241
Myrtle Ave 15234
Nakoma Dr 15228
Namy Dr 15220
Nancy Dr 15235
Nanette St 15221
Nansen St 15207
Nantasket St 15207
Nantucket Dr
100-121 15238
123-199 15238
196-198 15236
200-599 15236
Naomi Dr 15207
Napoleon St 15216
Napor Blvd 15205
Narcissus Ave 15204
Narrow Dr 15239
Nash Ave 15235
Nash St 15212
Nassau Dr 15239
Natchez St 15211
National Dr
1-299 15236
600-699 15235
Natrona Way 15201
Naugle St 15207
Nauman St 15223
Navahoe Dr 15228
Navajo Rd 15241
Navarro St 15206
Navato Pl 15228
Naylor St 15207
Nazareth Way 15229
Nebraska Ave 15225
Neeb St 15207
Neeld Ave 15216
Neff St 15211
N Negley Ave 15206
S Negley Ave
100-299 15206
300-999 15232
1000-1599 15217
Negley Run Blvd 15206
Neidel St 15220
Neilson Ave 15238
Nelbon Ave 15235
Nellis Dr 15220
Nelson Dr 15237
Nelson St 15206
Nelson Park Dr 15214
Nelson Run Rd
100-198 15237
200-599 15237
4000-4599 15214
Neola Cir & Dr 15237
Neptune St 15220
Nettie St 15212
Neulon Ave 15216
Nevada St 15218
Neville Ave 15202
Neville Rd 15225
Neville St 15224
N Neville St 15213
S Neville St 15213
Nevin Dr 15237
New Arlington Ave 15203
New Beaver Ave 15233
New Brighton Rd 15202
New Hampshire Dr 15212
New Haven Ave 15216
New Haven Ln 15225
New Texas Rd 15239
New York St 15220
Newburn Ave 15227
Newburn Dr 15216
Newcomer St 15204
Newett St 15210
Newgate Rd 15202
Newland Ln 15209
Newmeyer St 15218
Newport Dr
500-599 15235
600-600 15234
601-651 15235
602-652 15235
700-900 15234
902-998 15234
Newport Rd 15221
Newton St
1-3 15203
2-4 15221
6-99 15221
700-898 15203
Niagara Rd 15221
Niagara Sq 15213
Niagara St 15213
Niblick Dr 15236
Nicholas St 15210
Nichols Rd 15237
Nicholson Ave 15205
Nicholson St 15217
Nicole Ln 15236
Niggel St 15212
Nike Dr 15235
Nilden Ave 15234
Niles St 15203
Nill St 15209
Nimick Pl 15221
Nina Rd 15214
Nina Way 15210
Nineteen North Ct & Dr 15237
Nittany St 15220
Nix Dr 15236
Nixon Rd 15237
Nixon St 15233
Noah St 15207
Noble Ave 15205
Noble St
400-499 15232
1600-1999 15215
2000-2004 15215
2000-2002 15218
2004-2040 15218
2006-2018 15215
2018-2040 15218
2020-2100 15215
2042-2116 15218
2101-2199 15218
Noble Arms Ln 15205
Nobles Ln 15210
Noblestown Rd
1-7 15220
9-99 15220
20-28 15205
38-42 15220
101-103 15205
105-339 15205
600-700 15220
702-798 15220
800-1498 15205
1500-2800 15205
2802-2998 15205
Nock Dr 15237
Nocklyn Dr 15237
Nokomis St 15204
Nolan Ct 15208
Noll Ave 15205
Nollhill St 15207
Nolo Way 15206
Nora Way 15224
Norabell Ave 15226
Norbert St 15202
Nordica Dr 15237
Norfolk St 15217
Norine Dr 15227
Noring Ct 15237
Norma Dr 15236
Norma St 15205
Normahill Dr 15201
Norman Dr
100-199 15236
200-299 15239
Norman St 15214
Normandy Ct 15238
Normandy Pl 15212
Normlee Pl 15217
Norrington Dr 15236
Norris St 15212
Norsen Dr 15243
Norsis Dr 15220
Norte Way 15210
North Ave
929R-929R 15233
2-98 15209
100-150 15202
100-198 15209
123-123 15209
125-157 15202
159-196 15202
198-216 15202
200-1135 15209
215-221 15202
220-220 15209
222-222 15202
224-298 15209
300-499 15209
500-1125 15221
501-551 15209
620-644 15202
646-676 15202
676-676 15202
678-692 15202
678-712 15202
694-698 15202
736-736 15221
800-898 15209
909-919 15238
921-923 15238
925-1119 15238
1056-1088 15238
1137-1141 15209
1200-1299 15209
1300-1599 15221
1700-1899 15233
1125 1/2-1125 1/2 15221
E North Ave 15212
W North Ave
2-798 15212
800-828 15233
830-1499 15233
North Ct
19-19 15237
3600-3698 15205
North Dr 15238
North St
1-1 15214
300-398 15227
400-699 15227
Northcrest Dr 15226
Northern Pike 15235
Northfield Ave 15204
Northfield Dr 15237
Northgate Dr 15241
Northminster St 15212
Northridge Dr
100-199 15237
800-849 15216
851-899 15216
Northumberland St 15217
Northview Dr
100-199 15209
200-299 15237
Northview St 15203
Norton Rd 15241
Norton St 15211
Norton Way 15211
Norva Dr 15234
Norvell Dr
800-899 15235
1400-1499 15221
Norwalk St 15205
Norway Rd 15221
Norwich Ave
1-38 15229
40-98 15229
700-1099 15226
Norwin Rd 15236
Norwood Ave
600-1099 15202
2600-3100 15214
3102-3198 15214
Noster St 15212
Notre Dame Pl 15215
Nottingham Cir 15215
Nottingham Dr
100-199 15205
3200-3202 15235
3204-3265 15235
3267-3299 15235
Novelty St 15208
Nowalk Dr 15239
Nurnath St 15221
Nurnberger Dr 15236
Nusser St 15203
Nuttals Grove Rd 15239
Nuzum Ave 15210
Oak Ave
1-99 15209
100-104 15235
100-111 15209
106-143 15235
113-115 15209
145-145 15235
Oak Ct 15237
Oak Dr
1-99 15214
1400-1499 15234
Oak Ln 15225
Oak Rd 15239
Oak St
1-299 15202
300-399 15236
700-798 15238
801-899 15238
7700-7899 15237
9000-9199 15239
Oak Way 15228
Oak Forest Dr 15216
Oak Glen Rd 15237
Oak Grove St 15218
Oak Hill Dr
100-599 15213
1200-1298 15239
E Oak Hill Rd 15238
N Oak Hill Rd 15238
S Oak Hill Rd 15238
Oak Knoll Dr 15238
Oak Manor Dr 15220
Oak Manor Pl 15235
Oak Park Ct 15241
Oak Park Pl 15243
Oak Park Rd 15214
Oak Spring Dr 15238
Oakbrook Cir 15220
Oakcrest Dr 15209
Oakcrest Ln 15236
Oakcrest Rd 15235
Oakdale Ave 15234
Oakdale St
3700-3799 15212
3900-4199 15214
Oakdene St 15206
Oakfield Way 15210
Oakglen St 15204
Oakhill St 15212
Oakhurst Cir 15215
Oakhurst Ln 15215
Oakhurst Rd 15215
Oakhurst St 15210
Oakland Ave 15213
Oakland Ct 15213
Oakland Sq 15213
Oakland St 15223
Oaklawn Dr 15241
Oakleaf Dr 15207
Oakleaf Ln 15237
Oakleaf Rd 15227
Oakledge Ct 15241
Oakley Ave 15229
Oakley Way 15203
Oaklynn Ct 15220
Oakmont St 15205
Oakridge Dr 15227
Oakridge Ln 15237
Oakridge Rd
1-99 15229
100-200 15237
202-298 15237
Oakridge St 15226
Oakside Ln 15229
Oakton Rd 15227
Oakview Ave 15218
Oakview Dr 15237
Oakville Ct & Dr 15220
Oakwood Ave
1-399 15229
20-24 15202
58-398 15229
500-598 15202
601-699 15202
Oakwood Dr 15234
Oakwood Pl 15208
Oakwood Rd
1-99 15205
100-299 15237
Oakwood Sq 15209
Oakwood St
100-399 15209
500-899 15208
Oberlin Ave 15229
Oberlin St 15206
Oberon St 15204
Obey Ave 15205
Oblock Ave & Rd 15239
Obrien St 15209
Ocala St 15212
Ocala Trail Dr 15235
Ocenas Ave 15212
Ochiltree Way 15205
Odanah St 15212
Odessa Pl 15206
Odette St 15227
Odin St 15207
Oesterle Ln 15214
Oetting St 15204
Offley St 15233
Ogden Ave 15221
Oglethorpe St 15201
Ohara Pl 15201
Ohara St
3801-3899 15213
3999-3999 15260
4000-4098 15213
Ohara Manor Dr 15238
Ohara Woods Dr 15238
Ohio St
1-599 15209
2-98 15202
5500-5599 15225
E Ohio St
200-418 15212
419-419 15209
420-2198 15212
421-499 15212
501-503 15209
501-999 15212
1001-1099 15223
N Ohio St 15202
S Ohio St 15202
W Ohio St 15212
Ohio River Blvd
300-1099 15202
1101-8399 15202
4000-4098 15212
4100-8398 15202
Ohiopyle Dr 15239
Ohm St 15212
Oklahoma Ave 15216
Oklahoma St 15214
Olancha Ave 15227
Old Barn Rd 15239
Old Beulah Rd 15235
Old Boston Rd 15227
Old Camp Horne Rd 15237
Old Clairton Rd
2-8 15236
10-799 15236
4200-4299 15227
4900-5199 15236
Old Curry Hollow Rd 15236
Old Engineering Hall 15260
Old English Rd 15237
Old Farm Dr 15239
Old Farm Rd
200-499 15228
500-599 15234
Old Farm Trl 15238
Old Frankstown Rd 15239
Old Freeport Rd 15238
Old Gate Rd 15235
Old Gilkeson Rd 15228
Old Hickory Dr 15235
Old Hickory Rd 15243
Old Indian Trl 15238
Old Indian Trail Ct 15238
Old Kirkpatrick St 15219
Old Lebanon Church Rd 15236
Old Leechburg Rd 15239
Old Lesnett Rd 15241
Old Mcknight Rd 15237
Old Meadow Rd 15241
Old Mill Rd 15238
Old Oak Ct & Dr 15220
Old Orchard Cir 15205
Old Orchard Rd 15237
Old Orchard Trl 15238
Old Perry Hwy 15237
Old Pine Ln 15238
Old Soose Rd 15209
Old Steubenville Pike 15205
Old Timber Trl 15238
Old Washington Rd 15241
Old William Penn Hwy 15235
Olde Chapel Trl 15238
Olde Ingomar Ct 15237
Olivant Pl & St 15206
Olive St
8-99 15214
101-105 15214
300-899 15237
2101-2101 15214
Oliver Ave
100-199 15202
301-321 15222
323-339 15222
341-399 15222
400-499 15219
Oliver Ct 15239
Olivet Ave 15210
Olivia St 15218
Ollie St 15207
Oltman St 15204
Olympia Pl 15217
Olympia Rd 15211
Olympia St 15211
Olympic Rd 15236
Olympic Heights Dr 15235
Omaha St 15211
Omega Dr 15205
Omega Pl 15206
Omega St 15206
Oneida Ave 15237
Oneida Pl 15211
Oneida St 15211
Oneill Ln 15237
Onondago St 15218
Onyx St 15210
Ophelia St 15213
Oporto St 15203
Orangewood Ave 15216
Oranmore St 15201
Orator St 15204
Orbin St 15219
Orchard Ave
736R-736R 15202
1-99 15223
100-899 15202
111-199 15202
400-735 15202
E Orchard Ave 15202
Orchard Dr
2-14 15220
3-15 15236
17-17 15220
21-25 15236
80-80 15236
100-106 15229
104-106 15236
108-114 15229
108-422 15236
109-115 15235
116-118 15229
117-198 15235
190-282 15228
200-224 15235
201-229 15235
231-417 15228
284-284 15236
286-290 15228
292-292 15236
296-412 15228
308-308 15238
310-322 15238
324-326 15238
424-428 15236
500-599 15236
2400-2499 15241
Orchard Ln 15238
Orchard Pl 15210
Orchard Rd 15237
Orchard Sq 15229
Orchard St
1-99 15221
200-299 15225
Orchard Way 15218
Orchard Hill Dr
600-799 15238
5200-5399 15236
Orchard Manor Dr 15238
Orchard Spring Rd 15220
Orchardview Dr 15220
Orchid Ln 15243
Orchid Pl 15207
Orchid St 15207
Orchlee St 15212
Ordale Blvd 15228
Ordinance Ave 15216
Oregon Ave 15205
Oregon St 15204
Oregon Trl 15234
Orin St
1-399 15235
2900-2999 15210
Orinoco St 15207
Oriole Dr
203-205 15220

207-210 15220
212-214 15220
215-216 15243
217-217 15220
219-1199 15220
Orion Dr 15235
Orion St 15219
Orlando Ave 15229
Orlando Pl 15235
Orleans St 15214
Ormond Ave 15218
Ormsby Ave 15210
Orourke Dr 15236
Orphan St 15206
Orpwood St 15213
Orr Dr 15234
Orr Rd 15241
Orr St 15219
Orth Dr 15202
Orville Way 15224
Orvis Ave 15223
Orwell Way 15224
Osage Dr 15235
Osage Ln 15208
Osage Rd 15243
Osceola St 15224
Osgood St 15214
Oshkosh Dr 15231
Osprey Way 15207
Ossipee St 15219
Oswald St 15212
Oswego St 15212
Oswin St 15220
Otillia St 15210
Ott Dr 15236
Ottawa St 15211
Otterson St 15204
Ottis Way 15207
Otto St 15209
Our Way 15219
Outlook Dr
200-299 15228
2000-2099 15241
Outlook St 15227
Overbeck St 15212
Overbrook Blvd 15210
Overbrook Rd 15235
Overbrook Ter 15239
Overcliff Way 15212
Overdale Rd 15221
Overhill St
1-199 15210
2100-2198 15212
Overland Trl 15236
Overlook Ct 15222
Overlook Dr
1-30 15238
31-47 15216
32-48 15238
49-699 15216
Overlook St 15214
Overlook Glen Dr 15236
Overton Ln 15217
Overton St
200-299 15221
7300-7398 15218
Ovid St 15205
Owendale Ave 15227
Oxbow St 15205
Oxbridge Ct 15238
Oxbridge Dr 15237
Oxfield St 15212
Oxford Ave 15238
Oxford Blvd 15243
Oxford Ct 15237
Oxford Ctr 15219
Oxford Pl 15241
Oxford Rd 15202
Oxford St 15205
Ozan Way 15221
Ozark Dr 15239
Pacific Ave 15221
N Pacific Ave 15224
S Pacific Ave 15224
Paddock Ln 15236
Paden St 15221

Page Dr 15236
Page St 15233
Painters Dr 15228
Painters Run Rd
501-699 15228
1600-1704 15243
1705-2099 15241
Palace Ct & Dr 15227
Palen Way 15212
Palisade Ln 15214
Pallas Dr 15237
Palm Ave 15235
Palm Beach Ave 15216
Palmer Rd 15239
Palmer St 15218
Palmetto Dr 15235
Palo Alto St 15212
Pamela Dr
1-99 15209
100-199 15227
Pampena Ln 15239
Panama Way 15224
Panama Lodge Dr 15227
Pandora Way 15210
Panke St 15208
Pannier Rd 15237
Panno Dr 15237
Panther Hollow Rd 15213
Papercraft Park 15238
Par Dr 15236
Parade St 15207
Paragon Pl 15241
Parallel Ave 15210
Paree Dr 15239
Paris Rd 15235
Parise Rd 15221
Parish Ln 15213
Parish St 15220
Park Ave
7-7 15223
8-8 15223
10-38 15223
40-52 15223
42-198 15229
49-99 15229
200-234 15229
209-209 15202
211-240 15202
236-240 15229
242-298 15229
283-297 15221
299-599 15221
629-629 15202
631-647 15202
657-667 15221
669-696 15221
698-698 15221
900-999 15234
1000-1599 15221
7400-7499 15218
Park Blvd 15216
Park Pl
1-99 15205
100-699 15237
N Park Rd 15229
Park Sq 15238
Park St
1-299 15209
2001-2099 15236
Park Entrance Dr 15228
Park Hill Dr 15221
Park Lane Dr 15275
Park Manor Blvd
900-998 15205
1000-1935 15205
1936-1936 15244
1937-4099 15205
1938-4098 15205
Park Manor Dr 15205
Park Manor Pl 15235
Park Plaza Dr 15229
Park Ridge Pl 15221
Park Square Ln 15238
Park Way St 15235
Parkdale Ave 15227
Parke St 15205
Parkedge Rd 15220

Parker Dr 15216
Parker St
2-98 15223
100-299 15223
300-300 15209
302-499 15209
Parkfel Ave 15237
Parkfield St 15210
Parkhurst St 15212
Parklane Dr 15208
Parkline Dr 15227
Parklow St 15210
Parklyn St 15234
Parkman Ave
200-4298 15213
219-223 15260
225-4399 15213
Parkridge Dr 15235
Parkridge Ln 15228
Parkside Ave 15228
Parkside Ln 15236
Parkton Pl 15232
Parkview Ave
600-699 15202
3200-3799 15213
Parkview Blvd
600-999 15215
1000-1876 15217
1878-1888 15217
Parkview Dr
100-410 15236
411-499 15243
500-500 15236
500-500 15243
501-501 15236
501-501 15243
502-507 15236
506-506 15243
508-510 15236
509-509 15236
509-510 15243
511-523 15236
512-998 15243
525-999 15243
Parkview Rd 15237
Parkview St 15205
Parkvue Dr 15236
Parkway Ave 15235
Parkway Ctr 15220
Parkway Ctr W 15220
Parkway Dr 15228
Parkway Rd 15237
Parkway View Dr 15205
Parkwest Dr 15275
Parkwest Office Ctr 15275
Parkwood Rd 15210
Parliament Pl 15236
Parma Dr 15209
Parnell St 15207
Parquet St 15226
Parson St 15204
Partridge Dr 15241
Partridge Run Rd 15241
Parviss St 15212
Pary Ave 15227
Pasadena Ave 15221
N Pasadena Dr 15215
S Pasadena Dr 15215
Pasadena St 15211
Pasadena Drive Ext 15215
S Passage Dr 15236
Passavant Way 15238
Pat Haven Dr 15243
Path Way 15207
Patrice Ct 15221
Patricia Dr 15237
Patricia Rd 15215
Patricia Way 15225
Patrick Dr 15205
Patrick St 15209
Patriot Way 15215
Patterson Ave 15218
Patterson Rd 15220
Patterson St 15203
Patton Dr 15241
Patton St 15221

Paul Ct 15221
Paul St
43-197 15211
199-299 15211
9100-9199 15235
Paula Dr 15236
Pauley Ave 15207
Pauline Ave & Pl 15216
Paulowna St 15219
Paulson Ave 15206
Paur St 15211
Paxico Ave 15235
Paxton Pl 15201
Payne St 15235
Peach Aly 15202
Peach Dr 15236
Pear Hill Ln 15238
Pearce Rd 15234
Pearinso St 15233
Pearl Ave 15229
Pearl Dr 15227
Pearl Rd 15235
Pearl St
107-121 15224
123-499 15224
1100-1199 15221
Pebble Dr 15239
Pebble Stone Ct 15239
Pebblewood Ct 15237
Pecan Dr 15235
Peddler Pl 15212
Peebles Rd 15237
Peebles St 15221
Peekskill St
200-258 15212
259-2299 15214
Peermont Ave 15216
Pemberton St 15212
Pembroke Ct 15237
Pembroke Dr 15243
Pembroke Pl 15232
Pembrook Ct 15239
Penbryn Rd 15237
Penelope St 15211
Penfield Ct 15208
Penfield Pl
100-107 15208
101-111 15220
Penfort St 15214
Penham Ln & Pl 15208
Penhurst Dr 15235
Penhurst Rd 15202
Penn Ave
100-199 15210
200-200 15221
201-225 15210
202-206 15210
208-208 15221
210-222 15210
221-497 15221
224-224 15221
226-226 15210
300-499 15221
499-1901 15221
501-521 15222
523-601 15222
603-1243 15222
700-798 15221
800-1000 15222
1100-1198 15221
1200-1200 15222
1202-1214 15221
1250-1300 15222
1265-1299 15221
1301-1399 15221
1350-1398 15222
1400-1401 15222
1402-1498 15221
1403-1519 15222
1500-1520 15222
1536-1598 15221
1600-1602 15221
1601-1617 15222
1604-1620 15221
1619-1702 15222
1704-2898 15222
1705-1705 15221

1711-2899 15222
1903-1935 15221
2900-3899 15201
3900-5399 15224
5400-6599 15206
6700-7599 15208
7600-7799 15221
Penn Cir E 15206
Penn Cir N 15206
Penn Cir S 15206
Penn Cir W 15206
Penn Ctr W 15276
Penn Dr 15214
W Penn Pl 15224
Penn St
100-198 15215
200-299 15215
400-611 15227
604-604 15215
606-625 15215
612-612 15215
613-667 15227
616-698 15227
700-798 15215
800-1299 15215
Penn Bridge Ct 15221
Penn Center Blvd 15235
Penn Hills Dr 15235
Penn Vista Dr 15235
Pennant Dr 15239
Pennoak Dr 15235
Pennoak Manor Dr 15235
Pennock Rd 15212
Pennridge Ct 15235
Pennridge Rd 15211
Pennsbury Blvd 15205
Pennsview Ct 15205
Pennsylvania Ave
6-6 15202
68-68 15221
70-101 15221
103-107 15221
106-108 15202
128-128 15221
166-232 15202
234-240 15202
289-291 15221
293-399 15221
802-806 15233
808-1899 15233
Pennsylvania Blvd 15228
E Pennview Ave 15223
W Pennview Ave 15223
Pennview Dr 15235
Pennwood Ave
1-199 15218
200-799 15221
801-999 15221
Pennwood Dr 15235
Pennwood Pl 15295
Penny Dr 15235
Penrose Dr 15208
Pensdale St 15205
Pentland Ave 15227
Pentland Dr 15235
Penton Rd 15213
Peola Rd 15216
Peony Ave 15229
Peoples Rd 15237
Peoples Township Rd 15237
Peoria Way 15201
Peralta St 15212
Perchment St 15221
Percy Way 15201
Perez Way 15205
Perity Ln 15220
Perlick St 15223
Pernod St 15212
Perri Dr 15226
Perricrest Dr 15220
Perrilyn Ave 15226
Perrott St 15212
Perry Hwy
100-939 15229
940-1199 15237
4500-4898 15229
4900-5399 15229

5401-5499 15229
7700-9700 15237
Perry Ln 15229
Perry St
1-99 15219
19-40 15209
42-98 15209
200-299 15239
601-605 15219
607-631 15219
633-699 15219
Perry Knoll Pl 15237
Perrymont Rd 15237
Perrysville Ave
2-98 15202
1600-1799 15212
1801-1897 15214
1899-4299 15214
4500-5298 15229
5300-5399 15229
6800-7599 15202
Perrysville Rd 15229
Perrytown Pl 15237
Perryview Ave 15214
Perryvista Ave 15237
Pershing St 15235
Pet Pl 15239
Peter Dr 15235
Petermans Ln 15235
Peterson Pl 15241
Petunia Ave 15229
Petunia St 15210
Pheasant Cir 15241
Pheasant Dr
102-102 15238
103-123 15238
106-124 15235
125-127 15238
126-136 15235
200-399 15235
Phelan Way 15219
Philadelphia Ave 15216
Philander St 15218
Phillip Dr 15241
Phillippi Dr 15236
Phillips Ave
200-299 15225
5500-6499 15217
Phillips Dr 15241
Phillips Ln 15239
Phillips Pl 15217
Phineas St 15212
Phoenix St 15220
Phyllis Dr 15235
Pico St 15209
Picture Dr 15236
Piedmont Ave 15216
Pier St 15213
Pierce St 15232
Pierina Dr 15243
Piermont St 15211
Pierson Run Rd 15239
Pike St 15235
Pikeview Dr 15239
Pilgrim Aly 15215
Pilsen St 15212
Pin Oak Ct
1-69 15239
71-99 15237
Pin Oak Dr 15237
Pin Oak Pl 15220
Pinchtown Rd 15236
Pine Ave 15234
Pine Ct
100-199 15239
200-249 15237
Pine Rd 15237
Pine St
1-10 15235
3-57 15223
20-30 15223
300-399 15238
500-599 15235
701-799 15238
7700-7899 15237
9101-9299 15239
Pine Way 15225

Pine Creek Dr 15238
Pine Heights Pl 15237
Pine Hill Dr 15214
Pine Hill Ln 15238
Pine Hill Drive Ext 15214
Pine Line Dr 15237
Pine Shadows Dr 15216
Pine Valley Ct 15239
Pine Valley Dr
31-59 15235
600-799 15239
Pinecastle Ave 15234
Pinecrest Dr 15237
Pinehaven Dr 15241
Pinehurst Ave 15216
Pinehurst Ct 15237
Pinehurst Dr 15241
Pineridge Rd 15237
Pineridge St 15208
Pinetree Dr 15241
Pinetree Rd 15243
Pineview Dr 15241
Pinewood Ct 15202
Pinewood Dr 15243
Pinewood Sq 15235
Pinewood Ter 15237
Pinoak Rd 15243
Pintail Dr 15238
Pinto Dr 15239
Pioneer Ave
1-99 15229
1300-3199 15226
Piper Dr 15234
Pitcairn Pl 15232
Pitkin St 15214
Pitler St 15212
Pitt St 15221
Pittock St 15217
Pittsburgh St 15202
Pittview Ave
600-899 15209
1900-2299 15212
2300-2599 15209
2601-2699 15209
Pittview Rd 15237
Pius St 15203
Placid St 15207
Plainfield Ave
1-299 15202
5400-5499 15217
Plainview Ave 15226
Plaport St 15207
Plateau Dr 15237
Plateau St 15210
Platt Ave 15216
Pleasant Way 15201
Pleasant Hills Blvd 15236
Pleasant View Ct 15236
Pleasant View Ln 15238
Pleasantvue Cir 15241
Pleasantvue Dr 15227
Plereli Ave 15229
Pliney Way 15210
Plough St 15212
Plum St 15239
Plum Way 15201
Plum Creek Rd 15235
Plum Crest Dr 15239
Plum Industrial Park 15239
Plumdale Ct 15239
Plumer Ave 15202
Plummer St 15201
Plymouth Rd 15227
Plymouth Sq 15237
Plymouth St 15211
Pocahontas Pl 15237
Pocono Dr 15220
Pocono St 15218
Pocusset St 15217
Poe Dr 15235
Poe Way 15201
W Point Ave 15212
N Point Dr 15233
Point Breeze Pl 15208
Point Vue Dr 15237
Pointview Rd 15227

Pointview St 15206
Polaris Cir 15241
Polk Way 15206
Pondendi St 15223
Ponoka Rd 15241
Pontiac Ave 15237
Pontiac Rd 15241
Poor Richards Ln 15237
Poplar Ave 15234
Poplar Ct 15238
Poplar Dr
98A-98B 15228
1-100 15228
101-105 15238
102-106 15228
107-109 15238
110-110 15228
111-111 15238
112-112 15238
114-118 15228
120-199 15228
200-299 15209
Poplar St
1-41 15205
2-10 15235
43-1399 15205
87-87 15205
100-100 15223
116-126 15205
151-151 15223
200-598 15223
700-710 15238
712-716 15238
718-798 15238
745-797 15220
799-900 15220
902-998 15220
1400-1499 15205
Poplar Ridge Rd 15235
Poplargrove St 15210
Porterfield St 15212
Portia Dr 15236
Portland St & Way 15206
Portman St 15214
Portola St 15214
Portview Cir 15227
Post St 15201
Posvar Hl 15260
Potomac Ave
1-31 15220
33-41 15220
1400-2440 15216
2441-2441 15220
2442-2998 15216
2443-2999 15216
Potter St 15232
Powell St 15204
Powers Aly 15215
Powers Run Rd 15238
Powhattan St 15224
Ppg Pl
1-1 15272
1-6 15222
Prager St 15215
Prallana Dr 15241
Preble Ave 15233
Premier St 15201
Premo St 15206
Prencoll 15240
Prescott Dr
100-199 15235
8700-8799 15237
Prescott St 15207
President Way 15206
Presley Ct 15237
Presque Isle Dr 15239
Pressley St 15212
Preston Ave 15214
Preston St 15205
Pretense Way 15203
Price Way 15201
Pride Rd 15235
Pride St 15219
Primrose St 15203
Prince Andrew Ct 15237
Princess Ave 15216
Princess Ln 15236

Princeton Ave 15229
Princeton Blvd 15221
Princeton Dr 15235
Princeton Pl
301-499 15206
7200-7399 15218
Princeton Rd 15205
Printers Pl 15237
Priscilla Dr 15229
Pritchard St 15204
Private Rd 15239
Proctor Way 15210
Progress St 15212
Promenade St 15205
Prospect Ave
800-899 15215
1200-1300 15234
1302-1398 15234
2000-2099 15218
3800-3899 15234
3901-3999 15234
6800-6999 15202
E Prospect Ave 15205
W Prospect Ave 15205
Prospect Ct 15229
Prospect Cv 15229
Prospect Dr 15229
Prospect Rd
900-1599 15227
1700-1799 15236
Prospect St
1-31 15223
2-2 15211
3-117 15211
4-6 15211
8-8 15211
16-30 15223
32-70 15223
72-98 15223
110-118 15202
111-111 15211
115-117 15202
119-147 15211
120-122 15202
124-134 15202
149-161 15211
200-399 15211
401-499 15211
501-599 15223
Protectory Pl 15219
Provan Pl 15229
Providence Blvd 15237
Providence Dr 15239
Providence Point Blvd 15243
Province St 15212
Provost Rd
1-3 15227
4-98 15236
5-4099 15227
100-4098 15227
Proxim Way 15210
Pryor Way 15212
Pueblo Dr 15228
Pulawski Way 15219
Purchase Pl 15228
Purdue St 15212
Purity Rd 15235
Purse Way 15212
Pusey St 15214
Putnam St 15206
Pynchon St 15212
Pyramid Ave 15227
Pyrenees Rd 15239
Quail Dr 15235
Quail Hill Dr 15241
Quail Hill Rd
1-40 15214
1-199 15238
Quail Roost 15237
Quaill Ave 15202
Quaker Dr 15236
Quarry Rd 15237
Quarry St 15210
Queen St 15212
Queens Ct
1-99 15238
100-199 15237

Queensberry Cir 15234
Queensberry Ct 15237
S Queensberry Ct 15237
Queensboro Ave 15226
Queensbury St 15205
Queenston Dr 15235
Queenston St 15210
Questend Ave 15228
Quigg Dr 15241
Quincy St 15210
Quinn Dr
100-200 15275
6300-6399 15217
Quirin Ln 15207
Race St
1-99 15202
2-6 15218
18-54 15202
100-299 15218
1100-1199 15234
2700-2799 15235
7100-7699 15208
Racine Ave 15216
Radcliff Dr
100-199 15237
400-499 15235
Radcliffe St 15204
Radford Rd 15227
Radiant St 15210
Radisson Dr 15205
Radisson Rd 15227
Radium St 15214
Radner St 15212
Radnor Ave 15221
Rae Ave 15228
Raff St 15207
Rahe St 15210
Railroad St
2-98 15223
200-401 15235
402-404 15218
403-599 15235
420-698 15235
1100-1199 15236
2300-2405 15222
2407-2799 15222
2901-6197 15201
6199-6399 15201
Rainbow Ridge Ln 15238
Rainier Dr 15239
Raintree Dr 15236
Raleigh Ave 15216
Raleigh Ct 15237
Raleigh Pl 15239
Raleigh St 15217
Ralston Pl 15216
Ramada Dr 15241
Ramage Rd 15214
Ramey Dr 15220
Ramo St 15204
Ramon Dr 15238
Rampart St 15219
Ramsey St 15221
Ranchview Dr 15236
Range Dr 15236
Ranger Dr 15236
Rangley Dr 15209
Rankin Ave 15212
Ransom St 15214
Rapello St 15226
Rapidan Way 15206
Raven Dr 15243
Raven St 15210
Ravencrest Rd 15215
Ravenswood Ave 15202
Ravilla Ave 15210
Ravine St 15215
Rawley Dr 15243
Rawlins Run Rd 15238
Ray Ave 15226
Raymond St 15218
Readshaw Way 15236
Reagan Dr 15237
Realty Ave 15216
Reamer St 15226
Rebecca Ave 15221

Rebecca Ct 15237
Rebecca Dr 15237
Rebecca Ln 15236
Rebecca Sq 15209
Rebecca St
2-98 15205
3700-3899 15234
Recker Dr 15227
Rectenwald St 15210
Red Bird Point Ln 15202
Red Mill Dr 15241
Red Oak Ct 15237
Red Oak Dr
200-299 15239
800-999 15238
2400-2599 15220
Reddour St 15212
Redfern Dr 15241
Redlyn St 15210
Rednap St 15212
Redpath Trl 15241
Redrose Ave 15210
Redwood Ct 15202
Redwood Dr 15234
Redwood St 15210
Reece Dr 15227
Reed Dr 15205
Reed St
2-30 15219
32-99 15219
400-599 15221
1700-2499 15219
Reed Roberts Pl 15219
Reedsdale St
900-999 15212
1000-1599 15233
Reel Ave
1-199 15237
400-499 15229
Reese Ave 15223
Reese St 15211
Reetz St 15209
Regan Ave 15227
Regency Dr
400-799 15239
1100-8099 15237
Regent St 15236
Regina St
1-50 15203
95-95 15209
97-399 15209
Regis Ave 15236
Rehman St 15210
Reifert St 15210
Reiland St 15227
Reis Run Rd 15237
Reiss St 15212
Reiter Rd 15235
Reiter St 15206
Remington Dr
1900-2099 15221
7900-8899 15237
Renee Ct 15237
Renfer St 15237
Renfrew St 15206
Rennie Dr 15236
Renova St 15207
Rental Car Rd 15231
Renton Ave
200-399 15239
1700-1799 15229
Renton Rd 15239
Rentz Way 15210
Renwick St 15210
Republic St 15211
Resaca Pl 15212
Rescue St 15212
Reserve St 15209
Reuben St 15212
Reunion Pl 15219
Revere Dr 15236
Revere Way 15219
Revo Rd 15236
Rexford Dr 15241
Reynolds St
6600-6799 15206

6800-7199 15208
7201-7499 15208
Rheams Ave 15202
Rhett Dr 15241
Rhine Pl & St 15212
Rhode Island St 15220
Rhodes Ave
1-134 15220
109-109 15227
136-198 15220
Rialto Pl & St 15212
Ribb Way 15212
Richard Dr
100-127 15237
129-199 15237
1400-1599 15234
Richard Way 15214
Richardson Ave 15212
Richbarn Rd 15212
Richey Ave 15214
Richfield St 15234
Richland Ave 15229
Richland Dr 15235
Richland Ln
100-400 15208
402-498 15208
501-599 15221
Richland Pl 15208
Richland Rd 15228
N Richland St 15208
Richland Manor Dr 15208
Richmond Cir 15237
Richmond Dr 15215
Richmond St
1-99 15205
1101-1197 15218
1199-1399 15218
Rickenbaugh St 15212
Ricker Ct 15202
Rico Ln 15237
Riddile St 15212
Ridenour St 15205
Ridge Ave
3-5 15223
7-15 15223
107-113 15237
115-241 15237
121-127 15202
129-237 15202
132-138 15202
140-152 15202
200-220 15212
206-212 15221
214-261 15221
239-239 15202
243-291 15237
263-299 15221
284-298 15221
300-399 15221
400-404 15202
406-406 15202
459-481 15237
483-499 15237
601-699 15212
700-708 15202
710-712 15202
713-797 15212
714-798 15202
799-922 15212
924-950 15212
979-1009 15202
1011-1099 15202
1012-1098 15233
1100-1199 15233
Ridge Dr 15236
Ridge Rd
1-99 15221
112-136 15237
138-138 15237
200-299 15238
300-399 15221
600-699 15205
6751-6799 15236
Ridgecrest Dr 15235
Ridgedale Ln 15238
Ridgefell Ave 15237
Ridgefield Ave 15216

Ridgehaven Ln 15238
Ridgeland Dr
1-100 15238
102-198 15238
1100-1199 15212
Ridgeland Pl 15212
Ridgemont Dr 15220
Ridgemont Rd 15237
Ridgeside Rd 15237
Ridgetop Dr 15239
Ridgeview Ave 15235
Ridgeview Dr 15228
Ridgeville St 15217
Ridgevue Dr 15236
Ridgeway Ct 15228
Ridgeway St 15213
Ridgewood Ave 15229
Ridgewood Dr 15235
Ridgewood Rd
1-97 15237
99-200 15237
202-298 15237
1200-1299 15241
Ridgewood St 15214
Riding Trail Ln 15215
Riegel Dr 15209
Riehl Dr 15234
Rigel St 15212
Riggo Way 15233
Ringgold St 15220
Ringold Ave 15205
Ringwalt St 15216
Rinne St 15210
Rio Cir 15241
Riota Way 15210
Rippey Pl & St 15206
Rising Main Ave
200-299 15212
300-399 15214
600-699 15212
Rita Dr 15221
Ritzland Rd 15235
River Ave
100-200 15212
201-299 15215
202-1398 15212
1001-1299 15212
W River Ave 15212
River Rd 15238
River Heights Dr 15209
River Oaks Dr 15215
Riverfront Dr 15238
Rivermont Dr 15207
Riversea Rd 15233
Riverside Ct 15238
Riverside Mews 15203
Riverside Pl 15225
Riverside St 15219
Riverview Ave
1-99 15214
100-134 15238
101-199 15214
122-174 15202
129-141 15214
136-150 15238
152-158 15238
7800-7999 15218
W Riverview Ave 15202
Riverview Rd 15238
Riverview Ter 15215
Riverwatch Ct & Dr 15238
Riviera Dr 15209
Riviera Rd 15239
Roanoke St 15203
Robb Hollow Rd 15243
Robbins St 15236
Roberta Dr
100-199 15221
4800-4999 15236
Roberts Rd 15239
Roberts St 15219
Robertson Ave 15226
Robertson Dr 15237
Robertson Pl 15223
Robin Ct 15237
Robin Dr 15220

Robin Rd 15217
Robin Dell Dr 15215
Robina Dr 15221
Robinhood Rd
1-275 15220
698-698 15215
700-799 15215
Robinson Blvd
1900-2599 15221
2600-2899 15235
Robinson Ct 15213
Robinson Dr 15236
Robinson Plz 15205
Robinson Rd 15237
Robinson St 15213
Robinson Center Dr 15205
Robinwood Dr
595-597 15216
599-699 15216
701-709 15216
712-798 15220
Robson Dr 15241
Robyn Dr 15235
Rochelle St 15210
Rochester Rd
1-200 15229
100-190 15229
110-150 15237
250-268 15237
270-8649 15237
8651-8899 15237
Rock Haven Ln 15228
Rock Ridge Rd 15209
Rock Springs Rd 15228
Rockfield Cir & Rd 15243
Rockford Ave 15226
Rockhill Rd 15243
Rockingham Rd 15238
Rockland Ave 15216
Rockland Dr 15239
Rockledge St 15212
Rocklyn Dr 15205
Rocklynn Pl 15228
Rockwell Ln 15218
Rockwood Ave
100-299 15221
600-1099 15234
1101-1199 15234
Rockwood Dr
100-199 15238
4100-4199 15227
Rockyhill St 15204
Rodenbaugh Ave 15214
Roderick Dr 15237
Rodgers Ave 15205
Rodgers Dr 15238
Rodgers Dr W 15238
Rodgers St 15207
Rodi Rd 15235
Rodilin Dr 15235
Rodman St 15206
Rodney St 15212
Roessler Rd 15220
Roland Rd 15221
Roland St
1600-1698 15203
2900-3099 15227
Rolfe St 15221
Roll St 15210
Rolla St 15214
Rolling Dr 15229
Rolling Hills Ct 15239
Rolling Hills Rd 15236
Rolling Meadow Cir & Rd 15241
Rolling Rock Rd 15234
Rolshouse Rd 15237
Roma Way 15207
Romanhoff St 15212
Romeo St 15213
Romeyn St 15210
Romine St 15226
Roosevelt Ave
100-199 15214
400-499 15202
502-503 15215
504-512 15202

514-699 15202
Roosevelt Blvd 15237
Roosevelt Rd
100-299 15202
300-1799 15237
Roosevelt St 15235
Roosevelt Way 15215
Rope Way 15233
Rosalia Ave 15234
Rosalia Pl 15207
Rosalind Rd 15237
Rosary Way 15232
Rosbury Pl 15243
Roscoe St 15203
Rose Ave
101-137 15229
104-177 15235
138-138 15229
139-139 15229
179-181 15235
200-499 15235
Rose Cir 15241
Rose Dr
1-99 15235
2700-2740 15241
Rose Ln 15234
Rose St
1600-1699 15218
1800-2199 15219
Rose Arbor Pl 15207
Rose Garden Rd 15220
Rose Leaf Rd 15220
Rose Mary Hill Dr 15239
Roseanne Ave 15216
Roseberry Ln & St 15216
Rosecliff Dr 15209
Rosecrest Dr
1-199 15229
5000-5199 15201
Rosecrest Pl 15201
Rosedale St
400-534 15221
535-599 15208
Roseland Ave 15214
Roselawn Ave 15228
Roselawn Ter 15213
Roselle Ct & Dr 15207
Rosemary Rd 15221
Rosemont Ave
1-99 15228
800-899 15223
Rosemont Ln 15217
Rosemoor St 15217
E & W Roseridge St 15202
Roseton St 15210
Rosetta Ct 15221
Rosetta St
4800-5370 15224
5372-5398 15224
5400-5499 15206
Rosewood Ct 15236
Rosewood Dr
100-199 15235
400-404 15237
401-429 15236
431-599 15236
700-799 15239
3301-3399 15234
Rosewood St 15208
Rosina Way 15224
Roslyn Pl 15232
Roslyn St 15218
Ross Ave 15221
Ross Rd 15235
Ross St 15219
Ross Garden Rd 15206
Ross Hollow Rd 15239
Ross Municipal Rd 15237
Ross Park Dr 15237
Ross Park Mall Dr 15237
Rosser Dr 15239
Rossmoor Dr 15241
Rossmor Ct 15229
Rossmore Ave 15226
Rostock St 15212
Rostrevor Pl 15202
Rostron Dr 15241

Roswell Dr 15205
Roswin Dr 15226
Rothman St 15210
Rothpletz St 15212
Round Top St 15205
Roup Ave
100-299 15206
300-499 15232
Route 910 15238
Rowan St 15206
Rowley St 15219
Roxanna Way 15206
Roxbury Rd 15221
Royal Ave 15235
Royal Ct 15234
Royal Dr 15209
Royal St 15212
Royal Oak Ave 15235
Royal Oak Dr 15220
Royal Oak Rd 15220
Royal View Ct 15239
Royanna Dr 15241
Royce Ave
400-499 15216
600-699 15243
Roycrest Pl 15208
Roycroft Ave
1-199 15228
200-299 15234
Royston Rd 15238
Rubicon St 15211
Ruby St 15201
Rudolph St 15220
Rue Grande Vue St 15220
Rugby St 15206
Ruggles St 15214
W Run Rd 15207
Runnette St 15235
Running Brook Ln 15238
Runnymede Ave 15205
Rural Ct E 15221
Rural Ct W 15221
Rural St 15206
Ruralton St 15210
Rush St 15233
Rushmore Dr 15235
Ruskin Ave 15213
Ruskin Hl 15260
Russell Dr 15209
Russell Rd 15237
Russell St
1-99 15214
300-399 15209
Rustic St 15210
Rustic Ridge Dr 15239
Rutgers Rd 15205
Ruth Dr 15209
Ruth St
1-199 15211
200-299 15239
900-999 15243
Rutherford Ave 15216
Ruthfred Dr 15241
Ruthven St 15219
Ruthwood Ave 15227
Rutland St 15214
Rutledge Dr
100-200 15215
202-298 15215
1000-1099 15241
Rutledge St 15211
Ruxton St 15211
Ryan Ct 15205
Ryan Dr 15220
Rydal Ln 15237
Rydal St 15205
Ryland Dr 15237
Ryndwood Rd 15237
Sabbath Dr 15236
Sacramento Ave 15204
Sadowski Ave 15215
Sagamore St 15204
Sagamore Hill Rd 15239
Sage Dr
1-99 15235
400-499 15243

501-599 15243
Sagebrush Dr 15236
Sageman Ave 15226
Saginaw Dr 15237
Saginaw St 15204
Sagwa St 15212
Sailor Pl 15218
Saindiso St 15234
Saint Andrews Ct 15237
Saint Andrews Dr 15205
Saint Anne St 15234
Saint Charles Ct 15238
Saint Charles Pl 15215
Saint Clair Dr 15228
N Saint Clair St 15206
S Saint Clair St 15206
Saint Croix Dr 15235
Saint Gabriel Cir 15212
Saint Ives St 15212
Saint James Pl
1-99 15215
500-599 15232
3400-3498 15213
Saint James St 15232
Saint James Ter 15232
Saint John St 15239
Saint Johns Pl & Way 15201
Saint Joseph Dr 15209
Saint Joseph St 15210
Saint Joseph Way 15203
Saint Lawrence Ave 15218
Saint Leo St 15203
Saint Lucas St 15210
Saint Marie St 15206
Saint Marks Pl 15212
Saint Martin St 15203
Saint Marys Ln 15214
Saint Michael St 15203
Saint Norberts St 15234
Saint Patrick St 15210
Saint Paul St 15203
Saint Peter St 15209
Saint Susanna Dr 15235
Saint Thomas St 15203
Saint William Pl 15237
Salem Cir 15238
Salem Dr
200-299 15241
400-599 15243
2200-2399 15237
Salerma St 15220
Saline St
100-599 15207
601-799 15207
3800-4699 15217
Salisbury St 15210
Sally Ann Dr 15214
Salome Ave 15214
Salter Way 15212
Saltsburg Rd
6200-7599 15235
7600-10199 15239
Salvini Dr 15243
Samoa Dr 15239
Sample St 15209
Sampson St
1-199 15205
4-12 15223
30-198 15205
2000-2099 15221
2100-2199 15235
Sampsonia Way 15212
San Juan St 15235
San Pedro Pl & St 15212
Sanborn St 15204
Sanctus St 15220
Sanda Dr 15227
Sandalwood Ln 15237
Sanderson Ave 15227
Sandhurst Dr
100-199 15241
1500-1599 15237
Sandle Ave E & W 15237
Sandra Dr 15236
Sandrae Dr 15243
Sandridge Dr 15220

Sandstone Ct 15239
Sandune Ct & Dr 15239
Sandusky Ct & St 15212
Sandusky North St 15214
Sandwich St 15211
Sanford St 15204
Sangree Rd 15237
Sankey Ave & Ct 15227
Santa Rosa Ln 15237
Santiago St
1-99 15214
500-7399 15235
Santron Ave 15210
Sapling Way 15224
Sapphire Way 15224
Sarah St
2-98 15205
800-898 15223
900-998 15203
1000-2899 15203
2901-2999 15203
Saranac Ave 15216
Saratoga Dr
300-499 15236
800-9599 15237
Sardis Rd 15239
Sardis Way 15201
Sassafras St & Way 15201
Satellite Cir 15241
Saturn Way 15212
Savannah Ave
700-1099 15221
1100-1299 15218
Savoy St 15212
Saw Grass Ct 15237
Saw Mill Run Blvd
1-97 15226
99-805 15226
806-806 15220
807-899 15226
808-838 15226
840-900 15220
860-898 15226
902-908 15226
910-910 15220
912-928 15226
921-921 15220
930-930 15220
932-998 15226
1000-1000 15220
1001-1007 15226
1009-1017 15226
1019-1399 15226
1020-1032 15220
1044-1044 15226
1046-1060 15220
1100-1198 15226
1200-1298 15220
1400-2352 15210
2354-2398 15210
2400-2599 15234
2600-4254 15227
Sawyer St 15201
Saxman Rd 15205
Saxon Way
6400-6499 15206
7000-7199 15208
Saxonburg Blvd
900-999 15223
3400-3799 15238
Saxonwald Ave & Ln 15234
Saxony Dr 15241
Saybrook Dr 15235
Saylong Dr 15235
Scaife Hl 15260
Scarlett Dr 15241
Scarlett Ridge Dr 15237
Scathelocke Dr 15235
Sceneridge Ave 15227
Scenery Dr 15236
Scenery Rd 15221
Scenery Ridge Dr 15241
Scenic Dr 15236
Scenic View Dr 15241
Schaefer Rd 15209
Schaeffer Way 15211
Schafer St 15210

Schaffner Ctr 15202
Schang Rd 15236
Schar Ct 15209
Schars Ln 15237
Scheffel Rd 15237
Schell Ln 15237
Scheller Ln 15237
Schenk Dr 15215
Schenley Ave 15224
Schenley Dr
221-221 15213
5300-5398 15217
Schenley Park 15213
Schenley Rd 15217
Schenley Farms Ter 15213
Schenley Manor Dr 15201
Scherling St 15214
Schick St 15212
Schieck St 15227
Schimmer St 15212
Schlag Ct 15237
Schley Ave
1-199 15205
7300-7399 15218
Schley Ct 15218
Schley St 15235
Schmitt St 15209
Schnittgen St 15212
Scholar Dr 15236
School Ln 15236
School Rd 15239
School St
1-26 15223
27-99 15220
101-199 15220
200-214 15215
200-200 15220
201-299 15215
300-399 15209
1100-1164 15220
1101-1163 15220
1165-1299 15205
2300-2599 15235
N School St 15202
S School St 15202
School Way 15210
Schoolhouse Ln 15232
Schoyer Ave 15218
Schrauder Rd 15212
Schubert St 15212
Schuck Way 15210
Schuckert St 15210
Schuette Rd
3700-3799 15227
3800-3899 15236
Schuetzen Park Rd 15209
Schuler Rd 15237
Schuler St 15210
Schwartz Ave 15209
Schwerner Ct 15206
Schwitter Ave 15229
Science St 15210
Sciota St 15224
Scobbo Dr 15209
Scorer St 15207
Scorind Dr 15235
Scotia St 15205
Scott Ln 15217
Scott Rd
1-99 15228
100-248 15239
250-298 15239
267-267 15228
400-798 15228
Scott St 15209
Scott Way
900-998 15234
2400-2499 15218
Scott Frisco Way 15229
Scottdale Dr 15205
Scout Ave 15210
Scriba Pl 15212
Scrubgrass Rd 15243
Seabright St 15214
Seagirt St 15221
Seal St 15219

Seashalm St 15205
Seaton St 15226
Seavey Rd
2-68 15223
70-76 15223
78-206 15223
158-160 15223
162-199 15223
201-233 15223
208-208 15209
228-238 15223
300-899 15209
Seavey Highlands Dr 15223
Sebald Ln 15237
Sebring Ave 15216
Sebring Pl 15235
Secane St 15211
Sedalia Ave 15202
Sedan Way 15220
Seddon Rd 15218
Sedgwick St
1-199 15209
201-299 15209
1400-1799 15233
1900-2099 15212
Sedum Dr 15209
Seegar Cir & Rd 15241
Seel St 15223
Segar Rd 15243
Seidle St 15212
Seifried Ln 15215
Seine Way 15213
Selby Way 15203
Seldon Pl & St 15234
Selkirk Way 15208
Sellers St 15206
Selma St 15206
Selwyn St 15206
Semicir St 15214
Seminole Ave 15237
Seminole Ct 15235
Seminole Dr 15228
Seminole Rd 15241
Semple Ave 15202
Semple St 15213
Senate Dr 15236
Seneca Ave 15237
Seneca Dr 15228
Seneca Rd 15241
Seneca St 15219
Senior Dr 15227
Sennott Sq 15260
Sentinel Way 15206
Sentry Dr 15235
Sequoia Dr
400-599 15236
1500-1599 15241
Sequoia St 15237
Serene St 15212
Serpentine Dr 15243
Serrano Ave 15243
Service Way 15201
Session St 15207
Seton St 15227
Settlers Ridge Rd 15238
Settlers Ridge Center Dr 15205
Severn St 15217
Seville Ave 15214
Seward St 15211
Sewickley Oakmont Rd 15237
Seymour St 15233
Shade Ave 15202
Shadeland Ave 15212
Shadewell Ave 15227
Shadow Dr 15227
Shadow Ln 15238
Shadow Ridge Ct 15237
Shadow Ridge Dr 15238
Shadowlawn Ave 15216
Shadowlawn Cir 15236
Shadowlawn Dr 15236
Shady Ave
100-616 15206
618-678 15206

700-1299 15232
1300-3099 15217
Shady Dr E 15228
Shady Dr W 15228
Shady Ln
1-99 15235
100-199 15215
700-799 15228
Shady Avenue Ext 15217
Shady Forbes Ter 15217
Shady Hollow Rd 15239
Shady Knoll Dr 15220
Shady Run Ave 15234
Shadycourt Dr 15232
Shadycrest Ct, Dr, Pl & Rd 15216
Shadygrove Ave 15216
Shadyhill Rd 15205
Shadyside Ln 15232
Shadyview Pl 15216
Shadyway Dr 15227
Shadywood Dr 15235
Shaffer Pl 15202
Shaker Heights Dr 15238
Shakespeare St 15206
Shaler St
1-99 15209
112-117 15211
120-131 15209
200-399 15211
401-499 15211
601-699 15220
Shamokin St 15203
Shamrock Ct 15239
Shangri Ln 15237
Shangri La Cir & Ln 15239
Shank St 15212
Shannon Dr
100-118 15238
104-131 15237
133-133 15237
Shannopin Dr 15202
Sharbot Ct & Dr 15237
Sharon Ct 15235
Sharon Dr 15221
Sharon Ln 15236
Sharon St 15210
Sharps Hill Rd 15215
Shasta Dr 15239
Shaw Ave 15217
Shawano Way 15212
Shawhan Ave 15226
Shawnee Rd 15241
Shawnee St 15219
Sheena Dr 15239
Sheffield St 15233
Sheila Ct 15227
Sheila Dr 15220
Shelbourne Ave 15221
Shelbourne Dr 15239
Shelburne Ln 15217
Shelby Ln 15238
Shelby St 15212
Sheldon Ave 15220
Shell Way 15227
Shelly Dr 15216
Shelly St 15203
Shelton Ave 15214
Shenandoah Dr
100-399 15235
2500-2599 15241
Shepard Dr 15239
Sheraden Blvd 15204
Sheraton Rd 15237
Sherbrook Dr 15241
Sherbrook St 15217
Sheridan Ave 15202
N Sheridan Ave 15206
Sheridan Ct 15206
Sheridan Sq 15206
Sheridan St 15209
Sherlock St 15214
Sherman Ave
100-200 15223
202-298 15223
1100-1499 15212

W Sherman Ave 15209
Sherman St
1-29 15209
31-299 15209
106-108 15210
108-113 15209
110-136 15210
115-119 15209
138-160 15210
1100-1399 15221
Sherrie Dr 15239
Sherrod St 15201
Sherwin Ave 15234
Sherwood Ave 15204
Sherwood Dr
700-799 15215
4600-5399 15236
Sherwood Rd 15221
Sheryl Dr 15205
Sheryl Ln 15221
Shetland Ave 15206
Shields St 15207
Shiloh Ave 15202
Shiloh St 15211
Shipton St 15219
Shiras Ave 15216
Shire Ln 15243
Shire Pl 15226
Shireville Dr 15243
Shirl Dr 15238
Shirls St 15212
Shirray Dr 15237
S Shore Ct 15203
N Shore Ctr 15212
N Shore Dr 15212
Shoreham St 15212
Short Aly 15223
Short Ave 15223
Short St
1-11 15215
1-36 15223
38-98 15223
100-107 15237
109-199 15237
400-499 15239
1200-1298 15236
1300-1399 15236
7500-7599 15218
Short Canal St 15215
Shoup St 15209
Shreve St 15212
Sickles St 15221
S Side Ave 15212
Sidgefield Ln 15241
Sidney Ct 15203
Sidney St
2508A-2508B 15203
1-99 15205
1700-2900 15203
2902-3098 15203
Sieaforth Ave 15216
Siebert Rd 15237
Siebert St 15201
Siegel St 15209
Sierra Dr 15239
Sierra St 15203
Siesta Ct 15205
Siesta Dr
2500-2699 15241
5200-5299 15236
Sigel St 15212
Sigma Dr 15238
Sigsbee Way 15233
Sika Dr 15239
Silent Run Rd 15238
Sillview Dr 15243
Silver St 15209
Silver Lake Dr 15206
Silver Oak Dr & Pl 15220
Silver Reel Ave 15209
Silverdale St 15221
Silverton Ave 15206
Simen Ave 15212
Simms St 15211
Simon Ave 15237
Simona Dr 15201
Simonton St 15208
Simplon St 15202
Sinclair Dr 15234
Singer Pl 15221
Sinton Ave 15210
Sioux Rd 15241
Sipe St 15212
Siple St 15239
Sirius St 15214
Sisca St 15215
Skender Dr 15241
Sky Ridge Dr 15241
Skylark Cir 15234
Skyline Dr
100-199 15239
1600-1799 15227
Skyview Dr 15241
Skyvue Dr 15234
Slate St 15207
Slater Dr 15236
Sleepy Hollow Rd
100-269 15216
272-284 15228
286-551 15228
553-599 15228
800-1000 15234
1002-1198 15234
Sloan Ave 15221
Sloan Ct 15237
Sloan Way 15204
Sloop Rd 15237
Slope St 15204
Slovene St 15235
Small St 15220
Smallman St
201-1097 15222
1099-2899 15222
2900-3699 15201
Smilax St 15205
Smith Dr 15237
Smith Ln 15205
Smith Way
200-399 15211
4100-4122 15201
Smith Farm Ln 15238
Smithfield St 15222
Smithton Ave 15212
Smokey Wood Dr 15218
Snee Dr 15236
Snowden Dr 15229
Snowden St 15208
Snyder St
1-99 15223
2400-2455 15214
2457-2499 15214
Soffel St 15211
Soho St 15219
Solar St 15212
Sollinger Ln 15209
Solway St 15217
Somers Dr & St 15219
Somerset St
1-99 15210
7200-7399 15235
Somerville Dr 15243
Somerville St 15201
Songo St 15227
Sonny St 15221
Soose Rd 15209
Sophia St 15212
Sorell St 15212
Sorento St 15212
Soulier St 15227
South Ave 15221
South Ct
2-6 15239
9-9 15239
2000-2099 15205
South Dr 15238
N South Dr 15237
South Rd 15209
Southampton Dr 15241
Southcrest Ct & Dr 15226
Southern Ave
1-899 15211
600-604 15235
600-602 15211
604-728 15211
606-733 15235
730-734 15211
735-747 15235
Southern Hilands Dr 15241
Southfield Ct 15237
Southgate Dr 15241
Southridge Dr 15241
Southvale Rd 15237
Southview Dr 15226
Southvue Dr
100-499 15236
2400-2499 15241
Southwick Dr 15241
Southwood Dr 15241
Sovereign St 15214
Space Research
Coord 15260
Spahr St 15232
Spalding Cir 15228
Spang Aly 15223
Spangler Ave 15227
Spangler St 15236
Sparrow Ln 15215
Sparta St 15220
Speck St 15212
Spencer Ave 15227
Sperling Dr 15221
Spice St 15214
Spin Way 15206
Spinneweber St 15227
Spokane Ave 15210
N & S Sprague Ave 15202
Sprain St 15212
Spray Ln 15237
Spreading Oak Dr 15220
Spring Ave 15202
Spring St
2-4 15223
6-57 15223
8-27 15209
29-45 15209
59-59 15223
60-199 15223
2000-2999 15210
S Spring St 15223
Spring Way
800-999 15215
2100-2799 15222
2901-3297 15201
3299-3500 15201
3502-3598 15201
Spring Forest Dr 15238
Spring Garden Ave &
Rd 15212
Spring Grove Rd
100-199 15235
700-799 15215
Spring Hill Ct & Rd 15243
Spring Hollow Ct 15239
Spring Street Ext 15223
Spring Valley Dr 15236
Spring Valley Ln 15238
Spring Valley Rd 15243
Springdale Dr
400-699 15235
1000-5299 15236
Springfield St 15220
Springhouse Ln 15238
Springmeadow Ct 15236
Springmeadow Dr 15241
Springmont Dr 15241
Springvale Dr 15236
Springview Rd 15229
Spruce Ct 15229
Spruce St
2-10 15202
11-11 15223
12-98 15202
101-199 15202
500-598 15209
509-559 15209
513-513 15202
701-799 15238
900-999 15234
7700-7999 15237
Spruce Way
2600-2699 15222
2901-3299 15201
Spruce Run Rd 15202
Spruce Valley Dr 15229
Spruceton Ave 15228
Sprucewood Dr
2-98 15234
100-199 15209
Sprucewood St 15210
Squaw Run Rd E 15238
Squire Cir 15212
Squire Pl 15237
Squirrel Hill Ave 15217
St Simon Way 15237
Stadium Cir 15212
Stadium St 15204
Stafford Ct 15237
Stafford St 15204
Staffordshire Dr 15238
Staho St 15212
Stamm Ave 15210
Stancey Rd 15220
Standard Ave 15235
Standish Blvd 15228
Standish St 15206
Stanford Ave 15229
Stanford Rd
900-1029 15212
1031-1199 15212
1032-1036 15205
1038-1038 15212
1050-1080 15205
1100-1198 15212
Stanhope St 15204
Stanley St 15207
Stanton Ave
100-198 15209
200-1099 15209
4200-5299 15201
5300-6799 15206
7700-7799 15218
Stanton Ct E 15201
Stanton Ct N 15201
Stanton Ct W 15201
Stanton Ter 15201
Stanton Avenue Ext 15209
Stanwix St 15222
Stanwood St 15205
Star Ridge Dr 15241
Starch St 15210
Stark Dr 15239
Starkamp St 15226
N & S Starr Ave 15202
State Way 15224
Station St
1-99 15205
100-899 15235
1201-1299 15215
5801-5897 15206
5899-6299 15206
E & W Station Square
Dr 15219
Staunton Ave 15202
Staver St 15214
Stayton St 15212
Stebbins Ave 15226
Steck Way 15227
Stedman St 15233
Steele Ct 15207
Steelview Ave 15217
Steeplechase Ct 15236
Steiger St 15234
Steiner Dr 15236
Steiner St 15227
Stella St 15203
Stem St 15220
Stephen Foster Mem 15260
Sterling Dr 15214
Sterling St
1-17 15205
1-53 15203
2-14 15205
54-59 15203
61-67 15203
200-399 15210
400-1399 15203
1401-1505 15203
1500-1504 15210
1506-1699 15210
Sterrett St
1-222 15205
224-298 15205
600-648 15208
650-1399 15208
1401-1499 15208
Stetson St 15226
Steuben St 15220
E Steuben St 15205
W Steuben St 15205
Steubenville Pike 15205
Stevendale Dr 15221
Stevens Dr
102-108 15237
110-650 15237
201-299 15236
400-450 15237
436-450 15209
Stevens Ln 15221
Stevenson Pl 15206
Stevenson St 15219
Stewart Ave & Ln 15227
Stilley Rd 15227
Stilwell Ct 15228
Stilwell St 15214
Stirling Dr 15239
Stock St 15207
Stockholm St 15219
Stoebner Way 15206
Stokes Way 15212
Stolsey Dr 15237
Stolz St 15214
Stonedge Ct 15239
Stonehaven Ct 15239
Stonelea St 15212
Stoneledge Dr 15235
Stoner Rd 15237
Stoner Way 15221
Stoneville St 15221
Stoney Camp Ln 15238
Stotler Rd
1-19 15239
20-98 15235
21-67 15239
100-1099 15235
Stotlers Ln 15235
Stotz Ave 15205
Stowe Dr 15235
Stowe St 15205
Strachan Ave 15216
Strahley Pl 15220
Straka St 15204
Stranahan St
7200-7399 15206
7400-7412 15235
7401-7413 15206
7414-7499 15235
Stranmore St 15212
Strassburger Way 15210
Strata Way 15210
Stratford Ave
100-299 15206
300-399 15232
Stratford Ct 15237
Stratford Rd 15202
Stratmore Ave 15205
Stratton Ln 15206
Straubs Ln 15212
Strauss St 15214
Straw Ave 15202
Strawberry Way 15219
Streamside Dr 15237
Streets Run Rd
2-6 15207
200-212 15236
214-1000 15236
943-945 15207
1001-4899 15236
1002-4898 15236
4900-4998 15207
Strickler St 15204
Stringert Ln 15237
Strohm Dr 15238
Stromberg St 15203
Sturdy Oak Dr 15220
Sturgeon Ave 15202
Stuyvesant Rd 15237
Suburban Ave 15216
Success St 15212
Suffolk St 15214
Sugarloaf Dr 15239
Suismon St 15212
Sulgrave Rd 15211
Sullivan St 15224
Summer Pl 15243
Summer Duck Way 15238
Summer Haven Ct 15239
Summerdale St 15204
Summerlea St 15232
Summerset Dr 15217
Summit Ave 15202
Summit Dr
200-299 15238
400-499 15228
Summit St
1-99 15209
1400-1499 15221
4300-4399 15201
Summit Park Dr 15275
Sumner Ave
8-8 15221
10-34 15221
50-68 15202
70-87 15202
89-89 15202
100-150 15221
100-100 15202
101-199 15221
Sumner St 15203
Sun Ridge Dr 15241
Sun Valley Dr 15239
Sunbeam Way 15234
Suncrest St 15210
Sunday St 15212
Sundeman St 15212
Sunderland Dr 15237
Sunflower Ave 15202
Suninta St 15213
Sunny Dr
2-42 15236
3-27 15236
7-21 15237
44-299 15236
Sunnydale Rd 15243
Sunnyfield Dr 15241
Sunnyfield Ln 15235
Sunnyhill Dr
1-77 15228
78-88 15237
79-89 15228
90-109 15237
100-100 15228
110-110 15228
110-128 15237
111-299 15237
114-114 15228
200-298 15237
Sunnyland Ave 15227
Sunnyside Dr 15221
Sunnyside St 15207
Sunridge Dr 15234
Sunridge Rd 15238
Sunrise Ave 15221
Sunrise Dr
1-199 15236
1100-1199 15243
Sunset Ave
2300-2499 15212
2500-2699 15214
Sunset Dr
100-132 15237
112-118 15235
120-179 15235
134-142 15237
135-197 15235
181-345 15235
199-300 15235
302-330 15235
337-345 15228
347-599 15228
Sunset Ln
100-102 15238
110-117 15209
119-199 15209
Sunset Pl 15237
Sunset Rd 15237
Sunsetview Dr 15229
Sunview Dr 15227
Superior Ave
100-299 15202
1200-1599 15212
1400-1413 15212
1405-1409 15221
1415-1423 15212
1416-1420 15221
Sur Way 15210
Surban St 15204
Surfside Dr 15239
Surrey Ln 15241
Surrey Pl 15235
Susan Dr 15220
Susanna Ct 15207
Susquehanna St
1-99 15210
6901-7197 15208
7199-7899 15208
7900-8099 15221
Sussex Ave 15226
Suter St 15204
Sutherland Dr
1000-1099 15205
3700-3799 15213
Sutherland St 15204
Sutton Dr 15235
Sutton St 15214
Suzanne Dr 15235
Swallow Hill Cir, Ct &
Rd 15220
Swan Dr 15237
Swan View Dr 15237
Swaney St 15204
Swanson Ln 15241
Swanson St 15214
Swantek St 15204
Sweeney Way 15219
Sweet Gum Rd
101-197 15238
199-268 15238
800-899 15243
Sweet Water Ct & Ln 15238
Sweetbriar St 15211
Sweetbriar Village Trl 15211
Swinburne St 15213
Swissvale Ave 15221
E Swissvale Ave 15218
W Swissvale Ave 15218
Swope St 15206
Sycamore Dr
1-99 15235
101-185 15235
102-108 15235
102-144 15237
110-148 15235
148-148 15237
150-174 15235
176-198 15235
3300-3399 15234
Sycamore St
1-82 15223
25-27 15205
84-98 15223
99-99 15223
E Sycamore St 15211
W Sycamore St 15211
E Sycamore Ter 15211
Sylvan Ave
1-99 15207
700-999 15202
4400-4799 15207
Sylvan Dr 15237
Sylvan Rd 15221
Sylvan Ter 15221
Sylvan Walk 15202
Sylvandell Dr 15243
Sylvania Ave
1-108 15210
110-120 15210

131-131 15235
133-137 15235
139-139 15235
200-599 15210
Sylvania Dr
100-299 15236
400-499 15229
Sylvia Ave 15214
Sylvia Ln 15235
Syracuse Ave 15234
Syrian St 15210
Tabor St 15204
Tacoma St 15208
Tadmar Ave 15237
Taft Ave 15210
Taft Pl 15237
Taft Way 15221
Tahoe Dr 15239
Talco St 15214
Tall Tree Dr 15235
Tall Trees Dr 15241
Tally Dr 15237
Tamarack Ln 15237
Tamindin St 15208
Tampa Ave 15228
Tampico Ct 15239
Tanbark Dr 15237
Tanglewood Dr 15221
Tanglewood Rd 15237
Tank St 15212
Tannen Dr 15209
Taper Dr 15241
Tara Ct 15237
Tara Dr
1-99 15209
200-399 15236
600-625 15237
627-629 15237
Tarbell St 15226
Tarner St 15205
Tarpon Dr 15212
Tarragonna St 15210
Tartan Ct 15239
Tassel Ln 15236
Tasso St 15207
Taylor Ave 15202
N Taylor Ave 15212
Taylor St
1-99 15205
200-499 15224
Taylor Way 15221
Teakwood Ct 15209
Teal Dr
1-99 15238
1000-1099 15236
Teal Trce 15237
Tech Rd 15205
Technology Dr
100-100 15219
101-120 15275
121-197 15219
122-198 15275
199-2099 15219
Techview Ter 15213
Tecumseh St 15207
Teece Ave 15202
Tel Star Dr 15236
Telescope St 15203
Television Hl 15214
Tell St 15212
Temona Dr 15236
Temperance Dr 15237
Templeton Ave 15226
Tenner Way 15208
Tennessee Ave 15216
Tennis St 15206
Tennis Way 15221
Tennyson Ave 15213
Terence Dr 15236
Terminal Way 15219
Termon Ave 15212
Terphin Dr 15241
Terrace Ave 15202
Terrace Dr
1-59 15205
1-5 15209

1-11 15236
2-2 15209
2-10 15236
4-98 15205
401-599 15238
1000-1020 15234
1300-1499 15228
8700-8799 15237
Terrace St 15213
Terraceview Ave 15243
Terrie Dr 15241
Tesla St 15217
Tesla Way 15207
Teton Dr 15239
Texas Ave 15216
Texdale St 15216
Textor Ave 15202
Thackeray St 15213
Thackeray Building 15260
Thames Pl 15241
Thaw Hl 15260
Thayer St 15204
The Blvd 15210
The Gardens Dr 15238
The Knob 15202
The Maples 15215
The Oaks 15215
The Pines Dr 15243
The Trillium 15238
Thelma St 15212
Theodan Dr 15216
Theona St 15210
Theresa Dr 15215
Theresa St 15227
Thielman St 15210
Thistle Ct
300-399 15239
1700-1799 15237
Thomas Ave
300-399 15202
1100-1199 15236
Thomas Blvd 15208
Thomas Dr 15236
Thomas Ln 15235
Thomas St
1-99 15205
200-299 15221
500-599 15239
Thomaston Dr 15235
Thompson Ave 15234
Thompson Dr 15229
Thompson St 15206
Thompson Drive Ext 15229
Thompson Run Rd
100-425 15237
211-433 15235
221-497 15237
427-8299 15237
480-480 15235
500-544 15237
506-526 15235
554-8198 15237
Thorn Dr 15212
Thornberry Cir 15234
Thornberry Ct 15237
Thornberry Dr
100-178 15235
101-237 15235
101-247 15237
180-190 15235
192-298 15235
1001-2024 15237
Thornburg Rd 15205
Thorncliffe Dr 15205
Thorncrest Dr 15235
Thorndale St 15205
Thornewood Ct 15237
Thornridge Rd 15202
Thorntree Dr 15241
Thornwick Dr 15243
Thornwood Dr
1-99 15228
300-399 15239
1000-1099 15234
Thornycroft Ave 15228
Thornycroft Rd 15235
Thousand Oaks Dr 15241

Three Degree Rd 15237
Threnhauser Rd 15227
Thropp St 15212
Thrush Dr 15243
Thurner Dr 15236
Tidball Rd 15205
Tidemore Dr 15235
Tier Dr 15241
Tierra Pl 15237
Tiers St 15235
Tiffany Cir 15241
Tiffany Dr 15241
Tiffany Ln 15241
Tiffany Rdg 15241
Tiffany St 15212
Tiffin Dr 15209
Tilbury Ave 15217
Tilden St 15206
Tilford Rd 15235
Tilio Dr 15239
Tillotson Cir 15237
Tilton Dr 15241
Timber Ct 15238
Timber Trl 15237
Timber Ridge Dr 15239
Timber Ridge Rd 15238
Timber View Ln 15238
Timberland Ave 15226
Timberlane Dr
1-7 15238
9-11 15238
13-89 15238
90-199 15229
Timberline Ct 15217
Timberwood Ct 15239
Timberwood Dr 15241
Timothy Dr 15239
Tingley Ave 15202
Tinsbury St 15212
Tioga St 15208
Tipton St 15207
Titus St 15220
Tivoli Rd 15239
Toberg St 15212
Toboggan St 15212
Todd St 15221
Toft Ct 15237
Tokay St 15221
Tole St 15216
Toledo St 15204
Tolma Ave 15216
Tomahawk Dr 15215
Tomaino Dr 15220
Tomfran Dr 15236
Tommy Dr 15236
Tomoka Ave 15229
Toms Run Rd 15237
Tonapah St 15216
Toner St 15212
Tonette St 15218
Topsfield Rd 15241
Topview Dr 15209
Torley St 15224
Torrance St 15235
Torrens St 15206
Torwood Ln 15236
Toura Dr 15236
Tours St 15212
Tower Rd 15231
Towercrest Dr 15228
Towers Ter 15229
Towervue Dr 15227
Town View St 15209
Towne Square Way 15227
Township Rd 15229
Traci Dr 15237
Tracy Dr 15236
Tracy St 15233
Tragone Dr 15241
Trailview St 15220
Trance Dr 15234
Transport St 15234
Transvaal Ave 15212
Transverse Ave 15210
Tranter Ave 15220
Tranter St 15205

Travella Blvd 15235
Traverse Dr 15236
Travis Dr 15236
Traymore Ave
200-399 15216
1300-1499 15221
Tree Farm Rd 15238
Tree Line Ct 15237
Trelarai St 15217
Trelona St 15226
Tremont St 15235
Trent St 15219
Trenton Ave 15221
Trestle Rd 15239
Tretow St 15214
Tretter Dr 15227
Trevanion Ave 15218
Triana St 15210
Tridalls Dr 15275
Tridaria St 15214
Trillium Ln 15238
Trimble Rd 15237
Trimont Ln 15211
Trinity Cir 15219
Trinity St 15206
Trion Rd 15237
Tripod Way 15206
Tripoli St 15212
Tristan Dr 15209
Troit St 15227
Trolist Dr 15241
Trolley Ct 15237
Tropical Ave 15216
Trost Ave 15210
Trotwood Cir & Dr 15241
Trotwood Ridge Rd 15241
Trotwood West Dr 15241
Trout Dr 15212
Troutwood Dr 15237
Trowbridge St 15207
Troy St
1-99 15209
1900-1999 15212
Troy Hill Rd 15212
Truax Way 15212
Trumbull Dr 15205
Truro Pl 15213
Truxton Dr 15241
Try St 15219
Tucker St 15220
Tudor Ln 15205
Tulip Rd 15235
Tullymet St 15207
Tumbo St 15212
Tunnel St 15203
Tunnelview Dr 15235
Tunstall St 15207
Turnberry Dr 15241
Turner Ave 15221
Turner Pl 15213
Turrett St 15206
Turtle Way 15212
Tuscany Dr 15241
Tuscarora St
7500-7599 15208
7600-7799 15221
Tuscola St 15211
Tush Dr 15236
Tussey Cir 15237
Tustin St 15219
Tuxedo St 15204
Tuxey Ave 15227
Tweed St 15204
Twin Hills Dr 15216
Twin Maple Dr 15238
Twin Oak Dr 15235
Twin Oaks Dr 15237
Twin Oaks Rd 15243
Twin Pine Ct & Rd 15215
Twin Stream Dr 15238
Tybee St 15204
Tyburn Ln 15241
Tyler Dr 15236
Tyler Rd 15237
Tyler St 15237
Tyndall St 15204

Tyris Dr 15241
Tyro Way 15210
Tyrol Dr 15227
Tyson St 15221
N Tyson St 15208
S Tyson St 15221
Ulrich St 15234
Ulysses St 15211
Umpire Way 15201
E Undercliff Ave 15223
W Undercliff Ave 15223
Undercliff Rd 15221
Underhill St 15205
Underwood St 15227
Ung Dr 15235
Unger Ln 15217
Union Ave
39R-39R 15202
1-31 15205
8-198 15205
25-71 15202
29-31 15202
33-36 15205
38-430 15205
40-400 15202
81-199 15205
201-297 15202
299-351 15202
353-399 15202
401-429 15205
431-499 15205
500-599 15202
701-899 15212
7800-7999 15218
Union Pl 15225
Union St
200-299 15221
300-399 15215
400-499 15221
3600-3699 15234
Union Avenue Ext 15229
Unity Center Rd 15239
Universal Rd 15235
Universal St 15204
University Ave 15214
University Pl
101-127 15213
131-199 15260
University Drive C
--- 15240
University Drive C
1-199 15240
3700-3899 15213
Upland St
1-97 15209
99-100 15209
102-198 15209
6800-6898 15208
6900-7599 15208
Upland Ter 15235
Upper Dr 15214
Upper Rd 15228
Upper Arrowhead Rd 15237
Upper Saint Clair Dr 15241
Upper Spring St 15223
Upsal Pl 15206
Uptegraf St 15218
Upton Way 15219
Upview Ter 15201
Urbana Way 15201
Urbano Way 15205
Utah Ave 15225
Uvilla St 15220
Uxor Way 15203
Vale Ave 15239
Valentine St 15212
Valera Ave 15210
Valeview Dr 15235
Valiant Dr 15235
Valle Rue St 15220
Vallevista Ave & St 15234
Valley Ct
200-299 15237
1500-1599 15241
Valley Dr
2-48 15215
50-499 15215

900-1099 15237
3500-3600 15234
3602-3698 15234
Valley Ln 15238
Valley Rd 15237
Valley St
1-12 15205
8-8 15223
11-15 15223
14-14 15205
9200-9299 15235
Valley Fields Dr 15239
Valley Hi Dr 15229
Valley Hill Dr 15216
Valley Park Dr 15216
Valley Vale Dr 15209
Valley View Ave 15202
Valley View Ct 15237
Valley View Dr 15215
Valley View Rd 15237
Valley View St 15214
Valleyview Rd 15243
Valleyvue Dr 15237
Vallimont Dr 15234
Valmartin Dr 15235
Valmont St 15217
Valois St 15205
Valonia St 15220
Valora St
900-1102 15220
1104-1198 15220
1119-1127 15205
Van Dr 15237
Van Braam St 15219
Van Buren Cir 15229
Van Buren Dr 15237
E Van Buren Dr 15237
Van Buren St
1-99 15221
100-198 15214
101-101 15209
105-119 15214
122-122 15209
123-123 15209
125-173 15214
Van De Graaff
Building 15260
Van Dyke St 15237
Van Fleet Cir 15237
Van Wyck Ave 15227
Vanadium Rd 15243
Vance Dr 15235
Vancouver St 15205
Vancroft St 15219
Vandalia St 15210
Vanderbilt Dr 15243
Vanilla Way 15206
Vann Dr 15206
Vantassel St 15214
Vantine St
2100-2199 15221
9200-9299 15235
Vara Dr 15236
Vare St 15205
Varley St 15212
Varner Rd 15227
Varney St 15202
Varsity Rd 15218
Vassar Ave 15229
Vassar St 15206
Vaux Way 15211
Vee Lynn Dr 15228
Velte St 15235
Veman Rd 15227
Venango Ave 15209
Venango Dr 15237
Venango Pl 15237
Veneze Dr 15205
Venice Rd 15209
Vensel Way 15212
Ventura Dr 15236
Venture St 15214
Veranda Ln 15238
Verena St 15210
Veri Dr 15220
Vermillion Dr 15209

Vermont Ave 15234
Verna Dr 15209
Verna St 15220
Verner Ave & Ct 15212
Vernon Ave 15227
Vernon Dr 15228
Vernon St 15218
Verona Blvd & Rd 15235
Veronica Dr 15235
Veronica St 15212
Veryl Dr 15223
Vespucius St 15207
Veteran St 15214
Veto St 15212
Vetter Dr 15235
Vickers Dr 15236
Vickroy St 15219
Victoria Cir 15220
Victoria Ct 15235
Victoria Dr
1-147 15227
101-148 15227
103-105 15202
107-120 15202
122-124 15202
149-162 15227
Victoria St 15213
Victory Rd 15237
Vida Way 15227
Vidette St 15221
Vienna Dr 15235
Viennese Dr 15209
W View Ave 15229
W View Park Dr 15229
Villa Ct 15214
Villa Dr
1-99 15215
100-199 15214
1400-1499 15236
Villa Haven Dr 15236
Village Ct 15241
Village Dr
100-219 15227
221-299 15227
300-399 15215
500-599 15241
700-899 15237
901-1599 15237
1000-1550 15241
1556-1598 15237
2100-2199 15221
Village Rd 15205
Villanova Rd 15206
Villaview Dr 15236
Villawood Ave 15227
Vilsack St 15223
Vincent St 15210
Vincent Way 15237
Vinceton St 15214
Vine Aly 15221
Vine Ave 15223
Vine St
1-57 15223
1-99 15219
12-12 15223
14-398 15219
203-221 15218
275-275 15205
301-399 15219
1300-1398 15236
Vinecliffe St 15211
Vineland St 15234
Vinemont St 15205
Vinial St 15212
Vintage Way 15232
Vinton St 15204
Viola St 15214
Violet St 15229
Violet Way 15220
Virgila Pl 15213
Virginia Ave
1-10 15211
12-96 15211
101-119 15211
103-103 15215
105-225 15215
121-337 15211

316-318 15221
320-373 15221
339-345 15211
375-375 15221
400-418 15215
420-498 15215
600-798 15211
800-1499 15211
6400-6699 15202
Virginia Rd 15237
Virginia Ter 15229
Virginia Avenue Ext 15215
Virginia Manor Dr 15215
Viruth St 15212
Vista Cir 15238
Vista St
15-17 15202
60-60 15202
90-92 15223
94-199 15223
800-999 15212
Vista Park Dr 15205
Vistinge 15231
Vivian Dr 15237
Vivianna St 15225
Vixen St 15220
Vodeli St 15216
Voelkel Ave 15216
Volk St 15211
Volta St 15212
Von Lent Pl 15232
Von Stein Ln 15225
Voskamp St 15212
W Way 15207
Wabana St 15214
Wabash Ave 15234
Wabash St 15220
Wachter St 15210
Waddington Ave 15226
Wade St 15211
Wadlow St 15212
Wadsworth St 15213
Wagner Way 15221
Wagon Wheel Ln 15238
Waidler St 15227
Wainbell Ave 15216
Wainwright Ave 15227
Wainwright Dr 15228
Waite St 15210
Wakefield Dr 15236
Wakefield St 15213
Walbridge St 15220
Walcott St 15204
Walde St 15210
Waldeck St 15207
Walden St 15211
E & W Waldheim Rd ... 15215
Waldorf St 15214
Waldron St 15217
Waldwick Dr 15237
Walker Ave 15202
Wallace Ave 15221
Wallace Dr 15227
Wallace Rd 15209
Wallace Park Dr 15227
Wallingford Dr 15237
Wallingford St 15213
Walliston Ave 15202
Wally Dr 15237
Walnut Ave 15209
Walnut Ct 15238
Walnut Rd 15202
Walnut St
1-15 15223
2-50 15205
9-24 15202
17-42 15223
26-28 15202
56-56 15205
100-198 15229
105-105 15210
200-420 15210
206-212 15238
214-279 15238
243-247 15229
249-250 15229
252-252 15229
281-627 15238
300-399 15238
401-599 15238
408-410 15210
412-412 15238
422-601 15210
428-428 15210
450-498 15238
500-502 15210
506-612 15238
700-899 15221
900-999 15234
1000-1399 15221
1400-1599 15218
5400-5999 15232
6000-6399 15206
6800-6999 15225
9000-9199 15239
Walnut Ridge Dr 15238
Walpole Dr 15235
Walsh Rd 15205
Walter Ave & St 15210
Walters Ave 15209
Walters Dr 15231
Waltham Ave
200-299 15226
3200-3399 15216
Walther Ln 15241
Waltherman St 15229
Walton Ave 15210
Walton Ct 15215
Walton Rd 15236
Walz St 15212
Wandless St 15219
Wanker Dr 15214
Wapello St 15212
Warble St 15224
Ward St 15213
Warden St 15220
Wardsons St 15206
Wardwell St 15212
Wareman Ave 15226
Warfel St 15204
Warfield St 15212
Waring Ct 15213
Warlo St 15233
Warner St 15233
Warren St
1-99 15205
1500-1999 15212
E Warrington Ave 15210
W Warrington Ave
100-499 15210
600-699 15226
701-1099 15226
1300-1399 15210
Warriors Rd 15205
Warsaw St 15221
Warwick Dr 15241
Warwick Ter 15213
Washburn St 15212
Washington Ave
1-33 15202
35-199 15202
201-299 15202
7400-7599 15218
Washington Blvd
100-518 15237
800-1499 15206
Washington Dr 15229
Washington Ln 15237
Washington Pl 15219
Washington Rd
100-214 15221
200-318 15216
200-316 15221
216-410 15221
255-401 15216
418-424 15228
426-1609 15228
1611-1699 15228
1614-1698 15241
1700-2699 15241
2701-2749 15241
Washington St
1-197 15223
101-161 15218
118-130 15223
132-197 15223
163-165 15218
199-299 15223
Washington Way 15243
Washington Boulevard Ext
--- 15206
700-799 15237
Washington Heights Ave 15237
Washingtons Lndg 15222
Washville St 15204
Wasson Pl 15216
S Water St 15203
Waterford Ct
1700-1799 15241
3100-3299 15238
Waterford Dr
600-699 15234
3300-3499 15238
Waterford St 15224
Waterfront Dr & Pl 15222
Waterman Ave 15227
Waterside Pl 15222
Watkins Ave 15202
Watson Ave
1-99 15202
101-197 15238
199-299 15238
Watson Blvd 15214
Watson St 15219
Watt Ln
100-199 15221
700-799 15219
Watt St 15219
Watterson Ct 15241
Waverly Ave 15229
Waverly St
2000-2099 15218
2101-2599 15218
3100-3299 15234
7600-7799 15221
Wayne Rd 15206
Wayne St 15218
Wayside St 15210
Wealth St 15212
Weaver St 15220
Weber Dr 15238
Weber St 15221
Weber Way 15210
Webster Ave 15219
Webster Dr 15235
Webster Ter 15219
Wedgemere St 15226
Wedgewood Dr
100-199 15229
200-228 15227
201-227 15237
229-250 15237
251-299 15227
252-298 15237
9200-9299 15239
E Wedgewood Dr 15229
Wedgewood Ln 15215
Weedon Dr 15235
Weible St 15223
Weinman St 15221
Weir Dr 15215
Weiss Ln 15237
Weldin St 15206
Welfer St 15217
Well St 15211
Weller St 15204
Wellesley Ave
900-999 15202
5200-6399 15206
Wellesley Rd 15206
Welleston Way 15206
Wellington Dr
1-99 15229
1300-1399 15241
Wellington Rd 15221
Wellington St 15203
Wellington Apartments .. 15213
Wellington Woods Dr ... 15229
Wellsford St 15213
Wellsview Dr 15241
Welser Way 15212
Welsh Dr 15236
Welsh Way 15203
Wendelin St 15223
Wendover Pl & St 15217
Wenger St 15227
Wenke St 15210
Wentworth Ave
1-99 15229
500-699 15216
Wentworth Ct 15237
Wenzel Dr 15238
Wenzell Ave & Pl 15216
Werder St 15220
Werner Camp Rd 15238
Wernerberg Way 15201
Wertz Way 15224
Wescott Dr 15237
Wesley Ave 15221
Wesport Dr 15238
West Ave 15202
West Dr 15215
E West Dr 15237
West Rd 15209
West St 15221
Westborn St 15212
Westchester Dr
100-130 15215
102-104 15237
106-114 15237
132-180 15215
182-198 15237
3100-3199 15238
Westchester Pl 15215
Westchester St 15220
Western Ave
--- 15202
5-7 15202
12-30 15202
29-29 15220
37-39 15215
40-40 15202
41-315 15215
100-498 15215
110-111 15237
331-339 15237
401-499 15215
800-1499 15233
Westfield Ave 15229
Westfield St 15216
Westgate Dr
800-899 15241
2300-2399 15237
Westgate Rd 15231
Westhall St 15233
Westinghouse St 15216
Westland Dr 15217
Westminster Dr 15229
Westminster Pl
1-99 15209
5100-5399 15232
Westmont Ave 15210
Westmont Rd 15237
Westmoreland Ave 15218
Westmoreland St 15206
Westmoreland Farm Ln 15215
Weston Dr 15241
Weston Way 15220
Westover Rd 15228
Westpointe Dr 15205
Westview Ln 15237
Westward Ho Dr 15235
Westwood Ave 15209
Westwood Rd 15235
Westwood St 15211
Wettach St 15212
Wetzel Rd 15209
Wexford Ln 15235
Weyman Rd 15236
Wharton Ct, Sq & St ... 15203
Wheaton Dr 15236
Wheeler Ave 15205
N Wheeler St 15208
S Wheeler St 15221
Wheeling St 15207
Whipple St 15218
Whirlwood Dr 15235
Whispering Pines Dr 15238
Whitby Ln 15228
White Ave 15205
White St 15219
White Birch Cir 15220
White Birch Ct 15238
White Birch Dr 15235
White Fawn Ln 15238
White Gate Rd 15238
White Hampton Ln 15236
White Hill Dr 15219
White Oak Cir 15228
White Oak Ct
1600-1699 15237
4200-4299 15227
White Oak Dr 15237
White Pine Pl 15221
White Tail Ln 15209
Whited St
1800-2199 15210
2200-2499 15226
Whitehill Cir 15227
Whiteside Rd 15219
Whitetail Ln 15238
Whitewood Dr 15220
N & S Whitfield St 15206
Whitla St 15212
Whitley Dr 15237
Whitmore St 15234
Whitney Ave 15221
Whitney St 15213
Whitney Ter 15219
Whitridge St 15213
Whittier Dr 15235
Whittier St 15206
Whitworth St 15211
Wible Ln 15237
Wible Run Rd 15209
Wible Wood Ct 15209
Wichita Way 15219
Wick Dr 15237
Wick St 15219
Wickford Dr 15238
Wickliff St 15201
Wickline Ln 15212
Wicklow St 15224
Wickshire St 15212
Widgeon Dr 15238
Wiese St 15210
Wiggins St 15219
Wightman St 15217
Wil Tara Dr 15236
Wilbert St 15211
Wilbur St 15210
Wilburke Ave 15236
Wild Dr 15239
Wild Pl 15206
Wild Violet Dr 15239
Wildberry Rd 15238
Wildflower Ct 15202
Wildwood Ave 15227
Wilhelm Ave 15236
Wilhelm St 15220
Wiljohn St 15223
Wilkins Ave
700-1299 15221
5200-6799 15217
Wilkins Rd 15221
Wilkins Heights Rd 15217
Wilkinsburg Ave 15221
Wilksboro Ave 15212
Will Ln 15236
Willard Ave 15205
Willard Dr 15236
Willard St 15208
Willett Rd
2800-3669 15227
3670-3670 15236
3671-4099 15227
3672-4098 15227
Willett St 15205
William Ln 15238
William St
1-100 15229
100-599 15229
101-101 15237
102-202 15229
103-121 15237
111-285 15203
123-123 15237
201-217 15209
204-216 15209
264-300 15229
301-339 15209
304-320 15203
320-342 15209
345-345 15211
406-448 15211
424-436 15210
438-454 15210
450-452 15211
454-466 15211
456-464 15210
471-499 15229
1000-2899 15209
William Penn Ct 15221
William Penn Hwy
1942-1998 15221
2000-2199 15221
2200-3599 15235
William Penn Pl
500-520 15219
522-650 15219
652-698 15219
900-999 15222
William Pitt Un 15260
William Pitt Way 15238
Williams Ln 15238
Williams Pl 15221
Williamsburg Cir 15241
Williamsburg Pl 15235
Williamsburg Rd 15243
Willing St 15208
Willock Ave 15236
Willock Rd E
5000-5399 15236
1-4999 15227
W Willock Rd 15227
Willoughby Rd 15237
Willoughby St 15205
Willow Ave 15234
Willow Ct 15237
Willow Dr
100-199 15239
400-600 15243
602-698 15243
900-1099 15237
4600-4698 15236
4700-4999 15236
Willow Ln
1-99 15212
1000-1005 15237
1007-1099 15237
Willow Pl 15218
Willow Rd 15238
Willow St
1-10 15235
11-11 15202
13-199 15202
4000-4399 15201
Willow Farms Ln 15238
Willow Heath Dr 15234
Willow Run Rd 15238
Willow Village Dr 15239
Willowbrook Rd 15241
Willowcrest Dr 15214
Willowhaven Dr 15227
Willowood Dr 15214
Wills St 15211
Wilmar Dr 15238
Wilmar St 15211
Wilner Dr 15221
Wilson Ave
200-399 15237
2100-2300 15214
2302-2498 15214
Wilson Dr
1-99 15202
100-499 15235
500-3399 15227
Wilson Rd
1-99 15214
1100-1799 15236
Wilson St 15223
Wilson Way 15237
Wilson Street Ext 15223
Wilt St 15212
Wilton Way 15220
Wiltshire Dr 15241
Wiltsie St 15206
Wilvan Ln 15237
Wimar Cir 15209
Wimbledon Dr 15239
Wimer Cir & Dr 15237
Winchell St 15215
Winchester Dr
100-181 15239
183-189 15239
1800-1899 15241
2500-2691 15220
2693-2699 15220
8300-8799 15237
Windcrest Dr
1503-1507 15206
1509-1543 15206
1545-1545 15206
1553-1555 15237
1600-1699 15206
Windermere Ave 15216
Windermere Dr 15218
Winders St 15207
Windfall Way 15227
Windgap Ave
3100-3429 15205
3431-3499 15205
3600-4099 15204
Windgap Rd 15237
E & W Windhaven Rd .. 15205
Windmere Dr 15238
Windmere Rd 15202
Windmill Ct & Ln 15237
Windom St 15203
Windom Hill Pl 15203
Windover Dr 15205
Windridge Dr 15227
Windsor Ave 15221
Windsor Ct
1-99 15220
1500-1599 15241
3300-3699 15238
Windsor Dr
1-1 15239
100-199 15235
Windsor Rd
3-3 15215
5-40 15215
53-199 15227
Windsor St 15217
Windsor Way 15237
Windvale Dr 15236
Windvue Dr 15205
Windy Hill Dr 15239
Windy Oak Dr 15239
N & S Winebiddle St ... 15224
Winfield St 15206
Wingate Dr 15205
Wingate St 15210
Winhurst St 15212
Winifred Dr 15236
Winloch Ave 15205
Winner Way 15212
Winnerwood Rd 15237
Winona St 15220
Winschel St 15223
Winshire St 15212
Winslow Dr 15229
Winslow St 15206
Winston St 15207
Winter Ave 15229
Winterburn Ave 15207
Winterhaven Dr 15223
Winterhill St 15226
Winterset Dr 15209
Winterton St 15206
Winthrop Dr 15237

Winthrop St 15213
Winton St
400-499 15211
1500-1599 15221
Wisconsin Ave 15216
Wise Ln 15209
Wise Hill Rd 15238
Wisteria Ave 15228
Wisteria Dr 15235
Witherspoon St 15206
Witt St 15226
Wittman St 15220
Wittmer Ct 15237
Wittmer Pl 15237
Wittmer Rd 15237
Wittmer St 15212
Woessner St 15212
Wohleber St 15212
Wolf Dr 15236
Wolf Way 15213
Wolfe Dr 15236
Wolfendale St 15233
Wolford St 15226
Wolfrum St 15212
Wolpert Way 15212
Wood Dr
100-199 15237
400-499 15229
Wood St
1-7 15222
9-112 15222
114-610 15222
133-175 15223
201-601 15222
613-697 15221
618-620 15221
699-1599 15221
Wood Acres Ct 15237
Wood Duck Trl 15238
Wood Glen Dr 15235
Wood Park Dr 15209
Woodbine St 15201
Woodbourne Ave 15226
Woodbridge Ct & Dr 15237
Woodbrook Dr 15215
Woodcliff Cir 15243
Woodcliff Rd 15238
Woodcock Dr 15215
Woodcove Pl 15216
Woodcrest Dr 15205
Woodcrest Rd 15237
E & W Woodford Ave 15210
Woodgate Rd 15235
Woodhall Dr 15236
Woodhaven Ct 15209
Woodhaven Dr 15228
Woodhaven Ln 15237
Woodland Ave
1-20 15212
22-2698 15212
109-199 15238
1101-2699 15212
7000-7199 15202
Woodland Dr
1-139 15228
111-111 15236
113-198 15236
700-799 15238
Woodland Rd
--- 15232
22-70 15232
72-91 15232
93-95 15232
100-107 15238
108-112 15232
114-128 15232
200-298 15238
400-1300 15237
1000-1002 15238
1004-1028 15238
1030-1098 15238
1302-9700 15237
Woodland Rd N
9701-9777 15237
E Woodland Rd 15232
N Woodland Rd
100-198 15232

W Woodland Rd 15232
Woodland Ter 15229
Woodland Farms Rd 15238
Woodland Hills Dr 15235
Woodlands Cir 15241
Woodlawn Ave
100-299 15202
7300-7399 15218
Woodlawn Ct 15241
Woodlawn St
1-99 15205
1300-1499 15221
Woodlow St 15205
Woodmere Dr 15205
Woodmont Dr 15238
Woodmont St 15217
Woodridge Cir 15234
Woodridge Dr 15227
Woodrift Ln 15236
Woodrow Ave 15227
Woodruff St
300-361 15211
363-499 15211
753-1397 15220
1399-1599 15220
Woods Ave 15202
Woods Rd 15235
Woods Run Ave 15212
Woodsdale Dr 15241
Woodsdale Rd 15237
Woodshire Rd 15215
Woodside Rd 15221
Woodstock Ave 15218
Woodstock Place Ext 15218
Woodstone Dr 15235
Woodstream Dr 15238
Woodvalley Dr 15238
Woodview Dr 15237
Woodville Ave 15220
Woodvue Dr 15227
Woodward Ave 15226
Woodwell St 15217
Woodworth St
800-899 15221
5100-5199 15224
Woody Crest Dr 15234
Woolslayer Way
3600-3899 15201
3900-4499 15224
Wooster St 15219
Worcester Dr 15243
Worth St 15217
Worthington Rd 15238
Worthington St 15206
N Wren Dr 15243
Wren St 15236
Wright St 15221
Wrights Way 15203
Wurzell Ave 15214
Wyandotte St
26-28 15213
2000-2099 15219
2500-2599 15213
Wychelm St 15234
Wyckoff Ave 15204
Wylie Ave 15219
Wymore St 15220
Wyncotte St 15204
Wyndham Cir 15275
Wynette St 15204
Wyngold Dr 15237
Wynne Ave 15205
Wynne St 15209
Wynnewood Dr 15228
Wynnwood Dr 15215
Wynoka St 15210
Wyola St 15211
Wyoming St 15211
Wysox St 15210
Xavier Ln 15237
Yale Ave
1-299 15229
7400-7599 15225
Yale Dr 15210
Yale Rd 15205
Yale St 15214

Yanks Ln 15236
Yardley Way 15206
Yarrow Ln 15236
Yarrow Way 15213
Yellowstone Dr 15235
Yetta Ave 15212
Yettman Dr 15239
Yew St 15224
Yoder St 15207
Yorintri St 15224
York Dr 15214
York Rd 15241
York Way 15213
Yorkshire Dr
100-112 15238
101-119 15238
111-111 15208
113-6999 15208
Yorktown Pl 15235
Yosemite Dr 15235
Yost Blvd 15221
Young Dr 15227
Young St 15224
Younger Ave 15216
Youngridge Dr 15236
Youngwood Rd 15228
Zahniser St 15220
Zane Pl 15214
Zang Way 15212
Zara St 15210
Zaruba St 15210
Zenith Ct 15241
Zephyr Ave 15204
Zesta Dr 15205
Zeta Dr 15238
Zimmerman St 15210
Zoller St 15212
Zug Ave 15214
Zulema St 15213
Zupancic Dr 15236

NUMBERED STREETS

1st Ave
100-100 15222
106-106 15229
117-125 15222
129-133 15229
135-135 15222
137-163 15229
200-399 15222
400-699 15219
1st St
--- 15225
2-26 15215
70-99 15229
106-108 15215
110-112 15225
111-135 15229
111-399 15215
114-134 15225
118-198 15238
136-144 15225
200-299 15238
452-452 15227
900-999 15237
E 1st St 15238
2nd Ave
100-199 15229
600-3600 15219
3602-3698 15219
4100-5699 15207
2nd St
1-20 15215
4-98 15215
22-98 15215
100-200 15238
100-199 15237
100-399 15215
100-299 15225
202-222 15238
W 2nd St 15238
3rd Ave 15229
3rd Ave 15222
3rd Ave 15222
400-498 15219

3rd St
1-109 15215
100-299 15238
100-114 15229
101-199 15225
101-199 15229
111-111 15215
116-198 15225
318-398 15215
S 3rd St 15219
W 3rd St 15238
4th Ave
101-141 15229
200-341 15222
343-399 15222
400-599 15219
4th St
1-30 15215
9-9 15215
11-300 15215
32-110 15215
100-598 15238
100-299 15225
302-306 15215
700-702 15215
S 4th St 15219
W 4th St 15238
4th Street Ext 15221
5th Ave 15229
5th Ave 15229
5th Ave 15222
5th Ave 15222
101-131 15229
110-399 15222
133-137 15229
400-2299 15219
2300-3389 15213
3390-3390 15260
3391-3393 15213
3395-3395 15260
3397-4999 15213
4200-4204 15260
4400-4998 15213
5000-6300 15232
6301-6699 15206
6700-6898 15208
6701-6853 15206
6900-6999 15208
5th St
1-1 15215
99-121 15229
123-139 15215
205-215 15238
217-227 15215
239-241 15238
5600-5699 15236
S 5th St 15203
W 5th St 15238
6th Ave 15229
6th Ave 15229
6th Ave 15222
204-230 15229
300-327 15222
400-418 15219
6th Pl 15229
6th St
101-103 15222
107-109 15229
200-252 15238
202-226 15222
205-255 15238
212-222 15215
1200-1420 15234
5600-5699 15236
S 6th St 15203
7th Ave
300-399 15222
401-409 15219
7th St
1-99 15215
100-101 15222
106-116 15238
130-131 15222
200-208 15238
215-227 15215
224-298 15238
S 7th St 15203

8th Ave 15229
8th St
1-199 15222
200-212 15215
214-227 15215
216-218 15238
220-247 15238
249-251 15238
301-309 15215
311-399 15215
E 8th St 15215
S 8th St 15203
W 8th St 15215
9th Ave 15229
9th St
100-106 15229
107-118 15229
110-213 15222
120-122 15229
201-219 15215
202-224 15215
215-217 15222
221-225 15215
227-299 15215
301-307 15215
309-329 15215
331-399 15215
S 9th St 15203
W 9th St 15215
10th Ave 15229
10th St
101-117 15229
102-118 15229
105-223 15215
112-210 15215
171-173 15222
212-212 15222
212-226 15215
228-230 15215
300-399 15215
S 10th St 15203
11th St
1-99 15222
100-204 15215
101-199 15229
204-208 15215
S 11th St 15203
12th St
100-199 15222
201-225 15215
S 12th St 15203
13th St
1-99 15222
101-399 15215
102-110 15229
124-398 15215
S 13th St 15203
14th St
1-99 15222
100-199 15215
200-210 15222
211-299 15215
S 14th St 15203
15th St
1-199 15229
100-106 15229
102-106 15215
S 15th St 15203
16th St 15222
S 16th St 15203
17th St
1-99 15222
200-299 15215
S 17th St 15203
18th St
1-99 15222
100-299 15215
S 18th St 15203
S 18th Street Ext 15210
19th St
1-100 15215
100-118 15222
101-197 15215
S 19th St 15203
20th St
1-100 15222
200-299 15215

S 20th St 15203
21st St
1-99 15222
100-149 15215
150-199 15222
200-206 15215
201-299 15222
208-299 15215
301-399 15215
S 21st St 15203
22nd St
100-199 15215
200-298 15222
S 22nd St 15203
23rd St
100-116 15222
101-117 15215
S 23rd St 15203
23rd Street Ext 15215
24th St 15222
S 24th St 15203
25th St 15222
S 25th St 15203
26th St 15222
S 26th St 15203
27th St 15222
S 27th St 15203
28th St 15222
S 28th St 15203
29th St 15201
S 29th St 15203
30th St
1-99 15201
300-599 15219
S 30th St 15203
31st St 15201
32nd St 15201
33rd St 15201
34th St 15201
35th St
1-29 15201
31-36 15201
35-35 15202
38-198 15201
101-199 15201
36th St 15201
37th St 15201
38th St 15201
39th St 15201
40th St
2-98 15201
100-229 15201
231-299 15201
300-599 15224
41st St 15201
42nd St 15201
43rd St 15201
44th St 15201
45th St 15201
46th St 15201
47th St 15201
48th St 15201
49th St 15201
50th St 15201
51st St 15201
52nd St 15201
53rd St 15201
54th St 15201
55th St 15201
56th St 15201
57th St 15201
58th St 15201
62nd St 15201
29 1/2 St 15201
43 1/2 St 15201

PITTSTON PA

General Delivery 18640

POST OFFICE BOXES MAIN OFFICE STATIONS AND BRANCHES

Box No.s
All PO Boxes 18640

RURAL ROUTES

01, 04 18643

NAMED STREETS

Adams Ct 18643
Almond St 18641
Alta Vista Ter 18640
Alto Rd 18640
Ambrose St 18640
Anderson St 18640
Andrews Ct 18643
Angelina Ln 18643
Ann St 18643
Anthracite St 18643
Antrim Rd 18640
Apple Tree Rd 18643
Armstrong Rd 18640
Asbury Ln 18643
Ash Ct 18643
Ash St
1-99 18641
700-799 18643
Aster Ct 18643
Aston Farm Ln 18640
Aston Mountain Rd 18640
Atlantic Ave 18643
Atwell Dr 18641
Baer Ct 18643
Baker Rd 18640
Baltimore Ave 18643
Barber St 18643
Bass Ln 18643
Bear Creek Rd 18641
Begosh Aly 18640
Belin Vlg 18641
Bellus Ct 18643
Benedict St 18640
Bennett St
1-299 18643
400-499 18641
Berkeley St 18640
Berry St 18643
Birch Dr 18641
Birchwood Est 18643
Birney Ave 18641
Bishop Ln 18643
Blackman St 18643
Bluebell Ct 18643
Blueberry Ln 18640
Bolin St 18640
Bon Aire Ter 18640
Bond St 18643
Boston Ave 18643
Boston St 18640
Boyd St 18640
Brady St 18640
Brandenberg Ln 18640
Brann Ct 18643
Breezewood Dr 18640
Broad St 18640
Broadcast Ctr 18641
Brooks Dr 18640
Brown Rd 18640
Brown St 18643
Bryan Ln 18640
Bryden Ln & St 18640
Butler Aly, Rd & St 18640
Buttercup Ct 18643
Bypass Rd 18640
Byrd St 18643
Calvert St 18640
Cambridge Cir & Dr 18641
Campbell Rd 18641
Campground Rd 18643
Canyon Dr 18640
Capital Rd 18640
Carey Ln 18640
Carpenter St 18643
Carroll St
1-299 18640
800-899 18641
Cedar St 18643
Cemetery St
1-115 18640

100-144 18641
117-145 18640
146-198 18641
Center St
1-5 18640
Centerpoint Blvd 18640
Chapel Ln 18643
Chapel Rd 18640
Chapel St 18640
Chapman St
1-6 18641
66-80 18640
82-99 18640
E Chapman St 18640
W Chapman St 18640
Charles Cir, Pl & St 18640
Chase St 18643
Cherry Aly 18640
Cherry Dr 18643
Cherry St 18641
Chestnut Aly 18640
Chestnut St
1-3 18640
5-11 18640
12-24 18640
26-99 18640
100-700 18641
701-701 18641
702-702 18641
703-799 18641
801-899 18641
1000-1099 18643
Chestnut Hill Rd 18640
Chicory Ct 18643
Church Dr 18640
Church Rd 18643
Church St
1-199 18640
800-1199 18641
Circle Dr 18643
Clark St 18641
Clear Spring Ct 18643
Cleveland St 18640
Cliff St 18640
Clover Ct 18643
Clyde St 18643
Coal St 18640
Cole St 18640
E & W Columbus Ave 18640
Commerce Rd 18640
Commerce St 18641
Concorde Dr 18641
Coolidge Ave 18643
Coolidge St
1-99 18643
200-399 18641
Cornelia St 18640
Costello Cir 18641
Country Rd 18643
Country Corner Plz 18640
Craig St 18640
Crest St 18643
Crestmere Ter 18640
Cron St 18640
Crystal Creek Rd 18643
Culver Hill Rd 18643
Curran St 18640
Curry St 18640
Curtain St
1-99 18640
100-299 18641
Curtis St 18640
Daffodil Ct 18643
Daisy Ct 18643
Damon St 18643
Dandelion Ct 18643
Dawson St 18641
Defoe St 18640
Delaney St 18640
Delaware Ave 18643
Della Ln 18643
Delmount Ln 18640
Demark Rd 18640
Dennison St 18643
Depew St 18640
Dewitt St 18640
Diana Ln 18643
Dickinson St 18640
Dietrick Ln 18640
Dinniny St 18640
Division St 18640
Dolman St 18641
Donegal Park 18640
Donnas Way 18643
Doty St 18640
Dougherty Rd 18640
Drake St 18640
Drummond St 18640
East Ln & St 18640
Elizabeth St
1-299 18640
500-599 18643
Elm St
1-199 18643
100-399 18641
Emmas Ln 18643
Enterprise Way 18640
Erie St 18643
Esther St 18640
Evergreen Rd 18640
Everhart St 18641
Ewen St 18640
Excelsior St 18643
Exeter Ave 18643
Factory St 18641
Fairlawn Dr 18640
Fairway Dr 18643
Fanning St 18640
Fear St 18640
Flag St 18640
Florence St 18641
Flynn St 18641
Ford St 18640
Foundry St
1-99 18640
500-899 18643
Fourth St 18643
Franklin St 18643
Freeport Rd 18640
Fremont St 18643
Friend St 18640
Front St
1-199 18640
2-2 18640
300-499 18641
Frothingham St 18640
Fulton St 18640
Gable Crest Dr 18640
Gain St 18640
Gardenia Dr 18641
Gardner St 18640
Garfield St 18640
Gashi Rd 18643
Gaughan St 18640
Gayle Dr 18643
Gedding St 18641
Gedrich St 18641
George Dr & St 18640
George Kramer Rd 18640
Gidding St 18640
Gill St 18641
Gleason Dr 18641
Glen Mdws 18640
Glen Rock Rd 18640
Glendale Rd
105B-105D 18641
118A-118L 18640
105D-105G 18640
123A-123D 18640
94-110 18641
108-189 18640
112-124 18641
Grand Ln 18643
Grandview Dr 18640
Grant St
1-399 18643
25-29 18640
100-399 18641
401-499 18641
Gravity Rd 18641
Gravity St 18640
Greeley St 18641
Green St 18640
Greico Dr 18640
Griffith St 18640
Grove St
1-99 18641
100-199 18643
200-1599 18641
Hale St 18640
Hanger Rd 18641
Harding Ave 18643
Harding St
200-316 18641
318-398 18641
391-397 18643
399-499 18643
Harland St 18643
Hastie Ln 18643
Haston St 18640
Hawthorne St 18641
Heandela St 18640
Heather Highlands 18640
Hedding Ln 18643
Heidi Ln 18641
Hemlock St 18641
Hewitt Rd 18640
Hex St 18643
High St 18640
Highland Dr 18640
N Highland Dr 18640
S Highland Dr 18640
Highland St 18641
Hill St 18641
Hillpark Ave 18640
Hillside Ave 18641
Hilltop Rd 18640
Hobart St 18641
Holden St 18641
Hollow St 18641
Holly Ln 18643
Hoover St 18643
Hope St 18641
Horeent St 18641
Hospital St 18640
Howard St 18641
Howley Cir 18640
Hughes St 18640
Hunter St 18640
Hunters Cir 18643
Ida Cir 18643
Import Rd 18640
Independence Dr 18640
Industrial Dr 18640
Insignia Dr 18640
Irene St 18643
Isabelle Ct 18640
Ivy Ln 18641
Jackson St
100-104 18643
106-138 18643
130-398 18641
James Ct & St 18640
Jason St 18641
Jean Cir & St 18643
Jenkins Ct 18640
Jenkins St 18643
Jennings St 18640
Jepson St 18643
Jesse St 18643
John St
1-11 18640
2-744 18641
13-199 18640
746-750 18641
752-798 18641
Johns Rd 18643
Johnson St 18640
Jones St 18643
Kaufman Ct 18643
Keeler St 18643
Kelley Ln 18643
Kenley St 18640
Kennedy Blvd & St 18640
Kern St 18643
Keystone Ave 18640
Kitchen Ln 18643
Kokinda Dr 18641
La Grange St 18640
Lackawanna Ave
100-199 18643
100-399 18641
Lacoe St 18643
Laflin Rd 18640
Laird St 18640
Lambert St 18640
Lampman St 18641
Landon St 18640
Langan Rd 18640
Laurel Ct 18643
Laurel Plz 18640
Laurel St
20-799 18640
96-98 18641
100-199 18641
Laurie Ln 18640
Law St 18640
Layton St 18643
Ledge Ct 18640
Ledgeview Dr 18643
Lee Ln 18643
Lehigh St
100-299 18643
200-299 18641
Lenox Ct 18640
Leonard St 18640
Leslie Ln 18640
Lewis Rd 18643
Lewis St 18640
Liberty St
100-499 18643
300-499 18641
Lidy Rd 18641
Lily Ct 18643
Lincoln St
1-46 18640
36-38 18643
40-399 18643
48-64 18640
100-499 18641
Linden St
1-399 18643
800-899 18641
Lloyd St 18641
Lockville Rd 18643
Lolli Ln 18641
Lone St 18640
Lower Rock St 18640
Luzerne Ave 18643
Lynn Dr 18640
Lyons Aly 18640
Main St
250A-250R 18641
1-1499 18640
103-121 18641
123-609 18641
153-165 18641
167-1500 18641
611-623 18641
1502-1598 18641
N Main St 18640
S Main St 18640
Maple Ln 18640
Maple St
1-99 18640
1-199 18643
Marcy Rd 18643
Market St 18640
Martins Ct 18640
Marys Cir 18643
Mason Ct & St 18643
May St 18640
Mayfair Dr 18640
Mcalpine St 18641
Mccawley Ct 18643
Mckinley St 18643
Mclean St 18641
Mctigue St 18640
Meade St 18640
Mechanics Dr 18640
Melody Ln 18643
Memco Dr & Ln 18640
Memorial St 18643
Menhennett Ln 18643
Mercer St 18643
Mill St
1-299 18640
700-899 18641
Mill Hill Rd 18643
Mill Hill St 18640
Millcreek Rd 18641
Miller St
1-99 18643
1-11 18640
1-22 18640
24-28 18640
Milton St 18640
Miner St 18643
Mitchell Dr & St 18640
Monroe St 18641
Montgomery Ave 18643
Moosic Hts 18641
Morgan Ln
1-99 18640
1-99 18643
Morris St 18640
Mosier St 18643
Mount Zion Rd 18643
N & S Mountainview
Dr 18640
Moyer Ct 18643
Mt Lookout Trl 18643
Mullen St 18640
Mundy Ct 18643
Nafus St 18640
Nassau St 18643
Navy Way Rd 18641
New St
1-199 18640
101-199 18641
New Boston Rd 18640
Ninotti Ln 18643
Noah Ln 18643
Norman St 18640
North St 18643
Northview Rd 18640
Oak St
1-3 18641
5-15 18640
76-1199 18640
1201-1299 18640
E Oak St 18640
W Oak St 18640
Oberdorfer Rd 18643
Oconnell St 18640
Old Boston Rd 18640
Oldfield Dr 18640
Oliver Pl 18640
Oliveri Dr 18640
Orange St 18641
Orchard St
1-5 18640
6-299 18643
Orchid Dr 18641
Orme St 18640
Osborne Dr 18640
Overlook Dr 18640
Owen St 18640
Pacific Ave 18643
Packer Ave
1-439 18643
441-999 18643
624-698 18641
Packer St 18641
Paiges Dr 18640
Panama St 18640
Para Dr 18640
Park Dr 18641
Park Ln 18643
Park Pl 18641
Park St 18643
Parke St 18643
Parnell St 18640
Parsonage St 18640
Patrick Rd 18640
Pauline St 18643
Pecks Rd 18643
Penn Ave
1-199 18643
200-699 18641
Penox Plz 18640
Pepe Ct 18643
Perch Ln 18643
Philadelphia Ave 18643
Pine St
29B1-29B2 18640
1-1 18641
2-299 18640
100-698 18641
Pittston Ave
1-199 18640
200-615 18641
501-505 18641
512-698 18641
617-699 18641
Plachit St 18643
Plane St 18641
Plank St 18640
Pollock Dr 18640
Poole St 18640
Poppy Ln 18641
Powder Mill Rd 18640
Price St 18640
Primrose Ct 18643
Prospect Ln 18643
Prospect Pl 18640
Prospect St 18640
Quail Hill Dr 18641
Quality Rd 18641
Quiet Cv 18640
Race St 18643
Rachael Dr 18640
Radcliffe St 18640
Railroad St
1-99 18641
2-98 18640
101-499 18641
E Railroad St 18640
Red Ash Ct 18643
Regulators Ln 18641
Reid St 18640
Renfer Rd & St 18640
Research Dr 18640
Reservoir St 18640
Reynolds St 18640
Ridge Rd & St 18640
Rindgen Ln 18643
River Rd & St 18640
River Shores Ct 18643
Riverview Mnr 18640
Riverview Vlg 18643
Riverview Village Cir 18643
Roberts Rd & St 18640
Rock St 18640
Rockledge Dr 18640
Rocky Glen Rd 18641
Rohland Ln 18643
Romanowski Ln 18643
Roosevelt Ave & St 18643
Rose St 18640
Roselle Rd 18643
Route 315 Hwy 18640
Rowhouse Ln 18640
Rozelle Rd 18643
Rug Ln 18641
Russell St 18641
Rutledge Dr & St 18640
Saint Marks Ln 18640
Saint Marys St 18641
Salem St 18643
Sand St 18640
Sanovia St 18643
Sarf Rd 18640
Sathers Dr 18640
Scarboro St 18643
School St 18641
Schooley Ave & Rd 18643
Searfoss Rd 18643
Searle St 18640
Second St 18643
Semenza Dr 18640
Seneca St 18640
Serling St 18641
Shaft St 18640
Sharon Dr 18641
Sherinsky Rd 18643
Sherman St 18643
Short St 18643
Side Hill Acres Dr 18640
Siena Cir 18641
Silver Bell Dr 18643
Simpson St 18641
Skyline Dr 18640
Skytop Dr
2-2 18641
2-22 18643
4-399 18641
24-84 18643
86-98 18643
500-599 18643
Slocum Ave 18643
Smith St
1-99 18640
100-499 18641
Snapdragon Dr 18641
South St
1-299 18643
400-1399 18641
Spring Aly 18640
Spring Ct 18640
Spring St
2-98 18643
5-8 18640
7-15 18640
10-598 18640
17-523 18640
100-328 18643
100-1299 18641
330-398 18643
525-599 18640
Spruce St
100-600 18641
600-799 18643
602-698 18641
900-908 18641
910-1400 18641
1402-1498 18641
Stadium St 18643
Stanton St
1-499 18643
2-98 18640
100-400 18641
402-498 18641
Stark St 18640
State Route 92 Hwy 18643
Sterling St 18640
Stevens Ln 18643
Stone Ct 18640
Stout St 18640
Sturmer St 18643
Sullivan St 18643
Sunflower Ct 18643
E & W Sunrise Dr &
Ln 18640
Sunset Dr
200-299 18643
1100-1199 18640
Sunset Ln 18641
Suscon Rd 18640
Susquehanna Ave 18643
Sutton Creek Rd 18643
Swallow St 18640
Sweitzer Rd 18643
Swift St 18641
Taft Ave 18643
Tariff Rd 18640
Teasdale St 18640
Tedrick St 18640
Tennant St 18640
Terminal Dr 18641
Terrace Ave 18643
Theodore St 18643
Thistle St 18640
Thomas Ln 18640
Thomas St 18640
Thompson St 18640
Tinas Way 18643
Tompkins St 18640
Toni Ln 18643
Tower Ln 18643
N & S Township Blvd 18640
Towpath Ct 18640
Trayor St 18643

Troback Dr 18643
Tunkhannock Ave 18643
Tunnel St 18640
Underwood Ln 18640
Union St
1-3 18640
5-64 18640
7-9 18640
11-144 18640
146-198 18640
200-418 18643
420-420 18643
1/2-1/2 18640
Valley St
1-199 18643
600-699 18641
Valley View Ter 18640
Venetz St 18643
Village Rd 18643
Vilna Rd 18640
Vine St
1-299 18640
301-897 18641
899-1199 18641
Violet Ct 18643
Wall St 18640
Walnut St
1-699 18641
500-599 18643
800-999 18641
Warren St 18643
Warsaw St 18643
Washington St
1-99 18640
1-11 18643
2-8 18643
10-399 18643
13-125 18643
127-141 18643
Washington Ter 18640
Water St 18640
Waterford Dr 18641
Webster St 18640
Welsh St 18640
West St 18640
Westport Cir & Rd 18640
Wharf St 18640
White St 18641
Whitlock St 18643
Whitman Dr 18641
Wildflower Est 18643
Wilford St 18640
Wilkern St 18643
Wilkes Barre Ln 18643
William St
--- 18640
1-703 18640
701-701 18641
703-1399 18641
705-925 18640
W William St 18640
Willow Ln & Rd 18640
Willow Crest Dr 18640
Wilson Ave 18643
Wilson St
1-13 18641
2-6 18640
8-52 18640
54-98 18640
100-499 18643
Winans Ct 18641
Winter St 18640
Wisner St 18643
Wisteria Dr 18641
Wood St
1-59 18640
2-10 18640
2-10 18641
12-16 18641
12-53 18640
18-26 18641
61-99 18640
900-999 18641
Woodrow Ln 18640
Wvia Way 18640
Wynchurch Cir 18640
Wyoming Ave
200-949 18643
200-699 18641
951-959 18643
961-1999 18643
Yaletsko Ln 18643
Yates St 18640
Yatesville Rd 18640
York Ave
1-499 18643
501-597 18641
599-799 18641
801-899 18641
Yurish Rd 18643
Ziegler Rd 18640
Ziegler St 18641

NUMBERED STREETS

1st St
1-99 18641
2-22 18640
58-98 18641
E 1st St 18643
2nd St 18640
2nd St 18641
2nd St 18641
3rd St 18640
3rd St 18641
3rd St 18641
3rd St 18643
4th St 18640
4th St 18641
5th St 18643
6th St 18643

POTTSTOWN PA

General Delivery 19464

POST OFFICE BOXES MAIN OFFICE STATIONS AND BRANCHES

Box No.s
All PO Boxes 19464

NAMED STREETS

Aarons Way 19465
Acorn Way 19464
N & S Adams St 19464
Airport Rd 19464
Allison Dr 19464
Alyssa Ln 19465
Amanda Smith Dr 19464
Amoroso Ln 19464
Anneto Dr 19464
Anthony Dr 19464
Anthony Wayne Dr 19464
Apple St 19464
Applegate Ln 19464
Armand Hammer Blvd 19464
Ash St 19464
Aspen Dr 19464
Augusta Dr 19464
Autumnview Ln 19464
Bahr Rd 19464
Barbara Way 19464
Bard Rd 19465
Bards Way 19464
Bauman Cir 19465
Bayberry Ln 19465
Bealer Rd 19465
Beaumont Ln 19464
Becker Ln 19465
W Beech St 19464
Beechwood Ave 19464
Beechwood Ter 19465
Bell Aire Rd 19464
Belleview Ave 19464
Belmont St 19464
Berks St 19464
Bern Ct 19465
Bickel Rd 19465
Big Sky Ranch Dr 19464
Birch Ln 19465
Birdsong Way 19464
Bishop Rd 19465
Blackberry Dr 19464
Bleim Rd 19464
Blossom Ln & Way 19465
Blue Spruce Ct 19464
Blue Spruce Ln 19465
Boone Ct 19464
Boxwood Ct 19464
Bradley Way 19464
Bramblewood Ct 19464
Breezeview Ln 19465
Brentwood Dr 19465
Bretts Way 19465
Briana Dr 19464
Brianna Cir 19465
Briar Ln 19464
Briarwood Ln 19464
Broadmoor Rd 19464
Brooke Rd 19464
Brookside Ave & Rd 19464
Brookview Ln 19464
Brookwood Dr 19464
Brower Ln 19465
Brown St
800-899 19465
2200-2399 19464
Brownstone Dr 19465
Bruce Dr 19464
Brynne Ln 19464
Bryton Ave 19465
Buchert Rd 19464
Bucktown Xing 19465
Buckwalter Rd 19465
Bunker Way 19464
Burdan Dr 19464
Butler St 19464
Butternut Dr 19464
W Buttonwood Aly & St 19464
Byron Way 19464
Cadmus Rd 19465
Candelora Dr 19464
Carriage House Rd 19465
Catfish Ln 19465
Cedar St 19464
Cedar Hill Rd 19464
Cedar Ridge Dr 19465
E & W Cedarville Rd 19465
Cemetary Ln 19465
Centennial Ct 19464
Center Ave & St 19464
Chancery Ct 19465
Channing Ct 19465
N & S Charlotte St 19464
Cherry Ln & St 19464
Cherry Hill Ln 19465
Cherrytree Ln 19464
Cherrywood Ct 19464
Chester Dr 19465
Chestershire Pl 19465
Chestnut Ct 19465
Chestnut Ln 19465
Chestnut St 19464
W Chestnut St 19464
Chestnut Grove Rd 19465
Chestnut Hill Rd 19465
Christina Ct 19464
Christman Ct 19465
Circle Ct 19465
Circle Dr 19464
W Circle Dr 19465
Circle Of Progress Dr 19464
Clearview Rd & St 19464
Cloverhill Rd 19464
Cobb Hill Ln 19465
Cobbler Ln 19465
Coldsprings Rd 19465
Colebrookdale Rd 19464
College Dr 19464
Commerce Ct & Dr 19464
Commons Dr 19464
Concord Dr 19464
Conservation Ln 19465
Constitution Ave 19464
Continental Dr 19464
Coolidge Ave 19464
Cornerstone Dr 19465
Country Dr 19464
Country Ln 19465
Country Walk Dr 19465
County Park Rd 19465
Coventry Greene Ln 19465
Coventry Pointe Ln 19465
Coventryville Rd 19465
Coyne Ave 19465
Creamery Rd 19465
Creek Rd 19465
Creekside Dr 19464
Crest Ln 19465
Crest View Ln 19465
Crestview Cir 19465
Crestwood Dr 19464
Crimson Ln 19465
Cross Rd & St 19464
Crownview Rd 19465
Custer Ct 19464
Daisy Point Rd 19465
Danny Rd 19464
Darby Ct 19465
Dare Ln 19465
Daub Aly 19464
Dauphin Ct 19465
Deer Ridge Dr 19464
Deerfield Way 19464
Delmar Ave 19465
Dessere Ln 19465
Detweiler Rd 19465
Diamond Ct & St 19464
Diane Ct 19464
Dimity Ct 19465
Diprinzio Dr 19464
Dise Rd 19465
Do Jan Dr 19465
Doe Run Ln 19464
Dogwood Ct
400-999 19464
1100-1199 19465
Dogwood Ln 19464
Donald Dr 19464
Donna Ln 19464
Dorchester Ln 19465
Dori Ln 19465
Doris Dr 19464
Duckworth Dr 19464
Dunbar Rd 19465
Durham Ct 19464
Earl Dr 19465
Earls Ln 19465
East Ct & St 19464
Eaton Ct 19465
Ebelhare Rd 19465
Edgewood Dr & St 19464
El Dr 19465
Ellen Cir 19464
Ellis Woods Rd 19465
Elm St
1-265 19464
200-298 19465
267-299 19464
268-336 19465
301-309 19465
305-319 19464
315-317 19464
319-335 19465
337-399 19465
401-415 19464
417-599 19464
Elmwood Dr 19464
Emily Ln 19465
Erb Dr 19465
Essick Rd 19465
Evans Rd
201-339 19464
341-799 19464
1300-1899 19465
N Evans St 19464
S Evans St 19464
Evansbrooke Ln 19464
Evergreen Ln 19465
Evergreen Rd 19464
Fairview St 19464
Falcon Cir 19464
Fallbrook Ln 19464
Farmington Ave & Ct 19464
Farview Ln 19464
Faust Ln 19464
Favinger Rd 19465
Fawn Ln 19465
Feist Ave 19464
Fernbrook Ln 19465
Finley Cir 19464
Fisher Ave 19465
Foresman Dr 19464
Forest Glen Dr 19464
Fox Dr 19465
Fox Hollow Cir 19464
Foxgate Ln 19465
Foxtail Dr 19464
Foxview Rd 19465
Franklin Dr 19465
N Franklin St 19464
S Franklin St 19464
Freigh Ln 19465
French Creek Rd 19465
Fruitville Rd 19464
Fulmer Rd 19465
Futura Dr 19464
Gable Ave 19464
Gabriel Ct 19464
Garner Ave 19465
Gay St 19464
Gilbertsville Rd 19464
Glasgow St 19464
Glen Eagles Dr 19464
Glendale Ave 19464
Glenmar Dr 19465
Glocker Way 19465
Grace Rd 19464
Grace St 19464
Grandview Ave 19464
Grandview Cir 19465
Grandview Rd 19464
Grant St & Way 19464
Green Briar Ct 19464
Green View Dr 19464
Greenbriar Ln 19465
Gresh Dr 19464
Gross Rd 19464
S Grosstown Rd 19464
Grove St 19464
Grubb Rd 19464
Hale St 19464
Halteman Rd 19465
Hamilton St 19464
Hanover Dr 19464
N Hanover St 19464
S Hanover St
1-7 19464
9-99 19464
200-1699 19465
Harding St 19464
Harley Rd 19464
E & W Harmony Dr 19464
Harmonyville Rd 19465
Hartman Rd 19465
Harvey Ln 19465
Hause Ave 19464
Hawk St 19465
Hawthorne Ave 19464
Heather Ct 19465
Heather Ln 19464
Heather Pl 19464
Hemlock Row 19464
Henry St 19464
Heritage Dr 19464
Hershey Dr 19465
E & W High St 19464
Highland Rd 19464
Hill Camp Rd 19465
N & S Hills Blvd 19464
Hillside Dr 19464
Hillside Ln 19465
Hilltop Rd 19464
E & W Hoffecker Rd 19465
Holby Ln 19465
Holly Ct 19464
Holly Dr 19464
Holly Ln 19465
Hollyberry Ct 19464
Hollytree Ct 19464
Honeysuckle Ln 19465
Horseshoe Dr 19464
Horseshoe Ln 19465
E & W Howard St 19464
Hultz Ln 19465
Hunters Run Ln 19464
Hunters Run Rd 19465
Ian Dr 19465
Industrial Ave, Dr, Hwy & Pkwy 19464
Irene Ct 19464
Irwin Pl 19464
Isabella St 19464
Ivy Ln 19464
Jackson St 19464
Jay St 19464
Jays Ln 19464
Jefferson Ave & St 19464
Jem Ave 19464
Joanne Ct 19464
Johnson St 19464
Jones Blvd 19464
Jones Rd 19465
Julie Rd 19464
Juniper St 19464
Karen Dr 19464
Kauffman Rd 19464
Kay St 19464
Keen Rd 19465
N Keim St 19464
S Keim St
1-9 19464
11-99 19464
101-399 19465
700-1999 19465
E & W Keller Rd 19465
Kemp Rd 19465
Kennedy Ct 19464
Kenneth St 19464
Kenny Rd 19464
Kepler Rd 19464
Kerlin Ave 19465
Kerri Ct 19464
Keystone Blvd 19464
W King St 19464
Kline Ave 19465
Krepps Ln 19465
Kristen Cir 19465
Kristy Ct 19464
Kulp Rd 19465
Kummerer Rd 19464
Kutz Dr 19465
Labelle Ln 19465
Larkspur Ln 19465
Laura Ln 19464
Laurel Ln 19465
Laurel St 19464
Laurel Way 19464
Laurelwood Rd 19465
Law Ln 19465
Lee Ave & Dr 19464
Lemon St 19464
Lesher Aly 19464
Levengood Rd 19464
W Lightcap Rd 19464
Limerick Center Rd 19464
Lincoln Ave 19464
Linda Ln 19464
Lindberg Ave 19465
Linden St 19464
Lindley Ln 19465
Linfield Rd 19464
Linwood Cir 19465
Little Brook Ln 19465
Little Vine St 19464
Logan St 19464
Lois Ln 19465
Lomara Dr 19464
Longview Rd 19464
Loop Rd 19464
Lotus Dr 19464
Lower Fricks Lock Rd 19465
Lozark Rd 19464
Lubold Rd 19465
Lucy Ct 19464
Ludwig Ln 19464
Lynn Dr 19464
Maack Rd 19465
Maaco St 19464
Madison St 19464
E & W Main St 19465
Mallard Ct 19464
Malvern Dr 19465
Manatawny Dr & St 19464
Maple Dr & St 19464
Maple Glen Cir 19464
Maple Leaf Ln 19464
Maplewood Dr 19464
Marcus Dr 19465
Mark Dr & Ln 19465
Marshall Dr 19465
Master St 19464
Masters Dr 19464
Matthew Ln 19465
Maugers Mill Rd 19464
Maurer Rd 19465
May St 19464
Maywood Ln 19464
Meadow Aly 19464
Meadow Ln 19465
Meadow Wood Ave 19465
E & W Meadowbrook Rd 19465
Meadowview Dr 19464
Medical Dr 19464
Melville Dr 19465
Mervine St 19464
Micklitz Dr & Rd 19464
E & W Mill Creek Way 19465
Miller Rd 19465
Millstone Ln 19465
Mimosa Ln 19464
Mineral St 19464
Ming Dr 19464
Mintzer St 19464
Mirkwood Ct 19464
Mitch Rd 19464
Mitchell Dr 19465
Mock Rd 19464
Monroe Ave & St 19464
Montgomery St 19464
Morello Dr 19464
Morris St 19464
Moser Rd 19464
Mount Pleasant Rd 19465
N & S Mount Vernon St 19464
Mount Zion Ave 19465
E & W Moyer Rd 19464
Mulberry St 19464
Murray School Rd 19465
Myrtle St 19464
Nagle Rd 19464
Needhammer Rd 19464
Neiman Rd 19465
Nester Dr 19464
New St 19464
New Kepler Rd 19464
New Philadelphia Rd 19465
New Schuylkill Rd 19465
Nicholas Dr 19464
Noel Cir 19464
Norbury Ct 19464
North St 19464
Nottingham Rd 19465
Oak Dr & St 19464
Oak Crest Rd 19464
Oakdale Ave & Dr 19464
Oaktree Ct 19464
Old Glasgow St 19464
Old Orchard Dr 19464
Old Reading Pike 19464
Old Ridge Rd 19465
Old Schuylkill Rd 19465

Oleander Ln 19465
Olive Ln 19465
Orchard Ln & Way 19465
Orlando Rd 19464
Overlook Dr 19464
Par Cir 19464
Park Ct 19464
Park Dr
 700-798 19465
 900-1099 19464
S Park Rd 19464
Parkway Dr 19465
Patricia Ln 19464
Peach St 19464
Peachtree Cir 19464
Pearl St 19465
Pearson St 19465
Pebble Beach Ln 19464
Penn Rd 19464
N Penn St 19464
S Penn St
 1-123 19464
 230-298 19465
Pennsylvania Ave 19464
Peterman Rd 19465
Pheasant Ln 19465
Pigeon Creek Rd 19465
Pine Aly 19464
Pine Dr 19465
Pine St 19464
Pine Ford Rd 19464
Pine Hurst Dr 19464
Pinetree Ct 19464
Planted Stone Path 19465
N & S Pleasantview Rd 19464
Plum St 19464
Poplar St 19464
Porter Rd 19464
Porters Mill Rd 19465
Possum Hollow Rd 19464
Potter Dr 19464
Potts Ct & Dr 19464
Pottstown Pike 19465
Price Ln 19465
N Price St 19464
S Price St 19464
Primrose Ln 19464
Prince St 19464
Princeton Ave 19464
Prizer Rd 19465
Prospect St 19464
Prospect Hill Ln 19464
Pruss Hill Rd 19464
Pulaski St 19464
Putter Ln 19464
Quail Ln 19464
Queen St 19464
Quinter St 19464
E & W Race St 19464
Raleigh Ct 19464
Rambler Ave 19464
Randy Dr 19464
Reading Station Plz 19464
Reiff Ave 19465
Reynolds Ave 19464
Rhoads Rd 19464
Rice St 19464
Richards Cir 19465
W Ridge Pike 19464
Ridge Rd 19465
Ridgeview Dr 19465
Ridgeview Ln 19464
Rinehart Rd 19465
Ringing Rocks Park 19464
Rivendell Ln 19464
River Rd 19465
Riverside Dr 19465
Riverview Rd 19465
Robert Joseph Rd 19465
Roberta Dr 19465
Roberts Cir 19465
Roberts Dr 19464
Robin Ln 19465
Robins Nest Ln 19465
Robinson St 19464
Rock Run Rd 19465
Rockwood Dr 19464
N & S Roland St 19464
Romig Rd 19464
Root Ave 19465
Rose Ln 19465
Rose Valley Rd 19464
Rosedale Dr 19464
Rosewood Ct 19464
Rowan Aly 19464
Rupert Rd 19464
Ruth Ln 19465
Ryan St 19464
Saddlewood Dr 19465
Sage Dr 19465
Sageview Dr 19464
Saint Andrews Dr 19464
Saint Clair St 19464
Saint Peters Rd 19465
Sanatoga Rd
 100-1099 19465
 2301-2397 19464
 2399-3299 19464
 3301-3499 19464
N Sanatoga Rd 19464
S Sanatoga Rd
 2-398 19464
 1000-1145 19465
 1146-1146 19464
 1147-1299 19465
 1148-1298 19465
Sanatoga Station Rd 19464
Savage Rd 19465
N & S Savanna Dr 19465
Saw Mill Rd 19465
Saylor Ct & Rd 19464
Saylors Mill Rd 19465
N Schaffer Rd 19464
Scherfel Blvd 19465
Scholl Rd 19465
School Ln 19464
School Rd 19465
Schoolhouse Rd 19465
E & W Schuylkill Ave & Rd 19465
Schwenk Rd 19464
Scott St 19464
Sell Rd 19464
Sembling Ave 19464
Shadestone Dr 19465
Shady Ln 19464
Shane Dr 19464
Shaner Dr 19465
Sheep Hill Rd 19465
Sheffield Ln 19465
Shelly Ln 19464
Shenkel Rd 19465
Sheridan Ln & St 19464
Shire Dr 19465
Shoemaker Rd 19464
Shrum Rd 19465
Skytop Dr 19464
Smith Rd 19464
Snell Rd 19464
Snyder Rd 19464
South Ct & St 19464
Southview Dr 19465
Specht Rd 19464
Spiece Rd 19465
Spring St 19464
Spring Creek Ln 19465
Spring Hollow Dr 19465
Springhill Ln 19465
Springhouse Ln 19465
Spruce St 19464
State St 19464
Stauffer Rd 19465
Steinmetz Rd 19464
Stephen Ln 19465
Stockton Sq 19465
Stone Hill Dr 19464
Stratford Ct 19465
Stuart Dr 19464
Summer Ln 19465
Summer Grove Ln 19464
Summit Way 19464
Sunnybrook Rd 19464
Sunnyside Ave 19464
Sunnyslope Dr 19464
Sunrise Dr
 1-97 19464
 99-130 19464
 105-165 19465
 132-198 19464
 141-199 19464
Sunrise Ln 19465
Sunset Dr 19464
Swamp Pike 19464
Sweet Briar Ct 19464
Sweetwater Way 19464
Sweisford Ln 19465
Sycamore Blvd & Dr 19464
Sylvan Dr
 1-299 19465
 600-799 19464
Tanglewood Ct 19464
Tee Ct 19464
Temple Rd 19465
Terrace Dr 19465
Terrace Ln 19464
Terraced Hill Ct 19464
Thomas Oakes Dr 19465
Timber Ln 19464
Timberline Dr 19465
Timberview Dr 19464
Tisa Ln 19465
Town Square Rd 19465
Trinley St 19465
Tyler Ct 19464
Tyson St 19465
Union Aly 19464
Union Ave 19465
Unionville Rd 19465
Upland St 19464
Upland Sq Dr 19464
Upper Fricks Lock Rd 19465
E & W Urner St 19465
Vale Cir 19464
E, N & W Valley Ct, Ln & Rd 19464
Valley View Rd 19465
Vaughn Rd 19465
Vaune Ln 19465
Victoria Chase 19465
Villa Dr 19464
Village Ln 19465
E & W Vine St 19464
Virginia Ave 19464
Von Steuben Dr 19464
W Walnut St 19464
Walnut Ridge Est 19464
Walnut Springs Ln 19465
Warren St 19464
Warwick Cir 19465
Warwick Chase 19465
Warwick Furnace Rd 19465
N & S Washington St 19464
Wedge Ct 19464
Wedgewood Dr 19465
Wells Rd 19465
Welsh Ct & Dr 19464
Wendell Dr 19464
Wendler Cir 19465
Wendy Dr 19464
West St 19464
Whartnaby Ave 19465
White Pine Ln 19464
Whitespire Cir 19464
William Rd 19464
Willow Rd & St 19464
Willow Brook Ln 19465
Wilson St 19464
Winchester Ct 19465
Winding Rd 19464
Windsor Ct & Rd 19464
Wintergreen Ln 19465
Wood Lea Rd 19465
Wooded Way 19464
Woodgate Ln 19464
W Woodland Ave, Ct & Dr 19464
Woodmere Dr 19464
Woodmont Dr 19465
Woods Ln 19465
Worth Blvd 19465
Yarnall Rd 19464
Yarnell Rd 19465
Yerger Rd 19464
N York St 19464
S York St 19465
Young Rd 19465
Zara Dr 19464

NUMBERED STREETS

All Street Addresses 19464

READING PA

General Delivery 19612

POST OFFICE BOXES MAIN OFFICE STATIONS AND BRANCHES

Box No.s
A - E 19608
1 - 1092 19607
1 - 1723 19603
2001 - 2399 19608
3521 - 5436 19606
5761 - 7097 19610
7281 - 8671 19603
9000 - 9000 19610
10841 - 16400 19612
62801 - 63514 19606
62897 - 62897 19608

NAMED STREETS

Abington Dr 19610
Acacia Ave 19605
Acorn Ct 19605
Acorn Dr 19608
Acorn Ln 19605
Adams Dr 19606
Adams St
 1-99 19608
 2-4 19606
 20-98 19608
 200-300 19606
 302-398 19606
 2100-2199 19605
Ahrens Rd 19606
Air Museum Dr 19605
N Alabama Ave 19605
Albert Dr 19608
Albert Ln 19607
Albright Ave 19610
Alden Ln 19610
Aldine Ave 19606
Aldridge Ct 19606
Alicia Cir 19608
Alisan Rd 19606
Allegheny Ave 19601
Allen Ave 19605
Allen Dr 19606
Allenbrook Ln 19606
Allentown Pike 19605
Allison Rd 19601
Alpine Ct 19606
Alsace Ct 19606
Alsace Rd 19604
Alton Ave 19605
Amherst Ave 19609
Amity Cir 19605
Amity St
 1428A-1428F 19604
 101-199 19601
 801-897 19604
 899-1300 19604
 1302-1498 19604
Amy Ct 19607
Anderson Ave 19606
Andover Ave 19609
Andre Ct 19610
Andrea Ct 19607
Andrew Ct & Dr 19608
Angelica St 19611
Angora Rd 19606
Ann St 19611
Antietam Ave, Rd & Trce 19606
Antler Holw 19607
Antonio Dr 19605
Apache Dr 19608
Apple Dr
 800-899 19610
 4900-5099 19606
Apple Pl 19610
W Apron Dr 19605
Archer Ln 19607
Archery Club Ln 19607
Ardmore Ave
 1-299 19607
 3500-4099 19605
Argonne Rd 19601
Arlington St
 1-500 19611
 502-798 19611
 3300-3599 19605
 3601-3699 19605
Arnold Rd 19605
Arrowhead Trl 19608
N & S Arthur Dr 19608
Ashbourne Dr 19605
Ashfield Ct 19607
Ashley Ave 19606
Ashley Dr 19607
Ashley Ln 19608
Ashley Rd 19608
Aspen Ave 19608
Aster Ln 19606
Atlantic Ave 19608
Augusta Dr E 19608
Augusta Dr W 19608
Augusta Ln 19607
Autumn Ln 19605
Avenue A 19601
Avenue B 19601
Avenue C 19601
Avenue D 19601
Aviation Rd 19601
Avon Ave 19608
Avondale Dr 19610
Azalea Way 19606
Bainbridge Cir 19608
Baker Ln 19606
Baker Rd 19608
Baker St 19607
Balthaser Rd 19608
Baltic Ave 19608
Bancroft Ter 19607
Barberry Ave 19605
Barberry Rd
 1000-1099 19611
 1100-1199 19610
Bard Ave 19608
Bare Ave 19607
Bare Path Rd 19608
Barlow Ave 19601
Barnhardt Way 19611
Barrett Rd 19605
Barrington Dr 19607
Bartlett St 19611
Basket Rd 19606
Bawns Ct 19609
Bayberry Ln 19608
Beach St 19605
Beacon Ave, Dr, Rd & St 19608
Bear Blvd 19606
Beavens Rd 19608
Beaver Ln 19606
Becket Ct 19607
Bedford Ave 19607
Beech Ln 19606
Beech St
 100-299 19601
 1000-1099 19605
Beecham Rd 19606
Beechwood Dr 19606
Belair Ave 19607
Bell Aly 19602
Bell Dr 19609
Belle Alto Rd 19608
Bellefonte Ave 19607
E & W Bellevue Ave 19605
Belmont Ave
 1-99 19610
 500-899 19605
 1100-1199 19610
 2001-2099 19605
 2500-2598 19609
 2600-3199 19609
Beltline Ave 19605
Belvedere Ave 19611
Benners Ct 19602
Bennett St 19605
Bent Brook Cir 19606
Bentley Ct 19601
Berkley Rd & St 19605
Berkley Park Rd 19605
Berks Pl
 1-19 19610
 23-899 19609
Berks St
 835-837 19605
 1801-1899 19604
Berkshire Blvd 19610
Berkshire Ct 19610
Berkshire Dr 19601
Berkshire Pl 19601
Bern Rd 19610
Bern St
 100-400 19601
 402-598 19601
 1500-1899 19604
Bernard Dr 19605
Bernhart Ave 19605
Bernville Rd
 2405A-2405F 19605
 1-2125 19601
 2127-2299 19601
 2200-2298 19605
 2300-2799 19605
E & W Bertolet Pl 19605
W Berton St 19605
Berwick Ct 19606
Beverly Ave 19607
Beverly Ct 19607
Beverly Ln 19601
Beverly Pl 19611
Bewley Ln 19605
Beyer Ave 19605
Big Oak 19607
Billy Dr 19608
Bilmar Rd 19604
Bingaman Ct 19602
Bingaman Rd 19606
Bingaman St 19602
N Bingaman St 19606
S Bingaman St 19606
Birch St
 400-799 19604
 800-899 19605
 900-1599 19604
Birchmont Dr 19606
Birchwood Rd 19610
Birdie Ln 19607
Birdsong Ct 19607
Bittner Ave 19608
Blackwood Dr 19606
Blair Ave 19601
Blanbird Dr 19608
Blankenbiller Rd 19606
Bleeker Ave 19607
Blemker Rd 19606
Blessing Ln 19605
Blimline Rd 19608
Bliss Blvd 19607
Blue Gate Ln 19608
Blue Ridge Rd 19606
Bluebird Dr 19610
Bluejay Dr 19610
Boardwalk 19608
Boas Ln 19608
Bobolink Dr 19610
Boeing Ave 19601
Boeshore Cir 19605
Bordic Rd 19606
Bowers Rd 19605
Bowes Ln 19606
Bowman St 19605
Boxwood Ct 19606
Boyer Ln & St 19605
Boyers Rd 19605
Boyertown Pike 19606
Bradford Ave 19607
Bradley Ave 19608
Bran Rd 19608
Brandywine Ct & Rd 19610
Brassie Cir 19607
Brecon Ln 19607
Brentwood Dr
 1-99 19608
 500-598 19611
 600-699 19611
Bressler Ct 19610
Bressler Dr
 2100-2299 19610
 2300-2499 19609
Brevity Ln 19609
Briar Ln 19606
Briarwood Cir 19606
Bridge St 19601
Brighton Ave 19606
Brimway Ln 19606
Bristol Ct 19610
Broad St
 100-298 19608
 101-199 19607
 301-399 19608
 5200-5299 19606
E Broad St 19607
W Broad St 19607
Broadcasting Rd 19610
Broadway Ave 19606
Broadway Blvd 19607
N & S Brobst St 19607
Brook Hollow Dr 19608
Brooke Blvd 19607
Brookfield Ave 19608
Brookfield Ln 19607
Brookline Plz
 100-199 19607
 200-699 19611
Brookline St 19611
Brookstone Dr 19606
Brown St 19606
Brownsville Rd 19608
Bruckman Ave 19605
Brumbach St 19606
Buchanon Dr 19605
Buck Hvn 19607
Buckingham Dr
 2-18 19605
 30-99 19610
Buckman Ave 19610
Buckskin Dr 19607
Bungalow Park Rd 19606
Burkey Ct & Dr 19610
Burning Tree Ln 19607
Burnside Ave 19611
Burrows St 19608
Bushkill Ct 19606
Butler St 19601
Butter Ln 19606
Butternut Ct 19608
Buttonwood St
 100-299 19601
 300-325 19611
 326-328 19601
 327-333 19611
 330-342 19611
 341-397 19601
 399-899 19601
 401-499 19611
 901-921 19604
 923-1399 19604
W Buttonwood St 19601
Buzzard Rd 19608

Byram St 19606
N & S Cacoosing Ave & Dr 19608
Cactus Ln 19606
N Calais Dr 19605
Calco Ave 19608
Calkins Dr 19606
Calls Ct 19602
Calming Trl 19608
Calyn Ct & Dr 19607
Cambridge Ave
1-3 19609
5-199 19609
1700-2000 19610
2002-2098 19610
Cameron St
2-98 19606
300-899 19607
Campus Rd 19610
Canal St 19602
Canary Ln 19606
Canberra Ct 19608
Canterbury Cir 19607
Caramist Cir & Dr 19608
Caravelle Ln 19606
Carbon St 19601
Cardinal Pl & Rd 19610
Caribou Ct 19606
Carlisle Ave 19609
Carman Dr 19610
Carmina Dr 19608
Carolina Ave 19605
N Carolina Ave 19608
Carpenter St 19602
Carriage Ln 19607
N Carroll St 19611
Carsonia Ave 19606
Cassel Rd 19606
Castleton Dr 19607
Catherine St 19607
Cathy Ann Dr 19606
Cayuga Ct 19607
Cecil Ave 19609
Cedar Ln 19607
Cedar St 19601
Cedar Hill Dr 19605
Cedar Top Rd 19607
Cedarwood Rd 19610
Cemetery Ln 19606
Centennial Ln 19606
Center Ln & St 19606
Centre Ave
400-498 19601
500-1799 19601
1800-3199 19605
Centre St 19605
Century Blvd 19610
Cessna Ln 19601
Chalfont Pl 19606
Chapel Ter 19602
Chapel Hill Rd 19608
Charlemont Ct 19607
Charles Blvd 19608
Charles St 19606
Charles Reed Blvd 19605
Charleston Ln 19610
Charlotte Ave 19609
Chaser Ct 19607
Chelsea Cir 19606
Cheltenham Dr 19610
Cherry Ct 19606
Cherry Dr 19610
Cherry St
101-199 19611
201-297 19602
299-300 19602
302-332 19602
314-498 19611
317-397 19611
399-414 19611
416-598 19611
441-499 19602
500-700 19611
501-1099 19602
702-798 19611
Cherrydale Ave 19606
Cherrywood Rd 19610
Cheshire Ct 19608
Chester St 19601
Chesterwood Cir 19607
Chestnut St
1-100 19607
100-108 19606
101-297 19607
102-198 19607
107-197 19602
199-200 19602
200-298 19611
201-201 19607
202-208 19602
203-245 19611
234-238 19607
253-297 19602
299-305 19607
299-1299 19602
300-599 19611
3100-3699 19605
Chip Ln 19607
Chiselford Dr 19608
Christine Dr 19606
Christman Rd 19606
Christopher Dr 19610
Chrystine Dr 19609
Church Rd
100-198 19608
400-999 19607
1001-1099 19607
N Church Rd 19608
Church St
1-99 19607
100-118 19601
101-299 19607
122-198 19607
200-298 19601
300-1499 19601
Church Hill Rd 19606
Church Lane Rd 19606
Circle Ave & Dr 19606
City Line Ave 19604
Clair St 19607
Clarion St 19601
Clarissa Ln 19608
Clark Ave 19609
Clayborne Rd 19606
Clayton Ave 19610
Clearfield Ln 19608
E & W Clearview Dr 19608
Clematis St 19608
Cleveland Ave
100-299 19605
1100-1799 19610
1900-2699 19609
Clifton Ave 19611
Clinton St 19601
Cloister Ct 19608
Clover Dr 19610
Clover St 19604
Club Dr 19606
Club Ln 19607
Clymer St 19602
Cobblestone Run 19606
Cody Dr 19605
Colin Ct 19606
Colleen Ct 19610
College Ave 19604
Colonial Dr 19607
Colony Dr 19610
Colorado Ave 19608
Colston Ave 19605
Colt St 19608
Columbia Ave
1-99 19606
100-198 19601
200-299 19605
400-499 19601
500-1299 19608
1300-1399 19607
Commerce Dr
1-6 19607
7-7 19610
9-99 19610
Commerce St 19608
Commons Blvd 19605
Commons Ct 19607
Commonwealth Blvd 19607
Community Dr 19607
Concord Ln 19607
Concord Rd 19610
Conestoga Dr 19608
Congressional Cir 19607
Connecticut Ave 19608
Connor Ct 19608
Constitution Ave 19606
Coral Ln 19606
Corbit Dr 19607
Cornell Ave 19609
Cornell St 19606
Corporate Blvd 19608
Corporate Dr 19605
Cortelyou Ave 19607
Cortland Ave 19607
Cotswold Rd 19608
Cotton St
901-997 19602
999-1499 19602
1500-1899 19606
County St 19605
E Court Blvd 19609
W Court Blvd 19609
Court St
201-299 19601
401-429 19611
435-497 19601
499-634 19601
635-705 19611
636-1098 19601
751-1099 19601
602-604-602-604 19601
Courtleigh Pl 19606
Courtney Rea Cir 19606
Coventry Ln 19610
Craftsbury Ct 19605
Craig Ave 19609
Craig Dr 19606
Craley Ln 19608
Cranberry Rdg 19606
Creek Ct 19607
Creighton Cir 19607
Crescent Ave 19605
Crest Rd 19608
Crestline Dr 19606
Crestmont St 19611
Crestview Ave 19607
Crestview Dr 19608
Cricket Rd 19605
Cromwell Dr 19610
Crooked Ct 19606
Cross Keys Rd 19605
Crossing Dr 19610
Crossroads Blvd 19605
Crosswicks Dr 19605
Crowder Ave 19607
Croydon Ter 19601
Crystal Rock Rd 19605
Cullum Dr 19601
Culvert St 19602
Cumberland Ave 19606
Curtis Ave 19601
Curtis Rd
2900-2999 19609
3000-3199 19608
Curtiss Pl 19606
Cypress Ln 19610
Dairy Cir 19607
Daisy Ct 19608
Dalin Dr 19609
Dallas Ln 19608
Dallas Rd 19605
Dallearn Rd 19610
Danbury Ct 19605
Daniel Dr
700-799 19605
2800-3199 19602
Daniel St 19605
Daniels Ave 19607
Danor Dr 19605
Darien St 19601
Darlin Dr 19609
Dauphin Ave 19610
Dautrich Rd 19606
Davis Dr 19607
Day Lily Dr 19608
Deborah Dr
100-199 19610
500-599 19608
4700-4899 19606
Deer Run 19606
Deer Creek Rd 19608
Deer Hill Rd 19607
Deer Path Rd 19604
Deharts Ct 19604
Del Mar Dr 19606
Delaware Ave 19610
Delta Ave 19605
Demoss Rd 19606
Dengler St 19606
Dennis Dr
1-199 19606
201-299 19606
2000-2199 19601
Denton St 19605
Devon Dr 19606
Devon Ter 19607
Devonshire Dr 19610
Dewald Rd 19606
Dewberry Ave 19605
Diamond St 19607
Diane Ave 19608
Diane Ln 19606
Dickinson Dr 19605
Doe Run 19607
Dogleg Dr 19606
Dogwood Dr 19609
Dogwood Ln 19607
Doral Dr 19607
Dorchester Ave 19609
Dorchester Dr 19610
Douglass St
100-299 19601
300-398 19610
301-599 19601
331-397 19610
399-806 19610
400-598 19601
600-699 19610
701-799 19610
800-1299 19604
808-898 19610
925-925-925-927 19604
W Douglass St 19601
Dover Ct 19606
Downing Dr 19610
Downing St 19605
Dr Ln 19610
Dries Rd 19605
Drumheller Dr 19606
Duffield Ln 19608
Duke St 19605
Dumns Ct 19601
Dunham Dr 19606
Dunkle Dr 19605
Durham Dr 19610
Durwood Ct & Dr 19609
Duryea Ave 19605
Dutch Ct 19608
N & S Dwight St 19609
Eagle Ct 19605
Eagle Ln
1-5 19606
7-7 19606
19-51 19607
Eagles Ln 19608
Earl St 19605
Earl Gables Ct 19606
East Ave 19606
Eastwick Dr 19606
Eberly St 19611
Ebersole Rd 19605
Eckert Ave 19602
Ecks Ct 19601
Eddystone Ct 19605
Eden Ct 19610
Edgedale Ct 19610
Edgewood Dr 19606
Edinboro Ln 19605
Edison Ct & Dr 19605
Egle Rd 19601
Eisenbrown Rd 19605
Eisenbrown St
400-599 19605
600-699 19601
Eisenhauer Dr 19604
Eisenhower Ave 19605
Eisenhower Ct 19609
Elaria Dr 19608
Elder St 19604
Elderberry Dr 19606
Eli Ct 19607
Elizabeth Ave 19605
Elizabeth Dr 19608
Elk Ct 19606
Elk Ln 19607
Elkins Ave 19607
Elkton St 19605
Ellen Ave 19609
Ellery St 19611
Elliot Dr 19606
Ellsworth Dr 19608
Elm Ave 19605
Elm Pl 19609
Elm Rd 19605
Elm St
1-97 19606
99-100 19606
101-105 19606
102-108 19606
103-107 19601
109-151 19601
153-199 19601
200-264 19606
266-298 19606
300-700 19601
401-599 19611
702-836 19601
807-811 19605
812-812 19605
813-835 19601
814-835 19605
838-838 19605
840-998 19601
855-867 19605
901-999 19601
1000-1229 19604
1231-1235 19604
152-154-152-154 19601
539-39-539-41 19601
542-542-542-544 19601
E Elm St 19607
W Elm St
1-99 19607
100-129 19601
130-130 19607
131-131 19601
132-399 19607
Elmer Cir 19605
Elmwood Ave 19609
Elsie St 19607
Elwyn Ave 19608
Emerald Ave 19606
Emerald Ln 19610
Emerrenc Ave 19609
Emerson Ave
400-800 19605
802-898 19605
2600-2699 19608
Emily Ct 19606
W End Ave 19605
Endlich Ave 19606
Eric Ave 19607
Erie Ave 19601
Erie Dr 19608
Ernst Rd 19601
Estates Dr 19606
Esther Cir 19608
Ethan Dr 19610
Evans Ave
1-23 19610
26-26 19608
28-100 19608
101-103 19610
102-104 19608
105-106 19610
107-199 19608
108-698 19610
201-299 19601
401-499 19610
Evans Hill Rd 19608
Evergreen Ct 19610
Evergreen Dr 19610
Evergreen Hls 19608
Evergreen Rd 19611
Executive Cir 19606
Exeter Rd 19606
Exeter St
100-299 19601
900-1100 19604
1102-1198 19604
Fabers Rd 19606
Fairfield St 19605
Fairgrounds Way 19605
Fairlane Rd 19606
Fairmont Ave 19605
Fairmount Ave 19606
Fairview Ave
1001-1097 19610
1099-1100 19610
1102-1198 19610
1900-2699 19606
Fairview Dr 19605
Fairview Rd 19606
Fairview St
2-198 19605
200-599 19605
1300-1499 19602
1500-1809 19606
1811-1899 19606
2100-2499 19609
Fairway Dr 19606
Fairway Dr N 19606
Fairway Dr S 19606
Fairway Rd
1A-1F 19607
2A-2F 19607
3A-3F 19607
4A-4F 19607
5A-5F 19607
6A-6F 19607
7A-7F 19607
8A-8F 19607
9A-9F 19607
10A-10F 19607
11A-11F 19607
12A-12F 19607
13A-13F 19607
14A-14F 19607
15A-15F 19607
16A-16F 19607
30-50 19607
N Fairwood Ave 19608
Faller Ln 19605
Fallowfield Cir 19607
Farming Ridge Blvd 19606
Farr Pl 19611
Farr Rd
1300-1400 19611
1402-1498 19611
1500-1799 19610
Faust Rd 19608
Fawn Dr 19607
Fayette Ave 19607
Fayne St 19607
Fehrs Ct 19602
Felix Ct 19605
Fern Ave
100-699 19611
801-897 19607
899-1499 19607
1501-1599 19607
Fernleigh Pl 19606
Fernwood St 19604
Fidelity St 19604
Field St 19606
Fieldstone Rd 19608
Filbert Ave 19606
Filmore Ave 19609
Firethorn Ln 19608
Fischer Ln 19601
Fisher Rd 19601
Fishers Ct 19601
Fishers Ln 19606
Fix Ln 19607
Flanders Ln 19607
Flint Ridge Dr 19607
Florence St 19605
Floret Ave 19605
Florida Ave 19605
Florin Ave 19605
Flower Ln 19610
Forest Ave 19610
Forest Ct 19606
Forest Hill Cir 19606
Forrest Dr 19608
Forrest St
1600-1698 19602
1800-1899 19606
Forrest Lawn Ct 19606
Foster Ln 19605
Fountain Ave 19606
Fox Ct 19607
Fox Run 19606
Fox Glen Dr 19608
Fox Glove Ln 19606
Foxfield Ln 19608
Franklin Pl 19610
Franklin St
1-141 19607
101-151 19611
143-199 19607
150-198 19602
153-743 19611
201-399 19602
220-224 19611
230-238 19607
234-1298 19602
401-499 19611
501-615 19602
619-663 19611
701-1299 19602
745-799 19611
800-898 19610
900-944 19610
946-998 19610
1005-01-1005-03 19602
Fraver Dr 19605
Frederick St
400-699 19608
700-798 19607
Fredrick Blvd 19605
Freemansville Rd 19607
Fremont Ave & St 19605
Frey Rd 19606
Friedensburg Rd 19606
Fritz Ave 19607
Fritztown Rd 19608
N Front St 19601
S Front St 19602
Frontier Ave 19601
Frush Valley Rd 19605
Fulton St 19605
Funston Ave 19607
Gaelsong Ln 19610
Gage Ave 19610
Gail Cir 19610
Ganster St 19606
Garden Ln
1300-1399 19611
1400-1499 19610
2400-2499 19609
Garfield Ave
3209A-3209F 19605
Gass Ave 19605
Gateway Dr 19601
Gatskill St 19606
Gauby Rd 19606
Gaul Rd 19608
Gelsinger Rd 19608
Gene Ln 19607
George Ave 19610
George St
90-98 19605
100-501 19605
502-504 19606
503-599 19605
550-598 19605
600-698 19606
801-899 19601

Street	ZIP
Georgetown Dr	19605
Georgia Ave	19605
Gerald Ave	19607
Gerard Ave	19608
Gerhart Ln	19606
Gernant Ave	19608
Gerry St	19611
Gibraltar Rd	19606
Gilson Aly	19602
Ginger Ln	19606
Girard Ave	
1-300	19605
302-398	19605
1200-1599	19610
1901-1997	19609
1999-2799	19609
Gisella Dr	19608
Gladwyn Dr	19606
Glen Rd	19606
Glen Hollow Ct	19607
Glen Oley Dr	19606
Glenbrook Dr	19607
Glenfield Ct	19609
Glenn Ter	19606
Glenside Dr	19605
Glenwood Ct	19608
Goddard Ave	19608
Gold Ct & St	19607
Goldfinch Dr	19610
Golf Rd	19601
Golfview Ln	19606
Good St	19602
Goose Ln	19608
Gordon St	19601
Gosling Ct	19606
Gouglersville Rd	19608
Governor Dr	19607
Grace St	19611
Granary Rd	19608
Grand Blvd	19609
Grande Blvd	19608
Grande Valley Rd	19606
Grandell Ave	19605
Grandview Ave	19606
Grandview Blvd	
1-2999	19609
3000-3199	19608
Grandview Dr	19607
Granite Point Dr	19610
Grant Ave	19605
Grant St	19606
Granville Ave	19607
Grape St	
1-99	19611
100-198	19602
200-299	19602
500-598	19611
Gravel Hill Rd	19608
Gray St	19605
Great Bend Way	19608
Grecian Ter	19608
Green Ln	19601
Green Rd	19606
Green St	
801-825	19601
827-899	19601
900-1399	19604
1401-1499	19604
W Green St	19601
Green Ter	19601
Green House Ct	19605
Green Tree Rd	19606
Green Valley Rd	19608
Greenbriar Ct & Rd	19610
Greenview Ave	19601
Greenway Ter	19607
Greenwich St	
101-121	19601
123-530	19601
301-599	19610
532-604	19601
601-603	19610
605-609	19610
611-799	19610
628-798	19601
800-899	19601
900-1300	19604
1302-1398	19604
W Greenwich St	19601
Greenwood Mall	19610
Gregg Ave	
200-699	19611
901-1097	19607
1099-1699	19607
Gregg St	19607
Gretchen Dr	19607
E Grill Ave	19607
Gring Dr	
1900-2299	19610
2300-2399	19609
Grings Hill Rd	19608
Grizzly Rd	19608
Grouse Way	19606
Grouse Point Cir	19607
Grove St	19605
Grube Ln	19605
Guilford Ct	19606
Gulf Stream Dr	19607
Gunpowder Ln	19606
Haag Rd	19606
Haak St	19602
Hafer Rd	19606
Haig Blvd	19607
Hain Ave	19605
Hain Rd	19608
Hale Ct	19610
Hall Ave	19606
Halsey Ave	19609
Hamilton Pl	19610
Hampden Blvd	19604
Hampshire Ave	19606
Hampshire Rd	19608
S Hampton Dr	19610
Hampton Ln	19608
Hancock Blvd	
1-99	19607
101-197	19611
199-499	19611
501-599	19611
1400-1899	19607
Hanley Ln	19607
Hanley Pl	19611
Hannibal Ln	19605
Harbor Dr	19608
Harding Ave	19607
Harman Rd	19606
Harrison Ave	19605
Harry Ave	19607
Hartline Dr	19606
Hartman Rd	
1-199	19606
200-202	19605
201-203	19606
207-209	19605
220-1099	19606
Harvard Blvd	19609
Harvest Ln	19606
Harvey Ave	19606
Harwood Ln	19608
Hawthorn Ln	19606
Hawthorne Ave	19605
Hawthorne Ct	19610
Hawthorne Ct N	19610
Hawthorne Rd	19609
Hawthorne St	19611
Hayden Cir	19606
Hazel St	19611
Heaniant Rd	19606
Hearthstone Ct	19606
Hearthstone Dr	19606
Hearthstone Ln	19608
Heath Ave	19605
Heather Ct	19606
Heather Dr	19608
Heather Hts	19606
Heather Ln	
1-99	19601
100-202	19610
Heathrow Ct	19606
Heckmans Ct	19604
Hedgerow Ln	19606
Heffner Dr	19608
Heffner Ln	
9-99	19606
1000-1100	19605
1102-1198	19605
Heidelberg Ave	19606
Heine St	19606
Heister Blvd	19609
Helen Ln	19605
Helm Ln	19605
Hemlock Rd	19607
Hendel St	19607
Henley Pl	19606
Henry Cir	19608
Herington Dr	19608
Heritage Dr	19607
Heron Dr	19606
Hessian Blvd	19607
Hessian Rd	19602
Hettinger Rd	19609
Hickory Ln	
101-168	19610
1000-1199	19606
Hickory St	19604
Hidden Brook Way	19608
Hidden Pond Dr	19607
Hideaway Ct	19606
Hiesters Ln	19605
High Blvd	19607
E High Blvd	19607
High Rd	19610
High St	
1-100	19606
102-498	19606
2200-2298	19605
2300-2499	19605
S High St	19606
Highland Ave	19606
Highland St	
200-299	19611
2000-2599	19609
Highwood Ave	19607
Hilbert Ct	19606
Hilgert Ave	19607
Hill Ave	
300-398	19606
400-499	19606
501-599	19606
800-1099	19610
Hill Cir	19607
Hill Rd	
1200-1398	19602
1400-2099	19602
2300-2699	19606
Hill Terrace Dr	19608
Hilldale Ct	19605
Hilldale Rd	19606
Hillock Ln	19606
Hillpoint Cir	19608
Hillside Dr	19607
Hillside Rd	
1-99	19609
4300-4800	19606
4802-4898	19606
Hilltop Ave & Dr	19605
Hillvale Ave	19609
Hinnershitz Ct	19601
Hobart Ave	19610
Hoffer Ave	19605
Hoffmans Ct	19604
Holland Sq	
700-799	19611
800-899	19610
Holland St	19607
Hollenbach St	19601
Holly Dr	
44-1-44-10	19606
45-1-45-8	19606
46-1-46-8	19606
47-1-47-8	19606
48-1-48-8	19606
49-1-49-8	19606
50-1-50-8	19606
51-1-51-6	19606
52-1-52-8	19606
53-1-53-8	19606
54-1-54-8	19606
55-1-55-8	19606
56-1-56-8	19606
70-1-70-8	19606
71-1-71-8	19606
74-1-74-6	19606
Holly Rd	19602
Hollywood Ave, Ct & Dr	19606
Holtry St	19605
Hope Way	19607
Horseshoe Dr	19608
Horseshoe Ln	19607
Hoskins Pl	19602
Howard Blvd	19606
Howard Pl	19601
Howard St	19609
Hudson St	19601
Hughes Ln	19601
N & S Hull St	19608
W Huller Ln	19605
Hummingbird Rd	19610
Hunters Run Blvd	19606
Huron Blvd & Dr	19608
Huyett Dr	19608
Huyett St	19606
Hyde Park Ave	19605
Illinois Ave	19608
Imperial Dr	19607
Independence Ct & Dr	19609
Indiana Ave	19608
Inspiration Blvd	19607
Intervilla Ave	19609
Iron Cir	19607
Ironstone Dr	19606
Ironstone Ln	19608
Iroquois Ave	
3218A-3218H	19608
Ithaca St	19605
Ivy Ct	19610
Ivy Ln	19610
Ivy Rd	19610
Ivy St	19611
Ivy Hill Cir	19606
Jackson Ave	19606
Jackson St	19607
Jacksonwald Ave	19606
Jacob Dr	19608
James Ave	19606
James St	19608
James Way	19605
Jameson Pl	19601
Jana Ct	19607
Jay Ln	19609
Jefferson Ave	19609
Jefferson Blvd	19609
Jefferson Dr	19606
Jefferson St	
2-98	19605
100-112	19605
108-114	19601
114-131	19605
116-118	19601
120-124	19601
133-199	19605
200-600	19605
602-698	19605
Jeffrey Rd	19601
Jennifer Ct	19608
Jerome Pl	19609
Joan Ter	19611
John St	19607
John Glenn Ave	19607
John Henry Dr	19608
Johnson Ln	19605
Johnson St	19601
Johnston St	19608
Josephs Way	19607
Joshua Dr	19608
Junco Dr	19610
Juniata St	19611
Juniper Dr	19605
Kachel Blvd	19607
Kantner Ln N & S	19607
Kate Dr	19608
Katharine Dr	19608
Kathleen Ln	19610
Kathryn St	19601
Katylyn Ln	19605
Kay Ct	19609
Keats Dr	19608
Keener Rd	19608
Keiser Blvd	19610
Keller Ave	19608
Kelly Ct	19610
Kelly Ln	19606
Kendall Ct	19608
Kendall Dr	19606
Kenhorst Blvd	
400-999	19611
1300-1699	19607
N Kenhorst Blvd	19607
S Kenhorst Blvd	19607
Kenhorst Plz	19607
Kenny Dr	19608
Kenny St	19602
Kent Ave	19605
E Kent Rd	19605
W Kent Rd	19605
Kent Way	19611
Kentucky Ave	
301-324	19608
310-310	19605
Keppel Ave	19609
Kerr Rd	19606
Kerrick Rd	19607
Kevin Ct	19610
Keystone Rd	19606
Kickapoo Dr	19608
Killian Ave	19606
Kinder Dr	19605
King St	19605
Kings Blvd	19607
Kings Way	19606
Kingston Dr	19608
Kirkwood Ave	19608
Kissinger Ln	19610
Klapperthal Rd	19606
Klein Ave	19602
Kline Ave	19606
Kline St	19611
Knipe Ln	19607
Knoll Way	19608
Knollwood Dr	19608
Knollwood Ln	19606
Koch Rd	19605
Kocher Rd	19608
Kramer Ave & Ln	19606
Krick Ave & Ln	19608
Kutz Ct	19609
Kutztown Rd	
1700-1999	19604
2000-3633	19605
3635-3899	19605
Lackawanna St	19601
Lacrosse Ave	19607
Ladderback Ln	19606
Lady Diana Dr	19605
Lafayette Ave	19610
Lafayette St	19605
Lahall Ave & Ct	19605
Lahoma Ln	19601
Laird St	19609
Lake Ave	
100-598	19610
600-699	19610
701-799	19610
3600-3799	19606
Lake St	19606
Lakeview Ct	19608
Lakeview Dr	
10-16	19605
18-99	19605
800-898	19607
Lancaster Ave	
100-699	19611
700-1799	19607
E Lancaster Ave	19607
W Lancaster Ave	19607
Lancaster Pike	
2200-2500	19607
2502-2698	19607
3001-3497	19608
3499-4099	19608
Lancaster Pike W	19607
Lance Pl & Rd	19604
Landover Dr	19605
Landruhe Ln	19607
Langley Rd	19601
Lantana Ave	19605
Larchwood Rd	19610
Lark Ln	19608
Lasalle Dr	19609
Lash St	19607
Lauer Ct	19601
Lauers Ln	19610
Laura Ct	19608
Laurel Ave	19606
Laurel Ct	
101-154	19610
3505-3507	19605
Laurel Ln	
2-98	19607
2100-2199	19606
Laurel Rd	19609
Laurel St	
400-800	19602
802-898	19602
3400-3499	19605
3501-3503	19605
E Laurel St	19602
Laurel Run Ave	19605
Laurel Springs Ln	19606
Laurel Woods Dr	19607
Laurelee Ave	19605
Lavender Ln	19610
Lavern Ct	19607
W Lawn Ave	19609
Lawn Ter	19605
Lawndale Rd	19610
Lawrence Ave	19609
Leanne St	19605
Lee Ave	19607
Leesport Ave	19605
Legacy Blvd	19608
Lehigh Ave	19610
Lehigh St	19601
Leisczs Bridge Rd	19605
Leisure Ct	19610
Leiszs Bridge Rd	19605
Leland Ave	19609
Leland Way	19610
Lemon St	19602
Lenore Ct & Pl	19609
Lenox Ave	19606
Leonard Ln	19608
Leroy Ln	19608
Lester Ave	19607
Levan St	19606
Lewis Rd	19606
Lexington Dr	19610
Liberty Ave & St	19607
Liggett Ave	
900-1200	19611
1202-1298	19611
1300-1899	19607
Lilac Ln	
700-899	19606
1100-1299	19609
Limekiln Rd	19606
Limestone Dr	19606
Lincoln Ave	
100-199	19605
1100-1999	19610
2100-2499	19609
Lincoln Ct	
1600-1619	19605
2000-2099	19610
Lincoln Dr	
1-299	19606
501-597	19608
599-699	19608
701-799	19608
Lincoln Rd	19606
Lincoln St	19601
Linda Ln	
200-299	19606
2900-3199	19608
Lindale Dr	19609
Linden Ave	19605
Linden Ln	19611
Linden St	19604
Linkside Ct	19606
Linree Ave	19606
Lisa Ln	19606
Lisa Rd	19608
List Rd	19606
Little St	19605
Little Cherry St	19602
Little Clinton St	19601
Little Grape St	19602
Little Maple St	19601
Little Rock Rd	19605
Little Wunder St	19602
Littlefield Ave	19606
Lobelia Ave	19605
Loblolly Ln	19607
Lockheed Ave	19601
Locust St	19604
Logan Ave	
1-100	19609
101-103	19610
102-104	19609
105-206	19610
207-207	19609
208-398	19610
209-299	19610
301-399	19609
Logan St	19607
Lombard St	19604
Longview Dr	19608
Looking Glass Ln	19607
E Lorane Rd	19606
Lori Ct	19606
Lorraine Rd	19604
N & S Los Robles Ct	19606
Lost Ln	19607
Lost Tree Dr	19607
Love Rd	19607
Lowell Dr	19606
Lowrie St	19605
Lucinda Ln	19610
Lutz Dr	
2-98	19608
300-399	19606
Luzerne St	19601
Lyncrest Ave	19607
Lynn Ave & Ct	19606
Lynne Ave	19610
Lynoak Ave	19607
Macarthur Rd	19605
Maci Way	19606
Maderalm Ave	19607
Maderma St	19611
Madison Ave	
1-103	19605
105-199	19605
118-120	19601
122-198	19605
200-307	19605
202-310	19605
308-398	19601
309-599	19605
400-598	19605
600-1099	19601
Madison Dr	19606
Madison St	19607
Magnolia Ave	19605
Mail Route Rd	19608
Majestic Ln	19608
Mallard Dr	19606
Mansion Dr	19607
Maple Ave	
1-299	19607
3000-3099	19605
Maple Ct	19606
Maple Ln	19605
Maple St	19602
March St	19607
Marcor Dr	19608
Margaret Dr	19609
Margaret Ln	19605
Margaret St	
2-98	19605
500-951	19611
953-999	19611

1200-1499 19605
Maria Ave 19608
Marie Dr 19608
Marina Ln 19605
Marion St
501-599 19601
900-1299 19604
1301-1399 19604
3000-3499 19605
Marks Rd 19608
Marshall Ave
1-99 19606
100-199 19609
500-599 19606
Marshall Dr 19607
Martin Ave 19601
Martins Rd 19608
Marvin Dr 19608
Mashance Rd 19608
Master St 19602
Matthew Dr 19608
Matz Dr 19607
Mayapple Ln 19606
Mayberry Ave 19605
Mayer St 19606
Mayfair Rd 19610
Mayo Dr 19601
Mays Ave 19606
Maywood Ave 19608
Mcadoo Ave 19607
Mcarthur Ave 19607
Mcclellan St 19611
Mcilvain St 19602
Mckently St 19605
Mckinley Ave
100-198 19605
200-399 19605
2200-2530 19609
2532-2998 19609
Mcknight St 19601
Mcknights Gap Rd 19604
Meade St
901-997 19611
999-1299 19611
1300-1799 19607
Meade Ter 19607
Meadow Ct 19608
Meadow Dr 19605
Meadow Gln 19610
Meadow Ln
501-597 19605
599-699 19605
1900-1999 19610
7500-7599 19606
Meadow Glen Ln 19607
Meadow View Dr 19605
Meadowlark Rd
100-199 19606
1500-1799 19610
Medinah Dr 19607
Mediterranean Ave 19608
Mellowbrook Dr 19608
Melon Ln 19606
N Melrose Ave 19606
Mercer St 19601
N Meridian Blvd 19610
Merion Dr 19608
Merion Ln 19607
Merritt Pkwy
2500-2799 19609
2800-3199 19608
Merrybells Ave & Ct 19605
Merrymount Rd 19609
Mesa Dr 19608
Michael Dr 19608
Michele Ct & Dr 19606
Michigan Dr 19608
Midland Ave 19606
Mifflin Blvd 19607
Milford Ave 19607
Miller Dr 19608
Miller Rd 19608
Miller St 19602
N Miller St 19607
S Miller St 19607
Millers Ct 19601

Miltimore St 19601
Milton St 19604
Mimosa Ln 19606
Mineral Spring Rd 19602
Minor St 19602
Mint Tier Ct 19606
Misty Ln
1-99 19608
100-115 19606
100-110 19608
117-199 19606
Mitchell Ave 19605
Mitti Rd 19607
Mohawk Dr 19608
Mohegan Dr 19608
Mohns Hill Rd 19608
Moll Ave 19605
Molly Cir 19608
Monerall St 19602
Monroe Ave
1200-1499 19610
2101-2197 19609
2199-2399 19609
Monroe St
1-199 19605
1301-1397 19601
1399-1499 19601
Montclair Ave 19605
Montello Rd 19608
Montgomery Ave 19606
Montgomery St 19601
Montieth Ave 19609
Montrose Ave 19605
Montrose Blvd 19607
Montrose St 19605
Moonflower Ave 19606
Morgan Dr 19608
Morgantown Rd
2-98 19611
100-600 19611
602-698 19611
801-897 19607
899-2699 19607
Morris Pl 19607
Morrison Rd 19601
N & S Morwood Ave 19609
Moss St
1-299 19601
300-1699 19604
1701-1799 19604
Mount Penn Rd 19607
Mount Pine Ter 19606
Mountain Ct 19606
S Mountain Dr 19608
Mountain Home Rd 19608
Mountain Top Rd 19606
Mountain View Rd 19607
Moyer Ave & Rd 19606
Moyers Ln 19605
Muhlenberg St
400-599 19605
800-1499 19602
1501-1597 19606
1599-1799 19606
Muirfield Dr 19607
Mulberry St
1-199 19601
200-1699 19604
Mull Ave 19608
Mulligan Dr 19606
Muncy Ave 19607
Museum Rd
1-199 19605
2-298 19607
400-1399 19611
1400-1499 19610
1501-2011 19610
S Museum Rd 19607
Musket Ln 19607
Myrtle Ave
1-199 19606
1600-2099 19605
Nancy Cir 19606
Nantucket Dr 19605
Nash Rd 19608
Nassau Cir & Ct 19607
Netherwood Dr 19605

Neversink Aly 19602
E Neversink Rd 19606
W Neversink Rd 19606
Neversink St
2-198 19602
900-999 19606
Neversink Mountain
Rd 19606
New Castle Dr 19607
New Holland Ave &
Rd 19607
New York Ave 19608
Newkirk Ave 19607
Newlin Way 19607
Newport Ave 19611
Newport Way 19608
Nicol Dr 19606
Nicole Way 19608
Nicolls St 19604
Noble St
100-399 19611
2000-2599 19609
3100-3299 19605
3301-3499 19605
N Noble St 19611
S Noble St 19611
Nolan St 19605
Norman St 19609
Norona Ln 19607
North Ct 19601
Northfield Rd 19609
Northmont Blvd 19605
Norton Ave 19607
Nottingham Ct 19601
Oak Ave 19605
Oak Cir 19606
Oak Dr 19608
Oak Ln
100-499 19606
900-999 19610
1200-1400 19604
1402-1898 19604
Oak Pkwy 19606
Oak St
2-98 19606
3100-3799 19605
Oak Ter
200-299 19606
300-499 19611
Oak Grove Rd 19601
Oak Hill Ln 19610
Oakmont Ct 19607
Oberlin Ave 19608
Obold St 19611
Ochre St 19606
Octagon Ave 19608
Oesterling Dr 19605
Okmed Dr 19606
Old Bernville Rd 19605
Old Friedensburg Rd 19606
Old Fritztown Rd
1-600 19607
602-698 19607
700-704 19608
706-1499 19608
1501-1599 19608
Old Lancaster Pike
101-197 19607
199-600 19607
602-820 19607
900-2100 19608
2102-3798 19608
Old Lauers Ln 19610
Old Mill Ln & Rd 19610
Old Spies Church Rd 19606
Old Spring Valley Rd 19604
Old State Rd 19606
Old Wernersville Rd 19608
Old Wyomissing Rd
401-497 19611
499-1299 19611
1400-1999 19610
Oley St
100-399 19601
400-428 19610
401-497 19610
401-599 19601

430-598 19601
499-541 19610
543-545 19610
600-719 19610
721-799 19610
730-798 19604
800-1300 19604
1302-1398 19604
W Oley St 19601
Oley Turnpike Rd 19606
Olive St
100-299 19611
1600-1999 19604
Olympic Dr 19607
Oneida Dr 19608
Ontario Dr 19608
Ontelaunee Dr 19605
Opal Ave 19606
Open Hearth Dr 19607
Orange St 19602
Orchard Ct 19606
Orchard Ln 19606
Orchard Pl
100-199 19607
3300-3399 19605
5101-5199 19606
Orchard Rd
100-199 19605
201-299 19605
1200-1399 19611
1400-1499 19610
Orchard St 19606
Orchard View Rd 19606
Oriole Dr 19610
Oriole Ln 19606
Orton Ave 19611
Ossington Ave 19609
Oswego Ln 19605
Overhill Rd 19609
Overland Ave 19608
Overlook Dr 19606
Overview Ct 19607
Owls Nest Dr 19606
Oxford Ave 19609
Pacific Ave 19608
Painted Sky Rd 19606
Palm St 19604
Palmer Ave 19610
Palms Ct 19604
Pansy St 19611
Paper Mill Rd 19608
Papermill Rd 19610
Par Dr 19607
Park Ave
1-7 19605
2-48 19611
50-50 19608
52-100 19608
100-104 19611
100-198 19605
101-107 19607
101-199 19605
102-104 19608
105-185 19608
106-222 19611
109-134 19607
136-198 19607
200-212 19607
201-215 19608
214-218 19607
217-219 19607
220-222 19608
224-300 19608
302-398 19611
400-699 19611
701-799 19611
900-998 19607
Park Ln 19606
Park Pl
1-99 19609
1400-1404 19605
1406-1499 19605
2900-2999 19609
Park Plz 19610
Park Rd
1-99 19609
1100-1198 19605

1200-1299 19605
E Park Rd 19609
N Park Rd 19610
S Park Rd 19610
Park St 19606
Park Place Dr 19608
Parkside Ave 19607
Parkside Dr N 19610
Parkside Dr S
800-1299 19611
1300-1798 19610
Parkview Ave 19606
Parkview Dr 19610
Parkview Pl 19610
Parkview Rd
200-499 19606
500-898 19611
501-599 19606
900-999 19611
3600-3698 19606
Parkway Dr 19605
Parliament Dr 19610
Partridge Dr 19606
Patriot Pkwy 19605
Patton Ave 19611
Patton St 19606
Paul St 19607
Pauls Pl 19605
Peach Ln 19606
Peach St 19602
Peach Tree Ln 19608
Peachwood Dr 19608
Pear Ln 19606
Pear St 19601
Pearl St
1-99 19607
100-110 19602
111-199 19607
112-598 19602
201-599 19602
Pembroke Dr 19607
Pendergast Rd 19608
Penn Ave
158-296 19611
200-498 19611
298-451 19611
453-699 19611
500-799 19611
800-998 19610
927-1017 19610
1019-1700 19610
1701-1897 19609
1702-1798 19610
1899-3399 19609
3400-5000 19608
5002-5098 19608
Penn St
200-1098 19602
201-1099 19601
Penn Ter 19606
Penn Mawr Ct 19606
Penndale Ave 19606
Penns Ct & Dr 19606
Pennsylvania Ave
1-7 19607
9-403 19607
10-14 19605
16-24 19605
47-97 19606
99-221 19606
100-112 19608
114-124 19608
222-224 19607
223-285 19606
226-492 19606
301-313 19607
325-491 19606
405-409 19607
405-427 19605
500-599 19605
Pennwyn Pl 19607
Pennwyn Ter 19606
Pepper Ridge Dr 19606
Pequot Dr 19608
Perkasie Ave 19609
Perkiomen Ave
1100-1198 19602

1200-1799 19602
1800-6199 19606
5432-34-5432-38 19606
Perry St
500-599 19601
900-1499 19604
1501-1699 19604
Pershing Blvd
1-699 19607
1000-1299 19611
1300-1469 19607
1471-1499 19607
Persimmon Dr
1800-1899 19608
4900-5099 19606
Peters Rd 19601
Peters Way 19610
Petsch Rd 19606
Pheasant Rd 19607
Pheasant Run 19606
Pheasant Run N 19606
Philadelphia Ave 19607
Philmay Ter 19606
Phoebe Dr 19610
Pickwick Pl 19606
Pike St
500-599 19601
900-1415 19604
1417-1599 19604
Pillar Dr 19605
Pine Ave 19606
Pine St
1-199 19607
300-340 19602
341-353 19611
342-354 19602
355-400 19611
401-435 19611
402-406 19611
408-424 19602
426-699 19602
421 1/2-423 1/2 19602
Pine Cone Ln 19608
Pine Heights Rd 19605
Pine Hill Dr 19608
Pine Ridge Ln 19607
Pine Tree Ct 19607
Pine Tree Ln 19610
Pine Woods Ct 19607
Pinehurst Ct 19607
Pinewood Rd 19610
Playground Dr 19611
Plaza Dr 19605
Pleasant Run Dr 19607
Plestin St 19601
Plum Ct 19605
Plum St 19602
Plymouth Cir, Ct & Pl 19610
Poinciana Ave 19605
Pomander Ave 19606
Poplar Dr 19606
Poplar St 19601
Portland Ave 19609
Possum Ln 19606
Post Pl 19606
Potter Ln 19607
Pottsville Pike 19605
Prestwick Dr 19606
Primrose Ln
2-99 19608
100-148 19610
100-199 19608
Prince St 19605
Princeton Ave 19609
Printz St 19606
Prospect Ave 19611
Prospect Dr 19608
Prospect St 19606
N Prospect St 19606
W Prospect St 19606
Province Rd 19610
Ptarmigan Dr 19606
Puffin Dr 19606
Quail Hollow Dr 19606
Quail Ridge Dr 19607
Quarry Dr 19609
Quarry Rd 19605

Queen St
1-99 19608
1500-1599 19605
Queens Ct 19606
Quentin Ave 19607
Quince Dr 19606
Quincy Ct 19605
Rabbit Ln 19606
Radcliffe Ave 19609
Rainbow Ave 19605
Ralph Ave 19608
Ramsey Blvd 19607
Rand Dr 19606
Randee Ln 19607
Ranor Ct 19606
Ravens Ct 19606
Ravine Dr 19607
Ray Rd 19608
Raymond Ave & St 19605
Reading Ave
1-10 19607
11-21 19610
12-22 19607
23-26 19610
28-98 19610
100-230 19607
200-226 19611
228-299 19611
300-319 19611
320-399 19607
400-799 19611
1900-2399 19609
Reading Blvd
2-6 19610
8-1861 19610
1863-1899 19610
1892-1898 19609
1900-2799 19609
Reading Crest Ave 19605
Rebecca Dr 19608
Rebers Bridge Rd 19608
Red Bridge Rd 19605
Red Oak Rd 19605
Redwood Ave 19610
Redwood Dr 19606
Reed Ave 19610
Reed St 19601
Reedy Rd
101-297 19608
299-2399 19608
2400-2500 19609
2502-2698 19609
2900-3399 19608
Regency Dr
2000-2099 19610
2900-3799 19608
Regency Rd 19608
Rehr St 19606
Reichart Ave 19605
Reiff Pl 19606
Republic Ln 19601
Reservoir Rd
1-99 19606
1701-1897 19604
1899-2099 19604
Resh Ave 19610
Revere Blvd
1-299 19609
300-400 19608
402-698 19608
Rhodora Ave 19605
Richard Pl 19606
Richmond St
401-599 19605
1301-1347 19604
1349-1399 19604
Rick Rd
1-99 19607
1000-1099 19605
1101-1199 19605
Rickenbach Rd 19605
Ridge Ave & St 19607
Ridgeway St 19605
Ridgewood Ave 19610
Ridgewood Rd
1900-2198 19610
2200-2299 19610

Street	ZIP
5000-5099	19608
Ridgewood St	19607
Riegel Ave	19609
Riegel Rd	19608
Rill Rd	19606
Rim View Ln	19607
Rimby Way	19606
Rittenhouse Dr	19606
Ritter St	19601
Ritters Rd	19606
Ritz Ave	19606
River Rd	
801-1099	19601
2000-2098	19605
2100-4114	19605
4116-4120	19605
River Crest Dr	19605
River Oak Dr	19601
Riverfront Dr	19602
Riverside Dr	19605
Rivervale Rd	19605
Riverview Ave & Dr	19605
Robert Rd	19610
Robeson St	
100-599	19601
900-1300	19604
1302-1398	19604
Robin Ln	19606
Robin Rd	19610
Rock Rd	19606
Rock Haven Ct	19606
Rockland St	19604
Rocky Rd	19609
Romig Ave	19606
Roosevelt Ave	
200-399	19605
1102-1198	19606
1200-1299	19606
2400-2499	19605
Rose Ct	19607
Rose Ln	19606
Rose St	19601
Rose Virginia Rd	
1400-1499	19611
1500-1599	19610
Rosebud St	19605
Rosedale Ave	19605
Rosemary Dr	19608
Rosemead Ave	19608
Rosemont Ave	
1-199	19607
1301-1399	19604
Rosemont Blvd	19604
Rosemont Ct	19610
Rosenthal St	19601
Rosewood Ave	19605
Rosewood Ct	19610
Rosewood Pl	19605
Rothermel Blvd & St	19605
Roxberry Dr	19608
Royal Ct	19607
Royena Ave	19605
Ruby Ln	19608
Rummels Ct	19601
Running Creek Dr	19608
Russell Dr	19607
Ruth St	19608
Ryan Ct	19606
Saddle Ct	19608
Sadowski Dr	19606
Sage Ave	19605
Sage Dr	19608
Sagebrook Dr	19606
Saint Albans Dr	
2501-2697	19609
2699-2799	19609
2800-3099	19608
Saint Andrews Cir	19607
Saint Bernardine St	19607
Saint George St	19606
Saint Gian Ct	19608
Saint James Pl	19608
Saint Lawrence Ave	19606
Saint Nicholas St	19607
Saint Stephens Church Ln	19607
Saint Vincent Ct	19605
Salem Rd	19610
Salina St	19605
N Sandy Ln	19608
S Sandy Ln	19608
Sandy Way	19607
Sanibel Ln	19610
Santa Maria Dr	19606
Sauls Ct	19601
Savini Dr	19605
Sawgrass Dr	19606
Scarlet Ln	19608
Scenic Dr	19607
Schiller St	19601
Schlegel Dr	19605
Schoffers Rd	19606
Schonour Ln	19608
School Ln	19606
Schultz Ct	19602
Schuylkill Ave	19601
Scindo Ct	19604
Scotland Dr	19606
Scott Ct	19609
Scott St	
900-1299	19611
1300-1468	19607
1470-1498	19607
Scotty Way	19607
Securda Rd	19607
Sedona Ln	19610
Seiberts Ct	19609
Seidel Rd & St	19606
Seitz Rd	19601
Sell Ave	19608
Seminary Ave & Ct	19605
Sesser Ln	19606
Seven Springs Dr	19607
Shady Hollow Ln	19607
Shakespeare Dr	19608
Shearers Rd	19608
Sheerlund Rd	19607
Sheffield Ct	19601
Sheidy Ave	19605
Shelbourne Rd	19606
Shelby Rd	19604
Shellbark Dr	19608
Shelly Dr	19608
Sheridan St	19611
Sherwood Dr	19606
Sherwood Rd	19610
Sherwood St	19607
Shillington Rd	19608
Shilo St	19605
W Shore Dr	19605
Showers Ln	19605
Silk Dr	19611
Silver Swallow Rd	19606
Simmons Rd	19606
Simon Dr	19608
Singer Rd	19610
Sioux Ct	19608
Skyline Dr	19606
Skyview Ln	19608
Slater Rd	19605
Sledge Ave	19609
Snyder Rd	
200-499	19605
500-600	19609
501-599	19605
602-602	19609
619-639	19605
641-699	19605
700-898	19609
900-1199	19609
Snyder St	19601
Sofianos Ln	19605
Solvay Dr	19605
South Ct	19601
South St	19602
Southwick Ave	19608
Spies Church Rd	19606
Spinacker Ln	19605
Spohn Rd	19608
Spook Ln	19606
Spring Ave	19606
Spring Ln	19610
Spring St	
100-604	19601
606-698	19601
609-635	19610
665-667	19601
700-706	19604
701-735	19608
708-798	19604
709-711	19610
717-799	19604
800-899	19610
900-998	19604
901-999	19610
1000-1040	19604
1042-1044	19604
1045-1047	19610
1049-1068	19610
1070-1098	19610
1100-1165	19604
1166-1168	19610
1167-1299	19604
1200-1298	19604
2000-2499	19609
W Spring St	19601
Spring Crest Blvd	19608
Spring Garden St	19602
Spring Meadow Ln	19606
Spring Ridge Dr	19610
Spring Valley Rd	
1-97	19605
99-499	19605
500-598	19604
Springhouse Rd	19608
Springmont Dr	19610
Springside Dr E	19607
Spruce Ln	19610
Spruce St	
1-107	19607
6-6	19611
20-200	19607
109-111	19602
181-199	19607
201-217	19611
219-222	19611
224-398	19611
301-397	19611
301-397	19602
399-549	19611
399-446	19602
447-499	19611
448-1498	19602
501-699	19602
551-605	19611
701-899	19611
901-1499	19602
Spuhler Dr	19606
Squire Ct	19610
St Lucia Ct	19608
Stacey Dr	19605
Stanford Ave	19609
Starr Rd	19608
State St	19607
State Hill Rd	
1-15	19610
17-3122	19610
3124-3198	19610
3131-3197	19608
3199-3599	19608
3601-3699	19608
States Ave	19608
Steely Rd	19608
Steeple Chase Dr	19606
Steevers Ct	19607
Steiner Pl	19605
Stephanie Cir	19608
Stephen Rd	19601
N & S Sterley St	19607
Sterling Ave	19606
Steuben Rd	19602
Stevens Ave	
1-99	19609
200-399	19608
Stewart Ave	19608
Stingray Dr	19608
Stinson Dr	19605
Stokesay Castle Ln	19606
Stone Manor Dr	19607
Stone Ridge Rd	19608
Stonehenge Dr	19606
Stoner Ave	19606
Stony Run Dr	19606
Stoudts Ferry Rd	19605
Stoudts Ferry Bridge Rd	19605
Stratford Cir	19608
Strawberry Run	19606
Strong Aly	19602
Sturbridge Ct	
100-199	19610
2800-2899	19608
Sturbridge Dr	19610
Suburban Rd	19605
Suellen Dr	19605
Sugarloaf Ln	19607
Summer Hill Dr	19608
Summit Ave	
1-95	19605
96-121	19607
101-197	19611
122-198	19611
123-499	19607
199-399	19611
200-527	19607
200-222	19606
224-224	19606
300-308	19607
400-400	19611
401-499	19611
402-430	19607
500-504	19611
506-552	19611
507-511	19607
515-699	19611
529-625	19607
600-606	19607
618-632	19611
S Summit Ave	19607
Summit St	19611
Summit Chase Dr	19611
Sunny Ridge Rd	19605
Sunnyside Ave	19610
Sunrise Rd	19606
Sunset Ct	
1-10	19606
10-98	19608
11-99	19608
Sunset Dr	
1201-1299	19605
3000-3098	19608
3301-3399	19608
Sunset Rd	
300-599	19611
1100-1198	19608
Sunshine Rd	19601
Susanna Dr	19608
Sutton Cir	19606
Swallowtail Ct	19607
Sweitzer Rd	19608
Sycamore Dr	19606
Sycamore Rd	19611
Sylvan Dr	19606
Sylvan Pl	19608
Taft Ave	
2-2	19606
4-203	19606
201-217	19605
205-299	19606
212-214	19605
228-298	19606
300-398	19605
Tamarack Trl	19607
Tanager Dr	19610
Tanglewood Dr	19607
Tarragon Ct	19606
Tasker Ave	19607
Taylor Ave	19607
Taylor Dr	19606
Tee Cir	19607
Telford Ave	19609
Temple Dr	19608
Templin Ln	19608
Tennessee Ave	19608
Tennyson Ave	19608
Terrace Ave	19610
Tewkesbury Dr	19610
E & W Thistle Dr	19610
Thomas Pl	19608
Thorn St	19601
Thornbury Rd	19606
Thrush Rd	19610
Thymebrook Dr	19606
Timber Ln	19608
Timberline Dr	19610
Tiny Ln	19605
Tioga Ave	19607
Tippet Ct	19607
Tomlisa Ct	19608
Tranquility Ln	19607
Trebor Pl	19610
Tremont Ave	19607
N & S Trent Ave & Pl	19610
Tritch Ln	19608
Trooper Rd	19602
Trout Ln	19607
Trout St	19606
Tube Dr	19605
Tuckerton Ct & Rd	19605
Tulip Ct	19607
Tully Ln	19601
Tulpehocken Ave	19611
Tulpehocken Rd	19610
N Tulpehocken Rd	19601
S Tulpehocken Rd	19601
Tulpehocken St	19601
Turning Leaf Way	19605
Tyler Dr	19605
Tyrone Ave	19607
Unami Dr	19608
Union St	19604
Upland Ave	
1-599	19611
600-999	19607
Upland Rd	19609
Upper Van Reed Rd	19605
Valley Ct	19608
Valley Dr	19606
Valley Rd	19610
Valley Greene Cir	19610
Valley Stream Rd	19607
Valley View Ln	19606
Valley View Trailer Park	19605
Valmont Ct	19610
Van Buren St	19606
Van Reed Rd	
500-803	19610
805-823	19610
808-816	19605
861-899	19605
900-999	19610
1000-1040	19605
1001-1009	19610
1042-1199	19605
1700-1799	19608
1800-1898	19610
1900-2099	19610
2100-2298	19609
2300-2899	19609
2900-2998	19608
3000-3099	19608
Van Steffy Ave	19610
Vanguard Dr	19606
Ventnor Ave	19605
Verdun Dr	19605
Vermont Ave & Rd	19608
Verna Dr	19609
Versailles Ct	19605
Vesper Ave	19606
Vesta Pl	19605
Vester Pl	19608
Victoria Dr	19605
Victoria Ln	19610
Victory Cir	19605
Village Dr	19610
Village Center Dr	19607
Vine St	
800-899	19605
1400-1499	19606
1500-1699	19605
Vinemont Rd	19608
Vireo Dr	19610
Virginia Ave	
1-99	19608
2-8	19606
10-19	19606
100-199	19606
200-299	19605
Vista Ln	19606
Vista Rd	19610
Volunteer Way	19607
N Wagner Cir	19608
S Wagner Cir	19608
Wagner Ln	19601
Wagner Rd	19608
Wallaric Ave	19605
Walnut Rd	19606
Walnut St	
1-25	19606
27-99	19606
100-1099	19601
101-105	19606
400-699	19611
1101-1499	19604
E Walnut St	19607
W Walnut St	19607
Walton Ct	19606
Wanner Rd	19606
Wanshop Rd	19606
Warren Rd	19604
Warren St	19601
Warwick Ct	19606
Warwick Dr	19610
Washington Ave	19609
Washington Dr	19606
Washington Rd	19605
Washington St	
101A-101E	19607
1-100	19607
101-147	19607
101-229	19601
102-230	19607
231-1099	19601
228-226-228-228	19601
Wassner Dr	19609
Water Rd	19608
Water St	
1-100	19605
102-198	19605
400-499	19607
Waterford Ln	19606
N & S Waverly St	19607
Wayne Ave	
700-799	19611
800-1099	19610
Wayne St	19601
Weaver Rd	19608
Wedge Ln	
1-5	19604
7-63	19604
64-99	19607
Wedgewood Ter	19601
Wegman Rd	19606
Weidman Ave	19608
Weimer St	19602
Weimoor Ct	19606
Weiser St	19601
Wellington Ave	19609
Wellington Blvd	19610
Wellington Ct	19606
Wellington Rd	19607
Welsh Rd	19607
Wendy Rd	19601
Wernersville Rd	19608
Wesleyan Dr	19607
W Wesner Rd	19605
Wessex Ct	19606
Westbury Dr	19610
Westview Dr	
2600-2698	19610
3100-3299	19605
Westwood Rd	19610
Wexham Dr	19607
Wheatfield Rd	19608
Wheatland Ave	19607
White Oak Dr	19608
Whitehouse Rd	19602
Whitepine Gulch	19607
Whitetail Ln	
1-13	19607
1-99	19606
Whitfield Blvd & Ct	19609
Whitford Dr	19605
Whitner Rd	19605
Whitney Ave	19605
Whittier Ave	19608
Whitton Dr	19607
Wicker Ln	19607
Wickford Ct & Pl	19610
Wiest School Rd	19606
Wilbur Dr	19608
Wild Flower Ct	19607
Wilfox Ave	19605
William Ln	19604
William St	19607
Williams Ave	19606
Willingham Ave	19605
Willow Rd	19608
Willow St	
500-699	19602
5200-5299	19606
Willow Way	19606
Willow Creek Rd	19605
Willow Grove Ave	19605
Wilma Ave	19607
Wilshire Blvd	19608
Wilson Ave	19606
Wilson Pl	19607
Wilson St	
1-200	19609
201-2397	19605
202-298	19609
2399-2599	19605
Wilson School Ct & Ln	19608
Winchester Ct	19606
Windcroft Ct	19606
Winding Brook Dr	19608
Winding Brook Ln	19606
Windmill Rd	19608
Windsor Ct	19606
Windsor St	
100-344	19601
300-400	19610
346-598	19601
401-403	19610
402-498	19610
405-599	19601
700-798	19604
800-1299	19604
W Windsor St	19601
Wingate Ave	19607
Wingco Ln	19605
Winged Foot Dr	19607
Wingert Rd	19610
Wingspread Ct & Dr	19606
Wister Way	19606
Wisteria Ave	19606
Wisteria Ct	19608
Wisteria Ln	19608
Witman Rd	19605
Wolters Ln	19606
Wood Cir	19607
Wood Ln	19606
Wood St	19602
Woodchuck Ln	19606
Woodcock Ct	19606
Woodcrest Dr	19607
Woodland Ave	19606
Woodland Rd	19610
Woodpecker Ln	
1-199	19607
100-198	19606
Woodrow Ave	19608
Woods Way	19610
Woodside Ave	19609
Woodvale Ave	19606
Woodward Dr & St	19601
Wool Aly	19602
Wroxham Dr	19610
Wunder St	19602
Wyndham Hill Dr	19606
Wynnewood Ave	19608
Wyoming Ave	19610
Wyoming Dr	
2800A-2800F	19608

2801A-2801H 19608
2802A-2802F 19608
2803A-2803H 19608
2804A-2804H 19608
2805A-2805H 19608
2807A-2807J 19608
2809A-2809H 19608
2811A-2811H 19608
2813A-2813I 19608
2900E1-2900E2 19608
2902A-2902H 19608
2903A-2903F 19608
2905B-2905J 19608
2909A-2909H 19608
2806A1-2806A5 19608
2806B1-2806B5 19608
2806C1-2806C5 19608
2806D1-2806D4 19608
2806E1-2806E5 19608
2806F1-2806F5 19608
2806G1-2806G5 19608
2806H1-2806H5 19608
2900A1-2900A5 19608
2900B1-2900B5 19608
2900C1-2900C5 19608
2900D1-2900D5 19608
2900F1-2900F5 19608
2900G1-2900G5 19608
2900H1-2900H5 19608
2901A-2901M 19608
2907A-2907K 19608
2911A-2911K 19608
2815-3097 19608
3099-3116 19608
3118-3198 19608
Wyoming Dr N 19608
Wyoming Dr S 19608
N Wyomissing Ave 19607
S Wyomissing Ave 19607
Wyomissing Blvd 19610
E Wyomissing Blvd 19611
N Wyomissing Blvd 19610
W Wyomissing Blvd 19609
Wyomissing Ct 19610
Wyomissing Hills Blvd 19609
Yarnell St 19611
Yarrow Ave 19605
Yerger Blvd
1120-1124 19609
1201-1299 19608
York Rd 19610
York St 19605

NUMBERED STREETS

S 1st Ave 19611
S 2nd Ave 19611
2nd St 19607
N 2nd St 19601
S 2nd St 19602
N 3rd Ave 19611
S 3rd Ave 19611
N 3rd St 19601
S 3rd St 19602
S 4th Ave 19611
4th St 19607
N 4th St
2-98 19601
500-598 19610
501-599 19601
601-603 19610
623-1099 19601
800-808 19610
S 4th St 19602
S 5th Ave 19611
N 5th St
1-58 19601
59-1799 19601
59-59 19603
60-1898 19601
1910-1910 19605
S 5th St 19602
N 5th Street Hwy 19605
N 6th Ave 19611
S 6th Ave 19611
N 6th St
1-700 19601
701-717 19610
702-716 19601
719-727 19610
732-898 19601
S 6th St 19602
N 7th Ave 19611
S 7th Ave 19611
N 7th St 19610
S 7th St 19602
N 8th St
2-24 19601
26-699 19601
700-1010 19604
900-914 19610
916-923 19610
925-1099 19610
1012-1098 19604
618-600-618-620 19601
S 8th St 19602
N 9th St
1-499 19601
500-1700 19604
800-926 19610
1702-1798 19604
S 9th St 19602
N 10th St
1-299 19601
300-1799 19604
1801-1899 19604
833-831-833-835 19604
S 10th St 19602
N 11th St
8-22 19601
24-299 19601
300-2399 19604
2500-2598 19605
2701-2799 19605
S 11th St 19602
N 12th St
200-1899 19604
2501-2599 19605
S 12th St 19602
N 13th St
200-2099 19604
2100-2100 19612
2101-2199 19604
2136-2198 19604
S 13th St 19602
N 14th St 19604
S 14th St 19602
N 15th St 19604
S 15th St 19602
N 16th St 19604
200-399 19602
400-616 19606
N 17th St 19604
200-399 19602
400-636 19606
N 18th St 19604
S 18th St
200-298 19602
300-399 19602
400-498 19606
500-657 19606
659-675 19606
S 19th St 19606
S 20th St 19606
N & S 22nd 19606
N & S 23rd 19606
N & S 24th 19606
N & S 25th 19606
N 26th St 19606
N & S 27th 19606
W 33rd St 19606
E & W 34th 19606
E & W 35th 19606
E & W 36th 19606
E & W 37th 19606
E & W 38th 19606
E & W 39th 19606
E & W 40th 19606
W 46th St 19606
W 47th St 19606
W 48th St 19606
W 49th St 19606
S 14 1/2 St 19602
S 15 1/2 St 19606
S 16 1/2 St 19606
S 17 1/2 St
300-399 19602
513-677 19606
S 18 1/2 St 19606

SCRANTON PA

General Delivery 18505

POST OFFICE BOXES MAIN OFFICE STATIONS AND BRANCHES

Box No.s
A - L 18504
G - G 18501
1 - 1002 18501
1 - 645 18504
1061 - 1775 18501
1900 - 1900 18505
1959 - 2042 18501
3001 - 6709 18505
15000 - 15000 18501
20001 - 20240 18502

RURAL ROUTES

01 18504
02 18505

NAMED STREETS

Abby Way 18504
Academy Ln 18512
Academy St 18504
Acker Ave 18504
Adams Ave
100-399 18503
400-999 18510
1035-1297 18509
1299-2400 18509
2402-2598 18509
Adams Ct 18512
Adarlew St 18512
Albert St 18519
Albion St 18508
Albright Ave
800-898 18508
900-1199 18508
1400-1599 18509
Alder St 18505
Allen St 18512
Alpha Ct 18508
Ambrose St 18512
Amelia Ave 18509
Amherst Dr 18519
Amherst Park 18504
Amherst St 18504
Amity Ct 18509
Amnick Ct 18504
Andrew St 18512
Anthony St 18508
N & S Apple St 18512
April Ln 18505
Archbald St 18504
Ariel St 18505
Arlington Way 18504
Arnold Ave 18505
Arthur Ave 18510
Ash St
100-599 18509
600-608 18519
609-609 18519
609-611 18510
610-698 18519
619-699 18519
700-2699 18510
Aspen Dr 18505
Aswell Ct 18504
Atlanta Ave 18508
August Ave & Dr 18505
Augusta Ave 18508
Avery Pl 18510
Azalea Way 18505
Back St 18504
Bald Mountain Rd 18504
Baldassari Dr 18505
Ballau Ave 18508
Bank St 18519
Barnard St 18512
Barrett Ct 18509
Barring Ave 18508
Bartel St 18508
Barton St 18512
Bates St 18509
Batluck St 18505
Battin St 18512
Battle St 18508
Beacon Dr 18504
Beaumont Ave 18508
Beddoe Ct 18504
Bednar St 18512
Beech St 18505
Bellman St 18512
Belmont Ter 18508
Belvedere Dr 18505
Bengar Dr & Pl 18505
Bennett St 18508
Bergen Ct 18505
Birch St 18505
Birdie Ln 18519
Birney Ave 18505
Blair Ave 18508
N Blakely St 18512
S Blakely St
111-117 18512
119-599 18512
600-799 18510
Blatter Pl 18505
Block St 18508
Bloom Ave 18508
Blucher Ave 18505
Bogart Pl 18503
Boland Ct 18505
Boulevard Ave
100-204 18512
206-300 18512
301-309 18519
311-899 18519
1800-2599 18509
2601-3099 18509
3400-3498 18512
Boundary St 18519
Bowman St 18519
Boyle St 18512
Brady St 18510
Branch St 18512
Breaker St 18519
Breaker Creek Rd 18519
Breck St 18505
Brenda Ln 18512
Brick Ave 18508
Brick St 18512
Bridge St 18503
Briggs St 18504
Brighton Ave 18509
Bristol Ct 18509
Broadway St 18505
N & S Bromley Ave 18504
Brook St
300-825 18505
830-830 18519
832-839 18519
840-840 18505
841-899 18519
842-842 18519
844-844 18505
846-852 18519
900-998 18505
1000-1600 18505
1602-1698 18505
Brown Ave 18509
Brown Ct 18512
Bruno Dr 18512
Bryn Mawr St 18504
Buenzli Ct 18510
Bulwer St 18504
Bundy St 18508
Bunker Hill St 18510
Burke St
300-499 18505
500-699 18512
501-505 18505
Bush St 18510
Butler St 18512
Calvin St 18512
N & S Cameron Ave 18504
Campbell St 18505
Cannon St 18508
Capouse Ave 18509
Carlton Ct 18504
Carmalt St 18519
Caroline Ave 18504
Cascade Mnr 18505
Cavalier Dr 18519
Cayuga St 18508
Cedar 18503
Cedar Ave 18505
Cemetary St 18505
Center St
201-207 18503
300-422 18508
400-498 18512
500-1000 18512
500-516 18503
509-509 18512
511-720 18512
515-516 18508
722-798 18512
1002-1098 18512
Champion Cir 18512
Charles St
1-599 18512
100-499 18508
1001-1099 18512
Cherry St
100-399 18512
200-299 18519
301-1802 18505
Chesterfield Ln 18504
Chestnut St 18512
Christ Ct 18504
Christopher Dr 18504
Church Ave 18508
Church St 18512
Clairmont Rd 18519
Clam House Rd 18504
Clark Pl 18504
Clark St 18512
Clay Ave
400-1399 18510
1500-1899 18509
Clearview St 18508
Cleveland Ave 18505
Cliff St 18503
Clover St 18508
Coar Pl 18505
Cobb Ave 18505
Colan Ct 18504
Colfax Ave 18510
College Ave 18509
Colliery Ave 18505
Colliery Rd 18519
Collins Ct 18512
Columbia St 18509
Comegys Ave 18509
Comegys Pl 18505
Commerce Blvd 18519
Commercial St 18519
Community Dr 18504
Connell St 18505
Conroy St 18505
Cooney St 18512
Cooper St 18508
Coppernick St 18512
Corbett Ave 18504
E Corey St 18505
Cornell St 18504
Corner St 18512
Cosgrove Pl 18504
Costello Ct 18510
Cottage Ave 18508
Council St 18509
Court St
500-1299 18508
1500-1613 18504
1615-1615 18504
Coyne Ave 18505
Craig Rd 18519
Crane St 18505
Crestedge Mnr 18505
Crisp Ave 18504
Cronkey Ave 18505
Cross Dr
1-99 18505
100-198 18512
Crossin Ct 18504
Crown Ave 18505
Crown Circle Dr 18505
Curtis Ln 18508
Cusick Ave 18508
Cypress St 18512
Dale Ave & Dr 18504
Dartmouth St 18504
David Ter 18505
Davis St 18505
Dawn Dr 18505
De Sales Ave 18504
Deacon St 18509
Dean Ct & St 18509
Debbie Dr
1-99 18512
100-299 18505
December Dr 18505
N & S Decker Ct 18504
Deerfield Rd 18504
Delaware St
400-499 18512
600-1899 18509
1900-2099 18512
Dencenta St 18508
Depot St 18509
Derby Ave 18505
Derrig St 18512
Detty St 18509
N Dewey Ave 18504
S Dewey Ave 18504
Dewey St
300-399 18512
400-599 18519
Dexter Ave 18504
Diamond Ave 18508
Dickens St 18504
Dickson Ave 18509
Dimmick Ave 18509
Dimmick St
100-199 18512
800-1299 18519
Division St 18504
Dix Ct 18509
Dogwood Cir 18504
Donnelly Ct 18505
Donny Dr 18505
Dorothy St 18504
Doud Ave 18505
E Drinker St 18512
W Drinker St
100-399 18512
400-499 18509
Drinker Tpke 18512
Dudley St 18512
Duffer Dr 18519
Duncan St 18505
Dunda Dr 18512
Dundaff St 18519
Dunham Dr 18512
Dunmore St 18512
Dupont Ct 18503
Durkin Ave 18508
Eagen Ave 18505
Eagle Ln 18519
Edgar St 18512
Edith Ave 18508
Edna Ave 18508
N & S Edwards Ct 18504
El Harem Dr 18505
Electric St
1-1899 18509
1900-2099 18512
Eliza St 18508
Elizabeth St
100-399 18512
1400-1799 18504
Elm St 18519
E Elm St
100-198 18505
100-399 18512
200-1999 18505
W Elm St
200-699 18512
201-203 18505
500-1399 18504
Elmhurst Blvd 18505
Emerald Dr 18512
Emily Ave 18504
Emmett St 18505
Engle Ct 18510
Enterprise St 18519
Erie St
100-399 18510
400-499 18512
1101-1199 18512
Esther St 18512
Euclid Ave 18504
Eureka Ave 18508
Evans Ct 18504
Evelyn St 18509
N & S Everett Ave 18504
Eynon St 18504
Fainesti Ave 18503
Fairfield St 18509
Fairview Ave 18504
Farber Ct 18510
Farr St 18504
Faust Ave 18504
Fawnwood Dr 18504
February Dr 18505
Fellows St
300-399 18505
501-597 18504
599-1500 18504
1502-1698 18504
Ferdinand St 18508
Ferguson Pl 18509
Field St 18512
Fig St 18505
N & S Fillmore Ave 18504
Finn St 18509
Fisk St 18509
Florentine Pl 18512
Florida Ave 18505
Florin St 18509
Flynn St 18512
Foote St 18512
Fordham Ct 18509
Forenert St 18519
Forest Ct 18509
Forest Glen Dr 18504
Foster St 18508
Frances Ave 18504
Frank Ave 18508
Frank St 18512
Frank Way 18504
Franklin Ave 18503
Franklin St 18512
Franko St 18512
Frieda St 18519
Frink St 18504
Front St 18505
Froude Ave 18505
Fulton St 18508
Gallagher Ct 18505
Galvin Pl 18505
Gardner Ave 18509
N & S Garfield Ave 18504
Garwood Dr 18505
Gaston Pl 18508
Genet St 18505
George Ave 18508
George St 18512
Geraldine Ct 18504
Gerard St 18504
Gibbons St
100-399 18512
401-497 18505

499-1034 18505
1036-1054 18505
E Gibson St
300-599 18509
600-1900 18510
1902-1998 18510
W Gibson St 18504
Gilbert St 18508
Gilligan St 18508
Gilotti Dr 18509
Gilroy St
100-117 18505
100-106 18512
108-199 18512
119-199 18505
Glenn St 18509
Glenstone Rd 18519
Glinko St 18504
Golden Ave 18508
Goodman St 18512
Gordon Ave 18508
Gordon Pl 18510
Gorge St 18508
Grace St 18509
Grand Ave & Cir 18505
Grandview St 18509
N Grant Ave 18504
S Grant Ave 18504
Grant Ct 18519
Grant St 18519
Gravity St 18510
Green Pl 18509
Green St
100-299 18512
300-399 18508
301-399 18512
Green Ridge St
1-1899 18509
1900-2099 18512
Greenbush St 18508
Greenwood Ave 18505
Gregory Pl 18504
Grier St 18519
Griff Ave 18504
Griffin St 18508
Grimes Ave & Ct 18505
Grove St 18508
E Grove St 18510
W Grove St
100-299 18509
300-499 18510
Gunster Ave 18508
Hall St 18512
Hallstead St 18519
Hamilton Ave 18504
Hamilton St 18519
Hamm Ct 18505
Hampton St 18504
Hand Pl 18504
Harding St 18510
Harmony Ct 18509
Harper St 18512
Harriet St
100-199 18512
1200-1299 18519
Harrison Ave 18510
Harrison St 18512
Haverly St 18512
Hawthorne St 18504
Heangtow Ave 18509
Heermans Ave 18509
Helen St 18512
Hemlock St 18505
Hennigan St 18512
Henry St 18508
Herbert St 18505
Hertz Ct 18505
Hickory St 18505
High St 18508
Hill St
100-600 18512
200-299 18508
800-899 18512
Hiller Ave 18505
Hillside Mnr 18505
Hitchcock Ct 18510
Holcum Dr 18504
Hollister Ave 18508
Hollow Ave 18508
Holly Rd 18509
Homestead St 18512
Honesdale Ct 18509
Hope Way 18504
N & S Horatio Ave 18504
Howard Pl 18509
Howell St 18504
Huckleberry Hl 18505
Hudson Ave 18504
Hughes Ct 18504
Hulse St 18512
Huntington Dr 18519
N & S Hyde Park Ave 18504
N Irving Ave 18510
S Irving Ave 18505
Jackson St
400-999 18519
1000-2799 18504
Jadwin St 18509
James Ave 18510
James St 18519
Jamestown Way Cir 18504
Jane St 18512
January Ln 18505
Jefferson Ave
100-299 18503
300-1000 18510
1002-1098 18510
1300-2299 18509
Jennie St 18519
Jermyn St 18519
Jessup St 18512
Johler Ave 18508
John Ave 18510
Johnson St 18519
Jones St
300-399 18512
3000-3199 18505
Joseph Ave 18510
Joy Ct 18509
Julia St 18508
July Dr 18505
June Dr 18505
Kane St 18505
Karen Dr 18505
Kellum Ct 18510
Kelly Ave 18508
Kelly Way 18504
Kemmering Ct 18508
Kennedy Blvd 18504
Kennedy St 18508
Kerstetter Ct 18504
N Keyser Ave
100-1599 18504
1600-1899 18508
S Keyser Ave 18504
Keystone Ct 18512
Keystone Industrial Park 18512
Kimberlee Dr 18505
Kingsbury Rd 18509
Kirst Ct 18505
Kirtland St 18508
Knolltop Mnr 18505
Knox Rd 18505
Knox And Lake Scranton Rd 18505
Kossuth Ave 18512
Kossuth St 18508
Kozy Dr 18504
Kressler Ct
300-398 18503
801-899 18510
Kurtz St 18510
Lackawanna Ave 18503
W Lackawanna Ave
601-605 18503
620-626 18503
900-1099 18504
Lafayette St 18504
Lake St 18510
Lake Scranton Rd 18505
Lakeview Dr 18505
Lakewood Mnr 18505
Landis St 18504
Langstaff Pl 18508
Larch St 18509
Lauer Ave 18504
Laurel Dr 18505
Laurel St
400-499 18508
500-599 18512
501-599 18508
600-638 18519
601-699 18512
640-799 18519
Laurel Creek Dr 18519
Lavelle Ct 18505
Lawall St 18508
Laybourne St 18508
Leach Ave 18508
Lee Ct 18509
Leggett St 18508
Legion Dr 18512
Lemon St 18508
Leon Ct 18519
Leslie Dr 18505
Lewis Ave & St 18508
Lilac Ln 18505
N Lincoln Ave
100-899 18504
1400-1599 18508
S Lincoln Ave 18504
Lincoln St 18519
Linda Ln 18504
Linden St
100-699 18503
700-1799 18510
W Linden St
600-799 18503
900-1001 18504
1003-1099 18504
Line St 18512
Link St 18519
Little League Blvd 18504
Little Spike Way 18504
Lloyd St 18508
E Locust St 18505
W Locust St 18504
Loftus St 18512
Lonergan Pl 18504
Lontanch St 18510
Lookout Dr 18504
Loomis Ave 18504
Loop Ave 18508
Lords Ct 18509
Los Robles St 18508
Love Rd 18508
Lowery St 18505
Lucky Run Rd 18504
Lukasik Dr 18519
Luke Ave 18510
Luzerne St
300-499 18505
500-501 18504
502-504 18505
503-2701 18504
506-2698 18504
Lynwood Ave 18505
Lynwood Dr 18505
Lynwood St 18512
Madison Ave
201-299 18503
300-1099 18510
1301-2299 18509
1600-1699 18509
Mahon Ct 18510
N Main Ave
100-899 18504
900-998 18508
1000-3499 18508
S Main Ave 18504
Main St 18519
Maloney St 18512
Manila Pl 18504
Maple St
1-99 18512
200-228 18519
229-231 18505
229-231 18519
230-298 18519
233-299 18519
300-1599 18505
March Dr & Hl 18505
Marcus St 18512
Margaret Ave & St 18508
Marion St 18509
Marjorie Dr
100-199 18505
400-699 18512
Mark Ave 18510
E Market St
1-9 18509
2-22 18508
24-99 18508
100-799 18509
W Market St 18508
Marshwood Rd 18512
Marvine Ave 18508
Mary Ln 18505
Mary St
300-413 18519
415-429 18519
436-444 18508
446-499 18508
501-511 18508
506-510 18519
512-516 18519
517-517 18508
518-518 18519
519-599 18508
601-603 18508
601-631 18519
605-605 18519
607-609 18508
608-608 18519
610-625 18519
626-628 18508
627-627 18519
630-699 18508
700-799 18519
900-999 18512
Mary Ann St 18504
Masters St 18510
Matthew Ave 18510
May Dr 18505
Mccarthy St 18505
Mccormick Ct 18509
Mcdonough Ave 18508
Mcdonough St 18505
Mcguinness Ct 18505
Mckenna Ct
400-899 18510
901-999 18510
1300-1399 18509
Mclean St 18508
Meade Ave 18508
Meade St 18512
Meadow Ave & Mnr 18505
Meehan St 18519
Melnes St 18519
Memo Ln 18508
Memorial Dr 18512
Meridian Ave 18504
N & S Merrifield Ave 18504
Meylert Ave 18509
Mia Cara Dr 18505
Middle St
101-199 18508
1101-1199 18519
Mifflin Ave 18503
Mike Munchak Way 18508
Mill St 18512
Millard St 18519
Millenium St 18512
Millett St 18512
Mineral Ave 18509
Mohawk St 18508
Moir Ct 18510
Moltke Ave 18505
Monahan Ave 18512
Monroe Ave
200-398 18510
400-1099 18510
1100-1799 18509
Monsey Ave 18509
Monterey Rd 18505
Moosic St 18505
Moran Ct 18505
Morel St 18509
Morgan Hwy 18508
Morgan St 18519
Morgan Manor Dr 18508
Moritz St 18512
Morris Ave 18504
Mortimer St 18512
Mount Margaret Dr 18505
Mount Vernon Ave 18508
Mountain Mnr 18505
E Mountain Rd 18505
W Mountain Rd 18504
Mountain Lake Rd 18505
Mountain Laurel Dr 18505
Mountain View Way 18508
Mruck St 18512
Mt Pleasant Dr 18503
Mulberry St
100-499 18503
500-598 18510
600-1823 18510
1825-1999 18510
Murphy Ct 18505
Murray St 18512
Myrtle St
500-598 18509
600-698 18510
700-2299 18510
Nancy Dr 18505
Naphin Hill Rd 18512
Nay Aug Ave 18509
Nay Aug Pl 18510
Neptune Pl 18505
New St 18509
New York St 18509
Newton Rd 18504
Nichols St 18505
Nicole Dr 18512
Norfolk Way 18504
North St 18512
Norton Ave 18504
Norwalk Way 18504
Oak Ave 18505
Oak Ln 18505
Oak St
100-199 18508
200-399 18512
201-211 18508
210-210 18519
211-229 18519
213-213 18519
215-215 18508
219-225 18519
222-224 18508
226-230 18508
231-233 18519
232-1098 18508
301-923 18508
925-925 18515
927-1199 18508
Oakford Ct
200-299 18503
500-598 18509
Oakwood Dr 18504
Oakwood Pl 18510
Oconnor Pl 18505
October Dr 18505
Odell St 18519
Ohara St 18505
Oleckna St 18512
Olendike St 18512
Olga St 18519
Olive St
300-398 18509
400-499 18509
700-1899 18510
W Olive St 18508
Oliver Pl 18504
Olyphant Ave 18509
Oneill Hwy 18512
Oraliso St 18505
Oram St 18504
Orchard St 18505
Oswald Ave 18505
Overbrook Cir 18504
Oxford St 18504
Palm St 18505
Palmer Cir 18519
Pancoast St
416A-416B 18519
101-499 18512
300-999 18519
Parallel Dr 18504
E Park Ave 18504
W Park Ave 18504
Park Dr 18505
Park Gdns 18509
Park St
100-200 18510
202-298 18510
801-897 18509
899-1099 18509
1101-1199 18509
Parkdale Dr 18519
Parkedge Ln 18504
E Parker St 18509
W Parker St 18508
Parrott Ave 18504
Partridge Ave 18508
Pattison Ave 18504
Paul Ave 18510
Pawnee Ave 18508
Pear St 18505
Pearl St 18512
Peggy Pkwy 18512
Peller Ave 18505
Pen Y Bryn Dr 18505
Pendel St 18512
Penman St 18505
Penn Ave
100-499 18503
500-898 18509
900-1799 18509
Pennypacker Ave 18519
Penwood Dr 18505
Pequest Dr 18505
Perry Ave 18508
Pettibone St 18504
Pettit St 18519
Phelps St 18509
Phillips Dr 18505
Phillips St 18512
Philo St
600-1299 18508
1600-1698 18504
Philomena Dr 18512
Phinney St 18505
Pierce St 18508
Pike St 18508
Pine St
100-199 18512
501-599 18509
700-798 18510
800-1899 18510
E Pine St 18512
W Pine St 18512
Pittston Ave 18505
Pleasant Ave 18504
Plum Pl 18509
Pond Ave 18508
Poplar St
1-99 18509
101-199 18509
200-299 18519
301-499 18509
800-1099 18510
1101-1199 18510
W Poplar St 18509
Porter Ave 18504
Potter St 18512
Powderly Ct 18504
Prescott Ave & Pl 18510
Preston Pl 18504
Price Rd 18504
Price St
700-899 18519
901-911 18504
901-951 18519
913-917 18504
919-3199 18504
920-944 18519
1000-3198 18504
Prospect Ave 18505
Prospect St 18512
Providence Rd 18508
Putnam St 18508
Quay Ave 18504
Quincy Ave
400-1399 18510
1500-1799 18509
1801-1899 18509
Race St 18509
Railroad Ave
200-499 18505
1300-1399 18519
Raines St 18509
Ralph Ave 18508
Ramona Dr 18512
Ravine St 18508
N Rebecca Ave
100-1299 18504
1400-1499 18508
S Rebecca Ave 18504
Rebecca St 18512
Reese St 18508
Reeves St 18512
Regan Pl 18505
Reilly St 18512
Remington Ave 18505
Reservoir Dr 18512
Return Ave 18508
Reynolds Ave 18504
Rhonda Dr 18505
Richmont St 18509
Richter Dr 18510
Ridge Ave & Row 18510
Ridgerun Mnr 18505
Ridgeview Dr
1-233 18504
100-199 18512
235-299 18504
Ridgewood Ave 18505
Rigg St 18512
Ripple St 18505
River St
100-199 18512
101-197 18505
199-299 18505
301-1199 18505
402-410 18519
412-412 18505
416-418 18519
422-424 18505
422-536 18519
426-426 18519
428-430 18505
434-434 18519
438-438 18505
446-498 18519
500-1098 18505
Riverside Dr 18509
Roanoke Ln 18504
Robb Pl 18509
Roberts Ct 18504
Robinson St 18504
Roche Ct 18509
Rock St 18504
Rockwell Ave
2001-2197 18508
2199-2400 18508
2402-3198 18508
2415-2425 18519
3201-3299 18508
Roland Ave 18504
Rollin Ave 18505
Roosevelt Ave 18512
Roosevelt St 18505
Rosanna Ave 18509
Rose Dr 18512
Roselynn St 18510
Rosen Ct 18505
Ross Ave 18509
Ross St 18512
Ruane Ave 18508
Ruddy Pl 18508
Rundle St 18504
Ruth Ave 18509
Ryan St 18512
Ryerson Ave 18509

Saddler Ave 18510
Sadie St 18519
Saginaw St 18505
Saint Ann St 18504
Saint Francis Cabrini Ave 18504
Salico Ln 18512
Sand St 18510
Sanders St 18505
Sanderson Ave 18509
Sanderson St 18512
Sandie Ln 18519
Scanlon Ave 18508
Scenic Ln 18508
Schimpff Ct 18505
Schlager Ave & St 18504
School St 18508
School Side Dr 18512
Schultz Ct 18510
Scott Rd
700-1105 18519
1107-1199 18519
1156-1198 18508
Scranton St 18504
Scranton Carbondale Hwy 18508
Scranton Pocono Hwy 18505
Sebring Rd 18519
N Sekol Ave 18504
Seminary St 18509
Seneca St 18508
September Dr 18505
Seymour Ave 18505
Shaffer St 18519
Shawnee Ave 18509
Shea Pl 18505
N & S Sherman Ave 18504
Sherwood Ave 18512
Shirley Ln 18512
Shoemaker St 18512
Short Ave 18508
Short Ln 18505
Short St 18512
Siebecker St 18505
Silex St 18509
Silver Ave 18508
Simplex Dr 18504
Simpson St 18512
Skytop Mnr 18505
Skyview Dr 18505
Sloan St 18504
Slocum Ave 18505
Smallacombe Dr 18508
Smith Ln 18504
Smith Pl 18509
Smith St
100-731 18512
600-899 18504
733-799 18512
Snook St 18505
Snyder Ave 18504
Soldiers Ct 18504
Somers St 18512
N South Rd 18504
South St 18512
Spartan Dr 18512
Spring Ln 18508
Spring St
100-399 18508
300-399 18512
Spruce St 18503
Stafford Ave 18505
Stanton St 18508
Stark Pl 18504
State St 18512
Steckel St 18512
Steele St 18508
Stephen Ave 18505
Sterling St 18508
Stipp Ct 18510
Storrs St 18519
Straub St 18512
Summit Trl 18508
Summit Pointe 18508
N Sumner Ave
100-999 18504
1000-1799 18508
S Sumner Ave 18504
Sunset Dr
1-99 18505
100-308 18512
310-398 18512
Sunset St 18509
Sussex Rd 18519
Swartz St 18512
Sweeney Ave 18508
Swetland St 18504
E Swinick Dr 18512
Sycamore Ln 18505
Tall Trees Dr 18505
Taylor Ave 18510
Templeton Dr 18519
Terrace Dr 18505
Terrace Ln 18508
Terrace Mnr 18505
Terrace St 18512
Thackery St 18504
The Mall At Steamtown 18503
Theodore St 18508
Thomas Dr 18512
Throop St
1-199 18508
100-999 18512
801-829 18519
831-1399 18519
Thunderbird Dr 18505
Tiffany Dr 18505
Tigue St 18512
Tioga Ave 18509
Townhouse Blvd 18508
Tracy Ln 18505
Tripp Ave 18512
Tripp St 18508
Underwood Rd 18512
Union Ave 18510
Union St 18519
University Ave 18509
University Dr 18512
Valley Mnr 18505
N & S Van Buren Ave 18504
Varhley St 18512
Varsity Dr 18512
Veterans Dr
1A-1E 18519
Victory Ln 18512
Viewmont Dr 18519
Viewmont Est 18508
Viewmont Mall 18508
Vine St
200-399 18503
500-501 18509
503-599 18509
601-697 18510
699-1899 18510
Vipond Ave 18505
Von Storch Ave 18509
Waldorf Ln 18505
Wales St 18508
Walker St 18519
Walnut St
1-499 18509
100-199 18512
Walsh St 18505
Wanda St 18512
Ward St 18512
Warner St 18505
Warren St 18508
E Warren St 18512
W Warren St 18512
Washburn St 18504
N Washington Ave
100-228 18503
230-498 18503
235-235 18501
235-499 18503
501-713 18509
715-2499 18509
2501-2599 18509
S Washington Ave
100-150 18503
200-1200 18505
1202-1998 18505
Washington Rd 18509
Washington St 18512
Watkins St 18508
Watres Dr 18505
Watrous Ave 18510
Watson St 18504
Wayne Ave 18508
N Webster Ave
200-298 18510
300-1399 18510
1500-1999 18509
S Webster Ave 18505
Webster Dr 18509
Wedge Dr 18519
Wellington Rd 18505
Wells St 18508
Wheeler Ave
200-1299 18510
1300-1498 18512
1501-1599 18512
White Birch Dr 18504
Whitetail Dr 18504
Wilbur St 18508
William Dr 18505
William St
100-140 18510
141-145 18508
141-211 18510
147-327 18508
213-312 18510
329-339 18508
400-899 18510
Williamsburg Ln 18504
Willow St
98-98 18512
100-404 18512
300-1299 18505
406-498 18512
Wilson Ct 18519
Winchester Way 18504
Winfield Ave 18505
Winona Ave 18508
Wint Ave 18509
Wintermantle Ave 18505
Winton St 18512
Witko St 18519
Wood St
900-1400 18508
1402-1598 18508
1600-1698 18504
Woodlawn St
700-898 18512
800-1499 18509
Woodside Mnr 18505
Wright Ct 18503
Wurtz Ave 18509
Wymbs Pl 18504
Wyoming Ave
100-499 18503
500-2299 18509
S Wyoming Ave 18505
Yard Ave 18508
Yesu Dr & Ln 18505

NUMBERED STREETS

1st Ave 18508
2nd Ave 18508
2nd St
400-599 18512
800-898 18510
3rd Ave
100-198 18508
300-398 18505
400-599 18505
601-699 18505
3rd St
400-699 18512
801-899 18510
4th Ave 18505
4th St 18512
5th Ave 18505
S 5th Ave 18504
5th St 18512
N 6th Ave 18503
S 6th Ave 18504
6th St 18512
N 7th Ave 18503
S 7th Ave 18505
N 8th Ave 18503
S 8th Ave 18504
N & S 9th 18504
10th Ave 18504
12th Ave 18504
13th Ave 18504
14th Ave 18504
15th Ave 18504
16th Ave 18504
17th Ave 18504
18th Ave 18504
19th Ave 18504
20th Ave 18504
21st Ave 18504

SOUTHEASTERN PA

General Delivery 19399

POST OFFICE BOXES MAIN OFFICE STATIONS AND BRANCHES

Box No.s
1 - 304 19399
316 - 316 19397
325 - 997 19399
1000 - 1137 19398
1241 - 2517 19399
3001 - 8307 19398

NAMED STREETS

All Street Addresses 19399

STATE COLLEGE PA

General Delivery 16804

POST OFFICE BOXES MAIN OFFICE STATIONS AND BRANCHES

Box No.s
11 - 4000 16804
8001 - 13349 16805

NAMED STREETS

E & W Aaron Dr 16803
Abbott Ln 16801
Abby Pl 16803
Abercorn St 16803
Aberdeen Ln 16801
Abermuir Hts 16803
Abington Cir 16801
Acacia Dr 16803
Acorn Ln 16803
Adams Ave 16803
Aikens Pl 16801
Airport Rd 16801
Alder Ct 16803
Alexander Dr 16803
N Allen St 16803
S Allen St 16801
Alma Mater Ct & Dr 16803
Alto Ln 16803
Amblewood Way 16803
Amelia Ave 16801
Amherst Dr 16801
Apple Aly 16801
Apple Green Cir 16803
Appletree Cir 16803
Arbor Way 16803
Asbury Ln 16801
Ash Ave 16801
Ashburton Ct 16803
Ashwicken Ct N & S 16801
Asper Way 16803
N Atherton St
100-299 16801
401-497 16803
499-2599 16803
S Atherton St 16801
Atlee Cir 16803
August Aly 16803
Autumnwood Dr 16801
Avebury Cir 16803
Ayrshire Way 16803
Azalea Dr 16803
B Aly 16801
Ballybunion Rd 16801
Balmoral Cir & Way 16801
Banffshire Hts 16803
Banyan Dr 16801
N & S Barkway Ln 16803
Barley Way 16801
N & S Barnard St 16801
Barnstable Ln 16803
Bathgate Dr 16801
Bayberry Dr 16801
Bayfield Ct 16801
Bayletts St 16801
Beagle Run Ct 16801
Beaumanor Rd 16803
Beaumont Dr 16801
E & W Beaver Ave 16801
Bellaire Ave 16801
Bellvue Cir 16803
Belmont Cir 16803
Benjamin Ct 16803
Benner Pike 16801
Bergman Blvd 16803
Berkshire Dr 16803
Bernel Rd 16803
Big Hollow Rd 16801
Bigler Road Ext 16803
Birch Ct 16801
Birchtree Ct 16801
Black Bear Ln 16803
Blair Rd 16801
Bloomsdorf Dr 16801
Blue Course Dr
200-499 16803
1000-1799 16801
Blue Jay Ave 16801
N Boal Aly 16803
Bolton Ave 16803
Bottorf Dr 16801
Bradford Ct 16801
Bradley Ave 16801
E & W Branch Rd 16801
Brandywine Dr 16801
Breezewood Dr 16801
Briarwood Ln 16803
Bristol Ave 16801
Brittany Dr 16803
Broadmoor Ln 16801
Brushwood Dr 16801
Buchanan Ave 16801
Buchenhorst Rd 16801
N & S Buckhout St 16801
N Burrowes St
200-298 16801
300-399 16801
500-699 16803
S Burrowes St 16801
Butterfly Ave 16801
N & S Butz St 16801
C Aly 16801
E Calder Way
100-203 16801
202-202 16805
204-598 16801
205-599 16801
W Calder Way 16801
Cambridge Dr 16803
Camelot Ln 16803
Campbell Rd 16801
Candlebush Pl 16803
Candleford Hts 16803
Candlewood Dr 16803
Canterbury Dr 16803
Cardinal Ln 16803
Carnegie Dr 16803
Carogin Dr 16803
Carolean Industrial Dr 16801
Cato Ave 16801
Cedar Ln 16801
Centandi Dr 16803
Centre Ave & Ln 16801
Charles St 16801
Charleston Dr 16801
Chateaux Cir 16803
Chatham Ct 16803
Chaumont Ave 16801
Chelsea Ln 16801
E & W Cherry Ln 16803
N & S Cherry Hill Rd 16803
Cherry Ridge Rd 16803
Chestnut Ridge Dr 16803
Chickory Ln 16803
Chownings Ct 16801
Christopher Ln 16803
Circle Dr 16801
Circle Pl 16803
Circleville Rd 16803
Clair Ln 16801
Claremont Ave 16801
Clarence Ave 16803
Clay Ln 16801
E & W Clearview Ave 16803
Clemson Ct 16803
Cliffside Dr 16801
E & W Clinton Ave 16803
Clover Rd 16801
Clyde Ave 16801
Coal Aly 16801
Cobble Ct 16803
Cogan Cir 16801
Colby Ln 16801
E & W College Ave 16801
College View Rd 16801
Colonial Ct 16801
Colonnade Blvd & Way 16803
Commercial Blvd 16801
Concord Dr 16801
Conover Ln 16801
Constitution Ave 16801
Copper Leaf Ln 16801
Corinna Ct 16803
S Corl Cir & St 16801
Cornflower Ln 16803
Cornwall Rd 16803
Cottonwood Ave 16801
Country Club Ln 16803
Country Club Rd 16801
Country Glenn Ln 16801
Coventry Ln 16803
Crabapple Ct & Dr 16801
Cranberry Ln 16803
Crandall Dr 16803
Creekside Dr 16801
Crescent Ct 16801
Cresson Aly 16801
Crestmont Ave 16801
Cricklewood Cir & Dr 16803
Cromer Dr 16803
Curtin St 16803
Cypress Way 16801
Dahlia Dr 16803
Dartmouth Ln 16803
Decibel Rd 16801
Deerfield Dr 16803
Denton Ave 16803
Devonshire Dr 16803
Dewsbury Hts 16803
Dogwood Cir 16803
E & W Doris Ave 16801
Dorum Ave 16801
Douglas Dr 16803
Dover Cir 16801
Dreibelbis St 16801
Driftwood Dr 16803
Earl Dr 16803
Easterly Dr & Pkwy 16801
Edgewood Cir 16801
Edith St 16803
Edwards St 16801
Elderberry Ln 16803
Elizabeth Rd 16801
Ellen Ave 16801
Ellis Pl 16801
Ellman Ln 16801
Elm Rd & St 16801
Elm Shade Dr 16801
Elmwood St 16801
Enterprise Dr 16801
Ernest Ln 16803
Evergreen Ln & Rd 16801
Exeter Ct 16803
F Aly 16803
Fairchild Ln 16801
Fairfield Cir & Dr 16801
Fairlawn Ave 16801
E & W Fairmount Ave 16801
Fairway Rd 16803
Fairwood Ln 16803
Falconpointe Dr 16801
Far Hills Ave 16803
Farm Ln 16801
Farmstead Ln 16803
Ferguson Ave 16803
Fernleaf Ct 16801
Fernwood Ct 16803
Fieldstone Dr 16801
Fillmore Rd 16803
Fir Dr 16801
Floral Pl 16803
Florence Way 16801
E & W Foster Ave 16801
Fox Hill Rd 16803
Fox Hollow Rd 16803
N Foxpointe Dr 16803
S Foxpointe Dr 16801
Franklin St 16803
Franklin Manor Ln 16803
S Fraser St
100-300 16801
237-237 16804
302-798 16801
401-799 16801
Fraternity Row 16801
Fredericksburg Ct 16803
Friendly Cir 16803
Fry Dr 16801
Fultons Run Rd 16803
Gala Dr 16801
Galen Dr 16803
S Garner St 16801
Gas Light Cir 16801
Gateway Dr 16801
Gerald St 16801
Ghaner Dr 16803
Gibbons St 16801
N & S Gill St 16801
Glengarry Ln 16801
Glenn Cir & Rd 16803
Glenwood Cir 16803
Golden Rod Rd 16803
Goldfinch Dr 16801
Golfview Ave 16801
Grace Ct & St 16801
Grandview Rd 16801
Gray Fox Ln 16803
Green Acres Ln 16801
Green Tech Dr 16803
Greenbriar Dr 16801
Greenfield Cir 16801
Greenwood Cir 16803
Gregor Cir & Way 16801
Grimsby Hts 16803
Gwenedd Ln 16801
H Aly 16801
Hadden Ct 16801
Halerthe Dr 16801
E & W Hamilton Ave 16801
Hampshire Cir 16803
Hampton Ct 16803
Harley Aly 16801
Harris Dr 16801
E Harris Dr 16801

Harris St 16803
Hart Cir 16801
Hartman Farm Ln 16801
Hartswick Ave 16803
Harvest Cir 16803
Harvest Ridge Dr 16803
Harvest Run Rd N 16801
Haverford Cir 16803
Hawbaker Industrial Dr 16803
Hawknest Ct & Rd 16801
Hawthorn Dr 16801
Haymaker Cir & Rd 16801
Heather Cir 16801
Hedgerow Dr 16801
Heister St 16801
Hemlock Hill Rd 16803
Hess Ln & Rd 16801
Hetzel St 16801
Hickory Ln & Rd 16801
Hickory Hill Dr 16803
High St 16801
High Meadow Ct & Ln 16803
High Point Cv 16801
High Ridge Cir 16803
High Tech Rd 16803
W Highland Aly 16801
Highland Ave 16801
Highland Dr 16803
Highlandon Ct 16801
Hill Aly & Dr 16801
Hillcrest Ave 16803
E & W Hillside Ave 16803
Hilltop Ave 16801
Hilltop Trailer Park 16801
Hillview Ave 16801
Holly Aly, Cir & Ct 16801
Holly Ridge Dr 16801
Holmes St 16803
Homan Ave 16801
Honeydew Ln 16803
Honors Ln 16803
Horizon Dr 16801
Hosta Cir 16803
Houserville Rd 16801
Hoy St 16801
E Hubler Rd 16801
Humes Aly 16801
Hummingbird Ave 16801
Hunter Ave 16801
Huntington Ln 16803
I Aly 16801
Independence Ave 16801
Innovation Blvd 16803
N & S Inverary Pl 16801
E & W Irvin Ave 16801
Ivy Hill Dr 16801
Jackson Ave, Cir & St 16803
Jalice Cir 16801
James Ave 16801
Jay Ln 16801
Jefferson Ave 16801
Johnson Ter 16803
Joyce Dr 16801
Jules Dr 16801
Julian Dr 16801
Juniper Dr 16801
Justine Lodge Way 16801
Keller St 16801
Kelly Aly 16801
Kemmerer Rd 16801
Kenley Ct 16803
Kennard Rd 16801
Kennedy St 16801
Kennelworth Ct 16801
Kephart St 16803
Kings Ct 16801
Knob Hill Rd 16803
Koebner Cir 16801
Kradel Ln 16803
Kristina Cir 16803
Kuhns Ln 16801
Lanceshire Ln 16803
Lark Aly 16801
Larkspur Ln 16803
Lauck St 16803
Laurel Ln 16803
Leawood Ln 16803
Legion Ln 16801
Lehman Way 16803
Leisure Ln 16801
Lenor Dr 16801
Lester St 16801
Levashire Hts 16803
Lexington Cir 16801
Lightner St 16803
Lilac Ln 16803
Lillian Cir 16801
Limerock Ter 16801
Lincoln Ave 16801
Linden Rd 16801
Linn St 16803
Linnet Ln 16803
Lions Hill Rd 16803
Little Lion Dr 16803
Little Rock Ln 16801
Locust Ln 16801
Logan Ave 16801
Lois Ln 16801
Longbarn Rd 16803
Longfellow Ct & Ln 16803
Longmeadow Ln 16803
Lowder St 16801
Lower Grandview Rd 16801
Lowes Blvd 16803
E & W Lytle Ave 16801
M Aly 16801
Macduff Cir 16801
Madison St 16801
Magnolia Cir 16801
Majestic View Cir & Rd 16801
Mallard Ave 16801
Manor Ct & Dr 16801
Mansfield St 16801
Maple Ln & Rd 16801
Marigold Aly 16801
Marjorie Mae St 16803
Marshall Blvd 16803
Martin St & Ter 16803
Mary Ellen Ln 16803
E & W Marylyn Ave 16801
Matthew Cir 16801
Mayberry Ln 16801
Mcallister Aly & St 16801
Mcbath St 16801
Mccann Dr 16801
Mcclary Ct E & W 16801
E Mccormick Ave 16801
Mckee St 16803
Mckivison Ct 16803
Meadow Ln 16801
Meadowhawk Ln 16801
Meadowsweet Dr 16801
Meadowview Ct & Dr 16801
Meckley Rd 16801
Megan Dr 16803
Melissa Ln 16803
Merry Hill Rd 16801
Metz Ave 16801
Middle St 16801
Millbrook Way 16801
Miller Aly 16801
Millson Cir 16801
Minute Man Rd 16803
Misty Hill Dr 16801
Mitch Ave 16801
E & W Mitchell Ave 16803
Mitchell Farm Ln 16801
Mobile Ave 16801
Monarch Ave 16801
Monroe Ave 16801
Morningside Cir 16803
Moses Thompson Ln 16801
Mossey Glen Rd 16801
Mountain Rd 16801
Mountain Laurel Dr 16801
Mountain View Ave 16801
Muncy Rd 16801
Murphy Ln 16801
Nantucket Cir 16803
Nettle Ln 16803
New Aly 16801
Nimitz Ave 16801
E & W Nittany Ave 16801
Nittany View Cir 16801
N Nixon Rd 16803
S Nixon Rd 16801
Norle St 16801
Norma St 16801
E & W North Hills Pl 16803
Northampton St 16803
Northbrook Ln 16803
Northland Ctr 16803
Northwick Blvd 16803
Norwood Ln 16803
Oak Ln 16801
N Oak Ln 16803
Oak St 16803
Oak Leaf Ct & Dr 16803
Oak Pointe Cir 16801
Oak Ridge Ave 16801
Oakhurst Ln 16801
Oakley Dr 16803
Oakmont Rd 16801
Oakwood Ave 16803
Oakwood Cir 16801
Oakwood Dr 16801
October Dr 16801
Old Block Rd 16801
Old Boalsburg Rd 16801
Old Evergreen Ln 16801
Old Farm Ln 16803
Old Gatesburg Rd 16803
Old Houserville Rd 16801
Old Mill Rd 16801
Oneida St 16801
Orange Aly 16801
Orchard Rd 16801
Orlando Ave 16803
N & S Osmond St 16801
E, S & W Outer Dr 16801
Owens Dr 16801
Oxford Cir 16803
Pamela Cir 16801
Panorama Dr 16801
E & W Park Ave & Ln 16803
Park Center Blvd 16801
Park Crest Ln 16803
Park Forest Ave 16803
E & W Park Hills Ave 16803
Partridge Ln 16803
Patrick Cir 16801
Patriot Ln 16803
N & S Patterson St 16801
Patton Ln & Plz 16801
Pearson Aly 16801
Penbrook Ln 16801
Penfield Rd 16801
E Pennsylvania Ave 16801
Penny Ln 16803
Penrose Cir 16803
Persia Rd 16801
Pickwick Ave 16803
Piersol Ln 16801
Pierson Dr 16803
Pike St 16801
Pikeview Rd 16801
Pine Cliff Rd 16801
Pine Grove Rd 16801
Pine Hall Ct & Rd 16801
Pine Hurst Ct & Dr 16803
Plaza Dr 16801
Pleasant Hill Rd 16803
E Pollock Rd 16801
Portsmouth Rd 16803
Prairie Rose Ln 16801
Premiere Dr 16801
Presidents Dr 16803
Princeton Dr 16803
E & W Prospect Ave 16801
Puddintown Rd 16801
S Pugh St 16801
Quail Run Rd 16801
Quality Way 16801
Quick Farm Ln 16801
Quincy Ave 16801
Radnor Rd 16801
Railroad Ave 16801
Rainlo St 16801
Raleigh Ave 16801
Randy Ln 16801
Raven Hollow Rd 16801
Reagan Cir 16801
Red Lion Dr 16801
Red Oak Ln 16803
Red Willow Rd 16801
Redgate Rd 16801
Redwood Ln 16801
Reese Rd 16801
Regent Ct 16801
Regina Cir 16803
Research Dr 16801
Rhaubert Cir 16801
Ridge Ave 16803
Ridge Master Dr 16803
Ridgeview Rd 16801
Ridgewood Cir 16803
Ringneck Rd 16801
Rishel Ln 16801
Robin Aly & Rd 16801
Rock Rd 16801
Rock Forge Rd 16803
Rolling Ridge Dr 16801
Ronan Dr 16801
Roosevelt Ave 16801
Rosa Ln 16801
Rosemont Dr 16801
Roundhay Ct 16801
Royal Cir & Rd 16801
Roylen Cir 16801
Sadie Ln 16801
Sagamore Dr 16803
Sandpiper Dr 16801
Sandra Cir 16801
Sandy Dr 16803
Sandy Ridge Rd 16803
Saratoga Dr 16801
Sassafras Ct 16803
Sawgrass Cir 16801
Saxton Dr 16801
Scarlet Oak Cir 16803
Scenery Ct & Dr 16801
Scholl St 16801
School Dr 16803
Science St 16801
Science Park Ct 16801
Science Park Rd 16803
Scott Rd 16801
Seaton Dr 16801
Selders Cir 16801
Seneca Cir 16801
Setter Run Ln 16801
Severn Dr 16803
Seymore Ave 16803
E & W Shadow Ln 16803
Shady Dr 16801
Shagbark Ct 16803
Shamrock Ave 16801
Shannon Ln 16803
Shawn Cir 16801
Sheffield Ct & Dr 16801
Sheldon Dr 16801
Shellers Bnd 16801
Shiloh Rd 16801
Shingletown Rd 16801
Shoferd Ln 16801
Sierra Ln 16803
Slab Cabin Rd 16801
Sleepy Hollow Dr 16803
Smithfield Cir & St 16801
E & W South Hills Ave 16801
Southgate Dr 16801
Southridge Plz 16801
Sowards Pl 16803
Sowers St 16801
N & S Sparks St 16801
Spencer Ln 16801
Spring St 16801
Spring Creek Ln 16801
Spring Hill Ln 16801
Spring Lea Dr 16801
Spring Valley Rd 16801
Spruce Dr 16801
Squirrel Dr 16801
Stafford Cir 16801
Stanbury Ln 16803
Standing Stone Ln 16803
Stewart Dr 16801
Stonebridge Dr 16801
Stoneledge Rd 16803
Stoney Ln 16801
Storch Rd 16801
Stratford Ct & Dr 16801
Strouse Ave 16803
Struble Rd 16801
Stuart St 16801
Suburban Ave 16803
Sunday Dr 16801
Sunrise Ter 16801
Sunset Rd 16803
Surrey Ln 16803
Susan Ln 16801
Suzy Cir 16801
Sycamore Dr 16801
Sylvan Dr 16803
Tall Cedar Cir 16803
Tall Oaks Dr 16801
Tanager Dr 16803
Tara Cir 16803
Taylor St 16803
Teaberry Cir & Ln 16803
Teal Ln 16803
Thistlewood Way 16801
Thomas St 16803
Thorn Aly 16801
Thornton Rd 16801
Thrush Aly 16801
Timber Ln 16801
Timber Ridge Rd 16801
Tionesta Ct 16803
Toftrees Ave 16803
Toter Ln 16803
Tradition Dr 16803
Tradition Cove Ln 16803
Treetops Dr 16801
E Trout Rd 16801
Tug Cir 16801
Tulip Rd 16801
Tulira Ln 16801
Tussey Ln 16801
Twigs Ln 16801
University Dr 16801
Vairo Blvd 16803
Valley Vista Dr 16803
Varsity Ln 16803
Victory Blvd 16803
Villa Crest Dr 16801
Village Dr 16803
Village Heights Dr 16801
Villandry Blvd 16801
Vineyard Hvn 16803
Vivian Way 16801
Waddle Rd 16803
Walker Dr 16801
Walnut St 16801
Walnut Grove Dr 16801
Walnut Spring Ln 16801
Waltz Ave 16801
E Waring Ave 16801
Warnock Rd 16801
Washington Ave & Pl 16801
Watkins Rd 16801
Watson Rd 16801
Waupelani Dr 16801
Waupelani Drive Ext 16801
Wayland Pl 16803
Waypoint Cir 16801
Weaver St 16803
Webster Dr 16801
Wellington Dr 16801
Wells Ter 16801
Westerly Pkwy 16801
Westgate Dr 16803
Westminster Ct 16803
Westover Dr 16801
Westview Ave 16803
Westwood Cir 16803
Wetherburn Dr 16801
Weymouth Cir 16803
Wheatfield Dr 16801
Wheel Cir 16803
E & W Whitehall Rd 16801
Whitetail Ln 16801
Widmann Cir 16803
Wild Rose Way 16801
Wildot Dr 16801
Willard Cir & St 16803
William St 16801
Williamsburg Ct & Dr 16801
Willow Ave & Cir 16801
Wilson Aly 16801
Wiltree Ct 16801
Wilts Ln 16803
Wiltshire Dr 16803
Winchester Ct 16801
Windmere Dr 16801
Windrush Rd 16801
Windsor Ct 16801
Windtryst Ave 16803
Winterberry Dr 16803
Wintergreen Cir 16801
Wolfs Ln 16803
Wood Aly 16801
Woodberry Cir 16803
Wooded Way 16803
Woodland Dr 16803
Woodledge Cir & Dr 16803
Woods Rd 16801
Woodside Dr 16801
Woodycrest St 16803
Wren Aly 16801
Wyndlawn Ln 16801
Yardal Rd 16801
Yorkshire Cir 16803
Zorich Rd 16803

NUMBERED STREETS

1st Ave 16801
2nd Ave 16803
5th Ave 16803

VALLEY FORGE PA

General Delivery 19481

POST OFFICE BOXES MAIN OFFICE STATIONS AND BRANCHES

Box No.s
2 - 590 19481
603 - 2987 19482
80001 - 80865 19484

NAMED STREETS

Allendale Rd 19484
Valley Forge Rd
1721-1721 19481
1721-1721 19482

WARRENDALE PA

General Delivery 15086

POST OFFICE BOXES MAIN OFFICE STATIONS AND BRANCHES

Box No.s
1 - 558 15086
700 - 2000 15095
2001 - 2104 15086

NAMED STREETS

Allegheny Dr 15086
Brush Creek Rd
300-300 15086
300-302 15095
301-897 15086
899-999 15086
Commonwealth Dr 15086
Ericsson Dr 15086
Gay Ln 15086
Global View Dr 15086
Johnson Rd 15086
Keystone Dr 15086
Maple Dr 15086
Marshall Dr 15086
Mount Pleasant Rd 15086
Northgate Dr 15086
Pennwood Pl 15086
Perry Hwy 15086
Pinewood Ln 15086
Slade Ln 15086
Thorn Hill Rd 15086
Vanconer Dr 15086
Warren Rd 15086
Warrendale Bayne Rd 15086
Warrendale Village Dr 15086
Williamsburg Pl 15086
Woodland Rd 15086

WEST CHESTER PA

General Delivery 19380

POST OFFICE BOXES MAIN OFFICE STATIONS AND BRANCHES

Box No.s
1 - 1001 19381
1201 - 2750 19380
3001 - 3580 19381
4000 - 5352 19380
9998 - 9998 19382

NAMED STREETS

Achcom Way 19380
N Adams St 19380
S Adams St 19382
Adams Way 19382
Addison Pl 19382
Adele Aly 19382
Afton Way 19380
Airport Rd 19380
Albermarle Grv 19380
Alcott Cir 19380
Alexander Ln 19382
Alison Dr 19380
Allan Ln 19380
Allandale Ln 19380
Allegiance Dr 19382
Allerton Rd 19382
Allison Dr 19380
Alyssa Cir 19380
Amalfi Dr 19380
Amanda Ln 19380
Amber Ln 19382
Amelia Dr 19382
American Blvd 19380
Amstel Way 19380
Anderson Ave 19380
Andover Ct 19382
Andrew Dr 19380
Anglesey Ter 19380
Anna Rd 19380
Anne Dr 19380
Anthony Ln & Way 19382
Apple Hill Dr 19380
Appleberry Way 19382
Appleblossom Cir 19380
Applegate Dr 19382
Appleville Rd 19380
Apricot Ln 19380
Arden Ct 19382

Ardleigh Cir 19380
Ardrossan Ave 19382
Arlington Ave 19380
Arrowhead Ct & Dr 19382
Artillery Point Rd 19382
E & W Ashbridge Rd & St 19380
N & S Ashbrooke Dr 19380
Ashley Rd 19382
Ashton Way 19380
Aspen Ct 19380
Astor Sq 19380
Atlee Dr 19380
Audubon Rd 19382
Augusta Dr 19382
Aurora Dr 19380
Autopark Blvd 19382
Autumn Way 19380
Autumn View Way 19380
Avery Pl 19382
Ayer Ct 19382
Bainbridge Dr 19382
Bala Ter E & W 19380
Bala Farms 19382
Baldwin Dr 19380
Ballintree Ln 19382
Banbury Cir 19380
Bancroft Dr 19380
Bane Way 19380
Bantery Rd 19380
Barbara Dr 19382
Barker Cir & Dr 19380
Barkway Ln 19380
Barn Hill Rd 19382
E & W Barnard St 19382
Barnsworth Ln 19382
Barnview Ln 19382
Barry Rd 19382
Bartrams Ln 19382
Basin Rd 19382
Battle Dr 19382
Baylowell Dr 19380
Baywood Rd 19382
Beagle Rd 19382
Beam Rd 19380
Beau Dr 19380
Beaumont Cir 19380
Beech Ln 19382
Beechwood Rd 19382
Bell Flower Ln 19380
Bellbrook Dr 19382
Bellefair Ln 19382
Belmont Ave 19380
Belvidere Cir 19380
N & S Benjamin Dr 19382
Bent Oak Trl 19380
Bent Tree Dr 19380
Berkley Ln 19380
Berry Ln 19382
Berwick Dr 19382
Beversrede Trl 19382
Bicking Dr 19382
E & W Biddle St 19380
Bidefore Ct 19382
Birchwood Dr 19380
Birmingham Rd 19382
Birnam Pl 19380
Bittersweet Dr 19382
Bittersweet Ln 19380
Blanford Ln 19380
Blenheim Rd 19382
Blue Rock Rd 19382
Bobolink Ln 19382
Bolingbroke Rd 19382
S Bolmar St 19382
Bonnie Blink Dr 19380
E & W Boot Rd 19380
Bottom Ln 19382
Boulder Ln 19382
Bow Tree Dr 19380
Bowen Way 19380
Bowers Dr 19382
Bowman Ave 19380
Box Elder Dr 19380
Bracken Ct 19382

N Bradford Ave
2-98 19382
100-220 19382
222-298 19382
300-300 19380
S Bradford Ave 19382
Bradford Ter 19382
Braeburn Ct 19382
Bragg Hill Rd 19382
Bramble Ln 19380
W Branch Ln 19382
Brandyridge Dr 19382
Brandywine Ave 19380
Brandywine Dr 19382
Brandywine Pkwy 19380
Brandywine Rd 19382
N Brandywine St 19380
S Brandywine St 19382
Braxton Ln 19382
Brecknock Ter 19380
Breeze Wood Ln 19382
Brettingham Ct 19382
Brian Dr 19380
Briar Wood Cir & Ct 19380
S Bridge Rd 19382
Bridgewater Dr 19380
Bridle Ln 19382
Bridle Path 19380
Brinton Ave & Cir 19380
Brinton Lake Rd 19382
Brinton Place Rd 19380
Brinton Run Rd 19382
Brinton Woods Rd 19382
Brintons Bridge Rd 19382
Brittany Pl 19380
Broad St 19382
Broad Run Rd
200-699 19382
800-898 19380
900-1099 19380
Broadway 19382
Brooke Dr 19380
Brookfield Way 19382
Brookhill Rd 19380
Brookmeade Dr 19380
Brooks Rd 19382
Brookside Ct 19380
Buck Ln 19382
Buckeye Ln 19382
Bucktail Way 19382
Burke Rd 19380
Burning Bush Ln 19380
Butternut Cir 19382
Cabin Club Ln 19382
Caleb Dr 19382
Calhoun Ln 19380
Camaro Run Dr 19380
Cambridge Ct 19380
Camp Linden Rd 19382
Candy Ln 19382
Candytuft Ln 19380
Cann Rd 19382
Cannon Hill Dr 19382
Canterbury Ct & Dr 19380
Cardiff Ter 19380
Cardigan Ter 19380
Cardinal Ave 19380
Cardinal Dr 19382
Carlson Ave 19382
Carlton Ln 19382
Carlyle Rd 19382
Carmac Rd 19382
Carnation Ln 19382
Carol Cir 19380
Carolannes Way 19382
Carolina Ave 19380
Carolyn Dr 19382
Carpenter Ln 19382
Carriage Ln 19382
Carrie Ln 19382
Carroll Brown Way 19382
Carroll Hill Dr 19382
Carter Dr & Pl 19382
Casey Ln 19382
Cashel Ln 19380
Cassatt Ct 19380

Caswallen Dr 19380
Cavalier Ln 19380
Cavanaugh Ct 19382
Cedar Ave 19382
Cedar Mill Ln 19382
Cedar Ridge Rd 19380
Cedarwood Ave 19380
Centennial Dr 19382
Center St 19382
Centre School Way 19382
Ceredo Ave 19380
Chadd Ct 19382
Chadds Cv 19382
Chambers Ln 19382
Chambord Pl 19380
Chandlee Dr 19382
Chandler Dr 19380
Chaps Ln 19382
Charles Rd 19382
Charlotte Way 19380
Chateau Dr 19382
Chatham Way 19380
Chatwood Ave 19382
Chelsea Cir 19380
Cherry Ln 19380
Cherry St 19382
Cherry Farm Ln 19382
Cheshire Cir & Rd 19380
Chessie Ct 19380
W Chester Pike 19382
N Chester Rd 19380
S Chester Rd 19382
Chesterdale Farm Ln 19382
Chesterville Way 19382
E & W Chestnut Aly, Ct & St 19380
Chestnut Hollow Ln 19380
Cheyney Dr & Rd 19382
Chickadee Ln 19382
Chiswick Dr 19380
Chrislena Ln 19380
Christine Ln 19380
Church Ave 19382
N Church St 19380
S Church St 19382
Churchill Downs 19380
Cider Knoll Way 19382
Circle Ave & Dr 19382
Circle Top Ln 19382
Clarke St 19380
Clarks Ln 19382
Clayton Rd 19382
Clearbrook Rd 19380
Clearview Rd 19382
Clinton Aly 19382
Clipper Mill Dr 19382
Clock Tower Dr 19380
Cloud Ln 19382
Cloud Pl 19380
Clover Ln 19380
Clover Hill Dr 19382
Clover Ridge Dr 19380
Cloverly Ln 19380
Coach Hill Ct 19382
Cobblestone Ct 19380
Cockburn Dr 19382
Cohasset Ln 19380
Cold Springs Dr 19382
College Ave 19382
Collins Dr 19380
Colonial Dr 19382
Colonial Ln 19380
Colonial Way 19382
Coltsfoot Dr 19382
Colwyn Ter 19380
N Concord Rd 19380
S Concord Rd 19382
Conifer Dr 19380
Coniston Dr 19380
Connor Rd 19382
Constitution Dr 19380
Continental Dr 19380
Continental Line Ln 19382
Cooper Cir 19380
Copeland School Rd 19380
Copes Ln 19380

Cork Cir 19380
Cornwallis Dr 19380
Corrine Rd 19382
Corwen Ter W 19380
Cotswald Ct 19382
Cotswold Ln 19380
Cottage Ln 19382
Cougar Dr 19382
Country Ln 19380
Country Club Rd 19382
Countryside Dr 19380
Court House Aly 19380
Courtland Pl 19380
Courtney Cir 19382
S Coventry Ln 19382
Crabapple Ln 19380
Cranberry Ln 19380
Cratin Ln 19380
Creamery Ln 19382
Creek Rd 19382
N Creek Rd
201-397 19382
399-499 19382
501-599 19382
600-799 19380
S Creek Rd 19382
W Creek Rd 19382
Creekview Cir 19382
Crescent Dr 19382
Crest Dr 19382
Crestview Dr 19382
Cricket Ln 19380
Cricklewood Rd 19382
Cromwell Ln 19380
Crop Ct 19382
Crosspointe Dr 19380
Crownpointe Ln 19380
Crows Nest Cir 19382
E & W Cub Hunt Ln 19380
Culbertson Cir 19382
Cumbrian Ct 19382
Cynthia Ln 19382
Cypress Ln 19380
Daisy Ln 19382
Daly Dr 19382
Daniel Davis Ln 19382
Danielle Way 19382
Darlington Dr 19382
N Darlington St 19380
S Darlington St 19382
David Ln 19382
Davidson Rd 19382
Davis Cir 19380
Dawn Dr 19382
Day Spring Ln 19382
Dean Ct & St 19382
Debaptiste Ln 19382
Deblyn V Ln 19382
Debras Way 19382
Deer Ln 19380
Deer Crossing Rd 19382
Deer Pointe Rd 19382
N & S Deerwood Dr 19382
Delancey Pl 19380
Delaware Ave 19380
Delicious Dr 19380
Delmar Ave 19382
Denbi Ct 19382
Denbigh Ter 19380
Denton Hollow Rd 19382
Derby Dr 19382
Derry Ln 19380
Devereaux Cir 19380
Devon Ln & Way 19380
Devonshire Cir 19380
Diane Dr 19382
Dickens Dr 19380
Dilworth Farm Ln 19382
Dilworthtown Rd & Xing 19382
Dodgson Rd 19382
Doe Run Ct 19382
Dogwood Dr 19380
Dogwood Ln 19382
Dogwood Hill Rd 19380
Dorothy Ln 19380

Dorset Dr 19382
Douglas Dr 19380
Downing Ave 19380
Downingtown Pike 19380
Dressage Ct 19382
Dunmoore Ln 19380
Dunning Dr 19382
Dunsinane Dr 19380
Dunvegan Rd 19382
Dunwoody Dr 19380
Durant Ct 19380
Durham Ct 19382
Dutton Mill Rd 19380
Dutts Ml E 19382
Eagle Rd 19382
Easter Cir & Dr 19382
Eastwick Cir 19380
Eaton Way 19380
Echo Hill Rd 19382
Edgemill Way 19382
Edgemont Dr 19380
Edgewater Dr 19380
Edgewood Rd 19382
Edinburgh Dr 19382
Edith Rd 19380
Edkin Ave 19382
Edmondson Dr 19382
Edward Ln 19382
Edwin Cir 19382
Elbow Ln 19380
Elderberry Ln 19380
Eldridge Dr 19380
Eleni Ln 19382
Elizabeth St 19380
Elk Ln 19382
Ellis Cir & Ln 19380
Elm Ave 19382
Elmwood Ave 19380
Elton Cir 19382
Embree Ln 19380
Emily Cir 19382
Empress Rd 19382
Enterprise Dr 19380
Erin Dr 19380
Eskin Pl 19380
Essex Ct 19380
Estate Dr 19380
Eton Ct 19382
Evan Ct 19380
E & W Evans St 19380
Everest Cir 19382
Evergreen Ct 19382
N Everhart Ave 19380
S Everhart Ave 19382
Evesham Ct 19382
Evie Ln 19382
Exeter Dr 19380
Fairbrook Dr 19380
Fairfield Ct 19382
Fairmont Dr 19382
Fairview Ave 19380
Fairview Dr 19382
Fairway Dr 19382
Falcon Ln 19382
Farm Ln 19382
Farmington Ln 19380
Farmstead Dr 19382
Farmview Dr 19382
Farrell Dr 19380
Farren Ln 19380
Faucett Dr 19382
Faustina Dr 19382
Favonius Way 19382
Fawn Ct 19382
Ferncliffe Ln 19380
Fernhill Rd 19380
Fielding Dr 19382
Fieldpoint Dr 19382
Fieldstone Dr 19382
Firethorne Dr 19382
Flagg Ln 19382
Folly Hill Rd 19382
Foothill Dr 19382
Ford Cir 19380
Forelock Ct 19382
Forest Rd 19382

Forsythe Ln 19382
Four In Hand Ct 19382
Fowler Dr 19382
Fox Pl 19382
Fox Xing 19380
Fox Chase Dr 19380
Fox Hollow Ln 19382
Fox Knoll Ln 19380
Fox Meadow Ln 19382
Foxglove Ln 19380
Francis Cir 19382
Frank Rd 19380
Franklin Dr 19382
N Franklin St 19380
S Franklin St 19382
Franklin Way 19380
Frederick Dr 19380
Freemont Dr 19382
Fringetree Dr 19382
Full Cry Ct 19380
Furr Ave 19380
Gages Ln 19382
Gail Rd 19380
Galeriso Rd 19380
Galway Dr 19380
S Garden Cir 19382
Garfield Ave 19380
Garlington Cir 19380
Garrett Ln 19380
Gary Ter 19380
Gated Ln 19380
Gates Dr 19380
Gateswood Dr 19380
Gateway Ln 19380
Gawthrops Ct 19382
E Gay St
6-10 19380
12-102 19380
101-101 19381
103-799 19380
104-798 19380
W Gay St 19380
General Allen Dr 19382
General Cornwallis Dr 19382
General Greene Dr 19382
General Howe Dr 19382
General Lafayette Blvd 19382
General Sterling Dr 19382
General Stevens Dr 19382
General Sullivan Dr 19382
General Wayne Dr 19382
General Weedon Dr 19382
Generals Way 19382
Georgia Ln 19380
Giunta Ln 19382
Glamorgan Ter 19380
Glen Ave 19382
Glen Echo Rd 19380
Glenbrook Ln 19380
Glendale Ln 19382
E Glenmont Ln 19380
S Glenside Rd 19380
Glenwood Ln 19380
Goodwin Ln 19382
Goshen Pkwy & Rd 19380
Granby Way 19380
E Grand Oak Ln 19380
Granite Aly 19380
Grant Rd 19382
Great Rd 19380
Great Oak Cir 19380
Green Ave 19380
Green Ln 19382
Green Acres Ln 19380
Green Bank Ave 19380
Green Hill Ave 19380
Green Tree Dr 19382
Green Tree Ln 19380
Greenbriar Dr 19382
Greene Countrie Dr 19380
Greenhill Rd 19380
Greenview Dr 19382
Gregory Ln 19380
Greystone Dr 19380
Grist Mill Ln 19380
Groton Ct 19382

Ground Hog College Rd 19382
Grove Ave & Rd 19380
Grovenor Ct 19380
Grubbs Mill Rd 19380
Guthrie Rd 19380
Gypsie Ln 19380
Hadleigh Dr 19380
Hagerty Blvd 19382
Haines Mill Rd 19382
Halifax Ct 19382
Hall Rd 19380
Hallowell Dr 19382
Halls Ln 19380
Halvorsen Dr 19382
Hamilton Dr 19380
Hamlet Hill Dr 19380
Hampshire Ct 19380
Hampshire Pl 19382
Hampstead Pl 19382
Hampton Ct 19380
Hannah Penn Ct 19382
Hannum Ave 19380
Hanover Dr 19382
Hansen Dr 19380
Happy Creek Ln 19380
Harmony Aly & Cir 19380
Harmony Hill Rd 19380
Harriman Ct 19380
Harrison Rd E & W 19380
Hartford Sq 19380
Harvest Ln 19380
Harvey Rd 19382
Hawthorne Ln 19380
Heartsease Dr 19382
Heather Ln 19380
Heather Ridge Cir 19382
Heatherton Ln 19380
Hedgerow Ln 19380
Hemlock Aly 19382
Hemlock Hill Ln 19380
Heritage Dr 19382
Herron Ln 19380
Hershey Mill Rd 19380
Hersheys Dr 19380
Hessian Cir 19382
Hibberd Ln 19380
Hickory Hill Rd 19382
Hidden Hollow Ln 19380
Hidden Pond Way 19382
Hidden Valley Ln 19382
Hiddenview Dr 19380
Hideout Ct 19382
N High St 19380
S High St 19382
High Meadow Ln 19380
Highgate Rd 19380
Highgrove Dr 19380
Highland Ave 19380
Highland Rd
2-98 19382
100-399 19382
500-550 19380
552-598 19380
Highland Farm Rd 19382
Highpoint Dr 19382
Highspire Dr 19382
Hightop Rd 19382
Highview Cir 19382
N Hill Dr 19380
Hill St 19382
Hillary Ct 19382
Hillcrest Rd 19380
Hilloch Dr 19380
Hillsdale Rd 19382
Hillside Ave & Dr 19380
E & W Hilltop Rd 19382
Hinchley Run 19382
Hollow Run Ln 19380
Holly Rd 19382
Hollyberry Ln 19380
Hollyview Ln 19380
Holmes Dr 19382
Homestead Dr 19382
Honeysuckle Ct 19380
Hoopes Park Ln 19380

Hoskin Pl 19380
Howard Rd 19380
Huber Pl 19382
Hummingbird Ln 19382
Hunt Dr 19382
Hunters Cir & Ln 19380
Hunting Hill Ln 19382
Huntington Ct 19380
Huntrise Ln 19382
Huntsman Ln 19382
Huntteam Ln 19382
Hydrangea Ct 19380
Hyllwynd Ct & Dr 19382
Independence Dr 19382
Indian Hannah Rd 19382
Inverness Dr 19380
Irene Dr 19380
Isaac Taylor Dr 19382
Isabel Ln 19380
Ivy Ln 19380
Ivy Rock Rd 19382
Jack Russell Ln 19380
Jackson Ln 19380
Jaclyn Dr 19380
Jacqueline Dr 19382
Jaeger Cir 19382
James Dr
200-299 19380
600-699 19382
Jamestown Way 19380
Jefferies Ave 19382
Jefferies Bridge Rd 19382
Jefferson Way 19380
Jefferson Downs 19380
Jenissa Dr 19382
Jennifer Ln 19382
Jeroma Ln 19382
Jessica Ln 19380
Joeck Cir & Dr 19382
John Anthony Dr 19382
Johnnys Way 19382
Jolene Dr 19382
Jonathan Rd 19380
Jones Ln 19382
Jordan Rd 19382
Joseph Dr 19380
Joshua Dr 19380
Joy Ln 19382
Judson Dr 19380
Julieanna Dr 19380
Jumper Ln 19382
Justin Dr & Ln 19382
Kadar Dr 19382
Karen Ln 19380
Katherine Ln 19380
Katie Way 19380
Kay Cir 19382
Kelly Ann Dr 19382
Kenmara Dr 19380
Kennett Way 19380
Kent Ct 19380
Kerwood Rd 19382
Keswick Way 19382
Keystone Aly 19382
Kilduff Cir 19382
Killarney Ln 19382
Killern Ln 19380
Killington Cir 19380
Kimberly Ln 19382
Kimes Ave 19380
King Rd 19380
King George Ct 19380
Kingsway Rd 19382
Kinterra Ct 19382
Kirby Dr 19380
Kirkcaldy Dr 19382
Kirkland Ave 19380
Knolls Rd 19382
Knollwood Dr 19380
Kolbe Ln 19382
Lacey St 19382
Lady Kathryn Ct 19380
E Lafayette Dr 19382
W Lafayette Dr 19382
E Lafayette St 19380
W Lafayette St 19380
Lake Dr 19382
Lake George Cir 19382
Lakeview Dr 19382
Lambourne Rd 19382
Larc Ln 19382
Larch Ln 19380
Larchwood Rd 19382
Larkin Bailey Rd 19382
Lauber Rd 19382
Laura Ln 19380
Laurel Dr 19380
Lawrence Dr 19380
Laydon Ln 19380
Lea Dr 19382
Leadline Ln 19382
Leeds Ct 19382
Legacy Ln 19382
Legion Dr 19380
Lenape Rd 19382
Lenape Farm Ln 19382
Lenape Unionville Rd 19382
Lenni Dr 19382
Lennon Way 19380
Leslie Ln 19382
Lewis Ln 19380
Lexington Ave 19382
Lian Dr 19382
Liberty Pl & Sq 19382
Limner Ct 19382
Lincoln Ave & Dr 19380
Linda Dr 19380
Linda Vista Dr 19380
Linden Ln 19380
Linden St 19380
Line Rd 19380
Links Dr 19380
Lintell Dr 19382
Lisa Dr 19380
Little Ridge Dr 19382
Little Shiloh Rd 19382
Live Oak Ln 19380
Llewellyn Cir 19380
Lochwood Ln 19380
Lockerbie Ln 19382
Locksley Dr 19380
Locust Aly 19380
Locust Cir 19380
Locust Ct 19382
Locust Ln E 19380
Locust Ln N 19380
Locust Ln S 19380
Locust St 19382
Locust Grove Rd 19382
Lofting Ln 19382
Londonderry Dr 19382
Long Ln 19380
Longford Rd 19380
Longview Dr 19380
Lorient Dr 19380
Lotus Ln 19380
Louise Ln 19382
Lucky Hill Rd 19382
Luther Ln 19380
Lydia Ln 19382
Lyme Ct 19382
Lynetree Dr 19380
Lynn Cir 19380
W Lynn Dr 19380
Macelroy Dr 19380
Machinery Rd 19380
Mackenzie Dr 19380
Macpherson Dr 19380
Macroom Ave 19382
Maentel Dr 19382
Magnolia St 19382
Mallard Rd 19382
Manchester Ct 19380
Manley Ave 19380
Manley Rd
1400-1514 19382
1515-1517 19380
1516-1518 19382
1519-1799 19380
Manor Dr 19380
Manorwood Dr 19382
Mansion House Dr 19382
Mansion View Dr 19382
Mantel Dr 19382
Maple Ave 19380
Maple Ln 19382
Maple Ridge Way 19382
Maplewood Rd 19382
Margaret Ln 19380
Margate Ct 19380
Margo Ln 19380
Marguerite Ave 19382
Marie Rd 19380
Marie Rochelle Dr 19382
Mark Dr 19380
Marker Dr 19382
E & W Market St 19382
E Market And Westtown
Rd 19382
Marlboro Rd 19382
Marlene Dr 19380
Marlin Dr 19382
Marple Dr 19382
Marrones Ct 19382
E & W Marshall Dr &
St 19380
Marshallton Thorndale
Rd 19380
Martlet Rise 19380
Martone Rd 19382
Mary Fran Dr 19382
Mary Jane Ln 19380
Marydell Dr 19382
N & S Maryland Ave 19380
Masters Ct 19380
Mather Ln 19382
N Matlack St 19380
S Matlack St 19382
Maule Ln 19382
Mayapple Ln 19380
Mayfair Cir 19380
Mayfield Ave 19380
Mccardle Dr 19380
Mccool Blvd 19380
Mcdaniel Dr 19380
Mcdermott Dr 19380
Mcgregor Dr 19380
Mcintosh Ln 19380
Mcintosh Rd 19380
Mcmullan Farm Ln 19382
Meadow Dr 19380
Meadow Ln 19382
Meadow Croft Cir 19382
Meadow Glen Dr 19380
Meadowbrook Ln 19380
Meadowcroft Rd 19382
Meadowview Ln 19382
Mechanics Aly & St 19382
Meeting House Ln 19382
Meetinghouse Rd 19382
Meghan Ct 19382
Melba Ln 19380
Melissa Ln 19380
Melvin Dr 19380
Memory Ln 19380
Mercer Ln 19380
Mercers Mill Ln 19382
Merion Ter 19380
Merrifield Dr 19380
Merrill Rd 19382
Merrit Cir 19380
Metro Ct 19380
Mews Ln 19382
Michael Ln 19380
Michaels Aly 19380
Michele Dr 19380
Middle Aly 19380
Midvale Rd 19380
Miles Rd 19380
Militia Hill Dr 19382
Mill Rd 19380
Mill Creek Dr 19380
Milleson Ln 19380
Millrace Ln 19380
Mimosa Tree Ln 19380
E & W Miner St 19382
Misak Dr 19380
Misty Meadow Dr 19382
Molly Ln 19382
Monmouth Ter 19380
Montbard Dr 19382
Monte Vista Dr 19380
Monteray Ln & St 19380
Montgomery Ave 19380
Montvale Cir 19380
Morgan Cir 19380
Morning Glory Dr 19380
Morris Rd 19382
Morstein Rd 19380
Mount Bradford Way 19382
Mountain View Dr 19382
Muirfield Dr 19382
Murdock Dr 19380
Musket Ct 19382
Mutsu Ln 19382
Mystery Ln 19382
Natalie Dr 19382
Nathan Hale Dr 19382
Nathaniel Dr 19380
Nectar Ln 19382
Netherfield Ln 19380
N New St 19380
S New St 19382
New Jersey Ave 19380
New Kent Dr 19380
New York Ave 19380
Newbury Ln 19380
Newmarket Ct 19382
Nicholas Dr 19380
E & W Nields St 19382
E & W Niels Ln 19382
Nobb Hill Dr 19380
Norfolk Ave 19382
Norma Ln 19382
Normandy Ct 19382
Norris Ln 19380
Northbrook Rd 19382
Northgate Rd 19382
Norwood Rd 19380
Nottingham Cir & Dr 19380
Oak Cir 19380
Oak Ln 19382
Oak Creek Dr 19380
Oak Leaf Ln 19382
Oak Tree Hollow Rd 19382
Oakbourne Rd 19382
Oakland Rd 19382
Oaklea Ln 19382
Oakmont Ct & Ln 19380
Oakwood Ave 19380
Oermead Ln 19380
Old Bailey Ln 19382
Old Barn Dr 19382
Old Fern Hill Rd 19382
Old Greenhill Rd 19380
Old Orchard Ln 19382
Old Phoenixville Pike 19380
Old Pottstown Pike 19380
Old West Chester
Pike 19382
Old Westtown Rd 19382
Old Wilmington Pike 19382
Old Woods Rd 19382
Olivia Ct 19382
Orchard Ave 19382
Oriole Dr 19380
Osage Ln 19382
Overhill Cir & Rd 19382
Overlook Cir 19382
Owen Rd 19380
Oxford Rd 19380
Paddock Cir & Ln 19382
Padula 19382
Paine Dr 19382
Painters Xing 19382
Palomino Dr 19382
Paoli Pike 19380
Park Ave & Ln 19380
Parke Hollow Ln 19382
Parkerville Rd 19382
Parkside Ave 19382
Parry Cir 19380
Partridge Ln 19382
Patrice Ln 19380
Patrick Ave 19380
Patrick Henry Cir 19382
Patriot Pl 19382
Patterson Ln 19380
Patton Aly & Ave 19380
Paul Ln 19380
Paxson Dr 19382
Peacefull Ln 19380
Peach Tree Dr 19380
Peale Dr 19382
Pebblewood Rd 19380
Pembroke Dr 19380
Pendula Ct 19380
Penn Dr 19382
E Penn Dr 19380
N Penn Dr 19380
S Penn Dr 19380
W Penn Dr 19380
Penn Ln 19382
N Penn St 19380
S Penn St 19382
Penn Oaks Dr 19382
Penns Way 19382
Penns Grant Dr 19382
Pennsbury Dr 19382
Pennsylvania Ave 19380
Penny Ln 19380
Pepper Mill Ln 19380
Perry Dr 19380
Peter Christopher Dr 19382
Pheasant Path 19382
Pheasant Run Rd
100-299 19380
700-899 19382
Phoenixville Pike 19380
Picket Way 19382
Piedmont Rd 19382
Pietro Pl 19382
Pine Cir & Dr 19380
Pine Ridge Rd 19382
Pine Rock Rd 19380
Pine Valley Cir 19382
Pineview Dr 19380
Pintail Ct 19382
Pippin Ln 19380
E & W Pleasant Grove
Rd 19382
Plum Run Dr 19382
Plumly Rd 19382
Plumtry Dr 19382
Plymouth Ct 19380
Pocopson Rd 19382
Polo Run 19380
Pomona Hill Dr 19382
Pond View Dr 19382
Ponds Edge Rd 19382
Pony Ct 19382
Poplar St 19382
Pottstown Pike 19380
Powell Ln 19380
Prairie Ln 19380
Pratt Ln 19382
E & W Prescott Aly 19380
Price St 19382
Prichard Ave 19382
Primrose Ln 19380
Princeton Ln 19380
Private Dr 19382
Prospect Ave 19380
Pulaski Dr 19380
S Pullman Dr 19380
Pump House Ln 19382
Pynchon Hall Rd 19382
Quail Ct 19382
Quail Run Ln 19382
Quaker Rdg 19380
Queen Dr 19380
Queen Ln 19382
Queens Way 19382
Queens Rangers Ln 19382
Quincy Pl 19382
Radek Ct 19382
Radley Dr 19382
Radnor Ter 19380
Raewyck Dr 19380
Railway Sq 19380
Raleigh Dr 19380
Raspberry Ln 19382
Ravens Ln 19382
Raymond Dr 19380
Reading Ct 19380
Red Bridge Ln 19382
Red Coat Ct 19380
Red Fox Ln 19380
Red Hawk Ln 19382
Red Lion Rd 19382
Red Maple Dr 19380
Redtail Ct 19382
Redwood Ct 19380
Regimental Dr 19382
Reims Ln 19382
Reisling Ln 19382
Rennard Ln 19380
Renwick Dr 19382
Reservoir Rd 19380
Retford Ln 19380
Revere Rd 19382
Revolutionary Dr 19382
Rexton Dr 19380
Reynolds Ln 19380
E & W Rhodes Ave 19382
Richard Dr 19380
Richfield Rd 19380
Richmond Rd 19380
Ridge Rd 19382
Ridge Crest Dr 19382
Ridgehaven Rd 19382
Ridgewood Ln 19382
Ridings Way 19382
Ridley Creek Cv & Ln 19380
Riflery Dr 19382
Riverbend Ln 19382
Roberts Ln 19382
Robin Dr 19382
Robins Nest Ln 19382
Robynwood Ln 19380
Rock Creek Rd 19382
Rockland Ave 19382
Rockwood Dr 19380
Rodney Dr 19382
Rolling Dr 19380
Rolling Rd 19382
Rollinview Dr 19382
Rome Rd 19380
Romford Ct 19380
Rosary Ln 19382
Rose Ln 19380
E & W Rosedale Ave 19382
Rosewood Dr 19382
Roslyn Ave 19382
Roundelay Ln 19382
Roundhouse Ct 19380
Route 162 19382
Royal Berkshire Cir 19380
Royal View Dr 19382
Rue Ln 19380
Russell Ln 19382
Saber Rd 19382
E Sage Rd 19382
Sage Hill Ln 19382
Saint Andrews Ln 19382
Saint Annes Way 19382
Saint Finegan Dr 19382
Saint James Rd 19380
Salem Walk 19382
Samuel Rd 19380
Sandy Ln 19382
Saratoga Dr 19380
Sassafras Cir 19382
Saunders Ct & Ln 19380
Saville Ln 19380
Sawtimber Trl 19380
Scaleby Ln 19382
Scarborough Ct 19380
Scattergood Ln 19380
School Ln 19382
School House Ln 19382
Schuyler Dr 19380
Scofield Ln 19380
Sconnelltown Rd 19382
Scotch Way 19382
Scott Dr 19380
Scotts Aly 19380
Seal Ln 19380
Serpentine Dr 19382
Shadebrush Rdg 19382
Shadow Farm Rd 19380
Shady Grove Way 19382
Shadyside Rd 19380
Shagbark Dr 19382
Shaker Ln 19380
Sharon Aly & Cir 19382
Sharpless St 19382
Shaumont Dr 19382
Sheffield Ln 19380
Shenandoah Ln 19380
Shenton Rd 19380
Sherbrook Dr 19382
Sheridan Dr 19382
Sherwood Dr 19380
Shiloh Rd 19382
Shiloh Hill Dr 19382
Ship Rd 19380
Shippen Ln 19382
Short Ln 19380
Shropshire Dr 19382
Side Saddle Pl 19382
Silverbell Ct 19380
Silverwood Dr 19382
Sissinghurst Dr 19382
Skelp Level Rd 19380
Skiles Blvd 19382
Sleepy Hollow Ln 19380
Sloan Rd 19382
Smallwood Ct 19380
Smiths Ct 19382
Smoke House Rd 19382
Snowberry Way 19380
Snyder Ave 19382
Somerset Pl 19382
Sonnet Ln 19380
Sorber Dr 19380
Southerland Ct 19380
Southern Dr 19380
Southgate Rd 19382
Spackmans Ln 19380
N & S Speakman Ln 19380
Spindle Ln 19380
Spring Ct & Ln 19382
Spring Grove Ln 19382
Spring House Ln 19380
Spring Line Dr 19382
Spring Meadow Dr 19382
Spring Oak Dr 19382
Spring Valley Ln 19380
Springton Ln 19380
Springview Ct 19382
Springwood Dr 19382
Spruce Aly, Ave, Ct &
Dr 19382
Spur Ln 19382
Squire Cheney Dr 19382
Squires Dr & Pl 19382
St Andrews Dr 19380
Stable Ln 19382
Staghorn Way 19380
Stallion Ln 19380
Stanton Ave 19382
Station Pl 19380
Station Way 19382
Stayman St 19380
Steward Ln 19382
Stewart Dr 19380
Still Rd 19382
Stillwood Ln 19380
Stirling Ct 19380
Stirrup Cir 19382
Stockton Ct 19382
Stone Fence Rd 19382
Stonegate Ct 19380
Stoneham Dr 19382
Stonewall Ln 19382
Stoney Run Dr 19382
Stoneybrook Ln 19382
Story Rd 19380
Stourbridge Ct 19380
E Strasburg Rd 19380
W Strasburg Rd 19382

E & W Street Rd 19382
Sturbridge Ln 19380
Suffolk Downs 19380
Sugarmans Ct 19382
Sugars Bridge Rd 19380
Sullivan Cir 19380
Summit House 19382
Sumner Way 19382
Sundance Dr 19380
Sunhigh Dr 19380
Sunney Brook Ln 19382
Sunset Ln 19380
Sunset Hollow Rd 19380
Supplee Way 19382
Surrey Rd 19382
Susan Dr 19380
Sussex Rd 19380
Suzanne Dr 19380
Swallow Ln 19380
Sweet Briar Rd 19380
Swinburne Rd 19382
Sycamore Dr 19380
Sylvan Dr 19380
Sylvan Rd 19382
Sylvania Ln 19380
Tacie Lynn Dr 19382
Talcose Ln 19380
Tall Pines Dr 19380
Talleyrand Rd 19382
Tallmadge Dr 19380
Tanager Ln 19382
Tanglewood Dr 19380
Tarbert Dr 19382
Tattersall Way 19380
Taylor Ave 19380
Taylor Chase Ln 19382
Taylors Mill Rd 19380
Telegraph Rd
1100-1563 19380
1564-1599 19382
Thicket Ct 19380
Thistle Ln 19380
Thistlewood Ln 19380
Thomas Ave 19380
Thomas Ct 19382
Thornbury Rd 19382
Thorncroft Dr 19380
Thorne Dr 19382
Thrush Ln 19382
Tigue Rd 19382
Tilden Cir 19382
Timber Ln 19380
Timberland Dr 19380
Timberline Trl 19382
Todd Way 19380
Topaz Dr 19382
Torrey Pine Ct 19380
Toulon Ct 19382
Tower Ln 19380
Tower Course Rd 19382
Towne Dr 19380
Trafalgar Ln 19380
Trail Run Ln 19382
Traylor Dr 19382
Tree Ln 19380
Treetops Ln 19380
Trellis Ln 19382
Trinity Dr 19382
Trio Ln 19382
Trolley Way 19382
Troon Ln 19380
Tuckaway Trl 19380
N & S Tulip Dr 19380
Tullamore Dr 19382
Tunbridge Rd 19382
Turks Head Ln 19382
E & W Turnberry Ct 19382
Turnbrae Ln 19382
Turner Ave & Ln 19380
Turnhill Ct 19380
Twaddell Dr 19382
Twickensham Ct 19382
Twin Oaks Ln 19380
Twin Pond Dr 19382
Tyson Dr 19382
Ulster Cir, Ct, Ln, Pl, Ter & Way 19380
E & W Union St 19382
Unionville Wawaset Rd 19382
Upton Cir 19380
Vale Dr 19382
Valley Cir 19380
Valley Dr 19382
Valley Rd 19382
Valley Creek Rd 19380
Vance Ave 19380
Vassar Ct 19380
Veronica Rd 19380
Victoria Ln 19380
Viredarl Dr 19380
E & W Virginia Ave 19380
Vista Dr 19380
Von Steuben Dr 19380
Wagonwheel Ln 19380
Walden Dr 19380
N Walnut St 19380
S Walnut St 19382
Walnut Hill Rd 19382
Walnut Springs Ct 19380
Waltham Ct 19380
Waltz Rd 19380
Ward Ave 19380
Ware Cir 19382
Warpath Rd 19382
Warren Rd 19382
Warwick Rd 19380
Washington Ln 19382
N Washington Rdg 19382
S Washington Rdg 19382
E Washington St 19380
W Washington St 19380
Waterford Rd 19380
Waterglen Cir, Dr & Ln 19382
Waterview Rd 19380
Waterwillow Rd 19380
Waverly Pl 19382
Wawaset Rd 19382
Wawaset Farm Ln 19382
Wayne Ct 19380
Wayne Dr 19382
N Wayne St 19380
S Wayne St 19382
Weatherhill Dr 19382
Wedgewood Ln 19380
Weedon Ct 19380
Weldon Dr 19380
Wellesley Ter 19382
Wellington Rd 19380
Wells Ter 19380
Wencin Ter & Way 19382
Wesley Ct 19380
Wesmoore Dr 19382
S Westbourne Rd 19382
Westbrook Dr 19382
Westcroft Pl 19382
Westerly Way 19382
Weston Way 19380
S Westtown Cir, Rd & Way 19382
Westtown Thornton Rd 19382
Westwood Dr 19382
Wexford Cir & Dr 19380
Whispering Oaks Dr 19382
Whispering Pine Dr 19380
White Chimney Rd 19382
White Wood Way 19382
Whiteland Dr 19380
Whiteman Way 19380
Whitetail Ln 19382
S Whitford Rd 19380
Whiticar Ln 19380
Whittleby Ct 19382
Wickerton Dr 19382
Wiggins Way 19380
Wildwood Ave 19382
William Ebbs Ln 19380
William Penn Blvd 19382
Williams Way 19380
Williamsburg Dr 19382
Willow Way 19380
Willowbrook Ln 19382
Wilmington Pike 19382
Wilmont Mews 19382
Wilnor Dr 19382
Wilson Ave 19382
Wilson Cir 19382
Wilson Dr 19380
Wilson Ln 19382
Wimbleton Ct 19380
Winchester Ct 19382
Wind Song Rd 19382
Windermere Rd 19380
Windovr Way 19382
Windridge Dr 19380
Windsor Dr 19380
Windstem Ln 19380
Windy Hill Rd 19382
Windy Knoll Rd 19382
Wineberry Ln 19380
Winesap Ln & Way 19380
Winston Ln 19382
Winterbridge Ln 19382
Winthrop Cir 19380
Winturford Dr 19382
Wisteria Ln 19380
Withers Way 19382
Wollerton St 19382
Wood Ln 19382
E & W Woodbank Way 19380
Woodbine Rd 19382
Woodbridge Way 19380
Woodcrest Cir 19380
Woodcrest Rd 19382
Wooded Knls 19382
Wooded Way 19380
Woodhaven Rd 19382
Woodland Rd 19382
Woodmint Dr 19380
Woodpine Rd 19380
Woods Edge Rd 19382
Woodstock Ln 19382
Woodtone Rd 19382
Woodview Ln 19380
Woodward Dr 19380
Worington Dr 19382
N Worthington St 19380
S Worthington St 19382
Wrangley Ct 19380
Wren Ln 19382
Wrights Ln E 19380
Wycklow Rd 19380
Wylie Rd 19382
Wyllpen Dr 19380
Wyndham Ln 19380
Wyntrebrooke Dr 19380
Yankee Dr 19380
Yardley Ct & Dr 19380
Yarmouth Dr 19380
Yorkminster Rd 19382
Yorkshire Way 19382
Yorktown Ave 19382
Youngs Rd 19380
Zachary Dr 19382
Zephyr Glen Ct 19380
Zephyr Hill At Troon Ln 19380

NUMBERED STREETS

3 Oak Ln 19382
3 Fox Ln 19380
4 Streams Dr 19382
N 5 Points Rd 19380
S 5 Points Rd 19382

WEST MIFFLIN PA

General Delivery 15122

POST OFFICE BOXES MAIN OFFICE STATIONS AND BRANCHES

Box No.s
All PO Boxes 15122

RURAL ROUTES

01 15122

NAMED STREETS

A Dr 15122
Adams Ave 15122
Addison Ave 15122
Alberta Cir & Dr 15122
Alder Way 15122
Allegheny County Airport 15122
Amblers Ln 15122
Anborn Dr 15122
Andover Ct 15122
Anna Ave 15122
Antoinette St 15122
Ascension Dr E & W 15122
Ashwood Court Dr 15122
Aspen St 15122
Avon Rd 15122
B Dr 15122
Ball Ave 15122
Bantam St 15122
Beech St 15122
Bellwood Dr & Rd 15122
Belmont Ave 15122
Bettis Rd 15122
Beverly Dr 15122
Blackberry St 15122
Blueberry Dr 15122
Bluemont Dr 15122
Bluff St 15122
Bost Dr 15122
Bowes Ave 15122
Brice St 15122
Brick Hollow Rd 15122
Brierly Dr & Ln 15122
Brinway Dr 15122
Buchanan Ave 15122
Buttermilk Hollow Rd 15122
Byard Ave 15122
Camp Hollow Rd 15122
Campbell Cir 15122
Carnegie St 15122
Carolina Ave 15122
Castle Dr 15122
Cedar St 15122
Center Ave & St 15122
Centerview St 15122
Century Dr 15122
Cerasi Dr 15122
Cherry St 15122
Church St 15122
Clairton Rd
1600-3074 15122
3075-3075 15123
3076-7098 15122
3077-7099 15122
Clark St 15122
Cleveland Ave 15122
Clover Ln 15122
Clubvue Dr 15122
Coal Rd 15122
Commonwealth Ave 15122
Conlin St 15122
Constitution Ave 15122
Corbin St 15122
Creston Dr 15122
Curry Hollow Rd 15122
Cypress St 15122
D Dr 15122
Dana Dr 15122
Dawson Dr 15122
Debaldo Dr 15122
Dennison Dr 15122
Diller Ave 15122
Division St 15122
Donna Ave 15122
Dory St 15122
Douglas St 15122
Dover Ln 15122
Duchess Ave 15122
Dundee Dr 15122
Dunlap St 15122
Duquesne Ave 15122
E Dr 15122
East Ave 15122
Eastman St 15122
Easy St 15122
Edgewater Dr 15122
Edgewood Ave 15122
Edison St 15122
Elcona Ln 15122
Eliza St 15122
Elizabeth St 15122
Elm St 15122
Elm Street Ext 15122
Elmore Ave 15122
Elmwood Ave 15122
Elwell Ave 15122
Evans Ave 15122
Everlawn St 15122
Flading Ln 15122
Fleetwood Dr 15122
Ford St 15122
Foster Rd 15122
Francis St 15122
Frank St 15122
Garfield St 15122
Gina Dr 15122
Glencairn St 15122
Glencoe Dr 15122
Glenn St 15122
Glenny Ln 15122
Glenny Lane Ext 15122
Golfview Ln 15122
Gordons Ln 15122
Grandview Ave 15122
Grant St 15122
Grant Avenue Ext 15122
Greensprings Ave 15122
Haldane St 15122
Hampton Rd 15122
Hawkins Ave 15122
Hazel St 15122
Heilman St 15122
Helen St 15122
Helena St 15122
Henry St 15122
Henrys Ln 15122
Herrod St 15122
High St 15122
Highland Ave 15122
Hoffman Blvd 15122
Holiday Dr 15122
Holly Park Dr 15122
Home St 15122
Homestead Ave 15122
Homestead Duquesne Rd 15122
Homeville Rd 15122
Huber Ln 15122
Huston Dr 15122
Inland Ave 15122
Iowa Ave 15122
Irene St 15122
Irwin Run Rd 15122
Jamestown Ln 15122
Jane St 15122
Jefferson Dr 15122
Jewel St 15122
Jo Ann Dr 15122
Joyce Dr 15122
June Dr 15122
Juniper Dr 15122
Kane Way 15122
Kansas Ave 15122
Kaywood Dr 15122
Kelly Ln 15122
Kenneth Ave 15122
Kenny St 15122
Kennywood Blvd 15122
Kentucky Blue Dr 15122
Kenwood Pl 15122
Kings Rd 15122
Kingston Ln 15122
Krill St 15122
Laura St 15122
Lawrence St 15122
Layton Ln 15122
Lebanon Rd 15122
Lebanon Church Rd 15122
Lebanon Manor Dr 15122
Lebanon School Rd 15122
Lee St 15122
N Lewis Run Rd 15122
Lincoln Ave 15122
Lisa Dr 15122
Livingston Rd 15122
Lombardy Dr 15122
Longvue Dr 15122
Lower Bull Run Rd 15122
Lutz Ln 15122
Madison Ave 15122
Main Entrance Dr 15122
Maine Ave 15122
Majka Dr 15122
Maple St 15122
Marilyn Dr 15122
Marlette Dr 15122
Martin St 15122
Mary St 15122
Maryland Ave 15122
Mayfield Ln 15122
Mcclure Ave 15122
Mcginley Ave 15122
Mcgowan Ave 15122
Meadow Dr 15122
Meadowlark Ln 15122
Mellon St 15122
Melody Dr 15122
Mercury Ave 15122
Merion Dr 15122
Michael St 15122
Michellina Dr 15122
Michigan Ave 15122
Midway Dr 15122
Mifflin Mnr & St 15122
Mifflin Hills Dr 15122
Miller Rd 15122
Millport Rd 15122
Monroe Ave 15122
Montclair Dr 15122
Morton Ave 15122
Mountain View Dr 15122
Mountaineer Ln 15122
Muldowney Ave 15122
Neel St 15122
New England Rd 15122
Noble Dr 15122
Nordeen Dr 15122
North Ave 15122
Northgate Dr 15122
Oak St 15122
Oakdene St 15122
Ohio Ave 15122
Old Elizabeth Rd 15122
Omar St 15122
Oregon Ave 15122
Outlook Dr 15122
Oxford Dr 15122
Palmer Ln 15122
Park Ave 15122
Parkside Dr 15122
Patton Ave 15122
Paules Ln 15122
Peach St 15122
Pennsylvania Ave 15122
Phillip Murray Rd 15122
Pine Run Rd 15122
Pittsburgh Mckeesport Blvd 15122
Pleasant Ave 15122
Polk Ave 15122
Poplar St 15122
Purdy St 15122
Randall St 15122
Reuben Dr 15122
Rhodes Ave 15122
Roberta Dr 15122
Roberts St 15122
Rodeo Dr 15122
Romany Dr 15122
Rossmoor St 15122
Royal Dr 15122
Ruxton Ave 15122
Saint Agnes Ct & Ln 15122
Saint Germaine Dr 15122
Salem Ln 15122
Sanials Ln 15122
Saniel Dr 15122
Sarah St 15122
Satinwood Dr 15122
School St 15122
Seneca Ct 15122
Shady Ln 15122
Shadynook St 15122
Shadyside Dr 15122
Shaker Dr 15122
Shara Dr 15122
Sharp Ave 15122
Shasta Ln 15122
Shope Dr 15122
Short St 15122
Skylark Ave 15122
Skyline Dr 15122
Skyport Rd 15122
Skyview Dr 15122
Smiths Ln 15122
Sorg Ln 15122
South Ave & St 15122
Spring St 15122
Spring Valley Rd 15122
Steiner Ave 15122
Sunnyside Dr 15122
Sunset Dr 15122
Sylvan Ave 15122
Taft Ave 15122
Terrace Ave 15122
Texas Ave 15122
Thistle Dr 15122
Thomas St 15122
Thompson Run Rd 15122
Timothy Dr 15122
Utah Ave 15122
Vale Dr 15122
Valeview Dr 15122
Valley St 15122
Verelarl Ave 15122
Vermont Ave 15122
Victoria St 15122
Village Ln 15122
Vindale Dr 15122
Virginia Ave 15122
Vistaview St 15122
Walker Dr 15122
Water St 15122
Webster Ave 15122
West Ave & St 15122
Whigham St 15122
Whitaker St 15122
Willard Ave 15122
Williams Dr 15122
Willow Dr 15122
Wilson St 15122
Wood St 15122
Woodhill Rd 15122
Woodland Dr 15122
Woodward Dr 15122
Worton Blvd 15122

NUMBERED STREETS

All Street Addresses 15122

WILKES BARRE PA

General Delivery 18703

POST OFFICE BOXES MAIN OFFICE STATIONS AND BRANCHES

Box No.s
AA - AZ 18703
A - P 18773
A - A 18705
B - Y 18703

33AA - 33AA	18703
BA - BA	18703
1 - 1805	18703
20 - 39	18711
28 - 28	18773
730 - 730	18711
900 - 1108	18773
1541 - 1940	18705
2001 - 2961	18703
3050 - 4800	18773
5002 - 5340	18710
5475 - 7665	18773
7800 - 7800	18703
7800 - 9900	18773

NAMED STREETS

Abbott St	
1-5	18705
7-199	18705
10-26	18702
29-29	18702
Abraham Ave	18706
Academy Rd	18706
Academy St	
21-25	18702
27-333	18702
300-326	18706
328-330	18706
332-338	18706
335-399	18702
W Academy St	18702
Adams St	
3-3	18706
5-9	18706
11-17	18706
18-18	18705
20-36	18705
38-98	18705
Airy St	18702
Aleeda Blvd	18702
Alexander St	18702
Alexie Rd	18706
Allenberry Dr	18706
Almond Ln & St	18702
Alpine Ct	18702
Alta Rd	18706
Amber Ln	18702
Amesbury St	18705
Amherst Ave	18702
Anastasia Ct	18702
Anchorage Rd	18706
Andastes Dr	18702
Anderson St	18702
Andover St	18702
Andrew Dr	18706
E & W Ann St	18705
Anthracite St	18702
Applewood Dr	18706
Arch St	18702
Arena Hub Plz	18702
Ash St	18702
Ashley Ln	18702
Ashley St	18706
E Ashwood Dr	18702
Atherton St	18705
Atkin Ln	18702
Auburn St	18702
Augusta St	18702
Auman Ln	18706
Austin Ave	18705
Avon St	18702
Azalea Rd	18702
Bailey St	18705
Bald Mountain Rd	18702
Balsam Rd	18702
Baltimore Dr	18702
Bank St	
1-99	18702
1-49	18705
Barnes St	18706
Barney St	
1-320	18702
321-399	18706
322-398	18702
Barnum Pl	18701
Barr Ln	18706
Bauer St	18706
Bear Creek Blvd	18702
E & W Beatty St	18705
Beaumont St	
1-99	18702
201-297	18706
299-499	18706
Beaver Ct	18702
N Beech Rd	18705
S Beech Rd	18705
W Beech Rd	18705
Beech St	18702
Beechwood Dr	18702
Beekman St	18702
Bell Ln	18702
Belles Ave	18706
E Bennett St	18701
E & W Bergh St	18705
Bertels Ln	18702
Bethel St	18702
Betsy Ross Dr	18706
Birch Ave	18705
Birch St	
1-13	18702
14-34	18705
15-199	18702
Birchwood Ct	18702
Black St	18706
Blackman St	18702
Blanchard St	18705
Blossom Rd	18702
Bluebird Ct	18706
Boland Ave	18706
Bowman St	18702
Boyle Ln	18702
Boyle St	18706
Brader Dr & St	18705
Bradford St	18702
Brazil St	18705
Breaker Rd	18706
Brians Pl	18702
Briar Creek Rd	18702
Brislin St	18706
Broadhead Ave	18706
Broadway St	18702
Brogan Cir & St	18705
Brook St	
2-198	18702
148-148	18706
150-151	18706
153-153	18706
200-299	18702
Brookside St	18705
Brown St	
1-299	18702
1-99	18706
101-111	18706
112-199	18706
Bruce Ln	18702
Bryson Pl	18705
Bunker Dr	18706
Burke St	18705
Burrier St	18705
Burt St	18705
Butler Ln	18701
Butler St	18702
Buttonwood Ave	18702
Caffrey St	18702
Calvin St	18705
Carbon Ln	18702
Carey Ave	
1-799	18702
638-640	18706
642-699	18706
Carey St	18706
E Carey St	18705
W Carey St	18705
Carlisle St	18702
Carolina Dr	18705
Carpenter Ln	18705
Casey Ave	18702
Catherine St	18705
Catlin Ave	18702
Cedar Ln	18702
Cedar Rd	18705
Cedar St	18702
Cedarwood Dr	
1-134	18702
136-198	18702
500-599	18706
Cemetery Rd	18705
Cemetery St	
1-99	18705
1-63	18706
65-149	18706
W Cemetery St	18706
Center St	
1-43	18705
1-54	18706
56-56	18706
200-399	18702
401-405	18702
1001-1029	18706
1031-1099	18706
1101-1109	18706
Central Ln	18705
Chamberlain St	18705
Chandler St	18705
Chapel St	18702
Charles St	
1-21	18705
1-19	18706
2-22	18705
21-77	18702
21-25	18706
27-199	18706
79-1199	18702
E Charles St	18705
W Charles St	18705
Chase Ln	18705
Chase St	18702
Cherokee Sq	18702
Cherry St	18702
Cherrywood Dr	18702
Cheryl St	18705
Chester St	
1-99	18705
1-99	18706
Chestnut St	
1-25	18702
2-168	18706
27-100	18702
102-796	18702
108-108	18706
110-299	18706
170-800	18706
500-599	18706
802-898	18706
E Chestnut St	18705
W Chestnut St	18705
Chestnutwood Dr	18702
Chilwick St	18705
Church Ln	18706
Church St	
1-541	18702
543-543	18702
700-799	18706
Circle Ct	18702
Circle Dr	18706
Cist St	18706
Clark St	18705
Clarks Ln	18705
Clarks Cross Rd	18706
Claymont Ave	18706
Cleveland St	18705
Clifton Ct	18706
Clinton Dr	18706
Clyde Ln	18705
Coal St	18702
Coalville St	18706
Cody St	18705
Colley St	18706
Collins St	18702
Colonels Rd	18706
Columbia Ave	18706
Columbus Ave	18702
Commerce Blvd	18702
Company Row	18702
Concord Dr	18702
Congo Ln	18702
Conlon Ln	18705
Constitution Ave	18706
Conwell St	18702
Conyngham Ave	18702
Conyngham St	18706
Cook St	
1-199	18705
1-99	18706
Coon St	18705
Corbett Ln	18702
Corey St	18702
Cork Ln	18702
Corlear St	18702
Cottage Ave	18705
Cotton Ave	18705
Coulter St	18706
Countrywood Dr	18706
Court St	
1-99	18706
100-199	18702
Courtright Ave	18702
Courtright St	
67-87	18705
163-175	18702
177-214	18702
216-398	18702
Covell St	18702
Creekside Dr	18702
Crescent Ave	18702
Crescent Dr	18705
Crescent Rd	18702
Crest Hill Dr	18706
Cross Ln	18702
Crow St	18705
Crown Ln	18702
Crystal Rd	18702
Crystal St	18706
Cub Cove Rd	18702
Culvert St	18706
Cummiskey St	18702
Cunningham St	18702
Custer St	18702
Cypress St	18705
Dagobert St	18702
Dana St	18702
Darling St	18702
Dauphin St	18702
David Rd	18706
Davis Pl	18702
Davis St	18706
Dees Way	18706
Delaney St	18706
Delaware St	18705
Derby St	18702
Dewey Ln	18705
Dexter St	18706
Diamond Ave	18706
N Diamond St	18702
S Diamond St	18702
Diana St	18705
Diebel St	18702
Dillon St	18705
Dingwall St	18705
E Division St	18706
Dock Ln	18702
Dodson Ln	18702
Dogwood Dr	18702
Donald Ct	18702
Donato Dr	18706
Dougher Ln	18702
Downing St	18706
Downs Dr	18705
Driftwood Dr	18705
Dundee Apts	18706
Dupont Rd	18706
Eagle Ct	18706
East Ave	18702
Eastview Dr	18705
Edison St	18702
Elder St	18702
Eleanor St	18702
Elizabeth St	
1-22	18705
2-16	18702
18-199	18702
24-98	18705
Elk Ln	18702
Elk St	18706
Elm St	18706
E Elm St	18705
W Elm St	18705
Elma Dr	18706
Elmwood Dr	18702
Emily St	18705
N & S Empire Ct & St	18702
E End Blvd	
1111-1111	18711
1111-1555	18702
1201-1499	18702
1551-1551	18711
1600-2599	18702
E End Ctr	18702
W End Rd	18706
Enterprise St	18702
Espy St	18705
Essex Ln	18702
Eugene Dr	18702
Evans Ln	18702
Everett St	18705
Evergreen Rd	18706
Everhart St	18706
Factory St	18705
Fairfield Dr	18702
Fairway Dr	18702
Fall St	18706
Farley Ln	18702
Farrell Ln & St	18705
Fellows Ave	18706
Fernwood Dr	18702
Ferry Rd	18706
Filbert Ln	18702
Finn St	
1-172	18705
174-198	18705
400-499	18702
Fir Ln	18705
Firwood Ave	18702
Firwood Dr	18706
Flaherty Dr	18706
Flick St	18705
Flood Dr	18705
Fogel Ln	18702
Fordham Rd	18702
Forest Rd	
700-799	18702
3100-3699	18706
Forrest St	18702
Fox Ridge Ct	18702
Francis St	18702
Frank St	18706
N Franklin St	
10-20	18701
22-53	18701
54-54	18711
55-203	18701
64-198	18701
500-654	18702
655-799	18705
S Franklin St	
204A-204B	18701
1-100	18701
15-15	18711
101-299	18701
102-298	18701
300-999	18702
Frederick Ct	18706
Frederick St	
1-99	18706
15-17	18702
19-99	18702
Freed St	18706
Freeman St	18702
Front St	18706
N & S Fulton St	18702
Gail Dr	18702
Gallagher Dr	18705
Garber St	18706
Garden Dr & Rd	18705
Gardner Ave	18705
Garman St	18706
Garnet Ln	18706
Garrahan St	18706
Gates St	18702
Gatti St	18705
George Ave	18705
E & W Germania St	18706
Gildersleeve St	18701
Gilligan St	18702
Gills Ln	18705
Girard St	18702
Gladstone Ln	18706
Glen St	18702
Glynn Ct	18706
Goeringer Ave	18706
Golf Course Rd	18702
Gordon Ave	18702
Gore St	18705
Gouge St	18705
Govier St	18705
Grace Dr	18705
Graham Ave	18706
Grandview Ave	18706
N & S Grant St	18702
Gravel St	18705
Great Valley Blvd	18706
Grebe St	18702
Green Ln	18702
Green St	18706
Greenwalt St	18706
Gregory St	18702
Griffith Ln	18702
Grove Ln	18702
Grove St	
1-199	18702
201-299	18706
300-399	18706
Haefele St	18706
Haines St	18705
Haldeman St	18702
Halliday Ct	18706
Hamilton St	18702
Hancock St	18705
N Hancock St	18702
S Hancock St	18702
Hannis St	18706
Hanover St	
1-202	18702
203-297	18706
204-298	18702
299-399	18706
400-998	18706
1000-1099	18706
1100-1198	18706
Hanover Vlg	18706
Harkins Ln	18702
Harriet St	18705
Harris St	18702
Harrison St	18706
Harry St	18705
Hart St	18702
E & W Hartford St	18706
Haverford Dr	18702
Hawthorne St	18705
Hayes Ln	18702
Hazle St	
100-713	18702
715-715	18702
716-799	18706
Hazleton St	18706
Heinz Dr	18702
Helen St	18705
Hemlock Rd	18702
Hemlock St	
2-10	18702
3-8	18705
10-12	18705
12-155	18702
106-131	18706
133-135	18706
Henry St	
1-49	18702
2-16	18705
18-199	18705
Hickory Rd & St	18702
Hickorywood Dr	18702
Hicks Ln	18705
High Blvd	18702
High St	
1-3	18705
46-52	18706
54-599	18706
200-210	18706
Highland Dr	
3-3	18706
5-5	18705
5-41	18706
7-99	18705
43-57	18706
Highland Park Blvd	18702
Highway 315	18711
Highway 315 Blvd	18702
Hill St	
10-28	18702
11-15	18706
17-18	18706
20-30	18706
26-28	18705
30-199	18702
30-40	18705
300-399	18706
Hillard St	18702
Hillbrook Dr	18702
Hillcrest Rd	18702
Hilldale Ave	18705
Hillman St	18705
Hillside St	
1-103	18702
63-63	18705
65-70	18705
72-72	18705
105-107	18702
146-148	18706
Holland St	18702
W Hollenback Ave	18702
Hollenback St	18705
E Hollenback St	18705
Holly St	18706
Hollywood Ave	18705
Hopkins St	18705
Hortense St	18702
Horton St	18702
Howard St	18702
Huber St	18702
Hudson Rd	18705
Huff St	18705
Hughes St	18702
Hurley St	18705
Huston St	18702
Hutson St	18702
Independence Blvd	18706
Indian Creek Dr	18702
Industrial Dr	18706
Inman Ave	18706
Iroquois Ave	18702
Irving Pl	18702
J Campbell Collins Dr	18702
E & W Jackson St	18701
James St	18706
Janet Dr	18706
Jason Dr	18702
Jasper Ln	18702
Jay Dr	18702
Jay St	18705
Jean St	18702
Jeanette St	18702
Jefferson Ln	18701
Jenks Ln	18702
Jfl Memorial Dr	18702
Joe St	18706
John St	18702
Johnson St	
1-99	18705
200-451	18702
453-499	18702
Jones St	
1-27	18705
2-6	18702
8-299	18702
29-39	18705
41-99	18705
300-398	18706
Jordan Ln	18702
Joseph Ln	18702
Joshua Ct	18705
Jumper Rd	18702
Juniper Dr	18705
Juniper Rd	18702

Kado St 18705
Keating St 18702
Keith St 18706
Kelly Ave 18705
Kelly St 18702
Kennedy Dr 18705
Kent Ln 18702
Ketchum St 18702
Keystone Rd 18706
Kidder St 18702
Kings Rd 18706
Kirkendall Ave 18702
Kniffen St 18706
Knight St 18705
Knox St 18706
Kopko Dr 18706
Kresge St 18705
Kropp St 18702
Kulp Ave 18702
Kyra Way 18702
Lace Mill Ln 18702
E & W Lafayette Pl 18702
Laflin Rd 18702
Lagoon Dr 18702
Laird St
1-200 18705
201-297 18702
202-298 18705
299-399 18702
Lakeview Pl 18702
Lan Creek Rd 18702
Lanning Ln 18702
Larch Ln 18702
Lasley Ave 18706
Laurel St
1-99 18702
1-54 18705
200-299 18706
Laurel Run Est 18706
Laurel Run Rd
1-2999 18702
3000-3999 18706
Laurelbrook Dr 18702
Laurelwood Dr 18702
Lawrence St 18702
Lee Park Ave 18706
Lehigh Ct & St 18702
Lenape Ct 18702
Leonard St 18702
Leopold St 18706
Leslie Ln 18702
Leuder St 18706
Lewis St
16-20 18706
22-44 18706
28-50 18705
52-98 18705
Lexington Ct 18702
E & W Liberty St 18706
Liddon St 18705
Lincoln Dr 18706
Lincoln Plz 18702
E Linden St 18705
W Linden St 18702
Litchey Dr 18702
Little St 18706
Livingston St 18706
Lloyds Ln 18702
Lock St 18705
Lockhart St 18702
Locust St 18702
Logan St 18702
Lombardo Ct & Dr 18702
Loomis Park 18706
Loomis St 18702
Loop Rd 18702
Louis St 18705
Loxley St 18706
Luzerne St
1-99 18706
200-298 18702
Lynch Ln 18702
Lyndwood Ave 18706
Mack St 18705
Madison St
1-219 18702
220-599 18705
Maffett St
1-103 18702
1-103 18705
104-116 18705
105-117 18702
118-323 18705
300-306 18706
308-330 18706
325-399 18705
Magnolia St 18702
Maiden Ln 18705
Main Rd 18706
Main St
176A-176B 18702
1-203 18702
500-927 18706
929-975 18706
E Main St
1-444 18705
445-599 18702
601-699 18702
N Main St
1-15 18701
1-681 18705
1-199 18706
17-17 18702
19-21 18711
20-22 18702
24-30 18701
25-25 18702
41-41 18711
43-52 18702
53-73 18701
54-60 18702
70-70 18711
79-79 18711
87-89 18701
91-93 18701
95-177 18701
178-422 18702
424-426 18705
428-748 18705
683-727 18705
751-751 18702
753-757 18702
759-855 18702
55 1/2-55 1/2 18702
S Main St
1-13 18705
1-293 18701
1-165 18706
15-199 18705
166-3199 18706
295-655 18701
300-300 18703
300-300 18710
352-654 18701
701-701 18702
703-922 18702
Mallery Pl 18702
Manchester Dr 18702
Manhattan St 18706
Maple Ln 18702
Maple Rd 18702
Maple St
1-3 18706
4-38 18702
40-66 18702
W Maple St 18702
Maplewood Dr 18702
Mara Ln 18702
Marcy Ct 18706
Marcy St 18702
Margaret St 18705
Marion Ave 18706
Marjorie Ave 18702
Mark Dr 18706
Mark Hill Dr 18706
Market St
1-99 18702
280-298 18704
E Market St
1-149 18701
40-40 18711
40-98 18701
151-197 18702
199-279 18702
281-299 18702
W Market St
1-9 18701
8-8 18711
10-44 18701
11-99 18701
Marlboro Ave 18702
Martin St
1-99 18706
1-11 18705
13-29 18705
31-99 18705
Mary St 18706
Matson Ave 18705
Maxwell St
1-99 18702
1-99 18706
May St 18702
Mayer St 18702
Mayflower Xing 18702
Mayock St 18705
Mccabe St 18706
Mccarragher St 18702
Mccullough Rd 18702
Mcfarland St 18702
Mcgoverns Hl 18706
Mcgowan St 18702
Mchale St 18705
Mclean St 18702
N & S Meade St 18702
Meadow Run Rd 18702
Meadowbrook Ct 18702
Melrose Ave 18702
Mercedes Dr 18702
Mercer St 18705
Merlino Dr 18705
E & W Merritt St 18705
Metcalf St 18702
Meyers Ct 18701
Michael Rd 18702
Michaeline Dr 18702
Michelle St 18705
Midland Ct 18702
Mill St 18705
Mill Creek Rd 18702
Miller St 18705
Minden Pl 18705
Miner St
1-130 18705
19-119 18702
132-198 18705
Mineral St 18705
Mitchell St
3-3 18702
3-13 18705
5-51 18702
15-25 18705
Monahan Ct 18706
Monarch Rd 18706
Monroe St 18702
Morgan Dr 18705
Morris Ln 18702
Motorworld Dr 18702
Mott St 18706
E Mountain Blvd 18702
E Mountain Dr 18711
Mountain Oaks Dr 18706
E Mountain Ridge
Mhp 18702
Moyallen St 18702
Mundy St 18702
Murray St 18702
Musket Dr 18706
Myrtle Ln 18702
Myrtle St 18706
Nanticoke St 18706
Napoli St 18702
New St
3-199 18705
15-27 18702
29-99 18702
New Alexander St 18702
New Commerce Blvd 18706
New Elizabeth St 18702
New Frederick St 18702
New Grant St 18702
New Grove St 18702
New Hancock St 18702
New Mallery Pl 18702
New Market St 18702
Newman St 18706
E & W Newport St 18706
Nicholson St
5-11 18705
13-37 18705
17-299 18702
39-41 18705
Nicole Dr 18702
Ninotti St 18705
Nittany Ln 18702
Noble Ln 18702
North Ave 18702
North St 18705
E North St 18701
W North St
1-99 18701
113-113 18711
Northampton Ct 18702
E Northampton St
1-156 18701
157-197 18702
199-510 18702
511-511 18711
512-854 18702
555-853 18702
1001-1097 18706
1099-1399 18706
W Northampton St 18701
Norwood Ave 18706
Oak Ctr 18702
Oak Ln 18706
Oak St
1-1 18705
2-14 18702
3-72 18705
15-33 18706
16-199 18702
74-78 18705
100-106 18706
108-399 18706
S Oak St 18705
Oaklawn Ave 18706
Oakley Ln 18705
Oakwood Dr & Ln 18702
Obrien Dr 18705
Odonnell St 18702
Old Ashley Rd 18706
Old East End Blvd 18702
Old Hazleton St 18706
Old Mill Rd 18702
Old Pickaway Rd 18702
Old Pittston Blvd 18702
Old River Rd 18702
Olin St 18705
Olive St 18706
Oliver Ln 18706
Oliver St 18705
Omalley St 18705
Oneil Ave & St 18702
Opal Ln 18702
Oradistr St 18702
Orchard St
1-99 18702
500-599 18706
Oregon St 18702
Oxford St 18706
Park Ave 18702
Park Rd 18702
Park St 18706
Parkin St 18705
Parkview Cir 18702
Parkview Dr 18705
E & W Parkway Rd 18702
Parrish Rd 18706
Parrish St 18702
Passan Dr 18702
Patrick Henry Dr 18706
Paul Revere Dr 18706
Peachtree Ln 18706
Peachwood Dr 18702
N Peadwal Sq 18711
Pearl St 18702
Pearson St 18706
Pebbles Ln 18705
Pelza St 18705
Penn St
1-99 18702
200-299 18706
N Pennsylvania Ave
1-17 18701
19-53 18701
55-199 18701
96-96 18711
100-198 18701
222-244 18702
246-500 18702
501-899 18705
S Pennsylvania Ave 18701
Penny Ln 18702
Penrose St 18702
Perkins St 18705
Pershing St 18702
Pethick Dr 18702
Pfouts St 18706
Phillips St 18706
Phoenix St 18702
Pike Rd 18702
Pincorel St 18705
Pine Rd
4-17 18705
19-19 18705
40-199 18702
Pine St
1-13 18702
15-100 18702
102-698 18702
400-499 18706
Pine Ridge Dr 18705
Pine Run Rd 18706
Pinecrest Dr 18702
Pinewood Dr 18702
Pittston Blvd 18702
Planes Ave 18706
Plymouth Ave
1-499 18702
400-499 18706
Plymouth St 18706
Poplar St
2-10 18705
6-6 18702
8-300 18702
12-67 18705
69-69 18705
302-398 18702
Powell St 18705
President Rd 18706
S Preston St 18706
Price St 18705
Priestly St 18702
Prince St 18706
Princeton Ct 18702
Prospect St
1-3 18706
4-299 18702
Public Sq
1-66 18701
67-67 18711
68-98 18701
71-99 18701
67-69-67-69 18701
Pulaski St
1-199 18706
200-299 18702
Puritan Ln 18702
Quarry Rd 18706
Rabbit Run Ln 18702
Race St 18702
Railroad St 18705
Ralph St 18705
Ray St 18706
Raymond Dr 18706
Rear Nicholson St 18702
Red Coat Ln 18706
Red Fox Ln 18706
Redwood Dr 18702
Rees St 18702
Reese St 18702
Regal St 18706
Regent St 18702
S Regent St 18706
Regina St 18706
Reliance Dr 18702
Reno Ln 18702
Reservoir St 18702
Revere Ct 18702
Richard St
1-99 18702
1-99 18706
Richmont Ave 18702
Ridge Rd
1-399 18706
3800-3899 18702
Ridge St 18706
Ridgewood Rd 18702
Riley St 18706
Rita St 18702
River Rd 18706
N River St
2-124 18705
19-97 18702
100-102 18702
133-133 18711
133-133 18702
151-575 18702
200-200 18711
200-200 18702
216-598 18702
635-699 18705
1125-1499 18702
S River St
1-17 18705
2-232 18702
19-342 18705
234-599 18702
344-398 18705
W River St 18702
Riverside Dr 18702
Riverview Dr 18705
Robert St 18702
Robinson Cir 18706
Rodgers Ave 18706
Roosevelt Ter 18702
Rose Ave 18705
Rose Ln 18702
Ross St 18706
E Ross St 18701
W Ross St 18701
Route 309 18706
Rowe St 18706
Rowland St 18702
Royal St 18706
Ruddle St 18702
Rutter St 18706
Rutz St 18706
Saint Clair St 18705
Saint David St 18705
Saint James St 18705
Saint John St 18705
Saint Mary St 18705
E & W Saint Marys
Rd 18706
Salem Dr 18702
Samantha Dr 18705
Sambourne St 18701
Sand St 18705
Sandra St 18705
Sandspring Rd 18702
Sans Souci Pkwy 18706
Sans Souci Trailer
Park 18706
Sarah St 18705
Saratoga Ct 18702
Savoy Dr 18702
E & W Saylor Ave 18702
Schechter Dr 18702
School Ln 18706
School St
1-99 18705
1-99 18706
Schoolhouse Ln 18702
Schuler St 18702
Scott St
8-10 18705
12-19 18705
20-22 18702
21-63 18705
26-52 18705
54-54 18702
58-68 18705
84-98 18702
100-599 18702
700-1599 18705
Scureman St 18706
Seminary Rd 18706
Seminole Ave 18702
Seneca St 18702
Settlement Rd 18702
Seymour St 18702
Shannon St 18702
Shantytown Rd 18702
Shawnee St 18706
Sheldon St 18702
Sheridan Mnr 18702
Sheridan St
2-6 18702
8-106 18702
11-29 18705
31-38 18705
40-40 18705
108-198 18702
S Sheridan St 18702
N & S Sherman St 18702
Shiber Ln 18702
Shiffer Ln 18705
Short St 18702
E & W Sidney St 18705
Simon Block Ave 18706
Simpson St 18702
Sively St 18706
Skidmore St 18705
Skyview Dr 18705
Slattery Dr 18705
Slattery St 18702
Slope St
1-48 18705
11-12 18706
50-98 18705
300-399 18706
Smith Ct 18706
Smith St 18702
Smythe St 18706
Sobieski St 18706
Solomon St
1-199 18706
1-99 18702
8-12 18706
18-20 18702
24-28 18706
30-46 18702
50-52 18702
54-56 18702
60-198 18706
Somerset Dr 18706
South St 18706
E South St
1-99 18701
201-215 18702
217-499 18702
W South St 18701
Spencer Ln 18706
Spencer St 18702
Spring St
1-299 18702
1-399 18706
Springbrook Dr 18702
Springfield Ave 18706
Spruce Ave 18705
Spruce St 18702
Sprucewood Dr 18702
Stanley St
1-99 18702
1-99 18706
Stanton St 18702
E Stanton St 18705
W Stanton St 18705
Stark St
1-1 18702
3-38 18702
12-36 18705
38-99 18705
40-42 18702
101-199 18705

Street	ZIP
N State St	18701
Steele St	18706
Sterling Ave	18702
Steve St	18706
Stevens Rd	18702
Stewart Rd	18706
Stocker St	18705
Stoney Creek Rd	18702
Stoneyside Dr	18706
Strand St	18706
Stucker St	18705
Sturdevant St	18702
Sullivan St	18702
Summit St	18702
Sunrise Dr	18705
Sunset Dr	
1-99	18702
100-199	18706
Susquehanna St	18702
Susquehannock Dr	18702
Swanson Rd	18702
Sycamore St	18705
Sylvan Rd	18702
Sylvanus St	18702
Taft St	
1-99	18702
200-299	18706
Tamara Hl	18706
Tamarac Rd	18702
Tannery St	18702
Tanya Dr	18706
Taylor Ln	18705
Tenbrook St	18702
Terrace Ave	18705
Terrace Dr	18705
Terrace St	18702
Thayer St	18702
E Thomas St	18705
Thompson St	18702
Thornhurst Rd	18702
Timpson St	18706
Tomko Ave	18706
Trailwood Lake Rd	18702
Trenton Ct	18702
Trethaway St	18705
Tronerre St	18706
Tryba Ln	18706
Tulip Dr	18705
Twinbrook Rd	18702
Ugi Ctr	18711
Union St	
1-81	18705
83-99	18705
100-142	18702
101-101	18705
103-134	18705
136-140	18705
144-176	18702
E Union St	18701
W Union St	18701
Van Horn St	18706
Vanessa Cir & Dr	18706
Vine St	
1-99	18706
12-99	18702
1000-1011	18706
Virginia Dr	18705
Vulcan St	18702
Waddell St	18705
Wall St	18702
Waller St	18702
Walnut St	
1-21	18702
23-47	18702
49-99	18702
104-298	18706
N Walnut St	18702
S Walnut St	18702
Walnutwood Dr	18702
Walters Way	18702
Warner St	18705
Warren St	18702
N Washington St	
2-12	18701
14-206	18701
207-308	18702
310-312	18702
314-1499	18705
S Washington St	
1-200	18701
202-298	18701
205-205	18711
207-293	18701
Water St	
2-2	18711
5-5	18711
35-189	18702
300-398	18706
Watson St	18702
Wayne St	18702
Wedgewood Dr	18702
Weir Ln	18705
Weitz Rd	18702
Welles Ave	18706
N Welles St	18702
S Welles St	18702
West Ave	18702
Westminster Rd & St	18702
Weston Ln	18702
Whispering Way	18702
Whitemere Ln	18706
Widener Dr	18702
Wilcox Dr	18705
Wilcox St	
2-6	18706
8-12	18706
10-32	18705
14-98	18706
34-58	18705
60-198	18705
Wildflower Dr	18702
Wilkes Ln	18702
N Wilkes Barre Blvd	18702
S Wilkes Barre Blvd	18702
Wilkes Barre St	
500-700	18706
702-1002	18706
1000-1000	18711
Wilkes Barre Township Blvd & Cmns	18702
Wilkes Barre Township Market Pl	18702
Wilkeswood Dr	18702
William St	18705
Willow St	
2-58	18702
60-1199	18702
300-400	18706
402-498	18706
Wilson St	18705
Winter Ln	18702
Wood St	18702
Woodbury St	18706
Woodcrest Dr	18702
Woodland Rd	
100-698	18706
500-599	18702
700-899	18706
Woodside Dr	18705
Woodview Rd	18706
Woodward St	18705
Woody Rd	18702
Worrall St	18702
Worth Ln	18702
Wrights Cors	18705
Wyndtree Dr	18702
Wyndwood Dr	18705
Wyoming St	
1-56	18706
2-8	18702
7-7	18705
9-26	18705
10-98	18702
28-98	18705
58-98	18706
100-100	18702
111-399	18705
400-499	18706
Wyoming Valley Mall	
K1-K99	18702
1-87	18702
88-88	18711
88-755	18702
89-399	18702
100-398	18702
Yale St	18705
York Ln	18702
Young St	18706
Zack St	18706
Zinn Ct	18702

NUMBERED STREETS

Street	ZIP
1st St	18705
1st St	18706
2nd St	18702
2nd St	18706

WILLIAMSPORT PA

Street	ZIP
General Delivery	17701

POST OFFICE BOXES MAIN OFFICE STATIONS AND BRANCHES

Box No.s	ZIP
1 - 2516	17703
3001 - 4176	17701
5001 - 5180	17702
7777 - 7777	17701
9998 - 9998	17703
17705 - 17705	17701

NAMED STREETS

Street	ZIP
Aberdeen Rd	17701
Academy St	17701
Acme Pl	17701
Adams St	17701
Addies Ln	17702
Aderhold Ln	17701
Albert Pl	17701
Alexander Ave	17701
Alexis Dr	17701
Allen Ave	17702
Allen St	
100-199	17702
400-499	17701
501-699	17701
Almond Ct & St	17701
Alta Vista Dr	17701
Alvin Ave	17701
Ames Pl	17701
Andrews Ln & Pl	17701
Anna Rd	17701
Anne St	17701
Anthony St	17701
Antlers Ln	17701
Apple Ln	17702
Apple St	17701
Arch St	17701
S Arch St	17702
Arlington St	17702
Armanda Rd	17701
Arnold St	17701
Ashwood Ct	17701
Aubrey Ct & Pl	17701
Avalon Pkwy	17701
Aztec Ln	17701
Bachman Ln	17702
Baier Ln	17702
Baker St	17701
Bald Eagle Ave	17702
Baldwin St	17701
Banister Pl	17701
Barbours Cemetery Rd	17701
Basin St	17701
Bastian Ave	17702
Bayard St	17702
Bayard St Ext	17702
Be Daro Dr	17702
Beauty Ave	17701
Becht Rd	17701
Becker Hill Rd	17701
Beeber St	17701
Beech St	17702
Beechnut Pkwy	17701
Belmont Ave	17701
Belvedere Dr	17701
Benedict St	17701
Bennardi Development Rd	17702
Bennett Dr & St	17701
Bent Rd	17701
Bentley Dr	17701
Berger St	17701
Berkshire Pl	17701
Berndt Ave	17701
Berry Ave	17701
Bertin Hts	17702
Beverly Ave	17701
Big Run Rd	17702
Birkle Ct	17701
Blackberry Aly	17701
Blackbird Aly	17702
Blaine St	17701
Blair St	17701
Blair Street Ext	17701
Blairs Dam Rd	17701
Blanchard Ave	17701
Blank Ln	17702
Blehl Aly	17701
Bloomingrove Rd	17701
Bloomingrove Road Anx	17701
Blue Jay Aly	17702
Blueberry Ln	17701
Bodene Ln	17702
Bon Ln	17701
Bonair Dr	17701
Borderline Dr & Rd	17702
Bottle Run Rd	17701
Bowen Dr	17701
Bower Ln	
1-99	17702
2-12	17701
42-98	17702
Bower Rd	17701
Boyd Ct & St	17701
Braine St	17701
Brandon Ave & Pl	17701
Breininger Ln	17702
Bridge St	17701
Brion Pl	17702
Brittany Pkwy	17701
Brook St	17702
Brooke Ln	17702
Brooks Ave	17701
Brown Ave & St	17702
Bryan Rd	17701
Bubb St	17702
Bucks Rd	17701
Buffington Rd	17702
Bush Hill Rd	17701
Busler Ln	17702
Butternut Dr	17701
Butters Rd	17701
Buttorf Ln	17702
Buttorff Ln	17702
Bybrook Rd	17701
Cabbage Hollow Rd	17701
Caldwell Ave	17701
Calvert Ave	17701
Calvin Dr	17701
Cambridge St	17702
Campbell St	17701
E Canal St	17701
Canterbury Rd	17701
Cardinal Ln	17701
Carl Wenner Ln	17702
Carlton Ter	17701
Casey Dr	17701
Catawissa Ave	17701
Catherine Dr & St	17701
Ce Ce Rd	17702
Cemetery Rd & St	17701
Center Pl & St	17701
Central Ave	17701
E Central Ave	17702
W Central Ave	17702
Centreline Ave	17701
Chadlee Dr	17702
Charles St	
200-499	17702
1100-1199	17701
Charlotte Ave	17702
Charlotte St	17701
Chatham Ln, Park & St	17701
Chatham Park Dr	17701
Chelsea Pl	17701
Cherokee Ln	17701
Cherry St	17701
Chester Rd & St	17701
Chestnut St	17701
Childs Ave & Dr	17702
Chiswick Rd	17701
Church St	17702
E Church St	17701
W Church St	17701
Circle Dr & Rd	17701
Clarendon St	17702
Clarion Dr	17701
Clark St	
300-599	17702
700-922	17701
924-998	17701
Clayton Ave	17701
Cliffside Dr	17701
Clinton St	17702
Cochran Ave	17702
Cohick Rd	17702
Cold Watertown Rd	17702
College Ave & Pl	17701
Columbus Ave	17702
Colvin Rd	17701
Commerce Park Dr	17701
Comp Rd	17702
Corbin Rosa Dr	17702
W Cottage Ave	17701
Country Club Dr	17701
Country Club Ln	
101-299	17702
1400-1599	17701
Court Aly & St	17701
Crawford Ln	17701
Creekside Ln	17701
Crestfield Dr	17701
Crestview Dr	17701
Crestwood Cir	17701
Crisman Rd	17702
Cross Mountain Ln	17702
Cummings St	17701
Curtin St	17702
Danneker Dr	17701
Dartmouth St	17702
Daughertys Run Rd	17701
David Ave	17701
Dawne Dr	17701
Day St	17701
Deckman Hollow Rd	17701
Deer Dr	17702
Deer Path Ln	17701
Deerfield Dr	17701
Demorest St	17701
Depot St	17701
Devon Rd	17701
Dewey Ave	17701
Diamond St	17701
Dincher Ln	17702
Division Rd	17701
Dix St	17701
Doebler Ln	17701
Dogwood Ln	
1-165	17701
167-199	17701
196-198	17702
200-298	17701
201-297	17702
299-300	17702
301-499	17701
302-398	17702
Doris Ave	17701
Dove St	17701
Dubois St	17701
Dudek Rd	17701
Duke St	17701
Dunbar Rd	17701
Dunkleberger Rd	17701
Dunwoody Rd	17701
East St	17701
Eck Cir	17701
Eck Ln	17702
Eckmont Ave	17702
Eddy St	17701
Edercrest Rd	17701
Edgewood Ave	17702
Edler Rd	17701
E & W Edwin St	17701
Eldred St	17701
Elizabeth St	17701
Ellinger St	17701
Elliott St	17701
Elm St	17702
Elmira St	17701
Elwood Cres & Rd	17701
Emery St	17701
Emick Dr	17701
Emick Farm Rd	17701
Engel Ln	17702
Engle Mill Ln	17701
Engle Run Dr	17701
English Farm Rd	17701
Ertel Rd	17701
Euclid Ave	17702
Eureka Pl	17701
Evergreen Rd	17701
Fairmont Ave	17702
Fairview Ave & Ter	17701
Faxon Cir & Pkwy	17701
Federal Ave	17701
Fieldcrest Dr	17701
Fink Ave	17701
First Rd	17701
Fisher St	17702
Flannigan Ave	17701
Fleming St	17702
Flock Pl	17701
Florence St	17701
Fluman Ln & Rd	17701
Foresman St	17701
Forest Ln	17701
Forrest St	17702
Four Mile Dr	17701
Fox St	17701
Fox Hollow Rd	17701
Franklin St	17701
Frederick Ave	17701
Fredna Ave	17701
Freed Pl	17701
Freedom Rd	17701
French Settlement Rd	17702
Frey Ave	17701
Fritz Ln	17701
W Front St	17702
Fuller Ln	17702
Fullerton Ave	17701
Funston Ave	17701
Furey St	17702
Furnace St	17701
Garden St	17701
Garden View Plz	17701
Gearhart Ln	17701
George St	
300-699	17702
1000-1199	17701
Germania St	17701
Giles Ln	17702
Ginny Ln	17701
Girio Ter	17702
Glen Echo Rd	17701
Glenwood Ave	17701
Glynn Ave	17701
Goldy Ln	17701
Good Aly	17701
Gordon St	17702
Government Pl	17701
Grace St	17701
Grafius St	17701
Graham Rd	17701
Grammer Rd	17701
Grampian Blvd	17701
Grand Ct & St	17701
Grandview Pl	17702
Grandview Rd	17701
Grant St	17701
Green Ave & St	17701
Greenock Rd	17701
Grier St	17701
Grimes Ln	17701
Grimesville Rd	17701
Grininger Rd	17701
Grove St	
100-299	17702
300-1599	17701
1601-1699	17701
Guinter Ave	17701
Hadley St	17701
Hadtner Ave	17701
Halls Ln	17701
Hammond Pl	17701
Hancock St	17701
Harding Ave	17701
Harris Pl	17701
Harrison Ave	17701
Harvard Ave	17702
Harvard Ct	17701
Harvey Rd	17701
Hastings St	17702
Hatfield St	17701
Hawthorne Ave	17701
Hayes Ave	17701
Hays Ln	17701
Hazel Dr	17701
Hazelbrook Ln	17701
Heather Ln	17701
Heavenly Hollow Rd	17701
Heller Ave	17701
Helminiak Ave & St	17701
Hemlock Ln	17702
Hemlock Rd	17701
Hemlock Grove Ln	17702
Henrietta St	17701
Henry St	17702
Hepburn St	
200-622	17701
621-621	17703
624-1698	17701
631-1699	17701
Herdic St	17701
Heritage Hill Ln	17701
Herlocker Ln	17701
Heshbon Rd & St	17701
Hiawatha Blvd	17701
Hickory Ln	17702
Hidden Crest Ln	17701
Hidden Hollow Ln	17701
Hidden Valley Rd	17701
High St	17701
High Pines Rd	17701
Highfields Dr	17701
Highland Ave	17702
W Highland Ave	17702
Highland Ter	17701
Hill St	17702
Hill Top Rd	17701
Hillcrest Ln	17701
Hiller Rd	17701
E, N & W Hills Cres & Dr	17701
Hillsdale Dr	17701
Hillside Ave	17701
Hillside Dr	17702
Hillview Ave	17701
Hinaman Hts	17701
Hines St	17702
Hinkal Ln	17702
Hively Pl	17701
Hollywood Cir	17701
Holt Rd	17701
Holy Cross Ln	17701
Homewood Ave	17701
Hoover Rd & St	17701
Hoppestown Rd	17701
Horn Ave	17701
Howard St	17701
S Howard St	17702
Huffman Ave & St	17701

Street	ZIP
Hughes St	17701
Huling Ln	17702
Ida Ln	17702
Industrial Rd	17701
Inwood Rd	17701
Iona Aly	17701
Isabella Ct & St	17701
Ivy Crest Ln	17701
Jacks Hollow Rd	17702
Jackson St	17701
Jacob Rd	17702
Jaculin Ave	17702
Jake Wenner Ln	17702
James Rd	17701
Jamison Ave	17701
Janet Ave	17701
Janzy Ln	17701
Jefferson Ln	17701
Jerome Ave	17701
Johnson Dr	17702
Johnston Pl & St	17701
Kaiser Ave	17702
Kane St	17702
Keller Ave & Loop	17701
Kennedy Ct	17701
Kenneth Ave	17701
Kenwood Ave & Rd	17701
Keyser Cir	17701
Keyte Ave	17701
Kimble Hill Rd	17701
King Ct & St	17701
Kinley Rd	17701
Knoll Rd	17702
Kramer Ct	17701
Krouse Ave	17701
Kurtz Rd	17701
Labrador Ln	17701
Lacey St	17701
Lacomic St	17701
Lafayette Pkwy	17701
Lambert Ln	17701
Laurel St	17701
Laurel Run Cir	17701
Lawson St	17701
Leader Dr	17701
Lehman Rd	17702
Leona Ln	17701
Lewis Rd	17701
Liberty Dr & Ln	17701
Lick Run Rd	17701
Light St	17701
Lincoln Ave	17701
W Lincoln Ave	17702
Lincoln Dr	17701
Lincoln St	17701
Linda Ln	17701
Linden St	17702
Linn St	17701
Linwood Ave	17701
Little Bear Creek Rd	17701
Little League Blvd	17701
Livermore Rd	17701
E Lloyd St	17701
Lockcuff Rd	17701
Locust St	17701
Log Run Rd	17701
Logue St	17701
Lois Ln	17701
Longview Dr	17701
Lorson Dr & Rd	17702
Lose Ave & Pkwy	17701
Loudenslager Rd	17701
Louisa St	17701
Love Dr	17701
Lowe St	17702
Lower Barbours Rd	17701
Lower Manor Rd	17701
Lower Water St	17701
Lowmiller Rd	17701
Loyalsock Dr	17701
Loyalsock Manor Rd	17701
Loyalsock Pines Ln	17701
Lumber St	17701
Lundy Dr & Ln	17701
Lycoming St	17701
Lycoming Creek Rd	17701
Lyla Ln	17701
Lymehurst Pkwy	17701
Lyons Ave	17701
Mahaffey Ln & St	17701
Main St	17702
Malvin Pl	17701
Malvina Rd	17701
Mankey Pl	17701
Manleys Ln	17702
Mansel Ave	17701
Maple Ave, Ln & St	17701
Maple Grove Cir	17701
Mark Ave & Ln	17701
Market St	17701
S Market St	17702
Marlin Aly	17702
Marlin Pkwy	17701
Marshall Ave, Ct & Ln	17701
Marvin Cir & Ln	17701
Mary St	17701
Marydale Ave	17701
Matthews Blvd	17702
Maxwell Pl	17701
May Ave	17701
Maybee Hill Rd	17701
Mayer Rd	17701
Maynard Aly	17701
Maynard St	17701
S Maynard St	17702
Mcconnell Dr	17701
Mccormick Ave	17702
Mccoy St	17701
Mckeag Dr	17701
Mckinney St	17701
Mcminn Ave	17701
Meade St	17701
Meadow St	17702
Melody Ln	17701
Memorial Ave	17701
Menne Aly	17701
Merrill Ave	17701
Middle Aly	17701
Mifflin Pl	17701
Mill Ln	17701
Mill Rd	17702
Miller Ave & St	17701
Miller Hill Rd	17701
Millers Ln	17701
Misner Rd	17701
Misty Ridge Cir	17701
Mock Run Rd	17701
Monroe Pl	17701
Montgomery Pike	17702
Moore Ave	17701
Moores Ln	17702
Morgan Ave	17701
Morgan Valley Rd	17702
Morrison Dr	17701
Morse Dr	17701
Mosquito Valley Rd	17702
Mosser Ave	17701
Mosser Avenue Ext	17701
Mossy Oak Rd	17702
Motters Ln	17701
Mount Carmel St	17701
Mount Royal Hts	17701
Mountain Ave	17701
E Mountain Ave	17702
W Mountain Ave	17702
Mountain Rd	17701
Mountain Laurel Ln	17702
Mountain Spring Ln	17702
Mountainstone Ln	17702
Mountainview Dr	17702
Mulberry St	17701
Myers Rd	17701
Myrtle Ave	17701
New Lawn Ave	17701
Newberry St	17701
Newcomer Ave	17701
Nez Perce Rd	17701
Nicely Ln	17701
Nichols Pl	17701
Nicola Crossway	17701
Nisbet Ter	17702
Norman St	17701
North St	17701
Northway Rd	17701
Northway Road Ext	17701
Northwood Dr	17701
Norwood Dr	17701
Nottingham Rd	17701
Nubby Ln	17702
Oak St	17702
Oak Ridge Pl	17701
Oak View Dr	17701
Oakes Ave	17701
Oakland Ave	17701
Oakmont Dr	17701
Oberlin Ave	17701
Old Church Ln	17702
Old Edler Rd	17701
Old Montgomery Pike Rd	17702
Oldt Dr	17701
Oliver Ave & St	17701
Oneil Aly & Ave	17701
Orchard Pl	17701
Ort Aly	17701
Overbrook Rd	17701
Overhill Rd	17701
Packer St	17701
Paige Ln	17701
Palmer Hill Rd	17701
Palmer Industrial Rd	17701
Park Ave, Ct, Dr, Ln, Pl & St	17701
Parkwood Pl & St	17701
Pearl St	17701
Pearson Ave	17701
Pebblewood Ln	17701
Penn St	17701
Pennsylvania Ave	17701
Pentridge Cv	17701
Percy St	17702
Perry Nigart Rd	17702
Pfirman Rd	17702
W Pheasant Aly	17702
Phillips Hill Dr	17701
Phillips Park Dr	17702
Pine St	17701
Pine Crest Dr	17702
Pine Grove Cir	17701
Pine Summit Rd	17701
Pinecrest Dr	17701
Pintoner Rd	17702
Plantation Ln	17702
Pleasant Hill Ln	17702
Pleasant Hill Rd	17701
Pleasant Hills Rd	17701
Poco Ln & Ter	17701
Poco Farm Rd	17701
Poco Farm Road Ext	17701
Poplar St	17701
Princeton Ave	17701
Princeton Avenue Ext	17701
Private 164 Rd	17702
Proctor Rd	17701
Prospect Ave & Ln	17701
Quality Ln & St	17701
Queen St	17701
Quigel Ln	17701
Race St	17701
Railway St	17701
Randall Cir	17701
Raven Aly	17702
Ravine Dr & Rd	17701
Reach Rd	17701
Reading Ave	17701
Reed St	17701
Reighard Ave	17701
Reservoir Rd	17701
Retreat Rd	17702
Reynolds St	17702
Rhoads Aly	17701
Rice Ln	17701
Richard Ave	17701
Ridge Ave & St	17701
Ridgedale Ave	17701
Ritchey St	17701
Rivendell Rd	17701
River Ave	17701
River Rd	17702
Riverside Dr	17702
Riverview Dr	17702
Roderick Rd	17701
Roosevelt Ave	17701
Rose St	17701
Rosemary Ln	17701
Roseville Rd	17701
Ross St	17701
Rosser Ln	17702
Round Hill Rd	17701
Round Knob Ln	17701
Round Top Rd	17701
Rowley Pl	17701
Royal Ave	17701
Rural Ave	17701
Russell Ave	17701
Ruthies Ln	17701
Ryan St	17701
Saar Dr	17702
Saint Boniface St	17701
Saint Davids Rd	17701
Saint James Pl	17701
Sallonti St	17701
Sandpiper Aly	17702
Sarama Ln	17701
Scaife Rd	17701
Scenic View Ln	17701
School Aly	17701
School House Rd	17701
Scott Ln & St	17701
Scoville Pl	17701
Sechler Cir	17701
Seitzer Rd	17701
Selkirk Rd	17701
Seneca Ave	17701
Seth St	17701
Shady Ln	17701
Shady Brook Ln	17702
Shaffer St	17702
Shaw Pl & Rd	17701
Sheridan St	17701
Sherman St	17701
Sherwood Ave & Ln	17702
Shiffler Ave	17701
Sholder Ave & Rd	17701
Short St	17701
Shumbat Ln	17701
Shurer Ln	17702
Sidney St	17702
Simpson Ln	17702
Skylark Way	17702
Smokey Ln	17701
Smokey Corners Rd	17701
Sortman Ave	17702
South Aly & St	17701
E & W Southern Ave	17702
Southmont Ave	17702
E & W Southview Ave	17701
Spring Ln	17701
Spring St	17702
Spring Garden St	17701
Spring Grove Dr	17701
Spring Run Rd	17701
Springhouse Ln	17701
Spruce St	17701
Stahl Ave	17701
Stanley Ln	17702
Stanton St	17702
Stark Ln	17701
State St	17701
S State Route 44	17702
State Route 654	17702
State Route 87	17701
State Route 973 E	17701
Steel Way Rd	17701
Steinbacher Ln	17702
Steppe Ln	17702
Steppe Brothers Dr	17702
Sterling Ave	17701
Stevens St	17701
Stewart Rd	17702
Stillmeadow Ln	17701
Stone Ln	17701
Stopper Rd	17702
Strafford Rd	17701
Stroble Ln	17702
Strouse Rd	17701
Sulphur Springs Rd	17702
Summer St	17702
Summit Rd	17701
Sunny Ter	17701
Sunnyside Rd	17702
Susquehanna St	17701
Sutton Ave	17701
Swan Aly	17702
Sweeley Ave	17701
Sylvan Dr	17702
Sylvan Dell Rd	17702
Sylvan Dell Park Rd	17702
Tabbs Dr	17701
Taggertys Run Rd	17702
Tall Oaks Ln	17701
Tallman Ave	17702
Taylor Pl	17701
Teal Aly	17702
Terrace Ln & Pl	17701
Thomas Ave, Rd & St	17701
Thompson Aly	17701
Thompson St	17702
Tiffany Dr	17701
Timber Ln	17702
Tinsman Ave	17701
Towncrest Rd	17701
Trenton Ave & Pl	17701
Trinity Pl	17701
Tucker St	17701
Turkey Farm Rd	17701
Union Ave	17701
Upland Rd	17701
Upper Manor Rd	17701
Us Highway 15	17702
Vallamont Dr & Ln	17701
Valley Rd & St	17702
Valley Heights Dr	17701
Valley View Ave	17701
Valley View Ln	17702
Vander Ln	17702
Vernon Ave	17701
Vesta Ave	17701
Via Bella St	17701
Vikings Ct	17701
E & W Village Dr	17702
Vine Ave	17701
Vista Rd	17701
Wagner Rd	17701
Wahoo Dr	17701
Waldman Dr	17701
Walker St	17701
Wallis Run Rd	17701
Walnut St	17701
Walnut Run Ln	17702
Waltz Ave, Ln & Pl	17701
Ward St	17701
Warren Ave	17701
Warrensville Rd	17701
Washington Blvd	17701
Waterdale Rd	17702
Watson St	17701
Wayne Ave	17701
Webb St	17701
Wedgewood Knl	17701
Weller Dr	17701
Wells Rd	17702
Westbury Pl	17701
Westland Ave	17702
Westminster Dr	17701
Wheatfield Dr	17701
Wheatland Ave	17701
Wheeland Dr	17701
Whipple Rd	17701
White Oak Ln	17701
Whitford Ave	17702
Whitman St	17701
Whitney St	17701
E & W Wilcox Rd	17701
Wildwood Blvd	17701
William St	17701
Williams Rd	17701
Williamson Rd	17701
E & W Willow St	17701
Willow Brook Rd	17701
Willow Trace Rd	17701
Wilson St	17701
Windfield Dr	17701
Winner Rd	17701
Winter St	17702
Winthrop St	17702
Wisteria Ln	17701
Wither Hollow Ln	17701
Wolfe Pl	17701
Wood St	17701
Woodbryn Dr	17701
Woodland Ave	17701
S Woodland Ave	17702
Woodland Dr	17702
Woodlyn Ter	17701
Woodmont Ave	17701
Woodruff Ave	17701
Woodside Ave	17702
Woodward St	17701
Woolever Ln	17701
Wren Aly	17702
Wreyburn Pl	17701
Wrong Rd	17702
Wyndham Ct	17701
Wyndmere Dr	17701
Wynwood Ln	17701
Wyoming St	17701
Yale Ave	17701
Zuni Ln	17701

NUMBERED STREETS

Street	ZIP
1st Ave	17702
1st Ave	17702
1st Ave	17702
600-1199	17701
E 1st Ave	17702
W 1st Ave	17702
1st St	17701
2nd Ave	
1-99	17702
600-999	17701
E 2nd Ave	17702
W 2nd Ave	17702
2nd St	17701
E & W 3rd Ave & St	17701
E & W 4th Ave & St	17701
5th Ave & St	17701
5th Ave & St	17702
6th Ave	17701
E 6th Ave	17702
W 6th Ave	17702
6th St	17701
7th Ave	17701
E 7th Ave	17702
W 7th Ave	17702
E 7th St	17701
W 7th St	17701
8th Ave	17701
W 8th Ave	17702
9th Ave	17701
W 9th Ave	17702
10th Ave	17701

YORK PA

General Delivery	17405

POST OFFICE BOXES MAIN OFFICE STATIONS AND BRANCHES

Box No.s	ZIP
A - A	17407
1 - 299	17407
1 - 1349	17405
320 - 360	17407
1441 - 2932	17405
3001 - 3958	17402
5001 - 5185	17405
7001 - 7791	17404
12001 - 12012	17402
15012 - 15648	17405
20001 - 22206	17402

RURAL ROUTES

Route	ZIP
08, 38	17403

NAMED STREETS

Street	ZIP
Abbey Ln	17402
Abbie Rd	17408
Aberdeen Rd	17406
Academy Rd	17406
Acco Dr	17402
Accomac Rd	17406
Adam St	17404
Adams Rd	17406
N Adams St	17404
S Adams St	17404
Adamson Ln	17406
Addison Ct	17404
Alana Dr	17402
N & S Albemarle St	17403
Albright Ave	17404
Alcott Rd	17406
Alder Ct	17408
Alder Way	17406
Allegheny Dr	17402
Alliance Ave	17406
Allison Dr	17402
Aloe Ct	17402
Alpha Dr	17408
N Alpine Dr	17408
S Alpine Dr	17408
Alpine Rd	17406
Altland Ave	17404
Alton Ln	17402
N & S Alwine Ave	17408
Alyce Cir	17402
Amad Dr	17403
Amanda Ln	17406
Ambleside Dr	17402
Ameda Dr	17407
Amethyst Rd	17408
Anderson Ln	17403
E & W Andes Rd	17406
Andintan Rd	17402
Andrew Dr	17404
Andrews St	17404
Angel Dr	17404
Angela Ln	17402
Angus Ln	17408
Anna May St	17404
Annette Dr	17403
Anthony Ln	17406
Antler Dr	17406
Apple Butter Ln	17408
Apple Hill Ln	17402
Appleford Way	17402
Applewine Ct	17404
Aqua Ct	17403
Arbor Ln	17406
Arch St	
100-199	17401
200-299	17403
Ardmore Ln	17402
Argyle Dr	17406
E Arlene Dr	17406
Arlington Rd	17403
Arlington St	17402
Armory Ln	17408
Arnold Ln	17406
Arnold Rd	17408
Arsenal Rd	
1-199	17404
200-400	17402
402-698	17402
601-799	17406
Arthur St	17406
Arthurs Ct	17408
Artman Ave	17406
Ashgrove Ln	17403
Ashland Dr	17408
Ashleigh Dr	17402
Ashley Way	17402

Aslan Ct & Dr 17404
Associates Dr 17403
Aster Dr 17408
Atlantic Ave 17404
Auburn Rd 17402
Audlyn Dr 17408
Augusta Cir 17402
Augusta Ct
100-199 17404
1100-1199 17408
Austin Ln 17408
Autumnwood Ave 17404
Aylesbury Ln 17404
Azalea Dr 17408
Baer Ridge Rd 17406
Baer Valley Ln 17406
Bahn Ave 17408
Bairs Rd 17408
N Baker Rd 17408
Baldsmere Dr 17403
Balsa St 17404
N Banintan St 17401
Bank Ln 17408
Bannister St
1300-1398 17404
1400-2199 17404
2200-2700 17408
2702-2798 17408
Barachel Dr 17402
Barcardi Cir 17404
Barcroft Rd 17406
Barkhill Rd 17404
Barkwood Ln 17406
Barley Rd 17408
Baron Dr 17408
Barrington Dr 17408
Barrister Dr 17404
Barrow Ln 17403
Barshinger Ave 17403
Bartlett Dr 17406
Barton Cir 17408
Barwood Rd 17406
Basil Ct 17402
Basswood Rd 17408
Bayberry Ct 17403
Bayberry Dr 17404
Bayberry Ln 17403
Beacon Rd 17402
Beadsley Rd 17406
Bear Rd 17406
Beaumont Rd 17403
E Beaver St 17406
N Beaver St
1-499 17401
500-2299 17404
20-10-20-10 17401
S Beaver St
1-799 17401
800-999 17403
34-36-34-36 17401
7-9-7-9 17401
W Beaver St 17406
Beaverton Dr 17402
Beck Rd 17403
Becker Way 17401
Becket Rd 17402
Bedford Pl 17408
Bedford Rd 17404
Bedfordshire Dr 17402
Bee Jay Dr 17404
Bee Tree Rd 17403
Beeler Ave 17408
Beidler Rd 17406
Belair Way 17404
Belaire Ln 17404
Bellaire Dr 17402
Belle Ln 17406
Belle Rd 17402
Bellevue Dr 17403
N & S Belmont St 17403
N Belvidere Ave
1-299 17401
400-698 17404
700-799 17404
S Belvidere Ave 17401
Bentley Ln 17404
Bentwood Ln 17408
Bentz Ct 17404
Bentzel Mill Rd 17404
Bergman St 17403
Berkley Rd 17402
E Berlin Ct & Rd 17408
Bernays Dr 17404
Bert Ct 17404
Berwick St 17404
Bierman Ave 17401
S Biesecker Rd 17408
Binder Ln 17406
Birch Rd 17408
Birchwood Rd 17402
Biscayne Ln 17404
Bishops Cir 17402
Bitternut Blvd 17404
Black Bridge Rd
1701-2099 17402
2601-2697 17406
2699-2999 17406
Blackfriar Ln 17402
Blackgum Ct 17406
Blackthorne Ct 17406
Blake Ct 17408
Blenheim Ct 17403
Blessing Blvd 17406
Bloomingdale Ct 17402
Blossom Valley Dr 17402
Blue Bird Ln 17402
Blue Ridge Dr 17402
Bluestone Rd 17406
Blunston Ln 17406
Board Rd 17406
Boddington Pl 17402
Bon Aire Dr 17408
Bonbar Rd 17403
Bond Ave 17403
Bonneview Rd 17406
Booth Ave 17403
Borom Rd 17404
E Boundary Ave
31-33 17401
35-130 17401
132-198 17401
200-1099 17403
W Boundary Ave 17401
Bovary Dr 17402
Bowman Rd 17408
Box Hill Ln 17403
Boxwood Ln 17402
Braden Dr 17404
Bradford Dr 17402
Brady Rd 17404
Braeburn Ct 17404
Brafferton Ct 17404
E Branch Dr 17407
Brandywine Ln 17404
Braxton Ln 17408
Brechin Ln 17403
Breezeview Dr 17404
Breezewood Rd 17408
Breezy Vista Ln 17406
Bremer Rd 17406
Brenda Rd 17408
Brentwood Dr 17403
Bretton Ln 17408
Brian Ln 17404
Briargate Dr 17404
Briarwood Ct 17408
Bridle Ct 17404
Bridlewood Way 17402
Brigadier Dr 17404
Briggs Cir 17402
Brighkin Dr 17402
Brighton Dr 17402
Brillhart Station Rd 17403
Bristol Dr 17403
Britain Dr 17402
Brittany Ct 17408
Brittany Dr 17404
Broad St 17408
N Broad St
1-700 17403
1-99 17406
101-199 17406
702-798 17403
39-35-39-35 17403
S Broad St
1-399 17406
1-1299 17403
Brockie Dr & Ln 17403
N & W Brook Cir 17403
Brookedge Ln 17402
Brookfield Dr 17404
Brooklyn Ave 17401
Brooklyn Dr 17406
Brookmar Dr 17408
Brooks Robinson Way 17401
Brookside Ave 17408
Brookside Ln 17402
Brookway Dr 17403
Brookwood Dr N & S 17403
Brougher Ln 17408
Brown Ln 17406
Broxton Ln 17402
Bruaw Dr 17406
Brummer Ln 17406
Bryan Ave 17408
Buchanan Dr 17402
Bucktail Ln 17408
Buckthorn Dr 17406
Bull Rd 17408
Bunny Ln 17406
Bunting Dr 17403
Burgard St 17404
Burgs Ln 17406
Burning Tree Ct 17404
Burton Dr 17404
Buser Farm Ln 17406
Butcher Ct 17404
Butler Ave 17403
Butter Rd 17404
E Butter Rd
100-465 17404
495-1499 17406
Butterfly Commons Dr 17402
Butternut Ln 17408
Buttonwood Ln 17406
Cabin Creek Rd 17406
Caldwell Dr 17402
Callie Dr 17404
Calvert St 17403
Camberlay Dr 17402
Cambridge Rd 17402
Camelot Arms 17406
Camp Betty Washington Rd 17402
Campbell Rd 17402
Canada Dr 17402
Canadochly Cir & Rd 17406
E Canal Rd 17404
Canal Road Ext 17406
Canary Cir & Ct 17404
Candle Ln 17404
Candlelight Dr 17402
Candlewyck Ct 17402
Canford Rd 17406
Cannon Ct 17408
Canterbury Ln 17406
Canyon Dr 17406
Cape Climb 17408
Cape Horn Rd 17402
Capital Dr 17406
Cardinal Dr 17403
Carl St 17403
Carlisle Ave
1-100 17401
102-198 17401
200-799 17404
1500-1698 17408
1700-1899 17408
Carlisle Ct 17408
Carlisle Rd
2899A-2899D 17408
800-898 17404
900-1299 17404
1400-2829 17408
2831-2899 17408
Carllyn Dr 17403
Carlton Ct 17402
Carlton Pl 17408
Carnegie Rd 17402
Carol Ave & Rd 17402
Carousel Dr 17406
Carriage Ct 17403
Carriage Ln 17406
Carriage Hill Ln 17406
Carriage Run Rd 17408
Carroll Rd 17403
Casey Ln 17402
Cashew Ct 17404
Caspian Ct & Dr 17404
Castanea Ct 17402
Castle Pond Dr 17402
Catherine St 17408
Cayuga Ln 17402
Cedar Rd 17408
Cedar St 17401
Cedar Run Dr 17404
Cedar Village Dr 17406
Cedarlyn Dr 17408
Cedarwood Dr 17402
Cemetery Ln 17406
Cemetery Rd 17408
Center Ct 17404
Central Ave 17406
Chablis Way 17404
Chadbourne Dr 17404
Chambers Rd & Rdg 17402
Chanceford Ave 17404
Chancellor Rd 17403
Chapel Dr 17404
Chapelwood Dr 17402
Chardonnay Dr 17404
Chardrie Dr 17402
Charles Cir 17406
E Charles Ln 17401
W Charles Ln 17401
Charleston Ln 17408
Chelsea Way 17406
Cheltenham Rd 17402
Cheradwa Dr 17407
Cherimoya St 17404
E Cherry Ave 17406
Cherry Ln 17406
N Cherry Ln
1-99 17401
126-126 17407
S Cherry Ln 17401
Cherry St 17402
Cherry Blossom Ct 17402
Cherry Hills Rd 17404
Cherry Manor Dr 17402
E Cherrywine Dr 17404
Chesapeake Rd 17402
Chesley Rd 17403
Chesterbrook Dr 17406
Chestnut Hl 17408
Chestnut Ln 17403
Chestnut Rd 17408
Chestnut St 17403
Chestnut Hill Rd 17402
Chestnut Run Rd 17402
Chimney Rock Rd 17406
Chippenham Dr 17408
N Christensen Rd 17402
Chronister St 17406
Chronister Farm Rd 17402
E Church Ave 17401
W Church Ave 17401
Church Rd
2109A-2109B 17408
1-499 17406
500-1499 17404
1500-2699 17408
Church St
1-99 17407
1-99 17406
701-799 17406
E Church St 17402
W Church St 17402
Churchill Dr 17403
Cimmeron Rd 17402
Cinema Dr 17402
N Circle Blvd 17406
Circle Ct 17402
Circle Dr
1-16 17407
1-99 17402
100-199 17406
City View Rd 17406
Claire Ave 17406
Clairian Dr 17403
Clare Ln 17402
W Clark Ln 17401
E Clarke Ave
101-199 17401
201-297 17403
299-800 17403
802-820 17403
W Clarke Ave 17401
Clarks Way 17403
Clarkson Dr 17403
Clary Way 17404
Clayoma Ave 17408
Claystone Rd 17408
Clayton Ave 17401
Clear Springs Blvd 17406
Clearbrook Blvd 17406
Clearmount Rd 17403
Clearview Dr 17404
Clearview Rd 17406
Clearview Way 17403
Cleveland Ave 17401
N & S Clinton St 17404
Clover Dr 17406
Clover Ln 17403
Cloverleaf Rd 17406
Club Farm Rd 17403
Clubhouse Rd 17403
Clugston Rd 17404
Clydesdale Dr 17402
Cobblestone Ln 17408
Codorun Ln 17408
Coffee Mill Ln 17406
Coldspring Rd 17404
E College Ave
1-199 17401
200-214 17403
216-400 17403
402-498 17403
W College Ave
2-98 17401
100-999 17401
1000-1499 17404
1700-2598 17408
2600-3399 17408
Colonial Ave 17403
Colony Dr
601-697 17404
699-799 17404
1700-1798 17408
Colt Ct 17402
Columbia Ave
1-99 17403
1101-1299 17404
Cometlight Dr 17402
Commerce Dr 17408
Commerce Way 17406
Community Pl 17404
Company St 17401
Compton Ln 17402
Concord Ave
100-199 17406
3800-3899 17402
Concord Rd 17402
Conewago Ave 17404
Conifer Ct & Ln 17406
Constantine Ln 17402
Continental Rd 17404
Cookes House Ln 17401
Cooper Pl 17401
Copenhaffer Rd 17404
Copper Beach Dr 17403
Copper Beech Dr 17403
Copperwood Ct 17408
Coraderl Rd 17404
Corbin Rd 17403
Cortland Dr 17403
Cortleigh Dr 17402
E Cottage Pl
1-27 17401
29-199 17401
200-399 17403
W Cottage Pl 17401
Cottage Hill Rd 17401
Cottonwood Rd 17408
Country Ln 17406
Country Rd
607-715 17403
717-719 17403
721-799 17403
1700-1799 17408
Country By Way 17402
Country Club Rd 17403
Country Manor Dr 17408
Country Ridge Dr 17408
Countryside Ln 17408
Course Rd 17402
N Court Ave
1-399 17401
901-1499 17404
S Court Ave 17401
Courtland St 17403
Cousler Cir 17404
Coventry Ct 17406
Coventry At Waterford 17402
Cranberry Ln W 17402
Cranbrook Dr 17402
Cranmere Ln 17402
Crawford Ct 17406
Creek Ln 17406
Creekwood Dr 17407
Crescent Rd
1200-1399 17402
1700-2099 17403
Crest St 17408
Crest Way 17403
E Crestlyn Dr 17402
W Crestlyn Dr 17402
Crestlyn Rd 17403
Creston Rd 17403
Crestview Dr 17402
Crestwood Ln 17402
Crocus Ln 17408
Croll School Rd 17403
E & W Crone Rd 17406
Crooked Wind Ln 17404
Cropthorne Ln 17402
Cross Farm Ln
100-198 17404
200-299 17406
Crossbrook Dr 17406
Crossfield Ln 17406
Crosslyn Dr 17404
Crossway Dr 17402
Crown Pointe Dr 17402
Crows Nest Ln 17403
Croyden Rd 17408
Crystal Ln 17402
Cypress Dr 17408
Daisy Rd 17402
Daleview Ct 17403
Dallas Dr 17406
Dallas St 17403
Dana Ct 17406
Dandelion Dr 17404
Dandridge Dr 17403
Danielle Ct 17404
Darby Ln 17402
Dark Hollow Rd 17406
Darlene St 17402
Darlington Rd 17408
Darrow Rd 17404
Dartmouth Rd 17404
Daugherty Rd 17404
David Cir 17406
Davidson Dr 17402
Davies Dr 17402
Dawn Ln 17406
Dawnlight Dr 17402
Daylight Dr 17402
Days Mill Rd
400-500 17403
502-598 17403
3100-3198 17408
3200-3399 17408
3401-3499 17408
Deamerlyn Dr 17406
Dearborn Ln 17402
Debbie Dr 17403
Deep Run Ln 17406
Deer Chase Ln 17403
Deer Ford Way 17408
Deer Forest Rd 17406
Deer Leap Ln 17403
Deerfield Ln 17403
Deerhill Dr 17406
Deininger Rd 17406
Delaware Ave 17404
Denny Ln 17406
Derry Ct 17406
Derry Rd 17403
Detwiler Ct 17403
Detwiler Dr 17404
Devers Rd 17404
Devon Rd 17403
Dew Drop Ct 17403
Dew Drop Rd
27-31 17403
33-100 17403
101-163 17402
165-399 17402
Dewberry Rd 17404
Dewey Ave & St 17404
N Diamond St 17404
Dietz Rd 17402
Dietz Estates Dr 17404
Dill Rd 17404
Dixie Dr 17402
Doersam Ct 17406
Dogwood Cir 17403
Dogwood Ct 17406
Dogwood Dr 17406
Dolls Ln 17406
Dolomite Dr 17408
Domenick Dr 17402
Donlenik 17402
Donna Ln 17403
Donnelly St 17403
Dorchester Dr 17408
Doris Ln 17406
Dorsett Ln 17402
Dove Dr 17408
Downing St 17408
Dressage Ct 17404
Drexel St 17404
Druck Valley Rd 17406
Ducktown Rd 17406
Duella Ct 17404
Dugan Ln 17406
Duke St 17403
N Duke St
1-299 17401
301-399 17401
701-797 17404
799-1499 17404
S Duke St
1-799 17401
800-1499 17403
1501-1599 17403
Dulcy Dr 17404
Dunbar Rd 17408
Dundee Rd 17406
Dunkard Valley Rd 17403
Dunster Rd 17403
Dupont Ave 17403
Duquesne Rd 17402
Durham Rd 17402
Dutton Ct 17402
Duvall Ave 17404
Duxbury Dr 17404
Dyan Dr 17402
Dylan Dr 17404
Eagles Lndg 17406
Eagleton Dr 17407
Earl Way 17401
N East St
1-299 17403
301-399 17403
1401-1497 17406
1499-1899 17406
Eastern Blvd 17402
Eastgate Dr 17402

Eastland Ave 17406
Eastwood Dr 17402
Eaton St 17402
Eberts Ln
1100-1299 17402
1700-1999 17406
N Eberts Ln 17403
Ebony Dr 17402
Eden Rd
1201-1297 17402
1299-1399 17402
1401-1499 17402
2100-2199 17406
Edenbridge Rd 17402
Edgar St 17403
Edgecomb Ave 17403
Edgehill Rd 17403
Edgewood Dr 17403
Edgewood Ln 17403
Edgewood Rd 17402
Edinburgh Rd 17406
Edison St 17403
Edmund Ave 17404
Edward Rd 17403
Edwards Ave 17406
Eisenhower Dr 17402
El Dorado 17402
Elaine Pl 17403
Elderslie Ln 17403
Eldine Ave 17408
Elham Dr 17406
Eli Dr 17404
Elim St 17408
Elkridge Ln 17404
Elliott Ln 17403
Elm St 17403
Elm Ter
200-300 17401
302-498 17401
600-799 17404
Elm St And Albemarle St 17403
Elmhurst Ct 17408
Elmwood Blvd 17403
Emerald Ave 17408
Emig Rd & St 17406
N & S Emigs Mill Rd 17408
Emiray Ct 17403
Emmanuel Dr 17408
English Way 17402
Ensminger Dr 17407
Equestrian Dr 17402
Erlen Dr 17402
Esbenshade Rd 17408
Espresso Way 17406
Estate Dr 17408
Eton Ln 17402
Evan Dr 17404
Everett Rd 17403
Evergreen Dr 17402
Evergreen Ln 17408
Evunbreth Dr 17404
Exeter Dr N & S 17403
Exton Ln 17402
Ezios Way 17402
Fading Way 17406
Fahringer Dr 17406
Fahs St 17404
Fair Ln 17408
Fair Acres Dr 17403
Fairfax Dr 17403
Fairfax Rd 17404
Fairfield Ave 17408
Fairlane Dr 17404
Fairmount Pl 17401
Fairview Dr & Ter 17403
Fairway Dr
2200-2450 17408
2400-2448 17408
2450-2490 17408
2479-2692 17402
2492-2500 17408
2694-2790 17402
Fake Rd 17406
Fake Hollow Rd 17406
Falls Grove Ln 17404
Farefield Ct 17402
Farm Dr 17402
Farm Ln
150-200 17402
2100-2199 17408
Farm Cross Way 17408
Farm House Ln 17408
Farm Lane Cir 17408
Farmbrook Ln 17406
Farmhill Dr 17406
Farmington Dr 17407
Farmstead Way 17408
Farmtrail Rd 17406
Farmview Dr & Rd 17408
Farnham Ln 17408
Farquhar Dr 17403
Fauth Ln 17406
Faversham Way 17402
Fawn Ct 17406
N & S Fayette St 17404
Federal Rd 17408
Felty Ave 17403
Fern Pl 17404
Ferncreek Ln 17404
Ferree Ln 17406
Ferree Hill Rd 17403
Fickes Way 17403
Fieldbrook Cir & Dr 17403
Fieldstone Ct 17402
Fiesta Dr 17403
Filbert St 17404
Finch Dr 17404
N & S Findlay St 17402
Fineview Rd 17406
Finks Dr 17404
Fireside Ct & Rd 17404
Fisher Dr 17404
Fitzkee Ln 17402
Fitzpatrick Ln
400-499 17406
6411-6429 17403
Fleming Pl 17408
Flora Ln 17403
Florida Ave 17404
Flour Mill Rd 17406
Folkemer Cir 17404
Folkstone Ct & Way 17402
Forbes Ln 17408
Forest Rd 17402
Forest Hill Cir & Rd 17406
Forge Ln 17406
Forrest Ln 17402
Forrest Rd 17408
N Forrest St 17404
S Forrest St 17404
E Forry Ave 17406
W Forry Ave 17406
Forry St 17408
Fountain Dr 17402
Fox Ln 17406
Fox Ridge Ln 17406
Fox Run Dr 17403
Foxshire Dr 17402
Foxtail Dr 17404
Foxwald Ln 17406
Frank Dr 17402
Franklin St 17407
N Franklin St 17403
Franklin Way 17403
Fredrick Ct 17403
Freedom Way 17402
Frelen Rd 17404
Freys Ln 17406
Freysville Rd 17406
Friar Rd 17408
Friends Cir 17408
Friendship Ave 17406
Friesian Rd 17406
Front St
200-699 17404
1401-1499 17402
Frontenac Ct 17403
Frysville Rd 17406
Fulton St 17403
Furnace Rd 17406
Futurity Dr 17404
N Gabrielle Ct 17408
Galtee Ct 17402
Garfield St 17401
Garnet Rd 17403
Garrett Rd 17404
Garrison Dr 17404
Gartner Ln 17402
E Gas Ave
1-100 17401
102-198 17401
200-398 17403
W Gas Ave 17401
Gatehouse Ln E & W 17402
Gateway Rd 17403
W Gay St 17401
Gea Dr 17406
Geesey Ct 17404
Geiselman Dr 17407
Gemstone Ln 17404
E George St 17408
N George St
1-11 17401
13-499 17401
500-2100 17404
2102-2198 17404
2200-3099 17406
401-405-401-405 17401
S George St
1-199 17401
200-200 17403
200-200 17405
201-799 17401
202-798 17401
800-2899 17403
W George St 17408
Gillespie Dr 17404
Ginger Cir 17402
Ginger Dr 17408
Girard Ave 17403
Gladfelter St 17403
Glen Pl 17403
Glen Hollow Dr 17406
Glen View Dr 17403
Glendale Rd 17403
Gleneagles Dr 17404
Glenleigh Dr 17404
Glenmore Way 17402
Glenwood Dr 17403
Gloria Dr 17407
Goddard Dr 17402
Golden Way 17402
Golden Dale Dr 17406
Golden Eagle Dr 17408
Golden Villas Dr 17408
Goldens Path 17408
Golf Dr 17408
Golf Club Rd 17403
Gora Rd N & S 17404
Gosling Dr 17406
N & S Gotwalt St 17404
Governors Pl At Waterf 17402
Graffius Rd 17404
Graham St 17402
Grandview Ave 17408
Grandview Rd
700-1129 17403
1130-1130 17408
1131-2399 17403
1132-2398 17403
Grandview Park Dr 17408
Grant Dr
400-499 17406
4900-4999 17408
Grant Ln 17406
Grant St 17401
Grantley Ct 17403
Grantley Rd 17403
Grantley St 17401
Graybill Rd 17408
Green St 17401
Green Spring Rd 17403
Green Springs Rd
1-699 17404
700-772 17406
774-1199 17406
Green Valley Rd 17403
Greenbriar Dr 17407
E Greenbriar Dr 17407
Greenbriar Rd 17404
Greendale Rd 17403
Greenhill Rd 17403
Greenleaf Ct & Rd 17406
Greenmeadow Dr 17408
Greenspring Dr 17402
Greensprings Dr 17402
Greenwood Rd
1-50 17404
501-597 17408
599-2999 17408
Grenlyn Rd 17402
Greystone Rd 17402
Greywood Dr 17402
Grim Ln 17406
Gross Ct 17404
Grouse Ln 17404
Grumbacher Rd 17406
Guildford Ln 17404
Gulton Rd 17404
Gun Club Rd 17406
Gunnison Rd 17404
Guy St 17406
Gwen Dr 17404
Hackberry Ln 17404
Hadley Dr 17408
Hagarman Dr 17408
Haines Rd 17402
Hake St 17406
Hall Ln 17406
Halstead Ln 17404
Hambiltonian Way 17404
Hambledon Ct 17402
Hamilton Ave 17401
Hamilton St 17406
Hammond Rd 17406
Hampden Dr 17408
Hampshire Dr 17404
Hampstead Ct 17403
Hampton Rd 17408
S Hampton At Waterford 17402
Hanover Rd 17408
Harding Ct 17403
Hardwick Pl 17404
Harford Cir 17404
N & S Harlan St 17402
Harley Davidson Dr 17402
Harmony Hill Ln 17402
Harold St 17406
N Harrison St
1-199 17403
1300-1498 17406
1500-1699 17406
S Harrison St 17403
Harrowgate Rd 17402
Hartford Rd 17402
N Hartley St
1-299 17401
301-399 17401
400-1100 17404
1102-1198 17404
S Hartley St 17401
N & S Hartman St 17403
Harvest Dr 17404
Harvest Field Ln 17403
Hastings Blvd 17402
Hatchery Rd 17406
Hauser School Rd 17406
Haven Dr 17406
Haviland Rd 17408
Hawthorne Rd 17406
N Hawthorne St 17404
S Hawthorne St 17401
Hay St
100-199 17401
201-697 17403
699-799 17403
801-1099 17403
Haybrook Dr 17406
Hayden Heights Rd 17408
Hayley Rd 17404
Haymarket Ct 17406
Haymeadow Dr 17406
Hayshire Dr 17406
Hayward Rd 17408
Hearthridge Ln 17404
Hearthstone Ct 17402
Heather Dr
2700-2799 17402
3389-3499 17408
Heather Rd 17408
Heather Way 17404
Heavenlight Cir 17402
Hedgegate Ln 17404
Heidelberg Ave 17404
W Heiges St 17404
Heindel Rd
1100-1200 17408
1202-1298 17408
3500-3599 17402
Heistand Rd 17402
Heller Ln 17406
Hemlock Dr 17408
Hempfield Dr 17408
Hengst Ct 17406
Henrietta St 17408
Henry Ln 17402
Hepplewhite Dr 17404
Heritage Dr 17402
Heritage Ln 17403
Heritage Hills Cir & Dr 17402
Herman Ct 17406
Herman Dr 17408
Herman St 17404
Hershey Ct 17404
Hess Rd 17404
Hess Farm Rd 17403
Hialeah Ct 17408
Hickory Hill Ln 17402
Hickory Ridge Cir 17404
Hidden Farm Ln 17406
Hidden Hill Farm Ln 17403
High St 17408
High Rock Ln 17406
N Highland Ave 17404
S Highland Ave 17404
Highland Rd 17403
Highland Ter 17403
Highlands Path 17402
Hill St 17403
Hill N Dale Ct & Dr 17403
Hill Top Ln 17403
Hill View Rd 17406
Hillcrest Rd 17403
Hillcroft Ln 17403
Hillery Ct 17402
Hillock Ln 17403
N Hills Rd
1-97 17402
99-1000 17402
1002-1298 17402
1300-1698 17406
1700-1999 17406
Hillside Ct 17406
Hillside Dr
1-99 17407
1000-1099 17403
1101-1199 17403
Hillside Ln 17403
Hillside Ter 17408
Hilltop Dr
1600-1698 17406
1700-1799 17406
2901-2999 17408
Hilltop Pl 17403
Hilltop Rd 17408
Hilton Ave 17408
Hoffman Ln 17403
Hoffman Rd 17403
Hogans Cv 17404
Hoke St 17404
Hokes Mill Rd
1-200 17404
202-298 17404
1201-1297 17408
1299-1399 17408
1401-1535 17408
Holbrook Rd 17402
Holly Ct 17406
Holly Ln 17402
Hollywood Dr, Pkwy & Ter 17403
Holyoke Dr 17402
Homedale Rd 17403
Homeland Rd 17403
Homestead Rd 17402
Homewood Dr 17403
Homewood Rd 17402
Honey Run Dr 17408
Honey Valley Rd 17403
E Hope Ave 17401
W Hope Ave 17401
Hope Ln 17406
Horn Rd 17406
Houghten Ln 17406
Houston Ln 17406
N Howard Ave 17404
N Howard St 17401
S Howard St 17401
Howards End 17403
Hudson Dr 17402
Hudson St 17403
Hull Dr 17404
Hummel Dr 17404
Hunt Club Dr 17402
Hunter Creek Dr 17406
Hunters Crest Dr 17402
Huntfield Dr 17404
Hunting Park Ct & Ln 17402
Huntley Ct 17408
Idylwyld Rd 17406
Imperial Dr 17403
Indian Rock Dam Rd
1-1501 17403
1503-1625 17403
2255-2467 17408
2469-3599 17408
Industrial Hwy 17402
Industrial Rd 17406
Innovation Dr 17402
Interchange Pl 17406
Ironstone Dr 17406
Ironstone Hill Rd 17403
Ironwood Way 17404
Iroquois Dr 17406
Irving Rd 17403
Irwin Ct 17404
Ivory Rd 17402
Ivy Ln & St 17402
Ivy Pump Ln 17408
Ivyside Dr 17402
E Jackson St
1-199 17401
200-222 17403
224-400 17403
402-1298 17403
W Jackson St 17401
James Dr 17404
James Way 17406
Jamestown Ln 17408
Jamison Dr 17402
Jasper Ave 17404
Jayme Dr 17402
Jean Lo Way 17406
Jefferson Ave 17401
Jeffrey Ln 17402
Jennifer Rd 17404
Jessamine Way 17408
Jesse Ln 17404
Jessop Pl
500-799 17401
800-899 17403
Jewel Dr 17404
Joan Dr 17404
Jody Dr 17402
Johns Rd 17402
Jolo Way 17403
Jonquil Rd 17403
Joppa Rd 17403
Joseph Rd 17408
Joshua Dr 17404
Judith Ct 17408
Jug Rd 17404
June St 17404
Juniper Dr 17408
Juniper St 17401
Kain Rd 17408
Kalreda Rd 17406
Karens Way 17402
Karyl Ln 17404
Kauffman Ln 17406
Kbs Rd 17408
Keeney Dr 17403
Keeney Ln 17406
N & S Keesey St 17402
Keller Ave & Rd 17406
Kelly Cir 17402
Kelly Dr 17404
Kelly Ln 17406
Kenneth Rd
1301-1399 17404
1400-1999 17408
2001-2099 17408
Kensington Ct 17402
Kent Rd 17402
Kentwell Dr 17406
Kentwood Ln 17403
Kern Dr 17408
Kern Rd 17406
Kerria Dr 17404
N & S Kershaw St 17402
Kestrel Ln 17406
Kevin Dr 17408
Keymar Dr 17402
Keystone Dr 17406
Keyway Dr 17402
Kildore Ct 17404
Kimes Rd 17402
E King St
1-199 17401
200-1399 17403
W King St
1-999 17401
1000-1900 17404
1902-2198 17404
King Richards Ct N & S 17408
E Kings Ct 17403
Kings Arms Ln 17402
Kings Arms At Waterfor 17402
Kings Mill Rd
200-428 17401
430-498 17401
701-1027 17403
1029-1079 17403
1081-1099 17403
Kingsbriar Way 17404
Kingston Ct & Rd 17402
Kingswood Dr 17403
Kinross Ave 17402
Kipling Ln 17406
Kirch Rd 17402
Kirkham Dr 17402
Knob Run 17408
Knob Creek Ln 17402
Knobhill Rd 17403
Knoll Dr 17408
Knoll Ln 17406
Knottingham Ln 17408
Kochenour Ln 17404
Koontz Ln 17408
Kotur Ave 17408
Kreidler Ave 17402
Kreidler Rd 17403
Kreis Ln 17406
Kresta Dr 17403
Kreutz Creek Ave & Rd 17406
Kunkel Ln 17408
Kurtz Ave 17401
Kyle Rd 17404
Kylemore Way 17402
Lady Bug Ln 17402
Lafayette St
2-198 17401
200-299 17401
1000-1100 17404
1102-1198 17404
Lake Rd 17403

Street	ZIP
Lake View Ln	17406
Lakefield Rd	17402
Lakeview Dr	17403
Lambeth Walk	17403
Lamour St	17403
Lancaster Ave	17403
Lancer Ln	17404
Landon Ln	17403
Langshire Dr	17404
Lanie Ct	17402
Larchmont Dr	17404
Lark Cir & Dr	17404
Larkspur Ln S	17403
Latimer St	17404
Laughman Ln	17408
Laura Ln	17402
Laurel Dr	
300-399	17406
1112-1118	17404
1120-1128	17404
1130-1140	17404
Laurel Ln	17402
Laurel St	17404
Laurel Ter	17406
Laurel Oak Ln	17403
Lawncrest Dr	17402
Lawson Ct	17408
Leader Dr	17407
Leaders Heights Rd	
1-157	17403
158-180	17402
182-299	17402
301-399	17402
Leaf St	17404
Leafydale Dr	17403
Leaman Ln	17406
Ledge Dr	17408
Lee Ct	17406
N Lee St	
1-99	17406
2-98	17403
S Lee St	
1-99	17403
2-298	17406
300-399	17406
Leeds Rd	17403
Lees Ln	17406
Leeward Ct	17403
Leewood Ln	17406
Legacy Ln	17402
Lehigh Rd	17402
N & S Lehman Dr & St	17403
Lehr Dr	17404
Leigh Dr	17406
Lemon St	
1800-1848	17408
1850-1898	17404
2000-2098	17408
2100-2600	17408
2602-3098	17408
Lena Dr	17408
Lenox Pl	17408
Lentzlyn Dr	17403
Leonard St	17404
Leslynn Rd	17403
Lester Ave	17408
Lewisberry Rd	17404
Lexington Rd	17402
Lexington St	17403
Lexton Dr	17404
Liberty Ct	17403
Libhart Mill Rd	17406
Liborio Ln	17402
Lightner Rd	17404
Lilac Rd	17408
Lincoln Dr	17404
Lincoln Hwy	17406
Lincoln Hwy W	17408
Lincoln St	
101-199	17404
400-699	17401
Lincolnway Ct & Dr	17408
Lincolnwood Dr	17408
Lindberg Ave	17401
Linden Ave	17404
Linden Rd	17408
Linton Ter	17402
Lisa Cir	17406
Lisa Ln	17402
Lismore Blvd	17402
Little John Dr	17408
Live Oak Ln	17406
Livingston Rd	17404
Livingstone Dr	17402
Local Way	17403
Locust Ln	17408
E Locust Ln	17406
W Locust Ln	17406
Locust Rd	17403
E Locust St	17403
W Locust St	
600-999	17401
1000-1300	17404
1302-1498	17404
Locust Grove Rd	17402
Locust Point Rd	17406
Locust Run Dr	17404
Log Rd	17403
Log Cabin Rd	17408
Logan Rd	17408
Logan Heights Rd	17403
Loman Ave & Dr	17408
Long Dr	17406
Long Point Dr	17402
Longstown Rd	17402
Longview Rd	17406
Lookout Ct	17408
Lorenzo Ct	17402
Lori Dr	17404
Loucks Pl	17404
Loucks Rd	
300-1200	17404
1202-1298	17404
1401-1497	17408
1499-2499	17408
Loucks St	17403
Loucks Mill Rd	
600-799	17403
800-999	17402
1001-1099	17402
Louise Ave	17403
Lovegren Ct	17404
Lower Glades Rd	17406
Lucy Ln	17404
Ludlow Ave	17403
Lustig Ln	17401
Lycan Dr	17408
Lydon Ln	17406
Lyle Cir	
1-35	17402
100-199	17403
Lyn Cir	17403
Lynbrook Dr N & S	17402
Lynch Way	17403
Lyndale Rd	17402
Lyndhurst Rd	17402
Lynwood Dr & Ln	17402
Mackenzi Ln	17408
Madison Ave	17404
Maggie Cir	17402
Main St	17406
N Main St	
1-251	17407
1-12	17408
14-108	17408
25-25	17403
61-107	17408
128-138	17403
167-169	17403
171-177	17408
179-199	17408
200-204	17408
201-209	17403
206-221	17408
211-216	17403
218-234	17403
221-247	17408
223-341	17408
249-298	17408
253-257	17407
300-322	17408
301-337	17403
339-363	17403
365-399	17403
205-207-205-207	17407
207-205-207-205	17407
S Main St	
1-21	17407
1-100	17408
23-151	17407
102-198	17408
Maine Ave	17403
Manchester Ct	17408
Manchester St	
100-199	17401
700-799	17404
N & S Manheim St	17402
Manor Ct	17408
Manor Rd	
1-99	17403
1800-1999	17406
2100-2599	17408
Manor St	
300-799	17401
800-899	17403
Maphelia Rd	17406
Maple Rd	
1-99	17403
2100-2399	17408
Maple St	17407
E Maple St	
1-199	17401
200-1300	17403
1302-1498	17403
W Maple St	17401
Maple Crest Blvd	17406
Maple Run Dr	17404
Maplewood Dr	17403
Marble Ct	17402
Marbrook Ln	17404
Mardale Dr	17403
Margaret St	17408
Margate Rd	17408
Marian Way	17408
Marianne Dr	17406
Maribel Ln	17403
Marigold Rd	17408
Marion Rd	17406
Marion St	17408
Mark Dr	17402
E Market St	
1-199	17401
1-599	17406
200-1700	17403
1701-4099	17402
5000-5000	17406
W Market St	
1-700	17406
1-199	17401
160-160	17405
200-998	17401
201-999	17401
702-798	17406
1000-3699	17404
3901-3997	17408
3999-4899	17408
107-109-107-109	17401
273-267-273-267	17401
287-285-287-285	17401
288-286-288-286	17401
328-330-328-330	17401
369-363-369-363	17401
Markey St	17402
Markle Rd	17408
Marlborough Dr	17403
Marlow Dr	17402
E Marshall Ave	17403
Marshall Ct	17402
N Marshall St	17402
S Marshall St	17402
Martin Dr & Rd	17408
Martingale Dr	17404
Marvell Dr	17402
Maryland Ave	17404
E Mason Ave	17403
W Mason Ave	
200-298	17401
300-800	17401
802-898	17401
1880-2198	17404
Masonic Dr	17406
Matthew Dr	17404
Maurice St	17404
May Ln	17406
May Rd	17406
May St	17404
May Apple Dr	17402
Mayfair Ln	17408
Mayfield St	17406
Maywood Rd	17402
Mccoy Ln	17406
Mcdonald Ln	17401
Mckenzie St	
500-799	17401
800-920	17403
922-998	17403
Mckinley Dr	17403
Meade St	17404
Meadow Ct	17402
Meadow Ln	17402
Meadow Rd	17406
Meadow St	17407
Meadow Cross Way	17402
Meadow Hill Dr	17402
Meadowbrook Ave & Blvd	17406
Meadowview Dr	17402
Melinda Dr	17408
Melrie Dr	17403
Melrose Ln	17402
Memory Ln	17402
Memory Lane Ext	
1201-1297	17402
1299-1599	17402
1600-1999	17406
Meridian Ln	17402
Merion Rd	17403
Merlot Ct	17404
Merrill Rd	17403
Merrin Rd	17402
Mesa Ln	17408
Messersmith Rd	17408
Messman Ln	17406
Mia Brae Dr	17406
Michael Ln	
2500-2599	17404
6100-6199	17406
Michelle Dr	17408
Middle St	17408
Middleview Dr	17402
Midland Ave	17403
Midpine Dr	17404
Milford Ln	17402
S Mill Rd	17402
Mill St	17406
Mill Creek Rd	17404
Mill Run Rd	17404
Millcreek Rd	17404
Miller Dr	17402
Miller Ln	17401
Millers Spring Rd	17406
Mills St	17402
Millstone Rd	17406
Mimi Ct	17402
Mimosa Dr	17402
Mineral Dr	17408
Minton Dr	17402
Mirlyn Dr	17406
Misty Dr	17408
Mockingbird Ln	17403
Moffett Ln	17403
Monarch Dr	17403
Monocacy Rd	17404
Monroe St	17404
Monteview Dr	17404
Monticello Pl	17408
Monument Rd	17403
Monya Ct	17404
Moonlight Dr	17408
Morgan Ln	17406
Morningside Dr	17402
Moul St	17402
Mount Herman Blvd	17406
Mount Pisgah Rd	17406
Mount Rose Ave	
900-1799	17403
1801-1899	17403
2300-2899	17402
Mount Zion Rd	
1-1599	17402
1600-2500	17406
2502-2998	17406
Mountain Rd	17402
Mountain Laurel Ln	
600-799	17402
5172-5236	17406
Mountain View Dr	17404
Mountain Vista Ct	17402
Mourning Dove Ln	17406
Mulberry St	17403
Mundis Mill Rd	17406
Mundis Race Rd	17406
Murifield Dr	17404
Murray Pl	17403
Myers Ave	17408
Myers Ln	17403
Nancy Ave	17402
Namia Ct & Dr	17404
Natalie Dr	17402
Neater St	17401
Needham Cir E & W	17404
Neighbors Ln	17406
Nena Dr	17408
Neonlight Dr	17402
Ness Rd	17402
Neu Rd	17404
New Ct	17404
New Fairview Church Rd	17403
N Newberry St	
307A-307B	17401
1-399	17401
401-499	17401
501-699	17404
9-11-9-11	17401
S Newberry St	
1-799	17401
800-899	17403
53-51-53-51	17401
Newlin Rd	17403
E & W Newton Ave	17401
Niagara Ln	17408
Nicholas Ln	17402
Nightlight Dr	17402
Niles Ln & Rd	17403
Nina Dr	17402
Nixon Dr	17403
Nolan Dr	17404
Noonan Rd	17404
Nora Ln	17406
Norhurst Rd	17402
Norman Rd	17406
Normandie Dr	17408
North Dr	17408
North Rd	17403
North St	17403
E North St	17401
W North St	17401
Northbriar Dr	17404
N & S Northern Way	17402
Northland Ave	17406
Northridge Ln	17406
Northview Rd	17406
Northvue Ln	17408
Norway St	17403
Norwood Ave	17403
Norwood Pl	17408
Norwood Rd	17406
Noss Rd	17408
Nugent Way	17402
Nursery Ln	17404
Oak Ln	17401
Oak Rd	17402
Oak St	17402
Oak Knoll Ln	17403
Oak Manor Dr	17402
Oak Ridge Dr	17402
Oak View Ln	17406
Oakdale Dr	17403
Oakes Ave	17404
Oakham Dr	17402
Oakleigh Dr	17402
Oakley Dr	17408
Oakwood Ct	17407
Oakwood Ln	17403
Oatfield Ct	17408
Oatman St	17404
Oberlin Dr	17404
N & S Ogontz St	17403
Old Baltimore Pike	17403
Old Church Ln	17406
Old Colony Rd	17402
Old Dutch Ln	17402
Old Farm Ln	
1-107	17406
109-113	17406
1301-1397	17403
1399-1699	17403
Old Frontier Ln	17406
Old Garden Ln	17403
Old Joseph Rd	17408
Old Mill Dr	17407
Old Mill Inn Rd	17404
Old Orchard Ln	17403
Old Orchard Rd	
101-107	17403
109-119	17403
121-125	17403
4000-4399	17402
Old Stone Way	17406
Old Taxville Rd	17404
Olde Field Dr	17408
Olive St	17403
Olivia Ct	17404
Olmstead Way	17404
Olson St	17403
Olympia Ave	17404
Onyx Rd	17408
Opal Rd	17408
Opportunity Ln	17406
Orange St	
200-398	17406
1400-2099	17404
2101-2199	17404
Orchard Hills Dr	17402
Ore Ln	17406
Ore Bank Rd	17406
Oriole Dr	17403
Ottar Ln	17404
Overbrook Ave	17404
Overbrook Cir	17403
Overbrook Dr	17404
Overlook St	17403
Overview Dr	17406
Owen Rd	17403
Owl Valley Rd	17406
N Oxford St	
12-24	17402
23-25	17404
27-31	17404
30-32	17402
33-99	17404
36-38	17402
40-40	17404
42-98	17402
100-150	17402
151-153	17404
151-155	17402
152-198	17402
157-199	17402
201-399	17404
500-698	17404
S Oxford St	17404
Pacific Ave	17404
Palmer Ave	17408
Palomino Dr	17402
Pampas Dr	17404
Paradise Ln	17407
Paradise Rd	17406
Park Ave	17406
Park Ln	
1-99	17403
4000-4998	17406
Park Pl	17401
Park St	
---	17407
1-22	17407
24-98	17407
200-499	17401
2200-2398	17408
Parklyn Dr	17406
Parkside Ave	17406
Parkton Ln	17408
Parkview Rd	17406
Parkway Blvd	17404
Parkwood Dr	17404
Patriot St	17408
Pattison St	17403
Paul St	17406
Paula Dr	17402
Pauline Dr	
100-100	17402
101-101	17408
103-105	17408
107-199	17408
108-108	17402
114-114	17408
150-198	17402
200-276	17402
278-298	17402
Pauline Ln	17406
Paulownia Ln	17404
Paulson Dr	17406
Peace Ln	17406
Peach Orchard Holw	17402
N Pearl St	17404
Pearson Dr	17408
Pebble Ridge Dr	17402
Pelham Dr	17406
Pemberton Pl	17408
Penn Blvd	17402
N Penn St	17401
S Penn St	17401
Penn State Dr	17404
Pennsylvania Ave	17404
Penny Ln	17402
Penwood Rd	17406
Peppermill Ln	17404
Percheron Dr	17406
Perry Ave	17408
Perry Ln	17403
Perry Pl	17401
N Pershing Ave	
1-499	17401
500-799	17404
S Pershing Ave	
1-799	17401
800-999	17403
Persimmon Dr	17404
Peyton Rd	17403
Pheasant Run Rd	17406
E Philadelphia St	
1-199	17401
200-1599	17403
1601-1699	17403
1900-1998	17402
2000-2199	17402
2201-2399	17402
696-698-696-698	17403
W Philadelphia St	
1-799	17401
1300-2599	17404
2601-2699	17404
Philip Ct	17404
Picking Rd	17406
Piedmont Cir & Dr	17404
Pilgrim Rd	17406
Pin Oak Dr	
1-1	17406
1900-1999	17402
2407-2435	17406
2437-2531	17406
2533-2599	17406
Pine Ct	17408
Pine Dr	17406
Pine Ln	17406
Pine Rd	
1-99	17403
2200-2499	17408
Pine St	
1-22	17406
1-99	17407
N Pine St	
1-299	17403

900-1499 ... 17404
S Pine St
1-1299 ... 17403
2300-2399 ... 17402
Pine Creek Ln ... 17404
Pine Grove Cir & Rd ... 17403
Pine Grove Commons ... 17403
Pine Hill Ln
300-399 ... 17403
900-999 ... 17406
Pine Hollow Rd ... 17408
Pine Springs Blvd ... 17408
Pine Springs Blvd Ext ... 17408
Pine View Ln ... 17403
Pinehurst Pl ... 17408
Pinehurst Rd ... 17402
Pineview Dr ... 17408
Pinewood Ln ... 17402
Pinnacle Ct ... 17408
Placid Dr ... 17402
Plain Way ... 17408
Plantation Ln ... 17406
Pleader Ln ... 17402
N & S Pleasant Ave ... 17407
Pleasant Acres Rd ... 17402
Pleasant Valley Rd
2300-2398 ... 17402
2400-2799 ... 17402
2801-2999 ... 17402
3500-4999 ... 17406
Pleasant View Dr ... 17406
Plymouth Rd ... 17402
Pocono Dr ... 17402
Poe Ln ... 17406
Poff Rd ... 17406
N Point Cir & Dr ... 17406
Point Ridge Dr ... 17402
Pond Dr ... 17402
Ponds Ct ... 17404
Poplar Ave ... 17403
E Poplar St ... 17403
W Poplar St
601-697 ... 17401
699-999 ... 17401
1000-1399 ... 17404
1401-1699 ... 17404
W Poplar Ter ... 17404
Poplars Rd ... 17408
Poses Pl ... 17406
Potomac Ave ... 17408
Powder Mill Rd
1600-1800 ... 17403
1801-1805 ... 17402
1802-1806 ... 17403
1807-1999 ... 17402
Powder Ridge Ln ... 17404
Power St ... 17404
Prayer Mission Rd ... 17406
Prescott Rd ... 17403
Primrose Ln
1000-1099 ... 17402
2500-2699 ... 17404
2700-2799 ... 17402
2700-2899 ... 17404
E Princess St
1-199 ... 17401
200-1199 ... 17403
1201-1299 ... 17403
W Princess St
1-999 ... 17401
1000-1799 ... 17404
Princeton Rd ... 17402
Priority Rd ... 17404
Prospect Ave ... 17408
E Prospect Rd
2800-3600 ... 17402
3602-3898 ... 17402
3900-4098 ... 17406
4100-5205 ... 17406
5207-5227 ... 17406
E Prospect St ... 17403
N Prospect St ... 17406
S Prospect St ... 17406
Putters Cv ... 17408
Quail Ln ... 17408
Quail Run Rd ... 17406
Quaker Ct ... 17408
Quaker Dr ... 17402
Quartz Ridge Dr ... 17408
N Queen St
1-499 ... 17403
900-1499 ... 17402
1501-1599 ... 17404
S Queen St
1-2145 ... 17403
2147-2149 ... 17403
2150-2699 ... 17402
2700-2732 ... 17403
2734-2736 ... 17403
360-354-360-354 ... 17403
Queensdale Dr ... 17403
Queenswood Dr ... 17403
Quickel Rd ... 17404
Raborn Ln ... 17406
Rachel Dr ... 17404
Radnor Rd ... 17402
Rainbow Cir ... 17408
Rainier Dr ... 17402
Raintree Rd ... 17404
Raleigh Dr ... 17402
Ramblewood Rd ... 17408
Rambling Ln ... 17406
Ramsgate Ct ... 17404
Randolph Dr ... 17403
Randow Rd ... 17403
Range Rd ... 17406
Rannoch Ln ... 17403
Rathton Rd ... 17403
Raylight Dr ... 17402
Rayma Dr ... 17407
Rebecca Ln ... 17403
Red Front Rd ... 17406
Red Rock Rd ... 17406
Redbud Ct ... 17404
Redwood Rd ... 17408
Regency Ln ... 17402
Regents Glen Blvd ... 17403
Reinecke Pl ... 17403
Revere Rd ... 17402
Rex Dr ... 17402
Reynolds Mill Rd ... 17403
Rhonda Dr ... 17408
Richard St ... 17408
Richardson Rd ... 17408
N Richland Ave ... 17404
S Richland Ave
1-399 ... 17404
600-628 ... 17403
630-999 ... 17403
Richwill Dr & Ln ... 17404
Riddle Rd ... 17406
Ridge Ave ... 17403
Ridge Ct ... 17402
Ridge Rd
300-399 ... 17402
2100-2299 ... 17406
Ridgefield Ct ... 17408
Ridgefield Dr ... 17403
Ridgeview Dr ... 17402
Ridgeview Ln ... 17406
Ridgeway Dr ... 17404
Ridgewood Rd ... 17406
Riding Club Dr ... 17404
Riding Silks Ln ... 17404
Ridinger Ln ... 17406
Ridings Way ... 17408
Ridley Dr ... 17402
Rillian Ln ... 17404
Rimrock Rd ... 17402
Rinehart Ln ... 17408
Rishel Dr ... 17406
Rita Rd ... 17402
River Dr ... 17406
River Farm Rd ... 17406
Riverview Ct ... 17406
Robin Cir & Rd ... 17404
Robin Ann Ct ... 17406
Robin Hill Cir ... 17404
Robinhood Dr ... 17408
Robinwood Rd ... 17402
N & S Rockburn St ... 17402
E Rockdale Ave ... 17403
Rockhill Ln ... 17406
Rockwood Ave ... 17406
Rocky Ridge Ct ... 17406
Rodney Rd ... 17408
Rolling Meadow Ct ... 17408
Roman Ct ... 17404
Roosevelt Ave
100-499 ... 17401
500-1499 ... 17404
1601-1697 ... 17408
1699-2799 ... 17408
2801-2899 ... 17408
Rosalia Cir ... 17402
Rose Ave ... 17401
Rose Ct ... 17406
Rose Ln ... 17403
Rosebay Dr ... 17408
Rosebrook Dr ... 17402
Roselyn Dr ... 17402
Rosemill Ct ... 17403
Rosepointe Dr ... 17404
Rosewood Ln ... 17403
Round Hill Rd ... 17402
Round Pebble Ct ... 17402
Roxboro Rd ... 17402
Royal St ... 17408
N Royal St ... 17402
S Royal St
2-36 ... 17401
38-99 ... 17401
100-999 ... 17402
Royal Ct At Waterford ... 17402
Rudy Rd ... 17406
Run Way ... 17406
Ruppert Rd ... 17408
Rushmore Dr ... 17402
N & S Russell St ... 17402
Rustique Dr ... 17408
Ruth Dr ... 17403
Ruth St ... 17408
Rutland Ave ... 17406
Ruxton Rd ... 17403
Ryan Run Rd ... 17404
Saddleback Rd ... 17408
Sagamore Dr ... 17406
Sage Dr
500-508 ... 17402
1100-1199 ... 17408
Saint Andrews Ct
1100-1199 ... 17408
2600-2699 ... 17402
Saint Andrews Way ... 17404
Saint Charles Way ... 17402
Saint Johns Ct ... 17406
Saint Paul St ... 17401
Salem Ave ... 17401
Salem Ct ... 17407
Salem Rd
1301-1397 ... 17404
1399-1499 ... 17404
3700-3799 ... 17408
3801-3999 ... 17408
S Salem Church Rd ... 17408
Salem Springs Dr ... 17408
Salisbury St ... 17408
Sam Spur ... 17406
San Gabriel Dr ... 17406
Sand Bank Hill Rd ... 17403
Sandalwood Ct ... 17404
Sandhurst Dr ... 17406
Sandra Dr ... 17402
Sandstone Ln ... 17404
Sandy Ln ... 17406
Sapphire Rd ... 17408
Saratoga Rd ... 17402
Sarazen Way ... 17404
Sarver Rd ... 17406
Satellite Dr ... 17402
Scarboro Dr ... 17403
Scarlet Dr ... 17408
Scenic Ln ... 17406
Schaefer Ln ... 17401
Schmuck Rd ... 17406
School Rd ... 17407
School St
1-400 ... 17402
700-798 ... 17401
2100-2299 ... 17408
Schoolhouse Ln
100-199 ... 17406
2400-2599 ... 17402
Schultz Way ... 17402
Scotch Dr ... 17404
Scott Rd ... 17403
N Scott St ... 17404
Scout Ridge Ln ... 17406
Seabiscuit St
300-399 ... 17406
2700-2799 ... 17402
Security Dr ... 17402
Seitz Ln ... 17406
Seminole Dr ... 17403
Seneca Dr ... 17408
Seneca Ridge Dr ... 17403
N & S Sentinel Ln ... 17403
September Way ... 17403
Sequoia St ... 17404
Setter Run Ct ... 17408
Seven Valleys Rd ... 17408
N & S Seward St ... 17404
Shaanti Ln ... 17403
Shady Dell Rd ... 17403
Shady Tree Ct ... 17402
Shaffer Ln ... 17407
Shagbark Ct ... 17406
Shannon Ln ... 17406
Sharoden Dr ... 17408
Sharon Dr ... 17403
Sharpshin Ln ... 17406
Shasta Dr ... 17402
Shawan Ln ... 17406
Shawna Ave ... 17402
Sheep Bridge Rd ... 17406
Shelbourne Dr ... 17403
Shenandoah Ln ... 17404
Shennys Dr ... 17408
Shereck Ln ... 17406
Sheridan Rd ... 17406
S Sheridan St ... 17401
N Sherman St
1-499 ... 17403
700-1199 ... 17402
1201-1299 ... 17402
1301-1397 ... 17406
1399-2899 ... 17406
2901-2999 ... 17402
290-298-290-298 ... 17403
S Sherman St ... 17403
N Sherman Street Ext ... 17406
Sherry Dr ... 17404
Sherwood Dr
301-399 ... 17403
4000-4099 ... 17408
Sherwood Rd ... 17408
Shetland Ln ... 17406
Shilling Dr ... 17404
Shiloh Dr ... 17408
Shire Ln ... 17406
Shoe House Rd ... 17406
Shulton Dr ... 17406
Sienna Dr ... 17406
Sierra Dr ... 17402
Sigsbee Ave ... 17404
Silver Screen Dr ... 17402
Silver Spur Dr ... 17402
Silverwood Dr ... 17402
Simpson St ... 17403
Sinking Springs Ln
200-298 ... 17406
300-399 ... 17406
400-799 ... 17404
Sitler Ln ... 17402
Skipton Cir ... 17402
Skunk Hollow Ln ... 17406
Skylark Dr ... 17403
Skylight Dr ... 17402
Skyline Dr
1-99 ... 17404
600-799 ... 17406
Skyview Dr ... 17406
Slate Ridge Dr ... 17408
Slatehill Rd ... 17408
Slater Hill Ln E & W ... 17406
Sleepyhollow Rd ... 17403
Sloane Cir ... 17404
W & E Sloway Cir & Dr ... 17402
Small St ... 17404
Smallbrook Ln ... 17403
Smile Way ... 17404
Smith Dr ... 17408
Smith Rd ... 17406
Smith St
2-99 ... 17407
300-398 ... 17401
400-499 ... 17401
500-799 ... 17404
Smith Hill Rd ... 17408
Smyser Rd ... 17406
Smyser St ... 17401
Snaffle Ln ... 17404
Snyder Ln ... 17406
N Snyder Pl ... 17401
Soapstone Ln ... 17404
Solarlight Dr ... 17402
Somerset Ln ... 17403
Sonoma Ln ... 17404
E Sorrel St ... 17404
Sorrel Ridge Ln ... 17406
South Dr ... 17408
E South St
1-199 ... 17401
201-297 ... 17403
299-1299 ... 17403
W South St ... 17401
Southbrook Dr ... 17403
Southern Rd ... 17403
Southern Hills Rd ... 17403
Southfield Dr ... 17403
Southview Dr ... 17402
Southwynd Ct ... 17403
Spahn Ave ... 17403
Spangler Cir ... 17406
Spangler Ln
201-299 ... 17403
5300-5399 ... 17406
Sparrow Dr ... 17408
Sparton Rd ... 17403
Spencer Ct ... 17408
Spondin Dr ... 17402
Sprenkle Ct & Ln ... 17408
Spring Ln ... 17403
Spring Rd ... 17406
Spring St ... 17408
Spring Lake Ter ... 17406
Spring Ridge Dr ... 17408
Springdale Rd ... 17403
Springetts Dr ... 17406
E & W Springettsbury Ave ... 17403
Springfield Dr ... 17408
Springwood Rd
1901-1997 ... 17403
1999-2199 ... 17403
2201-2299 ... 17403
2300-2699 ... 17402
Spruce Ct ... 17408
Spyker Ln ... 17406
Stanford Dr ... 17402
Stanley Pl ... 17403
Stanton St ... 17404
Stanyon Rd ... 17403
Starcross Rd ... 17403
Starfire Dr ... 17403
Starlight Dr ... 17402
Starling Ln ... 17406
Starview Dr ... 17402
State St ... 17404
N State St ... 17403
Steeple Chase Dr ... 17402
Stella Ave ... 17403
Stephen Ave ... 17408
Sterling Dr ... 17404
Steven Dr ... 17406
Stevens Ave ... 17401
Stevenson Ct ... 17402
Stevenson Dr ... 17404
Stewart St ... 17408
Stillcreek Ln ... 17406
Stillmeadow Ln ... 17404
Stitt Dr ... 17408
Stone Ave ... 17401
Stone Creek Dr ... 17406
Stone Gate Dr ... 17406
Stone Hill Dr ... 17402
Stone Ridge Rd ... 17402
Stone Run Dr ... 17402
Stonefield Cir ... 17402
Stonegate Ct & Rd ... 17408
Stonehaven Way ... 17403
Stonehedge Ln ... 17406
Stonehenge Dr ... 17404
Stonewall Ave ... 17403
Stonewood Dr ... 17407
Stonewood Rd ... 17402
Stony Brook Dr ... 17402
Stony Run Way ... 17406
Stoverstown Rd ... 17408
Stratford Rd ... 17403
N & S Strathcona Dr ... 17403
Strawberry Flds ... 17406
Strawberry Ln
700-798 ... 17404
1101-1299 ... 17408
Stream View Ln ... 17403
Stricklers Ln ... 17406
Stricklers School Rd ... 17406
Stuart Dr ... 17402
Suburban Rd ... 17403
Sultan Supreme Way ... 17402
Summer House Ln ... 17408
Summit Cir, Dr, Rd & Ter N & S ... 17403
Summit Run Ct ... 17408
N & S Sumner St ... 17404
Sundale Dr ... 17402
Sunlight Dr ... 17402
Sunny Hill Cir ... 17406
Sunnyside Rd ... 17408
Sunset Ln ... 17408
Sunset Rd ... 17406
Surrey Dr ... 17406
Surrey Ln ... 17402
Surrey Run Ct ... 17408
Susquehanna Ave ... 17403
Susquehanna Trl ... 17407
Susquehanna Trl S ... 17403
N Susquehanna Trl
1701-1797 ... 17404
1799-2400 ... 17404
2402-2598 ... 17404
2650-3599 ... 17406
3600-4199 ... 17404
4200-5400 ... 17406
5402-5498 ... 17406
Susquehanna Plaza Dr ... 17406
Sussex Cir ... 17408
Sutton Rd ... 17403
Sweet Gum Cir & Ln ... 17406
Sweitzer Dr ... 17407
Swith Ct ... 17404
Sycamore Ln ... 17406
Sycamore Rd ... 17408
Sycamore Ter ... 17403
Sylvan Ct ... 17406
Sylvan Dr ... 17402
Taft Ave ... 17404
Talisman Ct ... 17404
Tall Oaks Ln
2100-2199 ... 17403
2200-2299 ... 17406
Tanglewood Ln ... 17406
Tara Ln
2500-2599 ... 17404
2700-2800 ... 17408
2802-2898 ... 17408
Taralee Dr ... 17406
Tarpley Dr ... 17402
Tate Way ... 17402
Taunton Dr ... 17402
Taxville Rd ... 17408
Taylor Dr ... 17404
Taylor Rd ... 17406
Tenby Ct ... 17402
Terrace Rd ... 17404
Teslin Rd ... 17404
Test Rd ... 17404
Texas Ave ... 17404
Thackston Ln ... 17401
Thames Ave ... 17408
Theater Ln ... 17402
Thelon Dr ... 17408
Thomas Dr & St ... 17404
Thornbridge Rd E & W ... 17408
Thoroughbred Ct ... 17408
Throne Ave ... 17402
Thunderhill Rd ... 17402
Tiburon Dr ... 17408
Timber Crest Dr ... 17408
Timberlane Dr ... 17404
Tioga St ... 17404
Toann Rd ... 17403
Tollgate Rd ... 17403
Tome Farms Ln ... 17406
Tonden Dr ... 17402
Tonys Dr ... 17408
Topaz Rd ... 17408
Topper St ... 17406
Toronita St ... 17402
Torrington Dr ... 17402
Tower Rd ... 17406
Town Center Dr ... 17408
Townsend Ct ... 17402
Tracey School Rd ... 17406
Track Ln ... 17406
Travis Ct ... 17403
Traymore Vlg ... 17402
N & S Tremont St ... 17403
Trevor Rd ... 17404
Tri Hill Dr & Rd ... 17403
Trinity Rd ... 17408
Trolley Rd ... 17408
Trooper Ct ... 17403
Trotter Ridge Ct ... 17408
Trout Run Rd ... 17406
Trowbridge Rd ... 17402
Tulip Ln ... 17406
Tulip Tree Ln ... 17406
Tulsa Rd ... 17406
Tunnel Hill Rd ... 17408
Turnberry Ct
1401-1499 ... 17403
2500-2599 ... 17404
Turnberry Ln ... 17403
Tuscarora Dr ... 17403
Twigden Ct ... 17403
Twilight Dr ... 17402
Twilight Ln ... 17406
Twin Ln ... 17402
Twinbrook Dr ... 17408
Tyler Run Rd ... 17403
Union St ... 17401
United Ave ... 17407
Upland Rd ... 17403
Upperidge Ln ... 17403
Valley Rd
1-299 ... 17407
301-491 ... 17407
496-496 ... 17403
500-511 ... 17404
513-535 ... 17404
553-565 ... 17403
567-1252 ... 17403
1254-1798 ... 17403
Valley Acres Rd ... 17406
Valley Brook Dr ... 17402
Valley View Cir ... 17408
Valley View Dr ... 17406
Valley View Rd
1-3 ... 17403
5-7 ... 17403
900-999 ... 17406
1000-1099 ... 17406
1100-1399 ... 17403
Valley Vista Dr ... 17406
Valmere Path ... 17403
Vander Ave ... 17403
Verdan Dr N & S ... 17403
N & S Vernon St ... 17402

Vicki Dr 17403
Villa Ter 17403
Village Cir, Rd & Way E & W 17404
Vinmar Dr 17402
Vinton Dr 17402
Vireo Rd 17403
Virginia Ave 17403
Vogelsong Rd 17404
Volk Ln 17403
Walden Ct 17404
Waldorf Dr 17404
Wallace St
300-1299 17403
1700-2199 17402
605-601-605-601 17403
Wallicks Rd 17406
Walnut Ln & St 17403
Walnut Bottom Rd 17408
Walnut Springs Rd 17406
Walt Way 17403
Walter Rd 17402
Walter St 17408
Walters Hatchery Rd 17408
Wantz Ln 17406
Warren Rd 17406
Warren St 17403
Warwick Rd 17408
Washington Ct 17402
Washington Rd 17402
Washington St 17401
Water St
1-25 17407
2-14 17407
5-21 17403
23-23 17407
24-24 17408
25-25 17403
26-26 17407
28-28 17403
29-35 17407
36-36 17408
40-40 17407
49-49 17408
51-99 17408
291-2597 17403
2599-2799 17403
Waterford Professional Ctr 17402
Waters Rd 17403
Waverly Ct 17402
Wayne Ave 17403
Weatherburn Dr 17402
Webster Ave 17404
Webster Dr 17402
Webster Dr E 17402
Webster Dr N 17402
Wedgewood Way 17408
Weire Rd 17404
Weisgerber Way 17404
Weldon Ct & Dr 17404
Wellington Dr
500-599 17402
1311-1397 17408
Wellington St 17403
Wellsley Ct 17402
Wentworth Rd 17408
West Rd 17403
N West St
1-200 17401
202-398 17401
400-699 17404
S West St 17401
Westgate Dr 17408
Westminster Dr 17408
Westover Ln 17403
Westview Mnr 17408
Westwind Ln 17404
Westwood Ct 17402
Westwood Dr 17404
Westwood Rd 17403
Wetherburn Ct & Dr 17404
Wexford Ln 17404
Weymouth Ct 17404
Wharton Rd 17402
Wheatfield Dr 17408
Wheatfield St 17403
Wheatfield Way 17403
Wheatlyn Dr 17403
Wheatlyn Rd 17402
Wheaton St 17403
Whispering Pines Rd 17403
Whispering Springs Dr 17408
White Dr 17408
White St 17404
White Fence Ln 17408
White Oak Dr 17406
White Rose Ln
400-499 17402
1400-1499 17404
Whiteford Rd 17402
Whitehurst Ct 17404
Whitetail Ln 17406
Whitney Dr 17402
Wicklow Dr 17404
Wildasin Dr 17407
Wildcat Ln 17406
Wilde Ln 17406
Wildon Dr 17403
Willeta Ct 17402
Williams Rd
1400-1499 17402
1900-1998 17406
N Williams St 17404
S Williams St 17404
Williamsburg Dr 17402
Williamstown Cir 17404
Willis Ln & Rd 17404
Willomette Ct 17402
Willow Ct
500-599 17402
1100-1199 17408
Willow Rd 17408
Willow St 17406
Willow Ridge Ct & Dr 17404
Willow Springs Cir & Ln 17406
Willow Wood Ct 17406
Willowbrook Way 17403
Wilshire Dr 17402
Wilson Ave 17404
Wilson Ct 17403
N Wilson Ln 17406
S Wilson Ln 17406
Wilt Dr 17408
Wiltshire Rd 17403
Windcliff Dr 17403
Windcrest Rd 17408
Windemere Ct 17402
Winding Rd 17408
Winding Oak Dr 17403
Windsor Rd
1-97 17402
99-599 17402
3401-3499 17406
Windsor St 17403
Winemiller Ln 17408
Wingfield Dr 17406
Winsford Ln 17404
Winship Rd 17406
Winston Dr 17408
Winterberry Ct 17408
Winterberry Dr 17406
Winterberry Ln 17406
Wintergreen Ln 17406
Wire Rd 17402
Wise Rd 17403
Wishing Well Ct 17408
Witmer Rd
1-199 17404
600-799 17402
800-1299 17406
1301-1399 17406
Witness Rd 17403
Wogan Rd 17404
Wolfs Church Rd 17408
Wood Ln 17408
Wood St 17404
Woodberry Rd
700-710 17403
712-899 17403
1200-1498 17408
1500-3499 17408
3501-3599 17408
Woodbridge Ct 17406
Woodbridge Rd 17402
Woodcrest Dr 17402
Woodland Ave 17404
Woodland Ct 17403
Woodland Dr
1-99 17407
100-1199 17403
100-118 17407
120-120 17407
Woodland Rd 17403
Woodland View Dr 17406
Woodlawn Ave 17408
Woodlyn Ter 17402
Woodmont Dr 17404
Woodmyers Rd 17403
Woods Dr 17402
Woodshead Ter 17403
Woodside Dr 17402
Woodside Rd 17406
Woodspring Dr & Ln 17402
Woodstone Ct 17402
Woodstream Dr 17406
Woodsview Ln 17406
Woodthrush Ln 17403
Woodward Dr 17406
Woodwick Cir 17402
Worth St 17404
Wren Ter 17403
Wyndham Dr 17403
Wyndhurst Ct 17408
Wyndsong Dr 17403
Wyndward Ct 17403
Wyngate Dr 17403
Wyntre Brooke Dr 17403
Wynwood Ct & Rd 17402
N & S Yale St 17403
Yarshire Rd 17404
York Rd 17407
York St 17403
York Crossing Dr 17408
Yorkana Rd 17406
Yorkanna Rd 17406
Yorklyn Gate 17402
Yorkshire Ter 17403
Yorktowne Dr 17408
N & S Zarfoss Dr 17404
Zimmerman Dr 17408
Zinns Quarry Rd 17404
Zoar Ave 17404

NUMBERED STREETS

1st Ave
1300-1799 17403
3200-3299 17402
1st St 17406
2nd Ave
1300-1799 17403
1801-1897 17402
1899-1900 17402
1902-1998 17402
E 2nd Ave 17404
2nd St 17406
3rd Ave
1400-1799 17403
1800-2400 17402
2402-3298 17402
E 3rd Ave 17404
3rd St 17406
4th Ave 17403
E 4th Ave 17404
5th Ave
1500-1799 17403
2900-3000 17402
E 5th Ave 17404
6th Ave 17403
E 6th Ave 17404
W 6th Ave 17404
7th Ave 17403
E 7th Ave 17404
W 7th Ave 17404
E & W 8th 17404
9th Ave 17402
E 9th Ave 17404
W 9th Ave 17404
10th Ave 17402
E 10th Ave 17404
W 10th Ave 17404
11th Ave 17402
E 11th Ave 17404
W 11th Ave 17404

Puerto Rico

Puerto Rico

3 DIGIT ZIP CODE MAP

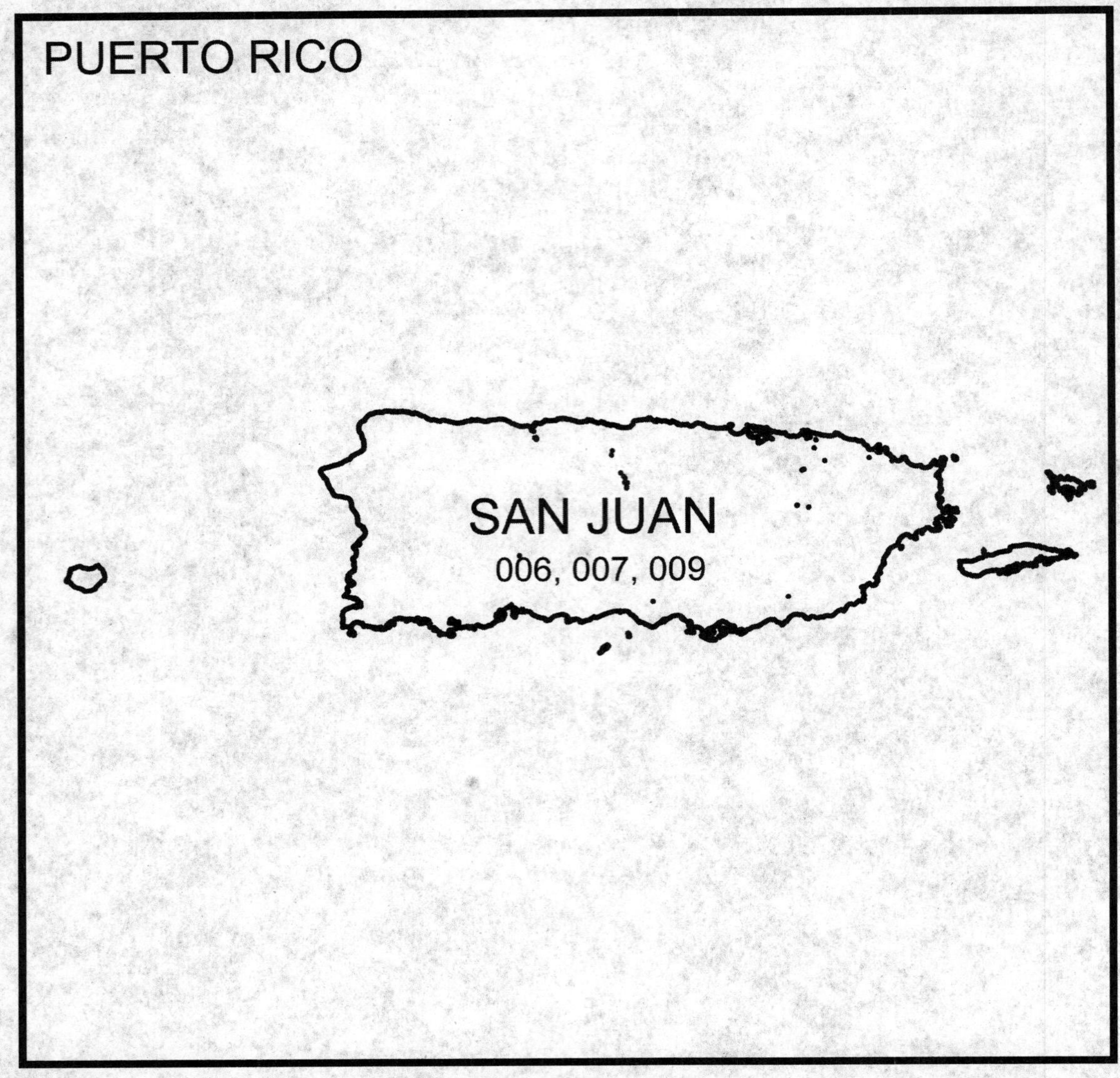

Puerto Rico

(Abbreviation: PR)

Post Office, County	ZIP Code

Places with more than one ZIP code are listed in capital letters, See pages indicated.

Adjuntas, Adjuntas 00601
Adjuntas, Lares 00631
Aguada, Aguada 00602
AGUADILLA, Aguadilla
(See Page 3294)
Aguas Buenas, Aguas Buenas 00703
Aguirre, Salinas 00704
Aibonito, Aibonito 00705
Anasco, Anasco 00610
Angeles, Utuado 00611
ARECIBO, Arecibo
(See Page 3294)
Arroyo, Arroyo 00714
Bajadero, Arecibo 00616
Barceloneta, Barceloneta 00617
Barranquitas, Barranquitas 00794
Barrio Obrero
(See San Juan)
BAYAMON, Bayamon
(See Page 3294)
Bo Obrero, San Juan 00915
Boqueron, Cabo Rojo 00622
Cabo Rojo, Cabo Rojo 00623
CAGUAS, Caguas
(See Page 3300)
Camuy, Camuy 00627
Canovanas, Canovanas 00729
Caparra
(See San Juan)
Caparra Hills
(See San Juan)
Caparra Terrace
(See San Juan)
CAROLINA, Carolina
(See Page 3303)
Castaner, Lares 00631
CATANO, Catano
(See Page 3307)
CAYEY, Cayey
(See Page 3307)
Ceiba, Ceiba 00735
Ceiba, Ceiba 00742
Ciales, Ciales 00638
Cidra, Cidra 00739
Coamo, Coamo 00769
College Park, San Juan 00921
Comerio, Comerio 00782
Condado, San Juan 00907
Corozal, Corozal 00783
Coto Laurel, Ponce 00780
Culebra, Culebra 00775
Cupey
(See San Juan)
Dorado, Dorado 00646
Ensenada, Guanica 00647
Fajardo, Fajardo 00738
Fernandez Juncos
(See San Juan)
Florida, Florida 00650
Fort Buchanan, Guaynabo 00934
Garrochales, Arecibo 00652
Guanica, Guanica 00653
GUAYAMA, Guayama
(See Page 3307)
Guayanilla, Guayanilla 00656
GUAYNABO, Guaynabo
(See Page 3307)
Gurabo, Gurabo 00778
Hatillo, Hatillo 00659
Hato Rey
(See San Juan)
Hormigueros, Hormigueros 00660
HUMACAO, Humacao
(See Page 3309)
Isabela, Isabela 00662
Isla Verde, San Juan 00913
Jayuya, Jayuya 00664
Juana Diaz, Juana Diaz 00795
Juncos, Juncos 00777
La Plata, Aibonito 00786
Lajas, Lajas 00667
Lares, Lares 00669
Las Marias, Las Marias 00670
Las Piedras, Las Piedras 00771
Levittown, Toa Baja 00949
Loiza, Loiza 00772
Luquillo, Luquillo 00773
Manati, Manati 00674
Maricao, Maricao 00606
Maunabo, Maunabo 00707
MAYAGUEZ, Mayaguez
(See Page 3309)
Mercedita, Ponce 00715
Mercedita, Ponce 00716
Minillas
(See San Juan)
Miramar, San Juan 00907
Moca, Moca 00676
Morovis, Morovis 00687
Naguabo, Naguabo 00718
Naranjito, Naranjito 00719
Old San Juan
(See San Juan)
Orocovis, Orocovis 00720
Palmer, Rio Grande 00721
Patillas, Patillas 00723
Penuelas, Penuelas 00624
PONCE, Ponce
(See Page 3311)
Pto Nuevo
(See San Juan)
Puerta De Tierra, San Juan 00906
Puerto Nuevo
(See San Juan)
Puerto Real, Fajardo 00740
Punta Santiago, Humacao 00741
Quebradillas, Quebradillas 00678
Ramey
(See Aguadilla)
Rincon, Rincon 00677
Rio Blanco, Naguabo 00744
Rio Grande, Rio Grande 00721
Rio Grande, Rio Grande 00745
Rio Piedras
(See San Juan)
Roosevelt Roads, Ceiba 00735
Rosario, San German 00636
Sabana Grande, Sabana Grande 00637
Sabana Hoyos, Arecibo 00688
Sabana Seca, Toa Baja 00952
Saint Just, Trujillo Alto 00978
Salinas, Salinas 00751
San Antonio, Aguadilla 00690
San German, San German 00683
San Jose
(See San Juan)
SAN JUAN, San Juan
(See Page 3314)
San Lorenzo, San Lorenzo 00754
San Sebastian, San Sebastian 00685
Santa Isabel, Santa Isabel 00757
Santurce
(See San Juan)
TOA ALTA, Toa Alta
(See Page 3321)
TOA BAJA, Toa Baja
(See Page 3321)
TRUJILLO ALTO, Trujillo Alto
(See Page 3321)
Utuado, Utuado 00641
Vega Alta, Vega Alta 00692
VEGA BAJA, Vega Baja
(See Page 3321)
Viejo San Juan
(See San Juan)
Vieques, Vieques 00765
Villalba, Villalba 00766
Yabucoa, Yabucoa 00767
Yauco, Yauco 00698

AGUADILLA PR

General Delivery 00605

POST OFFICE BOXES MAIN OFFICE STATIONS AND BRANCHES

Box No.s
1 - 5968 ... 00605
6001 - 6150 ... 00604
7000 - 60401 ... 00605
250001 - 250660 ... 00604

HIGHWAY CONTRACTS

01, 02, 03, 04, 05, 06, 07, 08, 09 ... 00603

NAMED STREETS

All Street Addresses 00603

ARECIBO PR

General Delivery 00613

POST OFFICE BOXES MAIN OFFICE STATIONS AND BRANCHES

Box No.s
1 - 9994 ... 00613
140001 - 145260 ... 00614

HIGHWAY CONTRACTS

01, 02, 03, 04, 05, 06, 07, 08 ... 00612

NAMED STREETS

All Street Addresses 00612

BAYAMON PR

General Delivery 00958

POST OFFICE BOXES MAIN OFFICE STATIONS AND BRANCHES

Box No.s
1 - 3200 ... 00960
3201 - 4321 ... 00958
6001 - 9560 ... 00960
40000 - 40003 ... 00958
55001 - 609440 ... 00960

RURAL ROUTES

04, 05, 08, 11, 12, 14 .. 00956

HIGHWAY CONTRACTS

67, 69, 71 ... 00956

NAMED STREETS

Altos De Panorama 00957
Ave A
1-49 ... 00956
50-99 ... 00959
Ave Aguas Buenas 00959
Ave Betances ... 00959
Ave Carbonell ... 00959
Ave Carlos Javier Andaluz ... 00956
Ave Casa Linda ... 00959
Ave Cementerio Nacional ... 00961
Ave Comerio
A1-A99 ... 00957
1500-1599 ... 00961
Ave Hermanas Davila .. 00957
Ave Hostos ... 00956
Ave Irlanda ... 00956
Ave La Ceiba ... 00956
Ave Las Cumbres ... 00957
Ave Laurel
E1-E99 ... 00956
Z1-Z99 ... 00956
2A1-2A99 ... 00956
2E1-2E99 ... 00956
2M1-2M99 ... 00956
2U1-2U99 ... 00956
3A1-3A99 ... 00956
3M1-3M99 ... 00956
3R1-3R99 ... 00956
D1-D99 ... 00956
G1-G99 ... 00956
L1-L99 ... 00956
M1-M99 ... 00956
AQ1-AQ99 ... 00956
AR1-AR99 ... 00956
AO1-AO99 ... 00956
200A-299A ... 00956
1-297 ... 00956
4-4 ... 00956
7-199 ... 00956
200-299 ... 00959
299-399 ... 00956
Ave Lomas Verdes ... 00956
Ave Los Almendros ... 00956
Ave Los Cedros ... 00956
Ave Los Cerezos ... 00956
Ave Los Dominicos ... 00957
Ave Los Filtros ... 00959
Ave Los Millones ... 00956
Ave Los Pinos ... 00956
Ave Los Robles ... 00956
Ave Los Sauces ... 00956
Ave Magnolia ... 00956
Ave Main ... 00959
Ave Millones ... 00957
Ave Minillas ... 00956
Ave North Main ... 00961
Ave Orquidea ... 00959
Ave Principal ... 00956
Ave Ramon Luis Rivera
201-205 ... 00956
500-500 ... 00961
500-500 ... 00959
501-507 ... 00961
509-599 ... 00961
550-1098 ... 00959
1600-1600 ... 00961
3000-3013 ... 00956
3015-3097 ... 00956
Ave Ramon R Rodriguez ... 00959
Ave Rio Hondo ... 00961
Ave Ruiz Soler ... 00959
Ave San Agustin ... 00959
Ave Santa Juanita ... 00956
Ave Tnte N Martinez ... 00959
Ave West Main ... 00961
Bayamon Country Clb .. 00957
Bayamon Gdns Shopp Ctr ... 00957
Bda Cedeno ... 00959
Bda Los Viejitos ... 00961
Bda Maestre ... 00961
Bda Parkhurst ... 00959
Bella Vista Hts ... 00957
Bella Vista Commercial Ctr ... 00957
Blvd Las Palmas ... 00956
Bo Juan Sanchez ... 00959
Bo Nuevo ... 00956
Bosque Sereno ... 00957
Boulevard Dr ... 00959
Brisas De Panorama ... 00957
Calle E
F1-F99 ... 00957
400A-499A ... 00959
1-99 ... 00956
2-98 ... 00961
100-199 ... 00957
400-499 ... 00959
Calle Plz ... 00956
Calle 1
D1-D99 ... 00957
D1-D99 ... 00959
G1-G99 ... 00959
NN1-NN99 ... 00959
OO1-OO99 ... 00959
PP1-PP99 ... 00959
F1-F99 ... 00957
G1-G99 ... 00957
C1-C5 ... 00956
A1-A99 ... 00956
E32A-E32A ... 00956
AI1-AI99 ... 00956
D1-D99 ... 00956
H1-H99 ... 00957
CO1-CO99 ... 00957
O1-O99 ... 00957
Q1-Q99 ... 00957
G1-G99 ... 00959
G1-G99 ... 00959
H1-H99 ... 00959
D1-D99 ... 00959
D1-D99 ... 00959
V1-V99 ... 00959
Y1-Y99 ... 00959
Z1-Z99 ... 00959
F1-F99 ... 00959
H1-H99 ... 00959
D1-D99 ... 00959
F1-F99 ... 00959
G1-G99 ... 00959
H1-H99 ... 00959
E1B-E99B ... 00957
D1-D99 ... 00961
E1-E99 ... 00961
G1-G99 ... 00961
H4A-H5A ... 00957
N50-N99 ... 00957
E13-E99 ... 00957
D1-D12 ... 00956
E1-E15 ... 00956
C1-C2 ... 00956
D8-D9 ... 00956
D1-D49 ... 00956
C1-C15 ... 00956
A1-A4 ... 00959
B17-B22 ... 00959
A22-A42 ... 00956
B1-B21 ... 00956
C1-C99 ... 00959
I1-I99 ... 00959
C1-C99 ... 00959
I1-I99 ... 00959
J1-J99 ... 00959
K1-K99 ... 00959
T2A-T2B ... 00957
H6A-H6B ... 00957
A1-A2 ... 00956
E1C-E99C ... 00957
X1-X99 ... 00959
X1-X99 ... 00959
X1-X99 ... 00959
E1-E13 ... 00959
E3-E3 ... 00959
A1-A99 ... 00959
B1-B99 ... 00957
L1-L99 ... 00957
O1-O99 ... 00957
A1-A99 ... 00956
B1-B99 ... 00956
A1-A99 ... 00957
C1-C99 ... 00957
D1-D99 ... 00957
A4-A99 ... 00959
B11-B99 ... 00959
J1-J99 ... 00959
E14-E98 ... 00959
E1-E99 ... 00959
E1-E99 ... 00959
B1-B99 ... 00961
F1-F99 ... 00956
A1-A99 ... 00961
H1-H99 ... 00961
C1-C99 ... 00957
E1-E99 ... 00959
K1-K99 ... 00959
A1-A99 ... 00959
B1-B99 ... 00959
C1-C99 ... 00959
D1-D99 ... 00957
E1-E99 ... 00957
L1-L99 ... 00957
M1-M99 ... 00957
B1-B99 ... 00956
C1-C99 ... 00956
F1-F99 ... 00956
B1-B995 ... 00956
E1-E99 ... 00956
C1-C99 ... 00956
A1-A99 ... 00957
D1-D99 ... 00957
C1-C99 ... 00957
T1-T3 ... 00957
U1A-U24A ... 00957
T5-T99 ... 00957
C1-C99 ... 00956
D1-D99 ... 00956
F1-F99 ... 00956
E2-E98 ... 00956
B1-B99 ... 00957
K1-K99 ... 00957
L1-L99 ... 00957
M1-M99 ... 00957
N1-N99 ... 00957
A1-A99 ... 00957
B1-B99 ... 00957
A29-A99 ... 00959
B24-B99 ... 00959
A1A-A99A ... 00959
J1-J99 ... 00959
A1-A99 ... 00959
C1-C99 ... 00959
A1-A99 ... 00959
B1-B99 ... 00959
D1-D99 ... 00956
E1-E32 ... 00956
C1A-C1A ... 00956
F1-F99 ... 00956
N1-N7 ... 00957
A1-A21 ... 00956
A6-A99 ... 00959
A15-A18 ... 00959
B5-B17 ... 00959
A1-A24 ... 00959
A26-A28 ... 00959
K20-K98 ... 00959
K1-K19 ... 00959
U21-U99 ... 00957
T3A-T3A ... 00957
C14-C99 ... 00957
U11-U19 ... 00957
W7-W99 ... 00957
A1-A9 ... 00959
A11-A99 ... 00959
A1-A4 ... 00961
B9-B12 ... 00961
7-52 ... 00956
8-100 ... 00959
100-100 ... 00959
200-298 ... 00956
1-1-1-9 ... 00957
1-10-1-99 ... 00961
2-1-2-99 ... 00957
9-1-9-99 ... 00959
Calle 1 E ... 00961
A1-A99 ... 00957
B1-B99 ... 00957
1-24 ... 00961
26-38 ... 00961
Calle 1 Final ... 00956
Calle 10
Y1-Y99 ... 00957
A1-A99 ... 00957
I1-I99 ... 00956
J1-J99 ... 00956
AA1-AA99 ... 00959
BB1-BB99 ... 00959
E44A-E44C ... 00956
GA1-GA99 ... 00956
S1-S99 ... 00956
L1-L99 ... 00957
JA1-JA99 ... 00957
KK1-KK99 ... 00957
F1-F99 ... 00957
T1-T99 ... 00959
U1-U99 ... 00959
V1-V99 ... 00959
X1-X99 ... 00959
AB1-AB99 ... 00959
TT1-TT99 ... 00959
K1-K99 ... 00956
A1-1-A1-99 ... 00957
B1-1-B1-99 ... 00957
H1B-H99B ... 00957
E30-E99 ... 00956
C40-C199 ... 00959
P1-P28 ... 00959
L1-L7 ... 00959
L1-L6 ... 00961
BA1-BA99 ... 00959
P1-P99 ... 00957
Q1-Q99 ... 00957
Z1-Z99 ... 00957
E1-E99 ... 00957
M1-M99 ... 00957
P1-P99 ... 00959
Q1-Q99 ... 00959
G1-G99 ... 00959
G1-G99 ... 00956
G1-G99 ... 00956
H1-H99 ... 00956
O1-O99 ... 00956
S1A-S15A ... 00956
H1-H99 ... 00957
H1A-H99A ... 00957
G1-G99 ... 00957
H1-H99 ... 00957
Z1-Z99 ... 00959
H1-H99 ... 00959
K1-K99 ... 00959
O1-O99 ... 00959
E1-E99 ... 00961
F1-F99 ... 00961
Z1-Z99 ... 00956
C1-C24 ... 00959
M1-M6 ... 00961
100-199 ... 00959
14-1-14-99 ... 00959
15-1-15-99 ... 00959
16-1-16-99 ... 00961
17-1-17-99 ... 00959
18-1-18-99 ... 00959
22-7-22-13 ... 00957
23-1-23-8 ... 00957
Calle 10 Interior ... 00957
Calle 10a
C1-C99 ... 00957
H1-H99 ... 00957
K1-K99 ... 00961
H12B-H12B ... 00957
H1A-H99A ... 00957
G1-G99 ... 00957
G1-G47 ... 00957
G31A-G31Z ... 00957
Calle 11
Q1-Q99 ... 00957
Z1-Z99 ... 00957
AA1-AA99 ... 00957
BB1-BB99 ... 00959
CC1-CC99 ... 00959
H1-H99 ... 00956
U1-U99 ... 00957
V1-V99 ... 00957
O1-O99 ... 00957
EE1-EE99 ... 00957
HH1-HH99 ... 00957
RR1-RR99 ... 00957
A1-A99 ... 00957
T1-T99 ... 00959
S1-S99 ... 00959
AG1-AG99 ... 00959
AH1-AH99 ... 00959
AJ1-AJ99 ... 00959
AK1-AK99 ... 00959
AL1-AL99 ... 00959
AR1-AR99 ... 00959
AS1-AS99 ... 00959
F1-F99 ... 00959
U15A-U15B ... 00957
V5A-V7A ... 00957
N20-N99 ... 00957
M1-M10 ... 00957
M13-M99 ... 00957
I1-I99 ... 00959
I1-I11 ... 00957
O1-O99 ... 00959
R1-R99 ... 00957
J1-J99 ... 00957
H1-H99 ... 00959
I1-I99 ... 00959
G12-G43 ... 00957
G1-G99 ... 00956
H1-H99 ... 00956
K1-K99 ... 00956
L1-L99 ... 00956
T1-T99 ... 00957
U1A-U14A ... 00957
J15-J99 ... 00957
B1-B99 ... 00957
J1-J99 ... 00957
I13-I99 ... 00957
R1-R99 ... 00959
AH2A-AH98A ... 00959
AJ52A-AJ98A ... 00959
AG1A-AG99A ... 00959
AJ1A-AJ25A ... 00959
AK1A-AK99A ... 00959
AR1A-AR99A ... 00959
L8-L99 ... 00959
M1-M99 ... 00959
K1-K99 ... 00961
L1-L99 ... 00961
M1-M99 ... 00961
N11-N14 ... 00957
N1-N9 ... 00957
P16-P16 ... 00957
J1-J34 ... 00956
B1-B14 ... 00959
P1-P99 ... 00957
AL19A-AL99A ... 00959
AL1A-AL17A ... 00959
B20-B99 ... 00959
N1-N6 ... 00961
1-99 ... 00961
100-199 ... 00957
100-198 ... 00959
11-1-11-99 ... 00961
23-9-23-17 ... 00957
24-1-24-10 ... 00957
24-11-24-11 ... 00957
24-8-24-8 ... 00957
29-1-29-99 ... 00959
Calle 11a
G1-G99 ... 00957
Q1-Q99 ... 00957
Z1-Z99 ... 00957
K1-K99 ... 00961
K23-1-K23-99 ... 00957
L2-1-L2-99 ... 00957
300-399 ... 00957
Calle 12
R1-R99 ... 00957
AA1-AA99 ... 00957
BB1-BB99 ... 00957
H1-H99 ... 00956
U1-U99 ... 00957
RR1-RR99 ... 00957
SS1-SS99 ... 00957
D1-D99 ... 00957
V1-V99 ... 00959
W1-W99 ... 00959
X1-X99 ... 00959
Y1-Y99 ... 00959
T1-T99 ... 00959
AJ1-AJ99 ... 00959
AS1-AS99 ... 00959
AX1-AX99 ... 00959
I1-I99 ... 00959
B1-B99 ... 00959
G1-G99 ... 00961
AB1-AB99 ... 00959
J11A-J11A ... 00956
P1-P99 ... 00959
AR1-AR99 ... 00959
N20-N99 ... 00957
O1-O7 ... 00961
R1-R99 ... 00959
S1-S99 ... 00957
A1-A99 ... 00959
A1-A99 ... 00959
J1-J99 ... 00956
M1-M99 ... 00956
E1-E99 ... 00956
F1-F99 ... 00956
T1-T99 ... 00957
V1-V99 ... 00957
O2-O99 ... 00957
A1-A99 ... 00957
Q1-Q99 ... 00957
S1-S99 ... 00957
W1-W99 ... 00957
Y1-Y99 ... 00957
Z1-Z99 ... 00957
R1-R99 ... 00957
E1-E99 ... 00957
S1-S99 ... 00959
AK1A-AK10A ... 00959
AJ2A-AJ98A ... 00959
AK12A-AK16A ... 00959
AR4A-AR4A ... 00959
AR1A-AR1A ... 00959
J1-J99 ... 00959
M1-M99 ... 00959
Q1-Q99 ... 00959
F1-F99 ... 00961
J1-J99 ... 00956
AK1-AK16 ... 00959
N1-N8 ... 00959
N7-N99 ... 00961
1-399 ... 00957
100-250 ... 00957
12-1-12-99 ... 00961
28-1-28-99 ... 00959
29-1-29-99 ... 00959
4-21-4-27 ... 00957
Calle 12 Final ... 00957
Calle 12a
J2-1-J2-99 ... 00957
K23-1-K23-99 ... 00957
XX1-XX99 ... 00959
YY1-YY99 ... 00959
K23-1A-K23-99A ... 00957
Calle 12b ... 00957
Calle 13
S1-S99 ... 00957
BB1-BB99 ... 00957
CC1-CC99 ... 00957
F1-F99 ... 00959
K1-K99 ... 00956
B1-B99 ... 00956
F1-F99 ... 00957
M1-M99 ... 00957
Y1-Y99 ... 00957
CA1-CA99 ... 00957
D1-D99 ... 00957
G1-G99 ... 00957
P1-P99 ... 00957
C1-C99 ... 00957
W1-W99 ... 00959
X1-X99 ... 00959
U1-U99 ... 00959
G1-G99 ... 00959
K1-K99 ... 00959
N1-N99 ... 00959
B1-B99 ... 00959
YA-YZ ... 00957
G10INT-G10INT ... 00957
G17A-G17B ... 00957
S1-S15 ... 00957
B1-B9 ... 00957
F12B-F12B ... 00957
O8-O99 ... 00961
P1-P8 ... 00961
K34A-K34B ... 00957
C5-C5 ... 00957

M1-M99 00959
Q1-Q99 00959
S1-S99 00959
N2-N99 00957
J1-J99 00957
K1-K99 00957
C1-C99 00959
T1-T99 00957
J1-J99 00956
T1-T99 00956
A1-A99 00956
K1-K99 00956
G1-G99 00957
I1-I99 00957
S1A-S10A 00957
Q1-Q99 00957
B1-B99 00957
C1-C99 00957
A1-A99 00957
I1-I99 00957
J1-J99 00957
Q1-Q99 00957
E2-E98 00957
H1-H99 00957
B13-B24 00957
B26-B98 00957
T1-T99 00959
O1-O99 00959
P1-P99 00961
G16B-G16B 00957
F11-F99 00959
K1-K72 00957
13-1-13-99 00961
24-12-24-24 00957
27-1-27-99 00959
28-1-28-99 00959
Calle 13a
L1-L99 00959
N1-N99 00959
K1-K99 00961
J2-1-J2-99 00957
K21-1-K21-99 00957
M1-M99 00959
Calle 14
W1-W99 00957
CC1-CC99 00957
DD1-DD99 00957
EE1-EE99 00957
FF1-FF99 00957
GG1-GG99 00957
HH1-HH99 00957
JJ1-JJ99 00957
G1-G99 00959
L1-L99 00956
J1-J99 00956
M1-M99 00956
N1-N99 00956
F1-F99 00956
B1-B99 00957
I1-I99 00957
J1-J99 00957
Q1-Q99 00957
SS1-SS99 00957
TT1-TT99 00957
C1-C99 00957
S1-S99 00957
Y1-Y99 00957
Z1-Z99 00959
NN1-NN99 00959
AM1-AM99 00959
AN1-AN99 00959
AO1-AO99 00959
AQ1-AQ99 00959
U1-U99 00959
O1-O99 00959
P1-P99 00959
D1-D99 00959
OO1-OO99 00959
PP1-PP99 00959
AM1A-AM1A 00959
L14A-L15A 00956
A15A-A15A 00957
YY1-YY99 00959
D3-D7 00957
V14-V99 00956
V1-V13 00959
B20A-B21A 00957

HH7A-HH7B 00957
JJ7A-JJ7B 00957
X1-X99 00957
K1-K99 00957
T1-T99 00957
L1-L15 00957
K1-K99 00956
G1-G99 00956
A8-A28 00957
L1-L99 00957
M1-M99 00957
R1-R99 00957
D1-D99 00957
R1-R99 00957
I1-I13 00957
U1-U99 00959
G1-G99 00961
A26B-A26B 00957
A14INT-A17INT 00957
B24B-B99B 00957
T21-T99 00959
X13-X99 00959
XX1-XX6 00959
P8-P99 00961
Q1-Q7 00961
100-199 00959
14-1-14-99 00961
26-1-26-99 00959
27-1-27-99 00959
7-33-7-55 00957
Calle 14 W 00957
Calle 14a
K1-K99 00961
F2-1-F2-99 00957
G2-1-G2-99 00957
Calle 15
W1-W99 00957
M1-M99 00957
C1-C99 00957
I1-I99 00957
K1-K99 00957
R1-R99 00957
S1-S99 00957
T1-T99 00957
Y1-Y99 00957
AA1-AA99 00959
CC1-CC99 00959
W1-W99 00959
B1-B99 00959
AF1-AF99 00959
T1-T99 00959
U1-U99 00957
BB1-BB99 00957
L16-L99 00957
V14-V99 00959
G8-G99 00959
R1-R7 00961
V1-V99 00957
H1-H99 00959
G1-G99 00959
P1-P99 00956
H1-H99 00957
L1-L99 00957
R1-R99 00957
P1-P99 00959
H1-H14 00959
A1-A3 00959
D17-D18 00959
E1-E17 00959
A22-A99 00959
H17-H99 00959
D21-D99 00959
E1-E18 00959
Q2-Q10 00959
Q8-Q99 00961
200-399 00959
15-1-15-99 00961
25-1-25-99 00959
26-1-26-99 00959
4-39-4-49 00957
5-14-5-28 00957
6-1-6-13 00957
Calle 15a
K1-K99 00961
C2-1-C2-99 00957
G2-1-G2-99 00957
Calle 16
N1-N99 00957

F1-F99 00956
G1-G99 00956
H1-H99 00956
M1-M99 00956
N1-N99 00956
P1-P99 00956
V1-V99 00957
AA1-AA99 00959
W1-W99 00959
X1-X99 00959
AO1-AO99 00959
AP1-AP99 00959
P1-P99 00959
R1-R99 00959
C1-C99 00959
P1-P99 00961
NN1-NN99 00959
Q50-Q99 00956
BB1-BB99 00957
H1A-H99A 00956
J1-J99 00959
J1-J99 00957
Q1-Q99 00959
Q11-Q99 00959
C14A-C14A 00959
C15A-C99A 00959
R8-R99 00961
S1-S7 00961
24-1-24-99 00959
25-1-25-99 00959
6-14-6-27 00957
7-1-7-14 00957
Calle 16a 00957
Calle 17
O1-O99 00957
R1-R99 00956
S1-S99 00956
V1-V99 00956
X1-X99 00956
F1-F99 00957
G1-G99 00957
W1-W99 00957
X1-X99 00957
Z1-Z99 00959
BB1-BB99 00959
CC1-CC99 00959
Y1-Y99 00959
K1-K99 00959
L1-L99 00959
AP1-AP99 00959
AQ1-AQ99 00959
Q24-Q99 00956
U1-U18 00957
V1-V39 00957
T1-T9 00961
N1-N99 00957
Q1-Q99 00956
R1-R99 00956
S1-S99 00956
U1-U99 00956
N1-N99 00959
R1-R99 00959
S1-S99 00959
R1-R99 00959
S1-S99 00959
U1-U99 00959
T1-T99 00961
Z1-Z99 00956
T1-T60 00959
S8-S99 00961
15-1-15-99 00959
18-1-18-99 00959
19-1-19-99 00959
20-1-20-99 00959
21-1-21-99 00959
27-1-27-99 00957
32-1-32-99 00957
33-1-33-99 00957
34-1-34-99 00957
46-1-46-99 00959
48-1-48-99 00959
7-15-7-15 00957
7-16-7-32 00957
7-21-7-23 00957
8-1-8-10 00957
9-4-9-9 00957
Calle 17a 00957

Calle 18
Q1-Q99 00956
G1-G99 00956
H1-H99 00956
E1-E99 00957
F1-F99 00957
V1-V99 00957
W1-W99 00957
Z1-Z99 00957
CC1-CC99 00957
DD1-DD99 00959
EE1-EE99 00959
FF1-FF99 00959
R1-R99 00959
S1-S99 00959
S1-S99 00959
T1-T99 00959
Q1-Q99 00961
R1-R99 00961
S1-S99 00961
V1-V99 00961
WW1-WW99 00959
V1-V99 00959
W1-W99 00959
O1-O99 00957
P1-P99 00957
P1-P99 00956
P1-P99 00956
Q1-Q99 00956
U1-U99 00959
U1-U99 00961
R1-R36 00956
O17-O99 00956
QQ2-QQ14 00959
22-1-22-99 00961
22-1-22-99 00959
23-1-23-99 00959
Calle 18a
P1-P99 00956
Q1-Q99 00956
E2-1-E2-99 00957
G2-1-G2-99 00957
Calle 19
Q1-Q99 00957
O1-O99 00956
D1-D99 00956
E1-E99 00956
F1-F99 00956
G1-G99 00956
K1-K99 00956
L1-L99 00956
M1-M99 00956
E1-E99 00957
W1-W99 00957
X1-X99 00957
WW1-WW99 00957
XX1-XX99 00957
Z1-Z99 00957
GG1-GG99 00959
M1-M99 00959
O1-O99 00959
G1-G99 00959
B1-B99 00959
T1-T99 00959
U1-U99 00959
C1-C99 00956
P1-P49 00956
W1-W99 00959
X1-X99 00959
Z1-Z99 00957
N1-N99 00959
P1-P99 00957
N1-N99 00957
Y1-Y99 00957
Y1-Y99 00957
100-198 00959
300-398 00957
10-1-10-14 00957
21-1-21-99 00959
21-1-21-13 00961
22-1-22-99 00959
23-1-23-99 00959
8-11-8-21 00957
9-1-9-3 00957
Calle 1a
FF1-FF99 00957
G1-G99 00956

Q1-Q99 00956
T1-T99 00959
A1-A99 00959
E1-E99 00959
Calle 1a W 00961
Calle 1b W 00961
Calle 1c W 00961
Calle 1d W 00961
Calle 1f W 00961
Calle 2
E1-E99 00957
F1-F99 00957
F1-F99 00959
NN1-NN99 00959
PP1-PP99 00959
H1-H99 00957
I1-I99 00957
A1-A99 00956
C1-C99 00956
A1-A99 00957
Q1-Q99 00957
R1-R99 00957
B1-B99 00957
M1-M99 00957
N1-N99 00957
A1-A99 00959
I1-I99 00959
HH1-HH99 00959
II1-II99 00959
A1-A99 00959
U1-U99 00959
W1-W99 00959
D1-D99 00959
E1-E99 00959
D1-D99 00959
A1-A99 00959
D1-D99 00959
C1-C99 00961
P1A-P99A 00957
E1-E99 00956
A2A-A2A 00956
D1-D99 00959
P9A-P9A 00957
A1-1-A1-1 00956
A1-1A-A1-1A 00956
A1A-A99A 00956
D1-D99 00961
D1-D99 00959
A1-A99 00959
D2-D7 00956
M11A-M11B 00957
N7A-N7B 00957
X1-X99 00959
A1-A12 00956
D1-D99 00956
B27-B99 00959
B1-B16 00959
D10B-D10B 00957
C9A-C9B 00956
D7A-D7A 00956
C1-C99 00959
C1-C99 00959
C1-C99 00959
C1-C99 00959
C1-C99 00957
D1-D99 00957
P1-P99 00957
Q1-Q99 00957
E1-E99 00957
A10-A99 00956
B15-B99 00956
C1-C99 00956
A1-A99 00957
B1-B99 00957
D1-D99 00957
E1-E99 00957
F1-F99 00957
H1-H99 00959
I1-I99 00959
E1-E99 00961
C5-C99 00956
D1-D99 00956
D1-D99 00959
D1-D99 00957
A1-A99 00959
D1-D99 00959
K1-K99 00957

A1-A99 00956
B1-B99 00956
D1-D99 00956
B1-B27 00956
C1-C99 00956
D1-D7 00956
D9-D99 00956
B1-B99 00956
B1-B99 00957
C1-C99 00957
D1-D99 00957
B4-B99 00956
C1-C99 00956
D1-D99 00956
C1-C99 00957
C11-C99 00957
C1-C99 00957
K1-K99 00957
L1-L99 00957
P1-P99 00957
E1-E99 00959
L1-L99 00959
D50B-D59B 00959
B2-B98 00959
E1-E99 00959
A1-A99 00961
A1-A99 00961
E1-E99 00961
A1-A99 00956
B1-B99 00956
201A-295A 00959
J12A-J12A 00959
B13-B99 00959
J16-J16 00959
J1-J5 00959
J8-J99 00959
B21-B99 00959
G1-G8 00959
G1-G14 00959
H24-H99 00959
B31-B36 00959
B1-B10 00959
B1-B25 00959
G15-G16 00959
H5-H9 00959
B7-B99 00959
G1-G14 00959
D1-D11 00961
E1-E8 00961
29-199 00957
100-198 00961
200-200 00959
283-311 00959
2-1-2-21 00957
2-1-2-18 00961
3-1-3-10 00957
7-56-7-59 00957
Calle 2 E 00961
B1-B99 00957
D1-D99 00957
D17A-D17B 00957
1-1 00961
3-18 00961
20-22 00961
Calle 20
Q1-Q99 00957
S100-S199 00957
S1-S99 00956
N1-N99 00956
V1-V99 00956
Z1-Z99 00957
BB1-BB99 00957
YY1-YY99 00957
ZZ1-ZZ99 00957
V1-V99 00957
AA1-AA99 00957
B1-B99 00959
C1-C99 00959
F1-F99 00959
T1-T99 00961
U1-U99 00961
W1-W99 00961
Y1-Y99 00961
D1-D99 00959
R97A-R97D 00957
AA13-AA28 00957
R1-R49 00956

E1-E99 00959
X1-X99 00959
Y1-Y99 00959
R1-R199 00957
Y1-Y99 00957
2500-2598 00956
20-1-20-99 00961
25-1-25-99 00959
30-1-30-99 00959
4-28-4-38 00957
52-1-52-99 00959
54-1-54-99 00959
Calle 21
T100-T199 00957
AA1-AA99 00956
AB1-AB99 00956
AE1-AE99 00956
AF1-AF99 00956
D1-D99 00956
N1-N99 00957
O1-O99 00957
S1-S99 00957
X1-X99 00957
Y1-Y99 00957
Z1-Z99 00957
AA1-AA99 00957
EE1-EE99 00957
WW1-WW99 00957
ZA1-ZA99 00957
ZB1-ZB99 00957
ZC1-ZC99 00957
A1-A99 00959
V1-V99 00961
ABB1-ABB99 00956
AF1A-AF99A 00956
ZA1A-ZA99A 00957
ZB1A-ZB99A 00957
Q1-Q49 00957
F17-F99 00956
W1-W99 00956
X1-X99 00956
CD1-CD99 00957
N1-N99 00959
O1-O99 00959
A1-A99 00959
B1-B99 00959
E1-E99 00959
F1-F99 00959
H1-H99 00959
Q1-Q99 00957
H1-H99 00956
B1-B99 00959
C1-C2 00959
AA1A-AA99A 00956
AB1A-AB99A 00956
AKK1-AKK99 00956
P1-P15 00957
P62-P99 00957
101-199 00957
200-299 00959
200-298 00957
2000-2016 00956
10-15-10-30 00957
11-1-11-13 00957
11-8-11-14 00957
18-12-18-99 00961
19-1-19-99 00961
51-1-51-99 00959
Calle 21a 00957
Calle 22
S100-S199 00957
T100-T199 00957
AC1-AC99 00956
AD1-AD99 00956
H1-H99 00956
I1-I99 00956
Z1-Z99 00957
HA1-HA99 00957
HI1-HI99 00957
II1-II99 00957
CD1-CD99 00957
E1-E99 00959
U1-U99 00961
T1-T99 00961
AA1-AA99 00961
BB1-BB99 00961
MM1-MM99 00959

L1-L99 00959
JJ1-JJ18 00956
JJ16-JJ99 00957
C15-C99 00959
D1-D99 00959
V20-V99 00961
D2-D11 00959
100-198 00959
17-1-17-19 00961
17-20-17-98 00961
18-1-18-11 00961
37-1-37-99 00959
38-1-38-99 00959
39-1-39-99 00959
40-1-40-99 00959
47-1-47-99 00959
48-1-48-99 00959
9-10-9-28 00957
Calle 22a 00957
Calle 23
R100-R199 00957
S100-S199 00957
AD1-AD99 00956
AE1-AE99 00956
AO1-AO99 00956
AP1-AP99 00956
T1-T99 00956
U1-U99 00956
CA1-CA99 00957
M1-M99 00959
N1-N99 00959
O1-O99 00959
P1-P99 00959
Q1-Q99 00959
D1-D99 00959
K1-K99 00959
AH1-AH99 00961
AB1-AB99 00956
XX1-XX99 00956
YY1-YY99 00956
J1-J99 00959
V1-V99 00959
AF1A-AF99A 00956
AO14A-AO14A 00956
AO15B-AO15B 00956
C1-C99 00959
AI1-AI99 00961
AQ1-AQ99 00961
S1-S99 00959
AF1-AF99 00961
AF1-AF99 00956
100-199 00957
300-399 00957
11-15-11-30 00957
12-1-12-11 00957
23-1-23-99 00961
24-1-24-99 00961
36-1-36-99 00959
37-1-37-99 00959
40-1-40-99 00959
41-1-41-99 00959
45-1-45-99 00959
46-1-46-99 00959
48-1-48-99 00959
49-1-49-99 00959
Calle 23a 00957
Calle 24
U1-U99 00957
AG1-AG99 00956
A1-A99 00956
HH1-HH99 00957
II1-II99 00957
CD1-CD99 00957
CE1-CE99 00957
P1-P99 00959
AA1-AA99 00961
BB1-BB99 00961
CC1-CC99 00961
AB1-AB99 00956
AJ1-AJ99 00956
AQ1-AQ99 00956
AU1-AU99 00956
RR1-RR99 00959
VV1-VV99 00959
O49A-O49F 00957
O1-O99 00959
T100-T199 00957
Y277A-Y277A 00957
O1-O99 00957
Y200-Y284 00957
Y286-Y300 00957
BB4-BB99 00959
CC1-CC99 00959
CC1A-CC99A 00959
DD1-DD6 00959
1-1 00956
90-98 00961
100-100 00957
100-198 00961
12-12-12-21 00957
13-1-13-10 00957
35-1-35-99 00959
36-1-36-99 00959
41-1-41-99 00959
42-1-42-99 00959
44-1-44-99 00959
45-1-45-99 00959
49-1-49-99 00959
50-1-50-99 00959
73-1-73-99 00961
74-1-74-99 00961
75-1-75-99 00961
Calle 25
V1-V99 00957
AG1-AG99 00956
AH1-AH99 00956
V1-V99 00956
FF1-FF99 00957
HH1-HH99 00957
Q1-Q99 00959
S1-S99 00959
K1-K99 00959
AA1-AA99 00961
CC1-CC99 00961
DD1-DD99 00961
BB1-BB99 00956
CC1-CC99 00956
26A-1-26A-99 00961
26B-1-26B-99 00961
B1-B99 00959
M1-M99 00961
GG1-GG29 00957
25-5A-25-5B 00961
25-8A-25-8B 00961
25-10A-25-10B 00961
25-11A-25-11B 00961
R1-R99 00959
AH1A-AH99A 00956
GG38-GG99 00956
Y1-Y22 00957
BB1-BB3 00959
BB8-BB98 00959
C13-C99 00959
25C-15-25C-99 00961
AA6-AA14 00959
301-399 00957
400-422 00957
13-11-13-23 00957
15-1-15-7 00957
25-1-25-99 00961
26-1-26-99 00961
31-1-31-99 00959
34-1-34-99 00959
35-1-35-99 00959
42-1-42-99 00959
43-1-43-99 00959
44-1-44-99 00959
45-1-45-99 00957
50-1-50-99 00959
51-1-51-99 00959
Calle 25a 00961
Calle 25b 00961
Calle 26
V1-V99 00957
W1-W99 00957
AJ1-AJ99 00956
I1-I99 00956
J1-J99 00956
D1-D99 00957
E1-E99 00957
FF1-FF99 00957
S1-S99 00959
J1-J99 00959
K1-K99 00959
L1-L99 00959
AA1-AA99 00961
AB1-AB99 00961
GG1-GG99 00961
HH1-HH99 00961
JJ1-JJ99 00956
KK1-KK99 00956
LL1-LL99 00959
AH1-AH9 00961
R1-R99 00959
L1A-L99A 00959
AH1-AH99 00956
26-1-26-99 00961
27-1-27-99 00961
33-1-33-99 00959
34-1-34-99 00959
Calle 27
W1-W99 00957
X1-X99 00957
B1-B99 00957
FF1-FF99 00957
GG1-GG99 00957
DH1-DH99 00957
P1-P99 00959
S1-S99 00959
I1-I99 00959
AG1-AG99 00961
JJ1-JJ99 00961
LL1-LL99 00961
ALL1-ALL99 00956
II1-II99 00956
26A-1-26A-99 00961
26B-1-26B-99 00961
M1-M99 00959
U1-U99 00959
33-34A-33-34A 00959
DG1-DG99 00957
AKK1-AKK99 00956
15-8-15-10 00957
16-1-16-8 00957
32-1-32-99 00959
33-1-33-99 00959
Calle 27a 00956
Calle 28
U1-U99 00957
V200-V299 00957
X1-X99 00957
J1-J99 00956
D1-D99 00957
DF1-DF99 00957
DG1-DG99 00957
AB1-AB99 00961
AC1-AC99 00961
AKK1-AKK99 00956
AF1-AF99 00956
DD1-DD99 00956
EE1-EE99 00956
LL1-LL99 00956
SS1-SS99 00959
UU1-UU99 00959
LL1B-LL99B 00956
S1-S99 00959
14-1-14-28 00957
19-3-19-5 00957
28-1-28-99 00961
29-1-29-99 00961
31-1-31-99 00959
32-1-32-99 00959
Calle 28 E 00956
Calle 29
Y1-Y399 00957
Z1-Z99 00957
DD1-DD99 00957
EE1-EE99 00957
DA1-DA99 00957
DB1-DB99 00957
DC1-DC99 00957
DE1-DE99 00957
DF1-DF99 00957
R1-R99 00959
HH1-HH99 00956
II1-II99 00956
200-299 00957
16-9-16-25 00957
17-1-17-19 00957
30-1-30-99 00961
31-1-31-99 00961
48-1-48-99 00959
50-1-50-99 00961
Calle 2a
EE1-EE99 00957
FF1-FF99 00957
U1-U99 00959
B1-B99 00961
B1-B99 00959
Calle 2a E 00961
Calle 2b E 00961
Calle 2c E 00961
Calle 2d E 00961
Calle 3
E1-E99 00957
G1-G99 00957
H1-H99 00957
Q1-Q99 00957
R1-R99 00957
PP1-PP99 00959
I1-I99 00957
J1-J99 00957
G1-G99 00956
BB1-BB99 00956
NN1-NN99 00956
OO1-OO99 00956
J1-J99 00956
N1-N99 00956
O1-O99 00956
A1-A99 00957
NN1-NN99 00957
OO1-OO99 00957
L1-L99 00957
U1-U99 00957
W1-W99 00957
Z1-Z99 00957
E1-E99 00959
R1-R99 00959
W1-W99 00959
X1-X99 00959
A1-A99 00959
A1-A99 00956
A1-A99 00961
B16A-B16B 00959
F16A-F16B 00957
C1-C30 00956
D8-D99 00956
C30-C99 00959
B1-B18 00959
B1-B7 00959
B23-B25 00959
F16INT-F16INT 00957
B6-B99 00957
F14A-F14B 00957
G19A-G19A 00957
F1-F99 00957
D1-D99 00957
D1-D99 00956
E1-E99 00956
C1-C99 00957
D1-D99 00957
F1-F99 00959
H1-H99 00959
B1-B99 00959
C1-C99 00959
B1-B99 00959
D1-D99 00959
H1-H99 00959
D7-D99 00956
E1-E99 00956
C1-C99 00957
H1-H99 00959
J1-J99 00959
K1-K99 00957
C1-C99 00956
E1-E99 00956
D2-D98 00956
C1-C99 00956
B1-B99 00956
C1-C99 00956
B1-B99 00956
B1-B99 00957
C1-C20 00957
F1-F99 00957
G1-G99 00957
B1-B99 00956
C1-C99 00956
C1-C99 00957
B1A-B15A 00957
C1-C99 00957
K1-K99 00957
J1-J99 00959
K1-K99 00959
B1-B99 00959
D1-D99 00959
W1A-W99A 00959
C1-C99 00959
D1-D99 00959
J1-J99 00959
F1-F99 00959
H1-H99 00959
D1-D99 00959
AD10-AD99 00957
F1-F35 00956
G34-G99 00959
G1-G99 00959
C8-C29 00959
F1-F10 00959
G1-G11 00959
C11-C19 00959
C1-C1 00959
G1-G28 00959
C1-C12 00959
B15-B99 00961
C1-C16 00961
C1-C8 00961
D1-D10 00961
B1-B10 00961
B1-B7 00961
C1-C29 00961
42-199 00957
100-100 00957
100-112 00956
1-1-1-99 00961
1-9-1-16 00957
10-1-10-99 00959
2-20-2-99 00961
3-1-3-99 00961
3-17-3-20 00957
4-1-4-4 00957
5-1-5-13 00957
9-1-9-99 00959
Calle 3 E 00961
A1-A99 00957
D1-D99 00957
E1-E99 00957
J1-J99 00957
AB1-AB99 00957
E1A-E1A 00957
BB1-BB99 00957
AB1A-AB99A 00957
D1A-D4A 00957
AB19B-AB23B 00957
1-12 00961
14-14 00961
Calle 3 Final 00957
Calle 30
Y300-Y399 00957
AO1-AO99 00956
AP1-AP99 00956
BA1-BA99 00957
BG1-BG99 00957
BH1-BH99 00957
AC1-AC99 00961
AD1-AD99 00961
AL1-AL99 00956
DD1-DD99 00956
LL1-LL99 00956
MM1-MM99 00956
A1-A99 00956
F1-F99 00956
L1-L99 00956
AQ1-AQ25 00956
AQ1A-AQ99A 00956
UU2-UU99 00956
17-20-17-26 00957
18-1-18-8 00957
32-1-32-99 00961
Calle 30a 00959
Calle 31
CC1-CC99 00957
DD1-DD99 00957
UU1-UU99 00957
AA1-AA99 00957
AJ1-AJ99 00957
BB1-BB99 00957
BJ1-BJ99 00957
BL1-BL99 00957
BM1-BM99 00957
DA1-DA99 00957
DB1-DB99 00957
JJ1-JJ99 00959
KK1-KK99 00959
LL1-LL99 00959
PP1-PP99 00959
P1-P99 00959
Q1-Q99 00959
AJ1-AJ99 00961
AN1-AN99 00961
AU1-AU99 00961
BB1-BB99 00961
ZA1-ZA99 00961
ZH1-ZH99 00961
GG1-GG99 00956
HH1-HH99 00956
18-9-18-14 00957
19-1-19-2 00957
33-1-33-99 00961
34-1-34-99 00961
Calle 32
V1-V99 00956
Y1-Y99 00956
AA1-AA99 00957
BB1-BB99 00957
EE1-EE99 00957
DB1-DB99 00957
KK1-KK99 00959
AD1-AD99 00961
AE1-AE99 00961
ZF1-ZF99 00961
ZG1-ZG99 00961
MM1-MM99 00956
NN20-NN99 00956
NN1-NN99 00959
25-1-25-99 00957
26-1-26-99 00957
36-2-36-99 00961
37-1-37-13 00961
37-11-37-11 00961
37-14-37-98 00961
52-1-52-99 00959
53-1-53-99 00959
54-1-54-99 00959
56-1-56-99 00959
57-1-57-99 00959
Calle 33
BB1-BB99 00957
CC1-CC99 00957
BA1-BA99 00957
BC1-BC99 00957
BG1-BG99 00957
LL1-LL99 00959
AN1-AN99 00961
AO1-AO99 00961
ZG1-ZG99 00961
FF1-FF99 00956
GG1-GG99 00956
PP1-PP99 00959
ZF1-ZF99 00961
XX7-XX99 00959
27-1-27-99 00957
36-1-36-99 00961
37-1-37-99 00961
38-1-38-99 00961
55-1-55-99 00959
56-1-56-99 00959
57-1-57-99 00959
Calle 33 E 00956
Calle 34
Z1-Z99 00956
BF1-BF99 00957
BH1-BH99 00957
BI1-BI99 00957
LL1-LL99 00959
MM1-MM99 00959
AE1-AE99 00961
AF1-AF99 00961
AG1-AG99 00961
ZD1-ZD99 00961
ZJ1-ZJ99 00961
NN1-NN99 00956
OO1-OO99 00956
PP1-PP99 00956
QQ1-QQ99 00956
F1-F99 00956
Y10-Y99 00956
Y1-Y99 00956
26-1-26-99 00957
28-1-28-99 00957
35-1-35-99 00961
Calle 35
BI1-BI99 00957
BJ1-BJ99 00957
M1-M99 00957
P1-P99 00957
MM1-MM99 00959
OO1-OO99 00959
AB1-AB99 00959
AO1-AO99 00961
AP1-AP99 00961
ZC1-ZC99 00961
ZD1-ZD99 00961
AE1-AE99 00956
AF1-AF99 00956
EE1-EE99 00956
FF1-FF99 00956
RR1-RR99 00956
SS1-SS99 00956
WW1-WW99 00959
RR1-RR99 00959
SS1-SS99 00959
PP1-PP99 00959
39-25A-39-25A 00961
OO9A-OO99A 00959
QQ1-QQ99 00959
28-1-28-99 00957
31-1-31-99 00957
33-1-33-99 00961
39-1-39-99 00961
Calle 35a 00961
Calle 35b 00961
Calle 35c 00961
Calle 36
OO1-OO99 00959
ZA1-ZA99 00961
ZC1-ZC99 00961
ZE1-ZE99 00961
ZH1-ZH99 00961
OO1-OO99 00956
PP1-PP99 00956
25-1-25-99 00957
30-1-30-99 00957
48-1-48-99 00961
49-1-49-99 00961
Calle 37
BF1-BF99 00957
FF1-FF99 00959
AP1-AP99 00961
AQ1-AQ99 00961
AR1-AR99 00961
ZJ1-ZJ99 00961
L1-L99 00956
AG1-AG99 00956
AL1-AL99 00956
TT1-TT99 00956
EE1-EE99 00959
GG1-GG99 00959
DD30-DD99 00956
DD1-DD29 00959
AS1-AS99 00956
UU48-UU48 00956
26-1-26-99 00957
29-1-29-99 00957
40-1-40-99 00961
42-1-42-99 00961
Calle 38
BB1-BB99 00957
BE1-BE99 00957
AJ1-AJ99 00961
AK1-AK99 00961
29-1-29-99 00957
31-1-31-99 00957
44-1-44-99 00961
Calle 38 N 00956
Calle 38a 00961
Calle 39
A1-A99 00956
BA1-BA99 00957
BC1-BC99 00957

BD1-BD99 00957
AR1-AR99 00961
AS1-AS99 00961
AX1-AX99 00961
AZ1-AZ99 00961
AG1-AG99 00956
AH1-AH99 00956
TT1-TT99 00956
X1-X99 00959
UU6B-UU6B 00956
41-13A-41-13D 00961
UU1-UU99 00956
W14-W24 00959
27-1-27-99 00957
31-1-31-99 00957
32-1-32-99 00957
41-1-41-99 00961
43-1-43-99 00961
Calle 3a
DD1-DD99 00957
EE1-EE99 00957
BB1-BB99 00956
OO1-OO99 00956
C1-C99 00957
Z1-Z99 00959
D1-D99 00959
U1-U99 00959
J1-J99 00956
B1-B99 00957
B6-B9 00961
1-199 00959
Calle 3a E 00961
Calle 3b 00956
Calle 4
J1-J99 00957
K1-K99 00957
B1-B99 00957
KK1-KK99 00959
LL1-LL99 00959
MM1-MM99 00959
A1-A99 00957
D1-D99 00956
C1-C34 00956
E1-E99 00956
I1-I99 00957
D1-D99 00957
R1-R99 00957
E1-E99 00957
O1-O99 00957
L1-L99 00959
DF1-DF99 00959
Y1-Y99 00959
H1-H99 00959
K1-K99 00959
B1-B99 00959
F1-F99 00959
L1-L99 00959
XA-XZ 00957
A1-A99 00961
E12A-E12B 00959
B1-B4 00956
B10-B99 00956
S9-S99 00957
JJ1-JJ99 00959
E1-E16 00959
E4-E12 00959
B10-B20 00961
Q1-Q99 00959
I26A-I26A 00957
G1-G99 00957
H1-H99 00957
R1-R99 00957
S1-S99 00957
C1-C99 00957
B5-B99 00956
F1-F99 00956
G1-G99 00956
C1-C99 00959
E1-E99 00956
F1-F99 00956
B1-B99 00957
E1-E99 00956
Q1-Q99 00956
F1-F99 00957
X1-X99 00957
C1-C99 00957
K1-K99 00957
L1-L99 00957
H1-H99 00957
J1-J99 00957
K1-K99 00957
J1-J99 00959
K1-K99 00959
Q21A-Q99A 00959
C1-C99 00959
X1-X99 00959
I1A-I99A 00959
B1-B99 00959
C1-C99 00959
D1-D99 00959
L1B-L99B 00959
J1A-J99A 00959
B1-B99 00959
C1-C99 00959
L1-L99 00959
C1-C99 00959
J16INT-J16INT 00959
I9-I99 00959
F1-F10 00959
A1-A22 00959
I18-I99 00959
J5-J99 00959
A10-A99 00959
E26-E99 00959
I18-I99 00959
J20-J99 00959
K1-K13 00959
I1-I10 00959
J1-J19 00959
E14-E20 00959
D12-D16 00959
E1-E9 00959
D10-D18 00959
E1-E10 00959
D10-D18 00959
E1-E1 00959
D20-D38 00959
B25-B99 00961
D20-D28 00959
C1-C7 00961
B1-B6 00961
C1-C4 00961
D11-D99 00961
E19-E99 00961
1-39 00959
1-50 00959
2-50 00957
56-199 00957
11-23-11-99 00959
2-4-2-8 00957
3-11-3-16 00957
4-1-4-99 00961
8-1-8-13 00959
9-22-9-99 00959
Calle 4 E 00961
Calle 40
BA1-BA99 00957
BD1-BD99 00957
BE1-BE99 00957
BF1-BF99 00957
AK1-AK99 00961
AL1-AL99 00961
45-1-45-99 00961
Calle 41
A1-A99 00956
BL1-BL99 00957
BM1-BM99 00957
BN1-BN99 00957
AS1-AS99 00961
AT1-AT99 00961
AH1-AH99 00956
AN1-AN99 00956
AP1-AP99 00956
UU1-UU99 00956
CC1-CC99 00959
DD1-DD99 00959
GG1-GG99 00959
HH1-HH99 00959
100-198 00957
3-39-3-44 00956
4-1-4-48 00956
46-1-46-99 00961
47-1-47-99 00961
54-1-54-99 00957
Calle 42
BN1-BN99 00957
BO1-BO99 00957
AL1-AL99 00961
AM1-AM99 00961
26A-1-26A-99 00961
A1-A99 00961
100-199 00961
33-1-33-99 00957
34-1-34-99 00957
35-1-35-99 00957
4-18-4-24 00956
45-1-45-99 00961
Calle 42a 00957
Calle 43
BO1-BO99 00957
BQ1-BQ99 00957
AU1-AU99 00961
AV1-AV99 00961
AB1-AB99 00956
AC1-AC99 00956
X1-X99 00959
Y1-Y99 00959
100-199 00961
2-1-2-2 00956
3-23-3-38 00956
34-1-34-99 00957
Calle 43a 00959
Calle 44
BQ1-BQ99 00957
AI1-AI99 00961
2-3-2-57 00956
35-1-35-99 00957
39-1-39-99 00957
54-1-54-99 00957
55-1-55-99 00961
56-1-56-99 00961
65-1-65-99 00961
Calle 45
AV1-AV99 00961
AY1-AY99 00961
AC1-AC99 00956
AD1-AD99 00956
BB1-BB99 00959
CC1-CC99 00959
HH1-HH99 00959
II1-II99 00959
1-2 00956
2-27-2-34 00956
39-1-39-99 00957
40-1-40-99 00957
54-1-54-99 00961
55-1-55-99 00961
57-1-57-99 00961
66-1-66-99 00961
70-1-70-99 00961
72-1-72-99 00961
Calle 45a 00957
Calle 46
AQ1-AQ99 00961
3-2-3-11 00956
40-1-40-99 00957
43-1-43-99 00957
55-1-55-99 00961
Calle 47
A1-A99 00956
AY1-AY99 00961
AN1-AN99 00956
AP1-AP99 00956
AQ1-AQ99 00956
AR1-AR99 00956
Y1-Y99 00959
Z1-Z99 00959
AX1-AX99 00961
1-7-1-20 00956
37-1-37-99 00957
54-1-54-99 00961
Calle 47a 00959
Calle 48
AO1-AO99 00956
1-1-1-29 00956
33-37-33-99 00957
36-1-36-99 00957
53-1-53-99 00961
Calle 48a 00957
Calle 49
AA1-AA99 00957
AC1-AC99 00957
AD1-AD99 00957
AZ1-AZ99 00961
BA1-BA99 00961
GA1-GA99 00956
GB1-GB99 00956
Z1-Z99 00959
AA1-AA99 00959
BB1-BB99 00959
II1-II99 00959
AB1-AB50 00957
36-1-36-99 00957
38-1-38-99 00957
51-1-51-99 00961
52-1-52-99 00961
Calle 49a 00959
Calle 4a 00961
Calle 5
U1-U99 00957
V1-V99 00957
L1-L99 00957
O1-O99 00956
D1-D99 00956
I1-I99 00957
OO1-OO99 00957
PP1-PP99 00957
P1-P99 00957
Q1-Q99 00957
AK1-AK99 00959
DF1-DF99 00959
AA1-AA99 00959
AB1-AB99 00959
AD1-AD99 00959
K1-K99 00959
L1-L99 00959
G1-G99 00961
H1-H99 00961
EE1-EE99 00959
LL1-LL99 00959
KK1-KK99 00959
D1-D99 00959
M1-M99 00957
100A-199A 00957
C1-C99 00961
D1-D99 00961
N1-N99 00959
G30-G99 00956
C21-C99 00956
G1-G29 00956
B1-B9 00959
E17-E99 00959
F1-F18 00959
B10-B99 00959
H1-H13 00959
H4-H23 00961
S16A-S19A 00957
J21A-J21B 00959
AC1-AC99 00959
D1-D99 00959
C1-C99 00959
D1-D99 00959
J1A-J99A 00957
K1-K99 00957
F1-F99 00957
G1-G99 00957
I1-I99 00959
H1-H99 00959
H1-H99 00959
G1-G99 00959
H1-H99 00959
M1-M98 00956
C1-C99 00956
G1-G99 00957
E7-E99 00959
E13-E99 00959
I1-I99 00959
H4-H4 00959
H1-H1 00959
N1-N14 00956
F1-F13 00956
H2-H3 00959
J13-J99 00957
K24-K99 00957
J1-J3 00957
S1-S15 00957
E14-E99 00957
G1-G7 00957
K1-K17 00957
S16-S99 00957
E1-E9 00957
J1-J10 00957
J1-J99 00961
K1-K99 00961
E15INT-E15INT 00957
H10-H99 00959
J1-J10 00959
C12-C18 00959
A11-A20 00959
J18-J99 00959
G1-G9 00959
G1-G8 00959
C1-C38 00959
I13-I99 00959
F4-F99 00959
E1-E16 00959
F1-F9 00959
G15-G99 00959
E1-E10 00961
F1-F27 00961
1-99 00957
100-110 00959
101-199 00957
300-300 00961
3-1-3-99 00957
4-1-4-99 00957
5-1-5-99 00961
6-1-6-99 00959
8-14-8-99 00959
Calle 5 E 00961
Calle 50
AD1-AD99 00957
AH1-AH99 00957
AQ1-AQ99 00957
AR1-AR99 00957
AO1-AO99 00961
GC1-GC99 00956
AR1-AR99 00961
AH1A-AH1C 00957
38-1-38-99 00957
41-1-41-99 00957
5-1-5-6 00956
58-1-58-99 00961
6-1-6-22 00956
64-1-64-99 00961
65-1-65-99 00961
Calle 51
AA1-AA99 00957
AE1-AE99 00957
AJ1-AJ99 00957
AN1-AN99 00957
BA1-BA99 00961
GD1-GD99 00956
GE1-GE99 00956
BC1-BC99 00961
100-198 00961
33-1-33-99 00957
64-1-64-99 00961
65-1-65-99 00961
Calle 52
AE1-AE99 00957
AF1-AF99 00957
AI1-AI99 00957
AV1-AV99 00961
AX1-AX99 00961
41-1-41-99 00957
42-1-42-99 00957
63-1-63-99 00961
64-1-64-99 00961
65-1-65-99 00961
Calle 53
AF1-AF99 00957
AG1-AG99 00957
12-1-12-99 00956
14-16-14-24 00956
44-1-44-99 00957
50-1-50-99 00957
51-1-51-99 00957
61-1-61-99 00961
63-1-63-99 00961
Calle 54
AG1-AG99 00957
AH1-AH99 00957
11-1A-11-99A 00956
13-17A-13-17A 00956
14-1A-14-1A 00956
11-1-11-5 00956
13-1-13-29 00956
14-1-14-15 00956
46-1-46-99 00957
50-1-50-99 00957
51-1-51-99 00957
54-1-54-99 00957
56-1-56-99 00961
62-1-62-99 00961
63-1-63-99 00961
Calle 55
11-1-11-99 00956
12-1-12-99 00956
49-1-49-99 00957
59-1-59-99 00961
60-1-60-99 00961
Calle 56
AL1-AL99 00957
BB1-BB99 00961
BB1A-BB99A 00961
46-1-46-99 00957
47-1-47-99 00957
60-1-60-99 00961
Calle 57 00957
Calle 57a 00957
Calle 58 00957
Calle 59
AO1-AO99 00957
AP1-AP99 00957
49-1-49-99 00957
52-1-52-99 00957
71-1-71-99 00961
Calle 6
P1-P99 00959
L1-L99 00956
N1-N99 00956
NN1-NN99 00956
I1-I99 00957
J1-J99 00957
PP1-PP99 00957
QQ1-QQ99 00957
DE1-DE99 00957
DF1-DF99 00957
S1-S99 00957
H1-H13 00957
AF1-AF99 00959
J1-J99 00959
C1-C99 00961
JJ1-JJ99 00959
KK1-KK99 00959
AC1-AC99 00959
G1-G99 00956
Z1-Z99 00956
K39A-K46A 00957
C1-C16 00956
C11-C21 00956
F1-F99 00961
D1-D17 00956
DC1-DC99 00957
C1-C11 00959
F19-F99 00959
G1-G20 00959
F1-F99 00959
K43B-K43C 00957
M18A-M18A 00957
C1-C99 00957
M1-M99 00957
G1-G99 00957
H1-H99 00957
J1-J99 00957
J1-J99 00957
C1-C99 00956
G1-G99 00957
H1-H99 00957
F1-F99 00959
G1-G99 00959
F1-F99 00959
F1-F99 00959
M1-M99 00956
F1-F99 00956
G1-G99 00956
C39-C99 00956
D1-D99 00956
M1-M99 00956
D1-D99 00956
K1-K99 00957
M1-M99 00957
F1-F99 00957
G1-G99 00957
E1-E99 00957
F12-F99 00957
H2-H11 00957
F2-F10 00957
H1-H1 00957
H13-H99 00957
B1-B99 00959
D1-D99 00959
D1-D99 00959
G1-G99 00959
I2-I98 00959
G1-G99 00959
C1-C99 00956
H16-H99 00956
F1-F73 00956
B1-B40 00959
E10-E18 00959
F1-F11 00959
E35-E99 00959
A1-A10 00959
K1-K15 00959
B49-B99 00959
C53-C99 00959
D19-D99 00959
E1-E13 00959
G11-G99 00959
H15-H99 00959
F1-F17 00959
H1-H2 00959
G17-G99 00959
H1-H7 00959
K16-K99 00959
H14-H25 00959
I1-I12 00959
D1-D11 00961
D1-D8 00961
K42B-K42B 00957
100-399 00957
200-299 00961
200-299 00959
20-1-20-6 00957
21-1-21-5 00957
21-12-21-12 00957
29-1-29-99 00961
30-1-30-99 00961
6-1-6-99 00961
6-1-6-99 00959
Calle 6 E 00961
Calle 60
AP1-AP99 00957
AQ1-AQ99 00957
51-1-51-99 00957
52-1-52-99 00957
53-1-53-99 00957
68-1-68-99 00961
70-1-70-99 00961
Calle 60a 00957
Calle 61
AM1-AM99 00957
AR1-AR99 00957
AS1-AS99 00957
AT1-AT99 00957
67-1-67-99 00961
69-1-69-99 00961
Calle 62 00957
Calle 63
AI1-AI99 00957
74-1-74-99 00961
76-1-76-99 00961
77-1-77-99 00961
Calle 64
AL1-AL99 00957
AM1-AM99 00957
75-1-75-99 00961
76-1-76-99 00961
77-1-77-99 00961
Calle 65 00961
Calle 67 00961
Calle 68 00961
Calle 69 00961
Calle 6a 00957
Calle 7
C1-C99 00957
D1-D99 00957

F1-F99 00957
L1-L99 00956
BB1-BB99 00959
F1-F99 00956
D1-D99 00956
M1-M99 00956
N1-N99 00956
M1-M99 00957
A1-A99 00957
E1-E99 00957
O1-O99 00957
Y1-Y99 00959
AD1-AD99 00959
AE1-AE99 00959
H1-H99 00959
E1-E99 00959
FF1-FF99 00959
M1-M99 00961
N1-N99 00961
Q1-Q99 00961
CC1-CC99 00959
AE1A-AE1A 00959
AE6A-AE6A 00959
M1-M99 00959
N1-N99 00959
G1-G99 00961
MB1-MB99 00959
X6-X99 00957
G21-G99 00959
GG1-GG19 00959
I13-I24 00959
J1-J15 00959
R1-R9 00961
F8A-F8A 00957
N1-N99 00957
F1-F99 00957
H1-H99 00957
I1-I99 00957
H1-H99 00957
C1-C99 00957
E1-E99 00959
F1-F99 00959
D1-D99 00959
B1-B99 00959
D1-D99 00959
N1-N99 00959
GG1-GG99 00959
E1-E99 00956
E1-E99 00956
R1-R99 00957
I1-I99 00957
J1-J99 00957
P1-P99 00957
F1-F99 00959
X1-X99 00959
A1B-A98B 00959
I1-I99 00959
K1-K99 00959
E1-E99 00959
F1-F99 00961
F1-F99 00961
K64A-K64A 00957
20-1A-20-1Z 00957
K1-K16 00956
I1-I13 00957
K18-K70 00957
F1-F8 00957
K1-K17 00957
I30-I32 00957
DD1-DD22 00959
A25-A99 00959
G1-G9 00959
G2-G6 00959
E14-E99 00959
A1-A23 00959
F15-F99 00959
G22-G99 00959
B12-B99 00959
B2-B10 00959
E11-E99 00961
1-99 00961
10-30 00959
100-199 00961
100-150 00957
190-299 00957
11-1-11-20 00959
20-19-20-20 00957
6-13-6-99 00959
7-1-7-99 00959
8-1-8-99 00961
9-1-9-99 00959
Calle 7 Interior 00957
Calle 70 00961
Calle 73 00961
Calle 76 00961
Calle 78 00961
Calle 79 00961
Calle 7a
O1-O99 00957
R1-R99 00957
B1-B99 00961
O26A-O26A 00957
N14A-N14A 00957
N2-N98 00957
E16-E99 00961
Calle 8
I1-I99 00956
DD1-DD99 00959
EE1-EE99 00959
GG1-GG99 00959
HH1-HH99 00959
FF1-FF99 00956
D1-D99 00956
L1-L99 00957
O1-O99 00957
LL1-LL99 00957
MM1-MM99 00957
CL1-CL99 00957
CM1-CM99 00957
W1-W99 00956
I1-I99 00959
F40A-F42A 00957
N11A-N11A 00957
O19A-O19A 00957
E1-E12 00956
I1-I12 00957
A11-A99 00959
D15-D99 00959
F1-F11 00957
N10A-N10C 00957
N1-N99 00957
B1-B99 00957
C1-C99 00957
E1-E99 00957
K1-K99 00957
J1-J99 00956
E1-E99 00956
F1-F99 00956
E1-E99 00956
200A-299A 00957
H1-H99 00957
H26-H98 00957
H1-H99 00959
F1-F99 00959
O1-O99 00959
F1-F99 00956
E10-E10 00956
E3-E3 00956
K13-K99 00956
F32-F99 00957
J25-J99 00957
N1-N4 00957
N5-N99 00957
J1-J8 00957
M1-M17 00959
H14-H24 00957
I15-I99 00957
E10-E19 00957
J14-J99 00959
C1-C13 00959
D14-D26 00959
J1-J4 00959
H22-H99 00959
O1-O23 00959
A1-A10 00959
B34-B99 00959
G1-G7 00959
H1-H8 00959
N16-N99 00959
D12-D22 00961
E1-E11 00961
G14-G99 00961
19-47 00961
200-299 00957
12-1-12-99 00959
13-1-13-99 00959
16-1-16-99 00959
19-1-19-99 00959
20-1-20-99 00959
21-11-21-11 00957
21-6-21-6 00957
21-7-21-10 00957
22-1-22-6 00957
9-1-9-99 00961
Calle 80 00961
Calle 81 00961
Calle 82 00961
Calle 83 00961
Calle 84 00961
Calle 8a
EE1-EE99 00956
GG1-GG99 00956
O1-O99 00957
M1-M99 00957
X1-X99 00959
O16A-O16A 00957
200-299 00957
Calle 9
Y1-Y99 00957
A1-A99 00957
B1-B99 00957
E1-E99 00957
F1-F99 00957
I1-I99 00956
AA1-AA99 00959
CC1-CC99 00959
DD1-DD99 00959
J1-J99 00956
FF1-FF99 00956
GG1-GG99 00956
F1-F99 00956
G1-G99 00956
GA1-GA99 00956
L1-L99 00956
J1-J99 00957
KK1-KK99 00957
LL1-LL99 00957
L1-L99 00957
CK1-CK99 00957
J1-J199 00959
AE1-AE99 00959
AG1-AG99 00959
AH1-AH99 00959
AQ1-AQ99 00959
AR1-AR99 00959
L1-L99 00961
N1-N99 00961
GG1A-GG99A 00956
E2-1-E2-99 00957
F2-1-F2-99 00957
Q1-Q99 00959
AG10A-AG10A 00959
AG1A-AG1A 00959
AX1A-AX1A 00959
I20-I99 00957
EE1-EE18 00956
M1-M10 00956
EE19-EE99 00959
B50-B99 00959
M11-M99 00959
P1-P99 00957
H1-H99 00956
X1-X99 00959
H1-H99 00957
K1-K99 00957
B1-B99 00959
C1-C99 00959
B1-B49 00959
O1-O99 00959
P1-P99 00959
A1-A99 00959
L1-L99 00959
L1-L99 00957
K1-K99 00957
I1-I99 00957
K1-K99 00957
O1-O99 00957
A1-A99 00959
F1-F99 00959
G1-G99 00959
H1-H99 00959
L1-L99 00959
A1-A99 00959
AH1A-AH99A 00959
K1-K99 00959
G1-G99 00959
K31B-K31B 00959
N8-N99 00957
I1-I7 00957
GG1-GG30 00957
E1-E22 00959
C14-C99 00959
E19-E99 00959
C1-C10 00959
H17-H99 00961
100-199 00957
200-399 00957
13-1-13-99 00959
14-1-14-99 00959
17-1-17-99 00959
19-1-19-99 00959
23-1-23-99 00959
24-1-24-99 00959
4-12-4-20 00957
52-1-52-99 00959
Calle 9 W 00957
Calle 9a 00956
Calle 9b 00956
Calle A
L1-L99 00957
N1-N99 00957
U1-U99 00957
AA1-AA99 00957
CC1-CC99 00957
DD1-DD99 00957
J1-J99 00957
K1-K99 00957
O1-O99 00959
P1-P99 00959
Q1-Q99 00959
R1-R99 00959
B1-B99 00959
L14A-L14A 00957
A1-A26 00957
A9-A9 00959
A1-A99 00959
C1-C99 00959
A1-A13 00957
L1-L99 00959
B1-B99 00959
A2-1-A2-99 00957
B2-1-B2-99 00957
C2-1-C2-99 00957
D2-1-D2-99 00957
B1-B99 00956
D1-D99 00956
A1-A99 00959
D1-D99 00959
A1-A99 00961
L1-L99 00957
A1-A99 00957
M1-M99 00959
O2A-O98A 00959
Q1A-Q99A 00959
C1-C99 00956
A1B-A99B 00957
A1-A16 00956
M6-M99 00957
1-50 00959
1-136 00961
2-25 00959
15-18 00956
27-33 00959
101-197 00959
110-132 00961
134-199 00961
138-140 00961
199-200 00959
201-399 00961
202-298 00959
400-499 00959
Calle A50 00956
Calle Aa 00957
Calle Abad N 00956
Calle Abedul 00956
Calle Abeto 00956
Calle Acacia 00956
Calle Adara 00956
Calle Adelfa 00956
Calle Adondia 00956
Calle Aguirre 00956
Calle Alameda 00956
Calle Alamo 00956
Calle Alcazar 00961
Calle Aleli
G22-G99 00956
G6-G17 00956
100-199 00959
Calle Alexandria 00959
Calle Alfa 00956
Calle Alfa Final 00956
Calle Alicia 00957
Calle Almacigo 00956
Calle Almendra 00956
Calle Almendro 00956
Calle Almendros 00961
Calle Alum Tio 00961
Calle Amalia 00957
Calle Amapola
C1-C99 00956
M1-M99 00956
S1-S99 00956
T1-T99 00956
A1-A99 00959
F1-F99 00959
H1-H99 00959
3C1-3C99 00956
3D1-3D99 00956
J1-J99 00956
B1-B99 00956
D1-D99 00956
G1-G99 00956
H1-H99 00956
B1-B99 00959
C1-C99 00959
G1-G99 00959
3B18-3B99 00959
1-99 00956
100-199 00959
Calle Amarata 00956
Calle Amatista 00961
Calle Ambar 00957
Calle Ana 00959
Calle Andalucia 00957
Calle Andino 00957
Calle Andorra 00956
Calle Angelina 00956
Calle Anones 00959
Calle Antares 00956
Calle Anthony 00957
Calle Antigua 00959
Calle Antonio Principe 00961
Calle Apolo 00956
Calle Aquamarina 00961
Calle Aragon
E1-E99 00956
F1-F99 00956
K1-K99 00956
A1-A99 00961
Calle Areca 00956
Calle Ares 00956
Calle Argol 00956
Calle Argos 00956
Calle Aries 00956
Calle Aristides Chavier 00961
Calle Arturus 00956
Calle Astromelia 00956
Calle Asturia 00961
Calle Asturias
B1-B99 00957
C1-C99 00957
D1-D99 00957
E100-E199 00957
1-99 00959
Calle Atenas
EE1-EE99 00956
OO1-OO99 00956
A1-A99 00959
B1-B99 00959
DC1-DC99 00956
DE1-DE99 00956
DF1-DF99 00956
A1A-A99A 00959
1-599 00959
Calle Atenea 00956
Calle Atun 00956
Calle Avalon 00961
Calle Azalea 00956
Calle Azucena
D1-D99 00956
H1-H99 00956
J1-J99 00956
H9A-H9B 00956
100-199 00959
Calle B
M1-M99 00957
N1-N99 00957
I1-I99 00957
E1-E99 00956
B1-B99 00957
A1-A99 00959
E1-E99 00959
N1-N98 00959
C2-1-C2-99 00957
D2-1-D2-99 00957
E2-1-E2-99 00957
B1-B99 00959
C1-C99 00957
C7-C98 00959
C1-C3 00959
C5-C99 00959
1-36 00961
2-12 00959
14-53 00959
14-37 00959
19-60 00956
37-145 00961
38-98 00961
55-55 00959
200-299 00957
200-498 00961
Calle Babilonia 00956
Calle Baldorioty De
Castro 00961
Calle Barbosa 00961
Calle Barcelona 00959
Calle Barracuda 00956
Calle Batavia 00956
Calle Baviera 00956
Calle Bb 00957
Calle Begonia
G30-G99 00956
F30-F99 00956
G1-G5 00956
200-299 00959
Calle Belize 00959
Calle Bellisima 00956
Calle Bermuda 00956
Calle Bernardino 00956
Calle Betances 00961
Calle Bignonia 00956
Calle Bilbao 00957
Calle Biscayne 00956
Calle Bismarkia 00956
Calle Blanca 00957
Calle Boabal 00956
Calle Bogota
OO1-OO99 00956
PP1-PP99 00956
200-899 00959
Calle Bonaparte 00956
Calle Bonito 00956
Calle Borbon 00956
Calle Borgona 00956
Calle Boundary 00959
Calle Brasil 00959
Calle Bromelias 00959
Calle Buckingham 00956
Calle Buenos Aires 00959
Calle C
G1-G99 00957
J1-J99 00957
K1-K99 00957
N1-N99 00957
AA1-AA99 00957
BB1-BB99 00957
DD1-DD99 00957
R1-R99 00959
400A-499A 00959
C1-C99 00959
D19A-D19D 00959
P1-P99 00957
P1-P99 00959
C1-C99 00961
D1-D99 00959
P1-P99 00957
C1-C99 00957
C5-C99 00959
O1-O99 00959
1-99 00961
1-17 00959
19-99 00959
27-53 00956
56-98 00956
400-499 00961
25-1-25-99 00957
Calle Cadiz 00956
Calle Cafetero 00959
Calle Cali 00959
Calle Cambodia 00956
Calle Campanilla 00956
Calle Campeche 00956
Calle Capella 00956
Calle Capeto 00956
Calle Capitan Correa 00959
Calle Caracas 00959
Calle Caribe 00959
Calle Carite 00956
Calle Carlos Signet 00961
Calle Carmen 00957
Calle Carola 00957
Calle Cartagena 00956
Calle Casia 00956
Calle Castiglioni 00957
Calle Castilla
F1-F99 00956
R1-1-R1-99 00961
R2-1-R2-99 00961
Calle Castor 00956
Calle Cataluna 00956
Calle Cataluna Final 00956
Calle Caunabo 00957
Calle Cedro N 00956
Calle Ceibas 00961
Calle Central 00959
Calle Cereza 00956
Calle Cerros 00961
Calle Chile 00959
Calle Cinthya 00959
Calle Cipress 00956
Calle Cisne 00956
Calle Ciudad De Las
Lomas 00959
Calle Ciudad Del
Oriente 00959
Calle Ciudad Del
Pepino 00959
Calle Ciudad Del
Turabo 00959
Calle Clavel 00956
Calle Clavelillo 00956
Calle Clinica 00959
Calle Coco Plumoroso 00956
Calle Colibri 00956
Calle Colinas 00961
Calle Colombina 00956
Calle Colon 00957
Calle Columba 00956
Calle Comerio
49-97 00959
99-448 00959
450-498 00959
453-497 00957
465-469 00957
499-599 00957
Calle Coral
J1-J99 00956
K1-K99 00956
M1-M99 00956
T1-T99 00956
U1-U99 00956
V1-V99 00956
V1-V99 00957
Calle Coralillo 00956
Calle Corcega 00956
Calle Cordilleras 00961
Calle Cordova 00961
Calle Crisantemo 00956
Calle Cristina 00957

Calle Cronos 00956
Calle Cruz De Malta 00956
Calle Cuartel 00959
Calle Cuarzo 00961
Calle Cuba 00959
Calle Cumberland 00956
Calle Curacao 00959
Calle D
C1-C99 00957
D1-D99 00957
G1-G99 00957
H1-H99 00957
K1-K99 00957
L1-L99 00957
S1-S99 00959
BB1-BB99 00957
F2-1-F2-99 00957
G2-1-G2-99 00957
2-298 00961
200-498 00957
300-471 00959
401-428 00959
473-499 00959
Calle Dakar 00956
Calle Damasco 00956
Calle Dante 00956
Calle Davila 00959
Calle De La Vera 00961
Calle Degetau 00961
Calle Del Carmen 00959
Calle Del Vivi 00959
Calle Delfin 00956
Calle Delfinio 00956
Calle Delphi 00959
Calle Dened 00956
Calle Diamante 00957
Calle Diana 00959
Calle Dilenia 00956
Calle Dinuba 00956
Calle Dominica 00959
Calle Dorado
200-400 00959
402-598 00959
501-698 00956
Calle Dr Domingo Perez Ortiz 00956
Calle Dr Ferrer 00961
Calle Dr Veve 00961
Calle Duende 00956
Calle Durazno 00956
Calle Echinata 00956
Calle Ecuador 00959
Calle Edinburgo 00956
Calle Edmee 00959
Calle El Pardo 00957
Calle Elba 00956
Calle Elliottii 00956
Calle Elmira 00956
Calle Elodea 00956
Calle Emilia 00959
Calle Emperatriz 00956
Calle Encina 00956
Calle Ephesus 00959
Calle Escocia 00956
Calle Esmeralda 00957
Calle Espana 00956
Calle Estancias 00956
Calle Esteban Padilla
60A-60E 00959
1-99 00961
2-60 00959
62-199 00959
Calle Esteban Quintana 00959
Calle Estefandota 00956
Calle Esther 00957
Calle Estonia 00956
Calle Etna 00956
Calle Eucalipto 00956
Calle Eucaliptos 00961
Calle Eugenio Duarte 00959
Calle Euphrates 00959
Calle Evans 00959
Calle Everalda 00957
Calle F
BB1-BB99 00957
V1-V99 00959
W1-W99 00959
X1-X99 00959
FM1-FM99 00959
AI1-AI99 00959
1A-99A 00959
1-99 00959
17-116 00956
61-65 00956
67-99 00956
100-148 00961
100-100 00956
118-199 00959
150-151 00961
153-199 00961
200-299 00957
201-399 00959
Calle Faisan 00959
Calle Federico Montilla N 00956
Calle Fenix 00956
Calle Ferrer Y Guardia 00959
Calle Flamboyan 00956
Calle Flamboyanes 00961
Calle Flamenco 00956
Calle Flamingo 00959
Calle Formosa 00956
Calle Francia 00956
Calle Fresa 00956
Calle Fresno 00956
Calle G
AA1-AA99 00957
BB1-BB99 00957
CC1-CC99 00957
P1-P99 00957
BB1A-BB99A 00957
100-299 00961
Calle Galicia 00956
Calle Garcia 00961
Calle Gardenia
B1-B99 00956
D1-D99 00956
2E1-2E99 00956
Y1-Y99 00956
Z1-Z99 00956
100-199 00959
Calle Gema 00956
Calle Gemini 00956
Calle Gemini Final 00956
Calle Genova
DM1-DM99 00956
1-99 00959
Calle Geranio
A1-A99 00956
G1-G99 00956
200-299 00959
Calle Gerbera 00956
Calle Gerona 00961
Calle Gioconda 00956
Calle Giralda 00956
Calle Girasol
2E1-2E99 00956
2K1-2K99 00956
2M1-2M99 00956
3F1-3F99 00956
3P1-3P99 00956
3D2-3D99 00956
2P1-2P19 00956
3H18-3H99 00956
1-99 00957
100-199 00959
Calle Glabra 00956
Calle Gladys 00959
Calle Gloucester 00956
Calle Gorrion 00956
Calle Graciela 00957
Calle Granada 00957
Calle Granadilla 00956
Calle Granate 00961
Calle Guacamayo 00956
Calle Guanahani 00957
Calle Guarionex 00957
Calle Guatemala 00956
Calle Guayama 00956
Calle Guilarte 00956
Calle Guillermina 00957
Calle H
BB1-BB99 00957
CC1-CC99 00957
DD1-DD99 00957
GG1-GG99 00957
HH1-HH99 00957
JJ1-JJ99 00957
P1-P99 00957
H1-H99 00959
Calle Habana 00959
Calle Haiti 00956
Calle Hanover 00956
Calle Hector Ramos Rivera 00956
Calle Hera 00956
Calle Hermes 00956
Calle Hibisco 00956
Calle Hidalgo 00956
Calle Hiedra 00956
Calle Higuerillos 00961
Calle Higuey 00957
Calle Honduras 00956
Calle Horda 00956
Calle Hortensia
2M1-2M99 00956
2N1-2N99 00956
100-199 00959
Calle Hungria 00956
Calle I
EE1-EE99 00957
JJ1-JJ99 00957
I1-I99 00959
S1-S99 00959
95-97 00961
99-199 00961
Calle India 00956
Calle Ines Davila Semprit 00961
Calle Interior 00957
Calle Irene 00959
Calle Isabel 00957
Calle Isabel Ii 00961
Calle Isis 00956
Calle Isla Nena 00959
Calle Islam 00956
Calle Islandia 00959
Calle Isleta 00959
Calle J 00957
Calle Jabillo 00956
Calle Jacinto 00956
Calle Jacqueline 00957
Calle Jade 00956
Calle Jaime Pericas 00961
Calle Jalisco 00956
Calle Jaragua 00956
Calle Jazmin
C1-C99 00959
D1-D99 00959
2U1-2U99 00956
2X1-2X99 00956
2Z1-2Z99 00956
1-100 00956
Calle Jobos
CA1-CA99 00961
CB1-CB99 00961
CC1-CC99 00961
3N1-3N99 00956
3P1-3P99 00956
CA2A-CA98A 00961
Calle Joglar Herrera 00959
Calle Jordania 00956
Calle Jordania Final 00956
Calle Josefina
D1-D99 00957
E1-E99 00957
F1-F99 00957
G1-G99 00957
AL1-AL99 00959
AM1-AM99 00959
E1A-E99A 00957
Calle Jt Pinero 00956
Calle Juan Lines Ramos 00961
Calle Julia 00959
Calle Julio Alvarado 00961
Calle Juno 00956
Calle Junquitos 00956
Calle Juriel 00956
Calle K 00959
Calle Kent 00956
Calle Kenya 00956
Calle Kermes 00956
Calle Korea 00961
Calle La Cambija 00961
Calle La Liga 00959
Calle La Pluma 00959
Calle Lancaster 00956
Calle Laredo 00956
Calle Las Colinas 00959
Calle Las Delicias 00959
Calle Las Flores 00959
Calle Las Marias 00959
Calle Las Mercedes 00961
Calle Las Rosas 00961
Calle Laurel 00956
Calle Leon 00956
Calle Leonor Figueroa 00961
Calle Libano 00956
Calle Libano Final 00956
Calle Lima 00959
Calle Lira 00956
Calle Lirio
3C1-3C99 00956
D1-D99 00959
E1-E99 00959
WF1-WF99 00959
3B2-3B99 00956
200-299 00959
Calle Litio 00956
Calle Llanuras 00961
Calle Lomas 00961
Calle Lorena 00956
Calle Los Burgos 00959
Calle Los Millones 00957
Calle Los Olivos 00961
Calle Loto 00956
Calle Luis Munoz Rivera 00959
Calle Luxemburgo 00956
Calle M Teresa De Calcutta 00961
Calle Macarthur 00956
Calle Maceo 00961
Calle Madrid
A1-A99 00957
1-99 00959
300-499 00959
Calle Main 00957
Calle Manuel Martinez 00961
Calle Manuel Rossi 00961
Calle Manzanera 00961
Calle Manzanilla 00956
Calle Maraca 00956
Calle Margarita
G1-G99 00957
F1-F99 00959
J1-J99 00959
E1-E99 00959
E1-E99 00957
F1-F99 00957
1-61 00956
63-99 00956
100-199 00959
Calle Marginal
U1-U99 00957
EE1-EE99 00956
J1-J99 00957
L1-L99 00957
CC1-CC99 00957
F1-F99 00959
A1-A99 00959
BB1-BB99 00957
J9A-J9C 00957
J11INT-J11INT 00957
CC1A-CC13A 00957
B1-B99 00959
V200-V299 00957
A1-A99 00961
J1A-J99A 00957
CC2B-CC98B 00957
B1-B99 00959
C1-C99 00961
D1-D99 00961
E1-E99 00961
E1A-E99A 00961
A5B-A99B 00961
Y1-Y99 00957
A1-A99 00957
G1-G99 00956
A1-A99 00957
B1-B99 00957
C1-C99 00957
A1-A99 00959
C1-C99 00959
D1-D99 00959
E1-E99 00959
C1-C99 00959
D1-D99 00959
E1-E99 00959
G1-G99 00959
1-16 00959
17-17 00959
100-199 00957
100-100 00959
500-598 00956
600-699 00959
1990-1998 00957
51-1-51-99 00959
Calle Marginal N 00959
Calle Maria 00956
Calle Marien 00957
Calle Marina 00961
Calle Mario Canales 00956
Calle Marlin 00956
Calle Marsella 00956
Calle Marti 00961
Calle Matiz 00956
Calle Memorial Dr 00961
Calle Mero 00956
Calle Miosotis 00956
Calle Mitra 00956
Calle Mizar 00956
Calle Ml Gomez 00956
Calle Montanas 00961
Calle Montes 00961
Calle Morena 00956
Calle Municipal 00959
Calle Munoz Rivera 00959
Calle Nacar 00961
Calle Nancy 00957
Calle Napoles 00956
Calle Navarra 00956
Calle Nevado 00956
Calle Ninfa 00956
Calle Ocal 00956
Calle Oliva 00956
Calle Olivo 00961
Calle Olmo 00956
Calle Ongay 00961
Calle Onice 00956
Calle Onix 00957
Calle Ontario 00956
Calle Opalo 00961
Calle Oquendo 00959
Calle Oriente 00956
Calle Orion 00956
Calle Orleans 00956
Calle Orquidea 00956
Calle Pablo Salas 00959
Calle Padre Mariano 00959
Calle Pales Matos 00956
Calle Palestina 00956
Calle Palestina Final 00956
Calle Palma 00956
Calle Palma Real 00956
Calle Palmer 00961
Calle Palustris 00956
Calle Panca 00956
Calle Panorama 00957
Calle Panorama Gold 00956
Calle Parana 00956
Calle Pargo 00956
Calle Parque 00961
Calle Partenon 00959
Calle Pasadena 00956
Calle Pascuas 00956
Calle Pavo Real 00959
Calle Pavona 00956
Calle Pedreira N 00956
Calle Pegazo 00956
Calle Pelicano 00956
Calle Pensacola 00956
Calle Perla 00957
Calle Perla Del S 00959
Calle Peru 00956
Calle Pesquera 00959
Calle Peto 00956
Calle Petrea 00956
Calle Petunia 00956
Calle Pez Vela 00956
Calle Pino 00961
Calle Piquito Marcano 00959
Calle Pirineos 00961
Calle Planicies 00961
Calle Platino 00961
Calle Playera 00956
Calle Polaris 00956
Calle Polirubia 00956
Calle Ponpon 00956
Calle Pontevedra 00961
Calle Praderas 00961
Calle Prados 00961
Calle Principal
C1-C99 00957
D1-D99 00957
E1-E99 00957
F1-F99 00957
J1-J99 00957
K1-K99 00957
L1-L99 00957
M1-M99 00957
N1-N99 00957
O1-O99 00957
P1-P99 00957
AA1-AA99 00957
M9A-M9A 00957
D1A-D99A 00957
O4A-O4C 00957
C10A-C10B 00957
I2INT-I2INT 00957
E21A-E21C 00957
O2INT-O2INT 00957
I1A-I99A 00957
Q1A-Q99A 00957
B1-B99 00956
C1-C99 00956
B1-B99 00957
I1-Q1 00957
I2-I99 00957
Q2-Q99 00957
L1A-L99A 00957
300-399 00956
Calle Quina 00956
Calle Quintana 00956
Calle Ramon Miranda 00959
Calle Ramos 00957
Calle Rasel 00956
Calle Real 00956
Calle Reno 00956
Calle Ricardo Ramos 00957
Calle Rigel 00956
Calle Rio Amazonas 00961
Calle Rio Bairoa 00961
Calle Rio Bauta 00961
Calle Rio Bayamon 00961
Calle Rio Blanco 00961
Calle Rio Botijas 00961
Calle Rio Caguitas 00961
Calle Rio Camuy 00961
Calle Rio Canas 00961
Calle Rio Caonillas 00961
Calle Rio Casey 00961
Calle Rio Cialitos 00961
Calle Rio Cocal 00961
Calle Rio Corozal 00961
Calle Rio Cupey 00961
Calle Rio Duey 00961
Calle Rio Espiritu Santo 00961
Calle Rio Fajardo 00961
Calle Rio Grande De Loiza 00961
Calle Rio Guadiana 00961
Calle Rio Guavate 00961
Calle Rio Herrera 00961
Calle Rio Humacao 00961
Calle Rio Ingenio 00961
Calle Rio Jajome 00961
Calle Rio La Plata 00961
Calle Rio Lajas 00961
Calle Rio Mameyes 00961
Calle Rio Manati 00961
Calle Rio Maravilla 00961
Calle Rio Morovis 00961
Calle Rio Nilo 00961
Calle Rio Orinoco 00961
Calle Rio Orocovis 00961
Calle Rio Portugues 00961
Calle Rio Sonador 00961
Calle Rio Tallaboa 00961
Calle Rio Turabo 00961
Calle Rita 00959
Calle Riviera 00956
Calle Robalo 00956
Calle Robel 00956
Calle Roble 00956
Calle Robles
B1-B99 00956
C1-C99 00956
D1-D99 00956
E1-E99 00956
EC1-EC99 00961
ED1-ED99 00961
EE1-EE99 00961
Calle Rodas 00959
Calle Rosa
A1-A99 00959
B1-B99 00959
4F1-4F99 00956
4K1-4K99 00956
Calle Rosario 00956
Calle Rubi 00957
Calle Ruda 00956
Calle Ruisenor 00956
Calle Sabalo 00956
Calle Sabana Del Palmar 00959
Calle Sagitario 00956
Calle Salamanca 00961
Calle Salvia 00956
Calle San Agustin 00957
Calle San Alfonso 00957
Calle San Blas 00959
Calle San Carlos 00957
Calle San Francisco 00957
Calle San Gregorio 00957
Calle San Juan Bautista 00959
Calle San Mateo 00957
Calle San Miguel 00959
Calle San Pedro 00957
Calle San Rafael 00957
Calle San Raimundo 00957
Calle Sandy 00957
Calle Santa Cruz 00961
Calle Santander 00956
Calle Santiago 00956
Calle Santo Domingo De Guzma 00957
Calle Santo Tomas De Aquino 00957
Calle Sauce
EA1-EA99 00961
EC1-EC99 00961
4K1-4K99 00956
Calle Savoya 00956
Calle Segovia 00961
Calle Serotina 00956
Calle Sevilla
B1-B99 00957
C1-C99 00957
1-99 00959
400-499 00959
Calle Sierra 00956
Calle Sirio 00956
Calle Sofia
B1-B99 00956
G200-G299 00956
H200-H299 00956
AJ1-AJ99 00959
AL1-AL99 00959
Calle Sonia 00959
Calle Sultana Del W 00959
Calle Susa 00956

Calle Susana 00959
Calle Sylvia Rexach 00961
Calle Tamesis 00956
Calle Taragona 00961
Calle Tiagosan 00956
Calle Tilo 00961
Calle Toledo 00956
Calle Toluca 00956
Calle Topacio 00957
Calle Toronto 00956
Calle Torrech N 00956
Calle Trinidad 00959
Calle Trinitaria 00956
Calle Tucan 00956
Calle Tudor 00956
Calle Tula 00956
Calle Tulipan 00956
Calle Tulipan 1 00959
Calle Tulipan 2 00959
Calle Turquesa 00957
Calle Ucar 00956
Calle Uruguay 00959
Calle Utuado 00956
Calle Uva 00956
Calle Valencia 00959
Calle Valois 00956
Calle Valparaiso 00959
Calle Venecia
G1-G99 00956
EE1-EE99 00956
PP1-PP99 00956
700-799 00959
Calle Venus 00956
Calle Verbena 00956
Calle Via Periferica 00959
Calle Victoria 00956
Calle Villa Real 00956
Calle Violeta
Q1-Q99 00956
R1-R99 00956
S1-S99 00956
T1-T99 00956
V1-V99 00956
G1-G99 00959
H1-H99 00959
I1-I99 00959
200-299 00959
Calle Visalia 00956
Calle Vista Hermosa 00959
Calle Vizcaya
A1-A99 00961
C1-C99 00961
700-899 00959
Calle Washintonia 00956
Calle Wellington 00956
Calle Windsor 00956
Calle X 00959
Calle Yagrumo 00956
Calle Yokohama 00956
Calle York 00956
Calle Zafiro 00957
Calle Zaragoza 00961
Calle Zaraza 00956
Calle Zeus
K1-K99 00956
M1-M99 00956
N1-N99 00956
1-199 00959
Calle Zinia 00956
Calle24 00959
Camino Cirilo Villalba 00956
Camino De Amapolas 00961
Camino De Begonias 00961
Camino De Dalias 00961
Camino De Gardenias 00961
Camino De Las Rosas 00961
Camino De Lilas 00961
Camino De Lirios 00961
Camino De Nardos 00961
Camino Del Chalet 00961
Camino Del Hostal 00961
Camino Del Meson 00961
Camino El Paraiso 00956
Camino Esteban Cruz 00956
Camino La Palma 00956
Camino Las Americas 00959

Camino Los Burgos 00956
Camino Los Diaz 00956
Camino Valentin 00956
Carr 168 00961
Carr 174
1-99 00956
1-99 00959
100-100 00959
102-199 00959
11-1-11-99 00959
20-1-20-99 00959
21-1-21-99 00959
58-1-58-99 00959
Carr 177 00959
Carr 2
1001-1995 00959
1100-1198 00961
1302-1498 00959
1400-1498 00961
1500-1898 00961
1501-1599 00959
1906-1964 00959
1990-1996 00961
1998-2000 00961
2001-2499 00959
2002-2498 00961
2350-2398 00961
Carr 22
1-199 00959
202-298 00961
Carr 28 00961
Carr 29 00961
Carr 5 00961
Carr 830
200-298 00957
300-499 00957
501-1097 00957
800-898 00956
1000-2098 00957
Carr 831 00956
Carr 861
A1-A99 00957
X1-X99 00957
B1-B99 00957
L1-L99 00957
500-598 00956
Carr 862 00959
Carr 864 00959
Carr 871 00961
Carr 872 00961
Carr 879 00956
Carr 8855 00961
Carr Dr John W Harris 00957
Casa Linda Vlg 00959
Chalets Las Cumbres 00956
Colinas De Cerro
Gordo 00956
Cond Alegria S 00957
Cond Bayamonte 00956
Cond San Fernando
Gdns 00957
Cond Santa Juanita
Housing 00956
Cond Sunset Vw 00959
Coop La Hacienda 00956
Coop Villa Navarra 00956
Edif Jeannie 00957
El Cortijo Shopp Ctr 00956
El Frutal 00959
Estancias Del Josco 00959
Ext Quintas De
Flamingo 00959
Flamingo Apartments 00959
Habra Estrecha 00961
Hacienda Las
Carmelitas 00956
Industrial Correa 00961
Irlanda Apts 00956
La Milagrosa Shopp
Ctr 00959
Marginal Ruiz Soler 00961
Missent 00957
Parkeast 00961
Parkwest 00961
Parq De La Salle 00961
Parq Del Sol 00959
Paseo 10 00956

Paseo 5 00956
Paseo 6 00956
Paseo 7 00956
Paseo 8 00956
Paseo 9 00956
Paseo A 00956
Paseo B 00956
Paseo C 00956
Paseo D 00956
Paseo Del Claro 00961
Paseo Del Monte 00961
Paseo Del Parque 00961
Paseo Del Rio 00961
Paseo Del Valle 00961
Paseo F 00956
Paseo Monaco 00956
Paseo Rio Hondo 00961
Paseo Rossy 00959
Paseo San Pablo 00961
Paseo Santa Juanita 00956
Plaza 1 00961
Plaza 10 00961
Plaza 11 00961
Plaza 12 00961
Plaza 13 00961
Plaza 14 00961
Plaza 15 00961
Plaza 16 00961
Plaza 17 00961
Plaza 18 00961
Plaza 19 00961
Plaza 2 00961
Plaza 20 00961
Plaza 21 00961
Plaza 22 00961
Plaza 23 00961
Plaza 24 00961
Plaza 25 00961
Plaza 26 00961
Plaza 27 00961
Plaza 28 00961
Plaza 29 00961
Plaza 3 00961
Plaza 30 00961
Plaza 31 00961
Plaza 32 00961
Plaza 34 00961
Plaza 35 00961
Plaza 36 00961
Plaza 37 00961
Plaza 38 00961
Plaza 39 00961
Plaza 4 00961
Plaza 40 00961
Plaza 41 00961
Plaza 42 00961
Plaza 43 00961
Plaza 44 00961
Plaza 5 00961
Plaza 6 00961
Plaza 7 00961
Plaza 8 00961
Plaza 9 00961
Plaza Catorce 00961
Plaza Cinco 00961
Plaza Cuatro 00961
Plaza Diecinueve 00961
Plaza Dieciocho 00961
Plaza Dieciseis 00961
Plaza Diecisiete 00961
Plaza Diez 00961
Plaza Doce 00961
Plaza Dos 00961
Plaza Nueve 00961
Plaza Ocho 00961
Plaza Once 00961
Plaza Quince 00961
Plaza Seis 00961
Plaza Siete 00961
Plaza Trece 00961
Plaza Tres 00961
Plaza Uno 00961
Plaza Veinte 00961
Plaza Veintidos 00961
Plaza Veintiuno 00961
Proyecto Los Millones 00957

Qta Del Rio 00961
Quintas Del Parque 00959
Res Alhambra 00957
Res Barbosa 00957
Res Los Dominicos 00957
Res Magnolia Gdns 00956
Res San Fernando
Apt 00957
Res Sierra Linda 00957
Rexville Plz 00957
Royal Gardens Shopp
Ctr 00957
Samara Hls 00956
Santa Juanita Shopp
Ctr 00956
Sect Adrian Ortiz 00956
Sect Algarin 00956
Sect Atanacio 00956
Sect Avila Morales 00956
Sect Chorreras 00956
Sect De Jesus 00956
Sect El Gandul 00956
Sect El Tarzan 00956
Sect Gascot 00956
Sect Gonzalez 00956
Sect Kuilan 00956
Sect La Ceiba 00956
Sect La Lomita 00956
Sect Lorenzo Oyola 00956
Sect Los Rosas 00956
Sect Padilla 00959
Sect Pagan 00956
Sect Santana 00959
Sector Colon
Gonzalez 00956
Sector Espinoza 00956
Sector Flor Sanchez 00956
Senda De La Posada 00961
Teranger 00961
Tintillo Hills Chalets 00961
Torre Sanchez Erazo 00959
Urb Los Almendros 00961
Urb San Miguel 00959
Urb Sans Souci Ct 00957
Valle De Sta Olaya 00956
Vereda De Las Flores 00961
Vereda Del Monte 00961
Vereda Del Rio
B1-B99 00961
1-99 00959
Vereda Real 00961
Vereda Tropical 00961
Via Bogota 00961
Via Caracas 00961
Via Rexville 00957
Via San Jose 00961
Via San Juan 00961
Via Santo Domingo 00961
Victory Shopp Ctr 00957
Villa Warsel 00956
Villas De Ciudad
Jardin 00957
Villas De Hato Tejas 00959
Villas De La Fuente 00959
Villas De Monterey 00957
Vista De La Bahia 00957
Vista Del Mar 00957
Vista Del Morro 00957
Vistas De Panorama 00957
Zaya Verde 00959

CAGUAS PR

General Delivery 00726

POST OFFICE BOXES MAIN OFFICE STATIONS AND BRANCHES

Box No.s
All PO Boxes 00726

HIGHWAY CONTRACTS

01, 03, 05, 06, 08, 09,
10, 11 00725
02, 04, 06, 07 00727

NAMED STREETS

Alambra 00725
Ave Boulevar 00725
Ave Chumley 00727
Ave Degetau
F1-F99 00725
D1-D99 00725
A1-A18 00725
A1-A99 00727
1-41 00727
42-100 00725
102-500 00725
Ave Del Espiritu Santo 00725
Ave El Troche 00725
Ave Jose Garrido 00725
Ave Jose Mercado 00725
Ave Jose Villares 00725
Ave Los Nunez 00725
Ave Los Parques 00727
Ave Luis Munoz Marin 00725
Ave Parque Central 00727
Ave Pino 00725
Ave Puerto Rico 00727
Ave Rafael Cordero 00725
Ave Ricky Seda 00727
Ave San Pedro 00725
Ave Shufford 00727
Ave Troche 00725
Belarank 00727
Bonneville Apts 00725
Bonneville Terrace
Apts 00725
Boriken Park 00725
Boulevard Alambra En
Granada 00725
Brisas Del Parque I 00725
Calle E
E100-E199 00725
D1-D99 00727
E1-E99 00727
R11-1-R11-99 00727
R12-1-R12-99 00727
101-185 00725
187-299 00725
H1-H99 00727
I1-I99 00727
400-599 00725
801-999 00725
Calle S 00725
Calle 1
C9-C19 00725
R1-R99 00725
J1-J99 00725
B1-B25 00725
A1-A24 00725
B6-B16 00725
C1-C18 00725
D1-D28 00725
F1-F18 00725
G1-G14 00725
A1-A11 00725
D1-D7 00725
Q1-Q8 00725
A1-A34 00725
B1-B14 00725
C1-C19 00725
D4-D17 00725
E1-E23 00725
F1-F13 00725
F1-F12 00725
G14-G29 00725
H14-H24 00725
C1-C8 00725
O1-O2 00725
A1-A16 00725
B6-B6 00725
C4-C9 00725
A3-A13 00725
A1-A99 00725

E11-E20 00727
F6-F8 00727
G7-G16 00727
D1-D7 00727
E12-E18 00727
F7-F11 00727
A1-A7 00727
B8-B11 00727
A1-1-A1-99 00727
A2-A99 00727
B1-B22 00727
C1-C1 00727
4G1-4G99 00727
4K1-4K99 00727
4P1-4P99 00727
4T1-4T99 00727
C7-C11 00727
D1-D49 00727
BY1-BY99 00725
BZ1-BZ99 00725
1-99 00725
100-100 00725
Calle 10
CN1-CN99 00725
Q14-Q17 00725
R1-R3 00725
J1-J11 00725
K9-K17 00725
K10-K28 00725
N1-N5 00725
O9-O10 00725
J6-J11 00725
G1-G17 00725
H7-H9 00725
T13-T26 00725
U1-U12 00725
J24-J27 00727
M10-M18 00727
N1-N9 00727
4U14-4U26 00727
4X2-4X21 00727
X1-X1 00727
H33-H52 00727
I1-I9 00727
H12-H14 00727
L1-L5 00727
L6-L11 00727
CQ1-CQ99 00725
Calle 10a
X1-X10 00725
Z1-Z7 00725
H10-H10 00725
SS1-SS99 00727
Calle 11
Y1-Y15 00725
L16-L31 00725
CS11-CS20 00725
K1-K8 00725
L10-L24 00725
I12-I21 00725
K9-K17 00725
L2-L13 00725
M1-M5 00725
C1-C1 00725
P8-P8 00725
P1-P8 00725
Q19-Q25 00725
K1-K17 00725
J28-J31 00727
N10-N18 00727
O1-O9 00727
CC1-CC99 00727
FF1-FF99 00727
JJ1-JJ99 00727
I10-I18 00727
J1-J9 00727
P1-P9 00725
Q14-Q26 00725
U1-U2 00725
300-399 00725
Calle 11a 00725
Calle 11b 00725
Calle 12
Y16-Y17 00725
L2-L9 00725
M1-M10 00725
L17-L25 00725

R1-R14 00725
I1-I6 00725
K9-K14 00725
P1-P1 00725
Z8-Z12 00725
BB29-BB31 00725
II2-II7 00725
JJ1-JJ13 00725
KK14-KK26 00725
J1-J25 00725
L1-L15 00725
CW11-CW19 00725
CY1-CY10 00725
Z7-1-Z7-8 00727
Z8-1-Z8-8 00727
Z8-1A-Z8-1A 00727
Y1-Y5 00727
AA4-AA16 00727
BB1-BB13 00727
G10-G18 00727
H1-H20 00727
R1-R99 00725
Calle 12a
Y1-Y99 00727
AA1-AA3 00727
CW1-CW10 00725
Calle 12b 00725
Calle 13
I5-I6 00725
T1-T10 00725
U9-U16 00725
M22-M42 00725
R7-R10 00725
K1-K8 00725
L23-L36 00725
DB10-DB18 00725
DC1-DC11 00725
Z8-1-Z8-99 00727
Z9-1-Z9-99 00727
BB14-BB26 00727
EE1-EE99 00727
E35-E54 00727
F1-F9 00727
M1-M11 00725
Q1-Q13 00725
R11-R20 00725
R11-1-R11-99 00725
Calle 13a
DB1-DB9 00725
DD1-DD99 00725
CY11-CY19 00725
Calle 13b 00725
Calle 14
U1-U8 00725
L14-L16 00725
M11-M19 00725
R1-R4 00725
X10-X11 00725
DD11-DD20 00725
DF1-DF9 00725
L1-L22 00725
N22-N43 00725
Z6-1-Z6-99 00727
Z7-1-Z7-99 00727
EE13-EE23 00727
GG1-GG11 00727
F10-F18 00727
G1-G9 00727
Calle 14a 00725
Calle 14b 00725
Calle 15
V1-V7 00725
X1-X11 00725
Q1-Q7 00725
R11-R13 00725
M1-M10 00725
N1-N39 00725
N1-N35 00725
O1-O9 00725
X12-X14 00725
Z5-1-Z5-10 00727
Z6-1-Z6-19 00727
GG12-GG22 00727
HH29-HH39 00727
D11-D19 00727
R1-R11 00725
R10-1-R10-6 00725

S14-S26 00725
S14-1-S14-3 00725
EE1-EE11 00725
GG1B-GG1B 00725
DF10-DF18 00725
N38A-N38A 00725
N37A-N37A 00725
E1-E23 00727
Calle 15a
HH1-HH99 00727
DE8-DE13 00725
DL1-DL4 00725
Calle 16
X1-X5 00725
X12-X16 00725
L26-L35 00725
Q8-Q14 00725
N1-N9 00725
O1-O20 00725
P24-P33 00725
AA12-AA14 00725
O3-O8 00725
P9-P16 00725
N1A-N1A 00725
P1-P4 00727
HH15-HH28 00727
LL11-LL24 00727
B25-B43 00727
C1-C10 00727
PP5-PP11 00727
Calle 16a 00727
Calle 16b 00727
Calle 17
Q9-Q18 00725
R1-R9 00725
L1-L47 00725
N1-N10 00725
O10-O16 00725
P5-P23 00725
2M20-2M50 00727
2M48A-2M48C 00727
2N1-2N22 00727
2N11A-2N14A 00727
2Q1-2Q14 00727
2Q12A-2Q13A 00727
2T73-2T84 00727
2X1-2X20 00727
2Y1-2Y8 00727
X9-X27 00727
LL1-LL10 00727
MM1-MM6 00727
C11-C20 00727
D1-D10 00727
S1-S99 00725
S13-1-S13-99 00725
T11-T20 00725
T11-1-T11-4 00725
LL1A-LL1A 00727
2M31A-2M37A 00727
Calle 17a 00727
Calle 18
X6-X9 00725
I13-I24 00725
R15-R24 00725
N11-N21 00725
Q1-Q19 00725
S1-S3 00725
AA1-AA11 00725
BB1-BB11 00725
CC26-CC47 00725
FF1-FF26 00725
GG1-GG2 00725
II8-II19 00725
JJ14-JJ26 00725
M6-M23 00725
X28-X36 00727
Y21-Y24 00727
Z10-Z18 00727
MM1-MM99 00727
NN1-NN99 00727
W1-W14 00727
X7-X12 00727
X1-X4 00725
BR5-BR7 00725
BS1-BS6 00725
Calle 19
T4-T22 00725
U4-U12 00725
R5-R8 00725
FF27-FF44 00725
GG3-GG21 00725
2O1-2O20 00727
2Q13-2Q28 00727
2Q15A-2Q15A 00727
2W1-2W15 00727
Y17-Y20 00727
Z1-Z9 00727
Z1-1-Z1-18 00727
NN7-NN99 00727
PP1-PP99 00727
X1-X6 00727
Y18-Y32 00727
2N23-2N40 00727
2N41-2N89 00727
T1-T11 00725
T10-1-T10-5 00725
TT1-TT20 00725
BP6-BP10 00725
BR1-BR4 00725
Calle 19a 00727
Calle 1a 00727
Calle 2
U1-U99 00725
V1-V99 00725
H1-H4 00725
B1-B5 00725
F7-F10 00725
G1-G22 00725
A19-A36 00725
B1-B12 00725
E1-E6 00725
F19-F38 00725
B10-B29 00725
B7-B9 00725
C1-C3 00725
D1-D21 00725
H2-H6 00725
K1-K99 00725
K32A-K32C 00725
A1-A99 00725
E1-E10 00727
H1-H11 00727
C1-C24 00727
D15-D52 00727
C12-C16 00727
D17-D21 00727
A1-4-A1-5 00727
B1-B99 00727
C2-C9 00727
4C1-4C99 00727
4G1-4G99 00727
A15-A35 00727
B19-B24 00727
E24-E34 00727
H21-H32 00727
K21-K31 00727
L2-L37 00727
M8-M11 00727
A1-A99 00725
A1A-A99A 00725
B1-B99 00725
B2A-B99A 00725
C19-C24 00725
G1-G1 00725
BX1-BX99 00725
BY1-BY99 00725
Calle 20
S1-S12 00725
T1-T52 00725
Y13-Y16 00727
Z1-1-Z1-9 00727
Z2-1-Z2-9 00727
V1-V9 00727
W23-W41 00727
2N1-2N99 00727
Z1-Z4 00725
AA1-AA5 00725
FF1-FF7 00725
BN6-BN12 00725
BP1-BP5 00725
1-99 00725
Calle 21
KK1-KK10 00725
LL9-LL18 00725
2O1-2O99 00727
2P1-2P12 00727
Y1-Y12 00727
T1-T22 00727
U11-U21 00727
CC11-CC20 00725
CC19A-CC19A 00725
NN1-NN8 00725
BL1-BL99 00725
1-8 00725
97-99 00725
Calle 21a 00725
Calle 21b 00725
Calle 22
V7-V21 00725
BB12-BB28 00725
KK11-KK13 00725
T1-T8 00727
U1-U8 00727
T23-T25 00727
U1-U10 00727
2P1-2P99 00727
S1-S99 00727
4E1-4E99 00727
4F1-4F99 00727
V1-V99 00727
LL1-LL9 00725
BB1-BB6 00725
BH1A-BH1D 00725
BJ1-BJ10 00725
2N52-2N99 00727
1-99 00725
Calle 23
FF1-FF99 00725
CC2-CC25 00725
DD1-DD21 00725
2O1-2O99 00727
U1-U99 00727
V1-V99 00727
4D1-4D23 00727
4E2-4E15 00727
R1-R99 00727
S1-S99 00727
T1-T99 00727
S17-S20 00727
CC1-CC10 00725
CC1A-CC1A 00725
DD14-DD26 00725
BG1-BG99 00725
BJ1-BJ99 00725
EE1-EE8 00725
Calle 23a 00727
Calle 24
2M1-2M99 00727
2M48A-2M48Z 00727
2R1-2R99 00727
2S1-2S99 00727
2T1-2T99 00727
2U1-2U99 00727
2V1-2V99 00727
S21-S99 00727
V1-V99 00727
X1-X99 00727
4C1-4C99 00727
4D1-4D99 00727
S1-S12 00727
T1-T99 00727
BB1-BB99 00725
GG1-GG99 00725
GG1A-GG1A 00725
BE1-BE99 00725
BG1-BG99 00725
Calle 24a 00727
Calle 25
T1-T99 00725
U1-U99 00725
Z1-Z99 00725
S18-S25 00725
ZZ26-ZZ36 00725
ZZ1-ZZ99 00725
2S1-2S99 00727
R17-R34 00727
S1-S12 00727
4C1-4C99 00727
R13-R24 00727
T60-T63 00727
Y1-Y99 00725
DD1-DD99 00725
EE1-EE99 00725
EE20A-EE20A 00725
BB1-BB99 00725
BD1-BD99 00725
100-199 00727
Calle 25a 00725
Calle 25b 00725
Calle 26
T1-T99 00725
Z1-Z99 00725
XX1-XX99 00725
2S1-2S99 00727
R1-R99 00727
NN1-NN99 00725
AX1-AX99 00725
AZ1-AZ99 00725
100-199 00727
Calle 27
2R1-2R99 00727
2S1-2S99 00727
2T1-2T99 00727
K1-K99 00727
R1-R99 00727
AV1-AV99 00725
AX1-AX99 00725
AY1-AY99 00725
Calle 28
K31-K59 00727
T1-T99 00727
T1-1-T1-99 00727
Z2-1-Z2-99 00727
A1-A99 00727
B1-B99 00727
C1-C99 00727
F1-F99 00727
H1-H99 00727
J1-J99 00727
K1-K2 00727
LA1-LA99 00725
AS1-AS99 00725
AV1-AV99 00725
100-199 00727
Calle 29
2M48D-2M48I 00727
2T1-2T99 00727
2T62A-2T63A 00727
2U1-2U99 00727
2U17A-2U18A 00727
2Y1-2Y99 00727
LB1-LB99 00727
LC1-LC99 00727
AR1-AR99 00725
AS1-AS99 00725
AT1-AT99 00725
Calle 2a 00725
Calle 3
S1-S99 00725
T1-T99 00725
X1-X99 00725
D29-D56 00725
E1-E27 00725
G15-G28 00725
H1-H11 00725
I13-I17 00725
C1-C17 00725
C21-C40 00725
D1-D22 00725
A2-A22 00725
B2-B12 00725
A1-17-A1-22 00725
A18-A32 00725
E1-E10 00725
F1-F14 00725
A1-A99 00725
C13-C99 00727
G1-G18 00727
I1-I11 00727
D8-D14 00727
E1-E11 00727
B1-B59 00727
C8-C9 00727
K1-K12 00727
4G41-4G56 00727
4H1-4H15 00727
A1-A13 00727
B1-B18 00727
Y1-Y99 00727
Z1-Z99 00727
C1-C9 00725
D1-D16 00725
G1A-G99A 00725
G1B-G99B 00725
DD1-DD4 00725
B13-B24 00725
B25-B26 00725
BU1-BU99 00725
BV1-BV99 00725
BW1-BW99 00725
BX2-BX99 00725
CA1-CA99 00725
CB1-CB99 00725
Calle 30
2T1-2T99 00727
2T61A-2T61A 00727
R9-1-R9-99 00727
LD1-LD99 00727
R3-1-R3-99 00727
AP1-AP99 00725
AR1-AR99 00725
AT1-AT99 00725
Calle 31
R4-1-R4-99 00727
R5-1-R5-99 00727
G1-G99 00727
H1-H99 00727
LG1-LG99 00727
LH1-LH99 00727
LM1-LM99 00727
AN1-AN99 00725
AP1-AP99 00725
Calle 31b 00725
Calle 32
A1-A99 00727
C1-C99 00727
D1-D99 00727
R2-1-R2-99 00727
R5-1-R5-99 00727
R6-1-R6-99 00727
LF1-LF99 00727
AL1-AL99 00725
AM1-AM99 00725
Calle 32a 00725
Calle 32b 00725
Calle 33
AH1-AH99 00725
AJ1-AJ99 00725
R6-1-R6-99 00727
R7-1-R7-99 00727
R7-1A-R7-1A 00727
LG1-LG99 00727
LJ1-LJ99 00727
Calle 33a 00725
Calle 33b 00725
Calle 34
N1-N99 00725
P1-P99 00725
R13-1-R13-99 00727
R15-1-R15-99 00727
LJ1-LJ99 00727
LK1-LK99 00727
R6-1-R6-99 00727
R7-1-R7-99 00727
Calle 34a 00727
Calle 35 00727
Calle 36
A1-A99 00725
E1-E99 00725
C1-C99 00727
D1-D99 00727
Calle 37
E4-E5 00725
F1-F99 00725
A1-A99 00727
E35-E47 00727
H1-H99 00727
I1-I99 00727
Calle 38
F3-F4 00725
G1-G99 00725
E1-E99 00727
F1-F8 00727
Calle 39
G1-G99 00725
E1-E99 00727
Calle 3a 00727
Calle 4
D1-1-D1-99 00725
I1-I12 00725
D8-D13 00725
E1-E6 00725
I1-I4 00725
D4-D14 00725
E7-E11 00725
M1-M34 00725
P1-P9 00725
R1-R10 00725
I5-I12 00725
A1-A17 00725
B13-B24 00725
CD1-CD99 00725
CC1-CC99 00725
F1-F99 00727
C9-C15 00727
D1-D7 00727
4H16-4H30 00727
4J1-4J15 00727
K43-K43 00727
P1-P15 00727
T1-T99 00727
W1-W99 00727
Y1-Y99 00727
Z1-Z99 00727
B1-B99 00725
B1A-B99A 00725
C1-C99 00725
C1A-C18A 00725
F1A-F14A 00725
G1A-G7A 00725
E28-E29 00725
F13-F27 00725
G1-G13 00725
G1-G8 00725
F12-F20 00725
F1-F15 00725
H1-H22 00725
Calle 40
DN1-DN99 00725
DP1-DP99 00725
G1-G99 00727
H1-H99 00727
K1-K99 00727
A1-A99 00727
J1-J99 00727
100-199 00727
Calle 40a 00725
Calle 41
I1-I99 00727
L1-L99 00727
J1-J1 00727
J2-J99 00727
DP1-DP99 00725
DT1-DT99 00725
Calle 42
L1-L99 00727
DQ1-DQ99 00725
DR1-DR99 00725
Calle 43
A2-1-A2-99 00727
A3-1-A3-99 00727
A4-1-A4-99 00727
M1-M99 00727
N1-N99 00727
DR1-DR99 00725
DS1-DS99 00725
DT1-DT99 00725
Calle 43a 00725
Calle 44 00727
Calle 45 00727
Calle 46 00727
Calle 4a
D1-D99 00727
C1-1-C1-99 00727
BI-1-BI-99 00725
GG1-GG99 00725
HH1-HH99 00725
Calle 5
F1-F6 00725
N1-N99 00725
O1-O99 00725
S1-S99 00725
T1-T99 00725
V1-V99 00725
D1-1-D1-99 00725
E6-E11 00725
H1-H7 00725
L1-L9 00725
B15-B36 00725
G1-G11 00725
J15-J22 00725
B1-B12 00725
C13-C24 00725
CD1-CD99 00725
CF1-CF99 00725
F9-F17 00727
F1-F6 00727
G1-G14 00727
D8-D16 00727
E1-E99 00727
F1-F4 00727
4J16-4J30 00727
4L1-4L15 00727
M1-M7 00727
Q1-Q99 00727
F1-F99 00725
B11-B34 00725
H5-H14 00725
K32-K44 00727
Calle 500 00725
Calle 5a
J1-J99 00725
4M1-4M99 00727
Calle 6
T1-T99 00725
G8A-G14A 00725
I1A-I8A 00725
K10A-K16A 00725
C13-C13 00725
S1-S99 00725
G1-G13 00725
I1-I3 00725
J8-J11 00725
K1-K36 00725
L10-L32 00725
F5-F10 00725
D1-D6 00725
R10-R21 00725
K9-K16 00725
G8-G15 00725
I1-I9 00725
J1-J5 00725
K9-K17 00725
L1-L5 00725
C1-C12 00725
D22-D42 00725
F15-F18 00725
CF1-CF99 00725
E16-E16 00725
J1-J9 00725
C1-C6 00727
B1-B3 00727
E10-E17 00727
F5-F16 00727
4L16-4L30 00727
4N1-4N15 00727
A1-A2 00727
O1-O99 00727
Q1-Q99 00727
F1-F44 00725
CH1-CH99 00725
Calle 600 00725
Calle 7
H1-H99 00725
K1-K8 00725
K1A-K7A 00725
P11A-P11A 00725
S17-S40 00725
I7-I9 00725
J1-J5 00725
B22-B34 00725
C14-C24 00725
J2-J14 00725
T4-T13 00725
L8-L15 00725
I1-I99 00725
I9A-I99A 00725
F21-F31 00725
E11-E19 00725

K1-K8 00725
CJ1-CJ99 00725
P1-P13 00725
E9-E15 00725
A1-A8 00727
B1-B9 00727
A1-A8 00727
F27-F35 00727
I1-I9 00727
J12-J15 00727
4N16-4N30 00727
4Q1-4Q15 00727
L45-L53 00727
O1-O11 00727
D5-D6 00725
Calle 700 00725
Calle 7a
CH1-CH99 00725
4R1-4R99 00727
CJ1-CJ99 00725
200-299 00725
Calle 8
G1-G99 00725
B1-B99 00725
I1-I4 00725
H1-H4 00725
I4-I6 00725
M1-M8 00725
H1-H16 00725
I1-I11 00725
J16-J30 00725
K1-K8 00725
D7-D12 00725
E2-E8 00725
L1-L7 00725
M7-M13 00725
H1-H13 00725
F3-F10 00725
CM1-CM99 00725
D22-D46 00727
K1-K27 00727
E6-E10 00727
I10-I18 00727
J1-J99 00727
L1-L9 00727
4Q16-4Q30 00727
4S1-4S14 00727
L38-L44 00727
M1-M15 00727
100-199 00725
Calle 800 00725
Calle 9
K8-K27 00725
G15-G29 00725
J1-J15 00725
C1-C99 00725
P2-P7 00725
Q3-Q14 00725
R4-R9 00725
M1-M6 00725
N6-N11 00725
I12-I14 00725
G7-G15 00725
F19-F55 00725
T1-T12 00725
W1-W9 00725
CM1-CM99 00725
J11-J22 00725
F22-F37 00727
I6-I10 00727
J1-J3 00727
J1-J99 00727
L10-L18 00727
M1-M9 00727
4S15-4S28 00727
4U1-4U13 00727
J10-J18 00727
K1-K20 00727
N1-N99 00725
O1-O99 00725
P10-P18 00725
U1-U99 00725
U3-1-U3-2 00725
CN1-CN99 00725
Calle 900 00725
Calle 9a 00727
Calle A
A1-A5 00725
A6-A18 00725
B1-B99 00727
R12-1-R12-99 00727
R13-1-R13-99 00727
R15-1-R15-99 00727
R16-1-R16-99 00727
A20-A39 00725
A1-A17 00727
1-1 00725
17-1097 00725
1099-1289 00725
1274-1-1274-3 00725
Calle Abacoa 00727
Calle Abeto 00725
Calle Abraham Lincoln 00725
Calle Acerina 00725
Calle Acerola 00725
Calle Acosta 00725
Calle Adjuntas 00727
Calle Aguadilla 00725
Calle Aguas Buenas 00727
Calle Agueybana
BV1-BV99 00725
BB1-BB99 00727
CC1-CC99 00727
BX1-BX99 00725
BY1-BY99 00725
Calle Aguila 00727
Calle Aibonito 00727
Calle Alabama 00725
Calle Albacete 00727
Calle Alejandrina 00725
Calle Aleli 00725
Calle Alicante 00727
Calle Alicia Moreda 00727
Calle Aljibe
C1-C99 00725
BB1-BB99 00725
1-99 00727
Calle Almacigo 00727
Calle Almacigos 00727
Calle Almendro 00725
Calle Almeria 00727
Calle Amatista 00725
Calle Ambar 00727
Calle Amercia 00725
Calle America 00725
Calle Amor 00727
Calle Anasco 00727
Calle Andalucia 00727
Calle Andrew Jackson 00725
Calle Angel L Ortiz 00725
Calle Angelino
Fuentes 00727
Calle Angelitos 00725
Calle Anoranza 00727
Calle Antillas 00727
Calle Antonio Garcia 00725
Calle Antonio Jimenez 00727
Calle Antonio Rojas 00727
Calle Antulios 00727
Calle Aquamarina 00725
Calle Arado 00725
Calle Aragon
Q1-Q99 00725
R1-R99 00725
1-99 00727
Calle Arajibo 00727
Calle Aramana 00725
Calle Aranjuez 00727
Calle Arawak 00725
Calle Arcada 00727
Calle Ardiente 00727
Calle Arecibo 00725
Calle Areyto 00725
Calle Argentina 00725
Calle Arturo Correa 00727
Calle Arturo Mas 00727
Calle Asturias 00727
Calle Atenas 00725
Calle Augusto
Rodriguez 00725
Calle Aureola 00727
Calle Austria 00727
Calle Ausubo 00727
Calle Avila 00727
Calle Aymaco 00727
Calle Aymanio 00727
Calle Azada 00725
Calle Azucena 00725
Calle B
B5-B99 00727
C9-C17 00727
A1-A99 00727
B1-B6 00727
C1-C8 00727
D1-D99 00727
R14-1-R14-99 00727
R15-1-R15-99 00727
B71-B71 00725
100-199 00725
Calle Badajoz 00727
Calle Bagazalez 00725
Calle Baldorioty 00725
Calle Barajas 00725
Calle Barcelona 00727
Calle Barranco 00725
Calle Barranquitas 00727
Calle Bartolome
Esteras 00725
Calle Baston 00725
Calle Batey 00725
Calle Baviera 00725
Calle Bayamon 00725
Calle Beato Jose Ma
Escriva 00725
Calle Belen 00725
Calle Belgica 00727
Calle Benito Rodriguez 00727
Calle Benjamin
Harrison 00725
Calle Bernardin Torres 00725
Calle Bernardino
Torres 00725
Calle Betances 00725
Calle Betances Final 00725
Calle Bilbao 00727
Calle Billy Suarez 00725
Calle Boagame 00725
Calle Bohio 00725
Calle Bohique 00725
Calle Bolivia 00725
Calle Bonanza 00727
Calle Bonaparte 00725
Calle Borbon 00727
Calle Borgona 00727
Calle Botello 00727
Calle Bou 00725
Calle Brasil 00725
Calle Bretana 00725
Calle Brillante 00725
Calle Bromelia 00727
Calle Bucano Gigante 00727
Calle Bucare 00725
Calle Buckingham 00725
Calle Buren 00725
Calle C
C99-C99 00725
C7-C12 00727
D1-D99 00727
E1-E99 00727
F1-F99 00727
F18A-F18A 00727
R13-1-R13-99 00727
R14-1-R14-99 00727
11-111 00725
112-112 00725
113-199 00725
114-199 00725
Calle C1 00727
Calle Cabuya 00725
Calle Cacique 00725
Calle Cadaques 00727
Calle Caguax 00725
Calle Caimito 00725
Calle Camino 00725
Calle Campeche 00725
Calle Campio Alonso 00725
Calle Campoamor 00725
Calle Camuy 00727
Calle Canarias 00727
Calle Canario 00727
Calle Caney 00725
Calle Canovanas 00727
Calle Cantalicio
Rodriguez 00727
Calle Canuela 00725
Calle Caonilla 00725
Calle Capuchino 00725
Calle Caracas 00725
Calle Carbonera 00725
Calle Caridad 00727
Calle Carite
1-99 00727
1001-1099 00725
Calle Carlomagno 00725
Calle Carlos M
Medina 00727
Calle Carlos Osorio 00727
Calle Carraizo 00725
Calle Carreta 00725
Calle Casabe 00725
Calle Casimiro Ortiz 00727
Calle Castellan 00727
Calle Castilla 00725
Calle Cayey 00727
Calle Cedro 00725
Calle Ceiba 00727
Calle Celestino Sola 00727
Calle Celis Aguilera 00725
Calle Cemi 00725
Calle Chablis 00725
Calle Chile 00725
Calle Chipre 00727
Calle Chiringa 00725
Calle Cibeles 00727
Calle Cibuco 00725
Calle Cidra 00727
Calle Cielito 00727
Calle Cipres 00725
Calle Circon 00725
Calle Cisne 00727
Calle Clavel 00725
Calle Coa 00725
Calle Coamo 00725
Calle Colesibi 00725
Calle Colibri 00727
Calle Colombia 00725
Calle Colorado 00727
Calle Comerio 00727
Calle Consuelo
Torrent 00725
Calle Conuco 00725
Calle Coqui Churi 00725
Calle Coqui De La
Montana 00725
Calle Coqui Grillo 00725
Calle Coqui Guajon 00725
Calle Coqui Hedrick 00725
Calle Coqui Llanero 00725
Calle Coqui Melodioso 00725
Calle Coqui Mona 00725
Calle Coqui Pitito 00725
Calle Coral 00725
Calle Corazon 00725
Calle Corchado 00725
Calle Cordova
1-199 00727
300-399 00727
Calle Corpus Christi 00727
Calle Costa Rica 00725
Calle Crisantemos 00727
Calle Crisolita 00725
Calle Cristino
Rodriguez 00725
Calle Cristo Rey 00727
Calle Cristobal Colon 00725
Calle Cuenca 00727
Calle Cumberland 00725
Calle D
B1-B99 00725
D1-D6 00725
C1-C99 00727
D7-D99 00727
E1-E99 00727
F1-F99 00727
G1-G99 00727
H1-H99 00727
R12-1-R12-99 00727
R13-1-R13-99 00727
A1-A2 00725
A3-A99 00725
100-142 00725
144-148 00725
Calle Da Vinci 00725
Calle Daguao 00727
Calle Dali 00725
Calle Dalia 00725
Calle Dalmacia 00727
Calle Damasco 00727
Calle De La
Agrigultura 00725
Calle De La
Constitucion 00725
Calle De La Fidelidad 00725
Calle De La Industria 00725
Calle De La Santisima
Trini 00725
Calle De Las
Haciendas 00725
Calle De Los Castillos 00725
Calle De Los Palacios 00725
Calle Decima 00725
Calle Del Buen Retiro 00725
Calle Del Comercio 00725
Calle Del Lago 00725
Calle Del Milenio 00725
Calle Del Recreo 00725
Calle Demetrio
Aguayo 00725
Calle Diamante 00725
Calle Diana 00725
Calle Dita 00725
Calle Domingo Lasa 00725
Calle Dorado 00727
Calle Dos Bocas 00725
Calle Dr Goyco 00725
Calle Dr Marti 00725
Calle Dr Rufo 00725
Calle Dublin 00725
Calle Duho 00725
Calle Ecuador 00725
Calle Eden 00727
Calle Edinburgo 00725
Calle El Ferrol 00727
Calle El Josco 00725
Calle El Yunque 00727
Calle Emajagua 00725
Calle Emma Rosa
Vicente 00727
Calle Enrique Moreno 00727
Calle Ensuenos 00725
Calle Esmeralda 00725
Calle Espana
CU1-CU99 00725
K1-K99 00727
L1-L99 00727
M1-M99 00727
R1-R99 00727
S1-S99 00727
DA1-DA99 00725
DJ1-DJ99 00725
DK1-DK99 00725
Calle Esperanza 00727
Calle Espino Real 00727
Calle Estambul 00725
Calle Este 00727
Calle Estrella 00725
Calle Estuardo 00725
Calle Eucalipto 00727
Calle Eugenio M
Hostos 00725
Calle Ext Cristobal
Colon 00725
Calle Ext Munoz
Rivera 00725
Calle F
E1-E99 00727
F1-F99 00727
C1-C99 00727
Q1-Q99 00727
R1-R99 00727
S1-S99 00727
R10-1-R10-99 00727
R11-1-R11-99 00727
100-170 00725
172-198 00725
200-298 00725
2009-2009 00725
Calle F D Roosevelt 00725
Calle F1 00727
Calle Faisan 00727
Calle Fajardo 00727
Calle Fe 00727
Calle Federico 00727
Calle Felicidad 00727
Calle Fernando Pla 00725
Calle Fernando
Primero 00725
Calle Ferrara 00727
Calle Flamboyan 00725
Calle Flandes 00725
Calle Florencia 00725
Calle Florencio
Romero 00725
Calle Forastieri 00725
Calle Formon 00725
Calle Francia 00727
Calle Francisco Cotto 00725
Calle Francisco
Mendez 00727
Calle Fraternidad 00727
Calle Frontera 00727
Calle G
F1-F99 00727
G1-G99 00727
A1-A99 00727
B1-B99 00727
C1-C99 00727
D1-D99 00727
P1-P99 00727
Q1-Q99 00727
R9-1-R9-99 00727
R10-1-R10-99 00727
100-190 00725
192-198 00725
200-299 00725
Calle Gales 00725
Calle Galicia 00727
Calle Garabato 00725
Calle Gardenia
G1-G9 00727
H1-H99 00727
1-99 00725
Calle Garzas 00725
Calle Gaútier Benitez 00725
Calle Gaviota 00727
Calle Genova 00725
Calle Georgetti 00725
Calle Gerona 00727
Calle Gijon 00727
Calle Gilberto Rolon 00725
Calle Girasol 00725
Calle Gladiola 00725
Calle Gloria 00727
Calle Gloucester 00725
Calle Gorrion 00725
Calle Goyco 00725
Calle Granada
G1-G99 00725
H1-H99 00725
1-99 00725
Calle Granadillo 00727
Calle Granate 00725
Calle Grecia 00727
Calle Guacabo 00727
Calle Guajataca 00725
Calle Guama 00725
Calle Guanina 00725
Calle Guardiana 00725
Calle Guarico 00725
Calle Guarionex
BK1-BK99 00725
BL1-BL99 00725
AA1-AA99 00727
BB1-BB99 00727
Calle Guatibiri 00725
Calle Guayabal 00725
Calle Guayacan 00725
Calle Guayama 00725
Calle Guayanilla 00727
Calle Guaynabo 00727
Calle Guaynia 00727
Calle Guayo 00725
Calle Guilarte 00727
Calle Gurabo 00727
Calle Guyniabon 00727
Calle H
F1-F99 00725
D1-D17 00725
G1-G99 00727
H1-H99 00727
B1-B99 00727
D19-D99 00727
E1-E99 00727
O1-O99 00727
P1-P99 00727
R1-1-R1-99 00727
R3-1-R3-99 00727
R8-1-R8-99 00727
R9-1-R9-99 00727
100-199 00725
Calle Hamaca 00725
Calle Hanover 00725
Calle Harry S Truman 00725
Calle Hawaii 00725
Calle Hector R Bunker 00725
Calle Herbert Hoover 00725
Calle Hermogenes
Alvarez 00725
Calle Hiedra 00725
Calle Higuerillo 00727
Calle Higuero
200-299 00727
900-1099 00725
Calle Holanda 00727
Calle Honduras 00725
Calle Hormigueros 00727
Calle Humacao 00725
Calle Humildad 00727
Calle I
551INT-551INT 00725
H1-H99 00727
I1-I99 00727
F1-F99 00727
M1-M99 00727
N1-N99 00727
A1-A99 00725
B1-B99 00725
100-199 00725
500-699 00725
Calle I1 00727
Calle Igualdad 00727
Calle Ilusion 00727
Calle Indiana 00725
Calle Inglaterra 00727
Calle Intendente
Ramirez 00725
Calle Israel 00725
Calle Izcoa Diaz 00725
Calle J
B1-B99 00725
C1-C99 00725
I1-I99 00727
J1-J99 00727
G1-G99 00727
R3-1-R3-99 00727
R4-1-R4-99 00727
JR1-1-JR1-99 00727
JR8-1-JR8-99 00727
700-799 00725
Calle J1 00727
Calle Jacho 00725
Calle Jade 00725
Calle James Madison 00725
Calle Jardines 00725
Calle Jaspe 00725
Calle Jataca 00725
Calle Jazmin 00725
Calle Jerez 00725
Calle Jerusalem 00725
Calle Jesus Fernandez 00727
Calle Jimenez Cruz 00725
Calle Jimenez Garcia 00725
Calle Jimenez Sicardo 00725
Calle Jobos 00727
Calle John F Kennedy 00725
Calle John Quincy
Adams 00725

Street	ZIP
Calle Jorge Haddock	00725
Calle Jose Celso Barbosa	00725
Calle Jose D Sola	00727
Calle Jose E Pedreira	00725
Calle Jose Grillo	00725
Calle Jose I Quinton	00727
Calle Jose M Solis	00727
Calle Jose Mercado	00725
Calle Jose Reguero	00727
Calle Jose Rios	00725
Calle Jose Villares	00725
Calle Jossie Perez	00727
Calle Juan Delau Rivera	00725
Calle Juan M Morales	00727
Calle Juan Pena Reyes	00725
Calle Julio Aldrich	00727
Calle Jumacao	00727
Calle Juncos	00727
Calle Jupiter	00725
Calle Juracan	00725
Calle Juventud	00727
Calle K	
G1-G99	00725
J1-J99	00727
R3-1-R3-99	00727
R4-1-R4-99	00727
701-945	00725
947-947	00725
Calle K Int	00725
Calle Kansas	00725
Calle Kent	00725
Calle Kingston	00725
Calle L	00725
Calle La Via	00725
Calle La Borinquena	00725
Calle La Central	00725
Calle La Coruna	00727
Calle La Mancha	00727
Calle La Nina	00725
Calle La Paz	00725
Calle La Pinta	00725
Calle Lajas	00727
Calle Lancaster	00725
Calle Lanzalote	00727
Calle Lares	00727
Calle Las Flores	00725
Calle Las Orquideas	00725
Calle Las Piedras	00727
Calle Laudelino Aponte	00725
Calle Laura Martel	00727
Calle Laurel	00725
Calle Laurel Sabino	00727
Calle Leon	00725
Calle Lerida	00727
Calle Lima	00725
Calle Lirio	00725
Calle Ll	00725
Calle Logrono	00727
Calle Lope Flores	00725
Calle Lorena	00725
Calle Lorraine	00725
Calle Los 3 Brincos	00725
Calle Los Criollos	00725
Calle Los Gonzalez	00725
Calle Lucero	00725
Calle Luis Gonzalez Pena	00725
Calle Luis Lozada	00725
Calle Luis Vigoreaux	00727
Calle Luisa Campos	00727
Calle Luixa	00725
Calle Luna	00725
Calle Luquillo	00727
Calle Luxemburgo	00725
Calle M	00725
Calle Madarcos	00727
Calle Madeira	00725
Calle Madeline Willensen	00727
Calle Madrid	
1-99	00725
300-399	00727
Calle Magnolia	00725
Calle Majagua	00727
Calle Malaga	00727
Calle Mamey	00727
Calle Mango	00725
Calle Manuel Perez Duran	00727
Calle Manuel Soto Aponte	00725
Calle Marcelino Sola	00725
Calle Margarita	00725
Calle Maria Garcia Roque	00727
Calle Marte	00725
Calle Martillo	00725
Calle Maunabo	00727
Calle Maureen	00725
Calle Mayaguez	00725
Calle Maymi	00725
Calle Mejico	00725
Calle Mencey	00727
Calle Menorca	00727
Calle Mercurio	00725
Calle Michigan	00725
Calle Miguel A Gomez	00727
Calle Miguel F Chiques	00725
Calle Milagros Carrillo	00727
Calle Milo Borges	00727
Calle Miramelinda	
C1-C99	00727
D1-D99	00727
400-499	00725
Calle Mirto	00725
Calle Mis Amores	00725
Calle Modesto Sola	00725
Calle Molinillo	00725
Calle Mona Marti	00727
Calle Monaco	00725
Calle Monet	00725
Calle Monroe	00725
Calle Monsenor Berrios	00725
Calle Montana	00725
Calle Monteaguado	00727
Calle Montreal	00725
Calle Morell Campos	00725
Calle Moscu	00725
Calle Munoz Rivera	00725
Calle Murica	00727
Calle Myrna Delgado	00727
Calle Myrna Vazquez	00727
Calle Naboria	00725
Calle Nago	00725
Calle Naguabo	00725
Calle Napoleon	00727
Calle Napoles	00727
Calle Naranjito	00727
Calle Nardo	00725
Calle Nazario	00725
Calle Nebraska	00725
Calle Neisy	00725
Calle Nelson Millan	00727
Calle Neptuno	00725
Calle Nevada	00725
Calle Nicaragua	00725
Calle Nitaino	00725
Calle Nobleza	00727
Calle Normandia	00727
Calle Noruega	00727
Calle Nueva	00725
Calle O	00725
Calle Ohio	00725
Calle Oller	00725
Calle Onice	00725
Calle Opalo	00725
Calle Oporto	00725
Calle Oregon	00725
Calle Orense	00727
Calle Orleans	00725
Calle Orotava	00727
Calle Orquidea	00725
Calle Oslo	00725
Calle Otoao	00725
Calle Ovalo	00727
Calle Oviedo	00727
Calle P	00725
Calle Pablo J Hereter	00727
Calle Padial	00725
Calle Padilla El Caribe	00725
Calle Pala	00725
Calle Palma	00725
Calle Palma De Mallorca	00727
Calle Palma Real	00725
Calle Palmita De San Juan	00725
Calle Pamplona	00727
Calle Panama	00725
Calle Paris	00725
Calle Parq Del Condado	00727
Calle Paseo	00725
Calle Pedro Flores	00725
Calle Penuelas	00727
Calle Pepita Garced	00725
Calle Perfecto Torres	00727
Calle Peridot	00725
Calle Peyo Merce	00725
Calle Pfc Carlos J Lozada	00727
Calle Picaflor	00727
Calle Picasso	00725
Calle Pico	00725
Calle Pilon	00725
Calle Pina	00725
Calle Pinuela	00725
Calle Pitirre	00727
Calle Playera	00725
Calle Pomarosas	00727
Calle Ponce	00725
Calle Ponce De Leon	00725
Calle Pontevedra	00727
Calle Portugal	00727
Calle Praga	00725
Calle Principal	00727
Calle Prolongacion C Aguiler	00725
Calle Prosperidad	00727
Calle Provenza	00725
Calle Q	00725
Calle Quebec	00725
Calle Quebradillas	00727
Calle Quijote	00727
Calle Quinque	00725
Calle Quisqueya	00725
Calle R	00725
Calle R Sotomayor	00727
Calle Rafael Cordero	00725
Calle Rafael Hernandez	00725
Calle Rafael Polo	00727
Calle Ramon Melendez	00727
Calle Ramon Ramos	00725
Calle Ramon Santini	00725
Calle Rectitud	00727
Calle Reina De Las Flores	00725
Calle Reina Isabel	00725
Calle Reinita	00725
Calle Rey Baltazar	00727
Calle Rey Gaspar	00727
Calle Rey Merchor	00727
Calle Riqueza	00727
Calle Rita	00725
Calle Roberto Rivera Negron	00727
Calle Roble	
F1-F99	00725
L1-L99	00725
M1-M99	00725
F18A-F18A	00725
E10-E99	00725
D1-D99	00725
E1-E13	00727
M9A1-M9A2	00727
Calle Robles	00725
Calle Rodrigo De Triana	00725
Calle Roma	00725
Calle Rosa	00725
Calle Rubi	00725
Calle Ruisenor	00727
Calle Ruisenor Azul	00727
Calle Ruiz Belvis	00725
Calle Sabana Grande	00727
Calle Sable	00725
Calle Sagrada Familia	00727
Calle Sagrado Corazon	00727
Calle Sajonia	00727
Calle Salinas	00727
Calle Salustiana Colon	00727
Calle Salustiano Colon	00725
Calle San Agustin	00725
Calle San Alberto	00725
Calle San Alejo	00725
Calle San Alfonso	00725
Calle San Andres	00725
Calle San Antonio	00725
Calle San Bartolome	00725
Calle San Bernardo	00725
Calle San Carlos	00725
Calle San Clemente	00725
Calle San Esteban	00725
Calle San Felipe	00725
Calle San Fernando	00725
Calle San Florencio	00725
Calle San Francisco	00725
Calle San Gabriel	00725
Calle San Ignacio	00725
Calle San Isidro	00725
Calle San Joaquin	00725
Calle San Jose	00725
Calle San Juan	00725
Calle San Lorenzo	00727
Calle San Lucas	00725
Calle San Luis	00725
Calle San Marcos	00725
Calle San Mateo	00725
Calle San Miguel	00725
Calle San Onofre	00725
Calle San Pablo	00725
Calle San Pedro	00725
Calle San Rafael	00725
Calle San Ramon	00725
Calle San Vicente	00725
Calle Sanjurjo	00727
Calle Santa Ana	00725
Calle Santa Cecilia	00725
Calle Santa Clara	00725
Calle Santa Elena	00725
Calle Santa Gertrudis	00725
Calle Santa Ines	00725
Calle Santa Isabel	00725
Calle Santa Lucia	00725
Calle Santa Margarita	00725
Calle Santa Maria	00725
Calle Santa Marta	00725
Calle Santa Rita	00725
Calle Santa Rosa	00725
Calle Santander	00727
Calle Santiago	00725
Calle Santiago Final	00725
Calle Santillana	00727
Calle Santo Domingo	00725
Calle Sara	00725
Calle Saturno	00725
Calle Savoya	00727
Calle Sendero	00725
Calle Sevilla	00727
Calle Sharon	00725
Calle Sol	00725
Calle Suiza	00727
Calle T	00725
Calle Tabonuco	00727
Calle Taino	00725
Calle Tala	00725
Calle Tapia	00725
Calle Tarragona	00727
Calle Teide	00727
Calle Tenerife	00727
Calle Terminal	00725
Calle Teyo Gracia	00725
Calle Thomas Jefferson	00725
Calle Tio Leopo	00725
Calle Toa	00727
Calle Toledo	00727
Calle Topacio	00725
Calle Tormenta	00725
Calle Tortola	00727
Calle Troche	00725
Calle Trompo	00725
Calle Tudor	00725
Calle Tulipan	
D1-D99	00727
E1-E99	00727
200-399	00727
300-399	00725
Calle Turabo	00727
Calle Turey	00725
Calle Turmalina	00725
Calle Turpial	00727
Calle Turquesa	00725
Calle U	00725
Calle Ucar	00725
Calle Ulices Grant	00725
Calle Urayoan	00727
Calle Utah	00725
Calle Valencia	00727
Calle Van Gogh	00725
Calle Venecia	00725
Calle Venus	00725
Calle Veracruz	00725
Calle Verdad	00727
Calle Verde Luz	00725
Calle Vereda	00725
Calle Vicente Munoz	00727
Calle Victor Torres Lizardi	00727
Calle Vidal Y Rios	00725
Calle Viena	00725
Calle Vieques	00727
Calle Vigo	00727
Calle Villa Franca	00727
Calle Villanova	00727
Calle Violeta	00725
Calle Virginia	00725
Calle Virtud	00727
Calle Vizcarrondo	00725
Calle Vizcarrondo Final	00725
Calle Washington	00725
Calle William Harding	00725
Calle William Santiago	00727
Calle Wilson	00725
Calle Windsor	00725
Calle Worcester	00727
Calle X	00725
Calle Yabucoa	00727
Calle Yagrumo	00727
Calle Yagua	00725
Calle Yaguez	00725
Calle Yahueca	00727
Calle Yaurel	00725
Calle Yocahu	00725
Calle York	00725
Calle Yucayeque	00725
Calle Yugo	00725
Calle Yuisa	00727
Calle Yunta	00725
Calle Yuquiyu	00725
Calle Zamora	00727
Calle Zaragoza	00727
Calle Zorzal	00727
Calle Zuez	00725
Callejon Bonanza	00727
Callejuela Munoz Rivera	00725
Camino Brisas Del Rio	00725
Carr 1	
C1-C99	00725
A1-A14	00725
A14-A15	00725
B1-B22	00725
B1-B99	00727
B14A-B15A	00727
1-99	00725
100-199	00725
300-399	00725
400-499	00727
500-599	00727
Carr 156	00727
Carr 172	00727
Carr 183	00725
Carr 784	00727
Carr 789	00725
Carr 796	00725
Cond Brisas De San Alfonso	00725
Cond Caguas Tower	00725
Cond Jom	00725
Cond Los Flamboyanes	00725
Cond Los Pinos	00725
Cond Parq De Bonneville	00727
Cond Puerta Del Parque	00727
Cond Santa Juana	00725
Cond Vista Del Rio	00727
Cond Vista Del Valle	00727
Cond Vista Real	00727
Cond Vista Real Ii	00727
Dondenes	00725
El Mirador Apts	00727
Est Del Rey	00725
Est Santa Teresa	00727
Estancias Del Lago	00725
Ext Bunker	00725
Golden Gate Ii	00727
Grand Blvd Los Prados	00727
Jard Condado Moderno	00725
La Industria	00725
Mansiones De Bairoa	00727
Parq Central 64	00727
Parq Central 65	00727
Parq De Bolonia	00727
Parq De Colon	00727
Parq De La Alianza	00727
Parq De La Fuente	00727
Parq De La Luna	00727
Parq De La Luz	00727
Parq De Las Delicias	00727
Parq De Las Flores	00727
Parq De Las Monjas	00727
Parq De Las Palomas	00727
Parq De Los Angeles	00727
Parq De Los Heroes	00727
Parq De Los Recuerdos	00727
Parq De Los Romances	00727
Parq Del Cisne	00727
Parq Del Condado	00727
Parq Del Lucero	00727
Parq Del Rey	00727
Parq Del Sol	00727
Parq Del Tesoro	00727
Parq San Antonio	00727
Parque Del Retiro	00725
Paseo Caracoles	00727
Paseo De La Palma Real	00727
Paseo Degetau	00727
Paseo Del Flamboyan	00727
Paseo Del Parque	00727
Paseo Del Rio	00725
Paseo El Verde	00725
Paseo Las Catalinas	00725
Plaza Canoas	00727
Plaza Caribe	00727
Plaza Carioca	00727
Plaza Cordillera	00727
Plaza Criolla	00727
Plaza Madrigal	00727
Plaza Mirasoles	00727
Plaza Molienda	00727
Plaza Montesino	00727
Plaza Morivivi	00727
Plaza Mosaico	00727
Portales Reales	00725
Prolongacion Em Hostos	00725
Quintas Las Americas	00725
Res Bonneville Hts	00727
Res Gautier Benitez	00725
Res San Carlos	00725
Res Turabo Hts	00727
Res Vistas Del Turabo	00727
Rio Bairoa	00725
Rio Blanco	00725
Rio Caguitas	00725
Rio Cibuco	00725
Rio Grande De Loiza	00725
Rio Guajataca	00725
Rio Guamani	00725
Rio Guanajibo	00725
Rio Guayanes	00725
Rio Indio	00725
Rio Jacaguas	00725
Rio La Plata	00725
Rio Portugues	00725
Rio Rosario	00725
Rio Tallaboa	00725
Rio Tanama	00725
Rio Yaguez	00725
Sect Bucana	00727
Sector La Loma	00727
Shufford Ct	00727
Turabo Clusters	00727
Urb Caguas Real	00725
Urb Camino Real	00727
Urb El Valle	00727
Urb La Esmeralda	00727
Urb La Serrania	00725
Urb Lakeview Est	00725
Urb Las Carolinas	00727
Urb Serenna	00727
Via Cafetal	00727
Via Campesino	00727
Via Campina	00727
Via Canada	00727
Via Canaveral	00727
Via Constanza	00727
Via Cristalina	00727
Via Cundeamor	00727
Via De La Colina	00725
Via De La Ermita	00727
Via De La Montana	00725
Via De La Vereda	00725
Via Decampo	00727
Via Del Cielo	00725
Via Del Guayabal	00727
Via Del Llano	00727
Via Del Parque	00725
Via Del Rio	00725
Via Del Rocio	00725
Via Del Sol	
100-199	00725
600-799	00727
Via Destello	00727
Via El Redonder	00727
Via Eucalipto	00727
Via Farolero	00727
Via Flamboyanes	00727
Via Grande	00727
Via Guajana	00727
Via Jacarandas	00727
Via Maizales	00727
Via Matinal	00727
Via Medialuna	00727
Via Medieval	00727
Via Miradero	00727
Via Morenilla	00727
Via Naranjales	00727
Via Olivos	00727
Via Palmasola	00727
Via Pintada	00727
Via Placida	00727
Via Platanal	00727
Via Primavera	00727
Via Valle San Luis	00725
Villa Nueva Apts	00727
Villa Vigia	00727

CAROLINA PR

Street	ZIP
General Delivery	00984

POST OFFICE BOXES MAIN OFFICE STATIONS AND BRANCHES

Box No.s	ZIP
1 - 1398	00986

1401 - 6030 00984
6022 - 6022 00988
6023 - 6028 00986
6400 - 6400 00984
7001 - 8220 00986
8700 - 10140 00988
79001 - 79901 00984
810001 - 815008 00981

RURAL ROUTES

01 00979

HIGHWAY CONTRACTS

01, 02, 03, 04 00987

NAMED STREETS

Ave 65 Infanteria
3200-3599 00982
5800-5896 00987
5898-8700 00987
10000-10058 00985
10059-11097 00987
11099-16326 00987
Ave A 00987
Ave C 00987
Ave Calderon 00985
Ave D 00987
Ave De Diego 00987
Ave El Comandante 00982
Ave Fidalgo Diaz 00983
Ave Fragoso 00983
Ave Galicia 00983
Ave Girasol 00987
Ave Gobernadores 00979
Ave Isla Verde 00979
Ave Iturregui
200-398 00987
500-600 00982
600-899 00982
602-21328 00982
Ave Jose A Tony Santana 00979
Ave Laguna 00979
Ave Los Gobernadores 00979
Ave Monserrate 00985
Ave Paseo De Los Gigantes 00982
Ave Pontezuela 00983
Ave Rafael Carrion 00983
Ave Roberto Clemente 00985
Ave Roberto Sanchez Vilella
GJ1-GJ99 00982
GK1-GK99 00982
GL1-GL99 00982
GO1-GO99 00982
GP1-GP99 00982
GQ1-GQ99 00982
PA1-PA99 00982
1000-11698 00982
8000-8099 00982
8100-9898 00983
9900-32653 00983
11700-11726 00982
11728-11730 00982
32655-32659 00983
Ave Rosendo Vela Acosta 00987
Ave Salvador V Caro 00979
Ave San Marcos 00982
Ave Sanchez Castano 00985
Ave Sanchez Osorio 00983
Blvd Media Luna 00987
Bo Colo 00987
Calle E
D1-D99 00985
E1-E99 00985
A1-A99 00987
D1-D99 00987
E1-E99 00987
F1-F99 00987
600-608 00987
Calle 1
L1-L99 00985
O1-O99 00985
A1-A99 00983
B1-B99 00983
H1-H99 00983
M1-M99 00983
N1-N99 00983
O1-O99 00983
C1-C99 00985
H1-H99 00985
I1-I99 00985
J1-J99 00985
A1-A99 00985
B1-B99 00985
G1-G99 00985
E1-E99 00987
F1-F99 00987
GI1-GI99 00987
HI1-HI99 00987
AT1-AT99 00983
M13A-M13A 00983
A1-A99 00982
B1-B99 00982
B17A-B17B 00982
C1-C99 00982
B1-B26 00987
B22-B24 00987
A16-A16 00983
AR1-AR99 00983
AS1-AS99 00983
A1-A6 00985
F32-F43 00985
D26-D27 00987
A1-A14 00987
D1-D6 00987
A1-A9 00987
B1-B8 00987
A1-A99 00985
F1-F99 00985
A1-A17 00987
A4-A99 00987
300-399 00987
1000-1199 00985
2000-2000 00985
Calle 10
O1-O99 00983
P1-P99 00983
J1-J99 00987
K1-K99 00987
B1-B99 00987
F1-F99 00987
N1-N99 00987
O1-O99 00987
N8A-N8A 00987
O4A-O4A 00987
Q1-Q99 00987
100-199 00983
10-1-10-13 00983
30-1-30-99 00985
31-1-31-99 00985
4-1-4-99 00985
5-1-5-99 00983
6-1-6-99 00983
7-1-7-4 00983
8-29-8-35 00983
9-37-9-46 00983
Calle 100 00985
Calle 100a 00985
Calle 101 00983
Calle 102
BA1-BA99 00983
BB1-BB99 00983
100-1-100-99 00985
105-1-105-99 00985
106-1-106-99 00985
Calle 103 00985
Calle 104
BB1-BB99 00983
BC1-BC99 00983
103-1-103-99 00985
104-10-104-99 00985
Calle 105 00985
Calle 106
BC1-BC99 00983
BD1-BD99 00983
101-1-101-99 00985
102-1-102-99 00985
Calle 107 00985
Calle 108 00983
Calle 108a 00983
Calle 109 00983
Calle 11
K1-K99 00987
L1-L99 00987
B1-B99 00987
H1-H99 00987
I1-I99 00987
O1-O99 00987
I1-I99 00983
F1-F99 00987
KK1-KK99 00983
D1-D99 00983
E1-E99 00983
33-1-33-99 00985
Calle 110 00983
Calle 111 00983
Calle 112 00983
Calle 113 00983
Calle 114 00983
Calle 115 00983
Calle 116 00983
Calle 117 00983
Calle 118 00983
Calle 119 00983
Calle 11a 00983
Calle 11b 00983
Calle 12
J1-J99 00983
N1-N99 00983
L1-L99 00987
G1-G99 00987
H1-H99 00987
I10-I99 00983
P1-P99 00983
P11A-P15A 00983
R1-R99 00983
R1A-R9A 00983
32-1-32-99 00985
8-1-8-14 00983
9-1-9-18 00983
Calle 120 00983
Calle 121 00983
Calle 122 00983
Calle 123 00983
Calle 124 00983
Calle 125 00983
Calle 126 00983
Calle 127 00983
Calle 128 00983
Calle 129 00983
Calle 13
J1-J99 00983
K1-K99 00983
N1-N99 00983
UA1-UA99 00987
G1-G99 00987
L1-L99 00987
I1-I99 00987
J1-J99 00987
K1-K99 00987
B1-B99 00987
N31-N31 00987
E1-E99 00985
G1-G99 00985
34-1-34-99 00985
8-15-8-28 00983
9-19-9-36 00983
Calle 130 00983
Calle 131 00983
Calle 132 00983
Calle 133 00983
Calle 134 00983
Calle 135 00983
Calle 136 00983
Calle 137 00983
Calle 138 00983
Calle 139 00983
Calle 14
K1-K99 00983
L1-L99 00983
N1-N99 00983
C1-C99 00987
J1-J99 00987
B1-B99 00987
R1-R99 00983
R13A-R20A 00983
S1-S99 00983
10-14-10-99 00983
35-1-35-99 00985
36-1-36-99 00985
7-5-7-6 00983
9-47-9-60 00983
Calle 140 00983
Calle 141 00983
Calle 141 Final 00983
Calle 142 00983
Calle 143 00983
Calle 144 00983
Calle 145 00983
Calle 146 00983
Calle 147 00983
Calle 148 00983
Calle 149 00983
Calle 15
L1-L99 00983
M1-M99 00983
N1-N99 00983
E1-E99 00987
UA1-UA99 00987
G1-G99 00983
H1-H99 00983
21-1-21-99 00983
22-1-22-99 00983
35-1-35-99 00985
Calle 151 00983
Calle 153 00983
Calle 155 00983
Calle 157 00983
Calle 16
AA1-AA99 00983
M1-M99 00983
N1-N99 00983
P1-P99 00983
K1-K99 00987
L1-L99 00987
AA5A-AA12A 00983
S1-S99 00983
Z1-Z99 00983
AB1-AB99 00983
AB10A-AB11A 00983
22-1-22-99 00983
23-1-23-99 00983
35-1-35-99 00985
36-1-36-99 00985
Calle 161 00983
Calle 163 00983
Calle 165 00983
Calle 167 00983
Calle 17
R1-R99 00983
T1-T99 00983
BB1-BB99 00983
H1-H99 00983
K1-K99 00983
20-1-20-99 00983
21-1-21-99 00983
21-1-21-99 00985
Calle 18
Z1-Z99 00983
AC1-AC99 00983
T1-T99 00983
U1-U99 00983
L1-L99 00987
M1-M99 00987
AA1-AA99 00983
AC1A-AC6A 00983
AB1-AB99 00983
18-1-18-99 00983
19-1-19-99 00983
22-1-22-99 00983
Calle 19
U1-U99 00983
V1-V99 00983
M1-M99 00987
O1-O99 00987
T1-T99 00987
U1-U99 00987
K1-K99 00983
L1-L99 00983
19-1-19-99 00983
19-1-19-99 00985
20-1-20-99 00983
20-1-20-99 00985
Calle 1a 00982
Calle 2
C1-C99 00982
D1-D99 00982
A1-A99 00983
AW1-AW99 00983
B1-B99 00983
B1-B99 00985
C1-C99 00985
EI1-EI99 00987
E1-E99 00987
C1-C99 00987
E1-E99 00985
N1-N99 00983
B15-B21 00987
D7-D12 00987
B1-B39 00985
D1-D21 00985
B9-B15 00987
D1-D8 00987
D1-D99 00985
C1-C10 00983
C1-C1 00985
1-1-1-99 00983
3-1-3-99 00983
Calle 20
V1-V99 00983
W1-W99 00983
AA1-AA99 00983
AB1-AB99 00983
AB12A-AB12A 00983
AA18A-AA35A 00983
17-1-17-99 00983
18-1-18-99 00983
18-1-18-99 00985
19-1-19-9 00985
Calle 201
GC1-GC99 00982
GD1-GD99 00982
GE1-GE99 00982
GJ1-GJ99 00982
GK1-GK99 00982
GL1-GL99 00982
DA1-DA99 00983
DK1-DK99 00983
DK20A-DK20A 00983
Calle 202 00983
Calle 203
GO1-GO99 00982
GP1-GP99 00982
GS1-GS99 00982
DA1-DA99 00983
DL1-DL99 00983
Calle 204
GQ1-GQ99 00982
GT1-GT99 00982
DF1-DF99 00983
DG1-DG99 00983
Calle 206 00982
Calle 207
GT1-GT99 00982
GW1-GW99 00982
DL1-DL99 00983
DB1-DB99 00983
DA1-DA99 00983
Calle 208 00982
Calle 209 00983
Calle 21
W1-W99 00983
X1-X99 00983
O1-O99 00987
L1-L99 00983
M1-M99 00983
16-1-16-99 00983
Calle 210 00982
Calle 211 00983
Calle 213 00983
Calle 215
HA1-HA99 00982
HB1-HB99 00982
DD1-DD99 00983
DE1-DE99 00983
Calle 216 00982
Calle 217
HA1-HA99 00982
HC1-HC99 00982
DE1-DE99 00983
DF1-DF99 00983
DH1-DH99 00983
Calle 218 00982
Calle 219 00982
Calle 22
Y1-Y99 00983
Z1-Z99 00983
O1-O99 00987
P1-P99 00987
Q1-Q99 00987
AC1-AC99 00983
AC7A-AC12A 00983
O31A-O31A 00987
AD1-AD99 00983
15-1-15-99 00983
17-1-17-99 00983
17-1-17-99 00985
18-1-18-99 00985
Calle 220 00982
Calle 221 00982
Calle 222 00982
Calle 223 00982
Calle 224 00982
Calle 225 00982
Calle 226 00982
Calle 227 00982
Calle 227a 00982
Calle 227b 00982
Calle 228 00982
Calle 229 00982
Calle 23
M1-M99 00983
Z1-Z99 00983
Q1-Q99 00983
15-1-15-99 00985
16-1-16-99 00983
16-1-16-99 00985
17-1-17-99 00983
17-1-17-99 00985
18-1-18-99 00985
Calle 230 00982
Calle 231 00982
Calle 232 00982
Calle 234 00982
Calle 235 00982
Calle 236 00982
Calle 237 00982
Calle 238 00982
Calle 239 00982
Calle 23a 00983
Calle 24
R1-R99 00983
R1-R99 00987
Q1-Q99 00987
11-1-11-99 00985
14-1-14-99 00983
15-1-15-99 00983
15-1-15-99 00985
16-1-16-99 00983
49-1-49-99 00985
51-1-51-99 00985
53-1-53-99 00985
75-1-75-99 00985
76-1-76-41 00985
Calle 240 00982
Calle 241 00982
Calle 242 00982
Calle 242a 00982
Calle 243 00982
Calle 244 00982
Calle 245 00982
Calle 246 00982
Calle 247 00982
Calle 248 00982
Calle 249 00982
Calle 25
R1-R99 00983
Q1-Q99 00987
S1-S99 00987
J1-J99 00983
M1-M99 00983
N1-N99 00983
14-1-14-99 00985
Calle 252 00982
Calle 253 00982
Calle 254 00982
Calle 255 00982
Calle 258 00982
Calle 259 00982
Calle 26
M1-M99 00987
T1-T99 00987
AG1-AG99 00983
AM1-AM99 00983
S1-S5 00983
S6-S8 00983
13-1-13-99 00985
14-1-14-99 00983
15-1-15-99 00983
Calle 260 00982
Calle 264 00982
Calle 266 00982
Calle 267 00982
Calle 269 00982
Calle 27
AD1-AD99 00983
AD1A-AD5A 00983
S1-S99 00987
V1-V99 00987
N1-N99 00983
P1-P99 00983
P1A-P2A 00983
AA1-AA99 00983
AA29A-AA29A 00983
P4A-P4A 00983
N11A-N14A 00983
S9-S99 00983
12-1-12-99 00985
13-1-13-99 00983
14-1-14-99 00983
Calle 270 00982
Calle 271 00982
Calle 272 00982
Calle 273 00982
Calle 274 00982
Calle 275 00982
Calle 276 00982
Calle 28
DD1-DD99 00983
FF1-FF99 00983
V1-V99 00987
10-1-10-99 00985
12-1-12-99 00983
13-1-13-99 00983
9-1-9-99 00985
Calle 29
FF1-FF99 00983
GG1-GG99 00983
D1-D99 00987
T1-T99 00987
V1-V99 00987
AC1-AC99 00987
1-1-1-99 00985
11-1-11-99 00985
12-1-12-99 00983
3-1-3-99 00985
8-1-8-99 00985
Calle 2a 00985
Calle 2b 00985
Calle 2c 00985
Calle 3
D1-D99 00982
A1-A99 00983
D1-D99 00985
B1-B99 00987
C1-C99 00987
A1-A99 00987
EI1-EI99 00987
E1-E99 00987
F1-F99 00987
E1-E99 00985
F1-F99 00985
N1-N99 00983
AB1-AB99 00987
B40-B43 00985
B17-B18 00985
B1-B17 00985
O1-O99 00983
C1-C24 00985
AA1-AA99 00987

FI1-FI99 ... 00987
C11-C99 ... 00983
D1-D10 ... 00983
C2-C99 ... 00985
1-1-1-99 ... 00983
3-1-3-99 ... 00983
Calle 30
GG1-GG99 ... 00983
HH1-HH99 ... 00983
AB1-AB99 ... 00987
AC1-AC99 ... 00987
T1-T99 ... 00987
U1-U99 ... 00987
V1-V99 ... 00987
2-1-2-99 ... 00983
29-1-29-99 ... 00983
30-1-30-9 ... 00983
6-1-6-99 ... 00985
7-1-7-99 ... 00985
Calle 31
HH1-HH99 ... 00983
JJ1-JJ99 ... 00983
AB1-AB99 ... 00987
AD1-AD99 ... 00983
3-1-3-99 ... 00985
30-10-30-99 ... 00983
31-1-31-99 ... 00983
4-1-4-99 ... 00985
Calle 32
DD1-DD99 ... 00983
EE1-EE99 ... 00983
AD1-AD99 ... 00987
AE1-AE99 ... 00987
AN1-AN99 ... 00983
1-1-1-99 ... 00983
2-1-2-99 ... 00985
29-1-29-99 ... 00983
5-1-5-99 ... 00985
Calle 32a ... 00987
Calle 32b ... 00987
Calle 33
P1-P99 ... 00983
EE1-EE99 ... 00983
II1-II99 ... 00983
AE1-AE99 ... 00987
AG1-AG99 ... 00987
2A1-2A99 ... 00987
2B1-2B99 ... 00987
2C1-2C99 ... 00987
2C18A-2C18A ... 00987
2A16A-2A16A ... 00987
T1-T99 ... 00983
2-1-2-99 ... 00985
27-1-27-99 ... 00983
29-1-29-99 ... 00983
5-1-5-99 ... 00985
Calle 34
JJ1-JJ99 ... 00983
AE1-AE99 ... 00987
AF1-AF99 ... 00987
AN1-AN99 ... 00983
AN13A-AN14A ... 00983
AP1-AP99 ... 00983
AP2A-AP2A ... 00983
25-1-25-99 ... 00983
26-1-26-99 ... 00983
28-1-28-99 ... 00983
38-1-38-99 ... 00985
39-1-39-99 ... 00985
41-1-41-99 ... 00985
42-1-42-99 ... 00985
Calle 35
A1-A99 ... 00987
B1-B99 ... 00987
2G1-2G99 ... 00987
2G18A-2G18A ... 00987
Q1-Q99 ... 00983
AE1-AE99 ... 00983
AF1-AF99 ... 00983
AF12A-AF13A ... 00983
37A-1-37A-36 ... 00985
2E1-2E99 ... 00987
2F1-2F99 ... 00987
2E16A-2E16A ... 00987
2F2A-2F2A ... 00987
24-1-24-99 ... 00983
26-1-26-99 ... 00983
27-1-27-99 ... 00983
37-1-37-99 ... 00985
43-1-43-99 ... 00985
44-1-44-99 ... 00985
Calle 35a ... 00985
Calle 35b ... 00985
Calle 36
A1-A99 ... 00987
B1-B99 ... 00987
D1-D99 ... 00987
E1-E99 ... 00987
AP1-AP99 ... 00983
AP10A-AP10A ... 00983
AQ1-AQ99 ... 00983
37-1-37-99 ... 00985
38-1-38-99 ... 00985
40-1-40-99 ... 00985
Calle 37
C1-C99 ... 00987
D1-D99 ... 00987
F1-F99 ... 00987
2G1-2G99 ... 00987
2G23A-2G23A ... 00987
2I1-2I99 ... 00987
E1-E99 ... 00987
G1-G99 ... 00987
AF1-AF99 ... 00983
AF10A-AF11A ... 00983
AH1-AH99 ... 00983
AH9A-AH9A ... 00983
39-1-39-99 ... 00985
40-1-40-99 ... 00985
44-1-44-99 ... 00985
Calle 38
H1-H99 ... 00987
J1-J99 ... 00987
K1-K99 ... 00987
Q1-Q99 ... 00987
R1-R99 ... 00987
S1-S99 ... 00987
2H1-2H99 ... 00987
2I1-2I99 ... 00987
AQ1-AQ99 ... 00983
AR1-AR99 ... 00983
37-1-37-99 ... 00985
41-1-41-99 ... 00985
Calle 38a ... 00987
Calle 38b ... 00983
Calle 38c ... 00983
Calle 39
J1-J99 ... 00987
L1-L99 ... 00987
M1-M99 ... 00987
2H1-2H99 ... 00987
AH1-AH99 ... 00983
AJ1-AJ99 ... 00983
42-1-42-99 ... 00985
43-1-43-99 ... 00985
Calle 4
A1-A99 ... 00982
B1-B99 ... 00982
C1-C99 ... 00982
O1-O99 ... 00983
A1-A99 ... 00985
B1-B99 ... 00985
D1-D99 ... 00985
E1-E99 ... 00985
F1-F99 ... 00985
C1-C99 ... 00987
D1-D99 ... 00987
F1-F99 ... 00987
FF1-FF99 ... 00987
N1-N99 ... 00983
AR1-AR99 ... 00983
D22-D41 ... 00983
E1-E21 ... 00985
GI1-GI99 ... 00987
FI1-FI99 ... 00987
D11-D99 ... 00983
E1-E11 ... 00983
1000-1199 ... 00985
1-1-1-99 ... 00983
3-1-3-99 ... 00983
Calle 40
H1-H99 ... 00987
S1-S99 ... 00987
T1-T99 ... 00987
2H1-2H99 ... 00987
47-1-47-99 ... 00985
48-1-48-99 ... 00985
Calle 400 ... 00982
Calle 401
MA1-MA99 ... 00982
100-199 ... 00985
133-1-133-99 ... 00985
134-1-134-99 ... 00985
135-1-135-99 ... 00985
139-1-139-99 ... 00985
143-1-143-99 ... 00985
147-1-147-6 ... 00985
167-1-167-99 ... 00985
168-1-168-99 ... 00985
172-1-172-99 ... 00985
173-1-173-99 ... 00985
Calle 402
MD1-MD99 ... 00982
133-1-133-99 ... 00985
Calle 403
MN1-MN99 ... 00982
137-1-137-99 ... 00985
138-1-138-99 ... 00985
Calle 404
ME1-ME99 ... 00982
135-1-135-99 ... 00985
139-1-139-99 ... 00985
Calle 405
MT1-MT99 ... 00982
134-1-134-99 ... 00985
136-1-136-99 ... 00985
Calle 406
MG1-MG99 ... 00982
136-1-136-99 ... 00985
137-1-137-99 ... 00985
Calle 407
MU1-MU99 ... 00982
138-1-138-99 ... 00985
140-1-140-99 ... 00985
Calle 408
MH1-MH99 ... 00982
149-1-149-99 ... 00985
Calle 409
MV1-MV99 ... 00982
141-1-141-99 ... 00985
142-1-142-99 ... 00985
Calle 41
J1-J99 ... 00987
K1-K99 ... 00987
2H1-2H99 ... 00987
2K1-2K99 ... 00987
2P1-2P99 ... 00987
2H6A-2H6A ... 00987
2M18-2M32 ... 00987
AJ1-AJ99 ... 00983
AK1-AK99 ... 00983
45-1-45-99 ... 00985
46-1-46-99 ... 00985
50-1-50-99 ... 00985
Calle 410
MI1-MI99 ... 00982
139-1-139-99 ... 00985
143-1-143-99 ... 00985
Calle 411
MW1-MW99 ... 00982
140-1-140-99 ... 00985
141-1-141-99 ... 00985
Calle 412
MJ1-MJ99 ... 00982
142-1-142-99 ... 00985
144-1-144-99 ... 00985
Calle 413
MO1-MO99 ... 00982
149-1-149-99 ... 00985
Calle 414
MK1-MK99 ... 00982
145-1-145-99 ... 00985
146-1-146-99 ... 00985
Calle 415
NA1-NA99 ... 00982
MX1-MX99 ... 00982
143-1-143-99 ... 00985
147-1-147-99 ... 00985
Calle 416
ML1-ML99 ... 00982
144-1-144-99 ... 00985
145-1-145-99 ... 00985
Calle 417
NB1-NB99 ... 00982
146-1-146-99 ... 00985
148-1-148-99 ... 00985
Calle 418 ... 00982
Calle 419 ... 00985
Calle 41a ... 00987
Calle 42
K1-K99 ... 00987
L1-L99 ... 00987
2D1-2D99 ... 00987
2R1-2R99 ... 00987
2S1-2S99 ... 00987
2R16A-2R16A ... 00987
45-1-45-99 ... 00985
48-1-48-99 ... 00985
49-1-49-99 ... 00985
Calle 420
MM1-MM99 ... 00982
160-1-160-99 ... 00985
161-1-161-99 ... 00985
Calle 420a ... 00985
Calle 421 ... 00985
Calle 422
MN1-MN99 ... 00982
161-1-161-99 ... 00985
162-1-162-99 ... 00985
Calle 423 ... 00985
Calle 424
MO1-MO99 ... 00982
150-1-150-99 ... 00985
Calle 426
MP1-MP99 ... 00982
154-1-154-99 ... 00985
159-1-159-99 ... 00985
Calle 427 ... 00985
Calle 428
MQ1-MQ99 ... 00982
156-1-156-99 ... 00985
157-1-157-99 ... 00985
Calle 429 ... 00985
Calle 43
P1-P99 ... 00987
Q1-Q99 ... 00987
2P1-2P99 ... 00987
AK1-AK99 ... 00983
AL1-AL99 ... 00983
300-300 ... 00987
46-1-46-99 ... 00985
47-1-47-99 ... 00985
Calle 430
MR1-MR99 ... 00982
153-1-153-99 ... 00985
155-1-155-99 ... 00985
Calle 431 ... 00985
Calle 432
MS1-MS99 ... 00982
151-1-151-99 ... 00985
152-1-152-99 ... 00985
Calle 433 ... 00985
Calle 434
MX1-MX99 ... 00982
154-1-154-99 ... 00985
Calle 435 ... 00985
Calle 436
MY1-MY99 ... 00982
168A1-168A99 ... 00985
168-1-168-99 ... 00985
169-1-169-99 ... 00985
Calle 437 ... 00985
Calle 438
MZ1-MZ99 ... 00982
171-1-171-99 ... 00985
172-1-172-99 ... 00985
174-1-174-99 ... 00985
181-1-181-99 ... 00985
Calle 439 ... 00985
Calle 44
N1-N99 ... 00987
P1-P99 ... 00987
51-1-51-99 ... 00985
52-1-52-99 ... 00985
Calle 440
NA1-NA99 ... 00982
179-1-179-99 ... 00985
180-1-180-99 ... 00985
Calle 441 ... 00985
Calle 442
NB1-NB99 ... 00982
177-1-177-99 ... 00985
178-1-178-99 ... 00985
Calle 443 ... 00985
Calle 444 ... 00982
Calle 446 ... 00982
Calle 448 ... 00982
Calle 45
I1-I99 ... 00987
T1-T99 ... 00987
U1-U99 ... 00987
AL1-AL99 ... 00983
Calle 46
2T16-2T26 ... 00987
59-1-59-99 ... 00985
60-1-60-99 ... 00985
63-1-63-99 ... 00985
Calle 46a ... 00983
Calle 46b ... 00983
Calle 47 ... 00985
Calle 48 ... 00985
Calle 482 ... 00982
Calle 4a ... 00987
Calle 5
G1-G99 ... 00982
A1-A99 ... 00983
O1-O99 ... 00983
P1-P99 ... 00983
R1-R199 ... 00983
G1-G99 ... 00985
E1-E99 ... 00985
F1-F99 ... 00985
D1-D99 ... 00987
E1-E99 ... 00987
A1-A99 ... 00987
CI1-CI99 ... 00987
DI1-DI99 ... 00987
HI1-HI99 ... 00987
G1-G99 ... 00987
H1-H99 ... 00987
H1-H99 ... 00982
DI17A-DI17A ... 00987
I1-I99 ... 00985
L1-L99 ... 00985
C1-C99 ... 00987
H4A-H4B ... 00987
B1-B99 ... 00983
C1-C99 ... 00985
E12-E99 ... 00983
F1-F11 ... 00983
1000-1199 ... 00985
2-1-2-99 ... 00983
24-1-24-99 ... 00983
25-1-25-99 ... 00985
3-1-3-99 ... 00983
6-1-6-99 ... 00983
7-1-7-99 ... 00983
Calle 50 ... 00985
Calle 500
OA1-OA99 ... 00982
219-1-219-99 ... 00985
Calle 501
OD1-OD99 ... 00982
216-1-216-99 ... 00985
218-1-218-99 ... 00985
219-1-219-99 ... 00985
Calle 502
OB1-OB99 ... 00982
OC1-OC99 ... 00982
212-1-212-99 ... 00985
217-1-217-99 ... 00985
218-1-218-99 ... 00985
Calle 503
OB1-OB99 ... 00982
212-1-212-99 ... 00985
213-1-213-99 ... 00985
214-1-214-99 ... 00985
Calle 504 ... 00982
Calle 505
OF1-OF99 ... 00982
212-1-212-99 ... 00985
215-1-215-99 ... 00985
216-1-216-99 ... 00985
217-1-217-99 ... 00985
Calle 506
OJ1-OJ99 ... 00982
OK1-OK99 ... 00982
214-1-214-99 ... 00985
215-1-215-99 ... 00985
Calle 507
OI1-OI99 ... 00982
207-1-207-99 ... 00985
210-1-210-99 ... 00985
Calle 508
OL1-OL99 ... 00982
OK1-OK99 ... 00982
210-1-210-99 ... 00985
211-1-211-99 ... 00985
212-1-212-27 ... 00985
213-1-213-99 ... 00985
Calle 509
OU1-OU99 ... 00982
211-1-211-99 ... 00985
Calle 51 ... 00985
Calle 510
OM1-OM99 ... 00982
ON1-ON99 ... 00982
205-1-205-99 ... 00985
208-1-208-99 ... 00985
Calle 511
OL1-OL99 ... 00982
209-1-209-99 ... 00985
210-1-210-99 ... 00985
Calle 512
ON1-ON99 ... 00982
OO1-OO99 ... 00982
208-1-208-99 ... 00985
209-1-209-99 ... 00985
Calle 513
OO1-OO99 ... 00982
OM1-OM99 ... 00982
204-1-204-99 ... 00985
206-1-206-99 ... 00985
Calle 514
OE1-OE99 ... 00982
205-1-205-99 ... 00985
206-1-206-99 ... 00985
Calle 515
OS1-OS99 ... 00982
192-1-192-99 ... 00985
199-1-199-99 ... 00985
203-1-203-99 ... 00985
204-1-204-99 ... 00985
207-1-207-99 ... 00985
Calle 516
OF1-OF99 ... 00982
OG1-OG99 ... 00982
200-299 ... 00985
188-1-188-99 ... 00985
212-1-212-99 ... 00985
217-1-217-99 ... 00985
Calle 517 ... 00985
Calle 518
OG1-OG99 ... 00982
OH1-OH99 ... 00982
184-1-184-99 ... 00985
186-1-186-99 ... 00985
Calle 519
QA1-QA99 ... 00982
QB1-QB99 ... 00982
QC1-QC99 ... 00982
184-1-184-99 ... 00985
186-1-186-99 ... 00985
187-1-187-99 ... 00985
Calle 51a ... 00987
Calle 52 ... 00985
Calle 520
OQ1-OQ99 ... 00982
OR1-OR99 ... 00982
186-1-186-99 ... 00985
187-1-187-99 ... 00985
Calle 521
QC1-QC99 ... 00982
QD1-QD99 ... 00982
188-1-188-99 ... 00985
189-1-189-99 ... 00985
190-1-190-99 ... 00985
192-1-192-99 ... 00985
Calle 522
OR1-OR99 ... 00982
OS1-OS99 ... 00982
188-1-188-99 ... 00985
190-1-190-99 ... 00985
191-1-191-99 ... 00985
192-1-192-99 ... 00985
Calle 523
QE1-QE99 ... 00982
188-1-188-99 ... 00985
190-1-190-99 ... 00985
191-1-191-99 ... 00985
Calle 524
OT1-OT99 ... 00982
190-1-190-99 ... 00985
191-1-191-99 ... 00985
Calle 525
QF1-QF99 ... 00982
QG1-QG99 ... 00982
193-1-193-99 ... 00985
Calle 526
QA1-QA99 ... 00982
193-1-193-99 ... 00985
194-1-194-99 ... 00985
197-1-197-99 ... 00985
198-1-198-99 ... 00985
199-1-199-99 ... 00985
Calle 527
QG1-QG99 ... 00982
QH1-QH99 ... 00982
194-1-194-99 ... 00985
197-1-197-99 ... 00985
Calle 528 ... 00985
Calle 529
QI1-QI99 ... 00982
194-1-194-99 ... 00985
196-1-196-99 ... 00985
200-1-200-99 ... 00985
Calle 52a ... 00987
Calle 53 ... 00985
Calle 530
QB1-QB99 ... 00982
QD1-QD99 ... 00982
195-1-195-99 ... 00985
196-1-196-99 ... 00985
Calle 531
QJ1-QJ99 ... 00982
QK1-QK99 ... 00982
201-1-201-99 ... 00985
Calle 532
QF1-QF99 ... 00982
QH1-QH99 ... 00982
200-1-200-99 ... 00985
203-1-203-99 ... 00985
Calle 533
QL1-QL99 ... 00982
QK1-QK99 ... 00982
202-1-202-99 ... 00985
203-1-203-99 ... 00985
Calle 534
QJ1-QJ99 ... 00982
201-1-201-99 ... 00985
202-1-202-99 ... 00985
Calle 535
QN1-QN99 ... 00982
QO1-QO99 ... 00982
200-299 ... 00985
195-1-195-99 ... 00985
Calle 536 ... 00982
Calle 538 ... 00982
Calle 53a ... 00987
Calle 54 ... 00985
Calle 55
2H1-2H99 ... 00987
2M1-2M99 ... 00987
2I1-2I99 ... 00987
2H43A-2H43A ... 00987
67-31-67-99 ... 00985
68-1-68-32 ... 00985
Calle 56
2D1-2D99 ... 00987
2F1-2F99 ... 00987
2L1-2L99 ... 00987
2M33-2M99 ... 00987
68-33-68-99 ... 00985
69-1-69-24 ... 00985
Calle 56a ... 00987
Calle 57
NN1-NN99 ... 00987
2B1-2B99 ... 00987
69-25-69-99 ... 00985
70-1-70-21 ... 00985

Calle 58
NN1-NN99 00987
C1-C99 00987
J1-J99 00987
MM1-MM99 00987
70-22-70-99 00985
71-1-71-24 00985
Calle 58a 00987
Calle 59 00985
Calle 6
E1-E99 00982
G1-G99 00982
D1-D99 00985
E1-E99 00985
B1-B99 00985
G1-G99 00985
H1-H99 00985
GI1-GI99 00987
H1-H99 00987
K1-K99 00987
P1-P99 00983
H5A-H5A 00987
F1-F11 00983
F12-F99 00983
2-12A-2-12A 00983
100-198 00983
2-1-2-99 00983
24-1-24-99 00985
25-1-25-99 00985
26-1-26-99 00985
28-1-28-99 00985
29-1-29-99 00985
Calle 60
2I1-2I99 00987
72-16-72-99 00985
73-1-73-11 00985
Calle 600 00985
Calle 601 00985
Calle 602 00985
Calle 603 00985
Calle 604 00985
Calle 605 00985
Calle 606 00985
Calle 607 00985
Calle 608 00985
Calle 609 00985
Calle 61 00985
Calle 610 00985
Calle 611 00985
Calle 612 00985
Calle 613 00985
Calle 614 00985
Calle 615 00985
Calle 616 00985
Calle 617 00985
Calle 618 00985
Calle 619 00985
Calle 62 00985
Calle 620 00985
Calle 63
2I1-2I99 00987
2J1-2J99 00987
122-1-122-99 00985
123-1-123-99 00985
Calle 64
2K1-2K99 00987
2I51-2I65 00987
120-1-120-99 00985
121-1-121-99 00985
122-1-122-99 00985
123-1-123-99 00985
Calle 65 00985
Calle 67 00985
Calle 69 00985
Calle 7
P1-P99 00983
R1-R199 00983
E1-E99 00985
F1-F99 00985
C1-C99 00985
H1-H99 00985
I1-I99 00985
H1-H99 00987
I1-I99 00987
C1-C99 00987
K1-K99 00987
L1-L99 00987
B1-B99 00983
C1-C99 00983
G1-G10 00983
100-168 00985
170-299 00985
27-1-27-99 00985
28-1-28-99 00985
Calle 70 00985
Calle 71 00985
Calle 72 00985
Calle 73 00985
Calle 73b 00985
Calle 73c 00985
Calle 74 00985
Calle 75 00985
Calle 76 00985
Calle 77 00985
Calle 78 00985
Calle 79 00985
Calle 8
R1-R99 00983
F1-F99 00985
I1-I99 00987
B1-B99 00987
F1-F99 00987
G1-G99 00987
L1-L99 00987
M1-M99 00987
G11-G18 00983
100-299 00985
100-199 00983
30-1-30-99 00985
31-1-31-99 00985
4-1-4-99 00983
5-1-5-99 00983
Calle 80 00985
Calle 81 00985
Calle 82 00985
Calle 83 00985
Calle 84 00985
Calle 85 00985
Calle 86 00985
Calle 87 00985
Calle 88 00985
Calle 89 00985
Calle 8a 00985
Calle 9
H1-H99 00985
I1-I99 00985
H1-H99 00987
J1-J99 00987
D1-D99 00987
M1-M99 00987
N1-N99 00987
G8-G16 00985
G1-G21 00985
G19-G99 00983
C1-C99 00983
D1-D99 00983
158-699 00985
30-1-30-99 00985
4-1-4-99 00983
5-1-5-99 00983
Calle 90 00985
Calle 90a 00985
Calle 91 00985
Calle 92 00985
Calle 93 00985
Calle 94 00985
Calle 95 00985
Calle 96 00985
Calle 97 00985
Calle 98 00985
Calle 99 00985
Calle 99a 00985
Calle 9a 00985
Calle A
H1-H99 00985
122A-1-122A-99 00985
122B-1-122B-99 00985
11800-11813 00983
11815-11815 00983
122-1-122-99 00985
Calle Acacia 00983
Calle Acuario 00979
Calle Agustin Cabrera .. 00985
Calle Alamo 00983
Calle Alborada 00987
Calle Aleli 00985
Calle Alicante 00983
Calle Almendro
CD1-CD99 00983
CQ1-CQ99 00983
CR1-CR99 00983
100-199 00983
101-1399 00987
196-230 00987
Calle Almeria 00983
Calle Almirante 00987
Calle Amadeo E 00985
Calle Amapola
S1-S99 00985
T1-T99 00985
1-6 00979
7-23 00979
8-30 00979
25-99 00979
100-199 00987
200-299 00987
Calle Anastacio Villeg .. 00987
Calle Andalucia 00983
Calle Andorra 00983
Calle Andres Arus E 00985
Calle Andromeda 00979
Calle Angel Rivero
Mendez 00987
Calle Anon 00983
Calle Antonio J Landrau
N 00985
Calle Antonio Landrau
N 00985
Calle Aquamarina 00987
Calle Aragon 00983
Calle Argentina 00987
Calle Aries 00979
Calle Arrufat
Dominguez 00985
Calle Astros 00979
Calle Atun 00983
Calle Austral 00979
Calle Ausubo 00983
Calle Avila 00983
Calle Azalea 00987
Calle Azucena
M1-M99 00985
N1-N99 00985
100-199 00987
400-599 00987
Calle B
A1-A99 00985
B1-B99 00985
C1-C99 00983
11827-11835 00983
Calle Bachiller 00987
Calle Barcelona 00983
Calle Barracuda 00983
Calle Bazar 00987
Calle Begonia
X1-X99 00985
2-98 00979
16-16 00979
300-599 00987
Calle Bernardo Garcia
N 00985
Calle Beso De Mar 00987
Calle Bilbao 00983
Calle Bonelli 00987
Calle Brazil 00987
Calle Brisa Del
Paraiso 00987
Calle Bromelia 00987
Calle C
C1-C99 00987
B1-B99 00985
C1-C99 00985
A1-A99 00987
B1-B99 00987
8B1-1-8B1-3 00983
8B2-2-8B2-2 00983
Calle Cacimar 00987
Calle Cadiz 00983
Calle Caguax 00987
Calle Calais 00982
Calle Calcita 00987
Calle Camarero 00987
Calle Camino Real 00987
Calle Campeche 00987
Calle Campestre 00987
Calle Campina 00987
Calle Canaria 00985
Calle Canario 00987
Calle Cancer 00979
Calle Caoba
G1-G99 00983
H1-H99 00983
I1-I99 00983
E1-E99 00983
F1-F99 00983
201-399 00987
Calle Capela 00979
Calle Capri 00982
Calle Capricornio 00979
Calle Casimiro Febres .. 00987
Calle Castellon 00983
Calle Castilla 00983
Calle Cataluna 00983
Calle Cedro 00983
Calle Ceiba 00983
Calle Celestial 00979
Calle Cemi 00987
Calle Centauro 00979
Calle Cerezo 00983
Calle Cerezos 00985
Calle Cerro Chico 00987
Calle Cerro Dona
Juana 00987
Calle Cerro La Santa ... 00987
Calle Cerro Maravilla ... 00987
Calle Cerro Morales 00987
Calle Cerro Penuelas ... 00987
Calle Cerro Pio 00987
Calle Cerro Punta 00987
Calle Cerro Taita 00987
Calle Cipres
C1-C99 00983
1-35 00985
37-99 00985
Calle Ciudad Real 00983
Calle Clavel
L1-L99 00985
300-399 00987
400-699 00987
Calle Clemente
Delgado 00985
Calle Clemente
Fernandez 00985
Calle Cofresi 00987
Calle Cojoba 00987
Calle Colaborador 00987
Calle Colombia 00987
Calle Colon 00985
Calle Cometa 00979
Calle Coqui Blanco 00987
Calle Coral 00987
Calle Cordoba 00987
Calle Cordova 00983
Calle Cosmos 00979
Calle Cotto Hernandez . 00985
Calle Crisostoma
Castro 00987
Calle Cuatro Ruedas ... 00983
Calle Cundeamor 00987
Calle D
C1-C99 00985
D1-D99 00985
C1-C99 00987
D1-D99 00987
8B2-1-8B2-99 00983
Calle Daguao 00987
Calle Dalia
N1-N99 00985
1-32 00979
15-15 00979
34-98 00979
100-199 00987
Calle Darsena 00987
Calle De Diego 00985
Calle Del Rio 00985
Calle Delgado 00985
Calle Delicias 00985
Calle Diamante 00987
Calle Diaz Way 00979
Calle Diego 00985
Calle Domingo Caceres
E 00985
Calle Don Carlos
Rodriguez 00987
Calle Don Glory 00987
Calle Don Jose Calvo .. 00987
Calle Dr C Fernandez .. 00985
Calle Dr Manuel
Martinez 00987
Calle Drako 00979
Calle Ducal 00982
Calle Dulce Sueno 00987
Calle E Vizcarrondo 00987
Calle East Rose 00987
Calle Eduardo
Kercado 00987
Calle El Aguila 00987
Calle El Palmar 00979
Calle El Palmar Sur 00979
Calle El Titan 00987
Calle Enrique Vazquez . 00982
Calle Eridano 00979
Calle Ernesto
Rodriguez 00987
Calle Escolastico Diaz .. 00987
Calle Escorpio 00979
Calle Esmeralda 00987
Calle Estados Unidos ... 00987
Calle Estrella 00979
Calle Estrella Del
Norte 00979
Calle Esturion 00983
Calle Eucalipto
O1-O99 00983
1-199 00987
Calle Eusebio
Gonzalez 00985
Calle F 00985
Calle Fabril 00987
Calle Farallon 00987
Calle Felix Rivera 00985
Calle Fenix 00979
Calle Feria 00987
Calle Fernandez
Juncos 00985
Calle Ferpier 00987
Calle Ferrol 00983
Calle Filadelfia 00987
Calle Firmamento 00979
Calle Flamboyan
B1-B99 00983
Y1-Y99 00983
AP1-AP99 00983
AZ1-AZ99 00983
100-199 00985
200-699 00987
201-299 00985
Calle Flor De Sierra 00987
Calle Florentino
Roman 00987
Calle Floridiano 00987
Calle Fraile 00987
Calle G 00985
Calle Galaxia 00979
Calle Galeon 00987
Calle Galgo Jr 00987
Calle Galleguito 00987
Calle Gardenia
P1-P99 00985
Q1-Q99 00985
1-99 00987
2-12 00979
11-33 00979
14-35 00979
35-99 00979
Calle Geminis 00979
Calle Generalife 00987
Calle Geranio 00987
Calle Gerona 00983
Calle Gibraltar
501-599 00985
1301-1399 00983
Calle Gijon 00985
Calle Gildita 00983
Calle Girona 00979
Calle Gladiola
N1-N99 00985
O1-O99 00985
1-99 00987
Calle Govich 00987
Calle Grace 00982
Calle Gralte 00987
Calle Granada
U1-U99 00985
G1-G99 00983
1-299 00985
1-299 00983
Calle Granadilla 00983
Calle Granito 00987
Calle Grave 00987
Calle Greda 00987
Calle Grimaldi 00982
Calle Grus 00979
Calle Guadalajara 00983
Calle Guajataca 00987
Calle Guama 00983
Calle Guamani 00987
Calle Guarionex 00987
Calle Guatemala 00987
Calle Guayacan 00987
Calle H 00985
Calle H Rodriguez 00985
Calle Hermanos
Rodriguez Ema 00979
Calle Hermanos
Ruppert 00987
Calle Hermogenes
Figueroa 00987
Calle Hernan Besosa ... 00982
Calle Higuero 00983
Calle Hnos Rodriguez
Ema 00979
Calle Honduras 00987
Calle Hortencia 00987
Calle Hucar
Q1-Q99 00983
R1-R99 00983
301-499 00987
Calle Hydra 00979
Calle I 00987
Calle Iglesias 00985
Calle Ignacio Arzuaga
E 00985
Calle Igneito 00987
Calle Imperial 00987
Calle Indones 00987
Calle Indus 00979
Calle Infante 00982
Calle Ingenio 00985
Calle Inocencio Cruz ... 00985
Calle Isla Verde 00983
Calle Islena 00987
Calle Israel 00987
Calle Israeli 00987
Calle Italia 00982
Calle J 00987
Calle Jacinta Lacens ... 00987
Calle Jacinto 00987
Calle Jade 00987
Calle Jaen 00983
Calle Jagua 00983
Calle Jamaica 00987
Calle Jazmin
R1-R99 00985
S1-S99 00985
400-499 00987
Calle Jazmin Del Mar .. 00987
Calle Jesus Allende 00987
Calle Jesus T Pinero ... 00987
Calle Jesus Velazquez . 00987
Calle Joaquina 00979
Calle Jobos 00983
Calle Jose S
Quinones 00985
Calle Jumacao 00987
Calle Jupiter 00979
Calle K 00987
Calle Kansas 00987
Calle Kelimar 00987
Calle Kelly 00982
Calle La Ceramica 00983
Calle La Paz 00985
Calle La Riviera 00982
Calle La Torre 00987
Calle La Torrecilla 00987
Calle Laja 00987
Calle Las Flores 00985
Calle Las Marias
C1-C99 00983
D1-D99 00983
M1-M99 00983
N1-N99 00983
B12-B99 00983
1001-1399 00985
Calle Las Rosas 00985
Calle Laurel
S1-S99 00983
T1-T99 00983
1-99 00985
501-599 00985
Calle Legamo 00987
Calle Leo 00979
Calle Leopoldo
Jimenez 00987
Calle Lerida 00983
Calle Libra 00979
Calle Lila 00987
Calle Lima 00987
Calle Lino De Paz 00987
Calle Lira 00979
Calle Lirio
1-9 00979
2-8 00979
100-211 00987
236-299 00987
Calle Lirios 00985
Calle Lluvia De Coral .. 00987
Calle Loma Ancha 00987
Calle Lomas Verdes 00987
Calle Lorencita 00983
Calle Los Alpes 00982
Calle Los Picachos 00987
Calle Lucero 00979
Calle Luis Felipe 00987
Calle Luis Vigo 00987
Calle Luna 00979
Calle Madrid 00983
Calle Madrilena 00987
Calle Magnolia 00985
Calle Malaga 00983
Calle Malagueta 00987
Calle Mallorca 00983
Calle Mango 00987
Calle Mango Final 00987
Calle Manuela Walker .. 00987
Calle Mar Amarillo 00979
Calle Mar Arabigo 00979
Calle Mar Baltico 00979
Calle Mar Caribe 00979
Calle Mar De Bering 00979
Calle Mar De China 00979
Calle Mar De Irlanda ... 00979
Calle Mar De Japon ... 00979
Calle Mar Del Coral 00979
Calle Mar Del Norte 00979
Calle Mar
Mediterraneo 00979
Calle Marbella
201-699 00985
1101-1599 00983
Calle Margarita 00985
Calle Marginal 00983
Calle Marginal
Villamar 00979
Calle Maria De La
Paz 00987
Calle Marlin 00983
Calle Marmol 00987
Calle Marquesa 00987
Calle Marte 00979
Calle Mediterraneo 00982
Calle Merida 00985
Calle Mexico 00987
Calle Milagros
Cabezas 00987
Calle Miosotis 00987

Street	ZIP
Calle Molinillo	00985
Calle Monaco	00982
Calle Monte Alegre	00987
Calle Monte Britton	00987
Calle Monte Guilarte	00987
Calle Monte Membrillo	00987
Calle Montebello	00987
Calle Montenegro	
P1-P99	00987
U1-U99	00987
N1-N99	00987
599-699	00982
Calle Morera	00983
Calle Mulato	00985
Calle Munoz Rivera N	00985
Calle Murcia	00983
Calle Naranjo	
AK1-AK99	00983
BD1-BD99	00983
500-599	00987
Calle Narciso Font E	00985
Calle Natividad Landrau	00987
Calle Navarra	00983
Calle Nepomusemo	00987
Calle Neptuno	00979
Calle Nicaragua	00987
Calle Nispero	00983
Calle Niza	00982
Calle Nogal	00983
Calle Oklahoma	00987
Calle Olmo	00987
Calle Onix	00987
Calle Opalo	00987
Calle Orion	00979
Calle Orocobix	00987
Calle Orquidea	
W1-W99	00985
100-199	00987
270-399	00987
Calle Ortegon	00983
Calle Pablo Gonzalez	00985
Calle Pablo Pizarro	00987
Calle Pablo Velazquez	00985
Calle Palma De Coco	00979
Calle Palma De Corozo	00979
Calle Palma De Maraca	00979
Calle Palma De Sierra	00979
Calle Palma De Sombrero	00979
Calle Palma Real	
1-99	00979
100-199	00985
Calle Palmera	00979
Calle Pandora	00987
Calle Parque	00985
Calle Parque Alegre	00983
Calle Parque Asturias	00983
Calle Parque Bolonia	00983
Calle Parque Borinquen	00983
Calle Parque Central	00983
Calle Parque Colon	00983
Calle Parque De La Alianza	00983
Calle Parque De La Fuente	00983
Calle Parque De La Luna	00983
Calle Parque De Las Flores	00983
Calle Parque De Las Palomas	00983
Calle Parque De Los Lirios	00983
Calle Parque De Los Recuerdo	00983
Calle Parque Del Condado	00983
Calle Parque Del Tesoro	00983
Calle Parque Florido	00983
Calle Parque Hermoso	00983
Calle Parque Maria Luisa	00983
Calle Parque Munoz Rivera	00983
Calle Parque Napoleon	00983
Calle Parque Real	00983
Calle Parque Rosaleda	00983
Calle Parque San Jose	00983
Calle Parquesito	00985
Calle Paseo Real	00987
Calle Patty	00983
Calle Pedro Arzuaga E	00985
Calle Pegaso	00979
Calle Perez Villegas	00985
Calle Perla Fina	00987
Calle Perseo	00979
Calle Peru	00987
Calle Petunia	
U1-U99	00985
394-402	00987
Calle Pico Del Este	00987
Calle Pino	00983
Calle Pinos	00985
Calle Pinto	00987
Calle Pisa Flores	00987
Calle Piscis	00979
Calle Plantio	00987
Calle Pomarrosa	00983
Calle Pontevedra	00983
Calle Portugal	00983
Calle Pradera	00987
Calle Princesa	00982
Calle Principal	00985
Calle Principe	00982
Calle Progreso	00985
Calle Providencia	00987
Calle Quebrada	00985
Calle Quinones	00985
Calle Quito	00987
Calle Ramada	00987
Calle Ramon Negron	00985
Calle Ramon Quinones	00983
Calle Ramos Rodriguez	00985
Calle Reina De Las Flores	00987
Calle Republica Dominica	00987
Calle Rev Haydee Castro	00985
Calle Rialto	00982
Calle Ribera Enamorada	00987
Calle Rigel	00979
Calle Rio Danubio	00982
Calle Rivera	00985
Calle Robalo	00983
Calle Roberto Alberty Torre	00987
Calle Roble	00987
Calle Robles	
X1-X99	00983
Y1-Y99	00983
B1-B99	00983
1-199	00985
120-140	00983
Calle Roca	00987
Calle Rodriguez Ema	00983
Calle Rodriguez Oquendo	00985
Calle Roman Rivera	00987
Calle Rosa	
V1-V99	00985
W1-W99	00985
1-30	00979
31-31	00979
32-98	00979
36-36	00979
200-399	00987
Calle Rosa Imperial	00987
Calle Rosales	00983
Calle Rosario	00985
Calle Rosarito	00983
Calle Sabalo	00983
Calle Sagitario	00979
Calle Salvador Brau E	00985
Calle San Carlos	00982
Calle San Damian	00982
Calle San Fernando	00982
Calle San Jose	00985
Calle San Luis	00987
Calle Sanchez Rohena	00985
Calle Santa Maria	00982
Calle Sara	00982
Calle Saturnina	00987
Calle Sauce	00987
Calle Segovia	00983
Calle Segundo Delgado	00987
Calle Selenita	00987
Calle Serpentina	00987
Calle Sevilla	00983
Calle Silvina	00987
Calle Sirio	00979
Calle Sol	00979
Calle Sonajero	00987
Calle South Main	00983
Calle Tartak	00979
Calle Tauro	00979
Calle Tegucigalpa	00987
Calle Teruel	00983
Calle The Kid	00987
Calle Tiburcio Berty	00987
Calle Ticalito	00987
Calle Tikal	00987
Calle Tincy	00987
Calle Toledo	00985
Calle Tomas De Jesus	00987
Calle Tomasa Ortiz	00987
Calle Tony Pizarro	00983
Calle Torrecilla	00987
Calle Torremolino	00985
Calle Trinitaria	
K1-K99	00985
L1-L99	00985
N1-N99	00985
P1-P99	00985
100-799	00987
248-299	00987
Calle Trinity	00982
Calle Tulipan	
AC1-AC99	00983
BA1-BA99	00983
200-299	00987
Calle U	00983
Calle Ulises Ortiz	00985
Calle Urano	00979
Calle Urayoan	00987
Calle Uruguay	00987
Calle V Villegas	00987
Calle Valencia	00983
Calle Valladolid	00983
Calle Venus	00979
Calle Veracruz	00987
Calle Vereda	00987
Calle Vergel	00987
Calle Vicente Bultron	00985
Calle Victor Salaman	00987
Calle Victoria	00985
Calle Violeta	
Y1-Y99	00985
Z1-Z99	00985
W1-W99	00985
1-99	00987
9-23	00979
15-21	00979
34-900	00982
500-699	00985
902-4000	00982
Calle Virgo	00979
Calle West Rose	00987
Calle Wiso G	00987
Calle Yagrumo	00983
Calle Yaurel	00987
Calle Ycaro	00987
Calle Yuisa	00987
Calle Yunquesito	00987
Calle Zafiro	00987
Calle Zamora	00983
Calle Zaragoza	00983
Calle Zinnia	00987
Camino Kercado	00987
Camino La Loma	00987
Camino Monico Rivera	00987
Campo Rico Shopp Ctr	00982
Cape Farewell	00979
Cape Kennedy	00979
Cape Race	00979
Cape Sable	00979
Cape Yubi	00979
Carolina Comercial Pk	00987
Carolina Housing	00987
Carr 187	00979
Carr 190	
D1-D99	00982
D5A-D5B	00982
33A-33Z	00983
33CC-39CC	00983
33FF-40FF	00983
33KK-33KK	00983
33NN-33NN	00983
33CCC-33CCC	00983
35A-35Z	00983
38A-38Z	00983
39A-39Z	00983
39GG-40GG	00983
33JJ-33JJ	00983
33EE-40EE	00983
33HH-40HH	00983
36A-36Z	00983
37A-37Z	00983
40II-40II	00983
34B-34H	00983
35BB-41BB	00983
39AA-40AA	00983
44A-44L	00983
40A-40Z	00983
1-71	00983
73-499	00983
100-298	00987
240-3198	00983
700-799	00982
4000-5099	00979
4130-4199	00983
20243-20243	00983
30085-30087	00982
40110-40212	00983
Carr 3	00987
Carr 848	00987
Carr 853	00987
Carr 857	00987
Carr 860	00987
Carr 874	
A1-A99	00985
1-99	00985
153-999	00985
301-799	00985
803-805	00987
810-820	00987
1501-1785	00985
Carr 8860	00987
Carr 887	00987
Chalets De San Fernando	00987
Club Costa Marina 1	00983
Club Costa Marina 2	00983
Cond Andalucia	00987
Cond Balcones De Monte Real	00987
Cond Garden Vw	00985
Cond Golden Tower	00983
Cond Jard De San Fernando	00987
Cond Los Naranjales	00985
Cond Lucerna	00983
Cond Metromonte	00987
Cond Parq Juliana	00987
Cond Pontezuela	00983
Cond Rio Vis	00987
Cond San Fernando Vlg	00987
Cond Torrecillas	00983
Cond Veredas Del Rio	00987
Cond Vistamar Princess	00983
Country Club Shopp Plz	00982
Ctro Comercial Borinquen	00982
Fontana Twrs	00982
Marginal Baldorioty	00979
Marginal Biascochea	00979
Marginal Campo Rico	00985
Marginal Celestial	00979
Marginal Country Clb	00982
Marginal Del Parque	00987
Marginal Sanchez Castano	00985
Medina Shopp Ctr	00982
Palacios Del Escorial	00987
Parq Los Modelos	00982
Parque Boliviano	00983
Res Catanito Gdns	00985
Res El Coral	00985
Res El Faro	00985
Res Felipe S Osorio	00985
Res Las Esmeraldas	00985
Res Loma Alta	00987
Res Los Mirtos	00987
Res Sabana Abajo	00982
Res Santa Catalina	00987
Res Torres De Sabana	00983
Roberto Clemente Hsing	00987
Sect El Pajuil	00983
Sect La 44	00982
Vereda Del Bosque	00987
Vereda Del Lago	00987
Vereda Del Parque	00987
Vereda Del Prado	00987
Via 1	00983
Via 10	00983
Via 11	00983
Via 12	00983
Via 13	00983
Via 13a	00983
Via 14	00983
Via 15	00983
Via 16	00983
Via 17	00983
Via 18	00983
Via 19	00983
Via 2	00983
Via 20	00983
Via 21	00983
Via 22	00983
Via 23	00983
Via 24	00983
Via 25	00983
Via 26	00983
Via 27	00983
Via 28	00983
Via 29	00983
Via 3	00983
Via 30	00983
Via 31	00983
Via 32	00983
Via 33	00983
Via 34	00983
Via 35	00983
Via 36	00983
Via 37	00983
Via 38	00983
Via 39	00983
Via 4	00983
Via 40	00983
Via 41	00983
Via 42	00983
Via 43	00983
Via 44	00983
Via 45	00983
Via 46	00983
Via 47	00983
Via 48	00983
Via 49	00983
Via 5	00983
Via 50	00983
Via 51	00983
Via 52	00983
Via 53	00983
Via 54	00983
Via 55	00983
Via 56	00983
Via 57	00983
Via 58	00983
Via 59	00983
Via 6	00983
Via 60	00983
Via 61	00983
Via 62	00983
Via 63	00983
Via 64	00983
Via 65	00983
Via 66	00983
Via 67	00983
Via 68	00983
Via 7	00983
Via 8	00983
Via 9	00983
Via Adelina	00983
Via Angelica	00983
Via Blanca	00983
Via Caterina	00983
Via Cecilia	00983
Via Diana	00983
Via Donatella	00983
Via Elena	00983
Via Emilia	00983
Via Fabiana	00983
Via Georgina	00983
Via Isabel	00983
Via Josefina	00983
Via Leticia	00983
Via Lourdes	00983
Via Lucia	00983
Via Myrta	00983
Victoria Industrial Park	00987
Villas El Diamantino	00987

CATANO PR

General Delivery 00963

POST OFFICE BOXES MAIN OFFICE STATIONS AND BRANCHES

Box No.s
All PO Boxes 00963

NAMED STREETS

All Street Addresses 00962

CAYEY PR

General Delivery 00737

POST OFFICE BOXES MAIN OFFICE STATIONS AND BRANCHES

Box No.s
All PO Boxes 00737

HIGHWAY CONTRACTS

43, 44, 45, 71, 73, 74 00736

NAMED STREETS

All Street Addresses 00736

GUAYAMA PR

General Delivery 00785

POST OFFICE BOXES MAIN OFFICE STATIONS AND BRANCHES

Box No.s
All PO Boxes 00785

RURAL ROUTES

01, 02 00784

HIGHWAY CONTRACTS

02 00784

NAMED STREETS

All Street Addresses 00784

GUAYNABO PR

General Delivery 00970

POST OFFICE BOXES MAIN OFFICE STATIONS AND BRANCHES

Box No.s
All PO Boxes 00970

HIGHWAY CONTRACTS

01, 02, 03, 04, 05, 06 00971

NAMED STREETS

Street	ZIP
Ave Wall	00966
Ave Alejandrino	00969
Ave Apolo	00969
Ave Arbolote	00969
Ave B	00969
Ave E Ramos Antonini	00965
Ave Esmeralda	00969
Ave Fd Roosevelt	00968
Ave Las Colinas	00969
Ave Las Cumbres	00969
Ave Lincoln	00969
Ave Lopategui	00969
Ave Los Filtros	00971
Ave Luis Vigoreaux	00966
Ave Marginal Kennedy	00968
Ave Mexico	00969
Ave Ortegon	00966
Ave Palma Real	00969
Ave Ponce De Leon	00965
Ave Ramirez De Arellano	00966
Ave San Ignacio	00969
Ave San Patricio	00968
Ave Santa Ana	
1-99	00969
100-146	00971
101-399	00969
150-398	00969
13-1-13-99	00969
14-1-14-99	00969
16-1-16-99	00969
4-1-4-99	00969
5-1-5-99	00969
Ave Victor Braeger	00966
Ave Washington	00969
Baldwin Walk	00969
Calle E	
G1-G99	00969
H1-H99	00969

E1-E6 00966
F1-F6 00966
19-51 00965
53-53 00965
300-499 00969
Calle N 00965
Calle Un
H1-H99 00966
I1-I99 00966
J1A-J1A 00966
P1-P99 00966
Q1-Q99 00966
J14-J14 00966
L8-L14 00966
M1-M2 00966
N2-N3 00966
O1-O6 00966
1-99 00966
2-4 00965
7-11 00971
7-9 00965
13-59 00971
400-499 00969
Calle 1
D1-D99 00966
Calle 1
F1-F99 00966
H1-H99 00966
P1-P99 00966
Q1-Q99 00969
R1-R99 00969
W1-W99 00969
E1-E99 00969
C1-C99 00966
G1-G99 00966
G1-G99 00969
B1-B99 00969
E1-E13 00966
B1-B22 00966
H1-H8 00966
B23-B99 00966
E10-E18 00966
A1-A20 00969
J4-J20 00966
A1-A13 00969
J1-J99 00966
1-16 00966
1-1 00968
1-13 00968
2-18 00968
14-23 00966
28-28 00969
101-110 00965
600-699 00966
2070-2099 00966
1-1-1-99 00969
2-1-2-99 00969
3-1-3-6 00969
Calle 10
F1-F99 00966
G1-G99 00966
K1-K99 00969
L1-L99 00969
40-40 00969
10-1-10-99 00969
5-32-5-46 00969
Calle 10a 00969
Calle 10b 00969
Calle 11
G1-G99 00966
B1-B99 00969
F1-F99 00969
M1-M99 00969
L9-L11 00969
10-1-10-99 00969
11-1-11-99 00969
Calle 12 00969
Calle 13 00969
Calle 14 00969
Calle 15 00969
Calle 16 00969
Calle 17 00969
Calle 18 00969
Calle 19 00969
Calle 1a 00969
Calle 2
B1-B99 00966
J1-J99 00969
IA1-IA99 00969
S1-S99 00969
T1-T99 00969
U1-U99 00969
D1-D99 00969
E1-E99 00969
H1-H99 00966
I1-I99 00966
A1-A9 00966
A39-A99 00966
B1-B15 00969
C1-C9 00969
B15-B26 00969
C1-C16 00969
A21-A28 00969
C16A-C16B 00969
126A-126B 00969
1-5063 00966
1-32 00966
1-17 00968
118-140 00965
16-1-16-99 00969
2-1-2-99 00969
3-1-3-99 00969
6-1-6-99 00969
7-1-7-99 00969
Calle 20 00969
Calle 21 00969
Calle 22 00969
Calle 23 00969
Calle 25 00969
Calle 27 00969
Calle 2a 00969
Calle 3
C1-C99 00966
D1-D99 00966
I1-I99 00966
DI1-DI99 00966
T1-T99 00969
V1-V99 00969
A1-A99 00969
B1-B99 00969
D1-D5 00969
C9-C16 00969
C10-C16 00969
D4-D14 00969
1-13 00966
8-13 00966
80-99 00966
111-117 00965
11-1-11-99 00969
6-1-6-99 00969
Calle 4
H1-H99 00966
A1-A99 00966
C1-C99 00966
D1-D99 00966
D1-D99 00969
E1-E99 00969
P1-P99 00969
Q1-Q99 00969
B1-B99 00969
H1-H99 00969
C1-C99 00969
18A-18B 00966
A1-A99 00969
B1-B99 00966
1-99 00966
100-199 00966
16-1-16-99 00969
17-1-17-99 00969
Calle 5
E1-E99 00969
H1-H99 00969
O1-O99 00969
R1-R99 00969
S1-S99 00969
U1-U99 00969
W1-W99 00969
D1-D99 00966
D1-D9 00966
D7-D16 00966
F1-F6 00966
A19-A99 00969
B10-B99 00969
A1-A18 00969
B1-B9 00969
F4-F13 00969
E1-E9 00966
J1-J2 00966
C9-C17 00966
G1-G3 00966
H25-H48 00966
I1-I18 00966
DI1-DI44 00966
B13-B24 00966
18-1-18-99 00969
Calle 5a 00969
Calle 6
B1-B99 00966
F1-F99 00966
K1-K99 00966
L1-L99 00966
G1-G99 00966
A1-A99 00966
I1-I99 00969
N1-N99 00969
U1-U99 00969
A1-A99 00969
B1-B99 00969
D1-D99 00966
H1-H99 00966
Calle 6a 00966
Calle 7
C1-C99 00966
D1-D99 00966
L1-L99 00966
G1-G99 00966
J1-J99 00966
G1-G99 00969
H1-H99 00969
A1-A99 00969
190-207 00968
15-1-15-99 00969
16-1-16-99 00969
4-1-4-99 00969
Calle 8
D1-D99 00966
N1-N99 00966
P1-P99 00966
F1-F99 00966
I1-I99 00969
J1-J99 00969
L1-L99 00969
A1-A99 00969
B1-B99 00969
E1-E20 00966
G4-G28 00966
E1-E18 00966
G3-G99 00966
45-47 00966
49-99 00966
15-1-15-99 00969
16-1-16-99 00969
17-1-17-99 00969
Calle 9
M1-M99 00966
N1-N99 00966
E1-E99 00966
C1-C99 00966
D1-D99 00966
G1-G99 00969
H1-H99 00969
F3-F5 00966
F1-F14 00966
11-1-11-99 00969
5-1-5-99 00969
Calle A
M1-M99 00969
N1-N99 00969
G1-G99 00969
M1A-M1A 00969
A1-A99 00969
A1-A11 00969
A1-A20 00966
C9-C99 00966
C1-C8 00966
A1-A40 00966
A48-A54 00966
A42-A46 00966
A13-A99 00966
E1-E12 00969
22INT-80INT 00965
1-81 00965
44-44 00966
49-49 00966
99-99 00969
100-200 00968
201-214 00965
Calle Aberdeen 00969
Calle Acapulco 00966
Calle Acasia 00968
Calle Acerina
1-22 00965
2-39 00969
24-38 00965
41-51 00969
Calle Acropolis 00969
Calle Acuarela 00969
Calle Adams 00969
Calle Adonidia 00969
Calle Adonis 00969
Calle Akron 00969
Calle Alabama 00969
Calle Alameda
A1-A99 00966
B1-B99 00966
1-99 00969
Calle Alaska 00969
Calle Alba 00969
Calle Alborada 00969
Calle Aleli 00969
Calle Alfonso Xiii 00969
Calle Alheli 00969
Calle Alkazar 00966
Calle Almendro
N1-N99 00969
75-196 00971
Calle Alpierre 00969
Calle Amapola 00969
Calle Amarilis 00968
Calle Amatista
1-2099 00969
92-199 00968
Calle Ambar 00969
Calle Amelia 00968
Calle Anamu 00969
Calle Antioquia 00969
Calle Antonio Barcelo 00965
Calle Apolo 00965
Calle Aquamarina 00969
Calle Arca De Noe 00969
Calle Arcadia 00969
Calle Areca 00969
Calle Argentina
I1-I99 00969
J1-J99 00969
M1-M99 00969
A1-A99 00966
B1-B99 00966
D1-D99 00966
E1-E99 00969
A1-A18 00969
Calle Arizona 00969
Calle Arpegio 00969
Calle Artemisa 00969
Calle Arturo R Mujica 00966
Calle Astarte 00969
Calle Asturias 00966
Calle Atalaya 00966
Calle Atenas 00969
Calle Aurora 00965
Calle Azahar 00969
Calle Azalea 00969
Calle Azucena 00969
Calle B
B1-B99 00966
C1-C99 00966
M1-M99 00966
H1-H99 00969
A1-A99 00966
B1-B99 00966
B7-B11 00966
B1-B5 00966
B1-B99 00966
B1-B58 00969
B35A-B35B 00969
BA-BC 00969
1-99 00965
100-172 00968
174-176 00968
178-250 00968
230-253 00965
Calle Balcones De Sevilla 00966
Calle Baldomar 00969
Calle Baldorioty
1-63 00969
2-6 00965
8-16 00965
18-48 00965
Calle Bamboo Dr 00966
Calle Barbosa 00969
Calle Barcelona 00966
Calle Basilio Catala 00971
Calle Beatriz 00968
Calle Begonia 00969
Calle Belen 00968
Calle Benitez 00969
Calle Betances
5-17 00969
19-31 00969
33-99 00969
52-52 00971
Calle Betania 00969
Calle Bilbao 00969
Calle Bizmarkia 00969
Calle Blue Hl 00966
Calle Boada 00965
Calle Bolivar Pagan 00965
Calle Bolivia 00969
Calle Borinquen 00965
Calle Brazil
H1-H99 00969
C1-C99 00966
D1-D99 00966
D10A-D10A 00966
A1-A99 00969
B8-B99 00966
50-50 00966
Calle Brillante 00969
Calle Brisaida 00969
Calle Bromelia 00969
Calle Bucare
M1-M99 00969
H1-H99 00968
I1-I99 00968
J1-J99 00968
Y2-Y20 00969
Calle Buchanan 00966
Calle Buen Samaritano 00966
Calle C
D1-D99 00966
N1-N99 00969
O1-O99 00969
C1A-C1A 00966
E1-E99 00966
C5-C8 00966
D1-D6 00966
181A-181A 00966
C1-C6 00966
C1-C99 00969
1-10 00965
12-98 00965
112-117 00969
125-125 00968
215-229 00965
300-500 00968
455-467 00969
469-471 00969
473-475 00969
Calle C Martinez 00969
Calle Calabura 00969
Calle California 00969
Calle Calistemon 00966
Calle Camelia 00969
Calle Campo Bello 00969
Calle Canales 00969
Calle Cancel 00969
Calle Cancio 00969
Calle Caoba 00966
Calle Capri 00966
Calle Carazo
1-144 00969
146-180 00969
155-155 00971
Calle Caribe 00965
Calle Carlos I 00969
Calle Carvajal 00969
Calle Cascada 00969
Calle Castana 00968
Calle Cecilio Urbina 00969
Calle Cedro 00968
Calle Cereipo 00969
Calle Cerezo
1-99 00968
52-74 00971
Calle Cerrillos 00969
Calle Chalet De La Reina 00966
Calle Chile 00966
Calle Church Hl 00966
Calle Cipres 00966
Calle Claudia 00968
Calle Cleveland 00969
Calle Cloto 00969
Calle Club Dr 00966
Calle Coco Plumosa 00969
Calle Cola De Pescado 00969
Calle Cola De Zorro 00969
Calle Coll Y Toste 00965
Calle Collores 00969
Calle Colombia 00966
Calle Colorado 00969
Calle Colton 00969
Calle Condor 00969
Calle Coral
B1-B99 00968
C1-C99 00968
1-99 00965
Calle Corcega 00966
Calle Cordoba 00966
Calle Corta 00966
Calle Cortijo Alto 00966
Calle Cortijo Bajo 00966
Calle Crisalida 00969
Calle Cristalina 00969
Calle Crosandra 00969
Calle Cubitas 00969
Calle Cyca 00969
Calle D
D1-D99 00966
R1-R99 00969
B1-B99 00969
C1-C99 00969
E1-E99 00969
F1-F99 00969
G1-G99 00969
H1-H99 00969
R1A-R2A 00969
A20-A99 00966
A1-A19 00969
6INT-6INT 00965
2-4 00965
2-6 00966
6-21 00965
23-25 00965
Calle Dalia 00969
Calle Delfos 00969
Calle Delicias 00966
Calle Desembarcadero 00965
Calle Diamante
1-20 00969
7-70 00968
22-22 00969
Calle Diana 00968
Calle Diaz Navarro
1-19 00965
3-6 00969
8-28 00969
21-49 00965
Calle Diego Vega 00965
Calle Dildo 00969
Calle Domenech 00969
Calle Dora Soler 00969
Calle Dr Ramos Mimoso 00966
Calle Dr Toro 00966
Calle Duque De Kent 00969
Calle Duque Windsor 00969
Calle Durazno 00968
Calle E Int 00965
Calle Ebano 00968
Calle Ecuador 00969
Calle El Torito 00969
Calle El Vigia 00969
Calle El Yunque 00969
Calle Elemi 00969
Calle Emajagua 00969
Calle Emilia 00966
Calle Emiliano Chinea 00971
Calle Emma 00968
Calle Enrique Viii 00969
Calle Ensenada 00969
Calle Escarlata 00969
Calle Esmeralda
1-12 00965
7-22 00969
14-98 00965
24-24 00969
37-50 00968
Calle Espana
B1-B99 00966
D1-D99 00966
C1-C99 00969
D1-D99 00969
F1-F99 00969
Calle Esparta 00969
Calle Esperanza 00966
Calle Esteves 00969
Calle Eucalipto 00968
Calle Eugene 00966
Calle F
J1-J99 00966
H1-H99 00966
A1-A99 00969
51A-51A 00965
1-10 00969
25-51 00966
1000-1199 00969
Calle Fagot 00969
Calle Falcon 00969
Calle Febe 00969
Calle Febles 00969
Calle Felipe I 00969
Calle Fernando I 00969
Calle Filipo Di Plana 00966
Calle Flamboyan
N1-N99 00969
O1-O99 00969
A1-A99 00966
5A-5Z 00966
1-99 00966
Calle Florencia 00966
Calle Florida 00969
Calle Fontana 00971
Calle Forest Hl 00966
Calle Frances 00968
Calle Francia 00966
Calle Fray Angelico 00969
Calle Fray Geronimo 00969
Calle Fray Inigo 00969
Calle Fresno 00968
Calle G
1-16 00965
2-8 00966
10-44 00966
1100-1199 00969
Calle Garcia 00969
Calle Garden Mdw 00966
Calle Gardenia 00965
Calle Garfield 00969
Calle Gea 00969
Calle Genova 00966
Calle Geronimo Sevilla 00966
Calle Girasol 00969
Calle Gladiola 00969
Calle Gloxinia 00969
Calle Gonzalez Giusti 00968
Calle Granada 00966
Calle Grant 00969
Calle Green Hl & Vly 00966
Calle Guacima 00969
Calle Guadalupe 00969
Calle Guayabo 00971
Calle Guayacan 00966
Calle Guilarte 00969
Calle Guillermo Saldana 00965

Calle H
H1-H99 00966
H21A-H21Z 00966
H28B-H28B 00966
1-99 00965
Calle Hamilton 00969
Calle Harding 00969
Calle Harrison 00969
Calle Hastings 00966
Calle Hercules 00969
Calle Hermandad 00965
Calle Hermosilla 00969
Calle Hiedra 00969
Calle Hill Dr 00966
Calle Homero 00969
Calle Honduras 00969
Calle Hucar 00969
Calle Humacao 00969
Calle I
A1-A99 00969
C1-C99 00969
D1-D99 00969
I1-I99 00966
B11-B11 00969
B5-B9 00969
1-99 00965
Calle Ibiza 00966
Calle Iglesia 00966
Calle Irun 00966
Calle Isabel La
Catolica 00969
Calle Itaca 00969
Calle J 00966
Calle Jacinto Galib 00968
Calle Jackson 00969
Calle Jade 00968
Calle Jaguas 00969
Calle Jaime Rodriguez 00969
Calle Jardin 00966
Calle Jazmin 00969
Calle Jefferson 00969
Calle Jerez 00966
Calle Jerusalem 00965
Calle Jobos 00971
Calle Jose C Barbosa 00965
Calle Jose De Diego
36INT-64INT 00965
44A-44Z 00965
1-85 00965
8-12 00969
14-19 00969
87-99 00965
Calle Jose J Acosta 00965
Calle Jose Julian
Acosta 00969
Calle Jose Lopez 00965
Calle Juan C Borbon 00969
Calle Juan H Lopez 00965
Calle Juan Martinez 00971
Calle Juan Ramos 00969
Calle Juan Roman 00965
Calle Juancho Lopez 00965
Calle K
K1-K99 00966
K1A-K1B 00966
2-3 00965
1100-1199 00969
Calle L
L1-L1 00966
G1-G7 00966
L3-L17 00966
L19-L21 00966
B0-B0 00969
1-9 00966
1-13 00965
1000-1199 00969
Calle La Caridad 00966
Calle La Fe 00966
Calle La Gaviota 00969
Calle La Marquesa 00969
Calle La Santa 00969
Calle La Tortola 00969
Calle Lady Palm 00969
Calle Laredo 00969
Calle Las Aguilas 00969
Calle Las Alondras 00969
Calle Las Flores
E1-E99 00969
H1-H99 00969
I1-I99 00969
1-299 00966
Calle Las Garzas 00969
Calle Las Golondrinas 00969
Calle Las Marias 00966
Calle Las Mesas 00969
Calle Las Palmas 00965
Calle Las Palomas 00969
Calle Laurel 00969
Calle Lerna 00969
Calle Lila 00969
Calle Lima 00969
Calle Limonero 00971
Calle Lirio 00969
Calle Loma Alta 00966
Calle Los Frailes 00969
Calle Los Gavilanes 00969
Calle Los Llanos 00966
Calle Los Mirlos 00969
Calle Los Picachos 00969
Calle Los Prados 00969
Calle Los Robles 00966
Calle Luhn 00966
Calle Luisita 00969
Calle M
E1-E99 00969
M2-M8 00966
1-6 00965
1-27 00969
1000-1199 00969
Calle M Champanat 00969
Calle M Rivera Ferrer 00968
Calle Madison 00969
Calle Madrid
G1-G99 00969
H1-H99 00969
18-1-18-99 00966
2-1-2-99 00966
3-1-3-99 00966
5-1-5-99 00966
Calle Maga 00969
Calle Main 00969
Calle Malaga 00966
Calle Malaya 00969
Calle Mango 00971
Calle Manuel Ocasio 00966
Calle Margarita 00969
Calle Marginal
K1-K99 00969
B1-B99 00969
A1-A18 00966
A1-A2 00969
1-10 00965
100-130 00969
Calle Marginal 177 00969
Calle Maritima 00965
Calle Martinez Nadal 00965
Calle Matienzo Cintron 00965
Calle Mayaguez 00969
Calle Mckinley 00969
Calle Meadow Ln 00966
Calle Melaleuca 00969
Calle Mercurio 00969
Calle Mexico 00969
Calle Milan 00966
Calle Milan Padro 00965
Calle Mileto 00969
Calle Minerva 00969
Calle Miramonte
E1-E99 00966
IA1-IA99 00966
B1-B99 00966
C1-C99 00966
NA1-NA99 00966
MA1-MA99 00966
1-99 00966
Calle Monroe 00969
Calle Monserrate
Colon 00965
Calle Monte Del
Estado 00969
Calle Monte Rey 00969
Calle Montebello 00966
Calle Montellano 00969
Calle Mora 00968
Calle Mt Pierre 00969
Calle Munet Ct 00968
Calle Munoz Rivera
1-15 00969
1-16 00965
17-25 00969
18-22 00965
Calle Napoles 00966
Calle Naranjo 00971
Calle Nebraska 00969
Calle Neptuno 00969
Calle Nevada 00969
Calle Nogal
C1-C99 00968
G1-G99 00968
F1-F99 00968
I1-I99 00968
A1-A99 00968
B2-B2 00968
B1-B1 00968
1-81 00968
87-1999 00968
125-199 00969
Calle Noruega 00969
Calle Nueva
E1-E99 00969
F1-F99 00969
1-10 00966
Calle Olimpo 00969
Calle Onfala 00969
Calle Onix 00969
Calle Opalo 00969
Calle Oreste Sevilla 00966
Calle Orfeo 00969
Calle Orquidea
1-1 00969
1-4 00966
Calle Oviedo 00966
Calle P
1-99 00965
1000-1099 00969
Calle Pajuil 00971
Calle Palm Cir 00968
Calle Palma De Coco 00969
Calle Palma De
Corozo 00969
Calle Palma De
Mariposa 00969
Calle Palma Real
R1-R99 00969
Q1-Q99 00969
S1-S99 00969
1-99 00966
Calle Palma Sola 00966
Calle Palos Grandes 00966
Calle Parentesis 00969
Calle Park Ln 00966
Calle Parkside 1 00968
Calle Parkside 2 00968
Calle Parkside 3 00968
Calle Parkside 4 00968
Calle Parkside 5 00968
Calle Parkside 6 00968
Calle Parnaso 00969
Calle Parque 00965
Calle Pascua 00969
Calle Paseo De La
Reina 00969
Calle Paseo Del
Parque 00966
Calle Pastora 00966
Calle Patio Hl 00966
Calle Patricia 00966
Calle Pedregal 00971
Calle Pedro V
Pedrosa 00966
Calle Pentagrama 00969
Calle Perla 00969
Calle Petronita Alamo
Solis 00966
Calle Phoenix 00969
Calle Pichipen 00968
Calle Pino 00969
Calle Pino Del Rio 00966
Calle Playera 00969
Calle Pomarrosa 00969
Calle Ponce 00969
Calle Princesa Ana 00969
Calle Princesa Cristina 00969
Calle Princesa Diana 00969
Calle Princesa
Margarita 00969
Calle Principal
1-21 00966
1-15 00965
1-17 00969
Calle Principe Alberto 00969
Calle Principe Andres 00969
Calle Principe Carlos 00969
Calle Principe De
Asturias 00969
Calle Principe De
Gales 00969
Calle Principe Eduardo 00969
Calle Principe
Guillermo 00969
Calle Principe Raniero 00969
Calle Progreso 00966
Calle Quenepa 00971
Calle Quimera 00969
Calle Rafael
Hernandez 00969
Calle Ramon Cosme 00971
Calle Ramon Murga 00971
Calle Ramos Antonini 00965
Calle Raphis 00969
Calle Rdgo De Triana 00965
Calle Regina Medina 00969
Calle Reina Alexandra 00969
Calle Reina Ana 00969
Calle Reina Beatriz 00969
Calle Reina Carlota 00969
Calle Reina Carolina 00969
Calle Reina Catalina 00969
Calle Reina Cristina 00969
Calle Reina De Las
Flores
S1-S99 00969
T1-T99 00969
1-99 00966
Calle Reina Eugenia 00969
Calle Reina Isabel 00969
Calle Reina Isabel I 00969
Calle Reina Margarita 00969
Calle Reina Maria 00969
Calle Reina Maria
Antonieta 00969
Calle Reina Sofia 00969
Calle Reina Victoria 00969
Calle Reparto Pinero 00969
Calle Rey Arturo 00969
Calle Rey Carlos 00969
Calle Rey Constantino 00969
Calle Rey Eduardo 00969
Calle Rey Federico 00969
Calle Rey Felipe 00969
Calle Rey Fernando 00969
Calle Rey Francisco 00969
Calle Rey Gustavo 00969
Calle Rey Jorge 00969
Calle Rey Jorge V 00969
Calle Rey Luis 00969
Calle Rey Ricardo 00969
Calle Ridgewood 00966
Calle Riverside 00971
Calle Roberto Arana 00969
Calle Roble 00966
Calle Roble Blanco 00969
Calle Roebellini 00969
Calle Roma 00966
Calle Romerillo 00966
Calle Rosa 00969
Calle Rosalina
Martinez 00965
Calle Rubi
A1-A99 00969
B1-B99 00969
C1-C99 00969
D1-D99 00969
1-99 00965
100-199 00968
Calle Rufino
Rodriguez 00969
Calle Ruisenor 00969
Calle Ruiz Belvis 00965
Calle Sabila 00969
Calle Salamanca 00966
Calle Salvia 00969
Calle San Antonio 00969
Calle San Jacinto 00969
Calle San Jose 00969
Calle San Martin 00968
Calle San Miguel 00966
Calle San Sebastian 00966
Calle Sandalo 00969
Calle Santa Rosa De
Lima 00965
Calle Santander 00966
Calle Santiago Iglesias 00965
Calle Saturno 00969
Calle Sauco 00969
Calle Segovia 00966
Calle Sendero 00965
Calle Serrania 00966
Calle Sevilla 00966
Calle Sevilla Biltmore 00966
Calle Sicilia 00966
Calle Sirce 00969
Calle Sonata 00969
Calle Sun Vly 00966
Calle Sunset 00966
Calle Tabonuco 00968
Calle Taina 00969
Calle Tamarindo 00968
Calle Tanagra 00969
Calle Tapia 00969
Calle Taylor 00969
Calle Tejas 00969
Calle Teresa 00969
Calle Tintillo 00966
Calle Toledo 00966
Calle Topacio
A1-A99 00968
B1-B99 00968
D1-D99 00968
2000-2113 00969
2114-2199 00969
Calle Topaz 00969
Calle Tornasol 00969
Calle Torrecillas 00969
Calle Tropical 00969
Calle Tulipan 00969
Calle Turey 00969
Calle Turquesa
100-299 00968
2000-2098 00969
2100-2109 00969
2110-2199 00969
Calle Ucar 00969
Calle Valencia 00966
Calle Vanda 00966
Calle Venecia 00966
Calle Venus 00969
Calle Veracruz 00969
Calle Viajera 00969
Calle Villa Alta 00969
Calle Villa Flores 00969
Calle Villa Iris 00969
Calle Villa Rita 00969
Calle Villegas 00971
Calle Violeta 00969
Calle Vista Linda 00969
Calle Washingtonia 00969
Calle Wilson
M1-M99 00969
N1-N99 00969
C1-C99 00966
1A-1A 00966
1-13 00966
15-23 00966
Calle X 00965
Calle Yagrumo
H1-H99 00968
C1-C99 00969
D1-D99 00969
E1-E99 00969
F1-F99 00969
G1-G99 00968
Calle Yagua 00966
Calle Yarey 00966
Calle Zafiro
1-7 00969
1-39 00969
76-199 00968
Calle Zeus 00969
Calle Zuania 00966
Camino Los Baez 00971
Carr 165
2-2 00968
4-40 00968
42-198 00968
61-61 00965
Carr 177
2-2 00966
50-98 00969
2001-2599 00969
Carr 19 00966
Carr 199 00969
Carr 2 00966
Carr 20 00966
Carr 21 00966
Carr 28 00965
Carr 8177 00966
Carr 833
1-10 00969
12-16 00969
26-98 00971
197-197 00971
Carr 834 00971
Carr 837
300-399 00969
401-499 00971
Carr 838 00969
Carr 841 00969
Carr 873 00969
Carr 8834 00971
Eastside Ct 00969
El Alamo Dr 00969
Federal Dr 00965
Las Villas Townhouses 00969
Marginal Buchanan 00966
Northview Ct 00969
Parkville Ct 00969
Paseo De La
Alhambra 00966
Paseo Mediterraneo 00966
Res La Rosaleda 00969
Res Zenon Diaz
Valcarcel 00965
Southview Ct 00969
Valle De Torrimar 00966
Valle Escondido 00971
Via Alcazar 00969
Via Alessi 00969
Via Bernardo 00969
Via Capobore 00969
Via Escorial 00969
Via Louvre 00969
Via Portica 00969
Via San Gabriele 00969
Via San Paolo 00969
Via San Rufino 00969
Via Santa Catalina 00969
Via Versalles 00969

HUMACAO PR

General Delivery 00791

POST OFFICE BOXES MAIN OFFICE STATIONS AND BRANCHES

Box No.s
All PO Boxes 00792

HIGHWAY CONTRACTS

01, 02, 03, 04, 11, 12,
15 00791

NAMED STREETS

All Street Addresses 00791

MAYAGUEZ PR

General Delivery 00681

POST OFFICE BOXES MAIN OFFICE STATIONS AND BRANCHES

Box No.s
All PO Boxes 00681

HIGHWAY CONTRACTS

02, 03, 04, 05, 06, 07 00680

NAMED STREETS

Ave Algarrobo 00682
Ave Borinquen 00680
Ave Condominio 00680
Ave Dunscombe 00682
Ave Efrain Rivera 00680
Ave Gonzalez
Clemente 00682
Ave Hiram D Cabassa 00680
Ave Hostos
200-898 00682
301-599 00680
521-799 00682
801-899 00680
900-950 00682
951-999 00680
952-3098 00682
2001-3099 00682
Ave Jardines 00682
Ave La Arboleda 00680
Ave Los Corazones 00680
Ave Los Maestros 00682
Ave Pedro Albizu
Campo 00680
Ave Porvenir 00680
Ave Santitos Colon 00680
Ave Sta Teresa
Journet 00682
Bda Martell 00680
Bda Nadal 00680
Bella Vista Gdns 00680
Blvd Alfonso Valdes 00680
Blvd Del Carmen 00682
Blvd Edualdo Baez
Garcia 00680
Blvd Guanajibo 00682
Calle 00682
Calle 1 00680
Calle 2 00680
Calle 3 00680
Calle 65 De Infanteria 00682
Calle A 00682
Calle A Ramirez 00680
Calle A Ramirez Silva 00680
Calle Abacoa 00680
Calle Abraham Lincoln 00682
Calle Acapulco 00682
Calle Acasia 00680
Calle Acuario 00682
Calle Aduana 00682
Calle Aguacate 00680
Calle Agueybana 00680
Calle Aguila 00680
Calle Agustin Stahl 00682
Calle Ahleli 00682
Calle Alameda 00680
Calle Alborada 00682
Calle Alcatraz 00682
Calle Alcazar 00680
Calle Alejandro Tapia 00682
Calle Alemany 00680

Calle Alfonso Gonzalez 00680
Calle Alfredo Quintana 00680
Calle Alhambra 00680
Calle Alicia Moreda 00680
Calle Almirante 00682
Calle Alora 00680
Calle Altiery 00682
Calle Alvarez Quintero 00682
Calle Amapola 00680
Calle Amatista 00682
Calle America 00680
Calle Amor 00680
Calle Ana Luisa Sanchez 00682
Calle Andalucia 00680
Calle Andres Camara 00680
Calle Angel Fajardo 00680
Calle Angelica 00680
Calle Anibal Marrero 00680
Calle Anthurium 00680
Calle Antonia Cabassa 00680
Calle Antonio Blanes 00682
Calle Antonio Cruz Ayala 00680
Calle Antonio Paoli 00682
Calle Antonio R Barcelo 00680
Calle Aquilino Monteverde 00680
Calle Aracibo 00680
Calle Araez 00680
Calle Aragon 00680
Calle Aramana 00680
Calle Aramis 00680
Calle Arcangel 00680
Calle Archilla Cabrera 00680
Calle Arenal 00680
Calle Argentina 00682
Calle Aries 00682
Calle Arnaldo Sevilla 00680
Calle Arturo Gigante 00680
Calle Asia 00680
Calle Asomante 00682
Calle Asturias 00680
Calle Atabey 00680
Calle Atalaya 00682
Calle Ausencia 00680
Calle Azorin 00682
Calle B 00682
Calle Balbino Trinta 00680
Calle Balboa 00680
Calle Baldorioty 00680
Calle Bambu 00680
Calle Barbosa 00680
Calle Bartolo Rivera 00682
Calle Begonia 00682
Calle Bel Del Valle 00680
Calle Bellas Lomas 00682
Calle Benavide 00680
Calle Benigno Contreras 00682
Calle Benito Perez Galdoz 00682
Calle Betances 00680
Calle Bimini 00680
Calle Bogota 00682
Calle Bondad 00680
Calle Bonet 00682
Calle Boquilla 00682
Calle Boriquen 00680
Calle Bosque 00680
Calle Brazil 00682
Calle Broadway 00680
Calle Bromelia 00680
Calle Buena Vis 00680
Calle Buenos Aires 00682
Calle Burgos 00680
Calle C 00682
Calle Cabo Gomez 00680
Calle Cadaquez 00680
Calle Cadiz 00680
Calle Caguax 00680
Calle Candelaria 00682
Calle Cantera 00680
Calle Caparra 00680
Calle Capestany 00680
Calle Capisfally 00680
Calle Capitan Espada 00680
Calle Capricornio 00682
Calle Capulin 00682
Calle Caracas 00682
Calle Caracol 00682
Calle Carbonell 00680
Calle Carey 00682
Calle Caridad 00680
Calle Carlos Baco Soria 00682
Calle Carlos Casanova 00682
Calle Carlos Chardon 00682
Calle Carlos E Chardon 00682
Calle Carmelo Alemar 00682
Calle Carmelo Martinez 00682
Calle Carmen 00680
Calle Carmen E Vilella 00680
Calle Carolina
B1-B99 00682
B1A-B99A 00682
A1-A99 00682
A1A-A99A 00682
1-99 00680
Calle Carrau 00680
Calle Carrion Maduro 00680
Calle Casandra 00680
Calle Cascada 00680
Calle Castilla 00680
Calle Casuarina 00680
Calle Cataluna 00680
Calle Cayetano 00680
Calle Cecilia V De Raldiris 00680
Calle Ceiba 00680
Calle Celestina 00680
Calle Celestino Rodriguez 00680
Calle Celso Torres Ramirez 00682
Calle Cerro La Santa 00682
Calle Cerro Lindo 00680
Calle Cesarina Gonze 00680
Calle Charles Foote 00680
Calle Chevremont 00682
Calle Chile 00682
Calle Cielito 00680
Calle Cipey 00680
Calle Cipres 00680
Calle Claudio Carrero 00682
Calle Clavel 00680
Calle Clemente Ramirez 00680
Calle Cofresi 00680
Calle Colina 00682
Calle Coll Y Toste 00682
Calle Collores 00682
Calle Comprension 00680
Calle Concordia 00682
Calle Conde 00680
Calle Condor 00682
Calle Confraternidad 00680
Calle Contraste 00680
Calle Coqui 00682
Calle Coral 00682
Calle Cordillera 00682
Calle Cordova 00680
Calle Coronel Soto 00680
Calle Corte 00680
Calle Cristobal Colon 00680
Calle Cristobal Sotomayor 00682
Calle Cristy
1-120 00680
121-299 00682
Calle Cruz 00682
Calle Cruz Castillo 00680
Calle Cruz Maria 00682
Calle Cruz Roja 00680
Calle Cumpiano 00682
Calle Cupey 00682
Calle D 00682
Calle Dalias 00682
Calle De Diego E 00680
Calle De Hostos 00680
Calle De La Candelaria 00682
Calle Del Cristo 00682
Calle Delicias 00680
Calle Desengano 00680
Calle Diego Colon 00682
Calle Diego Salcedo 00682
Calle Domingo Acosta 00680
Calle Domingo Ortiz 00682
Calle Domingo Silva 00682
Calle Doncella 00680
Calle Dr Augusto Perea 00682
Calle Dr B Gaudier Texidor 00682
Calle Dr Basora N 00680
Calle Dr Escabi 00680
Calle Dr Jimenez 00680
Calle Dr Jorge Larranaga 00682
Calle Dr Lassise 00680
Calle Dr Nelson Perea 00680
Calle Dr Orsini 00680
Calle Dr Pedro Perea 00680
Calle Dr Ramon E Betances 00680
Calle Dr Rivera Olan 00680
Calle Dr Vadi 00680
Calle Dr Veve 00682
Calle Dr Villamil 00682
Calle Dra Loida Figueroa 00680
Calle Duarte 00682
Calle Dulce Palito 00680
Calle Dulievre 00680
Calle E Bravo De Rivero 00680
Calle E De Irizarry 00680
Calle Eden 00682
Calle Eduardo Riera 00680
Calle Eduardo Trabal 00680
Calle El Mango 00680
Calle Elena Segarra 00682
Calle Elias Valdespino 00680
Calle Eliseo F Guillot 00682
Calle Emeterio Ramirez 00682
Calle Enrique Dorrego 00680
Calle Enrique Franco 00682
Calle Enrique Gutierrez 00680
Calle Enrique Koppisch 00682
Calle Enrique Padilla 00682
Calle Enrique Seda 00682
Calle Enrique Simon 00680
Calle Enrique Vazquez Baez 00680
Calle Ensanche 00680
Calle Ensueno 00682
Calle Epifanio Ortiz 00680
Calle Epifanio Vidal 00682
Calle Escorial 00680
Calle Esteban Ferrer 00680
Calle Estrecha 00680
Calle Ethel Marin 00682
Calle Eugenio Cesani 00682
Calle Eugenio Cuevas 00682
Calle Europa 00680
Calle Ext Alora 00680
Calle F 00682
Calle F Martinez De Matos 00680
Calle Fabregas 00680
Calle Farallon 00682
Calle Fatima 00680
Calle Federico Degetau 00682
Calle Felices Dias 00680
Calle Felicidad 00680
Calle Felix Castillo 00680
Calle Felix R Gonzalez 00680
Calle Fermin Guzman 00682
Calle Fidel Castillo 00682
Calle Flamboyan 00682
Calle Flor De Maga 00682
Calle Flor Del Valle 00680
Calle Florida 00680
Calle Fomento 00682
Calle Forestier 00680
Calle Fortunet 00680
Calle Fraile 00682
Calle Francisco De Matos 00680
Calle Francisco Galanes 00680
Calle Francisco M Quinones 00682
Calle Francisco Oller 00682
Calle Frank Souffront 00680
Calle Frankie Ruiz 00680
Calle G 00682
Calle G Odiot Machado 00682
Calle G Pales Matos 00682
Calle Galicia 00680
Calle Garcia Quevedo 00680
Calle Garcia Sanjurjo 00680
Calle Gardenia 00682
Calle Garfield 00682
Calle Garnier 00680
Calle Garnier Int 00680
Calle Gautier Benitez 00680
Calle Gaviota 00682
Calle Geminis 00682
Calle Gen Contreras 00680
Calle Gen Del Valle 00680
Calle Gen Mcarthur 00680
Calle Gen Patton 00680
Calle Georgetti 00680
Calle Geranio 00682
Calle Gilberto Jeque Rodrigu 00680
Calle Giralda 00680
Calle Gonzalez Martinez 00680
Calle Granada 00680
Calle Granate 00680
Calle Gregoria Vargas 00680
Calle Guadarrama 00682
Calle Guainia 00680
Calle Guarionex 00680
Calle Guayacan 00680
Calle Guenard 00680
Calle Guilarte 00680
Calle Guillermo Gajate 00680
Calle Guillermo Muller 00682
Calle H 00682
Calle H Diaz Navarro 00682
Calle Habacuc 00680
Calle Habana 00682
Calle Harry S Truman 00682
Calle Hernan Cortez 00682
Calle Heyliger 00682
Calle Hipolito Arroyo 00682
Calle Hm Towner 00682
Calle Hnos Rodriguez 00680
Calle Hnos Segarra 00680
Calle Hucar 00680
Calle I 00682
Calle Idilio 00680
Calle Iglesia N 00680
Calle Ignacio Flores 00680
Calle Ing Arturo Davila 00682
Calle Ingenio 00680
Calle Inmaculada 00682
Calle Iris 00682
Calle Isaac Plz 00680
Calle Isaac Diaz 00680
Calle J 00682
Calle J Aponte De Silva 00680
Calle J Arroyo Mestre 00680
Calle J Campeche Jordan 00682
Calle J Ortiz De Pena 00680
Calle J Vascaran Quintero 00680
Calle Ja Gautier 00680
Calle Jaguita 00680
Calle Jaime Rodriguez 00682
Calle Jardines 00682
Calle Jardines Del Obispado 00682
Calle Jesus Esteves 00682
Calle Joaquin Monteagudo 00682
Calle Jorge Mucaro Rosas 00680
Calle Jose Abad Bonilla 00682
Calle Jose Antonio Figueroa 00680
Calle Jose Bellaflores 00682
Calle Jose E Arraras 00682
Calle Jose E Sanabria 00682
Calle Jose G Padilla 00682
Calle Jose G Tizol 00682
Calle Jose Gitany Frangie 00682
Calle Jose J Acosta 00682
Calle Jose M Silva 00680
Calle Jose Maria Monge 00682
Calle Jose Menendez 00680
Calle Jose P Morales 00682
Calle Jose Pepito Cesani 00680
Calle Jose Ramirez 00680
Calle Jose S Alegria 00682
Calle Jose Sabater 00682
Calle Josefina F Rua 00680
Calle Juan B Lojo 00682
Calle Juan Baez Ruiz 00682
Calle Juan Mari Ramos 00680
Calle Juan Marin 00680
Calle Juan R Gonzalez 00680
Calle Juan Rodriguez 00682
Calle Juan Rullan 00680
Calle Juan Valentin 00682
Calle Juan Vicenty 00680
Calle Juanita 00682
Calle Juanita Barbosa 00680
Calle Juape 00680
Calle Julian Blanco Sosa 00682
Calle Julio Baloiz 00680
Calle Julio Martinez 00680
Calle Julio N Matos 00682
Calle Julio Vizcarrondo 00682
Calle Justiniano 00680
Calle K 00682
Calle Korea 00680
Calle L 00682
Calle L Mojica Valentin 00680
Calle La Via 00682
Calle La Bolera 00682
Calle La Borinquena 00680
Calle La Esperanza 00680
Calle La Floresta 00682
Calle La Hiedra 00682
Calle La Loma 00680
Calle La Milagrosa 00680
Calle La Mora 00682
Calle La Nina 00682
Calle La Paz 00680
Calle La Pinta 00682
Calle La Resecadora 00682
Calle La Torre 00682
Calle La Tuna 00680
Calle Laliza 00682
Calle Las Azucenas 00682
Calle Las Caiseas 00682
Calle Las Dalias 00680
Calle Las Flores 00680
Calle Las Marias 00680
Calle Las Mesas 00682
Calle Las Orquideas 00682
Calle Las Pascuas 00682
Calle Las Rosas 00682
Calle Laura Honore 00680
Calle Laurel 00680
Calle Lavezzary 00682
Calle Lealtad 00680
Calle Leon 00680
Calle Leopoldo Feliu 00680
Calle Liana 00680
Calle Liceo 00680
Calle Lino Minguela 00682
Calle Lirio 00682
Calle Lisboa 00680
Calle Llorens Torres 00682
Calle Loja 00680
Calle Loma Bonita 00680
Calle Lope De Vega 00682
Calle Lorca 00680
Calle Los Adoquines 00680
Calle Los Alamos 00682
Calle Los Caobos 00680
Calle Los Cruz 00680
Calle Los Flamboyanes 00682
Calle Los Ingenieros 00682
Calle Los Irizarry 00680
Calle Los Lirios 00682
Calle Los Miosotis 00682
Calle Los Nardos 00682
Calle Los Pinos 00680
Calle Los Robles 00682
Calle Los Tainos 00682
Calle Los Torres 00680
Calle Los Tulipanes 00682
Calle Los Velez 00682
Calle Lourdes Sallaberry 00680
Calle Lucy Boscana 00680
Calle Luis Castellon 00680
Calle Luis De Celis 00682
Calle Luis Monzon 00682
Calle Luis Ortiz 00680
Calle Luis Ortiz Valle 00680
Calle Luis Pales Matos 00682
Calle Luis R Vicenty 00680
Calle Luis Stefani 00682
Calle Luis Vilella 00680
Calle Luis Xiv 00682
Calle M 00682
Calle M Rodriguez Feliciano 00680
Calle Madeline Williamsen 00680
Calle Madrid 00680
Calle Magallanes 00682
Calle Magnolia 00682
Calle Malaga 00680
Calle Mallorca 00680
Calle Manantiales 00680
Calle Mano Sico 00680
Calle Manolo Garcia 00680
Calle Manuel A Barreto 00682
Calle Manuel Blanco 00682
Calle Manuel Cintron 00680
Calle Manuel Corchado 00682
Calle Manuel M Samas 00682
Calle Manuel Marin 00682
Calle Manuel Monge 00682
Calle Manuel Pirallo 00682
Calle Manuel Ramon 00682
Calle Marcos A Comas 00680
Calle Margarita 00682
Calle Margarita Vilella 00680
Calle Marginot 00682
Calle Maria Luisa Arcelay 00680
Calle Maria Teresa Aveillez 00682
Calle Mariana Bracetti 00680
Calle Mariano Abril 00680
Calle Marleen 00680
Calle Marquesa 00682
Calle Martinez Guasp 00680
Calle Matienzo Cintron 00680
Calle Matildo Caban 00682
Calle Maximino Barbosa 00680
Calle Mckinley E 00680
Calle Meditacion 00680
Calle Mejico 00682
Calle Mendez Vigo E 00680
Calle Mercedes Suau 00680
Calle Miguel A Santin 00680
Calle Miguel Cervantes 00682
Calle Miguel De Unamuno 00682
Calle Miguel M Munoz 00682
Calle Miguel Maymon 00680
Calle Milagrosa 00680
Calle Mineral 00680
Calle Minerva 00680
Calle Miraflores 00680
Calle Miramar
1-99 00680
200-299 00682
Calle Mis Amores 00680
Calle Mona Marti 00680
Calle Montalvo 00682
Calle Monte Del Estado 00682
Calle Monte Sinai 00682
Calle Montecristo 00682
Calle Montoso 00682
Calle Morell Campos 00680
Calle Mudejar 00680
Calle Munoz Rivera E 00680
Calle N Medina Gonzalez 00682
Calle N Mencha Arroyo 00680
Calle Nan Ramirez 00680
Calle Narcisos 00680
Calle Nardo 00682
Calle Navamar 00680
Calle Nelson Colon 00682
Calle Nelson Cortina 00680
Calle Nelson Ramirez 00682
Calle Nenadich 00680
Calle Nene Cole 00682
Calle Neptuno 00680
Calle Nogal 00682
Calle Nuevo Londres S 00680
Calle Oasis 00680
Calle Obispado 00682
Calle Olga Nolla 00680
Calle Oliva Polanco 00680
Calle Oliviery 00680
Calle Opalo 00682
Calle Oriente 00680
Calle Orquideas 00680
Calle Otoao 00680
Calle Oviedo 00680
Calle Pablo Casals 00680
Calle Pablo Flores 00680
Calle Pablo Maiz 00680
Calle Pablo Morales 00682
Calle Pablo Rojas 00682
Calle Pabon Maristany 00680
Calle Pachin Marin 00682
Calle Padre Aguilera 00680
Calle Palencia 00682
Calle Palma Real 00682
Calle Papo Boggie 00680
Calle Paraiso 00682
Calle Parque 00682
Calle Pascua 00682
Calle Pascual Valle 00680
Calle Pedro A De Alarcon 00682
Calle Pedro Enriquez 00680
Calle Pedro Muniz 00680
Calle Pelayo 00680
Calle Penaranda 00680
Calle Peral N 00680
Calle Perpetuo Socorro 00682
Calle Picacho 00682
Calle Pilar Defillo 00680
Calle Pineiro 00680

Calle Pirineo 00682
Calle Pirinola 00680
Calle Piscis 00682
Calle Pitirre 00682
Calle Playera 00682
Calle Polvorin 00680
Calle Portugal 00680
Calle Pravia 00680
Calle Primavera 00682
Calle Primm 00680
Calle Princesa 00682
Calle Principe 00680
Calle Providencia
  B1-B99 00680
  C1-C99 00680
  801-819 00682
  821-899 00682
Calle Puntita 00682
Calle Pusan 00680
Calle Quintana 00682
Calle Quintita 00682
Calle R De Arellano 00682
Calle R Martinez Nadal 00682
Calle R Martinez Torres 00682
Calle R Ramirez Pabon 00682
Calle R Sanchez Justiniano 00680
Calle Rafael Cintron 00682
Calle Rafael Hernandez 00682
Calle Rafael Mangual 00682
Calle Rafael Nazario 00682
Calle Rafael Quinones Vidal 00680
Calle Rafael Soler Ribas 00680
Calle Rafael Velez 00682
Calle Raimundo Ortiz 00680
Calle Ramirez Cuerda 00680
Calle Ramirez Silva 00682
Calle Ramon Bayron 00682
Calle Ramon E Ramirez Quiles 00682
Calle Ramon Freyre 00680
Calle Ramon Martinez 00682
Calle Ramon Ortiz 00680
Calle Ramon Power 00682
Calle Ramon Roque Valentin 00680
Calle Ramon Valdes 00680
Calle Ramonita 00682
Calle Ramos Antonini E 00680
Calle Ramos Antonini Int 00680
Calle Reina 00680
Calle Reina Del Sol 00682
Calle Reina Isabel 00682
Calle Reinaldo Santiago 00680
Calle Reinita 00682
Calle Relampago 00680
Calle Rey Fernando De Aragon 00682
Calle Riachuelo 00680
Calle Rialto 00682
Calle Riera Palmer 00680
Calle Rio N 00680
Calle Rius Rivera 00680
Calle Roberto Cole 00680
Calle Robles 00680
Calle Rochelaise 00682
Calle Rodrigo De Triana 00682
Calle Rodriguez De Tio 00682
Calle Rodulfo Labiosa 00682
Calle Romaguera 00682
Calle Ronda 00680
Calle Roosevelt E 00680
Calle Rosalia 00680
Calle Rubi 00682
Calle Sagitario 00682
Calle Saint Thomas 00680
Calle Salamanca 00680
Calle Salud N 00680
Calle Salvador Brau 00682
Calle Salvador Mestre 00680
Calle Salvador Tio 00682
Calle Salvador Vilella 00682
Calle San Agustin 00680
Calle San Alfonso 00680
Calle San Antonio 00680
Calle San Dionisio 00680
Calle San Expedito 00682
Calle San Felipe 00682
Calle San Fernando 00680
Calle San Gerardo
  1-99 00680
  5000-5099 00682
Calle San Geronimo 00680
Calle San Ignacio 00680
Calle San Jose
  1-49 00680
  50-199 00682
Calle San Juan N 00682
Calle San Marcos 00680
Calle San Martin 00680
Calle San Miguel 00680
Calle San Pablo 00682
Calle San Pedro 00682
Calle San Rafael 00680
Calle San Salvador 00680
Calle San Vcte De Paul 00682
Calle San Vicente E 00680
Calle Santa Barbara 00682
Calle Santa Catalina 00680
Calle Santa Clara 00682
Calle Santa Fe 00682
Calle Santa Isabel 00680
Calle Santa Juanita 00682
Calle Santa Lucia 00680
Calle Santa Maria 00680
Calle Santa Rita 00682
Calle Santa Rosa 00680
Calle Santa Teresa 00680
Calle Santa Teresita 00680
Calle Santervas 00680
Calle Santiago Iglesias Pant 00682
Calle Santiago Llorens 00680
Calle Santiago Mari Ramos 00680
Calle Santiago R Palmer E 00680
Calle Santiago Ruiz 00680
Calle Santo Tomas 00680
Calle Santos Chocano 00682
Calle Sauce 00682
Calle Secundino Miguela 00680
Calle Segovia 00680
Calle Serenidad 00680
Calle Sevilla 00680
Calle Sierra Cayey 00682
Calle Sierra Morena 00682
Calle Sierra Nevada 00682
Calle Simon Bolivar 00680
Calle Simon Carlo 00682
Calle Simon Madera 00680
Calle Solimar 00680
Calle Souffront 00680
Calle Suau 00680
Calle Tablon 00682
Calle Tamarindo 00680
Calle Tamarindo Norte Int 00680
Calle Tauro 00682
Calle Tendal 00680
Calle Tenerife 00680
Calle Tetuan N 00680
Calle Theopolis 00680
Calle Thomas A Edison 00682
Calle Toledo 00680
Calle Tolosa 00680
Calle Tomas Carlo 00682
Calle Topacio 00682
Calle Torrecillas 00682
Calle Torrimar 00682
Calle Tulio Larrinaga 00682
Calle Tulipa 00682
Calle Turabo 00680
Calle Turquesa 00682
Calle Uroyan 00682
Calle Valencia 00680
Calle Valladolid 00680
Calle Vendrix 00680
Calle Venecia 00680
Calle Venus La Chorra 00680
Calle Vicenta Mendez 00682
Calle Vicente Yanez Pinzon 00682
Calle Victor Honore 00682
Calle Villa Detallista 00680
Calle Virginia 00680
Calle Vista Alegre 00680
Calle Vista Bahia 00680
Calle Vistamar 00682
Calle Washington 00680
Calle Wenceslao Colon 00680
Calle Wenceslao Perez 00682
Calle William F Brennan 00682
Calle William Irizarry 00680
Calle Wilson 00680
Calle Yagrumo 00680
Calle Yahueca 00680
Calle Yamil Galib 00682
Calle Yaurel 00682
Calle Yunque 00682
Calle Zafiro 00682
Calle Zamora 00680
Calle Zaragoza 00682
Calle Zoilo Rivera 00680
Callejon Hormigueros 00680
Callejon Rio Piedras 00680
Camino Bechara 00680
Camino Clinica Espanola 00680
Camino Cristo De Los Mila 00682
Camino El Guayo 00680
Camino La Cuchilla 00680
Camino Los Ayala 00680
Camino Los Berrios 00680
Camino Los Rosados 00682
Camino Los Vazquez 00682
Camino Maguayo 00680
Camino Martell 00680
Camino Ortiz 00680
Camino Pablo Martinez 00680
Camino Pedro Fernandez 00680
Camino Ruben Mas 00680
Camino Sonsire 00680
Camino Victor Perez Rodrigue 00682
Camino Zoologico 00680
Carr 102 00682
Carr 104 00682
Carr 108 00680
Carr 3341 00682
Carr 341 00682
Carr 342 00682
Carr 348 00680
Carr 349 00680
Carr 351 00682
Carr 380 00680
Carr 64 00682
Carr Rio Hondo 00680
Cols De Alturas De Mayaguez 00682
Cond Petromar 00682
Cumbres De Miradero 00682
Cumbres Las Mesas 00680
Est Miradero 00682
Est San Benito 00680
Jard De Borinquen 00682
Jard De Mayaguez 00680
Mancenwo 00680
Mans Las Mesas 00680
Parq Forestal 00682
Pasaje Collado 00680
Pasaje Las Delicias 00680
Paseo Del Sol 00682
Paseo Las Colinas 00680
Pelican Park 00682
Qtas De San Francisco 00680
Qtas De Santa Maria 00682
Qtas Del Bambu 00680
Repto Feliciana 00680
Repto Mercado 00680
Repto Senorial 00680
Res Candelaria 00682
Res Carmen 00682
Res Columbus Lndg 00682
Res Cuesta Las Piedras 00680
Res Eleonor Roosevelt 00680
Res Flamboyan Gdns 00680
Res Igualdad 00682
Res Kennedy 00682
Res Mar Y Sol 00682
Res Mayaguez Gdns 00680
Res Yaguez 00680
Sect Cuba 00682
Sect La Ceiba 00682
Sect Montoya 00682
Sect Pitillo 00682
Sect Salto Al Chivo 00682
Senderos Del Valle 00680
Sonsire Chalets 00682
Urb College Gdns 00682
Urb El Retiro 00682
Urb La Rueda 00682
Urb Las Hortencias 00682
Urb Los Carteros 00682
Urb Nu Sigma 00682
Urb Private Ct 00682
Urb Valle Sur 00680
Urb Vista Del Mar 00682
Villa Acevedo 00680
Villa Angel 00680
Villa Benny 00680
Villa Blanca 00680
Villa Candelaria 00680
Villa Cristina 00680
Villa De Ensenat 00682
Villa Del Capitan 00682
Villa Fontana 00682
Villa Garcia 00682
Villa Gracia 00680
Villa Lala 00680
Villa Las Violetas 00682
Villa Martinez 00682
Villa Ramirez 00682
Villa San Francisco 00680
Villa Soledad 00680
Villa Sonsire 00680
Villa Tuli 00682
Villas De Algarrobo 00682
Villas De Santa Maria 00680

PONCE PR

General Delivery 00732

POST OFFICE BOXES MAIN OFFICE STATIONS AND BRANCHES

Box No.s
7001 - 32280 00732
35001 - 35780 00734
330001 - 336960 00733

HIGHWAY CONTRACTS

06, 07, 08, 09 00731

NAMED STREETS

Alts De Jacaranda 00730
Andarken 00731
Antigua Carr 1 00716
Ave E 00730
Ave A 00730
Ave Ana Maria Oneill 00728
Ave Anita Moseley 00730
Ave B 00730
Ave Baramaya 00728
Ave Caribe 00716
Ave Circunvalacion 00728
Ave Constancia 00716
Ave Eduardo Ruberte
  1500-1699 00716
  1701-2099 00716
  2100-2198 00716
  2201-2285 00717
  2287-2399 00717
  2500-2599 00728
  3000-3199 00728
Ave Emilio Fagot
  1-3038 00716
  2900-2999 00716
  3000-3006 00716
  3039-3099 00716
  3100-3198 00730
  3200-3399 00730
Ave Fd Roosevelt
  2800-3189 00717
  3190-3198 00717
  3191-3199 00717
  3200-3299 00728
Ave Federal 00730
Ave Generalife 00716
Ave Hillcrest 00716
Ave Hostos
  800-1099 00716
  1101-1299 00717
Ave Hungria 00716
Ave Interior 00728
Ave Jose De Diego 00716
Ave Julio E Monagas
  1900-1999 00716
  3100-3199 00717
Ave La Ceiba
  300-599 00717
  600-698 00717
  601-615 00717
  612-630 00717
  619-699 00717
  700-742 00717
  801-999 00717
  1000-1099 00716
Ave Las Brisas 00728
Ave Los Caobos 00716
Ave Los Meros 00716
Ave Manati 00716
Ave Maruca 00728
Ave Munoz Rivera 00717
Ave Obispado 00716
Ave Padre Noel 00716
Ave Parque 00728
Ave Ponce De Leon 00728
Ave Punto Oro 00728
Ave Rafael Cordero Santiago 00716
Ave Rafael Lugo Gonzalez 00717
Ave Rochdale 00728
Ave Sancho 00716
Ave Santiago Andrade 00728
Ave Santiago De Los Caballer 00716
Ave Tito Castro 00716
Bda Caribe 00716
Bda Lajes 00716
Biredald 00730
Blvd Luis A Ferre
  1792-1806 00728
  1808-1999 00728
  2000-2599 00717
  2100-2198 00717
  2600-2799 00717
  2601-2899 00717
  2800-2898 00717
Blvd Miguel Pou 00717
Blvd Ruth Fernandez 00730
Bo Bucana 00716
Bo Lomas 00716
Bo San Anton 00717
Brisas Del Caribe 00728
Bulevar Pescao 00730
Calle E
  L1-L199 00728
  L43A-L57A 00728
  Q1-Q199 00728
  E13-E24 00716
  F1-F16 00716
  Q85A-Q86A 00728
  18-35 00716
Calle Un 00730
Calle 1
  E6-E10 00730
  B3-B7 00730
  E10-E99 00730
  H1-H19 00730
  B1-B37 00730
  C1-C9 00730
  J1-J11 00730
  AD1-AD99 00730
  AE1-AE99 00730
  A1-A16 00716
  A1-A2 00730
  H1-H99 00716
  A1-A25 00730
  1-31 00730
  5-5 00730
  7-55 00730
  57-77 00730
  100-399 00728
  200-599 00730
  210-298 00728
Calle 10
  L1-L8 00728
  M1-M5 00728
  H1-H99 00716
  I40-I99 00730
  K6-K8 00730
  L4-L6 00730
  K1-K13 00730
  AM1-AM99 00730
  AT1-AT99 00730
  AU1-AU99 00730
  8INT-8INT 00730
  L1-L99 00716
  M1-M99 00716
  I1-I99 00716
  J1-J99 00716
  1-2 00730
  4-99 00730
  100-199 00728
Calle 11
  O1-O99 00728
  I1-I30 00716
  XX1-XX99 00716
  I18-I24 00716
  I39-I99 00730
  L7-L10 00730
  K14-K25 00730
  L7-L8 00730
  E1-E99 00728
  E29A-E40A 00728
  AM1-AM99 00730
  AN1-AN99 00730
  AP1-AP99 00730
  AX1-AX99 00730
  M1-M16 00728
  100-199 00728
Calle 11/2 00730
Calle 12
  P1-P99 00728
  J1-J99 00716
  K1-K99 00716
  H1-H29 00716
  I9-I14 00716
  I29-I35 00730
  M4-M7 00730
  L1-L6 00730
  M1-M99 00730
  N1-N99 00730
  145INT-145INT 00728
  AQ1-AQ99 00730
  AR1-AR99 00730
  O1-O99 00728
  99B-99E 00728
  104A-104D 00728
  1-199 00728
  101-299 00728
Calle 13
  I1-I99 00716
  K1-K99 00716
  L1-L19 00716
  M1-M99 00716
  M8-M11 00730
  N2-N13 00730
  AS1-AS99 00730
  AT1-AT99 00730
  AW1-AW99 00730
  100-199 00728
Calle 14
  L1-L99 00716
  M33-M99 00716
  N1-N99 00730
  O1-O12 00730
  AR1-AR99 00730
  AT1-AT99 00730
  100-198 00728
Calle 15
  M1-M99 00716
  N1-N19 00716
  R1-R99 00716
  S1-S99 00716
  N20-N99 00730
  Q4-Q99 00730
  AU1-AU99 00730
  AV1-AV99 00730
  N18A-N18C 00716
  T1-T98 00716
  100-299 00728
Calle 16
  N1-N99 00716
  O1-O99 00716
  S1-S99 00730
  T1-T99 00730
  100-199 00728
Calle 17
  N1-N99 00716
  P1-P99 00716
  Q1-Q99 00730
  T12-T99 00716
  PP1-PP99 00716
  XX1-XX99 00716
  U1-U99 00730
  100-198 00728
Calle 17 De Enero 00716
Calle 18
  O1-O99 00716
  R1-R99 00716
  V1-V99 00730
  Q1-Q99 00716
  T1-T99 00716
Calle 19
  Q1-Q99 00716
  R1-R99 00716
  Y1-Y99 00730
  100-199 00728
Calle 1ro De Mayo 00716
Calle 2
  N1-N99 00716
  S1-S99 00716
  A2-A6 00730
  B1-B12 00730
  C3-C8 00730
  D1-D6 00730
  AE1-AE99 00730
  AH1-AH99 00730
  AJ1-AJ99 00730
  AK1-AK99 00730
  AL1-AL99 00730
  A1-A18 00730
  B1-B10 00730
  C1-C4 00730
  R1-R14 00716
  1-25 00730
  1-99 00716
  2-12 00730
  14-98 00730
  27-33 00730
  101-101 00728

103-449 00728
122-122 00730
124-200 00730
245-599 00730
Calle 20
Q1-Q99 00716
U1-U99 00730
100-199 00728
Calle 21
Q1-Q99 00716
S1-S99 00716
Z1-Z99 00730
AA1-AA99 00730
100-199 00728
Calle 22
R1-R99 00716
S1-S99 00730
Calle 23
O18-O25 00716
Q1-Q99 00716
R1-R99 00716
R1-R6 00728
S1-S11 00728
T1-T99 00728
Q8-Q37 00730
S8-S99 00730
BB1-BB99 00730
101-199 00716
Calle 24
T1-T99 00716
Q1-Q99 00728
Calle 25
U7-U99 00728
V1-V16 00728
UU1-UU99 00716
VV1-VV99 00716
XX1-XX99 00716
BJ1-BJ99 00730
BK1-BK99 00730
PP1-PP99 00716
Calle 25 De Enero 00730
Calle 25 De Julio
100-199 00716
2000-2099 00728
Calle 26
U1-U99 00728
X1-X99 00728
RR1-RR99 00716
XX1-XX99 00716
Calle 27
U1-U99 00728
W1-W99 00728
X1-X99 00728
UU1-UU99 00716
VV1-VV99 00716
WW1-WW99 00716
ZZ1-ZZ99 00716
Calle 28
Y1-Y99 00728
Z1-Z99 00728
AA1-AA99 00728
BB1-BB99 00728
CC1-CC99 00728
DD1-DD99 00728
JJ1-JJ99 00716
RR1-RR99 00716
XX1-XX99 00716
Calle 29 00728
Calle 29a 00728
Calle 29b 00728
Calle 29c 00728
Calle 3
152A-152B 00730
B1-B16 00716
D2-D11 00730
E21-E99 00730
D7-D15 00730
E1-E9 00730
AF1-AF99 00730
C5-C14 00730
D1-D25 00730
F1-F9 00730
H1-H22 00730
J23-J99 00730
C1-C51 00716
C52-C99 00716
B1-B16 00716
A17-A99 00716
G1-G99 00716
H1-H99 00716
D1-D99 00716
E1-E99 00716
F1-F99 00716
1-75 00730
1-26 00716
3-22 00730
14-14 00716
24-34 00730
29-33 00730
77-81 00730
96-96 00730
98-499 00730
101-105 00728
107-109 00728
300-349 00730
Calle 30 00728
Calle 31 00728
Calle 32 00728
Calle 33 00728
Calle 34 00728
Calle 35 00728
Calle 36 00728
Calle 37 00728
Calle 38 00728
Calle 39 00728
Calle 39a 00728
Calle 4
1B-99B 00730
C1-C13 00716
D10-D25 00716
E23-E99 00730
F1-F12 00730
E10-E18 00730
F1-F9 00730
AE1-AE99 00730
AF1-AF99 00730
AV1-AV99 00730
AX1-AX99 00730
D26-D48 00730
G1-G20 00730
H20-H99 00730
C1-C4 00716
D1-D7 00716
F1-F9 00716
G11-G20 00716
E1-E99 00730
B1-B99 00716
1-30 00730
1-67 00716
1-77 00730
32-40 00730
68-99 00716
76-156 00730
102-299 00728
155-155 00730
157-199 00730
158-400 00730
201-299 00730
Calle 4 De Julio
194A-194A 00716
1-194 00716
2600-2699 00728
Calle 40 00728
Calle 41 00728
Calle 42 00728
Calle 44 00728
Calle 45 00728
Calle 46 00728
Calle 48 00728
Calle 49 00728
Calle 4a 00728
Calle 5
B1-B99 00730
C1-C18 00730
D1-D15 00730
E1-E99 00730
F10-F19 00730
G1-G10 00730
AC1-AC99 00730
AD1-AD99 00730
AK1-AK99 00730
J1-J99 00730
G1-G9 00730
H2-H7 00730
C1-C99 00716
D1-D99 00716
E1-E99 00716
F1-F99 00716
5INT-5INT 00730
1-1 00730
1-120 00730
1-199 00716
3-23 00730
24-24 00730
25-25 00730
26-40 00730
101-113 00728
122-126 00730
128-399 00730
200-299 00730
Calle 50 00728
Calle 51 00728
Calle 53 00728
Calle 54 00728
Calle 55 00728
Calle 56 00728
Calle 57 00728
Calle 58 00728
Calle 5a 00730
Calle 6
8A-8B 00730
A1-A99 00716
B1-B99 00716
D1-D9 00716
E17-E18 00716
F11-F20 00716
G4-G5 00716
J1-J99 00716
K1-K99 00716
O1-O99 00716
G18-G19 00730
H11-H17 00730
I4-I99 00730
G11-G20 00730
H1-H10 00730
AA1-AA19 00730
AB1-AB99 00730
AD1-AD99 00730
G1-G8 00716
G18A-G18C 00730
G19A-G19B 00730
1-21 00730
2-96 00730
23-29 00730
91-117 00716
98-116 00730
101-109 00728
147-168 00730
300-399 00716
Calle 7
Q1-Q7 00730
R1-R99 00730
I3-I99 00730
K1-K99 00730
L1-L99 00730
M1-M99 00730
N38-N40 00730
P1-P99 00730
Q1-Q3 00730
H11-H99 00730
I1-I11 00730
U1-U99 00730
V1-V99 00730
Y1-Y99 00730
Z1-Z99 00730
AB1-AB25 00730
AC1-AC99 00730
T1-T99 00730
C1-C99 00716
1-3 00730
5-40 00730
21-28 00730
42-52 00730
90-299 00730
100-119 00728
Calle 7a 00730
Calle 8
L1-L99 00728
G1-G3 00716
Q1-Q99 00716
H6-H10 00716
I1-I99 00730
J1-J2 00730
I12-I49 00730
AC10-AC99 00730
AK1-AK99 00730
25INT-25INT 00730
5INT-7INT 00730
16INT-18INT 00730
1-1 00730
3-36 00730
9-15 00730
17-99 00730
38-50 00730
100-199 00728
Calle 81/2 00730
Calle 8a 00728
Calle 8b 00728
Calle 9
M1-M99 00728
N1-N99 00728
I1-I16 00716
12INT-12INT 00730
G1-G99 00716
H12-H14 00716
I1-I25 00716
J15-J16 00716
K4-K6 00716
O1-O99 00716
I50-I99 00730
J3-J5 00730
K4-K5 00730
J12-J22 00730
A1-A99 00728
B1-B10 00728
D1-D14 00728
R1A-R99A 00728
S1-S99 00728
T1-T99 00728
AJ1-AJ99 00730
AL1-AL99 00730
AM1-AM99 00730
AN1-AN99 00730
J1-J99 00728
N1A-N1D 00728
A14A-A14A 00728
F1-F3 00716
G9-G16 00716
2-17 00730
3-26 00730
19-21 00730
100-399 00728
Calle A
A1-A11 00730
B8-B8 00730
57INT-57INT 00730
A11A-A11D 00730
A1-A99 00716
C1-C99 00716
23INT-47INT 00730
44INT-55INT 00730
7-12 00730
20-61 00730
100-399 00730
Calle A R Barcelo 00728
Calle A1 00730
Calle A2 00730
Calle A3 00730
Calle Aa 00716
Calle Abelardo Eloisa 00730
Calle Abolicion 00717
Calle Acacia 00716
Calle Aceitillo 00716
Calle Acerina 00728
Calle Acerola 00716
Calle Acorazonada 00728
Calle Acuario N 00716
Calle Acueducto 00730
Calle Afgani 00728
Calle Afrodita 00716
Calle Agua 00730
Calle Aguamarina 00728
Calle Agueybana 00728
Calle Agustin Daviu 00717
Calle Alamar 00716
Calle Albahaca 00728
Calle Albaicin 00716
Calle Albizia 00716
Calle Alcatraz 00728
Calle Alcazar 00716
Calle Alejandro Ordonez 00728
Calle Alelies 00730
Calle Algarrobo 00716
Calle Algas 00716
Calle Alicante 00730
Calle Alma Sublime 00730
Calle Almacigo 00716
Calle Almeida 00728
Calle Almeja 00717
Calle Almenas 00716
Calle Almeria 00728
Calle Almudena 00730
Calle Aloa 00717
Calle Altagracia 00717
Calle Altamisa 00716
Calle Altura 00730
Calle Alumbre 00728
Calle Amalia Paoli 00728
Calle Amanda 00717
Calle Amanecer 00716
Calle Amapola 00730
Calle Amarilis 00730
Calle Amatista 00728
Calle Amazonas 00728
Calle Ambar 00716
Calle America 00730
Calle America Capo 00717
Calle Amistad 00730
Calle Andino 00717
Calle Andres Gonzalez Matos 00730
Calle Angel Conejo Garcia 00730
Calle Angel Perez Lugo 00716
Calle Angelina 00717
Calle Anibal 00717
Calle Anon 00716
Calle Antares 00717
Calle Antonia Saez 00728
Calle Antonio Egipciano 00717
Calle Antonio Perez Pierret 00728
Calle Aquino 00717
Calle Arado 00728
Calle Aragon 00730
Calle Araguaney 00730
Calle Arboleda 00716
Calle Arcoiris 00716
Calle Arenas 00730
Calle Ares 00716
Calle Areyto 00728
Calle Arias 00716
Calle Aries 00716
Calle Arpa 00728
Calle Arrayanes 00716
Calle Arrecife 00716
Calle Artemis 00716
Calle Arturo Pasarell 00717
Calle Arturo Somohano 00728
Calle Aserrado 00728
Calle Astromelia 00730
Calle Asturias 00716
Calle Atocha 00730
Calle Aureola 00717
Calle Aurora 00717
Calle Ausencia 00730
Calle Austral 00728
Calle Ausubo 00716
Calle Avila 00730
Calle Azabache 00716
Calle B
39A-39B 00730
B1-B30 00716
C6-C19 00716
27INT-73INT 00730
2-99 00730
90-135 00716
200-299 00730
Calle B1 00730
Calle B2 00730
Calle B3 00730
Calle B4 00730
Calle Bagazo 00728
Calle Balaju 00716
Calle Balboa 00728
Calle Baldorioty 00717
Calle Ballena 00716
Calle Baluarte 00730
Calle Bambu 00716
Calle Baramaya 00728
Calle Barcelona 00730
Calle Barnes 00730
Calle Baronesa 00716
Calle Beato Francisco Palau 00728
Calle Begonia 00716
Calle Belen 00716
Calle Berlin 00730
Calle Bertoly 00730
Calle Betances 00730
Calle Betun 00730
Calle Bianca 00731
Calle Biriji 00716
Calle Birr 00728
Calle Bivalvo 00728
Calle Bobby Capo 00728
Calle Bocachica 00717
Calle Bogota 00717
Calle Bolivia 00717
Calle Bonaire 00716
Calle Bonanza 00730
Calle Bondad 00730
Calle Bonita 00717
Calle Bravo 00728
Calle Brillante 00730
Calle Bronco 00730
Calle Bucare 00716
Calle Buen Humor 00730
Calle Buena Vis 00717
Calle Buenos Aires 00717
Calle Burgao 00716
Calle C
C1-C45 00730
C17-C31 00730
C52-C56 00730
C47-C49 00730
C51-C99 00730
A1-A32 00716
D1-D8 00716
C13INT-C31INT 00730
77-199 00716
100-399 00730
Calle C1 00730
Calle C2 00730
Calle C3 00730
Calle C4 00730
Calle C5 00730
Calle Cacimar 00716
Calle Cadiz 00728
Calle Cafe 00716
Calle Caguana 00716
Calle Caimito 00716
Calle California 00730
Calle Caliope 00716
Calle Calma 00717
Calle Camaron 00716
Calle Campeche 00717
Calle Campos 00717
Calle Canario 00716
Calle Cancer 00716
Calle Candido Fernandez 00728
Calle Candido Hoyos 00717
Calle Candorosa 00730
Calle Caney 00716
Calle Caoba 00716
Calle Capellan 00730
Calle Capitan Correa 00717
Calle Capricornio 00716
Calle Capt Correa 00730
Calle Caracas 00717
Calle Carambola 00716
Calle Caridad 00730
Calle Carlos Cartagena 00717
Calle Carlos Casanova 00717
Calle Carlos E Chardon 00728
Calle Carmelitas Descalzos 00728
Calle Carmelo Seglar 00728
Calle Carmen Pacheco 00728
Calle Carmen Sola Pereira 00730
Calle Carnaval 00717
Calle Carpintero 00716
Calle Carreta 00728
Calle Carrucho 00716
Calle Cascada 00716
Calle Castania 00731
Calle Castellana 00730
Calle Castillo 00730
Calle Caudal 00716
Calle Caviar 00716
Calle Cedi 00728
Calle Cementerio Civil 00730
Calle Central 00730
Calle Cerro Punta 00716
Calle Chalet 00717
Calle Chaparral 00730
Calle Chayanne 00730
Calle Chelin 00728
Calle Chile 00717
Calle China 00716
Calle Cidra 00716
Calle Ciguena 00728
Calle Cima 00730
Calle Cipreses 00730
Calle Cisco 00730
Calle Cisne 00716
Calle Clara Lugo De Cendra 00728
Calle Clarisas 00730
Calle Clavel 00716
Calle Clavelino 00716
Calle Clavellina 00730
Calle Clerigo 00728
Calle Clio 00716
Calle Cobre 00730
Calle Cocollo 00728
Calle Cofresi 00728
Calle Cojoba 00716
Calle Colina 00730
Calle Colirrubia 00716
Calle Colombia 00717
Calle Colon 00730
Calle Colorado 00728
Calle Coloso 00717
Calle Comercio 00730
Calle Comparsa 00717
Calle Concha 00728
Calle Concordia
8000-8199 00717
8200-8299 00730
Calle Condado 00730
Calle Conquista 00717
Calle Convento 00730
Calle Coral 00728
Calle Cordillera 00730
Calle Cordova 00728
Calle Corona 00731
Calle Corozo 00716
Calle Corsario 00728
Calle Cortada 00717
Calle Cosme Tizol 00717
Calle Costa Coral 00717
Calle Covadonga 00730
Calle Cripton 00728
Calle Crisantemos 00730
Calle Cristal 00728
Calle Cristina 00730
Calle Cristo Rey 00730
Calle Cristobal Colon 00730
Calle Cromo 00728
Calle Cruzado 00728
Calle Cuba 00717
Calle Cumbre 00716
Calle Cupey 00716
Calle D
19INT-19INT 00730
D1-D99 00716

E1-E99 00716
1-38 00730
35-399 00730
36-99 00716
40-44 00730
2200-2299 00730
Calle D2 00730
Calle Dalasi 00728
Calle Dalia 00716
Calle Dalila 00730
Calle Damas 00717
Calle Damasco 00728
Calle Damaso Del Toro 00728
Calle Daniela 00728
Calle Danubio 00728
Calle Delfin 00716
Calle Delta 00728
Calle Dened 00717
Calle Despedida 00728
Calle Diamante 00730
Calle Diamela 00728
Calle Dilenia 00728
Calle Diluvio 00728
Calle Dinar 00728
Calle Diploma 00728
Calle Dirham 00728
Calle Dispensario 00716
Calle Distrito
2800-2899 00728
2800-2842 00730
2844-2899 00730
Calle Divina Providencia 00717
Calle Dobra 00728
Calle Doce De Octubre 00730
Calle Dolar 00731
Calle Dolores P Marchado 00728
Calle Domingo Lopez Rivera 00730
Calle Don Diego 00716
Calle Don Quijote 00716
Calle Dona Juana 00716
Calle Doncella 00728
Calle Dorado 00716
Calle Dos De Mayo 00730
Calle Dr Bartolomei 00728
Calle Dr Eusebio Corona 00717
Calle Dr Ferran 00717
Calle Dr Jaime C Diaz 00717
Calle Dr Jose Celso Barbosa 00728
Calle Dr Jose J Henna 00717
Calle Dr Lopez Nussa 00717
Calle Dr Lorenzo A Balasquid 00716
Calle Dr Manuel Pila 00728
Calle Dr Manuel Z Gandia 00717
Calle Dr Pedro Albizu Campos 00716
Calle Dr Santaella 00717
Calle Dr Tommayrac 00717
Calle Dr Ulises Clavell 00716
Calle Dr Virgilio Biaggi 00717
Calle Drama 00728
Calle Duende 00728
Calle Dulcinea 00730
Calle Duquesa 00716
Calle Durazno 00728
Calle E Pujals 00717
Calle E10 00730
Calle E11 00730
Calle E12 00730
Calle E4 00730
Calle E5 00730
Calle E6 00730
Calle E7a 00730
Calle E7b 00730
Calle E9 00730
Calle East Main 00728
Calle Eclipse 00716
Calle Eduardo Cuevas 00717
Calle Eduardo Newman Gandia 00728
Calle Efigenio Coco Ferrer 00728
Calle El Anaez 00728
Calle El Angel 00728
Calle El Belford 00728
Calle El Bud 00728
Calle El Cademus 00728
Calle El Cerro 00730
Calle El Charles 00728
Calle El Condor 00728
Calle El Correo 00728
Calle El Gallardo 00728
Calle El Gato 00730
Calle El Greco 00730
Calle El Lago 00730
Calle El Llano 00730
Calle El Monte 00716
Calle El Relampago 00728
Calle El Reyent 00728
Calle El Sereno 00728
Calle El Temido 00728
Calle El Ventura 00728
Calle El Vigia 00730
Calle El Yeso 00730
Calle Eladio Mattei 00728
Calle Elias Barbosa 00728
Calle Emajagua 00730
Calle Emilio J Pasarell 00728
Calle Emperatriz 00716
Calle Enrique Laguerre 00730
Calle Ensueno 00717
Calle Eros 00716
Calle Escorpio 00716
Calle Escudo
2000-2099 00728
2401-2404 00731
Calle Esmeralda 00730
Calle Espada 00716
Calle Esperanza
2100-2175 00717
2176-2176 00730
2177-2177 00717
2178-2199 00730
Calle Estrella 00730
Calle Eterna 00716
Calle Eureka 00717
Calle Ext Jajome 00730
Calle Ext San Rafael 00730
Calle Extremadura 00730
Calle F 00728
Calle Falcon 00716
Calle Fatima 00730
Calle Fe 00730
Calle Federico Ramos 00717
Calle Felices Dias 00730
Calle Ferrocarril 00717
Calle Fidela Mathew 00728
Calle Figaro 00730
Calle Firmamento 00717
Calle Flamboyan 00716
Calle Flamingo 00716
Calle Flor 00728
Calle Florin 00731
Calle Fogos 00730
Calle Fortuna 00717
Calle Fragancia 00717
Calle Fraile 00716
Calle Francisco G Marin 00728
Calle Francisco Garcia 00716
Calle Francisco Oller 00730
Calle Francisco P Coimbre 00728
Calle Francisco Valls 00730
Calle Francisco Vasallo 00728
Calle Franco 00728
Calle Frontispicio 00730
Calle G 00728
Calle Ga 00728
Calle Gaita 00728
Calle Galan 00728
Calle Galaxia 00717
Calle Galeria 00728
Calle Galilea 00728
Calle Gallardia 00728
Calle Gallardo 00728
Calle Galope 00728
Calle Gamboa 00728
Calle Gardel 00728
Calle Gardenia 00716
Calle Garita 00728
Calle Gaucho 00728
Calle Gaudi 00730
Calle Gaviota 00716
Calle Geminis 00716
Calle Genesis 00728
Calle Gengibre 00730
Calle Genio 00728
Calle Genuino 00728
Calle Gerena 00728
Calle German Rieckehoff Samp 00716
Calle Gibraltar 00730
Calle Gimnasia 00728
Calle Girasol 00716
Calle Gitano 00728
Calle Glacial 00728
Calle Global 00728
Calle Gloria 00730
Calle Gobernadores 00728
Calle Goce 00728
Calle Golondrina 00728
Calle Gorrion 00716
Calle Gotero 00728
Calle Gran Via 00717
Calle Granada 00716
Calle Granate 00728
Calle Granizo 00728
Calle Gregorio Sabater 00728
Calle Grima 00728
Calle Grosella 00716
Calle Guabairo 00728
Calle Guacamayo 00728
Calle Guadalquivir 00728
Calle Guadalupe 00730
Calle Guadiana 00728
Calle Guajana 00730
Calle Guajira 00728
Calle Guama 00716
Calle Guamani 00730
Calle Guanabano 00716
Calle Guanina 00728
Calle Guara 00716
Calle Guaraca 00728
Calle Guaraguao 00716
Calle Guarani 00716
Calle Guardian 00728
Calle Guarionex 00728
Calle Guasima 00730
Calle Guavina 00716
Calle Guayabo 00716
Calle Guayacan 00716
Calle Guayanes 00730
Calle Guilarte 00716
Calle Guillermo Venegas 00728
Calle H 00728
Calle Hermanos Schmidt 00730
Calle Herminia Tormes 00728
Calle Hibiscus 00716
Calle Hidra 00717
Calle Hucar
57A-57B 00716
1-99 00730
1-99 00716
Calle Huelva 00728
Calle I 00728
Calle Ideal 00730
Calle Idilio 00730
Calle Iglesia 00716
Calle Igualdad 00717
Calle Inabon 00728
Calle Industrial 00730
Calle Infanta 00716
Calle Ingenio 00728
Calle Intendente Ramirez 00730
Calle Inti 00728
Calle Isabel 00730
Calle Isabel Segunda 00716
Calle J 00728
Calle J Cortada Quintana 00728
Calle J Gil De La Madrid 00730
Calle Jacaguas 00728
Calle Jacinto Gutierrez 00717
Calle Jacobo Morales 00730
Calle Jaen 00728
Calle Jaguey 00716
Calle Jaime Pericas 00717
Calle Jajome 00730
Calle James E Mcmanus 00717
Calle Jardin Ponciana 00730
Calle Jardines 00730
Calle Jazmin
500-516 00728
1700-1799 00716
Calle Jerez 00716
Calle Jesus T Pineiro 00728
Calle Jobos 00717
Calle Jose A Salaman 00716
Calle Jose Del Toro 00728
Calle Jose Mcdonald 00728
Calle Jose Pocho Labrador 00716
Calle Josefina Moll 00728
Calle Josemaria Escriva 00716
Calle Joseph Benitez 00728
Calle Juan Alindato Garcia 00716
Calle Juan Boria 00728
Calle Juan Cabrel Llul 00728
Calle Juan Davila 00728
Calle Juan De Dios Conde 00728
Calle Juan De Jesus 00728
Calle Juan Guilbe 00716
Calle Juan H Cintron 00730
Calle Juan J Cartagena 00728
Calle Juan Julio Burgos 00728
Calle Juan Martinez 00716
Calle Juan Ortiz De La Renta 00728
Calle Juan Rios Ovalle 00717
Calle Juan Rondon 00728
Calle Juan Santaella 00717
Calle Juan Seix 00730
Calle Juan Xxiii 00728
Calle Juey 00716
Calle Julia De Burgos 00728
Calle Julian Rodriguez 00716
Calle Julio C Arteaga 00717
Calle Julio Medina Moreno 00716
Calle Justo Martinez 00717
Calle K 00728
Calle Kina 00728
Calle Kwacha 00728
Calle Kwanza 00728
Calle Kyat 00728
Calle L 00728
Calle La Almiranta 00728
Calle La Candelaria 00728
Calle La Capitana 00728
Calle La Centella 00728
Calle La Constitucion 00728
Calle La Cosmopolita 00728
Calle La Cruz
1-99 00716
3200-3399 00717
3301-3341 00717
Calle La Diana 00728
Calle La Fuente 00717
Calle La Golondrina 00728
Calle La Joya 00730
Calle La Merced 00728
Calle La Milagrosa 00730
Calle La Monserrate 00730
Calle La Montana 00728
Calle La Nina 00728
Calle La Pinta 00728
Calle La Plata 00730
Calle La Redondela 00728
Calle La Roca 00730
Calle La Salle 00728
Calle La Santa 00716
Calle La Superior 00728
Calle Lady Di 00716
Calle Lafayette 00717
Calle Laffite 00728
Calle Laguna 00716
Calle Lanceoda 00728
Calle Langosta 00716
Calle Laramie 00730
Calle Laredo 00730
Calle Las Carrozas 00717
Calle Las Casas 00730
Calle Las Flores
68A-70A 00716
1-99 00730
87-162 00716
Calle Las Martinez 00730
Calle Las Piedras 00730
Calle Laurel 00716
Calle Lempira 00728
Calle Leo 00716
Calle Leon 00730
Calle Leon Norte 00730
Calle Leone 00728
Calle Lev 00728
Calle Libra 00716
Calle Librado Net 00728
Calle Lidice 00730
Calle Lilas 00716
Calle Lilly 00716
Calle Lima 00716
Calle Linares 00728
Calle Lindaraja 00716
Calle Lineal 00728
Calle Lira 00717
Calle Lisboa 00730
Calle Llanura 00730
Calle Lola Rodriguez De Tio 00728
Calle Lolita Tizol 00730
Calle Loma 00730
Calle Loma Bonita
1-99 00730
1-199 00716
Calle Lorca 00728
Calle Lorencita Ferrer 00728
Calle Lorenza Bizo 00716
Calle Los Canos 00717
Calle Los Cedros 00728
Calle Los Cerezos 00728
Calle Los Hucares 00728
Calle Los Lopez 00717
Calle Los Millonarios 00728
Calle Los Olivos 00728
Calle Los Olmos 00728
Calle Los Pinos 00728
Calle Los Portones 00730
Calle Los Potes 00716
Calle Los Quenepos 00730
Calle Los Robles 00728
Calle Los Rosales 00730
Calle Loti 00728
Calle Lucas Amadeo 00717
Calle Lucero 00717
Calle Luis A Morales 00730
Calle Luis Llorens Torres 00728
Calle Luis Torres Nadal 00728
Calle Luminosa 00716
Calle Luna 00717
Calle Lydia E Rodriguez 00728
Calle Mabo 00728
Calle Mackenzie 00728
Calle Maga 00716
Calle Magnolia 00730
Calle Malaga 00728
Calle Manatee 00716
Calle Mantarraya 00716
Calle Manuel Domenech 00728
Calle Manuel G Tavares 00728
Calle Manuel M Sama 00728
Calle Manuel Torres Torres 00730
Calle Maravilla 00716
Calle Marbella 00716
Calle Marco Aleman 00728
Calle Margarita 00728
Calle Marginal 00730
Calle Maria Cadilla 00728
Calle Marimar 00728
Calle Marina
9100-9199 00717
9200-9299 00730
Calle Mario C Canales 00728
Calle Marlin 00716
Calle Marquesa 00716
Calle Marsella 00728
Calle Martin Corchado 00717
Calle Marzo Cabrera 00717
Calle Mayor
1-19 00730
21-199 00730
2600-2699 00717
Calle Mayor Cantera 00730
Calle Meana 00730
Calle Mejorana 00728
Calle Melaza 00728
Calle Melero 00730
Calle Membrillo 00716
Calle Mendez Vigo
24-30 00730
32-199 00730
7000-7099 00717
Calle Mendez Vigo Ext 00730
Calle Menta 00728
Calle Mercurio 00730
Calle Messier 00717
Calle Miguel A Gonzalez 00728
Calle Miguel Pou 00728
Calle Miguel Rivera Texidor 00730
Calle Millito Navarro 00730
Calle Minero 00716
Calle Minorca 00731
Calle Miosotis 00730
Calle Miramar N 00730
Calle Mirasol 00717
Calle Mississippi 00728
Calle Moca 00716
Calle Modesto Rivera 00717
Calle Modesto Roubert 00717
Calle Mojacar 00728
Calle Molina 00730
Calle Monaco 00716
Calle Monasterio 00730
Calle Monsita Ferrer 00728
Calle Montalvo 00730
Calle Montaner 00730
Calle Monterrey 00716
Calle Mora 00730
Calle Motillo 00716
Calle Munoz Rivera 00716
Calle Murcia 00730
Calle N13 00730
Calle N14 00730
Calle N15 00730
Calle N16 00730
Calle N17 00730
Calle N18 00730
Calle N19 00730
Calle N20 00730
Calle N21 00730
Calle Nacar 00716
Calle Naira 00728
Calle Naranjo 00716
Calle Narciso Serrano 00728
Calle Natacion 00728
Calle Naval 00716
Calle Navarra
EX1-EX99 00716
A20-A99 00716
E1-E99 00716
1200-1299 00730
1500-1599 00730
1600-1698 00730
1800-2099 00716
Calle Nazaret 00717
Calle Nevada 00716
Calle Niagara 00716
Calle Nilo 00728
Calle Ninfa 00716
Calle Noble 00716
Calle Nogal 00716
Calle Novas 00717
Calle Novedades 00730
Calle Novicia 00730
Calle Nube 00716
Calle Nuclear 00716
Calle Nueva Atenas 00730
Calle Nuevo Lek 00728
Calle Nuevo Norte 00730
Calle Nuevo Ponce 00717
Calle Obispado 00716
Calle Oeste 00717
Calle Omani 00728
Calle Opalo 00728
Calle Orca 00716
Calle Orion 00717
Calle Oro 00730
Calle Orquidea 00716
Calle Ostion 00716
Calle Ostra 00717
Calle Otero 00730
Calle Ouguilla 00728
Calle Pabellones 00730
Calle Pacifico 00728
Calle Padre Jeronimo Usera 00728
Calle Padre Jose Mateo 00730
Calle Padre Santiago Guerra 00728
Calle Paisaje 00716
Calle Pajuil 00716
Calle Palma 00716
Calle Palma De Lluvia 00728
Calle Palma De Sierra 00728
Calle Palma Real 00716
Calle Paloma 00716
Calle Paquito Montaner 00717
Calle Parana 00728
Calle Pargo 00716
Calle Pedregal 00716
Calle Pedro Flores 00728
Calle Pedro M Caratini 00717
Calle Pedro Mendez
700-799 00730
1200-1299 00728
Calle Pedro P Cepeda 00717
Calle Pedro Roman Sabater 00730
Calle Pedro Schuck 00728
Calle Pelicano 00716
Calle Peltada 00728
Calle Pendula 00716
Calle Perla 00728
Calle Perpetuo Socorro 00717
Calle Perseo 00717
Calle Pescadilla 00716
Calle Peseta De Espana 00728
Calle Peso 00728
Calle Petalo 00728
Calle Petardo 00730
Calle Picachos 00730
Calle Picaflor 00716
Calle Pico Dulce 00730
Calle Piscis 00716
Calle Pitirre 00728
Calle Placeres 00730

Calle Platino 00730
Calle Plazuela 00717
Calle Podocarpus 00716
Calle Pomarrosa 00716
Calle Pompones 00730
Calle Poncena 00728
Calle Pontevedra 00716
Calle Portugues 00730
Calle Pradera 00730
Calle Prados 00730
Calle Primer Aniversario 00716
Calle Principal
A1-A99 00716
B1-B99 00716
D1-D99 00716
F1-F99 00716
G1-G99 00716
8-14 00730
16-76 00730
40-299 00730
77-399 00730
2700-2722 00728
2701-2721 00728
2723-2799 00728
Calle Progreso
17INT-17INT 00730
4A-4B 00730
1-199 00716
1-43 00730
45-73 00730
Calle Prol Tricoche 00730
Calle Prol Vives 00730
Calle Protestante 00730
Calle Provi Torres 00717
Calle Puerto Rico 00730
Calle Puerto Viejo 00716
Calle Pula 00728
Calle Pulpo 00716
Calle Quetzal 00728
Calle Quinto Aniversario 00716
Calle Quique Lucca 00730
Calle Rafael Hernandez 00728
Calle Rafael Martinez Nadal 00728
Calle Rafael Moreno 00716
Calle Rafael R Esbri 00728
Calle Ramon Power 00717
Calle Ramon R Velez 00716
Calle Ramos Antonini 00728
Calle Reina 00730
Calle Reina De Las Flores 00716
Calle Reinamora 00716
Calle Reniforme 00728
Calle Riachuelo 00716
Calle Rial 00728
Calle Rigel 00717
Calle Riollano 00717
Calle Rito Morel Campos 00717
Calle Rivas 00730
Calle Riverside 00730
Calle Riyal 00728
Calle Roberto Baracoa Collad 00716
Calle Roberto Clemente 00716
Calle Rodulfo Del Valle 00728
Calle Romaguera 00730
Calle Romboidal 00728
Calle Rosa 00728
Calle Rosales 00730
Calle Rosario 00730
Calle Rosas 00730
Calle Rosendo M Cintron 00728
Calle Rosich 00730
Calle Ruanova 00730
Calle Rubi 00728
Calle Rublos 00731
Calle Ruisenor 00716
Calle Rupia
2000-2099 00731
2000-2099 00728
Calle S3 00730
Calle Sabalo 00716
Calle Sabana 00730
Calle Sabanera 00716
Calle Sabiduria 00717
Calle Sabio 00717
Calle Sacra 00716
Calle Sacramento 00717
Calle Sacristia 00717
Calle Sagitada 00728
Calle Sagitario 00716
Calle Salamanca 00716
Calle Saledon 00716
Calle Salerno 00716
Calle Saliente 00716
Calle Salmon 00716
Calle Salou 00716
Calle Salpicon 00717
Calle Salud
1300-1399 00717
1400-1599 00730
Calle Salvador Dijols 00716
Calle Samaria 00716
Calle Samoa 00716
Calle San Alejandro 00730
Calle San Alfonso 00730
Calle San Alvaro 00730
Calle San Andres 00730
Calle San Antonio 00730
Calle San Blas 00730
Calle San Bruno 00730
Calle San Carlos 00730
Calle San Ciprian 00730
Calle San Claudio 00730
Calle San Cosme 00730
Calle San Damian 00730
Calle San Dionisio 00730
Calle San Edmundo 00730
Calle San Esteban 00730
Calle San Expedito 00730
Calle San Felipe 00730
Calle San Fernando 00730
Calle San Francisco 00717
Calle San Gerardo 00730
Calle San Geronimo 00730
Calle San Isaac 00730
Calle San Joaquin 00730
Calle San Juan 00730
Calle San Judas 00730
Calle San Marcos 00730
Calle San Miguel 00730
Calle San Pablo 00730
Calle San Pedro 00730
Calle San Rafael 00730
Calle San Rogelio 00730
Calle Santa Alodia 00730
Calle Santa Ana 00730
Calle Santa Anastacia 00730
Calle Santa Catalina 00730
Calle Santa Cecilia 00730
Calle Santa Fe 00730
Calle Santa Genoveva 00730
Calle Santa Ines 00730
Calle Santa Juanita 00730
Calle Santa Lucia 00730
Calle Santa Luisa 00730
Calle Santa Marta 00716
Calle Santa Monica 00730
Calle Santa Narcisa 00730
Calle Santa Paula 00730
Calle Santa Rita 00730
Calle Santa Suzana 00730
Calle Santiago Oppenheimer 00728
Calle Santillana 00728
Calle Sardina 00716
Calle Sauco 00716
Calle Segovia 00716
Calle Sendero 00716
Calle Senorial 00730
Calle Sentina 00716
Calle Serenata 00717
Calle Seti 00716
Calle Sevilla 00716
Calle Shangai 00730
Calle Shequel 00728
Calle Sicilia 00716
Calle Siclo 00728
Calle Sierra 00716
Calle Siervas De Maria 00730
Calle Silvia Rexach 00728
Calle Sirena 00716
Calle Sirio 00717
Calle Sol 00730
Calle Sol De Canada 00730
Calle Soldevila 00716
Calle Soledad Llorens 00728
Calle Solimar 00716
Calle Solis 00716
Calle Soller 00717
Calle Sonia 00717
Calle Sor M Rosa Rivera 00728
Calle Soria 00716
Calle Sucre 00728
Calle Sultana 00717
Calle Sur 00717
Calle Surco 00728
Calle Syli 00728
Calle Tablado 00716
Calle Tabonuco 00716
Calle Tacita 00728
Calle Taino 00716
Calle Taita 00716
Calle Taka 00728
Calle Tala 00728
Calle Tamarindo 00716
Calle Tamborin 00728
Calle Tamesis 00728
Calle Tanama 00728
Calle Tarragona 00716
Calle Tartagos 00730
Calle Tauro 00716
Calle Tejerina 00716
Calle Tejido 00728
Calle Temor 00728
Calle Templado 00728
Calle Tenaz 00728
Calle Tendal 00716
Calle Tenerife 00716
Calle Tenor 00728
Calle Ternura 00728
Calle Terranova 00716
Calle Tetuan 00716
Calle Tiaret 00716
Calle Tiben 00716
Calle Tiburon 00716
Calle Tite Curet Alonzo 00730
Calle Tobar 00716
Calle Toledo 00716
Calle Tolosa 00716
Calle Tomas Alcala 00730
Calle Topacio 00728
Calle Torre 00730
Calle Torrecillas 00716
Calle Torres 00717
Calle Toscania 00716
Calle Trampolin 00728
Calle Trapiche 00728
Calle Tricia 00716
Calle Tricoche 00730
Calle Trigo 00716
Calle Trinitaria 00716
Calle Tropical 00716
Calle Trucha 00716
Calle Trujillo 00730
Calle Tudela 00716
Calle Tulipanes 00730
Calle Turabo 00716
Calle Turin 00716
Calle Turina 00716
Calle Turpial 00716
Calle Turquesa 00728
Calle Tutin Rosado 00716
Calle Ulpiano Colon 00728
Calle Union Final 00730
Calle Universidad 00717
Calle Urayoan 00728
Calle Ursula Cardona 00728
Calle Valdivieso 00716
Calle Valladolid 00730
Calle Vannina 00717
Calle Varsovia 00717
Calle Vatu 00728
Calle Velazquez 00730
Calle Venus 00730
Calle Verbena 00728
Calle Verdun 00717
Calle Vereda 00716
Calle Veronica Acevedo Sepul 00730
Calle Victor Gutierrez 00728
Calle Victoria 00730
Calle Villa
305INT-323INT 00730
268A-268D 00730
100-387 00730
389-397 00730
399-599 00728
401-417 00728
419-441 00728
Calle Villa Madrid 00730
Calle Virginia 00730
Calle Virgo 00716
Calle Virtud 00730
Calle Vista Del Cobre 00728
Calle Vista Dorada 00728
Calle Vista Plateada 00728
Calle Viva La Pepa 00730
Calle Vivas Valdivieso 00728
Calle Vives 00730
Calle Vizcaya 00716
Calle W22a 00730
Calle W22b 00730
Calle W23 00730
Calle W24a 00730
Calle W24b 00730
Calle W25 00730
Calle W26 00730
Calle W27 00730
Calle Washington 00730
Calle West Main 00728
Calle Wilson 00717
Calle Wong 00728
Calle Yagrumo 00716
Calle Yaguez
1-2999 00730
2300-2399 00728
Calle Yen 00728
Calle Yerba Buena 00728
Calle Yuan 00728
Calle Yucatan 00728
Calle Yunque 00728
Calle Yuquiyu 00728
Calle Zafiro 00728
Calle Zaire 00728
Calle Zaragoza 00730
Calle Zarina 00716
Calle Zorzal 00728
Calle Zumbador 00728
Calle Zurbaran 00730
Callejon Avispa 00730
Callejon Besitos 00730
Callejon Borinquen 00730
Callejon Brea 00716
Callejon Campana 00730
Callejon Cangrejo
239INT-241INT 00730
217INT-237INT 00730
243INT-247INT 00730
1-3 00728
5-99 00728
200-299 00730
Callejon Chardon 00716
Callejon Comercio 00730
Callejon Del Rio 00716
Callejon El Tiro 00716
Callejon Fagot
9INT-9INT 00730
1-499 00730
1300-1399 00717
Callejon Higuerito 00730
Callejon Juan Ramon 00716
Callejon La Mora 00730
Callejon Lang 00717
Callejon Las Martinez 00730
Callejon Lin 00717
Callejon Los Novios 00730
Callejon Magdalena 00730
Callejon Medina 00717
Callejon Mucaro 00717
Callejon Negrito 00728
Callejon Palito 00716
Callejon Pao 00730
Callejon Patio Hernandez 00730
Callejon Patio Rosa 00717
Callejon Placeres 00730
Callejon Puerto Arturo 00730
Callejon Rodriguez 00730
Callejon Sabater 00717
Callejon Sevilla 00730
Callejon Tricoche 00730
Callejon Vigo 00716
Camino Viejo 00728
Canas Ind Park 00728
Carr 1 00716
Carr 123 00728
Carr 132 00728
Carr 505 00730
Carr 591 00728
Carr Campo De Golf 00730
Carr Guayanilla 00717
Carr Vigia Vieja 00730
Chalets Del Bulevar 00716
Clerrani 00717
Cond La Ceiba 00717
Cond Los Flamboyanes 00716
Cond Tibes Town House 00730
El Tuque Industrial Park 00728
Estancias Del Sur 00728
Ext Dr Pila 00716
Ext El Yeso 00730
Gianna Laura Apts I 00716
Gianna Laura Apts Ii 00716
Grancoma 00728
Ind San Rafael 00716
Las Americas Housing 00717
Los Caobos Industrial Park 00716
Marginal Conchita Dapena 00717
Noridenc 00716
Pasaje Oliver 00730
Paseo Alhambra 00716
Paseo Arias 00730
Paseo Artesanal 00716
Paseo Atocha 00730
Paseo Azucena 00730
Paseo Buena Vis 00717
Paseo Caracoles 00717
Paseo Caracoles Int 00717
Paseo Cundeamor 00730
Paseo De La Loma 00716
Paseo De La Pradera 00716
Paseo De La Reina 00716
Paseo De La Sierra 00716
Paseo De La Vega 00716
Paseo De Pesca 00728
Paseo Del Cerro 00716
Paseo Del Llano 00716
Paseo Del Principe 00716
Paseo Del Puerto 00716
Paseo Del Rey 00716
Paseo Del Valle 00716
Paseo Del Veterano 00716
Paseo Don Onofre 00730
Paseo El Tuque 00728
Paseo Fagot 00716
Paseo Floresta 00730
Paseo Hector Lavoe 00717
Paseo Hormigueros 00730
Paseo La Colonia 00717
Paseo La Feria 00730
Paseo La Guancha 00716
Paseo La Vega 00716
Paseo Las Monjitas 00730
Paseo Mercedita 00717
Paseo Morel Campos 00728
Paseo Nardos 00730
Paseo Perla Del Sur 00717
Paseo Polyantha 00730
Paseo Real 00716
Paseo Rocio Del Cielo 00730
Paseo Sauri 00716
Paseo Talantalan 00730
Paseo Trebol 00730
Paseo Versatil 00716
Paseo Vila 00716
Paseo Villa Flores 00716
Paseo Zinnia 00730
Patio Moreno 00717
Ponce Byp
1700-1898 00716
1900-2000 00716
2001-2599 00717
2002-2598 00716
2600-3600 00728
3602-3798 00728
3701-3797 00728
3799-3898 00728
Repto El Valle 00728
Repto Lomas Del Sol 00728
Res Aristides Chavier 00728
Res Dr Pila 00716
Res E Ramos Antonini 00716
Res Gandara 00717
Res La Ceiba 00716
Res Lirios Del Sur 00716
Res Lopez Nussa 00717
Res Los Rosales 00730
Res Miramar Housing 00728
Res Pedro J Rosaly 00717
Res Perla Del Caribe 00730
Res Ponce De Leon 00717
Res Ponce Housing 00730
Res Portuguez 00730
Res Santiago Iglesias 00730
Res Tormos Diego 00730
Res Villa Del Caribe 00728
Res Villa Elena 00730
Res Villa Machuelo 00730
Riberas Del Bucana Iii 00731
Sabanetas Ind Pk 00716
Sect Las Batatas 00728
Sect Los Chinos 00730
Sect Playita 00730
Villa Ponce Housing 00730
Villa Ramonita 00728
Zona Ind Reparada 1 00716
Zona Ind Reparada 2 00716

SAN JUAN PR

General Delivery 00936

POST OFFICE BOXES MAIN OFFICE STATIONS AND BRANCHES

Box No.s
1000 - 1009 00955
2100 - 2641 00922
6001 - 6899 00914
7001 - 7899 00916
8000 - 8999 00910
9000 - 10260 00908
10001 - 12011 00922
11001 - 11881 00910
12001 - 12386 00914
13000 - 13999 00908
14001 - 14593 00916
15011 - 15091 00902
16001 - 16894 00908
19000 - 19980 00910
20001 - 21540 00928
20961 - 20996 00910
21301 - 23500 00931
25001 - 28002 00928
29001 - 31360 00929
33001 - 33200 00933
37001 - 38100 00937
40001 - 42008 00940
50004 - 50072 00902
70100 - 72010 00936
190001 - 195777 00919
270001 - 270460 00928
360001 - 368180 00936
9020001 - 9027515 00902
9065001 - 9067517 00906
9227511 - 9227516 00922
9300001 - 9300960 00928

RURAL ROUTES

02, 03, 06, 07, 09, 10, 16, 17, 18, 35, 36, 37 00926

NAMED STREETS

Andoners 00921
Apartments Santa Ana 00927
Ave E 00915
Ave 65 Infanteria
A1-A99 00926
17-29 00926
49-61 00923
63-499 00923
300-398 00926
400-499 00926
424-424 00926
470-498 00923
700-1199 00924
1100-1134 00924
Ave A 00915
Ave Alterial B 00918
Ave Americo Miranda
340-498 00927
401-405 00927
900-1299 00921
1000-1098 00921
1300-1599 00921
1600-1799 00921
Ave Ana G Mendez 00926
Ave Andalucia
300-749 00920
750-799 00921
Ave Arterial Hostos 00918
Ave Ashford
800-898 00907
900-1499 00907
1500-1599 00911
1485-1-1485-99 00907
Ave Avelino Vicente 00909
Ave Baldorioty De Castro
600-698 00907
1900-1998 00912
Ave Barbosa
257INT-257INT 00917
200-309 00917
238-262 00917
252-264 00917
264-308 00917
310-698 00917
311-335 00917
425-701 00923
579-1069 00923
735-739 00915
1000-1098 00925
1801-1869 00912
Ave Borinquen 00915
Ave Borinquen Final 00915
Ave Caimito 00926
Ave Carlos Chardon 00918
Ave Condado 00907
Ave D 00915
Ave De Diego
1-188 00927
1-75 00911
60-114 00907
81-95 00927
103-105 00911
122-127 00921
126-126 00907
127-199 00911
128-128 00921
129-199 00921

150-150 00907
190-1698 00927
201-201 00927
250-799 00920
299-307 00909
309-329 00909
331-399 00909
751-900 00921
901-939 00921
902-928 00921
930-938 00921
940-999 00921
Ave De La Constitucion 00901
Ave Delcasse 00907
Ave Dona Felisa Rincon De 00926
Ave Eduardo Conde
1700-2015 00912
2017-2051 00912
2050-2050 00915
2052-2426 00915
2428-2498 00915
Ave Emiliano Pol 00926
Ave Escorial 00920
Ave F 00915
Ave Fd Roosevelt
102-106 00918
108-505 00918
150-248 00918
250-398 00918
507-583 00918
585-585 00936
601-699 00918
900-1400 00920
1200-1398 00920
1400-1487 00920
1402-1498 00920
1489-1499 00920
Ave Fernandez Juncos
2-98 00901
100-499 00901
501-599 00901
600-1299 00907
1300-1999 00909
Ave Gandara 00925
Ave Gilberto Monroig
1800-2022 00912
2024-2050 00912
2055-2055 00915
2057-2299 00915
Ave H 00915
Ave Hostos 00918
Ave I 00915
Ave J 00915
Ave Jesus T Pinero
200-200 00918
201-299 00927
202-310 00927
258-398 00918
282-286 00927
312-329 00927
500-600 00918
900-1998 00921
1001-1905 00920
Ave La Sierra 00926
Ave Las Brisas 00926
Ave Las Mansiones 00924
Ave Las Palmas 00907
Ave Las Palomas 00926
Ave Lomas Verdes 00927
Ave Los Chalets 00926
Ave Los Parques 00926
Ave Los Romeros 00926
Ave Magdalena 00907
Ave Marginal Barbosa 00923
Ave Monte Carlo 00924
Ave Montehiedra 00926
Ave Munoz Rivera
5-51 00901
44-50 00918
54-98 00901
73-247 00918
204-224 00918
249-271 00918
273-399 00918
296-352 00901
396-402 00918
401-401 00901
401-425 00918
402-402 00901
404-698 00918
433-499 00901
501-699 00918
556-648 00918
701-1199 00925
876-998 00927
1000-1298 00927
1001-1101 00925
Ave Nemesio R Canales 00918
Ave Park Gdns 00926
Ave Paseo Real 00926
Ave Paz Granela 00921
Ave Plaza Las Americas 00918
Ave Ponce De Leon
1-611 00917
2-574 00918
403-577 00917
604-606 00907
610-610 00918
613-613 00907
613-615 00917
619-619 00907
619-619 00917
621-621 00907
623-623 00917
625-625 00907
625-627 00917
650-650 00907
650-650 00918
651-651 00917
651-651 00907
652-655 00907
654-662 00918
655-655 00917
657-667 00907
669-671 00907
673-701 00907
702-750 00918
703-703 00917
705-705 00907
705-735 00917
762-762 00907
776-776 00925
800-805 00907
804-806 00925
807-1001 00907
808-1000 00907
1000-1023 00925
1025-1061 00925
1050-1072 00925
1050-1050 00907
1052-1054 00907
1056-1065 00907
1067-1103 00907
1100-1108 00925
1105-1107 00907
1109-1117 00907
1110-1122 00925
1119-1149 00907
1124-1130 00925
1151-1151 00925
1153-1197 00907
1199-1434 00907
1200-1229 00926
1231-1299 00926
1301-1387 00926
1389-1391 00926
1393-1399 00926
1436-1492 00907
1455-1457 00926
1459-1621 00926
1500-1561 00909
1563-1899 00909
1590-1590 00926
1600-1998 00909
1623-1661 00926
1717-1769 00926
1903-1999 00915
Ave Principal 00924
Ave Rafael Hernandez Marin 00924
Ave Ramon B Lopez 00923
Ave Rexach 00915
Ave Roberto H Todd 00907
Ave Roberto Sanchez Vilella 00924
Ave Sagrado Corazon 00915
Ave San Alfonso 00921
Ave San Ignacio 00921
Ave San Patricio
601-633 00920
635-650 00920
652-698 00920
700-899 00921
829-849 00921
900-1098 00921
1400-1499 00921
Ave Simon Madera 00924
Ave Universidad 00925
Ave Victor M Labiosa 00926
Ave Winston Churchill 00926
Baninsou 00901
Beastern 00912
Blvd De La Fuente 00926
Blvd De La Montana 00926
Blvd Ramallo 00926
Blvd Sagrado Corazon 00909
Blvd San Miguel 00926
Bo Tortugo 00926
Boulevard Del Morro 00901
Butheana 00924
Caleta De Las Monjas 00901
Caleta De San Juan 00901
Calle E
G1-G99 00926
BG1-BG99 00926
F1-1-F1-99 00926
G1-1-G1-99 00926
A4-A6 00926
D9-D18 00926
E1-E11 00926
90-99 00924
101-103 00924
203-299 00917
Calle N 00917
Calle Un
64B-64B 00915
1-99 00915
200-210 00918
212-298 00918
600-610 00907
612-799 00907
Calle 1
C1-C99 00921
Calle 1
D1-D99 00921
F1-F99 00921
H1-H99 00921
F1-F99 00924
B3-B4 00924
H1-H99 00924
J1-J99 00924
A2-A6 00926
K1-K99 00926
G1-G99 00926
H1-H99 00926
I1-I99 00926
E1-E99 00926
B1-B99 00927
B1-B99 00921
358A-358E 00924
K18A-K18A 00926
B5-B7 00926
B1-B4 00926
B1-B5 00926
C13-C13 00926
A3-A24 00926
B1-B7 00926
B16-B20 00926
A2-A7 00926
B1-B12 00926
D1-D12 00926
D1-D10 00926
D4-D13 00926
A12-A22 00921
A1-A43 00924
B1-B20 00924
C1-C6 00924
D1-D11 00924
A10-A99 00921
A9-A13 00926
C13-C99 00927
A1-A15 00924
A1-A13 00926
B16-B36 00926
C1-C6 00926
338A-338G 00924
343B-343C 00924
345A-345G 00924
B4-B18 00926
D1-D5 00926
C1-C10 00923
D9-D99 00923
E1-E99 00923
339A-339C 00924
344B-344D 00924
B2-B62 00926
B8-B12 00926
C18-C39 00926
C40-C40 00926
A1-A24 00926
B21-B39 00926
A1-A3 00926
B1-B10 00926
B1A-B1A 00926
C12-C21 00926
C37-C44 00926
B1-B14 00924
A1-A10 00926
1-47 00920
1-16 00926
1-7 00926
2-23 00926
2-99 00926
11-99 00924
14-26 00927
17-25 00924
49-99 00920
53-57 00920
64-78 00926
91-118 00926
100-100 00926
125-127 00926
129-151 00926
136-198 00917
153-175 00926
200-299 00924
300-399 00915
300-370 00924
400-400 00924
403-526 00923
405-405 00924
528-528 00923
700-799 00915
701-771 00920
1038-1055 00924
1060-1062 00927
1064-1099 00927
1101-1199 00927
1201-1299 00924
Calle 1 NE 00920
Calle 10
Y1-Y99 00924
K1-K99 00924
L1-L99 00924
N1-N99 00924
O1-O99 00924
D1-D99 00926
F1-F99 00926
N1-N99 00926
C1-C99 00926
N7-N12 00926
D14-D19 00926
M7-M99 00926
M2-M10 00926
116INT-122INT 00917
M1-M4 00926
126INT-126INT 00917
159INT-159INT 00917
B13-B49 00926
B1-B12 00926
1-1 00926
3-299 00926
50-99 00924
100-134 00917
101-109 00924
114-128 00917
135-145 00917
136-146 00917
250-250 00926
401-427 00915
429-437 00915
438-440 00924
439-799 00915
450-798 00915
800-1398 00924
1000-1099 00927
Calle 10 NE 00920
Calle 10a 00924
Calle 11
L1-L99 00924
M1-M99 00924
I1-I99 00926
J1-J99 00926
C1-C99 00926
E1-E99 00926
G1-G99 00926
H1-H99 00926
S1-1-S1-99 00926
S2-1-S2-99 00926
387A-387B 00924
7INT-9INT 00917
698INT-698INT 00917
738INT-738INT 00915
1-1 00917
1-99 00926
3-182 00917
15-131 00917
30-391 00917
133-702 00917
184-1098 00917
300-399 00924
393-393 00917
400-799 00915
900-1198 00924
1000-1024 00923
1024-1099 00927
1026-1098 00923
1200-1299 00924
Calle 11 NE 00920
Calle 12
M1-M99 00924
N1-N99 00924
N1-N99 00926
O1-O99 00926
C1-C99 00926
L1-L99 00926
S1-S99 00926
3-99 00924
200-399 00926
400-799 00915
801-899 00924
901-997 00923
999-1099 00923
1037-1075 00927
1077-1085 00927
Calle 12 NE 00920
Calle 12 De Octubre 00918
Calle 12a 00924
Calle 13
Q1-Q99 00926
C1-C99 00926
H1-H99 00926
I1-I99 00926
Z1-Z99 00926
650-699 00924
901-997 00923
999-1049 00923
1050-1199 00927
1200-1299 00926
1250-1299 00924
Calle 13 NE 00920
Calle 13a 00924
Calle 14
A1-A99 00926
D1-D99 00926
S1-S99 00926
O1-O99 00926
I1-I99 00926
189A-189B 00924
193A-193D 00924
GI1-GI99 00924
194A-194A 00924
A-G 00926
188A-188D 00924
E1-E99 00926
P7-P99 00926
1-1 00926
184-192 00924
194-194 00924
600-799 00915
801-899 00924
1000-1099 00927
Calle 14 NE 00920
Calle 15
P1-P99 00924
B1-B99 00926
F1-F99 00926
G1-G99 00926
J1-J99 00926
L1-L99 00926
M1-M6 00926
M1-M99 00926
O1-O99 00923
P1-P6 00926
1-619 00924
101-199 00926
800-1299 00924
1000-1199 00927
1201-1259 00926
1261-1265 00926
1267-1269 00926
Calle 15 NE 00920
Calle 15a 00924
Calle 16
S1-S99 00924
T1-T99 00924
B1-B99 00926
C1-C99 00926
J1-J99 00926
K1-K99 00926
199A-199D 00924
191B-191B 00924
399A-399G 00924
400A-400I 00924
188-194 00924
196-199 00924
301-399 00927
399-400 00924
Calle 16 NE 00920
Calle 16a 00924
Calle 17
T1-T99 00924
U1-U99 00924
C1-C99 00926
D1-D99 00926
G1-G99 00926
K1-K99 00926
L1-L99 00926
O1-O99 00926
119B-119C 00924
4-258 00926
20-399 00924
800-1299 00924
1000-1115 00927
1117-1199 00927
Calle 17 NE 00920
Calle 18
U1-U99 00924
V1-V99 00924
K1-K99 00926
Z1-1-Z1-99 00924
43A-43B 00924
44-68 00924
70-699 00924
300-1099 00927
490-599 00915
800-1398 00924
Calle 18 NE 00920
Calle 19
V1-V99 00924
F1-F99 00926
G1-G99 00926
L1-L99 00926
M1-M99 00926
O10-O99 00924
O1-O9 00926
S14-S21 00926
300-399 00924
800-1299 00924
1000-1099 00927
Calle 19 NE 00920
Calle 1a 00924
Calle 1t 00926
Calle 2
D1-D99 00924
D1-D4 00924
A1-A99 00924
H1-H99 00926
A1-1-A1-99 00924
350A-350D 00924
D4-D7 00926
C10-C17 00926
C1-C5 00926
D1-D3 00926
C1-C12 00926
B5-B7 00926
C1-C14 00926
B6-B16 00926
D6-D10 00926
B18-B20 00926
B8-B16 00926
A1-A7 00926
B21-B23 00926
C1-C6 00924
C9-C11 00924
B20-B99 00924
C7-C19 00924
A1-A16 00927
C1-C5 00927
B13-B22 00921
C1-C10 00921
F1-F99 00926
B10-B29 00926
E3-E8 00926
B1-B13 00923
C11-C26 00923
F1-F7 00923
F1-F99 00924
9A-9H 00924
A1-A8 00926
D1-D8 00926
A12-A22 00926
B1-B16 00926
C1-C4 00926
B30-B99 00926
C51-C99 00926
C1-C11 00926
C45-C57 00926
D58-D75 00926
350INT-350INT 00924
1-78 00926
7-9 00924
9-99 00926
14-28 00926
17-22 00927
30-47 00926
66-79 00926
100-134 00917
100-126 00927
100-298 00926
135-199 00917
136-198 00917
300-399 00924
400-515 00923
435-440 00926
439-455 00924
520-532 00923
701-703 00915
705-707 00915
707-799 00915
709-719 00915
801-847 00924
849-1259 00924
1000-1029 00925
1031-1257 00924
1259-1399 00924
4398-4398 00926
Calle 2 NE 00920
Calle 20
CC1-CC99 00924
D1-D99 00926
F1-F99 00926
M1-M99 00926
N1-N99 00926
36A-36B 00924

35A-35C 00924
37-99 00924
300-399 00927
800-1399 00924
Calle 20 NE 00920
Calle 21
M1-M99 00926
N1-N99 00926
O1-O99 00926
499A-499B 00924
S1-S24 00926
497-599 00924
1300-1399 00924
Calle 21 NE 00920
Calle 22
224A-224B 00924
225A-225C 00924
228A-228B 00924
229A-229B 00924
100-300 00924
300-399 00927
302-450 00924
Calle 22 SW 00921
Calle 22a 00924
Calle 23 00924
Calle 23a 00924
Calle 24
85A-85C 00924
97A-97A 00924
84-98 00924
300-399 00927
Calle 24 SW 00921
Calle 25 00924
Calle 26
398A-398G 00924
200-299 00924
300-397 00927
398-398 00924
399-399 00927
Calle 26 SE 00921
Calle 27 00924
Calle 28
326-349 00924
350-399 00927
Calle 28 SE 00921
Calle 29 00924
Calle 29a 00924
Calle 2a 00926
Calle 3
G1-G99 00924
C13-C24 00926
C1-C7 00926
D1-D6 00926
C7-C12 00926
D1-D5 00926
C1-C8 00926
B1-B6 00926
D18-D19 00926
B34-B35 00926
D1-D7 00926
B1-B3 00921
D15-D28 00921
E1-E14 00921
F7-F29 00921
J1-J5 00921
E8-E14 00924
F30-F99 00924
B1-B3 00924
C1-C2 00924
H9-H15 00924
B30-B99 00926
C22-C59 00926
E1-E3 00926
F1-F6 00926
B7-B29 00927
C6-C12 00927
347A-347G 00924
H1-H99 00923
H10A-H10A 00923
I1-I99 00923
I13A-I15A 00923
A1-A99 00926
C1-C9 00926
D1-D6 00926
C60-C99 00926
D77-D99 00926
J1-J99 00926

S2-1-S2-99 00926
S3-1-S3-99 00926
S4-1-S4-99 00926
346A-346F 00924
164INT-164INT 00917
C7-C11 00921
C11-C19 00921
5-13 00927
50-59 00921
68-79 00926
100-199 00917
100-199 00926
300-312 00926
314-350 00926
346-348 00924
350-351 00924
352-398 00926
415-415 00923
417-510 00923
498-499 00923
512-540 00923
600-699 00924
800-1299 00924
1000-1199 00927
1000-1014 00925
1016-1023 00925
1025-1099 00925
1200-1208 00926
1210-1239 00926
Calle 3 NE 00920
Calle 3 Final 00921
Calle 30
266B-266C 00924
267A-267D 00924
250B-250C 00924
250-254 00924
256-270 00924
300-399 00927
Calle 30 SE 00921
Calle 31 00924
Calle 32
200-325 00924
300-338 00927
301-399 00927
600-699 00924
1000-1098 00921
Calle 32 SW 00921
Calle 33 00924
Calle 33a 00924
Calle 34 00924
Calle 34a 00924
Calle 35 00924
Calle 36 00924
Calle 36b 00924
Calle 37 00924
Calle 37a 00924
Calle 38 SE 00921
Calle 39 00924
Calle 3a 00926
Calle 3b 00926
Calle 3t 00926
Calle 4
F1-F99 00924
E1-E8 00926
K1-K99 00926
L1-L99 00926
M1-M99 00926
N1-N99 00926
B1-B99 00926
S1-1-S1-99 00926
S2-1-S2-99 00926
S3-1-S3-99 00926
E7-E10 00926
386A-386C 00924
428A-428D 00924
I9-I12 00926
I1-I3 00926
J6-J26 00926
F7-F8 00924
G1-G4 00924
G1-G5 00926
D7-D8 00926
H1-H13 00926
I16-I25 00926
J1-J15 00926
A1-A99 00923
G1-G10 00923

H1-H20 00923
GA6-GA6 00923
D7-D13 00926
E1-E9 00926
G1-G18 00924
H13-H99 00926
358A-358F 00924
343A-343G 00924
27-39 00927
39-83 00917
40-72 00921
62-73 00917
73-80 00926
85-199 00917
300-399 00927
342-348 00924
344-344 00924
350-499 00924
400-499 00926
601-699 00924
719-799 00915
801-819 00924
821-847 00924
849-1299 00924
1000-1099 00925
Calle 4 NE 00920
Calle 40
D1-D99 00924
E1-E99 00924
F1-F99 00924
40-40 00923
200-298 00924
Calle 40 SE 00921
Calle 40 Final 00924
Calle 41
G1-G99 00924
146B-146C 00924
155B-155D 00924
157B-157E 00924
183A-183A 00924
141-184 00924
186-190 00924
440-498 00926
1001-1097 00927
1099-1199 00927
Calle 41 SE 00921
Calle 42 00924
Calle 42a
3B1-3B99 00926
100-199 00924
Calle 43
G1-G99 00924
H1-H99 00924
K1-K99 00924
220A-220B 00924
280A-280A 00924
200-281 00924
300-399 00926
Calle 43 SE 00921
Calle 44
F1-F99 00924
H1-H99 00924
300-399 00924
600-724 00926
726-728 00926
Calle 44 SE 00921
Calle 44a 00926
Calle 45
H1-H99 00924
217A-217C 00924
221B-221C 00924
201A-201B 00924
208A-208B 00924
204A-204C 00924
185A-185B 00924
210INT-210INT 00924
100-500 00924
186-299 00926
502-598 00924
Calle 45 SE 00921
Calle 45a 00924
Calle 46
A1-A99 00923
100-199 00926
1801-1889 00926
1891-1999 00926
Calle 46 SE 00921

Calle 47
100-299 00926
140-149 00924
1800-1886 00926
1888-1999 00926
Calle 47 SE 00921
Calle 48 00926
Calle 49
152-599 00924
220-240 00924
239-299 00926
341-343 00924
Calle 49 SE 00921
Calle 5
E1-E99 00921
J1-J99 00921
K1-K99 00926
L1-L99 00926
D11-D14 00926
E1-E2 00926
E1-E17 00926
I1-I99 00926
D13-D99 00926
B4-B6 00921
B50-B99 00926
C8-C99 00926
J1-J99 00926
B7-B49 00926
D1-D10 00926
H17-H99 00926
I10-I15 00926
J1-J5 00926
A8-A99 00926
B1-B6 00926
D1-D14 00924
F1-F99 00924
E10-E19 00926
F1-F99 00926
76INT-76INT 00917
76FINAL-76FINAL 00917
98A-98B 00924
99A-99B 00924
H1-H16 00926
85INT-85INT 00917
S9-15-S9-99 00926
108A-108A 00924
78A-78A 00917
83A-83A 00917
1-73 00926
1-99 00901
74-99 00926
74-79 00917
76-199 00917
81-108 00924
81-83 00917
600-799 00915
850-1299 00924
1000-1024 00925
1000-1000 00926
1024-1199 00927
1200-1238 00926
1229-1229 00926
Calle 5 NE 00920
Calle 5 Rafael Villegas 00926
Calle 5 T 00926
Calle 50 00926
Calle 51 00926
Calle 52 00924
Calle 53 SE 00921
Calle 53b 00926
Calle 54 00924
Calle 55 00924
Calle 56 SE 00921
Calle 57 SE 00921
Calle 58 SE 00921
Calle 5a 00926
Calle 6
I1-I99 00926
A1-A99 00926
S7-1-S7-99 00926
S5-1-S5-99 00926
S6-1-S6-99 00926
J9-J99 00926
L1-L8 00926
F1-F99 00924
B50-B99 00926
E1-E8 00926

K1-K14 00926
E9-E99 00926
F1-F9 00926
J1-J10 00926
K7-K99 00926
L3-L99 00926
B1-B49 00926
C1-C99 00924
401D-403D 00924
90INT-92INT 00917
439INT-439INT 00926
F1-F22 00926
G1-G99 00926
96A-96A 00917
462B-462B 00926
AE1-AE99 00926
H1-H15 00926
O1-O5 00926
10-14 00926
84-84 00917
84-139 00917
86-97 00917
99-99 00917
100-122 00924
100-105 00917
123-199 00924
141-199 00917
300-399 00927
301-305 00926
307-309 00926
311-463 00926
465-499 00926
600-799 00915
901-999 00924
1000-1099 00925
Calle 6 NE 00920
Calle 60
BA6A-BA7A 00926
BA4-BA99 00926
BC1-BC15 00926
600-699 00924
Calle 61 00926
Calle 61a 00926
Calle 62 00926
Calle 63 00926
Calle 64 00926
Calle 65 00926
Calle 65a 00926
Calle 68 00926
Calle 69 00926
Calle 7
H1-H99 00924
E1-E99 00924
G1-G99 00926
H1-H99 00926
I1-I99 00926
J1-J99 00926
349A-349B 00924
357A-357B 00924
E9-E14 00926
F1-F10 00926
L1-L4 00926
M1-M9 00926
M10-M99 00926
E1-E9 00926
F1-F7 00926
F11-F99 00924
348A-348F 00924
347F-347G 00924
346B-346B 00924
375A-375C 00924
86A-86B 00924
1-9 00924
1-99 00917
36-99 00926
50-399 00924
1000-1079 00925
1080-1199 00927
1200-1240 00926
1241-1299 00924
1300-1398 00924
Calle 7 NE 00920
Calle 7a
D1-D99 00926
A1-1-A1-99 00924
A2-1-A2-99 00924
A3-1-A3-99 00924

D1-D99 00924
A12-A13 00924
Calle 7g 00924
Calle 8
Y1-Y99 00924
B1-B99 00924
E1-E99 00924
J1-J99 00924
L1-L99 00926
G1-G99 00926
O1-O99 00926
C1-C99 00926
D1-D99 00926
S7-1-S7-99 00926
S8-1-S8-99 00926
M11-M99 00926
M1-M10 00926
H11-H99 00924
J10-J16 00926
H1-H10 00926
B1-B99 00924
18-20 00917
22-33 00917
143-145 00924
147-340 00924
159-199 00917
200-261 00925
360-399 00926
600-799 00915
1000-1099 00927
1000-1018 00925
1200-1399 00924
Calle 8 NE 00920
Calle 8a 00924
Calle 8e 00926
Calle 9
F1-F99 00926
K1-K99 00926
L1-L99 00926
C1-C99 00926
D1-D99 00926
M1-M99 00926
J6-J99 00924
K1-K8 00924
I1-I9 00926
O6-O8 00926
N1-N99 00926
N1-N99 00926
49-66 00917
53-63 00924
600-699 00924
1000-1099 00925
1100-1199 00927
1200-1299 00924
Calle 9 NE 00920
Calle A
G1-G99 00926
BA1-BA99 00926
BB1-BB99 00926
B1-B25 00926
BB17A-BB18A 00926
A1-1-A1-99 00926
A1-1A-A1-1A 00926
B1-1-B1-99 00926
D1-D99 00926
B27-B37 00926
C30-C99 00926
B1-B9 00926
E1-E9 00926
C1-C29 00926
C1-1-C1-99 00926
A1-A14 00926
A1-A14 00926
B1-B16 00926
A1-A11 00926
A1-A99 00924
B1-B99 00924
A20-A99 00926
E65-E99 00926
1-30 00926
1-68 00907
32-32 00926
42-545 00917
84-86 00926
88-94 00926
100-299 00926
140-141 00924

165-165 00924
208-299 00917
390-398 00920
400-598 00920
418-418 00920
547-653 00917
1700-1705 00926
Calle A Arche Diaz 00924
Calle A De Los Reyes 00924
Calle A Ganivet 00926
Calle A Machado 00926
Calle Abolicion 00918
Calle Aboy 00907
Calle Acacia
K1-K99 00926
1-3 00920
5-5 00920
7-8 00920
10-98 00920
740-1199 00924
1800-1899 00927
Calle Acadia 00926
Calle Acapulco 00920
Calle Acerina 00926
Calle Acerola 00926
Calle Acuario 00926
Calle Acueductos 00926
Calle Adams
600-699 00926
1600-1799 00920
Calle Adolfo Calderon 00907
Calle Adoquines 00926
Calle Adriana 00926
Calle Africa 00909
Calle Afrodita 00926
Calle Agosto Rivera 00918
Calle Aguadilla
1-3 00917
5-51 00917
52-52 00907
52-52 00917
53-53 00917
54-98 00917
54-54 00907
55-55 00917
55-55 00907
57-57 00907
Calle Aguas Calientes 00926
Calle Agueybana 00918
Calle Aibonito 00909
Calle Aida 00926
Calle Alabama 00926
Calle Alameda 00923
Calle Alaska 00926
Calle Albacete 00923
Calle Albania 00920
Calle Albeniz 00924
Calle Alberto Valenzuela 00926
Calle Alcala 00921
Calle Alcaniz 00923
Calle Alcazar 00923
Calle Alda 00926
Calle Aldea 00907
Calle Aldebaran 00920
Calle Alegria 00924
Calle Alejandria 00920
Calle Alejo Cruzado 00924
Calle Aleli 00927
Calle Alesia 00920
Calle Alfaro 00915
Calle Alfredo Carbonell 00918
Calle Alfredo Galvez 00926
Calle Algarrobo 00924
Calle Algarvez 00923
Calle Alhambra 00917
Calle Alheli 00926
Calle Alicante 00920
Calle Almaden 00923
Calle Almagro 00923
Calle Almendares 00907
Calle Almendro
A1-A99 00926
C1-C99 00926
1-99 00913
Calle Almeria 00923

Calle Almijarra 00923
Calle Almirante 00926
Calle Almirante Pinzon 00918
Calle Almonte 00926
Calle Alondra 00924
Calle Alora 00926
Calle Alozaina 00923
Calle Alpes 00920
Calle Alto 00926
Calle Alto Int 00926
Calle Alvarado 00918
Calle Amalia 00912
Calle Amalia Marin 00925
Calle Amalio Roldan 00924
Calle Amapola
1-6 00927
8-99 00926
Calle Amarillo 00926
Calle Amarillo Int 00926
Calle Amatista 00926
Calle Amazonas 00926
Calle Ambar 00926
Calle Amberes 00920
Calle America
1-5 00907
2-398 00917
6-148 00917
7-99 00917
7-99 00907
150-156 00917
158-198 00917
400-417 00917
419-499 00917
1400-1599 00909
Calle Americo Salas 00909
Calle Amparo 00915
Calle Amur 00921
Calle Ana Castelar 00912
Calle Ana De Cauzos 00924
Calle Ana De Lanzos 00924
Calle Ana Otero 00924
Calle Ana Roque
Duprey 00918
Calle Anapolis 00926
Calle Anasco
100-198 00911
800-840 00925
841-845 00925
842-848 00925
850-898 00925
Calle Andes 00926
Calle Andorra 00920
Calle Andres Bello 00926
Calle Andromeda 00926
Calle Angel Buonomo 00918
Calle Angel Martinez 00924
Calle Angel Mislan 00924
Calle Angeles
Gonzalez 00925
Calle Angora 00920
Calle Anguesis 00926
Calle Anon 00924
Calle Antartico 00920
Calle Antillana 00913
Calle Antillas 00920
Calle Antolin Nin 00918
Calle Antonia Martinez 00924
Calle Antonio Arias
Cruz 00924
Calle Antonio Arroyo 00921
Calle Antonio De Asis 00915
Calle Antonio Luciano 00924
Calle Antonio Sarriera 00923
Calle Antonsanti 00912
Calle Apeninos 00920
Calle Aponte
1-99 00915
100-199 00911
200-399 00912
Calle Aponte Final 00915
Calle Aquamarina 00926
Calle Arabia 00920
Calle Aragon 00920
Calle Aranjuez 00923
Calle Arboretum 00927
Calle Ardenas 00920
Calle Arecibo
1-99 00917
300-399 00926
601-699 00907
Calle Arecife 00924
Calle Argel 00920
Calle Argelia 00920
Calle Argentina 00915
Calle Ariel 00923
Calle Aristides Chavier 00924
Calle Arizmendi 00925
Calle Arizona 00926
Calle Arkansas 00926
Calle Arnau
Igarravides 00924
Calle Arnedo 00923
Calle Arrigoitia 00918
Calle Arroyo
J1-J99 00926
A1-A99 00926
B1-B99 00926
C1-C99 00926
S9-1-S9-99 00926
3-7 00918
9-99 00918
Calle Arterial B 00918
Calle Artico 00920
Calle Arturo Pasarell 00924
Calle Aruz
120-199 00917
900-999 00909
Calle Arzuaga 00925
Calle Asabache 00926
Calle Asenjo 00926
Calle Ashford 00923
Calle Asomante 00920
Calle Aster 00926
Calle Astoret 00926
Calle Astorga 00923
Calle Astoria 00926
Calle Astromelia 00926
Calle Asturias 00923
Calle Asuncion 00920
Calle Atenas
300-399 00920
1297-1340 00926
1342-1398 00926
Calle Atlanta 00926
Calle Atlantic Pl 00911
Calle Atlas 00920
Calle Augusta 00926
Calle Aurora 00907
Calle Austral 00920
Calle Austria 00920
Calle Ausubo 00926
Calle Avila 00923
Calle Ayacucho 00926
Calle Azabache 00924
Calle Azalea 00926
Calle Azores 00924
Calle Azorin 00926
Calle Azucena
C1-C99 00926
1-99 00927
Calle B
B1-1-B1-99 00926
D1-1-D1-99 00926
D1-D99 00926
F1-F99 00926
A1-1-A1-99 00926
B26-B99 00926
A1-A99 00926
C1-C13 00926
BC1-BC46 00926
D50-D99 00926
B12-B19 00926
A9-A99 00924
B1-B99 00924
D1-D99 00924
E1-E99 00924
18INT-20INT 00917
C14-C26 00926
E1-E74 00926
A1-A99 00926
B60-B99 00926
C1-C49 00926
B1-B50 00926
1-663 00917
2-94 00924
22-28 00926
96-148 00924
149-199 00924
163-171 00917
173-299 00917
566-592 00917
594-621 00917
600-799 00920
2200-2399 00915
Calle B Graciani 00926
Calle Badajoz 00923
Calle Badia 00918
Calle Baena 00923
Calle Baez 00917
Calle Bagur 00923
Calle Bahamas 00920
Calle Bahia 00920
Calle Bailen 00926
Calle Balboa 00925
Calle Balcanes 00920
Calle Baldorioty De
Castro
770INT-770INT 00925
700-749 00918
750-853 00925
751-799 00918
854-858 00925
855-899 00925
860-898 00925
Calle Baldrich 00912
Calle Baleares 00920
Calle Balseiro 00925
Calle Bambu 00926
Calle Barbados 00924
Calle Barbe 00912
Calle Barbosa
615INT-615INT 00915
2-98 00901
600-698 00915
607-697 00915
699-711 00915
713-765 00915
1866-1872 00912
1874-2027 00912
2028-2056 00915
2058-2273 00915
2275-2299 00915
Calle Barcelona 00907
Calle Barnard 00926
Calle Barranquitas
1-54 00907
56-98 00907
500-599 00923
Calle Bartolome Las
Casas 00915
Calle Bayahonda 00924
Calle Bayamon
1-5 00926
7-99 00918
300-899 00926
409-469 00926
Calle Bayona 00920
Calle Beacon 00926
Calle Becasina 00924
Calle Bechara 00920
Calle Begonia
1-44 00926
1700-1899 00926
1830-1899 00927
Calle Belaval 00909
Calle Belcaire 00920
Calle Belen 00920
Calle Belen Burgos 00921
Calle Belen Zequeira 00924
Calle Belgica 00917
Calle Bella Vis 00915
Calle Bellevue 00915
Calle Bellisima
1-99 00926
200-1699 00927
233-299 00927
Calle Belmonte 00923
Calle Benavente
401-430 00923
431-514 00923
500-1799 00926
516-536 00923
Calle Beneficencia 00901
Calle Benigno Reyes 00918
Calle Benitez Castano
100-199 00911
200-202 00912
204-399 00912
Calle Benito Alonso 00907
Calle Benito Feijoo 00926
Calle Bermuda 00924
Calle Berwin 00920
Calle Besosa 00918
Calle Betances
2-50 00917
19-49 00917
51-199 00917
100-227 00911
250-399 00915
Calle Biblos 00926
Calle Bien Te Veo 00926
Calle Bisbal 00923
Calle Bizet 00924
Calle Blanca 00907
Calle Blanca Rexach 00915
Calle Blanes 00923
Calle Blay 00920
Calle Bogota 00920
Calle Bohemia 00920
Calle Bolivar
201-1299 00926
300-499 00912
600-799 00909
Calle Bolivar Pagan 00924
Calle Bolivia 00917
Calle Bolonia 00920
Calle Bonafoux 00918
Calle Bondad 00924
Calle Borgona 00923
Calle Bori 00927
Calle Borinquena 00925
Calle Borneo 00924
Calle Bosque 00912
Calle Bouret 00912
Calle Braeger 00911
Calle Braulio Dueno 00925
Calle Bravante 00923
Calle Brazil 00915
Calle Brema 00927
Calle Brumbaugh
100-398 00901
400-499 00901
1000-1164 00925
1166-1198 00925
1178-1198 00926
1200-1255 00926
1257-1261 00926
Calle Bruselas 00920
Calle Bucare 00913
Calle Buchanan 00925
Calle Budapest 00921
Calle Buen Amor 00924
Calle Buen Consejo 00926
Calle Buena Suerte 00923
Calle Buenaventura 00915
Calle Buenos Aires
2-4 00917
6-99 00917
600-799 00915
901-977 00923
979-1000 00923
1002-1098 00923
2000-2099 00911
Calle Bulgaria 00920
Calle Burgos 00923
Calle Buzardo 00924
Calle C
A1-A99 00926
BC1-BC99 00926
BE1-BE99 00926
D1-1-D1-99 00926
E1-1-E1-99 00926
F1-1-F1-99 00926
C1-C10 00926
BD1-BD49 00926
D1-D4 00926
D1-D23 00926
C50-C99 00926
D1-D99 00924
B1-B14 00926
BG1-BG6 00926
D1-D54 00926
C1-C19 00926
20-30 00926
100-199 00924
159-161 00917
163-259 00917
261-263 00917
700-799 00920
1200-1299 00926
2300-2399 00915
Calle C De La Torre 00924
Calle Cabo Felipe
Rodriguez 00924
Calle Cabo H Alverio 00918
Calle Cabrera 00925
Calle Caceres 00923
Calle Cacique
1900-2099 00911
2100-2399 00913
Calle Cactus 00924
Calle Cadiz 00920
Calle Cafeto 00924
Calle Caguas 00926
Calle Cairo 00920
Calle Calaf 00923
Calle Calandria 00924
Calle Calderon De La
Barca 00926
Calle Cali 00920
Calle California 00926
Calle Calma 00923
Calle Calve 00927
Calle Calzada
C1-C99 00926
F1-F99 00926
G1-G99 00926
300-399 00923
Calle Camaguey 00920
Calle Cambray 00923
Calle Cambridge 00927
Calle Camelia 00927
Calle Camelia Soto 00925
Calle Campanilla 00926
Calle Campeche 00920
Calle Campina 00920
Calle Campo Alegre 00907
Calle Camus 00926
Calle Canada
G1-G99 00926
H1-H99 00926
M1-M99 00926
L1-L99 00926
1100-1399 00920
Calle Canales 00926
Calle Canales Int 00926
Calle Canals 00907
Calle Canarias
1-79 00926
1100-1299 00920
Calle Cancer 00926
Calle Candina 00907
Calle Canet 00923
Calle Canillas 00923
Calle Canovanas 00912
Calle Cantizales 00926
Calle Caoba
H1-H99 00926
H6A-H6A 00926
2-4 00913
6-99 00913
Calle Caparra 00926
Calle Capetillo
100-269 00925
270-399 00923
271-299 00925
Calle Capitan Espada 00918
Calle Capitol 00907
Calle Capri 00926
Calle Capricornio 00926
Calle Capt Amezquita 00926
Calle Capt Berreteaga 00901
Calle Caracas 00915
Calle Cardenas 00920
Calle Caribe
1-1299 00907
400-599 00917
Calle Caridad 00924
Calle Carite 00926
Calle Carlos Bertero 00924
Calle Carlos De Jesus 00907
Calle Carlos Delgado 00924
Calle Carlos T
Ramsden 00924
Calle Carlota Matienzo 00918
Calle Carmen 00917
Calle Carmen Buzello 00924
Calle Carmen
Hernandez 00924
Calle Carmen
Sanabria 00924
Calle Carolina
300-499 00926
500-599 00917
1600-1612 00912
1614-1799 00912
Calle Carpintero 00926
Calle Carrara 00920
Calle Carrion Maduro
100-184 00926
186-299 00926
600-999 00909
Calle Cartagena 00920
Calle Cascada 00926
Calle Casia 00921
Calle Casimiro
Duchesne 00924
Calle Casimiro
Figueroa 00907
Calle Casino 00920
Calle Casiopea 00923
Calle Castelar 00911
Calle Castellon 00923
Calle Castilla 00920
Calle Castro Vinas
100-174 00911
175-399 00912
Calle Castuera 00923
Calle Cataluna
700-799 00909
1200-1299 00920
Calle Catania 00924
Calle Cataratas 00926
Calle Cauce 00926
Calle Cavalieri 00927
Calle Cayey
300-399 00926
1901-1999 00909
Calle Cayo Hueso 1 00923
Calle Cayo Hueso 2 00923
Calle Cayo Hueso 3 00923
Calle Ceciliana 00926
Calle Cecilio Lebron 00924
Calle Cefiro 00926
Calle Ceiba
1201-1201 00926
1203-1299 00926
2207-2207 00915
2209-2299 00915
Calle Ceilan 00924
Calle Celia Cestero 00924
Calle Celis Aguilera 00925
Calle Centauro 00920
Calle Central 00907
Calle Cerdena 00920
Calle Ceres 00923
Calle Cerra 00907
Calle Cerra Andino 00907
Calle Cervantes
W5-1-W5-99 00926
W7-1-W7-99 00926
1-99 00907
Calle Cesar Castillo 00918
Calle Cesar Gonzalez 00918
Calle Cesar Roman 00918
Calle Cesar Silva 00918
Calle Ceuta 00923
Calle Chales 00924
Calle Chamariz 00924
Calle Chapultepec 00926
Calle Chatumel 00923
Calle Chestnut Hl 00926
Calle Chevere 00923
Calle Chihuahua 00926
Calle Chile 00917
Calle Chipre 00920
Calle Ciales
1-99 00917
1800-1898 00911
Calle Cibeles 00926
Calle Cien Hojas 00926
Calle Cima 00926
Calle Cipres 00924
Calle Circeo 00926
Calle Cisne 00923
Calle Citadel 00926
Calle Citera 00926
Calle Clara Lair 00901
Calle Clavel
L1-L99 00927
M1-M99 00927
1-83 00926
500-576 00926
578-599 00926
1700-1799 00926
Calle Clemenceau 00907
Calle Clemson 00927
Calle Coamo 00917
Calle Cobalto 00926
Calle Cobana 00926
Calle Codorniz 00924
Calle Coin 00926
Calle Cojimar 00920
Calle Coll 00923
Calle Coll Y Toste 00918
Calle Collins 00920
Calle Collores 00913
Calle Colmenar 00926
Calle Colomer 00907
Calle Colon
1-99 00915
101-147 00926
149-1198 00926
151-1597 00911
1599-1799 00911
Calle Colonia 00921
Calle Colonial 00926
Calle Colorado 00926
Calle Colton 00915
Calle Columbia 00927
Calle Comercio
100-498 00901
900-1011 00907
1013-1099 00907
Calle Compostela 00921
Calle Concepcion 00909
Calle Concha Espina 00926
Calle Concord 00926
Calle Concordia 00907
Calle Condado 00907
Calle Confianza 00924
Calle Consolacion 00924
Calle Constancia 00920
Calle Constitucion
300-398 00920
301-397 00920
399-799 00920
2300-2399 00915
Calle Consuelo Carbo 00925
Calle Consuelo
Gonzalez 00924
Calle Consuelo Matos 00924
Calle Conveniencia 00907
Calle Convento 00912
Calle Coral
G1-G99 00926
H1-H99 00926
2-7 00924
Calle Coralina 00926
Calle Corazon 00926
Calle Corcega 00920
Calle Corchado 00907
Calle Cordero 00911
Calle Cordillera 00926
Calle Cordova 00920
Calle Corfu 00924
Calle Cornell 00927

Calle Corona 00911
Calle Coronel Irizarry ... 00909
Calle Corozal 00917
Calle Corriente 00926
Calle Corrientes 00920
Calle Corta 00915
Calle Cortijo 00915
Calle Coruna 00920
Calle Costa Azul 00926
Calle Costa Rica 00917
Calle Court 3 00926
Calle Court 4 00926
Calle Cozumel 00923
Calle Cracovia 00921
Calle Cremona 00920
Calle Creuz 00923
Calle Crisantemo 00927
Calle Cuadra 00917
Calle Cuba 00917
Calle Cuba Final 00917
Calle Cuenca
F1-F99 00926
G1-G99 00926
600-699 00920
Calle Cuernavaca 00926
Calle Cuevillas 00907
Calle Culto 00907
Calle Cundeamor 00913
Calle Cupey Gdns 00926
Calle Cupido 00926
Calle Curazao 00924
Calle D
C1-1-C1-99 00926
C1-13A-C1-13A 00926
E1-1-E1-99 00926
F1-1-F1-99 00926
H1-1-H1-99 00926
J1-1-J1-99 00926
F1-F99 00926
D1-D29 00926
E71A-E71A 00926
A1-A50 00926
E10-E49 00926
E1-E99 00926
B1-B99 00926
30-49 00926
60-90 00917
92-594 00917
200-250 00917
252-299 00917
589-589 00917
800-899 00920
2300-2311 00915
2313-2399 00915
Calle D Bousquet 00924
Calle D Cabrera 00925
Calle D Penaloza 00926
Calle D1 00926
Calle Daisy 00926
Calle Dakota 00926
Calle Dalia 00926
Calle Dallas 00926
Calle Dalmacia 00920
Calle Damasco 00920
Calle Danubio 00920
Calle Darien 00920
Calle De Diego
305INT-305INT 00923
599INT-599INT 00924
2-259 00925
261-267 00923
269-523 00923
525-525 00923
550-676 00924
575-575 00924
678-698 00924
Calle De La Cruz 00901
Calle De La Fortaleza .. 00901
Calle De La Luna 00901
Calle De La Rosa 00907
Calle De La Tanca 00901
Calle De La Virtud 00901
Calle De Odonnell 00901
Calle De San
Francisco 00901
Calle De San Jose 00901
Calle De San Justo 00901

Calle De San
Sebastian 00901
Calle De Tetuan 00901
Calle Decatur 00920
Calle Degetau
100-227 00911
229-249 00911
250-499 00915
1101-1199 00924
1114-1118 00923
Calle Del Carmen
1000-1099 00907
1101-1104 00925
1106-1198 00925
1191-1205 00907
1207-1399 00907
Calle Del Mercado 00901
Calle Del Muelle 00901
Calle Del Parque
100-199 00911
200-202 00912
204-499 00912
601-697 00909
699-899 00909
Calle Del Pilar 00925
Calle Del Recinto S 00901
Calle Del Santo Cristo .. 00901
Calle Del Sol 00901
Calle Del Valle
100-219 00911
220-399 00912
400-499 00915
Calle Delbrey
100-199 00911
200-208 00912
210-399 00912
Calle Deledda 00926
Calle Delhi 00920
Calle Delicias
60-99 00926
100-199 00907
1200-1299 00920
1301-1399 00920
Calle Delta 00920
Calle Demetrio O Daly . 00924
Calle Denotiera 00924
Calle Denton 00912
Calle Denver 00920
Calle Detroit 00926
Calle Diamante
1-54 00924
800-899 00926
Calle Diamela
1600-1674 00927
1676-1899 00927
1700-1800 00926
Calle Diana 00923
Calle Diego Cuellar 00926
Calle Diego Morguey ... 00926
Calle Diego Salazar 00926
Calle Diego Salcedo 00926
Calle Dieppa 00920
Calle Diez De Andino
100-199 00911
200-499 00912
Calle Dignidad 00924
Calle Disneyland 00926
Calle Dolores
3INT-3INT 00915
1-99 00915
100-134 00917
700-799 00915
Calle Domingo Cruz 00924
Calle Dominica 00924
Calle Doncella 00913
Calle Dorado
660A-660F 00924
600-652 00924
654-1199 00924
1300-1399 00920
1800-1899 00911
Calle Dos Hermanos ... 00907
Calle Dos Palmas 00912
Calle Dover 00920
Calle Dr Lopez
Sicardo 00923

Calle Dr M Guzman
Rodriguez 00923
Calle Dr Pavia
Fernandez 00909
Calle Dr Stahl 00918
Calle Dresde 00920
Calle Duarte Final 00917
Calle Duarte Interior 00917
Calle Duay 00920
Calle Dublin 00920
Calle Duclet 00917
Calle Duero 00920
Calle Duffaut 00907
Calle Duina 00921
Calle Duke 00927
Calle Dunas 00920
Calle Dunquerque 00920
Calle Durazno 00920
Calle Durbec 00924
Calle Durcal 00923
Calle E Dors 00926
Calle E Fernandez
Vanga 00926
Calle E Sanchez
Lopez 00921
Calle Earle 00907
Calle Ebano 00920
Calle Ebro 00926
Calle Echegaray 00926
Calle Ecuador 00917
Calle Eddie Gracia 00918
Calle Eden 00920
Calle Edinburgo 00920
Calle Edison 00927
Calle Eduardo Alvarez .. 00907
Calle Eduardo Baza 00926
Calle Eider 00924
Calle El Che 00926
Calle El Guano 00915
Calle El Morro 00926
Calle El Yunque 00926
Calle Elba 00920
Calle Elena 00911
Calle Eleonor
Roosevelt 00918
Calle Elida 00920
Calle Elisa Cerra 00907
Calle Elisa Colberg 00907
Calle Elizondo 00923
Calle Elliot 00926
Calle Elma 00920
Calle Elmira 00920
Calle Eloy Morales 00923
Calle Emajagua 00913
Calle Emancipacion 00924
Calle Emanuelli 00917
Calle Emilio R
Delgado 00924
Calle Emory 00926
Calle Encarnacion 00920
Calle Encina 00920
Calle Eneas 00926
Calle Enrique Amadeo .. 00918
Calle Ensenada
300-499 00920
501-599 00907
Calle Ernesto Cerra 00907
Calle Ernesto
Vigoreaux 00915
Calle Escocia 00920
Calle Escorpion 00926
Calle Escuela 00917
Calle Esmeralda
1-99 00924
400-498 00920
800-899 00926
Calle Esmirna 00920
Calle Espana
300-529 00917
550-600 00917
1900-2099 00911
Calle Esperanza 00920
Calle Espioncela 00924
Calle Esquilin
1900-2049 00912
2050-2099 00915

Calle Estado 00907
Calle Estancia 00920
Calle Esteban
Gonzalez 00925
Calle Esteban Ortiz 00921
Calle Esteban Padilla ... 00921
Calle Estocolmo 00920
Calle Estonia 00920
Calle Estornino 00924
Calle Estrella 00907
Calle Estuario 00920
Calle Eternidades 00926
Calle Etna 00920
Calle Eucalipto
G1-G99 00926
700-799 00920
Calle Eufrates 00926
Calle Everest 00926
Calle Everglades 00926
Calle F
BF1-BF99 00926
BE1-BE99 00926
BF1A-BF99A 00926
76-78 00917
80-615 00917
201-240 00917
242-298 00917
602-609 00917
Calle F De Rojas 00926
Calle F Sauvalle 00924
Calle F Vizcarrondo 00926
Calle Fajardo 00915
Calle Falcon 00926
Calle Faraday 00927
Calle Faragan 00926
Calle Farrar 00927
Calle Faure 00927
Calle Fco Barrio
Nuevo 00926
Calle Federico Costa ... 00918
Calle Felicidad 00924
Calle Felipe Gutierrez .. 00924
Calle Felipe R Goyco ... 00915
Calle Felipe Roey 00924
Calle Felix Clemente ... 00926
Calle Felix De Azara ... 00924
Calle Felix Hernandez .. 00924
Calle Fenix 00924
Calle Feria 00909
Calle Fermin Zedo 00926
Calle Fernandez
Campos 00907
Calle Fernando Calder . 00918
Calle Fernando Callejo . 00924
Calle Fernando G
Acosta 00921
Calle Fernando
Primero 00918
Calle Ferrara 00924
Calle Ferrer 00915
Calle Ferrocarril
121-199 00909
201-299 00909
1000-1099 00925
Calle Ferrol 00923
Calle Fidalgo Diaz 00912
Calle Fidela Cruz 00926
Calle Figueras 00926
Calle Figueroa
327-327 00923
329-329 00923
331-1004 00923
384-388 00915
390-398 00915
1006-1098 00923
Calle Fiji 00924
Calle Filipinas 00924
Calle Finisterol 00923
Calle Finlay 00909
Calle Flamboyan
H1-H99 00926
I1-I99 00926
P1-P99 00926
1101-1199 00926
2000-2099 00915
Calle Flamboyan Del Rio
100-229 00911

230-499 00912
Calle Flamingo 00924
Calle Flandes 00923
Calle Flor De Lis 00927
Calle Florencia 00924
Calle Flores 00926
Calle Florida 00923
Calle Forbes 00924
Calle Fordham 00927
Calle Formosa 00924
Calle Forte 00913
Calle Fortuna 00911
Calle Foulton 00927
Calle Francia
100INT-102INT 00917
177INT-177INT 00917
107INT-109INT 00917
70-86 00917
88-199 00917
94-106 00917
204-390 00917
392-597 00917
599-599 00917
1501-1599 00911
Calle Francia Final 00917
Calle Francisco Blasini . 00924
Calle Francisco
Casalduc 00924
Calle Francisco
Cassans 00926
Calle Francisco Lar
Roca 00924
Calle Francisco P
Cortes 00924
Calle Francisco
Quindos 00926
Calle Francisco Sein
A1-A99 00917
12-12 00917
100-100 00926
300-599 00917
Calle Francisco Soler ... 00924
Calle Francisco Zuniga . 00926
Calle Franco 00926
Calle Frank Becerra 00918
Calle Franqueza 00924
Calle Fray A
Marchena 00926
Calle Fray Angel
Vazquez 00924
Calle Fray Granada 00926
Calle Frazer 00921
Calle Fresa 00926
Calle Friburgo 00921
Calle Frontera 00926
Calle Fuerte 00912
Calle G
BA1-BA99 00926
99-655 00917
1900-1999 00915
Calle G Corvalan 00926
Calle G De Arteaga 00924
Calle G De La Vega ... 00924
Calle G Garcia
Moreno 00925
Calle G Maranon 00926
Calle G Rios Morales ... 00923
Calle Galapagos 00924
Calle Gales 00924
Calle Galileo 00927
Calle Gallegos 00926
Calle Gambia 00926
Calle Ganges 00926
Calle Garcia Cepeda ... 00917
Calle Garcia Ledesma .. 00924
Calle Garcia Lorca 00926
Calle Gardel 00917
Calle Gardenia
CC1-CC99 00926
DD1-DD99 00926
P1-P99 00927
O10A-O10B 00927
P2A-P2B 00927
P3A-P3B 00927
O2-O99 00927
1600-1779 00927
1780-1899 00926

Calle Garfield 00926
Calle Garona 00926
Calle Garza 00926
Calle Gaucin 00926
Calle Gautier Benitez
2-50 00917
52-199 00917
200-799 00915
Calle Gaviota
1-16 00926
900-999 00924
Calle Gema 00926
Calle Geminis 00926
Calle Gen Del Valle
999-1099 00924
2101-2197 00913
2199-2299 00913
Calle Gen Esteves 00901
Calle Gen Mcarthur 00901
Calle Gen Patton 00913
Calle Gen Valero 00924
Calle Generalife 00926
Calle Genova 00921
Calle Genoveva De
Lago 00924
Calle Georgetown 00927
Calle Georgetti
1-199 00925
1300-1499 00909
Calle Georgina 00926
Calle Geranio 00927
Calle Gerardo Mejias ... 00923
Calle Gerardo Selles
Sola 00923
Calle German Moyer ... 00918
Calle Gerona 00923
Calle Gertrudis 00911
Calle Gettysburg 00926
Calle Gibraltar 00923
Calle Gigi 00927
Calle Gila 00926
Calle Glacier 00926
Calle Gladiola 00926
Calle Glasgow 00921
Calle Gloria Castaner ... 00924
Calle Glorimar 00926
Calle Golondrina 00924
Calle Gonzalez 00925
Calle Gonzalo Berceo .. 00926
Calle Gonzalo
Gallegos 00926
Calle Gonzalo Philippi .. 00923
Calle Gorrion 00926
Calle Granada 00913
Calle Granate 00926
Calle Grand Cyn 00926
Calle Gratitud 00924
Calle Greenwood 00920
Calle Gregorio
Hernandez 00924
Calle Grenoble 00921
Calle Groenlandia 00924
Calle Grosella 00926
Calle Guadalajara 00923
Calle Guadalquivir 00926
Calle Guadalupe 00924
Calle Guadiana 00926
Calle Guajataca 00926
Calle Guam 00924
Calle Guama 00927
Calle Guamani 00926
Calle Guanajibo 00926
Calle Guaracanal 00926
Calle Guaraguao 00926
Calle Guarionex 00918
Calle Guatemala 00921
Calle Guayaba 00926
Calle Guayacan 00926
Calle Guayama
53INT-53INT 00917
70INT-70INT 00917
2-2 00917
4-99 00917
100-212 00917
101-213 00917
214-300 00917

302-398 00917
556-556 00918
Calle Guayanes 00926
Calle Guayanilla 00923
Calle Guaynabo 00917
Calle Guernica 00926
Calle Guerrero Noble ... 00913
Calle Guillermo Ortiz
Glez 00920
Calle Guipuzcoa 00923
Calle Gurabo 00917
Calle Gustavo
Becquer 00926
Calle Gutemberg 00927
Calle H 00917
Calle H Mariani
Peralta 00920
Calle Habana 00921
Calle Halcon 00924
Calle Harvard 00927
Calle Hatillo 00918
Calle Haydee Rexach .. 00915
Calle Hebrides 00924
Calle Hector Salaman .. 00918
Calle Hector Urdaneta .. 00915
Calle Henna 00915
Calle Hermes 00923
Calle Hermosillo 00926
Calle Hernandez 00907
Calle Herrera 00911
Calle Hibiscus 00927
Calle Hicaco 00926
Calle Hidalgo 00926
Calle Higuero 00926
Calle Hija Del Caribe ... 00918
Calle Hillside 00920
Calle Himalaya 00926
Calle Hipodromo 00909
Calle Histella 00913
Calle Hoare 00907
Calle Holanda 00917
Calle Hollywod Dr 00926
Calle Holy Cross 00926
Calle Honduras 00917
Calle Hoover 00926
Calle Horas 00926
Calle Hortensia 00926
Calle Hostos 00927
Calle Hotspring 00926
Calle Howard 00927
Calle Hucar 00926
Calle Huelva 00926
Calle Huesca 00923
Calle Humacao
900-1199 00925
1400-1499 00909
Calle Humboldt 00924
Calle Hypolais 00924
Calle I Andreu De
Aguilar 00918
Calle I De Luzan 00926
Calle Ibiza 00926
Calle Iglesias 00912
Calle Igualdad 00912
Calle Iguazu 00926
Calle Imperial 00901
Calle Independence 00926
Calle Independencia 00918
Calle Indo 00926
Calle Inga 00913
Calle Inglaterra 00915
Calle Inmaculada 00915
Calle Interamericana 00927
Calle Iris 00926
Calle Irlanda
6-8 00917
800-899 00924
Calle Isabel La
Catolica 00918
Calle Isabela 00912
Calle Isaura Arnau 00924
Calle Isidoro Colon 00926
Calle Ismael Colon 00918
Calle Ismael Rivera
1-211 00911
213-213 00911

234-238 00912
240-399 00912
400-499 00915
Calle Istar 00926
Calle Italia
300-599 00917
1900-2099 00911
Calle Iturriaga 00907
Calle Izcoa Diaz 00926
Calle J 00917
Calle J Benvenuti 00921
Calle J Boscan 00926
Calle J Ferrer Y Ferrer 00921
Calle J Gil De La Madrid 00924
Calle J Lopez Lopez 00925
Calle J R Gautier 00921
Calle Ja Marcano 00918
Calle Jacaranda 00913
Calle Jaen 00923
Calle Jaguas 00926
Calle Jaime Drew 00923
Calle Jajome 00926
Calle Jalapa 00926
Calle Jamaica 00917
Calle James Bond 00924
Calle Janda 00923
Calle Janer 00925
Calle Jarandilla 00923
Calle Jasper 00926
Calle Java 00924
Calle Jazmin
DD1-DD99 00926
EE1-EE99 00926
1-1799 00927
400-499 00926
Calle Jefferson
100-199 00911
612-699 00926
Calle Jerez 00923
Calle Jeritza 00927
Calle Jerusalem
438INT-438INT 00924
401-499 00924
500-598 00923
501-579 00923
501-699 00924
581-599 00923
Calle Jesus M Munoz 00924
Calle Jesus Tizol 00907
Calle Jijona 00926
Calle Jilguero 00926
Calle Joffre 00907
Calle John Albert 00920
Calle John Ray 00924
Calle Jordan 00909
Calle Jorge Manrrique 00926
Calle Jorge Romany 00925
Calle Jose A Canals 00918
Calle Jose Abad 00924
Calle Jose B Acevedo 00923
Calle Jose Brisson 00924
Calle Jose De Jossieu 00924
Calle Jose F Diaz 00926
Calle Jose Fernandez 00918
Calle Jose Fidalgo Diaz 00926
Calle Jose Gregorio Garcia 00921
Calle Jose H Alprey 00921
Calle Jose H Cora 00909
Calle Jose M Espinosa 00926
Calle Jose Marti
2-52 00917
54-199 00917
601-697 00907
699-999 00907
Calle Jose Oliver 00918
Calle Jose Padin 00918
Calle Jose Quinones 00926
Calle Jose Quinton 00924
Calle Jose R Acosta 00918
Calle Jose Ramon Figueroa 00907
Calle Jose Sabogal 00926
Calle Jose Severo Quinones 00915
Calle Jose Tizol 00901
Calle Jose Zorrilla 00926
Calle Josefa Cabrera 00925
Calle Josefa Mendia 00923
Calle Josefina Pares 00924
Calle Jovillo 00926
Calle Juan A Davila 00918
Calle Juan Antonio Corretjer 00901
Calle Juan B Huyke 00918
Calle Juan B Rodriguez 00918
Calle Juan B Roman 00924
Calle Juan B Ugalde 00926
Calle Juan Baiz 00924
Calle Juan Calaf 00918
Calle Juan Casado 00926
Calle Juan D Lefebres 00926
Calle Juan Esquivel 00926
Calle Juan Gil 00926
Calle Juan J Jimenez 00918
Calle Juan Jose Osuna 00923
Calle Juan Kepler 00926
Calle Juan P Duarte 00917
Calle Juan Pena Reyes 00924
Calle Juan R Jimenez 00926
Calle Juan Suarez 00926
Calle Juana Diaz 00917
Calle Julia 00917
Calle Julian Bengochea 00924
Calle Julian Blanco 00925
Calle Julio Andino 00924
Calle Julio Aybar 00921
Calle Julio C Arteaga 00924
Calle Julio Gonzalez 00924
Calle Julio Lopez Lopez 00918
Calle Julio Ruedas 00926
Calle Juncal 00926
Calle Juncos
1-99 00917
200-349 00915
350-879 00926
Calle Junin 00926
Calle Junquera 00926
Calle Jupiter 00926
Calle Kennedy 00926
Calle Kings Ct 00911
Calle Kingston 00921
Calle Krueger 00926
Calle Krug 00911
Calle Kurices 00924
Calle L Romanach 00926
Calle La Brisa 00924
Calle La Casa Blanca 00926
Calle La Catedral 00926
Calle La Ceramica 00918
Calle La Gallera 00923
Calle La Garita 00926
Calle La Milagrosa 00915
Calle La Nueva Palma 00907
Calle La Paz
1-99 00925
101-299 00925
600-799 00907
Calle La Plata 00920
Calle La Princesa 00926
Calle La Puntilla 00901
Calle La Rabida 00918
Calle La Rogativa 00926
Calle La Rosa
591-591 00917
593-699 00917
900-998 00907
1000-1050 00907
1052-1052 00907
Calle Labra 00907
Calle Labrador 00924
Calle Lafayette
300-399 00917
700-899 00909
901-999 00909
Calle Laguna 00915
Calle Laguna A 00917
Calle Laguna B 00917
Calle Lares 00917
Calle Larrinaga 00918
Calle Las Colinas 00926
Calle Las Croabas 00926
Calle Las Flores
100-199 00911
200-399 00912
400-498 00923
1000-1199 00907
Calle Las Lomas 00926
Calle Las Marias
100-186 00927
181-215 00927
188-899 00927
901-999 00927
1500-1599 00911
Calle Las Mercedes 00915
Calle Las Palmas
1-99 00911
1000-1011 00923
1013-1099 00923
1301-1397 00909
1399-1499 00909
Calle Las Palomas
1-199 00911
200-299 00912
Calle Las Rocas 00926
Calle Las Vegas 00926
Calle Las Villas 00924
Calle Las Violetas 00915
Calle Latimer 00907
Calle Laura 00911
Calle Laurel 00913
Calle Laviana 00923
Calle Lealtad
1000-1017 00907
1002-1002 00923
1004-1038 00923
1018-1018 00923
1019-1077 00907
1040-1040 00923
1050-1098 00907
Calle Ledru 00924
Calle Lena 00926
Calle Leo 00926
Calle Leon 00926
Calle Leon Acuna 00911
Calle Lepanto 00926
Calle Lerida 00923
Calle Lesbos 00926
Calle Libertad 00923
Calle Libra 00926
Calle Lilas 00927
Calle Lilly 00926
Calle Lima 00915
Calle Limoncillo 00927
Calle Linacero 00924
Calle Linares 00923
Calle Lince 00923
Calle Lincoln 00926
Calle Lino Padron Rivera 00926
Calle Lippit 00915
Calle Lira 00923
Calle Lirio 00926
Calle Lirios 00927
Calle Livorna 00924
Calle Llanez 00926
Calle Llausetina 00924
Calle Llorens Torres 00917
Calle Lloveras
600-698 00909
800-899 00907
Calle Loaiza Cordero 00918
Calle Lodi 00924
Calle Logrono 00923
Calle Loira 00926
Calle Loiza
300-399 00926
1500-2101 00911
2103-2149 00911
2151-2499 00913
Calle Lola Rodriguez De Tio 00924
Calle Lombardia 00924
Calle Lope De Rueda 00926
Calle Lope De Vega 00926
Calle Lopez Landron 00911
Calle Lopez Sicardo 00923
Calle Lorenzo Noa 00924
Calle Los Andes 00926
Calle Los Angeles
700-799 00909
1000-1099 00923
Calle Los Banos 00911
Calle Los Caobos 00927
Calle Los Castillos 00924
Calle Los Cayos 00924
Calle Los Corozos 00915
Calle Los Flamboyanes 00927
Calle Los Marianistas 00925
Calle Los Mirtos 00927
Calle Los Mitas 00917
Calle Los Naranjos 00907
Calle Los Palacios 00924
Calle Los Picachos 00926
Calle Los Pinos
25-99 00926
101-161 00907
163-399 00907
401-449 00917
Calle Los Pirineos 00926
Calle Los Rios 00917
Calle Los Robles 00926
Calle Los Santos 00915
Calle Los Tanques 00926
Calle Lotus 00926
Calle Lovaina 00921
Calle Luchetti 00907
Calle Lugo Vinas 00901
Calle Luis Almansa 00926
Calle Luis Blanco Romano 00925
Calle Luis Caballer 00924
Calle Luis Cordova Chirino 00924
Calle Luis De Gongora 00926
Calle Luis F Machicote 00924
Calle Luis Gonzalez 00918
Calle Luis Muniz Souffront 00923
Calle Luis Munoz Colon 00924
Calle Luis Nec 00924
Calle Luis Pardo 00924
Calle Luis R Miranda 00924
Calle Luisa 00907
Calle Luisa Capetillo 00921
Calle Luisa Gutierrez 00923
Calle Luna
1-99 00926
94-199 00917
Calle Luquillo 00926
Calle Lutz 00915
Calle Luz Castelar 00912
Calle Luzon 00924
Calle M 00917
Calle M Maldonado 00926
Calle M Rodriguez Serra 00907
Calle Madagascar 00924
Calle Madeira 00924
Calle Madison 00926
Calle Madreselva 00926
Calle Madrid
1-99 00907
900-998 00925
901-999 00925
1000-1099 00925
Calle Maestro Cordero 00917
Calle Magdalena 00915
Calle Magnolia
FF1-FF99 00926
GG1-GG99 00926
GG5A-GG5B 00926
GG15A-GG15B 00926
GG16A-GG16B 00926
GG17A-GG17B 00926
GG18A-GG18B 00926
GG19A-GG19B 00926
2000-2099 00915
Calle Majestad 00926
Calle Malaga
1-99 00911
401-499 00923
Calle Malaquita 00926
Calle Mallorca
1-199 00917
700-799 00907
Calle Malva 00927
Calle Malvis 00924
Calle Mamey 00926
Calle Managua 00921
Calle Manantial 00926
Calle Manati
1-99 00917
1700-1798 00912
Calle Manila 00925
Calle Manso 00926
Calle Manuel Camunas 00918
Calle Manuel Corchado
100-163 00911
165-177 00911
178-198 00912
200-399 00912
Calle Manuel Domenech 00918
Calle Manuel F Rossy 00918
Calle Manuel Guerra 00924
Calle Manuel M Zama 00926
Calle Manuel Ocasio 00921
Calle Manuel Samaniego 00926
Calle Manuel Texidor 00921
Calle Manzanillo 00926
Calle Maracaibo 00926
Calle Marbella
1-49 00926
50-99 00907
Calle Marcano 00923
Calle Marcial 00925
Calle Marconi 00927
Calle Marfil 00926
Calle Margarida 00925
Calle Margarita
N1-N99 00927
P1-P99 00927
1-49 00926
50-199 00925
Calle Marginal
A60-A99 00924
D1-D99 00926
A1-A99 00921
3B-3E 00926
A1-A2 00926
A12-A59 00926
B1-B99 00924
A2-1-A2-24 00924
A1-A2 00924
1-99 00923
1-899 00926
2-4 00921
18-18 00924
1401-1499 00921
1900-1998 00927
Calle Maria Benitez 00924
Calle Maria Cadilla 00924
Calle Maria Giusti 00924
Calle Maria Isabel 00913
Calle Maria Llovet 00918
Calle Maria Moczo 00911
Calle Maria R Bustamante 00924
Calle Mariana 00907
Calle Mariana Bracetti 00925
Calle Mariano Abril 00924
Calle Mariano Ramirez Bages 00907
Calle Maribel 00911
Calle Marina
1-50 00913
50-99 00926
52-2298 00913
Calle Marquesa
M1-M99 00926
N1-N99 00926
O1-O99 00926
700-799 00924
Calle Marseilles 00907
Calle Martin Fernandez 00901
Calle Martin Guiluz 00926
Calle Martin Travieso
1400-1499 00907
1500-1599 00911
Calle Martinete 00926
Calle Martinica 00924
Calle Martino 00915
Calle Mary Wood 00926
Calle Matias Ledesma 00901
Calle Matienzo Cintron 00917
Calle Maximo Alomar 00923
Calle Maximo Gomez 00918
Calle Mayaguez 00917
Calle Mayol 00909
Calle Mckinley 00907
Calle Mcleary
1700-2099 00911
2100-2299 00913
Calle Mejias 00925
Calle Mendoza 00926
Calle Menfias 00926
Calle Mercedes Sola 00924
Calle Merhoff 00915
Calle Merida 00926
Calle Mesina 00924
Calle Mexico 00917
Calle Middle 00926
Calle Miguel Xiorro 00924
Calle Milan 00924
Calle Mimosa 00927
Calle Mindanao 00924
Calle Minerva 00923
Calle Miosotis 00927
Calle Mirador 00926
Calle Miramar 00907
Calle Mirlo 00924
Calle Mirsonia 00911
Calle Mississipi 00926
Calle Mizar 00923
Calle Modena 00921
Calle Modesta 00924
Calle Molina 00911
Calle Molucas 00924
Calle Monforte 00926
Calle Monsenor Torres 00925
Calle Monserrate 00907
Calle Monsita 00911
Calle Montana 00926
Calle Monte Britton 00926
Calle Montebello 00926
Calle Montellano 00923
Calle Monterrey
AX1-AX99 00926
AK1-AK30 00926
1-199 00920
Calle Montevideo 00921
Calle Montgomery 00926
Calle Montilla 00918
Calle Mora 00925
Calle Moradilla 00926
Calle Morales 00909
Calle Morelia 00926
Calle Morell Campos 00915
Calle Morovis 00901
Calle Motril 00926
Calle Mozart 00924
Calle Murgia 00909
Calle Nairn 00907
Calle Napoles 00924
Calle Naranjal 00924
Calle Naranjo 00926
Calle Narciso 00927
Calle Nardo 00927
Calle Navarra 00923
Calle Navarro 00918
Calle Navas 00907
Calle Navio 00923
Calle Neblin 00924
Calle Nebraska 00926
Calle Negron Flores 00918
Calle Nemesio Canales 00917
Calle Neptuno 00926
Calle Nevada 00926
Calle Nevarez 00927
Calle New London 00912
Calle Nicolas Aguayo 00924
Calle Nieper 00926
Calle Nilo 00926
Calle Nin 00915
Calle Nispero 00926
Calle Niza
1-99 00926
501-597 00924
599-699 00924
Calle Noble 00926
Calle Nogal 00926
Calle Nora Lk 00926
Calle Norzagaray 00901
Calle Notre Dame 00927
Calle Nueva
162C-162D 00917
174A-174D 00917
174INT-174INT 00917
406A-406A 00917
157INT-157INT 00917
125-200 00917
202-406 00917
400-499 00915
600-699 00917
1500-1522 00909
1524-1524 00909
Calle Nuevo Laredo 00926
Calle Nunez Prieto 00915
Calle Obi 00926
Calle Obregon 00926
Calle Ochoa 00918
Calle Ohio 00926
Calle Ojeda 00907
Calle Oklahoma 00926
Calle Olga Esperanza 00924
Calle Olimpic 00920
Calle Olimpo 00907
Calle Olivia Paoli 00924
Calle Olivos 00920
Calle Olmo 00924
Calle Olot 00923
Calle Oneill 00918
Calle Onide 00926
Calle Opalo 00926
Calle Oquendo 00909
Calle Orbeta 00907
Calle Orchid 00926
Calle Orduna 00923
Calle Oregon 00926
Calle Orense 00923
Calle Orgiva 00926
Calle Orinoco 00926
Calle Orion 00923
Calle Orlando 00926
Calle Orocovis 00925
Calle Orquidea 00927
Calle Orta 00907
Calle Ortega V Gasset 00926
Calle Ortegon 00926
Calle Ottawa 00921
Calle Oviedo 00921
Calle Oxford
H1-H99 00926
251-255 00927
Calle Ozama 00926
Calle P Pillot Garcia 00921
Calle P Rivera Martinez 00917
Calle Pabellones 00911
Calle Pablo Saez 00924
Calle Pacheco 00917
Calle Pachin Marin 00917
Calle Pacific 00911
Calle Padre B Boil 00926
Calle Padre Berrios 00917
Calle Padre Brawny 00924

Calle Padre Colon
100-269 00925
270-399 00923
Calle Padre Hoff 00901
Calle Padre Jose Maria
Casta 00924
Calle Padre Las
Casas 00918
Calle Padre Rufo 00917
Calle Padres
Capuchino 00925
Calle Padua 00921
Calle Pafos 00926
Calle Paganini 00926
Calle Pajuil 00926
Calle Palacios 00915
Calle Palermo 00924
Calle Palestina 00917
Calle Palma 00907
Calle Palma Real 00927
Calle Palmeras 00901
Calle Pampero 00924
Calle Pamplona 00923
Calle Paoli
200-299 00917
400-424 00918
426-498 00918
Calle Paraguay 00917
Calle Parana 00926
Calle Parcha 00926
Calle Paris 00917
Calle Park Blvd 00913
Calle Parnaso 00920
Calle Parque
100-269 00925
270-319 00923
321-399 00923
Calle Pasadena 00926
Calle Pascal 00927
Calle Pascua 00927
Calle Pasionaria 00927
Calle Pasternak 00926
Calle Pasteur 00925
Calle Patillas 00917
Calle Patria Tio 00924
Calle Pecos 00926
Calle Pedernales 00926
Calle Pedro Bigay 00918
Calle Pedro De Castro 00909
Calle Pedro Diaz
Correa 00923
Calle Pedro Espada 00918
Calle Pedro Figari 00926
Calle Pedro Margarit 00926
Calle Pedro Mejia 00926
Calle Pedro San
Miguel 00921
Calle Pedro Suarez
Cintron 00926
Calle Pegaso 00926
Calle Pelayo 00901
Calle Pelegrina 00925
Calle Peliux 00926
Calle Pellin Rodriguez 00915
Calle Penalara 00923
Calle Penarrubia 00923
Calle Penasco 00926
Calle Pendula 00926
Calle Penuelas 00918
Calle Pepe Diaz 00917
Calle Perafan Rivera 00926
Calle Perdiz 00924
Calle Pereira Leal 00923
Calle Perez 00911
Calle Perez Galdos 00918
Calle Perla 00926
Calle Perseo 00920
Calle Peru 00918
Calle Perurgia 00924
Calle Perusa 00921
Calle Pesante
401INT-499INT 00912
100-199 00911
200-1899 00912
Calle Pesqueria 00926
Calle Petunia
Z1-Z99 00927

K1-K99 00927
L1-L99 00927
P1-P99 00927
Q1-Q99 00927
C1-C99 00926
1-97 00927
99-1999 00927
Calle Piamonte 00924
Calle Picacho 00926
Calle Piccioni 00907
Calle Piedras Negras 00926
Calle Pina
1-199 00926
2300-2399 00915
Calle Pinero 00925
Calle Pinta 00918
Calle Pintor
Campeche 00918
Calle Pintor Jorge
Rechany 00912
Calle Pio Baroja 00926
Calle Pirandello 00926
Calle Pirineo 00926
Calle Piscis 00926
Calle Pitirre 00926
Calle Placid Court 1 00907
Calle Placid Court 2 00907
Calle Platanillo 00927
Calle Platero 00926
Calle Playera 00927
Calle Playero 00924
Calle Plaza 1 00926
Calle Plaza 2 00926
Calle Poincare 00911
Calle Polar 00926
Calle Polaris 00923
Calle Pomarrosa
100-199 00911
111-116 00926
200-299 00912
Calle Ponce 00917
Calle Pons 00909
Calle Pontevedra 00923
Calle Poppy 00926
Calle Popular 00917
Calle Portugues 00926
Calle Potomac 00926
Calle Pradera 00926
Calle Presidente
Ramirez 00918
Calle Primavera 00907
Calle Princesa 00926
Calle Principal
1-176 00926
2-18 00926
20-99 00926
101-107 00926
2200-2317 00915
2319-2319 00915
4659-4659 00926
Calle Principe De Luz 00926
Calle Prof Augusto
Rodrigue 00909
Calle Progreso
1-29 00907
30-98 00909
301-349 00923
351-399 00923
1100-1199 00907
Calle Prolongacion
Francia 00917
Calle Pruna 00923
Calle Puebla 00923
Calle Puente Final 00927
Calle Puerto Arturo 00907
Calle Puerto Principe 00921
Calle Puerto Vallarta 00926
Calle Puigdoller 00911
Calle Pumarada 00912
Calle Purus 00926
Calle Quebrada
Arenas 00926
Calle Quenepa 00926
Calle Quetzal 00924
Calle Quisqueya 00917
Calle Quito 00921
Calle R Gandia 00918

Calle R Lopez
Landron 00921
Calle R Menendez
Pidal 00926
Calle Radiante 00926
Calle Rafael Alers
1-225 00911
227-239 00911
240-399 00912
Calle Rafael Alonso
Torres 00921
Calle Rafael Arcelay 00924
Calle Rafael Berdejo 00926
Calle Rafael Castillo 00923
Calle Rafael Cepeda 00915
Calle Rafael Cordero 00901
Calle Rafael Garcia 00918
Calle Rafael Gimenez 00926
Calle Rafael Lamar 00918
Calle Rafael Mercado 00924
Calle Rafael Santana 00926
Calle Ramirez Pabon 00925
Calle Ramon Elvira 00923
Calle Ramon Garay 00924
Calle Ramon
Gonzalez 00926
Calle Ramon Power 00901
Calle Ramon Ramos 00918
Calle Rampla Del
Almirante 00911
Calle Raspinel 00924
Calle Ravel 00924
Calle Refugio 00907
Calle Reina De Las
Flores 00927
Calle Reina Mora 00926
Calle Reinita 00924
Calle Republica 00909
Calle Reseda 00927
Calle Resolucion 00920
Calle Rev Luis A
Orengo 00909
Calle Revdo Francisco
Colon 00925
Calle Rey 00926
Calle Rhin 00926
Calle Riaza 00923
Calle Ribot 00907
Calle Ricardo Skerret 00918
Calle Riera 00909
Calle Rimac 00926
Calle Rincon 00923
Calle Rio De Janeiro 00915
Calle Rio Grande
200-399 00915
300-399 00926
Calle Rioja 00923
Calle Rius Rivera 00918
Calle Rivadavia 00923
Calle Roberto
Clemente 00926
Calle Roberto Rivera 00923
Calle Roberts 00907
Calle Roble 00925
Calle Robledo 00917
Calle Robles
C1-C99 00926
B13-B99 00926
1-168 00925
170-198 00925
200-399 00923
250-998 00907
1000-1099 00907
Calle Rochester 00927
Calle Rocky Mtn 00926
Calle Rodano 00926
Calle Rodeo Dr 00926
Calle Rodrigo De
Triana 00918
Calle Rodriguez Serra 00907
Calle Rodriguez Vera 00921
Calle Roman 00918
Calle Romerillo 00927
Calle Ronda 00926
Calle Ronda Interior 00926
Calle Roosevelt
1-99 00907

489-506 00926
600-799 00907
Calle Rosa 00927
Calle Rosaleda 00926
Calle Rosales 00909
Calle Rosario
100-204 00911
206-208 00911
210-299 00912
Calle Rosario Andraca 00924
Calle Rosario Timothe 00923
Calle Rose 00926
Calle Roselane 00915
Calle Rosendo Viterbo 00924
Calle Rubi
17-99 00924
700-799 00926
Calle Rubicon 00926
Calle Rucabado 00907
Calle Rufino Tamayo 00926
Calle Ruisenor
100-199 00926
801-873 00924
875-999 00924
Calle Ruiz Belvis
1-199 00917
200-399 00915
Calle Rvdo Domingo
Marrero 00925
Calle S Cuevas
Bustamante 00918
Calle Sabatini 00926
Calle Sacarelo 00924
Calle Sacedon 00923
Calle Sagrado
Corazon 00909
Calle Salamanca 00927
Calle Saldana
1-99 00925
300-399 00912
400-498 00909
Calle Salerno 00921
Calle Salgado 00912
Calle Salinas 00907
Calle Salomon 00924
Calle Saltillo 00926
Calle Saluen 00926
Calle Salva 00907
Calle Salvador Brau 00917
Calle Salvador Pratts 00907
Calle Salven 00926
Calle Samoa 00924
Calle San Agustin 00901
Calle San Alejandro 00927
Calle San Alfonso 00921
Calle San Alvaro 00926
Calle San Andres 00901
Calle San Antonio
100-299 00917
400-641 00915
643-699 00915
1800-1863 00912
1864-1899 00909
Calle San Bernardino 00926
Calle San Bernardo 00921
Calle San Bruno 00926
Calle San Carlos
1-12 00926
14-98 00926
1400-1499 00921
2300-2399 00915
Calle San Ciprian 00915
Calle San Claudio 00926
Calle San Cosme 00927
Calle San Cristobal 00926
Calle San Damian 00921
Calle San Diego 00927
Calle San Edmundo 00927
Calle San Enrique 00921
Calle San Esteban 00927
Calle San Etanislao 00927
Calle San Felipe
1-99 00926
900-984 00923
986-1099 00923
Calle San Felix 00921
Calle San Gabriel 00926

Calle San Genaro 00926
Calle San Geronimo 00901
Calle San Gregorio 00921
Calle San Guillermo 00927
Calle San Isaac 00927
Calle San Jacinto 00921
Calle San Jacobo 00926
Calle San Javier 00926
Calle San Jeremias 00926
Calle San Joaquin 00926
Calle San Jofiel 00926
Calle San Jorge
100-174 00911
176-198 00911
200-499 00912
601-799 00909
Calle San Jose
2416INT-2416INT 00915
2387INT-2387INT 00915
28-77 00926
200-299 00925
600-799 00909
1900-2499 00915
Calle San Jose N 00917
Calle San Jovino 00926
Calle San Juan
100-199 00917
201-215 00917
206-210 00917
300-399 00926
600-698 00907
700-799 00915
700-1000 00907
1002-1006 00907
1500-1599 00909
Calle San Juan
Bautista 00901
Calle San Julian 00926
Calle San Justo 00926
Calle San Leandro 00926
Calle San Lino 00926
Calle San Lino Final 00926
Calle San Lorenzo 00926
Calle San Lucas 00921
Calle San Luis
100-130 00926
132-1900 00926
200-299 00920
300-398 00920
Calle San Mateo 00912
Calle San Mauro 00926
Calle San Melchor 00927
Calle San Miguel
1-61 00911
63-69 00911
1100-1199 00915
Calle San Pablo 00926
Calle San Pedro 00926
Calle San Pio 00917
Calle San Rafael
188INT-188INT 00926
1-99 00907
45-82 00926
100-299 00926
1300-1599 00909
Calle San Rafael Int 00926
Calle San Ramon 00907
Calle San Ricardo 00926
Calle San Roberto
1-99 00927
996-998 00926
1000-1012 00926
Calle San Rodolfo 00927
Calle San Salvador 00921
Calle San Sebastian
1-99 00926
500-599 00917
601-609 00917
Calle San Tomas 00926
Calle San Uriel 00926
Calle San Valentin 00926
Calle San Vicente 00915
Calle San Vidal 00926
Calle Sanchez 00909
Calle Sandalio Alonso 00921
Calle Santa Agueda 00926
Calle Santa Alodia 00921

Calle Santa Ana
1-99 00911
1600-1699 00909
Calle Santa Anastacia 00926
Calle Santa Angela 00926
Calle Santa Barbara 00921
Calle Santa Beda 00926
Calle Santa Bibiana 00926
Calle Santa Brigida 00926
Calle Santa Catalina 00921
Calle Santa Cecilia
1-189 00911
190-200 00912
201-215 00911
202-398 00912
237-399 00912
Calle Santa Clara 00926
Calle Santa Eduvigis 00926
Calle Santa Elena
1601-1799 00921
2300-2398 00915
2400-2499 00915
Calle Santa Eulalia 00926
Calle Santa Fe 00921
Calle Santa
Guadalupe 00921
Calle Santa Ines 00921
Calle Santa Isabel 00926
Calle Santa Juana 00921
Calle Santa Luisa 00921
Calle Santa Maria 00918
Calle Santa Marta 00926
Calle Santa Monica 00921
Calle Santa Narcisa 00921
Calle Santa Praxedes 00926
Calle Santa Rosa
A1-A99 00926
C2-C98 00926
B20-B20 00926
1-1 00926
21-299 00926
1600-1699 00921
Calle Santa Susana 00921
Calle Santa Teresa 00921
Calle Santa Ursula 00926
Calle Santander 00925
Calle Santiago
Carreras 00921
Calle Santiago Iglesias
1-82 00917
61-67 00907
69-73 00907
84-88 00917
Calle Santiam 00924
Calle Santo Domingo 00921
Calle Sara Isabel
Spencer 00924
Calle Sarasate 00924
Calle Sarracin 00923
Calle Sarria 00923
Calle Sauco
42-46 00926
100-1949 00927
Calle Savoya 00924
Calle Schuck Ct 00917
Calle Sea Vw 00907
Calle Sebastian Olano 00926
Calle Segarra
1-99 00917
100-399 00920
Calle Segovia 00923
Calle Segre 00926
Calle Sentina 00923
Calle Sequoya 00926
Calle Sevilla 00917
Calle Sgto Luis
Medina 00918
Calle Sherman 00920
Calle Sicilia
C-1-C-20 00923
1-499 00923
300-416 00923
418-444 00923
1100-1198 00924
Calle Siena 00921
Calle Sierra Linda 00926
Calle Sierra Morena 00926

Calle Sinai 00920
Calle Sinsonte 00924
Calle Siracusa 00924
Calle Sirio 00920
Calle Soberano 00926
Calle Sol
1-35 00926
100-112 00917
114-120 00917
122-198 00917
Calle Sola 00907
Calle Soldado Alcides
Reyes 00923
Calle Soldado Cruz 00913
Calle Soldado S
Libran 00923
Calle Soldado Serrano 00911
Calle Soledad 00907
Calle Solferino 00924
Calle Soller 00923
Calle Sonora 00926
Calle Sorbona 00927
Calle Soria 00923
Calle Sorrento 00924
Calle Sta Catalina 00926
Calle Suau 00907
Calle Sucre 00926
Calle Suiza 00917
Calle Sunflower 00926
Calle Sungari 00926
Calle Sunlight 00920
Calle Sunny Ct 00911
Calle T Cesar
Gonzalez 00921
Calle Tadeo Rivera 00901
Calle Taft
1-199 00911
200-299 00912
600-699 00926
1700-1798 00911
Calle Tagore 00926
Calle Tamarindo
102-110 00926
1200-1298 00924
Calle Tamaulipa 00926
Calle Tamesis 00926
Calle Tampa 00926
Calle Tanoa 00923
Calle Tapia
372INT-372INT 00912
1-229 00911
242-244 00912
246-399 00912
400-799 00915
Calle Tarragona 00923
Calle Tauladina 00924
Calle Tauro 00926
Calle Tavarez
400-599 00915
1100-1199 00925
Calle Tegucigalpa 00921
Calle Tehuacan 00926
Calle Tejas 00926
Calle Temple 00927
Calle Teniente
Lavergne 00913
Calle Teniente Matta 00913
Calle Teniente Rivera 00913
Calle Teodoro Aguilar 00923
Calle Teresa Capo 00924
Calle Teresa Jornet 00926
Calle Terranova 00924
Calle Teruel 00923
Calle Texidor 00917
Calle Theis 00926
Calle Thimothee 00923
Calle Thomas Barbour 00924
Calle Tiber 00926
Calle Tigris 00926
Calle Tijuana 00926
Calle Tinto 00926
Calle Tirso De Molina 00926
Calle Tito Rodriguez 00915
Calle Tivoli 00926
Calle Tizol 00925
Calle Tnte Felix
Beveraggi 00923

Calle Tnte Pablo
Ramirez 00923
Calle Tocantis 00926
Calle Toledo 00923
Calle Tolima 00926
Calle Tolosa 00921
Calle Toloy 00926
Calle Toluca 00926
Calle Tomas Agrait 00924
Calle Topacio 00926
Calle Torcaza 00924
Calle Tormina 00924
Calle Torrecilla 00920
Calle Torrelaguna 00923
Calle Torreon 00926
Calle Torres Cintron 00921
Calle Tortola 00926
Calle Tortosa 00926
Calle Toscania 00924
Calle Tossa Del Mar 00907
Calle Tous Soto 00918
Calle Trafalgar 00923
Calle Tranquilidad
1-99 00901
100-199 00917
Calle Traveris 00921
Calle Traviata 00926
Calle Trenton 00926
Calle Tres Hermanos 00907
Calle Trevi
B1-B99 00926
F1-F99 00926
A1-A99 00924
C1-C99 00924
D1-D99 00924
F1-F99 00924
Calle Treviso 00924
Calle Trianon 00926
Calle Trier 00921
Calle Trieste 00924
Calle Trigo 00907
Calle Triguero 00924
Calle Trinidad 00917
Calle Trinidad Orellana 00923
Calle Trinidad Padilla 00924
Calle Trinitaria 00927
Calle Trinity 00926
Calle Trujillo 00926
Calle Trujillo Alto 00917
Calle Tubingen 00921
Calle Tudela 00926
Calle Tulane 00927
Calle Tulip 00926
Calle Tulipan 00927
Calle Tulsa 00926
Calle Turia 00923
Calle Turin 00924
Calle Turina 00924
Calle Turpial
222-235 00926
800-898 00924
Calle Turquesa 00926
Calle Ubeda 00923
Calle Upsala 00921
Calle Ural 00926
Calle Uraneta 00924
Calle Urdiales 00923
Calle Uruguay 00917
Calle Uruguay Int 00917
Calle Utah 00926
Calle Utrera 00926
Calle Utuado 00917
Calle Valcarcel 00923
Calle Valdes 00901
Calle Valencia 00907
Calle Valladolid 00923
Calle Vallejo
1000-1159 00925
1170-1237 00926
1239-1299 00926
Calle Valparaiso 00915
Calle Valverde 00923
Calle Vara 00912
Calle Vasallo 00911
Calle Vatoria 00926
Calle Vedruna 00927

Calle Vega Santos 00921
Calle Vela 00918
Calle Vendig 00907
Calle Venecia 00917
Calle Verbena 00927
Calle Verdaza 00924
Calle Verde 00926
Calle Verdejo 00907
Calle Verderon 00924
Calle Verdi 00924
Calle Verdun 00926
Calle Vereda 00926
Calle Vergel 00923
Calle Vermont 00926
Calle Verona 00924
Calle Versalles 00926
Calle Vesta 00923
Calle Vicenza 00921
Calle Victor A
Fernandez 00927
Calle Victor Figueroa 00907
Calle Victor Lopez 00909
Calle Victor Morales 00924
Calle Victor Rosario 00924
Calle Victoria
1400-1499 00915
1500-1599 00912
1600-1698 00909
1700-1706 00909
1708-1798 00909
Calle Viena 00921
Calle Vieques
1-99 00917
1100-1199 00907
Calle Vila Mayo 00907
Calle Villa Castin 00923
Calle Villa Internacional
I 00913
Calle Villa Internacional
Ii 00913
Calle Villa Real 00915
Calle Villa Verde 00907
Calle Villalba 00923
Calle Villamil 00907
Calle Vinyater 00924
Calle Violeta
GG1-GG99 00926
TT1A-TT1B 00926
TT2A-TT2B 00926
TT3A-TT3B 00926
TT4A-TT4B 00926
TT5A-TT5B 00926
TT6A-TT6B 00926
TT7A-TT7B 00926
100-128 00927
101-127 00927
129-1700 00927
1702-1798 00927
Calle Virgo 00926
Calle Vistula 00926
Calle Vizcarrondo 00915
Calle Volga 00926
Calle Volta 00927
Calle Volturno 00924
Calle W Bosch 00924
Calle Washington
1-199 00907
14-699 00926
Calle Waymouth 00907
Calle Webb 00915
Calle Weser 00926
Calle William Jones
400-599 00915
1000-1199 00925
Calle Williams 00915
Calle Wilson 00907
Calle Xevell 00924
Calle Xsipibu 00926
Calle Xurla 00924
Calle Yaboa Real 00924
Calle Yabucoa 00917
Calle Yaguez 00926
Calle Yale 00927
Calle Yangtze 00926
Calle Yardley Pl 00911
Calle Yauco 00912

Calle Yellowstone 00926
Calle Yensey 00926
Calle York 00926
Calle Yorkshire 00926
Calle Yosemite 00926
Calle Yukon 00926
Calle Yunque 00920
Calle Zafiro
1-99 00924
700-899 00926
Calle Zaida 00924
Calle Zambeze 00926
Calle Zamora 00923
Calle Zenobia 00926
Calle Zion 00926
Calle Zorzal 00926
Calle Zumbador 00924
Callejon E 00926
Callejon 1 00917
Callejon 2 00917
Callejon 3 00917
Callejon 6 00917
Callejon 6 Interior 00917
Callejon 7 00917
Callejon 8 00917
Callejon A
53-58 00926
60-60 00926
200-296 00917
600-699 00917
Callejon Aguacate 00907
Callejon Aponte 00911
Callejon Aruz 00917
Callejon B
50-72 00926
74-99 00926
100-199 00917
Callejon Baez 00918
Callejon Baja Bata 00907
Callejon Bellevue 00915
Callejon Blanco 00907
Callejon C 00917
Callejon Carolina 00915
Callejon Checo 00915
Callejon Concordia 00911
Callejon D
297-1223 00926
500-599 00917
1225-1232 00926
Callejon De La Capilla 00901
Callejon Del Carmen 00912
Callejon Del Hospital 00901
Callejon Del Toro 00901
Callejon Dooley 00912
Callejon El Coco 00907
Callejon El Nene 00915
Callejon El Pilar 00915
Callejon Esperanza 00915
Callejon Esquife 00915
Callejon Figueroa 00915
Callejon G 00917
Callejon Guasp 00923
Callejon H 00917
Callejon Hernandez 00912
Callejon K 00917
Callejon L 00917
Callejon Lebron 00915
Callejon Los Pinos 00915
Callejon Lutz 00915
Callejon M 00917
Callejon Montanez 00907
Callejon Naguabo 00915
Callejon O 00917
Callejon Oriente 00915
Callejon Pachin Marin 00917
Callejon Palmita 00915
Callejon Pedroza 00907
Callejon Portalatin 00917
Callejon Progreso 00909
Callejon Quinones 00912
Callejon Republica 00915
Callejon Rosario
1000-1099 00923
1800-1899 00912
Callejon Saliente 00915
Callejon San Ciprian 00915

Callejon San Hipolito 00915
Callejon San Hipolito
2 00915
Callejon San Juan 00907
Callejon Soriano 00915
Callejon Tamarindo 00915
Callejon Tapia 00926
Callejon Tavares 00926
Callejon Tranquilidad 00915
Callejon Vega Baja 00911
Callejon Verdejo 00912
Camino Alejandrino 00926
Camino Avelino Lopez 00926
Camino Caloca 00926
Camino Dario Collazo 00926
Camino Del Lago 00926
Camino Del Rio 00926
Camino Diaz Aponte 00926
Camino Dolores Cruz 00926
Camino El Mudo 00926
Camino Esquilin 00926
Camino Esteban Cotto 00926
Camino Felix Roman 00926
Camino Figueroa 00926
Camino Francisco
Rivera 00926
Camino Gabino
Rodriguez 00926
Camino Jose Castro 00926
Camino Juan
Hernandez 00926
Camino Julito
Melendez 00926
Camino Las Lomas 00926
Camino Las
Margaritas 00926
Camino Las Palmas 00926
Camino Las Rosas 00926
Camino Lomas Del
Viento 00926
Camino Los Agostos 00926
Camino Los Andinos 00926
Camino Los Cruce 00926
Camino Los Figueroa 00926
Camino Los Gonzalez 00926
Camino Los Mercados 00926
Camino Los Navarro 00926
Camino Los Pizarro 00926
Camino Los Pomales 00926
Camino Los
Velazquez 00926
Camino Mangual 00926
Camino Pablo Ortiz 00926
Camino Pedro Angulo
Rivera 00926
Camino Real 00926
Camino Saldana 00926
Camino Tomas
Morales 00926
Cantera 00915
Carmen Hills Dr 00926
Carr 1 00926
Carr 175 00926
Carr 176 00926
Carr 177 00926
Carr 21
T3-1-T3-99 00921
U3-1-U3-99 00921
Q3-1-Q3-99 00921
S3-1-S3-99 00921
201-399 00927
1409-1787 00921
1779-1785 00921
1788-1788 00921
1789-1799 00921
Carr 28 00920
Carr 833 00921
Carr 842 00926
Carr 843 00926
Carr 844 00926
Carr 845 00926
Carr 849 00924
Carr 873 00926
Carr 877 00926
Carr 8838 00926
Carrion Ct 00911

Centro De Estudiantes 00925
Centro Gubernamental 00940
Centro Medico
Metropolitano 00921
Chalets De Santa
Maria 00927
Citibank Dr 00926
Ciudad Campo 00926
Com Los Bravos De
Boston 00915
Comunidad Borinquen 00920
Comunidad El Retiro 00924
Cond College Park 00921
Cond College Park A 00921
Cond El Mirador 00915
Cond Jard De San
Ignacio 00927
Cond Jard San
Francisco 00927
Cond Pem Ct 00926
Cond Quintana A 00917
Cond Quintana B 00917
Cond Villa
Panamericana 00924
Convention Blvd 00907
Decennial Census 00918
El Falansterio 00901
Escalinata De Las
Monjas 00901
Est De Campo Llano 00924
Fairview Shopp Ctr 00926
Family Ct 00911
Grand Paseo Blvd 00926
Hacienda Del Lago 00926
Handarel 00913
Horenest 00927
Jameralt 00911
Jard De Country Clb 00924
La Perla 00901
Laderas De San Juan 00926
Las Cumbres Shopp
Ctr 00926
Los Cantizales 00926
Marginal Ave Fd
Roosevelt 00917
Marginal Baldorioty 00912
Marginal Hoare 00907
Marginal Jf Kennedy 00920
Marginal Jt Pinero 00921
Mouthenw 00915
Ocean Walk 00911
Paraldel 00925
Parque Del Oriente 00926
Parque Las Ramblas 00926
Parque Medici 00926
Parque Tivoli 00926
Parque Vondel 00926
Paseo 00923
Paseo 1 00924
Paseo 10 00924
Paseo 11 00924
Paseo 2 00924
Paseo 3 00924
Paseo 4 00924
Paseo 5 00924
Paseo 6 00924
Paseo 7 00924
Paseo 8 00924
Paseo 9 00924
Paseo Colectora 00909
Paseo Concepcion De
Gracia 00901
Paseo Covadonga 00901
Paseo De Colon 00901
Paseo De La Princesa 00901
Paseo Don Juan 00907
Paseo El Conde 00915
Paseo Sereno 00926
Pintral 00909
Plaza Cinco 00926
Plaza Cuatro 00926
Plaza Diez 00926
Plaza Doce 00926
Plaza Dos 00926
Plaza Nueve 00926
Plaza Ocho 00926

Plaza Once 00926
Plaza Seis 00926
Plaza Siete 00926
Plaza Tres 00926
Plaza Uno 00926
Postage Due St 00907
Ramal 842 00926
Res Bartolome Las
Casas 00915
Res Cordero Davila 00917
Res Facultad Upr 00923
Res Jard Campo Rico 00924
Res Jard Selles 00924
Res Las Margaritas 00915
Res Llorens Torres 00913
Res Los Penas 00924
Res Mira Palmeras 00915
Res Monte Park 00924
Res Nemesio R
Canales 00918
Res Puerta De Tierra 00901
Res San Agustin 00901
Res San Antonio 00901
Res San Fernando 00927
Res San Jose Proyecto
13 00923
Res San Jose Proyecto
16 00923
Res San Jose Proyecto
17 00923
Res San Juan
Bautista 00909
Res San Martin 00924
Res Villa Espana 00921
Rio Piedras Vly 00926
Riverside Blvd 00926
Roseville Dr 00926
San Juan Park I 00909
San Juan Park Ii 00909
Sect Minao 00926
Summit Blvd 00926
Sunrise Blvd 00926
Sunset Blvd 00926
Terrazas De Carraizo 00926
Urb Brisas Del Valle 00926
Valle De Collores 00926
Valle De Lajas 00926
Valle Del Toa 00926
Valle Del Turabo 00926
Valley Blvd 00926
Veredas Los Laureles 00926
Via Cimas 00924
Via Cordilleras 00924
Via Cumbres 00924
Via Del Parque 00924
Via Del Valle 00924
Via Horizonte 00924
Via Laderas 00924
Via Las Alturas 00924
Via Llanuras 00924
Via Panoramica 00924
Villa Dagmarita 00926
Villa De Las Americas 00927
Villa Kennedy 00915
Villas Del Parque 00909
Waleark 00920
Welderic 00923

TOA ALTA PR

General Delivery 00954

POST OFFICE BOXES MAIN OFFICE STATIONS AND BRANCHES

Box No.s
All PO Boxes 00954

RURAL ROUTES

01, 02, 03, 04, 05, 06,
07 00953

NAMED STREETS

All Street Addresses 00953

TOA BAJA PR

General Delivery 00950

POST OFFICE BOXES MAIN OFFICE STATIONS AND BRANCHES

Box No.s
1 - 2559 00951
1904 - 1904 00950
2600 - 8282 00951
50001 - 52360 00950

HIGHWAY CONTRACTS

01 00949

NAMED STREETS

All Street Addresses 00949

TRUJILLO ALTO PR

POST OFFICE BOXES MAIN OFFICE STATIONS AND BRANCHES

Box No.s
All PO Boxes 00977

HIGHWAY CONTRACTS

61, 645 00976

NAMED STREETS

All Street Addresses 00976

VEGA BAJA PR

General Delivery 00694

POST OFFICE BOXES MAIN OFFICE STATIONS AND BRANCHES

Box No.s
All PO Boxes 00694

HIGHWAY CONTRACTS

01, 02, 03, 04, 05 00693

NAMED STREETS

All Street Addresses 00693

Rhode Island

People QuickFacts	Rhode Island	USA
Population, 2013 estimate	1,051,511	316,128,839
Population, 2010 (April 1) estimates base	1,052,567	308,747,716
Population, percent change, April 1, 2010 to July 1, 2013	-0.1%	2.4%
Population, 2010	1,052,567	308,745,538
Persons under 5 years, percent, 2013	5.2%	6.3%
Persons under 18 years, percent, 2013	20.4%	23.3%
Persons 65 years and over, percent, 2013	15.5%	14.1%
Female persons, percent, 2013	51.6%	50.8%
White alone, percent, 2013 (a)	85.6%	77.7%
Black or African American alone, percent, 2013 (a)	7.5%	13.2%
American Indian and Alaska Native alone, percent, 2013 (a)	0.9%	1.2%
Asian alone, percent, 2013 (a)	3.3%	5.3%
Native Hawaiian and Other Pacific Islander alone, percent, 2013 (a)	0.2%	0.2%
Two or More Races, percent, 2013	2.5%	2.4%
Hispanic or Latino, percent, 2013 (b)	13.6%	17.1%
White alone, not Hispanic or Latino, percent, 2013	75.3%	62.6%
Living in same house 1 year & over, percent, 2008-2012	86.3%	84.8%
Foreign born persons, percent, 2008-2012	13.0%	12.9%
Language other than English spoken at home, pct age 5+, 2008-2012	21.0%	20.5%
High school graduate or higher, percent of persons age 25+, 2008-2012	84.8%	85.7%
Bachelor's degree or higher, percent of persons age 25+, 2008-2012	30.8%	28.5%
Veterans, 2008-2012	74,982	21,853,912
Mean travel time to work (minutes), workers age 16+, 2008-2012	23.4	25.4
Housing units, 2013	461,640	132,802,859
Homeownership rate, 2008-2012	61.2%	65.5%
Housing units in multi-unit structures, percent, 2008-2012	40.7%	25.9%
Median value of owner-occupied housing units, 2008-2012	$259,400	$181,400
Households, 2008-2012	410,639	115,226,802
Persons per household, 2008-2012	2.46	2.61
Per capita money income in past 12 months (2012 dollars), 2008-2012	$30,005	$28,051
Median household income, 2008-2012	$56,102	$53,046
Persons below poverty level, percent, 2008-2012	13.2%	14.9%

Business QuickFacts	Rhode Island	USA
Private nonfarm establishments, 2012	28,034	7,431,808
Private nonfarm employment, 2012	402,977	115,938,468
Private nonfarm employment, percent change, 2011-2012	-0.8%	2.2%
Nonemployer establishments, 2012	73,154	22,735,915
Total number of firms, 2007	96,822	27,092,908
Black-owned firms, percent, 2007	3.3%	7.1%
American Indian- and Alaska Native-owned firms, percent, 2007	0.4%	0.9%
Asian-owned firms, percent, 2007	2.1%	5.7%
Native Hawaiian and Other Pacific Islander-owned firms, percent, 2007	0.0%	0.1%
Hispanic-owned firms, percent, 2007	6.0%	8.3%
Women-owned firms, percent, 2007	27.3%	28.8%
Manufacturers shipments, 2007 ($1000)	12,061,517	5,319,456,312
Merchant wholesaler sales, 2007 ($1000)	9,182,788	4,174,286,516
Retail sales, 2007 ($1000)	12,286,485	3,917,663,456
Retail sales per capita, 2007	$11,646	$12,990
Accommodation and food services sales, 2007 ($1000)	2,148,674	613,795,732
Building permits, 2012	731	829,658

Geography QuickFacts	Rhode Island	USA
Land area in square miles, 2010	1,033.81	3,531,905.43
Persons per square mile, 2010	1,018.1	87.4
FIPS Code	44	

(a) Includes persons reporting only one race.
(b) Hispanics may be of any race, so also are included in applicable race categories.
FN: Footnote on this item for this area in place of data
NA: Not available
D: Suppressed to avoid disclosure of confidential information
X: Not applicable
S: Suppressed; does not meet publication standards
Z: Value greater than zero but less than half unit of measure shown
F: Fewer than 100 firms
Source: US Census Bureau State & County QuickFacts

Rhode Island

3 DIGIT ZIP CODE MAP

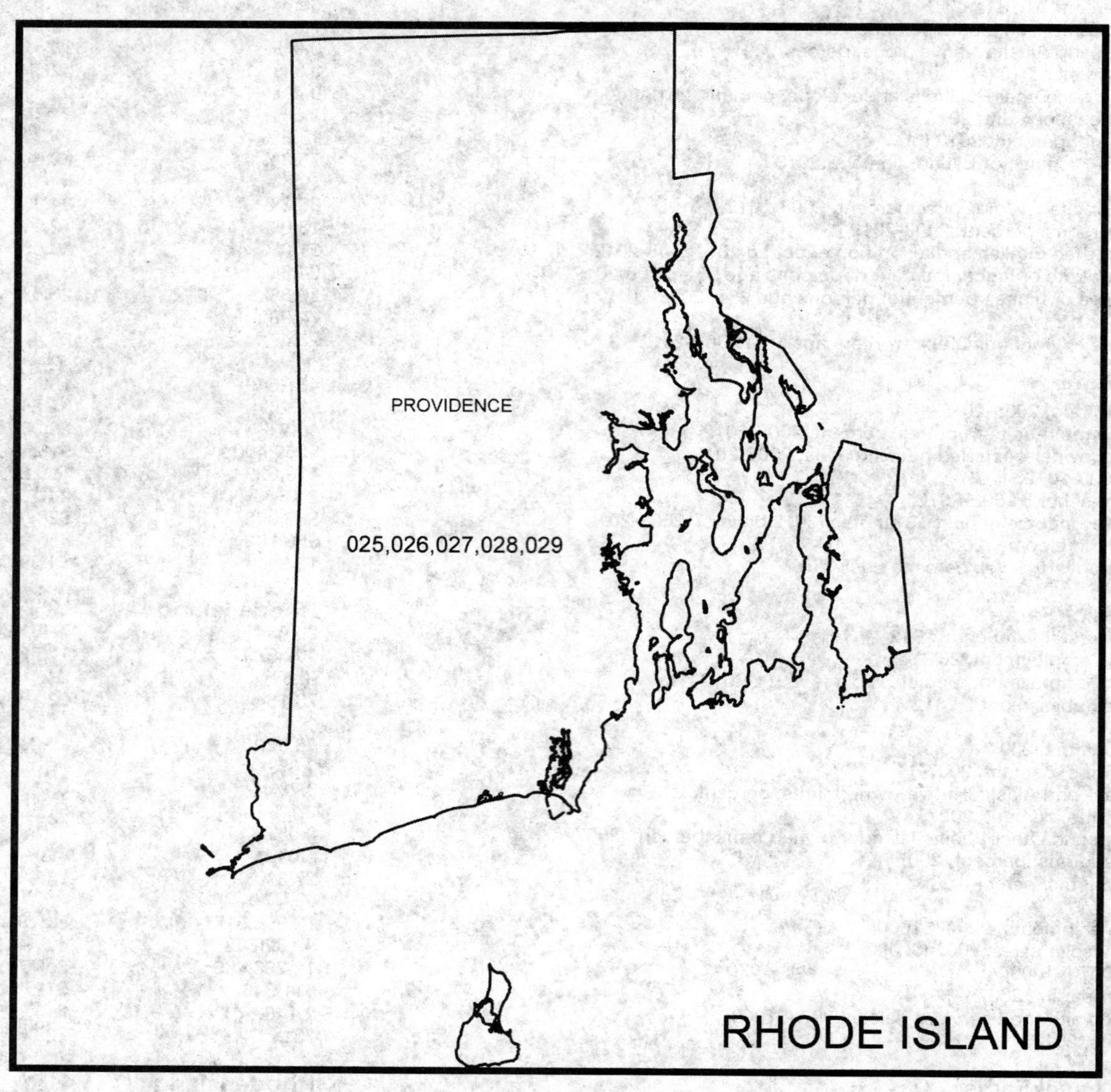

Rhode Island

(Abbreviation: RI)

Post Office, County	ZIP Code

Places with more than one ZIP code are listed in capital letters, See pages indicated.

Post Office, County	ZIP Code
Adamsville, Newport	02801
Albion, Providence	02802
Ashaway, Washington	02804
Barrington, Bristol	02806
Block Island, Washington	02807
Bradford, Washington	02808
Bristol, Bristol	02809
Burrillville, Providence	02830
Carolina, Washington	02812
Central Falls, Providence	02863
Charlestown, Washington	02813
Chepachet, Providence	02814
Clayville, Providence	02815
Coventry, Kent	02816
Coventry, Kent	02827
CRANSTON, Providence (See Page 3326)	
Cumberland, Providence	02864
East Greenwich, Kent	02818
East Providence, Providence	02914
Escoheag, Washington	02822
Exeter, Washington	02822
Fiskeville, Providence	02823
Forestdale, Providence	02824
Foster, Providence	02825
Glendale, Providence	02826
Greene, Kent	02827
Greenville, Providence	02828
Harmony, Providence	02829
Harrisville, Providence	02830
Hope, Providence	02831
Hope Valley, Washington	02832
Hopkinton, Washington	02833
Jamestown, Newport	02835
Johnston, Providence	02919
Kenyon, Washington	02836
Kingston, Washington	02881
Lincoln, Providence	02865
Little Compton, Newport	02837
Manville, Providence	02838
Mapleville, Providence	02839
Middletown, Newport	02842
Narragansett, Washington	02879
Narragansett, Washington	02882
New Shoreham, Washington	02807
NEWPORT, Newport (See Page 3328)	
North Kingstown, Washington	02852
North Providence, Providence	02904
North Scituate, Providence	02857
North Smithfield, Providence	02896
Oakland, Providence	02858
Pascoag, Providence	02859
PAWTUCKET, Providence (See Page 3329)	
Peace Dale, Washington	02879
Peace Dale, Washington	02883
Point Judith, Washington	02882
Portsmouth, Newport	02871
PROVIDENCE, Providence (See Page 3330)	
Prudence Island, Bristol	02872
Richmond, Washington	02812
Riverside, Providence	02915
Rockville, Washington	02873
Rumford, Providence	02916
Saunderstown, Washington	02874
Scituate, Providence	02857
Shannock, Washington	02875
Slatersville, Providence	02876
Slocum, Washington	02877
Smithfield, Providence	02917
South Kingstown (See Wakefield)	
Tiverton, Newport	02878
WAKEFIELD, Washington (See Page 3334)	
Warren, Bristol	02885
WARWICK, Kent (See Page 3336)	
West Greenwich, Kent	02817
West Kingston, Washington	02892
West Warwick, Kent	02893
Westerly, Washington	02891
Wood River Junction, Washington	02894
Woonsocket, Providence	02895
Wyoming, Washington	02898

CRANSTON RI

POST OFFICE BOXES MAIN OFFICE STATIONS AND BRANCHES

Box No.s
3501 - 3800 02910
8001 - 8998 02920
9950 - 10480 02910
20001 - 22120 02920
100001 - 100998 02910

NAMED STREETS

A St 02920
Abbott St 02920
Aborn St 02905
Adams St 02920
Adie St 02920
Aetna St 02910
Agawam Trl 02921
Albert Ave 02905
Alder Dr 02905
Alderbrook Dr 02920
Aldrich Ave 02920
Alexander St 02910
Algonquin Trl 02921
Alhambra Cir 02905
Allard St 02920
Allen Ave 02910
Alpine Estates Dr 02921
Althea Dr 02920
Alto St 02920
Alton St 02910
Amalia Ave 02910
Amanda Ct & St 02920
Amber St 02910
Ambrose St 02920
America St 02920
Amflex Dr 02921
Amherst Rd 02920
Amy Ct & Dr 02921
Angela Ave 02921
Angell Ave 02920
Ann Ct 02921
Annual Dr 02920
Anstis St 02905
Anthony Dr 02921
Aplin St 02920
Apple Blossom Ln 02921
Apple Hill Dr 02921
Apple House Dr 02921
Applegate Rd 02920
Appleton St 02910
Applewood Rd 02920
Aqueduct Rd 02910
Arbor St 02921
Arcadia Ave 02910
Argyle St 02920
Arlington Ave 02920
Armington St 02905
Arnold Ave 02905
Arrow Gln & Way 02921
Arrowfield Rd 02921
Arthur St 02910
Ash Ave 02910
Ashbrook Dr 02921
Ashburton Dr 02921
Ashland Rd 02921
Ashley St 02920
Ashmont St 02905
Asia St 02920
Aspen Dr 02920
Astle St 02905
Atwood Ave 02920
Auburn St 02910
Aumond St 02905
Aurora Ave 02905
Ausdale Rd 02910
Autumn St 02910
Avery Rd 02910
Avon Rd 02905
Azalea Ct & Dr 02921
B St 02920
Bagley Ave 02920
Bailey St 02920
Bain St 02920
Bakewell Ct 02921
Bald Hill Rd 02920
Baldino Dr 02920
Baldwin Orchard Dr 02920
Balsam Ct 02920
Baneberry Dr 02921
Bank St 02920
Barndoor Ln 02921
Barney St 02920
Barnsdale Rd 02910
Barrett St 02910
Bartlett Ave 02905
Basil Xing 02921
Basswood Rd 02910
Batcheller Ave 02920
Bateman Ave 02920
Bay St 02905
Bayamo Ln 02905
Bayberry Rd 02920
Beachmont Ave 02905
Beacon Cir & St 02910
Beaver Creek Ct 02921
Beckwith St 02910
Bedford Rd 02910
Bedson Rd 02910
Beech Ave 02910
Beechwood Dr 02921
Beeckman Ave 02920
Begonia Dr 02920
E & W Bel Air Rd 02920
Belcrest Rd 02920
Belgium St 02920
Belle Isle Way 02921
Bellefont St 02905
Bellevue Dr 02920
Belmont Rd 02910
Belvedere Dr 02920
Benjamin Ave 02920
Bennett Ave 02920
Bennington Rd 02920
Berkley St 02910
Berkshire Rd 02910
Bernard St 02920
Bernice Dr 02920
Berry St 02920
Berwick Ln 02905
Bethel St 02920
Betsey Williams Dr 02905
Bev Cir 02920
Beverly St 02920
Bicknell Ave 02920
Birch St 02920
Birch View Ct 02921
Birchfield Rd 02905
Birchview Dr 02920
Birchwood Dr 02920
Black Oak Ct 02921
Blackamore Ave 02910
Blaine St 02920
Blais Ave 02920
Blaisdell St 02910
Blossom Dr 02920
Blue Bonnet Rd 02920
Blue Gentian Rd 02921
Blue Jay Dr 02920
W Blue Ridge Rd 02920
Blueberry Ln 02921
W Bluebird Ln 02921
Bluff Ave 02905
Bobolink Dr 02920
Bolton St 02920
Bow St 02905
Bowen St 02905
Bower St 02905
Boxwood Ave 02910
Boylston Dr 02921
Bracken St 02920
Bradford Rd 02910
Bradshaw St 02910
Braeburn Cir 02921
Branch Ave 02910
Brandon Rd 02910
Brayton Ave 02920
Brettonwoods Dr 02920
Brewster Rd 02910
Briar Hill Dr 02921
Briarbrooke Ln 02921
Briarcliffe Rd 02910
Briarwood Rd 02920
Bridge St 02905
Bridgton Ct & Rd 02910
Briggs St 02920
Brimfield Rd 02920
Britton St 02920
Broad St 02905
Broadmoor Rd 02910
Brookdale Ave 02921
Brookfield Dr 02920
Brooks St 02920
Brookside Dr 02910
Brookview Dr 02921
Brookwood Rd 02910
Browne St 02920
Bryant Rd 02910
Budlong Rd 02920
Burbank St 02910
Burdick Dr 02920
Burlingame Rd 02921
Burnham Ave
1-44 02920
45-99 02910
Burnside St 02910
Burr St 02920
Burton St 02920
Butler St 02920
Buttercup Rd 02920
Buttonwood Dr 02920
Buxton Dr 02921
Byron St 02920
C St 02920
Cadillac Ave 02910
Cady St 02920
Calaman Rd 02910
Calder St 02920
Calef St 02920
Calvin Ave 02905
Cambio Ct 02921
Camelia Dr 02920
Candle Dr 02920
Candy Ln 02921
Cannon St 02920
Canonchet Trl 02921
Canterbury Ct 02920
Canton Ct 02921
Capeway Rd 02920
Caporal St 02910
Capuano Ave 02920
Caraway Dr 02921
Cardi Cir 02920
Cardinal Rd 02921
Carlisle St 02920
Carlo Ct 02921
Carlsbad St 02920
Carlton St 02910
Carman St 02910
Carmina Cir 02921
Carnation Dr 02920
Carole Ct 02921
Carolina St 02920
Caronia St 02920
Carpathia Rd 02920
Carriage Rd 02920
Carrie Ann Dr 02921
Cartier St 02920
Carver Rd 02920
Case Ave 02910
Casino Ave 02920
Cassandra Ct 02921
Castle Dr 02920
Castleton Dr 02921
Cavalry St 02920
Cedar St 02910
Cedarwood Dr 02920
Celestia Ave 02920
Central St 02905
Century Ln 02921
Chaloner Ct 02921
Chandler Ave 02910
Chapel View Blvd 02920
Chaple Dr 02920
Chappy St 02920
Charcalee Dr 02921
Charles St 02920
Charlotte St 02910
Chase Dr 02920
Chatham Rd 02920
Cherry Rd 02905
Cherrydale Ct 02920
Cheryls Way 02921
Cheshire Dr 02921
Chester Ave 02920
Chestnut Ave 02910
Chestnut Hill Ave 02920
Chicory Ln 02921
Chiswick Rd 02905
Church St 02920
Church Hill Dr 02920
Cindy Ln 02921
Circuit Dr 02905
City View Pkwy 02921
Clarence St 02910
N & S Clarendon St 02910
Clarion St 02920
Clark Ave 02920
Classic Ct 02921
Claudia Dr 02921
Clay St 02920
Clear View Dr 02921
Clemence St 02920
Cleveland Ave 02920
Clifden Ave 02905
Cliff Ave 02920
Cliffdale Ave 02905
Cliffside Dr 02920
Cloverdale Rd 02905
Coastway Plz 02910
Cobblestone Ter 02921
Cohasset Ln 02921
Coldbrook Ct & Dr 02920
Collingwood Dr 02921
Colonial Ave 02910
Colony St 02920
Columbia Ave 02905
Columbus Blvd 02910
Colwell St 02920
Commercial St 02905
Community Dr 02905
S Comstock Pkwy 02921
Concord Ave 02910
Conley Ave 02921
Connecticut St 02920
Coolspring Dr 02920
Coombs St 02920
Cornell St 02920
Corral Ct 02921
Cortland Ln 02920
Cory Ave 02920
Cottage Cir & St 02910
Cottonwood Dr 02921
Coulters Rd 02920
Council Rock Rd 02921
Country Ln 02921
Country Meadow Dr 02921
Country View Dr 02921
Countryside Dr 02921
Cranberry Ter 02921
Cranston St 02920
Crawford St 02910
Crescent Ave 02910
Crest Dr 02921
Crestwood Rd 02920
Crocus Dr 02920
Crossway Rd 02910
Crothers Ave 02910
Cruz St 02920
Curry Rd 02920
Curtis St 02920
Cutting Ave 02920
Cypress Dr 02920
Cyr St 02905
Daisy Ct 02920
Dale Ave 02910
Dallas Ave 02905
Daniels Way 02921
Dart St 02920
Dartmouth Rd 02920
David Dr 02920
Davis Ave & Ct 02910
Dean Pkwy & St 02920
Dean Ridge Blvd, Ct & Dr 02920
Debbie Dr 02921
Deborah Way 02910
Deer Run 02921
Deerfield Rd 02920
Dekalb St 02910
Dellwood Rd 02920
Delta St 02920
Delway Rd 02910
Dennis Ave 02905
Denver Ave 02905
Depot Ave 02920
Derby Ln 02921
Derbyshire Dr 02921
Dercole Dr 02920
Dixwell Ave 02910
Doane St 02910
Dogwood Dr 02921
Donna Dr 02921
Dora St 02920
Doric Ave 02910
Douglas St 02910
Dove Ct 02921
Dover St 02920
Doylston Dr 02905
Dresden St 02910
Drowne St 02905
Dunedin St 02920
Dunham Ave 02905
Dutchess Dr 02921
Dwight St 02921
Dyer Ave 02920
Eagle Rd 02920
East St 02920
Echo Ln 02921
Eddy St 02920
Eden Crest Cir & Dr 02920
Eden Park Dr 02910
Edge St 02905
Edgemere Dr 02905
Edgewood Ave & Blvd 02905
Egan Rd 02910
Eilein Ave 02920
Elberta St 02910
Eldorado St 02910
Eldridge St 02910
Elena St 02920
Eliot Rd 02910
Elite Dr 02921
Ellen Ln 02921
Ellison St 02920
Ellwood Ave 02910
Elm Cir & Dr 02920
Elmhurst Ave 02920
Elmwood Ave 02910
Elsie St 02910
Elton Cir 02921
Elwyn St 02920
Endicott St 02910
Enos Cir 02921
Enterprise St 02920
Eric Ct 02921
Essex St 02910
Esther St 02920
Euston Ave 02910
Eva Ln 02921
Evangeline Dr 02910
Evans Way 02920
Everbloom Dr 02920
Everett Rd 02920
Evergreen Ct & St 02910
Everly St 02920
Exchange St 02920
Ezekiel St 02920
Fairbanks St 02910
Fairfield Rd 02910
Fairlawn St 02910
Fairview Ave 02905
Fairway Dr 02920
Fairweather Ave 02910
Fairwood Dr 02920
Falcon Ln 02921
Fales St 02920
Falmouth Rd 02920
Farm St 02920
Farmington Ave 02920
Farragut Ave 02905
Farragut St 02910
Farrar St 02920
Farwell St 02920
Fay St 02920
Felicia Dr 02920
Fenner St 02910
Fernbrook Ct & Dr 02920
Ferncrest Ave 02905
Fernwood Dr 02920
Fiat Ave 02910
Field St 02920
Fielding Rd 02910
Finch Ct 02921
Firethorn Ln 02920
Firglade Dr 02920
Fleming Rd 02920
Fletcher Ave 02920
Flint Ave 02910
Florida Ave 02920
Flower St 02920
Flynn Ave 02920
Fordson Ave 02910
Forest Ave 02910
Forsythia Ln 02921
Fort Ave 02905
Fortini St 02920
Fountain Ave 02920
Fox Run 02921
Fox Ridge Dr 02921
Foxglove Dr 02920
Frances Ave 02910
Frances Dr 02920
Franconia Dr 02920
Frankfort St 02910
Franklin Ave 02920
Freedom Dr 02920
Freehold Ave 02920
Freeway Dr 02920
Friendly Rd 02910
Fringetree Dr 02921
Fruit St 02920
Furlong St 02920
Furnace Hill Rd 02921
Fyffe Ave 02920
Gaglione Ct 02921
Gail Ave 02905
Gallup Ave 02910
Galveston St 02910
Gansett Ave
1-39 02920
40-299 02910
Garden Ct 02920
Garden St 02910
Garden City Dr 02920
Garden Hills Ct, Dr & Pkwy 02920
Gardner Ave 02910
Garfield Ave 02920
Garland Ave 02910
Garrison St 02920
Garvey Rd 02920
Gaunt Dr 02920
Gearys Dr 02920
George St 02905
Geranium Cir 02920
Gianna Dr 02921
Gina Ct 02921
Ginger Cir 02921
Gladstone St 02920
Gleason St 02910
Glen Ave 02905
Glen Rd 02920
Glen Hills Dr 02920
Glen Ridge Rd 02920
Glen View Dr 02920
Glencoe Ln 02920
Glengrove Ave 02910
Glenham Rd 02921
Glenmere Dr 02920
Glenwood Ave 02910
Goddard Rd 02920
Goeckel Ave 02910
Gordon St 02910
Gould Rd 02921
Governor St 02920
Grace St 02910
Grand Ave 02905
Grant Ave 02920
Grantland Rd 02910
Grape Ct & St 02920
Gray Birch Dr 02921
Gray Coach Ln 02921
Graysonia Dr 02905
Green Ct 02920
Green Bush Dr 02921
Greendale Ct 02920
Greene Ave 02920
Greenfield St 02920
Greening Ln 02920
Greenview Rd 02920
Greenway St 02910
Greenwood St 02910
Greylock Ave 02910
Griswold Ave 02910
Grove Ave 02910
Groverdale Rd 02905
Haddon Hill Rd 02905
Hagen Ave 02920
Hall Pl 02905
W Hamden Rd 02920
Hamilton Rd 02910
Hampshire Rd 02910
Handy Ave 02910
Hans St 02910
Harbour Ter 02905
Harcourt St 02920
Harding Ave 02905
Hardpoint Rd 02920
Hardy St 02920
Harmon Ave 02910
Harmony St 02920
Harper Ave 02910
Harrington Rd 02920
Harris Ave 02920
Harris Driftway St 02920
Harrison Ave 02920
Harry St 02907
W Harry St 02920
Harvard Ct & St 02920
Harvest St 02920
Harwich Rd 02920
Harwood St 02910
Haven Ave 02920
Hawthorne Ave 02910
Hayes St 02920
Hayward St 02910
Hazel Bush Dr 02921
Hazelton St 02920
Hazelwood St 02910
Heath Ave 02910
Heather St 02920
Hemalin Rd 02910
Hemlock Ave 02910
Henry St 02905
Heritage Ct 02921
Herod St 02921
Hersey Rd 02910
Hervey St 02920
Hibiscus Dr 02920
Hickory Dr 02921
High Gate Rd 02920
High Meadow Ct 02921
High School Ave 02910
High View Dr 02921
Highland St 02920
Highwood Ter 02920
Hilda St 02920
W, E & S Hill Cir & Dr 02920
Hillcrest Dr N 02921
Hillock Rd 02921
Hillsdale Dr 02920
Hillside Ave & Rd 02920
Hilltop Dr 02920
Hillview Rd 02920
Hillwood St 02920

Hines Farm Rd 02921
Hobson Ave 02910
Hodsell St 02910
Hoffman Ave 02920
Holburn Ave 02910
Holgate St 02920
Holland St 02920
Hollins Dr 02920
Hollow Tree Dr 02920
Holly St 02910
Holly Hill Ln 02921
Hollyhock Dr 02920
Homeside Dr 02905
Homestead Ave 02920
Honey Lou Ct 02921
Honeysuckle Dr 02921
Hope Rd 02921
Hope Hill Ter 02921
Hopewell Ave 02920
Horielli St 02920
Horizon Dr 02921
Hornbeam Dr 02921
Hornbine St 02910
Hosey Dr 02920
Howard Ave & St 02920
Howland Rd 02910
Hubbard St 02920
Hudson Pl 02905
Humbert Ave 02910
Hummingbird Ln 02921
Hybrid Dr 02920
Hyde St 02920
Imperial Ave 02920
Independence Way 02921
Indian Rd 02905
Indian Trl 02921
Industrial Rd 02920
Ingleside Ave 02905
Intervale Rd 02910
Invernia Rd 02920
Ionia St 02921
Iris Dr 02921
Iroquois Trl 02921
Irving St 02910
Ivanhoe St 02910
Ivy Ave 02905
Ivy Hollow Ct 02921
Jackson Rd 02920
Jacqueline Ct 02921
Janet Dr 02921
Jasmine Ct 02920
Jay Ct 02921
Jennie St 02920
Jennifer Cir 02921
Jennings Ave 02920
Jessica Ct 02920
John St 02920
John Hazen White Sr
Way 02920
Jonathan Way 02920
Jordan Ave 02910
Joseph Henry Ln 02921
E Josephine St 02910
Judge St 02910
Julia St 02910
Juliana Dr 02921
June Ave 02920
Juniper Dr 02920
Justin Way 02910
Katelan Ct 02921
Kearney St 02920
Kearsarge Dr 02920
Keith Ave 02910
Keller Ave 02920
Kenmore St 02905
Kennedy Ave 02920
Kenney Dr 02920
Kensington Rd 02905
Kent Pl 02905
Kenyon Rd 02910
Kermit Ave 02920
Kiki Cir 02921
Kimberly Ln N 02921
King Ave 02905
King Cir 02920
Kingwood Ave 02920
Kneeland St 02905
Knight St 02920
Knollwood Ave 02910
Knowles St 02910
Koster St 02910
Koutsogiane Dr 02920
Kristin Dr 02921
La Grange St 02910
Lace Cir 02921
Laconia Rd 02920
Lake St 02910
Lake Garden Dr 02920
Lake View Rd 02920
Lakeland Rd 02910
Lakeside Ave 02910
Lakeview Dr 02910
Lambert St 02910
Lang Ct 02921
Lantern Ln 02921
Larch St 02920
Lark Ave 02920
Larkspur Dr 02920
Laten Knight Rd 02921
Laura Cir 02920
Laurel Hill Ave 02920
Laurelhurst Rd 02920
Lauren Ct 02921
Laurens St 02910
Law Ave 02910
Lawnacre Dr 02920
Lawrence St 02920
Leah Dr 02921
Leawood Dr 02920
Lebaron Ct 02921
Ledgewood Dr 02920
Lee St 02920
Legion Way 02910
Lenox Rd 02920
Leslie St 02910
Lexington Ave 02910
Leyden St 02910
Libera St 02920
Lilac Cir 02920
Lillian Ln 02920
Lily Dr 02920
Lincoln Ave 02920
Lincoln Park Ave 02920
Linden Ave 02910
Lindsay Ln 02921
Lippitt Ave 02921
Lockmere Rd 02910
Lockwood St 02905
Locust Glen Ct & Dr 02921
Lodge St 02920
Lofty Rd 02921
Lolly Ln 02920
Long Ct 02920
Longhill Dr 02920
Longview Dr 02920
Lookoff Rd 02905
Lookout Ave 02920
Loomis St 02920
Loretta St 02910
Loring St 02920
Lou Cir 02920
Lovevine Dr 02920
Lowell St 02910
Luigi St 02920
Lyndon Rd 02905
Lynn Ave 02905
Macbeth St 02920
Macera Dr 02920
Macintosh Dr 02921
Macklin St 02920
Macon St 02920
Madison Ave 02920
Magazine St 02920
Magnolia St 02910
Malcolm St 02910
Malden St 02910
Mallory Ct 02910
Malvern Ave 02905
Manhasset St 02910
Manilla Ave 02920
Manor Rd 02920
Maple St 02910
Maple Farms Rd 02921
Mapleton St 02910
Mapleview Dr 02910
Maplewood Ave 02920
Marcy St 02905
Marden St 02910
Margaret St 02907
Marigold Ct 02920
Marion Ave 02905
Marjoram Dr 02921
Mark Dr 02920
Marlborough St 02910
Marlow St 02920
Marshall Rd 02920
Mary Ann Dr 02921
Mary Jo Ct 02921
Mason Ave 02910
Massachusetts St 02920
Massasoit Ave 02905
Mather Ave 02905
Mathewson St 02920
Mauran St 02910
Maxim St 02910
May Dr 02920
Mayberry St 02920
Mayfair Rd 02905
Mayfield Ave 02920
Mayflower Dr 02905
Mccabe St 02920
Meadow Ave 02920
Meadow Lark Dr 02921
Meadow View Dr 02920
Mecca St 02910
Melody Ln 02920
Melrose St 02910
Melton St 02920
Meredith Dr 02920
Merit Dr 02920
Merrill Rd 02920
Meshanticut Dr 02920
Meshanticut Valley
Pkwy 02920
Metro Park Dr 02910
Metropolitan Ave 02920
Mica Ave 02920
Michael Dr 02920
Midland Dr 02920
Midler St 02910
Midvale Ave 02920
Midway Rd 02920
Midwood St 02910
Miles Ave 02920
Milford St 02910
Mill St 02905
Milton Ave 02905
Minola St 02910
Mirick Ave 02920
Mitchell Cir 02921
Moccasin Trl 02921
Mockingbird Dr 02920
Mohawk Trl 02921
Mollie Dr 02921
Molter St 02910
Montgomery Ave 02905
Monument St 02910
Moon St 02920
Moore Ave 02910
Moorland Ave 02905
Morgan St 02920
Morningside Ct 02921
Mount View Dr 02920
Mountain Laurel Dr 02920
Mozart St 02920
Mulberry Dr 02921
Murad St 02920
Muriel St 02910
Myrtle Ave 02910
Mystery Farms Dr 02921
Narragansett Blvd &
St 02905
Natick Ave & Cir 02921
Nelson Rd 02921
Neptune St 02920
Netherlands Ave 02905
New Depot Ave 02920
New Hampshire St 02920
New London Ave 02920
Newbury St 02920
Newbury Village Dr 02921
Newell Rd 02910
Newmarket St 02910
Newwood Dr 02920
Niantic Ave 02910
Nichols St 02920
Nickerson St 02910
Nina Ct 02921
Noble St 02920
Norelank St 02910
Norfolk St 02910
Norman Ave 02910
Normandy Dr 02920
North St 02920
Northup St 02905
Norton Ave 02920
Norwood Ave 02905
Nowell Rd 02910
Oak St 02910
Oak Hill Dr 02920
Oak Tree Ln 02920
Oak View Dr 02921
Oakland Ave 02910
Oaklawn Ave 02920
Oaklawn Manor Dr 02920
Oakridge Dr 02921
Oakwind Ter 02920
Oakwood Dr 02920
Ocean Ave 02905
Ocean View Dr 02921
Ochil Pl 02905
Old Oak Ave 02920
Old Park Ave 02910
Old Phenix Ave 02921
Old Spring Rd 02920
Olivia Dr 02921
Olney Arnold Rd 02921
Oneida St 02920
Ontario Ave 02920
Opal St 02905
Orchard Dr 02920
Orchard St 02910
Orchard Valley Dr 02921
Oregon Ave 02920
Oriole Ave 02920
Orlando Ave 02910
Overbrook Dr 02920
Overhill Rd 02920
Overland Ave 02910
Owl Ct 02921
Oxford St 02920
Packard St 02910
Paddock Dr 02921
Paige Cir 02921
Paine Ave 02910
Paliotta Pkwy 02921
Palmer Ave 02920
Paradiso Way 02921
Park Ave
1116A-1116B 02910
1-360 02905
361-1302 02910
1303-1499 02920
Park Forest Rd 02920
Park View Blvd 02910
Parkman St 02910
Parkside Cir 02905
Parkside Dr 02910
Parkway Ave 02905
Pasture Way 02921
Pasture View Ln 02921
Paul St 02920
Pavilion Ave & Ct 02920
Pawtuxet Ave 02905
Pearce Ave 02910
Pearl Ave 02905
Peerless St 02910
Pendleton St 02920
Pengrove St 02920
Penny Ln 02921
Pepper Mill Ln 02921
Perennial Dr 02920
Perkins Ave 02910
Permain Rd 02920
Perpali Ln 02920
Pershing St 02910
Pettaconsett Ave 02920
Peveril Rd 02921
Pheasant Ct & Dr 02920
Pheasant Hill Ln 02921
Phenix Ave
1-489 02920
490-2299 02921
Phenix Ridge Dr 02921
Phillips Ct 02921
Philmont Ave 02910
Piedmont St 02910
Pierce Pl 02905
Pilgrim Dr 02905
E Pine Rd 02921
Pine St 02910
Pine Hill Dr 02921
Pine Ridge Dr 02921
Pinewood Dr 02920
Pippin St 02920
Pippin Orchard Rd 02921
Plainfield Cir 02920
Plainfield Pike
1400-1720 02920
1722-2884 02921
Plainfield St 02920
Plant St 02920
Plantation Dr 02920
Plaza St 02920
Pleasant St 02910
Pleasant Hill Rd 02910
Pleasure Dr 02921
Plymouth St 02920
Polo Cir 02921
Pomham St 02910
Pond St 02910
Pond View Rd 02920
Pontiac Ave
79-87 02910
89-900 02910
901-909 02920
902-910 02910
911-1799 02920
Poplar Cir & Dr 02920
Poppy Cir & Dr 02920
Potter St 02910
Power Rd 02920
Preston Ave 02920
Preston Dr 02910
Primrose Dr 02921
Princess Ave 02920
Priscilla Dr 02921
Prospect St 02910
Puritan Ave 02920
Quail Hollow Rd 02920
Quail Ridge Rd 02921
Queen St 02920
Rainbow Rd 02920
Ralls Dr 02920
Randall St 02920
Randolph St 02920
Rangeley Rd 02920
Raven Cir 02921
Rawlinson Ave 02920
Raymond Dr 02921
Red Barn Ct 02920
Red Berry Cir 02921
Red Cedar Dr 02920
Red Hawk Dr 02921
Red Oak Dr 02921
Red Robin Rd 02920
Redbud Ter 02921
Redfern Dr 02920
Redwood Dr 02920
Reed Ave 02910
Reeves Pl 02920
Regal Way 02921
Regan Ct 02920
Regina Dr 02921
Reservoir Ave
401-1120 02910
1121-1399 02920
Restwood Rd 02920
Rhode Island St 02920
Rhodes Ave & Pl 02905
Richard St 02910
Richfield Ave 02910
Richland Rd 02910
Ridge St 02920
Ridgevale Ct 02921
Ridgeway Rd 02920
Ridgewood Rd 02921
River St 02905
Riverfarm Rd 02910
Riverside Ave 02910
Robert Cir 02905
Robin Hood Rd 02921
Robinlyn Dr 02921
Robson St 02920
Rock Hill Dr 02920
Rockcrest Dr 02920
Rockland Ave 02910
Rockwood Ave 02920
Roger Williams Cir 02905
Roland Ave & Ct 02920
Rolfe Sq 02910
Rome Ct & Dr 02921
Rondo St 02920
Rose St 02920
Rose Bush Cir 02921
Rose Hill Dr 02920
Roseland Ave 02905
Rosemary St 02920
Roseview Dr 02920
Rosewood Ave 02905
Roslyn Ave 02910
Ross Simons Dr 02920
Rossi Ln 02921
Rotondo Ave 02920
Rowe Dr 02921
Royal Ave 02920
Royal Crest Dr 02921
Royer St 02920
Ruby St 02905
Rugby St 02910
Ruggieri Cir 02920
Rushton Dr 02905
Ruskin St 02920
W Russe St 02910
Russet Way 02920
Rutland St 02920
Ruxton St 02910
Ruzzi St 02920
Ryder Ave 02920
Sabra St 02910
Sachem Dr 02920
Sagamore Rd 02920
Sage Dr 02921
Sailor Way 02921
Saint Marys Dr 02920
Salem Ave 02920
Salisbury Ct 02905
Samuel Ct 02920
Sanctuary Dr 02921
Sandstone Cir 02921
Saxonia Rd 02920
Scaralia Rd 02921
Scenic Dr 02920
Scituate Ave 02921
Scituate Farms Dr 02921
Scituate Vista Dr 02921
Scotland Rd 02920
Scott St 02920
Searle Ave 02920
Seaview Ave 02905
Sefton Dr 02905
Selkirk Rd 02905
Selma St 02920
Seminole Trl 02921
Seneca St 02920
Seymour Ave 02910
Sharon St 02910
Sharpe Dr 02920
Shaw Ave 02905
Shean St 02920
Sheffield Rd 02920
Sheldon St 02905
Sherman Ave 02920
Sherwood St 02920
Shirley Blvd 02910
Short Rd 02920
Short Hill Dr 02920
Shortway Rd 02910
Sidney Thomas Dr 02920
Silo Dr 02921
Sinclair Ave 02907
Slate Hill Rd 02920
Slater Rd 02920
Smith St 02905
Snowdrop Dr 02920
Sockanosset Cross Rd 02920
Somar St 02910
Somerset Rd 02910
Sophia Dr 02921
Soprano Cir 02920
South St 02920
Southern St 02920
Southern Industrial Dr 02921
Sparrow Ln 02921
Speck Ave 02910
E Spectacle St 02910
Spenstone Rd 02910
Split Creek Ct 02921
Sprague Ave 02910
Spring St 02910
Spring Meadow Ct 02921
Springwood St 02905
Spruce Ave 02910
Spurwink Pl 02910
Squantum St 02920
Stacey Dr 02920
Stafford Ct 02920
Stam Ave 02920
Stamp Farm Rd 02921
Standish Ave 02920
Star Ln 02920
Starline Way 02921
Starling Dr 02920
State St 02920
Station St 02910
Stayton St 02920
Stevens Rd 02910
Stone Dr 02920
Stonebridge Ct 02921
Stoneham Ct & St 02920
Stony Acre Dr 02920
Stony Brook Dr 02920
Stratford Rd 02905
Strathcona Rd 02910
Strathmore Pl & Rd 02905
Strawberry Ln 02921
Stream Dr 02921
Stuart Rd 02920
Suez St 02920
Sugar Hill Ct 02921
Summer St 02910
Summit Dr 02920
Sumner Ave 02920
Sundale Rd 02921
Sunkist Cir 02920
Sunrise Rd 02920
Sunset Ter 02905
Sunset Ridge Dr 02920
Surrey Dr 02920
Susan Dr 02920
Sutton Pl 02910
Swallow Dr 02920
Swan Ct 02921
Swanton St 02910
Sweet Corn Dr 02921
Sweet Fern Dr 02921
Sweet Meadow Dr 02920
Sweet Pea Dr 02921
Sweetbriar Dr 02920
Swift St 02905
Sycamore Dr 02921
Sylvan Ave 02905
Tabor St 02920
Tacoma St 02920
Taft St 02905
Talbot Mnr 02905
Tallman Ave 02910
Tampa St 02920
Taylor St 02920
Tennyson Rd 02910
Tepee Trl 02921
Terra Ct 02920

Terrace Ave 02920
Thistle Dr 02920
Thomas Ln 02921
Thomas St 02920
Thunder Trl 02921
Thyme Dr 02921
Tiffany St 02920
Tilden St 02920
Tisdale St 02920
Tobyhanna St 02910
Togansett Rd 02910
Tomahawk Trl 02921
Tome St 02920
Topeka St 02920
Tophill Cir & Dr 02920
Towne St 02920
Transit St 02920
Traverse Rd 02920
Traymore St 02920
Tremont St 02920
Tricia Cir 02921
Tucker Ave 02905
Tudor St 02920
Tulip Cir 02920
Tupelo Hill Dr 02920
Turin St 02910
Turner Ave 02920
Tweed St 02920
Twin Birch Dr 02921
Unity St 02920
Urbana St 02920
Urquhart St 02920
Usher Ave 02920
Utter St 02920
Uxbridge St 02920
N Vale Ave 02910
Valente Dr 02920
Valerie Ct 02921
Vallangt Dr 02921
Vallette St 02920
Valley St 02920
Valley View Cir & Dr ... 02921
Vallone Rd 02920
Varson St 02920
Vera St 02920
Verdant Dr 02920
Vermont St 02920
Versailles St 02920
Vervena St 02920
Victoria Ave 02920
Victory St 02910
E, N, W & S View Ave & Ter 02920
Vigilant St 02920
Viking Rd 02910
Villa Ave 02905
Village Ave & Ct 02920
Vincent Way 02921
Vinton Ave 02920
Violet Dr 02920
Wain St 02920
Waite Ave 02905
Wakefield Ave 02920
Walden Way 02921
Waldron Ave 02910
Wales St 02920
Walker St 02920
Walnut Ave 02921
Walnut Grove Ave 02920
Walter St 02910
Warfield Ave 02920
Warman Ave 02920
Warren Ave & Ct 02920
Warwick Ave 02905
Washington Ave 02920
Water Fall Way 02921
Waterman Ave 02910
Watkins Ave 02920
Wayland Ave 02920
Wayside Dr 02920
Weaver St 02920
Webb St 02920
Webber Ave 02920
Webster Ave 02920
Wedge St 02920
Weingeroff Blvd 02910
Weir St 02920
Welfare Ave 02910
Well Ave 02910
Wellington Ave 02910
Wellspring Dr 02920
Wentworth Ave 02905
Wessex St 02910
West Rd 02920
Westbrook Rd 02920
Westcott Ave 02910
Western Hills Ln 02921
Western Industrial Dr ... 02921
Western Promenade 02905
Westfield Dr 02920
Westland Ct 02921
Westmore St 02910
Weston Ave 02920
Westwood Ave 02905
Wheatland Ave 02910
Wheeler Ave 02905
Wheelock Ave 02920
Whipple Ave 02920
Whispering Pines Dr 02921
White Birch Rd 02920
White Oak Ln 02920
Whitehead St 02920
Whitewood Dr 02920
Whiting St 02920
Wholesale Way 02920
Wickham Ct 02921
Wilbur Ave
  1-191 02920
  192-699 02921
Wild Berry Dr 02920
Wildacre Dr 02920
Wildflower Dr 02921
Wildwood Dr 02920
Williams Ave 02905
Williams Way 02921
Willis St 02910
Williston St 02920
Willow Dr & Rd 02920
Wilma Schesler Ln 02920
Wilshire Ln 02921
Windsor Rd 02905
Windwood Rd 02920
Wine St 02920
Winthrop St 02910
Winton St 02910
Wisteria Ln 02920
Woburn St 02910
Wollaston St 02910
Woodbine St 02910
Woodbury Rd 02905
Woodcrest Ct 02921
Woodhaven Ct 02920
Woodhill Dr 02920
Woodland Ave 02920
Woodlawn Dr 02920
Woodmont Dr 02920
Woodridge Rd 02920
Woodrow Ave 02920
Woodside St 02920
Woodstock Ln 02920
Woodview Dr 02920
Worthington Rd 02920
Yard St 02920
Yeoman Ave 02920
Youlden Ave 02910
Zane St 02920
Zenith Dr 02920
Zinnia Dr 02920

NUMBERED STREETS

All Street Addresses 02910

NEWPORT RI

General Delivery 02840

POST OFFICE BOXES MAIN OFFICE STATIONS AND BRANCHES

Box No.s
1 - 3994 02840
5001 - 5360 02841

NAMED STREETS

Aborn St 02840
Admiral Kalbfus Rd 02840
Albro St 02840
Almy Ct & St 02840
Alpond Dr 02840
America 02840
Americas Cup Ave 02840
Andrew St 02840
Ann St 02840
Annandale Rd & Ter ... 02840
Annwood Ter 02840
Anthony Pl & St 02840
Appleby St 02840
Apthorp Ave 02840
Armstrong Pl 02840
Arnold Ave 02840
Ashurst Pl 02840
Atlantic Ave & St 02840
Ayrault St 02840
Bacheller St 02840
Bainbridge Rd 02840
Bancroft Ave 02840
Bannisters Wharf 02840
N & S Baptist St 02840
Barbara St 02840
Barclay Sq 02840
Barney Ct & St 02840
Bartlett Ct 02840
Bateman Ave 02840
Battery St 02840
Bayside Ave 02840
Bayview Ave 02840
Beach Ave 02840
Beacon Ct & St 02840
Beacon Hill Rd 02840
Bedlow Ave & Pl 02840
Beech Tree St 02840
Bellevue Ave & Ct 02840
Berkeley Ave & Ter 02840
Binney St 02840
Blackwell Pl 02840
Bliss Rd 02840
Bliss Mine Rd 02840
Bliven Ct 02840
Boss Ct 02840
Bosworth Ct 02840
Boughton Rd 02840
Bowens Lndg 02840
Bowens Wharf 02840
E Bowery Ct & St 02840
Bowler Ln 02840
Bowser Ct 02840
Bradford Ave 02840
Braman St 02840
Brandt St 02840
Brenton Rd 02840
Brewer St 02840
Bridge St 02840
Brightman St 02840
Brinley St 02840
Broadway 02840
Brooks Ave 02840
Brown And Howard Wharf 02840
Buchanan Ct 02840
Bull St 02840
Bulldog Blvd 02841
Burdick Ave 02840
Burnside Ave 02840
Bush St 02840
Bushnell St
  1-1296 02841
  1297-1298 02840
  1298-1298 02841
  1299-1299 02841
  1300-1376 02840
  1301-1375 02840
Butler St 02840
Byrnes St 02840
Caleb Earl St 02840
Callender Ave 02840
Calvert St 02840
Canonicus Ave 02840
Capella S 02840
Caperton St 02840
Capodanno Dr 02841
Carey St 02840
Carroll Ave 02840
Casey Ct 02840
Casino Ter 02840
Castle Hill Ave 02840
Caswell Ave 02840
Catherine St 02840
Central St 02840
Centre St 02840
Chadwick St 02840
Champlin Pl & St 02840
Chandler St 02841
Channing Pl & St 02840
Chapel St & Ter 02840
Charles St 02840
Chartier Cir 02840
Chase St 02840
Chastellux Ave 02840
Cherry St 02840
Cherry Creek Rd 02840
Chestnut St 02840
Christies Lndg 02840
Church St 02840
Clarke St 02840
Clay Ct & St 02840
Cliff Ave & Ter 02840
Clinton Ave & St 02840
Cloyne Ct 02840
Coddington Cv, Park & St 02840
Coddington Park Dr 02841
Coddington Wharf 02840
Coggeshall Ave 02840
Collins St 02840
Colonial St 02840
Columbus Rd 02840
Commercial Wharf 02840
Commonwealth Ave 02840
Congdon Ave 02840
Connection St 02840
Connell Hwy 02840
Conrad Ct 02840
Corne St 02840
Cottage St 02840
County St 02840
Court House Sq 02840
Covell St 02840
Cowie St 02840
Cowsill Ln 02840
Cozzens Ct 02840
Cranston Ave 02840
Cross St 02840
Cummings Rd 02840
Curry Ave 02840
Cushing Rd 02841
Cypress St 02840
Damon St 02840
Dana St 02840
Daniel St 02840
Dartmouth St 02840
Dauser Cir 02841
Davis Ct 02840
Dean Ave 02840
Dearborn St 02840
Deblois St 02840
Defenders Row 02840
Defense Hwy 02841
Dennison St 02840
Dexter Ct & St 02840
Division St 02840
Dixon St 02840
Dodge Ct 02840
Doris Ter 02840
Downing St 02840
Dr Marcus Wheatland Blvd 02840
Dresser St 02840
Dudley Ave 02840
Duke St 02840
Dyers Gate 02840
Eadie St 02840
Earl Ave 02840
East St 02840
Eastnor Ct & Rd 02840
Eastnor Rd Ext 02840
Easton St 02841
Edgar Ct 02840
Edward St 02840
Elizabeth St 02840
Ella Ter 02840
Ellery Rd 02840
Elliot Pl 02840
Elliot St 02841
Ellwood Pl 02840
Elm St 02840
Enterprise Ct 02840
Equality Park W 02840
Equality Park Pl 02840
Ernest St 02840
Eustis Ave 02840
W Evans St 02840
Evarts St 02840
Everett St 02840
W Extension St 02840
Fahey St 02840
Fair St 02840
Farewell St 02840
Faxon Grn 02840
Feke St 02840
Fenner Ave 02840
Festival Fld 02840
Fillmore St 02840
Findlay Pl 02840
Fir St 02840
Flemish Downs 02840
Florence Ave 02840
Fort Adams Dr 02840
Fountain St 02840
Fowler Ave 02840
Francis St 02840
Franklin St 02840
Freebody St 02840
Freeborn St 02840
Friends Dr 02840
Friendship Pl & St 02840
Fulton St 02841
Gammell Rd 02840
Gardiner St 02840
Garfield St 02840
George St 02840
Gibbs Ave 02840
Gibson Park Pl 02840
Gidley St 02840
Gillies Ct 02840
Gilroy St 02840
Girard Ave 02840
Gladding Ct 02840
Gleadeld St 02840
Goat Is 02840
Goddard Row 02840
Golden Hill St 02840
Goodwin St 02840
Goose Neck Cove Ln .. 02840
Gooseberry Rd 02840
Gordon St 02840
Gould St 02840
Grafton St 02840
Grant Ct 02840
Gray Ter 02840
Green Ln, Pl & St 02840
Greenlaw Blvd 02840
Greenough Pl 02840
Griswald Pl 02840
Guerney Ct 02840
Guinn Ct 02840
Guthrie St 02840
Hacker Ave 02841
Halidon Ave & Ter 02840
Hall Ave 02840
Halsey St 02840
Hammersmith Rd 02840
Hammett Pl 02840
Hammond St 02840
Harbor View Dr 02840
Harold St 02840
Harrington St 02840
Harrison Ave & Ln 02840
Harvard St 02840
Haskell Ave 02840
Hayden Ct 02840
Hazard Ave, Rd & St ... 02840
Heath St 02840
High St 02840
Highland Pl 02840
Hillside Ave 02840
Hobbs St 02840
Hoffman Pl 02840
Holland St 02840
Holten Ave 02840
Homer St 02840
Hope St 02840
Hopkins Ave 02840
Hoppin Rd 02840
Horseman Ter 02840
Houston Ave 02840
W Howard St 02840
Howe Ave 02840
Howell St 02841
Hozier St 02840
Hunt Ct 02840
Hunter Ave 02840
Intrepid Ct 02840
Jackson Ct & Rd 02840
Janet Ter 02840
Jeffrey Rd 02840
John St 02840
John H Chafee Blvd 02840
Johnson Ct 02840
Katzman Pl 02840
Kay Blvd, St & Ter 02840
Keeher Ave 02840
Kempsen St 02840
Kerins Ter 02840
Key Ct 02840
Kilburn Ct 02840
King St 02840
King Philip Rd 02840
Kingston Ave 02840
Kirwins Ln 02840
Kollmeyer St 02841
Kyle Ter 02840
Lakeview Ave 02840
Lasalle Pl 02840
Laura Pl 02840
Lawrence Ave 02840
Leal Ter 02840
Ledge Rd 02840
Ledyard St 02840
Lee Ave 02840
Lees Wharf 02840
Leonard Ter 02840
Leroy Ave 02840
Liberty St 02840
Lincoln St 02840
Linden Gate Ln 02840
Lois Ln 02840
Long Lane Ct 02840
Long Wharf Mall 02840
Longwood Pl 02840
Lowndes St 02840
Loyola Ter 02840
Lucas Ave 02840
Luce Ave 02841
Madeline Dr 02840
Madison Ct 02840
Mahan St 02840
Maher Ct 02840
Maitland Ct 02840
Malbone Rd 02840
Mann Ave 02840
Manning Ter 02840
Maple Ave 02840
Marchant St 02840
Marin St 02840
Marina Plz 02840
Marine Ave 02840
Marion St 02840
Market Sq 02840
W Marlborough St 02840
Marsh St 02840
Martin St 02840
Mary St 02840
Mary Jane Ln 02840
Mayberry Ct 02840
Mcallister St 02840
Mccormick Rd 02840
Meeting St 02840
Meikle Ave 02840
Memorial Blvd W 02840
Merton Rd 02840
Meyerkord Ave 02841
Michael Ter 02840
Middleton Ave 02840
Milburn Ct 02840
Mill St 02840
Moorland Rd 02840
Morgan St 02840
Morton Ave & Pl 02840
Mount Vernon St 02840
Mumford Ave 02840
Murray Pl 02840
W Narragansett Ave ... 02840
Newport Ave & Grn 02840
Newton Ct 02840
Nicol Ter 02840
Norman St 02840
Oak St 02840
Oakwood Ter 02840
Ocean Ave 02840
Ocean Heights Rd 02840
Ocean Lawn Ln 02840
Ochre Point Ave 02840
Old Beach Rd 02840
Old Fort Rd 02840
Osborne Ct 02840
Palmer St 02840
Park St 02840
Parker Ave 02840
Parkholm 02840
Pearl St 02840
Peary St
  1-656 02841
  657-657 02840
  658-1998 02841
  659-1999 02841
Peckham Ave & Ct 02840
Pelham St 02840
Pell St 02840
Pen Craig Pl 02840
Pennacook St 02840
Perry Rd
  I-J 02840
  1-1258 02841
  1260-1290 02840
Perry St 02840
Perry Mill Wharf 02840
Pier 2 02841
Pier Access Rd 02841
Pine St 02840
Pleasant St 02840
Polk Ct 02840
Pond Ave 02840
Pope St 02840
Poplar St 02840
Porter Ave
  1-70 02840
  71-71 02841
  72-98 02840
  73-99 02840
  112-1378 02841
Potter St 02840
Powel Ave 02840
Prairie Ave 02840
Prescott Pl 02840
Prescott Hall Rd 02840
Prices Nck 02840
Princeton St 02840
Prospect Hill St 02840
Queen Anne Sq 02840
Ranger Rd 02840
Record St 02840
Red Cross Ave & Ter .. 02840
Redwood St 02840
Reliance Row 02840
Resolute Rd 02840
Rhode Island Ave S 02840
Richmond Pl 02840
Ridge Rd 02840
Riggs Rd
  A-F 02840

1-2 02841
4-98 02841
River Ln 02840
Robert H Douglas Ln 02840
Robinson St 02840
Rosa Ter 02840
Rose St 02840
Roseneath Ave 02840
Rovensky Ave 02840
Rowland Rd 02840
Ruggles Ave 02840
Russell Ave 02840
Russo Ct 02840
Sagamore St 02840
Sanford St 02840
Sayers Wharf 02840
School St 02840
Scotts Wharf 02840
Seaview Ave 02840
Sgt Green Way 02840
Sgt Weidemann 02840
Sharon Ct 02840
Sheffield Ave 02840
Shepard Ave 02840
Sherman St 02840
Shields St 02840
Shiloh Ct 02840
Shimoda Way 02840
Simmons St 02840
Simonpietri Dr 02841
Sims St 02840
Slocum St 02840
Smith Ave 02840
Smith Rd
H-H 02840
1-99 02841
Southmayd St 02840
Spouting Rock Dr 02840
Spring St 02840
Spring Wharf 02840
Stacey St 02840
Stephen Dr 02840
Stevenson Pl 02840
Stewart Ct & St 02840
Stockholm St 02840
Stoddard Ct 02840
Stone St 02840
Sullivan St 02840
Summer St 02840
Sunnyside Pl 02840
Sunset Blvd 02840
Sunshine Ct 02840
Swans Wharf Row 02840
Swinburne Row 02840
Sycamore St 02840
Sylvan St & Ter 02840
Taber St 02840
Taylor Dr 02841
Tews Ct 02840
Thames St 02840
Thomas St 02840
Thurston Ave 02840
Tilden Ave 02840
Tilley Ave 02840
Toppa Blvd 02840
Touro St 02840
Touro Park St W 02840
Training Station Rd 02840
Tyler St 02840
Underwood Ct 02840
Union St 02840
Van Zandt Ave 02840
Vanderbilt Ave 02840
Vaughan Ave 02840
Vaughan St 02841
Vernon Ave 02840
Veterans Cir 02840
Vicksburg Pl 02840
Victoria Ave 02840
Waites Wharf 02840
Walnut St 02840
Ward Ave 02840
Warner Pl & St 02840
Washington Sq & St 02840
Watson St 02840
Weatherly Ave 02840
Weaver Ave 02840
Webster Ct & St 02840
Welarie St 02841
Wellington Ave 02840
Wesley St 02840
West St 02840
Wetmore Ave 02840
Wheatland Ct 02840
Whipple St
1-1254 02841
1134-1252 02840
1254-1286 02840
1256-1298 02841
1285-1285 02841
1288-1354 02840
1301-1353 02840
White St 02840
Whitfield Pl 02840
Whitwell Ave & Pl 02840
Wickham Rd 02840
Wilbur Ave & St 02840
William St 02840
Willow St 02840
Winans Ave 02840
Winslow St 02840
Xavier Ter 02840
Yale St 02840
York St 02840
Young St 02840
Yznaga Ave 02840

NUMBERED STREETS

All Street Addresses 02840

PAWTUCKET RI

General Delivery 02860

POST OFFICE BOXES MAIN OFFICE STATIONS AND BRANCHES

Box No.s
A - E 02862
A - R 02861
1 - 1120 02862
1 - 1 02860
1141 - 1999 02862
2001 - 5018 02861
5301 - 9236 02862
9999 - 9999 02861

NAMED STREETS

Abbott St 02860
Abram St 02860
Acorn St 02860
Adin St 02861
Aigan Pl 02860
Aiken St 02861
Albert St 02861
Alden St 02861
Alexander Mcgregor Rd 02861
Alfa Dr 02860
Alfred St 02861
Alfred Stone Rd 02860
Alice St 02860
Allen Ave 02860
Ames St 02861
Amey St 02860
Amherst Ave 02860
Anawan Rd 02861
Anderton Ave 02860
Andrew Ferland Way 02860
Angle St 02860
Ann Mary St 02860
Annette Ave 02861
Annie St 02861
Anthony Ave 02860
Appleton Ave 02860
Arbor St 02860
Arch St 02860
Archer St 02861
Argol St 02860
Arland Dr 02861
Arlington St 02860
Armistice Blvd
1-284 02860
285-287 02861
286-288 02860
289-999 02861
Arthur St 02860
Ash St 02860
Ashburne St 02861
Ashton St 02860
Atwood Ave 02860
Auburn St 02860
Avon St 02860
Bacon St 02860
Bagley St 02860
Balbo St 02860
Balch St 02861
Baldwin St 02860
Ballou St 02860
Ballston Ave 02861
Barnard St 02861
Barnes St 02860
Barney Ave 02860
Bart Dr 02861
Barton St 02860
Bassett St 02861
Bates St 02861
Baxter St 02861
Bayley St 02860
Beatty St 02861
Bedford Rd 02860
Beech St 02860
Beecher St 02860
Beechwood Ave 02860
Belgrade Ave 02861
Bella Ave 02860
Bellevue Ave 02861
Bellmore Dr 02861
Belmont St 02860
N & S Bend St 02860
Benedict St 02861
Benefit St 02861
Benjamin St 02861
Bensley St 02860
Berndt St 02861
Berry Spring St 02860
Beverage Hill Ave
1-279 02860
280-799 02861
Birch St 02860
Birchland Ave 02860
Bishop St 02860
Blackburn St 02861
Blackstone Ave 02860
Blaisdell Ave 02860
Blake St 02860
Blodgett Ave 02860
Bloodgood St 02861
Bloomfield St 02861
Bloomingdale Ave 02860
Booth Ave 02861
Borden St 02861
Boutwell St 02860
Bowen St 02861
Bowers St 02860
Bowles Ct 02860
Boyce Ave 02861
Bradley St 02861
Branch St 02861
Brewster St 02860
Bristol Ave 02861
Broad St 02860
Broadway
1-716 02860
Broadway
717-719 02861
718-720 02860
721-899 02861
Brook Ct 02861
Brookdale Blvd 02861
Brown St 02860
Buchanan St 02860
Bucklin St 02861
Buffum St 02860
Bullock St 02860
Burgess Ave 02861
Burke St 02861
Busby St 02860
Byron Ave 02861
Cala Dr 02861
Calder St 02861
Camac St 02861
Cambria Ct 02860
Cameron St 02861
Campbell St
1-1 02860
2-199 02861
Campbell Ter 02860
Capital St 02860
Capwell Ave 02860
Cardosi Ct 02861
Carnation St 02860
W Carpenter St 02860
Carson St 02860
Carter Ave 02861
Carver St 02860
Catherine St 02861
Cato Ave 02860
Cedar St 02860
Cedarbrook Rd 02861
Cedarcrest Dr 02861
Central Ave
1-386 02860
387-1200 02861
1202-1298 02861
Centre St 02860
Chandler Ave 02860
Chaplin St 02861
Charles St 02860
Charlton Ave 02860
Charpentier Ave 02861
Chase St 02861
Cherry St 02860
Chestnut St 02860
Church St 02860
Clark Ave 02860
Clarner St 02861
Clay St 02860
Clayton St 02861
Cleveland St 02860
Clews St 02861
Clifford St 02860
Clinton St 02861
Clover St 02860
Clyde St 02860
W Cole St 02860
Coleman St 02860
Colfax St 02860
Collins Ave 02860
Columbia Ave 02860
Columbine Ave 02861
Columbus Ave
1-179 02860
180-499 02861
Colvin St 02861
Commerce St 02860
Comstock St 02860
Conant St 02860
Concord St 02860
Congress St 02860
Consolation Ave 02861
Cooke St 02860
Cooper St 02860
Cornell Ave 02860
Corrente Ave & Ct 02861
Cottage St
1-357 02860
358-999 02861
County St 02861
Court St 02861
Courtney Ave 02861
Cove St 02861
Coyle Ave
1-89 02860
90-299 02861
Crane St 02860
Crescent Rd 02861
Crest Dr 02861
Crystal Pl 02861
Cumberland St 02861
Cushman St 02861
W Cute St 02860
Daggett Ave 02861
Dale St 02860
Daley Ct 02861
Daniels St 02860
Darlingdale Ave 02861
Darrow St 02860
Dartmouth St 02860
Davis St 02860
Dawson St 02861
Day St 02860
Dean St 02861
Delta Dr 02860
Deming St 02861
Denver St 02860
Derby St 02860
Desmarais Ave 02861
Dewey Ave 02861
Dexter Ct & St 02860
Diana Dr 02861
Dickens St 02861
Division St
1-524 02860
525-569 02861
526-570 02860
571-699 02861
Dix Ave 02860
Dodge St 02860
Don Ct 02861
Dora St 02860
Doran Dr 02861
Dorrance St 02860
Dorset Rd 02860
Dover St 02860
Downes Ave 02861
Draper St 02861
Drolet Ave 02860
Dryden Ave 02860
Dudley St 02860
Duncan St 02861
Dunnell Ave & Ln 02860
East Ave & St 02860
Eaton St 02861
Eddington St 02861
Edendale Ave 02861
Edgemere Rd 02861
Elder St 02860
Eldridge St 02860
Elizabeth St 02861
Elmcrest Dr 02861
Emory St 02861
Empire St 02861
Enfield St 02861
Englewood Ave 02860
Esten Ave 02860
Eventan St 02860
Everett St 02861
Evergreen St 02861
Exchange Ct & St 02860
Exeter Ave 02860
Fairlawn Ave 02860
Fairmont Ave 02860
Fairview Ave 02860
Farnum St 02861
Farrell St 02861
Federal St 02861
Felsmere Ave 02861
Fenner St 02860
Fenwood Ave 02860
Fern St 02860
Ferncrest Dr 02861
Ferris St 02861
Field St 02860
Fillmore St 02860
Finch Ave 02860
Fiume St 02860
Fleet St 02861
Flint St 02861
Floral Park Blvd 02861
Florence St 02860
Follett St 02860
W Forest Ave 02860
Fortin Ave 02860
Foss Ave 02860
Foster St 02861
Fountain St 02860
Fowler Ave 02860
Francis Ave 02860
Frank St 02860
Franklin St 02860
Fred St 02860
Freeman St 02861
Freight St 02860
French St 02860
Front St 02860
Fruit St 02860
Fuller St 02861
Galego Ct 02860
Garden St 02860
Gardner St 02861
Garrity St 02861
Gates St 02861
Geneva St 02860
George St 02860
Gerald St 02860
Germania St 02860
Gill Ave 02860
Gilmore St 02861
Glen Meadows Dr 02861
Glenwood Ave 02860
Gloria St 02861
Goff Ave 02860
Gooding St 02860
Gorizia St 02860
Gould St 02861
Grace St 02860
Grand Ave 02861
Grand View Rd 02860
Grant St 02861
Greeley St 02861
Green Lane Rd 02861
Greene St 02860
Greenfield St 02861
Greenslitt Ave 02861
Grenville St 02860
Grosvenor Ave 02860
Grotto Ave 02860
Grove St 02860
Halliday St 02861
Hamlet St 02861
Hancock St 02860
Hand St 02861
Hanover Ave 02861
Harcourt Ave 02861
Harding St 02861
Harris St 02861
Harrison St 02860
Harvard St 02860
Harvey St 02860
Hastings Ave 02861
Hatfield St 02861
Hawes St 02860
Hayward St 02860
Hazard St 02860
Hazel St 02860
Heaton St 02860
Herold Way 02861
Hicks St 02860
High St 02860
Highland St 02860
Hill St 02860
Hillcrest Ave 02860
Hillside Ave 02860
Hilton St 02860
Hobson Ave 02860
Holland Ave 02860
Home St 02861
Homestead St 02860
Hope St 02860
Howard Ave 02860
Hudson St 02861
Hughes Ave 02861
Humboldt Ave 02860
Humes St 02860
Hunts Ave 02861
Hurley Ave 02860
Hutchinson Ave 02861
Hyde Ave 02861
India St 02860
Irving Ct 02860
Ivy St 02860
Jackson St 02860
James St 02860
Jane St 02860
Japonica St 02860
Jeffers St 02860
Jefferson Ave 02860
Joan Dr 02861
John St
1-16 02860
17-199 02861
Johnson St 02860
Jones Ave 02861
Julian St 02861
Jutras St 02861
Karen Dr 02861
Katama Rd 02861
Kelarrid St 02861
Kelton St 02861
Kenilworth Way 02860
Kenmore St 02861
Kent St 02860
Kenyon Ave 02861
Keough St 02860
Kepler St 02860
Kids Way 02860
Kimball Ave 02860
King St 02860
King Philip Rd 02861
Kirk Dr 02861
Knowles St 02860
Kossuth St 02860
Lafayette St 02860
Lake St 02860
Lakeview Ave 02860
Lanesboro St 02861
Langdon Ave 02861
Lanni Dr 02861
Larch St 02860
Lauder Ave 02860
Laurel St 02860
W Lawn Ave 02860
Lawrence St 02860
Lawton St 02860
Lee St 02861
Legion Dr 02860
Legris Ave 02861
Leicester Way 02860
Lewis St 02860
Liberty St 02861
Lilac St 02860
Lincoln Ave 02861
Linden St 02861
Lindesta Rd 02861
Link St 02861
Linton St 02861
Linwood Ave 02860
Littlefield St 02861
Liverpool Ave 02861
Lloyd St 02860
Lloyd Phillips Ct 02861
Lockbridge St 02860
Locust St 02860
Lodi St 02861
London Ave 02861
Longfellow St 02861
Longley Ct 02860
Lonsdale Ave 02860
Loring Pkwy 02861
Lorraine St 02860
Lowden St 02860
Lowell Ave 02861
Lucas St 02860
Lupine St 02860
Lyman St 02860
Lyon St 02860
Mabel St 02860
Madison St 02861
Magill St 02860
Magnolia St 02860
Main St 02860
Makin St 02861
Malvern Ave 02861
Manchester St 02860

Manistee St ... 02861
Manning St ... 02860
Manton St ... 02861
Manuel St ... 02861
Maple St ... 02860
Maplecrest Dr ... 02861
Maplewood Dr ... 02861
Marbury Ave ... 02860
Marconi St ... 02860
Margaret St ... 02860
Marion Ter ... 02860
Martha St ... 02860
Martin Ct ... 02860
Martin St ... 02861
Mary St ... 02860
Maryland Ave ... 02860
Mason St ... 02860
Massasoit Ave ... 02861
Mavis St ... 02860
May St ... 02860
Mayfield St ... 02861
Maynard St ... 02860
Mcaloon St ... 02861
Mccabe Ave ... 02861
Mccallum Ave ... 02860
Meadow St ... 02860
Melrose Ave ... 02860
Melton St ... 02860
Memorial Dr ... 02860
Mendon Ave ... 02861
Merrick St ... 02860
Merry St ... 02860
Middle St ... 02860
Midway Ave ... 02860
Miles Ave ... 02861
Mill St ... 02861
Miller St ... 02860
Mineral Spring Ave ... 02860
Moeller Pl ... 02860
Monroe St ... 02861
Montgomery St
  1-41 ... 02860
  40-40 ... 02862
  42-198 ... 02860
  43-199 ... 02860
Monticello Pl & Rd ... 02861
Morris Ave ... 02860
Moshassuck St ... 02860
Moshassuck Valley Ind Hwy ... 02860
Moss St ... 02860
Mount Vernon Blvd ... 02861
Mowry St ... 02861
Mulberry St ... 02860
Myrtle St ... 02860
Nancy St ... 02860
Narragansett Ave ... 02861
Narragansett Park Dr ... 02861
Nashua St ... 02860
Nassau St ... 02860
Nathaniel Ave ... 02860
Naushon Ct & Rd ... 02861
New Ct ... 02860
Newell Ave ... 02860
Newman Rd ... 02860
Newport Ave ... 02861
Newton St ... 02860
Nickerson St ... 02860
Norfolk Ave ... 02861
Norman Ave ... 02860
Norris Ave ... 02861
Norton St ... 02860
Notre Dame Ave ... 02860
Nottingham Way ... 02860
Nye St ... 02861
Oak Hill Ave ... 02860
Oakdale Ave ... 02860
Oakland Ave ... 02861
Olive St ... 02860
Olympia Ave ... 02861
Oneida St ... 02860
Orchard St ... 02860
Ordway St ... 02861
Oregon Ave ... 02861
Orient Ave ... 02861
Oriole Ave ... 02860
Orms St ... 02861
Orth St ... 02860
Oswald St ... 02861
Overland Ave ... 02860
Owen Ave ... 02860
Packer St ... 02861
Paisley St ... 02860
Palm St ... 02860
Paris St ... 02860
Park Pl & St ... 02860
Parker Dr ... 02861
Parkside Ave ... 02861
Parkview Dr ... 02861
Patt St ... 02860
Patterson Ave ... 02860
Paul St ... 02861
Paulhus Ct ... 02861
Pawtucket Ave ... 02860
Pearl St ... 02860
Pearson Ave ... 02860
Peckham St ... 02861
Pembroke Ave ... 02860
Pequot Rd ... 02861
Perrin Ave ... 02861
Piave St ... 02860
Pidge Ave ... 02860
Pierce St ... 02860
Pine St ... 02860
Pine Grove St ... 02861
Pinecrest Dr ... 02861
Plain St ... 02860
Pleasant St ... 02860
Poirier St ... 02861
Pollard Ave ... 02861
Polo St ... 02860
Pommenville St ... 02861
Pond St ... 02860
Potter St ... 02860
Power Rd ... 02860
Preneta St ... 02861
Prentice Ave ... 02860
Primrose St ... 02860
Prince St ... 02860
Princeton Ave ... 02860
Privet St ... 02860
Progress St ... 02860
Prospect St ... 02860
Pullen Ave ... 02861
Quincy Ave ... 02860
Raleigh Ave ... 02860
Randall St ... 02860
Raymond Ave ... 02860
Redwood Ave ... 02861
Reservoir Ave ... 02860
Revere St ... 02861
Rhode Island Ave ... 02860
Rhodes St ... 02860
Rice St ... 02861
Ridge St ... 02860
Ridgewood Rd ... 02861
Riley St ... 02861
Riverview Ave ... 02860
Robert St ... 02861
Roberta Ave ... 02860
Robinson Ave ... 02861
Roblen Dr ... 02860
Rocco Ave ... 02860
Rock Ave ... 02861
Rome St ... 02860
Roosevelt Ave
  1-978 ... 02860
  979-1299 ... 02861
Rose Dr ... 02861
Rosella Ave ... 02861
Rosemere Rd ... 02861
Rosemont Ave ... 02861
Rosewood St ... 02860
Rowe Ave ... 02861
Rowland St ... 02860
Rufus St ... 02860
Ruth St ... 02861
Sabin St ... 02860
Sachem St ... 02861
Saint Marys Way ... 02860
Samuel Ave ... 02860
San Antonio Way ... 02860
Sando St ... 02860
Sanford St ... 02860
Saratoga Ave ... 02861
Saunders St ... 02860
Sayles Ave ... 02860
Scarborough Rd ... 02861
Schiller St ... 02860
Schofield St ... 02860
School St ... 02860
Scott St ... 02860
Seabiscuit Pl ... 02861
Seba Kent Rd ... 02861
Selkirk St ... 02860
Senate St ... 02861
Seneca Ave ... 02860
Sharon Ave ... 02860
Shaw Ave ... 02860
Sheffield Ave ... 02860
Sherman St ... 02860
Shoreham Ct ... 02860
Short St ... 02861
Sisson St ... 02860
Slade St ... 02861
Slater St ... 02860
Slater Park Ave ... 02861
Smithfield Ave ... 02860
Snow St ... 02861
South St ... 02860
Spencer St ... 02860
Spring Ct & St ... 02860
Stafford St ... 02861
Stanley St ... 02861
Star St ... 02860
State St ... 02861
Stearns St ... 02861
Stedman Ave ... 02860
Stephanie Dr ... 02860
Sterling St ... 02860
Sterry St ... 02860
Stuart St ... 02860
Suffolk Ave ... 02861
Summer St ... 02860
Summit St ... 02860
Sumner St ... 02860
Swan St ... 02860
Sweet Ave ... 02861
Taft St ... 02860
Talcott Ave ... 02860
Tally St ... 02861
Tashmoo Way ... 02861
Terrace Ave ... 02860
Thomas Ave ... 02860
Thornley St ... 02860
Thornton St ... 02860
Thurber St ... 02861
Thurston St ... 02860
Tidewater St ... 02860
Tim Healey Way ... 02860
Tingley St ... 02861
Tobie Ave ... 02861
Toledo Ave ... 02860
Tower St ... 02860
Trenton St ... 02860
Trieste St ... 02860
Tweed St ... 02861
Tyler St ... 02860
Underwood St ... 02860
N & S Union St ... 02860
Unity St ... 02860
Urban Ave ... 02860
Utton Ave ... 02860
Vale St ... 02860
Varnum Ave ... 02860
Vernon St ... 02860
Vincent Ave ... 02860
Vine St ... 02861
Vineyard St ... 02860
Vivian Ave ... 02860
Walcott St
  1-402 ... 02860
  403-403 ... 02861
  404-404 ... 02860
  405-599 ... 02861
Waldo St ... 02860
Walker St ... 02860
Walnut St ... 02860
Waltham St ... 02860
War Admiral Pl ... 02861
Warren Ave ... 02860
Warwick Rd ... 02861
Wasaga Rd ... 02861
Washburn St ... 02861
Washington St ... 02860
Waterman St ... 02861
Webb St ... 02860
Webster St
  1-51 ... 02860
  52-299 ... 02861
Weeden St ... 02860
Weldon St ... 02861
Wellesley Ave ... 02860
Wendell St ... 02861
West Ave ... 02860
Wheeler St ... 02861
Whipple St ... 02860
Whirlaway Pl ... 02861
White St ... 02860
Whitford Ave ... 02860
Whitman St ... 02860
Whittier Rd ... 02861
Wilcox Ave ... 02860
Willard St ... 02861
Williams St ... 02860
Willington Rd ... 02861
Williston Way ... 02861
Willow Ave ... 02860
Wilmarth Ct ... 02860
Wilson St ... 02861
Wilton Ave ... 02861
Windmill St ... 02860
Windsor Ct & Rd ... 02861
Winter St ... 02860
Winthrop Ave ... 02861
Wood St ... 02860
Woodbine St
  1-271 ... 02860
  272-399 ... 02861
Woodbury St ... 02861
Woodhaven Rd ... 02861
Woodland St ... 02860
Woodlawn Ave ... 02860
Woodside Ave ... 02861
Yale Ave ... 02860
York Ave
  1-410 ... 02860
  411-1199 ... 02861
Young St ... 02860

NUMBERED STREETS

All Street Addresses ... 02861

PROVIDENCE RI

General Delivery ... 02904

POST OFFICE BOXES MAIN OFFICE STATIONS AND BRANCHES

Box No.s
A - R ... 02901
1 - 1825 ... 02901
2000 - 2299 ... 02905
2301 - 2900 ... 02906
3201 - 3500 ... 02909
5601 - 5999 ... 02903
6001 - 9949 ... 02940
23001 - 23680 ... 02903
25001 - 25989 ... 02905
27001 - 27999 ... 02907
28001 - 28910 ... 02908
29001 - 29994 ... 02909
40001 - 44141 ... 02940
60001 - 60010 ... 02906
72601 - 73340 ... 02907
320109 - 339009 ... 02909
603001 - 603460 ... 02906

NAMED STREETS

A St ... 02907
Abbott St ... 02906
Abbott Park Pl ... 02903
Abbottsford Ct ... 02906
Abe Ct ... 02908
Aborn St ... 02903
Abram St ... 02904
Academy Ave ... 02908
Acorn St ... 02903
Actinia St ... 02909
Ada St
  1-99 ... 02904
  2-14 ... 02909
  16-99 ... 02909
Adams St
  1-8 ... 02911
  7-47 ... 02904
  49-82 ... 02904
  84-98 ... 02904
Addeo St ... 02908
Addison Pl ... 02909
Adelaide Ave
  1-199 ... 02911
  1-499 ... 02907
Adelphi Ave ... 02906
Adie St ... 02903
Admiral St
  1-808 ... 02908
  809-999 ... 02904
Africa St ... 02903
Agnes St ... 02909
Ahwahnee Ave ... 02911
Ainsworth St ... 02904
Alabama Ave ... 02905
Alachest St ... 02903
Alaska St ... 02904
Albany St ... 02904
Albert Ave ... 02911
Albro St ... 02903
Alcaranci Dr ... 02904
Alden St ... 02909
Aldine St ... 02909
Aldrich St
  1-99 ... 02911
  1-199 ... 02905
Aldrich Ter ... 02906
Aleppo St ... 02909
Alexander St
  1-199 ... 02904
  1-80 ... 02907
Alfred Dr ... 02911
Alfred Stone Rd ... 02906
Alger Ave ... 02907
Algonquin St ... 02907
Alicant St ... 02908
Allegheny Ave ... 02904
Allen Ave ... 02911
Allendale Ave ... 02911
Allens Ave
  1-225 ... 02903
  226-242 ... 02905
  227-243 ... 02903
  244-899 ... 02905
Allison Ave ... 02911
Allston St ... 02908
Alma St ... 02908
Almira Ave ... 02909
Almy St ... 02909
Alpha Ct ... 02911
Alphonso St ... 02905
Althea St
  1-167 ... 02907
  168-299 ... 02909
Alton Rd ... 02906
Alton St ... 02908
Alumni Ave ... 02906
Alverson Ave ... 02909
Alves Way ... 02903
Alvin St ... 02907
Amanda Ct & Way ... 02904
Amboy St ... 02904
Ambrose St
  1-199 ... 02904
  1-99 ... 02908
Amelia Ct ... 02904
America St ... 02903
Ames St ... 02909
Amherst St ... 02909
Amity St ... 02908
Amory St ... 02904
Amsterdam St ... 02909
Amy St ... 02906
Anchor St ... 02908
Andem St ... 02908
Anderson St ... 02909
Anderton Ave ... 02904
Andover St ... 02904
Andrew St ... 02909
Andy St ... 02904
Angela Ct ... 02904
Angell Ave ... 02911
Angell Ct ... 02906
Angell Rd ... 02904
Angell St
  1-3 ... 02903
  4-54 ... 02906
  5-55 ... 02903
  56-799 ... 02906
S Angell St ... 02906
Angelo Ave ... 02904
Ann St
  1-199 ... 02904
  1-99 ... 02903
Annie St ... 02908
Ansel Ave ... 02907
Anthony Ave
  1-58 ... 02907
  59-99 ... 02909
Appian St ... 02908
Applegate Ln ... 02905
Appleton St ... 02909
April Ct ... 02908
Arbor Dr ... 02908
Arch St ... 02907
Ardmore Ave ... 02908
Ardoene St ... 02907
Ardwick St ... 02911
Argol St ... 02904
Ark Ct ... 02908
Arline St ... 02908
Arlington Ave ... 02906
Armand Dr ... 02904
Armenia St ... 02909
Armington Ave ... 02908
Armstrong Ave ... 02903
Arnold Ct ... 02904
Arnold St ... 02906
Arro St ... 02904
Arthur Ave ... 02904
Ascham St ... 02904
Ash Ln ... 02911
Ashburton St ... 02904
Asherado St ... 02904
Ashmont St ... 02905
Ashton St ... 02904
Astral Ave ... 02906
Asylum Rd ... 02904
Atkins St ... 02908
Atlantic Ave
  1-99 ... 02904
  1-299 ... 02907
Atlantic Blvd ... 02911
Atlas St ... 02904
Atwells Ave
  1-366 ... 02903
  367-375 ... 02909
  368-376 ... 02903
  377-1199 ... 02909
Atwood Ave ... 02904
Atwood St ... 02909
Audrey St ... 02909
Audubon Ave ... 02908
August St ... 02908
Augusta Ave ... 02904
Augusta St ... 02908
Aurelia Dr ... 02909
Aurora St ... 02908
Autumn St ... 02905
Aventine Ave ... 02904
Avenue Of The Arts ... 02903
Avon St
  1-99 ... 02911
  1-99 ... 02909
Ayrault St ... 02908
Azad Ct ... 02904
Babcock St ... 02905
Badger Rd ... 02908
Baffin Ct ... 02905
Bagalia Rd ... 02904
Bailey Blvd ... 02905
Bailey Ct ... 02909
Bainbridge Ave ... 02909
Baird Ave ... 02904
Baker St ... 02905
Balcom St ... 02907
Baldwin Ct ... 02907
Balmoral Ave ... 02908
Balston St ... 02911
Baltimore St ... 02909
Balton Rd ... 02906
Bancroft St ... 02909
Barbara St ... 02909
Barbara Ann Dr ... 02911
Barberry Hill Rd ... 02906
Barbour Dr ... 02906
Barden St ... 02909
Barker Ave ... 02911
Barker St ... 02903
Barnaby St ... 02904
Barnes St ... 02906
Barone Ct ... 02904
Barrett Ave ... 02904
Barrows St ... 02909
Barry Ct ... 02904
Barry Rd ... 02909
Barstow St ... 02909
Barton St ... 02909
Bassett St
  1-99 ... 02904
  1-99 ... 02903
Bassi Ln ... 02909
Basswood Ave ... 02908
Batcheller Ave ... 02904
Bath St ... 02908
Battey St ... 02903
Baxter St ... 02905
Bay St ... 02905
Bay View Ave ... 02905
Bayard St ... 02906
Beach St ... 02904
Beacon Ave ... 02903
Beaufort St ... 02908
Beckside Rd ... 02911
Beetle St ... 02909
Bel Air Dr ... 02911
Belair Ave ... 02906
Belcourt Ave ... 02911
Belknap St ... 02903
Bell St ... 02909
Bellevue Ave
  1-199 ... 02911
  1-299 ... 02907
Belmont Ave ... 02908
Belmore Rd ... 02904
Beloit St ... 02908
Belvidere Blvd ... 02911
Bend St ... 02909
Benedict St
  1-99 ... 02904
  1-125 ... 02907
  126-299 ... 02909
Benefit St
  1-100 ... 02904
  101-599 ... 02903
Benevolent St ... 02906
Benjamin Dr ... 02904
Bennett St ... 02904
Benton St ... 02909
Bergen St ... 02908
Berkley St ... 02908
Berkshire St ... 02908
Berlin St ... 02908
Bernard St ... 02905
Bernon St ... 02908
Berwick Ave ... 02911
Beta Ct ... 02911

Betteridge Ct 02909
Bevelin Rd 02906
Beverly Ann Dr 02911
Bianco Ct 02909
Bicentennial Way 02911
Biltmore Ave 02908
Bingham St 02904
Birchwood Dr 02904
Bismark St 02904
Bissell St 02907
Blackstone Blvd 02906
Blackstone St
1-86 02903
87-290 02905
291-499 02907
Blaine St 02904
Bluff St 02908
Blundell St 02905
Bodell Ave 02909
Bogman St 02905
Bolton Ave 02908
Bonaparte St 02904
Bond St 02903
Book Ct 02908
Borah St 02904
Borden St 02903
Borinquen St 02905
Bosworth St 02909
Bough St 02909
Boulston Ln 02908
Boundary Ave 02909
Bourne Ave 02911
Bourne St 02904
Bowditch Pl 02903
Bowdoin St 02909
Bowen St
1-50 02903
51-299 02906
Bowlet St 02909
Boyd St 02908
Boylston Ave 02906
Bradford St 02903
Bradley St 02908
Brae St 02911
Braman St 02906
Branch Ave 02904
Brattle St 02907
Brayton Ave 02903
Brenton Ave 02906
Brentwood Ave 02908
Brewster St 02906
Briar Hill Rd 02904
Briarwood Dr 02911
Bridge St 02903
Bridgham St
1-101 02907
102-172 02909
103-173 02907
174-199 02909
Briggs St 02905
Brighton St 02909
Brightwood Ave 02908
Brinkley St 02909
Bristol Ave 02909
Bristow St 02904
Broad St
2-50 02903
52-278 02903
279-934 02907
935-1516 02905
1518-1520 02905
Broadway
1-310 02903
Broadway
311-699 02909
Brockton St 02904
Brook St
1-99 02911
1-110 02903
111-499 02906
Brookdale Rd 02904
Brookfarm Rd 02904
Brookfield St 02909
Brookside Ave
1-99 02911
1-99 02906

S Brookside Ave 02911
Brookway Rd 02906
Broom St 02905
Brown Ave 02911
Brown St
1-99 02904
1-299 02906
Brownell St 02908
Brush Hill Rd 02909
Bryant St 02908
Buchanan St 02904
Bucklin St 02907
Buell Ct 02908
Buffalo Ct 02909
Burchard St 02909
Burleigh St 02904
Burlington St 02906
Burnett St 02907
Burns St 02904
Burnside St
1-199 02911
1-299 02905
Burrows St 02907
Burrs Ln 02904
Burton St 02904
Butler Ave & Dr 02906
Buttonhole Dr 02909
Bye St 02911
Byfield St 02905
Byron St 02911
Cabot St 02906
Cactus St 02905
Cadillac Dr 02907
Cady St 02903
Cahill St 02905
Cahir St 02903
Calais St 02908
Caldar Rd 02904
Calder St 02907
Calhoun Ave 02907
California Ave 02905
Calla St 02905
Callan St 02908
Calverley St 02908
Cambridge St 02908
Camden Ave 02908
Camp St 02906
Campbell Ave 02904
Canal St & Walk 02903
Candace St 02908
Candy Ct 02911
Canete St 02904
Canonchet St 02908
Canton St 02908
Capitol Hl
1-3 02908
2-2 02903
Capitol View Ave 02908
Capron St 02909
Carder St 02904
Cargill St 02903
Carl Ave 02904
Carl St 02909
Carleton St 02908
Carlisle St 02907
Carmine Dr 02911
Carnac St 02904
Carol Ct 02909
Carol Ann Cir & Dr 02911
Carolina Ave 02905
Caroline St 02904
Carovilli St 02904
Carpenter St
1-259 02903
260-399 02909
Carr St 02905
Carriage Way 02904
Carrington Ave 02906
Carter St
1-99 02904
1-199 02907
Carteret St 02908
Carver Ct 02906
Case Ln 02909
Cass St 02905
Cassisi Ct 02904

Catalpa Rd 02906
Cathedral Ave 02908
Cathedral Sq 02903
Cato St 02908
Caxton St 02904
Cedar St
1-99 02911
1-199 02903
Celia St 02909
Cemetery St 02904
Center Pl 02903
Central Ave
1-199 02911
200-299 02904
Central St 02907
Centredale Ave 02911
Century Cir 02911
Ceres St 02908
Chace Ave & Dr 02906
Chad Brown St 02908
Chaffee St 02909
Chalkstone Ave
1-1326 02908
1327-1327 02909
1328-1328 02908
1329-1799 02909
Chambers St 02907
Chandler St 02911
Channing Ave 02906
Chapin Ave 02909
Chapman St 02905
Charlene Rd 02911
Charles St 02904
Charlesfield Ct & St 02906
Charlotte St 02904
Chatham St 02904
Chaucer St 02908
Cheeves St 02903
Chenango Ave 02904
Cherry St 02911
Cheshire St 02908
Chester Ave
1-53 02905
54-199 02907
Chestnut St
1-99 02904
1-299 02903
Christopher St 02904
Church St 02904
Citizens Plz 02903
City View Cir 02911
Claremont Ave 02908
Clarence St
1-99 02904
1-299 02909
Clarendon Ave 02906
Clark St 02911
Clarke Ln 02906
Clarkson St 02908
Claverick St 02903
Clear Meadow Dr 02911
Clematis St 02908
Clemence St 02903
Clement St 02904
Cleveland St
1-199 02904
1-299 02909
Cliff St 02908
Clifford St
1-99 02904
5-11 02903
13-299 02903
W Clifford St 02907
Cloud St 02909
Clove St 02908
Clyde St 02908
Clym St 02908
Coes St 02904
Coggeshall St 02908
Cold Spring Ave 02911
Cold Spring St 02906
Cole Ave 02906
Cole Farm Ct 02906
Coleman St 02904
Colfax St 02905
College Rd 02908

College St 02903
Collingwood Dr 02904
Collyer St 02904
Colonial Dr 02904
Colonial Rd 02906
Colton Dr 02904
Columbus Ave 02911
Columbus St 02908
Commercial Way 02904
Commodore St 02904
Common St 02908
Communications Pl 02903
Como St 02904
Compton St 02908
Comstock Ave 02907
Conca St 02904
Concannon St 02904
Concord St 02904
Conduit St 02903
Congdon St 02906
Congress Ave
1-99 02911
1-299 02907
Conifer Dr 02904
Constitution Hl 02904
Constitution St 02907
Convent St 02908
Cooke St 02906
Cookson Pl 02903
Cooper St 02904
Cora St 02911
Corina St 02908
Corinth St 02907
Corliss Park 02908
Corliss St
1-25 02904
24-24 02940
26-298 02904
27-299 02904
Cornplanter Row 02907
Cornwall St 02908
Cortez St 02909
Cosmo Dr 02904
Cottage Ave 02911
Country Pkwy 02911
Countryside Dr 02904
County St 02904
N Court St 02903
S Court St 02906
Courtland St 02909
Cove Ct 02911
Covell St 02909
Cowper Ct 02909
Craigie St 02911
Cranberry Rd 02911
Crandall St 02908
Cranston St
1-50 02903
51-800 02907
Crary St 02903
Creighton St 02906
Cresant Dr 02904
Crescent St 02907
Crest Ave 02904
Creston Way 02906
Crimea St 02908
Cromwell St 02907
Cross St
1-99 02911
2-198 02904
Crout St 02903
Crown St 02909
Crowninshield St 02909
Croyland Rd 02905
Cumberland St 02908
Cumerford St 02909
Curtis St 02909
Cusano St 02911
Cushing St
1-99 02904
49-150 02906
E Cushing St 02906
W Cushing St 02906
Custom House St 02903
Cutler St 02909
Cutters Grn 02904

Cynthia Dr 02911
Cypress Ct 02911
Cypress St 02906
Daboll St 02907
Dail Dr 02911
Daisy St 02908
Dakota St 02904
Dale St 02909
Dallas St 02904
Damian Ct 02911
Dan St 02908
Dana St 02906
Danby St 02904
Danforth St 02908
Dangelis Dr 02911
Daniel Ave 02909
Dante St 02908
Darlento St 02908
Dartmouth Ave 02907
Dave Gavitt Way 02905
David St 02904
Davis St 02904
N Davis St 02908
Davol Sq 02903
Dawley Ave 02911
Dayton Ct 02905
De Pasquale Ave 02903
De Pinedo St 02904
De Soto St 02909
Dean St 02903
Dearborn Ave 02911
Dearborn St 02909
Deborah St 02909
Decatur Ave 02904
Dedham Ave 02909
Deerfield Ter 02907
Defoe Pl 02906
Delaine St 02909
Delhi St 02908
Delmar St 02907
Denison St 02904
Depew St 02907
Derby Ave 02904
Derry St 02908
Detroit Ave 02907
Devereux St 02909
Devine St 02905
Devon St 02904
Devonshire St 02908
Dewey Ave 02911
Dewey St
1-31 02909
31-33 02907
33-39 02909
34-38 02909
35-39 02907
40-99 02909
Dexter St
1-140 02909
141-599 02907
Dexterdale Rd 02906
Di Filippo Ct 02904
Di Guilio Dr 02911
Di Mario Dr 02904
Diamond St 02907
Diane Dr 02904
Dickens St 02908
Dickinson Ave 02904
Dike St 02909
Diman Pl 02906
Division St 02909
Dixon St
1-99 02904
1-199 02907
Doane Ave 02906
Dodge St
1-99 02904
1-199 02907
Dome St 02908
Don Ave 02904
Donelson St 02908
Dora St
1-299 02909
2-4 02904
Dorchester Ave 02909
Dorman Ave 02904

Dorothy Ave 02904
Dorr St 02908
Dorrance Plz & St 02903
Dosco Dr 02904
Douglas Ave
1-981 02908
982-1109 02904
1110-1899 02904
Douglas Ter 02904
Dove St 02906
Dover St 02908
Downing St 02907
Doyle Ave 02906
Doyle Dr 02911
Dresser St 02909
Drew St 02908
Drill St 02908
Dryden Ln 02904
Dudley St
2-225 02905
226-399 02907
Duke St 02908
Dunbar Ave 02904
Dunbar St 02909
Duncan Ave & Dr 02906
Dunford St 02909
Dupont Dr 02907
Durham St 02908
Dutchess Ave 02904
Dutton St 02909
Duxbury St 02909
Dwight St 02906
Dyer St
1-99 02911
1-299 02903
Eagle St
1-40 02908
41-99 02909
Eames St 02906
Earl St 02907
Early St
1-115 02905
116-299 02907
East Ave 02911
East Dr 02904
East St
1-51 02906
52-99 02903
Easter St 02904
Easton St 02908
Eastwood Ave 02909
Eaton St 02908
Eben St 02904
Eddy St
1-99 02911
1-758 02903
759-1399 02905
Edendale Ave 02911
Edgehill Rd 02906
Edgemere Ave 02909
Edgeworth Ave 02904
Edison Ave 02906
Edith St 02908
Edna St 02909
Edward St 02904
Elbow St 02903
Elder Pl 02909
Elena St 02904
Elgin St 02906
Eliot Ave 02904
Eliza St 02909
Elizabeth Dr 02904
Elizabeth St 02903
Ellen Ln 02904
Ellenfield St 02905
Ellery St 02909
Elm St
1-99 02911
1-199 02903
Elma St 02905
Elmcrest Ave
1-60 02908
61-61 02911
Elmcroft Ave 02908
Elmdale Ave 02909
Elmgrove Ave 02906

Elmhurst Ave 02908
Elmira St 02904
Elmo St 02911
N Elmore Ave 02911
Elmway St 02906
Elmwood Ave 02907
Elton St 02906
Elvira St 02904
Emanuel St 02911
Emeline St 02906
Emerson St 02907
Emilys Way 02904
Emmett St 02903
Empire Plz & St 02903
Enfield Ave 02908
Enterprise Row 02903
Enterprise St 02904
Erastus St
1-61 02909
62-199 02908
Eric Pl 02911
Erie St 02908
Ernest St 02905
Esten St 02908
Esther Dr 02911
Ethan St 02909
Euclid Ave 02906
Eudora St 02903
Eugene St 02909
Europe St 02903
Eutaw St 02903
Eva St 02908
Evelyn St 02909
Everett Ave 02906
Everett St 02911
Evergreen Pkwy 02904
Evergreen St 02906
Everson St 02904
Exchange St 02903
W Exchange St 02903
Exchange Ter
1-299 02903
2-2 02901
2-298 02903
Exeter St 02906
Fair St 02908
Fairbanks St 02908
Fairfield Ave 02909
Fairmount Ave 02908
Fairoaks Ave 02908
Fairview Ave 02904
Fairview St
1-200 02908
201-299 02909
Falco St 02911
Falconer St 02907
Fales St 02907
Fallon Ave 02908
Falls Pl 02903
Famiglietti Dr 02904
Farm St 02908
Farmington Ave 02909
Farnum Ave 02911
Fatima Dr 02904
Faunce Dr 02906
Federal St
1-215 02903
216-299 02909
Felix St 02908
Felix Mirando Way 02904
Fenner St 02903
Fenway St 02911
Fera St 02904
Fern St 02908
Fernando St 02908
Ferncliff Ave 02911
Ferncrest Blvd 02911
Fields Point Dr 02905
Fillmore St 02908
Financial Plz 02903
Finch Ave 02904
Fiore St 02908
Firglade Ave 02906
Fisher St
1-99 02911
1-99 02906

Fisk St 02905
Fitzhugh St 02904
Flancoun Ave 02911
Flora St 02904
Florence St
1-99 02904
1-199 02909
Flower St 02909
Foch Ave 02904
Fones Aly 02906
Forbes St 02908
Ford St
1-138 02907
139-199 02909
Forest St
1-99 02911
1-199 02906
Forest View Dr 02904
Forestry Cir 02907
Forestwood Dr 02904
Forsyth St 02908
Fosdyke St 02906
W Fountain St 02903
Fowler St 02909
Fox Pl 02903
Francis Ave 02904
Francis St 02903
Frank Rd 02911
Frank St 02903
Franklin Sq 02903
Franklin St
1-99 02904
1-99 02903
Frederick St
1-99 02904
1-99 02908
Freedom Rd 02909
Freeman Pkwy 02906
Freese St 02908
Fremont St 02906
French St 02905
Fricker St 02903
Friendship St
1-199 02904
1-365 02903
366-499 02907
W Friendship St 02907
E Frontage Rd 02904
Frost St 02904
Fruit Hill Ave
1-106 02909
107-113 02911
108-114 02909
115-799 02911
Fuller St 02907
Fulton St 02903
Funston Ave 02908
Furnace St 02903
Gage St 02909
Gainer Ave 02911
Gale Ct 02904
Galileo Ave 02909
Gallatin St 02907
Gallup St 02905
Gamma Ct 02911
Gano St
1-70 02903
71-299 02906
Gardner Ave 02911
Garfield Ave 02908
Garfield St 02904
Garibaldi St 02911
Garnet St 02903
Gaspee St 02903
Gaudet St 02911
Gay St 02905
Gem St 02904
Gemelli Dr 02904
General St 02904
Geneva St 02908
Gennaro Pl 02909
Genoa St 02904
Gentian Ave 02908
Geoffreys Ct 02908
George St
1-99 02911
1-299 02906
E George St 02906
George M Cohan Blvd 02903
Georgia Ave 02905
Gerardi St 02909
Gesler St 02909
Gibbon Ct 02909
Gibbs St 02904
Gifford St 02909
Gilbert St 02909
Gillen Ave & St 02904
Gilmore St 02907
Gladstone St 02905
Glasgow St 02908
Glen Dr 02906
Glen St 02911
Glenbridge Ave 02909
Glendale Ave 02906
Glenham St 02907
Globe St 02903
Glossop St 02911
Gloucester St 02908
Glover St 02908
Goddard St 02908
Goldsmith St
1-99 02904
1-99 02906
Golemba Ln 02905
Gompers St 02904
Gordon Ave 02905
Gorton St 02906
Goulding St 02906
Gov Notte Way 02904
Governor St 02906
Grafton St 02904
Graham St 02906
Grancour St 02906
Grand Ave
1-99 02904
141-299 02905
Grand St 02907
Grand Broadway 02908
Grand View St 02906
Grant St 02909
Grape St 02908
Gray St
1-99 02904
1-299 02909
Great View Ave 02904
Greaton Dr 02906
Greco Ln 02909
Greeley St 02904
Greene St 02903
Greenfield Ave 02911
Greenville Ave 02911
Greenwich St 02907
Greenwood St 02909
Greystone Ave 02911
Gridley St 02904
Grimwood St 02909
Grosvenor Ave
1-99 02908
217-217 02904
219-299 02904
Groton St 02909
Grotto Ave 02906
Grove Ave 02911
Grove St 02909
Grover St
1-99 02911
2-18 02909
20-99 02909
Gulf St 02906
Gwinnett Ct 02907
Hagan St 02904
Hale St 02909
Hall St 02904
Halsey St
1-99 02911
1-199 02906
Halton St 02907
Hamilton St 02907
Hamlin St
1-99 02904
1-199 02907
Hammond St 02909
Hampshire St 02904
Hampton St 02904
Hancock St 02905
Handy St 02909
Hannah St 02909
Hanover St 02907
Hanson St 02911
Harborside Blvd 02905
Harbourside Dr 02905
Harian Rd 02906
Harkness St 02909
Harlam St 02909
Harmony Dr 02909
Harold St 02908
Harriet St 02905
Harris Ave
1-250 02903
251-799 02909
Harrison St
1-127 02909
128-299 02907
Hart St 02906
Hartford Ave 02909
Hartshorn Rd 02906
Harvard Ave 02907
Harvest St 02908
Harwich Rd 02906
Harwol Ct 02904
Hasbro Pl 02903
Haskins St 02903
Haslam St 02904
Hathaway St 02907
Hatherly St 02911
Hauxhurst St 02909
Havana St 02904
Hawkins Blvd 02911
Hawkins Cir 02911
Hawkins St
1-198 02908
199-399 02904
Hawthorne Pl 02904
Hawthorne St
1-199 02904
1-99 02907
Hayes St 02908
Hayward St 02907
Hazael St 02908
Hazard Ave 02906
Health Ave 02908
Heath St 02909
Hebron St 02904
Helen St 02911
Helm St 02904
Helme St 02909
Hemlock St 02908
Hempstead St 02907
Henderson St 02903
Hendrick St 02908
Hennessey Ave 02911
Henrietta St 02904
Henry St 02909
Herbert St 02909
Hereford St 02908
Heritage Cir 02904
Herschel St 02909
Hewitt St 02909
Hickory Rd 02904
Hidden St 02906
Higgins Ave 02908
High St 02904
High Service Ave
1-176 02911
177-299 02904
Highland Ave
1-99 02911
1-399 02906
Hilarity St 02909
Hilary Dr 02908
Hill St
1-1 02911
2-4 02904
5-5 02911
6-98 02904
7-99 02904
100-108 02911
Hillard St 02909
Hillcrest Ave 02909
Hillhurst Ave 02909
Hillside Ave 02906
Hillside Dr
1-86 02904
87-87 02911
88-88 02904
89-199 02911
Hilltop Ave 02908
Hilltop Dr 02904
Hillview Ave 02908
Hillview Dr 02904
Hilton St 02905
Hobart Ave 02906
Hobson Ave 02911
Holden Ct & St 02908
Hollis St 02907
Holly St 02906
Hollywood Rd 02909
Home Ave 02908
Homefield Ave 02908
Homer St 02905
Homes St 02904
Homeside Dr 02905
Homestead Ave 02907
Homewood Ave 02911
Hooker St 02908
Hooper Pl 02908
Hope St
1-99 02911
1-50 02903
51-1199 02906
Hopedale Rd 02906
Hopewell Ave 02904
Hopkins St 02903
Hoppin St 02903
Horace St 02909
Horton St 02904
Hospital St 02903
Houghton St 02904
Houston St 02905
N Howard Ave 02911
Howe St 02911
Howell St 02906
Huber Ave 02909
Hudson St 02909
Hugo St 02904
Huldah St 02909
Humbert Ave 02904
Humbert St 02911
Humboldt Ave 02906
Humes St 02907
Hunters Run 02904
Huntington Ave
1-399 02909
402-798 02907
Hurdis St 02904
Huron St 02908
Husted Ct 02905
Huxley Ave 02908
Hyacinth St 02904
Hyat St 02909
Hylestead St 02905
Hymer St 02908
Ianthe St 02904
Ida St 02909
Imera St 02909
Imperial Pl 02903
India St 02903
Indiana Ave 02905
Infield Ct 02911
Inkerman St 02908
Intervale Ave 02911
Intervale Rd 02906
Iona St 02908
N Iowa St 02904
Iris Ln 02911
Iron Horse Way 02908
Irving Ave 02906
Irving St 02904
Isabella Ave 02908
Italy St 02908
Ivan St 02904
Ives St
1-75 02903
76-399 02906
Ivone Ct 02909
Ivy St 02906
Jackson St 02904
Jackson Walkway 02903
Jacksonia Dr 02911
Jacqueline Dr 02909
James St 02903
Jane St 02904
Janes St 02905
Jared Ct 02911
Jasper St 02904
Jastram St 02908
Jefferson St 02908
Jeffres St 02904
Jenckes St 02906
Jenkins St 02906
Jenny Dr 02911
Jessica Cir 02911
Jewell St 02909
Jewett St 02908
Jillson St 02905
Job St 02904
John St
1-299 02904
1-199 02906
John F Kennedy Cir 02904
Johnson St 02905
Jones St 02903
Josa St 02904
Joseph St 02904
Josephine St 02904
Joslin St
1-199 02909
2-4 02911
6-60 02911
Joy St 02908
Joyce Dr 02911
Judith St 02909
Julia Dr 02911
Julian St 02909
Julie Ann Ct 02904
Junction St 02907
June St
1-99 02904
1-199 02908
Justice St
1-99 02911
1-99 02908
Karen Dr 02911
Keene St 02906
Kelley St 02909
Kendall St 02907
Kennedy Dr 02904
Kennedy Plz 02903
Kentland Ave
1-99 02904
100-106 02908
101-105 02908
107-199 02908
Kenwood St
1-29 02907
2-48 02909
31-299 02907
78-298 02907
Kenyon St 02903
Kepler St 02908
Kiley St 02911
Killingly St 02909
Kimball St 02908
Kimberly Ct 02911
Kinfield St 02909
King St
1-99 02911
1-99 02909
King Philip St 02909
Kingston Ave 02906
Kinsley Ave
1-6 02903
8-398 02903
400-598 02909
Kipling St 02907
Klondike St 02909
Knapp Ave 02904
Knight St 02909
Knoll Pl 02904
Knowles St 02906
Kossuth St 02909
Kristen Ct 02904
Kristen Dr 02911
La Bonte Rd 02911
La Salle Dr 02908
La Salle Sq 02903
La Vaughn St 02909
Laban St 02909
Lafayette St 02903
Lake Dr 02904
Lakeside St 02904
E & W Lakeview Dr 02904
Lakewood St 02911
Lancashire St 02908
Lancaster St 02906
Langdon St 02904
Langham Rd 02906
Langsberries Ave 02911
Lantagne Ave 02911
Larch St 02906
S Larchmont Ave & St 02911
Lark St 02909
Laura St 02907
Laurel Ave 02906
Laurel Ct 02906
Laurel Dr 02911
Laurel St 02911
Laurel Hill Ave 02909
Lauriston St 02906
Lawn St 02908
Lawnacre Dr 02911
Lawrence Rd 02911
Lawrence St
1-99 02904
1-99 02909
Layton St 02911
Leah St
1-99 02911
1-299 02908
Leander St 02909
Lecia Dr 02909
Ledge St 02904
Lee Ave 02904
Lee St 02903
Lees Farm Commons
Dr 02904
Legion Memorial Dr 02909
Lehigh St 02905
Leland St 02908
Lena St
1-99 02904
1-99 02909
Lennon St 02908
Lenox Ave 02907
Leo Ave 02904
Leslie Dr 02908
Lester St 02907
Lewis St
1-205 02904
1-99 02906
207-299 02904
Lexington Ave
1-299 02904
1-299 02907
Libia St 02909
Library Ct 02909
Liege St 02908
Lillian Ave 02905
Lily St 02909
Lincoln Ave
1-99 02904
1-199 02906
Lincoln St 02911
Linda Ct 02904
Linden Dr 02906
Linden St 02907
Lindy Ave 02908
Link St 02911
Linton St 02908
Linwood Ave
1-99 02911
1-116 02909
117-299 02907
Lippitt St 02906
Lisbon St 02908
Lisi Ln 02904
Livingston St 02904
Lloyd Ave & Ln 02906
Lockwood St
1-206 02903
207-399 02907
Locust Ave 02911
S Locust Ave 02911
Locust St 02906
Lois Ave 02908
Lojai Blvd 02904
Lombardi St 02904
Longblock St 02904
Longfellow St & Ter 02907
Longmeadow Dr 02904
Longmont St 02908
Longo St 02909
Longue Vue Ave 02904
Longwood Ave
1-99 02911
1-199 02908
Lookout Ave 02911
Lopez St 02908
Loreto St 02904
Lori Dr 02911
Lorimer Ave 02906
Loring Ave 02906
Loring Ln 02904
Lorraine Ave 02906
Lotus Pl 02908
Louis Ave 02907
Louisa St 02905
Louisburg Pl 02909
Louisquissett Pike 02904
Loveday St 02908
Lowell Ave 02909
Loxley Rd 02908
Lubec St 02904
Lucille St 02908
Lucy St 02909
Luke St 02904
Luna St 02904
Luongo Sq 02903
Luzon Ave 02906
Lydia Ave 02904
Lydia St 02908
Lyman Ave 02911
Lyman St 02903
Lynch St
1-5 02909
6-299 02908
Lynde St 02908
Lyndhurst Ave 02908
Lynn Ave 02911
Lynn St 02907
Lyon Ct 02903
Lytherland Pl 02909
Macgregor St 02904
Maclaine Dr 02904
Madison St
1-99 02911
1-99 02907
Mafalda St 02904
Magdalene St 02909
Magee St 02906
Magellan St 02906
Magnolia St 02909
N Main St
2-321 02903
322-498 02904
500-1399 02904
S Main St 02903
Mainella St 02904
Malbone St 02908
Malcolm St 02904
Malvern St 02904
Manchester Pl 02903
Manchester Way 02908
Manchester Farm Rd 02904
Manhattan St 02904
Manila St
1-99 02911
1-99 02904
Manning St
1-99 02911
1-199 02906
E Manning St 02906

Street	ZIP
Manomet St	02909
Mansfield St	02908
Manton Ave & Ct	02909
Maple St	
1-99	02911
1-99	02903
Maplecrest Ave	02911
Maplehurst Ave	02908
Marblehead Ave	02904
Marcello St	02909
March St	02908
Marconi St	
1-99	02904
1-99	02909
Margrave Ave	02906
Marie Ct	02904
Marietta St	
1-99	02911
1-99	02904
Marigold Cir	02904
Marilyn Dr	02904
Marion Ave	02905
Marisa Ln	02904
Mark Dr	02904
Market Sq	02903
Marlborough Ave	02907
Marshall St	02909
Martin Ave	02904
Marvin St	02909
Mary Ann Ct	02904
Mashapaug St	02907
Mason St	02903
Massachusetts Ave	02905
Massie Ave	02905
Masso Dr	02904
Mathewson St	02903
Matilda St	02904
Matson Ave	02909
Matteo Dr	02904
Mattie St	02909
Maude St	02908
Mawney St	02907
Maxcy Dr	02906
May St	02904
Mayflower Dr	02905
Mayflower St	02906
Maynard St	
1-99	02904
2-20	02909
22-99	02909
Mcarthur Dr	02911
Mcavoy St	02903
Mccann Pl	02906
Mcclellan St	02909
Mcguire Rd	02904
Mckinley St	
1-99	02904
1-99	02907
Mcmillen St	02904
Meader St	02909
Meadow Ave	02911
Meadow Rd	02904
Meadow St	02903
Meadow View Blvd	02904
Meadowbrook Rd	02911
Mecca St	02904
Mechanics Ave	02904
Medway St	02906
Meeting St	
1-50	02903
51-299	02906
Melissa St	02909
Melrose St	02907
Memorial Blvd	02903
Memorial Rd	02906
Mendon St	02904
Meni Ct	02905
Meola Ave	02904
Merchant St	02911
Mercy St	02909
Meridian St	02908
Merino St	02909
Merrenwo St	02905
Merrimac St	02904
Merritt Ave	02911
Messenger St	02903
Messer St	02909
Messina St	02908
Metcalf Ave	02911
Metcalf St	02904
Methyl St	02906
Metropolitan Rd	02908
Michele Dr	02904
Michigan Ave	02905
Middle Dr	02904
Middle St	
1-99	02903
1-99	02911
Middleton St	02909
Midland St	02911
Milano St	02904
Miles Ave	
1-99	02911
1-99	02906
Milk St	02905
Mill St	02911
Millard Ave	02911
Millard St	02905
Miller Ave	02905
Milo St	02909
Milton St	02911
Miner St	
1-99	02904
1-199	02905
Mineral Spring Ave	
935-2000	02904
2001-2299	02911
Mink Rd	02908
Minnesota St	02904
Minto St	02908
Mission Pl	02908
Mitchell St	02907
Modena Ave	02908
Modesta St	02904
Mohawk St	02906
Molloy St	02908
Molter St	02910
Mongenais St	02909
Monitor St	02904
Monongahela Ave	02911
Montague St	02906
Monte Carmele St	02904
Montgomery Ave	02905
Monticello St	02904
Montrose St	02908
Moore St	02907
Moorefield St	02909
Moorland Ave	02908
Morgan Ave	02911
Morgan St	02907
Morning Star Row	02907
Morrill Ln	02904
Morris Ave	02906
Morrison St	02906
Morton St	02905
Moses Brown St	02906
Mott St	02909
Mount Ave	02906
Mount Hope Ave	02906
Mount Pleasant Ave	02908
Mount Vernon St	02907
Mountain St	02903
Mowry St	02908
Moy St	02904
Muriel Ave	02911
Murphy Ct	02911
Murray St	
1-99	02911
1-199	02909
Mutual Pl	02906
Mutual St	02905
Myra St	02909
Myrtle St	02907
Mystic St	02905
Nahant St	02904
Nancy St	02909
Naples Ave	02908
Narragansett Ave	02907
Narragansett Blvd	02905
Nashua St	02904
Navaho St	02907
Nebraska St	02905
Needle Grv	02904
Nellie St	02904
Nelson St	
1-99	02911
1-399	02908
Nelson Ter	02904
Nemo St	02904
Netop Dr	02907
New St	02904
New York Ave	02905
Newark St	02908
Newbury St	02904
Newcomb St	02908
Newport St	02904
Newton St	
1-99	02911
1-99	02903
Niagara St	02907
Niantic Ave	02907
Nicholas Brown Yards	02904
Ninigret Ave	02907
Nipmuc Trl	02904
Nisbet St	02906
Nolan St	02908
Norman Dr	02904
North Ave	02906
Northup Ave	02904
Norwich Ave	02905
Noto Dr	02904
Noyes Ave	02907
Oak Pt	02904
Oak St	
1-99	02911
1-299	02909
Oak Grove Blvd	02911
Oak Knoll Ct	02904
Oak Park Dr	02904
Oakcrest Dr	02904
Oakdale St	02908
Oakhurst Ave	02911
Oakland Ave	02908
Oakleigh Ave	02911
Oakwood Ave	02909
Oakwood Dr	02911
Obed Ave	02904
Obediah Brown Rd	02909
Observatory Ave	
1-99	02911
1-99	02906
Ocean St	02905
Oconnell St	02905
Oconnor St	02905
Octavia St	02909
Ogden St	02906
Ohara Ave	02904
Ohio Ave	02905
Okie St	02908
Old Rd	02908
Old Tannery Rd	02906
Oldham St	02903
Olive St	02906
Oliver St	02904
Olmsted Way	02904
Olney Ave	02911
Olney St	
1-99	02904
1-399	02906
Olneyville Sq	02909
Olympia Ave	02911
Oneil St	02904
Ontario St	02907
Ophelia St	02909
Opper St	02904
Orange St	02903
Orchard Ave	02906
E Orchard Ave	02906
Orchard Ln	02904
Orchard Pl	02906
Orchard St	02911
Orchard Hill Rd	02911
Oregon Ave	02911
Oregon St	02908
Orford St	02904
Oriental St	02908
Oriole Ave	02906
Orlando Dr	02904
Orms St	
1-50	02904
51-499	02908
Ortoleva Dr	02909
Osborn St	02908
Overhill Rd	02906
Overlook Cir	02904
Owen St	02909
Oxford St	02905
Packard Ave	02911
Padelford St	02906
Page St	02903
Palfrey Pl	02909
Pallas St	02903
Palm Ct	02909
Palm St	02904
Palmer Dr	02904
Palou Dr	02904
Paolino St	02909
Parade St	
1-127	02909
128-199	02907
Parente St	02904
Park Ln	02907
Park Row	02903
Park Row E	02903
Park Row W	02903
Park St	
1-99	02904
83-85	02903
W Park St	02908
Parkhill Rd	02911
Parkis Ave	02907
Parkman St	02907
Parkside Rd	02906
Parkview Ave	02905
Parkway Ave	02908
Parnell St	02909
Parsonage St	02903
Partridge St	02908
Pasteur St	02908
Paterson St	02906
Patricia Dr	02904
Paul St	02904
Pavilion Ave	02905
Pawnee St	02907
Payton St	02905
Peace St	02907
Peach Ave	02906
Peach Hill Ave	02911
Pearl Ave	02904
Pearl St	
1-110	02905
111-399	02907
Peck St	02903
Peckham Ave	02908
Pekin St	02908
Pelham Pkwy	02911
Pelham St	02909
Pemberton St	02908
Pembroke Ave	02908
Penelope Pl	02903
Penn St	02909
Pennsylvania Ave	02905
Penrose Ave	02906
Penrose St	02911
Pensaukee Ave	02911
Pequot St	02903
Perkins St	02907
Peter St	02904
Peter Pan Way	02904
Petteys Ave	02909
Phebe St	02904
Phillips St	
1-99	02906
2-14	02911
16-99	02911
Piave St	02904
Piedmont St	02909
Pierce St	02909
Pike St	02903
Pilsudski St	02909
Pine St	
1-99	02911
1-420	02903
421-599	02907
Pinehurst Ave	02908
Pinewood Dr	02904
Pitman St	
1-99	02911
1-299	02906
Plain St	
1-130	02903
131-399	02905
Plainfield St	02909
Planet St	02903
Pleasant Ave	02911
S Pleasant Ave	02911
Pleasant Ct	02906
Pleasant St	02906
Pleasant Valley Pkwy	02908
Pleasant View Dr	02904
Plenty St	02907
Plum St	02905
Plymouth Rd	02904
Plymouth St	02907
Plympton St	02904
Pocasset Ave	02909
Poe St	02905
Point St	02903
Polly Dr	02911
Polly St	02909
Pomfret St	02904
Pomona Ave	02908
Ponagansett Ave	02909
Pond Ct	02904
Pontiac Ave	02907
Pope St	
1-99	02904
1-99	02909
Poplar St	02906
Porter St	02905
Portland St	02907
Potter Dr	02907
Potters Ave	
1-330	02905
331-899	02907
Power St	
1-50	02903
51-299	02906
Powhattan St	02909
Prairie Ave	02905
Pratt St	02906
Prentice St	02911
Prescott St	02908
President Ave	02906
Preston St	02906
Price St	02907
Primrose Ln	02904
Primrose St	02909
Princeton Ave	02907
Printery St	02904
Priscilla Ave	02909
Proctor Pl	02906
Progress Ave	
1-99	02911
1-299	02909
Promenade St	02908
Prospect St	
1-99	02904
3-39	02906
41-199	02906
Prosper St	02904
Providence Pl	02903
Providence St	02907
Providence Washington Plz	02903
Prudence Ave	02909
Public St	
1-200	02903
201-404	02905
405-799	02907
Pumgansett St	02908
Puritan St	
1-99	02904
1-99	02907
Putnam St	02909
Quail Ridge Rd	02904
Quarry St	02904
Queen St	02909
Quince St	02905
Quincy St	02908
Rachel St	02905
Radcliffe Ave	02908
Ralph St	02909
Ralston St	02904
Randall Rd	02904
Randall Sq	02904
Randall St	
1-99	02911
2-198	02904
Rangeley Ave	02908
Rankin Ave	02908
Raphael Ave	02904
Raritan Ave	02909
Rathbone St	02908
Ravenswood Ave	02908
Ray Dr & St	02906
Raymond Ave	02911
Raymond Rd	02911
Raymond St	02908
Rayna Rd	02904
Reade St	02904
Recreation Way	02904
Red Cedar Ln	02904
Redfern St	02911
Redwing St	02907
Redwood Dr	02911
Redwood St	02908
Regency Plz	02903
Regent Ave	02908
Remington St	02904
Rena St	02911
Reservoir Ave	02907
Reynolds Ave	
1-99	02911
1-299	02905
Rhode Island Ave	02906
Rhodes St	
1-202	02903
203-299	02905
Rialto St	02908
Ricci Dr	02911
Rice St	02907
Richard Rd	02911
Richland St	02909
Richmond Sq	02906
Richmond St	02903
Richter St	02908
Ricom Way	02909
Ridge St	02909
Ridgeway Ave	02909
Rill St	02908
Ring St	02909
Ringgold St	02903
River Ave	02908
W River Pkwy	02904
River Rd	02904
E River St	02906
W River St	02904
Riverdale St	02909
Riverview Dr	02904
Roanoke St	02908
Robert Dr	02911
Roberta St	02904
Robin St	
1-99	02908
1-3	02904
5-99	02904
Robins Way	02904
Robinson St	02905
Rochambeau Ave	02906
Rockingham St	02908
Rockland Ave	02908
Rockwell Ave	02911
Rockwell St	02904
Roda Dr	02909
Rodman St	02907
Roger St	02906
Roger Williams Ave	02907
Roger Williams Ct	02907
Roger Williams Grn	02904
Rome Ave	
1-99	02904
1-199	02908
N Rome Ave	02904
Ronnie Dr	02911
Roosevelt St	
1-99	02904
1-299	02909
Rosario Dr	02909
Rose Ct	02906
Rose St	02904
Rosebank Ave & Dr	02908
Rosedale St	
1-99	02911
1-199	02909
Rosemont Ter	02911
Rosewood Dr	02904
Roslyn Ave	02908
Rosner Ave	02904
Rossi Dr	02904
Rounds Ave	02907
Rowan St	02908
Rowley St	02909
Royal Ave	02904
Royal St	02906
Royal Little Dr	02904
Ruby St	02909
Rugby St	02905
Ruggles St	02908
Rushmore Ave	02909
Ruskin St	02907
Russell St	02907
Russo St	02904
Ruth Ave	02904
Rutherglen Ave	02907
Ruthven St	02906
Rutland St	02907
Ryan Ln	02911
Rye St	02909
Sabin St	02903
Sack St	02911
Sackett St	02907
Sacramento St	02909
Saddle Grn	02904
Sadler St	02911
Saint James St	02907
Saint Johns Cir	02911
Saint Marys Rd	02911
Saint Thomas St	02911
Salem Dr	02904
Salem St	02907
Salina St	02908
Salisbury St	02905
Salmon St	02909
Salter St	02908
Salvan St	02911
Salvati Way	02909
Samoset Ave	02908
Sampson Ave	02911
San Giovanni Dr	02911
Sandringham Ave	02908
Sanford St	02909
Santiago St	02907
Santini St	02904
Santomarco Dr	02904
Sarah St	02906
Saratoga St	02905
Sargent Ave	02906
Sassafras St	02907
Save The Bay Dr	02905
Savin St	02911
Savings St	02907
Savoy St	
1-99	02911
1-199	02906
Sawin Ave	02911
Sawyer St	02907
Saxe St	02909
Sayles St	02905
Schofield St	02903
School St	02909
Seabury St	02907
Seamans Ave	02904
Seamans St	02908
Searle St	02905
Sears Ave	02908
Sedan St	02904
Seekell St	02903
Seekonk St	02906
Selwyn Way	02908
Service Rd	02905

Sessions St 02906
Seton St 02909
Sevier St 02909
Seymour St 02905
Shafter St 02909
Sharon Dr 02904
Sharon St 02908
Shaw St 02904
Sheffield Ave 02911
Sheldon St 02906
Shepard Ave 02904
Sherburne St 02905
Sheridan St 02909
Sherman Ave 02911
Sherman St 02904
Sherri Dr 02911
Sherwood Ave 02911
Sherwood St 02908
Shiloh St 02904
Ship St 02903
Shipyard St 02905
Sibley St 02907
Sibyl St 02909
Silver Lake Ave 02909
Silver Spring St 02904
Simmons St 02909
Simpson St 02911
Sims Ave 02909
Sinclair Ave 02907
Siravo St 02904
Sisson St 02909
Slater Ave 02906
Slocum St 02909
Smart St 02904
Smith Hl 02903
Smith St
  2-140 02903
  141-1331 02908
  1332-1338 02911
  1333-1339 02908
  1340-2199 02911
Smithfield Ave & Rd 02904
Snow St 02903
Social St 02904
Solar St 02903
Somerset St 02907
Sonoma Ct 02909
Sophia St 02909
Sorrell Rd 02904
Sorrento St 02909
South Ln 02904
South St 02903
Sparkbrook Rd 02911
Sparrow St 02908
Spencer St 02909
Spicer St
  1-99 02904
  1-199 02905
Spokane St 02904
Spooner St 02907
Sprague St 02907
Spring St 02904
Springdale Ave 02904
Springfield St 02909
Spruce St 02903
Squanto St 02904
Stadden St 02907
Stadium Rd 02906
Stamford Ave 02907
Standish Ave
  1-99 02911
  1-199 02908
Stanfield St 02909
Stanhope St 02904
Staniford St 02905
Stanley St 02904
Stansbury St 02908
Stanton St 02909
Stanwood St 02907
Star St 02904
State St 02908
Steele St 02906
Steeple St 02903
Steere Ave
  1-99 02911
  1-99 02909
Stella Dr 02911
Stella St 02909
Stenton Ave 02906
Stephanie Dr 02904
Stephen Hopkins Ct 02904
Sterling Ave 02909
Steuben St 02909
Stevens St 02911
Stewart St 02903
Stillwater Ave 02908
Stimson Ave 02906
Stockwell St 02909
Stokes St 02909
Stone St & Trl 02904
Stonelaw Ave 02908
Stukely St 02909
Sudbury St 02904
Suffolk St 02908
Sullivan St 02904
Summer St 02903
Summit Ave
  1-99 02911
  1-299 02906
Sumter St 02907
Sunbury St 02908
Sunflower Cir 02911
Sunrise Dr 02908
Sunset Ave
  1-200 02911
  1-199 02909
  349-499 02904
Superior St
  1-125 02907
  126-199 02909
Superior View Blvd 02911
Sussex St 02908
Sutton St 02903
Swan Ct 02904
Swan St
  1-99 02911
  1-399 02905
Swanee St 02904
Sweet St 02911
Sweetbriar St 02908
Swift St 02904
Swiss St 02909
Sybaris St 02909
Sycamore St 02909
Sykes Pl 02909
Sykes St 02911
Sylvia Ave 02911
Syracuse St 02909
Taber Ave 02906
Taft Ave
  1-99 02904
  1-199 02906
Tag Dr 02911
Talbot St 02904
Tanglewood Ln 02904
Tanner St 02907
Tappan St 02908
Tara St 02904
Tarklin St 02904
Taylor St
  1-99 02911
  1-199 02907
Tecumseh St 02906
Tell St 02909
Temple Ct & St 02905
Tennessee Ave 02905
Tennyson Ln 02905
Terino Dr 02911
Terminal Rd 02905
Terminal Way 02903
Ternay Gdns 02904
Terrace Ave 02909
Terry St 02904
Testa Dr 02911
Tew Pl 02906
Texas Ave 02904
Thackeray St 02907
Thayer St 02906
Thelma St 02904
Theresa Ct 02909
Thomas St
  1-99 02911
  1-99 02903
Thomas Olney Cmn 02904
Thomas P Whitten Way 02903
Thomas Spann Way 02908
Thompson St 02903
Thornton St 02909
Throop Aly & St 02903
Thurber St 02904
Thurbers Ave 02905
Thurston St 02907
Tiber St 02909
Ticknor St 02909
Tidd St 02908
Tiffany St
  1-299 02904
  1-99 02908
Timber St 02904
Time St 02904
Times Way 02908
Tingley Ln 02904
Tingley St 02903
Tobey St 02909
Tockwotton St 02903
Tomcat Ter 02911
Top St 02906
Top Hill Rd 02904
Toronto Ave 02905
Touro St 02904
Towanda Dr 02911
Transit St
  1-59 02903
  60-299 02906
E Transit St 02906
Trask St 02905
Traverse St
  1-6 02906
  7-99 02903
Tremont St 02904
Trent St 02908
Trenton St 02906
Trinidad St 02908
Trinity Pkwy 02908
Trinity Sq 02907
Tripoli St 02909
Troy St 02909
Turcone St 02911
Turks Head Pl 02903
Turner St 02908
Turnessa Dr & Grn 02904
Tuscola Ave 02904
Tuxedo Ave 02909
Twins Ln 02904
Tyler St 02904
Tyndall Ave 02908
Udell St 02904
Union Ave
  1-99 02904
  1-799 02909
Union St 02903
Union Sta 02903
Unit St 02909
United St 02904
University Ave 02906
Updike St 02907
Upton Ave 02906
Urban Ave 02904
Utter St 02904
Vacca St 02911
Vale St 02908
Valley St
  1-280 02909
  281-799 02908
Valley Green Ct 02904
Van Ausdall St 02909
Van Buren St 02905
Vandewater St 02908
Vandieman Ave 02909
Vangtond St 02909
Vantredg St 02907
Vassar Ave 02906
Vaughan St 02904
Veazie St
  1-200 02908
  201-699 02904
Venice St 02908
Ventura St 02908
Venturi Grn 02904
Verdi St 02904
Verdic Ave 02909
Vermont Ave 02905
Verndale Ave 02905
Vernon St 02903
Vesta St 02908
Veto St 02908
Vicksburg St 02904
Victor St
  1-99 02911
  1-99 02908
Victor Emanuel Ave 02904
Victoria St
  1-99 02911
  1-199 02909
W View Ave 02911
View St
  1-99 02908
  1-99 02904
N View Ter 02911
Villa Ave
  1-299 02904
  1-99 02906
Villa Dr 02911
Vincent Ave 02904
Vincent St 02908
Vineland Ave 02911
Vineyard St 02907
Vinton St 02909
Vinyard Ln 02911
Viola St 02909
Violet St 02908
Vireo St 02904
Virginia Ave 02905
Virginia Ln 02908
Vivian Ave 02904
Volturno St 02904
Wabun Ave 02908
Wade St 02903
Wadsworth St
  1-165 02907
  166-299 02909
Wainwright St 02908
Waite St 02908
Wakefield Ave 02909
Waldo St
  1-99 02904
  1-176 02907
  177-299 02909
Wallace St 02909
Waller St 02908
Walnut St
  1-99 02904
  1-99 02903
Walter Ave 02911
Walton St 02908
Wanda Ct 02904
Wanskuck Ave 02904
Ward Ave 02904
Wardlaw Ave & Ct 02908
Ware Ct 02907
Warren Ave 02911
Warren St 02907
Warren Way 02905
Warrington St 02907
Washakie Ave 02911
Washburn St 02908
Washington Ave 02905
Washington Pl 02903
Washington St
  1-99 02904
  1-599 02903
Wasiota Ave 02911
Watauga St 02911
Water St 02911
S Water St 02903
Water View Ln 02904
Waterman Ave 02911
Waterman St
  1-30 02903
  31-399 02906
Watson St 02904
Waverly St
  1-158 02907
  159-299 02909
Wayland Ave & Sq 02906
Wayne St 02908
Wealth Ave 02908
Webb St 02908
Webster Ave 02909
Wedge Row 02904
Weeden St 02903
Weiss Ct 02905
Wellesley Ave 02911
Wendell St
  1-99 02911
  1-299 02909
Wendi Dr 02911
Wenscott Ln 02904
Wentworth Ave 02905
Wentworth St 02904
Wesleyan Ave 02907
West Dr 02904
West St
  1-99 02904
  1-99 02903
Westcott Ave 02909
Westerly Ave 02909
Western St 02906
Westfield St 02907
Westford Rd 02906
Westminster St
  1-1075 02903
  1076-1107 02909
  1108-1108 02907
  1109-1999 02909
  1110-1998 02909
Westwood Manor Dr 02909
Weybosset Hl & St 02903
Weymouth St 02906
What Cheer Ave 02909
Wheaton St 02906
Whelan Rd 02909
Whipple Ave 02911
Whipple Ct 02911
Whipple St 02908
White Ct 02911
Whitehall St 02909
Whitford Ave 02908
Whiting St 02906
Whitmarsh St 02907
Whitney St 02907
Whittemore Pl 02909
Whittier Ave 02909
Wickenden St 02903
Wickham St 02903
Wild St 02904
Wildwood Ave 02907
Wiley St 02908
Wilkens St 02906
Willard Ave
  1-265 02905
  266-399 02907
Willard St 02904
Willern St 02911
William Ellery Pl 02904
Williams St
  1-35 02903
  36-399 02906
Willow St
  1-99 02911
  1-199 02909
Wilna St 02904
Wilson St 02907
Winchester St 02904
Windmill St 02904
Winfield Ct & Rd 02906
Wingate Rd 02906
Winona St
  1-99 02911
  1-99 02904
Winrooth Ave 02908
Winsor St 02908
Winsted St 02906
Winter St 02903
Winthrop Ave 02908
Wisdom Ave 02908
Wolcott St 02908
Wolfe St 02909
Wood St 02909
Woodbine St
  1-99 02911
  1-199 02906
Woodbury St 02906
Woodcliffe Ave 02911
Woodfall St 02909
Woodhaven Blvd 02911
Woodland Ter 02906
Woodlawn Ave
  1-9 02911
  10-499 02904
Woodman St 02907
Woodmont St 02907
Woodside Dr 02904
Woodside Rd 02909
Woodward Rd 02904
Woonasquatucket Ave 02911
Worcester Ave 02911
Wright St 02911
Wriston Dr 02906
Wyatt St 02905
Wyndham Ave 02908
Wythe Ave 02904
Yale Ave 02908
Yarmouth St 02907
York St 02906
Yorkshire St 02908
Yorktown Pl 02908
Young Ave 02908
Young St 02904
Young Orchard Ave 02906
Zambarano Ave 02911
Zella St 02908
Zipporah St 02911
Zoar St 02911
Zone St 02908

NUMBERED STREETS

All Street Addresses 02906

WAKEFIELD RI

General Delivery 02879

POST OFFICE BOXES MAIN OFFICE STATIONS AND BRANCHES

Box No.s
All PO Boxes 02880

NAMED STREETS

Abalone Dr E 02879
Abalone Dr W 02879
Abalone Rd 02882
Acorn Ct 02879
Admirals Way 02882
Alan Ave 02882
Albatross Dr E & W 02882
Albro Ln 02879
Alcides Dr 02879
Alder Rd 02879
Alexander Ct 02879
Alexander Dr 02882
Algonquin Rd & Trl 02882
Allagash Trl 02882
Allen Ave 02879
Allisons Ave 02879
Amancio St 02879
Ambleside Rd 02882
Amey St 02882
Amos St 02879
Anawan Ave & Dr 02882
Anchorage Rd 02882
Andre Ave 02879
Angela Ln 02879
Angell Rd 02882
Anglers Ct 02882
Anna Olivo Ct 02882
Anne Hoxsie Ln 02882
Antique Rd 02879
Arbeth Rd 02879
Arbor Way 02879
Arciero Ct 02882
Arnold Ave 02882
Arnold St 02879
Aroostook Trl 02882
Arrow Head Trl 02879
Arrow Wood Trl 02879
Arrowhead Rd 02882
Asa Pond Rd 02879
Ash St 02879
Ashbrook Rd 02882
Ashley Ct 02882
Ashton Ln 02882
Aspen Dr 02882
Aspen Rd 02879
Atlantic Ave
  1-99 02882
  1-199 02879
Atlantic St 02879
Auburn Rd 02879
Audobon Dr 02879
Aurora Ct 02879
Austin St 02879
Ave D 02882
Avice St 02882
Azalea Rd 02882
Baker Rd 02882
Baldwin Ct 02882
Balsam Rd 02879
Baltimore Ave 02882
Barnacle Dr E 02879
Barnacle Dr W 02879
Barnacle Rd 02882
Barney Ave 02879
Basin Rd 02882
Bass Rd 02879
Bass Rock Rd 02882
S & W Bay Dr 02882
Bayberry Ave 02879
Bayberry Rd 02882
Bayberry Hill Rd 02882
Bayfield Dr 02879
Bayview Dr 02882
Beach Ave 02882
Beach Dr 02879
Beach Row 02879
Beach St 02882
Beach Plum Dr E 02879
Beach Plum Dr W 02879
Beach Plum Rd 02882
Bedford Cir 02882
Bedford Dr 02879
Beech Rd 02882
Beech Hill Rd 02879
Beech Tree Pl 02879
Bellevue Ct 02882
Belmont Ave 02879
Benefit Rd 02879
Benjamin Rd 02882
Berglund Ave 02879
Bethany Rd 02879
Betty Dr 02882
Betty Hill Rd 02882
Big Water Rd 02879
Bill Sweet Way 02882
Billington Ave 02879
Birch Rd 02879
Birch St 02882
Birchwood Dr
  1-99 02882
  1-199 02879
Bishop Rd 02882
Bittersweet Ln 02879
Bittersweet Farm Way 02879
Blackberry Hill Dr 02879
Blanchard Pl 02879
Blindbrook Dr 02882
Bliss Rd 02879
Blooming Pl 02879
Blossom Ct 02879
Blossom Way 02882
Blue Heron Rd 02879
Blue Spruce Ln 02879
Blueberry Ln 02882

Bluff Hill Cove Farm 02882
Bonnet Point Rd 02882
Bonnet Shores Rd 02882
Bonnet View Dr 02882
Boon St 02882
Border Ave & Dr 02879
Boston Neck Rd 02882
Bow St 02879
Bow And Arrow Trl N & S 02879
Boxwood Ct 02879
Bramblewood Ln 02879
Branch Rd 02882
Branch St 02879
Brandywine Ln 02882
Brandywyne Ct 02879
Brant Rd N & S 02879
Breachway Rd 02882
Breakwater Rd 02879
Brecka Dr 02879
Briarwood Dr 02879
Bridgetown Rd 02882
Briggs Rd 02879
Bristol Rd 02882
Broad Hill Way 02879
Broad Rock Rd 02879
Broadmoor Rd 02879
Brook Rd 02882
Brook Farm Rd N & S 02879
Brooklyn Rd 02882
Brookwood Rd 02879
Brown St
1-99 02882
1-99 02879
Brown Bear Rd 02879
Browning Dr 02882
Browning St 02879
Brush Hill Rd 02882
Bud Browning Cir 02879
Burbank Ave 02882
Burnside Ave 02882
Calef Ave 02882
Calerani Rd 02879
Calypso Dr E & W 02879
Camden Ct 02879
Camden Rd 02882
Camp Fuller Rd 02879
Canonchet Way 02882
Canopus Ave 02882
Canterbury Rd 02879
Cantone Rd 02882
Captain Freebody Rd 02882
Cardinal Ln 02879
Cards Pond Rd 02879
Carol Ln 02882
Carol Ann Ave 02879
Carpenter Dr 02879
Carpenters Beach Rd 02879
Carver Ln 02882
Castle Rd 02882
Castlerea Way 02879
Caswell Ct 02882
Caswell St
1-199 02882
1-99 02879
Cavalier Rd 02882
Cedar St 02882
Cedar Hollow Rd 02879
Cedar Island Rd 02882
Celestial Dr 02882
Celestial Heights Dr 02879
Cemetery Ln 02879
Center Rd 02882
Central Ave
1-99 02882
1-99 02879
Central St
1-199 02882
1-199 02879
Champlin Ave 02879
Champlin Cove Rd 02882
Chancellorsville Blvd 02882
Channing Rd 02879
Chappell Rd & St 02879
Charles St 02879
Charlestown Blvd 02882
Chatham Rd 02879
Checkerberry Trl 02882
Cherry Ln 02879
Chestnut Ave & St 02882
Chestnut Hill Rd 02879
Choctaw Trl 02882
Christopher St 02879
Church St 02879
Circuit Dr 02882
Clara Ln 02882
Clarke Rd 02882
Claudia Dr 02882
Clearwater Dr 02882
Cleveland St 02879
Cliff Dr 02882
Clipper Cir 02879
Clubhouse Dr 02882
Coast Guard Ave 02879
Coddington Way 02879
Coffey Ave 02882
Collins St 02882
Colonel John Gardner Rd 02882
Columbia St 02879
Columbine Ct 02879
Comd Oliver Hazard Perry Hwy 02879
Comfort Ln 02879
Commons Corner Way 02879
Community Dr 02879
Conanicus Rd 02882
Conanicut Rd 02882
Conant Ave 02882
Conch Rd 02882
Congdon Dr 02879
Congdon St 02882
Congress Rd 02882
Continental Rd & St 02882
Cook Ave 02879
Corey Rd 02879
Cormorant Rd
1-99 02879
1-99 02882
Cornell Rd 02882
Country Side Rd 02882
S County Commons Way 02879
Courtland Dr 02882
Courtway St 02882
Cove Rd 02882
Cove St 02879
Cowesett Ave 02882
Cranberry Run 02879
Crane Ter 02882
Cree Trl 02882
Crest Ave
1-99 02882
1-199 02879
Crest Dr 02882
Crestwood Dr 02882
Cross Rd 02882
Crosshill Dr 02882
Cull Blvd 02882
Curtis Cir 02879
Curtis Corner Rd 02879
Cypress Ave 02882
Dale Carlia St 02879
Dam St 02879
Dania Dr 02882
Darlene Dr 02879
Dartmouth Ln 02879
Davids Way 02879
Davis St 02879
Davisville Ln 02882
Dawley Way 02879
Dawn Ct 02879
Day Lily Cir 02879
Daytona Ave 02882
Dean Knauss Dr 02882
Deangelis St 02882
Deborah St 02879
Deer Ridge Way 02879
Deer Trail Rd 02879
Defelice Rd 02882
Delray Dr 02882
Dendron Rd 02879
Denison Dr 02882
Desano Dr 02882
Dewberry Ln 02879
Diane Rd 02882
Dinonsie Way 02879
Dixon St 02882
Dobson Rd 02879
Dockray St 02879
Dolphin Rd 02882
Donna Ct 02879
Dory Ct 02879
Douglas Dr 02882
Dove Ter 02882
Dovetail Ln 02879
Driftway Rd 02879
Dry Creek Way 02879
Dudley Dr 02882
Dunes Ct & Rd 02882
Durkin Dr 02882
Eagle Nest Ter 02879
Eagles Nest Ter 02882
Earles Ct 02882
Eastern View Ave 02879
Easy St 02879
Ed A Ln 02882
Eddy Ln 02882
Edgewater Rd
1-199 02882
1-99 02879
Edgewood Farm Rd 02879
Edith Rd 02882
Edwards Ave 02879
Egret Ln 02879
Eire Rd 02882
Eisenhower Pl 02882
Elderberry Ln 02879
Eldred Ct 02879
Elizabeth Rd 02882
Elm Ave 02882
Elm Rd 02879
Elm St 02879
Elwood Ct 02879
Emerson Way 02879
Emery St 02882
Emma G Ln 02882
Emmett Ln 02879
Erin Dr 02879
Estampes Ct 02879
Evergreen Ct 02882
Exeter Blvd 02882
Fagan Ct 02879
Fairport Ave 02882
Fairway Ct & Dr 02882
Farrells Way 02879
Fayerweather Dr 02882
Fernleaf Trl 02882
S Ferry Rd 02882
Field Ter 02882
Fieldstone Dr 02879
Fiore Dr 02879
Fiore Industrial Dr 02879
Fir Dr 02882
Fire Lane 1 02879
Fire Lane 2 02879
Fire Lane 3 02879
Fire Lane 4 02879
Fire Lane 5 02879
Fire Lane 6 02879
Fire Lane 7 02879
Fish Rd 02882
Flintstone Rd 02882
Florence Rd 02882
Foddering Farm Rd 02882
Follett Rd 02882
N Fort Rd 02882
Foster Ln 02882
Foster Rd 02879
Foster Sheldon Rd 02879
Fox Ct 02879
Fox Dr 02879
Fox Ridge Cir 02882
Frances Ave 02882
Frank Low St 02882
Franks Neck Rd 02882
Freemans Trl 02882
Fresh Meadow Rd 02879
Front St 02879
Gale Dr 02879
Galleon Ct 02879
Galway Ct 02879
Gardencourt Dr 02882
Gardenia Ln 02882
Gardiner St 02882
Gaspee Rd 02882
Gateway Dr 02879
Genesee Way 02879
Gentian Dr 02879
George St 02879
George Schaeffer St 02879
Gibson Ave 02882
S Glen Ct 02879
Glendale Rd 02882
Glendaway Dr 02882
Glenwood Ave 02882
Glenwood Cir 02879
Glocester Rd 02882
Golden Rd 02882
E Golden Sands Dr 02879
Goose Island Rd 02882
Gooseberry Rd 02879
Gould St 02879
Grande Brook Cir 02879
Grande Isle Dr 02879
Grandeville Ct 02879
Grant Ave 02879
Gravelly Hill Rd 02879
Great Island Rd 02882
Green St 02879
Green Acres Dr 02882
Green Hill Ave 02879
Green Hill Beach Rd 02879
Green Hill Ocean Dr 02879
Green Kinyon Driftway 02882
Green Meadow Dr 02882
Greenbrier Rd 02882
Greene Ln 02882
Greenwich Rd 02882
Greenwood Dr 02879
Gregory St 02879
Greybirch Ct 02879
Gull Rd 02882
Gunning Rock Dr 02882
Hahn Ave 02879
Half Moon Trl 02879
Hampton Way 02879
Harbor Rd 02882
Harbour Island Rd 02882
Harcourt Ave 02879
Harrison Ave 02879
Hartford Ave 02879
Harvey Ln 02882
Hathaway Ln 02879
Haven St 02882
Hawthorne Ave 02882
Hazard Ave
1-99 02882
1-99 02879
Hazard St 02879
Healey Brook Ct 02879
Heather Hollow Dr 02879
Hemlock Ave 02882
Hemlock Rd 02879
Hemlock St 02882
Hendricks St 02879
Henry Case Way 02879
Herbert Dr 02882
Heron Way 02879
High St
1-99 02882
1-599 02879
High Meadow Ln 02879
High Ridge Dr 02879
Highland Ave
1-99 02882
1-299 02879
Highview Ave 02882
E Hill Rd & Way 02879
Hillcrest Rd 02879
Hills Pkwy 02882
Hillside Rd
1-99 02882
1-199 02879
Hilltop Ave 02879
Hillview Dr 02882
Hinkley Ln 02882
Hogan Ave 02882
Holden Rd 02879
Holiday Ct 02879
Holland Dr 02879
Holley St 02879
Holly Rd 02879
Hollywood Ave 02882
Homeland Ave 02882
Homestead Rd 02882
Hope Ct 02879
Hope Ln 02882
Hopkins Ln 02879
Horielde Rd 02882
Hotel Dr 02879
Houston Ave 02882
Howard Cir 02879
Hull St 02879
Hummingbird Holw 02879
Hunt Ave 02879
Hurley Cir 02879
Huron Ave 02882
Iacuele Dr 02879
Ice House Rd 02879
Ide St 02879
Ilex Rd 02882
Independence Ln 02879
Indian Trl N & S 02879
Indian Head Trl 02879
Indian Rock Farm Rd 02882
Indian Run Rd & Trl 02879
Indigo Point Rd 02879
Inez St 02882
Inglenook Ln 02879
Inkberry Dr 02879
Inkberry Trl 02882
Iroquois Rd 02882
Irvings Path 02882
Isabelle Dr 02882
Island Rd 02882
Island View Rd 02882
Isle Point Rd 02882
Jakes Way 02879
James St 02882
Jamestown Blvd 02882
Jean St 02879
Jenckes Ct 02882
Jennifer Ct 02882
Jennifer Dr 02879
Jenny Ln 02882
S Jerry Cv 02879
Jerry Brown Farm Rd 02879
Jessica Ln
1-99 02879
1-99 02882
John St
1-99 02882
1-99 02879
John Briggs Way 02879
John Brown Ln 02882
Johnny Cake Trl N & S 02879
Johnson Ave 02882
Johnson Pl 02879
Johnson St 02882
Jonathan Is 02882
Joy Ln 02882
Judith Ave 02882
Julia Ave 02882
Juliet Rd 02882
Juniper Rd 02879
Juniper Trl 02882
Jupeter St 02882
Kardway St 02882
Karee Ct 02879
Karen Ann Dr 02879
Karison St 02879
Kathy St 02882
Kathy Ann Dr 02882
Kelley Way 02879
Kendall Ct 02882
Kensington Ct N & S 02879
Kentara Grn 02882
Kenwood Ave 02879
Kenyon Ave 02879
Kenyon Woods Way 02879
Kersey Rd 02879
Kettle Pond Dr 02879
Kimball St 02879
Kimberley Dr 02879
King St 02882
King Philip Rd 02882
Kingfisher Rd
1-99 02882
1-99 02879
Kings Ridge Rd 02879
Kingston Ave 02879
Kingston Ln 02882
Kingstown Rd
981A-981B 02879
1-375 02882
376-550 02879
551-551 02880
552-2094 02882
553-2095 02879
Kingswood Ct 02879
Kinney Ave 02882
Knight St 02882
Knowlesway Ext 02882
Kogoli Way 02879
Kymbolde Way 02879
Lab Hill Dr 02879
Lafayette Ave 02879
Lahinch Rd 02879
Lake Ave 02879
Lake Rd 02882
Lake St 02879
Lakeside Dr 02882
Lakeview Dr 02882
Lakewood Dr 02879
Lakeworth Ave 02882
Lambert St 02882
Land N Sea Dr 02879
Laneway Ct 02882
Larch Ave 02882
Larkin St 02879
Larson Ln 02879
Lauderdale Dr 02882
Laura Ln 02882
Laurel Rd 02879
Laurel Ridge Rd 02879
Lawnacre Dr 02879
Lawrence Dr 02882
Leatherleaf Rd 02882
Ledge Rd 02879
Lee Rd 02879
Leeann Dr 02882
Leeward Ln 02879
Legend Rock Rd 02879
Leisure Dr 02879
Leonard Bodwell Rd 02882
Lewis Ln 02879
Liberty St 02879
Lilly Ln 02882
Lincoln Way 02882
Linden Rd 02882
Lindsley Dr 02882
Little Comfort Way 02879
Little Pond Rd 02879
Little Woods Path 02879
Locust Ct 02882
Long Cove Rd 02882
Longview Ct 02879
Longview Dr 02882
Lookout Ln 02879
Lorelei Dr E & W 02879
Louise Ave 02882
Lower Farm Rd 02879
Lupine Ct 02879
Lupine Trl 02882
Mac Alder St 02882
Macarthur Blvd 02879
Main St 02879
Major Arnold Rd 02882
Major Cleathe Runway 02882
Mallard Dr & Rd 02882
Mallory Ln 02879
Manning Dr 02882
Manor Dr 02882
Mansion Ave 02882
Maple Ave 02882
Maple Dr 02879
Maple St 02879
Maplehurst Dr 02882
Margaret St 02882
Marian Ave 02882
Marine Dr 02882
Marine Rd 02879
Marsh Ln 02882
Marten Ave 02882
Martin Ct & Rd 02882
Martingale Ln 02882
Massasoit Ct 02882
Mast Ct 02879
Mathewson St 02882
Matunuck Beach Rd 02879
Matunuck School House Rd 02879
Mautucket Rd 02879
Maywood Rd 02882
Mcburney Ave 02882
Mcmillen Way 02882
Meadow Ave 02879
S Meadow Dr 02882
Meadow Ln 02882
Meadow Rd 02882
Meadow St 02879
Meadowbrook Way
1-99 02882
1-199 02879
Mechanic St 02879
Melbourne Dr 02882
Mellbridge Dr 02879
Melville Ln 02882
Memorial Sq 02882
Merriweather Ave 02882
Metaterraine Ave 02879
Mettatuxet Rd 02882
Middle Rd
1-99 02882
1-99 02879
Middle St 02879
Middlebridge Rd
1-119 02882
120-1299 02879
Midway Rd 02882
Milkay Way 02882
Mill Field Ct 02879
Mill Pond Rd 02879
Millstone Rd 02879
Ministerial Rd 02879
Miss Kane Ln 02882
Misty Ct 02879
Mitchell Ave 02879
Mitchell Rd 02882
Mittendorf Rd 02879
Mockingbird Ln 02879
Mohawk Trl 02882
Mollusk Dr 02882
Mollusk Dr E 02879
Mollusk Dr W 02879
Molson Ct 02879
Montauk Rd 02882
Moonstone Beach Rd 02879
Mooresfield Rd 02882
Moosehead Trl 02882
Moraine Ct 02879
Morgan Dr 02882
Mount View Rd 02882
Mourning Dove Ln 02879
Mulberry Dr 02879
Mumford Rd 02882
Muratore Ln 02882
Mystic Dr 02879
Namcook Rd 02882
Narragansett Ave 02882
Narragansett Ave E 02879
Narragansett Ave W 02879
Narragansett Ct 02882
Narrows Rd 02882
Nassau Rd 02882
Nautilus Dr E 02879
Nautilus Dr W 02879
Nautilus Rd 02882
Nepaug Rd 02882
Neptune Dr E & W 02879

Netop Rd 02882
Newport Ln & Row 02882
Newton Ave 02882
Nichols Ave 02882
Ninigret Ave 02879
Ninigret Rd 02882
Noble St 02882
Noel Ct 02879
Normandy Rd 02879
North Dr 02882
North Rd 02879
Northup St 02879
Nye St 02879
Oak Ave 02882
Oak Rd 02879
Oak St 02879
Oak Hill Rd
1-99 02882
1-99 02879
Oakdell St 02879
Oakwoods Dr 02879
Ocean Ave 02879
Ocean Rd 02882
Ocean Look 02882
Ocean Spray Ave 02882
Ocean View Dr
1-99 02882
1-99 02879
Ocean View Park 02879
Ocean Village Ct 02879
Oceanside Pl 02882
Offshore Rd 02882
Old Boston Neck Rd 02882
Old Garden Way 02879
Old Mountain Rd 02879
Old Pine Rd 02882
Old Point Judith Rd 02882
Old Post Rd 02879
Old Rose Hill Rd 02879
Old Shannock Rd 02879
Old Succotash Rd 02879
Old Tower Hill Rd 02879
Old Town Trl 02882
Oliver Dr 02879
Omer Dr 02879
Onondega Rd 02882
Orchard Ave
1-99 02882
1-199 02879
Orlando Dr 02882
Osceola Ave 02882
Ospray Rd 02882
Osprey Rd 02879
Oswego Trl 02882
Othmar St 02882
Ottawa Trl 02882
Otter Acres Way 02879
Overhill Rd 02879
Overlook Cir & Rd 02882
Oxeye Trl 02882
Oyster Rd 02882
Paddock Ct 02879
Paddy Hill Rd 02879
Palisades Blvd 02879
Palm Beach Ave 02882
Park Ave 02879
Parkman Rd 02882
Partridge Ln 02879
N Pasture Ln 02879
Paterson Ct 02882
Patton Ave 02879
Paul Ave 02879
Pawnee Trl 02882
Peace Pipe Trl N & S 02879
Peaked Rock Ln 02882
Peaked Rock Rd
1-199 02882
20-499 02879
Pearls Way 02879
Peckham Ave 02879
Pendleton Pl 02882
Penguin Dr 02882
Peninsula Rd 02879
Pennsylvania Ave 02882
Penny Ln 02879
Penobscot Trl 02882

Percy Ln 02879
Periwinkle Rd 02882
Perkins Ave 02882
Perriwinkle Dr E & W 02879
Perry Ave 02879
Perrywinkle Rd 02879
Pershing Ave 02879
Petal Ln 02879
Peterson Ct 02882
Petrel Dr 02879
Pettaquamscutt Ave 02882
Philip Dr 02882
S Pier Rd 02882
Pier Market Pl 02882
Pike St 02879
Pilgrim Ave 02882
Pine Ave 02882
Pine Ct 02879
Pine St 02879
Pine Hill Rd 02879
Pine Knoll Ln 02879
Pine Tree Ln 02879
Pine Tree Point Rd 02882
Pinehurst St 02879
Piping Plover Dr 02882
Pitch Pine Pl 02879
Pleasant Ave 02882
Pleasant St
1-99 02882
1-99 02879
Pocono Rd 02882
Point Ave 02879
Point Judith Rd 02882
Pollock Ave 02879
Polo Club Rd 02882
Pomfret Rd 02882
Ponagansett Pkwy 02882
Pond Dr 02879
E Pond Rd 02882
Pond St 02879
Pond View Rd 02882
Pontiac Rd 02882
Port Ave 02879
Post Rd 02879
Potter Rd 02879
Preservation Way 02879
President Dr 02882
Presque Isle Trl 02882
Prospect Ave
1-99 02882
1-99 02879
Prospect Ct 02882
Prospect Rd 02879
Quagnut Dr 02879
Quiet Way 02879
Radial Dr 02879
Railroad St 02879
Ram Head Rd 02882
Ray Trainor Dr 02882
Raymond Dr 02882
Reactor Rd 02882
Red Feather Trl N & S 02879
Red House Rd 02879
Red Oak Way 02879
Redberry Dr 02879
Redwood Dr
1-99 02882
1-99 02879
Rhode Island Ave 02882
Richard Smith Rd 02882
Ridge Dr 02882
Ridge Rd 02879
Ridge Crest Ln 02879
Ridgewood Ln 02879
Riptide Rd 02882
River Ave 02879
N River Dr 02882
S River Dr 02882
River St 02879
River Heights Dr 02882
River View Rd 02879
Riverside Dr
1-99 02882
1-299 02879
Riviera Dr 02882

Robert Frost Way 02879
Robertson Rd 02882
Robinson St
1-199 02882
1-299 02879
Rockland Dr 02879
Rockland St 02882
Rockwood Ln 02879
Rocky Rd 02879
Rocky Brook Way 02879
Rodman St
1-199 02882
1-399 02879
Rolling Rock Trl 02879
Rose Cir 02879
Rose Ct 02882
Rose Hill Rd 02879
Rosebriar Ave 02879
Rosewood Ave 02882
Roxbury Rd 02882
Roys Rd 02879
Ruth Ann Rd 02882
Rye Point Rd 02879
Sabbatia Trl 02879
Sachem Rd 02882
Saint Dominic Rd 02879
Saint James Rd 02882
Sakonnet Blvd 02882
Salem Trl 02882
Salt Pond Rd 02879
Saltaire Ave 02882
Samuel Rodman St 02879
Sand Hill Cove Rd 02882
Sand Piper Dr 02879
Sand Plains Rd & Trl 02879
Sand Sprite Dr 02879
Sand Trail Rd 02879
Sandpiper Rd 02882
Sandra Ct 02882
Sandy Beach Rd 02882
Sandy Bottom Shores Dr 02879
Sarasota Ave 02882
Sassafras Trl 02882
Saugatucket Rd 02879
Saybrook Ave 02882
Scallop Rd 02882
Scallop Shell Dr 02879
Scallop Shell Rd 02882
Schaeffer St 02879
School Ln & St 02879
School House Rd 02882
Schooner Dr 02879
Schooner Cove Rd 02882
Sea Crest Dr 02882
E Sea Crest Dr 02879
Sea Lea Dr 02882
Sea View Ave 02879
Seabonnet Dr 02882
Seabreeze Ter 02879
Seacrest Dr W 02879
Seagate Dr 02882
Seagrass Dr 02879
Seaport Dr 02882
Seaside Ave 02879
Sebago Trl 02882
Secluded Dr
1-599 02882
1-99 02879
Sedge Ct 02882
Segar Ct 02879
Sentinal Dr 02879
Serenity Way 02879
Sewell Rd 02882
Sextant Ln 02882
Shadberry Trl 02879
Shadbush Rd
1-99 02882
1-99 02879
Shadbush Trl 02879
Shadow Farm Way 02879
Shagbark Rd 02882
Shannock Rd 02879
Shannon Rd 02879
Sheldon Point Rd 02882
Shelldrake Rd 02879

Shepherd Dr 02879
Sherman Ct & Rd 02879
E Shore Dr & Rd 02882
Shorty Way 02879
Silva St 02879
Silver Lake Ave 02879
Sleepy Hollow Ln 02879
Slope Ave 02879
Smith St 02879
Snipe Rd 02882
Snug Harbor Ln 02879
Sophia Ct 02879
South Rd 02879
South Trl 02882
Southern View Dr 02882
Southwest Rd 02882
Southwinds Dr 02879
Spartina Cove Way 02879
Spencer Ct 02879
Spice Bush Trl 02882
Spindrift Dr E 02879
Spindrift Dr W 02879
Spindrift Rd 02882
Spinnaker Ct 02882
Spring St
1-99 02882
1-199 02879
Spring Brook Rd 02882
Springcove Rd 02882
Spruce Ave 02882
Spruce Ct 02879
Spruce Rd 02879
Stanton Ave 02882
Starboard Ter 02882
Starfish Dr 02882
Starflower Ct 02879
Starlight Dr 02879
Starr Dr W 02882
State St 02882
Stedman Ct & Rd 02879
Steeplebush Dr 02879
Stellar Way 02879
Steven Cir 02879
Stevenson Way 02882
Stewart Way 02882
Stone Bridge Dr 02879
Stone Soup Farm Rd 02879
Stoneway Rd 02879
Stoney Acres Way 02879
Stoney Farm Way 02879
Stratford Ave 02882
Strathmore St 02882
Straw Ln 02879
Succotash Rd 02879
Sumac Trl 02882
Summer St
1-99 02882
1-99 02879
Summit Ave
1-199 02879
1-99 02882
Summit Rd 02882
Sundance Trl 02879
Sunnybrook Farm Rd 02879
Sunset Ave 02879
Sunset Blvd 02882
Sunset Dr 02879
Sunset Rd 02882
Sunset Shore Dr 02882
Sunset View Blvd 02879
Surfside Ave & Dr 02879
Susan Cir 02879
Swampfire Dr 02879
Sweet Allen Farm Rd 02879
Sweet Fern Ln 02879
Sweet Meadows Ct 02882
Sycamore Ln 02879
Sydney Ln 02882
Sylvan Rd 02882
Table Rock Rd 02879
Talia Ct 02882
Tallow Hill Pt 02882
Tanglewood Trl 02882
Tara Way 02879
Tarleton Rd 02879
Tarzwell Dr 02882

Taylor St 02882
Teal Dr & Rd 02879
Teal Pond Rd 02882
Tefft Ridge Ln 02879
Tellier Rd 02882
Temple Ln 02882
Tern Dr 02879
Tern Rd
1-99 02882
1-99 02879
101-199 02879
Terra Dr 02882
Thayer Ave 02882
Therese St 02882
Thewlis Woods Way 02879
Thoreau Ln 02879
Thornapple Rd 02882
Thule Cove Rd 02882
Tidal St 02879
Tidewater Dr E 02879
Tidewater Dr W 02879
Tidewater Rd 02882
Tiny Ln 02882
Tom Walsh Ln 02882
Tomahawk Trl N & S 02879
Torrey Rd 02879
Tower Hill Rd 02879
Tower View Ct 02882
Town Farm Rd 02879
Treasure Rd 02882
Tri Pond Ct 02879
Triton Dr E & W 02879
Tucker Ave
1-99 02879
1-99 02882
Tucker Ln 02879
Tuckertown Rd 02879
Tupelo Rd 02879
Tupelo Trl 02882
Turner Cove Way 02879
Twin Peninsula Ave 02879
Twin Pond Cir 02882
Uncle Sams Ln 02879
Upper Farm Way 02879
Upper Pond Rd 02879
Upper Terrace Cir 02879
Vanderbilt Dr 02882
Vernstrom Rd 02882
Viburnam Rd 02882
Victoria Ln 02879
Victory St 02879
W View Dr 02879
N View Rd 02882
Village Ln 02882
Village Square Dr 02879
Wager Ln 02879
Wakefield Ave 02879
Walcott Ave 02882
Walden Way 02879
Walnut St 02882
Walts Way 02882
Wampum Rd 02882
Wampum Trl N 02879
Wampum Trl S 02879
Wanda St 02882
Wandsworth St 02882
Warner Ave 02879
Wash Pond Rd 02879
Washington St 02879
Watch Hill Way 02879
Water St 02879
Watson Ave 02882
Wayland Trl 02882
Wayne St 02882
Wayside Meadow Rd 02879
Weathervane Rd 02879
Webster Ave 02882
Webster Trl 02879
N & S Weeden Rd 02879
Wendy Ln 02879
Wesquage Dr 02882
West St 02879
Westchester Way 02882
Westcote Dr 02879
Westcote Close 02879
Westlake Ave 02882

Westmoreland St 02882
Westside Rd 02879
Westwind Rd 02879
Whale Rock Rd 02882
What Cheer Ct & Rd 02882
Wheatfield Cove Rd 02882
Whippoorwill Dr 02879
White Birch Trl 02879
White Cap Rd 02882
White Falls Trl 02879
White Oak Ct 02879
White Pond Rd 02879
White Swan Dr 02882
Whitewood Dr 02879
Whitford St 02879
Whitney Ct 02882
Wild Flower Trl 02879
Wild Goose Ln 02882
Wild Goose Rd 02879
Wild Rose Ct 02879
Wilderness Dr 02882
Wilderness Trl 02879
Wildfield Farm Rd 02882
Wildwood Rd 02882
Willard Ave 02879
William Schmid Dr & Rd 02879
Willow Ave 02882
Wilson Dr 02882
Wilson St 02879
Winchester Dr 02879
Windermere Rd 02882
Windmill Dr 02879
Windsor Rd 02879
Windswept Dr 02879
Windward Cir 02882
Windward Rd 02879
Windwood Valley Rd 02879
Wingate Rd 02879
Winter St 02879
Winterberry Ln 02879
Wintman Dr 02879
Wishing Well Cir 02879
Withington Rd 02882
Wolfe Rd 02882
Wood Ave 02882
Wood Ln 02879
Wood Hill Rd 02882
Wood Hollow Rd 02879
Woodbine Rd 02879
Woodland Trl 02879
Woodmans Trl 02879
Woodmark Way 02879
Woodmist Cir 02879
Woodridge Rd 02882
Woodruff Ave
1-99 02882
100-110 02879
101-125 02882
112-504 02879
S Woods Dr 02879
Woodsia Trl 02879
Woodstock Ln 02879
Woodward Ave 02882
Wordens Pond Rd 02879
Wright Ave 02879
Wyndham Way 02879
Yankee Trl 02879
Yarmouth Cir 02879
Yellowbirch Rd 02882
Zinns Dr 02879

NUMBERED STREETS

All Street Addresses 02882

WARWICK RI

General Delivery 02886

POST OFFICE BOXES MAIN OFFICE STATIONS AND BRANCHES

Box No.s
300 - 7911 02887
8101 - 8999 02888
9001 - 9709 02889
81000 - 81080 02888

NAMED STREETS

Abbey Ave 02888
Abbott Ave 02886
Aberdeen Ave 02888
Aborn Ave 02888
Access Rd 02886
Acorn Ave 02888
Acura Dr 02886
Adams St 02888
Adelaide Ave 02886
Adler Ct 02886
Adrian St 02886
Agawam Ave 02889
Airport Rd
1-315 02889
316-699 02886
701-799 02886
Airtower Dr 02886
Airway Rd 02886
Alabama Ave 02888
Alanna Ct 02886
Albany Rd 02888
Albert Rd 02889
Alden Ave 02889
Aldrich Ave 02889
Alfred St 02889
Algonquin Dr 02888
Alhambra Rd 02886
Alice Ave 02886
Alicia Cir 02886
Allard St 02889
Allegheny Ave 02888
Allen Ave 02889
Almy St 02886
Alpine St 02889
Althea Rd 02889
Altieri Way 02886
Alto St 02886
Alvin St 02886
N Alvira Ave 02888
Amanda Ct 02889
Ambassador Ave 02889
Americo Dr 02889
Amherst Rd 02889
Amore Rd 02886
Amsterdam Ave 02889
Anchorage Rd 02889
N Anderson Ave 02888
Andover Dr 02886
Andrew Comstock Rd 02886
Angell Ct 02889
Ann St 02889
Ann Mary Brown Dr 02888
Anne C Holst Ct 02886
Anoka Rd 02889
Anscot Ct 02889
Ansell Ave 02886
Ansonia Rd 02889
Anthony St 02886
Anton Ct 02889
Apollo St 02888
Apple Tree Ln 02888
Aquarius Dr 02889
Archdale Dr 02889
Arden Ct 02889
Ardway Ave 02889
Aries Ct 02886
Arizona Ave 02888
Arlee St 02889
Arlington Ave 02889
Armory Dr 02889
Armstrong Ave 02889
Arnolds Neck Dr 02886
Arrow Ave 02886
Arrowhead Way 02886
Arthur St 02888
Arthur W Devine Blvd 02886
Ash St 02888
Ashmont St 02886
Ashwood Cir 02886
Aspen Way 02886

Aspinet Dr 02888
Aster St 02888
Astral St 02888
Asylum Rd 02886
Atkins St 02886
S Atlantic Ave 02888
Audrey St 02886
Audubon Rd 02888
Aurora Dr 02889
Avon Ave 02889
Bagley Rd 02888
Bailey St 02886
Baker St 02886
Bakers Creek Rd 02886
Balcom Ave 02889
Bald Hill Rd 02886
Baldwin Rd 02886
Ballou Rd 02888
Balsam St 02888
Bancroft Ave 02889
Bangor St 02886
Bank St 02888
Barber Ave 02886
Barberry St 02889
Barden Ave 02888
Barker St 02888
Barnard Rd 02886
Baron Ct 02888
Barre Ct 02886
Barren Hill Dr 02886
Barstow Rd 02888
Bartlett Dr 02886
Barton Ave 02889
Bassett Ave 02889
Bates Ave 02886
Baxter St 02888
Bay Ave 02889
Bay Lawn Ave 02888
Bay Shore Blvd 02888
Bay State Ave 02888
Bay Vista Pl 02886
Bayberry Way 02889
Bayonne Ave 02889
Bayside Ave 02888
Baywood St 02886
Beach Ave 02889
Beach Park Ave 02886
Beacon Ave 02889
Beacon Ctr 02886
Beacon Hill Dr 02886
Beatrice Ave & Ter 02889
Beaver Ave 02889
Becker St 02886
Bedford Ave 02886
Beechcrest St 02888
Belfort Ave 02889
Bellair Ave 02886
Belle Ave 02889
Bellevue Ave 02889
Bellman Ave 02889
Bellows St 02888
Belt St 02889
Belvedere Dr 02889
Benbridge Ave 02888
Bend St 02889
Benedict Rd 02888
Benefit St 02886
Bennett St 02889
N Benson Ave 02888
Bentley Rd 02888
Berisont Ave 02889
Bethel St 02889
Betsey Williams Dr 02889
Bigelow Cir 02888
Bignall St 02888
Bingham St 02886
Birch St 02888
Birch Glen Ave 02886
Birchwood Ave 02889
Birkshire Dr 02886
Bishop Rd 02888
Black St 02888
Black Creek Ln 02888
Blackburn St 02889
Blackstone Ave 02889
Blade St 02886
Blake St 02889
Blanchard Ave 02888
Bleachery Ct 02886
Bloor St 02889
Blossom Ct 02886
Blue Hill Dr 02886
Blue Ridge Rd 02889
Bluff Ave 02889
Bly St 02888
Boccia Ct 02888
Bokar St 02886
Bolster Ave 02889
Bolton St 02888
Booth Ave 02888
Boulder View Dr 02886
Bourbon Pl 02888
Bourne St 02889
Bowen Briggs Ave 02886
Bowler Rd 02889
Bowman Dr 02889
Boylston St 02889
Bradley Ave 02889
Bragger St 02889
Branch Rd 02888
Brand Ave 02886
Brandon St 02888
Brayton Ave 02886
Breana Ln 02886
Bremen Ave 02889
Brendard Ave 02889
Brentwood Ave 02886
Brett Ct 02886
Brewster Dr 02889
Brian Dr 02886
Brianwood Ct 02886
Briarcliff Ave 02889
Bridal Ave 02886
Brier Ct 02886
Bright Water Dr 02886
Brighton Ave & Way 02886
Brightside Ave 02889
Brinton Ave 02889
Broad St 02888
Broadbent St 02886
Broadview Ave 02889
Brook St 02889
Brook Spring Dr 02889
Brookdale Ave 02889
Brookfield Blvd 02888
Brookline Dr 02886
Brookwood Rd 02889
Brow St 02889
Brownell St 02889
Brownlee Blvd 02886
Bruce Ln 02886
Brunswick Dr 02886
Brush Neck Ave 02889
Bryantville Ct 02886
Buckeye Rd 02889
Bucklin Ave 02888
Budlong Ave 02888
W Budlong Farm Rd 02886
Buena Vista Ave 02889
Bugbee Ave 02889
Bunker St 02886
Bunting Rd 02889
Burbank Dr 02886
Burgess Dr 02886
Burgoyne Dr 02889
Burnett Rd 02889
Burnside St 02886
Burr Ave 02889
Burt St 02886
Burton St 02886
Bush Ave 02889
Butler Ct 02888
Buttonwoods Ave 02886
Buttonwoods
Campground 02886
By The Way St 02888
Byfield St 02888
Byron Blvd 02888
Cactus St 02886
Cadora Ave 02886
Cady Ave 02889
Cahir Ct 02889
Calcott St 02889
Calderwood Dr 02886
Calef St 02886
Calhoun Ave 02886
California Ave 02888
Call St 02889
Calvert Ct 02888
Cambridge Ave 02889
Cameron Ct 02888
Camp St 02889
Candle Hill Ct 02886
Canfield Ave & Ct 02889
Canna St 02888
Canonchet Ave & Ln 02888
Cantibury Ct 02889
Capen St 02889
Capeway Rd 02886
Capron Farm Dr 02886
Carant Rd 02889
Carder Rd 02889
Cardinal St 02886
Carlisle St 02889
Carlton Ave 02889
Carnation Dr 02888
Carney Rd 02889
Carolyn St 02886
Carpenter St 02886
Carriage Dr 02886
Carriage Hill Dr 02886
Carrie Brown Ave 02888
Carrs Ln 02886
Carson Ave 02886
Cartney Dr 02888
Carvin Ct 02886
Case St 02886
Castle Way 02889
Castle Rocks Rd 02886
Catalpa Rd 02889
Cates Lndg 02886
Cathcart St 02889
Cathedral Rd 02889
Cavalcade Blvd 02889
Caverly St 02886
Cedar Bay Dr 02888
Cedar Pond Dr 02886
Cedar Swamp Rd 02889
Centennial St 02886
Center Ct 02886
Centerville Rd 02886
Central St 02886
Chambly Ave 02889
Channel Vw 02889
Channing St 02889
Chapel St 02889
Chapin Ave 02889
Chapmans Ave 02886
Charles St 02889
Charlestown Ave 02889
Chatham Cir 02886
Chatworth Ave 02886
Chelmsford Ave 02889
Cherry St 02888
Chester Ave 02889
Chesterfield Ave 02889
Chestnut St 02888
Chevy Ct 02886
Child Ln 02886
Chiswick Rd 02889
Christie Rd 02886
Church Ave 02889
Churubusco Dr 02889
Cindy Ln 02886
Cindy James Cir 02889
Circuit Dr 02889
Claflin Rd 02886
Clara Ave 02889
Claris St 02889
Clarke St 02886
Claypool Dr 02886
Clayton Rd 02886
Clearwater St 02886
Cleveland Ave 02888
Cliff Rd 02889
Clifford St 02889
Clifton Ave 02889
Clinton Ave 02886
Clorane St 02889
Cloverfield Ave 02889
Clyde Ave 02889
N & S Cobble Hill Rd 02886
Coburn St 02889
Cogonet Ave 02889
Coin St 02889
Colby St 02888
Coldbrook Rd 02888
Cole Ave 02886
Cole Farm Rd 02889
Coleman St 02889
Colesonian Dr 02888
Colfax St 02886
Colgate St 02888
College St 02886
College Hill Rd 02886
Collingwood Dr 02886
Colonial Ave 02886
Colony Ave 02889
Colorado Ave 02888
Columbia Ave 02888
Comma St 02889
Commerce Dr 02886
Commodore Ave 02886
Commonwealth Ave 02886
Community Rd 02889
Congress St 02889
Conn St 02888
Connecticut Ave 02888
Contour Rd 02886
Cooke Pl 02888
Cooper Ave 02886
Corin St 02886
Cornell Ave 02889
Corona Ct & St 02889
Coronado Rd 02886
Corwin St 02889
Cosett Rd 02886
Cottage St 02886
Cottage Grove Ave 02889
Count Fleet Ave 02889
Country Ln 02886
N Country Club Dr 02888
Country View Dr 02889
Cove Ave 02889
Covel Cir 02888
Covington Dr 02886
Cowesett Rd 02886
Cowesett Green Dr 02886
Coyle St 02886
Craig Rd 02886
Crandall Ct 02889
Crane St 02889
Crawford Ave 02889
Cread Pl 02888
Creamer Ave 02889
Creekwood Dr 02886
Crescendo Dr 02889
Crest Ave 02889
Creston Way 02886
Crestwood Rd 02886
Criterion Ave 02889
Crockett St 02889
Crocus St 02886
Cromwell Ave 02889
Cross St 02886
Cross Road Dr 02889
Crossing Ct 02888
Crossings Blvd 02886
Crowfield Dr 02889
Crown St 02889
Cruise St 02889
Crystal Dr 02889
Cumberland Rd 02886
Curry Pl 02889
Curtis St 02889
Cushing Rd 02888
Custer St 02889
Cypress St 02888
Daboll Ct 02889
Dahlia St 02889
Dallas Ave 02888
Dalton Cir 02889
Damon Ave 02889
Dan St 02889
Danforth St 02888
Darby St 02888
Darling St 02886
Darrow Dr 02886
Dartmouth Ave 02888
Davidson Rd 02886
Davis Cir 02886
Dawn Ln 02886
Dawson Ave 02888
Day St 02886
Dayton Ave 02889
Deacon Ave 02886
Dean Ct 02889
Debbie Ct 02888
Deborah Rd 02888
Dedham Rd 02888
Deerfield Dr 02886
Dees Cir 02889
Defiance Rd 02889
Deirdra Ct 02889
Delaine St 02886
Delaware Ave 02888
Delwood Rd 02889
Desmar Ct 02889
Desota Ave 02888
Devon Ct 02889
Dewey Ave 02886
Dexterdale Dr 02886
Diamond Hill Rd 02886
Diane Dr 02889
Dickens St 02886
Diploma St 02888
Dixie Ave 02889
Dodge St 02886
Dolores Ct 02889
Dongay Ave 02886
Doris Ave 02889
Dorrance St 02886
Dory Rd 02886
Douglas Rd 02886
Dover Rd 02888
Downing Ln 02886
Drake Rd 02888
Draper Ave 02889
Drift Rd 02889
Drowne St 02888
Druid Rd 02888
Drum Rock Ave 02886
Drumsna Ct 02886
Drybrook Rd 02889
Dryden Blvd 02886
Duchess St 02888
Dudley Ave 02889
Duluth Ave 02889
Dunbar Ct 02886
Duncan Cir & Rd 02886
Dundas Ave 02889
Dunmore Rd 02889
Dutch Ct 02888
Duxbury Ct 02886
Eagle Ave 02889
Earl St 02886
Earlham Way 02889
Early Ave 02889
East Ave 02886
Eastgate Dr 02886
Eastman St 02886
Easton Ave 02886
Echo Dr 02889
Economy Ave 02889
Edaville Ct 02886
Eden St 02889
Edgehill Rd 02889
Edgeknoll Ave 02888
Edgemere Ave 02889
Edgemont St 02888
Edgewater Dr 02886
Edison St 02889
Edman St 02886
Edmond Cir & Dr 02886
Edythe St 02889
Elberta St 02889
Eldridge Ave 02886
Eleanor St 02888
Electronics Dr 02886
Elgin St 02889
Elite Dr 02889
Elkland Rd 02886
Elks Ln 02886
Ellery St 02889
Elliot Ave 02889
Ellsworth St 02886
Elm St 02888
Elmbrook Dr 02889
Elmdale Ave 02889
Elmer Ave 02886
Elmhurst St 02889
Elmore St 02886
Elmwood Ave 02888
Elton Ave 02889
Elwin St 02889
Emerson Ave 02889
Emery Ct 02886
Emily Ln 02886
Emmons Ave 02888
Endicott Dr 02886
Enfield Rd 02886
Englewood Ln 02888
Ennis Pl 02888
Enterprise Rd 02886
Ernest Ave 02889
Errol St 02888
Esquire Ave 02889
Essex Rd 02888
Estelle Blvd 02889
Ethan St 02888
Ethel Ave 02886
Eton Ave 02889
Etta St 02889
Euclid Ave 02889
Eva St 02888
Everglade Ave 02886
Evergreen Ave 02888
Everill St 02889
Everleth Ave 02886
Ewing Ct 02889
Fair St 02888
Fairfax Dr 02888
Fairfield Ct 02889
Fairhaven Ave 02889
Fairview Rd 02888
Fairway Ln 02889
Falbourt St 02889
Falcon Ave 02889
Farmland Rd 02889
Farnum Rd 02888
Faroe Ct 02889
Fashion Dr 02886
Fatima Rd 02886
Felicia Ct 02889
Fern St 02889
Ferncliff Ave 02886
Ferrier Dr 02888
Fessenden St 02886
Fieldstone Rd 02886
Fieldview Dr 02886
Fillmore St 02888
Fir Glade Dr 02886
Fisher Ave 02886
Fishs Ln 02886
Flagg Ave 02886
Flamingo Dr 02886
Fleet Ave 02888
Fletcher St 02889
Florin St 02889
Floyd Rd 02888
Folly Lndg 02886
Forbes St 02886
Ford Ln 02888
Forrest St 02889
Foster St 02889
Fostmere Ct 02889
Founder Ave 02886
Fountain Ave 02886
Fowler Ave 02888
Fox Ridge Cres 02886
Foxcroft Ave 02889
Francis St 02889
Frawley St 02889
Frederick St 02888
Freeborne St 02889
Freeman St 02886
Fresno Rd 02886
Frey St 02886
Friar Tuck Rd 02886
Friendly Dr 02888
Friendship Ave 02889
Frontier Rd 02889
Frost Ave 02888
Fuller St 02889
Fullerton Rd 02886
Fulton St 02889
Gage St 02889
Gainsville Dr 02886
Galant Dr 02886
Gallway St 02889
Garden St 02888
Gardiner St 02888
Garfield Ave 02889
Gary St 02888
Gaspee Point Dr 02888
Gateway Ct 02889
Gauvin Dr 02886
Gavel Ave 02888
Gayton Ave 02889
Gazebo View Dr 02886
General Hawkins Dr 02888
George Cir & St 02888
George Arden Ave 02886
Gerald St 02886
Gertrude Ave 02886
Gibbons Ave 02889
Gilbane St 02886
Gilbert St 02886
Gillan Ave 02886
Gillmore St 02886
Gillooly Dr 02888
Ginger St 02886
Gladys Ct 02886
Glass St 02886
Glen Dr 02889
Glen Farm Ct 02889
Glen Meadows Ct 02886
Glenbrook Rd 02889
Glenco Rd 02889
Glendale Ave 02889
Glenham Ave 02886
Glenwood Dr 02889
Globe St 02886
Gloria Dr 02886
Gloucester St 02886
Goodrich Ave 02886
Gordon Ave 02889
Gorham Ave 02886
Gorton Holden Ter 02886
Gorton Lake Blvd 02886
Gould Ave 02888
Grace Ave 02889
Graham Ave 02889
Grand Ave 02889
Grand View Dr 02886
Granger Ct 02889
Granite St 02886
Grant St 02886
Grassmere St 02889
Gray St 02889
Graybar Rd 02888
Graymore Ave 02886
Grayson Ave 02888
Graystone St 02886
Great Hill Dr 02886
Great Oak Dr 02886
Greble St 02886
Greco Ln 02886
W Greeley Ave & Cir 02886
Green Acre Ave 02888
Green Meadow Dr 02886
Green River Ave 02889
Greene St 02886
Greenfield Ave 02886
Greening Ln 02889
Greenlawn St 02886
Greenpost Ln 02889
Greenwich Ave 02886
Greenwood Ave 02886
Grenore St 02888
Greylawn Ave 02889
Griffin Dr 02886

Grimshaw Pl 02889
Gristmill Rd 02889
Grotto Ave 02888
Grove Ave 02889
Grovedale St 02888
Groveland Ave 02886
Guild Ave 02889
Guilford Dr 02886
Gulf St 02886
Hackman Pl 02889
Hade Ct 02889
Hagerstown Rd 02886
Hague Rd 02889
Haley Rd 02889
Halifax Dr 02886
Hallene Rd
- 1-110 02888
- 111-299 02886

Hallmark Dr 02886
Hallworth Dr 02886
Halsey Dr 02889
Hamilton Ave 02886
Hamlin Ave 02889
Hampton Ave 02889
Hannah Dr 02888
Hanover St 02886
Harborview Dr 02889
Hardig Rd 02886
Harding Ave 02888
Hardwick St 02889
Hargraves St 02889
Harkness St 02888
Harmony Ct 02889
Harold St 02888
Harrington Ave 02888
Harris Ave 02889
Harrison Ave 02888
Harrop Ave 02886
Hart Ave 02889
Hartford Pl 02888
Harvard Ave 02889
Harvest Rd 02888
Hasbrouck Ave 02888
Haswill St 02889
Haven St 02889
Haverford Rd 02886
Haverhill Ave 02886
Hawksley Ave 02889
Hawley Ave 02889
Hawser St 02889
Hawthorne Ave 02886
Hayes St 02886
Hayward Rd 02888
Hazard Ave 02889
Health Ln 02886
Heath Ave 02888
Hedgerow Dr 02886
Hedley Dr 02889
Heights Ave 02889
Helen Ave 02886
Hemlock Ave 02886
Hendricken Ct 02889
Henry St 02889
Henzie St 02886
Herff Jones Way 02888
Hermit Dr 02889
Hess Ave 02889
Hewett St 02889
Hiawatha St 02888
Hibiscus Ln 02886
High St 02886
Highland Ave 02886
Higney Ave 02889
Hilary St 02886
Hilburt St 02886
Hillard Ave 02889
Hillcrest Ave 02889
Hillside Dr 02889
Hilton Rd 02889
Hobbs Rd 02889
Holden St 02889
Holiday Ave 02888
Hollis Ave 02886
Hollow Ct 02886
Hollywood Ave 02888
Holmes Rd 02888

Holt St 02889
Holyoke Ave 02889
Home Ave 02889
Home Loan Plz 02886
Homeland Ave 02886
Homestead Ave 02889
Honeysuckle Rd 02888
Hope Ave 02889
Hornet Rd 02886
Horse Neck Rd 02889
Houston Dr 02886
Howard Ave 02889
Howie Ave 02888
Howland Ave 02888
Hoxsie Ave 02889
Hoyle Ave 02888
Hoyt St 02886
Huckleberry Ct 02888
Hudson Ln 02886
Hull St 02888
Humes Ave 02886
Hunt Ave 02886
Hunter St 02889
Hurley Ave 02889
Huron St 02889
Hutchinson St 02886
Idaho Ave 02888
Illinois Ave 02888
Imera Ave 02886
Imperial Dr 02886
Independence Dr 02888
Indian Hill Rd 02886
Industrial Ave 02888
Inez Ave 02886
Ingalls St 02889
Ingersoll Ave 02886
Inman Ave 02886
International Way 02886
Irene St 02886
Irma Ave 02886
Irondale St 02886
Ironwood Ct 02886
Iroquois Dr 02888
Irving Rd 02888
Island St 02888
Island View Dr 02886
Ithica St 02889
Ivan Ave 02889
Jackson St 02888
Jacqueline Ct 02889
Jambray Ave 02886
James St 02886
Janet Dr 02886
Janice Rd 02886
Jefferson Blvd
- 1-349 02888
- 350-1399 02886

Jefferson St 02888
Jefferson Park Rd 02888
Jennie Ln 02889
Jennison Rd 02889
Jeri Lynn Cir 02886
Jerome Ave 02889
Jerry St 02886
Jewett St 02886
Jillian Ct 02889
Joanna Dr 02886
Joelle Ct 02889
John St 02889
Johnson Ave 02886
Jonathan Ct 02888
Joseph Ct 02889
Joshua Ct 02889
Joyce Glen St 02886
Judge St 02886
Judith Ave 02889
Julian Rd 02889
Juliet St 02886
Junction St 02889
June Ave 02889
Juniper Ave 02886
Kalmer Rd 02886
Kane Ave 02889
Kansas Ave 02888
Karen Dr 02886
Katelyn Ct 02886

Katherine Ct 02889
Kay St 02888
Kearns Ave 02888
Keeley Ave 02886
Keller Ave 02889
Kendall Ln 02888
Kennedy Dr 02889
Kenneth Ave 02889
Kent Ave 02886
Kentucky Ave 02888
Kenway Ave 02889
Kenwood St 02889
Kenyon Ave 02886
Kernick St 02886
Kerri Lyn Rd 02889
Kettle St 02886
Keystone Dr 02889
Killdeer Rd 02888
Killey Ave 02889
Kilvert St 02886
King St 02886
King Philip Cir 02888
Kingston St 02888
Kirby Ave 02889
Kiwanee Rd 02888
Knight St 02886
Knowles Dr 02888
Kristen Ct 02888
La Salle Dr 02886
Lachance Ave 02889
Ladderlook Rd 02886
Lafayette Rd 02889
Lake St 02886
Lake Shore Dr 02889
Lakecrest Cir & Dr 02889
Lakeknole Rd 02889
Lakeside Ave 02888
Lakewood Ave 02888
Lambert Lind Hwy 02886
Lancaster Ave 02886
Landmark Rd 02886
Landon Rd 02888
Lane E 02888
Lane 1 02888
Lane 2 02888
Lane 3 02888
Lane 4 02888
Lane 5 02888
Lane 6 02888
Lane 7 02888
Lane 8 02888
Lane 9 02888
Lane G 02888
Langley St 02889
Lansdowne Rd 02888
Lansing Ave 02888
Lantern Ln 02886
Larchmont Rd 02886
Larchwood Dr 02886
Largo Rd 02886
Larkin Ave 02886
Larkspur Rd 02886
Larochelle Ave 02889
Larson Dr 02886
Lauderdale Blvd 02886
Laura St 02888
Lauren Ct 02889
Lavan St 02888
Law St 02888
Lawn Ave 02888
Lawrence Ave 02888
Lazywood Ln 02886
Ledgemont Dr 02886
Lee Ave 02889
Leigh St 02889
Leland Ave 02889
Lemac St 02889
Leon E Whipple Rd 02889
Leonard Ave 02886
Lerner St 02886
Leroy Ave 02889
Leslie Rd 02886
Levesque St 02886
Lewis St 02886
Lewiston St 02889
Lighthouse Ln 02889

Lilac St 02889
Lillian Ct 02886
Lima St 02889
Limestone St 02889
Linbrook Dr 02889
Lincoln Ave 02888
Linda Cir 02886
Lindell St 02888
Lindy Ave 02889
Link St 02886
Lippitt Ave 02889
Lisa Ln 02889
Lisa Marie Cir 02886
Lister St 02886
Little Ln 02886
Liverpool St 02886
Lloyd Ave 02889
Lockhart Ave 02886
Lockhaven Rd 02889
Lockwood St 02889
Locust Ave 02886
Lodi Ct 02886
Logan St 02889
Long St 02886
Long View Dr 02886
Longmeadow Ave 02889
Longwood Ave 02888
Lori Ann Way 02886
Loring Rd 02889
Lorna Ave 02886
Louisiana Ave 02888
Love Ln 02886
Loveday St 02889
Lovell Ave 02889
Lowe Ave 02889
Lucile St 02886
Lufkin Ct 02888
Luther Ave 02886
Lyall Ave 02889
Lydick Ave 02888
Lyman Ave 02888
Lyndale Ave 02889
Lyndon Ave 02889
Macarthur Dr 02889
Macera Cir 02886
Mach Dr 02886
Madison St 02888
Magnolia St 02889
Main Ave 02886
Main Channel 02889
Majestic Ave 02888
Major Potter Rd 02886
Malbone St 02888
Manchester St 02888
Mann St 02888
Manning St 02889
Manolla Ave 02888
Manomet Ct 02886
Manor Dr 02888
Manse Ct 02888
Manson Ave 02888
Maple St 02888
Maplehurst Ave 02889
Maplewood Ave 02888
Marblehead St 02889
Marigold Dr 02889
Marina View Ter 02889
Marine Ave 02888
Marjorie Ln 02886
Mark Allen Dr 02886
Marla Ct 02886
Marlow Rd 02889
Marple St 02888
Marquette Dr 02888
Mars Ave 02889
Marshall Ave 02889
Martine St 02889
Martingale Dr 02886
Marvin St 02886
Mary Beth Dr 02886
Maryland Ave 02888
Mashuena Dr 02886
Massachusetts Ave 02888
Massasoit Dr 02886
Masthead Dr 02886
Matteson Ave 02886

Mawney Ave 02886
May Ave 02889
Mayfair Rd 02888
Mayflower Ave 02889
Mayor Ln 02889
Maywood Ave 02889
Mcgarry Ave 02889
Mckay Ct 02889
Mckinley St 02886
Meader St 02888
Meadow St 02886
Meadow View Ave 02889
Meadowbrook Ave 02889
Meaghan Brooke Ln 02888
Medford St 02889
Medway Ave 02889
Meetinghouse Ln 02886
Melbourn Rd 02886
Mellon Rd 02889
Melrose Ave 02889
Meridan St 02889
Merle St 02889
Merrymount Dr 02888
Messenger Dr 02888
Messer St 02886
Metcalf St 02888
Metro Center Blvd 02886
Metropolitan Dr 02886
Meyers Ct 02889
Mia Ct 02886
Miantonomo Dr 02888
Michael Dr 02889
Michelle Cir 02886
Michigan Ave 02888
Middlefield Dr 02889
Midgely Ave 02886
Midget Ave 02886
Midway Dr 02886
Mill Cove Rd 02889
Mill Wheel Rd 02886
Millard Ave 02889
Miller Ave 02889
Milton Rd 02888
Miner St 02886
Minnesota Ave 02888
Missouri Dr 02886
Mitchell Ct 02889
Moccasin Dr 02889
Model Ave 02889
Modena Dr 02886
Mohawk Ave 02889
Monk Rd 02889
Monroe St 02888
Montana Ave 02888
Montcalm Rd 02889
Montebello Rd 02886
Monterey Rd 02889
Montgomery St 02886
Moore St 02889
Morgan Ave 02889
Morning Glory Dr 02889
Morris St 02889
Morse Ave 02886
Morton Dr 02888
Moulton Cir 02886
Mullen Rd 02888
Murray St 02886
Music Ln 02886
Myrtle Ave 02889
Mystic Dr 02889
Nakomis Dr 02886
Namquid Dr 02888
Nanci Karen Dr 02886
Naples Ave 02888
Narragansett Pkwy 02888
Narragansett Bay Ave 02889
Nash Ave 02889
Natalie Ln 02886
Nathan Rd 02886
W Natick Ave & Rd 02886
Naughton Ave 02886
Nausauket Rd 02886
Naushon Ave 02888
Negansett Ave 02888
Nelson St 02888
New Britain Dr 02889

New England Way 02886
New London Ave 02886
New York Ave 02888
Newfield Ave 02888
Newton Ave 02889
Nichol Ave 02886
Nicolas Ln 02886
Nightingale Ave 02889
Ninigret St 02889
Nolbeth Dr 02888
Norfolk Rd 02886
Normandy Dr 02886
North St 02886
Northampton St 02888
Northbridge Ave 02886
Northup St 02889
Norwood Ave 02888
Novelty Rd 02889
Noyes St 02886
Oak St 02886
Oak Hill Ave 02886
Oak Park Rd 02886
Oak Tree Ave 02886
Oakdale St 02888
Oakhurst Ave 02889
Oakland Ave 02889
Oakland Beach Ave 02889
Oakridge Ct 02886
Oakside St 02889
Obadiah Ave 02889
Oberlin Dr 02886
Observatory Rd 02888
Ocean Ave 02889
Octave St 02886
Ode Ct 02886
Odonnell Ave 02886
Ogden Ave 02889
Ohio Ave 02888
Okeefe Ln 02888
Okinawa Ave 02889
Old Homestead Rd 02889
Old Lyme Dr 02886
Old Mill Blvd 02889
Old Oak Dr 02886
Old Warwick Ave 02889
Oldham St 02886
Oliver St 02888
Olson Ct 02888
Omaha Blvd 02889
Oniska St 02889
Onset St 02889
Ontario Ave 02888
Opper Ave 02889
Orchard Ave 02886
Oregon Ave 02888
Orient St 02886
Orleans Ct 02886
Orly Dr 02889
Orms St 02889
Ormsby Ave 02886
Orrin St 02889
Osage Dr 02888
Osborne St 02886
Osceola Ave 02888
Osprey Ct 02889
Otis St 02889
Ottawa Ave 02889
Outlet Ave 02886
Overbrook Ave 02889
Overhead Way 02888
Overton St 02888
Owens St 02889
Oxford Ave 02889
Pace Blvd 02886
Packard Ave 02886
Paddock Dr 02886
Page St 02889
Paine St 02889
Palace Ave 02886
Palm Blvd N 02888
Palmer Ave 02889
Pamela Cir 02886
Panto Rd 02886
Parade Rd 02886
Park Ave 02889
Park View Ave 02888

Parkhurst Rd 02889
Parkside Dr 02888
Parkway Cir & Dr 02886
Parsonage Dr 02889
Partition St 02888
Pasadena Ct 02888
Pasco Cir 02886
Passeonquis Dr 02888
Paterson Ave 02886
Patience Ct 02888
Patricia Ct 02889
Patrick Way 02886
Patriot Ct 02888
Paul Ave 02886
Pavilion Ave 02888
Pawtuxet Ave 02888
Payton Ave 02889
Peabody Dr 02889
Peace St 02888
Peaceful Ln 02886
Peacock Rd 02886
Peadinso Ave 02888
Pearl Ave 02889
N Pearson Dr 02888
Pecan St 02888
Peck Ln 02888
Peeptoad Rd 02888
Pell Ave 02888
Pembroke Ave 02889
Pender Ave 02889
Pender John Ct 02886
Pennsylvania Ave 02888
Pensacola St 02888
Pequot Ave 02889
Pera St 02886
Perkins St 02886
Perry Ave 02888
Petansett Ct 02888
Peter St 02886
Pettaconsett Ave 02888
Pettigrew Dr 02886
Pettis Dr 02889
Pevear Ave 02886
Pheasant Ave 02886
Phillips Ave 02888
Pierce Ave 02888
Pilgrim Cir, Dr & Pkwy 02888
Pilla Dr 02886
Pine St 02888
Pine Edge Ct 02889
Pinegrove Ave 02889
Pinehurst Ave 02889
Pinnery Ave 02886
Pioneer Ave 02888
Pitman Rd 02886
Place Ave 02888
Plain St 02886
Plan Way 02886
Plantation St 02886
Pleasant St 02886
Pleasant View Rd 02888
Plenty St 02889
Pocahontas Dr 02888
Pocasset Ct 02886
Pocono Dr 02888
Point Ave 02888
Polk Rd 02889
Pond View Dr 02886
W Pontiac St 02886
Poplar Ave 02889
Poppy Pl 02886
Port Cir 02889
Portsmouth Ave 02888
Posnegansett Ave 02888
Possner Ave 02889
Post Rd
- 1-1776 02888
- 1777-3204 02886
- 3205-3205 02887
- 3206-4100 02886
- 3207-4099 02886

Potomac Rd 02888
Potters Ave 02886
Powell St 02888
Power Ave 02888
Powhatan St 02889

Pratt Cir 02888
Preston Dr 02886
Prince St 02888
• Princeton Ave 02889
Prior St 02889
Priscilla Ave 02889
Proctor Ave 02888
Progress St 02889
Promenade Ave 02886
Prospect St 02886
Providence St 02886
Prudence Ct 02888
Puritan Dr 02888
Putnam St 02888
Quaid Ln 02886
Quail Ridge Ln 02886
Quaker Ln 02886
Quarry Rd 02889
Quimby St 02889
Quinlan Ct 02886
Quinton St 02888
Quisset Ct 02886
Quonset Ave 02889
Railroad Row 02886
Rainbow Ct 02889
Ralston St 02888
Ramblewood Dr 02889
Rancocos Dr 02888
Rand St 02889
Randall Ave 02889
Range Rd 02889
Raymond St 02888
Red Chimney Dr 02886
Red Oak Cir 02886
Reed St 02886
Reeland Ave 02889
Regent Rd 02886
Relph St 02888
Remington St 02888
Remy Cir 02886
Reynolds Ave 02889
Rhode Island Ave 02889
Rice St 02886
Richfield St 02886
Richmond Dr 02888
Ridge Rd 02889
Ridgeway Ave 02889
Ring Ave 02888
Rip Van Winkle Cir 02886
Rita St 02889
River St 02888
River Vue Ave 02889
Riverdale Ct 02886
Riverside Ave 02889
Robin Hill Rd 02886
Robins Way 02889
Rock Ave 02889
Rocky Beach Rd 02889
Rocky Point Ave 02889
Rodney Rd 02889
Roger Williams Cir 02888
Rogers Rd 02888
Rollins Rd 02889
Rome Ave 02886
Ronaele Dr 02889
Roosevelt St 02888
Rosalind Ct 02886
Rose St 02888
Rosegarden St 02888
Roseland Ave 02888
Rosemere Ave 02889
Rosewood Ave 02888
Rossi St 02886
Round Hill Ct 02886
Rowe Ave 02889
Royal Ave 02889
Royland Rd 02888
Ruby St 02889
Rustic Way 02886
Rutherford Ave & Ct 02886
Rutland St 02888
Ryan Ave 02889
Sabin St 02888
Sable St 02889
Sachem Ave 02888
Sackett St 02886

Sagamore St 02889
Sage Dr 02886
Saint Claire Ave 02889
Saint George Ct 02888
Salisbury St 02889
Salix St 02889
Samuel Gorton Ave 02889
Sand Pond Rd 02888
Sandlewood Ave 02886
Sandro Cir & Dr 02886
Sandy Ln 02889
Sandy Brook Ct 02886
Santa Maria Dr 02886
Sarah Ln 02889
Sarah Teft Dr 02889
Saratoga Rd 02886
Sargent St 02888
Savoy St 02889
Saxony Dr 02886
Sayles Ave 02889
Scandia Ave 02888
Scarsdale Rd 02886
Scenic Dr 02886
School St 02889
Scolly St 02889
Scott Ave 02888
Scranton Ave 02888
Sea View Dr 02889
Seabreeze Ln & Ter 02886
Seacrest Ln 02889
Searle St 02889
Seaside Ct 02889
Sefton Ave 02889
Seminole St 02889
Senator St 02888
Seneca St 02886
Serenity Ct 02888
Service Ave 02886
Sevilla Ave 02889
Shadbush Rd 02888
Shadow Brook Dr 02886
Shady Oak Rd 02886
Shalom Dr 02886
Shamrock Dr 02886
Shand Ave 02889
Shannon Dr 02889
Sharon St 02886
Shattock Ave 02886
Shawomet Ave 02889
Sheffield St 02889
Sheldon Ave 02888
Shenandoah Rd 02886
Sheppard Dr 02886
Sherwood Ave 02888
Ship St 02889
Shippee Ave 02886
Shippen Ave 02888
Shirley St 02888
Shore Ave 02889
S Shore Ave 02889
W Shore Rd
1-2784 02889
2785-2837 02886
2786-2838 02889
2839-3699 02886
N Shore St 02889
Short St 02889
Silby St 02889
Silent Dr 02886
Silver St 02889
Silver Birch Rd 02888
Silver Lake Ave 02886
Slater Ave 02889
Sleepy Hollow Farm Rd 02886
Slocum St 02888
Smile Ct 02889
Smith Ct & St 02886
Snow Rd 02888
Social Dr 02889
Solar Dr 02886
Sophia Dr 02886
Soule St 02886
Spadina Ave 02889
Sparrow Ln 02889
Spectacle Ave 02888

Speer St 02888
Spencer Hill Ct 02886
Spinnaker Ln 02886
Spofford Ave 02888
Spooner Ave 02889
Sprague Ave 02889
Spring Garden St 02888
Spring Green Rd 02888
Spring Grove Ave 02889
Spruce St 02889
Spywood Ave 02888
Squantum Dr 02888
Stafford St 02886
Standish Ave 02889
Stanfield St 02889
Stanford St 02888
Stanmore Rd 02889
Staples Ave 02886
Star St 02888
State St 02889
State Park Ave 02886
Station St 02886
Steele Ave 02889
Step Cir 02889
Stephanie Ct 02889
Stephens Ave 02886
Sterling Ave 02889
Stetson St 02889
Stewart St 02889
Stillwater Dr 02889
Stiness Dr 02886
Stoddard Pl 02888
Stokes St 02889
Stone Ave 02889
Stonedale Rd 02889
Strand Ave 02889
Stratford Ln 02886
Strawberry Field Rd 02886
Stubtoe Dr 02886
Studley Ave 02889
Sturbridge Dr 02886
Suburban Pkwy 02889
Sudbury St 02886
Sue St 02886
Summerland Rd 02886
Summit St 02888
Sumner Ave 02888
Sundance St 02886
Sunny Cove Dr 02889
Sunny View Ct 02886
Sunnyside Dr 02889
Sunset Ave 02889
Superior St 02886
Surf Ave 02889
Sutter Ave 02886
Sutton Ave 02889
Sweet St 02889
Sweet Meadow Dr 02889
Sweetbriar Ct 02888
Sweetfern Rd 02888
Sweetwater St 02889
Sycamore Ave 02886
Sykes St 02886
Sylvan Pl 02888
Sylvia Dr 02886
Symonds Ave 02889
Taft Ave 02886
Talcott Ave 02889
Tampa Ave 02889
Tanner Ave 02886
Taplow St 02889
Tarawa Dr 02886
Tarleton St 02889
Taylor Ln 02886
Tea House Ln 02889
Teakwood Dr 02886
Tell St 02889
Temple Ave 02888
Tennessee Ave 02888
Tennyson Rd 02888
Terrace Ave 02889
Tex Ct 02886
Texas Ave 02889
Thames Ave 02886
Thatch Ct 02889
Thayer Pl 02888

Theodore Ave 02886
Thomas St 02886
Thor Pl 02888
Thrush Rd 02886
Thurber St 02886
Thurman St 02886
Ticonderoga Dr 02889
Tidewater Dr 02889
Tiernan Ave 02886
Tiffany Ave 02889
Tilden Ave 02889
Tillinghast Ave 02886
Timberline Rd 02886
Tingley St 02886
Titus Ln 02888
Tivoli Ct 02886
Tobey Ct 02886
Todd St 02888
Toledo Ave 02888
Toll Gate Rd 02886
Tomahawk Ct 02886
Torrington Cir & Dr 02889
Tourtelot Ave 02889
Transit St 02889
Trask St 02888
Tremont St 02888
Trent Ave 02889
Trinity St 02886
Tropical Ct 02889
Troy Ave 02889
Tucker St 02888
Tunis Rd 02889
Turner St 02886
Turtle Creek Dr 02886
Twin Oak Dr 02889
Tyler St 02889
Uncas St 02889
Underwood Ave 02888
Union Ave 02889
Unity Ct 02889
Universal Blvd 02886
Uphill Ave 02886
Urban Ave 02888
Utica Ct & Dr 02886
Vale St 02889
Valentine Cir 02886
Valley Ave 02886
Van Buren St 02888
Van Zandt Ave 02889
Vancouver Ave 02888
Vanderbilt Rd 02886
Vanstone Ave 02889
Vaughn Ave 02886
Vega Dr 02889
Venturi Ave 02888
Vera St 02886
Verdant Ln 02886
Vermont Ave 02888
Verndale St 02889
Vernon St 02889
Veterans Memorial Dr 02886
Viceroy Rd 02886
Vickery St 02888
Victory St 02889
View Ave 02886
E View St 02888
W View St 02889
Viewesta Ct & Rd 02886
Villa Ave 02886
Village Cir 02888
Vineyard Rd 02889
Viscount Rd 02889
Vista Rd 02888
Vistrive Ave 02886
Vohlander St 02889
Waco Ct & Rd 02889
Wade St 02889
Wadsworth St 02889
Waite St 02886
Waldo Rd 02889
Waldron Ave 02888
Walker Rd 02889
Wallace Ave 02886
Walnut St 02889
Walnut Glen Dr 02886
Walter St 02889

Walton Ave 02886
Wampum Dr 02886
Warner Ave 02889
Warner Brook Dr 02889
Warren Ave 02889
Warwick Ave
316-1499 02888
1500-2999 02889
Warwick Industrial Dr 02886
Warwick Lake Ave 02889
Warwick Neck Ave 02889
Washington St 02888
Water St 02886
Waterfront Dr 02889
Waterman Ave 02889
Waterman St 02888
Waterview Ave 02889
Watson St 02889
Wauregan Dr 02888
Waverly St 02889
Way Ave 02888
Waycross Dr 02888
Wayne St 02889
Webb Ave 02889
Weber Ave 02886
Webster St 02889
Weetamoe Dr 02888
Weir Rd 02886
Welch Rd 02889
Welfare Ave 02888
Wellington Ave 02886
Wells Ave 02889
Wellspring Dr 02886
Wendell Rd 02888
Wentworth Ave 02889
Wesleyan Ave 02886
West St 02886
Westbrook Rd 02886
Westchester Way 02886
Westfield Rd 02888
Westford Ave 02889
Westonia Ln 02889
Westwood Dr 02889
Wethersfield Dr 02886
Whalen Ave 02889
Wharf Rd 02889
Wheaton Ave 02888
Wheeler St 02889
Whipple Ave 02889
Whippoorwill Rd 02888
Whispering Ln 02886
White Ave 02889
White Acorn Cir 02886
White Rock Rd 02889
Whitehall Dr 02886
Whitford St
1-153 02889
154-299 02886
Whitin Ave 02888
Wicks Ct 02886
Wilbur Ave 02889
Wilclar St 02886
Wilcox St 02889
Wild Flower Cir 02889
Wilde Field Dr 02889
Wildrose Ct 02888
Wildwood Ave 02889
Willard St 02889
Williamsburg Cir & Dr 02886
Willing Ave 02888
Williston Rd 02889
Willow Glen Cir 02889
Wilmar St 02886
Wilson Ave 02889
Wilton St 02889
Winchell Rd 02889
Windermere Way 02886
Windward Cir 02889
Wingate Ave & Ct 02888
Winifred Ave 02889
Winman Ct 02886
N Winnisquam Dr 02886
Winslow Ave 02886
Winston Ave & Ct 02886
Winter Ave 02889
Winthrop Rd 02888

Woburn Ave 02888
Woguagonet Ave 02889
Wood St 02889
Woodbine Ave 02886
Woodbury St 02889
Woodcrest Rd 02889
Woodfield Dr 02886
Woodland Rd 02889
Woodridge Dr 02889
Woodstock Dr 02889
Woodwind Ct 02886
Worth St 02889
Worthington Rd 02889
Wriston Ave 02888
Wuddall Ave 02889
Wyoming Ave 02888
Xavier Ct 02888
Yale Ave 02888
Yates Ave 02889
Yellowstone Ave 02888
Young Ave 02889
Young Orchard Ave 02888
Yucatan Dr 02889
Zachariah Pl 02889
Zinnia St 02886
Zircon St 02886

NUMBERED STREETS

2nd Ave 02888
2nd Point Rd 02889
3rd Ave 02888
4th Ave 02888
5th Ave 02888
6th Ave 02888
8th Ave 02886
9th Ave 02886
10th Ave 02886
11th Ave 02886
12th Ave 02886
13th Ave 02886
14th Ave 02886
15th Ave 02886

South Carolina

People QuickFacts	South Carolina	USA
Population, 2013 estimate	4,774,839	316,128,839
Population, 2010 (April 1) estimates base	4,625,360	308,747,716
Population, percent change, April 1, 2010 to July 1, 2013	3.2%	2.4%
Population, 2010	4,625,364	308,745,538
Persons under 5 years, percent, 2013	6.1%	6.3%
Persons under 18 years, percent, 2013	22.6%	23.3%
Persons 65 years and over, percent, 2013	15.2%	14.1%
Female persons, percent, 2013	51.3%	50.8%
White alone, percent, 2013 (a)	68.3%	77.7%
Black or African American alone, percent, 2013 (a)	27.9%	13.2%
American Indian and Alaska Native alone, percent, 2013 (a)	0.5%	1.2%
Asian alone, percent, 2013 (a)	1.5%	5.3%
Native Hawaiian and Other Pacific Islander alone, percent, 2013 (a)	0.1%	0.2%
Two or More Races, percent, 2013	1.7%	2.4%
Hispanic or Latino, percent, 2013 (b)	5.3%	17.1%
White alone, not Hispanic or Latino, percent, 2013	63.9%	62.6%
Living in same house 1 year & over, percent, 2008-2012	84.7%	84.8%
Foreign born persons, percent, 2008-2012	4.8%	12.9%
Language other than English spoken at home, pct age 5+, 2008-2012	6.8%	20.5%
High school graduate or higher, percent of persons age 25+, 2008-2012	84.0%	85.7%
Bachelor's degree or higher, percent of persons age 25+, 2008-2012	24.6%	28.5%
Veterans, 2008-2012	396,873	21,853,912
Mean travel time to work (minutes), workers age 16+, 2008-2012	23.4	25.4
Housing units, 2013	2,158,652	132,802,859
Homeownership rate, 2008-2012	69.5%	65.5%
Housing units in multi-unit structures, percent, 2008-2012	17.7%	25.9%
Median value of owner-occupied housing units, 2008-2012	$137,400	$181,400
Households, 2008-2012	1,768,255	115,226,802
Persons per household, 2008-2012	2.54	2.61
Per capita money income in past 12 months (2012 dollars), 2008-2012	$23,906	$28,051
Median household income, 2008-2012	$44,623	$53,046
Persons below poverty level, percent, 2008-2012	17.6%	14.9%

Business QuickFacts	South Carolina	USA
Private nonfarm establishments, 2012	101,228	7,431,808
Private nonfarm employment, 2012	1,548,516	115,938,468
Private nonfarm employment, percent change, 2011-2012	1.8%	2.2%
Nonemployer establishments, 2012	304,327	22,735,915
Total number of firms, 2007	360,397	27,092,908
Black-owned firms, percent, 2007	12.1%	7.1%
American Indian- and Alaska Native-owned firms, percent, 2007	0.5%	0.9%
Asian-owned firms, percent, 2007	1.8%	5.7%
Native Hawaiian and Other Pacific Islander-owned firms, percent, 2007	0.1%	0.1%
Hispanic-owned firms, percent, 2007	1.7%	8.3%
Women-owned firms, percent, 2007	27.6%	28.8%
Manufacturers shipments, 2007 ($1000)	93,977,455	5,319,456,312
Merchant wholesaler sales, 2007 ($1000)	40,498,047	4,174,286,516
Retail sales, 2007 ($1000)	54,298,410	3,917,663,456
Retail sales per capita, 2007	$12,273	$12,990
Accommodation and food services sales, 2007 ($1000)	8,383,463	613,795,732
Building permits, 2012	18,708	829,658

Geography QuickFacts	South Carolina	USA
Land area in square miles, 2010	30,060.70	3,531,905.43
Persons per square mile, 2010	153.9	87.4
FIPS Code	45	

(a) Includes persons reporting only one race.
(b) Hispanics may be of any race, so also are included in applicable race categories.
FN: Footnote on this item for this area in place of data
NA: Not available
D: Suppressed to avoid disclosure of confidential information
X: Not applicable
S: Suppressed; does not meet publication standards
Z: Value greater than zero but less than half unit of measure shown
F: Fewer than 100 firms
Source: US Census Bureau State & County QuickFacts

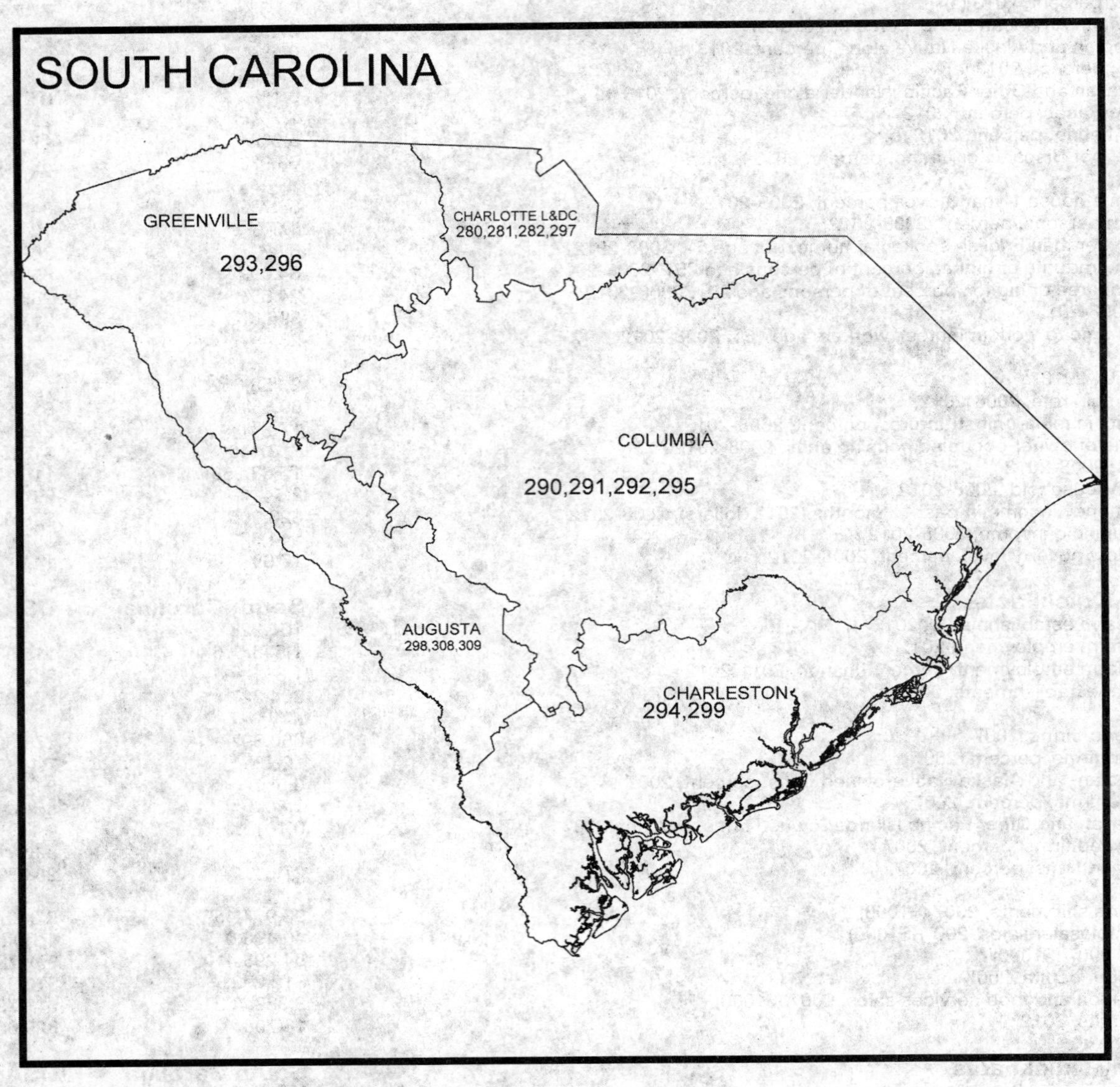

SOUTH CAROLINA
GREENVILLE
293,296
CHARLOTTE L&DC
280,281,282,297
COLUMBIA
290,291,292,295
AUGUSTA
298,308,309
CHARLESTON
294,299

South Carolina

(Abbreviation: SC)

Post Office, County — ZIP Code

Places with more than one ZIP code are listed in capital letters, See pages indicated.

Abbeville, Abbeville 29620
Adams Run, Charleston 29426
AIKEN, Aiken
(See Page 3344)
Alcolu, Clarendon 29001
Allendale, Allendale 29810
Alvin, Berkeley 29479
ANDERSON, Anderson
(See Page 3347)
Andrews, Georgetown 29510
Arcadia, Spartanburg 29320
Atlantic Beach, Horry 29582
Awendaw, Charleston 29429
Aynor, Horry 29511
Aynor, Horry 29544
Ballentine, Richland 29002
Bamberg, Bamberg 29003
Barnwell, Barnwell 29812
Batesburg, Lexington 29006
Batesburg-Leesville,
Lexington 29006
Bath, Aiken 29816
BEAUFORT, Beaufort
(See Page 3352)
Beech Island, Aiken 29841
Beech Island, Aiken 29842
Belton, Anderson 29627
Belvedere, Aiken 29841
Bennettsville, Marlboro 29512
Bethera, Berkeley 29430
Bethune, Kershaw 29009
Bishopville, Lee 29010
Blacksburg, Cherokee 29702
Blackstock, Chester 29014
Blackville, Barnwell 29817
Blair, Fairfield 29015
Blenheim, Marlboro 29516
Bluffton, Beaufort 29909
Bluffton, Beaufort 29910
Blythewood, Richland 29016
Boiling Springs,
Spartanburg 29316
Bonneau, Berkeley 29431
Borden, Sumter 29128
Bowling Green, York 29703
Bowman, Orangeburg 29018
Bradley, Greenwood 29819
Branchville, Orangeburg 29432
Brittons Neck, Marion 29546
Brunson, Hampton 29911
Bucksport, Horry 29527
Buffalo, Union 29321
Cades, Williamsburg 29518
Cainhoy, Berkeley 29492
Calhoun Falls, Abbeville 29628
CAMDEN, Kershaw
(See Page 3354)
Cameron, Calhoun 29030
Campobello, Spartanburg 29322
Canadys, Colleton 29433
Carlisle, Union 29031
Carnes Crossroads,
Dorchester 29483
Cassatt, Kershaw 29032
Catawba, York 29704
Cateechee, Pickens 29667
Cayce, Lexington 29033
Cayce, Lexington 29171
Centenary, Marion 29519
Central, Pickens 29630
Chapin, Lexington 29036
Chappells, Newberry 29037
CHARLESTON, Charleston
(See Page 3355)
Charleston Afb, Charleston ... 29404
Cheraw, Chesterfield 29520
Cherokee Falls, Cherokee 29702
Cherry Grove Beach, Horry .. 29582
Chesnee, Spartanburg 29323
Chester, Chester 29706
Chesterfield, Chesterfield 29709
Clarks Hill, Mccormick 29821
Clearwater, Aiken 29822
Clearwater, Aiken 29841
CLEMSON, Pickens
(See Page 3360)
Cleveland, Greenville 29635
Clifton, Spartanburg 29324
Clinton, Laurens 29325
Clio, Marlboro 29525
Clover, York 29710
COLUMBIA, Richland
(See Page 3361)
Conestee, Greenville 29636
Converse, Spartanburg 29329
CONWAY, Horry
(See Page 3369)
Coosawhatchie, Jasper 29912
Coosawhatchie, Jasper 29936
Cope, Orangeburg 29038
Cordesville, Berkeley 29434
Cordova, Orangeburg 29039
Cottageville, Colleton 29435
Coward, Florence 29530
Cowpens, Spartanburg 29330
Crocketville, Hampton 29913
Cross, Berkeley 29436
Cross Anchor, Spartanburg ... 29331
Cross Hill, Laurens 29332
Dale, Beaufort 29914
Dalzell, Sumter 29040
Daniel Island, Berkeley 29492
DARLINGTON, Darlington
(See Page 3372)
Daufuskie Island, Beaufort ... 29915
Davis Station, Clarendon 29041
Denmark, Bamberg 29042
Dewees Island, Charleston ... 29451
Dillon, Dillon 29536
Donalds, Abbeville 29638
Dorchester, Dorchester 29437
Drayton, Spartanburg 29333
Due West, Abbeville 29639
Duncan, Spartanburg 29334
Early Branch, Hampton 29916
EASLEY, Pickens
(See Page 3374)
Eastover, Richland 29044
Edgefield, Edgefield 29824
Edgemoor, Chester 29712
Edisto, Colleton 29438
Edisto Island, Colleton 29438
Effingham, Florence 29541
Ehrhardt, Bamberg 29081
Elgin, Kershaw 29045
Elko, Barnwell 29826
Elliott, Lee 29046
Elloree, Orangeburg 29047
Enoree, Spartanburg 29335
Estill, Hampton 29918
Estill, Hampton 29939
Eutawville, Orangeburg 29048
Fair Play, Oconee 29643
Fairfax, Allendale 29827
Fairforest, Spartanburg 29336
Fingerville, Spartanburg 29338
FLORENCE, Florence
(See Page 3377)
Floyd Dale, Dillon 29536
Folly Beach, Charleston 29439
Fork, Dillon 29543
Fort Lawn, Chester 29714
FORT MILL, Lancaster
(See Page 3380)
Fort Motte, Calhoun 29135
Fountain Inn, Greenville 29644
Fripp Island, Beaufort 29920
Furman, Hampton 29921
Gable, Clarendon 29051
Gadsden, Richland 29052
GAFFNEY, Cherokee
(See Page 3384)
Galivants Ferry, Horry 29544
Garnett, Hampton 29922
Gaston, Lexington 29053
GEORGETOWN, Georgetown
(See Page 3386)
Gifford, Hampton 29923
Gilbert, Lexington 29054
Glendale, Spartanburg 29346
Glenn Springs, Spartanburg .. 29374
Gloverville, Aiken 29828
Goose Creek, Berkeley 29445
Gramling, Spartanburg 29348
Graniteville, Aiken 29829
Gray Court, Laurens 29645
Great Falls, Chester 29055
Greeleyville, Williamsburg 29056
Green Pond, Colleton 29446
Green Sea, Horry 29545
Greenpond, Colleton 29446
GREENVILLE, Greenville
(See Page 3388)
GREENWOOD, Greenwood
(See Page 3395)
GREER, Greenville
(See Page 3397)
Gresham, Marion 29546
Grover, Dorchester 29447
Hamer, Dillon 29547
Hampton, Hampton 29924
Hanahan, Berkeley 29410
Hardeeville, Jasper 29927
Harleyville, Dorchester 29448
HARTSVILLE, Darlington
(See Page 3400)
Heath Springs, Lancaster 29058
Hemingway, Williamsburg 29554
Hickory Grove, York 29717
Hilda, Barnwell 29813
Hilton Head, Beaufort 29925
HILTON HEAD ISLAND,
Beaufort
(See Page 3400)
Hodges, Greenwood 29653
Holly Hill, Orangeburg 29059
Hollywood, Charleston 29449
Honea Path, Anderson 29654
Hopkins, Richland 29061
Horatio, Sumter 29062
Huger, Berkeley 29450
Indian Land, Lancaster 29707
Inman, Spartanburg 29349
Irmo, Richland 29063
Islandton, Colleton 29929
Isle Of Palms, Charleston 29451
Iva, Anderson 29655
Jackson, Aiken 29831
Jacksonboro, Colleton 29452
Jamestown, Berkeley 29453
Jefferson, Chesterfield 29718
Jenkinsville, Fairfield 29065
Jericho, Charleston 29426
Joanna, Laurens 29351
JOHNS ISLAND, Charleston
(See Page 3402)
Johnsonville, Florence 29555
Johnston, Edgefield 29832
Joint Base Charleston,
Charleston 29404
Jonesville, Union 29353
Kershaw, Lancaster 29067
Kiawah Island, Charleston 29455
Kinards, Newberry 29355
Kings Creek, Cherokee 29702
Kingstree, Williamsburg 29556
Kline, Barnwell 29812
Knightsville, Dorchester 29483
La France, Anderson 29656
Ladson, Berkeley 29456
Ladson, Dorchester 29485
Ladys Island, Beaufort 29907
Lake City, Florence 29560
Lake View, Dillon 29563
Lake Wylie, York 29710
Lamar, Darlington 29069
LANCASTER, Lancaster
(See Page 3404)
Lando, Chester 29724
Lando, Chester 29729
Landrum, Spartanburg 29356
Lane, Williamsburg 29564
Langley, Aiken 29834
Latta, Dillon 29565
Laurens, Laurens 29360
Leesville, Lexington 29070
LEXINGTON, Lexington
(See Page 3406)
Liberty, Pickens 29657
Liberty Hill, Kershaw 29074
Lincolnville, Dorchester 29485
Litchfield, Georgetown 29585
Little Mountain, Newberry 29075
Little River, Horry 29566
Little Rock, Dillon 29567
Livingston, Orangeburg 29107
Lobeco, Beaufort 29931
Lockhart, Union 29364
Lodge, Colleton 29082
Lone Star, Calhoun 29030
Long Creek, Oconee 29658
Longs, Horry 29568
Loris, Horry 29569
Lowndesville, Abbeville 29659
Lugoff, Kershaw 29078
Luray, Hampton 29932
Lydia, Darlington 29079
Lyman, Spartanburg 29365
Lynchburg, Lee 29080
Madison, Oconee 29693
Manning, Clarendon 29102
Marietta, Greenville 29661
Marion, Marion 29571
Martin, Allendale 29836
Mauldin, Greenville 29662
Mayesville, Sumter 29104
Mayo, Spartanburg 29368
Mc Bee, Chesterfield 29101
Mc Clellanville, Charleston ... 29458
Mc Coll, Marlboro 29570
Mc Connells, York 29726
Mc Cormick, Mccormick 29835
Meggett, Charleston 29449
Miley, Hampton 29933
Modoc, Mccormick 29838
Moncks Corner, Berkeley 29430
Moncks Corner, Berkeley 29461
Monetta, Aiken 29105
Monticello, Fairfield 29065
Montmorenci, Aiken 29839
Moore, Spartanburg 29369
Mount Carmel, Mccormick 29840
Mount Croghan, Chesterfield . 29727
MOUNT PLEASANT,
Charleston
(See Page 3409)
Mountain Rest, Oconee 29664
Mountville, Laurens 29370
Mullins, Marion 29574
Murrells Inlet, Horry 29576
MYRTLE BEACH, Horry
(See Page 3411)
N Litchfield, Georgetown 29585
Neeses, Orangeburg 29107
Nesmith, Williamsburg 29580
New Ellenton, Aiken 29809
New Zion, Clarendon 29111
Newberry, Newberry 29108
Newry, Oconee 29665
Nichols, Horry 29581
Ninety Six, Greenwood 29666
Norris, Pickens 29667
North, Orangeburg 29112
NORTH AUGUSTA, Aiken
(See Page 3416)
NORTH CHARLESTON,
Charleston
(See Page 3419)
NORTH MYRTLE BEACH,
Horry
(See Page 3421)
Norway, Orangeburg 29113
Ocean Drive, Horry 29582
Okatie, Beaufort 29909
Olanta, Florence 29114
Olar, Bamberg 29843
ORANGEBURG, Orangeburg
(See Page 3422)
Oswego, Sumter 29150
Pacolet, Spartanburg 29372
Pacolet Mills, Spartanburg 29373
Pageland, Chesterfield 29728
Pamplico, Florence 29583
Parksville, Mccormick 29844
Parksville, Mccormick 29845
Parris Island, Beaufort 29905
Patrick, Chesterfield 29584
Pauline, Spartanburg 29374
Pawleys Island, Georgetown .. 29585
Paxville, Clarendon 29102
Peak, Newberry 29122
Pelion, Lexington 29123
Pelzer, Anderson 29669
Pendleton, Anderson 29670
Perry, Aiken 29137
Pickens, Pickens 29671
Piedmont, Greenville 29673
Pineland, Jasper 29934
Pineville, Berkeley 29468
Pinewood, Sumter 29125
Pinopolis, Berkeley 29469
Plum Branch, Mccormick 29845
Pomaria, Newberry 29126
Port Royal, Beaufort 29935
Poston, Florence 29555
Powdersville, Greenville 29611
Prosperity, Newberry 29127
Quinby, Florence 29506
Rains, Marion 29589
Ravenel, Charleston 29470
Reevesville, Dorchester 29471
Reidville, Spartanburg 29375
Rembert, Sumter 29128
Richburg, Chester 29729
Richland, Oconee 29675
Ridge Spring, Saluda 29129
Ridgeland, Jasper 29936
Ridgeville, Dorchester 29472
Ridgeway, Fairfield 29130
Rimini, Sumter 29125
Rion, Fairfield 29132
Ritter, Colleton 29488
River Hills, York 29710
ROCK HILL, York
(See Page 3425)
Roebuck, Spartanburg 29376
Round O, Colleton 29474
Rowesville, Orangeburg 29133
Ruby, Chesterfield 29741
Ruffin, Colleton 29475
Russellville, Berkeley 29476
Saint Charles, Sumter 29104
Saint George, Dorchester 29477
Saint Helena Island,
Beaufort 29920
Saint Matthews, Calhoun 29135
Saint Stephen, Berkeley 29479
Salem, Oconee 29676
Salley, Aiken 29137
Salters, Williamsburg 29590
Saluda, Saluda 29138
Sandy Springs, Anderson 29677
Santee, Orangeburg 29142
Sardinia, Clarendon 29143
Scotia, Hampton 29939
Scranton, Florence 29591
Seabrook, Beaufort 29940
Seabrook Island, Charleston .. 29455
Sellers, Marion 29592
SENECA, Oconee
(See Page 3428)
Sharon, York 29742
Shaw Afb, Sumter 29152
Sheldon, Beaufort 29941
Shoals Junction, Abbeville ... 29638
Shulerville, Berkeley 29453
Silverstreet, Newberry 29145
SIMPSONVILLE, Greenville
(See Page 3432)
Six Mile, Pickens 29682
Slater, Greenville 29683
Smoaks, Colleton 29481
Smyrna, York 29743
Society Hill, Darlington 29593
South Of The Border, Dillon .. 29547
SPARTANBURG, Spartanburg
(See Page 3435)
Springfield, Orangeburg 29146
Starr, Anderson 29684
Startex, Spartanburg 29377
State Park, Richland 29147
Sullivans Island, Charleston .. 29482
Summerton, Clarendon 29148
SUMMERVILLE, Dorchester
(See Page 3440)
SUMTER, Sumter
(See Page 3444)
Sunset, Pickens 29685
Surfside Beach
(See Myrtle Beach)
Swansea, Lexington 29160
Sycamore, Allendale 29846
Tamassee, Oconee 29686
Tatum, Marlboro 29594
Taylors, Greenville 29687
Tega Cay, York 29708
Tigerville, Greenville 29688
Tillman, Jasper 29943
Timmonsville, Florence 29161
Townville, Anderson 29689
Travelers Rest, Greenville 29690
Trenton, Edgefield 29847
Trio, Williamsburg 29590
Troy, Greenwood 29848
Turbeville, Clarendon 29162
Ulmer, Allendale 29849
Una, Spartanburg 29378
Union, Union 29379
Van Wyck, Lancaster 29744
Vance, Orangeburg 29163
Varnville, Hampton 29944
Vaucluse, Aiken 29801
Vaucluse, Aiken 29850
Wadmalaw Island,
Charleston 29487
Wagener, Aiken 29164
Walhalla, Oconee 29691
Wallace, Marlboro 29596
Walterboro, Colleton 29488
Wando, Berkeley 29492
Ward, Saluda 29166
Ware Shoals, Greenwood 29692
Warrenville, Aiken 29851
Waterloo, Laurens 29384
Wedgefield, Sumter 29168
Wellford, Spartanburg 29385
WEST COLUMBIA, Lexington
(See Page 3447)
West Union, Oconee 29696
Westminster, Oconee 29693
Westville, Kershaw 29175
White Oak, Fairfield 29180
White Rock, Richland 29177
White Stone, Spartanburg 29386
Whitmire, Newberry 29178
Williams, Colleton 29493
Williamston, Anderson 29697
Williston, Barnwell 29853
Windsor, Aiken 29856
Winnsboro, Fairfield 29180
Wisacky, Lee 29010
Woodruff, Spartanburg 29388
Yemassee, Hampton 29945
Yonges Island, Charleston 29449
York, York 29745

AIKEN SC

General Delivery 29801

POST OFFICE BOXES MAIN OFFICE STATIONS AND BRANCHES

Box No.s
312A - 312A 29802
581A - 581A 29802
EE - EE 29802
AA - AA 29802
CC - CC 29802
A - U 29802
1 - 3840 29802
5001 - 7397 29804
8000 - 8000 29802

NAMED STREETS

Ab Miles Dr 29805
Abbeville Ave NE & NW 29801
Aberdeen Dr 29803
Abigail Ln SW 29803
Ace Ct 29803
Acorn Ln 29801
Adams Ave & Rd 29803
Affirmed Ln 29803
Agave Ln 29803
Agile Ct 29803
S Aiken Blvd SE 29803
Aiken Ln NW 29801
S Aiken Ln 29803
Aiken Mall Dr 29803
Aiken Rescue Ln NE 29801
Air Park Blvd 29805
Airco Blvd 29801
Airport View Dr 29805
Alan Ave 29801
Albert Ln 29803
Alderman St NE 29801
Aldrich St NE 29801
Alex Johnson Dr 29805
Alfonzo Ln 29805
Alfred St NE 29801
Alicia Dr 29801
Allison St 29801
Alpha Dr 29803
Alpine Dr 29803
Alvin Dr 29801
Alwood Dr 29803
Alydar Ln 29803
Amanda Ct 29803
Amberly Cir 29803
Amity Ln 29803
Anchor Ct 29803
Ancient Oak Ln 29805
Anderson Mill Rd 29803
Anderson Pond Rd 29803
Andrews Cir 29803
Ansel Dr 29803
Ansley Dr 29803
Antietam Dr 29803
Antler Pass 29805
Anzalone Ct 29803
Anzelle Trailer Ct 29803
Apac Rd 29801
Apollo Dr 29805
Appleseed Ln 29801
Arbor Ct & Ter 29801
Arborgate Ln 29803
Arbutus Dr SW 29801
Arbutus Hills Dr 29801
Archdale Dr 29803
Arcturus Dr 29803
Ascot Dr 29803
Ashbrook Ct 29803
Ashbury Dr 29803
Ashen Farm Rd 29805
Ashepoo Dr 29803
Ashwood Dr 29801
Aspen Ct 29803
Asphalt Plant Rd 29801
Assembly St NW 29801
Association Dr 29803
Athol Ave 29803
Atlas Dr 29803
Atomic Rd 29803
Audubon Dr SE
1200-1399 29803
1400-1599 29801
Augusta Rd 29801
Augustus Rd 29801
Aumond Pl 29803
Aurora Pl 29801
Aurora Park Dr 29801
Aurum Way 29801
Avery Ln 29801
Aviation Blvd 29805
Ayala Ln 29803
Azalea Pl SE 29801
B And S Dr 29803
Babble Pt 29803
Backwoods Ln 29801
Bacon Rd 29805
Bainbridge Dr 29803
Bald Cypress Ct 29803
Baldwin Rd 29805
Balfour Ct 29803
Balltown Dr 29801
Balsam Ln 29803
Baltimore St 29803
Bamberg Ave 29801
Band Box Ave 29801
Banks Rd 29803
Banks Ter SE 29801
Banks Mill Rd
800-1099 29801
1100-5099 29803
Banks Mill Rd SE 29801
Banksia Rd 29803
Baptist Ct 29801
Barbara Ln SE 29801
Barbaro Ct 29803
Barn Owl Rd 29805
Barnard Ave SE 29801
Barnwell Ave NE & NW 29801
Barretts Church Way 29803
Barrington Farms Dr 29803
Barron Way 29803
Barton Brothers Ln 29801
Barton Cove Dr 29805
Barway Dr 29803
Bass Pond Rd 29805
Basswood Dr 29803
Bates Rd 29801
Battle Ct 29803
Baxley Pl 29803
Bay Cove Rd 29805
Bay Meadows Dr SW 29803
Bay Tree Ct 29803
Beacon Ct 29805
Beams Rd 29801
Bear Cir 29801
Bears Rock Rd 29801
Beaten Path Rd 29801
Beatrice Ln 29801
Beatty Ln 29803
Beaufort St NE & SE 29801
Beauregard Ln 29803
Beaver Cv 29803
Beaver Branch Rd 29801
Beaver Creek Ln 29803
Beaverbrook Ct 29803
Beaverdam Rd 29805
Beckner Trl 29803
Beckwood Trl 29803
Bedford Pl 29803
Bee Ln 29801
Beehive Ln 29805
Belair Ter 29801
Belford Grove Dr 29801
Bell Clapper Ct 29803
Bella Vista Ln 29803
Bellatrix Dr 29803
Belle Mead Dr 29803
Bellewood Dr 29803
Bellreive Dr 29803
Belmont St 29801
Beloit St 29805
Benedict St 29801
Benji Cir 29801
Bennett Ave 29801
Bennie Rd 29801
Bennington Ln 29803
Bent Arrow Rd 29801
Bentley Ct 29803
Beresford Loop 29801
Berkley St SE 29801
Berrie Rd SW 29801
Berringer Dr 29803
Bertram Trl 29803
Berwick Ct 29803
Beryl Dr 29803
Bethany Ln 29805
Bethel Church Rd 29801
Betty Ct 29803
Bevington Dr 29803
Bidborough Ct 29803
Big Tree Rd 29805
Bimini Ln 29803
Birch St 29803
Birch Tree Cir 29803
Bird In Hand Pl 29803
Birkdale Ct E & W 29803
Biscayne Rd 29803
Bissell Rd 29801
Blackberry Ln 29805
Blackheath Ct 29803
Blair Dr 29803
Blarenne Rd 29805
Blazing Trl 29805
Blough Ct 29803
Bluebird Ln 29801
Bluegrass Dr 29803
Bluetick Trl 29805
Bluff Pointe Way 29803
Boardman Rd 29803
Bob Bell Ct 29801
Bobwhite Dr 29801
Boggy Branch Rd 29805
Bold Ruler Dr 29803
Bolton Ct 29803
Bonner St SE 29801
Bonnie Ln 29803
Bonnie Blue Dr 29801
Boothe Rd 29801
Bordeaux Pl SW 29801
Bose Dr 29801
Boss Hogg Ln 29803
Boston St 29803
Bouknight Rd 29805
E Boundary Ave SE 29801
Boxelder Dr 29803
Boxwood Rd 29803
Boyd Pond Rd 29803
Boys Ct 29801
Boysenberry Ln 29803
Brad Cir 29805
Bradby Ln 29801
Bradley Mill Rd 29805
Bramble Ridge Rd 29803
Brampton Way 29803
Branchwater Ln 29803
Brandon Rd 29801
Brandy Rd SE 29801
Brandywine Way 29803
Bransome Blvd 29803
Brant Ct NE 29801
Brashum Dr 29803
Brayboy Rd 29803
Breanne Ct 29803
Breeze Hill Dr 29803
Brentwood Pl NE 29801
Brer Rabbit Rd 29801
Brewer Dr 29803
Brewster Way 29803
Brickling Ct 29803
Bridge Creek Trl 29801
Bridge Crest Ct 29803
Bridle Ln 29803
Bridle Creek Trl 29803
Bridlewood Dr 29803
Brightwood Dr 29803
Bristlecone Dr 29803
Bristol Ave & Pass 29801
Brittnee Ct 29805
Broad Oak Ln 29801
Broadwater Loop 29801
Broadway St 29803
Brogdon Branch Ct 29801
Brookhaven Dr 29803
Brookline Ct & Dr 29803
Brooks Ave 29803
Broughton Dr 29803
Brown Ln 29801
Brownlee St 29803
Brucewood St NW 29801
Brunswick Ln 29803
Brynhill Ct 29803
Buck Passer Ln 29803
Buck Point Ct 29803
Buckey Ln 29805
Buckhar Ln 29803
Buckhead Ct 29803
Buckhorn Pt 29803
Buckley Ave 29803
Bud Ln 29805
Buddy Ln 29805
Bulbury Woods Dr 29803
Buldra Ln 29803
Bumpsas Pl 29805
Bunche Ter NE 29801
Bungalow Ct 29803
Bungalow Village Way 29803
Burden Cir 29803
Burden Lake Rd 29803
Burgess Dr 29801
Burgundy Rd SW 29801
Burkwood Pl SW 29801
Burlington St 29801
Burnette Dr 29801
Burnham Ct 29803
Burris Rd 29805
Busby Rd 29801
Busch Acres Ln 29803
Business Ct 29801
Butler Cir & Rd 29801
Butternut Ct 29803
Byrnes Rd & St SW 29801
C And H Ln 29803
Cabinet Dr 29801
Cablevision Rd NW 29801
Cadence Ct 29803
Caitlyn Dr 29803
Calderwood Dr 29801
Caldwell Ct 29803
Calhoun Pl SE 29801
Callahan Ter 29801
Calton Trl 29801
Calumet Ct 29803
Camacho Ct 29803
Camberly Ct 29801
Cambridge St 29801
Camellia St NE 29801
Cameron Aly 29803
Camp Gravatt Rd 29805
Camp Long Rd 29805
Camp Marie Dr 29801
Campanile Ct 29801
Candlewood Rd 29803
Candy Ln 29801
Canterbury Ct SE 29801
Canvas Back Cir 29801
Cape Fox Cir 29803
Capella Dr 29803
Capers Path 29803
Capital Dr 29803
Cardigan Dr 29803
Cardinal Cir, Ct, Dr & Pl 29803
Carillon Ct 29803
Carlyle Pl 29803
Carnoustie Ct 29801
N & S Carolina Ave & Dr SW 29801
Carpenter Dr & Ln 29801
Carriage Dr 29803
Carriage Hill Pl 29801
Carrington Pl 29803
Carver Ter NE 29801
Casa Lake Dr 29803
Casaba Dr 29803
Casena Dr SW 29801
Castle Way 29801
Castlesteads Dr 29803
Catawba St 29801
Catenary Blvd 29801
Cathedral Isle 29801
Caw Caw Ct 29803
Cedar Dr 29801
Cedar Rd 29803
Cedar St 29803
Cedar Meadows Rd 29803
Cedar Ridge Dr 29803
Cedarwood Park 29803
S Centennial Ave 29803
Central Building Rd 29803
Centre South Blvd 29803
Century Ln 29803
Cetch Ct 29803
Chabot Ln 29803
Chafee Springs Dr 29801
Chaffee Ave SW 29801
Chamberley Pl 29803
Chamomile Ct 29803
Champagne Dr 29803
Champion Way 29801
Champion Pine Ln 29803
Chappells Rd 29803
Chardonnay Ln 29803
Charismatic Dr 29803
Charles Towne Pl 29803
Charleston Hwy & St SE 29801
Charleston Row Blvd 29803
Charnwood Forest Cir 29803
Charrelm Rd 29801
Chase Ln 29803
Chasin Way 29803
Chatfield St NE 29801
Chatham St SE 29801
Chavous Rd 29803
Checkered Way 29803
Chelsea Ct 29803
Cheltenham Dr 29803
Cherbourg Pl SW 29801
Cherokee Ave, Rd & St 29801
Cherry Dr 29803
Cherry Hills Dr 29803
Chesterfield St N & S 29801
Chestnut Ct 29803
Chestnut Hollow Ln 29803
Chewacla Ln 29803
Chewink Way 29801
Chilton Pl 29801
Chime Bell Church Rd 29803
Chime Bell Park Dr 29803
Chinkapin Ct 29803
Chipper Run 29803
Chloe Ln 29803
Chris Dr 29803
Christee Pl 29803
Christopher Downs Ct 29803
Chug Bug Ln 29803
Chukker Creek Rd 29803
Church St
1-99 29801
100-199 29803
200-224 29801
201-225 29803
226-241 29801
242-298 29803
243-1199 29801
300-1198 29801
8000-8199 29803
Churchill Cir 29803
Cilles Manor Dr 29803
Cinnamon Dr 29803
Citadel Dr 29803
Citation Dr 29803
Claflin Dr 29801
Clarendon Pl 29801
Clark Rd SW 29803
Clary Hill Dr 29805
Classic Ln 29805
Claw And Paw Ct 29803
Clayburne Pl 29803
Clear Creek Ct 29803
Clemson Dr 29803
Cleora Murray Dr 29801
Cliatt Dr 29803
Clifton St 29803
Clifton Weeks Rd 29803
Climbing Rose Dr 29803
Cloud Trl 29803
Clovis Pl 29801
Club Dr 29803
Club Villas Dr E & W 29803
Coach Light Way 29803
Coachman Dr 29803
Cobbs Way 29803
Cocoa Dr 29801
Coconut Ct 29801
Cody Ln 29803
Coker Dr 29803
Coker Springs Rd SW 29801
Colbert Bridge Rd 29803
Coleman Bridge Rd 29805
Colibri Ln 29805
College Station Dr 29801
Colleton Ave SE & SW 29801
Collier St 29803
Collins Ave 29801
Colonial Dr 29801
Colony Pkwy 29803
Colston Ave 29801
Columbia Ave NE 29801
Columbia Ave NW 29801
Columbia Hwy N
1400-1408 29801
1410-1799 29801
1800-3299 29805
Combine Ct 29803
Combs Dr 29801
Comfort Point Ct 29803
Commerce Ct 29803
Common Wealth Way 29803
Commons Ct 29803
Community Dr 29803
Confederate Rd 29801
Congaree Ave NW 29801
Conger Dr 29803
Congress Dr NW 29801
Connies Way 29801
Contract Dr 29801
Contreras Ln 29803
Converse Dr 29803
Cooks Bridge Rd 29805
Cooley St 29803
Cooper Dr 29803
Copperhead Rd 29801
Coral Reef Rd 29801
Cornells Pl 29803
Corner Stroll Ln 29801
Cornerstone Dr 29801
Cornish St NE 29801
Corona Run 29803
Corporate Pkwy 29803
Corry Ln 29801
Cottonwood Cir & Dr 29803
Cottonwood Creek Ln 29803
Council Cir 29801
Country Living Rd 29801
County Down Ct 29803
Courtillians Rd 29801
Coward Rd 29803
Cox Ave NW 29801
Cozier Ct 29803
Crab Trl 29805
Craft Ln 29803
Crane Ct 29803
Crawford Ave 29801
Creek Ct 29803
Creek View Ct 29803
Creekridge Rd 29803
Creekside Dr 29803
Crepe Myrtle Dr 29803
Crescent Pt 29803
Crestwood Dr 29803
Croft Ave NE 29801
Croft Mill Rd 29801
Crooked Creek Rd 29805
Crosby Rd 29803
Crosland Dr NE 29801
Cross Country Cir 29801
Cross Creek Dr 29803
Crossroads Park Dr 29803
Crossways Pl SE 29801
Crump Dr 29803
Cubs Hamlet Ct 29803
Cullum Trail Rd 29803
Cumbee Trail Rd 29805
Cumberland Ln SE 29801
Currycomb Dr 29803
Curzon Ct 29801
Cushman Dr 29801
Cushman Rd 29805
Cutler Ct 29803
Cypress Ln 29803
Daja Dr 29801
Dallas Cir 29801
Dalmatian Dr 29803
Damon St 29801
Daniel Dr 29803
Daniel Boone Dr 29803
Dannan Ct 29805
Danzig Ln 29803
Darien Dr 29803
Darlington Dr 29803
Dasher Cir 29803
Date Palm Cir 29803
Davenport Ln 29803
Daves Way 29801
David St 29803
Davis Ter NW 29801
Dawhoo Pl 29805
Day Rd 29805
Daylily Pl 29801
Dean Family Ln 29801
Deep Run Rd 29803
Deer Run Rd 29803
Deerwood Ct & Dr 29803
Deloach Way 29803
Deneb Dr 29803
Denise Ct 29801
Denver Rd 29803
Derby Ln 29801
Derrick St 29805
Desoto Dr 29803
Destiny Ln 29805
Devereux Dr 29803
Devonshire Dr 29803
Dewberry Ln 29803
Dewitt Dr 29801
Dexter St NE 29801
Diane St 29801
Dibble Rd SW 29801
Dickson Pl 29801
Dillon Ave NW 29801
Divine Monroe Pl 29803
Dogwood Rd 29803
Dominion Dr 29803
Donegal Dr 29803
Donnel Dr 29803
Doral Dr 29803
Dottie Rd 29803
Double Eagle Ct 29803
Double Springs Rd 29803
Double Tree Dr 29803
Dougherty Rd 29803
Douglas Dr 29803
Downing St SW 29801
Dragstrip Rd 29803
Drapery Dr 29805
Drayton Ct 29801
Drayton Hall Blvd 29803
Driftwood Cir & Ct 29801
Dry Branch Ct & Rd 29803
Duchess Ln 29803
Duckwood Ln 29805
Duke Dr 29801
Dumbridge Rd 29803
Dunbarton Cir SE 29801
Dunham Forest Way 29803

Dunovant Ct 29803
Dupont Dr NE & NW ... 29801
Dupree Pl SW 29801
Durham St NW 29801
Dusty Ln 29803
Dutchess Rd 29801
Dwyer Ln 29801
Dyches Rd & St 29801
Eagle Point Ct 29801
Eagles Nest Ln 29803
Earl Church Rd 29805
Earlmont Dr 29803
Early Ct 29803
Eastbrook Park Dr 29801
Eastern Pl NE 29801
Eastgate Dr 29803
Eastwood Ct 29801
Easy St 29801
Easy Wind 29803
Ebbwater Dr 29803
Eboney Rd 29801
Eclipse Loop 29801
Eden Ct 29803
Edengale Way 29803
Edgefield Ave & Hwy ... 29801
Edgemont St 29801
Edisto Ave 29801
Edisto Rd 29805
Edrie St NE 29801
Edrie Oaks Cir 29801
Eider Cir NE 29801
Elbert St 29803
Elim Ln 29801
Elk Dr 29805
Ella Cir 29801
Ellenton St SE 29803
Ellis Ct 29803
Elm St 29803
Elon St 29803
Elwood Dr 29803
Emerald Rdg 29803
Emerson Rd 29801
Enclave Dr 29803
End Rd 29801
Englewood Rd 29803
English Oak Ln 29801
English Park Dr 29801
Enterprise Ave 29803
Eola Ct 29801
Epona Ln 29801
Equestrian Ct 29803
Equestrian Way 29805
Equine Ct 29803
Equinox Loop 29803
Erindale Ct 29803
Erskine Ln & Sq 29803
Essex Ct 29803
Estates Dr 29803
Ester Dr 29801
Eu Williemae Ln 29801
Eugene Ct 29803
Eutaw St 29801
Evans Rd 29803
Eve St 29803
Evergreen Dr 29801
Express Ln 29803
Fabian Dr 29803
Fairfield Ct & St 29801
Fairway Rd SW 29801
Fairway Rdg 29803
Falcon Hill Dr 29803
Fappiano Ct 29803
Farmer Rd 29805
Farmfield Rd 29805
Farmingdale Ct 29805
Farmstead Dr 29803
Farrington Pt 29803
Fauburg St SW 29801
Fawnwood Dr E & W 29803
Fays Garden Ln 29805
Fellowship Ln 29801
Fermata Pl SW 29801
Ferndown Ct 29803
Fernwood Ct 29803
Fields Rd 29801
Fifth Ave 29801

Fincher Ct 29805
Fingle Glen Ct 29803
Fire Tower Rd 29803
First Ave 29801
Flag Ln 29805
Flat Trail Ct 29803
Flatland Dr 29805
Flintlock Curve Rd 29805
Florence St NW & SW . 29801
Florida Ave 29801
Flower Break Rd 29803
Folly Hill Ln 29801
Ford Farm Loop 29803
Fore St 29803
Foreman Floyd Cir 29803
Forest Dr 29801
Forest Bluffs Rd 29803
Forest Hill Dr SW 29801
Forest Pines Rd 29803
Forest Ridge Dr 29803
Forest Trail Ct 29805
Forest View Rd 29803
Formosa Ln 29805
Forrest Holley Way 29805
Forward Ct 29805
Fowler Way 29801
Fox Rd 29805
Fox Bluff Ln 29803
Fox Haven Ct & Dr 29803
Fox Lea Trl 29803
Fox Pond Rd 29801
Fox Tail Ct 29803
Fox Trace Ct 29803
Foxdale Ct 29803
Foxhound Run Rd 29803
Foxs Lair 29803
Foxwood Dr 29803
Frankel Rd 29801
Franks Dr 29801
Fred Jones Ln NE 29801
Freedom Ln 29803
Freiday Ln 29801
Friendship Rd 29803
Fringetree Loop 29803
Frontage Rd 29801
E Frontage Rd 29805
W Frontage Rd 29805
Full Moon Dr 29801
Fulmer Rd 29805
Funderburg Trl 29805
Furman Dr 29803
Gadwall Ln 29803
Galaxy St 29803
Gallant Hill Dr 29803
Gamble Rd 29801
Gamboa Pl 29803
Garden Springs Ct 29803
Garnet Ln 29803
Gaston St 29801
Gate Post Ln 29803
Gateway Dr 29803
Gatewood Dr & Pt 29801
Gator Ln 29801
Gayle Ave NW 29801
Gentle Breeze Ct 29805
Georgann Ln 29803
George St NE 29801
Germany Pl 29801
Geronimo Way 29801
Gibbon Ln 29803
Gilbert St SE 29801
Gin Rd SE 29801
Ginger Ln 29803
Gippy Ct 29803
Given St 29805
Glade Springs Ct 29803
Glass Pl 29803
Glass Rope Ln 29805
Glassbore Rd 29805
Gleenwood Dr 29803
Glen Arbor Ct 29801
Glen Haven Cir 29803
Glencarin Dr 29803
Glencoe Ln 29803
Gleneagles Dr 29803
Glenlevit Dr 29803

Glenn Pl 29803
Glenside Ln 29803
Glenview Dr 29803
Glenwood Dr 29803
Gobbler Ct 29801
Golden Ln 29801
Golden Arrow Pl 29801
Golden Bridge Ct 29803
Golden Oak Dr 29803
Golden Pond Ct 29803
Goldview Dr 29801
Golphin Ln 29803
Gone West Ct 29803
Good Hope Farms Rd .. 29803
Good Springs Rd 29801
Goode Ln 29803
Gooseneck Rd 29805
Governors Ln NW 29801
Grace Ave & Cir SE & SW 29801
Grady Pond Rd 29805
Grady Williams Cir 29805
Grand Oak Way 29801
Grandiflora Cir 29803
Grandmothers Pl 29801
Granger Dr 29803
Granny Ln 29805
Grantham Ct 29803
Grantto Ln 29803
Grasmere Ct 29803
Grassy Creek Ln 29803
Gray Mare Hollow Rd .. 29803
Graylyn Lakes Dr 29803
Graystone Ct 29801
Green Rd 29803
Green St 29801
Green Ash Ct 29803
Green Hill Rd 29801
Green Oak Dr 29803
Green Oaks Rd 29803
Green Pond Rd 29803
Green Tree Ln 29801
Greenbush Rd 29803
Greengate Cir 29803
Greenville St NW & SW 29801
Greenwich Dr 29803
Greenwood St SW 29801
Gregg Ave & Hwy 29801
Gregory Rd 29805
Greyhound Cir 29803
Griffin Ave 29803
Griffin Park Dr 29801
Griggs St 29803
Grindiddys Farm Rd 29801
Gull Ln 29803
Gun Range Rd 29801
Gunter Rd 29803
Gwinnett St NE 29801
Gyles Rd SW 29803
Gyles Storey Rd 29805
Hackberry Ln 29803
Haddington Way 29803
Hagen Ct 29803
Hahn Ave NE 29801
Halcomb Rd 29801
Hall Dr SW 29801
Hall Hill Rd 29801
Hallman Loop 29803
Hameanto Rd 29803
Hamelin Rd 29805
Hamilton Dr 29803
Hamilton Branch Way .. 29803
Hammond Rd SW 29803
Hampton Ave NE & NW 29801
Hamstead Pl 29803
Hancock Rd 29801
Hanger Way 29805
Hankinson St 29803
Hanlon Woods Ct 29803
Harbor Dr 29801
Harco Dr 29803
Harden Dr 29801
Harding Acres Rd 29801
Hardwood Ct 29803

Harewood Ct 29803
Harold Ln NW 29801
Harriett St 29803
Harrow Cir 29803
Hartford Ct 29803
Hartwell Dr 29803
Harvest Ln 29803
Harvey Ct 29805
Hasty Rd 29803
Hatchaway Bridge Rd
- 1000-1699 29801
- 1700-1899 29805

Haven Pl 29801
Hayden Rd 29805
Hayne Ave SW 29801
Haywire Pl 29801
Hazel Dr 29801
Heartwood Pass 29803
Heather Way 29803
Heathwood Dr 29803
Heavenly Ln 29805
E Hedge Rd 29801
Hedgerow Ct 29803
Hedgewood Dr 29805
Helmsdale Dr 29803
Hemingford Way 29803
Hemlock Ct & Dr 29803
Henley Ln 29801
Hennessy Dr 29803
Henry St 29803
Herbert Ct 29801
Herndon Dairy Rd 29803
Heron Lake Trl 29803
Herron Pl 29801
Hickory Bnd & Rd 29803
Hickory Nut St 29805
Hickory Ridge Rd 29803
Hidden Field Ct 29803
Hidden Haven Dr 29803
Hidden Mountain Ln 29805
Hidden Pond Rd 29801
High Meadow Loop 29803
High Town Trl 29803
Highberry Ct 29803
Highgrove Ct 29805
Highland Forest Dr 29803
Highland Park Dr & Ter SW 29801
Highland Reserve Ct ... 29803
Hightower Ln 29805
Hill Ave NW 29801
Hill Rd 29803
Hillcrest Rd SW 29801
Hillhead Ct 29801
Hills End Rd 29803
Hills Woodland Ln SW . 29801
Hillsboro Dr 29801
Hillsborough Ln 29803
Hillsdale Dr 29803
Hillshire Ct 29803
Hillside Dr 29801
Hilltop Ave 29801
Hillview Cir 29801
Hilton St 29803
Hitchcock Dr SW 29803
Hitchcock Pkwy 29801
Hitchcock Rd 29803
Hitching Post Dr 29803
Hiwassee Run 29803
Hobcaw Ct 29803
Hodges Bay Dr 29803
Holden Dr 29805
Holley Estates Dr 29803
Holley Haven Dr 29803
Holley Lake Cir & Rd .. 29803
Holley Ridge Rd 29803
Hollow Creek Farm Rd 29803
Hollow Hill Dr 29803
Hollow Tree Dr 29803
Holly Ln SW 29801
Holmes Dr 29803
Home Rd 29803
Homestead Ln SE 29801
Honey Ridge Ln 29801
Honeysuckle Ct 29803

Hoods Ln SW 29801
Hopeland Farm Dr 29803
Horizon St 29801
Horned Owl Rd 29805
Horry St NE & SE 29801
Horse Health Blvd 29801
Horse Trail Rd 29805
Horseshoe Bnd 29803
Horseshoe Bend Rd 29801
Houndslake Dr 29803
Hourglass Ln 29805
House Finch Hl 29801
Huckleberry Ct & Dr ... 29803
Hudson Rd 29801
Hunt Rd 29805
Huntcliff Pt & Trce ... 29803
Hunters Run Dr 29803
Hunting Hills Dr 29803
Huntington Ct 29803
Huntley St 29803
Huntsman Dr 29803
Hurlingham Dr 29801
Huron Dr 29803
Hutto Pond Rd 29805
Hyde Rd 29803
Idlewild Dr 29803
Ilex Ln 29803
Implement Rd 29803
Independent Blvd 29803
Indian Creek Trl 29803
Indian Springs Rd 29801
Inez Ln 29805
Interlachen Ct SW 29803
Inverary Ct 29803
Inverness St E & W 29803
Inwood Dr 29803
Iris Ln 29801
Irish Bank Ln 29803
Ironbark Ct 29803
Ironwood Trce 29801
Iroquois St 29801
Irving Dr 29801
Iselin Way 29803
Ivy Cir 29803
J And H Park Rd 29805
J And S Dr 29803
Jack Jones St 29801
Jack Russell Ln 29803
Jackson Ave & Dr SE .. 29803
Jade St 29805
Jake Pl 29801
James Rd 29803
James Town Ct NE 29801
Janet Rd 29803
Jasmine Ridge Rd 29801
Jasper St SW 29801
Jcs Country Ln 29801
Jefferson Ave 29803
Jefferson Ter NE 29801
Jefferson Davis Hwy ... 29801
Jehossee Dr SE 29801
Jennifer Dr 29803
Jerrys Folly Rd 29803
Jessica St 29801
Joann Dr 29801
Jockey Trl 29801
Joe R Ln 29801
Joe Walker Ct 29801
John Elliot Ln 29801
John Scott Rd 29803
Johnny St 29803
Johns Park Ln 29803
Johnson Rd 29803
Johnson Dam Rd 29801
Johnson Mill Dr 29805
Jones Ave & St NW 29801
Josef Hofmann Ter 29801
Joseph Dr 29805
Josh Ln 29801
Joshua Ln 29801
Joyce St 29801
Joyce Branch Rd 29805
Joyner Pond Rd 29803
Juanita Dr 29801
Judith Cir 29801
Julie Ann Ct 29801

June Bug Ln 29801
Juniper Loop 29803
Jw Trl 29801
Kalmia Cir 29801
Kalmia Forest Dr 29801
Kalmia Hill Rd 29801
Kaminer Rd 29801
Kangaroo Ct 29801
Kansas Way 29805
Kaolin Dr & Rd 29801
Kasey Ln 29803
Kasper Ln 29803
Kathryn St 29801
Kedron Church Rd 29805
Keeper Ln 29803
Keith St 29801
Kellogg Dr 29803
Kellsboro Run 29801
Kelly Dr 29803
Kelly Acres Ln 29803
Kemper Downs Dr 29803
Kendallwood Ct 29803
Kenmont St 29801
Kennebec St 29801
Kensington Ct 29803
Kenya Dr 29801
Kerr Dr SW 29803
Kershaw Pl & St 29801
Khaki Ct 29803
Kiawah Trl 29803
Kimball Pond Rd 29803
Kimberlie Dr 29801
Kimberly Dr 29801
Kimberwick Ct 29803
Kimwood Ct 29803
Kincade Ct 29805
King St 29801
King Edward Way 29803
Kings Grant Dr 29803
Kings Sport Way NW ... 29801
Kingston Ct 29803
Kingston Heath Ct 29803
Kinross Ct 29803
Kinte Ave 29801
Kipling Rd 29805
Kipper Ct 29805
Kirkwood Dr 29803
Kismet Dr 29803
Kiwi Ct 29801
Kline St NW 29801
Knollview Dr 29803
Knox Ave 29801
Kojains Pl 29801
Kousa Ln 29803
L And L Ln 29801
Ladiah Ln 29803
Lady Bank Ln 29803
Lady Banks Rd 29803
Lady Bug Dr 29801
Lafaye St 29803
Lagoon Lair 29803
Lain St 29801
Lake Duncan Ln 29801
Lake Forest Ln 29803
Lake Shore Dr 29801
Lake Vincent Rd 29801
Lakeshore Ct 29801
Lakeside Dr 29803
Lamont Ln 29805
Lamp Post Loop 29803
Lamplight St 29801
Lancaster St NW & SW 29801
Lance Dr 29803
Lander Ln 29803
Landing Dr 29801
Landsford Ct 29803
Landview Ct 29803
Langdon Rd 29805
Langfuhr Ln 29803
Larchmont Pl 29801
Laughlin Loop 29805
Laurel Dr SW 29801
Laurel Oak Dr 29803
Laurel Ridge Cir 29803

Laurens St NW
- 100-306 29801
- 301-309 29802
- 307-999 29801
- 308-1098 29801

Laurens St SW 29801
Lavender Ln 29803
Lawhead Ln 29803
Lawrence St 29803
Laws Dr 29801
Lawson Rd 29801
Leadership Dr 29801
Leann Ct NW 29801
Leanne Dr 29805
Lee Ln SW 29801
Legacy Ln 29803
Legare Rd SW 29803
Levels Church Rd W ... 29801
Lewis Ln 29803
Lexington Ct 29803
Liberty Ln NW 29801
Ligon St NW 29801
Lila Rd 29801
Lilypond Ct 29803
Lime Ln 29801
Limerick Dr 29803
Limestone Ct 29801
Lincoln Ave 29801
Linda Ln 29801
Linden St NW & SW 29801
Lindrick Ct 29803
Lindsey Dr 29801
Linler Ln 29805
Little Tepee Ln 29801
Live Oak Ct & Rd 29803
Lloydtown Rd 29801
Locke Ln SE 29801
Log Cabin Rd 29805
Loganberry Ct 29803
Lokey Dr 29801
London Ct 29803
Lone Oak Dr 29803
Long Branch Ct 29801
Long Creek Dr 29803
Long Shadow Dr 29803
Longleaf Ct & Dr 29803
Longmeadow Ct 29803
Longridge Loop 29803
Longwood Dr 29803
Longwood Green Ct 29803
Loren St 29801
Lorraine Dr SW 29801
Lott St 29801
Lotus Ln 29801
Loudoun Dr 29803
Lowe Pl 29803
Lucas Ln SW 29803
Lundee Ct & Dr 29803
Lyndhurst Ct 29803
Lynn Dr 29803
Lynwood Dr 29803
Lyon Dr SE 29801
Macaw Ct 29801
Macbean Loop 29801
Mack Donald Ln 29805
Mackey Scott Rd 29801
Madison Ave 29803
Mae Acres Ct 29801
Magnolia Dr 29803
Magnolia St 29803
Magnolia St SE 29801
Magnolia Lake Ct, Ln & Rd 29803
Maidstone Way 29803
Main Dr 29801
Main St 29803
Majestic Oak Way 29801
Major Rd 29803
Mallard Lake Dr 29803
Malpass Farm Rd 29803
Mamies Ln 29803
Manor Ln 29803
Maple St 29803
Maranatha Dr 29803
Maredo Dr 29803
Maria Ln 29805

Street	ZIP
Marigold Dr	29803
Marion St NE & SE	29801
Marion St Ext SE	29801
Marion Young Ct	29801
Mark Anthony Dr	29801
Market Pl	29803
Marlboro St NE & SE	29801
Marmalade Ln	29805
Marmiton Ct	29803
Martin Rd & St	29801
Martin Hollow Rd	29803
Martinez Ln	29801
Martingale Ln	29803
Marvin Dr	29803
Mary Ann Dr	29801
Mason Way	29801
Matanzas Ct	29801
Matt Ln	29805
Matties Country Ct	29803
Maurice Ter	29801
Maxine Ln	29805
Maxwell Rd	29803
May Royal Dr	29801
Maybelle Ln	29803
Mayfield Rd	29801
Mccall Ln	29805
Mccloud St	29803
Mccormick St NW	29801
Mccormick Street Ext	29801
Mcdaniel Sapp Ct	29803
Mcdougal Rd	29805
Mcintosh Loop	29805
Mckenzie Ln	29801
Mcmillian St	29801
Mcswain Dr	29801
Mcvey Rd	29803
Mead Ave	29801
Meadow Dr	29801
Meadow Trace Ct	29805
Meadow Wood Pl	29801
N Meadows Dr	29805
Meadows Ridge Ct	29803
Meares St	29803
Medical Park Dr	29801
Medinah Dr	29801
Medwell Hill Rd	29803
Meeting Pl	29803
Melissa Ct	29803
Melrose Dr	29801
Melville Ln SW	29801
Mepkin Ct	29803
Mercy Place Dr	29801
Merlot Pl	29803
Merrifield Ct	29803
Merritts Bridge Rd	29805
Metts Park Cir	29805
Michael Ct	29801
Michoacan Ln	29803
E & W Middlebury Ln	29803
Midlothian Ct E & W	29803
Midway Cir	29803
Mike Cir	29801
Milestone Cir	29803
Milion Ave	29803
Mill Springs Rd	29801
Millbrook Ave	29803
Miller Dr	29801
Millerton Dr	29803
Millrace Cir	29805
Mimosa Cir	29801
Minikahda Ct	29803
Miracle Dr	29801
Mississippi Ave	29801
Missy Ln	29801
Mistland Loop	29803
Misty Morning Ct	29805
Misty Oak Ln	29803
Mixon Rd	29801
Mockernut Cir	29803
Mockingbird Ln	29803
Modoc Ln	29803
Mohawk Dr	29801
Molly Dr	29805
Monetta St SE	29801
Montcastle Dr	29803
Monterey Dr	29803
Montmorenci Rd	29801
Moody St	29803
Moon Shadow St	29803
Moonlight Dr	29803
Moore Rd	29805
Morgan St	29803
Morgan St NW	29801
Moriah St	29801
Morning Ln	29803
Morning Glow Ln	29803
Morningside Dr	29801
Morris Rd	29805
Morris Bottom Dr	29801
Morris Hill Rd	29805
Morris Pond Rd	29801
Morton Ave NE	29801
Moseley Pond Rd	29805
Mosley Rd	29801
Mossback Cir	29803
Mossy Tree Ln	29803
Most Times Trl	29803
Moultrie Dr	29803
Mountain Laurel Dr	29801
Muddy Branch Rd	29805
Muirfield Ct	29803
Mulberry Ct	29803
Mull St	29803
Munday Rd	29803
Murrah Ave	29803
Murray Ct	29803
Mynah Bird Ln	29801
Nancy Ln SE	29803
Nandina Ct	29801
Natures Ln	29803
Nautilus St	29805
Navajo Trail Ln	29805
Nectarine Ln	29801
Ned Ln	29803
Negrete Village Ln	29801
Neibling Dr	29801
Neilson St	29803
Neomia Dr	29803
Nettleton Ct	29803
New Ln SW	29801
New Booth Rd	29801
New Bridge Rd	
1-599	29801
600-1399	29805
New Haven Ln SW	29803
New Holland Rd	29805
New Seigler Cir	29805
New York St	29803
Newberry St NW & SW	29801
Newfield Ln	29801
Newman Cir	29803
Nicholson Dr & Ln	29801
Nickletop Rd	29803
Nickroy Dr	29801
Nicole Dr	29805
No Mad Ct	29805
Noahs Ark Dr	29803
Nogales Pl	29803
Nokesville Cir	29803
Nondron St	29803
Norfolk Dr	29803
Norman Pl	29803
Normandy Ln	29801
North St	29803
Northbrook Dr	29805
Northern Way	29801
Northern Danger Ct	29803
Northgate Cir	29801
Northland Blvd	29801
Northwest Dr	29801
Northwood Dr	29803
Nottingham Dr SE	29801
Nutmeg Ct	29803
Oak Ln	29803
Oak Pl	29801
Oak St NW	29801
Oak Brook Dr	29801
Oak Grove Rd	29803
Oak Leaf Ln	29801
Oak Meadow Ln	29803
Oak Valley Ln	29803
Oakcrest Ln	29803
Oakland Hills St	29803
Oakman Dr	29803
Oakmont Ln	29803
Oakwood Dr	29801
Ocean Grove Rd	29805
Ochlocknee Ln	29803
Odom St	29803
Off Springs Rd	29801
Ola Hitt Ln	29803
Old Airport Rd	29801
Old Allen Rd	29803
Old Barnwell Rd	29803
Old Bell Rd	29801
Old Camp Long Rd	29805
Old China Springs Rd	29801
Old Country Rd	29801
Old Cowpath Way	29805
Old Dairy Rd	29803
Old Dibble Rd	29803
Old Dominion Rd	29803
Old Double Springs Rd	29803
Old Draw Bridge Rd	29803
Old Ellis Sq	29803
Old Farm Rd	29801
Old Friar Rd	29801
Old Graniteville Hwy	29801
Old Graymare Hollow Rd	29803
Old Jordan Rd	29805
Old Kennel Rd	29805
Old Kimbill Trl	29805
Old Lawson Rd	29801
Old Levels Trl	29803
Old Lloydtown Rd	29801
Old Market St	29803
Old Meadows Dr	29801
Old Paddock Ln	29803
Old Pope Rd	29801
Old Powderhouse Rd	29803
Old Thicket Pl	29803
Old Tory Trl	29801
Old Town Rd	29803
Old Wagener Rd	29801
Oleander Dr SE	29801
Opal Dr	29803
Orangeburg St NE & SE	29801
Oriole St	29803
Osbon Dr	29801
Outaways Rd	29803
Outback Way	29803
Outing Club Rd	29801
Overlook Ct	29805
Overlook Dr SW	29801
Owens St	29803
Owens Pond Rd	29805
Oxmoor Cir	29803
Pacer Cmns	29801
Pacer Crossings	29801
Pacer Downs Way	29801
Pacer Park Ln	29801
Paddock Club Pkwy	29803
Paddocks Bnd	29803
Page St	29801
Paine Trl	29805
Palisades Dr	29803
Palm Dr S	29803
Palmetto Ln SW	29801
Palmetto Farms Rd	29805
Palmira Ln	29803
Paloma Ln	29805
Panorama Pl	29803
Pardue Ln	29801
Paris Dr	29801
Park Ave SE & SW	29801
Parkside Dr	29803
Parksville Ln	29803
Parkway S	29803
Parque Ln	29803
Parrot St	29801
Parsons Cir & Ln	29803
Partridge Ct & Dr	29803
Partridge Bend Rd	29803
Pascalis Pl	29803
Pat Bells Cir	29805
Pathfinder Ln	29803
Pats Village Rd	29803
Patterson Ln	29803
Pawnee St	29803
Payton Pl	29805
Peace Dr	29801
Peach Orchard Pl NW	29801
Peacock Ct	29803
Pebble Ln	29801
Pebble Beach Ct	29803
Pecan Grove Ct	29805
Peconic Ct	29803
Pedro Dr	29805
Pellet Dr	29801
Pembrook Ct	29803
Pendleton St NW & SW	29801
Pendula Ct	29803
Peninsula Pt	29803
Penland Pl	29805
Penmar St	29803
Penny St	29803
Pepper Hill Way	29801
Peppermint Pl	29803
Periwinkle Ct	29803
Perrin St NW	29801
Perth Ct N & S	29803
Petaca Ln	29805
Peters Way	29805
Petite St	29803
Petticoat Ln	29803
Pheasant Run Dr	29803
Phillips St	29801
Photinia Dr	29803
Physician Dr	29801
Pickens Ave NW	29801
Pickett Ln	29803
Pin Oak Dr	29801
Pinckney Pl	29803
Pine Ave SE	29803
Pine Dr NW	29801
Pine St	29801
Pine Hill Dr	29801
Pine Hollow Dr	29803
E Pine Log Rd	29803
Pine Needle Cir & Rd	29803
Pine Shadow Way	29803
Pinecrest Ave	29801
Pinehurst Ave SE	29801
Pineland Ter SW	29801
Ping Way	29803
Pink Dogwood Cir	29803
Pintail Dr	29803
Pinyon Pine Loop	29803
Pioneer Pl	29801
Pioneer Rd	29805
Pipeline Rd	29801
Piper Rd	29805
Place Cir	29805
Plantation Dr	29803
E & W Pleasant Colony Dr	29803
Pleasant Oak Dr	29803
Pleasant Spring Ct	29805
Plunkett Ave NW	29801
Plymouth Dr	29801
Poe Cottage Pl	29805
Polaris Dr	29803
Polo Dr SE	29801
Ponder Ct	29803
Pontoon Sapp Dr	29803
Pony Trl	29803
Poplar Pl	29803
Poplar Branch Rd	29805
Poplar Hill Ct	29803
Poplar Springs Rd	29805
Poppy Ct	29801
Porter Trl	29803
Portofino Ln SW	29801
Powder House Rd	29801
Powderhouse Rd SE	29803
Powell Pond Rd	29801
Prairie Clover Run	29803
President Dr NW	29801
Prestwick Ct	29803
Prestwood Hts	29803
Price Ave	29803
Prickly Pear Ct	29801
Prides Xing	29801
Priester Ln	29803
Princess Ln	29801
Prosperity Ln	29801
Proud Pacer Dr	29801
Psalms Cir	29803
Quail Bend Rd	29801
Quail Hollow Ct	29803
Quaker Ridge Rd	29803
Quarry Pass	29803
Queens Ct	29803
Quiet Oak Ct	29803
R And B Way	29801
Rabom Rd	29805
Racehorse Way	29803
Raintree Ct	29803
Ramblewood Rd	29803
Ranchero St	29805
Rancho Pine Rd	29803
Randolph St	29803
Range Rd	29803
Raspberry Ln	29805
Raven Cir	29801
Raven Hollow Trl	29803
Ravenel St	29801
Ravenglass Ct	29803
Ravenwood Ct	29803
Ray Ln SE	29801
Raymond St	29801
Reading Ct	29803
Rebel Rd	29801
Recreation Dr	29803
Red Bird Ln	29805
Red Cedar Rd	29803
Red Leaf Ln	29803
Red Oak Dr	29801
Red Oak Ln	29803
Red Tip Ln	29801
Redd Cir & St	29801
Redd Street Ext	29801
Redds Branch Rd	29801
Redwood Dr	29803
Reedy Fork Rd	29805
Reid Dr & Ln	29801
Rein Dr	29803
Remington Pl	29803
Representative Dr	29801
Reserve Club Dr	29803
Residence Dr	29801
Retreat Pl	29801
Retro Dr	29801
Reynolds Pond Rd	
1000-1026	29801
1028-1299	29801
1300-1799	29805
Rhinestone Dr	29801
Rhododendron Pl SE	29801
Rhone St SW	29801
Rich Rd	29801
Richardson Ln	29801
Richardsons Lake Rd	29803
Richland Ave E & W	29801
Rico Ln	29801
Ridan Way	29803
Ridge Ave NW	29801
Ridgecrest Ave & Rd SW	29801
Ridgemont Dr	29803
Ridgemoor Dr	29803
Ridgewood Ln	29801
Riding Ridge Ct	29801
Riley St	29803
Rinehart Way	29803
Risen Star Ln	29805
Riva Ridge Ln	29803
River Birch Rd	29803
River Ridge Rd	29805
Riverbirch Dr	29803
Riviera Ct & Rd	29803
Robert M Bell Pkwy	29801
Robin Rd	29803
Robinhood Trl	29803
Robinson St	29801
Robinwood Dr	29803
Rock Maple Ct	29803
Rocking Horse Ln	29801
Rodgers Rd	29801
Rogers Ter	29801
Rogers County Ln	29803
Rolling Hills Rd	29803
Rolling Rock Rd	29803
E & W Rollingwood Rd	29801
Rookbranch Ct	29803
Roosevelt Ct	29801
Rose Hl	29801
Rose Chase Cir	29805
Rosemary Dr	29803
Rosemont Dr	29801
Roses Run	29803
Rosier Cir	29801
Rosin Ct	29803
Roslyn Cir	29803
Roundabout Rd	29805
Roundhill Ct	29803
Rouse Pl	29801
Rowdy Friends Rd	29801
Rowe Ln	29803
Royal Adelaide Ct	29803
Royal Oak Ct	29801
Rubins Cottage Ln	29801
Rudy Mason Pkwy	29801
Ruffian Rd	29803
Running Brook Ct	29805
Running Fox Ln	29803
Rushton Rd	29801
Russellpine Ct	29803
Russellwood Ct	29803
Ruth Ln	29803
Rutherford Pl	29803
Rutland Dr NE & NW	29801
Rutledge Rd SW	29801
Rye Field Rd	29801
Sabal Dr	29803
Saddlebred Loop	29801
Saddlejump Pl	29801
Saint Andrews Way	29803
Saint Annes Ct	29803
Saint Charles Ave	29801
Saint Johns Church Rd	29803
Salley St	29803
Saluda St NE	29801
San Juan Ln	29803
Sand Bend Rd	29801
Sand Fox Pl	29803
Sand Mountain Dr	29801
Sand River Ct	29801
Sandbed Ln	29805
Sandcroft Ct	29801
Sandhurst Pl SW	29801
Sandpiper Pl	29803
Sandshifter Ct	29803
Sandstone Blvd	29803
Sandy Ln	29801
Sandy Run	29803
Sandy Knoll Ln	29805
Sandy Springs Rd	29805
Santee Ave	29801
Sarahsetter Trl	29803
Saratoga St	29801
Sassafras Ct	29803
Sassafras Rd	
100-199	29803
2100-2199	29801
Satomi Way	29803
Saturn Way	29801
Savannah Dr	29803
Saw Pine Dr	29801
Sawyer Ln SW	29803
Scarborough Pass	29801
Scarlet Oak Pl	29803
Scholar Loop	29801
Schroder Ave NE	29801
Scotch Ln	29801
Scotch Pine Ct	29803
Scott Simmons Cir	29803
Scotts Ranch Rd	29801
Screaming Eagle Ct	29801
Screech Owl Trl	29805
Sea Grass Ln	29803
Seabiscuit Ln	29803
Sean St	29803
Seattle Slew Ln	29803
Sebastian Ct	29803
Secession Ln	29805
Secretariat Ln	29803
Seminole Ave & St	29801
Senate Dr NW	29801
Seneca Ave	29801
Senn St	29801
Sequoia St	29801
Serenity Ct	29801
Sessions Dr	29803
Seven Oaks Dr	29803
Sewee Dr	29803
Shadow Dr	29801
Shadow Oak Pl	29803
Shadow Pines Dr	29803
Shadow Ridge Ln	29801
Shadowood Dr	29801
Shady Ln NW	29801
Shady Pines Dr	29801
Shady Rest Rd	29803
Shagbark Ct	29803
Shakerag Rd	29803
Shannon Ln	29803
Shark Dr	29801
Sharyn Ln	29803
Shawnee Dr	29803
Shaws Crest Dr	29801
Shaws Fork Rd	29805
Sheephead Path	29805
Shelby Dr	29803
Shell Bluff Dr	29803
Shell Stone Trl	29803
Shenandoah St	29801
Shennecock Ct	29803
Sherry Dr	29803
Sherry Dr SE	29801
Sherwood Pl SE	29801
Shiloh Church Rd	
3500-3999	29805
4100-4599	29801
Shiloh Estates Rd	29805
Shiloh Heights Rd	29801
Shore Dr	29801
Short Ct & St	29803
Short Iron Dr	29803
Shrewsbury Ln	29803
Shumpert Pl	29805
Shuvee Cir	29803
Sierra Dr	29803
Silver Bluff Rd	
100-751	29803
750-760	29804
752-3698	29803
753-3699	29803
Silver Maple Ct	29803
Silver Meadow Ct	29803
Silverleaf Way	29803
N Silverton St	29803
Sim Gantt Rd	29805
Simonside Ct	29803
Simplicity Ln	29801
Sims Wood Rd	29803
Singletree Ln	29803
Sirius Dr	29803
Sizemore Cir & Rd	29803
Skylark Ln	29801
Skywatch Dr	29801
Sleepy Hollow Farm Rd	29803
Smallridge St	29803
Smith Ln	29801
Smiths Lawn Dr	29801
Smoot Dr	29803
Snipes Rd	29801
Snipes Pond Rd	29805
Society Hill Dr	29803
Solann St SE	29801
Solstice Meadow Ln	29803
Sommer St NE	29801
Sonoma Pl	29803
Sonora Ct	29801

Sorrel Trl 29803
South St 29803
Southbank Dr 29803
Southeastern Ln 29801
Southmeadows Blvd 29803
Southpark Cmns 29803
Southwood Ct 29803
Spains Trl 29805
Spalding Lake Cir 29803
Spann Ln 29805
Sparkleberry Ln 29803
Spaulding Dr 29803
Sperrin Cir 29803
Spike Ln 29801
Spirit Ln 29801
Sporthorse Ln 29803
Sporting Way 29801
Spring Dr 29801
Spring Fever Ln 29803
Spring Forest Cir 29803
Spring Stone Ct 29803
Spring Valley Ct & Dr 29803
Springfield Church Rd 29801
Springhouse Dr 29803
Springlake Rd 29801
Springside Ln 29801
Springwood Dr 29803
Spruce St 29803
Spyglass Dr 29803
Squire St 29803
Stable Dr 29801
Staghorn Ct 29801
Starbuck Dr 29803
Starling Ct 29805
Starlite St 29803
Station Ln 29803
Staubes Ln 29801
Steadman Rd 29801
Steeple Ridge Rd 29803
Steeplechase Rd 29803
Sterling Grove Cir 29803
Stetson Ln 29803
Stewart Dr 29801
Stiefel Rd 29805
Stinger Ln 29801
Stockton St 29801
Stone Dr 29801
Stonegate Dr 29803
Stonehaven Dr 29803
Stonington Ln SW 29803
Stono Ct 29801
Storm Branch Rd 29803
Storm Branch Leg 29803
Storm Song Ct 29803
Story St 29801
N Stream Dr 29805
Strutter Trl 29801
Studebaker Dr 29801
Suffolk Dr 29803
Sugar Maple Cir 29803
Sugar Mill Pl 29801
Sugarberry Rd 29803
Sugarwood Dr 29803
Sumac Ct 29803
Summer Lakes Dr 29805
Summer Place Dr 29801
Summer Squall Ln 29803
Summer Wind Ct 29805
Summer Winds Cir 29803
Summerall Ct 29801
Summerhill Ave 29801
Summerset Ct 29803
Summerwood Way 29803
Summit Dr 29801
Sumter St NE & SE 29801
Sunderland Rd 29803
Sundy Ave NE 29801
Sunnyside Cir & Ln 29803
Sunridge Rd 29803
Sunset Dr 29801
Sunshine Cir & Ct 29803
Surrey Cir 29801
Surrey Park Dr 29803
Sussex Ct 29803
Sweet Bee Ln 29803
Sweet Gum Ct 29803
Sweet Gum Ln 29803
Sweet Gum Rd 29805
Sweetbay Dr 29803
Sweetgum Ln 29801
Swing Way 29801
Sybal Ln 29801
Sycamore Dr 29803
T Ln 29801
T And S Dr 29801
T Lane Cir 29801
Tab Dr 29803
Tahoe Dr 29803
Talatha Church Rd 29803
Tall John Ln 29805
Tall Pine Dr 29803
Tamil Dr 29803
Tar Heel Rd 29803
Tarton Pass 29801
Taylor Dr 29801
Taylor St 29803
Taylor Springs Dr 29801
Tea Olive Ct 29803
Tea Rose Dr 29803
Teague St NW 29801
Teal Ct 29803
Teds Way 29801
Teke Ln 29803
Telegraph Dr 29801
Tennessee Ave NW 29801
Terrapin Trl 29801
Terry Dr 29801
The Aly 29801
The Cors 29803
The Bunkers 29803
Thomas St
100-199 29803
1000-1099 29801
Thornapple St 29805
Thornhill Ct & Dr 29803
Thoroughbred Run 29803
Thorpe Ln SE 29801
Three Creek Run 29803
Three Farms Rd 29805
Three Notch Rd 29805
Three Runs Creek Way 29803
Three Runs Plantation Dr 29803
Tiger Ln 29805
Timber Run 29801
Timberchase Ln 29803
Timberlane Rd SE 29801
Timberton Pl 29803
Tin Roof Ln 29803
Tin Whistle Ln 29803
Titanic Rd 29805
Tiznow Dr 29803
Toadstool Trl 29803
Toby Ave & Ext 29801
Tolt Trl 29801
Tom Cat Ln 29803
Tomahawk Dr 29801
Tommy Ln 29801
Toole St NW 29801
Toolebeck Rd 29803
Toomer Ln 29803
Tower Pl 29801
Town Creek Rd 29803
Tracewood Pl 29803
Tradd Ln 29805
Trade Ct 29805
Trafalgar St SW 29801
Trail Pt 29803
Trail Ridge Ct & Rd 29803
Trailwood Ave 29803
Travellers Ln 29803
Treadway Bridge Rd 29803
Tree Top Pl 29803
Trellis Ct 29803
Trenton Pl 29801
Trestle Ct 29801
Tri C Dr 29801
Trials Trl 29803
Tricemont St 29801
Triple H Farm Ln 29803
Triple Tree Ln SW 29803
Trippi Ln 29803
Trolley Line Rd 29801
Trolley Run Blvd 29801
Troon Way 29803
Trotters Run Ct 29803
Trowell Rd 29801
Troy Ln 29801
Tulane Dr 29803
Tulip Poplar Ct 29803
Tundra Trl 29801
Tupelo Ct 29803
Turbyfill Ln 29801
Turnberry Ct N & S 29803
Turpin Ln 29803
Turtle Pond Ct 29803
Twiffy Ln 29805
Twilight Ln 29801
Twin Creek Farm Rd 29805
Twin Lakes Rd 29803
Twin Ponds Ln 29803
Two Notch Rd SE
500-899 29801
900-1899 29803
Tyler St 29803
Tyler Hill Rd 29801
Umbria Ct 29803
Unbridled Ct 29803
Union St NE & SE 29801
Union Baptist Rd 29801
Union Church Ln 29801
University Ln & Pkwy 29801
Valley Dr 29803
Valley Rd 29801
Valley Green Dr SW 29801
Valley View Ct & St 29801
Valleydale Ln 29803
Van Bryan Dr 29801
Vanderbilt Dr 29803
Varden Dr 29803
Vass St 29805
Vaucluse Rd 29801
Veline Ln 29805
Vella Dr 29803
Ventura Ln 29805
Veranda Ln 29803
Verbena Dr 29803
Vfw Rd 29803
Vicars Ln 29805
Victoria Dr NW 29801
Village Dr 29803
Village Green Blvd 29803
Vincent Ave NE 29801
Vine St 29803
Vines Dogwood Dr 29803
Vintage Vale Rd 29805
Violets Dr 29801
Virginia Ave 29801
Virgo Ct 29803
Vista Dr 29801
Vivion Dr & Pl 29803
Voorhees St 29801
Wadley Dr 29801
Wagener Rd
2400-3499 29801
3500-4599 29805
Waites St 29803
Wake Robin Loop 29803
Walden Pond Ct 29803
Waldon Brook Way 29803
Walker Ave SE 29801
Walkers Pine Ln 29803
Wallace Green St 29801
Walters Way 29801
Walton Ct 29805
Walton Heath Ct & Way 29803
Wando Ridge Rd 29801
War Eagle Pl 29805
Ward Cir 29801
Warehouse Rd 29801
Wash A Way Dr 29801
Washboard Rd 29801
Washington Cir 29801
Washington Dr 29803
Water Locust Ct 29803
Water Oak Ct & Dr SW 29803
Waterbridge Ln 29803
Wateree Pl 29803
Waterloo St SW 29801
Waters Edge Dr 29803
Watkins Ln 29803
Watsonia Dr 29803
Waverly Ln 29803
Wax Myrtle Cir & Ct 29803
Waxhaw Dr 29803
Weatherwood Ct 29803
Weaver St 29801
Wedgewood Ct & Dr 29803
Weeks Rd 29805
Wellshod Ln 29803
Wentworth Cir 29803
Wesley Dr 29803
Wesson Dr 29803
West Rd 29801
Westbrook Farms Trl 29805
Westcliff Dr SW 29801
Westdale Ave 29801
Westmont Dr 29801
Westo Rd 29801
Westover Dr 29803
Westwinds Dr 29801
Westwood Dr 29803
Wethersfield Dr 29801
Wexford Ct 29803
Weyanoke Ct 29803
Weyerhaeuser Rd 29801
Weyhill Pl 29801
Weymouth Pl 29803
Wheat Rd 29801
Wheeler Dr SW 29803
Whipporwill Ct 29803
Whiskey Rd
400-1199 29801
1200-5099 29803
5101-5199 29803
Whispering Branch Ct 29805
Whispering Pines Ter 29801
Whistling Straits Ln 29803
White Birch Ct 29803
White Cedar Way 29803
White Herron Cir 29801
White Pond Rd 29803
White Willow Pl 29803
Whitecap Pl 29803
Whitehall Pl SE 29801
Whitemarsh Dr 29803
Whithorn Ct 29803
Whitney Dr 29803
Widener Rd 29803
Wild Berry Rd 29801
Wild Oak Ln 29803
Wilderness Rd 29805
Wildhaven Dr 29803
Wilds Ave 29803
Wildwood Rd 29801
Willard Ter 29801
Williams Dr 29803
Williams Ln 29801
Williams Park Ln 29803
Williams Sand Ln 29803
Williamsburg St NE & SE 29801
Willing Ln 29801
Willis Ct 29801
Willis Hill Rd 29801
Williston Rd 29801
Willow Lake Ct & Dr 29803
Willow Leaf Pl 29801
Willow Oak Loop 29803
Willow Run Rd 29801
Willow Trace Pl 29803
Willow Woods Dr 29803
Wilson Young Dr 29801
Winchester Ln 29803
Windchime Ct 29803
Windermere Way 29803
Windham Blvd & Way 29805
Windmill Dr 29801
Windsor Pl SE 29801
Winged Elm Cir 29803
Winged Foot Dr 29803
Winthrop Dr 29803
Wire Rd
1-500 29801
501-597 29805
502-598 29801
599-3099 29805
Wise Creek Ln 29801
Wise Hollow Rd 29803
Wishing Well Ln 29801
Wisteria Dr 29803
Wofford Cir 29803
Wood Pond Ln 29801
Woodbine Rd 29803
Woodbridge Dr 29801
Woodfield Rd 29803
Woodhill Pl 29803
Woodlake Dr 29803
Woodland Dr 29801
Woodland Drive Ext 29803
Woodmont Ct 29801
Woodruff Ct 29803
Woods Bend Dr 29803
Woods Edge Ct 29803
Woodsia Ln 29803
Woodside Executive Ct 29803
Woodside Plantation Dr 29803
Woodthrush Ln 29803
Woodvale Ln 29801
Woodvalley Dr 29803
Woodvine Rd 29803
Woodward Dr & St 29803
Woodwardia Gln 29803
Woodwind Way 29803
Wren Pl 29803
Wrights Mill Rd 29801
Wyatt Ln 29803
Wyman St NE 29801
Wynnewood Ln 29801
Yarrow Way 29803
Yates St NE 29801
Yellow Pine Rd 29803
Yellow Ribbon Rd 29803
Yemassee Ave 29801
Yonce Ln 29803
York St NE & SE 29801
Youmans Ln 29803
Zachmann St 29803
Zambrano Ct 29803
Zane Trace Rd 29805
Zekia Dr 29801
Zelkova Ct 29803

NUMBERED STREETS

All Street Addresses 29801

ANDERSON SC

General Delivery 29621

POST OFFICE BOXES MAIN OFFICE STATIONS AND BRANCHES

Box No.s
1 - 4460 29622
5001 - 6279 29623
8002 - 8022 29622
13001 - 15028 29624

NAMED STREETS

A St 29625
A Lane Dr 29625
A M Ellison Rd 29621
Abbeville Hwy
2900-7899 29624
8200-9299 29621
Abercrombie Rd 29626
Aberdeen Dr 29621
Abigail Ln 29621
Abington Ct 29621
Acker Rd 29624
Acorn Dr 29621
Adams Ave 29624
Addis Cir 29626
Adger Dr 29624
Admiral Ct 29621
Agnew Rd 29626
Air Defender Way 29625
Airline Rd 29624
Airport Rd 29626
Alan Ct 29625
Alarelak St 29624
Alene Hills Way 29625
Algonquin Ave 29626
Alice Dr 29625
Alisha Dr 29621
Allen Ave 29624
Allenby Rd 29621
Allendale Cir 29626
Alliance Pkwy 29621
Allison Cir 29625
Allison Square Dr 29624
Allston St 29624
Aloha Dr 29625
Alpha St 29625
Altamont Ct 29621
Amanda Dr 29621
Ambassador Dr 29625
Amber Dr 29621
Amberwood Dr 29621
American Way 29621
American Airline Rd 29624
Amity Rd 29621
Amity Road Ext 29621
Amy St 29626
Anchor Pt 29625
Andalusian Trl 29621
Anderson Ave 29625
Anderson Beach Blvd 29621
Anderson Business Park 29621
Anderson Independent Mail Blvd 29625
Andi Ln 29626
Andrea Pt 29625
Angie Dr 29624
Animal Shelter Dr 29624
Anmed Foundation Dr 29621
Ann Ct & Rd 29625
Anna Ln 29625
Annandale Dr 29621
Anne Hutto Rd 29625
Anthony Dr 29626
Antiguay Dr 29621
Appian Way 29625
Applebee Ln 29626
Appledown Ct 29621
Appleton St 29625
Arabian Way 29626
Arbor Ln 29621
Arborwood Dr 29621
Arcadia Dr 29621
Archdale Way 29621
Arden Chase 29621
Arlington Ave 29621
Armstrong St 29624
Arnold Dr 29625
Arnold Rd 29625
Arrowhead Pt 29625
Arrowood Dr 29626
Asaville Church Rd 29621
Asaville School Rd 29621
Asbury Ct 29624
Asbury Park Rd 29625
Ashburn Dr 29621
Ashby Ct 29625
Ashland Chemical 29625
Ashlawn Ct 29625
Ashley Ave 29624
Ashley Rd 29621
Ashley Downs 29621
Ashton Ln 29621
Ashwood Dr 29624
Ashwood Ln 29625
Aspen Way 29626
Auburn Ave 29626
Augusta National 29621
Austin Dr 29624
Autumn Oaks 29621
Avant Cir & Rd 29625
Avenue Of Oaks 29621
Avondale Rd 29624
Awaken Ct 29625
Axman Dr 29625
Axman Rd 29626
Aycock Dr 29621
Azalea Dr 29625
B St 29625
Babb St 29621
Bailey Rd 29624
Bailey St 29621
Bainbridge Dr 29625
Baker St 29625
Ball St 29625
Ballentine Rd 29621
Balloon Ln 29625
Balloonfest Blvd 29625
Balmoral Rd 29625
Baltic Ave 29621
Bamboo Dr 29621
Banabus Ln 29621
Banfield Ct 29621
Bannister Ln 29626
Bannister St 29621
Barcliff Ln 29621
Barefoot Trl 29621
Barnard E Bee Ave 29625
Barnes Ave 29625
Barnett Cir 29625
Barrett Cir 29621
Bash Ln 29625
Baum Ln 29624
Bauml Ln 29624
Baybrooke Ln 29621
Bayhill Cir 29625
Bayshore Ln 29621
Bayview Ln 29625
Beachwood Ave 29621
Beagle Run 29625
Beamer Dr 29621
Bean Mill Way 29625
Bear Creek Rd 29621
Beaty Sq 29624
Beauregard Ave 29625
Beaver Run & Trl 29625
Beaver Creek Rd 29624
Beaver Lake Rd 29625
Becker Ln 29625
Beckman Dr 29624
Becky St 29626
Bedford Dr 29621
Bedford Forest Ave 29625
Beech Ln 29621
Beecher St 29625
Beechwood Pkwy 29621
Belaire Cir 29621
Belford Ct & Dr 29625
Belhaven Rd 29621
Belk Dr 29621
Belleadi Rd 29626
Bellview Rd 29621
Belmont Dr 29624
Belspring Ln 29621
E Beltline Blvd 29621
W Beltline Blvd 29625
Beltline Connector 29621
Belton Hwy 29621
Belton St 29624
Benjamin St 29625
Bennett Dr 29621
E & W Benson St 29624
Berkley Dr 29625
Berkshire Hl 29621
Bermuda Dr 29621
Bern Cir 29626
Berry Ln 29624
Bertha Dr 29625
Bertharee Ct 29625
Best Ln 29624

Beta St 29625
Betty St 29624
Beulah Dr 29625
Beverly Ln 29626
Bevlyn Rd 29621
Bib Way 29626
Bickford Cir 29625
Big Vw 29621
Big Oak Rd 29626
Biggs St 29625
Bill Harbin Cir 29621
Binewood Ln 29625
Birch St 29625
Bitterweed Ln 29621
Black Bass Rd 29626
Blackberry Ln 29625
Blair St 29625
Blanding Dr 29625
Blanding St 29624
Bleckley St 29625
Bleckley Street Ext 29625
Blue Heron Trl 29625
Bluebird Ln 29621
Blume Rd 29625
Blumefield Rd 29625
Boat Ramp 29621
Bob White Ln 29625
Boggs St 29625
Bolt Dr 29621
Bonaire Pt 29621
Bonham Ct 29621
Booker St 29624
Boscobel Rd 29625
Boseman Rd 29621
Boston St 29625
N & S Boulevard Hts 29621
Boundary St 29625
Bowden Rd 29626
Bowen Dr 29621
Bowen Rd 29621
Bowen St 29625
Bowman Ave 29625
Boxwood Ln 29621
Boyce Ave & St 29625
Boyd St 29624
Brackenberry Dr 29621
Bradford Trl 29625
Bradford Way 29621
Bradley Ave, Park & Rd 29621
Brady Dr 29626
Braeburn Dr 29621
Bramble Ridge Rd 29621
Brandywine Ln 29625
Bree Dr 29621
Brenda Dr 29625
Brentwood Cir 29625
Brenwood Dr 29624
Brewton Ct 29621
Briar Creek Ln 29621
Briar Creek Trl 29625
Briar Patch Rd 29621
Briarwood St 29621
Bridgeview Dr 29625
Brighton Rd 29621
Brissey St 29624
Bristol Ct 29625
Brittania Cir 29621
Brittany Park 29621
Brittlewood Way 29625
Britton St 29621
Broad St 29621
Broad Leaf Ln 29621
Broadbent Way 29625
Broadwater Cir & Dr 29626
Broadway Heights Rd 29621
Broadway Lake Rd 29621
Broadway School Rd 29621
Broadwell Ave 29625
Broadwell Mill Rd 29626
Brock St 29624
Brogan Ave 29625
Bronco Dr 29624
Brook Allen Dr 29625
Brook Forest Dr 29621
Brookgreen Cir, Ct & Dr 29625
Brookhaven Ct & Dr 29624
Brookhollow Rd 29621
Brooklyn Ave 29624
Brookmeade Dr 29624
Brookridge Dr
100-199 29624
300-399 29625
Brooks St 29624
Brookside Dr 29625
Brookview Dr 29621
Brookwood Ct 29621
Brown Rd
100-1699 29621
2000-2099 29625
Brown St 29624
Brown Well Trl 29621
Broyles St 29624
Bryant Rd 29621
Bryson Rd
100-199 29625
2000-2099 29621
Bubanna Rd 29626
Buck Tree Ln 29621
Buckeye Trl 29626
Buckingham Ct 29621
Buckland Dr 29621
Bud Ln 29625
Buena Vista Ave 29624
Buford Ave 29621
Burdine Dr & Rd 29624
Burning Tree Rd 29621
Burns Bridge Cir & Rd 29625
Burns Bridge Road Ext 29625
Burris St 29625
Burson Rd 29624
Burt Dr 29621
Burton Dr & Rd 29625
Burts Ct 29624
Burts Garage Rd 29626
Busby Rd 29626
Busby Dairy Rd 29626
Buteos Way 29621
Butler St 29624
Buttercup Trl 29621
Byrd Ln 29624
C St 29625
Cabin Cove Rd 29625
Cala Way 29625
Calais Dr 29625
Caldwell Ln 29626
Caleb Ct 29625
Calhoun Dr 29621
E Calhoun St 29621
W Calhoun St 29625
Calico Rd 29625
Callow Hill Way 29621
Calm Cv 29626
Calrossie Rd 29621
Calvary Home Cir 29621
Calvert St 29624
Calvin Est 29621
Cambridge Cv 29621
Cambridge Rd 29625
Camden Dr 29624
Camellia Dr 29625
Camelot Dr 29624
Cameo Ct 29621
Cameron Way 29621
Camfield Rd 29621
Camp Lou Ann 29621
Campbell Rd & St 29621
Camson Rd 29625
Canary Dr 29626
Candi Dr 29625
Candice Ashley Trl 29625
Candlewood Dr 29625
Canebrake Dr 29621
Cann Rd 29625
Canna Lily Ln 29625
Canter Ln 29626
Canterbury Rd 29621
Canton Ln 29621
Canvas Back Ct 29626
Capeview Ln 29626
Capic Rd 29625
Capitol Way 29626
Captains Way 29625
Cara Ct 29625
Cardinal Cir 29621
Cardinal Ct 29625
Cardinal Ln 29626
Cardinal Park Dr 29621
Carey St 29624
Caribou Cv 29621
Carl Anderson Way 29625
Carling Dr 29625
Carlisle Pl 29621
Carlton Ct 29621
Carnoustie Cir 29621
Carole Ave 29625
Carolina Cir 29621
Carpenter Rd 29621
Carpenter St 29624
Carrick Ct 29624
Carroll St 29624
Carson St 29625
Carswell Dr 29624
Cartee Rd 29625
Carter Rd 29626
Carter Hall Dr 29621
Carter Oak Rdg 29621
Carter Oaks Dr 29621
Carter Woods Dr 29621
Carver St 29624
Casa Del Rd 29625
Casa Del Rio Dr 29625
Case Ln 29624
Casey St 29624
Cason Dr 29624
Cassandra Turn 29621
Casselberry Ct 29621
Cassena Dr 29626
Castle Springs Rd 29621
Catawba Ave 29626
Cater St 29621
Cathcart Dr 29624
Cathey Rd 29621
Catlett St 29624
Catrina Ln 29625
Caughlin Ave 29624
Cavas Cir 29626
Caversham Ln 29621
Cayman Way 29621
Cc Trl 29621
Cedar Ln 29621
Cedar Rd 29624
Cedar Rdg 29621
Cedar St 29626
Cedar Crest Trl 29621
Cedar Pond Rd 29621
Cedarwood Ln 29626
Center Ave 29624
Centerville Rd 29625
Central Ave 29625
Cetona Ct 29621
Chad Ct 29621
Chadwick Rd 29621
Challenge Ct 29624
Chambers Rd 29626
Chamblee Rd 29626
Chantilly Ln 29625
Chapel Ave 29625
Chapelwood Dr 29626
Chapman Rd
100-299 29625
1600-1699 29621
Chardonnay Dr 29621
Charles Dr 29624
Charlestowne Way 29621
Charley Dr 29625
Charping Ln 29621
Charter Rd 29625
Charter Oak Dr 29625
Chase Ave 29625
Chasen Ct 29621
Chasewater Dr 29621
Chastain Rd 29621
Chastine Dr 29621
Chateau Rd 29625
Chauga Dr 29626
Chaumont Rd 29625
Cheek St 29624
Cherokee Cir
100-199 29621
1000-1699 29625
Cherokee St 29626
Cherokee Trl 29626
Cherry Ave 29621
Cherry Dr 29625
Cherry Grove Blvd 29625
Cherry Seed Rd 29625
Cherry Tree Ct 29621
Cherry Tree Rd 29625
Chestnut Blvd 29625
Chestnut Dr 29624
Chestnut Ln 29625
Cheswych Dr 29621
Chetwood Dr 29621
Cheyenne St 29626
Chianti Ln 29621
Chief Dr 29624
Chipwood Dr 29624
Choctaw St 29626
Christine Ln 29624
Christopher Dr 29626
Christopher T Way 29626
Chuck Dr 29624
Chucka Luck Dr 29621
E & W Church St 29624
Churchwell Ave 29624
Cindy Dr
100-199 29624
1500-1599 29621
Cindy Ln 29621
Cinema Ave & Ctr 29621
Citation Ct 29621
Civic Center Blvd 29625
Civic Center Boulevard Ext 29625
Clairmont Ln 29626
Clara Ln 29624
Clarence Ave 29624
Clarendon Dr 29621
Clarke Ln 29621
Clarke Stream Dr 29621
Claudine Dr 29624
Clear Pond Way 29626
Clearview Dr 29625
Clemson Blvd
3400-3421 29621
3420-3420 29623
3422-4698 29621
3423-4699 29621
Clemson Research Blvd 29625
Cleveland Ave 29624
Cleveland Ct 29624
Cleveland Dr 29626
Cleveland Rd 29626
Cliftons Landing Dr 29625
Clinkscales Dr 29626
Clinkscales Rd 29624
Clinkscales St 29625
Clinton Dr 29621
Clover Patch Way 29621
Cloverdale Dr 29626
Cloverhill Dr 29624
Club Dr
500-799 29626
1801-1999 29625
Club Pt 29626
Coachman Ct & Dr 29625
Cobblestone Ct & Path 29621
Cobbs Way 29621
Cobbs Glen Dr 29621
Cochran Block 29625
Cody Ct 29626
Coe Rd 29624
Coffee Ct 29625
Coker Rd 29626
Cola Hawkins Rd 29621
Cold Berry Dr 29624
Cold Water Ln 29624
Cole Cir & Dr 29625
College Ave & Hts 29621
Collett Dr 29621
Collett Ln 29626
Collingwood Dr 29621
Colonial Dr 29621
Colonial Pl 29625
Colony Ct 29621
Colorado Ln 29626
Comanche St 29626
Combine Ln 29624
Comet St 29621
Commerce Blvd 29625
Commons Pkwy 29621
Commonwealth Ln 29621
Community Park Dr 29621
Compass Pt 29625
Computer Ct 29625
Concord Ave, Cir & Rd 29621
Construction Way 29625
Continental St 29625
Control Dr 29625
Cool Springs Dr 29626
Coosa Ln 29621
Cornelia Rd 29621
Corning St 29624
Corrine St 29626
Cortez Rd 29626
Cortland Ln 29625
Corto St 29625
Cothran Cir 29625
Cottage Ln 29624
Country Mdws 29626
Country Club Ln 29625
Country Creek Dr 29625
Country Garden Ln 29626
Country View Rd 29621
County Home Rd 29625
Courtney Dr 29625
Courtyard Dr 29621
Cove Cir 29626
Cove Trl 29621
Covered Bridge Pkwy 29621
Covington Ct 29621
Cox Ave & Rd 29621
Crabapple Chase 29625
Craft Rd 29621
Craig Dr 29624
Crain Ct 29624
Crawford St 29624
Crayton St 29621
Creamer Rd 29625
Creekside Ct 29621
Creekwalk Dr 29625
Crepe Myrtle Ln 29625
Crescent Dr 29624
Crest Cir 29626
Cresta Verde Rd 29621
Crestview Rd 29621
Creswell Ave 29621
Cretewood Dr 29621
Cricket Ln 29621
Crighten Ct 29621
Cringle Ln 29625
Cripple Creek Rd 29626
Crocker St 29624
Cromer Rd 29624
Crooked Creek Ct 29626
Crosby Dr 29621
Cross Pt & St 29625
Crosscreek Dr 29621
Crossland St 29624
Crossridge Ln 29621
Crowther Dr 29621
Crystal Ln 29621
Cumberland Way 29621
Cunningham Dr 29624
Curtis St 29624
Cutliff Ln 29625
Cynthia Dr 29625
Cypress Ln 29621
Cypress Run 29625
D St 29625
D L Dr 29624
Dakota Ln 29626
Dalrymple Rd 29621
Danbury Ln 29624
Dandelion Trl 29621
Daniel Dr 29626
Daniel St 29625
Daniels Ave 29625
Danny Boy Ln 29626
Darby Ln 29624
Darby Way 29626
Darracott Dr 29624
Darson Dr 29621
David Lee Coffee Pl 29625
Davis Cir 29625
Davis Dr 29621
Davis Ln 29621
Day Rd 29626
De Leon Dr 29626
Dean Rd 29625
Debos Ln 29626
Debra Ave 29626
Deep Creek Church Rd 29626
Deep Water Pt 29621
Deer Creek Trl 29621
Deer Run Rd 29626
Deerfield Dr 29621
Deerwood Rd 29621
Deerwood Trl 29624
Delaware Dr 29625
Delia St 29624
Dellwood Cir & Ln 29621
Deloach Dr 29625
Delta Rd 29621
Denver Rd 29625
Denver Cove Rd 29625
Derrick Ln 29626
Derrydown Way 29624
Destination Blvd 29621
Devon Way 29621
Dewars Trl 29621
Diamond Pt 29625
Diamond St 29624
Dianna St 29624
Dickens Ave 29621
Dickerson Rd 29626
Dixie Dr 29624
Dixon Ave, Dr & Rd 29625
Dobbins Ave 29625
Dobbins Bridge Rd 29626
Dockside Way 29625
Doe Run 29621
Dogwood St 29625
Dogwood Trce 29621
Dohi Ama Ln 29624
Dolphin Pt 29625
Don Ave 29624
Donaldson Rd 29621
Donan Ct 29625
Donaree Cir & Dr 29625
Donhill Rd 29625
Dooley St 29624
Dora Dr 29624
Doris Ave 29626
Doris Mcgill Jones Rd 29624
Dostak Dr 29621
Double Oak Ct 29621
Doubletree Dr 29625
Douglas St 29624
Dove Dr 29625
Dove Holw 29626
Dove Tree Ln 29621
Dover Ct 29625
Dowell Rd 29626
Downie Ln 29621
Dr Martin Rd 29621
Dragon Aly 29625
Drake Cir 29624
Drakeford Ct 29621
Drakes Xing 29625
Drayton Cir 29621
Dresden Ln 29625
Driftwood Dr 29621
Driftwood Ln 29626
Driftwood Way 29625
Drucker Rdg 29625
Druid Hills Dr 29621
Dublin Ct 29621
Duckett Cir 29621
Duckett Rd 29625
Duckworth Ln 29621
Ducworth Down 29621
Dudley Rd 29624
Due West Hwy
100-499 29624
500-2032 29621
2034-2098 29621
Dugout Cove Rd 29626
Duke St 29624
Dunaway Ct 29621
Duncan St 29625
Dundee Ct 29621
Dunecrest Rd 29625
Dunhill Ct & Dr 29625
Dunlap Rd 29621
Dunn Rd 29625
Duraleigh Rd 29621
Dursely Dr 29621
Duvall Way 29624
Dyar Dr 29621
E St 29625
Eagles Nest 29625
Eagleview 29625
Earl White Dr 29626
E Earle St 29621
W Earle St 29625
Eastwood St 29621
Easy Gap Rd 29621
Eathern Dr 29625
Echo Cir 29625
Echo Holw 29621
Echo Trl 29621
Edenbrooke Cir 29621
Edgebrook Dr 29621
Edgewater Dr 29626
Edgewater Way 29621
Edgewood Ave 29625
Edinburg Dr 29625
Edinburgh Trl 29625
Edisto Rd 29621
Edith Dr & St 29626
Edwards Dr 29626
Egret Pt 29626
Eisenhower Rd 29625
Elderberry Ln 29625
Electric City Blvd 29621
Elgin Dr 29621
Elizabeth Ln 29621
Elizabeth St
400-499 29621
700-1199 29624
Ella St 29621
Ellen St 29624
Ellenburg Dr 29626
Elliott Cir 29621
Ellison St 29624
Ellsworth Ln 29621
Elm Ave 29625
Elma Rd 29625
Elmhurst Ln 29621
Elrod Cir 29625
Elrod Rd 29624
Embassy Dr 29625
Emily Dr 29625
Emma St 29626
W End Ave 29625
England Way 29625
Engram Ln 29621
Erskine Rd 29621
Eskew Cir 29621
Essex Dr 29621
Estes Dr 29621
Ethelise Cir 29626
Eureka Dr 29621
Evans St 29621
Evanston Ct 29621
Evergreen Rd 29621
Evergreen St 29625
Everytime Dr 29626
Evonshire Blvd 29621
Exeter Ct 29621
Extended Ln 29625
Extertal Dr 29625
F St 29625

Fagg Rd 29621
Fair St 29625
Fairfax St 29625
Fairfield Dr 29621
Fairhaven Dr 29626
Fairlane Dr 29624
Fairmont Rd 29621
Fairview St 29624
Fairway Grn 29621
Falcons Lndg 29625
Fall St 29624
Fallon Ln 29625
Fallstaff St 29624
N Fant St 29621
S Fant St 29624
Fants Grove Cir & Rd 29625
Farmer St 29621
Farmington Dr 29621
Farmington Rd 29626
Fates Way 29621
Fawn Hill Dr 29621
Faye Dr 29624
Featherfilled Ct 29625
Federal St 29625
Fennell Pt & Rd 29625
Fenwick Way 29621
Fernwood Cir 29626
Fernwood Ct 29621
Ferry St 29626
Few Ct 29621
Fieldcrest Dr 29625
Fielding Dr 29625
Fields Ave 29625
Fieldstone Way 29621
Financial Blvd 29621
Findley Cir 29626
Finley St 29625
Firethorn Rd 29621
First Creek Rd 29621
Fisher Rd 29625
Fisher Jenkins Rd 29625
Fishermans Club Dr 29626
Five Forks Rd 29621
Five Knoll Ct 29621
Flat Bridge Rd 29621
Flat Rock Rd 29624
Fleet Dr 29625
Fleming Dr 29621
Fletcher St 29625
Florence Ct 29621
Flowe Rd 29624
Flynn Dr 29626
Fonya Ln 29625
Forest Ave 29625
Forest Ln 29621
Forest Cove Rd 29626
Forest Hill Dr 29621
N Fork Dr 29621
Forrester Rd 29621
Fort Hill Ct 29624
Foster St 29625
Fountainbleu Blvd 29625
Fowler Rd 29625
Fox Trl 29621
Fox Creek Rd 29621
Fox Fire Rd 29621
Fox Valley Rd 29621
Foxcroft Way 29621
Frampton St 29624
Frances St 29621
Frances Cannon Dr 29621
Franklin Rd 29625
E Franklin St 29624
W Franklin St 29624
E Fredericks St 29621
W Fredericks St 29625
Fretwell Dr 29626
Fretwell St 29621
Friend St 29621
Friendship Ln 29624
Fritz Dr 29621
Frontage Rd 29621
Fullbrights Plus Dr 29624
Fulwer St 29624
Furman Rd 29621
Furman Gambrell Rd 29621

Fyffe Dr 29625
G St 29625
G W M Dr 29626
Gabrielle St 29621
Gadsden Sq & St 29624
Gaffney Rd 29626
Gaineswood Rd 29625
Gallant Ln 29621
Galloping Ghost Rd 29626
Gambrell Rd 29625
Gamewell Ct 29621
Gantt Ave 29625
Gap Hill Rd 29625
Garden Gate Dr 29621
Garden Park Dr 29621
Garden Way Dr 29625
Gardenia Ct 29625
Gareloch Ln 29625
Garrett Dr 29625
Garrett Maxwell Rd 29626
Garrison Rd 29625
Gary Rd 29625
Gary St 29624
Gates St 29625
Gavotte Ln 29621
Gayland Dr 29621
Gaylord Ln 29625
Geer Dr 29621
Geisberg Dr 29624
Gemstone Trl 29625
Genchari Rd 29621
General Vandergrift Trl 29624
Genesis Cir 29625
Gentry Dr & Rd 29621
George Albert Lake Rd 29624
George B Timmerman Dr 29621
George Edward Dr 29624
George Mcclain Ln 29625
George Merck Rd 29626
George Smith Mill Rd 29625
Gerrard Rd 29625
Gerrard Point Rd 29626
Getsinger Dr 29621
Getsinger Rd 29625
Ghent Dr 29621
Gibson Rd 29625
Giladiola Ln 29625
Gilbert St 29625
Giles St 29621
Gillwood Dr 29624
Gilmer Cir 29626
Gilmer Dr 29621
Gilmer Rd 29621
Gilmer St 29621
Gilreath Rd 29621
Glade Spgs 29621
Glazed Oaks Dr 29625
Glen Arbor Dr 29625
Glen Eden Ln 29626
Glenaire Rd 29626
Glendale Rd 29624
Glenn Rd 29626
Glenn St 29625
Glenna Dr 29626
Glenwood Ave 29625
Glintz Dr 29621
Glory Ln 29626
Gold Standard Way 29621
Golden Eagle Ln 29621
Golden Hickory Dr 29621
Golf Widow Dr 29621
Goodrum Ln 29624
Goodwin Cir 29626
Gordon Cir & St 29626
N Gossett St 29621
S Gossett St 29624
Governors Blvd 29621
Grace Dr 29625
Graceview E & W 29625
Grady Rd 29624
Grady Hall Rd 29626
Graham Rd 29625
Grandma Dr 29624
Grandview Ter 29626

Granite Ln 29626
Grant St 29624
Grassy Knoll Way 29621
Grate Rd 29625
Gray Dr 29626
Gray St 29624
Graylyn Ct & Dr 29621
Graymoss Ln 29621
Grayson Ct 29625
Great Oaks Dr 29625
Green St 29625
Green Chase E & W 29621
Green Cherry Rd 29621
Green Hill Dr 29621
Green Oaks Dr 29624
Green Pond Rd 29626
Green Teal Ln 29621
Green Tree Rd 29625
Green Valley Rd 29621
Green Willow Trl 29621
Greenacres 29621
Greenbriar Ln 29625
Greenbriar Rd 29621
Greenfield Dr 29621
Greenforest Dr 29625
Greenland Rd 29626
Greenleaf Dr 29626
Greenmeadow Cir 29626
Greentree Cir 29624
Greenview Dr & Ln 29625
E Greenville St 29621
W Greenville St 29625
Greenway Dr 29625
Greenwood Ave 29621
Greer Heights Rd 29624
Gregory Ct 29626
Grimes St 29624
Grindstone Way 29625
Grove Rd 29621
Grove Park Dr 29621
Groveland Ct 29626
Guest Cir 29625
Guilbault Dr 29621
N & S Gunter Cir & St 29624
Gurley St 29625
Guy Rd 29625
Guy St 29624
H St 29625
Hack St 29624
Hales Dr 29625
Haley Rd 29621
Halifax Cir 29625
Hall Rd
100-799 29624
5000-5099 29621
Hall St 29624
Hall White Dr 29626
Hamilton Dr 29621
N & S Hammett St 29624
Hammett Acres 29621
Hammond Cir 29621
Hammond School Rd 29621
E & W Hampton St 29624
Haney Rd 29621
Hanks Cir 29621
Hanks Rd 29625
Hanks Gin Rd 29621
Hanna Rd 29621
Hannah Cir 29621
Hanover Cir & Rd 29621
Harbin Dr & Rd 29626
N Harbor Dr 29625
Harbor Gate 29621
Harborough Rd 29625
Harbour Point Dr 29626
Harbour Springs Way 29626
Hard Hillhouse Dr 29626
Harden Rd 29621
Harkness St 29624
Harley Davidson Dr 29626
Harlond Dr 29621
Harmony Rd 29624
Harpers Way 29621
Harrell Dr 29624
Harriett Cir 29621
Harrington Dr 29625

Harrington Rd 29624
Harris Rd 29625
Harris St 29624
Harris Bridge Rd 29621
N Harrison Rd 29625
Harrison Harbor Way 29625
Harry Dr 29624
Hart Rd 29621
Hartford Ct 29621
Hartview Cir 29625
Hartwell Villas 29626
Harvard Dr 29621
Harvester Ct 29626
Harvesters Walk 29621
Hatten Rd 29621
Haven Rdg 29621
Havenbell Ln 29621
Hawk Ridge Dr 29621
Hawkins Ln 29621
Hawkins Rd 29621
Hawkins St 29625
Hawnes Pl 29621
Hawthorne Dr 29625
Hawthorne Ln 29621
Hay Barn Dr 29626
Hayes Rd & St 29624
Haymarket Rd 29625
Haynie Rd 29625
Haynie St 29624
Hazel Ave 29626
Hazelwood Ave 29626
Healthy Way 29621
Hearthstone Dr 29621
Heather Trl 29621
Heatherbrook Ct 29625
Heidi Dr 29626
Helen Dr 29626
Hembree Rd 29625
Hembree Creek Rd 29625
Hemlock Ave 29625
Hen Coop Rd 29621
Henry Ave 29625
Henry Dr 29621
Henry Cullins Rd 29621
Herd Park Ct 29621
Heritage Dr 29621
Hermitage Dr
100-199 29624
5000-5099 29625
Heyward Rd 29621
Hiawatha Dr 29621
Hickory Ln 29624
Hickory Rd 29626
Hickory Forest Dr 29626
Hickory Hollow Rd 29621
Hidden Falls Dr 29621
Hidden Lake Dr 29625
High St 29624
High C Dr 29621
High Field Ct 29626
High Shoals Rd 29621
E Highland Ave 29621
W Highland Ave 29625
Highway 187
5000-7699 29625
Highway 187 S
100-2499 29626
2500-2599 29624
2600-4399 29626
Highway 24
3200-5199 29626
5200-5899 29625
Highway 252 29621
Highway 28 Byp 29624
Highway 29 N 29621
Highway 29 S 29626
Highway 29 Byp N 29621
Highway 413 29621
Highway 76 29621
Highway 81 S 29624
N Highway 81 29621
Hill Rd 29621
Hill St 29624
Hillcrest Cir 29624
Hillcrest Ct 29621
Hilldale Dr 29625

Hillhouse Rd 29626
Hillman Dr 29624
Hillsborough Dr 29621
Hillside Dr 29625
Hilltop Cir 29626
Hilltop Dr 29621
Hillview Cir 29621
Hinton Dr 29626
Hiott Rd 29625
Hix Rd 29625
Hobby Ln 29621
Hobson Rd 29621
Hokie Dr 29626
Holden Ln 29626
Holland Dr 29624
N & S Holly St 29625
Holly Creek Dr 29621
Holly Hill Dr 29621
Holly Knoll Dr 29626
Holly Ridge Dr 29621
Holman St 29624
Homestead Rd 29621
Homewood St 29625
Honea Path Park Rd 29625
Honey Creek Rd 29621
Honeysuckle Ln 29624
Hooper Dr 29624
Hopewell Rd & Rdg 29621
Horse Shoe Bnd 29625
Horse Shoe Trl 29621
Howard Ln 29621
Howard Mcgee Rd 29621
Howell Dr 29624
Howland Dr 29626
Hoyt Dr 29626
Hub Dr 29621
Huckleberry Ln 29625
Hudgens St
100-199 29624
200-599 29621
Hudson Cir 29625
Hugh St 29624
Huitt Rd 29626
Humbert St 29624
Hummingbird Ln 29625
Hunt St 29624
Hunter Dr & St 29625
Hunters Ln & Trl 29625
Huntington Dr 29625
Huntington Rd 29626
Huron Ln 29621
Hurricane Cir & Rd 29621
Hurst Ave 29625
N I St 29625
Ila St 29624
Independence Path 29621
Indian Trl 29625
Indigo Cir 29625
Inez St 29625
Inland Dr 29625
Inlet Dr 29625
Inlet Pointe Dr 29625
Inman Dr 29625
Interlaken Way 29626
Interstate Blvd 29621
Inway Dr 29621
Issac Ct 29625
Iva St 29626
Ivy Cir 29621
J St 29625
Jack Frost Rd 29621
Jackson Cir 29625
Jackson Rd 29626
Jackson Sq 29625
Jackson St 29625
Jacobs Rd 29625
James Ct 29624
James St 29625
James Hare Rd 29626
James Lawrence Orr Dr 29621
Janice Cir 29626
Janice Dr 29624
Jarrett Rd 29626
Jasmin Dr 29626
Jasper St 29624

Jaynes St 29624
Jean Ave 29626
Jeanne Dr 29624
Jeb Stuart Ave 29625
N Jefferson Ave 29621
S Jefferson Ave 29624
Jeffery Dr 29621
Jerry Dr 29624
Jim Ed Rice Pkwy 29625
Jimmie Ln 29621
Joe Dyar Rd 29621
Joe Wheeler Dr 29625
Joey St 29626
Johanna Cir 29621
John Ave 29626
John St 29624
John Ginn Blvd 29625
John Rutledge St 29621
Johnson Ave 29621
Johnson St 29624
Johnson Trl 29625
Jolly Acres 29621
Jonagold Ct 29621
Jonathans Joy Cir 29626
Jones Dr 29626
Jones Rd 29624
Jones St 29625
Jones Creek Cir 29621
Jordan Cir 29625
Joseph St 29625
Joy Cir 29621
Jule Martin Rd 29621
Julia Cir 29625
Julia St 29624
Julian Beaty Rd 29621
June St 29624
June Way 29621
Juniper Ave 29625
Justice Ln 29621
K St 29625
Kalye Dr 29624
Karen Ln 29626
Karen St 29621
Kari Ln 29626
Kates St 29625
Kauffman Dr 29626
Kay Dr
700-799 29621
1000-1299 29624
Kaye Dr 29624
Keasler Cir & Rd 29625
Keith Ave 29625
Keith Dr 29621
Keithwood Dr 29621
Kelly St 29625
Kelsey Dr 29626
Ken Hill Ln 29624
Kennedy St 29624
Kenneth Dr 29626
Kensington Ct 29621
Kent Way 29621
Kenwood Dr 29625
Kestrel Ct 29621
Keys St 29624
Keystone Dr 29621
Ki Ki Ce Ce Ln 29621
Kiev Ct 29626
Kilsprings Rd 29621
Kimberly Rd 29621
Kinert Cir 29624
King Dr 29621
King St
100-199 29624
200-1099 29625
King Arthur Dr 29621
King Cove Dr 29621
Kingfisher Ct 29626
Kings Ct & Rd 29621
Kings Mill Ct 29621
Kingsboro Rd 29626
Kingsgate Way 29621
Kingshill Dr 29625
Kingsley Rd 29621
Kingston Way 29625
Kingswood Ter 29621
Kirkwood Dr 29624

Kirven Dr 29624
Knightsbridge Ln 29621
Knollwood Dr 29625
Knotts Lndg 29626
Knowlandwood Cir 29624
Knox Rd 29625
Knoxwood Ct 29621
Kokomo Way 29625
Kosma Dr 29626
Krismark Trl 29621
Kristie Dr 29624
Kudzu Rd 29621
L St 29625
L C Hanks Rd 29621
Lacy Ln 29621
Ladys Ln 29621
Lafayette St 29624
Lafrance Rd 29625
Lake Forest Cir 29625
Lake Ridge Ln 29626
Lake Secession Rd 29621
Lake Side Rd 29625
Lakecrest Rd 29625
Lakefront Dr 29626
Lakeland Dr 29626
Lakemont Dr 29626
Lakepoint Dr 29626
Lakeshore Dr 29625
Lakeside Dr 29621
Lakeview Dr 29626
Lakewood Dr
100-499 29621
1000-1099 29625
Lakewood Ln
100-199 29626
200-1699 29625
Lancaster Dr 29621
Lance Rd 29624
Lancelot Ct 29625
Landau Ln 29625
Lands End 29626
Lane Ave 29621
Lanford St 29624
Langwell Dr 29621
Lanier Ave 29624
Lanier Pruitt Rd 29621
Largo Ct 29625
Lari Ln 29625
Lark Ln 29625
Latham Dr 29621
Latimer Rd
100-399 29626
1000-1199 29625
Laura St 29621
Laurel Ave 29625
Laurel Crk 29621
Laurel Hts 29621
Laurel Ridge Rd 29621
Laurelwood Dr 29621
Lauren Flynn Dr 29626
Laurens Ct & Dr 29621
Lawrence Rd 29624
Lawrence Beatty Rd 29626
Lawson Rd 29621
Lazy St 29626
Leah Ln 29626
Leatherman Ct 29621
Leawood Ave 29621
Leconte Rd 29621
Lee Dr 29626
Lee St 29625
Lee Dobbins Rd 29626
Lee Shoals Rd 29621
Leeward Rd 29625
Leftwich Ln 29621
Lehman Way 29621
Leilani Ln 29621
Lemans Dr 29626
Lena St 29624
Leon Dr 29621
Level Land Rd 29621
Lever Ct 29625
Lewis St 29624
Lexington Way 29621
Liberty Ct 29621
Liberty Dr 29624

Liberty Hwy 29621
Liberty Roe 29626
Liddell Ave 29621
Lide Fant Ave 29624
Life Style Ln 29621
Lifechoice Ln 29621
Ligon Dr 29621
Ligon St 29624
Lilac St 29625
Limelight Dr 29621
Lincoln Ave 29624
Linda Dr 29626
Linda Ln 29621
Lindale Rd 29621
Linden St 29625
Lindsay St 29624
Linkside Dr 29621
Linley St 29625
Linmar Cir 29621
Linwa Blvd 29621
Lisa Dr 29625
Lissa Ln 29625
Little Creek Dr & Rd 29621
Little John Trl 29621
Little Mountain Rd 29626
Live Oak Ct 29621
Lloyd Dr & Rd 29621
Loblolly Dr 29625
Locke Cir 29621
Lockwood Dr 29621
Lofton Ct 29621
Logans Dr 29626
Lois Dr 29624
Lomax Dr 29624
Londonberry Dr 29621
Lone Oak Rd 29621
Lonely Oak Dr 29625
Long Forest Cir 29625
Long Needle Way 29621
Longview Dr 29621
Lookover Dr 29621
Lost Acres Rd 29625
Lost Lake Rd 29625
Loualgia Dr 29626
Loudwater Dr 29621
Louise Cir 29625
Lowry Rd 29621
Lullwater Dr 29624
Lullwater Pkwy 29625
Luton And Hatties Pl 29625
Lyndhurst Dr 29621
Lyndon Ave 29624
Lynn Ave 29621
Lynn St 29624
N & S Lyons St 29624
Lyonswood Dr 29624
Lyttleton Way 29621
M St 29625
Mabry St 29624
Maffett Cir 29625
Magaha Dr 29621
Maggie Ln 29625
N Main St
1900B-1900B 29622
100-3399 29621
S Main St 29624
S Main Street Ext 29624
Mallard Ct & Ln 29625
Manana Trl 29625
Manchester Cir 29625
Manley Dr
100-199 29624
200-599 29626
N Manning St 29621
S Manning St 29624
Manse Jolly Rd 29621
Maple Ct 29621
Maple Dr 29621
Maple St 29625
Maplewood Rd 29625
Mar Mac Rd 29626
Marcdon Pl 29621
Marchbanks Ave 29621
Margaretta Cir 29621
Margate Rd 29621
Maria Dr 29625

Marian Dr 29621
Marie St 29624
Marina Rd 29625
Marion St 29621
Mariposa Cir 29621
Mark Ln 29625
E & W Market St 29624
Market Place Dr 29621
Markhams Chase 29621
Marlon Ave 29624
Marne St 29624
Marsh Creek Dr 29626
Marsha Ln 29625
Marshall Ave 29621
Marshall Ct 29621
Marshall Rd 29626
Martha Dr 29624
Martin Ave 29625
Martin Dr 29624
Martin Rd 29626
Martin Luther King Jr Blvd 29625
Martins Pt E 29626
Mary Ct & St 29624
Mary Beth Dr 29624
Mason Dr 29625
Masters Blvd 29626
Masters Dr
100-308 29624
309-699 29626
Matisse Way 29624
Matt And Bev Blvd 29625
Matt Brown Rd 29624
Matthews Dr 29625
Mattison Rd 29626
E Mauldin St 29621
W Mauldin St 29625
Maxie Dr 29624
Maxwell Ave 29624
Mayci Way 29625
Mayfield Dr 29625
Mcadams St 29625
Mcalister Dr 29625
Mcbane Ct 29621
Mcclain Rd 29626
Mcclain Lake Dr 29625
Mcclellan Rd 29621
Mcclure Dr 29625
Mcclure Rd 29626
Mccollum St 29624
Mcconnell Springs Rd 29621
Mccowan Farm Rd 29626
Mccown St 29621
Mccoy St 29626
Mccue St 29624
Mccullough Dr 29626
Mccully St 29624
Mccurley Cir & St 29626
N Mcduffie St 29621
S Mcduffie St 29624
S Mcduffie Street Ext 29624
Mcfalls Cir 29621
Mcgee Cir 29626
Mcgee Ct 29621
Mcgee Rd
100-799 29625
3000-3299 29621
Mcgill Rd 29626
Mckenzie Dr 29624
Mckinley Dr 29621
Mckinney St 29621
Mclees Rd 29621
Mcleod Dr 29621
Mcneil Dr 29624
Mcphail Farms Cir 29621
Meadow Ln 29621
Meadow Walk 29626
Meadow Hills Dr 29624
Meadow Park Dr 29625
Meadowbrook Cir 29624
Meadowbrook Dr 29626
Meadowcreek 29621
Meadowland Dr 29624
Meadowood Dr 29626
Meadows Edge Ct 29621
Medford Ct 29626

Mediterranean Ave 29621
Meeting St 29621
Melbourne Dr 29621
Melia Ln 29625
Meljo Dr 29626
Melody Trl 29621
Melrose Ln 29626
Melvin Dr 29626
Memory Ln 29621
Mercury Ln 29621
Merriman Trl 29621
Meta St 29625
Metro Dr 29625
Metz Rd 29621
Mi Lues Ct & Dr 29626
Michael Mountain Rd 29624
Michelin Blvd
100-699 29625
700-1409 29626
Michelle Rd 29624
Mid Town Sq 29621
Middle Brooke Dr 29621
Middleton Ct 29621
Middleton Rd 29624
Middleton Shores Dr 29621
Middlewood Ln 29621
Midlake Heights Dr 29626
Midway Dr 29625
Midway Rd 29621
Midwood Dr 29625
Milan St 29624
Mildred St 29621
Milford Rd 29621
Milldenhall Rd 29625
Miller Cir 29625
Miller Dr 29621
Miller Rd 29625
Miller Lark Rd 29624
Millgate Rd 29621
Milton Rd 29624
Mimosa Ct 29625
Mimosa Trl 29624
Ming Ln 29625
Mini Bell Ln 29621
Minor St 29624
Mirabella Way 29625
Miracle Mile Dr 29621
Mistlebe Ln 29625
Mitchell St 29624
Moats Fowler Rd 29626
Mockingbird Rd 29625
Mohawk St 29626
Molly Rd 29626
Monitor Dr
100-199 29624
200-999 29626
Monroe St 29624
Monroe White Rd 29624
Montague St 29624
Montgomery Dr 29621
Monti Dr 29625
Monticello Cir 29624
Moon Ct 29625
E Moore St 29624
W Moore St
109A-109A 29624
100-109 29624
110-199 29626
Moorehead Dr 29621
Moorland Dr 29625
Morningside Dr 29625
Morris Dr 29626
Morris Ln 29625
Morris Rd 29625
E Morris St 29624
W Morris St 29624
Morton Dr 29625
Moss Dr 29625
Moss Oak Rd 29621
Motes Rd 29621
Moultrie Sq 29621
Mount Tabor Rd 29625
Mount Vernon Rd 29624
Mountain Creek Church Rd 29626
Mountain Oak Ct 29625

Mountain Springs Rd 29621
Mountain View Rd 29626
Mountainview Pl 29626
Muddy Toes Dr 29626
Muirfield Dr 29625
Mulberry Ave 29625
Mullikin Dr 29625
Mullinax Dr 29625
Muncie Dr 29624
Murdock Rd 29621
Muriel Ln 29626
Murphy Rd & St 29626
N Murray Ave 29625
S Murray Ave 29624
S Murray Avenue Ext 29624
Mutual Dr 29621
Myers St 29624
Myrtlewood 29621
Mystic Vineyard Ln 29621
Nalley Dr 29621
Nardin Ave 29624
Nashmore Rd 29625
Nates Berry Rd 29624
Natures Trl 29625
Nautical Way 29625
Neal St 29621
Nelson Dr 29621
Nesbitt Ct 29621
Neville Way 29621
New St 29624
New Court Rd 29625
New Hope Rd
100-1199 29626
1200-1399 29625
New Pond Rd
2300-2999 29624
3000-3599 29626
New Prospect Church Rd 29625
New Salem Dr 29625
Newcastle Dr 29625
Newell St 29624
Newington Cir 29621
Newport Ct 29624
Newton Ln 29624
Nicklaus Dr 29621
Nina Cir 29626
Nixon St 29625
Nob Hl 29626
Noel Ct 29625
Norbert Ln 29624
Norfolk Cir 29625
Norman St 29625
Norris Ln 29626
Norris Rd 29626
Norris St 29624
North Ave 29625
E North Ave 29625
W North Ave 29625
North St 29621
Northampton Rd 29621
Northfield Dr 29625
Northgate Dr 29625
Northlake Dr 29625
Northridge Dr 29621
Northview Ave 29625
Northwest Dr 29625
Nottingham Ct & Way 29621
Nunnally Rd 29625
Nursery Dr 29621
Nursery Ln 29626
O St 29625
Oak Dr 29625
Oak Is 29621
Oak Gate Dr 29625
Oak Hill Dr 29621
Oak Knoll Ter 29625
Oak Shores Rd 29625
Oak Tree Dr 29624
Oak Valley Trl 29625
Oakcliff Ter 29625
Oakland Ave 29621
Oakmont Dr 29621
Oakridge Ct 29621
Oakridge Dr 29625
Oakwood Ave 29625

Oakwood Estates Dr 29621
Obannon Ct 29621
Ocentang Rd 29625
Ohara Dr 29626
Old Abbeville Hwy 29624
Old Asbury Rd
100-1099 29625
1100-1599 29626
Old Belton Rd 29624
Old Colony Ct & Rd 29621
Old Denver Rd 29625
Old Denver School Rd 29625
Old Dirt Rd 29625
Old Emerson Bridge Rd 29621
Old Gantt Mill Rd 29625
Old Green Pond Rd 29625
Old Ivy Rd 29621
Old Mill Rd
4200-4699 29621
4700-4799 29625
Old North Church Rd 29621
Old Oak Trl 29621
Old Pearman Dairy Rd 29625
Old Port Rd 29625
Old Portman Rd
3800-4299 29626
4300-4499 29625
Old Roberts Church Rd 29626
Old Shoals Rd 29625
Old Smith Mill Rd 29625
Old Spring Dr 29625
Old Stone Dr 29621
Old Trail Dr 29626
Old Village Dr 29621
Old Webb Rd 29626
Old Williamston Rd 29621
Olde Towne Dr 29621
Oleander Dr 29621
Olin Dr 29624
Olivarri Dr 29621
Olive Br 29626
Olive St 29625
Oliver St 29624
Oneal Ct & Dr 29625
Ora Ln 29625
Orchard Ln 29621
E Orr St 29621
W Orr St 29625
Osborne Ave 29621
Ottawa Cir 29626
Overbrook St 29626
Overland Dr 29625
Overview Ter 29621
Owen Dr 29624
Owens Cir 29625
Oxford Dr 29625
Oxmoor Dr 29625
P St 29625
P And N Ct & Dr 29621
Paddock Rd 29621
Page Dr 29625
Palancar Ct 29621
Palm Ct 29621
Palm Branch Way 29621
Palmer St 29626
Palmetto Ln & St 29625
Paradise Ln 29625
Park Ave 29621
Park Dr 29625
E Park Dr 29621
N Park Dr 29625
S Park Dr 29624
W Park Dr 29625
Park St 29625
Park Way 29625
Parker Ln 29625
Parkside Dr 29621
Parkwood Cir, Ct & Dr 29625
Parnell Rd 29621
Partridge Ct 29625
Partridge Ln 29621
Patagonia Rd 29625
Patrick St 29624
Patriot Ct 29621

Patterson Ave 29621
Patterson Rd 29625
Patterson St 29624
Paul Revere Trl 29621
Pauls Lndg 29621
Pawleys Ct 29625
Peachtree St 29621
Pearl Harbor Way 29626
Pearman St 29624
Pearman Dairy Rd 29625
Peartree Ln 29625
Pebble Ln 29621
Pecan Dr 29624
Pelham Ln 29621
Pelican Ln 29625
Pembroke Ln 29625
Peninsula Dr 29626
Pennell Rd 29626
Pennelly St 29626
Penninger Dr 29621
Peoples Way 29626
Peppermill Ct 29621
Peppertree 29621
Peridot Cir 29626
Perpetual Sq 29621
Perry Cir 29624
Persimmon Ln 29626
Pheasant Ridge Dr 29626
Phil Watson Rd 29625
W Phillips Rd & St 29625
Phoenix St 29624
Phyllis Dr 29621
Picadilly Ct 29625
Pickens Cir 29624
Pickens St 29621
Piedmont Ave 29625
Pikes Rdg 29626
Pindo Ct 29621
Pine Ln 29621
Pine St 29625
Pine Bark Rd 29625
Pine Cone Trl 29621
Pine Crest Rd 29626
Pine Grove Rd 29624
Pine Hill Ct 29625
Pine Needle Cir & Trl 29625
Pine Top Cir 29626
Pine Tree Ln 29625
Pineapple Cir 29625
Pinecroft Dr 29621
Pinedale Rd 29626
Pineforest Dr 29625
Pinehollow Dr 29621
Pinehurst Dr 29625
Pinehurst Ln 29621
Pinion Ln 29621
Pinoca Dr 29626
Pintail Rd 29626
Pioneer Dr 29621
Pioneer Ln 29625
Pisgah Dr 29624
Pitts Rd 29626
Plain St 29624
Plainfield Dr 29624
Plainview Rd 29626
Plantation Pt 29625
Plantation Rd 29621
Plaza Way 29621
Pleasant Valley Dr 29621
Pleasantburg Rd 29625
Plum Ln & Rdg 29621
Plum Leaf Ct & Ln 29626
Pocalla Way 29624
S Point Cir 29626
N Point Dr 29621
W Point Dr
100-199 29621
200-299 29624
Pointe Crk & Dr 29625
Points End 29625
Polaris St 29621
Pollard Dr 29626
Pomona Dr 29625
Pompano Dr 29625
Ponce Deleon Dr 29621
Pony Trl 29621

Pope Dr 29625
Poplar Ave 29625
Poplar Ln
100-399 29624
2201-2297 29621
2299-2599 29621
Poppy Ln 29625
Port Anne Cv 29625
Port Royal Rd 29621
Portside Way 29625
Posey St 29624
Post Oak Way 29624
Postelle Dr 29621
Potomac Rd 29624
Powell Rd 29625
Power St 29621
Powers Ferry Rd 29626
Prairie Ln 29624
Preamble Ct 29621
Precious Pl 29621
Premiere Ct 29621
Prescott Dr 29621
Preserve Ln 29621
Presher Rd 29625
Preston Dr 29621
Prestwick Dr 29621
N Prevost St 29625
S Prevost St 29624
Price St 29621
N & S Prince St 29624
Princess Ave 29621
Princess Ln 29625
Pristine Dr 29621
Pritchards Dr 29625
Professional Ct 29621
Prospect Ct 29625
Providence Pt 29626
Providence Church Rd 29626
Providence Villas 29626
Pruitt St 29624
Public Well Rd 29626
Putt Putt Dr 29625
Q St 29625
Quail Run 29621
Quail Hollow Rd 29621
Quail Ridge Rd 29625
Quarry St 29624
Queen Ct & Dr 29625
Queensdale End 29621
Quiet Way 29626
Quinn St 29625
R St 29625
Radcliff Way 29621
Raeburn Way 29621
Railroad Cir 29625
Railroad St 29624
Rainbow Rd 29621
Rainbows End 29626
Rambling Path 29621
Ramsey Rd 29621
Ranchwood Dr 29625
Range View Cir & Rd 29626
Rankin Ct 29621
Rantowles Rd 29621
Raptor Ct 29621
Raspberry Ln 29621
Ravenal Rd 29621
Ravenswood Dr
100-199 29626
1000-1399 29625
Ray St 29624
Rayben Ln 29624
Raymond Ave 29625
Rear High St 29624
Rear Lewis St 29624
Rear Pickens St 29621
Rear Stephens St 29625
Reaves Pl 29625
Red Oak Dr 29625
Redbud Ln 29625
Redwood Ave 29621
Reed Ct 29624
Reed Pl 29621
Reed Rd 29621
E Reed Rd 29621
E Reed St 29624

Street	ZIP
W Reed St	29624
Regatta Dr	29625
Regency Cir	29625
Regent Ct & Rd	29621
Remington Rd	29621
Renee Way	29626
Revere Ct & St	29624
Revie Dr	29626
Revival Center Rd	29625
Rexton Dr	29621
Reynolds St	29625
Rhodehaven Dr	29625
Rhodes Cir	29621
Rhoe Cir	29621
Rice Cir & Ln	29625
Rice Cemetery Rd	29621
Rice Park Dr	29621
Rich Dr	29624
Richey Cir & St	29625
Richfield Dr	29625
Richland Dr	29626
Richland Cove Rd	29626
Richland Creek Rd	29626
Richland Point Rd	29626
Richmond Ave	29624
Rideau Rd	29625
Ridge Rd	29625
Ridgecrest Ave	29621
Ridgeway Rd	29625
Ridgeway Trl	29621
Ridgewood Ave	29625
Riley St	29624
Rio Way	29625
Ripley Cir	29621
Riser Rd	29624
Rivanna Dr	29625
Rivendell Dr	29621
E River St	
100-1799	29624
2000-3999	29621
W River St	29624
River Club Dr	29621
River Forks Rd	29626
River Heights Cir	29621
River Oak Dr	29624
Riverview Dr	29624
Riviera Cir	29621
Rivolli Dr	29625
Roach Cir	29625
Roadway St	29624
Robbins Dr	29621
Robert De Brus Cir	29621
Roberts Dr & St	29621
Roberts Church Rd	29626
Robertson Rd	29621
Robin Dr	
100-299	29621
1000-1099	29626
Robin Hood Ln	29621
Rock Creek Rd	29625
Rockefeller Dr	29624
Rocky Top Rd	29621
Roddy Ln	29625
Rogers Rd	29621
Rogers St	29625
Rohan Dr	29621
Rolling Green Rd	29621
Rolling Hill Dr	29621
Rolling M Dr	29626
Rolling Meadows Ct	29621
Rontree Dr	29625
Roof Rd	29624
Rooks Dr	29625
Roosevelt Ct	29624
E Roosevelt Dr	29624
W Roosevelt Dr	
100-205	29624
206-499	29626
Roosevelt Thompson Rd	29621
Rosabella Dr	29625
Rose Dr & Hl	29624
Rose Petal Ct	29626
Rose Valley Blvd	29625
Rosemary Cir	29621
Rosemont Dr	29624
Rosewood Dr	29625
Round About Trl	29625
Roundrock Ln	29621
Roush St	29625
Rowland Rd	29625
Roxbury Ct	29625
Royal American Rd	29625
Royal Birkdale Ct	29621
Royal Dor Noch Ct	29621
Royal Oaks Dr	29625
Royal Troon Ct	29621
Rozema Cir	29621
Rubin Ave	29624
Rucker Rd	29626
Rudolph Ct	29625
Runway Ln	29626
Rush St	29621
Russell Dr	29624
Rustic Ln	29621
Rutledge Way	29621
Ryan Rd	29625
Ryder Ln	29625
Sable Ln	29626
Saddle Brk	29625
Saddle Trl	29621
Sadlers Dr	29626
Sadlers Creek Rd	29626
Sago Ct	29621
Saint Charles Way	29621
Saint Clair Rd	29626
Saint James Ct	29621
Saint Paul St	29624
Salem St	29624
Salem Church Rd	
900-999	29621
1000-1399	29625
Sam Gerrard Rd	29626
Sam Mcgee Rd	29621
Samuel Camp Rd	29624
San Mateo Dr	29625
Sand Palm Way	29621
Sanders Dr & St	29624
Sandlewood Dr	29621
Sandy Crk	29625
Sandy Holw	29621
Sandy Point Dr	29625
Sandy Springs Ct & Rd	29625
Sandy Station Ct	29626
Sansbury Dr	29621
Sapphire Pt	29626
Sapphire Vly	29621
Sarah Dr	29621
Savannah Ct & Dr	29621
Sawmill Rd	29621
Saxony Dr	29621
Sayre St	29624
Scarborough Rd	29626
Scenic Rd	29621
Schmid Plaza Rd	29624
Scott Dr	
100-599	29625
1100-1299	29624
Scott Rd	29621
Scotts Bridge Rd	29621
Sea Palms Dr	29621
Seagull Ln	29625
Searay Dr	29624
Sears St	29621
Sebastian Dr	29621
Secession Way	29625
Second St	29621
Sedgefield Ct	29621
Selwyn Dr	29625
Seminole Ave & Ct	29626
Senate Pkwy	29621
Sentimental Ln	29625
Sentry Ct & Ln	29621
Serena Cir	29621
Service Rd	29625
Severn St	29626
Shackleburg Rd	29621
Shadow Ln	29625
Shadow Creek Ln	29621
Shady Ln	29625
Shady Creek Trl	29625
Shakleton Dr	29625
Shalimar Dr	29621
Shamrock Ln	29621
Shannon Ct	29626
Shannon Dr	29625
Shannon Way	29621
Sharonwood Dr	29621
Sharp Dr	29625
Sharpe St	29621
Shawnee Ave	29626
Shaws Creek Dr	29624
Sheffield Dr	29625
Sheldon Dr	29621
Shelter Pt	29626
Shennandoah Dr	29625
Sherard Dr	29624
Sherard St	29621
Sherman Dr	29624
Sherry Dr	29621
Sherwood Dr	29621
Shiflet Rd	29624
Shiloh Church Rd	29624
Shipyard Cir	29621
Shire Dr	29621
Shirlane Dr	29621
Shirley Cir	
100-599	29625
1000-1099	29621
Shirley Dr	29621
Shirley St	29621
Shirley Store Rd	29621
Shoalview Dr	29625
E Shockley Ferry Rd	29624
W Shockley Ferry Rd	
100-299	29624
400-1299	29626
N Shore Dr	29625
Shore Line Dr	29626
Short St	29624
Short And Sweet Rd	29624
Short Cut Rd	29621
Siena Dr	29621
Silo Ln	29625
Silver Lane Cir	29626
Silver Stone Cir	29626
Simmons St	29625
Simpson Dr	29624
Simpson Rd	29621
Simpson St	29625
Sims St	29624
Singer Rd	29625
Singleton Rd	29625
Sioux St	29625
Sirrine St	29624
Slater Rd	29621
Slaton Ct	29621
Sloan Ave	29621
Sloans Ferry Rd	29626
Sm Lyerly Rd	29621
Smith Cir	29625
Smith Dr	29625
Smith St	29624
Smithfield Dr	29621
Smithland Bnd	29621
Smithmore St	29621
Sneed Rd	29626
Snipes St	29625
Snow Rd	29621
Snowden Ln	29626
Snug Hbr	29625
Soaring Hawk Ct	29621
Society St	29621
Somerset Ln	29625
Sophie Ln	29626
Soren Ln	29621
Southern Acres	29625
Southwood Dr & St	29624
Spanish Wls	29621
Speedway Dr	29621
Spencer St	29624
Spring Cir	29621
Spring Rd	29625
Spring St	29625
Spring Vly	29621
Spring Back Way	29621
Spring Hill Rd	29626
Spring Park Dr	29625
Springbrook Dr	29621
Springdale Rd	29621
Springfield Rd	29626
Springfield Villas	29626
Springside Cir	29625
Springview Dr	29625
Spruce Crk	29625
Squirrel Dr	29626
Stacy Ct	29625
Stafford Rd	29626
Stagecoach Dr	29625
Stanbury Ct	29621
Stancil Rd	29625
Standridge Rd	29625
Stanmoore Dr	29621
Starboard Way	29625
Starboard Side	29625
Starkes St	29625
State St	29625
Station Dr	29621
Stephen King Dr	29621
Stephens Rd	29621
Stephens St	29625
Sterling Dr	29626
Sterling Silver Dr	29626
Stetson Dr	29625
Stewart Cir	29624
Stewart St	29626
Stone Dr	29625
Stone Cottage Dr	29621
Stone Creek Dr	
100-199	29626
700-899	29621
Stoneham Cir	29626
Stonehaven Dr	
100-499	29625
1000-6099	29626
Stonehurst Dr	29621
Stoneleigh Ct	29621
Straight Dr	29625
Stratford Dr	29621
Stratton Ln	29621
Strawberry Ln	29625
Strawberry Pl	29624
Strawberry Rd	29626
Streams Way	29625
Streater Ln	29625
Strickland Ave	29625
Stringer Rd	29621
Sugar Hl	29624
Sugar Creek Ln	29625
Sugar Pine Rd	29626
Sullivan Ln	
100-115	29625
117-299	29626
Sullivan Rd	29625
Sullivan St	29624
Sumac St	29624
Summer Ln	29626
Summer Pl	29621
Summerfield Ln	29621
Summerwalk Ct	29625
Summitt Ave	29621
Sumter St	29621
Sun Chase Rd	29621
Sundowner Blvd	29626
Sunny Ln	29625
Sunny Hill Ln	29626
Sunny Shore Ln	29621
Sunrise Vw	29621
Sunrise Harbor Dr	29621
Sunset Dr	29625
Sunset Ln	29626
Sunset Pt	29626
Sunset Forest Rd	29626
Sunset Hills Dr	29626
Supreme Industrial Dr	29621
Surfside Dr	29625
Surrey Ln	29621
Susan St	29624
Susan B Ln	29621
Sussex Way	29625
Sutton Pl	29621
Swain St	29625
Sweet Spgs	29625
Sweet Farm Rd	29621
Sweet Gum Trl	29621
Sweet Willow Pond	29624
Sweetbriar Cir	29626
Sweetgrass Trl	29625
Swinton Rd	29626
Sycamore Dr	29621
Sycamore St	29625
Sydney Ct	29625
Sylvester Dr	29621
Tabitha Ct	29625
Tall Pines Rd	29625
Tall Ship Dr	29625
Talley Ct	29621
Talon Ct	29621
Tanglewood Ave & Dr	29621
Tarcus Ct	29626
Tarheel Ln	29625
Tarleton Rd	29626
Tarrytown Ln	29621
Tate Dr	29626
Tate St	29624
Taylor St	29625
Taylors Trl	29621
Tea Leaf Ct	29626
Tea Rose Ct	29625
Teakwood Dr	29625
Technology Dr	29625
Teeside Ct & Dr	29625
Templeton Ave	29624
Teresa Ave	29626
Terrace Dr & Ln	29621
Terry Ave	29625
Thaxton Place Ct	29625
Theodore Ct	29621
Thomas St	29624
Thomas Welborn Rd	29625
Thomason Cir	29626
Thompson Rd	
100-499	29624
1000-1099	29621
Thorncliff Pl	29625
Thornehill Dr	29621
Threlkeld Blvd	29621
Tiara Ct	29625
Tidewater	29625
Tiffany Dr	29625
Tiger Ln	29626
Tillotson Rd	29621
Timber Ln	29621
Timber Rock Rd	29621
Timberlake Rd	29625
Tindall Ave	29621
Tinsley Dr	29621
Todd Rd	29626
Todd St	29624
Toliver Ln	29626
Tolkien Dr	29621
Tolly St	29624
Tomahawk Trl	29621
Topaz Pt	29626
Topsail Dr	29625
Torch Cir	29626
N Towers St	29625
S Towers St	29624
Towhee Trl	29625
Town Creek Dr	29621
Towne Creek Trl	29621
Townsend St	29625
Townsley Ct	29624
Tradd St	29625
Traflagar Rd	29621
Trail Rd	29621
Trail End Rd	29626
Trammell Rd	29621
Travis Ln & Rd	29626
Traywick Dr	29621
Tribble St	29625
Trident Ct	29621
Triple Oak Dr	29625
Tropical Way	29621
Trotter Rd	29626
Troy Hunter Ct	29621
Trudy Ln	29621
True Temper Rd	29624
Trump Pointe	29626
Trusler Rd	29626
Trussel View Rd	29625
Tucker Dr	29621
Tucker Trl	29625
Tully Dr	29621
Turbine Ct	29624
Turnberry Rd	29621
Tuscany Dr	29621
Twelve Oaks Dr	29621
Twig Ln	29624
Twin Lake Dr	29621
Twin Lakes Ct & Dr	29621
Twin Oaks Dr	29621
Ulmer St	29624
Upland Way	29621
Upper View Ter	29625
V W Ct	29624
Valentine St	29624
Valley Ct, Dr & Rd	29625
Valley Dale Dr	29625
Van Martin Rd	29621
Vanadore Cir	29625
Vandale Pl	29626
Vandiver Rd	29621
Vandiver St	29624
Vanguard Rd	29625
Vanwood Dr	29621
Varennes Church Rd	29624
Vaughn St	29624
Ventura St	29621
Verona Ct	29624
Versailles Ave	29625
Vesey Dr	29624
Vesper Dr	29621
Veterans St	29625
Viaroma Dr	29621
Vickery Dr	29626
Vicki Ct	29624
Victor Cir	29625
Victoria Cir	29621
Victorian Dr	29625
Video Warehouse Way	29624
Vienna Ct	29625
E View Ave	29621
Viking Ct	29625
Villa Ct	29621
Village Dr	29624
Village Boundary	29621
Village Main	29621
Vine St	29621
Virginia Cir	29621
Visage Dr	29626
Vista Dr & Trl	29624
Vista Rose Ct	29621
Vista Verde Dr	29621
Vogel Ext	29624
Vogel Ridge Dr	29624
Voyles Rd	29625
Waccamaw Trl	29621
Waco Rdg	29621
Waites Ln	29626
Walden Pkwy	29621
Waldo Way	29621
Walker Cir	29621
Walker Dr	29625
Walker Rd	29621
Walker Way	29621
Walls Dr	29621
Walnut Ave	29625
Walnut Dr	29624
N Walnut Dr	29621
Walnut Way	29626
Walter Dr	29621
Walter Brown Way	29621
Walter Chamblee Rd	29626
Wanstead Ct	29621
Wardlaw St	29624
Ware Cir	29625
Ware Circle Ext	29625
Warner Rd	29625
S Warner Rd	29626
Warren Dr	29621
Warriors Path	29621
Warwick St	29621
Washington St	29624
Water Oak Way	29621
Waterford Ct	29621
Waterman Way	29621
Watermarke Ln	29625
Waters Ln	29626
Watkins Rd	29625
Watkins Road Ext	29625
Watson Ave	29625
Watson St	29624
Waverly Rd	29625
Waybrook Dr	29624
Waycaster Rd	29621
Waynes Ct	29625
Weatherstone Way	29621
Webb Rd	29621
Webb St	29624
Wedgefield Ct	29625
Wedgewood Dr	29621
Welborn Dr	29621
Welborn Oaks Way	29621
Welco St	29621
Weldon Way	29626
Wellington Ct & St	29624
Wells Rd	29625
Wellwood Dr	29621
Wendover Way	29621
Wentworth Ct	29625
Wentzky Cir	29621
Wentzky Rd	29624
Wenzick St	29625
E West Pkwy	29621
Westchester Dr	29621
Westgate Rd	29626
Westminister Ct	29625
Westminster Ave	29625
Westover Rd	29626
Westridge Ct	29625
Westview Ave	29625
Westway Ct	29624
Westwind Rd	29625
Westwind Way	29626
Westwind Harbour Dr	29626
Westwood Cir & Dr	29626
Wetland Way	29621
Wexford Dr	29621
Wham Rd	29625
Wharf Ct	29625
Wheaton Dr	29625
Whirlaway Cir	29621
Whisper Ln	29621
Whisper Wood Ln	29621
Whispering Pnes	29626
Whispering Pines Dr	29621
White Rd	29625
White St	29624
White City Park Rd	29625
White Oak Dr	29621
White Street Ext	
1900-2299	29624
2300-2599	29621
Whitehall Ave	29621
Whitehall Rd	
100-2999	29625
3000-4099	29626
Whiten Rd	29621
Whitetail Trl	29625
Whitewater Ln	29621
Whitfield Dr	29624
Whitfield Pt	29626
Whitner Dr	29621
E Whitner St	29624
W Whitner St	
100-2599	29624
2600-3199	29626
Whitney Way	29625
Whitten Rd	29621
Wicker Ln	29621
Wieuca Ct	29625
Wigfall Dr	29621
Wilbrooke Way	29621
Wild Cherry Ct	29626
Wild Oak Run	29625
Wild Vine Path	29621
Wildcat Clfs	29621
Wilderness Ln & Trl	29626
Wildwood Dr	29621
Wiles Dr	29625

Wilkes Way 29621
Will Graham Dr 29625
William Walker Dr & Rd 29625
Williams Rd
1-99 29621
100-299 29626
1000-1299 29625
Williams St 29621
Williamsburg Dr & Rd 29621
Williamston Rd 29621
Willie Bennett Dr 29621
Willie Mae Ct 29626
Willie Rice Rd 29621
Williford Rd 29626
Willow Ct, Pl & Run 29621
Willow Springs Rd 29621
Willow Wood Ln 29625
Willowbend Dr 29621
Wilmac Dr 29626
Wilmont St 29624
Wilson Ave 29624
Wilson Rd 29625
Wilson St 29621
Wilson Way 29621
Wiltshire Ct 29621
Winchester Dr 29624
Windcrest Ln 29626
Windemere Way 29625
Windham Dr 29621
Winding Brk 29621
Winding Creek Rd 29621
Winding River Dr 29625
Windjammer Way
100-248 29626
249-299 29625
Windmill Trl 29626
Windsong Ct 29621
Windsor Dr 29621
Windsor Oaks 29621
Windward Trl 29621
Windward Way 29625
Windwood Dr 29621
Windy Hill Dr 29621
Winesap Cir 29621
Winfield Dr 29624
Wington Ct 29626
Winmar Dr 29621
Winslow Dr 29621
Winston Dr 29624
Wintergreen Ct 29625
Wishire Dr 29621
Wolf Creek Rd 29621
Wood St 29624
Wood Duck Rd 29621
Wood Valley Dr 29621
Woodbine Cir 29621
Woodbridge Cir & Ct 29621
Woodburn Ave 29625
Woodcone Trl 29624
Woodcreek Rd 29621
Woodcrest Dr 29625
Woodfern Cir 29625
Woodfield Dr 29621
Woodforest Ln 29626
Woodlake Rd 29621
Woodland Dr & Way 29621
Woodlawn Ave 29625
Woodmont Cir 29624
Woodoak Dr 29621
Woodridge Ct & Dr 29621
Woodrow Cir 29621
Woods Way 29625
Woodshore Dr 29625
Woodside Ave 29625
Woodson Dr 29625
Woodvale Rd 29624
Woodview Dr 29624
Woody Acres Ct & Dr 29625
Worsham Ln 29621
Worthington Ct 29621
Wren Rd 29621
Wren Way 29625
Wright School Rd 29621
Wt Agnew Cir 29621
Wycombe Dr 29621
Yarbrough Dr 29621
Yates Cir 29621
Yellow Pine Dr 29626
Ymca Camp Rd 29625
York St 29625
Yorkshire Dr 29625
Zana Ln 29621
Zebulon Dr 29624
Zellwood Ln 29624
Zeno St 29625
Zoysia Ct 29624

BEAUFORT SC

General Delivery 29902

POST OFFICE BOXES MAIN OFFICE STATIONS AND BRANCHES

Box No.s
6092B - 6092C 29902
6093B - 6093C 29902
6094B - 6094C 29902
6095B - 6095C 29902
6096B - 6096C 29902
6097B - 6097C 29902
6098B - 6098C 29902
6101B - 6101C 29902
6102B - 6102C 29902
6103B - 6103C 29902
6104B - 6104C 29902
6111B - 6111C 29902
6112B - 6112C 29902
6113B - 6113C 29902
6114B - 6114C 29902
6115B - 6115C 29902
6116B - 6116C 29902
6117C - 6117C 29902
6121B - 6121C 29902
6122B - 6122C 29902
6123B - 6123C 29902
6124B - 6124C 29902
6125B - 6125C 29902
6126B - 6126C 29902
6127B - 6127C 29902
6128B - 6128C 29902
6131B - 6131C 29902
6132B - 6132C 29902
6133B - 6133C 29902
6134B - 6134C 29902
6141B - 6141C 29902
6142B - 6142C 29902
6143B - 6143C 29902
6144B - 6144C 29902
6145B - 6145C 29902
6146B - 6146C 29902
6147C - 6147C 29902
6151A - 6161A 29902
6161C - 6161C 29902
6162A - 6162C 29902
6163A - 6163C 29902
6164A - 6164C 29902
6165C - 6168C 29902
6171A - 6171C 29902
6172A - 6172C 29902
6173A - 6173C 29902
6174A - 6174C 29902
6182A - 6182C 29902
6183A - 6183C 29902
6184A - 6184C 29902
6185A - 6185C 29902
6186A - 6186C 29902
6187A - 6187C 29902
6188A - 6191A 29902
6191C - 6191C 29902
6192A - 6192C 29902
6193A - 6193C 29902
6194A - 6194C 29902
6195C - 6198C 29902
6201A - 6201C 29902
6202A - 6202C 29902
6203A - 6203C 29902
6204A - 6204C 29902
6212A - 6212C 29902
6213A - 6213C 29902
6214A - 6214C 29902
6215A - 6215C 29902
6216A - 6216C 29902
6217A - 6217C 29902
6218A - 6296A 29902
6001B - 6091B 29902
6091C - 6091C 29902
6175A - 6181A 29902
6181C - 6181C 29902
6205A - 6211A 29902
6211C - 6211C 29902
1 - 2620 29901
4001 - 8096 29903
9001 - 66199 29904

HIGHWAY CONTRACTS

06, 07, 10 29907

NAMED STREETS

Abbey Ln 29902
Abbey Row 29906
Abelia St 29906
Abner Ln 29902
Acorn Dr 29906
Acorn Hill Ave 29902
Acres Dr 29902
Adams Cir 29902
Adams Way 29906
Addison St 29907
Admiration Ave 29906
Adventure St 29902
Afton Cir 29906
Airport Cir 29907
Ajuga Dr 29906
Alaska St 29902
Albacore St 29906
Albatross Dr 29906
Albert St 29902
Alexander Dr 29902
Alexander Way 29906
Alexandra Loop 29906
Alfred Alston Ct 29907
Alligator Aly & Ln 29907
Allison Rd 29902
Alston Rd 29907
Alston Field Dr 29906
W Althea St 29906
Alumni Rd 29907
Amapola Dr 29907
Ambrose Run 29906
Amelly Dr 29907
Anchorage Dr 29907
Anchorage Way 29902
Angel Ln 29906
Angel Oak Ln 29907
Anns Point Dr 29906
Appaloosa Ct 29906
Appleby Ln 29906
Applemint Ln 29906
Arbor Victory Rd 29907
Ard Rd 29906
Ardmore Ave 29907
Argonne Dr 29902
Arnold Dr 29902
Arnold Ln 29906
Arum Cir N & S 29907
Ash St
1-500 29906
502-518 29906
1700-1799 29902
Ashdale Dr 29907
Ashley Dr 29907
Ashton Pointe Blvd 29906
Ashwood Cir 29906
Aspen St 29906
Assembly Row 29906
Aster St
1-599 29906
1500-1799 29902
Atkins Blf 29907
Attaway Ln 29907
Audubon Rd 29907
Audusta Pl 29902
Autumn Cir 29906
Avalon Dr 29907
Azalea Dr
1-899 29906
2500-2599 29902
B Glover Ln 29906
Badgers Bnd 29902
Baggett St 29902
Bajala Dr E & W 29907
Ballard Cir 29902
Balsam St 29906
Banyan Dr 29906
Barbara Ln 29907
Barnwell Blf 29902
Barnwell Dr 29907
Barnwell St 29902
Barracuda Dr 29906
Barrett Ln 29907
Bartram Dr 29902
Battery Ln 29902
Battery Chase 29902
Battery Creek Rd 29902
Battery Creek Club Dr 29902
Battery Green Ct 29902
Battery Point Ln 29902
Bay Cir 29906
Bay Dr 29907
Bay St 29902
Bay Breeze Ln 29907
Bay Pines Rd 29906
Bayard St 29902
Baynard Rd 29906
Be Wheatley Dr 29902
Beau Ct 29907
Beauregard Ct 29902
Beautyberry Ln 29907
Beavers Den 29902
Beckley St 29902
Beeburst Rd 29906
Beech St 29906
Beirut Cv 29902
E Belakens Cv E 29907
Bella Way 29906
Belle Isle Farms 29907
Belleview Blf & Cir E, N & W 29902
Ben Allen Rd 29906
Ben And Flossie Dr 29907
Bengals Blvd 29906
Bennett Point Rd 29907
Bent Oak Rd 29907
Better Than Ever St 29907
Biddie Ln 29906
Big Rd 29906
Big Ash Ln 29907
Big Barnwell Is 29906
Big Ben Ln 29907
Big John Rd 29906
Big Leaf Bnd 29907
Billy Hill Rd 29906
Binaker Ct 29902
Birch Dr & Rd 29906
Bishop Rd 29906
Black Oak Cir 29902
Black Skimmer Ct & Dr 29907
Blackburn Pierce Dr 29906
Blacksmith Cir 29906
Bladen St 29902
Bladen Street Ln 29902
Blanche Ct 29907
Blue Dolphin Dr 29906
Blue Heron Cir 29907
Bluebell Ln 29906
Blueberry Ct 29906
Bluebird Ln 29906
Bluestem Dr 29902
W Bluff 29906
S Bluff Ln 29907
Bluff Rd 29907
Blythewood Rd 29907
Bobwhite Ct 29907
Bobwhite Dr 29906
Bogus Ln 29906
Bonaire Cir 29906
Bosnia Ave 29902
Bostick Cir 29902
Bouganville St 29902
Boulevard E & W 29907
Boulevard De France 29902
Boundary St
700-2399 29902
2400-2899 29906
Bowling Ln 29902
Boyds Neck Ct 29902
Boyer St 29902
Braden Rd 29906
Bradford Ct 29902
Braeburn Ln 29907
Brandy Station Ct 29907
Brasstown Way 29906
Bray St 29902
Breeze Way 29907
Brenda Ln 29906
Briar Rose Ln 29906
Briarpatch Ln 29907
Briarwood Ln 29906
Brickman Way 29907
Brickyard Hills Ct & Dr 29907
Brickyard Point Rd N & S 29907
Bridge Pt 29906
Brighton Ln 29902
Brighton Trce 29906
Brilliant Ln 29906
Brindlewood Dr 29907
Brinks Pl 29906
Brisbane Dr 29902
Broad St 29902
Broad Oaks Cir, Ct, Dr & Ln 29906
Broad River Blvd & Dr 29906
Brook Side 29906
Brookins Path 29906
Broome Ln N 29902
Broomfield Dr & Ln 29907
Broomsedge Ln 29907
Brotherhood Rd & Way 29902
Bruce K Smalls Dr 29906
Bryan Dr 29902
Buck Rd 29907
Bull Ln & St 29902
Bull Run Ct 29907
Burbage Ln 29906
Burckmyer Dr 29907
Burlington Cir 29906
Burlington Land Rd 29906
Burnside St 29902
Burroughs Ave 29902
Burton Creek Dr 29902
Burton Hill Rd 29906
Burton Wells Rd 29906
Busby Dr 29906
Butterfield Ln 29907
Cadage Ln 29907
Calhoun St 29902
Calico Ct 29906
Calypso Ln 29906
Camellia Dr 29906
Camellia Rd 29902
Cameroon Dr 29907
Campbell Rd 29906
Canavan Pl 29906
Candida Dr 29906
Candleberry Ln 29902
Cane Way 29907
Canton Row 29906
Cape Gloucester 29902
Cape Haitian Dr 29906
Capehart Cir, Dr & Ln 29906
Capers St 29902
Capwing Dr 29902
Cardinal Ln 29906
Carissa Ln 29907
Carolina Ave 29906
Carolina Ln 29907
Carolina Village Cir 29906
Carolyn Dr 29907
Caron Cir 29902
Carriage Run 29906
Carteret St 29902
Casanovas Way 29907
Cassena Dr 29907
Castle Rock Rd 29906
Caswell Ave 29902
Catawba Way 29906
Cattail Ct 29907
Causey Way 29907
Cavalry Ln 29906
Cavu Ln 29906
Cedar Creek Cir 29906
Cedar Crest Cir 29907
Cedar Grove Cir 29902
Cedar Point Dr 29907
Cedarbrook St 29906
Celadon Dr 29907
Cely Ln 29907
Cemetary Rd 29907
Center Dr E 29902
Center Dr W 29902
Center Ln 29907
Centerview Dr 29902
Central Dr 29907
Charity Dr 29906
Charles St
100-502 29902
501-505 29901
503-1499 29902
504-1498 29902
Charlesfort St 29902
Charleston Dr 29906
Charlotte Amalie Dr 29906
Cheashil Rd 29906
Checkerboard Blvd 29906
Cherokee Rd 29902
Cherokee Farms Rd 29906
Cherokee Oaks Ln 29906
Cherry Blvd 29902
Chesapeake Bay Rd 29902
Chesterfield Dr 29906
Chesterfield Lake Dr 29906
Chickadee Ln 29907
Chinaback Dr 29907
Chipps Ln 29907
Chloe Ct 29907
Chloes Way 29907
Chowan Creek Blf 29907
Chris Ln 29906
Christine Dr 29907
Chu Lai Dr 29902
Church St 29902
Churchdale Dr 29906
Claires Point Rd 29907
Clarendon Ct & Rd 29906
Clarendon Plantation Dr 29906
Clarendon Shores Dr 29906
Clark Ln 29902
Clark St 29907
Clearwater Way 29906
Cleveland Dr 29906
Cloverwood Rd 29906
Clovis Ct 29906
Club Rd 29907
Clydesdale Cir 29906
Coates Ln 29902
Cobia Dr 29906
Cockle Ln 29906
Coinbow Loop 29906
Cole Dr 29907
Coleman Ln 29902
Colleton Dr 29906
Collin Campbell 29906
Colonial Ave 29906
Colony Ct 29906
Colony Gardens Rd 29907
Columbia Dr 29906
Commons Cir 29902
Conch Point Ln 29907
Conestoga Loop 29906
Congaree Way 29902
Congress St 29902
Coosaw Club Dr 29907
Coosaw Island Ct & Dr 29907
Coosaw Point Blvd 29907
Coosaw River Dr 29907
Copeland Dr 29902
Coquinas Ct & Ln 29906
Cordata Ct 29907
Cordgrass Loop 29907
Corner Loop 29906
Cotesworth Ln 29906
Cottage Farm Dr 29902
Cottage Walk Cir 29907
Cotton Ct 29907
Cotton Eye Ct 29902
Cougar Dr 29907
Country Rd 29906
Country Club Dr 29907
Country Manor Rd 29906
County Shed Rd 29906
Cove Rd 29907
Craig Ln 29906
Craven St 29902
Creek Rd 29906
Creekview Dr 29907
N Crescent 29906
Crescent Moon Bnd 29906
Cricket Ln 29906
Croaker Ln 29907
Crossgate Loop 29906
Crows Nest Ave 29907
Crusaders Xing 29906
Cuba St 29902
Culebra Dr 29906
Cuthbert St 29902
Cydette Ln 29906
Cypress St 29906
W D Walsh Ln 29906
Dahlia Dr 29906
Daisy Ln 29907
Dak To Dr 29902
Danang Ave 29902
Dante Cir 29906
Darby Dr 29902
Darity Ln 29906
David Wayne Ln 29907
Davidson Rd 29906
Dawn St 29906
Dawson Landing Dr 29902
Deanne Dr 29902
Debby Ln 29906
Deepwood Ln 29906
Deer Run 29906
Dela Gaye Pt 29902
Deloach Ave 29906
Delta Ln 29906
Dempster St 29907
Dennis Ln 29906
Depot Rd 29902
Deschamps Ln 29906
Dessaussure St 29902
Deveaux Ln 29907
Diana Ln 29907
Distant Island Dr 29907
Division St 29907
Dock Builders Dr 29907
Doe Dr 29907
Dog Creek Rd 29907
Dogwood St 29906
Dolly Ln 29907
Dolphin St 29906
Dolphin Point Dr 29907
Dolphin Row Dr 29906
Dolphin View Pt 29907
Dolphin Watch Pt 29907
Donaldson Dr 29906
Donaldson Camp Rd 29906
Dong Ha St 29902
Dorchester Dr 29906
Dore Dr 29907
Dorinsou Blvd 29904
Dove Ln 29906
Dover Ln 29902
Dow Rd 29907
Dowitcher Ct 29907
Dowlingwood Dr 29902
Downing Dr 29907

Dreamcatcher Ln 29906
Duck Branch Ct 29902
Duke St 29902
Duncan Dr 29902
Dusty Cir 29906
Eagle Ln 29906
Eagle Pointe Ln 29906
Eagle Ridge Rd 29906
Eagle Roy Ln 29907
Eagle Trace Ct 29907
East St 29902
Eastern Rd 29906
N & S Eastover 29906
Edgehill Ln 29906
Edith Ln 29902
Edward Ct 29906
Egret Ct & Dr 29907
Elderberry Dr 29906
Eleanore Fine Rd 29906
Elisabeth Cv 29907
Eliza Ln 29907
Elizabeth Ln 29902
Elizabeth Samuel Ln 29907
Elliott Dr 29906
Elliott St 29902
Ellis Pl 29906
Elm St 29902
Elton Ln 29902
Emerald St 29907
Emily Ln 29902
Emmons St 29902
Enduring Freedom Pkwy 29906
Enoree Way 29906
Ermine Dr 29902
Esteli Dr 29906
Estelle Rd 29906
Ethel Grant Ln 29907
Eugene Dr 29907
Euhaw St 29902
Eustis Landing Rd 29907
Eve Crk 29906
Eventide Way N & S 29907
Evergreen Ln 29906
F And B Rd 29907
F L Brown Ln 29907
Factory Creek Ct & Rd 29907
Faculty Dr 29907
Fair Rd 29906
Fairfield Rd 29907
Faith Sta 29906
Falling Leaf Ln 29906
Falls Rd 29906
Familial Ln 29907
Farm Wagon Rd 29907
Faye Ln 29907
Federal St 29902
Fen Ln 29907
Fernswood Ln 29907
Ferrets End 29902
Ferry Dr 29907
Fiddler Dr 29907
Fiddler Pond Loop 29907
Fiddlerville Cv 29906
Fieldcrest Cir 29906
Fig Dr 29907
Firebranch Ln 29906
Five Oaks Cir 29902
Flamingo Cir 29906
Flamingo Cv 29907
Flamingo Dr 29906
Fleetwood Ln 29906
Fleming Ln 29906
Flora Cir 29907
Flycatcher Ln 29907
Flyway Dr 29907
Folson Ct 29907
Forest Park 29902
Forest Fields Rd 29906
Forks Of Ivy Ln 29906
Forrest Ln 29902
Fort Lyttleton 29906
Fort Lyttleton Rd 29902
Fort Marion Rd 29902
Four Winds Ave 29907

Foxglove St 29906
Frame Ave 29906
Frances Ct 29907
Francis Davant 29906
Francis Marion Cir 29907
Franklin Dr 29906
Fraser Dr 29902
Fraser St 29907
Frazier Village Dr 29906
Fred Walker Dr 29907
Freddies Dr 29907
Frederick Dr 29906
Freeman Dr 29907
Freemont Ct & Ln 29906
Friendship Ln 29907
Fripp St 29902
Fuller Pkwy & St 29902
Fulwood Ln 29906
Gadson Ln 29906
Gadwall Dr E & W 29907
Gail St 29906
Gamecock Way 29906
Gannet Point Rd 29907
Garden Grove Ct 29907
Gardenia Dr 29906
Gator Ln 29907
Gautier Pl 29902
Gavis Ln 29907
Gay Dr 29907
Geechie Rd 29907
Geiger Blvd 29904
Gene Allen Rd 29906
Gillens Gray Ln 29906
Gladstone Pl 29906
Glass Rd 29906
Glaze Dr 29906
Glebe St 29902
Glendale Ln 29902
Glory Rd 29906
Godfrey St 29902
Godwin Rd 29906
Goethe Hill Rd 29906
Golden Pond Ln 29907
Gollihugh Blvd 29906
Goodwin St 29906
Governer Blake Ct 29907
Governors Trce 29907
Grace Park 29906
Grackle Ln 29906
Grafton Dr 29902
Grand Oaks Way 29907
Grande Oaks 29906
Grandiflora Ln 29907
Grant St 29906
Grays Hill Acres 29906
Grayson St 29902
Great Bend Dr 29906
Green Acres 29906
Green Family Dr 29906
Green Pointe Ln 29906
Green Pond Dr 29906
Green Winged Teal Dr N & S 29907
Greene St 29902
Greenlawn Cir & Dr 29902
Greenleaf Ln 29906
Greenway Ln 29907
Grober Hill Rd 29906
Grove Rd 29907
Guadalcanal St 29902
Guam Cir 29902
Gumwood Dr 29907
Habersham Ave & Park 29906
Hagood Ln 29906
Hale Dr 29906
Hamar St 29902
Hamilton St 29902
Hamlet Row 29906
Hammy Path 29907
Hampton Dr 29906
Hamrick Dr 29906
Hancock St 29902
Hanna Ave 29906
Hanover Ln 29902
Harbison Pl 29906

Harborview Cir & Dr 29907
Harding St 29902
Harford 29906
Harold Dr 29906
Harper Ln 29906
Harrington St 29902
Harris Rd 29902
Harvest Ln 29907
Harvey Rd 29902
Harveys Bnd 29906
W Haven 29906
Hawks Lndg 29906
Hawthorne Rd 29902
Hay St 29902
Hayek St 29907
Hazel Rd 29906
Hazel Farm Rd 29907
Heather St 29906
Hendersons Way 29907
Hermitage Rd 29902
Hermitage Pointe 29902
Heron Way 29902
Heronwyck Plantation Dr 29906
Hester Ln 29907
Hewlett Rd 29907
Heyward St 29902
Hickory Rd 29907
Hickory St 29906
Hidden Ct 29907
High Tide Dr 29906
Highpoint 29907
Hilanda Ct & Dr 29906
Hilda Ave 29907
Hodge Dr 29906
Hogarth St 29902
Holbrook Dr 29902
Hollingsworth Run 29906
Holly Hall Rd 29907
Holmes Rd 29902
Honeysuckle Ln 29907
Hookstra Dr 29902
Hopwood Ln 29907
Hornsborough Ct 29902
Horton Ct, Ln, Rd & Trl 29906
Hosea Rd 29906
Houston Dr 29907
Howard Dr 29906
Hudson Dr 29907
Huguenin Dr 29902
Humbolt Cir 29907
Huron Dr 29902
Ice House Rd 29906
Ihly Rd 29906
Ihly Farm Rd 29906
Indigo Loop 29907
Industrial Village Rd 29906
Inlet Rd 29907
Inwood Ct 29906
Inwood Plantation Dr 29906
Iris Ln 29906
Irongate Dr 29906
Island Breeze Ln 29907
Island Tank Rd 29906
Islands Ave 29902
Islands Cir 29902
Islands Cswy 29907
Isralite Church Rd 29907
Ivy Ln 29902
Iwo Jima St 29902
J W Ln 29907
Jade St 29907
James St 29902
James F Byrnes St 29907
James Green Ln 29907
James Habersham 29906
Jane Way 29902
Janna St 29906
Jasmine Ct 29907
Jasmine St 29906
Jasper Ln 29907
Jasperstone Cir 29906
Jay St 29906
Jefferson Dr 29906
Jennings Rd 29906

Jerry Ln 29906
Jersey Dairy Farm Rd 29902
Jeter Rd 29906
Joann St 29906
Joe Allen Dr 29906
Joe Frazier Rd 29906
John St 29906
John Calhoun St 29907
John Davis Ct 29906
John Galt Rd 29906
Johnnies Loop 29906
Johnny Morrall Cir 29902
Johns Pl 29906
Johnson Landing Rd 29907
Jones Ave 29902
Jonesfield Pl & Rd 29906
Joppa Rd 29906
Jordan Dr 29906
Josephine Dr 29906
Joshua Cir & Ct 29902
Joyner St 29902
Judge Island Dr 29907
Julep St 29906
W K Alston Dr 29906
Kader St 29906
Kaminsky Ln 29906
Katelyns Way 29907
Katherine Ct 29902
Katie Rivers Rd 29906
Kato Ln 29906
Katy Cir 29907
Kemmerlin Ln 29907
Kennedy Cir 29906
King St 29902
Kings Cross Ct 29902
Knight Ln 29907
Knollwood Ln 29907
Kojo Dr 29902
Korea Ave 29902
Kuwait Ave 29902
L H Nelson Dr 29906
La Chere St 29902
Lady Elizabeth Dr 29907
Ladys Walk 29907
Ladys Island Dr 29907
Lafayette St 29902
Lagaree Ct 29902
Lake Ct 29907
Lake Melton St 29906
Lake Point Dr 29907
Lamon Dr 29906
Landing Dr 29907
Landon Ln & Way 29906
Langhorne Dr 29902
Laudonniere St 29902
Laughing Gull Dr 29907
Laurel St E & W 29906
E & W Laurel Bay Blvd & Rd 29906
Laurel Hill Ln 29907
Laurens St 29902
Lawing Dr 29906
Lawson Rd 29907
Le Chene Cir 29906
Le Moyne Ct & Dr 29907
Legare St 29902
Lemon Ln 29906
Leo Green Rd 29906
Leola Pl 29906
Lexxus Ln 29906
Linda St 29906
Linda Sue Ct 29907
Linton Ln 29902
Lisbon Way 29907
Little Ln 29906
Little Capers Rd 29907
Little Creek Rd 29907
Little Jane Way 29906
Live Oak Cir 29902
Logeorge Ln 29907
Loggerhead Trl 29907
Logwood Path 29907
Lonesome Ct 29906
Long Point Dr 29907
Long Pond Dr N 29907
Longstaple Ct 29907

Loretta Ln 29906
Lost Island Rd 29907
N & S Loudon 29906
Lovejoy St 29902
Lucerne Ave 29907
Lucy Dr 29907
Lucy Creek Dr 29907
Lucy Creek Farm Rd 29907
Luella St 29906
Lukes Ln 29906
Lupo Dr 29907
Lyford Pl 29902
Madeline Ln 29907
Magnolia St 29906
Magnolia Bluff Cir 29902
Makin St 29902
Mallard Ct 29907
Mallard Ln 29906
Mamie Frazier Ln 29906
E & W Manor 29906
Manta Ln 29902
Marauders Bay 29906
Marguerita Ct 29906
Marina Blvd 29902
Marina Village Ln 29902
Mark Ave 29906
Market 29906
Marley Dr 29906
Marquis Way 29907
Marsh Dr 29907
Marsh Harbor Dr 29907
Marsh Hawk Dr 29907
Marshall Ln 29907
Marshellen Dr 29902
Marshfront Dr 29902
Marshtacky Dr & Run 29906
Marshview Dr 29907
Martha Ann Way 29907
Mary Elizabeth Dr 29907
Mary Stuart Ln 29907
Mauldin Ct 29902
Maxine Ln 29906
Mayberry Ln 29907
Mayfair Ct 29907
Mccalley Ct 29906
Mcchesney Ln 29902
Mcguire Ct 29902
Mcintrye Cir 29906
Mckee Rd 29907
Mcknight Sr Dr 29907
Mcteer Cir 29902
Meadowbrook Dr S 29907
Meadowbrook Farm Rd 29907
Meadowlark St 29907
Meagan Dr 29907
Meander Ln 29906
Meeting St 29907
Mellow Breeze Ln 29907
Merchants Ln 29907
Meridian Rd 29907
Meridith Ln 29907
Meritta Ave 29902
Micah Loop 29906
Mickey D Ln 29907
Mid South Dr 29906
Middle Rd 29907
Middle River Rd 29906
Middleton St 29902
Middleton Recreation Dr 29906
Midtown Dr 29906
Milkweed Ln 29907
Milledge Village Rd 29906
Miller Dr E & W 29907
Millers Pond Dr 29907
Milton Way 29907
Mink Point Blvd 29902
Mint Farm Dr 29906
Miranda Cir 29906
Mises Rd 29907
Mission Way 29906
Misty Dr 29906
Moccasin Gap 29907
Mockingbird Dr 29907
Monson St 29902

Moody Dr 29907
Moody Sons Ln 29906
Moonlighters Cv 29906
Morgan St 29902
Morgan River Dr N & S 29907
Morning Glory Dr 29906
Morning Mist Dr 29906
Morrall Dr 29906
Morris St 29902
Moses Rd 29906
Moss St 29902
Mossy Oaks Rd 29902
Moultrie Cir 29906
Moultrie Ct 29907
Moultrie Pl 29906
Mount Grace 29906
Moyd Ln 29907
Mr Douglas Ln 29907
Mroz Rd 29906
Mullet Aly 29907
Mulrain Rd 29906
Mum Grace 29906
Munch Dr 29906
Murray Dr 29906
Mustelidae Rd 29902
Myrtle St 29902
Mystic Cir & Dr 29902
Najas Ln 29907
Nak Tong Dr 29902
Narcissus Ln 29902
National Blvd 29907
E National Blvd 29907
W National Blvd 29907
National St 29902
Neddlegrass Dr 29902
Needlerush Ct 29907
Needles Rd 29906
Neil Rd 29906
New St 29902
Newcastle St 29902
Newpoint Rd 29907
Nicaragua St 29902
Nighthawk Ln 29907
No Balance Due Ln 29902
Norman Dr 29906
North St 29902
Northview Dr 29906
Northwoods Ln 29907
Noye Wiggins Dr 29906
Nyssa Ln 29907
Oak Bluff Ct 29906
Oak Grove Cir 29906
Oak Haven St 29902
Oak Pond Psge 29906
Oak View Dr 29902
Oaklawn St 29902
Oakmont Dr 29906
Oakview Dr 29902
Oakwood Dr 29907
Oconnell St 29902
Ogden Ct 29907
Okinawa St 29902
Old Barn Rd 29907
Old Bethel 29906
Old Country Dr 29906
Old Distant Island Rd 29907
Old Ferry Cv 29907
Old Jericho Rd 129A-129B 29902
Old Plantation Dr 29907
Old Salem Rd 29902
Old Trail Rd 29902
`Oldellon St 29902
Oleander Dr 29907
Omega Ln 29906
Oneal Rd 29907
Oscar Mack Rd 29906
Osmunda Dr 29907
Osprey Rd 29907
Otter Cir 29902
Outreach Ln 29906
Over Dm 29906
Oxeye Ln 29907
Oyster Catcher Rd 29907
Oyster Cove Rd 29902

Oyster Factory Rd 29907
Paige Dr 29906
Palm Dr 29902
Palm Point Rd 29907
Palmer Ln 29902
Palmetto Cir 29906
Palmetto Dr 29902
Palmetto Pl 29902
Palmetto St 29902
Palmetto Breeze Cir 29907
Palmetto Grove Ln 29907
Palmetto Ridge St 29906
Palmetto Sands Ct 29902
Palomino Dr 29906
Panama St 29902
Paradise Ln 29906
Park Ave 29902
Park Bnd 29906
Park Sq N 29907
Park Sq S 29907
Parker Dr 29906
Parkway 29907
Parris Island Gtwy 29906
Partridge Cir 29907
Patricia Ct 29907
Patrick Dr 29902
Patriot Ct 29906
Patterson Rd 29906
Paukie Island Rd 29906
Paul Dr 29902
Paul Heyward Rd 29907
Peace Haven Dr 29906
Peaceful Way 29906
Peacock Run 29906
Pearl St 29902
Pecan St 29906
Pelelieu St 29902
Pelican Cir 29906
Pennyroyal Way 29906
Pepper Vine Ln 29906
Perryclear Dr 29906
Petigru Dr 29902
Peytons Way 29907
Phillips St 29902
Phoebe Pass 29906
Piccadilly Cir 29907
Pick Pocket Plantation Dr 29902
Pickens St 29907
Pigeon Point Rd 29902
Pigler Cv 29907
Pilot St 29902
Pin Drop Ln 29902
Pinckney Blvd & St 29902
Pinckney Retreat 29902
Pine Ct 29902
Pine Cove St 29902
Pine Grove Rd 29906
Pine Haven St 29902
Pine Martin Rd 29902
Pine Run Trl 29907
Pinecrest Ln 29906
Pinewood Cir 29906
Pinto Ct 29906
Plantation Dr 29902
Planters Cir 29907
Pleasant Farm Ct, Dr, Ln & Ter 29906
Pleasant Place Ct & Dr 29907
Pleasant Point Dr 29907
Pleasant View Ln 29902
Plough Pt 29902
Plum Tree Ln 29907
N & S Point Trl 29907
Pointe Cv 29906
Polite Dr 29906
Polk St 29902
Pond Side 29902
Ponvert Dr 29902
Pony Ave 29906
Pope Rd 29907
Poppy Hill Cir & Rd 29906
Porcher Pinkney 29906
Port Republic St 29902
Possum Hill Rd 29906

Powell Dr 29906
Pratt Progeny Rd 29907
Prescient Ave 29907
Prescott Ct & Dr 29902
Presnell Cir 29902
Prince St 29902
Professional Village Cir 29907
Providence Rd 29906
Pulaski Ct & Dr 29906
Punch Bowl St 29902
Purdy Way 29907
Purrysburg Dr 29907
Purslane Dr 29907
Quail Dr 29906
Quail Ridge Cir, Dr & Loop N & S 29906
Qualls Rd 29906
Quang Tri Way 29902
Quarter Horse Rd 29906
Queen St 29902
Quiet Cove Way 29907
R J Oneill Dr 29906
Rabon Ln 29906
Ramsey Loop & Rd 29906
Ratel Cir, Ct & Dr 29902
Ray Cir 29902
Raymond Ct 29907
Rebeccas Way 29907
Red Oak Dr 29907
Red Tip Rd 29907
Redwood Ln 29907
Reeds Rd 29907
Register Rd 29906
Reid Ct 29907
Relative Ln 29907
Rentz St 29906
Rerock Rd 29906
Retreat Plantation 29902
Reynolds St 29902
Rhoda St 29902
Ribaut Rd 29902
Rice Rd 29906
Ridenour Pl 29902
N Ridge Pl 29906
Ridge Rd 29907
Riley Rd 29906
Rising Tide Dr 29902
River Dr 29907
E River Dr 29907
W River Dr 29907
River Pl 29906
River Rock Way 29902
Riverbank Dr 29902
Riverchase Blvd 29906
Riverfront Pl 29902
Rivers Ct 29907
Rivers Hill Rd 29906
Riverside Dr & Ln 29902
Riverview Dr 29907
Robert Smalls Pkwy
41C1-41C2 29906
1-100 29906
11-11 29903
101-899 29906
102-898 29906
Roberts Ln & Rd 29906
Robin Dr & Way 29907
Rock Springs Dr 29907
Rockville Way 29902
Rodgers St 29902
Rogers Dr 29902
Rolling Waters Way 29902
Roosevelt Ave 29906
Roper St 29902
Rosa Cove Ln 29907
Rose Mary Dr 29906
Roseida Rd 29906
Roseida Road Ext 29906
Rough River Rd 29906
Roundabout Loop 29906
Rowell Ln 29902
Royal Dr 29906
N Royal Oaks Dr 29902
Royal Pines Blvd 29907
Royal Star Dr 29907
Rue Du Bois 29907
Ruelle Du Belle 29907
Rugrack Rd 29906
Rush St 29907
Saigon Ave 29902
Saint Charles Pl 29907
Saint James Pl 29907
Saint Mihiel Rd 29902
Saint Pauls Church Rd 29906
Saint Phillips Blvd 29906
Saipan St 29902
Salem Dr & Rd 29902
Salem Farm Rd 29902
Salicornia Dr 29907
Salt Creek Dr E & W 29906
Salt Marsh Cv 29907
Saluda Way 29906
Sammie Ln 29906
Sams Way 29907
Sams Point Rd 29907
San Miguel Dr 29906
San Pedro De Marcoris Dr 29906
Sandel Ln 29902
Sandhill Dr 29906
Sandpiper Dr E & W 29907
Sandra Dr 29906
Sandstone Cir 29906
Sandy Ln 29907
Sandy Ridge Rd 29902
Sangster Rd 29907
Santee Ln 29906
Satilla Blvd 29902
Sauls Dr 29906
Saunders Rd 29902
Savannah Hwy 29906
Sawgrass Ct & Dr 29907
Schein Loop 29906
Scheper Ln 29902
Scipio Rd 29906
Scotch Pine Dr 29902
Scott St 29902
Scurpus Ct 29907
Sea Breeze Way 29907
Sea Gull Dr 29907
Sea Gull Villa Ln 29906
Sea Island Pkwy 29907
Seabrook Pl 29907
Secession Dr 29907
Sedgewick Pl 29907
Self Storage Rd 29906
Seneca Way 29906
Seoul St 29902
Settlers Cv 29907
Shad Tree Ln 29907
Shadow Moss Dr 29906
Shallop Ln 29906
Shallowbrook Ln 29907
Shallowford Downs 29907
Shanghai St 29902
Shanklin Rd 29906
Shannon Ln 29906
Sharisse Way 29907
Shea Ln 29906
Sheffield Ave & Ct 29907
Shelby Ln 29907
Shell Park Cir 29906
Shell Point Rd 29906
Shell Point Rec Park 29906
Sheppard Rd W 29907
Sheridan Rd 29907
Sherman Dr 29907
Sherwood Ln 29907
Shiney Leaf Ct 29907
Shire Dr 29907
Short St 29902
Short Cut 29906
Shorts Landing Rd 29907
Shuri Dr 29902
Sidewinder St 29906
Silver Eagle Way 29906
Simmons Family Rd 29906
Simms St 29902
Singleton Dr 29907
Singleton Hill Cir & Ct 29906
Skoshi Ct 29906
Sky Ct 29907
Smalls Hill Rd 29906
Smart Adams Ln 29906
Smith Rd 29906
Smoketree Ln 29907
Snapper Ln 29907
Sommer Lake Dr 29902
Sonya Faye Ln 29906
South Dr 29902
South Park 29906
Southern Magnolia Dr 29907
Southside Blvd 29902
Spanish Ct 29902
Spanish Moss Dr 29902
Spanish Point Dr 29902
Sparkleberry Dr 29907
Spartina St 29907
Spearmint Cir 29906
Spectable St 29902
Spoonbill Dr 29907
Spring Knob Cir 29907
Springfield Rd 29907
Squash Ct 29906
Squirrel Run 29907
St James Cir 29907
Staffwood Rd 29906
Staigers Way 29907
Stanley Rd 29906
Stanley Farm Rd 29906
Star Magnolia Ct & Dr 29907
Starlight Ln 29907
Steever Ln 29907
Stellata Ln 29907
Stevens Ln 29907
Stevic Ct 29907
Still Shadow Dr 29906
Stillwell Ln 29906
Stone Marten Cir & Dr 29902
Stoney Island Dr 29907
Stono Ct 29902
Storage Rd 29906
Stratford Ln 29902
W Street Ext 29902
Stuart St 29902
Stuart Town Ct & Rd 29902
Sturdevant Dr 29902
Sugar Loaf St 29902
Summer Dr 29906
Summerfield Ct 29907
Sunburst Ln 29906
Sundown Bnd 29906
Sunfish Ct 29902
Sunmist Dr 29907
Sunny Pl 29907
Sunrise Blvd 29907
Sunset Blf 29907
Sunset Blvd 29907
Sunset Cir 29906
Sunset Cir N 29906
Sunset Cir S 29906
Sunset Ct 29902
Sunshine Ln 29906
Surf Dr 29907
Susan Ct 29907
Sussex Ct 29907
Suzanne Ave 29906
Swamp Fox Trl 29906
Sweet Grass Dr 29907
Sweet Olive Dr 29907
Switchgrass Dr 29902
Sycamore St 29902
Tabby Rd 29902
Taft St 29902
Tailwind Trl 29907
Talbird Rd 29902
Talisman Ln 29906
Tallwood Ln 29906
Tammy Ln 29906
Tanglewood Dr 29902
Tarawa St 29902
Tarra Ct 29906
Taylor Dr 29907
Taylor St 29906
Tekoa Ln 29902
Telfair Dr 29907
The Hill Rd 29907
The Horseshoe 29907
Thomas Atkins Rd 29907
Thomas Sumter St 29907
Thomasina Dr 29906
Thoroughbred Cir 29906
Three Pence Ln 29906
Thunder Pumper Rd E & W 29907
Thunderbolts Ln 29906
Tidal St 29902
Tidal Walk Dr & Ln 29907
Tidewatch Cir 29907
Tidewater St 29907
Timber Trl 29907
Tinian St 29902
Tipan Ln 29906
Toad Hall 29907
Todd Dr 29902
Token Ln 29907
Tomlow Trce 29906
Tomotley Ct 29906
Toppers Ln 29906
Toro Ln 29906
Town Crier 29906
Trails End 29907
Trask Pkwy 29906
Trask Farm Rd 29906
Treadlands 29906
Treasure End Ln 29907
Tripoli St 29902
Tronie Ln 29907
Trotters Loop 29907
Tsing Tao Dr 29906
Tucker Ave 29907
Tugaloo Dr 29906
Tulagi St 29902
Turnstone Dr N & S 29907
Turtle Ln 29907
Tuscarora Ave 29907
Tuscarora Trl 29906
Tuxedo Dr 29907
Twin Lakes Rd 29902
Union St 29902
Vanita Dr 29906
Varsity St 29907
Vaux Rd 29906
Vella Lavella Dr 29906
Venice Ct 29907
Verdier Rd 29902
Verdier Bluff Rd 29902
Via Venado 29906
Village Row 29906
Viola Smalls Ln 29907
Von Harten St 29902
Waccamaw Way 29906
Waddell Rd 29902
Wade Hampton Dr 29907
Waight St 29902
Wake Blvd 29902
Walker Cir 29906
Wallace Rd 29907
Walling Grove Rd 29907
Walnut St 29906
Walnut Hill St 29907
Walsh Dr E & W 29906
Walter Dr 29906
Walton Way 29906
Warren Ln 29906
Washington St 29902
Washington Family Rd 29906
Water St 29902
Waterbird Dr 29907
Wateree Ct 29902
Waterford Ct 29907
Waters Edge Ct 29902
Waterside Dr 29907
Waveland Ave 29907
Waverly Way 29902
Wayfield Rd 29902
Wayside Ln 29902
Wearien Ln 29906
Weatherford Dr 29906
Webb Ct 29906
Webb Rd 29906
Webb Way 29907
Wegeon Ln 29906
Wellena Ct 29906
Wesley Ave 29906
West St 29902
Westboro Rd 29906
Western Trce 29907
Westgate Cir 29906
Westminister Pl 29907
Westview Ave 29902
Westvine Dr 29902
Westwood Cir 29906
Whelk Rd 29906
White Dogwood Rd 29907
White Hall Ct 29906
White Hall Dr 29907
White Heron Dr 29907
White Horse Rd 29907
White Pine Rd 29906
White Pond Blvd 29902
Whites Dr & Ln 29906
Whitewater Way 29906
Whitewing Dr 29906
Whitfield St 29902
Wickecliff Pl 29906
Wiggins Rd 29907
Wildcat Ln 29906
Wildwood Ln 29907
William St 29907
Williams St 29902
Willie Moody Ln 29906
Willis Rd 29902
Willow Point Rd 29906
Wilmington St 29902
Wilson Dr 29902
Winding Way 29907
Windsong Rd 29906
Windy Point Dr 29907
Winn Ln 29906
Winn Farm Rd 29906
Winsor Rd 29906
Wintergreen Dr 29906
Winthrope St 29907
Winyah Way 29906
Wolverine Dr 29902
Wood Duck Ln 29907
Wood Ibis Trl 29907
Woodbine Dr 29907
Woodlake Dr 29907
Woodland Ridge Cir 29907
Woods Ln 29907
Woodward Ave 29902
Wren Ln 29906
Wrenhaven Ln 29902
Wrights Point Cir & Ln 29902
Yacht Club Dr 29907
Yalu Dr 29906
Youmans Dr 29907
Zamboango Dr 29906
Zehm Ln 29906

NUMBERED STREETS

All Street Addresses 29902

CAMDEN SC

General Delivery 29020

POST OFFICE BOXES MAIN OFFICE STATIONS AND BRANCHES

Box No.s
1 - 1784 29021
2001 - 3668 29020
7000 - 7075 29021

NAMED STREETS

Academy Ct & Dr 29020
Acorn Ln 29020
Addto Rd 29020
Airline Dr 29020
Albert St 29020
Alexander St 29020
Alice Dr 29020
Amberhill Ct 29020
Amelia St 29020
An Dun Ln 29020
Ancrum Rd 29020
Anglewood Ln 29020
Anns Ct 29020
Antioch Rd 29020
Apple Ln 29020
Arnett Dr 29020
Arrowwood Rd W 29020
Ascot Dr 29020
Atoka Trl 29020
B St 29020
Bailey St 29020
Ball Park Rd 29020
Ballfield Rd 29020
Balsam Rd 29020
Bantam Trl 29020
Barfield St 29020
Barn Owl Rd 29020
Baron Dekalb Rd 29020
Barrett St 29020
Bateman Blvd 29020
Battleship Rd 29020
Battleship Road Ext 29020
Bay Ln 29020
Bayou Rd 29020
Beam Ln 29020
Beard St 29020
Beaufort Rd 29020
Beaver Creek Rd 29020
Beaverdam Rd 29020
Belmont Dr 29020
Belton Ct, Dr, Ln, Rd & St 29020
Belton Cemetery Rd 29020
Belton Shade Village Rd 29020
Benttree Ln 29020
Berry Ln 29020
Beulah Church Rd 29020
Beverly Hills Rd 29020
Bina Ln 29020
Bishopville Hwy 29020
Black Duck Rd 29020
Black Locust Ln 29020
Black Oak Ln 29020
Black River Rd 29020
Bloomsbury Cir 29020
Blue Heron Ln 29020
Blueberry Ln 29020
Bobwhite Cir 29020
Bolden St 29020
Bomburgh Rd 29020
Booker Rd 29020
S Boundary Rd 29020
Bowden Rd 29020
Boyd Rd 29020
Boykin Rd 29020
Boykin Rd Ext 29020
Bradley Rd 29020
N & S Brailsford Rd 29020
Bramblewood Plantation Rd 29020
Branham Ave 29020
Breeze Hill Ln 29020
Brevard Ln & Pl 29020
Brewer Springs Rd 29020
Briar Patch Rd 29020
Bridle Path Rd 29020
S Broad St 29020
Brook Dr 29020
Brookdale Ln 29020
Brookgreen Ct 29020
Brookwood Rd 29020
Broome Dr & Ln 29020
Brown Dr, Rd, St & Trl 29020
Bruce Dr 29020
Bull St 29020
Burbage St 29020
Burndale Ln 29020
Burns Ln 29020
Burroughs Rd 29020
Butternut Ln & Rd 29020
Calhoun St 29020
Calvins Rd 29020
Camden Ave & Hwy 29020
Campbell St 29020
Campus Dr 29020
Canada Dr 29020
Canterbury Ct & Ln 29020
Cantey Ln & Pkwy 29020
Cantey Hill Ln 29020
Cardinal Cir 29020
Carefree Oaks Ln 29020
Carl A Horton Rd 29020
Carlisle Ln 29020
Carlos Ln & St 29020
Carriage House Ln 29020
Carrison St 29020
Carter Dr, Ln & St 29020
Cash Dr 29020
Cassidy Rd 29020
Catawba Ct 29020
Catawba Timber Rd 29020
Cedar Pl 29020
Cedar Cove Rd 29020
Cedar Cove Road Ext 29020
Cedarsprings Ln 29020
Century Blvd 29020
Champion St 29020
Chance Ln 29020
Chancefield Plantation Ln 29020
Charlotte Thompson Sch Rd 29020
Chase Cir 29020
Chesnut St 29020
Chestnut Ferry Rd 29020
Chewning St 29020
Cheyenne Trl 29020
Chicora Trl 29020
Chillingham Rd 29020
Choke Berry Ln 29020
Christmas Pl 29020
Chukar Rd 29020
Church St 29020
Clay Rd 29020
Clearwater Ln 29020
Clearwater Lake Rd 29020
Cleveland School Rd 29020
Clyburn Ln & St 29020
Coach Hill Rd 29020
Cody Trl 29020
Coffeetree Ln 29020
Collins Cir 29020
Colonial Lake Dr 29020
Colony Dr 29020
Commerce Aly 29020
Community Center Rd 29020
Concord Dr 29020
Conway Cir 29020
Cooks Ct 29020
Cool Springs Dr 29020
Cooper St 29020
Copeland Cir 29020
Corbett Rd 29020
Corbett Mill Rd 29020
Corkwood Ln 29020
Cornwallis Ave 29020
Cottesmore Ln 29020
Cottonwood Ln 29020
Country Manor Rd 29020
Court St 29020
Court Inn Ln 29020
Crab Apple Rd 29020
Creed Rd 29020
Crescent Cir & Rd 29020
Crestmont Dr 29020
Crestwood Dr 29020
Crickle Creek Ln 29020
Crofts Mill Rd 29020
Cross Ln 29020
Crowfoot Ln 29020
Cubs Path 29020
Cureton Rd & St 29020
Cypress Rd 29020

Daisy Ln 29020
Damascus Church Rd 29020
Daniels St 29020
Davie Ln 29020
Davis St 29020
Deak Ln 29020
Deerfield Rd 29020
E Dekalb St
1-543 29020
542-598 29020
542-542 29021
545-599 29020
W Dekalb St 29020
Dekalb School Rd 29020
Deloache St 29020
Denton St 29020
Desaussure St 29020
Dibble St 29020
Dicey Ln 29020
Dicey Creek Rd 29020
Dicey Ford Rd 29020
Dillon Ln 29020
Dixon Ln 29020
Doby St 29020
Docks Rd 29020
Douglas St 29020
Dove Rd 29020
Dr Humphries Rd 29020
Drake Ct 29020
Dubose Ct 29020
Duck Cove Rd 29020
Duell St 29020
Dunn Ave 29020
Dusty Ln & Rd 29020
Eagles Nest Rd 29020
East Ln 29020
Easy St 29020
Ebenezer Church Rd 29020
Edinburgh Castle Ln 29020
Egret Cv 29020
Egypt Rd 29020
Ehrenclou Dr 29020
Elder Rd 29020
Elizabeth St 29020
Elkridge Dr 29020
Elkwood Ln 29020
Ellen Rd 29020
Elmore St 29020
W End St 29020
English St 29020
Essex Ct 29020
Estate Pl 29020
Evergreen Ct 29020
Fair St 29020
Fairfax Dr 29020
Fairlawn Dr 29020
Fairleaf Cir 29020
Family Ln 29020
Favor Rd 29020
Field Rd & St 29020
Field Trial Rd 29020
Fire Tower Rd 29020
Fire Tower Farm Rd 29020
Fishing Ln 29020
Flat Rock Rd 29020
Flint Hill Rd 29020
Flynn Ln 29020
Forest Dr 29020
Fort Ln & Rd 29020
Fouts St 29020
Fox Fire Ln 29020
Fox Haven Ln 29020
Foxwood Ln 29020
Franklin St 29020
Friendship Rd 29020
Frogden Ct 29020
Frost Rd 29020
Gaines Church Rd 29020
Galloway Rd 29020
Garden St 29020
Gardner St 29020
Garrison Ct 29020
Gary Rd & St 29020
Gates Ct & St 29020
Gazebo Ct 29020
Genesis Ln 29020
Geno Branch Rd 29020
George Wright St 29020
Gin House Ln 29020
Godwin Dr 29020
Goff St 29020
Golden Dr 29020
Goodale Ave 29020
Goodwin Jenkins Ln 29020
Gordon St 29020
Green Street Ext 29020
Greenbriar Rd 29020
Greene St 29020
Griswold Rd 29020
Hackamore Ln 29020
Hacks Rd 29020
Haier Blvd 29020
Haile Ln & St 29020
Halley Rd 29020
E & W Hampton Park & St 29020
Hanger Ln 29020
Harbor View Rd 29020
Harriett Dr 29020
Hasty Ln & Rd 29020
Hatfield Dr 29020
Hatten St 29020
Hawkwood Dr 29020
Hawthorne Dr 29020
Hazelhurst St 29020
Hazelwood Dr 29020
Healthy Pine Rd 29020
Hengst Blvd 29020
Henry St 29020
Heritage Dr 29020
Hermitage St 29020
Hermitage Farm Rd 29020
Hermitage Pond Rd 29020
Hickory Hill Rd & Way 29020
Highland Ave 29020
Highway 1 N 29020
S Hill Ln 29020
Hillsdale Dr & Ln 29020
Hilton St 29020
Hiltons Ln 29020
Hinsdale Ln 29020
Hobkirk Ct 29020
Holland Ln 29020
Holly Pl 29020
Homeward Dr 29020
Horse Pasture Rd 29020
Horton Ln 29020
Horton Acres Ln 29020
Horton Cove Rd 29020
Hound Hollow Rd 29020
Hummingbird Ln 29020
Humphries Rd 29020
Hunt Trce 29020
Hunt Cup Ln 29020
Hunter Ln 29020
Hunter Hill Rd 29020
Hunting Inc Rd 29020
Hunts End Ln 29020
Indigo Ct 29020
Ivybush Trl 29020
Jackies Ln 29020
Jackson St 29020
Jamestown Rd 29020
Jefferson Davis Hwy 29020
Jeffrey Turn Rd 29020
John G Richards Rd 29020
Johnson Ln 29020
Jordan Ln & St 29020
Jordan Cemetary Rd 29020
Joy Rd 29020
Jumelle Springs Rd 29020
Juneberry Rd 29020
Kamschatka Ln 29020
Kanawha Trl 29020
Kaybee Ct 29020
Kelly Rd 29020
Kendall St 29020
Kennedy Dr & St 29020
Kent Pl 29020
Kershaw Hwy 29020
King St 29020
Kings Ave 29020
Kings Chase Rd 29020
Kiowa Trl 29020
Kirkland St 29020
Kirkland Cemetary Rd 29020
Kirkover Ln 29020
Kirkwood Cir, Ln & St 29020
Knights Hill Rd 29020
Knotty Pine Rd 29020
Kornegay Cir & Ct 29020
Lafayette St & Way 29020
Lake Mallard Ln 29020
Lakeshore Dr & Rd 29020
Lakeview Ave 29020
Land St 29020
Lauray Ln 29020
Laurel Pl 29020
Laurens Ct & St 29020
Lausanne Dr 29020
Law St 29020
Lawhorn Rd 29020
Lawton Ct 29020
E Lee Ct, Rd & St 29020
Leisure Rd 29020
Leonard Cir 29020
Lewis St 29020
Liberty Hill Rd 29020
Lila D Ln 29020
Little St 29020
Little Creek Rd 29020
Lloyd St 29020
Lloyds Woods Dr 29020
Lockhart Rd 29020
Logan Rd 29020
Logans Ln 29020
Lonesome Pine Trl 29020
Lorick Horton Rd 29020
Lovett Rd 29020
Loy Rd 29020
Lucknow Rd 29020
Lydford Ln 29020
Lynch Ln 29020
Lyndhurst Dr 29020
Lynn Ave 29020
Lynwood St 29020
Lystra Rd 29020
Lyttleton St 29020
M West Rd 29020
Mackey St 29020
Maggie Ave 29020
Maiden Ct 29020
Mallard Ln & Rd 29020
Malvern Hill Dr 29020
Manchester Trl 29020
Maple Ln 29020
Marietta Lake Rd 29020
Marina Way 29020
Market St 29020
Maroney St 29020
Marsh Hawk Rd 29020
Mary Ln 29020
Mathis Ct 29020
Mattison St 29020
May Ln 29020
Mccarley Dr 29020
Mccartha St 29020
Mccaskill Rd 29020
Mccleod Ln 29020
Mcleod Ct & Rd 29020
Mcrae Rd 29020
Meadowbrook Dr 29020
Medfield Dr 29020
Meeting St 29020
Merry Way 29020
Methodist Camp Rd 29020
Mill Ln & St 29020
Mill Bank Rd 29020
Miller Rd 29020
Mission Ln 29020
Misty Oak Ln 29020
Mitchell Dr 29020
Mohawk Dr 29020
Monroe St 29020
Montessori Way 29020
Monument Sq 29020
Moore Rd 29020
Moultrie Rd 29020
Mount Olivet Rd 29020
Mount Zion Rd 29020
Mount Zion Cemetery Rd 29020
Mustang Rd 29020
Nancy Ct 29020
Napper Rd 29020
Nautical Dr 29020
Navaho Trl 29020
Neal Switch Rd 29020
Nelson St 29020
Newcastle Ln 29020
Niagara Dr 29020
Norden Dr 29020
Norris Ave 29020
North Ln 29020
Northgate Dr 29020
Nursery Dr 29020
Oak Ln 29020
Oak Hill Ln 29020
Old Mill Ln 29020
Old Rail Rd 29020
Old River Rd 29020
Old Stagecoach Rd 29020
Omega Dr 29020
Outlaw Rd 29020
Owens Rd 29020
Palmetto Arms Dr 29020
Park Cir & Rd 29020
Pate Rd 29020
Pathfinder Trl 29020
Peck Woods Rd 29020
Perkins Ln 29020
Pickett St 29020
Pickett Thomas Rd 29020
Pin Oak Ct 29020
Pine Rd & St 29020
Pine Bark Rd 29020
Pine Creek Ave & Ln 29020
Pine Crest St 29020
Pine Oak Rd 29020
Pine Ridge Rd 29020
Pine Top Rd 29020
Pinehurst Dr 29020
Pineview St 29020
Pipeline Rd 29020
Pitts St 29020
Pleasant Rdg 29020
Plum Ln 29020
Poinsietta Trl 29020
Polo Ln 29020
Polson Rd 29020
Pony Ln 29020
Poplar Ln 29020
Powell St 29020
Precipice Rd 29020
Preserve Ave 29020
Price St 29020
Pritchard Ct 29020
Puddle Ln 29020
Purdy Stretch Ln 29020
Quail Dr & Rd 29020
Queen St 29020
Raccoon Run 29020
Railroad Ave 29020
Raindance Ln 29020
Rapid Run Rd 29020
Ray St 29020
Rectory Sq 29020
Red Rd 29020
Red Fox Rd 29020
Red Hill Rd 29020
Red Oak Ln 29020
Revere Cir 29020
Richardson Rd 29020
Ridgecrest Dr 29020
Rippondon St 29020
River Rd 29020
Riverwinds Ct 29020
Robbin Dr 29020
Roberts Ave, St & Way 29020
Robinson Rd 29020
Robinson Watkins Rd 29020
Roosevelt Dr 29020
Roundtop Ln 29020
Rowe St 29020
Rowland Ln 29020
Ruddy Duck Rd 29020
Running Fox Rd 29020
Rush Ln & St 29020
Russell Rd 29020
Rutledge St 29020
Rye Ln 29020
Saddle Dr 29020
Sailing Club Ln & Rd 29020
Saint Rd 29020
Saint Matthews Rd 29020
Saint Paul Ln & Rd 29020
Saint Paul Church Cir 29020
Sairenc Rd 29020
Salem Church Rd 29020
Salmond St 29020
Sams Ln 29020
Sanders Creek Rd 29020
Sandspur Rd 29020
Sandway Dr 29020
Sandy Ln 29020
Sandy Springs Dr 29020
Sarsfield Ave 29020
Savage Ave & St 29020
Saxon Pl 29020
Scarlett Ln 29020
Scenic Dr 29020
Scott St 29020
Screech Owl Rd 29020
Seegars Cir 29020
Seegars Mill Rd 29020
Seneca Dr 29020
Shady Ln 29020
Shannon Ct, Ln & St 29020
Shawnee Trl 29020
Sherob Ln 29020
Sherwood Ln 29020
Shipboard Rd 29020
Shiver Pond Rd 29020
Short St 29020
Shorty Ct 29020
Shoshone Dr 29020
Simmons Dr 29020
Sinclair Ln & St 29020
Skyview Dr 29020
Smallwood Trce 29020
Smith Dr & St 29020
Smiths Lawn 29020
Smyrl Cir 29020
Snowy Owl Rd 29020
South Ln 29020
Southern Cedar Ln 29020
Southern Oak Dr 29020
Southgate Dr 29020
Sparkleberry Ln 29020
Split Oak Ct 29020
Spring Ln 29020
Spring Hill Rd 29020
Springdale Dr 29020
Staley Rd 29020
Steeplechase Industrial Blvd 29020
Sterling Green Ct 29020
Stevens Cir 29020
Stewart St 29020
Still House Rd 29020
Stokes Rd 29020
Stowers St 29020
Stretch Dr 29020
Summit Ridge Dr 29020
Sumter Hwy 29020
Sunnyhill Dr 29020
Swift Creek Kennels Rd 29020
Sycamore Ln, Pl & Rd 29020
Temperance Hill Ct 29020
Tennessee Ln 29020
Thomas St 29020
Thompson Rd & St 29020
Thomspon Rd 29020
Tickle Hill Rd 29020
Tiffany Trl 29020
Tillman St 29020
Timber Ln 29020
Timber Creek Rd 29020
Timberline Dr 29020
Tipsy Trl 29020
Tombfield Rd 29020
Town And Country Lk 29020
Trails End Rd 29020
Trapp Mill Rd 29020
Tremble Branch Rd 29020
Trimnal Ave 29020
Trinity Ct 29020
Triple J Rd 29020
Truesdale Rd & St 29020
Tucker St 29020
Tudor Ln 29020
Tupelo Pl 29020
Union St 29020
Upton Cir & Ct 29020
Valley Ct 29020
Vaughns Mill Pond Rd 29020
Villepigue Ext 29020
Vineyard Dr 29020
Virginia Dr 29020
Vocational Ln 29020
Wall St 29020
Walnut St 29020
Warwick St 29020
Washington Ln 29020
Wateree Ave, Blvd & St 29020
Watts Ln & Way 29020
Wells Rd 29020
Welsh St 29020
Westvaco Rd 29020
Wheeler Rd 29020
Whippoorwill Rd 29020
Whispering Pine Trl 29020
White Rd & St 29020
White Oak Ln & Rd 29020
White Pines Cir, Dr & Ln 29020
Widgeon Cv 29020
Wild Turkey Ln & Rd 29020
Wilder St 29020
Will Ln 29020
Williams Ct, Rd & St 29020
Wilson St 29020
Windsor Dr 29020
Windy Ln 29020
Windy Hill Rd 29020
Wisdom Dr 29020
Wolf Ln 29020
Wood Ln 29020
Wood Duck Rd 29020
Woodgate Rd 29020
Woodlawn Ct & Dr 29020
Woodside Dr 29020
Woodstock Ln 29020
Wren Ln 29020
Wylie St 29020
Yellow Locust Trl 29020
Yelton Dr 29020
E York St 29020

NUMBERED STREETS

All Street Addresses 29020

CHARLESTON SC

General Delivery 29402

POST OFFICE BOXES MAIN OFFICE STATIONS AND BRANCHES

Box No.s
B - X 29402
1 - 1885 29402
12001 - 14578 29422
20001 - 22874 29413
29422 - 29422 29422
30000 - 32446 29417
80001 - 81138 29416
130003 - 2941398 29413
2941698 - 2941698 29416
2941798 - 2941798 29417

NAMED STREETS

Abeam Way 29414
Able St 29407
Acacia St 29407
Achurch Ave 29403
Ackerman Ct 29403
Adaline St 29406
Addison St 29403
Addlestone Ave 29403
Adele St 29407
N & S Adgers Wharf 29401
Affirmation Blvd 29412
Afterthoughts Dr 29492
Afton Ave 29407
Agatha St 29407
Agnes Rd 29414
Aiken St 29403
N & S Ainsdale Dr 29414
Akers St 29407
Albacore Ave 29406
Albemarle Rd 29407
Alberta Ave 29403
Alden Dr 29407
Alexander St
1-50 29401
51-199 29403
Alice Dr 29407
All Seymour Ln 29412
N & S Allan Park 29403
Allatoona Ct 29406
Alleghany St 29407
Allen Brown Ln 29412
Allgood Rd 29407
Allison Ct 29407
Allison Cove Dr 29412
Allway St 29403
Alma St 29407
Alpheretta Ct 29414
Alric Ct 29412
Alstonridge Ln 29492
Altman St 29407
Alton St 29406
Amanda Dr 29412
Amanda Park Ln 29412
Ambassador Ln 29414
Amber Ln 29407
Amberbrook Ln 29414
Amberhill Way 29414
Amberjack Ln 29492
Amberly Rd 29407
Ambrose Aly 29401
Amelia Ave 29403
America St 29403
Amherst St 29403
Ammersee Ct 29414
Amoco Dr 29492
Amos Ct 29412
Amy Elsey Dr 29407
Anchor Rd 29412
Ancrum Rd 29407
Ancrum Hill Rd 29407
N And South Rd 29412
E And West Rd 29412
S Anderson Ave 29412
Andrew Ln 29492
Angelfish Ct 29412
Anita Dr 29407
Ann St 29403
Anson St 29401
Anthony Way 29492
S Antler Dr 29406
Apex Ln 29412
Apollo Rd 29407
Applebee Way 29414
Aquaduct St 29414
Aquarium Wharf 29401
Arabian Dr 29407
Arbor Trce 29414
Arborwood Dr 29412
Arcadian Park & Way 29407
Archdale St 29401

Street	ZIP
Area Way	29492
Argonne St	29407
Arlington Dr	29414
Armistice Pt	29412
Armstrong Ave	29407
Arrow Wind Ter	29414
Arsburn Rd	29412
Arthur Dr	29412
Arthur Gaillard Ln	29414
Aruba Cir	29412
Asbury Pl	29407
Asby Dr	29492
Ascot Aly	29401
Ashdale Dr	29407
Ashe St	29403
Asheford Place Dr	29414
Ashland Dr	29407
Ashley Ave	
2-10	29401
12-137	29401
170-180	29403
182-1342	29403
Ashley Blvd	29401
W Ashley Cir	29414
Ashley Cooper Ln	29414
Ashley Crossing Dr & Ln	29414
Ashley Ferry Rd	29414
Ashley Garden Blvd	29414
Ashley Hall Rd	29407
Ashley Hall Plantation Rd	29407
Ashley Point Dr	29407
Ashley River Rd	
1100-1971	29407
1964-1964	29416
1972-2198	29407
1973-2199	29407
2200-4400	29414
4402-4530	29414
Ashley Town Center Dr	29414
Ashley Villa Cir	29414
Ashmead Pl	29403
Ashmont Dr	29492
Ashton St	29403
Ashworth Ln	29412
Assembly Dr	29414
Aston Pl	29401
Athens Ct	29403
Atlantic St	29401
Atlantic Palms Ln	29406
N Atlantic Wharf	29401
Attaway St	29406
Aubrey Dr	29412
Auburn Dr	29406
Audubon Ave	29407
Augustus St	29492
E Avalon Cir	29407
Avenue A	29412
Avenue B	29412
Aviary Way	29412
Avon Ct	29407
Avondale Ave	29407
Ayers Dr	29412
Aylsford Ct	29412
Babbitt St	29414
Back Creek Rd	29412
Back Pond Ct	29492
Backman Rd	29412
Backwater Ct	29412
Bainbridge Dr	29407
Bairds Cv	29414
Baldwin Rd	29406
Balfour Dr	29492
Balfoure Dr	29407
Ballston Ct	29406
Balsam St	29407
Baltimore St	29492
Bamberg Cir	29492
Bamboo Dr	29407
Banbury Ct & Rd	29414
Banner Rd	29414
Bantry Cir	29414
Barbados Dr	29492
Barbados Way	29412
Barbour Dr	29414
Barcreek Rd	29412
Barfield St	29492
Barnaby St	29492
Barre St	29401
Barrett Rd	29407
Barrington Ln	29414
Bass Ln	29412
Bass Alley Rd	29492
Bassett Ct	29412
Batavia Rd	29414
Battalion Dr	29412
Batten Dr	29414
Battery Ave	29407
W Battery Ln	29407
Battery Pl	29401
E Battery St	29401
S Battery St	29401
Battery Brown Ct	29412
Battery Glover Ct	29412
Battery Haig Ct	29412
Battery Island Dr	29412
Battery Kirby Ct	29412
Battery Reynolds Ct	29412
Battery Stevens Ct	29412
Battery Wagner Rd	29412
Battery Weed Ct	29412
Battle Ground Rd	29412
Battlesea Rd	29407
Battlewood Ave	29407
E Bay St	
40-44	29401
46-399	29401
400-558	29403
557-557	29413
560-798	29403
601-799	29403
Bay Creek Dr	29414
Bayhill Dr	29414
Bayview Farms Blvd	29412
Beardsley Rd	29407
Beaten Path	29412
Beaufain St	29401
Beauregard St	29412
Beck Ln	29492
Beckon St	29492
Becky Rd	29414
Bedford Dr	29407
Bedons Aly	29401
Bee St	
---	29403
1-99	29403
101-137	29401
139-199	29401
Beech Hill Dr	29492
Beechcraft St	29407
Beechnut St	29414
Beechwood Rd	29414
Beekman St	29492
Bees Ferry Rd	29414
Belfast Rd	29407
Belgrade Ave & Ct	29407
Bellinger St	29492
Bellpointe Ln	29492
Bellwood Rd	29412
Belvue Rd	29407
Ben Rd	29412
Ben Graham Rd	29412
Benada St	29407
Bender St	29407
Benefitfocus Way	29492
Benhelen Rd	29412
Bennett St	29401
Bennington Dr	29492
Benson St	29403
Bent Hickory Rd	29414
Bent Twig Ln	29407
Bentgrass Ct	29412
Benton Bend Rd	29412
Beresford Run	29492
Beresford Creek St	29492
Beresford Woods Ln	29492
Berkeley Rd	29407
Berkshire Dr	29492
Bermuda St	29412
Bermuda Stone Rd	29414
Berwick Cir	29407
Bethlehem Blvd	29401
Betsy Rd	29407
Beverly Rd	29407
Bevis Rd	29414
Bibury Ct	29414
Bidwell Cir	29414
Bill Bailey Ln	29412
Billfish Ct	29412
Bills Ct	29407
Biltmore Dr	29412
Bimini Dr	29414
Birchdale Dr	29412
Birchwood St	29407
Birdhaven Ln	29492
Birkdale Ct	29414
Birkenhead Dr	29414
Birmingham Ct	29407
Birthright St	29407
Bishop Dr	29414
Bishop Gadsden Way	29412
Blackburn Cir	29407
Blackshear Ct	29406
Blackwatch Ct	29414
Blaine Ct	29407
Blairmore Dr	29414
Blake St	29403
Blakeway St	29492
Blaze Ln	29412
Blitchridge Rd	29407
Blitzen Ct	29406
Blockade Ln	29412
Blockade Runner Ct	29414
Blue Crab Ln	29492
Blue Dragonfly Dr	29414
Blue Jasmine Ln	29414
Blue Marlin Dr	29412
Blue Sky Ln	29492
Bluefish Cir	29412
Bluewater Way	29414
Bluffview Ln	29492
Boardman Rd	29407
Boardwalk Dr	29414
Boat Dock Ct	29492
Bob White Dr	29412
Boeing Ave	29407
Bogard St	29403
Bolden Ln	29492
Bolton Rd	29414
Bolton St	29406
Bonanza Rd	29414
Bonham Dr	29412
Bonieta Harrold Dr	29414
Boom Vang Ln	29414
Boone Hall Dr	29407
Bossis Dr	29407
Boulder Ct	29406
Bounty Ln	29412
Bounty St	29492
Bounty Square Dr	29492
Bowens Island Rd	29412
Boyce Ct	29412
Boyces Wharf	29401
Boyer Ct	29403
Brabant St	29407
Bracky Ct	29403
Bradbury Ln	29492
Bradford Ave	29412
Bradham Rd	29412
Brady St	29492
Brandam Ln	29492
Brant Rd	29414
Brantley Dr	29412
Bravo St	29401
Braxton Ave	29407
Breakwater Ct	29412
Bredon Ct	29414
Breezeway Cir	29492
Brennon St	29407
Bresee St	29412
Brevard Rd	29414
Brewster Ct	29403
Brian Rd	29407
Brianna Ln	29412
Briarcliff Dr	29407
Briarfield Ave	29412
Briargate Ct	29414
Briarwood Dr	29414
Brigade St	29403
Brigadier Dr	29407
Brigadoon Pl	29414
Brigantine Dr	29412
Brighton Cir	29414
Brighton Rd	29407
Brisbane Dr	29407
Bristol Cir	29407
Broad St	
143A-143B	29401
1-104	29401
83-83	29402
105-399	29401
106-398	29401
Brockington Ave	29407
Brockman Cir & Dr	29412
Brody Ave	29407
Brogun Ln	29414
Brook Hollow Ct	29414
Brookbank Ave	29412
Brookfield St	29407
Brookforest Dr	29406
Broughton Rd	29407
Brown Dr	29412
Brown And Smith Ln	29412
Brown Pelican Dr	29492
Brown Pelican Ln	29412
Browning Rd	29407
Bruce St	29412
Bryce Ct	29492
Bryce Rd	29412
Bryjo Pl	29407
Buck Run Ct	29406
Buckeley Cir	29414
Buckingham Dr	29407
Bucknell Dr	29406
Buckner St	29412
Bucksley Ln	29492
Buffware Ct	29492
Bull St	29401
Bull Creek Ln	29414
Bulldog Dr	29406
Bulline St	29492
Bunches Pl	29407
Bunkhouse Dr	29414
Buoy Ln	29414
Bur Clare Rd	29412
Burgess St	29407
Burgess Dr	29412
Burlington Ave	29414
Burnett Dr	29412
Burnham Ct	29414
Burnham St	29492
Burningtree Rd	29412
Burnley Rd	29414
Burns Ln	29401
Burris Rd	29414
Butte St	29414
Butternut St	29414
Byron Rd	29407
C St	29403
Cabell St	29407
Cabot St	29412
Cabrill Dr	29414
Cainhoy Rd	29492
Cainhoy Landing Rd	29492
Cainhoy Village Rd	29492
Caisson Ct	29414
Calais Pt	29492
Calamari Ct	29406
Calhoun St	29401
Califf Rd	29406
Calvinmary Ln	29492
Cambria Cir	29414
Camelia Rd	29407
Camellia Walk Ct	29412
Camelot Dr	29407
Camerton St	29407
Camp Rd	29412
Campbell Dr	29407
Campion Hall Rd	29407
Canal St	
2-98	29401
2100-2399	29412
Canary Dr	29414
Candela Grove Dr	29414
Cannon St	29403
Canopy Cv	29412
Canterbury Rd	29407
Canty Ln	29407
Cape St	29492
Cape Romain Rd	29492
Capers Rd & St	29412
Caperton Way	29412
Capri Dr	29407
Captain Bill Ln	29492
Captiva Row	29407
Carla St	29412
Carlin Ave	29412
Carlisle Rd	29412
Carlson Ct	29403
Carmel Dr	29412
Carnegie Ave	29407
Carol St	29412
Carolina St	29403
Carolina Bay Dr	29414
Carondolet St	29403
Carpenter St	29412
Carrere Ct	29403
Carriage Ln	29407
Carrie St	29407
Carson Dr	29407
Carter Rd	29406
Carterett Ave	29407
Carters Grove Rd	29414
Cartright St	29492
Cartwright Dr	29414
Carverwood Ln	29407
Casa Bianca Dr	29407
Cashew St	29407
Casrope Ln	29412
Cassina Rd	29407
Castle Ave	29407
N Castle Ln	29414
E Castle Pl	29414
Castle Pinckney Dr	29412
Castlebank Pl	29414
Castlebrook Pl	29414
Castleford Ct	29414
Castlegate Ct	29414
Castlegreen Ct	29414
Castlehill Ct	29414
Castlelake Ct	29414
Castlereagh Rd	29414
Castleview Ct	29414
Castlewood Blvd	29414
Cat Tail Row	29407
Catalina Dr	29412
Catawba Rd	29414
Catbird Retreat	29412
Cathedral Ln	29414
Catterton Dr	29414
Cattle St	29492
Cattle Ranch St	29492
Cavalier Ave	29407
Cecil Cir	29412
Cecilia Dr	29407
Cecilia Cove Dr	29412
Cedar Ln	29414
Cedar St	29403
Cedar Hill Rd	29412
Cedar Petal Ln	29414
Cedar Point Dr	29412
Cedarhurst Ave	29407
Celanese Ln	29412
Center Park St	29492
Centervilla Ln	29412
Centerwood Dr	29412
Central Park Rd	29412
Century Pl	29412
Certificate Ct	29414
Cessna Ave	29407
Cestus Ln	29414
Chadwick Dr	29407
Chairmaker Ct	29414
Chalmers St	29401
Chalmers Way	29492
Champaign Ln	29412
Chancellory Ln	29414
Chandler St	29412
N & S Channel Ct	29412
Channing St	29407
Chapel St	29403
Charing Cross Rd	29407
Charles St	29403
Charlesfort Aly	29403
Charleston Center Dr	29401
Charleston Regional Pkwy	29492
Charlestowne Ct	29401
Charlestowne Dr	29407
Charlestowne Rd	29407
Charlie Hall Blvd	29414
Charlotte St	29403
Charlton Ln	29407
Charlyn Dr	29407
Chatuge Ct	29406
Chavis Rd	29412
Chelsea Ct	29407
Cheltenham Ln	29414
Chelwood Cir	29407
Cheraw Dr	29412
Cherokee Hall Ln	29414
Cherry St	29401
Chesapeake Dr	29406
Cheshire Dr	29412
Chestnut Oak Ln	29414
Cheves Dr	29412
Chickadee Ave	29407
Chickasaw Dr	29414
Chicorie Way	29412
Chipley Ter	29412
Chisolm St	29401
Chloe Ln	29406
Christian Rd	29407
Chuka Ct	29412
Church St	29401
Church Creek Dr	29414
Circle Oaks Dr	29492
Citadel Haven Dr	29414
Clam Shell Row	29412
Clara Ln	29406
Clark Ave	29412
Clark Sound Cir	29412
Clay Ln	29414
Clayton Dr & St	29414
Clearspring Dr	29412
Clearview Dr	29412
Clements Ferry Rd	29492
Clemson St	29403
Cleveland St	29403
Clifford St	29401
Clifton St	29406
Climbing Tree Ct	29414
Clipper St	29412
Cloudbreak Ct	29492
Clouter Ct	29492
Clouter Creek Dr	29492
Clover St	29414
Club View Ct	29412
Clyde St	29407
Coburg Rd	29407
Cochran Ct	29407
Cochran St	29492
Codners Ferry St	29492
Coffey Ct	29414
Coker Ave	29412
Cold Harbor Way	29414
Coleridge St	29407
Colleton Dr	29407
Collette St	29412
Collingwood Ave	29407
Collins Hill Ln	29492
Colonial St	29401
Colony Dr	29407
Columbus St	29403
Colyem Rd	29407
Combahee St	29412
Comesee Ln	29492
Coming St	
1-37	29401
39-89	29401
91-399	29403
Commencement Ln	29406
Commercial Row	29412
Compass Pt	29412
Conch Cor	29412
Concord St	29401
Condon Dr	29412
Cone St	29401
Confederate Cir	29407
Congress St	29403
Conifer Dr	29412
Conroy St	29403
Conservancy Ln	29414
Constant Dr	29412
Cook St	29406
Cooke St	29492
Cool Blow St	29403
Cooper St	29403
Cooper Judge Ln	29412
Coopers Basin Cir	29414
Coosaw Dr	29407
Copperas Hill Dr	29406
Cordes St	29401
Cordwainer Ct	29414
Corinne St	29403
Cork Rd	29407
Corlis Dr	29414
Corn Planters St	29492
Cornell St	29407
Cornerstone Ct	29412
Cornflower Ct	29414
Cornish Ave	29412
Cornsilk Dr	29414
Cornucopia Way	29414
Cornwallis Rd	29412
Corral Dr	29414
Cotswold Ct	29414
Cottage Rd	29412
Cotton House Rd	29412
Cotton Planters Ct	29412
Cottonwood St	29403
Couch Ln	29414
Council St	29401
Country Club Dr & Ln	29412
Country Lake Ct	29414
Court St	29403
Court House Sq	29401
Courtenay Dr	29403
Courtland Ave	29403
Coventry Cir	29407
Covey Ln	29412
Coxroost Ln	29492
Crab Walk	29412
Crabb St	29407
Cranbrook Dr	29414
Crape Myrtle Dr	29412
Craven Ave	29407
Creek Back St	29492
Creek House Ln	29492
Creek Landing St	29492
Creek Side Way	29492
Creekfront Ln	29492
Creeks Bluff Ct	29414
Creeks Edge	29412
Creekside Dr	29412
Creekstone Dr	29406
Crestwood Pl	29412
Cristalino Cir	29414
Cristaliono Cir	29414
Croghan Spur	29407
Croghan Landing Dr	29414
Cromwell Aly	29401
Cromwell Dr	29412
Cross St	29407
Crossbow Ct	29414
Crosscreek Dr	29412
Crossfield Ln	29492
Crossing St	29492
Crown Pointe St	29492
Crowned Kinglet Retreat	29412
Crull Dr	29407
Crystal Lake Dr	29412
Crystal Shore Ct	29412
Cuffy Ln	29412
Culpepper Cir	29407
Culver Ave	29407
Cumberland St	29401
Cunningham St	29492
Currier St	29492

Street	ZIP
Curtiss Ave	29407
Cutchin Ct	29414
Cuthbert St	29412
Cutter Dr	29412
Cynthia Ln	29407
Cypress St	29403
Cypress Branch Ct	29414
Cypress Walk Way	29492
Dade Dr	29407
Daggett St	29492
N & S Dallerton Cir	29414
Dalton St	
1-199	29492
1900-2099	29406
Daniel St	29407
Daniel Ellis Dr	29412
Daniel Island Dr	29492
Daniel Whaley Dr	29412
Daniels Landing Dr	29492
Danny St	29412
Dantzler Dr	29406
Darcy Ct	29414
Darien Dr	29414
Darlington Ave	29403
Darter Rd	29414
Dartmoor Cir	29407
Dartmouth Dr	29414
W Darwin St	29412
Davan Dr	29407
Davidson Ave	29407
Dawn Dr	29412
Dawn Hill Dr	29414
Dawson Rd	29412
Day Lily Ln	29412
Daytona Dr	29407
Deanna Ln	29492
Debbenshire Dr	29407
Deek Ln	29412
Deene St	29412
Deepwood Dr	29412
Deer Path Way	29414
Deerfield Dr	29414
Delahow St	29492
Delaney Dr	29412
Deleston St	29412
Dell Rd	29407
Delmar St	29407
Derby St	29407
Derbyshire Ct	29414
Dereef Ct	29403
Despestre St	29492
Desportes Ct	29403
Devereaux Ave	29403
Devils Elbow	29407
Devons St	29412
Devonshire Dr	29407
Dewey St	29403
Dexter Ln	29412
Diana St	29407
Dick Singleton Rd	29412
Dickens St	29407
Dill Ave	29412
Dills Bluff Ct & Rd	29412
Dillway St	29407
Dingle St	29403
Doane Way	29492
Dobbin Rd	29414
Dobester Ave	29412
Dogwood Rd	29414
Doldridge St	29492
Dollie Cir	29412
Dolmane Dr	29407
Dolphin Watch Dr	29414
Dominion Ct	29414
Donahue Dr	29407
Doncaster Dr	29414
Donner Ave	29406
Donnie Ln	29412
Doris Dr	29414
Dorothy Dr	29414
Dorset Ln	29407
Dotterers Run	29414
Double Fox Rd	29414
Double Oak Dr	29414
Doughty St	29403
Douglass Ave	29407
Dove Haven Ct	29414
Dove Run Dr	29412
Dowden Ct & St	29407
Downer Dr	29412
Downing St	29407
Downwood Pl	29412
Drake St	29403
Drawbridge Ct	29414
Drew Ln	29492
Drews Aly	29403
Drexell Dr	29407
Driftwood Dr	29412
Droos Way	29414
Druid Rd	29407
Drummond Ct	29414
Dry Creek Ln	29414
Dryden Ln	29407
Duck Hawk Retreat	29412
Ducs Ct	29403
Duffers Ct	29414
Duffy Rd	29407
Dulsey Rd	29407
Dunbar St	29407
Dunbarton Dr	29407
Duncan St	29403
Dunham St	29492
Dunlap St	29406
Dunnemann Ave	29403
Dunnes Ln	29407
Dunoon Dr	29414
Dunvegan Dr	29414
Dupont Rd	29407
Duren Ct	29414
Durham Pl	29407
Durkee St	29414
Duvall St	29412
E St	29403
Eades Ln	29414
Eagle Creek Dr	29414
Eagle Landing Blvd	29406
Eagle View Dr	29414
Eaglewood Trl	29412
Eallystockert Rd	29414
Earl Ct	29407
East St	29407
Eddy Willie Ln	29412
Edentree Pl	29412
Edenwood Ct	29407
E Edgewater Dr	29407
Edgewood Dr	29407
Edinburgh Rd	29407
Edisto Ave	29412
Edmonds Dr	29412
Edsent Ave	29407
Edward D Singleton	
Dr	29412
Egret Ln	29414
Egret Crest Ln	29414
Elfe St	29492
Elfes Field Ln	29492
N & S Elgin Ct	29414
Elias Ln	29412
Elissa Dr	29414
Eliza Ct	29407
Elizabeth Ln W	29407
Elizabeth St	29403
Elk St	29406
Ella Ln	29492
E Elliott St	29401
Ellis St	29407
Ellis Creek Lndg	29412
Ellis Oak Dr	29412
Ellison Run	29412
Elm Rd	29414
Elmwood St	29403
Elsey Dr	29407
Elsinore Ct	29406
Elton Ct	29407
Emanuel Ln	29412
Emden St	29406
Emerald Fern Dr	29406
Emerald Forest Pkwy	29414
Emerson St	29412
Emily Dr	29407
Emily Brown Rd	29412
Emory Ave	29407
Encampment Rd	29412
End St	29407
Endo Dr	29407
Engel St	29403
N & S England Ct &	
St	29414
Enoree Ln	29412
N & S Enston Ave	29403
Ephesian Ct	29492
Erskine Ave & Ct	29414
Essex Farms Dr	29414
E Estates Blvd	29414
Ethel Rd	29406
Etiwan Ave	29414
Etiwan Park St	29492
Eton Rd	29407
Euclid Dr	29492
Eugene Gibbs St	29412
Evans Rd	29412
Eve Cir	29414
Evening Shade Dr	29414
Evergreen St	29407
Exchange St	29401
Executive Cir	29407
Executive Hall Rd	29407
Exeter Ct	29407
F St	29403
Faber St	29401
Fain St	29406
Fair Spring Dr	29414
Fairbanks Oak Aly	29492
Fairchild St	29492
Fairfax Ct	29407
Fairfield Ave	29407
Fairway Dr	29412
Fairwind Dr	29406
Falkirk Dr	29407
Falmouth St	29407
Famhill Trl	29492
Family Cir	29407
Family Cemetery Rd	29492
Farmers Market Dr	29414
Farmfield Ave	29407
Farmington Rd	29412
Farnham Rd	29412
Farr St	29492
Fassitt Rd	29406
Father Grants Ct	29403
Fawn St	29406
Federal St	29401
Feldman Ct	29492
Felix St	29403
Fenwick Dr	29407
Ferguson Rd	29412
Fernwood Dr	29406
Ferris And Cyrus Rd	29412
Ferry Crossing Cir	29414
Ferry Point Dr	29492
Ferryman Ln	29492
Fiall St	29407
Fiddle Way	29412
Fiddler Crab Ln	29492
Fiddler Crab Way	29414
Fiddler Creek Dr	29412
Fiddler Island Ln	29412
Fidling Rd	29414
Fieldfare Way	29414
Fields Cir	29412
Fields Pl	29403
Fieldstone Cir	29414
Fife Ln	29414
Finley Rd	29492
First Mate Ct	29412
Firth St	29407
Fishburne St	29403
Fitzroy Dr	29414
Five Oaks Ct & Dr	29412
Flamingo Dr	29414
Flat Bloom Dr	29414
Fleming Rd	29412
Flint St	29412
Flood St	29403
Floral Bank Ln	29414
Florence Ln	29407
Flower Creek Way	29414
Floyd Dr	29414
Flyingfish Cir	29412
Fogarty Ln	29492
Folly Rd	
200-600	29412
579-579	29422
601-2299	29412
602-2298	29412
Folly Creek Way	29412
Folly Road Blvd	29407
Forbes Ave	29407
Ford Ct	29401
Forde Row	29412
Fordham Rd	29492
Forest Ln	29412
Forest Creek Ct	29414
Forest Dew Ct	29414
Forest Glen Dr	29414
Forest Lakes Blvd	29414
Forestwood Dr	29407
Formosa Dr	29407
Fort Johnson Rd	29412
Fort Lamar Rd	29412
Fort Lamar Road Ext	29412
Fort Pemberton Dr	29412
Fort Royal Ave & Ct	29407
Fort Sumter Dr	29412
Fortune Ln	29412
Foster St	29407
Fox Lake Ct	29414
Fox Ridge Ct	29414
Fox Trot Rd	29414
Foxcroft Rd	29412
Foxhall Rd	29414
Fragrant Ln	29414
Frampton Ave & St	29412
Francis St	29403
Francis Marion Dr	29412
Frank St	29407
Franklin St	29401
Franklin Gaillard Rd	29412
Franklin Retreat Ct	29492
Frayed Knot Aly	29414
Fred St	29412
Freedom Dr	29414
Freedom Peak Ln	29412
Freer St	29412
Frelisou Ave	29406
Fremont St	29412
Friendly Cir	29414
Fruitwood Ave	29414
Fuller St	29406
Fulton St	29401
Furman Dr	29414
Furman Farm Pl	29492
Furr St	29406
Fuseler Rd	29407
Gable St	29406
Gadsden Ct	29403
Gadsden St	29401
Gallberry St	29414
Galleon Rd	29412
Galloway Ln	29412
Gamecock Ave	29407
Gammon St	29414
Garco St	29406
Garden St	29407
Garden Corner Ct	29407
Garden Creek Rd	29414
Gardenia Rd	29407
Gardenwalk Ct	29414
Gardner Rd	29407
Garrison St	29412
Garth Dr	29414
Gate House Ct	29414
Gateway Walk	29401
Gatewood St	29492
Gator Trak	29414
Gaylord St	29406
Geddes Ave	29407
Gendron St	29401
George St	29401
Gettysburg Dr	29412
N & S Gevert Dr	29412
Gibbes St	
---	29401
1-99	29401
500-699	29492
1/2-1/2	29401
Gibbon St	29492
Gilbert St	29412
Gillon St	29401
Gilmore Ct	29412
Gilmore Rd	29407
Gin House Ct	29412
Ginned Cotton St	29492
Gippy Ln	29407
Gladden St	29412
Glazed Brick St	29492
Glebe St	29401
Glen Oaks Ct	29414
Glendale Dr	29414
Glengary Ct	29414
Glenkirk Dr	29414
Glenn Mcconnell Pkwy	29414
Glenwood Ave	29403
W Glow Dr	29407
Godber St	29412
N Godfrey Park Pl	29407
Golfview Dr	29412
Gomer Ln	29412
Goodlet Cir	29412
Gordon St	29403
Gracewood Dr	29414
Gracie Lee Ln	29412
Graham St	29406
Grand Concourse St	29412
Grand Council St	29492
Grand Park Blvd	29492
Grande Oaks Blvd	29414
Grant Hill Rd	29407
Gray Ct	29401
Great Castle Pl	29414
Great Hall Ct	29414
Grech St	29407
Green Park Ave	29414
Green Valley Ln	29412
Greenann Ct	29492
Greenbay Dr	29406
Greenbriar Ln	29412
Greenhill Rd	29412
Greenhill St	29401
Greenmore Dr	29407
Gregg Dr	29412
Griffindorff Blvd	29406
N & S Grimball Ave &	
Rd	29412
Grimball Farm Ln	29412
Grimball Road Ext	29412
Grimsley Dr	29412
Ground Pine Dr	29414
Grove Ln	29492
Grove St	29403
Grove Park Dr	29414
Guerard Rd	29407
Guerins Bridge Rd	29492
Guerry Ave	29414
Guess St	29406
Guignard St	29401
Gullane Dr	29414
Gunboat Ln	29492
Gunclub Rd	29414
Gunn Ave	29407
Gunpowder Dr	29412
Gunwale Ln	29414
H St	29403
Habakkuk Ln	29492
Haddon Hall Dr	29414
Hagerman St	29406
Hagerty Dr	29414
Hagood Ave	29403
Hainsworth Dr	29414
Halbert Dr	29406
Hale St	29412
Haley Ct	29406
Halfshell Ln	29414
Halfway Creek Rd	29492
Halo Ln	29407
Halsey Blvd & St	29401
Halstead St	29414
Hammock Ln	29492
Hampden Ct	29403
Hampshire Rd	29412
E Hampstead Sq	29403
N Hampton Dr	29407
S Hampton Dr	29407
Hampton Pl	29403
Hampton Bluff Rd	29414
Hanahan Rd	29406
Hanckel St	29412
Handel Ln	29407
N Hanover St	29403
Happy Hollow Cir	29414
Hara Ln	29414
Harbor Cove Ln	29412
Harbor Creek Pl	29412
Harbor Mist Ct	29492
Harbor Oaks Dr	29412
Harbor Place Dr	29412
Harbor Trace Cir	29412
Harbor View Cir, Ln &	
Rd	29412
Harbor Woods Cir	29412
Harborsun Dr	29412
Harbortowne Rd	29412
Harcourt Ln	29414
Harlech Way	29414
Harlem Ct	29403
Harleston Pl	29401
Harmony St	29407
Harper St	29406
Harrell Square Ctr	29407
Harrill Ct	29412
Harris St	29403
W Harrison Ave & Rd	29407
Harrods Ln	29412
Harrow St	29407
Hartland St	29414
Harvard Rd	29414
Hasell Ct	29492
Hasell St	29401
Hastie Rd	29492
Hasting Ct	29414
Hasting St	29407
Haswell St	29492
Hatchers Run Dr	29414
Hattie Cir	29492
Hawks Cay Ct	29414
Hayden Glenn Dr	29406
Hayne St	
1-99	29401
2100-2299	29406
Haywick Ct	29414
Hazel Rd	29407
Hazelhurst St	29492
Hazelwood Dr	29407
Hazzard Ln	29412
Hearthside Dr	29414
Heather Glen Dr	29414
Heathwood Dr	29407
Heatley Rd	29406
Hector Ln	29492
Heidels Way	29412
Heidie Ln	29492
S Held Cir	29412
Heldsberg Dr	29414
Hemmingway Dr	29414
Hempstead Ct	29414
Henderson Rd	29412
Henley Rd	29412
Henrietta St	29403
Henry Tecklenburg Dr	29414
Hepburn St	29412
Hepplewhite St	29414
Heriot St	29403
Heritage Park Rd	29407
Herman Ln	29492
Hermitage Ave	29412
Herndon Dr	29414
Heron Watch Ct	29414
Herraire Dr	29407
Hershal Cir	29492
Hester St	29403
Hester Park St	29492
Heyward Cv	29412
Hialeah Ct	29414
Hibiscus Ln	29414
Hickory St	29407
Hidden Bottom Ln	29492
Hidden Fields Way	29412
High St	29407
High Cotton Ct	29406
High Nest Ln	29412
Highland Ave	29412
Hightide Dr	29414
Highway 41	29492
Highwood Cir	29412
Hillary Ct	29403
Hillcreek Blvd	29412
Hillman St	29412
Hillridge Rd	29492
Hillsboro Dr	29407
N Hillside Dr	29407
Hilt St	29406
Hinson Ave	29412
Hitching Post Rd	29414
Hobart Ave	29407
Hobonny Ln	29407
Hockley Blvd	29414
Hoff Ave	29407
Holliday St	29414
Hollings Rd	29412
Holly Creek Rd	29412
Hollyberry Rd	29412
Hollywood Dr	29407
Holt St	29403
Holton Pl	29407
Homel Pl	29403
Honeyhill Rd	29412
Honeysuckle Ln	29412
Honeywell Ct	29414
Hood St	29412
Hooper St	29492
Hopewell Ln	29492
Horizon St	29403
Horlbeck Aly	29401
Horse Island Ln	29412
Hoss Rd	29414
Houghton Dr	29412
Howard Mary Dr	29412
Howle Ave	29412
Hoylake Ct	29414
Hudson Ln	29492
Huffman Ln	29406
Huger St	29403
Huguenot Ave	29407
Humphrey Ct	29403
Hunley Ave	29412
Hunt St	29414
Hunt Club Run	29414
Hunt Park Rd	29414
Hunter Creek Ct & Dr	29414
Hunters Forest Dr	29414
Hunters Rest Ct & Dr	29414
Huntington Dr	29407
Huntley Dr	29407
Hurtes Island Dr	29407
Hutson St	29403
Hutton Ct & Pl	29407
Hutty St	29492
I St	29403
Idbury Ln	29414
Idlewood Ln	29414
Immigration St	29403
Indaba Way	29414
Indian St	29403
Indian Corn St	29492
Indian Mound Trl	29407
Indigo Marsh Cir	29492
Indigo Planters Ln	29492
Indigo Point Dr	29407
Ingram Rd	29407
Inland Ave	29412
Innisbrook Ct	29414
Inspection St	29401
Inverary Ct	29414
Inverness Dr	29412
Ipswich Ct	29403
Iron St	29406
Iron Bottom Ln	29492
Isabell Ln	29492
Isabella St	29403
Island Dr	29407
Island Club Dr	29492
Island Park Dr	29492

Island View Ct 29492
Islington Ct 29403
Ismael Rd 29412
Ithecaw Ct 29492
Ithecaw Creek St 29492
Ivy Cir 29414
Ivy Hall Rd 29407
Ivy Isle Dr 29412
Izard Ct 29414
Jack Primus Rd 29492
Jackrig Aly 29403
Jackson St 29403
Jackwood Ct 29407
Jacobs Aly 29401
Jalap Ln 29492
Jamaica Dr 29407
James Dr 29412
James Prioleau Rd 29412
Jamesbury Rd 29492
Jamestown Rd 29407
Jametta Ln 29492
Jamsie Cove Dr 29412
Jane Cir 29412
Jaques Ct 29492
Jason St 29406
Jasper St 29403
Jawol Dr 29414
Jaywood Cir 29407
Jean St 29407
Jeb Stuart Rd 29412
Jedediah Ct 29412
Jeff Gaillard Ln 29412
Jeffery Rd 29412
Jeffords St 29412
Jenkins Rd 29407
Jenny Lind St 29406
Jenys St 29492
Jerdone St 29412
Jerome Ct 29414
Jerry Dr 29407
Jervey Ave 29407
Jervey Point Rd 29492
Jessamine Rd 29407
Jessen Ln 29492
Jessica Ct 29406
Jet Park Rd 29406
Jim Isle Dr 29412
Joan St 29407
Jobee Dr 29414
Jocassee Dr 29406
Joe Richardson Rd 29412
Joe Rivers Rd 29412
Joe Washington Rd 29492
Joes Family Ln 29492
Joey Cir 29412
John St 29403
Johnson Rd 29407
Johnson St 29403
Johnson Ridge Pl 29492
Jonash Rd 29412
Jordan Ct 29492
Jordan St 29412
Joseph St 29412
Joshua Dr 29407
Josie Ln 29492
Joy Ave 29407
Joyner Ln 29492
Judith St 29403
Julia St 29412
Julian Clark Rd 29412
Juniper St 29407
Justin Ave 29407
Keats Rd 29407
Keble Rd 29407
Kell Pl 29412
Kelsey Blvd 29492
Kemper Ave 29412
Kempton Ave 29412
Kendall Dr 29414
Kenilworth Ave 29403
Kennedy Ct & St 29403
Kenneth Dr 29406
Kensington Dr 29407
Kentwood Cir 29412
N & S Kenwood Dr 29406
Kenyon St 29407
Kerry St 29406
Key Ct 29412
Kiki Way 29407
Killians St 29403
Kilmarnok Way 29414
Kimbell Rd 29406
Kimono Way 29492
Kincom Dr 29412
Kindred Ln 29492
King St
1-381 29401
382-1399 29403
1401-1449 29403
King Charles Ct 29414
King Edward Dr 29414
King George St 29492
King Richard Dr 29407
Kings Mill Ct 29414
Kingswood Dr 29412
Kipling Rd 29407
Kira Way 29492
Kirkland Ln 29401
Kirkless Abbey Dr 29407
Kissemee Dr 29406
Kith Ct 29492
Kittridge Dr 29412
Klister Ln 29492
Knightsmore Pl 29414
Knotty Pine Rd 29412
Koger Dr 29412
Kracke St 29403
Kruger Ave 29407
Kushiwah Creek Ct & Dr 29412
Kyle Pl 29403
Lacross Rd 29406
N & S Ladd Ct 29492
Ladson St 29401
Lady Ashley St 29412
Lady Cooper St 29412
Lady Jordan Ln 29412
Lafar St 29492
Lake Ave 29414
Lake Frances Dr 29412
Lake Marion Dr 29406
Lake Moultrie Dr 29406
Lake Myrtle Dr 29414
Lakefront Dr 29412
Lakeshore Dr 29412
Lamar St 29407
Lamb St 29414
Lamboll St 29401
Lamont Rd 29407
Lampton Rd 29407
Lancashire St 29412
N & S Lander Ln 29414
Landgrave Ave 29414
Landlubber Ln 29414
Lands End Dr 29407
Landsdowne Dr 29412
Lango Ave 29407
Lani Ct 29414
Lansfaire Dr 29414
Lantana Dr 29407
Lantern St 29414
Lapps Ct 29403
Larissa Dr 29414
Larkwood Rd 29412
Larnes St 29403
Laroche St 29412
Larry St 29406
Lasalle St 29407
Latham Cir 29407
Laura Creek Rd 29412
Laurel Ave 29403
Laurel Leaf Ln 29412
Laurelwood Dr 29414
Laurens St 29401
Lavington Rd 29407
Lawton Pl 29412
Lawton Harbor Dr 29412
Lazarette Ln 29414
Lazy River Dr 29414
Lazylake Ct 29412
Leafwood Rd 29412
League St 29412
N & S Leavitt Ct 29492
Lebanon Ln 29412
Lebby St 29412
Lee St 29403
Leeward Ave 29412
Legare St 29401
Legrand Blvd 29492
Leichester Rd 29407
Leiderman St 29406
Leila Ln 29414
Leinbach Dr 29407
Leith Ln 29414
Lemon Ln 29492
Lemon Tree Ln 29412
S & W Lenevar Dr 29407
Lenox St 29403
Lenwood Blvd 29401
Leo Ln 29403
Levin Ct 29414
Liberty St 29401
Lighthouse Blvd 29412
Limbaker St 29412
Limehouse St 29401
Limestone Blvd 29414
Linc Ln 29492
Lindberg St 29412
Linden Cir 29407
Lindendale Ave 29407
Lindrick Ct 29414
Line St 29403
Linguard St 29401
Lining Ct & Ln 29407
Litchfield Dr 29406
Little Barley Ln 29492
Little David Ct 29412
Little John Dr 29407
Little Pumpkin Ln 29492
Little Rock Blvd 29412
Little Sydneys Way 29406
Live Oak Ave 29407
Liverpool Dr 29414
Loch Carrun Ter 29414
Lochaven Dr 29414
Lochmore Ter 29414
Lockheed St 29407
Locksley Dr 29407
Lockwood Blvd 29403
Lockwood Dr 29401
Locust St 29407
Lodge Aly 29401
Logan St 29401
Lolandra Ave 29407
London Ct & Dr 29412
Long Bow Ct 29414
Longbranch Dr 29414
Longfellow Rd 29407
Longitude Ln 29401
Longkeep Ln 29492
Longstreet Dr 29414
Longview Ct 29414
Longwood Ln 29412
Lord Ashley Dr 29407
Lord Calvert Dr 29407
Lorne Ct 29414
Lotus Ln 29412
Louise P Gardner St 29412
Louisville St 29492
Lowland Ln 29412
Lowndes St 29401
Lowndes Pointe Dr 29403
Lucia St 29492
Lucky Rd 29412
Ludwell St 29407
Luke St 29414
Lula St 29407
Lumber St 29412
Luna Ct 29414
Lydia Dr 29412
Lynne Ave 29412
Lynton St 29412
Lynwood Dr 29414
Lytham Ct 29414
Lyttleton St 29407
Macbeth Creek Dr 29414
Maclaura Hall Ave 29414
Macqueen Ave 29407
Madagascar Ct 29407
Madelyn St 29406
W Madison Ave 29412
Magazine St 29401
Magnolia Ave 29403
Magnolia Rd 29407
Magnolia Ferry Rd 29414
Magnolia Plantation Rd 29414
Magwood Dr 29414
Mahi Mahi Way 29406
Mahone Ct 29492
Maiden Ln 29401
Main St 29407
Maintenance Way 29406
Majestic Oak Dr 29412
Mallory Dr 29414
Mamie St 29407
Manassas Dr 29414
Manchester Rd 29407
Manderley Ct 29414
Manigault Pl 29407
Manor Blvd 29407
Manor House Dr 29412
Manorwood Ln 29414
Mansfield St 29407
Maple St 29403
Maple Leaf Ct 29414
Maple Oak Ln 29414
Maplecrest Dr 29412
Mapleton Ave 29412
Maranda Holmes St 29403
Marbel Ln 29403
Marble Arch Ct 29407
Marginal Rd 29414
Marias Ct 29414
Marietta St 29406
Marina Dr 29492
Mariner Dr 29412
Mariners Fry 29414
Marion St 29403
Maritime Ln 29492
Market St 29401
Markfield Dr 29407
Markham Rd 29414
Marlin Ln 29412
Marlow Dr 29403
Marquise Ln 29492
Marsh St 29401
Marsh Creek Dr 29414
Marsh Flower Ln 29414
Marsh Grass Way 29492
Marsh Harbor Ln 29492
Marsh Lake Ct 29414
Marsh Oaks Dr 29407
Marsh Point Dr 29412
Marshfaire Pl 29414
Marshland Dr 29414
Marshview Dr 29412
Marson St 29406
Martello Dr 29412
Martin Luther King Blvd 29407
Martins Path 29414
Martins Creek Ln 29492
Marvin Ave 29407
Mary St 29403
Mary Ader Ave 29414
Mary Ellen Dr 29403
Mary Murray Dr 29403
Mary River Ln 29412
Mary Roper Ln 29412
E & W Marymont Ln 29414
Maverick St 29403
Mawood Ave 29406
Max Baker Blvd 29406
Maxcy St 29412
Maybank Hwy 29412
Maybelles Ln 29414
Mayfield Ct 29406
N & S Mayflower Dr 29412
Maygrass Ct 29492
Maylen Rd 29407
Maywick Ct 29414
Mazyck Rd
1100-1199 29407
7200-7399 29406
Mcclain St 29407
Mccutchen St 29412
Mcdougall Dr 29414
Mcelveen St 29412
Mcenery Aly 29412
Mcgregor St 29406
Mchenry Ave 29412
Mcintyre Rd 29412
Mckee Ct 29414
Mcleod Ave 29412
Mcleod Rd 29414
Mcneil Washington Rd 29412
Meadow Breeze Ln 29414
Meadow Grove Way 29412
Meadow Trace Ct 29414
Meadowlawn Dr 29407
Meander Row 29412
Means St 29412
Medical Plaza Dr 29406
Medway Rd 29412
Meeting St
753A-753B 29403
Megans Bay Ln 29492
Mellichamp Dr 29412
Mellish Ct 29492
Mellowood Pl 29412
Melnick Dr 29406
Melody Ln 29414
Melrose Dr 29414
Melville Rd 29406
Melvin Ct 29406
Memes Way 29492
Memminger Ave 29407
Memorial Dr 29414
Memory Ln 29407
Menola Ave 29414
Menotti St 29401
Mentella Cove Dr 29414
Mepkin Rd 29407
Merchant St 29492
Meritha Ln 29492
Merton Rd 29407
Meyers Rd 29407
Michel Pl 29401
Middle Atlantic Wharf 29401
Middleburry Ln 29414
Middleton Pl 29403
Middleton Oaks Rd 29414
Middleton Place Exit Rd 29414
Middlewood Dr 29412
Midland Dr 29406
Midland Park Rd 29406
Midvale Ave 29412
Mike Heyward Ln 29414
Mikell Dr 29412
Miles Dr 29407
Military Way 29414
Mill Point Rd 29412
Millcreek Dr 29407
Milner Ct 29492
Mim Ave 29407
Minnie St 29407
Minott St 29412
Mission Ave 29414
Misty Lake Dr 29412
Mitchell Wharf St 29492
Mizzen Mast Dr 29407
Mockingbird Ln 29414
Mohawk Ave 29412
Mona Ave 29414
Monarch Ct 29414
Monica Ln 29492
Montagu Ct & St 29401
Montclair St 29407
Montford Ave 29403
Montgomery Rd 29412
Montgrove Ct 29414
Monticello Dr 29412
Montreat Ct 29414
Moonlight Dr 29414
Moore Dr 29407
Mooring Dr 29412
Morgan Campbell Ct 29407
Morning Dove Ln 29414
Morris St 29403
Morrison Dr 29403
Morton Ave 29407
Moses Ct 29403
Mosquito Beach Rd 29412
N & S Moss Oak Ln 29414
Motley Ln 29401
Motorola Ln 29492
Moultrie Ct & St 29403
Mount Pleasant St 29403
Mount Vernon Dr 29412
Mowler Ct 29414
Mueller Dr 29407
Muirfield Pkwy 29414
Mulberry St 29407
Mulmar St 29407
Mulroy Ct 29414
Murphy Ct 29403
N Murray Ave 29406
Murray Blvd 29401
Murray Hill Dr 29407
Mutual Dr 29414
Myrtis Ln 29406
Nabors Dr 29412
Nad Rd 29406
Nashmor Rd 29407
N Nassau St 29403
Nathaniel Dr 29412
Nautical Chart Dr 29414
Needlegrass Ln 29412
Nelliefield Trl 29492
Nelliefield Creek Dr 29492
Nemours Dr 29407
Netherton Ct 29492
Nevonna Dr 29406
New St 29401
New Castle St 29407
New Town Ln 29407
Newbury St 29412
Newport Ct 29492
Nicholson St 29407
S Nicole Pl 29414
Norfolk Dr 29412
Norman St 29403
Norris Ave 29407
Northbridge Dr 29407
Northbrook Blvd 29406
Northfield Ct 29414
Northlake Ct 29414
Northpark Blvd 29406
Northside Dr 29407
Norton St 29414
Norview Cir & Dr 29407
Note Ln 29414
Notlee Pl 29407
Nottingham Dr 29407
Nuffield Rd 29407
Nunan St 29403
Nursery Rd 29414
Nye St 29407
Oak St 29407
W Oak Forest Dr 29407
Oak Island Dr 29412
Oak Overhang St 29492
Oak Point Rd 29412
Oak Turn Rd 29412
Oakcrest Dr 29412
Oakdale Pl 29407
Oakfield Dr 29412
Oakland Rd 29414
Oakmont Ln 29412
Oakview Ln 29492
Oates Ln 29412
Oatly Cir 29414
Ocean Neighbors Blvd 29412
Oceanview Ct 29492
Oceanview Rd 29412
W Oceanview Rd 29412
Oeland St 29403
Ogden Rd 29407
Ogier St 29403
Oglethorpe Dr 29414
Old Battery Cir 29412
Old Brick Ln 29492
Old Bridgeview Ln 29403
Old English Dr 29407
Old Folly Beach Rd 29412
Old Fort Ave 29414
Old Hazelwood Rd 29406
Old Military Rd 29412
Old Orchard Rd 29412
Old Oscar Walker Rd 29412
Old Parsonage Rd 29414
Old Plantation Rd 29412
Old Point Rd 29412
Old Sol Legare Rd 29412
Old Summer House Rd 29412
Old Towne Rd 29407
Ole Oak Dr 29492
Oleander Ct 29414
Oliver Ct 29403
Olivia Ln 29492
Olney Rd 29414
One Love St 29412
Oolong Tea Ct 29492
Opal Ave 29407
Ophir Dr 29407
Orange St 29401
Orange Branch Rd 29407
Orange Grove Rd 29407
Orange Grove Shores Dr 29407
Ordinance Pt 29412
Orleans Rd 29407
Orrs Ct 29403
Orvin St 29406
Oswego St 29403
Otis Ave 29414
Otranto Blvd & Rd 29406
Overboard Ln 29414
Overdell Dr 29407
Overrun St 29414
Owen St 29414
Oxbow Dr 29412
Oxford Pl 29414
Oxford St 29407
Oxon Hill Ct 29406
Oyster Cor 29412
Oyster Point Row 29412
Packard Ct 29414
Paddington Cir 29407
Paddlecreek Ave 29412
Paddy Pl 29407
Pageland Rd 29412
Pagett St 29492
Paige Ct 29403
Paladin Ln 29406
Palermo Pl 29406
Pally Man Ln 29412
Palm St 29492
Palm Cove Dr 29492
Palmer Dr 29414
Palmer Creek Bnd 29412
Palmetto Is 29412
Palmetto Rd 29407
Palmetto Park Rd 29407
Palomino Ct 29407
Palustrine Ct 29414
Par Ct 29414
Paran Oaks Dr 29414
Parana St 29406
Paris Williams Rd 29412
Parish Rd 29407
S Park Cir 29407
N Park Ext 29406
N Park Ln 29406
Park Crossing Dr 29492
Parkdale Dr 29414
Parkdale Ln 29492
Parkland Preserve Ln 29412
Parklawn Dr 29414
Parkshore Dr 29407
Parkstone Dr 29414
Parkway Dr 29412
Parkwood Ave 29403
Parkwood Estates Dr 29407
Parnell Ln 29407
Parrot Creek Way 29412
Parrot Point Dr 29412
Parrothead St 29403
Parsonage Ln & Rd 29414

Parsons Cor 29414
Parthol Rd 29492
Patterson Ave 29412
Paul Ave 29406
Paul Revere Ct & Dr 29412
Paula Dr 29407
Pauline Ave 29412
Paw Paw Pl & St 29412
Pawtucket St 29414
Payne Ct 29403
Peach Blossom Ln 29492
Peachtree St 29403
Pearlott St 29407
Pearlware Ct 29492
Peas Hill Rd 29412
Peas Island Rd 29412
Pebble Rd 29407
Pebble Creek Ct 29414
Peecksen Ct 29403
Peeks Pike 29407
Peele Pl 29401
Pemberton View Dr 29412
Pembrooke Dr 29407
Pendleton St 29403
Peninsula Dr 29412
Peninsula Cove Dr 29492
Penn Ave 29407
Pentland Dr 29412
Penwood Pl 29412
Pepperwood Ct 29414
Pequod Aly 29414
Percy St 29403
Peregrine Dr 29412
Perrine St 29414
Perrineau Ln 29492
Perry St 29403
Petersfield Place Dr 29412
Philadelphia Aly 29401
Physicians Dr 29414
Picard Way 29412
Piccadilly Cir & Dr 29412
Pickering Ln 29414
Pickett St 29412
Pickop Miles Ct 29406
Pickwick St 29407
Piedmont Ave
  1-99 29403
  4800-5199 29406
Pier View St 29492
Pierce St 29492
Pierpont Ave 29414
Pinckney St 29401
Pinckney Park Dr 29407
Pine St 29492
Pine Pitch St 29492
Pine Terrace Ct 29414
N & S Pinebark Ln 29407
Pinecrest Rd 29407
Pinefield Dr 29492
Pinehurst Ave 29414
Pineneedle Way 29492
Pineview Rd 29407
Pinnacle Ln 29412
Pintail Dr 29414
Piper Dr 29407
Pitt St
  1-60 29401
  61-99 29403
Pittsford Cir 29412
Pixley St 29414
Plainfield Dr 29407
Plainview Rd 29414
Plantation Court Dr 29406
Planters Dr 29414
Planters Trace Dr 29412
Playground Rd 29407
Pleasant Cove Ct 29412
Pleasant Garden Dr 29414
Pleasant Grove Ln 29407
Pleasant Hill Dr 29414
Plumridge Ct 29414
Plymouth Ave 29412
Poets Cor 29412
Poinsett St 29403
Poinsetta Rd 29407
Point Of Light Ln 29412

Pointe Coupee Ln 29414
Polony Pl 29414
Pompie Cir 29492
Ponce De Leon Ave & Ct 29407
Ponderosa Dr 29414
Pony Ln 29407
Pooshee Dr 29407
W Poplar St 29403
Poplar Ridge Rd 29406
Port Cir 29412
Portabella Ln 29412
Porters Ct 29403
Portside Way 29407
Portsmouth Cir 29407
Postal Crescent Ct 29492
Poston Rd 29407
Poulnot Ln 29401
Powell Rd 29406
Pratt St 29407
Preakness Stakes 29414
Prentiss St 29412
Prescott St 29412
President Pl & St 29403
Preston Rd 29412
Prevatt Ct 29414
Prices Aly 29401
Priestly St 29412
Prince Alan Ct 29414
Prince John Dr 29407
Princess St 29401
Prioleau St 29401
Pristine View Rd 29414
Privateer Ln 29492
Prospect Dr 29406
Providence St 29492
Proximity Dr 29414
Pryor Ct 29407
Psalms Ln 29492
Ptarmigan St 29412
Pullman St 29406
Purcell Ln 29492
Purity Dr 29406
Putnam Dr 29412
Putney Ct 29412
Quail Dr 29412
Quail Hollow Ct 29414
Queen St 29401
Queen Julieanne Ct 29414
Queenscastle Ct 29414
Quick Rabbit Loop 29414
Rab Rd 29406
Race St 29403
Radcliffe Pl & St 29403
Radcliffe Place Dr 29414
Radio Ln 29492
Rafeal Ln 29412
Rafers Aly 29401
Ragos Ln 29412
Rahn Rd 29407
Railroad Ave 29406
Rainbow Rd 29412
Rainsong Dr 29412
Ralston Creek St 29492
Rampart Pt 29412
Ramsay St 29412
Raoul Wallenberg Blvd 29407
Rapture Ln 29492
Ravenel Dr 29407
Ravenswood Dr 29412
Raymond Ave 29406
Raymond Way 29407
Razorback Ln 29414
Realm St 29406
Rebellion Rd 29407
Rebellion Farms Pl 29492
Red Gate Rd 29412
Red Oak Dr 29406
Red Sky Dr 29414
Reddick St 29412
Redford Rd 29492
Redstone Way 29492
Reflectance Dr 29492
Refuge Run 29412
Regatta Rd 29412
Regency Elm Dr 29406

Regina St 29412
Regis Ct 29407
Reid St 29403
E, N & W Relyea Ave 29412
Rembert Rd 29412
Remount Rd 29406
Renwood Dr 29412
Republic Dr 29492
Restoration Ct 29414
Revere Rd 29412
Reverend Joseph Heyward Rd 29414
Rhett Butler Dr 29414
Rhoden Island Dr 29492
Rhodes St 29414
Rhonda Jerome Ct 29406
Rice Ct & Dr 29407
Rice Drive Ext 29407
Rice Hollow Ct 29407
Rice Mill Pl 29492
Rice Pond Rd 29414
Rich Goss Ln 29412
Richard Mccloud Ln 29412
Richardson Rd 29412
Richmond St 29407
Ridgewood Ave 29414
Rigging Ct 29414
Riker St 29403
Riley Rd 29412
Rio St 29406
Ripley Dr 29412
Ripley Pointe Dr 29407
Ripplemoor Ln 29414
Riser Dr 29412
Risher St 29407
Ritter Dr 29412
River Bay Ln 29492
River Bend Dr 29412
River Breeze Dr 29407
River Front Dr 29407
River Green Pl 29492
River Grove Ave 29492
River Haven Cir 29412
River Landing Dr 29492
River Park Ct & Way 29414
River Reach Way 29407
Riverbend Trl 29492
Riverboat Pass 29492
Rivercrest Dr 29412
Riverdale Dr 29407
Riverland Dr 29412
Riverland Woods Pl 29412
Rivermont Pl 29414
Rivers Edge Way 29492
Rivers Point Row 29412
Rivers Reach Dr 29492
Rivershore Rd 29492
Riverside Dr 29403
Roanoke Dr 29406
Robert E Lee Blvd 29412
Roberts Rd 29412
Robin Rooke Way 29412
W Robinhood Dr 29407
Rochelle Ave 29407
Rockville Ct 29414
Rodgers Aly 29403
N Romney St 29403
Ronald Ln 29412
Ronda Dr 29406
Rondo St 29414
Rookery Ln 29414
Ropemakers Ln 29401
Roper Rd 29412
Rose Ln 29403
Rose Marie Dr 29414
Rose Park Dr 29412
Rosebush Ln 29412
Rosedale Dr 29407
Rosehaven St 29414
Rosemont St 29403
Roslyn Dr 29414
Rotherwood Dr 29407
Round Tree Ln 29414
Roundtable Ct 29414
Roustabout Way 29414
Royal Assembly Dr 29492

Royal Castle Ln 29414
Royal Empress Ct 29414
Royal Palm Blvd 29407
Rue Dr 29414
Rugby Ln 29407
Rutherford Way 29414
Rutledge Ave
  2-129 29401
  130-150 29403
  152-1399 29403
Rutledge Blvd 29401
Ryton Dr 29414
Sabrina Cir 29412
Sage Way 29414
Sage Bird Vw 29412
Sailmaker St 29492
Saint Andrews Blvd 29407
Saint Augustine Dr 29407
Saint Charles Ct 29407
Saint Clair Dr 29407
Saint David Ln 29414
Saint Dennis Dr 29407
Saint Helenas Pt 29407
Saint Hubert Way 29414
Saint Ives Rd 29406
Saint James Dr 29412
Saint Johns Church Rd 29492
Saint Julian Dr 29407
Saint Lukes Dr 29412
Saint Margaret St 29403
Saint Michaels Aly 29401
Saint Peters Ln 29414
Saint Philip St 29403
Saint Teresa Dr 29407
Saint Thomas Island Dr 29492
Saintsbury Cove Dr 29414
Sal Ln 29406
Salamander Creek Ln 29406
Salisbury St 29407
Sallie St 29412
Sallys Aly 29407
Salt Marsh Cv 29412
Sam Rittenberg Blvd 29407
Samson Rd 29412
Samuel Rd 29412
Samuel Grant Pl 29407
San Juan Ave 29407
San Miguel Rd 29407
San Souci St 29403
Sand Art Rd 29414
Sand Harbor Ln 29412
W Sandcroft Dr 29407
Sanders Rd 29414
Sanders Farm Ln 29492
Sandlewood Ct 29414
Sandshell Dr 29492
Sandstone Pl 29492
Sandyver Ct 29407
Sanford Dr 29414
Sanford Rd 29407
Santee St 29412
Sarah St 29407
Sarah Lincoln Rd 29492
Sasanqua Ln 29407
Savage Rd
  600-995 29414
  996-1598 29407
  1600-2099 29407
Savage St 29401
Savannah Hwy
  802A-802B 29407
  200-2099 29407
  2100-3399 29414
Saville Row 29414
Sawgrass Rd 29412
Saxony Dr 29412
Sayle Rd 29407
Schaffer St 29412
Scholar Ln 29406
Schooner Rd 29412
Schooner St 29492
Sconesill Ln 29414
Scott St 29492
Scott Hill Rd 29412

Scuba Dr 29414
Scudder Rd 29412
Sea Aire Dr 29412
Sea Bass Cv 29412
Sea Cotton Cir 29412
Sea Cove Ct 29412
Sea Eagle Watch 29412
Sea Robin Ct 29412
Sea Water Dr 29412
Seabago Dr 29414
Seabird Ct 29414
Seabrook Ave 29412
Seacroft Rd 29412
Seafarer Way 29412
Seanced Dr 29414
Seaside Ln 29412
Seaside Plantation Dr 29412
Seaward Dr 29412
Seawind Dr 29407
Secessionville Rd 29412
Sedge Ct 29412
Seignious Dr 29407
Selah St 29406
Sellkirk Dr 29414
Seloris Ct 29407
Semaht St 29412
Senate St 29403
Sequoia St 29407
Serenity Way 29412
Seroy St 29412
Seton Pl 29407
Settlers St 29492
Seven Farms Dr 29492
Sexton Dr 29412
Shadow Ln 29406
Shadow Arbor Cir 29414
Shadow Ferry Dr 29414
Shadow Mist Ln 29492
Shadow Oak Dr 29406
Shadow Pointe Dr 29414
Shadowmoss Pkwy 29414
Shady Ln 29407
Shaftsbury Ln 29401
Shamrock Ln 29412
Shand St 29403
Shandon St 29412
Sharon Ave 29407
Shawn Dr 29414
Sheffield St 29407
Shelby Ray Ct 29414
Sheldon Rd 29407
Shell Sand Cir 29412
Shelley Rd 29407
Shelter Cv 29414
Shem Butler Ct 29414
Sheppard St 29403
Sheridan Rd 29407
N Sherwood Dr 29407
Shiloh Ln 29414
Shipton Ct 29414
Shipwright St 29492
Shiraz Ln 29414
N Shore Dr 29412
S Shore Dr 29407
E Shore Ln
  200-399 29407
  400-499 29414
Shoreham Rd 29412
Shorepark Ct 29407
Short Ct 29407
Short St
  1-99 29401
  1400-1499 29412
Shortwood St 29412
Shrewsbury Rd 29407
Shrimp St 29412
Shuttle Ct 29407
Sienna Pl 29414
Signal Point Rd 29412
Sigsbee Rd 29412
Silver Leaf Cir 29412
Simmons Forge St 29492
Simons St 29403
Simonton Mews 29403
Simpkins St 29412
Sinclair Cir 29406

Sir Scott Pl 29414
Sires St 29403
Siri Ct 29407
Skeeboe Ct 29492
Skiff St 29412
Skinner Ave 29407
Skyeman Dr 29414
Skylark Dr 29407
Sloan Dr 29412
Sloop St 29412
Smalls Aly 29403
Smith Pl 29401
Smith St
  51A-51C 29401
  1-99 29401
  100-199 29403
  98 1/2-98 1/2 29401
Smythe St 29492
Soaring Ln 29412
Society St 29401
Sol Legare Rd 29412
Soling Ct 29414
Solomon Ct 29414
Sols Ln 29492
Somerset Cir 29407
Sothel Ave 29407
South St 29403
Southgate Dr 29407
Southport Dr 29407
Spanish Moss Ct 29412
Sparrow St 29412
Spearfish Cir 29412
Spell St 29403
Spencer St 29407
Spinnaker Ln 29407
Spivey Ct 29406
Spoleto Ln E 29406
Sportsman Island Dr 29492
Sprague St 29412
Spring St 29403
Spring Garden St 29414
Spring Tide Dr 29414
Springbok Ln 29492
Springmire Ct 29414
Springwater Ct 29412
Sprocket Ln 29406
Stadium Dr 29406
Stafford Rd 29406
Staffordshire Dr 29407
Stalin Smalls Ln 29412
Stall Rd 29406
Stallion Ct 29407
Standish St 29412
Stanyarne Dr 29414
Star Dr 29406
Starboard Rd 29412
Starwood Ct 29412
State St 29401
Stebbins Ct & St 29412
Steele Magnolia Ave 29414
Stefan Dr 29412
N Sterling Dr 29412
Stevenson Dr 29414
N Stiles Dr 29412
Stiles Bee Ave 29412
Still Shadow Dr 29414
Stillhouse Ln 29492
Stillwater Dr & Pl 29412
Stingray Blvd 29406
Stinson Dr 29407
Stockbridge Dr 29414
Stocker Dr 29407
Stolls Aly 29401
Stone Crab Ct 29412
Stone Creek Dr 29414
Stone Post Rd 29412
Stoneboro Ct 29412
Stonebridge Way 29412
Stonefield Ave 29412
Stoneham Aly 29414
Stonehedge Rd 29407
Stonewood Dr 29412
Stoney St 29407
Stono Dr 29412
Stono Edge Dr 29412
Stono River Dr 29412

Storen St 29406
Straight St 29407
Stratford Rd 29407
Strawberry Ln 29403
Stroble Ln 29403
Stuart St 29403
Studdingsail Ln 29412
Studebaker Ct 29414
Stutz Ct 29414
Sugar Magnolia Way 29414
Sugarbush Way 29414
Sulgrave Rd 29414
Sullivan St 29407
Sumar St 29407
Summer Leaves Ct 29414
Summer Rain Ct 29414
Summerfield Ct 29414
Summerhaven Pl 29492
Sumter St 29403
Sun Beam Way 29414
Sunburst Ct 29406
Sunfish Cir 29412
Sunnyside Ave 29403
Sunnyvale Ave 29414
Sunset Dr 29407
Sunstone St 29412
Surfside Ct 29412
Surr St 29492
Susan Dr 29407
Susan Brown Ln 29412
Sussex Rd 29407
Sutherland Ave & Ct 29403
Sutton St 29412
Swallow Dr 29414
Swamp Angel Ct 29412
Swamp Fox Ln 29412
Swan Ave 29414
Swan Dr 29492
Swanson Ave 29412
Sweetbay Rd 29412
Sweetgrass Creek Rd 29412
Sweetgum Rd 29414
Swift Ave 29407
Swinton St 29412
Swordfish Cir 29412
Sycamore Ave
  1-79 29407
  78-78 29417
  80-1098 29407
  81-1099 29407
Sycamore Shade St 29414
Sylvan Shores Dr 29414
Symmes Dr 29407
Taberwood Cir 29407
Tacony Rd 29414
Tahoe St 29407
Taliaferro Ave 29412
Talison Ave 29492
Tall Fern Ct 29406
Tall Oak Ave 29407
Tall Sail Dr 29414
Tallwood Rd 29412
Talon Ct 29403
Tamarack St 29407
Tanglewood Ave 29407
Tara Rd 29407
Targave Rd 29412
Tarleton Dr 29407
Tartan Ct 29414
Tatum St 29412
Taylorcraft Dr 29407
Taym Dr 29492
Tayside Ct 29414
Tea Farm Way 29492
Teaberry Path 29414
Teague St 29407
Teakwood Rd 29414
Teal Ave 29412
Teal Marsh Rd 29412
Technical Pkwy 29406
Technology Dr 29492
Ted Ave 29406
Telfair Way 29412
Tennent St 29412
Terns Nest Rd 29412
Terrabrook Ln 29412

Terrace Dr 29406
Terrell St 29414
Thaxton St 29414
Theresa Dr 29412
Thomas St 29403
Thomas Cary Ct 29492
Thomas Glenn Ct 29412
Thoreau St 29406
Thrasher Thicket Rd 29412
Three Oaks Ave 29407
Three Pence Ln 29414
Three Trees Rd 29412
Thrift Ln 29492
Thrower St 29492
Tibbett Ct 29414
Tidal Basin Ct 29412
Tidal Creek Cv 29412
Tidal Rice Ct 29492
Tidal View Ln 29412
Tides End Rd 29412
Tidway Cir 29407
Tiffany Dr 29414
Tigershark Ave 29406
Till Rd 29414
Tiller Rd 29412
Timber St 29406
Timberleaf Ct 29407
Timmerman Dr 29407
Timothy St 29407
Tobias Gadson Blvd 29407
Todd St 29403
Tomedjan Cir 29414
Tomoka Dr 29407
Tomotley Ct 29407
Topside Dr 29414
Torrey Pine Ct 29414
Toura Ct & Ln 29414
Tovey Rd 29407
E Tower Ct 29414
Tower Battery Rd 29412
Town Creek Dr 29407
Town Gate Pl 29414
Townpark Ln 29412
Townsend Pl 29492
Townsend Rd 29406
Trachelle Ln 29407
N & S Tracy St 29403
Tradd St 29401
Tradewind Ln 29492
Trafalgar St 29412
Trail Hollow Ct & Dr 29414
Trailee Dr 29407
Trailmore Dr 29407
Tram Ct 29403
Tramway Dr 29414
Tranquil Dr 29407
Transom Ct 29407
Trapier Dr 29412
Trapman St 29401
Travers Ct & Dr 29412
Travis Ln 29492
Treasury Bend Dr 29412
Treebark Dr 29414
Treescape Dr 29414
Treetop Ct 29414
Trenholm Dr 29412
Trent St 29414
Trey Ct 29406
Tribeca Ct & Dr 29414
Trident Ct 29406
Trillium Path 29414
N & S Trinity Dr 29407
Tripe St 29407
Truluck Dr 29414
Trumbo St 29401
Tucker Dr 29414
Tudor Pl 29407
E Tulane Rd 29406
Tulleys Aly 29403
Turkey Pen Rd 29412
Tuxbury Farm Rd 29492
Twain Ct 29412
Twelve Oak Dr 29414
Twin Oaks Dr 29414
Twin Ponds Ln 29492
Two Loch Pl 29414
Two Oaks Dr 29414
Tyler Ln 29492
Tynes Ave 29412
Tynte St 29407
Tyron Cir 29414
Underlie Ln 29492
Unity Aly 29401
Up On The Hill Rd 29412
Vale Rd 29407
Valentine Way 29414
Valley Rd 29412
Valley Forge Dr 29412
Vanderbilt Dr 29414
Vanderhorst Ct 29492
Vanderhorst St 29403
Vardel St 29412
Vassar Dr 29407
Vaucluse Rd 29414
Vendue Range 29401
Venningridge Ln 29492
Verdier Blvd 29414
Veritas St 29414
Vernon St 29401
Vespers Dr 29414
Vestry Dr 29414
Vicharad St 29401
Victoria Rd 29492
Victory Ln 29406
Village Rd 29407
Village Castle Ct 29414
Village Crossing Dr 29492
Vine St 29407
Virginia Oak Ct 29414
Viscount St 29492
Vista Ct 29406
Vista Perch Ln 29412
Vonzetta Ct 29492
Wabeek Way 29414
S Waccamaw Ct 29406
Wade Hampton Dr 29412
Wading Heron Rd 29412
Wadsbury Ln 29414
Wagner Ave 29403
Wainwright Rd 29406
Waites Dr 29412
Waldman Dr 29406
Walk Easy Ln 29407
Walkers Landing Rd 29412
Wall St 29401
Wallace Dr 29412
Wallace Ln 29407
Wallace School Rd 29407
Wallen Rd 29412
Wallerton Ave 29407
Walleye Cor 29414
Wallingford Ct 29414
Walnut St 29403
Walnut Creek Rd 29414
Walsingham Way 29412
Waltham Rd 29406
Wambaw Ave 29412
Wambaw Crk 29492
Wampler Dr 29412
Wando Rd 29492
Wando Creek Ln 29492
Wando Landing St 29492
Wando Reach Rd 29492
Wando Shores Dr 29492
Wando View St 29492
Wantoot Blvd 29407
Wappoo Dr
  1500-1799 29407
  2000-2299 29412
Wappoo Rd 29407
Wappoo Creek Dr & Pl 29412
Wappoo Hall Rd 29412
Wappoo Landing Cir 29412
Wardlaw Ct 29414
Waring Hall Ln 29414
Warren St 29403
Wasbee Range 29401
Washington St
  1-28 29401
  29-99 29403
Washitonia Way 29492
Water St 29401
Water Edge Dr 29492
Water Turkey Retreat 29412
Waterbrook Dr 29414
Waterbury Ct 29412
Wateree Dr 29407
Waterfront Plantation Dr 29412
Waterline Dr 29414
Waterloo Ct & St 29412
Watermelon Run 29412
Waters Edge Ct 29414
Waters Inlet Cir 29492
Waterstone Ln 29414
Waterville Pl 29414
Watroo Pt 29492
Wayah Dr 29414
Wayfarer Ln 29412
Wayne Scott Ct 29414
Weatherstone Rd 29414
Weaver St 29403
Wedgefield Rd 29407
Wedgepark Rd 29407
Wedgewood St 29407
Weeping Willow Way 29414
Weepoolow Trl 29407
Weims Ct 29401
Weir St 29412
Welch Ave 29412
Wellington Ct & Dr 29412
Wendy Ln 29407
Wensley Dr 29414
Wentworth St 29401
Wescott Ct 29403
Wesley Dr 29407
Wespanee Dr 29407
Wespanee Place Ct 29407
Wesson Ave 29403
West St 29401
Westchase Dr 29407
E, N, S & W Westchester Dr 29414
Westerly Ln 29414
Westfield Rd 29407
Westminster Rd 29407
Westmoreland Ave 29412
Weston Ave 29407
Westover Dr 29407
Westridge Cir 29412
Westrivers Rd 29412
Westside Dr 29412
Westway Dr 29412
Westwood Dr 29412
Wexford Rd 29414
Wexford Sound Dr 29412
Wharfside St 29401
Whispering Cypress 29414
Whispering Marsh Dr 29412
Whitby Ln 29414
Whitcomb Dr 29406
White Dr 29407
White Birch Ln 29414
White Chapel Cir 29412
White Heron Ln 29414
White House Blvd 29412
White Marlin Dr 29412
White Oak Dr 29407
White Oleander Ct 29414
White Point Blvd & Ct 29412
White Salt Ln 29492
White Tail Path 29414
Whitefalls Ln 29492
Whitmarsh Dr 29407
Wicklowe Dr 29414
Wicks Ave 29412
Wide Water Ct 29412
Wideman Dr 29406
Wigeon Ln 29412
Wild Flower Ln 29414
Wild Rich Way 29412
Wild Wing Ln 29412
Wildcat Blvd 29414
Wilder Rd 29412
Wildwood Rd 29412
William Ackerman Ln 29407
William E Murray Blvd 29414
William Kennerty Dr 29407
Williams Rd 29412
Williamsburg Ln 29414
Williman St 29403
Willingham Ct 29412
Willis Goodwin Cir 29407
Willow Lake Rd 29412
Willtown St 29492
Wilshire Dr 29407
Wilson St 29401
Wilton St 29412
Wimbee Dr 29407
E & W Wimbledon Ct & Dr 29412
Winborn Dr 29412
Winchester Dr 29407
Windermere Blvd 29407
Winding Creek Ct 29492
Windmill Creek Rd 29414
Windrush Ct 29412
Windsor Dr 29407
Windward Ct & Rd 29412
Winfield Way 29414
Winners Cir 29414
Winslow Dr 29412
Winston St 29407
Wisteria Rd 29407
E Witter St 29412
Wofford Rd 29414
Wolk Dr 29414
Wood Ave 29414
Wood Ride Ct 29414
Woodall Ct 29403
Woodcliff St 29414
Woodcrest Ave 29407
Woodford St 29492
Woodhaven Dr 29407
Woodhill Ter 29412
Woodland Rd 29414
Woodland Shores Rd 29412
Woodleaf Ct 29407
N & S Woodmere Dr 29407
Woodside Dr 29412
Woodview Ln 29412
Woodward Rd 29407
Woolfe St 29403
Wragg Sq 29403
Wraggborough Ln 29403
Wrecklers Race Ln 29414
Wyecreek Ave 29412
Wylie Dr 29406
Wyndham Rd 29412
Xavier St 29414
Yadkin Cir 29406
Yale Dr 29412
Yankee Dr 29412
Yates Ave 29412
Yaupon Dr 29492
Yeadon Ave 29407
Yeamans Rd 29407
Yearling Dr 29406
Yellow House Pl 29492
Yerby Farm Rd 29406
Yew St 29407
Yoricham St 29403
Yorktown Dr 29412
Zig Zag Aly 29401

NUMBERED STREETS

1st Dr 29407
2nd Dr 29407
3rd Ave 29403
5th Ave
  1-299 29403
  800-1399 29407
5th St 29412
6th Ave 29403
8th Ave 29403
9th Ave 29403
10th Ave 29403
11th Ave 29403
12th Ave 29403

CLEMSON SC

General Delivery 29631

POST OFFICE BOXES MAIN OFFICE STATIONS AND BRANCHES

Box No.s
All PO Boxes 29633

NAMED STREETS

Abel Rd 29631
Addison Ln 29631
Aileen Ln 29631
Airport Rd 29631
Albermarle Dr 29631
Allee St 29631
Anderson Hwy 29631
Anna Maria Blvd 29631
Aquatics Dr 29631
Argon St 29631
Ashley Rd 29631
Augusta Rd 29631
Azalea Dr 29631
Banks St 29631
Barre St 29631
Bayberry Ln 29631
Benson Blvd 29631
Bentbrook Ln 29631
Berkeley Ct & Dr 29631
Berkeley Place Cir 29631
Berry St 29631
Birch Pl 29631
Blue Ridge Dr 29631
Boggs St 29631
Booker Springs Rd 29631
Bradley St 29631
Briarwood Ct 29631
Broad St 29631
Brook St 29631
Brookhaven Dr 29631
Brookview Way 29631
E Brookwood Dr 29631
Butler St 29631
Calhoun St 29631
Cambridge Dr 29631
Camelot Rd 29631
Canoy Ln 29631
Cardinal Dr 29631
Carlton Ln 29631
Carolina Ct & Dr 29631
Carolus Dr 29631
Carrie Ln 29631
Carteret Ct 29631
Castle Ct 29631
Catawbah Rd 29631
Cedar Ln 29631
Chapman Hill Rd 29631
Charissa Dr 29631
Charleston Ave 29631
Chattooga Ln 29631
Cherokee Rd 29631
Cherry Rd 29631
Church St 29631
Clarendon Dr 29631
Clemson Ave & St 29631
Clemson Park Rd 29631
Clemson Place Cir 29631
Cochran Rd 29631
College Ave
  300-520 29631
  519-519 29633
  521-1199 29631
  522-1198 29631
College St 29631
College Heights Blvd 29631
Colleton Ct 29631
Combahee Ct 29631
Cottonwood Ln 29631
Country Walk Cir & Ln 29631
Crawford Ct 29631
Creekside Dr 29631
Creekview Dr 29631
Crest Cir 29631
Crestwood Dr 29631
Curtis Cir 29631
Daleview Cir 29631
Daniel Dr 29631
Dargan Ln 29631
Dawson St 29631
Devonshire Ct 29631
Dogwood Dr 29631
Dogwood Terrace Ln 29631
Dove Cir 29631
Downs Blvd & Loop 29631
Duke St 29631
Dupree St 29631
Earle St 29631
Edgewood Ave 29631
Elm St 29631
Entomology Ln 29631
Epting Cir 29631
Essex Dr 29631
Evans Pl 29631
Evergreen Dr 29631
Fabrica St 29631
Fern Cir 29631
Fife Dr 29631
Finley St 29631
Folger St 29631
Forest Ln 29631
Fort Rutledge Rd 29631
Foy Creek Dr 29631
Freedom Dr 29631
Frontage Rd 29631
Fruster St 29631
Gantt St 29631
Georgetown St 29631
Goldman St 29631
Goode Ln 29631
Grace St 29631
Greenlee Pl 29631
Gregory St 29631
Grove Dr 29631
Hamilton Dr 29631
Hardin Ave 29631
Hawthorne St 29631
Hazelwood Dr 29631
Hedgerow Ln 29631
Helton St 29631
Henderson Dr 29631
Hickory Way 29631
Highland Dr 29631
Hill Pine Ct 29631
Hillcrest Ave 29631
Holden Dr 29631
Holiday Ave 29631
Holly Ave 29631
Hopewell Rd 29631
Houston St 29631
Howard Ave 29631
Hunnicutt Ln 29631
Hunter Ave & St 29631
Hyde Ln 29631
Issaqueena Trl 29631
Jenkins Pl 29631
Karen Ct & Dr 29631
Keith St 29631
Keller Blvd 29631
Kelly Rd 29631
Kendra Pl 29631
Keowee Trl 29631
Keystone Ln 29631
Kiawah Ct 29631
Kings Way 29631
Knight Cir 29631
Knollwood Dr 29631
Knox Rd 29631
Lakeside Ct 29631
Lakeview Cir 29631
Lancelot Dr 29631
Lark Cir 29631
Laurel Ln 29631
Lawrence Rd 29631
Lee St 29631
E Lewis Rd 29631
Liberty Dr 29631
Ligon St 29631
Lincoln Dr 29631
Lindsay Rd 29631
Little Ln 29631
Littlejohn St 29631
Locust St 29631
Magnolia Way 29631
Manley Dr 29631
Maple Blvd 29631
Market St 29631
Martin St 29631
Mccollum St 29631
Mcgee St 29631
Mitchell Ave 29631
Monaco Cir 29631
Monte Carlo Cir 29631
Moorman Ln 29631
Mountain Laurel Dr 29631
Mountain View Ln 29631
Mulberry Ave 29631
Natural Resources Dr 29631
Nettles Rd 29631
Nettles Park Rd 29631
Oak St 29631
Old Central Rd 29631
Old Cherry Rd 29631
Old Greenville Hwy 29631
Old Stone Church Rd 29631
Oneida Ct 29631
Orange Ct 29631
Owens Dr 29631
N Palmetto Blvd 29631
Paw Path Ln 29631
Payne Ln 29631
Peand Dr 29631
Pendleton Rd 29631
Penson St 29631
Pershing Ave 29631
Pickens St 29631
Pickens Farm Rd 29631
Pine St 29631
Pine Ridge Ln 29631
Pinnacle St 29631
Pleasant View Dr 29631
Poe St 29631
Poole Ln 29631
Poplar Dr 29631
Pressley Dr 29631
Prince Albert St 29631
Prince Ranier St 29631
Princess Ln 29631
Princess Caroline St 29631
Princess Grace Ave 29631
Purple Ct 29631
Queens Ct 29631
Raven Ln 29631
Red Hill Ct 29631
Red Maple Way 29631
Reese St 29631
Reid St 29631
Rice St 29631
Ridgecrest Dr 29631
Ridgeview Dr 29631
Riding Rd 29631
Riggs Dr 29631
Rippleview Dr 29631
Riverbirch Run 29631
Riverpoint Dr 29631
Robin St 29631
Robinson St 29631
Rock Creek Rd 29631
Roslyn Dr 29631
Santee Trl 29631
Satula Ln 29631
Sedgefield Dr 29631
Sedgewood Ct 29631
Shadowood Dr 29631
Shady Ln 29631
Shaftsbury Rd 29631
Shaw St 29631
Shaw Street Ext 29631
Shorecrest Dr 29631
Sikes Ave 29631
Simpson St 29631
Singleton St 29631
Skyview Dr 29631
Sloan St 29631

Snider Ln 29631
Spencer St 29631
Squire Cir 29631
Stardust Ln 29631
Stephens Rd 29631
Stone Cir 29631
Stonebridge Dr 29631
Stoney Creek Dr 29631
Strawberry Ln 29631
Strode Cir 29631
Sugar Maple Ct 29631
Summer Walk 29631
Summey St 29631
Sunset Ave 29631
Sycamore Dr 29631
Tamassee Dr 29631
Tant St 29631
Taylor St 29631
Thomas St 29631
Thomas Green Blvd 29631
Thurmond Ln 29631
Tiger Blvd 29631
Twelve Mile Park Rd 29631
Upper Highland Dr 29631
Valley View Ct & Dr 29631
Village Walk Ln 29631
Vineyard Rd 29631
Vista Cir, Dr & Ter 29631
Walker St 29631
Wall St 29631
Wescott Dr 29631
Wesley St 29631
West Ln 29631
White Ln 29631
Wigington St 29631
Wild Cherry Ln 29631
Willow St 29631
Winchester Ct 29631
Winyah Ct 29631
Woodland Way 29631
Wren St 29631
Wyatt Ave 29631
Wyntuck Ct 29631
Young St 29631

COLUMBIA SC

General Delivery 29202

POST OFFICE BOXES MAIN OFFICE STATIONS AND BRANCHES

Box No.s
A - B 29202
R - R 29250
1 - 2852 29202
497 - 497 29207
3001 - 3999 29230
4001 - 4999 29240
5001 - 5998 29250
6000 - 6994 29260
7001 - 8918 29202
9001 - 9998 29290
9997 - 9997 29228
10001 - 10460 29207
11000 - 13118 29211
13342 - 13593 29201
21001 - 21999 29221
23001 - 25818 29224
29203 - 29205 29202
29207 - 29207 29207
30001 - 30840 29230
40001 - 40179 29240
50001 - 51918 29250
61001 - 61215 29260
90000 - 91124 29290
100101 - 100300 29290
100520 - 100520 29250
100603 - 100605 29260
100900 - 100902 29290
101100 - 101115 29211
102100 - 102111 29221
102400 - 102425 29224
210001 - 213138 29221
280001 - 280778 29228
290001 - 292520 29229
600601 - 600601 29260
929000 - 929998 29292

RURAL ROUTES

01, 05, 09, 43 29203
02, 06, 11, 14, 17, 32 29212
07 29223
03, 08, 12, 13, 15, 16, 18, 19 29229

NAMED STREETS

Aaron Dr 29203
Abberton Ct 29229
Abbeville St 29201
Abbeydale Way 29229
Abbeyhill Ct & Dr 29229
Abbeywalk Ln 29229
Abbott Rd 29201
Abe Cir 29223
Abelia Rd 29205
Aberdeen Ave 29203
Abernathy St 29209
Abingdon Rd 29203
Abraham St 29203
Acacia Ln 29229
Academy St 29203
Academy Way 29206
Accolades Dr 29229
Acme St 29201
Acropolis Ct 29209
Acton Ct 29212
Acuba Ct 29229
Adams Ct 29206
Adams Grv 29203
Adams St 29203
Addington Rd 29223
Addlestone Ct 29209
Addy Ct 29203
Adeline Dr 29205
Adella St 29210
Adger Rd
 700-1599 29205
 1600-1699 29204
Aerie Ct 29212
Afton Ct 29212
Afton Ln 29229
Aiken St 29201
Aiken Hunt Cir 29223
Aintree Dr 29223
Airline Dr 29205
Airport Blvd 29205
N & S Airy Hall Ct 29209
Alabama St 29201
Alatera Ct 29229
Alba Dr 29209
Albemarle St 29203
Albert Allen Rd 29203
Albion Rd 29205
Albritton Rd 29204
Alconbury Ct 29210
Alcott Dr 29203
Aldbury Ct & Rd 29212
Aldershot Way 29229
Alderston Way 29229
Alelia Ct & Ln 29229
Alexander Cir 29206
Alford Dr 29203
Algrave Way 29229
Alida St 29203
Alisia Way 29212
Alison Way 29229
Allaire Ct N & S 29229
Allans Mill Dr 29223
Allen St 29203
Allen Benedict Ct 29204
Allens Way 29205
Allison Brook Ct 29212
Alma Rd 29209
Almeda Dr 29223
Alpha Ct 29223
Alpine Cir & Rd 29223
Alpine Road Ext 29223
Alston Rd 29205
Alta Vista Dr 29223
Alta Vista Rd 29203
Alton Pl 29210
Amaryllis Dr 29229
Amber Ct 29212
Ambergate Ln 29229
Amberley Rd 29203
Amberly Ct 29212
Ambling Cir 29210
Ambrose Cir 29210
Amelia Forest Ln 29209
Amelia Oaks Way 29209
American Italian Way 29209
Ames Rd 29203
Amherst Ave 29205
Amick Dr 29206
Amstar Ct & Rd 29212
Amsterdam Dr 29210
Anchor Bnd 29212
Anchor Ct 29229
Anden Hall Dr 29229
Anders Dr & Way 29203
Anderson St
 2400-2498 29207
 4700-4899 29203
Andrews Rd 29201
Angel Garden Way 29223
Angus Dr & Rd 29223
Anita Ln 29229
Annacy Park Dr 29223
Annondale Ct & Rd 29212
Ansel St 29204
Ansley Ct 29209
Anson Dr 29229
Ansonborough Rd 29229
Anthony Ave 29201
Antioch Pl 29209
Antler Ct & Way 29229
Anwood Dr 29209
Apache Dr 29203
Apple Valley Ct & Rd 29210
Appleby Ln 29223
Applegate Ln 29209
Applehill Ct 29229
Aragon Ct 29229
Aralia Dr 29205
Arbor Dr 29206
Arbor Falls Dr 29229
Arbor Lake Dr 29223
Arbor Place Dr 29229
Arbor Vista Ct 29229
Arborgate Cir & Ct 29212
Arborland Ct 29212
Arborview Ct 29212
Arborvine Ct 29212
Arbutus Dr 29205
Arcadia Cv & Rd 29206
Arcadia Lake Dr 29223
Arcadia Lakes Dr E 29206
Arcadia Springs Cir 29206
Arcadia Woods Rd 29206
Archdale Rd 29209
Archers Ct & Ln 29212
Archie Dr 29223
Arcola Dr 29223
Ardincaple Dr 29203
Ardmore Rd 29223
Ardmount Rd 29212
Argent Ct 29203
Argyll Rd 29212
Arlene Dr 29204
Arlington St 29203
Armour St 29203
Arnold Palmer Ct 29229
Arrow Ct 29212
Arrow Field Rd 29209
Arrowhead Dr 29223
N Arrowwood Rd 29210
Arsenal Academy Pl 29201
Arsenal Hill Ct 29201
Artic Ct & Loop 29212
Artic Court Ext 29212
Artisan Dr 29229
Arundel Ln 29209
Arwen Ln 29212
Asbury Dr 29209
Ascot Ct 29210
Ash Bay Rd 29229
Ash Ridge Ct 29229
Ash Tree Rd 29229
Ashbury St 29223
Ashby Rd 29204
Ashewicke Dr 29229
Ashewood Commons Dr 29209
Ashewood Lake Dr 29209
Ashford Ln 29210
Ashland Dr 29229
Ashland Rd 29210
Ashland Park Ln 29210
Ashley Ct 29204
Ashley St 29203
Ashley Brook Ct 29229
Ashley Crest Dr 29229
Ashley Hall Ct & Rd 29229
Ashley Place Ct & Rd 29229
Ashleys Pl 29209
Ashmore Pl 29229
Ashridge Ct 29212
Ashton St 29204
Ashton Hill Dr 29229
Ashwell Ct 29223
Ashwood Rd 29206
Ashworth Ln 29206
Aspen Ct 29212
Aspen Ln 29212
Aspen Trl 29206
Aspinwall Rd 29203
Assembly St
 101-1600 29201
 1601-2099 29201
 1601-1601 29202
 1602-2098 29201
S Assembly St 29201
Assurance Rd 29210
Aster Cir & St 29201
Atascadero Dr 29206
Athena Dr 29223
Atlantic Dr 29210
Atlas Ct, Rd & Way 29209
Atrium Way 29223
Atrium Ridge Ct 29223
Atterbury Dr 29203
Aubrey St 29229
Auburn Rd 29212
Auburn St 29204
Auburncrest Ct 29229
Audrey Ln 29223
Audubon Ave 29223
Austin St 29209
Austree Ct & Dr 29229
Autumn Cir 29206
Autumn Glen Ct & Rd 29229
Autumn Run Cir & Way 29229
Avalee Ave 29210
Avalon Dr 29209
Avebury Ln 29229
Avenel Ct 29229
Avery Ln 29212
Avery Place Dr 29212
Averyt Ave 29210
Avian Trl 29206
Avington Ct & Ln 29229
Avocet Ct 29203
Avondale Dr 29203
Aylesford Pl 29210
Ayrshire Ave 29203
Azalea Dr 29205
Babe Reaves Rd 29203
Babington Way 29229
Baccharis Dr 29229
Back Bay Ct 29229
Baden Ct 29212
Baffin Bay Rd 29212
Bagnal Dr 29204
Bagpipe Rd 29223
Bailey Ct 29206
Bailey St 29203
Baine St 29203
Baker Ct 29206
Baker House Ct & Rd 29223
Bakers Point Ct & Rd 29223
Bakersfield Rd 29210
Bakerton Ct & Rd 29212
Bald Eagle Ct 29203
Baldur Ct 29229
Baldwin Rd 29204
Balfour Ct 29203
Ballemia Rd 29223
Ballenton Rd 29203
Bally Bunion Ln 29229
Ballymore Ct 29229
Balmoral Rd 29209
Balsam Rd 29210
Baltusrol Ct 29223
Banbury Rd 29210
Bancroff Rd 29223
Bancroft Ct 29206
Banner Hill Rd 29209
Bannockburn Dr 29206
Barbara Dr 29223
Barber St 29203
Barberry Ct & Ln 29212
Barclay Ct 29223
Barclay Ln 29210
Barhamville Rd 29204
Barker Dr 29206
Barksdale Dr 29203
Barlow Rd 29201
Barmettler Pl 29210
Barmount Dr 29210
Barn Owl Ct 29209
Barnes St 29201
Barnes Springs Rd 29204
Barnet Ct 29212
Barnetby Way 29229
Barney Ln 29223
Barnhart Rd 29204
Barnley Ct 29229
Barnsbury Rd 29203
Barnsley Rd 29212
Barnwell St
 200-499 29205
 700-1999 29201
Barony Cir, Ct & Dr 29203
Barony Place Cir & Dr 29229
Barrett St 29201
Barrington Dr 29203
Barrister Dr 29223
Barton St 29203
Barton Bend Ln 29206
Barton Creek Ct 29229
Barwick St 29205
Basil St 29209
Basinghouse Rd 29212
Bassett Loop 29229
Bassler St 29204
Bates St 29201
Batson Ct 29206
Battery Walk Ct 29212
Battleford Rd 29210
Bauer Cir 29203
Baxter Dr 29223
Bay St 29205
N Bay Xing 29229
S Bay Xing 29229
Bay Harbor Cir 29212
Bay Hill Ln 29201
Bay Laurel Pl 29201
Bay Shell Dr 29229
Bay Springs Rd 29223
Bay Tree Ln 29210
Bayberry Ct 29206
Baybridge Dr 29229
Bayfield Rd 29223
Baymore Ln 29212
Baynard Ct 29223
Baysdale Dr 29229
Bayside Rd 29212
Baytree Ct 29223
Bayview Dr 29204
Baywater Dr 29209
Beacon Ct & Ln 29229
Beacon Hill Ct & Rd 29210
Bear St 29204
Beardmore Ct 29223
Beatty Rd 29210
Beatty Downs Rd 29210
Beaufort St 29201
Beaumont Ct & St 29203
Beaver Creek Cir, Ct & Dr 29223
Beaver Dale Dr 29203
Beaver Dam Ct 29223
Beaver Dam Rd
 100-299 29223
 1100-1799 29212
N Beaver Dam Rd 29212
Beaverbrook Dr 29203
Beckett Cir 29212
Beckley Dr 29209
Beckman Rd 29203
Beckton Ct 29229
Becky Ct 29203
Bedford Ct 29209
Bedford Dr 29203
Bedford Way 29209
Bee Haven Rd 29223
Bee Ridge Cir & Rd 29223
Beech Glen Dr 29229
Beechaven Rd 29204
Beechwood Dr 29212
Beecliff Dr 29205
Belaire St 29210
Bella Ct 29210
Bella Vista Dr 29223
Belle Claire Dr 29203
Belle Grove Cir 29229
Belleclave Rd 29223
Bellefield Ln 29206
Belleford Ridge Rd 29223
Bellehaven Dr 29203
Bellelake Ct 29223
Bellevalley Ln 29223
Belleview Cir & St 29201
Bellingham Rd 29203
Bellmeade Pl 29209
Bellway Ct 29229
Bellwood Rd 29205
Belmont Dr
 1300-1500 29205
 1502-1598 29205
 1600-1999 29206
Belterdale Ave 29209
Beltline Blvd 29205
N Beltline Blvd
 1600-1899 29206
 1901-1997 29204
 1999-3599 29204
S Beltline Blvd
 200-1799 29205
 2000-3099 29201
W Beltline Blvd
 3300-3799 29203
 3800-4299 29204
Belvedere Dr 29204
Ben Brush Ct 29229
E Bend Ct 29223
Bendemeer Dr 29209
Benedict St 29203
Bengston St 29210
Benjamin Ct 29206
Bennett Ct 29229
Bennie Dr 29203
Benning Rd 29207
Bennington Cir & Ct 29229
Benson Rd 29209
Bent Bough Cir 29212
Bent Granite Pl 29212
Bent Pine Dr 29212
Bent Ridge Rd 29223
Bent Tree Ln 29210
Bentley Ct & Dr 29210
Benton St 29201
Bentwood Ct & Ln 29229
Berea Rd 29201
Beresford Pl 29210
Berkeley Rd 29205
Berkeley Forest Ct & Dr 29209
Berkeley Ridge Dr 29229
Berks Ct 29212
Berkshire Dr
 200-399 29223
 1800-1999 29210
Berl Mar Rd 29212
Bermuda Hills Rd 29223
Bernardin Ave 29204
Berry St 29204
Berry Ridge Cir & Ct 29229
Berry Tree Ln 29223
Berryhill Rd 29210
Bertha Ave 29203
Berwick Ct & Rd 29212
Beth Hope Ln 29210
Bethel Camp Rd 29223
Bethel Church Rd 29206
Bethune Ct 29203
Betsy Dr 29210
Bettys Ln 29210
Beverly Dr 29204
Biddle Rd 29212
Big Game Loop 29229
Big Leaf Cir & Ct 29229
Bill St 29209
Billings St 29203
Bilton Rd 29212
Birch Glenn Ct 29209
Birch Hollow Dr 29229
Birch Ridge Dr 29229
Birchbark 29229
Birchfield Dr 29203
Birchton Ct 29209
Birchwood Dr 29203
Bird Springs Ct 29223
Birdsong Dr 29223
Bisbane Rd 29203
Biscayne Rd 29212
Bishop Ave 29203
Bishopgate Rd 29212
Bitternut Rd 29209
Black Friars Rd 29209
Black Gum Rd 29209
Black Pine Ct 29229
Blackloon Dr 29229
Blackwell Cir 29209
Blaine St 29209
Blair Rd 29201
Blakeley Rd 29209
Blakeley St 29203
Blakesmoor Rd 29223
Blanchelle Ct 29203
Blanding St
 200-298 29201
 300-1999 29201
 2000-2099 29204
Blarney Dr 29223
Blazing Star Trl 29223
Bliss Ln 29229
Blondell Cir 29204
Bloomwood Rd 29205
Blossom St
 300-1899 29201
 1900-4499 29205
Blue Bill Ct 29229
Blue Church Ct 29212
Blue Heron Rd 29229
Blue Ridge Ter 29203
Blue Savannah St 29229
Blue Springs Ct 29229
Blue Willow Way 29229
Bluebead Ct 29229
Bluebird Dr & Ln 29204
Bluefield Dr 29210
Bluemont Ct 29229
Bluff Rd
 1-2699 29201
 2900-5799 29209
Bluff Industrial Blvd 29201
Bluff Oaks Rd 29209
Bluff Pointe 29212
Blume Ct 29204
Blyth Ct 29210
Blythe Glen Ln 29206

Street	ZIP
Blythecreek Ct	29210
Bob Brooks Ct	29210
Bolden Cir	29204
N & S Bolen Hall Ct	29209
Bolette Ln	29229
Bolton Rd & St	29209
Bombay Dr	29209
Bombing Range Pt & Rd	29229
Bon Air Dr	29203
Bondendi St	29205
S Bonham Rd	29205
Bonner Ave	29204
Bonnie Forest Blvd	29210
Bonnington Dr	29229
Bonnyridge Rd	29223
Booker St	29203
Boone Ct	29206
Boone St	29204
Booth St	29204
Bordeaux Ln	29210
Boston St	29203
Boston Commons Ct	29212
Bostwick Rdg	29229
Boswell Rd	29203
Bosworth Field Ct & Rd	29212
Botney Way	29212
Bouchet Ct	29203
Boulder Creek Trl	29212
E Boundary Rd	29223
Boundbrook Ln	29206
Bouquet Ct	29210
Bournemouth Way	29229
Bower Pkwy	29212
Bowland Ct	29212
Bowling Ave	29203
Box Turtle Ct	29229
Boxwood Dr	29205
Boyden Arbor Rd	29207
Boyer Dr	29204
Boylston Rd	29203
Brackenridge Rd	29206
Bradbury Dr	29203
Braddock Pt	29209
Bradford Ln	29223
Bradford Knoll Ct	29223
Bradford Ridge Ct & Ln	29223
Bradington Way	29229
Bradley Ct	29206
Bradley Dr	29204
Brady St	29204
Braewick Rd	29212
Bragg St	
2300-2399	29207
2400-2499	29209
Braham St	29204
Braiden Manor Rd	29209
Brampton Cir	29206
Branch Ln	29212
S Branch Rd	29223
W Branch Rd	29223
Branch Hill Ln	29223
Branchview Dr	29229
Brandon Ave	29209
Brandon Hall Rd	29229
Brandywine Dr	29212
Brandywine Ln	29206
Brannigan Ln	29229
Branning Dr	29209
Branson Ct	29223
Brantley St	29210
Brasington Ln	29209
Brass Lantern Way	29212
Brassie Ct	29229
Bratton St	29205
Brayton Aly	29204
Breda Ct	29212
Breeland St	29210
Breezewood Ct	29212
Bremer Ct	29206
Brenda Rd	29204
Brennen Rd	29206
Brent Ford Cir & Rd	29212
Brentfield Dr	29203
Brenthaven Rd	29206
Brentland Ct	29212
Brentwood Ct & Dr	29206
Brevard St	29210
Brewer St	29203
Briar Ct N & S	29223
Briarberry Rd	29223
Briarcreek Ct	29212
Briarfield Rd	29206
Briargate Cir	
1000-1119	29210
1120-1298	29210
1120-1120	29221
1121-1299	29210
Briarwood Rd	29206
S Brick Rd	29229
Brick Iron Rd	29203
Brickingham Way	29229
Brickyard Rd	29203
N Brickyard Rd	29223
Bridal Path Ct	29229
Bridgecreek Dr	29229
Bridgeton Rd	29210
Bridgeview Ct	29229
Bridgewood Rd	29206
Bridle Trl	29203
Briercliff Dr	29203
Bright Ave	29205
Brighton Ct	29203
S Brighton Rd	29223
Brighton Hill Cir & Rd	29223
Brinkley Ln	29210
Bristol Dr	29204
Brittany Way	29212
Brittany Park Ln & Rd	29229
Britton Ln	29209
Broad St	29203
Broad River Rd	
600-4799	29210
4800-5799	29212
Broadland Ave	29203
Broadmore St	29203
Broadview Ct	29212
E Broadway St	29201
Brockington Dr	29206
Brockwall Dr	29206
Brogdon Dr	29209
Broken Hill Rd	29212
Bronston Ct	29229
Bronte Rd	29210
Bronx Rd	29204
Brook Hollow Dr	29229
Brook Pines Dr	29210
Brook Valley Rd	29223
Brookfield Rd	
6600-6899	29206
6901-6999	29206
7000-8199	29223
Brookfield Heights Ct & Rd	29223
Brookgreen Cir, Ct & Dr	29210
Brookhirst Ct	29223
Brookland Cir	29204
Brookline Ct	29229
Brookman Rd	29210
Brookmist	29229
Brookmont Ln	29203
Brookridge Dr	29203
Brooks St	29203
Brooks Palmer Pl	29203
Brooksby Ct	29209
Brooksdale Dr	29229
Brookshire Dr	29210
Brookside Cir	29206
Brookspring Cir & Rd	29223
Brookview Rd	29212
Brookwood Ct	29204
Brookwood Dr	29201
Broomfield St	29203
Brown Ave	29206
Browning Ln	29212
Browning Rd	29210
Bruce St	
700-799	29223
6500-6599	29209
Brunswick Dr	29203
Brushwood Ct	29229
Bruton Rd	29203
Bryan St	29201
Bryant Ct	29206
Bryson Rd	29205
Bryton Trce	29210
E & W Buchanan Dr	29206
Buck Ridge Dr	29229
Buckeye Ct	29229
Buckfield Dr	29206
Buckhaven Way	29229
Buckingham Cir & Rd	29205
Buckman Ct	29229
Buckner Rd	29203
Buckner Park Dr	29203
Buckskin Ct	29203
Budon Ct	29204
Bull St	
100-398	29205
602-698	29201
700-2799	29201
S Bull St	29205
Bumgardner Ct	29204
Bur Oak Ln	29229
Burbank St	29210
Burberry Dr & Ln	29229
Burdell Dr	29209
Burdock Cir	29201
Burfodi Ct	29223
Burgee Ct	29229
Burke Ave	29203
Burley Ct	29204
Burmaster Dr	29229
Burnette Dr	29210
Burney Dr	29205
Burning Tree Ln	29210
Burnsdowne Rd	29210
Burnside Ave & Dr	29209
Burnwood Ct	29203
Burt Rd	29206
Burton St	29204
Burton Heights Cir	29203
Burton Holmes Ct	29206
Burwell Ln	29205
Busby St	29203
Bush Rd	29229
Bush River Ct	29210
Bush River Rd	
100-3799	29210
5100-6299	29212
Business Park Blvd	29203
Butler St	29205
Butternut Ln	29210
Buttonbush Ct	29229
Buxton Dr	29223
Byrd Ave	29203
Byrnes Dr	29204
Byron Pl	29212
Byron Rd	29209
Bywood Dr	29223
C J Jackson Cir	29203
Cabot Ave	29203
Cactus Ave	29210
Cades Ct	29212
Cadia Dr	29223
Cairnbrook Ct & Dr	29210
Calabash Ln	29223
Caladium Dr	29212
Caladium Way	29229
Caleb Ct	29203
Caledonia Ln	29209
Calendar Ct	29206
Calhoun St	
100-1800	29201
1802-1998	29201
2000-2099	29204
California Dr	29205
Calk St	29204
Calley Ct	29223
Calloway Ct	29223
Calvary Dr	29203
Calvin Dr	29223
Calway Aly	29205
Cam Ln	29229
Camay Ct	29209
Camberley Ct	29223
Cambill St	29203
Cambout St	29210
Cambridge Ln	29204
Cambridge Lane Rd	29223
Cambridge Oaks Ct & Dr	29223
Camden Chase	29223
Camellia St	29205
Camelot St	29203
Cameron Ct	29205
Cameron Rd	29204
Cami Forest Ln	29209
Camino Ct	29209
Camlin Ct	29229
Camp Ground Cir & Rd	29203
E, W & N Campanella Dr & Ext	29203
Camrose Ct	29229
Canal Ct & Dr	29210
Canal Place Cir, Dr & Way	29201
Canal Yard	29210
Canalside St	29201
Cancomar St	29203
Candi Ln	29210
Candleberry Cir	29201
Candlelite Dr	29209
Candlewood Ln	29209
Candon Ct	29229
Candwenn Ct	29204
Candytuft Ln	29223
Cane Brake Cir & Dr	29223
Cane Break Ct	29229
Cane Lake Dr	29203
Canemill	29229
Cannon St	29205
Cannon Dale Ct & Rd	29212
Cannon Grove Ct	29206
Canonero Ct	29229
Canterbury Ct	29210
Canterbury Rd	29204
Canterfield Rd	29212
Capers Ave	29205
Capers Rd	29206
Capital Ct	29212
Capitol Pl	29205
Cardamon Ct	29203
Cardiff St	29209
Cardigan Ct	29210
Cardinal St	29201
Cardington Ct & Dr	29209
Cardross Ln	29209
Carey Ct	29206
Carillon Ct	29204
Carl Rd	29210
Carl Weed Ct	29212
Carlisle St	29205
Carlow Dr	29209
Carlton Dr	29223
Carlyle Cir	29206
Carmel St	29203
Carnaby Ct	29223
Carnegie St	29204
Carnes St	29204
Carol Ann Dr	29223
Carola Ave	29203
Carolina St	29201
Carolina Ridge Dr	29229
Carolina Rose Ct & Dr	29209
Caroline Rd	29209
Caroline Jones Rd	29203
Carousel Cir	29203
Carraway Dr	29229
Carriage Ln	29212
Carriage House Rd	29206
Carriage Oaks Ct & Dr	29229
Carriage Trace Ct	29212
Carrie Anderson Rd	29203
Carrison Rd	29210
Carroll Dr	29204
Carson Dr	29204
Carswell Dr	29209
Carter St	29204
Carter Hill Dr	29206
Carteret St	29203
Cartwright Dr	29223
Carty Ct & Dr	29203
Carver St	29203
Cary Ln	29206
Casey Ct	29205
Cassia Ct	29209
Cassina Cir & Rd	29205
E & W Casterton Dr	29229
Castle Rd	29210
Castle Cary Ct	29209
Castle Hall Ct & Ln	29209
Castle Pinckney Rd	29223
Castle Ridge Ct & Dr	29229
Castleburg Ln	29229
Castlebury Dr	29229
Castleton Ln	29223
Catalina Ct	29223
Catalpa Ct & Ln	29229
Catawba Cir	29201
Catawba St	
200-1399	29201
1600-1899	29205
Catesby Cir	29206
Catherine Ave	29203
Cato Dr	29201
Caughman Rd	29209
Caughman Rd N	29203
Caughman Park Dr	29209
Caughman Ridge Rd	29209
Cavalier Ct	29205
Caymus Ct	29229
Cedar St	29201
Cedar Ter	29209
Cedar Edge Ct	29203
Cedar Field Ct & Ln	29212
Cedar Glen Ln	29223
Cedar Ridge Rd	29206
Cedar Springs Rd	29206
Cedar Top Ln	29212
Cedarbrook Ct & Dr	29212
Cedarwood Ln	29205
Celia Saxon St	29204
Celtic Rd	29210
Cendariv Rd	29209
Centennial Dr	29229
Center Ct	29212
Center St	29204
Center Point Cir & Rd	29210
Centeridge Dr	29229
Centerview Dr	29210
Century Dr	29212
Cermack St	29223
Chablis Dr	29210
Chadwell Rd	29223
Chadwick Ct	29223
Chalfont Ct & Ln	29229
Chalice Ln	29229
Challedon Ct & Dr	29212
Chalmers Ln	29229
Chamberlain Dr	29210
Chambly Dr	29209
Chancery Ln	29229
Chandler Ave & Ct	29210
Chaney St	29204
Channel Dr	29229
Chantilly Dr	29210
E Chapel Rd	29205
Chapelwood Dr	29229
Chappelle St	29203
Char Oak Ct & Dr	29212
Charbonneau	29210
Charles St	29203
Charles Ferry Dr	29209
Charles Towne Ct & Dr	29209
Charleston Estates Ln	29223
Charleswood Dr	29223
Charley Horse Rd	29223
Charlotte St	29203
Charlton St	29203
Charmont Dr	29223
Charnock Way	29209
Charring Dr	29203
Chartel Cir	29203
Charter Ct	29209
Charter House Cir & Rd	29212
Chartwell Rd	29210
Charwood Dr	29223
Chasewood Ct	29203
Chateau Dr	29204
N Chateau Dr	29223
Chaterelle Way	29229
Chatham Ave	29205
Chatham Trce	29229
Chatsworth Rd	29223
Chaucer Dr	29229
Chaunticleer Rd	29223
Chelmsford Ct & Way	29229
N & S Chelsea Cir & Rd	29223
Cheltenham Ln	29223
Chelton Ct	29212
Chelveston Dr	29210
Cherokee St	29201
Cherry St	29205
Cherry Blossom Ln	29203
Cherry Hill Dr	29204
Cherry Laurel Dr	29204
Cherry Stone Dr	29229
Cheryl Dr	29210
Chesapeake Ct	29223
Chesham Ct	29209
Cheshire Dr	29210
Chesnee Dr	29203
Chesney Ln	29209
Chesnut Rd	29206
Chester St	29201
Chesterfield Dr	29203
Chesterfield Sq	29210
Chestnut St	29204
Chestnut Woods Ct & Ln	29212
Cheval St	29209
Chevis St	29205
Chickasaw Ct	29229
Chicopee Dr	29210
Chicora St	29206
Childs Ln & St	29201
Chilhowie Rd	29209
S Chimney Ln	29209
Chimney Hill Rd	29209
Chimneyridge Dr	29229
China Rose Ct	29229
Chinaberry Dr	29204
Chinquapin Cir, Ct & Rd	29212
Chippenham Cir	29210
Chippewa Dr	29210
Chipping Ln	29223
Christian St	29203
Christie Rd	29209
Christopher St	29209
Chukker Hill Ct	29223
Church St	29201
Churchill Cir	29206
Churchland Dr	29229
Cinderella Ct	29223
Cindy Ct & Dr	29223
Circle Dr	29206
Citadel Ave	29206
City Club Dr	29201
Claey Ct	29223
Clairborne Pl	29229
Clairton Ct & St	29203
Claremont Dr	29205
Clarendon St	29203
Clark St	29201
Clark Ridge Rd	29223
Claudia Dr	29223
Clay Ridge Rd	29223
Clayton St	29229
Clear Water Pt	29212
Clearidge Ct	29229
Clearmeadow Dr	29229
Clearview Ct, Dr & Ter	29212
Clearwater Rd	29223
Clearwell Ct	29229
Clearwood Ct	29212
Cleaton Rd	29206
Clement Rd	29203
Clemson Ave	29206
Clemson Rd	29229
Clemson Frontage Rd	29229
Cleveland St	29203
Cleyera Ct	29229
Clif Kinder Rd	29209
Clifford Dr	29223
Cliffside Cir & Dr	29209
Clifton St	29209
Clinton St	29223
Clipper Way	29229
Clive St	29204
Cloister Pl	29210
Clover Bay Dr	29203
Clover Crest Ct	29229
Cloverdale Dr	29209
Club Rd	29203
Club House Rd	29203
Clusters Ct	29210
Clyburn St	29203
Coachmaker Cir & Rd	29209
Coachmen Ct	29229
Coachtrail Ct & Ln	29223
Coatesdale Cir & Rd	29209
Cobb St	29204
Cobb Hall Ct	29223
Cobblestone Ct	29229
Cobham Rd	29212
Coco Rd	29210
Cody St	29203
Cogburn Ct & Rd	29229
Coggins Pt	29209
Coker St	29206
Cokesbury Dr	29203
Cokesdale Rd	29212
Coland Ct	29223
Colchester Dr	29223
Cold Branch Ct & Dr	29223
Coldstream Ct & Dr	29212
Coleman St	29205
Coles Rd	29203
Coley Rd	29209
Colin Kelly Dr	29204
College St	
500-1999	29201
2000-2299	29205
College View Ct	29212
Colleton St	29203
Collins Ct & Dr	29212
Colonial Dr	29203
Colonial Brook Dr	29209
Colonial Commons Ln	29209
Colonial Life Blvd W	29210
Colony Dr	29203
Colony House Ct	29212
Colony Park Cir & Dr	29229
Columbia Ave	29201
Columbia College Dr	29203
Columbia Mall Blvd	29223
Columbia Northeast Dr	29223
Columbiana Cir & Dr	29212
Commerce Dr	29205
Commerce Dr NE	29223
Commercial Dr	29212
Commissary Way	29207
Commonwealth Blvd	29209
Concord Dr	29204
Concourse Dr	29223
Conestoga Cir	29223
Coney St	29204
W Confederate Ave	29201
Congaree Ave	29205
Congaree Pointe Dr	29209
Conifer Ct	29229
Conners St	29204
Connie Dr	29210
Conover Rd	29210
Conrad Cir	29212
Constable Ln	29223
Converse St	29206
Conveyor St	29203
Cook Ave	29203
Coolstream Dr	29223
Cooper Ave	29205

Coopersmith 29229
Copper Ridge Rd 29212
Copperfield Ct 29209
Copperhill Ct & Ln 29229
Copperwood Ct 29229
Cora Dr & Ln 29203
Coral Ct 29229
Coral Vine Ln 29223
Coralbean Way 29229
Corbett St 29209
Corby Ct 29229
Cordata Ct 29229
Cordova Dr 29203
Corison Loop 29229
Corley St 29212
Corley Ford Rd 29203
Cornelius Dr 29203
Cornflower Dr 29229
Cornhill Rd 29210
Corning Rd 29205
Cornwall Rd 29204
Coronado Dr 29203
Coronet Dr 29206
Corporate Ln 29223
Corporate Park Blvd 29223
Cort Rd 29203
Cosentino Ct 29229
Cotesworth Dr 29229
Cotoneaster Dr 29229
Cottage Path 29212
Cottage Lake Way 29209
Cotton Hope Ln 29209
Cottonplace Ln 29201
Cottontail Ct N & S 29229
Cottonwood Ln 29210
Cottonwood Way 29229
Coulter Pine Ct & Ln 29229
Country Club Ct & Dr 29206
Country Mill Rd 29229
Country Place Ct 29212
Country Squire Dr 29212
Country Town Dr 29212
Courtland Dr 29223
Courtney Rd 29206
Courtridge St 29203
Courtwood Dr 29206
Courtyard Ln 29223
Courtyard Homes Dr 29209
Covair St 29203
Cove Ct 29212
Cove View Ct & Pt 29212
Covenant Rd 29204
Cowdray Park 29223
Cox St 29204
Coxsfield Ct 29212
Crabtree Rd 29206
Craig Rd 29204
Cramer Dr 29203
Cranbrook Ln 29223
Crane Branch Ct 29212
Crane Branch Ln 29229
Crane Church Rd 29203
Crane Creek Ct & Dr 29203
Cranewater Ct & Dr 29212
Cranley Ct & Rd 29229
Crape Myrtle Ln 29206
Craven St 29203
Crawford Rd 29203
Creative Dr 29210
Creek Dr 29210
Creek Knoll Ln 29212
Creek Manor Ln 29206
Creek Vista Way 29206
Creek Way Ct & Ln 29209
Creekfield Ct 29229
Creekleaf Ct 29212
Creekside Way 29210
Creekview Dr 29212
Creekwood Dr 29223
Crescent Ln 29212
Crescent St 29206
Crest St 29203
Crest Haven Dr 29229
Crestbrook Rd 29223
Cresthill Dr 29223
Crestland Dr 29210
Crestlite Dr 29209
Crestmont Rd 29229
Crestmore Dr 29209
Crestview Ave 29223
Crestview Rd 29212
Crestwater Dr 29229
Crestwood Dr 29205
Creton Rd 29210
Crews Dr 29210
Cricket Ct 29209
Cricket Rdg 29210
Cricket Hill Rd 29223
Cricket Tree Ln 29210
Crimson Ct 29229
Crockett Ct & Rd 29212
Crofton Way 29223
Cromer Ave 29203
Cromwell Manor Dr 29210
Crooked Creek Pl 29229
Crooked Stick Ct 29229
Crosland Ln 29223
N Cross Ct 29223
Cross Hill Rd 29205
Crossbow Ct, Dr & Pl 29212
Crossbow Lakes Ct 29212
Crossbrook Rd 29212
Crosscreek Ct & Dr 29212
Crossfield Rd 29206
Crossing Ct & Dr 29229
Crossvine Ct 29229
Crowe Ct 29210
Crown Point Rd 29209
Crowson Rd 29205
Crystal Dr 29206
Cucumber Tree Ct 29212
Cullasaja Cir 29223
Cullum St 29209
Culpepper Cir 29209
Cumberland Dr 29203
Cunningham Rd 29210
Currant Ln 29210
Currituck Dr 29210
Curry St 29204
Curtis St 29210
Curvewood Rd 29229
Cushman Dr
1700-2399 29204
2400-2499 29203
Custer Loop 29206
Custer St 29210
Cutlers Ct 29212
Cutters Cove Ct 29212
Cyclamen Ct 29212
Cypress St 29205
Cypress Cove Rd 29229
Cypress Ridge Cir 29229
Dahlia Rd 29205
Dahoon Dr 29229
Dairy St 29203
Dakota St 29203
Dale Dr 29203
Dale Valley Rd 29223
Dallas Cir 29206
Dalloz Rd 29204
Daly St 29205
Damson Ln 29209
Dana Ct 29229
Danbury Dr 29203
Danby Ct 29212
Dandridge Ct 29209
Danfield Dr 29204
Daniel Dr 29206
Daniel St 29207
Dantzler Dr 29229
E Darby Ln 29205
Darby St 29203
Dare Cir 29206
Dargan Ct 29212
Darley Ct 29223
Darlington St 29201
Darlington Oak Ct 29229
Darnell Rd 29212
Dart St 29204
Dartmoore Ln 29223
Dartmouth Ave 29203
Datura Rd 29205
Daulton Dr 29223
Davant Pl 29209
David Dr 29229
David St 29203
Davidson St 29209
Davies Dr 29223
Davis Jenkins Rd 29229
Davis Smith Rd 29203
Dawning Ln 29223
Dawson Rd 29223
Dayton St 29203
Dean Hall Ct & Ln 29209
Deans Ln 29205
Dearborn Rd 29204
Deborah Dr 29209
Decker Blvd 29206
Decker Park Rd 29206
Deer Harbour Ct 29229
Deer Hound Trl 29223
Deer Lake Dr 29229
Deer Pass Way 29229
Deer Trail Ct 29223
Deerfield Dr 29204
Deerpath Ct 29229
Deertrot Ct 29229
Deerwood St 29205
Deerwood Run Dr & Trl 29223
Delane Dr 29204
Delano Dr 29204
Delaware St 29201
Delft Ln 29210
Delilah St 29203
Dell Dr 29209
Della Mae Ct 29203
Dellwood Dr 29206
Deloach Dr 29209
Delta Dr 29209
Delverton Rd 29203
Den Hague Ct 29223
Denby Cir 29229
Denman Loop 29229
Denmark St 29201
Dennis Dr 29204
Denny Rd 29203
Dent Dr 29203
Denton Dr 29203
Depot St 29201
Deptford Dr 29212
Derbyshire Ln 29210
Destin Rd 29212
Detreville Ave 29204
Devereaux Rd 29205
Devine St
500-1199 29201
1201-1899 29201
2000-4699 29205
4700-4799 29209
Devoe Dr 29223
Devon Rd 29209
Devonshire Cir 29204
Devonshire Dr 29204
Devonshire Ln 29212
Devonwood Ct 29212
Devonwood Dr 29210
Dial St 29204
Diamond Ln 29210
Diane Dr 29210
Dibble Ln 29223
Dickens Crst 29229
Dickson Ave 29203
Dill Ct 29204
Dillon St 29205
Dinton Ct & Rd 29212
Dinwood Cir 29204
Dixiana Rd 29292
Dixie Ave 29203
Dixie Rd 29207
Dixon Dr 29203
Doby Dr 29203
Doctor Cir 29203
Dodge St 29204
Dogwood St 29205
Dolly St 29223
Dominion Dr 29209
Dominion Hills Trl 29209
Donar Ct & Dr 29229
Donau Dr 29229
Donavan Dr 29210
Donegal Ct 29223
Donna Dr 29203
Donzi Ct 29203
Doral Ct 29229
Dorchester St 29203
Dorichlee Ln 29223
Doris Ct & Dr 29210
Dorrah St 29203
Dorset Dr 29210
Dory Ct 29229
Dothan Rd 29210
Douglas St 29203
Douglas Fir Ln 29229
Doulton Way 29212
Dove Ln 29210
Dove Park Cir & Rd 29223
Dove Ridge Ct & Rd 29223
Dove Tail Rd 29209
Dove Wood Ct 29229
Dovecreek 29229
Dover St 29201
Doverside Dr 29212
Dowgate Hl 29229
Downes Grove Rd 29209
Downing St 29209
Downs Dr 29209
Drake St 29209
Drakewood Dr 29212
Drayton St 29201
Dreher St 29205
Dreher Shoals Rd 29212
Dresden Cir 29203
Drew Park 29204
Drexel St 29204
Drexel Lake Dr 29223
Dreyfuss Rd 29201
Driftwood Dr 29210
Drury Ln 29212
Dryden Ln 29212
Dual Dr 29203
Duart Ln 29210
Dubard St 29204
Dubard Boyle Rd 29203
Dublin Rd 29209
Dubose Dr 29204
Duck Pond Rd 29223
Duffie Ct 29229
Duke Ave 29203
Dukes Hill Rd 29203
Dulaney Bnd, Ct & Pl 29229
Dumbarton Rd 29212
Dumont St 29201
Dunaway Ct 29210
Dunbarton Dr 29223
Duncan St 29205
Dundee Ln 29203
Dunmore Ct 29210
Dunn St 29204
Dunnagon St 29210
Dunnock Ct 29229
Dunoon Ct 29229
Dunston Rd 29209
Dunvegan Dr 29209
Dupont Dr 29223
Durango Ave & Cir 29203
Durant St 29203
Durham Creek Ct 29229
Dutch Branch Rd 29210
Dutch Square Blvd & Mall 29210
Duval St 29201
Eagle Feather Loop 29206
Eagle Park Dr 29206
Eagle Pointe Dr 29229
Earlewood Dr 29201
Early St 29207
Eascott Pl 29229
Eason Ct 29209
Eastbourne Ct 29223
Eastbranch Ct & Rd 29223
Eastbrook Rd 29206
Easter St 29203
Easter Pine Ct 29229
Eastfair Dr 29209
Eastfern Ct 29212
Eastgrove Ct 29212
Eastlawn Dr 29210
Eastman St 29203
Eastminster Dr 29204
Eastmont Dr 29209
Eastover St 29203
Eastpine Ct & Pl 29212
Eastshore Rd 29206
Eastway Dr
100-299 29201
2900-3099 29209
Eastwood Dr 29206
Easy St 29205
Eaton St 29205
Eau Claire St 29203
Echo Springs Ct 29223
Eddy St 29203
Eden St 29201
Edenhall Dr 29229
Edens Point Rd 29212
Edgecliff Way 29229
Edgefield St 29201
Edgehill Rd 29204
Edgemore Rd 29223
Edgerow Ct 29229
Edgerton Ct 29205
Edgewater Dr 29223
Edgewood Ave 29204
Edinburgh Rd 29204
Edison St 29204
S Edisto Ave 29205
Edmond Dr 29205
Edward Ct
100-499 29205
2100-2199 29209
Edward View Rd 29203
Ehrlich St 29201
Eileen St 29209
Eisenhower Dr 29203
El Hunter Rd 29203
Elberta St 29210
Elcan St 29204
Elderberry Ln 29229
Elders Pond Cir, Ct & Dr 29229
Eldorado Ct 29203
Elise Dr 29210
Elite St 29223
Elizabeth Ave 29205
Elizabeth Darby Ln 29205
Elk Hill Rd 29203
Elkhorn Ln 29229
Elleant Rd 29210
Ellerbe St 29204
Ellery Ct 29223
Elliot Ave 29203
Ellis St 29203
Ellison Rd 29206
Ellisor St 29212
Elm Ave 29205
Elm Abode Ter 29210
Elmgren St 29210
Elmhaven Rd 29204
Elmhurst Rd 29203
Elmira St 29204
Elmon St 29203
Elmont Dr 29203
Elmore St 29203
Elmtree Rd 29209
Elmwood Ave
301-497 29201
499-1499 29201
2102-2198 29204
2200-2500 29204
2502-2698 29204
Elmwood Ct 29204
Elsing Green St 29204
Elton Ct 29229
Elton Meetze Ln 29212
Elwyn Ln 29210
Ely St 29203
Emerald Lake Rd 29209
Emerald Valley Rd 29210
Emily Ln 29223
Emory Ct & Ln 29212
Emsworth Dr 29209
Enclave Ct, Loop & Way 29223
Enfield Dr 29212
English Ave 29204
Engrid Ct 29223
Enlow Ct 29223
Ennismore Common Ln 29229
Enoree Ave 29205
Ensor Ave 29203
Enterprise Ct 29229
Epsilon Cir 29223
Erie St 29201
Erskine St 29206
Ervin St 29204
Esplanade Ln 29229
Essayons Way 29207
Essex Rd 29204
Estes Swamp Rd 29209
Ethel St 29203
Ethels Ave 29203
Etiwan Ave 29205
Euclid Ave 29203
Eugene St 29209
Eunice Ave 29203
Eureka St 29205
Evans Ct 29206
S Evans St 29201
Evansbrook Ct 29223
Eve Dr 29210
Evelyn Ct & Dr 29210
Everett St 29223
Evergreen Dr 29204
Evian Pl 29204
Ewell Rd 29207
E Exchange Blvd 29209
Executive Center Dr 29210
Executive Pointe Blvd 29210
Exeter Ln 29223
Exmoor Rd 29204
Exton Shore Dr 29209
F M Young Ave 29204
Fair St 29203
Fair Hills Loop 29209
Fair Morgan Ct 29203
Fair Oaks Dr 29203
Fairbranch Ct 29212
Faircrest Way 29229
Fairfield Rd 29203
Fairforest Ct & Rd 29212
Fairglen Ln 29223
Fairhaven Dr 29210
Fairlake Ct 29212
Fairlamb Ave 29223
Fairlawn Ct 29203
Fairleaf Ct 29212
Fairmont Rd 29209
Fairview Dr 29205
Fairway Ln 29210
Fairwold St 29223
Fairwood Dr 29209
Faison Ct 29206
Faison Dr 29203
Falcon Dr 29204
Fallen Leaf Ct & Dr 29229
Fallen Oak Dr 29229
Falling Springs Rd 29203
Falls Mill Ln 29229
Fallstaff Ct & Rd 29229
Falmouth Rise Rd 29229
Fanning St 29204
Faraway Dr 29223
Farmington Rd 29223
Farmview St 29203
Farrier Ct 29229
Farrington Way 29210
Farrow Rd 29203
Farrow Pointe Ln 29203
Farrowood Dr 29223
Fashion Dr 29229
Faulkland Rd 29210
Faunas Rd 29203
Faust Ave & St 29223
Faversham Cres, Ct & Ln 29229
Fawnhill Ct 29229
Fawnwood Ct 29203
Faye Ave 29204
Felton St 29204
Fenrir Dr 29229
Fenwick Ct 29223
Fenwick Hall Ct 29209
Ferguson St 29201
Fern Ave 29203
Fernandina Ct 29212
Fernandina Rd
3200-3798 29210
3800-3999 29210
4000-5098 29212
5100-5200 29212
5202-5298 29212
Fernleaf Rd 29206
Ferntree Ct 29210
Fernview Dr 29229
Fernwood Rd 29206
Ferrel Ln 29212
Ferrell Dr 29204
S Field Dr 29229
Fieldrush Ct 29229
Fieldwood Dr 29223
Fifeshire Ct & Dr 29212
Fillmore St 29203
Finch Wood Dr 29229
Finley Rd 29203
Finn Ct 29223
Finsbury Ct & Rd 29212
Finwood Ct 29212
Fire Thorn Ln 29223
Firebranch St 29212
Firebrick Ln 29229
Firebridge Rd 29223
Firelane Rd 29223
Fireside Dr 29212
Firestone Ct 29229
Fish Haul Rd 29209
Fisher Ave 29209
Fishers Mill Dr 29206
Fishers Shore Rd 29223
Fishers Wood Ct & Dr 29223
Fiske St 29203
Fitzgibbon Dr 29209
Flamingo Dr
1000-1299 29203
2500-2699 29209
Flamingo Rd 29212
Flat Chimney Loop 29209
Fleetwood Dr 29209
Flint St 29212
Flintgate Ct 29212
Flintlake Rd 29223
Flintwood Ct 29229
Flodden Ct 29212
Flora Cir 29223
Flora Dr 29223
Flora St 29201
Flora Way 29223
Flora Springs Cir 29223
Floran St 29203
Florawood Dr 29204
Florence St 29201
Florida St 29201
Floyd Dr 29203
Folkstone Ct & Rd 29223
Folly Ct & Ln 29209
Fonta Vista St 29204
Fontaine Pl & Rd 29223
Fontaine Center Dr 29223
Fontana Dr 29209
Fonthill Ct & Dr 29229
Foot Point Rd 29209
Fords Ct 29229
Fore Ave 29229
Forest Dr
2400-4199 29204
4200-4899 29206
4840-4840 29260
4900-5698 29206
4901-5699 29206
Forest Ln 29209

Forest Edge Rd 29212
Forest Fern Ct & Rd 29212
Forest Green Dr 29209
Forest Grove Cir & Ln 29210
Forest Hills Ct 29204
Forest Lake Pl 29206
Forest Park Rd 29209
Forest Ridge Ln 29206
Forest Trace Ct, Dr & Way 29204
Forest Trail Ct 29212
Forestgate Ct 29212
Forestgrove Ct 29212
Forestland Ct 29212
Forestview Cir & Ct 29212
Forestwood Dr 29223
Forielar St 29204
S Fork Pl 29223
Formby Dr 29223
Formosa Dr 29206
Forney St 29207
Forrister St 29223
Fort Jackson 29207
Fort Jackson Blvd
4300-4399 29205
4400-4999 29209
Forum Dr 29229
Foster St 29203
Founders Lake Ct 29229
Founders Ridge Ct & Rd 29229
Fountain Lake Ct, Pl & Rd 29209
Fowler St 29223
Fox Chase Rd 29223
Fox Cove Ct 29229
Fox Glove Ln 29210
Fox Grove Cir 29229
Fox Haven Dr 29229
Fox Knolls Ct 29229
Fox Manor Ct 29229
Fox Run Ln 29210
Fox Squirrel Cir 29209
Fox Trail Dr 29223
Fox Trot Dr 29229
Fox Wind Way 29229
Foxcroft Rd 29223
Foxfire Dr 29212
Foxhall Rd 29204
Foxhill Ct 29223
Foxhunt Rd 29223
Frampton Ct 29212
Fran Dr 29203
Frances St 29209
Frandall Ave 29223
Frank Anderson Cir 29203
Franklin St 29201
Frasier St 29201
Frasier Bay Ct & Rd 29229
Frasier Fir Ln 29229
Fraternity Cir 29201
Fredricksburg Way 29210
Freshley Ct 29212
Freshwater Dr 29229
Freya Ct 29229
Friendly Ln 29210
Friendly Woods Rd 29203
Frost Ave 29203
Frostwood Ct & Dr 29212
Frye Rd 29203
Fuchsia Ct 29223
Fuller Ave 29203
Fulton St 29205
Furman Ave 29206
Furman Smith Loop & Rd 29206
Furwood Cir 29203
Gabriel St 29203
Gadsden St 29201
Gaitwood Ct 29212
Gala Dr 29209
Galbra St 29209
Gale Dr 29210
Gale River Rd 29223
Gallivan Dr 29229
Galway Ln 29209
Gamewell Dr 29206
Garadone St 29201
Garden Dr & Plz 29204
Garden Forest Rd 29209
Garden Path Ln 29210
Garden Springs Rd 29209
Garden Valley Ln 29210
Gardendale Ct & Dr 29210
Gardenhill Dr 29229
Gardenwood Ct 29209
Garland St 29201
Garmony Cir & Rd 29212
Garner Ln 29210
Garner Springs Ct 29209
Garners Ferry Rd
4800-7405 29209
7406-8298 29209
7406-7406 29290
7407-8299 29209
Garvey Cir 29203
Gary St 29203
Gaskins Ct 29206
Gaslight Ln 29212
Gate Post Ln 29223
Gateway Ln 29210
Gateway Corners Park 29203
Gateway Corporate Blvd 29203
Gatewood Way 29229
Gatwick Ct 29223
Gauley Dr 29212
Gavilan Ave 29203
Gavin Dr 29223
Gavinshire Rd 29209
Gayle Pond Trce 29209
Gayley St 29209
Geiger Ave 29201
Genessee Valley Rd 29223
Geology Rd 29212
George Rogers Blvd 29201
George Sumner Dr 29212
Georgia St 29201
Georgia Elam Ln 29204
Geraldine Rd 29203
Germany St 29204
Gervais St
700A-700E 29201
200-1999 29201
2000-3099 29204
Gibbes Ct 29201
Gibson St 29203
Gilden Hawke Way 29229
Giles Ct 29212
Gill St 29205
Gill Creek Ct & Rd 29206
Gills Creek Pkwy 29209
Gills Crossing Ct & Rd 29223
Gilmer Ct 29206
Gingerbread Ct N & S 29229
Gingerleaf Ct 29229
Gingeroot Way 29203
Ginkgo Ct 29229
Girardeau Ave 29204
Gisbourne Ln 29209
Gist St 29201
Glacier Way 29229
Gladden St 29205
Gladiolus Dr 29229
Glasgow Dr 29209
Glen Green Dr 29203
Glen Knoll Ct, Dr & Pl 29229
Glen Oaks Rd 29210
Glen Rose Ct 29212
Glenbrooke Cir & Ct 29204
Glencrest Dr 29204
Glencroft Dr 29210
Glendale Rd 29209
Glendevon Cir, Ct & Way 29229
Glendon Rd 29203
Glenfield Rd 29206
Glengarry Dr 29209
Glenhaven Dr 29205
Glenlake Rd 29223
Glenlea Rd 29203
Glenmount St 29212
Glenn Ave 29203
Glennvale Ct 29223
Glenridge Ct & Rd 29212
Glenshannon Dr 29223
Glenshire Dr 29203
Glenthorne Rd 29203
Glenwood Ct, Pl & Rd 29204
Glenwood Springs Ct 29229
Gloria Trl 29203
Glossop Cir 29212
Gnadenhunt Rd 29209
Godbold Ct 29204
Goff Rd 29229
Going St 29201
Gold St 29203
Goldbranch Rd 29206
Golden Ct 29203
Golden Arrow Rd 29207
Golden Ingot Ln 29229
Golden Oak Cir 29203
Goldstone Dr 29212
Gonzales Ave 29203
Goodrich St 29223
Gordon Dr 29223
Gordon St 29204
Gordon Bowman St 29204
Governor Pond Rd 29203
Governors Hl 29201
Grace St 29201
Grace Hill Rd 29204
Gracemount Ln 29229
Gracern Rd 29210
Graces Way 29229
Gracewood Dr 29229
Graeme Dr 29206
Grahams Aly 29205
N Grampian Hills Rd 29223
Granary Ct 29203
Granbury Ct & Ln 29229
Granby Ln 29201
Grand Ct & St 29203
Grandflora Ln 29212
Grandview Cir & Ct 29229
Grant St 29203
Granville Rd 29209
Gray St 29209
Gray Fox Blvd 29223
Graylock Ct 29212
Graymont Ave & Cir 29205
Grays Inn Rd 29210
Great North Ct & Rd 29223
Greemount Cir 29209
Green Glen Dr 29223
Green Meade Ct 29223
Green Petal Ct 29229
Green Pines Rd 29212
Green Rose Ct & Rd 29229
Green Springs Cir, Ct & Dr 29223
Green Tree Cir & Dr 29203
Greenbow Ct 29212
Greenbriar Dr
100-199 29212
3600-3799 29206
Greenbrook Ct 29210
Greenbrook Rd 29223
Greene Ave 29207
Greene St
500-1999 29201
2000-2111 29205
2108-2108 29250
2112-2598 29205
2113-2599 29205
Greeneedle Rd 29229
Greenfield Rd 29223
Greengate Dr 29223
Greengate Park Rd 29223
Greenhill Rd 29206
Greenhouse Ct 29212
Greenlawn Dr 29209
Greenleaf Rd 29206
Greenmill Rd 29223
Greenoaks Rd 29206
Greenore Dr 29210
Greenpines Rd 29206
Greenridge Ln 29210
Greenstone Way 29212
Greenvalley Ln 29210
Greenville Cir 29210
Greenway Dr 29206
Greenwood Rd 29205
Greenwyche Ave 29210
Gregg Pkwy 29206
Gregg St
800-1999 29201
4400-4499 29207
S Gregg St 29205
Grenadier Dr 29210
Grey Crest Ct 29212
Grey Moss Ct 29229
Greybark Dr 29209
Greys Ct 29209
Greystone Blvd 29210
Grice Ct 29212
Grinders Mill Rd 29223
Gristina Ct 29229
Gristmill Ct 29223
Grosse Point Dr 29206
Grove St 29203
Grove Hall Ct & Ln 29212
Grove Park Ln 29210
Groves Wood Ct & Pl 29212
Guard Tower Ln 29209
Guernsey Dr 29203
Guild Hall Dr 29212
Guilford Green Ct 29212
Gusty Ct 29212
Gyle Ct 29223
Habitat Ct 29223
Haddington Dr 29229
Hagood Ave
1100-1599 29205
1600-1699 29204
Hair St 29209
Hale St 29203
Haley Dr 29206
Hall St 29203
Hall Dunlap Rd 29203
Hallbrook Dr 29209
Halleck Ln 29229
Halliebug Ln 29203
Halling Ct & Dr 29229
Halton Ct 29223
Halyard Ct 29229
Hamby St 29203
Hamilton Dr 29203
Hamilton Place Cir, Ct & Rd 29229
Hamlet Park Dr 29209
Hammond Ave 29204
Hampshire Dr 29210
Hampstead Ct 29229
N Hampton Ct 29209
S Hampton Ct 29209
Hampton Pkwy 29207
Hampton Pl 29209
Hampton St
400-1999 29201
2000-2399 29204
E Hampton Way 29229
W Hampton Way 29229
Hampton Creek Ct & Way 29209
Hampton Crest Trl 29209
Hampton Forest Dr 29209
Hampton Hill Rd 29209
Hampton Leas Ln 29209
Hampton Oaks Pl 29212
Hampton Ridge Rd 29209
Hampton Springs Ct 29209
Hampton Trace Ct & Ln 29209
Hamptons Grant Ct & Way 29209
Hamptonwood Ct & Way 29209
Hamrick St 29201
Hanbury Dr 29203
Hancock St 29205
W Hanover Ave 29203
Hansford Ave 29206
Hanson Ave 29204
Harban Ct 29212
Harbin Ct 29206
Harbison Blvd & Way 29212
Harbison Club Ct 29212
Harbison Station Cir 29212
Harbor Dr 29229
Harbor Vista Dr 29229
Harborside Cir & Ln 29229
Harbour Pointe Dr 29229
Hard Scrabble Rd
1-2299 29203
2300-4299 29223
4300-5099 29229
Harden St
101-1199 29205
1200-2099 29204
2100-3099 29203
4300-4399 29207
S Harden St 29205
Harden Street Ext
1400-1499 29201
3100-3599 29203
Hardwicke Rd 29210
Hardwood Ct & Dr 29229
Harietta Ave 29209
Harlem St 29209
Harmon Rd 29203
Harold St 29223
Harper Ct & St 29204
Harrells Pl 29203
Harriett Dr 29209
Harrington Ct & Ln 29223
Harrison Rd 29204
Harrogate Rd 29210
Harrow Dr 29210
Hart St 29203
Hartford St 29204
Hartley Ct 29206
Hartwood Cir 29212
Harvard Ave 29205
Harvest Ln 29203
Harvest Ridge Dr 29229
Harvey St 29201
Harwell Dr 29223
Haskell Ave 29204
Hastings Aly 29201
Hastings Point Dr 29203
Hatcher Dr 29203
Hatfield St 29204
Hathcock Ct 29210
Hatrick Ct & Rd 29209
Hatten Rd 29203
Hattie Rd 29203
Hattie Gibson Rd 29209
Havana Ct 29206
N Haven Ct 29203
Haven Dr 29209
Haven Ridge Ct & Pl 29212
Havenoak Ct 29212
Haverford Cir & Dr 29203
Haviland Cir 29210
Hawkeye Ct 29206
Hawks Nest Ct 29212
Hawthorne Ave 29203
Hayden Ln 29229
Haymarket Rd 29210
Haynesworth Rd 29205
Haywick Ct 29229
Hazel St 29223
Hazelhurst Rd 29203
Hazelwood Rd 29209
Head St 29204
Hearn Dr 29223
Hearthstone Rd 29210
Heartleaf Dr 29229
Heath Hill Rd 29206
Heather Green Dr 29229
Heather Springs Rd 29223
Heatherlaurel Ct 29223
Heatherstone Ct & Rd 29212
Heatherwood Rd 29205
Heathwood Cir 29205
Heidt St
600-1199 29205
1200-2099 29204
Heises Pond Way 29229
Helena Cir 29209
Helena Rd 29206
Helms St 29203
Helmsdale Ct 29229
Helton Dr 29229
Hemlock Dr 29201
Hemphill St 29205
Hempstead Pl 29229
Hempsted Rd 29210
Henderson St
300-499 29205
601-697 29201
699-1999 29201
Hendrix St 29203
Heneriso Rd 29206
Henry St 29204
Henry Curtis St 29209
Herbert St 29205
Hergett Dr 29203
Heritage Cir 29203
Heritage Ln 29223
Heritage Hills Ct & Dr 29203
Heritage Village Ln 29212
Heron Ct & Dr 29203
Heron Glen Dr 29229
Heron Pond Ct 29223
Hertford Dr 29210
Hester Ct 29223
Hester Green Ct 29223
Hester Woods Dr 29223
Heyward St
300-1299 29201
1500-1598 29205
1600-3899 29205
Heyward Brockington Ct, Rd & Way 29203
Hi Sierra Dr 29210
Hibernia St 29223
Hibiscus St 29205
Hickory St 29205
Hickory Forest Dr 29209
Hickory Hill Dr 29210
Hickory Knoll Rd 29203
Hickory Nut Ln 29223
Hickory Ridge Dr 29209
Hickory Trace Ct 29209
Hickory Woods Ct 29223
Hicoria Ct 29209
Hidden Pines Ln & Rd 29229
Hidden Point Dr 29229
Hidden Sands Ct 29229
High Cir & St 29203
High Glen Ct 29229
High Hampton Dr 29209
High Knoll Rd 29223
High Valley Trl 29203
Highbourne Ct 29204
Highbrook Dr 29212
Highgate Cir, Ct, Rd & Trl 29223
Highhill Ct & Dr 29209
Highland Center Dr 29203
Highland Creek Ct & Ln 29212
N & S Highland Forest Dr 29203
Highland Park Dr 29204
Highland Point Dr 29229
Highpoint Ct 29212
Highview Dr 29223
Highwood Ct 29210
Hiland Ct 29229
Hileah Cir & Dr 29209
N Hill Ct 29223
Hill St 29207
Hillandale Rd 29223
Hillbeck Dr 29210
Hillcrest Ave & Ct 29203
Hillmark Dr 29210
N & S Hillock Ct 29223
Hillpine Ct & Rd 29212
Hillridge Ct & Way 29229
Hillsborough Rd 29212
Hillshire Ct 29212
Hillside Rd 29206
Hillstar Ct 29206
Hillstone Ct 29212
Hilltop Dr & Pl 29203
Hillvale Ct & Dr 29203
Hillview Ct 29229
Hillwood Ct 29204
Hilo St 29209
Hilton St 29205
Hinton St 29203
Hobkirk Rd 29223
Hobonny Ln 29209
Hodges St 29203
Hodson Hall Dr 29229
Hogans Run 29229
Holborn Ct 29210
Holiday Cir 29206
Holliday Ct & Rd 29223
Hollingwood Dr 29223
Holloway Rd 29209
Hollowtree Ct 29212
S Holly St 29205
Holly Ridge Ct & Ln 29229
Holly Spring Rd 29212
Holly Thorn Ct 29229
Holly Tree Ct 29204
Hollywood Ct 29205
Hollywood Dr 29205
Hollywood Rd 29212
Holmes Ave 29203
Holt Dr 29205
Homestead St 29205
Honey Tree Rd 29209
Honeysuckle Trl 29229
Hood St 29207
Hope Ave 29205
Hope Rd 29203
Hornsby Rd 29203
Horry St 29203
Horse Guards Ln 29229
Horseshoe Cir & Dr 29223
Hounds Ct N & S 29223
House St
900-1199 29205
1200-1399 29204
Houston St 29203
Howard Cir 29210
Howard St 29205
Howe St 29205
Howell Ave & Ct 29203
Hoyt St 29223
Huffman Dr 29209
Huffstetler Dr 29210
Huger St 29201
Hughes St 29204
Hulda Ave 29203
Humane Ln 29209
Humble Dr 29223
Humphrey Dr 29223
Hunt Ct 29206
Hunt Club Rd 29223
Huntcliff Ct & Dr 29229
N & S Hunters Ct 29206
Hunters Blind Dr 29212
Hunters Pond Dr 29229
Huntington Ave 29205
Huntwick Ct 29206
Hurlingham Dr 29223
Huron St 29205
Hurst St 29203
Huspah Ln 29209
Hutchinson St 29203
Hutto Ct 29204
Hyatt Ave 29203
Hydrangea St 29205
Hydrick St 29203
Hyer Ct 29223
Ida Ln 29203
Idalia Dr 29206
Idlebrook Cir 29229
Idlewilde Blvd 29201
Ila Ln 29206
Ilex St 29205
Imboden St 29206
Independence Blvd 29210
India St 29223
Indian Mound Rd 29209
Indigo Chase 29229

Indigo Lake Ct 29229
Indigo Ridge Ct & Dr 29229
Indigo Springs Ct & Dr 29229
Inglesby Dr 29223
Inglewood Dr 29204
Inkberry Ct 29229
Inland Dr 29210
Inlet Way 29229
Innis Ct 29223
Innsbrook Dr 29210
Innsbruck Dr 29212
Inway Ct & Dr 29223
Ione St 29229
Irby Ave 29203
Irmo Dr 29212
Iron Spot Cir 29223
Ironcrest Ct & Way 29212
Irongate Dr 29223
Ironweed Ct 29229
Ironwood Way 29209
Irvine Ct 29212
Irwin Park Cir & Dr 29201
Isaac St 29203
Isabel St 29203
Islay Ln 29210
Isles Way 29229
Ithan Cir 29223
Ithica St 29204
Ivanhoe Dr 29210
Ivy Ln 29204
Ivy Hall Dr 29206
Ivy Square Dr & Way 29229
Ixworth Grn 29229
Jabay Dr 29229
Jackson Ave 29203
Jackson Blvd 29207
Jacob Rd 29210
Jacobs Dr 29229
Jacobsville Rd 29209
Jaggers Plz 29204
Jamaica St 29223
James St 29203
Jamil Rd
  100-599 29210
  601-697 29212
  699-700 29212
  702-798 29212
Janice Dr 29210
Jasmine Ln 29203
Jasmine Place Ct & Dr 29203
Javelin Ct 29212
Jaybird Ln 29223
Jaydeen Ct 29204
Jayne Ln 29210
Jeanette Dr 29223
Jefferson Pl 29212
Jefferson St 29201
Jefferson Allen Dr 29210
Jennings Ct 29204
Jerome Dr 29203
Jerrie Ln 29209
Jeter St 29203
Jilda Dr 29229
Jim Hamilton Blvd 29205
Jimmy Love Ln 29212
Joan St 29203
Jodo Dr 29203
Joe Frazier Ct 29209
Joe Louis Dr 29201
John Edward St 29209
John End Rd 29203
John Francis Ct 29204
John Mark Dial Dr 29209
John Wesley Rd 29209
Johnson Ave 29203
Johnson St 29207
Joiner Rd 29209
Jones St 29203
Jonwall Ct 29206
Jordan St 29206
Jordan Point Rd 29212
Jordan Springs Cir 29229
Joseph Wesley Rd 29209
Joshua St 29205
Joyce Ct 29203
Joye Cir 29206
Juarez Ct 29206
Judges Ct 29229
Judy St 29223
Julia St 29209
Julius Dixon Ln 29203
June Dr 29223
Juneau Rd 29210
Junebug Ct 29209
Juniper St 29203
Justice Sq 29201
Kaiser Ave 29204
Kaiser Hill Rd 29203
Kalmia Dr 29205
Kaminer Dr 29206
Kaminer Way Pkwy 29210
Karnvilla Ct 29229
Katherine Park Ct 29206
Kathleen Ct & Dr 29210
Kathwood Dr 29206
Katy St 29203
Kawana Rd 29205
Kay St 29210
Kayak Ct 29212
Keats Ct 29212
Keats St 29204
Keeler Dr 29229
Keenan Dr 29201
Kelford Dr 29209
Kellwood Way 29229
Kelsey St 29203
Kemberly St 29209
Kemper St 29207
Kemsing Rd 29212
Kendall Ct 29204
Kendrick Ct & Rd 29229
Kenilworth Rd 29205
Kenmore Dr 29209
Kenmore Park Dr 29223
Kenmure Ct 29229
Kenna Dr 29212
Kennebeck Ct 29229
Kennedy St 29205
Kenny Ct 29204
Kensington Pl 29209
Kensington Rd 29203
Kent St 29203
Kentucky St 29201
Kerryton Rd 29223
Kersey Rd 29212
Kershaw Rd 29207
Kershaw St 29205
Keswick Ct 29229
Keswick Rd 29210
Kettering Ct & Dr 29210
Kew Cir 29223
Key Rd 29201
Kiawah Ave 29205
Kiawah Rd 29212
S Kilbourne Ct 29205
Kilbourne Rd
  100-4199 29205
  4200-4999 29206
  5000-5199 29209
S Kilbourne Rd 29205
Kilbourne Hill Rd 29205
Kilbrannon Dr 29210
Kildare Dr 29209
Kilkee Cir 29223
Killian Loop 29203
Killian Rd 29203
E Killian Rd 29229
W Killian Rd 29203
Killian Arch 29203
Killian Baptist Cemetery Rd 29203
Killian Commons Pkwy 29203
Killian Green Ct & Dr 29229
Killian Lakes Dr 29203
E & W Killian Station Ct & Dr 29229
Killington Ct & Ln 29212
Kinard Ct 29201
Kinder Rd 29212
Kinderway Ave 29203
S King St 29205
King Arthur Ct 29223
King Charles Rd 29209
King George Way 29210
Kingbird Ct 29229
Kingfisher Ln 29203
Kingmaker Ct 29223
Kingnut Dr 29209
Kings St & Way 29223
Kings Down Ln 29203
N & S Kings Grant Dr 29209
Kings Mill Rd 29206
Kingsbridge Rd 29210
Kingsgate Dr 29205
Kingston Rd 29204
Kingston Ridge Dr 29209
Kingston Trace Ct & Rd 29229
Kingstree Ct 29203
Kingswood Dr 29205
Kinlaugh Ct 29204
Kinlock Ct 29223
Kinrose Ct 29229
Kipling Dr 29205
Kirby St 29205
Kirkbrook Ct 29212
Kirkland St 29203
Kirkman Ct 29209
Kirkwall Ct 29229
Kirkwood Rd 29205
Kismet St 29210
Kline Ct 29223
Kline St 29205
Kneece Rd 29223
Knight Ave 29206
Knight Rd 29207
Knight Valley Cir 29209
Knightbridge Rd 29223
Knightner St 29203
Knoll Rd 29203
Knollwood Ct & Dr 29209
Knowles Loop 29229
Kobold Ln 29229
Kolob St 29205
Koon Rd 29203
Koon Store Rd 29203
Kortright St 29203
Koslin St 29210
Koulter Dr 29210
La Brew Dr S 29203
La Clair Dr 29209
Labruce Ln 29205
Laburnum Dr 29205
Lacy St 29201
Ladd St 29203
Lady St
  300-1999 29201
  2000-2499 29204
Lake Ave 29206
Lake Ct 29206
E Lake Ct 29209
N Lake Dr 29212
E Lake Trl 29209
Lake Arcadia Ln 29206
Lake Carolina Blvd, Dr & Way 29229
Lake Elizabeth Dr 29203
Lake Forest Rd 29209
Lake Front Ct & Dr 29212
N & S Lake Marion Cir 29223
Lake Mist Ct 29229
Lake Murray Blvd 29212
Lake Point Rd 29206
N Lake Pointe Dr 29229
Lake Village Dr 29229
Lake Vista Ct 29229
Lake Way Ln 29209
Lakecrest Dr 29206
Lakeland Dr 29204
Lakeridge Pkwy 29203
Lakeshore Dr 29206
W Lakeside Ave 29203
Lakeview Cir 29206
Lakewood Ave 29201
Lakeworth Dr 29212
Lamar St
  3700-4029 29203
  4026-4026 29230
  4030-4098 29203
  4031-4099 29203
Lambeth Ct 29210
Lambeth Dr 29209
Lambeth Walk 29229
Lambright Cir 29203
Lame Horse Rd 29223
Lamplighter Ct 29229
Lancaster St 29201
Lance Dr 29212
Lancelot Ln 29223
Lancer Ct 29203
Lancer Dr 29212
Lancewood Rd 29210
Lander St 29206
Landgrave Rd 29206
Landmark Dr
  1-41 29210
  3600-3799 29204
Landon Place Dr 29229
Landoshire Ct 29212
Landrace Ct 29209
Landrum Dr 29206
Lanesborough Dr 29210
Lang Ct & Rd 29204
Langley Ct 29203
Langsdale Rd 29212
Langwater St 29203
Lanier Ave 29205
Lanneau Ct 29212
Lansing Cir 29203
Lantana Dr 29205
Lantern Rd 29229
Larchmont Dr 29223
Larchwood Dr 29203
Laredo Dr 29210
Large Oak Loop 29209
Larger St 29203
Larkhall Rd 29223
Larkin Ct 29203
Larkspur Ct 29212
Larkspur Ln 29229
Larkspur Rd 29212
Larry Ct 29203
Latonea Dr 29210
Lauderdale Rd 29203
Laudmon Cir 29203
Laureate Dr 29206
Laurel St
  300-398 29201
  400-1999 29201
  2000-2799 29204
Laurel Bay Ln 29229
Laurel Bluff Ct 29229
Laurel Branch Way 29212
Laurel Field Ct 29229
Laurel Hill Ln 29201
Laurel Ridge Dr 29223
Laurel Rise Ct & Ln 29229
Laurel Springs Rd 29206
Laurelhurst Ave 29210
Laurens St
  701-797 29201
  799-1099 29201
  1100-1500 29204
  1502-1598 29204
Laurie Ln 29205
Lauriston Dr 29229
Lavender St 29203
Lavington Ct 29209
Law Ln 29203
Lawand Dr 29210
Lawrence St 29210
Lawson Dr 29229
Lawton St 29203
Layton Way 29229
Lazy Acres Dr 29209
Leabrook Rd 29223
Leaf Cir 29203
Leaf Crest Ct 29210
Leaning Tree Ct & Rd 29223
Leaside Dr 29223
Leawood Ct 29206
Leconte Ct 29205
Lee Rd
  100-599 29229
  1700-4799 29207
  5600-5699 29206
  5700-10199 29207
Lee St 29205
Lee Hills Dr 29209
Lee Ridge Ct & Dr 29229
Leeds St 29210
Leesburg Rd 29209
Leeside Cir 29223
Leeward Loop 29209
Leeward Rd 29212
Legare Ln 29204
Legend Pt 29229
Legend Oaks Ct & Dr 29229
Legge Ct 29206
Legion Dr 29229
Legion Plaza Rd 29210
Legrand Rd 29223
Lehigh Ct 29223
Leila Ln 29223
Leisure Ln 29210
Leith Rd 29212
Leitner Rd 29209
Lelias Ct 29206
Lemans Ct & Ln 29209
Lennox Ct 29204
Leslie Loch Ln 29212
Lester Dr 29203
Letitia St 29203
Leton Dr 29210
Leventis Dr 29209
Lever Acres Rd 29203
Levington Ln 29209
Levity St 29203
Lewes Cir 29212
Lewis St 29203
Lewisham Ct & Rd 29210
Lexington Pointe Dr 29229
Leyden Ln 29210
Lib Lucas Rd 29203
Liberty St 29203
Liberty Hill Ave 29204
Lightwood Knot Rd 29223
Ligustrum Ln 29209
Lilac Ln 29223
Lilevil Ct 29205
Lilly Ave 29204
Limehouse Reach Rd 29210
Limerock Ln 29209
Limestone St 29206
Linbrook Dr 29204
Lincoln Pkwy 29203
Lincoln Rd 29203
Lincoln St 29201
Lincoln Inn Rd 29212
Lincolnshire Blvd & Sq 29203
Lincolnshire North Dr 29203
Lincreek Dr 29212
Linda St 29210
Lindale Ct 29204
Lindella St 29203
Linden St 29203
Lindenwood Dr 29204
Lindevon Ln 29223
Lindsay St 29201
Lingstrom Ln 29212
Linnet Ct 29229
Linsbury Cir 29210
Linwood Rd 29205
Lionburg Ct 29229
Lionsgate Dr 29223
Lippwell Ct 29229
Lipscombe Ln 29229
Liston Ln 29203
Litchfield Dr 29209
Little St 29204
Little John Dr 29209
Live Oak Ct & St 29205
Loch Dr 29210
Loch Ln 29223
Loch Lane Cir 29223
Lochleven Rd 29209
Lochmore Dr 29209
Lochweed Ct & Dr 29212
Lockewood Ln 29206
Lockleven Dr 29223
Lockner Cir, Ct & Rd 29212
Lockshire Cir, Ct & Rd 29212
Locust Rd 29223
Lofty Pine Ct & Dr 29212
Logan Rd 29229
Loggerhead Dr 29229
Lois Ct 29210
Loki Ct 29229
London Ln 29223
London Gray Dr 29229
Londonberry Cir 29210
Lone Dr 29203
Lonesome Pine Rd & Trl 29203
Long Glen Ct 29229
Long Meadow Ln 29223
Long Needle Ct & Rd 29229
Long Pointe Ln 29229
Long Ridge Dr 29229
Long Shadow Ln 29223
Longbow Ct 29212
Longbrook Rd 29206
Longcreek Dr 29210
Longleaf Rd 29205
Longreen Pkwy 29229
Longtown Rd 29229
Longtown Commons Dr 29229
Longtown Place Dr 29229
Longwood Rd 29209
Lonsford Dr 29206
Loquat Ct & Dr 29205
Lord Byron Ln 29209
Lord Nelson Ct 29209
Lorick Ave & Cir 29203
Lost Creek Ct, Dr & Pl 29212
Lost Tree Ct, Dr & Ln 29223
Lotus St 29205
Lou Ln 29203
Louis Lee Ln 29229
Louisa St 29204
Love St 29204
Lovett Ct 29229
Lowder Rd 29204
Lowell Ln 29209
Lowndes Rd 29205
Lozada Ct 29206
Lucille Dr 29204
Lucius Rd 29201
Lucy Ln 29229
Ludwell Rd 29209
Luke St 29203
Lupine Rd 29229
Luster Ln 29210
Luther Rd 29210
Luvalie St 29203
Lydgate Dr 29210
Lykesland Ct & Trl 29209
Lyles St 29201
Lyme Bay 29212
Lyndhurst Ct & Rd 29212
Lynhaven Dr 29204
Lynn St 29210
Lyon St 29204
Mabar St 29206
Mabron Rd 29209
Macdougall St 29201
Macgregor Dr 29206
Mackay St 29203
Mackays Pt 29209
Macon Rd 29209
Madera Dr 29203
Madison Rd 29204
Maggie Hipp Rd 29210
Magnolia St 29204
Magnolia Bay Ct 29229
Magnolia Bluff Dr 29229
Magnolia Glen Ln 29205
Magnolia Park Cir 29206
Magnolia Point Dr 29212
Magnolia Springs Ct 29209
Magrath St 29203
Magruder Ave 29207
Mahalo Ln 29204
Maiden Ln
  500-599 29204
  1100-1198 29205
  1200-1299 29205
Main St 29201
N Main St
  2800-3199 29201
  3300-6999 29203
Maingate Dr 29223
Mainsail Ct 29229
Majestic Cir, Ct & Dr 29223
Makeway Dr 29201
Malcolm Dr 29204
Malibu Ct & Dr 29209
Malisa Dr 29229
Mallard Landing Ct & Way 29209
Mallard Pointe Ct 29229
Mallet Hill Ct & Rd 29223
Manchester Rd 29204
Manchester Park Ct 29229
Mandel Dr 29210
Mangrove Trl 29229
Mangum St 29210
Mann Rd 29223
Manning Ave 29204
Manor Ave 29205
Manor View Ct 29212
Manorwood Ct 29212
Manse St 29203
Mansfield Ln 29203
Manzanita Ct 29203
S Maple St 29205
Maple Springs Ct 29223
Mapleleaf Dr 29229
Mapleside Dr 29229
Mapleview Ct & Dr 29212
Maplewood Dr 29205
Marathon Dr 29209
Marbrent Ct 29204
Marbun Rd 29223
March Ln 29229
Marchant Ave 29203
Marchbank Pkwy 29229
Marchese St 29223
Marco Polo Ct 29209
Margate St 29203
Margrave Rd 29203
Margurette St 29204
Marie Cir 29203
Marie St 29209
Marietta St 29204
Mariners Cir & Row 29212
Mariners Cove Dr 29229
Mariners Point Way 29229
Marion Ave 29207
Marion St
  1000-1234 29201
  1233-1233 29211
  1235-2999 29201
  1236-2998 29201
S Marion St 29205
Mark St 29203
Mark Buyck Way 29201
Market St 29201
Markham Ct & Rd 29229
Markham Rise 29229
Marksbury Dr 29203
Marlboro St 29201
Marley Dr 29210
Marling Dr 29204
Marlowe Ln 29209
Marrob Ct 29203
Mars Dr 29209
Marsh Hawk Ln 29229
Marsh Pointe Dr 29229
Marshall St 29203
Marshdeer Way 29229
Marsteller Ct & St 29203
Marston Moor Ln 29212
Martha St 29203
Marthas Glen Rd 29209
Martin Rd 29223
Martin St 29204
Martindale Rd 29223

Mary St 29209
Mary Hill Dr 29210
Marydale Ln 29210
Maryfield Dr 29229
Maryland St 29201
Mason Rd 29203
Mason Ridge Cir & Ct 29229
Massingale Rd 29210
Matthews St 29204
Mauldin Ave 29203
Mauney Ct & Dr 29201
Maurice St 29204
Maxcy St 29201
Maxwell Ln 29203
May Dr 29223
May Oak Cir, Ct & Rd 29229
Maybank St 29204
Maybelle Ct 29204
Mayer St 29203
Mayfair Dr 29209
Mayfield St 29203
Mayhaw Dr 29206
Mayland Ct 29209
Maywood Dr 29209
Mcalister St 29204
Mcarthur Ave 29204
Mcbride Ct 29229
Mccaw Rd 29204
Mcdonald St 29204
Mcduffie Ave 29204
Mcfadden St 29204
Mckinley St 29203
Mckinney Ct 29206
Mcleod Ct 29206
Mcleod Rd 29203
Mclester Ct 29203
Mcmanaway Ct 29206
Mcmillan Cir 29212
Mcnamara Ln 29229
Mcnaughton Dr 29223
Mcneely Rd 29223
Mcqueen St 29203
Mcrae St 29203
Mcwhorter Ct 29206
Mead Ct 29203
E Meadow Ct 29210
Meadow St 29205
Meadow Creek Dr 29203
Meadow Spring Dr 29229
Meadowbrook Dr 29223
Meadowbury Dr 29203
Meadowlake Ct & Dr 29203
Meadowland Ct 29210
Meadowlark Dr 29204
Meadowmist 29229
Meadowood Rd 29206
Means Ave 29210
Medical Dr 29203
NE Medical Park 29223
Medical Park Rd 29203
Medina Ct 29223
Medlins Dr 29209
Medway Rd 29205
Meech St 29210
Melbourne Dr 29203
Melinda Rd 29203
Melissa Ln 29210
Mellowood Dr 29209
Melody Ln 29210
Melrose Ct 29229
Melrose Hts 29205
Melville Cir & Rd 29212
Menlo Dr 29210
Merc Ct 29201
Mercer St 29204
Merchants Dr 29212
Mercury St 29209
Meredith Dr 29212
Meredith Ln 29205
Meredith Sq 29223
Merganser Ct 29203
Meridian Ct 29212
Merridun Ln 29209
Merril Leaf Ct 29229
Merrill Rd 29209
Merrimac Dr 29209
Merry Wood Rd 29210
Metal Park Dr 29209
Metro Ln 29209
Metso Way 29229
Metze Rd 29210
Meyer Ln 29229
Michigan St 29205
Mickens Rd 29201
Middle St 29223
Middleburg Dr 29204
Middlesex Rd 29210
Middleton Ct & St 29203
Midgard Ct 29229
Midland Dr 29204
Mikell Ln 29205
Mildred Ave 29203
Miles Rd 29223
Miles Park Ct & Dr 29223
Milford Rd 29206
Mill Creek Pkwy 29209
Mill Field Rd 29223
Millbrook Rd 29223
Miller Ave 29203
Millet Ridge Ct 29223
Millhouse Cir & Ct 29223
Millpond 29204
Mills Dr 29204
Mills Rd 29206
Millstone Ct 29223
Millwood Ave 29205
N Millwood Ave 29204
Milton Ln 29209
Mimosa Rd 29205
Mindenti Rd 29223
Minerva St 29209
Miot St 29204
Miramar Dr 29203
W Miriam Ave & Ct 29203
Mirror Lake Rd 29209
Mistwoode Rd 29210
Misty Morning Dr 29229
Misty Oak Rd 29223
Misty Ridge Ct 29229
Misty Vale Cir & Ln 29210
Mitchell St 29205
Mockernut Ln 29209
Mockingbird Rd 29204
Moet Dr 29210
Monarch Ln 29229
Monckton Blvd 29206
Mondamin Rd 29210
Monmouth Ct 29209
Monroe St 29205
Montadale Dr 29209
N Montague Dr 29203
Montague Rd 29209
Montclair Dr 29206
Montcrest Ct & Rd 29210
Monteith St 29203
Monterey Ct & Pl 29206
Montgomery Ave 29205
Montgomery Ln 29209
Montgomery Rd 29203
Monticello Rd & Trl 29203
Montlake Ave 29203
Montreat Ct 29209
Mood Ct 29206
Moody View Ct 29223
Moolah Dr 29223
Moone Cross Dr 29209
Moonglo Cir 29223
Moonlight Dr 29210
Moore Hopkins Ln 29210
Moores Creek Dr 29209
Moorland Dr 29223
Morning Echo Dr 29229
Morning Ridge Ct 29229
Morninghill Dr 29210
Morninglo Ln 29223
Morningside Dr 29210
Morningwalk 29229
Moseby St 29207
Moses St 29203
Moss Ave 29205
Moss Field Ct & Rd 29229
Moss Springs Rd 29209
Mosshill Rd 29206
Mosswood Rd 29206
Mossy Oaks Ct 29203
Moultrie Ct 29223
Mount Pilgrim Church
Rd 29223
Mount Vernon St 29203
Mountain Dr 29203
Mountain Laurel Ct &
Ln 29223
Mountainbrook Dr 29209
Muir St 29203
Muirfield Dr 29212
Mulberry Ln 29201
Muller Ave 29203
E Muller Ave 29203
Muller Ct 29206
Munsen Spring Dr 29209
Murchison Dr 29229
Murdock Rd 29203
Murray St 29205
Murrayhill Cir 29212
Murrayview Dr 29212
Murraywood Ct & Dr 29212
Muse Ct 29206
Musgroves Mill Ln 29209
Musket Ln 29223
Myers Cv & St 29203
Myles Ave 29203
Myrtle Ct 29205
Myrtle Bank Pl 29209
Mystic Way Dr 29229
Myton Ct & Rd 29212
Nancy Ave 29223
Nandina Rd 29206
Nannie Kelly Rd 29203
Nannyberry Ln 29210
Natchez Ct 29229
Nates Rd 29223
National Guard Rd 29201
Nationsbank 29222
Nautique Cir 29229
Nearview Ave 29223
Nell St 29223
Nelson Ave 29206
Nelson Rd 29203
Nelsons Ferry Ct 29209
Nephi St 29205
Neptune Dr 29209
Nestle Ct 29209
Nevada St 29201
Nevamar Dr 29223
New Grant Ct 29209
New Holland Cir 29203
New Holland Ct 29210
New Holland Dr 29203
New Lake Dr 29210
New Life Fitness Dr 29229
New Way Ct & Rd 29223
New York Ave 29204
Newbond Way 29212
Newburgh Dr 29203
Newcastle Dr 29223
Newcourt Pl 29229
Newell Rd 29209
Newgate End 29229
Newland Rd 29229
Newman Ave 29201
Newnham Dr 29210
Newpark Pl 29212
Newport Dr 29223
Newport Hall Ln 29209
Newquay Ct 29229
Newstead Ct & Way 29229
Newstead Rise 29229
Newworth Ct 29229
Niblick Ct 29223
Nicie Byrd Way 29209
Nicklaus Ln 29229
Night Hawk Way 29229
Night Heron Ct 29229
Nightingale Dr 29229
Nina Lee Dr 29203
Nine Alters Ct 29212
Nipper Creek Rd 29203
Noah Ct 29209
Nob Hill Rd 29210
Nobility Dr 29210
Noble Ave 29203
Norman St 29203
Normandy Rd 29210
Norris St 29209
Norse Dr & Way 29229
Northbrown Ct & Rd 29229
Northeast Dr 29203
Northfern Ct 29212
Northfield Ct 29229
Northgate Rd 29223
Northgrove Ct 29212
Northlake Rd 29223
Northman Dr 29210
Northpine Ct 29212
Northridge Rd 29206
Northshore Rd 29206
Northway Rd 29201
Northwood St 29201
Norton Hope Ct 29212
Norwood Rd 29206
Nottingham Ct
1-99 29209
100-199 29210
Nottingham Rd 29210
E Nottingham Rd 29210
Nottingwood Dr 29210
Nubbin Ridge Rd 29203
Nunamaker Dr 29210
Nursery Rd 29212
Nursery Hill Rd 29212
Nursery Ridge Ln 29212
Nut Hatch Ct 29223
N Oak Ct 29212
S Oak Ct 29212
Oak St
800-1199 29205
1200-2199 29204
Oak Bluff Ct 29223
Oak Cove Ct & Dr 29229
Oak Creek Cir 29223
Oak Edge Ct 29212
Oak Hollow Ct
1-99 29209
100-199 29212
Oak Manor Dr 29229
Oak Park Dr 29223
Oakbrook Ct & Dr 29223
Oakbrook Village Ct &
Rd 29223
Oakcrest Dr & Rd 29223
Oakdale St 29201
Oakfield Rd 29206
Oakgrove Ct 29209
Oakhaven Rd 29204
Oakhill Rd 29206
Oakland Ave 29203
Oakleaf Rd 29206
Oakley Cir, Ct & Dr 29223
Oakman Ct & Ln 29209
Oakmont Dr 29223
Oakridge Dr 29204
Oakside Ln 29223
Oakview Rd 29204
Oakway Dr 29223
Oakwood Dr 29206
Oberlin Rd 29212
Oberon Pl 29223
Ocelot Trl 29203
Oceola St 29205
Oconee St 29201
Odin Ct 29229
Office Park Ct & Rd 29223
Ogden St 29204
Ohara Ct 29204
Ohio St 29201
Old Arms Ct 29212
Old Brass Dr 29229
Old Clayton Ct 29205
Old Clemson Rd 29229
Old Coach Dr 29203
Old Colony Rd 29209
Old Dairy Dr 29201
Old Fairfield Rd 29203
Old Farm Rd 29223
Old Field Ct & Rd 29223
Old Friars Rd 29210
Old Garners Ferry Rd 29209
Old Hampton Ln 29209
Old Home Pl 29212
Old Hopkins Rd 29209
Old Iron Rd 29229
Old Lamplighter Rd 29206
Old Leesburg Rd 29209
Old Legrand Rd 29223
Old Manor Rd 29210
Old Mill Cir & Ct 29206
Old Neck Rd 29206
Old Oak Dr 29203
Old Park Cir & Dr 29229
Old Percival Rd 29223
Old Pond Ln & Way 29212
Old Ridge Ct 29212
Old Satchelford Rd 29223
Old Saybrook Dr 29210
Old Selwood Trce 29212
Old Shandon Cir 29205
Old Sheperd Rd 29210
Old Sloan Rd 29223
Old South Dr 29209
Old Still Rd W 29223
Old Stone Rd 29229
Old Trace Ct 29209
Old Veterans Rd 29209
Old Willowby St 29223
Old Wood Ct, Dr & Pl 29212
Old Woodlands Ct &
Rd 29209
Olde Knight Pkwy 29209
Olde Springs Cir, Ct &
Rd 29223
Oleander Mill Ct, Dr &
Way 29229
Olga Dr 29229
Olive Dr 29203
Olive St 29205
Olympia Ave 29201
Omarest Dr 29210
Omega Dr 29223
Oneil Ct 29223
Ontario St 29204
Opus Ct 29209
Orangeburg St 29204
Orchard Cir 29206
Oriole Rd 29204
Orr St 29204
Oscar St 29204
Osprey Pond Ct 29223
Ostlund Dr 29210
Ostrich Cir 29229
Otranto Ln 29209
S Ott Rd 29205
Otter Trail Ct 29203
Ouida St 29223
Outlet Pointe Blvd 29210
Outrigger Ln 29212
Ovanta Rd 29209
Overbranch Dr 29223
Overbrook Dr 29205
Overcreek Rd 29206
Overdale Dr 29223
Overhill Rd 29223
Overland Dr 29203
Owens Rd
200-299 29206
900-1299 29203
6900-6999 29206
Oxford Rd 29209
Oxford Commons Way 29209
P C Richards Ln 29203
Paces Brook Ave 29212
Paces Run Blvd & Ct 29223
Paddington Rd 29203
Paddock Pl 29223
Padgett Rd 29209
Page St 29205
Paisley Ln 29210
Palace Dr 29210
Palace Green Ct 29210
Palatine Rd 29209
Palisades Cir 29223
Pall Mall St 29201
W Palm Dr 29212
Palm Ln 29203
Palm Hill Ct & Dr 29212
Palm Lake Dr 29212
Palm Point Dr 29212
Palm Tree Ln 29210
Palmer Rd 29205
Palmetto Ave & Plz 29203
Palmetto Health Pkwy 29212
Palmetto Park Cir 29229
Palmetto Springs Dr 29229
Palmland Dr 29209
Palston Ct 29210
Pamela Dr 29209
Pamlico Cir 29206
Paperbark Ct 29209
Paramount Dr 29209
Paris Rd 29210
Park Cir & St 29201
Park Central Dr 29203
Park Lake Cir 29223
Park Shore Dr E 29223
Park Springs Rd 29223
Park Terrace Dr 29212
Parker Ln 29206
Parker St 29201
S Parker St 29201
Parkhaven Ct 29209
Parkingson Dr 29223
Parklane Rd 29223
Parkman Dr 29206
Parkridge Dr 29212
Parkside Dr 29203
Parkview Dr 29223
Parkway Cir 29203
Parkwood Dr 29204
Parliament Dr 29223
Parliament Lake Ct &
Dr 29223
Parnell Ct 29229
Parrish Dr 29206
Parsons Mill Ln 29229
Partridge Dr 29206
E & W Passage Ct 29212
Pasture Ln 29201
Patio Dr & Pl 29212
Patricia Dr 29209
Patrick Dr 29203
Pats Dr 29203
Patterson Rd 29209
Paul St 29203
Pavilion Tower Cir 29201
Pavillion Ave 29205
Paxton St 29204
Payne St 29203
Payton Pl 29203
Peaceful Ln 29223
Peachtree Cir 29206
Peachwood Dr 29203
Peacock Path 29203
Peale St 29203
Pearl St 29203
Pebble Creek Rd 29223
Pebble Gate 29212
Peeples St 29203
Pelham Dr 29209
Pelican Cir & Dr 29203
Pell St 29209
Pembroke Ave 29205
Pembury Ct 29223
Pendleton St
400-1999 29201
2100-2599 29205
Penhurst Ct 29229
Peninsula Way 29229
Pennfield Dr 29223
Pennington Rd 29209
Pennington Square
Way 29209
Pennridge Ct 29229
Pennsylvania Ave 29204
Pennywell Ct 29229
Penrose Dr 29203
Pepper St 29209
Peppercorn Ln 29223
Pepperwood Ct 29229
Percival Rd
100-799 29206
1000-3699 29223
3800-4799 29229
Percival Woods Rd 29223
Peregrine Ct 29203
Perry Ct 29206
Perry Oaks Ln 29229
Pershing Rd 29206
Persimmon St 29205
Petal Ct 29203
Peter Paul Ct 29209
Petigru St 29204
Petworth Ct & Dr 29229
Peyton Rd 29209
Pheasant Ct 29204
Phelps St 29205
Phillips Ct 29206
Phillips St 29203
Philmont Dr 29223
Phoenix Ct 29209
Picadilly St 29201
Pickens Ave 29207
Pickens St
100-499 29205
500-1999 29201
S Pickens St 29205
Pickett St 29205
Pickett Hill Rd 29203
Pickwick Dr 29223
Piedmont Ave 29203
Piedmont Rdg 29229
Pin Oak Ct 29229
Pinckney Dr 29209
Pincushion Ln & Rd 29209
Pindo Palm Ln 29203
Pine Ct 29203
Pine St
700-1199 29205
1200-1500 29204
1502-1598 29204
Pine Belt Rd 29204
Pine Bluff Rd 29229
Pine Cliff Ct 29209
Pine Cone Ct & Dr 29204
Pine Forest Cir 29204
Pine Forest Ct 29210
Pine Forest Dr 29204
Pine Forest Trl 29210
Pine Grove Ct 29206
Pine Island Rd 29212
Pine Landing Ct 29229
Pine Lee Rd 29223
Pine Lilly Dr 29229
Pine Mast Ct 29209
Pine Oak Dr 29223
Pine Shadow Ct & Trl 29210
Pine Springs Rd 29210
Pine Tops Rd 29210
Pine Tree Cir 29206
Pine Valley Rd 29206
Pinebranch Rd 29206
Pinebrook Rd 29206
Pineclave Cir & Ct 29229
Pinecrest Ct 29204
Pinecroft Ct 29229
Pinedale Dr 29223
Pinefield Rd 29206
Pinegate Ct 29223
Pinehaven Ct 29205
Pinehill Rd 29206
Pinehurst Rd 29204
Pinelake Rd 29223
Pineland Dr 29203
Pinelane Rd 29223
Pinemont Dr 29206
Pineneedle Rd 29203
Pineridge Rd 29206
Pinestraw Rd 29206
Pinevale Dr 29203
Pineview Dr 29209
Pinewood Dr 29205
Piney Grove Rd 29210
Piney Woods Rd
100-599 29212

600-1199 29210
Pinnacle Dr 29212
Pinnacle Point Ct & Dr . 29223
Pinnacle Ridge Dr 29229
Pinnata Rd 29223
Pinson St 29203
Pintail Ln 29229
Pisgah Dr 29209
Pisgah Church Rd 29203
Pitney Rd 29212
Pittsdowne Rd 29210
Plain St 29204
Plainfield Rd 29206
Planters Dr 29209
Pleasant Ridge Dr 29209
Pleasant Springs Ct 29212
Plover Ct 29203
Plowden Rd 29205
Plumbers Rd 29203
Plumer Dr 29204
Plyler Ln 29229
Plymouth Rock Rd 29209
Poachers Ln 29223
Poe St 29201
Poinsett Loop 29209
Poinsettia St 29205
Point Comfort 29209
Polo Rd 29223
Polo Hill Ct & Rd 29223
Polo Park Ct 29223
Polo Ridge Cir 29223
Pond Oak Ct & Ln 29212
Pond Ridge Rd E 29223
Pond Shore Pl 29209
Ponte Vedra Dr 29206
Pontiac Ave 29223
Pope St 29201
Poplar Grove Ln 29203
Poplar Ridge Rd 29206
Poplar Springs Ct 29223
Portchester Ct & Dr 29203
Porter Dr 29209
Porter St 29203
Portobello Ct & Rd 29206
Possum Run 29223
Post Oak Ct & Way 29212
Powell Rd 29203
Prause Ct 29206
Prentice Ave 29205
Prescott Rd 29203
Preserve Ln 29209
Press Lindler Rd 29212
Pressley St 29209
Prestley Dr 29203
Preston St 29205
Preston Green Ct & Dr 29209
Preston Hills Ct & Dr ... 29210
Prestwick Cir 29223
Price Ave 29201
Prices Ct 29212
Pridmore St 29209
Prince Charles Ct 29209
Prince Edward Ct 29209
Prince Wales Dr 29209
Princess St 29205
Princeton St 29205
Pringle Rd 29209
Privet Ct 29203
Professional Park Rd ... 29229
Promenade Pl 29229
Promentory Rd 29209
S Prospect St 29205
Providence St 29204
Providence Crossing Dr 29203
Providence Manor Ct ... 29203
Providence Plantation Cir & Ct 29203
Pruitt Dr 29204
Pryor Ct 29204
Pulaski St 29201
Puritan Rd 29209
Putnam St 29204
Quail Ln 29206
Quail Vly E 29212
Quail Vly W 29212
Quail Trace Dr 29212
Quaker Rd 29223
Quality Ct 29229
Quantas Dr 29223
S Queen St 29205
Queen Anne Ct 29210
Queens Way Dr 29209
Queensbury Ct 29212
Quiet Ln 29223
Quill Ct & Dr 29212
Quinby Pl 29209
Quincannon Rd 29212
Quinine Hl & Ln 29204
Quinton Ln 29229
Quitman St 29204
Quoin Ct 29229
Rabon Rd
100-699 29223
700-799 29203
Rabon Croft Rd 29209
Rabon Farms Ln 29223
Rabon Pond Dr 29223
Rabon Springs Rd 29223
Radcliffe Rd 29206
Radcot Ct 29229
Radio Ln 29210
Ragsdale Dr 29209
Rail Fence Dr 29212
Railroad Ave 29203
Rainsborough Way 29229
Raintree Dr 29212
Ramblewood Dr 29209
Ramona St 29209
Ramsgate Dr 29210
Ranch Rd 29206
Ranchero Dr 29223
Randall Ave 29203
Randolph St 29203
Ransom Dr 29206
Rapids Ct & Rd 29212
Ratchford Way 29229
Rauch Dr 29209
Raven Hill Rd 29204
S Ravenel St 29205
Ravenwing Ct 29209
Ravenwood Rd 29206
Rawl St 29203
Rawlins Ln 29223
Rawlinson Rd 29209
Rawlinson Place Rd 29209
Raymond St 29223
Read St 29204
Reamer Ave 29206
Red Berry Ct 29229
Red Cedar Dr 29229
Red Cliff Rd 29212
Red Coat Ln 29223
Red Fox Ct 29223
Red Hill Rd 29203
Red Ivy Ln 29229
Red Maple Ct 29229
Red Oak Rd 29223
Red Thorn Ct 29229
Redbud Dr 29210
Redridge Ter 29203
Redstone Way 29212
Redwood Ct 29223
Reeder Ct 29209
Reeder Point Dr 29209
Reeves Cir 29223
Regal Ct & Dr 29212
Regatta Ct, Pt & Rd 29212
Regency Dr & Pl 29212
Regency Park Dr 29210
Regents Ct 29209
Reidy Ct 29223
Rembert St 29201
Rembert Martin Park ... 29210
Remington Dr 29223
Renaissance Way 29204
Research Dr 29203
Reseda Dr 29223
Restredg St 29207
Retreat Ln 29209
Revelstoke Dr 29203
Rexton Ct 29229
Reynolds Dr 29204
Rhame Rd 29229
Rhea St 29203
Rhett Rd 29210
Rhett St 29203
Rice Ct & St 29205
Rice Bent Way 29229
Rice Creek Farms Rd .. 29229
Rice Meadow Cir & Way 29229
Rice Pointe Ct 29203
Rice Terrace Dr 29229
Ricemill Fry 29229
Richard St 29209
Richcreek Rd 29203
Richfield Dr 29201
Richland St
301-397 29201
399-1999 29201
2300-2599 29204
Richland Medical Park Dr 29203
Rickenbaker Rd 29205
Ricky Ln 29229
Ridarr Dr 29229
N Ridge Rd 29223
Ridge Lake Dr 29209
Ridge Point Rd 29223
Ridge Pond Dr 29229
Ridge Shot Rd 29212
Ridge Spring Dr 29229
Ridge Trail Dr 29229
Ridgecrest Ct 29229
Ridgedale St 29203
Ridgeley Pl 29210
Ridgemont Dr 29212
Ridgemont St 29203
Ridgeside Ct 29229
Ridgetop Ct 29229
Ridgeway St 29203
Ridgewood Ave 29203
Ridgewood Camp Rd ... 29203
Riding Ridge Rd 29223
Rigby Dr 29204
Riley Ct & St 29201
Rio Rose Cir 29205
Ripley Station Cir & Rd 29212
Ripplemeyer Ave 29203
Ripplerock Rd 29210
Risdon Way 29223
Risley Rd 29223
Rivendale Ct & Dr 29229
River Dr 29201
River Rd 29212
River Birch Ln 29206
River Birch Rd 29229
River Bluff Blvd, Ct & Way 29210
River Ridge Rd 29210
River Valley Dr 29201
Riverhill Cir 29210
Rivermont Dr 29210
Riverside Cir 29210
Riverview Ct 29201
Riverwind Dr 29210
Riviera Rd 29205
Rivkin Blvd 29223
Roberson St 29203
Robert Springs Rd 29204
Roberts St 29203
Roberts Land Rd 29223
Robin Rd 29204
Robin Hood Ct 29205
Robin Nest Rd 29223
Robins Egg Ct & Dr 29229
Robinwood Rd 29206
Robney Ct & Dr 29209
Rock Springs Rd 29223
Rockbridge Rd 29206
Rockcreek Dr 29203
Rockerfella Ln 29223
Rockhaven Dr 29223
Rockingham Ct & Rd ... 29223
Rockland Rd 29210
Rockwood Rd 29209
Rocky Branch Ln 29209
Rocky Creek Trl 29212
Rocky Point Dr 29212
Rockyknoll Dr 29203
Rockymount Rd 29203
Rockyview Dr 29203
Rodborough Rd 29212
Rolling Green Ln 29210
Rolling Hills Ct & Rd ... 29210
Rolling Knoll Dr 29229
Rolling Pines Dr 29206
Rolling Pines Rd 29210
Rolling Rock Rd 29212
Rollingview Ln 29210
Rollingwood Trl 29210
Romain Dr 29210
Rome Rd 29212
Romeo Johnson Rd 29203
Romford Rd 29203
Ronald Ln 29203
Ronnie St 29203
Ronson St 29209
Roof St 29223
Rook Branch Ln 29209
Roosevelt St 29203
Roper St 29206
Roper Pond Cir 29206
Roscoe St 29204
Rose Dr 29205
Rose Branch Ct & Ln .. 29229
Rose Cottage Ln 29203
Rose Creek Ct & Ln ... 29229
Rose Hill Ct 29210
Rose Trailer Park 29203
Roseangel Ct 29229
Rosebank Ct & Dr 29209
Roseberry Ln 29223
Rosebud St 29203
Rosedale Arch 29203
Roselle Dr 29210
Rosepine Dr 29223
Rosewood Dr
600-1399 29201
1401-1797 29205
1799-4399 29205
4400-4499 29209
Rosewood Hills Dr 29205
Roslyn Dr 29206
Ross Rd 29223
Rothberry Ct 29229
Round Table Ct 29209
Roundtop Rd 29205
Rowe Cir 29212
Roxann Rd 29223
Roxboro Dr 29223
Royal Crest Dr 29229
Royal Curtis Dr 29212
N & S Royal Fern Ln .. 29203
Royal Palm Blvd 29212
Royal Woods Rd 29210
Royalgate Dr 29223
Royster St 29205
Rugby Rd 29203
Rumar St 29203
Running Brook Rd 29223
Running Fox Ct & Rd .. 29223
Running Ridge Ct 29223
Rushfoil Dr 29229
Rushmore Rd 29210
Rushwood Ct 29209
Russell St 29203
Rustic Ct 29210
Rusting Oak Dr 29209
Rusty Barn Rd 29212
Ruth St 29203
Ruthberry Ct 29229
Ruther Glen Ct 29210
Rutland Ct 29206
Rutledge Pl 29212
Rutledge St 29204
Rutledge Hill Rd 29209
Ryan Ave 29203
Rye Creek Dr 29212
Saddlechase Ln 29223
Saddlefield Rd 29203
Saddleridge Rd 29223
Saddletrail Rd 29203
Saddlewood Pl 29210
Sagamare Rd 29229
Sagebrook Rd 29223
Sageland Pl 29223
Sago Palm Dr 29212
Sail Pt 29229
Sail Point Ct & Way 29212
Sailing Club Dr 29229
Saint Andrews Ct 29210
Saint Andrews Rd
7223B-7223C 29212
100-4599 29210
6000-7299 29212
Saint Anthony Rd 29223
Saint Claire Dr 29206
Saint George St 29223
Saint Ives Rd 29223
Saint James Rd 29210
Saint James St 29205
Saint Julian Pl 29204
Saint Louis Ave, Ct & St 29204
Saint Margaret St 29209
Saint Michaels Ln 29212
Saint Michaels Rd 29210
Saint Patrick Rd 29210
Saint Phillips St 29204
Sal Sue Ct 29203
Salem Dr 29203
Sallie Baxter Rd 29209
S Saluda Ave 29205
Saluda Ferry Rd 29212
Saluda River Rd 29210
Salusbury Ln 29229
Sam Snead Ct 29229
Samol Cir 29203
Sams Crossing Rd 29229
Samson Cir 29203
Sand Iris Ct 29229
Sand Spur Rd 29223
Sandale Dr 29206
Sandalewood Ct & Ln .. 29212
Sandhill Rd 29206
Sandhurst Rd 29210
Sandmyrtle Cir 29229
Sandpine Cir, Ct & Rd . 29229
Sandpiper Ln 29203
Sandra Dr 29209
Sands St 29201
Sandstone Ct & Rd 29212
Sandwedge Ct 29203
Sandwood Dr 29206
Sandy Glen Ct 29223
Sandy Knoll Ct 29209
Sandy Lake Rd 29229
Sandy Ridge Rd 29206
Sandy Shore Rd 29206
Sandy Springs Ct 29210
Sanford Dr 29206
Sanibel Cir 29223
Santee Ave 29205
Sapling Dr 29210
Sara Dr 29223
Sara Matthews Rd 29203
Saramont Rd 29205
Sasanqua Cir 29209
Sassafras Springs Dr ... 29229
Satchelford Rd 29206
Saturn Ln 29209
Saturn Pkwy 29212
Savannah Dr 29203
Sawdust Ct 29209
Sawgrass Ct 29229
Sawtimber Ln 29209
Sawtooth Ln 29229
Saxon Shore Rd 29209
Saxonbury Dr 29223
Saye Cut 29209
Scales Ave 29207
Scaleybark Dr 29210
Scarlet Ct 29223
Scarlet Sage Ln 29223
Scarsdale Dr 29203
Schofield Ln 29229
School House Rd 29204
School Yard Ct 29209
Schooner Ct 29229
Schooner Ln 29212
Science Ct 29203
Scioto Dr 29203
Scotch Pine Rd 29209
Scotsman Rd 29223
Scott St 29201
Scottish Ct 29229
Scottsdale Ct 29229
Screech Owl Ct 29209
Scrubby Oaks Ln 29223
Scurry St 29204
Sea Gull Ln 29203
Sea Hawk Ct & Ln 29203
Seaboard Aly 29201
Seaboard Ave 29203
Seabury St 29203
Seafarer Ln 29212
Seals Rd 29203
Seawright Rd 29210
Seay Ct 29206
Sebring Dr 29212
Sedgefield Rd 29210
Sedgewood Dr 29203
Seehorne Ct 29229
Selmun St 29210
E & W Selwood Ct & Ln 29212
Seminole Rd 29210
Semmes Rd 29207
Senate St
300-1999 29201
2000-2700 29205
2702-2798 29205
Seneca Ave 29205
Senegal Ln 29229
Sepia Ct 29229
Sequoia Rd 29206
Sesqui Ct & Trl 29223
Seton Rd 29212
Seton Hall Ct & Dr 29223
Setting Sun Ln 29212
Seven Oaks Ln 29210
Seven Springs Rd 29223
Sewick Cir 29223
Sexton Ct 29206
Shadetree Ct 29212
Shadow Pt 29229
Shadow Creek Ct 29209
Shadow Grey Ct 29223
Shadow Lawn Rd 29206
Shadow Mist Ln 29210
Shadowbrook Dr 29210
N Shadowbrook Dr 29223
Shadowleaf Ct 29212
Shadowood Ct & Dr 29212
Shadowpine Rd 29212
Shady Ln 29206
Shady Mist Dr 29229
Shaftesbury Ln 29209
Shagbark Ave 29209
Shakespeare Ln & Rd .. 29223
Shale Ln 29223
Shalimar Dr 29206
Shallow Brook Dr 29223
Shallow Pond Rd 29206
Shamley Green Dr 29229
Shamrock Ct 29205
S Shandon Pl & St 29205
Shannon Springs Rd ... 29206
Shannondale Ct 29209
Sharebrook Ln 29212
Shareditch Rd 29210
Sharon Cir 29205
Sharpe Rd 29203
Shaw St 29203
W Shawnee Rd 29210
Shealy St 29203
Sheath Dr 29212
Sheffey Ct 29209
Sheffield Rd 29204
Shelby Dr 29223
Sheldon Ln 29209
Sheldon Pl 29223
Shelley Rd 29209
Shellnut Ave 29209
Shellwood Ct 29229
Shellywood Ln 29212
Shelter Cove Ct 29212
Shelton Dr 29212
Sheraton Rd 29209
Sherborne Cir 29212
Sherborne Ct 29229
Sherborne Ln 29229
Sherbrook Ct & Dr 29223
Sheridan Dr 29223
Sheringham Rd 29212
Sherry Ct 29223
Sherwood Rd 29204
Sheryl Ln 29204
S Shields Rd 29223
Shiran St 29209
Shirley St 29205
Shirlington Rd 29210
Shivers Rd 29210
Shop Rd
1000-2499 29201
2500-2899 29209
Shop Grove Dr 29209
Shore View Dr 29212
Shorebrook Dr 29206
N Shorecrest Dr & Rd .. 29209
Shoreditch Dr 29209
Shoreham Ct 29210
Shoreline Dr
1-99 29229
100-399 29212
Shorewood Ct & Way .. 29212
Short St 29205
Shortbow Ct 29212
Shortstream Ct & Rd ... 29212
Shoup Ct 29206
Shropshire Dr 29209
Shuler Cir, Ct & Rd 29212
Sidney Rd 29210
Siegfried Ln 29229
Sierra Ct 29204
Sigma Ct 29223
Sigmund Cir 29204
N & S Silas Brook Ct .. 29203
Silo Ct 29201
Silver St 29201
Silver Crest Dr 29223
Silver Fox Ln 29212
Silver Lake Cir 29212
Silver Lake Rd E 29223
Silver Oak Cir 29203
Silver Palm Dr 29212
Silver Pine Ct 29229
Silver Springs Ln 29229
Silverbell Ct 29229
Silverleaf Ct 29209
Silvermill Ct & Rd 29210
Silverwood Trl 29229
Simmon Tree Ln 29201
Simpkins Ln 29204
Simpson St 29203
Sims Aly 29205
Sims Ave 29205
S Sims Ave 29205
Sims Ct 29206
Sinclair Dr 29203
Singleton Dr 29203
Sinkler Rd 29206
Skiff Ln 29229
Skii Ln 29206
Skipwith Ave 29209
Skyland Ct & Dr 29210
Skylark Dr 29209
Skyview Dr 29203
Slab Pile Rd 29203
Slash Pine Ln 29203
Slatestone Trl 29203
Slighs Ave
2000-2099 29203
2100-2399 29204
Sloan Ct 29223
Sloan Rd 29223
Sloan St 29205
Smallwood Cir & Rd 29223

Smith St 29209
Smithfield Rd 29223
Smiths Market Ct & Rd 29212
Smitty Rd 29212
Snow Rd 29223
Social Cir 29229
Softwood Ln 29229
Solidago Ct 29229
Solomon St 29203
Somerton Ct
- 1-99 29209
- 600-699 29212

Somerton Pl 29209
Sommerset Dr 29223
Sonata Ct 29203
Songbird Dr 29209
Sonny Ct 29223
Sorenson Dr 29229
Sorrel Tree Dr 29223
South St 29203
Southbury Dr & Ln 29209
Southdown Dr 29209
Southern Dr 29201
Southern Pine Rd 29229
Southfern Ct 29212
Southgrove Ct 29212
Southlake Ct & Rd 29223
Southpine Ct 29212
Southport Dr 29229
Southwark Cir 29223
Southwell Ct 29209
Southwell Rd 29210
Southwood Dr 29205
Spalding Ave 29203
Spanish Trl 29210
Spann St 29204
Sparkleberry Ln 29229
Sparkleberry Crossing Rd 29229
Sparkleberry Lane Ext 29223
Sparkleberry Springs Ct 29229
Sparkman Dr 29209
Spartan Dr 29212
Spencer St 29204
Spindrift Ln 29209
Spinnakers Reach Dr 29229
Spirea Ct 29223
Splendora Dr 29223
Spotswood Ct & Dr 29210
Sprig Ct 29223
Spring Ct 29223
Spring Branch Rd 29206
Spring Flower Rd 29223
Spring Glade Cir 29206
Spring Lake Rd 29206
Spring Oak Ln 29229
Spring Point Dr 29229
Spring Valley Ct & Rd 29223
Springate Dr 29209
Springbank Dr 29223
Springbrook Rd 29223
Springcrest Dr 29223
Springfield Ave 29223
Springhaven Dr 29210
Springhill Rd 29204
Springhouse Dr 29210
Springhurst Dr 29223
Springlawn Rd 29223
Springpond Rd 29223
W, E, N & S Springs Ct & Rd 29223
Springsdans Ln 29229
Springtree Dr 29223
Springview St 29223
Springwater Dr 29223
Springway Dr 29209
Springwell Rd 29210
Springwood Rd 29206
Springwoods Lake Dr & Pt 29223
Spritz Ln 29203
Sprott St 29223
Spruce Way 29229
Spyglass Ct 29229
Squire Rd 29223
St Andrews Place Ct & Dr 29210
St Andrews Terrace Rd 29210
Stablegate 29229
S Stadium Rd 29201
Stafford Rd 29223
Staffordshire Rd 29203
Staffort Ct 29223
Stagbriar 29229
Stamford Bridge Rd 29212
Stamhope Ct 29229
Standish St 29203
Stanford St 29203
Stanley St 29204
Stanton Dr 29204
Starboard Way 29209
Stark St 29205
Starlight Dr 29210
Statler Rd 29210
Staunton Ct 29229
Steadfast St 29203
Steadham Rd 29203
Stebondale Rd 29203
Steeple Dr 29229
Steeplechase N & S 29209
Stephen St 29209
Stephenson Ln 29212
Stepney Ct 29210
Stepp Dr 29204
Sterling Bridge Rd 29212
Sterling Cove Rd 29229
Sterling Cross Ct & Dr 29229
Sterling Hills Cir 29229
Sterling Ridge Ct 29229
Sterling Valley Ct 29229
Stevens Rd 29205
Stevenson St 29203
Steward Dr 29210
Stillwater Dr 29212
Stimson Ln 29229
Stirlington Rd 29212
Stockmoor Ct & Rd 29212
Stockport Rd 29229
Stone St 29209
Stone Column Way 29212
Stone Market Ct & Rd 29212
Stone Pine Ct 29229
Stonebriar Rd 29212
Stonegate Dr 29223
Stonehaven Dr 29209
Stoneheath Dr 29223
N & S Stonehedge Dr 29210
Stonemark Ln 29210
Stoneridge Dr 29210
Stoneroot Dr 29229
Stoney Creek Rd 29209
Stoneybridge Rd 29223
Stonsay Rd 29212
Stoopwood Ct 29210
Stork Rd 29206
Storkland Ave 29206
Stratford Rd 29204
Stratton Ct 29210
Strom Thurmond Blvd 29207
Stromsdale Rd 29210
Stuart Ave 29207
Stucawa Dr 29210
Stueber Dr 29229
Sturbridge Ln 29212
Styron Ct 29203
Suber Rd 29210
Suber St 29205
Suffolk St 29203
Sugar Hill Ln & Pt 29201
Sugar Mill Ct & Rd 29229
Sugar Pine Ct 29229
Sulgrave Dr 29210
Sulton St 29201
Summer Ct 29229
Summer Bend Rd 29229
Summer Crest Rd 29223
Summer Park Rd 29223
Summer Ridge Rd 29223
Summer Side Cir 29223
Summer Vale Ct & Dr 29223
Summer Vista Dr 29223
Summerall Ln 29229
Summerhill Dr 29203
Summerlea Dr & Ln 29203
Summerville Ave 29201
Summit Ave 29203
Summit Pkwy 29229
Summit Pl 29204
Summit Sq 29229
Summit Ter 29229
Summit Centre Cir & Dr 29229
Summit Hills Cir 29229
Summit Ridge Cir & Dr 29229
Summit Springs Dr 29229
Summit Terrace Ct 29229
Summit Townes Way 29229
Sumner Ct 29210
Sumter Ave 29207
Sumter St 29201
S Sumter St 29201
Sunbelt Blvd & Ct 29203
Sunbury Ln 29205
Sunchaser Dr 29229
Sundowne Ct & Pl 29209
Sunglow Ct 29223
Sunnybrook Ct 29212
Sunnydale Ct & Dr 29223
Sunnyside Dr 29204
Sunrise Ave 29205
Sunset Dr 29203
Sunset View Ct 29229
Suntrace Ct 29229
Sunturf Cir 29223
Sunview Cir & Dr 29209
Superior St 29205
Surfwood Dr 29209
Surrey Ct 29212
Surrey Ln 29229
Surrey St 29203
Susan Rd 29210
Sutters Mill Ct & Rd 29229
Sutton Pl 29210
Swallow Ct 29203
Swallowtail Ct & Ln 29229
Swan Ct & Ln 29203
Swandale Dr 29203
Sweet Bay Dr 29209
Sweet Branch Ct 29212
Sweet Grass Ln 29203
Sweet Gum Ct & Rd 29223
Sweet Jasmine Ct 29229
Sweet Knoll Ct 29229
Sweetbay Trl 29206
N Sweetbriar Ln 29223
W Sweetbriar Ln 29223
Sweetbriar Rd 29205
Sweetoak Ct & Dr 29223
Sweetwater Springs Rd 29229
Sweetwood Cir 29212
Swinton Rd 29209
Sycamore Ave 29203
Sylvan Dr 29206
Sysco Ct 29209
Systems Ln 29212
T S Martin Ct & Dr 29204
Tabor Dr 29203
Tall Pines Cir 29205
Tall Shadows Ln 29229
Tall Timber Ln 29203
Talltree Ln 29229
Tama Rd 29209
Tamara Way 29229
Tamarack Dr 29209
Tambridge Ct 29229
Tammy Dr 29223
Tanglewood Rd
- 1500-1599 29205
- 1600-1699 29204

Tara Cir, Ct, Ln & Trl 29210
Tarpon Springs Rd 29223
Tarragon Dr 29203
Tartan Rd 29212
Tat Rd 29223
Tavern Fare Rd 29223
Tavineer Dr 29209
Tawny Branch Ct & Rd 29212
Taylor St
- 300-1999 29201
- 2000-2399 29204

Taylor Chapel Rd 29203
Taylors Hill Dr 29201
Tea Olive Rd 29223
Tea Rose Ct 29229
Teaberry Dr 29229
Teague Rd 29209
Teague Park Ct 29209
Teakwood Ln 29223
Teal Way 29229
Teardrop Ln 29229
Technology Cir 29203
Ted St 29203
Tee Ct 29212
Tekesbury Ct 29212
Telfair Ct & Way 29212
Telford Ln 29203
Tempo Ct 29205
Tendrill Ct 29210
Tennyson Dr 29212
Tennyson St 29223
Terrace Way 29205
Terrapin Trce 29229
Terrel Ct 29206
Terri Ln 29203
Terry St 29209
Texas St 29201
Thames Ct 29209
The Blvd 29209
Thicket Ln 29204
Thimbleberry Ct 29212
Thomas Ct 29206
Thomaston Ct & Dr 29229
Thor Dr 29210
Thorn Bush Ct 29229
Thorn Tree Ln 29212
Thornberry Ct 29229
Thorndale Ct 29223
Thorndyke Dr 29204
Thornewood Ct 29212
Thornfield Ct & Rd 29229
Thornhill Dr 29229
Thornhill Rd 29212
Thornridge Rd 29223
Thornwell Ct 29205
Thornwood Rd 29205
Three Bears Rd 29223
Thurmond Mall 29201
Thurmond St 29204
Thurston St 29209
Thyme Cir 29223
Tideland Ct 29212
Tiftgreen Cir 29223
Tillbury Dr 29203
Tillman St 29206
Timber Ct 29210
Timber Crest Dr 29229
Timbercreek Ct 29212
Timberhill Ct 29212
Timberlake Ct 29212
Timberlane Dr 29205
Timberleaf Ct 29212
Timberline Ln 29203
Timberpoint Ct 29212
Timbertrace Ct 29212
Timbertrail Ct 29212
Timle Ln 29206
Timmons St 29209
Timothy Dr 29210
Timrod St 29203
Tims Rd 29203
Tindell Ct 29229
Toad Rd 29209
Toal St 29203
Todd Branch Dr 29223
Token St 29203
Tolliver St 29201
Tolson Ln 29212
Tomafield Ct 29229
Tomaka Rd 29205
E, N & W Tombee Ct, Ln & Pl 29209
Tomentosa Dr 29209
Tommy Cir 29204
Tomotley Ct 29209
Toms Chase 29229
Top Forest Dr 29209
Top Sail Ct 29229
Topknoll Ct 29212
Torbay Rd 29212
Toronto Rd 29204
Torrington Ct 29229
Tortoise Trl 29229
Torwood Dr 29203
Touchfield Ct 29229
Touring Rd 29212
Tower Ct 29212
Tower Ln 29210
Towhee Ct 29229
Towhee Dr 29209
Town Center Pl 29229
Townes Rd 29210
Townhome Ct 29210
Townsend St 29203
Trace Ct & Ln 29223
Tradd Ct & St 29209
Trader Mill Rd 29223
Traditions Cir, Ct, Dr & Way 29229
Trafalgar Ct 29209
Trafalgar Dr 29210
Trailwood Ln 29209
Tram Ct & Rd 29210
Traveler Ln 29209
Travis Ct 29204
Tree St 29205
Treeside Dr 29204
Treeslope Ct 29212
Tremain St 29204
Tremont Ave 29203
Trenholm Rd
- 2700-2798 29204
- 2800-3499 29204
- 3700-5199 29206

N Trenholm Rd 29206
Trenholm Road Ext 29223
Trenton Dr 29203
Trentridge Ct 29229
Trentwood Dr 29223
Trice Ct 29209
Trillium Rd 29229
Trimblestone Ct 29209
Trinity Dr 29209
Troon Ct 29229
Trotter Rd 29209
Trotwood Dr 29209
Trowbridge Ct & Rd 29229
Truax Ln 29204
True St 29209
Trull St 29204
Truman St 29204
Tryon St 29201
Tubman Ct 29203
Tuckahoe Ct 29209
Tudor Rd 29210
Tugaloo Ave 29205
Tupelo Trl 29206
Tupelo Farms Rd 29209
Turkey Point Cir 29223
Turnberry Ct 29223
Turnbridge Ln 29223
Turnstone Way 29229
Turtle Creek Dr & Way 29229
Tuxedo Rd 29209
Tweed Ct 29223
Twickenham Ct 29209
Twig Ln 29229
Twin Creek Ct 29212
Twin Eagles Dr 29203
Twin Lakes Rd 29209
Twin Oaks Cir 29209
Twin Oaks Ln 29209
Twin Oaks Pl 29210
Twin Oaks Way 29209
N Twin Oaks Way 29209
S Twin Oaks Way 29209
Two Notch Rd
- 10299A-10299C 29229
- 1600-2699 29204
- 2638-2638 29240
- 2700-5498 29204
- 2701-5499 29204
- 5500-8504 29223
- 8505-10135 29223
- 8505-8505 29224
- 8506-10134 29223
- 10136-10399 29229
- 10244-1-10244-4 29229

Two Oak Ct 29212
Tyborne Cir & Ct 29210
Tyeu Trl 29210
Tyler St 29205
Tyler Hill Ct 29212
Tyson St 29209
Ulmer Rd 29209
Union St 29201
Universal Dr 29209
Upland Dr 29204
Upper Cove Rd 29223
Upper Loop Way 29212
Upper Pond Rd 29223
Upton Ct 29209
Urban Mhp 29223
Valcour Rd 29212
Valerie Rd 29203
Valhalla Cir, Ct & Dr 29229
Valkyrie Blvd & Cir 29229
Vallejo Cir 29206
Valley Rd 29204
Valley End Ct 29229
Valley Heights Ln 29223
Valley Springs Rd 29223
Valleybridge Rd 29223
Valleybrook Rd 29206
Valleywood Ct 29212
Valmire Dr 29212
Van Der Horst Dr 29229
Van Heise St 29204
Van Lingle Ave 29210
Vandover Cir 29209
Vann St 29203
Vanwood Dr 29206
Varn St 29203
Vega Dr 29223
Ventura Ct 29223
Venus Rd 29209
Vera Cir 29204
Vermillion Dr 29209
Verner St 29204
Vernon Ct & St 29203
Versailles Ct 29204
Veterans Rd 29209
Veterans Pointe Ln 29209
Victoria St 29201
Victory St 29204
Victory Landing Loop 29206
Viking Ct & Dr 29229
Village Ct 29209
Village Ln
- 200-299 29209
- 801-899 29212

Village Pl 29209
Village Walk 29209
Village Way 29209
Village Creek Dr 29210
Village Farm Rd 29223
Vincenne Rd 29212
Vine St 29201
Vinewood Pl 29223
Vineyards Crossing Ct & Dr 29229
Vintage Ln 29210
Viola Ct 29229
Virginia St 29201
Visonerl Rd 29212
Voss Ave 29223
Waban Ct 29212
S Waccamaw Ave 29205
Wactor St 29209
Wade Dr 29203
Wade St 29210
Wages Rd 29203
Wagner Trl 29229
Waites Rd 29204
Wake Forest Dr 29206
Wakefield Rd 29203
Walcott St 29201
Walden Ct 29204
Wales Rd 29223
S Walker St 29205
Walker Solomon Way 29204
Walking Horse Ct & Way 29223
Wallace St 29201
Waller Ave 29203
Walnut Ct 29212
Walnut Ln 29212
Walnut St 29205
Walters Ln 29209
Waltham Abby Rd 29212
Walton Rd 29203
Wando St 29205
Ward Ct 29223
Warly Ct 29229
Warner Dr 29223
Warren Dr 29210
Warwick Ct 29229
Washington Rd 29207
N Washington Rd 29203
Washington St
- 700-1999 29201
- 2000-2599 29204

Water St 29203
Water Hickory Way 29229
Water View Ct & Dr 29212
Water Wheel Way 29229
Waterbrook Dr 29212
Wateree Ave 29205
Waterford Dr 29203
Waterhill Dr 29212
Watermark Pl 29210
Waterton Way 29229
Waterville Ct & Dr 29229
Waterway Trce 29229
Waterwood Dr 29212
Watson Way 29229
Waverly St 29204
E & W Waverly Place Ct & Dr 29229
Waxberry Cir 29201
W Way Ln 29212
Way St 29203
Waybrook Ct 29212
Wayland Ct 29229
Wayne St 29201
Wayside Dr 29203
Wayworth Ct 29212
Webb Ct 29204
Webber St 29203
Webster St 29205
Weddell St 29223
Wedgefield Rd 29206
Wedgewood Dr & Way 29206
Weed Dr 29212
Weeks Ct 29206
Weeping Cherry Ln 29212
Weir Dr 29223
Weiss Dr 29209
Welborn Rd 29209
Welch Rd 29223
Weldwood Ct 29223
Welland St 29203
Wellbrook Rd 29223
Wellesley Dr 29203
Wellington Dr 29204
Wells Ct 29206
Welwyn Pl 29212
Wembley Ct 29212
Wembley St 29209
Wendell Dr 29210
Wentworth Dr 29203
Wescott Pl 29229
Wescott Rd 29212
Wesley Dr 29204
Wessex Ln 29223

Wessinger Ln & Rd ... 29203
West Ave ... 29203
West Ct ... 29212
Westbridge Rd ... 29223
Westbrook Rd ... 29206
Westbury Dr ... 29201
Westbury Ln ... 29212
Westbury Pl ... 29212
Westchester Ct & Dr ... 29210
Western Pointe Dr ... 29229
Westfern Ct ... 29212
Westfield Rd ... 29206
Westgrove Ct ... 29212
Westlake Rd ... 29223
Westland Pine Ct ... 29229
Westlawn Rd ... 29210
Westminster Dr ... 29204
Westmore Dr ... 29223
Westmoreland Rd ... 29229
Weston Ave ... 29203
Westover Rd ... 29210
Westpark Blvd ... 29210
Westpine Ct ... 29212
Westport Dr ... 29223
Westridge Rd ... 29229
Westshire Ct ... 29209
Westshire Pl ... 29210
Westshore Rd ... 29206
Westwood Ave ... 29203
Wetherill Dr ... 29209
Wexford Ct & Ln ... 29212
Wexhurst Ct & Rd ... 29212
Wexwood Ct & Rd ... 29210
Weybourne Way ... 29223
Whaley St
200-1299 ... 29201
1300-1699 ... 29205
Wharton Ln ... 29229
Wheat St
500-1200 ... 29201
1202-1698 ... 29201
1700-3799 ... 29205
Wheat Grass Ct ... 29223
Wheatridge Ct ... 29223
Wheatstone ... 29229
Wheeler Rd ... 29204
Wheeler St ... 29207
Whispering Pine Rd ... 29203
Whispering Pines Cir ... 29205
Whitaker Rd ... 29223
White St ... 29203
White Birch Cir ... 29223
White Cedar Dr ... 29229
White Dove Ct ... 29212
White Falls Cir & Dr ... 29212
White Gables Dr & Pl ... 29229
White Pine Rd ... 29223
White Wing Ct & Dr ... 29229
Whiteford Rd ... 29210
Whitehall Rd ... 29204
Whitehouse Rd ... 29209
Whitehurst Way ... 29229
Whiteoak Rd ... 29206
Whitfield Ct ... 29229
Whitlock St ... 29209
Whitman St ... 29205
Whitmell Ave ... 29223
Whitney St ... 29201
Whittaker Dr ... 29206
Whittington Ct ... 29210
Whitton Ln ... 29229
Whitwood Cir ... 29212
Whixley Ln ... 29223
Wickersell Ct ... 29212
Wickham Ln ... 29229
Widgean Dr ... 29203
Wil Stel Rd ... 29210
Wilamore Ct ... 29223
Wild Azalea Ct ... 29223
Wild Cherry Rd ... 29223
Wild Fern Rd ... 29229
Wild Indigo Ct ... 29229
Wild Iris Ct ... 29209
Wild Olive Ct & Dr ... 29229
Wild Rose Ct ... 29229
Wildcat Rd ... 29209
Wildcat Way ... 29207
Wildeoak Ct & Trl ... 29223
Wildewood Club Ct ... 29223
Wildewood Crest Ct & Way ... 29223
Wildewood Downs Cir, Pt & Way ... 29223
Wildewood Park Dr ... 29223
Wildleaf Ct ... 29212
Wildlife Ln ... 29209
Wildlife Pkwy ... 29210
Wildsmere Ave ... 29203
Wildwood Ave ... 29203
Wildwood Centre Dr ... 29229
Wiley St ... 29205
Wilkes Rd ... 29203
Wilkinson Dr & Ln ... 29229
Wilkshire Dr ... 29210
Will Henry Ct ... 29210
Willa Dr ... 29209
Willdin Rd ... 29223
Willease Cir ... 29203
Willett Rd ... 29206
William And Mary Ct
100-199 ... 29205
1100-1199 ... 29210
William Duffie Rd ... 29203
William Hardin Rd ... 29223
William Tuller Dr ... 29205
S Williams St ... 29201
Williamsburg Dr ... 29203
Williamstown Ct & Way ... 29212
Willie Mccants Rd ... 29203
Willingham Dr ... 29206
Willis St ... 29204
Willow St ... 29203
Willow Bend Ct
1-99 ... 29223
500-599 ... 29212
Willow Bend Dr ... 29212
Willow Creek Dr & Ln ... 29212
Willow Hurst Ct ... 29209
Willow Oak Dr ... 29223
Willow Ridge Rd ... 29206
Willow Tree Dr ... 29209
Willow Winds Dr ... 29210
Willowby St ... 29223
Wilmette Rd ... 29203
Wilmot Ave ... 29205
Wilshire Dr ... 29209
Wilson Blvd ... 29203
Wilson Ct ... 29206
Wilton Hill Rd ... 29212
Wiltown Ct ... 29212
Wilts Ct ... 29212
Wiltshire Cir, Ct & Way ... 29229
Wimbledon Ct ... 29210
Wincay Rd ... 29223
Winchester Ave ... 29203
Wincrest Ln ... 29223
Windale Dr ... 29223
Windemere Ave ... 29203
Winding Way ... 29212
Winding Creek Ln ... 29229
Windjammer Ln ... 29229
Windmill Ct ... 29210
Windmill Orchard Rd ... 29223
Windover St ... 29204
Windridge Rd ... 29223
Windsong Island Ln ... 29212
Windsong Point Ln ... 29212
Windsor Cv ... 29223
Windsor Rd ... 29204
Windsor Brook Rd ... 29223
Windsor Lake Blvd & Way ... 29223
Windsor Point Rd ... 29223
Windsor Shores Dr ... 29223
Windsor Trace Dr ... 29209
Windsor Village Dr ... 29223
Windsorcrest Rd ... 29229
Windstone Dr ... 29212
Windwan Dr ... 29209
Windward Ct ... 29229
Windward Ln ... 29212
Windward Way ... 29212
Windward Point Ct & Rd ... 29212
Windwood Pl ... 29204
Windy Dr ... 29209
Windy Knl ... 29229
Windy Run Dr ... 29212
Winfield Rd ... 29209
Winford Pl ... 29229
Wing Stripe Ct ... 29229
Wingard St ... 29209
Wingate Pl ... 29229
Wingfield Ct ... 29212
Winhill Rd ... 29203
Winmet Dr ... 29203
Winners Cir ... 29229
Winnsboro Rd ... 29203
Winsham Dr ... 29229
Winslow Ct & Way ... 29229
Winsor Hills Dr ... 29204
Winstaire Dr ... 29210
Winston Rd ... 29209
Winter Park Ave ... 29203
Winter Park Dr ... 29209
Winterberry Ln ... 29223
Wintergreen Rd ... 29229
Winterwood Ct & Rd ... 29203
Winthrop Ave ... 29206
Winyah Dr ... 29203
Wise Ct ... 29209
Wisteria Ln ... 29206
Witherspoon Dr ... 29206
Wittering Dr ... 29206
Wofford Ave ... 29206
Wolf Cir ... 29204
Wolverham Ct ... 29212
Wolverton Ct ... 29229
Wood Ct ... 29210
Wood Duck Rd ... 29223
Wood Moor Pl ... 29212
Wood Ride Ct & Ln ... 29209
Wood Turtle Ct ... 29229
Woodale Cir ... 29203
Woodbine Ct & Dr ... 29206
Woodbranch Rd ... 29206
Woodbrier St ... 29203
N & S Woodburn Ln ... 29212
Woodbury Dr ... 29209
Woodcreek Ct ... 29212
Woodcrest Dr ... 29203
N Woodcross Dr ... 29212
Woodfern Ct ... 29212
Woodfield Dr ... 29223
Woodfin Ct ... 29229
Woodford Rd ... 29209
Woodgate Dr ... 29223
Woodhaven Rd ... 29203
Woodhill Cir ... 29209
Woodlake Dr ... 29206
N Woodlake Dr ... 29229
Woodland Dr ... 29205
Woodland Hls E ... 29210
Woodland Hls W ... 29210
Woodland Hills Rd ... 29210
Woodland Village Dr ... 29210
Woodlands W ... 29229
Woodlands Ridge Ct, Ln & Rd ... 29229
Woodlands Village Ct & Dr ... 29229
Woodlawn Ave ... 29209
Woodleaf Ct ... 29212
Woodleigh Rd ... 29206
Woodleigh Park Dr ... 29229
Woodlock Ln ... 29229
Woodmere Dr ... 29204
Woodmont Dr ... 29204
Woodpine Ct ... 29212
Woodpond Ct ... 29212
Woodridge Dr ... 29203
S Woodrow St ... 29205
Woodsboro Dr ... 29210
Woodshaw Ct ... 29212
Woodshore Cir, Ct & Dr ... 29223
Woodside Ave ... 29203
Woodside Haven Dr ... 29206
Woodsong Ln ... 29210
Woodspring Ct ... 29212
Woodstock Dr ... 29223
N & S Woodstream Rd ... 29212
Woodsview Ln ... 29223
Woodtrail Ct & Dr ... 29210
Woodtree Ct ... 29212
Woodvale Cir ... 29203
Woodvalley Ct & Dr ... 29212
Woodvine Rd ... 29206
Woodway Ln
100-299 ... 29210
2900-3099 ... 29223
Woodwind Ct ... 29209
Woodwinds Ct & Dr ... 29212
Woodwinds West Ct & Dr ... 29212
Worchester Ct ... 29209
Wordsworth Dr ... 29209
Wordsworth Pl ... 29212
Wormwood Ln ... 29209
Worthington Pkwy ... 29229
Worthy Dr ... 29204
Wotan Ct, Ln & Rd ... 29229
Wrenwood Ln ... 29206
Wright St ... 29203
Wycombe Rd ... 29212
Wyndham Rd
1400-1599 ... 29205
1600-1699 ... 29204
Wynette Way ... 29229
Wynfield Ct ... 29210
Wynn Way ... 29210
Wynnewood Rd ... 29223
Yacht Cove Rd ... 29212
Yale Ave ... 29205
Yarborough Ct ... 29206
Yarmouth Dr ... 29210
Yarrow Ln ... 29223
Yellow Flag Ct ... 29223
York Dr ... 29204
Yorkhouse Rd ... 29223
Yorkshire Dr ... 29209
Yorkton Ct ... 29229
Yorktown Ct ... 29209
Youman St ... 29204
Young Dr ... 29210
Youth Service Dr ... 29205
Zanark Ct & Dr ... 29212
Zeigler St ... 29205
Zephyr St ... 29212
Zeppelin Ln ... 29209
Zimalcrest Dr ... 29210
Zinnia Ct ... 29223
Zion Ave ... 29201

NUMBERED STREETS

1st Ave ... 29209
1st Street South Ext ... 29209
2nd Ave ... 29209
4835 ... 29207
5482 ... 29207

CONWAY SC

General Delivery ... 29526

POST OFFICE BOXES MAIN OFFICE STATIONS AND BRANCHES

Box No.s
All PO Boxes ... 29528

NAMED STREETS

A St ... 29526
A And M Ln ... 29526
A C Ln ... 29526
Aaron St ... 29526
Abba Ct ... 29526
Abberbury Dr ... 29527
Abrams Ct ... 29526
Academy Dr ... 29526
Accomp Dr ... 29526
Acie Ave ... 29527
Adeline Ct ... 29526
Adoniram Dr ... 29526
Adrian Hwy & Pkwy ... 29526
Adrianna Cir ... 29526
Afifi Ct ... 29526
Airport Rd ... 29527
Alahambra Ct ... 29526
Alcazar Ct ... 29527
Alford Rd ... 29526
Allen Dr & St ... 29526
Allen Dew Rd ... 29527
Allentown Dr ... 29526
Allied Dr ... 29526
Alligator Ct ... 29526
Allison Ct ... 29526
Aloe St ... 29527
Alston Aly ... 29527
Altman Cir ... 29526
Alton Rd ... 29526
Amanda Way ... 29526
Amber Ln ... 29526
Amber Nicole Rd ... 29526
Ambrose Aly ... 29526
S And J Pl ... 29526
Anderson St ... 29526
Anhinga Ct ... 29526
Anjali Ct ... 29526
Ann St ... 29526
Antioch Rd ... 29527
Apex Dr ... 29526
Aponte Dr ... 29527
Appaloosa Trl ... 29526
Apple Ln ... 29527
Applewhite Ln ... 29526
April Rd ... 29527
Aquila Ct ... 29527
Arabia Ct ... 29526
Archie Ln ... 29526
Arnie Cir ... 29526
Asbury Rd ... 29527
Ashley Cir ... 29526
Ashlyn Creek Dr ... 29527
Ashwood Cir ... 29526
Athens Dr ... 29526
Atlantic Ave ... 29526
Auburn Rd ... 29526
August Rd ... 29527
Augustus Dr ... 29527
Aurora Dr ... 29527
Austin Ave ... 29527
Austrian Pine Dr ... 29526
Autry Ave ... 29526
Avant Ln ... 29526
Ayrie Ct ... 29527
Azalea Dr ... 29526
Azaloak Rd ... 29526
B St ... 29526
B B Watson Rd ... 29526
Bald Eagles Dr ... 29527
Banbury Dr ... 29527
Bancroft Dr ... 29527
Bantry Ln ... 29526
Barberry Dr ... 29526
Barker St ... 29526
Barking Dog Ln ... 29527
Barlow Ct ... 29526
Barnfield Rd ... 29526
Barnyard Ln ... 29527
Barons Bluff Dr ... 29526
Barret Rd ... 29526
Barry Ln ... 29527
Bartley Dr ... 29527
Bashor Rd ... 29526
Bass Dr ... 29526
Basswood Ct ... 29526
Bates Dr ... 29526
Bay Blossom Dr ... 29527
Bayfield Ln ... 29527
Bayside Ave ... 29527
Beagle Trl ... 29526
Bear Bluff Dr & Rd ... 29526
Bear Grass Rdg ... 29526
Beatlegeous Dr ... 29527
Beaty St ... 29526
Beau St ... 29527
Beaver Creek Ct ... 29526
Beaver Pond Rd ... 29526
Beaver Run Dr ... 29527
Beechwood Ct ... 29526
Belair Ln ... 29526
Belk Rd ... 29526
Bell St ... 29526
Belladora Rd ... 29527
Bellamy Rd ... 29526
Bellatrix Ct ... 29527
Belle Ridge Ct ... 29526
Belton Dr ... 29526
Ben St ... 29526
Benchmade Rd ... 29527
Bens Ct ... 29527
Bent Wood Cir ... 29526
Berley Mc Rd ... 29526
Berry Tree Ln ... 29526
Beth Dr ... 29527
Bethel Dr ... 29526
Bethune Dr ... 29527
Betty St ... 29527
Beulah Cir ... 29527
Beverly Rd ... 29527
Beverly Richard St ... 29526
Big Bull Landing Rd ... 29527
Big Gutter Ln ... 29526
Bill Mack Blvd ... 29526
Birch Ave & Ln ... 29526
Birchwood Ln ... 29526
Bishop Pine Dr ... 29526
Black Cherry Way ... 29526
Black Harbor Dr ... 29526
Black Lab Trl ... 29527
Black Moss Dr ... 29526
Black Skimmer Dr ... 29526
Black Top Ln ... 29527
Blackmon Dr ... 29527
Bladen Ct ... 29526
Blain Ln ... 29527
Blair Ct ... 29526
Blake St ... 29526
Blanche Ln ... 29527
Blaze Trl ... 29527
Blenheim Ct ... 29526
Blinkhorn Rd ... 29526
Blossom St ... 29526
Blount St ... 29527
Blue Bell Ln ... 29527
Blue Gull Dr ... 29527
Blue Hole Ct ... 29526
Blue Jay Ln ... 29526
Blue Juniper Ct ... 29527
Bluebird Loop ... 29526
Bluewater Rd ... 29527
Board Landing Cir & Rd ... 29526
Bob Ct ... 29526
Boggy Rd ... 29526
Bohemia Ct ... 29526
Bonnie Ln ... 29526
Booth Cir ... 29527
Bosephus Ln ... 29526
Bottle Branch Rd ... 29527
Boundary St ... 29526
Boxwood Ln ... 29526
Boyd Rd ... 29526
Boydville Dr ... 29526
Bradford Dr ... 29526
Bramber Pl ... 29527
Brandon Ln ... 29526
Bratcher Rd ... 29526
Braves Ln ... 29526
Briarwood Ln ... 29526
Brickyard Pl ... 29527
Bridgebrook Ln ... 29527
Bridgette Ln ... 29527
Bridgewater Dr ... 29526
Brinson Ct ... 29527
Brison Ct ... 29527
Britt Ct ... 29526
Brittany Ln ... 29527
Broadway St ... 29527
Brock Ln ... 29526
Bromell Ct ... 29527
Bronco Aly ... 29526
Brook Ln ... 29526
Brookdale Ln ... 29526
Brookland Dr ... 29526
Brooklane Ct ... 29527
Brookshade Ct ... 29526
Brown Dr ... 29526
Brown St ... 29527
Brown Swamp Rd ... 29527
Browns Chapel Ave ... 29527
Browns Way Shortcut Rd ... 29527
W Brownway Cir ... 29527
Bryant Park Ct ... 29527
Bryants Landing Rd ... 29526
Brye Aly ... 29526
Buccaneers Cv ... 29526
Buchanan Ln ... 29526
Buck St ... 29526
Buck Bay Cir E ... 29526
Bucksport Rd ... 29527
Bucksport Heights Ct ... 29527
Bucksview Rd ... 29527
Bucksville Dr ... 29527
Bulk Plant Rd ... 29526
Bull Creek Cir ... 29527
Bulldozer Ln ... 29526
Bunyan Ln ... 29527
Burgundy Ln ... 29527
Burning Ridge Rd ... 29526
Burriss Rd ... 29526
Burroughs St ... 29526
Busbee St ... 29526
Bussey Ln ... 29526
Busy Corner Rd ... 29527
Butler Dr ... 29527
Buttercup Ln ... 29526
Butternut Cir ... 29526
Byrd Rd ... 29526
Cabbage Patch Ln ... 29527
Cabernet Ln ... 29526
Cadbury Ct ... 29527
Cadogan Ct ... 29526
Cain Wilson Rd ... 29526
Caines Ct ... 29526
Caines Landing Rd ... 29526
Caleb Rd ... 29526
Calhoun Rd
1200-1399 ... 29526
1500-1699 ... 29527
Camellia Ln ... 29526
Camelot St ... 29526
Canal Ter ... 29526
Candice Pl ... 29526
Candlewood Dr ... 29526
Cane Branch Church Rd ... 29527
Caniki Dr ... 29526
Canine Dr ... 29526
Cannie Ln ... 29526
Cannon Pond Rd ... 29527
Canterbury Ln ... 29526
Cantillo Ct ... 29526
Canyon Dr ... 29526
Capella Ct ... 29527
Cardinal Dr ... 29526
Carl Rd ... 29526
Carleita Cir ... 29527
Carolina Rd ... 29526
Carolina Springs Ct ... 29527
Carolina Wren Rd ... 29527
Carolyn St ... 29526
Carriage Rd ... 29527
Carroll Todd Rd ... 29526
Cart Crossing Dr ... 29526
Carter Ln ... 29526
Cassie Ln ... 29527
Castlewood Ct, Dr & Ln ... 29526
Cat Tail Bay Dr ... 29527

Catapults Ct ... 29526
Caulder Ln ... 29526
Causey Rd ... 29526
Causey St ... 29527
Causey Farm Rd ... 29527
Cavalier Rd ... 29526
Cedar Ln ... 29527
Cedar Ridge Ln ... 29526
Century Cir ... 29526
Cessna Dr ... 29527
Chadmon Ave ... 29527
Chana Cir ... 29526
Chaneybriar Ln ... 29526
Channel View Dr ... 29527
Chanticleer Dr ... 29526
Chantilly Ln ... 29526
Charisma Dr ... 29526
Charity Ln ... 29527
Charlies Rd ... 29527
Chasewood Ln ... 29526
Chateau Dr ... 29526
Chavis Rd ... 29526
Chelsey Cir ... 29526
Chelsey Lake Dr ... 29526
Cherokee St ... 29527
Cherry St ... 29527
Cherry Blossom Ct ... 29526
Cherry Buck Trl ... 29526
Chester Ln ... 29526
Chestnut Rd ... 29526
Cheticamp Ct ... 29527
Chevy Chase Dr ... 29526
Cheyenne Rd ... 29526
Chicora Blvd ... 29526
Chinaberry Dr ... 29527
Chow Ln ... 29526
Chresoulis Ln ... 29527
Christian Rd ... 29526
Christmas Tree Ln ... 29526
Christopher Columbus
Rd ... 29526
Church St
301-397 ... 29527
399-409 ... 29527
410-498 ... 29526
411-499 ... 29527
500-2999 ... 29526
3001-3353 ... 29526
Churchill Dr ... 29527
Citadel Dr & Ln ... 29526
Civil War Rd ... 29526
Clamour Ct ... 29526
Clara Ln ... 29527
Claremont Ct ... 29526
Claridy Rd ... 29526
Clay Ridge Rd ... 29526
Clayton St ... 29526
Clemson Cir & Rd ... 29526
Cleveland Dr ... 29526
Cloverbrook Cir ... 29526
Cloverfield Ln ... 29526
Club House Rd ... 29526
Clydesdale Dr ... 29526
Coastal Oaks Dr ... 29527
Cobblestone Ln ... 29526
Cobra Ct ... 29526
Cochran St ... 29526
Cocksfoot Ln ... 29527
E & W Coker Ln ... 29526
Cole Rd ... 29526
Colette Ct ... 29526
College Rd ... 29526
Colletta Ct ... 29527
Collins St ... 29526
Collins Park St ... 29526
Collins-Jollie Rd ... 29526
Colonial Ln ... 29526
Colony Rd ... 29526
Colton Cir ... 29526
Columbia St ... 29526
Comfort Ct ... 29527
Comfrey Ln ... 29527
Commonwealth Cir ... 29526
Compton Ln ... 29526
Con El Cir ... 29526
Confederate Dr ... 29526
Conner Ln ... 29527
Converse Dr ... 29526
Conway Plantation Dr ... 29526
Cooper Ln & St ... 29527
Cooper Place Dr ... 29527
Copperhead Rd ... 29527
Coral Ct ... 29526
Coral Crest Dr ... 29527
Corban Pl ... 29526
Corbett Dr ... 29526
Corbin Tanner Dr ... 29527
Cordoba Dr ... 29526
Corinne Ln ... 29526
Cornwall Cir ... 29526
Cory Rd ... 29527
Cosmos Ct ... 29527
Cottage Ln ... 29526
Cottage Creek Cir ... 29527
Cottonwood Ln ... 29526
E Country Club Dr ... 29526
Country Manor Dr ... 29526
Courtyard Dr ... 29526
Cove Rd ... 29527
Covery Ln ... 29526
Cowboy Ln ... 29526
E & W Cox Ferry Cir &
Rd ... 29526
Crabtree Dr ... 29526
Craig St ... 29527
Cranesbill Ct ... 29527
Crawford Ln ... 29526
Creek Dr ... 29526
Creel St ... 29527
Crescent Dr ... 29526
Crestwood Rd ... 29527
Creyk Ct ... 29526
Cricket Ct ... 29526
Crocus Ln ... 29527
Crosswinds Ln ... 29526
Crusade Cir ... 29526
Cul De Sac Ln ... 29527
Cultra Rd ... 29526
Currie St ... 29526
Cutlip Ct ... 29527
Cymmer Ct ... 29527
Cynthia Dr ... 29526
Cypress Cir ... 29526
Cypress Flat Ct ... 29526
Cypress Knee Ct ... 29526
Cypress Swamp Rd ... 29527
Cyprus Ct ... 29526
D St ... 29527
Daffodil Dr ... 29527
Dahlia Ct ... 29527
Daisy Ln ... 29526
Dales Rd ... 29526
Dana Ln ... 29527
Daniel Rd ... 29527
Danner Dr ... 29526
Daphane Dr ... 29526
Daresbury Ln ... 29526
Dargan Cir ... 29526
Darling Lake Rd ... 29527
Dartmoor Ct ... 29526
David Rd ... 29526
Davidson Rd ... 29526
Dawson Bluff Pl ... 29526
Dawson Graham Rd ... 29527
Dayton Dr ... 29527
Daytona St ... 29526
Deanna Ln ... 29526
Dearwood Ln ... 29527
Deborah Cir ... 29527
Declaration Ct ... 29526
Deer Trl ... 29526
Deer Dog Ln ... 29526
Deer Ridge Ct ... 29527
Deere Dr ... 29527
Delayna Ct ... 29527
Deliverance Dr ... 29527
Denali Dr ... 29526
Denine Dr ... 29526
Dennis Ln ... 29527
Depot Rd ... 29526
Derby Cir ... 29526
Derbyshire Ct & Ln ... 29526
Derrick Ln ... 29526
Destiny Ln ... 29526
Devin Park Dr ... 29527
Dew Ln ... 29526
Dewberry Dr ... 29527
Dewitt St ... 29527
Dexter Ln ... 29526
Diamond Ln ... 29526
Didapper Dr ... 29527
Dillon St ... 29527
Dilmar Dr ... 29526
Dirty Branch Rd ... 29527
Dobros Rd ... 29526
Dock Rd ... 29526
Dogwood Cir & Dr ... 29526
Dollie Ln ... 29526
Donahue Dr ... 29527
Donald St ... 29527
Dongola Hwy ... 29527
Doodle Hill Ln ... 29526
Dorchester Rd ... 29527
Doris Ln ... 29527
Dorset Pl ... 29526
Dossies Rd ... 29526
Dots Ct ... 29526
Double A Ln ... 29526
Double Oak Rd ... 29527
Dover Dr ... 29527
Doyle Ln ... 29526
Dozier Cir ... 29527
Dragonwings Way ... 29526
Drawbridge Dr ... 29526
Drew Ln ... 29526
Dub Ln ... 29526
Dublin Dr ... 29527
Duck Cove Rd ... 29526
Duckett St ... 29526
Dudley Ln ... 29526
Dukes Rd ... 29526
Dunbarton Ln ... 29526
Duncan Ln ... 29527
Dunlap Cir & Ct ... 29526
Dunn Acres Cir & Dr ... 29526
Dunn Short Cut Rd ... 29527
Dunraven Ct ... 29527
Durant St ... 29527
Dusenbury Pl ... 29527
Dutchman Dr ... 29527
E St ... 29526
Eagles St ... 29527
Eaglet Cir ... 29527
Earnhardt St ... 29526
Eastlynn Dr ... 29526
Eastwoods Dr ... 29526
Easy St ... 29526
Ebenezer Rd ... 29527
Echaw Dr ... 29526
Ecum Secum Pl ... 29527
Eddy Rd ... 29526
Edge Rd ... 29526
Edgewood Cir ... 29527
Edison Cir ... 29526
Edwards Ln ... 29526
El Bethel Rd ... 29527
El Paso Dr ... 29526
Elbow Rd ... 29527
Eldon Rd ... 29526
Electric Dr ... 29527
Elics Rd ... 29526
Elijah St ... 29527
Elizabeth St ... 29526
Elkford Dr ... 29526
Ellie Ln ... 29527
Ellis Dr ... 29526
Elm St ... 29526
Elsies Ct ... 29527
Elvington Rd ... 29526
Elvis Farm Rd ... 29526
Elwood Cir ... 29527
Embassy Ln ... 29526
Emerald Ct ... 29526
Emily Estate Dr ... 29527
Emily Springs Dr ... 29527
Emory St ... 29527
Enoch Rd ... 29526
Environmental Pkwy ... 29526
Erics Ln ... 29526
Erin Ct ... 29526
Ernest Rd ... 29526
Ernest Finney Ave ... 29527
Erskine Dr ... 29526
Esdale Ln ... 29526
Esmon Ln ... 29527
Estate Dr ... 29526
Esther Ct ... 29526
Eula Dr ... 29526
Eva Rd ... 29527
Evelyn Dr ... 29527
Everbreeze Rd N ... 29527
Everette St ... 29526
Fair Hill Ct ... 29527
Fairforest Ct ... 29526
Fairview Ln ... 29527
Fairway Ln ... 29526
Faith Dr ... 29527
Falls Creek Ct ... 29526
Family Ln ... 29527
Family Farm Rd ... 29526
Fannie B Rd ... 29526
Farmwood Cir ... 29527
Farrar Dr ... 29526
Faulk Cir ... 29527
Faulk Rd ... 29526
Faulk Landing Rd ... 29526
Fawn Rd ... 29527
Fawn Run ... 29526
Fern Ridge Rd ... 29527
Ferryfield Rd ... 29526
Fieldwoods Dr ... 29526
Filly Ct ... 29526
Firehouse Rd ... 29527
Fladger St ... 29527
Flamingo Rd ... 29526
Florence St ... 29527
Flossie Rd ... 29527
Floyd St ... 29526
Fonza St ... 29526
Ford Cir ... 29526
Ford Taylor Rd ... 29527
Forest Dr ... 29526
Forest Acres Ln ... 29527
Forest Lake Dr ... 29526
Forest Loop Rd ... 29527
Forest View Rd
1300-1499 ... 29526
1500-1799 ... 29526
Formosa Dr ... 29527
Forney St ... 29527
Fortress Ct ... 29526
Foster Ave ... 29527
Founders Dr ... 29526
Four Mile Rd ... 29526
Fowler Rd ... 29526
Fox Chase Dr ... 29527
Fox Hollow Rd ... 29526
Fox Tail Pine Dr ... 29526
Frail Ln ... 29526
Francis Marion Pl ... 29527
Franklin Dr ... 29527
Franks Ln ... 29526
Frazier Rd ... 29527
Fredrick Ct ... 29526
Freds Ln ... 29527
Freeman Dr ... 29526
French Collins Rd ... 29526
Friendship St ... 29527
Fruitwood St ... 29527
Fulmer St ... 29526
Furman Cir ... 29526
W G Rd ... 29526
Gailard Dr ... 29527
Gale Ave ... 29526
Gallinule Dr ... 29527
Galloway Dr ... 29526
Gamecock Ave ... 29526
Garden Ln ... 29527
Gardenia Ln ... 29526
Garkenta Rd ... 29527
Gary Rd ... 29526
Gary Lake Blvd ... 29526
Gasoline Aly ... 29527
Gatehouse Ct ... 29526
Gator Aly ... 29527
Gator Ct ... 29526
Gemini Cir ... 29527
Gene St ... 29526
George Ln ... 29527
Georgia Mae Loop ... 29527
Geranium Rd ... 29527
Gilbert Rd ... 29527
Gladys Ln ... 29527
Glagow Cir ... 29527
Glasgow Cir ... 29527
Glass Hill Dr ... 29526
Glenmoor Dr ... 29526
Glenwood Dr ... 29526
Glossy Ibis Dr ... 29526
Glover Rd ... 29527
Gobblers Run ... 29527
Godfrey Ave ... 29526
Godwin Paradise Ln ... 29526
Golden Eagle Dr ... 29527
Golden Key Rd ... 29526
Golden Leaf Rd ... 29526
Goldhill Rd ... 29526
Golf Course Rd ... 29526
Gordon Ln ... 29526
Gore Rd ... 29526
Goswick Ct ... 29526
Gowans Rd ... 29526
Grace Dr ... 29527
Graduate Rd ... 29526
Graham Rd ... 29526
Grahamville Rd ... 29526
Grainger Rd ... 29527
Grassy Ln ... 29526
Gravelley Gulley Cir, Dr
& Ln ... 29526
Gray Lake Blvd ... 29526
Gray Oaks Dr ... 29526
Great Oak Dr ... 29526
Green St ... 29527
Green Fir Loop ... 29527
Green Meadow Dr ... 29527
Green Pond Cir ... 29527
Greencrest Ct ... 29526
Greenleaf Dr ... 29526
Greenwich Dr ... 29526
Greenwood Dr ... 29527
Grier Crossing Dr ... 29526
Grissett Rd ... 29526
Gully Ct ... 29526
Gully Store Ct ... 29526
Gumbo Ln ... 29526
Gunsmoke Trl ... 29526
Haba Ln ... 29527
Hagwood Cir ... 29526
Hair Nook Rd ... 29526
Haley Ln ... 29527
Haley Brooke Dr ... 29526
Half Penny Loop ... 29526
Hall Rd ... 29526
Halle Lake Ct ... 29527
Hallie Martin Rd ... 29527
Hamilton Way ... 29526
Hamp Ned Rd ... 29526
Hampton Rd ... 29527
Hampton Ridge Rd ... 29527
Hannahrae Ct ... 29526
Hardee Ave & Ln ... 29526
Hardees Ferry Rd ... 29526
Harden Dr ... 29526
Hardwick Rd ... 29526
Hare St ... 29526
Harley Weaver Ln ... 29526
Harold Dr ... 29527
Harper Rd ... 29527
Harris Short Cut Rd ... 29526
Hart St ... 29526
Harvest Dr ... 29527
Harvest View Ave ... 29527
Hatteras Dr ... 29526
Hattie Ct ... 29527
Havenwood Path ... 29526
Hawksmoor Dr ... 29526
Hawthorne Dr ... 29526
Hazel Rd ... 29526
Hearl Ln ... 29527
Heather Dr ... 29527
Heather Heath Ln ... 29526
Helen Rd ... 29527
Helms Way ... 29526
Hemingway St ... 29527
Hemingway Chapel Rd ... 29527
Hendricks Short Cut
Rd ... 29527
Henrietta Blfs ... 29527
Henry Rd ... 29526
Henry C Ln ... 29527
Henry Heritage Dr ... 29527
Heritage Rd ... 29527
Heritage Downs Dr ... 29526
Herringbone Ct ... 29526
Hickman Dr ... 29527
Hickman Ln ... 29526
Hickory Cir ... 29527
Hickory Dr ... 29526
Hickory Fox Ct ... 29526
Hickory Hill Cir ... 29526
Hickory Springs Ct ... 29527
Hicks Cir ... 29526
Hidden Pl ... 29526
Hidden Oak Dr ... 29527
High Point Church Rd ... 29527
Highway 1124 ... 29526
Highway 134 ... 29527
Highway 139 ... 29526
Highway 19 ... 29526
Highway 319 E ... 29526
Highway 366 ... 29526
Highway 378 ... 29527
Highway 471 ... 29526
Highway 472 ... 29526
E & W Highway 501 ... 29526
Highway 501 Business ... 29526
Highway 544 Opas ... 29526
Highway 545 ... 29526
Highway 548 ... 29527
Highway 642 ... 29527
Highway 65 ... 29526
Highway 66 ... 29527
Highway 668 ... 29527
Highway 701 N ... 29526
Highway 701 S ... 29527
Highway 804 ... 29527
Highway 813 ... 29526
Highway 90 ... 29526
Highway 905 ... 29526
Highway 931 ... 29526
Highway 981 ... 29527
Hiland Ave
1500-1699 ... 29526
1700-1799 ... 29527
Hill Ct ... 29526
Hill St ... 29527
Hillmont Ct ... 29526
Hillsborough Dr ... 29526
Hillside Dr ... 29526
Hilly Ln ... 29527
Hippo Ct ... 29526
Hodges Rd ... 29527
Holcombe Ln ... 29527
Holly Ln ... 29526
Holly Springs Ct ... 29526
Hollywood Ln ... 29526
Holmes Ct N & S ... 29526
Holt Cir & Rd ... 29526
Home Plantation Rd ... 29526
W Homewood Rd ... 29526
Honeysuckle Ln ... 29527
Honors Rd ... 29526
Hoot N Hollar Ln ... 29526
Hope Cir ... 29527
Hopes Crossing Ct ... 29526
Hopscotch Ln ... 29526
Horry Rd ... 29526
Horry St ... 29527
Horseshoe Cir ... 29527
Hubs Ln ... 29527
Huckleberry Ln ... 29526
Hucks Ln ... 29526
Hucks Rd ... 29526
Hudnall Rd ... 29526
Hughes Ln ... 29526
Hugo Rd ... 29527
Hummingbird Ln ... 29527
Hunter Way ... 29526
Hunters Creek Dr ... 29527
Hunting Swamp Rd ... 29527
Huntington Cir ... 29526
Huntington Ct ... 29527
Huntwood Dr ... 29527
Husted Rd ... 29526
Huston Rd ... 29526
Hydrangea Dr ... 29527
Hyman Ln ... 29526
Ibis Ln ... 29527
Ida Ln ... 29527
Indigo Run ... 29526
Industrial Park Rd ... 29526
Ingonish Ct ... 29527
Inheritance Rd ... 29527
Inland Dr ... 29526
Inlet Ln ... 29526
Inman Cir ... 29526
International Dr ... 29526
Ireland Dr ... 29527
Irene Ct ... 29526
Iris St ... 29526
Isaac Rd ... 29526
Isabella Dr ... 29527
Isla St ... 29527
Island Rd ... 29526
Island Oak Dr ... 29526
Issac Dr ... 29526
Ivy Rd ... 29526
Ivy Glen Dr ... 29526
Ivy Lea Dr ... 29526
E J Dr ... 29526
J And S Countryside
Rd ... 29527
J And T Cir ... 29527
J Reuben Long Ave ... 29526
J T Barfield Ln ... 29527
Jack Pine Ln ... 29526
Jackie Rd ... 29527
Jackson Cir & Ln ... 29526
Jackson Bluff Rd ... 29526
Jacquelyns Ct ... 29527
Jaffa Ct ... 29526
Jake Cv ... 29527
Jama Rd ... 29526
James St ... 29527
James Farm Rd ... 29527
Jamestown Rd ... 29526
Jamie Ln ... 29526
Jamie D Ln ... 29527
Janette St ... 29527
Jasmine Dr ... 29527
Jason Ln ... 29526
Jay Rd ... 29526
Jefferson Cir ... 29527
Jefferson Way ... 29526
Jeffords Dr ... 29527
Jem Dr ... 29527
Jenkins Dr ... 29527
Jenna Macy Dr ... 29526
Jeopardy Ln ... 29526
Jerry Barnhill Blvd ... 29527
Jerusalem Rd ... 29527
Jessamine St ... 29526
Jessica Lakes Dr ... 29526
Jessie Ln ... 29526
Jewel Ln ... 29527
Jill Ct ... 29526
Jody Ln ... 29527
Joe Ben Trl ... 29526
John St
1700-1799 ... 29527
2700-2799 ... 29526
John Doctor Rd ... 29526
John Quincy Cir ... 29526
Johnathon Ln ... 29527
Johnson Ln & St ... 29527
Johnson Shelly Rd ... 29526
Johnson Shortcut Rd ... 29527
W Johnston Rd ... 29527
Jolly Rd ... 29526
Jon Cox Rd ... 29527
Jones St ... 29526

- Jordan Cir 29527
- Jordan Lake Rd 29527
- Joseph Ln 29527
- Jousting Ct 29526
- Joy Rd 29527
- Joy Ride Dr 29526
- Julia Ct 29526
- July Rd 29527
- June Rd 29527
- Juneberry Ln 29526
- Jungle Rd 29526
- Juniper Dr 29526
- Juniper Bay Rd 29527
- Juniper Ridge Rd 29527
- Kara Dr 29527
- Kates Bay Hwy 29527
- Kelly Rd 29526
- Kellys Cove Dr 29526
- Kenneth St 29526
- Kenney Ridge Rd 29526
- Kenworth Cir 29526
- Kenya Ct 29526
- Kerl Rd 29526
- Kermit Ln 29526
- Kerri Cir 29526
- Keysfield Cir 29527
- Kheishei Rd 29526
- Kim Cir 29526
- Kimberly Dr 29526
- Kin Ln 29527
- Kinfolk Rd 29527
- King St 29526
- Kings Rd 29526
- Kingston Ct & St 29526
- Kingston Lake Dr 29526
- Kingston Oaks Dr 29526
- Kingswood Dr 29526
- Kinlaw Ln 29527
- Kinsington Ct 29526
- Kirkland Dr 29526
- Kiskadee Loop 29526
- Kitty Ln 29527
- Knotty Branch Rd 29527
- Kourtni Ln 29527
- Kristen Cir 29526
- Krystal Ln 29527
- L C Dunn Ct 29526
- Labonte St 29526
- Ladson St 29527
- Lake Ann Dr 29527
- Lake Estates Ct 29526
- Lake Way Dr 29527
- Lakeland Dr 29526
- Lakeside Dr 29526
- Lakeside Crossing Dr 29526
- Lakewood Ave 29526
- Lalton Dr 29526
- Lambert Rd 29526
- Lancelot Ln 29526
- Lander Dr 29526
- Landing Rd 29527
- Landmark Rd 29527
- Lanes Dr 29526
- Langston Dr 29526
- Lantana Ln 29526
- Laris Ln 29527
- Laurel St 29526
- Laurelwood Ln 29526
- Lawnwood Dr 29527
- Lawrimore Ln 29527
- Lazy Pine Dr 29527
- Leatherman Rd 29527
- Lee St 29526
- Lee Hucks Ln 29527
- Leebury Ln 29526
- Lees Landing Cir 29526
- Legacy Way 29526
- Legion St 29526
- Lendrim Lake Dr 29526
- Lenox Dr 29526
- Leona Ln 29527
- Leonard Ave 29527
- Leonard Avenue Ext 29527
- Leopard Ct 29526
- Lesia Ln 29526
- Lettie Ln 29526
- Levi Ln 29527
- Leviner Ln 29527
- Lewis St 29526
- Lexus Ln 29526
- Leybourne Ct 29526
- Libbys Ln 29526
- Liberty Ln 29527
- Lighthouse Church Rd 29527
- Lily Pond Ct 29526
- Limbaugh Ln 29526
- Limestone Ln 29526
- Limpkin Dr 29526
- Lincoln Ln 29526
- Lincoln Park Dr 29527
- Linda Dr 29526
- Linda Lou Ct 29527
- Linden Cir 29526
- Liriope Ln 29526
- Lisa Ln 29526
- Lite Rd 29526
- Little St 29526
- Little Bit Mo Ln 29526
- Little Buck Rd 29527
- Little Hill Dr 29527
- Little Lake Ln 29527
- Little Lamb Rd 29527
- Live Oak St 29527
- Liz Ln 29527
- Loblolly Ln 29526
- Lochwood Ln 29526
- Londonberry Ct 29526
- Lone Star St 29526
- Long Ave, Rd & St 29526
- Long Avenue Ext 29526
- Long Branch Rd 29526
- Long Lake Cir 29527
- Long Leaf Pine Dr 29526
- Longwood Ln 29527
- Lonzy Ln 29526
- Looking Glass Ct 29526
- Lora Ln 29527
- Love Ln 29527
- Lovell Ct 29526
- Lu Lu Ln 29526
- Lucas Bay Rd 29527
- Lucy Ln 29526
- Luke Ct 29527
- Lumberjack Ln 29526
- Lundy Ave 29526
- Lundy Short Cut Rd 29527
- Lydick Ln 29527
- Lynette Ct 29526
- Lynn Ct 29526
- Macala Dr & Rd 29527
- Macallan Ct 29526
- Macarthur Dr 29527
- Mack Rd 29526
- Madelyn Ln 29526
- Madge Ct 29526
- Madison Way 29526
- Mae Rd 29526
- Magnolia Ave 29527
- Magnum Dr 29527
- Magrath Ave 29526
- Mahalia Dr 29527
- Main St
  - 200-2571 29526
  - 2570-2570 29528
  - 2572-2612 29526
  - 2573-2671 29526
- Malinda Ct 29526
- Mallard Ct 29526
- Mama Cecil Rd 29526
- Manassas Dr 29526
- Manor Ln 29526
- Maple Ave 29527
- Maple Leaf Dr 29526
- Maple Oak Dr 29526
- Maple Run Rd 29526
- Maplewood Cir 29526
- March Rd 29527
- Marengo Dr 29526
- Marie Ct 29526
- Marigold Rd 29527
- Marina Dr 29526
- Marion St 29527
- Marissa Dr 29526
- Marjory Cir 29527
- Mark Dr 29527
- Marley Ct 29526
- Marley St 29527
- Marsh Dr 29527
- Martha Anns Rd 29526
- Martin Ln 29526
- Martin Luther Dr 29527
- Martinfield Ct 29527
- Martinfield Plantation Dr 29527
- Martins Lake Rd 29527
- Mary Rd 29527
- Maulden St 29527
- Maxine Rd 29526
- May Rd 29527
- Mayberry Ln 29526
- Mayfair Ter 29526
- Mayfield Dr 29526
- Mccall Loop 29526
- Mcclain Farm Ct 29526
- Mccown Dr 29526
- Mccray Aly & Rd 29527
- Mcdermott St 29526
- Mcdougall Dr 29526
- Mcdowell Rd 29526
- Mckeithan St 29526
- Mckeiver St 29527
- Mckinley Way 29526
- Mckinley Short Cut Rd 29526
- Mckoy Pl 29527
- Mcmillan Ln 29526
- Mcmurray Rd 29526
- Mcnair Ln 29526
- Mcneill St 29526
- Mcqueen St 29527
- Meadowbrook Dr 29526
- Meadowlark Cir 29527
- Mecca Ct 29526
- Medieval Dr 29526
- Medlen Pkwy 29526
- Medley Ln 29526
- Melon Hill Rd 29526
- Melson St 29526
- Memory Ln 29527
- Mercedes Dr 29526
- Mercer Dr 29526
- Merrimac Dr 29527
- Merritt Rd 29526
- Merrybell Ln 29527
- Merrymount Dr 29526
- Merrywood Rd 29526
- Middle Bay Dr 29527
- Middle Ridge Ave 29526
- Middleton Rd 29527
- Midtown Village Dr 29526
- Midvale Dr 29527
- Mikes Rd 29526
- Miles Standish Ct 29526
- Mill Berry Ln 29526
- Mill Branch Rd 29526
- Mill Hill Rd 29526
- Mill Pond Rd 29527
- Milledge Dr 29526
- Miller Rd 29526
- Millsite Dr 29526
- Mimosa Ct 29527
- Mineral Springs Rd 29527
- Minnie Mae Dr 29526
- Minsteris Dr 29526
- Miracle Dr & Ln 29527
- Mishoe Rd 29527
- Missouria Ln 29526
- Misty Morning Dr 29527
- Mitchell Dr 29527
- Mobile Rd 29527
- Moccasin Ct 29526
- Mocha Ct 29526
- Molly Ln 29527
- Monterey Ave 29527
- Monti Dr 29526
- Moon Bridge Ct 29526
- Moore Ln 29526
- Morgan Rd 29526
- Morning Dale St 29526
- Morningside Dr 29526
- Morris Rd 29526
- Morris Carter Ct & Rd 29527
- Mosdell Dr 29527
- Moss Cir 29526
- Mount Pisgah Cemetery Rd 29526
- Mount Triumph Ln 29527
- Movile Rd 29527
- Ms Maggie Ln 29526
- Mulberry St 29527
- Mule Trace Dr 29526
- Mums Dr 29526
- Murphy Way 29526
- Murray Johnson Rd 29526
- Murrells Landing Rd 29526
- Muscovy Pl 29526
- Myrtle St 29527
- Myrtle Grande Dr 29526
- Myrtle Greens Dr 29526
- Myrtle Ridge Dr 29526
- Myrtle Trace Dr 29526
- Myrtle Trace Drive Ext 29526
- Nancy Ln 29526
- Naomi Ave 29526
- Naples Dr 29526
- Ned Ln 29527
- Neely Dr 29527
- Neighbor Ln 29527
- New Rd 29527
- New Dawn Rd 29526
- New Grace Ln 29527
- New Home Cir 29526
- New Jamie Rd 29527
- New River Rd 29527
- Nic Nat Pl 29527
- Nicholas St 29527
- Nichole Ln 29527
- Night Owl Ln 29527
- Ninety Park Dr 29526
- Nixon Ave 29527
- Norman St 29526
- Norris Rd 29526
- Northfork Dr 29526
- Northlake Dr 29526
- Norton St 29527
- Notting Hill Ct 29526
- Nottingham Estate Dr 29526
- Nottingham Lakes Ct & Rd 29526
- Nowhere Rd 29526
- Nursery Rd 29526
- Nuzzo Ln 29526
- Oak St 29526
- Oak Grove Rd 29527
- Oak Landing Dr 29527
- Oak Lea Dr 29526
- Oak Log Lake Rd 29526
- Oak Pond Ct 29526
- Oak Tree Ln 29526
- Oakey Estates Dr 29527
- Oakham Dr 29527
- Oakland Ave 29526
- Oakmont Ln 29526
- S Oaks St 29526
- Oasis Pt 29526
- Oconee Ave 29527
- Odell Ln 29526
- Odiham Pl 29527
- Oglethorpe Dr 29527
- Old Altman Rd 29526
- Old Bucksville Rd 29527
- Old Clearpond Rd 29526
- Old Coquina Rd 29526
- Old Dog Bluff Rd 29527
- Old Dunn Ln 29526
- Old Farm Rd 29527
- Old Groves Ln 29526
- Old Hickory Dr 29526
- Old Highway 472 29526
- Old Highway 701 29526
- Old Highway 90 29526
- Old Irish Rd 29526
- Old Little River Rd 29526
- Old Magnolia Dr 29526
- Old Magnolia Ln 29527
- Old Nelson Rd 29526
- Old Packhouse Rd 29527
- Old Pireway Rd 29526
- Old Plantation Rd 29527
- Old Railroad Rd 29527
- Old Reaves Ferry Rd 29526
- Old Tram Rd 29527
- Olde Forde Rd 29526
- Ole Alston Ave 29527
- Ole Amanda Rd 29527
- Ole Bellamy Dr 29527
- Ole Cedar Ln 29526
- Ole David Rd 29527
- Ole King St 29526
- Ole Kristol Rd 29527
- Ole Larry Cir 29527
- Ole Lee Dr 29527
- Ole Moore Dr 29527
- Ole Nobleman Ct 29527
- Ole Pam Rd 29527
- Ole Woodward Ave 29526
- Olin Rd 29526
- Olympus Ln 29526
- Orange Blossom Trl 29526
- Osprey Ln 29527
- Ossie Ln 29527
- Otter Ct 29526
- Outreach Dr 29526
- Owens Ln 29527
- Pace Cir 29527
- Padgett Ln 29526
- Page Dr 29526
- Pageland St 29526
- Palace Ct 29526
- Palasade Ct 29526
- Palm Dr 29526
- Palmetto St 29527
- Pampass Ln 29527
- Pandora Dr 29526
- Pansy Rd 29526
- Pantheon Dr 29526
- Paradise Rd 29527
- Paradise Estates Dr 29526
- Park Ave 29526
- Park Ctr 29527
- Park Hill Dr 29526
- Park View Rd 29526
- Parker Rd 29526
- Parmley Dr 29527
- Partridge Ln 29527
- Party Pines Rd 29526
- Patricia Ct & Dr 29526
- Patriots Hollow Way 29526
- Patterson Dr 29526
- Paul St 29527
- Paula Ct 29526
- Pauley Swamp Rd 29527
- N Pawley Rd 29527
- Payne Ct 29526
- Peace Ct 29527
- Peaceful Ln 29526
- Peacock Dr 29527
- Pearl St 29527
- Pearlwood Ln 29526
- Peavy Dr 29527
- Pebble Ln 29526
- Pecan Ln 29526
- Pecan Grove Blvd 29527
- Peckin Hill Rd 29527
- Pee Dee Hwy 29527
- Peninsula Ct 29526
- Penny Ct 29526
- Penson Dr 29527
- Pepperberry Ct 29526
- Pepperwood Dr 29526
- Perriwinkle Ct 29526
- Perry St 29527
- Perseverance Dr 29526
- Persimmon Rd 29527
- Persivant Dr 29526
- Pet Farm Ln 29527
- Peter Horry Ct 29526
- Phipps Ln 29526
- Phoenix Dr 29526
- Pickens St 29527
- Pickney Ct 29526
- Pine Loop & St 29526
- Pine Crest Cir 29526
- Pine Loop Rd 29526
- Pine Ridge Cir & St 29527
- Pinehaven Ln 29526
- Pinehurst Ln 29526
- Pineland Lake Dr 29526
- Pinetops Dr 29526
- Pinewood Cir 29526
- Pink Ln 29527
- Pioneer Rd 29526
- Piperridge Dr 29526
- Pital Ln 29526
- Pitch Landing Dr & Rd 29527
- Pittman St 29527
- Plantation Cir 29526
- Plum Tree Ln 29526
- Plumber Rd 29527
- Pocono St 29526
- Poinsettia Dr 29526
- Polaris Ct 29527
- Ponderosa Park 29526
- Pope Martin Rd 29527
- Poplar St 29527
- Port Harrelson Rd 29527
- Porter St 29526
- Pottery Landing Dr 29527
- Pottz Trl 29526
- Powell St 29526
- Preakness Cir 29526
- Presbyterian Dr 29526
- Prestbury Dr 29526
- Price Rd 29526
- Price Park Ln 29526
- Primrose Ln 29527
- Privetts Rd 29526
- Professional Park Dr 29526
- Pulaski St 29527
- Pumpkin Ash Loop 29527
- Punch Bowl Rd 29527
- Putney Ct 29526
- Python Cir 29526
- Quail Run 29526
- Quarter Penny Way 29526
- Quiet Ave 29526
- Rabbit Ln 29526
- Rabon Dr 29526
- Racepath Ave
  - 1300-1699 29526
  - 1700-1999 29527
- Radio Ln 29527
- Railroad Dr 29527
- Rainbow Rd 29526
- Rainer St 29527
- Rainsbrook Ct 29526
- Raintree Ln 29526
- Rainwood Rd 29526
- Ralston Ct 29527
- Ram Rd 29527
- Rambling Rose Dr 29527
- Randall Rd 29527
- Ransom St 29526
- Rasberry Ln 29527
- Raven Ln 29526
- Raven Cliff Ct 29526
- Ray Ln 29527
- Raymond St 29526
- Reba Rd 29527
- Rebel Ridge Rd 29526
- Recycle Rd 29526
- Red Bird Ln 29526
- Red Elf Ln 29527
- Redbud Ln 29527
- Reddick Rd 29526
- Redmond Ct 29526
- Redwood Ln 29527
- Regal Rd 29526
- Regency Dr 29526
- Regina Rd 29527
- Register Dr 29527
- Residence Blvd 29526
- Restful Ln 29527
- Reta St 29526
- Rheuark Dr 29527
- Rhine Ct 29526
- Rhodes Rd 29526
- Rhue St 29527
- Richardson St 29526
- Ridge St 29527
- Ridge Point Dr 29526
- Ridgefield Cir 29526
- Ridgewood Dr 29526
- River Rd 29526
- River Country Dr 29526
- River Front N & S 29527
- River Pine Dr 29526
- Riverbirch Dr 29526
- Rivers Edge Dr 29526
- Rivers End Ct 29526
- Riverside Dr 29526
- Rivertown Blvd & Dr 29526
- Riverwatch Dr 29527
- Ro Phen Rd 29526
- Robert Laney Dr 29527
- Robin Rd 29527
- Rocky Ln 29526
- Rodney Rd 29526
- Roena Dr 29527
- Roleighn Rd 29526
- Rolling Hills Dr 29526
- Rolling Terrace Dr 29526
- Ronald Phillips Ave 29527
- Roscoe Rd 29527
- Rose St 29527
- Rose Moss Rd 29527
- Rosebud Dr 29526
- Rosehaven Dr 29527
- Rosehip Ct 29527
- Rosella Ln 29526
- Rosetta Dr 29526
- Roundabout St 29527
- Rowe Pond Rd 29526
- Rowells Ct 29526
- Royals Cir 29526
- Ruby Ln 29527
- Rudder Ct 29526
- Rufus St 29527
- Rush Rd 29526
- Rushmore Dr 29526
- Russell Rd 29526
- Rusty Rd 29526
- Rutledge St 29527
- Sabrina Ln 29526
- Sadie Cir 29526
- Safari Ln 29526
- Sagittarius Ct 29527
- Saint Andrews Ln 29526
- Saint Paul Dr 29526
- Salem St 29526
- Salem Church Rd 29527
- Sam W Ave 29527
- Sanctuary Blvd 29526
- Sand Dollar Dr 29526
- Sand Hill Dr 29526
- Sand Ridge Rd 29526
- Sanderson Dr 29526
- Sandpiper Ln & Rd 29526
- Sandy Oaks Cir 29527
- Sarah Dr 29526
- Sassafras Ln 29526
- Sasser Ln 29527
- Satelite Cir 29526
- Savannah Bluff Rd 29526
- Sawyer St 29527
- Scott Cir 29527
- Sean River Rd 29526
- Seaside Dr 29526
- Security Ln 29527
- Sedgefield St 29527
- Sellers Rd 29526
- Serenity Pl 29526
- Sessions St 29526
- Shady Ln 29526
- Shady Grove Rd 29527
- Shady Moss Ct 29527
- Shaftesbury Ln 29526
- Shalimar Dr 29526
- Shallow Pond Dr 29526
- Shalom Dr 29526
- Shamrock Dr 29526
- Shanlee Dr 29526
- Shannon Pl 29526

Sharon Ct 29526
Shawn Ln 29527
Sheffield Rd 29526
Sheldon Ct 29526
Shell Rd 29526
Shephard Rd 29527
Sherman Pl 29527
Sherry Ave 29527
Sherry Dr 29526
Sherwood Dr 29526
Shoffner Rd 29526
Short Aly 29527
Sidewheeler Rd 29527
Sigma Rd 29526
Silly Ln 29526
Silver Moon Ct 29526
Silver Peak Dr 29526
Silverstone Ct 29526
Sinbad Ln 29527
Sing Ave 29527
Singing Pines Dr 29527
Singleton St 29527
Singleton Ridge Rd 29526
Sioux Swamp Dr 29527
Siwel Rd 29526
Skipper Rd 29526
Skyline Dr 29526
Sleepy Hollow Ln 29527
Small Dr 29526
Smiley Ln 29526
Smith St 29526
Smithfield Dr 29526
Smokehouse Cir 29527
Snider St 29526
Snowhill Dr 29526
Society Dr 29527
Soho Ct 29526
Soldier Rd 29526
Sophie Rd 29526
Southern Living Ln 29527
Spain Ln 29527
Spankie Cir 29527
Spencerswood Dr 29526
Spivey Ave & Dr 29527
Spoleto Ln 29526
Spoonbill Dr 29526
Spring Beauty Dr 29527
Spring Garden Rd 29527
Spring Lake Dr 29526
Spyderco Rd 29527
Squirrel Ridge Rd 29526
Stack House Dr 29526
Stallion Ct 29526
Stalvey Rd 29527
Stalveys Antique Ln 29526
Stamford Rd 29527
Stanley St 29526
Stanway Dr 29526
Starr Dr 29526
Starview Rd 29526
Steamer Trace Rd 29527
Steele Ct 29526
Steep Landing Rd 29526
Steritt Swamp Rd 29526
Stern Dr 29526
Still Meadow Dr 29527
Still Pond Rd 29526
Stilley Cir 29526
Stillwagon Ln 29526
Stonehinge Ct 29526
Stoney Grove Ct 29526
Stoneybrook Dr 29526
Stormy Ln 29527
Straight A Way 29526
Street Rod Ln 29527
Strickland Rd 29526
Stroud Rd 29527
Sudan Ct 29526
Sugar Maple Ln 29526
Suggs St 29527
Summer Dr 29526
Sunbury Dr 29527
Sunflower Dr 29527
Sunmeadow Dr 29526
Sunrise Dr 29527
Sunset Dr 29526
Suzanne Dr 29526
Swamp Fox Dr 29527
Sweet St 29526
Sweetbriar Ln 29526
Sweetpine Ln 29527
Swinton Rd 29527
Switch Rd 29526
Sycamore St 29527
Talon Dr 29527
Tampa Ln 29527
Tanga Ln 29526
Tattlesbury Dr 29526
Taylor Sq 29527
Technology Rd 29526
Tee Jay Ct 29527
Telfair Ct 29526
Temple St 29527
Terrace Ln 29527
Tez Ln 29527
Thomas Rd 29526
Thompson St 29527
Thoroughbred Dr 29526
Three Mile Rd 29527
Three Oak Ln 29526
Three R Dr 29526
Tidway Cir 29527
Tiffany Ln 29526
Tiger Bay Pl 29527
Tiger Grand Dr 29526
Tigger Loop 29527
Tigris Ct 29526
Tillmond Dr 29526
Tilly Ct 29526
Tilly Lake Rd 29526
Tilly Pine Dr 29526
Tilly Swamp Rd 29526
Timber Ridge Rd 29526
Timberline Dr 29526
Timrod Rd 29527
Tin Top Aly 29527
Tinkertown Ave 29527
Tisdale St 29526
Tobacco Rd 29527
Todd Blvd 29526
Todd Ludlam Ln 29526
Tolar Ln 29526
Tolley Rd 29526
Tom Trout Dr 29526
Tower Dr 29526
Townsend Ln 29527
Track Hoe Dr 29527
Tracy Dr 29527
Tranquil Rd 29527
Trapp Ln 29526
Traviana Rd 29526
Trawler Bay Ct 29526
Treatment Rd 29527
Trestle Way 29526
Trierlen Rd 29526
Troutman Cir 29526
Troy Ln 29527
Truman Rd 29526
Tulley Ct 29527
Turkey Ct 29526
Turn Bridge Ln 29526
Turtle St 29527
Turtle Creek Dr 29526
Tweety Ave 29527
Twin Oaks Dr 29526
Twinbrook Ct 29526
Two Pine Dr 29526
Union Rd 29527
University Blvd, Cir & Dr 29526
University Forest Cir & Dr 29526
University Plaza Dr 29526
Upper Mill Rd 29527
Upper Saddle Cir 29526
Utermark Dr 29526
Valenti Dr 29527
Vallie Rd 29526
Varnies Cir 29527
Vassal Ct 29526
Velma Rd 29527
Ventura Rd 29526
Victory Ln 29526
Village St 29526
Vineyard Lake Cir 29527
Vogue Rd 29526
Wa Wa Ct 29526
Waccamaw Cir & Dr 29526
Waccamaw Bend Rd 29527
Waccamaw Lake Dr 29526
Waccamaw Medical Park Ct & Dr 29526
Waccamaw River Dr 29526
Wagon Wheel Ct 29527
Wahee Pl 29527
Wake Forest Rd 29526
Walden Lake Rd 29526
Walking Fern Ct 29526
Wall Ln 29527
Walnut Cir 29526
Waltrip Ct 29526
Wanda Ln 29526
Wandering Way 29526
Wando Rd 29527
Ward Cir 29527
Warf Dr 29526
Warm Springs Ln 29527
Warren Springs Dr 29527
Warwick Cir 29526
Washington Ave 29526
Waterman Ln 29526
Watershed Dr 29527
Waterside Dr 29527
Watson Dr 29527
Watts Rd 29526
Wayna Marie Ln 29527
Wayside Rd 29527
Weaver Rd 29527
Webb St 29527
Wedding Ln 29526
Wedgefield Dr 29526
Wedgewood Ln 29526
Weldon Ln 29526
Welkin Ct 29526
Wellfound Ct 29526
Wellman Ct 29526
Wellspring Dr 29526
Wendy Ln 29526
Wesley Dr 29527
West Rd 29527
Westbrook Dr 29526
Westmoreland Rd 29526
Weston Dr 29526
Westridge Blvd 29527
Westville Dr 29526
Wet Cir 29526
Wetlands Industrial Dr 29526
Whispering Woods Rd 29526
White Fox Ct 29526
White Oak Forest Pl 29527
White Rose Ln 29527
White Sand Ln 29526
White Water Loop 29526
Whittemore St 29527
Whitts Aly 29526
Whooping Crane Dr 29526
Wigeon Dr 29526
Wilbur Rd 29527
Wilbur Dunn Pl 29526
Wilcot Branch Ct 29526
Wild Blueberry Ln 29527
Wild Life Ln 29527
Wild Wing Blvd 29527
Wilderness Rd 29526
Wildhorse Cir & Dr 29526
Will Park Ln 29526
Willard Rd 29526
Willet Cv 29526
William Bradford Pl 29526
William Finlayson Rd 29526
Williams St 29526
Williamson Lake Cir 29526
Williamson Park Dr 29526
Willie James Rd 29526
Willie Joes Ct 29527
Willow Ct & Rd 29526
Willow Brook Rd 29526
Willow Green Dr 29526
Willow Oak Dr 29526
Willow Springs Rd 29527
Wilson Ln 29526
Winburn Rd 29527
Wincrest Ct 29526
Wind Ridge Rd 29526
Wind Tree Ln 29526
Windemere Ct 29526
Winding Rd 29526
Windmeadows Dr 29526
Windsor Springs Rd 29527
Windy Hill Dr 29526
Winter Rain Dr 29527
Winterberry Ct 29526
Winterwood Ln 29527
Winthrop Ln 29526
Winyah Rd 29526
Wise Rd 29526
Wisteria Ave 29526
Wofford Cir, Ln & Rd 29526
Wolf Trl 29527
Wonderland Dr 29526
Woodall Ct 29526
Woodbriar Bnd 29527
Woodcock Dr 29526
Woodcreek Ln 29527
Woodduck Ct 29526
Woodfield Cir & Dr 29526
Woodford Ct 29526
Woodholme Dr 29526
Woodhurst Dr 29527
Woodland St 29526
Woodlawn Dr 29526
Woodman Dr 29526
Woodruff Ct 29526
Woodstork Dr 29526
Woodward Dr 29527
Woodwinds Dr 29526
Woody Ln 29526
Wren Ln 29527
Wright Blvd
300-422 29526
423-1900 29527
1902-1998 29527
Wylie Ct 29526
Wynford Dr 29526
Yawnoc Dr 29526
Yeager Ave 29526
Yellow Rose Ct 29526
Young St 29527
Youpon Dr 29526
Za Ga Zig Ln 29526
Zaccheus Ln 29527

NUMBERED STREETS

1st Ave 29526
2nd Ave 29526
2nd Loop Rd 29526
3rd Ave 29526
4th Ave
900-1699 29526
1700-3399 29527
5th Ave
800-1699 29526
1700-1800 29527
6th Ave
800-1699 29526
1700-2299 29527
7th Ave
900-1699 29526
1900-2299 29527
8th Ave
1300-1599 29526
2100-2399 29527
9th Ave
500-1609 29526
1610-3299 29527
10th Ave 29526
11th Ave 29526
12th Ave 29526
13th Ave 29526
14th Ave 29526
15th Ave & Ct 29526
16th Ave
500-1399 29526
1400-1799 29527
17th Ave 29526
18th Ave 29526
100th St 29526

DARLINGTON SC

General Delivery 29532

POST OFFICE BOXES MAIN OFFICE STATIONS AND BRANCHES

Box No.s
All PO Boxes 29540

NAMED STREETS

A Ave 29532
Abbott Rd 29540
Abby Dr 29532
Abe Lincoln St 29532
Advance Ln 29532
Air Force Ct 29540
Airline Dr 29532
Alabama Dr 29532
Albert Dr 29540
Alexander St 29532
Alice Ln 29532
Allen St 29532
Allentown St 29532
Amanda Ln 29540
Amazing Run 29532
Ambergate Dr 29540
Amberwood Dr 29532
Amoretta Dr 29532
Anderson Dr & Rd 29532
Anderson Farm Rd 29532
Andy Ln 29532
Angel Wing Dr 29540
Angelica Cir 29532
Anhow St 29532
Apartment Cir 29540
Apple St 29532
Applegate Ln 29532
April Dr 29532
Arabian St 29532
Arapaho Cir 29532
Arlington St 29532
Arnold St 29532
Asbury St 29532
Ash St 29532
Ashley Oaks Dr 29540
Athol St 29532
Atlantic St 29532
Auburn School Rd 29540
Auburndale Rd 29540
Auction Ave 29532
Augusta Dr 29532
Autrey St 29532
Awesome Dr 29532
Azalea Dr 29532
B Ave 29532
Back St 29532
Bacote St 29532
Baltimore Cir 29532
Barbara Dr 29532
Barclay Rd 29532
Barcus Dr 29532
Barfield Rd 29532
Baron Dr 29532
Basswood Dr 29540
Bastion Blvd 29540
Bayberry Dr 29532
Bayfield Dr 29532
Bear Den Rd 29540
Beatrice St 29532
Beaver Dr 29532
Beaverdam Ct 29532
Becky Ln 29540
Bell Acres Dr 29532
Bellhaven Dr 29532
Belvin St 29532
Bennett Dr 29532
Bennie Aly 29532
Bernice St 29540
Berts Dr 29532
Bessie Dr 29540
Beth Dr 29540
Bethea Rd 29532
Beverly Dr 29532
Big Foot Ln 29532
Big Pine Rd 29540
E Billy Farrow Hwy 29532
Bird Bath Ln 29532
Birdsnest Rd 29532
Bishop Dr 29540
Black Creek Rd 29540
Blackmon Ln 29532
Blackwell Cir 29532
Blue St 29532
Blue Mist Dr 29532
Bluebird Ln 29540
Bob Cat Dr 29532
Bogan Ln 29532
Boiling Springs Rd 29532
Bonaparte Dr 29532
Bonfire Rd 29532
Bonnoitt St 29532
Boots Ln 29540
Borders Dr 29532
Borough St 29532
Bowens St 29532
Boyd St 29532
Bracey Ave 29532
Brad Dr 29532
Brandon Dr 29532
Branham Dr 29532
Branhams Airport Rd 29532
Braves Ave 29540
Braxton Cir 29532
Brearly St 29532
Breezewood Dr 29540
Bridle Path Ln 29532
Bristow Farm Rd 29532
Brittain Rd 29532
E & W Broad St 29532
Brockington Rd 29532
Bronco Rd 29532
Brooks Dr 29540
Brookwood Cir 29540
Brown St 29532
Bruce St 29532
Brunson St 29532
Bryant St 29540
Bubbly Brook Dr 29532
Buchanan St N & S 29532
Buddy Ln 29532
Bull Rd 29532
Bunnys Dr 29532
Burkitts Ln 29532
Byrd Ave 29532
C Ave 29532
Cabin Trl 29532
Cacamar Ln 29540
Cagle St 29532
Cain St 29532
Calhoun St 29532
Camellia Ct 29532
Camellia Hill Dr 29532
Camp Rd 29532
Campbell Ln 29532
Candleberry Dr 29532
Candlelight Dr 29532
Cannon Dr 29532
Capricorn Dr 29540
Carl Cir 29532
Carley Ave 29532
Carol Dr 29532
Carolina Dr 29532
Carolina Breeze Dr 29532
Caroline Cir 29532
Case St 29532
Cashua St 29532
Cashua Ferry Rd 29532
Catfish Dr 29532
Catherine St 29532
Cedar Ct 29532
Cedar Ln 29540
Cedar Ridge Rd 29540
Cedarwood Ct 29532
S Center Rd 29532
Central St 29532
Central Pointe Park 29532
Chain St 29532
Chalmers Dr & St 29532
Champ Dr 29540
Charan Rd 29540
Charles Dr 29540
N Charleston Rd 29540
S Charleston Rd 29532
Charleston Way 29532
Chasity Dr 29532
Cherry St 29532
Cherry Grove Rd 29540
Chesterfield Lumber Dr 29532
Chestnut St 29532
Chickadee Ln 29540
Childrens Farm Rd 29532
Chinaberry St 29532
Chip Run Dr 29540
Chippendale Ln 29532
Christian Ct 29532
Churchill St 29532
Circle Dr 29532
City Ln 29532
Clants Dr 29532
Clara Rd 29532
Clarice Ln 29532
Clay Pit Dr 29540
Cleveland St 29532
Clifton Ln 29540
Clover St 29540
Coefield Ave 29532
Coggeshall Rd 29532
Coker St 29532
Coleman Dr 29532
Columbian St 29532
Comfort Ln 29532
Conder Cir 29532
Cone St 29532
Confederate St 29540
Converse Ct 29540
Cookie Hill Cir 29532
Cool Brook Dr 29532
Coon Hunter Dr 29540
Coop Dr 29532
Cooper Dr 29532
Copeland Dr 29532
Corn Patch St 29532
Corner Ln 29532
Cornerboard Ln 29532
Corporation Way 29532
Cotton St 29532
Cotton Patch Rd 29532
Cottonfield Ln 29532
Cottonwood Dr 29540
Country Ct 29532
Country Club Rd 29532
Country Manor Rd 29532
Country Squire Rd 29540
Couplin Pl 29532
Court St 29532
Couture Dr 29532
Crabapple Dr 29540
Craft Rd 29532
Crane Ln 29540
Creek Crossing Rd 29540
Creekview Dr 29540
Crickintree Ln 29532
Cross St 29532
Crosswinds Dr 29532
Crowley St 29532
Crystal Springs Dr 29540
Cunningham Ct 29532
Curtis Dr 29540
Cypress St 29532
D Ave 29532
Daisy St 29532
Damon Dr 29532
Daniel St 29532
Darandow Rd 29532
N & S Dargan St 29532

Dargan Farms Rd 29532
Darlington Ave 29532
Daventry Dr 29532
David St 29532
Davis St 29532
Davis Farm Rd 29532
Dawns Dr 29532
Deerfield Rd 29532
Delaware Dr 29532
Denise Dr 29532
Derby Dr 29532
Devaughan Dr 29532
Dewitt Cir 29532
Diamond Way 29532
Diana Dr 29532
Dingo Ln 29532
Divinity Rd 29532
Dixie Dr 29532
Dixon Dr 29532
Docs House Rd 29540
Dogwood Ave 29532
Donald Ln 29532
Doneraile St 29532
Dontia Ave 29540
Dorla Rd 29532
Dotts Cir 29532
Dove Ct 29532
Dove Trail Rd 29540
Dovesville Hwy 29540
Drakes Nest Ln 29532
Dreamland Trl 29540
Drew Dr 29540
Dubose St 29532
Duck Cove Dr 29532
Dust Bath Rd 29540
Dutch St 29532
Dutton Ln 29532
Duval Ln 29532
E Ave 29532
Earl St 29532
Easler Rd 29532
Eastburn Ct 29532
Ebenezer Rd 29532
Echo Acres Dr 29532
Eddie Dr 29540
Edith St 29532
Edna St 29532
Edwards Ave 29532
Elbow Rd 29532
Eldon Dr 29532
Elissa Dr 29540
Ellarela Rd 29540
Elliott St 29532
Ellison Ave 29532
Elm St 29532
Elma Cir 29532
Elvin Dr 29532
Emmaus Rd 29540
Erinvine Ct 29532
N & S Ervin St 29532
Ervin Pasture Dr 29532
Evander Dr 29540
Evangeline Dr 29532
Evans St 29532
Evelyn Cir 29540
Everlasting Branch Rd 29540
Exchange St 29532
Express Ln 29532
F Ave 29532
Fairway Dr 29532
Faith Ln 29532
Family St 29540
Fantasy Ln 29532
Farm St 29532
Farmhouse Ln 29540
Farmwood Cottage Dr 29532
Farrow Ridge Ct 29540
Faulkner Dr 29532
Fawn Dr 29532
Feather Rd 29540
Field Pond Rd 29540
Flat Creek Rd 29540
Flatnose Rd 29540
Fleet Cir 29532
Fleming St 29532
Flora Dr 29532
Florida Dr 29532
Flounder Fun Rd 29532
Flowers St 29532
Floyds Rd 29540
Flycatcher Ln 29540
Flynn Cir 29532
Forest Dr 29540
Fountain St 29532
Fox Hollow Dr 29532
Franklin St 29532
Franway Dr 29532
Freeman St 29532
Friendly St 29532
Friendship St 29532
Fulton Rd 29532
Funderburke St 29532
G Ave 29532
G Graham Segars Pkwy 29540
Gandy St 29532
Gandy Farm Rd 29540
Gann Dr 29532
Gardner St 29532
Garnet St 29532
Gat Dr 29540
Gathering Place Ln 29540
Gee Money Dr 29540
Gemini Dr 29532
Geneva Dr 29532
Gentle Rd 29532
George And Hayes Ln 29532
Georgeanna Ln 29532
Georgetown Rd 29532
Georgia Dr 29532
Gilchrist Rd
300-599 29532
600-1499 29540
Glenwood Dr 29540
Gloria Dr 29532
Go Kart Ln 29532
Godbold Dr 29532
Goodson Farm Rd 29540
Goose Rd 29540
N Governor Williams Hwy
100-1099 29532
1100-4699 29540
S Governor Williams Hwy 29532
Grace St 29532
Graham Dr 29540
Grand Dr 29532
Grandpa Rd 29532
Gray Dr 29532
Grayson Cir 29532
Great Cypress Rd 29540
Green Dr 29532
Green Pines Cir 29540
Green Street Rd 29532
Greenfield Rd 29540
Greenview Dr 29532
Greenway Dr 29532
Grove St 29532
Guess St 29532
Gumtree Dr 29532
Gunther Dr 29532
Gus Dr 29532
Gwendolyn Dr 29532
H Ave 29532
Halston Rd 29540
Ham Rd 29532
Hamlin Dr 29532
E & W Hampton St 29532
Hanger Access Rd 29540
Hank Haynie Dr 29532
Harllee Dr 29532
Harmony Dr 29532
Harmony Hall Dr 29540
Harper St 29532
Harry Byrd Hwy 29532
Hart St 29532
Hartsville Hwy 29540
Harvest Ln 29532
Hayfield Rd 29532
Haynesworth Aly 29532
Heather Dr 29540
Heathwood Dr 29540
Helton St 29532
Henry St 29532
Heron Pointe Dr 29532
Hewitt St 29532
Hickory St 29532
Hickory Hill Rd 29540
Hidden Ln 29540
High Cotton St 29532
High Hill Rd 29532
Highland Dr 29532
Hill Creek Rd 29532
Hill Park Dr 29532
Hodges Dr 29532
Hoffmeyer Rd 29532
Hollomans Dr 29540
Holly Cir 29532
Holy Ln 29540
Home Ave 29532
Home Park Ln 29532
Home Place Rd 29540
Homebound Ln 29540
Honeybee Dr 29532
Honeydew Rd 29532
Honeysuckle Rd 29540
Hoole St 29532
Hope Rd 29532
E & W Horse Branch Trl 29540
Horseshoe Bend Dr 29532
Horseshoe Lake Dr 29532
Hospitality Trl 29532
Howard St 29532
Howle Ave 29532
Howle Park St 29532
Hubbard Dr 29532
Huckleberry St 29532
Hudson Ln 29532
Huggins Farm Rd 29532
Hummingbird Ln 29540
Humphries Rd 29532
Hunter St 29532
Hyde Park Rd 29532
Icoe Ln 29532
Imperial Dr 29540
Indian Branch Rd 29532
Indigo Dr 29540
Industrial Way 29532
Ingram Ct 29532
Inspiration Way 29532
Irene Ln 29532
Iroquois St 29532
Irrigation Way 29532
Isaac Ln 29540
Iseman Rd 29532
Isgett Rd 29540
Ivey Ct 29540
Jackson St 29532
Jacobs Dr 29532
Jade St 29532
James St 29532
James Paul Dr 29532
Jamestown Ave 29532
Jamonica Ln 29540
Jans Dr 29532
Jefferson St 29532
Jeffery St 29532
Jeffords Mill Rd 29540
Jeffries Creek Rd 29532
Jenkins Dr 29532
Jennifer Ln 29532
Jernigan Ln 29540
Jerome St 29532
Jessamine St 29532
Jessie Ln 29532
Jetts Way Dr 29540
Jewel Dr 29532
Jimmy Ln 29532
Joe Louis Blvd 29532
John Deere Rd 29532
Johns Ln 29532
Johnson St 29532
Joja Rd 29532
Jones Rd 29532
Jordan St 29532
Joseph Hill St 29532
Josephine Rd 29532
Journeys End Rd 29540
Joy St 29532
Joy Star Ct 29532
Judor Ct 29540
Judson Dr 29532
Juleswood Dr 29532
Jupiter Dr 29532
Jupiter Venus St 29532
Justice Rd 29540
Kant Ave 29532
Kate Ln 29532
Keith Cir 29540
Kelly Dr 29540
Kenilworth Cir 29532
Kennedy St 29540
Kentucky Dr 29532
Keywest Dr 29532
Kimberly Dr 29532
Kindness Ln 29532
King Dr 29532
King Edwards St 29532
Kingfisher Dr 29532
Kirby Dr 29540
Kirven St 29532
Kitty Hawk Dr 29532
Knight St 29532
Knight Heron Ln 29532
Knotty Pine Rd 29532
Kodiak Dr 29540
L M S Dream Cir 29532
Ladys Ln 29532
Lake Grove Dr 29532
Lake Red Wing Dr 29532
Lake Swamp Rd 29532
Lakeland Dr 29540
Lamar Hwy 29532
Lands End Dr 29532
Langley Dr 29540
Langston Rd 29532
Lantern Dr 29532
Laredo Ln 29532
Larrys Dr 29532
Larymore Dr 29540
Laurel Ave 29532
Laurelwood Dr 29540
Laurentis Ln 29532
Lavendar St 29532
Law St 29532
Law Plantation Rd 29540
Lawson Rd 29532
Lawton Ln 29532
Lazy Pines Rd 29540
Leavensworth Rd 29540
Lee St 29532
Legrand Dr 29532
Lemon Dr 29540
Lennon Ave 29532
Leo Dr 29540
Leon Blvd 29532
Les Dr 29532
Lewis Dr 29532
Liberty St 29532
Lide St 29532
Lide Springs Rd 29540
Lighthouse Rd 29532
Lighty St 29532
Limit St 29532
Lincoln Blvd 29532
Little Branch Dr 29532
Lizzy Ln 29540
Lochend Dr 29532
Lofty Pines Dr 29540
Log Cabin Rd 29532
Log Jam Dr 29532
London Fog Dr 29540
Long Marsh Rd 29532
Longleaf Dr 29540
Lonnie Dr 29532
Lookout Dr 29540
Louise Rd 29540
Loupo Pl 29532
Lucas St 29532
Lucky Penny Ln 29532
Lunn Rd 29532
Magnolia St 29532
Mahlon St 29532
N Main St
100-1199 29532
1200-1499 29540
S Main St 29532
Major Dr 29540
Mallard Duck Dr 29532
Mandy Ln 29540
Margaret Dr 29532
Marie Dr 29540
Mark Pond Dr 29532
Mars Dr 29532
Marshall St 29532
Martin St 29532
Mary Dr 29532
Mary Jay Ln 29532
Maryland Dr 29532
Masters Way 29532
N & S Mccall St 29532
Mccowns Millpond Rd 29540
Mccoy Dr 29532
Mcdaniel Ln 29532
Mcinnis St 29532
Mcinville Dr 29540
E & W Mciver Rd 29532
Mcneil Rd 29540
Meadow Ln 29532
Meadow Lark Ln 29540
Meadowview Dr 29532
Mechanicsville Hwy 29540
Medford Dr 29532
Mercury Dr 29532
Merit Ln 29532
Merzelle Ln 29532
Middle Branch Rd 29532
Miller Rd 29532
Milling St 29532
Millstream Rd 29540
Millwood Ave 29540
Min Lou Cir 29532
Mineral Springs Rd
100-599 29532
600-1899 29540
Mission Home Cir 29532
Misty Ln 29532
Mohican Dr 29540
Monroe Dr 29532
Mont Clare Rd 29540
Moonshadow Ln 29540
Moore St 29532
Moore Airport Rd 29532
Morocco St 29532
Moses Dr 29532
Mount Sinai Dr 29540
Muldoon Ln 29532
Murphys Law Cir 29532
Murrayhill Rd 29532
Murraywood Rd 29532
Mustang Rd 29532
My Lady Cir 29532
N & S Myrtle Dr 29532
Myrtlewood Dr 29540
Mystic Pines Dr 29540
Nancys Dr 29532
Nathan St 29532
Navarre Rd 29532
Nephi Rd 29532
Nest Rd 29540
Nettles Rd 29532
Nettlewood Rd 29532
New Hopewell Rd 29540
Nez Perce Dr 29532
Nicole Cir 29532
Nolan Dr 29532
Nora Dr 29532
Norbeck Ln 29540
Nordell St 29532
Norman Dr 29540
North St 29532
Norwood Cir 29532
Nursery Rd 29532
Oak St 29532
Oak Commons Dr 29540
Oakland Dr 29540
Oaklyn Rd 29532
Oakview Dr 29532
Oakwood St 29532
Oasis Island Ln 29532
Ocie St 29532
Odom St 29532
Oklahoma Dr 29532
Old Florence Rd 29532
Old Lamar Hwy 29532
Old Millpond Rd 29540
Oleander Dr
500-999 29532
1000-1699 29540
Oneal Cir 29540
Opal St 29532
Orange St 29532
Ours Ct 29540
Outback Ln 29532
Owens Dr 29532
Owl Cir 29540
Oxford Dr 29532
Packhouse Rd 29540
Padgett Ln 29532
Palmetto Cir & Rd 29532
Pan Rd 29532
Pandys Dr 29532
Parallel Rd 29532
Park St 29532
Parker Dr 29540
Parrott St 29532
Patience St 29532
Paul St 29532
Pawnee Dr 29532
Peach St 29532
Peachland Dr 29540
Peachtree Dr 29532
Peacock Dr 29532
Pearl St 29532
Pebble Dr 29532
Pecan Ln 29532
Pee Dee Landing Dr 29532
Pelican Ln 29540
Peniel Ln 29532
Penn Rd 29532
Pepper Dr 29532
Periwinkle St 29532
Pettit St 29532
Pheasant Dr 29532
Philadelphia St 29532
Phillips St 29532
Phoebe Ln 29532
Pierce Dr 29540
Pilgrim Dr 29540
Pine St 29532
Pine Log Cir 29540
Pinedale Dr
100-799 29532
800-1899 29540
Pineforest Ln 29540
Pinehaven Ave 29532
Pineview Dr 29532
Pineville Rd 29532
Pinewood Dr 29532
Pink Dogwood St 29532
Pit Rd 29540
Planters Dr 29532
Player St 29532
Plum St 29532
Pocket Rd 29532
Pond Ln 29540
Ponderosa Dr 29532
Pone St 29532
Popular St 29532
Post And Point Farm Rd 29532
Potato House Rd 29532
Powerline Dr 29540
Precious Ln 29532
President St 29540
Preston Ln 29532
Price Ct 29532
Private Rd 29532
Prophet Dr 29540
Providence Dr 29532
Public Sq 29532
Quack Rd 29532
Quail Hollow Dr 29532
Quality Ln 29532
Quiet Brook Rd 29540
Quincy Ln 29540
Raccoon Dr 29532
Race Track Rd 29532
Railroad Ave 29532
Rally Cir 29532
Ramona Dr 29532
Randy Rd 29540
Rasma Dr 29540
Raspberry Ln 29532
Raven Ct 29532
Rays Dr 29532
Ready Dr 29532
Red St 29532
Red Camellia Dr 29532
Red Cedar St 29532
Red Tip Ln 29540
Redwood St 29532
Register Dr 29540
Reid St 29532
Remount Rd 29540
Reservoir St 29532
Resolution Ln 29532
Rhodes Community Rd 29540
Richards Ave 29532
Richmond St 29532
Ricky Dr 29532
Ridge Rd 29532
Ridgeway Dr 29532
Rio Dr 29532
Riverview Rd 29532
Roanoke Dr 29532
Robert Dr 29532
Robin Ln 29532
Robin Woods Ln 29540
Rocking Chair Dr 29532
Roena Ln 29540
Rogers Rd 29532
Romance Dr 29540
Rosa St 29532
Rosalee Dr 29532
Rose Bud Ln 29540
Ross St 29532
Round O Rd 29540
Royce Rd 29540
Ruby St 29532
Ruff Rd 29540
Rummell Rd 29532
Running Brook Rd 29540
Russell St 29532
Ruth Dr 29540
Saint Johns St 29532
Saleeby Loop 29532
Sallie St 29532
Salt Pepper Ranch Rd 29540
Samuel Dr 29532
Samuel Rd 29540
Samuel Benjamin Ave 29532
Sandbar Rd 29532
Sanders St 29532
Sandridge Dr 29532
Sandy Pine Ln 29540
Sandy Spring Ln 29540
Sanfran Cir 29532
Sapphire St 29532
Sarges Pl 29532
Sartor Dr 29532
Saturn Dr 29532
Scipio Dr 29540
Seed Tick Dr 29540
Segars Ct 29532
Selena Dr 29540
Settlement Dr 29532
E Seven Pines St 29532
Shady Ln 29532
Shanndora Dr 29532
Sharon Woods Dr 29532
Shawnee Dr 29532
Shearin St 29532
Sheffield Dr 29532
Sheldon Dr 29532
Shilow Dr 29540
Shirley St 29540
Short Coker St 29532
Shoshone Dr 29532
Shuler St 29532

Silverpine Ln 29540
Silverqueen Rd 29532
Simon Dr 29532
Sir Adams Ln 29532
Siskron St 29532
Skeets Farm Rd 29540
Skinner Dr 29532
Skyview Dr 29532
Slingshot Dr 29532
E & W Smith Ave 29532
Society Hill Rd
 100-499 29532
 500-3033 29540
Sohneman Dr 29532
Soulful Ln 29532
Southborough Rd 29532
Southern Pine St 29532
Southfork Dr 29532
N & S Spain St 29532
Spanish Moss Ln 29532
Sparks St 29532
Spears St 29532
Spillway Dr 29532
Spring St 29532
Spring Acres Dr 29532
Spring Heights Cir 29532
Springfield Cir 29532
Springflowers Rd 29532
Springview Dr 29532
N Springville Rd 29540
S Springville Rd 29532
Sprout Rd 29532
Squirt Dr 29540
Stallion Rd 29532
Stanley Cir 29532
Steel Mill Rd 29540
Stem St 29532
Stillfork Rd 29532
Stillwater Dr 29532
Stone Rd 29532
Stoney Hill Dr 29540
Strawberry Cir 29532
Strickland Ter 29532
Sturgeon Dr 29532
Sturkie Dr 29540
Sugar Shack Rd 29532
Sunburst Dr 29532
Sunflower Ct 29532
Sunny Ln 29532
Sunset Dr 29532
Sunset Cottage Ln 29532
Survival Dr 29532
Susan Dr 29532
Sweet Bay Dr 29540
Swinton Ln 29532
N & S Sycamore St 29532
Sylvia Ln 29532
Syracuse St 29532
Syracuse Community Rd 29532
Tall Pines Dr 29540
Tallokas Trl 29532
Tallulah St 29532
Tamara Ln 29532
Tamlu Dr 29532
Tapper Dr 29532
Technology Dr 29532
Tedder St 29532
Tee Cir 29532
Teebo Ln 29532
Tega Dr 29532
Tennessee Dr 29532
Terrell St 29532
Thank You Blvd 29532
Theressa Dr 29532
Theron Cove Ct 29532
Thomas Dr 29532
Thompson Dr 29532
Thrasher Ct 29532
Tiffany Ln 29532
Tifton Dr 29532
Timber Dr 29532
Timmonsville Hwy 29532
Tims Dr 29532
Tina Ln 29532
Tish Dr 29540
Tobias Dr 29532
Tom Dr 29532
Tom Brooks Dr 29540
Tonda Ln 29532
Toy Ln 29532
Trackside Dr 29532
Trestle St 29532
Trexler St 29532
Treys Dr 29532
Trimble Rd 29532
Trinity Gate Ln 29532
Trudie Ave 29532
Trussel Falls Rd 29540
Tulip Dr 29532
Tunnel Rd 29532
Turkey Run Ln 29540
Turning Point Dr 29532
Turnpike Rd 29532
Turtle Hill Dr 29540
Twilight Ln 29532
Twin Oaks Ct 29540
N & S Twitty St 29532
Valley Creek Dr 29540
Vance Dr 29540
Vaughan St 29532
Venus Dr 29532
Vi Cliff Rd 29532
Victory Dr 29532
Viola Ln 29532
Virgil Wells Cir 29532
Virginia Dr 29532
Waddell Dr 29532
Wagon Rd 29532
Waiter Ln 29532
Walking Horse Way 29532
Wallace Park Ln 29540
Wallflower Ln 29540
Walton Dr 29532
Ward St 29532
N & S Warley St 29532
Washington St 29532
Watchmans Ln 29532
Watercrest Dr 29532
Wateree Rd 29532
Watford St 29532
Watkins St 29532
Watson St 29532
Watts Pl 29532
Way Off Rd 29532
Weaver St 29532
Wedgewood Dr 29532
Welling Farm Rd 29532
Wellman Rd 29532
Wells St 29532
Wesley Church St 29532
Westside Ave 29532
Wetlands Dr 29532
Wheat Field Dr 29540
Wheeler Siding Rd 29532
Whipple St 29532
Whippoorwill Dr 29540
Whiskey Rd 29532
Whispering Pines Dr 29532
Whit St 29532
White Magnolia Ave 29532
Whites Cir 29532
Wild Cat Ln 29532
Wild Cherry Ln 29532
Wildcat Ln 29532
Wilds St 29532
Wildshall Rd 29540
Wilkinson Ln 29540
Willcox St 29532
Williams Dr 29532
Williamson Pl 29532
S Williamson Park Dr 29532
Willistine Ave 29540
Willowtree Rd 29540
Wilson St 29532
Wilson Village Dr 29532
Windham Dr 29532
Winding Oaks Rd 29532
Windsor Dr 29532
E & W Wine St 29532
Wing Haven Dr 29532
Wingate St 29532
Winlark Dr 29540
Winston Ct & St 29532
Wintergreen Dr 29532
Wire Rd 29532
Wither Spoon Way 29532
Wonderful Dr 29532
Wood Chuck Dr 29532
Wood Creek Rd 29532
Wood Duck Dr 29532
Wood Hill Ln 29532
Woodard Farm Rd 29540
Woodhaven Dr 29532
Woodland Dr 29532
Woods St 29532
Woods Dargan Rd 29532
Woodspond Dr 29540
Woodstream Dr 29532
Wrenfield Rd 29532
Wyandot St 29532
Yankee Dr 29532
Yarboro Ln 29532
Yellow Hammer Ct 29532
York Sq 29532
Young St 29532
Young Farm St 29532
Yow Byrd Ave 29540
Yoyo Dr 29540
Zackview Dr 29540

NUMBERED STREETS

All Street Addresses 29532

EASLEY SC

General Delivery 29640

POST OFFICE BOXES MAIN OFFICE STATIONS AND BRANCHES

Box No.s
All PO Boxes 29641

NAMED STREETS

E, W & N A Ave & St 29640
Abbey Rd 29642
Abigail Ln 29640
Acorn Hill Ct 29640
Acquillious Ln 29642
N & S Adams Ct 29642
Addington Dr 29640
Addis St 29640
Adger Rd
 100-199 29640
 200-499 29642
Agnes Ct 29640
Ahlstrom Way 29640
Airy Springs Rd 29642
Albatross Rd 29640
Albertson Dr 29642
Alethia St 29642
Alex Dr 29640
Alfred Rd 29640
Alicia Ln 29640
Allan St 29640
Allana Ln 29640
Allison Ct 29642
Alpen Rd 29642
Alpine Dr 29640
Altman Dr 29640
Ambergate Ct 29642
Amberly Ct 29642
Amberway Rd 29640
Amesbury Ln 29642
Amherst Way 29642
Ammons Way 29640
Amy Ln 29640
Anastasia Ct 29642
S And S Dr 29640
Anders Ln 29640
Anderson Hwy & Rd 29642
Andover Turn 29642
Andrea Cir & Ln 29642
Andrew Ave 29640
Andrews Cor 29642
Andy Ct 29642
Angelwing Dr 29642
Angie Ln 29642
Anna St 29640
Anne Dr 29640
Annenberg Ln 29642
Annex Way 29642
Ansel Ct 29642
Anthony Rd 29640
Antioch Rd 29640
Anton Dr 29642
Anzio St 29640
Apple Hill Rd 29642
April Dr 29642
Arcadian Ln 29642
Argonne Dr 29640
W Arial St 29640
Ariel Way 29642
Arizona Rd 29642
Arlen Ave 29642
Arlington Ave 29640
Armistead Ln 29642
Arrendale Ct & Ln 29640
Arron Dr 29640
Arrowhead Trl 29642
Arrowridge Dr 29640
Arthur Dr 29642
Asbury Cir 29640
Ascot Ct & Dr 29642
Ash Ct 29642
Ashbury Ct 29642
Ashford Ct 29642
Ashley Ct 29642
Ashmore Ln 29642
Ashton Ct 29642
Ashwood Ln 29640
Aspenwood Ln 29642
Associate Dr 29642
Astor St 29642
Atlantic Ave 29642
Audley Ct 29642
Audubon Acres Dr 29642
Augusta St 29640
Austin Ave 29640
Auston Woods Cir 29640
Autumn Ln 29642
Avalon Cir 29640
Avalon Ln 29640
Avendell Dr 29642
Avery Ct 29642
Avery Dr 29640
E, W, N & S B Ave & St 29640
Bagwell Dr & St 29640
Bailey Brown Rd 29640
Baker Ct & Rd 29640
Bakerville Rd 29642
Baldwin Pl 29642
Ballard Ct 29642
N Ballard Dr 29640
Ballard Hill Rd 29642
Ballentine Rd & St 29642
Balsam Ct 29640
Balsam Dr 29642
Banks Rd 29640
Bannister St 29640
Barbrey Dr 29642
Barfield Dr 29642
Barkley St 29640
Barlet Ln 29640
Barnett Way 29640
Barr Rd 29640
Barrington Ct 29642
Barton St 29640
Batson Pate Dr 29640
Baynard St 29640
Baywood Ct & Dr 29642
Beachwood St 29642
Beacon Hill Ct 29640
Beagle Run 29642
Beaver Dam Rd 29640
Beaver Pond Ct 29640
Bedford Rd 29642
Bell St 29640
Bella Vista Dr 29640
Bellewood Dr 29640
Belmont Cir 29642
Belt Rd 29640
Ben Dr 29642
Bennington Ct & Ln 29642
Bent Tree St 29642
Bent Twig Rd 29642
Bent Willow Way 29642
Bentcreek Ct 29642
Benton Park Dr 29642
Berkley Dr 29642
Berkley Ln 29640
Berkshire Ct 29642
Bermuda Dr 29640
Berryfield Ct 29642
Berryhill Dr 29642
Berwick Ct 29642
Betty Mae Ln 29640
Beverly Dr 29640
Bhattacharjee Blvd 29640
Big Foot Dr 29642
Bigby St 29642
Bill And Lee Rd 29642
Billet Ct 29642
Biltmore Cir 29642
Biltmore Rd 29640
Birchwood St 29642
Bishop Dr 29640
Bj Dr 29640
Black Rd 29642
Black Snake Rd 29640
Blair St 29640
Blake Dr 29642
Blake P Garrett Dr 29642
Blazes Dr 29642
Blossom Ct 29642
Blue Bird Ln 29640
Blue Ridge St 29640
Blue Wing Ln 29642
Bluestone Ct 29642
Bob White Ct 29642
Bobbie Ln 29642
Boff Dr 29640
Boggs Way 29640
Bolding St 29640
Bolt Ln 29640
Bonanza Ln 29642
Bonaventure Ct & Gln 29640
Bonita Dr 29642
Bonnie Brae Ct 29640
Booker T Cir 29640
Boone Dr 29640
Boulder Ct 29642
Bovine Ln 29640
Bowen Rd 29640
Bowers Ln 29640
Boxwood Ct & Ln 29640
Bracken Ln 29642
Brackett Dr 29640
Bradford Ct 29640
Bradley Ave 29640
Bradley Page Ct 29640
Brandon Ct
 101-103 29640
 105-199 29642
 200-299 29642
Brandywood Dr 29640
Brayden Dr 29640
Breanna Ct 29640
Breazeale Rd 29640
Brecken Ct 29642
Breezedale Rd 29640
Breezewood Ln 29642
Brenley Ln 29642
Brevard Dr 29640
Briarwood Dr 29642
Briarwood Rd 29640
Bridgewater Dr 29642
Briggs Dr 29642
Brighton Cir 29642
Brightside Ln 29642
Bristol Ct 29642
Brittany Ct 29642
Brockman Dr 29640
Bromwell Way 29642
Brookfall Ct & Dr 29642
Brookshire Dr 29642
Brookstone Dr 29642
Brookview Cir 29642
Brookway Dr 29642
Brookwood Dr 29642
Broome Ln 29640
Brothers Rd 29640
Brown Dr 29642
Brushy Creek Rd 29642
Buck Dr 29640
Buck Hill Way 29642
Buck Horn Ln 29642
Buckingham Ct & Rd 29640
Buckle Dr 29640
Buckshot Dr 29640
Buckskin Rd 29640
Buckthorn Ct 29642
Bud Nalley Dr 29642
Buddin St 29640
Buddys Trl 29640
Buena Vista Dr 29640
Bugle Horne Ct 29642
Bunch Ct 29640
Burdine Dr 29640
Burdine Creek Dr 29640
Burns Ave & Rd 29640
Burts Rd 29640
Butler Rd 29642
Buxton Ct 29642
E, W, N & S C Ave & St 29640
W C Avenue Ext 29640
C E Ellison Rd 29640
Cabin Rd 29640
Caden Ln 29640
Cadillac Ct 29640
Cage Cove Ln 29642
Calhoun Memorial Hwy 29640
Calico Ln 29640
California Dr 29642
Calvert Ct 29642
Cambridge Ct & Dr 29642
Camelot Ct 29640
Cameo Ct 29640
Cameron Ct 29642
Camille St 29642
Campbell Ave 29640
Campden Ct 29642
Camperdown Ct 29642
Canaan Dr 29640
Cane Creek Ct 29642
Cannery Rd 29640
Cannon Ln 29640
Canterbury Dr 29642
Cantle Ct 29642
Canvasback Ct & Way 29642
Capps Hill Dr 29640
Caradale Way 29642
Cardiff Ct 29642
Cardinal Dr 29642
Cardinal Woods Ct & Way 29642
Carla Ct 29642
Carlissa Ct 29640
Carmel Church Rd 29642
Carmel Woods Dr 29640
Carmen Ln 29640
Carmen Way 29642
Carnoustie Dr 29642
Carolina Ave 29640
Carolina Center Dr 29642
Caroline Dr 29640
Carolyn Rd 29640
Caron Ln 29642
Carriage Path 29642
Carrie Ln 29642
Carson Ct & Rd 29642
Carter Ave 29640
Carthage Dr 29640
Cassidy Ln 29640
Catalina Cir 29640
Catawba Dr 29640
Cate Ct 29642
Cater Dr 29642
Caterpillar Dr 29640
Cedar Cir & Ln 29642
Cedar Brook Cir 29640
Cedar Creek Ct 29640
N Cedar Rock Rd 29640
Cedar Rock Church Rd 29640
Cedar Tree Ct 29642
Celebrity Blvd 29642
Cely Rd 29642
Centerfield Ln 29642
Century Oaks Dr 29642
Chadwick Ct 29642
Champion Ln 29640
Chandler Rd 29640
Chanticleer Ct 29642
Chaparral Way 29640
Chapman Ln 29642
Charles St 29640
Charlie Dr 29640
Charlton Cir 29642
Chase Dr 29642
Chatham Ct 29642
Chatsworth Ct 29642
Chedfrey Lar Dr 29642
Chelmsford Dr 29642
Chelsea Ct 29642
Cherish Dr 29642
Cherokee Rd 29642
Cherokee Trl 29640
Cherry Dr 29640
Chesire Ct 29642
Chesterfield Ct 29640
Chestnut Ct & Dr 29642
Chickadee Trl 29642
Childress Rd 29640
China Berry Ct 29640
Chinkapin Ct 29642
Chinquapin Rd 29640
Chipley Trl 29642
Christopher Ln 29640
Church Rd 29640
E Church Rd 29640
W Church Rd 29642
Church St 29640
Churchill Way 29640
Cimmaron Ln 29640
Cindy Ln 29642
Circle Rd 29642
Cisson Dr 29642
City Ct 29642
Civic Ct 29642
Claire Ln 29642
Claremont Ct 29642
Clarence Ave 29640
Clarendon Dr 29642
Clark Ln 29640
Clarks Hill Dr 29640
Claude Dr 29642
Claude Leslie Rd 29640
Clay St 29642
Clear Creek Rd 29640
Clear Dawn Dr 29640
Clear View Dr 29640
N & S Clearstone Ct & Dr 29642
Cleveland St 29640
Cliffstone Dr 29640
Clover Ct 29640
Clovervale Dr 29640
Cobb St 29640
Cobblestone Trce 29642
Cochran Ln 29640
Coconut St 29640
Cold Stream Ct 29640
Colleen Dr 29640
Colleton Ct 29642
Collins Rd & St 29642
Colonel Johnson Rd 29642
Colonial Ct & Dr 29642
Columbine Ct 29642
Commerce Blvd 29642
Commons Dr 29642

Cone Ridge Dr 29640
Connie Rd 29642
Connifer Ct 29640
Conway Dr 29640
Cooper Ln 29642
Coppermine Dr 29642
Coppice Ct 29640
Corner Wood St 29640
Cornerstone Ct & Rd 29640
Corrine St 29642
Cottage Gate Ln 29642
Cotton Ln 29642
Cottonwood Ct 29640
Couch Ln 29642
Couch St 29640
Country Ct & Ln 29642
Country Estates Dr 29642
Country Lakes Rd 29642
Country Side Dr 29642
Court Dr 29642
Courtney Dr 29640
Covenant Dr 29640
Covington Ct 29642
Cox Cv 29640
Craig St 29640
Cranberry Way 29642
Crane Thomas Rd 29640
Cravat Ct 29642
Crawford Lake Dr 29642
Creedmore Ln 29642
Creek Dr 29642
Creek Falls Xing 29640
Creek Side Ct 29642
Creek Trail Dr 29642
Creekside Way 29642
Crenshaw St 29640
Crepe Myrtle Ct 29640
Crescent St 29640
Crest Ct, Dr, Ln & Way 29640
Crestview Rd 29642
Crestwood Ct
100-199 29640
200-299 29642
Cribbs Way 29640
Cricket Ln 29640
Crimson Holw 29640
Crofton Ct 29642
Cross Ct 29642
Cross Hill Rd 29640
Cross Roads Church Rd 29640
Crosswell Acres Ct 29640
Crosswell School Rd 29640
E & W Croydon Ct 29642
Crumpton Ln 29640
Culley Trl 29640
Culpepper Ln 29642
Cumberland Ave 29640
Curtis Ln 29640
Cynthia Ln 29642
Cypress Ln 29640
W, N & S D Ave & St 29640
W D Avenue Ext 29640
Dacusville Hwy 29640
Dacusville School Cir 29640
Daisy Dr 29640
Daisy Trl 29642
N & S Dale Dr 29640
Dallas Ln 29640
Dalton Hill Rd 29640
Dana Dr 29642
Dance Ct 29640
Dancer Dr 29642
Daniel Dr 29642
Danielle Ct 29640
Danon Dr 29640
Danway Ct 29640
Daphne Ct 29640
Darby Way 29640
Darleen Ave 29640
Dartford Ct 29642
Dave And Vernon Dr 29642
David St 29640
Davidson Dr 29642
Davis Rd & St 29640

Dawn Ct 29640
Day St 29640
Days Inn Dr 29640
Dayton Dr 29642
Dayton School Rd 29642
Dearborn Ln 29640
Debra Cir 29642
Deck Dr 29640
Deer Creek Ct 29642
Deer Creek Rd 29640
Deer Wood 29642
Deerfield Ct & Run 29640
Del Rio Dr 29640
Del Riso Cir 29642
Dellwood Ct & Dr 29642
Denim Ct 29640
Denise Rd 29642
Dennis Dr 29640
Denton Dr 29640
Derby Ct 29640
Devenger Ct 29642
Devereux Ct 29642
Devilwood Ct 29642
Devon Ct 29640
Dewberry Ct 29642
Dewberry Trl 29640
Dewdrop Ln 29640
Diane Dr 29640
Diedra Dr 29640
Dillard Ct & Dr 29642
Divine Dr 29640
Diwa Dr 29640
Doberman Trl 29640
Dobson Ln 29640
Dodds Rd 29640
Dogwood Ct & Ln 29642
Dogwood Ridge Rd 29640
Donald Dr 29642
Donna Ln 29642
Dora Ln 29640
Dorcas Dr 29640
Doris Dr 29640
Dorisville Dr 29640
Dorr Cir 29640
Double Oaks Ct 29640
Dove Hill Cir & Ct 29640
Dover Close 29640
Dowling St 29640
Drake Dr 29640
Dreamweaver Ln 29640
Driftwood Ct 29640
Duchess Ln 29640
Due West Cir 29640
Dugan Rd 29642
Duke St 29640
Duncan Rd 29640
Dunklin St 29640
Durham Rd 29640
Dustin St 29642
Dusty Dr 29640
Duvall St 29640
Duxbury Ln 29642
S & W E Ave & St 29640
Eagles View Ct 29642
Earls Bridge Rd 29640
Eastpark Way 29642
Eastwood Ct 29640
Easy St 29640
Echo Cir 29642
Eddie Ave 29640
Edenberry Ct & Way 29642
Edens Rd 29640
Edgelawn Dr 29640
Edgemont St 29642
Edgewood Ave 29642
Edgewood Ct 29642
Edgewood Rd 29640
Edinburgh Ln 29640
Eisenhower St 29642
Elaine Ct 29640
Elaine Dr 29642
Elbert Ct 29640
Elbert Clark Dr 29640
Elizabeth Ct 29642
Elizabeth St 29640
Elizabeth City Dr 29642

Ella Dr 29640
Ellenburg Dr 29640
Elliott Ln 29640
Ellison Cir 29640
Ellison Dr 29642
Elljean Rd 29640
Elljean Heights Rd 29640
Elm Ct 29642
Elmwood St 29642
Elouise St 29640
Elrod St 29642
Emory Dr 29640
Enon Church Rd 29640
Enterprise Dr 29642
Equestrian Trl 29642
Estates Dr 29642
Esther Dr 29642
Estill Ct 29642
Esuary Rd 29640
Ethels Ln 29642
Eva Pl 29640
Evans Rd 29640
Evelyn Rd 29640
Evergreen St 29642
Excelsior Dr 29640
Exeter Close 29642
Fairfax Rd 29642
Fairfield Ct 29640
Fairview Ct 29642
Fairview Dr 29640
Fairway Oaks Ln 29642
Faith Dr 29640
Falcon Dr 29640
Farm Terrace Ct 29642
Farmer St 29640
Farmington Rd 29640
Farrier Ct 29642
Farrs Rd 29640
Farrs Bridge Rd 29640
Farthing Dr 29640
Fawn Ln 29640
Faye Cir 29640
Fayer Dr 29640
Feldman Dr 29640
Felix Ct 29640
Fern St 29640
Fernwood Dr 29640
Fieldstone Dr 29642
Finley Cir 29640
Finley Rd 29642
Fir Ct 29642
Fire Station Rd 29642
Firelight Ct & Ln 29642
Firestone Ct 29642
Fish Camp Rd 29642
N Fishtrap Rd 29642
Five Oaks Dr 29640
Five Ponds Ln 29640
Flagstone Dr 29642
Fledgling Way 29642
Fleet Ln 29640
Fleetwood Dr 29640
Flintlock Dr 29640
Florida Cir 29640
Floyd Cir 29640
Folger Ave 29640
Foliage Ct 29642
Folkstone Ct 29640
Ford Truck Trl 29640
Forest Dr 29642
Forest Rdg 29640
Forest Hill Dr 29642
Forest Park Dr 29642
Forest Woods Dr 29642
Foster Ave 29640
Four Lakes Dr 29642
Fox Chase Rd 29640
Foxglove Dr 29640
Foxhall Ct 29640
Frances St 29642
Francis Rd 29640
Frank St 29642
Frank Parrott Rd 29640
Franklin Dr 29642
Franklin Finley Rd 29640
Franklin Square Way 29642

Freebird Ln 29640
Freeman Rd 29642
Freeman Bridge Rd 29640
Freshwater Ln 29642
Frinnie Ln 29640
Front St 29640
Frontier Dr 29640
Fruit Mountain Rd 29640
Fuller Dr 29640
Gadwall Dr 29642
Gail St 29642
Galax Ct 29642
Galaxy Way 29640
Galerie Dr 29642
Galilee Church Rd 29642
Gallagher Trce 29642
Gamble Ln 29640
Gander Pl 29642
Garden Ct 29642
Garden Rd 29640
Gardenia Ct 29640
Garland Cir 29642
Garlington Ct 29642
Garren Rd 29640
Garrett St 29640
Garrison St 29640
Gary Ct 29640
Gatewood Ct 29642
Gayle Ridge Dr 29642
Gelola Dr 29640
Gemstone Trl 29640
Genell Ln 29642
Gentry Ct 29640
Gentry Memorial Hwy 29640
George St 29642
Georges Knl 29640
Georges Creek Dr 29640
Georgetown Rd & Way 29640
Georgewood Ct, Dr & Way 29640
German Cir 29640
Giants Ridge Rd 29642
Gibson Rd 29640
Gill Ln 29640
Gilliland Ave 29640
Gin Rd 29640
Ginger Ln 29642
Gingham Ct 29640
Ginkgo Ct 29642
Glazed Oak Dr 29642
Glazed Springs Ct 29642
Glazner St 29640
Glen Abbey Ct 29642
Glen Arbor Ct 29642
Glen Laurel Dr 29642
Glenda Ln 29642
Glendale Ln 29640
Glenn St 29642
Glenn Burnie Dr 29642
Glenwood Rd 29640
Glory Rd 29640
Golden Willow Ct 29642
Goldenbranch Dr 29642
Grace Ave & Dr 29640
Graham St 29640
Grand Hollow Rd 29642
Grandview Dr 29642
Grannys Village Dr 29642
Grant St 29640
Grant Valley Rd 29640
N & S Gray Haven Ln 29642
Green Crest Way 29640
Green Maple Dr 29640
Green Meadow Ln 29642
Green Pine Way 29642
Green Ridge Dr 29642
Green Wave Blvd 29642
Green Wing Ct 29642
Greenleaf Ln 29642
Greenvale Dr 29642
Greenville Hwy 29640
Greenway Dr 29642
Greenwood Ct 29642
Griffin Dr 29642
Griffin Rd 29640

Griffin Mill Rd 29640
Griffwood Lynn Dr 29640
Grigsby Ave 29640
Grimes Ct 29642
Grouse Ct 29642
Grover Ln 29640
Guiding Light Dr 29640
Guilford Dr 29642
Gulf St 29640
Gunter Ct 29642
Habersham Ct & Ln 29642
Hagood St 29640
Hagood Park Dr 29640
Hale St 29642
Haley Mill Rd 29640
Halifax Rd 29642
Hall Rd 29642
Hallmark Cir & Ln 29640
Halston Rdg 29642
Hamburg Rd 29640
Hamilton Ct 29642
Hamilton Pkwy 29642
Hamilton St 29640
W Hamilton St 29640
Hamilton Forest Dr 29640
Hamlin Rd 29642
Hampton Ct 29642
Hampton Rd 29640
Hanford Close 29642
Hank Dr 29640
Hanson Ln 29642
Hantzel Dr 29640
Happy Trl 29640
Happy Hollow Cir 29640
Harding Hendricks Rd 29640
Hardwood Ct 29640
Hardy Trl 29640
Harewood Ct 29642
Harlem St 29640
Harley Ct 29642
Harmony Hl 29640
Harris Trl 29640
Harrison Rd 29642
Harrogate Ln 29642
Harry Stanley Dr 29640
Hartsfield Ct & Dr 29642
Harvard Cmn 29642
Harvard Ln 29640
Harvest Dr 29640
Harvester Row 29642
Harvey Rd 29642
Harwick Ct 29642
Hasting Cir 29642
Hatters Ct 29642
Hattie Rd 29642
Haven Rst 29642
Haverhill Cir & Ln 29642
Hawk Ln 29640
Hawksbill Dr 29642
Hayes Rd 29642
Haynes Creek Cir 29642
Haywood Rd 29640
Haywood Acres Dr 29640
Hazel Dr 29640
Hearth Stone Ct 29640
Heath Cir 29640
Heatherbrooke Ct 29640
Heatherwood Dr 29642
Heathwood Ln, Pl & Rd 29640
Heaton Cir 29640
Heavens Way 29640
Heidi Ln 29642
Helen Dr 29642
Henderson Rd 29642
N Hendricks Ln 29640
Hendricks Rd 29642
Henline Dr 29640
Henry St 29640
Henry Jones Dr 29640
Henry Wood Dr 29640
Henrydale Dr 29642
Heritage Ln 29642
Heritage Rd 29640
Herringbone Run 29642
Herron Ln 29640

Herta St 29640
W Hester Dr 29642
Hester Store Rd 29642
Hibiscus Dr 29642
Hickory Dr 29642
Hickory Run Dr 29642
Hickory Wood Ct 29640
Hicks Ct 29642
Hidden Acres Dr 29640
Hidden Creek Dr 29642
Hidden Lake Dr 29642
Hideaway Hills Ln 29640
High Lawn Ave 29642
High Ridge Ct 29642
Highbourne Ct 29642
Highland Cir & Rd 29640
Highway 153 29642
Highway 81 N 29642
Highway 86 29642
Hiles St 29642
E Hill Dr 29640
Hill Rd 29642
Hill St 29640
Hill View Ct 29642
Hillandale Ct & Dr 29642
Hillcrest Cir & Dr 29640
Hillside Cir 29640
Hilltop Rd 29640
Hillway Dr 29640
Hinkle Ct & Dr 29642
Hinton Rd 29640
Hitt Rd 29640
Hobby Ct 29640
Holborne Dr 29642
Hollings Dr 29640
Hollingsworth Dr 29640
Hollow Ln 29642
Hollow Oaks Ln 29642
Holly Ct & Dr 29640
Holly Bush Rd 29640
Holly Hollow Ln 29640
Holly Tree Ct 29640
Hollywood St 29640
Home Place Dr 29640
Homeland Ct 29640
Homestead Dr 29640
Homestead Rd 29642
Honeybee Ln 29642
Honeymoon Hl 29640
Honeysuckle Ln 29640
Hood Rd 29640
Hope Dr 29642
Hornbuckle Dr 29642
Horseshoe Bend Rd 29642
Hosta Ln 29642
Hot Rod Hl 29640
Hounds Tooth Ct 29642
Houston Farm Dr 29642
Howard Ct 29640
Hoyt Fulmer Dr 29640
Hudson St 29640
Hummingbird Ct & Ln 29640
Hunt Rd 29642
Huntcliff Ct 29642
Hunters Hl 29640
Huntington Ct & Rd 29642
Hunts Bridge Rd 29640
Hyde Dr 29640
Independence Way 29640
Indigo Ln & Path 29642
Ingleoak Ln 29640
Innis Brook Dr 29642
Inverness Way 29642
Ireland Rd 29642
Iris Dr 29642
Isaiah St 29640
Isley Ct 29640
Ivy Woods Dr 29642
J C Mcdonald Dr 29640
J Pearle Ct 29642
Jackie Dr 29640
Jackson Ct 29642
Jackson St 29640
Jala Lake Dr 29642
James Rd & St 29642
James Creek Pt 29640

Jameson Rd 29640
Jamestown Rd 29640
Jamestown Trl 29642
N Jamestowne Dr 29640
Jamie St 29642
Jasper St 29640
Jeanette St 29640
Jearl Dr 29640
Jenkins Way 29640
Jennings Dr 29642
Jenny Ln 29640
Jeremiah St 29640
Jericho Rd 29640
Jericho Creek Ct 29640
Jericho Ridge Trl 29640
Jersey Way 29640
Jesse Dr 29642
Jessica Ct 29640
Jewell Rd 29642
Jim Hunt Rd 29640
Jimmy Dr 29640
Joan Dr 29642
Joes Ct 29642
John St 29640
John Deere Ln 29640
John Mcconnell Rd 29640
John Paul Ln 29642
Johnathon Ln 29640
Johnson Rd 29642
Johnson St 29640
Jones Ave 29640
Jordan Rd 29640
Jordan Close 29642
Joshua St 29640
Joy Glenn Dr 29642
Ju Jo Ln 29640
Julian Ct 29642
Julie Rd 29642
Justin Ct 29640
Jyniece Ct 29640
Kaci Ct 29640
Kaleope Rd 29642
Kalmia Pl 29640
Karhula Ct 29640
Katherine St 29640
Kathryn Dr 29640
Katie Ln 29640
Kay Dr 29640
Kayaker Way 29642
Kaye St 29640
Kayla Ln 29642
Keagan Ct 29642
Kelly Ct & Ln 29642
Ken Cir 29640
Kendal Ct 29642
Kennedy St 29642
Kennelworth Way 29642
Kennicott Ln 29640
Kensington Rd 29642
Kensington Lake Dr 29642
Kettering Ct 29642
Ketura Dr 29642
Killarney Way 29642
Kilma Tree Ct 29640
Kimberly Dr & Ln 29642
Kimi Ct 29642
Kinfolk Cir 29642
W King Cir & St 29640
Kingsberry Dr 29642
Kingsfield Close 29640
Kingsman Ct & Ln 29642
Kingswood Way 29640
Kinston Dr 29640
Knob Creek Ct 29642
Knoxtowne Rd 29642
Kristin Dr 29640
La Ln 29640
La Vista Dr 29642
La Von Ln 29642
Laboone Rd 29642
Lacy Ln 29642
Ladybank Ct 29640
Lafayette Rd 29640
Lake Rd 29642
Lake Forest Cir 29642
Lake Wood Ct 29642

Lakeshore Dr 29642
Lakeview Dr 29642
Lamar St 29640
Landis Rd 29642
Landmark Ct 29640
Landover Dr 29642
Lane Dr 29642
Lanford Ln 29640
Lantern Ridge Dr 29642
Latham Ln, Rd, St & Ter 29640
Laura Ln 29642
Laurel Rd 29642
Lavonne Ave 29642
Lawrence Way 29640
Lazy River Ln 29640
Le Ann Dr 29642
League St 29640
Ledgewood Way 29642
Lee Ct & Rd 29642
Legion St 29642
Lehigh Ln 29640
Leisure Dr 29640
Lemuel Ln 29642
Lena Dr 29640
Lenhardt Rd 29640
Lennox Ln 29642
Lentz Ln 29640
Leppards Ln 29640
Lesley Ct 29642
Lewis St 29640
Lia Way 29642
Liberty Dr 29640
Lida Falls Rd 29640
Lila Dr 29640
Lily St 29640
Limbaugh Dr 29642
Limited Ct 29640
Lincoln Ct 29640
Linda Ln 29642
Linden Hall Ln 29640
Lindsey Ct 29642
Linville Ln 29640
Linwood St 29640
Lisa Ct 29640
Little Man Ct 29640
Little Pond Rd 29640
Liz Ln 29642
Lloyd Ave 29640
Loblolly Ct 29640
Lobo Dr 29640
Lockmere Ct 29642
Lockwood Ave 29642
Logan Ln 29640
Lola Ln 29640
Long Creek Dr 29640
Longview Ter 29642
Longwood Ln 29642
Looney Ln 29640
Looper Rd 29640
Loraine Cir 29640
Lou Ave 29640
Louise Lake Rd 29640
Louns Dr 29640
Lucille Ave 29640
Lucky St 29640
Luke Ct 29640
Lula Dr 29640
Lumber Mill Dr 29642
Lutsen Dr 29642
Lynch Ct 29640
Lynn Cir 29640
Mad Ln 29640
Madgie Ln 29640
Madison St 29642
Mae Ave 29640
Maggi Valley Ln 29640
Magnolia Ave 29642
E, NE, NW & W Main St 29640
Major Ct 29642
Mallard Dr 29642
Mallard Creek Ct 29640
Malvern Hl 29642
Mandy Trl 29640
Maple Ct 29642
Maple St 29640
Maple Way 29640
Margaret St 29640
Marine Dr 29640
Mark Ave 29642
Mark St 29640
Mark Twain Ln 29640
Marshfield Ct 29642
Martin Rd & St 29640
Mary Ann St 29640
Mary Jane Dr 29642
Mary Jo Dr 29640
Maryland Ave 29640
Marys Mountain Rd 29640
Massingale Ln 29642
Masters Woods Way 29640
Mathis Dr 29640
Mauldin Rd 29640
May St 29640
Mayberry Dr 29640
Maycaw Dr 29642
Mayes St 29640
Mayfair Cir 29640
Mayfield Ln 29640
Mayfield Rd 29642
Mayflower Ct 29642
S Mcalister Rd & Trce 29642
Mcalister Lake Ct & Dr 29642
Mcarthur St 29642
Mcbee Ave 29640
Mccall Ln 29640
Mccollum St 29640
Mccoy St 29640
Mccrea Ct 29640
Mccue St 29642
Mcdaniel Ave 29640
Mcduffie Dr 29640
Mcfarlin St 29640
Mcgaha Rd 29640
Mcgregor Ln 29642
Mckell Ct 29640
Mckensie St 29640
Mckissick Rd 29640
Mcrogers Dr 29640
Mcscott Ct 29640
Mcwhorter Rd 29642
Meadow Ln 29642
Meadow Creek Ct 29642
Meadow Ridge Rd 29642
Meadow Woods Ct 29642
Meadowood Dr 29640
Meadowridge Dr 29642
Meagan Ln 29640
Medinah Dr 29642
Meeker Ct 29642
Mel Dr 29640
Melissa Rd 29640
Melrose Dr 29640
Memory Ln 29640
Mendel Dr 29640
Mendel H Stewart Dr 29642
Mercury Ct 29642
Meredith Ct 29640
Merri Ln 29642
Merrimeadows Rd 29642
Merritt Dr 29642
Merton Dr 29642
Mesa Path Rd 29642
Messervy Dr 29642
Michael Ct 29642
Middle Dr 29642
Midland Dr 29640
Mikenah Ct 29640
Milford Bridges Ln 29640
Mill Pond Rd 29642
N Mill Pond Rd 29640
Miller Rd 29640
Millsboro Ct 29640
Millwood Ct 29640
Mini Dr 29640
Mini Storage Ln 29640
Mission Dr 29642
Missy Jo Dr 29642
Mistletoe Ln 29640
Misty Oak Ct 29640
Mlj Smt 29640
Mockingbird Ln 29640
Momart Dr 29640
Montague Dr 29640
Montaigne Dr 29640
Montana Rd 29640
Montclair Ct 29642
Moody Dr 29642
Moonlight Ln 29640
Moore Dr 29642
Morey Ln 29642
Morning Creek Dr 29640
Morning View Ct 29642
Morningside Dr 29640
Morton Ln 29642
Mossie Smith Rd 29642
Moultrie Ct 29640
Mount Airy Church Rd 29642
Mount Calvary Church Rd 29642
Mount Forest Cir 29640
Mount Frontenac Way 29642
N Mount Tabor Church Rd 29640
Mountain Bridge Trl 29640
Mountain Crest Dr 29640
Mountain View Dr 29640
Mountainrock Vw 29642
Mud Run Rd 29640
Muirfield Dr 29642
Mulberry Ln & Rd 29640
Mull St 29640
Murdock Ln 29642
Muscadine Ln 29640
Mustang Dr 29640
Mystery Creek Ct 29640
Nalley St 29640
Nancy Dr 29642
Nancy Miller Dr 29640
Nandina Heights Blvd 29640
Natalie Ct 29642
Nations Way 29642
Nature Trl 29640
Neal St 29642
Nell Dr 29642
Nellstone Ct 29642
Neptune Ct 29642
Nesbitt Ln 29642
Nestle Trl 29640
Nevell Dr 29642
New Court Ln 29640
New Haven Ct 29640
Newberry Ct 29642
Newcastle Ct 29642
Newfound Ln 29642
Newman Dr 29642
Nicholas Ct 29640
Nickle Springs Dr 29642
Night Dr 29640
Nikol Ln 29642
Noble Rd 29640
Nolans Way 29640
Nora Ave 29640
Norman Dr 29640
Norris Ave 29640
Norte Vista Dr 29640
Northway Dr 29642
Norton St 29640
Norwood Dr 29642
Nottingham Ct, Ln & Way 29640
Nu Life Park 29640
Nursery Rd 29640
Oak Cir & St 29640
Oak Knoll Dr 29640
Oak Springs Ct 29640
Oakcreek Dr 29642
Oakdale Ln 29640
Oakfield Ave 29640
W Oakland Rd 29640
Oaklane Dr 29642
Oakvale Dr 29642
Oakwood Dr 29640
Oakwood St 29642
Oates Ave & St 29640
Odessa Dr 29640
Odom Rd 29642
Ola Ave 29640
Ola Dr 29642
Old Anderson Hwy 29642
Old Cedar Rock Rd 29640
Old Cuffy Creek Ln 29642
Old Dacusville Rd 29640
Old Easley Hwy 29640
Old Easley Bridge Rd 29642
Old Easley Pickens Hwy 29640
Old Forest Ln & Rd 29640
Old Greenville Hwy 29642
Old Greenville Highway Ext 29642
Old Liberty Rd 29640
Old Market Sq 29640
Old Mill Rd 29642
N Old Mill Rd 29640
N Old Pendleton Rd 29642
Old Pond St 29640
Old Saluda Dam Rd 29640
Old Sawmill Rd 29640
Old Stagecoach Rd 29642
Old Vinland School Rd 29640
Oldham Ct 29642
Olga Ln 29642
Olive St 29640
Omar St 29640
Oneal Rd 29640
Onyx Ln 29640
Orchard Rd 29640
Orchid Dr 29642
Orr Rd 29642
Orr Hill Rd 29642
Oshields Rd 29640
Othol Ct 29642
Overlook Ct 29642
Owen Ln 29640
Owings Rd 29640
Owl Ln 29640
Oxford Ct 29642
Pace St 29640
Pace Bridge Rd 29640
Pace Valley Rd 29640
Page Dr 29642
Palmetto Way 29642
Pamela Dr 29642
Papa Eds Ct 29640
Paradise Cv 29640
Park Ct 29642
Park Dr 29640
Park St 29640
Park Way 29640
Park Crossing Dr 29640
Park West Cir 29642
Parker Ln 29642
Parkway Dr 29640
Partridge Ct & Way 29640
Passage Way 29642
Patchwork Ln 29640
Pathfinder Cir 29640
Patio Rd 29642
Patrick Ave 29642
Patriot Dr 29640
Paulette Ln 29640
Peaceful Ln 29640
Peachtree St 29640
Pear St 29640
Pearle Dr 29642
Pearson Cir 29640
Pearson Rd 29642
Pearson Terrace Dr 29642
Peartree Ln 29640
Pebble Ct 29642
Pebble Brook Ct & Dr 29642
Pecan Ct 29640
Pecan Tree Cir 29640
Pelzer Hwy 29642
Pendleton Ct 29640
N Pendleton St 29640
S Pendleton St
100-811 29640
810-810 29641
812-898 29640
813-899 29640
900-1199 29642
Penny Ln 29640
Peoples Dr 29642
Pepper Rd 29642
Peppercorn Way 29642
Periwinkle Ln 29640
Perry Hill Rd 29640
Pete James Rd 29640
Petunia Dr 29640
Philbert Rd 29642
Phillips Ave 29640
Philpot Plantation Dr 29640
Pickens St 29640
Piedmont Rd 29642
Pierce Ln 29640
Pilgrim Dr 29640
Pin Oak Ct 29642
Pine Aly 29640
Pine Rd 29642
Pine St 29640
Pine Forest Ct 29640
Pine Forest Dr 29642
Pine Knoll Dr 29642
Pine Lake Dr 29642
Pine Mountain Dr 29640
Pine Ridge Dr 29642
Pineapple St 29640
Pineknob Rd 29640
Pinetree Ln 29640
Pineview Dr 29642
Pinewood Ct 29642
Pinewood Dr 29640
Pink Dr 29640
Pinnacle Ct & Ln 29642
Pintail Ln 29642
Pisgah Rd 29642
Pistol Club Rd 29640
Placid Forest Way 29640
Plantation Dr 29642
Planters Ct 29642
Planters Way 29640
Planters Walk Dr 29642
Players Dr 29642
Pleasant Dr 29642
Poinsett Cir 29640
Poinsettia Ct & Dr 29642
Polly Dr 29640
Polynesian Dr 29640
Pond Dr 29640
Ponder Cemetery Rd 29640
Pondstone Ct 29642
Pope Field Rd 29642
Poplar St & Way 29640
Poplar Springs Dr 29642
Poppy Ct 29642
Porcher Ln 29642
Portsmouth Ln 29642
Powdersville Rd 29642
Powdersville Main Ext 29642
Powell St 29640
E Powers Dr 29640
N & W Presbyterian Ln 29642
Prescot Ct 29642
Preston St 29640
Prestwick Ct 29642
Pretty Place Dr 29640
Primrose Ct 29642
Prince George Rd 29640
Prince Perry Rd 29640
Princeton Dr 29640
Private Dr 29640
Providence Way 29642
Prudacus Dr 29640
Pug Dr 29642
Purpose Dr 29642
Putt Putt Dr 29640
Quail Trl 29642
Quail Haven Ct & Dr 29642
Quiet Ln 29640
Quiet Acres Dr & Ln 29642
Quinfield Ct 29642
Rabbit Trl 29642
Rackley Ln 29642
Rackley Mill Rd 29640
Radcliff Dr 29640
Rae Cir 29642
Railroad St 29640
Rainbow Trl 29640
Raines Ct & Rd 29640
Rainfall Way 29642
Raintree Ct 29642
Rampey St 29640
Randall Rd 29642
Ray St 29640
Rayfield Ct & Dr 29640
Rebecca Dr 29642
Red Berry Ln 29642
Red Bird Dr 29640
Red Gate Rd 29640
Red Leaf Ct 29642
Red Maple Cir 29642
Red Oak Ct 29640
Red River Rd 29640
Red Row St 29640
Red Wing Ct 29642
Redbay Ct 29640
Redding Rd 29640
Redfern Ct 29640
Redmon Dr 29640
Redwood Ct 29640
Redwood Dr 29642
Reef Ct 29642
Reeves Ln 29642
Regency St 29640
Reianna Ln 29640
Rhetts Run 29642
N & S Rhome Ct 29642
Rice Rd & St 29640
Richard St 29640
Richland Ct & Dr 29642
Riddles Dr 29640
Ridge Rd 29642
Ridge Point Rd 29640
Ridgecrest Dr 29640
Ridgefield Cir 29640
Ridgeland Cir 29640
Ridgemont Ct 29642
Ridgeway Ct 29640
Ridgewood St 29642
Riding Park 29640
Riley Rd 29642
Ripplelake Dr 29640
River View Ct 29640
Riveroak Trl 29640
Rivers Edge Dr 29642
Riverstone Ct 29640
Robbie Ct 29642
Robert P Jeanes Rd 29640
Robinall Dr 29642
Robinson Ave 29640
Robinson Rd 29642
Rochester Ct & Rd 29640
Rochford Dr 29642
Rock Creek Xing 29642
Rock Sound Rd 29640
Rock Springs Rd 29642
Rock View St 29640
Rockbridge Close 29640
Rockbrook Ct 29642
Rockmont Rd 29640
Rocky Ln 29640
Rocky Top Trl 29640
Roe Ln 29640
Rogers St 29640
Rolling Green Dr 29640
Rolling Hills Cir 29640
Rolling Oak Dr 29642
Rollingwood Dr & Way 29640
Rooker Ln 29640
Roosevelt Dr 29642
Roper Rd & St 29640
Rose Ann Ct 29642
Rosemary Ln 29640
Rosemont Ct 29640
Rosewood Dr 29640
Ross Ave 29640
Rosselli Dr 29640
Rotterdam Rd 29640
Rounded Wing Dr 29642
Rowley Ct 29642
Royal Fern Ln 29642
Ruby Dr 29642
Runion St 29640
Russell St 29640
Rusty Ln 29642
Ruth Dr 29640
Rutledge St 29640
Ryan St 29640
Sabra Dr 29642
Saco Lowell Rd 29640
Saddlehorn Ln 29642
Sadie Dr 29640
Sage Ct 29640
Sahalee Dr 29640
Saint Helens Ln 29642
Saint Lo Cir 29640
Saint Lukes Cir 29642
Saint Paul Rd 29642
Saluda Dam Rd 29640
Saluda View Cir & Dr 29640
Samuel Cir 29642
San Ford Dr 29640
Sandalwood Dr 29640
Sanders Dr 29642
Sandfield Ln 29642
Sandy Ln 29640
Sapphire Ln 29640
Sassafras Dr 29642
Satin St 29640
Satterfield Rd 29642
Saturn Ct 29642
Sawberry Cir 29640
Sawtooth Ct 29642
Sawtooth Oak Ln 29640
School Rd 29640
Scotland Rd 29640
Scott Ave 29640
Seawright Dr 29640
Sedgewood Ct 29642
Sellers Dr 29642
Selsea Dr 29642
Selwood Ct 29642
Semper Fidelis Rd 29640
Sequoia Ct 29640
Sergent Ln 29640
Sesame Ct 29640
Seven Pines Ln 29640
N & S Severn Cir 29642
Sha Dr 29640
Shade Tree Cir 29640
Shadow Oaks Dr 29642
Shadowbrook Ct 29640
Shady Ln 29640
Shady Oaks St 29640
Shaffner Dr 29640
Shaina Ln 29640
Shallowford Rd 29640
Shaminc Rd 29642
Shamrock Ct 29642
Shangrila Dr 29640
Shannah Ln 29642
Shannon Dr 29642
Sharky Dr 29640
Sharon Ln 29640
Sheffield Ct & Rd 29642
Shefwood Dr 29642
Shenandoah Ct, Dr & Ln 29642
Shepherds Rdg 29640
Sheriff Mill Rd 29642
Sheringham Dr 29642
Sherman Rd 29642
Sherry Ln 29640
Sherwood Rd 29640
Sherwood St 29640
Shiloh Cir 29642
Shirley Ct 29640
Shirley Ridge Dr 29640
Shoal Creek Way 29642
Shoals Creek Church Rd 29640
Shop Ct 29640
Shorter St 29640
Sierra Dr 29642
Siloam Rd 29642
Silver Lake Dr 29640
Simpson Dr 29640

Sindy Park Ct 29640
Sitton Cir 29642
Sitton Dr 29640
Sitton Rd 29642
Sitton Hill Rd 29642
Skyland Dr 29640
Slickum Rd 29640
Smith Grove Rd 29640
Smith Hill Rd 29640
Smithfield St 29640
Smoak Dr 29642
Snipe Ln 29642
Snyder Rd 29640
Sommerset Ln 29642
Sondra Ave 29642
Sonora Dr 29640
Southern Center Ct & Way 29642
Southern Oaks Dr 29642
Southway St 29640
Spirit Mountain Ln 29642
Spotted Wing Ct 29642
Spring Dr 29642
Spring St 29640
Spring Point Dr 29640
Springdale Ln 29642
Springfield Cir 29642
Springwater Ct 29642
Stable Ln 29640
Stancil St 29640
Stanridge Ct 29640
Stapleford Ct 29642
Star View St 29640
Stegall Rd 29642
Stella Dora Dr 29642
Sterling Ct 29640
Stewart Dr 29640
Still Creek Ct 29640
Still Meadow Ln 29642
Stokes Dr 29640
Stone Ave 29640
Stone Briar Ln 29642
Stone Hedge Ct 29642
Stone Meadow Ct & Way 29642
Stonegate Ct 29642
Stonehaven Ln 29642
Stonehurst Ln 29640
Stonewall Ct & Dr 29642
Stonewall Farm Rd 29640
Stoney Creek Ct 29642
Storage Ln 29642
Store Rd 29640
Stratford Ct & Dr 29642
Stratton Ct 29640
Strawberry Ln 29642
Sturbridge Ct 29642
Styles Ct 29642
Sugar Dr 29640
Sugarhill Trl 29642
Sula Dr 29640
Summer Dr & St 29642
Summer Hill Ct 29642
Summercrest Ct 29642
Summit Dr 29640
Sun Blvd 29642
Sun Chase Dr 29642
Sun Meadow Ln 29640
E & W Sundance Dr 29642
Sunflower Ln 29640
Sunningdale Ct & Dr 29642
Sunset Ct 29642
Sunset Dr
100-399 29640
5000-5199 29642
Sunshadow Cir & Dr 29642
Sunshine Way 29642
Surrey Ct 29642
Sutherland Rd 29640
Sweetbay Ln 29642
Sweetbriar Way 29640
Sweetbud Ct 29640
Sycamore Ln 29640
Sylvan Ct 29640
Sylvia Rd 29642
Syracuse Rd 29642
T And H Blake Dr 29640
Tadpole Ln 29640
Taletha Ln 29640
Tall Oaks Ct 29642
Tall Pine Dr 29640
Tanglewood Dr 29642
Tanner Ct 29640
Tara Ct & Dr 29642
Tarrington Ln 29642
Taxiway Ave 29640
Teague Ct & Dr 29640
Teakwood Dr 29640
Teal Ct & Dr 29642
Tecora Ct 29642
Terra Oaks Ct 29642
E Terrace Dr 29640
Terrace Rd 29642
Terri Acres 29642
Thalia Ln 29642
Thistlewood Dr 29640
Thom Trl 29642
Thomas Mill Ct & Rd 29640
Thompson Trl 29642
Thornbury Rdg 29640
Thornwood Ct 29640
Three And Twenty Rd 29642
Three Bridges Rd 29642
Three Cs Ln 29640
Three J Rd 29642
Three Pond Rd 29642
Tiffany Dr 29640
Tiffany Kane Ln 29642
Tigue Dr 29640
Til House Ct 29642
Timber Trace Way 29642
Timberlane Dr 29642
Timberwood Ct & Ln 29640
Timbrooke Way 29642
Timer Trl 29640
Timmerman Ct 29642
Tinsel Ct 29640
Tinsley Dr 29642
Tiny Ct 29640
Tobie Ln 29642
Tomahawk Dr 29640
Tortuga Ln 29642
Townsend Dr 29640
Tractor Dr 29640
Tracy Ct 29642
Trail Hvn 29640
Tranquil Ln 29642
Travis Ct 29642
Tree Top Ln 29642
Trent Ct 29642
Trescott Ln 29642
Trey Ct 29640
Triggers Trce 29640
Trina Ct 29642
Tripp Ln 29642
Troy St 29640
Truman St 29642
Tucker Ln 29640
Tucker Rd 29642
Tulip Tree Ct 29642
Tupelo Ln 29642
Turkey Trot Ct 29640
Turner St 29640
Turner Trl 29642
Turner Hill Rd 29642
Turning Leaf Ln 29640
Turpin Dr 29640
Twin Oaks Ct & Dr 29640
Twin Pond Rd 29640
Two Notch Trl 29642
Tyler Ct
100-199 29640
200-299 29642
Umbrella Ct 29642
Upper Lake Dr 29642
Upward Way 29642
Utility St 29640
Valley Rd 29640
Van Henry Ln 29642
Venesky Way 29642
Venus Ct 29642
Vermont Ave 29640
Versailles Ln 29642
Victoria Ln 29640
View Place Ct 29640
Villa Ct 29640
Village Ln 29642
Vine St 29640
Vinland Ct 29640
Vinland Farms Dr 29640
Virginia Cir & Ln 29640
Vista Cir 29642
Von Hollen Dr 29642
Vreeland Ln 29642
Wagon Trl 29642
Wagon Ford Rd 29640
Walden Ln 29642
Walker St 29640
Walker Ellison Rd 29642
Walkers Way 29642
Wallace Dr 29640
Walnut Hl 29642
Walnut Hill Dr 29642
Walter St 29642
Ware Ln 29642
Ware St 29640
Warren Dr 29640
Warriche Rd 29640
Warrington Dr 29642
Washington Ave
100-399 29640
400-499 29642
Waterford Way 29642
Waterside Dr 29640
Waterstone Dr 29640
Watkins Rd 29642
N Watson Rd 29642
Waverly St 29642
Waynes Dr 29640
Wedgewood Ct & Dr 29640
Weeping Willow Dr 29642
Weeping Willow Ln 29640
Welborn Cir 29642
Wellesley Pl 29642
Wellington Rd 29642
Wells St 29642
Wenlock Ct 29642
Wentworth Ct 29642
Wescot Way 29642
Wessex Dr 29642
West Ct 29642
Westbrooke Ln 29642
Westchester Ct 29640
Westchester Rd 29640
Westchester Way 29640
Westminster Ln 29640
Weston Estates Dr 29642
Wexford Way 29642
Whetstone Ln 29640
Whisper Lake Ct 29640
White Oak Ct 29640
White Oak Dr 29642
White Willow Ct 29642
Whitmire Rd 29640
Whitten St 29640
Wickersham Way 29642
Wicklow Ct 29642
Widgeon Ln 29640
Wigeon Way 29642
Wilbur St 29640
Wild Briar Ct 29642
Wild Canary Ln 29640
Wild Wing Ct & Way 29642
Wildberry Ct 29642
Williams Ave
100-599 29642
600-699 29640
N Williamsburg Ct 29640
Williamsburg Way 29642
Willie Mae Ct 29640
Willow Ct 29642
Willow Pl 29640
Willow Lake Ct 29642
Willow Point Way 29642
Willow Springs Dr 29640
Willow Wind Ct 29642
Wilrobin Ln 29640
Wilshire Dr 29642
Wilson Rd 29642
Wiltshire Ct 29642
Wimberly Ln 29642
Wimberly Farms Ln 29642
Windamere Ct & Rd 29640
Windermere Ct 29642
Windham Ln 29642
Windover Ln 29640
Windsor Ct 29642
Windy Hill Ln 29640
W Winston Way 29640
Winterwood Ln 29642
Wisteria Way 29640
Wolf Creek Rd 29640
Wood Hopper Ct 29642
Woodberry Cir 29642
Woodbine Trl 29640
Woodbridge Ct 29642
Woodbury Dr 29640
Woodcock Ct 29642
Woodcross Way 29642
Woodfield Dr 29642
Woodhaven Ct 29642
Woodhaven Rd 29640
Woodhill Dr 29640
Woodland Ave 29640
Woodland Cir 29640
Woodland Dr 29642
W Woodland Rd 29640
Woodstone Dr 29642
Woodstream Ln 29640
Woodview Ct 29640
Woodward Way 29640
Woodworkers Ln 29640
Woody Ln 29640
Worcester Ln 29642
Wren Ct 29642
Wren Crossing Ct & Ln 29642
Wrentree Dr 29642
Wrenway Ct 29642
Wt Ln 29640
Wt Wyatt Rd 29642
Wyatt Ave 29640
Wyatt Oaks Ct 29642
Wylie Ct 29640
Yeoman Dr 29640
York Ct 29642
Yorkshire Ct 29642
Yorktown Ct 29642
N Yorktowne Dr 29640
Yount Ct 29642
Zane Cir 29640
Zelkova Rd 29642
Zion St 29640
Zion Church Rd 29642
Zion Heights Cir & Ct 29642
Zion School Rd 29642
Zip Ct 29640

NUMBERED STREETS

E, W, N & S 1st Ave & St 29640
E, W, N & S 2nd Ave & St 29640
E, W, N & S 3rd Ave & St 29640
W, N & S 4th Ave & St 29640
W 5th Ave 29640
N 5th St 29640
S 5th St
100-1099 29640
1100-1399 29642
W, N & S 6th Ave & St 29640
W, N & S 7th Ave & St 29640
S & W 8th Ave & St 29640
S 9th St 29640
21st St 29640
22nd St 29640
23rd St 29640
24th St 29640
25th St 29640
26th St 29640
27th St 29640
28th St 29640
29th St 29640
30th St 29640
31st St 29640

FLORENCE SC

General Delivery 29501

POST OFFICE BOXES MAIN OFFICE STATIONS AND BRANCHES

Box No.s
2 - 2635 29503
3001 - 7780 29502
9998 - 9998 29503
12001 - 14336 29504
15001 - 15494 29506
100501 - 299997 29502

NAMED STREETS

A St 29506
Aaron Cir 29506
Abandon Rd 29501
Abbey Way 29501
Abbington Hall Dr 29501
Aberdeen Ct & Dr 29501
Abernathy Dr 29505
Abraham Ln 29505
Acorn Ct 29501
N Adair Dr 29501
Adams Ave 29501
S Addison St 29501
Adler Ln 29501
Adrian Ln 29506
Advent Ln 29506
N & S Aiken Dr 29501
Alabama Ln 29501
Albemarle Blvd 29501
Alberti Dr 29501
Aldersgate Ct 29501
Aldridge Ln 29506
Aldwich Pl 29501
Alex Lee Blvd 29506
N & S Alexander St 29501
Alice Dr 29505
S Aline St 29506
N Allegheny Rdg 29506
Allies Ct 29506
Alligator Rd 29501
Allison St 29505
Alpine Dr 29501
N Alpine Trl 29506
Als Ln 29505
Alston Ct 29506
Alton Cir 29501
Amanda Cir 29505
Amber Ln 29501
Amberleigh Ct 29505
American Dr 29505
N Ames Ave 29506
Ames Bury Pointe 29501
E Amherst Dr 29506
Anderson Farm Rd 29501
W Andover Rd 29501
Andrew Ct 29505
Anita Cir 29505
Annelle Dr 29505
Ansley St 29505
Anson St 29501
Antique Cir 29506
Apple Valley Dr 29505
April Aly 29506
Arbor Dr 29501
Archie Ln 29505
Ard St 29505
Ares Ln 29506
Arin St 29501
Arizona Way 29501
Arlington Cir 29501
S Armstrong Ave 29505
Arrowhead Cir 29501
Arrowood Dr 29501
Arthur Rd 29505
S Arundel Dr 29501
Ascot Dr 29501
E Ashby Rd 29506
W Ashby Rd 29501
Ashley Ct 29505
Ashley Hall Dr 29501
Ashton Dr 29501
Ashwood Ln 29501
Aspen St 29501
Aster Dr 29501
Athens St 29501
W Athens St 29506
Atlanta Ter 29505
Atlee Ct 29506
W Attwood Ave 29505
Aubrey Ln 29506
Aunt Prissey Ct 29505
Austin Ln 29505
Author Dr 29501
Autumn Ln 29501
Autumn Oaks Ln 29505
Avent St 29505
Avery Ln 29505
Avington Ct 29505
Avondale Dr 29501
Azalea Ln 29501
Babar Ln 29501
Baccus Ln 29506
Back Forty Dr 29505
Backswamp Dr 29506
Backwoods Dr 29506
Badger Ln 29506
Badger Rd 29501
Bagpipe Cir 29505
Bailey Ln 29506
Bair Ct 29505
Baker Ave 29501
Balbec Dr 29501
S Ballard St 29506
E Baltic Rd 29506
Banbury Cir 29501
Bancroft Rd 29501
Bankers Ct 29505
Bannockburn Rd 29505
Barclay Dr 29501
Barfield Dr 29501
Barkley Ave 29505
Barnes St 29501
Barnwell Dr 29501
Barr Ln 29506
S Barringer St 29506
S Barrington Dr 29501
Bartell Cir 29505
Bartley Ct 29505
Bateman Dr 29501
Battery Ln 29505
Battery Park Dr 29506
Battle Ln 29505
Battleboro Ct 29505
Baxter Ct 29505
Bayberry Cir 29501
Bayswater Rd 29506
Baytree Dr 29501
Bazen Ln 29505
Beauvieu Dr 29501
Beauvoir Dr 29501
Beaver Pointe Dr 29501
N Beaverdam Dr 29501
Beck Ln 29506
Beckett Dr 29505
Beckford St 29501
Beckys Pkwy 29506
Beddingfield Hall 29501
Bedford Ln 29501
Beechlawn Ct 29505
Beechwood Rd 29501
Bell St 29506
Bellaire Dr 29505
Belle Rose Cir 29501
Bellemeade Cir 29501
Bellevue Dr 29501
Bellingham Ct 29501
W Belmont Cir 29501
N Beltline Dr 29501
Ben Hogan Cir 29506
Benjamin Blvd 29501
E Bennett Dr 29506
E Benshire Ave 29505
Benton Rd 29505
Bentree Ln 29501
Berkley Ave 29505
Berry Ln 29501
Beth Ct 29501
Bethel Rd 29506
Bettys Ln 29506
Beverly Dr 29501
Bill Crisp Blvd 29506
Billy Green Rd 29505
Birch Cir 29501
Birkdale Ct 29501
Bishop Dr 29505
Bishops Gate 29505
E Black Creek Rd 29506
W Black Creek Rd 29501
Black Friars Ct 29501
Black Heath Dr 29505
Blackberry Ln 29506
Blackmon Rd 29501
Blaire Ct 29501
Blanchard Rd 29506
Blanche Ln 29505
Blass Dr 29505
Blenheim Ln 29501
Blitsgel Dr 29501
Blochton Ln 29501
Blue Cap Rd 29506
Blue Heron Cir 29501
Blue Pond Rd 29506
Bluff Rd 29506
Boardwalk 29505
Bogart St 29501
Bondells Rd 29505
Bonnie Dr 29501
E Bonnie Ln 29505
W Booker St 29506
Boone Cir 29501
Bordaria Ct 29505
S Botany Dr 29501
Boulder Dr 29501
Boxwood Ave 29501
N Boyd Ct & St 29506
Bradberry Ln 29506
N Bradford St 29506
Branch Rd 29505
N Brand St 29506
Brandon Dr 29505
Brandon Woods Rd 29505
S Brandy Cir 29505
Branford Rd 29505
Brava Dr 29501
Breckridge Cir 29505
S Brehenan Dr 29505
Brettwood Rd 29501
Brian Ct 29501
Briarcliff Dr 29501
S Briarleigh Rd 29501
E Briarwood Dr 29505
Brickhill Dr 29501
Brickhouse Rd 29506
Bridgeport Ct 29501
Bridgewood Dr 29501
Bridle Cir 29505
Brigadoone Ln 29505
Brightwood Dr 29505
Brinkleigh Ln 29505
Bristol St 29501
N Bristow St 29506
Britannia St 29501
Brittany Dr 29501
E Broach St 29505
Broad Dr 29505
Broadleaf Trl 29506
Brock Cir 29501
Brockington Ln 29501
Brockton Ln 29501
Brogdon St 29501

Bromfield St 29501
Bromley Hall 29501
Bronco Rd 29501
Brookfield Rd 29505
W Brookgreen Dr 29501
Brookhaven Ln 29505
W Brookshire Ct 29501
Brookwood Dr 29501
Brother Town Ln 29506
Broughton Blvd 29501
S Brown St 29506
S Bruins Ln 29505
N Brunson St 29506
S Brunswick Ct 29501
Brunwood Dr 29501
Bryson Dr 29501
Buchanan Dr 29505
Buckeye Dr 29505
N Buckingham Rd 29506
Buckshot Rd 29501
Bunch St 29501
N Buncombe Rd 29506
Bunker Hill Rd 29506
Burris Rd 29501
Buster Trl 29505
E Butler Ln 29505
Butterfly Lake Dr 29505
Byrd Ln 29506
Byrnes Blvd 29506
Cabin Dr 29506
Cabrillo Dr 29505
Cade Ct 29505
Caesar Ln 29505
Calder Ln 29506
Caledonia Ct 29501
N & S Calhoun Dr 29501
California Rd 29501
Calumet Ct 29501
Calverts Ct 29505
Calvin Cir 29505
W Cambridge Dr 29501
Camellia Cir 29501
Camelot Ct 29505
Cameron Ln 29501
Camlin Ln 29501
Camp Wiggins Rd 29506
E Campbell St 29506
E Campground Rd 29506
Canal Dr 29501
S Canal Dr 29505
Canberra Pl 29501
Candy Ln 29501
E Candy Ln 29505
Cane Branch Rd 29505
Cannon St 29501
Canterbury Rd 29505
Canvas Back 29505
Capers Ct 29505
Capri Dr 29506
Cardinal Cir 29505
N Carnaby Cir 29506
Carnell Dr 29505
N & S Carolina Dr 29501
Carolina Wren Ct 29501
E Carolyn Ave 29505
Carriage Ln 29505
Carriage Place Dr 29505
Carrigan Ct 29505
Carroll Dr 29506
Carson Dr 29506
Carter St 29501
Carter Corner Rd 29506
Carver Cir & St 29501
Cascade Ave 29505
N & S Cashua Dr 29501
Castleberry Dr 29505
Catawba River Dr 29501
Caterpillar Ln 29506
Catfish Cir 29506
Cato Rd 29505
W Caudle Ave 29505
Cauley Cir 29505
Cecil Rd 29501
E Cedar St 29506
W Cedar St 29501
Cedar Falls Ln 29505
Cedar Lawn Ct 29505
Cedarwood Cir 29501
Celebration Blvd 29501
E Cemetery St 29506
E Center St 29506
Central Dr 29501
Century Dr 29501
Chadwick Dr 29501
Chain Ln 29505
Chalmers Row 29501
Championship Dr 29501
Chancery Ct 29505
Chancery Ln 29506
Chandler Cir 29505
Channel Dr 29505
Chantz Ct 29501
E Chapel View Dr 29505
Charity Dr 29506
Charles St 29506
S Charleston Rd 29501
Charlestowne Blvd 29505
Charlotte St 29506
Charters Dr 29501
Chase St 29501
Chase Park Cir 29501
Chatfield Dr 29505
Chatham Pl 29501
Chaucer Dr 29505
Cheer Ln 29505
N Chelsea Dr 29501
Cheraw Dr 29501
Cheraw River Dr 29501
Cherokee Rd 29501
Cherry Ln 29505
Cherrywood Rd 29501
Cheryl Ct 29501
Cheshire Ln 29505
W Chesterfield St 29501
Chestnut St 29501
E Cheves St 29506
W Cheves St 29501
Chickadee Ct 29501
Chinaberry Rd 29506
Chippenham Ln 29501
Chisolm Trl 29505
Choate Ln 29505
Chomper Ct 29505
Chris Ave 29506
Christine Ln 29501
S Christopher Ln 29506
N Church St 29506
S Church St
200-1299 29506
1300-1599 29505
W Churchill Pl 29501
Cicero Ln 29505
E Circle Ln 29506
Citadel St 29505
Citizen Ln 29501
Claiborne Pl 29505
Claremont Ave 29501
Clarendon Ave 29505
Clareview Dr 29505
Clark Memorial Dr 29506
W Clarke Rd 29501
Claude Douglas Cir 29501
Claussen Rd 29505
Claymont Ct 29501
Clayton Ct 29505
Clearfield Cir 29506
Clearwater Ct 29505
Clearwater Dr 29501
Clement St 29501
Cloisters Dr 29505
Clyde St 29506
Cobblestone Ct 29501
Cobblestone St 29506
Cocoa Ln 29506
N & S Coit St 29501
Coker St 29506
Cokesbury Ct 29501
Colchester Pl 29501
College Lake Dr 29506
Colonial Rd 29501
Colony Ln 29501
Colton Dr 29506
W Comanchee Dr 29501
Combray Cir 29501
Commander St 29506
Congaree Dr 29501
Conner Dr 29501
Constance Dr 29506
Constantine Dr 29505
Constitution Dr 29501
Converse Dr 29501
S Converse Dr 29505
Conyers Ave 29505
E Cooper Cir 29506
Cooper Ln 29501
Corbett Pl 29501
Cormac St 29505
Cotswold St 29501
Cottingham Rd 29505
Cottontail Ln 29506
Cottonwood Dr 29501
Cougar Trl 29505
Count Ave 29501
Country Club Blvd 29501
Country Side Ln 29505
S Court Ave 29506
Courthouse Sq 29501
Courtland Ave 29505
Courtney St 29501
Cove Pointe Dr 29501
Coventry Ln 29501
Coventry St 29506
Covington St 29501
Cowpens Cir 29501
Cox St 29506
Cox Farm Rd 29506
S Crabtree Ct 29505
Crandall Hall 29501
Cravenhurst Ct 29501
E Crawford Ave 29505
Creamoor Ln 29505
Creek Dr 29506
Creekside Ct & Dr 29506
Crepe Myrtle Rd 29505
Crescent Cir 29506
Cresthive Ct 29505
Crestview Dr 29501
E Crestwood Ave 29505
Crestwood Dr 29501
Crickentree Ln 29501
E Cricklewood Dr 29505
Crinoline Ct 29505
Critcher Rd 29501
Cromer Ln 29506
Cromwell Dr 29506
Crooked Creek Dr 29506
Crown Cir 29506
Crown Rd 29505
Cucumber Aly 29501
Culbreth Ct 29501
Cullowee Ln 29501
Cumberland Dr 29501
Curry Ln 29501
Cypress Rd 29505
Cypress Bend Rd 29506
N & S Dabney Dr 29501
S Dale Dr 29505
Damon Dr 29505
S Daniels St 29506
Danny Rd 29501
Danvers Ct 29501
E Danville Dr 29505
Darden Dr 29501
N & S Dargan St 29506
Dark Rd 29501
E Darlington St 29506
W Darlington St 29501
Darris Ln 29505
David H Mcleod Blvd 29501
Davidson St 29506
Davis Rd 29501
Dawn St 29505
Day St 29506
Deberry Blvd 29501
Declaration Dr 29501
Deena Ln 29506
N Deepwoods Ln 29506
Deerfield Dr 29505
Deerwood Pl 29501
Deforest Ln 29506
Dejongh St 29501
Delaware River Dr 29501
Delica Ln 29501
Dell Joe Cir 29505
Dellwood Ln 29505
W Delmae Dr 29501
Dempsey Rd 29505
Derby Cv 29505
Derby Dr 29501
Deschamps Dr 29501
Desean Dr 29501
Desi Ln 29506
Desmond Dr 29501
Devon Rd 29505
Devonshire Dr 29505
Dexter Dr 29505
Diamond Head Loop 29505
Dickman St 29501
Diggs Ave 29506
S Dingle Dr 29505
Divine St 29506
Dix Ln 29505
Dixie St 29501
Dogwood Ln 29506
W Dogwood Chase Ct 29501
Dominion Ct 29501
Dorado Dr 29505
Dorchester Rd 29501
Dordie Cir 29506
Dorn Ln 29505
Dorset Dr 29501
Doub Ln 29505
Double Dee Ln 29506
N Douglas St 29501
W Dover Dr 29501
W Downing St 29501
Doyle Ln 29505
Dozier Blvd 29501
Drake Shore Dr 29501
Drayton Ave 29505
Dresden Dr 29501
W Driftwood Ave 29501
Drury Ln 29506
Duck Pond Rd 29506
Duckhunter Point Dr 29501
Dudley Dr 29505
Dunaway Dr 29506
Dunbar St 29501
Dunbarton Dr 29501
Duncan Dr 29505
S Dunes Dr 29501
Dunhill Ct 29501
Dunston Dr 29501
Dunton Dr 29506
Dunvegan Rd 29501
Dunwoody Rd 29501
Dupont Dr 29506
Durant Dr 29501
Dusenbury Dr 29501
Duxbury Ln 29501
Dylan Rd 29506
Eaddy Cir 29505
W Eagle St 29501
Eagle Point Dr 29501
Earl Ct 29501
Easterling Cir 29506
Eastman Branch Rd 29505
E Eastway Dr 29506
Eaton Cir 29501
Ebenezer Rd 29501
Ebenezer Chase Dr 29501
Eden Ct 29505
Edenbridge Hall 29501
Edenderry Way 29501
W Edgefield Rd 29501
Edgerton Ln 29506
Edgeware Ct 29501
Edgewood Ave 29501
N Edisto Dr 29501
S Edisto Dr
100-1299 29501
1300-1499 29505
Edsel Rd 29506
Edwards Cir 29501
E Edwards Ct 29505
Effies Ln 29505
Egret Dr 29501
Elaine Cir 29505
Elderberry Dr 29505
Eleanor Dr 29505
Elijah Ludd Rd 29501
N Elizabeth St 29506
Ellie Ln 29506
Ellington Cv 29505
Elliott Ave 29501
Ellis Dr 29501
E Elm St 29506
W Elm St 29501
Elmgrove Ave 29506
Elmore St 29501
Elwood Rd 29501
Emerson Ave 29505
W Emery Ln 29501
N Emma Ln 29506
S Enchanted Ln 29505
Encino Dr 29505
English Ln 29501
Enterprise Dr 29501
Equestrian Ct 29505
Eric Dr 29506
E Ervin Ct & St 29506
Eureka Rd 29506
S Evander Dr 29506
E Evans St 29506
W Evans St
100-1902 29501
1901-1901 29502
1903-2299 29501
1904-2298 29501
Evergreene Rd 29501
Exeter Pl 29501
Fair Oaks Ln 29506
Fairfax Rd 29501
Fairfield Cir 29501
Fairhaven St 29501
Fairlane Dr 29505
S Fairview St 29506
Fairway Dr 29501
Falcon Way 29501
Farm Quarter Rd 29501
Farmingdale Rd 29505
Farmoor Ct 29501
Farmwood Dr 29501
Faulkner Ct 29501
N Fenwick Cir 29506
Fern Bank Rd 29505
Fernleaf Ln 29501
Ferrell St 29501
Fieldale Rd 29501
Fieldcrest Dr 29501
Fiesta Ln 29506
Fillmore Ct 29505
Fireball Ln 29501
Firestone Dr 29501
N & S Firetower Rd 29506
Fishermans Ln 29506
Fitz Randolph Cir 29505
Flag Dr 29505
Flamingo Rd 29506
S Flanders Rd 29505
N Flea Market Rd 29506
Fleetwood Dr 29505
Fletcher St 29501
Flint Lock Cv 29501
Florence Harllee Blvd 29506
Florence Park Dr 29501
Florida Dr 29501
Flowers Rd 29505
S Floyd Cir 29501
Follin Ln 29505
Ford Ln 29505
Fore Rd 29506
W Forest Lake Dr 29501
Forestry Commission
Dr 29501
Fortune St 29506
Founder Dr 29501
Fountain Cir 29501
Four Seasons Rd 29505
Fox Run 29505
Fox Turn Rd 29501
Foxhall Dr 29501
W Foxtail Ln 29501
Foxtrot Dr 29501
Fran Dr 29506
Francis Marion Rd
100-2899 29506
3000-4799 29505
Frank Monroe Dr 29505
N & S Franklin Dr 29501
N Fraser St 29506
Freedom Blvd
1200-1299 29506
1400-2399 29505
Freeman St 29506
Freemont St 29505
W Freight Rd 29501
French Rd 29501
Friars Gate Ct 29505
Furches Ave 29505
Furman Dr 29501
Gable Ter 29505
Gable Ridge Dr 29501
Gail Dr 29501
N & S Gaillard St 29506
Gandy Path Ln 29501
Garden Hills Dr 29505
Garedall Dr 29501
Garland Dr 29501
Garrett Cir 29505
W Gate Pl 29501
Gateway Rd 29501
General William W Dr 29506
W Gentry Dr 29501
Georgetown Rd 29506
Georgia Ln 29501
Gibbs Ave 29501
Gilbert Dr 29506
Gilcrest Rd 29501
Ginny Ct 29501
Gladstone St 29501
Gladys Cir 29505
Glencove Dr 29506
E Glendale Dr 29506
Glenmore Way 29505
Glenns Park Rd 29505
Glenns Way Ct 29505
Glenwood Rd 29505
Godbold Ln 29506
Godwin Ln 29501
Goff Ct 29501
Gold Dr 29505
Golden Way 29505
Golden Pond Ln 29506
Golf Terrace Blvd 29501
Good Boy Rd 29501
Goose Pond Ln 29506
E Grace Dr 29505
Graham St 29501
Grandview Dr 29501
Gray Kat Ln 29501
Green St 29501
Green Acres Rd 29505
Green Meadow Ln 29501
Greenland Dr 29505
Greenleaf Ln 29505
Greenview Dr 29501
Greenway Dr 29501
Greenwing Teal 29505
S Greer Rd 29506
Gregg Ave 29501
Grey Oaks Dr 29505
Greystone Cir & Dr 29501
N & S Griffin St 29506
N Grove Park Dr 29501
N & S Guerry St 29501
Guildford Cir 29501
Gulf Cv 29501
H And M Ln 29506
Habersham Sq 29501
Habitat Ln 29501
Haiasi Dr 29501
Hallie Dr 29505
S Hallmark Dr 29505
Ham Ct 29501
Hamer Cir 29501
Hamilton Ave 29505
Hamlet St 29506
Hamlin St 29506
Hamm Bone Ln 29501
Hammock Ct 29501
Hampton Ct & Dr 29505
W Hampton Pointe Dr 29501
E Handy Ln 29506
Hannah Dr 29505
S Hanover Rd 29501
Harbor Creek Dr 29501
Harborough Ct 29501
Harbour Ln 29505
Hardin St 29505
N Harlem St 29506
Harleston Green Dr 29505
Harley Ln 29506
Harmon Farm Rd 29506
Harmony St 29501
Harrell St 29501
Harriett Dr 29501
Harris Ct 29501
Hart Rd 29501
Harvard Way 29501
N Harvest Ln 29501
W Haskell Ave 29501
Haven Straits Rd 29505
Hawthorne Dr 29501
Hayden Ct 29505
Hazel Dr 29501
Head Dr 29506
Heard St 29506
Heather Dr 29501
Heatherwood Cir 29501
Heathway Dr 29501
Helen St 29505
Hemingway Ave
400-499 29506
500-599 29501
Henry St 29506
Hepborn Blvd 29501
Heritage Ln 29505
Heritage Pointe Ct 29501
Hermies Ln 29505
Hermitage Ln 29501
W Heron Dr 29501
Herring Pl 29506
S Herrington Ct 29501
E Hewitt St 29505
Heyward Ct 29506
Hialeah Ct 29505
Hibernian Dr 29505
Hickory St 29501
Hickory Grove Cir 29501
Hickory Nut Ridge Dr 29501
Hicks Dr 29501
Hicks Ln 29506
Hidden Valley Ln 29506
W Higgins St 29501
E High Hampton Rd 29506
Highgate St 29505
Highland Ave 29501
Highland Bluff Ct 29506
Highlander Ct 29505
Highway 76 29501
Hill Dr & Rd 29505
W Hillcrest Dr & Ter 29501
Hillside Ave
1100-1299 29505
1300-1699 29501
Hilltop Ln 29506
Hinds Ln 29506
Hinson St 29506
Hobart Dr 29501
Hoffmeyer Rd 29501
Holiday Dr 29505
Hollings Ave 29506
S Holloman Dr 29501
S Hollow Cove Rd 29506
Holloway Dr & Ln 29501
Holly Cir 29501
Holly Ln 29505
Hollyberry Ln 29501
Hollybrook Cir 29505
E Holmes St 29506
N & S Homestead Dr 29501

E Homewood Ave 29505
Hondros Cir 29505
Honeysuckle Ln 29506
Honor Cv 29501
Hoole Hill Ln 29506
Hopkins Ct 29505
Hopper Ln 29501
Horlbeck St 29505
Horseshoe Cir 29505
Hospitality Blvd 29501
Houndsfield Dr 29506
Howard St 29506
E Howe Springs Rd 29505
Howell Ln 29501
E Hoyt St 29506
Hucks Ln 29505
Hudson Dr 29506
Hug Me Ct 29506
E Hughes Cir 29506
Hummingbird Rd 29505
Hunt Rd 29506
Hunter St 29505
Hunters Run 29505
Hunters Ridge Rd 29506
Huntinghill Farm Rd 29501
E Huntington Dr 29506
Hutchinson Ave 29505
Hutton Ct 29506
Hyde Cir 29501
Hyler Ln 29506
Hyman St 29506
Ilene Ln 29506
Independence Ave 29501
Indian Dr 29501
Indian River Dr 29501
Indigo Pl 29501
E Industrial Park Blvd 29505
Industry Blvd 29501
Inglewood Dr 29501
Ingram St 29501
Inland Ct 29501
Inlet Ct 29505
Interstate Blvd 29501
Inverness Dr 29505
Iona Dr 29505
N Irby St 29501
S Irby St
100-1199 29501
1200-4499 29505
Iris Dr 29501
Isaiah St 29505
Isgett Rd 29505
Ivanhoe Dr 29505
N & S Ives St 29506
Ivy Ln 29501
Ivywood Rd 29501
Jackson Ave 29501
Jade Dr 29506
James St 29506
James Jones Ave
1200-1299 29506
1300-1399 29505
Jamestown Rd 29506
Jamestown Cemetery Rd 29506
Janes Ln 29501
W Janice Ter 29501
Japonica Ln 29501
Jarrott St 29506
Jasmine Ln 29501
Jason Dr 29505
Jassamine Ln 29506
Java Rd 29505
Jebaily Cir 29505
Jefferies Ln 29505
Jefferson Dr 29501
Jefferson St 29506
N & S Jeffords St 29506
Jennifers Ln 29506
Jerome St 29501
Jerry Ln 29505
Jessie Ln 29505
Jethros Ln 29501
Jevon Ln 29501
W Joan Rd 29501
W Jody Rd 29501

John C Calhoun Rd 29506
John Paxton Ln 29501
Johns St 29506
Johnson Rd 29506
Jones Rd 29505
Joseph Cir 29501
Joyce Ln 29501
Juanita Dr 29501
Judea Ln 29506
Judy Ln 29501
Julie Ann Dr 29505
Juliet Dr 29505
Julip Ln 29505
July Aly 29506
June Ln 29506
Juniper Rd 29501
Justine Rd 29506
Kalmia St 29501
Kamlar Dr 29506
Kansas Dr 29505
Karen Ct 29505
Kates Garden Ln 29505
Katherines Ct 29505
Kathwood Ct 29501
Kebro Ln 29506
Keels Rd 29506
Keirra Ave 29501
Keith Cir 29505
Kelly Dr 29506
Kelly Farm Rd 29501
S Kemp St 29506
Kenfield Ln 29505
Kenley Hall 29501
Kennedy Cir 29501
Kensington St 29505
Kent Cir 29505
Kentucky Dr 29505
Kentwood Dr 29505
Kenwood Ave 29501
W Kenzie Ave 29505
Kershaw St 29506
W Keswick Rd 29501
Key Largo Ct 29501
N Kim Rd 29506
Kimberly Ln 29505
Kimmie Ln 29506
Kincaid Ct 29505
King Ave 29501
N King David Dr 29506
E King George Dr 29506
E King Henry Dr 29506
Kingfisher Ln 29501
Kings Rd 29506
Kings Gate Ct 29501
Kingston Dr 29505
Kinloch Ct 29501
Kintyre Rd 29501
W Kirby Dr 29501
Kirby Farm Dr 29506
Kirkwood Ct 29505
Kirshy Blvd 29506
Kiss Me Ln 29506
Kitty Ln 29501
Knightsbridge Rd 29501
S Knollwood Rd 29501
Knotts Landing Rd 29506
N Koppers Rd 29506
Kristens Channel 29501
Kuker St 29501
Lacy Ct 29505
S Lady St 29501
Lafayette Cir 29501
W Lake Dr 29501
Lake Oakdale Dr 29501
Lake Russell Dr 29501
Lake Wateree Dr 29501
Lakeshore Dr 29501
Lakeside Dr 29505
Lakeview Dr 29505
N Lakewood Dr 29501
Lakota Dr 29505
Lamb Rd 29505
Lampley Way 29501
Lance Dr 29501
Lancelot Dr 29505
Lancer Dr 29506

Lane Rd 29506
E Lanford Rd 29506
Langland Ct 29505
S Langley Dr 29501
S Lansdale Dr 29506
N Lansdowne Dr 29501
Larkspur Rd 29501
Laufer Dr 29501
Laurel Cir 29506
Laurel Ln 29506
Laurel Pl 29506
E Laurel St 29506
W Laurel St 29501
Laurens Cir 29501
S Laurie Cir 29505
E Lauter Ave 29506
Lawrence Dr 29506
Lawson St 29501
Lawton Dr 29501
Layton St 29506
Lazar Pl 29501
Lazy Ln 29506
Lee Dr & Ln 29501
Left Bank Dr 29501
Legacy Ln 29501
W Leggs Cir 29501
Leigh Ln 29505
Lemont Dr 29505
Lenhart Way 29505
Leola Hill Dr 29506
Lester Ave 29501
S Levy St 29506
Lewis Ln 29506
Leyland Dr 29501
Liberty Dr 29501
E Liberty St 29506
W Liberty St 29506
Liberty Chapel Rd 29506
Light St 29506
Lilah Marie Way 29505
Lilas Ct 29501
W Lillian Dr 29501
Lilo Ln 29505
Lincoln St 29506
E Linda Dr 29506
Lindberg Dr 29501
Linden Dr 29505
Lindsey Dr 29501
Liston Street Dr 29501
Live Oak Cir 29501
Livery Ct 29505
Loblolly Pass 29506
Lockhaven Dr 29501
Lofty Way 29505
Log Cabin Rd 29501
Londonberry Dr 29505
Longbranch Rd 29506
Longfellow Dr 29505
Longview Ln 29505
Longwood Dr 29505
Loni Kaye Ln 29501
Loquat Dr 29505
Lorraine Ave 29501
W Louise Rd 29501
Louisiana Ln 29501
Lowell St 29506
E Lucas St 29506
W Lucas St 29501
Lucius Cir 29506
Lucy Ln 29505
Lula Ct 29506
Lunn Dr 29501
Lupine Dr 29501
Lymington Ct 29501
Lynch St 29506
Lynwood Dr 29501
Macgregor Ln 29506
Macon Dr 29506
E Macree Ter 29505
Madden Ln 29501
Madeira Ln 29505
Madison Ave 29501
Mae Dr 29505
Maggie Way 29505
Magna Carta Rd 29501
Magnolia Dr & St 29506

S Main St 29501
Malabar St 29501
Malcray Ln 29505
Malden Dr 29505
Malissa Mae Rd 29506
Mallard Ln 29501
Mallard Hen Rd 29505
Malloy St 29506
Manchester Ave 29505
Mandeville Rd 29501
Manigault Ct 29501
E Manning St 29505
Manor Cir 29501
Manorway Dr 29501
Maple St
100-199 29506
2300-2399 29501
Maple Chase Ln 29501
Margaret Dr 29501
N Marigold St 29506
Marion Ave 29505
E Marion St 29506
W Marion St 29501
Marion Green Rd 29506
Mariposa Dr 29501
E & W Marlboro St 29506
Marlington Rd 29505
Marlow Ave 29506
Mars Hill Cir
1400-1599 29505
1600-1899 29501
Marsh Ave 29505
Marshall Ave 29501
Masters Cir 29501
Mater Ln 29505
E Maxwell St 29506
Mayberry Ln 29501
S Mayfair Ter 29501
S Mayhill Ln 29506
Maynard Ave 29505
Mays Pl 29506
W Mcarthur Ave 29501
S Mccall Blvd 29506
Mcclellan St 29505
Mcconnell Ln 29506
W Mccown Dr 29501
Mccracken Dr 29505
S Mccurdy Rd 29506
Mcdonald Blvd 29506
E Mcelveen Ter 29505
Mcfarland St 29506
Mcintosh Woods Rd 29501
E Mciver Rd
200-799 29506
1200-2599 29501
W Mciver Rd 29501
Mckeithan Rd 29501
Mckenney Ct 29501
Mckinleys Ln 29506
Mclaurin Dr 29501
Mclellan Ln 29501
Mcleod Aly & St 29501
Mclure Ct 29505
Mcmaster Ave 29506
Mcmillian Ln 29501
Mcneil Dr 29501
Mcpherson Farm Rd 29505
N & S Mcqueen St 29501
Mcwhite Cir 29505
W Meade Cir 29505
Meadors Rd 29501
W Meadow Ln 29501
Meadow Green Pl 29501
Meadowbrook Dr 29501
S Meadows Farm Rd 29505
Mears Dr 29501
Mechanic St 29506
Mechanicsville Rd 29501
Medford Ln 29505
Medinah Ct 29501
Megan Rd 29505
Melanie Ct 29505
Melon St 29501
Melrose Ave 29505
Memory Ln 29501
Mercedes Way 29506

Mercury Ln 29506
Mercy Cir 29501
Meredith Dr 29505
Meridian St 29505
Merlin Pl 29505
Merrill Hall 29501
Merriweather Ln 29501
Michelle Ct 29505
Middle Dr 29501
Middleberg Way 29505
Middlecoff Ln 29506
Middleton Rd 29501
Middleton St 29506
Milan Rd 29506
Miles Rd 29505
Milestone Ln 29505
Milford Ln 29501
Millbank Dr 29501
Millbrook Dr 29505
Millcrest Dr 29501
Miller St 29506
Millridge Dr 29505
Millstone Cir & Rd 29505
S Millwood Dr 29505
Milwaukee Dr 29501
Mimosa Dr 29501
Minden St 29506
Ministry Ln 29506
S Miriam Ave 29506
Missle St 29506
Misty View Ln 29506
Mobley Ln 29501
Mockingbird Cir 29501
Mohawk Dr 29501
Mohawk River Dr 29501
Mollhoff Ct 29506
Monquie Ave 29501
Montague Pl 29501
E Montclair Way 29505
Monterey Dr 29501
Moonlight Ct 29505
Moose Ln 29501
W Morningside Rd 29505
Morris St 29506
Mortimer St 29506
Moses Ln 29501
Moss Dr 29505
Mosswood Dr 29501
Mountain Laurel Ct 29505
Muirfield Pl 29505
Muldrow St 29501
Muldrows Ln 29505
Mullins St 29506
S Murray Hill Dr 29501
Muses Bridge Rd 29501
N Mustang Rd 29506
Myrtle Dr 29505
S Mystic Ct 29501
E N B Baroody St 29506
W N B Baroody St
100-199 29506
200-1499 29501
Nails Pl 29501
Nance Rd 29501
Nantucket Dr 29501
Nathaniel Ln 29506
National Ave 29501
E National Cemetery Rd 29506
Nature Trl 29501
Navajo Cir 29506
Nellie St 29505
Nelson Ln 29505
Nena Ln 29506
N & S New St 29506
W New Castle Rd 29501
New Forrest Dr 29505
New Gate Ct 29501
New Hope Dr 29501
Newman Ave 29506
Newport Dr 29506
Nicklaus Ct 29506
Nighthawk Dr 29501
Nob Hill Dr 29505
Noble St 29506
Nome St 29501

Norfolk St 29506
Norman Murray Cir 29506
N Norwood Ln 29506
Nottingham Dr 29505
Nottinghill Ct 29501
Nute St 29506
Oak Dr 29501
S Oak Rd 29505
Oak St 29506
Oak Bend Ln 29501
Oak Chase Ln 29501
Oak Forest Blvd 29501
Oak Hei Ln 29505
Oakdale Rd & Ter 29501
Oakdale Green St 29501
Oakland Ave 29506
Oakmont Ave 29501
Oaktree St 29501
Oakwood Ln 29501
N Obrian Rd 29506
N Ogden St 29501
Ohara Dr 29505
Old Ball Diamond Rd 29505
Old Ebenezer Rd 29501
Old Ivey Ln 29501
E Old Marion Hwy 29506
Old Mars Bluff Rd 29506
Old Muldrows Mill Rd 29501
N Old River Rd 29505
Old Wallace Gregg Rd 29506
Old Woodlands Rd 29505
Olde Colony Dr 29505
Olde Mill Rd 29505
Oldfield Cir 29501
Oleander Dr 29501
Olive St 29506
S Oliver Dr 29505
Olympic Ct 29501
E Openwood Ln 29505
Orange Cir 29506
Orchard Dr 29501
Orlando Ct 29505
Osprey Dr 29501
Ossie Ln 29505
Otis Way 29501
Overhill Dr 29505
Oxford St 29501
Page Ct 29505
Palm Ct 29501
Palmer Dr 29506
E Palmetto St 29506
W Palmetto St 29501
Palmetto Heights Dr 29501
Palmetto Shores Dr 29501
Palomar Pkwy 29506
Pamplico Hwy 29505
Pansy Ln 29506
Papa Dr 29506
Paper Mill Rd
200-3499 29506
3500-3999 29505
7300-7399 29506
Paradise Ct 29505
Park Ave 29501
Park Pl
600-699 29501
2800-2999 29505
S Parker Dr 29501
Parkland Dr 29501
Parkview Cir 29501
Parkwood Dr 29505
Parliament Cir 29501
Parrott Dr 29501
Parsons Gate 29501
Partridge Cir & Dr 29505
Patrick Dr 29501
Patriot Ln 29506
Patterson St 29501
Patton Dr 29501
Pawley St 29506
Payton Ln 29505
Peaceful Cir 29506
Peachtree St 29505
Peanut Cir 29506
Pearl Cir 29506
Peatree Ct 29505

Pebble Rd 29501
Pecan St 29501
Pecan Grove Rd 29505
Pee Dee Dr 29501
W Pelican Ln 29501
Pendleton Ct 29505
S Peninsula Rd 29501
Pennsylvania St 29501
Pensacola Ct 29505
Penshurst Dr 29506
Pepper Tree Rd 29506
W Percy Dr 29501
Perdue Ln 29506
Periwinkle Ln 29501
Perkins Rd 29501
Perth St 29501
Peterbilt Rd 29501
N & S Pettigrew St 29501
Philadelphia Pl 29501
Phoenix Rd 29506
Piano Rd 29501
W Piccadilly Dr 29501
Pickett Dr 29501
Pickford Ln 29501
S Piedmont St 29506
Pike Pl 29501
Pilchard Ct 29505
Pilgrim Dr 29501
Pinckney Ave 29505
Pindo Ct 29501
E Pine St 29506
W Pine St 29501
Pine Acres Dr 29501
N Pine Court Cir 29506
Pine Forest Dr 29505
Pine Grove Rd 29501
Pine Haven Dr 29506
Pine Hill Ct 29506
Pine Hollow Dr 29501
W Pine Lake Dr 29506
Pine Needles Rd 29501
Pineapple Gate Dr 29501
Pineland Ave 29501
Pineland Dr 29505
Pinetree Dr 29501
Pisgah Rd 29501
Pitty Pat Dr 29505
Place De Julian 29501
W Placid St 29501
Plantation Dr 29505
Platt St 29505
Player Ct 29506
W Pleasant Dr 29501
Plum Dr 29501
Pocket Rd 29506
Poinsett Dr 29505
N Poinsett Dr 29501
N Point Dr 29501
Point View Dr 29501
W Pointe Dr 29501
Pond Rd
900-1199 29506
3900-3999 29501
Poor Farm Rd 29505
Poplar St 29501
Poplar Chase Ln 29501
E Poston Ave 29505
Powell Ln 29506
Power St 29501
Preakness Ln 29501
Press Rd 29501
Preston St 29501
Prestwick Dr 29501
N Price Rd 29506
Price St 29501
Primrose St 29505
Prince St 29506
Prince Alston Cv 29501
Progress St 29501
Prosperity Ct & Way 29501
Prout Dr 29506
Providence Ct 29505
Pumpkin Ln 29505
S Purvis Dr 29505
Quail Arbor Cir 29506
Quail Pointe Dr 29501

Quaker Ridge Dr 29505
Quartz Ln 29506
Queen Ann Rd 29501
Queen Elizabeth Way .. 29506
Queens Rd 29501
Queens Ferry Rd 29505
Quinby Cir, Ln & Plz ... 29506
Quincy Rd 29506
Qvc Rd 29501
R Bar M Ranch Rd 29501
R S Hepburn Rd 29501
Rabbit Wood Ln 29505
W Radio Dr 29501
Raiford Ln 29505
Railroad Ave 29506
Rainbow Dr 29501
Rainford Rd 29501
Rainier St 29505
Ralston Ct 29505
Rambler Rd 29501
Ranch Rd 29506
Random Ln 29501
Range Way 29501
Rankin Plantation Rd ... 29506
Ratliff Ln 29501
Raven Dr 29505
N & S Ravenel St 29506
Raymond Ln 29505
Reb Ln 29506
Rebecca St 29501
Rebel Ln 29505
Red Doe Rd 29506
Red Tip Cir 29505
Red Wing Ln 29501
Redbird Rd 29505
Redbreast Pt 29506
E Redbud Ln 29505
Redwood Dr 29501
Reed Ct 29506
Regency Ct 29505
Regent St 29506
Regional Rd 29501
Reid Ln 29501
Renee Cir 29506
Renee Ct 29501
Renee Dr 29501
Republic Ave 29501
Restview Rd 29506
Revell Dr 29501
Rhett Ct 29505
Rhodes Ln 29505
Rice St 29501
Rice Hope Cv 29501
Rice Planters Ln 29501
Richbourg Ln 29505
Richmond Hills Dr 29505
E Rico Dr 29505
Ridarenc Rd 29506
W Ridgecrest Cir 29501
Ridgeland Dr 29501
Ridgewood Dr 29501
River Birch Rd 29506
River Forest Dr 29505
River Neck Rd 29506
S Riverdale Ave 29505
Rivergate Dr 29501
Roberta Cir 29505
Roberts St 29506
S Robeson Ave 29505
Rock Creek Rd 29505
Rocking Chair Rd 29505
Rockmore St 29501
Rockwood Ln 29506
N Rocky Way Dr 29506
Roda Dr 29501
Rodanthe Cir 29501
Rogers Ct 29506
N Rogers St 29501
Rogers Bridge Rd 29506
Rollins Ave 29505
Romsey Pl 29501
Roosevelt St 29501
Rose Dr 29501
Rose St 29506
Rosedale St 29501
Rosemary Ave 29505
Rosemount Dr 29505
W Roseneath Rd 29501
Rosewood Dr 29501
E Roughfork St 29506
W Roughfork St
100-499 29506
500-799 29501
Roxbaro Pl 29505
Roxboro Ct 29501
Royal St 29506
Rugby Ln 29501
Running Deer Dr 29501
Rustling Bark Dr 29505
Rutherford Dr 29505
Rutledge Ave 29505
Rutledge Manor Dr 29501
Ryan Dr 29501
Ryefield St 29506
Saddle Ct 29505
Sahalee Ln 29501
Saint Andrews Blvd 29505
Saint Andrews Rd 29501
Saint Anthony Ave 29505
Saint Beulah Rd 29506
S Saint Claire Dr 29501
Saint George Dr 29505
Saint James Ct & Ln 29501
Saint John Dr 29505
N Salem Dr 29506
Sally Cir 29501
Sally Hill Farms Blvd 29501
Saluda Dr 29501
E Sam Harrell Rd 29506
W Sam Harrell Rd 29501
Sam Snead Ct 29506
E Sammys Ln 29506
Sanborn St 29501
Sand Pit Rd 29506
Sanderling Dr 29505
E & W Sandhurst Dr 29505
Sandifer Ln 29505
Sandpiper Ln 29505
Sandra Ter 29501
Sandwood Ave 29506
Sandy Ln 29501
Santee Dr 29501
Santee River Dr 29501
S Santiago Dr 29501
Sarah Ln 29506
Sarah Estate Ln 29505
Sarasota Ct 29505
Sarazen Ct 29506
W Saunders St 29501
Saurus Ct 29505
Sawgrass Dr 29505
Sawyer Ln 29501
Saxon Dr 29501
Saxony Way 29506
E Scarlett Ln 29505
N Schlitz Dr 29501
N Schofield St 29501
Scotland Dr 29506
Scott Dr 29505
Scout Ln 29501
Scriven Dr 29501
Sebery Ln 29505
Sebrell St 29505
Secretariat Dr 29505
Sedgebrook Dr 29505
Seminole Ave 29501
Seminole River Dr 29501
Seneca Dr 29501
Seneca River Dr 29501
Senior Way 29505
Sewanee Ave 29501
Seward St 29506
Seymore Dr 29505
Shadeland Cir 29501
Shadow Burch Rd 29505
Shadow Creek Dr 29505
Shadwell Ct 29501
Shady Oak Ln 29506
Shamrock Dr 29505
Shandon Dr 29501
Sharing Ln 29506
Sharon Rd 29506
Sheffield Dr & Ln 29505
E Shenandoah Ln 29506
Sherwood Dr 29501
Shingle Oak Dr 29506
Shore Ln 29505
Shorebird Ln 29501
Short Ln 29501
Shortpost Ln 29506
S Shouboe St 29506
Shrek Way 29505
Shuler Rd 29506
Sidney Ave 29505
N Sierra Range 29501
E Siesta Dr 29505
Silver Leaf Rd 29505
Silverstone Dr 29506
Silverthorn St 29505
Simmons St 29501
Singlewood Dr 29501
Sioux River Dr 29501
E Skylane Dr 29506
Skylark Dr 29501
Sliger Cv 29501
Smith Dr 29501
Sneed Rd 29501
Somerset Pl 29501
Sopkin Ave 29506
E South Village Blvd 29505
Southborough Rd 29501
Southbrook Cir 29505
Southside Cir 29505
Southwood Ct 29505
Spanish Oak Dr 29506
Sparkleberry Ln 29506
Spears Rd 29505
Spencer Ln 29501
Spicewood Dr 29505
Spike Ct 29505
Split Rail Dr 29506
E Spring St 29505
Spring Farm Rd 29505
Spring Hill Rd 29501
Springbranch Rd 29501
W Springdale Dr 29501
N Springdale Pl 29506
W Springfield Dr 29501
Springvalley Dr 29501
Springwood Dr 29501
Spruce St 29501
Spud Ln 29505
Stackley St 29506
S Stadium Rd 29506
Stafford Ct 29501
Stag Horn Ln 29506
S Stanley Dr 29501
Starlight Ln 29505
Starwood Dr 29501
Steel Rd 29506
Steen Dr 29506
Steeple View Dr 29505
Steeplechase Dr 29501
Steerfork Dr 29501
Stephanie Ln 29505
Stephen Cir 29506
Stephenson Dr 29506
Sterling Dr 29501
Stillwater Ln 29501
Stillwell Dr 29505
Stockade Dr 29506
Stockbridge Ln 29505
Stockton Dr 29501
Stokes Aly & Rd 29501
E Stone Ln 29506
Stonehenge Ln 29501
Stoneybrook Ter 29501
Strada Amore 29501
Strada Angelo 29501
Strada Gianna 29501
Strada Mateo 29501
Strada Rosa 29501
Strada Santa 29501
Stratford Cir 29505
Stratton Dr 29501
Stricklen Dr 29505
Stripplewood Dr 29505
Suburban Rd 29501
W Suburbia St 29501
Success Way 29501
E Suena Dr 29505
Suffolk Pl 29501
Sugar Creek Cir 29501
Sumac Dr 29505
Summergate Dr 29501
Summertree Dr 29506
E Summit Cir 29506
W Sumter St 29501
Sun Vue Dr 29506
S Sundance St 29506
Sunny Point Rd 29501
Sunnyside Rd 29501
N & S Sunset Dr 29501
Sunset Acres Ln 29501
Sunshine Ave 29506
Superior Ln 29506
Susan Dr 29501
Sussex Ct 29501
Swamp Fox Dr 29506
Swan Cir & Pt 29501
Sweetbriar St 29505
Sweetgrass Dr 29501
W Swinney Dr 29501
Sycamore Dr 29501
Sylvan Dr 29505
Tall Oaks Dr 29506
Tallulah St 29501
Tampa Ct 29505
Tanager Dr 29501
Tanglewood Cir 29501
Tara Dr 29505
Taylor Ct 29501
Taylor Rd 29506
Taylor Hill Cir 29506
Teaberry Dr 29501
Teal Ln 29501
Teapot Ln 29501
Technology Pl 29501
Teddy Ln 29505
Tee Ct 29501
Tennessee Ter 29501
Tennyson Dr 29501
Terminal Dr 29506
S Terrace Dr 29506
Terry Ct 29505
Tetbury St 29501
Texas Rd 29501
Theatre Cir 29501
Therell Dr 29501
Thicket Pl 29501
Thistle Ct 29505
Thomas Rd 29501
Thompson St 29501
Thornberry Dr 29505
Thornblade Dr 29501
E Thorncliff Rd 29505
Thoroughbred St 29505
Threadgill Dr 29501
Three Bees Ln 29501
Thunderbird Dr 29501
Tidewater Ct 29501
E Tierra Dr 29505
Tiffany Dr 29501
Tilly Dr 29501
Timberlake Dr 29501
Timberlane Dr 29506
Timberwood Rd 29506
Timmons St 29506
Timrod Park Dr 29501
Tingen Aly 29501
Tivoli Dr 29501
N Tobin Dr 29501
Toledo Rd 29505
Toledo Scale Rd 29505
Tommy Dr 29506
Took Pl 29505
Traces Dr 29501
Tradd Ct 29506
Trade Ct & St 29501
N Trailer Rd 29506
Travis Ct 29501
Treasure Cv 29505
Trellis Ln 29501
S Tremont Rd 29506
Trent Dr 29505
Trenton St 29501
Trey Chase Dr 29506
Triangle Ln 29506
Trillium Ct 29501
Trilly Ln 29505
Trinidad Ct 29506
N Trinity St 29501
Triple Crown Dr 29505
Troon Dr 29501
Trotter Rd 29501
Trotwood Dr 29501
Truman St 29506
Tudor Ln 29505
Tuggie Ln 29505
Tumbleweed Dr 29506
Tunridge Rd 29501
Turnberry Pl & Rd 29501
Turner Rd
600-699 29501
900-1499 29506
Turnpike Rd 29501
Tutson Aly 29501
Tv Rd 29501
Twiggs Rd 29505
Twin Cir 29505
Twin Bridge Dr 29505
Twin Church Rd 29501
Union Aly 29506
Utah Ct 29501
Valparaiso Dr 29501
S Vance Dr 29505
Vardon Way 29506
Ventura Ct 29506
Veranda Way 29501
Vespers Ct 29505
Via Ponticello 29501
Via Salvatore 29501
Viburnum Dr 29505
Victoria Ct 29501
Victory Ct 29505
Vince Cir 29505
N Vine Dr 29506
Vintage Dr 29501
Virginia Acres 29505
E Vista St 29506
W Vista St
100-499 29506
500-699 29501
Vivian Ln 29501
Vonda Kay Ln 29506
Wachovia Bluff Dr 29506
Wachovia Hills Dr 29506
Wade St 29501
Wainwright Ct 29501
Wake Robin Ct 29505
E & W Wakefield Ave 29505
Walden St 29501
Waldens Pond 29501
Wall St 29501
S Wallace Rd 29506
Walnut St 29506
Walter Dr 29505
Wanda Cv 29501
Wannamaker Ave 29501
N Ward Cir 29506
Warley St 29501
Warner St 29501
Warwick Ln 29501
Washington St
400-499 29506
500-699 29501
Watauga Cir 29506
Waterford Dr 29501
Waterfowl Way 29501
Waterfront Dr 29501
Waterman Ave 29506
Watermark Rd 29506
Waters Ave 29501
Watersedge Ln 29501
Waterway Dr 29501
Waverly Ave 29501
Waverly Woods Dr 29505
Wax Myrtle Dr 29501
Waxwing Dr 29505
Weatherford Ln 29506
Wedgefield Rd 29501
Welch Dr 29505
Wellesly Ct 29505
S Wellington Dr 29506
Wellon Ln 29505
Wenonah Dr 29501
Wensley Ct 29501
Wentworth Dr 29501
Wesley Ct 29501
West Ct 29505
Westbrook Dr 29501
Westbury Ct 29501
Westchester Dr 29501
Westfield Dr 29501
E Westford Rd 29506
S Westminister Dr 29501
Westmoreland Ave 29505
Westview Dr 29501
Westwind Dr 29501
Westwood Dr 29501
Wethersfield Dr 29501
Whirlaway Ave 29505
S White Palm Ct 29506
S Whitehall Cir 29501
N Whitehall Dr 29506
Whitehall Shores Rd 29501
Whiterail Dr 29501
Whitestone Dr 29505
Whitman Ave 29501
W Whittier Cir 29501
E Whittington Forest
Rd 29506
Wickerwood Rd 29505
Wilcus Ln 29505
Wildcat Rd 29506
Wildwood Dr 29506
Wiley Ln 29506
Wilford Dr 29505
Wiljay Ln 29506
Willard Henry Rd 29505
William Ln 29501
Williams Blvd 29501
Williamsburg Cir 29506
N Williamson Rd 29506
Willis Cir 29501
N Williston Rd 29506
W Willow Dr 29501
Willow Creek Rd 29505
Willow Trace Dr 29501
Willwood Dr 29501
Wilshire Ct 29505
Wilson Rd & St 29506
N Wiltshire Dr 29501
Wimbledon Ave 29505
S Winburn Dr 29501
Winding Creek Ln 29506
Windover Rd 29501
S Windsong Dr 29501
Windsor Rd 29505
Windsor Forest Dr 29501
Windy Plains Dr 29501
Wingate Ave 29506
E Winlark Dr 29506
Winning Colors Dr 29505
Winslow Ct 29501
Winston St 29501
Winterbrook Dr 29505
Winterbury Rd 29506
Winterwood Rd 29505
Winthrop Dr 29501
Wisteria Dr 29501
Wood Duck Ln 29505
Wood Lake Dr 29506
Woodall Ct 29505
W Woodbine Ave 29501
Woodbridge Rd 29501
E Woodburn Dr 29506
S Woodcreek Ln 29506
Woodfield Rd 29505
Woodland Dr 29501
Woodlawn Ct 29505
Woodmore Cir 29505
Woodridge Ln 29501
Woods Dr 29505
Woods Rd 29501
Woodstone Dr 29501
Woodvale Dr 29501
Woodville Rd 29506
Woodward St 29501
Woody Jones Blvd 29501
Wreathwood Ln 29505
Wren Creek Ct 29501
Wrenfield Rd 29501
Wrenwood Rd 29505
Wright Ln 29506
Yancey Dr 29505
Yankee Ct 29501
Yeargin Cv 29501
Yellowstone Dr 29505
Ymca Ln 29505
York St 29506
Yorkshire Ct 29505
Yosemite Ct 29505
Young Charles Dr 29501
Youpon St 29501
Yucker Dr 29501
Yukon Rd 29505
Yvonne St 29506
Zaharias Ct 29506

NUMBERED STREETS

S 1st St 29506
S 2nd St 29506
2nd Loop Rd 29504
2nd Loop Rd 29505
2nd Loop Rd 29505
2nd Loop Rd 29505
1700-2899 29501
S 3rd St 29506
3rd Loop Rd 29505
1800-2599 29501
S 4th St 29506
S 5th St 29506
S 6th St 29506
50th St 29506

FORT MILL SC

General Delivery 29715

POST OFFICE BOXES MAIN OFFICE STATIONS AND BRANCHES

Box No.s
1 - 2119 29716
3001 - 3538 29708
3010 - 9998 29716
9998 - 9998 29715

NAMED STREETS

A O Jones Blvd 29715
Abbotsford Dr 29715
Abbottsbury Dr 29707
Abigdon Way 29715
Abilene Ln 29715
Abode Ln 29707
Academy St 29715
Adair Marble St 29708
Adams Ridge Dr 29715
Adie Ln 29707
Agate Ct 29708
Agnes Douglas Rd 29707
Agusta Ct 29707
Alana Ct 29708
Albany St 29715
Albany Park Dr 29715
Albatross Ln 29707
Albert Ct 29707
Alder Ct 29708
Alderman Ln
500-598 29707
500-598 29715
501-599 29707
501-599 29715
Alexandrite Way 29708

Street	ZIP
Alfred Ln	29708
All Saints Way	29707
Allendale Dr	29707
Allison St	29715
Allspice Rd	29708
Alsace Ln	29708
Altovista Ct	29708
Altura Rd	29708
Amaranth Dr	29708
Amaryllis Ct	29708
Amber Woods Dr	29708
Amberlea Ln	29715
Amberly Xing	29708
Ambleside Dr	29707
Amelia Dr	29715
Amethyst Cir	29708
Amistead Ave	29708
Anchorage Ln	29708
Anchura Rd	29708
Anderson St	29715
Andover Ln	29708
Andrew Ln	29707
Andrew L Tucker Rd	29715
Angel Carrie Ln	29707
Angela Ct	29715
Angelica Ln	29708
Ann Shaw Ave	29708
Annatto Way	29708
Ansley Walk Ln	29715
Apple Tree Ln	29715
Applegate Rd	29715
Appleseed Cir	29715
Applevalley Way	29715
Arbor Place Dr	29707
Archie St	29715
Ardrey St	29715
Argentum Ave	29707
Arrieta Ct	29707
Arrington Rd	29707
E & W Arrow Lake Ct	29707
Arrowpoint Ln	29707
Arthur Rd	29707
Arundale Ln	29707
Asbury Ln	29707
Ashbin Ct	29707
Ashbrooke Dr	29715
Ashby Ln	29707
Ashford Way	29708
Ashleigh Ct	29715
Ashley Rd	29707
Ashley Arbor	29715
Ashley Glen Way	29707
Ashlyn Cir	29707
Assembly Dr	29708
Athena Pl	29715
S Atlantic Dr	29708
Audubon Lake Blvd	29707
Augusta Ct	29707
Autumn Hill Ln	29707
Autumn Moon Dr	29715
Autumn Ridge Ln	29708
Avenue Of The Carolinas	29708
Avery St	29715
Avon Ct	29707
Aycoth Rd	29707
Ayers Rd	29715
Azalea Dr	29707
Azurine Cir	29708
Backer Ln	29707
Badlands Ct	29707
Balboa Ct	29715
Ballard Ct & Ln	29715
Balsam Bark Ln	29708
Baltusrol Dr	29707
Bamborough Dr	29715
Bancroft Ct	29707
Banks Rd & St	29715
Banksridge Rd	29715
Bannerman Ln	29715
Bannock Dr	29715
Barber Rock Blvd	29707
Barberville Rd	29707
Barcroft Ln	29715
Barnett Woods	29708
Barrington Ridge Dr	29707
Bass St	29715
Bassett Dr	29707
Bath Ct	29708
Baxter Ln	29715
Bayneswood Ln	29707
Baywoods Dr	29708
Beach Club Ln	29708
Beachwood Cove Dr	29708
Beacon Ct	29708
Beacon Knoll Ln	29708
Bearwood Ln	29707
Beaver Run	29708
Beck St	29715
Becker Ave	29715
Becknell St	29715
Beech Dr	29715
Beechnut Ct	29708
Beille Ln	29708
Belair Dr	29707
Belews St	29707
Belfield Ln	29715
Bellflower Dr	29715
Bellhaven Chase Way	29707
Belo Ct	29715
Belt Ln	29707
Ben Casey Dr	29708
Ben Lee Rd	29715
Benedict Pl	29707
Benelli Ln	29707
Benjamen Latrobe Cir	29708
Bennett Rd	29715
Bent Leaf Ct	29708
Bentgrass Ln	29708
Berg Cir	29715
Bergamot St	29708
Bermuda Run Dr	29708
Berry St	29715
Bertram Rd	29708
Bessbrook Dr	29708
Bethany Green Ct	29708
Bethpage Dr	29707
Bidford Ct	29707
Big Rock Ct	29708
Biltmore Dr	29707
Birkhall Ct	29715
Birkhill Ln	29707
Birkshire Hts	29708
Birnamwood Ct	29715
Biscayne Ct	29707
Bison Ct	29707
Black Ash Rd	29707
Black Hawk Ln	29708
Black Heath Dr	29707
Black Horse Run Rd	29707
Black Mountain Dr	29708
Black Oasis Cir	29708
Blackberry Walk	29715
Blackburn Ct	29707
Blackwelder Rd	29707
Blandina Ct	29708
Blandwood Ct	29715
Blossom Ter	29715
Blowing Rock Cv	29708
Blue Field Ln	29708
Blue Jay Pass	29708
Blue Ridge Dr	29707
Bluebell Way	29708
Bolick Rd	29707
Bolick Road Ext	29707
Bollin Cir	29715
Bolton Rd	29707
Bon Villa Way	29707
Bontrager Trl	29715
Bora Bora Dr	29708
Botley Ct	29708
Boudins Ln	29707
Bounty Ln	29708
Bourgess Ct	29707
Boyer Rd	29708
Bozeman Dr	29715
Bracket St	29708
Braliste Dr	29708
Bramblett	29715
Brecken Hill Ln	29708
Brian Kelley Ln	29708
Briarberry Ct	29708
Briarwood Cir	29715
Brickdust Ct	29708
Brickyard Rd	29715
Bridge Hampton Club Dr	29707
Bridge Mill Trl	29707
Bridgepoint Dr	29715
Bridle Path	29708
Brienza Beach Way	29715
Brighton Ln	29715
Brimstone Dr	29707
Brittany Ln	29708
Brixham Pl	29708
Brixton Cir	29708
Broad Ln	29707
Brodie Ln	29707
Broken Brook Way	29708
Bromley Village Dr	29708
Bronze Leaf Dr	29707
Brook Dr	29708
Brook Bluff Ln	29707
Brookbend Ct	29715
Brookchase Blvd	29707
Brookmead Dr	29715
Brooks Mill Dr	29708
Brookshaw Run	29715
Brookshire Dr	29715
Brookside Dr	29715
Brookstone Ln	29707
Broughton Ln	29707
Brown St	29715
Bryson Rd	29707
Bubbling Creek Ct	29715
Buck St	29715
Buck Skin Ct	29707
Buckingham Dr	29707
Buckland Ct	29707
Buckner Hl	29715
Buffalo Park Dr	29715
Bull Finch Bnd	29708
Bunchberry Ct	29715
Burchwood Dr	29707
Butler Pl	29715
Buttercup Way	29715
Buttermere Rd	29715
Bw Thomas Dr	29708
Cabin Creek Ct	29715
Cabin View Way	29707
Cabot Way	29715
Cadbury Ln	29715
Caddell Rd	29707
Caddy St	29715
Cadogan Ct	29708
Caernarvon Ct	29715
Caggy Ln	29707
Cahill Ln	29715
Caille Ct	29708
Calaboose Ln	29707
Calder Ct	29707
Calfee Ct	29715
Calhoun St	29715
Calico Ct	29708
Caliper Pl	29708
Calla Lily St	29707
Callahan Rd	29715
Calliwell Ct	29708
Calloway Dr	29715
Calloway Pines Dr	29708
Calming Way	29708
Calvary Ct	29715
Calvin Hall Rd	29707
Calwayne Dr	29707
Camber Woods	29708
Cambridge Ct	29708
Camden Ln	29707
Camden Woods Dr	29707
Camp Cox Cir	29708
Candlewick Dr	29715
Canonero Ln	29707
Canterbury Xing	29708
Cantrell Ave	29715
Canyon Trl	29715
Caprington Dr	29707
Capris Ln	29707
Captains Ct	29708
Cara Ct	29708
Cardan Ct	29708
Carlisle Ct	29715
Carnation Ln	29707
Carnoustie Ct	29707
Carnwarth Ln	29707
Caroland Dr	29708
Carolina Commons Dr	29707
Carolina Lakes Way	29707
Carolina Place Dr	29708
Carolina Wren Ln	29707
Caroline Way	29715
Caroline Acres Rd	29707
Carowinds Blvd	29708
Carowood Dr	29708
Cascading Pines Dr	29708
Caseys Side Way	29708
Caspar Way	29708
Castlewatch Dr	29708
Cat Tail Blf	29708
Catamaran Dr	29708
Catherine Lothie Way	29708
Cathys Ct	29715
Cause Way Ln	29715
Cebu Ct	29708
Cecil Jones Rd	29707
Cedar Holw	29707
Cedar Holw S	29715
Cedar Ln	29707
Cedar Trace Rd	29707
Cedarbrook Ln	29707
Celandine Way	29708
Celtic Ln	29707
Central Ave	29708
Centre Cir	29715
Chadwell Ct	29707
Chancelot Ln	29708
Channings Way	29707
Chapel Ln	29707
Charleston Ct	29707
Charlotte Hwy	
100-10198	29707
101-199	29715
201-10199	29707
Charlotte Park Dr	29707
Charost Way	29707
Charterhouse Ln	29715
Chartwell Ln	29708
Chase Ct	29708
Chasewater Dr	29707
Chastain Way	29707
Chatham Dr	29707
Chatsworth Dr	29707
Chaucer Cir	29708
Chelsea Day Ln	29708
Chelton Ln	29715
Cherry Blossom Cir	29707
Cherry Blossom Ct	29715
Cheryl Ln	29707
Chesterfield Canal	29708
Chestnut Ave	29708
Chestnut Hill Dr	29708
E & W Cheval Dr	29708
Chevis Ct	29708
Chicopee Dr	29708
Chimney Rock Ln	29708
Chipper Ct	29707
Choate Ave	29708
Chorus Rd	29715
Cilantro Ct	29708
Cinda St	29715
Citron Ave	29708
Clarence Julian Ave	29708
Clarion Dr	29707
Clark Elliott St	29708
Classified Ct	29715
Clear Spring Ct	29708
Clebourne St	29715
Clems Branch Rd	29707
Clifflure Ln	29708
E & W Close St	29715
Clover Hill Rd	29707
Club Range Dr	29715
Club View Dr	29708
Clydesdales Ct	29715
Cobblestone Ct	29708
Cobra Ln	29707
Coburn Ct	29715
Coddin Ln	29707
Cody Ct	29715
Colbert Way	29715
Cole Creek Dr	29707
Collin House Dr	29715
Collins Rd	29707
Colnago Pl	29715
Colonel Springs Way	29708
Colt Ct	29707
Coltharp Rd	29715
Colville Ln	29708
Commons Ct	29708
Conant Cir	29708
Coneflower Pl	29708
Confederate St	29715
Congaree Ct	29707
Congressional Ct	29707
Congressional Ln	29708
Cononero Pl	29707
Constitution Hill Pl	29707
Convention Dr	29715
Conway Ct	29715
Cook Dr	29707
Cool Mist Ct	29707
Cool Spring Ct	29707
Cool Water Ct	29715
Cooleewee Ct	29715
Coolidge St	29715
Copper Creek Ln	29715
Copperstone Ln	29708
Coralbell Way	29708
Coralstone Dr	29708
Corbret Rd	29707
Cormorant Ct	29707
Coronet Cir	29715
Corval Ln	29707
Cougar Point Ct	29707
Council House Rd	29708
Country Acres Dr	29707
Country Brook Way	29708
Country Club Dr	29715
Country Haven Ln	29708
Country Lodge Rd	29708
Country Overlook Dr	29715
Courtney Ln	29707
Cove Ln	29708
Cove Point Ln	29708
Coventry Ct	29708
Coyote Ln	29715
Crabtree Ct	29708
Cramer Cir	29707
Cranberry Cir	29715
Cranborne Chase	29708
Crandon Rd	29707
Crater Lake Dr	29707
Creek View Ct	29707
Creekside Ct	29707
Creekside Dr	29715
Crescent Bay Ct	29715
Crescent Ridge Dr	29715
Cressingham Dr	29707
Crestfield Ln	29708
Cresthaven Dr	29715
Cresthill Ln	29715
Crestmont Dr	29708
Crofton Dr	29715
Crooked Pine Ln	29707
Crossroads Plz	29708
Crosswater Ln	29708
Crosswind Dr	29707
Crowded Roots Rd	29715
Crown Dr	29708
Crown Ridge Dr	29708
Crown Vista Dr	29707
Croxton Rd	29715
Croyden Ct	29715
Crystal Ln	29707
Crystal Springs Ct	29715
Culp Farms Dr	29715
Cumberland Ct	29707
Cusabo Ln	29707
Cuxhaven Ct	29715
Cuyo Ct	29708
Cyclone Dr	29707
Daffodil Ct	29707
Dairy Barn Ln	29715
Daisy Chain Ct	29715
Dall Petus Rd	29707
Daly Cir	29715
Dam Rd	29708
Dana Ct & Ln	29707
Danbury Ln	29708
Danby Rd	29707
Danielle Way	29715
Danson Dr	29715
Daphne Cir	29708
Dartington Dr	29707
Dashers Den	29708
Dave Gibson Blvd	29708
Dave Williams Rd	29707
David Ct	29715
Dawn Ct	29715
Dawn Mist Ln	29708
Dealtry Ln	29707
Dean Dr	29708
Debonair Dr	29707
Deep Cove Dr	29708
Deep Water Ln	29715
Deer Creek Dr	29708
Deer Forest Dr	29707
Deerbrook Ln	29708
Deerfield Dr	
2200-2499	29715
2500-2699	29708
Del Webb Blvd	29707
Delta Dr	29715
Derricks Xing	29708
Derringer Ave	29707
Des Prez Ave	29707
Desert Rose Ct	29708
Deville Ct	29707
Dewey Ct	29715
Diamond Head Cir	29708
Doby Ct	29715
Doby Creek Ct	29715
Dobys Bridge Rd	
1-3799	29715
3800-4599	29707
Doe Ridge Ln	
1400-1498	29707
1400-1498	29715
1401-1499	29707
1401-1499	29715
Dog Leg Trce	29708
Dogwood Ct	29715
Dogwood Ln	
100-121	29715
122-198	29707
123-199	29715
Dogwood Acres Rd	29707
Dogwood Bay Ln	29708
Dogwood Hills Ct & St	29715
Dogwood Trail Ln	29707
Donaldson St	29707
N & S Dorchester Trce	29707
Dorsett Downs	29708
Double Oaks Rd	29715
Dove Trce	29708
Dove Field Dr	29707
Dovekie Ln	29707
Doves Rd	29708
Downing Dr	29708
Downman Ct	29715
S Downs Way	29708
Drake Park Ave	29708
Drane Cir	29715
Drayton Ct	29708
Drayton Ln	29707
Dream Catcher Cir	29715
Drew Ave	29708
Driftwood Cir	29708
Drummond Ave	29707
Dry Run Rd	29708
Dubriels Way	29708
Duck Pond Ct	29715
Duclair Ln	29707
Dunbar Ln	29707
Duncan Chase Ln	29707
Dundee Ln	29707
Dunes Ct	29715
Dunipace Ct	29707
Dunlin Dr	29707
Dunrobin Pl	29707
Dunwoody Ave	29715
Dunwoody Dr	29707
Durand Rd	29715
Dynasty Ct	29708
Eagle Ln	29707
Eagle Lake Dr	29707
Eagles Cv	29708
Eagles Nest Ln	29707
Earl Dr	29715
Easywater Ln	29707
Eaton Ct	29708
Ebulant Ct	29708
Ed Thompson Rd	29715
Eddy Dr	29715
Edenfield Ln	29707
Edge Hill Dr	29715
Edgewater Way	29708
Edgewater Corp Pkwy	29707
Edie Rose Ln	29708
Edinburgh Ln	29707
Edisto Way	29707
Edward Ln	29707
Elberta Ln	29715
Elders Story Rd	29708
Elis Way	29708
Elizabeth Ln	29707
Elizabeth Berry Ct	29708
Ellen Ln	29707
Elliott St E & W	29715
Elm St	29715
Elmhurst Dr	29715
Elmsbrook Ln	29707
Elswick Ct	29708
Elven Dr	29707
Embassy Dr	29715
Emerald Pines Dr	29708
Emry Ln	29707
Endora Ln	29707
Enfield Ct	29707
English Ivey Ct	29715
Eppington South Dr	29708
Epps Rd & St	29715
Epps Farm Rd	29715
Erskine Ln	29707
Ervin St	29715
Essie Cir	29708
Esther Ct	29708
Evans Trace Ln	29708
Evening Mist Dr	29708
Everett Ln	29707
Everglades Ct	29707
Everlasting St	29707
Executive Pt	29708
Exodus Ct	29715
Fahleh Cv	29708
Faile St	29715
Fair Oaks Dr	29708
Fairburn Ct	29708
Fairntosh Dr	29715
Fairview Rd	29707
Fairway Dr	29715
Fairway Point Dr	29708
Fairwind Ct	29708
Faison Ave	29708
Fallen Timber Ln	29708
Falling Leaf St	29707
Falls Creek Ct	29715
Fants Grove Ln	29707
Farben Way	29715
Farley Rd	29715
Farm Branch Dr	29715
Farmcrest Ct	29708
Farmhouse Rd	29715
Farmlake Ln	29708
Farmstead Ln	29708
Fawnwood Ln	29708
Faye Ann Dr	29715
Featherson Rd	29715
Felts Pkwy	29715
Fenworth Ct	29715
Ferguson Ln	29707
Fern Forest Ct	29715
Fern Run Ct	29715

Fernleigh Pl 29707
Festival Dr 29708
Fifth Baxter Xing 29708
Finch Loop 29715
Finches Ct 29707
Finsbury Ln 29708
Fire Water Ln 29707
Firefly Ln 29715
First Baxter Xing 29708
Fischer Rd 29715
Fisher Ln 29707
Flint Hill Rd 29715
Flour Mills Ct 29715
Flycatchers Ct 29707
Foggy Meadow Ln 29708
Folly Ln 29707
Foothills Way 29708
E Foralto Rdg N 29707
Forbes Rd 29707
Forest Dr 29715
Forest Gdn 29708
Forest Home Dr 29708
Forest Ridge Dr 29715
Forest Walk Ln 29708
Forest Way Dr 29715
Forrest St 29715
Fort Mill Hwy 29707
Fort Mill Pkwy 29715
Fort Mill Sq 29715
Fortson Dr 29707
Fossil Stone Ln 29708
Founders St 29708
Fountain Ct 29715
Fourth Baxter Xing 29708
Fowler Brook Ct 29707
Fox Hvn 29707
Fox Cub Way 29707
Fox Hill Ct 29708
Fox Paw Run 29707
Fox Ridge Ln 29707
Fox Run Dr 29715
E & W Foxwood Ct 29707
Foxwood Village Dr 29715
Frances Cir 29708
Frank Carter Rd S 29715
Fred Nims Rd 29715
Freeman Dr 29715
Fresia Dr 29708
Friendfield Dr 29715
Fritts Ave 29715
Front St 29708
Frost Meadow Way 29707
Furman Ct 29708
Gabriel Ct 29715
Gadwell Pl 29707
Gage Ct 29715
Galette Ln 29707
Gamesford Ln 29715
Gant Rd 29707
Garden Grove Rd 29708
Gardendale Rd 29708
Gardenia St 29708
Garnet Ct 29708
Garrison Farm Rd N 29715
Garys Cir 29708
Gasper Ln 29707
Gates Mills Dr 29708
Gauguin Ln 29708
Gentlewinds Ct 29708
Georgetown Cir 29715
Gethsemane Ct 29715
Geyser Ct 29715
Giles Ln 29707
Gillig Dr 29715
Gilmore St 29715
Gilroy Dr 29707
Ginger Ln 29715
Gladiola Way 29708
Gladiolus St 29707
Glandon Ct 29708
Glen Allen Way 29715
Glen Cove Dr 29708
Glen Laurel Dr 29707
Glen Oaks Rd 29715
Glen Walk Dr 29708
Glenmore Ct 29707
Glenville Dr 29715
Glide Ln 29707
Gloriosa Ct 29708
Glory Ct 29715
Gold Finch Cir 29715
Gold Hill Rd
200-751 29715
788-2299 29708
Gold Rush Ct 29708
Golden Cascade Ln 29707
Golf Vista Ln 29715
Golfview Crest Dr 29708
Gordon Dr 29707
Gower St 29708
Grace St 29715
Gracefield Ln 29707
Grady Hope Rd 29708
Gragg House Rd 29715
Granby Dr 29708
Grandview Dr 29707
Granite Cir 29707
Grant Ct 29707
Grant Farm Dr 29708
Grantham Ct 29707
Gray Mist Ct 29707
Grayrock Rd 29708
Great Basin Ln 29707
Great Smoky Pl 29707
Great Wagon Rd 29715
Green Front Ct 29708
Green Pond Rd 29707
Greenview Ct 29708
Greenway Dr 29715
Greenway Industrial Dr 29708
E & W Gregg St 29715
Gregor Ct 29707
Gretna Green Way 29708
Grey Rd 29708
Grey Rock Dr 29708
Greyfield Gln 29707
Grier St 29715
Grimball Ln 29715
Grimley Ln 29707
Gringley Hill Rd 29708
Grove Park Ln 29707
Hadden Hall Blvd 29715
Haddington Dr 29707
Haddonfield Dr 29708
Hahn Ct 29715
Haire Rd 29715
Haley Ct 29708
Haley Ln 29707
Hallett St 29715
Halyard Ln 29708
Hambley House Ln 29715
Hamilton Rd 29708
Hamilton Forest Dr 29708
Hamilton Place Dr 29708
Hamlin Rd 29715
Hammond Rd 29715
Hampton Hills Ct 29715
Hamstead Ln 29707
Hannon Farm Rd 29715
Hanover Ct 29707
Harbor Ct 29708
Harcourt Xing 29707
Harlech Ct 29715
Harper Keefe Rd 29707
Harrington Ct 29715
Harris Rd
1200-1499 29715
1500-1999 29708
Harris St 29715
Harrisburg Rd 29707
Hartmann Ct 29715
E & W Hartwell Ln &
Pl 29707
Harvest Pointe Dr 29708
Harvester Ave 29708
Hastings Pl 29707
Hatchway Rd 29707
Hatton Ter 29708
Haven Ct 29707
Haverstock Hill Dr 29715
Haviland Ln 29707
Hawick Ln 29707
Hawks Eye Ct 29708
Hawks View Dr 29707
Haybrook St 29707
Haymarket Pl 29708
Hayword Ln 29715
Hazelwood Ct 29715
Heather Chase Dr 29707
Heavens Ct 29715
Hedgerow Dr 29707
Hemingford Grey 29708
Hemmingway Ln 29708
Hendon Row Way 29715
Henry St 29715
Henry Harris Rd 29707
Henry Harrison Blvd 29715
Hensley Rd 29715
Heritage Blvd, Ct &
Pkwy 29715
Heritage Grande 29715
Heron Harbor Dr 29708
Heron Run Dr 29708
Hickory Knob Ct 29715
Hickory Stick Dr 29715
Hickory View Dr 29707
Hickory Wood Ct 29715
Hidden Creek Ct 29707
Hidden Pasture Rd 29715
Hiddenbrook Way 29707
High Ridge Ct
2600-2699 29707
11000-11099 29708
Highgate Dr 29715
Highland Creek Cir 29707
Highway 160 E
900-1699 29715
Highway 160 E
3000-3051 29707
Highway 160 W
1000-1499 29715
1500-3499 29708
Highway 160 Byp 29715
Highway 21 Byp 29715
Highway 51 N 29715
E & W Hill St 29715
Hillcrest Dr
100-299 29715
1600-1799 29708
Hillview Ln 29715
Hilton Head Ct 29715
Hogan Ln 29707
Holbrook Rd 29707
Holiday Cove Dr 29708
Hollow Brook Ct 29707
Holly Dr 29715
Holly Knoll Ln 29715
Hollyhock Ln 29708
Hollyhurst Ln 29708
Honeybee Trl 29715
Honeywind Ct 29708
Hood Rd 29707
Hopkins Ln 29707
Hopkins Trace Ln 29707
Horoa Ct 29708
Horse Rd 29715
Horseshoe Cir 29707
Horseshoe Trl 29708
Horton Grove Rd 29715
Hosta Dr 29715
Howington Cir 29715
Hoxton Ct 29715
Hsbc Way 29707
Hubbard Ct 29708
Huber Ln 29715
Huckleberry Hill Dr 29715
Hudson Ln 29707
Hummingbird Ct 29715
Hunter Brooke Ln 29707
Hunter Oaks Ln 29715
Hunters Dance Rd 29708
Hunters Run Dr 29708
Huntington Dr 29707
Hyde Park Ln 29708
Ibis Ln 29707
Ichabod Ln 29715
Ideal Way 29715
Indian Hills Ln 29707
Indian Park Ln & Rd 29707
Indian Park Lane Rd 29707
Inlet Point Dr 29708
Inlet Shore Dr 29708
Interstate 77 29708
Island Cove Rd 29708
Island View Rd 29708
Isle Of Palms Ct 29708
Isom Rd 29708
Ivey Ct 29707
Ivy Field Dr 29715
Ivy Mill Rd 29715
Ivy Trail Way 29715
Jackie Bayne Rd 29707
Jackson St 29715
Jacobs Rdg 29715
Jade Ln 29708
Jasmine Dr 29707
Jason Ct 29715
Jasper Pl 29715
Jasper Ridge Dr 29707
Jefferson Pl 29708
Jenkins Dr 29707
Jenkins Park Ln 29707
Jennifer Ln 29707
Jessamine Way 29707
Jim Wilson Rd 29707
Joanna Ln 29707
Joe Louis St 29715
Johannes Ln 29707
John Earl Jones Ct 29708
John Scott Ln 29707
John Short Rd 29707
Johnna Ln 29707
Johnna Park Ln 29707
Jones Branch Rd 29715
Jones Wade Ct 29708
Jordon Crk 29707
Joshua Case Ct 29715
Joy Dr 29715
Julia St 29708
Jumprock Rd 29707
Juniper St 29715
Juniper Hills Ln 29707
Jw Wilson Rd 29715
Kaci Ln 29707
Kailua Cir 29708
Kaiser Way 29715
Kanawha Ct & St 29715
Karber Ln 29707
Karley Ct 29707
Karriker Ct 29707
Kashmir White Ln 29708
Katrina Ln 29707
Katy Ln 29708
Kaylied Dr 29707
Keara Ct 29708
Kearney Ln 29715
Kelly Ct 29715
Kelston Ln 29707
Kenbury Ct 29708
Kendall Trce 29707
Kendall Green Rd 29715
Kendallwood Ct 29715
Kennedy Dr 29707
Kennell Rd 29715
Kennet Ln 29707
Keowee Ln 29708
Kestrel Ln 29707
Keswick Ter 29707
Keystone Cir 29707
Kidd Rd 29708
Kiki Ct 29708
Kilberry Ln 29715
Kilburn Ln 29715
Kilchurn Dr 29707
Kilpatrick Ln 29708
Kimbrell Rd & Xing 29715
Kimbrell Heights Dr 29707
Kims Way 29715
Kingdom Way 29707
Kingfisher Dr 29707
Kings Ct 29708
Kings Bottom Dr 29715
Kingsley Park Dr 29715
Kingston Way 29715
Kinross Ln 29707
Kirkwall Ln 29707
Kite Dr 29715
Kitridge Bay Rd 29708
Kitty Hawk Ln 29707
Kiwi Pt 29708
Klein Rd 29715
Knightsbridge Rd 29708
Knightswood Rd 29708
Knob Creek Ln 29708
Knob Hill Ct 29715
Knollwood Ct 29715
Koala Cir 29708
Kohut Rd 29707
Kristie Ln 29707
Kura Ct 29708
Lachlan Dr 29715
Ladson Rd 29707
Lafinca Ct 29708
Lagan Ct 29715
Lake Drive Cir 29715
Lake Forest Dr 29708
Lake Point Dr 29708
Lake Shore Dr 29715
Lake View Dr 29715
Lake Vista Dr 29708
Lakebridge Dr 29715
Lakeland Trl 29708
Lakemont Blvd 29708
Lakes Blvd 29715
Lakeshore Dr 29708
Lakespur Way 29708
Lakeview Landing Rd 29707
Lamington Dr 29707
Lanai Ln 29708
Lanark Ln 29707
Lancashire Dr 29707
Lancaster Hwy 29707
Lancaster Estate Rd 29707
Lander Dr 29708
Landry Ln 29707
Lands End 29708
Landsdown Ct 29708
Lange Ct 29715
Langston Place Dr 29708
Lapis Ct 29708
Largo Ln 29707
Larkspur Ct 29707
Larkspur Way 29708
Latimer Ln 29715
Laurel Cir 29715
Laurel Fork Dr 29715
Laurel Glen Way 29707
Laurel Hills Rd 29707
Laurel Meadow Dr 29708
Laurelmont Ct 29707
Laurent Ave 29715
Lazenby Dr 29715
Lazywood Ln 29715
Leaf Ln 29707
Ledgestone Ct 29708
Lee Rd 29707
Lee St 29715
Leek Ct 29707
Leela Palace Way 29708
Leeward Ln 29708
Legacy Ln 29708
N & S Legacy Park
Blvd 29707
Legend Oaks Ct 29707
Legion Rd 29715
Legion Lake Rd 29715
Len Patterson Rd 29708
Lena Way 29708
Lengers Way 29707
Lennon Dr 29715
Leon Ln 29707
Leonidas St 29715
E & W Leroy St 29715
Lestina Dr 29715
Lighthouse Ave 29708
Lilac Ln 29707
Lillian Ln 29708
Lilly Pond Dr 29715
Lillywood Ln 29707
Lily Magnolia Ct 29707
Linden Tree Ln 29708
Lindsay Ct 29707
Link St 29715
Links View Dr 29707
Linkside Ct 29715
Lion Ln 29715
Little Bighorn Ct 29707
Little Creek Dr 29715
Little River Rd & Trl 29707
Live Oaks Ct 29715
Liverpool Ct 29707
Loch Stone St 29715
E & W Lockman St 29715
Lodge Rd 29707
Lois Ln 29707
Long Branch Ln 29707
Long House Ln 29707
Longspur Ln 29707
Longwood Dr 29708
Lonnie Dr 29715
Loretto Ln 29715
Lorraine Rd 29708
Lost Lake Trailer Park 29708
Louthan Hill Rd 29707
Lower Assembly Dr 29708
Luckadoo Rd 29715
Ludlow Ln 29715
Lulworth Ct 29715
Lurecliff Pl 29708
Lylic Woods Dr 29715
Lyman Oak Ct 29715
Lyndley Dr 29708
Lynnwood Farms Dr 29715
Mabry Pl 29707
Mack St 29715
Macmillan Park Dr 29707
Maddox Ct 29708
Madison Ct 29708
Madison Green Dr 29715
Magnolia Ct 29707
Magpie Ct 29707
Mai Kai Way 29708
Maiden Ln 29707
Main St 29715
Majestic Cir 29715
Majorie St 29715
Makayla Ct 29715
Mallard Dr 29707
Mallard Rdg 29708
Man O War Rd 29707
Manakin Pl 29707
Manawa Ln 29708
Manchester Ct 29707
Mandarin St 29707
Mandrake Ct
3300-3399 29708
37400-37499 29707
Maned Goose Ct 29707
Manila Bay Ln 29708
Manor House Ml 29708
Maple Cir & St 29715
Maple Ridge Ln 29715
E & W Marbella Ln 29707
Marblewood Ct 29708
Marcus St 29707
Mariah St 29715
Mariana Ct & Ln 29708
Marina Dr 29708
Mariners Ct 29708
Mark Trail Ln 29715
Marker Pl 29707
Market St 29708
Marks St 29708
Marquesas Ave 29708
Marsh Hen Ln 29708
Marshall St 29715
Marthas Vineyard 29707
Marvin Rd 29707
Marvin Meadows Rd 29707
Mary Ellen Dr 29708
Mary Louise Ct 29715
Mary Mack Ln 29715
Massey St 29715
Masterson Ct 29707
Matilda Key Ln 29707
Mava Ct 29707
Maxwell Mill Rd 29708
Mayfield Ct 29715
Mc Duffie Ln 29715
Mcalpine Cir 29707
Mccammon St 29715
Mcconnell Ct 29707
Mccoy Pl 29707
Mcfalls Dr 29707
Mcgee St 29715
Mchanna Pt 29708
Mckee Rd 29708
Mckenzie St 29715
Mckinney St 29715
Mcmanus Rd 29708
Mcminn Dr 29707
Meacham St 29715
Meadow Haven Cir 29707
Meadow Ridge Rd 29707
Meadow View Ct 29715
Meadow Wood Dr 29715
Meadowside Dr 29715
Medora Ln 29708
Meehan Ct 29715
Melbourne Dr 29708
Melrose Ct 29715
Mendenhall Ct 29715
Mercer St 29707
Merion Ln 29708
Merritt Rd 29715
Mesa Verde Dr 29707
Meyer Rd 29715
Michael Scott Xing 29708
Mickelson Way 29715
Middle Bridge St 29715
Midnight Blue Ln 29708
Milford Way 29708
Millbank Ct 29708
Millbrook Ln 29708
Mills Ln 29708
Millwood Dr 29715
Mimosa Ct 29707
Mimosa Ln 29715
Miners Cove Way 29708
Minstrels Way 29707
Mirage Pl 29715
Missi Ln 29708
Misty Plum Ct 29715
Misty Way Dr 29708
Molokai Dr 29708
Monacan Way 29707
Monorail Dr 29708
Monroe White St 29715
Monteray Oaks Cir 29715
Monticello Dr 29708
Montmorenci Xing 29715
Montpelier Ct 29715
Moray Way 29707
Morehead Ln 29707
Morel Ave 29715
Moreland Ct 29715
Morgan St 29715
Morning Mist End 29708
Morningside Dr 29708
Morris Hunt Dr 29708
Morrow Bradford St 29715
Moss Ridge Rd 29708
Mossy Hill Ln 29707
Moultrie Ct 29707
Mount Side Way 29715
Mountain Rdg 29707
Mountain Ridge Ct 29707
Mulberry Towers Apts 29715
Mulberry Village Ln 29715
Munn Rd E 29715
Murl Ln 29708
Murphy Ct 29715
Murphy Dr 29707
Murray St 29707
Murray Mack Rd 29715
Myers St 29715
Nantucket Rd 29707
Nations Commons St 29708
Nauvasse Trl 29715
Neighbor Ln 29715
Neptunes Lndg 29708
Nesbitt St 29715

Nestling Ln 29708
Netties Ln 29707
New Castle Dr 29707
New Gray Rock Rd 29708
New Harbour Ct 29707
Newberry Ln 29708
Newfield Dr 29707
Newport Dr 29707
Nichole Ln 29708
Nicklaus Ln 29715
Nigella Ct 29708
Nighthawk Dr 29707
Nightingale Way 29707
Nims Ln 29707
Nims St 29715
Nims Lake Rd 29715
Nims Spring Dr 29715
Nims Street Ext 29715
Nivens Landing Dr 29708
Nivens Park Dr 29708
Nivens Trailer Pk 29708
Norkett Rd 29707
Northfield Dr 29707
Northfield Ln 29708
Norwalk Ln 29707
Norwich Rd 29715
Nottingham Knl 29708
Nugget Ct 29708
O Henry Ln 29708
E & W Oak St 29715
Oak Forest Ln 29715
Oak Grove Ct 29715
Oak Hill Ln 29707
Oakbriar Cir 29715
Oakenshaw St 29715
Ocalle Ln 29707
Ola Dr 29707
Old Bailes Rd 29707
Old Cove Rd 29708
Old Farm Rd 29708
Old Hickory Ct 29715
Old Nation Rd 29715
Old Oak Ln 29715
Old Oak Hill Ct 29707
Old Pettus Pl 29707
Old Springs Rd 29715
Old Tara Ln 29708
Oleander Branch Ct 29715
Olin Yarborough Rd 29707
Olmstead St 29708
Olympic Ct 29707
Onyx Rdg 29708
Orchard Ct & Dr 29715
Orchid Ln 29707
Orchid Way 29708
Oriole Dr 29707
Orion Dr 29707
Osborne Farm Rd 29715
Our Place Dr 29708
Overhill Dr 29707
Owl Ct 29707
Oxford Hts 29715
Oxford Place Dr 29715
Paddington Walk 29708
Paddock Club Ln 29715
Pago Pago Dr 29708
Palau Ct 29708
Palawan Ct 29708
E & W Palermo Ct 29707
Palmetto Pl 29708
Palmetto Bay Dr 29715
Palmyra Dr 29708
Panthers Way 29708
Par One Ct 29715
Parchment Blvd 29708
Park Dr 29715
Parkers Fry 29715
Parks St 29715
Parkview Ct 29707
Partridge Trl 29708
Passage Dr 29708
Pate Dr 29715
Patterson Ln 29707
Patterson St 29715
Patterson Plantation Rd 29707
Peace Rd 29715
Peach Place Dr 29715
Peachtree Ln 29715
Peachwood Ct 29715
Peacock Run 29708
Peak Ct 29708
Pear Tree Ct 29715
Pebble Beach Ln 29715
Pebble Creek Xing 29715
Pedestal Ln 29715
Pee Dee Ct 29707
Pela Vista Ct 29715
Pelham Ln 29715
Pelican Ct 29708
Pembroke Ct 29707
Peridot Dr 29708
Perriwinkle Ln 29708
Perth Rd 29707
Petersburg Dr 29708
Pettus Ln, Pl & Rd 29707
Pettus Farm Rd 29707
Petunia Dr 29715
Pheasant Run 29708
Phifer St 29715
Phil Ct 29715
Phillips St 29715
Piccadilly Ln 29707
Pickney Blf 29715
Pierre Ln 29707
Pikeview Rd 29715
Pine Run 29708
Pine St 29715
Pine Bluff Ct 29708
Pine Bluff Way 29707
Pine Knoll Rd 29715
Pine Links Dr 29708
Pine Needles Ln 29708
Pine Ridge Ct 29715
Pine Valley Ct 29707
Pinecrest Rd & St 29715
Pinehurst Ln 29707
Pinetree Dr 29715
Pink Azalea Pl 29715
Pinto Ct 29707
Pitcairn Dr 29708
Placid Ct 29708
Platinum Dr 29708
Pleasant Rd 29708
Pleasant Lake Clb 29708
Pleasant Ridge Rd 29715
Pleasant Valley Dr 29707
Plum Branch Ln 29715
Point Carpenter Rd 29707
Point Clear Dr 29708
Point Wylie Ln 29708
Polly Collins Ct 29715
Pomegranate Pl 29708
Pond View Ln 29715
Ponderosa Dr 29707
Poplar St 29715
Porcher Ct 29715
N & S Portman Ln 29708
Portpatrick Pl 29708
Poseidon Way 29708
Possum Hollow Rd 29707
Potomac Ct 29707
Potter Place Rd 29708
Potts Ln 29707
Powell Pl 29708
Prayer Center Dr 29707
Prestmont Ct 29708
Preston Pl 29707
Preston Woods Way 29707
Preswick Dr 29707
Primrose Ct 29707
Primrose Walk 29715
Priory Ridge Dr 29707
Priscilla Ln 29715
Privette St 29715
Promenade Walk 29708
Prospect Ln 29708
Prowess Ln 29707
Pryor Dr 29707
Pursuit Dr 29707
Putman Ln 29715
Putting Dr 29715
Pyrite Cir 29708
Quail Run Ct 29707
Quailridge Ln 29708
Quailwood Dr 29715
Quaker Meadows Ln 29715
Quarry Overlook Dr 29715
Quartz Rdg 29708
Queen Annes Cv 29708
Queens Walk Ct 29707
Queensland Ct 29707
Quicksilver Trl 29708
Quiet Cv 29708
Quincy Rd 29715
R P C Rd 29708
Railroad Ave 29715
Ralph Bunch St 29715
Ralph Hood Rd 29707
Randolph St 29715
Rapids Rd 29715
Raven Crest Dr 29707
Ravenglass Dr 29715
Ravenwood Dr 29707
Ray Forrester Cir 29707
Raylen Pl 29707
Rea Cir 29715
Reagan Ln 29707
Red Fox Trl
1-99 29715
100-2599 29708
Red Oak Ct 29708
Red Square Ln 29707
N Red Tail Ct 29707
Red Ventures Dr 29707
Redbud Ln 29715
Redcoat Dr 29715
Redhaven Dr 29715
Redmayne Ln 29707
Regal Manor Ln 29715
Regatta Ct 29708
Regent Pkwy 29715
Reid Pointe Ave 29707
Reliance Ct 29708
Reserve Ln 29707
Retail Dr 29715
Reverdy Ct 29715
Revival Row 29708
Reynolds Dr 29707
Rhett Ct 29715
Rhodins Ln 29707
Rich St 29715
Richards Xing 29708
Ridge Rd 29715
Ridgebrook Dr 29715
Ridgeline Ln 29707
Riley Ln 29708
Ripple Rock Rd 29715
Rippling Brook Ct 29707
Rise Ln 29707
Rising Sun Ln 29707
Ritch St 29715
Rivendale Ct 29707
River Rd 29707
River Bend Blvd 29707
River Bend Dr 29708
River Chase Ln 29707
River Clay Rd 29708
River Lake Ct 29708
River Ridge Pl 29708
River Road Ext 29707
River Wood Dr 29715
Rivercrossing Dr 29715
Rivers Edge Dr 29715
Roanoke Dr 29715
Robert Gibson Dr 29708
Rochard Ln 29707
Rock Forest Way 29707
Rock Lake Gln 29715
Rockmont Dr 29708
Rocky Knoll St 29708
Rocky Point Ln 29708
Rocky Trail Ct 29715
Rolin Ave 29708
Rolling Park Ln 29715
Rose Ct 29715
Rose Tree Ln 29715
Rosebay Ct 29707
Rosebud Ct 29708
Rosemary Ln 29708
Rosemont Dr 29707
Ross Hl 29707
Ross Hill Rd 29707
Rosy Billed Ct 29707
Roxburgh St 29707
Royal Auburn Ave 29708
Royal Tern Ln 29707
Rubin Center Dr 29708
Running Fox Dr 29708
Ruth Lee Ct 29708
Ryans Pl 29715
Saddle Rd 29715
Saddle Ridge Rd 29708
Saddlewood Dr 29715
Sadlers Ridge Rd 29707
Sailview Dr 29708
Saint Andrews Ct 29707
Saint Clair St 29715
Saint George Rd 29708
Saint Helena Ct 29715
Saint Ives Ct 29708
Saint Michaels Way 29708
Salara Ln 29707
Salud Ln 29707
Sam Smith Rd 29708
Sam White Rd 29715
Samar Ct 29708
Samoa Ct 29708
Sand Paver Way 29708
Sandal Brook Rd 29707
Sanderling Ct 29707
Sanders St 29715
Sandle Rd S 29707
Sandpiper Ct 29707
Sandra Ln 29707
E & W Sandy Trl 29707
Sandy Green Ct 29715
Santee Ct 29707
Santee Ln 29708
Sapphire Ln 29708
Savannah Ln 29708
Savannah Place Dr 29715
Savile Ln 29715
Savona Ter 29708
Savoy Pl 29707
Scarlett Ln 29715
Schlumberger Dr 29715
School House Ln 29708
Scotch Pine Ln 29708
Scotland Ave 29707
Scullers Run 29708
Sea Island Blvd 29708
Seabrook Ln 29715
Second Baxter Xing 29708
Secret Path Dr 29708
Sedgewick Dr 29708
Sedona Pl 29708
Segundo Ln 29707
Seminole Dr 29707
Sentinel Way 29715
Sequoia Ct 29707
Serendipity Dr 29708
Settler Heights Dr 29708
Seven Coves Dr 29708
Shade Tree Cir 29715
Shadow Bend Dr 29708
Shadow Lawn Ct 29715
Shadow Moss Cir 29708
Shady Grove Xing 29708
Shady Hill Ct 29715
Shady Pine Cir 29715
Shadydale Ct 29708
Shaker Dr 29708
Shallow Branch Rd 29715
Shamrock Ct 29715
Sharon Lee Ave 29708
Sharonview St 29715
Sharples Dr 29715
Shaw Ct 29707
Sheba Rd 29715
Sheldon Brook Ln 29707
Shelley Mullis Rd 29707
Shellstone Pl 29708
Shelly Woods Dr 29707
Sheltered Cove Ct 29708
Shenandoah Dr 29707
Sherborne Dr 29715
Sherill Ln 29707
Sherri Ln 29715
Shinnecock Ln
300-399 29708
1300-1399 29707
Shirley Dr 29707
Shoreham Ln 29715
Shoreline Pkwy 29708
Short Link St 29715
Shutterfly Blvd 29708
Shuttles Way 29715
Sidney Johnson St 29715
Sienna Sand Way 29708
Sigel Dr 29715
Silver Arrow Ct 29715
Silver Cypress Ln 29708
Silver Fox Dr 29708
Silver Gull Dr 29708
Silver Mine Rd 29707
Silver Ridge Dr 29708
Silver Run Rd 29707
Silver Spring Rd 29715
Silverwood Dr 29715
Six Mile Creek Rd 29715
Sixth Baxter Xing 29708
Skipper St 29715
Sleepy Hollow Rd 29715
Sliding Rock Trl 29708
Smith Rd 29707
Smith St 29715
Smokey Hill Ln 29707
Smokey Quartz Ln 29708
Smythe Rd 29715
Snap Dragon Ln 29707
Snapper Pt 29708
Snead Rd 29715
Snowy Pines Ln 29707
Snuggles Ave 29708
Social Cir 29707
Society Ln 29707
Solandra Way 29708
Somerset Ter 29707
Somerton Dr 29715
Sommers Ln 29707
Sommerton Gln 29707
Song Bird Ct 29708
Song Sparrow Ln 29707
Sonnys Way 29708
Sooner Ln 29707
Sophia Ct 29708
Sora Ln 29715
Sourwood Ct 29707
Southmoor Ln 29707
Southridge Ln 29708
Southwinds Dr 29707
Spandril Ln 29708
Spanish Wells Ct 29708
Spice Rd 29707
Spicewood Pines Rd 29708
Spinnaker Dr 29708
Sportsman Dr 29715
Spratt St 29715
Spring Branch Rd 29715
Springbrite Way 29715
Springcrest Dr 29715
Springfield Pkwy 29715
Springhill Farm Rd 29715
Springmaid Ave 29715
Springs St 29715
Spruce Pine Ct 29715
St Pauli St 29715
Stacey Ln 29707
Stacy Howie Rd 29707
Stan Hope Dr 29715
Starlight Dr 29715
Starling Ln 29707
Starnes Pointe Ct 29715
Stateview Blvd 29715
Steel Brook Way 29708
Steele Cir, Rd & St 29715
Steele Meadows Dr 29715
Steeple Chase Ln 29707
Stegall Ln 29715
Stepping Stone Dr 29708
Sterling Ct 29707
Still Ave 29715
Still Water Ln 29707
Stillbrook Ave 29708
Stirling Ln 29707
Stirling Heights Ln 29715
Stock Ln 29707
Stockbridge Dr 29708
Stone Village Dr 29708
Stonecrest Blvd 29708
Stonekirk Ln 29707
Stonewater Ct 29707
Stoney Creek Ln 29707
Stoneybrook Dr 29708
Straddle Site Ln 29708
Straightaway Ln 29707
Stratford Run Dr 29708
Strawberry Knoll Dr 29715
Stream Ln 29707
Streamhaven Dr 29707
Stroud Ln 29707
Stuart Ln 29707
Sugar Creek Xing 29715
Sugar Maple Dr 29708
Sugar Pond Ct 29715
Sugar Ridge Ct 29708
Sugarberry Ct 29715
Summer Fog End 29708
Summerlake Dr 29715
E & W Summersby St 29715
Sumner St 29715
Sun City Blvd 29707
Sun Dance Dr 29707
Sun Valley Ln 29715
Sunfish Ln 29708
Sunflower Ct 29707
Sunland Dr 29715
Sunny Acres Mhp Rd 29707
Sunny Valley Ct 29707
Sunrise Meadow Rd 29707
Sunset Cir 29715
Sunset Hollow Rd 29707
Sunset Rose Dr 29708
Sutters Mill Way 29708
Sutton Rd N 29708
Sutton Rd S
100-499 29708
500-799 29715
Sutton Ridge Ln 29708
Suttonview Rd 29708
Suwarrow Cir & Ct 29708
Swamp Fox Dr 29715
Swarm Ln 29707
Sweeney Ln 29707
Sweet Peach Ln 29715
Sweetgum Dr 29715
Sweetleaf Dr 29707
Swordleaf Hl 29715
Sycamore Creek Rd 29708
Tadlock Dr 29707
Tail Race Ln 29715
Taku Ct 29708
Talking Stick Ln 29708
Tall Hickory Ct 29715
Tall Oaks Dr & Trl 29715
Tana Tea Cir 29708
Tanager Ct 29707
Taney Way 29707
Tanglewood Dr 29707
Tanner Crossing Ln 29707
Tanzanite Cir 29708
Tara Tea Dr 29708
Tatton Ln 29707
Tatton Hall Rd 29715
Tay St 29707
Teal Ct 29707
Tee Ridge Ct 29715
Tega Cay Dr 29708
Telephone St 29715
Tempo Ln 29707
Tennis Villa Dr 29715
Tepa Pl 29708
E & W Tern Ct 29707
Terrier Ln 29707
Terrys Rd 29715
Third Baxter St 29708
Thistle Ln 29707
Thomas Ave 29715
Thorn Creek Ln 29708
Thornhill St 29715
Thousand Oaks Rd 29707
Thrashers Ct 29707
Three Horse Ln 29707
Tidal Way 29708
Tifton Ct 29708
Tillman Steen Rd 29707
Timber Falls Dr 29707
Timber Wolf Trl 29715
Timberlake Dr 29708
Timberwood Dr 29708
Tinder Box Ln 29708
Tintinhull Dr 29707
Tinura Ct 29708
Tips Ln 29707
Tom Hall Plz 29715
Tom Hall St
100-200 29715
201-1599 29715
201-201 29716
202-1598 29715
9800-9899 29707
E Tom Hall St 29707
Topsail Cir 29708
Torrence Branch Dr 29708
Torrey Pines Ln 29715
Township Dr 29715
Tracy Ct 29708
Trailhead Ln 29708
Trailridge Dr 29708
Train Chaser Pl 29707
Travertine Ln 29708
Treasure Ct 29708
Tree Branch Ct 29715
Tregonwell Trce 29708
Trenholm Trl 29715
Trillium Way 29708
Trinity Ct 29707
Trinity Ridge Pkwy 29715
Triton Dr 29708
Trot Ave 29707
Truman Dr 29707
Trumpet Ct 29715
Tuckerton Dr 29708
Tulagi Ct 29708
Tulip Ct 29707
Tupelo Ln 29707
Turnridge Ct 29708
Turquoise Way 29708
Turtle Bay Ct 29708
Twiddy St 29707
Twin Lakes Trailer Park 29715
Twin Maple Dr 29707
Tybee Dr 29715
Tyger Brook Ln 29707
Tyler Ct 29707
Tylers Way 29715
Tyne Ct 29707
Ulster Ct 29707
Ultegra Ct 29715
Unity St 29715
Us Highway 521 N 29707
Valley Rd 29707
Valley Hill Rd 29707
Vance Baker Rd 29707
Vandora Springs Rd 29708
Veloce Trl 29715
Verbena Ct 29708
Vermount Way 29707
Vernon St 29715
Vevey Ln 29707
Victorian Way 29708
Victory Ct 29715
Villa Ter 29715
Villa Lake Dr 29708
Villa View Ct 29707
Villa Walk Ln 29707
Village Dr 29708
Village West Dr 29715
Vinecrest Dr 29707
Vineyard Rd 29708

Vineyard Wood Trl 29715
Viola St 29715
Violet Ct 29708
Virginia Ln 29707
Virginia Lee Ct 29708
Vista Rd 29708
Vogel Way 29715
Voyageurs Way 29707
Wade Carnes Rd 29707
Wagner Ave 29715
Walden Park Dr 29715
Wales Ave 29715
Walker St 29715
Walker Street Ext 29715
Wallace Lake Rd 29707
Wallace Park Ln 29707
Walnut Ln 29715
Waridere Rd 29715
Waring Ct 29707
Warpers Ln 29715
Warrior Ave 29707
Warwick Way 29708
Washington St 29715
Water Trace Dr 29708
Waterford Pl 29708
Waterview Ln 29715
Watford St 29715
Watling St 29715
Watson St 29715
Watsonia St 29707
Wave Crest Dr 29708
Waxwing Ct 29707
Wayside Dr 29715
Weavers Xing 29715
Webbs Mill Dr 29715
Weber Ct 29715
Wedgewood Ln 29707
Wellridge Dr 29708
Wells Ln 29707
Wellspring Dr 29715
Wessex Way 29708
Wessington Manor Ln 29715
Westerleigh Rd 29715
Westside Dr 29715
Westwind Dr 29707
Wheatfield Dr 29707
Whimbrel Cir 29707
Whippoorwill Ln 29707
Whispering Oaks Ln 29708
Whistling Straits Dr 29707
Whistling Straits Ln 29708
N & S White St 29715
White Bluff Dr 29708
White Branch Ct 29715
White Bridge Ln 29715
White Chappell Ct 29715
White Springs Rd 29708
White Swan Ct 29708
Whitecedar Ln 29707
Whitegrove Dr 29715
Whitehead Ct 29708
Whites Rd 29715
Whiteside Dr 29707
Whitetail Dr 29708
Whitley Rd 29708
Whitley Mills Rd 29708
Whitmyre Ct 29715
Whitney Ct 29715
Whittingham Dr 29707
Wigeon Ln 29707
Wilburn Park Ln 29707
Wildbrook Trce & Walk 29708
Wildflower Ct 29707
Wilkes Place Dr 29715
Williams Rd 29715
Williamson St 29715
Willing Ct 29707
Willis Ct 29708
Willow Ridge Rd 29707
Willowbrook Dr 29708
Wilma Dr 29715
Wilmington Cir 29715
Wilshire Cir 29708
Wilson Dr 29707
Wilson St 29715
Wilson Business Pkwy 29708
Wilson Park Ln 29707
Wimbleton Wood Dr 29708
Winchester St 29707
Windell Dr 29708
Windell Senior Cir 29708
Windgate Ct 29708
Winding Brook Ct 29715
Winding Grove Way 29707
Winding Trail Ln 29708
Windjammer Dr 29708
Windrift Dr 29708
Windsong Bay Ln 29708
Windsor Gate Dr 29708
Windsor Trace Dr 29707
Windward Dr 29708
Windy Oaks Rd 29708
Winners Cir 29707
Wiregrass Dr 29707
Wisteria Walk Way 29715
Withers St 29715
Woburn Abbey Dr 29715
Wolf Ln 29715
Wolverine Ln 29707
Wood Duck Ln 29707
Woodbend Trl 29708
Woodcroft Dr 29708
Woodhaven Dr 29708
Woodholm Ct 29708
Woodlake Ln 29708
Woodleaf Ln 29715
Woodridge Dr 29715
Woodview Ct 29707
Woodville Ln 29707
Woolen Way 29708
World Reach Dr 29707
Xandra Ct 29707
Yarborough Rd 29707
Yellow Springs Dr 29707
Yellowstone Dr 29707
York Southern Rd 29715
Yorkshire Ct 29707
Yorktowne St 29715
Yosemite Way 29707
Yukon Ct 29707
Zackary Ln 29708
Zenith Ave 29715
Zimmer Rd 29707
Zimmerman Dr 29708
Zoar Rd 29708

NUMBERED STREETS

1st Pl 29707
1st St N 29708
1st St S 29708
521 Corporate Ctr Dr 29707

GAFFNEY SC

General Delivery 29341

POST OFFICE BOXES MAIN OFFICE STATIONS AND BRANCHES

Box No.s
1 - 5000 29342
8001 - 8360 29340

NAMED STREETS

A And T Dr 29341
Aaltonen Dr 29341
Abernathy Dr 29341
Abingdon Rd 29340
Adair Ln 29340
Adam St 29340
Administrative Dr 29340
Ahmad St 29341
Alanda Dr 29341
Albert Dr 29341
Alexander St 29340
Alice St 29340
Allen Ct 29341
E Allen St 29340
W Allen St 29340
Allison Dr 29341
Allison Creek Rd 29341
Allison Hill Dr 29340
Alma St 29340
Alpine Dr 29341
Amanda Dr 29341
Amber Leaf Dr 29341
Amity Dr 29341
Ammons Rd 29341
Angel Meadows Dr 29341
Angelicus Ln 29341
Annette St 29340
Annie Ave 29341
Anns Trl 29341
Anthony St 29340
Antler Trl 29340
Apache Dr 29340
Appaloosa Trl 29341
Apple Aly 29340
Archer Rd 29340
Arlington Ave 29340
Arrowhead Rd 29340
Arrowood Dr 29340
Arthur Dr 29341
Ashley Ln & St 29340
Ashmore Ave 29341
Ashworth School Rd 29341
Atkinson Rd 29341
Aubrey Ln 29340
Austin Dr 29340
Autumn Cir 29341
Avondale Dr 29341
Azalea St 29340
Bailey St 29340
Bailey Bridge Rd 29341
Baker Rd 29341
Baldwin Dr 29340
Ballenger Rd 29340
Bancroft Rd 29340
Barbara Ave 29341
Barclay Ave 29341
Barry St 29340
Bates Rd 29340
Baxter Rd 29341
Bay Rd 29340
Beason Rd 29341
Beaver Creek Dr 29341
Beaver Dam Rd 29341
Beaver Dam School Rd 29340
Beaver Park Dr 29341
Beaver Ridge Rd 29341
Beech St 29340
Bellcrest Dr 29341
Belle Estate Dr 29340
Belmont Cir 29341
Beltline Rd 29341
Belue Rd 29341
Bens Farm Rd 29341
Bent Ln 29341
Bent Twig Ct 29340
Berry Dr 29340
Bessies Rd 29341
Bettys Trl 29340
Big Oak Cir 29341
Billy Goat Bridge Rd 29340
Birch St 29340
Birchwood Ct 29341
E Birnie St 29340
W Birnie St
100-199 29340
200-499 29341
Blackberry Trl 29341
Blackwell Farm Rd 29341
Blake Rd 29340
Blake Chandler Dr 29341
Blalock Ln 29341
Blanton Dr 29341
Blanton Estate Rd 29341
Blanton Meadows Dr 29341
Blue Branch Rd 29340
Bluestone Dr 29341
Bo Ln 29340
Boat Landing Dr 29341
Bobs Ln 29340
Boiling Springs Hwy 29341
Bolivar St 29341
Bonner Rd 29341
Bonner Lake Rd 29340
Bostic Rd 29340
Bouvier Way 29341
Boyd St 29341
Boyd Floyd Dr 29340
Bradbury Ct 29341
Bramblewood Dr 29340
Brandie Dr 29340
Bratton Dr & Trl 29340
Breezewood Dr 29340
Brendon Dr 29340
Briarcreek Trl 29340
Briarwood Ln & Trl 29340
Brick House Rd 29340
Bridges Farm Rd 29341
Brights Rd 29340
Brittany Rd 29341
Broad St 29341
Brook Dr 29340
Brook Stone Ln 29341
Brookhaven Dr 29341
Brookshire Dr 29341
Brookside Dr 29340
Brookwood Dr 29341
Brookwood Ln 29340
Brown St 29341
Browning Rd 29341
Browns Dr 29341
Browns Creek Rd 29340
Bryant St 29341
Bubba Dr 29340
Buck Trl 29340
Buck Ridge Rd 29340
Buck Shoals Rd 29341
Buckson St 29341
Buddy Dr 29340
Buds Trl 29341
E Buford St 29340
W Buford St
100-199 29340
200-2499 29341
Buford Street Aly 29340
Buice Rd 29341
Bunche St 29341
Burgess Rd 29341
Burnett St 29341
Burnt Gin Rd 29340
Byars Farm Rd 29341
Cabin Creek Rd 29341
Caggiano Dr 29341
Calton Dr 29341
Cambridge Cir 29341
Camellia Cir 29341
Camelot Dr 29341
Cameron Ln 29341
Camp Dr 29340
Camp Ferry Rd 29341
Campus Dr 29341
Candlewood Ln 29341
Canty Way 29341
E Carlisle St 29340
W Carlisle St 29341
Carls Rd 29341
Carolina Ridge Rd 29341
Carolyn Dr 29341
Carpenter Ln 29341
Carriage Pl 29341
Carrie Dr 29341
Carroll Estate Rd 29340
Carson Dr 29341
Carter Heights Dr 29340
Carver St 29341
Cash Rd 29341
Cashmere Dr 29340
Castle Ct 29340
Castlewood Rd 29341
Catawba Rd 29341
Catherine St 29341
Cathy Lee Dr 29340
Cats Creek Rd 29340
Causey Ct 29340
Cavalier Dr 29341
Cedar St 29340
Cedar Post Rd 29341
Cellwood Pl 29340
Chambers Rd 29341
Champion Ferry Rd 29341
Chance Dr 29341
Chandler Dr 29340
Charles Hayes Rd 29340
Chatham Ave 29340
Chaucer Dr 29341
Chellelin Dr 29341
Cherokee Ave 29340
Cherokee Plz 29341
Cherokee Creek Rd 29341
Cherokee National Hwy 29341
Cherokee Ridge Dr 29341
Cherry St 29340
Chesnee Hwy 29341
Chestnut St 29340
Chestnut Ridge Rd 29340
Cheval Trl 29341
Cheyenne Rd 29341
Childers Rd 29340
Christi Jean Dr 29340
Christopher Rd 29340
Church St 29340
Claiborne St 29340
Claire Manning Ln 29341
Clara B Jolly Rd 29341
Claremont St 29341
Clark Dr 29341
Clary Dr 29341
Clary Ln 29341
Clary St 29340
Clayton Dr 29340
Clear Acres Dr 29341
Clear Field Dr 29341
Cliffside Hwy 29341
Cline Rd 29340
Club House Rd 29341
Club View Dr 29340
Coach Hill Dr 29340
Cobblestone Dr 29340
Cobblestone Xing 29341
Coburn St 29340
Coggins Blvd 29341
Cole Creek Rd 29341
College Dr 29340
Colonial Ave 29340
Columbus Dr 29340
Commerce Dr 29340
Concord Ave 29340
Concord Hts 29341
Concord Rd 29340
Concord Acres Dr 29341
Concord Baptist Acres Dr 29341
Connecticut Ave 29341
Conner Dr 29341
Cooper St 29341
Copeland Rd 29341
Coral Stone Rd 29340
Corinth Rd 29340
Corona Dr 29341
Corporate Dr 29341
Corry St 29340
Cotton Creek Trl 29341
Country Ln 29341
Country Club Rd 29340
Country View Dr 29341
Courthouse Aly 29340
Coventry Ct 29340
Covered Bridge Rd 29341
Coyl Rd 29340
Coyl Hill Rd 29340
Cozy Ln 29340
Creek Hill Dr 29341
Creek Stone Rd 29341
Creek View Ln 29341
Creekside Ln 29341
Crescent Cir 29340
Cresthaven Dr 29341
Crestmont Dr 29340
Crestview Dr 29340
Crosby St 29340
Cross St 29341
Crosscreek Ln 29340
Crown Cir 29341
Cudd St 29340
Curry St 29340
Curtis Dr 29341
Cypress Dr 29340
Daniel Morgan School Rd 29341
Darby Rd 29340
Darwin Rd 29340
David Pelzer Blvd 29341
Davis St & Trl 29341
Davis Estate Rd 29340
Deal St 29340
Dean St 29341
Debra Dr 29340
Deer Haven Dr 29340
Deer Ridge Rd 29340
Deer Run Dr 29341
Deer Track Ln 29341
Deerwood Ln 29340
Delaware Ct 29341
Den Hill Trl 29341
Dennis Dr 29340
Desert Primrose Pl 29341
Destiny Dr 29341
E & W Diesel Dr 29341
Doe Dr 29340
Dogwood Dr 29340
Dora Ave 29341
Doris Ln 29341
Dots Dr 29340
Double Bridge Rd 29340
Douglas Heights Dr 29341
Downey Hawthorne Pl 29341
E Dr Lm Rosemond Ln 29340
W Dr Lm Rosemond Ln 29341
Dr Martin Luther King Jr St 29341
Drayton Trl 29340
Draytonville Hts & Rd 29340
Draytonville Church Rd 29340
Drucilla Dr 29340
Dry Fork Rd 29340
Duffers Dr 29341
Durham Aly 29340
Dusty Trl 29340
Earl Rd 29340
Earls Ridge Rd 29341
Easler Rd 29341
Eastbrook Rd 29340
Eastview St 29340
Eastwood Cir 29341
Easy St 29340
Ebenezer Rd 29340
Echo Dr 29341
Echoles Rd 29340
Eden Dr 29341
Edgehill Dr 29341
Edgewater Dr 29340
Edgewood Dr 29340
Edna Ln 29341
Edward Rd 29340
Edwards Ave 29341
El Paso Dr 29341
Elbethel Rd 29340
Elizabeth Rd 29341
Elliott Dr 29341
Ellis Ferry Ave & Rd 29341
Elm St 29341
Elmore St 29340
Elmwood Dr 29341
Emerald Dr 29341
Emerson Rd 29341
Emmas Ln 29340
Ephrom Dr 29340
Erika Ln 29341
Escambia Ave 29340
Estate Ridge Rd 29340
Estelle Rd 29341
Estes Rd 29341
Eubanks Rd 29341
Euphra Dr 29340
Evans St 29340
Evergreen Rd 29340
Express Ln 29341
Ezra Ln 29340
Factory Shops Blvd 29341
Fairfield Dr 29341
E Fairview Ave 29340
W Fairview Ave 29341
Fairview Rd 29341
Fairway Dr 29341
Faith Hl 29340
Farm Wind Rd 29341
Farmington Rd 29341
Farrington Dr 29341
Farview Dr 29340
Fatima Dr 29341
Fatz Dr 29341
Fawn Trl 29340
Fawnhurst Dr 29341
Fernwood Dr 29340
Ferry Rd 29341
Fielding Rd 29340
Fieldstone Dr 29340
Filbert St 29340
Filter Plant Rd 29340
Fishermans Ln 29341
Fleming Rd 29341
Flint St 29340
Flint Hill Rd 29340
Florence St 29340
E Floyd Baker Blvd 29340
W Floyd Baker Blvd
100-199 29340
200-298 29341
300-1799 29341
1801-1899 29341
Foot Hill Dr 29340
Ford Rd 29340
Forest Dr 29341
Forest Hills Dr 29340
Forest Lane Dr 29340
Forestdale Dr 29341
Fort St 29341
Fortanberry Rd 29340
Foster Rd 29341
Fowler Aly 29341
Fowler Rd 29340
E & W Fowler Farm Rd 29341
Fox Run Ct 29340
Foxfire Dr 29340
E Frederick St 29341
W Frederick St
100-199 29340
200-599 29341
Freds Rd 29340
Freemont Dr 29340
Freeport Dr 29341
Freezer St 29340
Frontier Dr 29341
Frye Rd 29340
Fuller Ln 29340
Furnace Rd 29341
Furnace Mill Rd 29341
Gaffney Ave 29341
Gaffney Ferry Rd 29340
Gallman Rd 29341
Gardner Rd & St 29341
Garner Rd 29340
Garnett Dr 29340
Garrett Dr 29341
Garrison St 29340
Garvin Lake Rd 29340
Gaston Shoals Rd 29341
N Gate Rd 29341
Gateway Dr 29341
Gees Rd 29341
General Dr 29341
Gentle Ln 29341
George Way 29341
Gerald Dr 29341
Gertrude St 29340

Gettys Dr 29341
Gettys Farm Rd 29341
Glencrest Dr 29340
Glendale Rd 29340
Gloria Ln 29341
Goforth Dr 29340
Gold Mine Rd 29340
Gold Ridge Rd 29340
Golden Ln 29341
Goldmine Springs Rd 29340
Gordon Rd 29341
Goucher Creek Rd 29340
Goucher Green Bethel Rd 29340
Goucher School Rd 29340
Gowdeysville Rd 29340
Grace Rd & St 29340
Graces Way 29341
Grambling Ferry Rd 29341
N & S Granard St 29341
Granite Dr 29340
Grassy Knoll Rd 29341
Grassy Pond Rd 29341
Grassy Pond Creek Rd 29341
Grayson Ln 29340
Graystone Dr 29341
Great Meadows Rd 29340
Green St 29340
Green Acres Rd 29341
Green Park Dr 29341
Green River Rd 29341
Greenbriar Dr 29341
Greenfield Rd 29340
Greenland Dr 29341
Greenway St 29340
Gregory Rd 29340
Grestern Rd 29341
Griffith St 29340
Grindall Ford Rd 29340
Grove Ave 29340
Grubb St 29340
Guest Ridge Rd 29340
Gulley Rd 29340
Guthrie St 29340
Hackberry Cir & Dr 29340
Hall Rd 29340
Hames Rd 29340
Hamlet Rd 29340
Hampshire Dr 29341
Hampton Ave, Blvd, Ct & Dr 29341
Hamrick St 29340
Hannon Dr 29341
Hardin Dr 29340
Harrington Rd 29341
Harris Trl 29341
Harrison St 29340
Harvest Dr 29341
Harvey Rd 29340
Hatcher Dr 29341
Hawkins Reynolds Rd 29341
Hayes Rd 29341
Hazelnut Dr 29340
Hemlock Rd 29340
Henderson Dr 29341
Henderson St 29341
Henderson Place Dr 29341
Heritage Ln 29341
Hess Ln 29340
Hetty Hill St 29340
Hickory St 29340
Hickory Grove Rd 29340
Hicks Rd 29340
Hidden Acres Dr 29341
Hidden Springs Ct 29341
Hidden Valley Dr 29340
High Point Rd 29341
Hill St 29340
Hill Top Dr 29341
Hillcrest Dr 29340
Hillsdale St 29340
Hillside Dr 29340
Holland St 29341
Holly St 29340
Holly Hill Dr 29341
Hollywoods Dr 29341
Holmes Rd & St 29341
Honeysuckle Ln 29341
Hope Acres Dr 29341
Hopes Trl 29341
Hopper Dr 29341
Hortons Acres 29341
Howell Ferry Rd 29340
Huggin Rd 29340
Humpey Rd 29340
Humphries Cir 29341
Humphries Rd 29341
Humphries St 29340
Hunter Dr 29341
Hunters Creek Rd 29341
Huntington Dr & Rd 29341
Huntington Square Dr 29341
Huskey Dr 29341
Hyatt St 29341
Ida Ln 29341
Idlewood Rd 29340
Illinois Cir 29341
Indian Hill St 29340
Indiana Cir 29341
Irene Park Dr 29341
Iris Ln 29341
Iron Ore Rd 29341
Isabel Dr 29340
Ivine Rd 29341
Jackson St 29340
James Rd & St 29341
Jane St 29341
Jasmine Dr 29341
Jason Owensby Dr 29340
Jasper Dr 29340
Jeans Dr 29340
Jefferies Rd 29340
E Jefferies St 29340
W Jefferies St
101-199 29340
200-299 29341
Jefferson St 29340
Jenkins St 29341
Jennies Ln 29341
Jesse Trl 29341
Jimmy Rd 29340
John St 29340
Johns Trl 29341
N & S Johnson St 29340
Jolly Dr & Rd 29341
Jonah Rd 29341
Joy Ave 29340
Joy Dale Ln 29341
Joyce St 29340
Jr Farm Rd 29340
Judson Rd 29340
Junie Rd 29341
E Junior High Rd 29340
Karens Way 29341
Katie Ln 29340
Kay St 29340
Keeney Dr 29341
Kelly St 29341
Kendrick St 29341
Kennedy St 29341
Kent Wood Rd 29340
Kents Trl 29341
Killion Dr 29340
King St 29341
Kings Rd 29340
E Kings Rdg 29341
W Kings Rdg 29341
Kirby Rd 29340
Knollcrest Dr 29340
Koonce Ln 29341
Kraft Ave, Rd & St 29340
Kristin Dr 29341
Lacewood Rd 29341
Lake Dr 29341
Lake Cherokee Rd 29340
Lake Tree Rd 29340
Lake Whelchel Dr 29341
Lakeshore Dr 29341
Lakeside Dr 29341
Lakeside Ln 29340
Lakeview Dr 29340
Lakewinds Dr 29341
Lakewood Dr 29340
Lakewood Acres Dr 29341
Lamplighter Cv 29340
Lane Dr 29340
Lansdell Dr 29340
Lapalma Dr 29341
Laroi Rd 29340
Laurel Cv 29341
Laurel Ln 29341
Laurel St 29340
Lawson Ln 29340
Lazywood Dr 29341
Leadmine Rd & St 29340
Leadmine Meadows Dr 29340
Ledge Stone Ln 29341
Lee St 29340
Lees Farm Rd 29340
Lehi Rd 29340
Lemaster Cir & Rd 29341
Lemmons Ln 29341
Lemuels Rd 29341
Lenora Dr 29340
Lester Dr 29340
Lettie Rd 29341
Liberty St 29340
Lillie Dr 29341
N & S Limestone St 29340
Limestone Springs Rd 29340
Lincoln Dr 29341
Lincoln St 29340
Lindas Dr 29341
Linder Ln & Rd 29341
Lindley Rd 29341
Link Rd 29340
Lionshead Way 29341
Lipscomb Cir & St 29340
Lipscomb Farm Rd 29340
Lisas Ln 29341
Little Dr 29340
Little Creek Dr 29341
Little Egypt Rd 29341
Little Lowrys Rd 29340
Little View Dr 29340
Little Wolf Ln 29341
Littlejohn Rd 29340
Littlejohn St 29340
Lockhart Ln 29341
Log Cabin Rd 29340
N & S Logan St 29341
Lois Dr 29341
London Ln 29340
Lora Acres Dr 29341
Lori Rd 29340
Los Pinos Rd 29341
Love Springs Rd 29341
Lovers Lane Rd 29340
Lowrys Rd 29340
Lyman St 29340
Lynn Ln 29341
Mabry Dr & Ln 29341
Macedonia Rd 29341
Maddox Rd 29340
Made St 29340
Madison Ave 29340
Magg Rd 29341
Maggie Dr 29341
Magnolia St 29340
Mall Dr 29340
Mallard Ln 29341
Malone Rd 29341
Maloney Dr 29341
Maple Dr 29341
Maplewood Dr 29341
Marc Anthony Dr 29340
Margaret Ave 29341
Margie Rd 29340
Marietta Rd & St 29340
Marion Ave 29341
Markys Rd 29341
Marlin Dr 29341
Marlowe Dr 29341
Marrison Rd 29341
Martin Ln & St 29341
Martin Acres 29341
Martins Lake Rd 29340
Marvin Rd 29340
Mascot Dr 29341
Matthew Rd 29341
Mattie St 29341
Mattie Jones Rd 29340
Maude Rd 29340
Mayfield Rd 29340
Mcarthur St 29340
Mccluney Dr 29340
Mccoy Cir 29341
Mccraw Ln, Rd & Trl 29341
Mcdowell Rd 29341
Mcgill Dr 29341
Mcgraw St 29340
Mckowns Mountain Rd 29340
Meadow Ln 29340
W Meadow St
100-198 29340
200-299 29341
Meadow Wood Dr 29341
Meadowview Rd 29341
Medical Center Dr 29340
Medley Rd 29340
Meehan Rd 29340
Meeting House Rd 29341
Megan Dr 29340
Mendels Dr 29340
Merrifield Ct 29340
Mesopotamia Rd 29340
Michael James Rd 29340
Michigan Ave 29341
Midway Rd & Ter 29341
Mike Ct 29341
Mikes Creek Rd 29341
Mildred Ave 29341
Mill St 29341
Mill Gin Rd 29341
Mill Stone Rd 29341
Millen Farm Rd 29340
Millies Rd 29341
Millwood Ln 29340
Mimosa Dr 29341
Minkum Rd 29340
Mintz Farm Rd 29341
Misty Ln 29340
Mohea Ave 29341
Monroe Rd 29341
Monroe St 29340
E Montgomery St 29340
W Montgomery St 29341
Monticello St 29340
Montpelier St 29341
Mooney Dr 29340
Moores Farm Rd 29341
Morgan Cir & Dr 29341
Morgan Creek Rd 29341
Morgan Cross Rd 29341
Morgan Park Dr 29340
Morris Dr 29341
Morris Farm Rd 29340
Moss St 29340
Mosswood Rd 29341
Motts Rd 29340
Mountain Laurel Trl 29341
Mountain Top Rd 29340
Mountain View Rd 29341
Mulligan Dr 29341
Mullinax Ln 29341
Mullinax Farm Rd 29341
Musgrove St 29340
Myras Rd 29341
Nancy Ln 29341
Nancy Creek Rd 29341
Nans Rd 29341
Nations Ave 29340
Natures Trl 29341
Nc Stateline Rd 29341
Nectarine Ln 29341
Nehemiah Ln 29340
Nellies Dr 29340
Nesbitt St 29340
New St 29340
New Mexico Dr 29341
New Painter Dr 29341
New Pleasant Rd 29341
Niles Ln 29340
Ninety Nine Ferry Rd 29340
Nob Hl 29340
Noble Rd 29341
Norman Blvd 29341
Northside Dr 29341
Northwood Dr 29340
Northy St 29340
E & W Nott St 29340
Nursery Rd 29341
Oak St 29340
Oak Brook Ln 29341
Oak Creek Cir 29341
Oak Forest Cir 29341
Oak Ridge Rd 29341
Oakland Ave 29341
Oakview Dr 29341
Oakview St 29340
Oakwood Dr 29341
Oglesby Valley Rd 29341
Old Barn Rd 29340
Old Bridge Rd 29340
Old Detour Rd 29340
Old Georgia Hwy
1300-1799 29341
1800-3699 29340
Old Mckown Farm Rd 29340
Old Metal Rd 29341
Old Mill Rd 29341
Old Plantation Rd 29340
Old Post Rd 29341
Old Pros Dr 29341
Old Race Track Rd 29340
Olde Springs Ct 29340
Olee Rd 29341
N & S Oliver St 29341
Olivers Way 29341
Omni Rd 29341
E & W Oneal St 29340
Osage Cir & Dr 29340
Osment St 29340
Overbrook Dr 29341
Overhill Dr 29340
Owens Ln 29340
Oxford St 29341
Ozell Ave 29340
Pacolet Hwy 29340
Padgett Dr 29341
N Palma Ct 29341
S Palma Ct 29341
Palma Dr 29340
Palmetto St 29340
Pamela Dr 29340
Pan American Dr 29341
Panaview Dr 29341
Park Ct 29341
Park Gate Rd 29341
Park Place Dr 29341
Parris St & Trl 29340
Patrick Rd 29340
Pauline Dr 29341
Pauls Rd 29341
Paw Paw Dr 29340
Peachoid Rd 29341
Peachtree St 29341
Peachview Blvd 29341
Pearl Dr 29340
Pebblestone Rd 29340
Pecan St 29340
Peeler St 29341
Peeler Creek Rd 29340
Peeler Ridge Rd 29340
Pennington Ln 29341
Peoples Creek Rd 29340
Perrine Dr 29341
Perry St 29341
Peterson Rd 29340
Pettit Ct 29341
Petty Dr 29341
N Petty St 29340
S Petty St 29340
E Phillips Ave 29341
W Phillips Ave 29341
Phillips Dr 29341
Phillips Ln 29340
Phillips Farm Rd 29341
Pickle Springs Rd 29341
Piedmont St 29340
Pierce Ln 29341
Pine St 29340
Pine Ridge Dr 29341
Pine Village Dr 29340
Pinecrest Dr 29341
Pinepoint Dr 29341
Pineville Rd 29341
Pinewood Dr 29340
Piney Knob Dr 29340
Pipeline Dr 29340
Plantation Dr 29340
Planters Dr 29341
Pleasant Grove Rd 29340
Pleasant Meadows Dr 29341
Pleasant School Rd 29341
Ponderosa Rd 29340
Pondfield Rd 29340
Pooles Rd 29341
Poor Mans Farm Rd 29340
Poplar St 29341
Poplar Ridge Dr 29341
N & S Poplar Springs Dr 29341
Porter St 29340
Potter Rd 29341
Powell Rd 29340
Preston Way 29341
Price Ln 29341
Prince Rd 29341
Professional Park 29340
Progressive Dr 29340
Providence Rd 29341
Providence Creek Rd 29341
Pryor St 29341
Public Works Dr 29341
Pumping Station Rd 29340
Quail Run 29341
Quarry Dr 29340
Queens Rd 29341
Quint Ct 29341
Rabbit Run 29341
W Race St 29341
Railroad Ave 29340
Rainbow Dr 29340
Raintree Ln 29340
Ramsey Hts 29340
Ramsey St 29341
Randolph Rd 29341
Randys Dr 29340
Rector Dr 29340
Redbud Ln 29340
Redwood Cir & Dr 29341
Regency Ct 29341
Rehobeth Rd 29340
Renee Dr 29341
Rest St 29340
Richardson St 29340
Rick Byars Dr 29340
Riddle Rd 29340
Ridgeway Rd 29340
Rita St 29340
River Dr 29340
River Tree Rd 29341
River Valley Dr 29340
Riverbrook Dr 29341
Robbs Ln 29340
Robbs School Rd 29341
Roberta Dr 29340
Roberts Aly 29341
Roberts Farm Rd 29340
Robinhood Dr 29340
E Robinson St 29340
W Robinson St
100-198 29340
201-223 29340
225-599 29341
Rocky Branch Rd 29340
Rodeo Dr 29340
Rodgers St 29341
Roger Rd 29341
Roland Farm Rd 29340
Rolling Hill Cir 29340
Rolling Mill Rd 29340
Rosa Acres Dr 29341
Rose St 29340
Rosewood Ln 29340
Ross St 29340
Ross Hill Rd 29341
Round Tree Rd 29340
Roy Dr 29340
Royal Dr 29340
Roys Farm Rd 29340
Ruppe Dr 29341
Russell St 29340
Ruth Dr 29341
E Rutledge Ave 29340
W Rutledge Ave
100-199 29340
200-1899 29341
Ryan Dr 29341
Rye St 29340
Saddle Dr 29340
Sage Ln 29341
Salem Rd 29340
Sallie Dr 29341
Sams Rd & St 29340
Sandy Ln 29340
Sardis Rd 29340
Sarratt Ave 29341
Sarratt Rd 29341
Sarratt Trl 29340
Sarratt Creek Rd 29341
Sarratt School Rd 29341
Saxon Dr 29341
Say St 29340
School Rd 29341
Scoggins Rd 29340
Scruggs Ln, Rd & Trl 29341
Self Dr 29340
Serene Dr 29340
Settlemeyer St 29340
Shady Ln 29341
Shady Grove Rd 29341
Shalimar Dr 29341
Shannon Ave 29341
Sharon Dr 29340
Shelby Hwy
100-499 29340
500-1099 29341
Sheraton Loop 29341
Sherman Dr 29340
Sherwood Dr 29340
Short Aly 29341
Short Peeler St 29341
Shrine Club Rd 29340
Sierra St 29341
Silica Springs Rd 29340
Silver Cir 29340
Silverton Rd 29341
Sioux Rd 29341
Sizemore Rd 29340
Skinnys Rd 29340
Skull Shoals Rd 29340
Sloan Rd 29340
Small Farm Rd 29341
Smiley Dr 29341
Smith Rd 29341
W Smith St 29341
Smith Ford Rd 29340
Smoke Ridge Rd 29340
Soap Stone Rd 29340
Songbird Ln 29341
Sossoman Loop 29340
N & S Sparks St 29340
Spears Aly 29340
Speedway Rd 29340
Spencer Cir 29340
Spillway Rd 29341
Splawn Rd 29340
Sportsman Ln 29341
Spring St 29340
Spring Lake Rd 29340
Spring Valley Rd 29341
Springfield Dr 29341
Springwood Dr 29340
Spruce St 29340
Stacy Dr 29341
Stagecoach Rd 29340
Starr Ridge Rd 29340
State Line Rd 29341

Stein City Rd 29340
Stephenson St 29340
Sterling Lakes Dr 29341
E & W Stillwater Rd 29341
Stonecrest Ln 29341
Stoneridge Dr 29341
Storm Ct 29341
Strawberry Rd 29341
Stroupe Estate Rd 29340
Stuard St 29341
Suck Creek Church Rd 29341
Suez St 29341
Sullivan Dr 29340
Summer Dr 29340
Sunny Dale Ln 29341
Sunrise Dr 29341
Sunset Dr 29340
Susans Rd 29341
Susie Parker Rd 29341
Swan Rd 29341
Swanger Rd 29341
Sweet Gum Rd 29340
Swofford Trl 29341
Sycamore St 29340
Tammy Dr 29340
Tansi Trl 29340
Taylors Ln 29340
Teague Rd 29340
Teal Dr 29341
Temple St 29340
Thicketty Ln 29341
Thicketty Creek Farm Dr 29340
Thicketty Mountain Trl 29341
Thomas St 29340
Thompson Ln & St 29340
Tiffany Park & Ter 29341
Tillmon Rd 29341
Timber St 29341
Timberbrook Rd 29340
Timken Rd 29341
Tindall Ter 29340
Tindall Mill Rd 29340
Tobias Creek Rd 29340
Toby Ct 29340
Topaz Ln 29341
Tracy Dr 29341
Trails End 29340
Tram Ct 29341
Tramlaw Dr 29340
Trenton Rd 29340
Triangle Rd 29340
Trio Rd 29341
Trout View Rd 29341
Tumbleweed Dr 29340
Turkey Ridge Rd 29340
Turner Trl 29340
Twin Acres Rd 29341
Twin Bridge Rd 29341
Twin Lake Rd 29341
Twin Oaks Dr 29341
Twin State Dr 29341
Union Hwy & St 29340
Upchurch Rd 29340
Vadar Cir 29340
Valerie Dr 29340
Valley Ct 29341
Valley Pond Rd 29340
Van Buren St 29340
Vance St 29340
Vaughn Rd 29341
Veralerr Rd 29340
E Verdia Rd 29341
Vermont Dr 29341
Vernie Rd 29341
Vernon St 29340
Vestas Rd 29340
Victoria Ln 29340
Victoria Rd 29341
Victory Ct 29340
Victory Trail Rd 29340
Vienna Rd 29340
E View Dr 29340
Villa Dr 29340
Vine St 29340

Vinesett Dr 29340
Virginia Ave 29341
Vivian Dr 29340
Walker Farm Rd 29340
Wall St 29340
Walnut St 29340
Walnut Hill Farm Rd 29340
Walters Rd 29341
Walton Dr 29341
Warren Dr 29340
Warrior Dr 29341
Wash Away Bridge Rd 29340
Washington Ave 29340
Watson Glenn Rd 29340
Watts Dr 29341
Web Blanton Ct 29341
Webber Rd 29341
Webster Dr & St 29340
West Ln 29340
Westbrook Dr 29340
Westfield Dr 29340
Westland Dr 29341
Westmont Dr 29340
Whelchel Rd 29341
Whig Hill Rd 29340
Whippoorwill Dr 29340
Whispering Pines Rd 29341
White Oak Dr & Rd 29341
White Plains Rd 29340
Whites Rd 29340
Whittenburg Dr 29340
Wilcox Ave 29341
Wildwood Ln 29341
Wilkie Rd 29340
Wilkie Trl 29341
Wilkins St 29340
Wilkins Farm Rd 29340
Wilkinsville Hwy 29340
William Way 29341
Williams Rd 29341
Willingham Rd 29341
Willis Plz & St 29341
Willow St 29340
Wilmac Rd 29341
Winchester Dr 29341
Wind Hill Rd 29340
Windburg Dr 29341
Windslow Ave 29341
Windy Hill Rd 29341
Withrow Acre Dr 29341
Wofford Rd 29340
Wolf Den Ln 29340
Wolfhaven Dr 29340
Wood St 29341
Woodland Rd 29341
Woodlawn Dr 29340
Woods Cross Rd 29341
Woodside Dr 29340
Woodview Dr 29341
Worthmore Dr 29340
Worths Trl 29340
Wylie St 29340
Yale St 29341
York Dr 29340
Young St 29341
Zacks Ln 29340
Zelure Rd 29341

NUMBERED STREETS

1st Ave & St 29340
2nd Ave & St 29340
3rd Ave 29340
E 3rd St 29340
W 3rd St 29341
4th Ave & St 29340
5th St 29340
6th St 29340
7th St 29340
8th St 29340
W 9th 29340
10th St 29340
11th St 29340
12th St 29340
13th St 29340
14th St 29340
15th St 29340
16th St 29340
17th St 29340

GEORGETOWN SC

General Delivery 29442

POST OFFICE BOXES MAIN OFFICE STATIONS AND BRANCHES

Box No.s
All PO Boxes 29442

NAMED STREETS

A Ave & St 29440
Abbeville Rd 29440
Abel Way 29440
Abraham Pl 29440
Academy Ave 29440
Acorn Trl 29440
Adair Dr 29440
Aerie Ct 29440
Airport Rd 29440
Albatross Rd 29440
Alden Rd 29440
N & S Alex Alford Dr 29440
Allen Ln 29440
Allston St 29440
Alma St 29440
Alpha Pl 29440
Amanda Dr 29440
Amelia Dr 29440
Amos Rd 29440
Amys Pl 29440
Andrew Dr 29440
Anna Dr 29440
Annandale Rd 29440
Annett Ln 29440
Annie Bell Dr 29440
Annie Village Rd 29440
Anthuan Maybank St 29440
Antioch Loop 29440
Antonio Dr 29440
Antwine Dr 29440
Apache Rd 29440
Apollo Trl 29440
Apricot Ln 29440
Arapaho Dr 29440
Arcadia Plantation Dr 29440
Armstrong Dr 29440
Arundel Ave 29440
Asbury St 29440
Ascott Pl 29440
Ash St 29440
Athens Loop 29440
Avant Ct 29440
Aviation Blvd 29440
Azalea Cir 29440
B St 29440
Backfield Rd 29440
Bald Eagle Ct 29440
Ballard Pl 29440
Ballyhoo St 29440
Bamboo Loop 29440
Banana Bunch Ln 29440
Bantu Ln 29440
Baptism Ln 29440
Barbara Ln 29440
Barony Vw 29440
Bates Hill Rd 29440
Battery White Ct 29440
Battie Loop 29440
Baxley Trl 29440
E & S Bay St 29440
Baylor Trl 29440
Bayview Dr 29440
Beachwalker Ct 29440
Bear Loop 29440
Beaty St 29440

Beaufort Ct 29440
Beck St 29440
Beechcraft Ln 29440
Belladonna Ct 29440
Belle Isle Rd 29440
Bellefield Rd 29440
Belleflower Way 29440
Belton Loop 29440
Ben Jay Pl 29440
Ben Rufus Dr 29440
Beneventum Rd 29440
Benfield Ct 29440
Benton Williams Rd 29440
Benvenue Ave 29440
Bertie Ave 29440
Bessillieu Dr 29440
Bethals Rd 29440
Better Way 29440
Big Bay Ln 29440
Big Cone Ln 29440
Big Red Rd 29440
Bigelow Dr 29440
Bills Dr 29440
Billyfield Ave 29440
Birch St 29440
Bird Watch Ct 29440
Birthright Ave 29440
Black River Rd 29440
Black Water Loop 29440
Bland Dr 29440
Blessed Ln 29440
Blossom Ln 29440
Blue Heron Rd 29440
Blueberry Ln 29440
Bluebird St 29440
Bluegill St 29440
Bogg Ln 29440
Bohicket Dr 29440
Bolick St 29440
Bonds St 29440
Bonnyneck Dr 29440
Bootsie Ln 29440
Bossie Ln 29440
Bossie Lee Rd 29440
Bourne St 29440
Boykin Rd 29440
Bragdon Ave 29440
Bramco Way 29440
Branch Dr 29440
Brandon Way 29440
Brandy Ln 29440
Brave Dr 29440
Breakwater Ct 29440
Brian Trl 29440
Brick Chimney Rd 29440
Bridge View Rd 29440
Brier St 29440
Brinkley St 29440
Britt St 29440
Britton Ave 29440
Brixton Ln 29440
Broad St 29440
Brock St 29440
Bromell Ave 29440
Brook St 29440
Broomsage Trl 29440
Brothers Ln 29440
Browns Ferry Rd 29440
Brownville Ave 29440
Bryant Rd 29440
Buck Dr 29440
Bud Rd 29440
Buffalo Ct 29440
Bulldog Way 29440
Burdette Loop 29440
Burgin Pl 29440
Bush St 29440
Butts St 29440
C St 29440
Caesar Dr 29440
Cagle Rd 29440
Calais Ave 29440
Calhoun Dr 29440
Calvin Hardee Rd 29440
Camelia Cir 29440
Campbell Ct 29440

Canal St 29440
Candace Ln 29440
Candlewood Dr 29440
Cannon St 29440
Canteen Dr 29440
Canton Ct 29440
Canvasback Cv 29440
Captain Anthony White Ln 29440
Carbelle Dr 29440
Carlos Dr 29440
Carnation St 29440
Carnell Loop 29440
Carrie Rd 29440
Carvers Bay Rd 29440
Castlepine Dr 29440
Catfish Ln 29440
Cedar St 29440
Cemetary Ct 29440
Center Rd 29440
Cephus Ln 29440
Challies Aly 29440
Chapin Pl 29440
Charlies Pl 29440
Charlotte St
1100-1196 29440
1101-1197 29440
1101-1101 29442
Chasewood Dr 29440
Chatsworth Ct 29440
Chavis Landing Ct 29440
Cheraw Way 29440
Cherokee Dr 29440
Cherry St 29440
Childers Ln 29440
China Grove Ln 29440
Chinaberry Pl 29440
Chippewa Ln 29440
Choppee Rd 29440
N Christmas Ln 29440
Chronicles Dr 29440
Church St 29440
Church Of God Way 29440
Cinnamon Dr 29440
Circle Dr 29440
Citrus Ln 29440
Clear Springs Ln 29440
Cleburn St 29440
Cleland St 29440
Clifford Vereen Rd 29440
Clio Pl 29440
Clover St 29440
Clubhouse Ln 29440
Clyde Ln 29440
Cody Ln 29440
Cokerville Rd 29440
Collington Way 29440
Collins St 29440
Collins Meadow Dr 29440
Colonial St 29440
Colony Club Dr 29440
Colony Pointe Dr 29440
Columbus Rd 29440
Comanche Dr 29440
Congaree Ln 29440
N & S Congdon St 29440
Cook St 29440
Cookies Pl 29440
Coolwater Dr 29440
Cooper Ln & St 29440
Cordelua Ct 29440
Corkwood Ln 29440
Corner Loop 29440
Cotillion Ct 29440
County Line Rd 29440
Cove Ln 29440
Cow Path Ln 29440
Cox Trl 29440
Crabhall Rd 29440
Craftsman Ln 29440
Crappie Ct 29440
Cree Trl 29440
Creek Bend St 29440
Crescent Dr 29440
Cribb Ct 29440
Crow Hill Dr 29440

Cuffie Ln 29440
Curly Ln 29440
Cusack Ct 29440
Cuttino St 29440
Cypress St 29440
D St 29440
D Alvin Ln 29440
Dab Dr 29440
Daffodil Dr 29440
Daisy St 29440
Dalton Rd 29440
Damarka Dr 29440
Dana Ln 29440
Dandelion Ct 29440
Daniel Morrall Ln 29440
Darby Ct 29440
Darthez Rd 29440
Datanna Ct 29440
David W Ray Dr 29440
Davis St 29440
Dawhoo Lake Rd 29440
Dawson St 29440
Deas Dr 29440
Debordieu Blvd 29440
Deck Loop 29440
Deer Run Ave 29440
Deer Springs Loop 29440
Deerfield Pl 29440
Dekalb St 29440
Dell Pl 29440
Delta Dr 29440
Dene Ct 29440
Dennison Trl 29440
Devine St 29440
Dexter Rd 29440
Diamond Ln 29440
Diann St 29440
Dill St 29440
Dillon Dr 29440
Dingle Ct 29440
Dirleton Rd 29440
Disher St 29440
Doar Ln 29440
Dock St 29440
Doe Ln 29440
Doiley Dr 29440
Donham Ave 29440
Double A Ct 29440
Dove St 29440
Dover Plantation Dr 29440
Dozier St 29440
Drayton St 29440
Driftwood Ave 29440
Duckpond Pl 29440
Duke St 29440
Dumont Dr 29440
Dunbar Rd 29440
Dune Oaks Dr 29440
Durwood St 29440
Dusenberry St 29440
Dutch Ct 29440
E St 29440
Eaddy Rd 29440
Earl Rd 29440
Earnhardt Ln 29440
Easley Pl 29440
Eastland Way 29440
Easy St 29440
Ed Miller Way 29440
Edgewater Dr 29440
Edisto Ln 29440
Edwards Trl 29440
Egret Cir 29440
Elizabeth St 29440
Ellen Rd 29440
Ellis Landing Rd 29440
Elm St 29440
Elouise Rd 29440
Emanuel St 29440
Emily Ct 29440
Emma Ln 29440
Empire Ct 29440
English Ln 29440
Enterprise St 29440
Equestrian Dr 29440
Ernestine Dr 29440

Esau Ct 29440
Estate Ln 29440
Estherville Dr 29440
Estill Dr 29440
Ethel Trl 29440
Evans Pl 29440
Evelyn Collins Ct 29440
Ever Lee Pl 29440
Evert Dr 29440
Exchange Dr & St 29440
Exodus Dr 29440
Ezra Way 29440
F W Anderson Dr 29440
Faber Ave 29440
Fair Ln 29440
Faith Way 29440
Faithful Way 29440
Falcon Ct 29440
Fancy Ln 29440
Farrelly St 29440
Feagen Dr 29440
Feather Dr 29440
Fennel Ct 29440
Fern St 29440
Ferry Landing Rd 29440
Fiddlers Loop 29440
Fieldcrest Rd 29440
Finch Dr 29440
Fir Dr 29440
Firehouse St 29440
Fishermans Ln 29440
Flock St 29440
Flora St 29440
Floranada Ln 29440
Fogel St 29440
Ford Village Rd 29440
Forest Ave 29440
Fountain Ln 29440
Fox Pond Dr 29440
Foxfire Ct 29440
Francis Marion Dr 29440
Francis Parker Rd 29440
Frank Cribb Rd 29440
Frank Williams Dr 29440
Franklin Loop 29440
N & S Fraser St 29440
Frederick Dr 29440
Freeman Dr 29440
Friendfield Rd 29440
Front St 29440
Frost Cir 29440
Fuller Ct 29440
Funnye Ln 29440
Fuzzy Dr 29440
Fyfee Ct 29440
Gabriel St 29440
Gaffney Ct 29440
Gapway Rd 29440
Gar Ct 29440
Garden Ave 29440
Gardenia Cir 29440
Garrison Rd 29440
Gasque St 29440
Gause Ln 29440
Gaylord Trl 29440
Gene Hill Dr 29440
Genesis Dr 29440
Geneva Ln 29440
George Washington Trl 29440
Georgetown Hwy 29440
Geronimo Ln 29440
Gibson St 29440
Gilbert St 29440
Gillyard Ave 29440
Gladding Pl 29440
Glenda Loop 29440
Glenny Loop 29440
Glenwood St 29440
Going St 29440
Goldfinch Dr 29440
Golf Dr 29440
Good Hope Pl 29440
Gordon St 29440
Governor Boone Ln 29440
Governor Johnston Rd 29440

Grafton Dr 29440
Graham Ln 29440
Grand Oak Dr 29440
Grant Dr 29440
Gravel Gulley Rd 29440
Graves Station St 29440
Greedy Ave 29440
Green Acres Dr 29440
Green Meadow Cir 29440
Greentown Rd 29440
Greenwich Dr 29440
Gresham Dr 29440
Grimes St 29440
Grissett Dr 29440
Gum Branch Ct 29440
H Ave & Ln 29440
H Mcconnell Ct 29440
Haig Ct 29440
Halloween Way 29440
Halsey Ave 29440
Hampton Ct & St 29440
Hams Ln 29440
Handy Hill Dr 29440
Harbor St 29440
Harmony Hills Dr 29440
Harold Dr 29440
Harrelson Rd 29440
Harris Landing Rd 29440
Harvest Moon Dr 29440
Harvey Ct 29440
Hasty Point Dr 29440
Hatties Ct 29440
Haven Dr 29440
Hawk Ct 29440
Hawkins St 29440
Hayfield Rd 29440
Haynes Pl 29440
N & S Hazard St 29440
Heathstead Ln 29440
Hebrew Ct 29440
Helena St 29440
Hemingway Ln 29440
Henrietta Ln 29440
Henry St 29440
Herbert Way 29440
Heriot Rd 29440
Heron Cv 29440
Herriott Farms Dr 29440
Hesterville Rd 29440
Hewitt Ln 29440
Heyward St 29440
Hezekiah Pl 29440
Hickory Dr 29440
Hidden River Rd 29440
Highland Rd 29440
Highmarket St 29440
Hill St 29440
Hillcrest Ct 29440
Hilliard St 29440
Hilton Ln 29440
Hinds St 29440
Hoagan Ln 29440
Hobcaw Rd 29440
Hodge Dr 29440
Hole Ave 29440
Holmes Dr 29440
Holt Ln 29440
Holy Ln 29440
Honey Hill St 29440
Hope Ln 29440
Hopsewee Rd 29440
Horry St 29440
Howard St 29440
Huffman Dr 29440
Huger Dr 29440
Humes Dr 29440
Hummingbird Ave 29440
Hunter Ln 29440
Ibis Ave 29440
Ida Dr 29440
Idols Ln 29440
Imperial Dr 29440
Indian Creek Ln 29440
Indian Hut Rd 29440
Indigo Ave 29440
Industrial Dr 29440
Inlet Creek Ln 29440
International Dr 29440
Iris St 29440
Isaiah St 29440
S Island Rd 29440
Izard Pl 29440
Jackson Village Rd 29440
Jacobs Ave 29440
Jacquelyn Dr 29440
James Lee Pl 29440
James Milton Rd 29440
Jasper St 29440
Jaycee Cir 29440
Jeff Dr 29440
Jena Ct 29440
Jeremiah Dr 29440
Jericho Ct 29440
Jerome Dr 29440
Jessamine Ave 29440
Jessica Dr 29440
Jessie Trl 29440
Jiles Rd 29440
Jim Ln 29440
Joanna Guillard Ln 29440
Jobie Classroom Dr 29440
Jock Trl 29440
Joe Dr 29440
Joe Senior Dr 29440
Joe Smith St 29440
John St 29440
John Green Ln 29440
John Moultrie Dr & Rd 29440
John Waites Ct 29440
Johnnys River Rd 29440
Johnson Rd 29440
Johnstone Ln 29440
Joseph Pl 29440
Josie Way 29440
Judges Rd 29440
Julian Ct & St 29440
July Ln 29440
Junior St 29440
Juniper Pl 29440
Jutland Ln 29440
K C Ct 29440
N & S Kaminski St 29440
Karlton Ln 29440
Katherine Ct 29440
Kaufman St 29440
Keever St 29440
Kenneth Ln 29440
Kensington Blvd 29440
Kent Rd 29440
Kepton Ct 29440
Kershaw Pl 29440
Kiawah Rd 29440
Kilsock Dr 29440
Kimmel Rd 29440
King St 29440
King George Rd 29440
Kingsbury Pl 29440
Kinloch St 29440
Kirby Ct 29440
Kirkwood Ln 29440
Kisha Dr 29440
Kitty Jay Ln 29440
Knowlin Rd 29440
Ladson Ln 29440
Lafayette Cir & St 29440
Lakeside Dr 29440
Lakewood Ave 29440
Lamb Rd 29440
Lambert Loop 29440
Lance Dr 29440
Land Fill Rd 29440
Landgrave St 29440
Lanes Creek Dr 29440
Lanford Ln 29440
Lantana Cir 29440
Latta Pl 29440
Lawhorn Loop 29440
Lawrence Dr 29440
Lazarus Ln 29440
Lear Ln 29440
Ledan Dr 29440
Lee St 29440
Leeward Ct 29440
Lefty Ln 29440
Legion St 29440
Lehman Pl 29440
Leigge Dr 29440
Leland St 29440
Leon St 29440
Lessie Loop 29440
Lethia Dr 29440
Levi Ln 29440
Liberty St 29440
Lilly Ave 29440
Lincoln St 29440
Lincolnshire Dr 29440
Linen Loop 29440
Lionel Dr 29440
Little Brook Dr 29440
Little Point Ln 29440
Live Oak Ln 29440
Livingston Rd 29440
Loblolly St 29440
Lobo Loop 29440
London Ln 29440
Long Ct 29440
Long Branch Dr 29440
Longfellow Ln 29440
Lookout Ln 29440
Lorena Dr 29440
Loril St 29440
Loris Ave 29440
Lot Dr 29440
Louis Rd 29440
Lowrimore Dr 29440
Lucas St 29440
Lucius Dr 29440
Lucy Grier Rd 29440
Luke St 29440
Lula Ct 29440
Lumberton Dr 29440
Lurleen Loop 29440
Luther Trl 29440
Luvan Blvd 29440
Luz Dr 29440
Lynch St 29440
M E Ln 29440
Madison Dr 29440
Mae Pl 29440
Magdelene Ct 29440
Maggie Mae Pl 29440
Magill Ln 29440
Magnolia Dr 29440
Mahan St 29440
Maidenbush Rd 29440
Mallard Cir 29440
Mammoth Rd 29440
Manelhala Ct 29440
Manigault Ct 29440
Mansfield Rd 29440
Maple St 29440
Marcella St 29440
Marigold St 29440
Marina Dr 29440
Marion St 29440
Mark St 29440
Marsh St 29440
Marsh Lake Dr 29440
Marshview Ln 29440
Martin St 29440
Mary Hines Ln 29440
Matthew St 29440
Maurice Ct 29440
Mawtwo Dr 29440
Mayer St 29440
Mayrant Bluff Ln 29440
Mazie Ln 29440
Mccaffrey Ct 29440
Mccain Dr 29440
Mccants Ave 29440
Mcclary Ln 29440
Mccray Ln 29440
Mcdonald Rd 29440
Meadow Ln 29440
Meadowlark Ct 29440
S Meeting St 29440
Meggett Dr 29440
Melrose Trl 29440
Melvina Dr 29440
Memorial Ln 29440
Mercer Ave & Rd 29440
Meredith Ct 29440
Meria Dr 29440
Merriman Rd 29440
Mesa Dr 29440
Messiah Dr 29440
Micah Rd 29440
Middleton St 29440
Midway Rd 29440
Milton Hall Dr 29440
Mims Ln 29440
Mineral Pl 29440
Mingo Bluff Ln 29440
Minister Dr 29440
Mintwood Dr 29440
Missroon St 29440
Mistletoe Ln 29440
Misty Ln 29440
Mitchell Way 29440
Mobile Ct 29440
Mohican Dr 29440
Montford Dr 29440
Moody Pl 29440
Moonfish St 29440
Mormon Ln 29440
Morris Ln 29440
Morrison St 29440
Moss St 29440
Mossdale Ln 29440
Mount Zion Ave 29440
Mouresina Rd 29440
Moury Dr 29440
Muskogee Dr 29440
Muster Shad Rd 29440
Musterfield Ln 29440
Muy Grande Way 29440
Myers Dr 29440
Myrtle St 29440
Myrtle Wood Ln 29440
Naja Ln 29440
Natalie Ct 29440
Nate Dr 29440
Nautica Way 29440
Navaho Trl 29440
Neighbor Dr 29440
Nemiah Ave 29440
Nicole Ln 29440
Nightingale Rd 29440
Nimmer Ln 29440
Nita Dr 29440
Noah Loop 29440
Noahs Mill Rd 29440
North St 29440
Novia Pl 29440
Nowell St 29440
Nushell St 29440
Oak St 29440
Oak Haven Dr 29440
Oak Hill Dr 29440
Oak Ridge Ln 29440
Oakley St 29440
Oaks Plantation Rd 29440
Oatland Rd 29440
Ocean Hwy 29440
Ocean Green Dr 29440
Ocean Park Loop 29440
Old Carriage Loop 29440
Old Charleston Rd 29440
Old Gunn Way 29440
Old Kinloch Rd 29440
Old Mingo Trl 29440
Old Pee Dee Rd 29440
Old Town Ave 29440
Olive St 29440
Orange St 29440
Osprey Way 29440
Overton Ln 29440
Oxford Ln 29440
Palm Aly & St 29440
Palmetto St 29440
Papas Pl 29440
Papo Dr 29440
Paprika Way 29440
Paradise Ln 29440
Paris Ln 29440
Park Blvd & St 29440
Patches Pl 29440
Pate Ct 29440
Patriot Ct 29440
Paul And Sadie Ln 29440
Paul Mcrae Trl 29440
Pawnee Dr 29440
Peace Lily Ln 29440
Peaceful Ridge St 29440
Peaches Ln 29440
Peachtree St 29440
Pearline Ct 29440
Pecan Ct 29440
Pee Dee Rd 29440
Pelican Reef Dr 29440
Penncine Ct 29440
Pennsylvania Ave 29440
Pennyroyal Rd 29440
Pepperberry Way 29440
Peppermint Ln 29440
Permit Ct 29440
Perry Rd 29440
Peru Rd 29440
Peter Horry Ct 29440
Pharoah St 29440
Pheasant Loop 29440
Philippi Ln 29440
Phillip Loop 29440
Pickens St 29440
Pickerel Rd 29440
Pier St 29440
Pinckney Rd 29440
Pine St 29440
Pine Grove Ln 29440
Pineberry St 29440
Pinewood St 29440
Pioneer Loop 29440
Piper Ln 29440
Pisgah Dr 29440
Plantersville Rd 29440
Player St 29440
Plover Dr 29440
Poinsettia St 29440
Polo Ln 29440
Pond St 29440
Pool Pl 29440
Poplar St 29440
Porter Rd 29440
Porthampton Dr 29440
Possum Trot Pl 29440
Postfoot Cir 29440
Powell Rd 29440
Power Ave 29440
Prince St 29440
Pringle Ferry Rd 29440
Prior Dr 29440
Prospect Point Loop 29440
Proverbs Ln 29440
Psalms Ln 29440
Pumphouse Landing Rd 29440
Pumpkinseed Ct 29440
Pyatt St 29440
Quail Run 29440
Queen St 29440
Queen Esther Dr 29440
Quince Pl 29440
Rachel Loop 29440
Racquet Ct 29440
Raeford Ct 29440
Railroad Ave & St 29440
Rainbow Dr 29440
Rainey Dr 29440
Ramsey Grove Rd 29440
Rebel Ln 29440
Redear Ct 29440
Redfin Loop 29440
Redick Ave 29440
Redwood St 29440
Reed Ct 29440
Reginas Pl 29440
Reown Dr 29440
Reservoir St 29440
Retreat Ln 29440
Rice St 29440
Rice Planters Way 29440
Ricefield Pl 29440
Richmond Dr 29440
N & S Ridge St 29440
Rimini Dr 29440
Ringneck Ct 29440
Rio Vista Ave 29440
Rion St 29440
Rivens Ln 29440
River Rd 29440
Riverhouse Rd 29440
Riverview St 29440
Robert Conway Ct 29440
Roberts Rd 29440
Robin Dr 29440
Romans Dr 29440
Rosasusan Dr 29440
Rose Ave 29440
Rose Hill Rd 29440
Rosebank Ave 29440
Rosemary St 29440
Rosemont St 29440
Rosetter Ct 29440
Royal Pines Dr 29440
Royal Tern Ct 29440
Rubin Ave 29440
Ruffin Ct 29440
Rufus Loop 29440
Ruice Dr 29440
Rural Hall Dr 29440
Russ Ln 29440
Rustic Ln 29440
Rustwood Dr 29440
Rutledge St 29440
Ryan Morant Ln 29440
Sabal Ct 29440
Sabine Dr 29440
Saint Annes Church Rd 29440
Saint Bryan Dr 29440
Saint James St 29440
Saint Luke Trl 29440
Saints Delight Rd 29440
Salisbury Dr 29440
Saluda Dr 29440
Sampit Ln 29440
Samuel Dr 29440
Samworth Loop 29440
Sanderling Ave 29440
Sanders Way 29440
Sandpiper Ln 29440
Sangamon Ave 29440
Santee Landing Rd 29440
N Santee River Rd 29440
Sarah Dr 29440
Sarg Mary Ct 29440
Sargent Ct 29440
Sassanqua Dr 29440
Sasser Ave 29440
Saul Dr 29440
Savannah St 29440
Saville St 29440
Screven St 29440
Sea Biscuit Ct 29440
Sea Island Dr 29440
Seaboard St 29440
Seabrook Ct 29440
Seawind Ct 29440
Sedge St 29440
Sedley Ct 29440
Seitter St 29440
Seleaner Dr 29440
Seminole Ln 29440
Sequoia Ln 29440
Serenity Park Ln 29440
S Sesame Ln 29440
Severin Pl 29440
Shackleford Pl 29440
Shackleford Park Loop 29440
Shad Ct 29440
Shade St 29440
Sharon Pl 29440
Shearwater Ct 29440
Sheba Dr 29440
Shellcracker Ln 29440
Shiloh Ln 29440
Shingle Dr 29440
Shopwall St 29440
Short St 29440
Shortcut Dr 29440
Shortleaf Dr 29440
Shotgun Ct 29440
Siau Ln 29440
Silas Ln 29440
Silent Hollow Ln 29440
Simms St 29440
Simone Dr 29440
Singleton Ave 29440
Sirfield St 29440
Siwa Ln 29440
Sloan St 29440
Smith St 29440
Smitty Ln 29440
Snooks Ct 29440
Snow Hill St 29440
Sollie Cir 29440
Soloman Ln 29440
Sorrell Dr 29440
South Blvd 29440
Spanish Moss Dr 29440
Sparrow Dr 29440
Spring St 29440
Spring Pond Ln 29440
Springwood Trl 29440
Spruce St 29440
Stacy Ct 29440
Stafford Dr 29440
Staghorn Trl 29440
Stanley Ct 29440
Starling Pl 29440
State St 29440
Steam Plant Dr 29440
Stevenson St 29440
Stina St 29440
Stoney Brooke Ln 29440
Stono Ln & Rd 29440
Sudie Ln 29440
Sugar Hill Rd 29440
Summer Duck Cv 29440
Summer Haven Ct 29440
Summerwood Ln 29440
Summit Ave 29440
Sumter St 29440
Sundance Ln 29440
Sunfish St 29440
Susan Ln 29440
Sutton Rd 29440
Swallow Ave 29440
Swamp Fox Ln 29440
Swan Point Trl 29440
Swann Ln 29440
Sweet Grass Ln 29440
Sweet Pea Ln 29440
Swift Pl 29440
Sycamore St 29440
T And G Ln 29440
Tabby Ln 29440
Tabor Rd 29440
Tail Water Trl 29440
Tallahassee Rd 29440
Tanager Dr 29440
Tansy Ln 29440
Tara Hall Rd 29440
Tatum Ln 29440
Teal Trl 29440
Tee Trl 29440
Tegs Ln 29440
Telfair Rd 29440
Terry Ln 29440
Thatchpalm Ct 29440
Thelma Ln 29440
Thomas Dr 29440
Thompson St 29440
Thrush Ct 29440
Ticket Dr 29440
Tiffany Ln 29440
Timberbrook Ln 29440
Timothy Pl 29440
Timrod St 29440
Tisby Ct 29440
Titmouse Dr 29440
Tom Edwards Rd 29440

Tom Giles Ln 29440
Tom Johnson Rd 29440
Tony Dr 29440
Topsaw Rd 29440
Towbridge Rd 29440
Tower St 29440
Towhee St 29440
Tradd Rd 29440
Tradewind Ct 29440
Tranquility Ln 29440
Traverson Ln 29440
Trebor Ln 29440
Trey Ave 29440
Trinity Rd 29440
Triple A Trl 29440
Tripp Ln 29440
Trotter Trl 29440
Trout St 29440
Trudie Ln 29440
Tulip St 29440
Turkey Dr 29440
Tuskegee Ln 29440
Two Pond Rd 29440
Upper Topsaw Rd 29440
Valleydale Rd 29440
Van Vlake Dr 29440
Vance Dr 29440
Velvetseed Ln 29440
Vereen Rd 29440
Vernard Ln 29440
Veronica Rd 29440
Verry Ct 29440
Victoria Ln 29440
Village Rd 29440
Vine Ct 29440
Violet St 29440
W Virginia Dr & Rd 29440
Voss Trl 29440
Vy Ct 29440
Waccamaw Rd 29440
Walker Rd 29440
Wallace Pate Dr S 29440
Walnut Ave 29440
Warbler St 29440
Ward St 29440
Warham Dr 29440
Warmouth Dr 29440
Washington St 29440
Washington Hill Dr 29440
Wateree Rd & Trl 29440
Waterford Dr 29440
Waterloo Dr 29440
Waxwing St 29440
Wayne St 29440
Wearing Dr 29440
Weaver Loop 29440
Wedgefield Rd 29440
Wedgefield Village Rd 29440
West St 29440
Weymouth Dr 29440
Whiskey Ln 29440
Whispering Pines Dr 29440
White Dove Ln 29440
White Oak Ct 29440
Whitehall Ave 29440
Whitehouse Rd 29440
Whites Bridge Dr 29440
Whites Creek Rd 29440
Whiteville Dr 29440
Whiting Ln 29440
Whitmire Ave 29440
Whitton St 29440
Wicklow Hall Dr 29440
Widgeon Rd 29440
Wild Horse Rd 29440
Wildewood Ave 29440
Wildlife Dr 29440
Wilkinson St 29440
William St 29440
William Screven St 29440
Willie Rd 29440
Willietown Ct 29440
Willowbank Rd 29440
Windsong Dr 29440
Windsor Dr 29440
Windum Dr 29440
Winns Ln 29440
Winyah St 29440
Winyah Bay Dr 29440
Wishbone Ln 29440
Withers St 29440
Wolf Dr 29440
Wood St 29440
Wood Chip Ln 29440
Wood Duck Ln 29440
Wood Stork Ln 29440
Woodland Ave 29440
Woodside Trl 29440
Woodstock St 29440
Wraggs Ferry Rd 29440
Wren St 29440
Wright Skinner Dr 29440
Xavier Ct 29440
Yadkin Ave 29440
Yauhannah Lake Dr 29440
Yawkey Way S 29440
Yellow Rose Ln 29440
Yellowthroat Rd 29440
York Dr 29440
Zack Ln 29440
Zeb Ford Dr 29440

NUMBERED STREETS

All Street Addresses 29440

GREENVILLE SC

General Delivery 29602

POST OFFICE BOXES MAIN OFFICE STATIONS AND BRANCHES

Box No.s
1 - 3478 29602
3501 - 4998 29608
5000 - 7016 29606
8001 - 9986 29604
10002 - 10934 29603
11001 - 11356 29604
12001 - 12394 29612
14001 - 15320 29610
16000 - 18004 29606
19000 - 21000 29602
24000 - 27339 29616
31001 - 32318 29608
709510 - 709595 29607

NAMED STREETS

A St
1-199 29611
200-299 29609
Abbot Trl 29605
Abby Cir 29607
Abelia Dr 29617
Aberdare Ct & Ln 29615
Aberdeen Dr 29605
Aberdeen Drive Ext 29605
Abingdon Way 29615
Abney St 29611
Abraham Dr 29605
N & S Academy St 29601
Ace Dr 29605
Ackerman Ct 29607
Ackley Rd 29607
Ackley Road Ext 29607
Aconee St 29611
Acorn Ct 29609
N Acres Dr 29609
Ad Asbury Rd 29605
Addie Ct 29605
Addis Dr 29617
Adelaide Dr 29615
Adele St 29609
Adger St 29605
Adley Way 29607
Adrianna St 29607
Affirmed Ct 29617
Afton Ave & Ct 29601
Agnes St 29617
Agnew Rd
1-99 29611
100-499 29617
Agora Pl 29615
Aiken Cir 29617
Aiken St 29611
Airline Dr 29605
Airpark Ct 29607
Airport Rd 29607
Airport Road Ext 29607
Airview Dr 29607
Aisha St 29607
Aklavik Ct 29605
Akron Dr 29605
Alabama Ave 29611
Aladdin St 29609
Alameda St 29607
Alamo St 29617
Alaska Ave 29607
Albain Cir 29617
Alberta Ave 29617
Alco St 29609
Alcove Ct 29607
Alde St 29607
Alden Ct 29611
Aldridge Dr 29607
Alex Ct 29609
Alexander St 29609
Alford Ct 29615
Algonquin Trl 29607
Alice Ave & St 29611
Alice Farr Dr 29617
All Star Way 29615
Allen St 29605
Allendale Ln 29607
Alleta Ave 29607
Allison St 29601
Allwood Ct 29607
Alm Way 29601
Alma St 29617
Almena Dr 29617
Aloha Dr 29611
Alpha Dr 29605
Alpine Way 29609
Alston St 29617
Altacrest Dr 29605
Altamont Ct & Rd 29609
Altamont Forest Dr 29609
Altamont Ridge Rd 29609
Altamont Terrace Ln 29609
Alva St 29605
Alvin Dr 29605
Amber Dr 29607
Amberly Ct 29617
N America Way 29615
American Ct 29609
Amherst Ave 29605
Amity Ln 29609
Anacoca Ln 29611
Anchor Rd 29617
Anchorage Dr 29607
Ancient Way 29607
Anders Rd 29617
Anderson Rd
700-1399 29601
1400-11899 29611
Anderson St 29601
Andover Rd 29615
Andrea Ln 29615
Andrews St 29601
Andromeda Ct 29615
Angel Oak Ct 29615
Aniwetauk St 29607
Annacey Pl 29607
Annette Dr 29615
Anniston Way 29617
Ansel St 29601
Anthony Dr 29611
Anthony Pl 29605
Antioch Dr 29605
Antioch Church Rd 29605
E & W Antrim Dr 29607
Apa Way 29611
Apex Ct 29617
Apopka Ave 29609
Appaloosa Dr 29611
Appletree Ct 29615
Applewood Dr 29615
Apricot Ln 29607
Arbor St 29617
Arboretum Ln 29617
Arborland Way 29615
Arbutus Trl 29607
Arcadia Cir 29605
Arcadia Dr 29609
Arch St 29611
Arch Street Ext 29617
Arden St 29607
Arden Street Ext 29607
Arezzo Dr 29609
Argonne Dr 29605
Arizona Ave 29605
Arlene Dr 29617
Arlington Ave 29601
Arnold St 29611
Arrington Ave 29617
Arrow Head Rd 29609
Arrowhead Ct 29605
Arrowood Dr 29611
Arthur Ave 29605
Arundel Rd 29615
Asbury Ave 29601
Ashbook Ln 29605
Ashburn Pl 29615
Ashby Dr 29609
Ashby Park Ln 29607
Ashe Dr 29617
Ashford Ave 29609
Ashgrove Ln 29607
Ashland Dr 29611
Ashley Ave 29609
Ashmore St 29607
Ashmore Bridge Rd
500-799 29607
800-1199 29605
Ashton Ave 29609
Ashwicke Ln 29615
Ashwood Ave 29607
Assembly Dr
1-99 29617
100-399 29609
Asteria St 29607
Astor St 29615
Athelone Ave & Ct 29605
Atlas St 29601
Attu St 29609
Atwood St 29601
Auburn Cir 29607
Auburn St 29609
Audrey Ln 29615
Audubon Rd 29609
Augusta Ct 29605
Augusta Dr 29605
E Augusta Pl 29605
W Augusta Pl 29605
Augusta Rd 29605
Augusta St
1726A-1726B 29605
1-499 29601
500-3299 29605
Augusta Ter 29605
Augusta Arbor Way 29605
Austin St 29607
Autumn Dr 29611
Autumn Creek Way 29615
Averill St 29601
Avery St 29617
Aviation Ln 29607
Avice Dale Dr 29611
Avon Dr 29605
Avon St 29617
E Avondale Dr 29609
Awendaw Way 29607
Ayrshire Dr 29615
Azalea Ct
1-399 29615
500-599 29611
Azalea Hill Dr 29607
Azure Vw 29607
B St
1-199 29611
200-299 29609
Babbs Holw 29607
Bachman Ct 29605
Backwater Way 29611
Bacon St 29601
Badger Ct & St 29605
Bagwell Ave 29611
Bagwell Cir 29605
Bagwell Rd 29615
Bailey St 29609
Bainbridge Dr 29611
Baker Rd 29605
Baker St 29611
Baker Street Ext 29611
Bald Rock Dr 29609
Baldric Dr 29605
N Baldwin Rd 29607
Baldwin St 29611
Balentine Dr 29605
Balfer Ct & Dr 29615
Ballarat Ct 29605
Ballenger St 29609
Balmoral Ct 29611
Balsam Dr 29607
Bamber Green Ct 29615
Banking Way Dr 29615
Bankside Ln 29609
Banner Dr 29611
Barbara Ave 29615
Barbours Ln 29607
Barcelona Dr 29605
Barkingham Ln 29607
Barksdale Grn 29607
Barksdale Ln 29611
Barksdale Rd 29607
Barley Barn Ct 29607
Barlia Way 29607
Barnwell St 29601
Barnwood Cir 29607
Barr Cir 29611
Barrett St 29601
Barrier Way 29607
Barton St 29617
Bartons Aly 29601
Bartram Grv 29605
Barwood Cir 29611
Basil Ct 29611
Bates Line 29601
Batesview Dr 29607
Batson Dr 29617
Battery Blvd & Park 29615
Battle Abby Ct 29607
Baxter St 29607
Bayberry Ct 29617
Bayne Dr 29617
Bayou St 29601
Baywood Ave 29607
Beacon Dr 29615
E Beacon Dr 29615
Beacon Ln 29611
Beacon St 29605
N Beacon St 29609
Bear Dr 29605
Bear Grass Ct 29605
Beatrice St 29611
Beattie Pl 29601
Beattie St 29611
Beaufort St 29615
Beaumont Creek Ln 29609
N & S Beaver Ln 29605
Beck Ave 29605
Beckenham Ln 29609
Becker St 29607
Becket Ct 29605
Beech St 29601
Beechridge Way 29607
Beechtree Blvd 29605
Beechwood Ave 29607
Belaire Dr 29601
Belgrade Dr 29615
Belk St 29611
Bell Rd 29607
Bella Citta Ct 29609
Bellarine Dr 29605
Belle Ct 29605
Belle Meade Ct 29605
Belle Terre Ct 29609
Bellport Dr 29607
Bellwood Farm Ln 29607
Belmont Ave 29601
Belmont Stakes Way 29615
E & W Belvedere Rd 29605
Belvoir Ct 29607
E & W Belvue Rd 29609
Ben St 29601
Ben Hamby Dr & Ln 29615
Bennett St
2-4 29601
6-199 29601
200-899 29609
1100-1199 29611
Bent Bridge Rd 29611
Bent Twig Dr 29605
Bentwood Dr 29609
Berea Dr & Ln 29617
Berea Forest Cir & Spur 29617
Berea Heights Rd 29617
Berea Middle School Rd 29617
Beringer Ct 29615
Berkley Ave 29609
Berkmans Ln 29605
Berkshire Ave 29615
Bermuda Ct 29609
Berry Ave 29617
Berry Dr 29607
Berryhill Ct & Rd 29615
Bertrand Ter 29617
Best Dr 29611
Beth Dr 29609
Bethel St 29607
Bethuel Church Rd 29605
Betty Spencer Dr 29607
Beverly Ave 29605
Beverly Ln 29609
Beverly Rd 29609
Bexhill Ct 29609
Bi Lo Blvd 29607
Biddeford Pl 29609
Biddle St 29607
Bigby St 29607
Biltmore Dr 29601
Birch River Rd 29611
Birchbark Dr 29611
Birchbriar Way 29605
Birchwood Dr 29605
Birdfield Dr 29607
Birkhall Cir 29605
Birnam Ct 29615
Birnie St
1-399 29601
400-799 29611
Birnie Street Ext 29611
Biscayne Dr 29615
Black Hawk Rd 29611
Black Knob Ct 29609
Blackberry Valley Rd 29617
Blackbird Ln 29611
Blackburn St 29607
Blackford Ct 29609
Blackmore Dr 29615
Blacks Dr 29615
Blackstone Dr 29617
Blackwood St 29611
Blair St 29607
Blake St 29605
Blanche Rd 29617
Blassingame Rd 29605
Blease St 29609
Bleckley Ave 29607
Blenheim Ct 29607
Block House Rd 29615
Blossom Dr 29605
Blue Jay Ct 29607
Blue Lake Rd 29617
Blue Mist Dr 29611
Blue Mountain Dr 29617
E Blue Ridge Dr 29609
W Blue Ridge Dr
600-1199 29609
1200-3599 29611
Blue Slate Ct 29607
Blueforest Ln 29611
Bluff Dr 29605
Bluff Point Ct 29605
Bluff Ridge Ct 29617
Bluffside Dr 29611
Blythe Dr 29605
Blythewood Dr 29607
Bob St 29611
Bobby Jones Ct 29609
Bobs Aly 29611
Boggs Dr 29617
Boggs St 29601
Boland Ct 29615
Boland St 29607
Boling Cir 29609
Boling Rd 29611
Boling Road Ext 29611
Bolt St 29605
Bolton Dr 29607
Bonaventure Cir 29607
Bonaventure Dr 29615
Bond Ln 29607
Bonito St 29605
Bonnie Woods Dr 29605
Booker Aly 29607
Borden Cir 29617
Bostic St 29609
Boswell Ct 29617
Botany Rd 29615
Bouchillion Dr 29615
Boulder Rd 29607
Box Tree Way 29605
Boxford Ct 29605
Boxthorne Ct 29615
Boxwood Ln 29601
Boyce Ave 29601
Boyce Springs Ave 29607
Boykins Ct 29617
Bradberry Cir 29615
Braden Ct 29617
Bradford Ct & Pl 29615
Bradford North Way 29617
Bradley Blvd 29609
Bradley Ct 29615
Bradley St 29611
Bradshaw St 29601
Braelock Ct 29615
Braemar Ter 29607
Bragg St 29611
Braley Ct 29615
Bramble Ct 29615
Bramco Dr 29615
E Bramlett Rd
200-499 29601
500-799 29611
W Bramlett Rd 29611
Branch St 29605
Branchester Ct 29607
Brandywine Ct 29615
Branif Ln 29611
Brannon St 29611
Bransfield Ct & Rd 29615
Brantford Ln 29605
Branwood St 29611
Braves Ave 29607
Breazeale Est 29605
Breckenridge Ct 29615
Breezewood Ct 29607
Brendan Way 29615
Brentbrook Way 29609
Brentwood Cir 29605
Brentwood Dr 29609
Brevard St 29607
Brians Rd 29607
Briar St 29601
Briarcliff Dr 29607
Briarcreek Pl 29615
Briargate Pl 29615
Briarglen Pl 29615
Briarridge Ct 29615
Briarrun Pl 29615
Briarview Cir 29615

Briarwood Blvd 29615
Bridgeport Dr 29615
Bridges Dr 29611
Bridgeton Ct & Dr 29615
Bridgewater Ct & Dr 29615
Bridle Path Ln 29615
Bridwell Ave 29607
Briggs Ave 29601
Bright Water Ln 29609
Brimfield Ct 29605
Briton Ct & Way 29615
Brittany Dr 29615
E & W Broad St 29601
Broadford Rd 29615
Broadmoor Dr 29615
Broadus Ave 29601
Broadway Dr 29611
Brock Dr 29605
Brockman Aly 29601
Brockman Ave 29609
Brockman Rd 29615
Brockman Hill Rd 29617
Brockmore Dr 29605
Bromsgrove Dr 29609
Brook Dr 29607
Brookdale Ave 29607
Brookfield Blvd & Pkwy 29607
Brookfield Oaks Dr 29607
Brookford Ct 29615
Brookforest Dr 29605
Brookline Ct 29605
Brooks Ave 29617
Brookside Ave 29607
Brookside Cir 29609
Brookside Way 29605
Brookstone Grn 29609
Brookview Cir & Dr 29605
Brookway Dr 29605
N Brookwood Dr 29605
Broomfield Dr 29617
Broughton Dr 29609
N Brown St 29601
Brownstone Cir 29615
Brownwood Dr 29611
Brozzini Ct 29615
Bruce Rd 29605
Bruce St 29607
Brunson St 29607
Brunswick Ave 29609
Brush St 29607
Bryant St 29611
Brynhurst Cir & Ct 29615
Bryson St 29611
Buckeye Ln 29611
Buckhannon Rd 29607
S & E Buckhorn Dr, Rd & St 29609
Buckingham Rd 29607
Buckland Way 29615
Buckner Ct & St 29601
Buckskin Rd 29607
Bud St 29617
Buena Vista Ave 29607
Buena Vista Way 29615
Buff St 29609
Buffalo Dr 29605
Buist Ave 29609
Buncombe Rd 29609
Buncombe St 29601
Bunker Dr 29609
Burbank Dr 29605
Burbridge Ct 29605
Burdette St 29611
Burdine Dr & Rd 29617
Burgess Ave 29609
Burgundy Dr 29615
Burke St 29615
Burmaster Dr 29605
Burning Bush Ln & Rd 29607
Burns Cir & St 29605
Burty Rd 29605
Business Park Ct 29605
Butler Ave 29601
Butler Rd 29617
E Butler Rd 29607
W Butler Rd 29607
Butler Row 29601
Butler Springs Rd 29615
Butternut Dr 29605
Buxton Ct 29611
Bynum St 29605
Byrd Blvd 29605
Byrdland Dr 29607
Byron Ct 29605
Bywater Pl 29617
C St
  1-99 29611
  100-199 29609
Cabot Ct 29607
Cagle St 29601
Cain St 29611
Calder St 29611
Caledon Ct 29615
Calhoun Ave 29617
N Calhoun St 29601
S Calhoun St 29601
Calhoun Memorial Hwy 29611
Caliston Ct 29615
Callahan Ave 29617
Callaway Ct 29605
Calle Pl 29607
Calmar Ct 29617
Calumet Ct 29615
Calvert St 29611
Calvin St 29601
Cambridge Ave 29617
Cambridge Dr 29605
Camden Ln 29605
Camelback Rd 29617
Camelot Ln 29611
Cameron Ln 29615
Camille Ave 29605
Cammer Ave 29605
Campbell St 29607
E & W Camperdown Way 29601
Candlewyck Ln 29615
Canners Ct 29605
Cannock Ct 29609
Cannon Cir 29607
Cannon Dr 29605
Canso St 29607
Cantera Cir 29615
Canterbury Dr 29609
Canvasback Trl 29617
Canyon Ct 29607
Cape Charles Ct & Dr 29615
Capers St 29605
Capertree Ct 29615
Capewood Ct 29609
Capitol Ct 29601
Capri Ct 29609
Caraway Ct 29615
Cardinal Dr 29609
Cardinal Creek Dr 29607
Cardona Ct 29611
Cardwell St 29605
Caren St 29611
Carilion Ln 29617
Carl Ct 29611
Carl Kohrt Dr 29617
Carlton Ave 29611
Carmel St 29607
Caroleton Way 29615
Carolina Ave 29607
W Carolina Ave 29611
Carolina Point Pkwy 29607
E & W Caroline St 29611
Carpenter St 29611
Carpin Dr 29611
Carriage Ct & Dr 29609
Carrie Ct & Dr 29615
Carroll Ln 29605
Carson St 29601
Cartee Ave 29605
Carter Dr & St 29607
Carver St 29611
Cary St 29609
Cascade Ct 29611
Casey St 29601
Cashmere Dr 29605
Castell Dr 29617
E & W Castle Dr 29605
Castlemaine Dr 29617
Castleton Way 29615
Castlewood Dr 29615
Catalan St 29607
Catalina Dr 29609
Cataloo Ct 29609
Catawba Ave & St 29611
Cateechee Ave 29605
Catesby Vale 29605
Catherine Ave 29605
Cathey St 29609
Cathey Street Ext 29609
Catlin Cir 29607
Cauley Dr 29609
Cavalier Dr 29607
Cedar Ave 29605
Cedar Ct 29607
Cedar Berry Ln 29611
Cedar Brook Ct 29611
Cedar Crossing Ln 29615
Cedar Lane Ct 29601
Cedar Lane Rd
  1-199 29601
  200-699 29611
  700-1999 29617
Cedar Pines Dr 29615
Cedarcroft Dr 29615
Celand St 29607
Celestial Ct 29605
Celriver Dr 29605
Cemetery St 29601
Center St
  1-99 29607
  100-199 29611
E Center St 29611
Central Ave 29601
Central Ct 29609
Centre Blvd & Ct 29605
Century Cir & Dr 29607
Cessna Ct 29607
Chadwyck Ct 29615
Chalet Pl 29607
Chalmers Rd 29605
Chamberlain Ct 29605
Chamblee Blvd 29615
Chamonix Ct 29607
Champions Pt 29609
Champlain Dr 29611
Chancellor Dr 29611
Chandler St 29609
Chandon Ct 29615
Chaney St 29607
Channel Dr 29611
Channing Dr 29617
Chanticleer Dr 29605
Chantilly Ct & Dr 29615
Chapel Rd 29605
Chapin St 29605
Chapman Pl, Rd & St 29605
Charcross Ct 29615
Chardon Pl 29607
Charis Dr 29615
Charlbury St 29607
Charlene Dr 29615
N Charles Dr 29605
S Charles Dr 29605
Charles St 29611
Charleston Oak Ln 29615
Charlestonplace Ct 29615
Charlotte St 29607
Chasta Ave 29615
N & S Chastain Dr 29617
Chateau Dr 29615
Chatelaine Dr 29615
Chatham Dr 29605
E & W Chaucer Rd 29617
Chelsea Cir 29605
Chendins Rd 29617
Cherie Ct 29611
Cherokee Dr
  1-699 29615
  1000-1299 29605
Cherry Ave 29605
Cherry St 29601
Cherry Hill Rd 29607
Cherry Laurel Ct 29617
Cherrydale Dr 29609
Cherrylane Dr 29617
Cherub Ct 29615
Cheryl Dr 29611
Chesden Hall Ct 29607
Chester St 29611
Chesterfield Rd 29605
Chestnut St
  19A-19B 29607
  1-99 29607
  100-199 29605
Chestnut Ridge Rd 29609
Cheswick Dr 29607
Chetsworth Ln 29607
Chevoit Dr 29609
Chianti Dr 29609
Chick Springs Rd 29609
Chickasaw Dr 29617
Chicora Ave 29605
Chicora Ct 29611
Childress Cir 29617
Chinquapin Ln 29615
Chipley Ln 29605
Chippendale Ct & Dr 29615
Chipping Ct 29607
Chipwood Ln 29615
Chisolm Trl 29607
Chloe Pl 29605
Choice Hill Rd 29609
Christiane Way 29607
Christina Ln 29609
Christine Ct 29605
Christopher St 29617
Chrome Dr 29615
Chukar Way 29617
Church St 29609
N Church St 29601
S Church St
  1-1099 29601
  1100-1499 29605
Churchill Cir 29605
Churchill Downs 29615
Cinderella Ln 29617
E Circle Ave 29607
W Circle Ave 29607
Circle Dr 29617
Circle Rd 29617
Citation Way 29615
City View St 29611
Claire Ln 29607
Clairewood Ct 29615
Claremont Dr 29609
Claremore Ave 29607
Clarendon Ave 29609
Claret Dr 29609
Clark Dr 29617
Clark St 29607
Claussen Ave 29601
Claxton Dr 29617
Clay St 29609
Clearfield Rd 29607
Clearview Ave 29605
Clemson Ave 29611
Cleo St 29601
Cleveirvine Ave 29607
Cleveland Ct 29607
Cleveland St
  1350A-1350C 29607
  1-9 29601
  11-999 29601
  1000-1599 29607
E & W Cleveland Bay Ct 29615
Cleveland Park Dr 29601
Cleveland Street Ext 29607
Cliffside Dr 29605
Clifton Acres 29609
Cloudless Cir 29607
Clover St 29617
Cloverdale Ln 29607
Cloverleaf Ct 29611
Club Cir 29611
Club Dr
  22A-22B 29605
  5-5 29605
  7-299 29605
  500-699 29611
Club Loop 29605
Club Rd 29609
Club Forest Ln 29605
Club View Dr 29609
Coach Hill Dr 29615
Coan St 29617
Coatbridge Rd 29615
Cobb St 29611
Cobb Hall Ct 29607
Cobble Glen Ct 29607
Cobblestone Ct & Rd 29615
Cochran Dr 29611
Cody St 29609
E & W Coffee St 29601
Colburn Rd 29617
Cold Branch Way 29609
Cold Springs Rd 29607
Cole Rd 29611
Coleman Ct 29609
Coley Way 29615
Colfax Ln 29617
Colgate Ave 29617
Coligny Ct 29607
College St 29601
Collegiate Cir 29609
Collina Ct 29609
Collingsworth Ln 29615
Collingwood Dr 29615
Collins Creek Rd 29607
Collins Crest Ct 29607
Collins Ridge Dr 29607
Collinson Rd 29605
Colmar Ct 29609
Colonial Ave
  1-399 29611
  400-599 29617
Colorado St 29607
Colt Dr 29611
Columbia Ave 29617
Columbia Cir 29607
Column St 29601
Colvin Rd 29615
Comesee Ct 29605
Commerce Ctr 29615
Commerce Rd 29611
Commercial Dr 29607
Commons Way 29611
Commonwealth Dr 29615
Community Rd 29605
Compton Dr 29615
Concord St 29609
Condurso Dr 29611
Cone St 29609
Cone Crest Ct 29609
Cone Elementary School Ln 29609
Conestee Ave
  17A-17A 29605
  1-18 29605
  19-19 29604
  20-198 29605
  21-199 29605
Conestee Rd
  1-299 29607
  300-599 29605
Conestee Lake Rd 29607
Congaree Rd 29607
Congress St 29609
Conley St 29605
Connecticut Ct 29605
Connecticut Dr 29615
Continental Dr 29615
Converse St 29607
Conway Dr 29615
Conwell St 29601
Conyers St 29609
Cook St 29601
Cool Springs Dr 29609
Coolbrook Dr 29605
Cooley St 29605
Coolidge Ave 29607
Cooper St 29611
Cope Cir 29617
Copeland Ct 29607
Coquina Ct 29617
Coral Ct 29611
Coralvine Ct 29611
Cordova Ln 29605
Corn Rd 29607
Cornelia St 29609
Cornell Ct 29611
Corner Ct 29605
Corrine Dr 29607
Cortez St 29611
Cortona Cir 29609
Cothran St
  1-99 29605
  100-199 29617
Cottingham Cir 29617
Cotton St 29609
Cottonpatch Ct 29607
Cougar Ln 29609
Country Club Dr 29605
Country Squire Ct 29615
County Cork Dr 29611
Couples Ct 29609
E & W Court St 29601
Courtland Dr 29617
Courtney Cir 29617
Coventry Ln 29609
Coventry Rd 29615
Covey Hill Ct & Ln 29615
Covington Ct & Rd 29617
Cowan Ct 29607
Cox St
  300-398 29601
  800-899 29609
Coxe Dr 29609
Coxton Mill Ct 29605
Crabapple Ct 29605
Crag River Dr 29617
Craigwood Ct & Rd 29607
E & W Cranberry Ln 29615
Cranbrook Ct 29617
Crandall Dr 29607
Crandon Dr 29615
Crane Ave 29617
Craven St 29611
Crawford Glen Ct 29615
Crawford Hill Rd 29617
Creek Dr & Ln 29607
Creek Arbor Ct 29607
Creek Forest Dr 29615
Creek Shore Dr 29605
Creek View Ct 29609
Creekdale Ct 29615
Creekpoint Dr 29617
Creekridge Rd 29607
Creeks Edge Ct 29615
Creekside Dr 29605
Creekside Way 29609
Creekside Park Ct 29615
Creekstone Ct 29609
Creektop Ct 29605
Creekview Ct 29615
Creekview Dr 29607
Creekwood Ct 29607
Creole St 29611
Crepe Myrtle Ct 29607
Crescent Ave
  1-499 29605
  500-899 29601
Crescent Ct 29605
Crescent Creek Ct 29605
Crescent Ridge Dr 29615
Crest Ln 29609
Crest St 29617
Crestbrook Dr 29607
Crested Spring Ct 29605
Crestfield Rd 29605
Crestline Rd 29609
Crestmont Way 29615
Crestmore Dr 29611
Crestone Dr 29611
Crestview Dr 29609
Crestwood Dr 29609
Crestwood Forest Dr 29609
Crestwyck Ln 29615
Crevasse Ln 29617
Crigler St 29607
Croft St 29609
Crofton Dr 29605
Cromwell Ave 29605
Crook St 29601
Crosby Cir & Ln 29605
Cross Ct, Holw & Rdg 29607
Cross Club Dr 29607
Cross Field Rd 29607
Cross Glenn 29607
Cross Park Ct 29605
Cross Pointe 29607
Cross Yard 29607
Crossbow Way 29607
Crosscreek Ln 29615
E & W Crossridge Dr 29617
Crosstree Ct 29609
S Crosswell Dr 29611
Croydon Way 29609
Crucible Ct 29605
Crystal Ave 29605
Crystal Springs Ln & Rd 29615
Cumbahee Trl 29611
Cumberland Ave 29607
Cupola Ct 29615
Cureton Rd 29607
Cureton St 29605
Current Dr 29611
Currier Dr 29617
Curtis Dr & Rd 29611
Custom Mill Ct 29609
Cutler Way 29615
Cuttino Cir 29609
Cynthia Dr 29605
Cypress Rdg 29609
Cypress St
  1-199 29609
  300-399 29611
Cypress Cove Ct 29611
Cypress Run Dr 29615
Cyrus Ct 29609
D St
  1-99 29611
  100-199 29609
Da Vinci Blvd 29609
Dabbs Ct 29609
Dacus Dr 29605
Daffodil Ln 29611
Dagenham Dr 29615
Dahlglen Ave 29607
Dairy Dr 29607
Daisy Dr 29605
Dakota Rd 29617
Dale Dr 29607
Dalegrove Ct 29607
Dallas Rd 29607
Dameron Ave 29607
Danbury Ct & Dr 29615
Dandelion Ct 29611
Danhardt St 29605
Daniel Ave 29611
W Darby Ct & Rd 29609
Dargan St 29611
Darien Way 29615
Darlington Ave 29609
Darnell Ln 29609
Darrell Dr 29615
Darwin Ave 29607
Datastream Plz 29605
David St 29609
Davidson Rd 29609
N Davis Dr 29611
S Davis Dr 29611
Davis St 29609
Davis Drive Ext 29611
Davis Keats Dr 29607
Dawnwood Dr 29615
Dawson Rd 29609
Daybrook Ct 29605
De Braham Ct 29605
Deacon St 29605
Dean St 29605
Dearsley Ct 29609

Deborah Ln 29611
Debsyl Way 29611
Decamp St 29601
Decatur St 29607
E Decatur St 29617
W Decatur St 29617
Deckers Way 29607
Deer Cross Ct 29607
Deer Ridge Ct 29607
Deerfield Rd 29605
Deering St 29605
Deerpath Ct 29617
Degolian Ct 29609
S Del Norte Blvd, Ct, Ln & Rd 29615
Delaware St 29605
Dellwood Dr 29609
Delmar Ave 29609
Delores St 29605
Delray Cir 29617
Delta Dr 29617
Demopolis Ct 29615
Dempsey St 29605
Denali Ct 29605
Denver St 29609
Deoyley Ave 29605
Dera St 29615
Derwood Cir 29617
Descent Ct 29617
Devon Cir 29611
Devonshire Ln 29617
Devonshire Rd 29607
Dewberry Ln 29615
Dewey St 29601
Diby Dr 29609
Dill St 29601
Dillingham Ct 29605
Dillon Dr 29609
Dime Ct & St 29607
Dinwiddle Dr 29617
Diploma Dr 29609
Directors Dr 29615
Divot Way 29609
Dixie Ave 29607
Dixie Cir 29605
Dixon St 29605
Dobbs St 29605
Doctors Dr 29605
Doe St 29611
Doelling Ct 29609
Dogan St 29607
Dogwood Ln
2-98 29607
100-199 29611
Dolce Vita Ct 29609
Dolphin St 29605
Dominick Ct 29605
Don Dr 29607
Donaldson Rd 29605
Donaldson St 29611
Donatello Ct 29609
Donavan Pl 29607
Doneghan St 29611
Donington Dr 29615
Donkle Rd 29609
Donnybrook Ave 29609
Donwood Dr 29611
E & W Dorchester Blvd 29605
Dorn Ave 29601
Dorr Dr 29605
Dorsett Ct 29609
Dorsey Ave & Blvd 29611
Dothan Ct 29607
Douglas Dr 29605
Douthit Cir & St 29601
Dove Ter 29605
Dove Tree Ct & Rd 29615
Doverdale Ct & Rd 29615
Downington Ct 29615
Downs Rd 29617
Doyle Dr 29615
Dr David C Francis St 29601
Draper St 29611
Drayton Ave 29601
Dreamland Way 29609
Drew St 29617
Drexel Ave 29615
Driver Ave 29605
Dronfield Ct & Dr 29609
Druid St 29609
Drummond Ct 29605
Dubard St 29615
Dublin Ct & Rd 29615
Duck Pond Ct 29611
Duffer Ct 29609
Duke St
1-99 29605
100-199 29609
Dukeland Dr 29617
Dunbar St 29601
Duncan Rd 29617
W Duncan Rd 29617
Duncan St 29601
Duncan Chapel Rd 29617
Duncan Creek Rd 29609
Dundee Ln 29617
Dunean St 29611
Dunlap Dr 29605
Dunrovin St 29607
Dupont Dr 29607
Durham Dr 29615
Durham St 29611
Duvall Dr 29607
Duvernet Dr 29617
Dwaines Ct 29611
Dyer St 29611
Dykeson Ave 29609
Dylan Rdg 29609
E St 29611
Eagle Ave 29605
Eagle Ridge Ln 29615
Earle Dr 29611
E Earle St 29609
W Earle St 29609
Earnhardt St 29609
Earnshaw Ave 29617
Easley Bridge Rd 29611
East Ave 29601
Eastbourne Rd 29611
Eastcliffe Way 29611
Easterlin Way 29607
Eastlan Dr & Pl 29607
Eastview Dr 29605
Eastwood Ct 29607
Ebaugh Ave 29607
Eberhardt Ct 29611
Echelon Rd 29605
Echols Dr 29605
Echols St
1-97 29601
99-399 29601
400-499 29609
Eden Dr & Way 29617
Edge Ct 29609
Edgefield Rd 29605
Edgemont Ave
1-299 29611
300-1099 29617
Edgeview Trl 29609
Edgewater Ln 29609
Edgewood Dr 29605
Edgewood Rd 29615
Edgeworth St 29607
Edinburgh Ct 29607
Edisto St 29605
Edwards Rd 29615
Edwards St 29609
Egret Ct 29611
Eisenhower Dr 29607
El Paso Dr 29617
Elcon Dr 29605
Elder St 29607
Elder Street Ext 29607
Eldorado Dr 29617
Elf Ln 29617
Elgin Ct 29605
Eli St 29617
Elizabeth Dr 29615
Elizabeth St 29609
Elkhorn Dr 29617
N & S Ella Ave 29607
Ellendale Ave 29609
Ellesmere Dr 29615
Elletson Dr 29607
Ellison St 29607
Ellwood Ct 29607
Elm St 29605
Elmhurst Rd 29611
Elmira St 29615
Elmley Ct 29607
Elmore St 29601
Elmwood Ave 29611
Elrod St 29609
Elsie Ave 29605
Embassy Ct 29601
Emery St 29605
Emile St 29617
Emma St 29609
Emmaline St 29611
Emory St 29609
Empire Ave 29611
Enchanted Cir 29617
Enclave Paris Dr 29609
Endel St 29611
Enfield Way 29615
Engel Dr 29617
Engineer St 29605
Englewood Dr 29605
English Ivy Ln 29609
Enka Ct 29609
Enterprise Blvd 29615
Erskine St 29607
Essex Ct 29609
Estanolle St 29615
N & S Estate Dr 29605
Estelle St 29601
Ethel St 29601
Ethelridge Dr 29609
Etowah Dr 29617
Eugene St 29617
Eugene Walker Ln 29607
Eula St 29609
Eunice Ave 29611
Eunice Dr 29617
Evans St 29611
Evelyn Ave 29607
Evelyn Dr 29605
Evelyn Dr Ext 29605
Evergreen St 29609
Evonvale Ct 29605
Exchange St 29605
Executive Center Dr 29615
Exeter Way 29617
Exposition Dr 29607
Faculty Row 29609
Fair St 29609
Fairbanks St 29609
Fairbrook Ln 29617
Fairchild Way 29607
Fairfax Dr 29617
E & S Fairfield Rd 29605
Fairforest Way 29607
Fairhope Ln 29617
Fairlane Cir 29607
Fairlawn Cir 29617
Fairmont Ave & Dr 29605
Fairoaks Ct & Dr 29615
Fairview Ave 29601
Fairview Dr 29609
Fairway Ln 29609
Fairwood Dr 29617
Faith Dr 29617
Falcon Crest Dr 29607
Falling Rock Way 29615
Falls St 29601
Fallsburg Ct 29615
Family Ln 29611
Faraway Pl 29615
Farewell St 29611
Fargo Cir 29611
Faris Cir 29605
E Faris Rd
1-649 29605
650-899 29607
W Faris Rd 29605
Farley Ave 29605
Farmington Rd 29605
Farrell Kirk Ln 29615
Farren Ct 29607
Farringdon Dr 29615
Farrs Bridge Rd
1-499 29617
500-1399 29611
Faversham Cir 29607
Fawn Lake Pl 29607
Fayethel Dr 29617
Feaster Rd 29615
Featherstone Dr 29617
Fedex Way 29605
Fenland Dr 29615
Fenway Ln 29605
Fenwick Ct & Ln 29617
Ferguson St 29601
Fern Ct 29611
Fern St 29601
Fern Valley Ln 29611
Ferncreek Ln 29615
Ferncrest Ct & Dr 29605
Fernwood Ln 29607
Ferol Dr 29611
Fiddlers Ct 29617
Field St 29601
Fielding Way 29615
E & W Fieldsparrow Ct 29615
Fieldstone Pl 29615
Fillery Dr 29615
Finchers Aly 29601
Finley St 29611
Finnish Ct 29615
Fire Island Way 29607
Firehouse St 29605
Firnstone Ct 29607
First St 29605
Fisher Dr 29607
Fisher Rd 29615
Fisherman Ln 29615
S Fishtrap Rd 29611
Five Oak Pl 29609
Flamingo Dr 29609
Flanders Ct 29607
Fleetwood Dr 29605
Fleming St 29607
Fletcher St 29611
Flicker Dr & Pt 29609
Flight Ct 29605
Flint Dr 29609
Flintlock Ct 29611
Flora Ave 29611
Florence Ave 29609
N Florida Ave 29611
S Florida Ave 29611
Florida St 29605
Flower Dr 29605
Fludd St 29601
Fluor Daniel Dr 29607
Foister St 29609
N & S Folkshire Ct 29611
Folkstone St 29605
Fontaine Rd 29607
Fontana Dr 29609
Foot Hills Rd 29617
Fore Ave 29607
Forest Cir 29617
Forest Ln 29605
Forest St 29601
Forest View Dr 29605
Fork Shoals Rd 29605
Forrest Haven Ct 29609
Forrester Dr 29607
Forrester Creek Dr & Way 29607
Fortner Ave & St 29611
Fortune St 29605
Foster Ct 29609
Foster Dr 29611
Foster St 29609
Fountainview Ter 29607
Four Oak Way 29609
Fowler Cir 29607
Fowlerville Rd 29617
Fox Ct 29605
Foxcroft Rd 29615
Foxglove Ct 29615
Foxhall Rd 29605
Foxtrot Ct 29615
Frady Rd 29611
Francis Ave 29611
Francis St 29601
Frangipani Way 29609
Frank St
1-399 29601
2-98 29609
100-398 29601
N Franklin Rd
815A-815C 29617
1-699 29609
700-1299 29617
S Franklin Rd 29609
Frederick St 29607
Fredricksburg Dr 29615
Freeman Dr 29611
Freeport Dr 29615
Freestone St 29605
Freetown Cir 29611
French Ln 29605
Friartuck Rd 29607
Frontage Rd
300-718 29611
720-998 29611
801-1003 29615
1005-1099 29615
1100-1299 29611
5500-6800 29605
6802-6898 29605
Frontus St 29605
Frost St 29611
Frosty Meadow Ct 29615
Fruitville Rd 29607
Fuller St 29605
Fulton Ct 29615
Fulton St 29611
Furman Rd 29609
Furman St 29611
Furman College Way 29601
Furman Hall Ct & Rd 29609
Furman View Dr 29609
Gables Way 29615
Gabriel Dr 29611
Gage Ct 29611
Galax Ct & Dr 29617
Galaxy Ct 29605
Galena Ct 29605
Gallant Fox Way 29615
Gallivan St 29609
Gallon St 29605
Gallop Ct 29617
Galphin Dr 29609
Gandy St 29607
Gantt Dr 29605
Gantt St 29609
E Gantt St 29605
N Garden Cir 29615
N Garden Ct 29615
Garden Ter 29609
Garden Trl 29605
Gardenia Dr 29617
Garlington Rd 29615
Garraux St 29609
Garren Dr 29611
Garrett St 29607
Garrison Rd 29611
Gascony Dr 29609
Gatehouse Dr 29617
Gates St 29611
Gateway Blvd 29607
Gateway Dr 29615
Gatling Ave 29605
Gavins Point Rd 29615
Gay St
1-99 29607
100-199 29617
Gaylord St 29611
N Gaywood Dr 29615
Gelsemium Pl 29615
Genesis Ct 29601
Genessee St 29617
Geneva Ct 29607
Genoa Ct 29611
Gentle Winds Way 29605
Gentry St 29611
George St 29611
George Allen Dr 29615
N & S Georgia Ave 29611
Georgianna Ln 29605
Germander Ct 29615
Germane Dr 29615
Gethsemane Dr 29611
Gettysburg St 29605
Geystan Dr 29607
Ghana Dr 29605
Gibbs St 29601
Gibson Ct 29615
Gibson Dr 29617
Gibson Rd 29617
Gilbert Ct 29605
Gilder Creek Dr 29607
Gilderbrook Rd 29615
Gilman Ave 29605
Gilreath St 29609
Gilstrap Dr 29609
Giverny Ct 29607
Glacier Dr 29617
Gladesworth Dr 29615
Gladys Dr 29607
Gladys Ln 29611
Glasgow Ct 29607
Glass St 29609
Glassy Wing Cir 29607
Glen Burnie St 29605
Glen Forest Dr 29607
Glen Haven Ct 29611
Glenbrooke Way 29615
Glenda Ln 29607
Glendale St 29605
Glenlea Ln 29617
Glenmont Ln 29607
Glenmore Dr 29617
Glenn Rd & St 29607
Glenrose Ave 29617
Glens Choice Ct 29609
Glenwaye Dr 29615
Glenwood Ln 29605
Glenwood Rd 29615
Glenwood Lane Ext 29605
Glinda Ann Ct 29607
Global Dr 29607
Gloucester Ferry Rd 29607
Goblet Ct 29609
Goings St 29611
Golden Bear Ct 29609
Goldendale Ct 29607
Goldfield St 29611
Goldsmith St 29609
Golf View Ln 29609
Gondola Ct 29609
Good St 29617
Goodrich St 29611
Goodwin St 29609
Gordon St 29611
Gordon Street Ext 29611
Gosnell Cir 29609
Gossamer Pl 29607
Gower St
308A-308B 29611
1-299 29601
300-599 29611
Grace St 29601
Graceland St 29611
Grahl Ct 29611
Gramercy Ct 29617
Granada Dr 29605
Grand Ave 29607
Grand Vista Dr 29609
Granite Ln 29607
Grape Vine Ct 29607
Grassy Ct 29607
Graves Dr 29609
Graylewis Ct 29607
Graystone Ct 29611
Graystone Rd 29615
Graythorn Ln 29607
Great Glen Ct & Rd 29615
Greatview Ln 29611
Green Ave
1-799 29601
800-1199 29605
Green Arbor Ln 29615
Green Farm Dr 29607
Green Fern Dr 29611
Green Heron Rd 29607
Green Lake Rd 29607
Green Leaf Dr 29617
Green Meadow Ln 29609
Green Valley Rd 29617
Greenacre Rd 29607
Greenbriar St 29609
Greencove Dr 29605
Greenedge Ln 29609
Greenfield Ct & Dr 29615
Greenland Dr 29615
Greenlee Hill Ct 29615
Greenpine Way 29607
Greenport Way 29607
Greensboro Ct 29617
Greentree Rd 29607
Greenview Cir & Dr 29609
Greenvista Ln 29609
Greenwood Ave 29615
Grenoble Ct 29609
Grey St 29605
Grey Beard Ct 29609
Gridley St 29609
Griffin Dr 29607
Griffin Rd 29607
Griffin St 29601
Griffin Lake Rd 29607
Griffith Rd 29607
Griggs Dr 29611
Groce Ave 29611
Groce Rd 29617
Groovy Way 29617
Grouse Ridge Way 29617
Grove Rd 29605
Grove Valley Way 29605
Guess St 29605
Gurley Ave 29605
Guyton St 29615
Haddington Ln 29609
Hadley Pl 29607
Hagood St 29601
Hala Ct 29609
Hale St 29605
Haley Ct 29607
Half Mile Pl & Way 29609
Halidon Rd 29607
Halifax Dr 29615
Hall Ct 29609
Hall Rd 29609
Hall St 29607
Hallcox St 29609
Halsey Dr 29605
Halton Rd 29607
Halton Green Way 29607
Halton Village Cir 29607
Hamby Dr 29607
Hamilton Ave 29601
Hamlet Dr 29615
Hammett St 29609
Hammett Street Ext 29609
Hammond St 29601
Hampton Ave 29601
Hampton Ct 29609
Hampton Avenue Ext 29601
Hampton Farms Trl 29617
Hampton Grove Way 29617
Hanging Moss Ln 29615
Hanover St 29611
Hanson Ct 29615
Hanson Pl 29607
Happy Ave 29609
N Harbor Dr 29611
Harbor Oaks Dr 29609
Harcourt Dr 29601
Hardale Ln 29607
Harding Dr 29609
Hardwick Dr 29617
Hardwood Rd 29607
Harlem Sq 29611
Harley Barn Ct & Dr 29611

Street	ZIP
Harpswell Pl	29615
Harrington Ave	29607
Harris Ave	29611
Harris Ln	29607
Harris St	29601
W Harris St	29611
Harrison Ave	29617
Hartline Ct	29605
Hartness Dr	29615
Hartsell St	29601
Harvard Ave	29611
Harvard Dr	29605
Harvard St	29611
Harvest Ct & Ln	29601
Harvestwood Pl	29605
Harvley St	29609
Hatch St	29611
Hathaway Cir	29617
Haughty Ct	29609
N & S Haven Dr	29617
Haviland Ave	29607
Hawkins Ct	29609
Hawkins Rd	29615
Hawkins St	29611
Hawkins Creek Ct & Rd	29609
Hawkins Glen Way	29617
Hawthorne Ln	29605
Hawthorne Park Ct	29615
Haynesworth Rd	29617
Haynesworth St	29611
Haynie Ct & St	29605
Haywood Rd	
649A-649B	29607
1-799	29607
900-1399	29615
Haywood Crossing Rd	29607
Heard Dr	29605
Hearthstone Ct & Ln	29615
Heartwood Way	29607
Heather Way	29605
Heatherbrook Rd	29615
Heatherly Dr	29611
Heathrow Rd	29605
Heavenly Way	29615
Hedge St	29609
Hedgerow Cir	29611
Hedgerow Dr	29607
Hellams St	29611
Hellene St	29617
Helm Ct	29617
Hemlock Dr	29601
Henderson Ave	29605
Henderson Rd	29607
Henderson St	29611
Hendricks St	29607
Hendrix Dr	29607
Henri Dunant Dr	29605
Henrietta St	29601
Henry Dr	29605
Henry St	
1-99	29605
100-199	29609
Henrydale Ave	29605
Heralinc St	29611
Herbert St	29609
Hercules Way	29605
Heritage Ct	29615
Heritage Club Dr	29615
Heritage Green Pl	29601
Hermitage Rd	29615
Hester Rd	29609
Hialeah Rd	29607
Hiawatha Dr	29615
Hibourne Ct	29615
Hickory Ln	29617
Hickory Rdg	29609
Hickory Branch Dr	29611
Hickory Hill Ln	29609
Hickory Hollow Ct	29607
Hicks Ct & Rd	29605
Hidden Corner Ct	29601
Hidden Hills Ct & Dr	29605
Hidden River Pl	29605
Hidden Turn Way	29609
High St	29605
High Farm Rd	29607
High Hat Cir	29617
High Hawk Ct	29615
High Hill St	29605
High Valley Blvd	29605
Highbourne Dr	29615
Highcrest Dr	29617
Highland Dr	29605
Highlawn Ave	
1-299	29611
300-599	29617
Highview Dr	29609
S Highway 14	29615
Highway 153	29611
N Highway 25 Byp	29617
Hill St	
1-399	29611
2-198	29605
300-398	29611
Hillandale Cir & Rd	29609
Hillcrest Cir	29609
E Hillcrest Dr	29609
W Hillcrest Dr	29609
Hillcrest St	29605
Hillhouse St	29605
Hillrose Ave	29609
Hillsborough Dr	29615
Hillside Cir	29607
Hillside Dr	29607
Hillside Ln	29605
Hilltop Ave & Dr	29609
Hillview Dr	29615
Hilly St	
1-199	29601
200-399	29607
Hilton St	29607
Hindman Dr	29609
Hitchcock Ln	29615
Hitching Post Ln	29615
Hiwassee Dr	29617
Hodgens Dr	29617
Hodges Dr	29611
Hogan Dr	29605
Hogarth St	29617
Hoke Smith Blvd	29615
Holbrook Trl	29605
Holder Ln	29605
Holgate Ct & Dr	29615
Holiday St	29611
Holley Ln	29611
Hollie Bush Rd	29617
Hollingsworth Dr	29607
Hollis St	29611
Hollow Hill Rd	29607
Hollow Tree Way	29605
Holloway Cir	29609
Holly Cir	29607
Holly Hill Ct	29609
Hollyridge Ct	29607
Hollywood Cir	29607
Hollywood Dr	29611
Holmes Dr	
1-399	29609
500-599	29605
Holston Dr	29607
Holtzclaw Dr	29617
Honbarrier Dr	29615
Honeysuckle Dr	29609
Honour St	29611
Hood Rd	29611
Hope St	29601
Hope Bridge Way	29611
Horivenc Rd	29609
Horse Shoe Cir	29605
Horseman Ln	29615
Horton St	29601
Hosteller Ln	29605
Houston St	29601
Howard St	29611
Howe St	29601
Howell Cir, Ct & Rd	29615
Howlong Ave	29609
Hoyt St	29611
Huckleberry Cir	29611
Huckleberry Rdg	29609
Hudson Aly	29601
Hudson Grv	29615
Hudson Rd	29615
Hudson St	29609
N Hudson St	29601
S Hudson St	29601
Huff Dr	29611
Huff Line	29601
Hughes Rd	29611
Hull Dr	29605
Hummers Ct	29615
Hummingbird Cir	29615
Hummingbird Rdg	29605
Hunley Ln	29605
Hunt St	29611
Huntcrest Ct	29605
Hunters Cir	29617
Hunters Ct	29617
Hunters Run	29615
Hunters Trl	29615
Hunters Way	29617
Hunting Hollow Rd	29615
Huntington Cir	29607
Huntington Ct	29615
Huntington Rd	29615
Hunts Bridge Rd	29617
Huntsfield Dr	29607
Hutchins St	29605
Hutton Ct	29607
Hyde St	29601
Hydro Ct	29611
Hyland Rd	29615
E & W Hypericum Ln	29615
Idaho St	29605
Idlewild Ave	29605
Idlewood Dr	29609
Ila Ct	29611
Impact Dr	29605
Imperial Dr	29615
Independence Blvd, Dr & Pt	29615
Indian Springs Dr	29615
Indian Wood Ln	29605
Indigo Dr	29617
Industrial Dr	29607
Ineeda Dr	29605
Inez Ln	29605
Ingleoak Ln	29615
Ingleside Way	29615
Inglewood Dr	29609
Inglewood Way	29615
Innovation Dr	29607
Insignia Pl	29601
Interchange Blvd	29607
International Ct	29607
International Dr	29615
Interstate Blvd & Ct	29615
Interstate 185	
500-5499	29605
Interstate 185	
5500-6999	29607
Interurban Ave	29609
Inverness Ct	29617
Iola St	29611
Irene Cir	29617
Iris Ct	29611
Iron Gate Dr	29615
N & S Irvine St	29601
Isaac Ln	29615
Isbell Ct & Ln	29607
E Issac Dr	29615
Ivanhoe Cir	29615
Iverson St	29615
Ivory Glen Ct	29611
Ivy St	29601
Ivy Trl	29615
Ivy Lawn Pl	29605
Ivy Log Ct	29609
Ivybrooke Ave	29615
Ivydale Dr	29609
Ivystone Dr	29615
Jaben Dr	29611
Jackson St	29609
Jacobs Dr & Rd	29605
Jacquline Ln	29607
Jake Snake Ct	29609
Jamaica Rd	29607
James Dr	29605
James St	29609
Jamestown Dr	29615
Jamison St	29611
Janice Ct	29611
Japanese Dogwood Ln	29601
Jasmine Dr	29611
Jasper Dr	29605
Jassamine Ct	29611
Jay Dr	29611
Jay St	29601
Jean Ave & Dr	29611
Jedwood Dr	29607
Jeff Cir	29611
Jeffery Ct	29607
Jenkins St	29601
Jenkinson Ct	29605
Jennifer Ct	29609
Jennings Dr	29605
Jerome Dr	29611
Jersey Ct	29605
Jervey Ave	29607
Jervey Rd	29609
Jessamine Ct	29615
Jeter St	29601
Jib Ct	29611
Jim Logan Ct	29611
Jimmy Doolittle Dr	29607
Jocassee Ct	29609
Joe Dr	29611
Joe Louis St	29611
John Mccarroll Way	29607
Jolly St	29617
Jonagold Ct	29607
Jones Ave	
1-199	29601
200-499	29605
Jones Cir	29617
Jones St	29611
Jonquil Ln	29617
Juanita Ct	29611
Judge Martin Ct	29611
Judson Rd	29611
Judson St	29601
Judson Mill Rd	29611
Judy St	29601
Julesking Ct	29609
Julian Ave & St	29611
Junaluska Way	29609
Junction Ct	29611
June Ln	29605
Juneau Ct	29605
Juniper St	29607
Juniper Bend Cir	29615
K Mart Plz	29605
Kalmia Ct	29605
Kalmia Creek Dr	29607
Kanuga Ct	29609
Kardell St	29609
Karen Dr	29607
Kascar Plz	29605
Kathryan Cir & Ct	29605
Katie Dr & Ln	29617
Kavanagh Ct	29611
Kay Ct & Dr	29605
Keat Ave	29601
Keeler Mill Rd	29617
Keith Ave	29611
Keith Dr	29607
Kellett Dr	29607
Kellett Park Dr	29607
Kellogg Ave	29611
Kelly Ave	29601
Kelso Ct	29615
Kempsey Way	29607
Kenai Ct	29605
Kendal Green Dr	29607
E Kenilworth Ct & Dr	29615
Kenlauren Ave	29607
Kennedy Dr	29605
N Kensington Rd	29617
Kent Ln	29609
Kentland Ln	29611
Kentucky Ct	29615
Kentucky Derby Ct	29615
Kenwood Ln	29609
Keowee Ave	29605
Kerns Ave	29609
Kershaw Ct	29607
Ketchitan Ct	29605
Ketron Ct	29607
Kettering Ct	29607
Keys Dr	29615
Kilberry Blvd	29605
Kilgore St	29611
Kilkenney Ct	29615
Kim St	29605
Kimbell Ct	29617
Kimborough St	29607
Kinderwood Ct	29609
King St	29601
King George Rd	29615
Kings Ct & Rd	29605
Kingsbury Rd & Way	29617
Kingsridge Ct & Dr	29615
Kingsview St	29611
Kingswood Dr	29611
Kirk Blvd	29601
Kirkwood Ln	29607
Kitson St	29611
Kittery Dr	29615
Kitty Hawk Rd	29605
Knoll Cir	29609
Knollview Dr	29611
Knollwood Dr & Ln	29607
Knox St	29605
Knoxbury Ter	29601
Kojak Ct	29605
Kondros Cir	29611
Konnarock Cir	29617
Koswell Dr	29611
Kristen Way	29607
La Juan Dr	29617
La Rosa Ln	29611
La Salle Ln	29611
La Vista Ct	29601
Lacey Ave	29607
Ladbroke Ct & Rd	29615
Ladson St	29605
Lady St	29605
Lady Marion Ln	29607
Lafayette St	29601
Lake Dr	29611
Lake Circle Dr	
11-399	29609
400-499	29605
Lake Como Ct	29609
Lake Fairfield Dr	29615
Lake Fairfield Drive Ext	29615
Lake Forest Dr	29609
Lake Ridge Dr	29611
Lake Shore Dr	29605
Lake Summit Dr	29615
Lakecrest Dr	
1-199	29609
500-599	29611
Lakemont Dr	29611
Lakeside Cir	29615
Lakeside Ct	29615
Lakeside Dr	29617
Lakeside Rd	29611
Lakeside Ter	29615
Lakeside Branch Ct	29611
Lakeside Grove Ln	29611
Lakeview Cir	29617
Lakeview Dr	
1-199	29617
1100-1299	29611
Lakewood Dr	29607
Lama Way	29605
Lamar Cir	29605
Lambourn Way	29615
Lame Duck Dr	29611
Lamont Ln	29611
Lana Dr	29611
Lancashire Ct	29615
Lancaster Ln	29605
Lander St	29607
Landsdown Ave	29601
Landwood Ave	29607
Lane Ave	29607
Lanewood Dr	29607
Lanford Dr	29605
Langdon St	29611
Langley Dr	29605
Langston Dr	29617
E Lanneau Dr	29605
Lansfair Way	29607
Laramie Dr	29617
Lark Dr	29609
Lark St	29607
Larkspur Dr	29617
Larry Ct	29611
Latham Dr	29617
Latherton Ct	29607
Latimer St	29617
Lattice Pl	29615
Laura Ln	29605
Laurel Dr	29607
Laurel Rdg	29609
Laurel St	29609
Laurel Creek Ln	29607
Laurel Falls Way	29609
Laurel Fork Ct	29609
Laurel Meadows Pkwy	29607
Laurel View Ln	29607
Laurelberry Ln	29607
Laurens Rd	
1-1520	29607
1521-1521	29606
1522-3698	29607
1523-3699	29607
N Laurens St	29601
S Laurens St	29601
Lavinia Ave	29601
Lavonia Ave	29609
Lawnview Ct	29617
Lawnwood Ct	29607
Lawson Way	29605
Lawton Ave	29601
Layton Dr	29617
N & S Leach St	29601
Leacroft Dr	29615
Leacroft Way	29611
Leaping Brook Way	29605
Leatherton Way	29615
Lebar Ct	29615
Leconte Woods	29605
Ledbetter St	29611
Ledbury Ln	29609
Ledford Dr	29605
Ledge Run Ct	29617
Ledgemont Dr	29607
Ledgewood Way	29609
Lee St	29601
Lee Haven Ct	29611
Legacy Ln	29607
Legacy Park Rd	29607
Legrand Blvd	29607
Lehman Moseley Rdg	29609
Leland Cir	29617
Lemington Ct	29609
Lemon St	29611
Lenhardt Ct	29611
Lenhardt Dr	29611
Lenhardt Rd	29611
E Lenhardt Rd	29605
Lenore Ave	29617
Lenox Ave	29607
Leo Lewis St	29609
Leonard Dr	29611
Leone Ave	29617
Lepore Ln	29611
Lermann Dr	29605
Lester Ave	29617
Lewis Dr	29605
E Lewis Plz	29605
S Lewis Plz	29605
W Lewis Plz	29605
Lewis St	29611
Lexington Place Way	29615
Leyswood Dr	29615
Liberty Ln	29607
Liberty St	29611
Library Dr	29609
Ligon St	29605
Lila St	29609
Lilac St	29617
Lily St	29617
Lincoln St	29601
Linda Ave	29605
Linda Ln	29617
Lindasue Ln	29609
Lindberg Ave	29601
Linden Dr	29617
Lindmont Dr	29607
Lindsay Ave	29607
Lindsay St	29611
Link St	29611
Linnet Dr	29609
Linton St	29611
Linwood Ave	29615
Lions Club Rd	29617
Lisa Dr	29615
Litten Way	29615
Little Buck Ct	29609
Little Creek Dr	29609
Little Pond Dr	29607
Little Yellow Cir	29607
Littlejohn Glen Ct	29615
Livingston Ter	29607
Lloyd St	29601
Loblolly Cir & Ln	29607
Loch Lomand Dr	29615
Lockhart Dr	29605
Lockheed Martin Blvd	29605
Lockman Dr	29611
Lockwood Ave	29607
Locomotive Way	29605
Locust St	29609
Loebs Ct	29607
Lofty Ridge Rd	29609
Log Shoals Rd	
200-209	29605
210-242	29607
244-999	29607
Logan St	29601
Loganberry Cir	29609
Logue Ct	29615
Lois Ave	29611
Lois St	29601
Lombard Ln	29605
Lomond Ln	29607
Lone Tree Ct	29605
Lone Willow Ct	29605
Long Forest Dr	29617
Long Hill St	29605
Longland Dr	29609
Longleaf Ct	29609
Longtail Ct	29607
Longview Ter	29605
Lookout Ln	29609
Loom St	29609
Loop St	29609
Looper St	29611
Lora Ct & Ln	29617
Lord Fairfax Dr	29605
Lotus Ct	29609
Louise Ave	29617
Louisville Dr	29607
Love St	29609
Lovett Dr	29607
Low Hill St	29605
Lowery Dr	29605
Lowndes Ave	29607
Lowndes Hill Rd	29607
Lownsville Ct	29611
Lowood Ln	29605
Lowther Hall Ln	29615
Lucca Dr	29609
Lucille Ave	29605
Lucille Dr	29611
Ludlow St	29607
Lued Robinson Ct	29611
Luke Ln	29605
Lula Ln	29611
Lullwater Rd	29607
Lulu Ln	29611
Lupo St	29605
Luray Dr	29617
Luther Dr	29607
Lydia St	29605

Street	ZIP
Lynbrook Ct	29607
Lynch Dr	29605
Lynchburg Dr	29617
Lynchester Ln & Rd	29615
Lyncrest St	29611
Lynell Pl	29607
Lynhurst Dr	29611
Lynn St	29605
Lyra St	29601
Mack St	29609
Mackenzie Dr	29605
Maco St & Ter	29607
Madden St	29605
Madren Ct	29615
Mae Dr	29617
Maggie St	29605
Mahon St	29609
Main St	29605
E Main St	29611
N Main St	
1-699	29601
700-1899	29609
S Main St	29601
W Main St	29611
Maitland Dr	29617
Majestic Oak Ct	29609
Majesty Ct	29615
Malibu Ct	29611
Mall Connector Rd	29607
Mallard Ct	29617
Mallard St	29601
Mallory St	29609
Mallowrose Ln	29615
Malone St	29605
Maloy St	29601
Malvern Pl	29615
Man O War Ct	29615
Manassas Dr	29617
Mancke Dr	29605
Mangum Dr	29607
Manhassett Ct	29607
Manly Dr	29609
Manly St	29601
Manning St	29601
Mansell Ct & St	29601
Maple Cir	29607
Maple St	29609
Maple Creek Cir	29607
Maple Lake St	29609
Maple Leaf Ct	29611
Maple Tree Ct	29615
Maplecrest Dr	29615
Maplecroft St	29609
Mapleton Dr	29607
Maplewood Dr	29615
Marainso Dr	29605
Maravista Ave	29617
Marbella Cir	29617
Marble St	29611
Marcal St	29611
Marchant Rd	29615
Marchant St	29617
Marchbanks Dr	29617
Marcus Dr	29615
Margaret Ct	29601
Margaux Way	29615
Maria Louisa Ln	29609
Marie St	29609
Marigold Ct	29615
Marine Rd	29617
E Marion Rd	29617
W Marion Rd	29617
Marion St	29611
Mariscat Pl	29605
Mark Dr	29611
Market Place Dr	29607
Market Point Dr	29607
N & S Markley St	29601
Marlboro Dr	29605
Mars Hill St	29611
Marsailles Aly, Ct & St	29601
Marsala Ct	29609
Marshall Ave	29601
Marshall Ct	29605
Marshall Bridge Dr	29605
Martin Dr	29617
Martin Rd	29607
Martin Row	29601
Martin St	29601
Maruca Dr	29609
Marue Dr	29605
Mary St	29611
Mary Knob	29607
Maryland Ave	29611
Mascot Ct	29611
Mason St	29611
Matera Ct	29609
Matilda Ct	29611
Matthew Ct	29611
Matton Ct	29607
Maudie St	29605
Mauldin Cir	29609
Mauldin Rd	
1-549	29605
550-1099	29607
Mauldin St	29601
Maxeva Ln	29611
Maxie Ave	29611
Maxwell Ave	29605
Maxwell Cir	29615
May Ave	29601
Mayberry St	29601
Maycox Ct	29617
Maydell Ave	29607
Mayfair Ln	29609
Mayfield St	29601
Mayflower Ave	29605
Mayo Dr	29605
Mcadoo Ave	29607
Mcalister Rd	29607
Mcarthur St	29611
E & W Mcbee Ave	29601
Mcbeth St	29611
Mccall Rd	29607
Mccall St	29601
Mccarter Ave	29615
Mccrary St	29609
Mccuen St	29605
Mccullough St	29607
Mcdade St	29611
Mcdaniel Ave	
2-499	29601
500-999	29605
Mcdaniel Ct	29605
Mcdaniel Greene	29601
Mcdaniel Oaks Ln	29605
Mcdavid Way	29601
Mcdonald St	29609
Mcdougall Ct	29607
Mcdowell St	29611
Mcduffie Ct	29611
Mcgarity St	29605
Mcgee St	29601
Mchan St	29605
Mcintosh Way	29607
Mciver St	29601
Mckay St	29605
Mckenna Cir	29615
Mckenna Commons Ct	29615
Mckinley Dr	29611
Mckinney Ln	29615
Mckinney Rd	29609
Mckoy St	29609
Mclean St	29611
Mclendon Dr	29611
Mcleod St	29601
Mcmakin Dr	29617
Mcneese Dr	29605
Mcneil Ct	29609
Mcpherson Ln	29605
Mcprice Ct	29615
Mcswain Dr	29615
Meadors Ave	29605
Meadow Ln	29615
Meadow St	29601
Meadow Brook Rd	29617
Meadow Crest Cir	29609
Meadow Wood Dr	29615
Meadowlands Way	29615
Meadowsweet Ln	29615
Means St	29601
Meareney St	29601
Meddabrook Dr	29617
Medfield Ct	29605
Medical Path Rd	29605
Medical Ridge Dr	29605
Medshore Way	29605
Meeting Pl	29615
Meherrin Ct	29617
Melanie Ln	29609
Melbourne Ln	29615
Melody Ln	29617
Melrose Ave	29611
Melrose Rd	29605
Melville Ave	29605
Melvin Dr	29605
N & S Memminger St	29601
Memorial Medical Ct & Dr	29605
Mendel Dr	29609
Meredith Ln	29607
Merimac Ct	29609
Merlocke Dr	29607
Merrifield Ct, Dr & Pl	29615
Merrilat Ave	29617
Merrill Ln	29611
Merritt Ct	29617
Merritt View Ter	29609
Merriweather St	
1-99	29609
2-98	29617
100-199	29617
Merriwoods Dr	29611
Merry Dale Ln	29617
Merry Oaks Ct	29615
Mesa Dr	29609
Metropolitan Dr	29609
Metts St	29609
Meyers Ct	29609
Meyers Dr	29605
Micasa Ct	29615
Michael Dr	29611
Michaux Ct & Dr	29605
Michelin Rd	29605
Michigan St	29605
Midcroft Ct	29607
Middle Rd	29607
Middlecreek Way	29607
Middleton Ln	29607
Middleton St	29601
Midland St	29607
Midvale St	29615
Midway Dr & Rd	29605
Milan Dr	29609
Miler Ln	29607
Miles Ct	29611
Milestone Way	29615
Milford Ln	29605
Mill St	29609
Mill Park Ct	29611
Millbrooke Cir & Ct	29609
Milledge Rd	29605
Millennium Blvd	29607
Miller Rd & St	29607
Millport Cir	29607
Mills Ave	29605
Millsmith Ct	29617
Millstone Grit Ct	29607
Milstead Way	29615
Milton Dr	29605
Milton St	29609
Mimosa Dr	29615
Mims Ave	29607
Mims Ln	29615
Minus St	29601
Minus Chapel Ln	29601
Miracle Dr	29605
Mission St	29605
Missy Dr	29605
Mistletoe Dr	29617
Misty Ln	29615
Misty Creek Ct & Ln	29611
Misty Crest Cir	29615
Misty Meadow Dr	29615
Misty View Ct	29615
Mitchell Rd	29615
Mizzenmast Ct	29617
Mockingbird Hl	29605
Moffat Dr	29615
Mohawk Dr	29609
Molano Ct	29607
Mona Way	29611
Monaghan Ave	29617
Monaghan Meadow Rd	29611
Monaview Cir, Ct & St	29617
Monet Dr	29609
Monroe St	29601
Montague Cir, Dr & Rd	29617
Montana St	29611
Montauk Dr	29607
E & W Montclair Ave	29609
Montebello Dr	29609
Monteith Cir	29605
Monterey Ln	29615
Montero Ln	29615
Montglen Ct	29607
Montgomery Ave	
1-99	29609
100-199	29601
Montgomery St	29609
Monticello Ave	29607
Montis Dr	29617
Montreux Dr	29607
Montrose Dr	29607
Montverde Dr	29609
Moody St	29611
Mooney Rd	29609
Moonlit Dr	29605
Moonshell Ct	29617
Moore Ct	29615
Moore Ln	29615
Moore Rd	29615
Moore St	29605
Mooremont Ave	29605
Mora St	29609
Mordecai St	29601
E Morgan St	29611
W Morgan St	29611
Morgan Way	29615
Morganshire Dr	29609
Moriches Ct	29607
Morning Creek Pl	29607
Morning Ivy Rd	29607
Morningdale Dr	29609
Morningside Dr	29605
Morris St	29609
Morristown Dr	29609
Morwell Rd	29615
Mosher St	29609
Moss Ave	29617
Moss Creek Ct	29609
Mosspoint Dr	29617
Motor Boat Club Rd	29611
Moultrie St	29605
Mount Eustis St	29607
Mount Pleasant Ave	29617
Mount Vere Dr	29607
Mount Vista Ave	29605
Mount Zion Ave	29607
Mountain Brook Trl	29609
E Mountain Creek Rd	29609
W Mountain Creek Church Rd	29609
Mountain Face Ct	29617
Mountain Trace Ct	29609
Mountain View Cir	29609
Mountain View Ct	29611
Mountainside Way	29609
E & W Mountainview Ave	29609
Mourning Dove Ln	29607
Muddy Ford Rd	29615
Mulberry St	29601
Mulligan St	29609
Mullinax Dr	29607
Murphy Ln	29607
Murrell Rd	29605
Myers Ln	29611
Mylon Ray Hopkins Ct	29607
Myron Ln	29605
Nancy Dr	29617
Nandina Dr	29605
Napoli Ct	29609
Nassau St	29601
Natahala Ct	29609
Nature Trl	29609
Neal Ct & St	29601
Nearfield Ct	29615
Neely St	29609
Nelson St	29601
Neves Dr	29607
Neville Cir	29617
New St	29611
New Altamont Ter	29609
New Castle Way	29615
New Commerce Ct	29607
New Dunham Bridge Rd	29611
New Easley Hwy	29611
New Forest Ct	29615
New Haven Dr	29615
New Hope St	29611
New Perry Rd	29617
New Plaza Dr	29617
Newberry St	29617
Newfort Pl	29607
Newland Ave	29609
Newman St	29601
Newtonmore Rd	29615
Nichol St	29607
Nicholas Dr	29617
Nicholtown Rd	29607
Nicklaus Dr	29605
Nightingale Ln	29607
Nimitz St	29609
Nimmons Shead Ct	29617
Nitsill Ct	29605
Nix Cir	29617
Nobska Dr	29611
Nolin Dr	29611
Nora Dr	29609
Norman Pl	29615
Normandy Rd	29615
E North St	
2013A-2013B	29607
1-1199	29601
1201-1297	29607
1299-2399	29607
2400-4399	29615
W North St	29601
Northbrook Way	29615
Northcliff Way	29617
Northside Cir	29609
Northwood Ave	29609
Norwell Ln	29605
Norwich Dr	29609
Norwood Pl	29601
Norwood St	29611
Notchwood Ct & Dr	29611
Notre Dame Dr	29617
Nottingham Rd	29607
Novatak Ct	29605
Nuggett St	29609
Nut Leaf Ln	29605
O Jones St	29609
Oak Dr, Ln & St	29611
Oak Bridge Pl	29605
Oak Brook Ln	29611
Oak Creek Ln	29615
Oak Crest Ct	29605
N Oak Forest Dr	29617
S Oak Forest Dr	29607
Oak Glen Ct & Dr	29607
Oak Grove Lake Rd	29615
Oak Hill Dr	29617
Oak Hollow Ct	29607
Oak Pointe Ct	29615
Oak Ridge Pl	29615
Oak Springs Dr	29615
Oakdale Dr	29617
Oakhurst Ave	29609
Oakland Ave	29601
Oakland Dr	29607
Oakleaf Rd	29609
Oakvale Rd	29611
Oakview Dr	29605
Oakway Cir	29615
Oakwood Ct	29607
Oakwood Dr	29609
Oba Rd	29611
Oconee Ave	29617
Oconner Ct	29609
Odessa St	29601
Odom Cir	29611
Oeland Dr	29609
Office St	29611
Ogden Dr	29617
Ohio Loop	29605
Oil Mill Rd	29611
Old Airport Rd	29607
Old Altamont Rd	29609
Old Altamont Ridge Rd	29609
Old Anderson Rd N, S & W	29611
Old Augusta Rd	29605
Old Bent Bridge Rd	29611
Old Blassingame Rd	29605
Old Bleachery Rd	29609
Old Bramlett Rd	29611
Old Buncombe Rd	
1000-1199	29617
1800-3299	29609
3300-5199	29617
5200-6499	29609
Old Cedar Lane Rd	29617
Old Congaree Rd	29607
Old Country Rd	29607
Old Dunham Bridge Rd	29611
Old Easley Hwy	29611
Old Easley Bridge Rd	29611
Old Fairforest Way	29607
Old Farm Ln	29605
Old Farrs Bridge Rd	29611
Old Fork Shoals Rd	29605
Old Grove Rd	29605
Old Hall Dr	29607
Old Hickory Pt	29607
Old Highway 81	29611
Old Homestead Rd	29611
Old Howell Rd	29615
Old Hunts Bridge Rd	29617
Old Log Shoals Rd	29607
Old Mauldin Rd	29607
Old Mcelhaney Rd	29617
Old Mill Rd	29607
Old Mountain Creek Rd	29609
Old Murrell Rd	29605
Old Paris Mountain Rd	29609
Old Parker Rd	29609
Old Pendleton Rd	29611
Old Piedmont Hwy	29605
S Old Piedmont Hwy	29611
Old Rockhouse Rd	29609
Old Saluda Dam Rd	29611
Old Sentell Rd	29611
Old Standing Springs Rd	29605
Old Sulphur Springs Rd	29607
Old Tanyard Rd	29609
Old Taxi Way	29605
Old Taylor Ct	29615
Old Trail Rd	29607
Old Tyler Ct	29615
Old White Horse Rd	29617
S Old White Horse Rd	29611
Olde Orchard Ln	29615
Oldenberg Ct	29615
Omar St	29609
One Oak St	29609
Oneal St	29601
Opportunity Pl	29607
Orange St	29609
Orchard Meadow Ln	29607
Orchard Park Dr	
50A-50B	29615
1-99	29615
100-100	29616
101-199	29615
102-198	29615
W Orchard Park Dr	29615
Orchid Dr	29617
Orders St	29609
Oregon St	29605
Orient Dr	29607
Oriole St	29609
Orion St	29605
Orlando Ave	29609
Orleans Ct	29615
Orr St	29605
Osage Dr	29605
Oscar St	29601
Osceola Dr	29605
Osteen St	29611
Otago Pl	29605
Otis St	29605
Ottaray St	29611
Ottaway Dr	29605
Overbrook Cir, Ct & Rd	29607
Overcreek Rd	29607
Overlook Ct	29609
Overlook Dr	29605
Overton Ave & Ct	29617
Owasso Dr	29615
Owens Ct & St	29611
Oxford St	29607
P And N Dr	29611
Pace St	29609
Pacific Ave	29605
Pack St	29611
Paddington Ave	29609
Paddock Club Dr	29615
Page Dr	29611
Page Ln	29607
Paisley Ct	29607
Paladin Ct	29617
Palisades Way	29617
Palladio Dr	29617
Palm St	29607
Palmetto Ave	
300-499	29611
500-799	29617
Palmyra Ave	29605
Pamela Dr	29611
Panorama Ct	29611
Paper Mill Rd	29605
Par Dr	29609
Parade Dr	29605
Paradise Ct	29607
Paris Creek Ct	29617
Paris Glen Way	29609
Paris Mountain Ave	29609
Paris Point Ct & Dr	29609
Paris View Dr	29609
E Park Ave	29601
W Park Ave	29601
Park Cir	29605
Park Ct	29605
N Park Dr	29609
S Park Dr	29607
Park Plz	29607
Park St	29605
Park Creek Dr	29605
Park Lane Ct	29607
Park Place Ct	29607
Park Vista Way	29617
Park West Blvd	29611
Park Woodruff Dr	29607
Parkdale Dr	29611
Parker Cir	29601
E Parker Rd	29611
N Parker Rd	29609
S Parker Rd	29609
W Parker Rd	
1-899	29611
900-2499	29617
Parker Cone Way	29609
Parker Ivey Dr	29607
Parker Ridge Ln	29609
Parkhaven Way	29607
Parkhurst Ave	29609
Parkins Pl	29607
Parkins Glen Ct	29607
Parkins Grove Ct	29607
Parkins Lake Ct & Rd	29607
E Parkins Mill Ct & Rd	29607

Parkins Pointe Way 29607
Parkside Dr 29609
Parkston Ave 29605
Parkstone Ct & Dr 29609
Parkway E & S 29615
Parkwood Dr 29609
Parliament Rd 29615
Parris Ave 29605
Parrish Ct 29607
Partridge Dr 29609
Partridge Ln 29601
Pasadena Ave 29605
Pate Dr 29609
Patewood Ct & Dr 29615
Pathway Dr 29611
Patio Way 29609
Patricia Ave 29617
Patrol Club Rd 29609
Patterson St 29601
Patti Dr 29611
Patton Dr 29605
Patton Rd 29605
Patton St 29601
Paul Beacham Way 29609
Payne St 29601
Peace St 29611
Peachtree St 29611
Pear St 29609
Pearce Ave 29607
Pearl Ave 29601
Pearls Ln 29605
Pecan Dr & Ter 29605
Peconic Ct 29607
Pecos Dr 29617
Peden St 29601
Peggy Ct 29611
Pelham Rd 29615
Pelham Commons
Blvd 29615
Pelham Davis Cir 29615
Pelham Park Way 29615
Pelham Ridge Dr 29615
Pelham Springs Pl 29615
Pelham Townes Dr 29615
Pelham View Dr 29615
Pelican Pl 29605
Pelzer St 29611
Pemberton Ct & Dr 29611
Penarth Dr 29617
Pender Dr 29611
Pendleton Rd 29611
Pendleton St
500-1154 29601
1155-1399 29611
Penn St 29605
Pennbrooke Ln 29607
Pennine Dr 29605
Pennsylvania Ave 29612
Pennwood Ln 29609
Penrose Ave 29605
Pepper Ln 29611
Pepper Harrow Ct 29607
Pepperwood Dr 29611
Percy Ave 29609
Perigon Ct 29607
Perimeter Rd 29605
Periwinkle Ct 29615
Perrin St
1-9 29607
11-199 29607
500-599 29611
Perry Ave
16A-16B 29601
1-499 29601
500-599 29611
Perry Rd
1-899 29609
900-999 29617
E Perry Rd 29609
Persimmon Ln 29609
Perthwood Pl 29617
Pete Hollis Blvd 29601
Petiver Ln 29605
Pettee St 29611
Pettigru St 29601
Pheasant Ct & Trl 29607

Phillips Ave 29609
Phillips Ln 29605
Phillips Trl 29609
Phoenix Ave 29605
Phoenix Ct 29607
Phoenix Bluff Ct 29607
Piazza Plz 29601
Picardy Dr 29605
Pickens Dr 29611
Pickett St 29609
Piedmont Ave 29611
Piedmont Hwy 29605
Piedmont Grove Park 29611
Piedmont Park Rd 29609
Piedmont Park Road
Ext 29609
Pierre Ct 29617
Pigeon Pt 29607
Pilgrim Rd 29607
Pilgrims Point Rd 29615
Pilot Rd 29609
Pimlico Ct & Rd 29607
Pimmit Pl 29607
Pinckney St
1-899 29601
900-999 29609
Pine St
1-99 29611
1-99 29601
100-399 29601
Pine Creek Ct & Dr 29605
Pine Creek Court Ext 29605
Pine Crest Dr 29605
Pine Forest Dr 29601
Pine Forest Drive Ext
300-335 29601
336-398 29605
337-399 29601
Pine Gate Ct & Dr 29607
Pine Grove Ln 29617
Pine Knoll Dr 29609
E, S & W Pine Lake
Cir 29605
Pine Ridge Dr 29605
Pine Shoals Ct 29617
Pine Spring Ct 29609
Pine Straw Way 29607
Pine View Dr 29617
Pine Walk Dr 29615
Pine Wood Dr 29607
Pineapple Pointe 29607
Pinebrook Dr 29611
Pinedale Dr 29609
Pinefield Dr 29605
Pinehurst Dr 29609
Pinehurst Green Way 29609
Pinewood Ln 29611
Piney Dr & Rd 29611
Piney Grove Rd 29607
Piney Mountain Rd 29609
Piney Woods Ln 29605
Pink Blossom Ct 29607
Pinsley Cir 29617
Pintonto Rd 29607
Piper Ln 29607
Pisgah Cir & Dr 29609
Pittler Dr 29607
Pittman Cir 29617
Pittman Dr 29609
Plainfield Cir 29605
N & S Plainview Dr 29611
Plano Dr 29617
Plant St 29607
Plant Drive Ext 29607
Plantation Rd 29605
Planterswood Ct 29615
Plassey Ln 29609
Pleasant Grove St 29611
Pleasant Ridge Ave 29605
N Pleasantburg Dr
1-1499 29607
1500-2430 29609
2431-2431 29608
2432-3298 29609
2433-3299 29609

S Pleasantburg Dr
1-1099 29607
1100-1599 29605
Pleasantdale Cir 29607
Plum Dr 29605
Plum Creek Ln 29607
Plumbridge Ln 29615
Plyler Dr 29617
Plymouth Ave 29607
Pocahatchie Trl 29611
Poe St 29611
Poinsett Ave 29601
Poinsett Hwy 29609
Point Hope Ct 29605
Pointe Cir 29615
Pointer Ln 29607
Polk Blvd 29611
Ponce De Leon Dr 29605
E Pond Dr 29611
Pond Bluff Ln 29607
Ponderosa Rd 29607
Ponders Ct 29615
Ponders Ray Ln 29615
Pope Ln 29605
Poplar St 29611
Poplar Grove Ct 29607
Poplar Hill Ln 29615
Porcher Cir 29605
Port Rd 29617
Port Royal Dr 29615
Portofino Ct 29609
Portsmouth Dr 29617
Post Oak Rd 29605
Potomac Ave 29605
Powdersville Main 29611
Powell Dr 29617
Power St 29611
Prado Way 29607
Prancer Ave 29605
Precipice Pl 29617
E & W Prentiss Ave 29605
Prescott St 29607
Prestbury Dr 29605
Prestige Ct 29615
Prestwick Dr 29605
Primrose Ln 29607
Primrose St 29601
Prince Ave 29605
Prince Charming Dr 29617
Princess Ave 29611
Princeton Ave 29607
Profs Pl 29609
Progress Rd 29607
Progressive Ct 29611
Promenade Dr 29609
Promontory Ct 29615
Propst Ct 29609
Prospect St 29611
Prosperity Ave & Ct 29605
Provence St 29607
Providence Ct & Sq 29615
Provo Dr 29617
Pruitt Dr 29607
Pueblo Dr 29617
Quail Run 29605
Quail Trl 29609
Quail Creek Ct & Ln 29615
Quail Hill Ct & Dr 29607
Quail Meadow Ln 29617
Quality Way 29605
Quarter Ct 29607
Queen Aly & St 29611
W Queen Ann Rd 29615
Queens Way 29615
Queensbury Dr & Rd 29617
Quest Dr 29605
Questover Dr 29607
Quincy St 29601
Quinlan Dr 29617
Quoite Ct 29617
Racine Ct 29617
Racing Ln 29611
Raes Creek Dr 29609
Ragon Ln 29609
Ragsdale Rd 29611
Railroad St 29607

Rain Flower Dr 29615
Rainbow Ct & Dr 29617
Rainey Rd 29609
Rainstone Dr 29615
Raintree Ln 29615
Ramblewood Ln 29615
Ramseur Ct 29607
Ramsey Dr 29607
Ranch Rd 29607
Randall St 29609
Randolph St 29605
Randwood Ct 29617
Rangeview Cir 29617
Rapid River Trl 29615
Rasor Dr 29617
Raven Rd 29615
Raven Fork Ct 29609
Ravenel St 29611
Ray St
1-99 29611
100-299 29609
Ray Martin Ln 29611
Rayburn St 29617
Rayford Ln 29609
Reach St 29611
Rear Gower St 29611
Rearden Dr 29605
Rebecca St 29607
Red Bud Ln 29617
W Red Fox Ct & Trl 29615
Red Oak Rd 29615
Redcliffe Rd 29615
Redman Dr 29609
Redspire Dr 29617
Redstone Rd 29611
Redwood Dr 29611
Reedy St 29611
Reedy Falls Dr 29605
Reedy Fork Rd 29605
Reedy Pointe Dr 29605
Reedy River Way 29605
Reedy Springs Ln 29605
Reedy View Dr 29601
Reeves Ave & St 29605
Regency Hill Dr 29607
Regent Dr 29617
Regent Park Ct 29607
Reid St 29609
Remington Ct 29607
Renrick Dr 29609
Research Dr 29607
Retriever Ln 29607
Rhett St 29601
Rhonda Ct 29617
Rice St 29605
Richard St 29601
Richards Ave 29617
S Richardson St 29601
Richbourg Ct & Rd 29615
Richfield Dr 29615
Richland Way 29607
Richland Creek Dr 29609
Richmond Dr 29617
Richwood Dr 29607
Riddle Rd 29607
Riddle St 29601
Ridenour Ave 29617
Ridge Rd
114A-114A 29617
116A-116A 29607
1-99 29617
101-102 29607
104-105 29617
106-106 29607
108-108 29617
110-110 29607
112-112 29617
114-114 29607
114-114 29617
115-115 29607
115-115 29617
116-116 29607
116-116 29617
124-152 29607
154-156 29607
158-198 29607

200-299 29617
700-2299 29607
Ridge St 29605
Ridge Bay Ct 29611
Ridge Pine Pl 29605
Ridgebrook Way 29605
Ridgecrest Dr 29609
Ridgeland Dr 29601
E & W Ridgemount Ct 29617
Ridgeover Dr 29617
Ridgeside Ct 29617
Ridgeway Ave 29607
Ridgeway Dr
1-1 29605
3-38 29605
23-25 29607
40-48 29605
41-45 29605
100-299 29607
Ridgewood Dr
1-99 29615
500-599 29607
Ridley Piper Ln 29609
Riggs St 29611
Riglaw Ln 29605
Riley Rd 29611
Riley St 29601
Riley Smith Dr 29615
Rio Vista Dr 29617
Ripley St 29601
Rison Rd 29611
Riva Ridge Way 29615
Rivanna Ln 29607
River Ct 29617
River Rd 29611
River St 29601
River Bend Rd 29617
River Forest Ln 29615
River Meadows Ct 29605
River Oaks Dr 29611
River Run Ct 29605
River Valley Ln 29605
River Watch Dr 29605
Riverbed Dr 29605
Riverbreeze Rd 29611
Riverplace 29601
Riverplace Dr 29611
Riverside Dr 29605
Riverview Cir & Dr 29611
Riverwood Cir, Ct &
Rd 29617
Riviera Dr 29615
Rivoli Ln 29615
Roanoke Way 29607
Robbins Dr 29611
Roberta Dr 29615
Robin Ln 29605
Robin Rd 29609
Robin Hood Rd 29607
Robinson Ct 29611
Robinson Rd 29611
Robinson St 29609
Rochester St 29611
Rock Creek Ct & Dr 29605
Rock Garden Ln 29609
Rock Hill Ct 29607
Rock Side Ct 29615
Rockbridge Rd 29607
Rockcliff St 29617
Rockhampton Dr 29607
Rockingham Rd 29607
Rockledge Dr 29609
Rockmont Rd 29615
Rockrose Ct 29615
Rockview Ct 29611
N Rockview Dr 29609
S Rockview Dr 29609
Rockwood Dr 29605
Rocky Pt 29615
Rocky Chase Dr 29615
Rocky Creek Ln & Rd 29615
Rocky Ford Ct 29615
Rocky Knoll Dr 29605
Rocky Point Way 29615
Rocky Slope Rd 29607
Rocky Top Dr 29615

Rodney Ave 29617
Roe Ct 29617
Roe Rd 29611
Roe Ford Rd 29617
Rogers Ave 29617
Rolleston Dr 29615
Rolling Green Cir 29615
Rolling Meadows Ave 29605
Rollingbridge Dr 29615
Rollingreen Rd 29615
Roman Ln 29601
Ron Ln 29611
Ron Edge Rd 29607
Roosevelt Ave 29607
Roper Corners Cir 29615
Roper Creek Dr 29615
Roper Mountain Ct 29615
Roper Mountain Rd
1-99 29607
100-2000 29615
2002-2198 29615
Roper Mountain Road
Ext 29615
Rose Ave 29601
Rose Cir 29607
Rose Wood Dr 29607
Rosebank Way 29615
Rosebay Dr 29615
Rosemary Ln 29615
Rosemond Dr 29605
Rosewood Way 29609
Ross St 29611
Rothwell Dr 29607
Round About Way 29609
E & W Round Hill Rd 29617
Round Knob St 29601
S Round Pond Rd 29607
Rowley St 29601
Roxbury Ct 29617
Royal Ct 29611
Royal Oak Ct & Rd 29607
Ruby Dr 29617
Ruffian Way 29615
Runnymede Rd 29615
Rushden Dr 29615
Rushmore Dr 29615
Ruskin Sq 29607
Russell Ave 29609
Rutherford Rd & St 29609
Rutledge Ave 29617
Rutledge Way 29615
Rutledge Lake Rd 29617
Ryans Run Ct 29615
Ryedale Ct 29615
Ryland Dr 29611
Saad Ln 29605
E & W Sable Ct 29617
Sable Glen Dr 29615
Sabrina Ct 29615
Saco St 29611
Saddlebrook Ln 29607
Saddlewood Ln 29615
Sadler Way 29607
Sagamore Ln 29607
Sage St 29609
Sage Street Spur 29609
Saint Andrews Ct &
Way 29607
Saint Augustine Dr 29615
Saint Clair St 29601
Saint Francis Dr 29601
Saint Helena Ct 29607
Saint Josephs Dr 29607
Saint Pauls Dr 29601
Salem Ct 29617
Salters Rd 29607
Saluda Rdg 29611
Saluda Dam Rd 29611
Saluda Fern Ct 29611
E Saluda Lake Cir &
Rd 29611
Sametta Cir 29611
Sandalwood Ct & Ln 29611
Sanderling Dr & Ln 29607
Sanders Ln 29609
Sandown Ln 29615

Sandpiper Ln 29607
Sandpiper Way 29605
Sandra Ave 29611
Sandtrap Ct 29609
Sandy Ln 29605
Sanford Ct 29605
Sangamo Dr 29611
Santa Maria Ct 29609
Santa Monica Ln 29605
Santuck St 29611
Saponee Dr 29617
Saran Dr 29611
Saros Ct 29607
Sasanqua Dr 29615
Satterfield Dr 29611
Saul Rd 29615
Savannah St 29617
Savona Dr 29609
Savoy Ct 29607
Sawgrass Ct 29609
Sawley Ct 29607
Sawyer Dr 29605
Saxon Falls Ct 29607
Saxum Way 29611
Scalybark Rd 29617
Scarlett St 29607
Scenic Dr 29609
School St 29601
Scogin Dr 29615
Scotland Cir 29615
Scott Dr 29611
Scott St
1-99 29607
100-299 29609
Scott Street Judson 29611
Scottie Ct 29617
Scotts Moor 29615
Scottsdale Dr 29615
Scottswood Rd 29615
Scout Rd 29611
Seaborn Line 29601
Seabrook Ct 29607
Seabury Dr 29615
Seaton Ct 29615
Seattle Slew Ln 29617
Seawright Ln 29605
Secretariat Way 29615
Security Dr 29611
Sedgefield Dr 29615
Selma St 29609
Selwyn Dr 29615
Seminar Dr 29609
Seminole Dr 29605
Senator Pettus Ave 29617
Sennet Dr 29609
Sentell Rd 29611
Sequin Ct 29615
Sequoia Dr 29605
Serenity Ln 29605
Service Dr 29607
Setfair Ln 29615
Seth St 29605
Setter Ln 29607
E Settlement Rd 29617
E & W Seven Oaks
Dr 29605
Sevier St
1-199 29605
1800-1999 29609
Sewanee Ave 29609
Seyle St 29605
Shada Ln 29611
Shadow Way 29615
Shadwell St 29607
Shady Ln
1-3 29605
2-4 29615
6-299 29615
Shady Acres Cir 29611
Shady Brook Ln 29615
Shadydale Ct 29615
Shairpin Ln 29607
Shale Ct 29607
Shallowford Rd 29607
Shamrock Cir 29611

Shamrock Ln
 1-99 29609
 100-199 29615
Shannon Dr 29615
Shannon Creek Ct 29615
Shannon Lake Cir 29615
Shannon Ridge Ct 29615
Shark Ct 29609
Sharon Dr
 1-99 29607
 100-199 29617
Shaw St 29609
Shay Ave 29605
Shelburne Rd 29607
Shellcracker Ct 29611
Shelton Rd 29611
Shemwood Ln 29605
Shenandoah Dr 29615
Shepard Dr 29609
Sheraton Ave & Ct 29615
Sherborne Ct & Dr 29615
Sherman Ln 29605
Sherwood St 29601
Shiloh Ln 29607
Shiloh Bend Rd 29609
Shinleaf Ct & Dr 29615
Shirley St 29601
Shoally Ln 29607
Shoppers Dr 29607
Shore Dr 29611
Short Leaf Pine Cir 29609
Short Minus St 29601
Shubuta Ct & Dr 29617
Shumagin Ct 29605
Side Ln 29611
Sidney St 29609
Siena Dr 29609
Silver Run Ln 29607
Silver Spur Ct 29605
Silvery Blue Ct 29607
Simmons Ave 29607
Simmons Ct 29609
W Simpson St 29605
Singing Pines Dr 29611
Singleton Cir 29617
Sioux Dr 29605
Sir Abbott St 29607
Sirrine Dr 29605
Sirrine St 29611
Sistine Ct 29609
Sitka Ave 29607
Sitton Dr 29611
Sizemore Ct 29611
Sizemore St 29609
Skid Row 29605
Skyland Ave 29617
Skyland Dr 29607
Skyview Dr 29607
Slazenger Dr 29605
Sleepy Hollow Dr 29609
Sleepy Orange Cir 29607
Smilax Ct 29617
Smith Rd 29615
Smith St
 1-99 29611
 100-199 29605
Smith Hines Rd 29607
Smith Hollow Dr 29615
Smokerise Ct 29607
Smythe Ave 29605
Smythe St 29611
Snipes Rd 29615
Snow St 29607
Snowbird Ln 29605
Solar Dr 29605
Somerset St 29611
Somerville Ct 29605
Sorono Dr 29609
Sorrell Dr 29611
Sorrento Dr 29609
South Dr 29609
South St 29611
Southbourne Ct 29607
Southern Height Dr 29607
Southfield Dr 29607
Southland Ave 29601
Southpointe Dr 29607
Southridge Ct 29607
Southwick Ln 29615
Southwood Dr 29605
Sovern Dr 29607
Spaniel Ct 29607
Spanish Oak Dr 29615
Spartanburg Ct, Ln & St 29607
Spaulding Farm Rd 29615
Spaulding Lake Dr 29615
Spearman Cir 29611
Spears Dr 29605
Speed St 29611
Spencer St 29611
Spicey Dr 29607
Spindletop Ct 29615
Spinnaker Ct 29611
Spoleto Ct 29609
Spring St
 500-599 29611
 700-799 29609
 800-899 29605
N Spring St 29601
S Spring St 29601
Spring Falls Ct 29607
Spring Forest Ct & Rd 29615
Spring Valley Rd 29615
Spring Walk Way 29605
Springbrook Dr 29605
Springcrest Ct 29607
Springdale Dr 29609
Springer St 29601
Springfield Ave 29611
Springhouse Way 29607
Springmont Ct 29605
Springside Ave 29611
Spruce Ct 29611
Spruce St
 1-8 29611
 9-99 29607
 10-398 29611
 101-399 29611
Spyglass Ct 29609
Stablechase Dr 29617
E & W Stablegate Rd 29615
Stables Rd 29611
Stacy Dr 29617
Stadium Dr 29609
Stadium View Dr 29609
Stafford St 29605
Stag St 29607
Stage Ct 29611
Stall St 29609
Stallings Rd
 1-599 29611
 1200-1399 29609
Stallion Rd 29617
Standing Springs Rd 29605
Stanford Ct & Rd 29617
Stanley Dr 29611
Stapleford Park Dr 29607
Star Ct 29605
Star Dr 29611
Starboard Ct 29617
Starburst Ln 29617
Starling Ct 29607
Starnes St 29609
Starsdale Cir 29609
State Park Rd 29609
Station Ct 29601
Staton Dr 29611
Staunton Ct 29611
Staunton Bridge Rd 29611
Steel City St 29605
Stegall Cir 29611
Stella Ave 29609
Stenhouse Dr 29607
Stephane St 29609
Stephens Ln 29609
Stephenson Ave 29617
Sterling St 29601
Sterling Bridge Rd 29611
Stern Ct 29617
Stevens St 29605
Stevenson Ln 29611
Stewart St 29605
Stillwater Dr 29611
Stillwood Dr 29607
Stokes Ct & St 29611
E Stone Ave
 1-399 29609
 400-999 29601
W Stone Ave 29609
Stone Holw 29605
Stone Lake Ct & Dr 29609
Stone Meadow Rd 29615
Stone Plaza Dr 29609
Stone Shield Ct & Way 29609
Stonebrook Farm Way 29615
Stonefield Ct 29615
Stonehaven Dr 29607
Stonehedge Dr 29615
Stonewall Ln 29615
Stoney Creek Dr 29607
Stoney Point Dr 29605
Stono Dr 29609
Stonybrook Dr 29615
Stradley Ter 29617
Stratford Rd 29605
Stratham St 29609
Stratton Pl 29615
Strawberry Dr 29617
Stream Run Ct 29617
Sturbridge Ct & Dr 29615
Sturtevant St 29611
Styles Rd 29607
Suffolk Dr 29617
Suffolk Downs Way 29615
Sugarberry Ct & Dr 29615
Sullivan St 29605
Sullivan Street Ext 29605
Sulphur Springs Dr & Rd 29617
Sumlar Dr 29607
Sumlar Hall Dr 29607
Summergrass Dr 29617
Summergreen Way 29607
Summerside Dr 29615
Summerville Way 29609
Summit Dr 29609
Summitbluff Dr 29617
Sumner St 29601
Sumter St 29617
S Sumter St 29611
Sun Garden Ct 29615
Sunbriar Dr 29615
Sunderland Ct & Dr 29611
Sundew Ct 29615
Sunflower St 29601
Sunnydale Dr 29609
Sunnyside Ln 29615
Sunnyview Dr 29611
Sunrise Valley Rd 29617
Sunset Dr
 1-5 29611
 4-4 29605
 6-100 29605
 100-100 29611
 102-102 29605
 103-104 29611
 105-105 29605
 105-107 29611
 106-110 29611
 109-109 29605
 109-109 29611
 111-111 29611
 111-111 29605
 114-114 29605
 116-200 29605
 200-203 29611
 204-206 29605
 205-599 29611
 206-206 29611
 208-208 29605
 208-598 29611
Sunset Ln 29607
Sunset St 29609
Sunset Glory Ln 29617
Sunshine Ave 29609
Surrywood Dr 29607
Sutherland Hill Dr 29615
Swallowtail Pl 29607
Swamp Fire Ct 29611
Swansgate Pl 29605
Swanson Ct 29609
Swathmore Ct 29615
Sweet Shade Way 29605
Sweetbriar Rd 29615
Sweetgum Rd 29617
Sweetland Ct 29607
Sweetwater Ct 29611
Swindon Cir & Ct 29615
Swinton Dr 29607
Sycamore Dr 29607
Sycamore St 29601
Sylvan Dr & Way 29605
Sylvania Ave 29609
Sylvatus Ct 29617
Symbolic Ct 29617
Tabor St 29609
Tagus Ct 29607
Tailwater Way 29611
Tall Oaks Dr 29611
Talley St 29609
Tallin Ct 29607
E & W Tallulah Dr 29605
Tamala Gwinnett Dr 29609
Tamarack Trl 29609
Tamburlaine Ct 29609
Tammy Ray Dr 29615
Tampa St 29609
Tanacross Way 29605
Tanaga Ct 29605
Tanglewood Dr 29611
Tanner Rd 29607
Tanner Chase Way 29607
Tanyard Rd 29609
Tar Blvd 29605
Tasha Dr 29605
Task Industrial Ct 29607
Tassel Trl 29609
Tawba Ln 29617
Taylor Rd 29607
Taylor St
 1-99 29605
 100-199 29601
Tazewell Dr 29617
Teal Trl 29605
Tee Time Ct 29609
Telfair St 29609
Temple St 29601
Templewood Dr 29611
Tenney Cir 29617
Tennwood Dr 29609
Terilyn Ct 29611
Terminal Rd 29605
Terra Ct & Ln 29615
Terra Creek Ct 29615
Terra Lea Ln 29615
Terra Oak Dr 29615
Terra Woods Ln 29615
Terrace Dr 29607
Terrain Dr 29605
Terramont Dr 29615
Terrell Ave 29609
Terry Ct 29605
N & S Texas Ave 29611
N & S Textile Ave 29611
The Pkwy 29615
The Smt 29609
Theodore Cir, Ct & Dr 29611
Theresa Dr 29605
E & W Thistle Ct & Ln 29615
Thistle Brook Ct 29615
Thomas St
 1-99 29611
 101-199 29617
Thompson Dr 29607
Thornbury Ct 29607
Thornton Ave 29609
Thornwood Ln 29605
Thousand Oaks Blvd 29607
Thrasher Ct 29607
Three Bridges Rd 29611
Three Forks Ct & Pl 29609
Three Notch Rd 29605
Three Oak Cir 29609
Three Springs Trl 29615
Thrift St 29609
Thriftside Dr 29609
Thruston St
 1-99 29605
 100-199 29601
Thurgood Dr 29607
Thyme Pl 29607
Tigris Way 29607
Tilbury Way 29609
Tillman Ct 29607
Timber Ct 29617
Timber Dr 29611
Timber Ln 29609
Timber Leaf Dr 29605
Timberlake Dr 29615
Timlin Dr 29607
Timmons Dr 29607
Timrod Way 29607
Tindal Ave 29605
Tindal Rd 29617
Tinsberry Dr 29607
Tinsley Ct 29615
Tiverton Dr 29615
Todds Trl 29617
Tolbert Dr 29607
Toledo St 29609
Tomassee Ave 29605
Topsail Ct 29611
Topsfield Ct 29605
Toscano Ct 29615
Toulouse Pl 29615
Tower Dr
 1-199 29607
 201-299 29605
Tower Rd 29609
Townes St
 2-98 29601
 100-599 29601
 600-999 29609
Townes Creek Ct 29609
Townes Square Ln 29609
Townes Street Ext 29609
Towson Dr 29615
Toy St 29601
Traction St 29611
Trafalgar Rd 29617
Trail Oaks Dr 29615
Trailhead Ct 29617
Trails Edge Ct 29617
Trails End 29607
Trailside Ln 29607
Trammell Rd 29617
Tranquil Ave 29615
Transit Dr 29607
Travertine Ct 29615
Travis St 29607
Traxler St 29607
Tray Dr 29605
Traybon Ct 29611
Traynham Blvd 29609
Traynham St 29605
Treadstone Way 29615
Treebrooke Dr 29607
Trellis St 29615
Tremont Ave 29605
Trenholm Rd 29615
Tresanton Ct 29607
Trescott St 29601
Tricia Ct 29611
Trinity Way 29617
S Trinity Way 29611
Triple Crown Ct 29615
Tripps Cir 29605
Trish Ct 29611
Tristan Ridge Ct 29611
Tropicana Ct 29609
Trotter Aly & St 29605
Tryon Ave 29609
Tuckahoe Ct 29607
Tucker Ln & Rd 29615
Tucson Dr 29617
E & W Tugaloo Ct 29609
Tulane Ave 29617
Tulip St 29609
Tupelo Ct 29609
Turben Ct 29607
Turin Ct 29607
Turner Cir 29609
Turningstone Ct 29611
Turpin Dr 29611
Turtle Creek Dr 29615
Turtle Dove Ct 29617
Tuskegee Ave 29607
Tussock Rd 29615
Twelve Oaks Ter 29615
Twickenham Dr 29615
Twin Creek Cv 29615
Twin Lake Rd 29609
Twin Oaks Ct 29615
Twin Springs Dr 29605
Twinbrook Dr 29607
Two Notch Rd 29605
Two Oak Ln 29609
Tyler St 29605
Tyne Ct 29607
Understone Dr 29609
Underwood Ave 29607
Uneeda Ct & Dr 29605
Union Church Rd 29605
United Way 29607
University Rdg & St 29601
Upper Meadow Way 29609
Urban St 29605
Utica St 29607
Vale St 29617
Valentine St 29601
Valerie Dr 29615
Valley Ln & St 29611
Valley Oak Dr 29617
Valley View Ln 29605
N & S Vance St 29611
Vanderbilt Cir 29609
Vannoy St 29601
Vantinti Rd 29615
Vantross Ln 29607
Vardry Ct 29611
Vardry St 29601
Varsity Row 29609
Vaughn Rd 29615
Vedado Ln 29611
Velma Rd 29609
Venning Ct 29609
S Venture Dr 29615
Venus Ct 29609
Verdae Blvd 29607
Verdin Rd 29607
Verdun Ave 29609
Vermont St 29611
Verner Dr 29617
Verner Creek Ct 29609
Verner Springs Rd 29609
Vero St 29607
Veronese Dr 29609
Vesta Dr 29611
Via Delrosa Dr 29607
Vicchio Dr 29609
Vicki Cir 29615
Vickilyn Ct 29611
Vicksburg Dr 29617
Victor St 29609
Victory Ave 29601
View Point Dr 29609
Viewmont Dr 29609
Villa Rd 29615
Villaggio Dr 29609
Vine St 29609
Vine Hill Rd 29607
Vineyard Ln 29615
Vinson Dr 29617
Vintage Ave 29607
Vintage Hill Dr 29609
Viola St 29601
Violet Ct 29615
Virginia Ave
 2-8 29611
 10-299 29611
 400-499 29607
Virnelle St 29607
Vista Dr 29617
Vocational Dr 29605
Von Hollen Dr 29617
Waccamaw Ave & Cir 29605
Waco St 29611
Waddell Rd 29609
Wade Hampton Blvd
 1-1899 29609
 1900-2799 29615
Wahoo Ln 29611
Waite St 29607
Wakefield Ct 29615
Wakefield Ln 29609
Wakefield St 29601
Wakewood Way 29609
Walcott St 29609
Walden Creek Way 29615
Walker Ct 29615
Walking Ct 29607
Wallace St 29605
Wallingford Rd 29609
Walnut Dr 29601
Walnut St 29607
Walnut Creek Way 29611
Walnut Hall Ln 29615
Wanda Ln 29605
War Admiral Way 29617
Wardlaw St 29601
Wardview Ave 29617
Ware St 29601
Warner St 29605
Warren Ct 29607
N & S Warwick Rd 29617
N Washington Ave 29611
S Washington Ave 29611
Washington Ct 29607
Washington Park 29601
E Washington St
 1-299 29601
 300-1298 29601
 300-300 29603
 301-1299 29601
 1300-1799 29607
W Washington St
 1-599 29601
 600-602 29602
 600-600 29602
 600-600 29603
 601-1899 29601
 602-1898 29601
Watch Hill Ct 29607
Water St 29609
Waterbrook Dr 29607
Waters Ave 29605
Waters Edge Dr 29609
Waterway Ct 29615
Watkins Rd 29617
Watkins Bridge Rd 29617
Watson Ave 29601
Watson Dr 29611
Watson Aviation Rd 29607
Watts Ave & Ct 29601
Waverly Ct 29605
Waverly Dr 29611
Waxhaw Way 29611
Wayline Ct 29605
Wayne St 29609
Weatherby Ct & Dr 29615
Webb Rd 29607
Webb St 29605
Webster Rd 29607
Webster St 29601
Wedgewater Ct 29609
Wedgewood Dr 29609
Welborn St 29601
Welch St 29605
E & S Welcome Ave, Rd & St 29611
Welcome Avenue Ext 29611
Welcome View Dr 29611
Weldon St 29609
Wellesley Way 29615
Welling Cir 29607
Wellington Ave 29609
Welsh Cobb Ct 29615
Welter Ln 29609
Welwyn Ct 29615
Wembley Rd 29607

Street	ZIP
Wendover Dr	29615
Wentworth St	29605
Wenwood Cir, Ct & Rd	29607
Werts St	29605
Wesc Dr	29617
West Ave, Blvd & St	29611
Westbrook Dr & Ln	29605
Westchester Rd	29615
Westcliffe Way	29611
Westcreek Way	29607
Westfield St	29601
Westminster Dr	29605
Weston Brook Way	29607
Westover Pl	29615
Westview Ave	29609
Wetherill Rd	29615
Weybridge Ct	29615
Whaley Dr	29609
Whaling Way	29615
Wheat Cressing Ct	29607
Wheatberry Ct	29611
Wheatley Pl	29607
Wheatridge Dr	29617
Wheatstone Ct	29617
Whiller Dr	29605
Whirlaway Ct	29615
Whispering Hollow Rd	29615
Whitbread Ct	29615
White Cir	29611
White Dogwood Dr	29611
White Empress Dr	29617
White Hawk Ct	29607
White Horse Ct	29605
White Horse Rd	
300-2499	29605
2500-7499	29611
7500-7500	29610
7501-7899	29611
7502-7898	29611
7900-8999	29617
White Horse Road Ext	29605
White Oak Dr	29607
White Oak Rd	29609
White Pine Ln	29617
White Rapids Way	29617
White Tail Ct	29607
Whitehall St	29609
Whitehaven Dr	29611
Whitehouse Ct	29617
Whitethorn Ln	29607
Whitin St	29611
Whitlee Ct	29607
Whitmire Dr	29605
Whitmire St	29611
Whitner St	29601
Whitsett St	29601
Whitten St	29605
Whittington Ct & Dr	29615
Whixley Ln	29607
Whyteman Way	29617
Wieuca Ct	29609
Wilbanks St	29611
E & W Wilburn Ave	29611
Wilcun Dr	29617
Wild Dogwood Way	29605
Wild Indigo Cir	29607
Wild Thorn Ln	29615
Wild Turkey Way	29617
Wildaire Ln	29615
Wilderness Ln	29607
Wildflower Ct	29615
Wildrose Ln	29617
Wildwood Rd	29615
Wilkins St	29605
Willard St	
1-196	29601
197-399	29611
Willenhall Ln	29611
William Rhodes Rd	29611
Williams Dr	29605
Williams St	29601
Williamsburg Dr	29605
Willie Mae Dr	29607
Willis Ave	29611
Willow Dr	29609
Willow Springs Dr	29607
Willowleaf Ct	29617
Wilma Dr	29617
Wilmington Rd	29615
Wilmont Ln	29605
Wilshire Dr	29609
Wilson St	29611
Wilton St	
1-199	29601
200-699	29609
Wimborne Dr	29615
Windbrooke Cir	29615
Windcrest Dr	29615
Windemere Dr	29615
Windfaire Pass Ct	29609
Windfield Rd	29607
Winding Brook Ct	29617
Windjammer Ln	29617
Windmill Way	29615
Windmont Dr	29607
Windrush Ln	29607
Windsong Dr	29615
Windsor Dr	29609
Windstone Ct & Dr	29615
Windthistle Dr	29615
Windy Ct	29615
Windy Bluff Dr	29617
Wineberry Way	29615
N & S Wingate Rd	29605
Winn St	29601
Winners Ct	29617
Winsford Dr	29609
Winterberry Ct	29607
Winthrop Ave	29607
Winyah St	29605
Wiscasset Way	29615
Wiuka Ave	29607
Wolf Creek Ct	29609
Wollaston Dr	29617
Wolseley Rd	29615
Wonderwood Dr	29615
Wood St	29611
Wood Pointe Dr	29615
Woodall Rd	29617
Woodberry Dr	29615
Woodberry Way	29609
Woodbine Rd	29609
Woodbriar Ct	29617
Woodbridge Ln	29607
Woodcove Ct	29615
Woodcrest Cir	29615
Woodfern Cir & Ct	29615
Woodfin Ave	29605
N & S Woodgreen Way	29615
Woodhaven Dr	29609
Woodington Dr	29607
Woodland Dr	29617
Woodland Ln	29615
Woodland Way	
2-98	29601
100-199	29601
200-500	29607
502-522	29607
Woodland Way Cir	29601
Woodlark St	29607
Woodlawn Ave	29611
Woodmede Way	29605
Woodmont Cir & Ln	29605
Woodridge Cir	29607
Woodridge Dr	29611
Woodrow Ave	29605
Woodrow St	29611
Woodruff Rd	29607
Woodruff Industrial Ln	29607
Woodruff Oaks Ln	29607
Woods Crossing Rd	29607
Woods Edge Ct	29615
Woods Lake Rd	29607
Woodsford Dr	29615
Woodside Ave	29611
Woodside Cir	29609
Woodside Xing	29607
Woodsmoke Ct	29607
Woodstream Ct	29609
Woodtrace Cir	29615
Woodvale Ave	29605
Woodvalley Ct	29617
Woodville Ave	29607
Woodward St	29611
Workman Dr	29607
Worley Rd	29609
Wormy Ln	29605
Worth St	29617
Wrangler Ct	29605
Wren Dr	29609
Wren Way	29605
Wrenn St	29609
Wright Ln	29611
Wrigley St	29605
Wyndham Ct	29615
Wynn Cir	29617
Yacht Club Dr	29609
Yakutata Dr	29605
Yale St	29611
Yancey Dr	29615
Yarmouth Ct	29611
Yearling Rd	29617
Yellowstone Dr	29617
Yeoman St	29605
N Ymca St	29611
Yonah Ct	29609
York Cir	29605
York Dr	29611
Yorkshire Ct & Dr	29615
Yorkswell Ln	29607
Young Ct	29615
Young St	
1-99	29601
100-299	29609
Yown Rd	29611
Yukon Dr	29605
Zara St	29607
Zarline St	29611
Zelma Dr	29617
Zet Ct	29611
Zora Dr	29607

NUMBERED STREETS

Street	ZIP
1st Ave	
1-299	29605
1100-1199	29611
1200-1299	29609
1st St	29611
2nd Ave	29609
800-899	29605
900-999	29611
2nd St	29611
3rd Ave	
1-99	29611
100-199	29605
200-299	29609
3rd St	
2-298	29611
3-3	29605
5-299	29611
300-399	29605
4th Ave	
1-99	29611
400-499	29605
500-599	29609
4th St	
1-199	29611
600-699	29605
4th Street Ext	29611
5th Ave	
1-99	29609
1400-1499	29611
5th St	
1-99	29605
1500-1599	29611
E 5th St	29611
W 5th St	29611
6th Ave	
1-99	29609
1600-1699	29605
6th St	
1-599	29611
700-999	29605
N 6th St	29611
S 6th St	29611
W 6th St	29611
7th Ave	29609
7th St	
1-99	29611
1700-1799	29605
E 7th St	29611
E & W 8th Ave & St	29611
9th St	29611
9th Street Ext	29611
10th St	29611
11th St	29611
20th St	29611
21st St	29611
23rd St	29611

GREENWOOD SC

General Delivery	29646

POST OFFICE BOXES MAIN OFFICE STATIONS AND BRANCHES

Box No.s	ZIP
A - C	29648
1 - 1820	29648
2001 - 2408	29646
3001 - 5046	29648
5031 - 5046	29649
5306 - 5307	29648
49001 - 52999	29649

NAMED STREETS

Street	ZIP
Abbey Ct, Dr & Ln	29649
Abbington Ln	29649
Abbott Ave	29646
Abercrombie Pt	29649
Abney St	29646
Academy Ave	29646
Acorn Ct & Ln	29646
Acres Rd N	29649
Adams Dr & Run	29646
Addison Ave	29649
Adrian Ave	29649
Agnew Rd	29649
Airport Rd	29649
Airport Industrial Park	29649
Alabama Ave	29646
Alex Way	29649
E & W Alexander Ave & Rd	29646
Allen Ave & St	29649
Allendale St	29646
Alliance St	29646
Allison Dr	29649
Alma St	29649
Alpine Way	29649
Althea St	29646
Ames St N & S	29646
Amherst Dr	29649
Amity Ct	29646
Ammonwood Dr	29649
Anagnost Ct	29649
Anchor Rd	29646
Anderson Cir	29649
Anderson Dr	29646
Anderson St	29646
Andrews Ave	29646
Anita Way	29646
Annette Way	29646
Ansley Ct	29649
Apache Dr	29646
Appaloosa Ln	29646
Appian Way	29649
Applegate Ct	29646
Arabian Rd	29646
Arbor Ct	29649
Arlington Ln	29646
Arnold Ct	29646
Arroyo Ct	29646
Arthurs Pt	29649
Ashcroft Dr	29646
Ashford Pl	29646
Ashley Ln	29649
Ashton Ct	29649
Ashwood St	29646
Attaway Way	29649
Auburn Ln	29649
Augusta Cir	29646
Auld Rd N & S	29649
Autry Dr	29646
Autumn Ct	29646
Autumn Trce	29649
Avid Rd	29649
Avondale Rd	29649
Azalea Dr	29646
Backwater Rd	29649
Bailey Cir	29646
Bailey St	29649
Baldwin Ave	29649
Balsam Ln	29646
Bamboo Ct	29649
Baptist Ave & Ct	29646
Barksdale St	29649
Barkwood Ct	29646
Barkwood Dr	29649
Barkwood Ln	29646
Barley Dr	29649
Barrett Dr	29649
Barrington Ct	29649
Bass St	29649
Battery Dr	29646
Bay Ct	29646
Beacon St	29649
Beadle Ave	29646
Bearcat Blvd	29649
Beattie Dr	29649
Beaudrot Rd	29649
Beaufort St	29646
Beaver Creek Ln	29646
Beaverdam Creek Rd	29646
Bedford Rd	29649
Beech Ct	29649
Beech Lake Rd	29649
Beech Run Dr	29649
Beechwood Cir	29646
Belcourt Dr	29649
Bell Cir	29646
Bellcrest Dr	29649
Belle Meade Rd	29649
Belle Oaks Ct & Dr	29646
Belle Pines Ct & Dr	29646
Benjamin St	29646
Benson St	29649
Bent Rd	29649
Bent Creek Rd	29649
Bermuda Dr	29649
Bethune St N & S	29646
Beulah Church Rd	29646
Bevington Ct	29649
Billee St	29649
Biltmore St	29649
Bintage Rd	29649
Birch Trl	29649
Birchtree Dr	29649
Biscayne Dr	29649
Blackberry Patch Rd	29646
Blackwell Rd	29649
Blake St	29649
Blakedale Cir	29649
Blossom Ln	29649
Blue Heron Ct	29646
Bluff Rd	29649
Blyth Ave	29649
Blyth Rd	29649
Boardwalk	29649
Bolt Ave	29646
Bolton St	29649
Bonanza Dr	29649
Bond Ave	29649
Bonham Ct	29649
Booker St	29646
Boreitta Dr	29649
Boston Terrier Rd	29646
Botany Ct	29649
Bowie St	29646
Bowles Ave	29649
Brannon St	29646
Brazington Ct	29649
Bream St	29649
Breazeale Rd	29646
Breezewood Rd	29646
Brentwood Dr	29646
Brewer Ave	29646
Briarwood Rd	29646
Brice St	29649
Bridge Point Rd	29649
Bridle Ct	29646
Briggs Ave	29649
Brighton Ct	29646
Brissie Ave	29646
Broadway Ave	29646
Broken Ridge Ct & Dr	29646
Brooke Ct	29649
Brookfield Dr	29646
Brookhaven Dr	29646
Brooklane Dr	29649
Brooks St	29646
Brooks Stuart Dr	29649
Brookside Dr	29646
Brookwood Ln	29646
Brown Ave	29646
Brown Town Rd	29646
Bryan Dorn Rd	29646
Bryant Dr	29646
Bryte St	29649
Bucklevel Rd	29649
Buggy Ct	29646
Bumble Bee Ln	29649
Bunche Ave	29646
Burgess Dr	29646
Burnett Rd	29646
Burnham Ct	29649
Butler St	29646
Butler Place Dr	29649
Buxton Ct	29646
Bypass 225 S	29646
Bypass 25 NE	
100-899	29646
900-1199	29649
Bypass 25 SE	29646
Bypass 72 NE & NW	29649
Byrd St W	29646
Cabin Rd	29646
Cabot Ct E & W	29649
Cadillac Ct	29646
Calhoun Ave	29649
Calhoun Rd	29649
Calhoun Rd E	29646
Callison Dr & Hwy	29646
Cambridge Ave E	29646
Cambridge Ave W	
100-599	29646
600-1199	29649
Camden St	29646
Camelia Dr	29646
Campbell St	29646
Cane Ct	29649
Cannon Rd	29646
Canyon Dr	29646
Cape Pl	29649
Capital St	29649
Capsugel Ct	29646
Captains Choice	29649
Cardinal Rd	29646
Carlton St	29649
Carnoustie Ct	29646
Carolina Ave & St	29646
Carp St	29649
Carriage Ct	29646
Carver St	29646
Cascade Ct	29649
Cassell Cir	29649
Caymen Ct	29649
Cedar Ct & Dr	29649
Cedar Lake Ct	29649
Cemetery Rd	29646
Centepede Ct	29646
Center Rd	29646
Center St	29649
Central Ave	29646
Cessna Ave	29649
Chace Ave	29646
Chadford Ct	29649
Champion Grn	29649
Channing Dr	29646
Chapman Ct	29646
Chappel St	29646
Charles Rd & St	29649
Charleston Way N & S	29649
Chase Ln	29649
Chatham Ct & Dr	29649
Chauncy Ct	29649
Cheekwood Ct & Rd	29649
Chelsea Sq	29649
Cherokee Dr	29646
Cherry Ct	29646
Chesterfield Ct	29646
Chestnut Ct	29646
Chestnut Rdg	29649
Chinquapin Rd	29646
Chipley Ave & Rd	29646
Chipping Ct	29649
Christian Rd	29649
Church Ave	29646
Cindy Ln	29646
Circle Dr	29646
Circular Ave	29646
Clairmont Dr	29649
Clark Ave	29649
Clegg Ct	29649
Clem Rd	29649
Cleveland Ct	29649
Clifton St	29649
Club Dr	29646
Cobb Rd	29649
Cobblestone Ln	29649
Coker Rd	29649
Cokesbury Rd	29649
Cokesbury St	
101-199	29646
200-1099	29646
Cole St	29646
Coleman Dr & St	29649
Colonial Dr	29649
Colony Ct	29649
Colson St	29649
Columbia Ave	29646
Commerce Cir	29646
Commons Dr	29649
Community Ct	29649
Connector Way	29649
Connors Dr	29646
Cooper Rd & St	29646
Coosaw Run	29649
Corley St	29646
Cornelia Cir	29646
Cornerstone Ct & Dr	29649
Corrie Ct	29646
Cothran Ave & Dr	29649
Cottonwood St	29646
Country Acres Rd	29646
Country Club Dr	29646
Country Village Ct	29649
Countryside Dr	29646
County Farm Rd	29646
Court Ave E & W	29646
Cove Rd	29646
Coventry Dr	29649
Covey Ct	29649
Cowhead Creek Rd	29646
Crabapple Way	29649
Crawford Ave	29649
N Creek Blvd	29649
Creek Rd E	29646
Creek Rd W	29646
Creekside Ct	29649
Crescent Dr	29646
Crescent Rd	29649
Crestmont Dr	29649
Crestview Dr	29646
Creswell Ave E & W	29646
Crews St	29649
Cricket Ridge Ct	29646
Crooked Rd	29646
Crosby Rd	29646
Cross St	29646
Crosscreek Connector	29649

Cude Rd 29646
Culbertson Ct 29649
Culbertson Dr 29646
Cullum St 29649
Curl Ct & Dr 29649
Curl Creek Rd 29649
Curtail Ln 29646
Curtis Ave 29646
Cypress Ave 29646
Cypress Holw 29649
Dallas Ct 29646
Daniel Ct 29649
Danny Dr 29649
Dargan Ave 29646
Darinchi Rd 29646
Darlene Dr 29646
Darlington St 29646
Davenport Ave E & W 29649
Davis Ave & St 29646
Deadfall Rd E & W 29649
Deal Rd 29646
Deans Aly 29646
Debbie B Ct 29646
Decker Dr 29646
Deer Creek Rd 29649
Deer Run Ln 29646
Deerwood Ln 29646
Dendenti Rd 29649
Devon Ct & Park 29649
Devore Rd 29649
Dianer Ct 29649
Dinghy 29649
Divot Trl 29649
Dixieland Ave 29646
Dogwood Dr 29646
Donegal Dr 29646
Dorchester St 29646
Dorsey Ct 29649
Dotson St 29649
Douglas Ct 29646
Dove Rd 29649
Dowling Cir 29646
Draper Ave 29646
Drew Ave 29646
Driftwood Dr 29649
Dry Branch Ct 29649
Dublin Rd 29646
Duff St 29646
Dukes Ave 29646
Dunbar Dr 29649
Duncan Ave 29646
Dupont Cir 29649
Durst Ave & Ln 29649
Dustin Way 29649
Dusty Rd 29646
Duvall Ln 29646
Eagle Rd 29646
Eagle Trce 29649
Earl Ct 29649
East Ave 29646
Eastman St 29649
Edgefield St 29646
Edinborough Cir 29649
Edisto St 29646
Edward Ave 29649
Effie Dr 29649
Effie Drive Ext 29649
Egret Ln 29649
Elementary Ave 29646
Elizabeth Ave 29646
Elk Ln 29649
Ellenberg Ave 29646
Elliott St 29649
Ellis Dr 29646
Ellison Ave 29649
Elm Ct 29646
Emerald Rd 29646
Emerald Farm Rd 29646
Emili Ln 29646
Empire Cir 29646
English Ct 29649
Enterprise Ct 29649
Epting Ave 29646
Erica Pl 29649
Erin Way 29649
Ernies End 29649

Essex Ct 29649
Ethel St 29646
Evans St 29646
Evans Pond Rd 29649
Eve St 29646
Evergreen Dr 29649
Everleen Ct 29649
Explorer Ln 29649
Fair Oaks Ln 29646
Fairforest Dr 29646
Fairview St 29649
Fairway Ct 29649
Fairway Lakes Rd 29649
Faith Home Rd 29649
Faulkner St 29646
Fawn Ln 29646
Fawn Brook Dr 29646
Feather Run Trl 29646
Feed Mill Rd 29646
Felder St 29649
Fenwick Ct 29649
Ferncliff Dr 29649
Ferry Cove Rd 29649
Fincannon Dr 29649
Findlay Dr 29646
Firethorn Rd 29649
Fisher St 29646
Fishpond Cir & Ct 29649
Florence St 29646
Florida Ave 29646
Flowers Rd 29649
Folly Bend Dr 29649
Folly Farm Rd 29649
Forest Dr 29646
Forest Dr E 29646
Forest Dr W 29646
Forest Ln 29649
Forest Park Dr 29649
Forsythia Ln 29646
Fortune St 29646
Foster Ave 29646
Foundry Rd 29646
Foxcroft Dr 29646
Foxmeadow Ct 29649
Foxtrail Rd 29649
Frances St 29646
Franklin Dr & St 29646
Freeway Rd 29649
Friendfield Ln 29649
Fuller St 29649
Fulton St 29649
Furman St 29649
Gage St 29646
Galilee Rd 29646
Gambrell St 29649
Gantt Rd 29649
Garner Hts 29649
Garrett Dr 29649
Gary Ct 29649
Gatewood Dr 29646
Gatlin St 29649
Genesis Cir 29646
Gentry Run 29649
Georgia Ave 29646
Gilbert St 29646
Giles Ave 29646
Gilliam Ave & Ct 29646
Ginn St 29649
Glen Eagle Ct 29646
Glencrest Ct 29646
Glendale Ave 29649
Glenridge Cir 29646
Glenwood St 29649
Goode Ave 29646
Grace St & Ter 29649
Gracemont Dr 29646
Graham Dr 29649
Grand Prix Ct 29646
Grange Rd 29646
Granite Ct 29649
Grannys Ln 29646
Grant St 29649
Graves St 29646
Gray St 29646
Graydon Ave 29649
Green Oaks Rd 29649

Greenbriar Dr & Rd 29649
Greene St 29646
Greenside Dr 29649
Greenway Dr 29649
Greenwood St 29646
Gregor Mendel Cir 29646
Grendel Ave E & W 29649
Grenola Ave 29646
Grier St 29646
Griffin Ave & Pl 29646
Grimes St 29646
Grove St 29646
Gulf St 29646
Gum Ave 29646
Hackett Ave 29646
Hagood Rd 29649
Hailey Ct 29649
Halcyon Ct 29649
Hall Ave 29646
Haltiwanger Rd 29649
Hammond Rd 29649
Hampton Ave 29646
Hampton Rd 29649
Harborside Dr 29649
Hardwood Loop 29646
Harless St 29646
Harper Ln & St 29649
Harris Rd 29649
Harrison Aly 29646
Harvest Ln 29649
Harvey Ave 29646
Hatchers Pass 29646
Hawkins Ave 29646
Hawthorne Ct 29646
Haze St 29649
Hazelwood Ct 29649
Headwater Dr 29649
Heather Ln 29649
Heathwood Dr 29649
Heddy Rd 29646
Helix Rd 29649
Hemlock Ct 29649
Henderson Ave & St 29646
Henrietta Ave E & W 29649
Herbert Ct 29649
Herin Dr 29649
Heritage West Ct 29649
Hickory Ln 29646
Hidden Lake Ct 29646
High St 29649
Highland Dr 29649
Highland Forest Dr 29646
Highland Park Dr 29649
Highside St 29646
Highway 178 S 29646
Highway 221 S 29646
Highway 246 N 29649
Highway 246 S
100-1299 29649
Highway 246 S
1300-2399 29646
Highway 25 S 29646
Highway 72 W 29649
Highway 72 221 E 29649
N Hill Rd 29646
Hill And Dale Dr 29646
Hillcrest Dr 29646
Hillcrest Farm Rd 29649
Hilley St 29649
Hillside Dr 29649
Hillside Rd 29646
Hilltop Ave 29649
Hillyard St 29646
Hinton Ct 29649
Hitching Post Rd 29646
Hitt St 29649
Hoffman Ct 29649
Holloway Ave 29646
Holly Ave 29649
Holman St 29649
Holmes Rd 29649
Holmes St 29649
Horizon Ct & Way 29649
Hospital St N & S 29646
Hospitality Blvd 29649
Huckleberry Pl 29649

Hughes Rd 29646
Hulsey Dr 29646
Hunt St 29649
Hunter Rd & St 29646
Hunters Creek Blvd 29649
Hunters Village Dr 29649
Hunting Rd 29646
Hutira Ln 29649
Hutson St 29649
Hyatt St 29649
Independence Way 29646
Indigo Way 29649
Industrial Dr 29646
Iroquois Dr 29646
Irvines Cir 29646
Isabella Ct 29649
Ivester Ct 29646
Ivy Ln 29649
Ivy Hall Ln 29649
Jackson Ave 29646
Jacob St 29649
James St 29646
Jamison St N 29646
Janet St 29646
Janeway 29649
Jasmine Ct 29646
Jay Bird Ln 29649
Jebosha Dr 29646
Jefferson St 29646
Jenkins Springs Rd 29646
Jennings Ave 29649
Jesup Ct 29649
Joanna Ln 29649
Joe Bernat Dr 29646
Joe Louis Blvd 29646
Joe Wells Rd 29649
Joel Ave 29649
Johns Rd 29649
Johnson St 29649
Jones St 29649
Jordan St 29649
Juniper Ct 29646
Karen Way 29649
Karlie Ct 29649
Kateway
1500-2399 29646
2400-2599 29649
Kathwood Dr 29649
Kathy Hill Rd 29646
Katie Ct 29649
Kayak Pt 29649
Kaye Dr 29649
Keisler Dr 29649
Kelley Rd 29649
Kelli Dr 29649
Kenilworth Dr 29649
Kennedy Ct 29646
Kensington Dr 29649
Kentucky Ave & Ct 29646
Kimberly Ln 29649
Kimbrook Dr 29649
King Cir 29646
Kings Ct 29646
Kings Grant 29649
Kingston Rd 29649
Kingswood Ct 29646
Kinkade Dr 29649
Kirksey Dr E & W 29646
Kitson St
100-199 29649
200-799 29646
Klugh St 29649
Knotty Pine Ct 29646
Kuchta Rd 29649
La Port Dr 29649
Lacy Ct 29649
Laguna Ln 29646
Lake St 29646
Lake Clubhouse Ln 29649
Lake Forest Rd 29649
Lake Pointe Cir 29649
Lakeport Dr 29649
Lakeshore Dr 29649
Lakeview Dr 29646
Lakeview Rd 29649
Lakewood Dr 29649

Lamar Ave 29646
Lancaster Rd 29649
Lander St 29649
Lands End 29649
Lanett St 29649
Langley Rd 29649
Lanham St 29649
Lanier Wood Rd 29649
Larkin Dr 29646
Larkspur Ln 29649
Larry Dr 29649
Laurel Ave E & W 29649
Laurel Ridge Pl &
Way 29649
Lauren Cir 29649
Laurens St 29646
Lawson St 29649
Lawton St 29649
Lazy O Ranch Rd 29649
Lebanon Church Rd 29646
Lee St 29646
Legend Ct 29649
Lelia Dr 29646
Lemon Tree Rd 29646
Leonard St 29649
Leslie Dr 29646
Lewis Trce 29649
Leyland Ct 29649
Ligon Rd 29649
Lilly Ln 29649
Limerick Rd 29649
Lincoln Ave 29646
Linda Ln 29649
Lindsey Ave 29646
Liner Dr & St 29646
Links Ln 29649
Lisa Dr 29646
Lites St 29649
Little St 29646
Live Oak Ct 29649
Loblolly Cir 29649
Locksley Dr 29649
Lodge Dr 29646
Logan Ct & Rd 29646
Lollis Rd 29649
Londonberry Ct 29649
Long Ave 29649
Longleaf Ct 29649
Longwood Ln 29649
Lorenzo Rd 29646
Lou Ellen Dr 29646
Louvenia Ave 29646
Lovely Ln 29646
Lowe Ave 29646
Lowell Ave 29646
Lucille Dr 29649
Lupo Dr 29649
Luton Pl N & S 29649
Lyman Ave 29646
Lynn St 29646
Mabrey Ct 29646
Macedonia Ave 29646
Madison St 29649
Magnolia Ave
100-203 29646
202-202 29648
204-498 29646
205-499 29646
Magnolia Dr 29646
Main St 29646
Mainsail Dr 29649
Major Dr 29646
Mallard Ct 29649
Manning Ct & Rd 29649
Maple Ct 29646
Maplewood Ct 29646
Marble Ct 29649
Margaret St 29646
Marietta Dr 29646
Marion Ave 29646
Marshall Cir, Rd & St 29646
Mason St 29646
Masters Ct & Dr 29649
Mathews Heights Rd 29646
Mathis Rd 29649
Mathis St N 29646

Mathis St S 29646
Mauldin Rd 29649
Maxwell Ave 29646
Maxwelton Dr 29646
Mayapple St 29649
Mays St 29646
Mcadams Rd 29646
Mccord Rd 29646
Mccormick Hwy 29646
Mcdowell St 29649
Mcferrin Rd 29646
Mcghee Ave & Ct 29649
Mckee Rd 29649
Mckellar Ct 29649
Mckellar Dr 29646
Mclees Ave 29646
Mcneill Ave 29649
Mcquay Ct 29646
Meadow St 29646
Meadowbrook Dr 29649
Meadowview Ln 29646
Meeks Aly 29646
Meeting St 29649
Melanie Ct 29649
Melody Ln 29649
Melrose Ter 29649
Memorial Ln 29646
Merriman Ave 29646
Merrywood Dr 29649
Metro Dr 29646
Middle St 29649
Milford Springs Rd 29649
Mill Ave 29646
Mill Rd N 29649
Mill Rd S 29646
Milling Ct 29649
Milton St 29649
Milwee Ave & Ct 29646
Mimis Mnr 29649
Mimosa Ct 29646
Mineral Ave & Ct 29646
Minor Dr 29649
Mistletoe Way 29649
Montague Ave 29649
Montague Avenue Ext 29649
Montclair Dr 29649
Montgomery Ave 29646
Monument St 29646
Moore St 29649
Morgan Ave 29646
Morningside Dr 29649
Morrow Rd 29646
Morse Ct 29646
Morton Rd 29646
Mosley Rd 29646
Moss Creek Dr & Ln 29646
Mount Moriah Rd 29646
Mountain Shore Dr 29649
Mulberry St 29646
Myrtle St 29646
Nautical Way 29649
Neel St 29646
Nelson St 29649
New St 29646
New Market Rd & St 29646
New York Ct 29646
Newcastle Rd 29649
Newport Dr 29649
Ninety Six Hwy 29646
Nix Ct 29646
Nixon Cir 29646
Norman Rd 29646
Norris Rd 29646
North St 29649
Northgate St 29649
Northhampton Ct 29649
Northlake Dr 29649
Northside Dr E & W 29649
Northwoods Rd 29649
Norwich Sq 29649
Norwood Ave 29646
Nottingham Ln 29649
Oak Ave 29646
Oak Creek Dr 29649
Oak Forest Dr 29646
Oak Ridge Dr 29649

Oakdale Dr 29649
Oakhaven Ct 29646
Oakhill St 29649
Oakland St 29646
Oaklane Dr 29646
Oakmonte Cir 29649
Oakview Ct 29649
Oakwood Dr 29649
Oakwood Rd 29646
Oakwood Farms Ct 29649
Oglesby Ave 29646
Ohio Ct 29646
Old Abbeville Hwy 29649
Old Brickyard Rd 29649
Old Greenwood Hwy &
Rd 29649
Old Highway 246 S 29646
Old Laurens Rd 29649
Old Mount Moriah Rd 29646
Old Ninety Six Hwy 29646
Old Oak Dr 29649
Old Sample St 29649
Old Wingert Rd 29649
Old Woodlawn Rd 29646
Olde Pucketts Ferry
Rd 29649
Omega St 29646
Orange Ave 29646
Orchard Dr 29649
Orchard Park Dr 29649
Oregon Ave 29646
Orlando Ct 29646
Osborne Ave 29649
Outrigger 29649
Ouzts Rd 29646
Overbrook Dr & Rd 29649
Overland Dr 29646
Overlook Dr 29649
Owens St 29646
Oxford Rd 29649
Oxnard Ct 29649
Packer Ave 29646
Paddock Ln 29649
Page Dr & Rd 29646
Pageland Ave 29646
Paige Pl 29649
Palmer Pl 29649
Palmetto Ct 29646
Pam Ave 29649
Pampas Dr 29649
Panacea Rd 29646
Panola Ave 29646
Par Pl 29649
Paradise Ct 29646
Park Aly, Ave & Ter 29646
Parker Ave 29649
Parkland Place Rd 29646
Parkview Pl 29646
Parkway 29646
Parkwood Ct & Rd 29646
Partridge Rd 29649
Pascal Dr 29649
Patrick Rd 29646
Patton St 29649
Peachtree St 29646
Pearl St 29649
Pebble Ln 29649
Pecan Dr 29646
Pelican Dr 29649
Pelzer St 29649
Pembroke Rd 29646
Pence Rd 29646
Peninsula Way 29649
Penn Ave 29646
Pennington Ln N & S 29649
Pepperhill Ln 29649
Perch St 29649
Percival Ave 29646
Perrin Ave 29646
Perry Dr 29646
Persimmon Ct 29649
Phillips Cir 29649
Phoenix Rd & St 29646
Piedmont Ave 29646
Pierce Ave 29649
Pin Oak Dr 29649

Pine Cir & Dr 29649
Pine Bark Ln 29649
Pine Forest Dr 29649
Pine Hill Dr 29646
Pine Tree Dr 29649
Pinecrest Dr 29649
Pinehurst Dr 29646
Pineneedle Ln 29649
Pineview Dr & Rd 29646
Pinion Dr 29649
Pinsonville Rd 29646
Piper St 29649
Pitts Cir 29649
Placid View Ct 29649
Plantation Dr 29649
Planters Ct 29649
Plowden Ave 29646
N & S Pond Ct 29649
Pope St 29649
Poplar Dr 29649
Poppy Ln 29649
Port Tack 29649
Portland Cir 29649
Portsmouth Rd 29649
Posey St 29646
Possum Hollow Rd 29646
Powers Ave 29646
Premier Dr 29646
Pressley St 29646
Prestwick Ct 29646
Price Dr 29646
Princess Ct 29646
Pristine Dr 29646
Promised Land St 29646
Prosperity Dr 29646
Puckett Ferry Rd 29649
Pucketts Cv 29649
Pucketts Pointe Rd 29649
Pullham Rd 29646
Pump House Rd 29649
Quail Run Ct 29646
Quarry Rd 29649
Quarter Creek Rd 29649
Queens Ct 29649
Quince St 29646
Radden Ct 29649
Raintree Ln 29649
Ranch Ct 29646
Ravenel Rd 29649
Ravine Ct 29646
Raye Rd 29649
Rebecca Dr 29646
Reds Rd 29649
Redwood St 29646
Reedy Cove Ct, Ln & Pl 29649
Reflections Dr 29646
Reynolds Ave 29649
Reynolds Park Dr 29646
Rhett Ct 29649
Rice Rd 29649
Richard St 29649
Richardson Dr 29649
Ridge Pt & Rd 29649
Ridgemont Dr 29649
Ridgeway Dr & St 29649
Ridgewood Cir 29649
Riley Ave & Rd 29646
River Birch Ct 29649
Rivers Run & St 29649
Roberts Dr 29649
Robinson Ave 29646
Rock Church Rd NW & SE 29649
Rock Creek Dr 29646
Rock House Rd 29646
Rock Knoll Dr 29649
Rockcreek Blvd 29649
Roman Cir 29649
Ron Mcnair St 29646
Ronnie Dr 29649
Rose Ave 29646
Roseland Dr 29649
Rosemont Dr 29646
Roswell Rd 29646
Royal Oak Dr 29649

Rumford Ct 29649
Runnymeade St 29649
Russell St 29646
Rutledge Rd 29649
Ryders Cup 29649
Rye Ct 29649
Sable Ln 29649
Saco Ave 29646
Saddle Hill Rd 29646
Saddlebrook Ln 29646
Sagewood Rd 29646
Saint Andrews Ln 29646
Saint Augustine Dr 29646
Saint Barts Ct 29649
Saint Kitts Ct 29649
Salak Rd 29646
Saluca Ct 29646
Sam St 29646
Sample Rd 29646
Sand Trap Ln 29649
Sanders Ct, Dr & St 29649
Sandshore Dr 29649
Sandy Ln 29649
Sanka St 29646
Sara Dr 29646
Sargent Rd 29649
Satcher Dr 29646
Savannah Ct 29646
Savayo Dr 29649
Sawgrass Pl 29649
Scenic Ct 29649
Scotch Cross Rd E & W 29646
Seaboard Ave 29646
Segers Dr 29649
Seminole Dr 29646
Settlers Dr 29646
Seymour Dr 29646
Shadowood Ln 29649
Shalott Ct 29649
Shamrock Dr 29649
Shannon St 29646
Shaun Rd 29649
Shearbrook Dr 29646
Sheffield Rd 29646
Sheldon Ave 29649
Sherard Rd 29646
Sherwood Dr 29646
Sherwood Ln 29649
Shoreline Dr 29649
Short St 29646
Shortleaf Ct 29649
Shrine Club Rd 29649
Sidney Dr 29646
Siloam Acres Dr 29646
Siloam Church Rd 29646
Simpkins Rd 29646
Sims Rd 29649
Singleton Ct & St 29646
Singletree Rd 29646
Sivell Rd 29646
Sleepy Hollow Rd 29646
Sloan Ave 29646
Smith St 29646
Smythe Ave 29649
Snyder Rd 29646
South St 29646
Southern Ave 29646
Sparrow Rd 29649
Spencer Ct 29646
Spinnaker Pt 29649
Spray Shed Rd 29646
Spring St 29646
Spring Lake Dr 29646
Spring Valley Rd 29649
Spring Woods Trl 29646
Springfield Church Rd 29649
Sproles Ave E & W 29646
Sprott St 29649
Spruce Ct 29649
Spyglass Dr 29649
Squires Ct 29646
Squirrel Tree Rd 29646
Stafford Dr 29649
Stanley Ave 29649
Starboard Tack 29649

Stellar Ct 29649
Stevens Ave 29646
Still Dr 29646
Still Creek Rd 29646
Stillwell Rd 29646
Stockman St 29646
Stoker Rd 29646
Stone Oak Ln 29646
Stonebrook Ct 29646
Stonehaven Dr 29649
Stoneridge Ct 29649
Stonewood Dr 29649
Stoney Point Rd 29649
Stratford Rd 29649
Stratton Ter 29649
Strong St 29646
Stroud Ct 29646
Subdivision St 29646
Suburban Dr 29646
Sullivan Ct & St 29646
Summerhill Dr 29649
Summitt Ct & St 29646
Sumpter Ct 29649
Sumter St 29646
Sunnyside Dr 29646
Sunrise Cir 29646
Sunset Dr 29646
Surrey Ct 29646
Sutton Ct 29646
Sweetwater Rd 29646
Swing About 29649
Sycamore Dr 29646
Sylvan Rd 29649
Tabor St 29646
Taggart Ave 29646
Tall Pines Trl 29646
Tally Ho Dr 29649
Tanglewood Dr 29646
Tanyard Ave 29646
Tarrant St 29646
Taylor St 29646
Tedards Store Rd 29646
Tennessee Ct 29646
Terminal Rd 29649
Terrace Way 29649
Thames Ct 29649
Thistle Ct 29646
Thomason Pt 29649
Thompson Dr 29646
Thornblade Dr 29649
Thornbrook Ct 29646
Thornhill Ct & Rd 29649
Tifton Dr E & W 29646
Timber Lane Dr 29646
Timberwood Rd 29646
Timmerman Rd 29646
Tin Cup Aly 29646
Tompkins St 29646
Towers Dr 29649
Towne St 29646
Trace Chain Rd 29646
Trafalgar Sq 29649
Trakas Ave 29649
Tranquil Rd 29646
Trestle Rd 29649
Troon Ct 29649
Trotters 8 29649
Trout St N & S 29646
Truett Ave 29646
Truman St 29646
Tryon Ct 29649
Tucker Rd 29649
Turnberry Ct 29646
Tuscany Ln 29649
Twin Ponds Ct 29649
Twisted Oak Ct & Dr 29646
N & S University St 29646
Utopia Acres Rd 29646
Valley Rd 29646
Valley Brook Rd 29646
Vanguard Rd 29646
Vaughn St 29646
Venture Ct 29649
Verdae Ct 29649
Victory Rd 29646
Village Rd 29649

Vine St 29646
Vinecrest Ct 29649
Vintage Ct 29646
Violet Ct 29649
Virginia Ave 29646
Vista Dr 29646
Wade Ave 29646
Wagon Tree Ln 29646
Walker Ave 29649
Waller Ave 29649
Walnut St 29646
Ware St 29646
Warren Rd 29646
Washington Ave 29646
Water Plant Rd 29649
Waters Edge Rd 29649
Watford Ave 29649
Watson St 29646
Wayhill Dr 29649
We Smith Rd 29649
Webb St 29649
Wedgewood Ct 29649
Weimer Cir 29646
Welborn Ln 29646
Weldon Ave 29646
Wellington Dr 29649
Wells Ave & Rd 29646
Wendover Rd 29649
Wenmount Ct 29646
Wentworth Dr 29649
Westbrook Dr 29649
Westgate Dr 29646
Westpointe Dr 29646
Westview St 29646
Wexford Pl 29649
Whatley Dr 29649
Wheat Dr 29649
Wheatfield Dr 29649
Whispering Pines Ln 29646
White Rd 29646
White Oak Ave 29646
White Oak Ln
100-199 29646
700-799 29649
Whitehall Rd 29646
Wideman Dr 29646
Wilbanks Cir 29649
Wilbert St 29646
Wiley Ct & Rd 29649
Willard Rd 29649
Williams Ave 29649
Willowbrook Rd 29649
Willowdale Ct 29646
Willson St 29646
Wilton St 29649
Wimbledon Ct 29646
Wincey Rd 29646
Winchester Ct 29646
Wind Valley Rd 29649
Windfield Ct 29649
Winding Creek Ct & Dr 29649
Windjammer 29649
Windmill Cir 29649
Windsor Oaks Ct 29646
Windtree Ct & Rd 29649
Wingert Rd 29649
Winston Ct W 29649
Winter Way 29649
Winter Ridge Ct 29649
Wisewood Cir 29646
Wisteria Ct 29649
Woodbine Ct 29649
Woodbury Dr 29646
Woodcreek Dr 29649
Woodcrest Ct & St 29646
Woodfields St 29646
Woodhaven Ct 29649
Woodland Dr 29646
Woodland St 29649
Woodland Way 29646
Woodlawn Park 29649
Woodlawn Rd
100-1599 29646
1600-2499 29649
Woodlawn St 29649

Woodlock Ln 29646
Woodridge Rd 29646
Woodrow Ave 29646
Woods Ter 29646
Woodson Ct 29646
Wright Ave 29646
Wyatt Ct 29649
Yorke Dr 29649
Yosemite Dr 29649
Young St 29646
Yvonne Ave 29646
Zion St 29646
Zoysia Ct 29649

NUMBERED STREETS

All Street Addresses 29646

GREER SC

General Delivery 29650

POST OFFICE BOXES MAIN OFFICE STATIONS AND BRANCHES

Box No.s
All PO Boxes 29652

NAMED STREETS

Aaron Tippin Dr 29650
Abigail Ln 29651
Abington Hall Ct 29650
Able St 29650
Abner Creek Rd 29651
Abners Run Dr 29651
Abners Trail Rd 29651
Acorn Dr 29651
Adara Ct 29651
Admiral Ln 29650
Ager Ct 29650
Aimee Len Dr 29651
Air Park Dr 29651
E Airport Rd 29651
Alan Kent Ln 29651
Albert St 29651
Alderberry Dr 29651
Aldgate Way 29650
Alexander Rd 29650
Allenwood Ln 29650
Amanda Dr 29651
Amandajo St 29651
Amarillo Trl 29651
Amber Crest Ct 29651
Amber Oaks Dr 29651
Ambergate Ct 29650
Ambrose Trl 29650
American Legion Rd 29651
Amethyst Dr 29650
Amy Gray St 29651
Andella Dr 29651
Anderson St 29650
Anderson Mill Rd 29651
Anderson Ridge Rd 29651
Andon Ln 29651
Anita St 29651
Annabelle Ct 29650
Annandale Ave & Ct 29651
Annenberg Ln 29650
Ansel School Rd 29651
Ansley Ct 29650
N & S Antigo Ct 29650
Antigua Way 29650
Apalache St 29651
Apalache Duncan Rd 29651
Apollo Ave 29651
Appling Ct 29651
Arbolado Way 29651
Arborlea Ct 29651
Arch Dr 29651
Argo Dr 29651

Arkell Dr 29651
E Arlington Ave 29651
W Arlington Ave 29650
Arlington Rd 29651
Armstrong Ct 29651
Ascot Dr 29651
Ascot Ridge Ln 29650
Ashby Cross Ct 29651
Ashlan Woods Ct 29651
Ashland Dr 29651
Ashler Dr 29650
Ashley Commons Ct 29651
Ashmore Rd 29650
Ashmore St 29651
Ashworth Ln 29650
Aspen Ct & Dr 29651
Aster Dr 29651
Atherton Ct & Way 29650
Austin Ln & St 29651
Austin Woods Ct 29651
Autry Dr 29651
Autumn Dr 29651
Autumn Rd 29650
Autumn Hill Rd 29651
Avalon Chase Cir 29650
Avens Hill Dr 29651
Aviation Pkwy 29651
Avis Ct 29651
Azure Ln 29651
B St 29651
Babb Rd 29651
Babe Wood Rd 29651
Bailess Ct 29650
Bailey Rd 29651
Baileyview St 29651
Bainbridge Ct 29651
Ballenger Ave 29650
Ballenger Rd 29651
Ballyhoo Ct 29651
Banister Ct 29650
Barbare Ave 29650
Barberry Ln 29651
Barley Mill Dr 29651
Barnett Rd & St 29651
Barnstable Ct 29650
Baronne Ct 29650
Barrington Cir 29651
Barrington Park Dr 29650
Barry Ct 29651
Barry Dr 29650
Bascom Ct 29650
Batesville Ct 29650
Batesville Rd 29651
S Batesville Rd 29650
Bateswood Ct & Dr 29651
Baucom Park Dr 29650
Bayberry Rd 29650
Bayberry Ridge Ct 29651
Bayswater Ln 29651
Beacham Rd 29651
E Bearden St 29651
W Bearden St 29650
Beauregard Ct 29651
Beaver Track Dr 29651
Becky Don Dr 29651
Becky Gibson Rd 29651
Beech Cliff Ln 29651
Beech Springs Rd 29651
Beechwood Dr 29651
Beeco Rd 29650
Belfast Ct 29650
Belfrey Dr 29650
Belk Ct 29651
Bell Heather Ln 29650
Bellagio Way 29651
Bellamy Close 29651
Bellows Falls Dr 29650
Belton Ave 29650
Belue Rd 29651
Bengal Ct 29651
Benjamin Ave 29651
Bennett St 29651
Bennett Center Dr 29650
S Bennetts Bridge Rd 29651
Bennetts Crossing Ct 29651
Bennington Rd & Way 29650

Bens Creek Rd 29651
Benson Rd 29650
Bent Creek Dr 29650
Bent Creek Run Dr 29651
Bent Hook Way 29651
Bent Oak Rd 29650
Bentley Way 29650
Beralers Rd 29651
Bernice Snow Rd 29651
Berry Ave 29651
Berry Rd 29650
Berry Mill Rd 29651
Berry Pond Rd 29651
Berry Shoals Rd 29651
Berry Tree Ct 29651
Berrywood Ct 29650
Bert Ct & Dr 29651
Bessie Ave & Ct 29651
Beth St 29651
N Beverly Ln 29650
S Beverly Ln 29650
Beverly Rd 29651
Biblebrook Dr 29651
Big Dipper 29651
Big Fox Ln 29650
Bill Dr 29651
Biltmore Ln 29650
Birch Tree Rd 29651
Birchleaf Ln 29650
Birchwood Ct 29651
Bird St 29651
Bishop Ave 29651
Blackwatch Way 29650
Blackwell Rd 29651
Blanding Ln 29650
Blanton Ln 29650
Bloomfield Ln 29650
Blue Gill Dr 29651
Blue Horizon Ct 29651
N & S Blue Ridge Cir, Dr & Way 29651
Blueberry Hl 29651
Bluebird Ln 29650
Bob Ledford Dr 29651
Bobby Ave 29651
Bobo St 29650
Boiling Springs Rd 29650
Boling Cir 29651
Bomar Rd 29651
Bookman Ct 29650
Boone Rd 29651
Botswains Ct 29650
Boulder Creek Way 29651
Bowers Cir 29650
Boxford Ct 29650
Boxleaf Ct 29650
Boxwood Ln 29650
Bradley St 29650
Bradstock Dr 29650
Bradwell Way 29650
Braelock Dr 29650
Bramer Rd 29651
Bramlett Rd & St 29651
Brandi Starr Ct 29651
Brannon Ave
100-199 29650
200-399 29651
Brannon Dr 29651
S Brannon Rd 29650
Brassington Pl 29651
Breeds Hill Way 29650
Breezewood Ct 29651
Breton Dr 29650
Briar Creek Rd 29650
Briar Ridge Way 29651
Briarberry Ct 29651
Briarcliff Way 29651
Briarpark Dr 29651
Bricewood Dr 29650
Bridgecreek Dr 29651
Bridgestone Ct 29651
Bridle Way 29650
Brigadoon Ct 29650
Brigantine Ln 29650
Brigham Creek Ct & Dr 29650

Street	ZIP
Bright Rd	29651
Brightfield Ln	29651
Brightmore Dr	29650
Broadus St	29651
Brockman Rd	29651
Brockman St	29650
Brockman Mcclimon Rd	29651
Brockway Ln	29651
Brookdale Dr	29651
Brookshire Rd	29651
Brookton Ct & Way	29651
Brookwood Dr	29651
Broomstraw Ct	29651
Brown Rd	29651
Brown St	29650
Brown Canyon Ct	29651
Brown Wood Rd	29651
Browning Dr	29650
Brunner Ct	29650
Brushy Creek Rd	29650
Brushy Hollow Ln	29650
Brushy Meadows Dr	29650
Brystolayne Ct	29651
Buckhorn Rd	29651
Buddy Ave	29651
Bullard Ct	29651
N Buncombe Rd	29651
S Buncombe Rd	
1-999	29650
1000-1599	29651
Buncombe St	29650
Bunker Hill Rd	29650
Burch Dr	29651
Burgess Ct	29651
Burgess Dr	29650
Burgess St	29650
Burgoyne Ct	29650
Burl Hollow Ln	29651
Burlington Ave	29650
Burlwood Ct & Dr	29651
Burnett Dr	29651
Burnett Duncan Rd	29651
Burns Rd	29651
Burnsview Dr	29651
Burton Rd	29651
Bushberry Way	29650
Business Pkwy	29651
Butternut Cir	29651
Byars St	29651
C St	
100-199	29650
200-299	29651
C And S Dr	29651
Caddell Dr	29650
Caedmon Ct	29650
Calcite Dr	29650
Calderwood Ct	29651
Caldwell St	29651
Caleb Dr	29651
Caliber Ridge Dr	29651
Calina Hts	29651
Calmwater Ct	29650
Calvary St	29650
Camp Rd	29651
Campbell Ave	29651
Campbell Lake Rd	29651
Campion Rd	29650
Camrose Dr	29651
Canebrake Dr	29650
Cannon Ave, Rd & St	29651
Cannongate Dr	29650
Canteen Ave	29650
Canton Ct	29651
Cape Ann Ave	29650
Caperton Way	29651
Captains Ct	29650
Capucine Ct	29651
Care Ln	29651
Carey Ave & Dr	29651
Carissa Ct	29650
Carlyle Pointe Dr	29650
Carmilla Dr	29651
Carole Dr	29651
Carolee Way	29651
Carolina Ave	29650
Carolyn Ct	29651
Carriage Dr	29651
Carriage Park Cir	29650
Cascade Dr	29651
Casey Lee Ln	29651
Cassette Ct	29650
Castellan Dr	29650
Castle Creek Dr	29651
Castlestone Dr	29650
Cathedral Vw	29650
Cayanne Ct	29651
Caz Ln	29651
Ccc Camp Rd	29651
Cedar Ln	29651
Cedar Grove Rd	29650
Cedar Rock Dr	29650
Cedar Wood Ln	29651
N & S Cedarbluff Ct	29650
E, N & W Celestial Dr	29651
Center Dr & St	29651
Century Pl	29651
Chad Dr	29651
Chanbury Ct	29650
Chandler Ct & Rd	29651
Chandler Creek Ln	29651
Chandler Crest Ct	29651
Chapel Rd	29651
Chartwell Dr	29650
E & W Chase Ct	29651
Chasie Ln	29651
Chatley Way	29651
Chatman St	29650
Chatsworth Rd	29651
Cheek Rd	29651
Chelsea Ln	29650
Cherry Ln	29651
Cherry Field Ct	29651
Cherrywood Trl	29650
Chesterfield St	29650
Chesterton Ct	29650
Chestnut Ave	29651
Chestnut Springs Ct	29651
Chestnut Woods Ct	29651
Chick Springs Rd	29650
Chilton Pl	29650
Chipping Ct	29650
Chosen Ct	29650
E Church St	29651
W Church St	29650
Churchfield Ct	29651
Churchill Ave	29651
Cierra Ln	29651
Circle Dr	29650
Circle Rd	29651
Circle Grove Ct	29650
Cirrus Ct	29650
Clare Bank Dr	29650
Clarity Ct	29650
Clark Ave	29651
Claude Collins Rd	29651
Claudia St	29651
Clay Ave	29650
Clay Thorn Ct	29651
Claybrooke Dr	29650
Claymore Ct	29650
Clayton St	29650
Clear Springs Ct	29651
Clearbrook Ct	29650
Clearridge Way	29651
Clearview Cir & Dr	29651
Clearview Drive Ext	29651
Clement Rd	29650
Cliffside Dr	29651
Cliffview Ct	29650
Cliffwood Ct & Ln	29650
Clifton Way	29650
Clines Ln	29651
Cloverglen Dr	29650
Coachman Ln	29651
Coal Pit Rd	29651
Cockrell Rd	29651
Cody Dr	29651
Coffield Dr	29650
Cogin Dr	29651
Cohen Ct	29651
Colby Ct	29650
Colchester Ct	29650
Coldbrook Dr	29651
Cole Creek Ct	29651
E Coleman Rd	29650
Coleman Grove Ct	29650
Collier Ln	29651
Collins Dr	29651
Colonel Storrs Ct	29650
Colonial Dr	29651
Commerce Dr	29650
Community Dr	29651
Companion Ct	29651
Comstock Ct	29650
Concourse Way	29650
Confederate Ln	29651
Connecticut Ave	29650
Conner Dr	29651
Constantine Way	29650
Conway Dr	29651
Cool Creek Dr & Ln	29651
Cooper Dr	29651
Copeland Rd	29651
Copper Ct	29651
Cork Dr	29650
Cornelson Dr	29651
Cosmic Ct	29651
Cosmos Ln	29651
Cottage Creek Cir	29650
Cotter Ln	29650
Cotton Rd	29651
Cotton Hill Ln	29651
Coulter Ct	29650
Country Ln	29651
Country Club Dr & Rd	29651
Country Cove Ln	29651
Country Knolls Dr	29651
Country Mist Dr	29651
Countryglen Ct	29651
Courtland Way	29651
Covey Ct	29650
Cox Dr & Rd	29651
Craftsman Ct	29650
Craigmillar Pl	29650
Crain Dr	29651
Cranmore Ct	29650
Creedmoor Dr	29650
Creek Crossing Way	29651
Creekshore Dr	29650
Creekside Ct & Rd	29650
Creekwater Way	29651
Crepe Myrtle Dr	29651
Crepe Myrtle Way	29650
Crest St	29650
Crest Oak Ct	29651
Crestview Cir	29651
Crestwood Dr	29651
Crimson Ct	29650
Cripple Creek Rd	29651
Cross Lake Ln	29651
Cross Meadow Ct	29651
Crossland Way	29651
Crosswinds Ct, St & Way	29650
Crown Point Ct	29650
Crusoe Cv	29651
Crystal Ln	29650
Cudd Dr	29651
Cullen Ct	29650
Cumberland Dr	29651
Cumulus Ct	29650
Cunningham Dr	29650
Cunningham Point Ct	29651
Curtis Dr	29651
Cypress Valley Rd	29651
D St	
100-120	29650
145-199	29651
Dales Ct	29650
Dan St	29651
Dan Dougs Pl	29651
Daniel Ave	29651
Danny Lynn Dr	29651
Dartmoor Dr	29650
Darvis St	29651
Davenport Ave	29650
David Ave & Rd	29651
Davis Ave	29651
Davis Cir	29650
Davis Rd	29651
Davis St	29651
Davis Allen Rd	29651
Davola Pl	29650
Dawes Dr	29650
Dawn Dr	29650
Dayside Ct	29651
De Kalb Dr	29650
Dean Rd	29651
Dean Crain Rd	29651
Dean Lake Rd	29650
Dean Ross Rd	29651
Debbie Ave	29651
Deeangela Ct	29651
Deepwood Dr	29651
Deerfield Dr	29650
Delagrave Rd	29651
Delano Ave	29650
Delicata Ln	29650
Dellany Ct	29651
Delward Way	29651
Denmark Dr	29650
Dent Rd	29651
Depot St	29651
Derby Trl	29651
Derry Ln	29650
Devenger Pl, Pt & Rd	29650
Devenhill Ct	29650
Devenhollow Dr	29650
Devenridge Ct & Dr	29650
Dever Knoll Ln	29651
Dewey Rd	29651
Deyoung Rd	29651
Deyoung Meadows Dr	29651
Diamond Hill Ct	29651
Dill Ave	
1-99	29651
100-199	29650
N Dill Ave	29651
Dill St	29651
Dill Creek Ct	29650
Dillard Dr & Rd	29650
Dillard Creek Ct	29651
Dills Farm Way	29651
Distribution Ct	29650
N & S Dobson Rd	29651
Dobson Shed Rd	29651
Docker Way	29650
Doeskin Hl	29650
Dogwood Dr	29651
Donahue Rd	29651
Donaldson Ave	29651
Donbeck Ct	29651
Douglas Dr	29651
Dovie Dr	29651
Downey Hill Ln	29650
Downing Pl	29650
Drace Ave	29650
Dragway Rd	29651
Drakemont Ct	29651
Draw Bridge Ct	29651
Drennan Dr	29651
Driftwood Dr	29651
Dry Pocket Rd	29650
Duer Way	29651
Duke St	29650
Dunbar Ct	29651
Duncan Ave	29651
Duquesne Dr	29650
Durand Ct	29650
Durham Rd	29651
Durham Snow Rd	29651
Dusk Sky Ln	29651
Dusty Oak Ln	29651
Dutchman Ct	29651
Dylan Crest Trl	29651
Earl St	29651
East Ave	29651
Eastern Mdw	29650
Eastland Dr	29651
Eastover Dr	29651
Ebbitt Ct	29651
Ebenezer Rd	29651
Echo Cir	29651
Eckley Ct	29651
Edwards Ave	29650
Edwards Lake Dr & Rd	29651
Edwin Dr	29650
El Centro Dr	29651
El Craigo Dr	29651
Elcon Dr	29650
Elevation Ct	29651
Elise Dr	29650
Elizabeth Sarah Blvd	29650
Ellington Creek Ln	29651
Elmer St	29651
Elmshorn Dr	29650
Emma Bryant Way	29651
Endless Dr	29651
Enoree Cir & Rd	29650
Enoree View Dr	29650
Ephraim Few Rd	29651
Ermon Ct	29651
Executive Dr	29651
Exodus Way	29651
F St	29650
Fairhaven Dr	29651
E Fairview Ave	29651
W Fairview Ave	29650
Fairview Ct	29651
Fairview Pl	29651
Fairview Rd	29651
Fairview Road Ext	29651
Fairway Estates Rd	29651
Falcon Ridge Way	29650
Falling Waters Way	29651
Farm Dell Ct	29651
Farm Hill Rd	29651
Farm Valley Ct	29650
Farmers Cir	29651
Farrar Ln	29650
Fate Dill Rd	29651
Father Hugo Dr	29650
Faulkner Cir	29651
Faux Dr	29650
Fawnbrook Dr	29650
Faye Ct	29651
Feldspar Ln	29650
Fence Rd	29651
Fenwick Pl	29650
Fernridge Ct	29651
Fernwood Dr	29651
Few St	29650
Fews Bridge Rd	29651
Fews Chapel Rd	29651
Fieldhaven Ct	29651
Finley Ave	29651
Firethorne Ct & Dr	29650
Fisher Rd	29651
Fitts Rd & Spur	29651
Fitzgerald Way	29651
Five Oaks Dr	29651
Flat Ct	29651
Flat Tail Way	29651
Flatwood Rd	29651
Fleming Dr	29650
Flint Ln	29651
Flowerwood Dr	29651
Flynn Rd	29651
Fond Hart St	29651
Ford Cir	29651
Ford Ct	29651
Ford Rd	29651
N Ford Rd	29651
Ford St	29650
Forest Ct	29651
Forest St	
100-299	29650
300-399	29651
Forest Cove Ln	29651
Forest Creek Cir	29651
Forest Valley Way	29651
Forrester Rd & St	29651
Foster Cir	29651
Four Meadows Ln	29650
Fox Farm Way	29651
Fox Hunt Ln	29651
Fox Run Cir	29651
Foxfield Way	29651
Francis St	29651
Franklin Meadow Way	29651
Franklin Oaks Ln	29651
Frederick St	29651
Freedom Ct	29650
Freedom Pond Rd	29650
Freeman Farm Rd	29651
Fritzsimons Ct	29651
Frohawk St	29651
E Frontage Rd	29651
Fuller St	29650
Furwood Ct	29650
Futura Ct	29650
Gaffney Ct	29650
Gail Ave	29651
Galena Ln	29651
Galeton Ct	29651
Galewood Dr	29651
Gallivan St	29650
Galway Dr	29650
E & W Gap Creek Cir & Rd	29651
Garbor Ct	29650
Garden Rose Ct	29651
Gary Armstrong Rd	29651
Gassaway Ct	29650
Gateway Dr	29651
Gaujard Ct	29650
Geer St	29650
Gemini Way	29651
Genoble Rd	29651
Georgia Belle Ln	29650
Germander Ct	29650
Germantown Ct	29650
Gibbs Shoals Rd	29650
Gibson Oaks Dr	29651
Gibson Woods Trl	29651
Gilbert St	29651
Gilliam Rd	29651
Gin House Rd	29651
Gladstone Way	29650
Gladwin Ct	29651
S Glassy Mountain Rd	29651
Glassyrock Ct	29650
Glastonbury Dr	29651
Glen Dr	29651
Glen Abbey Way	29650
Glen Willow Ct	29650
Glenaire Dr	29650
Glencreek Dr	29650
Glencrest Ct	29650
Glenfield Ct	29650
Glenrise Ct	29650
Glens Crossing Ct	29650
Godfrey Rd	29651
Golden Ln	29651
Golden Tanager Ct	29651
Golden Wings Ct & Way	29650
Goldenstar Ln	29651
Goldfinch Cir	29650
Goldsturm Ln	29650
Golf St	29650
Good Taylor Ct	29651
Goodman Ct	29651
Goodridge Ct	29651
Governors Ct & Sq	29650
Gracefield Ct	29650
Grafton Ct	29650
Grand Teton Dr	29650
Grandmont Ct	29650
Grandy Ct	29651
Granite Woods Way	29650
Gratiot Ln	29651
Graviton Rd	29650
Gravley Rd	29651
Green Ct	29651
Green Rd	29651
Green St	29650
Greendale Ln	29651
Greene Dr	29651
Greenleaf Dr	29651
Greer Ct	29650
E Greer St	
100-199	29651
200-299	29650
Greer Pelham Rd	29651
Gregory Dr	29650
Grey Stone Ct	29650
Griffith Creek Dr	29651
Griffith Hill Way	29651
Griffith Knoll Way	29651
Grinders Cir	29650
Grove Pt & St	29651
Grubbs Rd	29651
Gsp Dr	29651
Gsp Logistics Pkwy	29651
E & W Hackney Rd	29650
Haddon Ln	29651
Hadrian Ln	29650
Halcyon Cir	29650
Hallo Dr	29651
Hamby Ct	29651
Hammett Rd	29650
S Hammett Rd	29651
Hammett Bridge Rd	29650
Hammett Grove Ln	29650
Hammett Pond Ct	29650
Hammetts Glen Way	29650
Hammond Ave & Ct	29651
Hampstead Pl	29650
Hampton Rd	29651
Hampton Ridge Dr	29651
Hampton Road Ext	29651
Hancock Ln	29650
Hannu Ct	29651
Hansa Ln	29650
Harbin Ave	29651
Harbrooke Cir	29651
Hardin St	29651
Harkins Bluff Dr	29651
Harold Ct	29651
Harris Dr & St	29651
Hartman Rd	29651
Hartsdale Ct & Ln	29650
Harvey Rd	29651
Haskell Ct	29651
Haven Dr	29651
Hawkins Rd	29651
Hawksbeak Rdg	29650
Hayfield Ln	29650
Haynes St	29650
Heart Ct	29651
Heather Rose Ct	29651
Hedgewood Ct & Ter	29650
Henderson Cir	29650
Henderson Rd	29651
Henderson Gap Rd	29650
Hendrix Rd	29651
Henley Ct	29650
Henry Clark Ln	29651
Henson Pl	29650
Hermosa Ct	29650
Hessell Ct	29650
Hickory Ln	29651
Hickory Rock Ln	29651
High St	29651
High Meadow Ct	29650
High Meadows Ln	29651
High Tech Ct	29650
Highfield Ct	29650
Highgate Cir	29650
Highland Ave & Dr	29651
Highland Parc Dr	29650
Highmount Dr	29651
N Highway 101 S	29651
N Highway 14	29651
S Highway 14	29650
Highway 357	29651
Hill Dr & St	29651
Hill Pass Ct	29650
Hillcrest Dr W	29651
Hillington Pl	29651
E Hills Dr	29650
Hillsdale Dr	29650
Hillside Dr	29651
Hillside Glen Dr	29650
Hilton St	29650
Hingham Way	29650
Hobcaw Dr	29650
Holiday Rd	29651
Hollington Ct	29651

Holly Cir & Ln 29651
Holly Circle Ext 29651
Holly Creek Dr 29651
Holly Vista Dr 29650
Homer Cir 29651
Hood Rd 29650
Hoptree Dr 29650
Horton Grove Rd 29651
Howe Rd 29651
E Howell Rd 29651
N Howell Rd 29651
Howell Spur 29651
N Howell St 29650
S Howell St 29650
Hubbard Ln 29651
Hubert St 29650
Hudson Rd & Way 29650
Hudson Farm Rd 29650
Hudson Water Rd 29651
Hunt St 29650
Hunters Landing Dr 29651
Hunting Hill Cir 29650
Huntress Dr 29651
I St 29651
Inderich Rd 29650
Indigo Ct 29651
Industrial Ct 29651
Industrial Park Rd 29651
Inglesby St 29650
International Commerce Blvd 29651
Intrepid Ct 29650
Inwood Ct 29650
Irving St 29651
Isaqueena Dr 29651
Island Ct 29650
Ivy Springs Dr 29650
J St 29651
J Verne Smith Pkwy 29651
Ja Brooke Dr 29651
Jackson St
100-199 29650
1000-1299 29651
Jade Tree Ct 29650
Jaden Ct 29651
Jaguar Ln 29651
James Ave 29650
James Rd 29650
N James Rd 29651
E James St 29651
W James St 29650
Jameswood Ct 29651
Jarmel Way 29650
Jason St 29651
Jay Marie Dr 29651
Jefferson Dr 29651
Jenny Rd 29651
Jessica Way 29651
Joe Leonard Rd 29651
John St 29651
John Suddeth Rd 29651
Johnnie St 29650
Johnnys Lake Rd 29651
Johns Rd 29650
Johnson Ave & Rd 29651
Joines Ct 29651
Jones Ave 29650
Jordan Rd 29651
Jordan Oak Way 29651
Josh Ct 29651
Jude Ct 29651
Judges Ln 29651
Judson Ave 29651
Judy Way 29651
S Jug Factory Rd 29651
Juneberry Ct 29651
Juniper Leaf Way 29651
Justin Dr 29651
Kaleigh Dr 29651
Kates Ct 29650
Kayes Ct 29651
Kaylas Dr 29651
Kaylyn Way 29650
Keating Dr 29650
Keelin Ln 29650
Keeneland Way 29651

Keith St 29651
Kelly Ave 29650
Kelsea Taylor Dr 29651
Kelvyn St 29651
Kemper Ln 29651
Kendrick St 29651
Kennesaw Way 29650
Kentmont Ln 29651
Killarney Ln 29650
Kimbrells Cove Ln 29651
E & S King Rd & St 29651
Kings Mountain Dr 29650
Kingscreek Dr 29650
Kingston Ct 29651
Kingsway Ct 29651
Kinross Row 29650
Kirby St 29651
Kirkpatrick Ct 29650
Kist Rd 29651
Kluge Rd 29650
Knob Creek Ct 29651
Knoll Ridge Dr 29650
Knot Cir 29651
Kramer Ct 29650
Kruger Ln 29650
Kylemore Ln 29650
Lady Banks Ln 29650
Lady Hillingdon Ct 29650
N & S Lady Slipper Ln 29650
Ladykirk Ln 29650
Lafay Way 29650
Lake Ave 29650
Lake Dr 29651
Lake Pl 29651
Lake Cunningham Cir & Rd 29651
Lake Harbor Ct 29651
Lake Robinson Pt 29651
Lake Water Ct 29650
Lakecrest Dr 29651
Lakeforest Dr 29651
Lakeland Dr 29651
Lakemont Dr 29651
Lakeview Cir & Dr 29651
Lakewood Cir 29651
Lamar St 29651
Lamira Ave 29651
Lamp Light Dr 29650
Lamplighter Dr 29651
Lancaster Ave 29650
Landing Ferry Way 29650
Landmark Dr 29651
Landrum Dr 29651
Landstone Ct 29650
Lanford St 29650
Lantern Dr & Ln 29651
Laramie Peak Ln 29651
Laredo Ct 29651
Latigo Ct 29650
Latour Way 29650
Laurel Ln & Rd 29651
Laurel Lake Dr 29651
Laurelhurst Ct 29650
Lauren Leigh Ct 29651
Lauriston Pl 29650
Lawing Ln 29651
Lawndale Dr 29651
Lawton St 29651
Leach St 29651
Leatherwood Ct 29651
Leatherwood Dr 29650
Lebanon Ct 29651
Ledgestone Way 29651
Lee Cir 29650
N Lee Cir 29651
Lee St
100-198 29650
1100-1199 29651
Leesburg Peak 29651
Leeward Ter 29650
Leona Dr 29651
Leonard Rd 29651
Lex Ct 29651
Liberty Hill Rd 29651
Lightwood Knot Rd 29651
Lillians Ln 29651

Lindall St 29651
Lindbergh Ct 29651
N & S Line Rd & St 29651
N & S Line Street Ext 29651
Lismore Park Dr 29650
Lister Rd 29651
Little Dipper 29651
Little Fox Ct 29650
Littlefield St 29651
Live Oak Ct 29651
Lockerbie Ct 29650
Locust Dr 29651
Locust Hill Rd 29651
Lodgewood Trl 29651
Log Ct 29651
London Ct 29650
Londonderry Ct 29650
Lone Tree Cir 29651
Long Pineview Ct 29651
Long Pond Ct 29651
Longstreet Ct & Dr 29650
Longview Ter 29650
Loquat Ct 29650
Lorla St 29651
Lynn St 29651
Lytle Ct & St 29650
Madison Ave 29651
Madison Haven Dr 29651
E & W Magill Ct 29651
Magnolia Creek Ct 29651
Mahaffey Rd 29651
N Main St
100-699 29650
700-1199 29651
S Main St 29650
Malinda Dr 29651
Manatee Ct 29651
N Manley Dr 29651
Manley Crain Rd 29651
Manly Ct 29651
Maple Dr & Pl 29651
Maplewood Cir 29651
Marah Ln 29651
March Ct 29651
March Winds Ct 29650
Marchant St 29651
Marcie Rush Ln 29651
Margie Rd 29650
Mariah Dr 29651
Mariner Ct 29650
Marion Ave 29650
Marlis Ct 29650
Marnie Ln 29651
Marsh Spring Ct 29650
Marshland Ln 29650
Martin Ct & Dr 29651
Mary St 29651
Mary Grove Ln 29651
Mary Louise Dr 29650
Mary Rose Ln 29650
Maryland Ave 29650
Mason St 29651
Matalin Ct 29651
Matlock Cir 29651
Matt Ct 29651
Mattie Ln 29651
Mattman Cir 29651
Matts Lake Rd 29651
Maximus Dr 29651
Mayfield St 29651
Mays Bridge Rd 29651
Mcabee Ct & Rd 29651
Mccall St 29650
Mcclure Smith Rd 29651
Mcdade Ave 29651
Mcdaniel Ave 29651
N & S Mcelhaney Ct & Rd 29651
Mcelrath Rd 29651
Mckissick St 29650
Mcneely Cir 29651
Meadow Breeze Ct 29650
Meadow Clary Dr 29650
Meadow Creek Ct 29650
Meadow Grove Way 29650
Meadow Haze Ct 29650

Meadow Hill Way 29650
Meadow Lake Trl 29650
Meadow Mist Trl 29650
Meadow Oak Ct 29650
Meadow Pond Ct 29650
Meadow Ridge Dr 29651
Meadow Springs Ln 29650
Meadow Trace Ct 29651
Meadow Vale Ct 29651
Meadowglen Pl 29651
Medallion Ct 29650
Medford Dr 29650
Medical Pkwy 29650
Medora Dr 29650
Meilland Dr 29650
Melisa Ct 29651
Mellow Way 29651
Memorial Dr 29650
Memorial Drive Ext 29651
Meritage St 29651
Metro Ct 29650
Middle Brook Ct & Rd 29650
Middleberry Ct 29650
Middlehouse Way 29650
Middleton Way 29650
Milford Dr 29651
Milford Church Rd 29651
Milky Way 29651
Mill Rocks Dr 29651
N & S Miller St 29650
Millervale Rd 29650
Mills Ave 29651
Mimosa Dr 29650
Minert Ct 29651
Mint Ct 29651
Mirabella Pkwy 29650
Mirramont Pl 29650
Misty Dawn Ct 29651
Misty Oaks Dr 29651
Mitchell Dr 29650
E & W Miter Saw Ct 29651
Moat Ln 29651
Mockingbird Ln 29650
Monmouth Ct 29650
Montclair Rd 29651
Montpelier Dr 29650
Moorcroft Way 29650
Moore St 29651
Moore Street Ext 29651
Morgan Ct 29650
Morgan Rd 29651
Morgan St 29651
Morgan Pond Dr 29650
Morgan Woods Ct 29651
Moriah Ln 29651
Morning Star Ct 29651
Morningside Ave 29650
Morningside Dr 29651
Morrow St 29650
Moss St 29651
Mossy Oak Ln 29651
Mostella Rd 29651
Mosteller Dr 29651
Motherwell Dr 29651
Motor Way 29651
Mound Ct 29650
Mount Lebanon Church Rd 29651
Mount Vernon Cir & Rd 29651
Mountain Height Ct 29651
Mountain Valley Dr 29651
Mountain View Ave 29650
Mountain View Ct 29651
S Mountain View Rd 29651
Mulberry St 29650
Mullinax Dr 29651
Murdock Ln 29651
Muse Cir & Dr 29651
Myrtle Way 29651
Nalley Rd 29651
Natalie Ct 29651
Nature Trail Dr 29651
Nautical Dr 29650
Neely Mill Rd 29651
New Bruce Rd 29651

New Tarleton Way 29650
New Woodruff Rd 29651
Newfanes Way 29650
Nichole Pl 29651
Nichols Dr 29650
Nigh Oak Trce 29651
Nimbus Ct 29650
Noble St 29651
Noe Rd 29651
Nopal Ct 29651
Norfolk Ave 29650
North Ave 29650
Northcote Ct 29650
Northridge Ct & Rd 29650
Northview Dr 29651
Northway Ct 29651
Notting Hill Ln 29651
Oak Dr 29650
Oak Pl 29650
Oak St 29651
Oak Forest Dr 29650
Oak Haven Ct 29651
Oak Ridge Ct 29650
Oak Springs Dr 29651
Oak Wind Cir 29651
Oakdale Ave 29651
Oakland Ave 29650
Oban Ct 29651
Old Ansel School Rd 29651
Old Boiling Springs Rd 29650
Old Hickory Dr 29651
Old Highway 14 S
1600-1899 29651
N Old Highway 14 29651
S Old Highway 14
2600-2899 29650
Old Indian Trl 29650
Old Jones Rd 29651
Old Orchard Rd 29650
Old Province Way 29650
Old Rutherford Rd 29651
Old Salem Ave 29650
Old Spartanburg Rd 29650
Old Tiger Bridge Rd 29651
Old Wagon Rd 29651
Old Waterworks Rd 29651
Old Woodruff Rd 29651
Olivine Way 29650
Omniwood Ct 29651
Oneal Rd 29651
Oneal Church Rd & St 29651
Oneal Village Ave 29651
Opal Ct 29651
Ora Vista Brae 29651
Oran Ct 29651
Overbrook Dr 29650
Overcup Ct 29650
Owens Rd 29651
Packer Ct 29651
Paddle Pond Pl 29651
Paddock Ct, Dr & Ln 29650
Palmer St 29651
Palmetto Cir, Ct & Dr 29651
Panorama Cir 29651
Panther Ct 29651
Papa Ct 29650
Paris St 29650
Park Ave 29651
Park Hill Ct & Dr 29651
Park Ridge Cir 29651
Parker St 29650
Parksouth Dr 29651
Parkwalk Dr 29650
Parkway Commons Way 29650
Partridge Ln 29650
Patriot Ln 29651
Patterson Rd 29651
Peach Blossom Ct 29650
Peach Packers Ct 29650
W Peach Ridge Dr 29651
Peach Valley Ct 29651
Peach Wood Trl 29651
Peachland Dr 29651
Peachtree Dr & Ln 29651
Pearl Cir 29651

Pearson Rd 29651
Pearson Lake Rd 29651
Pebblebrook Ct 29651
Pelham Ct 29650
Pelham Rd 29650
Pelham St 29651
Pelham Falls Dr 29651
Pelham Industrial Park Dr 29650
Pelham Square Way 29650
Pen Oak Ct 29650
Penelope Ln 29650
Pennington Rd 29651
Pennsylvania Ave
413A-413B 29650
100-505 29650
504-504 29652
506-598 29650
507-599 29650
Penny Ave 29651
Penny Meadow Ct 29650
Pennypacker Ct 29650
Pentland Ct 29651
Pepper Bush Dr 29651
Pepperbush Ct 29650
Peppercorn Ct 29650
Perdita Way 29650
Perkins Ct 29651
Perry Ave & Rd 29651
Peter Mccord Ln 29651
Peterman Pl 29650
E & W Phillips Ln & Rd 29650
Phillips Mccall Rd 29651
Physicians Dr 29650
Pileus Dr 29650
Pin Aly 29651
Pine Dr 29651
Pine St 29650
Pine Forest Dr 29651
Pine Hill Dr 29651
Pine Ridge Dr 29651
Pine Street Ext 29651
Pine Trail Ct 29651
Pinecrest Dr 29651
Pinewood Dr 29651
Pink Dill Mill Rd 29651
Plantation Dr & Rd 29651
Pleasant Dr & Hts 29651
Pleasant Brook Ct 29651
Pleasant Hill Rd 29651
Pleasant Knoll Ln 29651
Pleasant Oak Ct 29651
Plum Mill Ct 29650
E Poinsett St 29651
W Poinsett St 29650
E Poinsett Street Ext 29651
Ponder Rd 29651
Poole Rd 29651
Poplar Dr 29651
Poplar Drive Ext 29651
Portrush Dr 29651
Post Dr 29650
Prairie Knoll Ct 29651
Preakness Ct 29651
Preston Dr 29651
Prince Cir & St 29651
Princess Cir 29651
Princess Glen Dr 29650
Pristine Ct & Dr 29650
Quail Creek Dr 29650
Quail Run Dr 29651
Quincy Dr 29650
Racing Rd 29651
Randall St 29651
Ravenell St 29651
Rawlins Ct 29651
Rayland Pl 29651
Rayna Ct & Dr 29651
Red Haven Ct 29650
Red Holly Ridge Ct 29651
Red Quail Ln 29651
Red Raven Dr 29651
Red Shirt Ct 29651
Red Spruce Ln 29651
Reddington Dr 29650

Redgold Ct 29650
Redwater Way 29651
Redwing Ct 29651
Reese Ave 29651
Regency Commons Dr 29650
Regional Dr 29651
Reid Rd 29651
Reidville Rd 29651
Reidville Sharon Rd 29651
Rene Ct 29651
Revere Ct 29650
Rhett St 29651
Richey Dr 29651
Richfield Ter 29650
Richglen Way 29650
Ridge Rd 29651
Ridge Road Ext 29651
Ridgeburg Ct 29651
Ridgecrest Cir 29651
Ridgefield Park Dr 29651
Ridgewood Dr 29651
Riello Dr 29650
Riley Hill Ct 29650
Ripton Ct 29650
River Rd
700-1099 29651
2000-2299 29650
River St 29651
River Birch Way 29650
River Oaks Rd 29650
River Way Dr 29651
Riverbanks Ct 29651
Riverside Ct 29650
Riverside Chase Cir 29650
Riverside Towne Cir 29650
Riverstone Way 29651
Riverton Ct 29650
Rivertrail Ct 29651
Roberts Cir 29650
Robin Hood Ln 29651
Robins St 29651
Robinson Rd 29651
Robinson St 29650
Robinson View Ln 29651
Rock Rd 29651
Rockbrook Ct 29650
Rockcrest Dr 29650
Rockport Ave 29650
Rockridge Dr 29651
Rodgers Rd 29650
Roe Rd & St 29651
Rogers Cir 29650
Rollingreen Rd 29651
Roscoe Dr 29651
Rosebud Ct & Ln 29650
Rosedale Dr 29651
Rosehaven Way 29651
Roselite Cir 29650
Rotan St 29651
Rowland Ct 29650
Royal Oak Ct 29650
Royal Troon Ct 29650
Rubaiyat Ct 29650
Rubiwood Cir 29651
Ruby Elizabeth Dr 29651
Ruddy Creek Cir 29651
Rugosa Way 29650
Runion Dr 29651
Running Deer Ct 29650
Running Springs Ct 29650
Rustcraft Dr 29651
N Rutherford Rd 29651
Ryans Corporate Way 29650
Saber Ct 29651
Saddle Creek Ct 29651
Saddle Tree Ct 29650
Sage Brush Ct 29651
Sage Creek Way 29650
Sagey Ct 29651
Saint Charles Pl 29650
Saint Croix Ct 29651
Saint Helaine Pl 29650
Saint James Place Dr 29650
Saint Thomas Ct 29651
Samuel Rd 29651
San Bruno Ct 29651

Sandy Creek Ct 29650
Sandy Run Dr 29651
Saratoga Dr 29650
Satterfield Rd 29651
Saturn Ln 29651
Saucer Ct 29650
Savage Ct 29651
Scarborough Dr 29650
Scattershot Ln 29650
Scenic Dr 29651
Schiller Dr 29651
School St 29651
Scofield Ct 29650
Scotch Rose Ln 29650
Scott Ct 29651
Scottbine Ct 29651
Scruggs Cir 29651
Seaboard Dr 29651
Seaside Ln 29650
Seaver Ct 29651
Seaward Ct 29650
Serendipity Gate 29651
Service Center Rd 29651
Setinel Ct 29650
Seven Pines Ct 29651
Shadetree Ct 29651
Shady Ln 29651
Shady Creek Ct 29650
Shady Glen Dr 29651
Shady Hollow Ln 29651
E & W Shallowstone Rd 29650
Shandwick Dr 29650
Shane Dr 29651
Sharon Dr & Rd 29651
Sharon Church Rd 29651
Sheffield Rd 29651
E & W Shefford Ct, Ln & St 29650
Sheila Ave 29651
E Shelter Ct & Dr 29650
Shelwood Ct 29651
Sherard Ct 29650
Sheridan Pl 29650
Sherman St 29650
Sherwood Ave 29651
Shetland Way 29650
Shipyard Ln 29650
Shoals Rd 29651
Shore Vista Ln 29651
Shortie St 29651
Sidra Way 29650
N & S Silver Beech Ln 29651
Silver Creek Ct & Rd 29650
Silver Knoll Ct 29651
Silver Meadow Ln 29651
Silver Pine Ct 29650
N Silver Ridge Ct & Dr 29651
Silver Tip Ct 29651
N & S Silver View Ln 29651
E & W Silverleaf St 29650
Sizemore St 29651
Skyland Cir & Dr 29651
Skylark Cir 29650
Skyline Rd 29651
Slate Ln 29650
Smith Ct 29651
Smith Waters Dr 29651
Snow Rd & St 29651
Soma Ct 29651
Somerset Pl 29650
Sonia Dr 29650
South Ave 29650
Southern Ln 29651
Southwind Way 29651
Spanish Moss Ln 29650
Sparkleberry Ct 29651
Sparrow Hawk Ct 29650
Spartan Ct 29650
S Spearman Dr 29651
Spindleback Way 29651
E & W Spindletree Way 29650
Spring St 29650
Spring Crossing Cir 29650
Springdale Ave 29650
Springhead Way 29650
Sproughton Ct 29650
Spruce Ave 29651
Sprucewood Ct 29651
Squirrel Hollow Ct 29651
N & S Staghorn Ln 29650
Stanford Rd 29651
Steadman Way 29650
Steeple Ridge Ct 29650
Steepleview Ct 29651
Stewart Ave 29650
Still Ln 29651
Still Creek Ct 29650
Stillhouse Rdg 29650
Stockbridge Dr 29650
Stokes Rd & St 29651
Stone Creek Rd 29650
Stone Hill Ct 29650
Stone Ridge Ct & Rd 29650
Stone Valley Ct 29650
Stonecrest Rd 29650
Stonewash Way 29650
Strathmore Dr 29650
Stratus Ct 29650
Strawfield Ct 29651
Stream Crossing Way 29650
Stringer Rd 29651
Styles Mill Rd 29651
Suber Rd 29651
E Suber Rd 29650
N Suber Rd 29651
S Suber Rd 29650
Suber Mill Rd 29650
Suburban Park Dr 29650
Sudbury Pl 29650
Suddeth Rd 29651
Suffolk Ct 29650
Sugar Cane Ct 29650
Sugar Creek Ct, Ln & Rd 29650
Sugar Lake Ct 29650
Sugar Mill Ct, Rd & Way 29650
Sugar Pine Ct 29651
Sugar Time Ln 29651
Sugar Valley Ct 29650
Sugarfield Ct 29650
Summer Creek Ct 29650
Summer Rose Ct 29651
Summer Valley Ct 29650
Summerlea Ln 29651
Summerplace Ct, Dr & Way 29650
Summit Dr 29651
Sumter St 29650
Sun Flare Ct 29650
Sun Meadow Rd 29650
Sunapee Ct 29651
Sunbelt Ct 29650
Sunbelt Business Park Dr 29650
Sunfield Ct 29650
Sunnybrook Ln 29650
Sunnydale Dr 29651
Sunnyglen Ct & Dr 29651
Sunnyside Cir & Dr 29651
Sunrise Dr 29651
Sunset Ave 29650
Superior Way 29651
Susana Dr 29651
Sussex Pl 29650
Swade Way 29650
Swamp Fox Trl 29650
Swan River Ct 29650
Swedes Run 29650
Sweet Juliet Way 29650
Sweetbriar Ct 29650
Sweetwater Ct & Rd 29650
Sylvan Dr 29650
Sylvia St 29651
Tabor Ln 29651
Tack Ln 29650
Talavera Ln 29651
Tale Ct 29650
Tall Pines Ctr 29651
Talus Dr 29650
Tamaron Way 29650
Tamelia Ct 29651
Tampico Ct 29651
Tanager Cir & Ct 29650
Tandem Dr 29650
Tapp Rd 29651
Tarleton Way 29650
Taylor Rd 29651
Teaberry Ct 29651
Tedwall Ct 29650
Teepee Dr 29651
Terminal St 29651
Terra Lake Dr 29650
Terra Plains Dr 29651
Terrence Ct 29650
Thatcher Ln 29650
The Pkwy 29650
Thompson Rd 29651
Thompson St 29650
Thorington Ct 29651
Thornblade Blvd 29650
Thornbush Ct 29651
Thurmond Ct 29651
S Ticonderoga Dr 29650
Timber Trl 29651
Timberidge Dr 29650
Timberlane Rd 29651
Timberwood Rdg 29651
Timmons Dr 29651
Titan Ct 29651
Todd Ct 29651
Tomotley Ct 29651
Tonya Ann Ln 29651
Torchwood Ct 29651
Tot Howell Rd 29651
Tracy Trl 29651
Trade St 29651
Tralee Ln 29650
Trask Ct 29650
Traymore Way 29650
Treetops Ct 29650
Tremont Ave 29650
Trenton Ln 29651
Trevor Ct 29651
Treyburn Ct 29650
Treyford Dr 29650
Tryon St
100-199 29650
200-799 29651
Tungsten Blvd 29651
Tupelo Dr 29651
Turnberry Pl 29650
Turner St 29651
Turner Hill Rd 29651
Tuscany Ct & Way 29650
Tuxedo Ln 29651
Twin Magnolia Dr 29650
Twin Oaks Dr 29651
Twin Silo Ct 29651
S & W Tyger Ct & Dr 29651
E Tyger Bridge Rd 29651
Tyler Ridge Dr 29651
Unicoi Dr 29650
United Cir 29651
Upper View Ct 29651
Valentine Ln 29651
Valley Dr & Ln 29651
Valley Creek Dr 29651
Valley Fall Ct 29650
Valley Forge Dr 29650
Valley Glen Ct 29650
Valleybrook Ln 29651
Van Patton Rd 29651
Vandelay Way 29650
Vandiventer Dr 29650
Vanity Way 29651
Varnson Ln 29650
Vasti Dr 29651
Vaughn Ave 29650
Vaughn Rd 29651
W Vaughn Rd 29651
Vaughn St 29651
Vega Ln 29651
Vera Cir 29651
Vernon St 29650
Victor Ave, Ct & St 29651
Victor Avenue Ext 29651
Victor Hill Rd 29651
Victoria Ln & St 29651
View Forest Ct 29651
Viking Dr 29651
Village Ct & Dr 29651
Village Green Cir 29650
Vine Ct 29651
Virginia Ave 29650
Vista Pointe Dr 29651
Waddell Rd 29651
E Wade Hampton Blvd 29651
W Wade Hampton Blvd 29650
Wadsworth Ct 29651
Wallace Town Dr 29651
Wallhaven Dr 29651
Walls Rd 29651
Walton Ct 29651
Wando Way 29650
Ward St 29651
Ward Oak Ct 29651
Warriston Ct 29650
Water Mill Rd 29650
Waterbrook Ln 29651
Watercourse Way 29651
Waterfield Ct 29650
Waterford Ln 29650
Waterford Park Dr 29650
Waterloo Cir 29650
Waterwheel St 29651
Watkins Farm Dr 29651
Wax Myrtle Ct 29651
Waymon Dr 29651
Weeping Willow Ct 29651
Welcome Ave 29651
Wellhouse Rd 29651
Welsh Poppy Way 29650
Wenlock Ct 29650
Wennington Pl 29651
Werrington Ct 29651
West Rd 29650
Westcot Ct 29650
Westfield Ave 29651
Westmoreland Ave 29650
Westmoreland Rd 29651
Westover Dr 29651
Weybourne Dr 29650
Wheat Ct 29651
Wheatfield Dr 29651
Whilden Ct 29651
Whistler Dr 29651
White Cir 29651
White Oak Dr 29651
White Water Ct 29650
Whitekirk Way 29650
Whitewood Way 29650
Whitfield Way 29651
Wicker Park Ave 29651
Wild Eve Way 29650
Wild Ridge Ln 29650
Wilder Ct 29650
Wildlife Trl 29650
Wildwood Dr 29651
Will St 29651
Will Bomar Rd 29651
William Owens Way 29651
Williamsburg Dr 29651
Willow Rd 29651
Willowgreen Way 29651
Wills Cap Ct 29651
Wilson Ave 29651
Wilson Rd 29650
Wilson St 29651
Windsor Ct & Rd 29651
Windward Ct & Way 29650
Windward Peak Ct 29651
Windy Oak Way 29651
Wingbrook Ct 29651
N & S Wingfield Rd 29650
Winnjay Ct 29650
Winterthur Ct & Dr 29650
Winterwood Ct 29650
Woburn Ct 29651
Wolf Den Dr 29650
Wolfe Rd 29650
Wood Ave 29650
Wood Dr 29651
N Wood Ln 29651
Wood Chip Ln 29651
Wood Duck Way 29650
Wood Hollow Cir 29650
Wood Spring Ct 29651
Woodfield Dr 29651
Woodgrove Way 29651
Woodhaven Dr 29651
Woodland Dr 29651
Woodlawn Hills Dr 29651
Woodruff Dr 29651
Woods Rd 29650
Woods Chapel Rd 29651
Woodstock Ln 29650
Woodstrace Ct 29650
Woodvale Cir 29651
Woodward St 29651
Woodway Ct & Dr 29651
Woodwind Way 29651
Woody Creek Rd 29650
Woolridge Way 29650
Wrenwood Ct 29651
Wright Dr 29651
Wycliffe Dr 29650
Wyman Ct 29651
Xander Dr 29650
Yellow Ln 29651
Yellow Fin Ct 29651
Yellow Rose Ct 29651
Yorba Ln 29651
Zoar Heights Rd 29651
Zuber Rd 29651

NUMBERED STREETS

All Street Addresses 29651

HARTSVILLE SC

General Delivery 29550

POST OFFICE BOXES MAIN OFFICE STATIONS AND BRANCHES

Box No.s
All PO Boxes 29551

NAMED STREETS

All Street Addresses 29550

NUMBERED STREETS

N & S 1st 29550
N & S 2nd 29550
N 3rd St 29550
N 4th St 29550
S 4th St
100-501 29550
500-500 29551
502-2098 29550
503-2099 29550
N & S 5th 29550
N & S 6th 29550
7th St 29550
N & S 8th 29550
N & S 9th 29550
N & S 10th 29550
S 11th St 29550
14th St 29550

HILTON HEAD ISLAND SC

General Delivery 29928

POST OFFICE BOXES MAIN OFFICE STATIONS AND BRANCHES

Box No.s
1 - 2000 29938
3001 - 3544 29928
4000 - 8074 29938
21001 - 25000 29925

NAMED STREETS

Aberdeen Ct 29926
Abigail Ln 29928
Abraham Jones Ln 29926
Acorn Ln 29928
Adell Ln 29926
Adrianna Ln 29926
Adventure Galley Ln 29926
Aiken Pl 29926
Airport Rd 29926
Airy Hall Ct 29928
Albemarle Pl 29928
Alder Ln 29928
Alex Patterson Rd 29926
Alfred Ln 29926
Alice Perry Dr 29926
Allen Dr 29926
Amberjack Rd 29926
Amelia Cir, Cmn, Ct & Dr 29926
Anchorage Pt 29928
Angel Wing Dr 29926
Anglers Pond Ct & Ln 29926
Anna Ct 29926
Annabella Ln 29926
Ansley Ct 29926
Archer Rd 29926
Armada St 29926
Arrow Rd 29928
Arrow Wood Ct & Rd 29926
Arthur Hills Ct 29928
Ashton Cove Dr 29928
Atlantic Pt 29928
Audubon Pl 29928
Audubon Pond Rd 29928
Auld Brass Ct 29928
Automoblie Pl 29926
Avalon Way 29926
Avocet St 29928
Azalea St 29928
Bald Eagle Rd W 29928
Baldwin Ln 29926
Balmoral Pl 29926
Balsams Ct 29926
Bank Swallow Lagoon 29926
Barcelona Rd N 29928
Barksdale Ct 29926
Barnacle Rd 29928
Barony Ln 29928
Barrier Beach Cv 29928
Bateau Rd 29928
Battery Rd 29928
Bay Pines Dr & Rd 29928
Bayberry Ln 29928
Baygall Rd 29926
Bayley Point Ln 29926
Baynard Cove Rd 29928
Baynard Park Rd 29928
Baynard Peninsula 29928
S Beach Ln 29928
Beach City Rd 29926
E, S & W Beach Lagoon Rd & Vl 29928
Beach Market 29928
Beachside Dr 29928
Beachwalk 29928
Beachwood Dr 29928
Bear Creek Dr 29926
Bear Island Rd 29926
Beaver Ln 29928
Beech Hill Ct 29928
Belfair Ct 29928
Bellhaven Way 29928
Belted Kingfisher 29928
Belton Ct 29926
Ben White Dr 29926
Benjamin Dr 29926
Bent Hook Ct 29926
Bent Tree Ln 29926
Benty Ct 29928
Berkshire Ct 29928
Bermuda Pointe Cir 29926
Bertram Pl 29928
Berwick Dr 29926
Bethea Dr 29926
Bethel Ct 29926
Betty P Ln 29926
Big Oak St 29926
Big Woods Dr 29926
Bill Fries Dr 29926
Birdsong Way 29926
Birkdale Ct 29926
Bittern St 29928
Black Duck Rd 29928
Black Gum Ln & Pl 29926
Black Mink Ln 29926
Black Rail Ln 29926
Black Skimmer Rd 29928
Black Tern Rd 29928
Black Watch Dr 29926
Blake Pl 29928
Blazing Star Ln 29926
Bligen Ln 29926
Blossum Pl 29926
Blue Crab Mnr 29926
Blue Heron Pt 29926
Blue Jay Way 29926
Blue Water Marina Dr 29926
Bluebell Ln & Trce 29926
Bobcat Ln 29926
Bobwhite Ln 29926
Bolen Hall Ln 29926
Bonny Hall Ct 29928
Bow Cir
1-7 29928
2-12 29938
8-98 29928
9-99 29928
Bowline Bay Ct 29926
Braddock Cv 29928
Braddock Bluff Dr 29928
Bradley Cir 29928
Bradley Beach Rd 29928
Brams Point Cir & Rd 29926
Branford Ln 29926
Brassie Ct 29928
Brewton Ct 29928
Bridgeport Ln 29928
Bridgetown Ln & Rd 29928
Bridle Ct 29928
Brigantine 29928
Brinson Hill Dr 29928
Brittany Pl 29928
Broad Creek Marina Way 29926
Broad Pointe Dr 29926
Bronco Xing 29926
Broomsedge Ct 29928
Brown Ct 29926
Brown Pelican Rd 29928
Brown Thrasher Rd 29928
Brunson Ct 29926
Bryant Rd 29926
Buckfield Ln 29926
Buckingham Lndg 29926
Burkes Beach Rd 29928
Burns Ct 29928
Bus Dr 29926
Butterfly Ln 29926
Button Bush Ct & Ln 29926
C Heinrichs Cir 29926
Cadogan Ct 29926
Caladium Ct 29926
Calibogue Cay Rd 29928

Street	ZIP
Calibogue Cay Villas	29928
Cambridge Cir	29928
Camden Ln	29926
Camellia St	29928
Campbell Dr	29928
Candy Doll Blf	29928
Cannon Row	29928
Canvasback Rd	29928
Capital Dr	29926
Capri Ln	29928
Captain Sims Dr	29926
Captains Quarters	29928
Caravell Ct	29928
Cardinal Ct & Rd	29926
Carma Ct	29926
Carnoustie Rd	29928
Carolina Isles Dr	29926
Carters Mnr	29928
Cartgate Dr	29928
Cassina Ln	29928
Castle Hall Ln	29928
Castlebridge Ct & Ln	29928
Cat Brier Ln	29926
Catalina Ct	29926
Catbird Ln	29928
Catboat	29928
Catesby Ln	29928
Cattail Ct	29926
Ceasar Pl	29926
Cedar Ct & Ln	29926
Cedar Wax Wing Rd	29928
Celosia Ln	29926
Centella Ct	29926
Central Ave	29926
Century Dr	29926
Chamber Of Commerce Dr	29928
Chantilly Ln	29926
Chaplin Dr	29926
Charlesfort Pl	29926
Chelsea Ct	29928
Cherry Hill Ln	29926
Cheryls Blf	29926
Chestnut Ln	29926
Chickadee Rd	29926
China Cockle Ln & Way	29926
Chinaberry Cir & Dr	29926
Chisolm Pl	29926
Christo Dr	29926
Christopher Dr	29928
Circlewood Dr	29926
Claire Dr	29928
Clara Sq	29926
Clarendon Ln	29928
Clearwater Ln	29926
Clifford Miller Dr	29926
Clove Hitch Ct	29926
Club Mnr	29928
Club Course Dr & Ln	29928
Clubhouse Dr	29928
Clyde Ln	29926
Cobblestone Ct	29928
Cobia Ct	29926
Cockle Ct	29928
Coggins Point Rd	29928
Coligny Plz & Vl	29928
College Center Dr	29928
Colleton Dr	29926
Collier Ct	29926
Collier Beach Rd	29928
Colonial Dr	29926
Colonnade Clb & Dr	29928
Columbine Ln	29928
Combahee Rd	29928
Compass Pt	29928
Conrad Rd	29926
Conservancy Ct	29926
Cooperative St & Way	29926
Coopers Hawk Rd	29926
Coquina Rd	29928
Cora Lee Ln	29926
Cordillo Pkwy	29928
Cordillo Cabanas	29928
Corey Trce	29926
Corpus Christie Pl	29928
Corrine Ln	29928
Cotesworth Pl	29926
Cottage Ct	29928
Cotton Ln	29928
Cotton Hall Ln	29928
Cotton Point Cir	29926
Cottonwood Ln	29926
Cougar Run	29926
Country Club Ct	29926
Courtyard Cmn	29926
Coventry Ln	29928
Covington Ct, Park & Pl	29928
Crabline Ct	29928
Cranberry Ln	29926
Craven Pl	29928
Creek Cove Ln	29926
Crepe Myrtle Ct	29926
Crooked Pond Dr	29926
Crosstree Dr N	29926
Crosstree Patio	29926
Crosswinds Dr	29926
Curlew Rd	29926
Cusabo Pl	29926
Cutter Ct	29926
Cygnet Ct	29926
Cypress Marsh Dr	29926
Dahlgren Ln	29926
Dalmatian Ln	29928
Dalton Ct	29928
Daniel Dr	29928
Darling Rd	29926
Davant Ct	29926
Dawson Way	29926
Deallyon Ave	29928
Deep Fording Rd	29926
Deer Island Rd	29928
Deer Run Ln & Rd	29928
Deerfield Ct & Rd	29926
Deixler Ln	29926
Delander Ct	29928
Deldench Dr	29926
Delta Ln	29928
Demsey Ln	29926
Devils Elbow Ln	29926
Dewberry Ln	29928
Dewees Ln	29926
Diamondback Rd	29926
Dianahs Dr	29926
Dillon Rd	29926
Dinghy	29928
Dogwood Ln	29926
Dolphin Head Dr	29926
Dolphin Point Ln	29926
Donax Rd	29926
Doral Ct	29926
Doubloon Dr	29926
Dove St	29928
Down Wind	29928
Drayton Pl	29926
Driftwood Ln	29928
Drummond Ln	29926
Duck Field Rd	29926
Duck Hawk Rd	29926
Duey Hill Dr	29926
Dune Ln	29928
Dune House Ln	29928
Dunlin Pl	29926
Dunmore Ct	29926
Dunnigans Aly	29926
Durban Pl	29926
Dw Mcdonald Ln	29926
Eagin Ct	29926
Eagle Claw Dr & Ln	29926
Earl Ct	29928
Earline Ln	29926
Eastwind	29928
Edgewood Ct & Dr	29926
Egret St	29928
Elderberry Ln	29928
Elizabeth Dr	29926
Ellenita Dr	29926
Elliot Pl	29926
Ellis Ct	29926
Elmwood Ct	29926
Emergency Ct	29926
End Ct	29928
Ensis Rd	29928
Enterprise Ln	29926
Eugene Dr	29926
Evelina Rd	29926
Everglade Pl	29928
Evergreen Ln	29928
Exchange St	29926
Executive Park Rd	29928
Fairfax Ln	29928
Fairlawn Ct	29926
Fairway Ct & Ln	29928
Fairway Oaks	29928
Fairway Winds Pl	29928
Fairwood Vl	29928
Falcatta Rd	29928
Fallen Arrow Ct & Dr	29926
Fantail Ln	29926
Farmers Club Rd	29926
Fawn Ln	29928
Ferguson Ln	29926
Fern Ct	29928
Fernwood Ct & Trl	29926
Fetterbush Dr	29926
Fiddlers Cv	29928
Fiddlers Way	29926
Field Sparrow Ct & Rd	29926
Fife Ln	29928
Finch St	29926
Firethorn Ln	29926
Fish Haul Rd	29926
Fish Hawk	29926
Fishermans Bend Ct	29926
Flagg Rd	29928
Flagship Ln	29926
Flamingo St	29928
Florencia Ct	29926
Flotilla	29928
Flying King Ct	29926
Folly Field Rd	29928
Foot Point Rd	29928
Fording Island Rd	29926
Fording Island Road Ext	29926
Forest Cv & Dr	29928
N & S Forest Beach Ct, Dr & Vl	29928
Fort Howell Dr	29926
Fort Walker Dr	29928
Fox Ln	29928
Fox Den Ct	29926
Foxbriar Ct & Ln	29926
Foxglove Ct	29926
Foxgrape Rd	29926
Foxhunt Dr	29926
Freshwater Ln	29928
Friendfield Ct	29928
Full Sweep	29928
Fuller Pointe Dr	29926
Gadwall Rd	29926
Galleon	29928
Gannet St	29928
Gardenia St	29928
Gardner Dr	29926
E & W Garrison Pl	29928
Gaspee Ct	29926
Gateway Cir	29926
Genesta St	29928
Genoa Ct	29928
Georgianna Dr	29926
Ghost Crab Way	29928
Gibson Dr	29926
Ginger Beer Ct	29928
Gleneagle Grn & Ln	29928
Glenmoor Pl	29928
Gloucester Rd	29928
Gold Oak Ct & Dr	29926
Golden Bear Way	29926
Golden Hind Dr	29926
Goldfinch Ln	29928
Golf Cottages	29928
Good Hope Ct	29928
Gordonia Tree Ct	29926
Governors Ln & Rd	29928
Gracefield Rd	29928
Graham Ln	29926
Grandview Ct	29926
Grant Dr	29926
Grasslawn Ave	29928
Graves Rd	29928
Great Baracuda Ln	29926
Green Acres	29928
Green Heron Rd	29928
Green Wing Teal Rd	29928
Greens Rd	29928
Greenside Pl	29926
Greenwood Ct & Dr	29928
Grey Fox Ln	29926
Grey Widgeon Rd	29928
Grove Ct	29928
Gull Point Rd	29928
Gumtree Rd	29926
Gunnery Ln	29928
Gunpowder Pl	29928
Habitat Cir	29926
Hackney Pony Ln	29926
Hadley Ln	29926
Haig Point Ct	29928
Half Hitch Ct	29926
Half Penny Ln	29928
Hanahan Ln	29926
Harbortown Club Villas	29928
Harbour Psge E	29926
Harbour Passage Patio	29926
Harbour South Villas	29928
Harbourside Ln	29928
Harbourtown Grn	29928
Harleston Grn	29928
Harrogate Dr	29928
Hartford Pl	29928
Hatteras Ct	29926
Hatton Pl	29926
Haul Away	29928
Hawk Ct	29926
Headlands Dr	29926
Hearthwood Dr	29926
Heath Ct & Dr W	29928
Heather Ln	29926
Helmsman Way	29928
Henry Ln	29926
Heritage Ct & Rd	29928
Heritage Villas	29928
Hermit Crab Ct	29926
Hermit Thrush	29926
W Heron St	29926
Herring Gull Ln	29926
Heyward Pl	29928
Hickory Ln	29928
Hickory Cove Vl	29928
Hickory Forest Dr	29926
Hickory Knoll Pl	29926
Hickory Nut Ct	29926
High Bluff Rd	29926
High Water	29928
Highbush Dr	29926
Highrigger	29928
Hiltech Park Ln	29926
Hobnoy Ct	29928
Hobonny Pl	29926
Hollyberry Ln	29928
Holmes Ln	29926
Honey Hill Ct	29928
Honey Horn Rd	29926
Honey Horn Plantation Rd	29926
Honey Locust Cir	29926
Honeysuckle Ct	29926
Horse Sugar Ln	29926
Horseman Ln	29926
Horvaths Peninsula	29928
Hospital Center Blvd & Cmns	29926
Hotel Cir	29928
Hudson Rd	29926
Humane Way	29926
Hummingbird Ct	29926
Hummock Pl	29928
Hunt Club Ct	29926
Hunter Rd	29926
Hydrangea Ln	29926
Ibis St	29928
Indian Trl	29926
Indian Hill Ln & Pt	29926
Indian Pipe Ln	29926
Indigo Ct	29926
Indigo Ln	29928
Indigo Run Dr	29926
Inland Harbour	29928
Interlochen Dr	29928
Iron Clad	29928
Isabal Ct	29926
Isabella Ct	29926
Island Dr	29926
Isle Of Pines Dr	29928
Ivory Gull Pl	29926
Ivy Rd	29928
Jacana Rd	29928
Jarvis Creek Ct, Ln & Way	29926
Jarvis Park Rd	29926
Jenkins Island Rd	29926
Jessamine Pl	29928
Jessica Dr	29926
Jib Sail Ct	29928
Jingle Shell Ln	29926
Jonesville Rd	29926
Joyce Ln	29926
Julia Dr	29926
Junior Trce	29926
Juniper Ln	29926
Junket	29928
Katie Miller Dr	29926
Kent Ct	29926
Ketch Ct	29928
Kids Way	29928
Killdeer Ln	29928
King Oak Ct	29926
King Rail Ct & Ln	29926
King William Ct	29926
Kingbird Ln	29926
Kingfisher St	29928
Kinglet Lagoon Rd	29926
Kings Ct	29926
Kings Tree Rd	29928
Kingston Cv & Rd	29926
Kingston Dunes Rd	29928
Knightsbridge Ln	29928
Knollwood Dr	29926
Knotts Way	29928
Korber Ct	29926
Ladson Ct	29926
Ladyslipper Ln	29926
Lafayette Pl	29926
Lagoon Rd	29928
Lake Forest Dr	29928
Lamotte Dr	29926
Lancaster Pl	29926
Lands End Ct	29928
Lands End Dr	29928
Lands End Rd	29928
Lands End Way	29928
Larium Pl	29926
Lark St	29926
Laughing Gull Rd	29928
Laurel Ln	29928
Lavington Rd	29928
Lawton Dr, Rd & Vl	29928
Lawyer Pl	29926
Leamington Ct, Ln & Pl	29928
Leatherwood Ct	29926
Lee Shr	29928
Leeward Psge	29928
Leg O Mutton	29926
Legacy Ct	29926
Lemon Grass Ct	29928
Lemoyne Ave	29928
Lenora Dr	29926
Lenox Ln	29926
Lh Tennis Clb	29928
Liberty Pl	29928
Lighthouse Ln & Rd	29928
Lighthouse 1 Villas	29928
Lighthouse Ii Villas	29928
Linden Pl	29928
Little Garden Path	29926
N & S Live Oak Rd	29928
Loblolly Ln	29926
Loblolly Rd	29928
Loggerhead Ct	29926
Long Boat	29928
Long Brow Rd	29928
Long Cove Dr	29928
Long Marsh Ln	29928
Longleaf Ln	29926
Lookout	29928
Loomis Ferry Rd	29928
Lost Way Mnr	29926
Low Water	29928
Mac Donough Ln	29926
Mackerel Dr	29926
Madison Ln	29926
Madrid Ct	29928
Magazine Pl	29928
Magnolia Cresent Rd	29928
N Main St	29926
Mall Blvd	29928
Mallard Rd	29928
Man O War	29928
Manatee Way	29926
Manor Court Ct & Ln	29926
Maplewood Ct	29926
Marblehead Rd	29928
Margarita Ct	29926
Marina Side Dr	29928
Mariners Way	29928
Market Place Dr	29928
Marsh Dr	29928
Marsh Hawk Ct	29926
Marsh Island Rd	29928
Marsh Owl Ct	29926
Marsh Point Dr	29926
Marsh Wren Rd	29928
Marshland Ln, Pl & Rd	29926
Marshview Dr	29928
Marshwinds	29928
Masters Ct	29928
Mathews Ct & Dr	29926
Matilda Dr	29926
Mcguire Ct	29926
Mcintosh Rd	29926
Mckays Point Rd	29928
Mead Ln	29926
Meadowlark Ln	29926
Mediterranean Ln	29926
Meeting St	29926
Merchant St	29926
Merganser Ct	29928
Merion Ct	29928
Middleton Pl	29928
Midstream	29928
Miller Rd	29926
Millwright Dr	29926
Mimosa St	29928
Mingo Green Rd	29926
Misty Cove Ln	29928
Misty Cove I	29928
Misty Cove Ii	29928
Misty Morning Dr	29926
Mitchell Landing Rd	29926
Mitchellville Pl & Rd	29926
Mizzenmast Ct & Ln	29928
Mockingbird Ln	29928
Monticello Dr	29926
Moonshell Rd	29928
Mooring Buoy	29928
E & W Morgan Ct	29926
Moss Creek Ct, Dr & Vlg	29926
Mossy Oaks Ln	29926
Muddy Creek Ct & Rd	29926
Muirfield Rd	29928
Mulberry Ct	29928
Murray Ave	29926
Museum St	29926
Musgrove Cir	29926
Mustang Ln	29926
Myrtle Ct	29926
Myrtle Ln	29928
Myrtle St	29926
Myrtle Bank Ln & Rd	29926
Myrtle Warbler Rd	29926
Mystic Dr	29926
Namon Rd	29926
Namon Landing Pl	29926
Narragansett Ln	29928
Nassau St	29928
Natures Way	29926
Nautilas Rd	29928
Nazarene Rd	29926
Ned Ct	29926
Neptune Ct	29926
New Orleans Rd	29928
Newhall Rd	29926
Newport Dr & Vl	29928
Niblick Ct	29928
Nichols Ct	29926
Night Hbr	29928
Night Heron Ln	29928
Night Heron Lakeside	29928
Nighthawk St	29928
Nina Dr	29926
Northridge Dr	29926
Northside Dr	29926
Nut Hatch Rd	29926
Oak Ct	29928
Oak Creek Dr	29928
Oak Marsh Dr	29926
Oak Park Dr	29926
Oak Point Lndg	29928
Oakman Branch Rd	29928
Oakview Rd	29926
Ocean Ln & Pt N	29928
Ocean Cove Clb	29928
Ocean Gate Vl	29928
Ocean One	29928
N & S Ocean Point Pl	29928
Oceanwood Trce	29928
Oconnor Rd	29926
Ocracoke Ln	29926
Off Shr	29928
Office Way	29928
Office Park Rd	29928
Oglethorpe Ln	29926
Oketee Ct	29926
Old Ferry Pt	29926
Old Fort Dr, Ln & Way	29926
Old House Creek Dr	29926
Old Military Rd	29928
Old Otter Hole Rd	29926
Old Wild Horse Rd	29926
Oleander St	29928
Orage Ln	29926
Ordnance Pl	29928
Orista Pl	29926
Osprey St	29928
Otranto Ct	29928
Otter Rd	29926
Otter Hole Rd	29926
Outerbridge Cir	29926
Outlaw Rd	29926
Outpost Ln	29928
Overlook Pl	29926
Oxford Dr	29928
Oyster Bateau Ct	29926
Oyster Bay Pl	29926
Oyster Catcher Rd	29928
Oyster Landing Ln & Rd	29928
Oyster Rake Ct & Ln	29926
Oyster Reef Cv & Dr	29926
Oyster Shell Ln	29926
Paddle Boat Ln	29928
Paddocks Blvd & Ct	29926
Painted Bunting Rd	29928
Palm Isle Ct	29926
Palm View Dr	29926
Palmetto Pkwy	29926
Palmetto Pl	29926
Palmetto Bay Rd	29928
Palmetto Beach Vl	29928
Palmetto Business Park Rd	29928
Park Ln & Rd	29928
Parkwood Dr	29928
Pauline Mnr	29926
Pearl Reef Ln	29926
Pearl Shell Mnr	29926

Pelican St 29928
Pelican Watch Ct & Way 29926
Pembroke Dr 29926
Pender Ln 29928
Pendergrass Ct 29928
Peninsula Dr 29926
Pensacola Pl 29928
Pepper Bush Ln 29926
Percheron Ln 29926
Peregrine Dr 29926
Perriwinkle Ln 29928
Persimmon Pl 29926
Pheasant Run 29926
Pheasant Run Ct 29926
Phillip Dr 29926
Phoebe Ln 29928
Pieces Of Eight Pl 29928
Pine Ct 29928
Pine Burr Rd E & W 29926
Pine Island Ct, Dr & Rd 29928
Pine Sky Ct 29926
Pine Warbler Cir 29926
Pinefield Rd 29926
Pineland Rd 29926
Pintail Ct 29928
Piping Plover Rd 29928
Plantation Dr 29928
Plantation Club Vl 29928
Planters Row 29928
Planters Wood Ct & Dr 29928
Plaza Dr 29926
Plumbridge Cir & Ln 29928
Point Comfort Cir, Clb & Rd 29928
Pond Dr 29926
Pope Ave 29928
Port Au Prince Rd 29928
Port Au Spain Rd 29928
N & S Port Royal Dr 29928
Port Tack 29928
Portside Dr 29928
Possum Ln 29928
Post Mill Rd 29926
Power Aly 29926
Prestwick Ct 29926
Primrose Ln 29926
Princeton Cir 29926
Promontory Ct 29928
Purple Martin Ln 29926
Pyxie Ln 29928
Quail St 29928
Quail Walk Ln 29926
Quartermaster Ln 29928
Queens Way 29928
Queens Folly Rd 29928
Quincy Ln 29928
Rainbow Ct 29926
Raintree Ln 29926
Rampart Ln 29928
Raquet Club Villas 29928
Rasta Dr 29926
Ravenwood Rd 29928
Rebecca Cir 29926
Red Bay Ct 29926
Red Cardinal Rd 29928
Red Maple Rd 29926
Red Oak Rd 29928
Red Tip Ct 29926
Redstart Ct & Path 29926
Reef Clb 29926
Reflection Cove Ct 29926
Regency Pkwy 29928
Reggies Rd 29926
Resolute Pl 29926
Retreat Ln 29928
Rhiner Dr 29926
Ribaut Dr 29926
Rice Ln 29928
Rice Mill Ln 29928
Richfield Way W 29926
Ridgewood Ln 29928
River Club Dr 29926
Roadrunner St 29928
Robbers Row 29928
Robin St 29928
Roma Ct 29928
Rookery Way 29926
Rosebank Ln 29928
Row Boat Rd 29928
Roxbury Cir 29928
Royal Crest Dr 29928
Royal Fortune Ct 29926
Royal James Dr 29926
Royal Pointe Dr 29926
Royal Tern Rd 29928
Ruddy Turnstone Rd 29928
Rum Row 29928
Rusty Rail Ln 29926
Rutledge Ct 29926
Sabal Ct 29926
Saddlewood Ct 29926
Sadie Cmn 29926
Sagebush Ln 29928
Sailmaster Cmn 29928
Sailstock Pt 29926
Sailwing Club Dr 29926
Saint Andrews Cmn & Pl 29928
Saint Augustine Pl 29928
Saint Croix Pl 29928
Saint George Rd 29928
Saint Johns Pl 29928
Saint Thomas Pl 29928
Salem Rd 29928
Sally Port Rd 29928
Salt Marsh Dr 29926
Salt Marsh Cottages 29926
Salt Spray Ln 29928
Salt Wind Way 29926
Sam Frazier Retreat 29926
Sams Point Ln 29926
Sandcastle Ct 29926
Sanddollar Rd 29926
Sanderling Ct & Ln 29926
Sandfiddler Rd 29928
Sandhill Crane Rd 29928
Sandpiper St 29928
Sandy Beach Trl 29928
Santa Maria Dr 29926
Sapos Pl 29926
Sara Ct 29926
Sassafras Ln 29926
Savannah Trl 29926
Saw Timber Dr 29926
Sawtooth Ct 29926
Saxton Ln 29926
Scarborough Head Rd 29928
Scaup Ct 29926
School Rd 29926
Schooner Ct 29928
Sea Ln 29928
Sea Breeze Ct 29928
Sea Cabins N 29928
Sea Front Ln 29928
Sea Hawk Ln 29928
Sea House W 29928
Sea Loft Villas 29928
Sea Oak Ln 29928
Sea Olive Rd 29928
Sea Otter Ct 29926
N & S Sea Pines Dr 29928
Sea Pines Country Club Ln 29928
Sea Robin Ct 29926
Sea Spray Ln 29926
Sea Trout Ct 29926
Seabrook Dr 29926
Seabrook Landing Dr 29926
Seagrass Landing Ct 29926
Seahorse Way 29926
Seaside Sparrow Rd 29928
Sedge Fern Dr 29926
Sentry Oak Ln 29926
Shadewood Ct & Ln 29926
Shaftsbury Ln 29926
Shamrock Cir 29926
Shear Water Ct & Dr 29926
Sheldon Ln 29926
Shell Ring Rd 29928
Shelley Ct 29928
Shelter Cove Ln 29928
Shepards Needle 29926
Sherman Dr & Pl 29928
Shipwatch Pt 29928
Shipyard Dr 29928
Shore Ct, Dr & Pl 29928
Shore Crest Ln 29928
Shoreline Dr 29928
Shrimp Ln 29926
Silver Fox Ln 29926
Silver Oak Cir & Dr 29926
Simmons Rd 29926
Singleton Pl 29928
Singleton Beach Rd 29928
Skull Creek Dr 29926
Slack Tide 29928
Smock Ml 29926
Snider Walk 29926
Snowy Egret Rd 29928
Song Sparrow Ln 29928
Sorgum Ln 29928
Southwind Dr 29928
Southwood Park Dr 29926
Sovereign Dr 29926
Spanish Moss Rd 29928
Spanish Pointe Dr 29926
Spanish Wells Rd 29926
Sparkleberry Ln 29926
Sparrow Hawk Ct 29926
Spartina Cres & Ct 29928
Spartina Point Dr 29926
Sparwheel Ln 29926
Spindle Ln 29926
Spinnaker Ct 29928
Spotted Sandpiper Rd 29928
Spridald Rd 29926
Spring Hill Ln 29926
Spruce Ct 29926
Sprunt Pond Rd 29926
Squire Pope Rd 29926
Squiresgate Rd 29926
Stable Gate Rd 29926
Starboard Tack 29928
Starfish Dr 29928
Steam Gun Pl 29928
Sterling Pt 29926
Stevens Ct 29926
Still Run Ramble 29926
Stillwater Ct & Ln 29926
Stingray Dr 29926
Stonegate Ct & Dr 29926
Stonewall Cir 29926
Stoney Creek Rd 29928
Stoney Creek Villas 29928
Stratford Ln 29926
Strath Ct 29928
Strawberry Hill Rd 29926
Stuart Pl 29926
Sugar Pine Ln 29926
Sullivans Ln 29926
Summer Breeze Ct 29926
Summerfield Ct 29926
Summers Ln 29926
Summit Dr 29926
Sunday Ford Dr 29926
Sundew Ct 29926
Sunflower Ct 29926
Sunningdale Ln 29926
Sunset Pl 29926
Surf Scoter Rd 29926
Surf Watch Way 29928
Surfwatch Way 29928
Surrey Ln 29926
Sussex Ln 29926
Sutherland Ct 29926
Sutherland Way 29926
Suttlers Row 29926
Sweet Bay Ln 29926
Sweet Grass Mnr 29926
Sweet Gum Ct & Ln 29926
Sweetwater Ln 29926
Swing About 29928
Sycamore Ln 29926
Sylvan Ln 29926
Tabby Rd 29928
Tabby Trl 29926
Tall Pines Rd 29926
Tanglewood Dr 29928
Tansyleaf Dr 29926
Target Rd 29926
Tarpon Trl 29926
Tattnall Pl 29928
Teal Ln 29926
Tealwood Ct 29926
Telford Ln 29926
The Anchorage 29928
The Breakers 29928
The Moorings 29928
Thomas Cohen Dr 29926
Thompson St 29926
Three Mast Ln 29928
Tidal Bluff Rd 29926
Tidepointe Way 29928
Tidewater Mnr 29926
Timber Ln 29926
Timber Marsh Ln 29926
Timbercrest Cir 29926
Tombee Ct 29928
Tomotley Ct 29928
Toppin Ct & Dr 29926
Topside 29928
Tower Ml 29926
Towhee Rd 29926
Town Center Ct 29928
Townhouse Mnr 29928
Trade Winds Trce 29928
Trails End Rd 29926
Tree Swallow Ct 29926
Trellis Ct 29926
Trent Jones Ln 29926
Trigger Fish Trl 29926
Trillium Ln 29926
Trimblestone Ln 29928
Trinh Palace Way 29926
Troon Dr 29926
Tucker Ridge Ct 29926
Tupelo Rd 29928
Turkey Hill Ln 29928
Turnberry Ln 29926
Turnbridge Dr 29926
Turret Shell Ln 29926
Turtle Dove Ln 29926
Turtle Lane Clb 29928
Twickenham Ln 29926
Twin Pines Ct & Rd 29928
Twisted Cay Ln 29926
Twisted Oak Ct 29926
Union Cemetery Rd 29926
Up Wind 29928
Urchin Mnr 29928
Valencia Rd 29928
Vanessa Ln 29926
Ventura Ln 29926
Verbena Ln 29926
Victoria Cir & Dr 29926
Victoria Square Dr & Xing 29926
Village At Wexford 29928
Village North Dr 29926
Vine St 29926
Viola Rd 29926
Virginia Rail Ln 29926
Viscount Ct 29928
Wagener Pl 29928
Wagon Rd 29928
Walking Horse St 29926
Wanderer Ln 29928
Warbler Ln 29926
Water Oak Dr & Vl 29928
Water Orchid Ct 29926
Water Thrush Pl 29926
Waters Edge 29928
Waterside Dr 29928
Waterway 29928
Waterway Ln 29926
Waterway Pl 29926
Wax Myrtle Ct & Ln 29926
Weather Shr 29928
Weaver Cmn 29926
Wedgefield Dr & Ln 29926
Wee Rd 29926
Wells East Dr 29926
Welsh Pony Ln 29926
Wentworth Pl 29928
Wexford Cir & Dr 29928
Wexford Club Dr 29928
Wexford On The Grn 29928
Wheeler Ln 29926
Whelk St 29928
Whispering Pines Ct 29926
Whistling Swan Rd 29926
White Hall Ct 29928
White Tail Deer Ln 29926
Whitney Pl 29926
Whooping Crane Way 29926
Wicklow Dr & Ln 29928
Widewater Rd 29926
Wilborn Rd 29926
Wild Azalea Ln 29926
Wild Heron Pt 29928
Wild Holly Ct 29926
Wild Horse Ln, Pl & Rd 29926
Wild Laurel Ln 29926
Wild Turkey Run 29926
Wildbird Ln 29926
Wilderness Pt 29926
Wildwood Ct & Rd 29928
Wilers Creek Way 29926
Wiley Ln 29926
Willet Rd 29926
William Dr 29926
William Hilton Pkwy
1-212 29926
201-215 29925
213-499 29926
214-498 29926
500-1099 29928
Willow Oak Ct & Rd 29928
Wimbledon Ct 29926
Wimbrel Ln 29926
Windflower Ct & Way 29926
Winding Trail Ln 29926
Windjammer Ct 29928
Windward Village Dr 29928
Windy Cove Ct 29926
Wing Shell Ln 29926
Winged Arrow Ct 29926
Wisteria Ln 29928
Witch Hazel Dr 29926
Wood Duck Ct & Rd 29928
Wood Ibis Rd 29928
Wood Thrush Ct 29926
Woodbine Pl & Rd 29928
Woodhaven Dr 29926
Woodland Sky Ct 29926
Woodstock Ct 29928
Woodward Ave 29928
Wren Dr 29928
Wright Pl 29926
Wyndemere Dr 29928
Yacht Club Dr 29926
Yacht Club Vl 29928
Yacht Cove Dr & Vl 29928
Yard Arm 29928
Yardley Ln 29928
Yellow Rail Ln 29926
Yorkshire Dr 29928
Yucca Dr 29926

JOHNS ISLAND SC

General Delivery 29457

POST OFFICE BOXES MAIN OFFICE STATIONS AND BRANCHES

Box No.s
All PO Boxes 29457

NAMED STREETS

Abbapoola Rd 29455
Abbotts Blvd 29455
Abram Rd 29455
Abundant Rd 29455
Academy Rd 29455
Acorn Drop Ln 29455
Airy Hall 29455
Alfred Freeman Rd 29455
Alvan Rd 29455
Amaranth Rd 29455
Amberjack Ct 29455
Ambor St 29455
E Amy Ln 29455
Ancient Oaks Ln 29455
Andell Way 29455
Andell Bluff Blvd 29455
Angel Oak Rd 29455
Angler Hall 29455
Anglers Pond Ln 29455
Anglers Retreat Rd 29455
Anhinga Ct 29455
Annabelle Rd 29455
Antilles Way 29455
Appaloosa Rd 29455
Ardwick Rd 29455
Arrowhead Hall 29455
Asarina Ln 29455
Atlantic Beach Ct 29455
Atrium Villa 29455
Audette Ave 29455
August Rd 29455
Augusta National Ct 29455
Auldreeke Rd 29455
Avant Rd 29455
Avocet Ln 29455
Back Pen Rd 29455
Bald Eagle Ln 29455
Bald Pate 29455
Bally Bunion Dr 29455
Balmoral Rd 29455
Bank Swallow Ln 29455
Barnes Dr 29455
Barracuda Rd 29455
Barton St 29455
Bass Creek Ln 29455
Bateau Trce 29455
Bay Forest Dr 29455
Bayou Rd 29455
Baywood Dr 29455
Beach Ct 29455
Beach Club Villa 29455
Beach Townhouses 29455
Beachcomber Run 29455
Beachwalker Dr 29455
Bear Swamp Rd 29455
Beaumont Rd 29455
Beauty Berry Ct 29455
Beckett Rd 29455
Bee Balm Rd 29455
Bees Ferry Rd 29455
Bell Flower Ln 29455
Belmeade Hall Rd 29455
Belted Kingfisher Rd 29455
Belvedere Rd 29455
Ben Mir Ct 29455
Benjamin Rd 29455
Benjamin Jenkins Rd 29455
Bent Creek Rd 29455
Bent Twig Dr 29455
Berkshire Hall 29455
Bernier Commons 29455
Berryhill Rd 29455
Bethlehem Ct 29455
Betsy Kerrison Pkwy 29455
Biering Rd 29455
Birds Key Rd 29455
Bittern Ct 29455
Black Duck Ct 29455
Black Swamp Rd 29455
Black Tupelo Ln 29455
Blackfish Rd 29455
Blackground Rd 29455
Blake Hill Rd 29455
Blanding Dr 29455
Blazer Horse Ct 29455
Blidgen Rd 29455
Blind Rd 29455
Blue Cross Ln 29455
Blue Gold Ln 29455
Blue Heron Dr 29455
Blue Heron Pond Rd 29455
Bluebill Ct 29455
Bluebird Rd 29455
Bohicket Rd 29455
Bohicket Creek Pl 29455
Bohicket Estates Dr 29455
Bonita Ct 29455
Bonneau Rd 29455
Bonnetts Dr 29455
Bower Ln 29455
Boyd N Hayes Rd 29455
Bozo Ln 29455
Branjess Dr 29455
Brenda Dr 29455
Brent St 29455
Briars Creek Ln 29455
Brickyard Rd 29455
Bridle Path Rd 29455
Bridle Trail Dr 29455
Brittlebush Ln 29455
Bronson Rd 29455
Broomsedge Ln 29455
Brownswood Rd 29455
Bryans Dairy Rd 29455
Bufflehead Dr 29455
Bull Thistle Ln 29455
Bulow Plantation Rd 29455
Bulow Point Rd 29455
Bulrush Ln 29455
Burden Creek Rd 29455
Burnswick Dr 29455
Burroughs Hall 29455
Calhoun Suggs Ln 29455
California Ln 29455
Camp Care Rd 29455
Camp Christopher Ln 29455
Canal Bridge Rd 29455
Canal Prism Rd 29455
Cane Slash Rd 29455
Canter Ln 29455
Cape Rd 29455
Captain Maynard Is 29455
Captain Sams Rd 29455
Captain Toms Xing 29455
Caroline Ln 29455
Caroline Rose Path 29455
Cast Net Rd 29455
Castlewick Ave 29455
Cat Tail Pond 29455
Catbrier Ct 29455
Catesbys Blf 29455
Cedar Springs Ln 29455
Cedar Waxwing Ct 29455
Celosia Aly 29455
Chaneybriar Ln 29455
Chardon Commons 29455
Charles Freer Ln 29455
Charlie Jones Blvd 29455
Chilhowee Dr 29455
Chinaberry Ln 29455
Chisolm Rd 29455
Christine Dr 29455
Clam Dr 29455
Clark Hills Cir 29455
Clay Hall 29455
Claybrook St 29455
Clear Marsh Rd 29455
Club Cottage Ln 29455
Cobby Creek Ln 29455
Cobia Ct 29455
Cohen Hill Rd 29455
Coles Dr 29455
Colossians Ct 29455
Comsee Ln 29455
Conifer Ln 29455
Constantine Ln 29455
Contentment Rd 29455
Cooke Rd 29455
Coon Hollow Dr 29455
Copperhead Trl 29455
Coquina Dr 29455
Coral Reef Dr 29455
Corbetts Aly 29455

Cord Grass Ct 29455
Cormorant Island Ln 29455
Cottage Plantation Rd 29455
Cotton Gin Rd 29455
Cotton Hall 29455
Courtland Rd 29455
Creek Watch Trce 29455
Creekbank Ln 29455
Crested Flycatcher 29455
Crooked Oak Ln 29455
Curlew Ct 29455
Curry Rd 29455
Cynthia Dr 29455
Cypress Cottage Ln 29455
Daniel Fludd Rd 29455
Daufuskie Place Ct 29455
David St 29455
Dawning Ln 29455
Deer Point Dr 29455
Deer Run Dr 29455
Diodia Ct 29455
Doctor Whaley Rd 29455
Dogpatch Ln 29455
Dominic Dr 29455
Donnelly Ln 29455
Doral Open 29455
Double Eagle Trce 29455
Dove Nest Ct 29455
Dragging Bottom Rd 29455
Dry St 29455
Duck Pond Rd 29455
Dune Loft Villas 29455
Dunecrest Trace Villa 29455
Duneside Dr 29455
Dungannon Hall 29455
Dunlin Ct 29455
Dunmovin Dr 29455
Dunwick Dr 29455
Eagle Point Rd 29455
Eagles Nest Ct 29455
Eckenrod Aly 29455
Eden Forest Rd 29455
Edenborough Rd 29455
N Edenvale Rd 29455
Edings Ct 29455
Edwins Xing 29455
Eenjy Ln 29455
Egret Pond Ct 29455
Elaine St 29455
Eliza Darby Ln 29455
Embassy Row Way 29455
Emmaus Rd 29455
Equinox Ct 29455
Ernest Levy Ln 29455
Esau Jenkins Rd 29455
Eugenia Ave 29455
Evans Way 29455
Evenings Bnd 29455
Everett St 29455
Exchange Landing Rd 29455
Exodus Way 29455
Ezra Ct 29455
Fagan Way 29455
Fairdell St 29455
Falcon Point Rd 29455
Falling Leaf Ct 29455
Faust Rd 29455
Felders Ln 29455
Feldman Rd 29455
Fenwick Fry 29455
Fenwick Hall Aly 29455
Fenwick Plantation Rd 29455
Fern Gully Ln 29455
Fernhill Dr 29455
Fetterbush Ln 29455
Fickling Hill Rd 29455
Fiddlers Reach 29455
Field Planters Rd 29455
Fish Hawk Ln 29455
Fletcher Hall 29455
Flossy Ln 29455
Flying Squirrel Ct 29455
Flyway Dr 29455
Forestay Ct 29455
Fort Trenholm Rd 29455
Fosters Glenn Dr 29455

Four Paws Path 29455
Foxglove Ln 29455
Foxlair Ct 29455
Francis Johnson Ln 29455
Fred Farm Rd 29455
Freeman Hill Rd 29455
Freshfields Dr 29455
Friendfield Hall 29455
Fripp Ln 29455
Frisco Ln 29455
Gadwall Ln 29455
Gallinule Ct 29455
Gardners Cir 29455
Gasque St 29455
Gatetree Rd 29455
General Cornwallis Dr 29455
Genesis St 29455
George Bellinger Rd 29455
Ghana St 29455
Gibbs Rd 29455
Gift Blvd 29455
Gillins Ln 29455
Givens Rd 29455
Gladstone Rd 29455
Glaze St 29455
Glen Abbey 29455
Glen Eagle Ct 29455
Glenbrook Ln 29455
Glossy Ibis Ln 29455
Glover Rd 29455
Gnarled Pnes 29455
Gnarled Oaks Ln 29455
Goldeneye Dr 29455
Goldenrod Ct 29455
Golf Cottage Ln 29455
Golf Oak Park 29455
Governors Dr 29455
Gracie Parrott Rd 29455
Gradydale Ln 29455
Grass Garden Ln 29455
Green Dolphin Way 29455
Green Heron Ct 29455
Green Meadow Dr 29455
Green Winged Teal Rd 29455
Greenland Rd 29455
Greensward Rd 29455
Gregg Ct 29455
Gregorie Commons 29455
Greta St 29455
Grey Fox Den Ct 29455
Grey Widgeon Ln 29455
Griffith Ln 29455
Grimshaw Rd 29455
Grover Dr 29455
Habitat Blvd 29455
Halle Rd 29455
Halona Ct 29455
Hamilton Rd 29455
Hamlett Ct 29455
Hammrick Ln 29455
Hanscombe Point Rd 29455
Harbor Pointe Cir 29455
Harris Hill Rd 29455
Harry Wilson Rd 29455
Harvester Ln 29455
Haulover Dr 29455
Haulover Pointe Cir 29455
Hay Rd 29455
Hayshire Ln 29455
Haystack Dr 29455
Hazymist Ln 29455
Headquarters Plantation Dr & Ln 29455
Heads Point Ct 29455
Heather Island Ln 29455
Hector Rd 29455
Hedge Row Ln 29455
Henry Singleton Rd 29455
Herman Rd 29455
Heron Marsh Cir 29455
Hickory Knl 29455
Hickory Hill Rd 29455
Hickory Springs Dr 29455
Hidden Oak Dr 29455
High Court Ln 29455

High Dunes Ln 29455
High Hammock Rd & Vlg 29455
High Meadow St 29455
Hilton Dr 29455
Hobson Dr 29455
Hoggard Ln 29455
Hollington Rd 29455
Holloway Ct 29455
Hollydale Ct 29455
Holmes Dr 29455
Hooded Merganser Ct 29455
Hope Plantation Dr 29455
Hopkinson Plantation Rd 29455
Horned Grebe Ct 29455
Hughes Rd 29455
Humbert Rd 29455
Hunters Oak Ln 29455
Hunting Rd 29455
Hut Rd 29455
Hydrangea Trl 29455
Indigo Palms Way 29455
Iron Duke Rd 29455
Isadora Ln 29455
Island Bridge Way 29455
Island Creek Trl 29455
Island Estates Dr 29455
J And R Rd 29455
Ja Nean Pl 29455
Jackstay Ct 29455
James Bay Rd 29455
Javier Ct 29455
Jay Dr 29455
Jenkins Farm Rd 29455
Jenkins Freeman Rd 29455
Jenkins Lagoon Dr N & S 29455
Jenkins Point Rd 29455
Jennifer Rd 29455
Jeronica Way 29455
Jesse Qualls Rd 29455
Jessie Elizabeth Rd 29455
Jewel St 29455
Jimmy Mitchell Ln 29455
Joe Ln 29455
Joe Wright Rd 29455
Johan Blvd 29455
John Boyer Rd 29455
John Fenwick Ln 29455
John Smalls Rd 29455
Johnnie Buncum Rd 29455
Johnson Scott Ln 29455
Johnstowne St 29455
Jules Dr 29455
Julius Taylor Rd 29455
Kano St 29455
Katoro Rd 29455
Kay St 29455
Kemway Rd 29455
Kenneth Ayers Rd 29455
Kestrel Ct 29455
Keswick Dr 29455
Kiawah Dr 29455
Kiawah Beach Dr 29455
Kiawah Island Pkwy 29455
Kiawah Island Club Dr 29455
Kill Dee Ct 29455
King Haven Ln 29455
Kings Is 29455
Kings Pine Dr 29455
Kit Freeman Ln 29455
Kitford Rd 29455
Koger Ln 29455
Krawcheck St 29455
Laboard Ln 29455
Lady Anna Ln 29455
Landfall Way 29455
Langston Dr 29455
Lanyard St 29455
Laplante Ln 29455
Laughing Gull Ct 29455
Laurel Point Ln 29455
Leentred Rd 29455
Legareville Rd 29455
Lemoyne Ln 29455

Leonard Dr 29455
Levi Lake Rd 29455
Lincrest Rd 29455
Little Creek Rd 29455
Little Rabbit Ln 29455
Live Oak Park 29455
Lloyed Rd 29455
Lobella Aly 29455
Loblolly Ln 29455
Log Cabin Rd 29455
Loggerhead Ct 29455
Long Bend Dr 29455
Lotties Ln 29455
Louis Miles Rd 29455
Low Oak Woods Rd 29455
Maddis Rd 29455
Magnolia Tree Ln 29455
Mahan Blvd 29455
Mahogany Rose Ct 29455
Main Rd 29455
Mallard Lake Dr 29455
Malope Aly 29455
Maple Grove Dr 29455
Marie Mcneil Rd 29455
Mariners Watch 29455
Maritime Forest Dr 29455
Marlin Rd 29455
Marsh Cv & Hvn 29455
Marsh Cottage Ln 29455
Marsh Edge Ln 29455
Marsh Elder Ct 29455
Marsh Hawk Ln 29455
Marsh Hen Dr 29455
Marsh Island Dr 29455
Marsh Oak Ln 29455
Marsh Wren Ct 29455
Marshfield Rd 29455
Marshgate Dr 29455
Mary Ann Point Rd 29455
Mary Hay Blvd 29455
Masters Ct 29455
Maybank Hwy
2400-2861 29455
2860-2860 29457
2862-3798 29455
2863-3799 29455
Maybry Dr 29455
Mayfair Ln 29455
Mcgill Ct 29455
Mcleod Mill Rd 29455
Mclernon Trce 29455
Mcpherson Lndg 29455
Meadowlark Dr 29455
Meeks Farm Rd 29455
Michelle Ln 29455
Middle Dam Ct 29455
Milgray Ln 29455
Moon Shadow Ln 29455
Moon Tide Ln 29455
Moonbeam Dr 29455
Moonglow Dr 29455
Moose Trl 29455
Morse Ave 29455
Moss Pointe Ct 29455
Muirfield Ln 29455
Mullet St 29455
Mullet Hall Rd 29455
Murraywood Rd 29455
Nancy Island Dr 29455
Nature View Cir 29455
Needlerush Rd 29455
Needwood Forest Dr 29455
Nepeta Ln 29455
Never No Dr 29455
New Hope Rd 29455
New Settlement Rd 29455
Ney St 29455
Nicholas Carteret Cir 29455
Nicklaus Ln 29455
Nigeria Ln 29455
Nitsa St 29455
Oak Branch Rd 29455
Oakley Dr 29455
Oakville Plantation Rd 29455
Obadiah Ct 29455
Ocean Course Dr 29455

Ocean Forest Ln 29455
Ocean Green Dr 29455
Ocean Marsh Rd 29455
Ocean Oaks Ct 29455
Ocean Palms Ct 29455
Ocean Winds Dr 29455
Old Cedar Ln 29455
Old Charleston Hwy 29455
Old Chisolm Rd 29455
Old Dock Rd 29455
Old Drake Ct & Dr 29455
Old Ferry Rd 29455
Old Forest Dr 29455
Old Hickory Xing 29455
Old Main Rd 29455
Old Oak Walk 29455
Old Pit Rd 29455
Old Pond Rd 29455
Old Wharf Rd 29455
Ortega Dr 29455
Osprey Cottage Ln 29455
Osprey Point Ln 29455
Ostrom Aly 29455
Oswald St 29455
Otter Is & Ln 29455
Overlook Dr 29455
Oyster Catcher Ct 29455
Oyster Rake 29455
Oyster Shell Rd 29455
Painswick Rd 29455
Painted Bunting Ln 29455
Palm Warbler Rd 29455
Palmcrest Dr 29455
Pamlico Ter 29455
Park Lake Dr 29455
Parkers Cemetery Rd 29455
Partner Rd 29455
Partnership Ln 29455
Partridge Walk Ct 29455
Patton Ave 29455
Paulette Dr 29455
Pelican Perch 29455
Pelican Watch Villas 29455
Penny Ln 29455
Pepper Vine 29455
Persimmon Ct 29455
Persimmon Pond Ct 29455
Peyton St 29455
Pine Barren Ln 29455
Pine Creek Rd 29455
Pine Needle Ln 29455
Pine Siskin Ct 29455
Pineland Dr 29455
Pinelog Ln 29455
Piping Plover Ln 29455
Plantation Lakes Dr 29455
Plantation Pointe Rd 29455
Platt Rd 29455
Pleasant Valley Dr 29455
Plow Ground Rd 29455
Point Field Rd 29455
Point Park Dr 29455
Polarus St 29455
Pompano Ct 29455
Pond Crossing Ct 29455
Pondview Rd 29455
Porchview Pl 29455
Possom Path Ct 29455
Pottinger Dr 29455
Preserve Rd 29455
Privateer Creek Rd 29455
Produce Ln 29455
Prosperity Rd 29455
Proverbs Ct 29455
Pumpkin Hill Rd 29455
Quail Ridge Ct 29455
Queens Cottage Ln 29455
Raccoon Key Ct 29455
Racquet Club Dr 29455
Raina St 29455
Rascal Run Ct 29455
Ravens Bluff Rd 29455
Ravens Point Rd 29455
Ravens View Rd 29455
Raynor Ln 29455
Readen Rd 29455

Rearick Rd 29455
Red Bay Rd 29455
Red Cedar Ln 29455
Redbud Ct 29455
Regal Oak Ln 29455
Reggie Rd 29455
Regimental Ln 29455
Remington Trl 29455
Resurrection Rd 29455
Retreat Dr 29455
Revelation Ct 29455
Rhetts Bluff Rd 29455
Riley Wright Rd 29455
Rio Vista Ln 29455
River Rd 29455
River Course Ln 29455
River Landing Rd 29455
River Marsh Ln 29455
Rivers Choice 29455
Roast Duck Ln 29455
Rolling Dune Rd 29455
Rookwood Pl 29455
Roper Rd 29455
Rosabelle Rd 29455
Rosas Ln 29455
Rose Hill Ln 29455
Rosebud Ct 29455
Royal Beach Dr 29455
Royal Colony Rd 29455
Royal Crown Blvd 29455
Royal Oak Dr 29455
Royal Pine Dr 29455
Ruby May Ln 29455
Ruddy Duck Ct 29455
Ruddy Turnstone 29455
Rushland Mews 29455
Rushland Grove Ln 29455
Rushland Landing Rd 29455
Ryder Cup Ct 29455
Sailfish Dr 29455
Saint Christopher Ln 29455
Saint Johns Dr 29455
Saint Johns Parrish Way 29455
Saint Pauls Parrish Ln 29455
Salt Cedar Ln 29455
Saltgrass Ct 29455
Salthouse Ln 29455
Saltmeadow Cv 29455
Salvo Ln 29455
Sanctuary Beach Dr 29455
Sand Alley Rd 29455
Sand Fiddler Ct 29455
Sanderling Ct 29455
Sandhill Rd 29455
Sandwedge Ct 29455
Santa Elena Way 29455
Sassy Dr 29455
Savanna Point Rd 29455
Savannah Hwy 29455
Sawgrass Ln 29455
Scaup Ct 29455
Scribus Ln 29455
Sea Elder Dr 29455
Sea Forest Dr 29455
Sea Island Estates Dr 29455
Sea Lavender Ct 29455
Sea Marsh Dr 29455
Sea Myrtle Ct 29455
Sea Rocket Ct 29455
Seabrook Farm Rd 29455
Seabrook Island Rd 29455
Seabrook Village Dr 29455
Sealoft Villa Dr 29455
Seaman Ln 29455
Seascape Ct 29455
Seaview Dr 29455
Segar St 29455
Seven Oaks Ln 29455
Shad Dr 29455
Shadberry Ln 29455
Shadow Pond Rd 29455
Shady Moss Ln 29455
Shady Oak Rd 29455
Sheen Dr 29455
Shell Creek Lndg 29455

Shell Island Trce 29455
Shipwatch Rd 29455
Shogry Pointe Rd 29455
Shoolbred Ct 29455
Shoran 29455
Shoreline Dr 29455
Shoveler Ct 29455
Silver Moss 29455
Silverbell Ln 29455
Simmons Rd 29455
Skimmer Ct 29455
Slawson Ln 29455
Snoqualmie Pl 29455
Snowy Egret Ln 29455
Soft Shell Rd 29455
Solom Rd 29455
Sonny Boy Ln 29455
Sora Rail Rd 29455
Southwick Dr 29455
Sparkleberry Ln 29455
Sparrow Dr 29455
Sparrow Hawk Rd 29455
Spartina Ct 29455
Spence Dr 29455
Spinnaker Beachhouse Vl 29455
Split Hickory Ct 29455
Spotted Sandpiper Ct 29455
Stable Trot Cir 29455
Staffwood Rd 29455
Stanley Dr 29455
Stanwick Dr 29455
Stardust Way 29455
Starfish Dr 29455
Startrail Ln 29455
Sterling Marsh Ln 29455
Still Life Dr 29455
Stono Watch Dr 29455
Stonoview Dr 29455
Storybrook Farms 29455
Straw Market 29455
Sugarberry Ln 29455
Summer Duck Way 29455
Summer Islands Ln 29455
Summer Tanager 29455
Summerall Rd 29455
Summerland Dr 29455
Summertrees Blvd 29455
Summerwind Cottages 29455
Sunbronze Ct 29455
Sundown Bnd 29455
Sunlet Bnd 29455
Sunnybrook Dr 29455
Sunnyside Farm Rd 29455
Surfscoter Ln 29455
Surfsong Rd 29455
Surfwatch Dr 29455
Suzanne St 29455
Swamp Land Way 29455
Sweet Gum Ct 29455
Sweetbriar Ct 29455
Sweetgrass Ln 29455
Sweetleaf Ln 29455
Sweetspire Ln 29455
Sweetwater Dr 29455
Swygert Blvd 29455
Tallow Tree Ln 29455
Tarbit Rd 29455
Tennis Club Villas 29455
Terrapin Ct 29455
Terrapin Island Ln 29455
Tesoro Dr 29455
The Haul Over 29455
The Lookout 29455
Thomas Jones Rd 29455
Thomas Whaley Rd 29455
Thompson Heyward Dr 29455
Thorn Chase Ln 29455
Thoroughbred Blvd 29455
Thorpe Constantine Ave 29455
Thrasher Ct 29455
Thunder Trl 29455
Tideland Dr 29455
Timothy Simmons Rd 29455

Tom Watson Ln 29455
Top Soil Rd 29455
Towne St 29455
Traywick Ave 29455
Treeduck Ct 29455
Treeloft Trce 29455
Trucklands Rd 29455
Trumpet Rd 29455
Trumpet Creeper Ln 29455
Turkey Hill Rd 29455
Turnberry Dr 29455
Turning Leaf Dr 29455
Turtle Beach Ln 29455
Turtle Landing Ct 29455
Turtle Point Ln 29455
Turtle Watch Ln 29455
Twitchell St 29455
Two Mile Run 29455
Up Da Creek Ct 29455
Updyke Dr 29455
Valcour Dr 29455
Valley Oak Rd 29455
Valnore Rd 29455
Vardell Legare Rd 29455
Vetch Ct 29455
Victoria Brooke Ln 29455
Victory Bay Ln 29455
Village Green Dr 29455
Viola Ct 29455
Virginia Rail Rd 29455
Waitesfield Rd 29455
Waldon Jones Rd 29455
Walker Cup 29455
Walker White Rd 29455
Walkers Ferry Ln & Pl 29455
Walpole Way 29455
Walter Dr 29455
Warbler Ct 29455
Watercrest Ln 29455
Waterfall Pl 29455
Waterleaf Rd 29455
Waverly Ln 29455
Wax Myrtle Ct 29455
Westphal Dr 29455
Whimbrel Rd 29455
Whippoorwill Ln 29455
Whippoorwill Farm Rd 29455
Whistler Rd 29455
Widows Ct 29455
Wild Plum Rd 29455
Wild Turkey Way 29455
Wildcat Pt 29455
Wilkin Ln 29455
William Freeman Ln 29455
Willow Pointe Ln 29455
Winding River Dr 29455
Wine Rd 29455
Winged Foot Ct 29455
Winnies Way 29455
Wittrell Rd 29455
Wood Duck Pl 29455
Woodbridge Dr 29455
Woodcock Ct 29455
Woodland Garden Ln 29455
Woodscape Ct 29455
Workhouse Ct 29455
Yellow Throat Ln 29455
Yost Ln 29455
Zachary George Ln 29455
Zelasko Dr 29455
Zurlo Way 29455

LANCASTER SC

General Delivery 29720

POST OFFICE BOXES MAIN OFFICE STATIONS AND BRANCHES

Box No.s
1 - 9050 29721
9998 - 9998 29720
34369 - 34369 29721

NAMED STREETS

Abbey Ct 29720
Acacia Rd 29720
Aces High Ln 29720
Activity Rd 29720
Adage Rd 29720
Adams Ln 29720
Adams Estate Rd 29720
Addington Dr 29720
Addison Rd 29720
Aero Ln 29720
Agree Ln 29720
Ahoy Ln 29720
Airdale Rd 29720
Airport Rd 29720
Aldridge Ln 29720
Alee Ln 29720
Alexander Ln 29720
Allen Ct 29720
Almetta St 29720
Alpha Rd 29720
Alston Dr 29720
Alton Ln 29720
Amber Way 29720
Amy Ln 29720
Anchor Rd 29720
Ander Vincent Rd 29720
Anderson Dr 29720
Andrew Jackson Park Rd 29720
Angus Ln 29720
Anna Howard Rd 29720
Antioch Cir 29720
Antler Rd 29720
NW Apartment Dr 29720
Apollo Ln 29720
Aqua Ln 29720
Arant Dr 29720
E & W Arch St 29720
Arrington Rd 29720
Arrowhead Dr 29720
Arrowood Ave 29720
Arundel St 29720
Ashley Way St 29720
Ashwood Ln 29720
Assention Rd 29720
Aster Ave 29720
Athena Rd 29720
Atlas Ln 29720
Autumn Oaks Dr 29720
Avelon Rd 29720
Avery Ln 29720
Aviation Blvd 29720
Azalea Rd 29720
Bacon St 29720
Bailey Rd 29720
Baker St 29720
Baker Place Rd 29720
Baldwin Dr 29720
Balkcum Rd 29720
Ballard St 29720
Balmy Ct 29720
Barbarosa Dr 29720
Bardell St 29720
Barker Ln 29720
Barnes Rd 29720
Barnett St 29720
E & W Barr St 29720
Barron Blvd 29720
Bartlett St 29720
Barton Rd 29720
Bath Ln 29720
Bay Ln 29720
Beacon Rd 29720
Beam Ln 29720
Beatrice Ln 29720
Beckham Ln 29720
Beckstead Ct 29720
Belk St 29720
Belmont St 29720
Belmont Circle Dr 29720
Ben Ln 29720
Ben Massey Rd 29720
Bencollo Rd 29720
Bennett Rd 29720
Benson Rd 29720
Bent Creek Dr 29720
Bentley Dr 29720
Berkeley Ln 29720
Berkley Way 29720
Bertha Knight Rd 29720
Bessie Hudson Rd 29720
Beth Dr 29720
Bethea Rd 29720
Bethel Rd 29720
Bethel Boat Landing Rd 29720
Bill Sweatt Rd 29720
Bill Thompson Rd 29720
Billings Dr 29720
Birch Pl 29720
Bird Ln 29720
Black Oak Cir 29720
Blackberry Ln 29720
Blackmon Ln & Rd 29720
Blackstone Dr 29720
Blairwood Ct 29720
Blakeney Pl 29720
Blalock Aly 29720
Blenheim Ct 29720
Bless Ln 29720
Blossom St 29720
Blue Ln 29720
Blue Heron Cir 29720
Bob Ormond Rd 29720
Bon Rea Dr 29720
Bonanza Trl 29720
Bowling Ln 29720
W Boxcar Rd 29720
Boxwood Ave 29720
Boykin Blvd 29720
Bradburn Dr 29720
Bradford Dr 29720
Brady Rd 29720
Branch St 29720
Brendale Dr 29720
Briarwood Ln & Rd 29720
Brice Ln 29720
Bridgewood Dr 29720
Bristol Pl 29720
Broken Circle Dr 29720
Brook Dr 29720
Brookfield Ln 29720
Brookhill Ln 29720
E & W Brooklyn Ave 29720
Brookwood Dr 29720
Broome Pl 29720
Brown Rd 29720
E Brown Ferry Rd 29720
Bruce Hough Ln 29720
Bubba Ln 29720
Buck Brasington Rd 29720
Buckelew St 29720
Bucks Dr 29720
Bud Harris Rd 29720
Buford Cir 29720
Buhrstone Ct 29720
Burgess Dr 29720
Burke Duncan Rd 29720
Burnette St 29720
Burning Bush Ln 29720
Caldwell Rd 29720
Calhoun St 29720
Calvert Estate Dr 29720
Cambridge Dr 29720
Camellia Ct 29720
Camp Dr 29720
Camp Creek Rd 29720
Campbell Lake Rd 29720
Cane Mill Rd 29720
Cannery Rd 29720
Canterbury Dr 29720
Capricorn Rd 29720
Captain Ln 29720
Carelock Rd 29720
Carlton Way 29720
Carmel Rd 29720
Carnes Aly 29720
Carnes Wilson Rd 29720
Carolina Ln 29720
Carolina Creek Ln 29720
Caroline Ct 29720
Carousel Ln 29720
Carrie Ln 29720
Carrington Dr 29720
Carter Rd 29720
Caskey Ln & Rd 29720
N & S Catawba St 29720
Catawba Ridge Blvd 29720
Catoe Rd 29720
Cattail Rd 29720
Cedar Ln & St 29720
Cedar Circle Rd 29720
Cedar Creek Rd 29720
Cedar Dale Ln 29720
Cedar Hills Ln 29720
Cedar Pine Lake Rd 29720
Cedar Terrace Dr 29720
Central Ave 29720
Chaffee Rd 29720
Chandler Pl 29720
Charles Ave 29720
Charles Pettus Rd 29720
Charlie Stacks Rd 29720
Charlotte Hwy 29720
Chase Madison Dr 29720
Chasebrook Ln 29720
Cherrystone Rd 29720
Chester Hwy & St 29720
Chesterfield Ave & Ct 29720
Chestnut Dr 29720
Chiffon St 29720
Childrens Ave 29720
Chinaberry Dr 29720
Chote Rd 29720
Church St 29720
Churchill Dr 29720
Cimmeron Rd 29720
Cinderella Cir 29720
Cindy Ln 29720
City Ave 29720
Claddah Way 29720
Clarendon Dr 29720
Clark Dr, Ln & Rd 29720
Claude Phillips Rd 29720
Clearwater Dr 29720
Cliff Rd 29720
Clinton Ave 29720
Clinton School Rd 29720
Clover St 29720
Club Ct 29720
Clyburn Dr & St 29720
Clyde Stogner Rd 29720
Cockatoo Way 29720
Cody St 29720
Coker Ln 29720
Colonial Ave 29720
Colonial Commons Ct 29720
Colony Rd 29720
Colorado Ct 29720
Colton Rdg & Way 29720
Comb Way 29720
Commerce Blvd 29720
Commodore Dr 29720
Community Ln 29720
Confederate Ave 29720
Connor St 29720
Continental Dr 29720
Converse St 29720
Coot Sistare Rd 29720
N Corner Estates Rd 29720
Cortland Dr 29720
Corvette Ln 29720
Cot Ln 29720
Cotesworth Ln 29720
Country Club Dr 29720
Country Meadows Ln 29720
Courtney Miles Rd 29720
Courtside Dr 29720
Cove View Ct 29720
Covenant Pl 29720
Craggy Oaks Ln 29720
Craig Ave 29720
Craig Farm Rd 29720
Craig Manor Rd 29720
Craigwood Ln 29720
Crawford Dr 29720
Creekside Park Ln 29720
Crenshaw Dr 29720
Crenson Dr 29720
Creola Rd 29720
Crescent Dr 29720
Crestfield Dr 29720
Crestview Ln 29720
Cricket Ln 29720
Cross St 29720
Cross Creek Estates Rd 29720
Crown Rd 29720
Culdesac Rd 29720
Culp St 29720
Culp Ferguson Rd 29720
Culp Landsford Rd 29720
Cunningham St 29720
Cureton Taylor Dr 29720
Curtis Trapps Ct 29720
Cushion Ln 29720
Cutlet Ln 29720
Cypress Cir 29720
Dahlia Rd 29720
Dalton Ridge Dr 29720
Danlee Dr 29720
Darlene Blvd 29720
Darter Ln 29720
Davis St 29720
Daystar Rd 29720
Daytime Rd 29720
Deason Ln 29720
Deaton Aly & Dr 29720
Decole Dr 29720
Deer Run Rd 29720
Deer Track Cir 29720
Deerfield Rd 29720
Deerwood Rd 29720
Defiant Ln 29720
Delta Dr 29720
Demount Rd 29720
Denton Hill Rd 29720
Deputy Brent Mccants Ave 29720
Derby Ln 29720
Dhec Rd 29720
Diamond Cir 29720
Dirt Rd 29720
Divine St 29720
Dixie School Rd 29720
Dixon Rd 29720
Dobson St 29720
E & W Doc Garris Rd 29720
Doc Holliday Cir 29720
Doctor David Rd 29720
Dogwood Ln 29720
Dolphin Rd 29720
Dome Ln 29720
Doster Rd 29720
Double Oak Rd 29720
Douglas Rd 29720
Douglas Heights Ln 29720
Douglas Way Ln 29720
Dover Ln 29720
Downey Dr 29720
Downing St 29720
Drew Dr 29720
N & S Driftwood Ln 29720
Dry Ln 29720
Drywood Cir 29720
Duckwood Rd 29720
Dudley Steele Rd 29720
Duke St 29720
E & W Dunlap St 29720
Dusty Pine Ln 29720
Dusty Trail Ln 29720
Dwight Starnes Rd 29720
Eagle Point Est 29720
Earnhardt Dr 29720
Eastview Ct & Dr 29720
Eastwood Trail Dr 29720
Echo Woods Dr 29720
Edgar Dr 29720
E & W Edgemont Ct & Dr 29720
Edgeport Dr 29720
Edgewood Ct 29720
Edsen Ct 29720
Egrets Ct 29720
Elijah Ln 29720
Elliott St 29720
Ellis Ln 29720
Ellison Cir 29720
Elm St 29720
Elmwood Ave 29720
Emerald Estates Rd 29720
Emma Cir 29720
Ernest Wright Rd 29720
Erwin St 29720
Ethel Dr 29720
Eton Ln 29720
Eula Ct & St 29720
Evans Dr 29720
Evergreen Rd 29720
Faile St 29720
Fairfield St 29720
Fairleaf Rd 29720
E & W Fairmeadow Dr 29720
Fairway Dr 29720
Faith St 29720
Farmbrook Rd 29720
Farthing Dr 29720
Fawn Ln 29720
Feature Rd 29720
Felly Ln 29720
Fender Ln 29720
N & S Ferguson St 29720
Fickling Dr 29720
Fiddle Dr 29720
Field Rd 29720
Fireman Ln 29720
Firetower Rd 29720
Firewood Rd 29720
Fisc Ln 29720
Flagstone Dr 29720
Flamingo Rd 29720
Flat Creek Rd 29720
Fleetwood Rd 29720
Fletcher Funderburk Rd 29720
Flint Dr 29720
Florence Cir 29720
Flowergate Farm Rd 29720
Flutter Dr 29720
Foote St 29720
Footlog Rd 29720
Forest Dr 29720
Forest Glen Dr 29720
Foster Heights Dr 29720
Fowler Rd 29720
Fox Ln 29720
Fox Run Rd 29720
Foxbrook Cir 29720
Foxdale Ct 29720
Foxes Pond Rd 29720
Foxfire Dr 29720
Foxmeade Ct 29720
Foxworth Ln 29720
Franandel Dr 29720
Frank St 29720
Frank Hallman Rd 29720
Franklin St 29720
Frazier St 29720
Freeman Way 29720
Freemont Dr 29720
N & S French St 29720
Friars Ct 29720
Froebe Dr 29720
Funderburk St 29720
Gamble Dr 29720
Gardener Ave 29720
Garnette Rd 29720
Gaslight Ave 29720
Gauley Dr 29720
E & W Gay St 29720
Gear Dr 29720
Gene Hudson Dr 29720
George Carnes Rd 29720
George Cook Rd 29720
George Howle Rd 29720
Georgetown Rd 29720
Gilliam Sowell Rd 29720
Gills Creek Dr 29720
Gillsbrook Rd 29720
Ginger Cake Rd 29720
Gladstone Rd 29720
Gladys Marie Dr 29720
Glenn Dr 29720
Glenwood Ave 29720
Gleny Pine Cir 29720
Gold Pl 29720
Golf Course Rd 29720
Gooch St 29720
Goose Down Ln 29720
Grace Ave 29720
Graham Dr 29720
Grain Bin Rd 29720
Gray Fox Ln 29720
Great Falls Hwy & Rd 29720
Green Rd 29720
Green Meadow Cir 29720
Green Peach Rd 29720
Greenbriar Dr 29720
Greenoak Dr 29720
Greenway Dr 29720
N & S Gregory St 29720
Greyfox Estates Rd 29720
Greystone Dr 29720
Griffin Rd 29720
Gunnars Ridge Rd 29720
Gypsy Ln 29720
Habitat Ln 29720
Hagins Rd 29720
Hailstone Ln 29720
Hall Ln 29720
Hallman Rd 29720
Halloway Ln 29720
Hammond Carnes Rd 29720
Hampton Rd 29720
Hampton Grace Ave 29720
Hance St 29720
Hancock Rd 29720
Happy Trl 29720
Hardee Ln 29720
Hardin St 29720
Hardwick Ln 29720
Harkey Rd 29720
Harmon Ln 29720
Harper Ln 29720
Harris St 29720
Harris Hill Rd 29720
Harrison Barr Rd 29720
Harvison Ct 29720
Havenwood Dr 29720
Hawthorne Rd 29720
Hayes Ln 29720
Haynes Ln 29720
Hayward Dr 29720
S Hazel St 29720
Healthcare Dr 29720
Heath Cir 29720
Heather Ln 29720
Heatherwood Ln 29720
Hector Rd 29720
Hegler Ln 29720
Helms Rd 29720
Henderson Rd 29720
Henry Pl 29720
Henry Harris Rd 29720
Hereford Way 29720
Herman Ashley Dr 29720
Hermit Rd 29720
Hermitage Rd 29720
Hershel Plyler Rd 29720
Heyward Hough Rd 29720
Hickory Dr 29720
Hickory Hill Dr 29720
High Lane Dr 29720
High Point Cir 29720
Highgate Ln 29720
Highway 521 Byp S 29720
Highway 9 Byp E & W 29720
Hillcrest Ave 29720
Hilldale Dr 29720
Hillside Ave 29720
Hilltop Ln 29720
Hilton Way Rd 29720

Hines Aly & St 29720
Holden Rd 29720
Holiday Rd 29720
Hollow Cir 29720
Holly Ln 29720
Holly Hill Rd 29720
Hollyberry Ln 29720
Hollybrook Ln 29720
Hollydale Cir 29720
Home Cir 29720
Home Place Ln 29720
Homestead Pl 29720
Honeycutt Rd 29720
Honeywood Rd 29720
E & W Hood St 29720
Hood Park Ln 29720
Hope Pl 29720
Hopkins Ln 29720
Hough Rd 29720
Howard Stacks Estate Rd 29720
Howle St 29720
Hubbard Dr 29720
Hudson St 29720
Hudson Street Ext 29720
N & S Hughes St 29720
Hunter St 29720
Hunters Ridge Rd 29720
Huntkins Rd 29720
Hurley Walters Rd 29720
Hyde St 29720
Industrial Park Rd 29720
Ira Roberts Rd 29720
Isom St 29720
Ixoria Rd 29720
Jacal Ln 29720
Jack Robertson Ln 29720
Jack Usher Rd 29720
N & S Jackson Rd 29720
Jacobs Ln 29720
James St 29720
Jamestowne Rd 29720
Jb Denton Rd 29720
Jefferson St 29720
Jenkins Hill Rd 29720
Jenna Ln 29720
Jerry Funderburk Rd 29720
Jessica Chad Ln 29720
Jl Gainer Rd 29720
Joe Funderburk Rd 29720
John St 29720
John Clyburn Rd 29720
John Everall Rd 29720
John L Hudson Sr Rd 29720
John Truesdale Rd 29720
Johnson Rd 29720
Jolly St 29720
Jonathan Ln 29720
Jordan St 29720
Joshua Tree Rd 29720
Jubilee Ln 29720
Juneau Rd 29720
Jw Roberts Rd 29720
Kacy Ln 29720
Karla Cir 29720
Katelyn Dr 29720
Kayla Ln 29720
Kaywood Dr 29720
Kelly Dr 29720
Kendlewood Dr 29720
Kent Dr 29720
Kershaw St 29720
Kershaw Camden Hwy 29720
Kerwick Ct 29720
Kettle Rd 29720
Kim St 29720
Kings Cir 29720
Kirk Air Base Rd 29720
Kirk Mccain Rd 29720
Kirkover Dr 29720
Knight Rd & St 29720
Knollcreek Dr 29720
Knollwood Apts Dr 29720
Knothead Dr 29720
Knottingwood Dr 29720
Knotty Pines Dr 29720
Kyrie Ln 29720
S Lake Dr 29720
Lake Shore Dr 29720
Lake Veronica Dr 29720
Lakefront Dr 29720
Lakeside Cir 29720
Lakeview Cir & St 29720
Lambert Dr 29720
Lamplight Rd 29720
Lancaster Byp E & W 29720
Lancer Ln 29720
Landsford Rd 29720
Laney Rd 29720
Langley Rd 29720
Lass St 29720
Laughridge St 29720
Laurel Ave & Ct 29720
Laurens Ct 29720
Lavoy Ct 29720
Lawanda Ln 29720
Lazy H Dr 29720
Lazy Oak Dr 29720
Lead Off Rd 29720
Lee St 29720
Lee Ormand Rd 29720
Lee Park Ln 29720
Lee Snipes Rd 29720
Legacy Rd 29720
Legend Rd 29720
W Leroy St 29720
Lewis Dr 29720
Linseed Ln 29720
Little John Dr 29720
Lloyd Reid Rd 29720
Loading Rd 29720
Locker Rd 29720
Lockwood Ln 29720
Locustwood Ave 29720
Loft Ln 29720
Logan Terry Rd 29720
Logging Rd 29720
Logo St 29720
Loraine Ln 29720
Lord Rd 29720
Lori St 29720
Louis Mcateer Rd 29720
Louis Springs Rd 29720
Louisa St 29720
Louisa Park Ln 29720
Louise St 29720
Love Dr 29720
Low Country Ln 29720
Lure Ln 29720
Lymon Reece Rd 29720
Lyndell Way 29720
Lyndon Dr 29720
Lynwood Dr 29720
Lynwood Circle Rd 29720
Macadams Rd 29720
Mackey Rd 29720
Maclean Ct 29720
Madison Ln 29720
Magnolia Dr & Ln 29720
Mahaffey Line Dr 29720
N Main St
100-500 29720
501-1299 29720
501-501 29721
502-1298 29720
S Main St 29720
Major Evans Rd 29720
Malvern Ln 29720
Mamoth Oaks Dr 29720
Mangum Dr 29720
W Manor Dr 29720
Mantell Rd 29720
Mantid Way 29720
Maple Ln 29720
Maplewood Ave 29720
Marble Ct 29720
Marie Dr 29720
Mariners Cove Ln 29720
Marion St & Way 29720
Marion Sims Dr 29720
Maritime Dr 29720
Mark Ln 29720
N & S Market St 29720
Marlborough Ct 29720
Marsh Rd 29720
Martin Ln 29720
Marty Ln 29720
Mary Cauthen Farm Rd 29720
Mary Lee Ln 29720
Mason St 29720
Massey Rd 29720
Masterson Ct 29720
Mayflower Dr 29720
Mcateer Park Ln 29720
Mccain Rd 29720
Mccardell St 29720
Mccowan Ln 29720
Mcilwain Rd 29720
Mckinney Ln 29720
Mcmanus Ln 29720
Mctown Rd 29720
E & W Meadow Dr 29720
Meadow Plaza Dr 29720
Meadowbrook Dr 29720
E & W Meeting St 29720
Melton Park Cir 29720
Memorial Dr 29720
Memorial Park Rd 29720
Mercy Ln 29720
Merribrook Ln 29720
Merritt Ln 29720
Michael Dr 29720
Michaw St 29720
Mickles Ln 29720
Mikala Ln 29720
Mill Race Ln 29720
Miller St 29720
Miller Ridge Ln 29720
Miller Street Ext 29720
Mills Ln 29720
Millstone Creek Rd 29720
Millwood Rd 29720
Mint St 29720
Misty Oak Dr 29720
Misty Woods Ln 29720
Mockingbird Ln 29720
Mole Hill Dr 29720
Monitor Ln 29720
Monroe Hwy 29720
Montecrest St 29720
Montgomery Rd 29720
Monticello Rd 29720
Moore St 29720
Moorefield Ln 29720
Moose Lodge Rd 29720
Morningside Dr 29720
Morris Rd 29720
Morris Hinson Rd 29720
Morrison Rd 29720
Moseley Private Dr 29720
Mosteller Dr 29720
Mount Laurel Rd 29720
Mountainbrook Rd 29720
Mourning Dove Ln 29720
Mulberry Ln 29720
Mullis Cir 29720
Mungo Rd 29720
Myers Cir 29720
Nc Potter Rd 29720
Needles Dr 29720
Neill Rd 29720
New Burns Ln 29720
New Cut Cir 29720
New Cut Church Rd 29720
New Hope Rd 29720
New Loch Ct 29720
New Miller St 29720
New Way Apartments 29720
Nichols Rd 29720
Nim Ln 29720
Nina Ct 29720
Niven Rd 29720
Nomad Ln 29720
Nope Ln 29720
Norfolk Rd 29720
Norland Ln 29720
Norman Ln 29720
Normandy Rd 29720
North Cir 29720
E & W North Corner Rd 29720
Northpark Sq 29720
Oak Creek Ct 29720
Oak Hill Church Rd 29720
Oakdale Dr 29720
Oakhaven Dr 29720
Oakland Dr 29720
Oakridge Rd 29720
Oakwood Ave 29720
Old Blackmon Ln 29720
Old Camden Hwy & Rd 29720
Old Camden Monroe Hwy 29720
Old Carter St 29720
Old Charles St 29720
Old Charlotte Rd 29720
Old Church Rd 29720
Old Dixie Rd 29720
Old Evans Cir 29720
Old Farm Rd 29720
Old Greenbriar Dr 29720
Old Gregory Ln & Rd 29720
Old Hickory Rd 29720
Old Hillside Dr 29720
Old Landsford Rd 29720
Old Lynwood Cir 29720
Old Oakland Cir 29720
Old Pardue Rd 29720
Old Ponderosa Rd 29720
Old Skipper Ave 29720
Old Still St 29720
Old Sullivan Rd 29720
Old Thompson Ave 29720
Old Water Works Rd 29720
Old Woodlawn Ave 29720
Omni Ct 29720
Orange Ave 29720
Osceola Rd 29720
Oxford Cir & Pl 29720
Pacer Rd 29720
Paddock Pl 29720
Pageland Hwy 29720
Palidin Rd 29720
Palmer Lloyd Rd 29720
Palmetto St 29720
Palmetto Kennel Ln 29720
Panther Rd 29720
Pardue Cir & St 29720
E Park Dr 29720
Parkman Ave 29720
Partridge Cir 29720
Partridge Hill Rd 29720
Pasture Ln 29720
Pate Terrace Dr 29720
Patricia St 29720
Patton St 29720
Paul Snipes Rd 29720
Peacewood Trail Rd 29720
Peach Farm Rd 29720
Peagler Dr 29720
Pearl Dr 29720
Pearson Ct 29720
Pecan Dr 29720
Pennington Dr 29720
N & S Penny St 29720
Peony Ln 29720
Pheasant Rd 29720
Phillips St 29720
Philthurman Rd 29720
Pickett Ln 29720
Pierson Dr 29720
N Pine St 29720
Pine Ridge Ln 29720
Pine Spring St 29720
Pinedale Rd 29720
Pinehill Cir 29720
Pinestraw St 29720
Pineview Dr 29720
Pineview Court Ln 29720
Pinewood Ave 29720
Pink Dogwood Ave 29720
Pink Plyler Rd 29720
Pinta Dr 29720
Pioneer Ln 29720
Plantation Rd 29720
Pleasant Rd 29720
Pleasant Dale Cir 29720
Pleasant Hill St 29720
Plexico Dr 29720
Plyler Rd & St 29720
Plyler Mill Rd 29720
Plymouth Dr 29720
Polston Dr 29720
Pond Ct 29720
Pond Ridge Ln 29720
Pop Ln 29720
Poppy Ln 29720
Porter Ranch Rd 29720
S Potter Rd 29720
Powderhorn Rd 29720
Powell Ave 29720
Preston Ln 29720
Prince Dr & Ln 29720
Providence Rd 29720
Quail Hill Ct 29720
Quality Dr 29720
Quarry Dr 29720
Quiet Acres Rd 29720
Quiet Creek Dr 29720
Ranson Rd 29720
Ray St 29720
E & W Rebound Rd 29720
Red Doc Rd 29720
Red Fox Rd 29720
Red Hill Rd 29720
Reece Rd 29720
Reeves Rd 29720
Rhonda Rd 29720
Rhyner Rd 29720
Rickenbacker St 29720
Ridgehaven Rd 29720
Ridgewood Acres Rd 29720
Riggs Pvt Dr 29720
Riley Cir 29720
Rillstone Dr 29720
Riverbend Rd 29720
Riveroak Ln 29720
Riverside Rd 29720
Roach Dr 29720
Robert Allen Rd 29720
Robert H Kirk Rd 29720
Robert Usher Rd 29720
Roberts Dr 29720
Robin Dr 29720
Robinson Rd 29720
Rock St 29720
Rock Chimney Cir 29720
Rock Hill Hwy 29720
Rock Springs Rd 29720
N Rocky River Rd 29720
Rocky Top Dr 29720
Roddey Dr 29720
Roebuck Dr 29720
Rogers Ln 29720
Roland Williams Rd 29720
Rollie Rd 29720
Rolling Hills Rd 29720
Rollings Roost Rd 29720
Rondo Ln 29720
Rope Ln 29720
Rose Ln 29720
Roseanna Ln 29720
Rosewood Ct & Ln 29720
Ross Rd 29720
Ross Cauthen Rd 29720
Rowell Rd 29720
Roy Carnes Rd 29720
Royida Dr 29720
Rucker Ln 29720
Rugby Rd 29720
Rus Tom Dr 29720
Rushing Rd 29720
Ruth St 29720
Ruthburn Ct 29720
Rutledge St 29720
Rutledge Acres Rd 29720
Saddle Rd 29720
Saddle Club Rd 29720
Saint Paul St 29720
Sandy Branch Ln 29720
Santa Barbara Dr 29720
Santa Rosa Ct 29720
Sara Dr 29720
Sardis Dr 29720
Sawgrass Ln 29720
Scallybark Ct 29720
Seaboard Cir 29720
Seagull Dr 29720
Sedgefield Dr 29720
Seminole Winds Ln 29720
Seneca Plaza Dr 29720
Sentry Rd 29720
Serenity Ln 29720
Seth Ln 29720
Setters Ln 29720
Seven Oaks Way 29720
Shady Ln 29720
Shady Lakes Est 29720
Shagbark Rd 29720
Shamrock Ave 29720
Sharon Ln 29720
Shehane Private Rd 29720
Shelton St 29720
Sherwood Cir 29720
Shiloh Dr 29720
Shiloh Ranch Rd 29720
W Shiloh Unity Rd 29720
Shore Dr 29720
Shoreline Dr 29720
Short Ln 29720
Sienna Ln 29720
Sigmon St 29720
Silkies Blvd 29720
Silver Fox Cir 29720
Sims Dr 29720
Sims Grove Way 29720
Six Mile Creek Rd 29720
Skipper Ave 29720
Small St 29720
Smiley Dr 29720
Smokey Joe Rd 29720
Smokey Starnes Rd 29720
Snow Dr 29720
Snug Harbor Rd 29720
Somerset Dr 29720
Songbird St 29720
South Ave 29720
Southport Ln 29720
Southside Cir 29720
Southwyck Dr 29720
Sowell St 29720
Spanish Villa Ln 29720
Sparkle Trl 29720
Sparrow Ln 29720
Split Oak Ln 29720
Spring Club Rd 29720
Spring Hill Church Rd 29720
Springbrook Ct 29720
Springdale Rd 29720
Springdale Road Ext 29720
Springdell Church Rd 29720
E & W Springs St 29720
Springwood Dr 29720
Stacks Rd 29720
Stallion Ln 29720
Standing Timber Rd 29720
Starcliff Cir 29720
Starmount Cir 29720
Starnes St 29720
Starwood Ln 29720
Steele St 29720
Steele Hill Rd 29720
Stevens Hill Rd 29720
Steward Rd 29720
Stewman St 29720
Stinson Rd 29720
Stogner Dr 29720
Stonebridge Ln 29720
Storage Rd 29720
Stormy Ln 29720
Strafford Dr 29720
Stribling Cir 29720
Strickland Ct 29720
Stroupe Rd 29720
Summit Ave 29720
Sumter St 29720
Sunday Pl 29720
Sunny Ln 29720
Sunnybrook Ln 29720
Sunnyside Dr 29720
Sunset Cir 29720
Sunshine Rd 29720
Survey St 29720
Sutter Ln 29720
Suttle Rd 29720
Sutton Ln 29720
Swiss Way 29720
Tabernacle Rd 29720
Tallon Pl 29720
Tam Ln 29720
Tara Trl 29720
Tarram Ct 29720
Taxahaw Rd 29720
Taxidermy Rd 29720
Taylor Dr & St 29720
Ten Oaks Dr 29720
Tenacity Ct 29720
Terra Ln 29720
Terrace Rd 29720
Thames Ct 29720
The Knoll Ln 29720
Thelma Ln 29720
Theron Cir 29720
Third Tee Rd 29720
Thomas Ln 29720
Thomasville St 29720
Thompson Rd 29720
Thornwell Rd 29720
Threatt St 29720
Threatt Park Ln 29720
Three Oaks Ln 29720
Tiger Paw Ln 29720
Tillman St 29720
Tilly Ln 29720
Tim Foster Ln 29720
Tin Ln 29720
Tirzah Church Rd 29720
Todd St 29720
Tom Laney Rd 29720
Tombeck Ln 29720
Tower Court Rd 29720
Townes Ave 29720
Traders Ct 29720
Tradesville Rd 29720
Tradewinds Ct 29720
Trailer Court Rd 29720
Trailstream Dr 29720
Tram Rd 29720
Travertine Dr 29720
Travis Ln 29720
Treetop Dr 29720
Trestle Ln 29720
Trevor Ct 29720
Tribal Rd 29720
Tripp Ln 29720
Truesdale Dr 29720
Tryon St 29720
Tuck Knight Ct 29720
Tully Ct 29720
Turtle Point Ct 29720
Twelve Mile Creek Rd 29720
Twilight Rd 29720
Twin Ln 29720
Union Church Rd 29720
Unity Church Rd 29720
University Dr 29720
University Park Dr 29720
Upson Dr 29720
Usher Rd 29720
Van Wyck Rd 29720
Venus Ln 29720
Vicks Dr 29720
Victoria St 29720
Videtta Dr 29720
Virginia St 29720
Vista Ln 29720
Volkmar Ln 29720
Waccamaw Dr 29720
Wade St 29720
Wadell Stinson Rd 29720

Walden Rd 29720
Walkabout Ln 29720
Wallace St 29720
Walnut Rd 29720
Walters Ln 29720
Warwick Pl 29720
Washington St 29720
Wateree St 29720
Waters Edge Ln 29720
Watson Dr 29720
Watts Dr 29720
Waverly Ct 29720
Waxhaw Hwy 29720
Waxhaw Village Rd 29720
Wayne Rd 29720
Wedgewood Rd 29720
Wendover Ln 29720
Westgate Cir 29720
Westglen Pl 29720
Westminister Dr 29720
Westmoreland Dr 29720
Westover Pl 29720
Westway Apartment Dr 29720
Westwood Rd 29720
Whaley St 29720
Wheels Of Peace Dr 29720
Whispering Pines Ln 29720
Whitaker Rd 29720
N & S White St 29720
White Buffalo Dr 29720
White Pine Ct 29720
Whittle St 29720
Wild Rose Ln 29720
Wildcat Rd 29720
Wilderness Ln 29720
Wildwood Rd 29720
William Carnes Rd 29720
Williams Cir & St 29720
Williams Estate Dr 29720
Willie Reed Rd 29720
Willie Usher Rd 29720
N & S Willow Lake Rd 29720
Willow Oak Cir 29720
Wilma Dr 29720
Wilson Dr 29720
Windsor Dr 29720
Windward Ln 29720
Windy Hill Ln 29720
Windy Oaks Way 29720
Winston Dr 29720
Winter Ln 29720
Winterberry Ln 29720
Winthrop Ave 29720
Wisdom Rd 29720
Wisteria Way 29720
Witherspoon St & Trl 29720
Woodbridge St 29720
Woodcreek Apartments Dr 29720
N & S Woodland Dr & Way 29720
Woodland Court Rd 29720
Woodlawn Ave 29720
Woodleaf Ln 29720
Woodley St 29720
W Woodmont Dr 29720
Woodrow Carnes Rd 29720
Woodrow Neal Rd 29720
Woodshire Dr 29720
Woodside Ln 29720
Woody Way 29720
Wrenwood Dr 29720
Wright Rd 29720
Wyatt Brown Rd 29720
N & S Wylie St 29720
Wylie Park Rd 29720
Yachstman Ct 29720
Yancey St 29720
Yancy Catoe Rd 29720
Yellow Jacket Dr 29720
N & S York St 29720
Zarrelli Rd 29720
Zeb Deese Rd 29720
Zion Rd 29720
Zion Hill Rd 29720
Zion Mhp Rd 29720

NUMBERED STREETS

All Street Addresses 29720

LEXINGTON SC

General Delivery 29072

POST OFFICE BOXES MAIN OFFICE STATIONS AND BRANCHES

Box No.s
1 - 9030 29071
84001 - 100005 29073

NAMED STREETS

A B Frye Rd 29073
Abbie Ct & Ln 29072
Aberdeen Dr 29072
Aberdour Ct 29072
Abingdon Dr 29073
Able Harmon Ln 29072
Absalom Ct 29072
Acorn Dr 29073
Adams Rd 29073
Adastra Ln 29072
Addie Lucas Rd 29073
Addison Ct 29072
Addy Ln 29072
Adkins Ln 29073
Aiken Craft Rd 29073
Alcott Ct 29072
Alderwood Ct 29072
Alfred Ct 29073
Allen St 29072
Allenbrooke Dr & Way 29072
Alliance Rd 29073
Alston Cir & Ct 29072
Alta Vista Ct 29073
Altonia Lee Dr 29072
Amber Chase Ct & Dr 29073
Amelia Ct & Dr 29072
American Legion Dr 29072
Amethyst Ln 29072
Amick St 29072
Anadale Ln 29072
Andover Ct 29072
Andrew Corley Rd 29072
Angel Ct 29073
Angel Oak Dr 29073
Annapolis Rd 29072
Appalachian Trl 29072
Appaloosa Dr 29072
Appaloosa Trl 29073
Arabian Rd 29073
Arbor Ln 29073
Arbor End Rd 29072
Arborshade Ct 29072
Ariel Cir 29072
Arietta Ct 29072
Arkhaven Ct 29073
Armanda Ct & Rd 29072
Arnwood Ct 29072
Arrie Ln 29073
Arrowwood Ct 29072
Arstook Ct 29072
Artisan Ct 29072
Arundel Ct 29073
Asa Rose Ln 29072
Ashdown Park Ct 29072
Ashe St 29073
Ashford St & Way 29072
Ashley Ct 29072
Ashley Hills Ct, Dr & Trl 29072
Ashley Oaks Ct & Dr 29072
Ashley Trace Ct & Dr 29072
Ashmore Ln 29072
Ashton Cir 29073
Ashworth Dr 29072
Aspen Glade Ct 29072
Aston Ln 29072
Athena Ln 29072
Augusta Hwy 29072
Augusta Rd
4200-4999 29073
5000-5499 29072
Aurora Ln 29072
Autumn Ln 29072
Autumn Oaks Ln 29073
Autumn Park Ct 29072
Autumn Stroll Ct 29072
Azalea Dr 29072
Bachman Dr 29073
Backman Ave 29073
Backman Rd 29073
Backman St 29072
Backman Grove Ct 29073
Badminton Ln 29072
Bagford Ct 29072
Bailey Island Cir 29072
Bakers End 29072
Baldric Ct 29072
Ball Park Rd 29072
Baneberry Dr, Ln & Loop 29073
Barberry Cir & Dr 29072
Barco Ct 29073
Barefoot Dr 29073
Barn Plank Ct & Rd 29072
Barnacle Cir & Rd 29072
Barnevelder Dr 29072
Barnstable Ct 29072
Barnwell Ct 29073
Baron Ct & Rd 29072
Barr Cir & Rd 29072
Barre St 29072
Barrett Dr 29072
Barretts Way 29072
Barrier Ln 29073
Barrington Dr 29072
Barrister Ct 29073
Bartram St & Way 29072
Basin Rock Ln 29073
Baskin Hills Ct & Rd 29072
Batten Ct 29072
Battenkill Ct 29073
Bay Pines Ct 29072
Bay Pointe 29073
Baywood Ct & Dr 29072
Beach Rd 29072
Bear Brook Ct 29072
Beauclaire Dr 29072
Beaumont Dr 29072
Beaver Creek Rd 29072
Beck Taylor Pl 29073
Beckenham St 29072
Beckley Ct 29072
Beckman Rd 29073
Bedford Ct 29073
Bedford Place Ct 29072
Beech Leaf Ct 29072
Beech Tree Ct 29073
Beechaven Rd 29072
Beechcreek Cir, Ct & Rd 29072
Beechwoods Dr 29072
Beecliff Ct & Ln 29073
Beekeeper Ct 29072
Belfry Ct & Dr 29072
Belinda Ct & Dr 29072
Bell Haven Ln 29072
Bella Vista Ct 29073
Belle Chase Dr 29072
Bellerive Dr 29073
Bellewood Dr 29072
Belmont Ct 29072
Belo Rd 29072
Belo Ridge Ct & Rd 29072
Belton Dr 29073
Beltrees Dr 29072
Bending Oak Ct 29073
Benjamin Dr 29073
Bennett Foley Ln 29073
Bennock Mill Ct 29072
Bent Needle Ct 29072
Bent Ridge Ct 29072
Bentley Ct & Dr 29072
Beringer Cir 29072
Berkman Ct 29072
Berly St 29072
Berrybrook Ln 29072
Berrywood Ct 29072
Beth Ln 29073
Bethany Church Rd 29073
Bethel Church Rd 29072
Bethpage Ct 29073
Betty Blvd 29073
Bickley Rd 29072
Big Thicket Ct 29072
Big Timber Dr 29073
Big Valley Ln 29073
Bill Williamson Ct 29072
Bimini Twist Cir 29072
Birch Knot Ct 29073
Birch Terrace Ct 29073
Birkdale Ct 29072
Bison Cir & Pl 29072
Black Ave 29072
Black Pine Ct 29073
Black Walnut Ct 29073
Black Walnut Dr 29073
Blackberry Ln 29073
Blackjack Oak Ln 29073
Blacksmith Ct & Rd 29073
Blaine Ln 29072
Blazer Dr 29073
Bledsoe Dr 29073
Blue Heron Ct 29072
Blue Lake Dr & Ln 29072
Blue Ledge Cir 29072
Blue Pine Ct & Ln 29073
Blue Quill Ct 29072
Blueberry Dr 29073
Bluebill Ct 29072
Bluefield Ct & Rd 29073
Bluff Ridge Rd 29073
Boardwalk Ln 29072
Boiling Springs Ln & Rd 29073
Bonhomme Cir 29072
Bonhomme Richard Rd 29072
Bonnie Jean Ct 29073
Bonnie View Ct 29073
Boone Rd 29073
Boykin Ln 29073
Bracken Dr 29072
Bradfield Ct 29072
Bradford Ct 29073
Brady Porth Rd 29072
Braekel Way 29072
Braker Ln 29073
Bramble Pl 29072
Bran Ct 29073
Branch Cir 29072
Branch Hill Rd 29073
Brandon Ct 29072
Branham View Rd 29072
Brass Ct 29072
Bream Pt 29072
Breezes Dr 29072
Brentwood Dr 29073
Brevard Pkwy 29073
Briarpatch Rd 29072
Brick Rd 29073
Brickyard Rd 29073
Bridgeport Ln 29072
Bridle Cir & Ct 29072
Bridle Trail Ln 29072
Bridleridge Rd 29072
Bridlewood Ct & Dr 29072
Brighton Ct 29072
Brinton Ct 29072
Britt Ct 29073
Broad Oak Ln 29073
Broadleaf Dr 29073
Broadreach Rd 29073
Brockton Ct 29072
Broken Ln 29072
Bronz Bluff Ct 29073
Bronze Dr 29072
Bronze Bluff Ct 29073
Brook Hollow Ct 29072
Brook Trout Ct 29072
Brookdale Cir 29072
Brookgreen Dr 29072
Brookhaven Ln 29073
Brookhill St E & W 29072
Brooklet Ct & Dr 29072
Brookside Pkwy 29072
Brooksong Dr 29073
Brown Blvd & Ln 29073
Browning Ct & Ext 29073
Browns River Rd 29072
Bruin Dr 29073
Bruner Rd 29072
Bruton Smith Rd 29072
Bryars Ct 29072
Buck Dr 29072
Buck Corley Ct & Rd 29073
Buckboard Rd 29072
Buckhaven Way 29072
Buckhead Ct 29072
Buckstone Trl 29073
Buckthorne Dr 29072
Bufflehead Pt 29072
Bundrick Rd 29072
Burbank Ct 29073
Burma Rd 29073
Burton Rd 29072
Business Park Dr 29072
E & W Butler St 29072
Butler Hill Ln 29073
Butterfly Ct 29072
Bywater Ct 29072
Cabana Way 29072
Cabin Creek Ct 29073
Cabot Bay Dr 29072
Caley Ct 29072
Calks Ferry Rd
1598A-1598C 29072
100-1699 29072
1700-3100 29073
3102-3148 29073
Cambridge Hill Dr 29072
Camden Ct 29072
Camelia Dr 29072
Cameron Ct 29072
Campbell Ct 29072
Canadian Rd 29073
Candy Cane Ln 29072
Cannon Knoll Rd 29073
Cannon Trail Ct & Rd 29073
Cantigny Ct 29073
Canting Way 29072
Canton Way 29072
Cape Ct 29072
Cape Jasmine Way 29073
Cape Romain Ct 29072
Caprice Ct 29072
Captains Watch 29072
Cardinal Ct & Dr 29073
Cardinal Pines Ct, Dr & Ln 29073
Caribou St 29072
Carl Ln 29073
Carlen Ave 29072
Carlton Ct 29073
Carnouste Ct 29072
Carola Ln 29073
Caroline Xing 29072
Caroline Hill Rd 29072
Caroline Springs Rd 29072
Carriage Hill Ct & Dr 29072
Carriage Lake Ct & Dr 29072
Carrie Clyde Ct 29072
Carroll Hill Dr 29072
Carter Ln 29073
Cascade Ct & Dr 29072
Casco Ct 29072
Castlefield Dr 29073
Castleville Ct 29073
Catawba Ct & Trl 29072
Cathy Ln 29073
Cats Paw 29072
Caughman Rd 29072
Caughman Farm Ln 29072
Cavalier Ln 29073
Caxton Ct 29072
Cecil Ln 29073
Cedar Rd 29073
Cedar Break Ct 29073
Cedar Green Dr 29073
Cedar Vale Dr 29073
Cedarcrest Dr
200-399 29072
400-499 29073
Center Dr 29072
Central St 29073
Century Farm Ct 29073
Century Hill Ct 29073
Chaddork Ct 29072
Chadwick Trl 29072
Chadwood Cir 29073
Chamfort Dr 29072
Chapman Ct 29072
Chaps Cir 29073
Chariot St 29072
Charles Ct 29072
Charter Ln 29072
Charter Oak Ct & Rd 29072
Chasan Hill Ct 29073
Chason Rd 29073
Chateau Dr 29073
Chattooga Pl 29072
Cherokee Trl 29072
Cherokee Hills Ct 29072
Cherokee Isle Ct 29072
Cherokee Pond Ct & Trl 29072
Cherokee Shores Dr 29072
Cherry Hall Dr 29072
Cherry Hill Ln 29072
Cherry Laurel Dr 29073
Cheryse Dr 29073
Cheshire Rd 29072
Chesterbrook Ln 29072
Chesterton Dr 29072
Chestnut St 29073
Chethan Cir 29073
Chisolm Cir, Ct & Way 29073
Chowning Pl 29072
Christian Ct 29072
Christie St 29072
N & S Church St 29072
Churchill Ct 29073
Churchview Ct & Loop 29073
Cinda Leigh Ct & Dr 29073
Cinnamon Ln 29073
Cinnamon Hills Ct & Ln 29072
E & W Circle Dr 29072
Circleview Dr 29072
Claiborne Ct 29073
Clark St 29072
Clarmont Ct 29072
Claude Ct 29073
Claudious St 29072
Claycut Rd 29073
Clear Creek Ct 29072
Clear Springs Trl 29072
Clearstream Valley Rd 29073
Clermont Lakes Ct & Dr 29073
Cleyera Dr 29073
Clovis Pt 29072
Clubside Ct & Dr 29072
Coachman Ct & Dr 29072
Coatbridge Ln 29072
Cobblers Glen Ct 29072
Cobbleview Dr 29072
Cobden Ct 29072
Cochin Ct & Trce 29072
Cog Hill Dr 29073
Coldridge Ct 29073
Colleton Ct 29072
Colony Ct 29072
Colony Hill Rd 29073
Colony Lakes Ct & Dr 29073
Coltsfoot Ct 29072
Columbia Ave 29072
Commonwealth Ct 29073
Community Dr 29073
Compass Ln 29073
Concrete Rd 29073
Condor Rte 29073
Confederate Ct 29073
Conifer Cir 29073
Conner Rd 29072
Connie Ct 29072
Cool Springs Ct & Rd 29073
Copper Ln 29072
Copper Bluff Rd 29073
Copper Head Rd 29073
Copper Queen Ct 29073
Coral Ct 29073
Coriander Ln 29073
Corley St 29072
Corley Manor Ct 29072
Corley Mill Rd 29072
Corley Woods Ct & Dr 29072
Cornerstone Ct & Ln 29073
Cornish Way 29073
Cottage Green Ln 29072
Cottage Woods Trl 29072
Cottingham Ct 29072
Country Rd 29073
Country Lake Ct & Dr 29072
Country Meadow Ln 29073
Country Oak Rd 29073
Counts Ferry Rd 29072
Courtside Dr 29073
Coventry Ct & Dr 29072
Coventry Lake Dr 29072
Coveside Dr 29072
Covey Ln 29073
Coxswain Rd 29072
Coxton Mill Ln 29073
Coy Ln 29072
Coyahago Ct 29073
Cranberry Ct 29072
Cranford Ct 29072
Crassula Dr 29073
Creek Branch Ct & Dr 29072
Creek Side Ct & Ln 29072
Cregar Ct 29072
Crepe Myrtle Cir 29073
Creps St 29072
Crescent Moon Ct 29072
Crescent Ridge Dr 29073
Crescent River Rd 29073
Creston Ct 29072
Crestridge Dr 29073
Crestwood Arch 29073
Crickhollow Cir 29073
Crimson Ct & Ln 29072
Crimson Oak Dr & Ln 29072
Cromer Rd 29073
Crooked Pine Ct 29073
Cross Rd & St 29073
Cross Hill Cir & Rd 29073
S Crout St 29072
Crout Place Rd 29073
Crown Colony Ct 29073
Crown Point Ct & Rd 29073
Crowne Pointe Dr 29072
Crumpton Ct 29073
Crystal Springs Dr 29073
Cuddles Ct 29072
Cumberland Dr 29072
Cumbre Ct 29073
Cunningham Rd 29073
Cypress Lake Ln 29072
Cypress Woods Ct 29072
Dahlia St 29072
Dalecrest Ct 29072
Dalin Ct 29072
Dana Ct 29072
Dandelion Ct 29072
Danwood Ave 29073
Daralynn Dr 29073
Darby Ambrose Rd 29072
Dari June Rd 29073
Darian Dr 29073
Dark Hollow Dr 29073
Darkwood Ct 29072
Davega Dr 29073

David Dr & Ln 29073
Davidson Rd 29072
Dawson Hill Ln 29072
Dawsons Park Dr & Way 29072
Daylily Ct & Dr 29072
Dean Ct 29073
Deanna Ct 29072
Deep Aly 29072
Deer Hill Rd 29073
Deer Meadow Ln 29073
Deer Moss Trl 29073
Deer Run Ln 29072
Deer Springs Trl 29073
Deerchase Ln 29072
Deerglade Ct & Run 29072
Deertrack Ct & Run 29073
Delane St 29073
Delshire Ln 29073
Dempsey Dr 29073
Dennis Cir 29073
Derrick St 29072
Devin Dr 29072
Deweeses Ct 29072
Dick Corley Rd 29073
Dickert Dr 29073
Dock St 29072
Doe Trail Ct, Dr & Ln 29073
Dogwood Ln & Trl 29072
Dogwood Place Ct 29072
Donald Dr 29073
Dooley Rd 29073
Dorchester Ct & Dr 29072
Double Eagle Cir 29073
Dove Dr 29073
Dove Cote Ln 29072
Dovefield Ln 29073
Dover Ct 29072
Draftswoods Rd 29073
Dragonfly Dr 29072
Drake Trce 29072
Drake Hill Dr 29072
Drayden Ct 29073
Dreher Ct & St 29072
Dresden Ct 29073
Drifters Ct 29072
Driftwood Dr 29072
Drooping Leaf Dr, Ln & Rd 29072
Dry Branch Ct 29073
Duchess Trl 29073
Due West Ct & Dr 29072
Duffie Dr 29072
Dungannon Dr 29072
Dunn Ln 29073
Dupre Mill Ct & Rd 29072
Dustin Ct 29072
Dusty Ct 29073
Dutch Ct 29073
Duvall Ct 29072
Eagleview Dr 29073
Eastmarch Dr 29073
Eastshore Dr 29072
Eastside Dr 29072
Eastwood Dr 29072
Echo Ct 29073
Edge St 29072
Edgehill Ct 29072
Edgerton Ln 29072
Edgewater Ln 29072
Edinburgh Way 29072
Edmund Hwy 29073
Efird St 29072
Egret Ct 29072
Elberta Dr 29073
Elderberry Ct 29072
Eleta Dr 29073
Elkhorn Ct 29072
Ellis Ave 29072
Elm Ct & St 29072
Elmer Rd 29072
Elmhurst Ct 29072
Elvington Ln 29073
Emanuel Church Rd 29073
Emerald Farm Rd 29073
Emerald Oak Dr 29072
Emma Dr 29073
Endicot St 29072
English Dr 29073
Erica Ct 29072
Erin Ct 29072
Estancia Ct 29073
Estate Ln 29072
Eugene Ct 29073
Eventani Rd 29072
Everleigh Ct 29072
Ezzell Ct 29072
Fabrister Ln 29072
Fairmount Ct 29072
Falcon Dr 29073
Fannie Ln 29073
Farm Chase Ct & Dr 29073
Farmdale Dr 29073
Farmhouse Ct & Loop 29072
Farming Creek Way 29072
Farmington Ct 29072
Farringdon Ct 29073
Faskin Ln 29072
Fawn Ct 29072
Feather Site Ln 29072
Feder Pl 29073
Fenwick Ct 29072
Fergon Rd 29072
Fern Creek Ct 29072
Fern Hall Dr 29072
Ferry Dr 29072
Fiddler Branch Ct & Rd 29072
Fieldcrest Ct 29072
Fields Ln 29073
Filhol Rd 29072
Firbough Ct 29073
Fire Tower Rd 29072
Firethorn Ct 29072
Fish Hatchery Rd 29073
Flagstaff Ln 29072
Flagstone Ct & Way 29072
Fleetwood Dr 29073
Flinchum Ct & Pl 29073
Flora Dr 29072
Flutter Dr 29072
Fly Cast Ct 29073
Flyer Ct 29073
Foley Ln 29072
Forbidden Ln 29072
Forecastle Ct 29072
Foremost Dr 29073
Forest Dr 29073
Forest Ln 29073
Forest Green Dr 29073
Fort St 29072
Founders Blvd, Ct & Rd 29073
Fourteen Mile Ln 29072
Fox St 29072
Fox Branch Rd 29072
Fox Chase 29072
Fox Trail Ln 29073
Foxglen Cir & Rd 29072
Foxhall Blvd & Dr 29073
Foxhill Ct & Pl 29073
Foxridge Run 29072
Foxworth Dr 29072
Frank St 29073
Freedom Dr 29072
Freestone Ln 29073
Freida Rd 29073
Fresh Spring Way 29072
Freys Ct & Ln 29073
Frontage Rd 29073
Frye Rd 29072
Frye Branch Rd 29072
Gable Rd 29072
Gamecock Rd 29073
Gander Ct 29072
Gantt St 29072
Garden Arbor Ct, Dr & Ln 29072
Garden Gate Way 29072
Garden Pond Dr 29073
Garden Trail Ln 29072
Gasque Ct 29072
Gates Cir & Dr 29072
Gemstone Ct 29072
Genetian Ct 29072
George St 29072
George Taylor Ct 29073
Georgia Ln 29072
Giaben Dr 29072
Gibson Ct & Rd 29072
Gibson Forest Ct & Dr 29072
Gillfield Ct 29072
Ginny Ln 29072
Glade Spring Dr 29072
Glasgo Ln 29072
Glassmaster Rd 29072
Glenbrooke Ct 29072
Glencove Ct 29072
Glenda Ct 29073
Glenellen Rd 29072
Glenforest Ct 29072
Glengary Ct 29072
Glenkirk Ln 29072
Glossy Green Ln 29072
Glynway Ave 29072
Gold Rd 29072
Golden Ln 29072
Golden Leaf Ln 29073
Golden Pond Dr 29073
Goldenrod Ct 29073
Goldleaf St 29073
Governors Grant Blvd 29072
Grace St 29072
Grafton Ln 29072
Grand Palm Cir 29072
Granny Dr 29072
Gravedigger Rd 29073
Green Acres Cir 29072
Green Fern Ct 29072
Greenbank Dr 29073
Greenetree Ln 29072
Greenside Ct & Dr 29072
Greenvale Ct & Dr 29072
Greenview Ct 29072
Greenwich Ct 29073
Grey St 29072
Grey Mare Ct 29072
Greybeard Ln 29072
Greycoat Ct 29072
Grist Mill Ct 29072
Grubb Ct 29073
Guildbrook Dr 29072
Gum Bluff Ct 29072
Gustav Ct 29072
Gwen Ct 29073
Hagen Ct 29072
Hallbick Ct 29072
Hallie Hills Pl 29072
Hallmark Dr 29072
Halsey Ct 29072
Hamilton St 29072
Hammock Dr 29072
Hampstead Ct 29072
S Hampton Ave 29073
Happy Ridge Rd 29073
Harbor Glen Dr 29072
Harbor Heights Dr 29072
Harbor Vista Cir 29072
Harbour Place Ct 29072
Harbra Ct 29072
Harmon St 29072
Harmon Creek Ct & Dr 29072
Harmon Hill Dr 29072
Harris St 29072
Harrison Pt 29072
Harvard Ct 29073
Harvel Koon Rd 29073
Harvest Grove Ln 29072
Harvest Hill Trl 29072
Harwich Ct 29072
Hatton Ct & Ln 29072
Haven Cove Ct 29072
Hawley Dr 29073
Hawthorne Ln 29072
Hayfield Ct & Ln 29072
Haygood Ave 29072
Haynesworth Pl 29072
Heartwood Ct & Dr 29073
Heather Glen Dr 29072
Heber Ln 29072
Hedge Grove Ln 29072
Hedgerow Ct 29072
Heffner Pl 29072
Heights Ave 29072
Helenwood Rd 29073
Hendrix St 29072
Hendrix Landing Rd 29072
Heritage Trl 29072
Hermitage Ct & Rd 29072
Herrick Ct 29072
Heyward Dr 29072
Hickory Glade Ct 29073
Hickory Hill Rd 29072
Hickory Meadow Ct & Rd 29072
Hickory Nut Hill Ln 29072
Hickory Swamp Ct 29072
Hickory Trace Dr 29072
Hidden Ln 29072
Hidden Springs Rd 29073
Hidden Valley Dr 29073
High Rd 29072
High Hill Rd 29072
High Ripple Rd 29072
Highcrest Ln 29072
Highland Cir 29072
Highland Dr 29073
Highway 378 29072
Highway 6 29073
Hill Lake Dr 29072
Hill Springs Ct & Dr 29073
Hillock Ct 29073
Hillside Cir 29073
Hilltop Rd 29073
Hillview Dr 29073
Hilly Rock Rd 29072
Hobden Ct 29073
Hogan Ct & Way 29072
Hollingsworth Ln 29072
Hollis Ct & Rd 29073
Hollow Cove Rd 29072
Holly Rd 29073
Holly Brook Dr 29072
Holly Ferry Ct 29072
Holly Harbor Ln 29072
Holly Leaf Ln 29072
Holly Tree St 29073
Home Prt 29072
Homestead Ln 29072
Honey Hill Ct 29072
Honey Tree Dr 29073
Honeybee Ct & Ln 29072
Honors Ct 29073
Hook Land Ln 29072
Hope Ferry Rd 29072
Hope Springs Rd 29072
Horace Ct 29073
Horseshoe Trl 29072
Hosta Ln 29072
Hounds Run Dr & Ln 29072
Howard St 29073
Huckleberry Ln 29072
Huggins St 29073
Hunley Dr 29072
Hunt Rd 29073
Hunters Trl 29073
Hunters Ridge Dr 29072
Huntington Cir 29072
Huntsman Ln 29072
Hurstwood Ct 29073
Huxley Ct 29072
Hyler Rd 29073
Indian Creek Trl 29072
Indian Land Rd 29072
Indian Mound Rd 29072
Industrial Blvd, Ct & Dr 29072
Inglewood Ct 29072
Innkeeper Dr 29072
Innovation Pl 29072
Inverness Ct & Dr 29072
Irene Way 29072
Iris St 29073
Iris Hill Dr 29072
Iron Horse Rd 29073
Ironstone Ln 29073
Irwin Rd 29073
Island View Ct 29072
Isobel Ct 29072
Ivey St 29073
Ivy Green Ln 29072
Ivy Hill Ct 29072
Ivy Park Ln 29072
J Rufus Rd 29073
Jakes Landing Rd 29072
Jamestowne Ct 29072
Jamie Lee Ln 29073
Janna Ct 29073
Jarrah Dr 29072
Jason Rd 29073
Jennifer Ct 29073
Jericho Ct 29072
Jessamine Rd 29073
Jessica Ct & Dr 29073
Jessie St 29072
Jewell St 29073
Jibe Ct 29072
Jillian Pl 29072
Jim Kleckley Rd 29072
Jim Spence Rd 29073
Jocassee Trce 29072
John Drayton Ct 29072
John Fox Ct 29072
John Preston Ct & Dr 29072
Jordan Way 29072
Josie Ct 29073
Joyce Ann Rd 29072
Juanita Dr 29072
Judy Dr 29072
Jules Rd 29073
Julia Ct 29072
June Dr 29073
Justin Rogers Ct 29072
Kaminer Ln 29072
Kaminer Mill Ct 29072
Karr Ct 29072
Katmai Ct 29073
Katrina Ct 29073
Kaymin Hill Ct 29073
Keegan Rock Ct 29073
Keith Ct 29073
Kelberry Ct 29073
Kellers Pond Ln 29072
Kellfad Dr 29073
Kellway Cir 29072
Kellwood Ct 29073
Kelsey Glen Ct & Dr 29072
Kennebec Ct 29072
Kenneth Dr 29073
Kentante Rd 29073
Kenwood Dr 29072
Kenzi Ct 29073
Keowee Dr 29072
Keystone Ct 29073
Kibler Ct 29073
King St 29072
King Lees Ct 29072
Kingbird St 29073
Kings Way 29073
Kings Grant Rd 29072
Kings Point Ct 29073
Kingston Ct 29073
Kingston Harbour Dr 29072
Kirby Ln 29072
Kissimmee Trl 29072
Kittal Rd 29073
Kittery Ct 29072
Kitti Wake Rd 29073
Kittie Dr 29072
Kleckley Ln 29072
Knoll Estates Ct & Dr 29073
Knoll Station Dr 29073
Knoll Wood Dr 29072
Knotts Cir, Ct & Rd 29073
Knotts Haven Loop & Trl 29073
Kwanzan Dr 29072
Kyle Rd 29073
Kyzer Rd 29073
Lace Bark Ln 29073
Lacy Springs Cir 29073
Lady Kathryns Ct 29072
Ladybug Ln 29072
S Lake Ct 29073
N Lake Dr 29072
S Lake Dr
- 1404A-1404B 29073
- 1657B-1657C 29073
- 2301A-2301C 29073
- 100-999 29072
- 1000-2899 29073

W Lake Dr 29073
Lake Harbor Dr 29072
Lake Murray Ct & Ter 29072
Lake Shire Dr 29073
Lake Villa Rd 29072
Lakeview Dr 29073
Lancelot Ct 29072
Lanchire St 29073
Land Of Lakes Blvd & Cir 29073
Landfill Ln 29073
Landford Ct 29073
Landing Dr 29072
Lanham Spring Dr & Way 29072
Lann Cir 29073
Lantern Hill Cir 29073
Lark Ln 29073
Larry Ct 29072
Laryn Ln 29072
Lassitter Ct 29072
Latherton Ct 29073
Laurel Dr 29072
Laurel Rd 29073
Laurel St 29073
Laurel Bluff Dr 29072
Laurel Creek Ln 29073
Laurel Ridge Ln 29072
Laurel Springs Trl 29072
Laurent Ct 29072
Lavender Ln 29072
Lawrence Dr 29073
Leafy Bend Ct 29073
Leaning Pine Ct & Trl 29072
Lee Kleckley Rd 29072
Leigh James Ct 29072
Lena Dr 29073
Leonard Dr 29072
Leondry Sox Rd 29073
Lessie Oswald Ct 29072
Letha Ln 29072
Leventis Ln 29072
Lewis Pond Ct 29073
Libby Ln 29072
Liberty Farm Blvd & Ct 29073
Liberty Hill Rd 29073
Library Hill Ln 29072
Lightning Bug Ln 29072
Lilly Pond Rd 29072
Linden Way 29072
Lindler St 29073
Linger Ct 29072
Linville Ct 29072
Linwood Dr 29072
Lion Ct 29073
Lisa Dr 29073
Little Dogwood Ct 29073
Little Hollow Ln 29072
Litton Dr 29073
Livebark Ct & Ln 29072
Liverman Rd 29072
Living Waters Blvd 29073
Loch Levin Ct & Ln 29072
Locksley Ct 29073
Lockwood Dr 29072
Log House Ct 29073
Loganberry Ct 29072
London Way 29073
Long Branch Rd 29072
Long Island Trl 29072
Longford Ct 29073
Longitude Ln 29073
Longleaf Ct 29072
Longmont Dr 29072
Longs Pond Rd
- 100-299 29072
- 300-799 29073

Longshadow Cir, Ct & Dr 29072
Longspur Ln 29073
Longview St 29073
Longwood Dr 29073
Lord And Tucker Ct 29073
Lord Michaels Ct 29072
Lori Ct 29072
Lorick Cir 29072
Loskin Ln 29073
Lost Branch Rd 29072
Lost Spring Rd 29072
Lothrop Hill Rd 29072
Louisa Ln 29073
Louise Ct 29073
Low Hill Ln 29072
Loyd Ct 29073
Luden Ct 29072
Luna Trl 29072
Lunsford Ln 29072
Lupine Ct 29072
Lyngate Ct 29072
Lynn Haven Ct 29073
Mac Cir 29073
Macaw Ln 29073
Mace Ct 29073
Macedon Dr 29073
Mackey Ln 29072
Maddie Ct 29073
Magnolia Ridge Ln 29073
Magnolia Tree Rd 29073
Maguire Dr 29073
Maiden Ln 29072
W Main 29071
E Main St 29072
W Main St 29072
Maize St 29072
Majestic Ct 29072
Malden Ct 29072
Mallard Pt 29072
Mallard Lakes Ct & Dr 29072
Mallard Shores Pl 29072
Mallory Dr 29072
Malton Ct 29072
Mana Vista Ct 29072
Manchester Park Ave 29073
Mansfield Cir 29073
Manus Cir 29073
Maple Rd 29073
Maple Leaf Way 29073
Maple Ridge Ct 29073
Maple Shade Ln 29073
Maple Tree Ct 29073
Maplewood Dr 29073
Marguerite Ct 29073
Maria Ln 29073
Mariannas Ct 29072
Marianne Ct 29073
Marina Ct 29072
Mariners Creek Ct & Dr 29072
Mariscat Pl 29073
Marissa Ln 29072
Maritime Trl 29072
Marjorie Ct 29073
Mark Ln 29073
Mark I Rd 29072
Marlee Ct 29072
Marsh Dr 29073
Martel Dr 29072
Martreb Pl 29072
Marty Ln 29073
Mason Rd 29073
Masters Way 29072
Mattox Rd 29072
Maxie Rd 29072
May Ken Ct 29073
May Morning Ct & Dr 29073
Mayapple Dr 29073
Mccarter Trl 29073
Mccartha Rd 29073
Mcgregor Cir 29072

Mclee Rd 29073
Meades Ct 29073
Meadow Pl 29072
Meadow Ridge Ct 29073
Meadow Saffron Dr 29073
Meadow Wood Ct & Dr 29073
Meadowbrook Ln 29072
Meadowfield Rd 29073
Meander Ln 29072
Meat Plant Rd 29073
Meetze Ave 29072
Meetze Rd 29073
Megan Ln 29073
Melann Pass 29073
Melwood Ct 29073
Memory Ln 29073
Menauhant Ct 29072
Mercator Ct 29073
Merion Dr 29073
Merrimac Ct 29072
Merry Dr 29072
Merry Willow Ct 29072
Merus Dr 29072
Mesa Verde Dr 29073
Mews Ct & Way 29072
Michael Rd & St 29072
Middlebrook Ct & Dr 29072
Midway Rd 29072
Midway Farms Dr 29072
Mill St 29072
Mill Creek Rd 29072
Mill Farm Ct & Dr 29072
Mill Haven Ln 29072
Mill House Ln 29072
Mill Stream Rd 29072
Mill Wheel Dr 29072
Miller St 29072
Mills Rd 29072
Mills Park Cir 29072
Millstone Ln 29072
Millwood Ave 29073
Millwright Dr 29072
Mineral Creek Ct 29073
Mineral Lake Rd 29073
Mineral Springs Cir 29073
Mineral Springs Ln 29073
Mineral Springs Rd
2400-2899 29072
2900-4399 29073
Mineral Waters Dr 29073
Minnie Fallaw Rd 29073
Minor Dr 29073
Mission Way 29073
Mist Ln 29073
Misty Dew Ln 29072
Misty Meadows Ct 29072
Misty Oaks Ct & Pl 29072
Misty Spring Ct 29072
Mockingbird Cir, Ct & Dr 29073
Molly Ct 29073
Monroe Ln 29072
Montauk Dr 29072
Montelena Dr 29072
Montfort Ln 29073
Montrose Ct & Dr 29072
Moontide Ct 29072
Mooring Ln 29072
Moose Trl 29072
Morgan Dr 29072
Morning Lake Ct & Dr 29072
Morning Shore Ct & Dr 29072
Morningwood Dr 29073
Mossborough Dr 29073
Mountain Laurel Ct 29072
Mourning Dove Ct 29072
Muddy Springs Rd 29073
Muirfield Way 29072
Mulberry Ridge Ct 29073
Murray Vista Cir 29072
Mustang Rd 29073
My Pl 29073
Myles Ct 29072
Narrow Way 29073
Natalie Ln 29072
Nautical Rd 29072
Nazareth Rd 29073
Neighbor Ln 29072
New St 29072
New Colony Ct 29073
New Market Cir & Dr 29073
New Orangeburg Rd 29073
Newmont Dr 29072
Newport Hill Ln 29072
Newridge Rd 29072
Newton Ct 29073
Nicole Ct 29073
Nightingale Ct 29072
Noah Lucas Rd 29073
Noble Ct 29072
Nolancrest Dr 29073
Northpoint Dr 29072
Northwood Rd 29072
Nut Tree Ct 29072
Nutmeg Rd 29073
Oak Dr 29073
Oak Bough Ct 29072
Oak Burne Ct 29073
Oak Haven Ct & Dr 29072
Oak Leaf Ln 29073
Oak Ridge Ln 29073
Oaklimb Rd 29073
Oakmeade Ct 29072
Oakpointe Dr & Ln 29072
Oaks Ct 29072
Oakwood Dr 29073
Obannon Way 29072
Odaniel Rd 29073
Old Armory Ct 29072
Old Barn Ct 29072
Old Barnwell Rd 29073
Old Carrington Pkwy 29072
Old Chapin Rd 29072
Old Charleston Rd 29073
Old Cherokee Rd 29072
Old Church Rd 29072
Old Field Ct 29072
Old Gate Rd 29073
Old Orangeburg Rd 29073
Old Price Rd 29072
Old Rapids Rd 29072
Old Sugar Hill Rd 29072
Olde Farm Ct & Rd 29072
Olde Hickory Ct 29072
Olde Oak Ct 29072
Olde Pine Trl 29072
Olde River Pkwy 29072
Oldham Way 29072
Oldtown Dr 29073
Ole Sox Dr 29073
Oliver Metz Rd 29072
Olivewood Dr 29073
Olivia Way 29072
Oma Dr 29073
Oneil Ln 29072
Opago Way 29073
Orange Ct 29073
Orange Pond Ct 29073
Orchard Grove Ln 29072
Orchard Place Ct 29072
Oron Ct 29072
Oscar Price Rd 29072
Oskee Rd 29073
Oswald St 29072
Otero Ln 29073
Otis Miller Ln 29073
Otto Hegman Ct 29072
Overhill Ct 29073
Overview Ct 29073
Owls Roost Run 29072
Oxford Ct & Rd 29072
Paden Hill Rd 29073
Palm Ct 29072
Palmer Dr 29072
Palmetto Cove Ln 29072
Palmetto Hall Ct & Dr 29072
Palmetto Park Blvd 29072
Panorama Dr & Pt 29072
Pantigo Ln 29072
Paps Dr 29073
Park Ct & Rd 29072
Park Meadow Dr 29072
Park Place Cir, Ct & Trl 29072
Park Ridge Way 29072
Parker St 29072
Parkhurst Ln 29072
Parkside Ct & Rd 29072
Parkview Ct 29072
Parsley Ct 29073
Pat Rd 29073
Patrick Dr 29073
Patrick David Ct 29073
Patterson Ct 29073
Payne Ln 29072
Paynehurst Dr 29072
Pea Ridge Ct 29072
Peach Hill Dr 29072
Peachtree Rock Rd 29073
Peak View Rd 29073
Pear Ct 29073
Pebble Beach Ct 29073
Pebble Place Ct 29072
Pebble Stone Dr 29072
Peek Dr 29073
Pennine Pl 29073
Penny Ln 29073
Penwood Ln 29072
Pepper Rd 29073
Pepper Harrow Ln 29073
Persimmon Ct & Ln 29072
Persimmon Tree Rd 29072
Pewter Dr 29072
Pheasant Glen Ct 29072
Phoenix Ct & Ln 29072
Pico Pl 29073
Pilgrim Church Rd 29072
Pilgrim Point Ct & Dr 29072
Pin Oak Ct & Dr 29073
Pine Dr 29073
Pine Cone Dr 29073
Pine Knot Ct 29073
Pine Mill Ct 29073
Pine Point Dr 29072
Pine Tree Dr 29073
Pinestraw Cir 29073
Pineview Dr 29073
Pink Camellia Ln 29072
Pinnacle Way 29073
Pintail Ct 29072
Piper Rd 29073
Pisgah Ct 29072
Pisgah Church Rd 29072
Pisgah Flats Cir & Ct 29072
Plantation Dr 29072
Plantation Oak Dr 29073
Platinum Dr 29072
Platt Springs Rd 29073
Pleasant Ct & Ln 29072
Pleasant Creek Ct 29073
Pleasant View Dr 29073
Plum Tree Ct 29073
Plummet Ct 29072
Plymouth Pass Ct, Dr & Way 29072
Poet Pl 29072
Poindexter Ct & Ln 29072
Point Dr 29072
Point South Ct & Ln 29073
N & W Pond Ct & Dr 29073
Pond Branch Rd 29073
Pond View Ln 29072
Ponds Ln 29072
Popes Ln 29072
Poplar Leaf Ct 29073
Poppy Trl 29072
Porsche Dr 29072
Porth Cir 29072
Portsmouth Dr 29072
Potano Ct & Dr 29072
Potters Way 29073
Powell Dr 29072
Power Point Ln 29072
Presque Isle Rd 29072
Prestwick Ct 29072
Prides Way Dr 29072
Puller Ct 29072
Putters Trl 29072
E Q Shull Ln 29073
Quail Trl 29072
Queenland Ct 29072
Queens Ct 29072
Quiet Grove Dr & Ln 29072
Quigley Ct 29073
Quin Oak Rd 29072
Quoin Ct 29073
Rabbit Rd 29072
Rabon Rd 29073
Railroad Ave 29072
Rainwater Dr 29072
Rama Ct & Ln 29072
Randy Rd 29072
Raspberry Hill Ct 29073
Rauch St 29072
Ravenglass Ct 29072
Rawl Rd 29072
Rawl St 29073
Raymond Cir 29072
Reading Ct 29073
Red Alder Ct 29073
Red Ash Ln 29072
Red Bank Dr 29073
Red Barn Ct & Rd 29072
Red Cedar Ct 29073
Red Leaf Ct 29073
Red Maple Ct 29073
Red Pine Dr 29073
Red Ribbie Rd 29073
Red Rover Ln 29072
Redmond Rd 29073
Reed Ave & Ct 29072
Reedy Pkwy 29072
Retreat Ct 29073
Rice Hill Ct 29072
Rich Lex Dr 29072
Richmond Farm Cir & Ct 29072
Ridge Rd 29073
Ridge St 29072
Ridge Terrace Ln 29073
Ridge Top Rd 29073
Ridgecreek Dr 29072
Ridgecrest Ct 29073
Ridgecrest Dr 29072
Ridgehill Dr 29073
Ridingfield Rd 29073
Riglaw Cir 29073
Rindle Dr 29072
Ringo Rd 29073
Ripple Ct 29072
Rivendell Dr 29073
River Xing 29072
River Camp Dr 29072
River Club Aly & Rd 29072
River Crossing Ct 29072
River Falls Ln 29072
Riverbirch Rd 29072
Riverchase Ct & Way 29072
Robbie Rd 29073
Robert Davis Rd 29072
Robert Hendrix Rd 29073
Roberts St 29072
Robin Rd 29073
Robin Woods Dr 29073
Rockridge Ct 29072
Rocky Cove Ct & Rd 29072
Rocky Well Rd 29073
Rogan Ln 29073
Rogers Ct 29072
Roland Dr 29073
Roland Fox Rd 29073
Rollingwood Dr 29072
Ronnie Walker Rd 29073
Roost Ct 29073
Roscoe Rd 29073
Rose Lake Rd 29073
Rose Sharon Dr 29072
Rosebank Ct 29073
Rosecrest Rd 29072
Rosewood Ct & Ln 29072
Round Hill Ln & Vly 29072
Round Knob Rd 29072
Rowland Pines Ct 29073
Royal Creek Dr 29072
Royal Lythan Cir & Dr 29072
Royal Oaks Ct & Ln 29072
Rudder Ct 29072
Rudwick Dr 29073
Ruff Acres Ln 29073
Rumford Pl 29072
Runnymede Ln 29072
Rustic Xing 29073
Rustic Manor Ct 29072
Ruth Vista Rd 29073
Rutherford Rd 29073
Ryan Ct 29073
Saddlebrooke Cir, Ct, Ln & Rd 29072
Saddlehorn Ln & Way 29073
Sag Harbor Ct 29072
Sagauro Ct & Dr 29073
Sage Tree Ct 29073
Sagemont Ct 29072
Sailing Ct 29072
Saint Claire Pl 29072
Saint Helena Ct 29072
Saint Johns Church Rd 29072
Saint Peters Rd 29072
Saks Ave 29072
Saltair Ct 29072
Saluda Pointe Dr 29072
Saluda Springs Ct & Rd 29072
San Palo Ct 29073
Sandbrier Ct 29073
Sandlapper Way 29072
Sandy Bank Dr 29072
Sandy Hill Rd 29072
Sandy Path Ln 29072
Sandy Peach Ln 29073
Sandy Pine Rd 29072
Sandy Point Rd 29072
Sandy Ridge Rd 29073
Sandy Springs Ct & Ln 29073
Sassafras Trl 29072
Satcher Rd 29072
Savannah Hills Dr 29073
Saxe Gotha Ln 29072
Saxons Ferry Dr 29072
Saxony Ct 29072
Scarborough Dr, Ln & Way 29072
Scarlet Oak Way 29072
Schell Dr 29072
School St 29072
Scoggins Dr 29073
Scotland Ct & Dr 29072
Seabrook Ct 29072
Sease Hill Rd 29073
Seases Cir 29072
Seaside Ct 29072
Seaygard Ln 29072
Seclusion Ct 29072
Secret Cove Ct & Dr 29072
Segwun Dr 29072
Seibles Ct 29072
Seleta Cir 29073
Sennville Ln 29073
Serendipity Way 29072
Serenity Ct & Dr 29072
Settlers Ct, Dr & Trl 29072
Settlers Bend Ct 29072
Shadow Ridge Ct 29072
Shady Creek Rd 29072
Shady Oak Dr 29073
Shag Bark Trl 29073
Shantel Ct 29073
Shanty Ln 29072
Sharon Lake Ct 29072
Sharpe Cir 29073
Shellcracker Rd 29072
Shelton Trail Ct 29073
Sherwood Dr 29073
Shetland Ln 29073
Shirway Ct & Rd 29073
Shoal Ct, Dr & Ter 29072
Shoal Creek Cir & Dr 29072
Shoalwood Dr 29072
Siddington Way 29072
Silva Ct 29073
Silver Leaf Dr 29073
Silver Maple Ct 29073
Silver Spring Ln 29073
Silver Wood Ln 29072
Silverbell Ln 29073
Silverberry Dr 29073
Silverbrook Ln 29073
Silvercreek Dr 29072
Silverstone Rd 29072
Simmons Ln 29073
Sir Edwards Ln 29072
Sixteen Mile Ct 29072
Skeeter Ridge Rd 29073
Sky Crest Ct
200-299 29073
400-499 29072
Skyview Dr 29073
Slater Hill Dr 29073
Smith St 29072
Smith Pond Rd 29072
Smoke Rise Ln 29072
Smokewood Ct 29073
Smokey Ct 29073
Smokey Joe Ct 29073
Snelgrove Landing Rd 29072
Snow Ct & Ln 29073
Soaring Eagle Rd 29073
Sommerford Ct 29072
Southberry Ln & Way 29072
Southbrook Dr & Way 29073
Southwood Dr 29073
Sparkleberry Ln 29073
Sparrow Point Ct & Rd 29073
E & W Sparrowood Run 29072
Spence Rd 29072
Spence Shores Ct 29072
Spillway Blvd & Ct 29072
Spindrift Ct 29072
Spinnaker Ct 29072
Spool Wheel Rd 29072
Spring Rd 29073
Spring St 29072
Spring Creek Ct 29072
Spring Farm Ln 29072
Spring Frost Dr 29072
Spring Hill Rd 29072
Spring Lake Dr 29072
Spring Mist Ct & Dr 29072
Spring Tyme Ct, Ln & Pl 29073
Spring View Ct 29072
Spring Water Dr 29072
Springwood Ct & Ln 29073
Spruce Glen Ct & Rd 29072
Squirrel Hollow Rd 29073
Stafford Ct 29073
Stagone Ln 29073
Stanley Ct 29073
Star Ln 29072
Star Hill Ct & Ln 29072
Starling Way 29073
Starling View Ct 29073
Statley Way Dr 29072
Steele Pond Rd 29073
Steeple Ct 29073
Steeplechase Rd 29072
Stephanie Dr 29073
Sterling Rd 29072
Sterling Lake Ct & Dr 29072
Stirrup Ln 29072
Stone Ledge Ct 29072
Stone Spring Ct 29072
Stonebury Ct 29073
Stonehaven Ct 29073
Stoneridge Dr 29072
Stoney Creek Ct & Ln 29072
Stoneybrook Ln 29072
Storey Rd 29072
Straight St 29072
Stuart Ln 29072
Stubblefield Rd 29073
Stump Rd 29073
Sturton Dr 29072
Summer Duck Trl 29072
Summer Gate Ct 29072
Summerfield Dr 29072
Sunflower Ct 29072
Sunningdale Dr 29072
Sunny Cove Ct 29072
Sunny View Ln 29073
Sunny Vista Dr 29073
Sunrise Farm Ct 29073
Sunset Blvd
4766B2-4766B5 29072
Sunset Bay Ln 29072
Sunset Point Dr 29072
Sunset Royal Ct 29073
Sunshine Dr 29072
Surfwood Ct 29073
Swanhaven Dr 29073
Swartz Rd 29072
Sweet Melody Ln 29073
Sweet Springs Ct & Dr 29073
Sweetbay Ct 29073
Sweetberry Ln 29073
Sweetwater Ct & Ln 29073
Swingset Ln 29072
Sycamore Tree Rd 29073
Tadpole Ct 29072
Tailwater Bnd 29072
Tall Palmetto Ln 29072
Tall Timber Trl 29072
Tami Ln 29073
Tanglewood Dr 29072
Tannock Ct 29072
Tar Box Ct & Trl 29073
Tarparlin Dr 29073
Tarragon Dr 29073
Tarrar Springs Rd 29072
Tarrington Cir 29072
Tarwood Ln 29073
Taylor Cir 29072
Taylor Dr 29072
Taylor Ln 29073
Taylors Cove Rd 29072
Tayser Ct 29072
Tea Olive Ave 29073
Teal Ct 29072
Teesdale Ct 29072
Tennis Court Ln 29072
Tennis View Ct 29073
Tennyson Dr 29073
Terra Dr 29073
Testo Dr 29073
Thackeray Ln 29073
Thicket Ct & Dr 29072
Thimbleberry Ln 29073
Thomas Hill Ct 29072
Thompson St 29072
Three Chop Run 29072
Three Oaks Dr 29073
Three Pond Ln 29073
Thunder Rd 29072
Thyme Dr 29073
Tidas St 29072
Tillman St 29072
Timber Chase Ct & Ln 29073
Timbergate Ct, Dr & Rd 29073
Timberline Ct 29072
Timbermill Dr & Xing 29073
Tintagel Ct 29072
Tisbury Ct 29072
Toboggan Ct 29072
Tolbert Ct & St 29072
Topaz Ct 29073
Torreyglen Dr 29072
Torrisdale Dr 29073
Toucan Way 29073
Toula Ln 29072
Towhee Ct 29072
Towser Ct 29073
N Trace Ct 29072
Trail Ln 29073
Trailside Ln 29072

- Tranquil Pt 29072
- Tranquility Ct 29072
- Traveler Trl 29073
- Travertine Xing 29072
- Trellis Ct 29072
- Tri Springs Ct 29073
- Triami Path 29072
- Triangle Rd 29072
- Trillium Ct 29072
- Tryon Trl 29072
- Tulip Way 29072
- Turkey Creek Ct 29073
- Turkey Farm Ct 29073
- Turnberry Ln 29072
- Turners Cir & Ct 29072
- Turtle Cove Ct 29072
- Twelve Mile Dr 29072
- Twelve Oaks Ln 29072
- Twilight Ln 29072
- Twin Hickory Ct 29072
- Twisted Oak Ct 29073
- Twisting Rd 29072
- Two Notch Rd
  - 100-2099 29073
  - 2100-3600 29072
  - 3602-3698 29072
  - 402-3-402-6 29073
- Tybo Dr 29072
- Tylers Trl 29073
- Underwood Ct & Dr 29072
- Vale Dr 29073
- Valley Ln 29073
- Valleydale Dr 29072
- Vanderbilt Rd 29072
- Vaughns Mh Park 29073
- Vera Rd 29072
- Veranda Ln 29072
- Verano Ct 29073
- Vernon Dr & St 29073
- Viclynn Run 29073
- Viking Ln 29073
- S Village Rd 29072
- Virginia Pine Ln 29073
- Vista Farm Ct 29073
- Vista Oaks Dr 29072
- Vista Springs Ave & Cir 29072
- Volley Ct 29073
- Vonda Dr 29073
- Vonda Kay Cir 29072
- Wagon Trl 29073
- Walking Ln 29073
- Wallace Cir & Way 29073
- Walnut Creek Cir, Ct & Dr 29073
- Walter Ln 29073
- Walter Hutto Ct 29072
- Walter Rawl Rd 29072
- Wandawood Ln 29073
- Wander Ct & Way 29072
- Wando Cir 29073
- Warner Woods Rd 29072
- Water Crest Dr 29072
- Water Oak Ct & Dr 29072
- Waterloo Dr 29072
- Waters Edge Ct & Dr 29072
- Watershed Ln 29072
- Waterstone Dr 29072
- Waterway Ct 29072
- Waverly Ct & Dr 29072
- Waverly Point Dr 29072
- Weatherby Ct 29072
- Weatherford Ct 29072
- Weatherstone Rd 29072
- Weaver Dr 29073
- Welsh Ct 29073
- Welsummer Way 29072
- Wesley Ct 29073
- Wessell Dr 29073
- Wessinger Dr 29072
- Westbrook Ct & Way 29072
- Westpointe Ct 29073
- Westside Dr 29072
- Westwood Dr & Ln 29073
- Whippoorwill Dr 29073
- Whisper Lake Dr 29072
- Whispering Winds Dr 29072
- Whisperwood Dr 29072
- White Ash Ct 29072
- White Birch Ct 29073
- White Caps Way 29072
- White Cedar Ct & Way 29073
- White Horse Cir & Rd 29073
- White Oak Ln 29073
- White Oleander Dr 29072
- White Rock Ct & Ln 29072
- Whitefield Ln 29072
- Whiteford Ct & Way 29072
- Whitewing Dr 29073
- Whitland Rd 29072
- Whitney Ln 29072
- Whitton Ct 29073
- Whixley Ln 29073
- Whooping Crane Way 29073
- Widgeon Dr 29072
- Wigfall Ct 29072
- Wigmore Ln 29072
- Wild Azalea Ct 29072
- Wild Oaks Trl 29072
- Wild Spring Ct & Rd 29072
- Wild West Ct 29073
- Wilderness Rd 29072
- Wildlife Cir, Ct & Rd 29072
- Wilhowie Dr 29073
- Will Dent Rd 29072
- Willow Dr 29072
- Willow Forks Ct & Rd 29073
- Willow Lake Rd 29072
- Willow Tree Ct 29073
- Wilma Ann Dr 29073
- Wilmington Ln 29072
- Wilmont Dr 29072
- Wilson St 29073
- Windmere Dr 29072
- Windsor Park Dr 29072
- Windstone Dr 29073
- Windy Hollow Dr 29073
- Windy Ridge Ln 29073
- Windy Trail Ct 29073
- Windy Wood Rd 29073
- Wing Hill Dr 29072
- Wingard Ave 29073
- Winners Cir 29072
- Winterberry Dr & Loop 29072
- Wintergreen Ct 29072
- Winyah Ct 29072
- Wire Rd 29072
- Wise Ferry Ct & Rd 29072
- Wisteria Way 29072
- Wolf Run Ct 29073
- Wolver Hampton Ct 29072
- Wolverton Mountain Ln 29073
- Wood Ct, Dr & Rd 29073
- Wood Cut Rd 29072
- Wood Dale Dr 29072
- Wood Eden Ct 29072
- Wood Ride Ln 29072
- Woodbay Ct & Dr 29072
- Woodberry Dr & Rd 29073
- Woodbridge Dr 29072
- Woodcraft Dr 29073
- Woodland Dr 29072
- Woodland Pond Dr 29073
- Woodlanders Pl 29073
- Woodmill Cir & Way 29072
- Woodmont Ct 29072
- Woodpark Ct 29072
- Woodruff Ct 29072
- Woodside Rd 29072
- Woodside Hill Ct 29072
- Woodstork Way 29073
- Woodview Ct 29073
- Woodvine Dr 29072
- Woodward Ct 29073
- Wrangell Ct 29073
- Wren Rd 29073
- N & S Wrenwood Cir, Ct, Dr & Way 29073
- Wyndotte Ct & Pl 29072
- Wynnsum Trl 29073
- Wyoming Rd 29073
- Yachting Cir & Rd 29072
- Yachtsman Pl 29072
- Yale Rd 29072
- Ymca Rd 29073
- York Commons 29072
- Yorkswell Ct 29072
- Yoshino Cir 29072
- Younginer Dr 29073
- Youpon Dr 29073
- Zenker Rd 29072
- Zoe Ct 29073

NUMBERED STREETS

- All Street Addresses 29072

MOUNT PLEASANT SC

- General Delivery 29465

POST OFFICE BOXES MAIN OFFICE STATIONS AND BRANCHES

Box No.s

- All PO Boxes 29465

NAMED STREETS

- Abcaw Way 29464
- Abercorn Trce 29466
- Adler Rd 29466
- Adluh St 29464
- Adrian Way 29466
- Aeton Rd 29466
- Alan Brooke Dr 29466
- Albatross Ln 29466
- Alderly Ln 29466
- Alexandra Dr 29464
- Alice Smalls Rd 29466
- Allbritton Blvd 29464
- Allen St 29464
- Alonzo Rouse Rd 29466
- Alston Rd 29464
- Ambassador Way 29464
- Ambling Way 29464
- Amenity Park Dr 29464
- Amesbury Ct 29466
- Anacostia Ave 29466
- Anchor Cir 29464
- Andover Way 29466
- Angel Wing Ct 29464
- Angus Ct 29464
- Ann St 29464
- Ann Edwards Ln 29464
- Ann Foster Ln 29464
- Anna Knapp Blvd & Ext 29464
- Annie Laura Ln 29466
- Ansley Ct 29466
- Antebellum Ln 29464
- Antigua Dr 29464
- Appling Dr 29464
- Arden Ct 29464
- Armory Dr 29466
- Armsway St 29464
- Arness St 29466
- Arundel Pl 29464
- Ashburn Ln 29464
- Ashburton Way 29466
- Ashton Shore Ln 29466
- Ashwycke St 29466
- Astley Rd 29464
- Astor Dr 29464
- Atlanta Dr 29464
- Atlantic St 29464
- Attley St 29466
- Attwood Cir 29464
- Audubon Pl 29464
- Auger Aly 29464
- Augsburg Dr 29464
- Austin Sq 29464
- Ayers Plantation Way 29466
- Azalea St 29464
- Azimuth Ct 29466
- Aztec Ln 29466
- W B Rd 29466
- Babington Way 29464
- Bagley Dr 29466
- Balcome Rd 29466
- Baldock Ct 29464
- Baldwin Park Dr 29466
- Balgrove Ct 29466
- Ball Ct 29466
- Ballast Pt 29466
- Ballyliffen Dr 29466
- Baltusrol Ln 29466
- Bamberg Jenkins Rd 29466
- Bampfield Dr 29464
- Bancroft Ln 29466
- Banded Tulip Ln 29464
- Bank St 29464
- Banning St 29466
- Barbadian Way 29464
- Barbara St 29464
- Barkla Ave 29466
- S Barksdale Rd 29464
- Barquentine Dr 29464
- Barrier Island Ct 29466
- Basildon Rd 29466
- Basketweave Dr 29466
- Bastian Rd 29464
- Battery Way 29464
- Battery Hill Ct 29466
- Bay Ct 29464
- Bay Crossing Rd 29464
- Bay Water Way 29464
- Bayfront Dr 29464
- Baytree Cir & Ct 29464
- Bayview Dr 29464
- Bb Ln 29464
- Beach St 29464
- Beaconsfield Rd 29466
- Bearing Ct 29466
- Beatrice Horry Ln 29466
- Beaucastel Rd 29464
- Beauford Pointe Vw 29464
- Beck Dr 29466
- Beckenham Dr 29466
- Beech Hill Ln 29464
- Belair Ct 29464
- Belcourt Ln 29466
- Belhaven Dr 29466
- Belk Dr 29464
- Belle Chez 29464
- Belle Hall Pkwy 29464
- Belle Isle Ave 29464
- Belle Point Dr 29464
- Belle Station Blvd 29464
- Bellview Dr 29464
- Belser Cir 29466
- Belvedere Ter 29464
- Belvue Cres 29464
- Ben Sawyer Blvd 29464
- Bending Oak Loop 29466
- Bennett St 29464
- Bennett Charles Rd 29466
- Bent Tree Ln 29464
- Beresford Ct 29464
- Bergenfield Rd 29466
- Bergeron Way 29464
- Bermuda Towne Row 29464
- Bernice Ln 29464
- Berry Creek Dr 29466
- Bessemer Rd 29466
- Big Fire Ct 29464
- Billings St 29466
- Black Oak Ct 29464
- Black River Dr 29466
- Black Rush Cir 29466
- Blackmoor St 29466
- Blackrail Ct 29464
- Blackstrap Pl 29464
- Blackstrap Retreat 29464
- Blalock St 29466
- Blessing Ct 29464
- Bloomfield Dr 29464
- Bloomingdale Ln 29466
- Blue Cascade Dr 29464
- Blue Crab Way 29464
- Blue Heron Run 29464
- Blue Jack Pt 29464
- Bluebird Dr 29464
- Bluff Ln 29466
- Blythewood Ct 29464
- Boat Landing Aly 29464
- Boathouse Close 29464
- Bobo Rd 29466
- Bonneau Ln 29464
- Bonnie Ln & St 29464
- Bonnywood Ct 29464
- Bose Ct 29466
- Boston Grill Rd 29466
- Bottle Brush Ct 29466
- Bowline Dr 29466
- Bowman Rd 29464
- Bradburn Dr 29466
- Braemore Dr 29464
- Bragg Dr 29466
- Bramson Ct 29466
- Branch Creek Dr 29466
- Brasie Ct 29466
- Brecon Rd 29464
- Breezy Point Dr & Ln 29466
- Brent Mill Ct 29466
- Brentley Rd 29466
- Brently Rd 29466
- Brentwood Ct 29464
- Brick Kiln Pkwy & Pt 29466
- Brick Landing Ct 29466
- Brickman Way 29466
- Brickmill Ln 29466
- Brickside Ln 29466
- Brickyard Pkwy 29466
- Bridge St 29464
- Bridge Point Cir 29464
- Bridgeport Dr 29466
- Bridgeside Blvd 29464
- Bridgetown Pass 29464
- Bridlewood Ln 29464
- Bristle Pine Ct 29464
- Bristol Ter 29464
- Broadway St 29464
- Brook Haven Ct 29464
- Brown Sugar Retreat 29464
- Bryden Ln 29466
- Buckhall Ct 29464
- Cadberry Ct 29464
- Cadence Dr 29466
- Cadet Ct 29466
- Cain Dr 29464
- Caitlins Way 29466
- Calais Dr 29464
- Calaveras Cir 29466
- Caldwell Ct 29466
- Calico Retreat 29464
- Caliper Oak Cir 29464
- Callan Rd 29466
- Calm Water Ct 29464
- Cambridge Lakes Dr 29464
- Camellia Dr 29464
- Camfield Ln 29466
- Canby Ct 29466
- Candlewood Dr 29464
- Cane Ct 29464
- Canebreak Ln 29466
- E & W Canning Dr 29464
- Canton Sq 29464
- Canvasback Ct 29464
- Canyon Ln 29466
- Canyon Oaks Dr 29464
- Cape Jasmine Ct 29464
- Cape May Ln 29466
- Capel St 29466
- Captain Waring Ct 29466
- Cardiff Rd 29464
- Cardinal Hill Dr N 29466
- Carmel Bay Dr 29466
- Carol Oaks Dr 29466
- Carolina Isle Dr 29466
- Carolina Jasmine Rd 29464
- Carolina Park Blvd 29466
- Carr St 29464
- Carriage Ln 29464
- Carrie Heyward Ln 29464
- Carter Ave 29464
- Casseque Province 29464
- Cassidy Ct 29464
- Castle Hall Rd 29464
- Catalpa Ct 29464
- Catamaran Ct 29466
- Causey Rd 29466
- Cavalier Ct 29464
- Cavalry Cir 29464
- Cawley Rd 29464
- Cedar Creek Ct 29466
- Center St 29464
- Center Lake Dr 29464
- Center Street Ext 29464
- Central Haven Dr 29464
- Chadbury Ln 29466
- Chambers Ln 29464
- Chamfort Rd 29466
- Channel Creek Ct 29464
- Channel View Ct 29466
- Chapel Ct 29466
- Charlotte Ln 29464
- Charlotte G Cir 29464
- Chart Ridge Dr 29466
- Charter Ct 29464
- Charter Oaks Dr 29466
- Chatelain Way 29464
- Chatfield St 29464
- Chatter Rd 29464
- Chelsea Park Blvd 29464
- Cherokee Rose Cir 29464
- Cherry St 29464
- Chersonese Round 29464
- Cheswick Ln 29466
- Chicco Ln 29464
- Children Rd 29466
- Chimney Bluff Dr 29464
- Chrismill Ln 29466
- Christ Church Ct 29466
- Chuck Dawley Blvd 29464
- Church St 29464
- Circle Ct 29464
- Cistern Aly 29464
- Citation Ct 29466
- N Civitas St 29464
- Clancy Rd 29466
- Clapper Ct 29464
- Claremont St 29466
- Clarendon Way 29466
- Clarity Rd 29464
- Clarksville Ct 29466
- Claymill Ln 29466
- Cleary Ln 29466
- Cliffwood Dr 29464
- Clover Pl 29466
- Club Dr & Ter 29464
- Clubhouse Ln 29466
- Coakley Rd 29466
- Coastal Crab Rd 29466
- Coastal Marsh Rd 29466
- Coatbridge Rd 29466
- Coaxum Rd 29466
- Cobblestone Way 29464
- Coddell Ct 29466
- Codorus Ct 29466
- Coinbow Cir & Dr 29464
- W Coleman Blvd 29464
- Colfax Ct 29466
- Collier St 29466
- Colonel Vanderhorst Cir 29466
- Colonial Dr 29464
- Colonnade Dr 29466
- Comingtee Ln 29464
- Commonwealth Dr & Rd 29466
- Conant Rd 29466
- Conch St 29466
- Contentment Cottage Ln 29466
- Coolidge St 29466
- Cooper River Dr 29464
- Copahee Rd 29464
- Copper Penny Ct 29466
- Coral St 29464
- Coral Vine Ct 29464
- Corinth Ct 29464
- Cormorant Ct 29466
- Cotesworth Ct 29464
- Cotillion Pl 29464
- Cottingham Dr 29464
- Cotton Pt 29464
- Cotton Bounty Ct 29466
- Cotton Creek Dr 29466
- Cottonfield Dr 29466
- Country Ln 29464
- Country Manor Dr 29466
- Country Place Rd 29464
- Country Store Rd 29464
- Country Wood Ct 29466
- Cove Bay Ln 29464
- Covenant Sq 29464
- Cowrie Ct 29464
- Crab Claw Cv 29466
- Crab Creek Ct 29466
- Crane Creek Dr 29466
- N Creek Dr 29466
- Creek Bend Wharf 29464
- Creekside Dr 29464
- Creole Pl 29464
- Creole Retreat 29464
- Croaton Xing 29466
- Crooked Pine Dr 29466
- Crooked Stick Ln 29466
- Cross Timbers Dr 29464
- E Crossing Ln 29466
- Crowell Ln 29466
- Crowfield Ln 29464
- Crown Ct 29466
- Crown Reach 29466
- Crystal Rd 29466
- Cullowhee Cir 29464
- Cummings Cir 29464
- Curran Pl 29466
- Cutler Ln 29466
- Cypress Ct 29466
- Cypress Pointe Dr 29466
- Daffodil Ln 29464
- Dan Rd 29466
- Daniel Legare Pl 29466
- Daniels Pointe Blvd 29466
- Darlington Ln 29464
- Darrell Creek Trl 29466
- Darts Cove Lndg & Way 29466
- Dataw Ct 29464
- Davant Cir 29464
- Davenport Dr 29464
- David Green Rd 29466
- Dawn View Ter 29464
- Dean Hall Ct 29464
- Dearsley Ct 29464
- Debbie St 29464
- Decoy Ct 29464
- Deene Park Cir 29466
- Deep Sea Cir 29464
- Deep Water Dr 29464
- Deer St 29464
- Deer Creek Rd 29466
- Deer Park Way 29466
- Deer Path Dr 29464
- Deer Sight Way 29466
- Deer Walk Ct & Way 29466
- Delacourt Ave 29464
- Deleisseline Blvd 29464
- Densmore Cir 29466
- Detyens Ct & Rd 29464
- Detyens Lamb Rd 29466
- Devol St 29466
- Diamond Blvd 29464
- Diddy Dr 29464
- Dingle Rd 29466
- Divot Ct 29466
- Downing Place Way 29466
- Downsberry Dr 29466
- Dragoon Dr 29464
- Draymohr Ct 29466
- Duany Rd 29464

Duckclam Ln ... 29464
Duke St ... 29464
Dunes Mill Ct & Way ... 29466
Dunes West Blvd ... 29466
Dunhill Ct ... 29466
Dupre Ln ... 29464
Dutch Iris Ct ... 29464
Eagle St ... 29464
Earl Johnson Ln ... 29466
Easthampton Dr ... 29464
Eastlake Rd ... 29464
Eastman Dr ... 29466
Eastover Dr ... 29464
Ebbtide Way ... 29464
Edenton Rd ... 29464
Edwards Dr ... 29464
Egrets Landing Ct ... 29466
Egrets Point Dr ... 29466
S Egypt Rd ... 29464
Eighty Oak Ave ... 29464
Elbow Aly ... 29464
Elijah Green Rd ... 29464
Elijah Smalls Rd ... 29466
Elizabeth Ct & St ... 29464
Ellen Ave ... 29464
Ellis St ... 29464
Ellsworth St ... 29466
Emerald Ter ... 29464
Emma Ln ... 29466
Enclave Dr ... 29464
Endicot Way ... 29466
English Ivy Ct ... 29464
Epic Ln ... 29466
Equestrian Dr ... 29464
Erckmann Dr ... 29464
Ethan St ... 29466
Etiwan Pointe Dr ... 29464
Evelina St ... 29464
Everhope Rd ... 29466
Evermart Dr ... 29466
Evian Way ... 29466
Ewall St ... 29464
Fair Sailing Rd ... 29466
Fairhope Rd ... 29464
Fairlawn Cir ... 29464
Fairmont Ave ... 29464
Fairway Place Ln ... 29464
Faison Rd ... 29466
Faith St ... 29466
Fallen Oak Dr ... 29466
Falling Creek Cir ... 29466
Falling Moss Dr ... 29466
Farm Quarter Rd ... 29464
Faulkner Dr ... 29466
Faye Ln ... 29464
Ferdinand Ct ... 29466
Fern House Walk ... 29464
Fernandina St ... 29464
Ferry St ... 29464
Fiddler Run Ct ... 29466
Fiddlers Den Ct ... 29464
Fiddlers Lake Ct ... 29464
Fiddlers Marsh Dr ... 29464
Fiddlers Point Ln ... 29464
Fig Vine Ct ... 29464
Firethorne Dr ... 29464
Fishermans Bnd ... 29464
Fitch Ct ... 29466
Flambeau Retreat ... 29464
Flannery Pl ... 29466
Floodtide Way ... 29464
Flowering Oak Way ... 29466
Forsythe Ln ... 29466
Fort Bliss Ct ... 29466
Fountain Ln ... 29464
Fountainhead Way ... 29466
Four Winds Pl ... 29466
Fowler Ct ... 29464
Fox Pond Dr ... 29464
Fox Tail Ln ... 29464
Frank Bonneau Rd ... 29466
Franke Dr ... 29464
Franklin Tower Dr ... 29466
Fraserburgh Way ... 29466
Fred Cooper Ct ... 29464
Freelock Dr ... 29464
Freeman St ... 29464
Freeman Scott Rd ... 29464
Fresh Meadow Ln ... 29466
Friend St ... 29464
Frogleg Ct ... 29466
Frogmore Rd ... 29464
Fulford Ct ... 29466
Fulham Rd ... 29466
Galera Ln ... 29464
Gangway Cut ... 29466
Garden Way ... 29464
Garden Hill Rd ... 29466
Garden Wall Walk ... 29464
Garland Rd ... 29464
Garmouth Ct ... 29466
Gaston Gate ... 29466
Gate Post Dr ... 29464
George Browder Blvd ... 29466
Georgetown Rd ... 29464
Georgiana St ... 29466
Gibby Greer Rd ... 29464
Gilberts Lndg ... 29466
Gilead Rd ... 29466
Ginglis Way ... 29464
Glen Erin Dr ... 29466
Glen Lake Ct ... 29464
Glencoe Dr ... 29464
Goblet Ave ... 29464
Goldie Rd ... 29466
Governors Ct & Rd ... 29464
Governors Point Ct ... 29464
Grace Ln ... 29466
Graddick Rd ... 29464
Grandview Ct ... 29464
Grape Ln ... 29466
Grass Marsh Dr ... 29466
Gray Battery Ct ... 29464
Great Hope Dr ... 29466
Greeley Rd ... 29466
Green Path Ln ... 29464
Greenshade Way ... 29464
Greenspoint Ct ... 29466
Greenview Ln ... 29464
Greenwich St ... 29466
Greer St ... 29464
Gregorie Ferry Rd ... 29466
Grey Marsh Rd ... 29466
Greystone Blvd ... 29464
Grimsby Bridge Rd ... 29466
Griswold St ... 29466
Groves Manor Ct ... 29464
Guilford Ct ... 29466
Gulf Dr ... 29466
Gunnison St ... 29466
Gurley St ... 29464
Gypsy Ln ... 29464
Habersham Rd ... 29466
Haddrell St ... 29464
Haig Ln ... 29466
Hale Rd ... 29464
Hall Point Rd ... 29466
Hallahan Ct ... 29464
Halls Pond Rd ... 29466
Hamlet Square Ln ... 29464
Hamlin Rd ... 29464
Hamlin Beach Rd ... 29466
Hamlin Park Cir ... 29466
Hammond Dr ... 29466
Hamp Fludd St ... 29464
Happyland Blvd ... 29466
Harbor Ln ... 29464
Harbor Bridge Ln ... 29464
Harbor Pointe Dr ... 29464
Harborgate Blvd & Dr ... 29464
Harbour Watch Ct & Way ... 29464
Hardware Aly ... 29464
Harleston Green Ln ... 29466
Harpers Ferry Way ... 29466
Harriets Island Ct ... 29466
Harrietta Ct ... 29464
Harriman St ... 29466
Harrington Ct ... 29466
Harry Habersham Rd ... 29464
Harry M Hallman Junior Blvd ... 29464
Harry Robinson Rd ... 29466
Hartford Village Way ... 29466
Hartfords Bluff Cir & Ln ... 29466
Harvest Way ... 29464
Harwick Rd ... 29464
Hatchway Dr ... 29466
Hatteras Sound ... 29464
Hattie St ... 29464
Havenshire Ct ... 29464
Haviland Ct ... 29466
Hawksbill Ct ... 29464
Hawthorne St ... 29464
Hazan Ct ... 29464
Hearthstone Way ... 29466
Heather Dr ... 29464
Heather Grove Ln ... 29466
Heathermoor Ct ... 29466
Heathland Way ... 29466
Heidelberg Dr ... 29464
Heidiho Way ... 29466
Henrietta Hartford Rd ... 29466
Heritage Cir ... 29464
Hermit Crab Way ... 29466
Heron Ave ... 29464
Heron Pointe Blvd ... 29464
Hiawatha St ... 29464
Hibben St ... 29464
Hibbens Grant Blvd ... 29464
Hickory Cv ... 29464
Hidden Blvd ... 29464
Hidden Bridge Dr ... 29464
Hidden Cove Dr ... 29464
Hidden Lakes Dr ... 29464
Hidden Marsh Rd ... 29466
Hideaway Bay Ln ... 29464
E & W Higgins Dr ... 29466
High Battery Cir ... 29464
High Pond Ln ... 29464
N Highway 17
1400-1999 ... 29464
2000-2000 ... 29466
2002-3699 ... 29466
Highway 41 ... 29466
Hill St ... 29464
Hindman Ave ... 29464
Historic Dr ... 29464
Hob St ... 29464
Hobcaw Dr ... 29464
Hobcaw Bluff Dr ... 29464
Hogans Aly ... 29466
Hollenberg Ln ... 29466
Holly Bend Dr ... 29466
Hollythorne Dr ... 29466
Holmgren St ... 29466
Home Farm Rd ... 29464
Honeysuckle Ct ... 29464
Hook Ln ... 29464
Hopeman Ln ... 29466
Hopetown Rd ... 29466
Hopewell Ct ... 29464
Hopsewee Ln ... 29464
Hopton Cir ... 29466
Horseshoe Bnd ... 29464
Hospital Dr ... 29464
Hospitality St ... 29464
Houston Northcutt Blvd ... 29464
Howard St ... 29464
Hubbell Dr ... 29466
Hugh Smith Ct ... 29466
Hungryneck Blvd ... 29464
Hunters Trce ... 29464
Hunters Run Dr ... 29464
Huro Rd ... 29466
Huxley Dr ... 29466
Hyer St ... 29464
Ibis Ct ... 29464
Ida Rd ... 29466
Ike Dr ... 29466
Ilex Ct ... 29464
Indian St ... 29464
Indigo Ct ... 29466
Indigo Bay Cir ... 29464
Infantry Dr ... 29466
Ingot Way ... 29464
Inland Creek Way ... 29464
Inlet Dr ... 29464
Inlet Cove Ct ... 29464
Innovation Dr & Way ... 29466
Intracoastal View Dr ... 29466
Ionsborough St ... 29464
Iron Bridge Dr ... 29466
Ironclad Aly ... 29466
Isaac Boston St ... 29464
Isaiah Smalls Rd ... 29466
Isaw Dr ... 29464
Island Walk E & W ... 29464
Island Overlook ... 29464
Island Point Ct ... 29464
Island View Dr ... 29464
Isle Of Hope ... 29464
Isle Of Palms Connector ... 29464
Iverson Rd ... 29464
Jabbers Dr ... 29464
Jacaranda Ct ... 29466
Jack Snipe Ln ... 29464
Jackson St ... 29464
Jakes Ln ... 29464
James Basford Pl ... 29466
N & S James Gregarie Rd ... 29466
Jane Jacobs St ... 29464
Japonica Rd ... 29464
Jardinere Walk ... 29464
Jefferson Rd ... 29466
S Jetties Ct ... 29466
Jewelwood Ln ... 29466
Jimmy Brewer Ln ... 29466
Joe Bryant Ct ... 29466
Joe Edwards Rd ... 29466
Joe Rouse Rd ... 29466
Joggling St ... 29464
John Ballam Rd ... 29466
John Bartram Pl ... 29466
John Boone Ct ... 29466
John Dilligard Ln ... 29464
John Galt Way ... 29464
Johnnie Dodds Blvd
200-1051 ... 29464
1050-1050 ... 29465
1052-1598 ... 29464
1053-1599 ... 29464
Jorrington St ... 29466
Joseph Glover Rd ... 29466
Josephine Rd ... 29466
Joyce Ave ... 29464
Judge Rd ... 29464
Judy Ct ... 29464
Julep Dr ... 29464
Julius Robertson Rd ... 29466
Kathryn St ... 29464
Kaycees Ct ... 29464
Kennison Ln ... 29466
Kent St ... 29464
Ketch Ct ... 29464
Kidmore Rd ... 29466
Kilarney Rd ... 29464
Kiln Ct ... 29466
Kiln Creek Cir ... 29466
Kiln Point Dr ... 29466
Kincade Dr ... 29464
King St ... 29464
King Bird Ct ... 29466
Kingdom Hall Rd ... 29466
Kinglet St ... 29466
Kings Ct ... 29464
Kings Gate Ct & Ln ... 29466
Kingsford Ln ... 29466
Kingston Ln ... 29464
Kinloch Ln ... 29464
Kinloss Country Ln ... 29466
Kip Ln ... 29464
Kirk Ct ... 29464
Klein St ... 29464
Klink Ln ... 29464
Knightbridge Ln ... 29466
Korbel Cir ... 29466
Krier Ln ... 29464
Kweteng Dr ... 29466
La Mesa Rd ... 29464
Labor Camp Rd ... 29464
Lacannon Ln ... 29464
Lackland Ct ... 29464
Lagoon Park Cir ... 29466
Lake Pt ... 29464
Lake Bluff Ct ... 29466
Lake Hunter Cir ... 29464
Lake Mallard Blvd ... 29464
Lakecrest Ct ... 29466
Lakenheath Dr ... 29464
N Lakeshore Dr ... 29466
Lakeside Dr ... 29464
Lakeview Dr ... 29464
Lancer Ln ... 29464
Landau Ln ... 29466
Landings Run ... 29464
Langford Rd ... 29464
Lansing Dr ... 29464
Lanterns Rst ... 29464
Lapwing Ln ... 29464
Larch Ln ... 29466
Latitude Ln ... 29466
Latrobe Ct ... 29466
Latroy Ave ... 29464
Lauda Dr ... 29464
Laurel Park Trl ... 29466
Laurel Springs Ln ... 29466
Lavalier Sq ... 29464
Law Ln ... 29464
Lazy Ln ... 29464
Lazy Lane Ct ... 29464
Leader Ln ... 29464
Leaning Oaks Ct ... 29466
Leatherleaf Ct ... 29466
Lee Shore Ln ... 29464
Leeann Ln ... 29464
Legends Ter ... 29464
Legends Club Dr ... 29466
Leisure Ln ... 29464
Leland Cres ... 29464
Leonard Fulghum Dr ... 29464
Leonard Stoney Rd ... 29464
Lettered Olive Ln ... 29464
Lewisfield Pl ... 29464
Lexington Dr ... 29466
Libbys Pt ... 29464
Liberty Ct ... 29464
Lieben Rd ... 29466
Lillie And Rebecca Ln ... 29464
Lindner Ln ... 29466
Lindsey Creek Dr ... 29466
Linksland Rd ... 29466
Linnen Ln ... 29466
Linns Pt ... 29464
Lions Head Dr ... 29464
Liriope Ln ... 29464
Little Palm Loop ... 29466
Live Oak Dr ... 29464
Llewellyn Rd ... 29464
Lochmere Ct ... 29466
Locklear Ln ... 29466
Loebs Ct ... 29464
Lohr Dr ... 29466
London Bridge Rd ... 29464
Lone Oak Pt ... 29466
Lone Tree Dr ... 29464
Long Cove Ct ... 29466
Long Grove Dr ... 29464
Long Point Rd ... 29464
Longview Rd ... 29464
Lonnie Cir ... 29464
Lookout Pt ... 29464
Loomis St ... 29466
Lorenzo St ... 29464
Louise Ter ... 29464
W Lowcountry Blvd ... 29464
Loyalist Ct & Ln ... 29466
Lucas St ... 29464
Lucinda Dr ... 29466
Lucys Ln ... 29466
Lyman Ln ... 29464
Lymington Dr ... 29464
Lynch Ct ... 29464
Lynda Ann Ln ... 29464
Mack Rd ... 29464
Mackenzie Ct ... 29466
Macoma Dr ... 29466
Madison Ct ... 29466
Maggie Rd ... 29464
Maggie Road Ext ... 29464
Magnolia St ... 29464
Magnolia Meadows Dr ... 29464
Magnolia Place Ct ... 29466
Magnolia Woods Dr ... 29464
Magwood Ln ... 29464
Mahan Ct ... 29466
Maidstone Dr ... 29466
Main Canal Ct & Dr ... 29464
Mainland Ct ... 29464
Majestic Roses Ct ... 29464
Majore St ... 29464
Malcolm Rd ... 29466
Mallard Ct ... 29464
Manor Ln ... 29464
Maple Hill Ln ... 29464
Maplewood Ln ... 29466
Marginal Rd ... 29466
Mariner Place Dr ... 29466
Market Center Blvd ... 29464
N Marsh Dr ... 29466
Marsh Breeze Ln ... 29466
Marsh Court Ln ... 29464
Marsh Grove Ave ... 29464
Marsh Harbor Ln ... 29464
Marsh Ibis Trl ... 29464
Marsh Rabbit Ct ... 29466
Marsh Walk Cir ... 29464
Marshgrass Blvd ... 29464
Marshview Dr ... 29464
Mary St ... 29464
Mashie Ct ... 29466
Masthead Dr ... 29466
Mataoka St ... 29464
Mathis Ferry Rd ... 29464
May Ln ... 29464
Mazzy Ln ... 29464
Mcadams Ct ... 29466
Mccants Dr ... 29464
Mcconnell Ln ... 29466
Mccormick St ... 29466
Mcdaniel Ln ... 29464
Mcgrath Darby Blvd ... 29464
Mciver St ... 29464
Mcknight Rd ... 29466
Mcleans Ct ... 29466
Mcmanus Rd ... 29466
Meader Ln ... 29464
Meadow Park Ln ... 29464
Meadowcroft Ln ... 29466
Medinah Dr ... 29466
Melincou Dr ... 29464
Melvin Bennett Rd ... 29464
Merchant Ct ... 29466
Mercury Rd ... 29466
Merganser Ct ... 29464
Merion Pl ... 29466
Merrifield Ct ... 29466
Merwether Ln ... 29466
Middle St ... 29464
Middleburg Ln ... 29464
Middlesex St ... 29466
Middleton Ct ... 29464
Midtown Ave ... 29464
Mill St ... 29464
Mill Grove Ct ... 29466
Millbrook Ct ... 29466
Milldenhall Rd ... 29464
Mises St ... 29464
Mobile St ... 29464
Molasses Ln ... 29464
Monaco Dr ... 29464
Monhegan Way ... 29464
Monk Pl ... 29466
Montclair Dr ... 29464
Montrose Rd ... 29464
Mooring Line Dr ... 29466
S Morgans Point Rd ... 29466
Morning Glory Ct ... 29466
Morningdale Dr ... 29466
Morrison St ... 29464
Moss Blf & Path ... 29464
Mossy Rd ... 29464
Mossy Oak Way ... 29464
Moultrie St ... 29464
Moultrieville Rd ... 29464
Mount Royall Dr ... 29464
Muirhead Rd ... 29464
Muirwood Cir ... 29464
Mulligan Dr ... 29466
Murduck Dr ... 29466
Musket Range St ... 29464
Myrick Rd ... 29464
Myrtle Ct ... 29464
Mystic Dr ... 29464
Nantahala Blvd ... 29464
Nassas St ... 29466
Natchez Cir ... 29464
National Dr ... 29466
Nautical Ln ... 29466
Navigators Run ... 29464
Needlerush Pkwy ... 29464
Nehamiah Rd ... 29466
Neighbors Way ... 29466
Nell Ct ... 29464
Nevis Trl ... 29464
New St ... 29464
New Market Dr ... 29464
New Parrish Way ... 29464
Nicholas Aly ... 29464
Nicolette Cir ... 29466
Night Heron Dr ... 29464
Nix Ct ... 29466
Noble Ln ... 29464
Nolen Way ... 29464
Nomad Ln ... 29464
Nora Ln ... 29464
Nye View Cir ... 29466
Oak Hill Ter ... 29466
Oak Manor Dr ... 29466
Oak Marsh Dr ... 29464
Oak Mill Ct ... 29466
Oak Park Dr ... 29464
Oak Point Landing Dr ... 29464
Oak Tree Ln ... 29464
Oakhaven Blvd ... 29464
Oakhurst Dr ... 29466
Oakland Market Rd ... 29466
Oaklanding Rd ... 29464
Oakleaf Dr ... 29464
Ocean Breeze Ct ... 29464
Oconee Loop ... 29466
Old Brickyard Rd ... 29466
Old Bridge Ct ... 29464
Old Carolina Ct ... 29464
Old Colony Rd ... 29464
Old Course Ln ... 29466
Old Georgetown Rd
912-998 ... 29464
1000-1399 ... 29464
2300-2599 ... 29466
Old Ivy Way ... 29466
Old Jay Ln ... 29466
Old Marsh Pkwy ... 29466
Old Mill Ln ... 29464
Old South Way ... 29464
Old Tabby Ln ... 29464
Old Tavern Ct ... 29464
Old Village Dr ... 29464
Old Wanus Dr ... 29466
Old Williamston Ct ... 29464
Olde Central Way ... 29464
Olde Salt Run ... 29464
Oliver Brown Rd ... 29466
Olympia Fields Ln ... 29466
Olympic Ln ... 29466
Omni Blvd ... 29466
On The Harbor Dr ... 29464
Order Ct ... 29466
Osmond Rd ... 29466
Osprey Ct ... 29464
Osullivan Dr ... 29464
Outreach Ln ... 29464
Overcreek Ct ... 29464
Overseer Pl ... 29464
Overseer Retreat ... 29464
Overview Ct ... 29464
Oxborough Cir ... 29466
Oxfordshire Ln ... 29466

Oyster View Ct 29466
Page Tree Ln 29464
Palisades Dr 29464
Palm St 29464
Palm Cove Way 29466
Palmetto Blf & St 29464
Palmetto Battery Way .. 29464
N & W Palmetto Fort Dr 29466
Palmetto Grande Dr 29464
Palmetto Hall Blvd 29466
Palmetto Isle Dr 29466
Palmetto Marsh Cir 29466
Palmetto Peninsula Dr .. 29466
Pandora Dr 29466
Panther Ct 29464
Paradise Lake Dr 29464
Parapet Ct 29464
Parc Vue Ave 29464
Parish Lndg 29466
Park Pond Cir 29466
E & W Park View Pl ... 29466
Park West Blvd 29466
Parkers Island Rd 29466
Parkers Landing Rd 29466
Parkfront Dr 29464
Parkton Rd 29464
Parkway Dr 29464
Parsonage Woods Ln .. 29466
Passfield Ln 29466
Pat St 29464
Pat Kelly Ln 29464
Patjens Ln 29464
Patriots Point Rd 29464
Pawley Rd 29464
Peaceful Way 29464
Pearl St 29464
Pegnail Cor 29464
Pelican Pl 29464
Pelzer Dr 29464
Pendergrass Ln 29464
Penders Blvd 29466
Penny Cir 29464
Penshell Pl 29464
Perching Ct 29464
Periwinkle Dr 29466
Periwinkle Spout Cv 29466
Perseverance St 29466
Peyton Moore Ct 29464
Pherigo St 29464
Phillips Park Dr 29464
S Piazza Ct 29464
Pierates Cruz 29464
Pignatelli Cres 29466
Pilots Pt 29464
Pilsdon Crst 29464
Pin Oak Cut 29466
Pine Hollow Rd 29464
Pine Island Vw 29464
Pine Shadow Ln 29464
Pinebrook Ct 29466
Pinecone Ct 29466
Piper Pt 29464
Pirates Cv 29464
Pitt St 29464
Plantation Ct & Ln 29464
Plantation View Ln 29464
Planters Curv, Loop, Pl & Rst 29464
Planters Pointe Blvd 29466
N & S Plaza Ct 29464
Pleasant Oaks Dr 29464
Pleasant Pines Rd 29464
Pleasant View Ct 29466
Pleasant Walk Ct 29466
Plover Ave 29464
Pluff Mud Aly 29464
Poaug Ln 29464
Pocahontas St 29464
N Point Ct 29464
W Point Dr 29466
N Point Ln 29464
Pointe Bluff Ct 29466
Ponsbury Rd 29464
Porchers Bluff Rd 29466
Port Harbor Ct 29464
Port Royal Rd 29464
Portico Park 29464
Post Oak Dr 29464
Powhatan Ave 29464
Premier Ln 29466
Prescient St 29464
Preservation Pl 29464
Presidio Dr 29466
Primus Dr 29466
Prince Ferry Ln 29466
Prince Nelson Ln 29466
Pritchards Point Dr 29464
Privateer Dr 29464
Professional Ln 29464
Promenade Ct 29466
Proprietors Pl 29466
Prospect Hill Dr 29464
Provincial Cir 29464
Pumpkin Ln 29464
Purple Martin Ct 29466
Pyracantha Ct 29466
Queen St 29464
Queen Anne Ct 29464
Queens Ct 29464
Queensborough Blvd ... 29464
Queensgate Way 29466
Quiet Rd 29464
Quinby Ct 29464
Quince St 29464
Ralston Ct 29464
Rambler Ln 29464
Ramblewood Cir 29464
Randall Dr 29464
Ranns Hill Rd 29464
Rebels Cp 29464
Recreation Way 29466
Red Coat Run 29464
Red Drum Rd 29466
Red Fern Ln 29466
Rees Row 29464
Reid St 29464
Resolute Ln 29464
Retreat Lndg 29464
Revetment Ln 29464
Revolution Dr 29464
Rhum Retreat 29464
Rialto Rd 29464
Rice Bay Dr 29464
Rice Field Cv 29464
Rice Field Ln 29466
Rice Hope Dr 29464
Rice Marsh Ct 29466
E & W Rice Planters Ct, Dr & Ln 29464
Richard Ln 29466
Richies Way 29464
Richter Way 29464
Ridge Rd 29464
Rifle Range Rd
1000-1999 29464
2100-3099 29466
Ringsted Ln 29466
Ringwood Rd 29466
River Bluff Ln 29466
River Lake Walk 29464
River Oak Dr 29464
River Otter Ct 29466
River Vista Way 29466
Rivers St 29464
Riverstation Ct 29466
Rivertowne Pkwy 29466
Rivertowne Country Club Dr 29466
Riverwood Dr 29466
Riviera Dr 29464
Robert Mills Cir 29464
Robin Rd 29464
Robyns Glen Dr 29464
Rockfish Ct 29466
Roddington St 29464
Rogers Ln 29464
Rose Ln 29464
Rose Hill Ln 29464
Rose Walk Ct 29466
Rose Wilder Ln 29464
Rosedown Pt 29466
Rosemead Rd 29464
Rosewood Ln 29464
Roswell Ct 29464
Royal Links Dr 29466
Royal Tern Ln 29464
Royal Trace Ln 29466
Royal Troon Ct 29466
Royalist Rd 29464
Royall Ave 29464
Royce Rd 29466
Royston Rd 29464
Ruby Dr 29464
Rue De Muckle 29464
Ruffin Rd 29466
Runaway Bay Ln 29466
Rush Haven Dr 29466
Russell Dr 29464
Saint Ellens Dr 29466
Sally Gaillard Ln 29466
Salt Wind Way 29466
Salterbeck Ct 29466
Salty Aly 29464
Salty Tide Cv 29464
Sam Edwards Rd 29466
Sam Snead Dr 29466
Sampa Rd 29464
Sand Marsh Ln 29466
Sandlake Dr 29464
Sandpiper Dr 29464
Sandy Point Ct & Ln ... 29466
Sandy Shore Ct 29466
Sanibel St 29464
Sanset Pl 29464
Saphire Ct 29466
Sappho Ct 29464
Sarazen Dr 29466
Sareda Cir 29464
Sassafrass Cir 29466
Saturday Rd 29464
Savoy St 29464
Sawgrass Ln 29464
Scallop Ct 29464
Scarlet Oak Ct 29466
Schirmer Ave 29464
School House Rd 29464
Schweers Ln 29464
Scotland Dr 29464
Scott St 29464
Scott Singleton Ln 29464
Scotts Creek Cir 29464
Scranton Dr 29466
Sea Dog Cir 29464
Sea Gull Dr 29464
Sea Island Crossing Ln 29464
Sea Oats Ct 29464
Sea Palms Cres 29464
Sea Pines Dr 29466
Seaborn Dr 29466
Seacoast Pkwy 29464
Seafood Dr 29464
Seaport Ln 29466
Searle Ct 29464
Seastrand Ln 29466
Seaway Ln 29464
Secession St 29464
Seewee Cir 29464
Sehoy Dr 29464
Seminole St 29464
Serendipity St 29464
Serotina Ct & Pt 29464
Sessions Way 29464
Settlers Rst E & W 29464
Sewee Fort Rd 29466
Sewee Indian Ct 29466
Shadow Dr 29464
Shadow Lake Cir 29464
Shady Grove Ln 29464
Shagbark Cir 29464
Shakerwood Cir 29464
Shannon Dr 29464
Shark Eye Aly 29464
Sharon Ct 29464
Shell Fish Ct 29466
Shell Point Ln 29464
Shell Ring Cir 29466
N & S Shelmore Blvd .. 29464
Shem Dr 29464
Shetland Ct 29464
Shields Ln 29466
Shilling Pl 29464
Shingleback Dr 29466
Shipping Ln 29464
E & W Shipyard Rd 29464
Shire Rd 29464
Shoals Dr 29464
Shoreside Way 29464
Short St 29464
Short Grass Ct 29466
Short River Ct 29464
Show Basket Way 29466
Shrimp Boat Ln 29464
Shutesbury St 29466
Silent Harbor Ct 29464
Silver Stone Dr 29466
Simmons St 29464
Simon Point Rd 29464
Sinlea Ave 29464
Sirop Ct 29464
Sisseton Ln 29466
Six Mile Rd 29466
Skyhawk Ct 29466
Slate Ln 29464
Slipper Shell Ct 29464
N & S Smokerise Way . 29466
Snap Dragon Ct 29464
Snee Farm Pkwy 29464
Snowden Rd 29464
Soliel Ct 29464
Somersby Ln 29466
Somerset Ct 29464
Somerset Hills Ct 29466
Somerton Ct 29464
Sonja Way 29466
Sound View Dr 29466
Southern Cottage Way . 29466
Southern Magnolia Ln .. 29464
Southern Oak Way 29466
Southlake Dr 29464
Southwark St 29464
Sovereign Ter 29464
Sowell St 29464
Spann St 29464
Spark St 29464
Speights St 29464
Spinner Cir 29464
Splitshot Cir 29464
Spoon Ct 29466
Spoonbill Ln 29464
Spotted Owl Dr 29464
Spring Hill Ln 29464
Spring Line Dr 29466
Springfield Rd 29464
Springwood Cir 29464
Sprucewood Ct 29464
Spyglass Pt 29464
Stamby Pl 29464
Station Point Ct 29466
Stay Sail Way 29464
Steven Gaillard Rd 29466
Stewardship Rd 29464
Stockade Ln 29466
Stockdale St 29464
Stockton Dr 29466
Stonewall Ct 29464
Strathene Ct 29466
Strathmore Ln 29464
Stratton Pl 29466
Stratton Ferry Ct 29464
Stringer Aly 29464
Stuart Engals Blvd 29464
Stucco Ln 29464
Sturbridge Rd 29466
Sugar Cane Way 29464
Sugar House Retreat ... 29464
Summers Creek Ct 29464
Summersill Ln 29464
Summerwood Dr 29466
Sunchaser Ln 29466
Sweet Garden Ct 29464
Sweet Myrtle Cir 29466
Sweetgrass Basket Pkwy 29466
Swinton Ct 29464
Tabor Rd 29466
Tailwind Ct 29464
Talisman Rd 29464
Tall Grass Cir 29466
Tall Pine Rd 29464
Tamarack Pine Ct 29464
Tambourine Ct 29466
Tarrington Ln 29464
Tea House Ln 29464
Tea Olive Trl 29464
Tea Planter Ln 29466
Tennyson Row 29464
Thayer Pl 29466
Thayer Hall Dr 29466
Theater Dr 29464
Thomas Barksdale Way 29466
Thomas Cairo Blvd 29466
Thornrose Ln 29466
Three Gates Dr 29464
Tidal Pt 29464
Tidal Currents Ln 29466
Tidal Marsh Ln 29466
Tidal Place Cir 29464
Tidal Reef Cir 29464
Tidal Terrace Ct 29464
Timothy Bostic Ln 29464
Tip Ln 29466
Tison Ln 29464
Tolbert Way 29466
Toler Dr 29464
Tombee Ct 29464
Tomota Ct 29464
Toomer Ln 29464
Toomer Kiln Cir 29466
Topaz Dr 29466
Topsail Ct 29464
Towana Coleman 29466
Tower Dr 29466
Towne Centre Way 29464
Traders Aly 29464
Tradewind Dr 29466
Tradition Cir 29466
Treadwell St 29466
Treasure Cv 29464
Trimbleston Pl 29464
Trip Line Dr 29466
Triple Oak Dr 29466
Triton Ct 29464
Trowman Ln 29464
Trumpet Vine Ct 29464
Tugman Ln 29464
Tupelo Bay Dr 29464
Turben Pl 29466
Turgot Ln 29466
Turnbuckle Pt 29466
Twickenham Pl 29464
Twilight Trl 29464
Two Cedar Way 29466
Two Island Ct 29466
Two Rivers Ct & Dr 29464
Ty Ln 29466
Tybee Pass 29466
Unwin Way 29464
Upland Pl 29464
E & W Vagabond Ln ... 29464
Vanguard Pl 29466
Vantage Pt 29466
Vasi Ct 29466
Venning Rd & St 29464
Ventura Pl 29464
Veranda Vw 29464
Veron Pl 29464
Vestige Sq 29464
Victoria Lake Dr 29466
Victory Ct 29466
Victory Pointe Dr 29466
Villa Maison 29464
Village Sq 29464
Village Creek Ln 29464
Village Rest Ct 29464
Vinca Vw 29464
Vincent Dr 29464
Virginia Rouse Rd 29466
Vision Rd 29464
Volunteer Ln 29464
Von Kolnitz Rd 29464
Wading Ct 29464
Wagner Creek Ct 29466
Wakendaw Blvd & Rd .. 29464
Walking Trail Ct 29466
Wallers Ferry Dr 29466
Walt Miller St 29464
Walton Heath Ct 29466
Wando Ln 29464
Wando Park Blvd 29464
Wando Place Dr 29464
Wando Plantation Way . 29466
Wando Reach Ct 29464
Wando River Way 29464
Wando View Ln 29464
Wandolea Dr 29464
Wappetaw Pl 29464
Ware Bottom Ln 29464
Warrick Ln 29464
Warrior Way 29466
Washrich Ln 29464
Water Oak Cut 29466
Waterfront Dr 29464
Waterlily Dr 29464
Watermark Blvd 29464
Waterpointe Cir 29466
Watershade Ct 29466
Waterside Ct 29466
Waterway Ct 29464
Waterway Arms Blvd ... 29464
Watoga Way 29466
Wavespray Ct 29466
Wayne St 29464
Wayward Ct 29466
Weaver Cir 29464
Wedge Hall Trce 29464
Wellbrooke Ln 29466
Wellesley Cir, Ct & Pl .. 29466
Wellford St 29464
Wellstead St 29466
Wendell Ct 29466
Westos Way 29464
Wexford Park 29466
Wharf Indigo Pl 29464
Whilden St 29464
Whipple Rd 29464
Whisker Pole Ln 29466
Whisper Grass Cir 29466
Whispering Oaks Trl 29466
White Deer Way 29466
White Flat Rd 29464
White Hall Dr 29466
Whites Cabin Rd 29466
Whiting St 29466
Whitsun Ct 29464
Wickersham Ct 29466
Wickfield Ct 29464
Wigfall Dr 29466
Wild Dogwood Way 29466
Wild Horse Ln 29464
Wild Olive Dr 29464
Willbrook Ln 29466
William St 29464
William Hapton Way 29466
William Ladson Rd 29466
Williams Mazyck Rd 29466
Williams Veneer Ct 29466
Williamson Dr 29464
Willington Ct 29466
Willoughby Ln 29466
Willow Branch Way 29464
Willow Pond Rd 29466
Willowdale Ct 29466
Willowick Ct 29466
Windchime Aly 29464
Winding Creek Ct 29464
Winding Ridge Ct 29466
Windsome Pl 29464
Wingo Way 29464
Winifred St 29464
Winnowing Way 29466
Winthrop St 29464
Winton Rd 29464
Wisteria Wall Dr 29464
Wittenberg Ct & Dr 29464
Wood Stork Pt 29466
Woodgreen Cir 29464
Woodlake Ct 29464
Woodland Ave 29464
Woodland Park Dr 29466
Woodland Pointe Pl 29464
Woodlock Rd 29464
Woodspring Rd 29466
Woodstream Rd 29466
Worthington Dr 29466
Worthy Ct 29466
Wosley Ct 29466
Wren Ave 29464
Wylls Nck 29464
Wynbrook Trce 29466
Wynford Ct 29464
Wyngate Cir 29466
Wynnwood Ct 29466
Yachtsman Dr 29466
Yonge St 29464
York St 29464
Yorktown Ct 29464
Yough Hall Rd 29466
Zacoma Rd 29466
Zinser St 29466

NUMBERED STREETS

All Street Addresses 29464

MYRTLE BEACH SC

General Delivery 29577

POST OFFICE BOXES MAIN OFFICE STATIONS AND BRANCHES

Box No.s
1 - 3986 29578
6761 - 7838 29572
8000 - 9676 29578
14001 - 16848 29587
30001 - 32454 29588
50001 - 51918 29579
70001 - 71258 29572
780001 - 780004 29578
870001 - 870777 29587

NAMED STREETS

Abalone Ct 29579
Abby Ln 29572
Abc Dr 29577
Abcaw Blvd 29579
Abercromby Ct 29579
Aberdeen Way 29579
Abergele Way 29572
Abingdon Dr 29579
Abrams Mobile Home Park 29577
Acadian Way 29588
Ackerman Dr 29579
Acline Ave 29577
Adaline Ct 29579
Adaringt Dr 29575
Addison Ct 29577
Afton Ct 29579
Agape Ct 29588
Ailsa Ct 29579
Airdrome St 29577
Alameda Ct 29579
Alberta Dr 29577
Alder St 29577
Alexander Ct 29588
Alexandria Ave 29577
Ali Ct 29588
Alice Bud Ln 29588
Allspice Ln 29579
Almeria Ct 29572

Alwoodley Ln 29579
Alyssum Ct 29579
Amalfi Pl 29572
Amber St 29577
Amberly Dr 29575
Amberwood Ct 29588
Ambling Way Dr 29579
Ambrosia Loop 29579
Amelia Pl 29588
American Way 29577
Ammons Ln 29588
Amore Ct 29572
Andover Dr 29575
Andrew Jack Mitchell Ln 29577
Andys Dr 29588
Angel Ct 29579
Ann St 29588
Annandale Dr 29577
Annese Dr 29588
Anson Ct 29575
Antebellum Dr 29579
Antigua Dr 29572
Antilles Ct 29577
Antler Ln 29579
Antler Ridge Cv 29588
Antonio Ln 29588
Apache Dr 29577
Apache Trl 29588
Apostle Ct 29588
Appaloosa Dr 29588
Appian Way 29588
Appleby Way 29572
Appledore Cir 29572
Applesauce Dr 29588
Appleton Way 29579
Applewood Ct 29588
April Gray Ln 29579
Aqua Vista Ct 29588
Aquarius Dr 29575
Arcadian Dr 29572
Archdale St 29588
Aries Ln 29575
Arignon Ct 29579
Armelise Dr 29579
Arran Ct 29579
Arrow Wood Ct 29579
Arrowhead Blvd 29579
Arrowhead Ct 29572
Arundel Rd 29577
Ascot Dr 29588
Ash St 29577
Ashboro Ct 29579
Ashdale Dr 29588
Ashepoo Creek Dr 29579
Ashfield Ct 29579
Ashford Ct 29588
Ashleaf Dr 29579
Ashley Ct 29588
Ashley Dr 29577
Ashley Cove Dr 29588
Ashley Park Dr 29579
Ashley River Rd 29588
Ashtabula Ct 29579
Ashton Cir 29588
Ashton Glenn Dr 29575
Ashwood Cir 29575
Ashwood Ln 29588
Aspen Dr 29577
Assembly Ln 29588
Aster Ct 29579
Atalaya Pl 29579
Atoll Dr 29588
Aubrey Ln 29588
Auburn Ln 29575
Augusta Cres 29588
Augusta Plantation Dr 29579
Austell Ct 29588
Autumn Pond Ct 29579
Autumnwood Rd 29588
Avalon Dr 29575
Avenue E 29577
Avenue C 29577
Avenue Of The Palms 29579
Avocado Ct & Dr 29579
Avocet Dr 29575
Avondale Dr 29588
Avx Dr 29577
Awendaw Ct 29579
Ayershire Ct & Ln 29575
Azalea Ct 29577
Azalea Dr 29575
N Azalea Dr 29575
Aztec Ct 29579
Babaco Ct 29579
Babylon Pine Dr 29579
Backstage Blvd 29579
Backwater Ct 29579
Backwoods Rd 29588
Baggott Ln 29588
Bagley Dr 29579
Baker Ct 29579
Baldwin Ln 29577
Balfour Ct 29575
Balmoral Ct 29588
Balmore Dr 29579
Balmwood Cir 29588
Balsam St 29577
Bamboo Ct 29579
Banks Dr 29588
N Bar Ct 29579
Barclay Dr 29579
Barcreek Ct 29579
Barkwood Dr 29575
Barn Owl Ct 29579
Baron Dr 29577
Barona Dr 29579
Barre Ct 29579
Barringer Rd 29577
Barrington Ln 29588
Barrister Ln 29577
Barton Loop 29579
Baslow Ct 29572
Bathurst Dr 29579
Battery Way Ct 29579
Battey Dr 29588
Battleway Ct 29579
E Bay Ct 29579
Bay Dr 29575
E Bay Dr 29588
Bay Ln 29588
Bay Rd 29588
Bay St 29577
Bay Covey 29588
Bay Forge Rd 29579
Bay Tree Ln 29575
Bayberry Ln 29572
Bayberry Pl 29579
Bayhaven Dr 29579
Baylight Ct 29579
Baywood Cir 29588
Beach Dr 29572
S Beach Dr 29575
Beach Pl 29577
Beach Club Dr 29572
Beachwalk Pl 29577
Bear Ln 29588
Bear Claw Ct 29588
Bear Dance Rd 29588
Bear Stand Trl 29588
Beauclair Ct 29579
Beaucoup Ct 29588
Beaufain Dr 29579
Beaumont Way 29577
Beaver Rd 29577
Beaver Road Ext 29577
Beaver Run Blvd 29575
Beeker Ct 29579
Bella Rd 29588
Bella Verde Ct 29579
Bella Vista Cir 29579
Belladonna Ct 29579
Bellamy Ln 29588
Bellamy St 29577
Bellasera Cir 29579
Belle Terre Blvd 29579
Belleglen Ct 29579
Bellegrove Dr 29579
Bellfield Ct 29579
Bellini Ct 29579
Bellis Dr 29579
Belmont Park Dr 29588
Belmonte Dr 29588
Belvidere Dr 29579
Ben Ln 29588
Benchmark Ct 29588
Benna Dr 29577
Benson Dr 29579
Bent Grass Dr 29575
Bent Tree Way 29588
Bent Twig Ct 29579
Bentcreek Ln 29579
Bentley Ct 29577
Bentwood Dr 29577
Bergeron Ct 29579
Berkshire Ave 29577
Berkshire Ct 29575
Berkshire Dr 29588
Bermuda Ct 29575
Bermuda Way 29577
Bermuda Way N 29577
Bermuda Grass Dr 29579
Berrywood Ct 29588
Bertha Dr 29588
N Berwick Dr 29575
Berwick Ln 29579
Best Western Trl 29588
Bethpage Dr 29579
Beverly St 29588
Big Bear Ct 29579
Big Block Rd 29588
Big Woods Ct 29588
Billy K Trl 29579
Biltmore Dr 29579
Bingham Ct 29588
Birch Ln 29572
Birch N Coppice Dr 29575
Birchwood Cir 29577
Bird Key Ct 29579
Birkdale Ln 29588
Birnamwood Ct 29579
Bittern Dr 29575
Bittersweet Ln 29579
Black Bear Rd 29588
Black Hawk Trl 29588
Black River Rd 29588
Black Smith Ln 29579
Black Willow Ct 29579
Blackberry Ln 29579
Blackburn Ct 29579
Blackheath Ct 29575
Blackjack Ln 29588
Blackstone Dr 29588
Blackwolf Dr 29579
Blackwood Ct 29588
Blade Beak Ln 29588
Blake Rd 29588
Blease Ct 29588
Bleckley Ave 29579
Block House Way 29577
Bloomwood Dr 29588
Blue St 29577
Blue Heron Blvd 29588
Blue Indigo Ln 29579
Blue Jay Dr 29588
Blue River Ct 29579
Blue Stem Dr 29588
Blue Tree Ct 29588
Blue Water Ln 29579
Bluebill Covey 29588
Bluebonnet Ct 29579
Bluefish Ct 29579
Bluff Dr 29577
Bluffton Ct 29579
Bluffview Dr 29579
Blynn Dr 29572
Blyth Ct 29572
Bobcat Ct 29575
Bobwhite Ln 29575
Bohicket Ct 29579
Bolton Ln 29575
Bonita Loop 29588
Bonnie Dr 29588
Bonnie Bridge Cir 29579
Boone Trl 29588
Boone Hall Dr 29579
Bougainvillea Dr 29577
Boundary St 29577
Bouquets Green Way 29579
Bovardia Pl 29577
Box Turtle Ct 29588
Boxwood Dr 29588
Boxwood St 29577
Boyne Dr 29588
Bradford Cir 29588
Bradley Cir 29579
Braemar Way 29579
Braewood Ct 29575
Bragg Dr 29588
Bramble Glen Dr 29579
Bramblewood Dr 29579
Bramblewood Lakes Dr 29588
Brampton Dr 29588
Branch St 29577
Branchwood Ct 29579
Brandenberry Dr 29575
Brandymill Blvd 29588
Branigan Ct 29579
Brassie Rd 29588
Breakers Dr 29579
Breakwater Dr 29579
Breckinridge Dr 29575
Breezewood Blvd 29588
Brenda Pl 29577
Brentford Pl 29579
Brentwood Dr 29572
Brewster Dr 29577
Briar Patch Ct 29579
Briar Vista Dr 29579
Briarberry Ln 29588
Briarwood Dr 29572
S Bridge Dr 29575
Bridgecreek Dr 29588
Bridgeport Dr 29577
Bridleford Dr 29588
Brighton Ave 29588
Brighton Hill Ave 29588
Brightwater Dr 29579
Britewater Ct 29579
British Ln 29579
Brixton Ct 29579
Broad River Rd 29588
S Broadway St 29577
Brock St 29588
Broken Anchor Way 29575
Bromley Ct 29579
Brookfield Dr 29588
Brookgate Dr 29579
Brookgreen Dr 29577
Brookhill Dr 29588
Brookline Dr 29579
Brookmont Dr 29588
Brooksher Dr 29588
Brookside Ln 29579
Brookstone Dr 29588
Brookton Cir 29588
Brookwater Ct 29588
Brothers Hill Rd 29588
Brown Pelican Dr 29577
Bryan Pl 29572
Bryant St 29572
Brynfield Dr 29588
Buck Ct 29579
Buck Hill Dr 29588
Buck Scrape Rd 29588
Buckeye Dr 29577
Buckeye Ln 29575
Buckingham Ave 29577
Buckingham Ln 29579
Buckley Ct 29579
Bucklin Loop 29579
Buddy Ln 29588
Builth Ct 29588
Buist Cir 29579
Bull Run Way 29579
Bunch Rd 29588
Bunny Trail Ct 29588
Bur Oak Ct 29579
Burcale Pl & Rd 29579
Burcale Road Cir 29579
Burchap Dr 29577
Burchwood Ln 29588
Burgess Oak Ln 29588
Burkridge West Dr 29588
Burroughs And Chapin Blvd 29577
Bush Dr 29579
Business St 29579
Butch Ln 29588
Buteo Ct 29588
Butkus Dr 29588
Butler Rd 29588
Button Buck Rd 29588
Buxton Dr 29579
Byrnes Ln 29588
Byrom Rd 29579
Cabana Rd 29572
Cabazon Dr 29579
Cabo Loop 29588
Cabots Creek Dr 29588
Cactus St 29577
Caddis Ct 29579
Cadiz Dr 29579
Caduceus Dr 29588
Caffrey Ct 29579
Cagney Ln 29577
Caldee Ct 29579
Caledonia Dr 29577
Calhoun Rd
300-6199 29577
6200-6299 29572
Callalily Ct 29579
Callie Dr 29588
Calypso Dr 29588
Cambridge Cir 29577
Camden Dr 29588
Camellia Dr 29577
Camellia Dr N 29575
Cameron Cir 29579
Campbell St 29577
Canal St 29577
Candlewick Ct 29575
Candy Ln 29575
Cane Pole Ct 29588
Canna Trl 29579
Cannon Rd 29577
Canterbury Ct 29572
Canterbury Dr 29579
Canterbury Ln 29577
Canvasback Trl 29588
Cape Landing Cir & Dr 29588
Capella Ln 29575
Capers Creek Dr 29579
Capital Field Ct 29588
Capri Ln 29579
Capricorn Dr 29575
Captain Ct 29579
Captiva Row 29579
Capua Ct 29588
Capulet Cir 29588
Cara Mia Ct 29577
Carbella Cir 29579
Cardinal Ave 29577
Cardinal Cres 29588
Caribbean Way S 29577
Caribou Trl 29588
Carlisle Way 29579
Carlton Dr 29577
Carnaby Loop 29579
Carnation Cir 29577
Carnegie Ave 29588
Carnes Ln 29577
Carnoustie Ct 29575
Carolina Ct 29588
Carolina Pl 29577
Carolina Chickadee Ct 29588
Carolina Commercial Dr 29579
Carolina Cove Dr 29577
Carolina Exchange Dr 29579
Carolina Farms Blvd 29579
Carolina Forest Blvd 29579
Carolina Lakes Blvd 29588
Carolina Woods Dr 29588
Carolina Wren Cres 29588
Caroline Cir 29572
Carolines Cove Ct 29588
Carolyn Dr 29588
Caromax Ct 29588
Caropine Dr 29575
Carra Ln 29579
Carrera St 29572
Carriage Row Ln 29577
Carrington Dr 29579
Carsten Ct 29579
Cart Ln 29577
Carter Cir 29579
Carvel Ct 29588
Carver St 29577
Caryle Ct 29579
Cascarilla Ct 29579
Casentino Ct 29579
Casita Ln 29579
Caspian Tern Dr 29588
Cassandra Ln 29577
Cassian Way 29588
Cassiopia Dr 29575
Castle Dr 29579
Castle Harbour Dr 29575
Castle Pinckney Dr 29579
Castleberry Pl 29588
Castleford Cir 29572
Catalonia Ct 29579
Catawba Ct & Trl 29588
Catawba River Rd 29588
Catbird Cir 29579
Catena Ln 29572
Cathedral Dr 29588
Catherine Ave 29575
Causeway Dr 29588
Causey St 29577
Cavandish Dr 29588
Cavaretta Ct 29575
Cayman Ct 29577
Cedar Dr 29577
Cedar Dr N 29575
Cedar Dr S 29575
Cedar Ln
1-99 29572
4200-4299 29588
Cedar Run 29588
Cedar St 29577
Cedar Grove Ln 29579
Cedar Hill Ln 29588
Cedar Trace Dr 29588
Cedarwood Cir 29572
Celebrity Cir 29577
Celene Ct 29579
Centennial Cir 29579
Center Dr 29572
Century St 29577
Chactaw Rd 29588
Chadbury Ln 29588
Chalmers Ct 29579
Chamberlin Rd 29588
Chandler Dr 29575
Chanticleer Village Dr 29579
Chapel Ln 29588
Chapel Hill Ct 29588
Chapel Ridge Cir 29588
Chapin Cir 29572
Chapman Pl 29577
Charleston Ct 29572
Charlotte Rd 29577
Chartwell Ct 29588
Chatham Dr 29579
Chattooga Ct 29588
Cherokee St 29577
Cherry Dr 29575
Cherry Ln 29572
Cherry Bark Ct 29579
Cherry Laurel 29588
Cherrywood Dr 29588
Chester St 29577
Chesterfield Ct
100-299 29575
400-499 29577
Chesterwood Ct 29579
Chestnut Dr 29577
Chestnut Rd 29572
Chestnut Ridge Dr 29572
Cheston Ct 29588
Cheyenne Rd 29588
Chianni Ln 29579
Chickasaw Ln 29579
Chinon Ct 29588
Chippendale Dr 29588
Chisholm Rd 29579
Christiana Ln 29579
Christie Mcauliffe Blvd 29579
Christopher Ln 29588
Church St 29577
Churchill Downs Dr 29579
Cimerron Dr 29588
Cinnamon Fern Ln 29588
Cipriana Dr 29572
Circle Dr 29575
Circle Ln 29588
Cirus Dr 29575
Citadel Ln 29577
Citation Way 29577
Claire Chapin Epps Dr 29577
Clambake Ct 29579
Clandon Ct & Dr 29579
Clardy Ln 29588
Claremont Ct 29577
Clarion Ct 29588
Clark St 29577
Clay Pond Village Ln 29579
Claypond Rd 29579
Clear Creek Cir 29588
Clearfield Dr 29588
Clearwater Dr 29575
Clearwater St 29577
Clematis Ct 29579
Cliffwood Dr 29572
Cloister Dr 29575
Cloisters Ln 29577
Clovis Cir 29579
Club Cir & Dr 29572
Club House Dr 29577
Cluster Ln 29579
Co Op Rd 29588
Coachman Ln 29575
Coalition Dr 29588
Coastal Ln 29577
Coastal Grand Cir 29577
Cobblers Ct 29579
Cobblestone Dr 29577
Cocas Dr 29579
Cocker Ct 29579
Coffee Tree Ct 29579
Coggin Ct 29579
Coinbow Ln 29579
Colby Ct 29588
Coldwater Cir 29588
Cole Ct 29577
College Green Way 29579
Collins St 29577
Colonial Cir & Dr 29572
Colony Dr 29575
Columbia Dr 29577
Commadores Ct 29575
Commerce Pl 29577
Commons Blvd 29572
S Commons Dr 29588
Compass Center Pl 29588
Conbraco Cir 29577
Concord Dr 29579
Cone Ln 29588
Congressional Dr 29579
Conifer Ct 29572
Connemara Dr 29579
Connie Ct 29588
Cook Cir 29577
Coomac Rd 29588
Cooper River Rd 29588
Coopers Ct 29579
Coopers Hawk Ct 29588
Coosaw Ct 29579
Copper Creek Ct 29579
Copperleaf Dr 29588
Coppersmith Ln 29579
Coral Beach Cir 29575
Coral Harbor Dr 29588
Corn Pickers Ln 29579
Corn Pile Rd 29588
Corn Planters Ln 29579
Cornerstone Ct & Ln 29588
Cornfield Ct 29579

Cornfield Rd 29588
Cornwall Dr 29588
Corporate Centre Dr 29577
Corrado St 29572
Corsico Ln 29579
Cortona Dr 29572
Costa Verda Dr 29572
Coteswood Dr 29572
Cottage Cir 29579
Cottage Ct 29572
Cottage Dr 29577
Cottage Oaks Cir 29579
Cottage Shell Dr 29579
Cotton Easter Ln 29588
Cottontail Trl 29588
Cottonwood Dr 29588
Countess Ct 29588
Country Club Dr 29577
Country Club View Dr 29588
Countryside Dr 29579
Courage Ln 29577
Courtyard Dr 29577
Cove Ct & Dr 29572
Covelo Ln 29579
Coventry Rd 29575
E Covington Ct & Dr 29579
Coyledom Ct 29577
Crab Pond Ct 29579
Crabtree Ln 29577
Cranbrook Ln 29579
Crane Dr 29572
Craven Dr 29579
Creekside Dr 29588
Creekwatch Rd 29588
Creekwood Cir 29588
Creon St 29588
Crepe Myrtle Ct 29577
Cresswind Blvd 29577
Crestwood Dr 29588
Crimson St 29577
Cromley Cir 29577
Crooked Pine Dr 29575
Cross Cut Trl 29579
Cross Gate Blvd 29575
Crossing Ct 29588
Crow Ln 29577
Crow Field Ct 29579
Crows Nest Ct 29579
Crumpet Ct 29579
Crusader Ct 29588
Crutchfield Ct 29579
Crystal Lake Dr 29575
Crystal Water Way 29579
Culbertson Ave 29577
Culcross Ct 29577
Culpepper Way 29579
Cumberland Ter 29572
Cumberland Terrace
Dr 29572
Curlew Dr 29575
Curtis Brown Ln 29577
Cutwing Loop 29579
Cycad Dr 29579
Cygnus Dr 29575
Cypress Cir 29577
Cypress Dr 29575
Cypress Ln 29572
Cypress Bay Ct 29579
Cypress Point Ct 29579
Cypress River Way 29588
Dahlia Ct 29577
Dandelion Ln 29579
Daniel Rd 29588
Daniella Dr 29579
Darby Ln
2199-2215 29577
4900-4930 29579
4932-4932 29579
Darlene Dr 29588
Dave Carr Ct 29588
David Ln 29588
Davis St 29577
Davis Shelley Cir 29588
Dawn Ct 29579
Daylily Cres 29588
De Lago Ct 29572

Debbie Ln 29588
Deep Blue Dr 29579
Deer Creek Rd 29575
Deer Park Ln 29575
Deer Run Ct 29575
Deer Run Dr 29579
Deer Trace Cir 29588
Deerfield Ave 29575
Deerfield Links Dr 29575
Delos Dr 29577
Delta Cir 29577
Deltura Dr 29588
Dendy Ct 29579
Dennison Ave 29577
Desert Wheatgrass Dr 29579
Destin Ct 29575
Deville St 29577
Devon Ct 29572
Devon Ln 29588
Devon Estate Ave 29588
Dew Drop Ct 29579
Dew North Ct 29579
Dewey Rd 29579
Diamond Ln 29577
Dick Pond Rd
1100-2000 29575
2001-2049 29588
2002-2398 29575
2051-2799 29575
2900-6699 29588
Dick Scobee Rd 29579
Dillingham Dr 29579
Dioon Dr 29579
Dipper 29575
Discovery Ln 29575
Ditchford Ct 29577
Dividend Loop 29577
Dizzy Ct 29575
Doar Pt 29577
Docksider Ct 29575
Doctors Ln 29579
Doe Ct 29579
Dog Pen Ct 29588
Dogwood Ave 29577
Dogwood Cir
400-499 29572
5500-5799 29588
Dogwood Ct
200-299 29579
900-999 29572
Dogwood Dr
1-1 29588
99-399 29575
N Dogwood Dr 29575
S Dogwood Dr 29575
Dogwood Ln 29572
Don Donald Ct 29588
Dooks Ct 29579
Dooleys Dr 29588
Dora Dr 29588
Doral Pl 29579
Dorman Cir 29577
Dornoch Ct & Pl 29579
Double Eagle Dr 29575
Dougs Trl 29579
Dove Ct 29579
Dove Haven Ln 29579
Dowenbury Dr 29588
Dowling St 29579
Downybrook Rd 29588
Dragonfly Dr 29579
Drake Ln 29575
Driftwood Dr 29572
Dry Gulley Ln 29575
Dry Valley Loop 29588
Drywall Dr 29577
Ducane Rd 29579
Duchess Ct 29588
Duck Ct 29577
Duck Blind Pl & Trl 29588
Duckview Dr 29575
Duel Ct 29588
Dunbar St 29577
Duncan Ave 29572
Dunes Cir & Dr 29572
Dunes Gables Ct & Dr 29572

Dunlon Ct 29588
Dunoway Ct 29579
Dunrobin Ln 29588
Dunsmuir Ln 29575
Dusty Trail Ln 29575
Eagle Ave 29572
Eagle Cres 29588
Eagle Creek Dr 29588
Eagle Crest Dr 29579
Eagle Terrace Ct 29579
Eagle Trace Dr 29579
Eagles Cliff Dr 29575
Earl St 29588
Earls Rd 29588
Eastbrook Rd 29577
Eastcott Dr 29579
Easton Ct 29579
Ebb Tide Harbour 29577
Ed Dr 29588
Ed Smith Ave 29588
Edenborough Dr 29588
Edge St 29577
Edgecreek Dr 29579
Edgerton Dr 29572
Edgewood Dr
1600-1799 29577
8500-8599 29588
Edisto Ct 29588
Edisto River Rd 29588
Egret 29575
El Camino Dr 29579
El Duce Pl 29588
Elderberry St 29577
Elgin Ct 29579
Elizabeth Rd 29577
Ella Ct 29588
Ella Kinley Cir 29588
Ellerbe Cir 29588
Ellington St 29577
Ellsworth Ct & Dr 29579
Elmore Dr 29579
Ely Trl 29588
Emerson Dr 29579
Emma St 29588
Emma Gause Pl 29588
Emory Rd 29577
Encampment Ct 29579
Endenshall Way 29579
Englemann Oak Dr 29579
Enoree Ct 29588
Enterprise Ave 29577
Enterprise Rd 29588
Erin Way 29577
Esher Ct 29579
Espana St 29579
Esperia Ln 29572
Essex Dr 29575
Essex Way 29577
Estepa Ct 29579
Ethan Dr 29577
Eton St 29579
Evans Ct 29579
Everett St 29588
Evergreen Cir 29575
Evergreen Ln 29572
Evergreen Way 29577
Evers Loop 29575
Excalaber Ct 29588
Executive Ave 29577
Factory Stores Blvd 29579
Fair Oaks Dr 29575
Fairmont Ln 29579
Fairway Rd 29572
Fairway Lakes Dr 29577
Fairway Ridge Dr 29575
Fairway Village Dr 29588
Fairwood Ter 29588
Fairyland Dr 29588
Faith Dr 29577
Falcon 29575
Falkirk St 29579
Fallen Timber Dr 29588
Family Ln 29588
Fantasy Way 29579
Fantasy Harbour Blvd 29579
Farlow St 29577

Farm Lake Dr 29579
Farmer Brown Ct 29579
Farmers Rest Dr 29579
Farmington Ct & Pl 29579
Farrow Pkwy 29577
Fawn Vista Dr N 29575
Fern Creek Ct 29588
Fernwood Rd 29579
Fetlock Dr 29588
Fiano Ct 29579
Ficus Dr 29579
Fiddlehead Way 29579
Fiddlers Run 29579
Fieldstone St 29579
Figure Eight Rd 29588
Finch Ln 29575
Finger Lake Dr 29588
Finnegan Ct 29579
Fire Ring Ct 29579
Firebird Ln 29577
Fish Hawk Ct 29579
Fisher Dr 29577
Flagg St 29577
Flagstone Dr 29588
Flamewood Ct 29588
Flamingo 29575
Flat Bay Cir 29588
E & W Flintlake Ct 29579
Floratino Ct 29579
Flowerdale Ct 29579
Fly Line Dr 29579
Folly Rd 29588
Folly Estates Dr 29588
Folly Ranch Ln 29588
Footy Dr 29588
Foral Dr 29588
Forest Dr 29577
Forestbrook Dr 29579
Forestbrook Rd
100-1999 29579
2000-4199 29588
Formby Ct 29588
Forsythia Ct 29588
Fort Moultrie Ct 29588
Foster Ave 29588
Fountain Ln 29577
Fountain Pointe Ln 29579
Fox Catcher Dr 29588
Fox Haven Blvd 29588
Fox Squirrel Dr 29588
Foxbrook Dr 29588
Foxcroft Ln 29577
Foxglove Ct 29579
Foxpath Loop 29588
Foxridge Dr 29588
Francis Ct 29577
Frank Mills Rd 29588
Fred Nash Blvd 29577
Freedom Cir 29588
Freedom Way 29577
Freewoods Rd 29588
Fresh Dr 29579
Freshwater Ct 29588
Friendship Ln 29588
Fripp Ct 29588
Frontage Rd
6100-6199 29577
6200-6299 29572
Frontage Rd E 29577
Frontier Dr 29577
Fulbourn Pl 29579
Futrell Dr 29577
Gabreski Ln 29577
Gadsden St 29588
Gaither Ct 29588
Gallant Ct 29588
Galley Harbour 29577
Gannet 29575
Ganton Way 29588
Gap Dr 29588
Garden Dr 29575
Gardner Lacy Rd 29579
Garrison St 29577
Garron Ct 29579
Gasparilla Ct 29588
Gasque Ln 29577

N & S Gate Rd 29572
Gateway Rd 29579
Gatewick Ct 29579
Gatewood Dr 29577
Gator Ln 29588
Gavin Ct 29588
Gazania Ln 29579
Geddings Dr 29588
Geletto Ct 29572
Gemini Dr 29575
Gemstone Ct 29588
Genoa Ct 29579
George Bishop Pkwy 29579
George Cox St 29577
Gervais Ln 29588
Gibson Ave 29575
Gina Ct 29588
Girvan Dr 29579
Gist Ln 29588
E & W Glades Dr 29588
Gladiola Ct 29588
Glamis Ct 29588
Glasgow Ct 29575
Glen Haven Dr 29588
Glenbrook Dr 29579
Gleneagles Dr 29588
Glenforest Rd 29579
Glenkeith Ct 29575
Glenmere Dr 29588
Glenn Ellen Way 29572
Glenns Bay Rd 29575
Glenwood Dr 29572
Glory Blvd 29579
Gloucester Pt & Ter 29572
Gloucester Point Ct 29572
Gloucester Terrace Cir 29572
Goff Creek Ct 29579
Gold Place Ln 29588
Golden Ct 29579
Golden Stone Dr 29579
Golden Willow Ct 29579
Goldwire Ln 29588
Golf Village Ln 29579
Goodwill Ct 29579
Goosecreek Dr 29588
Gordon Dr 29579
Gore Ln 29577
Gouchos Ln 29588
Governors Loop 29588
Grace Ln 29588
Graeagle Way 29588
Graham Ave 29577
Granada St 29579
Grand Palm Ct 29579
Granddaddy Dr 29577
Grande Dunes Blvd
100-1300 29572
1350-1499 29579
Grands Rd 29588
Grandview Dr 29588
Grannys Ln 29577
Grape Arbor 29588
Grapevine St 29579
Gravelley Ct 29588
Gravelley Shore Dr 29588
Gray Dr 29579
Gray Fox Trl 29588
Great Lakes Cir 29588
Great Scott Dr 29579
Green Bay Cir 29588
Green Bay Trl 29577
Green Fern Ln 29579
Green Lake Dr 29572
Greenbank Dr 29579
Greenleaf Cir 29579
Greens Blvd 29577
Greenslake Pt 29588
Grenfell Ct 29579
Gresham Ln 29588
Grey St 29577
Grey Hawk Ct 29588
Grey Squirrel Rd 29579
Grim Ln 29588
Grouse Ct 29588
Grousewood Dr 29588
Grove Park Dr 29575

Guest Ct 29572
Guinevere Cir 29588
Gulfstream Ct 29575
Gull 29575
Gullane Ct 29575
Gully Branch Ln 29572
Gumbo Limbo Ln 29579
Gunnel Rd 29588
Gussies Ct 29588
Gwen Dr 29588
Gypsy Ct 29575
Hack Ct 29575
Hackler St 29577
Hagood Ln 29588
Hague Dr 29588
Haig Dr 29579
Hallborough Dr 29575
Halyard Way 29579
Hamilton Oaks Ct 29588
Hammer Beck Dr 29579
Hammond Dr 29577
Hampton Cir 29577
Happy Woods Ct 29588
Harbor Aly 29577
Harbor Lights Dr 29575
Harbor Oaks Dr 29588
Harbor Watch Loop 29579
Harbour Blvd 29579
Harbour Lights Dr 29579
Harbour Reef Dr 29588
Harbour Towne Dr 29577
Harbour View Dr 29579
Harbour Village Dr 29575
Hard Rock Pkwy 29579
Harlequin Duck Ct 29588
Harlow Ct 29579
Harrelson Blvd 29577
Hartland Dr 29572
Hartsfield Pl 29577
Hartwood Ln 29579
Harvest Dr 29579
Harvest Run Way 29579
Harvester Cir 29579
Haskell Cir 29577
Hasty Point Dr 29577
Hathaway Ln 29575
Hatteras Ct 29588
Hatteras River Rd 29588
Haven Dr 29572
Havering Ave 29579
Hawk 29575
Hawk Run Ct 29575
Haworth Ct 29579
Hawthorne Ln 29572
Hay Hill Ln 29579
Hayfield Dr 29579
Hayseed Way 29579
Haystack Way 29579
Hazelnut Ridge Rd 29588
Hazelwood Dr 29575
Hearthstone Ct 29588
Heartwood Ln 29579
Heather Ln 29572
Heatherwood Ct 29588
Heathmuir Dr 29575
Heathridge Ct 29575
Heathrow Dr 29579
Hemingway St 29577
Hemlock Ave 29577
Henagan Ln 29588
Hendrick Ave 29577
Hennessy Ln 29577
Henry James Dr 29579
Henry Middleton Blvd 29588
Herbert Ln 29588
Heritage Ln 29588
Heritage Loop 29577
Heritage Point Dr 29588
Hermosa Ct 29579
Heron Ave 29572
Heron Cir 29579
Heron Pt 29588
Hewitt Pl 29577
Hibernia Rd 29579
Hibiscus Ave 29577
Hickory Cir 29577

Hickory Dr 29575
Hickory Ln 29572
Hickory Oak Ct 29579
Hidden Ct 29588
Hidden Acres Dr 29588
Hidden Bridge Ct 29579
Hidden Creek Ln 29579
Hidden Harbor Rd 29577
Hidden Woods Dr 29588
Hideaway Pt 29579
High Cir 29572
High St 29577
High Brass Trl 29588
High Brass Covey 29588
High Society Ct 29577
Highfield Loop 29579
N & S Highgrove Ct 29575
Highland Cir 29575
Highland Ct 29575
N Highland Way 29572
S Highland Way 29572
Highland Ridge Dr 29588
Highway 15 29577
Highway 17 N 29575
Highway 17 S 29575
Highway 17 Byp N 29577
Highway 17 Byp S
1900-3399 29577
3400-8898 29588
3401-4999 29577
5001-8999 29575
Highway 394 29575
Highway 396 29575
Highway 501
500-2899 29577
Highway 501
3000-3498 29579
3500-5099 29579
Highway 544 29588
Highway 643 29577
Highway 707 29588
Highway 73 29577
Highway 814 29588
Hilo Ct 29588
Hilton Rd 29572
Hinson Dr 29579
History Dr 29577
Hitchcock Way 29577
Hobart St 29579
Hobcaw Dr 29577
Hog Barn Hl 29588
Holland Willow Dr 29579
Hollings Ct 29588
Holly Cir 29588
Holly Dr 29577
Holly Ln 29572
Holly Berry Ct 29579
Holly Leaf Dr 29579
Holly Park Cir 29577
Hollybrooke Dr 29579
Hollywood Dr 29577
N Hollywood Dr 29575
S Hollywood Dr 29575
Holmestown Rd 29588
Holtzman St 29575
Home Place Cir 29588
Honey Bear Dr 29588
Honey Locust Ct 29588
Honeysuckle Ln 29588
Hopeland Ct 29579
Hopewell Rd 29588
Hopkins Cir 29575
Hopper Ct 29579
Hopsewee Dr 29577
Horizon River Dr 29588
Horne St 29577
Horseshoe Cir 29588
Horsetail Moss Ct 29588
Hospitality Ln 29579
Houndsfield Ave 29577
Howard Ave 29577
Huger St 29577
Hummingbird Ct 29579
Hummingbird St 29577
Hunley Ln 29579
Hunters Rd 29579

Hunters Trl 29588
Hunters Horn Ln 29588
Hunting Bow Trl 29579
Huntingdon Dr 29575
Hyatt Ln 29588
W Hyde Park 29572
Hydrangea Dr 29579
Ibis 29575
Ibis Ct 29572
Idlewood Dr 29588
Indian Oak Ln 29575
Indian Wood Ln 29588
Indianola Ct 29579
Indigo Ct 29588
Indigo Ln 29577
Inland Dr 29588
Innisbrook Ct 29579
International Dr 29579
Intracoastal Village Ct 29588
Intracoastal Way Dr 29579
Inverness Ct
100-107 29588
1300-1399 29575
Inwood Ct 29588
Ioma Cir 29588
Ira Dr 29579
Iris St 29577
Isabel Ct 29579
Islander Dr 29588
Isle Ct 29579
E Isle Of Palms Ave 29579
Isle Royale Dr 29577
Islington Ct 29579
Ivory Gull Ln 29588
Ivystone Dr 29588
Ivywood Dr 29575
Jacana 29575
Jacks Pl 29588
Jackson St 29577
Jacob Ln 29579
Jacqueline Ct 29577
Jade Dr 29579
Jamerthe St 29577
James St 29577
Jasmine Ave 29577
Jason Blvd 29577
Jay Gould Ln 29588
Jefferson Pl 29572
Jenn Dr 29577
Jennifer Ln 29588
Jennings Rd 29577
Jenny Ln 29588
Jensen Ln 29577
Jeremy Loop 29588
Jericho Ct 29579
Jesse St 29579
Jester Ln 29577
Jesters Ct 29572
Jet Port Rd 29577
Jeter Ln 29588
Jetport Industrial Dr 29577
Jib Ct 29579
Jimmy D Angelo Way 29572
Joann Ln 29588
Joe Mill Trl 29588
John Cooper Ct 29579
John Henry Ln 29579
John Luther Rd 29588
Johnny Ln 29588
Johns Ln 29588
Johnson Ave 29577
Johnson Rd 29588
Johnston Dr 29588
Jones Rd 29588
Jonquil Pl 29577
Joseph Rd 29588
Jubilee Cir 29579
Julious Ln 29588
Jumper Trail Cir 29588
June Bug Ct 29588
Juniper Dr
500-799 29575
500-599 29577
Juxa Dr 29579
Kalmia Ct 29579
Kama Ln 29588
Kane Ct 29577
Karen Ln 29588
Kashton Dr 29577
Kate Ln 29575
Kay Ln 29575
Kayla St 29577
Keel Ct 29579
Keith St 29588
Kennison Dr 29588
Kennoway Ct 29579
Kensington Ct 29577
Kensington Dr 29588
Kensington Ln 29577
Kent Ln 29579
Kenzgar Dr 29588
Kenzie Ct 29588
Kerwin Ct 29579
Kessinger Dr 29575
Kestrel Ct 29588
Ketch Ct 29577
Kevin Ln 29588
S Key Largo Cir 29577
Keystone Ln 29588
Kildare Ct 29588
Kilkee Dr 29579
Killarney Dr 29588
Kindred Dr 29588
King Dr & St 29577
King Arthur Dr 29588
Kingfisher 29575
Kinglet Ct 29588
Kings Cir 29572
Kings Dr 29588
N Kings Hwy
100-6199 29577
6200-10799 29572
S Kings Hwy
100-3400 29577
3402-4398 29577
4400-6099 29575
Kings Rd 29572
N Kings Highway Ext 29577
Kings Road Ext 29572
Kingsley Dr 29588
Kingston Rd 29572
Kingswood Dr 29572
Kinloch Dr 29577
Kippford Way 29579
Kirby Ct 29579
Kirkcaldy Cir 29575
Knights Ct 29572
Knobcone Ct 29579
Knoles St 29577
Knoll Ct 29588
Knollty Ct 29588
Knollwood Dr 29588
Knox Ln 29588
Kruzel St 29577
Kyle Ln 29577
La Costa Dr 29579
La Patos Dr 29588
Labrador Ct 29579
Lac Courte 29579
Lacy Dr 29588
Ladd Dr 29588
Ladybank Dr 29575
Ladyfish Dr 29588
Ladykirk Ln 29579
Lafayette Rd 29572
Lafon Ln 29588
Laguna Pt 29588
Lahinch Dr 29579
Lake Ct 29575
Lake Dr 29572
E Lake Dr 29575
Lake Ln 29575
N Lake Trl 29572
S Lake Trl 29572
Lake Arrowhead Rd 29572
Lake Front Blvd 29588
Lake Haven Dr 29572
Lake Park Dr 29588
Lake Shore Dr
400-10499 29572
500-599 29575
Lake View Cir 29575
Lakeside Dr 29575
Lakeside Trl 29577
Lakeview Ln 29575
Lakewood Cir & Dr 29575
Lamplighter Rd 29588
Landing Rd 29577
Lands End Blvd 29572
Laney St 29588
Lansdowne Ct 29572
Lansford Pl 29588
Lanterns Rest Rd 29579
Lark 29575
Lark Hill Dr 29577
Larkspur Ct 29579
Larry Ln 29588
Lars Ct 29588
Larue Ct 29579
Las Palmas Dr 29579
Laurel Ct 29572
Laurel Oak Ct 29579
Laurel Woods Dr 29588
Lauren Ln 29588
Laurice Dr 29577
Lavender Ln 29579
Layson Dr 29588
Lazy Willow Ln 29588
Leadoff Dr 29588
Leaf Ter 29577
Ledbury Ln 29579
Lee Ln 29588
Leeds Cir 29588
E & W Leeshire Blvd 29579
Legacy Ct 29575
Legacy Loop 29577
Legare Pl 29588
Legends Ave 29577
Legends Rd 29579
Legion St 29577
Leilani Cir 29588
Leisure Ln 29588
Lenue Cir 29579
Leo Dr 29575
Leon Cir 29577
Leonard Loop & Rd 29588
Leone Cir 29579
Leroy Ln 29577
Lexi Ln 29577
Lexington Pl 29588
Leyland Dr 29572
Liberty Oak Ln 29575
Libra Dr 29575
Lichen Ct 29588
Lighthouse Way 29577
Likely Pl 29577
Lilac Rd 29588
Lilly Naz Ln 29588
Limerick Rd 29579
Linden St 29577
Lindrick Ct 29579
Lindsey Rd 29588
Linen Dr 29577
Links Rd 29575
Linton Park Rd 29579
Lissie Ln 29577
Little Bear Ct 29579
Little Creek Rd 29572
Little Pee Dee Rd 29588
Little River Rd 29577
Live Oak Ct 29575
Live Oak Ln 29572
Livorn Loop 29579
Lizard Ln 29588
Lizzie Ln 29575
Loarre Ct 29588
Loblolly Ct
300-399 29572
2500-2599 29579
Loblolly Ln 29579
Loch Lomond Way 29575
Lochmoore Loop 29588
Lochview Ct & Dr 29588
Lockerbie Ct 29579
Loddin Ave 29579
Loggerhead Ct 29579
Loggers Run 29588
Lomond Ln 29579
London St 29577
Lone Oak Ln 29575
Long Line Ln 29579
Longchamps Ct 29579
Longleaf Dr
1500-1799 29575
5700-6099 29577
Longwood Lakes Dr 29579
Lonnie St 29588
Loon Ct 29575
Loquat Ct 29579
Louise Dr 29577
Low Country Pl 29577
Loyola Dr 29588
Lucky Ln 29588
Ludlow Loop 29579
Lugano Ct 29579
Luke Ln 29588
Lullwater Ct 29588
Lumber Ct 29588
Lumber St 29577
Lumber River Rd 29588
Luster Leaf Cir 29577
Luther Senior Ln 29577
Luttie Rd 29588
Lyerly Ct 29579
Lynches River Ct 29588
Lynco Ln 29575
Lyndhurst Ct 29579
Lyons Cove Dr 29577
Lytham Ct 29575
Mackie Cir 29579
Macklen Rd 29588
Maddington Place Dr 29575
Maddux Ln 29588
Maggie Parker Ln 29577
Magic Cir 29588
Magnolia Dr 29575
Magnolia Ln 29577
Magnolia St 29577
Magnolia Lake Dr 29577
Magnolia Pointe Ln 29577
Maiden Ln 29588
Main St 29577
Maintenance Dr 29588
Maison Cir 29575
Maison Ct 29572
Maison Dr 29572
Mako Ct 29577
Malabar Ct 29588
Malaga Cir 29579
Malibu Ln 29577
Mallard Cir 29579
Mallard Ln 29575
Mallard Covey 29588
Mallard Lake Cir 29575
Mallard Lake Dr 29577
Mallard View Pt 29588
Mammie Dr 29588
Manatee Ct 29575
Manchester Way 29575
Mancini Dr 29577
Manor Cir 29588
Manor Wood Dr 29588
Maple Dr 29575
Maple St 29577
Maplecrest Dr 29588
Margaret Rd 29588
Margate Cir 29572
Marina Pkwy 29572
Mariners Ct 29572
Mariners Way 29577
Marion Cir 29577
Maritimes Ct 29579
Market Ct 29577
Market Place Dr 29572
Marsala Dr 29572
Marsh Ct 29572
Marsh Hawk Dr 29588
Marsh Island Dr 29579
Marsh Rabbit Dr 29588
Marsh Tacky Loop 29588
Marsh Vista Ct 29579
Marshall St 29588
Marshfield Cir 29579
Marshland Ct 29572
Marshwood Dr 29579
Martin Cir 29579
Martin St 29577
Martina Ct 29579
Martinique 29572
Mary St 29577
Mary Ann Ct 29579
Mary Anna Ct 29577
Marylebone Dr 29579
Maryport Dr 29575
Mashie Dr 29577
Mason St 29588
Masters Ct 29577
Matanzas Dr 29577
Matheson Ln 29577
Maui Ct 29588
Maximus Ct 29588
Maybank Cir 29588
Mayfair St 29577
Maypop Cir 29588
Mccormick Rd 29579
Mcdaniel Dr 29579
Mcdonald Ct 29588
Mcdowell Shortcut Rd 29588
Mcduffie Dr 29588
Mcgarvey Ct 29579
Mcgee Dr 29588
Mckaylas Ct 29579
Mckendree Ln 29579
Mckinley Way 29577
Mclain Ct 29575
Mclamb Dr 29588
Mcleod Ln 29588
Mcmaster Dr 29575
Mcsweeney Ct 29588
Meadow Cres 29588
Meadow Oak Dr 29575
Meadowbrook Dr 29588
Meadowlark 29575
Meadowsweet Dr 29579
Medical Cir 29572
Mega Dr 29588
Megan Ann Ln 29579
Megashane Ln 29588
Melanie Ln 29577
Melody Ln 29575
Melrose Pl 29572
Memory Ln 29588
Menlo Park Ln 29588
Mercantile Pl 29577
Mercy Ct 29588
Meredith Ct 29588
Merlin Ct 29588
Merlot Ct 29579
Merton Ct 29579
Mesa Grande Dr 29579
Metherton Ct 29579
Meyers Ave 29588
Middle Gate Rd 29572
Middlebrook Ln 29579
Middleburg Dr 29579
Middleton View Dr 29579
Midiron Ct 29577
Midway Cir 29588
Milano Ct 29579
Miles Cir 29577
Mill St 29579
Mill Creek Rd 29588
Mill Pond Rd 29588
Mills Ln 29588
Millstone Dr 29588
Millwood Dr 29575
Mindy Ct 29577
Mingo Creek Dr 29579
Minim Ct 29579
Minner Ct 29575
Minwick Ct 29579
Miromar Way 29588
Mistletoe Ct 29579
Misty Ln 29588
Misty Oaks Pl 29579
Misty Pine Dr 29575
Mitchell Dr 29577
Mobile Ln 29588
Mockingbird Ave 29577
Modena Ct 29579
Monaco Cir 29579
Monroe Cir 29588
Montague Ln 29588
Montalcino Blvd 29579
Montclair Dr 29575
Montenegro Way 29579
Monterrosa Dr 29572
Montgomery Ln 29572
Monticello Dr 29577
Montrose Dr 29575
Montrose Ln 29579
Moonbeam Ct 29579
Moonlight Dr 29575
Moonstruck Ct 29579
Moore St 29577
Mooreland Dr 29588
Mordecai Ct 29575
Morlynn Dr 29577
Morning Frost Pl 29579
Morning Glory 29575
Morning Glory Ct 29579
Morning Star Ct 29579
Morris Pl 29588
Morton Cir 29579
Moser Dr 29577
Moss Dr 29575
Moss Bridge Ln 29579
Moss Creek Rd 29588
Moss Pond Rd 29588
Mossy Point Cv 29579
Moultrie Cir 29588
Moultrie Dr 29579
Mount Pleasant Dr 29579
Mountain Ash Cir & Ln 29579
Mr Joe White Ave 29577
Muirfield Rd 29588
Mulberry Cir 29579
Muldrow Ct 29588
Murray Ave 29577
Mustang St 29577
Myers Ln 29588
Mynatt Ct 29588
N Myrtle Dr 29575
S Myrtle Dr 29575
Myrtle Ln 29572
N Myrtle St 29577
S Myrtle St 29577
Myrtle Oak Dr 29575
Myrtle Pointe Dr 29577
Myrtlewood Ct 29572
Nadene Ln 29588
Nance St 29577
Nash St 29577
National Dr 29579
Naylor Ave 29577
Neal Ln 29588
Neath Ct 29588
Nectar Ct 29579
Needlerush Ct 29579
Neighbor Ln 29577
Nelson Ct 29572
Nevers St 29577
New Found Ln 29588
New Haven Ct 29579
New London Ct 29579
New River Rd 29588
Newburgh Ct 29579
Newcastle Loop 29588
Niblick Cir 29575
Nicole Trl 29588
Nigels Dr 29572
Night Heron Cres 29588
Night Heron Ln 29572
Nightingale Dr 29577
No Wake Ct 29575
Nollie Rd 29588
Northgate Blvd 29577
Northgate Dr 29588
Northumberland Way 29588
Norwich Ln 29588
Oak Cir 29577
Oak Dr 29577
N Oak Dr 29575
S Oak Dr 29575
N Oak St 29577
S Oak St 29577
W Oak Circle Dr 29588
Oak Forest Ln 29577
Oak Manor Ct & Dr 29588
Oak Ridge Pl 29572
Oakheart Rd 29579
Oakhurst Dr 29579
Oakmont Dr 29579
Oakmoor Dr 29579
Oakwood Ln 29572
Obd Way 29588
Ocala St 29577
N Ocean Blvd
1-1699 29575
100-6199 29577
6200-9099 29572
S Ocean Blvd
1-5099 29575
100-3299 29577
Ocean Way 29575
Ocean Creek Dr 29572
Ocean Front 29577
Ocean Palms Dr 29575
Ocean Sands Ct 29579
Ocean View Dr 29572
Oceanside Dr & Vlg 29575
Okatie Creek Ct 29579
Old Bridge Rd 29572
Old Bryan Dr 29577
Old Carriage Ct 29588
Old Castle Loop 29579
Old House Rd 29588
Old Kings Rd 29575
Old Pepper Rd 29579
Old Railroad Bed 29577
Old Socastee Hwy 29577
Old Village Dr 29588
Old Woods Rd 29588
Olde Towne Way 29588
Ole Marion Cir 29579
Oleander Dr 29577
Olivia St 29588
Ooneecan Ct 29579
Orange Ave 29577
Orangewood Ct 29588
Orchard Dr
100-199 29579
1700-1899 29577
Orchid Way 29577
Ordsall Ct 29579
Orion Dr 29575
Orr Ln 29588
Osage Dr 29579
Osceola St 29577
Osprey Rd 29588
Osprey Cove Loop 29588
Otter St 29577
Outlet Blvd 29579
Overcrest St 29579
Owens Dr & St 29577
Owners Club Ct 29577
Oxbow Dr 29579
Oxford Pl 29588
Oxner Ct 29579
Oyster Point Way 29579
Pachino Dr 29579
Paddington Ct 29588
Paddington St 29577
Pafko St 29588
Page St 29577
Painted Duck Ct 29588
Painted Trillium Ct 29579
Paleade Dr 29579
Palencia Ct 29579
Palisade Cir 29577
Palladium Dr 29575
Palm Ln 29577
Palm Cove Cir 29588
Palm Frond Dr 29588
Palmas Dr 29575
Palmer Ladd Ln 29572
Palmetto Dr
700-999 29575
3800-3899 29577
N Palmetto Dr 29575
Palmetto Ln 29572

Palmetto St 29579
Palmetto Trl 29577
S Palmetto Way 29575
Palmetto Glen Dr 29588
Palmetto Pointe Blvd 29588
Palmina Loop 29588
W Palms Dr 29579
Palo Verde Dr 29579
Pamlico Ct 29588
Pampas Dr
400-499 29575
800-3799 29577
Pampass Dr 29588
Pancho St 29577
Panola Ln 29588
Panthers Pkwy 29588
Pantherwood Dr 29579
Paradise Cir 29577
Parasol Ct 29579
Paris Ln 29577
Parish Way 29577
Park Ave 29572
Park Dr 29577
Park St 29572
Parkgreen Dr 29575
Parkland Dr 29579
Parkwood Dr 29572
Parsons Way 29575
Parsons Pond Dr 29588
Partridgeberry Rd 29579
Patrick St 29577
Patterson Dr 29572
Patty Ln 29588
Pauls Pl 29588
Pawpaw Ln 29579
Payton Dr 29588
Pea Patch Covey 29588
Peace Pipe Pl 29579
Peaceful Ln 29588
Peach Ct 29579
Peachtree Dr, Ln & Rd 29588
Peachwood Ct 29588
Pear Ct 29579
Pearl Ct 29577
Pearlie Ln 29588
Pebble Dr 29588
Pebble Beach Cres 29588
Pebble Creek Dr 29588
Pecan St 29577
Pegasus Dr 29575
Pelican Ave 29577
Pelican Lake Ct 29588
Pembridge Ct 29579
Pembroke Ct 29577
Pendant Cir 29577
Pendleton Pl 29588
Pennan Ln 29579
Pennington Loop 29588
Penny Ln 29577
Pennyroyal Ct 29579
Pennystone Trl 29575
Pepperbush Dr 29579
Pepperhill Cir 29588
Perdiz Covey 29588
Periwinkle Ct 29572
Periwinkle Pl 29577
Perry Cir 29577
E Perry Rd 29579
W Perry Rd 29579
Persimmon Ln 29579
Peyton Ct 29588
Pheasant Pointe Ct 29588
Phillip Ct 29579
Phillis Blvd 29577
Physicians Ct 29579
Pickens Ave 29577
Picket Fence Ln 29579
Piedmont Ave 29577
Piemonte Ln 29579
Pienza Dr 29579
Pierce Pl 29575
Piling Rd 29579
Pilot House Ct 29579
Pilothouse Dr 29577
Pinckney Ave 29577
Pine Cir 29572
Pine Dr
400-899 29575
900-1199 29577
Pine Holw 29588
Pine Ln 29588
Pine Island Rd 29577
Pine Lake Dr 29577
Pine Needle Dr 29572
Pine Needle Ln 29575
Pine Thicket St 29577
Pine Tree Ln 29572
Pine Valley Ln 29575
Pine View Ln 29575
W Pine Village Dr 29579
Pinecrest Dr 29572
Pinecrest Rd 29579
Pinegrove Dr 29577
Pinehurst Ln 29588
N Pinewood Dr 29575
S Pinewood Dr 29575
Pinewood Rd 29577
Pinfeather Trl 29588
Pinnacle Ln 29577
Pinner Pl 29577
Pintail Ct 29588
Pintintr Rd 29588
Pinto Ln 29588
Pinwheel Loop 29577
Pioneer Ln 29577
Piper Ct 29588
Pipers Ln 29575
Pipers Pointe Ln 29577
Pisces Ln 29575
Pistoia Ln 29579
Plantation Dr
500-1199 29575
1800-1899 29577
Plantation Rd 29588
Plantation Oaks Dr 29579
Planters Creek Dr 29579
Planters Row Way 29579
Platt Blvd 29575
Plattmoor Dr 29588
Plaza Pl 29577
Pleasant Point Ln 29579
Pleasant Run Rd 29588
Pleneren Dr 29572
Plover Ln 29588
Plum Ct 29579
Plumfield Ct 29579
Poinsett Rd 29577
Point Break Dr 29588
Pointer Ct 29579
Polly Ln 29588
Pomo Dr 29579
Pond Shoals Ct 29579
Poplar Dr 29577
N Poplar Dr 29575
S Poplar Dr 29575
Poplar Ln 29572
Poppi Point Ct 29579
Porcher Dr
5501-5505 29577
5507-5999 29577
6300-7999 29572
Port Dr 29577
Portico Loop 29577
Portland Dr 29577
Portrait Cir 29577
Portrush Trl 29579
Portsmith Dr 29588
Portstewart Cir 29579
Portwest Dr 29579
Posada Dr 29572
Post Oak Ct 29579
Postal Way 29579
Potomac Ct 29579
Potters Aly 29577
Pottery Dr 29579
Powder Mill Dr 29579
Powder Springs Loop 29588
Powell Ln 29577
Powhaton Dr 29577
Prather Park Dr 29588
Prato Loop 29579
Preservation Dr 29572
Presidential Dr 29575
Prestwick Rd 29588
Prestwick Club Dr 29575
Price Ln 29577
Pridgen Rd 29577
Primrose Ct 29579
Princess St 29588
Prioloe Dr 29588
Pritchard St 29588
Professional Dr 29577
Providence Dr 29572
Prudie Ln 29588
Pumpkin Patch Ln 29579
Putnam Dr 29577
Quail Cir 29579
Quail Run 29572
Quail Hollow Ln 29577
Quail Hollow Rd 29579
Queens Ct & Rd 29572
Queens Harbour Blvd 29588
Queensway Blvd 29572
Quinby Ct 29579
Quince Ave 29577
Quincy Hall Dr 29579
Quinn Rd 29579
R C Sarvis Rd 29588
Raccoon Ln 29575
Racepath St 29577
Racewater Dr 29588
Ragin St 29577
Rahnavard Blvd 29588
Railing Ln 29588
Rainbow Ave 29577
Raines Dr 29579
Rambler Ct 29588
Ramsey Dr 29577
Ranchette Cir 29588
Randall Ave 29577
Randor Ct 29579
Randy Cir & Ln 29588
Ravello Ct 29579
Raven St 29577
S Reach Ct 29588
Reavis Ln 29579
Recreation Rd 29588
Red Bird Ln 29588
Red Cedar Ave 29588
Red Fox Cir & Rd 29579
Red River Ct 29579
Red Rooster Ln 29579
Red Wing Ct 29588
Redden Ln 29577
Redwolf Trl 29579
Redwood Ave 29577
Redwood Dr 29588
Reed St 29577
Reed Brook Dr 29579
Reedy Ct 29588
Reedy River Rd 29588
Reef Ct & Rd 29588
Regency Oaks Dr 29579
Regent Ct 29588
Regent Ter N 29575
Regent Ter S 29575
Regina Ct 29572
Registry Dr 29588
Reid Ct 29588
Reindeer Moss Ct 29588
Remo Ct 29572
Renata Ln 29588
Renee Dr 29579
N Retail Ct 29577
Rexford Ct 29579
Rhoda Loop 29577
Rice Hope Ct 29577
Rice Mill Dr 29579
Richmond Park 29572
Ricks Industrial Park Dr 29588
Ridge Dr 29588
Ridge Crest Rd 29579
Right End Ct 29579
Riley Ct 29588
Rimsdale Dr 29575
Ringneck Trl 29588
Ripken Way 29577
Rittenhouse Rd 29588
River Rd 29588
River Bend Rd 29588
River Cliff Dr 29588
River Landing Blvd 29579
River Oaks Dr 29579
River Reach Dr 29588
River Run Dr 29588
Riverbrook Ct 29588
Riverside Dr 29579
Riverwalk Dr 29579
Riverward Dr 29588
Riverwood Farms Rd 29588
Rivolo Ct 29579
Robert M Grissom Pkwy 29577
Roberta Ln 29588
Robin Ave 29572
Robins Nest Way 29579
Rockdale St 29579
Rocko Dr 29579
Rockwater Cir 29588
Rocky Rd 29588
Rockymount Rd 29588
Rodeo Dr 29579
Rodney Dr 29588
Rogers Dr 29577
Ronald Mcnair Blvd 29579
Ronaldsby Ct 29579
Ronda Ct 29579
Ronnie Ct 29579
Rookery Dr 29588
Rosano Cir 29579
Roscoe Rd 29588
Rose Dr 29588
Rose Bud Ln 29588
Rose Water Loop 29588
Rosea Ln 29588
Rosehaven Dr 29577
Rosemary St 29577
Rosencrans Ln 29577
Rosewood Dr 29588
Roswell Ct 29579
Rothbury Cir 29572
Rotunda Ct 29588
Roundtree Rd 29588
Rourk St 29572
Royal Bluff Dr 29579
Royal Devon Dr 29575
Royal Fern Cres 29588
Royal Perth Ct 29575
Royal Pine Dr 29588
Royal Tern Ct 29588
Royals Pointe Ct 29588
Ruby Ln 29588
Rue De Jean Ave 29579
Rung Rd 29588
Running Deer Trl 29588
Rushing Wind Dr 29588
Rustic Ct 29588
Ruth Dr 29588
Ruthin Ln 29588
Rutledge Ln 29588
Ryan Ln 29579
Sabel Palmetto Ct 29588
Sabel Springs Way 29588
Sable Palm Way 29575
Saddlebrook Ct 29588
Saddlewood Cir 29579
Sadler Way 29579
Saffron Ct 29579
Sagittarius Dr 29575
Sago Ct 29579
Sago Palm Dr 29579
Sailors Ct 29577
Saint Andrews Ln 29588
Saint Annes Ct 29579
Saint Catherine Bay Ct 29575
Saint Charles Ave 29577
Saint Charles Cir 29588
Saint Clears Way 29572
Saint Croix Ct 29572
Saint Davids Ave 29588
Saint George Ln 29588
Saint Ives Rd 29588
Saint James Ave 29577
Saint James Park 29572
Saint James Rd 29588
Saint Julian Ln 29579
Saint Peters Church Rd 29588
Saint Thomas Cir 29577
Salem Rd 29588
Salleyport Dr 29579
Salt Kettle Bay Ct 29575
Salt Meadow Ln 29577
Saltwater St 29588
Saluda River Rd 29588
San Marcello Dr 29579
San Marks Ct 29572
Sancindy Ln 29572
Sancroft Ln 29588
Sand Fiddler Ct 29572
Sand Pebble Ln 29588
Sandberg St 29575
Sandbinder Dr 29579
Sandlake Ct 29579
Sandlewood 29575
Sandollar Dr 29575
Sandpebble 29575
Sandpiper Ct 29572
Sandpiper Dr 29588
Sandpiper Ln 29575
Sandridge Pl 29577
Sandringham Ct & Dr 29588
Sandy Ln 29575
Sandy Pine Dr 29575
Sandy Pines Ln 29588
Sanibel Cir 29588
Sanibel Ct 29577
Santee Cir 29588
Santee River Rd 29588
Santo Dr 29588
Sapling Ct 29588
Sarasota St 29577
Sardis Dr 29579
Satterwhite Way 29577
Saturday St 29577
Sauer Ct 29575
Savannah Sparrow Dr 29588
Savoy Dr 29579
Sawgrass Ct 29575
Sayebrook Pkwy 29588
Scala Ct 29579
Scallop Ct 29572
Scarecrow Way 29579
Scarlet Oak Ct 29579
Scattergun Trl 29588
Schooner Harbour 29577
Schulz Way 29572
Schwartz Plant Rd 29575
Scipio Ln 29588
Scorpio Ln 29575
Scotney Ln 29579
Scotsman Cres 29588
Scott Dr 29577
Scottie Ln 29588
Scottish Ct 29588
Scotts Mill Ct 29588
N Sea Bridge Ct 29575
Sea Eagle Ct 29588
Sea Oats Dr 29588
Sea Turtle Dr 29588
Seabert Rd 29579
Seaboard St 29577
Seaborn Dr 29579
Seabreeze Ln 29579
Seabury Ln 29579
Seacroft Dr 29575
Seafoam Ln 29577
Seagrass Loop 29588
Seagull Ct 29572
Seagull Landing Pl 29588
Seahawk Way 29577
Seahorse Ct 29575
Seahouse Ct 29575
Seascale Ln 29572
N & S Seaside Dr 29575
Seaside Sparrow Ct 29588
Seawatch Dr 29572
Seaweed Ct 29575
Sebastian Dr 29588
Sebring Ln 29588
Seclusion Ln 29577
Sedona Ct 29579
Senato Ct 29572
Seneca Ct 29588
Seneca Ridge Dr 29579
Seneca River Rd 29588
Serena Dr 29579
S Service Ct 29588
Sessions St 29577
Setter Ct 29579
Settlers Ct & Dr 29577
Seville Dr 29572
Shaddowood Ct 29579
Shadow Creek Ct 29588
Shady Branch Rd 29588
Shady Grove Cir 29579
Shady Grove Rd 29588
Shady Oak Ln 29575
Shady View Ln 29588
Shalom Dr 29588
Shannondora St 29577
Sharpe Ln 29577
Shavis Ct 29577
Shawnee Trl 29588
Shell Ct 29575
Shelley Dr 29577
Shelly St 29577
Shelter Cv 29577
Shem Creek Cir 29588
Sheridan Rd 29579
Sherrybrook Dr 29588
Shetland Ln 29577
Shine Ave 29577
Shipmaster Ave 29579
Ships Anchor Ct 29575
Shipwatch Way 29577
Shipwreck Ct 29575
Shipyard Rd 29577
Shipyard Walk 29579
Shiraz Ct 29579
Shire Way 29577
Shirley Dr 29588
Shoebridge Dr 29579
Shore Dr 29572
N Shore Dr 29579
Shore Ln 29575
Shoreline Dr 29577
Shoreward Dr 29579
Shuffleboard Ct 29572
Siena Blvd 29572
Signature Dr 29579
Silver Fox Trl 29588
Silver Maple Ct 29579
Silver Moon Ct 29579
Silver Spring Ln 29577
Silvercrest Dr 29579
Silverton Dr 29588
Simmons St 29577
Sims Dr 29588
Sindab Ln 29588
Sioux Trl 29588
Six Lakes Dr 29588
Six Point Covey 29588
Six Shot Ct 29588
Skimmer Bay Bnd 29572
Skipper Harbour 29577
Skyland Pines Dr 29588
Slash Pine Ct 29579
Sly Fox Trl 29588
Smalley Ct 29575
Smalls Dr 29588
Smith Blvd 29588
Snapdragon Ct 29579
Snee Ct 29579
Snorkel Way 29577
Snowy Egret Cres & Trl 29588
Snowy Owl Ct 29588
Socastee Blvd 29588
Society Hill Dr 29577
Soils Rd 29588
Solitary Sandpiper Ct 29588
Somerset Dr 29572
Somerworth Cir 29575
Sonland Dr 29588
Sorrel Cir 29575
Sorrento Cir 29579
Sosa Ct 29575
Sounders Trl 29588
Sourgrass Ln 29579
Southborough Ln 29588
Southbury Dr 29588
Southern Trl 29579
Southern Branch Dr 29588
Southern Cross 29579
Southern Pines Dr 29579
Southgate Pkwy 29579
Southpark Dr 29577
Southwood Dr 29575
Spalding Ct 29575
Spanish Oak Ct & Dr 29575
Sparkle Ct 29579
Sparrow Dr 29575
Sparrow Hollow Ln 29572
Spencer St 29579
Spice Bush Cres 29588
Spice Hill Ln 29575
Spirit Pl 29577
Spivey Ave 29577
Split Oak Ct 29588
Spring Ave 29575
Spring Creek Dr 29588
Springlake Dr 29579
Springs Ave 29577
Springside Dr 29588
Springwater Loop 29588
Spruce Dr
1300-1599 29575
3600-3999 29577
Sprucewood Ct 29588
Spyglass Ct 29575
Squealer Lake Trl 29588
Squealer Lake Covey 29588
Squires Ln 29588
Squires Rd 29577
Stableford Ct 29577
Stacey St 29577
Stafford Dr 29579
Stalvey Ave 29577
Stanton Pl 29579
Starbridge Dr 29575
Starcreek Cir 29588
Starling Dr 29588
Starlit Way 29579
Steeple Chase Dr 29588
Sterling Place Ct 29579
Stillwater Ct 29572
Stillwood Dr 29588
Stockholder Ave 29577
Stockton Dr 29579
Stone Mill Dr 29588
Stonebridge Dr 29588
Stonebrook Dr 29588
Stonemason Ct & Dr 29579
Stoney Burn Ln 29579
Stoney Falls Blvd 29579
N Strand Dr & Pkwy 29588
Strand Market Dr 29588
Strathmill Ct 29575
Stuart Square Cir 29577
Stump Blind Trl 29588
Sugar Creek Ct 29579
Sugar Mill Loop 29588
Sugar Tree Dr 29588
Summer Rose Ln 29579
Summerhill Ct & Dr 29579
Summersweet Ln 29579
Summerwood Ct 29579
Summit Trl 29579
Sumter Dr
5800-6199 29577
6200-6299 29572
Sun Light Dr 29588
Suncrest Dr 29577
Sundown Trl 29588
Sunflower Ct 29579
Sunnehanna Dr 29588
Sunning Dale Ct 29575
Sunningdale Ln 29588

Sunny Boy Ln 29588
Sunrise Dr 29575
Sunrise Trl 29575
Sunset Dr & Trl 29577
Surf Pine Dr 29575
Surf Scoter Dr 29588
Surfside Dr 29575
Surfside Industrial Park 29575
Surfview Pl 29572
Surgeons Dr 29579
Surrey Ln 29579
Susie Ln 29588
Sutter Dr 29575
Sutton Dr 29588
Swallow Ave 29577
Swan Ct 29577
Swann Cv 29577
Swanson Dr 29579
Swash Ct 29572
Sweet Bay Trl 29579
Sweet Gum Cres & Trl 29588
Sweet Home Church Rd 29588
E & W Sweetbriar Trl 29588
Sweetgum St 29577
Sycamore Ave 29577
Tabernacle Dr 29577
Talbot Cir 29577
Tall Pine Ln 29575
Tanner Ct 29588
Tano Way 29572
Tapscott St 29579
Tarpon Ct 29579
Tarpon Bay Rd 29579
Tartan Ln 29588
Tatum Ln 29577
Taurus Ln 29575
Tayport Ct 29579
Tea Rose St 29577
Teague Rd 29577
Teak Ct 29579
Teakwood Dr 29588
Teal Ct 29588
Temperance Dr 29577
Terminal St 29577
Tern Hall Dr 29588
Ternberry Dr 29588
Terra Vista Dr 29588
Terracina Cir 29588
Terre Verde Dr 29579
Terri Dr 29588
Thames Ct 29577
Theatre Dr 29579
Thistle Ln 29579
Thomas St 29588
Thompkins Rd 29588
Thompson Ct 29577
Thornbury Dr 29577
Thornwood Ct & Dr 29588
Thorton Ct 29579
Thrash Way 29577
Threshing Way 29579
Thunder Ct 29577
Thunderbolt Ave 29577
Tibton Cir 29588
Tiburon Dr 29588
Tibwin Ave 29579
Tidal Point Ln 29579
Tideland Ct 29579
Tidewater Rd 29579
Tiffany Ln 29577
Tiger Paw Ln 29588
Timberdoodle Cut 29588
Timberline St 29572
Timmerman Rd 29588
Timrod Dr 29575
Tinamou Ln 29588
Tindal St 29572
Tinkers Dr 29575
Tip Top Ct 29577
Tirrell Loop 29577
Todd Cir & St 29577
Tortoise Shell Dr 29579
Touhey Dr 29579
Tower St 29577
Towhee Ct 29588
Towne Centre Pkwy 29579
Townes Ct 29588
Trace Run 29588
Tradd St 29588
Trade St 29577
Tradition Ave 29577
Tralee Pl 29579
Trammell Rd 29588
Tranquility Ln 29577
Travis Ct 29588
Tree Cir 29575
Tree Top Ct & Ln 29588
Tremiti Ln 29579
Triana Ct 29572
Triple Crown Ct 29579
Triumph Dr 29577
Troon Ln 29588
Truman Ln 29577
Tuckahoe Rd 29579
Tulip Dr 29577
Tullamore Ct 29579
Tullick Dr 29575
Turkey Ridge Rd 29575
Turnberry Ct
104-115 29588
1300-1399 29575
Turtle Cove Dr 29579
Tuscany Grande Blvd 29579
Twin Lake Dr 29572
Twin Lakes Pt 29575
Twin Pond Ct 29579
Twinoak Ct 29572
Twisted Willow Ct 29579
Two Notch Rd 29572
Two Rivers Ct 29579
Tyger River Ct 29588
Tyner St 29588
Uniola Dr 29579
Ursa Major Dr 29575
Ursa Minor Dr 29575
Utopiate Ct 29579
Vacation Dr 29577
Valencia Cir 29572
Valene Ct 29572
Vannoy Ct 29579
Veneda Ct 29579
Veneto Ct 29572
Venezia Cir 29579
Venice Way 29577
Ventura Ct 29572
Vereen Ave 29577
Verona Dr 29572
Vesta Dr 29579
Viareggio Rd 29579
Victoria Ct 29588
Victoria Ln 29577
Victory Ln 29577
Viejas Dr 29579
W View Ct 29588
Viking Dr 29577
Villa Grande St 29579
Villa Mar Dr 29579
Villa Marbella Ct 29572
Villa Woods Dr 29579
Village Dr
100-199 29588
1860-1870 29575
Village Center Blvd 29579
Villarosa Dr 29572
Vine St 29577
Vintage Cir 29579
Virgo Ln 29575
Vista Del Mar Ln 29572
Vista Glen Dr 29579
Vista Wood Dr 29579
Volterra Way 29579
Volunteer Dr 29575
Waccamaw Blvd 29579
Waccamaw Pines Dr 29579
Waccamaw River Rd 29588
Waccamaw Village Dr 29579
Wacobee Dr 29579
Wading Bird Ln 29577
Wagon Wheel Ln 29575
Wagon Wheel Rd 29572
Wainwright Ave 29577
Walcott Dr 29579
Walden Ct 29588
Walker Ct 29577
E & W Walkerton Rd 29579
Wallingford Cir 29588
Walnut Ave 29577
Walton Heath Dr 29588
Wanabac Pl 29588
Wando River Rd 29579
Wardour Ct 29579
Warehouse St 29577
Warren St 29577
Warthog St 29577
Washington Cir 29572
Washington St 29577
Water Ave 29575
Water Banks Dr 29579
Water Grass Ct 29579
Waterbridge Blvd 29579
Waterbury Ln 29588
Wateree River Rd 29588
Waterford Dr 29577
Waterfront Way 29572
Watergate Dr 29588
Waterside Dr 29577
Waterton Ave 29579
Waterville Ct 29579
Waterway Ln 29572
Waterway Village Blvd 29579
Watts Ave & Ln 29577
Waverly Ave 29577
Wayland Cir 29588
Wayvland Dr 29575
Wedgewood St 29572
Weeks Dr 29588
Weeping Willow Dr 29579
Weikles Ln 29588
Welch Pass 29588
Welcome Dr 29579
Welk Ct 29572
Wellington Way 29577
Wellness Dr 29579
Wells Blvd 29588
Wendover Ct 29579
Wentworth Dr 29575
Wesley St 29579
Weslin Creek Dr 29588
E West Way 29588
Westbury Ct 29572
Westchester Ct 29579
Westferry Xing 29575
Westfield Dr 29577
Westhaven Dr 29579
Westhill Cir 29572
Westleton Dr 29572
Westminster Dr 29588
Westwind Dr 29579
Westwood Ln 29588
Wetherby Way 29572
Wexford Ct 29575
Weyburn St 29579
Whale Ave 29588
Whaler Harbour 29577
Whatuthink Rd 29588
Wheatfield Dr 29577
Whetstone Ln 29579
Whipple Run Loop 29588
Whisker Pole 29579
Whispering Winds Dr 29579
White St 29577
White Dove Ln 29579
White Hawk Ct 29588
White Heron Cres 29588
White Oak Ln 29577
White Pine Dr 29588
White River Dr 29579
White Tail Pl 29588
White Wing Cir 29579
Whitehaven Ct 29577
Whitty Dr 29579
Wickalow Way 29579
Wickham Dr 29579
Wigston Ct 29579
Wild Game Trl 29588
Wild Ginger Ct 29579
Wild Horse Ct 29579
Wild Iris Dr 29577
N Wild Rose Dr 29579
Wild Turkey Cir 29579
Wildflower Trl 29579
Wildwood Cir & Trl 29572
Wildwood Dunes Trl 29572
Willbrook Rd 29577
William St 29577
William Moultrie Cir 29588
Williamson Cir 29579
Willingham Dr 29579
Willoughby Ln 29577
N Willow Dr 29575
S Willow Dr 29575
Willow Ln 29575
Willow St 29577
Willow Trce 29572
Willow Bend Dr 29579
Willow Garth Cir 29572
Willow Ridge Rd 29588
Wilmonte Ct 29588
Winchester Ct 29577
Windchime Dr 29572
Winddrift Ct 29575
Windemere By The Sea 29572
Windermer By The Sea Cir 29572
Winding Oaks Ln 29588
Windmere Way 29575
Windmill Way 29579
Windrose Way 29577
Windsong Dr 29579
Windsor Rd 29588
Windsor Bay Blvd 29588
Windsor Green Way 29579
Windwalk Cir 29575
Windward Ct 29579
Windwood Xing 29575
Winged Foot Ct 29579
Winslow Ave 29588
Winter Wren Ct 29588
Winterberry Ln 29579
Wintergreen Pt 29588
Winyah Ct 29588
Winyah Bay Rd 29588
Wisteria Dr 29588
Withers Aly & Dr 29577
Withers Swash Dr 29577
Wood Duck Cv 29588
Wood Duck Ln 29579
Wood Lee Dr 29572
Woodbine Ct 29579
Woodburn Dr 29579
Woodchuck Rd 29588
Woodduck Ln 29575
Woodfield Dr 29588
Woodhaven Dr 29588
Woodland Dr
7600-7799 29572
8148-8399 29588
Woodmont Ln 29588
Woodside Ave 29577
Woodsong Dr 29579
Woodview Ln 29575
Woodwind Ct 29572
World Tour Blvd 29579
Worthington Cir 29588
Wren Ave 29572
Wrigley Dr 29588
Wyandot Ct 29579
Wyatt Ln 29577
Wycliffe Dr 29577
Wynfield Dr 29577
Yacht Dr 29577
Yahroy St 29579
Yancey Way 29577
Yaupon Cir
401-497 29577
499-799 29577
4800-5999 29575
Yaupon Dr 29577
N Yaupon Dr 29575
S Yaupon Dr 29575
Yellow Jasmine Ave 29588
Yellow Morel Way 29579
Yellowwood Ave 29577
York St 29577
Yorkshire Pkwy 29577
Yorktown Ct 29579
Young William Rd 29588
Youngwood Turn 29588
Yucca Ave 29577
Zeddie Ln 29588
Zinnia Dr 29579
Zion Dr 29588

NUMBERED STREETS

1st N & S 29575
1st N & S 29577
2nd N & S 29575
2nd N & S 29577
3rd N & S 29575
3rd N & S 29577
4th N & S 29575
4th N & S 29577
5th N & S 29575
5th N & S 29577
6th N & S 29575
6th N & S 29577
7th N & S 29575
7th N & S 29577
8th Ave N
100-799 29575
201-397 29577
399-1099 29577
8th Ave S
100-1099 29575
300-499 29577
9th N & S 29577
9th N & S 29575
10th N & S 29575
10th N & S 29577
10th Avenue Ext N 29577
11th Ave N 29575
11th Ave S 29577
12th N & S 29575
12th N & S 29577
13th N & S 29575
13th N & S 29577
14th N & S 29575
14th N & S 29577
15th N & S 29575
15th N & S 29577
16th Ave N
100-899 29575
300-600 29577
602-698 29577
16th Ave NW
900-1099 29575
16th Ave S
100-899 29575
300-499 29577
17th N & S 29575
17th N & S 29577
18th N & S 29577
19th N & S 29577
20th N & S 29577
21st N & S 29577
22nd N & S 29577
23rd N & S 29577
24th N & S 29577
25th N & S 29577
26th N & S 29577
27th N & S 29577
28th N & S 29577
29th N & S 29577
30th Ave N 29577
31st Ave N 29577
32nd Ave N 29577
33rd Ave N 29577
33rd Avenue Ext N 29577
34th Ave N 29577
35th Ave N 29577
36th Ave N 29577
37th Ave N 29577
38th Ave N 29577
39th Ave N 29577
40th Ave N 29577
41st Ave N 29577
42nd Ave N 29577
43rd Ave N 29577
44th Ave N 29577
45th Ave N 29577
46th Ave N 29577
47th Ave N 29577
48th Ave N 29577
48th Avenue Ext N 29577
50th Ave N 29577
52nd Ave N 29577
61st Ave N 29577
62nd Ave N 29572
63rd Ave N 29572
64th Ave N 29572
65th Ave N 29572
66th Ave N 29572
67th Ave N 29572
68th Ave N 29572
69th Ave N 29572
70th Ave N 29572
71st Ave N 29572
72nd Ave N 29572
73rd Ave N 29572
74th Ave N 29572
75th Ave N 29572
76th Ave N 29572
77th Ave N 29572
78th Ave N 29572
79th Ave N 29572
80th Ave N 29572
81st Ave N 29572
82nd Ave & Pkwy N 29572
707 Connector 29588

NORTH AUGUSTA SC

General Delivery 29841

POST OFFICE BOXES MAIN OFFICE STATIONS AND BRANCHES

Box No.s
6001 - 8220 29861
9995 - 9995 29841

NAMED STREETS

Adams Dr 29841
Adams Branch Rd 29860
Adamsville Spring Rd 29860
Aidan Ln 29841
Aiken Ave 29841
Albert Dr 29860
Alberta Ave & Dr 29860
Alexander Dr 29841
Allean Sq 29860
Allenwood Way 29841
Allway Dr 29841
Allwin Ln 29842
Allwin Overlook Ln 29842
Alpine Ave 29841
Alta Vista Ave 29841
Altamaha Dr 29841
Amazing Grace Ct 29860
Ambassador Dr 29841
Amberwood Ct 29841
Amelia Dr 29860
Amen Loop 29842
American Ln 29842
Amherst Dr 29841
Amos Ct 29841
Amy Cir 29841
S And M Ln 29841
Andover Ct 29841
Andrews Br 29860
Andy Ln 29842
Ann St 29860
Apache Dr 29841
Arcadia Ct 29841
Arch Dr 29841
Archer Ct 29841
Ardis Rd 29842
Argyle Ave 29841
Arianna Ln 29842
Arizona Ct 29841
E & W Arlington Hts 29841
Aroma Dr 29841
Arrie Ln 29842
Arrington Ave 29841
Arrow Wood Dr 29841
Arrowhead Lake Rd 29860
Ascauga Lake Rd 29841
Ashford Dr 29841
Ashley Cir 29841
Ashmore Dr 29842
Ashton Pointe Dr 29841
Ashwood Dr 29860
Aster Dr 29841
Astor Ct 29841
Atkinson Rd 29842
Atlantis Ave 29841
Atomic Rd
701-9997 29841
1748-12098 29842
9999-11099 29841
11101-11199 29841
12100-16199 29842
Audey Dr 29842
Audubon Cir & Rd 29841
Augusta Rd 29842
Austin St 29841
Austin Graybill Rd 29860
Autumn Chase Ln 29842
Avalon Ln 29842
Ayr Dr 29841
Azalea Dr 29842
Azalea Ln
1-99 29860
100-199 29842
Badger Creek Ln 29842
Bailey Dr 29842
Bakers Branch Dr 29860
Ballantine Ct 29860
Bama Ave 29841
Bamboo Ln 29842
Banks Dr 29860
Barbara Ln 29860
Baron Pl 29841
Bartlett Ln 29860
Barton Rd 29841
Bay St 29842
Beard Rd 29842
Beaulah Ave 29841
Beaumont Ct 29841
Beaver Pond Ct 29860
Beech Island Ave 29842
Beechdale Dr & Loop 29842
Beechwood St 29841
Beekeeper Pl 29842
Belair Ct & Rd 29841
Belfast Ct 29860
Belgium Cir 29841
Believers Path 29842
Bell Dr 29842
Bella Vita Way 29860
Belle Cir 29860
Bellingham Dr 29842
Belmont Ct 29841
Belvedere Rd 29842
Belvedere Clearwater Rd 29841
Belview Dr 29841
Bennett Ln 29841
Bentley Dr 29860
Bergen Rd
100-299 29841
400-799 29860
Berkley Ct 29841
Berry Ln 29842
Berrywood Ct 29860
Bethune Dr 29842
Beverly Cir 29841
Big Branch Ct & Ln 29860
Big Cone Dr 29860
Big Mama Ct 29841
Big Oak Dr 29860

Big Pine Rd 29841
Bight Ct 29841
Biltmore Dr 29841
Birch Cir 29841
Birch Dr 29860
Birch St 29841
Bismark Cir 29841
Blackburn Loop 29842
Blackhaw Dr 29860
Blackstone Camp Rd 29842
Blair Dr 29860
Blanch St 29860
Blanchard Rd 29841
Bleachery St 29842
Blessing Ln 29841
Blossom Dr 29860
Blossom St 29841
Blue Heron Ln 29841
Bluff Ave 29841
Bobbye Dr 29841
Bobolink Ave 29841
Boettjer Rd 29842
Bogus Hill Dr 29860
Bolin Ct & Rd 29841
Bonner Ln 29842
Bonnie Brook Dr 29860
Bordeaux St 29841
Borden Rd 29841
Border Dr 29841
Bowden Ct 29860
Boxing Kat Ct 29841
Boyd Pond Rd 29842
Boykin Dr & Rd 29842
Boylan St 29841
Brack Ln 29860
Bradberry Ln 29842
Bradford Dr 29860
Bradley Ct & Dr 29841
Bradleyville Rd 29841
Bramble Rd 29860
Branch Ct 29842
Breckenridge Dr 29841
Brenda Dr 29841
Briarcliff St 29841
Brickton Ct & Ln 29841
Bridle Path Rd 29860
Briggs Ave 29841
Briggs Ln 29860
Briggs Rd 29860
Briggs Haven Cir & Ext 29860
Brigham Rd 29841
Brittle Wood Ct 29860
Broadcast Dr 29841
Broadwalk Dr 29860
Broadwater Cir 29860
Broken Arrow Ct 29860
Broken Branch Rd 29841
Brookgreen Dr 29841
Brooks Dr 29841
Brookside Ave 29841
Brookview Ct 29841
Browning Dr 29860
Brownstone Dr 29842
Broxten Dr 29860
Bryant Ave 29841
Buckhall Dr 29841
Buckthorn Ct 29860
Budwell Ct 29860
E & W Buena Vista Ave 29841
Bumble Bee Ln 29842
Bunting Dr 29841
Burning Tree Pl 29860
Burnside Ave 29841
Burwick Run 29842
Busters Pl 29841
Butler Ave 29841
Butterfly Dr 29860
Byars Ln 29841
Byrnes Rd 29841
Byron Rd 29842
Cadada Ct 29841
Caden Ct 29841
Calbrieth Cir & Way 29860
Camellia Dr 29842
Campbellton Dr 29841
Campfire Ct 29860
Canary Ln 29841
Canary Lake Rd 29841
Cannon Mill Ct & Dr 29860
Canton Dr 29841
Capers Dr 29860
Caprice Ln 29842
Captain Johnsons Dr 29860
Cardinal Ln 29841
Caretta St 29841
Carls Ln 29860
Carmel St 29841
Carn Park Rd 29841
Carolina Ave & Pl 29841
Carolina Springs Rd 29841
Carolina Springs Spur Rd 29841
Carolyn Cir 29841
Carpenter Cv 29860
Carpentersville Rd 29841
Carr Cir 29841
Carriage Ln 29841
Carriee Ln 29860
Carriee Lane Ext 29860
Carver St 29842
Cary Ave 29841
Cary Dr 29842
Casa Linda Dr 29860
Casalina Dr 29860
Cascade Dr 29841
Casnette Rd 29842
Catawba Rd 29841
Catfish Ln 29842
Catland Woods 29860
Cavalry Run 29860
Ccc Rd 29842
Cedar Knl 29842
Ceferino Dr 29860
Celeste Ave 29841
Celeste Mobile Home Park Cir 29841
Cellus Park Rd 29841
Center St 29841
Chalet North Ct 29841
Chalet North Entrance Rd 29841
Chambers Dr 29842
Chandler Dr 29842
Chariot Ct 29841
Charity Ln 29841
Cherokee Dr 29841
Cherry Ave 29841
Cherry St 29842
Cherry Laurel Dr 29860
Cherry Tree Ln 29860
Chestnut Ave 29841
Chestnut Ln 29860
Cheves Creek Cir, Ct & Rd 29860
Cheyenne Cir 29841
Chicasaw Dr 29841
Chinaberry Dr 29842
Church Rd & St 29842
Cindy Dr 29842
Cindy Ln 29860
N Circle Dr 29842
Circle View St 29841
Circlewood Dr 29841
Clannerm Rd 29860
Claridge St 29860
Clay Ave 29841
Clay Ct 29860
Claypit Rd 29841
Clearmont Dr 29841
E & W Clifton Ave 29841
Clint Ct 29841
Clover Dr 29860
Clover Ridge Ct 29842
Cnw Rd 29842
Coastal Dr 29842
Cole St 29842
Collin Reeds Rd 29860
Colonel Shaws Way 29860
Colonial Ct 29841
Colorado Ct 29841
Columbus Ave 29841
Commercial Dr 29841
Community Rd 29860
Concord Ave & St 29841
Conifer Ct & Dr 29841
Cooper Loop 29860
Cooper Mill Rd 29860
Cooper Place Dr 29860
Copeland Cir 29860
Coral Way 29841
Corley Dr 29841
Coronet Dr 29860
Cotton Gin Ct 29860
Cottonwood Ct 29860
Coulter Dr 29841
Country Ln 29860
Country Club Hills Dr 29860
Country Manor Ln 29860
Country Place Dr 29841
Court A 29841
Court B 29841
Courtney Dr 29841
Courtyards Pl 29841
Coventry Cir & Ct 29860
Cowdry Park Rd 29842
Crawley Cir 29842
Crazy Horse Ln 29841
Creek Stone Dr 29860
Creekview Ct 29841
Creighton Dr 29860
Crescent Ct 29841
Crestlyn Dr 29841
Crestview Dr 29841
Cricket Ct 29860
Crossland Ave 29841
Crossroads Dr 29841
Crystal Lake Dr 29841
Culley Dr 29841
Cumberland Ave 29841
Cunningham Ct 29860
Cupid Ct 29841
Curry Ct 29860
Curry Dr 29841
Currytown Ln & Rd 29860
Currytowne Blvd 29860
Curtis Dr 29841
Cypress Dr 29841
Cypress Point Ln 29842
Dabbs Ln 29841
Daffodil Dr 29841
Damby Ct 29860
Dana Dr 29860
Daniels Ct 29860
Davis Simmons Ln 29842
Deans Dr 29842
Deepwood Pl 29841
Deer Trail Pt 29860
Deerwood Dr 29841
Delaughter Dr & Pt 29860
Delehanty Ct 29842
Devon Ct 29860
Diamond St 29842
Diamond Park Rd 29841
Dicks Ct & Dr 29842
Disher Ln 29841
Dittman Ct 29842
Divine Dr 29842
Dixie Clay Rd 29842
Dl Dr 29841
Dobson Rd 29842
Dobys Ct 29860
Dock Dr 29860
Dogwood Dr 29841
Dogwood Glen Ct & Dr 29860
Dorr Dr & St 29841
Dorsett Kenzie Rd 29842
Douglas Dr
100-199 29860
100-499 29842
Dove Ave, Ct & St 29841
Dove Lake Dr 29841
Dry Branch Way 29860
Dry Creek Trl 29842
Dunbar Ln 29842
Dunbarton Dr 29841
Duncan Rd 29841
Dundee Dr 29841
Dunn Dr 29842
Dupriest Cir 29860
Durango Pine Ln 29842
Durst Dr 29860
Dusty Ln 29860
Dyer Trl 29842
Eagle Rd 29860
Eagle Lake Rd 29841
Earls Ct 29860
East Ave 29841
Easy St 29842
Edgefield Rd
100-999 29841
1000-1799 29860
Edgewood Ave, Ct & Dr 29841
Edisto Ave 29842
Edisto Dr 29841
Edna St 29841
Edwards Dr 29860
Edwards Loop 29842
Elder St 29841
Elgin Ct 29842
Elizabeth Ave & St 29841
Elm St 29841
Elma Ln 29842
Elmore Way 29842
Elton Ave 29841
Emerald Dr 29841
Emma Ln 29841
Emory Dr 29842
Euclid Ave 29841
Eutaw Springs Trl 29860
Evelyn Ln 29841
Eventing Way 29842
Evergreen Ct 29841
Fairfield Ave 29841
Fairlane Ave & Dr 29841
Fairview Ave 29841
Fairview Rd 29842
Fairview St 29841
Fairway Ave 29841
Fairwood Ave 29841
Fallmouth Dr 29841
Farrington Way 29860
Faye Dr 29860
Feagin Dr 29860
Fieldcrest Dr 29841
Fiesta Dr 29842
Figtree Ct 29841
Finkledey Dr 29841
Finklin Rd 29842
Finley Dr 29860
Finley Drive Ext 29860
Fiord Dr 29841
Fir St 29841
Firethorn Dr 29860
Fitzsimmons Dr 29860
E Five Notch Rd 29841
W Five Notch Rd
100-499 29841
500-999 29860
Five Notch Spur 29841
Flamingo Rd 29841
Flatwood Ct 29860
Fleetwood Dr 29841
Flintlock Dr 29860
Flintrock Ct 29860
Floyd Ave 29841
E & W Forest Ave & Dr 29841
S Fork Bnd 29842
Fowke St 29842
Fowkewood Ct 29841
Fox Ave 29841
Fox Creek Dr 29860
Fox Lair Dr 29842
Fox Terrace Rd 29860
Fox Trail Dr 29860
Foxchase Cir 29860
Foxfire Ct 29860
Foxglove Ct 29860
Foxhil Ct & Dr 29860
Foxhunt Dr 29860
Foxwood Ct 29860
Frances Dr 29841
Frances St
500-599 29860
1000-1199 29841
Franklin Dr 29841
Free Indeed Blvd 29841
Freeland Dr 29860
Friendly Ln 29841
Friendship Ln 29860
Front St 29841
Frontage Rd 29860
Fulton St 29841
Gardenia Ct 29841
Gardner Rd 29860
Garrett Rd 29842
Garrett Town Rd 29860
Gasque Ln 29860
Gecko Trl 29841
Gentry Ln 29841
Georgetown Ct & Dr 29841
Georgia Ave 29841
Geraldine Ln 29860
Gerber Daisy Ln 29841
Gerhard Rdg 29860
Gibson Dr 29842
Gilmore Ave 29841
Gizmo Ct 29842
Gladiolus Way 29842
Gladys Dr 29842
Glastonbury Ct 29842
Glenmore Ave 29841
Glory Ln 29841
Goldman St 29841
Gone Away Ln 29842
Gordon St 29841
Goudy Ct 29841
Grady Ln 29842
Grand Prix Dr 29842
Grant Ave 29841
Grapevine Ln 29841
Graystone Dr 29842
Green Forest Ct & Dr 29841
Green Valley Cir 29842
Greenbriar Dr 29860
Greenland Dr 29841
Greenwood Dr 29841
Gregory Ct 29860
Gregory Lake Rd 29860
Griffin Ln 29860
Groesbeck Aly 29841
Groves Blvd 29841
Gustav Ct 29860
H And H St 29841
Haley Dr 29860
Hallelujah Ln 29841
Halo Ln 29842
Hamburg Rd 29841
Hammond Dr 29841
Hammond Rd 29842
Hammond Ferry Rd 29841
Hammond Place Cir, Ct & Way 29841
Hammond Pond Rd 29841
Hampton Ave, Cir & Ter 29841
Hampton Wills Dr 29841
Hannahs Ln 29860
Happiness Ln 29842
Happyland Cir 29841
Harlem St 29842
Harmony Pl 29842
Harts Ln 29842
Harvester Dr 29860
Haskell Rd 29841
Hastings Pl 29841
Hawthorne St 29841
Hayes Dr 29860
Hazel St 29841
Hazel Grove Rd 29842
Heatherwood Dr 29860
Heil Dr 29841
Helen Ln 29842
Hemlock Dr 29841
Henley Dr 29842
Henry Ave 29841
Heritage Ct 29841
Hermitage Ln 29860
Herndon Dairy Rd 29842
Heyward St 29842
Hibiscus Pl 29841
Hickory Ct 29841
Hickory Dr 29860
Hickory Pl 29841
Hickory Hill Dr 29860
Hickory Nut Lodge Rd 29860
Hidden Cir 29860
Hidden Hills Dr 29841
Hideaway Trl 29860
Highpointe Dr 29842
Highview Ave 29841
Hill St 29841
Hillcrest Ct & Dr 29841
N Hills Dr 29841
Hillside Dr & Pl 29841
Hilltop Ct 29842
Hillwood Ct 29841
Holiday Dr 29841
Holley Hill Dr 29841
Hollis Ave 29841
Holly Cir 29860
Holly Ln 29841
Holly Rd 29841
Holly Circle Br 29860
Hollywood Ln 29841
Homeward Bound Dr 29860
Horse Creek Rd 29842
Horseman Dr 29842
Horseshoe Rd 29841
Howard Johnson Ln 29842
Howard Mill Rd 29841
Huckabee St 29842
E & W Hugh Ct & St 29841
Hunters Xing 29841
Hunters Farm 29841
Hunters Forest Rd 29842
Hunters Gate Blvd 29841
Huntington Dr 29860
Hunts Grove Rd 29860
Hutchinson Dr 29841
Hyacinth Way 29841
Independent Hill Ln 29860
Indian Hill Ct 29860
Indian Mound Dr
300-399 29842
700-799 29841
Indian Ridge Dr 29860
Indian Rock Ct 29841
Indies Lndg 29841
Indigo Dr 29860
Innsbrook Cir 29842
Irene St 29841
Ivy Ln 29860
Jabba Rd 29842
Jackson Ave & Rd 29841
Jackson Grove Rd 29842
Jacob Dr 29841
Jake Rd 29842
James St 29841
James Booth Ct 29860
James E Andrews Ln 29842
Janie Cir 29842
January Ln 29841
Jarvis Ct 29841
Jay Ln 29860
Jeff St 29841
Jefferson Ln 29860
Jefferson Davis Hwy
4100-5699 29842
5700-6499 29841
Jeffrey St 29841
Jenkins Dr 29842
Jersey Ave 29841
Jesse Dee St 29841
John Foxs Run 29860
Johnson Cir 29860
Johnson Rd 29841
Johnstown Rd 29842
Jones St 29841
Jonquil Ln 29841
Jude Ln 29860
Judge Gantt Ct 29860
Julia Ave 29841
June St 29841
Karnes St 29841
Katherine Ave 29841
Keller St 29842
Kenilworth Dr 29860
Kennedy Dr 29860
Kerr St 29841
Kerry Ct 29860
Kershaw Dr & Pl 29841
Kesiah Ct 29860
Keystone Ct 29842
Kildare Dr 29860
Kimberly Ln 29860
Kingstree Rd 29841
Kingswood Ln 29860
Kip Ln 29841
Kirby Dr 29841
Kj Davis Dr 29842
Knight Ln 29860
Knobcone Ave 29841
Knollwood Blvd 29841
Knollwood Trl 29860
Knotts Lndg 29860
Knotty Pine Dr 29841
Knox Ave 29841
Koger Loop 29842
Kringlewood Ct 29841
Lacebark Pine Way 29842
Lady St 29841
Lake Ave 29841
Lake Catawba Dr 29841
Lake Forest Dr 29860
Lake Greenwood Dr 29841
Lake Hartwell Dr 29841
Lake Keowee Ct 29841
Lake Lanier Ct 29841
Lake Lure Dr 29841
Lake Marion Dr 29841
Lake Moultrie Dr 29841
Lake Murray Dr 29841
Lake Norman Dr 29841
Lake Santee Dr 29841
Lake Selisa Dr 29860
Lake Thurmond Ct 29841
Lakeside Dr 29841
Lakeview Dr 29841
Lakeview Ext 29860
Lakeview Rd 29860
Lakewood Cir & Dr 29841
Lamar Ct 29841
Lamar Dr 29842
Lamar St 29842
Lamback Way 29841
Landing Dr 29841
Landon Ln 29841
Lands End Ct 29860
Lang Hl 29860
Langfuhr Way 29860
Langley Rd 29842
Lanham Dr 29841
Lanham Ln 29860
Lanier Rd 29842
Lantana Ln 29841
Lark Ln 29860
Larry Dr 29842
Larry Dee St 29841
Laurel Lake Dr 29860
Laurel Oaks Dr 29860
Laurens St 29841
Laurie Dr 29842
Laverne Ave 29841
Lecompte Ave 29841
Lecroy Ave 29842
Lee Dr & St 29841
Lehigh Ave 29841
Leigh Place Dr 29841
Leonard Ln 29860
Lettye Ct 29860
Lewis Rd & Way 29842
Lexus Ct 29841
Leyland Pl 29841
Liberty Hill Rd 29841
Lighthouse Ln 29841
Lily Ave 29841
Limping Dog Ln 29841

Lincoln Way 29842
Linds Pond Cir 29860
Line Bars Dr 29860
Linnet Loop 29841
Lions Gate Dr 29860
Lismore Ct 29860
Little Ln 29860
Live Oak Ct 29860
Lizard Ln 29842
Loblolly Ct 29841
Locust Dr 29860
Lodgepole Ave 29841
Long Dr 29860
Longleaf Ct 29841
Longmeadow Rd 29860
Longstreet Pl & Xing 29860
Loop Dr 29842
Loper Dr 29841
Lorraine Dr 29841
Lorry Ct 29841
Lost Rd 29842
Louise Dr 29842
Lowe St 29841
Lucerne Ave 29841
Luckie Bear Ln 29841
Lucy Ave 29841
Lullaby Ln 29842
Lynwood Dr 29841
Macedonia Rd 29860
Macedonia Road Ext 29860
Macklin Ln 29860
Macmillan Dr 29842
Maddox Ave 29841
Madison Rd & St 29841
Mae St 29841
Maggie Valley Ln 29842
Magnolia Ct 29860
Maher St 29860
W Main St 29841
Malone Ave 29841
Manchester St 29842
Maple Dr 29860
Maplewood Dr 29841
Marbury Ln 29860
Margie Ln 29841
E Marion Ave 29841
Market Place Dr 29860
Marshall Ave 29841
E Martintown Rd 29841
W Martintown Rd
100-1299 29841
1301-1397 29860
1399-1999 29860
Mary Johnson Ct 29860
Mason Ct 29860
Matthew Dr 29860
Mayfield Ct & Dr 29860
Mayflower Rd 29842
Mccain Rd 29860
Mccallum Dr 29860
Mccaskill Rd 29841
Mcclain St 29842
Mcelmurray Rd 29842
Mckenzie Cir, Ct, Pl & St
E & W 29841
Mckenzie End 29841
Mckie Rd 29860
Mckinney St 29842
Mckinnon St 29841
Mcnair Dr 29841
Mealing Ave 29841
Mealing Ct 29860
Mealing Dr 29860
Mealing Rd 29860
Medie Ave 29841
Medlin St 29841
Melarrel Rd 29842
Melody Ln 29841
Memory Ln 29860
Meridian Ave 29841
Merovan Dr 29860
Merriwether Ct 29860
Merriwether Dr 29841
Metz Dr 29841
Miles Ct 29860
Militia Loop 29860
Mill Pass & Run 29860
Mill Branch Way 29860
Mill Stone Ln 29860
Miller St
100-399 29842
400-599 29860
Millrose Cir 29842
Millwood Ln 29860
Mim Woodring Dr 29860
Mims Rd 29860
Mims Grove Church
Rd 29860
Miracle Island Ln 29842
Mistletoe Ct 29860
Mitchell Dr 29860
Moccasin Way 29841
Mockingbird Ln 29841
Mokateen Ave 29841
Moms Ln 29860
Monterey Ave 29841
Montgomery Pl 29841
Moore Rd 29860
Moprior Ln 29860
Morgan Ave 29841
Morris Run 29860
Moss Cv 29841
Mossy Oak Cir 29841
Moton St 29841
Mount Vintage Plantation
Dr 29860
Mountside Dr 29841
Muffin Ln 29842
Mullens St 29860
Mullis St 29842
Murphy St 29860
Murrah Rd 29860
Murrah Forest Ct & Dr 29860
Murrah Road Ext 29860
Mystery Ln 29842
Mystic Hts 29860
Nail Rd 29842
Namon Ln 29842
Nappier Ln 29841
Nathanie Dr 29841
Navaho Dr 29841
Neighbor Ln 29842
Neo Dr 29842
New Castle Ave 29841
New Delaughter Dr 29860
New Morgan Ln 29841
New Windsor Way 29842
Newt Ct 29841
Nocturne Ln 29841
Norell Ln 29842
Norman St 29841
North Ct 29860
Northside Dr 29841
Northview St 29841
Northwood Ct 29841
Norway Dr 29841
Notchaway Ct 29860
Nut Grove Dr 29841
Oak Dr 29842
Oak Creek Dr 29860
Oak Crest Dr 29860
Oakbrook Dr 29860
Oakdale Ave 29841
Oakdale Dr 29842
Oakhurst Dr 29860
Oakland Dr 29860
Oakleaf Dr 29860
Observatory Ave 29841
Ogeechee Ct 29841
Old Aiken Rd
200-1099 29841
1100-1299 29842
Old Aiken Road Ext 29842
Old Chavous Rd 29842
Old Cherokee Dr 29842
Old Edgefield Rd 29841
Old Ferry Rd 29842
Old Graniteville Rd 29860
Old Jackson Hwy 29842
Old Magnolia Ln 29842
Old Martintown Rd
1-99 29860
700-733 29841
1300-1499 29860
Old Minor Bridge Rd 29842
Old Nail Rd 29842
Old Plantation Rd 29841
Old Ridge Rd 29841
Old South Rd 29842
Old Storm Branch Rd 29842
Old Sudlow Lake Rd 29841
Old Sudlow Lake Road
Ext 29841
Old Trail Rd 29842
Old Walden Well Rd 29841
Old Walnut Br 29860
Oliver Dr 29842
Olympian Hts 29860
Orange St 29841
Orchard Way 29860
Oriole Ave 29841
Osprey Pt 29841
Our Rd 29860
Overlook Ct 29841
Owens St 29842
Palmetto Ave 29841
Pampas Ln 29841
Pareende Dr 29841
Paris Ave 29841
Park Ave 29841
Parker Dr 29842
Partridge Ln 29841
Pat Dr 29841
Patricia Dr 29841
Paul Weston Dr 29841
Pavilion Lake Rd 29860
Peach Blossom St 29841
Pearson Ave 29841
Pecan Grove Rd 29860
Penn St 29860
Pepper Branch Rd 29842
Pershing Dr 29841
Persimmon Way 29842
Petal Pl 29860
Peter Carnes Dr 29860
Pheasant Ct 29841
Phenix Ct N 29860
Philpot Ln 29841
Phoenix St 29841
Piedmont Ave 29841
Pig Path Ln 29842
Pin Oak Dr 29841
Pindo Pass 29860
Pine St 29841
Pine Bark Ln 29860
Pine Butte Ln 29841
E & W Pine Grove
Ave 29841
Pine Log Pl & Rd 29842
Pine Tree Ln 29841
Pinecrest Dr 29841
Pinegrove Rd 29842
Pineland Dr 29842
N Pines Dr 29841
Pineview Ave 29841
Pineview Cir 29842
Pineview Dr 29841
Pinewood Ct & Rd 29841
Pinewoods Park Cir 29842
Pinnacle Ct 29842
Pinon Rd 29841
Pisgah Rd 29841
Plank Rd 29841
Plantation Ct & Dr 29841
Plantation Point Dr 29860
Plaza Pl 29841
Pleasant Ln 29860
Pleasant Lane Ext 29860
Pollen Ct 29842
Ponce De Leon Ave 29841
Ponderosa Dr 29841
Pooh Ln 29842
Post Oak Dr & Ln 29841
Post Office Ct 29860
Powell Pl 29860
Powerhouse Rd 29841
Powers Ct 29860
Prague St 29841
Pram Ct 29841
Pressley Ave 29841
Pretty Run Dr 29841
Pride Ave 29841
Prince William Dr 29841
Privacy Ln 29841
Psa Rd 29842
Puds Pl 29841
Quail Ct 29860
Rabbit Run 29860
Raborn Ct 29841
Rachel Rd 29842
Radiance Dr 29841
Radio Station Rd 29841
Railroad Ave 29841
Rainbow Falls Rd 29860
Rainforest Ln 29860
Randall Rd 29860
Randolph Ct 29860
Randy Dr 29860
Rapids Ct 29841
Raven Dr 29841
Reams Rd 29841
Rebecaas Ct 29860
Red Fox Ct 29841
Red Globe St 29860
Red Maple Ct 29841
Redbud Dr 29860
Redcliffe Rd 29842
Redwood Dr 29860
Rest Master Ln 29860
Revco Rd 29842
Revolutionary Way 29860
Rhomboid Pl 29841
Rhomboid Place Ext 29841
Rice Bottom Rd 29842
Richland Rd 29841
Rider Ln 29842
N Ridge Ct 29841
Ridge Rd
200-999 29860
1000-1099 29841
N Ridge Rd 29841
Ridgecliff Ct 29841
Ridgecrest Ave 29841
Ridgefield Dr 29841
Ridgeland Dr 29841
Riley Ct 29841
Rita Ave & Ct 29841
River Bluff Ct, Dr &
Rd 29841
River Club Ln 29841
River North Dr 29841
River Oak Dr 29841
River Pointe Dr 29860
River View Dr 29841
River Wind Dr 29841
Riverbend Ct & Dr 29842
Riverdale Dr 29842
Rivers Cir 29841
Riverside Blvd 29841
Riverview Park Dr 29841
Roan Ave 29841
Robin Rd 29841
Robinson Dr 29841
Robinson Estate Ln 29842
Roble Ave 29841
Rockbrook Ln 29841
Rockrose Dr 29860
Rockwood Dr 29841
Ron Rd 29842
Roper Ct N 29860
Roper Ranch Trl 29860
Rose Dr 29860
Rosel Dr 29841
Rosemary Ln & St 29841
Roundtree Rd 29842
Royal Pl 29860
Royalette Ave 29841
Ruby Rd 29860
Runnel Vw 29841
Running Creek Dr 29860
Rush St 29841
Rushton Ct 29841
Russell St 29842
Ryan Ranch Ct 29860
Saddle Soap Ln 29842
Sadie St 29841
Safari Dr 29842
Sage Ct 29860
Saint Anthony St 29860
Saint Edward Ct 29860
Saint James St 29841
Saint Johns Dr 29860
Saint Julian Pl 29860
Saint Marys Dr 29860
Saint Phillip Rd 29842
Salty Dog Ln 29860
Saluda Ct 29860
Salvation Ln 29842
Samuels Rd & St 29841
San Jose Rd 29841
San Salvador Dr 29841
Sand Bar Ferry Rd 29842
Sand Hill Ct 29841
Sand Pit Rd 29841
Sanders Dr 29841
Sandy Rd 29860
Sandy Hill Ct 29860
Sante Fe Ct 29841
Sapp Dr 29842
Sassafras Ln 29860
Savannah Way 29860
Savannah Barony Dr 29841
Savannah Pointe 29841
Savannah River Pl 29841
Scarborough Dr 29842
Scenic Ct 29841
Scenic Dr 29860
Scenic Foundations Dr 29841
Scenic Lakes Dr 29841
Schoolhouse Ln 29860
Science Hill School Ln 29860
Scoggins Rd 29860
Scott Dr 29841
Scottsville Rd 29842
Seaborn Dr 29841
Sedgewood Ct 29860
Selisa Dr 29860
Seminole Dr 29841
Serpentine Dr 29841
Setiers Ct 29841
Seton Cir 29841
Setters Ct 29841
Seymour Cir, Ct, Dr &
Pl 29841
Shaddohill Pl 29860
Shadow Ln 29841
Shadow Rock Dr 29860
Shadowmoor Ct 29841
Shammah Dr 29842
Shannon Dr 29860
Shasta Daisy Path 29841
Shawnee Dr 29841
Sheffield St 29841
Sheppard Dr 29860
Sheraton Dr 29842
Sheridan Ave 29841
Shining Starr Ln 29842
Shoals Way Ct 29841
Shooting Match Ln 29860
E Shoreline Dr 29841
Short St
1-99 29842
1100-1199 29841
Shortcut Rd 29860
Shortleaf Ct 29841
Shultz Rd 29841
Shultz Hill Dr 29842
Sidereal Ave E 29841
Sidney Ct 29841
Siesta Ln 29842
Sikes Ave 29841
Silos Rd 29842
Silver Fox Cir 29860
Silver Fox Way 29841
Silver Maple Dr 29860
Sinclair Dr 29841
Siskin Cir 29841
Skyview Dr 29841
Slash Ct 29841
Smith Hardy Rd 29842
Smoke Ridge Rd 29860
Smokey Cir 29860
Snow Hill Ct 29841
Socastee Dr 29841
Sombrero Ct 29842
Sourwood Dr 29860
Southern Pines Dr 29841
Southwood Dr 29841
Spann Hammond Rd 29842
Spartan Dr 29841
Spearhead Ct 29860
Spider Webb Rd 29842
Spiked Cannon Ct 29860
Spofford Row 29842
Spring Dr, Gdn & Rd 29841
E & W Spring Grove
Ave 29841
Spring Hill Ct 29860
Spring Lake Ct & Dr 29860
Spring Oak Ln 29841
Springdale Rd 29841
Springhaven Dr 29860
Springknob Cir 29860
Springwood Ct & Dr 29841
Spruce Ct
1000-1099 29841
1800-1899 29860
Spur Ct 29860
Square Circle Ranch
Rd 29860
Stanton Dr 29841
Stapleton Dr 29860
Star Bright Ln 29842
Stave Ct 29860
Steamboat Ct 29860
Stem Ct 29860
Stephens Est & Rd 29860
Stephens Mill Ct & Dr 29860
Sterling Dr 29841
Stevens Creek Dr 29860
Stevenson Ct 29842
Stevie Seymour St 29841
Stirrup Dr 29860
Stirrup Cup Ct 29841
Stonehill Farm Rd 29860
Storm Ct 29842
Storm Branch Rd 29842
Sudlow Hills Ct 29841
Sudlow Lake Rd 29841
Sudlow Ridge Rd 29841
Summerhill Rd 29841
Summerlake Dr 29860
E & W Summit Ave 29841
Summit Commons Ct 29841
Sumter St 29842
Sunfest Dr 29841
Sunrise Ct 29841
Sunset Cir 29860
Sunview Dr 29841
Swallow Lake Dr 29841
Swamp Rd 29842
Swathmore Ave 29841
Sweetwater Ct & Rd 29860
Sweetwater Creek Dr 29860
Swiss St 29841
Sycamore Dr & St 29841
Sylvan Rd 29860
Sylvester Ln 29842
Talisman Dr 29841
Tamarack Dr 29841
Tanager Rd 29841
Tanglewood Dr 29841
Tarleton Ct 29842
E Tavelle Ln 29842
Tavelle Plantation Dr 29842
Taylor Pond Rd 29860
Teal Ct 29841
Teapot Rd 29842
Teresa Ave 29841
Terrace Cir & Rd 29841
The Ledges 29841
Thistle Ct 29860
Thomas Rd 29842
Thomas Grove Ct 29842
Thomas Park Rd 29841
Thompson Ave 29841
Thornwood Dr 29860
Thurmond St & Way 29841
Tiger Lily Cir 29841
Tillman Ct 29860
Timberbrook Pl 29842
Timberidge Dr 29860
Timothy Crossing Ct 29860
Todd Ave 29841
Todds Landing Dr 29842
Tonya Dr 29842
Toole Cir 29842
Toole Plantation Rd 29842
Toronto Rd 29841
Torry Ave 29841
Tower Lndg 29842
Towhee Ave 29841
Townes Rd 29860
Townsend St 29842
Tracey Dr 29860
Trail Of Sand Ln 29842
Trailside Dr 29860
Tranquility Creek Dr 29841
Trimmier Pl 29841
Tulip Dr 29841
Turabi Ln 29842
Turkey Ridge Ct 29860
Turner St 29842
Twiggs Cir 29841
Twiggs Family Ln 29860
Twin Forks Dr 29860
Twin Hills Rd 29860
Twin Oaks Dr 29860
Twisted Needle Ct 29841
Two Oaks Rd 29842
Tyler Ave 29841
Urquhart Dr & Rd 29842
Van Rd 29860
Vancouver Rd 29841
Vankerkhoff Pl 29841
Velvet Ct 29842
Verdery Dr 29841
Vernon St 29842
Vet Ln 29860
Victoria Dr & Ln 29841
Vidot Ct 29841
View Pointe Ct 29841
Village Pkwy 29841
Vireo Dr 29841
Vixen Ln 29842
Waccamaw Dr 29841
Walker Ave 29841
Walking Horse Cir 29860
Wall St 29842
Walnut Ct & Ln 29860
Wando Dr 29841
Wapoo Dr 29841
Ware Dr 29841
Warren Ct 29860
Washington Ave 29842
Water Lilly Ln 29841
Water Oak Ct 29841
Waterford Ct 29860
Waters Rd 29842
Webbs Park Dr 29841
Webley St 29841
Weller Ln 29860
Wellington Rd 29841
Wells Rd 29841
Wesley Dr 29842
West Ave, Dr & Ter 29841
Westobou Xing 29841
Weston St 29841
Westshire Pl 29841
Westwood Ct 29860
Wetland Way 29841
Whatley Dr 29841
Whiskey Rd 29860
Whispering Woods Dr 29860
White Oak Dr 29860
White Pine Ct & Dr 29841
Whitebark Ave 29841
Whitehall Rd 29841
Whitewood Way 29860
Whitlaws Rd 29841
Whitney Ct 29860
Whitt Ct 29841

Wilde Dr 29841
Wilderness Trl 29860
Wildmeade Ct 29841
Wildwood Dr 29841
Williams Way 29842
Willingham Dr 29842
Williston Rd 29842
Willow Ln & Run 29841
Willow Springs Dr 29841
Wilson Park Dr 29841
Winburn St 29841
Wind Rd 29860
Windsor Dr 29842
Windy Mill Ct & Dr 29841
Wineberry Ln 29841
Winnipeg Rd 29841
Winterberry Way 29860
Winterbrook Pl 29842
Winyah Dr 29841
Wise Dr 29842
Woldus Rd 29841
Womrath Ct & Rd 29841
Wood Dr 29860
Woodberry Ln E & W 29841
Woodcrest Dr, Pl & Way 29842
Woodland Dr 29841
E & W Woodlawn Ave, Ct & Ln 29841
Woodspring Ct 29860
Woodstone Way 29860
Woodvine Dr 29860
Wren Rd 29841
Yardley Dr 29841
Yaun Cir & Rd 29841
Yellow Wood Ct 29860
Yonder Way 29842
Yucca Ave 29860
Zenith Dr 29842

NUMBERED STREETS

All Street Addresses 29841

NORTH CHARLESTON SC

POST OFFICE BOXES MAIN OFFICE STATIONS AND BRANCHES

Box No.s
29419 - 29419 29419
40001 - 42876 29423
60001 - 63554 29419
70001 - 73360 29415
118000 - 119001 29423
150008 - 150021 29415
190005 - 190029 29419
237075 - 239998 29423
2940504 - 2941598 29415
2941905 - 2941905 29419

NAMED STREETS

A Ave 29406
Aamco Way 29406
Abby Dr 29418
Aberdeen Ave 29405
Abraham Ave 29405
Accabee Rd 29405
E & W Ada Ave 29405
Adair St 29405
Addykay Pl 29406
Admiral Dr 29405
Adonis Ave 29405
Aichele Dr 29406
Aintree Ave 29405
Air Cargo Ln 29418
Air Park Rd 29406
Airframe Dr 29418
Alabama Dr 29405
Alamo St 29405
Albert St 29418
Aldrich Ave 29406
Alexandria Dr 29420
Alexis Ct 29406
Alfonzo Cir 29406
Algonquin Rd 29405
All St 29418
S Allen Dr 29405
Allwood Ave 29418
Alpha St 29405
Alston Ave 29406
Altamaha Dr 29420
Altec Rd 29406
Althea Ave 29406
Alvie St 29418
Amaker St 29405
Amberlake Dr 29418
Amberwood Ln 29418
Amboy Ave 29406
N American St 29418
Amsterdam St 29418
Anadale Ct 29418
Andreas Way 29418
Andrews St 29418
Angel Ct 29420
Ann St 29418
Annette St 29406
Ansley Trl 29418
Anthony St 29405
Apache St 29405
N & S Apaloosa Ct 29420
Apartment Blvd 29418
Apollo Ct 29420
Appian Way 29420
Apple St 29405
Appleton Ave 29405
Appletree Ave 29418
April Ave 29406
April Pine Cir 29406
Aragon Ave & St 29405
Arant St 29405
Arapahoe St 29405
Arbor Glen Dr 29420
Arbutus Ave 29405
Archdale Blvd 29418
N Arco Ln 29418
Arthur Hills Cir 29420
Ashburne Ct 29418
Ashby Ave 29405
Ashcroft Ave 29405
Ashepoo Ln 29405
Ashley Phosphate Rd
2000-2499 29406
2500-5299 29418
Ashley Shores Dr 29405
Ashley View Ln 29405
Aspen Woods Ln 29420
Assembly St 29406
Associate Dr 29418
Aster St 29405
Athens Way 29420
Atkins St 29405
Atlanta St 29418
N Atlantic Ave 29405
Atlas St 29405
Aurora Dr 29420
Austin Ave & St 29405
Avenue B 29405
Avenue C N 29405
Avenue D 29405
Avenue F 29405
Avenue G 29405
Avenue H 29405
Avery Ave 29405
S & W Aviation Ave & Rd 29406
Azalea Dr 29405
Azalea Trail Dr 29405
Azaline Dr 29406
B Ave 29406
Bailey Dr 29405
Bainbridge Ave 29405
Baker Ave 29405
Baker Dr 29406
Baker Hospital Blvd 29405
Bakers Landing Dr 29418
Balmoral Ct 29418
Baltimore Pl 29418
Bamberg Ave 29405
Banco Rd 29418
Bankshire Trl 29420
Banyan St 29405
Barclay Ave 29418
Barnsley Dr 29420
Barnwell Ave 29405
Barony Park Cir 29405
Barracks Rd 29405
Barwick Rd 29418
Bassey Ct 29420
Battery Range 29420
Battle Forest Dr 29420
Battleview Ct 29420
Baxter St 29405
Bay Tree Ln 29418
Bayboro Ln 29420
Bayfield Dr 29418
Baylor Ave 29405
Beacon St 29405
Beaufort Ave 29405
Beaver St 29405
Becker St 29405
Beckton St 29420
Beech Ave 29405
Belford Ct 29420
Belle Oaks Dr 29405
Belling Rath Ct 29420
Belmont Ct 29406
Benchley Ct 29420
Benedict Ave 29418
Bengal Rd 29406
Bennett Yard Rd 29405
Bennington Pl 29420
Bent Creek Dr 29420
Bentwood Dr 29406
Berckman Rd 29405
Berda St 29405
Beret St 29418
Berkers Ct E & W 29420
Bernay Ct 29420
Berringer Blf 29418
Best Friend Rd 29418
Bethany St 29405
Betty Ct 29418
Bexley St 29405
Bideford Ct 29420
Biedler St 29418
Bienville Rd 29406
Big Ben Ct 29418
Bindon Cir 29418
Birch St 29405
Bird St 29405
Birdie Garrett St 29405
Birnam Ct 29420
Bishop Green Ln 29420
Bismarck Ct 29420
Bixby Ln 29405
Blacksmith Ct 29420
Blackstone Ct 29406
Blackwell Ave 29406
Blakeford Ct 29420
Blanton St 29405
Blue Ridge Trl 29418
E & W Bluegrass Dr 29420
Bluffwood Ave 29405
Blufton Ct 29418
N Boland Cir 29406
Bon Aire Blvd 29418
Bonaparte Dr 29418
Bonds Ave 29405
Bonds Wilson Dr 29405
Bonnecrest Ln 29420
Bonnie Marie Way 29405
Booker St 29405
Boots Ave 29406
Bordeaux Ct 29406
Bordelon Ave 29405
Borie St 29405
Botany Bay Blvd & Ct 29418
Boulevard Ln 29405
Bowen St 29418
Boxwood Ave 29405
Boykin Dr 29420
Braddock Ave 29405
Brairess Ave 29405
Bramble Ave 29406
Branch Ave 29406
Brandt St 29406
Brandywine Rd 29420
Brantford St 29418
Braswell St 29405
Bream Rd 29418
Breeders Cup Dr 29420
Briarstone Ct 29418
Bridge View Dr 29405
Bridle Path 29420
Brigham Ct 29406
Britain Ct 29418
Britton Ln 29418
Broadmarsh Ct 29418
Broadmoore Pl 29420
Brookdale Blvd 29418
Brookland Blvd 29418
Brookside Dr 29405
Brossy Cir 29418
Bryhawke Cir 29418
Buchanan St 29405
Buck Creek Ct 29420
Buck Pond Rd 29418
Buckfield Dr 29406
Budds Ave 29405
Buffalo St 29418
Buist Ave 29405
Burkeshire Ct 29420
Burnt Creek Ct 29420
Burton Ln 29405
Busch Ave 29405
Business Cir 29418
Buskirk Ave 29406
Butler St 29406
Button St 29418
Buttonwood Ct 29420
C B Ln 29405
Cadence Ct 29420
Cainwood Rd 29420
Callaway Ct 29420
Calvert St 29405
Calvin St 29418
Cambridge Ave 29405
Camden St 29405
Camp Gregg Ln 29418
Canary Ct 29420
Cancha Ln 29405
Cannondale Dr 29420
Cantwell St 29405
Capital Ct 29418
Captain Ave 29405
Cardinal Cir 29405
Cardinal Crest Blf 29418
Carlton St 29405
Carner Ave 29405
N Carolina Ave 29405
Carpentaria Ct 29420
Carver Ave 29405
Cashiers Ln 29405
Caspiana Ln 29420
Cassey St 29420
Castleberry Ct 29418
Casway Ln 29405
Cattells Blf 29420
Cedar Grove Dr 29420
Cedars Pkwy 29420
Cedarwood Rd 29406
Celestial Ct 29406
Celtic Dr & St 29405
N Center St 29406
Centre Pointe Dr 29418
Chaffee St 29405
Chamblee Ct 29420
Champion Way 29418
Chantilly Ln 29418
Charlene Dr 29405
Charleywood Lndg 29420
Charter Dr 29406
Chartwell Dr 29420
Chateau Ave 29405
Chatham Ave 29406
Chatsworth Ct 29406
Cheatham Dr 29418
Cherokee St 29405
Cherry Hill Ln 29405
Cherrywood Dr 29418
Cheryle Ln 29405
Chesterfield Rd 29405
Chestnut St 29405
Cheviot Dr 29418
Cheyenne St 29405
Chicopee Dr 29420
Chicora Ave 29405
Chicory Ln 29420
Childs Cove Cir 29418
Chimney Springs Ct 29420
Chippendale Rd 29420
Chitwood Dr 29405
Christiee Ct 29418
Christopher St 29405
Churchill Rd 29405
Churchill Downs 29420
Cider Ct 29420
Cindy Ln 29418
Cislo Ct 29406
City Hall Ln 29406
Clairmont Ln 29420
Clarkin Ave 29405
Clearbrook St 29405
Clearview Dr 29420
Clement Ave 29405
Clinton St 29405
Club Course Dr 29420
Clydesdale Ct 29420
Cobalt Ct 29418
Cochise St 29405
Cody St 29405
Cofer St 29405
Coldspring Dr 29406
Colie Morse Ln 29405
Coliseum Dr 29418
Colleton St 29405
Colonial Chatsworth Cir 29418
Columbia Ave 29405
Commanche St 29405
Command St 29406
Commander Rd 29405
Commissary St 29405
Comstock Ave 29405
E, N, S & W Constellation Dr 29418
Constitution Ave 29405
Continental Ct 29420
Converse St 29405
Conway St 29405
Coosaw Creek Blvd 29420
Copper Trce 29418
Coppergrove Dr 29420
Corabell Ave 29405
Coras Ct 29406
Corder St 29405
Cordial Aly 29405
Core Ave 29406
Corley Dr 29418
Cornwell Ave 29405
Corona St 29405
Corporate Rd 29405
Cortez St 29405
Cosgrove Ave 29405
Cosgrove Avenue Ext 29405
Cosmopolitan St 29405
Cotillion Dr 29405
Courtwood Rd 29406
Courtyard Sq 29405
Coventry Ct 29420
Covington Dr 29418
Craig Rd 29406
Crawford St 29405
Credit Union Ln 29406
Creighton St 29405
Creola Rd 29420
Crestline Dr 29405
Cricket Ct 29418
Crosby Ave 29405
Crosland Ct E & W 29420
Cross County Rd
7000-7076 29418
7075-7075 29423
7078-7498 29418
7101-7499 29418
Cross Park Dr 29418
Crossgate Blvd 29420
Crossroads Dr 29406
Crown Ave 29406
Cumbahee Ct 29418
Cumberland Way 29420
Cunnington Ave 29405
Curtisston Ct 29418
Cypress Grove Dr 29420
Dakota St 29406
Dale St 29405
Dalton Ave 29420
Dame Ct 29405
Dandelion Ave 29418
Darius Rucker Blvd 29418
Darlene St 29405
Date Palm Dr 29418
Dayton St 29405
Deacon St 29406
Dearborne Rd 29406
Deas Hill Ln 29405
Debonair St 29405
Decatur St 29405
Dee St 29418
Deep Blue Ln 29418
Deer Ridge Ln 29406
Deerwood Dr 29406
Deidrich St 29418
Delancey Cir 29406
Delano St 29405
Delaware Ave 29405
Delhi Rd 29406
Dellwood Ave 29405
Deloach St 29406
Delsey St 29405
Delta St 29406
Dempsey St 29406
Denham St 29420
Deryl St 29406
Design St 29418
Desmond Ave 29418
Desoto Dr 29420
Dewsbury Ln 29418
Dillinger Ave 29420
Discher St 29405
Disco Ave 29405
Discovery Rd 29420
Diston Ct 29420
Dobson St 29406
Dodge St 29405
Doe St 29406
Doe Walk Ln 29406
E & W Dolphin St 29405
Domino Ave 29405
Dorchester Ct 29418
Dorchester Rd
2100-4899 29405
4900-8399 29418
8400-9099 29420
Dorchester Manor Blvd 29420
Dorsey Ave 29405
Doscher Ave 29405
Dove Creek Rd 29418
Dover Ct & St 29405
Dover Creek St 29420
Dowling St 29405
Doyle Ave 29405
Draper St 29405
Drayton Ave 29420
Dreamliner Dr 29418
Drifters Way 29420
Drum St 29420
Dry Dock Ave 29405
Dublin Rd 29420
Dundee St 29420
Dundrum St 29418
Durant Ave 29405
Dutch Ct 29420
Dutton Ave 29406
Dwight Dr 29420
Dyemakers Rdg 29418
Dyess Ave 29405
Eagle Dr 29406
Eagle Lake Rd 29418
Eastbury Ct 29420
Easton St 29405
Eastway St 29418
Easy St 29406
Eberly Ave 29420
Ebony Ct 29420
Echo Ave 29405
Edbillellis Rd 29406
Edge Ave 29405
Edgebrook Cir 29418
Edith St 29418
Eileen St 29418
Elba Dr 29418
Elder Ave 29406
Elderberry Cir 29418
Eleanor Dr 29406
Elegans Dr 29405
Elliott Glen Ct 29418
Elm Springs Rd 29418
Elms Center Rd 29406
Elms Plantation Blvd 29406
Empire Ave 29405
English St 29405
Enterprise Dr 29420
E Enterprise St 29405
W Enterprise St 29405
Ephgenie Sq 29406
Erin Ct 29418
Essex St 29405
Eucalyptus Ave 29418
Eva St 29418
Evangeline Dr 29420
Evanshire Ln 29420
Evanston Blvd 29418
Evatt Ln 29405
Evelyn Dr 29418
Everglades Dr 29405
Excaliber Pl 29418
Expedition Dr 29420
Explorer Dr 29420
Ezekiel Ave 29405
Faber Rd 29405
Faber Place Dr 29405
E & W Fairway Woods Dr 29420
Falcon Rd 29406
Falla Ave 29405
Falling Leaf Ln 29420
Falling Pine Ct 29405
Falling Tide 29420
Fargo St 29418
Farmal St 29405
Fayetteville Rd 29418
Fellowship Rd 29418
Fennell Rd 29418
Fern Pl 29405
Fernland Way 29420
Ferrara Dr 29405
Fetteressa Ave 29418
Fifth St W 29405
Figtree Ave 29418
Fillie Ct 29420
Fillmore St 29405
Firestone Rd 29418
Firetree Ct 29420
Fite St 29405
Flanders Ave 29406
Flintwood Ct 29406
Flora Dr 29406
Florida Ave 29405
Flynn Dr 29405
Forest Ave 29405
N Forest Dr 29420
Forest Hills Dr 29418
Forseman St 29405
Fortune Dr 29418
Four Mile Ln 29405
Four Poles Park Dr 29405
Fowler Dr 29418
Fox Hollow Rd 29420
Foxwood Dr 29418
Fraiser St 29405
France Ave 29405

Franchise St	29418
Frank Mallett Ln	29405
Fretwell St	29406
Fuel Farm Rd	29418
Gabe St	29405
Gaffney St	29405
Gaillard Ln	29405
Gaines Mill Dr	29420
Gale Ave	29406
Gallatin Ln	29420
Gap Rd Blvd	29418
Garfield St	29405
Garland St	29420
Garrett Ave	29406
Gary Dr	29405
Gaslight Aly	29405
Gatewood St	29418
Gaynor Ave	29405
Gilston Ln	29420
Ginger Ln	29420
Glenford Rd	29406
Glenhaven Shores Dr	29420
Glenn St	29405
Glenshaw St	29405
Glouster St	29420
Goer Dr	29406
Goldberg Ave	29405
Goldenrod St	29405
Good St	29406
Goodiron Way	29418
Goodman St	29405
Gordon St	29405
Governors Walk	29418
Gracefield Ct	29420
Grassy Oak Trl	29420
Gravely Ave	29405
Grayson St	29405
Great Oak Dr	29418
Great River Dr	29418
Greenleaf Ct	29420
Greenleaf Rd	29405
Greenridge Rd	29406
Greggs Lndg	29420
Grimke St	29405
Groveland Ave	29405
Gullah Ave	29405
Gumm St	29405
Gumwood Blvd	29406
Gwinnett St	29418
Hackemann Ave	29405
Hackney Ct	29406
Hadley Ct	29406
Hainsworth Dr	29418
Halifax Way	29420
Halsey St	29405
Hampton Ave	29405
Hanford Mills Ln	29406
Hanniford Dr	29418
Hansard Dr	29406
Hardy Ave	29406
Harley St	29406
Harmon St	29405
Harris Mill Dr	29420
Hartford Cir	29405
Harvey Ave	29405
Hassell Ave	29405
Hatfield Ave	29405
Haverhill Cir	29420
Hawthorne Dr	29406
Hayter St	29405
Haywood St	29418
Headquarters Rd	29405
Heatherglen Ct	29420
Hedgewood St	29405
Helene Dr	29418
Helm Ave	29405
Henry St	29405
Herbert St	29405
Herons Walk	29420
Hickman St	29405
Hickory Creek Ct	29420
Hidden Bakers Trce	29418
Hidden Forest Ln	29420
High Maple Cir	29418
Highgate Ct	29418
Highland Ridge Ct	29420
Highland Terrace Dr	29406
Highpoint Dr	29406
Highpoint Rd	29405
Hilda St	29405
Hill Park Dr	29418
Hillandale Rd	29420
Hillcrest Dr	29405
Hillock Ave	29418
Hillview Ln	29420
Hillyard St	29405
Hobby St	29405
Hobson Ave	29405
Hock Ave	29405
Holbird Dr	29405
Holden St	29418
Holland St	29405
Hollow Ct	29406
Holly Knls	29420
Holly St	29405
Holmes Ave	29405
Honeysuckle Lake Dr	29420
Hope Cir	29405
Horsemint Trl	29420
Hotel Rd	29418
Hottinger Ave	29405
Houston St	29405
Hubbard St	29405
Hugo Ave	29405
Hull St	29405
Hunley Waters Cir	29405
Huntclife Ct	29418
Hunter St	29405
Hunters Ridge Ln	29420
Hyannis Ct	29420
Hyde Ave	29405
Hyde Park Village Ln	29405
Independent Ave	29405
Indian Summer Dr	29406
Indica Ct	29418
Indigo Commons Way	29418
Indigo Fields Blvd	29418
Indigo Makers Trce	29418
Indigo Ridge Dr	29420
Industrial Ave	29405
Industry Dr	29418
Intercept St	29406
International Blvd	29418
Investment Dr	29418
Ireland Dr	29420
Iris St	29405
Iron Rod Ct	29406
Ironwood Trl	29418
Iroquois St	29405
Irving Ave	29405
Isle Cir	29418
Ivory Ave	29405
Ivydale Dr	29405
Jackson Mill Ln	29420
Jacksonville Rd	29405
Jadewood Dr	29418
James Bell Dr	29406
Jasons Cv	29418
Jean Rebault Dr	29420
Jedi St	29406
Jeff St	29405
Jenkins Ave	29405
Jenys Ct	29420
Jeremiah Ct	29418
Jericho Ct	29418
Jerome Ct	29406
Jessen Ave	29406
Jillanda Dr	29418
N & W Jimtown Dr	29405
Jockey Ct	29405
John Cabot Dr	29420
Johnson Ln	29405
Jonah St	29406
Joppa Ave	29405
Junction Ln	29405
June St	29405
Juneau Ave	29405
Jury Ln	29406
Justice St	29405
Kamberley Ct	29420
Kamborne Ct	29420
Karen Dr	29405
Kay St	29418
Keever St	29405
Kellum Dr	29420
Kelly St	29405
Kennestone Ln	29420
Kent Ave	29405
Kephart St	29405
Kershaw St	29405
Key Thatch Ct	29420
Kilo St	29405
King Indigo Ct	29418
King Street Ext	29405
Kingfisher Ave	29405
Kings Grant Ln	29420
Kings River Dr	29420
Kingsworth Ave	29405
Kinston St	29418
Kinzer St	29405
Kirk Patrick Ln	29418
Kirkwood Ave	29406
Kirshtein St	29418
Kite Ave	29405
Kittery Ave	29420
Knightsbridge Dr	29418
Knollwood Dr	29418
Kraft Ave	29405
La Quinta Ln	29420
Lachapelle Bnd	29418
Lackawanna Blvd	29405
Lacy St	29406
Lady St	29420
Lafayette Ct	29406
Lake Dr	29405
Lake Palmetto Ln	29418
Lake Park Dr	29406
E Lakeland Dr	29406
Lakewood Dr	29406
Lambert St	29405
Lambs Rd	29418
Lancaster St	29405
Lancelot Hall	29418
Landerwood Ct	29420
Landing Pkwy	29420
Landmark Dr	29418
Lang Ridge Dr	29405
Langley St	29405
Langston Park	29420
Langston St	29406
Lansbury Ct	29420
Larchmont Dr	29418
Launa St	29405
Lauradell Ave	29406
Laurel Grove Ln	29420
Laurel Ridge Rd	29418
Lavender Ln	29420
Lawrence St	29405
Lawyers Ln	29418
Layton Ct	29420
Lear Ave	29418
Leary St	29406
Least Tern Ln	29405
Leath Ct	29406
Lee St	29418
Leeds Ave & Pl W	29405
Leesville St	29405
Lela Dr	29418
Leland St	29405
Lenape St	29405
Leola St	29405
Leslie St	29418
Lester St	29405
Leventis St	29405
Lewisfield Dr	29418
Lexington Ave	29405
E & W Liberty Park Cir	29405
Lilac Ave & St	29405
Lincoln Ave	
1-199	29418
1000-1099	29405
Lincoln Blvd	
8200-8399	29418
8500-8598	29420
Linda St	29405
Lindenwood Cir	29420
Lindler Dr	29420
Lindo Ter	29418
Linfield Ln	29418
Links Ct	29420
Linsley Dr	29418
Lisa St	29406
Little Ave	29405
Livonia Cv	29420
Lockerly Ct	29420
Lockhart St	29405
Loggers Run	29420
Londonderry Rd	29420
Long Meadow Dr	29420
Long Shadow Ln	29406
Longleaf Ave	29406
Longridge Rd	29418
Loop Rd	29406
Lorraine Dr	29406
Louis St	29405
Louise Dr	29405
Lowell Dr	29418
Lucille Dr	29406
Luella Ave	29405
Lumberton Rd	29418
Lupine St	29405
Lyall Ct	29406
Lynn Haven Ln	29420
Lysa Ave	29405
Mabeline Rd	29406
Machinist St	29405
Macon Ave	29405
Madden Dr	29405
Madonna St	29405
Magellan Dr	29420
Magnolia Ct	29420
Magpie Ave	29405
Majestic St	29420
Makana St	29405
Malden Ave	29420
Mall Dr	29406
Mangrove Dr	29418
Manley Ave	29405
Mansfield Blvd	29418
Marathon Ct	29418
Marblehead Ln	29405
Margaret Dr	29406
Margle Way	29420
Marie St	29406
Marigold St	29405
Marilyn Dr	29418
Marine Ave	29405
Mark St	29405
Marlboro Pl & Rd	29405
Marquis Rd	29405
Marseilles Dr	29418
Marsh Hall Dr	29418
Marsh Overlook	29420
Marsia Ln	29405
Martha Dr	29405
Matipan Ave	29405
Maxwell St	29405
Mccandy Ln	29420
Mccarthy St	29405
Mcchune Ct	29420
Mccormack Ave	29420
Mccrady St	29405
Mcdowell Ave	29405
Mckeever Ave	29405
Mcknight St	29418
Mcmillan Ave	
1101-1197	29405
1199-1700	29405
1702-2198	29405
2180-2180	29415
Mcneil St	29405
Mcritchie Ave	29405
Mcroy St	29418
Meadow Ave	29406
Meadowbrook Ct	29420
Mechanic St	29405
Medcom St	29406
Meeting Street Rd	29405
Melanie Ct	29418
Melbourne St	29405
Mendelwood Dr	29418
Mercia Ln	29418
Meridian Rd	29405
Merrimac St	29405
Michigan Ave	29418
Middle River Way	29420
Midwood Dr	29420
Milford St	29405
Mill Rd	29406
Mill Creek Dr	29420
Mill Ridge Ln	29418
Millerville Dr	29420
Millstone Dr	29420
Mimosa St	29405
Minor St	29406
Mint Ave & St	29405
Misroon St	29405
Miss King St	29405
Misty Oak Ct	29420
Mixson Ave	29405
Mole Ln	29406
Monitor St	29405
Monrovia St	29405
E Montague Ave	29405
W Montague Ave	29418
Monterey St	29405
Montview Rd	29418
Morgan Ave	29406
Morningside Dr	29405
Morris Baker Blvd	29406
Moss Ct	
4600-4699	29420
6700-6799	29418
Mosstree Rd	29405
Mott Ave	29405
Moultrie Ln	29418
Mountainbrook Ave	29420
Mulberry Ct	29418
Nantuckett Ave	29420
Napoleon Dr	29418
Natures Color Ln	29418
Navajo St	29405
Navy Way	29405
Nazarene St	29406
Necessary Ln	29405
Nellview Dr	29418
Nelson St	29418
Neomi St	29405
Nesbit Ave	29405
Nesting Pl	29420
Netherby Rd	29420
New St	29405
New England Ct & Dr	29420
New Ryder Rd	29406
Newmans Aly	29405
Newport Pl	29420
Niagara St	29405
Nibbs Ln	29418
Nightingale Mnr	29418
Nightingale Rd	29405
Noisette Blvd	29405
Norden St	29418
North Blvd	29405
Northhaven Dr	29420
Northside Dr	29420
Northtree Ln	29420
Northwoods Blvd	29406
Norwalk Dr	29420
Norwood St	29405
Nova Ct	29420
Nowell Ave	29406
Nummie Ct	29418
W Oak Grove Rd	29406
Oak Leaf Dr	29420
E Oakridge Cir	29420
N Oakridge Cir	29420
S Oakridge Cir	29420
Oakridge Dr	29418
Oakwood Ave	29405
Obrien St	29405
Oceanic St	29405
Odessa St	29405
Ohear Ave	29405
Old Carriage Ct	29420
Old Dominion Dr	29418
Old Hertz Rd	29418
Old London	29406
Old Park Rd	29405
Old Pine Cir	29405
Old Saybrook Rd	29418
Old School Dr	29405
Old University Blvd	29406
Oldridge Rd	29418
Olivia Dr	29418
Olympia Ave	29405
Orangeburg St	29405
Orchid Ave	29405
Ore St	29418
Oregon Ave	29405
Orr St	29405
Orvid St	29405
Osburn Ave	29420
Oscar Johnson Dr	29405
Osceola St	29405
Ospery St	29405
Ott St	29418
Ottawa Ave	29405
Outlook Dr	29418
Ovaldale Dr	29418
Overbrook Ave	29405
Overland Trl	29420
Ozark St	29418
Pace St	29405
Pacific St	29418
Padgett St	29405
Palm Cir	29418
E Palm View Cir	29418
Palmetto Bluff Dr	29418
Palmetto Commerce Pkwy	29420
Pamela Ln	29405
Pantego Ln	29420
Paragon St	29405
Paramount Dr	29405
Parchment Ave	29418
Park Ct	29418
Park Pl E	29405
Park Pl N	29405
Park Pl S	29405
Park Pl W	29405
Park Forest Pkwy	29418
Park Gate Dr	29418
Parker Dr	29405
Parklane Ct	29418
Parkshire Way	29418
Parkside Dr	29405
Parliament Dr	29418
Partridge Ave	29405
Pastor Ave	29406
Patricia St	29418
Patriot Blvd	
8300-8399	29418
8400-8599	29420
Paulson St	29406
Peace St	29405
Peacock Ave	29405
Pearly Ln	29405
Pearson St	29405
Peggy Dr	29418
Pennsylvania Ave	29406
Penobscott Dr	29420
Penshire Ct	29418
Peonie Ave	29405
Peppercorn Ln	29420
Pepperdam Ave	29418
Peppermill Ln & Pkwy	29418
Peppertree Ln	29420
Percival Ln	29420
Pershing St	29405
Persimmon Ave	29418
Persimmon Woods Dr	29420
Pheasant Run Dr	29420
Phyllis St	29405
Picardy Pl	29420
Pierside St	29405
Piggly Wiggly Dr	29405
Pine Field Ct	29405
Pine Forest Dr	29405
Pine Grove Dr	29405
Pine Ridge Cir	29405
Pine Run Ct	29405
Pine Walk Ct	29405
Pinehaven Dr	29405
Pinehurst St	29420
Pinetree Ln	29405
Pinoca Ln	29420
Pipefitter St	29405
Pirate St	29405
Pittman St	29405
Pittsburgh Ave	29405
Plantation Rd	29420
Planters Knls	29420
Plate St	29405
Plaza Ln	29420
Pleasant Ridge Dr	29420
Pledge St	29405
Plum St	29405
Plumbranch Ave	29418
Pocasset Cir	29420
Poindexter Rd	29420
Polar Dr	29405
Pollock St	29405
Polo Pt	29418
Pomfret St	29418
Poole St	29405
Poor Valley Rd	29405
Poplar Ln	29405
Poplin Ave	29405
Popperdam Creek Dr	29418
Porsche Blvd	29418
N Port Dr	29405
Porter Dr	29420
Post St	29405
Potomac St	29405
Power Dr	29418
Preakness Dr	29420
Preston Ave	29420
Prestwick Ct	29406
Primrose Ave	29405
Prince St	29406
Princeton St	29405
Pringle St	29405
Priscilla St	29405
Proctor St	29405
Professional Dr	29420
Prosperity Ln	29405
Proteus St	29405
Pryor St	29406
Purcell Dr	29418
Purdue Dr	29418
Quail Hollow Ct	29420
Quarter Horse Rd	29420
Quest Dr	29418
Quintin Grant Ln	29405
Quitman St	29405
Racquet Rd	29418
Radar Ave	29406
Rae St	29418
Ramsey St	29405
Ramsgate Rd	29406
Randall Ct	29420
Ranger Dr	29405
Raven Ave	29405
Read St	29406
Rebecca St	29406
Red Birch Cir	29418
Red Fork Ln	29420
Red Tip Ln	29420
Reddin Rd	29405
Redland Ave	29405
Redwood St	29405
Ree St	29418
Refuge Point Cir	29420
Register St	29405
Remington Dr	29418
Remount Rd	29406
Renee Dr	29418
Renneau Ave	29406
Rental Car Ln	29418
Rentz St	29418
Renwick Ave	29420
Rescue Rd	29405
Rex Ave	29405
Rexton St	29405
Reynolds Ave	29405
N Rhett Ave	
4800-5199	29405
5400-5699	29406
S Rhett Ave	29405
Rhett Park Dr	29405
Rice Ave	29405

Rice Basket Ln 29420
Rice Mill Dr 29420
Rich St 29405
Richardson Dr 29406
Richfield Dr 29418
Rickett Ave 29406
Rickey St 29405
Rickles St 29418
Ridgebrook Dr 29418
N Ridgebrook Dr 29420
Ridgeland Dr 29405
Ridgeway St 29405
Rising Tide 29420
River Bluff Pkwy 29420
River Chase Ct 29418
River Island Ct 29420
River Oak Ln 29418
River Oaks Dr 29420
River Run Ct 29420
Riverbirch Ln 29418
Rivers Ave
2800-4799 29405
4800-6400 29406
6401-8899 29406
6401-6401 29419
6402-8898 29406
Riverview Ave 29405
Riverwalk Dr 29405
Robertson Blvd 29406
Rock St 29420
Rock Creek Ct 29420
Rockingham St 29406
Rocky Mount Rd 29406
Roe St 29405
Rolling Fork Rd 29406
Rollins Ct 29406
Roosevelt St 29405
Rosin Dr 29418
Ross St 29418
Rosser Dr 29420
Rourk St 29405
Rowan Dr 29405
Rowsham Pl 29418
Roxboro Rd 29418
Roxbury Dr 29418
Royal Palm Ln 29420
Ruff Rd 29418
Rugheimer Ave 29405
Rumsey St 29405
Runnymeade Ln 29406
Ruskin Rd 29418
Russelldale Ave 29406
Ruth Dr 29406
Ryans Bluff Rd 29418
Sabal St 29406
Sabalridge Dr 29418
Saddle Creek Ct 29420
E & W Saddlebrook Dr 29420
Sage Borough Dr 29420
Sageborough Dr 29420
Saint Angela Dr 29418
Saint Francis St 29405
Saint Johns Ave 29405
Salamander Rd 29406
Salt Pointe Pkwy 29405
Salter Ln 29405
Saluda St 29405
Sanders Ave 29405
Sandida Ct 29418
Sandlapper Pkwy 29420
Sandy Run 29418
Sandy St 29405
Saranac St 29405
Saratoga Ct 29420
Saratoga Rd 29405
Sardis Ct 29406
Saul White Blvd 29418
Sawgrass Dr 29420
Sawmill Trace Ln 29420
Sawpit Gap 29418
Saxon Ave 29406
Scarpa St 29405
Scarsdale Dr 29418
Scott St 29405
Scottish Troon Ct 29420
Scotts Mill Dr 29420
Scottswood Dr 29418
Scottswood Drive Ext 29418
Sea Ray Dr 29405
Sea Watch Ln 29406
Sebastian Ct 29405
See Port Dr 29406
Seiberling Rd 29418
Selma St 29420
Senegal Ct 29420
Sentry Cir 29420
Sewanee Rd 29405
Seymour Ave 29405
Shadowcreek Ct 29406
Shadowglen Dr 29420
Shagbark Trl 29418
Shahid Row 29418
Shawnee St 29405
Shelton St 29406
Shentat Dr 29420
Sherbrooke Ln 29418
Sherwood St 29405
Shipbuilding Way 29405
Shipyard Creek Rd 29405
E, N, S & W Shirley Dr 29418
Short Aly 29405
Sierra Ct 29418
Signal Island Dr 29420
Silver St 29405
Silver Creek Ln 29420
Simms Ave 29405
Singley St 29405
Sinkler Ct 29418
Skillmaster Ct 29418
Slarrow St 29405
Smalls St 29405
Smoketree Ct 29420
Smokey St 29418
Snipe St 29405
Social Aly 29405
Sorentrue Ave 29405
Sorrell Ave 29406
South Blvd 29405
Southern St 29406
Southern Grove Ct 29406
Southrail Rd 29420
Southside Dr 29418
Spa Rd 29418
Spaniel Dr 29405
Spartan Blvd E 29418
Spartan Blvd N 29420
Spartan Blvd W 29418
Spaulding Dr 29406
Speissegger Dr 29405
N & S Split Oak 29420
Spring Branch Ct 29406
Spring Chapel Ln 29420
Spring Creek Rd 29418
Spring Farm Gate Cir 29418
Spruce Blvd 29406
Spruce St 29405
Spruill Ave 29405
Spur St 29405
Stanton Ct 29418
Stark Ln 29405
Starlett Ave 29420
Stelling Ave 29420
Sterrett St 29405
Stewart Ave 29406
Stith Ave 29405
Stokes Ave 29406
Stone Mill Ct 29420
Stone Pine Ct 29405
Stonebridge Dr 29420
Stonehaven Dr 29420
Stoney Poynt Ct 29405
Stonybrook Rd 29420
Storie St 29406
Stratton Dr 29420
Stromboli Ave & Ln 29405
Strong St 29405
Success St 29405
Sue St 29406
Suffolk St 29405
Summerfield Ct 29420
Summerville Ave 29405
Summey St 29405
Sumner Ave 29406
Sumters Run 29418
Sundial Ct 29418
Sunny Ln 29405
Sunrise Rd 29418
Sunrise St 29405
Superior St 29405
Supply St 29405
Suribachi Ave 29405
Surprise St 29405
E Surrey Dr 29405
Sutton Pl 29420
Suzanne Dr 29418
Sweet Gum Xing 29420
Sylvia St 29406
S T Simmons Dr 29405
Taft St 29405
Talisman St 29405
Talluah Rd 29405
Tanger Outlet Blvd 29418
Tanglewood Dr 29418
Tank Farm Loop 29405
Tant St 29405
Target St 29406
Taylor St 29406
Taylor Plantation Rd 29420
Tedder St 29420
Tee St 29418
Tellico Rd 29405
Temple St 29405
Terry Dr 29405
Thelen St 29406
Thomasina Mcpherson Blvd 29405
Thomasville Rd 29418
Thompson Ave 29405
Thompson St 29406
Thornback St 29405
Thornlee Dr 29405
Thoroughbred Dr 29420
Three Lakes Rd 29418
Tidewater Dr 29420
Tile Dr 29405
Tillman St 29405
Tim St 29405
Timbercreek Ln 29418
Timberidge Ct 29420
Timberline Trl 29418
Timbermarsh Ln 29420
Tipson St 29406
Token St 29405
Tolbert Way 29420
Torgerson Ave 29406
Trade St 29418
Trailside Ct 29418
Trailwood Dr 29418
Transfer St 29405
Transportation Ln 29405
Trescott St 29405
Trevor St 29420
Tricom St 29406
Tricorn Ct 29420
Tropicana Rd 29406
Troy St 29405
Trudy St 29418
Truman Ave 29405
Trump St 29420
Truxtun Ave 29405
Tulip St 29405
Turgis Ct 29420
Turnbull Ave 29405
Turner St 29406
Turning Tide 29420
Tuscany Dr 29406
Tuskegee Dr 29418
Tuxbury Ln 29405
Twiggs St 29405
Twisted Antler Dr 29406
Twitty St 29406
Tyler St 29406
Tyrian Path 29418
Ubank St 29405
University Blvd 29406
University Dr 29418
Upham St 29405
Upjohn Rd 29405
Valleyview Cir 29418
Van Buren Ave 29406
Van Smith Ave 29405
Vanderbrook Pl 29420
Vardell Ln 29420
Varner Ln 29405
Vector Ave 29406
Veneer Ave 29405
Ventura Dr 29405
Verde Ave 29405
Vermont Rd 29418
Vernon Pl 29418
Vesole St 29405
Vestige Ct 29418
Viaduct Rd 29405
Victoria Ave 29405
Victory Ave 29405
Vinewood Pl 29420
Violet Ave 29405
Virginia Ave
4600-4798 29405
4800-5199 29405
5255-5255 29406
5500-5698 29406
Vistavia Rd 29406
Vistiana Way 29420
Wabash St 29405
Wadesboro Rd 29418
Wae St 29418
Wagram Ln 29420
Wakefield Ct 29418
Waldheim St 29418
Wales Ct 29418
Walker Dr 29420
Walker St 29405
Walking Stick Ln 29420
Walnut St 29405
Walsham St 29420
Walton St 29418
Wando Rd 29405
Ward Ave 29406
Warm Ave 29420
Warsaw Rd 29418
Wasp St 29405
Water Ash Way 29420
Waterford Ct 29420
Waterview Cir & Dr 29418
Watkins Rd 29418
Watts St 29418
Waverly Place Cir & Ln 29418
Waxhaw Cir 29420
Wayfield Cir 29418
Weatherbark Cir 29418
Wecco St 29405
Weld St 29418
Wellorad Dr 29418
Wentzel St 29418
N Wesley Ct 29420
Westchester Pl 29418
Westview St 29418
Wetland Xing 29418
Weyhill Ct 29420
Whaley Way 29405
Wharf Landing Ct 29418
Wheaton St 29406
Whipper Barony Ln 29405
Whispering Elms Ct 29406
Whitehaven Dr 29420
Whitney Dr 29405
Whitwil Blvd 29418
Wicker Ct 29418
Wilbur St 29405
Wild Bird Ct 29420
Wild Fern Ct 29420
Wild Indigo Blf 29418
Wild Thicket Ln 29420
Wilderness Trl 29418
Wildwood Lndg 29420
William Moultrie Dr 29420
Williams Ave 29405
Willis Dr 29406
Willow Ct 29420
Willow Ln 29405
Willow Oak Cir 29418
Willoway Cir 29420
Winchester St 29420
Windfern Ct 29418
Windsor Ct 29418
Windsor Hill Blvd 29420
Winona St 29405
Withers Dr 29405
Witsell St 29406
Woodbine Ave 29406
Woodbreeze Dr 29420
Woodcreek Ct 29406
Woodfield Ct 29406
Woodfin Dr 29420
Woodland Walk 29420
Woodlawn Ave 29405
Woodstock Ave 29406
Woodwind Ct 29420
Wren St 29406
Wright Ave 29405
Wright St 29406
Wye Ln 29405
Wyncliff Rd 29418
Wynnefield Dr 29420
Yardley Dr 29405
Yorkshire Ln 29406
Younger Ave 29420

NUMBERED STREETS

N 2nd St 29405
4th St
1101-1299 29405
2500-2599 29406
5th St W 29405
7th St 29405
9th St 29405

NORTH MYRTLE BEACH SC

General Delivery 29597

POST OFFICE BOXES MAIN OFFICE STATIONS AND BRANCHES

Box No.s
1 - 1000 29597
1001 - 2479 29598
3001 - 4000 29582
4001 - 5858 29597
9001 - 9249 29582
10000 - 10005 29597

NAMED STREETS

Acorn Way 29582
Adam Ln 29582
Airport Blvd 29582
Albatross St 29582
Alicia Ct 29582
Allen St 29582
Ameron Ct 29582
Anne St 29582
Appleton Way 29582
Arbor Cir & Ln 29582
Ash St 29582
Ashland Ave 29582
Banyan Pl 29582
Barefoot Resort Dr 29582
Barefoot Resort Bridge Rd 29582
Barnwell St 29582
Baron Ln 29582
Barry St 29582
Basin St 29582
Battery Park Dr 29582
Bay St 29582
Bay Pines Ct 29582
N Beach Blvd 29582
Beach Walker Ln 29582
Beacon Ave 29582
Bellamy Rd 29582
Belle Dr 29582
Belvoir Ct 29582
Bentbill Cir 29582
Bentley Ln 29582
Bentwood Ct 29582
Bert Dr 29582
Beverly Ct 29582
Birchwood St 29582
Birdsong Ct 29582
Blossom St 29582
Blue Ridge Trl 29582
Brantly Ln 29582
Bridge View Ct 29582
Bridgecrest Dr 29582
Bridlewood Rd 29582
Brigantine Rd 29582
Broome Ter 29582
Brown Pelican Ct 29582
Bryan St 29582
Bucks Bluff Dr 29582
Buffkin Rd 29582
Burgee Ct 29582
Burris St 29582
Camp St 29582
Canal St 29582
Cane St 29582
Cantor Ct 29582
Cardinal Cir & Pl 29582
Carolina Cv 29582
Cashmere Ln 29582
Castlewood Ln 29582
Catalina Dr 29582
Causey Dr 29582
Cecelia St 29582
Cedar Ave & Ln 29582
Cenith Dr 29582
Chad St 29582
Channel St 29582
Channel Point Ln 29582
Charles St 29582
Cherry Tree Ln 29582
Chester Rd 29582
Chestnut Rd & St 29582
Church View Ln 29582
Cinzia Ln 29582
Circle Dr 29582
Clipper Rd 29582
Club Course Dr 29582
Club House Dr 29582
E Coast Ln 29582
Colony Dr 29582
Compass Pt 29582
Congtont Ave S 29582
Conway St 29582
Coquina Pointe Dr 29582
Coral Reef Dr 29582
Coral Sand Dr 29582
Cottage Cove Cir 29582
Cottesmoor Ct 29582
Cottonwood Ct 29582
Cox St 29582
Creek Front Rd 29582
Crosswinds Ave 29582
Curlew St 29582
Curley St 29582
Cypress Cv & Ln 29582
Dale St 29582
Dargan St 29582
David St 29582
Dew Ave 29582
Diane Cir 29582
Dogwood Ln & Pl 29582
Dory Ct 29582
Douglas St 29582
Duffy St 29582
Dunes St 29582
Dustin Ln 29582
Eastover Ln 29582
Ebbtide Dr 29582
Edge Dr 29582
Edgewood Ct & St 29582
Edith Ln 29582
Elena Ct 29582
Elicia Ct 29582
Elizabeth St 29582
Elm Ave 29582
Emanon St 29582
Embers Dr 29582
Emu Dr 29582
Enclave Ln 29582
Eyerly St 29582
Falcon Landing Cir 29582
Fern St 29582
Festival Ave 29582
Ffa Circle Rd 29582
Forest Dr 29582
Fox Hollow Way 29582
Foxfire Dr 29582
Foxworth Rd 29582
Frinks Ct 29582
Futch St 29582
Gann Ave 29582
Gardenia Ave 29582
Gayle St 29582
Gazebo Ct 29582
Gilbert Ln 29582
Gleaton St 29582
Golf Academy Way 29582
Golf Course Dr 29582
Golfview Dr 29582
Gray Heron Dr 29582
Greenhaven Dr 29582
Grove Ln 29582
Grovecrest Cir 29582
H C Lewis Ln 29582
Half Moon Ct 29582
Halyard Ct 29582
Handy St 29582
Harbor Dr 29582
Harbor Pointe Dr 29582
Harbourgate 29582
Hardy St 29582
Harmony Ln 29582
Harrelson Ave 29582
Harris Cove Ln 29582
Harrison St 29582
Havens Dr 29582
Havens Lake Dr 29582
Hedrick St 29582
Heidlsway Dr 29582
Hempsted Ct 29582
Heritage Dr 29582
Herndon Ln 29582
Heron St 29582
Herring Gull Cir 29582
Heshbon Dr 29582
Hickory St 29582
Hightide Dr 29582
Highway 17 N 29582
Highway 17 S
1-4100 29582
4009-4009 29598
4101-5099 29582
4102-5098 29582
Hilburn St 29582
Hill St 29582
Hill Top St 29582
Hillside Dr N & S 29582
Hilton Dr 29582
Holloway Cir 29582
Holly Dr & Way 29582
Horne Ave 29582
Hounds Way 29582
Hunter Ave 29582
Hunters Rest Dr 29582
Inland St 29582
Inlet Way 29582
Ironwood Dr 29582
S & E Island Ct, Dr & Loop 29582
Ivory St 29582
Ivy Pl 29582
Jacks Circle Rd 29582
James Island Ave 29582
Janet Ct 29582
Jason St 29582
Jerdon Cir 29582
Johnstone Pl 29582
Jordan Rd 29582

King St 29582
Kingfisher St 29582
L D Dr 29582
E & W Lake Dr, Ln & St 29582
Lake Egret Dr 29582
Lakeland Dr 29582
Landfall Dr 29582
Landing Rd 29582
Laura Ln 29582
Leatherleaf Dr 29582
Lester Ln 29582
Lewis Cir & St 29582
Lighthouse Dr 29582
Little Egret Rd 29582
Little River Neck Rd 29582
Live Oak Cir & Ct 29582
Loblolly Cir 29582
Long Creek Rd 29582
Longbridge Dr 29582
Loreno Dr 29582
Lowe Dr 29582
Lowtide Dr 29582
Lynn Ct 29582
Madiera Dr 29582
Madison Dr 29582
Maggie B Ln 29582
Magnolia Dr 29582
Main St 29582
Mallard St 29582
Mandy Pl 29582
Maple St 29582
Marina Bay Dr 29582
Mariners Rest Dr 29582
Marion Cir 29582
N Market St 29582
Marsh Ct 29582
Marsh Creek Dr 29582
Marsh Glen Dr 29582
Marsh Oaks Dr 29582
Marsh Point Pl 29582
Marthas Way 29582
Martin St 29582
Meris Ln 29582
Merrill Pl 29582
Metts Dr 29582
Moore St 29582
Moorings Way 29582
Morrall Dr 29582
Morris Ave S 29582
Moss St 29582
Mosswood Ct 29582
Mossy Oaks Dr 29582
Mount Vernon Dr 29582
Myrtle Ct 29582
N Myrtle Point Blvd 29582
Natures Way 29582
Newport Dr 29582
Nixon St 29582
Norment St 29582
Norris Ave 29582
Norvell St 29582
Oak Dr N & S 29582
Oak Lake Cir 29582
N & S Ocean Blvd 29582
Ocean Oaks Blvd 29582
Ocean Pines Ct 29582
Ocean Pointe Ct 29582
Old Appleton Way 29582
Old Highway 17 N 29582
Olde Mill Dr 29582
Olde Pine Dr 29582
Ora Ln 29582
Osprey St 29582
Osprey Pointe Ln 29582
Outrigger Rd 29582
Oyster Ln 29582
Oyster Catcher Dr 29582
Painted Tree Ln 29582
Palm St 29582
Palm Bay Dr 29582
Palmer St 29582
Palmetto Harbour Dr 29582
Par Ave 29582
Park St 29582
Parkway Dr 29582
Paul St 29582
Pearlie St 29582
Pelican St 29582
Perrin Dr 29582
Persimmon Ln 29582
Pete Dye Dr 29582
Pheasant Dr 29582
Phyllis St 29582
Pine St 29582
Pine Valley Rd 29582
Pinecrest St 29582
Planters Grove Ln 29582
Plumbridge Ln 29582
Poinsett Rd & St 29582
Pointe Marsh Ln 29582
Poole St 29582
W Port Dr 29582
Possum Trot Rd 29582
Premier Resort Blvd 29582
Prince William Rd 29582
Princess Dr 29582
Princess Anne Rd 29582
Ratoon Ln 29582
Rayford Rd 29582
Rice Cir 29582
Ridge Rd & St 29582
Ridgewood Dr 29582
Riptide Cir 29582
Riverside Dr 29582
Robin Cir 29582
Rock St 29582
Rosemary Ln 29582
Royal Oak Cir 29582
Saint Charles Rd 29582
Salt Creek Ct 29582
Sand Ct 29582
Sand Dollar Ct 29582
Sandcrest Dr 29582
Sanderling Dr 29582
Sandpiper St 29582
Schooner Dr 29582
Sea Horse Ct 29582
Sea Island Way 29582
Sea Mountain Hwy 29582
Sea Vista Ln 29582
Sea Winds Pl 29582
Seabird Ct 29582
Seabrook Ave 29582
Seabrook Plantation Way 29582
Seafarer Way 29582
Seagull Blvd 29582
Seashell Ln 29582
Seaside Dr 29582
Seaview St 29582
Seedling Ct 29582
Seminole Cir 29582
Session Ct 29582
Shadow Moss Pl 29582
Shell Creek Cir 29582
Shelly Ct 29582
Ship Wheel Dr 29582
Shore Dr 29582
Shorehaven Dr 29582
Small St 29582
Smith St 29582
Spartina Ct 29582
Spicewood Ct 29582
Spinetail Dr 29582
Spinnaker Dr 29582
Spoonbill Cir 29582
Spotted Owl Lndg 29582
Spring St 29582
Springland Ln 29582
Stan Ct 29582
Starcrest Cir 29582
Starwatch Dr 29582
Staysail Ln 29582
Stephens St 29582
Stonegate Dr 29582
Stoney Creek Ct 29582
Strand Ave & Cir 29582
Sulley Ave 29582
Summers Pl 29582
Summerwind Ct 29582
Sunset St & Ter 29582
Sunset Harbour Way 29582
Surf Ct & St 29582
Surf Estates Way 29582
Surf Pointe Dr 29582
Surfsong Way 29582
Surfwatch Dr 29582
Swan Lake Dr 29582
Sweetgum Ln 29582
Swift St 29582
Tabby Ln 29582
Tall Grass Dr 29582
Tams Dr 29582
Tanglewood Ave & Cv 29582
Tarpon Pond Rd 29582
Terminal St 29582
Terri Ct 29582
Thick Branch Rd 29582
Thomas Ave 29582
Thrasher Dr 29582
Tidewatch Way 29582
Tidewater Dr 29582
Tiffany Ln 29582
Tilghman Forest Dr 29582
Tillson Rd 29582
Timberidge Trl 29582
Toby Ct 29582
Todd Ln 29582
Tom E Chestnut Rd 29582
Topsail Ln 29582
Tortuga Ln 29582
Toucan Dr 29582
Townsend Rd 29582
Tradewind Ct 29582
Trisail Ln 29582
Turner Ave 29582
Turtle Ct 29582
Twin Oaks Dr 29582
Vereen Dr 29582
Via Palma Dr 29582
Victoria Falls Ln 29582
Villa Dr 29582
Wading Heron Rd 29582
Walnut St 29582
Water Oak Ln 29582
Watermark Ct 29582
Waters Edge Ct 29582
Waterside St 29582
Waterview Dr 29582
Waterway Dr & Loop 29582
Watson Dr 29582
Wave Rider Ln 29582
Wax Myrtle Ct 29582
Wayne St 29582
Weatherwood Dr 29582
Wedgewood Ct 29582
Whispering Cv 29582
Whistling Duck Dr 29582
White Iris Dr 29582
White Oak Ln 29582
White Oleander Dr 29582
White Point Rd 29582
White Tern Cir 29582
Whooping Crane Dr 29582
Wickham Cir 29582
Wildwood Trl 29582
Wiley Dr 29582
Willard Lake Dr 29582
Willet St 29582
Williams St 29582
Willow St 29582
Wind Chase Ct 29582
Winding River Rd 29582
Windy Ln 29582
Windy Heights Dr 29582
Windy Hill Rd 29582
Windy Pines Dr 29582
Wood St 29582
Woodland St 29582
Woodmere Ct 29582
Woodville Cir 29582
Wyndell Dr 29582
Ye Olde Kings Hwy 29582

NUMBERED STREETS

1st N & S 29582
2nd N & S 29582
3rd N & S 29582
4th N & S 29582
5th N & S 29582
6th Ave N 29582
6th Ave S
200-620 29582
621-621 29597
621-1199 29582
622-1198 29582
7th Ave & St 29582
8th Ave N 29582
9th N & S 29582
10th N & S 29582
11th N & S 29582
12th N & S 29582
13th N & S 29582
14th N & S 29582
15th N & S 29582
16th N & S 29582
17th N & S 29582
18th N & S 29582
19th Ave S 29582
20th N & S 29582
21st N & S 29582
22nd N & S 29582
23rd N & S 29582
24th N & S 29582
25th N & S 29582
26th N & S 29582
27th N & S 29582
28th N & S 29582
29th Ave N 29582
29th Ave S 29582
30th Ave N 29582
30th Ave S 29582
31st Ave N 29582
31st Ave S 29582
32nd Ave N 29582
32nd Ave S 29582
33rd N & S 29582
34th N & S 29582
35th N & S 29582
36th N & S 29582
37th N & S 29582
38th Ave S 29582
39th N & S 29582
40th Ave S 29582
41st Ave S 29582
42nd N & S 29582
43rd N & S 29582
44th Ave N 29582
45th N & S 29582
46th N & S 29582
47th N & S 29582
48th N & S 29582
49th Ave N 29582
50th Ave N 29582
51st Ave N 29582
52nd Ave N 29582
53rd Ave N 29582
54th Ave N 29582
55th Ave N 29582
56th Ave N 29582
57th Ave N 29582
58th Ave N 29582
59th Ave N 29582
60th Ave N 29582
61st Ave N 29582
62nd Ave N 29582
63rd Ave N 29582

ORANGEBURG SC

General Delivery 29115

POST OFFICE BOXES MAIN OFFICE STATIONS AND BRANCHES

Box No.s
All PO Boxes 29116

RURAL ROUTES

01, 02, 03, 07, 10, 13, 14, 16 29115
04, 05, 06, 08, 09, 11, 12, 15 29118

NAMED STREETS

Aaron St 29115
Abe Rd 29115
Aberdeen Rd 29118
Acacia Ln 29115
Adden St 29115
Adicks Rd 29115
Airport Rd 29115
Airport Mhp 29115
Airy Hall Dr 29118
Albert St 29115
Albertson St 29115
Albritton Rd 29115
Aldrefus Dr 29115
Alether St 29115
Alexander Dr 29118
Alexis Rd 29118
All American Ln 29115
Allen St 29115
Allison Ln 29118
Alva St 29115
Amaker St 29115
Ambassador Ln 29118
Ambrose St 29115
Amelia St & Vlg 29115
Amherst St 29115
Amity Ln 29115
Amy Lin Ct 29118
Amyamanda Ln 29118
Anderson St 29115
Angler Ln 29115
Anna St 29115
Annandale Cir 29118
Annapolis St 29115
Anne Ln 29115
Arctic Ct 29118
Aristocrat St 29115
Armstrong Ter 29115
Army Dr 29115
Arquette Ct 29115
Arthur St 29115
Arundel Dr 29118
Ashland Dr 29115
Ashley St 29115
Ashwood St 29115
Assembly Hall Way 29115
Associate Pkwy 29118
Astaire Ave 29118
Aster Ct 29118
Ataria St 29115
Atkinson St 29115
Atlantic Ave 29115
Aultman St 29115
Aundria Rd 29118
Austin St 29115
Australia Ct 29115
Autolane St 29115
Autumn St 29115
Avian Ct 29118
Ayers Rd 29115
Azalea Dr 29115
B St 29118
Bair Rd 29115
Baker St 29115
Ballard St 29115
Balloon Ln 29115
Bamberg Rd 29115
Banashee Cir 29115
Bariboo Rd 29115
Barnbury Dr 29118
Barnhart Rd 29115
Barrington Dr 29118
Barrow Ct 29115
Bates Rd 29115
Baugh St 29118
Baxter St 29115
Bay St 29118
Bayliner Ln 29118
Bayne St 29115
Beason Rd 29115
Beauregard St 29115
Beaver Ln 29118
Beech Dr 29115
Beef Jerky Dr 29115
Bellcrest Ct 29115
Belle Ter 29115
Belleville Rd
1200-2999 29115
3000-4299 29118
Bellinger Ln 29115
Bellmont St 29118
Belton Dr 29118
Benchwood Dr 29115
Benedict Rd 29118
Benedna St 29118
Benjamin Blvd 29118
Bennett St 29115
Benthomp Rd 29115
Bentwood Trl 29118
Berkeley Dr 29118
Berlin Dr 29118
Bermuda Dr 29115
Bernadette Ln 29115
Berry St 29115
Berrywood Rd 29115
Bessie Ln 29115
Bethany Rd 29115
Bethel Forest Rd 29115
Bethune Way 29118
Betsy Ln 29115
Better Living Ct 29118
Beulah St 29115
Beverly Dr 29115
Big Buck Blvd 29118
Bill Salley Rd 29115
Biltmore St 29115
Bimini Bay Rd 29115
Binnicker Bridge Rd 29115
Birch Dr 29115
Birdnest Dr 29118
Blair Ln 29115
Blanda Cir 29118
Bleakley St 29115
Blessing Rd 29118
Blossom Rd 29115
Blue Bird Ln 29115
Bob White Rd 29115
Bobby St 29115
Bochette Blvd 29118
Boise Rd 29118
Bonnette Rd 29115
Bonneville Dr 29115
Boone Rd 29115
Bostick Trl 29118
Boswell St 29115
Bottlebrush Rd 29118
Boulevard St 29115
Bowman Ave 29118
Boxer Dr 29118
Boxwood Ln 29115
Boyleston Pond Rd 29115
Bozard Rd 29115
Braddy St 29115
Bragg Blvd 29118
Bramble Ln 29115
Brandon St 29115
Brandywine Blvd 29118
Brantlywood Ln 29115
Breezy Dr 29115
Brent Dr 29115
Brentwood Dr & St 29115
Brewton St 29115
N & S Briarcliff Rd 29115
Briarwood St 29118
Brickle St 29118
Brigadier Ln 29115
Brigman Ct 29115
Bristol St 29115
Broad St 29115
Brookdale Dr 29115
Brookside Dr 29115
Broughton St 29115
Browdy St 29115
Brown St 29118
Brown Meadows Ct 29115
Bruce St 29115
Bruin Pkwy 29118
Brunson Ct 29115
Bryan Dr 29115
Buck Ridge Dr 29115
Buckley St 29115
Buds Dr 29115
Buford Ct 29118
Bull St NW 29115
Bumpy Rd 29118
Burke Rd 29118
Burley Dr 29118
Burnham Ln 29115
Bushy Dr 29118
Butterfly Ct 29118
By Pass St 29115
Cabot Dr 29118
Cactus Dr 29115
Cade Dr 29118
Caesar Ct 29115
Cainhoy St 29118
Cambridge Dr 29118
Cameron Rd 29115
Camp Rd 29118
Campus St 29115
Canaan Rd 29115
Cannon Bridge Rd 29115
Cantor Dr 29118
Capers Ln 29115
Cardinal St 29118
Carol Dr 29115
Carolina Ave & St 29115
Carraway St 29118
Carriageton Dr 29115
Carson St 29115
Cartwright Rd 29118
Casa Ct 29118
Cavalier Dr 29115
Caw Caw Dr 29118
Cedar Ln 29115
Cedar Rd 29118
Cedric St 29118
Cemetery St 29115
Central St 29115
Centre St 29115
Challenger Rd 29115
Champy Rd 29115
Chanticleer Ct 29118
Charity Ln 29115
Charleston Hwy 29115
Charlotte Cir 29115
Charmaine Ln 29118
Chatterbox Cir 29118
Cheeks Ln 29118
Cherokee St 29115
Cherry Ln 29115
Cherry Hill Rd 29115
Cherrywoods St 29115
Chester St 29118
Chestnut St 29115
Chevy Ln 29115
Chickashea Ln 29118
Chicora Wood Ct 29118
Chitwood St 29115
Chris Dr 29118
Church St 29115
Church Camp Rd 29115
Churchill Rd 29118
Cielo Rd 29115
Cimmaron St 29115
N, S & W Circle Dr 29118
Citadel Rd 29118
Clarendon Pl & St 29115
Clark St 29115
Clay St 29115
Clearview St 29115
Cleckley Blvd 29118
Cliffe St 29115
Clifton Cir 29118
Clinton St 29115
Cloister Cove Ln 29115
Cloverdale Ln 29115
Club Acres Blvd 29118
Cluster Ct 29118
Cobb Rd 29115

Coburg Ln 29115
Coconut Ct 29115
Cold Dr 29115
Coleman Ave 29115
College Ave 29115
Colleton St 29115
Colonial Dr 29115
Colony Dr 29115
Columbia Rd
800-1999 29115
2000-5999 29118
Community Park Rd 29118
Coneybury Ln 29118
Congress Ln 29115
Connor Ln 29118
Cook Rd 29118
Cooper Ct 29115
Cooter Rd 29115
Copper Rd 29115
Cordova Rd 29115
Cordust Ln 29118
Corina St 29115
Corona Dr 29115
Corporate Dr 29115
Cote Ct 29115
Cottonseed Dr 29118
Cottonwood Dr 29118
Coulter Rd 29118
Country Colony Dr 29115
Countrylane Dr 29115
Countryside Dr 29118
Courage Ln 29115
Court House Sq 29115
Cowcastle Ln 29115
Cozy Ln 29118
Crab Apple Ln 29115
Craggy Bluff Rd 29115
Craven Ln 29118
Crawford St 29115
Creek Meadow Cir 29115
Creekmoor Dr 29118
Crepe Myrtle Way 29115
Crescent Oaks Ct 29115
Crestline Dr 29115
Crestwood Dr 29115
Cricket Dr 29118
Criddle Ln 29118
Crider Ln 29118
Crosscreek Dr 29115
Crossing Cir 29115
Crossover Rd 29115
Crown Ave 29115
Cue St 29115
Culler St 29115
Cumberland Ct 29115
Cut Off Rd 29115
Dacosta Ln 29115
Dainty Cir 29115
Dale Dr 29118
Dalton Dr 29118
Dan Keowen Dr 29115
Daniel St 29118
Dantzler St 29115
Darby St 29115
Darlene Dr 29115
Darrell Rd 29115
Dash St 29115
Davis Rd 29115
Debra Ln 29118
Decatur St 29118
Dee St 29118
Deer Crossing Rd 29118
Deerbrook Ln 29115
Deerfield Dr 29118
Dekoven Ln 29118
Delano St 29115
Delaware Dr 29115
Deldere St 29115
Dell St 29115
Dellwood Dr 29115
Delmas St 29118
Dempsey Ct 29115
Den Dr 29118
Dena Ln 29115
Desota St 29115
Devine Ct 29115
Devonshire Dr 29118
Diamondhead Dr 29118
Dibble St 29118
Dickson St 29115
Dinkie Lee Ln 29115
Doc Elliott Retreat 29118
Docket St 29115
Dogwood Dr 29118
Donnetta Dr 29118
Donovan St 29115
Doodlebug Ln 29118
Dora Rd 29115
Dorchester St 29115
Dorothy Ct 29115
Dothan Rd 29115
Double S Dr 29115
Double W Rd 29118
Douglas Macarthur St 29115
Dove Point Dr 29118
Doyle St 29115
Dragonfly Ct 29118
Drexel St 29115
Dubois Dr 29118
Duck Branch Dr 29115
Dudley Dr 29115
Dukes St 29115
Duncan St 29115
Dunes St 29115
Dunham St 29118
Dunkirk Ct 29115
Dunning Rd 29118
Dunwoody St 29118
Dustin Dr 29115
Dusty Dr 29115
Dutton St 29115
Dynasty Dr 29115
Eagle Crest Dr 29118
Earline Ln 29118
Early St 29118
Eastbrook Dr 29115
Eastwood Cir 29118
Easy St 29118
Ed King Dr 29118
Eddie Ln 29115
Edens St 29115
Edgewater Ct 29118
Edgewood Dr 29118
Edisto Ave 29115
Egret Ln 29118
Elizabeth St 29118
Eljay Ct 29115
Elliott St 29115
Ellis Ave
400-1399 29115
1400-2099 29118
Elm St 29115
Elmwood Ave 29115
Elrem Rd 29118
Emmadell Dr 29118
Enderly St 29118
Endicott Ct & Dr 29118
England Dr 29118
Enterprise St 29115
Erika Ln 29118
Escondido Dr 29115
Essex Dr 29118
Estate Ct 29115
Esther Ln 29115
Eunice Ln 29118
Eutaw St 29115
Evan Ln 29115
Evergreen St 29115
Executive Ct 29115
Exotic Wine Dr 29115
Express Ln 29118
Faglier Cir 29115
Fair St 29115
Fairey St 29115
Fairfield St 29115
Fairview Rd 29115
Fairway Dr 29118
Fake Ln 29118
Fall St 29115
Fame Ln 29118
Fanfare Ln 29118
Fannie Mae Ln 29115
Farmstead Ln 29115
Farnum Rd 29118
Faulkner Rd 29115
Fawn Ln 29115
Felder St 29115
Fenton Ter 29115
Fernwood Dr 29115
Ferris St 29115
Fersner St 29115
Finley St 29115
Fire Fighter Ln 29115
Fire Tower Rd 29115
Firefly Ln 29118
Fischer St 29115
Five Chop Rd 29115
Flake Rd 29115
Flamingo Dr 29118
Fletcher St 29115
Flossie Ln 29118
Fluffy Cloud Dr 29115
Folly Rd 29115
Foot Way 29115
Forest Dr 29115
Forest Oaks Rd 29118
Fortune Rd 29115
Foster Rd 29115
Founders Ct 29118
Four Holes Rd 29115
Fowles Ct 29115
Fox Dr 29115
Fox Run Ct 29118
Foxberry Ct 29118
Foxfire Ln 29118
Francilla St 29115
Francis St 29118
Franklin St 29115
Frazier Ln 29115
Fred St 29118
Frederick St 29115
Freeland St 29115
Fresno Ct 29118
Frolic Meadows Ln 29115
Fruit Port Ln 29118
Fuller St 29115
Fulton St 29115
Fuquay Ln 29115
Gadsden St 29115
Galaxy Rd 29115
Garbon Rd 29118
Gardenia Dr 29115
Garmay St 29115
Gaucho Rd 29115
Geddings Ct 29115
Geiger Rd 29118
Genesis Rd 29115
Geneva Rd 29115
George St 29115
George Patton St 29115
George Pickett St 29115
Gibson St 29115
Ginger Lake Dr 29118
Ginn Ct 29115
Gizmo Rd 29115
Gladys St 29115
Glaze Ln 29115
Glen Gloria St 29118
Glenbrook Dr 29118
Glenfield Cir 29118
Glenrobinson Ln 29115
Glenwood Dr 29115
Glenzell Rd 29115
Glivens Ct 29118
Global Dr 29115
Globe Dr 29115
Gloria St 29115
Glover St 29115
Goff Ave 29115
Gold Dr 29118
Goldenleaf Ln 29118
Goldfish Ln 29115
Golson Dr 29115
Goodwin Rd 29115
Gopal Dr 29118
Gospel Hill Ct 29115
Governors Creek Dr 29118
Graham St 29118
Gramercy Ln 29115
Gramling Rd 29115
Granny Ct 29118
Grasshopper Ct 29118
Grassview Ln 29118
Graves Ln 29118
Great Branch Rd 29115
Green Aly & St 29115
Green Valley St 29115
Greenbriar Ct 29115
Greenbush Ct 29118
Greenhead Cir 29115
Greenhouse Rd 29115
Greenview Ln 29118
Greenville St 29115
Greenwood Ave 29115
Gregg St 29115
Griffith Dr 29118
Grizzly Grove Rd 29115
Grove Park Dr 29118
Gue Rd 29115
Gulbrandsen Rd 29115
Gussy Dr 29115
H And S Dr 29115
Haddock Rd 29115
Hadley St 29115
Halford Ln 29118
Halifax Cir 29115
Hamer Ln 29115
Hammock St 29115
Hamp Chase Cir 29115
Hampton Dr 29118
Hampton Rd 29115
Harbison Dr 29118
Harleywood Dr 29115
Harmon St 29115
Harold Rd 29115
Harper St 29115
Harrelson Ct 29115
Harris Dr & St 29118
Hart St 29115
Hartwell St 29118
Hartzog St 29115
Harvest Ln 29118
Harvey Ln 29118
Haskell Ln 29118
Hawk Chase Dr 29118
Hawthorne Trl 29115
Haynes St 29115
Heartsfire Rd 29118
Heatherwood St 29115
Heavens Rd 29115
Heckle St 29115
Heiligwood Rd 29118
Helping Hands Dr 29115
Henley St 29115
Herman Dr 29115
Herron St 29115
Heyblanchwell Ln 29118
Heyward Dr 29118
Hickory Dr 29115
Hickory Hill Rd 29115
Hickson Dr 29115
Hidden Valley Dr 29118
Hideaway Ln 29115
High St 29115
High Point Cir 29118
Highland St 29115
Highland Grove Ave 29115
Hilda Dr 29115
Hildebrand Rd 29115
Hill Dr & St 29118
Hill Coast Rd 29118
Hillcrest Ave & Ln 29118
Hillock Ct 29115
Hillsboro Rd
500-1099 29118
1100-1799 29115
Hillside St 29118
Hilltop Cir 29118
Hilly Dr 29115
Hilton St 29115
Hobcaw Ln 29118
Hodges Dr 29118
Hodson Dr 29115
Hoffman Dr 29118
Hollohugh Rd 29115
Holly St 29115
Holly Cove Ln 29115
Holly Creek Dr 29118
Holt Dr 29115
Homestead Rd 29115
Honeysuckle Dr 29115
Hoot Owl Ln 29118
Horger St 29115
Horseshoe Dr 29118
Horton St 29118
Hot Ln 29115
Houser St 29115
Hubbard St 29115
Hudson Rd 29118
Hughes St 29115
Hundley Rd 29118
Hunter Dr 29115
Huntington Dr 29118
Huson Cir 29115
Hutto St 29118
Hydrick Ave 29118
Ibonnay Rd 29115
Indigo Dr 29115
Indonesia Ln 29118
Industrial Blvd
100-199 29115
3600-4099 29118
Iricks Pond Rd 29115
Irvin St 29115
Ivy Rd 29115
J Mack Cir 29118
Jackson Dr 29118
Jade Cir 29115
Jaguar Ln 29118
Jake Rd 29115
James St 29115
Jameson Farm Rd 29115
Jamison Ave 29115
Jasmine Ct 29118
Jasper St 29115
Java Ln 29118
Jay Keitt Rd 29115
Jefferson St 29115
Jellnab Ct 29118
Jennifer Ln 29118
Jennifer St 29115
Jennings Ct 29115
Jensen St 29115
Jermaine Ln 29118
Jernigan Dr 29115
Jeshua Ln 29118
Jessica Rd 29118
Joe S Jeffords Hwy
SE 29115
John St 29115
John C Calhoun Dr 29115
John Wesley Dr 29118
Johnson St 29115
Jones Dr 29118
Jordan St 29115
Joseph St 29115
Joyce Ln 29115
Ju Ju Ln 29118
Juan Ln 29115
Judicial Cir 29115
Julian St 29115
July Dr 29118
Jumbo Rd 29115
Jurassaic Dr 29118
Kadee Ln 29118
Kal Ln 29115
Katherine St 29115
Kearse Dr 29115
Keener Ct 29118
Keepajoy Cir 29118
Keitt St 29115
Kellog Ave 29118
Kemmerlin Rd 29115
Kennedy Dr
400-499 29118
1800-1899 29115
Kennerly Rd 29118
Key Lime St 29115
Keyport Ct 29118
Kidz Ln 29118
Kinard St 29118
Kings Rd 29115
Kingsdown Rd 29115
Kinte Ct 29118
Kips Ln 29115
Kirby Ln 29115
Kirkland St 29118
Knight Dr 29115
Knollwood Ct 29118
Knotty Pine Ln 29115
Koller Rd 29118
Krakue Ln 29115
Kucks Ct 29115
Lafrance Dr 29115
Lake Cir, Dr & Rd 29115
Lake Edisto Rd 29118
Lake Marston Dr 29118
Lakeshore Dr 29115
Lakeside Dr 29115
Lakeside St 29118
Lakeview Dr 29115
Lakewood Dr 29118
Lamar St 29115
Lancaster St 29115
Lancelot Dr 29115
Landfill Rd 29118
Landing Way 29118
Lands End 29118
Langley Rd 29115
Langston St 29115
Laquinta Dr 29115
Laraleigh Rd 29115
Lariot Rd 29115
Lartique Dr 29118
Last Dr 29115
Lathan Dr 29118
Latimore St 29115
Laughing Gull Dr 29118
Laurel St 29115
Lawrence St 29115
Lawton Rd 29115
Lazy Way Dr 29115
Leahmon Ln 29115
Lecinda Ln 29118
Lee Blvd 29118
Leeway St 29118
Legare Ct 29118
Legendary Rd 29115
Lekehia Ln 29115
Leslie Cir 29115
Lewis Dunton St 29115
Lexington St 29115
Liberty St 29115
Lime Kiln Rd 29118
Limestone Rd 29118
Limit St 29115
Lin Dr 29115
Linda Ln 29115
Lindale St 29115
Lindberg Dr 29115
Links Ct 29115
Lisa Rd 29118
Litchfield Ct 29118
Little Creek Dr 29115
Little Debbie Ln 29115
Live Oak Dr 29118
Livingston Ter 29118
Livingway Dr 29115
Lizzie Ln 29115
Lloyd St 29115
Loadholt St 29115
Loblolly Ln 29115
Loch Ness Ct 29115
Log Cabin Rd 29115
Logan St 29115
Loispaul Cir 29118
Lombardi Ct 29118
Lone Goose Ln 29115
Longview Dr 29118
Longwood Dr 29118
Lottie Ln 29115
Lou Dr 29115
Louis St 29115
Louise Dr 29118
Love Ln 29115
Lovell St 29115
Lovely Cir 29115
Lowman St 29115
Lucky Leaf St 29115
Lucrence Ln 29118
Lucy Ln 29115
Luke St 29115
Lyons Rd 29115
Macedonia Rd 29115
Mack St 29115
Macon Dr 29118
Madear Ln 29115
Madison St 29115
Maedrine St 29115
Magnolia St
100-3399 29115
3600-3799 29118
Mahan St 29118
Mahogany Ln 29115
Main Ave 29115
Main Trail Rd 29118
Majesty Rd 29115
Major Ln 29115
Majority Rd 29118
Malibu Dr 29115
Malik Ln 29115
Mall Terrace Ct 29118
Mallard Dr 29118
Manisha Dr 29118
Manning St 29115
Mannlicher Dr 29115
Maple St 29115
March Ln 29115
Margot Ct 29115
Marie St 29118
Marigold Rd 29115
Market Dr & St 29115
Marlboro St 29115
Marlee Dr 29118
Marquette Rd 29115
Mars Cir 29115
Marshall St 29115
Martin Ave 29118
Mary Ellen Dr 29118
Mary Joye Ln 29118
Mason Dr 29118
Masters St 29115
Maurice Dr 29118
Maxcy St 29115
Maxwell St 29115
Mayes Rd 29115
Mays St 29115
Mcalpine St 29115
Mccants Dr 29118
Mcgugan Ln 29118
Mcintosh St 29118
Mckewn St 29115
Mclaine St 29115
Mclees St 29115
Mcmichael St 29115
Mcnabb Rd 29115
Mcqueen Blvd 29118
Mcquire Rd 29118
Meadowcrest Dr 29115
Meadowlark Dr 29118
Medes Cir 29115
Medford St 29115
Medway Dr 29118
Meeting St 29115
Melissa Ter 29115
Mels Ct 29115
Melvin Rd 29118
Mercedes Ct 29118
Merle Dr 29118
Methodist Oaks Dr 29115
Metts Rd 29118
Michael St 29118
Middlepen Rd 29115
Middleton St
700-1551 29115
1550-1550 29116
1552-2298 29115
1553-2299 29115
Mike Dr 29118
Mildred Dr 29118
Mill Ct & St 29115
Mill Branch Rd 29118

Millcreek Ln	29118
Millender Ln	29118
Millennium Dr	29115
Millwood Farm Rd	29118
Mimosa Dr	29115
Mincer Cir	29115
Mingo St	29115
Mishoes Ln	29118
Misty Pine Ln	29118
Mitchell Rd	29118
Mobile St	29115
Mockingbird Ln	29118
Modesto Dr	29118
Mollie St	29115
Monica Rd	29118
Monroe St	29115
Monterey Trl	29118
Montezuma Dr	29115
Monticello Rd	29115
Mookie Ln	29115
Moore Rd	29118
Moorecrum Rd	29118
Morais Ln	29118
Moravinger Dr	29118
Morgan Dr	29118
Morninghill Dr	29115
Moroge Ln	29118
Morris St	29115
Moseley St	29115
Moss St	29115
Mount Gilead Dr	29118
Mount Hope Dr	29118
Mudslide Ln	29118
Mulberry St	29118
Muller St	29115
Muna Ave	29115
Murden Dr	29115
Muriel St	29115
Murph Ct	29118
Murph Mill Rd	29118
Murphy Ln	29115
Murray Rd	29115
Myers Rd	29115
Myrtle Dr	29115
Nals Dr	29115
Nance St	29115
Nandina Trl	29118
Nansbrook Dr	29115
Narvalle Ln	29115
Nash Rd	29118
National St	29115
Nature Ln	29115
Navy Dr	29115
Neeses Hwy	29115
Nelson St	29118
New Hope Rd	29118
New Light Rd	29115
New Wilkinson Ave	29115
Newman St	29115
Nimmons Rd	29118
Nix St	29115
Norman St	29115
North Rd	29118
Northlake Dr	29118
Northridge St	29118
Northside St	29118
Northview Dr	29118
Northwood Ct	29118
Northwood Dr	29115
Norway Rd	29115
Nottingham St	29115
Novice Pond Rd	29115
Nuggett Dr	29115
Oak St	29115
Oakcreek Dr	29118
Oakland St	29115
Oaklane Dr	29115
Oakmont Dr	29118
Oakridge Dr	29115
Oakwood Dr	29115
Oasis Ln	29115
Oates St	29115
Ocain Ln	29118
Odell Dr	29115
Office Park Dr	29118
Ola Ln	29118
Old Cameron Rd	29115
Old Edisto Dr	29115
Old Elloree Rd	29115
Old Orchard Way	29115
Old Riley St	
1700-1899	29118
1900-1999	29115
2000-2399	29118
Oleander Dr	29118
E Orange Rd	29115
Orange Parish St	29118
Orangeburg Mall Cir	29115
Orangepark Dr	29115
Orangewood Dr	29115
Orlando Dr	29115
Ott St	29115
Our Rd	29115
Ourshan Ct	29118
Owens St	29115
Oxford Dr	29118
Padgett Ct	29115
Palm Harbor Dr	29115
Palmer Dr	29115
Palmetto Pkwy	29115
Pamela Ln	29118
Pampus Dr	29115
Pandanus Rd	29115
Par Ct	29115
Park St	29115
Parker St	29115
Parlerdale St	29115
Parlor Rd	29115
Partridge Rd	29118
Pasture Ln	29118
Pate St	29118
Patrick Loop	29118
Patriots Way	29118
Paula Dr	29115
Pauline Ct	29115
Peachtree Ct	29118
Pear Dr	29115
Pearl St	29115
Peasley St	29115
Peckleton St	29115
Pelham Ct	29118
Pembroke Ln	29118
Pendarvis St	29115
Pendulum Ln	29115
Peninsula Ct	29118
Penn Rd	29115
Pepper Ln	29115
Pepsie St	29115
Percheron Dr	29115
Perfume Ct	29115
Perriwinkle Ln	29115
Perry Dr	29115
Perry St	29118
Perryclear St	29115
Perwalt Ct	29115
Pheasant Ln	29115
Phoenix Rd	29118
Pie Dr	29118
Pike St	29115
Pin Oak St	29115
Pine Ln	29118
Pine Cove Dr	29118
Pine Loop Cir	29115
Pinebrook St	29115
Pinehill Rd	29115
Pinehurst St	29115
Pineland St	29115
Pineridge St	29118
Pineview Ln	29118
Pinnacle St	29118
Pitt Rd	29115
Plantation Dr	29118
Plow Rd	29115
Plum Cir	29118
Plum Tree Rd	29118
Plywood St	29115
Podar Rd	29115
Point View Dr	29115
Pompion Hill Dr	29118
Pond Rd	29115
Poplar St	29115
Pops Dr	29115
Poradia Rd	29118
Porter St	29118
Praise Dr	29118
Prakash Ct	29118
Praline Ct	29115
Prep St	29118
Prescott St	29115
Presidential Dr	29115
Prestige Ct	29115
Princess Ln	29115
Progressive Ln	29115
Promise Ln	29115
Prosperity Dr	29115
Providence Rd	29118
Provo Rd	29115
Pruitt Dr	29118
Public St	29115
Purple Leaf Dr	29115
Putter Path Rd	29118
Quail Ln	29115
Quail Run Dr	29115
Quality Dr	29115
Quasar St	29115
Quick St	29115
Quiet Haven Ln	29115
Quiet Valley Dr	29118
Rachil Ln	29115
Radio Ln	29115
Rainbow Ct	29115
Rainey Dr	29115
Rainfall Rd	29115
Rambling Ridge Rd	29115
Ramsgate Dr	29118
Rand St	29118
Rashimori Ln	29118
Ravenwood Dr	29118
Raymond Rd	29115
Raysor St	29115
Rebel Rd	29115
Recap Dr	29115
Red Bank Rd	29118
Redd Rd	29118
Redmon St	29118
Regional Pkwy	29118
Reid St	29115
Rembert St	29115
Representative Cir	29115
Retha Rd	29118
Retreat Ln	29118
Rhinehart St	29118
Rhoad St	29118
Rhododendron Dr	29115
Rhonda Rd	29115
Rice Dr	29115
Rick Ln	29115
Rickenbaker Rd	29115
Rider Rd	29115
Ridgewood Dr	29118
Ridley Dr	29115
Riggs St	29115
Riley St	29118
Ringneck Trl	29118
Rio Dr	29118
Rising Creek Rd	29115
Rivelon Rd	29115
River Ridge Dr	29115
Riverbank Dr	
1200-1599	29115
1600-4199	29118
Riverbirch Dr	29118
Riverpark Rd	29118
Rivers St	29115
Rivers Turn Rd	29115
Riverside Dr	29115
Roache Ct	29115
Robert St	29115
Robert E Lee St	29115
Robin Ln	29118
Robin Hill Rd	29115
Robinson St	29115
Rochelle Dr	29118
Rodney Rd	29115
Rodriguez Rd	29118
Rogers Dr	29118
Rollingwood Ct	29115
Rome St	29115
Ron Dr	29115
Rooster Ln	29115
Roper Cir	29115
Roquemore Dr	29115
Rosedale Dr	29115
Rosehaven Ln	29115
Rosemont Dr	29115
Rosewood Dr	29115
Rowe St	29115
Rowesville Rd	29115
Roy Rd	29118
Royal Dr	29115
Ruf Rd	29118
Rufus Rd	29115
Rugby Rd	29115
Rume Place Ct	29115
Rumph Rd	29118
Rupaul Dr	29115
Ruple Dr	29118
Russell St NE	29115
Rustic St	29118
Rutledge Ave	29115
Ryan Rd	29118
Sabree Ct	29115
Saddlebrook Dr	29118
Saint Ct	29115
Saint Andrews St	29115
Saint Ann St	29115
Saint David St	29115
Saint John St	29115
Saint Matthews Rd	
1725A-1725B	29118
1000-1399	29115
1400-4299	29118
Saint Paul St	29115
Salley St	29115
Samshop Rd	29115
Sand St	29115
Sandpiper Ln	29118
Sapp Dr	29115
Sarah Hannah Rd	29115
Saturn Way Rd	29115
Sav Will Acres Rd	29115
Savant St	29115
Sawaga St	29115
Sawyer St	29115
Saxon Dr	29115
Scallion Rd	29115
Schley St	29115
Scott St	29115
Scoville St	29115
Scuffletown Rd	29118
Seaboard St	29115
Seabrook St	29115
Seal St	29115
Sease Rd	29115
Seaside Dr	29118
Seawright St	29115
Seba St	29115
Sedgefield Dr	29118
Seif St	29115
Seldom Rest Dr	29118
Sellers Ave	29115
Seminole Dr	29115
Senate St	29118
Shadow Lawn Dr	29115
Shalidonia Ln	29118
Shalom Ln	29118
Shannon St	29118
Sharperson St	29115
Shedburn Dr	29115
Sheffield Dr	29118
Shelton Rd	29118
Sheppard Rd	29118
Sheridan St	29115
Sheriff Blvd	29118
Sherrie Ln	29115
Sherwood Dr	29115
Shifting Ln	29118
Shillings Bridge Rd	
100-899	29118
1000-3099	29115
Shirley St	29115
Shopping St	29115
Shore Dr	29118
Short Ave	29115
Shuler St	29115
Sierra Dr	29118
Sifly Rd	29118
Sifly St	29115
Silkwood St	29115
Simpson St	29118
Sims St	29115
Sister Ln	29118
Sistrunk Ln	29118
Siva Ave	29118
Skyland Ln	29118
Slab Landing Rd	29115
Slaughter Dr	29118
Sleep Inn Dr	29115
Slick Trl	29118
Sly Rd	29115
Smoak Aly	29115
Snaffle Ct	29115
Snapover Rd	29115
Solomon Ter	29115
Sonic Dr	29115
South St	29115
Southland Rd	29115
Sparkleberry Hill Rd	29118
Sparklewood Dr	29115
Sparrow Ln	29118
Spinx Ct	29118
Spring St	29115
Spring Hill Ln	29118
Spring Valley Cir	29118
Springdale Dr	29118
Sprinkle Ave	29115
Spruce Dr & St	29115
Spurgeon Dr	29115
Squirrel Run Ln	29115
St Julien Pl	29115
Stacey Bridge Rd	29118
Stagecoach Ln	29118
Staley St	29115
Stanfield Ct	29115
Stanley St	29115
Stanton Dr	29115
Starling Rd	29118
State Ct	29115
Sterling Ave & St	29115
Stevfelkel Dr	29115
Stillwater Rd	29118
Stillwood Cir	29118
Stilton Rd	29115
Stitchen Ln	29115
Stonewall Jackson Blvd	29115
Straight Dr	29115
Strawberry Ln	29118
Stroman St	29115
Stuart St	29115
Sullens St	29115
Sulton Ct	29115
Summer Creek Dr	29118
Summers Ave	29115
Summit Park Way	29118
Sunny Dr	29115
Sunnyside St	29115
Sunnyvale Ct	29115
Sunrise Ln	29115
Sunset St	29115
Sunshine Ln	29118
Sweet Maple Dr	29118
Swinton Rd	29115
Sylvan Ave	29115
Symphony St	29115
Tabby Ln	29115
Tall Pines Dr	29115
Tamara Ln	29115
Tanniger Ln	29118
Tarheel Ln	29115
Taylor Blvd	29118
Tea Ticket	29118
Teakwood Dr	29115
Teal St	29115
Tecza Dr	29115
Tega Cay Rd	29118
Terry St	29115
Theo Cir	29115
Thomas Eklund Cir	29115
Thomas Way Ct	29118
Thorn Dyke Rd	29115
Threson St	29115
Throne Dr	29115
Tiffy Ct	29115
Tilden Rd	29115
Till Rd	29115
Till Hill Rd	29115
Tillson Ln	29115
Timber Ln	29118
Timberline Dr	29118
Timrose Ln	29115
Tipsy Dr	29115
Tobago Rd	29115
Tolly Ganly Cir	29118
Tonyota Ct	29118
Tooky Ln	29118
Towhee Cir	29118
Trade St	29115
Tradewinds St	29115
N Trail Rd	29115
Trail One St	29115
Train Line Rd	29118
Tranquil Ln	29115
Trapnell Ln	29115
Trashill Rd	29115
Travers St	29115
Treadwell St	29115
Trebie Rd	29115
Treeing Walker Rd	29118
Trell Ln	29118
Tremoni Ln	29118
Treno Ln	29118
N Triangle St	29115
Tricia Ln	29115
Triple Rd	29118
Tripp Ln	29115
Trotter Ln	29118
Trouble Ln	29115
Truman Cir	29115
Tucker St	29115
Tudon Rd	29118
Tuesday Ln	29118
Tulip Ln	29115
Turkey Hill Ct	29118
Twelve Oaks Ln	29118
Twin Oaks Dr	29118
Twins Rd	29118
Tybee Ln	29115
Tyke Ct	29115
Tyler Rd	29115
Ulmer St	29115
Uncle Bud Rd	29118
Union St	29115
University Village Dr	29115
Urbana Ln	29118
Usha Ct	29118
Utaff Ln	29115
Utica Ave	29118
Valencia Dr	29118
Valerie Dr	29115
Valiant Dr	29115
Valley Dr	29115
Venus Ct	29115
Verdall Ln	29115
Victoria St	29115
Village Park Dr	29118
Vine St	29115
Virginia Rd	29115
Vista Ln	29115
Viveke Ave	29115
Vogt Ln	29118
Von Oshen Dr	29118
Voyager Rd	29115
Wade Ct	29115
Wagon Rd	29115
Walker Ave	29115
Wall St	29115
Walter Dr	29118
Wanda Ln	29115
Wannamaker Ln	29118
Wannamaker St	29115
Ward Ln	29118
Waring St	29115
Warley Rd	29115
Washington St	29115
Watch Rd	29118
Waterford Pkwy	29118
Waters St	29115
Waters Edge Rd	29115
Waterspring Rd	29118
Watson St	29115
Way Dr	29118
Waycross St	29118
Wayside Dr	29115
Weatherford Rd	29115
Webber Farm Rd	29115
Webster St	29115
Wedgewood Rd	29118
Wednesday Ct	29115
Weeping Willow Dr	29115
Wells Dr	29115
Wellsgrove Ln	29115
Wertz St	29115
West Ct	29118
Westchester St	29115
Westminister Dr	29118
Westwood Ave	29115
Wetpond Rd	29118
Wexford Dr	29118
Weybridge Ct	29115
Weycourt Rd	29115
Whaley St	29115
Wheeler St	29115
Whippoorwill Rd	29118
Whistle Top Ln	29118
White Ct	29115
White Oaks Cir	29118
Whitetail Ln	29115
Whitford Stage Rd	29115
Whitman St	29115
Whittaker Pkwy & St	29115
Widgeon Rd	29118
Wilcants Rd	29115
Wild Iris Dr	29115
Wildeway Ln	29115
Wildwood Dr	29115
Wiles St	29115
Wileswood Dr	29115
Wilkinson St	29115
William St	29115
Williams St	29115
Williamsburg Ct	29118
Willie Rd	29115
Willing Lakes Ct	29118
Willington Dr	29118
Willnet Dr	29118
Willow Rd	29115
Willow Bay Dr	29118
Wilson St	29115
Winchester Ln	29118
Windchime Ln	29118
Windmill Way	29118
Windsor St	29115
Windy Ln	29118
Windy Pines Rd	29115
Wingate St	29118
Wingfield St	29115
Winningham Rd	29118
Winslow St	29115
Winward Ave	29115
Wisteria Dr	29115
Wolfe Trl	29115
Wolfton Rd	29118
Woodberry Dr	29115
Woodbine Dr	29115
Woodland Dr	29118
Woodlawn Dr	29115
Woodolive St	29115
Woodpecker Blvd	29118
Woodridge Ln	29118
Woodrow Dr	29115
Woods St	29115
Work Pl	29115
Wren Rd	29118
Wright Rd	29115
Wyouida Ln	29115
Yellow Jasmine Rd	29115
Yorkshire Dr	29115
Youngstown Cir	29118
Yvette Rd	29118
Zeigler St	29115
Zion Church Rd	29115

NUMBERED STREETS

All Street Addresses 29115

ROCK HILL SC

General Delivery 29730

POST OFFICE BOXES MAIN OFFICE STATIONS AND BRANCHES

Box No.s
1 - 1500 29731
2441 - 8058 29732
9998 - 9998 29730
10001 - 13501 29731
35999 - 38280 29732

NAMED STREETS

Aaron Ave 29730
Abernathy St 29732
Abigale Ct 29730
Ablewood Rd 29730
Acorn Ct 29732
Adams St 29730
Addison Dr 29730
Adelaide Ct 29730
Adkins Ave 29732
Adkins Ridge Rd 29730
Adlee Ct 29732
Adnah Dr 29732
Adnah Church Rd 29732
Adnah Hills Ave 29732
Adrian St 29732
Age Old Way 29732
Aiken Ave 29730
Aiken Avenue Ext 29730
Airport Rd 29732
Airslee Ct 29732
Airway Dr 29732
Alabama Ct 29732
Alamance Ct 29732
Albert St 29730
Alberta Ct 29730
Albright Rd 29730
Alden Ct 29732
Aldersgate Rd 29732
Alexander Rd 29732
Allen St 29730
Allendale Cir 29732
Allis Chalmers Rd 29730
Allison Cir 29732
Allison Bluff Trl 29732
Alpha St 29732
Alpine Ridge Pl 29732
Alton Rd 29730
Alyce Ln 29732
Alysia Ct 29732
Amanda Ln 29730
Amazon Cir 29732
Amber Ln 29732
Amberside Dr 29732
Amelia Ave 29732
Amendment Ave 29732
Amherst Ct 29730
Amy Lee Ln 29732
Anderson Rd N & S 29730
Andora Dr 29732
Andrea Ct 29730
Andreone Way 29732
Anglewood Rd 29730
Ann Carson Ct 29732
Annafrel St 29730
Annalinde Ln 29732
Anne St 29730
Annie Ln 29730
Antney Ln 29732
Anvil Draw Pl 29730
Apple Valley Mobile Park 29730
April Showers Ln 29730
Aragon St 29730
Aragon Beach Rd 29732
Arbalest Ct 29730
Arbor Ct 29732
Arbor View Dr 29732
Arboretum Rd 29732
Arborgate Dr 29732
Arcade St 29730
Arch Dr 29730
Archer Dr 29730
Archive St 29730
Arden Ln 29732
Ardwyck Pl 29730
Aria Way 29732
Arklow Dr 29730
Arlington Ave 29730
Armory Rd 29730
Armstrong Dr 29730
Armstrong Ford Rd 29730
Arnold St 29730
Arrowhead Dr 29730
Arrowwood Ln 29732
Arthur Way 29732
Asbury Ct 29732
Ascot Ridge Rd 29732
Ashcroft Ln 29732
Ashley Ln 29730
Ashley Park Dr 29732
Ashley Woods Dr 29730
Ashmore Ct 29732
Ashridge Rd 29730
Ashton St 29730
Ashworth Dr 29732
Aspen Ter 29732
Aspendale Rd 29732
Atherton Way 29730
Atwood St 29730
Auburndale Ln 29732
Audubon Dr 29732
Augustus Ct 29730
Auten Rd 29730
Automall Pkwy 29732
Autumn Breeze Ct 29732
Autumn Creek Ct 29732
Autumn Lake Dr 29732
Autumnwood Dr 29730
Avalon Dr 29730
Avenue Of The Nations 29730
Avon Ct 29732
Azalea Rd 29730
Aziza Rd & St 29732
B J Jackson Rd 29732
Bagwell Cir 29732
Bailey Ave 29732
Baker St 29730
Baker Street Ext 29730
Baldwin Ct 29730
Ballintoy Ln 29730
Balmoral Dr 29732
Banbury Ln 29732
Bancroft Dr 29730
S Bank Dr 29732
Barber St 29730
Barkridge Ct 29730
Barksdale Ct 29732
Barnes St 29730
Barnett St 29732
Barney Rhett Cir 29732
Barnswallow Rd 29732
Barrett Ct 29732
Barringer Rd 29730
Barrington Ct 29732
Barron Point Rd 29732
Barronwood Rd 29732
Barrow Ct & St 29730
Barton Ln 29730
Barwick Ct 29730
Baskins Rd 29730
Bates St 29732
Bavand Cir 29732
Bay Rd 29732
Baylor Dr 29730
Bayshore Dr 29732
Beachwood Rd 29730
Beacon Hill Ct 29730
Beaconfield Ct 29730
Beastre Rd 29732
Beckham Ln 29732
Beckton Ct 29732
Beckworth Ave 29730
E Bedford Dr 29732
Beechaven Dr 29732
Begonia Way 29732
Belaire Dr 29732
Belfast Ct 29730
Belinda St 29732
Bellanova Ct 29732
Belle Chase 29732
Belle Meade Rd 29730
Belle Regal Cir 29732
Belleview Rd 29730
Bellridge Rd 29732
Belmar Ln 29732
Bending Bough Ln 29732
Bens Ct 29730
Benson Rd 29730
Benton Ln 29732
Beray Ct 29732
Berkeley Rd 29730
Berry St 29732
Berryhill Ct & Ln 29732
Berwick Dr 29730
Bethesda Rd 29732
Betsy Bob Rd 29730
Beverly Dr 29730
Bianca Ct 29730
Big Chief Ct 29730
Big Oak Ln 29732
Billess Ct 29732
Bills Cir 29730
Billy Claude Cir 29730
Billy Wilson Rd 29730
Bird St 29732
Birdie Ln 29732
Birk Glen Dr 29732
Birmingham Ct 29732
Bitter Brook Ct 29730
E & W Black St 29730
Black Alder Ct 29732
Blackmon St 29730
Blackstone Ln 29730
Blackwell St 29730
Blair Ct 29732
Blake St 29730
Blakeley Walk 29732
Blanchard Bnd 29730
Blanche Cir 29730
Bloomfield Rd 29732
Bloomsbury Dr 29730
Blossom Dr 29730
Blue Rd 29730
Blue Crush Ct 29732
Blue Heron Dr 29732
Blue Jasper Dr 29732
Blue Ridge Way 29732
Blue Wing Ct 29732
Bluegrass Ln 29732
Bluff Ct 29732
Boardwalk Run 29732
Boatshore Rd 29732
Bobbie Ln 29732
Bogey Ct 29730
Boggs St 29730
Bon Rea Dr 29732
Boney Rd 29730
Bonnybrook Cir 29732
Booker St 29730
Booker Washington St 29730
Bookout Rd 29730
Boots Ln 29730
Border Rd E & W 29730
Bose Ave 29730
Boss Wylie Dr 29732
Bow St 29730
Bowater Rd 29732
Bowser St 29730
Bradford Ct 29730
Bradley St 29730
Brakefield Pkwy 29730
Brakewood Dr 29732
Bramlett Rd 29730
Branch St 29732
Brand Rd 29732
Brandon Lee Ct 29730
Brandyhill Dr 29732
Branham Rd 29730
Bratton Dr 29732
Breckenridge Pl 29732
Breckenwood Dr 29732
Breen Cir 29732
Breezewood St 29732
Brentfield Dr 29732
Brer Rabbit Run 29730
Brewington Pkwy 29732
Briar Cir 29732
Briarcliff Rd 29730
Briarfield Rd 29730
Briarwood Dr 29732
Brice St 29730
Bridal Trl 29732
Bridge Knot Ct 29732
Bridge Stone Ln 29730
Bridges Dr 29730
Bridgewater Rd 29730
Bridgewood Dr 29732
Bridlewood Dr 29732
Brighton Ct 29730
Bristol Pkwy 29732
Brittany Ridge Pl 29732
Britton Ct 29732
Broadmore Ct 29730
Broken Oak Rd 29732
Bromley Rd 29732
Brookdale Dr 29732
Brookfield Ln 29730
Brookgreen Cir 29732
Brookpines Ct 29732
Brookridge Dr 29732
Brooks Ln 29730
Brookstone Way 29732
Brooktree Ln 29730
Brookview Ct 29732
Brookwood Cir & Ln 29732
Broome Pl 29730
Brown St 29730
Brown Sanders Rd 29730
Brownstone Dr 29730
Brunswick Dr 29730
Brush Creek Rd 29732
Bryan Ct 29730
Bryant Blvd 29732
Brynwood Dr 29732
Bubbling Brook Dr 29732
Buckeye Ter 29732
Buena Vista Ct 29732
Buford Ct 29732
Buice Cir 29730
Bumpy Hollow Trl 29732
Bungalow Dr 29732
Burbank Ct 29730
Burgis Creek Rd 29730
Burkett Rd & St 29730
Burls Ln 29732
Burnage Way 29730
Burton St 29732
Bushmill Rd 29730
Byars St 29730
Bynum Ave 29730
Byron Rd 29730
Caldwell Dr & St 29730
Calen Ln 29730
Calhoun St 29730
Calhoun Falls Dr 29732
Calliewood Dr 29730
Cambridge Cir 29730
Camden Ave 29732
Camellia Ct 29730
Camelot Dr 29730
Cameron Dr 29730
Cammie Jordan Ln 29730
Campcreek Pl 29730
Campsite Rd 29732
Canberra Dr 29732
Candlelight Dr 29732
Candlewood Ln 29730
Candy Ln 29730
Canfield Dr 29730
Cannon Dr 29730
Canoe Ct 29732
Canterbury Glen Ln 29730
Canvas Ave 29732
Cape Ct 29730
Cape Cod Way 29732
Capel Ct 29730
Capstone Ct 29732
Captain White Dr 29730
Caraway Dr 29732
Cardinal Dr 29732
Cardinal Hill Dr 29732
Cardinal Point Dr 29732
Cardiology Dr 29732
Carey Dr 29732
Carhart Rd 29730
Carly Ln 29732
Carmel Rd 29730
Carodon Ct 29732
Carolina Ave 29730
Carolina Avenue Ext 29730
Carollbrook Dr 29730
Carpenter Parker Ln 29730
Carriage Ct 29732
Carrie Estates Rd 29730
Carroll St 29730
Carrollton Pl 29730
Carrolwood Dr 29732
Carter Ct 29732
Cascade Ave 29732
Cashew Way 29732
Cassey Olin Cir 29730
Castle St 29732
Castle Pines Dr 29730
Castlegate Ct 29730
Castlewood Cir 29730
Catalina Ct 29730
S Catawba Ave, Dr & Rd 29730
Catawba Church Rd 29730
Catawba Shores Dr 29730
Catawba Wells Ct 29732
Catchpoint Dr 29732
Cathedral Mills Ln 29732
Catherine Dr & St 29730
Catoctin Rd 29732
Cauthen St 29730
Cavendale Dr 29732
Cavendish Ct 29732
Cayce Olin Dr 29730
Cedar St 29730
Cedar Grove Ln 29732
Cedar Line Dr 29730
Cedar Post Ln 29730
Cedarvale Rd 29732
Cedarview Ct 29732
Cedarvilla Dr 29730
Cedarwood Ln 29732
Celanese Rd
1100-1199 29730
1301-1397 29732
1399-4199 29732
Celriver Rd 29730
Cemetary Rd 29730
Centennial Dr 29732
Center St 29730
Chad Wesley Rd 29730
Chadwick Ct 29732
Challis Ct 29732
Chalmers Row 29732
Chamberland Ct 29732
Chamberside Dr 29730
Champion Rd 29730
Chandler Dr 29732
Channing Park Way 29732
Chanticleer Cir 29732
Chapel Gate Dr 29732
Chapel View Ct 29732
Chapman Cir 29732
E Chappell Rd 29730
Charles Ln 29730
Charles Able Rd 29730
Charleston Ter 29732
Charlie Horse Rd 29730
Charlotte Ave
201-309 29730
311-499 29730
434-498 29734
500-998 29730
501-999 29730
1000-1399 29732
S Charlotte Ave 29730
W Charlotte Ave 29730
Charrow Town Dr 29730
Charter Dr 29732
Chase Brook Dr 29732
Chatham Ave 29730
Chelsa Ct 29732
Chelveston Dr 29732
Cherokee Ave 29732
Cherry Rd
100-2600 29732
2601-2637 29730
2602-2638 29732
2639-3099 29730
S Cherry Rd 29732
Cherry St 29730
Cherry Hills Pl 29730
Cherry Laurel Ln 29730
Cherry Meadow Ln 29732
Cherryfield Pl 29732
Chesbrough Blvd 29732
Chester St 29730
Chestnut St 29730
Chestwood Ct 29732
Chickasaw Loop 29732
Chicora Rd 29730
Chipstile Turn 29732
Chipwood Ln 29730
Chris Ct 29732
Christian Way 29732
Christmas Dr 29732
Christopher Cir 29730
Christopher Ridge Ct 29732
Church Rd & St 29730
Churchill Dr 29732
Cinema Dr 29730
Circle B Lake Rd 29730
Claire Ln 29732
Clairmont St 29730
Clara St 29730
W Clarendon Ct & Pl 29732
Clarinda St 29730
Clark St 29730
Clarke St 29732
Clarkson St 29730
Claxton Dr 29732
Clay Hill Dr 29730
Clayton Ave 29732
Clearbrook Dr 29730
Clearlake Dr 29732
Clearview Rd 29732
Clearwater Rd 29730
Cleggan Rd 29730
Clemmon Sanders Cir 29732
Clemons Ct 29730
Clinton Ave 29730
Clouds Way 29732
Cloverhill Ln 29732
Clubhouse Dr 29732
Clubside Dr 29730
Coach House Ct 29732
Coatsworth Ln 29732
Cobbs Glen Ct 29732
Coffee Tree Ln 29732
Cog Hill Ct 29730
Colby Ave 29732
Cole Ave 29732
Colebrook Dr 29730
Colecreek Ln 29732
Coleman Ct 29732
Coleman Dove Pl 29730
College Ave 29730
College Avenue Ext
900-999 29730
1000-1099 29732
College Plaza Blvd 29730
Colleton Ct 29732
Collins Rd 29732
Colonial Dr 29730
Colony Rd 29730
Colton Ct 29730
Columbia Ave 29730
Colwick Ln 29732
Comer Rd 29732
Commerce Dr 29730
Community St 29730
N & S Confederate Ave 29730
Coniston Pl 29732
Conner Oaks Trl 29730
Constance Way 29730
Constitution Blvd 29732
Constitution Park Blvd 29732
Cool Creek Dr 29732
Coolsprings Ln 29730
Copeland Ct 29732
Copes Ct 29732
Copley Dr 29732
Copper Kettle Dr 29732
Copperhead Rd 29730
Cornelia Ln 29732
Cornelious Rd 29730
Cornelius Dr 29730
Cornell Dr 29730
Cornerstone Rd 29732
Coronet Ct 29730
Corporate Blvd 29730
Corwin Dr 29732
Cote Ln 29730
Cottage Rose Ln 29730
Cotton Field Rd 29732
Cotton Mill Vlg 29730
Cotton Patch Cir 29730
Cottonwood Ln 29730
Country Ct 29732
Country Club Dr & Rd 29730
Country Manor Ln 29730
Country Oaks Dr 29732
Country Pride Ln 29730
Countryview Ln 29730
Covenant Pl 29732
Coventry Ln 29732
Covered Bridge Ct 29732
Covington St 29732
Covington Place Ct 29732
Cowan Farm Rd 29730
Cowboys Cir 29732
Craft Dr 29730
Craig Rd 29730
Crane St 29730
Cranford St 29732
Cranium Dr 29732
Crannog Way 29732
Craven Hill Dr 29730
Crawford Rd 29730
Creek Ct & Xing 29732
Creek Bluff Rd 29732
Creekbridge Dr 29732
Creekside Dr 29732
Crescent Leaf Ln 29730
Crest St 29730
Crestdale Rd 29732
Crestside Dr 29732
Crestview Dr 29732
Croatoan Dr 29730
Crooked Stick Dr 29732
Crosby St 29732
Cross Creek Ct 29732
Crosspointe Dr 29730
Crosstrail Rdg 29732
Crow Foot Ct 29730
Crowders Rd 29732
Crown Pointe Dr 29730
Crows Nest Rd 29730
Crumpsall Ct 29730
Crystal Ln 29732
Crystal Creek Dr 29732
Crystal Lakes Dr 29732
Crystal Ridge Dr 29732
Cubla Ct 29732
Cullybackey Dr 29730
Culp Cir & St 29730
Cumberland Ct 29732
Cumbria Way 29732
Cummings St 29730

Cunningham Dr 29732
Cureton Ct & Dr 29732
Curlew Ct 29732
Curtis St 29730
Cushendall Ter 29730
Cuttawa St 29730
Cypress Cv 29732
Cypress St 29730
Cypress Point Dr 29730
Cypress Tree Dr 29730
Daffodil Rd 29730
Daisy St 29730
Dale Ct 29732
Dalebrook Ln 29730
Dalecrest Cir 29732
Dalehurst Rd 29732
Dalene Ave 29730
Dalkeith Ave 29732
Dan Dr 29732
Dansington Ave 29730
Dantzler Ct 29732
Darby Dr 29732
Darrington Ct 29732
Dartmouth Dr 29732
Darwin St 29732
Dave Lyle Blvd S 29730
Davenport Ct 29732
David Ct 29732
Davidson Woods Dr 29730
Davis St 29730
Dawnshire Ave 29732
Dawson Ct 29730
Day Lily Ln 29730
Dayton Rd 29732
Dead End Rd 29730
Deanne Dr 29730
Dearborn Dr 29732
Deas St 29732
Deberry Holw 29732
E & W Decatur Dr 29730
Deer Run 29730
Deer Lick Rd 29730
Deer Track Dr 29732
Deerwood Ct 29732
Delamere Ct 29732
Delfin Ct 29730
Dellas Way 29732
Demetria Run 29732
Denali Way 29732
Denwood Ln 29732
Destiny Dr 29730
Devine St 29730
Devonshire Dr 29732
Devore Pl 29730
Dewars Dr 29730
Dewitt Dr 29730
Diary Dr 29732
Dickerson Village Rd 29730
Didsbury Dr 29730
Dillard Rd 29730
Dillwin Rd 29732
Dilworth Ln 29732
Divot Pl 29732
Dixie Ln 29730
Doby Dr 29730
Dockside Dr 29732
Docs Dead End Rd 29730
Dogwood Cir & Dr 29732
Doncaster Dr 29732
Doral Ct 29730
Dorchester St 29732
Doris Cir 29730
Dorothy St 29732
Dotson St 29732
Dotty Ln 29730
Douglas Dr & St 29730
Dove Tree Ln 29732
Dover Ct & Dr 29732
Downey St 29730
Dr Frank Gaston Blvd 29732
Drake Ct 29732
Drake Pond Ln 29732
Drakeford Rd 29730
Drawbridge Ct 29732
Driftwood Ln 29732
Dublin Ct 29732

Duckett Ct 29730
Dude Rd 29730
Duffy Ct 29730
Duncan Ct 29730
Dunlap St 29730
Dunlap Roddey Rd 29730
Dunluce Dr 29730
Durant Dr 29732
Durham Ln 29730
Durwood Rd 29730
Dusk Dr 29732
Dutch Ct 29730
Dutch Elm Pl 29732
Dutchman Dr 29732
Eagle Dr 29732
Eagle Bluff Ct 29730
Eagle Heart Ln 29730
Eagle Lair Dr 29730
Eagle Ridge Dr 29732
Eagles Pl 29732
Eakle Dr 29730
Eastover Dr 29732
Eastshire Rd 29730
Eastview Rd 29732
Eastwood Dr 29730
Ebenezer Ave 29730
Ebenezer Rd 29732
Ebenezer Avenue Ext 29732
Ebinport Rd 29732
Ebinwood Rd 29732
Ebony Point Dr 29730
Echo Ln 29730
Ed Bookout Ln 29732
Eden Ter 29730
Eden Oaks Dr 29730
Eden Terrace Ext 29730
Edenvale Rd 29730
Edgemont St 29730
Edgewood Dr 29730
Edinburgh Dr 29730
Edwards St 29732
Egret Ct 29732
Eisenhower Rd 29730
Elder Rd 29732
Elderwood Rd 29732
Elgin Ct 29732
S Elizabeth Ln 29730
Elk Ave 29730
Elks Park Rd 29732
Ellen Ave 29730
Ellington Dr 29732
Ellis St 29730
Ellis Pond Dr 29730
Ellison Dr 29730
Elmwood Dr 29730
Emerald Ln 29730
Emerson Dr 29730
Emily Pl 29732
Emily Crest Ln 29732
Emma Grace Ln 29732
Emma Wood Ln 29732
Emmett St 29730
Emorywood Ln 29730
Enfield Dr 29732
English Trl 29732
Enola Dr 29732
Enon Ct 29732
Enterprise Rd 29730
Epting St 29732
Erby Rd 29732
Erinn Rd 29730
Essex Hall Dr 29730
Estes Ct & Dr 29732
Estuary Ct 29732
Ethan Ln 29732
Etta Vaughn Ln 29730
Eva Mae Ln 29732
Evamar Ct 29730
Evans Ave 29732
Evelyn St 29730
Evelyn George Rd 29730
Evening Pl 29732
Evergreen Cir 29730
Evergreen Ln 29730
Faile Rd 29732
Fair Way Rd 29730

Faires Rd 29730
Fairfield Ave 29732
Fairhaven Rd 29732
Fairhill Cir 29732
Fairlawn Ct 29732
Fairway Cir & Dr 29730
Faith Blvd 29730
Faith Caroline Blvd 29732
Falcon Hall Way 29730
Falconwood Cir 29732
Fall Line Way 29730
Falling Leaf Ct 29732
Falls Rd
600-1599 29730
1600-1699 29732
Fancrest Ct 29732
Fargo St 29732
Farlow St 29732
Farm Pond Ln 29732
Farmstead Rd 29732
Farmview Pl 29732
Farmwood Ln 29732
Farrow Dr 29732
Faulk Rd 29730
Faulkenberry Rd 29730
Faversham Ln 29730
Favorwood Dr 29730
Fawnborough Ct 29732
Fayrene Rd 29732
Featherstone Ct 29732
Feemster Ln 29730
Fencepost Ln 29730
Fennell St 29730
Fenton Pl 29732
Ferguson Dr 29730
Ferncliff Rd 29730
Ferndale Dr 29730
Ferris St 29732
Fewell St 29730
Fieldbrook Rd 29732
Fieldcrest Cir 29732
Fields Farm Rd 29730
Fieldstone Dr 29730
Fincher Rd 29732
Finley Ct, Rd & Sq 29730
Finley View Dr 29730
Fire Tower Rd 29730
Firethorn Ln 29732
Fishing Creek Rd 29730
Fishing Creek Church Rd 29730
Fletcher Ct 29732
Fling Rd 29730
Flint St 29730
Flint Hill St 29730
Flint Street Ext 29730
Flintwood Dr 29732
Floral Rd 29732
Florence St 29730
Floyd Ln & Rd 29730
Flynn Dr 29730
Forest Ln & Rd 29730
Forest Creek Dr 29730
Forest Glen Dr 29732
Forest Hills Cir 29732
Forest Lake Dr 29732
Forest Point Ln 29730
Forestbrook Ct 29732
Forestwood Rd 29732
E Fork Rd 29730
Fouche St 29730
Fowler Rd 29730
Fox Chase Rd 29730
Fox Creek Ln 29730
Fox Croft Rd 29730
Fox Crossing Ct 29730
Fox Haven Ln 29732
Fox Hunt Ct 29732
Foxlair Ct 29730
Foxmead Rd 29732
Foxridge Rd 29730
Frances St 29730
Frank St 29730
Frank Barnett Dr 29732
Franklin St 29732
Frayser St 29730

Friar Rd 29732
Friedheim Rd 29730
Friendship Dr 29730
Front Porch Dr 29732
Frontier Way 29730
Frostproof Trl 29730
Fudge St 29730
Furr St 29730
Gable Dr 29732
Gaffney Ln 29730
Gainey Dr 29730
Gallant Ct 29732
Galleria Blvd 29730
Galleria Pointe Cir 29730
Garden Way 29732
Garden Hill Ct 29732
Garden Place Ct 29732
N & S Garrison Rd 29730
Gate Ridge Dr 29730
Gatehouse Ct 29732
Gates Ave 29730
Gateview Ct 29732
Gatewood Dr 29730
Gathings Rd 29730
Gatsby Cir 29732
Gauldens Park Rd 29732
Gayle Dr 29732
Gentle Breeze Ln 29730
George Ln 29732
George Dunn Rd 29730
George Ratteree Rd 29730
Gerald Nichols Rd 29730
Gettys St 29730
Ghent Ct 29732
Gibson St 29732
Giga Dr 29730
Gill Way 29730
Gillespie Ln 29730
Gilmore Rd 29730
Gingercake Cir 29732
Gist Rd 29730
Givens Rd 29730
Givens Creek Trl 29730
Glade Rd 29730
Gladstone Ct 29730
Glasscock Rd 29730
Glen Echo Pl 29730
Glenarden Dr 29730
Glendale Dr 29732
Glenn St 29730
Glennhope Rd 29730
Glenstone Dr 29730
Glenview Ln 29730
Glenwood Dr 29732
Glyndora Dr 29730
Godfrey St 29730
Golden Bell Dr 29732
Golden Gate Ct 29732
Goldenrod Rd 29730
Goldflower Dr 29732
Goldsboro Ct 29730
Gone Roping Trl 29730
Goodplace Rd 29732
Gordon Ct 29730
Gordon Rd 29730
Goudlock Rd 29730
Grace St 29730
Grady Dr 29730
Graham St 29730
Grand Cir 29730
Grand Oak Dr 29732
Granville Rd 29732
Grayson Rd 29730
Green St 29730
Green Street Ext 29730
Green Valley Rd 29732
Greenarch Dr 29730
Greenbay Dr 29730
Greenbriar Ave 29730
Greenfield Dr 29732
Greenmeadow Dr 29732
Greenmoor Rd 29732
Greentree St 29730
Greenwood Ln & Rd 29730
Gregg Rd 29730
Gregson Ct 29732

Gresham Ct 29730
Grier St 29730
Grier Lesslie Rd 29730
Grier Mcguire Dr 29730
Griffith Cir 29732
Gristmill Dr 29732
Guilford Rd 29732
Guiness Pl 29730
Habitat Ct 29730
Hackberry Dr 29732
Haddington Ct 29730
Hagins St 29730
Hagler Dr 29730
Haigler St 29732
Haile St 29730
Hall St 29730
Hall Spencer Rd 29730
Hallman Dr 29732
Hallmark Dr 29730
Hallmark Xing 29732
Hammock Ln 29732
Hampshire Ave 29732
Hampton St 29730
Hampton Ridge Rd 29732
Hamptonwood Rd 29732
Hancock Union Ln 29732
Hands Mill Ext & Hwy 29732
Hannah Dr 29732
Hanover Ct 29732
Happy St 29730
Harbor Inn Rd 29732
Harbor Town Pl 29730
Hardin St 29730
Hardy Dr 29732
Harlinsdale Dr 29732
Harmony Rd 29730
Harmony Glen Cir 29730
Harper Gault Rd 29730
Harrell St 29730
Harrison St 29730
Hartford Ct 29732
Harvest Moon Ln 29732
Harvey Neely Rd 29730
Hastings Ct 29732
Hasty St 29730
Hathaway Dr 29730
Hawkfield Rd 29730
Hawthorne Ln 29730
Hawthorne Lane Ext 29730
Hayes Dr 29732
Haynes St 29730
Hazel Downe Way 29732
Headwaters Way 29730
Health Care Dr 29732
Hearn St 29732
Hearthstone Ct 29732
Heather Sq 29732
Heatherhill Rd 29732
Heathland Dr 29730
Heathridge Rd 29732
Heavens Gate Dr 29730
Heckle Blvd
100-899 29730
900-2899 29732
S Heckle Blvd 29730
Heckle Pine Cir 29730
Heisler Rd 29730
Helms St 29732
Hemlock Ave 29730
Hempstead Rd 29732
Henderson St 29730
Hepp Ln 29730
Heritage Pl 29730
S Herlong Ave & Ct 29732
Herlong Village Dr 29732
Hermitage Rd 29732
Herndon Farm Rd 29732
Herrons Ferry Rd 29730
Heyward St 29730
Hicklin Dr 29732
Hicklin Creek Rd 29730
Hickory Ln 29732
Hickory Hollow Dr 29732
Hickory Nut Ct 29732
Hickory Oaks Ln 29730
Hickory Ridge Rd 29732

Hicks St 29730
Hidden Creek Dr 29732
Hidden Hills Dr 29730
Hidden Valley Rd 29730
High St 29730
High Hills Ct 29732
High Pines Rd 29732
Highcrest Way 29730
Highland St 29730
Highlander Pkwy 29732
Hightide Dr 29732
Hightower Rd 29730
Highway 21 S 29730
Highway 324 29732
E Highway 324 29730
W Highway 324 29730
Highway 5 29730
Highwood Rd 29732
Hill St 29730
Hillcrest Ave 29732
Hillcroft Pl 29732
Hilldale Dr 29732
Hillsborough Ln 29732
Hillside Dr 29730
Hilltop Rd 29730
Hilton Rd 29732
Hinesdale Dr 29730
Hinson Ln 29732
Hitching Post Ln 29732
Hoffman Pl 29730
Hoke Ln 29730
Holdcroft Ln 29730
Holland Rd 29732
Hollis St 29732
Hollis Lakes Rd 29732
Holly Rd 29730
Hollyberry Ct 29730
Hollydale Dr 29730
Hollythorne Dr 29732
Holton Rd 29732
Home Ct 29732
Home Depot Blvd 29730
Homeplace Rd 29730
Homestead Rd 29732
Homeward Ln 29732
Honeysuckle Rd 29732
Honeysuckle Pond Rd 29732
Honeywood Ln 29730
Hood Center Rd 29730
Hope Dr & St 29730
Hopewell Rd 29730
Horizon Cir 29732
Horse Rd 29730
Horseman Dr 29730
Horton Ave 29732
Hospitality Dr 29732
Hough Cir 29730
Hovis Rd 29730
Howard St 29730
Howell Rd 29732
Hoyle St 29730
Hoyles Dr 29730
Hudspeth Ln 29732
Huey Rd 29730
Hull St 29730
Hummingbird Ln 29732
Hunt Club Ct 29732
Huntcliff Dr 29732
Hunter Ridge Rd 29732
Hunter Trail Ct 29730
Hunters Trl 29732
Hunters Creek Ln 29732
Hunting Ct 29732
Huntington Pl 29732
Huntmoor Dr 29732
Hunts Cir 29730
Hutchinson St 29730
Hyacinthia Ln 29730
Hyatt Ave 29732
Idlewild Dr 29732
Impulse Ln 29732
India Hook Rd 29732
Indian Trl 29730
Indigo Ct 29730
Ingleside Ct 29732
Inland Trace Ct 29732

Innsbrook Commons Cir 29730
Interconnect Dr 29730
Inverness Pl 29730
Inwood Dr 29732
Iredell St 29730
Irene St 29730
Iris Cir 29730
Iron Gate Ct 29732
Ironwood Ct 29732
Irwin St 29730
Isom Estates Dr 29730
Ivy St 29730
Ivy Arbor Cir 29732
Ivydale Ct 29732
Ivywood Dr 29732
Iyeye St 29730
Izard St 29730
Jack White Dr 29732
Jackson St 29730
Jake Pierce Dr 29730
James Ct 29732
Janay Ct 29732
Jason Lyle Dr 29730
Jedburgh Way 29730
Jefferson Ave 29730
Jenkins St 29732
Jennie Boyd Ct 29730
Jennings Rd 29730
Jenny Skip Ln 29732
Jenson Way 29730
Jessicas Way 29730
Joanies Ct 29732
Joe Louis Blvd 29730
John St 29732
John Branch Rd 29732
John Brown Rd 29730
John Roddey Rd 29730
John Ross Pkwy 29730
Johnny Boyd Rd 29730
Johnston St 29730
N & S Jones Ave 29730
S Jones Avenue Ext 29730
Jones Mill Ln 29730
Jonesberry Dr 29732
Jonquil Ct 29730
Joseph Ct 29732
Joshs Ct 29732
Joslin Park Rd 29732
Joslin Pointe Ln 29730
Joyce Ct 29732
Juanita Ave 29730
June Bug Ln 29730
Juniper Ln 29730
Juniper View Rd 29732
Kacie Dr 29730
Kallaramo Rd 29732
Kaneland Ct 29732
Karen Dr 29730
Karen Ln 29732
Karwood Dr 29730
Kathies Pond Rd 29730
Kathleen Dr 29730
Keels Ave 29730
Keiger St 29730
Keith Dr 29730
Kellibell Ln 29730
Kelly St 29732
Kemper Cir 29732
Kenbridge Ln 29732
Kendall Dr 29730
Kendlewood Dr 29732
Kenneth Dr 29730
Kensington Sq 29732
Kentwood Dr 29730
Kenwood Ln 29730
Kestrel Dr 29732
Keswick Ln 29732
Ketchen Farm Rd 29732
Kettlewell Rdg 29732
Kevin Ln 29732
Keys Ct 29730
Kiley Ct 29730
Kilgarnin Ct 29732
Kimble Ln 29732
Kimbrell St 29730

Kimbrook Ct & St 29730
Kincaid Ct 29730
King Dr 29730
Kinghurst Dr 29730
Kings Row Dr 29732
Kingsbridge Rd 29730
Kingsfield Rd 29732
Kingsley Rd 29732
Kingstree Ct 29730
Kingswood Dr 29732
Kingswood Drive Ext 29732
Kinsey Creek Ct 29730
Kintyre Rd 29730
Kirkstone Ln 29732
Knighton Aly 29730
Knighton Hill Rd 29732
Knollwood Ct 29732
Knotty Branch Trl 29730
Knotty Hill Dr 29732
Knotty Pine Ln 29732
Knox Ct 29730
Knox Pointe Ln 29732
Kousa Ct 29732
Kuykendall St 29730
Kyle Dr 29732
Lacebark Dr 29732
Lacy Ln 29732
Ladybarn Dr 29730
Lake Club Dr 29732
Lake Commons Dr 29732
Lake Edward Rd 29730
Lake Wylie Dr 29732
Lakefront Dr 29730
Lakehurst Dr 29732
Lakeland Dr 29730
Lakeshore Pkwy 29732
Lakeside Dr 29730
Lakeview Dr 29732
E & W Lakewood Dr 29732
Lamp Post Ln 29732
Lancaster Ave 29730
Land Fall Dr 29732
Landis Ct 29730
Landmark Dr 29732
Landon Ln 29730
Landry Ln 29732
Lands End Rd 29732
Laney Ter 29730
Langston St 29730
Lannie Ln 29730
Lark Ln 29730
Larkin Butler Ct 29730
Larkin Jackson Ct 29730
Larkridge Ct 29730
Larne Port Dr 29732
Latham Ct 29732
Laurel St 29730
Laurel Creek Dr 29732
Laurel Glen Dr 29732
Laurendale Ct 29732
Laurens St 29730
Lavington Ct 29732
Law Pl 29730
Lawonna Dr 29732
Lawton Dr 29730
Lazy Hawk Rd 29730
Leach Rd 29732
Leatherwood Ct 29730
N Lee St 29730
Legend Dr 29732
Legere Ct 29730
Lela Mae Ct 29730
Lenax Ct 29732
Lesslie Hwy & Rd 29730
Lesslie Dale Rd 29730
Lesslie Trail Dr 29730
Lesslie Woods Ct 29730
Level St 29730
Lewis St 29732
Lexie Ln 29732
Lexington Commons Dr 29732
Liberty St 29730
Liberty Bell Ct 29732
Lige St 29730
Lighthouse Ct 29732
Limehouse Ct 29732
Linda Ct 29732
Linda Rd 29730
Lindsay St 29730
Linkwood Rd 29730
Linwood Dr & St 29732
Lister St 29732
Litchfield Rd 29732
Little St 29730
Little Leaf Ln 29732
Little Rock Rd 29730
Liverpool Rd 29732
Lock Haven Rd 29732
Locke Ln 29730
Locust St 29730
Lomax St 29730
Lombardy Rd 29730
London Dr 29732
Londonberry Dr 29730
Lone Oak Cir 29732
Long St 29730
Long Meadow Rd 29730
Long Shadow Ln 29732
Longbriar Rd 29732
Longfield Rd 29732
Longhorn Dr 29732
Longsight Ln 29730
Longview Rd 29732
Looking Glass Ln 29732
Lookout Pt & Rdg 29732
Lord Dunluce St 29732
Lotts Pl 29732
Louie Rd 29732
Lovelace Rd 29730
Lowell Trce 29732
Lucas St 29730
Lucille Ln 29730
Lucky Ct & Ln 29730
Lumpkin Cir 29732
Lydia St 29730
Lyle St 29730
Lyle Boyd Rd 29730
Lynderboro Dr 29730
Lynhaven Rd 29732
Lynn Cir 29732
Lynville Ln 29730
Lynwood Ln 29730
Mabry Pkwy 29732
Macarthur St 29730
Macey Ln 29732
Macgeary Rd 29730
Maddy Ln 29732
Madeline Dr 29730
Madison St 29732
Madonna St 29730
Maggie Ln 29730
Magnolia Dr 29730
E Main St 29730
W Main St
100-999 29730
1000-3099 29732
Maitland Dr 29732
Mallaney Rd 29730
Mallard Dr 29732
Mallard Creek Dr 29732
Mallard Head Dr 29732
Mallory Dr 29730
Maloa Way 29732
Malone Pl 29732
Malvern Rd 29730
Mana Ct 29732
Manchester St 29730
Mancke Dr 29730
Mandarin Dr 29732
Mangum Rd 29730
Manley St 29730
Manning Pl 29730
Manor Close Dr 29730
Manteo St 29732
Maple St 29730
Maple Hill Ln 29732
Mapleleaf Ct 29732
Maplewood Ln 29732
Marett Blvd 29732
Marett Boulevard Ext 29732
Margaret St 29730
Margaret Scott Rd 29730
Mariemont Way 29732
Marine Dr 29730
Marion St
100-199 29732
200-399 29730
Market Hall Pl 29732
Marley Ct 29732
Marshall Rd & St 29730
Marsley Ln 29730
Marston Cir 29732
Martin Ave 29730
Mary Halley Dr 29730
Mary Knoll Ct 29730
Marydale Ln 29732
Mast Wind Trl 29732
Masters Dr 29732
Mathis Rd 29732
Matthews Dr 29732
Matthews Simril Rd 29732
Mauldin Dr 29732
Maxi St 29730
Mayfair Pl 29730
Maypine Commons Way 29732
Mays Ct 29730
Maywood Dr 29730
Mccall Meadows Dr 29730
Mcclain Rd 29732
Mcclure Cir 29730
Mcconnells Hwy 29732
Mccullough St 29730
Mcdow Dr 29730
Mcfadden St 29730
Mcgee Rd 29732
Mcgill St 29732
Mcgill Pond Ln 29732
Mckinnon Dr 29732
Mcnair St 29730
Mcquire Dr 29730
Mcshae Dr 29730
Mcswain Ln 29730
Meade St 29732
Meadow Ln 29732
Meadow Glen Ln 29730
Meadow Lakes Rd 29732
Meadowbrook Ln 29730
Meadowdale Rd 29732
Meadowland Dr 29730
Meadowlark Dr 29732
Mecca Trl 29730
Medical Park Dr 29732
Meeting Blvd 29730
Mega Dr 29730
Melchers Dr 29730
Melody Ln 29732
Melrose Dr 29730
Memorial Dr 29730
Memory Ln 29732
Menehune Ln 29730
Menzies Dr 29730
Meredith Ct 29732
Meridan Dr 29730
Merrie Meadow Ct 29732
Merrill Pl 29732
Mickle Ct 29730
Micro St 29730
Midbrook Dr 29732
Middleton Pl 29732
Midland Rd 29730
Midnight Cir 29732
Midvale Ave 29730
Midwood Rd 29732
Milhaven St 29730
Mill St 29730
Miller St 29730
Miller Pond Rd 29732
Millhouse Dr 29730
Milling Rd 29730
Mills Park Dr 29730
Millstone Pl 29730
Millstream Dr 29732
Milton Ave 29730
Mimosa Rd 29730
Mini St 29730
Minnie Ln 29732
Mint St 29730
Mintwood Ln 29730
Mistwood Rd 29732
Mitchum Rd 29730
Mobley Store Rd 29730
Mockingbird Ln 29730
Monroe St 29730
Montclair Dr 29732
Monterey Dr 29732
Montford St 29730
Montgomery Dr 29732
E & W Moore St 29730
Moores Crk 29732
Morgan St 29730
Morgans Bnd 29732
Morningside Dr 29730
Morris St 29730
Moss Tree Ct 29730
Moultrie Way 29732
Mount Gallant Rd
100-598 29730
600-999 29730
1000-1098 29732
1100-6199 29732
E Mount Gallant Rd 29730
Mount Holly Dr & Rd 29730
Mount Phillips St 29730
Mountain Laurel Way 29732
Ms Farm Rd 29730
Muirfield Ct 29730
Mulberry Cir 29730
Mulligan Ln 29732
Murrah Dr 29732
Museum Rd 29732
Myers St 29732
Myrtle Dr
700-990 29730
992-998 29730
1000-1199 29732
Nalley Rd 29732
Nantucket Way 29732
Naples Ln 29730
Nassaw Cir 29730
Natalie Ln 29730
Nations Ct 29730
Nations Ford Rd 29730
Natures Trail Ct 29732
Nautilus Rd 29730
Navajo Ct 29732
Neal St 29732
Neely Ct 29730
Neely Rd 29730
Neely Store Rd 29730
Neelys Creek Rd 29730
Neptune Dr 29730
Nestledown Ct 29732
Neville St 29730
New Sugereetown Ln 29730
Newcastle Dr 29732
Newland Ct 29730
Newport Lakes Dr 29732
Newton Ave 29732
Nicholson Ave 29732
Nighthawk Dr 29732
Nightingale Rd 29732
Noahs Ark Rd 29730
Nobel Way 29730
Noel Ct 29732
Noostee Town Dr 29730
Norfolk Ct 29730
Norman Dr 29732
Normandy Way 29732
Norris Dr 29730
North Ave 29730
Northbrook Dr 29732
Northgate Ln 29732
Northpark Dr 29732
Northway Dr 29730
Norway Ln 29732
Norwood Ave 29732
Norwood Ridge Dr 29732
Notable Ln 29732
Nottingham Ct 29732
Nuthatch Dr 29732
Oak Ct 29730
Oak Dr 29730
W Oak Dr 29732
Oak Branch Dr 29730
Oak Meadows Ct 29732
Oak Park Rd 29730
Oak Pond Rd 29730
Oakbourne Ln 29732
Oakdale Rd 29730
Oakhurst Dr 29732
Oakland Ave
100-900 29730
902-998 29730
1000-1099 29732
S Oakland Ave 29730
Oakmont Dr 29732
Oakridge Meadows Ct 29732
Oakview Way 29730
Oakwood Cir 29732
Oakwood Ln 29730
Oates St 29730
Oconee Ave 29732
Ogden Rd 29730
Old Cattlebarn Rd 29730
Old Chisholm Rd 29732
Old Coach Ln 29732
Old Eury Rd 29732
Old Field Rd 29730
Old Forge Rd 29730
Old Friendship Rd 29730
Old High Ct 29730
Old Pointe School Rd 29732
Old Rawlinson Rd 29732
Old Springdale Rd 29732
Old York Rd 29732
Olde Creek Rd 29732
Olde Oxford Ct 29732
Olde Towne Way 29732
Ole Simpson Pl 29730
Oleen Cove Rd 29732
Olewoods Ct & Dr 29732
Ollie St 29730
Olympus Rd 29732
Open Meadow Rd 29732
Orange St 29730
Orchard Ln 29730
Oriole Dr 29732
Ormston Cir 29732
Orr Dr 29730
Osceola Ave 29732
Otman Ct 29732
Ottawa Dr 29732
Our Rd 29730
Overbrook Dr 29730
Overlook Rd 29730
Overmountain Dr 29732
Overview Dr 29730
Oxford Dr 29730
Ozark Ct 29732
Ozell J Berry Ct 29730
Paces Landing Ave 29732
Paces River Ave 29732
Paddock Pkwy 29730
Page Ct 29730
Painted Lady Ct 29732
Palmers Pl 29730
Palmetto Dr 29732
Pampas Cir 29732
Paperbark Ln 29732
Par Four Dr 29732
Par Ring Farm Rd 29730
Paragon Way 29730
Paraham Rd S 29732
Park Ave & Dr 29730
Park Avenue Ext 29732
Park Meadow Dr 29732
Park Ridge Blvd 29732
Park View Ct 29732
Park Walk Pl 29732
Parker St 29730
Parkmont Ln 29730
Parkwood Dr 29730
Parris Rd 29732
Parrish Pt & St 29730
Partridge Berry Ln 29732
Passmore Dr 29730
Patagonia Ct 29732
Patio Pt 29732
Patriot Pkwy 29730
Patterson Ct 29730
Patton St 29730
Pavillion Ct 29732
Paw Paw Dr 29730
Paxton St 29732
Payge Dr 29730
Peaches Ct 29730
Peachtree Rd & St 29730
Pearl St 29730
Pearson Dr 29730
Pebble Rd 29730
Pebblebrook Ct 29732
Pecan Cir 29732
Pelham Ln 29732
Pelham Wood Dr 29732
Pendleton St 29730
Pennington Rd 29732
Pennington Meadows Cir 29732
Penny Ln 29732
Penny Oaks Cv 29732
Penshurst Rd 29730
Peppermill Dr 29732
Percival Rd 29730
Perry Rd 29730
Persimmon Pl 29732
Phelps St 29730
Phil Grant Rd 29730
Picadilly Ln 29732
Pickens Ct & St 29730
Pickett Rd 29732
Picnic Ct 29732
Piedmont Blvd 29732
Piedmont St 29730
Pierce Ct 29730
Pinckney St 29730
Pine Dale Ct 29730
Pine Grove Ct 29730
Pine Lane Cir 29732
Pine Terrace Dr 29730
Pinebough Ln 29732
Pinebranch St 29730
Pinebrook Dr 29730
Pineburr Ln 29730
Pinecrest Dr 29732
Pinehill Rd 29730
Pinehurst Dr 29732
Pinetuck Ln 29730
Pinevalley Rd 29732
Pineview St 29730
Pinewood Ln & Rd 29730
Pioneer Pl 29730
Piper Gln 29732
Piscataway Ct 29732
Pitts St 29730
Plainfield Dr 29732
Plantation Rd 29732
Plantation Hills Dr 29732
Planters Ct 29732
Plateau Ct 29730
Pleazer Rd 29730
Plum Tree Dr 29732
Plyler Dr 29730
Poag St 29730
Poe St 29730
Poinsett Dr 29730
Pointe Cir 29730
Polk Cir 29730
S Pond St 29730
Pondway Downs 29730
Pope St 29732
Poplar St 29730
Porter Rd 29730
Porter Black Rd 29730
Post Ln 29730
Post Oak Ln 29732
Poston Dr 29732
Potpourri Pt 29732
Powderhouse St 29730
Powell St 29730
Presidio Dr 29732
Prestwick Dr 29730
Pride St 29730
Priestly Dr 29732
Prince Ln 29730
Princeton Rd 29730
Professional Park Dr 29732
Progress Way 29730
Pump Station Dr 29730
Purple Martin Dr 29732
Pursley St 29732
Putters Ln 29732
Pyxie Moss Ct 29732
Quail Dr 29730
Quail Creek Dr 29732
Quail Meadow Rd 29730
Quail Rush Dr 29730
Quaint Ln 29730
Quality Cir 29730
Quantz St 29730
Queens Rd 29732
Queensbridge Ct 29732
Quiet Acres Cir & Rd 29732
Quiet Creek Pl 29732
Quiet Waters Ct 29730
Quinby Way 29732
Rabs Rd 29730
Rabun Cir & Ln 29730
Ragin Ln 29732
Railroad Ave 29730
Rainey St 29730
Rains Mdw 29732
Ramble Wood Ct 29730
Rambling Rose Ln 29732
E & W Rambo Rd 29730
Ramrod Rd 29730
Randle Ct 29730
Randolph Rd 29730
Randwick Dr 29730
Ratteree Cir 29730
Ratteree Farm Rd 29730
Rauch St 29730
Raven Dr 29732
Raven Cliff Ct 29732
Rawlings Pl 29730
Rawlinson Rd 29730
Rawlsville Rd 29730
Raymond Ln 29730
Reba Dr 29730
Rebekah Ln 29730
Red Cedar Ln 29730
Red Door Dr 29732
Red Fox Trl 29730
Red Oaks Dr 29730
Red River Rd 29730
Redwood Dr 29730
Redwood Rd 29730
Reece Cir 29730
Reese Rd 29730
Reese Roach Rd 29730
Regency Ct 29732
Reid Rd & St 29730
Rental Ct 29730
Reservation Rd 29730
Restless One Ln 29730
Reynolds St 29730
Rhea St 29730
Rhinehart St 29730
Rhonda Dr 29732
Rich St 29730
Richards Landing Dr 29730
Richards Way Dr 29732
Richland St 29730
Richmond Dr 29732
Ridge Ct 29730
Ridge Rd 29732
Ridgecrest Rd 29732
Ridgefield Ct 29732
Ridgemont Rd 29732
Ridgerock Ln 29732
Ridgeview Ct 29732
Ridgeway Ln 29732
Ridgewood Dr 29732
Ridgewood Dr N 29732
Ridgewood Ln 29730
Ridley St 29730
Rillaby Ave 29732
Rittenhouse Ln 29732
River Cv 29732
River Bottom Rd 29730
River Cove Rd 29732

River Oaks Ct 29730
River Pines Rd 29732
River Run Ct 29732
Riverchase Blvd 29732
Rivercrest Rd 29730
Riverdale Dr 29732
Riverglenn Ct 29732
Rivers St 29730
Riverside Dr 29730
Riverview Rd
700-999 29730
1000-1599 29732
Riverwalk Pkwy 29730
Riverwood Ct 29732
Riviera Pl 29730
Roanoke Creek Trl 29730
Robbett Ct 29732
Robbie Ln 29730
Roberts Rd 29732
Robertson Rd 29730
Robin Ln 29730
Robinson St 29730
Robinson Street Ext 29730
Robinwood Ct 29730
Rock St 29730
Rock Glen Dr 29732
Rock Grove Ave 29730
Rock Springs Way 29730
Rockdale St 29730
Rocket Rd 29732
Rocklyn Dr 29730
Rockwell Cir 29730
Rockwood Dr 29730
Roddey St 29730
Rogers Cir 29730
Rolling Green Dr 29730
Rolling Ridge Rd 29730
Rolling Stream Dr 29732
Rollingwood Cir 29732
Roper Rd 29732
Rose St 29730
Rose Garden Ct 29732
Rose Hill Dr 29730
Roseborough Rd 29730
Rosedale St 29732
Rosehaven Ln 29732
Rosemore Pl 29730
Rosewell Dr 29732
Rosewood Dr 29732
Rough Hewn Ln 29730
Round Hill Rd 29730
Roundtree Cir 29732
Roxburgh Ave 29732
W Roy St 29730
Roy Brown Rd 29732
Rue De Vl 29732
Runningbrook Ln 29732
Runnymede Dr 29732
Rush Ct 29730
Ruslin Rd 29730
Russell Rd 29732
Russell St 29730
Rustic Ridge Rd 29730
Rustlewood Way 29732
Rutledge Ave 29732
Sabin St 29730
Saddlebrook Dr 29730
Sadie Ln 29730
Saint Katherines Way 29732
Saluda Rd & St 29730
Sam Berry Rd 29732
Sampson St 29732
Sanborn St 29730
Sancreek Dr 29732
Sand Island Rd 29732
Sanderling Dr 29732
Sanders Rd 29730
Sanders St 29732
Sandlewood Dr 29730
Sandpiper Dr 29732
Sandra Ln 29730
Sandy Ct 29730
Sandy Ridge Run 29732
Sapaugh Ave 29732
Sarahs Ct 29732
Sasha Ct 29732
Sawgrass Dr 29732
Saybrook Ct 29732
Scaleybark Rd 29732
Scarboro Ln 29732
Scarlet Oak Dr 29732
Schoolside Dr 29730
Schuyler Dr 29730
Scoggins St 29730
Scotland Yard 29732
Scott St 29730
Scottie Ct 29730
Scotts Way 29732
Secession Way 29732
Sedgewood Dr 29732
Seldon Pl 29730
Selma St 29730
Selwyn Pl 29732
Seneca Pl 29732
Sensation Rd 29732
Sentry Ln 29730
Sequoia Dr 29732
Serenity Ln 29730
Sesame St 29732
Sethwood Dr 29732
Shadewood Ct 29732
Shadow Ln 29732
Shadow Oak Dr 29730
Shadow Pine Ct 29732
Shadowbrook Dr 29732
Shady Oak Ln 29730
Shadyside Ln 29732
Shamrock Ct 29730
Shandon Rd 29730
Shandonwood St 29730
Sharonwood Ln 29732
Shaw Ave 29730
Sheebar Pl 29732
Sheffingdell Rd 29730
Sheheen St 29730
Shelby Ct 29730
Shelby Ann Ln 29732
Shenandoah Cir 29730
Sheraton Way 29732
Sherham Way 29732
Sherwood Cir 29730
Shetland Ln 29730
Shiland Dr 29730
Shimmer Light Cir 29732
Shorewood Dr 29732
Shuman St 29730
Shurley St 29730
Sibley Rd 29730
Sidney St 29730
Silk Tree Ln 29732
Silver Ln 29732
Silver Leaf Cir 29732
Silver Stream Dr 29732
Simpson St 29730
Simrill St 29730
Sims Rd 29730
Singing Bird Ln 29730
Sirrine St 29730
Six Mile Crk 29730
Six Pines Dr 29730
Skyline Rd 29730
Slemish Rd 29730
Sloan Dr 29730
Smith St 29730
Smiths Cir 29730
Smoke House Ln 29732
Smokey Dr 29730
Snyder St 29730
Soft Winds Village Dr 29730
Sol Aberman Rd 29732
Somerdale Rd 29732
Somerset Ct 29732
Sonnet Ln 29730
Soulsville St 29730
Southcross Blvd 29730
Southeastern Rd 29730
Southern St 29730
Southern Cross Trl 29730
Southfork Rd 29730
Southland Dr 29730
Southside Rd 29730
Southway Dr 29730
Southwinds Ct 29730
Sparkston Ln 29732
Sparrow Dr 29732
Spencer St 29730
Spencer Ridge Rd 29730
Split Cedar Rd 29732
Spring Dr & St 29730
Spring Anding Dr 29730
Spring Box Ct 29732
Spring Landing Dr 29730
Spring View Ct 29730
Springbreeze Ct 29730
E, S & W Springdale
Rd 29730
Springer Ct 29730
Springpoint Rd 29732
Springsteen Rd 29730
Springvalley Rd 29730
Springwinds Dr 29730
Springwood Ln 29730
Sprouse St 29732
N & S Spruce St 29730
Spurs Ct 29732
Spyglass Way 29730
Squire Rd 29730
St Johns Ct 29730
Stadium St
600-999 29730
1000-1099 29732
Stalcup Rd 29730
Stan Stella Ct 29732
Standard St 29730
Stanley Dr 29730
Stanton Dr 29730
Starboard Rdg 29732
Starcrest Cir 29730
Starling Dr 29730
Starnes Dr 29730
State St 29730
State Street Ext 29730
Steed St 29732
Steele St 29730
Steele Village Rd 29730
Steen Cir 29730
Steeplechase Dr 29732
Stephanie Ln 29730
Stephen Carroll Rd 29732
Stephens St 29730
Stewart Ave 29730
Stone Pine Dr 29730
Stone Post Rd 29730
Stonehenge Dr 29730
Stonehill Pl 29730
Stonetrace Dr 29730
N & S Stonewall Ct &
St 29730
Stoney Ridge Ct 29730
Stoneybrook Ln 29730
Stoneycreek Ln 29730
Stoneypointe Dr 29732
Strait Rd 29730
Stratford Ln 29732
Strathclyde Way 29730
Strawberry Rd 29730
Stroupe St 29730
Stuart Carter Ave 29730
Sturgis Rd & St 29730
Sturgis Farm Rd 29730
Sugar Loaf Ln 29730
Sugar Tree Dr 29730
Sullivan St 29730
Summer Breeze 29730
Summer Creek Ct 29732
Summer House Way 29732
Summerlin Pl 29732
Summers Gln 29732
Summerstone Dr 29732
Summerwood Dr 29732
Summit View Dr 29732
Summitt St 29730
Sumner Dr 29732
Sumter Ave 29730
Sundance Trl 29730
Sunnybrook Dr 29730
Sunset Dr 29730
Sunset Rdg 29730
Sunset Point Dr 29732
Surrey Ln 29732
Susan Cir 29730
Swallowtail Ct 29732
Sweetbriar Ln 29732
Sweetgrass Ln 29732
Swens Dr 29732
W Swift Creek Rd 29732
Sylvia Cir 29730
Tabor Pl 29730
Tallgrass Blf 29732
Tanglewood Dr 29732
Tanner Commons Ln 29732
Tanner Ridge Ct 29730
Tarleton Ct 29732
Tarrington Dr 29730
Tate Rd 29732
Tavern Ct 29732
Taxiway J Dr 29732
Taylor St 29730
Taylors Creek Rd 29730
Tea Olive Ct 29732
Teaberry Ln 29732
Teal Ct 29732
Tealwood Dr 29732
Tenacity Ct 29732
Terrace Park 29730
Terrell Pl 29730
The Xing 29732
Thistledown Dr 29730
Thomas Ct 29730
Thomas Sam Dr 29732
Thornburg Rd 29730
Thornfield Ln 29730
Thornwell Ave 29730
Three D Systems Cir 29730
Tiana Way 29732
Tiffany Dr 29730
Tigler Ct 29730
Tillman St 29730
Timber Ln 29730
Timber Crossing Dr 29730
Timber Ridge Ln 29730
Timberlake Ct & Dr 29730
Timberline Dr 29730
Timberstone Ct 29732
Timothy Dr 29730
Tinker Ln 29730
Tinsley Way 29730
Tipperary Rd 29730
Tirzah Rd 29730
Titanic Rd 29730
Todd St 29730
Tom St 29730
Tom Barber Rd 29730
Tom Steven Rd 29730
Tomahawk Rdg 29730
Toms Turnaround 29730
Tools Fork Rd 29732
Torngat Way 29732
Torrington Cir 29730
Tortoiseshell Ln 29732
Townes Ct 29730
Townsend Dr & Ln 29730
Trade St N 29730
Trade Street Aly & Ext 29730
Tradition Way 29730
Trailmaster Rd 29730
Trailsend St 29730
Tree Line Dr 29730
Treemont Dr 29730
Trellis Dr 29730
Tremont Ave 29730
Trevor Ln 29730
Trexler Ln 29730
Tributary Dr 29732
Trimnal Ln 29730
Triple Creek Dr 29730
Trotter Ridge Ct 29732
Troute Dr 29730
Truffle Ct 29730
Tuckaway Rd 29730
Tucker St 29730
Tuckers Glenn Dr 29732
Tulip Tree Pl 29730
Turkey Ln 29730
Turkey Farm Rd 29732
Turnstone Ct 29732
Turtle Pond Rd 29730
Tweedale Ct 29730
Twin Lakes Rd 29730
Twitty Ct 29730
Two Pond Rd 29730
Tysons Forest Dr 29732
Ulverston Dr 29732
Union Ave 29730
University Dr 29730
Upper Cove Rd 29732
Urbana Rd 29730
Utah Trl 29732
Valann Farm Ct 29732
Vale Ct 29730
Valley Rd 29732
Valley Creek Rd 29730
Valleymere Rd 29732
Van Ness Rd 29730
Van Valin Dr 29732
Vandind Rd 29730
Veery Ln 29732
Vernsdale Rd 29730
Vian Ct 29732
Vickie Ln 29730
Victoria Dr 29732
Victoria Drive Ext 29732
Village Ct 29732
Village Green Ln 29730
Village Loop Dr 29732
Vinson Rd 29730
Vintage Ln 29730
Virginia St 29730
Virginia Dare Dr 29730
Vistawood Rd 29730
Volunteer Dr 29732
Wade St 29732
Wade Harris Rd 29730
Wagon Trl 29732
Wagon Wheel Ct 29732
Wagon Wheel Rd 29730
Wakefield Way 29730
Walcott Ct 29730
Walden Ct 29732
Walker Rd 29730
Walkers Mill Cir 29732
Walking Horse Ln 29730
Wall St 29730
Wallace Ct 29732
Wallick Ln 29732
Walnut St 29730
Walnut Hill Dr 29732
Walnut Ridge Rd 29730
Walshaw St 29732
Wamsutter Ln 29730
Ward Dr 29730
Warner St 29730
Warrington Pl 29732
Washington Ct & St 29730
Waterford Glen Way 29730
Waterford Park Dr 29730
Waterscape Ct 29730
Watson St 29732
Watts Ct 29730
Waverly Ave 29730
Wayland Rd 29730
Wayward Xing 29732
Weatherwood St 29732
Webster Ct 29730
Wedgefield Dr 29730
Wedgewood Ct 29732
Wedowee Ct 29732
Welborn St 29732
Welch St 29732
Wellington St 29732
Wells Ct 29732
Wendover Ct 29732
Wendy Rd 29730
Wensley Ct 29730
Wentworth Dr 29732
Wesley Wood Dr 29730
Westerwood Dr 29732
Westminster Dr 29732
Westover Cir 29732
Westridge Dr 29732
Westwind Dr 29732
Wexford Dr 29730
Wh Borders Rd 29732
Whaley Ct 29732
Whetstone Ct 29730
Whippoorwill Ln 29732
Whisonant Rd 29730
Whispering View Ln 29732
Whispering Winds Dr 29732
Whispering Woods Rd 29732
E & W White St 29730
White Admiral Ln 29732
White Dove Ct 29730
White Fawn Ln 29730
White Horse Rd 29730
White Oak Ln 29730
White Pine Ct 29732
White Ridge Dr 29732
White Water Dr 29732
Whitehall Ct 29732
Whitgreen St 29730
Whitner St 29730
Whitney Wood Ln 29732
Wideglide Ct 29730
Wigmore Ln 29732
Wild Oats Ct 29732
Wild Turkey Trl 29732
Wildcat Creek Rd 29730
Wildflower Ct 29732
Wildwood Dr & Trl 29732
Wilhurst Ct 29730
Wilkerson Rd 29730
Willard Ct 29732
Willet Dr 29730
William Lytle Pl 29730
Williams St 29732
Williamsburg Dr 29732
Williamson Rd & St 29730
Williford Rd 29730
Williford Woods Ln 29730
Willow Ln 29730
Willow St 29730
Willow Creek Rd 29730
Willowblue Run 29732
Willowbrae Rd 29732
Willowbrook Ave 29730
Willowhaven Ct 29732
Willowood Dr 29730
Willowood Pond Rd 29730
Willowspring Ln 29730
Willowwalk Rd 29730
Willwood Cir 29730
Wilmslow Rd 29730
N Wilson St 29730
S Wilson St
100-299 29730
206-206 29731
300-598 29730
301-599 29730
Wilson Sturgis Rd 29730
Wimbledon Ln 29732
Winchester Dr 29730
Winco Way 29732
Windchime Ln 29732
Windemere Rd 29732
Winden Rd 29732
Windfield Ct 29732
Winding Way 29732
Winding Branch Rd 29732
Winding Oak Rd 29732
Windsong Ln 29732
Windsor Ter 29732
Windsor Chase Ln 29732
Windsor Ridge Dr 29732
Windstone Ct 29732
Windy Cove Rd 29732
Windyrush Rd 29732
Winged Foot Ct 29730
Winnridge Rd 29730
Winrock Ln 29730
Winter Rd 29730
Winterberry Rd 29732
Wintercrest Dr 29732
Winthrop Dr 29732
Wisteria Ln 29730
Witherspoon Ave 29730
Wofford St 29730
Wolcott Pl 29730
Wolf Mccain Dr 29730
Wolf Trap Way 29732
Wonder Trl 29732
Wood St 29730
Wood Forest Dr 29732
Woodberry Rd 29732
Woodbranch Rd 29732
Woodbridge Dr 29732
Woodbrook Pl 29730
Woodcrest Cir 29732
Woodcutter Rd 29732
Woodfield Rd 29732
Woodgreen Rd 29730
Woodhaven Rd 29732
Woodhurst Dr 29732
Woodland Dr 29732
Woodleigh Dr 29732
Woodrun Ct 29732
Woods Fery Ln 29732
Woodsbay Ln 29732
Woodshire Ct 29730
Woodside Dr 29732
Woodside Village Dr 29730
Woodstock Cir 29730
Woodvale Dr 29730
Woodward Rd 29732
Woodway Ln 29732
Woodwind Dr 29732
Workman St 29730
World Changers Ln 29730
Worthington Way 29730
Worthington Xing 29732
Worthy Boys Rd 29730
Wren Dr 29732
Wrenfield Ml 29732
Wright St 29730
Wylie Ct 29730
Wylie St 29730
Wylie Cove Ln 29732
Wyndale Dr 29730
Wynnview Ct 29732
Yale St 29730
Yarrow St 29732
Yellow Rose Ct 29732
Yellowood Ct 29732
Yesebehena Cir 29730
Yesteryear Ct 29732
S York Ave 29730
York Hwy 29732
Yorkdale Dr 29730
Yorkmont Dr 29730
Yorkshire Dr 29730
Yorkston Dr 29730
Young Warrior Town
Dr 29730
Yukon Dr 29732
Zinker Rd 29732

NUMBERED STREETS

All Street Addresses 29730

SENECA SC

General Delivery 29678

POST OFFICE BOXES MAIN OFFICE STATIONS AND BRANCHES

Box No.s
1 - 4773 29679
8001 - 8536 29678

NAMED STREETS

A Hamby Dr 29678
Aaron Sloan Dr 29678
Abaco Ln 29672
Abbott St 29678

Aberlady Dr ... 29678
Ables Rd ... 29678
Accountants Cir ... 29678
N & S Acorn Way ... 29672
Adams St ... 29678
Agape Ln ... 29678
Airline Rd ... 29678
Airport Rd ... 29678
N Alan Dr ... 29672
Alberts Rd ... 29672
Alesia Dr ... 29678
Alex Sluder Dr ... 29678
Alexander Rd ... 29672
S Alexander Rd ... 29678
Alice Ln ... 29678
Allen Cir & St ... 29678
Allison Dr ... 29678
Almond Ave ... 29678
Alpine Dr ... 29672
Amarie Cv ... 29678
Amenity Way ... 29672
Ames St ... 29678
Amethyst Way ... 29672
Anderson Rd ... 29672
Andover Way ... 29672
Andrew Dr ... 29678
Andrew Pickens Dr ... 29678
Angelle Ln ... 29672
Angus Run ... 29672
Ann Dr ... 29678
Annsolar Dr ... 29678
Apollo Dr ... 29672
Apple Dr ... 29678
Applewood Center Pl ... 29678
April Dr ... 29678
Arbor Way ... 29672
Argo Rd ... 29678
Arlie Dr ... 29678
Arlington Dr & Hts ... 29672
Armstrong Rd ... 29678
Arnold St ... 29678
Arrowhead Trl ... 29672
Arrowood Cir ... 29672
Arterburn Park Rd ... 29678
Asbury Dr ... 29678
Ashbrook Cir ... 29678
Ashford Ct ... 29672
Ashford Bluff Dr ... 29678
Ashley Ln ... 29678
Ashley Oaks Ct ... 29672
E Ashton St ... 29678
Ashton Place Ct ... 29678
Austin Dr ... 29678
Autumn Way ... 29672
Autumn Trace Ln ... 29678
Avondale Dr ... 29672
Azalea Dr ... 29678
Azar Rd ... 29672
Azure Cove Ct ... 29672
B And H Ln ... 29678
B Minor St ... 29678
Babb Rd ... 29678
Back Lash Bay Dr ... 29678
Backwoods Trl ... 29678
Bailey Dr ... 29678
Baldwin Rd ... 29678
Barbaras Dr ... 29678
Barber Dr ... 29678
Barefoot Ln ... 29672
Barker Ln ... 29678
Barker Hill Dr ... 29672
Barn Rd ... 29672
Barn Hill Dr ... 29678
Barnes Rd ... 29672
Barron Ct ... 29672
Barton Hill Dr ... 29672
Baskin Dr ... 29678
Bass Cove Rd ... 29672
Baxter Dr ... 29678
W Bay View Dr ... 29672
Baypoint Dr ... 29672
N Bayshore Dr ... 29672
Bayview Ct ... 29672
Baywood Ct ... 29672
Beacon Ridge Dr ... 29678
N Beacon Shores Dr ... 29672

Beagle Dr ... 29678
Bear Track Dr ... 29678
N Bearden Rd & St ... 29678
Beatrice Dr ... 29678
Beaver Pond Rd ... 29678
Becknell Dr ... 29672
Bee St ... 29678
Beech Dr ... 29678
Beech View Ct ... 29672
Bell Dr ... 29678
Belle Pines Ct ... 29672
Bellview Way ... 29678
Bellwood Dr ... 29678
Ben Hilda Dr ... 29678
Benjamin Dr ... 29678
Bennye Dr ... 29672
Benson Cir ... 29678
Bent Brook Ln ... 29672
Bent Creek Ln ... 29678
Bent Oak Dr ... 29678
Bent Tree Dr ... 29678
Benton St ... 29672
Bergen St ... 29678
Berkshire Dr ... 29672
Bernwood Cir ... 29672
Berwick Ct ... 29672
Bessie Mae Ln ... 29672
Beta Ridge Dr ... 29672
Beth Ln ... 29672
Betts Wilson Ln ... 29678
Betty St ... 29672
E Beverly Dr ... 29672
Big Barn Ct ... 29672
Big Bass Dr ... 29678
Big Oak Dr ... 29672
Big Rock Dr ... 29678
Biggerstaff Rd ... 29672
Bilo Pl ... 29678
Bimini Dr ... 29672
Birch Dr ... 29678
Birchbark Ct ... 29672
Birchwood Dr ... 29672
Blackberry Rd ... 29672
Blacksmith Dr ... 29678
Blackwell Dr ... 29672
Blakely St ... 29678
Blassingame Ct ... 29672
Blue Ridge Blvd ... 29672
Blue Sky Blvd ... 29678
W Bluebird Ct & Dr ... 29672
Boardwalk Pl ... 29678
Boat Ramp Dr ... 29678
Bob Campbell Dr ... 29678
Bobcat Rdg ... 29678
Bobolink Ct & Dr ... 29672
Bogey Blvd ... 29678
Boggs Dr ... 29678
Bolick St ... 29672
Bonanza Dr ... 29672
Boondock Trl ... 29672
Boren Pl ... 29672
Borg Rd ... 29678
Boulders Dr ... 29678
Bountyland Rd ... 29672
Bourbon St ... 29672
Bowen Ln ... 29678
Bowen Farm Rd ... 29678
Boyces Dr ... 29678
Boys Acres Dr ... 29678
Bracken Lea Dr ... 29678
Brady Dr ... 29678
Brady Hill Dr ... 29678
Brambly Hedge Ln ... 29678
Branham Rd ... 29678
Breakwater Ln ... 29678
Breezy Pt ... 29672
Brentwood Dr ... 29678
Brewer Ln ... 29678
Briar Ct ... 29672
Briargate Ct ... 29672
Briarledge Dr ... 29672
Briarwood Dr ... 29672
Bridgeview Dr ... 29672
Bridgewater Dr ... 29672
Bright Leaf Ct ... 29672
Brittany Ln ... 29678

Britton Dr ... 29678
Broad Creek Ct ... 29678
Broadbill Dr ... 29678
S Brock Dr ... 29678
Brook Ln ... 29672
Brook Hollow Dr ... 29678
Brookfield Dr ... 29672
Brookhaven Cir ... 29672
Brookwood Dr ... 29678
E Brown Anx & St ... 29678
Brown Farm Rd ... 29678
Bruce Blvd ... 29672
Bruce Hill Blvd ... 29678
E Brucke Rd ... 29672
Bruner Dr ... 29678
Bryant Dr ... 29678
Bryian Ln ... 29678
Buchanan Trl ... 29678
Buck Dr ... 29678
Buck Owen Rd ... 29678
Buckeye Ln ... 29672
Bufflehead Way ... 29678
Bunny Hop Trl ... 29678
Burkett Rd ... 29672
S Burns Dr ... 29678
Burns Park Dr ... 29678
Burriss Ave ... 29672
Burrleton Dr ... 29678
Business Park Dr ... 29678
By Pass 123 ... 29678
Byre Ln ... 29678
Byrlie Way ... 29678
C J S Dr ... 29678
Cabin Rd ... 29672
Cain Dr ... 29672
Cajun Mountain Ln ... 29678
Calico Way ... 29672
Callicoat Ln ... 29678
Calm Oak Dr ... 29678
Camacahe Dr ... 29678
Camel Cir ... 29672
E & W Camelia Ln ... 29678
Camelot Dr ... 29672
Camilla Ln ... 29672
Campbell Dr ... 29678
Campbell Bridge Rd ... 29678
Campers Way ... 29672
Cane Creek Dr ... 29672
Cane Creek Harbor
Rd ... 29672
Cane Creek Landing
Rd ... 29672
Cannie Ct ... 29672
W Cannon Ct ... 29672
Cannon Rd ... 29678
Canterbury Ln ... 29672
Cantrell Acres Dr ... 29678
Canty Ln ... 29678
Canvasback Way ... 29678
Cape Hatteras Dr ... 29672
E & W Capewood Ave ... 29678
Cardinal Dr ... 29672
Carlen Dr ... 29678
Carnelda Dr ... 29672
Carol Ln ... 29672
Carolina Ave ... 29678
Carolina Cv ... 29672
Carolina Knoll Dr ... 29672
Carpenter Dr ... 29672
Carradine Rd ... 29678
Carriage Trce ... 29678
Carrigan Ct ... 29678
Carson Rd ... 29678
Cartee Rd ... 29678
Carter St ... 29672
Carter Park Dr ... 29678
Carver St ... 29678
Carver Park 1 Dr ... 29678
Carver Park 2 Cir ... 29678
Cary Dr ... 29678
Casteen Way ... 29678
Castle Dr ... 29678
Catawba Cir ... 29672
Catfish Cove Rd ... 29672
Catherine Ln ... 29678
Catherines Dr ... 29672

Caw Caw Ln ... 29678
Cawthon Dr ... 29678
Cayuga Ct ... 29672
Cedar Cove Dr & Rd ... 29672
Cedar Creek Ln ... 29678
Cedar Grove Ln ... 29678
Cedar Hill Dr ... 29672
Cedar Hollow Rd ... 29678
Cedar Post Ct ... 29672
Cedar Valley Ln ... 29678
Cedar View Farm Rd ... 29678
Cedarhill Farm Rd ... 29678
Cedaridge Ln ... 29672
Celtic Ct ... 29678
Central Dr ... 29672
Central Park Ln ... 29678
Century Plaza Dr ... 29678
Chad Will Rd ... 29678
Chads Dr ... 29678
Chambers Hill Rd ... 29672
Championship Dr ... 29678
Chana Dr ... 29672
Chandler Pl ... 29672
Chantilly Cir ... 29678
Chapman Pl ... 29678
Chapman Pond Ln ... 29678
Charles Dr ... 29678
Charlie B Farm Rd ... 29678
Charlies Way Rd ... 29672
Charlotte Ct ... 29678
Charter Oak Dr ... 29672
Chartwell Point Rd ... 29672
Chatham Dr ... 29678
Chele Ln ... 29672
Cherokee Dr ... 29672
Cherokee Path Dr ... 29678
W, N & S Cherry Rd &
St ... 29678
Cheryl St ... 29678
Chesswood Dr ... 29678
N Chestnut St ... 29678
Chestnut Ridge Dr ... 29672
Chetola Rd ... 29672
Chicken House Rd ... 29678
Childers Dr ... 29678
Childs Dr ... 29678
Chippewa Ct ... 29672
Chocolate Drop Ln ... 29672
Choctaw Trl ... 29672
Chris Ln ... 29678
Christenbury Rd ... 29672
Christi Ln ... 29678
Christopher Ln ... 29678
Cimarron Dr ... 29678
Circle Dr ... 29678
Circle A Farm Rd ... 29678
Circle Hill Dr ... 29672
Circle K Dr ... 29678
Claire Ct ... 29672
Clarence Cir ... 29672
Clark Dr ... 29678
W Clay Dr ... 29678
Clearlake Pt ... 29672
Clearview Dr ... 29672
Clearwater Dr ... 29672
Clearwater Point Dr ... 29672
W Clemson Blvd & St ... 29678
Clemson Marina Dr ... 29678
Clemson View Dr ... 29678
Clermont Cir ... 29678
Cleveland Dr & Rd ... 29678
Cliffwick Ln ... 29672
Clifton Ct ... 29672
Clingman Dr ... 29672
Clinkscale Rd ... 29678
Cloverdale Dr ... 29678
Clovis Dr ... 29672
Club Dr ... 29678
Club Paramount Dr ... 29678
Club View Dr ... 29678
Clyde Crenshaw Rd ... 29672
Clydesdale Rd ... 29678
Coaly Trl ... 29678
Cobb Dr ... 29678
Cobbs Body Shop Dr ... 29678
Code Cir ... 29678

Cody Rd ... 29678
Coldstream Ct ... 29672
Coleman St ... 29678
Coleridge Ct ... 29672
Collins Home Dr ... 29672
Colonial Plaza Dr ... 29678
Commons Blvd ... 29678
Concord Industrial Dr ... 29672
Coneross Ave ... 29678
Coneross Creek Rd ... 29672
Coneross Knob Dr ... 29678
Coneross Point Dr ... 29678
Connally Dr ... 29678
Connie Cir ... 29678
Cook Ln ... 29672
Cool Breeze Dr ... 29672
Coolview Dr ... 29672
Copeland Dr ... 29678
Copperhead Hl ... 29678
Copperstone Dr ... 29678
Corinth Dr ... 29672
Cottage Grove Ln ... 29678
Cottonwood Dr ... 29678
Country Ln ... 29678
Country Kin Rd ... 29672
Country Place Cir ... 29678
Country Village Dr ... 29678
Courtenay Smith Dr ... 29672
S Cove Ct & Rd ... 29672
Cove Side Rd ... 29672
Cove View Ct ... 29678
Covenant Way ... 29672
Coves End Pt ... 29672
Cox Rd ... 29678
Coyote Ln ... 29678
Cranwood Cv ... 29672
Crawford Dr ... 29678
Crawford Farm Rd ... 29678
Creek Dr ... 29678
Creek View Dr ... 29678
Creekridge Ct ... 29672
Creekside Dr ... 29678
Crenshaw Hilltop Dr ... 29678
Crepe Myrtle Dr ... 29678
E Crescent Dr ... 29678
W Cresent Dr ... 29678
N Crest Dr ... 29672
Crest Pointe Dr ... 29672
Crestridge Dr ... 29672
Crestview Ct ... 29672
N Crestview Dr ... 29678
S Crestview Dr ... 29678
Cricket Creek Dr ... 29678
Crismore Ln ... 29672
Criswell Dr ... 29672
Crocker Rd ... 29672
Crooked Creek Dr &
Rd ... 29672
Crooks Rd ... 29678
Crooks Farm Rd ... 29678
Crooks Haven Dr ... 29678
Cross Creek Dr ... 29678
Cross Farm Rd ... 29678
Cross Roads Dr ... 29678
Crossfire Ln ... 29678
Crossover Dr ... 29672
Crosswinds Ln ... 29678
Crowe Dr ... 29672
Cryovac Blvd ... 29678
Crystal Ln ... 29672
S Crystal Ln ... 29678
Crystal Bay Ct ... 29672
Cunningham Dr ... 29678
Curly Grant Dr ... 29678
Curry Dr ... 29678
Curtis Dr ... 29672
D St ... 29678
D Morris Way ... 29678
Daffodil Dr ... 29678
Daisy Ln ... 29678
Dalezel Ln ... 29678
Dalton Rd ... 29678
Daniel Ave ... 29678
S Danielle Ln ... 29678
Danube Cir ... 29678
Dare Dr ... 29672

Darleen Ln ... 29678
Dave Nix Rd ... 29678
Davis Creek Rd ... 29678
Davis Mill Rd ... 29678
Davis Mill Park Dr ... 29678
Dawg Trail Dr ... 29672
Dawn Dr ... 29678
Dawn Cove Rd ... 29678
Daybreak Ln ... 29678
Deadwood Loop ... 29678
Debra St ... 29678
N Debra St ... 29672
Deep Well Dr ... 29678
Deer Rdg ... 29678
Deer Trl ... 29672
Deer Hollow Ln ... 29678
Deer Knoll Dr ... 29678
Deer Park Dr ... 29672
Deer Ranch Dr ... 29678
Deer Run Ct ... 29678
Deerfield Ln ... 29678
Deerland Farm Ln ... 29678
Deerwood Ln ... 29678
Defore Rd ... 29678
Deliverance Dr ... 29678
Delivery Rd ... 29678
Delphi Dr ... 29672
Delta Ct ... 29672
N & S Depot St ... 29678
Devon Way ... 29672
Devonhurst Dr ... 29678
Dewberry Way ... 29672
Dewey Cir ... 29678
Dick Price Dr ... 29678
Dickard Rd ... 29672
Dickerson Lake Rd ... 29678
Dillard Hill Dr ... 29678
Dilligaf Dr ... 29678
Display Dr ... 29672
Dixie Dr ... 29672
Dobson Cove Dr ... 29678
Docks Dr ... 29678
Dodd Farm Rd ... 29672
Dodgins Ln ... 29672
Dog Leg Ln ... 29678
Dogan Dr ... 29678
Dogwood Dr ... 29678
Dogwood Cove Dr ... 29678
Dogwood Springs Dr ... 29678
Donald Rd ... 29678
Doris Dr ... 29678
Dorothy Dr ... 29678
Double Branch Rd ... 29678
Double Creek Ln ... 29678
Double G Farm Rd ... 29678
Double O Farm Rd ... 29678
Doug Berry Dr ... 29678
Doug Hollow Rd ... 29672
Douglas Dr ... 29678
Dove Trl ... 29678
Down Home Dr ... 29678
Doyle Dr ... 29678
Dr Mitchell Rd ... 29678
Driftwood Dr ... 29678
Driver Ct ... 29678
Dry Gulch Trl ... 29678
Dubois Cir ... 29672
Duke Dr ... 29672
Duncan Dr ... 29678
Duncan Acres Dr ... 29672
Duncan Ward Rd ... 29672
Dundee Ct ... 29678
Durango Trl ... 29678
Durham Brown Rd ... 29678
Dusty Dr ... 29678
Dusty Trail Dr ... 29678
Dyar Rd ... 29672
Dye Dr ... 29678
E St ... 29678
Eagle Pt ... 29672
Eagles Landing Ln ... 29672
Eagles Nest Dr ... 29678
Eagles View Dr ... 29678
Earle Dr ... 29678
Earls Mill Rd ... 29678
Easter Ln ... 29678

Eastlake Ct ... 29672
Eastview Ct ... 29672
Easy St ... 29678
Ebenezer Rd ... 29672
Echo Trl ... 29678
Echo Hill Trl ... 29678
Echota Trl ... 29672
Ed Pettigrew Dr ... 29678
Edens Ln ... 29678
Edgeview Ct ... 29672
Edgewater Dr ... 29678
Edgewood Dr ... 29678
Edinburgh Way ... 29678
Edmond Crane Dr ... 29678
Elaine Dr ... 29678
Elbert Adams Rd ... 29678
Elclay Dr ... 29672
Elizabeth Ln ... 29672
Elizabeth Cain Dr ... 29672
Ellena Dr ... 29672
Ellenburg Rd ... 29672
Elliott Dr ... 29678
Ellsworth Dr ... 29672
Elm St ... 29678
Elmtree Ln ... 29672
Elmwood Ct ... 29672
Emerald Rd ... 29678
Emerald Point Dr ... 29672
Engelhard Dr ... 29678
English Ct ... 29678
English Hill Rd ... 29672
Enoch Dr ... 29672
Enterprise Ln ... 29672
Equestrian Dr ... 29678
Eric Dr ... 29678
Euna Ln ... 29678
Evalona Dr ... 29678
Evatt Rd ... 29672
Evelyn Dr ... 29678
Evening Shade Dr ... 29678
Evergreen Cir ... 29678
Evergreen Forest Dr ... 29678
F St ... 29678
Fair Haven Ct ... 29672
Fairfield Dr ... 29678
Fairoaks Cir ... 29678
N & S Fairplay St ... 29678
Fairview Church Rd ... 29672
Fairview Cove Rd ... 29672
Fairwind Ct ... 29678
Faith Hill Dr ... 29678
Falling Leaf Ct ... 29672
Family Dr ... 29678
Fancy Dr ... 29678
Fawn Dr ... 29678
Feather And Hoof Dr ... 29672
Feathery Ln ... 29678
Fenwick Ct ... 29678
Fern Creek Cove Dr ... 29672
Fern Hollow Ct ... 29672
Fernbrook Ct ... 29672
Ferncliff Dr ... 29678
Ferngrove Ct ... 29672
Fernwood Dr ... 29678
Fiddlers Way ... 29678
Field Village Dr ... 29678
Fife Pl ... 29678
Filo Dr ... 29678
Fire Tower Rd ... 29678
Fisherman Ln ... 29672
Fishermans Cove Dr ... 29672
Fitzgerald Dr ... 29678
Flat Creek Rd ... 29672
Fleming Ln ... 29672
Flemsey Ln ... 29678
Floy Dr ... 29678
Flynns Point Rd ... 29678
Flythe Dr ... 29672
Ford Dr ... 29672
Fords Lakefront Dr ... 29678
Forest Dr ... 29672
Forest Creek Dr ... 29678
Forest Pine Ct ... 29672
Forest Springs Dr ... 29678
Fort Hill Dr ... 29678
N Forty Rd ... 29672

Foster Ridge Rd 29678
Four Views Ct 29672
Four Wheel Dr 29678
Fourwinds Trl 29672
Fox Grape Ct 29678
Fox Run Rd 29672
Fox Run Cottage Ln 29678
Fox Trail Ln 29672
Foxcreek Ct 29678
Foxfire Ct 29672
Foxx Farm Rd 29678
Frances Dr 29678
Frank Gaillard Rd 29678
Free Spirit Ln 29672
Freedom Dr 29678
Frenge Branch Rd 29672
S Friendship Rd 29678
Friendship Court Cir 29678
Friendship Loop Dr 29678
Friendship Pointe Dr 29678
Friendship Valley Rd 29678
Frontage Rd 29672
Frosty Hollow Dr 29678
Fun Time Dr 29678
Furrawn Ln 29678
Gabriel Dr 29672
Gadwall Way 29678
Gail Ct 29672
Gaines Dr 29678
Gallo Way 29678
Gamble Dr 29678
E Gammell St 29678
Gantt Dr 29672
Garden Cir 29672
Garrison Rd 29678
Garvin Rd 29678
Gaskins Dr 29678
Gaspe Blvd 29672
S Gate Dr 29678
Gate View Ct 29672
General Dozier Dr 29678
Gentry Rd 29678
Georgia Rd 29678
Gettysburg Dr 29672
Gibby Dr 29678
S Gibson Ln 29678
Gibson Rd 29672
Gilbert Rd 29678
Gillespie Rd 29678
Gilliam Dr 29678
Glamorgan Dr 29678
Glen Rd 29672
Glenngarry Pl 29678
Glenview Ct 29672
Gloria Ln 29678
Goddard Ave 29678
Golden Eye Dr 29678
Goldie Ln 29678
Goldwing Dr 29678
Golf Dr 29672
Goodine St 29678
Grace Way 29678
Grace Grove Dr 29678
Gracie St 29678
E & W Grady St 29678
Grady Rogers Ct 29678
Graham Rd 29678
Grand Hammock Dr 29672
Grand Overlook Dr 29678
Grand Summit Dr 29672
Grandpas Pl 29672
Grandview Dr 29672
Grandview Farm Rd 29672
Grange Hermitage Ct 29678
Granite Dr 29678
N Grant Pt & Rd 29678
Gravel Rd 29678
Great Oak Way 29678
Green Acres Rd 29678
Green Valley Ln 29672
Green View Ln 29672
E Greenbriar Dr & Ln 29678
Greenleaf Ct 29678
Greentree Ct 29672
Greenway Farm Rd 29672
Greenwich Dr 29672

Greken Dr 29678
Grey Fox Ln 29678
Grey Oaks Dr 29678
Grey Pebble Ct 29672
Greystoke Cv 29678
Greystone Ct 29672
Griffin Dr 29678
Groveview Ln 29672
Growest Dr 29678
Hackberry Ln 29678
Hagan St 29678
Hagood Dr 29678
Halls Dr 29678
Halpers Dr 29678
Hammock Ridge Dr 29672
Hammond Dr 29678
Hammond Land Dr 29672
Hampton Shores Dr 29672
Hanover Way 29672
Hanvey Dr 29672
Harbers Way 29672
Harbin Ln 29678
Harbin Acres Rd 29678
Harbin Hill Dr 29678
Harbor Dr 29672
Harbor View Ln 29672
N Harbour Dr 29672
Hardys Ln 29678
Harley Rd 29678
Harley Davidson Blvd 29678
Harmon Dr 29678
E, N & W Harper Ridge Dr & Rd 29678
Harpers Ferry Dr 29678
Harris Ct 29672
Harts Cir 29678
Harts Cove Way 29678
Harts Ridge Dr 29678
Hartwell Dr 29672
Hartwell Lake Dr 29678
Hatfield Dr 29678
Hattie Sue Hill Dr 29672
Haven Ln 29678
Hawk Blvd 29678
Hawkins Rd 29672
Hawkins Krabbe Ln 29672
Hawks Nest Rd 29672
Hawthorne Ln 29672
Haynes St 29678
Heads Dr 29672
Heartwood Dr 29672
Heath Dr 29678
Heather Ct 29678
Hebron Rd 29672
Heller Rd 29678
Hembree Pt 29672
Hemlock Dr 29678
Henderson Dr 29678
Henry Ave 29678
Heritage Pt 29672
Heritage Hills Dr 29678
Hermans Hideaway Ln 29672
Hermitage Mooring Dr 29672
Heron Cove Cir 29672
Hershel Dr 29672
Hiawassee Dr 29672
Hickory Ln 29678
Hickory Cove Rd 29672
Hickory Hill Ln 29678
Hickory Knoll Ln 29678
Hickory Nut Dr 29672
Hickory Tree Dr 29678
Hicks Ln 29678
Hidden Acres Dr 29678
Hidden Cove Ct 29672
Hidden Creek Ct 29678
High Bluff Rd 29678
High Falls Rd 29672
High Hammock Dr 29672
High Hill Rd 29678
High Point Ct 29672
High View Ct 29672
Highland Ct 29672
Highpointe Blvd 29678
Highridge Dr 29672
Hightower Hl 29672

Hill Top Dr 29672
Hillandale Rd 29672
Hillbilly Trl 29678
Hillcrest Ct 29678
S Hillcrest Dr 29678
Hillsborough Dr 29678
Hillside Ln 29678
Hillview Dr 29672
Hilton Cir 29672
His Way Cir 29672
Hitec Rd 29678
Hog Dr 29672
Hoilman Haven Dr 29672
Holbrooks Dr 29678
Holders Landing Rd 29672
Holdievale Dr 29672
S Holland Ave & St 29678
Holland Ridge Dr 29672
Holleman St 29678
Holley Park Dr 29678
Holliday Dr & Ln 29678
Holly Ct 29678
Hollydale Dr 29678
Home House Dr 29672
Home Stretch Dr 29672
Homeport Cv 29672
Homerville Rd 29678
Honea Dr & Ln 29678
Honeybee Ln 29678
Honeysuckle Dr 29672
Hope Ave 29678
Hopewell St 29678
Hopewell Church Dr 29678
Hopkins Rd 29678
Hornick Dr 29678
Horse Dr 29678
Horse Head Point Dr 29672
Horsechestnut Trl 29672
Horseman Dr 29672
Horseshoe Dr 29678
Houston St 29678
Houston Rice Rd 29678
Howling Ln 29678
Hoyt St 29678
Huckleberry Dr 29672
Hughes St 29672
Hugo Dr 29678
E Humbert St 29678
Hummingbird Trl 29672
Hunnicutt Cove Rd 29672
Hunt Rd 29672
Hunt Farm Rd 29678
N Hunter St 29678
Hyder Way 29678
Idlewild Dr 29678
Ilds Ln 29678
Imports Dr 29678
Indian Oaks Rd 29672
Indian Trail Rd 29672
Indigo Ln 29672
Industrial Park Pl 29678
Ingles Pl 29678
Inglewood Ct 29678
Inlet Dr 29672
Inlet Reach Dr 29672
Inwood Ct 29672
Ironside Cir 29672
Iroquois Dr 29672
Island Pt 29672
Island Pine Dr 29672
Island View Ln 29672
Ivy Ct 29678
Ivy Ridge Ct 29672
Ivy Spring Ct 29672
J And G Dr 29678
J Blackwell Dr 29672
J Cobb Dr 29678
J Hart Ln 29678
J P Stevens Rd 29678
J Shirley Farm Rd 29678
J Stone Cir 29678
Jackie Ln 29678
Jacobs Rd 29672
Jade Ln 29672
Jade Creek Ct 29672
Jadewood Dr 29678

Jaimica Ln 29672
Jaira Dr 29678
Jamerson Ave 29678
E James St 29678
James Adams Rd 29678
James Carver Rd 29678
Jamesway Dr 29678
Jamie Way 29678
Janda Rd 29672
Jantzen Ct 29672
Jasmine Ln 29672
Jason Dr 29678
Jasper Ln 29672
Jaymory Way 29678
Jedena Dr 29672
Jenkins Rd 29672
Jennifer Ln 29672
Jennings Ave 29678
Jere Ln 29672
Jerica Ln 29678
Jessica Dr 29678
Jetty Lighthouse 29672
Jim Joe Rd 29678
Jody Dr 29678
Joe Jen Dr 29678
Joe Lewis Rd 29678
John Okelly Dr 29678
Johnnie Dr 29678
Johnson Rd 29678
Johnson Cove Rd 29672
Jones Ave 29678
Jones Kinder Dr 29678
Jordan St 29678
Joy Ln 29672
Jrj Dr 29678
Jubie Ln 29672
Judy Dr 29678
Julian Dr 29672
Julian Davis Dr 29672
Julie Ln 29678
Julius St 29678
Jullia Dr 29678
June St 29678
Juniper Ct 29672
Junkyard Dr 29678
Justin Ln 29672
K Mac Dr 29678
Kamp Ct 29672
Kan Kan Dr 29678
Karen Dr 29678
Karmon Dr 29672
Karriker Rd 29678
Kate Dr 29672
Katelynn Ln 29672
Kathmaette Dr 29678
Kathrine Dr 29672
Kathys Dr 29678
Katies Rd 29678
Kaye St 29678
Keasler Dr 29678
Keaton Dr 29678
Keese Dr 29672
Keith Ln 29678
Keller Hill Dr 29672
Kelley Ridge Rd 29672
Kellie Scott Dr 29672
Kelly Dr 29678
Kelly Mill Rd 29672
Keoway Dr 29672
Keowee Trl 29672
Keowee Business Pkwy 29678
Keowee Knoll Dr 29672
Keowee Lakeshore Dr 29672
Keowee Marina Dr 29672
Keowee Pointe Dr 29672
Keowee River Rd 29672
Keowee Sailing Club Dr 29672
Keowee School Rd 29672
Kershaw Ln 29672
Keswick Pt 29678
Ketterman Dr 29672
Keystone Dr 29672
Khaki Campbell Way 29678
Kids Ln 29678

Kilpatrick Ave & Rd 29678
S King Dr & St 29678
King James Rd 29678
Kings Park Dr 29678
Kings Pointe Dr 29678
Kingsford Ct 29672
Kirby D Ln 29672
Kirk Dr 29678
Knoll View Dr 29678
Knollcrest Dr 29678
Knollwood Dr 29672
Knossus Ct 29672
Knox Rd 29672
Knox Campground Rd 29672
Knox Landing Dr 29672
Kokay Dr 29678
Kokomo Way 29672
Krabbe Ln 29678
L Barker Dr 29678
L Smith Dr 29672
Lace Ave 29678
Lacey Ln 29672
Lagoon Dr 29678
Laid Back Ln 29678
Laing Ct 29678
Lake Breeze Ln 29672
Lake Keowee Ln 29672
Lake Linda Rd 29678
Lake Point East Dr 29672
Lake Pointe Rd 29678
Lake Ridge Ln 29672
Lake Winds Ct 29672
Lakecrest Dr 29672
Lakefront Dr 29678
Lakeshore Ln 29678
E Lakeside Dr 29672
Lakestream Ct 29672
Lakeview Dr 29672
Lakewater Cv 29672
Lancaster St 29678
Landing Dr 29672
Landon Dr 29678
Landress Dr 29678
Lands Dr 29672
Lands End Rd 29678
Lanford Dr 29672
Laredo Dr 29672
Lariat Loop 29672
Laun Dr 29678
Laurel Ln 29678
Laurel Grove Ct 29678
Laurel Haven Ct 29678
Lauren Ln 29678
Lauren Paige Ln 29672
Lawrence Ave & Ln 29678
Lawrence Bridge Rd 29672
Le Cabins Ln 29678
Leafy Ln 29672
Leah Rae Ln 29678
Leas Courtyard Dr 29672
Lee Ln 29678
Leesa Hopkins Ln 29678
Legato Ln 29678
Leigh Ln 29678
Leila St 29678
Leland St 29678
N Leroy Rd 29672
Leslo Ln 29678
Lewisville Dr 29678
Library Ln 29678
Lighthouse Ct 29672
Lighting Dr 29672
Lightwind Ct 29672
Lila Doyle Dr 29672
Lilly Ct 29678
Lincoln Terrace Dr 29678
Linda Dr 29678
Lindon Pl 29678
Lindos Dr 29672
Lindsay Rd 29678
Lingefelt Ln 29678
Linking Rd 29672
Lisa Ln 29678
Little Ln 29672
Little Cove Dr 29678
Little Ponderosa Rd 29672

W Little River Dr 29672
Littles Dr 29678
Live Oak Ct 29672
Livingston Cir 29678
Lloyd St 29678
Loba Ct 29678
Loblolly Pine Dr 29678
Lochwood Ct 29672
Locust Dr 29678
Loftis Ln 29678
Logan Hill Rd 29672
Logans Way 29678
Logs Trl 29678
Lone Wolf Pl 29672
Lonesome Trl 29678
Long Ave 29678
Long Point Dr 29678
Long View Ridge Ln 29672
Longforest Dr 29672
Longshore Ave 29672
Longview Ct 29672
Longwood Dr 29672
E Lonsdale St 29678
Loran Pointe Cir 29672
Lori Dr 29678
Lori Jen Ln 29678
Lorianna Cir 29678
Lost Harbor Dr 29678
Louie Ln 29678
Louie Evatt Dr 29672
Lowie Cir 29678
Lowkirk Aly 29672
Lowry Ln 29678
Lumber Ln 29672
Lumpkin St 29678
Luther Land Rd 29672
Lynch Dr 29678
N Lyndsey Pt 29672
N & S Lynhurst Ct 29672
Lynne Dr 29678
Lynnhaven Dr 29678
M Peay Dr 29678
Machunt Dr 29678
Macie Ln 29678
Mack Dr 29678
Mackra Dr 29678
Madison Trl 29672
Madison Pointe Dr 29678
Magnolia Pl 29678
Magnolia Way 29672
Mahaffey Dr 29672
Main St 29678
E Main St
400-509 29678
508-508 29679
510-1298 29678
511-1299 29678
Major Rd 29672
Malibu Ct 29678
Mallard Way 29678
Mallard Bend Rd 29672
E Man Dr 29678
Mandalay Way 29672
Manila Dr 29672
Manley St 29678
Manor Ln 29678
Maple Ave 29678
Maple Grove Rd 29678
Mapleleaf Way 29672
Maplewood Ct 29672
Maranatha Ln 29672
Marcia Ct 29672
Marcus Way 29678
Mard Dr 29678
Margie Ct 29678
Maria Ln 29678
Marie Leslie Ln 29678
Marina Pointe Ct 29672
Market St 29678
Marks Pl 29678
Marshall Ave 29678
S Martin Dr 29678
Martin Ln 29672
Martin Creek Rd 29678
Martin Lake Dr 29678

Martins Creek Landing Rd 29678
Martins Pointe Dr 29678
E & W Martinshore Dr 29678
Marvin K Dr 29672
Marvin Speed Rd 29678
Mary Sue Ln 29678
Masaw Ln 29672
Mason Ln 29678
Massey Ln 29672
Maud Ln 29678
Maughan Trl 29672
Mauldin Dr 29678
Mauldin Mill Rd 29678
May Sam Dr 29678
Mayes Dr 29678
Mccall Cir 29678
S Mccarey St 29678
Mccarley Dr 29678
Mccellion Ave 29678
Mcclain Dr 29678
Mcclanahan Ln 29678
Mcclure Rd 29678
Mccracken Dr 29678
Mcdonald Point Rd 29672
Mcgregor Dr 29678
Mcjunkin Dr 29672
Mckee Dr 29678
Mckinley Ct 29678
Mclane Dr 29678
Mclane Farm Rd 29678
Mcphail Poultry Farm Rd 29678
Meade St 29672
Meadow Dr 29678
Meadowbrook Dr 29678
Meadowcrest Dr 29672
Meadowlark Ln 29672
Meadowood Dr 29678
Meares Dr 29672
Megans Way 29678
Meldau Rd 29678
Melody Ln 29678
Mema Ln 29678
Memorial Dr 29672
Mendy Ln 29678
Mensings Dr 29678
Merrimac Cir 29672
Mertie Dr 29678
Michelle Ln 29678
Middle Park Dr 29672
Midnight Ln 29678
Midway Ct 29672
Mikes Trl 29678
Mildred St 29678
Mildred Johnson Rd 29672
Mill Rd 29672
Millbrook Way 29678
Miller Ln 29678
Millie Ln 29678
Milliken Rd 29678
Millstone Ct 29678
Mimosa St 29678
Minoaki Dr 29678
Miracle Rd 29678
Misty Hill Ln 29678
Misty View Ct 29672
Mitchell Dr 29678
Mize Dr 29678
Ml Jones Dr 29672
Mockingbird St 29672
Mohawk Path 29678
Monroe Dr 29678
Monte Video Dr 29678
Moon Rice Dr 29678
Moonbeam Way 29672
Moore Park Ln 29678
Moores Rd 29678
Mooring Line Dr 29672
Morgan Ln 29678
Mormon St 29678
Mormon Church Rd 29678
Morning Dew Ln 29678
Morninglory Dr 29678
Morningside Dr 29678

Morningside Heights Dr 29678
Morris Dr 29678
Moselle Dr 29672
Moss St 29678
Moss Hill Cir 29678
N Mount Vernon Dr 29672
Mountain View Dr 29672
Mountain View Farm Rd 29678
Mountain View Pointe Dr 29672
Mourning Dove Ln 29678
Mudhole Rd 29678
Mug Hollow Dr 29672
Mulberry Dr 29678
Mulholland Dr 29672
Mulwee St 29678
Mundy Ln 29678
Municipal Dr 29672
Muscadine Ridge Dr 29672
Muscovy Way 29678
My Hill Rd 29672
My Way Ln 29678
Myers Ln 29678
Nabors Dr 29678
Nalley Rd 29672
Nantahala Dr 29672
Narrowhaven Ln 29678
Nautic Ct 29672
Nautilis Ct 29672
Navigators Pt 29672
Neal Rd 29672
Near Lake Cir 29678
Nebo Church Rd 29678
Nellwood Dr 29678
Nelms Ln 29678
Nelson Ln 29678
Nesting Pine Ct 29672
New Cut Rd 29672
New Heritage Trl 29678
New Holland St 29672
New Timber Trl 29672
Newry Rd 29672
Newton Rd 29678
Nicholson Cove Rd 29672
Nickles Rd 29678
Nicole Dr 29678
Nimmons Cir 29678
Nix Rd 29672
Nonna Ln 29678
Noras Dr 29672
Noriceburner Dr 29678
E & W North 1st St 29678
E & W North 2nd St 29678
E & W North 3rd St 29678
E & W North 4th St 29678
E North 5th St 29678
Northampton Rd 29672
Northridge Pointe Dr 29672
Northshores Dr 29672
Northside Cir 29672
Northview Farm Rd 29672
Northwest Dr 29678
Northwoods Dr 29678
Nottingham Ct 29672
Nowell Dr 29678
Nursery Dr 29678
W, N & S Oak Hwy & St 29678
Oak Branch Ct 29672
Oak Creek Rd 29678
Oak Crest Cir 29672
Oak Forest Trl 29678
Oak Glen Ct 29672
Oak Haven Ct 29672
Oak Hill Dr 29678
Oak Hollow Ct 29672
Oak Knoll Ct 29678
S Oak Pointe Dr 29672
Oak Ridge Cir 29678
Oak Shore Ct 29678
Oak Tree Dr 29678
Oak Valley Rd 29678
Oak View Dr 29678
Oakdale Ln 29672
Oakleaf Ct 29678
Oakway Dr 29678
Oakwood Ln 29672
Oconee Bell Ct 29672
Oconee Estates Rd 29672
Oconee Point Rd 29678
Oconee Square Dr 29678
Ogilvie Dr 29678
Oglesby Ln 29678
Ohenrys Ln 29678
Okelley Dr 29678
Ola Mae Dr 29672
Old Clemson Hwy 29672
Old Dominion Dr 29678
Old Grove Rd 29678
Old Hamilton Dr 29678
N & S Old Mill Rd 29678
Old Oak Dr 29678
Old Pickens Church Rd 29672
Old Reedy Fork Rd 29678
Old Salem Rd
200A-200C 29672
100-199 29678
200-699 29672
Old Walhalla Hwy 29672
Oleander Trl 29678
Olian Adit Dr 29678
Oliver Dr 29678
Omega Dr 29678
Omni Dr 29672
Orangewood Dr 29678
Orchard Ln 29672
Ostrich Dr 29678
Overbrook Dr 29678
Overlook Dr 29678
Overlook View Ln 29678
Overyonder Ln 29678
Owens Rd 29678
Oxford Cir 29678
Oyd Dr 29678
E Padgett St 29678
Palmer Dr 29678
Paradise Ln 29678
Paradise Place Trl 29678
Paramount Dr 29678
Park Dr 29672
Park Place Dr 29678
Park Ridge Dr 29672
Parkgrove Pl 29678
Parris Dr 29678
Patterson Cir & Rd 29678
Pattersons Hill Ln 29678
Paul Gillison Rd 29672
Paula Dr 29672
Pauline Dr 29678
Paw Paw Dr 29678
Peaceful Ln 29678
Peachtree Ln 29678
Pebble Creek Dr 29678
Pecan Grove Rd 29672
Peek Ln 29672
Peggy Dr 29672
Pelfrey St 29672
Pelham Creek Dr 29678
Pendleton Rd 29678
Penn Farm Ln 29678
Penny Ln 29678
Pepper Ct 29678
Periwinkle Dell 29672
Perkins Pl 29678
Perkins Creek Rd 29678
Perry Ave 29678
Persimmon Ln 29678
Peterson Rd 29678
Petty Rd 29672
Petty Cove Ln 29672
Petunia Dr 29678
Phillis Dr 29672
Pi Delta Cir 29678
E Pickens Hwy 29672
Pickens Mill Rd 29672
Pier Pointe 29672
Pig Pickin Rdg 29672
W Pine Ct 29672
Pine St 29678
N Pine St 29678
S Pine St 29678
Pine Acre Ct 29672
Pine Cliff Dr 29672
Pine Creek Ct 29672
Pine Forest Cir 29678
W Pine Grove Rd 29678
Pine Haven Ct 29672
Pine Meadows Dr 29678
Pine Oak Dr 29678
Pine Plantation Trl 29672
Pine Terrace Dr 29678
Pine Tree Dr 29672
Pine Valley Dr 29678
Pinecrest Dr 29678
Pinecroft Ct 29672
Pinehill Ln 29672
Pinehurst Ct 29672
Pineknoll Dr 29672
Pineland St 29672
Pineridge Rd 29672
Pineridge Pointe Dr 29672
Pinetop Ln 29672
Pinewood Dr 29678
Pinnacle Pointe Dr 29672
Pitts Ave 29678
Plantation Rd 29672
Planters Dr 29678
Pleasant Dr 29678
Pleasant Acres Dr 29678
Pleasant View Dr 29678
Ploma Dr 29678
Poco Path Ln 29678
Point Rd 29672
Pointe East Dr 29672
Pointe Harbor Dr 29672
Pointe West Dr 29672
Pointe Wildwood Dr 29672
Polk A Way Ln 29678
Pond Dr 29678
Pond View Dr 29672
Ponderosa Dr 29678
Poole Dr 29678
Pooles Hill Dr 29678
Poore Ridge Dr 29672
Pope Acre Ln 29678
N & S Poplar St 29678
Porsche Ln 29678
S Port Dr 29672
Port View Ct 29672
Porter Dr 29672
S Porter Dr 29678
Poss Ln 29678
Post Oak Ln 29672
Poteet Ln 29678
Poverty Valley Dr 29678
E Powell St 29678
Prater Dr 29678
Prater Farm Rd 29678
Precipitous Way 29678
Preservation Pt 29672
Presque Isle Pl 29672
Pressley Pl 29678
Preston Ridge Dr 29672
Price Dr 29678
Price Farm Rd 29678
Pridemore Dr 29678
Prince St 29678
Professional Park Dr 29678
Professionals Cir 29678
Promontory Rdg 29672
Providence Ct 29678
Providence Point Dr 29678
Providence Ridge Dr 29678
Pruitt Rd 29678
Pumper Dr 29678
Pumpkin St 29678
Pyracantha Dr 29672
Quail Trl 29678
Quail Ridge Rd 29678
Queen St 29678
Queen Annes Ln 29672
Queens Park Loop 29678
Quiet Ln 29678
Quiet Water Way 29672
W Quincy Rd 29678
R H Hunter Dr 29672
Rabbit Farm Rd 29678
Raceway Dr 29678
Rackley Aly 29678
N & S Radio Station Rd 29678
Radisson Rd 29678
Radnorshire Rd 29678
E & W Railroad St 29678
Rainbow Rd 29678
Rainbows End Dr 29678
Raines Dr 29672
Ralph Sheriff Rd 29678
Ram Cat Aly 29678
Rambo Dr 29678
Ramsey St 29678
S Ranch Rd 29678
S Randall Cir 29678
Randalls Dr 29678
Ranger Dr 29678
Rankin Dr 29678
Raven Pt 29672
Ravenel Cir 29678
Ravenel Center Pl 29678
Ravenel School Rd 29678
Ravens Hollow Way 29678
Ravens View Dr 29678
Ravenwood Dr 29678
Raymond Dr 29672
Rays Rd 29678
Rebel Rd 29678
Rectory Dr 29678
Red Bird Ln 29678
Red Cardinal Rd 29672
Red Feather Rd 29678
Red Hawk Dr 29678
Red Oak Ct 29672
Red Rose Ln 29672
Redbud St 29672
Redtip Cir & Dr 29678
E & W Reedy Fork Rd 29678
Reid Dr 29678
Relaxing Ln 29672
Renee Dr 29672
Restful Ln 29672
Restin Creek Way 29672
Return Church Rd 29678
Rhine Ct 29672
Rice Dr 29678
Richardson Dr 29678
Richland Rd 29672
Rick Dr 29672
Rick Kelley Ln 29678
Ricmar Ln 29678
Riddle Dr 29672
Ridge Dr 29678
N Ridge Dr 29672
Ridge Pointe Ct 29672
Ridgecrest Rd 29678
Ridgeline Ct 29678
Ridgeview Ln 29678
Ridgewood Ct 29672
Riley Dr 29678
Riley Hare Pl 29678
Rill Ct 29672
Ringneck Dr 29678
River Birch Ct 29672
Riverbank Ct 29678
Rivercrest Dr 29678
Rivers Dr 29678
Riversedge Ct 29678
Robert Allen Dr 29678
Robert Earle Dr 29678
Robin Dr 29678
Robinhood Dr 29678
Rochester Hwy 29672
W Rochester St 29678
Rock Ln 29678
W Rockcliff Ct 29672
Rockcrest Ct 29678
Rocking Chair Ln 29678
Rockingham Rd 29672
Rockstone Dr 29678
Rockwood Dr 29672
Rocky Dr 29678
Rocky Creek Dr 29678
Rocky Farm Rd 29678
Rocky Hill Dr 29678
Rocky Ridge Cir 29678
Rocky Top Ln 29678
Rodeo Dr 29678
Roderick Dr 29678
Rodgers Rd 29678
Rolling Hills Dr 29678
Rollingwood Dr 29672
Romaine Cir 29672
Rose Ln 29678
Rosedown Dr 29678
Rothell Dr 29678
Rouda St 29678
Round Spinney Dr 29672
Rowdy Cir 29678
Roxbury Dr 29672
Royal Summit Dr 29678
Rudder Rdg 29678
Ruford Dr 29678
Rugosa Dr 29672
Rushford Ln 29672
Russell Dr 29678
Rusty Ct 29678
Rutledge Ct 29678
Ryan Dr 29672
Sagewood Ln 29678
Sailview Dr 29672
Saluda Rd 29672
Sam Dr 29672
Sam Brown Rd 29678
Samantha Dr 29678
Samuel Dr 29678
Sandal Dr 29678
Sanders Dr 29678
Sandifer Blvd 29672
Sandra Ln 29672
Sandstone Dr 29678
Sandy Hill Dr 29672
Sankanaga Cir 29672
Sapphire Ct 29672
Savage Ln 29672
Savannah Dr 29678
Scarlett St 29678
Scenic Cir 29672
Scotland Rd 29672
Scott Dr 29678
Scott K Dr 29678
Screamin Hollow Dr 29672
Scroggs Dr 29678
Sears Ln 29678
Semperfi Dr 29672
Seneca Dr 29678
Seneca Creek Rd 29678
Seneca River Rd 29678
Seneca Springs Ldg 29672
Seniors Way 29678
Sequoya Way 29672
Serenity Bay Dr 29672
Serria Way 29672
Setting Sun Ct 29672
Seven Oaks Dr 29672
Shade Tree Ln 29678
Shadow Ln 29678
Shadow Oaks Dr 29672
Shadowick Way 29672
Shadowood Ct 29678
Shady Ln
100-199 29678
19000-19099 29672
Shady Ter 29678
Shady Cove Trl 29678
Shady Hill Ln 29672
Shady Lane Dr 29678
Shady Pine Dr 29678
Shadywood Ln 29678
Shagbark Ln 29678
Shallowford Way 29672
Shannon Ln 29678
Sharon Ln 29678
Shea Ln 29672
Sheep Farm Rd 29672
Sheila Ln 29678
Shelter Cove Dr 29672
W Shepherds Way 29678
Sherard St 29678
Sherry Ln 29672
Sherwood Dr 29678
Shiloh Rd 29678
Shining Times Rd 29678
Shinnecock Hl 29678
Shirley Dr 29678
Shirleys Farm Rd 29678
Shook Rd 29672
Shooting Star Way 29672
Shop Ln 29672
Shorecrest Dr 29672
Shoreline Dr 29672
Shores Dr 29672
Shoreview Dr 29672
Shorewinds Ct 29672
Short St 29678
Shoveler Way 29678
Shrine Club Rd 29672
Silo Aly 29672
Silver Pine Pl 29672
Silverstone Dr 29672
N Singing Pines Rd 29678
Singing Waters Dr 29672
Singleton Rd 29672
E Sirrine St 29678
Sisters Way 29672
S Sitton Mill Rd 29678
Sitton Shoals Rd 29678
E & W Sizemore Rd 29672
Skeeter Dr 29678
Skimmer Cove Ln 29672
Skyland Dr 29678
Slater Dr 29678
Sleepy Hollow Dr 29678
Sleepy Oak Ct 29672
Sloan St 29678
Smith Rd 29672
Smith Estate Dr 29678
Smoak Pond Rd 29678
Snow Creek Rd 29678
Snow Creek Church Rd 29678
Snow Creek Forest Dr 29678
Snug Harbor Rd 29678
Soaring Heights Dr 29672
Sommers Dr 29672
Sonlit Way 29672
Sonnys Dr 29672
Sosebee Rd 29678
Sourwood Dr 29678
E & W South 1st St 29678
E & W South 2nd St 29678
E & W South 3rd St 29678
E & W South 4th St 29678
E & W South 5th St 29678
E & W South 6th St 29678
E & W South 7th St 29678
E South 8th St 29678
Southern Oaks Dr 29672
Southview Ct 29672
Southwater Dr 29672
Southwind Ct 29672
Southwind Bay Dr 29672
Spanish Point Dr 29678
Sparks Way Dr 29678
Sparrow Dr 29678
Spearman Dr 29678
Spears Rd 29678
Speed Ave 29678
Spider Farm Ln 29678
Spider Oak Ln 29678
Spinnaker View Rd 29672
Split Oak Cir 29678
Spoon Rd 29672
Spotted Bull Ln 29672
Spotted Horse Rd 29672
Spring Ln 29678
Spring Run Dr 29672
E Spring Valley Rd 29672
E & W Springwood Dr 29672
Spruce Ave 29678
Sputs Ln 29678
Spyglass Ln 29678
Squirrelridge Rd 29672
Stacey Kelley Dr 29678
Stadium Dr 29678
Stamp Creek Landing Rd 29672
Stanton Dr 29672
N Star Ct 29672
Star View Dr 29672
Stardust Ln 29672
Starnes Dr 29678
Stearman Ln 29678
Steepleton Way 29672
Steer Run Ln 29678
Stephanie Ln 29672
Stephen Dr 29678
Stephens Farm Rd 29678
Stephy Ln 29672
Steve Nix Rd 29678
Still Farm Dr 29678
Still Waters Trl 29678
Stillwater Dr 29672
Stinnette Rd 29672
Stokes Dr 29672
Stone Dr 29672
Stone Creek Rd 29672
Stone Pond Way 29678
Stone Post Ct 29678
Stonebriar Park 29678
Stonebrook Dr 29672
Stonegate Dr 29678
Stonehaven Way 29672
Stonemill Dr 29678
Stoneridge Ct 29672
Stonewall Ct 29672
Stoney Rd 29678
Stork Way 29678
Stormy Ln 29678
Stratford Dr 29678
N Strawberry Farm Rd 29678
N & S Stribling St 29678
Sub Station Rd 29672
Sue Dr 29678
Sugar Valley Rd 29672
Sugarhill Rd 29672
Sullivans Way 29672
Sumac Dr 29678
Summer Breeze Way 29672
Summer Haven Ln 29672
Summer Walk Ct 29672
Summers Way 29672
Summersweet Ln 29672
N Summit Dr 29672
S Summit Dr 29672
Summit St 29678
Summit Ridge Dr 29672
Sun Meadow Ln 29678
Sunny Dr 29678
Sunny Dell Dr 29678
Sunnybrook Dr 29672
Sunnyview Dr 29672
Sunpointe Ct 29672
Sunrise Ln 29678
E Sunrise Ln 29672
Sunset Ct & Dr 29672
Sunset Bay Blvd 29672
Sunset Cove Ct 29672
Sunset Ridge Dr 29672
E & W Sunsetstrip Dr 29672
Sunshine Dr 29678
Sunview Dr 29678
Surgical Blvd 29672
Surrey Ln 29672
Swamp Fox Ln 29678
Swaney Dr 29678
Swaneys Landing Rd 29678
Swansea Ln 29672
Sweet Gum Pt 29678
Sweet Pea Ln 29678
Sweetwater Dr 29678
Sweetwater View Rd 29672
Sylvia Ln 29678
T Birds Ln 29678
T Harper Dr 29678
Tabitha Dr 29678
Talco Trl 29672
Tall Oak Trl 29678
Tall Oaks Farms Rd 29672
Tall Pine Trl 29678
Tall Willow Dr 29672

Talons Point Rd 29672
Talons Ridge Rd 29672
Tamarack Dr 29678
E Tamassee Dr 29672
Tanglewood Dr 29672
Tant Dr 29672
Tara Ln 29672
Tasha Ln 29678
Tavies Ln 29678
Teardrop Trl 29672
Tee Dr 29678
Tee Ben Trl 29672
Tee Land Dr 29678
Tequila Hts 29678
Terez Dr 29678
Terrace Dr 29672
Terrace Meadows Dr 29672
Terrace View Way 29678
Terry Dr 29678
Thatcher Rd 29678
The Hidden Dr 29678
The Old Farm Pl 29672
Thomas Dr 29678
Thomas Heights Cir 29678
Thomas Place Dr 29672
Thomson Dr 29678
Thorn Hill Dr 29678
Thrasher Ln 29678
Three Iron Dr 29678
Three Oaks Dr 29672
Thrift Ave 29678
Thunder Valley Rd 29678
Tiger Paw Dr 29678
Tiger Pride Ln 29678
Tiger Tail Rd 29678
Tiger Terrace Dr 29678
Timber Trl 29672
Timber Ridge Ln 29678
Timberlake Dr 29678
Timberlake One Cir 29678
Timberwood Ct 29672
Tinpan Aly 29672
Tokeena Rd 29678
Tokeena Nstra Dr 29678
Tokeena Path Dr 29678
Tokeena Sunset Ln 29678
Tollison Rd 29672
Tollkeepers Pl 29678
Topaz Ct 29672
Towe St 29678
N & S Townville St 29678
N & S Tradewind Way 29672
Trails End Ct 29672
Tralee Ln 29678
Trammell Dr 29672
Tranquail Ln 29672
Treaty St 29678
Treehaven Ct 29672
Treeline Dr 29672
Treetops Dr 29672
Triangle Dr 29672
Tribble St 29678
Trickenc Dr 29672
Triple J Dr 29678
Tucker Ln 29672
Tucker Farm Rd 29678
Tully Dr 29672
Tumblestone Dr 29678
Turnberry Loop 29678
Turner Rd 29678
Turtle Dove Ln 29678
Tuscany Ln 29672
Twilight Ct 29672
Twin Creeks Dr 29678
Twin Lakes Rd 29678
Twin Oaks Dr 29672
Twin Springs Dr 29678
Tyson Cir 29672
Union St 29672
Union Station Dr 29678
University Dr 29678
Ustorit Dr 29672
Utica St 29678
Valley Farm Rd 29678
Valley View Dr 29672
Vance Dr 29678
Vaughan Dr 29678
Veranda Ct 29672
Vereen St 29678
Vermont Dr 29672
Vernell Smith Dr 29678
Vickery Rd 29672
Victorian Ln 29672
Videra Ln 29678
Viewpoint Ct 29672
Villa Ln 29678
Village Creek Cir 29678
Village Park Dr 29678
Vinda Dr 29678
Vinson St 29678
Vinyard Way 29678
Violet Field Ln 29672
Vocational Dr 29672
Waco Way 29678
Wade Rd 29678
Wade Hampton Ln 29678
Wake Robin Ln 29672
Wakefield Dr 29678
Waldrop St 29672
Walker Pt 29672
Walker Way Dr 29672
N & S Walnut St 29678
Walnut Cove Ct 29672
Walters Dr 29678
Walters Morris Dr 29678
Wanda Dr 29678
War Woman Trl 29672
Ward Dr 29678
Ware St 29678
Warehouse Rd 29672
Warren Dr 29678
Warren Pitts Dr 29678
Wash Hole Dr 29678
Washington St 29678
Water Oak Ct 29672
Water Tower Rd 29678
Waterfall Rd 29672
E Waterford Dr 29672
Waterford Farms Ln 29672
Watermark Ct 29672
Watersedge Rd 29678
Watershed Rd 29678
Waterside Cv 29678
E Waterside Dr 29678
N Waterside Dr 29672
Waterview Ct 29672
Waterway Ln 29672
N Watson Ave 29678
Watson Dr 29672
Waverly Ct 29678
Wayne Cir 29678
Wayside Cir 29672
Webb Rd 29678
Webb Heights Cir 29678
Weeping Willow Dr 29672
Wellingford Pl 29672
Wellington Way 29678
Wells Hwy 29678
Wellshire Pl 29672
Wendover Ct 29672
Westbrook Dr 29672
E Westbrooks Rd 29678
Westchester Cir 29672
Western Cir 29678
Westhampton Dr 29672
Westlake Dr 29672
Westview Pt 29672
Westwind Ct 29672
Westwood Bay Dr 29672
Wetoda Rd 29678
Wharf Way 29672
Whippoorwill Dr 29672
Whiskey River Dr 29678
Whispering Ln 29672
Whispering Brook Dr 29672
Whispering Oaks Dr 29678
Whispering Stick Way 29678
White Rd 29678
White Harbour Rd 29672
White Oak Way 29678
White Oak Hill Dr 29678
White Owl Ln 29678
White Pine Ln 29672
Whitebark Rd 29678
Whitehead Dr 29678
Whitfield Ln 29678
Whitmire Dr 29678
Whitney Ln 29678
Whitten Dr 29678
Whittle Park Dr 29672
Whitworth Cir 29672
Wilbanks Rd 29678
Wild Azalea Pt 29672
Wild Fern Rd 29672
Wild Oak Ct 29672
Wild Rose Ln 29678
Wildflower Ct 29672
E Wildwood Ct 29678
Wildwood Pl 29672
William Jordan Dr 29678
Williams St 29678
Williamsburg Dr 29672
Willie Lee Dr 29678
Willow St 29678
Willow Branch Ln 29672
Willow Brook Ln 29678
Willow Creek Cir 29678
Willow Leaf Dr 29672
Willow Oak Ct 29672
Willow Tree Ln 29678
Willow Wood Ct 29672
Wilma Dr 29678
Wilson Dr 29678
Winchester Dr 29678
Wind Walker Ln 29678
Windchime Way 29678
Winding Ln 29672
Winding Branch Ln 29678
Winding Creek Ln 29672
Winding Oaks Dr 29672
Windlake Dr 29672
Windrush Ln 29672
Windsong Way 29672
Windsor Ct 29672
Windward Pt 29672
Windy Hill Ln 29678
Windy Oaks Ln 29678
Windy Pines Ln 29672
Winkler Rd 29678
Winners Circle Dr 29678
Winter Pine Ct 29672
Winterberry Ln 29678
Winterbrook Cir 29678
Wisteria Ln 29678
Wits End Trl 29678
Wolf Stake Church Rd 29672
Wolfe Ln 29678
Wood Farm Ln 29678
Wood Gate Dr 29678
Woodale Cir 29678
N Woodbury Rd 29672
Woodcreek Dr 29672
Woodduck Dr 29678
Woodfield Dr 29672
Woodglen Ct 29678
Woodland Dr 29678
Woodland Acres Ct 29678
Woodridge Dr 29672
Woods Rd 29678
Woods Edge Dr 29672
Woody Way 29672
Woody Terry Rd 29678
Woosey Trl 29672
Worley Rd 29678
Worth St 29672
Wrangler Way 29672
Wren Dr 29672
Wrights Cir 29678
Wrong Rd 29678
Wtl Rd 29678
Wyatt Ln 29672
Wyman Dr 29678
Wynmere Way 29672
Wynrose Pl 29678
Wynswept Pt 29672
Wynwood Ct 29672
Yarid St 29678
Yellow Jasmine Dr 29678
Yellow Pine Dr 29678
Yellowood Dr 29672
Yes Dear Ln 29672
Yittle Dr 29678
Ymca Cir 29678
Yorktown Dr 29672
Young Dr 29678
Zack Dr 29678
Zion Dr 29678
Zion Hill Rd 29678

SIMPSONVILLE SC

General Delivery 29681

POST OFFICE BOXES MAIN OFFICE STATIONS AND BRANCHES

Box No.s
1 - 5000 29681
80001 - 82338 29680

NAMED STREETS

Abbey Gardens Ln 29681
Abbotsford Dr 29681
Abercorn Way 29681
Abercrombie Ln 29681
Acacia Dr 29681
Academy St 29681
Acklen Dr 29681
Adams Creek Pl 29681
Adams Farm Rd 29681
Adams Lake Blvd 29681
Adams Mill Rd 29681
Adeline Ct 29681
Adirondack Way 29681
Advent Ln 29681
Agee St 29681
Agewood Ct & Dr 29680
Airdale Ln 29680
Airlie Ln 29681
Alamosa Ct 29681
Albertine Rd 29680
Alcott Ct 29681
Alcovy Ct 29680
Alder Dr 29680
Aldershot Way 29681
Alender Way 29681
Alexan Dr 29681
Alexander Manor Way 29680
Alexander Mill St 29680
Alice Ave 29681
Allagash Ln 29680
Allawood Ct 29681
Allegheny Run 29681
Allendale Abbey Ln 29681
N & S Almond Dr 29681
Altamira Way 29680
Amador Ct 29680
Amber Ln 29681
Amber Grain Dr 29680
Amberleaf Way 29681
Amesbury Dr 29681
Amiata Way 29681
Amstar Ct 29680
Amsterdam Ln 29681
Anderson Ridge Rd 29681
Andulusian Trl 29681
Angel Falls Dr 29681
Angeline Way 29681
Angie Ln 29681
Anglewood Dr 29680
Annas Pl 29681
Ansley Ct & Dr 29681
Ansley Crossing Ct 29681
Anson Ct 29681
Antioch St 29681
Appian Cir 29681
Apple Blossom Ln 29681
Applehill Way 29681
Appomattox Dr 29681
Arabian Way 29681
Arbor Keats Dr 29680
Arbordale Ln 29681
Archers Pl 29681
Ardberry Ct 29680
Argent Ct 29681
Argyle Ct 29681
Arkrose Ct 29680
Arlen Ave 29681
Armor Ct 29681
Arnold Mill Rd 29680
Artesian Ct 29681
Ash Pt 29681
Ashbury Dr 29681
Ashby Grove Dr 29681
Ashdown Dr 29680
Asheton Way 29681
Asheton Commons Ln 29681
Asheton Lakes Way 29681
Asheton Springs Way 29681
Ashfield Ct 29681
Ashford Oak Way 29680
Ashington Dr 29680
Ashley Oaks Dr 29680
Ashridge Way 29681
Ashwyn Ct 29680
Aspen Ct 29681
Aspenwood Dr 29680
Aster Dr 29681
Asterbrook Ct 29681
Atchison Way 29680
Austin Brook St 29680
Autumnwood Way 29681
Avalon Ct 29681
Avenel Ct 29681
Avocet Ln 29680
Ayers Dr 29681
Bailey Knoll Ct 29681
Balcome Blvd 29681
S Baldwin Rd 29680
Baldwin Creek Way 29680
Baldwin Pines Ct 29680
Baldwin Woods Cir 29680
Bamburgh Brae Ct 29681
Banbury Cir 29681
Baneberry Ct 29680
Bannerbrook Dr 29680
Barker Rd 29680
Barley Run 29681
Barlow Ct 29681
Barn Swallow Dr 29680
Barnyard Way 29681
Barony Way 29680
Barrett Chase Dr 29680
Bartles Ct 29681
Basalt Ct 29681
Bass Harbor Ct 29681
Batesville Rd 29681
Bathurst Ln 29681
Battery Point Cir 29681
Bauder Ct 29681
Baughman Ct 29681
Bay Hill Dr 29681
Bay Laurel Way 29681
Bay Springs Dr 29681
Bayboro Way 29680
Bayview Ct 29680
Baywood Hills Dr 29680
Beason Farm Ln 29681
Beattie St 29681
Beauclair Dr 29680
Beaudon Ct 29681
Beaumaris Ln 29681
Beaver Tail Dr 29681
Beaverdale Ct 29681
Bedfordton Ct 29681
Bedstraw Ct 29680
Beechwood Dr 29681
Belcourt Ct 29680
Belcross Ct & Dr 29681
Bell Dr 29681
Belle Dr 29680
Belle Oaks Dr 29680
Bellerive Pl 29681
Belleville Pl 29681
Bellflower Ct 29680
Bells Creek Dr 29681
Bellspring Ct 29680
Beneventum Ct 29681
Benion Way 29681
Benjamine Perry Ct 29681
S Bennetts Bridge Rd 29681
Benson St 29681
Bentbrush Dr 29680
Bentford Ct 29681
Bentwater Trl 29680
Benwood Dr 29680
Bergen Ln 29681
Berlander Ct 29680
Berryblue Ct 29680
Berwyn Ct 29681
Bethany Rd & St 29681
Bethel Rd & Way 29681
Bethel School Rd 29681
Bickleigh Ct 29681
Big Oak Ct 29681
Billings Mill Ct 29680
Bindon Ln 29680
Bingham Way 29680
Birch Ct 29681
Birch Hill Way 29681
Birchall Ln 29681
Birchstone Ct 29681
Birkdale Dr 29681
S Birkenstock Ct & Dr 29681
Bittercrest Ct 29680
Bittern Ct 29680
Black Rd 29680
Black Horse Run 29681
Black Oak Ct 29680
Black Pine Ct 29681
Blackhawk Dr 29680
Blacksburg Ct 29681
Blakely Rd 29680
Blant Ct 29681
Blue Danube Dr 29681
Blue Heron Cir 29680
Blue Sage Pl 29680
Bobcat Trl 29681
Boggart Ct 29681
Bonefield Dr 29680
Bonwood Ave 29680
Boothbay Ct 29681
Bordeaux Dr 29680
Border Ave 29680
Bottesford Ct 29680
Boxelder Ln 29680
Boyd Ave 29681
Boyd Bluff Ct 29681
Bradbourne Way 29680
Braeburn Dr 29681
Bramblewood Ter 29681
Bramford Way 29680
Bramlett St 29681
Branchview Ct 29680
Brandau Ln 29680
Brandon Ct & Way 29681
Braywood Ct 29680
Brazos Ln 29680
Brenau Pl 29681
Brendle Dr 29680
Brenleigh Ct 29680
Brentmoor Pl 29680
Brentwood Way 29680
Briarhill Dr 29680
Briarwood Ct, Dr & Ln 29681
Brick House Ct 29681
Bridge Crossing Dr 29681
Bridges Rd 29681
Bridlestone Ct 29680
Bridwell Ct 29681
Brielle Ct 29681
Brighthaven Ct 29681
Brightleaf Ct 29680
Bristlecone Ct 29680
Brittle Creek Ln 29680
Brixton Cir 29681
Broadstone Ct 29681
Broken Past Ct 29680
Broken Pine Ct 29681
Bromley Way 29681
Bronson Dr 29680
Brook Hollow Ct 29681
Brook Run Ct 29680
Brookhaven Way 29681
Brookmere Rd 29681
Brookwood Point Pl 29681
Broomcage Ct 29680
Brown Ln & Rd 29681
Bruce St 29681
Bruce Farm Cir & Rd 29681
Bruce Meadow Rd 29681
Brushwood Ln 29680
Bryce Cir 29681
Brydon Ct 29680
Bryson Dr 29681
Bryson Heights Dr 29681
Buckboard Ln 29681
Buckey Ct 29680
Buckfield Ct 29680
Buckhead Ln 29681
Buckler Ct 29681
Burdette Rd 29681
Burdock Ct & Way 29681
Burge Ct 29681
Burwood Dr 29681
Butler Dr 29681
Buttermilk Ct 29681
Buzzell Ct 29681
Byswick Ct 29680
Cabrini Ct 29680
Cachet Ct 29680
Cactus Ct 29681
Cadogan Dr 29681
Caitlin Ct 29680
Calavera Dr 29681
Calaverdi Ct 29681
Caleridge Dr 29680
Calgary Ct 29680
Callawassie Ct 29681
Callbeck Ln 29681
Callipoe Ct 29681
Camellia Ln 29681
Camelot Dr 29681
Cameron Creek Ln 29681
Camino Ln 29681
Candleston Pl 29681
Candor Pl 29681
Candyce Ct 29680
Canebreak Ln 29681
Canebridge Ct 29681
Caney Ct 29681
Canosa Ct 29681
Canterbury St 29680
Cape Neddick Ln 29681
Capewood Rd 29680
Capriole Ct 29681
Capstone Ct 29681
Carderock Ct 29680
Cardiff Ct 29681
Cardinal Ct 29681
Cardston Dr 29680
Carillon Ct 29681
Carlisle Dr 29681
Carolina Bay Ct 29681
Carriage Ln 29681
Carriage Hill Rd 29681
Carrick Dr 29681
Carrington Way 29681
Carruth St 29680
Carsons Pond Dr 29681
Cartecay Ct 29680
Carter Run Ct 29681
Carters Creek Ct 29681
Cassidy Ct 29680
Castle Hall Ct 29680
Castle Hollow Trl 29681
Castlebridge Ct 29681
Castlegate Ct 29681
Caswell Ln 29680
Catbriar Ct 29680
Cattle Ct 29681
Caventon Dr 29681
Cedar Donne Cir 29680
Cedar Glenn Way 29681
Cedar Ridge Ln 29681
Cedarcrest Ct 29680

Cedarhill Ct	29681
Centerpointe Blvd	29681
Chadbourne Ln	29681
Chadley Way	29681
Chafford Ct	29681
Chancellors Park Ct	29681
N & S Chancelor Dr	29681
Chancery Ln	29681
Chandler Lake Dr	29680
Chantemar	29681
Chantilly Rue Ct	29681
Chapel Hill Ln	29681
Chardmore Ct	29681
Chariot Ln	29681
Chase Woods Ct	29680
Chasemont Ln	29680
Chatburn Ct	29681
Chattahoochee St	29680
Chatwood Ct	29680
Chaulk Hill Ct	29681
Cheekwood Ct	29680
Chenoweth Dr	29681
Cherokee Ct & Dr	29680
Cherrystone Ct	29680
Chesley Dr	29680
Chessington Ln	29681
Chestatee Ct	29680
Chestnut Grove Ln	29680
Chestnut Hill Pl	29680
Chestnut Oaks Cir & Ct	29681
Chetfield Ct	29680
Chewink Ct	29680
Cheyenne Dr	29680
Chickamauga Ln	29681
Chicora Wood Ln	29681
Chinaberry Ln	29680
Choppee Ct	29681
Chowan Dr	29681
Chuckwood Ct & Dr	29680
Church Ln & St	29681
Churchwill Ct	29680
Cinnamon Ct	29681
Circle Dr	29681
Circle Slope Ct & Dr	29681
Claiborne Way	29681
Clairhill Ct	29680
Clancy Ct	29681
Clear Creek Ct	29680
Clear Lake Dr	29680
Clear Spring Rd	29681
Clevington Ct & Way	29681
Cleyera Ct	29681
Clifford Ct	29681
Clifton Grove Way	29681
Clingmore Ct	29681
Cloverdale Ct & Ln	29681
Club Dr	29681
Clydesdale Dr	29681
Coach Ln	29681
Coachman Dr	29681
Coachwhip Ct	29680
Coalmont Ct	29681
Cobbler Ln	29681
Cog Hill Dr	29681
Colewood Pl	29681
E & W College St	29681
Colleton Ct	29681
Collins Mills Ct	29681
Collinsbrooke Ct	29681
Colonial Ln	29681
Colonist Ct	29680
Colony Centre Way	29681
Coltsfoot Ct	29680
Concord Ct	29681
Connemara Pl	29681
Connors Creek Ct	29681
Cook St	29681
Cooper Dr	29681
Cooper Lake Rd	29681
Copper Knoll Cir	29681
Copperdale Dr	29681
Coral Bell Ct	29680
Coralvine Ct & Rd	29681
Corgi Dr	29680
Corinth St	29681
Corinthian Dr	29681
Corkwood Dr	29680
Cornerstone Ct	29681
Cornerton Pass	29680
Coronado Ct	29680
Corporate Dr	29681
Cothran Dr	29681
Cotton Bay Way	29681
Cotton Hall Ct	29680
Cottonwood Ct	29681
Country Side Ln	29681
Country View Dr	29681
Country Walk Ln	29680
Cox St	29681
Cranebill Dr	29680
Cranston Ct	29681
Creek Shoals Dr	29681
Creekbend Ct	29681
Crest St	29681
Crested Owl Pl	29680
Cresthaven Pl	29681
Crestridge Dr	29681
Cricken Tree Dr	29681
Crispin Ct	29681
Criterion Dr	29681
Crooked Ct	29680
Crossbill Dr	29680
Crossbrook Way	29681
Crossroads Cir	29680
Crossview Dr	29680
Crossvine Way	29680
Crowflock Ct	29680
Crown Empire Ct	29681
Crown Gate Ct	29681
Crowsnest Ct	29680
Cruisair Ct	29681
E & W Curtis St	29681
Cutting Horse Ct	29680
Cypresshill Ct	29680
Dairwood Dr	29680
Dalewood Dr	29680
Damascus Dr	29681
Dandie Dr	29680
Dansel Ct	29681
Dante Ln	29681
Danwood Ct	29680
Dapple Gray Ct	29680
Davenport Rd	29680
Dawn Ln	29680
Dawn Meadow Ct	29680
Debonair Way	29681
Decatur St	29681
Deep Springs Way	29681
Deer Run Ct	29681
Deer Spring Ln	29680
Deer Track Rd	29681
Deerwood Cir	29681
Delgado Way	29681
Delmar Dr	29680
Dempsey Glen Ln	29681
Dendon Ct	29680
Dennis Waldrop Way	29681
Depford Ct	29680
Derrick Ln	29680
Devereaux Ct	29681
Dianne Ave	29681
Digby Pl	29681
Digital Pl	29681
Dillard Rd	29681
Dillworth Ct	29681
Donegal Ct	29681
Doonbeg Ct	29681
Doral Way	29680
Dorian Dr	29680
Douglas Dr	29681
Dove Haven Dr	29681
Dovestone Dr	29681
Draymoor Ln	29681
Drayton Hall Rd	29681
Druid Hill Ct	29681
Dry Fork Ct	29680
Drystack Way	29681
Ducktrap Ct	29681
Duffie Rd	29681
Dumbarton Ave	29681
Dunberry Ct	29681
Dunbrook Dr	29680
Dunk Rd	29681
Dunleith Ct	29681
Dunrobin Ln	29681
Dunsborough Dr	29680
Dunwoody Dr	29681
Durbin Creek Rd	29681
Dusty Ln	29681
Dutchess Rd	29680
Duxbury Dr	29681
Dylan Oaks Dr	29681
Eagle Creek Dr	29681
Eaglecrest Ct	29681
Eagleston Ln	29680
Earleigh Ct	29681
Eastcrest Dr	29681
Easton Ct	29680
Eastview Cir & Dr	29681
Ebenway Ln	29680
Eden Derry Dr	29681
Edgeridge Ct	29680
Edgewood Dr	29681
Edmunds St	29681
Edwards Cir & St	29681
Eelgrass Ct	29680
Elderberry Ct	29681
Elias Ct	29680
Ellicott Hill Ln	29681
Ellis Mill St	29680
Elstar Loop Rd	29681
Emerald Way	29681
Emerald Park Ct	29681
Engelmann Ln	29680
English Meadow Dr	29681
English Oak Rd	29681
Epps Dr	29681
Equestrian Ct	29680
Estate Dr	29681
European Plum Ct	29681
Eventide Dr	29681
Evergreen Cir	29681
Everleigh Ct	29681
Fair Grove Dr	29681
E Fair Isle Ct & Dr	29681
Fairdale Dr	29681
E & W Fairgate Ct	29680
Fairground Rd	29680
Fairlane Dr	29680
Fairview Dr	29681
Fairview Rd	
400-599	29681
601-1599	29680
Fairview Lake Way	29680
Fairview Pointe Dr	29681
Fall Brook Ct	29681
E & W Fall River Way	29680
Falling Ridge Ct	29680
Falling Spring Ct	29681
Farm Brook Way	29681
Farm Club Dr	29680
Farm Mill Cir	29681
Farming Creek Dr	29680
Fauna Ct	29680
Faunawood Dr	29680
Fazio Ct	29681
Featherwood Ct	29680
Felhurst Ct	29681
Ferguson Rd	29681
E & W Fernwood Rd	29681
Ferryhill Dr	29681
Fieldcrest Ct	29681
Fieldmont Cir	29681
Fieldwood Ln	29681
Fife Ct	29681
Finch Dr	29680
Finley Hill Ct	29681
Finsbury Ln	29681
Firestone Way	29681
Firetower Rd	29680
Fishbrook Way	29681
Five Fork Plaza Ct	29681
Five Forks Rd	29681
Five Gait Turn	29681
Flagstone Ct	29681
Flat Shoals Ct	29680
Flintwood Dr	29681
Florence Dr	29681
Forest Lake Dr	29681
Forest Park Dr	29681
Fork Shoals Rd	29680
Fort Dr	29681
Fortuna Dr	29681
Fountain Inn Dr	29681
Fowler Rd	29681
Fox Trce	29680
Fox Chase Ct	29680
Fox Den Ln	29681
Fox Hollow Ct	29680
Foxbriar Ct	29681
Foxfire Dr	29680
Foxglen Ct	29680
Foxhound Ct & Rd	29680
Foxtrail Ct	29680
Foxwood Ct & Dr	29680
Foxworth Ct & Ln	29680
Frankfort Ct	29681
Franklin Ave	29681
Fredericksburg Dr	29681
Fremont Dr	29680
Frontage Rd	29681
Frostweed Ct	29680
Fruitwood Ct	29681
Fudora Cir	29681
Fugate Dr	29681
Fullerton Ct	29681
Fundy Ct	29681
Furlong Ct	29681
Gainey Ct	29681
Gala Ct	29681
Galendale Ct	29680
Gamesford Ct	29680
Ganibrille Ct	29681
Ganton Ct	29680
Garden Corners Ct	29681
Garden District Dr	29681
Garden Spring Dr	29681
Garfield Ln	29681
Garnett Way	29680
Garrison Rd	29681
S Garrison Rd	29680
Gary Ave	29681
Gatewood Ave	29681
Gatwick Ln	29681
Gelding Way	29680
Georges Hideaway	29681
E Georgia Rd	29681
W Georgia Rd	
100-499	29681
500-2399	29680
Gerald Dr	29681
Gettysburg Ct	29681
Gibbs Ter	29681
Gibby Ln	29681
Gilden Ln	29681
Gilder Trce	29681
Gilder Creek Dr	29681
Gilder Point Ct	29681
Gilderview Dr	29681
Gillin Dr	29680
Ginger Gold Dr	29681
Ginkgo Ct	29680
Glassglenn Dr	29681
Glen Hawk Ct	29680
Glen Ivy Dr	29681
Glen Meadows Dr	29680
Glenbow Ct	29680
Glenbriar Ct	29681
Glencove Ct	29681
Gleneagles Ct	29681
Glengrove Dr	29681
Glenlocke Ct	29680
Glenmora Rd	29680
Glenrock Ln	29681
Glenview Dr	29681
E & W Glohaven Pl	29681
Goatsbeard Ct	29680
Godfrey Rd	29681
Golden Acre Ct	29681
Golden Leaf Ln	29681
Golden Oak Ct	29681
Goldenrain Way	29680
Goldrush Ct	29681
Goldsmith Rd	29681
Golf Club Dr	29681
Goodwin Rd	29681
Gorham Ct	29680
Gosford Rd	29681
Governors Lake Way	29680
Graburn Dr	29681
Grackle Ct	29680
Graclan Ct	29680
Grading Pl	29681
Granary Dr	29681
Grand River Ln	29681
Grande Oaks Ct	29681
Grandview Dr	29680
Grayhawk Way	29681
Grayling Ct	29680
Graywood Ct	29680
Great Oaks Way	29680
Great Pines Dr	29681
Green St	29681
Green Bank Ln	29681
Green Hill Dr	29681
Green Oak Dr	29680
Greenapple Way	29681
Greenbranch Way	29680
Greenbriar Dr	29680
Greening Dr	29681
Greenside Ct	29681
Greenview Ct	29681
Greer Dr	29681
Grenadier Ct	29681
Gresham Rd	29681
Greyleaf Ct	29680
Griffith Ct	29681
Grimes Dr	29681
Groton Ct	29680
Grotto Pl	29681
Groveton Ct	29681
Guillory Rd	29681
Gunnison Dr	29681
Gunter Rd	29680
Gwinn St	29681
Gwinn Meadow Ct	29681
Habersham Ct	29681
Hackamore Ct	29681
Hackberry St	29680
Hague Ct	29681
Halehaven Dr	29681
Halstead Ct	29681
Hammel Ct	29680
Hammond Rd	29680
Hannah Ln	29680
Harlequin Ct	29681
Harness Trl	29681
Harpers Ferry Ct	29681
Harrisburg Dr	29681
Harrison Bridge Rd	
1-199	29681
200-799	29680
N Harrison Bridge Rd	29680
S Harrison Bridge Rd	29680
Harrison Oaks Dr	29680
Harrogate Ct	29681
Harts Ln	29681
Hartwell Dr	29681
Harwich Dr	29681
Hatcher Creek St	29681
Hatteras Ln	29680
Hawk Rd	29681
Hawkesbury Rd	29681
Hawkhurst Ct	29681
Hawks Perch Way	29681
Hawksbill Ln	29680
Hawthorne Dr	29680
Hawthorne Creek Ct	29681
Haymaker Ct	29680
Hayworth Dr	29680
Hazeldeen Pl	29680
Hazeltine Ct	29681
Headwater Ct	29680
Heathbury Ct	29681
Heather Falls Ln	29681
Heather Grove Ct	29681
Heather Stone Ct	29680
Heathercrest Ct	29681
Heatherfield Dr	29680
Heathermoor Way	29680
Heathfield Ct	29681
Hedge St	29681
Hedgefield Ct	29680
Helen St	29681
Hemingford Cir	29681
Hennepin Dr	29680
Henning Ct	29681
Heritage Ln	29681
Heritage Creek Rd	29681
Heritage Oak Way	29681
Heritage Point Dr	29681
Herndon Ct	29681
Hickory Dr & St	29681
Hickory Chip Ct	29681
Hickory Cove Ln	29681
Hickory Twig Way	29681
Hidden Fawn Pl	29680
Hidden Oak Ter	29681
Hidden Pond Ct	29680
Hideaway Ct	29680
High Crest Ct	29681
High Plains Rd	29681
Highgrove Ct	29681
Highway 14	29681
Highway 418	29680
Hiley Ct	29681
Hill Ln & St	29681
Hillcrest Ave & Dr	29681
Hillpine Dr	29681
Hillstone Dr	29680
Hilltop St	29681
Hinterland Rd	29681
Hipps Ave	29681
Hipps Dr	29681
Hipps Rd	29680
Holcombe Rd	29680
Holland Ct, Rd & St	29681
Holland East Ct	29681
Holland Trace Cir	29681
Hollingdale Ct	29681
Holly St & Trce	29681
Holly Center Way	29681
Holly Crest Cir	29681
Holly Fern Ct	29680
Holly Hill Ln	29681
Holly Leaf Ct	29681
Holly Park Dr & Ln	29681
N & S Holly Thorn Ct	29681
Holly Tree Ln	29681
Hollyberry Ct	29681
Hollybrook Way	29681
Hollyhock Dr	29681
Hollymont Ct	29681
Hollywoods Ln	29681
Homeplace Ct	29680
Honey Crisp Way	29681
Honey Horn Dr	29681
Horizon Dr	29681
Horsepen Way	29681
Hospital Dr	29681
Howard Cir & Dr	29681
Howards End Ct	29681
Howden Pl	29681
Hudders Creek Way	29680
Huddersfield Dr	29681
Hunslet Way	29680
Hunt Club Dr	29680
Hunter Rd	29681
Hunterdon Ct	29680
Hunters Hill Rd	29680
Hunters Moor Ct	29680
Hunters Woods Dr	29680
Hunting Creek Dr	29681
Hunting Ridge Ct	29680
Huntingtower Ln	29681
Huntley Ct	29680
Huntsboro Dr	29680
Huntsman Ct	29680
Hushpah Ct	29680
Hydrangea Way	29681
I 185	
7000-7999	29680
I 185	
8000-9999	29681
Idared Ct	29681
Impasse Ln	29681
Indian Laurel Ct	29680
Indian Mound Ct	29680
N & S Industrial Dr	29681
Innisbrook Ln	29681
Iodine State Beagle Rd	29681
Ipswich Ln	29681
Irish Moss Ct	29680
Irish Rose Ct	29681
Iron Bridge Way	29681
Ironwood Rd	29681
Iselin St	29681
Ivey Mountain Cv	29681
Iveyrose Ct	29681
Ivory Arch Ct	29681
Ivy Dr	29680
Ivy Trellis Ct	29681
Ivyberry Rd	29681
Jackson Rd	29680
Jamar Ct	29680
James Hudson Ct	29681
James Riceland Ct	29681
Janet Ct	29681
Jasmine Cove Cir	29680
Jenkins Bridge Rd	29680
Jenkins Farm Way	29680
Jenna Ln	29681
Jericho Ct	29680
Jester Ct	29681
Jillian Lee Ct	29681
Jitney Ct	29681
Jockey Ct	29681
Joggins Dr	29681
John St	29681
Johnson Dr	29681
Jonas Ct	29681
Jones Ave	29681
Jones Mill Rd	29681
Jones Peak Dr	29681
Jonesville Rd	29681
Jordan Crest Ct	29681
Joshuas Pl	29681
Josiah Ct	29681
Joyce Ln	29680
Jubilee Way	29681
Junegrass Dr	29680
Justin Ct	29680
Kallam Way	29681
Kangley Dr	29681
Kaplan Ct	29681
Karsten Creek Dr	29681
Kay Dr	29681
Keenan Creek Way	29680
Kelsey Glen Ln	29681
Kemet Way	29681
Kempton Dr	29680
Kennard Ct	29681
Kennebec Ln	29681
Kennel Ct	29681
Kenton Ct	29681
Kenton Finch Ct	29681
Kersey Gale Ct	29681
Keswick Trl	29681
Kettle Oak Way	29681
Keynan Ct	29680
Kilgore Cir & Ct	29681
Kilgore Farms Cir	29681
Killean Ct	29681
Kilmarsh Rd	29680
Kilsock Ct	29681
Kilvey Ct	29680
Kimble Dr	29680
Kinard Way	29681
Kincade Dr	29681
Kindletree Way	29681
Kindred Dr	29681
King Rd	29681
Kingfisher Dr	29680
Kinglet Ct	29681
Kings Grant Way	29681
Kings Heath Ln	29680
Kings Reserve Cir	29681
Kingsdale Ct	29680
Kingsgate Ct	29681
Kingsmoor Dr	29681

Kingswood Cir 29681
Kinlaw Ct 29681
Kinner Ct 29681
Kirkshire Ln 29680
Kirkwall Ct 29681
Knights Valley Dr 29681
Knightsbridge Dr 29681
Knoll Creek Dr 29680
Kurdistan Way 29680
Kwikaway Ct 29680
Lacebark Ct 29680
Ladean Ct 29680
Ladell Dr 29681
Ladson Lake Ln 29680
Lady Fern Way 29680
Ladybird Ct 29680
Ladysmith Dr 29681
Laguna Ln 29680
Lake Lennox Dr 29681
Lake Park Vw 29681
Lake Sunshine 29681
Lake Valley Ct 29681
Lakeshore Dr 29681
Lakeview Dr & Ter 29681
Lambeth Ct 29681
Lancaster St 29680
Lancelot Ct & Dr 29681
Land Grant Dr 29681
Landau Pl 29680
Landfall Ct 29681
Landing Ln 29681
Landridge Ct 29681
Lantana Ct 29681
Larchwood Dr 29680
Lark Ln 29681
Larose Ct 29681
Larson Dr 29681
Lasalle Pl 29680
Latrobe Dr 29681
Laurel Branch Ln 29681
Laurel Grove Dr 29681
Laurel Oak Trl 29681
Laurel Tree Ln 29681
Laurenville Ln 29680
Lavender Hill Ct 29681
Layken Ln 29680
Lazy Willow Dr 29680
Lazydays Ct 29680
Lea Gail Cir 29681
Leafmore Ct 29680
League Rd 29681
Leake Dr 29681
Lee St 29681
Lee Vaughn Rd 29681
Leeds Ct 29681
Legends Way 29681
Leigh Creek Dr 29681
Leighton Ct 29680
Leland Cypress Ct 29681
Lenten Rose Ct 29680
Leopard Rd 29681
Lexington Ct 29681
Lifesprings Ct 29680
Lilly St 29681
Limerick Ct 29681
Linfield Ct 29681
Linwood Ct 29681
Lionel Ct 29681
Lippizan Way 29681
Lismore St 29680
Little Leaf Ct 29681
Locik Ct 29680
Lockeland Park Dr 29681
Lockhorn Ln 29681
E Loden Ct & Dr 29681
Loma St 29681
Lombardy Ct 29681
Lone Oak Ave 29681
Lone Pine Ct 29680
Lone Rock Ct 29680
Long Acre Ln 29680
E & W Long Creek Ct 29680
Long Point Way 29681
Longmont Ln 29681
Longspur Ct 29680
Longstaff Pkwy 29680
Lonnie Ave 29681
Loraine Dr 29680
Lori Dr 29681
Lost Creek Ct 29681
Lost Lake Dr 29681
Lost Tree Ln 29681
Lovelace Ct 29681
Lyons Ct & Dr 29681
Macintyre St 29680
Madera Trl 29680
Magnolia Crest Dr 29681
Magnolia Place Ct 29681
N, NE, S & SE Main St 29681
Maindowe Dr 29681
Malibu Ln 29680
Mallard Ridge Pl 29680
Manassas Ct & Dr 29681
Manatee Ct 29681
Mangrove Ct 29680
Manheim Dr 29681
Manor Ct 29681
Manorwood Ct 29681
N & S Maple St 29681
Maple Brook Ct 29681
Maple Rock Ct 29681
Maple Wind Ln 29681
Marchfield Ct 29681
Mare Ct 29681
Marefair Ln 29680
Margate Ct 29681
Mariposa Ct 29680
Market Bay Ct 29681
Markswood Dr 29681
E & W Marley Ln 29681
Marquette Rd 29680
Marseille Dr 29680
Marswen Ct 29680
Martele Ct 29680
Martindale Dr 29681
Martins Hollow Ln 29680
Matteson Brook Ln 29681
Maurice Ln 29681
Maxine Ln 29680
Maxwell Rd 29681
Mayfield Rd 29681
Maywood Dr 29681
Mccall Rd 29680
Mccrary Ct 29681
Mcfadden Dr 29680
Mckinney Rd 29681
Mcrae Pl 29681
Meadow Blossom Way 29681
Meadow Field Ct 29681
Meadow Reserve Pl 29681
Meadowrise Ln 29681
Meaway Ct 29681
Medford Pl 29681
Medina Ln 29681
Mendenhall Ct 29681
Menlo Dr 29680
Ment Dr 29680
Mercer Dr 29681
Meringer Pl 29680
Merlin Ct 29680
Metrogate Ct 29681
Middlefield Ct 29680
Middlewick Ct 29681
Milam Rd 29681
Militia Ct 29680
Millbrook St 29681
Miller St 29680
Millstone Way 29681
Milo Ct 29680
Milway Dr 29681
Mineral Ct 29681
Minnow Ct 29681
Minots Ledge Ln 29681
Mitchell Spring Ct 29681
Modesto Ln 29681
Moncton Pl 29681
Monpetit Pl 29680
Monroe Dr 29681
Montalcino Way 29681
Montreat Ln 29681
Montvale Dr 29681
Moore Rd 29681
N Moore Rd 29680
Moore St 29681
Moores Ct 29681
Moorgate Dr 29681
Moorland Way 29681
Morell Dr 29681
Morgan Cir 29681
Morning Mist Ln 29680
Morning Tide Dr 29681
Morningrose Ln 29681
Mornington Ct 29681
Morton Ave & Rd 29681
Mosley Rd 29680
Moss Spring Ct 29680
Moss Wood Cir 29681
Mossy Ledge Ln 29681
Mount Calvary Way 29681
Mount Sinai Ln 29681
Mountain Rose Ct 29681
Muirfield Ct 29681
Musket Ct 29680
Mustang Cir 29681
Mystic Ct 29681
Mystique Falls Ct 29681
Nakkol Dr 29680
Nancy Dr 29681
Needles Dr 29680
Neely Crossing Ln 29680
Neely Farm Dr 29680
Neely Ferry Rd 29680
Neland Ct 29681
Nermal Ct 29681
Netherland Ln 29681
Nevin Ct 29681
New Castle Pl 29680
New Harrison Bridge Rd 29680
New Palace Ct 29681
Newbern Way 29680
Newgate Dr 29681
Niagara Pl 29681
Nibbins Ln 29680
Night Heron Dr 29680
Nina Ct 29681
Nittany Pl 29681
Noble Oaks Ln 29681
Nobska Light Ct 29681
Northfield Ln 29681
Norvin Ct 29680
Nottinghill Ct 29681
Oak Branch Dr 29681
Oak Crest Ct 29680
Oak Knob Ct 29681
Oak Meadow Dr 29681
Oak Valley Dr 29681
Oakboro Ln 29680
Oakfern Ct & Dr 29681
Oakhill Dr 29681
Oakland Ave 29681
Oaklawn Rd 29680
Oaklynn Ct 29681
Oakmont Ct 29681
Odie Dr 29681
Oglethorpe Ct 29681
Oglewood Dr 29681
E & W Okaloosa Way 29680
Old Field Dr 29680
Old Georgia Rd 29681
Old House Way 29681
Old Ivy Dr 29681
Old Laurens Rd 29681
Old Stage Rd 29681
Old Town Way 29681
Old Tree Ct 29681
Old White Dr 29681
Oliver Ct 29681
Onslow Ct 29680
Ontario Ct 29681
Onyx Pillar Ct 29681
Open Range Ln 29681
N & S Orchard Farms Ave 29681
Orleans Dr 29680
Oshields Way 29680
Ossabaw Loop 29681
Owl Ct 29680
Oxborough Pl 29680
Oxbow Ct 29680
Oxner Rd 29681
Oystercatcher Way 29681
Paddock Pl 29681
Paddock Run Ln 29681
Palm Springs Way 29681
Palmetto Dr 29681
Palomino Ct 29681
Paloro Pl 29681
Paqcolet Dr 29681
Paranor Dr 29681
Park Dr 29681
Parkcrest Ct 29681
Parker Slatton Rd 29681
Parkgate Ct 29680
Parkside Dr 29681
Parkview Dr 29681
Parnell Dr 29680
Pasture Pl 29681
Pasture View Ct 29680
Patriots Pride Ct 29680
Pawleys Dr 29681
Pecan Dr 29681
Pecan Hill Dr 29681
Pelham Rd 29681
Pemaquid Ct 29681
Pembark Ln 29681
Peninsula Ct 29681
Penn Ct 29680
S Penobscot Ct 29681
Penrith Ct 29681
Pepper Tree Ln 29680
Percheron Path 29681
Pergola Pl 29680
Perry Ave 29681
Petal Ct 29681
Peter Brook Ct 29681
Peters Creek Ct 29681
Peters Fork Ln 29681
Peters Glenn Ct 29681
Pfeiffer Ct 29681
Phaeton Ave 29680
Philwood Dr 29681
Pickens Ct 29680
Pickering Ln 29681
Picton Pl 29680
Pike Ct & St 29681
Pilger Pl 29681
Pima Ct 29680
Pine Dr & Ln 29681
Pine Bark Ct 29680
Pine Island Dr 29681
Pine Tree Dr 29680
Pinehaven Way 29681
Pinehurst St 29681
Pinellas Ct 29680
Pinion Ct 29681
Pinonwood Ct & Dr 29680
Pioneer Ct 29681
Placid Falls Ct 29681
Placid Forest Ct 29681
Plamondon Dr 29680
Plantation Dr 29681
Plateau Pl 29681
Platte Ln 29680
Player Way 29681
Pleasant Isle Ln 29681
N & S Pliney Cir 29681
Plum Hill Way 29680
Plum Orchard Ct 29681
Poinsettia Dr 29681
Poinsettia Drive Ext 29681
Polaski Ct 29681
Pollard Rd 29681
Polo Dr 29681
Pond Terrace Ln 29681
Pond View Ct 29680
Ponderosa Dr 29681
Pontrang Dr 29680
Poplar Dr 29681
Poplar Ridge Rd 29681
Poppy Meadow Ln 29681
Portabello Way 29681
Portland Falls Dr 29680
Powderhorn Rd 29681
Powers Garden Rd 29681
Pride Dr 29681
Prince Williams Ct 29681
Privello Pl 29681
Privet Ct 29680
Pronghorn Ct 29680
Purpleleaf Ct 29680
Putman St 29681
Putney Bridge Ln 29681
Quail Trl 29681
Quail Hollow Dr 29681
Quail Ridge Dr 29680
Quiet Cove Ct 29680
Quiet Creek Ct 29681
Rabon Ct 29681
Radcliffe Way 29681
Radford Ct 29680
Rainwood Dr 29681
Raisinwood Dr 29681
Raleigh Ct 29681
Ralph Hendricks Dr 29681
Ramapo Ct 29681
Ramble Rose Ct 29681
Ramsford Ln 29681
Ranger Ct 29680
Rapidan Ct 29681
Raritan Ct 29681
Rashford Way 29681
Raven Falls Ln 29681
Raven Rock Ct 29680
Ravenwood Ln 29681
Ray E Talley Ct 29680
Rebecca Ct & Ln 29681
Rebel Ct 29681
Red Bluff Rd 29681
Red Branch Ln 29681
Red Cedar Ct 29681
Red Fern Trl 29681
Red Finch Dr 29680
Red Gate Ct 29680
Red Jonathan Ct 29681
Red Oak Ct 29681
Red Orchard Rd 29681
Red Orchid Rd 29681
Red Robin Ct 29680
Red Rome Ct 29681
Red Tip Ct 29680
Redbarn Ct 29680
Redcoat Ct 29680
Redfree Dr 29681
Redglobe Ct 29681
Redgum Ct 29681
Redriff Way 29680
Redstart Ct 29680
Redstem Dr 29681
Redvales Rd 29681
Redwood St 29680
Reedy Acres Dr 29680
Reeves Dr 29681
Regal Way 29681
Regents Gate Ct 29681
Reinhardt Dr 29681
Remus Way 29681
Renforth Rd 29681
Revis Creek Ct 29681
Rhinegold Ct 29681
Ricelan Dr 29681
Richardson Rd 29680
Richardson St
100-609 29681
610-699 29680
Richfield Ln 29681
Richmond Ct 29681
Riddle Rd 29681
Ridge Gln & Way 29680
Ridgecrest Ct 29680
Ridgecrest Dr 29681
Ridgedale Way 29681
Ridgeleigh Way 29681
Rimrock Ct 29681
Rio Grande Pl 29680
River Point Ct 29681
River Summit Dr 29681
River Walk Blvd, Ct, Dr & Ter 29681
Riverchase Ct 29680
Riverdale Rd 29680
Rivereen Way 29680
Riverfront Ln 29681
Rivers Edge Cir 29680
Roanoke Hills Ct 29681
Roberts Rd 29681
Roberts Farm Rd 29681
Robin Rd 29681
Robinwood Dr 29681
Rockberry Ter 29681
Rockland Dr 29681
Rocky Creek Rd 29680
Roebuck Dr 29681
Rollingwood Dr 29681
Rollins St 29681
Romsey Cir 29681
Romulus Ln 29681
Roper Meadow Dr 29681
Roper Mountain Rd 29681
Rosa Ln 29681
Rose Ln 29681
Rose Petal Ct 29680
Roseberry Ln 29681
Rosemoss Ct 29680
Rosings Aly 29681
Rossway Dr 29681
Rothesay St 29681
Roundleaf Ct 29680
Rox Run 29681
Roxie Dr 29681
Roxton Loop 29681
Roy Thomason Rd 29681
Royal Dutch Ln 29681
Royal Oak Ct 29680
Ruby Bay Ln 29681
Ruby Lake Ln 29681
Rue Dr 29681
Rustling Creek Ct 29681
Rusty Ct 29680
Sabin Ct 29681
Saddle Club Ct 29680
Saddle Horse Ct 29681
Saddlemount Ln 29680
Saddletree Pl 29681
Sagramore Ct & Ln 29681
Saint Albans School Rd 29680
Saint Johns St 29680
Sakonnet Ct 29680
Salford Way 29681
Salthouse Rd 29680
Sampit Dr 29681
Sand Castle Dr 29681
Sand Hill Dr 29681
Sanders Pl 29681
Sandhurst Dr 29680
Sandridge Ct 29681
Sandusky Ln 29680
N & S Sandy Brook Way 29680
Sandy Point Ct 29680
Sanibel Oaks Dr 29680
Santa Cruz Way 29680
Santee Ct 29680
Sarah Ct 29680
Saranac Ln 29681
Sarazen Way 29681
Satterfield Rd 29681
Savage Hill Pl 29680
Sawtooth Ct 29680
Saybrook Rd 29681
Scanawah Ct 29681
Scarsdale St 29681
Schooner Ct 29680
Scituate Ct 29681
Scotsburn Ct 29681
Scottish Ave 29680
Scotts Bluff Dr 29681
Scuffletown Rd 29681
Sea Harbour Way 29681
Seashell Ct 29681
Sedgebrook Dr 29681
Seedleaf Ct 29680
Selkirk Ct 29681
Sellwood Cir 29680
Seminole Dr 29680
Semmelrock Dr 29680
Sentinel Ct 29681
Sentry Way 29680
Shaddock Dr 29680
Shadow Dr 29681
Shadow Mist Dr 29681
Shadow Point Ct 29681
Shadow Ridge Cir 29681
Shadowbrooke Ct 29681
Shadowcreek Ct 29681
Shadowdale Dr 29681
Shadowlawn Way 29680
Shadowmoss Ct 29681
Shadowood Ct & Dr 29681
Shadowrock Ct 29681
Shady Grove Dr 29681
Shagbark Cir & Ct 29680
Shalom Dr 29681
Shea Ct 29681
Sheepscot Ct 29681
Shefleys Rd 29680
Shelbrook Rd 29681
Shelby Ct 29681
Sheldrake Pl 29681
Sherman Dr 29680
Sherondale Ln 29680
Shillingford Ct 29681
Shiloh Ct 29681
Shippers Dr 29681
S Shirley Rd 29680
Sierra Ct 29680
Silver Brook Dr 29681
Silver Fox Trl 29681
Silverthorn Ct 29681
Skipping Stone Ct 29681
Skye Ct 29680
Sleepy River Rd 29681
Slow Creek Dr 29681
Smithwood Ct 29681
Smokehouse Dr 29681
Snap Creek Ct 29681
Snow Rd 29681
Somerleaf Way 29681
Somerset Forest Ln 29681
South St 29681
Southbridge Ct 29680
Southern Oaks Ct & Ln 29681
Spaar Ln 29680
Sparrow Point Ct 29680
Sparsewood St 29680
Spillers Rd 29680
Spring Ct 29680
Spring Forest Dr 29681
Spring Glen Dr 29680
Spring Lake Loop 29681
Spring Meadow Ct 29680
Spring Meadow Dr 29681
Spring Meadow Rd 29680
Spring Meadow Way 29680
Spring Moss Ct 29681
Spring Point Ct 29681
Spring Tree Dr 29681
Springdale Dr 29681
Springhaven Ct 29681
Springhill Dr 29681
Springleaf Ct 29681
Squires Creek Rd 29681
Squires Meadow Ct 29681
Squirrel Hill Ct 29680
St Lucie Dr 29681
Staffordshire Way 29681
E Standing Springs Ct & Rd 29680
Star Fish Ct 29681
Staregrass Ct 29680
Stayman Ct 29681
Steamboat Ct 29681
Steeplechase Ct 29681
Stenhouse Rd 29680
Stewart Rd 29681
Stillwater Ct 29681
Stokes Ct & Rd 29681
Stone Dale Dr 29681
Stonebridge Dr 29681

Stonebury Dr ... 29680
Stonegate Ct & Rd ... 29681
Stonemason Ct ... 29681
Stonemint Ct ... 29680
Stonewater Dr ... 29680
Stonewyck Dr ... 29681
Stoney Ridge Dr ... 29680
Stonoview Ct ... 29680
Straight Pines Ln ... 29681
Straiharn Pl ... 29680
Strasburg Dr ... 29681
Strathpine Dr ... 29681
Stratton Chapel Ct ... 29681
Sugar Hill Ct ... 29681
Sugar Oak Ct ... 29680
Sullivan Rd ... 29680
Summer Ln ... 29680
Summer Glen Dr ... 29681
Summer Hill Rd ... 29681
Summerchase Dr ... 29680
Summercrest Cir ... 29681
Summerfield Ct ... 29680
Summerhall Glen Ln ... 29681
Summerlin Pl ... 29680
Summerridge Ct ... 29681
Summerwalk Pl ... 29680
Summerwind Dr ... 29681
Sun Rose Ct ... 29680
Sunglow St ... 29681
Sunning Hill Rd ... 29681
Sunny Meadow Ln ... 29681
Sunnydale Dr ... 29680
Sunrise Ave ... 29681
Sunshine Dr ... 29681
Suwannee Ct ... 29680
Swamp Lily Ct ... 29681
Sweeney Rd ... 29680
Sweeney Creek Ct ... 29680
Sweeney Farm Rd ... 29680
Sweetspire Ln ... 29681
Sycamore Ridge Dr ... 29681
Sydney Ct ... 29680
Sylvan Oak Way ... 29681
Tahoe Dr ... 29681
Talley Ct ... 29680
Tamora Ct ... 29681
Tamwood Cir ... 29680
Taniere Ct ... 29680
Tankersley Dr ... 29681
Tantallon Ct ... 29681
Tate Chapman Rd ... 29681
Taunton Ct ... 29680
Tea Olive Pl ... 29680
Teakwood Cv ... 29680
Tearose Ln ... 29681
Teaticket Ct ... 29681
Tebblewood Ct & Dr ... 29680
Tellico St ... 29680
Tennyson Ct ... 29681
Terrabay ... 29681
Terrace Cir & Ln ... 29681
Teton Ct ... 29681
Thomas Ct & Ln ... 29681
Thorn Hill Ct ... 29681
Thornapple Way ... 29681
Thornberry Ct ... 29680
Thorncliff Ct ... 29681
Thornless Ct ... 29680
Thurber Way ... 29681
Tickfaw Ct ... 29681
Tiffan Ct ... 29680
Tilden Ct ... 29680
Timber Fence Trl ... 29681
Timber Walk Dr ... 29681
Timberfield Way ... 29680
Timberjack St ... 29680
Timberstone Way ... 29681
Timberview Ln ... 29681
Tippecanoe St ... 29680
Todd Cir ... 29681
Tolland Ct ... 29681
Tollgate Ct & Rd ... 29680
Tooley Rd ... 29681
Torrey Ct ... 29680
Tracy Ln ... 29681
E & W Trade St ... 29681
Trailer Park Rd ... 29681
Travel Air Ln ... 29681
Travelers Ct ... 29681
Trebor Ct ... 29681
Treecrest Ct ... 29680
Trident Ct ... 29680
Tripmont Ct ... 29680
Trotters Field Way ... 29681
Trotters Ridge Ln ... 29681
Trowbridge Ct ... 29681
Truett Pl ... 29681
Trumpet Wood Trl ... 29680
Trumpeter Ln ... 29680
Tulip Tree Ln ... 29680
Turnbridge Trl ... 29680
Turner Forest Ln ... 29681
Turnhouse Ln ... 29680
Turnstone Ct ... 29680
Turtle Ln ... 29681
Tuscany Falls Dr ... 29681
Tuttle Dr ... 29680
Twilight Pl ... 29681
Twin Falls Dr ... 29680
Twinings Dr ... 29681
Twinleaf Way ... 29680
Two Creeks Ct ... 29680
Two Gait Ln ... 29680
Tybee Dr ... 29681
Valcourt Cir ... 29680
Valhalla Ln ... 29681
Valley Bluff Ln ... 29680
Van Horn Pl ... 29681
Vaughns Mill Ct ... 29681
Velmere Dr ... 29681
Vendue Ct ... 29681
Venetian Ct ... 29681
Ventana Ct ... 29681
Veray Ct ... 29681
Verdana Ct ... 29680
Verdmont Blvd ... 29680
Verona Cir ... 29681
Versilia Ln ... 29681
Via Roma Ct ... 29681
Viburnum Ct ... 29680
Vicksburg Ct ... 29681
Videl Way ... 29681
View Point Knl ... 29680
Village Park Dr ... 29681
Vinewood Ct ... 29680
Wabash Ct ... 29680
Wadmalaw Ct ... 29680
Wagon Trl ... 29681
Wagon Wheel Dr ... 29681
Wagoncreek Dr ... 29681
Wakulla Ct ... 29680
Walker Way ... 29681
Walkingstick Way ... 29680
Walnut Grove Ct ... 29680
Walnut Trace Ct ... 29681
Walthall Ct ... 29680
Walwyn Ct ... 29681
Wandflower Ct ... 29680
Warbler Ct ... 29680
Warrenton Way ... 29681
Warsaw Dr ... 29681
Wasson Way ... 29680
Waterbury Ct ... 29680
Watercrest Ct ... 29680
Wateree Way ... 29680
Watergrove Dr ... 29681
Waters Reach Ln ... 29681
Waterstone Way ... 29680
Waterthrush Way ... 29680
Waterton Way ... 29680
Waterton Creek Ct ... 29681
Waverly Hall Ln ... 29681
Waxford Way ... 29681
Waxwing Ct ... 29681
Waycross Ln ... 29681
Weatherly Ct ... 29680
Weatherstone Ln ... 29680
Weaver Ln ... 29681
Webb St ... 29681
Webbington Pl ... 29681
Webbwood Dr ... 29680
Weddington Ln ... 29681
Wedgefield Ln ... 29681
Wellesly St ... 29680
Welsford Ct ... 29681
Wemberly Dr & Ln ... 29681
Wessex St ... 29681
West Cir ... 29681
Westbourne Dr ... 29681
Westbury Way ... 29680
Westminister Dr ... 29681
Westshire Dr ... 29681
Westwood Dr ... 29680
Weycroft Ct ... 29681
Whaleback Dr ... 29681
Wheatland Way ... 29681
Whetstone Ct ... 29680
Whiffletree Dr ... 29680
Whipporwill Ct ... 29680
White Dr ... 29681
White Crescent Ln ... 29681
White Meadow Ct ... 29681
White Pine Dr ... 29681
Whitehurst Way ... 29680
Whiteside Ct ... 29680
Whitworth Way ... 29681
Wickby Ct ... 29680
Wickersham Dr ... 29681
Wickhaven Dr ... 29681
Wilbon Cir ... 29681
Wild Cedar Pl ... 29681
Wild Horse Creek Dr ... 29680
Wild Meadow Dr ... 29681
Wild Oat Way ... 29680
Wild Rice Dr ... 29681
Wildcard Ct ... 29680
Wildor Hill Ct ... 29680
William Seth Ct ... 29681
Williams Cir ... 29681
Willis St ... 29681
Willow Ct & Ln ... 29680
Willow Branch Dr ... 29680
Willow Creek Ct ... 29681
Willow Forks Dr ... 29681
Willow Oak Ct ... 29681
Willow Valley Way ... 29680
Willowtree Ct & Dr ... 29680
Wilson Bridge Rd ... 29680
Windchime Ct ... 29681
Winding Creek Way ... 29680
Winding River Ln ... 29681
Windrose Ct ... 29681
Windsor Pkwy ... 29680
Windsor St ... 29681
Windsor Creek Ct ... 29681
Windsorgate Way ... 29681
Windy Ln ... 29681
Windy Meadow Way ... 29680
Wingcup Way ... 29680
Wingfoot Ct ... 29680
Winslow Way ... 29681
Winter Brook Ln ... 29681
Winyah Ct ... 29681
Winyah Bay Ct ... 29681
Wiseton Ct ... 29681
Wishing Well Ct ... 29681
Wisner Ct ... 29681
Withington Blvd ... 29681
Wolf Run Dr ... 29681
Wood Dr ... 29681
Woodbluff Pl ... 29680
Woodbridge Way ... 29681
Woodcliff Ct ... 29681
Wooddale Ct ... 29681
Woodford Way ... 29680
Woodglen Dr ... 29681
Woodhill Ln ... 29681
Woodland Ln ... 29681
Woodmark Ct ... 29681
Woodmore Ct ... 29680
Woodruff Rd ... 29681
Woodruff Lake Way ... 29681
Woodruff Park Ln ... 29681
Woodruff Place Cir ... 29681
Woodside Cir ... 29681
Woodside Rd ... 29680
Woodside Park Dr ... 29681
Woodstone Dr ... 29681
Woodtrail Ct ... 29681
Worchester Pl ... 29680
Worthington Ct ... 29681
Wren Way ... 29681
Wright Way Ln ... 29681
Wyndhaven Ct ... 29681
Wynhurst Way ... 29680
Wynterhall Dr ... 29681
Xavier Ct ... 29681
Yardley Ct ... 29681
Yellow Jasmine Dr ... 29681
Yellow Poplar Ct ... 29681
E & W Yellow Wood Ct & Dr ... 29680
Yellowrose Ct ... 29681
Yolon Way ... 29680
Yonce Ct ... 29681
Yorktown Ct ... 29681
Young Harris Dr ... 29681

SPARTANBURG SC

General Delivery ... 29306

POST OFFICE BOXES MAIN OFFICE STATIONS AND BRANCHES

Box No.s
1 - 3592 ... 29304
4001 - 4994 ... 29305
5001 - 7308 ... 29304
8001 - 9229 ... 29305
10000 - 11000 ... 29304
14585 - 14585 ... 29305
15398 - 15398 ... 29304
17034 - 172996 ... 29301

NAMED STREETS

Abbie Ln ... 29301
Abbott Ln ... 29307
Aberdeen Ln ... 29307
E & W Abington Way ... 29301
Abner Rd ... 29301
Access Rd ... 29303
Acole St ... 29301
Acorn Ridge Pl ... 29301
Ada Ln ... 29301
Adair Dr ... 29301
Adams Pl ... 29306
Adams Hill Dr ... 29307
Adelaide Dr ... 29301
Aden St ... 29303
Adger St ... 29301
Advent St ... 29302
Afton Dr ... 29301
Aimee St ... 29303
Airflow Dr ... 29306
Airport Rd ... 29306
Alabama St ... 29302
Alamo St ... 29303
Aleaf Ter ... 29302
Alexander Ave ... 29306
Alexander Dr ... 29303
S Alexander Dr ... 29301
Alice St ... 29303
Allen Ave, Ct & St ... 29303
Alley St ... 29301
Allison Dr ... 29306
Allston Rd ... 29307
Alma Byrd Ln ... 29301
Alpha Ct ... 29303
Alpine Trl ... 29303
Alta Dr ... 29301
Alton St ... 29303
Amaker Ln ... 29307
Ambiance Ct ... 29301
Amelia Ave ... 29302
Amelia St ... 29303
American Way ... 29303
Amesbury Ln ... 29301
Amherst Dr ... 29306
Ammons Rd ... 29306
Amos St ... 29306
Amy Ct ... 29307
Anastasia Ct ... 29301
Anchor St ... 29303
Anderson Dr ... 29302
Anderson St ... 29301
Anderson Drive Ext ... 29302
Anderson Mill Rd ... 29301
Andover Rd ... 29301
Andre Ct & Ln ... 29301
Andrew Ln ... 29307
Andrews Rd ... 29302
Andrews Creek Ln ... 29302
Andrews Farm Rd ... 29302
Angler Dr ... 29303
Anita Ct & Dr ... 29302
Ann Dr ... 29303
Anne St ... 29302
Ansel St ... 29306
Ansley Ct ... 29301
Anthony Rd ... 29301
Apache Ct ... 29303
Apartment Cir ... 29307
Apollo Dr ... 29301
Appian Dr ... 29306
Apple Rd ... 29303
Applewood Ln ... 29307
Appliance Dr ... 29301
Arbor Rd ... 29307
Arbour Ln ... 29307
Arbours Commons Ct ... 29307
Arcadia St ... 29301
Arcadia Main St ... 29301
Arch St
200-399 ... 29303
400-599 ... 29301
Archer Rd ... 29303
Archer St ... 29306
Archer Ridge Dr ... 29303
Arden Way ... 29302
Ardmore Rd ... 29306
Arial Cir ... 29301
E & W Arizona Ave ... 29306
Arkmain St ... 29306
Arkwright Dr ... 29306
Arling Dr ... 29301
Arlington St ... 29303
Arlo Ct ... 29306
Armstrong Dr ... 29301
Arrow Wood Rd ... 29301
Arrowhead Cir ... 29301
Ash St ... 29303
Ashbrook Way ... 29301
Ashbury Ct ... 29302
Asheville Hwy ... 29303
Ashford Ave ... 29307
Ashley St ... 29307
Ashwick Ct ... 29301
Aspen Ct ... 29306
Aspencreek Cir ... 29301
Aspenwood Dr ... 29307
Astor Rd ... 29301
Atchison Blvd ... 29306
Athens Ct ... 29303
Auburn Ct ... 29307
Audrey Dr ... 29307
Audubon Dr ... 29302
Augusta Rd ... 29301
Augustine Dr ... 29306
Aurora Ct ... 29303
Austin St ... 29301
Austrian Way ... 29303
Autumn Glen Dr ... 29303
Autumn Wood Ct ... 29302
Avalon Ct ... 29301
Avant St ... 29302
Avanti Dr ... 29303
Avery Pl ... 29301
Avon Dr ... 29303
Avondale Dr ... 29302
Azalea Ct ... 29301
Baby Rd ... 29303
Back St ... 29307
Bagwell Pl ... 29302
Bagwell Farm Rd ... 29302
Bailey St ... 29307
Bain Dr ... 29307
Balfour Rd ... 29306
Balsam St ... 29303
Baltimore St ... 29301
Balton Ct ... 29301
Barbado Ln ... 29303
Barbara St ... 29306
Barberry Ln ... 29302
Barclay Downs Dr ... 29301
Barnett Dr ... 29302
Barnwell Rd ... 29303
Baron Ct ... 29301
Barritt Ave ... 29301
Barrubaro Ln ... 29307
Basil Ct ... 29301
Bates Ct ... 29301
Bayberry Dr ... 29306
Beacham St ... 29301
Beacon St ... 29306
Beacon Light Rd ... 29307
Beamon Dr ... 29307
Bearden Rd ... 29306
Bearden Heights Rd ... 29306
Beatrice Dr ... 29301
Beaumont Ave ... 29303
Beaver Ct ... 29303
Beaver Springs Ct ... 29307
Bedford Rd ... 29301
Bedrock Rd ... 29303
Bee St ... 29301
Beech Aly & St ... 29303
Beech Hill Dr ... 29307
Beech Tree Ct ... 29302
Beechcreek Dr ... 29303
Beechwood Dr ... 29307
Belclaire Ct ... 29301
Bell St
1-99 ... 29301
300-499 ... 29303
Belle Flower Ct ... 29303
Belle Rose Ct ... 29301
Bellew Carver Rd ... 29301
Bellhaven Ln ... 29301
Bellingham Ct ... 29303
Bellwood Ct, Dr & Ln ... 29302
Belmarc Dr ... 29301
Belmont St ... 29303
Belton Dr ... 29301
Belvedere Dr ... 29301
Ben Abi Rd ... 29307
Benjamin Ct ... 29301
Benjamin Rd ... 29307
Benjamin Mays Dr ... 29307
Bennett Cir ... 29307
Bennett Dairy Rd ... 29307
N & S Bennington Dr ... 29307
Benson Ln ... 29301
Bent Creek Ln ... 29306
Bent Oak Way ... 29301
Bentley Ct ... 29303
Benton Ct ... 29301
Bentridge Dr ... 29301
Bentway Ln ... 29302
Bentwood Cir ... 29307
Berkley Ct ... 29301
Bernhardt Dr ... 29302
Best Dr ... 29303
Beta Ct ... 29303
Beta Club Way ... 29306
Beth Ct ... 29302
Bethel St ... 29306
Bethesda Dr & Rd ... 29302
Bethlehem Dr ... 29306
Bethpage Dr ... 29301
Beverly Dr ... 29303
Beverly Rd ... 29307
Beverly Hills Dr ... 29301
Biggerstaff Rd ... 29307
Birch Cir ... 29303
Birch Grv ... 29307
Birchrun Dr ... 29301
Birkdale Dr ... 29306
Birkhall Ct ... 29301
Bishop St ... 29303
Bj Legins St ... 29301
Black St ... 29306
Black Oak Ct ... 29306
Black Wolf Run ... 29306
E Blackstock Rd ... 29301
N Blackstock Rd
300-4399 ... 29301
4400-5799 ... 29303
S Blackstock Rd ... 29301
W Blackstock Rd ... 29301
Blackwood Dr ... 29307
Blairwood Ct ... 29303
Blake St ... 29302
Blanchard Rd ... 29306
Blanche Cir ... 29301
Blanton Pl ... 29303
Blue Bonnet Dr ... 29303
Blue Heron Rd ... 29307
Blue Ridge St ... 29302
Bluebird Ln ... 29303
Boatsman Ln ... 29301
Bohler Ln ... 29301
Boiling Springs Rd ... 29303
Bomar Ave ... 29306
Bon Air Ave ... 29303
Bonanza Dr ... 29307
Bondale Dr ... 29303
Bonita Lake Rd ... 29307
Bonner Rd ... 29303
Bonnie Brae Dr ... 29303
Booker Blvd ... 29301
Booker T Washington Dr ... 29306
Boot Hill Ct ... 29307
Borman Dr ... 29301
Bouldercrest Ct ... 29301
E Boundary Dr ... 29303
Bowers Ct ... 29301
Bowie Ct ... 29302
Boxwood Ln ... 29307
Boy St ... 29303
Boyd Rd & St ... 29302
Boyd Bridge Rd ... 29303
Boyd Cate Rd ... 29303
Braddock Rd ... 29306
Bradley Rd ... 29307
Bradley St ... 29303
Bramblewood Ln ... 29307
Branch St ... 29301
Brandermill Rd ... 29301
Brandie Ct ... 29301
Brandon Dr ... 29303
Brandywine Ln ... 29301
Brannon Ct ... 29301
E & W Branyon Heights Ave ... 29306
Bravo Ln ... 29301
Brawley St
200-375 ... 29301
376-690 ... 29303
692-698 ... 29303
Brayton Ct ... 29301
Breakaway Ave ... 29302
Breckenwood Dr ... 29301
Breeze St ... 29301
Brenton Ave ... 29303
Brentwood Dr ... 29302
Brewton Rd ... 29301
Brian Ct & Dr ... 29307
Briarcliff Rd ... 29301
Briarcreek Ct & Dr ... 29301
Briarwood Ct ... 29302
Briarwood Rd ... 29301
N Briarwood Rd ... 29301
Bridlewood Ln ... 29301
Brighton St ... 29306
Brimstone Ln ... 29301
Brinkley Pl ... 29301
Brisack Rd ... 29303
Brisbane Way ... 29301
Bristol Ct ... 29301
Bristow Ln ... 29301
Britt St ... 29301
Brixton Ct ... 29301
E & W Broad St ... 29306
Broadbrook Ln ... 29302

Broadcast Dr 29303
Broadmoor Dr 29306
Broadview Dr 29303
Brock St 29303
N Brookdale Dr 29303
Brookfield Rd 29302
Brookgreen Ct 29301
Brookhaven Dr 29302
Brookland Ct 29301
Brooklyn Rd 29307
Brooks Blvd 29307
Brookside Park 29301
Brookside Rd 29301
Brookside St 29303
Brookwood Ter 29306
Brown Ave 29306
Brown Rd 29302
Brown St 29303
Brown Sanders Rd 29307
Bruce Ave 29302
Bruckner Rd 29307
Brunson Rd 29303
Bruton Pl 29302
Bryant Rd 29303
Bub Downs Ct 29301
Buckeye St 29301
Buckskin Trl 29301
Buckstone Ln 29307
Buckthorn Rd 29301
Bud Arthur Bridge Rd 29307
Buffington Rd 29303
Bullington Rd 29306
Bunker St 29306
Bunny Run 29303
Burdette St 29307
Burgundy Ln 29303
Burke Ave 29306
Burkshire Ct 29301
Burnett Dr 29302
Burnett St 29303
Burns Rd 29307
Burns St 29302
Burton Rd 29302
Burton St 29301
Busbin Rd 29307
Butler Ct 29307
Butler St 29306
Butternut Rd 29306
Byars Ct 29307
Byron Ter 29301
Cabot Ct 29306
Cain Cir 29303
Caldwell Cir & Dr 29301
Calhoun Ave 29302
E & W Calhoun Crossing Ct 29307
Calhoun Estates Dr 29307
California Ave 29303
California Blvd 29306
Calvert St 29307
Cambridge Cir 29306
Cambridge Dr 29301
Camden Dr 29302
Camelot Ct & Dr 29301
Cameron Dr 29302
Camp St 29303
Campground Rd 29303
Campsen Villa Ct 29301
E & N Campus Blvd 29303
Campus Suites Dr 29303
Canaan Rd 29306
Canaan Church Rd 29306
Canaan Pointe Dr 29306
Candler Pl 29302
Candlewood Dr 29306
Cannon Dr 29307
Cannons Campground Rd 29307
Canterbury Rd 29302
Cantey Ct 29306
Capstone Ln 29301
Captain Tom Ct 29306
Cardinal St 29302
Cardoon Ct 29303
Carla St 29303
N & S Carleila Lake Way 29307
Carleton Cir 29301
Carlisle St 29306
Carlisle Bennett Rd 29307
Carlow Ct 29301
Carlton Ct & Dr 29302
Carman Rd 29303
Carmel Dr 29303
Carnahan Dr 29306
Carol Dr 29307
Carol Ln 29302
N & S Carolina Ave & Dr 29306
Carolina Club Dr 29306
Carolina Country Club Rd
1000-1499 29302
1500-3199 29306
Caroline St 29303
Carolyn Dr 29306
Caroway Ct 29303
Carpenter St 29301
Carpet Dr 29303
Carrie Ellis Ct 29301
Carrollwood Ln 29302
Carson Ave 29306
Cart Dr 29307
Cartee Dr 29306
Carver Mill Rd 29301
Case Ave 29301
Case Dr 29306
Case Rd 29307
Casey Ln 29301
Casper Dr 29307
Casual Dr 29303
Catawba St 29303
Cates Pond Ct 29301
Cateswood Dr 29302
Caughman Dr 29307
Caulder Ave & Cir 29306
Cecil Ct 29306
Cedar Ln 29303
Cedar St
1-99 29303
100-299 29307
Cedar Canyon Dr 29307
Cedar Crest Rd 29301
Cedar Island Ct 29306
Cedar Springs Ave, Dr, Pl & Rd 29302
Cedarwood Ave 29302
Celeste Ct 29301
Celestial St 29306
Cemetery St 29306
W Centennial St 29303
Center Dr 29303
Center St 29303
N Center St 29301
S Center St 29301
Centura Ct 29303
Chaffee Rd 29301
Chain Gang Hill Rd 29307
Champion Ave 29303
Chapel Ct 29301
Chapel St 29303
Chapman Cir 29307
Chapman Rd 29303
Charisma Dr 29303
Charity Dr 29301
Charlesworth Ave 29306
Charlevoix St 29303
Charlie Mae Campbell Ln 29306
Charna Ct 29301
Chasander St 29302
Chastine Dr 29301
E & W Chatelain Dr 29301
Chatham Cir 29306
Chaucer Way 29301
Cheek Rd 29303
Cheetum Ln 29301
Cherokee Cir & Dr 29307
Cherry Hill Cir & Rd 29307
Cherry Tree Ct 29301
Chervil Ct 29303
Chesnee Hwy
2034A-2034D 29303
600-2499 29303
2500-3199 29307
Chesnee Highway Ext 29303
Chester St 29301
Chestnut St 29302
Chestnut Oak Ter 29306
Chiefs Dr 29303
Childress Rd 29307
Chinquepin Ln 29303
Chrisben Dr 29301
Christine Ct 29307
Church St 29301
N Church St
948A-948B 29303
100-307 29306
308-1099 29303
S Church St
99-275 29306
250-250 29304
250-250 29305
276-998 29306
277-999 29306
S Church Street Ext 29306
N Church Street Pl 29303
Cimmon Seed Rd 29301
Cinder Ter 29307
Cinder Creek Ct & Rd 29307
Cinderridge Dr 29301
Cinnabar Ct 29301
Circle Rd 29303
Claiborne Ct 29301
Claremont Cir 29302
Clark Cir 29307
Clarke Camp Rd 29302
Clary Dr 29303
Claude Ln 29307
Clayton Rd
100-199 29302
200-599 29306
Clearlake Dr 29301
Clearview Dr 29307
Clement Line 29302
Clemson St 29307
Clevedale Ct 29301
Cleveland St 29301
E Cleveland St 29303
Cleveland Chapel Rd 29303
N & S Cleveland Park Dr 29303
Clifdale Rd 29307
Cliffrose Ct 29306
Cliffwood Dr 29301
Clifton Ave 29302
Clifton Glendale Rd 29307
Clifton Pine St 29307
Clifton Village Dr 29307
Clinchfield St 29303
Clint Ct 29307
Clinton St 29301
Clover Cir & Ln 29307
Cloverleaf Ln 29301
Clowney Ct 29301
S Club Dr 29302
Club Close Ln 29302
Club Meadows Ct 29302
Club Pointe Dr 29302
Club Terrace Dr 29302
Clyde St 29302
Coastline Rd 29301
Cobden Ct 29301
Coburn Dr 29302
Coggins Dr 29302
Coggins Farm Rd 29307
Coldbrook Dr 29306
Coldspring Dr 29301
Cole St 29301
Coleman Ct 29307
Coleman Hill Dr 29302
College Dr & St 29303
College Pointe Ln 29303
Collingwood Ln 29301
Collins Ave 29306
Collins Rd 29307
Colonial Hills Dr 29302
E & W Colony Dr 29303
Colony Forest Cir 29303
Color Dr 29307
Colton St 29301
E & W Columbia Ave 29306
Comer St 29307
Commerce St 29306
Commercial Rd 29303
Commons Dr 29302
Community College Dr 29303
Concord Ave 29306
Condren Ave 29302
Conifer Cir 29303
Conley St 29306
Connecticut Ave 29302
Conner St 29302
Connie Lynn Dr 29303
Conrad Dr 29301
Continental Dr 29302
Convair Dr 29301
Converse Cir 29302
N Converse St
100-130 29306
131-299 29302
S Converse St 29306
Conway Black Rd 29307
Cook St 29303
Cooksey Ave 29301
Cooksey Ct 29303
Cooper Ln 29301
Coopertown Rd 29307
Copper Line 29301
Cordova Rd 29303
E & W Corley Ln 29303
Cornelius Rd 29301
Cornell St 29306
Cornwallis Rd 29306
Coromandel Dr 29301
Corporate Dr 29303
Correll Ct 29307
Cothran Cir 29301
Cotton Dr 29307
Cotton Creek Dr 29302
Cotton Owens Dr 29303
Cotton Ridge Ln 29302
Cotton Top Ct 29302
Cottonwood Dr 29301
Country Club Ct & Rd 29302
County Rd 29301
Courier Pl 29307
Courtney Louise Ln 29307
Cove Pt & Run 29302
Coventry Ct 29301
Cowford Bridge Rd 29302
Cowpens Clifton Rd 29307
Cowpens Line 29307
Cowpens Pacolet Rd 29307
Cox St 29306
Crabapple Pl 29307
Crainwood Ln 29301
Crandall Way 29301
Crawford Cir 29301
Creekridge Dr 29301
Creekwood Dr 29302
Crescent Ave 29306
E Crescent Rd 29301
W Crescent Rd 29301
Crest Cir 29302
Crestline Dr 29301
Crestview Dr 29306
Crestview Ln 29301
Crestwood Pl 29306
Crews Dr 29307
Cricket Ln 29301
Crocker Ct, Dr & Rd 29307
Crockett St 29303
E & W Croft Cir 29302
Croft State Park Rd 29302
Cromwell Dr 29301
Crosby Ln 29303
Cross St 29303
Crowder St 29301
Crown Oak Ct 29301
Croydon Rd 29301
Crystal Dr 29302
Cumberland St 29303
Cummings St 29303
Cunningham St 29301
Curtis Harley Dr 29302
Cypress Ln & Vw 29307
Cypress Creek Dr 29307
Cypress Point Ct 29306
Dairy Ridge Rd 29302
Daisy Ln 29306
Dakota St 29303
Dale Dr 29307
Dalewood Dr 29302
Dallas Pl 29306
Dallie Dr 29301
Damson St 29303
Damson Plum Ct 29301
Dan River Rd 29307
Danbury Ct 29301
Dandelion Ln 29303
Daniel Ct 29303
E Daniel Morgan Ave
100-199 29306
200-599 29302
N Daniel Morgan Ave 29306
S Daniel Morgan Ave 29306
Danny Dr 29303
Darby Rd 29306
Dares Ferry Rd 29302
Darnell Dr 29306
Darryl Windham Dr 29301
Dartmoor Dr 29301
Davis Dr & Rd 29303
Davis Chapel Rd 29307
Dawn Redwood Dr 29307
Daytona Dr 29303
Dean Ct 29307
N Dean St 29302
S Dean St 29302
Debbie Dr 29303
Deborah Dr 29306
Deer Run Ct 29303
Deer Springs Rd 29302
Deerfield Dr & Way 29302
E & W Deerview Ln 29302
Dellwater Way 29306
Dellwood Dr 29301
Delmar Ct & Rd 29302
Delray Dr 29301
Delta Ct 29303
Denison St 29302
Denton Rd 29307
Derby Downs 29301
Derrick Rd 29303
Devaughan Dr 29307
Devon St 29303
Dewberry Rd 29307
Dewey Ave 29303
Dewridge Ct 29301
Dexter Rd 29303
Diamond Ln 29301
Diamond D Club Rd 29302
Dick Wilson Rd 29303
Dietz Dr 29307
Dillard St 29301
Dillon Cir, Dr & Pl 29307
Diversco Dr 29307
Dobson Ct 29307
Dobson Heights Rd 29307
Doctors Br 29307
Doctors Park Dr 29307
Dodd Ln 29303
Dogan Ct 29302
Dogwood Ave & Grv 29302
Dogwood Club Rd 29302
Doleman Dr 29301
Dolphin Dr 29307
Donald Rd 29307
Donald St 29303
Donavan Dr 29302
Donna Ln 29303
Doral Ct 29301
Dorley Dr 29307
Dorman Centre Dr 29301
Dorman Commerce Dr 29301
Dorothy St 29303
Dorset Dr 29307
Dove Ct 29307
Dover Rd 29301
Dovetail Ct 29303
Dr Oc Kirkland Ter 29306
Draymont Dr 29303
Drayton Ave 29302
Drayton Ct 29301
Drayton Rd 29307
Driftway Pl 29301
Druid St 29306
Drummond Cir 29301
Drummond St 29303
Dublin Ct 29301
Dunbar St 29306
Dunbarton Ct & Dr 29307
Duncan St 29306
Duncan Park Dr 29306
Dungannon Ct 29301
Dunnett Ct 29303
Dunwoody Dr 29307
Dunwoody Way 29301
Dupre Dr 29307
Dutch Elm Ct 29302
Duval Dr 29307
Eagle Nest Rd 29302
Earl Dr 29306
Earley St 29303
Easler Dr 29307
Eastlake Dr 29302
Eastside Dr 29307
Eastway Dr 29307
Eastwood Cir 29302
Eastwood Dr 29307
Ebel Ct 29302
Ebn Dr 29307
Edenbridge Ln 29301
Edgebrook Ct 29302
Edgecombe Rd 29307
Edgefield Cir & Rd 29302
Edgemont Ave 29301
Edger St 29303
Edgewood Ave
200-299 29303
1100-1299 29301
Edgewood Dr 29307
Edison Cir 29303
Edisto Dr 29302
Edna Dr 29303
Edwards Ave 29306
Edwards Blvd 29301
Egg A Day Farm Rd 29307
El Camino Real 29301
El Capitan St 29301
El Paso St 29303
Elcar Ln 29301
Elderberry Dr 29307
Elford Ter 29306
Elizabeth St 29302
Elizabeth Alexandra Cir 29307
Ella Ln 29303
Ellington Dr 29301
Elliott St 29306
Elm Ct 29301
Elm St 29303
Elm View Ter 29307
Elmina St 29303
Elmwood Dr 29303
Eloise Dr 29301
Emerald Ct & Way 29302
Emma Cudd Rd 29302
Emory Rd 29307
Endeavor St 29303
England Pl 29303
English Oak Ct 29306
Enola Station Rd 29307
Epton St 29301
Ernest L Collins Ave 29306
Essex Ridge Ct 29307
Ethel Rd 29301
Euclid Rd 29301
Euial Dr 29307
Evangel Rd 29301
Evans Park Cir 29301
Evening Dr 29301
Everett St 29306
Evins St 29303
Evvalane Dr 29302
Exchange St 29306
Exchange Village Dr E & W 29301
Ezell St 29306
Fain St 29307
Fairfax Ave 29303
Fairfax St 29301
Fairfield Ct 29306
Fairforest Rd
200-398 29301
8200-8899 29303
8900-9399 29301
Fairforest Clevedale Rd 29301
Fairgrounds Rd 29303
Fairlane Dr 29307
E Fairmont Ave & Cir 29301
N Fairview Ave
298A-298B 29302
100-399 29302
400-599 29303
S Fairview Ave 29302
Fairview St 29301
S Fairview Avenue Ext 29302
Fairview Church Rd 29303
Fairway Dr 29303
Fairwood Dr 29306
Falcon Way 29307
Falling Creek Rd 29301
Fallon Pl 29306
Family Dr 29307
Fann Ct 29301
Farley Ave 29301
Farley St 29303
Farley Avenue Ext 29301
Farnsworth Rd 29301
Farr Rd 29307
Farragut Dr 29302
Farrington Ln 29302
Ferguson Ct 29306
Fernbrook Cir 29307
Fernridge Dr 29307
Fernwood Dr
100-599 29307
700-799 29302
Fernwood Glendale Rd 29307
Fernwood Park Dr 29307
Fieldcrest Ln 29301
Fieldstone Rd 29301
Finch Rd 29307
Fine Rd 29303
Fir St 29303
Firethorn Ln 29307
Fisher Ave 29301
Fisher Dr 29303
Fitzgerald Rd 29307
Flat Cove Rd 29303
Flatview Way 29303
Flatwood Ln 29307
Flatwood Rd 29303
Fleetwood Cir 29306
Fleming St 29302
Flinders Way 29301
Flintridge Ct & Dr 29306
Florence St 29303
Florida Ave 29303
Florida Ct 29306
Floy St 29301
Floya Dr 29301
Floyd Cir 29301
Floyd Rd
100-399 29303
400-599 29307
Floyd St 29303
Floyd Heights Dr 29303
Floyd Road Ext 29307
Floyd Summits Blvd 29301
Flynn Ct 29301
Folly Ln 29303
Folsom St 29303
Fontana Ln 29302
Foothills Dr 29302
Forest Ave 29302
W Forest Dr 29301

Forest Run 29301
N Forest St
218A-218B 29301
549A-549B 29303
1-399 29301
400-599 29303
S Forest St 29306
Forest Hills Rd 29303
Forest Mill St 29301
Forest Oaks Way 29307
E & W Forest Run Ct 29301
Forestbrook Ln 29303
Forestview St 29301
Fort Prince Blvd 29301
Foster Dr & St 29301
Foster Mill Rd 29302
Four Mile Branch Ln & Rd 29302
Four Oaks Ln 29302
Fox Dr 29302
Foxborough Rd 29303
Foxcross Rd 29301
Foxhall Rd 29306
Frady Rd 29307
Frances Dr 29301
Francis Marion Dr 29302
Franke Dr 29307
Franklin Ave 29301
Franklin St
100-399 29303
500-599 29301
Franwill Dr 29307
Freddie Dr 29303
E & W Fremont Ave 29303
Fretwell St 29306
Frey Aly, Cir & Rd 29301
Frey Creek Rd 29301
Freys Dr 29301
Friar Tuck Rd 29302
Fripp Dr & Rd 29303
Front St 29301
Fryml Dr 29303
Fuller Rd 29306
Fulton Ave 29303
Fushia Dr 29301
Gable Ct 29307
Gadsden Ct 29302
Gail Ct 29307
Galaxie Pl 29307
Galisout Rd 29306
Garage Rd 29307
Garden Creek Ln 29307
Garden Grove Ct 29302
Gardenia Ln 29301
Gardner Rd 29307
Garner Rd 29303
Garrett Rd 29301
Garrett St 29302
Gaskins Rd 29306
Gaston Dr 29307
Geddes Rd & St 29303
Geneva Cir 29307
Genoble St 29301
Gentry Rd 29301
Gentry St 29303
George St 29306
George Arthur Dr 29307
George Fields Dr 29301
George Washington Carver Dr 29306
Georgia Ave 29306
Georgia St
100-398 29306
111-299 29307
301-399 29306
Gerow Ave 29302
Gibson Rd 29302
Gibson St 29306
Gilbertson Dr 29303
Giles Rd 29307
Gillette Ct 29302
Gillingham Rd 29301
Ginkgo Ln 29302
Gladys Ct 29301
Gladys Court Ext 29301
Glen Eagle Pl 29301
Glenbrook Dr 29307
Glendale St 29307
Glendalyn Ave, Cir, Pl & Ter 29302
Glenn Dr 29301
Glenn Springs Rd 29302
Glennwood Hills Dr 29307
Glenridge Rd 29301
Glenrock St 29302
Glenwood Dr 29303
Glover Rd 29303
Goat Dr 29306
Godfrey Ct 29301
Goforth St 29303
Goldmine Rd
100-2099 29307
2100-3699 29302
3701-4299 29302
Goodlet Cir 29301
Gordon Dr & St 29301
Gossett Rd 29307
Gowan St 29301
Gowens Rd 29306
Gower Rd 29303
Gramercy Blvd 29301
Granada Dr 29303
Granby Ct 29306
Grand Central Ave 29306
Grand Duke Dr 29301
Grandview Dr 29303
Granger Rd 29306
Granite Park Ln 29301
Grant Cir 29307
Gravely Ct 29303
Gray St 29307
Graylin Dr 29301
Graymouth Ct 29301
Graystone Dr 29301
Green St 29303
Green Pastures Dr 29302
Green River Rd 29307
Green Tree Ct 29302
Greenbriar Rd 29302
Greenbriar Ter 29307
Greencreek Rd 29301
Greenfield Dr 29303
Greengate Ln 29307
Greenhill Rd 29303
Greenlea St 29306
Greenleaf St 29302
Greenville St 29301
Greer Dr 29303
Gregory St 29301
Grey Ct 29302
Greylogs Ln 29302
Griffin St 29301
N & S Griffin Mill Ct 29307
Grissom Rd 29301
Grist Mill Ter 29307
Griswald Cir 29302
Grizzle Ct 29302
Groce Rd 29302
N Grove Medical Park Dr 29303
Guernsey Ln 29306
Guilford Pl 29302
Gus St 29302
Habersham Pl 29301
Habitat Way 29301
Hadden Heights Rd 29301
Hagood Ct 29307
Hale St 29302
Hale Street Ext 29302
Halibut Ln 29303
Halifax Ct 29302
Hall St 29302
Halsey Ave 29302
Hamilton Ave 29302
Hammermill Holw 29307
Hammett Rd 29307
Hammett Grove Rd 29307
Hampshire Ct 29301
E, W & S Hampton Ave, Ct & Dr 29306
Hancock Ave 29302
Hannah Coln Way 29306
Hannon Ct 29302
Hanover Pl 29306
Hardee Ct 29303
Harding Dr 29307
Harley Ct 29307
Harmon Dr 29303
Harmony Dr 29301
Harold Fleming Ct 29303
Harrell Dr 29307
Harris Cir 29307
Harris Pl 29306
Harris Rd 29302
Harrison Ln 29301
Hart St 29306
Hartnett Dr 29301
Harvard Dr 29306
Harvest Valley Ct 29303
Harvin St 29303
Harwood Ct 29301
Haslett St 29302
Hatchett Dr 29307
Hatchett St 29301
Haunted Holw 29307
Hawes Dr 29303
Hawk Creek Dr 29301
Hawkins Rd 29303
Hawkins Acres Rd 29307
Hawthorne Rd 29303
Hayes Rd 29302
Hayne St 29301
Haynewood Park 29301
Hazelwood Ave 29302
Headquarters Loop 29302
Hearon Cir 29303
Hearon Circle Plz 29303
Heath Ln 29301
Heather Dr 29301
Heathwood Dr 29307
Helen St 29301
Hemlock St 29301
Henderson St 29301
Hennington Rd 29302
Henry Ct 29306
Henry Pl 29306
Henry St 29301
E Henry St
101-117 29306
119-287 29306
288-499 29302
W Henry St 29306
Henson St 29307
Herald Journal Blvd 29303
Herbert St 29301
Heritage Ct & Dr 29307
Heritage Hills Dr 29307
Hesla Club Rd 29301
Hester Ave 29302
Heywood Ave
100-199 29302
200-799 29307
Hickman Ct 29307
Hickory Dr 29302
Hickory Hill Rd 29302
Hickory Park Ct 29303
Hidden Creek Cir 29306
Hidden Hill Rd 29301
Hidden Lake Dr 29303
Hidden Ridge Dr 29301
Hidden Springs Rd 29302
High Dr 29303
High St 29306
S High St 29307
N & S High Point Rd 29301
Highland Ave 29306
Highridge Dr 29307
Highview Rd 29302
Highway 56 29302
Hilda St 29306
Hill Rd 29307
Hill St 29306
W Hill St 29301
Hillandale Rd 29301
Hillbrook Dr 29307
Hillcrest Ave 29303
Hillcrest Blvd 29307
Hillcrest Commons Way 29307
Hillsboro Trce 29301
Hillside Dr 29303
Hilltop Ln 29306
Hilltop Rd 29302
Hillview St 29302
Hillview Street Hl 29307
Hillwood Ave 29303
Hilton St 29302
Hilton Hill Rd 29302
Hines Aly & St 29301
Hobart Way 29303
Hobbit Ln 29302
Hodge Dr 29303
Hodges Ct 29301
Hoechst Dr 29307
Holiday Blvd 29303
Holiday Dr 29301
Hollis Dr 29307
Holly Dr 29301
Holly Hill Dr 29301
Holly Park Cir 29303
Holly Run Ct 29303
Hollyberry Ln 29301
Hollycrest Ln 29301
Hollyridge Rd 29301
Hollywood St 29302
Holmes Dr 29303
Holt St 29301
Holtfield Ter 29303
Holy St 29307
Home St 29306
Homeland Dr 29303
Honey Hive Cir 29301
Honeysuckle Ln 29303
Honeysuckle Rd 29303
Honeysuckle Ter 29307
Hope Rd 29303
Hopkins St 29307
Hopper Fish Camp Rd 29307
Horace Smith Rd 29302
Horne St 29303
Horseshoe Cir 29307
Horseshoe St 29303
Horseshoe Lake Dr 29306
Hospital St 29302
Hospitality Dr 29303
Hounds Trl 29303
Houndsear Trl 29306
Houston Dr 29307
Houston St 29303
Howard St 29303
Hub Bub Way 29306
Hudson Dr 29303
Hudson St 29306
Hudson L Barksdale Blvd 29306
Hugh St 29301
Hughes Ln 29301
Hughston Pond Rd 29303
Humphrey St 29301
Hunt St 29301
Hunt Club Ln 29301
Hunter Philson Ln 29301
Hunters Trl 29301
Hunters Pointe Dr 29303
Huntington Dr 29302
Huskey Ct 29303
Hutcherson Farm Rd 29302
Huxley St 29303
Hydrick St 29306
Ian Ct 29306
Iditarod Trl 29307
Idlewood Cir & Ct 29307
Idlewylde Ct 29301
Image Dr 29303
Indian Creek Rd 29302
Indian Hill Ln 29307
Indian Springs Ln 29302
Indian Wells Dr 29306
Indigo Springs Run 29303
Inglewood Ave 29302
Innisbrook Ln 29306
International Dr 29303
Interstate Park 29303
Inverness Cir 29306
Inwood Ct 29302
Irby Ct & Rd 29301
Iris Ct 29307
Iron Ore Rd 29303
N & S Irwin Ave 29306
S Irwin Avenue Ext 29306
Isabella Dr 29303
Isom St 29303
Itaska Ct 29306
Ivey Ln 29302
Ivory Dr 29303
Ivy Ct, Pl & St 29302
Jack Foster Rd 29306
Jackie Ct 29307
Jackson Cir 29303
Jackson Rd 29306
Jackson St 29303
Jacob Dr 29303
James Ct 29302
James Dr 29301
James St 29301
James Anderson Ln 29301
James Dixon Ln 29301
James H Young St 29306
Janulis St 29301
Jasmine St 29303
Jeanette Ln 29301
Jeff Davis Dr 29303
Jefferies Ln 29303
Jefferson St 29303
Jenkins St 29303
Jennie Ct 29307
Jennings St 29303
Jeri Ct 29302
Jessie Fisher Ln 29307
Jewell Rd 29302
Jim Merritt Dr 29302
Joann Dr 29301
Joel O Bryant Dr 29307
John B White Sr Blvd
1526A-1526C 29301
763A-763D 29306
100-1499 29306
1500-1506 29301
1501-1507 29306
1508-1899 29301
John Dodd Rd 29303
John Henry Way 29302
John Lancaster Rd 29306
John Martin Rd 29303
Johnson Dr 29302
Johnson St 29301
Johnson Lake Rd 29302
Jolly St 29302
Jones Rd
100-598 29307
101-105 29303
107-599 29307
Jones St 29303
Jordan St 29301
Judd St 29301
Judith Ln 29301
Julian Bond Ln 29307
Julien Pl 29301
Junction Ridge Park 29306
Juniper Ct 29302
Justice Dr 29301
Kale Blvd 29303
Kalmia St 29306
Kaplan Ct 29307
Katelyn Dr 29303
Kearse Ct 29307
Keatly St 29302
Keats Dr 29301
Kellie Lane Dr 29301
Kelly Rd 29307
Keloy St 29301
Kelsey Ct 29301
Kelsey Creek Rd 29302
Keltner Ave & Cir 29302
Kenilworth Rd 29303
Kenmore Dr 29303
E Kennedy St
100-219 29306
220-238 29302
221-239 29306
240-499 29302
W Kennedy St 29306
Kennesaw Ct 29301
Kennet Ct 29301
Kennsey Dr 29303
Kenny Dr 29306
Kensington Dr 29306
Kent Pl 29307
Kent St 29301
Kentfield Ln 29303
Kentucky Ave 29306
Kenyon Ct 29301
Kerry Ct 29301
Keswick Farm Rd 29302
Kevin Dr 29303
Kikelly Dr 29303
Kimber Ln 29303
Kimberly Dr 29306
King Line 29302
Kingston St 29303
Kingswood Ave 29303
Kirby Cir 29302
Kirkwood Pl 29306
Knee Run 29307
Knighton Rd 29302
Knightsridge Rd 29303
Knob Hill Dr 29302
Knollwood Dr 29301
Knollwood Acres Rd 29303
Knottingwood Ln 29303
Knoxwood Ct 29303
Kreswell Cir 29302
Kunzig Dr 29302
La Salle Ct 29306
Labon Dr 29301
Lacey Ln 29301
Lacey Leaf Ct 29307
Ladonna Ln 29303
Lafayette St 29302
Lafferty Ct 29302
Lake Access Way 29307
Lake Forest Dr
1-99 29302
100-499 29307
Lake Park Dr 29301
Lakecrest Dr 29301
Lakeland Dr 29306
Lakeridge Dr 29302
Lakeridge Ln 29301
Lakeside Dr 29303
Lakeview Cir 29307
Lakeview Dr 29306
Lakeview Rd 29307
Lakeview Trailer Park Rd 29303
Lakewood Dr 29302
Lakewood Park Dr 29303
Lamotte St 29301
Lancaster Rd 29306
Lancer Ct 29301
Landers Rd 29303
Landis St 29302
Landis Park Ln 29302
Lanette Dr 29301
N Lanford Rd 29301
S Lanford Rd 29306
E Lanford St 29302
W Lanford St 29302
Langdon St 29302
Lanham Cir 29307
Lanier St 29303
Lanlake Rd 29301
Lansdale Dr 29302
Lanyon Ln 29301
Lapear Dr 29303
Larch Cir 29303
Larkin Park Dr 29301
Larkspur Ln 29301
Larry Dr 29303
Laurel Blf 29301
Laurel St 29303
Laurel Glen Cir 29301
Laurel Oak Ct 29306
Laurelwood Cir 29301
Lavendula St 29301
Lawrence Johnosn Sr Ln 29306
Lawson St 29307
Lawson Creek Dr 29303
Layton Dr 29301
Lea Ct 29307
Leafy Way 29307
League St 29306
Leah Dr 29303
Leawood Dr 29302
Ledford Cir & Rd 29303
Lee Rd 29306
Leeds Dr & Ln 29307
Lees Crossing Dr 29301
Leisure Ln 29307
Leland St 29303
Len Ct 29303
Lena Ln 29301
Leona Ct 29301
Leonard St 29303
Leslie Ln 29301
Lester Dr 29301
Lester Kingman Dr 29301
Lewis St 29302
Lewis Chapel Rd 29307
Liberty Ln 29303
N Liberty St
100-199 29306
600-899 29303
S Liberty St 29306
Library St 29306
Lighthorse Ln 29302
Lilac Ln 29303
Lillian Dr 29301
Limerick Ct 29301
Limestone Dr 29306
Lincoln Dr 29306
Lincoln School Rd 29301
Linder St 29302
Lindsey Ct 29302
Lindsey Dr 29301
Lister St 29303
Little Creek Rd 29303
Little Farm Dr 29302
Littlefield Dr 29303
Littlejohn Cir 29302
Littlejohn Ct 29303
Littlejohn Rd 29301
Loblolly Dr 29303
Loche Adele Dr 29307
Lockport Way 29301
Lockwood St 29307
Locust Ct & Grv 29303
Log Cabin Ln 29302
Logan St 29306
Lomond Ln 29307
Londonberry Dr 29301
Lone Oak Blvd, Rd & St 29303
Lonely St 29303
Long St 29307
Longbow Dr 29302
Longfellow Way 29301
Longleaf Dr 29302
Longleaf Rd 29301
Longview Dr 29303
Longwood Dr 29301
Loop Rd 29306
Loretta Dr 29301
Lori Cir 29303
Loring St 29302
Lorraine Ct 29307
Lowe Dr 29306
Lowell Ct 29301
Lowndes Dr 29307
Lucas Ct 29302
Lucerne Dr 29303
Lucille Ct 29307
Lucky Ln 29302
Lumis Ave 29302
Lundquist Dr 29301
Luther Pl 29301
Lyda Rd 29307
Lyndhurst St 29307
Lynhaven Dr 29303
Lynn Rd 29306

Lynwood Dr 29302
Lynwood Rd 29307
Lytle St 29301
Mabry Ct 29307
Mabry Dr 29307
Mabry Rd 29307
Mabry St 29301
Macfarlane Ct 29302
Machine Dr 29303
Macks Ct 29307
Madison Cir 29301
Madora Dr 29306
Magness Dr 29303
Magnolia St
409A-409B 29303
Magnolia Blossom Ct 29301
Magnolia Park Dr 29301
Maid Marion Ln 29302
E Main St
505A-505B 29302
203A-203C 29306
100-253 29306
254-999 29302
1000-2799 29307
253 1/2-253 1/2 29306
S Main St 29307
W Main St
523A-523B 29301
100-300 29306
301-1099 29301
E Main Street Ext 29307
Malibu Dr 29303
Manchester Dr 29301
Mandala Ln 29303
Manning St
1-99 29301
200-399 29303
Mansfield Dr 29307
Maple St 29302
Maple Hollow Dr 29303
Maplecroft St 29303
Maplelane St 29301
Mapleleaf Dr 29303
Mapletree Ln 29303
Marconi Dr 29303
Margo Dr 29301
Marina Ct 29303
Marion Ave 29306
Mark Ct 29301
Market St 29301
Marlboro Rd 29301
Marlette Ave 29303
Marlin Dr 29307
Martin Rd & St 29301
Martin Family Rd 29306
Martinez Rd 29302
Mary Ave 29303
Mary Ella Dr 29301
Mary J Clement St 29306
Maryland Ave 29307
Massachusetts Blvd 29306
Massey Dr 29307
Matchlock Commons 29302
Mathew Perry Pkwy 29306
Mathis Dairy Rd 29307
Mattingly Ct 29301
Maulden St 29302
Maverick Cir 29307
Maxine St 29302
Maxton St 29302
Maxwell Cir 29303
Maxwell Rd 29302
Maxwell St 29306
Mayburgh Ct 29301
Mayfair St 29303
Mayview St 29303
Maywood St 29303
Mcabee Ct 29301
Mcabee Rd 29306
Mcabee St 29301
Mcarthur St 29302
Mcchesney Rd 29306
Mcconnell Rd 29307
Mccracken Dr 29307
Mccravy Dr 29303
Mcdowell Dr & St 29303
Mogaha Dr 29307
Mcgee St 29306
Mcgriffin Ct 29301
Mcguire Rd 29303
Mcham Rd 29307
Mckay Ave 29302
Mckerier Rd 29301
Mcmillan St 29303
S Meadow Dr 29306
Meadow Ln 29307
Meadow St 29307
Meadowbrook Dr &
Rd 29307
Meadowinds Dr 29306
Meadowlark Ln 29306
Meander Ln 29302
Melbourne Ln 29301
Melissa Ct 29303
Melody Ln 29303
Melody Forest Ln 29301
Melton Ave 29303
Melvin Dr 29303
Melvin St 29307
Mercer St 29303
Merideth Cir 29306
Meridian River Run 29301
Merle Dr 29307
Merrimac Dr 29303
Merriotte Hl 29303
Merritt Rd 29307
Merrivale Ln 29301
Metcalf Ct 29306
Methodist Dr 29301
Metro Dr 29303
Michael Dr 29306
Michael St 29301
Middle Dr 29302
S Middle St 29307
Midnight Star Trl 29303
Midway Dr 29301
Midway Rd 29303
Mike Cir & Dr 29303
Milan St 29303
Miles Dr 29306
Milford Ln 29301
Milhaven Dr 29301
Mill Rd 29301
Mill St 29303
Millay Pl 29301
Millbrook Dr 29301
Miller Dr 29301
Miller Line 29307
Milliken Rd 29303
Mills Ave 29302
E Millstone Acres Dr 29302
Millwood Dr 29306
Mimosa Rd 29301
Mimosa St 29307
Mimosa Lake Rd 29302
Minter Ct 29302
Mintz Rd 29307
Mirabelle Ct 29301
Missouri Ln 29301
Missy Ln 29306
Misty Ln 29303
Mistybrook Dr 29302
Mitchell St 29307
Mobile Dr 29303
Moby Ct 29303
Mockingbird Ct & Ln 29307
Moffitt Ct 29301
Mohawk Dr 29301
Moneypit Ln 29306
Monk St 29301
Monks Grove Church
Rd 29303
Monroe Rd 29307
Monroe St 29301
Montagu Dr 29301
Montana St 29306
Montclair Ct 29301
Montgomery Cir & Dr 29302
Montview St 29307
Moonbeam Ln 29301
Moore Rd 29302
Moreland Ave 29302
Morning Cir & Dr 29301
Morningside Dr 29306
Morrow Ln & Rd 29303
Mossberry Rd 29306
Mosspoint Cir 29303
Mosswood Ln 29301
Mossy Creek Ct 29307
N & S Mossy Rock
Rd 29303
Mossycup Oak Ct 29306
Mount Calvery Church
Rd 29302
Mount Pleasant Rd 29307
Mount Zion Rd 29303
Mountainbrook Ln 29301
Muirfield Ct, Dr & Way 29306
Mulligan Rd 29302
Mulligan St 29303
Mullins Rd 29301
Mullins St 29303
Munchberry Way 29301
E & W Murph Rd & St 29302
Murray Ct 29307
Mustang Dr 29307
E & W Myles Ln 29303
Myrtle Ave & Ln 29303
Nahant St 29301
E & W Nancy Ln 29303
National Ave 29303
Nature View Ln 29302
Navaho Dr 29301
Nazareth Rd 29301
Nazareth Church Rd 29301
Neal Rd 29307
Nebo St 29302
Neely Ave 29302
Nehemiah Ct 29303
Nelson Ave 29302
Nevada St 29306
Neville St 29303
New St 29303
New Cut Cir 29303
New Cut Rd
100-198 29301
200-999 29301
1000-2999 29303
New Faith Ct 29301
New York Ave 29306
Newman Rd 29301
Nicholls Ct & Dr 29301
Nichols Mountain Rd 29307
Nix Hamlet Dr 29301
Nob Hill Rd 29307
Nodding Hill Rd 29302
Normandy Ave 29301
Norris Ct 29306
Norris Dr 29301
Norris Rd 29303
Norris St 29306
North St 29306
Northeast Dr 29303
Northstar St 29301
Northview St 29302
Norwood St 29302
Nottingham Rd 29302
O And W Dr 29302
Oak St 29306
Oak Creek Ct & Dr 29302
Oak Forest Rd 29301
Oak Grove Rd 29301
Oak Ridge St 29306
Oak Valley Rd 29302
Oakcrest Rd 29301
Oakdale Ct 29306
Oakhollow Ct 29302
Oakhurst Cir 29302
Oakland Ave 29302
Oakland Hills Ln 29306
Oakleaf Dr 29301
N & S Oakley Ln 29301
Oaktree Rd 29303
Oakview Dr 29306
Oakway Ave 29301
Oakwood Ave 29302
Oconee Dr 29301
Octavia Dr 29306
Oglesby Creek Ln 29303
Old Birch Rd 29301
Old Blackstock Rd 29301
Old Boiling Springs Rd 29303
Old Canaan Rd 29306
Old Canaan Road Ext 29306
Old Charlotte Rd 29307
Old Clifton Village Rd 29307
Old Converse Rd 29307
Old Cooper Mill Rd 29307
Old County Parrish Rd 29301
Old Dirt Rd 29307
Old Fish Camp Rd 29303
Old Glendale Rd 29302
Old Greenville Hwy &
Rd 29301
Old House Ln 29302
Old Howard Gap Rd 29303
Old Indian Trl 29301
Old Iron Works Rd 29302
Old Knox Ln & Rd 29302
Old Lowe Ct & Rd 29303
Old Mill Ct 29307
Old Pacolet Rd 29307
Old Petrie Rd 29302
Old Petrie Road Ext 29302
Old Reidville Rd 29301
Old River Rd 29301
Old Towne Rd 29301
Old Whitney Rd 29303
Old Wynd Ct 29301
Oleander Ln 29303
Olintond Rd 29307
Oliver St 29303
Olivia Dr 29302
Olney Ln 29307
Omega Ln 29303
Oneal Pl 29303
Orallary Rd 29303
Orchard Ln 29303
Orchard Park Blvd 29303
Ormond Dr 29306
Osage St 29303
Otis Blvd 29302
Outlet Rd 29303
Overbrook Cir 29306
Overhill Cir & Dr 29303
Overland Dr 29307
Overlook Ct 29301
Overview Ter 29307
Owens Ave 29303
Owens Dr 29303
Owens St 29306
Owl Ct 29303
Oxboro Ct 29306
Oxford Rd 29301
Page Rd 29301
Painter Rd 29302
Palisade St 29306
Palm Dr 29301
Palm Tree Dr 29301
Palmer St 29302
Palmetto St 29302
Palomino Dr 29307
Pamela Dr 29303
E Park Ave 29306
Park Dr 29307
E Park Dr 29302
N Park Dr 29302
S Park Dr 29302
W Park Dr 29306
Parkdale Dr 29302
Parker Dr 29303
Parkview Dr 29302
Parkwood Dr 29301
Parrish Rd 29303
Parsonage Ln 29303
Partridge Ct & Rd 29302
Parwin Rd 29303
Pastel Ct 29307
Patch Dr 29302
Pathway Ct 29307
Patillo Ct 29302
Patrick St 29301
Patterson Rd 29307
Patton Ave 29302
Pauline Hill Ct 29302
Pawnee Dr 29301
Payne Ct 29303
Peaceful Valley Rd 29307
Peach Valley Cir & Dr 29303
Peachshed Rd 29307
Peachtree Ln 29301
Peachtree Rd 29302
Peachtree St 29303
Peachwood Centre Dr 29301
Peanut Ct 29306
E & W Pearl St 29303
Pearl Ridge Pl 29302
Pearson Ctr 29301
Pearson St 29303
Pebble Ridge Dr 29303
Pebble Rock Cir 29307
Pebblebrook Ct 29301
Pecan Ct & Dr 29307
Pecan Tree Ct 29306
Pelham Ct 29301
Penarth Rd 29301
Pennell Dr & St 29307
Pennwood Dr 29306
Penny Bennett Rd 29307
Penola St 29301
Pepperidge Dr 29303
Peppermint St 29303
Pequeno Ct 29301
Peronneau St 29306
Perrin Dr 29307
Perry Rd 29303
Pershing St 29302
Persimmon Dr 29302
Persimmon Hl 29301
Petras Way 29307
Petrie Dr 29302
Pettit Rd 29307
Pheasant Dr 29302
Phifer Dr 29303
Phifer Line 29307
Phillips Dr & Rd 29307
Phyllis Wheatley Ct 29307
Picadilly Ct 29301
Pickerel Ln 29306
Piehoff St 29301
Pierce Crossing Ct 29307
Pierpont Ave 29303
Pierpont Avenue Ext 29303
Pilgrim Aly & St 29301
Pinckney Ct 29306
Pine Pt 29302
Pine St 29301
N Pine St
101-399 29302
600-2799 29303
S Pine St 29302
Pine Acres Dr 29307
Pine Creek Dr 29307
Pine Forest Rd 29303
Pine Forest Road Ext 29303
Pine Gap Rd 29303
Pine Grove Mnr 29303
Pine Lake Ct 29301
N Pine Lake Dr 29301
S Pine Lake Dr 29306
E & W Pine Ridge Aly,
Ct, Rd & Ter 29302
Pine Valley Ct 29306
Pinebranch Ave 29307
Pinebrook Rd 29301
Pinecrest Rd 29302
Pinedale Ct 29301
Pinegate Dr 29303
Pinehill Cir 29306
Pinehurst Dr 29306
Pinehurst St 29302
Pineneedle Dr 29306
S Pinepoint Dr 29302
Pineridge Dr 29303
Pinetree Cir 29307
Pineview Cir 29302
Pineview Dr 29307
Pineview Rd 29301
Pineville Rd 29307
Pinewood Pl 29303
Pinewood Rd 29302
N Pinnacle Ave & Dr 29303
Pinson Ct 29301
Pinto Ct 29307
Pioneer Pl 29301
Pioneer Fish Camp
Rd 29306
Pisgah Dr 29303
Placid Ct & Pl 29307
Plainview Dr 29307
Plainview Drive Ext 29307
Plantation Ct, Dr & Rd 29302
Pleasant Pt 29301
Pleasant Breezes Way 29307
Pleasant Ridge Ct 29303
Pleasant Valley Rd 29307
Plum Creek Rd 29307
Plume St 29302
Pogue St 29301
Poinsetta St 29301
W Pointe Dr 29301
Pointe West Dr 29301
Police Club Rd
1-399 29303
600-799 29307
Pollard Ln 29303
Ponce De Leon Ave 29302
Pond St 29303
Pooles Spring Rd 29307
Poplar St 29302
Poplar Creek Dr 29303
Poplar Leaf Dr 29301
Portrush Dr 29301
Poteat St 29307
Pottery Rd 29303
Powell Ct 29307
Powell Mill Rd 29301
Preston St 29303
Preswick Ct 29301
Primrose Dr 29301
Primrose Ln 29303
Prince St 29303
Prince Hall Ln 29306
Princeton St 29306
Proctor Dr 29303
Promised Land Dr 29306
Prospect Ave 29306
Providence Rd 29302
Pueblo St 29301
Putman Ct 29307
Putman Dr 29306
Pyle Ct 29306
Quail Dr 29302
Quarry Rd 29302
Quarter Rd 29302
Quartermaster Rd 29301
Quartz Dr 29306
Queensbury Way 29302
Quiet Acres Cir & Dr 29301
Quinn Ln 29307
R And D Dr 29301
Rachel Ct 29303
N & S Radcliff Way 29301
Radford Ln 29307
Railroad St 29306
Raindrop St 29303
Raintree Dr 29301
Raleigh Ct 29301
Ramblewood Rd 29302
Rambling Ridge Dr 29307
Ramsgate Dr 29301
Ranch Rd 29303
Randall Rd 29306
Randolph St 29301
Randys Dr 29306
Ranmar Ln 29307
Ransdell Dr 29307
Ranson Ave 29302
Ravenel St 29302
Ravenwood Ln 29301
Ravines Ln 29301
Ray Cir 29307
Ray Estates Rd 29306
Ray Hill Rd 29301
Real Estate Way 29302
Reba Dale Ct 29307
Rebecca Rd 29306
Red Fox Ct 29301
Red Wine Ct 29301
Redwood Ave 29302
Redwood Cir 29301
Reed Rd 29303
Reeves Ct & St 29301
Regency Rd 29307
Regent St 29302
Reggie Sanders Dr 29301
Reibling St 29303
Reidville Rd 29301
Retha Dr 29303
Rev Booker T Sears
St 29306
Rev Cm Johnson Ave 29306
Rev J Leon Pridgeon
Blvd 29306
Rev Wl Wilson Dr 29306
Revere Cir 29302
Reynolds Rd 29307
Reynolds St 29303
Rhett St 29301
Ribault St 29302
Rice Rd 29303
Rice St 29301
Richborough Dr 29307
Richmond Ct 29301
Ridge St 29303
Ridgecrest Ave & Dr 29301
Ridgedale Dr 29306
Ridgeview Dr 29303
Ridgeway Ave 29302
Ridgeway Rd 29301
Ridgewood Ave 29306
Rigby Ave 29306
Riley Ct 29303
Riva Rdg 29302
River Dr 29307
River Rd 29302
S River St 29307
N River Hills Dr 29303
Rivergate Trce 29303
Rivermill Ct 29301
Rivermont Dr 29302
Riverrun Dr 29303
Riverside Dr 29302
Riverview Dr 29307
Robbs Ave 29303
Roberts Meadow Loop 29307
Robertson Ct 29301
Robin Cir, Ct & St 29303
Robin Hood Dr 29302
Robingate Ct 29303
Robinson Dr 29301
Robinsview Ln 29301
Rock Bridge Rd 29307
Rock Springs Dr 29301
Rock Valley Rd 29301
Rockbrook Blvd 29307
Rocking Chair Ln 29307
Rockshire Ct 29303
Rockwood Dr 29301
Roger Rd 29306
Rogers Ln 29306
Rolling Meadow Ct 29303
Rolling Ridge Dr 29307
Rollins St 29303
Romaine Dr 29307
Ronnie Lee Dr 29303
Rookard Ct 29303
Rose St 29303
Rose Penny Ln 29301
Rosecrest Rd 29303
Rosemary Rd 29301
Rosemeade Ct 29301
Rosetta Ct 29301
Rosewood Ln 29302
Rosewood St 29303
Rosewood Ter 29307
Rosewood Park Dr 29301
Rosewood Street Hl 29307
Ross Rd 29301
Roswell Ter 29307
Round Ridge Ct & Rd 29302
Rowe St 29301

Rowland St	29303
Roy Williams Rd	29302
Royal Oak Dr	29302
Ruby Dr	29301
Rudisal St	29302
Runnymeade Ln	29301
Rupe Easler Dr	29307
Rupert Dr	29302
Rushing Rd	29302
Russ Mcabee Rd	29307
Russell St	29307
Russells Creek Rd	29301
Rutledge St	29302
Ryan Daniel Ct	29303
Rylon Ct	29301
Safeway Ave	29303
Sagamore Ct	29301
Saint Andrews Dr & St	29306
Saint Annes Ct	29301
Saint James Dr	29301
Saint John St	29301
E Saint John St	
100-200	29306
201-207	29302
202-208	29306
209-599	29302
W Saint John St	
100-279	29306
280-999	29301
Saint Mark Church Rd	29307
Saint Matthews Ln	29301
Salem St	29302
Sally St	29301
Saluda St	29301
Samara St	29303
Sand Dollar Cir	29301
Sand Pit Rd	29307
Sandifer Pl	29302
Sandifer Rd	29303
Sandstone Dr	29301
Sara Lynn Ct	29307
Saranac Dr	29307
Saratoga Ave	29302
Sassafras Ct	29301
Satterfield Ave	29301
Satterfield Ln	29306
Saugus Rd	29307
Savanna Plains Dr	29307
Savoy St	29301
Sawgrass Ct	29301
Saxon Ave & Hts	29301
Saybrook Ct	29301
Scarlet Oak Ct	29306
Scenic Dr	29302
Schirra Ct	29301
School Dr	29301
Scott St	
300-499	29303
2300-2499	29302
Scottswood Dr	29302
Scout Dr	29301
Screven Ct	29301
Screvens Rd	29306
Scruggs Ave	29303
Seabrook Dr	29306
Seafaring Ln	29303
Seal St	29301
Seay Ln	29306
Seay Rd	29307
Seay St	29306
Security Pl	29307
Sedgefield St	29303
Sedgewood Ct	29301
Sedgewood Ln	29307
Sellars Rd	29303
Seminole Ct & Dr	29301
Seneca Ct	29301
Sentel Cir	29301
Sequoia Dr	29306
Serena Dr	29303
Serendipity Ln	29301
Serene Ct	29301
Serene Valley Dr	29307
Serenity Springs Ln	29302
Serpentine Dr	29303
Servan Dr	29307
Seven Oaks Ln	29301
Seven Springs Rd	29307
Sevier Pl	29302
Sha Ln	29307
Shadicrest Ter	29301
Shadowood Ct & Dr	29301
Shady Ln	29302
Shady Acres Rd	29307
Shady Creek Rd	29301
Shafer Ct	29301
Shalann Dr	29301
Shamrock Country Dr	29307
Shannon Dr	29301
Shannon St	29307
Shannon Woods Dr	29301
Sharon Dr	29302
Sharondale Ct	29303
Shaw Ave	29306
Shawnee Ct	29301
Shea Marie St	29303
Sheffield Dr	29301
Shehan Dr	29303
Sheila Ln	29303
Shelby St	29301
Shell Ln	29307
Shell Rd	29303
Shelton Dr	29307
Shenandoah Dr	29301
Shepard Rd	29301
Sherbert Ct	29303
Sherborne Dr	29307
Sherbrooke Dr	29307
Sherwood Cir & Dr	29302
Shields Dr	29303
Shilo Dr	29306
Shirley St	29303
Shirlynn Ln	29307
Shirock Ln	29302
Shoally Brook Dr	29303
Shoemaker Pl	29302
Shook Rd	29303
E Shore Dr	29302
Shoreham Rd	29307
Shoresbrook Dr & Rd	29301
Short St	29303
Short Allen St	29303
Short Hill St	29303
Short Rice St	29301
Shortwood St	29301
Sibley St	29301
Sierra Rd	29301
Sierra Hills Dr	29301
Silver Hill St	29302
Silver Meadows Dr	29307
Silverdale Dr	29301
Silverton St	29307
Simmons St	29303
Simpson St	29302
Sims Ln	29307
Sims Chapel Rd	29306
Simuel Rd	
100-599	29303
600-1199	29301
Singing Woods Ln	29301
Skipping Stone Ln	29303
Skylyn Dr	29307
Skyview Dr	29303
Sleepy Hollow Ln	29306
Slippery Moss Dr	29303
Sloan St	29303
Sloans Grove Rd	29307
Slopingwood Ln	29301
Smith Cir	29303
Smythe St	29301
Society Hl	29306
Soft Breezes Ln	29307
Softail Dr	29302
Sojourners Way	29303
Somerset Ln	29302
Somerset Pl	29301
Somersett Dr	29301
Sonley Cir	29306
South Ave	29306
Southern Ave & St	29303
Southern Magnolia Ct	29301
Southgate Rd	29302
Southport Rd	
146A-146B	29306
1-2199	29306
2200-3599	29302
Southport Commerce Blvd	29306
Southport Ridge Dr	29306
Southstar St	29301
Southview Ave	29302
Southwest Dr	29303
Spartan Blvd	29301
Special Way	29301
Spencer Cir	29307
Spencer Evans Dr	29306
Spillway Ln	29307
Spires Ct	29306
Splendid Meadows Way	29307
Spring Dr	29302
Spring St	29301
N Spring St	29306
S Spring St	29306
Spring Hope Cir	29307
Spring Valley Dr	29301
Springdale Dr & Ln	29302
Springfield Rd	29303
Springhill Ave	29303
Springlake Dr	29302
Springwater Dr	29303
Springwood Dr	29302
Sprouse Rd	29307
Spruce St	29303
Stafford Ave	29302
Staley Dr	29306
Stan Perkins Rd	29307
Standing Stone Rd	29303
Stanley Ridge Dr	29302
Star St	29303
Starline Dr	29307
Starlite Ct	29303
Steflo Pl	29301
Stephen Grove Rd	29301
Stephens Rd	29302
Stevens St	29301
Stewart Rd & St	29306
Stillwater Ct	29301
Stinnette Ln	29301
Stockbridge Dr	29301
Stone Dr	29302
Stone St	29301
Stone Hill Dr	29307
Stone Oak Ct	29303
Stone Station Rd	29306
Stone Station Farm	29306
Stone Village Ct	29302
Stonecliff Way	29301
Stonecreek Dr	29303
Stoneridge Rd	29306
Stoney Ln & Pass	29307
Story St	29301
Strafford Rd	29301
Strange Ct	29301
Stribling Cir	29301
Studhorse Rd	29303
Successful Way	29303
Sullivan Ave	29303
Summer Ct	29302
Summercreek Dr	29307
Summerland Dr	29306
N & S Summit Crest Ct	29307
Summit Glen Ct	29307
Summit Hills Dr	29307
Summit Knolls Dr	29307
Summit Lake Ct	29307
Summit Park Ct	29307
Summit Trace Ct	29307
Sun And Sand Rd	29303
Sunbeam Rd	29303
Sundance Way	29302
Sundown Dr	29302
Sunline Pl	29307
Sunny St	29306
Sunnydale Cir	29303
Sunnyview Cir	29307
Sunridge Ct & Dr	29302
Sunrise Rd	29302
Sunset Cir	29301
Sunset Dr	29302
Sunset St	29307
Sunshine Dr	29307
Sunshine Ln	29301
Surf Ln	29303
Susanne St	29303
Sussex Ct	29301
Sutton Rd	29302
Swain St	29303
Swamp Fox Rd	29306
Swanee St	29303
Swansea Rd	29307
Sweet Gum Rd	29307
Sweet Meadows Dr	29307
Sweet William Rd	29301
Sweetbay Ter	29306
Sweetbriar Ct & Ln	29301
Sweetie Way	29306
Swindon Ct	29301
Sycamore Ct	29302
Sydnor Rd	
1-199	29307
200-299	29302
Sylvan Ct & Dr	29302
Tacco Ct	29303
Taggart Dr	29303
Talmadge Dr	29307
Tamara Way	29301
Tamarack Rd	29307
Tanglewood Ct	29303
N Tanglewylde Dr	29301
Taurus Cir	29307
Taylor Colquitt Rd	29303
Taylor Piedmont Rd	29303
Teaberry Rd	29303
Temple St	29301
Templeton Dr	29306
Tempo Ct	29307
Tennent St	29301
Tennessee Ave	29306
Tennyson Ct	29301
Tenosha Dr	29303
Terken Ct	29307
Terrace Rd	29301
Terrell St	29301
Texanna Dr	29303
Textile Rd	29301
Thackston Dr	29307
Tharon Dr	29303
Thaydra Dr	29307
Theiler Rd	29301
Thelma Dr	29301
Theodosia Dr	29301
Thomas Dr	29307
Thomas Rd	29302
Thomas St	29303
Thomas Adam Rd	29307
N Thompson St	29301
Thompson Chapel Rd	29307
Thorn Dr	29303
Thornhill Dr	29301
Thornton Ln	29301
Thornwood Dr	29302
Thunderbird Pl	29307
Thurgood Marshall Rd	29307
Tibbs Dr	29301
Tiffany Dr	29303
Tiger Paw Ct	29307
Tillotson Rd	29301
Timberoak Ln	29301
Timothy St	29306
Tindall St	29301
Tinsley Heights Dr	29303
Tinsley Ward Rd	29303
Tipperary Ln	29303
Toledo Pl	29303
Tommy Stocks Rd	29303
Top Ridge St	29307
Torino Dr	29307
Torrey Pine Ct	29306
Towles Ct	29307
N Town Dr	29303
N, S & W Townes Ct	29301
Townsend Ct	29302
Tradd St	29301
Trailwood Dr	29301
Tram Ct	29307
Tranquil Dr	29307
Tranquility Rd	29307
Traveller Dr	29303
Traversie Ct	29306
Travis Cir	29301
Traxler St	29303
Tremont Rd	29306
Trenton Cir	29302
Trimmier St	29303
Trinity Ave	29303
Trinity Dr	29306
Trogden Rd	29306
Trolley Car Way	29302
Trout Ct	29302
Tryon St	29301
Tucker Rd	29306
Tulip Poplar Ct	29301
Turkey Hill Dr	29302
Turnberry Dr	29306
Turner Rd	29303
Turnstone Ln	29301
Tweed St	29301
Twin Dr	29302
Twin Oaks Ct & Dr	29306
Twin Pond Dr	29307
Twin Springs Dr	29301
Twin Woods Dr	29307
Twining Ter	29307
Twitty St	29303
Tyger Lake Rd	29301
Tyler Ct	29301
Tyler Rose Ct	29301
Ucci Way	29303
Una Ct	29301
Uninchea Rd	29302
Union St	
100-299	29302
300-799	29306
800-1799	29302
Unity Rd	29307
University Way	29303
Upton Rd	29307
Upton St	29301
Upward Way	29303
Utah St	29303
Utilities Rd	29302
Vale St	29301
Valley St	29307
Valley Falls Rd	29303
Vance Dr	29301
Vanderbilt Ln & Rd	29301
Varner St	29306
Vass St	29303
Vaughn Hl	29307
Venture Blvd	29306
Veracruz Plz	29301
Verdae Dr	29301
Vermillian Dr	29306
Vermont Ave	29306
Verna Ct	29303
N Vernon St	29303
Viaduct Rd	29303
E & W Victoria Rd	29301
Village West Ct	29301
Vintage Dr	29307
Virginia St	29306
Virginia Pine Ct	29306
Vista Hill Dr	29302
Wadsworth Rd	29301
Waite Ave	29302
Wake Robin Cir	29301
Walden Cir	29301
N Walker St	29301
Wall Dr	29301
Wall St	29306
Wallace Ave	29302
Wallace Rd	29307
Walnut St	29303
Walnut Hill Ln	29302
Walnut Ridge Dr	29306
Walters St	29303
Wannamaker Ct	29302
Wardlaw Ave	29302
Warehouse Dr	29303
Warehouse St	29306
Warren St	29306
Warren H Abernathy Hwy	29301
Washburn Ct	29302
Washington Pl	29302
Washington Rd	29302
Washington St	29301
Washington Way	29301
Watermere Dr	29303
Watervale Dr	29301
Waterway Ct	29301
Watkins Ct & St	29301
Watson Rd	29303
Waverly Ct	29306
Wayland St	29303
Webb Dr	29303
Webber Rd, Walk & Way	29307
Weblin St	29306
Wedgewood Cir	29307
Wedgewood Dr	29302
Wedgewood Pl	29302
Weeping Oak Dr	29303
Weezes Way	29301
Weitz St	29301
Weldon St	29303
Wellesley Dr	29307
Wellington Rd	29302
Wells St	29306
Wendover Ct & Way	29302
Wentworth Dr	29301
Werner Ct	29307
Wesberry Cir	29301
Wesley St	29303
West Ave	29301
West Dr	29303
West Rd	
700-999	29306
1000-1299	29302
West St	29301
Westbrook Ct	29303
Westgate Mall Dr	29301
Westhaven Ct	29301
Westlake Dr	29303
Westminster Dr	29302
Westmoreland St	29301
Westover Dr	29306
Westview Blvd	29306
Wexford Ln	29301
Weymouth Dr	29302
Wheeler Ct	29306
Wheeler Rd	29302
White Ave	29303
White Horse Ct	29306
White Oak Rd	29301
White Oak St	29307
White Plains Rd	29307
White Springs Dr	29302
White Star Pt	29301
Whiteford Rd	29301
Whitener Ave	29306
Whitener Ct	29301
Whites Mill Way	29307
Whitestone Rd	29302
Whitestone Glendale Rd	29302
Whitlock Ln & St	29301
Whitlock Park Dr	29307
Whitman Ln	29301
Whitney Rd	29303
Whittier Pl	29303
Wickson Ct	29301
Wiggins St	29306
Wilder Dr	29301
Wilderness Ln	29306
Wildmere Way	29301
Wildwood Ct	29301
Wildwood Dr	29306
Wildwood Ln	29301
Wildwood St	29302
Wilkinson Ct	29301
William Jolley Dr	29303
Williams St	29301
Williamsburg Dr	29302
Willis Rd	29301
Willis Means Ln	29303
Willow Ln	29307
Willow Crossing Ln	29301
Willow Leaf Ct	29301
Willow Oaks Dr	29301
Willow Pines Ct	29303
Willow Pond Rd	29307
Willow Run Ter	29303
Willowbrook Dr	29301
Willowdale Dr	29303
Willowood Dr	29303
Willowpoint Ln	29303
Wilmont St	29306
Wilson Rd	29307
Wimberly Dr	29306
Winchester Pl	29301
Winco Ave	29303
Windemere Ln	29301
Windham Ct	29301
Windigo Rd	29306
Winding Way	29306
Windsor Ave	29306
Windy Ct	29301
Windyrush Rd	29301
Winfield Dr	29307
Winged Elm Ter	29306
Winged Foot Ct	29306
Wingo Heights Rd	29303
Winsmith Ave	29306
Winterberry Ct	29301
Winterhaven Rd	29301
Winton Ct	29306
Wise Ln	29303
Wisteria Ct	29307
Withers Ct	29302
Wo Ezell Blvd	29301
Wofford St	29301
Wofford Campus Dr	29303
Wood Row	29306
Wood St	29303
E Wood St	29303
W Wood St	29303
Wood Lily Ln	29307
Wood Row St	29306
W Wood Street Ext	29303
Woodberry Pl	29307
Woodbine Ct	29307
Woodbine Ter	29301
Woodburn Rd	29302
Woodburn Club Ln	29302
Woodburn Creek Rd	29302
Woodburn Ridge Rd	29302
E & W Woodbury Ln	29301
Woodcreek Dr	29303
Wooden Duck St	29303
Woodfield Cir	29303
E & W Woodglen Rd	29301
Woodgrove Trce	29301
Woodhaven Dr	29307
Woodlake Dr	29301
Woodland St	29302
Woodlawn Ave	29306
Woodley Rd	29306
Woodride Ct	29306
Woodridge Dr	29301
Woodside Ct	29301
Woodside Ln	29302
Woodson Ct	29303
Woodvale Dr	29303
Woodview Ave	29306
Woodward St	29302
Woodwind Ct & Dr	29302
Wooten Dr	29307
Worden Dr	29301
Worthington Cir	29303
Wrengate St	29303
Wrenwood Ln	29307
Wrightson Ave	29306
Wyatt Dr	29303
Wyatt Rd	29302
Wycliff Dr	29301
Yard Rd	29302
Yardley Ct	29306
Yeamans Hall Ct	29306
Yellow Brick Rd	29303

Yellow Poplar Ter 29306
Yolanda Dr 29301
York St 29301
Yorkshire Dr 29301
Zellen Dr 29303
Zephyr St 29301
Zima Park Rd 29301
Zimmerman Rd 29303
Zimmerman Lake Rd ... 29306
Zion Hill Rd 29307

NUMBERED STREETS

1st Ave 29302
W 2nd St 29301

SUMMERVILLE SC

General Delivery 29484

POST OFFICE BOXES MAIN OFFICE STATIONS AND BRANCHES

Box No.s
1 - 3576 29484
50001 - 52518 29485
840001 - 840001 29484

NAMED STREETS

Aaron Ln 29485
Abandon Ln 29483
Abbey Ln 29485
Abelia Ln 29483
Aberdeen Cir & Ct 29483
Abigale Ln 29483
Acadian Ln 29483
Action Ln 29483
Adaba Dixie Ln 29483
Adam Austin Ave 29483
Afton Ct 29485
Agnes Ln 29483
Airport Entrance Rd 29483
Alan Ct 29485
Albacore Ln 29485
Aleene Dr 29485
Alexander Cir 29483
Alexis Ct 29483
Alicia Dr 29483
Allana Trl 29483
Allison Ln 29483
Allspice Dr 29483
Almers Ln 29483
Almond St 29483
Alpha Cir 29483
Alpine Dr 29483
Alpine Rd 29485
Alston St N 29483
Alwyn Blvd 29485
Alydar Ct 29483
Alyssa Ln 29483
Amaranth Ave 29483
Amaretto Ct 29485
Amaryllis Ave 29483
Amber Rd 29483
Amberjack Way 29485
Amberwood Dr 29483
Amen Cor 29483
Ancrum Ln 29483
Anders Way 29483
Andrews Blvd 29485
Angel Watch Ln 29483
Angora Way 29485
Angus St 29483
Anhinga Ct 29485
Anna Ct 29485
Annandale Ct 29485
Annie Cir 29483
Anstead Dr 29485
Antebellum Way 29483
Antietam Ct 29483
Antique Ln 29483
Apache Dr 29483
Apple Blossom Ln 29483
Apryl Ln 29483
Arabian Dr 29483
Arbor Rd 29483
Arbor Oaks Dr 29485
Ardis St 29483
Argosy St 29483
Argyll Dr 29483
Ariel Ct 29485
Arnolds Farm Ln 29483
Arron Ln 29485
Arrowhead Dr 29483
Arrowridge Ct 29485
Arthurs Ridge Ln 29483
Ash Ct 29483
Ash Hill Rd 29483
Ashborough Ave 29485
Ashdown Dr 29483
Asher Loop 29483
Ashford Cir 29485
Ashland Dr 29483
Ashley Ct 29483
Ashley Dr 29485
Ashley Bluffs Rd 29485
Ashley River Dr & Rd .. 29485
Ashton Cv 29485
Ashview Ct 29483
Ashwood Ct & Dr 29483
Asphalt Dr 29483
Astor Ct 29483
Athol St 29485
Atlantic St 29483
Audubon Ct 29483
Augustine Ct 29483
Aulds Ln 29483
Austin Creek Ct 29483
Autumn Creek Trl 29483
Avalon Rd 29483
Aviary Ct 29483
Avoncliff Ct 29485
Avonshire Dr 29483
Axtell Ct & Dr 29485
Ayers Cir & Ct 29485
Ayscough Rd 29485
Azalea Dr
100-199 29485
1100-1299 29483
Azalea Square Blvd 29483
Azalee Ln 29483
Aztec Ct 29483
Babe Ln 29483
Back Bay Ct 29485
Back Creek Ct 29485
Back Tee Cir 29483
Bacons Bridge Rd 29485
Bagovich Ct 29483
Bailey Dr
100-399 29485
2200-2299 29483
Bainsbury Ln 29483
Bald Cypress Ct 29485
Baldwin Ln 29483
Ballantine Dr 29485
Balsam Cir 29485
Baltusrol Ct 29483
Bamert St 29483
Banburry Cross Ct 29483
Banbury Cross Ct 29485
Bandolier Ln 29483
Barberry St 29483
Barefoot Ln 29483
Barfield Dr 29483
Barlow St 29485
Barnes Way 29483
Barnwell St 29483
Barons Rd 29483
Barrington Ct 29483
Barrymore Ct 29485
Barshay Ct & Dr 29483
Barton Ln 29483
Basnett Dr 29485
Basswood Ave 29483
Bateaux Dr 29483
Bates Branch Rd 29483
Battery Edge Dr 29483
Bawn Dr 29485
Bay Colony Ct 29483
Bay Leaf Ct 29483
Bayberry Run 29485
Bayleaf Ct 29485
Bayonet Dr 29483
Bayou Xing 29485
Beacon Falls Ct 29483
Beacon Hill Ln 29485
Beagle Dr 29483
Bear Island Rd 29483
Beatrice Ln 29483
Beaty Ln 29483
Beau Ct 29485
Beaufort St 29483
Beaumont Ct 29485
Beauregard Ct 29485
Beauregard Rd 29483
Beautberry Rd 29483
Beaverton Ct 29485
Beck Ct & St 29483
Beckham Ln 29483
Bedford Ct 29483
Bee St 29483
Beech Hill Rd 29483
Beechwood Bay Ct 29485
Begovich Ct 29483
Belgium Way 29483
Beliks Way 29483
Bell Dr 29483
Belle Meade 29483
Belleglade Dr 29483
Bellerive Ln 29483
Bellflower Dr 29483
Bellwright Rd 29483
Belmont Ct 29485
Beltline Rd 29483
Bennie Ave 29483
Bent Green Ct 29485
Bentons Lodge Rd 29485
Bergen Rd 29483
Berkeley Cir 29483
Berkeley Farms Rd 29483
Berkeley Pointe Ct 29483
Bermuda Ct 29483
E Berry St 29483
Bertram Rd 29483
Berwick Dr 29483
Beth Ct 29483
Bethpage Ct 29483
Betsy Ln 29483
Beverly Dr 29483
Big Bird Ln 29483
Big Oak Ln 29483
Bill Park Dr 29483
Billowing Sails St 29483
Birch Ln 29483
N Birch St 29483
Birchwood Dr 29483
Birdcage Walk 29483
Birdie Ln 29483
Birmingham Dr 29483
Black Oak Blvd 29485
Black River Dr 29483
Blackberry Ln 29483
Blackfin Dr 29483
Blackpoint St 29483
Blackwalnut Dr 29483
Blackwater Dr 29483
Blackwell Ave 29483
Blair Rd 29483
Blake Dr 29485
Blanton Ln 29483
Blockade Dr 29483
Blockade Runner
Pkwy 29485
Blocker Ln 29483
Bloomsbury Pl 29485
Blossom Way 29483
Blue Bonnet St 29483
Blue Heron Dr 29483
Blue Jasmine Ln 29483
Bluebell Ave 29483
Blueberry Pl 29483
Bluebird Ln 29483
Bluepoint St 29483
Bluetick Ln 29483
Bluff Ln 29483
Blythe Ave 29485
Bo Ln 29483
Bo Barry Ln 29483
Bobs Lake Dr 29483
Bobwhite Ln 29485
Bonita Ct 29485
Bonneau Ct 29485
Bonnie Ln 29485
Boone Dr 29485
Boone St 29483
Boone Hill Pkwy & Rd .. 29483
Bosquet Ct 29485
W Boundary St 29485
Boundview Ct 29485
Bowles Dr 29485
Boxer Ln 29485
Boyle Way 29485
Bradd St 29483
Bradford Ct 29485
Bradley Daniel Blvd 29483
Braemar Ct 29483
Brailsford Blvd & Rd 29485
Braly Dr 29485
Bramblewood Dr 29485
Bramwell Dr 29485
Branch Creek Trl 29483
Brandon Dr 29485
Brandy Ct 29485
Brandywine Dr 29485
Brenda B Ln 29485
Brett Ln 29485
Brevard Ct 29485
Brewer Rd 29485
Briarpatch Ln 29485
Briarwood Ln 29485
Brick Kiln Dr 29485
Bridge Pointe Ln 29485
Bridgewater Ct 29485
Brighton Ln 29485
Bristol St 29485
Bristow Dr 29485
Brittany Ct 29485
W Broad St 29483
Broad River Dr 29485
Broadleaf Dr 29485
Broken Trl 29485
Brookhaven Rd 29485
Brooks Loop 29485
Brookstone Way 29485
Brothers Ln 29483
Brown Ct 29485
Brownfield Dr 29483
Brownhare Ct 29485
Browning Ln 29483
Bruce Ct 29485
Brutus Ln 29483
Bryan St 29483
Bryce Ct 29483
Buckeye Ln 29483
Buckfield Ln 29483
Buckingham Ave 29485
Buckler St 29483
Buckshot Ln 29483
Buckskin Dr 29483
Buckthorn Cir 29483
Bud Ln 29483
Budda Ln 29483
Buddys Ln 29483
Buffalo Ct 29483
Bull Run Dr 29483
Bunker Ct 29483
Bunting Ct 29485
Burbage Ln & Rd 29485
Buremda Run 29483
Burnham Rd 29485
Burnt Tree Ct 29485
Burrows Ln 29483
Burrstone Trl 29485
Burton Ave 29485
Bushy Ln 29483
Business Park Rd 29483
Butler St 29485
Buttercup Way 29485
Butterfly Ln 29483
E & W Butternut Rd 29483
Cable Ct & Dr 29483
Cableswynd Way 29485
Caboose Ct 29483
Caddy Ct 29485
Cady Dr 29483
Caffrey Ct 29485
E Cain St 29483
Calamus Pond Rd 29483
Calhoun St 29485
Calming Mist Lndg 29483
Cambell Ct 29483
Cambridge Rd 29485
Camelia Dr 29485
Cameo Ln 29483
Cameron St 29483
Canaberry Cir 29483
Canal St 29485
Candace Ct 29483
Candle Dr 29485
Candlelite Path 29483
Candlewood Ct 29485
Candover Ct 29485
Candy Ln 29483
Cane Acre Rd 29485
Cane Bay Blvd 29483
Cane Mill Ct 29485
Cane Mill Ln 29485
Cane Pole Ln 29485
Cannonball Ln 29483
Cannonsmill Ln 29485
Cantering Hills Ln 29485
Cantilever Ct 29483
Cantley Dr 29483
Canvasback Dr 29483
Caralana Cir 29485
Cardinal Dr 29485
Carlisle Ct 29485
Carlton Ct 29485
Carmelton Dr 29485
Carmon St 29485
Carnegie Ct 29485
Carnes Blvd 29483
Carnoustie Ct
100-199 29483
4800-4899 29485
E Carolina Ave 29483
W Carolina Ave
100-658 29483
659-659 29485
661-700 29483
701-701 29485
702-702 29483
703-720 29485
800-899 29485
Caroline Ln 29483
Carolinian Dr 29485
N & S Carousel Cir 29485
Carriage Ct 29483
Carriage Ln 29485
Carriage Way 29485
Carriage Ride Ln 29483
Carrie Ln 29483
Carrington Ct & Ln 29485
Carroll Ct & Ln 29485
Carrousel Ln 29485
Cartbridge Ct 29485
Carter Ln 29483
Carters Dr 29485
Cartpath Ct 29485
Carya Ct 29485
Caryota Ln 29485
Cassels Ln 29483
Castle Harbor Dr 29483
Catawba Dr 29485
Catbriar Ct 29485
Cates Ct 29483
Catherine St 29485
Cattail Ct 29483
Causeyside Ct 29485
Cavalier Dr 29485
Caveson Dr 29483
N & S Cedar St 29483
Cedarfield Ln 29483
Cedarlake Ln 29483
Celebrity Dr 29483
Cember Way 29483
Center St 29483
Central Ave 29483
Centre St 29483
Cercial Ct 29485
Chaddsford Ct 29485
Chadford Park Dr 29485
Chaff Ct 29485
Chalcott Pl 29485
Challedon Dr 29485
Chalmers Ct & Ln 29485
Champion Cir 29485
Chance Ln 29483
Chancellors Dr 29485
Chaparral Ln 29483
Charlesford Chase 29485
Charleston St 29485
Charlie Ln 29483
Charpia Ave 29483
Charter Oak Ct 29485
Chase Ct 29483
Chato Ct 29485
Chatsworth Pl 29485
Chattum Ct 29485
Chaussee Blvd 29483
Checkerboard Rd 29483
Chelsea Ct 29485
Cherokee Dr 29483
Cherokee Valley Ln 29483
Cherry Pl 29483
Cherry Blossom Dr 29485
Cherrywood Dr 29485
Chessington Cir 29485
Chestnut Ct 29483
Cheyenne Rd 29483
Chickesaw Ct 29483
Chiles Dr 29483
Chinners Ln 29483
Chinquapin Dr 29483
Chipping Sparrow Dr 29485
Chisolm Ct 29485
Chivalry St 29483
Chris Ln 29483
Christian Ln 29483
Christina Ln 29483
Christy Ln 29483
Chucker Ct & Dr 29485
Churchill Ct 29485
Cider Ct 29483
Cimmeron Ct 29485
Cinder Ct 29483
Cindy Dr 29485
Cinnamon Rd 29485
Circle Dr 29483
E Circle Dr 29483
W Circle Dr 29483
Civic Ctr 29485
Clara Ln 29483
Clark Ln 29483
Classic St 29483
Claussen St 29483
Claybourne Ct 29485
Clayton Ln 29483
Clayton Woods Ln 29483
Clear Springs Cir 29483
Cleburne Ct 29485
Clemson Dr 29483
Cleveland St 29483
Clifton Ct & St 29483
Clover Ave 29485
Clover Ln 29483
Clover St 29483
Club View Rd 29485
Clubhouse Rd 29483
Coachman Ln 29483
Coastal Bluff Way 29485
Cobb Ct 29485
Cobblestone Blvd &
Way 29483
Cobley Pl 29485
Cold Harbor Cir 29483
Coldstream Ct 29483
Colkitt St 29485
College Park Rd 29483
Colleton Ave 29483
Colonial Ct 29483
Colony Ct
100-199 29485
1000-1099 29483
E Colpat St 29483
Coltsgate Ct 29485
Columns Rd 29483
Comingtee Range 29485
Comiskey Park Cir 29485
N & S Commodore
Way 29483
Community Rd 29485
Compton Xing 29483
Conductor Ct 29483
Cone Ln 29483
Coneflower Ct 29483
Coney Ct 29483
Confederate Ct & Dr 29483
Congaree River Dr 29485
Congress St 29483
Congressional Blvd 29483
Cooper Dr 29483
Coopers Ct 29485
Coosawatchie St 29485
Copley Cir 29483
Copper Ln 29483
Coralie Dr 29483
Corby Ct 29485
Corey Blvd 29483
Cornerstone Ln 29483
Coronet St 29483
Corporate Way 29483
Corral Cir 29485
Corrientes Ct 29483
Corsair St 29483
Cosmo Ln 29483
Cosmos Rd 29483
Cotillion Cres 29483
Cottage Ct 29485
Cottage Grove Ct 29483
Cottage Path Ln 29485
Cotton Hill Rd 29483
Cotton Hope Ln 29483
Cottonwood Dr 29483
Countess Dr 29485
Country Ln 29483
Country Boy Ln 29483
Country Club Blvd 29483
Country Club Ln 29483
Countryside Way 29483
Course View Ct 29483
Courtland Dr 29483
Courtney Round 29483
Coventry Rd 29483
Covert Ln 29485
Covey Ct 29485
Covey Rise Ct 29485
Cowabunga Ct 29483
Cowboy Up Ln 29483
Coy Ct 29483
Coyote Ct 29483
Crabapple Ct 29483
Craig Ct 29483
Cranbourne Abbey 29485
Crane Ct 29483
Cranston Ln 29483
Crazyfeather Ln 29485
Creedmoore Rd 29483
Creek Bend Dr 29485
Creekside Dr 29485
Crescent Ct 29483
Crestview Dr 29485
Crestwood Dr 29483
Cromwell Ct 29485
Crooked Creek Ct 29483
Crooked Oak Rd 29485
Crooked Stick Ct 29483
Crosby Ln 29483
Cross Tie Ct 29483
Cross Timbers Dr 29485
Crossandra Ave 29483
Crosscreek Dr 29483
Crossing Water St 29485
Crunch St 29483
Cujo Ln 29483
Culloden Dr 29483

Cumbria Ct 29483
Curico Ln 29483
Curry St 29483
Cushman Trl 29483
Cuthbert Ln 29483
Cynthia Ln 29485
Cypress St 29483
Cypress Campground Rd 29483
Cypress Knee Ldg 29483
Cypress Point Dr 29483
Dabbling Duck Dr 29485
Dabney Ln 29483
Dacs Ln 29483
Daffodil St 29483
Dahlia Pl 29483
Daisy Cir 29483
Dalegarth Ct 29485
Damascus Dr 29483
Dan Miler Ln 29483
Dana Ct 29485
Danberry Dr 29485
Danby Woods Ct 29485
Dandelion St 29483
Dangerfield Rd 29485
Daniel Ln 29483
Daniel Ridge Dr 29485
Danielle Ln 29483
Danners Pl 29483
Dante Ln 29483
Dantzler Ln 29483
Danzid Dr 29483
Darter Dr 29483
Dawnshire Ct 29485
Dawson Branch Rd 29483
Daybreak Blvd 29483
Dean Dr 29483
Debbie Ln 29483
Debrooks Ln 29483
Decatur Dr 29483
December Ln 29485
Deep River Rd 29483
Deer St 29485
Deer Cross Ct 29483
Deer Path Trl 29483
Deer Run Rd 29483
Delafield Dr 29483
Delaney Cir 29485
Delemar Hwy 29485
Dell Dr 29483
Delong Ct 29483
Deming Way 29483
Denali Ct 29483
Dennis Fort Ln 29483
Denny Ct 29483
Dequincy Ln 29485
Dericote Ln 29485
Desi Ct 29485
Destin St 29483
Devon Ct 29485
Devon Rd 29483
Dewees Ln 29485
Diana Ct 29483
Dig It Rd 29483
Dirocco Ln 29485
Diving Duck Ln 29483
Divot Ln 29485
Dj Eboni Ln 29483
Dockwell Ln 29483
Doe Run Trl 29483
Dogpatch Acres Ln 29483
Dogwood Cir 29485
Dogwood Row 29483
Dogwood Ridge Rd 29485
Dollie Cir 29485
Dolphin Dr 29485
Donegal Ln 29483
Donna Dr 29483
Donning Dr 29483
Donovan Ct 29483
Dons Ln 29483
Dootsie Ct 29485
Dorchester Ave 29483
Dorchester Rd 29483
Dordal Ln 29483
Dorsetshire Downs 29485

E & W Doty Ave 29483
Douglas Ct 29485
Douglas Pl 29483
Douglas Wayne Rd 29483
Dove Ct & Ln 29485
Dovetail Cir 29483
Downing Dr 29485
Drake Ct 29483
Drayton Ct & Dr 29483
Dream St 29483
Dreamer Ln 29483
Driver Ave 29483
Drop Off Dr 29483
Droze Ln & Rd 29483
Duane Ln 29483
Dubard St 29483
Duboise Rd 29483
Dubose Farm Ln 29483
Dubose School Rd 29483
Ducane St 29483
Duchess Ct 29485
Duck Cir 29483
Duck Blind Ct 29483
Duck Pond Ct 29485
Duck Pond Ln 29483
Duck Tail Cir 29483
Duggins Ln 29483
Dukes Ct 29483
Dunbury Dr 29483
Duncan Ct & Ln 29483
Dundee St 29483
Dunmeyer Hill Rd 29485
Dunmeyer Loop Rd 29485
Dunmow Dr 29483
Dunning Rd 29483
Dupont Way 29485
Durr Ln 29485
Dutch Ln 29483
Duxback Ln 29483
Eagle Ct 29483
Eagle Dr 29485
Eagle Creek Dr 29483
Eagle Harbor Ln 29483
Eagle Ridge Rd 29485
Earl St 29483
Earl Dupriest Dr 29483
Early Ln 29483
Early Bird Ln 29483
Earmine Rd 29483
Eastern Isle Ave 29483
Eastover Cir 29483
Eastside St 29483
Eaton Way 29483
Echo Dr 29483
Eckles Ln 29483
Edenbridge Ln 29485
Edgebrook Dr 29483
E & W Edgefield Dr 29483
Edinburgh St 29483
Edisto Dr 29485
Edmund Ct 29483
Edward Ct 29483
Edythe Ct 29485
Egret Ln 29485
Eider Down Dr 29483
Elaine Blvd 29483
Electra Ln 29483
Elena Ct 29483
Elery Ter 29485
Eley Ln 29483
Elgin Ct 29483
Eliston St 29483
Eliza Ln 29483
Elizabeth St 29483
Elker Dr 29483
Elks Lodge Ln 29483
Ellen Ct 29483
Elliana Way 29483
Ellie Ct 29483
Ellington Dr 29485
Elliot Creek Ln 29485
Ellison Way 29483
Elm Cir 29485
Elm Hall Cir 29483
Elm Village Dr 29483
Embassy Dr 29483

Enclave Ter 29483
Endicott Ct 29483
Endicott St 29483
Englewood Ct 29483
English Rd 29483
Equestrian Ct 29483
Equine Dr 29483
Era Ln 29483
Ernies Way 29483
Essex Dr 29485
Estates Dr 29483
Estees St 29485
Estelle Ln 29483
Estero Ct 29483
Estes Ct 29485
Eternal Ln 29483
Ethel Ct 29485
Ethel Mae Ln 29483
Eucalyptus Ct 29483
Evance Ct 29485
Evelyn Joy Dr 29483
Evergreen Oak Dr 29485
Evesham Dr 29485
Ewell Ct 29483
Exeter Ct 29485
Expressway Dr 29483
F A A Dr 29483
Fabricators St 29483
Factors Walk 29483
Fair Spring Ct 29485
Fairington Dr 29483
Fairway Dr 29483
Fairway Forest Dr 29485
Faith Ln 29483
Faith Missionary Ln 29483
Falcon Dr 29483
Fall Creek Blvd 29483
Fannie Dr 29485
Farm Rd 29483
Farm Branch Ln 29483
Farm Crest Ct 29483
Farm Springs Rd 29483
Farmhill Dr 29483
Farmington Rd 29483
Fawn Ct 29483
Felder Branch Ln 29483
Felder Creek Rd 29483
Felicia Ct 29483
Felix Ln & St 29483
Fern Ct 29483
Fichtelhof Pl 29483
Fiddie St 29483
Field Planters Dr 29485
Fields Dr 29485
Fieldstone Trce 29485
Finucan Rd 29483
Fire Fly Ln 29483
Fireman Ln 29483
Firestone Ct 29485
W Fisher Rd 29483
Five Iron Cir 29483
Fladger Ln 29483
Flamingo Ln 29483
Flegle Ln 29483
Fletton Way 29483
Flicker Ln 29483
Flintlock Ln 29483
Flood Heirs Rd 29483
Flud St 29483
Flying Cloud Dr 29483
Flynn St 29483
Flyway Rd 29483
Folklore Dr 29483
Folkstone Way 29483
Ford Ct 29483
Forest Cir, Ct & Ln 29483
Forest Glen Ct 29483
Forest Hills Rd 29483
Forsythia Ave 29483
Fort St 29483
Fort Johnson Dr 29483
Fort Ripley Ln 29483
Fort Sullivan Ln 29483
Foster St 29483
Four Iron Ct & Dr 29483
Fox Run Ln 29483

Fox Squirrel Run 29483
Fox Valley Ct 29485
Foxcroft Ln 29485
Foxfire Ct 29483
Foxglove Ave 29483
Fralixhill Ln 29483
Francis Ln 29483
Franconia Dr 29485
Frank St 29483
Franklin Ct 29485
Fred St 29483
Fredericksburg Dr 29483
Fredrick Dr 29483
Freeport St 29483
Fremont Dr 29483
Fripp Ln 29483
Frisk Ln 29485
Froman Dr 29483
W Front St 29485
Frontage Rd 29483
Frys Way 29483
Furlong Rd 29483
Gabriel Ln 29483
Gadsden St 29483
Gahagan Rd 29483
Gaillard Ln 29483
Gailynn Ln 29483
Gains Mill Dr 29483
Gallashaw Rd 29483
Gally Ct 29483
Gambels Ln 29485
Garbon Dr 29483
Garden Ln 29483
Garden Grove Dr 29485
Garden Hill Rd 29483
Gardenia St 29483
Gaslight Blvd 29483
Gatehouse Dr 29483
Gathering Island Rd 29483
Gelzer Ln 29483
Genell Rd 29483
General Dennis Dr 29483
Generations Ln 29483
Gennies Cor 29483
George Keen Dr 29483
Gerald Ct 29485
Gerards Ln 29485
Germander Ave 29483
Germantown Rd 29483
Gertrudes Ln 29483
Gibbon Ct 29483
Gibbs Loop 29483
Gilleys Ct 29483
Gilpen Ct 29485
Gippy Dr 29483
Gladys Ln 29483
Glasgow Cir 29485
Glaze Dr 29483
Glebe Rd 29483
Glen St 29483
Glen Abby Dr 29483
Glen Eagle Dr 29483
Glen Forest Ct 29485
Glendale Ct 29483
Glendale Dr 29483
Glenlivet Ct 29483
Glenspring Dr 29483
Glouchester Ct 29483
Goings Dr 29483
Goldfinch Ln 29483
Golf Rd 29483
Golf View Ln 29483
Gordon Ct 29483
Gosling Xing 29483
Gospel Ln 29483
Grafton Ct 29483
Graham Ln 29483
Grand Palm Ln 29483
Grande Belle Ln 29483
Grandfather Ln 29483
Grandview Dr 29483
E Grant St 29485
Grantham Ct 29483
Grape Arbor Dr 29483
Grapevine Rd 29483
Grassy Hill Rd 29483

Grayson Ln 29485
Grazing Meadow Ct 29483
Great Oaks Dr 29483
E Green St 29485
Green Acres Dr 29483
Green Grass Rd 29483
Green Leaf Ct 29485
Green View Ct 29485
Greenbriar Dr 29485
Greenbriar Pl 29483
Greendale Ct 29485
Greene Ln 29485
Greenhill Pastures 29483
Greenhurst Ave 29485
Greenpoint Dr 29483
Greenwave Blvd 29483
Greenwood St 29485
Gresham Ct 29485
Greyback Rd 29483
Grouse Ct & Rd 29485
Grove Hall Ln 29483
Guilford Dr 29483
N Gum St
100-300 29483
301-1099 29483
301-301 29484
302-1098 29483
S Gum St 29483
Gunpowder Ct 29485
E & W Gustave Ct 29483
Habersham Ln 29485
Haberstraw Ct 29483
Halcyon Rd 29483
Hall Ct & Ln 29483
Ham Ln 29483
W Hamilton St 29485
Hamlet Rd 29485
Hammerbeck Rd 29483
Hammock St 29483
Hampton Ct 29483
Hampton Dr
100-299 29485
1000-1399 29483
N Hampton St 29483
S Hampton St 29483
Haney Ln 29483
Haney Branch Rd 29483
Hanging Moss Rd 29485
Hanover Ct 29485
Hansberry Ln 29483
Harbor Point Ct 29483
Hardee Ave 29485
Hardwood Ln 29483
Harlesden Ln 29485
Harmony Ln 29483
Harold Dr 29483
Harolee Ln 29485
Harpers Row 29483
Harpers Ferry Ln 29483
Harroway Rd 29485
Harter Dr 29485
N & S Hartford Dr 29483
Harth Pl 29485
Harthill Ave 29485
Hartin Blvd 29485
Hartley Hall Ct 29485
Harvest Way 29485
Harvest Moon Ct 29485
Harvey Acres Ln 29483
Harvey Farm Ln 29483
Harvey Plantation Ln 29483
Hasting Way 29485
Haulover Way 29485
Haupt St 29483
Havelock Ct 29483
Haven Cir 29483
Haverstraw Ct 29483
Hawthorne Ave 29483
Hayden Rd 29483
Hayes Rd 29483
Hazel Dr 29483
Hazeltine Bnd 29483
Hazelwood Ln 29483
Heart Ln 29483
Heart Pine Cir 29483
Hearthside Dr 29485

Heath Ct 29485
Heather Dr 29483
Heavens Way 29483
Heber Rd 29485
Hedge Way 29483
Helen Dr 29483
Helms Dr 29483
Hema Ln 29483
Hemingway Cir 29483
Hemlock St 29483
Hemphill Ct 29483
Henderson Rd 29483
Henry Myers Blvd 29483
Hensley Ln 29483
Heritage Ln 29483
Heritage Pl 29483
Heritage St 29485
Heritage Lake Dr 29485
Hershey Cir 29483
N & S Heyward Ct 29485
Hialeah Ct 29483
N & S Hickory St 29483
Hickory Ridge Way 29485
Hidden Palms Blvd 29485
High Bridge Rd 29485
High Country Dr 29483
High Grove Rd 29485
High Meadow Farms Rd 29483
Highland Ave & Dr 29483
Highway 17a S 29483
Highway 78 E 29483
Highwoods Plantation Ave 29485
Hill Dr 29483
Hillcrest Ln 29485
Hillsborough Pl 29485
Hillside View Ln 29483
History Ln 29485
Hitching Post Ln 29483
Hobbleskirt Ln 29483
Hodge Rd 29483
Hoffman Ln 29483
Holdsworth Dr 29485
Holiday Dr 29483
Holly Ave & St 29485
Holly Berry Ln 29485
Holly Inn Rd 29485
Hollyridge Ln 29483
Honeydew Dr 29483
Honeysuckle Ln 29485
Hope Dr 29483
Hope Ln 29483
Hope Hollow Ct 29483
Hopper Dr 29483
Hornet Dr 29483
Horseshoe Bay Ct 29483
Hortonrest Ct 29485
Hounddog Ln 29483
Huckleberry Ln 29485
Hughes St 29483
Hulton Ln 29485
Hummingbird Ln 29483
Hundred Oaks Pkwy 29483
Hunley Pl 29485
Hunsford St 29483
Hunt Club Dr 29485
Hunters Wood Dr 29485
Huntingridge Pl 29485
Huntington Cir 29485
Huntington Rd 29483
Huntsman Ct 29485
Hutchinson Ln 29483
Hutchs Ln 29483
Hutson Dr 29483
Hutson Grove Ln 29483
Hyacinth St 29483
Hydrangea St 29483
Ilderton Dr 29483
Indian Dr 29483
Indigo Ct 29485
Industrial Rd 29483
Inez Dr 29485
Innisbrook Bnd 29483
Innovation Dr 29483
International Cir 29483

Inverness Ct 29483
Inwood Dr & Pl 29485
Irby Dr 29483
Irene Ct 29485
Iris St 29483
Iron Ct & Rd 29483
Isaac Way 29483
Isabela Ct 29483
Island Rest Dr 29483
Islesworth Way 29485
Isley Ct 29485
Islington Ter 29485
Iveson Rd 29483
Ivy Ct 29483
Izard Ct 29485
Jack Ct 29485
Jackson St
100-199 29483
700-799 29485
Jahnz Ave 29485
James Ct, Rd & St 29483
Jamestown Dr 29483
Jandrell Rd 29485
Janice Dr 29485
Janie Ln 29485
Jarett Rd 29485
Jasimine Ct 29483
Jasmine Dr 29483
Jay Ct 29485
Jaymar Cir 29485
Jeanette Cir 29485
Jeanna St 29483
Jed Park Pl 29483
Jedburg Rd 29483
Jedi Ln 29483
Jenkins Dr 29483
Jennies Ridge Ln 29483
Jennifer Dr 29483
Jennings Dr 29483
Jerry Way 29485
Jessen St 29483
Jessica Ln 29483
Jigsaw Rd 29485
Jimbo Rd 29485
Jo Furr Ln 29485
Jockey Ct 29483
Joes Ln 29483
John Ct 29485
John Mckissick Way 29485
E & W Johnston St 29483
Jordan Simmons Rd 29483
Joseph Ct 29483
Joseph Ln 29485
Joshua Ln 29485
Joyce Ln 29483
Jubilee Crescent Ct 29485
Judith Dr 29483
Judy St 29485
Julius Rd 29483
Jupiter Ln 29485
Kapalua Run 29483
Kate Ln 29483
Kay Ln 29483
Kaycee Ln 29483
Keller Spring Ct 29485
Kellorne Dr 29483
Kemper Lakes Ct 29483
Kendall Ct 29485
Kenilworth Rd 29485
Kennel Ln 29483
Kenneth Ln 29483
Kensington Pl 29485
Kent Ct & Ln 29485
Keowee Ct 29483
Kershaw Ct & Rd 29483
Kestevan Ct 29485
Kestrel Dr 29485
Kette Creek Rd 29483
Kevin Ln 29483
Key Way Ln 29483
Kiawah Cir 29483
Kilarney Rd 29483
Killdeer Trl 29485
Kilpatrick Ct 29483
Kimberly Ln 29483
Kimberwicke Dr 29483

Kimeran Ln 29485
King St 29483
King Charles Cir & Ct 29485
King Mountain Dr 29483
Kings Ct & Way 29485
Kingsley Vale Ct 29485
Kingston Pl 29483
Kingswood Pl 29483
Kinross Ct 29485
Kirk Ct 29483
Kirksey Dr 29485
Kirkwall Dr 29485
Kirven Rd 29483
Kitt Rd 29483
Kittering Ct 29485
Knight Ave 29483
Knights Ln 29483
Knotty Pine Dr 29483
Koger Dr 29483
Krismarc Ln 29483
Kyle Ct 29485
La Costa Way 29483
Labrador Ct 29485
Ladson Rd 29485
Lahina Cv 29483
Laidback Ct 29483
Laird Ct 29483
Lake Dr 29483
Lake Jogassee Dr 29485
Lake Pointe Ave 29483
Lakeview Dr 29485
Lakewood Cir 29485
Lakewood Dr 29485
Lamplight Cir 29483
S Lamplighter Ln 29483
Lancashire Rd 29483
Lancaster Rd 29483
Lancer Dr 29485
Landau Rd 29485
Langley Dr 29485
Lantana Ln 29483
Lantern Rd 29485
Lark St 29483
Larkspur Ct 29485
Larry St 29485
Larson Dr 29485
N & S Laurel St 29483
Laurel Crest Way 29485
Laurels Curv 29485
Laurens Ct 29485
Law Blvd 29485
Lawrence Dr 29483
Lazy Acres Loop 29483
Leaning Pin Ct 29485
Lebsl Ct 29483
Lee St 29485
Legacy Ln
200-299 29483
1000-1099 29485
Legare St 29483
Legend Oak Way 29485
Legion Rd 29483
Leighton Ct 29483
Leisure Dr 29483
Lenora Dr 29485
Lenwood Dr 29485
Leroy Ct 29485
Lewis Ln 29483
Lewis And Clark Trl 29485
Lewisfield Ct 29485
Leyland Ct 29485
Liberty Ct 29485
E, N, S & W Liberty Meadows Dr 29485
Liddington Ct 29485
Lilac Dr & Ln 29483
Lilith Ln 29483
Lillyann Ln 29483
Lily Pl 29483
Limehouse Dr 29485
Limerick Cir 29483
Lincoln Ave 29485
Lincolnville Rd 29485
Linda Ln 29485
Lindera Preserve Blvd 29483
Lindsey Ln 29483
Lingos Dr 29485
Linning Rd 29483
Linwood Ln 29483
Lionel Ct & Ln 29483
Lipman St 29483
Lipton St 29483
Lisa Dr 29485
Little School Ct 29485
Littlejohn St 29483
Live Oak Rd 29485
Livels Cir 29485
N Loblolly Ln & St 29483
Loch Lomond St 29483
Lofton Ct 29483
Logan Dr 29483
Long Bourne Way 29485
Long Bow Rd 29485
Long Cove Bnd 29483
Long Drive Rd 29485
Longfield Rd 29483
Longford Dr 29485
Longleaf Dr & Rd 29483
Longstreet St 29483
Lorraine Dr 29485
Lost Creek Ct 29485
Lotus Ct 29483
Lotz Dr 29483
Louise St 29483
Love Ln 29483
Lowery Ln 29483
Lowndes Ln 29483
Lucretia Ln 29483
Luden Dr
100-299 29483
300-399 29485
E & W Luke Ave 29483
Lynch Ln 29483
Lynches River Dr 29485
Macallan Ct 29483
Macfarren Ln 29485
Macgregor Dr 29485
Mackerel Ln 29485
Madison Brooke Ln 29483
Magazine Ct 29485
N & S Magnolia St 29483
Magwood Dr 29485
Magwood Rd 29483
Maidstone Dr 29483
N & S Main St 29483
Major Dr 29485
Mako Ln 29483
Malibu Rd 29483
Mallard Rd 29483
Malori Ln 29485
Malvasia Ct 29485
Manchester Rd 29483
Mandarin Ct 29483
Manigault Dr 29483
Manning Ct 29485
Manor Dr 29485
Maple Dr 29485
N Maple St 29483
S Maple St 29483
Maple Grove Dr 29485
Maplewood Ridge Ct 29485
Mapperton Ct 29485
Marclay Ct 29483
Marie Ln 29483
Marie Rd 29483
Marion Ave 29483
Marion Ct 29485
Marion Rd 29483
Marion Way 29485
Marjoram St 29483
Markie Rd 29483
Markley Blvd 29485
Markleys Grove Blvd 29485
Marlain Rd 29483
Marlow Dr 29483
Marmet Ct 29485
Marquis Dr 29485
Marsengill Pl 29485
Marsh Island Way 29483
Marsh Pointe Rd 29485
Marsh Walk Ct 29485
Marshall Acres Dr 29483
Marshside Dr 29485
Martha Ct 29483
Martin Ln 29483
Martins Creek Blvd 29485
Marvin Gdns 29483
Mary St 29483
Mary Ann Dr 29483
Mary Celestia Dr 29485
Mary Ellie Dr 29483
Marymeade Dr 29483
Mason St 29483
Masters Ct 29485
Mateeba Frst & Ln 29485
Mateeba Gardens Rd 29485
Mateo Ct 29483
Mattie Ln 29483
Maxine Ln 29483
Maxwell Rd 29483
Mayfair Ct 29483
Mayfield St 29485
Mayme Ct 29483
Mayrant St 29483
Mcalhaney Dr 29483
Mcdaid Ct 29483
Mcdonald Ct 29485
Mcdougal Cir 29483
Mcduffie Ct 29483
Mcgee Rd 29485
Mcgregor Downs Ct 29483
Mckayla Rd 29483
Mclaurin Ave 29483
Mcmakin St 29483
Mcneal Ln 29485
Mcqueen Blvd 29483
Meadow Run Dr 29483
Meadow Wood Rd 29483
Meadowlark Ct 29483
Meadowview Trl 29485
Medford Dr 29483
E & W Medina St 29483
Medway Ct 29483
Medway Sq 29485
Meeting St 29485
Megan Ln 29485
Megwood Dr 29485
Melanie Ln 29485
Mellichamp Rd 29485
Melvyn St 29485
Mendenhall St 29483
Mentor St 29483
Mepkin Dr 29483
Merriweather Ct 29485
Meryton Ct 29485
Mesa Ct 29483
Michele Dr 29483
Middleburg Sq 29485
Middlesboro Ave 29483
Middleton Blvd 29485
Midland Pkwy 29485
Mikel Ct & Dr 29485
Miken Ln 29483
Miles Rd 29483
Miley Dr 29485
Milindas Ln 29485
Mill St 29485
Mill Pond Ct 29485
Millbrook Cir 29483
Millbrook Rd 29483
Miller Ct 29485
Miltons Branch Rd 29485
Mistletoe Ln 29483
Misty Cove Trl 29483
Mitchell Dr 29483
Mizzell Rd 29483
Moccasin Ct 29485
Mockingbird Ln 29483
Mohican Cir 29483
Molasses Mill Ct 29485
Monarch Dr & Ln 29483
Mondo Ct 29483
Montana Ln 29483
Moon Dance Ln 29485
Moon Shadow Ln 29485
Moorer Town Ln 29485
Moreto Cir 29485
Morgan Pl 29485
Morning Dew Ct 29485
Morning Glory Ct 29483
Morrow Ln 29485
Mosby Ct 29483
Mose Cir 29483
Moss Ct 29483
Moss Haven Ln 29483
Moss Pond Rd 29483
Mossy Rd 29483
Mossy Hill Ln 29483
Mossy Wood Rd 29483
Mount Mckinley Dr 29483
Mount Whitney Dr 29483
Muckenfuss Ln 29483
Muir Ct 29483
Muirfield Village Ct 29483
Mulberry Dr 29483
Mulberry Hl 29485
Mulholland Ct & Dr 29485
Mulligan Way 29485
Mundy Ln 29483
Murray Blvd 29483
Musket Ln & Loop 29483
Muskie Dr 29483
My Ln 29483
Myers Rd 29483
Myrtle Pl & Way 29483
Nacoma Ln 29483
Nancy Ln 29483
Nantucket Dr 29485
E Nash St 29485
Nathan Ct & Rd 29483
Nathaniel Rd 29485
Navaho Blvd & Cir 29483
Neal St 29483
Nelson Ct 29483
Netherfield Dr 29485
Nettles Ln 29483
New Ct 29485
New Ashley Blvd 29485
New Bridge Ln 29483
New Haven Ct 29485
New Hope Dr 29485
New Spring Ct 29485
New Valley Rd 29485
Newcastle Ct 29485
Newground Ln 29483
Newington Rd 29485
Newton Rd & Way 29483
Niblick Rd 29483
Nifty Bar Ln 29485
Night Hawk Ln 29485
Night Heron Ct 29485
Noble Dr 29485
Nonabel St 29483
North Ln 29483
Northpark Ave 29485
Nottingham Ct 29485
Nuttall Dr 29485
Nutty St 29485
Nyna Joy Way 29485
O Mar Sue Ln 29483
O Sullivan Ln 29483
O T Wallace Dr 29483
Oak Cir 29485
Oak Dr 29483
S Oak St 29483
Oak Haven Pl 29485
Oak Leaf Rd 29483
Oak Village Ln 29485
Oakbluff Rd 29483
Oakbrook Ln 29483
Oakdale Dr 29483
Oakridge Dr 29483
Oakwood Dr 29483
Obannon Ct 29485
Okatee Dr 29483
Old Bridge Ln 29483
Old Country Club Rd 29483
Old Course Rd 29483
Old Dairy Ln & Rd 29483
Old Dorchester Trl 29485
Old Glory Ln 29485
Old Golf Rd 29483
Old Holly Ln 29483
Old Landmark Ln 29483
Old Parsonage Rd 29483
Old Post Ln 29483
Old Postern Rd 29483
Old Summerville Rd 29483
Old Tavern Ln 29483
Old Tower Rd 29483
Old Trolley Rd 29485
Old Winter Rd 29483
Oldbury Rd 29485
Oleander Way 29485
Olin Cir 29485
Olympic Club Dr 29483
Omalley Dr 29483
Omni Dr 29483
Omoooo Ln 29483
Oolong Ln 29483
Oran Ln 29483
Orangeburg Rd 29483
Orbit Ln 29483
Orchard Ct 29485
Orchard Park Dr 29485
Oriole Ct & St 29485
Osage Way 29483
Out Of Bounds Dr 29485
Outrigger Ct 29485
Overcup Loop 29485
Owens Cir 29483
Owens Dr 29485
E Owens Dr 29485
Oxford Rd 29485
Oxford Way 29485
Oyster Bay Dr 29483
Pacolet St 29485
Paddock Way 29483
Padgett Cir 29483
Paisan Rd 29485
Paladin Dr 29485
Palm Ct 29483
Palmer Rd 29483
N & S Palmetto St 29483
Palmetto Point Dr 29485
Palzita Ln 29485
Pamela Ln 29483
Paradise Pt 29485
Paradox Pl 29483
Paris Ln 29485
Parish Parc Dr 29485
Park Ln 29483
W Park Ln 29483
Parkway Ave 29483
Parkwood Dr 29485
Parniece St 29483
Parris Ct 29483
Parrott Ave 29483
Parrum Ct 29483
Parsons Rd 29483
Partridge Cir 29485
W Partridge Run 29483
Partridge Creek Rd 29483
Patrick Ln 29483
Patriot Ln 29483
Patriot Pl 29485
Patron Pl 29485
Paul Dr 29485
Pavilion St 29485
Pawley Dr 29483
Peace Ave 29485
Peaceful Ln 29485
Peacher Ct 29483
Peachtree Dr 29485
Peacock Ln 29485
Peacock Pl 29485
Peake Ln 29483
Peartree Cir 29485
Pebble Creek Blvd 29485
Pebble Creek Rd 29485
Pebbles Ln 29485
Pecan Dr 29483
Pekoe Ct 29483
Pelham Dr 29483
Pelican Ct & Ln 29485
Pelzer Dr 29485
Pemberly Blvd 29483
Pemberton Rd 29485
Pendarvis Ln 29485
Peninsula Pointe 29485
Pennyroyal Ct 29483
Pernell Ct 29483
Perritte Cir 29485
Perry Dr & Ln 29483
Persian Ln 29485
Pete Ewers Dr 29483
Peters St 29483
Peters Creek Dr 29483
Peytons Way 29483
Pheasant Ln 29485
Phoebe Rd 29483
Photinia Ct 29483
Picadilly Loop 29483
Pickens St 29485
Pickett Ct 29483
Pickett Fence Ln 29485
Pidgeon Bay Rd 29483
Pierre Ct 29483
Pike Dr 29483
Pimpernel St 29483
E Pinckney St 29485
Pine Ct 29483
Pine Ln 29485
N Pine St 29483
S Pine St 29483
W Pine St 29483
Pine Bluff Dr 29483
Pine Forest Blvd 29483
Pine Grove Ave 29483
Pine Valley Dr 29483
Pinecrest Blvd 29483
Pineforest Blvd 29485
Pinehurst Ave 29483
Pineland Ln 29485
Pineridge Rd 29483
Pinethicket Dr 29485
Pinewood Ct & Dr 29485
W Pinnacle Way 29485
Pintail Dr 29483
Pinto Ln 29483
Pioneer Br & Pt 29483
Pipestone Dr 29485
Pittsburg Lndg 29485
Plain St 29483
Planet Rd 29483
Plank Ct 29483
Plantation Cir & Dr 29485
Plantation House Rd 29485
Planters Row Ln 29485
Players Cir 29485
Plumtree Ln 29483
Poconos Ct 29485
Poinsettia Ave 29483
S Pointe Blvd 29483
Pointe Cir 29483
Pointe Of Oaks Rd 29485
Pointer Dr & Ln 29485
Pond Hill Ct 29485
Pond Pine Trl 29485
Ponderosa Rd 29483
Pondside Ct 29485
Pony Ct 29483
Pooh Ln 29483
Popcorn Ln 29483
Poplar Cir 29483
Poplar Grove Pl 29483
Poppy Pl 29485
S & E Port Dr & Ln 29483
Portal Ct 29485
Postell Dr 29483
Pottery Cir 29485
Powell Dr 29483
Prairie Ln 29483
Pratt Ct 29485
President Cir 29483
Presidio Bnd 29483
Presley Ln 29483
Pressley Ave 29483
Pressley Hill Ln 29483
Prestwick Ct 29483
Prim Rose Path 29483
Primate Ln 29483
Prince Edward Dr 29483
Prince Thomas Rd 29483
Princess Ct 29485
Pringle Ln 29483
Pristine Ct 29485
Proprietors Ct 29485
Providence Way 29483
Pruitt St 29483
Pryors Ln 29485
Puddle Duck Cir 29485
Pullman Ave 29483
Purple Martin Trl 29485
Putnam St 29483
Putter Ct 29483
Pye Ln 29483
Quail Dr & Ln 29485
Quality Dr 29483
Quarter Horse Cir 29483
Queen Mary Ct 29485
Queens Ct 29485
Quendon Ct 29485
Quest St 29483
Quiet Ln 29483
Quiet Bay Ln 29483
Quinby St 29483
Quince Cir 29483
Quintan St 29483
Rabbit Hill Rd 29483
Rabbit Run Ln 29483
Race Club Rd 29483
Rackaway Dr 29483
Racquet Ln 29485
Radcliff Cir 29483
Rafter Ln 29483
Rail Dr 29483
E Railroad Ave 29485
Rainbow Rd 29483
Raith Rd 29485
Rambo Dr 29483
Ramelias Dr 29485
Rampart Rd 29483
Ramseys Ln 29483
E Randolph St 29483
Ranworth Ln 29485
Ravens Wood Rd 29485
Ravenwood Ct 29485
Rawlins Dr 29485
Reagan Dr 29483
Rebellion Rd 29483
Red Barn Ln 29483
Red Bay Ln & Rd 29485
Red Fox Run 29485
Red Hill Ct 29483
E, N, S & W Red Maple Cir 29485
Red Oak Cir 29483
Redpoint Ln 29483
Redwood Ct 29483
Reed St 29483
Reed Hall Rd 29483
Refiner Cir 29485
Regency Oaks Dr 29485
Regent Ct & St 29485
Reign Aly 29485
Remleys Pt 29485
Renau Blvd 29483
Reserve Way 29485
Retriever Ln 29485
Rexford Ct 29485
Reynard Ct 29485
Reynolds Rd 29483
Rhetts Way 29485
Rhonda Dr 29483
Ribbon Rd 29483
Richard Dr 29483
E Richardson Ave
100-399 29483
500-699 29485
W Richardson Ave 29483
E & W Richland St 29483
Riddle Ct 29485
Ridge Rd 29483
Ridge Church Rd 29483
Ridge Lake Dr 29483
Ridgedale Rd 29483
Ridgemont Way 29485
Ridgeway Way 29483
Ridgewood Ct 29485
Riley Dr & Ln 29483
Ripley Ct 29483

Ripple Rd	29483
Rising Mist Dr	29483
River Birch Rd	29485
River Ridge Dr	29485
Riverbed Ln	29483
Riverwood Ln	29485
Riviera Dr	29483
Roadster Row	29483
Robbie Ln	29485
Roberta Dr	29485
Roberts Rd	29483
Robeson Pl	29485
Robin Ct & St	29485
Robins Nest Way	29485
Rock Dr	29483
Rocking Horse Ln	29483
Rockport Ct	29483
Rockys Ln	29483
Rodeman Rd	29483
Rodeo Dr	29483
Rohan Trl	29483
Roiley Ln	29483
Rolling Meadows Dr	29485
Rookery Ct	29483
Rooster Ridge Rd	29485
Rosa St	29483
Rosalee Dr	29483
Rosario Dr	29483
Rose Dr	29483
Rose Ln	29485
Rose Creek Ln	29485
Rosedale Ct	29485
Rosings Dr	29483
Rowe Ln	29483
Royal Palm Way	29485
Royal Star Rd	29483
Royal Troon Ct	29483
Royle Rd	29483
Royle Cove Ct	29483
Ruby St	29483
Ruffin Ct & Rd	29483
Rundle Ln	29483
Running Branch Ln	29483
Runnymede Ln	29485
Russell St	29483
Rustlers Ct	29483
Ruston Pl	29485
Ruth Anne Dr	29483
Rutherford St	29483
Rutland Rd	29483
Sabal Ct	29483
Saber St	29483
Sacora Ln	29483
Saddle Ln & Trl	29483
Saddlehorn Rd	29483
Sage Ln	29483
Sagebrush Ln	29483
Sago Palm Ct	29483
Sailfish Way	29485
Saint Awdry St	29485
Saint Benets Pl	29485
Saint Claire Ln	29483
Saint Germain Dr	29483
Saint James Ave	29483
Saint James Pl	29485
Saint Phillips Row	29485
Salem Ct & Rd	29483
Salinas Ct	29483
Salisbury Dr	29483
Salkahatchie St	29485
Sally Ln	29483
Sallyport Ct	29485
Salt Meadow Ln	29483
Salters Ln	29485
Salterton St	29485
Sam Ln	29483
Samuels Ln	29485
Sanctuary Park Dr	29483
Sand Bunker Ct	29483
Sand Dollar Ln	29483
Sand Dune Trl	29483
Sandel Ln	29483
Sanderson Ln	29483
Sandhill Path	29483
Sandlewood Dr	29483
Sandman Dr	29483
Sandtrap Rd	29483
Sandtuck Cir	29483
Sandy Hook Ct	29483
Sandy Run Cir	29483
Sangaree Pkwy	29483
Sangaree Park Ct	29483
Santee Ct	29483
Santee Tower Rd	29483
Sarmiento Ln	29483
Sasportas Ln	29483
Sassafras Ln	29483
Sassafrass Ct	29485
Saturn Ct	29483
Savannah River Dr	29485
Savannah Round	29485
Sawmill Ct & Dr	29483
Sawtooth Ln	29483
Sawtry Pl	29485
Scalybark Rd	29485
Scarborough Ct	29485
Scarlet Ct	29485
Scaup Ct	29485
Schieble Way	29483
School House Ln	29483
Schooner Bend Ave	29483
Schoonover Dr	29483
Schultz Lake Rd	29483
Scotch Range Rd	29483
Scotland Dr	29483
Scott Ct	29483
Scrapbook Ln	29483
Sea Foam St	29483
Sea Lavender Ln	29483
Seasaw Ct	29485
Seavington Ct	29483
Sebring St	29483
Sedgewick Rd	29483
Seewee Ct	29483
Sellars Cir	29483
Semester Ln	29483
Seminole Dr	29483
Seminole Way	29483
Seneca River Dr	29485
Seneco St	29483
Senrab Blvd	29483
Sequoia Dr	29485
Serendipity Ln	29485
Serenity Cove Ln	29483
Setter Ln	29483
Seven Oaks Ln	29485
Shad Row	29485
Shadow Brook Dr	29485
Shady Ln	29483
Shady Pine Ln	29485
Shady Tree Ln	29483
Shadybrook Dr	29483
Shaftesbury Ln	29485
Shamrock Dr	29483
Shante Cir	29483
Shaun Ln	29483
She Crab Ct	29483
Shea St	29483
Shed Ln	29483
Sheep Island Rd	29483
Sheffield Ln	29483
Shelbourne Ct	29483
Shellmore Trl	29483
Shenandoah Ct	29483
Shenandoah Ln	29483
E & W Shepard Ln & St	29483
Sherry Ct	29485
Shiloh Ct	29483
Shinnecock Hill Ct	29485
Shirley Ct	29485
Shitanc Dr	29483
Shoal Creek Ct	29483
Shop Rd	29483
Short St	29483
Short Woods Ct	29483
Shoveler Pl	29485
Siesta Ln	29483
Sigma Dr	29483
Silver Cypress Cir	29485
Silverwood Ln	29483
Simmons Ave	29483
Sinclair Rd	29483
Sioux Ct	29483
Six Iron Ln	29483
Skeet Rd	29483
Skelton Rd	29483
Skid Pole Ln	29483
Skidaway Rd	29485
Slam Dunk Ln	29483
Slate Stone Dr	29483
Sleepy Hollow Ct	29483
Slidel St	29485
Smilax Ln	29483
W Smith St	29485
Smith Creek Ln	29483
Smithfield Ave	29483
Smooth Pebble Ct	29483
Smythe Dr	29485
Snead Ln	29485
Soaring Way	29483
Sojourner Ln	29483
Solar Cir	29483
Sommett Blvd	29483
Sonteeya Ln	29483
Southside St	29483
Spaniel Ln	29483
Spear St	29483
Spearhead Ct	29483
Spectrum Rd	29483
Split Pine Ct	29483
Spring Rd	29483
Spring St	29483
Spring House Rd	29483
Spring Meadows Dr	29485
Spring Water Rd	29483
Springbrook Ct	29485
Springdale Ct	29483
Springdale Dr	29485
Springfarm Pl	29485
Springview Ln	29485
Sprucewood Dr	29483
Spy Glass Hill Ct	29483
Spyglass Dr	29483
Squire Ct	29485
Squirrel Hollow Ct	29483
Stack Ln	29483
Stadium Cir	29483
Stafford Springs Ct	29483
Stagecoach Ln	29483
Staley Dr	29485
Staley Ln	29485
W Stall St	29485
Stallsville Rd	29485
Starlifter Dr	29483
Starline Dr	29483
Starling St	29483
Starr Rd	29483
Starter Horse Dr	29483
State Rd	29483
State Park Rd	29483
Stay Awhile Ln	29483
Steel Bridge Ln	29483
E & W Steele Dr	29483
Steep Bank Ln	29483
Steeple Point Ct	29485
Stephanie Cir	29483
Stephen Ct	29483
Sterling Ln	29483
Sternside Run Ave	29483
Stewart Pl	29485
Stinney Ln	29483
Stockbridge St	29483
Stockport Cir	29483
Stone Ct	29483
Stone Gate Ln	29483
Stonewall Ct	29483
Stonewall Dr	29483
Stoneybrook Ct	29485
Storey Rd	29483
Stratford Dr	29483
Streamside Rd	29485
Strobel Ln	29483
Stuart Ct	29485
Sugar Mill Ct	29485
Sugarmaple Ln	29483
Sugarpine Pl	29485
Sugarplum Dr	29485
Summer Place Ln	29483
Summer Ridge Dr	29485
Summer Trace Dr	29485
Summer View Rd	29483
Summercourt Dr	29485
Summerset Ln	29483
Summit Retreat Dr	29485
Sumner Rd	29485
Sumners Aly	29485
Sumpter Hill Dr	29483
Sumter Ave	29485
Sun Valley Ct	29483
Sunburst Way	29483
Sundance Ct	29483
Sunnyside Way	29483
Surrey Ave	29485
Surrey Dr	29483
Susan Dr	29485
Sutherland Pl	29483
Swan Dr	29483
Swanson Dr	29483
Sweat Ln	29483
Sweatman Ln	29483
Sweet Tea Ln	29483
Sweetbriar Rd	29485
Sweetgum Dr	29485
Swift Ct	29485
Swiftwater Way	29483
Swordfish Way	29485
Swordgate Ct	29485
Sycamore Dr	29485
Sylvan Ter	29483
T J Ln	29483
Tabby Ln	29485
Tabby Creek Cir	29483
Tabler Ln	29483
Tallow St	29483
Tally Ho Ct	29485
Tanager St	29483
Tandil Ct	29483
Tangier Pl	29485
Tapp Ln	29483
Tasker Dr	29483
Taylor Dr	29485
Tea Farm Rd	29483
Tea Olive Ct	29485
Teakwood Ct	29485
Teal Ct	29483
Teddy Ct	29485
Tee Pee Ct	29483
Teesdale Ct	29483
Telfair Ct	29483
Telford Ct	29483
Telscombe Ct	29485
Temuco Ln	29483
Ten Acre Way	29483
Tennyson Way	29485
Terrapin Cir	29483
Terry Ave	29485
Testie Ln	29483
Thames Ave	29485
Thelma Dr	29485
Thicket Ct	29485
Thomas Dr	29483
E Thomas St	29485
Thomaston Ave	29485
Thornhill Dr	29485
Thornton Dr	29485
Thoroughbred Ct	29485
Thorpe Rd	29483
Thousand Oaks Ct	29485
Thrasher Dr	29485
Three Iron Dr	29483
Three Wood Ln	29483
Thrush Ln	29485
Thunderbird Dr	29485
Thunderbolt Dr	29485
Tidal Creek Ct	29483
Tideland Industrial Park	29483
Tierra Loop	29483
Tiffany Ln	29485
Tiger Ln	29483
Tillman Branch Rd	29483
Tillmans Ln	29483
Tim Ln	29483
Timberlake Ct	29485
Timberlane Dr	29485
Timicuan Way	29483
Tin Can Aly	29483
Tinston Ct	29483
Tipp Ln	29483
Tiptoe Ln	29483
Toddler Trl	29485
Todds Way	29483
Tom Pike Ln	29485
Tom Wesley Ln	29483
Tomahawk Dr	29483
Tomaka Dr	29483
Tony Ln	29483
Torrey Ln	29485
Torrey Pines Dr	29483
Tortoise St	29483
Totem Ct	29483
Tothill Dr	29485
Toutant Ct	29483
Towhee Dr	29485
Town Woods Trce	29483
Towne Square Rd	29485
Townsend Way	29483
Trade Center Pkwy	29483
Trade Zone Blvd	29483
Traders Station Rd	29483
Trailway Dr	29483
Train Dr	29483
Tram Blvd & Ct	29483
Tranquil Waters Way	29483
Travelers Blvd	29485
Travelers Rest Blvd	29485
Treasure Ln	29483
Tree Branch Cir	29483
Tree Canopy Dr	29485
Trellis Ct	29483
Trenholm Dr	29483
Trescott Ct	29483
Trestlewood Dr	29483
Tricias Misty Ln	29483
Trickle Dr	29483
Trigard Ln	29483
Trillium Ave	29483
Trim Rose Ln	29483
Trinity Dr	29483
Tripp St	29485
Tristen Ct	29485
Trolley Aly	29483
Trotters Blvd	29485
Trotters Club Way	29483
Trotters Run Rd	29483
Truluck Ln	29483
Tryon Dr	29485
Tucker Rd	29483
Tudor Rd	29483
Tugboat Ln	29483
Tulip St	29483
Tulip Street Ext	29483
Tunnel Rd	29483
Tupalo Dr	29483
Tupelo Dr	29485
Tupper Ln	29483
Tupperway Dr	29483
Turkey Nest Ln	29483
E & W Turner St	29483
Turner Field Way	29485
Turtle Bay Ct	29483
Turtle Cove Rd	29483
Turtle Point Rd	29483
Turtle Pond Rd	29483
Tweed Ct	29483
Twig Ln	29483
Twin Lakes Dr	29483
Twin Tree Dr	29483
Two Wood Ct	29483
Two Woods Trce	29483
Tyger St	29485
Tyner Trl	29483
Tyrick Pl	29483
Tyron Rd	29483
Tyvola Dr	29483
U Of K Way	29485
Umbria Dr	29483
Upcerne Rd	29483
Upshur Ct	29483
Valentin Dr	29483
Varner St	29483
Varner Estate Ln	29483
Varnfield Dr	29483
Venice St	29483
Veno Ln	29483
Venture Dr	29483
Veranda Dr	29485
Verbena Ave	29483
Verlou Dr	29483
Vicksburg Dr	29483
Victor Ct	29483
Victoria Rd	29483
Victoria Pointe Ln	29485
Victory Ln	29483
Villa Sq	29485
Village Way	29483
Village Crier Ln	29485
Village Green Cir	29483
Village Stone Cir	29483
Vine St	29483
Vineyard Blvd	29483
Vintage Ln	29483
Violet Dr	29483
Virginia Ave	29485
Vision Ln	29483
Vista Ct	29485
Volk Ln	29485
Volunteer Ln	29483
Von Oshen Rd	29485
Wachovia Ct	29485
Waddling Way	29483
Wade Ct	29483
Wadmalaw Cir	29483
Wahoo Dr & Rd	29485
Wainwright Mnr	29485
Walden Ridge Way	29485
E & W Walker Dr	29483
E Walnut Cir	29485
W Walnut Cir	29485
N Walnut St	29483
S Walnut St	29483
Walnut Creek Rd	29483
Walnut Hill Dr	29485
Walton Pl	29485
Walton Grove Rd	29483
Wampee Curv	29485
Wancy Cir	29483
Wanda Ave & Dr	29485
Wando Dr	29483
Wannamaker Ave & Cir	29485
Wappoolah Dr	29483
War Trace Ct	29485
Warbler Ln & Way	29483
Ward Ln	29483
Wardfield Ln	29485
Wards Dr	29485
Waring Rd	29485
Waring St	29485
Waring Ter	29483
Warington St	29483
Warrell Cir	29485
Washington Town Rd	29483
Wassamassaw Rd	29483
Water St	29483
Waterford Ln	29483
Waterfront Park Dr	29483
Waterlily Way	29483
Waterside Landing Way	29485
Watson Rd	29485
Wax Myrtle Ln	29485
Waylon Dr	29483
Weathers Ct	29483
Weber Rd	29483
Webster St	29483
Weeping Willow	29483
Weir St	29483
Welcome Ct	29483
Wellington Rd	29485
Welwyn Rd	29485
Wendy Way	29485
Wescott Blvd	29485
Wescott Club Dr	29485
Wessex Ter	29485
Westbrooke Rd	29483
Westbury Ln	29483
Westbury Mews Dr	29485
Westminster Ave	29485
Westmoreland St	29483
Westoe St	29483
Weston Hall Dr	29485
Westside St	29483
Westvaco Rd	29483
Wexford Ct	29483
Wexton Ct	29485
Whaler Rd	29485
Wheatfield Dr	29485
Wheeler Rd	29483
Whickline Ln	29483
Whippoorwill Dr	29483
Whispering Trl	29485
Whispering Breeze Ln	29485
White Blvd	29483
White Church Ln	29485
White Fence Ln	29483
White Gables Dr	29483
White Heron Ln	29485
White Pine Way	29485
White Water Ct	29483
Whitehall Rd	29485
Whitehouse Rd	29483
Whitetail Ln	29483
Whitfield Ct	29485
Whitlow Blvd	29483
Whooping Crane Ln	29483
Wicker Ct	29485
Wickford Ct	29485
Wide Awake Cir	29483
Wigmore St	29485
Wigwam Way	29485
Wilcox Ct	29483
Wild Cherry Ln	29485
Wild Goose Trl	29483
Wilderness Ln	29483
Wildflower Way	29485
Wildgame Rd	29483
Wiley Bottom Ct	29485
Willard Ln	29483
Willet Dr	29483
William St	29483
Williams Family Dr	29483
Willis Ln	29483
Willow Ct	29483
Willow Brook Ln	29483
Willow Oaks Ln	29483
Willowbend Ln	29483
Wilson Dr & St	29483
Wilsons Creek Dr	29483
Wilton Dr	29483
Wilverine Dr	29485
Winding Brook Ln	29483
Winding Trail Ln	29483
Windjammer Dr	29483
Windjoy Ct	29483
Windsong Dr	29483
Windsor Ct	29485
Winged Foot Ct	29483
Winningham Rd	29483
Winslow Ln	29483
Winston Cir	29483
Winter Dr	29483
Wise Rd	29483
Wisteria Ct	29483
Witt Ln	29483
Wodin Pl	29483
Wolfhound Ln	29483
Wood Side Dr	29483
Woodbridge Dr	29483
Woodduck Dr	29483
Woodlake Dr	29485
Woodland Dr	29485
Woodlawn Cir	29483
Woodrow Rd	29483
Woodthrush Rd	29485
Woodward Blvd	29485
Woodwin Cir	29483
Wragg Ln	29483
Wren Ct	29483
Wrigley Blvd	29483
Wyatt Ln	29485

Wylie St 29483
Wyman Blvd 29485
Wyndham Dr 29485
Wynfield Forest Dr 29485
Yahweh Ln 29483
Yancy Rd 29485
Yarrow Ct 29485
Yaupon Holly Cir 29483
Yearling Dr 29483
Yellow Hawthorn Cir 29483
Yemassee St 29483
Yerby Rd 29483
Yonges Ct 29483
York Ct 29485
Yorkshire Dr 29483
Young Dr 29483
Zinnia Ct 29483

NUMBERED STREETS

E & W 1st North 29483
E & W 2nd North 29483
E & W 2nd South 29483
E 3rd North St
100-599 29483
600-799 29485
W 3rd North St 29483
E & W 3rd South 29483
E & W 4th North 29483
E & W 4th South 29483
E & W 5th North 29483
W 5th South St 29483
E & W 6th North 29483
E & W 6th South 29483
E & W 7th North 29483
E & W 8th North 29483
E & W 9th North 29483

SUMTER SC

General Delivery 29150

POST OFFICE BOXES MAIN OFFICE STATIONS AND BRANCHES

Box No.s
All PO Boxes 29151

NAMED STREETS

Abbey Hall Ct 29154
Abel Rd 29150
Aberlour Dr 29154
Abiathar Ct 29154
Acacia Dr 29150
Acme Ln 29150
Acres Ave & Cir 29153
Adams Ave 29150
Addison St 29153
Adger Ln 29154
Adirondack Ct 29153
Admiral Dr 29150
Adolf Cir 29153
Adrian Cir 29153
Agnes St 29153
Aidan Dr 29154
Aignathser 29153
Airport Rd 29153
Albemarle Ct 29154
Albert Dr 29150
Albert Spears Dr 29150
Alder St 29153
Aldersgate St 29150
Alexander Pl 29150
Alice Ct 29150
Alice Dr
1-1299 29150
1500-1699 29153
Aliyah Ct 29154
Allen Dr 29150
Allene Rd 29154
Alligator Branch Rd 29153
Allison Brook Ln 29153
Alma Dr 29150
Almond Rd 29154
Alpine Dr 29154
Althea Cir 29150
Alva Dr 29154
Amanda Cir 29154
Amberwood Dr 29150
Ambrose Dr 29153
Amelia Dr 29154
Amerson St 29153
Amherst Ct 29154
Amidala Ln 29153
Ammons Rd 29153
Amonn Rd 29153
Amos Ct 29154
Amy Ln 29154
Anabell Dr 29154
Anburn Dr 29154
Anderson St 29150
Andiron Dr 29150
Andrena Dr 29150
Andrews St 29150
Andria Ln 29154
Angel Oak Dr 29150
Aniline Ct 29154
Annapolis Way 29154
Anne Park 29150
Anson Ct 29150
Antlers Ct & Dr 29150
Antrim Ct 29154
Appaloosa Dr 29154
Apple St 29153
Apple Hill Ln 29153
Appliance Rd 29153
Arabian St 29154
Arborwood Dr 29154
Arbutus Ct 29150
Archdale Dr 29150
Ard Ln 29150
Arkansas Dr 29153
Arlington Rd 29153
Armstrong Blvd 29150
Arnaud St 29150
Arnold Ave 29150
Arrowhead Dr 29150
Artesian Dr 29150
Arthur Rd 29154
S Artillery Dr 29150
Ash St 29150
Ashby Rd 29154
Ashleigh Collins Trl 29150
Ashley St 29150
Ashlynn Way 29154
Ashtonmill Dr 29154
Athena Ct 29150
Atlantic St 29150
Atwell St 29153
Aubrey Cir 29153
August Dr 29154
Aull St 29153
Aurora Dr 29154
Authority Ln 29153
Avalon Ct & Dr 29154
Avin Rd 29154
Aylesbury Cv 29150
B P Dr 29153
Babette Rd 29154
Bagnal Dr 29150
Baigo Ct 29153
Bailey St 29150
Bainbridge Rd 29153
Baker St 29150
Balclutha Ln 29153
Bald Pate Cv 29150
Baldwin Dr 29150
Balmoral Ct 29154
Bamburgh Way 29154
Banaca Cir 29150
Bancroft Dr 29154
Banff Springs Ct 29150
Bank Ln 29154
Bar Zee Dr 29154
Barefoot Ct 29150
Barfield Rd 29154
Barkley Rd 29150
Barnette Dr 29150
Barney Ln 29153
Barnwell Dr 29154
Barrett Cir 29154
E & W Bartlette St 29150
Barton St 29150
Barwick Rd 29150
Bass St 29150
Bates Rd 29150
Batty Way 29154
Bay Blossom Ave 29150
Bay Springs Dr 29154
Bayside Dr 29154
Beachforest Dr & Way 29153
Beacon Ct & Dr 29154
Bear St 29153
Beaufain Dr 29150
Beck Ave 29150
Beckridge Dr 29154
Beckwood Rd 29153
E & W Bee St 29150
Beech Creek Dr 29154
Belflower Ln 29150
Believers Path 29150
Belk St 29153
Bell Rd 29153
Belles Mill Rd 29154
Belmont Dr 29150
Belton Ct 29150
Belvedere Cir 29154
Ben St 29150
Bendale Rd 29153
Benelli St 29150
Benjamin Ln 29150
Bennington Dr 29154
Benton Ct & Dr 29150
Bermuda Rd 29154
Bernice Ct 29154
Berry St 29153
Bertha Cir 29153
Best St 29150
Bethel Church Rd 29154
Betsy Ln 29150
Beulah Cuttino Rd
1800-3099 29150
3100-3299 29154
3300-3399 29150
Biddle Rd 29153
Biloba Cir 29153
Birkdale Cir 29154
Birnie Cir 29150
Bishop Dr 29153
Bismuth Dr N & S 29150
Bittersweet Ln 29153
Black Oak Ct 29154
Black Walnut Ct 29154
Blackberry Ln 29154
Blackwell Ct 29150
Blair Ln 29150
Blanche Rd 29154
Bland Ave 29150
N & S Blanding St 29150
Blenhein Ct 29154
Blossom View Rd 29153
Blueberry Cir 29154
Bluebird St 29153
Bluegrass Ct 29150
Boardwalk 29150
Bob White Dr 29154
Bobcat Trl 29153
Bobs Dr 29150
Boise Lewis Rd 29153
Bonnell Dr 29154
Bonview Dr 29150
Booker St 29150
Boone Ln 29153
Boots Branch Rd 29153
Bordeaux Ave 29153
Bors St 29154
Boulevard Rd 29153
Bowen Ct & Dr 29150
Bowman Dr 29150
Bracey Ct 29150
Bradd St 29150
Bradford St 29150
Bradham Blvd 29153
Bragg Way 29150
Bramble Ln 29154
Branch St 29150
Brand Ct & St 29150
Brandon Cir 29154
Brandy Ct 29154
Breezy Bay Ln 29150
Brent St 29150
Brentwood Dr 29150
E & W Brewington Rd 29153
Briar Bend Ct & St 29154
Briar Branch Rd 29150
Briarwood Dr 29150
Bridge Ct 29150
Bridgepointe Dr 29154
Brigatine Dr 29154
Brighton Ct 29154
Bristol Cir 29154
British Ln 29153
Brittany Dr 29154
Britton Rd 29153
Britton Brogdon Rd 29153
Broad Ct 29150
Broad St
112A-112C 29150
1-3399 29150
3400-6299 29154
Broadwater Dr 29150
Brockenton St 29150
Brogdon Cir 29153
Brogdon St 29150
Brookgreen Rd 29154
Brookland Dr 29154
Brooklyn St 29150
Brooks St 29150
Broome St 29154
Brost Ct 29154
Brothers Ln 29150
Brown Ct & St 29150
Brownfield Way 29150
Browning Ridge Dr 29154
Browntown Rd 29153
Bruce Cir 29154
Brunhill Ct, Ln & St 29150
Brunson St 29150
Brunswick Rd 29153
Brushwood Ct & Dr 29154
Brutsch Ave 29154
Bryant Rd 29153
Bryn Mawr Pl 29150
Bryson Ct 29153
Buchanan St 29153
Buckhorn Dr 29150
Buckingham Blvd 29153
Buckshot Ln 29153
Buford St 29150
Builders Rd 29154
Bullfrog Ln 29153
N Bultman Dr 29150
Bum Hill Ln 29154
Bunneau St 29153
Burgess Ct 29150
Burgess Glen Mhp 29154
Burkett Dr 29150
Burning Tree Rd 29154
Burns Dr 29150
Burntfield Rd 29153
Burress St 29150
Burrows Rd 29153
Bush Branch Rd 29154
Business Cir 29153
Butler Ln 29150
Buttercup St 29150
Butterworth Cir 29154
Byrd St 29153
C Farm Ln 29153
Cabelas Pl 29150
Cadbury St 29154
Cains Mill Rd 29154
Caitlynn Dr 29154
Caldwell St 29150
Caledonia Ct 29154
E & W Calhoun Dr, Pl & St 29150
E Calhoun Street Ext 29153
California Blvd 29153
Callen Dr 29150
Cambridge Dr & Sq 29150
Camden Rd 29153
Camellia St 29150
Cameron Ct 29154
Camp Branch Rd 29153
Campbell Ct 29154
E & W Canal St 29150
Canberra Dr 29153
Candlelite Ct 29154
Cannalilly Ln 29154
Canty Ln & St 29150
Canvasback Cv 29150
Capetown Dr 29153
Capital Ln 29154
Capri Dr 29150
Caradenc Rd 29154
Caraway Ct 29153
Cardinal St 29150
Carissa Dr 29154
Carl Ave 29150
Carlos Ct 29154
Carnegie St 29153
Carnoustie Dr 29154
Caroland Dr 29150
Carolina Ave 29150
Carolina Mhp 29154
Carolyn Dr 29154
Carriage Dr 29154
Carrol Dr 29150
Carter Rd 29150
Carver St 29150
Casey Ln 29153
Cashew Ln 29153
Caslee St 29153
Cassena Ct 29150
Castle Rock Dr 29153
Cathryn Ave 29153
Catie Cir, Ct & St 29150
Cayman Ct & St 29154
Cecil St 29150
Cedar Ave 29150
Cedarwood Cir & Dr 29154
Center St 29150
Cessna St 29150
Champaca Ct 29154
Champagne Ln 29153
Chandler St 29150
Chanson Ct & Ln 29154
Chappell Cir, Ct & St 29150
Charity Ln 29154
Charles Ln & St 29150
Charleston Ave 29154
E & W Charlotte Ave 29150
Chartwell Ct 29150
Chatwick Ct 29150
Chelsey Ct 29154
Cherokee Rd 29150
Cherry St 29150
Cherry Hill Ct 29150
Cherryvale Dr 29154
Cheryl Dr 29154
Chesterfield Dr 29154
Chestnut St 29150
Chestnut Mhp 29154
Cheyne St 29153
Chickasaw Dr 29150
Childrens Ln 29154
China Ln 29154
Chinaberry Ln & Rd 29153
Chinquapin Dr 29150
Chippewa Cir 29150
Chism Ln 29153
Chivalry St 29154
Choice Ct 29154
Chokos St 29150
Christina Apts 29150
Christine Dr 29150
Christopher Ct 29154
Church Ct & St 29150
Churchill Dr 29153
Circle J Mhp 29153
Circleview Dr 29154
Citrus Dr 29153
Clara Louise Kellogg Dr 29153
Claremont Ln & Rd 29154
Clay St 29154
Clematis Cir, Ct & Trl 29150
Clement Rd 29150
Cleveland St 29150
Clifton Rd 29153
Clinton St 29150
Clipper Rd 29154
Clover St 29154
Club Cir & Ln 29154
Club Forest Ct 29154
Coachman Dr 29154
Coastal Dr 29150
Cobblestone Rd 29154
Cockerill Rd 29154
Coffey St 29153
Colar Ln 29153
Colclough Plantation Rd 29153
Coldice Ct 29150
Coleman St 29153
Coley Ln 29150
E & W College St 29150
Collingwood Ct & Dr 29154
Collins St 29150
Colonial Dr 29150
Colony Cir & Rd 29153
Columbia Cir 29154
Comings Rd 29153
Commander Ct & Rd 29153
Commerce St 29150
Community St 29150
Companion Ct 29150
Computer Cir 29153
Concord Cir 29153
Concord Church Rd 29153
Cone St 29150
Confederate Rd 29154
Congruity Rd 29153
Constance St 29150
Constitution Dr 29154
Continental Dr 29154
Contractors Ct 29154
Converse St 29153
Conway Dr 29153
Conyers St 29150
Cook St 29150
Coon Ridge Rd 29154
Copeland St 29150
Copley Dr 29154
Coral Way 29150
Corbett St 29150
Corn Ct & Rd 29150
Cornell St 29154
Cornfield Dr 29154
Corona Ct 29153
Corporate Cir & Way 29154
Cory Dr 29153
Cosmo Ln 29154
Cottage Path 29153
Cottingham Dr 29154
Cotton Rd 29153
Cotton Acres Rd 29153
Cotton Tail Ln 29150
Council Ln & St 29150
Country Ln 29154
Country Springs Dr 29150
Country Squire Ct 29154
Courtney Ct 29154
Covent Garden Dr 29153
Covey Pt 29150
Covington St 29150
Cowboy Ln 29153
Cox Rd 29154
Cozy Ln 29153
Crabapple Ct 29150
Craig Rd 29153
Crandall Rd 29153
Crape Myrtle Cir 29154
Creed St 29150
Creek Side Dr 29150
Creekfield Rd 29154
Crescent Ave 29150
Crestwood Dr 29154
Croft St 29154
Cromer Dr 29150
Cross St 29154
Crossfield Rd 29154
Crosson Hunter Dr 29154
Crosswell Dr 29150
Crowndale Ct & Dr 29150
Crowson St 29150
Cubbage Rd 29153
Cubbryant Ln 29153
Cumberland Way 29150
Currituck Ct & Dr 29153
Curtis Dr 29153
Curtiswood Dr 29150
Cutleaf Dr 29150
Cuttino Rd 29150
Cuz Rd 29153
Cynthia Ln 29153
Cypress St 29150
D C Ln 29154
D Family Rd 29153
Dabbs St 29150
Dads Ln 29154
Daisy Dr 29150
Dale St 29153
Damascus Rd 29153
Dancona Dr 29150
Danny Ct & St 29154
Dant St 29150
Danville Ln 29153
Daphne St 29153
Dargan St 29150
S Darlington Hwy 29153
Dartmouth Dr 29153
Daufaskie Ct & Rd 29150
David Ct 29153
Davis St 29150
Dbar Cir 29154
Deacon St 29150
Debidue Ln 29150
Debora Dr 29150
Decatur St 29150
Declaration Blvd 29154
Degroot Rd 29154
Delage Ct 29154
Delaine St 29150
Delores Rd 29154
Delorme Ct 29150
Delray St 29154
Demetrius Ln 29153
Derek Dr 29154
Derwent Dr 29154
Deschamps Rd 29154
Desmond Dr 29150
Deveaux Rd 29154
Devonshire Dr 29154
Dew Dr 29153
Dewees Ct & St 29150
Diamond T Cir 29150
Dibert St 29153
Dicks St 29150
Dickson Ave 29153
Diebold Dr 29153
Dillon Trace St 29153
Dingle St 29150
Dink St 29150
Dixie Dr 29150
Dobson St 29150
Doby St 29150
Dock Rd 29153
Dogwood Dr 29150
Dollard Ct & Dr 29150
Don St 29150
Donnie St 29154
Dorcel St 29150
Dorethia St 29154
Dorn St 29150
Dorsey Dr 29154
Douglas St 29150
Dove St 29150
Dover Cir 29154
Dow Ln 29150
Dowling St 29153
Drake St 29153
Driftwood Ct 29154
Dubose St 29150

Dubose Siding Rd 29153
Duck St 29150
Ducom Dr 29154
Dugan St 29150
Duke Dr 29153
Dunbarton Dr 29154
Duncan St 29150
Dunk Dr 29153
Dunway Dr 29150
Durant Ln 29150
Dusty Cir & Rd 29150
Dutch Branch Rd 29154
Dwyer Rd 29150
Dyson Ct 29153
Eagle Rd 29154
Earl Ln 29150
Earle St 29150
Earline Ct 29153
Early St 29154
Earnhardt Ln 29154
East St 29150
Eastern School Rd 29153
Eastwood Dr 29153
Eaton Blvd 29153
Ebenezer Rd 29153
Echo Springs Ct 29154
Eddie Ln 29154
Edenwood Dr 29154
Edgar Dr 29150
Edgehill Rd 29154
Edgehill Apts 29154
Edgewater Dr 29150
Edgewood Dr 29150
Edisto Ct 29154
Edmunds Dr 29154
Edwards St 29150
Eisenhower Ct 29150
Elbow Cir 29153
Elder Ln 29153
Eleanor Dr 29154
Electric Dr 29153
Elfin Ave 29150
Elkhorn Cir & Trl 29154
Ellen Dr 29150
Ellerbee St 29150
Elrae Ln 29153
Em Ru Ct 29150
E & W Emerald Lake
Dr 29153
Emily Dr 29150
Engleside St 29150
English St 29150
English Turn Dr 29150
Enter St 29153
Erskine Ct 29154
Ervin Ln 29154
Escallonia Dr 29154
Essex Dr 29154
Estate Cir & St 29150
Eternity Ln 29154
Ethel Ln 29154
Eugene St 29153
Eureka Way 29153
Evans Ter 29150
Eveningshade Ln 29154
Evinrude Dr 29154
Excitement Ln 29154
Ezell Ct 29150
Fagan St 29150
Fair Ct 29150
Fair Forest Dr 29150
Fairfield St 29150
Fairlawn Dr 29154
Faith Way 29154
Faith Acres Mhp 29154
Falcon Dr 29150
Falling Water Ln 29154
Fantasy Cir 29154
Farmers Cir & Rd 29154
Farmview Ct 29153
Farrier Ct 29150
Father Ln 29153
Fawn Cir 29150
February Ln 29153
Felder St 29153
Fellow Ln 29154
Fenimore Dr 29150
Fern Ct 29150
Ferrell Rd 29153
Firestone Ct 29150
Fish Rd 29154
Flagg St 29153
Flagstick Ct 29154
Flake Dr 29153
Flamingo Rd 29153
Fleming St 29153
Fletcher Dr 29153
Floral Ave 29150
Florence Hwy 29153
Floride St 29153
Floyd Dr 29154
Foliage Ln 29150
Follin Dr 29154
Folsom St 29150
Fontana Dr 29154
Ford St 29154
Forest Dr 29154
Forest Lake Ct & Dr 29154
Fort St 29153
Fossil Ln 29153
Four Bridges Rd 29153
Foxcroft Cir 29154
Foxridge Ct 29150
Foxworth St 29150
E & W Foxworth Mill
Rd 29153
Frances Kinlock Cir 29154
Frank St 29150
Frank Clarke St 29150
Frank Hastie Ln 29150
Franklin Ln & St 29150
Frazier St 29154
Frederick Ct 29150
Freedom Blvd 29154
Freeman St 29150
French Williams Rd 29153
Fricker Ln 29150
Frisco Branch Rd 29154
Frodo Cir 29153
Frost Wood Ct 29154
Fulton St 29153
E Fulton St 29150
W Fulton St 29150
Furman Cv, Dr, Pl &
Rd 29154
G St 29150
Gabby Ln 29154
Gable Ct 29150
Gaddy Ct & St 29150
Gadson St 29150
Gadwall Cir 29150
Gafton Cir 29154
Gaines Rd 29153
Galahad Ln 29153
Galicia St 29154
Galloway Ln 29154
Gamble St 29150
Gandalf Cir 29153
Garden St 29150
Gardner Rd 29153
Garners Ferry Rd 29154
Garrett St 29150
Garrison Cir & St 29154
Gates St 29150
Gatewood St 29150
Gayle St 29150
Gaymon Rd 29153
Geddings Cir & Rd 29150
Genbyrd Rd 29150
Gene Dr 29154
Generette Rd 29153
Genoa Dr 29153
George Washington
Blvd 29154
Georgetown Ave 29154
Georgianna Dr 29150
Geraint Rd 29154
Gerald St 29150
Gertrude Ct & Dr 29150
Gibbons St 29153
Gibbs Dairy Rd 29154
Gilbert St 29150
Gilligan Rd 29154
Gin Branch Rd 29154
Gina Ln 29154
Ginger Ln 29154
Gingko Dr 29150
Ginhouse Dr 29154
Gion St 29150
Girard Dr 29150
Gladys Ln 29150
Glastonbury Rd 29154
Gleaton St 29150
Glen Abbey Ct 29150
Glendale Ct
1-97 29150
400-599 29153
Glenn St 29154
Glenwood Dr 29153
Glider Ct 29150
W & E Glouchester Ct &
Dr 29150
Godwin St 29153
Gold Ct 29154
Gold Wing Rd 29153
Golden Bay Dr 29154
Golden Rod Rd 29154
Goldeneye Rdg 29150
Golduck Rd 29150
Golfair Ct & Rd 29154
Golfcrest Rd 29154
Good Neighbor Mhp 29154
Goodson Rd 29153
Gordon St 29150
Gordonia Dr 29150
Goshen Cir & Rd 29153
Grace Ln 29153
Granada Dr 29154
Grandeur Ct 29154
Grange Rd 29150
Granite Ct 29153
Grantham St 29150
Granville Ct 29150
Gravel Rd 29153
Gray Fox Ct & Trl 29154
Graystone Dr 29150
Green Ln 29150
Green Swamp Rd 29150
Green View Pkwy 29150
Greenville Cir 29154
Grier St 29150
Griffin Ln & St 29154
Grimble Ct 29150
Gristmill Ln 29150
N & S Guignard Dr &
Pkwy 29150
Guildford St 29153
Guinea Run 29154
Gulf St 29150
Guyton Dr 29150
Gwendale Rd 29154
H St 29150
Habitat Ct & Dr 29153
Hackberry Ct 29150
Hagan St 29150
Hager St 29150
Haile St 29150
Haley Ave 29150
Hallman Ct 29153
Hallmark Ln 29154
Hammond Rd 29154
E & W Hampton Ave 29150
Hancock Dr 29154
Hannah Ct & St 29153
Hanover Ct 29150
Harborview Dr 29153
Harby Ave 29150
Hard Pack Rd 29154
Hardaway Ln 29153
Hardee Cv 29150
Harlequin Cv 29150
Harmony Ct 29153
Harper St 29153
Harrell Rd 29150
Harriett Rd 29153
Harris St 29150
Harrison St 29150
Harry Ave 29150
Hartwell Dr 29153
Harvey Dr 29150
N & S Harvin St 29150
Harwood Dr 29154
Hasel St 29150
Hastings Dr 29150
Hatfield St 29150
Hathaway Dr 29154
Hatteras Way 29153
Hattie Ln 29153
Hauser St
1-299 29150
303-399 29153
Haven Dr & Rd 29150
Havenwood Ct & Dr 29150
Hawkins Rd 29153
Hawkins St 29150
Hawks Cv 29150
Hawthorne St 29150
Haynsworth St 29150
Heather Ct & Ln 29154
Heavens Trl 29154
Hedgewood Dr 29154
Helen Ln 29150
Henderson St 29150
Henrietta St 29150
Henry Cir 29154
Herbal Way 29153
Herbert Cir 29150
Heritage Rd 29150
Hermitage Dr 29150
Hess Ln 29150
Heyward St 29150
Hialeah Pkwy 29154
Hickory Rd 29154
Hidden Bay Dr 29154
Hidden Haven Rd 29154
Hideaway Ct & Dr 29154
High St 29150
Highland Ave 29150
Highview St 29154
Highway 15 N 29153
Highway 261 N 29154
Highway 521 S 29153
Hill Rd 29153
Hill Lake Dr 29150
Hilldale Dr 29154
Hilliard Dr 29150
Hilltop St 29150
Hilton Rd 29150
Hinson St 29150
Hiperformance Ln 29154
Hobbit Way 29153
Hobson St 29153
Hodge St 29154
Holiday Dr 29153
Holloway St 29153
Holly Dr 29154
Holman Rd 29153
Holmes Gardner Rd 29153
Holy Ln 29150
Home Place Rd 29154
Homestead Rd 29153
Honeysuckle Ln 29150
Honeytree Dr 29150
Hope Ct 29154
Horace Ln 29150
Horizon Ct & Dr 29154
Horne Rd 29154
Horseshoe Cv 29150
Hort St 29153
Hospital Cir 29150
Houck St 29150
Howard St 29153
Hoyt Hts & St 29150
Hub Cap Ln 29154
Huckabee Rd 29150
Huddersfield Dr 29154
Hudson St 29150
Hudson Graham Rd 29150
Hugo Ln 29153
Hunt Club Ct & Rd 29154
E & W Hunter St 29153
Hunters Point Ct 29150
Huntington Ct 29154
Hurley Dr 29150
Huron Ct & Dr 29150
Hutchins St 29150
Hwy 15 S 29150
Hynes St 29150
Idaho Dr 29153
Ideal Cir 29154
Ideal Mhp 29154
Idlelake Ct 29150
Ikesha Rd 29153
Ikeylah Ln 29154
Illery Rd 29153
Imperial Way 29153
Inabinet Dr 29154
Independence Ave 29153
Indigo Cir & Dr 29154
Industrial Blvd 29150
Inglewood Dr 29150
Ingram St 29150
Innisbrook Ct 29150
Inverness Ct 29154
Isadore Nathaniel Dr 29154
Island Ct & Dr 29154
Ithica Dr 29154
Ivey St 29150
J J Ct 29150
J J Roberts Dr 29154
Jabari Ln 29153
Jackie Ln 29154
Jackson St 29150
Jacob Cir 29154
Jake Rd 29153
James St 29153
James Quincy Ct 29154
Jameson Pl 29154
Jan Ave 29153
Janie St 29154
Jasmine St 29150
Jb Ln 29153
Jed Ct 29150
Jefferson Rd 29153
Jenkins St 29150
Jennifer Ct 29153
Jensen Rd 29154
Jereco Rd 29153
Jerin Way 29150
Jernigan Trl 29154
Jerry St 29153
Jessamine Trl 29150
Jessamyn Rd 29153
Jessica Dr 29154
Jimmie St 29150
Joann Dr 29154
Joe Billy Rd 29153
John St 29150
John Franklin Rd 29154
Johnson Aly & Ln 29150
Jonathan St 29150
Jones St 29150
Jordan St 29150
Joseph St 29150
Josh Wells Ct & Rd 29154
Joyce St 29154
Jubilee Dr 29150
Julius Ln 29154
Junebug Ln 29154
Justin Ln 29153
K St 29150
Kaempfer Cir 29153
Kannon Dr 29150
Kari Dr 29154
Katherine Ct 29150
Kathlean Rd 29153
Katwallace Cir 29154
Katydid St 29154
Keegan Ln 29153
Keels Rd 29150
Keith Rd 29154
Kelly Ave 29150
Kelsey Rd 29153
Kelvin Ln 29150
Kendal Ave 29154
Kendrick St 29150
Kenilworth Ave 29150
Kent Pl & St 29150
Kentwood Ct & Dr 29154
Kenyon Ave 29150
Ketch Ave 29154
Kettlewood Ct 29153
Kevin Rd 29153
Kiawah Ln 29150
Kilgo St 29150
Killarney Ln 29150
Killdee Dr 29154
Kilpatrick Dr 29154
Kimani Ln 29153
Kindness Ln 29154
King St 29150
Kingdom Ave 29150
Kingman St 29150
N Kings Hwy 29154
Kings Pointe Ct & Dr 29154
Kingsbury Dr
200-599 29150
600-2199 29154
Kinsey Cir & Dr 29150
Klepin Ct 29154
Knightbridge Rd 29150
Kolb Rd 29154
Kopac Cv 29154
Kshawn Ln 29154
L St 29150
Lacosta Ct 29150
N & S Lafayette Dr 29150
Lagavulin Dr 29154
Lake Ashwood Rd 29153
N & S Lake Cherryvale
Dr 29154
Lake Shore Dr 29150
Lakeside Dr 29150
Lakeview Dr 29154
Lakewood Cir, Ct & Dr 29154
Lala Ln 29153
Lamorak St 29154
Lancaster Dr 29153
Landmark Ct & Dr 29154
Landscape Ln 29154
Lanel Dr 29150
Lanford Way 29153
Lang Jennings Dr 29150
Lantern Ln 29154
Larkin St 29150
Larry Ln 29153
Last Chance Dr 29154
Lathan Ct 29150
Lauderdale Ln 29154
Laurel St 29150
Laurens Ave 29154
Laval Ct 29150
Laverne St 29153
Law Range 29150
Lawrence St 29150
Lawson St 29150
Lawton Cir 29150
Lazy Ln 29150
Leach Dr 29154
Leaning Tree Rd 29153
Lee St 29150
Leeds Ct 29154
Lees Mhp 29153
Leflore Dr 29154
Lefty Ln 29153
Legare St 29150
Legette St 29150
Leland Ln 29150
Lemmon St 29150
Lenoir St 29150
Lenox Cir 29153
Lens Heavins Rd 29154
Leonard Brown Rd 29153
Lesesne Ct & Dr 29150
Lester St 29153
Letcher Rd 29153
Level Ln 29153
Levi St 29150
Leviner Ln 29153
Lewis Cir & Rd 29154
Lexus Ln 29153
E Liberty St
1-399 29150
400-999 29153
W Liberty St 29150
Lightingflats Ln 29154
Lightwood Rd 29154
Lilac Ct 29150
Lilbaby Ln 29153
Lillie Dr 29153
Lillington Dr 29150
Lime Ln 29150
Lin Do Ct 29150
Lin Ran Ln 29153
Lincoln Ave 29150
Lindella Rd 29154
Linden Ln 29154
Lindley Ave 29150
Line St 29153
Linwood St 29153
Lirope Way 29154
Lisa Dr 29154
Lisbon Dr 29154
Little John Ln 29153
Livingston St 29150
Livingwood Ln 29154
Lloyd Dr 29154
Lodebar Rd 29153
Logan St 29150
Logic Ln 29153
Lois Ln 29150
Loman Rd 29150
London Rd 29153
Lone Rogers Ln 29153
Long Barn Ct 29154
Longleaf Dr 29154
Longview Rd 29154
Longwood Dr 29154
Lookout Cv 29154
Lorene Dr 29154
Lorentz Dr 29154
Loretto Dr 29150
Loring Dr 29150
Loring Mill Rd 29150
Lost Creek Dr 29154
Louella Ln 29154
Louise Cir 29150
Love St 29150
Lowder Rd 29153
Lowerlake Ct & Dr 29150
Lowfalls Ln 29150
Lowoods Ln 29154
Lucas Ct & St 29153
Lucianlake Dr 29154
Lucky Ct 29154
Lulu Ln 29150
Luton St 29154
Lynam Rd 29154
Lynette Dr 29154
Lynn Ln 29153
M And N Rd 29153
Ma Ln 29153
Macy St 29153
N & S Magnolia St 29150
Magnum Dr 29150
Maidenhair Ln 29153
N Main St
2-310 29150
311-999 29150
311-311 29151
312-998 29150
1000-3399 29153
S Main St 29150
Mainersi Rd 29153
Maize St 29154
Malibu St 29154
Mallard Dr & Rst 29150
Mallory Ct & Dr 29154
Malone Dr 29154
Mana Dr 29154
Manchester Cir & Rd 29154
Mandarin Cir 29150
Maney St 29150
Manhattan Ave 29150
Manning Ave & Rd 29150
Maple St 29153
Maplecreek Dr 29154
Maplewood Dr 29150
March St 29154
Marden Rd 29154
Margie Ln 29150
Marie Dr 29153

Marigold Ct & St	29150
Marilyn Ave	29153
Marion Ave	29150
Marion Ln	29153
Market St	29150
Marlborough Ct & Dr	29154
Marley Ct	29150
Marsand Ln	29154
Marsden Pl	29154
Marshall St	29150
Marshall Cemetery Rd	29154
Martatison Ln	29153
Martha Ct	29150
Martin St	29153
Martinville Church Rd	29153
Marwood Dr	29154
E & W Mary St	29150
Marywood Ln	29153
Mason Rd	29150
Mason Croft Dr	29150
Massingale Ln	29153
Masters Dr	29154
Mathis St	29150
Matthew Singleton Cir	29154
Matthews Dr	29154
Mattison Ave	29150
Maxwell Ave	29150
May Ln	29154
Mayberry Ln	29153
Mayfield Dr	29154
Mayflower Ln	29150
N & S Mayrant Cir & Ct	29154
Mcarthur Dr	29150
Mccathern Ave	29154
Mccleary Ln	29150
Mccormick Dr	29150
Mccrays Mill Rd	
1961B2-1961B2	29150
400-1999	29150
2000-4599	29154
Mcduffie St	29150
Mcfaddin St	29150
Mcinnis Store Rd	29153
Mcintosh Ct	29154
Mckay St	29150
Mckeiver Rd	29153
Mclean St	29153
Mcleod St	29150
Mcqueen St	29150
Meadow Cir	29150
Meadow Ct	29154
Meadow Dr	29154
Meadowbrook Rd	29153
Meadowcroft Dr	29154
Medical Ct	29150
Meehan St	29150
Mellette St	29154
Melodie Ln	29153
Meltons Ln	29153
Melvin Ave	29153
Memorial Ave	29153
Mere Ct	29150
Merganzer Pt	29150
Mesquite Cv	29153
Mickens St	29153
Middle St	29150
Midway St	29154
Mikayla Ln	29153
Mikom Rd	29153
Mill House Rd	29154
Mill Run Ct	29154
Miller Ln & Rd	29150
Millstone Dr	29154
Millwood Rd	29150
N & S Milton Rd	29150
Mimarie Ln	29153
Mimosa Rd	29150
Mims Rd	29153
Mineral Cir	29153
Minutemen Ln	29154
Missouri St	29153
Mistletoe Ln	29154
Mitchell St	29150
Mitchum Ln	29154
Mockingbird Ln	29150
Mohican Dr	29150
Moise Dr	29150
Mona Ct	29154
Monoghan Ct	29154
Monroe St	29150
Montague Ct	29150
Montana Dr	29153
Montclare Rd	29154
Monte Carlo Ct	29150
Monte Carlo Ln	29153
Montecello Ln	29154
Monterey Dr	29154
Montgomery St	29154
Montpelier Ln	29154
Montreat St	29150
Mood Ave	29150
Mooneyham Rd	29153
Moonlite Dr	29153
Moore Rd	29153
E Moore St	29150
W Moore St	29150
Moorhill Estate Ct & Dr	29154
Mordred St	29154
Morehead Pl	29150
Morgan Ave	29150
Morningside Dr	29153
Morris Way Dr	29154
Morton St	29150
Moses Ln	29154
Moses Mhp	29154
Mossberg Dr	29150
Mothers Ln	29150
Mount Vernon Dr	29154
Muddy Water Ln	29154
Muirfield Ct	29150
Mulberry Church Rd	29153
Muller Dr	29153
Munn St	29153
Munn Brown Rd	29153
Muriel St	29154
Murphy St	29150
Murray St	29150
Muscovy Trl	29150
Musket Trl	29150
Myers St	29150
Myrtle St	29150
Myrtle Beach Hwy	29153
Naimah Ln	29153
Nancy Ct	29153
Nandina Dr	29153
Naomi Ct	29154
Nash St	29150
Nathaniel St	29150
National St	29150
Nautical Dr	29154
Nazarene Church Rd	29154
Neal St	29150
Neeley St	29150
Nelson St	29150
Nettles Rd	29154
Nevada Ct	29153
New Castle St	29154
E & W Newberry Ave	29150
Newlevy Dr	29154
Newman St	29150
Niblick Dr	29154
Nicholas Dr	29153
Nicholson Dr	29153
Nicole Ln	29153
Night Owl Ln	29154
Nimmich Ln	29150
Nixon Rd	29153
No More Rd	29153
North St	29150
Northgate Dr	29154
Northwestern Ave	29150
Nottingham Dr	29153
Nuzzle Ln	29153
Nyree Way	29154
Oak Rd	29154
Oak Brook Blvd	29150
Oak Haven Ct	29154
Oak Hill Rd	29154
Oakcrest Rd	29154
E Oakland Ave	29150
W Oakland Ave	
1-1999	29150
2000-2699	29154
Oakland Dr	29154
Oaklawn Mhp	29154
Oakridge Ct	29154
Oakview Dr	29150
Oasis Ct	29150
Oatfield Ct & Rd	29154
October Cir	29153
Oklahoma Dr	29153
Old Castle St	29154
Old Field Rd	29150
Old Ford Dr	29154
Old Goodson Rd	29153
Old Manning Rd	29150
Old Pocallo Rd	29150
Old Spring Ct & Rd	29154
Old Stone Rd	29150
Old W Liberty St	29150
Old Whites Mill Rd	29153
Old York Rd	29153
Oleander Ct & Dr	29154
Olin Goode Dr	29153
Olive St	29150
Omarest Rd	29153
Oneal Ln	29153
Ootie Ct	29153
Orange St	
1-99	29150
40-40	29153
42-99	29153
100-123	29150
107-115	29153
124-198	29153
125-199	29150
Orchard Pl	29150
Oriole Cir & Ct	29150
Orlando Cir	29154
Orvis Ct & St	29154
Osteen Ln & Rd	29154
Oswego Hwy	
1-749	29150
750-799	29153
800-899	29150
900-4099	29153
Ott St	29153
Owens Dr	29150
Oxford St	29150
P And P Ln	29153
Pack Rd	29150
Paddock Ct	29154
Padme Dr	29153
Page Dairy Rd	29153
Paige Dr	29154
Paisley Park	29150
Palmer Dr	29153
Palmetto St	29150
Palomino Cir	29154
Pantego Dr	29154
Paper Birch Ave	29150
Par Ct	29154
Paradise Ln	29153
Paralee Cir	29154
Parish St	29150
Park Ave	29150
Park Homes Ct	29153
Parker Dr	29150
Parliament Ct	29154
Parsons Ln	29154
Partridge Dr	29153
Paschal Ln	29153
Pat Dr	29150
Pathfinder Dr	29153
Patience Ln	29153
E & W Patricia Dr	29150
Patriot Pkwy	29154
Patton Dr	29153
Paul St	29153
Pauline Dr	29153
Pava Ln	29153
Pawleys Ln	29150
Pawn Shop Cir	29154
Peace St	29150
Peach St	29150
Peach Orchard Rd	29154
Peacock Dr	29154
Pear St	29150
Pearl Ct	29154
Pearson Rd	29150
Pebble Brook Rd	29153
Pecan Ct	29154
Pelfrey Rd	29153
Pelham Dr	29154
Pembroke Ct	29153
Pendar Ln	29153
Penn St	29150
Penny Ln	29154
Peppercorn Ln	29154
Pepperidge Ct & Dr	29154
Periwinkle Ct	29153
Perkins Ave	29150
Perry Blvd	29154
Pheasant Dr	29153
Phelps St	29150
Pheriba Ln	29153
Phifer St	29150
Philadelphia Way	29154
Phill Ford Rd	29153
Phillips St	29150
Photina St	29154
Physicians Ln	29150
Picardy Dr	29150
Pickens Ct	29150
Pickwick Ct	29154
N Pike E	29153
N Pike W	29153
S Pike E	
2-698	29150
S Pike E	
1202-1298	29153
1300-1399	29153
S Pike W	29150
Pinckney St	29150
Pine St	29150
Pine Manor Ct	29150
Pinecone Dr	29154
Pinecrest Dr	29153
Pinefield Rd	29154
Pinehill Mhp	29150
Pineneedle Ct	29150
Pinewood Rd	
1-399	29150
400-4600	29154
4602-4602	29154
Pinnacle Ct	29154
Pinson St	29150
Pintail Dr	29150
Pioneer Ct & Dr	29150
Pipkin Rd	29154
Pistol Ln	29150
Pittman Dr	29154
Pitts Rd	29154
Plainfield Ct	29154
Plains Mhp	29150
Plantation Dr	29154
Planters Dr	29154
Plemons Ln	29150
Plowden Rd	29153
Plowden Mill Rd	29153
Pocalla Rd	29150
Pocotaligo Dr	29150
Poinsett Dr	29150
Point Dr	29154
Polaris Dr	29150
Poley Bridge Ln	29153
Pond Loop Rd	29154
Poole Rd	29154
Poppy Ct	29150
Porcher Dr	29150
Porter St	29153
Portsmouth Dr	29150
Possum Hollow Way	29154
Potomac Dr	29153
Poulas St	29150
Powers St	29150
Powhatan Ct & Dr	29150
Pratt Ave	29153
Preot St	29150
Prescot Dr	29150
Preserve Ct	29150
President St	29150
Presidio Dr	29154
Pressley Rd	29153
Prestwick Ct	29150
Pridgen Ln	29154
Primrose Ct	29150
Pringle Dr	29150
Pritchard Ln	29150
Privateer Ln	29154
Professional Ct	29150
Progress St	29153
Promise Ln	29153
Prosser Ave	29153
Providence St	29150
Pulpit St	29150
Pumpkin Ln	29150
N & S Purdy St	29150
Putter Dr	29150
Pyracantha Rd	29154
Pyramid Ct	29154
Quail Run	29154
Quail Roost Ct	29154
Quandry Rd	29150
Quarter Mile Rd	29153
Que St	29153
Queen St	29150
Queen Chapel Rd	29153
Questria Dr	29154
Quiet Ct & Ln	29154
Raccoon Rd	29154
Race Track Rd	29153
Radcliff Dr	29150
Radical Rd	29153
Ragin Rd	29150
Rainbow Dr	29154
Rainey Ln	29150
Ramsey Rd	29154
Ramsgate Ct	29154
Rast St	29150
Ravenel St	29153
Ravenwood Dr	29154
Raybrown Dr	29154
Rayfarms Rd	29153
Raymond St	29150
Raymond Jenkins St	29153
Reams Ave	29153
Reaves St	29150
Rebecca Cv	29153
Red And White St	29150
Red Apple Ln	29153
E Red Bay Rd	
1-299	29150
300-499	29153
W Red Bay Rd	29150
Red Bud Park	29150
Redstone Dr	29154
Reed St	29150
Reese St	29150
Regency Ct	29154
Rembert Ln	29153
Rembert Church Rd	29153
Remington Dr	29154
Renda Ln	29153
Reona Ave	29154
Reptile Rd	29153
Reshema Ln	29153
Retriever Ln	29153
Revolutionary Way	29154
Reynolds Rd	29153
Rhea Dr	29150
Rhododendron St	29154
Ribbon Ct & Rd	29150
Richardson St	29150
Richburg Ct	29150
Richland Rd	29154
Richwood Dr	29153
Ridgehill Dr	29154
Ridgeway St	29153
Rifle Ln	29154
Riggs Rd	29153
Riles Ct	29154
Riley St	29150
Ripper Ln	29153
River Birch Dr	29150
Rivers Rd	29153
Riverside Dr	29153
Robbins Ave	29150
Robert Dinkins Rd	29150
Robert Perry Rd	29153
Robertha Ln	29154
Roberts Ln	29153
Robin Hood Ave	29153
Robinson Ln & St	29150
Robney Dr	29150
Roche Rd	29153
Rock St	29154
Rockdale Blvd & Ct	29154
Rodgwin Rd	29153
Rogers Ave	29150
Rolling Creek Dr	29153
Rolling Hill Ln	29150
Ronda St	29154
Roosevelt Cir & Rd	29150
Rose Dr	29154
Rose Ln	29150
Rosemary Ct	29150
Rosewood Dr	29154
Rovena St	29150
Rowland Ave	29150
Roxbury Ct	29150
Royal Ave	29150
Royal Colwood Ct	29150
Ruby Ln	29153
Ruger Dr	29150
Running Deer Ln	29153
Runnymede Blvd	29153
Rushmore Ct	29154
Russell Dr	29150
Ruth St	29153
Rutland Rd	29153
Rutledge St	29150
Rye St	29150
Rytts Mhp	29153
Sabre Dr	29153
Saddle Trail Dr	29154
Sadie Ln	29153
Sage St	29153
Saint Augustine Dr	29150
Saint Edmunds Dr	29150
Saint Julien Dr	29154
Saint Kennedy Rd	29154
Saint Marks Cir & Rd	29154
Saint Matthews Church Rd	29153
N & S Saint Pauls Church Rd	29154
N & S Salem Ave	29150
Salters Rd	29153
Salters Town Rd	29153
Saltwood Rd	29154
Sam Gillespie Blvd	29154
Sam Smith St	29150
Sampson St	29150
Samuel St	29150
Sand Iron Ct	29154
Sandalwood Ln	29154
Sanders Dr	29150
Sandhill Dr	29154
Sandspur Dr	29154
Sandy Run Dr	29153
Sanford Dr	29153
Sans Souci Rd	29154
Santa Fe Trl	29154
Santee Dr	29153
Saratoga St	29150
Saresden Cv	29150
Sassafras Dr	29150
Savage Run	29154
Sawgrass Ct	29150
Sawmill Dr	29150
Scales Rd	29154
Scapeore Ln	29153
School St	29150
Scoop Cir	29153
Scotkins Ct	29150
Seabrook Rd	29154
Seales Ln	29150
Search Ln	29153
Sears St	29150
Seay Ct	29154
Seddon Dr	29150
Seidler Dr	29154
Seilder Dr	29154
Selma Ln	29154
Seminole Rd	29150
Senate Ln	29154
September Dr	29154
Sequoia Dr	29154
Seven Oaks Ln	29150
Shadow Trl	29150
Shady Brook Ct	29154
Shaginaw Ct	29153
Shallowford Rd	29154
Shannon St	29150
Sharolyn St	29154
Shaw St	29153
Shaw Oaks Mhp	29154
Shedricks Ln	29153
Sheffield Ct	29154
Shem Cv N & S	29150
Shephard St	29150
Sherry Ln	29150
E & W Sherwood Dr	29153
Shetland St	29153
Shipwatch Dr	29154
Shirer St	29150
Shirley P Dr	29154
Shivone Ln	29153
Shoreland Dr	29154
Short St	29150
Short Leaf St	29154
Shuler Dr	29150
Sidjohn Rd	29154
Sierra St	29154
Sigmon Way	29154
Significant Dr	29154
Silo Rd	29150
Silver St	29150
Simmons Dr	29154
Simpson Rd	29153
Sims St	29150
Sing Dr	29154
Singleton Ln	29154
Sisters Ln	29150
Skardon St	29154
Sky Ln	29154
Slick Willie Dr	29154
Slidingrock Ln	29150
Smalls Dr	29154
Smiley Rd	29154
Snowden St	29150
Soeven Pl	29154
Solomon Rd	29153
Somerset Dr	29150
Sound St	29150
South St	29150
Southern Hills Ct & Dr	29150
Southgate Dr	29154
Spann St	29153
Sparkleberry Ct & Ln	29150
Spaulding Ave	29150
Spider Ct	29150
Spring Dr	29153
Spring St	29150
Spring Lake Ct & Dr	29154
Springdale Way	29150
Springvalley Cir & Dr	29154
Spruce Ln	29153
Stadium Rd	29154
Stamey Livestock Rd	29153
Stanford Dr	29154
Stanley Ct & Rd	29154
Stanton Ct	29153
Stark St	29150
Starks Ferry Rd	29154
State St	29150
Stateburg Hills Dr	29154
Stelle St	29150
Stephen Tindal Dr	29154
Steppingstone Path	29150
Sterling St	29153
Stern Dr	29150
Stewart St	29150
Stick Ln	29154
Stillwater Ct	29153
Stone Ln	29150
Stonecroft Dr	29154
Stonehedge Ct	29154
Stonewood Dr	29154

Storage Rd 29153
Storestreet Rd 29153
Strange St 29153
Stratford Dr 29154
Stratton Ct 29154
Stubberfield Dr 29154
Stuckey St 29150
Suber St 29154
Summer Ct 29153
Summit Dr 29150
Sumter Hwy 29153
N Sumter St 29150
S Sumter St 29150
Sun Valley Dr 29154
Sunflower Ct 29154
Sunhurst Ct 29154
Sunset St 29150
Susan St 29154
Susie Rembert St 29150
Sussex Dr 29150
Swallow Dr 29154
Swamp Fox Run 29150
Swamp Mill Cir 29154
Swan Lake Dr 29150
Sweet Olive Ct 29154
Sweetbriar Ct & Dr 29154
Swimming Pen Rd 29153
Swinton Rd 29153
Switchback Rd 29153
Sylvan Way 29150
Taffy Ln 29154
Tahoe Dr 29150
Tailback Rd 29153
Talisker Dr 29154
Talisman Dr 29154
Tall Oak Rd 29154
Tally Ln 29150
Tamarah Way 29154
Tameka Ln 29153
Tanager Trl 29150
Tanglewood Rd 29154
Tantay Trl 29154
Tara Dr 29150
Taylor St 29153
Teal St 29150
Tearcoat Branch Rd 29153
Temple Rd 29153
Terry Rd 29150
Terwood Mhp 29154
Teton Rd 29154
Thatcher Ct 29154
Theatre Dr 29150
Thelma St 29150
Theodore Rd 29154
Thistledown Ct & Dr 29154
Thomas Dr 29150
Thomas Sumter Hwy 29153
Thompson Ln 29153
Thorntree Dr 29150
Thumb Ln 29153
Thunderbolt Rd 29153
Tickleweed Ln 29150
Tidewater Dr 29150
Tie Dr 29153
Tifton Ct 29150
Tiger Ln 29154
Tiger Lily Rd 29153
Tiller Cir 29150
Timberlane Ct 29154
Timmerman St 29150
Timmons St 29153
Tindal Ct & Rd 29150
Titanic Ct 29154
Titus Cir 29150
Tobacco Rd 29153
Toby Ct 29153
Tolkien Ln 29153
Tondaleia Dr 29153
Toole St 29150
Toonsie Dr 29150
Torrey Pines Dr 29150
Tot Ln 29153
Town House Ct 29150
Township Dr 29153
Toxoway Dr 29154
Tradd Cir 29150
Trailmore Cir 29154
Trailwood Ct & Dr 29154
Tram Rd 29153
Travis Ct 29154
Treetop Ct & Ln 29154
Trigger Ln 29154
Trillium Ln 29154
Tripp Dr 29153
Tristan St 29154
Troy Ln 29154
Trufield Dr 29153
Truitt St 29150
Tryon St 29150
Tuckaway Dr 29154
Tucson Cir & Dr 29150
Tudor St 29150
Tulip St 29153
Tullah Dr 29153
Tumbleweed Ct 29150
Tupelo Ln 29153
Turkey St 29150
Turnberry Ct 29150
Turner Ln 29154
Turnrow Ct 29154
Twelve Bridges Rd 29150
Twilight Dr 29150
Twin Lakes Dr 29154
Tyler Ln 29153
Underwood Rd 29154
Union Camp Blvd 29154
Unity Ct 29153
University Dr 29150
Urban Dr 29150
Utah Cir 29153
Valleybrook Ct & Rd 29154
Van Buren St 29150
Vanterid St 29150
Vaughn St 29150
Velletrude Dr 29150
Veranda Dr 29150
Vernon Dr 29150
Vesper Ct 29150
Victory Dr 29150
Village Ct 29154
Vinca Ct & St 29154
Vining Rd & St 29150
Vintage Ct & Dr 29154
Virginia Dr 29150
Vitex Ct 29153
Vivian Rd 29150
Volunteer Ct 29150
Wactor St 29150
Wade St 29154
Wadford St 29150
Wagon Cir 29150
Wagram Dr 29154
Walcora Dr 29150
Walden Cir & Dr 29154
N & S Walker Ave & Ln 29150
Walking Horse Ln 29154
Wall St 29150
Wallace St 29150
Walmart Blvd 29150
Walsh Grv 29150
Walter Ave 29153
Walter Conyers Ln 29154
Walton St 29150
Wardland Rd 29154
Warehouse Blvd S 29150
Warley St 29150
Warren Ct & St 29150
Warwick Ct & Dr 29154
N & S Washington St 29150
Water Song Run 29150
Waterlily Dr 29154
Wateroak Ln 29150
Waterway Dr 29154
Waterwheel Dr 29154
Watkins St 29150
Watson Ct 29153
Watts Dr 29154
Waverly Cir & Dr 29150
Waycross Cir 29153
Wayne St 29150
Waynick St 29153
Weary Rd 29153
Weatherly Ct & Rd 29150
Webb Ave & St 29150
Wedgefield Rd 29154
Weeks St 29150
Weldon Dr 29150
Wellington Rd 29153
Wells Ct 29154
Wells Rd 29153
Wellsboro Ct 29154
Welman Cir 29153
Wen Le Ct & Dr 29150
Wendemere Dr 29153
Wesley Hall Ct 29154
E & W Wesmark Blvd & Ct 29150
West Ln 29150
Westbury Mill Rd 29153
Westfield Ct 29154
Westmoreland Rd 29154
Westwood Dr 29154
Whatley St 29154
Wheat St 29154
Wheeler St 29154
Wheelwright Ct 29150
Whiffet Ln 29150
Whipporwill Dr 29154
Whispering Pines Mhp 29154
Whitash Ct 29154
White St 29150
White Horse St 29150
White Oak Park 29150
White Pine Ct & Way 29154
Whitehall Dr 29154
Whites Mill Rd 29153
Whitney Dr 29154
Widgeon Way 29150
Widman Dr 29154
Wildberry Ln 29154
Wilder St 29150
Wilds Park Cir 29154
Wildwood Ave 29154
Wilkie St 29153
Willcroft Ct & Dr 29154
E & W Williams St 29150
Willis St 29150
Willow Dr 29150
Wilma Ave & Ct 29154
Wilshire Ct 29154
Wilson St 29150
Wilson Hall Rd 29150
Wilton Dr 29150
Wimbledon Ct 29154
Winchester Ct 29153
Winder Ln 29154
Windham Rd 29154
Windmill Dr 29150
Windrow Ct & Dr 29150
Windtree Dr 29154
Winfield Dr 29153
Wingate Ct 29154
Winkles Rd 29153
Winn St 29150
Winston Rd 29154
Winter Creek Rd 29153
Winterberry Rd 29154
Winyah St 29150
N Wise Dr
1-399 29150
500-1399 29153
S Wise Dr 29150
Wisteria Way 29150
Wolf Pack Ct 29150
Wood Rack Rd 29153
Wood Runn Ln 29153
Woodbine St 29150
Woodcreek Ln 29153
Woodcrest St 29154
Woodfield Ct & Ln 29150
Woodhaven Rd 29154
Woodland Ct 29150
Woodland Acres Mhp 29154
Woodlawn Ave & Ct 29150
Woodrow Rd 29153
Woods St 29153
Woodside Rd 29150
Woodville Cir 29154
Workmans Ln 29154
Worthington Ct 29154
Worthit Ln 29153
Wrangler Trl 29150
Wren St 29150
Wright St 29150
Wsk Farm Rd 29153
Wyoming Dr 29153
Ya Ya Way 29153
Yadkin Ct 29154
Yank Haven Dr 29153
Yankee Dr 29154
Yaupon St 29154
Yeadon St 29150
Yellowstone Cir 29154
York Ct 29154
Yosemite Cir 29154
Yuma Ct 29150
Zachary Rd 29154
Zada St 29150
Zoar Church Rd 29153

NUMBERED STREETS

All Street Addresses 29150

WEST COLUMBIA SC

General Delivery 29169

POST OFFICE BOXES MAIN OFFICE STATIONS AND BRANCHES

Box No.s
All PO Boxes 29171

RURAL ROUTES

01, 05, 07, 09 29170
02, 03, 04, 06, 08, 10 29172

NAMED STREETS

Abberly Village Cir 29169
Abelia Ct 29169
Adams St 29169
Adams Terrace Ct 29172
Adelbert Dr 29172
Adkins Cir 29172
Adler Rd 29170
Agape Dr 29169
Agape Village Ct 29169
Air Commerce Dr 29170
Airport Blvd
1600-1700 29169
1702-2098 29169
2100-2322 29170
2324-3399 29170
Albert Rd 29172
Alexander Rd 29169
Alexandria St 29169
Ali Dr 29172
Allendale Dr 29169
Alpine Dr 29169
Amaker Dr 29172
American Ave 29170
Amick St 29169
Andrea Ct 29169
Ann St 29169
Anthony Dr 29172
Antique Dr 29170
Apian Way 29170
Appleton Ct 29172
Appletree Ln 29170
April Rd 29172
Arborgate Dr 29172
Archive Ct 29169
Arehart St 29169
Argus Cir 29172
Arlington St 29169
Armstrong St 29170
Arthurdale Ct & Dr 29170
Asbury Ln 29169
Ashburton Ln 29170
Ashley Ct 29169
Ashley Brooke Ct 29170
Ashwood Cir 29169
Atlas Rd 29170
Augusta Rd
1200-2699 29169
2700-3999 29170
Augusta St 29169
Autumn Knoll Dr 29172
Autumnview Ct 29170
Aviation Way 29170
Ayer Ct 29169
B Ave 29169
B And C St 29172
B And M Rd 29170
Bachman Rd 29172
Baldwin St 29169
Ballard Ct 29172
Ballington Ct 29172
Banny Jones Ave 29170
Barbara Dr 29169
Barcelona Ct 29170
Barron St 29169
Base St 29170
Batchelor St 29169
Bavarian St 29172
Bay Blossom Ln 29170
Bayberry Ct 29170
Baywater Dr 29170
Beachwood Dr 29170
Beaver Ln 29169
Beckham St 29169
Beckman Rd 29170
Bel Air Dr 29170
Bell Cir 29170
Belvedere Cir 29172
Ben Bow Ct 29169
Bensmin Dr 29170
Berry Dr 29170
E Berry Rd 29172
W Berry Rd 29172
Beth Dr 29169
Beverly Dr 29169
Biloxi Sq 29170
Birchwood Ct 29169
Blackbird Dr 29169
Blackhawk Ct, Ter & Trl 29169
Blackjack Ct 29169
Blakely Ct 29170
Blalock Dr 29169
Bleeker Ln 29169
Blossom View Ct 29170
Blue Ridge Ter 29170
Blue Sky Dr 29172
Bob White Ln 29169
Bobsled Dr 29170
Bonnie St 29169
Boone St 29172
Boozer St 29169
Boston Ave 29170
Botanical Pkwy 29169
Boulder Top Ct 29169
Bradford Hill Dr 29170
Bradley Dr 29170
Bramblewood Cir 29172
Branch Rd 29170
Brandy Ln 29170
Branham St 29169
Bray Park Rd 29172
Briar Bush Ln 29172
Broad St 29169
Broken Arrow Trl 29170
Brookfield Cir & Dr 29172
Brooks Ave 29169
Brookwood Cir 29169
N Brown St 29169
Brutus Pass 29170
Buckeye Dr 29170
Buckskin Ct 29170
Budby Ct 29170
Buff St 29169
Buffwood Dr & Ln 29169
Bunker Dr 29172
Burkett St 29172
Burlie Ct & Dr 29169
Burlie Drive Ext 29169
Burnham St 29169
Burroughs Ave 29172
Bush St 29169
Byrdun Dr 29170
C Ave 29169
S C Episcopal Home 29169
C Trotter Rd 29169
Cactus Ct 29172
Caesars Rd 29170
Calcutta Dr 29172
Calico Ct 29172
Calvary Rd 29170
Calvin Ct 29170
Camelot Dr 29170
E & W Campus Rd 29170
Canaberry Dr 29170
Canary Dr 29169
Candlelight Dr 29170
Candlewick Ct 29169
Cap Wing Dr 29170
Capitol Sq 29169
Carberry Ct 29169
Cardinal Dr 29169
Carlin Dr 29169
Carlsbad Ct 29170
Carolina Cir & St 29170
Carpenter St 29169
Carrik Ct 29170
Carrington Dr 29169
Carroll Ct 29170
Carroll Dr 29169
Carrolton St 29169
Carterhill Dr 29172
Castle Dr 29169
Castlerock Ct 29170
Castrald St 29169
Catalina Dr 29170
Caughman St 29169
Caughman Hill Ct 29170
Cedar Field Ln 29170
Cedar Hill Ln 29170
Cedarlane Cir & Pkwy 29170
Center St 29169
Central Dr 29169
Centurion Pass 29170
Chapel Rd 29172
Charity Ln 29170
Charleston Hwy
100-1799 29169
2500-4199 29172
Charwood Ln 29170
Chase Dr 29172
Chasehunt Dr 29172
E & S Chateau Dr 29170
Chavis St 29169
Cherokee Dr & Ln 29169
Cherry Ln 29170
Cherry Grove Dr 29170
Cherrywood Cir 29170
Chestnut Oak Ct & Ln 29169
Chickadee Ct 29170
Chicorana Rd 29169
Chimney Swift Ln 29169
China St 29169
Chipmunk Ln 29169
Chris Cir & Dr 29169
Church St 29172
Churchdale Dr 29170
Ciera Cir 29170
Cimarron Trl 29170
City View Dr 29172
Cla Rik Ln 29170
Clearwing Ln 29169
Clinging Vine Dr 29169
Cloudburst Ct 29172
Clubhouse Dr 29172
Clyde Ct 29170
Clydesdale Ct 29172
Cofield Dr 29169
Colite Dr 29170
Collett St 29169
Collumwood Cir 29170
Colonial Dr 29172
Colony Park Ln 29172
Columbia Ave 29170
Comanchee Trl 29169
Congaree Dr 29172
Congaree Downs Ln 29170
Congaree Mill Ln 29169
Congaree Park Dr 29169
Conner Park Ln 29170
Constellation Trl 29172
Continental Dr 29170
Cooksmount Rd 29172
Coolbreeze Dr 29172
Coolbrook Dr 29172
Cooper Ct & St 29170
Coops Ct 29170
Corine Dr 29172
Corley Ct 29170
Coronado Rd 29170
Corporate Blvd 29169
Corral Ln 29170
Cottage Rd 29172
Cougar Dr 29169
Court Ave 29169
Court Of Leonardo 29170
Court Of Michaelangelo 29170
Court Of Mozart 29170
Court Of Saint Paul 29170
Court Of Saint Peters 29170
Courtney Dr 29172
Courtney Oak Dr 29170
Cousins Ln 29172
S Cove Dr 29170
Coyote Ct 29172
Craft St 29169
Craig St 29170
Craigsen Ln 29169
Crapps Ave 29169
Creekmount Ct 29169
Creekside Rd 29172
Creighton Dr 29172
Crest Dr 29170
Crestline Dr 29170
Crestwater Ct 29169
Crip Hill Rd 29170
N & S Cromwell St 29169
Crystal Ln 29170
Culbreth Ln 29170
D Ave 29169
Dacus Ln 29170
Daisy Ln 29169
Dakota Rd 29170
Dale St 29169
Dalewood Dr 29170
Daniel Rd 29170
Danwood Dr 29169
Darby Way 29170
Dargan St 29169
Davis Dr & Rd 29172
Davon Dr 29170
Dawn Dr 29170
Dawson Dr 29169
Debbie Dink Rd 29172
Decatur St 29169
Decree Ave 29169
Dee St 29170
Dee Ann St 29170
Deer Haven Ct 29169
Delmar St 29169
Delree Ct & St 29170
Denham Ave 29169
Derby Ct & Dr 29170
Derrick St 29169
Deveaux Ct 29172
Devinrock Ct 29170
Dew Ave 29169
Dew Drop Ln 29169
Dickson Hill Cir 29170
Dion St 29172
Divinci Rd 29170
Dixiana Rd 29172
Dogwood Cir 29170
Dogwood Ln 29170

Dogwood Rd 29172
Dolphin Ct 29172
Dora Rd 29170
Double Branch Ct &
Rd 29169
Dove Nest Ct 29170
Dove Trace Ct & Dr 29170
Dreher Rd
100-899 29169
2000-2099 29170
Dryden Ct 29170
Dubbs Ave 29169
Dudley Rd 29170
Dugan Ct 29169
Duke St 29169
Dunbar Rd 29172
W Dunbar Rd 29170
Durham Dr 29170
Dusty Ln 29172
Eagle Dr 29170
Eagle Nest Trl 29169
Eargle Dr 29170
Earl Ct 29169
Earline Dr 29170
Earls Way 29172
Ebony Ln 29170
Echo Vly 29170
Eddine Dr 29169
Edgewater Ln 29169
Edmund Hwy 29170
Egret Pond Ct 29169
Elizabeth Ln 29169
Elk St 29169
Elmira St 29170
Elmonte Cir 29170
Elnora Dr 29170
Elrod Ave 29172
Elsie Ct 29172
Emanuel Dr 29169
Emanuel Church Rd 29170
Emanuel Creek Dr 29170
Emerald Ln 29172
Empress Rd 29170
Enterprise Pkwy 29170
Ephrata Dr & Ln 29169
Epic Dr 29170
Epting St 29169
Ermine Rd 29170
Ervin St 29169
Essex Dr 29170
Estes St 29170
Evergreen Ave 29169
Exum Dr 29169
F Ave 29169
W Fairhill Dr 29170
Fairlane Dr 29169
Farmers Market Dr 29172
Favorite Ct 29170
Feather Run Ct & Trl 29169
Finlay Dr 29169
Fire Academy Rd 29170
Fish Hatchery Ln &
Rd 29172
Florentine Rd 29170
Floyd St 29172
Fontanna Ave 29169
Forest St 29169
Forestland Ct 29169
Foster Brothers Dr 29172
Fountain Ct 29169
Four Acre Dr 29170
Fox Crossing Rd 29170
Fox Hollow Cir 29170
Fox Lake Ct & Dr 29170
Fox Path Ct 29170
Foxwood Ct 29170
Franklin Rd & St S 29170
Friars Ct 29169
Frieden St 29172
Friendship Ct 29170
G Ave 29169
Gaffney St 29169
Gambrell St 29169
Gandy Ct 29169
Garage Rd 29170
Garden Ln 29172

Garden View Dr 29169
Gardenwalk Dr 29170
Gardners Ct 29172
Gardners Terrace Rd 29172
Gas Lamp Dr 29169
Gator Rd 29170
Geiger Rd 29172
Genesis Cir 29172
Genny St 29170
Gerri Ln 29170
Gillins Terrace Rd 29172
Gilmore Dr 29169
Gilvie Ave 29169
Girley St 29172
Glad St 29170
Glad Rik Ln 29170
Gladys Ct 29172
Glendale Dr & Rd 29170
Glenn Rd 29172
Glenn St 29169
Goff Ct 29172
Golden Ln 29172
Goldfinch Ln 29169
Graham St 29169
Grandview Ln 29172
Granny Ln 29172
Grans Cv 29170
Gray Fox Ct 29169
Gray Heron Ct 29169
Graydon Ct 29170
Green St 29172
Green Haven Dr 29170
Green Meadows Rd 29170
Greenfields Rd 29170
Greenway Ct 29170
Greenwood Ct 29170
Greenwood Dr 29170
Greenwood Rd 29169
Grimsby Ln 29170
Grove Ln 29172
Grove St 29169
Guilford St 29169
Gum St 29172
Gunter Cir & Dr 29169
H Ave 29169
Hadley Hall Rd 29172
Haleywood Ln 29170
Half Moon Dr 29172
Hall St 29169
Hallman St 29169
Hallsborough Dr 29170
Hammond Ave 29169
Hammonds Hill Dr 29169
Hampton Crest Dr 29170
Happy Trl 29172
Happy Ridge Dr 29170
Harbor Dr 29169
Harrington Ct 29170
Harrison Cir 29172
Hartford Pl 29172
Harvest Glen Ln 29169
Haverhill Ct 29169
Heather Dr 29169
Heatherfield Ct & Dr 29170
Heatherton Ct & St 29170
Heatherwood Cir 29169
Hebron Dr 29169
Heidi Ln 29172
Henbet Dr 29169
Hendrix Dr 29170
Hendrix St 29169
Henslowe Ln 29170
Henston Dr 29172
Herman St 29169
Hickory Hollow Ct 29169
Hickory Knob Cir & Ct 29170
Hidden Acres Ln 29172
High Meadows Ln 29170
Highgrove Cir & Ct 29170
Highland Dr 29170
Highway 321 29172
Hilldale Rd 29170
Hillside St 29169
Hillside Ter 29170
Hite St 29169
Hobby St 29170

Hoffman Dr 29170
Holinced Rd 29170
Holland Cir & St 29169
Holly Hill Dr 29169
Holly Ridge Ct & Ln 29169
Hollyberry Ln 29169
Hollydale Dr 29170
Holmes St 29169
N Hook Ave 29169
Hookdale Rd 29170
Hooklawn Dr 29169
Hooksen Cir 29170
Hoover Ln 29170
Hoover St 29169
Hopedale Rd 29170
E Hospital Dr 29169
Houston Way 29169
Howe St 29170
Howitzer Cir 29170
Huckabee Rd 29169
Hudson St 29169
Hugo St 29170
Hulon Cir & Ln 29169
Hulon Greene Pl 29169
Hummingbird Dr 29169
Hunters Mill Ct, Dr &
Ln 29170
Huntington Dr 29169
Hyland Cir 29172
Idlewood Cir 29170
Idlewood Dr 29169
Idlewood Park Dr 29170
Illinois Ave 29170
Indian River Dr 29170
Indigo Place Ct 29172
Inview Rd 29169
Isabelle Rd 29170
Isom Ln 29170
Ivyfield Rd 29170
J C Ln 29172
J L Lucas Rd 29172
Jackson Ct 29172
Jackson St 29169
Jadetree Ct 29169
Jamaica Dr 29169
James St 29169
Jamie Ct 29170
Janice Fe Trl 29169
Jaret Ct 29169
Jarrett Ln 29172
Jasper St 29169
Jay Dr 29172
Jayne Ln 29172
Jaywood Cir 29170
Jefferson St 29169
Jensen St 29169
Jereme Bay Ct & Rd 29170
Jessamine Rd 29169
John Davis Dr 29170
John Wayne Dr 29170
Jolly St 29172
Jones Ave 29169
Joseph Walker Dr 29169
Joye St 29169
Joyner Ave 29169
Judan Dr 29170
Jupiter St 29169
Karen Dr 29170
Katie Ct 29170
Kelsey Ct 29172
Kendra Ln 29170
Kensington Ct 29170
Kilberry Ct 29170
Kim St 29169
Kimberly Ln 29170
Kimeric Ct 29170
Kinghill Dr 29172
Kinglet Ln 29169
Kings Tree Acres Dr 29170
Kingsberry Ter 29169
Kinley Dr 29172
Kinsler Dr 29172
Kirkland St 29169
Kirkwood Dr 29170
Kitti Wake Dr 29170
Kitty Hawk Dr 29170

Klapman Rd 29169
Knapp St 29169
Kodak Ct 29172
Konica Ct 29172
Koon St 29169
Kristen Ct 29170
Kyzer Ct & Dr 29172
L Ave 29172
L A Tanna Blvd 29170
La Habra Ln 29170
Lacy St 29169
Lady St 29172
Lake Rd 29172
Lake Dogwood Dr 29170
Lake Frances Dr 29170
Lake Princeton Dr 29170
Lake Shire Dr 29170
Lakeshore Dr 29169
Lakeside Dr 29169
Lakeview Dr 29169
Lakewood Dr 29170
Lamar Ln 29170
Lancaster St 29169
Lander Dr 29169
Lane Dr 29169
Lanier Ave 29170
Laurel Crest Dr 29169
Laurel Graydon Rd 29170
Laurel Hill Dr 29170
Laurel Leaf Dr 29169
Laurel Meadows Dr 29169
Laurel Mist Ct & Ln 29170
Laurel Oak Dr 29169
Lawrence Rd 29170
Lazy Pines Dr 29169
Leander Dr 29172
Leaphart Rd & St 29169
Lee Cir & St 29170
Leica Ln 29172
Leila Shull Ln 29170
Lemmond Dr 29170
Lenore Dr 29170
Lesley Dr 29169
Lexington Dr 29170
Lexington St 29169
Lillie Ave 29172
Lincoln St 29170
Lindler Dr 29170
Lindy Ln 29172
N & S Line St 29169
Linnet Dr 29169
Little Brooke Ln 29172
Little Chris Ln 29172
Littlefield Rd 29169
Lloydwood Dr 29172
Lois Ln 29172
Lonely St 29170
Lonesome Ct 29172
Long St 29169
Long Iron Ct 29172
Longview Dr 29169
Lonnie Ct 29170
Lonsdale Dr 29170
Lookout Point Rd 29172
Loop Rd 29170
Loraine Ct 29169
Lorick Village Rd 29172
Lott Ct 29169
Lown Dr 29170
Lown St 29169
Lownsdale Rd 29170
Lowry Rd 29170
N & S Lucas St 29169
Luke St 29169
Lumberjack Dr 29170
Lyndale Dr 29170
Lynn Dr 29170
Lynn St 29172
Lynnwood Rd 29169
Macbeth Ct 29169
Mack Park Ct 29172
Mae St 29170
Main St 29170
Manning Dr 29169
Manuel St 29170
Marabou Cir & Dr 29169

N & S Marble St 29169
March Rd 29172
Marilyn Ln 29172
Marion St 29170
Marjorie Ln 29169
Mark Anthony Ct 29170
Marvin Ct 29170
Mary Dr
100-199 29172
2300-2399 29169
Maryville Dr 29170
Mathias Rd 29169
Mattie Ln 29170
Mayligh Ct 29172
Mccleod Ave 29172
Mcdonald Ave 29172
Mcintosh Ave 29172
Mcneil St 29170
Mcqueen St 29172
Mcswain Dr 29169
Mctavish Ave 29172
Meadow Ln 29169
Meadow Crest Dr 29172
Meadowview Ct 29169
E Medical Cir & Ln 29169
Meeting St 29169
Melody Dr 29169
Melon Dr 29170
Melton St 29170
Memorial Dr 29170
Menscer Dr 29170
Merchant Lake Rd 29170
Merry Dr 29169
Merryfield Ln 29170
Mesa Ln 29170
Methodist Park Rd 29170
Metropolitan Dr 29170
Miami St 29170
Micala Dr 29170
Michelle Dr 29169
Middle Loop Rd 29170
Middleton St 29169
Midlands Ct 29169
Midway St 29170
Milan Pass 29170
Mill Run 29169
Mimosa Crescent St 29169
Miner St 29170
Minolta Dr 29172
Miranda Rd 29172
Mission Rd 29170
Misty Ln 29172
Mobile Ave 29170
Mobile Park Way 29170
Moffatt St 29169
Mohawk Dr 29169
Mohegan Trl 29169
Monarch Ln 29169
Montclaire Cir & Ln 29170
Monticello St 29169
Monza Trl 29170
Morningdale Dr 29169
Morningside Dr 29169
Moulton Way 29170
Murrah Dr 29172
Myrtle Rd 29172
Nandon Pl 29170
Naples Pass 29170
Natalie Rd 29170
Natchez Trl 29169
Nathan Dr 29169
Neal Dr 29170
New Brookland Pl 29169
Newfield Cir, Ct & Dr 29170
Niblick Ct 29172
Nikon Cir 29172
Nitsill Ct 29170
Norman Dr 29170
North St 29170
Northview Rd 29169
Notre Dame Pass 29170
Oak St 29172
Oakdale Rd 29170
Oakhill Rd 29172
Oakland Ave 29169
Oakwood Dr 29169

Old Barnwell Rd 29170
Old Castle Ct 29170
Old Column Ct 29172
Old Dunbar Rd 29172
Old Indian Trl 29170
Old Pine Plain Rd 29172
Old Plantation Dr 29172
Old State Rd 29172
Old Wire Ct & Rd 29172
Oliver St 29169
Ontario Dr 29169
Orangeburg Dr 29169
Orchard Dr 29170
Orchard Ln 29172
Orchard Hill Dr 29170
Organic Ln 29172
Oriole Ln 29169
Osage Ave 29169
Oswald Rd 29170
Otago Way 29170
Otter Trl 29169
Outlaw Est 29172
Overland Dr 29172
Oweada Dr 29170
Owl Cir 29169
Paddlewheel Ct 29170
Pallet Dr 29172
Palo Verde Dr 29170
Papa Ln 29172
Park Cir & Ln 29170
Parkdale Dr 29170
Parkstone Ct & Way 29170
Parkstream Cir 29170
Parkwood Ct & Dr 29170
Parnell St 29169
Parrish Pond Ct & Dr 29170
N & S Parson St 29169
Partridge Ln 29170
Partridge Hill Dr 29172
Peaceful Ct & Ln 29170
Peachblossom Ct 29170
Peamar Cir & Dr 29169
Pebble Brook Rd 29170
Pebble Creek Ct & Dr 29170
Pella Ave 29170
Pembrook Dr 29170
Pentax Rd 29172
Perry St
100-199 29172
200-299 29169
Phillip Ct & Dr 29170
Piedmont Dr 29170
Pine St
200-399 29169
900-1699 29172
1800-2499 29170
Pine Cliff Ct 29172
Pine Croft Dr 29170
Pine Lake Dr 29169
Pine Ridge Dr 29172
Pine Shadow Ln 29170
Pinebluff Ct 29170
Pinecrest Ave 29170
Pinedale Rd 29170
Pinefield Rd 29170
Pinehurst Ct 29170
Pinenook Rd 29170
Pineview Rd 29169
Platt Springs Rd
1300-1536 29169
1535-1535 29171
1537-2599 29169
1538-2598 29169
2600-4999 29170
Pleasant Ridge Ln 29170
Pleasant Valley Rd 29172
Plum Ct 29170
Poinsett Pl 29169
Pompeii Pl 29170
Pond Dr
800-999 29170
1100-1399 29172
Pony Hill Rd 29169
Poole Rd 29170
Preakness Ct 29172
Preston St 29170

Price Cir 29169
Princeton Rd 29170
Produce Ln 29172
Professional Ave 29169
Quail Ln 29169
Quail Creek Dr 29169
Quail Field Rd 29170
Quail Hollow Ct & Ln 29169
Quail Lake Dr 29169
Quailridge Dr & Ln 29169
Quarter Trl 29172
Quartermaster St 29170
Queen Pkwy 29169
Quinton Ct 29170
Railroad Ave 29169
Rainbow Cir 29170
Rainbow Dr
2300-2545 29169
2546-2999 29170
Raleigh St 29169
Ramblin Rd
951A-951B 29170
100-999 29170
1000-1599 29172
Randall Dr 29172
Raven Trl 29169
Ravengill Ct 29169
Ravenscroft Rd 29172
Raw Hide Ct 29172
Red Wings Rd 29170
Redbird Ln 29169
Redbud Ct 29170
Redwood Dr 29169
Rem Ct 29169
Rembrant Dr 29172
Rest Haven Dr 29169
Reuben Cir 29169
Reynolds Dr 29172
Reynord Cir 29172
Ridge Ct & Dr 29170
Ridgewood Dr 29172
Rising Hopes Rd 29169
Riverbend Dr 29169
Riverside Dr 29169
Riverstone Ct 29169
Riverview Dr 29169
Riverwalk Cir 29169
Riviera Dr 29169
Ro Mar Ln 29170
Rob Roy Ct 29169
Robin Crest Dr 29169
Robin Forest Ct & Dr 29170
Rockford Ct 29172
Rockmount Dr 29169
Roe Young Blvd 29170
Rolling Hills Ct & Ln 29172
Rolling Meadows Ln 29172
Romaine Way 29172
Roman Way 29170
Romell Rd 29170
Roof St
1-99 29169
100-499 29170
500-599 29169
Rose Dr 29170
Rosedale Rd 29170
Rosiland Dr 29169
Ross St 29169
Rossclan Rd 29172
Rutland Ave 29169
Saddlecreek Ct 29169
Saint David Dr 29170
Saint Davids Church
Rd 29170
Saint James Ave 29172
Saint Mark Dr 29170
Saluda Trl 29169
Saluda Chase Way 29169
Saluda Mill Dr 29169
Saluda Ridge Ct 29169
Saluda River Dr 29169
Saluda View Ct 29169
Saluda Woods Ct & Pl 29169
Sams Elbow Rd 29170
San Gabriel Ct 29170
San Sus Dr 29170

Sana Cir 29170
Sandalwood Dr 29170
Sandel Ln 29169
Sandy Ln 29172
Sangaree Dr 29172
Santa Ana Pl 29170
Santa Barbara Ct 29170
Santa Clara Cir 29170
Sausage Ln 29170
Savanna Woods Cir, Ct & Ln 29170
Savannah Ln 29169
Sawgrass Ct 29172
Sawtimber Dr 29170
Saxe Gotha Rd 29172
Scarlet Leaf Ln 29169
Scenic Dr 29170
School Bus Rd 29172
Scotia Ct 29169
Scotstown Ln 29170
Scotts Ct 29172
Scrabble Rd 29170
Seay Dr 29170
Sedgewood Ln 29170
Seibel Rd 29170
Seminole Dr 29169
Senn St 29169
Service Dr 29170
Sewanee Dr 29169
Shadblow Ln 29170
Shadeland Cir 29170
Shadowfield Cir 29169
Shadowfield Dr 29169
Shadowfield Ln 29170
Shampy St 29170
Shannon Ct 29169
Shannondora St 29169
Sharon Cir 29169
Sharron St 29170
Shealy Cir 29170
Shealy Pine Pl 29170
Shelton Ct & Rd 29170
Sheraton Ln 29172
Sherrywood Dr 29169
Shirley St 29169
Shuler St 29169
Shull St 29169
Shumard Oak Ct 29169
Shumpert Rd & St 29172
Sierra Dr 29170
Sightler Dr 29170
Silstar Rd 29170
Silver Branch Rd 29170
Silver Wing Dr 29169
Singing Pines Dr 29170
Sioux Trl 29169
Sisken Ct, Dr & Ln 29169
Six Mile Creek Rd 29170
Skipperling Ln 29169
Skylight Dr 29170
Skyview Dr 29170
Smith Dr 29169
Sonia Dr 29170
Sortwell St 29169
South St 29169
Southall Rd 29172
Southeastern Way 29169
Southern Ct 29169
Southmen Ln 29170
Southview Ln 29170
Sox St 29169
Spanish Ct 29170
Spanish Leaf Ln 29169
Spanish Oak Dr 29169
Spires Dr 29170
Spring Dr 29170
Spring St 29169
Springcreek Ct 29170
Springdale Rd 29170
Springfield Dr 29169
Springs Ct 29170
Spruce Ln 29172
Stacy Lowmens Ct 29170
Stanton Ln 29170
Starcrest Rd 29172
Starlight Ave 29172
Starmount Dr 29172
Starview Ct & Dr 29172
State St 29169
Steele Dr 29169
Steele Rd 29170
E Steele Rd 29170
Still Hopes Dr 29169
Stockman Dr 29170
Stonecross Ct 29170
Stonewood Ct & Dr 29170
Stoney Brook Ct 29169
Sturkie Sq 29170
Sum Mor Dr 29169
Summer Lake Dr 29170
Summer View Ct 29170
Summer Walk Ct 29170
Summerpath Ct 29169
Summerplace Dr 29169
Summerwood Cir 29170
Summitbluff Ct 29170
Sumter St 29169
Sunbright Dr 29170
Sunbury Loop 29169
Sunset Blvd 29169
Sunset Ct 29169
Sunset Dr 29172
Super Dr 29172
Susan Rd 29170
Swallowtail Ln 29169
Swannanoa Dr 29170
Sweetbirch Dr & Ln 29169
Tampa St 29169
Tanya Ln 29170
Tarawood Ct & Dr 29169
Tarrytown Ln 29170
Taylor St 29169
Teakwood Ct 29169
Technology Dr 29170
Tennessee Walker Trl .. 29172
Terrace View Dr 29169
Thomas St 29170
Thompson Ave 29169
Thornton Ave 29169
Timber Ridge Dr 29169
Timberland Dr 29170
Tina Dr 29172
Tinsley Dr 29172
Tiovoli Ct 29170
Todd Cir 29172
Tony St 29172
Trade Zone Dr 29170
Trailmark Dr 29170
Trailstream Rd 29170
Tranwood St 29169
Travis Ct & Ln 29170
Trey Ct 29169
Turnfield Dr 29170
Twin Oak Ct 29170
Unicorn Trl 29172
Utopia Ln 29170
Valley View Rd 29172
Vanarsdale Dr 29169
Vantage Point Dr 29172
Varn Rd 29172
Venetian Rd 29170
Vermont Rd 29170
Vickdon Ln 29170
Victoria Dr 29170
Victoria St 29169
Villa Ct 29170
Vineyard Ct 29170
Vining Ln 29172
Vinson Ct 29172
Violet St 29169
Vista Way 29170
Vista View Ct & Dr 29172
Von Lee St 29172
Wade St 29169
Wall St 29169
Walnut Ter 29172
Walterboro St 29170
War Admiral Dr 29170
Watson Rd 29169
Wattling Rd 29170
Wayside Dr 29170
Wedge Dr 29172
Well Spring Dr 29172
Wessinger St 29169
West St 29169
Westfall Ct 29170
Westgate Dr 29170
Westhaven Dr 29169
Westmoreland Ln 29170
Westside Dr 29169
Westwood Cir 29170
Westwood St 29169
Whetsell Rd 29172
Whindo Rd 29172
Whippoorwill Dr 29169
Whisper Way 29169
Whispering Glen Cir & Ct 29170
Whispering Hope Ln 29170
White Ave 29169
White Knoll Rd & Way . 29170
White Oak Ln 29172
Whiteside Cir 29169
Wholesale Ln 29172
Wildflower Ln 29170
Wildlife Ln 29172
Williams Ave 29172
Williams Cir 29172
Williams St 29169
Willow Oaks Ln 29169
Wilma Dr 29169
Wilmuth Cir & Ct 29170
Wilton Rd 29170
Winchester Ct & Dr 29170
Windham Dr 29170
Windill Ln 29172
Windrush Ct 29172
Winshore Dr 29170
Wisconsin St 29170
Wisteria Dr 29169
N & S Witt St 29169
Woodberry Rd 29170
Woodby Ln 29172
Woodcock Trl 29169
Woodfield Rd 29169
Woodhaven Dr 29169
Woodhurst Ln 29170
Woodland Dr 29169
Woodsedge Ct 29172
Woodsen Cir 29170
Woodside Ct 29169
Woodside Pkwy 29170
S Woodside Pkwy 29170
Wooten Ct 29170
Worlin Dr 29172
Wren Dr 29169
Yardley Farms Ct & Dr 29170
Yashica Ct 29172
Yellow Fox Ct 29170
Zeigler Rd 29169

NUMBERED STREETS

2nd Ave 29169
5th St 29169
6th St 29169
7th Street Ext 29169
N 9th 29169
11th St 29169
N 12th 29169
12th Street Ext 29172
13th St 29169
16th St 29169
17th St 29169

South Dakota

People QuickFacts	South Dakota	USA
Population, 2013 estimate	844,877	316,128,839
Population, 2010 (April 1) estimates base	814,180	308,747,716
Population, percent change, April 1, 2010 to July 1, 2013	3.8%	2.4%
Population, 2010	814,180	308,745,538
Persons under 5 years, percent, 2013	7.1%	6.3%
Persons under 18 years, percent, 2013	24.6%	23.3%
Persons 65 years and over, percent, 2013	14.9%	14.1%
Female persons, percent, 2013	49.8%	50.8%
White alone, percent, 2013 (a)	85.9%	77.7%
Black or African American alone, percent, 2013 (a)	1.9%	13.2%
American Indian and Alaska Native alone, percent, 2013 (a)	8.9%	1.2%
Asian alone, percent, 2013 (a)	1.2%	5.3%
Native Hawaiian and Other Pacific Islander alone, percent, 2013 (a)	0.1%	0.2%
Two or More Races, percent, 2013	2.1%	2.4%
Hispanic or Latino, percent, 2013 (b)	3.4%	17.1%
White alone, not Hispanic or Latino, percent, 2013	83.3%	62.6%
Living in same house 1 year & over, percent, 2008-2012	83.9%	84.8%
Foreign born persons, percent, 2008-2012	2.6%	12.9%
Language other than English spoken at home, pct age 5+, 2008-2012	6.7%	20.5%
High school graduate or higher, percent of persons age 25+, 2008-2012	90.1%	85.7%
Bachelor's degree or higher, percent of persons age 25+, 2008-2012	26.0%	28.5%
Veterans, 2008-2012	69,787	21,853,912
Mean travel time to work (minutes), workers age 16+, 2008-2012	16.8	25.4
Housing units, 2013	370,291	132,802,859
Homeownership rate, 2008-2012	68.6%	65.5%
Housing units in multi-unit structures, percent, 2008-2012	18.6%	25.9%
Median value of owner-occupied housing units, 2008-2012	$129,800	$181,400
Households, 2008-2012	320,467	115,226,802
Persons per household, 2008-2012	2.44	2.61
Per capita money income in past 12 months (2012 dollars), 2008-2012	$25,570	$28,051
Median household income, 2008-2012	$49,091	$53,046
Persons below poverty level, percent, 2008-2012	13.8%	14.9%

Business QuickFacts	South Dakota	USA
Private nonfarm establishments, 2012	25,773	7,431,808
Private nonfarm employment, 2012	336,526	115,938,468
Private nonfarm employment, percent change, 2011-2012	3.0%	2.2%
Nonemployer establishments, 2012	61,973	22,735,915
Total number of firms, 2007	76,997	27,092,908
Black-owned firms, percent, 2007	0.3%	7.1%
American Indian- and Alaska Native-owned firms, percent, 2007	2.2%	0.9%
Asian-owned firms, percent, 2007	0.6%	5.7%
Native Hawaiian and Other Pacific Islander-owned firms, percent, 2007	0.0%	0.1%
Hispanic-owned firms, percent, 2007	0.8%	8.3%
Women-owned firms, percent, 2007	22.2%	28.8%
Manufacturers shipments, 2007 ($1000)	13,051,128	5,319,456,312
Merchant wholesaler sales, 2007 ($1000)	11,400,476	4,174,286,516
Retail sales, 2007 ($1000)	12,266,218	3,917,663,456
Retail sales per capita, 2007	$15,390	$12,990
Accommodation and food services sales, 2007 ($1000)	1,622,751	613,795,732
Building permits, 2012	4,178	829,658

Geography QuickFacts	South Dakota	USA
Land area in square miles, 2010	75,811.00	3,531,905.43
Persons per square mile, 2010	10.7	87.4
FIPS Code	46	

(a) Includes persons reporting only one race.
(b) Hispanics may be of any race, so also are included in applicable race categories.
FN: Footnote on this item for this area in place of data
NA: Not available
D: Suppressed to avoid disclosure of confidential information
X: Not applicable
S: Suppressed; does not meet publication standards
Z: Value greater than zero but less than half unit of measure shown
F: Fewer than 100 firms
Source: US Census Bureau State & County QuickFacts

South Dakota

3 DIGIT ZIP CODE MAP

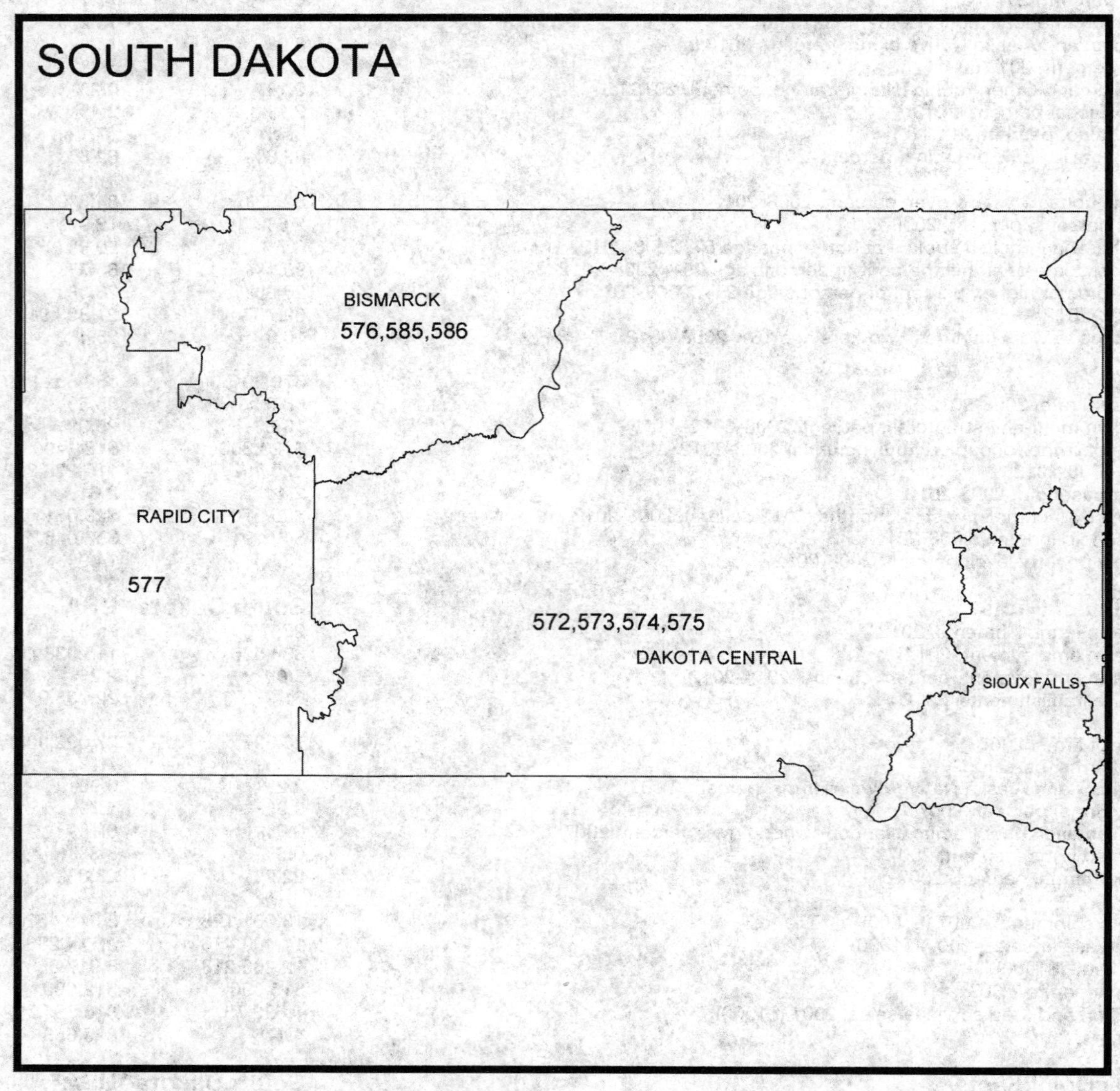

South Dakota

(Abbreviation: SD)

Places with more than one ZIP code are listed in capital letters, See pages indicated.

Post Office, County	ZIP Code
ABERDEEN, Brown (See Page 3454)	
Academy, Charles Mix	57369
Agar, Sully	57520
Agency Village, Roberts	57262
Akaska, Walworth	57420
Albee, Grant	57259
Alcester, Union	57001
Alexandria, Hanson	57311
Allen, Bennett	57714
Alpena, Jerauld	57312
Altamont, Deuel	57226
Amherst, Marshall	57421
Andover, Day	57422
Ardmore, Fall River	57735
Arlington, Kingsbury	57212
Armour, Douglas	57313
Artas, Mcpherson	57437
Artesian, Sanborn	57314
Ashton, Spink	57424
Astoria, Deuel	57213
Athol, Spink	57424
Aurora, Brookings	57002
Avon, Bon Homme	57315
Badger, Kingsbury	57214
Baltic, Minnehaha	57003
Bancroft, Kingsbury	57353
Barnard, Brown	57426
Batesland, Shannon	57716
Bath, Brown	57427
Belle Fourche, Butte	57717
Belvidere, Jackson	57521
Bemis, Deuel	57238
Beresford, Union	57004
Bethlehem, Meade	57769
Big Stone City, Grant	57216
Bison, Perkins	57620
Black Hawk, Meade	57718
Blunt, Hughes	57522
Bonesteel, Gregory	57317
Bowdle, Edmunds	57428
Box Elder, Pennington	57719
Bradley, Clark	57217
Brandon, Minnehaha	57005
Brandt, Deuel	57218
Brentford, Spink	57429
Bridgewater, Mccook	57319
Bristol, Day	57219
Britton, Marshall	57430
Brookings, Brookings	57006
Bruce, Brookings	57220
Bryant, Hamlin	57221
Buffalo, Harding	57720
Buffalo Gap, Custer	57722
Buffalo Ridge, Minnehaha	57107
Bullhead, Corson	57621
Burbank, Clay	57010
Burdock, Fall River	57735
Burke, Gregory	57523
Bushnell, Brookings	57276
Butler, Day	57219
Camp Crook, Harding	57724
Canistota, Mccook	57012
Canova, Miner	57321
Canton, Lincoln	57013
Caputa, Pennington	57725
Carpenter, Clark	57322
Carter, Tripp	57580
Carthage, Miner	57323
Castlewood, Hamlin	57223
Cavour, Beadle	57324
Cedarbutte, Mellette	57579
Centerville, Turner	57014
Central City, Lawrence	57754
Chamberlain, Brule	57325
Chancellor, Turner	57015
Chelsea, Spink	57465
Cherry Creek, Ziebach	57622
Chester, Lake	57016
Claire City, Roberts	57224
Claremont, Brown	57432
Clark, Clark	57225
Clear Lake, Deuel	57226
Clearfield, Tripp	57580
Colman, Moody	57017
Colome, Tripp	57528
Colton, Minnehaha	57018
Columbia, Brown	57433
Conde, Spink	57434
Corona, Roberts	57227
Corsica, Douglas	57328
Corson, Minnehaha	57005
Cottonwood, Pennington	57775
Crazy Horse, Custer	57730
Creighton, Pennington	57790
Cresbard, Faulk	57435
Crocker, Clark	57217
Crooks, Minnehaha	57020
Crooks, Minnehaha	57055
Custer, Custer	57730
Dakota Dunes, Union	57049
Dallas, Gregory	57529
Dante, Charles Mix	57329
Davis, Turner	57021
De Smet, Kingsbury	57231
Deadwood, Lawrence	57732
Dell Rapids, Minnehaha	57022
Delmont, Douglas	57330
Dempster, Hamlin	57234
Denby, Shannon	57716
Dewey, Fall River	57735
Dimock, Hutchinson	57331
Dixon, Gregory	57529
Doland, Spink	57436
Dolton, Mccook	57319
Draper, Jones	57531
Dupree, Ziebach	57623
Eagle Butte, Dewey	57625
Eden, Marshall	57232
Edgemont, Fall River	57735
Egan, Moody	57024
Elk Point, Union	57025
Elkton, Brookings	57026
Ellsworth Afb, Meade	57706
Elm Springs, Pennington	57791
Emery, Hanson	57332
Enning, Meade	57737
Erwin, Kingsbury	57233
Estelline, Hamlin	57234
Ethan, Davison	57334
Eureka, Mcpherson	57437
Fairburn, Custer	57738
Fairfax, Gregory	57335
Fairview, Lincoln	57027
Faith, Meade	57626
Farmer, Hanson	57311
Faulkton, Faulk	57438
Fedora, Miner	57337
Ferney, Brown	57439
Firesteel, Dewey	57633
Flandreau, Moody	57028
Florence, Codington	57235
Forestburg, Sanborn	57314
Fort Meade, Meade	57741
Fort Pierre, Stanley	57532
Fort Thompson, Buffalo	57339
Frankfort, Spink	57440
Frederick, Brown	57441
Freeman, Hutchinson	57029
Fruitdale, Butte	57717
Fulton, Hanson	57340
Gann Valley, Buffalo	57341
Garden City, Clark	57236
Garretson, Minnehaha	57030
Gary, Deuel	57237
Gayville, Yankton	57031
Geddes, Charles Mix	57342
Gettysburg, Potter	57442
Glad Valley, Perkins	57644
Glencross, Dewey	57630
Glenham, Walworth	57631
Goodwin, Deuel	57238
Gregory, Gregory	57533
Grenville, Day	57239
Groton, Brown	57445
Hamill, Tripp	57534
Harrisburg, Lincoln	57032
Harrison, Douglas	57344
Harrold, Hughes	57536
Hartford, Minnehaha	57033
Hayes, Stanley	57537
Hayti, Hamlin	57241
Hazel, Hamlin	57242
Hecla, Brown	57446
Henry, Codington	57243
Hereford, Meade	57785
Hermosa, Custer	57744
Herreid, Campbell	57632
Herrick, Gregory	57538
Hetland, Kingsbury	57212
Highmore, Hyde	57345
Hill City, Pennington	57745
Hitchcock, Beadle	57348
Holabird, Hyde	57540
Hosmer, Edmunds	57448
Hot Springs, Fall River	57747
Houghton, Brown	57449
Hoven, Potter	57450
Howard, Miner	57349
Howes, Meade	57748
Hudson, Lincoln	57034
Humboldt, Minnehaha	57035
Hurley, Turner	57036
Huron, Beadle	57350
Ideal, Tripp	57541
Interior, Jackson	57750
Iona, Gregory	57533
Ipswich, Edmunds	57451
Irene, Clay	57037
Iroquois, Kingsbury	57353
Isabel, Dewey	57633
Java, Walworth	57452
Jefferson, Union	57038
Kadoka, Jackson	57543
Kaylor, Hutchinson	57354
Keldron, Corson	57634
Kennebec, Lyman	57544
Keyapaha, Tripp	57580
Keystone, Pennington	57751
Kimball, Brule	57355
Kranzburg, Codington	57245
Kyle, Shannon	57752
La Plant, Dewey	57652
Labolt, Grant	57246
Lake Andes, Charles Mix	57356
Lake City, Marshall	57247
Lake Norden, Hamlin	57248
Lake Preston, Kingsbury	57249
Lane, Jerauld	57358
Langford, Marshall	57454
Lantry, Dewey	57636
Lead, Lawrence	57754
Lebanon, Potter	57455
Lemmon, Perkins	57638
Lennox, Lincoln	57039
Leola, Mcpherson	57456
Lesterville, Yankton	57040
Letcher, Sanborn	57359
Lily, Day	57274
Little Eagle, Corson	57639
Lodgepole, Perkins	57640
Long Lake, Mcpherson	57457
Long Valley, Jackson	57547
Loomis, Davison	57301
Lower Brule, Lyman	57548
Lowry, Walworth	57472
Lucas, Gregory	57523
Ludlow, Harding	57755
Lyons, Minnehaha	57041
Madison, Lake	57042
Manderson, Shannon	57756
Mansfield, Brown	57460
Marcus, Meade	57787
Marion, Turner	57043
Martin, Bennett	57551
Marty, Charles Mix	57361
Marvin, Grant	57251
Mc Intosh, Corson	57641
Mc Laughlin, Corson	57642
Mccook Lake, Union	57049
Meadow, Perkins	57644
Meckling, Clay	57069
Mellette, Spink	57461
Menno, Hutchinson	57045
Midland, Haakon	57552
Milbank, Grant	57252
Milesville, Haakon	57553
Millboro, Tripp	57580
Miller, Hand	57362
Mina, Edmunds	57451
Miranda, Faulk	57438
Mission, Todd	57555
Mission Hill, Yankton	57046
Mission Ridge, Stanley	57532
Mitchell, Davison	57301
Mobridge, Walworth	57601
Monroe, Turner	57047
Montrose, Mccook	57048
Morristown, Corson	57645
Mound City, Campbell	57646
Mount Vernon, Davison	57363
Mud Butte, Meade	57758
Murdo, Jones	57559
Nemo, Lawrence	57759
New Effington, Roberts	57255
New Holland, Douglas	57364
New Underwood, Pennington	57761
Newell, Butte	57760
Nisland, Butte	57762
Norbeck, Faulk	57438
Norris, Mellette	57560
North Sioux City, Union	57049
Northville, Spink	57465
Nunda, Lake	57050
Oacoma, Lyman	57365
Oelrichs, Fall River	57763
Oglala, Shannon	57764
Okaton, Jones	57562
Okreek, Todd	57563
Oldham, Kingsbury	57051
Olivet, Hutchinson	57052
Onaka, Faulk	57466
Onida, Sully	57564
Opal, Meade	57758
Oral, Fall River	57766
Orient, Hand	57467
Ortley, Roberts	57256
Ottumwa, Haakon	57552
Owanka, Pennington	57767
Parade, Dewey	57625
Parker, Turner	57053
Parkston, Hutchinson	57366
Parmelee, Todd	57566
Peever, Roberts	57257
Philip, Haakon	57567
Pickstown, Charles Mix	57367
Piedmont, Meade	57769
Pierpont, Day	57468
Pierre, Hughes	57501
Pine Ridge, Shannon	57770
Plainview, Meade	57748
Plankinton, Aurora	57368
Platte, Charles Mix	57369
Pollock, Campbell	57648
Porcupine, Shannon	57772
Prairie City, Perkins	57649
Presho, Lyman	57568
Pringle, Custer	57773
Provo, Fall River	57735
Pukwana, Brule	57370
Quinn, Pennington	57775
Ralph, Harding	57650
Ramona, Lake	57054
RAPID CITY, Pennington (See Page 3454)	
Ravinia, Charles Mix	57356
Raymond, Clark	57258
Red Owl, Meade	57787
Redfield, Spink	57469
Redig, Harding	57776
Ree Heights, Hand	57371
Reliance, Lyman	57569
Renner, Minnehaha	57020
Renner, Minnehaha	57055
Reva, Harding	57651
Revillo, Grant	57259
Ridgeview, Dewey	57652
Rochford, Pennington	57745
Rockerville, Pennington	57702
Rockham, Faulk	57470
Roscoe, Edmunds	57471
Rosebud, Todd	57570
Rosholt, Roberts	57260
Roslyn, Day	57261
Roswell, Miner	57349
Rowena, Minnehaha	57005
Running Water, Bon Homme	57062
Rutland, Lake	57057
Saint Charles, Gregory	57571
Saint Francis, Todd	57572
Saint Lawrence, Hand	57373
Saint Onge, Lawrence	57779
Salem, Mccook	57058
Scenic, Pennington	57780
Scotland, Bon Homme	57059
Selby, Walworth	57472
Seneca, Faulk	57473
Shadehill, Perkins	57638
Sherman, Minnehaha	57030
Silver City, Pennington	57702
Sinai, Brookings	57061
SIOUX FALLS, Minnehaha (See Page 3457)	
Sisseton, Roberts	57262
Sky Ranch, Harding	57724
Smithwick, Fall River	57782
South Shore, Codington	57263
Spearfish, Lawrence	57783
Spencer, Mccook	57374
Springfield, Bon Homme	57062
St Charles, Gregory	57571
Stephan, Hyde	57346
Stickney, Aurora	57375
Stockholm, Grant	57264
Stoneville, Meade	57787
Strandburg, Grant	57265
Stratford, Brown	57474
Sturgis, Meade	57785
Summerset, Meade	57718
Summit, Roberts	57266
Tabor, Bon Homme	57063
Tea, Lincoln	57064
Thunder Hawk, Perkins	57638
Timber Lake, Dewey	57656
Tolstoy, Potter	57475
Toronto, Deuel	57268
Trail City, Corson	57657
Trent, Moody	57065
Tripp, Hutchinson	57376
Tulare, Spink	57476
Turton, Spink	57477
Tuthill, Bennett	57574
Twin Brooks, Grant	57269
Tyndall, Bon Homme	57066
Union Center, Meade	57787
Utica, Yankton	57067
Vale, Butte	57788
Valley Springs, Minnehaha	57068
Veblen, Marshall	57270
Verdon, Spink	57434
Vermillion, Clay	57069
Vetal, Bennett	57551
Viborg, Turner	57070
Vienna, Clark	57271
Virgil, Beadle	57379
Vivian, Lyman	57576
Volga, Brookings	57071
Volin, Yankton	57072
Wagner, Charles Mix	57380
Wakonda, Clay	57073
Wakpala, Corson	57658
Walker, Corson	57659
Wall, Pennington	57790
Wallace, Codington	57272
Wanblee, Jackson	57577
Ward, Brookings	57026
Warner, Brown	57479
Wasta, Pennington	57791
Watauga, Corson	57660
Watertown, Codington	57201
Waubay, Day	57273
Waverly, Codington	57201
Webster, Day	57274
Wecota, Faulk	57438
Wentworth, Lake	57075
Wessington, Beadle	57381
Wessington Springs, Jerauld	57382
Westport, Brown	57481
Wetonka, Brown	57481
Wewela, Tripp	57580
White, Brookings	57276
White Lake, Aurora	57383
White Owl, Meade	57792
White River, Mellette	57579
Whitehorse, Dewey	57661
Whitewood, Lawrence	57793
Willow Lake, Clark	57278
Wilmot, Roberts	57279
Winfred, Lake	57076
Winner, Tripp	57580
Witten, Tripp	57584
Wolsey, Beadle	57384
Wood, Mellette	57585
Woonsocket, Sanborn	57385
Worthing, Lincoln	57077
Wounded Knee, Shannon	57794
Yale, Beadle	57386
Yankton, Yankton	57078
Zell, Spink	57469
Zeona, Meade	57758

ABERDEEN SD

General Delivery 57401

POST OFFICE BOXES MAIN OFFICE STATIONS AND BRANCHES

Box No.s
All PO Boxes 57402

NAMED STREETS

All Street Addresses 57401

NUMBERED STREETS

N & S 1st Ave, Curv & St NE, NW, SE & SW 57401
N & S 2nd Ave, Curv & St NE, NW, SE & SW 57401
N & S 3rd Ave, Curv & St NE, NW, SE & SW 57401
N & S 4th Ave, Curv & St NE, NW, SE & SW 57401
5th Ave NE 57401
5th Ave NW 57401
5th Ave SE 57401
5th Ave SW 57401
5th Curv 57401
N 5th St 57401
S 5th St
401-797 57401
1202-1202 57402
1300-2998 57401
S 6th Ave, Curv & St NE, NW, SE & SW 57401
S 7th Ave, Curv & St NE, NW, SE & SW 57401
S 8th Ave, Curv & St NE, NW, SE & SW 57401
S 9th Ave, Curv & St NE, SE & SW 57401
N & S 10th Ave & St NE, SE & SW 57401
S 11th Ave & St NE, NW, SE & SW 57401
S 12th Ave & St NE, NW, SE & SW 57401
S 13th Ave & St NW, SE & SW 57401
S 14th Ave & St NE, SE & SW 57401
S 15th Ave & St NE, NW, SE & SW 57401
S 16th Ave & St NE, NW, SE & SW 57401
S 17th Ave & St NE, SE & SW 57401
18th Ave NE 57401
19th Ave NE 57401
N 20th Ave & St NE, NW & SE 57401
21st Ave NE 57401
22nd Ave NE 57401
23rd Ave NE 57401
24th NE & NW 57401
27th Ave NE 57401
28th Ave NE 57401
29th Ave NE 57401
123rd St 57401
124th St 57401
125th St 57401
126th St 57401
127th St 57401
128th St 57401
129th St 57401
130th St 57401
131st St 57401
132nd St 57401
133rd SW 57401
134th SE 57401
135th St 57401
136th St 57401
137th St 57401
138th St 57401
139th St 57401
140th St 57401
141st St 57401
142nd St 57401
376th Ave 57401
377th Ave 57401
378th Ave 57401
379th Ave 57401
382nd Ave 57401
383rd Ave 57401
384th Ave 57401
385th Ave 57401
386th Ave 57401
S 387th 57401
388th Ave 57401
389th Ave 57401
390th S 57401
391st Ave 57401
392nd Ave 57401
393rd Ave 57401
394th Ave 57401
395th Ave 57401

RAPID CITY SD

General Delivery 57701

POST OFFICE BOXES MAIN OFFICE STATIONS AND BRANCHES

Box No.s
All PO Boxes 57709

NAMED STREETS

Aberdeen Ct 57703
Abilia St 57703
E Adams St 57701
Adjenty Ct 57702
Adonia Ln 57701
Adventure Trl 57702
Aero Rd 57702
Aeronauts Way 57702
Aigner Rd 57702
Ainsdale Ct 57702
S Airport Rd 57703
Alamo Dr 57702
Albert Ln 57703
Albertta Dr 57702
Aldren Rd 57702
Alfalfa Ct 57702
Alicia Ct 57701
Allen Ave 57701
Allie Ct 57701
Alma St 57701
Alpine Ct & Dr 57702
Alta Vista Ct & Dr 57701
Ambrose Dr 57701
Ambush Ranch Rd 57703
E Anaconda Rd 57701
Anamaria Dr 57701
Anamosa St 57701
E Anamosa St
101-327 57701
329-599 57701
601-799 57701
1701-1799 57703
Anderson Rd 57703
Antares Ct 57701
Antelope Creek Rd 57703
Antler Dr 57702
Apache Peak Ln 57702
Apollo Cir 57701
Apollo St 57703
Appaloosa Ln 57702
Apple Hill Ln 57703
Apple Tree Rd 57703
Apres Vous Ct 57703
Arabian Dr 57702
Arapahoe Ct 57702
Ardee Ave 57701
Arena Dr 57702
Argyle St 57702
Arizona St 57701
Arrow St 57702
Arrowhead Dr 57702
Arroyo Ct & Dr 57702
Arthur Pl 57701
Arvilla Ct 57701
Ascension Ct 57702
Ash Ave 57703
Ashland Rd 57701
Ashwood Ct 57702
Aspen Ave 57701
Aspen Dr 57702
Aster Ct 57702
Atlantic Dr 57703
Atlas St 57701
Auburn Dr 57701
Audubon Cir 57702
Augusta Dr 57703
Aurora Dr 57703
Autumn Pl 57702
Avenue A 57703
Aviation Rd 57703
Aztec Dr 57702
Back Country Trl 57703
Back Nine Dr 57703
Baker Park Rd 57702
Bald Eagle Ln 57701
Baldwin St 57702
Balmar Pl 57703
Balsam Ave 57701
Bandon Ln 57702
Bar Five Ranch Rd 57703
Barberry Cir & Ct 57702
Barney Rd 57702
Basham Rd 57702
Basswood St 57703
Bavarian Dr 57702
Beach Dr 57702
Beale St 57703
Bear Gulch Rd 57702
Bears Loose Rd 57702
Beaumont Ln 57703
Bel Aire Dr 57702
Belgarde Blvd 57702
Belgian Ct 57702
Belle Vista Ct 57701
Belleview Dr 57701
Bellewood Dr 57701
Belmont Dr 57702
Bendt Dr 57702
Bengal Dr 57701
Benjamin St 57703
Bennett Rd 57701
Berglund Rd 57701
Berniece St 57703
Berry Blvd & Spur 57702
N & S Berry Pine Rd 57702
Berry Pines Heights Dr 57702
Berwick Ct 57702
Bethpage Dr 57702
Beverly Dr 57701
Biernbaum Ln 57702
Big Bend Rd 57702
Big Piney Rd 57702
Big Sky Dr 57703
Bighorn Rd 57702
Bing Dr 57702
Birch Ave 57701
Birdie Ct & Ln 57702
Birkdale Dr 57702
Bison Point Rd 57701
Bitter Root Ct 57702
Bittersweet Rd 57702
Black Forest Pl & Rd 57702
Black Fox Rd 57701
Black Gap Ct & Rd 57703
Black Oak Pl 57702
Black Saddle Rd 57703
Blackbird Ct 57702
Blaine Ave 57701
Blake Ct & Rd N 57702
Blanche Dr 57703
Blue Grouse Way 57702
Blue Sky Trl 57702
Blue Stem Ct 57702
Blue Wing Rd 57702
Bluebird Ct 57701
Bluejay Dr 57701
Bobtail Gulch 57702
Boegel St 57701
Bogey Ct 57703
N Bogus Jim Rd 57702
Bone Path 57702
Bonita Ln 57703
Bonna Villa Dr 57701
Bonnie Ln 57703
Boulder St 57702
Boulder Hill Rd 57702
Box Elder Dr 57702
Bozeman Cir 57703
Bradsky Rd 57703
Brahman Ln 57703
Breckenridge Ct 57702
Brenner Pass 57702
Brentwood St 57701
Brett St 57702
Briarwood Ct 57702
Bridge Dr 57703
Bridge Ln 57702
Bridge View Dr 57701
Bristlecone Pl 57702
Broadmoor Cir, Ct & Dr 57702
Brockett Ln 57702
Bronco Ln 57701
Brooke St 57701
Brookshire Dr 57702
Brookside Ct & Dr 57702
Brown Ct 57702
Brush Creek Rd 57702
Buckhorn Dr 57702
Buckskin Ln 57703
Buddy Ct 57703
Buena Vista Dr 57702
Buffalo Berry St 57702
Bunco Ct 57701
Bunker Dr 57701
Burgess Rd 57702
Burns Cir & Dr 57702
Busted Five Ct & Ln 57702
Butte Cir & Ct 57703
Byrnwood Dr 57702
Byrum Ct 57703
Cabot Hill Rd 57701
Cactus Dr 57703
Cadillac Dr 57703
Calamity Rd 57702
Cale Ct 57701
Calle Baja St 57702
Calumet Rd 57702
N Cambell St 57701
Cambria Cir 57701
Cambridge Pl 57702
Cameron Dr 57702
Camp 15 Rd 57702
Campfire Dr 57702
Canal St 57701
Candle Stick Ct 57701
Candlelight Dr 57703
Candlewood Pl 57702
Canterberry Rd 57702
S Canyon Dr, Pl & Rd 57702
Canyon Lake Dr 57702
Canyon View Ct 57701
Capitol St 57702
Caputa Loop 57703
Carl Ave 57703
Carlin St 57703
Carmel Pt 57702
Carmen Ct 57702
Carnoustie Ct 57702
Carol St 57703
Carolyn Ct 57701
Carriage Hills Ct, Dr & Pl 57702
Carter Dr 57702
Castle Creek Dr 57702
Castle Heights Pl 57702
Cathedral Dr 57701
E Catron Blvd 57701
Cattle Dr 57703
Cavern Rd 57702
Cavern Crest Ct 57702
Cedar Dr 57702
N Cedar Crest Ct 57702
Cedar Ridge Pl 57702
Cedarwood Ct 57702
Celebration Way 57702
E Centennial Ct & St 57701
Centennial East Ct 57701
Central Blvd 57702
Centre St 57703
E Centre St 57701
Century Rd 57701
Cerro Ct 57702
Chalkstone Ct & Dr 57701
Champion Dr 57701
Chancery Ct & Ln 57702
Chaparral Dr 57702
Chapel Dr & Ln 57702
Chapel Valley Rd 57702
Charger Ct 57701
Chariot Pl 57702
Charmwood Dr 57701
Chateaux Ridge Ct 57702
N Cherry Ave 57701
Cherry Wood Dr 57703
Chevae Ct 57703
Cheyenne Blvd 57703
E Chicago St 57701
W Chicago St 57702
Chief Dr 57701
Chipmunk Ln & Pl 57702
Chokecherry Ln 57702
Chuckwagon Ct 57702
Churchill St 57701
Cimarron Hill Dr 57701
Cinnamon Ridge Dr 57702
Circle Dr 57702
Circlewood Ct & Dr 57703
City Springs Ct, Ln & Rd 57702
City View Dr 57701
Clark St
400-1300 57701
1302-1498 57701
1801-1899 57702
Clarkson Ln & Rd 57702
Clear Creek Rd 57702
Clearview Ln 57702
Cleghorn Canyon Ln & Rd 57702
Cleveland St 57701
Cliff Dr & Spur 57702
Cliff View Ln 57702
Clifton St 57702
Clover St 57702
Clover Ridge Ct & Dr 57701
Clower Ln 57702
Club Ct 57703
Clubhouse Dr 57702
Clydesdale Rd 57702
Coady Ct 57703
Coal Bank Ct & Dr 57701
Cobalt Dr 57701
Cobblestone Ct 57703
Coca Cola Ln 57702
Cog Hill Ln 57702
Cognac Ct 57701
E College Ave 57701
Colorado St 57701
Colt Ln 57701
Columbine Ct 57702
Columbus St 57701
Colvin Ct & St 57703
Comet Ct 57701
Commerce Rd 57702
Community Hall Rd 57702
Concourse Ct & Dr 57703
Coneflower Ct 57702
Conifer Ln 57702
Connemara Ln 57703
Connie Ct 57703
Conservation Way 57703
Cook Hangar Ln 57703
Copper Ln 57703
Copperdale Ct, Dr & Pl 57703
Copperfield Dr 57703
Copperhill Ct, Dr & Rdg 57702
Copperlane Ct 57703
Corbin Dr 57703
Cordes Ln 57701
Cornell Ct 57702
Corral Dr & Pl 57702
Cosmos Rd 57702
Cosport Ct 57702
Cottage Ct 57703
Cottonwood St 57702
Cougar Ct 57702
Country Ln 57702
Country Rd 57701
Country Rd W 57701
Country Club Ct & Dr 57702
Country View Pl 57702
Countryside Blvd 57702
Covenant Dr 57702
Covington St 57703
Cowboy Ct 57701
Coyote Flats Rd 57702
Craig St 57701
Crane Dr 57703
Crazy Horse St 57701
N Creek Dr 57703
N & S Creek View Rd 57702
Creekside View Ln 57701
Crescent Dr 57701
Crestridge Ct 57701
Crestview Dr
1-99 57701
600-699 57702
Crestwood Dr 57701
Crimson Ct 57701
Cripple Dove Ct 57702
Crocus Ln 57702
Cross Over Rd 57702
Crossbill Cir 57702
Crown Ct & Hl 57702
Croyle Ave & Ct 57702
Crusade Rd 57702
Cruz Dr 57702
Culvert St 57701
Currant Ct 57702
Curtis St 57701
E Custer St 57701
Custer Gulch Rd 57702
Custer Trails Rd 57702
Cyclone St 57703
Cypress Ct & St 57701
Daisy Ln 57702
Dakoming Dr 57702
Dakota Dr 57702
Dakota Craft Dr 57701
Dale Dr 57702
Daly Ct 57703
Dan Christy Ln 57701
Danbury Cir 57702
Dane Ln 57701
Danley Dr 57702
Danube Ln 57702
Dark Canyon Pl & Rd 57702
Davin Dr 57701
Dawkins Rd 57703
Dawn Ln 57703
Daybreak Ridge Rd 57702
Daylight Dr 57703
Deadman Gulch Rd 57702
Deadwood Ave 57702
Dealer Dr 57703
Dean Ln 57702
Debra Dr 57702
Deer Creek Ln 57702
Deer Valley Ct 57702
Degeest Dr 57703
Delor Ct 57702
E Denver St 57701
Derby Ln
4000-4399 57701
23501-23599 57703
Derringer Rd 57703
Diamond Ct 57703
Diamond Oak Pl 57702
Dice Ct 57701
Dilger Ave 57701
Discovery Cir 57701
E Disk Dr 57701
Distribution Ln 57701
Dogleg Dr 57702
Dogwood Ln 57702
Dolphin Ln 57701
Domivara Rd 57702
Donegal Way 57702
Doolittle St 57701
Doral Dr 57702
Dornoch Ct 57702
Dorothy Dr 57703
Double Eagle Ct 57702
Doubletree Rd 57702
Dover Ln & St 57702
Downing St 57701
Dream Bar Rd 57702
Dreamscape Rd 57702
Dry Creek Ct 57703
Dry Sage Ln 57702
Duckhorn St 57703
Duffer Dr 57702
Dugan St 57702
Dunbar Ct 57701
Dundee St 57702
Dunham Dr 57703
Dunn Rd 57703
Dunsmore Rd 57702
Dusty Trl 57702
Dyess Ave
1301-1399 57703
1800-2398 57701
2400-22499 57701
Dylan Dr 57703
Eagle Dr 57703
Eagle Rd 57701
Eagle Canyon Dr 57702
Earl Ct 57702
Earleen St 57701
East Blvd
314-500 57701
500-500 57709
600-698 57701
700-1699 57701
East Blvd N 57701
Easy St 57702
Echo Dr 57702
Echo Ridge Dr 57702
Echo Valley Ct 57702
Eclipse St 57703
Edelweiss Mountain Rd 57702
Eden Ln 57703
Edgewood Dr 57702
Edinborough Ct & Dr 57702
Edwards St 57703
Eglin St
801-897 57701
899-1749 57701
1750-1798 57703
1751-1799 57701
1800-3499 57703
3501-3899 57703
Eldene Ln 57701
Eli Dr 57701
E Elk St 57701
Elk Vale Rd
900-1000 57703
1002-3798 57703
22100-22499 57701
N Elk Vale Rd
1300-1400 57703
1402-1498 57703
2100-4898 57701
4900-5000 57701
5002-5898 57701
Elkhart Rd 57702
Elkhorn Ln 57701
Ellendale Dr 57703
Elm Ave 57701

Elmer St 57703
Elmhurst Dr 57702
Elysian Ct 57702
Ember Rd 57702
N Emerald Ridge Rd 57702
Emerson Ln 57701
Empey Dr 57702
Encampment Ln 57701
E Enchanted Pines Dr 57701
Enchantment Rd 57701
Ennen Dr 57703
Erickson Ranch Rd 57702
Estates Dr 57702
Estes Park Ct 57701
Esval Dr 57702
Ethan Ct 57703
Eunice Dr 57703
Evans Ct 57702
Everest Rd 57702
Evergreen Dr 57702
Exit Rd 57702
Explorer St 57701
Faa Rd 57703
Fairhaven Dr 57702
E Fairlane Dr 57701
Fairlawn Dr 57702
Fairmont Blvd 57701
E Fairmont Blvd 57701
Fairmont Ct 57701
Fairmont Pl 57701
E Fairmont St 57703
Fairview St 57701
Fairway Hills Dr 57702
Falcon Dr 57701
Falcon Ln 57702
Falling Rock Rd 57702
Falls Dr 57702
Farlow Ave 57701
Farview Dr 57702
Fawn Haven Ct 57702
Feather Pl 57701
Federal Ave 57702
Felicia St 57703
Ferntree Ct 57701
Field View Dr 57701
Fieldstone Dr 57703
Fillmore St 57701
Finch Ct 57702
Fir Ct & Dr 57701
Fire Station Rd 57703
First Thunder Rd 57702
Fischer Ct 57703
Flack Ln 57701
Flamingo Dr 57701
Flint Dr 57702
Flintlock Ct 57703
Flormann St 57701
E Flormann St 57701
W Flormann St 57702
Flume Ln 57702
Foothill Dr 57702
Forest Ct 57701
Forest Dr 57701
Forest Pl 57701
Forest Rd 57702
Forest St 57702
Forest Hills Dr 57701
Forest Park Cir & Ct 57702
Fort St 57703
Fort Hayes Rd 57702
Founders Bnd 57701
Founders Park Dr 57701
Fountain Pl 57701
Fountain Plaza Dr 57702
Fox Rd 57701
Fox Run Ct, Dr & Pl 57701
Fraley Ct 57701
E Franklin St 57701
Fredrick Ln 57702
Freedom Ct 57701
Freeland Ave 57701
Fremont St 57702
French Dr 57702
Frontier Dr 57702
Frontier Pl 57702
Frontier Rd 57703
Fulton St 57701
W Fulton St 57702
Gainsboro Dr 57701
Galaxy Dr 57701
Galena Dr 57702
Gallery Ln 57702
Galt Ct 57701
Garden Ln 57703
Garvin Ct 57702
Gary Owen Dr 57702
Geary Blvd 57702
Gemini St 57703
Gemstone Dr 57702
Gin Ct 57703
Gisi Rd 57701
Gladys St 57701
N Glen Pl 57702
S Glen Pl 57702
W Glen Pl 57702
Glen St 57703
Glen Haven Ct 57702
Glendale Ln 57702
E Glenshire Ct & Dr 57701
Glenside St 57703
N & S Glenview Pl 57702
Glenwood Dr 57702
Glory Ct 57702
Gnugnuska Dr 57701
Gold St 57701
Gold Creek Pl 57702
Golden Eagle Dr
2000-2099 57701
2500-2599 57702
Golden Hills Dr 57702
Golf Course Rd 57702
Gondola Rd 57702
Good Shepherd Way 57702
Gordon Gulch Rd 57702
Grace Way 57702
Gralders Dr 57703
Grand Blvd 57701
N & S Grand Vista Ct 57701
Grandview Dr 57701
Grant Cir 57703
Grapevine Ln 57703
Gray Fox Ct 57701
Grays Dr 57702
Green Dr 57703
Green Oak Ln 57703
Green Tree Ln 57703
Green Valley Dr 57703
Green Willow Dr 57703
Greenbriar St 57701
Greenfield Dr & Ln 57703
Greenleaf Ct 57702
Greenway St 57701
Greenwood Ln 57703
Grenoble Ct 57702
Grover Mountain Rd 57702
Guard Rd 57703
Guest Rd 57702
Gunderson Dr 57702
Gypsey Rd 57703
Haakon St 57703
Hacienda St 57703
Hacker Loop 57702
Hackney Ct 57702
Hagen Ct 57702
N Haines Ave & Ct 57701
Hale Pl 57701
Hall St 57702
Halley Ave 57701
Hallmark Ct 57702
Hamlin Cir & Ct 57703
Hampton Ct 57701
Hanks Dr 57701
Hanover Dr 57701
Hansen Ln 57703
Hansen Hangar Ln 57703
Happy Trl 57702
Happy Hollow St 57702
Harbor Pl 57701
Hardesty Rd 57702
Harding Ct 57703
Harley Dr & Ln 57702
Harmon Pl 57701
Harmony Ln 57702
Harmony Heights Ln
1201-1297 57701
1299-1399 57701
1401-1599 57701
1701-1897 57702
1899-2000 57702
2002-2098 57702
Harney Dr & Pl 57702
Harney View Dr 57703
Harper Dr 57702
Harrington Ct 57701
Hart Ranch Rd W 57702
Harter Dr 57702
Hartland Ct 57702
Harvard Ave 57702
Harvest Ln 57701
Harwood St 57703
Hat Mountain Dr 57702
Haven St 57703
Hawthorne Ave 57701
Haycamp Ln 57703
Hayloft Ln 57703
Haystack Ln 57703
Hazel Ln 57702
Hazeltine Ct 57703
Heald Trl 57702
Heart Ct 57703
Heather Dr 57702
Heather Ln 57703
Heidelberg Ln 57702
Heidiway Ct & Ln 57702
Heights Dr 57702
Helen Ct 57702
Helios St 57703
Hemlock St 57701
Henderson Dr 57701
Hendrix Ln 57701
Henry Ct 57701
Heritage Ln 57702
Herman St 57701
Hickory Dr 57701
Hidalgo Ct 57703
Hidden Springs Rd 57703
Hidden Timbers 57702
Hidden Valley Ln, Rd &
Trl 57702
Higgins Ln 57703
High St 57701
High Valley Dr 57702
Highland Ct 57701
Highland Loop 57702
Highland Hills Rd 57702
Highland Park Dr 57701
Highlight Dr 57703
S Highway 16
4100-4598 57701
S Highway 16
4600-5499 57701
5501-6399 57701
7000-13899 57702
Highway 385 57702
E Highway 44 57703
W Highway 44 57702
N Highway 79 57702
S Highway 79
2201-3097 57701
3099-3900 57701
3902-4498 57701
5001-5031 57702
5600-6298 57702
6500-6599 57701
7800-9398 57702
9400-23699 57702
Highwood Rd 57701
Hill St 57701
Hillcrest Dr 57701
Hillshire Ct 57701
Hillside Dr 57703
Hillsview Dr 57702
Hilltop Ln 57702
Hilltop Rd 57703
Hisega Dr & Rd 57702
Hoefer Ave & Ct 57701
Hogan Ct 57702
Hogan St 57703
Holcomb Ave 57701
Holiday Ln 57702
Holly Ct 57702
Holy Cow Ranch Rd 57703
Homestead St 57703
Horace Mann Dr 57701
Horse Creek Rd 57702
Horse Run Rd 57702
Horsecreek Rd 57702
Horsemans Ranch Rd 57702
Howard St 57701
Howie Dr 57703
Hughes Ct 57703
Hungarian Ct 57702
Hunter St 57703
Huntington Pl 57702
Hurst Ave 57701
Husker Pl 57701
Hyland Dr 57701
E Idaho St 57701
Idlehurst Ln 57702
Idlewild Ct 57702
Idlewood Dr 57701
Independence Ct 57701
E Indiana St 57701
Indigo Ct 57701
Industrial Ave 57702
Innsbruck Ct 57702
N Interstate 90 Service
Rd 57701
S Interstate 90 Service
Rd 57703
E Iowa St 57701
Ireland Pl 57702
Iris Dr 57702
Ivory Birch Pl 57702
Ivory Cliffs Ln 57702
Ivy Ave 57701
Ivy Mountain Ct 57702
J Ct 57703
J Pine Rd 57702
Jack Pine Dr 57703
Jackie Ln 57703
Jackson Blvd 57702
E Jackson St 57701
Jake Rd 57702
James Warren Dr 57701
Jane Dr 57702
Janet St
2100-2599 57702
6500-6599 57701
Jasmine Ln 57702
Jax Ct 57702
Jefferson St 57702
Jennifer St 57701
Jenny Gulch Rd 57702
Jericho Way 57702
Jess St 57703
Jet Dr 57703
Jewel Ct 57701
Jill Rd 57702
Jim St 57703
John St 57701
Johnston Ct, Dr & Ln 57703
Jolly Ln 57703
Joplin Ln 57701
Jordan Dr 57702
Joy Ave 57701
Judy Ave 57702
Julia Ct 57701
Junction Dr 57702
June Ct 57702
Juniper St 57702
Jupiter Ct 57701
Justice Ln 57703
Kabee Pl 57702
Kahler Ct 57701
Kansas City St 57701
E Kansas City St 57701
W Kansas City St 57702
Kary Ln 57701
Kateland St 57701
Kathryn Ave 57701
Katrina Ct 57702
Katy Ct 57703
Kellogg Pl 57701
Ken Ct 57701
Kennel Dr 57703
Kennemer Dr 57702
Kentucky Ln 57701
N & S Kepp Ct 57701
Kermit Ln 57703
Kerry Dr 57702
Kieffer Ranch Rd 57702
Kimbell Pl 57701
Kimberly Cir 57701
Kimberwick Ct 57703
Kimm St 57703
Kingbird Ct 57702
Kings Ct & Rd 57702
Kingswood Ct & Dr 57702
Kinney Ave 57702
Kiowa Ln 57701
Kirkeby Ln 57702
Kirkwood Dr 57702
Kitt Peak Rd 57702
Kitty Hawk Rd 57703
Klondike Rd 57702
Knight Ct 57702
Kno Pl 57701
E Knollwood Dr 57701
Knotty Pine Ct & Ln 57702
Knowledge Dr 57702
Knuckleduster Rd 57703
Knutson Ln 57702
Krebs Dr 57702
Kulpaca Pl 57701
Kyle St 57701
La Selva Dr 57701
Lacosta Dr 57703
Lacroix Ct 57703
N Lacrosse St 57701
Lakeview Dr 57702
Lamb Rd 57703
Lambeau Ct 57701
Lampert Ct 57701
Lamplight Dr 57703
Lanark Rd 57702
Lance St 57702
Lancer Dr 57703
Lange Rd 57702
Langenberg Ct 57702
Lariat Rd 57702
Lark Dr 57701
Latrobe Ave 57701
Laurel Ave 57701
Laurel Heights Dr 57701
Laveeda Dr 57702
Lawndale Dr 57702
Lawrence Ct & Dr 57701
Le Blanc Dr 57701
Lee Dr 57702
Legacy Ln 57703
Leland Ln 57702
Lemmon Ave 57701
Lennon Ln 57701
Leola Ln 57703
Leroy St 57703
E Liberty St 57701
Lien St 57702
Lightning Ridge Rd 57702
Lilac Ln 57701
Lime Creek Dr 57702
Limelight Ln 57702
Limestone Ln 57702
Lincoln Ave 57701
Lindbergh Ave 57701
Linden Ln 57702
Lindsey Dr 57702
Lion Dr 57701
Lions Paw Ct 57703
Lockwood Dr 57702
Locust St 57701
Lodge St 57702
Lodgepole Pl 57702
Log Porch Rd 57702
Lombardy Dr 57703
Lonetree Rd 57703
Long Acres 57703
Long View Rd 57703
Longhorn Ct 57703
Longview Dr 57703
Lookout Ln 57701
Lookout Mtn 57702
N & S Loretta Dr 57702
Lowery Pl 57701
Lowry Ln 57703
Lucky Ln 57701
Luna Ave 57701
Lunar Dr 57703
Lundin Ct 57702
Lynnwood Ave & Dr 57701
Lytle Ln 57703
Macarthur St 57701
Mack Dr 57703
Maddy Anne Ct 57701
Madison St 57701
E Madison St 57701
Madison Trl 57702
Maggie Way 57702
Magic Canyon Rd 57702
Magnolia Dr 57701
Maidstone Ct 57702
Main St
2-999 57701
9100-9499 57702
13400-13599 57702
E Main St 57701
E Main St N 57701
W Main St
1000-1298 57701
1301-1699 57701
1700-4999 57702
Majestic Trl 57702
Malibu Dr 57702
E Mall Dr 57701
Mallow St 57701
Mandalay Ln 57701
Mansfield Rd 57702
N Maple Ave 57701
Marathon Ct 57701
Marcia Ct 57702
Margaret Ct 57702
Marie Ct 57701
Markay Pl 57702
Marlin Dr
1701-1897 57701
1899-1999 57701
2001-2099 57701
2901-2997 57703
2999-3099 57703
Marquette Dr 57701
Martin Ln 57703
Marvel Mountain Rd 57702
Marvel Mountain Ridge
Rd 57702
Marvin Rd 57702
Mary Dr 57702
Matterhorn Dr 57702
May Ct 57703
Maywood Dr 57701
Mccurdy Gulch Rd 57702
E Meade St 57701
Meadow Ln 57703
Meadow Lane Ct 57703
Meadow Ridge Dr 57703
Meadowbrook Ct & Dr 57702
Meadowland Dr 57703
Meadowlark Dr 57702
E Meadowlark Dr 57701
Meadowview Ct 57702
Meadowwood Dr 57702
Medinah Ct 57702
Melano St 57701
Melcor Rd 57702
Melody Ln 57703
Memorial Rd 57702
Merchen Rd 57702
Mercury Dr 57703
Merion Ct 57702
Merlot Dr 57701
Merritt Rd 57702
Mesa Dr
1700-1899 57702
4200-4799 57701
4801-4999 57701
Meteor St 57703
Michelle Dr 57702
Michigan Ave 57701
Mickelson Dr 57703
Mickeriv St 57701
Middle Valley Dr 57701
Midway St 57701
Milehigh Ave 57701
Mill Rd 57702
Mill St 57701
Miller Ct & Dr 57702
Milwaukee St 57701
Minnekahta Dr 57702
Minnesota Pl 57701
Minnesota St 57701
E Minnesota St
101-197 57701
199-1100 57701
1102-1298 57701
2900-3098 57703
W Minnesota St 57701
Minnetonka Dr 57702
Minnewasta Ct, Pl &
Rd 57702
Minuteman Dr 57701
Miracle Pl & Rd 57702
Missing Ridge Dr 57701
Mission Hills Loop 57702
Missoula St 57703
Misty Woods Ln 57701
Mittenwald Ct 57702
Monarch Ct 57702
Mondo St 57703
E Monroe St 57701
Montage Dr 57701
E Montana St 57701
Monte Pl 57702
Monte Vista Dr 57702
Montebello Ct 57702
Moon St 57703
Moon Meadows Dr 57702
Moonlight Dr 57703
Morgan Ct 57702
Morning Star Ct 57703
Morning View Dr 57703
Morninglight Dr 57703
Morningside Dr 57701
Morningside Rd 57702
Morningview Dr 57702
Morris Ln 57703
Morse Pl 57702
Mory Rd 57702
Motherlode Dr 57702
Mothers Pl 57703
Mount Carmel St 57701
Mount Locke Ln 57702
Mount Palomar Ln 57702
Mount Royal Ln 57702
N Mount Rushmore
Rd 57701
Mountain Beaver Way 57702
Mountain Meadow Rd 57702
Mountain Park Rd 57702
Mountain Pine Ln 57702
Mountain Shadow Pl 57702
Mountain Springs Ct &
Ln 57702
Mountain View Ln 57701
Mountain View Rd
500-700 57702
655-659 57709
701-1999 57702
702-1798 57702
Muckler Ct 57703
Muirfield Dr 57702
Mulligan Ct 57703
Mulligan Mile 57702
Mullock St 57701
Munich Ln 57702
Mustang Ln 57703
Myrtle Ave 57701
Mystic Dr 57701
Mystic Mtn 57702
Nameless Cave Rd 57702
Naples Ct 57701
Nathan Ct 57701
National St 57702
National Guard Rd 57702

E Nebraska St 57701
Neck Yoke Rd 57702
N & S Neel St 57703
Neff St 57703
Neiger Ct 57702
Nemo Rd 57702
Neptune Dr 57701
Neva Way 57701
E Nevada Dr & St 57701
New England St 57703
E New York St 57701
Nicklaus Ct & Dr 57702
Nicole St 57701
Night Wind Ct 57703
Nike Loop & Rd 57701
Nonanna St 57702
Nordby Ln 57702
Normans Roost Rd 57702
Norris Peak Rd 57702
Norsemen Ln 57702
E North St 57701
Northbrook Dr 57702
Northeast Dr 57701
Northridge Dr 57701
Northstar Ct 57703
E Nowlin St 57701
Nugget Gulch Dr 57702
Nuthatch Rd 57702
Oak Ave & Dr 57701
E Oakland St 57701
Oakmont Ct 57702
Obrien St 57703
Odde Dr & Pl 57701
E Ohio St 57701
Oiler Ln 57701
Okpealuk Ct & St 57702
Old Farm Ct 57703
Old Folsom Rd 57703
Old Sheridan Rd 57702
Olde Orchard Rd 57702
Olive Ln 57703
Olympic Ct 57702
Omaha St 57701
E Omaha St 57701
W Omaha St
1000-1098 57701
1100-1199 57701
1201-1499 57701
2000-4100 57702
4102-4198 57702
Orchard Ln 57703
Oregon St 57701
Oriole Dr 57701
Oshkosh St 57701
Outfitter Rd 57701
Outlook Cir 57701
Overlook Dr 57702
Pacific Ln 57703
Packer Pl 57701
Pactola Ct & Dr 57702
Paddock Ct 57701
Padre Dr 57703
Pahasapa Rd 57701
Palamino Ln 57703
Palm Dr 57701
Palmer Ct, Dr, Ln & Rd 57702
Palo Verde Dr 57701
Panorama Cir 57701
Par Pl 57702
Paradise Ln 57702
Park Dr 57702
Park Hill Ct & Dr 57701
Parkridge Cir, Dr & Pl 57702
Parkview Dr 57701
Parkwood Rd 57701
Pat Pl 57703
Pathfinder Pl 57702
Patricia St 57703
Patriot Ln 57701
Patterson Dr 57703
Patton St 57701
Payton Ct 57702
Peace Path 57701
Peaceful Pines Rd 57702
Peanut Ln 57703
Pearl Harbor St 57701
Pebble Ln 57702
Pebble Beach Ct 57703
Pecan Ln 57703
Pelham Ct 57702
Pendar Ln 57701
Pendleton Dr 57701
Pennington St 57703
Penny Ln 57702
Penrose Pl 57702
Peregrine Pt 57702
Peridot Ln 57702
Perry Pl 57702
Pete Ln 57702
Peterson Rd 57701
Pevans Pkwy 57701
Phil Ct 57701
Philadelphia St 57701
E Philadelphia St
1-799 57701
801-1199 57701
1400-1498 57703
1500-1599 57703
Philip Dr 57702
Pierre Ln & St 57702
Pine Dr 57702
Pine St 57701
Pine Cliff Cir & Dr 57702
Pine Cone Ave 57702
Pine Cone Ln 57701
Pine Grove Rd 57702
Pine Haven Dr 57702
Pine Heights Dr 57701
Pine Hills Dr 57702
Pine Knoll Pl 57701
Pine Meadows Ct 57702
Pine Tree Dr 57702
Pine Valley Rd 57702
Pine View Dr 57702
Pinecrest Dr 57702
Pinedale Cir, Ct & Dr 57702
Pinedale Heights Dr 57702
Pinedale Ridge Rd 57702
Pinehurst Ct & Dr 57702
Pinewood Ct & Dr 57702
Pinon Pl 57702
Pinon Jay Cir 57702
Pioneer Ave 57702
Pioneer Cir 57702
Pioneer Dr 57703
Pioneer Trl N 57701
Pioneer Ridge Rd 57702
N & S Pitch Ct & Dr 57703
Placer Pl & Rd 57702
Placer Place Ct 57702
Plains Vista Ct 57701
Plant St 57702
Plateau Ln 57703
N Platt St 57702
Player Dr 57702
N & S Plaza Blvd & Dr 57702
Pleasant Dr 57702
Plum Creek Pl 57703
Plum Tree Ln 57702
Pluma Dr 57702
Plumbers Dr 57701
Pluto St 57703
Plymouth Dr 57703
Pointe West Pl 57702
Poker Dr 57703
Polaris Ct 57701
Ponderosa Ct 57702
Ponderosa Pl
1300-1399 57701
3200-3299 57702
Ponderosa Trl 57702
Pool Dr 57702
Poplar Ave 57701
Porthcawl Ct 57702
Portrush Rd 57702
Pot Rustle Loop 57702
Potter Ln 57703
Potter Rd 57702
Powderhorn Cir & Dr 57702
Power St 57702
Prairie Ave 57701
N & S Prairie Creek Rd 57702
Prairie Meadows Rd 57701
Prairie Rose Pl 57702
Prairie View Ct & Dr 57701
Preakness Ct 57701
Preston Pl & St 57703
Prestwick Rd 57702
Primrose Pl 57702
Princeton Ct 57702
Promise Rd 57701
Puckett Dr 57701
Pushing Pl 57702
Quad Ct 57703
Quail Dr 57702
Quarter Horse Dr 57703
Quartz Canyon Cir, Ct, Ln & Pl 57702
Queen Heights Ct 57702
Quiment Ct 57702
E Quincy St 57701
Racine St 57701
Radar Hill Rd 57703
Rainbow Ln 57703
Ram Ln 57701
Ranch View Ct 57702
Rand Rd 57702
Range Rd 57702
Range View Cir & Ct 57701
W Rapid St
1100-1498 57701
2600-2698 57702
2700-3499 57702
Rapp St 57701
Raspberry Ct 57702
Raveen Dr 57703
Raven Cir & Ct 57702
Rawhide Dr 57702
Ray Ann Ct 57702
Raymond Dr 57702
Receda St 57703
Recluse Ct 57701
Red Cliff Ter 57702
Red Cloud St 57701
Red Dale Dr 57702
Red Deer Rd 57702
Red Fern St 57702
Red Fox Ct 57702
Red Road Dr 57702
Red Rock Canyon Rd 57702
Redemption Rd 57703
Reder St 57702
Redrock Canyon Ranch Rd 57702
Redwing Ln 57703
Redwood Pl 57702
Redwood St 57701
Reed Ct 57703
Regency Ct 57702
Regional Way 57701
Remington Rd 57703
Rena Pl 57701
N Reservoir Rd 57703
Ridge Dr 57702
S Ridge Rd 57701
Ridge Heights Ct 57701
Ridgecrest Ct 57702
Ridgeland Loop 57702
Ridgemoor Dr 57702
Ridgeview Ct & Rd 57701
Ridgewood St 57702
Riley Ave & Ct 57701
Rimrock Ct, Dr & Hwy 57702
Rio Dr 57702
Riva Ridge Rd 57702
Riverview Ct 57702
Riviera Ct 57702
Robbins Dr 57701
Roberta St 57701
Roberts Ct 57703
Rockcress Ct 57702
Rocker Dr 57703
S Rockerville Rd 57702
Rockhill Rd 57703
Rockwood Rd 57702
Rocky Rd 57701
Rodeo Rd 57702
Rolling Hills Dr & Rd 57702
Roosevelt Ave 57701
Rosemary Ln 57702
Rosewood Ln 57703
Rosilee Ln 57701
Ross Ct 57703
Roubaix Dr 57702
Rounds St 57702
Roxbury Cir 57702
Rushmore St 57702
Russet Ln 57703
Rust Ridge Ct 57703
Rustling Pines Ln 57702
Rusty Spur Ct 57703
Ruthies Trl 57702
Ryther St 57702
Saddleback Ct 57703
Saddlenotch Trl 57702
Safe Haven Pl 57702
Sage Ave 57701
Sagewood St 57701
Sahalee Ct & Dr 57702
Saint Andrew St 57701
E Saint Andrew St
103-816 57701
818-998 57701
2300-2698 57703
Saint Anne St 57701
E Saint Anne St 57701
W Saint Anne St 57702
Saint Bury Ct 57703
Saint Charles St 57701
E Saint Charles St
103-1399 57701
2301-2497 57703
2499-2599 57703
Saint Cloud St 57701
E Saint Cloud St 57701
W Saint Cloud St 57702
Saint Francis St 57701
E Saint Francis St
100-1299 57701
2301-2497 57703
2499-2599 57703
2601-2699 57703
E Saint James St 57701
Saint Joseph St
2-18 57701
20-1220 57701
9101-9197 57702
9199-9499 57702
E Saint Joseph St 57701
E Saint Louis St 57701
W Saint Louis St 57702
Saint Martins Dr 57702
N Saint Onge St 57702
Saint Patrick St 57701
E Saint Patrick St
100-100 57701
102-1400 57701
1402-1498 57701
1500-2499 57703
2501-2599 57703
W Saint Patrick St 57702
Samco Rd 57702
Sammis Trl 57702
San Bernardo St 57703
San Francisco St 57701
San Marco Blvd 57702
Sanctuary Pl 57702
Sand Ct & Ln 57702
Sand Cherry Ln 57703
Sand Creek Ct 57703
Sanders Ranch Rd 57702
Sandlily Ct 57702
Sandra Ln 57701
Sandstone Ln 57701
Santana Ct 57701
Sapphire Ln 57702
Sarita Ct & St 57701
Saturn Dr 57703
Savannah St 57703
Savoy Cir 57701
Sawgrass Ct 57703
Sawmill Rd 57702
Scenic Dr 57702
Schaffer Rd 57702
Schamber St 57702
Schmitz Trl 57702
School Dr 57703
Schramberg Ct 57702
Schroeder Rd 57702
Scott St 57703
Scrub Oak Cir 57702
Seahawk Dr 57701
Secluded Ct 57702
Sedivy Ln 57703
Seeaire St 57702
Seger Dr 57701
Selkirk Pl 57702
Seminole Ln 57702
Sequoia Pl 57702
Serendipity Ln 57702
Serenity Ct 57703
Settlers Creek Pl 57701
Severson St 57702
Shad St 57703
Shadow Ct 57702
Shadow Mountain Ct 57702
Shannon Ct 57703
Sharlow Dr 57701
Sharp Dr & Ln 57703
Shaver St 57702
Shaw Ct 57703
Shayla Ct 57703
Sheffer St 57702
Shelter Dr 57702
Sheridan Loop 57702
Sheridan Heights Dr 57702
Sheridan Lake Rd 57702
Sherman St 57702
Sherry Ct 57703
Shetland Ln 57703
Shields Rd 57702
Shiloh Ct 57703
Shooting Star Trl 57702
Shore Dr 57702
Siding Ln 57702
Sienna Meadows Ln 57702
Sierra Ct & Pl 57702
E Signal Dr 57701
Sila Pl 57702
Silver St 57701
Silver Aspen Pl 57702
Silver City Rd 57702
Silver Fox Spur 57702
Silver Mountain Rd 57702
Silverleaf Ave 57701
Simpson Dr 57702
Sioux Ave 57701
Sitka St 57701
Sitting Bull St 57701
Sky St 57703
Skyline Dr 57701
Skyline Heights Ct 57701
Skyline Ranch Ct & Rd 57701
Skyview Dr 57702
Smith Ave 57701
Smokey Ridge Rd 57702
Snowberry Ct & Ln 57702
Snowmass Ct 57702
Soldier Field Ct 57701
Solitaire Dr 57703
Sonora Dr 57701
Sonquist Ln 57702
Soo San Dr 57702
Sophia Ct 57702
Sorrel Ct 57702
Sourdough Rd 57702
South St 57701
W South St 57702
Southpointe Dr 57701
Southside Dr 57703
Space Ave & Ct 57701
Spade Ct 57703
Sparrow Hawk Trl 57703
Spring Canyon Trl 57702
Springbrook Rd 57702
Springfield Rd 57703
Springsteen Ln 57701
Springtree Ct 57702
N Spruce St 57701
Sprucewood St 57703
Spyglass Ct 57702
Squire Ln 57702
Stacy St 57703
Stahl Ct 57701
Stanley Ct 57702
Star Ave 57701
N Star Rd 57702
Starlite Dr 57702
State St 57702
Station Loop 57703
Staton Pl 57702
Steamboat Cir 57702
Stearns Ct 57701
Steele Ave 57701
Steeler Ln 57701
Stellar Dr 57703
Stirling St 57702
Stirrup Ct 57702
Stockade Dr 57702
Stone Dr 57702
Stonecrest Dr 57702
Stonemeadow Rd 57702
Stoneridge Rd 57702
Stoney Brook Ct 57702
Stoney Creek Ct & Dr 57702
Storm Cir 57702
Storm Mountain Rd 57702
Stratmeyer Ct 57702
Strato Bowl Rd 57702
Strato Rim Dr 57702
Stratosphere Ln 57702
Strauss Ln 57702
E Stumer Rd 57701
Sturgis Rd & St 57702
Sully Ct 57703
Sum Pl 57701
Summer Creek Dr 57702
Summerfield Dr 57703
Summerset Dr 57702
Summit Blvd 57701
Sun Country Ln 57702
Sun Ridge Rd 57702
Sun Valley Dr 57702
Sunburst Dr 57702
Sundown Ct 57703
Sunlight Dr 57703
Sunny Hill Cir 57702
Sunny Springs Dr 57702
Sunnyside Dr 57701
Sunnyside Gulch Rd 57702
Sunnyvale Dr 57702
Sunset Dr 57702
Sunset Vista Rd 57702
Sunshine Trl 57702
Surfwood Dr 57701
Susan St 57701
Sutton Dr 57702
Sweet Clover Cir 57702
Sweetbriar St 57703
Swiss Dr 57702
Sycamore Pl 57702
Sycamore St 57701
Sydney Dr 57701
Taggart Rd 57701
Tahoe Peak Pl 57702
Tallent St 57701
E Tallent St
200-298 57701
300-1099 57701
1600-1799 57703
Tamara Ln 57702
Tamarack Dr 57701
Tanager Ct & Dr 57702
Taron Ct 57701
Tartan Ct 57701
Tatum Ct 57701
Taylor Ave 57701
Taylor Ranch Rd 57702
Teak Dr 57703
Teddy Bear Ln 57702
Teewinot Dr 57703
Telemark Ct 57702
Tepee St 57702
Terminal Rd 57703
Terra St 57703
N Terrace Dr & Pl 57701
Terracita Dr 57701
Terry Dr 57703
Teton Ln 57701
E Texas St 57701
Thames Cir 57702
Three Rivers Dr 57701
Thunderhead Falls Ln & Rd 57702
Timber Ln 57702
Timberlane Pl 57702
Timberline Ct, Rd & Trl 57702
Timmons Blvd 57703
Timothy St 57702
Tinton Ln 57703
Tish Blvd 57701
Titan Dr 57701
Tittle Springs Pl 57702
Tomaha Trl 57702
Tomaha Ridge Rd 57702
Tomahawk Dr 57702
Tompkins St 57701
Toni Ln 57703
Topaz Ln 57701
Tourist Rd 57702
Tower Ct & Rd 57701
Trae Ct 57701
Trail Dr 57703
S Trailview Dr 57702
Trailwood Ln 57703
Tranquil Trl 57701
Treeline Ct 57702
Triangle Trl 57702
Triple Crown Dr 57701
Triple S Dr 57702
Troon Ct 57702
Trooper King Rd 57702
Trout Ct 57702
Turbine Dr 57703
Turnberry Rd 57702
Turtle Creek Ct 57703
Tuscany Pl 57702
Twilight Dr 57703
Twin Elms Dr 57702
Twin Peak Ln 57702
Twin Springs Rd 57702
Tyler Ln 57701
Una Del Dr 57702
Universal Dr 57702
University Loop 57701
Upper Pines Dr 57701
Uranus Dr 57703
E Utah St 57701
Vale St 57702
Valentine St 57702
S Valley Dr 57703
Valley West Dr & Ln 57702
Van St 57701
E Van Buren St 57701
Vanishing Trail Ct 57702
Vantage Point Ct 57703
Vardon Ct 57702
Velvet Horn Pl 57702
Vick Dr 57702
Victoria Lake Rd 57702
Victory Ln 57702
Vienna Dr 57702
Viking Dr 57701
Villa Ridge Ct 57701
Village Dr 57701
Villaggio Ln 57702
Vilrickson Pl 57702
Vinecliff Dr 57703
Virginia Ln 57701
Vista Dr 57701
Vista Hills Dr 57702
Vista Ridge Rd 57701
Wallace St 57702
Walnut Dr 57701
Walter Pl 57701
Wamberg Ct 57702
Wambli Ct & Dr 57701

Ward Ct 57702
Warrington Ct 57702
Washington St 57702
E Waterloo St 57701
E Watertown St 57701
Waterville Ct 57702
Waxwing Ln 57702
Wayside Dr 57702
Weathervane Ln 57703
Wedgewood Dr 57702
Wellington Ct & Dr 57702
Wentworth Dr 57702
Wesleyan Blvd & Cir 57702
Wesson Rd 57703
West Blvd & St 57701
Westberry Ct & Dr 57702
Western Ave 57702
Westgate Dr & Pl 57702
Westpark Ln 57702
Westridge Rd 57702
Westview Estates Dr 57702
Westwind Dr 57702
Whaley Rd 57702
Wheaton Rd 57702
Wheel Inn Trl 57702
Whispering Pines Dr 57702
Whitewood St 57702
Wideview Dr 57702
Wild Flower Dr 57701
Wild Flower Ln 57702
Wild Irishman Rd 57702
Wild Life Rd 57702
Wilderness Cir & Trl 57702
Wilderness Canyon Rd 57702
Wildhorse Ct & Dr 57703
Wildwood Dr 57702
Wilkie Dr 57702
Williams St 57703
Willow Ave 57701
Willowbend Rd 57703
Willsie Ave 57701
Windhaven Dr 57703
Windmere Way 57703
Windmill Rd 57702
Windslow Dr & Pl 57701
Windsong Rd 57702
Windsor Dr 57702
Wineberry Ln 57703
Winfield Ct 57701
Wingate Ct 57701
Winged Foot Ct 57703
Winners Cir 57702
Winterset Dr 57702
Winton St 57703
Wisconsin Ave 57701
Wisteria Ct 57701
Wonderland Cir, Ct & Dr 57702
Wood Ave 57701
Woodbine Pl 57702
Woodcrest Ct 57702
Woodland Ct 57702
Woodlawn Dr 57701
Woodle Dr 57702
Woodridge Ct & Dr 57701
Woodrow St 57703
Woodrun Ln 57702
Woodstock Ct 57702
Wrangler Rd 57702
Wright Ct & St 57701
Wrinkle Valley Rd 57702
Wyoming 57702
Wyoming St 57701
E Wyoming St 57701
Yale Ct 57702
Yucca Dr 57702
Zamia St 57703
Zenker Pl 57702
Ziebach St 57703
Zinc St 57701
Zinnia St 57703

NUMBERED STREETS

1st Ave 57702
1st St 57701
N 1st St 57701
2nd Ave 57702
2nd St 57701
N 2nd St 57701
3rd Ave 57702
3rd St 57701
N 3rd St 57701
4th Ave 57702
4th St 57701
N 4th St 57701
5th Ave 57702
5th St 57701
N 5th St 57701
6th Ave 57702
6th St 57701
7th Ave 57702
7th St 57701
N 7th St 57701
7th Cavalry Trl 57702
9th Ave 57702
9th St 57701
11th St 57701
12th St 57701
E 27th St 57703
32nd St 57702
36th St 57702
37th St 57702
38th St 57702
N 39th 57702
N 40th St 57702
41st St 57702
N 42nd 57702
43rd Ct 57702
N 44th 57702
47th Ave W 57702
N 48th 57702
E 53rd St 57703
143rd Ave 57701
149th Ave 57703
153rd Ave 57703
154th Ave 57703
224th St 57701
225th St 57701
229th St 57703
237th St 57702

SIOUX FALLS SD

General Delivery 57101

POST OFFICE BOXES MAIN OFFICE STATIONS AND BRANCHES

Box No.s
1 - 3100 57101
5000 - 7590 57117
84001 - 86894 57118
87701 - 93134 57109

NAMED STREETS

N A Ave 57104
S Aaron Ave 57106
W Abbey Ln 57106
S Abbeystone Ct 57110
S Abbott Pl 57108
Aberdeen Ave & Cir 57106
S Acacia Cir 57106
S Acorn Ave 57105
Acorn Ct 57108
W Adalerso St 57106
E Adams St 57110
N Advantage Ave 57103
S Aftyn Ave 57108
N Aidan Ave 57107
S Alana Cir 57103
N Alaska Ave 57107
Albers Ave 57108
E Alder Ln 57105
S Alex Ct 57106
W Alexandra St 57106
W Algonquin St 57104
N Alguire Ave 57107
N Alicia Ave 57104
E Allen Dr 57103
W Alpha Pl 57106
S & E Alpine Ave & Cir 57110
W Alyssum St 57107
S Amanda Ct 57103
W Amber St 57107
E Amidon St 57104
S Amy Cir 57103
W Anchor Ln 57108
S Anderson Dr 57106
S Andrea Ave 57108
S Andrew Ave 57106
N Angel Ave 57104
E Angela Cir 57108
W Angie Pl 57105
S Anita Ave 57103
S Anna Ln 57106
W Annabelle St 57106
N Annika Ave 57107
S Annway Dr 57103
E Anoka Cir 57103
W Antelope Dr 57107
Anthem Cir & Dr 57110
S Anthony Ave 57106
W Antiqua St 57107
E Aplomado Blvd 57108
N Appaloosa Trl 57110
S Apple Pl 57105
E Apple Blossom Cir 57103
S April Pl 57105
W Arapahoe Cir 57106
Arbor Ave & Cir 57106
S Arcadia Rd 57105
E & N Archer Ave, Cir & Dr 57103
S & E Archstone Cir & St 57110
E Arctic Willow Cir 57110
S Arden Ave
4100-4899 57103
5000-5299 57108
S Arden Cir 57103
E Arrowhead Pass 57103
E Arrowhead Pkwy 57110
E Arrowhead Pl 57110
S Arthur Cir 57105
W Aruba St 57107
S Arway Dr 57106
S Ascot Ave 57103
S Ash Grove Ave
4100-4899 57103
4900-5499 57108
E Ash Grove Cir 57108
E Ashbury Pl 57110
W Ashcroft St 57106
N Ashland Dr 57104
W Ashley Cir 57104
S Ashorist Ave 57105
Aspen Cir, Dr & Hl 57105
E Aster Cir 57103
Auburn Hills Cir, Ct & St 57108
Audie Ave & Dr 57108
Aurora Ave & Cir 57107
Austin Ct 57108
S Austin Dr 57105
E Austin St 57103
E Autumn Ln 57105
Avalon Ave & Cir 57108
W Avera Dr 57108
W Aviary Pl 57107
N Aviation Ave 57104
S & E Avondale Ave, Cir & Ct 57110
N B Ave 57104
S Baha Ave 57106
N Bahnson Ave
600-1399 57103
1401-2099 57103
2200-2898 57104
S Bahnson Ave
200-4199 57103
4201-4399 57103
5200-5899 57108
E Bahnson Cir 57103
W Bailey St 57104
Baker Park Pl 57108
Bakker Cir & Pl 57108
W Bakker Park Dr 57106
Baldwin Ct & Dr 57108
S Ballymore Cir 57108
Baneberry Ave & Dr 57106
S Banyan Ave 57110
W Barbados St 57107
S Barbara Cir 57110
N Barnard Ave 57110
Baron Pl 57108
S Barret Pl 57106
S & W Barrington Cir, Dr & Pl 57108
E Basswood Ln 57110
W Batcheller Ln 57105
E Baxter Cir 57108
W Bayberry Cir 57108
E Beacon Pl 57103
N Beareens Ave 57104
Becky Rd 57108
S Bedford Ave 57103
S Beech Ave 57106
S Belfair Pl 57106
S Bell Cir 57108
S Bellepine Cir 57103
S Bellwood Ave 57108
E Belmont Cir 57103
E Belmont St
4400-4599 57103
4600-5399 57110
S & W Benelli Cir & Dr 57106
S Benjamin Dr 57103
E Bennett St 57103
W Bennett St 57104
E Benson Rd 57104
W Benson Rd 57107
N & W Bent Grass Ct & St 57107
Benton St 57107
W Bentreed Pl 57106
Bentwood Pl 57108
S & W Berkshire Blvd 57106
S Bernhaven Ave 57110
S & W Berretta Cir & Ln 57106
S Berry Cir 57105
S Bertina Cir 57103
S Beta Pl 57106
W Bethel Pl 57105
E Beverly St 57104
E Big Sky Pl 57110
S Big Timber Pl 57105
S Bill Dr 57110
S Bingen Ave 57110
S Birchwood Ave
3800-4799 57103
5000-5299 57108
W Birnhamwood Dr 57106
S Bishop Jones Pl 57103
E Bison Trl 57108
S & W Bitterroot Ct, Pl & St 57108
W Bittersweet Ln 57108
W Black Rock Cir 57108
Black Walnut Cir & St 57110
S Blackberry Dr 57108
W Blackhawk St 57104
S Blaine Ave 57103
E Blanche Pl 57103
N Blauvelt Ave 57103
S Blauvelt Ave
100-799 57103
1000-1099 57104
1101-1197 57105
1199-2699 57105
E Blazewood Dr 57110
N Blue Bell Ln 57107
Blue Sage Ln 57106
N Blue Spruce Pl 57110
W Bluebird Pl 57107
S Bluegrass Ct 57103
Bluegrass St 57107
E Blueridge Dr 57110
S & W Bluestem Cir & St 57106
N Bobhalla Dr 57107
N Bobwhite Pl 57107
S Bond Ave 57103
N Bonneville Pl 57104
W Bonnie Ct 57106
N Boulder Ave 57104
Boulder Creek Pl 57106
E Bourbon Pl 57110
Boxwood Pl & St 57107
W Boysenberry St 57106
E Brad St 57103
S & W Bradford Cir & Ct 57106
S Brady Ct 57103
E Braeburn Cir 57103
S Braemar Dr 57105
E Bragstad Dr 57103
W Bramble Cir 57108
Brande Ave & Pl 57108
Brandy Wine Cir & St 57108
S & W Braxton Cir & Dr 57108
Bream Ct, Dr & Pl 57107
N Breckenridge Cir 57110
S Breezeway Ave 57108
S Bremerton Pl 57106
S Brenda Pl 57108
E Brennan Dr 57110
Brentridge Cir & St 57108
S Brett Ave 57108
E Brewster St 57108
S Briar Cir 57108
E Briar Den Ct 57108
S Briarwood Ave
4300-4799 57103
5000-5299 57108
S Bridgeport Pl 57106
W Bridger St 57108
N & W Briggs Cir & Dr 57107
S & W Brighton Cir & Dr 57106
W Bristol Dr 57106
S Brittany Cir 57106
E Britton Cir 57103
S Broadband Ln 57108
W Broek Dr 57106
E Broken Arrow St 57103
N Broken Bow Ave 57103
E Brome Pl 57108
W Brook Haven Pl 57108
W Brookings St 57104
Brookline Cir & Dr 57103
W Brooks Pl 57106
E Brookshire Pl 57103
S Brookside Pl 57108
S Brookview Pl 57110
S Brown Pl 57105
S & W Browning Cir, Dr & St 57106
S Bruce Rd 57105
Brune Ave 57107
Buckeye St 57107
E Buckingham St 57108
N Bullet Pl 57103
N Bunker Pl 57103
S Bur Oak Pl 57108
S Burleigh Cir 57108
W Burnside St 57104
S Buttercup Trl 57110
N C Ave 57104
Cactus Dr 57110
Cactus Pl 57108
N Cactus Pl 57110
S & W Cain Ave & Cir 57106
E Cajun Pl 57110
N Caleb Ave 57103
N & S Caley Pl 57110
S Calico Pl 57108
E Callies Pl 57110
S Callington Cir 57108
S Cambridge Ave 57106
S Camden Ave 57106
S Camellia Ave 57110
S Cameo Way 57105
S Campbell Trl 57106
W Canary Dr & Pl 57107
W Cancedal St 57107
S Canterbury Pl 57106
S Canyon Ave 57110
S Capitol Ave 57110
Caraway Cir & Dr 57108
N Carbine Pl 57103
S Cardinal Dr
1900-2099 57105
26100-26199 57107
N & W Career Ave & Cir 57107
E Carlyle Cir 57108
W Carmel Ln 57108
Carnegie Cir & Pl 57106
E Carol St 57104
S Carolyn Ave
101-199 57107
2400-3299 57106
E Carra Pl 57108
S Carriage Ct & Ln 57108
S Carrick Ave 57106
S Carter Pl 57105
S Carver Cir 57108
W Cascade St 57108
N Casco Ave 57104
S Casea Cir 57108
S Cassandra Cir 57106
N Castle Dr 57107
E Castleroc Pl 57103
S Cathedral Ave 57103
S Cathy Ave 57106
W Cayman St 57107
Cedar Ln & Pl 57103
E Centennial Ln 57110
S Center Ave 57105
W Central Pl 57108
W Chad Cir 57106
W Chadwick Pl 57106
E Chambers St 57104
N Chapel Hill Rd 57103
S Chapelwood Ave 57110
S Charger Cir 57108
E & N Charleston Cir & Dr 57110
S Charlotte Ave 57103
S Charlotte Cir 57103
Charlotte Ct 57108
E Chatham St 57108
S Chatworth Cir 57108
N Cheers Pl 57107
W Chelsea Dr 57106
Cherapa Pl 57103
W Cherokee St 57104
E Cherry Ln 57105
S Cherry Lake Ave 57107
W Cherrywood Cir 57108
S & W Chesapeake Cir & Ln 57106
S Chestnut Cir 57103
Chestnut St 57107
Cheyenne Ct & Dr 57106
N & S Chicago Ave 57103
W Chickadee Pl 57107
Chicory Cir & Ln 57108
S Chinook Ave 57108
W Chippewa Cir 57106
S & W Christopher Ave & Pl 57106
S Chuck Dr 57108
S Churchill Ave 57103
S Cimarron Pl 57108
S Cinnabar Cir 57103
Cinnamon Cir & St 57108
Cinnamon Ridge Pl 57108
W Circle Dr 57106
E Claremont St 57110
E Clark St
1400-1498 57105
4501-4799 57110
S Clarkway Dr 57105
E Claudette Dr 57103
W Clay St 57106
S Clearbrook Ave 57106
E Clearwater Pl 57108
N & S Cleveland Ave 57103
Cliff Ave 57108
N Cliff Ave
100-1899 57103
2500-2998 57104
3000-6599 57104
6601-7799 57104
S Cliff Ave
300-598 57103
515-597 57104
599-1000 57104
1002-1098 57104
1100-2999 57105
3001-3499 57105
3700-4600 57103
4602-4898 57103
4900-5098 57108
5100-6399 57108
6401-7099 57108
Cloudas Ave 57104
S Cloudas Ave 57103
S Clover Ave 57110
S Clover Ln 57106
E Club View Dr 57110
S Clubhouse Rd 57108
S Coates Rd 57105
S Cobblestone Pl 57108
N Cockatiel Pl 57107
Cody Rd 57108
S Colleen Ln 57106
N Colorado Ave 57107
Columbia Cir & Dr 57103
S Comet Rd 57103
S Commerce Ave 57110
Commons Pl 57106
W Condor Pl 57107
N Conifer Pl 57107
N & S Conklin Ave 57103
S Connie Ave 57108
N Connor Trl 57103
S Cook Rd 57105
Copper Crest Cir & Trl 57110
S Copper Ridge Rd 57108
S Copperhead Dr 57108
Coral Cir & Ct 57103
N Cornflower Ave 57107
S Coromell Pl 57108
S Corporate Pl 57108
S Cortland Ave 57103
N & S Cory Pl 57110
W Costello Rd 57105
S & W Cottage Cir & Trl 57106
Cottonwood Ave 57107
S Cottonwood Pl 57106
W Coughran Ct 57106
Country Acres Dr 57106
S & W Courtyard Cir & Ln 57108
N Covell Ave 57104
S Covell Ave
100-899 57104
1400-3199 57105
3201-3299 57105
W Coventary Cir 57108
E Covey Cir 57108
S Crane Ave 57108
S Cranston Cir 57106
N Crape Pl 57107
Creekside Cir & Dr 57106
S Creole Pl 57110
S Crescent Dr 57106
E Crestview Dr 57103
S Crestwood Rd 57105
W Crimson St 57108
S Crossing Pl 57108
Crown Hill Cir & Dr 57106
S Crown Point Dr 57103
S Culbert Ave 57106
W Cushman St 57107
W Custer Ln 57106
E Cynthia Dr 57110

N Cypress Pl 57104
N D Ave 57104
S Daffodil Cir 57108
Dahlia Ct 57107
N Daisy Ave 57107
N Dakota Ave 57104
S Dakota Ave
100-899 57104
901-999 57104
1000-2300 57105
2302-2598 57105
S Dakota Pl 57105
Dale Cir & Dr 57110
S & W Dalston Cir & Ln 57108
E Dan Rdg 57110
E Dana Dr 57105
S Danberry Dr 57106
S Daniel Dr 57110
N Danielle Dr 57103
W Dante Pl 57107
W Darcie St 57106
W Dardanella Rd 57106
S Darryl Pl 57110
Dartmoor Ave & Cir 57106
S David Dr 57103
S & E Dawley Cir & Ct 57103
Dawson Ave 57107
S Day Ave 57103
W Deer Creek Dr 57106
E Deer Haven Pl 57105
Deer Hollow Cir & Rd 57110
S Deer Park Dr 57108
S Deerberry Trl 57106
S Deerfield Cir 57105
Deerfield Pl 57108
E Del Mar Cir 57103
W Delaware St 57104
W Delrich Dr 57107
W Delta Pl 57106
S Denton Ave 57108
S Desoto Ave 57110
N & S Detroit Ave 57110
W Devitt Dr 57108
S Devon Dr 57106
N & S Dewberry Ave & Cir 57110
E Diablo Cir 57108
S Diamond Cir 57108
S Diamond Pl 57106
E Dike Dr 57104
S Discovery Ave 57106
W Disney Pl 57104
N Ditch Rd 57104
S Dodge Ave 57106
N Dogwood Pl 57107
N Doland Pl 57107
W Domar Cir 57108
W Dome Pl 57105
Dominic Ave, Cir & St 57107
W Donahue Dr 57105
S Donegal Ave 57106
S Doodler Dr 57103
S & W Doral Ave, Ct & Trl 57108
S Dorothy Ave 57106
S Dorothy Cir 57106
Dorothy Dr 57107
S Douglas Pl 57106
E Dove Trl 57108
S & W Dover Cir & Dr 57106
W Dow Rummel St 57104
S Downing Ave 57106
S Dragonfly Dr 57110
W Dragonfly Dr 57107
S Drexel Dr 57106
Driftwood Cir 57108
S Dublin Ave 57106
N & S Dubuque Ave 57110
S Duchess Ave 57103
E Dudley Ln 57103
E Dugout Ln 57110
N Duluth Ave 57104
S Duluth Ave
100-999 57104
1000-4699 57105
4701-4799 57105
W Dunbar Trl 57108
S Dundee Dr 57106
S Dunham Cir 57106
Dunlap Ave & Ct 57106
Durango Cir & Dr 57110
Durham Ave & Cir 57108
N E Ave 57104
N Eagle Pl 57107
Eagle Ridge Cir & St 57108
N Eagles Nest Ave 57107
E Eastbridge Pl 57110
N Ebenezer Ave 57107
S Ebenezer Ave 57106
S Eden Cir 57106
Edgewood Pl & Rd 57103
S Edinborough Dr 57106
S Edinburg Pl 57108
N Edsel Dr 57110
S Edward Dr 57103
W Eide Dr 57107
Eisenhower Ave & Cir 57106
S & E El Dorado Ave, Cir, Ct & Dr 57108
W Elder Dr 57106
S Elderberry Cir 57108
W Eli Ct 57106
E Elizabeth Dr 57103
W Elkhorn St 57104
S Elkjer Cir 57103
N Ellis Rd 57107
S Ellis Rd 57106
N Ellison Ave 57103
E Elm St 57104
Elmen Pl 57108
S Elmstead Cir 57108
N Elmwood Ave 57104
S Elmwood Ave
100-699 57104
1201-1997 57105
1999-3899 57105
S Elmwood Pl 57105
E Elston Pl 57110
S Emerald Pl 57106
S Emery Ave 57106
W Emily St 57106
S Emma Ln 57106
W Emmitt Cir 57106
Empire Mall & Pl 57106
S Enterprise Ave 57110
W Epsilon Pl 57106
W Equestrian Pl 57106
S Equity Dr 57106
S Erica Dr 57108
E Erin Pl 57110
Essex Ct, Dr & Ter 57106
S Ester Dr 57103
W Eucalyptus Pl 57107
N Euclid Ave 57104
S Euclid Ave
101-899 57104
1100-1198 57105
1200-3299 57105
W & N Evergreen Cir & Dr 57107
N Evy Ave 57107
N F Ave 57104
E Fair Ln 57105
N Fairfax Ave
101-197 57103
199-899 57103
5400-5499 57104
S Fairfax Ave 57103
S Fairhall Ave 57106
N Fairway Cir 57110
N Fairway Dr 57110
Fairway Pl 57108
E Fairway Pl 57110
S Faith Ave
3501-3599 57110
5000-5199 57108
5201-5699 57108
W Falcon Pl 57107
E Falls Park Dr 57104
N Fanelle Ave 57103
S Faris Ave 57105
E & S Fawn Cir & Ct 57110
W Feathered Cir 57108
S & E Fernwood Ave & Dr 57110
E Fiddlewood Dr 57110
E Fieldstone Pl 57108
N Fiero Pl 57104
W Finch Pl 57107
N Fir Pl 57107
S Firefly Dr 57110
S & E Fireside Ave & Cir 57103
S Firestone Ln 57110
W Flamingo Pl 57107
W Flicker Dr 57107
S Florence Ave 57103
W Ford Cir 57106
N & S Foss Ave 57110
S Foster Ave 57103
E Fountain Cir 57103
S Fox Trl 57103
E Fox Run Pl 57103
W Foxdale St 57107
S Foxglove Pl 57110
N & S Franklin Ave 57103
E Freda Cir 57103
S Frederick Dr 57105
N French Ave
200-999 57103
5400-5599 57104
5601-6321 57104
S Frontier Trl 57108
W & N Galaxy Cir & Ln 57107
S Galway Ave 57106
W Garden Pl 57108
S Gardner Dr 57103
E Garfield Ave 57110
N Garfield Ave 57104
S Garfield Ave
100-999 57104
1401-1897 57105
1899-3399 57105
N Garfield Cir 57104
S Garfield Dr 57105
S Garnet Pl 57106
S Gary Dr 57103
S Gateway Blvd 57106
W Gateway Cir 57107
S Gateway Ln 57106
S Gazena Pl 57106
N Gemini Dr 57107
E Gemstone Cir 57103
S Genevieve Ave 57103
S George St 57110
S Gerbera Ave 57106
S Gibson Ave 57106
Gill Ave & Cir 57106
S Gina Pl 57106
Glen Eagle Cir & St 57108
S Glen Haven Pl 57108
W Glenbrook St 57108
S Glendale Ave
401-497 57104
499-999 57104
1000-3999 57105
S Glenview Rd
4000-4899 57103
4900-5299 57108
N Glenwood Cir 57103
E Gold Dust St 57104
E & N Gold Nugget Ave & Cir 57104
W Golden Pl 57106
S Golden Creek Pl 57106
W Golden Eagle St 57108
S Golden Willow Ave 57110
S Goldenrod Ln 57110
W Goldthread Cir 57108
Gordon Cir 57106
S Gordon Dr 57110
Grace Ave & Cir 57103
Graceland Ct & Pl 57106
S Grand Cir 57108
S & W Grand Arbor Cir, Ct & Pl 57108
S Grand Lodge Pl 57108
W Grand Point Cir 57108
S Grand Prairie Dr 57108
S Grandview Ave 57103
N Grange Ave 57104
S Grange Ave
100-899 57104
1000-1200 57105
1202-4099 57105
6801-7399 57108
N Granite Ln 57107
E Granny Smith Pl 57103
E Grant St 57110
S Grass Creek Dr 57108
S Gray Goose Cir 57110
S Graystone Ave
4400-4699 57103
4901-5199 57108
E Greenbrier Pl 57108
S Greenwood Ave 57106
W Grinn Pl 57106
S & W Grinnell Ave & Cir 57106
Grouse Point Pl 57108
W Grove Pl 57107
Groveland Ave & Dr 57110
N Gulby Ave 57104
N H Ave 57104
S Hackberry Cir 57103
S Hackrott Cir 57108
E Hagen Cir 57110
N Hainje Ave 57104
N Haley Ave 57104
S Hallmark Ln 57106
Hallow Ave & Cir 57106
N & S Hampton Ave 57110
W Hanger St 57104
E Hanna Cir 57110
E Hanover Ct 57110
S Hanson Pl 57108
S Haraldson Ave 57106
N Harlem Ave 57104
N Harley Pl 57103
E Harmodon St 57110
N Harmon Ave 57107
S & E Harmony Ct, Dr & St 57110
W Harpel Dr 57105
E Harriet Lea 57103
N & S Harrington Ave, Cir & Pl 57103
E Hartleaf Cir 57110
W Harvard Dr 57106
N Harvestore Rd 57107
S Harvey Dunn Dr 57103
E Harwood Cir 57103
W Hathaway Ln 57106
W Haugo Dr 57105
E Havenhill Dr 57110
N Hawthorne Ave 57104
S Hawthorne Ave
201-297 57104
299-999 57104
1000-3999 57105
4001-4099 57105
E Hayes Pl 57103
N Hazel Pl 57107
W Hazeltine Ln 57108
E Hearthstone Pl 57108
S & W Heatherridge Ave & Cir 57108
S Heatherwood Cir 57108
N Heights Ave 57104
E Hein Pl 57110
N Helen Ave 57104
S Hemingstone Trl 57108
W Hemlock Dr 57107
Hendon Cir & Ln 57108
Henry Pl 57108
W Heritage Pl 57106
E Hermosa Dr 57104
S Hickory Hill Rd 57103
S Hidden Pl 57106
E Hidden Valley Rd 57110
S High Cross Trl 57108
N Highland Ave
200-298 57103
300-1799 57103
2900-3299 57104
S Highland Ave 57103
N & S Highline Ave & Pl 57110
W Hillary Dr 57106
N Hillcrest Ave 57104
S Hills Rd 57103
S Hillside Dr 57110
N Hillside Pl 57107
E & S Hillview Cir & Rd 57110
E Hinks Ln 57104
W Hobbs Cir 57107
S Hoffman Pl 57108
S Hofstad Ave 57106
N Holbrook Ave 57107
S Holbrook Ave 57106
N Holiday Ave 57103
N Holland Ave 57107
N Holly Ave 57104
S Holly Ave
100-699 57104
1800-1898 57105
1900-3399 57105
S Holly Dr 57105
S Holt Ave 57103
S Homan Pl 57108
S Home Plate Ave 57110
W Homefield Dr 57106
N Homestead Cir 57103
S Honey Locust Ave 57110
S & W Honeysuckle Ct & Trl 57106
E, S & W Honors Cir, Dr & St 57108
S Horizon Cir 57106
Horizon Dr 57104
S Horizon Ln 57106
W Hovland Dr 57107
E Huber St 57110
N Hudson Ave 57104
S & W Hughes Ave & Pl 57108
N Hummingbird Ave 57107
S Hunters Cir 57103
Huntington Cir & St 57103
Hyannis Port Ln 57106
S Hyde Park 57106
S Hypointe Cir 57105
E I-90 Ln 57104
Independence Ave 57108
Indian Hills Ct 57108
Indian Ridge Ct 57108
N Indiana Ave
100-899 57103
5400-5499 57104
S Indiana Ave 57103
E Indigo Pl 57108
N Industrial Ave 57104
S Infield Ave 57110
W Innovation St 57107
E Inverness Dr 57108
W Ione St 57106
N Irene Pl 57107
E Iris Pl 57103
E Ironwood Cir 57103
S Isabel Pl 57108
N Islay Pl 57104
E Ivy Pl 57103
S Jackie Ave 57106
W Jacks St 57107
Jacob Cir & St 57106
W Jade Pl 57106
W Jade Berry Cir 57108
S Jana Pl 57106
S Jandl Dr 57106
Jane Ave 57104
E Jane Ln 57108
W & N Jans Cir & Dr 57107
S Jaren Lee Pl 57108
Jasmine Cir & Trl 57108
E Jasper Cir 57110
S Jay Cir 57103
N Jaycee Ln 57104
S Jayme Cir 57106
W Jeanne Dr 57106
S Jefferson Ave
100-699 57104
1001-1197 57105
1199-3399 57105
S Jeffrey Ave 57108
N Jenifer Pl 57107
E Jenny Cir 57108
N Jeremy Cir 57110
S Jersey Tess Dr 57108
Jesse James Cir, Ct & Dr 57103
N Jessica Ave
200-1999 57103
2900-3999 57104
4001-4099 57104
S Jessica Ave 57103
N Jessica Pl 57103
S John Ave 57106
N John Orr Dr 57104
W Johnson Pl 57105
S Joliet Ave 57110
W Jolyn Dr 57108
S Jonathan Ln 57103
S & W Jordan Cir, Ct & Dr 57106
S Joseph Pl 57106
S Josh Wyatt Dr 57108
W Jovan Cir 57108
S Joyce Dr 57110
S Judy Ave 57103
Julie Dr 57108
S June Ave 57106
S Juneau Ln 57106
N Juniper Pl 57107
W Justice St 57106
E Justin Dr 57108
N K Ave 57104
S Kalen Pl 57108
W Karen Dr 57106
W Karmya Cir 57106
W Kathleen St 57107
S Kathryn Ave 57106
S Katie Ave 57106
S Kaystone Dr 57103
E Kearney Pl 57110
S Keith Ln 57110
S Kelley Ave 57106
Kelsey Cir & St 57106
S Kennedy Ave 57103
E Kensington St 57108
W Kenwood Mnr 57104
S Kerry Ave 57106
E Kestral Pl 57108
S Keva Ave 57106
S Kevin Cir 57106
S Key Ave 57106
S Kierra Ct 57106
S & W Killarney Cir, Ct & St 57108
S Kinderhook Ave 57106
W King Arthur Dr 57106
Kingfisher Cir & Dr 57107
N Kings Trail Pl 57104
S Kingsberry Dr 57106
W Kingston Dr 57107
S Kingswood Way 57106
S Kinkade Ave 57103
S Kinser Cir 57110
W Kira Cir 57106
Kirkwood Cir & Pl 57106
N Kiwanis Ave
100-1300 57104
1302-1598 57104
5200-5298 57107
5300-25899 57107
S Kiwanis Ave
100-198 57104
200-900 57104
902-998 57104
1400-1798 57105
1800-3804 57105
3806-3898 57105
S Kiwanis Cir 57105
S Klein Ave 57106
E Klondike Trl 57103
N Knoll Dr 57110
W Kogel Dr 57107
S Kris Dr 57103
S Kristen Cir 57106
N Krohn Pl 57103
Kuehn Park Ave & Rd 57106
W Kuhle Dr 57107
S Kyle Ave 57103
N & S La Mesa Dr 57107
N & S La Salle Ave & Cir 57110
E Lacey Pl 57103
S Lafayette Pl 57110
N Lake Ave 57104
S Lake Ave
100-899 57104
1401-1597 57105
1599-3299 57105
E Lake Placid Cir 57110
W Lakeshore Blvd 57106
Lakeside Cir & Dr 57107
N Lakeview Rd 57110
N Lalley Ln 57107
N Lamesa Ave 57107
S & W Lancaster Cir, Dr & St 57106
S Landau Cir 57108
W Landon Ln 57107
W Landscape Pl 57108
S Landsdown Dr 57106
E Lanner Pl 57108
W Lantana Cir 57108
Laquinta Cir & St 57108
S Larch Ave 57106
W Larkin Dr 57105
S & W Larkspur Cir & Trl 57106
S Larry Ln 57103
Latigo Cir & Trl 57108
S Laurel Oak Dr 57103
S Laurie Dr 57103
W Lavern Wipf St 57106
Lazy Oaks Cir 57108
S Lazy Ridge Pl 57108
S Le Chateau Pl 57105
N Leadale Ave 57110
N Leaders Ave 57103
S & W Leah Cir & St 57106
S Ledgestone Pl 57108
Legacy Ct & St 57106
W Legion Dr 57104
Leighton Cir 57108
S Leinster Ave 57106
N Lewis Ave
200-1999 57103
2800-4515 57104
4517-4909 57104
S Lewis Ave
200-298 57103
300-4899 57103
4901-4997 57108
4999-5500 57108
5502-5598 57108
S Lewis Ct 57103
E Lexington Cir 57103
E Libby Ln 57108
S Liberty Pl 57106
Lighthouse Pl 57108
S Lilac Pl 57105
S Lillian Ave 57106
N Lily Pl 57103
S Limerick Cir 57108
E Limestone Cir 57110
N Lincoln Ave 57104
S Lincoln Ave
100-699 57104
1800-3399 57105
S Lincoln Rd 57105
N Linda Ave 57103
E Linden Ln 57110
S Lindenwald Dr 57106
S Linedrive Ave 57110
N Linwood Ct 57103

S Lisa Dr 57110
S Lisanne Ave 57103
S Little Brook Ln 57106
W Lobelia St 57106
S Lockwood Pl 57105
N Locust Ave 57103
S Locust Dr 57105
W Loganberry St 57106
S Lois Ln 57108
London Cir & Dr 57106
N Longview Ave 57107
S Lorne Ln 57106
E & W Lotta St 57105
Louise Ave 57108
N Louise Ave 57107
S Louise Ave
2300-2398 57106
2400-2500 57106
2501-4999 57106
2501-2501 57109
2502-4998 57106
5000-7499 57108
7501-7599 57108
N Louise Cir 57107
N Louise Dr 57107
N & S Lowell Ave 57103
S Lucerne Ave 57106
Ludlow Cir & Ln 57108
W Luke Dr 57106
S Lupine Pl 57110
N Lyme Grass Ave 57107
S & W Lyncrest Ave, Pl & Trl 57108
N Lyndale Ave 57104
S Lyndale Ave
100-699 57104
1000-3199 57105
S Lyons Ave 57106
N Lyons Blvd 57107
N M Ave 57104
N & S Mable Ave 57103
S Mac Arthur Ln 57108
S & W Mac Dougall Cir & St 57106
S Macey Ave 57106
S Madelyn Ln 57106
N Madison Cir 57103
E Madison St
2000-3699 57103
4501-4697 57110
4699-9599 57110
W Madison St
800-898 57104
900-2899 57104
3000-5498 57107
5500-8299 57107
Magnolia Ave & Cir 57103
N Main Ave 57104
S Main Ave
100-899 57104
1000-2899 57105
Majestic Dr 57108
S Majestic View Pl 57103
N Mallard Pl 57107
S Manchester Ct 57108
S & W Mandy Ave, Cir & Ct 57106
E Mangrove St 57110
W Manna Grass St 57107
E Manor Cir 57103
N Maple Ln 57107
E Maple St
301-399 57104
500-798 57104
5100-7599 57110
W Maple St 57107
S Marday Ave 57103
W Mardo Cir 57108
W Margaret Cir 57106
N Mari Car Dr 57107
S Maria Ave 57106
S Mariah Pl 57108
Mariana Ct & Dr 57103
N Marietta Pl 57107
S Marigold Ave 57110
N Marion Rd 57107
S Marion Rd
100-200 57107
202-398 57107
400-498 57106
500-5199 57106
5201-6999 57106
N Marker Dr 57110
N Markey Ave 57107
W Marlis St 57106
N Marlowe Ave 57110
N & S Marquette Ave & Cir 57110
Marsha St 57108
E Marson Dr 57103
S Marson Manor Cir 57103
N Martindale Rd 57107
S Mary Dr 57105
S Mary Beth Ave 57106
S Mary Knoll Dr 57105
S Matt Rd 57110
Matthew Cir & Dr 57103
Maverick Pl 57104
S Mayfair Dr 57106
N Mayfield Pl 57107
N Mayflower Pl 57103
N Maynard Ln 57110
S Mayo Ave 57106
E & S Maywood Dr 57110
E & W Mcclellan St 57104
E Mcintosh St 57103
S Mckenzie Pl 57106
S Mcknelly Ave 57106
S Mcmartin Ave 57108
Meadow Ave & Ln 57106
N Meadowbrook Ln 57110
S Meadowlark Cir 57108
Meadowlark Ln 57107
E Meadowlark Trl 57108
S Medina Cir 57108
S Megan Ave 57106
S Melanie Ln 57103
S Melrose Pl 57106
N Menlo Ave 57104
S Menlo Ave
100-900 57104
902-998 57104
1000-1298 57105
1300-2999 57105
S Meredith Ave 57108
W Meridian Pl 57106
W Mesa Pass 57106
S & E Mesquite Ave & Cir 57110
N Meyer Ln 57103
N Mgm Pl 57104
S & E Micah Cir & Ln 57103
W Miles Pl 57108
N Mineral Ave 57104
W Minnehaha Dr 57105
Minnesota Ave 57108
N Minnesota Ave 57104
S Minnesota Ave
100-100 57104
102-999 57104
1000-4799 57105
4800-6098 57108
6100-7400 57108
7402-7798 57108
W Miramar Cir 57108
E Mission St 57103
W Missouri St 57106
W Misty Glen Pl 57106
S Mockingbird Cir 57103
S Mogen Ave 57108
N Montana Ave 57107
S Monterey Pl 57108
N Montgomery Ct 57103
Monticello Ave & Ct 57106
S Montpelier Ave 57106
E Monument Pl 57104
S Moonflower Ave 57110
S & W Moor Cross Cir & Dr 57108
N Morrell Ave 57103
S Morrow Dr 57106
Morton Ct 57108
Mosby Cir & St 57108
Moss Stone Ave & Cir 57110
N Mossy Oak Ave 57103
S Mountain Ash Dr 57103
S Mueller Ave 57108
E Mulberry St 57103
W Mulberry St
1500-1598 57104
3201-3297 57107
3299-3399 57107
W Murphy Dr 57108
Mustang Ave & Cir 57108
E & N Mystic Cir & Dr 57110
W Nancy St 57106
S Nathan Ave 57103
N National Ave 57104
W National Guard Dr 57104
S Nature Run Pl 57108
Neener Cir 57104
S Nelson Cir 57106
N Nesmith Ave 57103
S Nevada Ave 57108
S & E Newcastle Ct & St 57110
S & W Newcomb Ave, Dr & St 57106
S Newport Pl 57106
S Newton Pl 57106
S Nicann Ct 57103
S Nicholas Ave 57106
W Nicole Dr 57105
W Nikita Dr 57106
W Noah Cir 57106
W Norie Pl 57106
W Norma Trl 57106
N North Dr 57104
S Northridge Cir 57105
Northstar Ln & Pl 57108
N Northview Ave 57107
S Norton Ave 57105
N Notley Ct 57110
N Nunda Pl 57107
W Nuthatch Pl 57107
E Nye St 57103
S Oak Cir 57103
N Oak Pl 57110
E Oak St
500-1499 57105
3200-4599 57103
W Oak St
1801-1897 57105
1899-2999 57105
3001-3099 57105
5400-5499 57106
5501-5699 57106
S Oak Ridge Ave 57103
N Oak Ridge Pl 57110
Oak Trail Pl 57108
Oakcrest Dr & Pl 57107
S Oakland Dr 57106
E Oakmont Pl 57110
N Oakview Pl 57110
E Oakwood Pl 57110
S Ogorman Dr 57105
N Ohio Ave 57107
N Oklahoma Ave 57107
S Old Brook Pl 57106
N Old Cabin Trl 57110
Old Farm Pl 57108
E Old Hickory Pl 57104
S & E Old Orchard Cir & Trl 57103
S Old Village Pl 57108
S & W Old Yankton Cir, Pl & Rd 57108
N Olde Wagon Rd 57110
W Oleanna Pl 57103
S Olive Dr 57103
S Ollerich Ave 57106
N Olympia Dr 57103
N & S Omaha Ave 57103
W Omega Pl 57106
S & E Orchard Ave & Pl 57103
S Orchid Ave 57110
W Oregon St 57107
W Oriole Cir 57106
N Orion Dr 57107
E Orleans Pl 57110
W Orwin Pl 57105
W Oscar Howe Cir 57106
S Ostro Ave 57108
S & E Otonka Pass, Rdg & Trl 57103
S Outfield Ave 57110
S Outlook Dr 57106
E Ovenc St 57110
S Overlook Dr 57103
S Overlund Pass 57110
W Owl Pl 57107
S Oxbow Ave 57106
Oxford Ave & Cir 57106
Paddington Cir & Trl 57110
S Paisley Ln 57108
Palametto Cir & St 57110
S Palisade Ln 57106
S Palmer Pl 57106
E Palomino Rd 57110
E Pam Rd 57105
E Pampas Pl 57110
N Pampas Grass Ave 57107
W Panama St 57106
W Panda Dr 57107
W Paradise Pl 57107
W Parakeet Pl 57107
N Paramount Pl 57104
S Park Ave 57105
E Park Dr 57105
Park Knl 57108
S Parklane Dr 57106
W Parkwood Ave & Cir 57108
W Parliament Dr 57106
Partridge St 57104
S Pasque Cir 57105
Pasque Ct 57108
W Pat St 57107
S Patrick Pl 57105
S Paulton Ave 57103
W Peacock Dr 57107
E Pearl St 57103
W Pebble Creek Rd 57106
N Pekin Pl 57107
N Pelican Pl 57107
S Pendar Ln 57105
W Penmarch Pl 57108
S Pennant Pl 57110
S & E Pennbrook Ave & Cir 57108
N Pennsylvania Ave 57107
N Penstemon Ave 57110
W Pentagon Pl 57107
E Peony Pl 57103
S & E Pepper Ridge Ave & Cir 57103
S Peregrine Pl 57108
S Perry Pl 57110
S Petro Ave 57107
W Pettigrew Ln 57106
S Pheasant Ln 57108
Phillip St 57105
N Phillips Ave 57104
S Phillips Ave
100-900 57104
902-998 57104
1000-3599 57105
N Pikes Peak Cir 57110
S Pillsberry Ave 57103
S Pin Oak Ct 57103
E Pine St 57103
S Pine Cone Pl 57105
S Pine Crest Pl 57106
E & N Pine Lake Dr & Rdg 57110
W Pine Meadows Pl 57107
E & S Pinehurst Cir, Ct & Dr 57108
N & W Pineridge Cir & Dr 57107
S Pinnacle Pl 57108
S Pintail Pl 57105
E Pioneer Trl 57103
E Piping Rock Ln 57108
S Plains Dr 57106
S Plandenw Ave 57108
S Plateau Trl 57106
Platinum Point Pl 57108
N Pleasantview Pl 57110
S Plucker Pl 57106
Plum Creek Cir & Rd 57105
E Plymouth Rd 57110
S Point Dr 57103
E Ponderosa Dr 57103
N Pontiac Pl 57104
E Pop Fly Pl 57110
S Poplar Dr 57105
S Portice Cir 57103
S Potomac Cir 57106
N Potsdam Ave 57104
N Potter Ave 57107
E, N & S Powder House Cir & Rd 57110
N Prairie Ave 57104
S Prairie Ave
100-899 57104
901-999 57104
1000-3299 57105
Prairie Dr 57106
S Prairie Creek Pl 57108
S Prairie Gardens Pl 57110
W Prairie Heart Pl 57108
W Prairie Rose St 57107
Prairie View Cir & Ct 57108
S Prairieside Pl 57108
E & N Presentation Ct & St 57104
W President St 57106
Preston Ln & Pl 57110
S Prestwick Pl 57106
N Primrose Pl 57107
S Prince Of Peace Pl 57103
S Princeton Ave 57106
W Pritchard Dr 57106
N Privet Pl 57107
E Producer Ln 57104
E Prospect St
1000-1200 57104
1202-1398 57104
2601-2697 57103
2699-2999 57103
5000-5299 57110
N Providence Ln 57110
S Purdue Ave 57106
N Purple Martin Ave 57107
W Quail Creek Cir 57108
S Quail Run Ave
4500-4899 57105
4900-4999 57108
5001-5099 57108
E Quail Run Cir 57108
N Quarry Ave 57104
S & E Quartzite Cir & Dr 57110
S & W Queens Ave & Cir 57106
Quiet Oak Cir & Trl 57108
E Quincey St 57110
S Racket Dr 57106
W Raegan St 57106
Rain Tree Rd 57108
Rainy Cir 57110
W Ralph Rogers Rd 57108
W Rambler Pl 57108
E Rampart Pl 57110
N Ranch Oak Pl 57110
S Randolph Ln 57106
N Raven Pl 57107
E Raven Oaks Cir 57103
S Raymond Cir 57106
W Rebecca St 57106
S Red Hill Cir 57108
E Red Oak Dr 57110
N & S Red Spruce Ave & Cir 57110
S Red Willow Ave 57110
N Redbird Pl 57107
N Redbud Pl 57107
S Redstone Ave 57108
S Redwood Ave 57106
Regal Ct 57108
S Regal Pl 57106
E Regency Ct 57103
S Regent Park Dr 57108
W Regina St 57106
S Reid St 57103
S Remington Cir 57106
S Remington Pl 57108
E Renee Pl 57110
N Reppert Ave 57107
N Republic Pl 57104
W Research Dr 57107
E Revere Dr 57110
Revilo Pl 57108
Reynolds Pl 57108
S Rhonda Ave 57108
W Ribbon Pl 57106
E Rice St
800-3499 57103
5000-7199 57110
W Rice St 57104
N Richard Pl 57103
N Richmond Cir 57103
N Ricochet Pl 57103
E Ridge Rd 57105
S & W Ridgestone Cir & Dr 57108
S Ridgeview Way 57105
S Risley Cir 57106
E River Blvd 57104
E & S River Bluff Cir & Rd 57110
River Oaks Cir & Dr 57105
S River Park Pl 57108
E River Ridge Pl 57103
E River Rock Cir 57110
S Riverdale Rd 57105
W Rivers Edge Way 57105
Riverside Pl 57108
S Riverview Ave 57110
S Riverview Hts 57105
S & W Riverward Dr & Pl 57106
N Rko Pl 57104
S Roberts Dr 57104
S Robin Dr
2900-2998 57105
26100-26199 57107
N Robindale Pl 57103
E Robur Dr 57104
N & S Rochelle Pl 57110
S Rock Creek Dr 57103
W Rocky Ridge Cir 57106
S Rohl Dr 57103
S Rolling Green Ave 57108
Rolling Thunder Ln 57108
N Romar Dr 57107
S & E Ronning Ct & Dr 57103
Roosevelt Ave & Cir 57106
W Rose St 57105
S & W Rose Crest Cir, Ct, Dr & Trl 57108
Rosemont Cir & Ln 57106
S Rotary Ct 57105
S & W Rough Rider Cir & Dr 57106
E Row Blvd 57108
S & W Royal Ct & St 57106
Royal Diamond Pl 57108
N Royal Oaks Rd 57110
S Ruby Pl 57106
Rudolph Ave 57107
W Runge Pl 57107
E Russell St 57103
W Russell St
200-2600 57104
2602-2604 57104
2900-3200 57107
3202-3398 57107
Russet Cir & Dr 57108
S Rutgers Ave 57106
S Ruth Ave 57106
E Ryan Pl 57110
E Saddle Creek Ct & Rd 57110
W Sagamore Cir 57106
E Sage Pl 57103
Sage St 57107
S Saguaro Ave 57110
S, E & W Saint Andrews Cir & Dr 57108
E & S Saint Charles Cir & Ln 57103
S Saint Francis Ln 57103
E Saint George Dr 57103
Saint James Cir & Dr 57106
S Saint Michaels Cir 57106
W Saint Orrie Cir 57106
N Saint Paul Ave
100-398 57103
400-1700 57103
1702-1798 57103
2900-3598 57104
3600-3604 57104
3606-3698 57104
S Saint Paul Ave 57103
E Saint Peter Cir 57103
E & S Salvation Dr & Pl 57108
S Samantha Dr 57106
S San Diego Ave 57106
N Sand Ave 57104
S Sand Cherry Cir 57108
W Sandalwood Pl 57107
N & S Sandberg Cir & Dr 57110
S Sandlot Ave 57110
E Sandpiper Trl 57108
Sandra Cir & Dr 57108
Sands St 57107
S Sandstone Cir 57103
Santa Rosa Cir & Pl 57108
W Sara Pl 57106
S Saratoga Pl 57110
S Sarmar Ave 57106
E Sassafras St 57110
N Savannah Dr 57103
S Sawgrass Cir 57108
S Scarlet Oak Trl 57110
E & S Scenic Ct & Way 57103
E Schave St 57110
W Schweigers Cir 57107
N Scotland Pl 57107
E Scranton St 57103
Sd Highway 11 57108
S Sd Highway 17 57106
Sd Highway 38 57107
E Sd Highway 42 57110
S Seabrook Cir 57108
S Secluded Pl 57103
W Selkirk Trl 57106
W Sencore Dr 57107
E Sequoia Trl 57103
E Serenity Pl 57108
S Serenity Trl 57103
S & W Sertoma Ave & Cir 57106
N Seubert Ave 57104
S Seven Oaks Dr 57108
S Severn Ln 57106
S Shadow Cir 57108
S & E Shadow Creek Ave & Ln 57108
Shadow Ridge Ave & Cir 57108
Shadow Wood Cir & Pl 57108
W Shady Hill St 57108
S Shafer Dr 57110
S Shamrock Cir 57106
S Shane Pl 57106
S Shannon Cir 57108
S Sharon Ave 57108
S Shaw Ave 57106
N Shawnee Ave 57103
Sheffield Ave & Cir 57106
E Shelby Pl 57104
S Sheldon Ln 57105

E & S Shellynn Dr 57103
E & N Shenandoah Cir & Trl 57103
E & N Shepherd Ave & St 57103
N Sherman Ave 57103
S Sherman Ave
300-499 57103
800-1099 57104
1100-2699 57105
2701-2799 57105
N Sherwood Ave 57103
S Shields Ave 57103
W Shipton St 57108
S & W Shirley Ave & Pl 57106
S & E Sierra Cir & Trl 57110
N Sigler Ave 57104
W Silver Pl 57106
S Silver Creek Cir 57106
E Silver Maple Cir 57110
E Silver Pond Pl 57108
W Silver Valley Dr 57106
E Silverbelle St 57110
S Silverpine Ct 57110
S Silverthorne Ave 57110
E Sioux St 57103
W Sioux St 57104
W Sioux K Ct 57106
S Sirocco Ave 57108
N & S Six Mile Rd 57110
S Skylane Dr 57106
W Skyline Dr 57107
E Slaten Ct 57103
E & S Slaten Park Cir & Dr 57103
Sleigh Creek Cir & Trl 57108
Slip Up Creek Rd 57104
W Snapdragon St 57106
S Sneve Ave 57103
W Snowberry Cir 57106
Snowberry St 57107
S Snowberry Trl 57106
Snowbird Cir 57108
S Snyder Cir 57106
N Solar Dr 57103
S Solberg Ave
4301-4499 57106
5000-5098 57108
5100-5200 57108
5202-5498 57108
S Solono Ave 57108
E Somerset Pl 57104
Songbird Cir & St 57107
W Sourwood Pl 57107
S Southeastern Ave
800-3898 57103
3900-4899 57103
26800-27099 57108
S Southern Cir 57103
S Southridge Dr 57105
S Southwind Ave 57106
S Spencer Blvd 57103
E Speyside Pl 57104
S Spice Hill Cir 57108
Split Creek Cir & Ct 57108
S & E Split Rock Blvd, Cir & Rd 57110
N Spring Ave 57104
S Spring Ave
100-999 57104
1001-1097 57105
1099-2699 57105
2701-3499 57105
W Spring Creek Pl 57108
N Springfield Pl 57107
E Spruce St 57103
Spruceleigh Ct & Ln 57105
S & W Spy Glass Cir & Dr 57108
E St Radigunds St 57110
S & W Stanford Ave & Dr 57106
Stanton Cir & Dr 57103
N Starlite Pl 57104
N Starr Pl 57104

S Statice Ave 57106
E Staudenmier Pl 57110
E Steamboat Trl 57110
Steeple Cir & St 57103
S Stephen Ave 57103
W Sterling Dr 57106
Sterling Oak Cir & Dr 57108
Steven Cir & Dr 57106
N Stewart Dr 57103
S & E Stoakes Ave & Cir 57110
S Stockwell Cir 57108
E Stockyards Pl 57103
S Stone Pl 57105
W Stonegate Dr 57108
E Stonehedge Ln 57103
Stoney Brook Trl 57108
Stoney Creek Cir & St 57106
S Stoney Pointe Ct 57106
S & W Strabane Cir, St & Trl 57106
S Stratford Cir 57106
W Stratton St 57108
E & S Street Car Cir, Pass & Pl 57110
S Suburban Dr 57110
W Sudbury St 57108
E & S Sugar Maple Cir & Dr 57110
E Summer Cir 57103
W Summer Creek Pl 57106
S Summerfield Pl 57108
N Summit Ave 57104
S Summit Ave
100-900 57104
902-998 57104
1000-3299 57105
N Sun Crest Rd 57107
Sun Meadow Ct 57108
N Sun Valley Pl 57110
S Sunburst Pl 57106
S Sundance Cir 57105
S Sunderland Ln 57108
S Sundowner Ave 57106
S Sundrop Ave 57110
S & W Sunflower Cir & Trl 57108
S Sunny Oak Cir 57108
S Sunny View Dr 57110
Sunny View Pl 57108
E Sunnybrook Dr 57105
Sunnycrest Dr 57105
W Sunnydale Pl 57106
S Sunnymede Cir 57108
E Sunrise Pl 57108
Sunset Blvd 57106
W Sunset Dr 57105
Surrell St 57104
S & W Surreyhill Cir & Ct 57108
N Swan Pl 57107
N Swanson Dr 57107
N Sweet Grass Ave 57107
S & W Sweetbriar Cir, Ct, Dr & Pl 57108
N Sweetman Pl 57107
S Sweetwater Pl 57108
S Swift Park Dr 57108
S Swiss Stone Cir 57108
Sycamore Ave 57108
N Sycamore Ave
100-1299 57110
1301-1499 57110
4500-4598 57104
S Sycamore Ave 57110
S Tabbert Cir 57103
S Tabor Pl 57106
E & N Tahoe St & Trl 57110
S Tallgrass Ave 57108
E Tamarac Dr 57103
W Tammy Pl 57107
E Tan Tara Cir 57108
W Tanager Pl 57107
S Tanglewood Ave 57106
S Tarragon Cir 57108

S & W Tayberry Ave & Cir 57106
E Taylor St 57110
S Teakwood Ave 57103
N Teal Pl 57107
S Techlink Cir 57106
S & W Technology Cir & Dr 57106
S Technopolis Dr 57106
W Tecumseh Ct 57106
Teem Dr & St 57107
S Tennis Ln
4400-4498 57106
4500-4999 57106
5000-5199 57108
N Terin Cir 57107
N Terrace Pl 57104
S Terry Ave 57106
E Terry Peak Ln 57110
W Thad Pl 57106
S & W Thatcher Cir & Dr 57106
S Thecla Ave 57106
S Theodore Ave 57106
Theresa Cir 57104
E Thomas Cir 57103
S Thompson Ave 57103
W Thompson Dr 57105
W Thora Cir 57108
E Thornwood Pl 57103
W Thrush Pl 57107
S Thunderbird Trl 57103
W Thurman Dr 57106
W Tickman St 57107
S Tierney Pl 57108
E Tiger Lilly St 57110
S Tim Trl 57110
S & W Timber Oak Cir & Trl 57108
N Timberline Ave
4700-4799 57110
4900-5499 57104
N Todd Pl 57107
E Tomar Ct 57105
E Tomar Ln 57105
E Tomar Pl 57105
E Tomar Rd 57105
S Tomar Rd
4400-4799 57105
4800-6899 57108
N Tombill Pl 57103
N Tonya Pl 57107
S Topaz Pl 57106
Torchwood Ln & Pl 57110
Torrey Pine Cir & Ln 57110
S Townpark Pl 57105
Townview Ave 57104
E Tracy Ln 57103
N Trade Ave 57107
W Tradewinds St 57108
Trading Post Rd 57108
S Trailsedge Cir 57108
W Trailview Cir 57108
E Tranquility Pl 57108
N Trapp Ave 57104
E Tree Top St 57108
E Trendenc St 57103
S Trenton Cir 57103
S Tribbey Trl 57106
E Tricia Ln 57103
W Trinity Pl 57108
S Triple Play Ave 57110
S Tuscan Club Cir 57108
S Tuscany Ct 57103
S Tuthill Ct 57103
W Tweed Trl 57106
Twin Oaks Est & Rd 57105
S Twin Ridge Rd
4600-4799 57105
4801-4897 57108
4899-5099 57108
N Twin Towers Cir 57103
S Twinleaf Dr 57108
Tyler Ave & Ct 57103
Unique Pl 57110
W Universal Pl 57104

W Urban Cir 57108
W Utica Pl 57107
Vail Cir & Dr 57110
S & W Valencia Cir & Dr 57108
W Valhalla Blvd 57106
E Valley Oaks Pl 57110
W Valley View Cir 57107
N Valley View Rd 57107
S Valley View Rd
201-499 57107
500-1798 57106
1800-3300 57106
3302-3398 57106
N Van Eps Ave
100-1100 57103
1102-1898 57103
2800-3098 57104
3601-3699 57104
S Van Eps Ave
100-298 57103
300-500 57103
502-598 57103
800-1099 57104
1100-2699 57105
N Velocity Ave 57104
Venita Ave & Cir 57108
W Verbena St 57107
S Veronica Pl 57105
W Victoria Dr 57106
W Victory Ln 57108
S Village Square Cir 57103
S Villanova Ave 57106
N Vincent Ave 57107
S Vintage Pl 57108
N Violet Pl 57103
S Vista Ln 57105
S & W Vista Park Ave & St 57106
S Vistas Ave 57106
E Wakefield Cir 57103
W Walden Dr 57106
N Walkanda Dr 57107
E Walker Way 57103
S Wallace Cir 57106
E Walnut St 57103
W Walnut St
300-398 57104
8500-8599 57107
N Walts Ave 57104
S Walts Ave
100-999 57104
1000-3200 57105
3202-3298 57105
N Warner Brothers Pl 57104
S Warren Pl 57105
S Wassom Ave 57106
W Watercress Cir 57108
W Waterford St 57106
S & W Waterstone Cir & Dr 57108
E Waterwood St 57110
N Watson Ave 57107
S Watson Ave 57106
N Wayland Ave
101-197 57103
199-2099 57103
2801-2897 57104
2899-3299 57104
S Wayland Ave
100-699 57103
900-1099 57104
1100-2199 57105
2201-2299 57105
S Wayland Ct 57105
N Wayland Pl 57103
Wayne Ave 57106
W Wayne Dr 57105
W Weather Ln 57104
N Weber Ave 57103
S Wedgeon Pl 57105
N Wedgewood Rd 57107
S Wegner Ave 57103
S Wellington Ave 57106
S Wells Ave 57108
N West Ave 57104

S West Ave
110-909 57104
1015-1409 57105
1411-4201 57105
4203-4211 57105
S Westbrooke Ln 57106
Western Ave 57108
N Western Ave
101-197 57104
199-903 57104
905-1205 57104
2200-5898 57107
5900-6501 57107
6503-6503 57107
S Western Ave
100-906 57104
908-910 57104
1006-1098 57105
1100-4101 57105
4800-4998 57108
5000-5903 57108
5905-8499 57108
S Westfield Trl 57108
W Westminster Dr 57106
S Westmoor Dr 57104
N Westport Ave 57107
S Westport Ave 57106
W Westview Rd 57107
S Westward Ho Pl 57105
S Westwind Ave 57108
S Wexford Ct 57106
Wheatland Ave & Ct 57106
S Whetstone Cir 57103
E Whisper Trl 57108
Whispering Cir & St 57108
W White Willow Cir 57108
S & W Whitechurch Cir & Ln 57108
S Whitewood Ave 57106
N Whitewood Cir 57107
Whitni Ave & Ln 57107
S & W Wicklow Ave, Ct & Ln 57108
E Wilcox St 57104
Wild Clover Cir 57107
E Wild Flower Cir 57110
S Wildwood Cir 57105
N Williams Ave 57104
S Williams Ave
100-999 57104
1400-3199 57105
E Williamsburg Ct 57103
N Willow Ave 57104
S Willow Ave
200-999 57104
1000-3800 57105
3802-3998 57105
S Willow Brook Pl 57108
S Willow Creek Pl 57106
E Willow Glen Cir 57110
E Willow Leaf St 57110
S Willow Meadow Pl 57106
Willow Ridge Cir & Pl 57110
E Willowwood St 57110
S Wilshir Pine Ave 57108
S & W Wilson Ave & Dr 57106
E Winchester Pl 57103
W Windrose Pl 57108
W Windsor Way 57106
S Windsor Way Cir 57106
Windswept Cir & Pl 57108
S & E Winncrest Ave & Cir 57103
E & S Winston Cir & Ln 57108
Winter Pl 57107
W Winterberry Cir 57106
Wiseman Cir & St 57106
E Wiswall Pl 57105
Witzke Ave & Pl 57108
W Wood Dr 57105
S Woodbine Ln 57103
W Woodcrest Way 57105
S Woodduck Pl 57105
E Woodland Hills Rd 57103
E Woodlawn Dr 57105

N Woodridge Ave 57107
E & S Woodsedge St & Trl 57108
Woodsong Pl 57108
S Woodwind Ave 57108
S Woodwind Ln 57103
E Worcester Pl 57108
S World Series Ave 57110
W Wren Pl 57107
N Wright Ave 57107
S Yellowstone Cir 57108
S Yellowstone Ln 57105
E York Cir 57110
E Yorkshire St 57108
W Yukon Trl 57107
W Zak Cir 57106
W Zephyr Pl 57108
W Zinnia Cir 57106

NUMBERED STREETS

N 1st Ave 57104
S 1st Ave
300-322 57104
324-999 57104
1000-3399 57105
3401-3499 57105
E 1st St 57103
W 1st St 57104
S 1st Avenue Cir 57105
N 2nd Ave 57104
S 2nd Ave
300-300 57104
320-320 57101
400-998 57104
1000-3299 57105
E 2nd St 57103
W 2nd St 57104
N 3rd Ave 57104
S 3rd Ave
300-398 57104
1000-2499 57105
E 3rd St
600-698 57103
4501-4597 57110
W 3rd St 57104
N 4th Ave
2000-4800 57104
4801-4801 57118
4802-4998 57104
S 4th Ave
400-498 57104
1000-3299 57105
E 4th St
600-1500 57103
4600-5099 57110
W 4th St 57104
S 5th Ave
500-698 57104
1001-1397 57105
W 5th Pl 57107
E 5th St 57103
W 5th St
100-408 57104
6500-6600 57107
N 6th Ave 57104
S 6th Ave
501-899 57104
1001-1097 57105
E 6th St
100-229 57104
300-700 57103
4600-4698 57110
W 6th St
100-398 57104
6700-6999 57107
N 7th Ave 57104
S 7th Ave
600-698 57104
1101-1197 57105
E 7th St
101-199 57104
600-4099 57103
W 7th St
400-2899 57104
6700-6999 57107

N 8th Ave 57104
S 8th Ave
601-699 57104
1600-3199 57105
E 8th St 57103
W 8th St
100-416 57104
418-2599 57104
5000-5098 57107
5100-6999 57107
N 9th Ave 57104
S 9th Ave
700-900 57104
1600-3199 57105
E 9th St
100-150 57104
1000-4499 57103
5100-5199 57110
W 9th St
101-197 57104
5100-5498 57107
N 10th Ave 57104
S 10th Ave
800-1000 57104
1600-3099 57105
E 10th St
100-299 57104
800-3999 57103
4500-4598 57110
W 10th St
101-197 57104
6200-6899 57107
E 11th St
100-198 57104
1300-1398 57103
1400-3499 57103
3501-3599 57103
W 11th St
100-398 57104
400-2999 57104
6500-6799 57107
E 12th St
100-198 57104
200-500 57104
502-598 57104
1201-1297 57103
5501-5599 57110
W 12th St
100-3199 57104
3900-7698 57107
4101-8499 57106
W 13th Pl 57106
E 13th St
100-198 57104
200-699 57104
1700-3799 57103
W 13th St
200-2699 57104
4201-4299 57106
W 14th Pl 57106
E 14th St
101-197 57104
199-1199 57104
1600-2999 57103
W 14th St
200-1399 57104
1401-1799 57104
4901-4997 57106
4999-5899 57106
W 15th Pl 57106
E 15th St
200-1199 57104
1801-2697 57103
4501-4597 57110
W 15th St
600-2500 57104
5301-5397 57106
W 16th Pl 57106
E 16th St
1000-1100 57104
2300-4000 57103
4500-4698 57110
W 16th St
400-2599 57104
4700-5398 57106
W 17th Pl 57106

E 17th St
901-997 57104
999-1599 57104
2300-3300 57103
3302-3398 57103
5100-5299 57110
W 17th St 57104
E 18th St
200-1798 57104
301-1499 57105
2200-4000 57103
4601-4897 57110
W 18th St
101-2399 57105
300-2698 57104
4900-5198 57106
E 19th St
101-197 57105
2200-2298 57103
4500-4598 57110
W 19th St
100-198 57105
8500-8698 57106
E 20th St 57105
E 20th St 57105
E 20th St 57105
2800-4499 57103
W 20th St
100-198 57105
200-2200 57105
2202-2298 57105
6901-8797 57106
8799-8999 57106
E 21st St
105-111 57105
113-1299 57105
1301-1399 57105
2800-2898 57103
2900-4099 57103
4501-4597 57110
4599-4600 57110
4602-4898 57110
W 21st St 57105
E 22nd St
1200-1298 57105
1300-1499 57105
2900-4399 57103
4600-5199 57110
W 22nd St
200-3200 57105
7000-7098 57106
E 23rd St
100-900 57105
2900-4499 57103
6100-6198 57110
6200-6299 57110
W 23rd St
101-197 57105
199-2899 57105
5300-5599 57106
E 24th St
101-797 57105
799-1900 57105
1902-1998 57105
2900-3298 57103
3300-4099 57103
W 24th St
100-2799 57105
5300-5499 57106
E 25th St 57105
3500-3999 57103
W 25th St
100-1499 57105
1501-1599 57105
5300-5499 57106
E 26th St
101-197 57105
199-1699 57105
1701-2199 57105
2701-2797 57103
4501-4597 57110
W 26th St
100-2799 57105
4601-4697 57106
E 27th St 57105
100-1999 57105
5700-5999 57106
E 28th St
201-297 57105
3100-3198 57103
5000-5298 57110
W 28th St
200-2899 57105
5700-5999 57106
E 29th Pl N 57104
E 29th St 57105
E 29th St N 57104
W 29th St 57105
E 30th St 57105
E 30th St N 57104
W 30th St 57105
E 31st Pl N 57104
E 31st St
101-197 57105
3200-3599 57103
E 31st St N 57104
W 31st St
101-197 57105
5400-5498 57106
E 32nd Pl N 57104
E 32nd St 57105
W 32nd St
1300-1398 57105
1400-1599 57105
1601-1699 57105
5300-9399 57106
E 33rd St
100-1600 57105
1602-1698 57105
2600-2698 57103
4500-4598 57110
E 33rd St N 57104
W 33rd St
100-3399 57105
5300-5400 57106
E 34th St 57105
E 34th St N 57104
W 34th St
300-2800 57105
2802-3098 57105
3800-5299 57106
W 34th St N 57107
E 35th St 57105
W 35th St
700-2599 57105
5000-5098 57106
5100-7299 57106
W 35th St N 57107
E 36th St
100-299 57105
3700-4499 57103
4500-4798 57110
4800-4999 57110
W 36th St
300-898 57105
900-999 57105
5300-5999 57106
W 37th Cir 57105
E 37th St 57103
W 37th St
100-2899 57105
4500-6099 57106
W 37th St N 57107
E 38th St
100-1299 57105
3001-3297 57103
3299-4499 57103
7700-8900 57110
8902-8998 57110
W 38th St
1100-1699 57105
4101-4197 57106
4199-5299 57106
E 39th St 57110
E 39th St N 57104
W 39th St
100-2899 57105
4500-4598 57106
4600-5599 57106
E 40th St
100-199 57105
201-499 57105
8600-8698 57110
8700-8799 57110
8801-8899 57110
E 40th St N 57104
W 40th St
100-399 57105
4700-6099 57106
E 41st St
100-900 57105
902-1098 57105
3400-3702 57103
4601-5897 57110
W 41st St
100-100 57105
3401-3497 57106
E 42nd St
3500-4298 57103
4300-4499 57103
4500-6799 57110
W 42nd St
100-2099 57105
7700-8399 57106
8401-8499 57106
W 43rd Pl 57106
E 43rd St 57110
W 43rd St
100-700 57105
702-798 57105
3201-3597 57106
3599-6599 57106
W 44th Pl 57105
E 44th St 57110
W 44th St
1700-1898 57105
5300-5498 57106
5500-8099 57106
E 45th St 57110
W 45th St
2001-2099 57105
4900-5800 57106
W 46th St
2200-2500 57105
2502-2598 57105
5300-5498 57106
5500-8499 57106
E 47th St 57110
W 47th St
2001-2099 57105
3401-4897 57106
E 48th St N 57104
W 48th St 57106
E 49th St
1300-3600 57103
3602-3798 57103
4500-6699 57110
W 49th St
2101-2197 57105
2199-2500 57105
2502-2798 57105
3200-3398 57106
3400-5999 57106
E 50th St N 57104
W 50th St
1700-1798 57105
1800-2299 57105
2301-2499 57105
5300-7500 57106
7502-7598 57106
E 51st St 57103
W 51st St
1200-1699 57105
1701-1799 57105
3301-5297 57106
5299-8299 57106
W 51st St N 57107
E 52nd St 57103
E 52nd St N 57104
W 52nd St 57106
E 53rd St 57110
W 53rd St 57106
E 54th St
1300-2219 57103
2221-2399 57103
4600-4798 57110
4801-5099 57110
E 54th St N 57104
W 54th St 57106
W 54th St N 57107
E 55th St 57103
W 55th St 57106
E 56th St
1200-1299 57105
1500-2299 57103
W 56th St 57106
57th St 57108
E 57th St 57108
E 57th St N 57104
W 57th St
301-397 57108
3600-4098 57106
4800-4898 57108
5300-5499 57106
E 58th St 57108
E 58th St N 57104
W 58th St
4300-4499 57108
5600-5798 57106
5800-6500 57106
6502-7598 57106
E 59th St 57108
W 59th St
3500-3898 57108
3900-4000 57108
4002-4498 57108
6200-6399 57106
6401-7399 57106
E 60th St N 57104
W 60th St 57106
W 60th St N
800-899 57104
1700-2198 57107
2200-7899 57107
E 61st St 57108
E 61st St N 57104
W 61st St 57106
W 61st St N 57107
E 62nd St 57108
W 62nd St 57106
W 62nd St N 57107
W 63rd Pl 57108
E 63rd St 57108
E 63rd St N 57104
W 63rd St 57106
E 64th St 57108
E 64th St N 57104
W 64th St 57106
E 65th St N 57104
W 65th St 57106
W 66th St 57106
W 66th St N 57107
E 67th St N 57104
W 67th St 57106
E 68th St N 57104
W 68th St 57106
W 68th St N 57107
69th St
46900-47099 57106
47100-47799 57108
E 69th St 57108
E 69th St N 57104
W 69th St 57108
E 70th Pl 57108
E 70th St 57108
E 70th St N 57104
W 70th St N 57107
E 71st St N 57104
W 71st St 57108
E 72nd St N 57104
W 72nd St N
800-899 57104
1800-2000 57107
E 73rd St 57108
W 74th St 57108
E & W 77th 57108
E 78th St N 57104
80th Pl & St 57108
E & W 81st Pl & St 57108
E & W 82nd Pl & St 57108
W 83rd St 57108
W 84th Pl 57108
E 84th St N 57104
W 84th St 57108
W 84th St N 57107
85th St
47000-47049 57106
47050-47799 57108
W 85th St 57108
W 86th St 57108
W 88th St 57108
W 89th St 57108
W 90th St 57108
91st Pl & St 57108
W 92nd St 57108
W 93rd St 57108
94th St 57108
W 95th 57108
98th St 57108
104th St 57108
257th St 57104
258th St 57107
47500-47899 57104
259th St 57107
260th St 57107
261st St 57107
262nd St 57107
263rd St 57107
264th St 57107
265th St 57107
46701-46899 57106
46702-46898 57107
266th St 57106
267th St 57106
268th St
46500-46899 57106
47801-47899 57108
269th St
46500-46899 57106
47800-47999 57108
270th St 57108
271st St 57108
272nd St 57108
466th Ave
26300-26499 57107
26500-26999 57106
467th Ave
25800-26499 57107
26500-26999 57106
468th Ave
25800-26299 57107
26700-26899 57106
469th Ave
25800-26099 57107
26800-26999 57106
470th Ave 57107
471st Ave
25800-26099 57107
27100-27199 57108
472nd Ave 57108
473rd Ave 57108
475th Ave 57104
476th Ave 57104
477th Ave 57104
478th Ave 57104
479th Ave 57108
480th Ave 57108

Tennessee

People QuickFacts	Tennessee	USA
Population, 2013 estimate	6,495,978	316,128,839
Population, 2010 (April 1) estimates base	6,346,113	308,747,716
Population, percent change, April 1, 2010 to July 1, 2013	2.4%	2.4%
Population, 2010	6,346,105	308,745,538
Persons under 5 years, percent, 2013	6.2%	6.3%
Persons under 18 years, percent, 2013	23.0%	23.3%
Persons 65 years and over, percent, 2013	14.7%	14.1%
Female persons, percent, 2013	51.2%	50.8%
White alone, percent, 2013 (a)	79.1%	77.7%
Black or African American alone, percent, 2013 (a)	17.0%	13.2%
American Indian and Alaska Native alone, percent, 2013 (a)	0.4%	1.2%
Asian alone, percent, 2013 (a)	1.6%	5.3%
Native Hawaiian and Other Pacific Islander alone, percent, 2013 (a)	0.1%	0.2%
Two or More Races, percent, 2013	1.7%	2.4%
Hispanic or Latino, percent, 2013 (b)	4.9%	17.1%
White alone, not Hispanic or Latino, percent, 2013	74.9%	62.6%
Living in same house 1 year & over, percent, 2008-2012	84.4%	84.8%
Foreign born persons, percent, 2008-2012	4.5%	12.9%
Language other than English spoken at home, pct age 5+, 2008-2012	6.6%	20.5%
High school graduate or higher, percent of persons age 25+, 2008-2012	83.9%	85.7%
Bachelor's degree or higher, percent of persons age 25+, 2008-2012	23.5%	28.5%
Veterans, 2008-2012	493,980	21,853,912
Mean travel time to work (minutes), workers age 16+, 2008-2012	24.1	25.4
Housing units, 2013	2,840,914	132,802,859
Homeownership rate, 2008-2012	68.4%	65.5%
Housing units in multi-unit structures, percent, 2008-2012	18.2%	25.9%
Median value of owner-occupied housing units, 2008-2012	$138,700	$181,400
Households, 2008-2012	2,468,841	115,226,802
Persons per household, 2008-2012	2.51	2.61
Per capita money income in past 12 months (2012 dollars), 2008-2012	$24,294	$28,051
Median household income, 2008-2012	$44,140	$53,046
Persons below poverty level, percent, 2008-2012	17.3%	14.9%

Business QuickFacts	Tennessee	USA
Private nonfarm establishments, 2012	130,592	7,431,808
Private nonfarm employment, 2012	2,344,047	115,938,468
Private nonfarm employment, percent change, 2011-2012	1.9%	2.2%
Nonemployer establishments, 2012	471,026	22,735,915
Total number of firms, 2007	545,348	27,092,908
Black-owned firms, percent, 2007	8.4%	7.1%
American Indian- and Alaska Native-owned firms, percent, 2007	0.5%	0.9%
Asian-owned firms, percent, 2007	2.0%	5.7%
Native Hawaiian and Other Pacific Islander-owned firms, percent, 2007	0.1%	0.1%
Hispanic-owned firms, percent, 2007	1.6%	8.3%
Women-owned firms, percent, 2007	25.9%	28.8%
Manufacturers shipments, 2007 ($1000)	140,447,760	5,319,456,312
Merchant wholesaler sales, 2007 ($1000)	80,116,528	4,174,286,516
Retail sales, 2007 ($1000)	77,547,291	3,917,663,456
Retail sales per capita, 2007	$12,563	$12,990
Accommodation and food services sales, 2007 ($1000)	10,626,759	613,795,732
Building permits, 2012	20,147	829,658

Geography QuickFacts	Tennessee	USA
Land area in square miles, 2010	41,234.90	3,531,905.43
Persons per square mile, 2010	153.9	87.4
FIPS Code	47	

(a) Includes persons reporting only one race.
(b) Hispanics may be of any race, so also are included in applicable race categories.
FN: Footnote on this item for this area in place of data
NA: Not available
D: Suppressed to avoid disclosure of confidential information
X: Not applicable
S: Suppressed; does not meet publication standards
Z: Value greater than zero but less than half unit of measure shown
F: Fewer than 100 firms
Source: US Census Bureau State & County QuickFacts

Tennessee

3 DIGIT ZIP CODE MAP

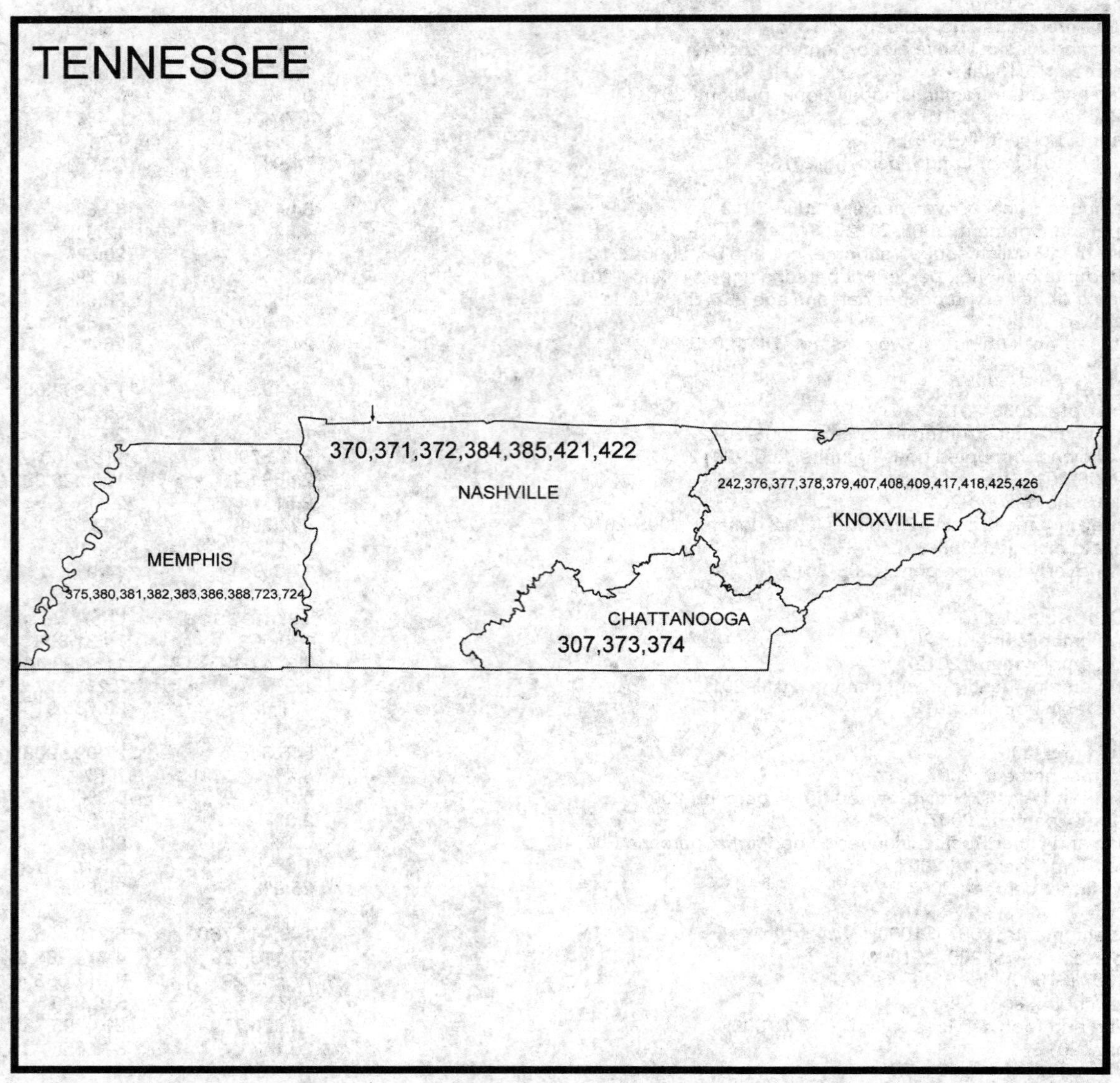

Tennessee

(Abbreviation: TN)

Post Office, County — ZIP Code

Places with more than one ZIP code are listed in capital letters, See pages indicated.

Adams, Robertson 37010
Adamsville, Mcnairy 38310
Afton, Greene 37616
Alamo, Crockett 38001
Alcoa, Blount 37701
Alexandria, Dekalb 37012
Algood, Putnam 38501
Allardt, Fentress 38504
Allons, Overton 38541
Allred, Overton 38542
Alpine, Overton 38543
Altamont, Grundy 37301
Andersonville, Anderson 37705
ANTIOCH, Davidson (See Page 3467)
Apison, Hamilton 37302
Ardmore, Giles 38449
Arlington, Shelby 38002
Arnold Afb, Coffee 37389
Arrington, Williamson 37014
Arthur, Claiborne 37707
Ashland City, Cheatham 37015
ATHENS, Mcminn (See Page 3468)
Atoka, Tipton 38004
Atwood, Carroll 38220
Auburntown, Cannon 37016
Bakewell, Hamilton 37304
Bakewell, Hamilton 37373
Baneberry, Jefferson 37890
Bartlett (See Memphis)
Bath Springs, Decatur 38311
Baxter, Putnam 38544
Bean Station, Grainger 37708
Beech Bluff, Madison 38313
Beechgrove, Coffee 37018
Beersheba Springs, Grundy 37305
Belfast, Marshall 37019
Bell Buckle, Bedford 37020
Bellevue, Davidson 37221
Bells, Crockett 38006
Belvidere, Franklin 37306
Benton, Polk 37307
Berry Hill, Davidson 37204
Bethel Springs, Mcnairy 38315
Bethpage, Sumner 37022
Big Rock, Stewart 37023
Big Sandy, Benton 38221
Birchwood, Hamilton 37308
Blaine, Grainger 37709
Bloomington Springs, Putnam 38545
Blountville, Sullivan 37617
Bluff City, Sullivan 37618
Bogota, Dyer 38007
Bolivar, Hardeman 38008
Bon Aqua, Hickman 37025
Bone Cave, Warren 38581
Braden, Fayette 38010
Bradford, Gibson 38316
Bradyville, Cannon 37026
BRENTWOOD, Williamson (See Page 3469)
Briceville, Anderson 37710
Brighton, Tipton 38011
BRISTOL, Sullivan (See Page 3471)
Brownsville, Haywood 38012
Bruceton, Carroll 38317
Brunswick, Shelby 38014
Brush Creek, Smith 38547
Buchanan, Henry 38222
Buena Vista, Carroll 38318
Buffalo Valley, Putnam 38548
Bulls Gap, Hawkins 37711
Bumpus Mills, Stewart 37028
Burlison, Tipton 38015
Burns, Dickson 37029
Butler, Johnson 37640
Bybee, Cocke 37713
Byrdstown, Pickett 38549
Calhoun, Mcminn 37309
Camden, Benton 38320
Campaign, Warren 38550
Cane Ridge, Davidson 37013
Carthage, Smith 37030
Caryville, Campbell 37714
Castalian Springs, Sumner 37031
Cedar Grove, Carroll 38321
Cedar Hill, Robertson 37032
Celina, Clay 38551
Centertown, Warren 37110
Centerville, Hickman 37033
Chapel Hill, Marshall 37034
Chapmansboro, Cheatham 37035
Charleston, Bradley 37310
Charlotte, Dickson 37036
CHATTANOOGA, Hamilton (See Page 3472)
Chestnut Mound, Smith 38552
Chewalla, Mcnairy 38393
Christiana, Rutherford 37037
Chuckey, Greene 37641
Church Hill, Hawkins 37642
Church Hill, Hawkins 37645
Clairfield, Claiborne 37715
Clarkrange, Fentress 38553
Clarksburg, Carroll 38324
CLARKSVILLE, Montgomery (See Page 3478)
CLEVELAND, Bradley (See Page 3483)
Clifton, Wayne 38425
CLINTON, Anderson (See Page 3486)
Coalfield, Morgan 37719
Coalmont, Grundy 37313
Coker Creek, Monroe 37314
College Dale, Hamilton 37363
College Grove, Williamson 37046
Collegedale, Hamilton 37315
COLLIERVILLE, Shelby (See Page 3486)
Collinwood, Wayne 38450
Colonial Heights, Sullivan 37663
COLUMBIA, Maury (See Page 3488)
Como, Henry 38223
Conasauga, Polk 37316
Concord (See Knoxville)
Concord Farragut, Knox 37922
COOKEVILLE, Putnam (See Page 3488)
Copperhill, Polk 37317
CORDOVA, Shelby (See Page 3490)
Cornersville, Marshall 37047
Corryton, Knox 37721
Cosby, Cocke 37722
Cottage Grove, Henry 38224
Cottontown, Sumner 37048
Counce, Hardin 38326
Covington, Tipton 38019
Cowan, Franklin 37318
Crab Orchard, Cumberland 37723
Crawford, Overton 38554
Crockett Mills, Crockett 38021
Cross Plains, Robertson 37049
CROSSVILLE, Cumberland (See Page 3493)
Crump, Hardin 38327
Culleoka, Maury 38451
Cumberland City, Stewart 37050
Cumberland Furnace, Dickson 37051
Cumberland Gap, Claiborne 37724
Cumberland Gp, Claiborne 37724
Cunningham, Montgomery 37052
Cypress Inn, Wayne 38452
Dandridge, Jefferson 37725
Darden, Henderson 38328
Dayton, Rhea 37321
Decatur, Meigs 37322
Decaturville, Decatur 38329
Decherd, Franklin 37324
Deer Lodge, Morgan 37726
Defeated, Smith 37030
Del Rio, Cocke 37727
Delano, Polk 37325
Dellrose, Lincoln 38453
Denmark, Madison 38391
Denver, Humphreys 37134
Devonia, Anderson 37710
Dickel, Coffee 37388
DICKSON, Dickson (See Page 3497)
Dixon Springs, Smith 37057
Dover, Stewart 37058
Dowelltown, Dekalb 37059
Doyle, White 38559
Dresden, Weakley 38225
Drummonds, Tipton 38023
Duck River, Hickman 38454
Ducktown, Polk 37326
Duff, Campbell 37729
Dukedom, Weakley 38226
Dunlap, Sequatchie 37327
Dyer, Gibson 38330
DYERSBURG, Dyer (See Page 3498)
Eads, Shelby 38028
Eagan, Claiborne 37730
Eagleville, Rutherford 37060
East Ridge, Hamilton 37412
Eastview, Mcnairy 38367
Eaton, Gibson 38331
Eidson, Hawkins 37731
Elgin, Scott 37732
Elgin, Morgan 37733
ELIZABETHTON, Carter (See Page 3499)
Elkton, Giles 38455
Ellendale, Shelby 38029
Elmwood, Smith 38560
Elora, Lincoln 37328
Englewood, Mcminn 37329
Enville, Chester 38332
Erin, Houston 37061
Erwin, Unicoi 37650
Estill Springs, Franklin 37330
Ethridge, Lawrence 38456
Etowah, Mcminn 37331
Eva, Benton 38333
Evensville, Rhea 37332
Fairfield Glade, Cumberland 38555
Fairview, Williamson 37062
Fall Branch, Washington 37656
Farner, Polk 37333
Farragut (See Knoxville)
Fayetteville, Lincoln 37334
Finger, Mcnairy 38334
Finley, Dyer 38030
Fisherville, Shelby 38017
Five Points, Lawrence 38457
Flag Pond, Unicoi 37657
Flatwoods, Perry 37096
Flintville, Lincoln 37335
Forest Hills, Davidson 37215
Fort Pillow, Lauderdale 38041
Fosterville, Rutherford 37063
Frankewing, Lincoln 38459
FRANKLIN, Williamson (See Page 3499)
Friendship, Crockett 38034
Friendsville, Blount 37737
Fruitvale, Crockett 38336
Gadsden, Crockett 38337
Gainesboro, Jackson 38562
Gallatin, Sumner 37066
Gallaway, Fayette 38036
Garland, Tipton 38019
Gassaway, Dekalb 37095
Gates, Lauderdale 38037
Gatlinburg, Sevier 37738
Georgetown, Meigs 37336
GERMANTOWN, Shelby (See Page 3502)
Gibson, Gibson 38338
Gilt Edge, Tipton 38015
Gladeville, Wilson 37071
Gleason, Weakley 38229
GOODLETTSVILLE, Davidson (See Page 3504)
Goodspring, Giles 38460
Gordonsville, Smith 38563
Grand Junction, Hardeman 38039
Grandview, Rhea 37337
Granville, Jackson 38564
Gray, Washington 37615
Graysville, Rhea 37338
Greenback, Loudon 37742
Greenbrier, Robertson 37073
GREENEVILLE, Greene (See Page 3504)
Greenfield, Weakley 38230
Grimsley, Fentress 38565
Gruetli Laager, Grundy 37339
Guild, Marion 37340
Guys, Mcnairy 38339
Halls, Lauderdale 38040
Hampshire, Maury 38461
Hampton, Carter 37658
Harriman, Roane 37748
Harrison, Hamilton 37341
Harrogate, Claiborne 37752
Hartford, Cocke 37753
Hartsville, Trousdale 37074
Heiskell, Knox 37754
Helenwood, Scott 37755
Henderson, Chester 38340
HENDERSONVILLE, Sumner (See Page 3507)
Henning, Lauderdale 38041
Henry, Henry 38231
Hermitage, Davidson 37076
Hickman, Smith 38567
Hickory Hill (See Memphis)
Hickory Valley, Hardeman 38042
Hilham, Overton 38568
Hillsboro, Coffee 37342
Hixson, Hamilton 37343
Hohenwald, Lewis 38462
Holladay, Benton 38341
Hollow Rock, Carroll 38342
Hornbeak, Obion 38232
Hornsby, Hardeman 38044
Humboldt, Gibson 38343
Huntingdon, Carroll 38344
Huntland, Franklin 37345
Huntsville, Scott 37756
Huron, Henderson 38345
Hurricane Mills, Humphreys 37078
Idlewild, Gibson 38346
Indian Mound, Stewart 37079
Iron City, Lawrence 38463
Jacks Creek, Chester 38347
Jacksboro, Campbell 37757
JACKSON, Madison (See Page 3508)
Jamestown, Fentress 38556
Jasper, Marion 37347
Jefferson City, Jefferson 37760
Jellico, Campbell 37762
Joelton, Davidson 37080
JOHNSON CITY, Washington (See Page 3511)
Jonesborough, Washington 37659
Karns, Knox 37921
Kelso, Lincoln 37348
Kenton, Gibson 38233
Kimball, Marion 37347
Kimberlin Heights, Knox 37920
Kimmins, Lewis 38462
KINGSPORT, Sullivan (See Page 3515)
Kingston, Roane 37763
Kingston Springs, Cheatham 37082
KNOXVILLE, Knox (See Page 3518)
Kodak, Sevier 37764
Kyles Ford, Hancock 37765
La Follette, Campbell 37729
La Follette, Campbell 37766
La Grange, Fayette 38046
La Vergne, Rutherford 37086
Laconia, Fayette 38045
Lafayette, Macon 37083
Lake City, Anderson 37769
Lakeland, Shelby 38002
Lakesite, Hamilton 37379
Lakewood, Davidson 37138
Lancaster, Smith 38569
Lancing, Morgan 37770
Lascassas, Rutherford 37085
Laurel Bloomery, Johnson 37680
Lavinia, Carroll 38348
Lawrenceburg, Lawrence 38464
LEBANON, Wilson (See Page 3532)
LENOIR CITY, Loudon (See Page 3534)
Lenox, Dyer 38047
Leoma, Lawrence 38468
Lewisburg, Marshall 37091
Lexington, Henderson 38351
Liberty, Dekalb 37095
Limestone, Washington 37681
Linden, Perry 37096
Livingston, Overton 38570
Lobelville, Perry 37097
Lone Mountain, Claiborne 37773
Lookout Mountain, Hamilton 37350
Loretto, Lawrence 38469
Loudon, Loudon 37774
Louisville, Blount 37777
Lowland, Hamblen 37778
Lupton City, Hamilton 37351
Luray, Chester 38352
Luttrell, Union 37779
Lutts, Wayne 38471
Lyles, Hickman 37098
Lynchburg, Moore 37352
Lynnville, Giles 38472
Macon, Fayette 38048
MADISON, Davidson (See Page 3535)
Madisonville, Monroe 37354
MANCHESTER, Coffee (See Page 3535)
Mansfield, Henry 38236
Martin, Weakley 38237
MARYVILLE, Blount (See Page 3535)
Mascot, Knox 37806
Mason, Tipton 38049
Mason, Fayette 38068
Maury City, Crockett 38050
Maynardville, Union 37807
Mc Donald, Bradley 37353
Mc Ewen, Humphreys 37101
Mc Kenzie, Carroll 38201
Mc Lemoresville, Carroll 38235
Mc Minnville (See Mcminnville)
MCMINNVILLE, Warren (See Page 3538)
Medina, Gibson 38355
Medon, Madison 38356
Melrose, Davidson 37204
MEMPHIS, Shelby (See Page 3538)
Mercer, Madison 38392
Michie, Mcnairy 38357
Middleton, Hardeman 38052
Midway, Greene 37809
Milan, Gibson 38358
Milledgeville, Mcnairy 38359
Milligan College, Carter 37682
MILLINGTON, Shelby (See Page 3554)
Milton, Rutherford 37118
Minor Hill, Giles 38473
Miston, Lake 38080
Mitchellville, Sumner 37119
Mohawk, Greene 37810
Monroe, Overton 38573
Monteagle, Grundy 37356
Monterey, Putnam 38574
Mooresburg, Hawkins 37811
Morley, Campbell 37766
Morris Chapel, Hardin 38361
Morrison, Warren 37357
MORRISTOWN, Hamblen (See Page 3555)
Moscow, Fayette 38057
Moscow, Fayette 38076
Mosheim, Greene 37818
Moss, Clay 38575
Mount Carmel, Hawkins 37645
MOUNT JULIET, Wilson (See Page 3557)
Mount Pleasant, Maury 38474
Mountain City, Johnson 37683
Mountain Home, Washington 37684
Mt Carmel, Hawkins 37645
Mtn Home, Washington 37684
Mulberry, Lincoln 37359
Munford, Tipton 38058
MURFREESBORO, Rutherford (See Page 3559)
NASHVILLE, Davidson (See Page 3563)
New Hope, Marion 37380
New Johnsonville, Humphreys 37134
New Market, Jefferson 37820
NEW TAZEWELL, Claiborne (See Page 3572)
Newbern, Dyer 38059
Newcomb, Campbell 37819
NEWPORT, Cocke (See Page 3572)
Niota, Mcminn 37826
Nolensville, Williamson 37135
Norene, Wilson 37136
Normandy, Bedford 37360
Norris, Anderson 37828
Nunnelly, Hickman 37137
Oak Hill, Davidson 37220
OAK RIDGE, Anderson (See Page 3572)
Oakdale, Morgan 37829
Oakfield, Madison 38362
Oakland, Fayette 38060
Oakland, Fayette 38076
Obion, Obion 38240
Ocoee, Polk 37361
Old Fort, Polk 37362
Old Hickory, Davidson 37138
Olivehill, Hardin 38475
Oliver Springs, Roane 37840
Oneida, Scott 37841
Only, Hickman 37140
Ooltewah, Hamilton 37363
Orlinda, Robertson 37141
Orme, Marion 37380
Ozone, Roane 37854
Pall Mall, Fentress 38577
Palmer, Grundy 37365
Palmersville, Weakley 38241
Palmyra, Montgomery 37142
Paris, Henry 38242
Parker Crossroads, Henderson 38388
Parrottsville, Cocke 37843
Parsons, Decatur 38363
Pegram, Cheatham 37143
Pelham, Grundy 37366
Petersburg, Lincoln 37144
Petros, Morgan 37845
Philadelphia, Loudon 37846
Pickwick Dam, Hardin 38365
PIGEON FORGE, Sevier (See Page 3573)
Pikeville, Bledsoe 37367
Piney Flats, Sullivan 37686
Pinson, Madison 38366
Pioneer, Campbell 37847
Piperton, Shelby 38017

Pittman Center, Sevier 37876
Pleasant Hill, Cumberland 38578
Pleasant Shade, Smith 37145
Pleasant View, Cheatham 37146
Pleasantville, Hickman 37033
Pocahontas, Hardeman 38061
Portland, Sumner 37148
Postelle, Polk 37317
Powder Springs, Grainger 37848
Powell, Knox 37849
Powells Crossroads, Sequatchie 37397
Primm Springs, Williamson ... 38476
Prospect, Giles 38477
Pruden, Claiborne 37851
Pulaski, Giles 38478
Puryear, Henry 38251
Quebeck, White 38579
Ramer, Mcnairy 38367
Ravenscroft, White 38583
Readyville, Cannon 37149
Reagan, Henderson 38368
Red Bank, Hamilton 37415
Red Boiling Springs, Macon . 37150
Reliance, Polk 37369
Riceville, Mcminn 37370
Rickman, Overton 38580
Riddleton, Smith 37151
Ridgely, Lake 38080
Ridgeside, Hamilton 37411
Ridgetop, Robertson 37152
Ripley, Lauderdale 38063
Rives, Obion 38253
Roan Mountain, Carter 37687
Robbins, Scott 37852
Rock Bridge, Sumner 37022
Rock Island, Warren 38581
Rockford, Blount 37853
Rockvale, Rutherford 37153
Rockwood, Roane 37854
Rogersville, Hawkins 37857
Rossville, Fayette 38066
Rossville, Fayette 38076
Royal, Bedford 37160
Rugby, Morgan 37733
Russellville, Hamblen 37860
Rutherford, Gibson 38369
Rutledge, Grainger 37861
Saint Andrews, Franklin 37375
Saint Joseph, Lawrence 38481
Sale Creek, Hamilton 37304
Sale Creek, Hamilton 37373
Saltillo, Hardin 38370
Samburg, Obion 38254
Santa Fe, Maury 38482
Sardis, Henderson 38371
Saulsbury, Hardeman 38067
Savannah, Hardin 38372
Scotts Hill, Decatur 38374
Selmer, Mcnairy 38375
Sequatchie, Marion 37374
SEVIERVILLE, Sevier (See Page 3574)
Sewanee, Franklin 37375
Seymour, Sevier 37865
Shady Valley, Johnson 37688
Sharon, Weakley 38255
Sharps Chapel, Union 37866
Shawanee, Claiborne 37867
SHELBYVILLE, Bedford (See Page 3578)
Sherwood, Franklin 37376
Shiloh, Hardin 38376
Signal Mountain, Hamilton 37377
Silerton, Hardeman 38377
Silver Point, Putnam 38582
Slayden, Dickson 37165
Smartt, Warren 37378
Smithville, Dekalb 37166
Smyrna, Rutherford 37167
Sneedville, Hancock 37869
So Carthage, Smith 37030
SODDY DAISY, Hamilton (See Page 3578)
Somerville, Fayette 38060
South Carthage, Smith 37030
South Fulton, Obion 38257
South Pittsburg, Marion 37380
Southside, Montgomery 37171
Sparta, White 38583
Speedwell, Claiborne 37870
Spencer, Van Buren 38585
Spring City, Rhea 37381
Spring Creek, Madison 38378
Spring Hill, Maury 37174
Springfield, Robertson 37172
Springville, Henry 38256
Stanton, Haywood 38069
Stantonville, Mcnairy 38379
Stewart, Houston 37175
Strawberry Plains, Jefferson .. 37871
Sugar Tree, Decatur 38380
Summertown, Lawrence 38483
Summitville, Coffee 37382
Sunbright, Morgan 37872
Surgoinsville, Hawkins 37873
Sweetwater, Monroe 37874
Taft, Lincoln 38488
Talbott, Hamblen 37877
Tallassee, Blount 37878
Tazewell, Claiborne 37879
Telford, Washington 37690
Tellico Plains, Monroe 37385
Ten Mile, Meigs 37880
Tennessee Ridge, Houston ... 37178
Thompsons Station, Williamson 37179
Thorn Hill, Grainger 37881
Three Way, Gibson 38343
Tigrett, Dyer 38070
Tipton, Tipton 38071
Tiptonville, Lake 38079
Toone, Hardeman 38381
Townsend, Blount 37882
Tracy City, Grundy 37387
Trade, Johnson 37691
Treadway, Grainger 37881
Trenton, Gibson 38382
Trezevant, Carroll 38258
Trimble, Dyer 38259
Troy, Obion 38260
Tullahoma, Coffee 37388
Tullahoma, Coffee 37389
Turtletown, Polk 37391
Tusculum, Greene 37745
Tusculum Coll, Greene 37743
Unicoi, Unicoi 37692
UNION CITY, Obion (See Page 3579)
Unionville, Bedford 37180
Vanleer, Dickson 37181
Viola, Warren 37394
Vonore, Monroe 37885
Walden, Hamilton 37377
Walland, Blount 37886
Walling, White 38587
Walnut Grove, Sumner 37048
Wartburg, Morgan 37887
Wartrace, Bedford 37183
Washburn, Grainger 37888
Watauga, Carter 37694
Watertown, Wilson 37184
Watts Bar Dam, Rhea 37381
Waverly, Humphreys 37185
Waynesboro, Wayne 38485
Westmoreland, Sumner 37186
Westpoint, Lawrence 38486
Westport, Carroll 38387
White Bluff, Dickson 37187
White House, Robertson 37188
White Pine, Jefferson 37890
Whites Creek, Davidson 37189
Whitesburg, Hamblen 37891
Whiteside, Marion 37396
Whiteville, Hardeman 38075
Whitleyville, Jackson 38588
Whitwell, Sequatchie 37397
Wilder, Overton 38589
Wildersville, Henderson 38388
Williamsport, Maury 38487
Williston, Fayette 38076
Winchester, Franklin 37398
Winfield, Scott 37892
Woodbury, Cannon 37190
Woodland Mills, Obion 38271
Woodlawn, Montgomery 37191
Wrigley, Hickman 37098
Wynnburg, Lake 38077
Yorkville, Gibson 38389
Yuma, Carroll 38390

ANTIOCH TN

General Delivery	37013

POST OFFICE BOXES MAIN OFFICE STATIONS AND BRANCHES

Box No.s	ZIP
All PO Boxes	37011

NAMED STREETS

Aaron Dr	37013
Abercorn Ct	37013
Aeolia Dr	37013
Aerie Lndg	37013
Agatha Ct	37013
Aileen Ct & Dr	37013
Ainsworth Cir	37013
Aldersgate Rd	37013
Aldwych Ct & Way	37013
Alexis Dr	37013
Algonquin Ct & Trl	37013
Alicia Ln	37013
Alpenglow Ct & Pt	37013
Alteras Dr	37013
Amber Crest Ct	37013
Amberton Ct	37013
Amberwine Ct	37013
Amelia Ct & Dr	37013
Anderson Rd	37013
Andrea Ct	37013
Anduin Ave	37013
Annalee Dr	37013
Annesbury Ln	37013
Ansley Ct	37013
Antioch Ct & Pike	37013
Antioch Woods Ct & Way	37013
Apache Trl	37013
Apollo Cir, Ct & Dr E & W	37013
Apple Blossom Ct	37013
Apple Orchard Trl	37013
Applejack Ct	37013
Appleseed Ct	37013
Applewood Ln	37013
Arapaho Bnd & Ct	37013
Arbor Pl	37013
Arbor Crest Blvd	37013
Arbor Knoll Blvd	37013
Arbor Ridge Dr	37013
Arcadia Cir & Ct	37013
Artelia Dr	37013
Arvington Way	37013
Ascot Dr	37013
Ash Ct	37013
Ash Forge Dr	37013
Ashby Dr & Pl	37013
Asheford Ct & Trce	37013
Ashwell Close	37013
Autumn Dr	37013
Ayers Dr	37013
Baby Ruth Ln	37013
Back Water Cir	37013
Backstretch Blvd	37013
Bakertown Ct & Rd	37013
Ballard Ct	37013
Banff Park Ct & Dr	37013
Banning Cir	37013
Barclay Square Cir, Ct & Dr	37013
Barella Ct & Dr	37013
Barkhill Pl	37013
Barkley Ct	37013
Barksdale Ln	37013
Barnbrook Cv	37013
Barnes Rd	37013
Barnes Bend Dr	37013
Barnes Cove Ct & Dr	37013
Bart Dr	37013
Battle Rd	37013
Bayridge Ct	37013
Bayshore Cv	37013
Bayswater Cir & Pl	37013
Beach St	37013
Beachfront Ave	37013
Beachmist Way	37013
Beazer Ln	37013
Beech Forge Dr	37013
Bell Rd	37013
Bell Crest Dr	37013
Bell Forge Ln E	
5300-5425	37013
5424-5424	37011
5426-5498	37013
5427-5499	37013
Bell Ridge Trce	37013
Bell Trace Cir, Ct, Cv, Dr & Ln	37013
Belle Oaks Ct, Dr & Pl	37013
Ben Alex Ct	37013
Benchmark Dr	37013
Bending Creek Dr	37013
Bent Wood Ct, Cv & Dr	37013
Bentfield Dr	37013
Benzing Rd	37013
Bess Ct N & S	37013
Big River Run	37013
Billingsgate Ct & Rd	37013
Birchbrook Ct & Dr	37013
Birchclay Pt N & S	37013
Birchmill Pt N & S	37013
Birdsong Chase	37013
Bishopsgate Rd	37013
Bison Ct	37013
Black Mountain Ct & Dr	37013
Black Oak Ct	37013
Blackpool Dr	37013
Blairfield Dr	37013
Blake Dr	37013
Blue Hole Ct, Rd & Way	37013
Blue Lake Cir & Trl	37013
Blue Mountain Ln	37013
Bluewillow Ct	37013
Bluffglen Ct	37013
Bluffhollow Gap	37013
Bob Burton Dr	37013
Bombadil Ln	37013
Bowfield Ct & Dr	37013
Bowwater Ln	37013
Bradburn Village Cir	37013
Bradley Ct	37013
Brandy Ct	37013
Brantley Ct & Dr	37013
Brass Oak Trce	37013
Brenda Cir, Ct & Ln	37013
Brentridge Cir, Dr & Pl	37013
Brian Cir	37013
Brianne Ct	37013
Bridge Creek Ln	37013
Bridgecrest Dr & Way	37013
Bridgeton Cv	37013
Bridgeton Cove Ct	37013
Bridgette Ct	37013
Bristol Mountain Ct	37013
Brittany Park Cir, Dr, Ln & Pl	37013
Broken Bow Dr	37013
Bromley Way	37013
Brook Dr	37013
Brook View Estates Dr	37013
Brookchase Ct	37013
Brookmont Cir	37013
Brookstone Ct	37013
Bruin Dr	37013
Bryant Ct	37013
Buckhorn Trl	37013
Buckpasser Ave & Ct	37013
Burkitt Rd	37013
Burlingame Ct	37013
Burnham Ln	37013
Burnt Pine Ct	37013
Burwick Ct & Pl	37013
Cabernet Trl	37013
Cadogan Ct & Way	37013
Cainbrook Ct & Xing	37013
Calais Cir & Ct	37013
Calder Ct	37013
Calderwood Dr	37013
Callabee Way	37013
Calumet Ct & Dr	37013
Calypso Ct	37013
Cambridge Dr & Pl	37013
Cambridge Close	37013
Camille Ct & Dr	37013
Candlecreek Way	37013
Candy Apple Cv	37013
Cane Ridge Rd	37013
Cane Springs Rd	37013
Canex Dr	37013
Canoe Ridge Pt	37013
Canyon Ridge Ct	37013
Cardigan Way	37013
Carl Miller Dr	37013
Castleton Ct	37013
Catawba Ct	37013
Catspaw Ct, Dr & Pl	37013
Cavendish Ct	37013
Cedar Ash Ct & Xing	37013
Cedar Pointe Pkwy	37013
Cedarcliff Cir, Ct & Rd	37013
Cedarcroft Ct & Dr	37013
Cedarhill Ct & Dr	37013
Cedarmont Dr	37013
Cedarview Dr	37013
Centreboard Ct	37013
Chadfield Ct & Way	37013
Chandler Cove Way	37013
Chaparal Ct	37013
Charlton Dr	37013
Charmaine Ct	37013
Chatterly Ct	37013
Chelsea Way	37013
Cheoah Ct	37013
Cherokee Ct & Pl	37013
Cherokee Hills Dr	37013
Cherry Hills Dr	37013
Cheshire Pass	37013
Chesterbrook Ct	37013
Chestnut Oak Dr	37013
Chestwick Ct	37013
Chetopa Ct	37013
Chimneytop Dr	37013
Chinook Dr	37013
Chrishall Ct	37013
Chutney Ct & Dr	37013
Cimarron Ct & Way	37013
Claircrest Dr	37013
Clapham Ct & Rd	37013
Clark Hill Xing	37013
Claybrook Ln	37013
Claycreek Pt	37013
Clingmans Ct	37013
Cloud Springs Ct	37013
Cloudfalls Trce	37013
Cloudgrove Pt	37013
Club Forge Dr	37013
Clubhouse Ct & Ln	37013
Coconut Ct	37013
Cold Spring Dr	37013
Coldfield Ct	37013
Colemont Ct, Dr, Pl & Ter	37013
Coleridge Ct & Dr	37013
Coles Branch Dr	37013
Collins Park Dr	37013
Collinwood Cor, Ct & Pl	37013
Colo Cv, Pl & Trl	37013
Coneflower Trl	37013
Copper Ridge Trl	37013
Coral Ct	37013
Cottage Grove Ct & Way	37013
Cottage Hill Dr	37013
Cottage View Ln	37013
Country Ct	37013
Country Hill Rd	37013
Country Lawn Ct & Dr	37013
Country Meadow Ct & Rd	37013
Country Ridge Ct & Dr	37013
Country Way Ct & Rd	37013
Countryside Dr	37013
Crab Apple Cv	37013
Craftwood Ct & Dr	37013
Creekedge Ct	37013
Cressent Glen Ct	37013
Crosshaven Ct	37013
Crossings Blvd, Cir & Pl	37013
Crystal Brook Dr	37013
Culbertson Rd	37013
Cummings Ct	37013
Cummings Park Dr	37013
Curran Ct	37013
Curtis Hollow Rd	37013
Cypress Leaf Ct	37013
Daffodil Ct	37013
Dahlgreen Ct	37013
Daisy Ct & Trl	37013
Dale View Dr	37013
Dali Ct	37013
Dana Way	37013
Danley Ct	37013
Darlene Dr	37013
Daybreak Dr	37013
Debra Dr	37013
Deer Valley Trl	37013
Deerhaven Ct & Dr	37013
Delia Dr	37013
Delvin Ct & Dr	37013
Denise Ct & Dr	37013
Derbyshire Ct & Dr	37013
Derrick Ct	37013
Diamondhead Ct	37013
Doriswood Ct	37013
Dory Dr	37013
Dove Creek Ct & Rd	37013
Dover Glen Dr	37013
Dowdy Ct & Dr	37013
Drawbridge Ct	37013
Dresden Ct	37013
Drewry Dr	37013
Dupree Point Dr	37013
Eagle View Blvd	37013
Eastport Ct	37013
Edencrest Ct & Dr	37013
Edenfield Ct	37013
Edge O Lake Dr	37013
Eli Dr	37013
Elijah Ryan Dr	37013
Elizabeths Ct	37013
Elkader Ct N & S	37013
Elkhorn Pt	37013
Ellen Way	37013
Ellsworth Pl	37013
Elmer Marshall Dr	37013
Emily Ct	37013
Erna Ct	37013
Esturbridge Ct	37013
Ethan Ln	37013
Evanfield Ct	37013
Evening Ave	37013
Eversholt Ct	37013
Fall Ct	37013
Fanning Dr	37013
Farrington Pl	37013
Fernhurst Ct	37013
Fieldoak Ct	37013
Fieldstone Ct & Dr	37013
Firelight Ct & Trl	37013
Flagstone Dr	37013
Folkstone Dr	37013
Forest Pl	37013
Forest Breeze Dr	37013
Forest Pointe Cir, Ln & Pl	37013
Forest View Dr	37013
Forrestal Way	37013
Four Lakes Dr	37013
Foxview Dr	37013
Franklin Limestone Rd	37013
Frodo Ln	37013
Gannett Peak Ln	37013
Garden View Ct	37013
Garrett Way Ct	37013
Gasser Dr	37013
Gillespie Ct & Dr	37013
Glade Ct	37013
E Glen Ct	37013
Gloryland Ln	37013
Golden Apple Dr	37013
Goldroom Way	37013
Gondola Dr	37013
Goodwin Rd	37013
Grace Falls Dr	37013
Grant Ridge Ln	37013
Grapeleaf Way	37013
Green Garden Ct	37013
Green Timbers Dr	37013
Green Trails Ct & Dr	37013
Greenhart Ct	37013
Greystone Ct & St	37013
Grovedale Trce	37013
Grovesnor Ct & Dr	37013
Halifax Ln	37013
Hamilton Ln & Xing	37013
Hamilton Church Rd	37013
Hamilton Glen Dr & Pl	37013
Hampstead N & S	37013
Hampton Blvd & Ct	37013
S Hampton Close	37013
Hannah Ridge Ct	37013
Harbor Lndg	37013
Harper Ridge Pl	37013
Hartfield Ct	37013
Harvest Ct	37013
Harvest Grove Dr	37013
Haskell Dr & Ln	37013
Haversham Ct	37013
Hawaiian Vw	37013
Hays Blackman Loop	37013
Haystack Ln	37013
Haywood Ln	37013
Hearthside Way	37013
Hickory Ct & Way	37013
Hickory Club Dr	37013
Hickory Forge Dr	37013
Hickory Glade Ct & Dr	37013
Hickory Grove Dr	37013
Hickory Highlands Dr	37013
Hickory Hollow Ln, Pkwy, Pl & Ter	37013
Hickory Lawn Ct	37013
Hickory Park Ct, Dr & Ln E & W	37013
Hickory Pass Ln	37013
Hickory Ridge Ct	37013
Hickory Rim Ct	37013
Hickory Timber Ct	37013
Hickory View Ct	37013
Hickory Way Ct	37013
Hickory Woods Ct, Dr & Way E	37013
Hidden Creek Dr	37013
High Meadow Ct	37013
Highland Ridge Ct & Dr	37013
Highlander Ct, Cv & Dr	37013
Hill Bennett Cir	37013
Hill Ridge Dr	37013
Hillshire Ct & Dr	37013
Hilo Ct	37013
Hobson Pike	37013
Homey Ct & Dr	37013
Honey Grove Ct & Dr	37013
Honolulu Rd	37013
Hunters Branch Rd	37013
Hunters Green Cir	37013
Huntingboro Ct & Trl	37013
Hurley Ct	37013
Hurricane Creek Blvd	37013
Irma Ct & Dr	37013
Isabelle Ln	37013
Jamerend Dr	37013
Jamie Cir	37013
Janice Dr	37013
Jason Dr	37013
Jenny Murff Dr	37013
Jenny Ruth Pt	37013
Jeri Ct	37013
Johnson Pass Ct & Dr	37013
Johnson Ridge Rd	37013
Josephine Ct	37013
Joust Ct	37013
Justin Towne Ct	37013
Kaeden Pointe Ct	37013
Kalvesta Ct	37013
Kanlow Dr	37013
Karen Ray Ct & Dr	37013
Katonka Ct & Dr	37013
Keeley Dr	37013
Kelsey Ct	37013
Kennebeck Pl	37013
Kenton Ct	37013
Kestenbaum Ct	37013
Kettering Close	37013
Kevinwood Ct	37013
Kimsaw Cir	37013
Kinwood Ct & Dr	37013
Knightsbridge Way	37013
Kolmia Trl	37013
Kothe Ct & Way	37013
Krohne Way	37013
Labrador Ln	37013
Lake Towne Dr	37013
Lakewalk Dr	37013
Lakewood Village Dr	37013
Lambeth Way	37013
Lancashire Dr	37013
Lassen Ct	37013
Laurel Oak Dr	37013
Laurenwood Dr	37013
Lava Ct	37013
Lavergne Couchville Pike	37013
Lawson Dr	37013
Leadenhall Ct	37013
Leafhollow Path	37013
Leafmill Ct	37013
Leatherbury Ct	37013
Leefield Dr	37013
Leeshan Ct	37013
Legacy Dr	37013
Legend Ct & Dr	37013
Leisure Ct & Ln	37013
Lenox Creekside Dr	37013
Lera Jones Dr	37013
Lindy Murff Ct	37013
Lipton Ct & Pl	37013
Logistics Way	37013
London Ct	37013
London Gardens Ct	37013
Londonview Pl	37013
Long Br	37013
Longhaven Xing	37013
Lonsway Cir & Ct	37013
Loralie Ln	37013
Lori Dr	37013
Lou Ct	37013
Louise Russell Dr	37013
Lower Park Pl	37013
Luann Ct & Dr	37013
Luke Ct & Dr	37013
Luker Ln	37013
Lydia Dr	37013
Maggie Ct & Dr	37013
Mallard Creek Ct	37013
Manatee Ct	37013
Maple Timber Ct & Dr	37013
Maple Top Dr	37013
Marhaden Dr	37013
Maritime Prt	37013
Marvell Ct	37013
Max Ct	37013
Maxine Dr	37013
Maxwell Pl & Rd	37013
Mcbride Rd	37013
Mccumber Dr	37013
Mclendon Ct & Dr	37013
Michele Dr	37013
Milbridge Ct & Dr	37013
Millbridge Bay	37013
Mimosa Ct	37013
Miners Cv	37013
Monroe Xing	37013
Monte Carlo Dr	37013
Monte Leone Ct	37013
Moonglow Ct	37013
Morning Ct & Rd	37013
Morningwood Ln & Pl	37013
Morris Gentry Blvd	37013
Moss Rd	37013
Moss Landing Dr	37013
Moss Spring Dr	37013
Mossdale Ct & Dr	37013
Mossy Oak Ct & Trl	37013
Mount Hood Dr	37013
Mount Mitchell Ct	37013
Mount View Cir & Rd	37013
Mount View Ridge Dr	37013
Mountain Dale Ct	37013
Mountain Laurel Dr	37013
Mountain Springs Dr	37013
Mountainhigh Dr	37013
Muci Dr	37013
Mulberry Hill Pl	37013
Murfreesboro Pike	37013
Murphywood Xing	37013
Muskhogean Ct	37013
Mystic Valley Ct	37013
Nala Ct	37013
Nantahala Ct	37013
Napa Pt E & W	37013
Nate Cv	37013
New Overlook Ct	37013
New Towne Ct & Rd	37013
New Windsor Ct	37013
Newington Cv	37013
Newlodge Ct	37013
Nightfall Ct	37013
Nolensville Pike	37013
Northway Cir	37013
Oak Barrel Dr & Ln	37013
Oak Chase Dr	37013
Oak Creek Dr	37013
Oak Forest Cir, Dr & Ln	37013
Oak Forge Dr	37013
E & W Oak Highland Ct & Dr	37013
Oak Ridge Ct	37013
Oak Springs Ct	37013
Oak Timber Ct, Dr & Pl	37013
Oak Trees Ct	37013
Oakview Ct	37013
Oakwood Forest Dr	37013
Oakwood Terrace Dr	37013
Ocala Dr	37013
Oceanfront Cir N & S	37013
October Woods Dr	37013
Ohara Dr	37013
Okee Trl	37013
Old Anderson Rd	37013
Old Burkitt Rd	37013
Old Forest Rd	37013
Old Franklin Rd	37013
Old Hickory Blvd	37013
Old Tusculum Rd	37013
Ole Nottingham Dr	37013
Olivia Dr	37013
Orchard Mountain Ct	37013
Ottenville Ave	37013
Overby Dr	37013
Owen Dr	37013
Owendale Dr	37013
Pacific Ct	37013
Paddington Ct & Way	37013
Painter Dr	37013
Palm Tree Ct	37013
Panamint Dr	37013
Park Royal Ln	37013
Park Trail Pt	37013
Parker Dr	37013
Parks Retreat Dr	37013
Parkstone Ln	37013
Paulson Ct, Pl & Way	37013
Payne Rd	37013
Peaceful Brook Dr	37013
Pebble Creek Cir, Ct & Dr E	37013
Peckham Ln	37013

Pekay Ct 37013
Pekoe Cir 37013
Penny Brink Dr 37013
Pepper Ridge Cir 37013
Peppertree Ct & Dr 37013
Pepperwood Ct & Dr 37013
Pettus Rd 37013
Pheasant Creek Ct 37013
Philhall Pkwy 37013
Piccadilly Row 37013
Piccadilly Sac 37013
Pin Hook Rd 37013
Pin Oak Ct & Dr 37013
Pine Glen Ct 37013
Pine Rock Ct 37013
Pineapple Ln 37013
Pinebrook Ct & Trl 37013
Pinelake Dr 37013
Pineorchard Pl 37013
Pinot Chase 37013
Pinwheel Ct & Dr 37013
Pippin Dr 37013
Placid Ct 37013
Pleasant Colony Ct & Dr 37013
Pleasant Ridge Rd 37013
Pocono Rd 37013
Point Break Cir & Dr 37013
Pointer Ct 37013
Ponderosa Way 37013
Pony Ridge Way 37013
Port Breeze Pl 37013
Port Hope Ct 37013
Port James Cir 37013
Post Oak Dr 37013
Preakness Dr 37013
Preserve Blvd 37013
Preston Ct & Rd 37013
Priestshore Bay 37013
Quails Nest Ct 37013
Quaise Moor E & W 37013
Quiet Creek Ct 37013
Rader Ct & Dr 37013
Rader Ridge Ct & Rd 37013
Rainey Dr 37013
Rainglen Cv 37013
Rainstone Pt 37013
Ramstone Way 37013
Ransom Village Way 37013
Ravenna Ct N & S 37013
Reagan Run 37013
Realtree Way 37013
Rebecca Trena Way 37013
Red Apple Rd 37013
Red Bark Ct 37013
Red Jacket Dr 37013
Reeves Rd 37013
Regents Park Cir 37013
Remmington Trce 37013
Retriever Ct & Pl 37013
Rice Rd 37013
Rice Hill Cir & Ct 37013
Richards Ct & Rd 37013
Ridgefalls Way 37013
Ridgeview Ct 37013
Ripple Cv 37013
Ristau Ct & Dr 37013
Rivendell Trce 37013
Robert Yoest Dr 37013
Rock Creek Dr 37013
Rock Glen Ct 37013
Rockglade Run 37013
Rockland Trl 37013
Rockridge Ct 37013
Rockview Ct 37013
Rocky Mountain Ct & Pkwy 37013
Rocky Top Ct & Dr 37013
Rogers Ct 37013
Rollingstone Dr 37013
Rosander Ln 37013
Round Rock Dr 37013
Roundwood Pl 37013
Roundwood Forest Ct, Dr & Ln 37013
Roxanne Ct & Dr 37013

Ruddell Ln 37013
Rugosa Ct 37013
Rural Hill Rd 37013
Russell Branch Ct 37013
Saddlecreek Way 37013
Safford View Dr 37013
Sailfish Ct 37013
Sailmist Pt 37013
Saint Cloud Dr 37013
Samwise Ln 37013
Sandbury Pt 37013
Sandia Peak Ct 37013
Sandpiper Ln 37013
Sandrose Ct 37013
Sands Ct 37013
Sandstone Dr 37013
Sandworth Cv 37013
Santee Ct 37013
Santeelah Way 37013
Saxony Lake Dr 37013
Scenic Lake Ct 37013
Schoolhouse Ct 37013
Seabisquit Dr 37013
Seasons Ct & Dr 37013
Seasons Lake Ct 37013
Sebetha Ct 37013
Secretariat Dr 37013
Septo Ct 37013
Shabnam Dr 37013
Shacklett Lane Ct 37013
Shadowbrook Ct & Trl 37013
Shady Tree Ln 37013
Shadyview Dr 37013
Shagbark Ct & Trl 37013
Shaker Ct 37013
Shakertown Ct, Cv & Rd 37013
Shakerville Ct 37013
Shallowbrook Trl N & S 37013
Shawa Trl 37013
Shaylin Loop 37013
Sheana Way 37013
Sheila Dr 37013
Shihmen Ct & Dr 37013
Shire Dr 37013
Shoemaker Ct & Dr 37013
Shoppe Ct 37013
S Shore Dr 37013
Shoreline Cir & Ln 37013
Shorewind Bay 37013
Shorewood Path 37013
Shufeld Ct 37013
Silvermoon Dr 37013
Singing Hills Dr 37013
Skinner Dr 37013
Skip Jack Dr 37013
Skyfalls Ct & Way 37013
Skygap Ct 37013
Skyglen Trce 37013
Skyshore Way 37013
Smedley Ln 37013
Smith Springs Pkwy & Rd 37013
Smokey Hill Rd 37013
Smokey Mountain Pl 37013
Snowglade Gap 37013
Somerset Valley Dr 37013
Sonoma Trce 37013
Sophie Dr 37013
Soulshine Pl 37013
Southbeach Cv 37013
Southern Way 37013
Spann Ct 37013
Split Oak Ct, Dr & Trl 37013
Spring Garden Ct 37013
Springmore Ct 37013
Springs Hill Way 37013
Springstead Trl 37013
Springtime Ct 37013
Sprucedale Dr 37013
Stanford Village Ct & Dr 37013
Stardale Way 37013
Starglen Trl 37013
Stecoah Ct & St 37013

Stephens Hill Ln 37013
Stephens Ridge Way 37013
Sterry Ct 37013
Stone Bridge Ct & Rd 37013
Stone Flower Ct 37013
Stonedale Way 37013
N & S Stonegate Dr 37013
Stoneshore Trce 37013
Stoneview Ct & Dr 37013
Stonewood Dr 37013
Stoney Brook Cir 37013
Straight Ln 37013
Strand Fleet Dr 37013
Streamdale Pt E & W 37013
Streamfield Ct & Pass 37013
Streamfire Cv 37013
Streamridge Ct E & W 37013
Sue Ct & Dr 37013
Sugar Cane Ln 37013
Sugar Magnolia Ln 37013
Sugaree Pt 37013
Summerbreeze Ln 37013
Summercrest Blvd, Ct, Cv & Trl 37013
Summertime Ct 37013
Sunbeam Dr 37013
Sundown Ct & Dr 37013
Sunnyvale Ct & Dr 37013
Sunnywood Ct & Dr 37013
Sunsail Dr 37013
Sunshine Ct & Dr 37013
Suzanne Dr 37013
Suzy Dr 37013
Swan Ridge Dr 37013
Sycamore Ct 37013
Syrah Dr 37013
Target Dr 37013
Tasmen Ct 37013
Tavistock Pl 37013
Tea Garden Way 37013
Tecumseh Ln 37013
Tee Pee Trce 37013
Tenonwood Ct 37013
Terragon Ct & Trl 37013
Terrapin Trl 37013
Thistle Down Ln 37013
Thomas Bay Ct 37013
Thomason Trl 37013
Thornehill Dr 37013
Three Stone Ct 37013
Timber Trl 37013
Timberlake Cir 37013
Tina Ct 37013
Tintop Ct 37013
Titan Ct 37013
Tomarand Ct & Rd 37013
Took Dr 37013
S Towne Ct 37013
Towne Ridge Dr 37013
Towne Valley Ct & Rd 37013
W Towne Village Ct & Rd 37013
Towneship Rd 37013
Traceton Cir & Ct 37013
Trailside Cir 37013
Trailwater Dr 37013
Trappers Rdg 37013
Treetop Dr 37013
Treeview Ct 37013
Tropic Isle Ct 37013
Tru Long Ct & Dr 37013
Tuckaleechee Ln 37013
Turfway Ln 37013
Tuscarora Ct & Dr 37013
Tusculum Ct & Rd 37013
Twin Oaks Ln 37013
Una Antioch Pike 37013
Upper Mill Dr 37013
Upsall Dr 37013
Valencia Ct 37013
Valley Way 37013
Valley Green Ct & Dr 37013
Vanguard Pl 37013
Vanna Ct 37013
Victoria Cir 37013
Victoria Station Ct 37013

Volcano Ct 37013
Volunteer Dr 37013
Wagondale Way 37013
Waikiki Blvd 37013
Walnut Crest Dr 37013
Wareham Ct 37013
Water Oak Ct 37013
Waterburg Ln 37013
Waterford Ct, Pl & Way 37013
Waywood Cir & Ct 37013
Weatherstone Cv E & W 37013
Weathertop Rd 37013
Wellenstein Way 37013
Wellfleet Ct 37013
Wells Ct 37013
Welshcrest Ct, Dr & Pl 37013
Westcliffe Cir & Ct 37013
Westridge Ct 37013
Whirlaway Dr 37013
White Mountain Ln 37013
Whitesail Ct 37013
Whitney Creek Dr 37013
Whittemore Ln 37013
Wild Apple Ct 37013
Wild Oaks Ct 37013
Wildgrove Ct & Dr 37013
Wilford Pack Ct & Dr 37013
E & W Winchester Dr, Pass & Pl 37013
Winchester Close 37013
Windcrest Trl 37013
Windsail Trl 37013
Windshore Way 37013
Windsor Brook Pl 37013
Windsor Green Ct & Dr 37013
Windsor Meadows Pass 37013
Winter Haven Ct 37013
Winton Dr 37013
Woburn Way 37013
Woodfern Ct 37013
Woodymore Ct, Dr & Pl 37013
Worthington Ave 37013
Xavier Ct & Dr 37013
Yellowstone Ct 37013
Yoest Cir 37013
Yosemite Ct 37013

ATHENS TN

General Delivery 37303

POST OFFICE BOXES MAIN OFFICE STATIONS AND BRANCHES

Box No.s
All PO Boxes 37371

NAMED STREETS

Ada St 37303
Adams St 37303
Aldridge Ln 37303
Alford St 37303
Alton St 37303
Anderson St 37303
Anton St 37303
Apache St 37303
Apple St 37303
Aqua St 37303
Ashley Ct 37303
Astrid St 37303
Athenian St 37303
Atlantic St 37303
Ava St 37303
Avalon St 37303
Baker St 37303
E & W Bank St 37303
Barnabas St 37303
Beech St 37303
Bell St 37303
Bellbrook Dr 37303
Bellview Rd 37303
Belmont Dr 37303
Benson Dr 37303
Benton Rd 37303
Berger St 37303
Betts St 37303
Blount St 37303
Blue Springs Rd 37303
Boaz St 37303
Breckenridge St 37303
Brentwood Dr 37303
Brewer St 37303
Brigadoon St 37303
Brown St 37303
Bryson St 37303
Bud St 37303
Burkett L Witt Blvd 37303
Burnsbrooke Dr 37303
Call Dr 37303
Callen Cv 37303
Canal St 37303
Canterbury St 37303
Cardinal St 37303
Carmen Dr 37303
Carter Rd 37303
Cartwright St 37303
Cawana St 37303
Ceaser St 37303
Cedar Springs Rd 37303
Central Ave 37303
Chapman St 37303
Charles St 37303
Charlotte St 37303
Cherokee St 37303
Cherry St 37303
Chesapeake Dr 37303
Chester St 37303
Chestnut Hill Dr 37303
Chilhowee St 37303
Church St 37303
Cindy St 37303
Circle Dr 37303
Clark St 37303
Clayton St 37303
Cleague St 37303
Clearwater Rd 37303
Cleveland Ave 37303
Clist St 37303
Coach Farmer Dr 37303
E & W College St 37303
Colonial Dr 37303
Congress Pkwy N & S 37303
Cook Dr 37303
Coosa St 37303
County Road 100 37303
County Road 102 37303
County Road 103 37303
County Road 104 37303
County Road 105 37303
County Road 106 37303
County Road 107 37303
County Road 108 37303
County Road 109 37303
County Road 110 37303
County Road 111 37303
County Road 112 37303
County Road 1120 37303
County Road 1121 37303
County Road 113 37303
County Road 114 37303
County Road 115 37303
County Road 116 37303
County Road 117 37303
County Road 119 37303
County Road 121 37303
County Road 122 37303
County Road 123 37303
County Road 124 37303
County Road 125 37303
County Road 126 37303
County Road 127 37303
County Road 128 37303
County Road 129 37303
County Road 130 37303
County Road 131 37303
County Road 132 37303
County Road 133 37303
County Road 134 37303
County Road 1340 37303
County Road 135 37303
County Road 136 37303
County Road 138 37303
County Road 139 37303
County Road 164 37303
County Road 165 37303
County Road 166 37303
County Road 167 37303
County Road 168 37303
County Road 169 37303
County Road 170 37303
County Road 171 37303
County Road 172 37303
County Road 173 37303
County Road 174 37303
County Road 175 37303
County Road 176 37303
County Road 177 37303
County Road 178 37303
County Road 180 37303
County Road 181 37303
County Road 184 37303
County Road 185 37303
County Road 187 37303
County Road 191 37303
County Road 194 37303
County Road 195 37303
County Road 196 37303
County Road 197 37303
County Road 198 37303
County Road 199 37303
County Road 200 37303
County Road 201 37303
County Road 202 37303
County Road 203 37303
County Road 204 37303
County Road 205 37303
County Road 207 37303
County Road 208 37303
County Road 209 37303
County Road 210 37303
County Road 212 37303
County Road 213 37303
County Road 214 37303
County Road 216 37303
County Road 218 37303
County Road 220 37303
County Road 221 37303
County Road 229 37303
County Road 242 37303
County Road 243 37303
County Road 244 37303
County Road 247 37303
County Road 248 37303
County Road 249 37303
County Road 250 37303
County Road 251 37303
County Road 252 37303
County Road 2520 37303
County Road 253 37303
County Road 254 37303
County Road 255 37303
County Road 257 37303
County Road 258 37303
County Road 259 37303
County Road 260 37303
County Road 2600 37303
County Road 267 37303
County Road 302 37303
County Road 3050 37303
County Road 3051 37303
County Road 332 37303
County Road 370 37303
County Road 371 37303
County Road 372 37303
County Road 373 37303
County Road 375 37303
County Road 378 37303
County Road 382 37303
County Road 383 37303
County Road 405 37303
County Road 406 37303
County Road 407 37303
County Road 415 37303
County Road 42 37303
County Road 420 37303
County Road 422 37303
County Road 423 37303
County Road 427 37303
County Road 434 37303
County Road 435 37303
County Road 436 37303
County Road 4360 37303
County Road 437 37303
County Road 438 37303
County Road 439 37303
County Road 44 37303
County Road 440 37303
County Road 441 37303
County Road 442 37303
County Road 443 37303
County Road 444 37303
County Road 445 37303
County Road 446 37303
County Road 447 37303
County Road 448 37303
County Road 449 37303
County Road 45 37303
County Road 450 37303
County Road 451 37303
County Road 452 37303
County Road 456 37303
County Road 46 37303
County Road 48 37303
County Road 49 37303
County Road 50 37303
County Road 51 37303
County Road 52 37303
County Road 523 37303
County Road 525 37303
County Road 526 37303
County Road 53 37303
County Road 54 37303
County Road 55 37303
County Road 550 37303
County Road 552 37303
County Road 554 37303
County Road 555 37303
County Road 556 37303
County Road 557 37303
County Road 558 37303
County Road 559 37303
County Road 56 37303
County Road 560 37303
County Road 561 37303
County Road 571 37303
County Road 580 37303
County Road 581 37303
County Road 582 37303
County Road 59 37303
County Road 60 37303
County Road 600 37303
County Road 601 37303
County Road 602 37303
County Road 603 37303
County Road 604 37303
County Road 605 37303
County Road 606 37303
County Road 607 37303
County Road 608 37303
County Road 609 37303
County Road 610 37303
County Road 611 37303
County Road 612 37303
County Road 613 37303
County Road 614 37303
County Road 615 37303
County Road 616 37303
County Road 617 37303
County Road 618 37303
County Road 632 37303
County Road 634 37303
County Road 635 37303
County Road 651 37303

County Road 652 37303
County Road 653 37303
County Road 654 37303
County Road 655 37303
County Road 656 37303
County Road 657 37303
County Road 658 37303
County Road 659 37303
County Road 660 37303
County Road 661 37303
County Road 662 37303
County Road 663 37303
County Road 666 37303
County Road 668 37303
County Road 669 37303
County Road 671 37303
County Road 672 37303
County Road 675 37303
County Road 679 37303
County Road 680 37303
County Road 688 37303
County Road 700 37303
County Road 7001 37303
County Road 7004 37303
County Road 702 37303
County Road 703 37303
County Road 7030 37303
County Road 704 37303
County Road 705 37303
County Road 706 37303
County Road 707 37303
County Road 708 37303
County Road 709 37303
County Road 711 37303
County Road 712 37303
County Road 713 37303
County Road 7130 37303
County Road 716 37303
County Road 717 37303
County Road 718 37303
County Road 722 37303
County Road 723 37303
County Road 750 37303
County Road 775 37303
County Road 776 37303
County Road 777 37303
County Road 778 37303
County Road 780 37303
County Road 782 37303
County Road 82 37303
County Road 83 37303
County Road 87 37303
County Road 88 37303
County Road 89 37303
County Road 92 37303
County Road 96 37303
County Road 99 37303
Courtney Dr 37303
Creek Pl 37303
Crestway Cir & Dr 37303
Crestwood Rd 37303
Cumberland Ave 37303
Cunningham Dr 37303
Dale St 37303
Davidson Rd 37303
Decatur Pike 37303
Delay St 37303
Delmar St 37303
Dennis St 37303
Denso Dr 37303
Dixon Ave 37303
Dodson St 37303
Dogwood Dr 37303
Dossett St 37303
Douglas St 37303
Dupitt St 37303
Dynasty Way 37303
East Ave 37303
Eastanallee Ave 37303
Eaves St 37303
Echo Cir 37303
Edgewood Dr 37303
Elizabeth St 37303
Elk St 37303
Elliott St 37303
Elmhurst Dr 37303
English Ln 37303
Ensminger St 37303
Epperson St 37303
Ervin St 37303
Euclid St 37303
Fairview Ave & Rd 37303
Fairway Dr 37303
Fisher St 37303
Forrest Ave 37303
Forrest Park Dr 37303
Fox St 37303
Fox Ridge Dr 37303
Francis St 37303
Frankfort St 37303
Frye St 37303
Fyke Dr 37303
Garden Dr 37303
Gay St 37303
George St 37303
George R Price Blvd 37303
Georgia Ave 37303
Gettys Ln 37303
Gideon St 37303
Glendale Ave 37303
Glenn St 37303
Gliden St 37303
Golf Crest Ln 37303
Grady St 37303
Graincol 37303
Green St 37303
Greenwood Dr 37303
Guille St 37303
Guthrie Rd 37303
Haines Rd 37303
Haley St 37303
Hamby St 37303
Hammerhill Rd 37303
Hammonds Rd 37303
Hanel St 37303
E Harper Johnson Dr 37303
Harris St 37303
Hawthorne St 37303
Hayleywood Dr 37303
Henderson St 37303
Hicks St 37303
High St 37303
Highland Ave 37303
Highway 11 N & S 37303
Highway 30 E & W 37303
Highway 305 37303
Highway 307 E 37303
Highway 39 E & W 37303
N & S Hill St 37303
Hillandale Dr 37303
Hillside Ln 37303
Hogan St 37303
Holiday Dr 37303
Holt St 37303
Hornsby St 37303
Housley Dr 37303
Houston St 37303
Howard St 37303
Hudson St 37303
Hughes St 37303
Hunters Ln 37303
Hunters Branch Rd 37303
Hutsell Dr 37303
Industrial Way 37303
Ingleside Ave 37303
Isahaya Ln 37303
Ivory Rd 37303
N & S Jackson St 37303
James St 37303
Jameson Rd 37303
Jamison Rd 37303
Jenkins Rd 37303
Joe Jaquish Dr 37303
John J Duncan Pkwy 37303
Johnson St 37303
Jones St 37303
Kathy St 37303
Keith Ln 37303
Kelly St 37303
Kenneth St 37303
Kensington St 37303
Kent St 37303
Kenwood Dr 37303
Kilgore St 37303
King St 37303
Knight Rd 37303
Knoxville Ave 37303
Lafayette St 37303
Lakefront St 37303
Lamar St 37303
Lark Ln & St 37303
Lawn St 37303
Lawrence St 37303
Lawson St 37303
Layman Rd 37303
Lee Dr & Hwy 37303
Lee Erwin Rd 37303
Legion Rd 37303
Leveck St NW 37303
Liberty Branch Ln 37303
Lime St 37303
Linden Cir 37303
Load Dr 37303
Lockmiller Blvd 37303
Long St 37303
Long Mill Rd 37303
Lovell St 37303
Lynman St 37303
Lynn Ave 37303
Lynnwood Dr 37303
E & W Madison Ave 37303
Mantle St 37303
Maple St 37303
Mason St 37303
S Matlock Ave 37303
Mccord Ave 37303
Mcell St 37303
Mcminn Ave 37303
N Meadows Dr 37303
Miami St 37303
Millard St 37303
Miller St 37303
Million St 37303
Milton Rd 37303
Monday St 37303
Moore St 37303
Morgan St 37303
Morning Pointe Ln 37303
Moses Cir & St 37303
Mount Verd Rd 37303
Mount Verd Connector 37303
Nash Dr 37303
Navajo Cir 37303
New Englewood Rd 37303
Nocatula Pl 37303
North Ave 37303
Northeastern Cir 37303
Northridge Dr 37303
Northside Dr 37303
Northwestern Ave 37303
Norton Rd 37303
Nova St 37303
Oak St 37303
Oakland Dr 37303
Ohio St 37303
Old Englewood Rd 37303
Old Niota Rd 37303
Old Riceville Rd 37303
Orchard Ln 37303
Overland Rd 37303
Oxnard Rd 37303
Palos St 37303
Park St 37303
Park Wilson Dr 37303
Peach St 37303
Perry St 37303
Pete St 37303
Pike St 37303
Pine St 37303
Pinecrest Dr 37303
Plaza Cir 37303
Pope St 37303
Powers Path 37303
Private Brand Way 37303
Puett Cir 37303
Quail Ridge Dr 37303
Railroad Ave 37303
Raven Cv & St 37303
Ray St 37303
Reading St 37303
Redfern Dr 37303
Richardson St 37303
Riddle St 37303
Ridgeway Cir 37303
Riggs St 37303
Robin St 37303
Rock St 37303
Rocky Mount Rd 37303
Rogers St 37303
Rose Dr & St 37303
Rosedale St 37303
Royal St 37303
Sage St 37303
Sanders Rd 37303
Saxton St 37303
Scenic Dr 37303
Scott St 37303
Seminole Ln 37303
Sequoia Dr 37303
Shadows Lawn Dr 37303
Shady Dr 37303
Sharp Rd 37303
Shawnee Trl 37303
Shell St 37303
Sherwood Ave 37303
Shoemaker St 37303
Short St 37303
Shreve Rd 37303
Shryer Rd 37303
Sioux St 37303
Slack Rd 37303
Sliger St 37303
Southern Pkwy 37303
Spence St 37303
Spring St 37303
Spring Place Blvd 37303
Springfield Dr 37303
Spruce St 37303
Stanford Dr 37303
Stansberry St 37303
Stanton Ln 37303
Stephanie Ln 37303
Sterling Rd 37303
Stiles St 37303
Sullins Rd 37303
Summitt St 37303
Sunset Dr 37303
Sunview Dr 37303
Sweetfield Valley Rd 37303
Taylor St 37303
Tell St 37303
Tellico Ave 37303
Tennal St 37303
Tennessee Ave 37303
Thompson St 37303
Tidence Ln 37303
Timber Creek Dr 37303
Timbercrest Dr 37303
Timothy St 37303
Topoca Trl 37303
Towanda Trl 37303
Union Rd 37303
Union Hill Ln 37303
Usry Blvd 37303
Ute St 37303
Valley Dr 37303
Van Dyke St 37303
Velma Rd 37303
E & W View St 37303
Viking Rd 37303
Village Ln 37303
Virginia Ave 37303
Vo Tech Dr 37303
Wabash St 37303
Walcon Ln 37303
Walker St 37303
Walnut Blvd 37303
Walter St 37303
Walthall St 37303
Warren St 37303
E & W Washington Ave 37303
Watson St 37303
Watts Rd 37303
Wayne Rd 37303
Webb St 37303
Westside St 37303
Whitaker Rd 37303
N White St 37303
S White St
1-299 37303
202-202 37371
300-1498 37303
301-1499 37303
Wilburn Dr 37303
Willet Dr 37303
Williams St 37303
Willow Trce 37303
Willow Springs Dr 37303
Wilson St 37303
Winder St 37303
Wood Creek Cir & Dr 37303
Woodacre Dr 37303
Woodlawn Cir 37303
Woodman St 37303
Woodward Ave & Park 37303
Yale Rd 37303
Young St 37303

BRENTWOOD TN

General Delivery 37027

POST OFFICE BOXES MAIN OFFICE STATIONS AND BRANCHES

Box No.s
All PO Boxes 37024

NAMED STREETS

Abbey Ct & Dr 37027
Abbottsford Rd 37027
Aberdeen Dr 37027
Abingdon Ct 37027
Addie Glenn Cir 37027
Adventure Ct 37027
Agincourt Way 37027
Alamo Rd 37027
Albemarle Ct & Ln 37027
Albert Dr 37027
Alcove Ct 37027
Allibar Pl 37027
Almadale Cir & Ct 37027
Altesse Way 37027
Amalfi Ct 37027
Amanda Ct 37027
Ambonnay Dr 37027
Ambrooke Ct 37027
Ambrose Ct 37027
American General Way 37027
Amethyst Ln 37027
Anders Dr 37027
Andrew Crockett Ct 37027
Angel Trce 37027
Ann Julian Ct 37027
Annandale Cv 37027
Ansley Ln 37027
Anthem Ct 37027
Apache Trl 37027
Apple Mill Ct 37027
Applerock Ct 37027
Appleton Ct 37027
Appomattox Dr 37027
Araby Dr 37027
Arbor Run Pl 37027
Arcaro Pl 37027
Arden Ct 37027
Arden Wood Pl 37027
Arlington Heights Dr 37027
Armstrong Pl 37027
Arnold Rd 37027
Arrowhead Ct & Dr 37027
Arrowhead Springs Ct 37027
Ascot Close 37027
Ashby Dr 37027
Ashford Ct & Pl 37027
Ashington Ct & Ln 37027
Ashley Run 37027
Atherton Ct & Dr 37027
Atrium Ct 37027
Auburn Ln 37027
Aurora Ct 37027
Autumn Pl 37027
Autumn Crossing Way 37027
Autumn Oaks Ct & Dr 37027
Avalon Dr 37027
Avery Ct 37027
Bakers Bridge Ave 37027
Balleroy Dr 37027
Banbury Ln, Pl, Row, Sta, Way & Xing 37027
Banbury Close 37027
Banshire Ct 37027
Barnstaple Ln 37027
Barrington Place Dr 37027
Bathwick Dr 37027
Baxter Ln 37027
Beauregard Ln 37027
Beech Creek Rd N & S 37027
Beech Grove Rd 37027
Beech Hill Rd 37027
Beech Tree Ln 37027
Beechville Ter 37027
Beechwood Ct 37027
Bel Air Pl 37027
Belle Glen Ln 37027
Belle Rive Dr 37027
Ben Nevis Ct 37027
Benziger Ter 37027
Berkley Dr 37027
Berkshire Ct 37027
Bernini Pl 37027
N Berrys Chapel Rd 37027
Big Horn Rdg 37027
Birchwood Ct 37027
Blackstone Ct 37027
Blakefield Dr 37027
Bliss Rd 37027
Bloomfield Way 37027
Bluff Rd 37027
Boone Trail Cir 37027
Boreal Ct 37027
Boswell Ct 37027
Bouchaine Pass 37027
Bowman Ln 37027
Boxmere Ct 37027
Brass Lantern Pl 37027
Brass Valley Dr 37027
Breaker Cir & Ct 37027
Brecon Rd 37027
Breithorn Cv 37027
Brelan Ct 37027
Brenthaven Dr 37027
Brentmeade Blvd 37027
Brenton Park Ct 37027
Brentvale Ln 37027
Brentview Ct 37027
Brentwood Blvd, Ct, Ln, Pkwy, Pt & Trce 37027
Brentwood Chase Dr 37027
Brentwood Commons Way 37027
Brentwood Meadows Cir 37027
Bridgeton Park Dr 37027
Bridle Pl 37027
Bridlewood Ln 37027
Bridlington Ct & Ln 37027
Brierly Ct 37027
Brightway Pl 37027
Bristol Ct 37027
Brittain Ct 37027
Bronwyn Ct 37027
Brookfield Ct & Dr 37027
Brookhaven Ct 37027
Brooks Chapel Rd
8000-8010 37027
8011-8011 37024
8011-8099 37027
8012-8098 37027
Brookview Dr 37027
Brownstone Dr 37027
Brunswick Dr 37027
Brushboro Ct & Dr 37027
Bryan Pl 37027
Buckhead Ct & Dr 37027
Bunker Hill Rd 37027
Burland Cres 37027
Burnham Park Dr & Ln 37027
Burnt Leaf Ct & Ln 37027
Butler Dr 37027
Cadillac Dr 37027
Calais Ct 37027
Calistoga Way 37027
Callaburn Pl 37027
Calloway Dr 37027
Calumet Ct 37027
Calverton Ln 37027
E & W Cambridge Ct 37027
Camel Back Ct 37027
Camelot Ct & Rd 37027
Canterbury Close 37027
Capstone Ct 37027
Carissa Dr 37027
Carl Seyfert Memorial Dr 37027
Carmel Ln 37027
Carol Ct 37027
Carondelet Pl 37027
Carouthers Pkwy 37027
Carphilly Ct 37027
Carriage Ct 37027
Carriage Hills Dr 37027
Carrisbrook Ln 37027
Castleford Ct 37027
Catlow Ct 37027
Cave Spring Dr 37027
Cecil Ct 37027
Center Ridge Ct 37027
Centerview Dr 37027
Century Ct 37027
Century Oak Ct 37027
Cerrisse Ct 37027
Chadwick Dr & Ln 37027
Charbay Cir 37027
Charity Dr 37027
Chartwell Ct 37027
Chatfield Ct 37027
Chatham Ct 37027
Chaucers Ct 37027
Chelsey Ct 37027
Chenoweth Pl 37027
Cherokee Ln 37027
Cherry Ct 37027
Cherrywood Dr 37027
Cherub Ct 37027
Chesapeake Dr 37027
Chestnut Ct & Dr 37027
Chestnut Springs Rd 37027
Chevoit Dr 37027
Chickasaw Ct & Dr 37027
Childe Harolds Cir & Ln 37027
Chiswell Ct 37027
Choctaw Trl 37027
Church St E 37027
Chuzzlewit Down 37027
Cimmaron Dr 37027
Clarkdun Ct 37027
Claybrook Park Cir 37027
Clear Spring Ct 37027
Clearfield Dr 37027
Clearview Cir & Dr 37027
Clearwater Dr 37027
Cliftee Dr 37027
Cloud Pt 37027
Cloverbrook Ct & Dr 37027
Clovercrest Ct & Dr 37027
Cloverfield Ct 37027
Cloverhill Dr 37027
Cloverland Dr & Pl 37027
Cloverland Park Dr & Pl 37027

Clovermeade Dr 37027
Cloverwood Dr 37027
Coachmans Ct 37027
Colfax Ct 37027
Colleton Way 37027
Colonel Winstead Dr 37027
Columbine Cir 37027
Commerce Way 37027
W Concord Pass & Rd 37027
Concord Hills Dr 37027
Concord Hunt Cir & Dr 37027
Concord Ridge Ct 37027
Continental Pl 37027
Cooks Ct 37027
Copperfield Ct & Way 37027
Copperstone Dr 37027
Coppola Ct 37027
Coralberry Dr 37027
Cornell Ct 37027
Cornwall Dr 37027
Coronet Ln 37027
Cotton Gin Ct 37027
Cottonport Dr 37027
Country Club Ct & Dr 37027
Courtyard Dr 37027
Covington Ct & Dr 37027
Coxboro Ct & Dr 37027
Creekside Xing 37027
E Creekview Ct 37027
N Creekwood Ct & Dr 37027
Crimson Clover Ct & Dr 37027
Crockett Rd 37027
Crockett Hills Blvd 37027
Crockett Springs Trl 37027
Crooked Stick Ln 37027
Cross Pointe Dr & Ln 37027
Crossroads Blvd 37027
Crystal Lake Dr 37027
Culpepper Ct 37027
Cumberwell Close 37027
Curlybark Pl 37027
Dahlia Dr 37027
Dairy Ln 37027
Dalewood Ct 37027
Dalton Ct 37027
Danforth Park Close 37027
Danville Pt 37027
Daphne Ct & Pl 37027
Darby Ct 37027
Davis Dr 37027
Deep Woods Trl 37027
Deer Point Dr 37027
Deer Track Ct 37027
Deerbourne Dr 37027
Deervale Ct 37027
Deerwood Ln 37027
Dekemont Ln 37027
Delamere Creek Ln 37027
Demery Ct 37027
Derby Glen Ln 37027
Devens Ct & Dr 37027
Dillard Ct 37027
Dogwood Ct & Pt 37027
Dolcetto Grv 37027
Donaway Ct 37027
Dorchester Cir 37027
Dorset Dr 37027
Dove Field Ct 37027
Doveland Ct 37027
Downing Ct 37027
Dozier Ct & Pl 37027
Duncan Ct 37027
Dunns Ln 37027
Dye Ct 37027
Dyer Ln 37027
Eagle Run Dr 37027
Eastbourne Dr 37027
Eastpark Dr 37027
Eastwood Dr 37027
Edenbrook Ct 37027
Edmondson Pike 37027
Elderton Ct 37027
Eldwick Dr 37027
Elgin Way 37027
Ella Ln 37027
Ellendale Dr 37027
Elmbrooke Blvd 37027
Elmhurst Ct 37027
Elmington Ct 37027
Elmsford Ct 37027
Enclave Ct 37027
Englishwood Ct 37027
Ennismore Ln 37027
Equestrian Ln 37027
Ethan Ln 37027
Evergreen Ct 37027
Ewell Ln 37027
Executive Center Dr 37027
Expedition Ct 37027
Exton Ln 37027
Fabert Cir 37027
Fall Ct E & W 37027
Falling Leaf Cir 37027
Fallswood Ln 37027
Falmouth Ct 37027
Far Fara Way 37027
Fawn Creek Ct & Rd 37027
Fayette Ct & Dr 37027
Fernwood Ct 37027
Fielding Crst 37027
Firefox Dr 37027
Fireside Cir, Ct & Dr 37027
Fischer Ct 37027
Flagpole Ct 37027
Flint Ct 37027
Flowerwood Ct 37027
Fontanella Dr 37027
Foothills Ct & Dr 37027
Ford Dr 37027
Forest Trl 37027
Forest Garden Dr 37027
Forest Lawn Dr 37027
Forest Park Dr 37027
Forsyth Park Dr 37027
Forsythia Dr 37027
Fort Gaines Pl 37027
Fort Morgan Pl 37027
Fort Sumter Pl 37027
Fountainbrooke Ct, Dr & Ter 37027
Fountainhead Ct & Dr 37027
Fox Ridge Dr 37027
Fox Run Dr 37027
Foxboro Ct & Dr 37027
Foxborough Sq E 37027
Foxland Dr 37027
Foxview Ct 37027
Franklin Rd 37027
Franklin Pike Cir 37027
Fredericksburg Way E & W 37027
Frierson Pl & St 37027
Frontier Ln 37027
Galleria Blvd 37027
Garnet Ct 37027
Garrett Park Pl 37027
Gasserway Cir & Ct 37027
General George Patton Dr 37027
General Mcarthur Dr 37027
Gentlewind Dr 37027
Georgeboro Ct 37027
Georgetown Pl 37027
Gervaise Ct 37027
Gesshe Ct 37027
Gessner Ln 37027
Gilbert Pl 37027
Ginger Ct 37027
Gingerwood Ct 37027
Glasgow Pl 37027
Glen Eden Ct 37027
Glen Ridge Dr 37027
Glenellen Way 37027
Glengarry Ln 37027
Glenstone Cir 37027
Glenview Dr 37027
Glover Ct & Dr 37027
Good Springs Ct & Rd 37027
Gordon Petty Ct & Dr 37027
Governors Way 37027
Gracelawn Ct & Dr 37027
Granberry Heights Dr 37027
Grand Haven Dr 37027
Grand Oak Way 37027
Grand Oaks Dr 37027
Granny White Pike 37027
Green Apple Ln 37027
Green Apple Turn 37027
Green Hill Blvd, Cir & Cv 37027
Greenleaf Ct 37027
Greensboro Ct 37027
Gretchen Ct 37027
Grey Pointe Ct & Dr 37027
Greylock Dr 37027
Greystoke Dr 37027
Grist Mill Ct 37027
Grove Ct 37027
Grove Hurst Ln 37027
Haber Dr 37027
Halford Pl 37027
Hamer Ct 37027
Hampton Reserve Dr 37027
Hannah Ct 37027
Harness Pl 37027
Harpeth Dr 37027
Harpeth Ridge Dr 37027
Harpeth River Dr 37027
Harrogate Dr 37027
Harvard Ct 37027
Haverhill Dr 37027
Hayes Pl 37027
Hayeswood Dr 37027
Hearthstone Cir & Ln 37027
Hearthstone Manor Cir & Ln 37027
Heather Cir, Ln, Pl, Spg & Way 37027
Heatherwood Dr 37027
Heathfield Cir 37027
Heathrow Blvd 37027
Heathrow Hills Ct & Dr 37027
Hedgewood Dr 37027
Helens Way 37027
Helmsdale Pl N & S 37027
Herbert Ct 37027
Hereford Ct 37027
Heritage Dr & Way 37027
Herschel Spears Cir 37027
Hickory Meadow Ct 37027
E & W Hickory Springs Ct & Rd 37027
Hidden Hollow Trl 37027
Hidden Oak Dr & Pl 37027
Hidden Valley Rd 37027
High Lea Rd 37027
High Oaks Ct 37027
High Valley Dr 37027
Highfield Ln 37027
Highland Rd 37027
Highland Bend Ct 37027
Highland View Pl 37027
Highpoint Ter 37027
Highwood Hill Rd 37027
Hill Rd 37027
Hilldale Dr 37027
Hillsboro Rd 37027
Hillsboro Valley Rd 37027
N, E, S & W Hillview Ct & Dr 37027
Hillwood Dr 37027
Hollow Spring Ct 37027
Holly Rd 37027
Holly Tree Farms Rd 37027
Holly Tree Gap Rd 37027
Holly View Ct 37027
Holt Lea Ct 37027
Homestead Rd 37027
Homestead Acres Ln 37027
Hood Dr & Pl 37027
Hugh Cates Pl 37027
Hunterboro Ct & Dr 37027
Hunters Ln 37027
Hunterwood Ct & Dr 37027
Husker Ct 37027
Hyde Ln 37027
Inavale Ln 37027
Indian Hawthorne Ct 37027
Indian Point Dr 37027
Innis Brook Ln 37027
Ironwood Ln 37027
Isabella Ln 37027
Ivy Crest Dr 37027
Jackson Ln 37027
James Robertson Ct 37027
Jamestown Park 37027
Jamie Ct 37027
Jasmin Park Dr 37027
Jefferson Davis Dr 37027
Jockey Club Ln 37027
Johnson Chapel Rd W 37027
Jones Ct & Pkwy 37027
Jones Hill Dr 37027
Jupiter Forest Dr 37027
Karen Ct 37027
Kathridge Ct 37027
Keeneland Dr 37027
Kelly Rd 37027
Kellywood Dr 37027
Kemah Ct 37027
Kendale Ct 37027
Kettering Trce 37027
Key Ct & Dr 37027
Kindra Ct 37027
Kingsboro Ct 37027
Kingsbury Dr 37027
Kipling Dr 37027
Kirby Pl 37027
Kirkwood Pl 37027
Knightsboro Ct 37027
Knightsbridge Park Close 37027
Knoll Ct 37027
Knox Ct & Dr 37027
Knox Valley Dr 37027
Kottas Ct 37027
Kristin Ln 37027
Lacebark Dr 37027
Lake Cir, Ct & Dr 37027
Lake Shore Dr 37027
Lakeview Ct 37027
Lancelot Rd 37027
Land Grant Pl 37027
Landings Blvd 37027
Landmark Pl 37027
S Lane Ct 37027
Langley Ct & Pl 37027
Lansdowne Approach 37027
Laurel Knoll Ct 37027
Laurelwood Dr 37027
Laurens Way 37027
Lavada Pl 37027
Leconte Park 37027
Legacy Cove Ln 37027
Leinster Ter 37027
Lenox Rd 37027
Lester Ct 37027
Lexington Dr 37027
Liberty Rd 37027
Liberty Church Rd & Trl 37027
Lighthouse Pl 37027
Lillian Ln 37027
Lineberger Ct 37027
Lipscomb Ct & Dr 37027
Little Gem Dr & Ln 37027
Littlestone Ct & Dr 37027
Lochinver Park Ln 37027
Lochmere Ct 37027
Locke Ct 37027
Lodestone Dr 37027
Log Cabin Trl 37027
Logwood Briar Cir 37027
Long Valley Rd 37027
Longstreet Cir & Dr 37027
Lookout Ridge Ct 37027
Lorme Ct 37027
Lost Hollow Cir, Ct & Dr 37027
Loudon Pl 37027
Lower Stow Ct 37027
Lowndes Ln 37027
Lucas Ct & Ln 37027
Lymington Ct 37027
Lynhurst Ct 37027
Lysander Ct & Ln 37027
Macaw Ct 37027
Magnolia Ridge Way 37027
Mallory Ln 37027
Manassas Cir, Ct & Dr 37027
Mandan Dr 37027
Manley Ln 37027
Manor Ct & Pl 37027
Manor View Cir & Ln 37027
Mansion Ct & Dr 37027
Maple Crest Ct 37027
Mapledale Ln 37027
Mapleton Ct 37027
Marcasite Dr 37027
Margarets Pl 37027
N & S Martha Ct 37027
Martingale Ct & Ln 37027
Maryland Ln & Way 37027
Maryland Farms 37027
Masonwood Ln 37027
Matthew Ct 37027
Maupin Rd 37027
Maxwell Ln & Xing 37027
Maycroft Knl 37027
Mayfield Ct, Pl & Sta 37027
Mayflower Cir 37027
Mcclanahan Dr 37027
Mcclendon Ct 37027
Mcgavock Rd 37027
Mcguire Ct 37027
Mckays Ct 37027
Mclean Ct 37027
Meadowlake Rd 37027
Meadowlark Ln 37027
Meadowlawn Dr 37027
Medalist Ct 37027
Micawber Ct 37027
Midlothian Dr 37027
Midway Cir 37027
Milbrook Ct & Rd 37027
Millsford Ct 37027
Millview Dr 37027
Millwood Ct 37027
Mint Spring Cir 37027
Missionary Dr, Ln & Way 37027
Mitchell Pl 37027
Monarch Ct & Way 37027
Monroe Ln 37027
Montclair Blvd 37027
Moonlight Trl 37027
Mooreland Blvd & Ct 37027
Moores Ct & Ln 37027
E Moran Rd 37027
Morgans Landing Ct 37027
Morning Glory Ct 37027
Morningside Ct 37027
Morningview Ct 37027
Mosley Dr 37027
Moss Rose Ct 37027
Mountain Ash Ct 37027
Mountview Pl 37027
Murray Ln 37027
Myers Park Ct & Ter 37027
Natchez Dr 37027
Navaho Dr 37027
Nevil Pt 37027
New Life Ln 37027
Newstead Ter 37027
Newton Nook 37027
Nialta Ln 37027
Nickleby Ct 37027
Nickleby Down 37027
Noel Dr 37027
Nolensville Rd 37027
Normandy Way 37027
Northfield Ln 37027
Northfork Dr 37027
Northumberland Dr 37027
Norton Ct 37027
Norwood Dr 37027
Nottaway Ln 37027
Nutmeg Ct 37027
Oak Brook Ter 37027
Oak Knoll Dr 37027
Oakes Dr 37027
Oakfield Grv & Way 37027
Oakhall Dr 37027
Oakhampton Pl 37027
Oakledge Dr 37027
Oakshire Ct 37027
Oakvale Dr 37027
Ochoa Ln 37027
Oden Ct 37027
Ohara Dr 37027
Old Brentwood Rd 37027
Old Brooks Rd 37027
Old Fowlkes Dr 37027
Old Hickory Blvd 37027
Old Moores Ln 37027
Old Orchard Rd 37027
Old Smyrna Rd 37027
Old Thrasher Ct 37027
Old Towne Dr 37027
Olde Towne Rd 37027
Oman Dr 37027
Onyx Ln 37027
Opal Ct 37027
Otter Creek Ct 37027
Ottershaw Ct 37027
Ottoe Ct 37027
Overall Dr 37027
Overbrook Point Ct 37027
Overcheck Ln 37027
Overlook Blvd & Cir 37027
Owen Rd 37027
Oxford Ct 37027
Oxmoor Ct 37027
Pachiner Dr 37027
Paddock Pl 37027
Palisades Ct 37027
Palmetto Ct 37027
Panorama Ct & Dr 37027
Parkcrest Ct 37027
Parker Pl 37027
Partridge Ct 37027
Patrice Dr 37027
Paxton Ct 37027
Peach Ct 37027
Pear Tree Cir 37027
Peebles Ct 37027
Pelham Dr 37027
Penicuik Ln 37027
Penn Warren Dr 37027
Pennines Cir 37027
Peter Taylor Park Dr 37027
Petersburg Ln 37027
Pewitt Dr 37027
Pheasant Run Ct & Trl 37027
Pickney Dr 37027
Pin Oak Cir & Ln 37027
Pine Terrace Dr 37027
Pinetree Ln 37027
Pinkerton Ct & Rd 37027
Pipers Ln 37027
Pisgah Park 37027
Placid Ct 37027
Plantation Ct & Dr 37027
Pleasant Water Ln 37027
Plum Nelly Cir 37027
Plymouth Dr 37027
Pointe Pl 37027
Pointe Cross Ln 37027
Pointer Pl 37027
Polk Cir 37027
Portofino Dr 37027
Portrush Ct & Pl 37027
Portsmouth Cv & Pl 37027
Post Oak Cir 37027
Postal Ct 37027
Potomac Ct & Ln 37027
Powell Ct & Pl 37027
Prada Dr 37027
Pratt Ct 37027
Prestmoor Pl 37027
Preston Pl 37027
Prestwick Pl 37027
Primm Dr 37027
Prince Phillip Cv 37027
Princeton Hills Dr 37027
Puryear Pl 37027
Putnam Ln 37027
Quail Valley Dr 37027
Queensboro Ct 37027
Queensbury Ct 37027
Quiet Ln 37027
Radiant Jewel Ct 37027
Radnor Glen Dr 37027
Radrick Rdg 37027
Ragsdale Rd 37027
Raintree Pkwy 37027
Ramsgate Ct 37027
Rausch Dr 37027
Raven Hollow Rd 37027
Ravenswood Farm Ln 37027
Red Feather Ln 37027
Red Oak Dr & Ln 37027
Red Sunset Ct 37027
Reed Ct & Dr 37027
Regent Dr 37027
Reins Ct 37027
Remington Dr 37027
Reston Ct 37027
Retreat Ln & Pass 37027
Rexford Ct 37027
Richbourg Park Dr 37027
Richland Woods Ln 37027
Richlawn Dr 37027
Ridge Farm Pl 37027
Ridgewood Ln & Pl 37027
Rittenberry Dr 37027
River Ct 37027
River Oaks Ct & Rd 37027
Roantree Dr 37027
Robby Ct 37027
Robert E Lee Ln 37027
Robinhood Rd 37027
Rockingham Run 37027
Rolling Creek Dr 37027
Rolling Fork Dr 37027
Romano Way 37027
Rosecrans Ct & Pl 37027
Rosella Ct 37027
Rosewood Ct & Dr 37027
Rosewood Valley Ct & Dr 37027
Rossi Rd 37027
Rosslare Cir 37027
Roxburgh Cv 37027
Rozell Ct 37027
Rue De Grande 37027
Saddle Ct 37027
Saddlebow Dr 37027
Saddlewood Ln 37027
Saint Edmunds Ct 37027
Saint Josephs Ct 37027
Saint Regis Ct 37027
Sam Houston Dr 37027
Sanctuary Pl 37027
Sapphire Ct 37027
Saratoga Dr & Pl 37027
Sassafrass Pl 37027
Sawgrass Ln 37027
Saxony Ct 37027
Scarlet Oak Ct 37027
Scarlet Ridge Ct & Dr 37027
Scenic View Ct 37027
Seaboard Ln 37027
Secretariat Ln 37027
Selkirk Ct 37027
Seminole Dr 37027
Settlement Ct 37027
Seven Springs Ct & Way 37027
Seward Ct & Rd 37027
Shadow Creek Dr 37027
Shadow Ridge Ct 37027
Shady Pl 37027
Shady Vale Ct 37027
Shadybrook Ct 37027
Shamrock Dr 37027
Sharondale Ct 37027

Shaw Ct 37027
Shawnee Ct & Trl 37027
Shays Ln 37027
Shenandoah Dr 37027
Sheridan Park Ct 37027
Sherwood Dr 37027
Sherwood Green Ct 37027
Shining Ore Dr 37027
Silverdale Ct 37027
Sinclair Cir 37027
Sioux Dr 37027
Skyline Dr 37027
Sleeping Valley Ct 37027
Smithson Ln 37027
Soho Ct 37027
Sonoma Ct & Trce 37027
Southerland Pl 37027
Southern Woods Dr 37027
Southgate Ct 37027
Split Log Rd 37027
Split Rail Dr 37027
Spring House Cir, Ct & Way 37027
Spring Valley Dr 37027
Springer Ct 37027
Spyglass Hl 37027
Stags Run Ct 37027
Stanfield Rd 37027
Stecoah St 37027
Steeplechase Dr 37027
Stephanie Ct 37027
Sterling Oaks Ct, Dr & Pl 37027
Sterns Xing 37027
Still Forest Dr 37027
Stillwater Cir 37027
Stone Box Ct & Ln 37027
Stone Brook Dr 37027
Stone Run Dr 37027
Stonegate Pl 37027
Stoneleigh Cir 37027
Stonewall Pl 37027
Stratton Pl 37027
Stryker Pl 37027
Stuart Ln 37027
Stubblefield Ct 37027
Suffolk Cres 37027
Sugarloaf Ln 37027
Sugarwood Ct & Dr 37027
Summit Ct 37027
Summit View Dr & Pl 37027
Sunbeam Ct 37027
Sunberry Ct 37027
Sunny Hill Rd 37027
Sunny Side Ct & Dr 37027
Sunnybrook Ct & Dr 37027
Sunset Rd & Trl 37027
Surrey Ct & Dr 37027
Suzanne Dr 37027
Sweetwater Ct & Dr 37027
Swynford Ct 37027
Sydney Ln 37027
Taggartwood Dr 37027
Tanglewood Ln 37027
Tapoco Ln 37027
Tara Dr 37027
Tarrington Ct 37027
Tartan Ct & Dr 37027
Tartan Crest Ct 37027
Tattersall Ct 37027
Tea Rose Ter 37027
Teakwood Ct 37027
Terri Sells Ln 37027
Thalman Dr 37027
Thorndale Dr 37027
Thornhill Cres 37027
Thoroughbred Ln & Way 37027
Thurrock Cir 37027
Thyme Ct 37027
Tilbury Cir 37027
Timber Ct & Dr 37027
Timber Ridge Cir, Ct & Dr 37027
Timbercrest Ct 37027
Tinney Pl 37027

Titans Ln 37027
Todgers Ct 37027
Torrey Pines Way 37027
Town Center Way 37027
Tradition Ln 37027
Trebor Ct 37027
Tree Line Ct 37027
Tree Ridge Cv 37027
Trotwood Cir & Mews 37027
Trotwood Down 37027
Trousdale Dr 37027
Tupper Pl 37027
Turnberry Cir, Pt & Way 37027
Turnbridge Ct & Dr 37027
Turner Ln 37027
Turning Leaf Pl 37027
Turquoise Ln 37027
Turtle Creek Dr 37027
Tuscany Way 37027
Twin Springs Ct & Dr 37027
Tyneside Cir 37027
Upper Stow Ct 37027
Vaden Blvd & Dr 37027
Valhalla Ln 37027
Valle Verde Dr 37027
Valley Ct & Dr 37027
Valley Brook Dr 37027
Valley Oak Dr 37027
Valley Springs Dr 37027
Valley View Cir & Rd 37027
Vellano Ct 37027
Versailles Ct 37027
Victoria Cv 37027
Victory Trl 37027
Villa View Ct 37027
Vineland Ct & Dr 37027
Virginia Way 37027
Vivians Way 37027
Volunteer Ct & Pkwy 37027
Wakefield Dr 37027
Waller Rd 37027
Walnut Bend Ln 37027
Walnut Hills Dr 37027
Walnut Park Dr 37027
Ward Cir 37027
Wardley Ln 37027
Wardley Park Ln 37027
Warner Ct & Rd 37027
Warrington Ct 37027
Watauga Pl 37027
Waterfall Rd 37027
Waterford Dr 37027
Waterton Ct 37027
Waxwood Ct & Dr 37027
Weatherly Dr 37027
Well Spring Ct 37027
Wellesley Way 37027
Wendover Gln 37027
Wentworth Pl 37027
Wescates Ct 37027
Wesley Ct 37027
Westbourne Dr 37027
Westbury Ct 37027
Westgate Cir 37027
Westheimer Dr 37027
Weston Ct & Dr 37027
Westpark Dr 37027
Westwood Pl 37027
Wexcroft Dr 37027
Weymouth Way 37027
Wheatfield Cir 37027
Wheatley Forest Dr 37027
Whippoorwill Ln 37027
Whispering Valley Dr 37027
Whispering Willow Ct 37027
White Chapel Ct 37027
White Oak Ct 37027
White Swans Xing 37027
Whittingham Dr 37027
Wicklow Dr 37027
N & S Wickshire Dr & Way 37027
Wikle Rd E & W 37027
Wild Wing Ct 37027
Wildwood Dr 37027

Wildwood Valley Dr 37027
Williams Grove Dr 37027
Williamsburg Cir, Ct & Rd 37027
Williamson Ct 37027
Willow Ct 37027
Willowick Dr 37027
Willowmet Dr & Ln 37027
Wilmington Way 37027
Wilshire Way 37027
Wilson Pike & Run 37027
Wilson Pike Cir 37027
Winchester Rd 37027
Winding Stream Way 37027
Windsong Ct 37027
Windstone Blvd 37027
Windy Hill Ct & Pl 37027
Winged Foot Pl 37027
Winners Cir N & S 37027
Winsley Pl 37027
Winston Dr 37027
Woodburn Dr 37027
Woodbury Ct 37027
Woodfield Ct 37027
Woodland Hills Dr 37027
Woodridge Ct 37027
N Woods Ct 37027
Woodside Dr 37027
Woodward Ct 37027
Woodward Hills Pl 37027
Wyckfield Pl 37027
Yale Ct 37027
Yellow Finch Ct 37027
Yorkshire Dr 37027

BRISTOL TN

General Delivery 37621

POST OFFICE BOXES MAIN OFFICE STATIONS AND BRANCHES

Box No.s
1 - 2234 37621
3001 - 4415 37625
7010 - 9002 37621

NAMED STREETS

Abbie Ln 37620
Academy Dr 37620
Ackley Cir 37620
S Acres Dr 37620
Adams Ln 37620
Akard Pl & St 37620
Alabama St 37620
Alder St 37620
Alders Pl 37620
Alders Place Ext 37620
Alex Ln 37620
Alhambra Dr 37620
Alisha St 37620
Alpine Private Dr 37620
Amanda Ln 37620
Amandas Private Dr 37620
Amber Dr 37620
Americana Dr 37620
Amhurst Ln 37620
Amity Dr 37620
Anderson St 37620
Andys Ln 37620
Ann St 37620
Arch St 37620
Arkansas Ave 37620
Arnold Rd & Way 37620
Ash St 37620
Ashewood Dr 37620
Askins Cir 37620
Auburn St 37620
Austin Dr & St 37620
Avoca Rd 37620

Ayrshire Rd 37620
Baines Dr 37620
Ball Rd 37620
Bank St 37620
Barber Rd 37620
Barker St 37620
Barker Street Ext 37620
Basham Hill Rd 37620
Basswood Dr 37620
Baumwood Ln 37620
Bay St 37620
Bealer Rd 37620
Bear Hollow Rd 37620
Beaver St 37620
Beckley Dr 37620
Beech Forest Rd 37620
Beech Knoll Rd 37620
Beecham St 37620
Beechwood Cir, Dr & Rd 37620
Beeler St 37620
Beidleman Rd 37620
Beidleman Creek Rd 37620
Belle Brook Dr & Rd 37620
Belmont Dr 37620
Belvedere Hts 37620
Bentley Rd 37620
Bethel Dr 37620
Big Valley Dr 37620
Bilco St 37620
Birch St 37620
Bird Rd 37620
Blackburn Cir & Dr 37620
Blackley Rd 37620
Blountville Hwy 37620
Blue Bonnet Dr 37620
Blue Ridge Dr 37620
Bluff City Hwy 37620
Boardwalk 37620
Booher Dr, Ln & Rd 37620
Booher Private Dr 37620
Booher Towne Private Dr 37620
Boswell Dr 37620
Boyd Ln & Rd 37620
Bradford Ln 37620
Braemar 37620
Bramm Ln & Rd 37620
Branch Ln 37620
Braswell Baker Rd 37620
Brentwood 37620
Brentwood Pvt Dr 37620
Brewer Rd 37620
Briarcliff Rd 37620
Brighton Pl 37620
Briscoe Cir 37620
Briscoe Circle Ext 37620
Bristol Caverns Hwy 37620
Bristol College Dr 37620
Bristol Heights Rd 37620
Bristol Metals Rd 37620
Bristol West Blvd 37620
Broad St 37620
Broad View Cir 37620
Brookshire Dr 37620
Brookside Dr 37620
Brookwood Dr 37620
Brown Ave & Dr 37620
Brown Private Dr 37620
Broyles Ln & Rd 37620
Buchanan Rd 37620
Bullock Hollow Rd 37620
Butler Dr 37620
Caldwell Dr 37620
Cambridge Cir 37620
Camelot Dr 37620
Camp Tom Howard Rd 37620
Campbells Private Dr 37620
Cannon Ave 37620
Cant Hook Hill Rd 37620
Canterbury Pl 37620
Carasil Rd 37620
Carden Hollow Rd 37620
Cardinal Ln 37620
Carla St 37620

Carlton Rd 37620
Carmack Cir 37620
Carolina Ave 37620
Carolyn Cir 37620
Carson Ln 37620
Cavern Rd 37620
E & W Cedar Ln, Rd & St 37620
Cedar Creek Rd 37620
Cedar Valley Rd 37620
Cedarbrook Cir 37620
E & W Central Dr 37620
Centre Dr 37620
Century Blvd 37620
Chambers St 37620
Chatham Rd 37620
Cherry St 37620
Cherrywood Ct & Ln 37620
Chesnut St 37620
Church Cir 37620
Churchill Cir 37620
Circle Ct, Dr & Rd 37620
Clark Dr, Ln & Rd 37620
Clark Cemetery Rd 37620
Clark Hill Rd 37620
Clarks Private Dr 37620
Clay St 37620
Cliffwood Dr 37620
Clifton Rd 37620
Cloudland Dr 37620
Cloverdale Pl 37620
Clyde Reser St 37620
Coble Ln 37620
Coffey St 37620
Cold Springs Church Rd 37620
Colebrook Ln 37620
College Ave 37620
Collingwood Dr 37620
Colony Dr 37620
Colooney Cir 37620
Columbia Rd 37620
Compton 37620
Concord Cir 37620
Cook Hollow Rd 37620
Corpus Christi Dr 37620
Cortland St 37620
Cory Lee Cir 37620
Country Meadows Cir 37620
Country Oaks Dr 37620
Coventry Ct 37620
Cowan St 37620
Cox St 37620
Creek Side Ct 37620
Crescent Dr 37620
Crestfield Dr 37620
Crestview St 37620
Crestwood Rd 37620
Crofton Dr 37620
Cross Community Rd 37620
Crosswhite Rd 37620
Crowe Rd 37620
E & W Crown Cir 37620
Crumley Aly 37620
Cunningham Rd 37620
Cypress St 37620
Dairy Cir 37620
Dale Pl 37620
Daniel Dr 37620
Dart Dr 37620
Dartmouth Dr 37620
Dead End Rd 37620
Dearstone Private Dr 37620
Deck Rd 37620
Deck Valley Ln & Rd 37620
Deer Harbour Rd 37620
Deer Meadows Rd 37620
Deer Run Private Dr 37620
Deerfield Dr 37620
Deerlick 37620
Defriece Private Dr 37620
Delaney St 37620
Delaware Ave 37620
Denton Rd 37620
Denton Valley Rd 37620
Dentons Ln 37620

Dentons Valley Rd 37620
Dishner Rd 37620
Donegal Way 37620
Douglas Ln 37620
Dover Ln 37620
Drake Rd 37620
Driftwood Ln 37620
Dulaney Rd 37620
Dumfries Rd 37620
Duncan Ln & St 37620
Duncan Private Dr 37620
Earlway Rd 37620
East Rd 37620
Eastside Dr 37620
Eaton Ln & Rd 37620
Eatons Private Dr 37620
Edgefield Rd 37620
Edgemere Dr 37620
Edgemont Ave 37620
Edgewood Rd 37620
El Paso Dr 37620
Elizabeth St 37620
Elk Rd 37620
Elm St 37620
Emmett Rd & Way 37620
English St 37620
Essies Private Dr 37620
Esther St 37620
Eula Private Dr 37620
Evergreen Pl 37620
Exide Dr 37620
Fairacres Dr 37620
Fairfield Dr 37620
Fairway Dr & Pl 37620
Fairwood Dr 37620
Farragut Rd 37620
Felty Private Dr 37620
Fernwoods Private Dr 37620
Fieldcrest Rd 37620
Flint St 37620
Florida Ave 37620
Foley Cir 37620
Forest Dr 37620
Forest Hills Dr 37620
Fox Hall Cir 37620
Freeman Dr 37620
Friendship Dr & Rd 37620
Gaffney Rd 37620
Galway Rd 37620
Garden Grove Dr 37620
Gentry Ct & Ln 37620
Georgia Ave 37620
Gifford Rd 37620
Gifford Private Dr 37620
Gilbert Ln 37620
Glen St 37620
Glendale St 37620
Glendor Dr 37620
Glenway Rd 37620
Glenwood Rd 37620
Godsey Rd 37620
Golf St 37620
Government Rd 37620
Grace St 37620
Grandor Ln & St 37620
Gray Rd & St 37620
Green Rd 37620
Green Hill Dr 37620
Green Springs Rd 37620
Greenfield Pl 37620
Greentree Dr 37620
Greenway Rd 37620
Greiner Dr 37620
Grove Park Dr 37620
Grove Park Drive Ext 37620
Grovedale Rd 37620
Grubb Ln 37620
H Barnett Private Dr 37620
Hale St 37620
Haley Walk 37620
E, S & W Hampton Ct & Dr 37620
Hannah Dr 37620
Harkleroad Ln 37620
Harr Rd 37620
Harrow 37620

Hatchall Way 37620
Haynes St 37620
Hazelwood St 37620
Helbert Pvt Dr 37620
Hemlock Ln, Rd & St 37620
Henards Private Dr 37620
Henry St 37620
Henry Anna Ln 37620
Henson Ln & Rd 37620
Henson Hill Rd 37620
Heritage Cir 37620
Hermitage Dr 37620
Heyford Dr 37620
Hickory Ln & Rd 37620
Hickory Tree Rd 37620
Hidden Valley Rd 37620
High Cir & St 37620
Highfield Rd 37620
Highland St 37620
Highridge St 37620
Highway 11 E & W 37620
Highway 126 37620
Highway 421 37620
Highway 44 37620
Hill Dr & St 37620
Hill Country Trl 37620
Hillbilly Private Dr 37620
Hillsboro Dr 37620
Hillside Ave 37620
Hilltop Rd & St 37620
Hillwoods Private Dr 37620
Hinkle Dr 37620
Hinkle Drive Ext 37620
Hob Knob Hollow Rd 37620
Holiday Dr 37620
Holly Ct 37620
Holmes St 37620
Holston Ave & Dr 37620
S Holston Dam Rd 37620
Holston Valley Golf Cr Rd 37620
S Holston View Dr & Trl 37620
Holston View Dam Rd 37620
Honaker Dr 37620
Honeysuckle Ln 37620
Hoot Owl Hollow Rd 37620
Horizon Dr 37620
Horton Dr 37620
Houston St 37620
Hunter Hills Cir 37620
Indian Trl 37620
Indian Hills Dr 37620
N Industrial Blvd & Dr 37620
Intermont Ln 37620
Island Rd 37620
Jackson St 37620
Jacob Creek Rd 37620
Jaybird Ct 37620
Johnson Chapel Rd 37620
Johnston Ave 37620
Jones Rd 37620
Jones Hollow Rd 37620
Jonesboro Rd 37620
Journeys End Private Dr 37620
Juniper Cir 37620
K Mart Dr 37620
Kanauga Private Dr 37620
Katie Ln 37620
Kegley Aly 37620
Keith Rd 37620
Kelly Ridge Rd 37620
Kelsey Dr 37620
Kendricks Hollow Rd 37620
Kennedy Rd 37620
Kentucky Ave 37620
Kenwood Ct 37620
Kestners Pvt Dr 37620
Kilcoote Way 37620
Kilmainhom Cir 37620
Kimberly St 37620
King Ln 37620
King College Rd 37620
Kings Meadow Cir 37620
Kingsbridge 37620

Kingsley Down Dr 37620
Kinkead Dr 37620
Kites Private Dr 37620
Knob Hill Dr 37620
Knob Park Rd 37620
Knollwood Rd 37620
Kohn St 37620
Lake View Estates Dr 37620
Lakenheath Dr 37620
Lakeshore Dr 37620
Lakeview St 37620
Lakeview Dock Rd 37620
Landmark Ln 37620
Langford Ln 37620
Laredo Dr 37620
Lark St 37620
Larkins St 37620
Laura Land & Ln 37620
Laurel Dr & Rd 37620
Lavinder Ln 37620
Lazy Acres 37620
Leafmore Ln 37620
Leona St 37620
Leonard Rd 37620
Leprechaun Way 37620
Leslie Ct 37620
Lick Branch Rd 37620
Lick Meadow Rd 37620
Lily St 37620
Lindas Way 37620
Link Rd 37620
Little Ln 37620
Little Switzerland Private Dr 37620
Little Valley Dr 37620
Littlewood Dr 37620
Locust Dr, Rd & St 37620
Locust Hill Ln 37620
Lolo St 37620
Lone Oak Ln 37620
Lone Oak Private Dr 37620
Long View Dr 37620
Longview Dr 37620
Longwood Rd 37620
Loudermilk Dr 37620
Lovedale Dr 37620
Lowry Ln 37620
Lynch St 37620
Lynfield Rd 37620
Lynn St 37620
Lynwood St 37620
Madeline Dr 37620
Main St 37620
Manchester Pl 37620
Maple Dr & St 37620
Maple Tree Dr 37620
Maplelawn Dr 37620
Mapleview Dr 37620
Marion Ave 37620
Marlene Dr 37620
Marlyn Dr 37620
Martin Luther King Jr Blvd 37620
Martindale Rd 37620
E Mary St 37620
Maryland Ave 37620
Massengill Rd 37620
Matt St 37620
Maxwell Dr 37620
Mayfield Dr 37620
Mccray St 37620
Mcdowell St 37620
Mcsherry Ln 37620
Meadow Dr, Rd & St 37620
Meadow Creek Rd 37620
Meadow Glen Dr 37620
Meadow View Rd 37620
Meadow Wood Dr 37620
Meadowcrest Dr 37620
Medical Park Blvd 37620
Melody Ln 37620
Melrose St 37620
Memorial Dr 37620
Memory Ln 37620
Merriwood Dr 37620
Mia Dr 37620
Midfield Dr 37620
Midred Guy Rd 37620
Midway Dr & St 37620
Midway Medical Park 37620
Mildred Guy Rd 37620
Millwood Rd 37620
Mimosa Rd 37620
Mission Dr 37620
Mockingbird Rd 37620
Moncier Cir 37620
Monroe Dr 37620
Monte Vista St 37620
Montvue Rd 37620
Monument Ridge Dr 37620
Moore Rd 37620
Morning St 37620
Morrell Rd 37620
Morrell Town Rd 37620
Morris St 37620
Morse Dr 37620
Mount Area Dr 37620
Mountain Breeze Ln 37620
Mountain View Dr 37620
Mountain Vista Dr 37620
Mulberry Ln 37620
Nascar Blvd 37620
Natalie St 37620
Neal Dr 37620
Nettie Hill Rd 37620
New Camp Ridge Rd 37620
Nita St 37620
Nordic Private Dr 37620
North St 37620
Norwood Dr 37620
Nottingham Pl 37620
Oak Rd 37620
Oak Forest Dr 37620
Oak View Cir 37620
Oakcrest Cir 37620
Oakland Dr 37620
Oakwood St 37620
Odell Rd 37620
Odessa Dr 37620
Offield Hollow Rd 37620
Offset Rd 37620
Old Beidleman Rd 37620
Old Carden Hollow Rd 37620
Old Dump Rd 37620
Old Hickory Tree Rd 37620
Old Jonesboro Rd 37620
Old Knobs Rd 37620
Old Shady Rd 37620
Old Stage Dr & Trl 37620
Olive St 37620
Ollis Estate Private Dr 37620
Orchard Dr & St 37620
Overbrook Dr 37620
Overlook Rd 37620
Paddle Creek Rd 37620
Painter Rd 37620
Painter Creek Rd 37620
N Paperville Rd 37620
Paramount Dr 37620
Park Dr 37620
Parks Rd 37620
Parkway Rd 37620
Parwood Private Dr 37620
Patty Branch Rd 37620
Pecos St 37620
Pemberton Ct & Rd 37620
Pendleton Dr 37620
Pennsylvania Ave 37620
Penrod Rd 37620
Peoples Rd 37620
Pershing Ave 37620
Peters Rd 37620
Peters Private Dr 37620
Phillips Ln 37620
Phillipswood Dr 37620
Phlox Crk 37620
Pine St 37620
Pine Hill Pvt Dr 37620
Pinecrest St 37620
Piney Hill Rd 37620
Pink Dogwood Cir 37620
Plainview Dr 37620
Plymouth Cir 37620
Poplar Cir & St 37620
Poplar Hill Ln 37620
Porenco Rd 37620
Potter Ln 37620
Pyle Rd 37620
Quail Ln & Run 37620
Queen St 37620
Queensgate 37620
Raceday Center Dr 37620
N & S Raceway Villa Dr 37620
Rachels Ln 37620
Ralph Peer St 37620
Ramey Rd 37620
Raytheon Rd 37620
Redbird Private Dr 37620
Redstone Dr 37620
Redwood Rd 37620
Reed Rd 37620
Reedy Creek Rd 37620
Renee Dr 37620
Rex Rd 37620
Reynolds St 37620
Richards Dr 37620
Richmond Heights Rd 37620
Ridge Rd 37620
Ridge Hill Rd 37620
Ridgecrest Rd 37620
Ridgedale Dr 37620
Ridgemont St 37620
Ridgeview Rd 37620
Ridgewood Rd 37620
River Bend Rd 37620
Riverside Rd 37620
Riverview Dr & Rd 37620
Robin Dr & Rd 37620
Robins Meadow Ln 37620
Robinson Walk 37620
Rock Dr & Rd 37620
Rock Hill Ln 37620
Rock Ledge 37620
Rock Rose Rd 37620
Rogers Rd 37620
Rogers Private Dr 37620
Rollers Aly 37620
Rooty Branch Rd 37620
Roscommon Dr 37620
Rose St 37620
Rosedale Ln 37620
Rosemont Dr 37620
Rosewood St 37620
Ross St 37620
Rouses Private Dr 37620
Rowan Dr 37620
Rush Dr 37620
Russell Ln 37620
Rust Rd 37620
Rustic St 37620
Ruth St 37620
Rutherford Ln 37620
Rutledge St 37620
Saint Albans Cir 37620
Saint James Pl 37620
Saint John St 37620
Saint Louis Ave 37620
San Antonio Dr 37620
Sand Bar Rd 37620
Santa Fe Dr 37620
Saul Rd 37620
Scenic Dr 37620
School Ln 37620
Seneker Rd 37620
Sequoia Ln 37620
Serenity Ridge Trl 37620
Shady Ln 37620
Shady Brook Dr 37620
Shady Ford Rd 37620
Shankle Mill Rd 37620
Shankle Private Dr 37620
Sharps Creek Rd 37620
Shelby Ln & St 37620
Sheri Dr 37620
Shirley Dr 37620
Sinking Springs Rd 37620
Sinking Springs Road Ext 37620
Skyland Dr 37620
Skyline Dr 37620
Skytrail Dr 37620
Slaughter St 37620
Sleepy Hollow Rd 37620
Sloan Dr 37620
Smith Hill Private Dr 37620
Smith Pvt Dr 37620
Sourwood Hills Rd 37620
South Rd 37620
Southern St 37620
Southside Ave 37620
Southview Rd 37620
Southwood Ln 37620
Spanish Oak Rd 37620
Sparger Rd 37620
Sparkling Brook Dr 37620
Speedway Blvd 37620
Sperry Cir 37620
Sperry View Dr 37620
Spring Dr 37620
Spring Brook Dr 37620
Spring Valley Rd 37620
Springdale Dr & Rd 37620
Springfield Dr 37620
Spruce St 37620
Stafford St 37620
Stage Coach Trl 37620
State St 37620
Steele Creek Dr & Rd 37620
Steele Creek Park Rd 37620
Steeles Rd 37620
Stevenswood Dr 37620
Stine St 37620
Stone Dr 37620
Stonecroft Cir & Rd 37620
Stonehenge Dr 37620
Suda St 37620
Sugar Hollow Dr 37620
Sullivan Ln 37620
Summer Time Dr 37620
Summerwood Dr 37620
Sunny Hills Dr 37620
Sunnybrook Dr 37620
Sunset St 37620
Sweet Hollow Rd 37620
Sycamore Dr 37620
E Tadlock Rd 37620
Tallman Rd 37620
Tallman Private Dr 37620
Tanase Lane Private Dr 37620
Tanase Private Dr 37620
Tanglewood Dr 37620
Taylor St 37620
Tennessee Ave 37620
Thomas Rd 37620
Tiffany Ln & Rd 37620
Tim Warren Rd 37620
Timberlane Rd 37620
Tipperary Cir 37620
Tipton Ln 37620
Tracy Ln 37620
Trail Ridge Rd 37620
Trammell Rd 37620
Travelers Way 37620
Tremont Ave & Pl 37620
Trey Cir 37620
Trinity Cove Private Dr 37620
Trivetts Private Dr 37620
Tudor Pl 37620
Tulip Grove Cir 37620
Tva Rd S 37620
Tween Hills Rd 37620
Tween Hills Forest Trl 37620
Twin Oaks Ln 37620
Tyler Dr 37620
Upland Way 37620
V I Ranch Rd 37620
Va Dead End 759 Rd 37620
Vale Ave & Cir 37620
Valley Dr 37620
Valley Pike Rd 37620
Valley View Dr 37620
Vance Dr 37620
Vance Tank Rd 37620
Victor Dr 37620
Virginia Ave 37620
Volunteer Pkwy
1-1499 37620
1430-1430 37625
1500-2898 37620
1501-2899 37620
Walkers Private Dr 37620
Wallace Ln & St 37620
Walnut Cir, Rd & Trl 37620
Walnut Hill Rd 37620
Walters Private Dr 37620
Wampler Rd 37620
Watauga Ave & Rd 37620
Watson Rd 37620
Weaver Pike 37620
Webb Ct 37620
Weber Rd 37620
Weise St 37620
Wellington St 37620
Westover Dr 37620
Westwood Place Private Dr 37620
Whipporwill Cir 37620
Whitaker Dr & St 37620
White Dogwood Ave 37620
Whitehall 37620
Whitney Ln 37620
Whitney Private Dr 37620
Wildwood Dr 37620
E & W Wilkshire Pl 37620
Williams Ln & St 37620
Willow St 37620
Wilson Ave 37620
Wimberly Cir & Way 37620
Winchester Ln 37620
Winding Rd & Way 37620
Windsor Ave 37620
Windy Hills Dr & Rd 37620
Winners Cir 37620
Witcher Private Dr 37620
Wolfdale Rd 37620
Wonder Valley Rd 37620
Woodbine Ln & Rd 37620
Woodbrook Ave 37620
Woodland Cir & Ct 37620
Woods Way Rd 37620
Woodside Dr 37620
Worley Dr 37620
Wren Rd 37620
Wright Ln 37620
Wyatt Cemetery Rd 37620
Wyatt Hollow Rd 37620
York Dr 37620
Yorkshire 37620

NUMBERED STREETS

1st Ave 37620
2nd Ave & St 37620
3 Oaks Dr 37620
3rd St 37620
4th St 37620
5th St 37620
6th St
1-110 37620
111-111 37621
112-3298 37620
113-3299 37620
6th Street Ext 37620
7th Ave & St 37620
8th St 37620
9th St 37620
10th St 37620
11th St 37620
12th St 37620
13th St 37620
14th St 37620
15th St 37620
16th St 37620
17th St 37620
18th St 37620
22nd St 37620
23rd St 37620
24th St 37620

CHATTANOOGA TN

General Delivery 37401

POST OFFICE BOXES MAIN OFFICE STATIONS AND BRANCHES

Box No.s
3009A - 3009A 37404
1 - 1749 37401
2001 - 2714 37409
3001 - 3859 37404
4001 - 4976 37405
5001 - 5997 37406
6001 - 6355 37401
8001 - 8996 37414
9001 - 9999 37412
9998 - 9998 37422
10901 - 10910 37409
11001 - 12047 37401
15001 - 15999 37415
16001 - 16996 37416
17001 - 17494 37415
19001 - 19438 37416
21001 - 21994 37424
22000 - 25699 37422
28001 - 28498 37424
60001 - 60227 37406
71501 - 73220 37407
80001 - 81344 37414
90001 - 91572 37412
180101 - 180208 37401
180400 - 180499 37404
180500 - 180599 37405
180600 - 180606 37406
180700 - 180799 37407
180901 - 180901 37409
181101 - 181101 37414
181200 - 181201 37412
181600 - 181600 37416
182200 - 188215 37422
190002 - 190002 37401

RURAL ROUTES

04 37409
04 37419

NAMED STREETS

Abelia Ln 37415
E & W Abercrombie Cir 37415
Abernathy St 37405
N Access Rd 37415
S Access Rd 37406
Acer Cir 37406
Ackerman St 37404
Acorn Ct 37415
Acorn Oaks Cir 37405
Acuff St 37406
Adair Ave 37412
Adams St 37408
Adamson Cir 37416
Addison Rd 37406
Adelia Dr 37416
Adkins Rd 37419
Adona Ln 37412
Afton Ln 37421
Agawela Dr 37406
Agnes Ave
1-99 37406
1600-1699 37411
Aiken Rd 37421
Aim Way 37411
Aimee Ln 37415
Airpark Dr 37421
Airport Rd 37421
Airways Blvd 37421
Akins Dr 37411
Alabama Ave 37409
Albany St 37405
Albemarle Ave 37411
Alden Ave 37405
Alexander Dr 37415
Alexis Cir 37406
Alford Hill Dr 37419
Alhambra Dr 37421
Alice Dr 37411
Alice St 37404
Allanco St 37409
Allancou Ave 37409
Allegheny Dr 37421
Allen St 37415
Allens Row 37403
Allgood Ct 37406
Allin St 37406
Allison Dr 37421
Almond Ridge Rd 37421
Alpine Dr 37415
Alta Vista Dr 37411
Altamaha St 37412
Altamira Dr 37412
Altamont Rd 37415
Althea St 37412
Alton Park Blvd 37410
Altoona Dr 37415
Amber Ave 37412
Amberley Trl 37421
Amhurst Ave 37411
Amin Dr 37421
Amnicola Hwy 37406
Amsterdam Ln 37421
Amy Ln 37421
Anderson Ave
1300-2999 37404
3600-5399 37412
Anderson Dr 37421
Anderson Ter 37421
Andover Pl 37421
Andrea Dr 37419
Andrews St 37406
Angela Dr 37410
Angela Ln 37419
Angie Dr & Ln 37421
Ani Ln 37419
Anita Dr 37411
Ansley Dr 37409
Antelope Trl 37415
Anthony Ln 37416
Appian Cir & Way 37415
Applebrook Ln 37421
Applegate Ln 37421
Appling St 37406
W Aquarium Way 37402
Arbell Ln 37421
Arbor Ln 37416
Arbor Leaf Ln 37421
Arbor Place Ln 37416
Arcadia Ave 37411
Archer Rd 37416
Arden Ave 37405
Ardian Rd & Trl 37412
Ariel Ln 37405
Arlena Cir 37421
Arlington Ave
500-799 37404
800-1899 37406
Arlington Ter 37410
Armour St 37412
Arno St 37406
Arnold Dr, Pl & St 37412
Arrowhead Trl 37411
Arrowrock Rd 37406
Arroyo Dr 37421
Asbury Dr 37411
Asbury Oak Ln 37419
Asbury Park St 37404
Ascension St 37410
Ash St 37402
Asherton Ln 37421
Ashford Dr 37421
Ashland Ter 37415
Ashley Mill Dr 37421
Ashley Oaks Dr 37421

Ashmore Ave 37415
Ashton St 37405
Ashton Ridge Dr 37421
Ashton Valley Dr 37421
Ashton View Dr 37421
Ashwood Ln & Ter 37415
Aspen Ln 37416
N & S Aster Ave 37419
Astor Ln 37412
Atlanta Ave 37421
Atlanta Dr 37415
Aubrey Ave 37411
Auburn St 37405
Auburndale Ave 37405
Auburndale Dr 37415
Audubon Dr 37411
Audubon Trl 37421
Ault Dr 37404
Austin Dr 37416
Austin St 37411
Autumn Dr 37415
Autumn Ln 37416
Autumn Chase Dr 37421
Autumn Wood Dr 37416
Avakian Dr 37421
Avalon Ave, Cir, Hl & Pl 37415
Avalon Acres Ct 37421
Aventine Way 37421
Averra St 37408
Averrani St 37408
Aviara Dr 37421
Avon Pl 37405
Avonlea Ln 37421
Awhila Dr 37421
Awtry St 37406
Azalea Dale Dr 37419
Azalean Dr 37415
Babbas Ln 37419
Bachman St 37406
Bacon Ln 37421
Bacon Trl 37412
Badger Ln 37416
Bailey Ave 37404
Bainbridge Rd 37415
Baker St 37405
Bal Harbor Cir & Dr 37416
Balcomb St 37409
Bald Eagle Cir 37419
Baldwin St
601-637 37403
639-1199 37403
1400-2499 37408
Bales Ave 37412
Bales Cir 37411
Ballard Dr & Pl 37421
Balsam Ln 37406
Bams Dr 37421
Bank St 37415
Banks Rd 37421
Bar Shore Dr 37416
Barbara Cir & Ln 37411
Barberry Ct 37421
Barker Rd 37415
Barnes Ct 37421
Barnie Fay Ln 37421
Barry Rd 37412
Barton Ave 37405
Basham St 37410
Baskette Way 37421
Bass Rd 37421
Basswood Dr & Ln 37416
Batters Place Rd 37421
Battery Dr 37406
Battery Pl 37403
Battlefield Trl 37409
Baxter St 37415
Bay Dr 37416
Bay Berry Dr 37421
Bay View Dr 37416
Baylor School Rd 37405
Beacon Ln 37421
Beason Dr 37405
Beautiful Pl 37415
Beck Ave 37405
Bedford Ave 37410
Beech St 37419
N Beech St
100-499 37404
2600-2699 37406
S Beech St 37404
Beeler Ave 37421
Bel Air Rd 37421
Belaire Dr 37411
W Bell Ave 37405
Bella Vista Dr 37421
Bellbrook Dr 37416
Belle Arbor Ave 37406
Belle Vista Ave & Dr 37411
Belleau Village Ln 37421
Belleau Woods Dr 37421
Belleview Ave 37409
Bellflower Cir 37411
Bellview Ave 37416
Belmeade Ave 37411
Belmont Ave 37409
Belvoir Ave
1-499 37411
600-999 37412
Belvoir Cir 37412
Belvoir Dr 37412
Belvoir Ter 37412
Belvoir Circle Dr 37412
Belvoir Crest Dr 37412
Belvoir Hills Cir & Dr 37412
Belvoir Pines Dr 37412
Bending Oak Dr 37421
Benham Cir & Dr 37421
Benjamin Ln 37415
Bennett Ave 37404
Bennett Rd 37412
Bennington Dr 37406
Benson Dr 37412
Bent Oak Rd 37421
Benton Ave 37406
Benton Dr
4200-4299 37406
4300-4399 37416
Berkley Cir 37405
Berkley Dr 37415
Berkshire Cir 37421
Bermerwood Dr 37421
Bermuda Ave & Ter 37412
Berry Patch Ln 37405
Berthas Pl 37421
Betts Rd 37411
Betty Ln 37412
Beulah Ave 37409
Beulah Dr 37412
Beverly Kay Dr 37416
Big Fork Rd 37405
Big Rock Rd 37405
Bill Reed Rd 37421
Biltmore Ave & Dr 37411
Bimini Pl 37412
Birch Dr 37421
Birchwood Dr 37406
Bird St 37406
Birdsmill Rd 37404
Birmingham Dr 37415
Birmingham Hwy 37419
N Bishop Dr 37416
Bitsy Ln 37415
Bivins Rd 37415
Black St 37405
Black Creek Dr 37419
Black Oak Cir 37415
Blackford St
900-1199 37403
1900-2399 37404
Blackhawk Trl 37412
Blackwell Dr 37412
Blackwell Farm Rd 37421
Blanchard St 37411
Blanton Dr 37412
Bledsoe Ter 37405
Bleen Pl 37421
Blessing Way 37419
Bliss Ave 37406
Block St 37411
Blocker Ln 37412
Bloom Rd 37412
Blossom Cir 37421
Blue Bird Dr 37405
Blue Jay Rd 37412
Blue Oak Dr 37416
Bluebird Cir 37412
Bluff Dr 37405
S Bluff Rd 37419
Bluff View Rd 37405
Bluff View St 37403
Bluffview Cir 37416
Blustery Way 37421
Bobby Dale Ln 37415
Bobwhite Ln 37421
Bohr Dr 37415
Bolton Ln 37421
Bon Air Cir 37404
Bonds Ter 37421
Bonneville Cir 37419
Bonnie Dr & Mnr 37416
Bonnie Lassie Dr 37411
Bonnie Way Dr 37411
Bonny Lake Ln 37416
Bonny Oaks Dr
4278A-4278B 37406
3401-3497 37406
3499-4299 37406
4300-6599 37416
6600-7499 37421
Bonnyshire Dr 37416
Bonnyvale Ln 37421
Boone St 37406
Booth Rd 37411
Boriss Dr 37416
Botsford Dr 37421
Bouton Dr 37415
Bowen Rd 37412
Bowman Ln 37416
Boyce St 37406
Boyd Pl 37404
Boyd St 37412
Boydston Rd 37419
Boylston St 37405
Boynton Dr 37402
Brack St 37412
Bradford Ave & Ct 37409
Bradt St 37406
Bragg St 37406
Brainerd Rd
3100-5900 37411
5901-5905 37421
5902-5906 37411
5907-5999 37421
E Brainerd Rd
6000-7699 37421
7610-7610 37424
7700-9698 37421
7701-9699 37421
Braly Pl 37415
Brandermill Ln 37421
Brandywine Ln 37415
Brannon Ave 37407
Brass Lantern Way 37415
Breckenridge Dr 37415
Breezewood Way 37421
Brelsford Rd 37405
Brenda Rd 37415
Brently Estates Dr 37421
Brently Woods Dr 37421
Brentwood Dr
100-399 37415
4700-4899 37416
Brianna Way 37421
Briar St 37412
Briarcliff Way 37406
Briarwood Cir & Dr 37416
Brickhouse Rd 37421
Brickwell Ln 37421
Bridgecreek Rd 37421
Bridgeview Dr 37415
Bridgewater Ln 37405
Briggs Ave 37415
Broad St
1-1499 37402
1500-3320 37408
3322-3348 37408
3350-3799 37409
Broadcreek Ct 37421
Brock Rd 37421
Brockhaven Rd 37404
Brogden Trl 37416
Bromley Ln 37419
Brookfield Ave
1-499 37411
500-899 37412
Brookfield Cir 37412
Brookhaven Cir 37421
Brookhollow Dr & Ln 37421
N & S Brooks Ave & Cir 37411
Brookside Dr 37421
Brookwood Dr
1-299 37411
2300-2399 37421
Broughton St 37411
W Brow Ter 37411
Brown Rd 37421
Brown St 37404
Browndell Dr 37419
Browns Aly 37406
Browns Chapel Rd 37415
Browns Ferry Rd 37419
Browntown Rd 37415
Brownview Dr 37415
Brownwood Dr 37404
Broyles Dr 37421
Bruning Ln 37415
Bryant Rd 37405
Bryant St 37406
Brynehill Ln 37415
Brynewood Ter 37415
Brynewood Park Dr, Ln & Rd 37415
Brynwood Dr & Ter 37415
Buccaneer Trl 37411
Buckingham Dr 37421
Buckley St 37404
Buena Vista Dr 37404
Buggy Ln 37421
Bunch St 37421
Bunker Hill Dr 37421
Burgess Rd 37419
Burgundy Cir 37421
Burke Ln 37405
Burns Ave 37412
Burns Trl 37419
Burnt Hickory Dr 37421
Burnt Mill Rd 37410
Burnwood Ln 37416
Burr St 37412
Burton St 37406
Bush Rd 37421
Bush St 37405
Business Park Dr 37419
Butterfly Dr 37406
Byrd Ave 37406
Cabin Rd 37404
Caden Dr & Ln 37406
Cagle Rd 37419
Cain Ave 37410
Caine Ln 37421
Calderwood Cir 37416
Caledonia Way 37415
Calhoun Ave
2700-2799 37404
2800-5099 37407
California Ave 37415
Callaway Ct 37421
Cambridge Dr 37411
Camden St 37406
Camden Oaks Dr 37406
Camean Ave 37404
Cameanc Ave 37404
Camelot Ln 37421
Cameron Cir 37402
Cameron Ln 37411
Cameron Hill Cir 37402
Camilla Dr 37421
Camp Jordan Pkwy & Rd 37412
Campbell St 37406
Candlewood Trl 37421
Caneadea Trl 37421
Canebreak Dr 37415
Cannon Ave
2300-2399 37408
2500-2999 37404
Cannondale Loop 37421
Canoe Ln 37416
Canterbury Rd 37421
Canyon Dr 37416
Capehart Ln 37412
Cappella St 37408
Caran Dr 37421
Caraway Turn 37415
Cardinal Cv 37421
Carey St 37404
Carl St 37410
Carl Swafford Dr 37419
Carl White Pl 37410
Carlisle Ln 37405
Carlton Ave 37415
Carnation St 37419
Caroline St 37409
Carolyn Ln 37411
Carousel Rd 37411
Carr St 37408
Carr Ter 37416
Carriage Xing 37421
Carriage Parc Dr 37421
Carroll Ln 37405
Carson Ave 37404
Carson Rd 37405
Carter Dr 37415
Carter Plz 37402
Carter St
900-1699 37402
1800-1899 37408
1901-1999 37408
Carter Lake Rd 37405
Cartwright St 37415
Caruthers Rd 37411
Carver Ln 37404
Carver St 37421
Cash Canyon Rd 37419
Castle Ave 37412
Castle Dr 37411
Castle Gate Dr 37421
Castleberry Ave 37412
Castleview Dr 37421
Castlewood Trl 37412
Cathowken Dr 37421
Cathy Ln 37412
Cavan Cir 37421
Cawood Ln 37421
Cecelia Dr 37416
Cecil Ln 37412
Cedar Ln 37421
Cedar St 37406
Cedar Creek Dr 37421
Cedar Glen Cir 37412
Cedar Tree Ct 37412
Cedar Wood Ct 37412
Cedarton Ct 37421
Celebration Way 37421
Celtic Dr 37416
Cemetery Ave 37408
Cemetery Ln 37421
Cemetery Rd 37412
Centennial Dr 37405
Center St
2200-2399 37421
3300-3499 37419
Centerview Ln 37419
Central Ave
100-899 37403
901-917 37403
918-926 37411
928-998 37411
1000-1100 37403
1101-1103 37411
1104-1198 37403
1105-1113 37411
1201-1297 37408
1299-1999 37408
3500-5599 37410
Central Dr 37421
Centro St 37419
Century Oaks Dr 37416
Chaffin Ln 37421
Chamberlain Ave 37404
N Chamberlain Ave 37406
Chambers Rd 37421
Chambliss St 37405
Champion Rd 37416
Chance Trl 37415
Chandler Ave & Pl 37410
Channel View Ln 37415
Chapman Rd 37421
Char Mac Ln 37419
Charbar Cir 37421
Charger Dr 37409
Charles Ave 37415
Charles Dr 37421
Charleston Sq 37421
Charlotte Ave
900-999 37421
2400-2499 37415
Chateau Ln 37411
Cheek St 37406
Cherished Vw 37415
Cherokee Ave 37412
Cherokee Blvd 37405
Cherry St
1-299 37403
401-597 37402
599-899 37402
Cherryton Dr 37411
Cherwood Ln 37406
Cheryl Ln 37415
Chesapeake Dr 37416
Cheshire Ln 37421
Chestnut Ln 37405
Chestnut St
100-600 37402
601-699 37450
602-1498 37402
701-1499 37402
1500-2599 37408
2601-2799 37408
Chestnut Hill Ln 37421
Chestnut Wood Ln 37421
Chevoit Dr 37411
Chianti Way 37421
Chiati Way 37421
Chickalilly Dr 37404
Chickamauga Ave 37406
Chickamauga Loop 37421
Chickamauga Rd 37421
Chickasaw Rd 37411
Chief Vann Rd 37406
Chilhowie St 37405
Chippewah Dr 37412
Chiswick Dr 37421
Choate Rd 37412
N Choctaw Dr 37411
S Choctaw Dr 37411
Choctaw Trl 37405
Christopher Rd 37416
Chula Creek Rd 37421
Chula Vista Dr 37411
Chumley Ln 37415
Church Rd 37421
Church St
3700-3999 37409
4600-4699 37410
Churchill Rd 37406
Churchill Downs Cir 37421
Cicero Trl 37421
Citico Ave
1300-2300 37404
2301-2499 37406
2302-2598 37404
2501-2599 37404
2700-2799 37406
City Green Way 37405
City View Ter 37421
Claremont Ave, Cir & Ct 37412
Clarendon St 37405
Clark Ave 37421
Clark St 37403
Claude Way 37415
Clay St 37406
S Clayton Ave 37412
Clayton Dr 37421
Clayton Avenue Ext 37412
Clear Brook Ct 37421
Clearfield Ln 37405
Clearview Ave 37404
Clearview Dr 37421
Clearwood Rd 37421
Clemons Rd 37412
Clermont Dr 37415
Cleveland Ave
2108A-2108B 37404
1100-1199 37403
1300-2199 37404
N Cliff Ln 37415
Cliff Top Ln 37419
Clifford Way 37419
Clift St 37405
Clifton Pl 37404
Clifton Ter 37407
Clifton Terrace Aly 37407
Cliftview Dr 37415
Cline Crst 37415
Cline Rd 37412
Cline St 37415
Clio Ave
2800-2999 37404
3100-4199 37407
Clipper Dr 37421
Close Rd 37412
Cloudburst Ln 37421
Cloudland Trl 37411
Cloudview Ln 37415
Clover St 37412
Club Dr 37411
Club House Dr 37416
Clyde Rd 37421
Coburn Cir & Dr 37415
Cody Cir 37406
Cogswell St 37406
Coker Cir 37415
Colby St 37405
Coleman Cir 37412
Colemere Dr 37416
Coleson Trl 37412
Collins Cir 37411
Collins St 37403
Colonial Dr 37411
Colonial Parkway Dr 37421
Columbia St 37402
Columbine Trl 37421
Colville St 37405
Colyar Dr 37404
Combs Dr 37405
Commerce St
1300-1399 37404
2300-2499 37408
Commercial Ln 37405
Commons Blvd 37421
Compress St 37405
Conahaney Trl 37406
Concord Cir 37421
N Concord Rd 37421
Concord St 37405
Cone Flower Trl 37421
Congo Ln 37421
Connell St 37412
Connelly Ln 37412
Conner Ln 37421
Conner St 37411
Constitution Dr 37405
Continental Dr 37405
Cooley St 37406
Coopers Edge Trl 37405
Coors Rd 37405
Copperhead Ln 37421
Coppinger Rd 37405
Cora Dr 37412
Corbley Dr 37411
Cordelia Ln 37416
Cornelia St 37408
Cornelison Rd 37411
Cornerstone Dr 37421
Cornwalls Way 37421
Corporate Pl 37419
Corral Trl 37421

Cotton Moore Rd 37405
Cottonwood Ln 37406
Cottonwood Rd 37421
Council Fire Dr 37421
Country Ln 37421
Countryside Dr 37406
Courage Way 37421
Court Dr 37412
E Court Dr 37404
Courthouse 37402
Courtney Ln 37415
Courtyard Cir 37415
Cove Ln 37415
Coventry Ln
8100-8199 37421
9100-9199 37416
Covey Ln 37421
Covington Dr 37412
Covington St 37407
Cowart St
1200-1399 37402
1400-2700 37408
2702-2798 37408
Crabtree Dr 37412
Craig Rd 37412
Crane Rd 37421
Cravens Rd & Ter 37409
Crawdad Holw 37421
Crawford St 37421
Creek Dr 37415
N Creek Rd 37406
S Creek Rd 37406
Creek Overlook 37415
Creek Stone Dr 37421
Creekside Rd 37406
Creekview Ln 37421
Creekwood Terrace Ln 37421
Crerar St 37415
Crescent Cir 37407
Crescent Park 37411
N Crest Ct 37404
Crest Dr 37415
E Crest Dr 37406
S Crest Pl 37404
E Crest Rd 37404
N Crest Rd
1-619 37404
620-2499 37406
S Crest Rd 37404
W Crest Rd 37404
S Crest Manor Ln 37404
Crest Terrace Dr 37404
Crestbrook Cir 37421
Crestfield Dr 37411
Cresthaven Dr 37412
Crestline Dr 37415
Crestone Cir 37411
Crestview Cir
100-299 37411
4500-4699 37415
Crestview Dr 37415
Crestway Dr 37411
Crestwood Ave 37415
Crestwood Dr
1700-1799 37405
1800-2799 37415
W Crewdson Ave 37405
Crisman St 37415
Croll Ct 37410
Cromwell Rd 37421
Cross St
100-199 37405
4200-4499 37416
Cross Creek Dr 37415
Cross Creek
Highlands 37415
Cross Winds Ln 37421
Crown Court Ln 37421
Croy Ln 37421
Crozier Ave 37405
Crutchfield St 37406
Culver St 37415
Cumberland Rd 37419
Cumberland St 37404
Cummings Hwy
1700-1799 37409
1900-4999 37419
Cummings Rd 37419
Cummings Cove Dr 37419
Curleque Dr 37411
Curtain Pole Rd 37406
Curtis Cir 37415
Curtis St 37406
Curve St 37405
Cuscowilla Trl 37415
Cushman St 37406
Custom House Sq 37402
Customer Delight Dr 37421
Cyndica Dr 37421
Cypress Street Ct 37402
D St 37405
Dabney Dr 37412
Dagnan Ln 37405
Dahlia St 37421
Daisy St 37406
Dal Brown Rd 37405
Dalders Rd 37419
Dalecrest Ct 37411
Dalefield Ln 37421
Daleview Ter 37411
Dalewood Dr 37411
E Dallas Rd 37405
Dalton St 37405
Damron Pl 37421
Danby Dr 37421
Dancing Fern Trl 37421
Daniel Dr 37412
Danube Dr 37421
Darlene Cir
100-199 37416
1300-1399 37412
Darryl Ln 37412
Dartmouth St 37405
Daugherty Ln 37421
Dauphin Way 37411
Davenport St 37406
David Cir 37421
David Ln 37421
David St 37419
Davidson Rd 37421
Davis Ave 37411
Davis Ln 37416
Day Lily Trl 37415
Day Long Pl 37421
Daydream Ln 37415
Dayton Blvd
1000-1899 37405
1900-6099 37415
E & W Daytona Dr 37415
De Fue St 37415
Debra Rd 37411
Dee Dr 37406
Deerfoot Dr 37406
Deermont Ct 37421
Delaine Ln 37416
Delano Dr 37406
Delawanna Ter 37405
Delaware Dr 37412
Delbert Ln 37421
Dell Trl 37411
Dellway Cir 37412
Dellwood Pl 37411
Delmont St 37405
Delong St 37410
Delray Ave 37405
Denham Rd 37406
Dennis St 37405
Denton Ln 37421
Derby Cir & St 37404
Derby Downs Dr 37421
Desales Ave 37404
Devel Ln 37405
Devonshire St 37405
Dewayne Rd 37416
Diamond St 37406
Diane Ln 37404
Discovery Dr 37416
Distribution Dr 37416
Divine Ave 37407
Dixie Ave 37409
Dixie Ln 37405
Dixon St 37421
Dodds Ave
300-2199 37404
2300-4799 37407
Dodie Dr 37421
Dodson Ave
400-799 37404
800-4099 37406
Dogwood Dr 37406
Dogwood Ln
100-199 37411
400-499 37405
4100-4199 37411
Dogwood Garden Ln 37421
Dogwood Season Dr 37421
Don Rob Ln 37411
Donaldson Rd
400-599 37411
600-999 37412
Dondende Ave 37407
Donna Ln 37404
Doolittle St 37406
Doral Ln 37416
Dorchester Rd 37405
Dorisa Ave 37411
Dorris St
2101-2197 37408
2199-2299 37408
3600-5399 37410
Dorroh Ln 37412
Dorsey St 37410
Dorthas Trl 37419
Douglas Dr 37412
Douglas St 37403
Dougs Dr 37419
Dove Ln 37421
Dover Ln 37412
Dower Rd 37419
Doyle St
1400-1499 37404
2800-2899 37407
Drake Parkway Rd 37416
Dreher Ln 37419
Drew Rd 37419
Druid Ln 37405
Drummond Dr 37411
Dry Branch Ct 37419
Duane Rd 37405
Dubsy Ln 37415
Dudley Rd 37421
Dugan Ave 37412
Dugdale St 37405
Duke Ln 37421
Dumac Rd 37416
Duncan Ave 37404
Dunlap Ave 37412
Dunwoody Dr 37421
Dupont St 37412
Dupre Rd 37421
Durand Ave 37406
Durham Dr 37421
Dutchess Ct 37421
Duvall St 37412
Dwight Ave & St 37406
Dyer St 37411
Eads St 37412
Eagle Bluff Trl 37416
Eagle Mere Rd 37421
Ealy Rd 37412
East Ave 37411
Eastgate Loop
1-697 37411
699-712 37411
711-711 37414
713-999 37411
714-898 37411
Eastglen Ct 37406
Easton Ave 37415
Eastview Ave 37411
Eastview Ct 37415
Eastway Ter 37412
Eastwood Ave 37411
Eastwood Dr 37416
Eaves Pl 37405
Eblen Dr 37421
Eddings St 37411
Edelweiss St 37409
Edgefield Dr & Ln 37421
Edgehill Ave 37405
Edgewater Rd 37416
Edgewood Cir & Ln 37405
Edgmon Dr 37421
Edgmon Forest Ln 37421
Edingburg Dr 37410
Edith Ln 37421
Edwards Ter 37412
Edwin Ln 37412
Edwina Ct 37412
Eileen Ln 37412
Elaine Cir & Trl 37421
Elam Ln 37421
Elbe Dr 37421
Elder St 37404
Elder Gap Pl 37419
Elder Mountain Rd 37419
Elderberry Ln 37411
Elderview Rd 37419
Eledge Rd 37412
Elena Dr 37406
Elinor St
400-799 37405
801-999 37405
918-928 37409
Elizabeth Crest Rd 37421
Elizabethton Ln 37421
Eller Rd 37416
Ellington Way 37421
Ellis Ave 37412
Ellis Park Ln 37419
Ellyn Ln 37411
N Elm St 37415
Elmar Dr 37421
Elmendorf Cir & St 37406
Elmore Ave 37415
Elmwood Dr
100-299 37411
800-899 37405
E Elmwood Dr 37405
W Elmwood Dr 37405
Emma St 37406
Emma Kate Dr 37406
Emory Dr
700-899 37415
6100-6198 37421
Enchanted Vw 37415
Enclave Rd 37415
Enclave Bay Dr 37415
E End Ave 37412
W End Ave
1-99 37419
1200-1399 37412
Endicott St 37405
Engel Ave 37421
Engert Dr 37411
Englewood Ave 37405
English Ave 37407
Enterprise Ln 37416
Enterprise Park Dr 37416
Enterprise South Blvd 37416
Eric Dr 37421
Esterbrook Ct & Dr 37412
Esther Ln 37421
Estrellita Cir 37421
Etowah St 37415
Eucalyptus Dr 37411
E & W Euclid Ave 37415
Evening Shadow Dr 37421
Eveningside Dr 37404
Everett Dr 37421
Everette St 37409
Evergreen Ct 37406
Evergreen Dr 37411
Ewing Dr 37415
Executive Oak Ln 37421
Explorer Ln 37421
Fagan St
900-1298 37408
1300-2299 37408
3700-5299 37410
Fair St 37415
Fairbluff Ln 37416
W Fairfax Dr 37415
Fairhills Dr 37405
Fairleigh St 37406
Fairmount Ave 37405
Fairoak Pl 37409
Fairpoint St 37405
Fairview Ave 37403
Fairview Dr 37406
Fairwood Ln 37416
Faith Rd 37406
Falcon Ln 37416
Fall Creek Rd 37416
Fallen Maple Dr 37421
Falmouth Rd 37405
Farris Rd 37421
Fawn Dr 37412
Fawn Ridge Dr 37416
Faxon St 37404
Faye Ave 37421
Federal St 37405
Fenchcroft Ln 37421
Ferent St 37406
Ferenti St 37406
Fern Ave 37419
Fern St 37411
Fern Leaf Ln 37421
Fernway Cir & Rd 37405
Fernwood Cir 37421
Festival Loop 37419
Fike Dr 37412
Finch Ln 37419
Fincher Ave 37412
Fire Pink Trl 37415
Firethorne Ln 37421
Fisher Ave 37406
Fisk Ave 37421
Fitehaven Dr 37415
Five Springs Dr 37419
Flarind St 37403
Flarinde St 37403
Fleeta Ln 37416
Flinn Dr 37412
Flora Cir 37415
Florida Ave 37409
Florida St 37421
Flowerbranch 37421
Flowerdale Dr 37421
Floyd Dr 37412
Flynn St 37403
Folts Cir & Dr 37415
Forest Ave 37405
Forest Rd 37406
Forest Acres Ln 37406
Forest Glen Dr 37415
Forest Green Dr 37412
Forest Highland Cir &
Dr 37415
Forest Shadows Dr 37421
Forgotten Trl 37406
Forsythe St 37415
Fort St
1200-1499 37402
1900-2199 37408
Fortwood Pl & St 37403
Foster Rd 37421
Foundation Way 37421
Founders Way 37416
Fountain Ave 37412
Fountain Cir 37412
Fountain Sq 37402
Foust St
1500-1699 37404
1700-2199 37407
Fox Dr 37404
Foxhall Ln 37421
Fralead Dr 37416
Fraleade Dr 37416
Frances Dr 37421
Francis St
1-99 37419
1800-1899 37406
3900-3999 37419
Frank Lawson Dr 37405
Franklin Dr
1200-1399 37421
3400-3599 37419
Franklin Pl 37412
Franklin St 37405
Franks Rd 37421
Frawley Rd 37412
Frawley St 37411
Frazier Ave 37405
Frazier Cir 37411
Frazier Dr 37421
Fred Will Cir 37411
Frederick Dr 37412
Fredrick St 37410
Freeman St 37406
Freudenburg Ln 37415
Friar Rd 37421
Frontage Rd 37405
Frost St 37406
Frosty Pine Trl 37405
Fruitland Dr 37412
Fuller Rd 37421
Fuller Glen Cir 37421
Fyffe Ave 37415
Gable Xing 37421
Gable Brook Dr 37421
Gable Ridge Ln 37421
Gadd Rd 37415
Gail Dr 37412
Galahad Rd 37421
Gale Ln 37421
Game Reserve Rd 37405
Ganasita Trl 37406
Garden Rd 37419
Garden Gate Ln 37416
Gardenspot Ln 37419
Gardner St 37411
Garfield Ave 37403
Garfield St 37404
Garner Cir 37412
Garner Rd 37406
Garner St 37412
Garnett Ave 37405
Gary Ln 37421
Gas St 37403
Gatehouse Xing 37421
Gateway Ave 37402
Gay St 37411
Gayda Ln 37421
Gayle Dr 37411
Gaylord Dr 37415
Gem Pl 37421
Geneal Ln 37406
General Thomas Blvd 37407
Genoa Dr 37421
Gentry Rd 37421
Georgetown Ln 37421
Georgetown Trace Ln 37421
Georgia Ave
301-599 37403
600-909 37402
910-910 37401
910-1098 37402
911-1099 37402
Germantown Cir 37412
N Germantown Rd 37411
S Germantown Rd
1-699 37411
700-899 37412
Geswein Ct 37412
Gibbons Rd 37421
Gibson St 37412
Gibson Pond Rd 37421
Gifford St 37408
Gilbert St 37406
Gillespie Rd & Ter 37411
Givens Rd 37421
Gladys Ln 37421
Glass St 37406
Gleason Cir & Dr 37412
Gleason Terrace Ct 37412
Glen Cir & Ct 37415
Glen Errol Way 37412
Glen Oaks Dr, Pl &
Ter 37412
Glenacre Ct 37411
Glenaire Dr 37416
Glenbury Dr 37421
Glencoe St 37406
Glencrofte Ln 37421
Glendale Dr 37405
Glendon Dr 37411
Glenfield Ln 37421
Glenhill Cir & Dr 37415
Glenmar Cir 37416
Glenn Fls 37409
Glenn Rd 37405
Glenron St 37415
Glenroy Ave 37405
Glenshire Ln 37421
Glenview St 37408
Glenwood Cir 37404
Glenwood Dr
100-799 37404
800-1299 37406
Glenwood Pkwy 37404
Gloucester Ln 37421
Glouster Ln 37416
Glover Rd 37416
Glowmont Dr 37412
Glyndon Dr 37409
Godsey Ln 37415
Goforth Ln 37421
Gold Wing Way 37416
Golden Pl 37415
Golf St 37405
Golfview Dr 37411
Goodson Ave 37405
Goodwin Rd 37421
Gordon Rd 37419
Gorge View Ln 37405
Gorse Ln 37421
Grace Ave 37406
Graceland Trl 37421
Graham Rd 37421
Graham St 37405
Granada Dr 37411
Granada St 37406
Grand Ave 37410
Grand Mountain Dr 37421
Granda Dr 37421
Grandview Ave
800-899 37405
1800-1899 37404
Graston Ave 37412
Gray Rd 37421
Grays Dr 37421
Graysville Rd 37421
Green Rd 37421
Green St 37408
Green Forest Dr & Ln 37406
Greenbriar Rd 37412
S Greenleaf St 37415
Greens Rd 37421
Greenslake Rd 37412
Greenview Dr 37411
Greenway Dr 37421
Greenway View Dr 37411
Greenwich Ave 37415
N Greenwood Ave 37404
S Greenwood Ave 37404
Greenwood Rd
800-1599 37411
1600-2099 37406
2101-2399 37406
Grey Oaks Ln 37421
Grider Way 37421
Grinder Creek Pl 37421
Grouse Ln 37421
Grove St
1100-1199 37402
2700-2799 37406
Grove Street Ct 37402
Guess Cir 37415
Guild Dr 37421
Guild St 37405
Guild Trl 37409
Guinevere Pkwy 37421
Gulf St 37408
Gunbarrel Rd 37421
Gundy Dr 37419
Gurley St 37405
Gw Davis Dr 37411
Hadley Dr 37416
Haisten Ct 37412
Hal Cir & Dr 37416
Hall St 37415

Halsey St 37410
Hamby Cir 37421
Hamilton Ave 37405
Hamilton Acres Cir 37421
Hamilton Brow Path 37421
Hamilton Camp Dr 37421
Hamilton Cove Dr 37421
Hamilton Mill Dr 37421
Hamilton Oaks Dr 37421
Hamilton Park Dr 37421
Hamilton Place Blvd 37421
Hamilton Run Dr 37421
Hamilton View St 37421
Hamilton Village Dr 37421
Hamlet Dr 37421
Hamm Rd 37405
Hampton St 37403
Hancock Cir 37416
Hancock Rd
4400-4699 37416
5900-6099 37421
7700-8199 37416
Hancock Ter 37416
Haney Dr 37411
Hanover St 37405
Hansley Dr 37416
Harbin Dr 37415
Harbor Cir & Ter 37416
Harbor Hills Ln & Rd 37416
Harbor Oaks Ln 37416
Harcourt Dr 37411
Hardin Dr 37412
Harding Rd 37415
Hardy St 37406
Hargraves Ave 37411
Harley Ln 37416
Harley St 37406
Harper St 37405
Harrah Ln 37412
Harris Dr 37412
Harris Ln
500-999 37412
3400-3499 37419
Harrison Pike
2300-2398 37406
2400-3299 37406
3300-6699 37416
Hartford Dr 37415
Hartman St 37405
Harvard St 37412
Harvest Oak Ln 37421
Harwood Dr 37415
Haven Acres Ln 37406
Haven Cove Ln 37421
Haven Crest Dr 37421
Haven Hill Dr & Ln 37412
Havendale Ln 37421
Hawk Run 37421
Hawkins St 37415
Hawks Nest Dr 37419
Hawthorne Ct 37406
N Hawthorne St
1098A-1098B 37406
100-899 37404
900-4099 37406
S Hawthorne St 37404
Haymore Ave 37411
Haynes Ln 37416
Haywood Ave 37415
Hazelwood Ave 37411
Healing Bluff Rd 37419
Healing Springs Rd 37419
Hearthstone Cir 37415
Heather St 37412
Heathfield Dr 37416
Heaton Dr 37421
Heaton St 37406
Hedgewood Dr 37405
Heidi Cir 37415
Heiskell Dr 37416
Helen Ln 37412
Hemingway Dr 37406
Hemlock Cir 37419
Hemphill Ave & Cir 37411
Henderson Ave 37405
Henderson Dr 37411

Henderson St 37406
Hendricks Blvd 37405
Hendricks St 37406
Heritage Dr 37416
Heritage Business Ct 37421
Heritage Landing Dr 37405
Heritage Park Dr 37416
Hetzel Ln 37415
Hewitt Ln 37421
Hibbler Cir 37412
Hickory Ln 37421
Hickory Pl 37404
Hickory St 37404
N Hickory St
100-899 37404
900-3199 37406
S Hickory St
500-1500 37404
1502-2306 37404
2301-2305 37407
2307-2799 37407
2800-2899 37404
2900-3099 37407
Hickory Brook Rd 37421
Hickory Creek Rd 37421
Hickory Hill Dr 37416
Hickory Hollow Ln 37421
Hickory Manor Cir 37421
Hickory Meadow Dr 37421
Hickory Ridge Dr 37421
Hickory Trace Cir 37421
Hickory Valley Rd 37421
Hickory View Ln 37421
Hicks Rd 37411
Hidden Creek Dr 37405
Hidden Forest Dr 37421
Hidden Hollow Dr 37416
Hidden Mountain Dr 37421
Hidden Shadows 37421
Hidden Trail Ln 37421
Higgs St 37406
High St 37403
High Oak Trl 37415
High Ridge Dr 37405
High Top Rd 37415
Highland Ave 37410
Highland Dr 37405
Highland Rd 37415
N & S Highland Park
Ave 37404
Highland Terrace Dr 37415
Highpoint Dr 37415
Highview Cir & Dr 37415
Highwater Trl 37419
Highway 27 37405
Highway 41 37419
Highway 58 37416
Highwood Dr 37415
Hill Rd 37415
Hill Pointe Ln 37405
Hillcrest Ave 37411
Hillcrest Dr 37405
Hillcrest Rd 37405
Hilldale Dr 37411
Hillndale Dr 37419
W Hills Rd 37419
Hillsboro Dr 37412
Hillsdale Cir 37416
Hillside Dr 37411
Hillsview Dr 37405
Hilltop Dr 37411
Hillwood Dr 37411
Hilton Dr 37412
Hiram Ave 37415
Hitchcock Rd 37421
Hixson Pike
900-1999 37405
2000-4399 37415
Holder Ln 37419
Holiday Dr 37412
Holiday Ln 37415
Holiday Hills Cir & Dr 37416
Holland Ln 37421
Hollar Trl 37407
N & S Holly St 37404
Holly Crest Dr 37421

Holly Hedge Ct 37405
Holly Hills Dr & Ln 37421
Holly Oak Ln 37421
Hollyberry Ln 37411
Holmes St 37408
N Holtzclaw Ave
100-999 37404
1200-1399 37406
S Holtzclaw Ave
600-2299 37404
2300-2399 37408
Home Dr 37410
Homecoming Dr 37421
Homer St 37406
Honest St 37421
Honey Ln 37415
Honeycut Ln 37412
Honeysuckle Dr 37411
Honor Cir 37416
Hooker Ave 37419
Hooker Rd
100-899 37410
1000-1299 37407
3800-4199 37410
4800-4999 37407
Hope Ln 37412
Hope Valley Trl 37421
Horse Creek Dr 37405
Hosea Ln 37404
Houser St 37405
Houston St
400-1099 37403
1100-1120 37402
1122-1198 37402
Howard Ave & Cir 37411
Howard Adair Rd 37416
N Howell Ave 37411
S Howell Ave
1-399 37411
400-499 37412
Howell Rd 37411
Howell Mill Dr 37421
Hoyt St
2900-3199 37404
3200-3999 37411
Hudson Rd & St 37405
Huff Pl 37404
Huffaker St 37410
Hughes Ave 37410
Hulsey St 37405
Hummingbird Ln 37412
Hundley Rd 37416
Hunt Ave 37411
Hunt Dr 37421
Hunt Club Rd 37421
Hunter Cir, Ct & Trl 37415
Huntley Ln 37421
Hurricane Creek Rd 37421
Hurricane Manor Trl 37421
Hurricane Ridge Cir &
Rd 37421
Hurst St 37412
Hurstwood Dr 37415
Hydas Ln 37421
Ichabod Ln 37405
Ida Bell Ln 37412
Idlewild Cir & Dr 37411
Igou Crossing Dr 37421
Igou Gap Rd 37421
Igou Place Dr 37421
Independence Ln 37421
Indian Trl 37412
Indigo Glen Ln 37419
Indus Way 37421
Industry Dr 37416
Inglenook Dr 37411
Inlet Harbor Ln 37416
Intermont Cir, Dr & Rd 37415
International Dr 37421
Inwood Ln 37416
Iris Dr & Rd 37412
Iron Wood Trl 37421
Irvin Rd 37416
Isabelle Rd 37411
Isbill Rd 37419
Island Ave 37405

Island Vista Way 37419
Ivy St 37404
Ivy Brook Ct 37421
Jacheri St 37405
Jacherin St 37405
Jackson Ave 37415
Jackson St 37404
Jacobs Ladder 37415
Jadie Ln 37405
James Ave
700-999 37421
2000-2299 37415
James Dr 37416
James Ln 37416
James Allen Trl 37421
Jamestown Rd 37416
Janeview Dr 37421
Jarnigan Ave 37405
Jarnigan Rd 37421
Jarren Ct & Dr 37415
Jarrett Rd 37416
Jarvis Ave 37411
Jasmine St 37421
Jason Dr 37412
Jasper Ln 37411
Jeanaga Trl 37406
Jefferson St 37408
Jeffery Dr 37416
Jeffery Ln 37410
Jenkins Rd 37421
Jennifer Dr & Ln 37421
Jennings Ln 37412
Jenny Lynn Dr 37412
Jerome Ave 37407
Jersey Pike
3000-4199 37421
4200-4900 37416
4902-4998 37416
Jesse Conner Rd 37421
Jim Snow Way 37421
Jocelyn Dr 37416
Jody Ln 37421
Joe Engel Dr 37421
John Arnold St 37412
John Douglass Dr 37421
John Henry Rd 37421
John Ross Rd 37412
John Sims Rd 37412
Johnny St 37406
Johnson Blvd 37415
Johnson St 37408
Johnston Ter 37415
Joiner Rd 37421
Jones St 37411
Joni Cir 37415
Jordan Dr 37421
Jordan Run Rd 37412
Joselin Ln 37415
Josh Ln 37416
Joshua Dr 37412
Joy Ln 37421
Joyce Ave 37415
Juandale Dr 37406
Jubilee Dr 37421
Judd Rd 37406
Judson Ln 37406
Judy Ann Dr 37406
Judys Ln 37419
Julian Rd 37421
Julian Ridge Rd 37421
Julie Ln 37421
Juniper St 37421
Justine Ln 37412
Karr St 37421
Karwill Ln 37412
Kathleen St 37411
Kathryn Ct 37421
Kathys Trl 37419
Kats Kove Ln 37421
Kay Cir 37421
Kayla Cir 37406
Keeble St 37412
Keith St 37405
Kelley Rd 37421
N Kelley St 37404
S Kelley St 37404

Kellys Ferry Ave, Pl &
Rd 37419
Kelso Ln 37421
Kemp Cir & Dr 37411
Kendale Dr 37411
Kenmoor Dr, Ln & Ter 37421
Kenner Ave 37415
Kensington Dr 37415
E & W Kent St 37405
Kenton Dr 37412
Kenton Ridge Cir 37421
Kenwood Ave & Cir 37411
Kenyon Rd 37416
Kerr St 37408
Kesler Ln 37421
Kestrel Ln 37419
Kettering Ct 37405
Kevin Ln 37421
Key West Ave 37412
Keystone Cir 37421
Kildare St 37415
Kilmer St
300-699 37404
800-999 37406
Kimberly Ann Ln 37421
Kimbro St 37415
King St 37403
NE King St 37421
King Arthur Rd 37421
King Court Ln 37421
Kings Rd 37416
Kings Cove Ln 37416
Kings Lake Ct 37416
Kings Point Rd 37416
Kingsbridge Rd 37416
Kingsley Ct 37421
Kingston St 37415
Kingwood Cir & Dr 37412
Kinser Cir 37421
Kinsey Dr 37421
Kippy Dr 37421
Kirby Ave 37404
Kirkland Ave 37410
Kirkman Rd 37421
Knickerbocker Ave 37405
Knoll Creek Cir 37415
Knollwood Dr & Ter 37415
Knollwood Hill Dr 37415
Koblentz Cir 37406
Koons Rd 37412
Krijen Ct 37421
Kyle St 37404
La Ln 37412
La Hugh St 37406
La Porte Dr 37415
Labeling Way 37419
Labrea Dr 37421
Ladd Ave & Ln 37405
Lady Slipper Rd 37421
Laguana Dr 37416
Laird Ln 37415
Lake Crest Cir 37416
Lake Haven Cir, Dr &
Ln 37416
Lake Hills Cir 37416
Lake Mist Dr 37421
Lake Resort Dr & Ter 37415
Lake Villa Ln 37416
Lake Vista Dr 37416
Lakeland Dr 37416
Lakeshore Dr
4700-4799 37415
6800-7299 37416
Lakeshore Ln 37415
Lakeshore Pkwy 37416
Lakeshore Ter 37415
Lamar Ave 37415
Lamon Rd 37416
Lamont Ln 37415
Lancaster Ave & Cir 37415
Lancer Ln 37421
Land St 37412
Lanier Ln 37415
Lanoir Cir & St 37412
Lanoka St 37405
Lansdell Rd 37412

Lantana Ln 37416
Lantern Ridge Ln 37421
Lara Ln 37416
Laramie Cir 37421
N & S Larchmont Ave 37411
Laredo Ave & Ct 37412
Lark Ln 37415
Larkin Ave 37411
Larkwood Ln 37421
Larry Dr 37411
Larry Ln 37412
Las Lomas Dr 37421
Latimore St 37406
Latta St 37406
Launcelot Rd 37421
Laura St 37406
Laurel Dr 37415
Laurel Ln 37412
Laurel Ridge Rd 37416
Laurelton Dr 37421
Laurelton Creek Ln 37421
Laurelwood Dr 37412
Laverne Dr 37421
Lavonia Ave 37415
Lawn St 37405
Lawn Street Pl 37405
Lawrence Rd 37405
Laws Ave 37411
Lawson St 37415
Lawton St 37415
Layfield Rd 37412
Lazard St 37412
Le Clercq Dr 37412
Lea Rd 37421
Leann Cir 37406
Learning Ln 37411
Learning Tree Ln 37415
Leavitt St 37408
E & W Leawood Ave 37415
Ledford St 37411
Lee Ave
3300-3399 37419
5300-5499 37410
Lee Hwy 37421
Lee Pkwy W 37421
Lee St 37412
Lee Parkway Dr 37421
Leemont Dr 37421
Leesburg Ct 37421
Legacy Park Ct 37421
Legends Way 37421
Lela Ln 37421
Lemon Tree Ln 37421
Lennox Ct 37421
Lenny Ln 37421
Lerch St 37411
Leroy Ln 37421
Leslie Ln 37411
Leslie Dell Ln 37421
Lester Ln 37421
Levi Rd 37415
Levi Cemetery Rd 37415
Lewis St 37404
Lexington St 37405
Liberty St 37405
Lifestyle Way 37421
Lightfoot Mill Rd
3807A-3807B 37406
2900-4099 37406
4100-4199 37416
Lilac Ave 37419
Lilac Ln 37411
Lillian Ct & Ln 37411
Lincoln St 37404
Lindberg Ave 37408
Lindcrest Cir 37415
Linden St 37405
Linden Hall Rd 37415
Lindsay Ave 37421
Lindsay Ct 37403
Lindsay St
200-699 37403
700-1099 37402
Line St
600-699 37411
700-1199 37404

Linear Ln 37409
Liner Ln 37421
Link Rd 37405
Linton Ave 37416
Lionheart Ln 37415
Lisa Dr 37412
Lisa Gaye Ln 37421
Live Oak Ln 37411
Lloyd Ln 37415
Lockhart Ln 37412
Lockington Ln 37416
Locksley Cir & Ln 37416
Lockwood Cir 37415
Lockwood Dr 37415
Lockwood St 37406
Lockwood Ter 37415
Loftis St 37406
Lois Ln 37416
Lolita Ln 37421
Lomnick St 37410
Lone Hill Rd 37416
Long Dr 37421
Long St
1500-2899 37408
2900-2999 37410
Long Street Aly 37408
Longholm Ct 37405
Longview Dr 37409
Longview Rd 37421
Lonsdale Dr 37411
Lookaway Trl 37406
Lookout St 37403
Lookout High St 37419
Lookout Lake Rd 37419
Lookout Mountain Blvd 37419
Loriven Dr 37411
Lorivend Dr 37411
Lost Mound Dr 37406
W Lottie Ln 37416
Louise Ave 37412
N Lovell Ave 37411
S Lovell Ave
1-399 37411
400-799 37412
Lovell Field Loop 37421
Lowell St 37415
Lower Craven Ter 37409
Lower Cravens Ter 37409
Lullwater Rd 37405
Luna Ln 37411
Lundy Ln 37412
Lupton Dr 37415
N & S Lyerly St 37404
Lynchburg Ave 37410
Lynda Cir & Dr 37405
Lyndhurst Dr 37405
Lyndon Ave 37415
Lynette Ct 37421
Lynnbrook Ave 37404
Lynnbrook Cir 37415
Lynncrest Dr 37411
N Lynncrest Dr 37411
N Lynncrest Ter 37416
S Lynncrest Ter 37416
Lynnland Ter 37411
Lynnolen Ln 37415
Lynnstone Dr 37405
Lynnwood Ave 37409
Lytle St 37405
Mabel St 37403
Mabry Pl 37415
Mac Ln 37421
N & S Mack Smith Rd 37412
Mackey Ave 37421
Mackey Branch Dr 37421
Madison St 37408
Madonna Ave 37412
Mae Dell Rd 37421
Magic Mountain Dr 37421
Magical Vw 37421
Magnolia Aly & St 37403
Magnolia Lake Dr 37421
Magnolia Leaf Ln 37421
Magnolia Vale Dr 37419
Mahala Ln 37421
Maiden Dr 37412

E Main St
1-1299 37408
1300-2899 37404
W Main St
2-24 37408
26-399 37408
400-1099 37402
Main Street Ext 37404
Majestic Hill Dr 37421
Malinta Ln 37416
Mallette Rd 37416
Mana Ln 37412
Manchester Dr 37415
Manilow Ln 37419
E & W Manning St 37405
Manning Cole Rd 37419
Manor Rd 37411
Mansion Cir 37405
Manufacturers Rd 37405
Maple Ln 37411
Maple St 37406
Maple Creek Ln 37411
Maple Hills Way 37406
Maple Street Ct 37402
Maple Terrace Ln 37406
Maple Tree Ln 37421
Maple Valley Dr 37421
Maplewood Ave 37411
Maplewood Dr 37421
Maplewood Ln
3500-3599 37412
7000-7099 37419
Mara Dr 37421
Marco Cir & Ct 37421
Margarita Ln 37412
Maria St 37411
Marietta Ave 37412
Marigold Dr 37421
Marijon Dr 37421
Marimont Dr 37421
Marion Ave 37412
Marion Cir 37415
Mark Ln 37421
Mark Twain Cir 37406
Market St 37402
N Market St 37405
S Market St
1500-2699 37408
2800-3099 37410
Marlboro Ave
1-499 37411
500-1499 37412
Marley Way 37412
Marlin Rd 37411
Marlow Dr 37415
Maromede Ln 37421
Marport Dr 37406
Marshall Ave 37415
Marshall St 37406
Martha Ave 37412
Martin Rd 37415
Martin St 37411
Martin Luther King
Blvd 37402
Mary Anna Dr 37412
Mary Dupre Dr 37421
Mary Hall Ln 37416
Mary Walker Pl 37411
Maryland Cir 37412
Maryland Dr 37412
Maryland St 37405
Marylin Ln 37411
Mason Dr
1-99 37415
3100-3199 37412
Massengale Rd 37419
Massengale Point Rd 37419
Matlock St 37405
Matthews Dr 37412
Maude St 37403
Mauldeth Rd 37415
Max Mountain Ln 37421
Maxwell Rd 37412
May St 37405
Mayfair Ave 37411
Maywood Ln 37416

Mc Kee Valley Trl 37421
Mcabee Ln 37415
Mcarthur Ave 37406
Mcbrien Ln 37419
Mcbrien Rd
1-399 37411
400-2199 37412
Mccahill Rd 37415
Mccall Rd 37412
Mccallie Ave
300-599 37402
600-1046 37403
1048-2851 37404
2853-2899 37404
Mcclure Ter 37415
Mcconnell Ln & St 37404
Mccool Dr 37406
Mccord Ave 37404
Mccutcheon Rd 37421
Mcdade Ln 37405
Mcdonald Dr 37421
Mcdonald Rd 37412
Mcdowell St 37411
Mcfarland Ave 37405
Mcgill Cemetary Rd 37419
Mcgowan Rd 37411
Mchann Dr 37412
Mckeel Ln 37405
Mckendrick Ln 37405
Mckinley St 37412
Mcmillan Row 37409
Mcnabb Rd & Way 37419
Mcnichol Ln 37421
Mcrae St 37406
Mcroy Dr 37405
Meade Cir 37406
Meadow Ln 37406
Meadow St 37405
Meadow Creek Way 37421
Meadow Falls Ln 37419
Meadow Lake Rd 37415
Meadow Stream Loop 37421
E Meadowbrook Dr 37415
W Meadowbrook Dr 37415
Meadowbrook Ln 37411
Meadowbrook Trl 37421
Meadowlark Ln 37421
Meadowlark Trl 37412
Mearain St 37450
Mearaing St 37450
Mee Mee Rd 37421
Meeting Pl 37421
Megan Ct 37421
Melinda Cir & Dr 37416
Melody Ln 37412
Melrose Dr 37421
Melton Dr & Ln 37416
Melville Ave 37412
Melwood Ln 37421
Memorial Dr 37415
Memphis Dr 37415
Menlo St 37411
Merida St 37412
Merlin Dr 37421
Meroney St 37405
Merriam St 37405
Merrill St 37412
Merrimac Cir 37412
Merriman Ave 37415
Merry Weather Dr 37421
Merrydale Dr 37404
Merrywood Ln 37416
Michael Ln 37411
Michelin Ln 37415
Michelle Ave 37412
Michigan Ave 37409
Middle Dr 37416
Midfield Dr 37421
Midland Pike 37411
E Midvale Ave 37415
W Midvale Ave 37405
Midwoode Dr 37411
Mike Edd Ln 37411
Mikemon Dr 37421
Military Rd 37409
Millard Lee Ln 37416

Millbro Cir 37412
Miller Ave 37405
Miller Dr 37411
Milne St 37406
Milton St 37411
Mimbro Ln 37412
Mimosa Cir 37416
Mimosa Dr 37415
Mimosa Trl 37416
Min Tom Dr 37421
Mink Place Dr 37416
Minnekahda Pl, Rd &
Trl 37405
Minor St 37405
Miriam Ln 37421
Misouni St 37402
Misounia St 37402
Mission Ave 37406
Mission Crest Ln 37404
N & S Mission Oaks
Dr 37412
Mission Ridge Oval 37412
Mission View Ave &
Ter 37411
Missionaire Ave 37412
Missionary Rdg 37404
W Mississippi Ave 37405
Misty Ln 37416
Misty Hollow Ln 37421
Misty Mountain Rd &
Trl 37421
Misty Ridge Dr 37416
Misty Way Ln 37421
Mitchell Ave 37408
Mixon St 37405
Mizel Ln 37421
E Ml King Blvd
100-199 37402
200-1099 37403
W Ml King Blvd 37402
Ml King Ct 37403
Moccasin Bend Rd 37405
Mockingbird Dr 37412
Mockingbird Ln 37405
Modern Industries
Pkwy 37419
Money Tree Ln 37405
Monroe St
2200-2399 37406
4100-4199 37412
Montaire Ln 37416
Montcrest Cir & Dr 37416
Monte Vista Dr 37411
Monterey Dr 37411
Montessori Way 37404
Montview Dr 37411
Monya Ln 37421
Moon St 37406
Moonbeam Trl 37421
Moonhollow Ln 37405
Moonstone Rd 37405
N Moore Ln 37411
N Moore Rd 37411
S Moore Rd
1-399 37411
400-1499 37412
Moore St 37411
Mooremont Ter 37411
Moorgate Dr 37421
Moreview Rd 37412
Morgan Ave 37404
E Morgan Ln 37415
N Morgan Ln 37415
Morin Rd 37421
Morning Grove Dr 37421
Morning Shadows Dr 37421
Morningside Dr 37404
Morris Ln 37421
Morris Glen Ct 37421
Morris Hill Rd 37421
Morrison Springs Rd 37415
Morton Cir & Dr 37415
Mosley Cir 37412
N Moss Ave 37419
S Moss Ave 37419
Moss Dr 37411

Moss Rd 37406
Moss St 37411
Mosswood Ln 37421
Mossy Oaks Dr 37406
Mount Belvoir Dr 37412
Mount Olivet Dr 37412
Mount Vernon Ave &
Cir 37405
E Mountain Ln 37421
Mountain Bluff Ln 37419
Mountain Breeze Dr 37421
Mountain Creek Rd
700-1299 37405
3100-5499 37415
Mountain Dale Ln 37421
Mountain Grove Dr 37421
Mountain Ridge Rd 37405
Mountain Shade Dr 37421
Mountain Shadows Dr 37421
Mountain Top Rd 37419
Mountain View Ave 37415
Mountain View Ct 37409
Mountain View Dr
3200-3399 37419
3600-3699 37406
Mueller Ave 37406
Muirfield Ln 37416
Mulberry St 37404
Munro Rd 37415
Murphy Rd 37416
Murray Hills Dr 37416
Murray Lake Ln 37416
Murray Ln Pvt 37421
Museum St 37406
Myra Ave 37412
Myrtle Ave
1-99 37419
2000-2099 37412
Myrtle Pl 37419
Myrtle St 37408
Mystic Trl 37415
Mystic Brook Ct 37421
Nakwisa Dr 37421
Nandena Dr 37411
Napier Rd 37421
Narragansette Ave 37415
N Natchez Rd 37405
National Ave 37404
Nautical Way 37416
Navajo Dr 37411
Needle Rush Ln 37415
Neighborhood Rd 37421
Nellie St 37404
Nelson Rd 37421
Nest Trl 37415
Nestledown Ct 37419
New Castle Ln 37421
New England Dr 37421
New Jersey Ave 37406
New York Ave 37406
E & W Newberry St 37415
Newby St 37402
Newell Ave 37404
Newport Dr 37412
Newton St 37406
Nichols Rd 37419
Nicklin Dr 37421
Night Hawk Rd 37421
Night Owl Ct 37419
Nile Rd 37421
Nimitz St 37406
Nip Way 37421
Noah St 37406
Noah Reid Rd
7200-7499 37421
7500-7799 37416
Noll St 37405
Nonova Ln 37415
Norcross Rd 37415
Norfolk Green Cir 37421
Norma Dr 37412
Normal Ave 37405
Norman Ln 37405
North Ave 37405
North Ter 37411
Northbriar Cir & Ln 37406

Northbridge Ln 37405
Northgate Mall & Park 37415
Northgate Commercial
Ctr 37415
Northgate Mall Dr 37415
Northgate Park Ln 37415
Northland Ln 37416
Northside Dr 37421
Northumberland Ln 37421
Northview Ave 37412
Northway Ln 37406
Northwind Dr 37416
Norwood Ave 37415
Notre Dame Ave 37412
Nottingham Dr 37412
Nottinghill 37405
Nowlin Ln 37421
Nurick Dr 37415
Nye Cir 37405
Nye Dr 37411
Oak Dr 37421
Oak Pl 37404
Oak St
100-199 37415
300-1199 37403
1401-1497 37404
1499-2799 37404
3000-3099 37419
Oak Burr Dr 37419
Oak Haven Dr 37421
Oak Hill Rd 37416
Oak Knoll Dr 37415
Oak Leaf Ln 37421
Oak Ridge Dr 37415
Oak Shadows Dr 37421
Oak Tree Dr 37415
Oak Valley Ln 37421
Oak View Dr 37421
Oakdale Ave 37412
Oaken Trl 37421
Oakhill Dr 37415
Oakland Ave 37410
Oakland Ter 37415
Oakmont St 37415
Oakwood Ave 37415
Oakwood Cir 37415
Oakwood Dr 37416
Oakwood Ln 37405
Obar Dr 37419
Obey St 37404
Observation Ln 37421
Occonechee Cir & Trl 37415
Ochs Hwy 37409
Ocoee St
2103A-2103B 37406
Ogletree Ave 37421
Ogrady Dr 37419
Ohio Ave 37406
Ohls Ave 37410
Olan Mills Dr 37421
Old Trl 37415
Old Birds Mill Rd 37421
Old Britain Cir 37421
Old Champion Rd 37416
Old Cleveland Pike 37421
Old Dayton Pike 37415
Old Elder Mountain
Rd 37419
Old Harrison Pike 37416
Old Hickory Valley Rd 37416
Old Lee Hwy 37421
Old Mission Rd 37411
Old Mountain Rd 37409
Old Pineville Rd 37405
Old Ringgold Rd
1400-1498 37404
1500-3199 37404
3200-3699 37412
Old Signal Mountain
Rd 37405
Old Stage Rd 37421
Old Stone Trl 37421
Old Tassel Trl 37421
Old Wauhatchie Pike
1700-2199 37409
2400-2699 37419

Olde Towne Ln 37415
Oleary St 37410
Olive St 37406
Oliver St 37405
Olmstead Dr 37412
Omalee Ave 37411
Oneal St 37403
Ontario St 37415
Opal Dr 37416
Orangewood Ave 37404
N Orchard Knob Ave
101-197 37404
199-899 37404
900-3599 37406
S Orchard Knob Ave
301-697 37404
699-2699 37404
2700-3499 37407
Orchard Valley Dr 37421
Orchard View Ave 37415
Orchid Ln 37409
Orear St 37406
Orgain Dr 37411
Oriole Dr 37411
Orlando Ave 37412
Orlando Dr 37415
Orlin Dr 37411
Ormand Dr 37415
Orr St 37405
Orton St 37406
Osborne Dr 37421
Osprey Way 37419
Oswego St 37406
Outlook Cir & Ln 37419
Over St 37411
Overbridge Ln 37405
Overlook Dr 37411
Overman St 37405
Overnite Dr 37421
Overton Dr 37415
Oweda Ter 37415
Oxford Rd 37405
W Oxford Rd 37415
Ozark Cir, Pl & Rd 37415
Paces Ferry Xing 37421
Paden Ln 37411
Palermo Dr 37421
Palmetto St 37403
Palms Ct 37421
Palo Verde Dr 37411
Palo Verde Ter 37404
Pan Gap Cir & Rd 37419
Panavista Ln 37421
Panorama Dr 37421
Paragon Dr 37415
Parham Dr 37412
Paris Metz Rd 37421
Park Ave
600-1099 37403
1400-1499 37408
Park Dr 37421
N & S Parkdale Ave 37411
Parker Ln 37419
Parkside Ln 37416
Parkview Dr 37411
Parkway Cir 37411
Parkway Dr 37406
Parkwood Ave 37404
Parlem Dr 37415
Parmenas Ln 37405
Passons Rd 37415
Patrick Pl 37421
Patten Pkwy 37402
Patten Chapel Rd 37419
Patterson Rd 37421
Patton Dr 37412
Patton Edwards Dr 37412
Paula Ln 37415
Pauline Cir 37421
Paulmar Dr 37415
Paw Trl 37416
Pawnee Trl 37411
Payne Rd
1900-1999 37421
18600-18699 37419
Peace St 37415

Peach Rd 37406
Peachbloom Dr 37411
Peachtree Rd & St 37404
Peak St 37405
Pearl St 37406
Pebble Creek Rd 37421
Pecan Springs Cir 37421
Peck Dr 37412
Peckinpaugh Dr 37416
Peeples St 37403
Peerless Ave 37405
Peggy Ln 37404
Pelican Dr 37416
Pembrook Ln 37421
Pennsylvania Ave
2900-2999 37406
3700-3999 37409
Peppermill Rd 37411
Perch Pass 37421
Peregrine Pl 37419
Perimeter Dr 37421
Perry St
1101-1199 37421
3500-3699 37411
Pershing Rd 37421
Persimmon Ln 37406
Peterson Dr 37421
Petty Rd 37421
Pheasant Ln 37421
Phelps St 37412
Phils Dr 37421
Phoenix Ave 37411
Phyllis Ln 37421
Pickering Ave 37415
Picture Ridge Dr 37421
Piedmont Cir 37415
Pierce Ave 37403
Pilot Pt 37416
Pin Oak Dr & Ter 37411
Pine Dr 37421
Pine St
600-600 37402
602-899 37402
4100-4499 37406
Pine Bluff Dr 37412
Pine Breeze Rd
1700-1799 37405
1800-1899 37415
Pine Brow Trl 37421
Pine Burr Ln 37419
Pine Cone Ln 37415
Pine Forest Ln 37415
Pine Grove Trl 37421
Pine Hurst View Ct 37416
Pine Manor Dr 37421
Pine Needles Trl 37421
Pine Ridge Rd 37405
Pine Top Ct 37412
Pine View Ln 37416
Pinecrest Dr 37421
Pinehurst Ave
100-399 37415
5900-6099 37421
Pinelawn Ave 37411
Pinelawn Dr 37421
Pinellas Ln 37412
Pineville Rd 37405
Pinewood Ave 37411
Pinewood Dr 37421
Pinewood Ter 37411
Pink Heather Trl 37415
Pinnacle Ln 37415
Pioneer Dr & Ln 37419
Pioneer Ridge Trl 37412
Pippin St 37415
Pirola St 37410
Pirtle Ave 37412
Pisgah Ave 37411
Plantation Dr 37416
Plaxco Dr 37421
Players Ct 37416
Players Run Ln 37416
Plaza Cir 37419
Pleasant St 37412
Plumwood Rd 37411
Plymouth St 37421

Poindexter Ave 37412
Point South Ln 37421
Pointe Center Dr 37421
Polk St
1300-2099 37408
3700-5299 37410
Polo Pl 37405
Polo Field Rd 37419
Polymer Dr 37421
Pontiac Dr 37412
Pope Dr 37404
Poplar St 37402
Poplar Street Ct 37402
Poralen Rd 37412
Poralent Rd 37412
Portland St 37406
Portview Cir 37421
Portview Pl 37404
Poss Dr 37408
Post Ave 37409
Potomac Dr 37421
Potter Ln 37415
Potts Rd 37416
Power Aly 37402
Power Corporation Dr 37405
Powers Ct 37416
Ppoole St 37415
Prater Rd 37412
Prayer Ln 37404
Premier Dr 37421
Premium Dr 37415
Preservation Dr 37416
Preserve Dr 37416
Preston Cir 37421
Preston St 37404
Price St 37409
Priceless Vw 37415
Prigmore Rd 37412
Primrose Ln 37421
Priscilla Dr 37421
Probasco Pl 37411
Prosperity Ln 37421
Provence St
3300-3899 37411
6100-6199 37421
Pulaski St 37410
Pumpkin Pie Ln 37409
Purple Hill Dr 37405
Pyron Ln 37412
N & S Quail Ln 37415
Quail Hollow Cir 37416
Quail Mountain Dr 37421
Quail Nest Cir 37421
Quail Run Dr 37421
Quarry Vw 37415
Queen Aire Ln 37415
Queen Ann Ln 37415
Queen Mary Ln 37415
Queens Dr 37406
Queens Rd 37416
Queens Lace Trl 37421
Quiet Creek Trl 37406
Quiet Pond Dr 37415
Quinn Adams St 37410
Quintus Loop 37421
Raccoon Trl 37419
Raccoon Mtn Rd 37419
Racoon Mountain Dr 37419
Radmoor Cir, Dr & Ln 37421
Rae Trl 37406
Rainbow Cir 37405
Rainbow Springs Dr 37416
Raines Ln 37419
Raintree Ln 37421
Ramona St 37405
Ranch Hills Rd 37421
Randolph Cir 37406
Randolph St 37404
Ranger Ln 37416
Rankin St 37421
Raulston St 37404
Raven Ln 37415
Raven Wolf Rd 37421
Ravencrest Dr 37421
E Ravenwood Dr 37415
Rawlings St 37406

Ray Jo Cir 37421
Raymond Ct 37421
Read Ave 37408
Reads Lake Rd 37415
Rebecca Dr 37412
Red Oak Dr 37415
Red Robin Ln 37421
Red Tail Ln 37421
Redding Rd 37415
Redlands Dr 37416
Redwood Dr 37421
Reece St 37404
Rees Ave 37411
Reeves Ave 37412
Reflecting Dr 37415
Regal Dr 37415
Regency Ct 37421
Reggie White Blvd
1600-1799 37402
1800-1999 37408
Reid Dr 37421
Remington Ct 37421
Renaissance Ct 37419
Renas Ter 37421
Reneau Way 37412
Renezet Dr 37416
Reserve Way 37421
Resource Dr 37416
Restoration Dr 37421
Reunion Dr 37421
Revere Cir 37421
Revington St 37406
Rhoda Ln 37416
Rhodes Rd 37421
Rhodes Farm Way 37421
Richard Ave 37404
Richmond Ln 37421
Ricky Dr 37411
Ridge Ave 37404
E Ridge Ave 37412
E Ridge Dr 37412
Ridge Rd 37411
Ridge St 37406
Ridge Crest Dr 37406
Ridgecrest Cir 37406
Ridgefield Cir 37412
Ridgemont Dr 37404
Ridgeside Rd 37411
Ridgestone Trl 37421
Ridgetop Dr 37421
Ridgevale Ave 37411
Ridgeway Dr 37415
Ridgeway Ter 37405
E Ridgewood Ave 37415
W Ridgewood Ave 37415
Ridgewood Dr 37404
Riding Trail Way 37405
Riggins Dr 37421
Righton Ln 37416
Ringgold Rd 37412
Rio Grande Rd 37421
Rivendell Ln 37421
River St 37405
S River St 37402
River Bend Rd 37419
River Canyon Rd 37405
River Canyon Trl 37419
River Forest Trl 37419
River Glade Dr 37416
River Gorge Dr 37419
E, S & W River Hills Cir
& Dr 37415
River Ridge Dr 37416
River Run Dr 37416
River Terminal Rd 37406
River View Oaks Rd 37405
Rivercrest Dr 37415
Riverfront Pkwy
100-1699 37402
1800-1999 37408
N Rivermont Cir, Pl &
Rd 37415
Riverport Rd 37406
Riverside Ave 37405
Riverside Dr
900-998 37403
1000-3299 37406
Riverside Ln 37406
Riverview Rd 37405
Rivervista Dr 37405
Riviera Rd 37421
Roanoke Ave
500-600 37404
602-898 37404
900-3099 37406
Robbins St 37404
Robbinsdale Ln 37415
Roberts Pl 37404
Roberts Rd 37416
Roberts St 37404
Robin Dr
100-999 37405
6800-6899 37421
Robin Ln 37421
Robin Glenn Dr 37421
Robin Roost Trl 37421
Robins Crest Rd 37415
Robinson Dr 37421
Robinwood Dr 37416
Rockford Ln 37411
Rockmeade Dr 37411
Rockshire Ln 37421
Rockway Dr 37411
Rocky Trl 37421
Rocky Cove Dr 37421
Rocky River Rd 37416
Rocky Shadows 37421
Rodeo Dr 37421
Rogers Rd 37411
Rolling Ridge Ct & Dr 37421
Rollingwood Dr 37406
Rondaboo Dr 37419
Roosevelt Rd 37412
Roper St 37412
Rosalee Ter 37416
Rosalind Ln 37416
Rose Cir 37419
Rose St 37412
Rose Ter 37404
Rosebrook Dr 37421
Rosebud Dr 37412
Rosedale Rd 37421
Roselawn Dr 37421
Rosemary Cir & Dr 37416
Rosemere Way 37421
Rosemont Dr 37411
Rosewood St 37405
Rossville Ave 37408
Rossville Blvd
2200-2599 37408
2600-2799 37404
2800-5099 37407
Rostis Ln 37421
Rotary Dr 37416
Rowden St 37404
Rowe Rd 37411
Rowewood Dr 37421
Roy St 37409
Royal Dr 37421
Royal Fern Trl 37421
Royal Mountain Dr 37421
Royal Shadows Dr 37421
Rubio St 37406
Ruby St 37406
S Rugby Pl 37412
N Runyan Dr 37405
Russell Ave & St 37405
Ruth St 37405
Ryan St 37404
Sable Dr 37416
Saddlebrook Dr 37405
Sadler Pl 37421
Safari Dr 37421
Safehaven Ct 37406
Sailmaker Cir 37416
Saint Elmo Ave
3000-3301 37408
3303-3399 37408
3400-5899 37409
Saint James Ave 37412
Saint Johns Ln 37421
Saint Lawrence Rd 37421

Saint Lucie Ct 37421
N Saint Marks Ave 37411
S Saint Marks Ave
1-399 37411
400-1199 37412
Saint Paul St 37404
Saint Thomas St 37412
Saluda St 37406
Samoyed Trl 37405
San Hsi Dr 37412
N Sanctuary Rd 37421
S Sanctuary Rd 37412
Sanders Dr 37415
Sanders Rd 37409
Sandpiper Ln 37421
Sanford Ave 37411
Santeelah St 37415
Sapulpa St 37406
Saratoga Ln 37421
Sargent Daly Dr 37421
Sargent Quick Dr 37421
Sasha Ln 37416
Sawgrass Ct 37416
Sawmill Trl 37415
Sawyer St 37405
S Scenic Hwy 37409
Scenic Waters Ln 37419
Schmidt Rd 37412
Schofield Ave 37412
School Dr 37411
School St 37403
Scott St 37412
Scrapeshin Trl 37421
Scruggs Rd 37412
Scruggs St 37403
Searle St 37406
Seasons Dr 37421
Secret Garden Dr 37421
Sedgewood Dr 37416
Sells Dr 37412
Selma St 37415
Semi Cir 37415
Seminary St 37410
N Seminole Dr 37411
S Seminole Dr
1-499 37411
500-1799 37412
Seminole Crest Ln 37412
Seneca Ave 37409
Sequoia Dr 37411
Severin Rd 37411
Sewanee Dr 37412
Shadow Pkwy 37421
Shadow Bend Cir 37421
Shadow Crossing Ln 37421
Shadow Point Cir 37421
Shadow Ridge Dr 37421
Shadow Valley Cir 37421
Shadow Walk Dr 37421
Shadowlawn Dr
3200-3300 37412
3301-3399 37404
3302-3598 37412
3401-3599 37412
E Shadowlawn Dr 37404
W Shadowlawn Dr 37404
Shady Cir 37405
Shady Cv 37421
Shady Dr 37412
Shady Ln 37404
Shady Branch Dr 37415
Shady Crest Dr 37415
Shady Fork Rd 37421
Shady Hollow Ln 37416
Shady Rest Rd 37421
Shady Ridge Ln 37405
Shady Vail Ln 37421
Shadyway Ln 37416
Shale St 37421
Shallowford Rd
1-199 37404
200-4799 37411
5900-6051 37421
6050-6050 37422
6052-8298 37421
6053-8299 37421
Shallowford Village Dr 37421
Shallowmeade Ln 37421
Shamrock Dr 37406
Shannon Ave 37411
Shanty Lake Dr 37419
Sharon Cir 37405
Sharondale Rd 37412
Sharp St 37404
Sharron Dr 37421
Shauff Pl 37409
Shaw Ave 37421
Shawhan Rd & Ter 37411
Shawnee Cir & Trl 37411
Shawtee Ln 37416
Shearer Cove Rd 37405
Shelborne Dr 37416
Shelby Cir 37412
Shenandoah Dr 37421
Shepherd Rd 37421
Shepherd View Cir &
Dr 37421
Sherida Ln 37416
Sheridan Ave 37406
Sheridan Ct 37406
Sheridan Rd 37412
Sherlin Dr 37412
Sherman St 37406
Sherwood Ave 37404
Sherwood Dr 37412
Shiloh Ln 37421
Shingle Rd 37409
Shinnecock Trl 37421
Shipp Ave 37410
Shirl Jo Ln 37412
Shirley Dr 37405
Shoals Ln 37416
Sholar Ave & Ct 37406
Shore Manor Ln 37416
Shoreline Dr 37416
Shorewood Dr 37416
Short St 37416
Shugart St 37415
Side Creek Way 37421
Siener Ln 37411
Signal Hills Dr 37405
Signal Mountain Rd 37405
Signal Shadow Ln 37405
Signal View St 37415
Silvels Ln 37409
Silverdale Rd 37421
Simmons Dr 37406
Simpson Ave 37415
Sims Dr 37415
Sims St 37406
Sioux Trl 37411
Sir John Ct 37421
Siskin Dr & Plz 37403
Skillet Gap Rd 37419
Skurlock Rd 37411
Skylark Trl 37416
Skyline Dr 37421
Skyview Dr 37416
Slater Rd 37412
Slayton Ave 37410
Slayton St 37408
Sleepy Hollow Rd
1100-1199 37419
3400-3599 37415
Sliger Cir 37415
Small St 37412
N & S Smith St 37412
Smittys Cir 37415
Smokerise Ln 37421
Smokewood Trl 37421
Snow St 37405
Social Cir 37415
Solitude Dr 37416
Solomon Seal Trl 37415
Somerville Ave 37405
Sonia Ln 37421
South St 37411
South Ter 37412
Southbridge Ln 37405
Southern St 37406
Southernwood Dr 37421
Southview St 37405

Spann Ct 37416
Spears Ave 37405
Spellman Rd 37421
Spencer Ave 37421
Spiderwebb Way 37415
Spindle Ct 37421
Spriggs St 37412
Spring St
100-199 37405
200-399 37403
400-599 37405
Spring Creek Rd
100-499 37411
900-1499 37412
Spring Garden Ln 37411
Spring Lake Ct & Rd 37415
Spring Valley Dr 37412
Spring Valley Ln 37415
Spring View Ln 37421
Springvale Rd 37412
Springview Dr 37421
Spruce St 37404
Spyglass Ct 37416
Squab Ln 37421
Stable View Cir 37405
Stagg Rd 37415
Standifer Dr 37416
Standifer Chase Dr 37421
Standifer Gap Rd 37421
Standifer Hills Dr 37421
Standifer Oaks Rd 37421
Stanfiel St 37406
Stanley Ave 37421
Starview Ln 37419
State St 37407
State Line Rd 37412
W State Line Rd 37407
Steeplechase Dr 37421
Stein Dr 37421
Stellar Vw 37405
Stephen Ln 37421
Stephens Rd 37419
Stephens St 37406
Sterling Ave 37405
Sterling Oaks Ln 37421
Stillwood Ln 37421
Stimpson Dr 37411
Stivers St 37405
Stockton Dr 37416
Stone Cir 37411
Stone St 37412
Stone Crest Cir 37421
Stone Mist Ln 37421
Stone Tip Ln 37421
Stone Trace Dr 37421
Stonebrook Dr 37415
Stonehenge Dr 37421
Stones River Rd 37421
Stoneway Ln 37421
Stoney Brook Ln 37415
Stoney Creek Dr 37421
Stoney Mountain Dr 37421
Storage Rd 37421
Stormy Hollow Rd 37421
Stratman Cir 37421
Stratton Place Dr 37421
Strawberry Ln 37405
Stringer St 37405
Stringers Ridge Rd 37405
Stuart St 37406
Stuart Ter 37415
E & W Stump St 37412
Suck Creek Ln & Rd 37405
Sullivan Ave 37412
Summer St 37405
Summertown Ct 37421
Summit Ave 37415
Summitt Ave 37412
Sumter Ave 37406
Sun Crest Ln 37421
Sunalay Ln 37421
Sunbeam Ave 37411
Sunbury Ave 37411
Sunflower Ln 37416
Sunlight Ln 37421
Sunny Dell Cir & Ln 37412

Sunny Shore Ln 37416
Sunnyfield Ln 37412
Sunnyside Ave 37409
Sunnyside Dr 37411
Sunray Dr 37412
Sunrise Ln 37411
Sunrise Ter 37412
Sunset Ave 37411
Sunset Rd 37405
Sunset Ter 37404
Sunset Mountain Dr 37421
Surry Cir 37421
Susan Carol Ln 37421
Sussex Ln 37421
Swallow Ln 37421
Swan Rd 37416
Swansons Ridge Rd 37421
Sweet St 37412
Sweet Pecan Ln 37421
N Sweetbriar Ave 37411
S Sweetbriar Ave
1-499 37411
500-799 37412
Sweetbriar Cir 37412
Sweetland Dr 37415
Swope Dr 37412
Sydney St 37408
Sylvan Ave 37411
Sylvan Dr 37411
Sylvan St 37405
Sylvia Cir 37416
Sylvia Trl 37421
Tacoa Ave & Cir 37411
Tacoma Ave 37415
Taft Ave 37408
Tag Rd 37416
Talatha St 37406
Tall Oak Ln 37421
Tall Pine Ln 37421
Tall Timber Trl 37415
Talladega Ave & Dr 37421
Talley Rd & Ter 37411
Tamara Ln 37421
Tamarack Cir & Trl 37412
Tampa St 37405
Tanager Cir & Ct 37412
Tanaka Trl 37404
Tanglewood Dr 37415
Tanner St 37410
Tarlton Ave 37410
Tarpon Trl 37416
Tatum Ln 37405
Tatum Rd 37421
Taylor St 37406
Teakwood Dr 37416
Tee Pee Dr 37406
Tee Way Cir 37416
Teeside Rd 37421
Teletha Ln 37415
Ten Oaks Dr 37412
Tennessee Ave 37409
Tennessee St 37419
Tennga Ln 37421
Terminal Rd 37405
Terra Verde Dr 37421
Terra Vista Dr 37416
Terrell St 37411
Terri Lynn Dr 37421
Terry Ct 37411
Test Dr 37421
Texas Ave 37409
Textile Ln 37419
Thelmeta Ave 37421
Thollar Ave 37410
Thollari Ave 37410
Thomas Ave 37409
Thomas St 37405
Thompson St 37405
Thornton Ave 37411
Through St 37411
Thrush Hollow Ln 37421
Thrushwood Dr 37415
Thueler St 37415
Thunderbird Dr 37406
Tiber Rd 37421
Tiffany Ln 37412

Tiftonia Dr 37419
Tiftonia View Rd 37419
Tiger Lily Trl 37415
Tiktin Dr 37415
Timber Knoll Dr 37421
Timbercrest Ln 37421
Timberlane Trl 37421
Timberlog Dr 37421
Tinsley Pl 37404
Tipton Ln 37419
Tom Weathers Dr 37415
Tom Wilson Trl 37412
Tomahawk Trl 37411
Tomben Ln 37416
Tombras Ave 37412
Topsail Greens Dr 37416
Torey Ct 37421
Touch Me Not Trl 37415
Towerway Dr 37406
Townsend Rd 37421
Traditions Dr 37415
Trafalgar Ct 37421
Trailer World Rd 37419
Trailhead Dr 37415
Trails End St 37415
Trailwood Dr 37416
Trammel Ln 37419
Tremont Pl & St 37405
Trenton St 37415
Tressie Ln 37416
Trewhitt St 37405
Triangle Farm Rd 37421
Tricia Dr 37416
Triple Crown Ct 37421
Triple Oaks Ln 37416
Tristram Rd 37421
Truman Ave 37412
Tucker St 37405
Tugaloo St 37406
N & S Tulip Ave 37419
Tunnel Blvd
1-1599 37411
1600-2899 37406
Tupelo Ct 37406
Turkey Foot Trl 37416
Turntable Rd 37421
Tuskegee Blvd 37421
N & S Tuxedo Ave & Cir 37411
Twin Brook Dr 37421
Ty Hi Dr 37421
Tyne Ridge Rd 37421
Tyner Rd 37421
Tyner Crossing Dr 37421
Unaka St 37415
Union Ave 37404
Union Sq 37402
Union Springs Rd 37415
University Pl & St 37403
Up The Creek Rd 37405
Upchurch Rd 37416
Upshaw Dr 37416
Uptain Rd 37411
Urban Trl 37405
Usher Dr 37410
Vaden Dr 37421
Vaden Village Dr 37421
Valentine Cir 37405
Valerian Dr 37415
Valley Dr & Trl 37415
Valley Bridge Dr & Rd 37415
Valley High Ln 37415
Valley View Dr 37415
Van Buren St 37415
Van Dyke St 37405
Van Ness Rd 37421
Van Winkle Cir 37415
Vance Ave 37404
Vance Cir 37421
Vance Rd 37421
Vannoy Dr 37411
Vantage Pt 37405
Vaughn Rd 37411
Velma St 37405
Vera Ln 37421
Vermont Ave 37404

Verona Dr 37421
Vester Ln 37412
Victoria St 37415
Victory Cir & St 37411
E View Dr 37404
Villa Green Ct 37416
Villa Rica Cir 37421
Village Lake Cir 37412
Vincent Rd 37416
Vine St
300-999 37403
1500-1698 37404
1700-2599 37404
Vinewood Dr 37406
Vineyard Ln 37421
Viola Dr 37415
Virginia Ave 37409
Vista Dr 37411
Vista Hills Dr 37416
Viston Ave 37411
Volkswagen Dr 37416
Vols Ln 37419
Volunteer Dr 37416
Vreeland St 37415
Vulcan Ln 37416
Waconda Ct, Ln & Rd 37416
Waconda Shore Dr 37416
Wade Dr 37412
Waheela Dr 37404
Wakerobin Dr 37412
Wakulla Dr 37412
Walden Ave 37421
Walker Rd 37421
Walker St
200-299 37421
1600-2199 37404
Wall St 37403
Walnut St
1-399 37403
500-799 37402
4200-4399 37406
Walsh Rd 37405
Walthall Ave 37407
Wando Dr 37412
Warbler Ln 37421
Warlick St 37421
Warren Dr & Pl 37419
Washington Cir 37416
Washington St 37408
Watauga St 37404
Water St 37410
Waterbury Ln 37421
Waterfront Ct & Dr 37419
Waterhaven Dr 37406
Waterhouse St 37412
Waterthrush Ln 37419
N & S Watkins St 37404
Watson Rd 37415
Watts Ave 37421
Wauchula St 37406
Wauhatchie Pike 37419
Wayne Ave 37405
Weather View Dr 37421
Weaver St 37412
Webb Cir 37415
Webb Rd 37416
Webb Oaks Ct 37416
Wedgewood Dr & Ln 37421
Weeks St 37405
Weigelia Dr 37416
Weldon Dr 37412
Wellington Ln 37421
Wells St 37405
Wellworth Ave 37412
Wentworth Ave 37412
Werner St 37415
Wert St 37405
Wessex Ln 37421
West Ave 37410
Westbridge Ln 37405
Wester St 37406
Westin Ct 37421
Westminister Circle Dr 37416
Westonia Dr 37412
Westover Ln 37405
Westridge Ave 37409

Westside Dr 37404
Westview Ave 37411
Westview Rd 37415
Westwood Ave 37405
Westwood Ct 37405
Westwood Ln 37415
Wetmore St 37406
Wexford Ln 37421
Whasha Ln 37405
Wheeler Ave 37406
Whirlaway Dr 37421
Whispering Oak Ln 37421
White Rd 37421
White Oak Rd 37415
White Springs Dr 37415
Whitehall Rd 37405
Whitehead Ave 37412
Whittaker Ave 37415
Wickley Rd 37415
Wiehl St 37403
Wilberforce St 37421
Wilcox Blvd
1600-2399 37406
3000-4299 37411
Wilcox Dr 37421
Wilcox Rd 37419
Wild Ginger Trl 37415
Wilder Rd & St 37406
Wildflower Cir & Ln 37419
Wildrose Ln 37419
Wildwind Trl 37421
Wiley Ave 37412
Wilhoit St
1500-1599 37408
2400-2499 37406
Wilkens Ln 37416
Wilkesview Dr 37416
Will Kelley Rd 37421
Willard Dr 37416
Willcrest Dr 37405
Williams Dr 37421
Williams St
1400-2799 37408
3000-3299 37410
Williamsburg Ln & Plz 37415
Willie Way 37419
Willingham Rd 37409
N Willow St
1-899 37404
900-999 37406
S Willow St 37404
Willow Brook Dr 37421
Willow Glen Rd 37421
Willow Lake Cir 37419
Willow Lawn Dr 37416
Willow Trace Dr 37421
Wilma Dr 37421
Wilshire Way 37405
Wilson Rd 37410
Wilson St
1500-2399 37406
4400-4498 37416
Wilsonia Ave 37411
Wilsonia Pl 37412
Wimberly Dr 37416
Wimberly Ln 37412
Wimbleton Pl 37421
Winchester St 37405
Wind Swept Dr 37421
Winding Way 37405
Winding Oaks Way 37405
Windmere Dr 37411
Windrose Cir 37421
Windrush Loop 37421
Windsor Ct 37411
Windsor St 37406
Windthrush Dr 37421
Windtower Dr 37402
Windy Ln 37421
Windy Hill Dr 37421
Windy Hollow Dr 37421
Winifred Dr 37415
Winniespan Rd 37416
Winston Rd 37405
Winter Ln 37419
Winter Garden Dr 37421

Winter Side Ln 37421
Winterberry Ln 37421
Winterview Ln 37409
Winthrop St 37405
Wisdom St 37406
Wolfe St 37415
Wonder Dr 37412
Wood Ave 37406
Wood Ln 37415
Woodard Cir 37412
Woodbrook Dr 37406
Woodbury Ave 37415
Woodfin Ave 37415
Woodfinch Trl 37421
Woodhill Dr 37405
Woodland Ave 37405
Woodland Rd 37405
Woodland Way 37419
Woodland View Cir 37410
Woodlawn Dr 37411
Woodmont Dr
3600-3699 37415
4000-4099 37412
Woodmore Cir, Ln, Pl & Ter 37411
Woodmore View Cir 37411
Woodrow Ave 37415
Woods Dr 37411
Woodside St 37407
Woodthrush Dr 37421
Woodvale Ave 37411
Woodward Ave 37404
Woody Holw 37421
Woolson Rd 37406
Wooten Rd 37416
Workman Rd
1-97 37410
99-1199 37410
1300-1599 37407
Worlick Way 37421
Worsham St 37412
Worthington St 37405
Wren Cir 37421
Wren Rd 37412
Wright St 37412
Wyandot St 37406
Wygoda Cir 37411
Wynnwood Rd 37412
Yale St 37412
Yellow Hammer Rd 37421
Yerbey Dr 37421
York St 37406
Yorkshire Ln 37415
Yorktown Rd 37416
Yother Ln 37415
Young Ave 37405
Young Rd 37406
Younger Cir 37415
Youngstown Rd 37406
Zena Dr 37419
Zephyr Dr 37416
Ziegler Rd 37421
Ziegler St 37405
Zinnia St 37421
Zorn Ln 37415

NUMBERED STREETS

1st Ave 37407
E 1st St 37403
2nd Ave 37407
E 2nd St 37403
W 2nd St 37402
3rd Ave
2800-3799 37407
4200-4399 37416
E 3rd St
1-99 37402
101-1199 37403
1200-2600 37404
2602-2698 37404
4th Ave
2300-2399 37404
2400-3999 37407
E 4th St
200-398 37403
400-950 37403
952-1098 37403
1800-2699 37404
W 4th St 37402
5th Ave 37407
E 5th St
1-99 37402
101-299 37402
400-1199 37403
1200-2699 37404
W 5th St 37402
6th Ave 37407
E 6th St 37402
W 6th St 37402
7th Ave 37407
E 7th St 37402
W 7th St 37402
8th Ave 37407
E 8th St
100-299 37402
300-1399 37403
W 8th St 37402
9th Ave 37407
10th Ave 37407
E 10th St
100-299 37402
300-1199 37403
W 10th St 37402
E 11th St
1-299 37402
300-1199 37403
W 11th St 37402
12th Ave
1900-2199 37404
2300-4799 37407
E 12th St
700-1099 37403
1300-2899 37404
W 12th St 37402
W 12th Street Ct 37402
13th Ave 37407
E 13th St
700-1299 37408
1300-2899 37404
W 13th St 37402
W 13th Street Ct 37402
14th Ave 37407
E 14th St
1-1199 37408
1201-1299 37408
1300-2799 37404
W 14th St 37402
W 14th Street Ct 37402
15th Ave
2300-2499 37404
2800-5099 37407
16th Ave 37407
E 16th St
1-1199 37408
1300-2699 37404
W 16th St 37408
17th Ave 37407
E 17th St
1-1099 37408
1300-2799 37404
W 17th St 37408
18th Ave 37407
E 18th St
200-699 37408
1300-2700 37404
2702-2798 37404
W 18th St 37408
E 18th Street Pl 37404
E 19th St 37408
1600-2699 37404
W 19th St 37408
E 20th St
1-499 37408
1600-2699 37404
W 20th St 37408
E 21st St 37404
W 21st St 37408
E & W 22nd 37408
E 23rd St 37408
1300-2199 37404
2200-2599 37407
E 24th St 37407

E 24th Street Pl
1800-1999 37404
2000-2199 37407
E 25th St
1-199 37408
201-299 37408
1600-1999 37404
2000-2799 37407
W 25th St 37408
E 25th Street Pl 37407
E 26th St 37407
W 26th St 37408
E 27th St
1200-1699 37404
1700-2299 37407
W 27th St 37408
E 28th St
1-399 37410
1200-1699 37404
1700-2999 37407
W 28th St 37408
E 29th St 37407
W 29th St 37410
E 30th St 37407
W 30th St 37410
E 31st St 37407
W 31st St
100-599 37410
1001-1297 37408
E 31st Street Pl 37407
E 32nd St 37407
E 33rd St 37407
400-1199 37410
1200-1299 37408
E 34th St 37407
W 34th St 37410
W 34th Street Cir 37410
E 35th St 37407
W 35th St 37410
E 35th Street Pl 37407
E 36th St 37407
W 36th St 37410
E 37th St
100-399 37410
1000-3199 37407
W 37th St
1-1099 37410
1200-1899 37409
E 38th St
1-199 37410
1000-3199 37407
3200-3399 37404
W 38th St
100-1299 37410
1700-1899 37409
W 38th Street Pl 37409
E 39th St 37407
900-1099 37410
1600-1799 37409
E 40th St 37407
100-999 37410
1100-1699 37409
E 41st St 37407
W 41st St 37410
E 42nd St
1-99 37410
1400-3399 37407
W 42nd St
400-899 37410
1400-1799 37409
E 43rd St 37407
700-899 37410
1400-1799 37409
E 44th St 37407
800-899 37410
1400-1699 37409
44th Street Pl 37407
E 45th St 37407
100-799 37410
1300-1599 37409
E 46th St
500-699 37410
1400-3299 37407
W 46th St
600-899 37410
1200-1599 37409
46th Street Aly 37409

E 46th Street Pl 37407
E 47th St 37407
200-899 37410
1500-1599 37409
E 48th St
700-899 37410
1400-2899 37407
W 48th St 37409
E 49th St
700-899 37410
1300-2999 37407
W 49th St 37409
E 50th St 37407
W 50th St 37409
E 51st St
700-799 37410
1400-3299 37407
W 51st St
1-99 37410
1400-1699 37409
E 52nd St 37410
W 52nd St 37409
W 53rd St
100-199 37410
1200-1799 37409
W 54th St 37409
W 55th St 37409
W 56th St 37409
W 57th St 37409
W 58th St 37409

CLARKSVILLE TN

General Delivery 37040

POST OFFICE BOXES MAIN OFFICE STATIONS AND BRANCHES

Box No.s
1 - 1982 37041
2001 - 2960 37042
3001 - 4060 37043
9998 - 9998 37041
20001 - 20958 37042
30001 - 33778 37040

NAMED STREETS

A St 37042
Abby Ln 37043
Abby Creek Dr 37042
Abby Lynn Cir 37043
Abbyton Pl 37043
Abeline Dr 37043
Aberdeen Rd 37043
Abigail Ct 37042
Abner Dr 37043
Abraham Dr 37042
Abrams Rd 37042
Academy Ave 37040
E & W Accipiter Cir 37043
Acorn Dr 37043
Acuff Rd 37043
Adams Ct 37040
Addison Dr 37042
Adkins St 37042
Adswood Rd 37042
Airborne St 37042
Airport Rd 37042
Aisle St 37040
Al Oerter Dr 37042
Alabama Ave 37042
Albert Dr 37042
Albright Cir & Rd 37043
Alex Rd 37040
Alex Overlook Way 37043
Alexander Blvd 37040
Alfred Dr 37043
Alfred Thun Rd 37040
Allen Rd 37042
W Allen Griffey Rd 37042

Allendale Dr 37043
Allenwood Dr 37043
Allison Dr 37042
Allison Lewis Rd 37040
Allmon Dr 37042
Alma Ln 37043
Alpine Dr 37040
Als Ln 37042
Alton Dr 37043
Aly Sheba Dr 37042
Amadeus Dr 37040
Amanda Dr 37042
Amber Ct & Way 37042
Amberley Dr 37043
Ambleside Dr 37040
Ambrose Dr 37042
Amesbury Ct 37043
Amy Ave 37042
Anchor Ct 37043
Anderson Dr 37040
Anderson Rd 37043
Andersonville Dr 37042
Andrew Dr 37043
Andrew Jackson Dr 37043
Angel Ct 37040
Angela Dr 37042
Angelise Ln 37042
Anita Ct & Dr 37043
Ann Dr 37040
Annalise Dr 37043
Annetta Ct 37042
Annie Dr 37042
Anthony Ct 37040
Antioch Rd 37040
Antioch Church Rd 37040
Apache Way 37042
Apex Dr 37040
Appellate Ct 37042
Apple Rd 37043
Apple Blossom Ct & Rd 37042
Apple Valley Rd 37043
Applegrove Cir 37040
Applemill Ct 37040
Appleton Dr 37042
Appleton Rd 37043
Applewood Cir 37040
Appomattox Ct 37043
Arbor Ct & St 37042
Archer Pl 37043
Archgate Ct 37043
Archwood Ct & Dr 37042
Arctic St 37040
Ardmoor Dr 37043
Arkadelphia Rd 37040
Arlington Pl 37043
Armistead Dr 37042
Arms Dr 37042
Armstrong Dr 37042
Arrow Ln 37043
Arrowfield Dr 37042
Arrowhead Ct 37042
Arrowood Ct & Dr 37042
Arthurs Ct 37040
Artie Manning Rd 37042
Arvin Dr 37042
S Ash Ridge Dr 37042
Ashbury Rd 37042
Ashebrooke Ln 37043
Ashland City Rd
1865A-1865Z 37043
1100-1599 37040
1600-5499 37043
Ashley Ct & Dr 37042
Ashley Oaks Dr 37042
Ashton Dr 37043
Ashwood Dr 37043
Aspen Dr 37042
Aster Dr 37042
Athena Dr 37042
Atlantic Blvd 37040
Attaway Rd 37040
Attaway East Rd 37040
Atwood Dr 37040
Auburn Dr 37043
Audrea Ln 37042
Audubon Woods Rd 37043
Augusta Pl 37043
Aurelia Lynn Dr 37043
Aurora Dr 37040
Austin Ct 37043
Austin Dr 37040
Austin Brian Ct 37043
Autumn Blvd & Dr 37042
Autumn Bluff Ct 37040
Autumnwood Blvd 37042
Avalon St 37042
Avebury Ct 37040
Avignon Way 37043
Avondale Dr 37040
Azalea Ct 37042
B St 37042
Back Nine Acres 37043
Backwind Ln 37040
Bagwell Dr 37040
Bagwell Rd 37043
Bailey St 37040
Bailywick Dr 37042
Bainbridge Dr 37043
Baker St 37040
Baldwin Pl 37043
Ballygar Ct & St 37043
Baltimore Dr 37043
Bamburg Dr 37040
Bancroft Cir, Ct & Dr 37043
Bandera Dr 37042
Banister Dr 37043
Barbara Dr 37043
Barbee Ln 37042
Barber Ct 37042
Barge Point Rd 37042
Barker St 37040
Barkers Mill Rd 37042
Barkley Dr 37043
Barkley Hills Cir & Rd 37040
Barkwood Ct & Dr 37040
Barnes Dr 37040
Barney Ln 37042
Barrett Dr 37043
Barry Dr 37040
Barrywood Cir E & W 37043
Basham Lks & Ln 37043
Bastogne St 37042
Batavia St 37040
Batchelor St 37043
Battle Creek Trl 37043
Batts Dr 37043
Batts Ln 37042
Bauling Ct & Ln 37040
Bay Ln 37042
Baylor Ct 37040
Baynesview Dr 37043
Bayview Dr 37040
Beacon Dr 37043
Bear Ct 37042
Bearden Rd 37043
Beasley Dr 37042
Beaumont St 37040
Beck Cir 37042
Beckett Dr 37042
Bedford Dr 37042
Beech Dr 37040
Beech St 37042
Beechwood Dr 37040
Bel Air Blvd 37042
Beldon Station Ln 37040
Bell Rd 37040
Bell Chase Way 37043
Bellamy Ct & Ln 37043
Belle Ct 37040
Bellingham Way 37043
Bellshire Dr 37043
Belmont Dr 37043
Belmont Rd 37040
Bend Rd 37040
Benjamin Dr 37040
Bennett Dr 37042
Bennington Ct 37042
Bentbrook Dr 37043
Bentley Ct 37042
Benton Ct 37042
Benton Park Pl 37040
Bentree Ct 37040
Benwood Dr 37042
Berkshire Dr 37042
Beth Dr 37042
Bevard Rd 37042
Beverly Hills Dr 37040
Bibb Dr 37042
Big Sam Ct 37042
Big Sky Dr 37040
Biglen Rd 37042
Billy Rinehart Rd 37043
Biltmore Pl 37042
Binks Dr 37042
Birdsong Trce 37040
Birnam Wood Trce 37043
Black Gum Ln 37043
Black Jack Way 37040
Blackberry Pl 37042
Blackbird Ct 37040
Blackman St 37040
Blaine Ct 37043
Blair Dr 37043
Blakemore Dr 37040
Blue Spruce Rd 37043
Blue Willow Ct 37042
Bluebonnet Dr 37042
Bluefield Ct 37040
Bluegrass Rd 37042
Bluff Dr 37043
Bo Ct 37042
Bo Peep Ln 37042
Bob White Dr 37042
Bobby Rd 37040
Bobcat Dr 37042
Bogard Ln 37040
Boillin Ln 37040
N & S Bombay Ct & Dr 37042
Bond St 37040
Bonellis Ln 37040
Bonnie Ct 37042
Bonnie Blue Ave 37042
Bonny Castle Rd 37040
Borrowdale Dr 37040
Bosca Ct 37040
Boscobel Ct 37040
Bourne Cir 37043
Bowers Ln 37042
Bowles Dr 37043
Boxcroft Ct & Rd 37042
Boxwood Ct 37043
E Boy Scout Rd 37040
W Boy Scout Rd 37040
Boyd Rinehart Rd 37043
Boyer Blvd 37043
Brad Ct 37043
Bradfield Dr 37042
Bradford Aly 37043
Bradley Ct 37043
Bradley St 37040
Bradley A Martin Rd 37042
Brady Dr 37042
Bramshaw Ct 37042
Branch Rd 37043
Branch Bend Rd 37040
Brandi Phillips Dr 37042
Brandywine Dr 37042
Brantley Ln 37043
Braxtons Run 37040
Breckinridge Rd 37042
Breeze Ln 37040
Breezemont Dr 37043
Brentwood Cir 37042
Bret Dr 37040
Brew Moss Dr & Way 37043
Brewster Dr 37042
Briar Hill Dr 37042
Briarcliff Rd 37043
Briarwood Ct, Dr & Rd 37040
Bridgette Dr 37042
Bridgewater Dr 37042
Bridgewood Rd 37040
Bridlewood Rd 37042
Brigade Dr 37043
Brigg Dr 37043
Brighton Dr 37043
Bristol Ct 37043
Brittney Ct 37042
Britton Springs Rd 37042
Broad Cir 37042
Broadmore Dr 37042
Broadripple Dr 37042
Brook Hill Dr 37042
Brook Hollow Rd 37040
Brook Mead Dr 37042
Brooke Valley Trce 37043
Brookfield Dr
2000-2099 37042
3400-3499 37043
Brookhaven Ter 37043
Brooks Aly 37040
Brookside Dr 37042
Brothers Rd 37043
Browning Ct & Way 37043
Brownsville Ct & Rd 37043
Bruce Jenner Dr 37042
Bruceton Dr 37042
Brunswick Dr 37043
Bryan Rd 37043
Bryson Ln 37043
Buchanon Dr 37042
Buck Dr 37040
Buck Rd 37043
Buckeye Ln 37042
Buckhorn Ct & Dr 37043
Buckingham Pl 37042
Buckshot Dr 37043
Bud Rd 37042
Buggy Cv 37043
Bullock Ct & Dr 37040
Bunker Hill Rd 37042
Bunny Ct 37043
Burch Rd 37042
Burchett Dr 37042
Burlington Ct 37043
Business Park Dr 37040
Butler Ln & Rd 37042
Buttercup Dr 37040
Buttermere Dr 37040
Butternut Dr 37042
Button Ct & Dr 37040
Butts Rd 37042
Byard Rd 37040
C. Booth Rd 37042
Cabana Dr 37042
Cabot Cv 37042
Cades Cv 37042
Cainlo Dr 37042
Cainridge Dr 37040
Cal Ct 37043
Caldwell Ln 37040
Calico Ct 37042
Calloway Dr 37042
N & S Callywood Ct 37040
Calumet Ct & Dr 37042
Calvert Dr 37042
Cambridge Rd 37043
Camden Xing 37040
Camelot Dr 37040
Cameo Ct 37042
Camino Dr 37042
Campbell Ct 37042
Candlewood Ct & Dr 37043
Cane Brake Rd 37040
Caney Ct & Ln 37040
Cannondale Dr 37042
Canterbury Rd 37043
Canvas Back Dr 37042
Canyon Pl 37042
Cardinal Dr & Ln 37043
Caribou Dr 37043
Carla Ct 37043
Carmack Ct & Dr 37042
Carnation Ct 37042
Carney Rd 37043
Caroline Dr 37042
Carousel Ct 37043
Carpenter St 37040
Carriage Ct 37043
Carriage Pl 37042
Carriage Way 37043
Carrie Dr 37042
Carrie Taylor Cir 37043
Carrigan Rd 37043
Carson Bailey Ct 37043
Carter Rd 37042
Cascade Dr 37042
Caskey Ct & Dr 37042
Castle Hts 37040
Castle Bar 37040
Castlerock Dr 37042
Castleton Ct 37043
Castlewood Dr 37042
Cavalier Dr 37040
Cave Rd 37043
Cave St 37042
Cave Mill Ct 37042
Cave Springs Rd 37042
Cayce Dr 37042
Cayuse Way 37042
Cb Rd 37040
Cedar Ct 37042
Cedar St 37040
Cedar Grove Ct 37040
Cedar Hill Dr 37040
Cedar Point Ct & Rd 37043
Cedar Springs Cir & Ct 37042
Cedar Valley Dr 37043
Cedarbend Cir, Ct & Rd 37043
Cedarbrook Dr 37040
Cedarcrest Dr 37042
Cedarcroft Dr 37043
Centennial Dr 37043
Center Ct 37040
Center Rd 37042
Center Pointe Dr 37040
Centerstone Cir 37040
Centerview Dr 37040
Central Ave 37040
Chadfield Dr 37043
Chadwick Dr 37040
Chalet Cir 37040
Challis Dr 37040
Chancery Ln 37042
Chaney Ln 37042
Channell Dr 37040
Channelview Ct & Dr 37040
Channing Pl 37043
Chapel St 37042
Chapel Hill Rd 37040
Chardea Ct & Dr 37040
Charlemagne Blvd 37042
N Charles Ave 37042
Charles Bell Rd
1300-1799 37040
1800-1899 37043
Charlestown Rd 37043
Charlie Akin Ln 37040
Charlotte Rd & St 37040
Chateauroux Dr 37042
Chatfield Dr 37043
Cheatham Dr 37042
Cheekwood Trl 37042
Chelsea Ct 37043
Cherokee Trl 37043
Cherry Ln 37042
Cherry Blossom Ln 37040
Cherry Point Ct 37042
Cherry Tree Dr 37042
Cherrybark Ln 37040
Cheryl Ct 37042
Chesapeake Ln 37040
Cheshire Rd 37043
Chesterfield Cir, Ct & Dr 37043
Chestnut Dr 37042
Chestnut Grove Ct & Way 37042
Chestnut Ridge Dr 37042
Cheyenne Ln 37042
Chickadee Ct 37042
Chickasaw Ct & Dr 37043
Childers St 37040
Chinook Cir 37042
Chinquapin Ln 37043
Chip N Dale Dr 37043
Choate Dr 37040
Chris Dr 37043
Chrisman Dr 37042
Christa Dr 37040
Christel Springs Ct & Dr 37043
Christine Dr 37042
Christopher Dr 37042
Christy Ct 37042
Chucker Ct & Dr 37042
Church Ct 37042
Church Rd 37040
Church St 37040
Churchill Ct 37042
Churchplace Ave 37040
Cider Dr 37040
Cimarron Ct 37042
Cinderella Ln 37042
Cindy Ct 37043
Cindy Jo Ct & Dr 37040
Circle Dr 37043
Circle Rd 37040
Circle Hill Dr 37042
Clara Ct 37040
Clarendon Trce 37043
Claridge Dr 37040
Clark Rd 37042
Clark St 37040
Classy Ct 37042
Clay Hills Dr 37043
Clay Lewis Rd 37040
Claymont Dr 37040
Claystone Ct 37040
Clayton Dr 37040
Clear Sky Ct 37043
Clear Springs Rd 37040
Clearfount Dr 37043
Clearview Dr 37043
Clearwater Ct & Dr 37042
Clearwood Ln 37040
Cleveland Dr 37042
Clifton Rd 37040
Clintwood Dr 37042
Cloamae Dr 37042
Cloe Ct 37042
Cloud Dr 37043
Clover Hill Dr 37043
Clover Hills Ct 37043
Cloverbrook Dr 37040
Cloverdale Dr 37040
Cloverwood Dr 37043
Clubhouse Ln 37043
Clyde Ct 37042
Clydesdale Ct & Dr 37043
Cobalt Dr 37040
Cobb Meadow Ln 37043
Cobbler Dr 37040
Cobblestone Ln 37042
Cobra Ln 37042
Coburn Rd 37042
Cody Ct 37043
Coke Rd 37040
Cola Dr 37043
Colby Cv 37042
Colin Ct 37043
E College St 37040
Collier Rd 37042
Collins View Way 37043
Collinwood Dr 37042
Colonial Ct 37043
Colt Dr 37042
Columbia St 37042
Comanche Ct 37042
Commerce St 37040
Commission Dr 37043
W Concord Dr 37042
Condor Ct 37042
Congressman Dr 37042
Coniston Dr 37040
Connemara Way 37040
Conrad Dr 37042
Conroy Ave 37040
Constitution Dr 37042
Convergys Way 37042
Cook Dr 37042
E & W Copeland Ct & Rd 37042
Copperfield Ct 37042
Copperstone Cir & Dr 37043
Core Dr 37040
Corinne Cir 37040
Corinth Ct 37040
Corlew Rd 37040
Cornelia Ct 37042
Cornish Way 37043
Cornwall Rd 37043
Corporate Dr 37040
Corporate Parkway Blvd 37040
Cory Dr 37040
Cotham Ln 37042
Cottingham Ct 37042
Cottonwood Ct & Dr 37040
Coulter St 37040
Country Ln 37043
Country Club Ct & Dr 37043
Country Fields Ln 37040
Countryside Dr 37043
Courthouse Ln 37040
Courtland Ave 37043
Courtney Dr 37042
Coventry Cir 37043
Covey Chase Rd 37043
Covey Rise Cir & Ct 37043
Covington St 37040
Cowboy Dr 37042
E & W Coy Cir 37043
Coyote Ct 37043
Crab Apple Dr 37043
Crabapple Ct & Ln 37040
Crabtree Cir 37040
Cracker Barrel Dr 37040
Craig Dr 37042
Craigmont Blvd 37043
Cranewell Ct 37042
Cranklen Cir 37042
Cranny Ct 37040
Creek Ct & Dr 37040
W Creek Coyote Trl 37042
Creek Stone Dr 37040
Creekside Dr 37042
Crest Dr 37043
Crestmont Ct 37042
Crestmore Dr 37040
Crestone Ct & Ln 37042
Crestview Dr 37042
Crestwood Dr 37043
Crisscross Ct 37040
Crockarell Rd 37043
Crocker Dr 37042
Crofton Pl 37043
Cross Ln 37040
Cross Ridge Dr 37040
Crossbow Ct 37043
Crossland Ave
1-1399 37040
1400-1500 37043
1502-1698 37043
Crossroads Dr 37040
Crosswind Ct 37043
Crystal Dr 37042
Cullom Way 37043
Culverson Ct 37040
Cumberland Dr & Ter 37040
Cumberland Drive Ext 37040
Cumberland Heights Rd 37040
Cummings Cir 37042
Cummings Creek Rd 37042
Cunningham Ln 37042
Cunningham Pl 37042
Cunningham Rdg 37040
Current Rd & St 37040
Cynthia Dr 37042
Cyprus Ct 37040
D St 37042
Dabney Ln 37043
Dailey Rd 37042
Dale Ter 37042
Dale Terrace Ct 37042
Dalewood Dr 37042

Dalton Dr	37043
Damion Dr	37042
Dana Ct	37043
Danbury Dr	37043
Dandelion Ct & Dr	37042
Danford Dr	37043
Daniel St	37040
Danielle Dr	37042
Danko Ln	37042
Darlene Dr	37042
Darlington Ct & Dr	37042
Darnell Pl & St	37042
Darrow Rd	37042
Darter Ln	37042
Dartmoore Dr	37043
Daughtry Ct	37043
Dave Dr	37042
David Dr	37040
David Ray Ct	37042
Davidson Dr	37040
Davidson Graveyard Rd	37043
Davis Dr, Ln & Rd	37040
Dawn Dr	37042
Dawn Ridge Ct	37042
Dawson Ave	37042
Dean Dr & Rd	37040
Debbie Dr	37042
Debra Dr	37040
Deepwood Cir, Ct, Dr & Trl	37042
Deer Ridge Dr	37042
Deer Trace Dr	37040
Deerfield Dr	37043
Deerhill Rd	37040
Deerstand Dr	37042
Deerview Ln	37043
Deerwood Cir & Rd	37043
Del Ray Dr	37040
Delano Dr	37043
Delaware Dr	37042
Delia Dr	37042
Delmar Dr	37040
Dennis Rd	37042
Denny Rd	37043
Denver Ct	37040
Derby Dr	37040
Derwent Dr	37040
Destin Dr	37040
Dewberry Rd	37042
Dewitt Dr	37043
Diane Ct	37043
Dillon Dr	37042
Dinsmore Rd	37040
Dirks Pl	37043
Dirt Rd	37040
Dixie Bee Rd	37043
Dixon Cir & Dr	37040
Doane Dr	37042
Dodd St	37040
Doe Dr	37043
Dogwood Ln	37043
Dogwood Trl	37042
Dolphin Ln	37043
Dominion Dr	37042
Donelson Dr	37042
Donna Ct & Dr	37042
Dorchester Cir	37043
Dortch St	37040
Dotsonville Rd	37042
Dotsonville Church Rd	37042
Double R Blvd	37042
Douglas Ln	37043
Dove Ct	37040
Dover Rd	37042
Dover Crossing Rd	37042
Downer Dr	37042
Dr Meade Ln	37042
Drane St	37040
Drawbridge Ct	37040
Dresden Way	37042
Drinkard Dr	37043
Drum Ct & Ln	37043
Dudley Rd	37043
Duke Ct	37043
Dumas Dr	37040
Dunbar Cave Rd	37043
W Dunbar Cave Rd	37042
Dunbar Dell Rd	37043
Dunbrook Dr	37043
Duncan St	37042
Dundee Dr	37043
Dunlop Ln	
200-1199	37040
1300-3499	37043
Dunwood Ct	37043
Dupuis Dr	37042
Durham Rd	37043
Durrett Dr	37042
Dury Ct	37043
Dwight Eisenhower Way	37042
Dyce Ct	37040
Dygert Ct	37042
E St	37042
Eads Ct	37043
Eagle St	37042
Eaglewood Ct	37042
Earl Rd	37043
Earl Slate Rd	37043
Earlington Ct	37043
East Rd	37040
Eastern Hills Dr	37043
Eastland Dr	37040
Eastwood Ct & Dr	37043
Economy Dr	37043
Edgehill Dr	37040
Edgemont Dr	37043
Edgewater Ln	37043
Edgewood Dr	37040
Edinburgh Way	37043
Edlin St	37043
Edmenson Rd	37040
Edmonds Way	37043
Edmondson Ln	37040
Edmondson Ferry Ct & Rd	37040
Edwards Ln & Rd	37043
Eggars Ct	37042
Egret Dr	37042
Eisenhower Rd	37042
Elaine Dr	37042
Elberta Dr	37042
Elder St	37040
Elderberry Dr	37043
Eldos Trace Cir & Trl	37042
Elfie Ct	37040
Elk Dr	37043
Elkmont Dr	37040
Ellen Dr	37042
Ellie Nat Dr	37040
Ellington Dr	37043
Ellington Ter	37040
Ellington Gait Dr	37043
Elliott Ct	37042
Ellsworth Ct & Dr	37043
Elm St	37040
Elm Hill Dr	37040
Elm Leaf Dr	37042
Elmhurst Ct	37043
W Elmwood Rd	37040
Elwood Dr	37040
Emerald Ct	37042
Emory St	37040
Emory Way	37043
Enclave Ct	37043
Endsworth Dr	37042
Eric Dr	37043
Erie Dr	37040
Erika Dr	37042
Ermine Dr	37043
Ernest St	37040
Ernest Shelton Dr	37040
Ernest Stewart Dr	37042
Erwin Rd	37043
Essex Dr	37043
Eubank Dr	37042
Eva Dr	37042
Evans Rd	37042
E Evans Rd	37043
Everett Dr	37040
Evergreen Ct	37040
Everwood Ct	37043
Excalibur Dr	37042
Excell Rd	37043
Executive Ave	37042
Exeter Ln	37043
Eysian Dr	37040
Fabian Pl	37043
Fair Brook Pl	37040
Fair Haven Dr	37043
Fairfax Dr	37043
Fairfield Dr	37042
Fairview Ln	37040
Fairway Dr	37043
Fairway Wingate	37043
Faith Dr	37042
Falcon Dr	37042
Falkland Cir	37042
Fallbrook Ln	37040
Fantasia Ct & Way	37043
Fantasy Ln	37043
Farmer Rd	37043
Farmington Bnd	37042
Farris Dr	37040
Faulkner Ct & Dr	37042
Fawn Dr	37043
Faye Dr	37040
Felts Dr	37043
Fennec Way	37042
Fenton Ct	37040
Fentress Ln & Loop	37040
Fergie Ct	37042
Fern Croft Ln	37043
Ferry Rd	37040
Fieldcrest Ln	37043
Fielding Ln	37043
Fieldstone Ct & Dr	37040
Fillmore Ct	37042
Fire Break Dr	37040
Fire Station Rd	37043
Fish Rd	37040
Fisher Ct	37042
Fitzgerald Dr	37042
Flagstone Ct & Dr	37042
Fleming Rd	37043
Flower Dr	37040
Floyd Rd	37042
Forbes Ave	37040
Ford St	37040
N Ford St	37043
Forest St	37040
Forest Glen Cir	37043
Forest Hills Dr	37040
E & W Fork Dr	37042
Formal Dr	37042
Forrest Dr	37040
Forrest Cove Ct	37040
Forrestdale Dr	37042
Fort Campbell Blvd	37042
Fortoria Dr	37042
Fortway Rd	37042
Fossil Dr	37040
Fountainbleau Rd	37042
Fox Den Ln	37040
Fox Hole Dr	37040
Fox Hound Dr	37040
Fox Meadow Way	37042
Fox Ridge Dr	37042
Fox Tail Ct & Dr	37040
Fox Trail Ct	37040
Fox Trot Dr	37042
Foxfield Dr	37042
Foxfire Rd	37043
Foxland Dr	37042
Foxmoor Dr	37042
Foxrun Ln	37042
Foxwood Rd	37043
Francesca Dr	37042
Francis Ln	37043
Franklin St	37040
Franklin Meadows Way	37042
Fredonia Rd	37043
Freedom Ct & Dr	37042
S Freestone Ct & Dr	37042
Freida Dr	37042
Friar Dr	37042
Fritz Cir	37042
Front St	37043
Frost Rd	37042
Frosty Morn Dr	37040
Fuji Ln	37040
Gable Ct	37042
Gableridge Ct	37042
Gaine Dr	37040
Gaine Lynn Dr	37040
Gala Ln	37040
Gale Dr	37040
Gallant Ct	37043
Galvin Dr	37042
Garden Ter	37043
Gardendale Ln	37040
Garfield Way	37042
Garnet Dr	37042
Garrettsburg Rd	37042
Garth Dr	37040
Garwood Dr	37040
Gary Ct	37043
Gary Hills Dr	37043
Gateau Dr	37043
Gateway Ln	37043
Gatewood Ln	37043
Gatlin St	37040
Gatsby Ct	37042
Gaylewood Dr	37043
Gemstone Ct	37042
General Neyland Dr	37042
Georgetown Rd	37043
Georgia Ave	37040
Gerald Dr	37043
Gettysburg St	37042
Gholson Rd	37043
Gibson Dr	37043
Giles Rd	37042
Gill St	37040
Ginger Dr	37043
Ginkgo Dr	37042
Gino Dr	37042
Gip Manning Rd	37042
Givens Ln	37040
Glade St	37040
Glastonbury Ct	37043
Glen Cove Dr	37043
Glen Ellen Way	37040
Glenbrooke Dr	37043
Glendale Cir & Dr	37043
Glenhurst Way	37040
Glenn St	37040
Glenndon Allen Dr	37043
Glennon Dr	37042
Glenraven Dr	37043
E Glenridge Ln	37043
Glenstone Springs Dr	37043
Glenwood Dr	37040
Glory Dr	37043
Gold Ln	37043
Gold Leaf Ln	37040
Golden Dr	37040
Golden Bell Ln	37043
Golden Eagle Way	37040
Goldeneye Ct	37042
Golf Club Ln	
1656A-1656Z	37043
Golfview Pl	37043
Gomer Rd	37042
Goodlett Dr	37042
Gordon Pl	37040
Gracelawn Dr	37040
Gracewood Ct	37043
Gracey Ave	37040
Graham Ln	37042
Graham Cemetery Rd	37043
Grand Forrest Ln	37043
Granger Ln	37042
Granny Ct	37040
Granny White Rd	37040
Grant St	37043
Grassland Dr	37043
Grassmire Ct & Dr	37042
Gratton Rd	37043
Gray Fox Dr	37040
Gray Hawk Ct & Trl	37043
Green Acres Dr	37042
Green Briar Dr	37040
Green Grove Way	37043
Green Valley Ct	37042
Greenboro Ct	37043
Greenfield Dr	37040
Greenland Ct	37042
Greenland Farms Dr	37040
Greenleaf Ln	37040
Greenspoint Ct & Dr	37042
Greenwood Ave & Ct	37040
Griffin Cir	37040
Grovewood Ct	37040
Guarterpath Dr	37042
Guildfield Dr	37043
Guildfield Church Rd	37043
Guinevere Ct	37040
Gunpoint Dr	37042
Gupton Aly, Cir, Ct & Ln	37040
Gusty Ct & Ln	37043
Guthrie Hwy	37040
Guthrie Rd	37043
Hadley Dr & Rd	37042
Haggard Dr	37043
Hallbrook Dr	37042
Halliburton Rd	37043
Hamilton St	37040
Hamlet Ct & Dr	37040
Hampshire Ct & Dr	37043
S Hampton Pl	37040
Hampton Station Rd	37040
Hamstead Ct	37040
Hand Ct & Dr	37042
Hanley Ct	37043
Hannah Elizabeth Ct	37042
Hannover Ct	37043
Hannum St	37040
E & W Happy Hollow Dr	37040
Harding Dr	37042
Hardwood Dr	37040
Harnett Ct	37043
Harold Dr	37040
Harper Rd	37043
Harpeth Ct	37043
Harrell Ln	37043
Harrier Ct	37042
Harriet Dr	37040
Hartford Ct	37043
Harvest Dr & Rdg	37040
Harvest Ridge Ln	37040
Harvill Dr & Rd	37043
Hassell Dr	37040
Hatcher Ln	37043
Hattington Dr	37042
Haven Dr	37042
Havendale Ct	37042
E Hawkins Ln	37043
Hawkins Rd	37040
Hawthorn Dr	37043
Hay Market Rd	37043
Hayden Dr	37043
Hayes Ln	37043
Hayes Rd	37043
Hayes St	37040
Haynes St	37043
Haystack Rd	37043
Haywood Ct	37042
Hazel Dr	37043
Hazelnut Ct	37042
Hazelwood Rd	37043
Heandeli Rd	37043
Heartstone Ct	37043
Heather Dr	37042
Heather Denise Ct	37042
Heatherhurst Ct	37043
Heatherwood Trce	37040
Hedge Apple Dr	37040
Hedgerow Ln	37043
Hedgewood Rd	37042
Helen St	37040
Helton Dr	37042
Hemlock Dr	37040
E Henderson Way	37042
Hendricks Ct	37040
Hengestone Ct	37040
Henry Place Blvd	37042
Heritage Dr	37043
Heritage Pt	37043
Heritage Pointe Cir	37042
Hermitage Rd	37042
Herndon Ct & Dr	37043
Herning Dr	37042
Heron Ridge Ct	37040
Hickory Hts & Trce	37040
Hickory Glen Ct & Dr	37040
Hickory Grove Blvd	37040
Hickory Hill Dr	37040
Hickory Point Rd	37043
Hickory Wild Ct	37040
Hickorywood Dr	37043
Hidden Ridge Ct	37043
Hidden Spring Dr	37042
Hidden Valley Dr	37040
Hietts Ln	37043
W High St	37040
High Lea Rd	37040
High Point Rd	37042
Highland Cir	37043
Highway Dr	37040
Highway 12 N	37043
Highway 149	37040
Highway 41a Byp S	37043
Highway 48	37040
Highway 76	37043
Hill Rd	37040
Hillcrest Cir & Dr	37043
Hilldale Ln	37043
Hillman Dr	37040
Hillsboro Rd	37042
Hillshire Dr	37043
Hilltop Ct	37042
Hilltop Dr	37040
Hilltop Rd	37043
Hilltop View Rd	37040
Hillwood Ct	37043
Hillwood Dr	37040
N Hinton Rd	37043
Hitcher Dr	37042
Hiter St	37040
Hogan Ln & Rd	37043
Hogue Dr & Rd	37040
Holden Dr	37042
Holiday Dr	37040
Holleman Dr	37042
Hollis Rdg	37043
Holly Cir & Pt	37043
Holly Rock Ct & Dr	37040
Holt Ln & Rd	37043
Home Ave	37040
Homeplace Ct	37043
Hondo Dr	37042
Honeysuckle Ln	37040
Honeywood Ct	37040
Hopkinsville Hwy	37042
Horace Crow Dr	37043
Hornberger Ln	37040
Hornbuckle Rd	37043
Horseshoe Cave Dr	37042
Hot Shot Dr	37042
Houston Fielder Rd	37043
Howard St	37040
Howell Dr	37042
Hoy Ct	37042
Hudson Dr	37042
Huey Cir	37042
Huggins Ln & Rd	37040
Hundred Oaks Dr	37043
Hunt Crest Ct	37043
Huntco Dr	37043
Hunter Ln	37043
Hunters Run	37043
Hunting Creek Ct	37042
Huntington Dr	37043
Hurst St	37040
Huskey Dr	37040
Hutcheson Ln	37040
Hutchins Camp Trce	37043
Hyde Park	37043
Hyman St	37040
Idaho Springs Rd	37043
Idlewild St	37042
Idlewood Dr	37043
Independence Dr	37043
Indian Hills Ct & Dr	37043
Industrial Dr	37040
Industrial Park Dr	37040
Inglewood Dr	37040
International Blvd	37040
Inver Ln	37042
Irene Dr	37043
Iris Ct & Ln	37042
Irishman Way	37042
Iron Wood Cir & Ct	37043
Iron Workers Rd	37043
Ironhorse Way	37042
Iroquois Rd	37043
Irving Ln	37040
Isaac Ct & Dr	37040
Ishee Dr	37042
Ivy Ln	37042
Ivy Bend Cir	37043
Ivy Brook Way	37043
J L Thompson Ln	37040
N Ja Tate Dr	37043
Jace Dr	37040
Jack Miller Blvd	37042
Jackie Lorraine Dr	37042
Jackson Rd	37042
Jacob Ct	37043
Jacqueline Ct	37042
Jacquie Dr	37042
Jake Ct	37042
James Ave & Dr	37042
Jamestown Pl	37042
Jan Dr	37043
Jana Dr	37043
Janet Way Dr	37042
Janie Ln	37042
Jardco Dr	37040
Jared Ct	37042
Jared Ray Dr	37042
Jarrell Ridge Rd	37043
Jarrell Ridge Farms Rd	37043
Jasmine Dr	37043
Jason Cir	37040
Jay Cir	37040
Jean Ct	37043
Jefferson St	37040
Jeffery Dr	37043
Jen Hollow Rd	37040
Jenny Ct & Ln	37042
Jessica Dr	37043
Jewel Dr	37042
Jim Ct	37043
Jim Johnson Rd	37040
Jim Thorpe Dr	37042
Jockey Dr	37042
Jody Dr	37042
Joe Mccraw Rd	37040
Joey Dr	37042
John Duke Tyler Blvd	37043
John Haley Rd	37043
John Sevier Ave	37040
Johnson Cir	37040
E Johnson Cir	37040
Johnson Rd	37043
Johnson St	37043
Jolene Ct	37040
Jon Dr	37043
Jones Rd	37043
Jordan Dr & Rd	37042
Joshua Dr	37042
Jostin Dr	37040
N & S Jot Dr	37040
Joy Dr	37043
Judge Cir	37043
Judge Tyler Dr	37043
Judith Ct & Dr	37043
Judy Lynn Dr	37042
Julie Dr	37042
Julius Hollis Rd	37043
Justene Ct	37040
Justice Dr	37043
Justin Douglas Ct	37042
Kaitlyn Virginia Ct	37042
Karen Ct	37043

Karmaflux Way 37043
Kathleen Ct 37043
Kathryn Ct 37042
Kathy Dr 37040
Katie Ct 37043
Kay Rd 37042
Kayla Ct 37043
Keech Dr 37042
Keeper Ct 37042
Keesee Rd 37040
Keith Dr 37043
Kellia Dr 37042
Kellogg St 37040
Kelly Ln 37040
Kelsey Dr 37042
Kendall Dr 37042
Kender Rhea Ct 37043
Kendra Ct N & S 37040
Kendrick St 37043
Kennedy Ln & Rd 37040
Kenney Dr 37042
Kensington Ct 37043
Kentucky Ave 37042
Kenwood Dr 37043
Keswick Ct 37040
Kettering Ct 37040
Kettle Ct 37043
Keyland Dr 37040
Keysburg Rd 37043
Keystone Ct & Dr 37042
Kicker Ct 37040
Killarney Ct 37042
Killebrew Rd 37043
Killington Ct & Dr S 37040
Kim Dr 37043
Kimberly Dr 37043
Kimbrough Ct & Rd 37043
King Rd 37042
King St 37040
King Cole Dr 37042
Kingfisher Dr 37042
Kings Deer Ct & Dr 37042
Kingsbury Ct, Dr & Rd 37040
Kingston Dr 37042
Kingswood Ct & Dr 37043
Kirby Dr 37042
Kirkwood Rd 37043
Kleeman Dr 37040
Kline Aly 37040
Knob Ct 37043
E & W Knollwood Cir 37043
Knox Ln 37042
Koch Rd 37043
Kraft St 37040
Kristie Michelle Ln 37042
Kyle Dr 37043
L Bumpus Rd 37040
Lacy Ln 37043
Ladd Dr
1-99 37040
2100-2399 37043
Lady Alice Ct 37042
Lady Marion Dr 37042
Lafayette Ct & Rd 37042
Lafayette Point Cir & Ct 37042
Lahna Ct 37043
Lake Court Dr 37043
Lake Pointe Dr 37043
Lakeview Rd 37040
Lakewood Dr 37043
Lamont Ct & Ln 37042
Lancashire Ct & Dr 37043
S Lancaster Rd 37042
Lancelot Ln 37040
Lancer Ct 37043
Landing Way 37040
Landon Rd 37043
Landrum Pl 37043
Langdale Ct 37040
Langford Rd 37043
Lannom Rd 37040
Lansinger Ln 37042
Lark Dr 37040
Larry Rd 37043
Larson Ln 37043

Lasalle St 37042
Laura Dr 37042
Laurel Dr 37043
Laurelwood Ct & Trl 37043
Laurent Ln 37040
Lavender Cir & Ct 37042
Lawn St 37040
Lawry Ln 37043
Layton Rd 37043
Lazy Jake Ct 37042
Lealand Ct, Dr & Ter 37042
Ledbetter Ln 37043
Legacy Ct & Dr 37043
Legion St 37040
Leigh Ct 37042
Leigh Ann Dr 37042
Leighton Ct 37043
Lena Ct 37043
Lennox Rd 37042
Leonard Dr 37042
Leonard Rd 37043
E Leonard Rd 37043
Leprechaun Ln 37042
Leslie Ave 37042
Leslie Wood Dr 37040
Lewis Ln 37040
Lewter Dr 37042
Lexington Dr 37042
Liberty Pkwy 37040
Liberty Bell Ln 37040
N & S Liberty Church Rd 37042
W Lilac Ct & Ln 37042
Lillian Dr 37040
Lillie Belle Ln 37042
Lily Way 37043
Limerick Ln 37042
Lincoln Dr & St 37040
Linda Ln 37042
Linden Dr 37042
Lindsey Dr 37042
Lintwood Dr 37042
Lion Dr 37042
Lisa Ct 37043
Lisle Dr 37042
Little Barn Dr 37043
Little Bird Way 37042
Little Bobcat Ln 37042
Little Grove Ln 37042
Little Hope Rd 37043
Little John Pl 37042
Little Springs Rd 37040
Lock B Dr 37040
Lock B Rd N 37043
Lock B Rd S 37040
Lockert Pl 37043
Locust Dr 37040
Locust Rd 37043
Locust St 37042
Lodge Dr 37043
Lois Ln 37043
Long Beech Dr 37042
Longbow Ct 37042
Longview Ct 37043
Longwood Ct & Ln 37043
Lookout Dr 37040
Loon Dr 37042
Loren Cir 37042
Lorie Ln 37042
Lou Ann Ln 37042
Louis Ussery Rd 37043
Louise Ln 37042
Louisiana Ave 37042
Loupin Dr 37042
Love Ct & St 37040
Lowes Dr W 37040
Lucas Ln 37040
Lucas Wayne Dr 37042
Lucy Ct & Ln 37043
Luke Dr 37043
Lulworth Cv 37043
Luran Rd 37040
Lutz Ln 37042
Luxury Dr 37043
Lyme Dr 37043
Lynes St 37040

Lynnwood Cir 37040
Lynx Dr 37042
Macarther Way 37042
Mackenzie Ct & Dr 37042
Maddox Ct 37040
Madeline Ct 37042
Madison St
1455A-1455Z 37040
200-307 37040
306-306 37041
308-1598 37040
309-1599 37040
1600-2799 37043
Madison Ter 37040
Madison Ter Ct 37040
Magnolia Ct 37042
Magnolia Dr 37042
N Magnolia Dr 37042
Magnolia Sq 37043
Main St 37040
Malibu Dr 37043
Maliki Dr 37042
Malkowski Rd 37043
Mallard Ct & Dr 37042
Mallory Dr 37042
Mammy Ln 37042
Man O War Blvd & Ct 37042
Manchester Ct 37043
Mann Cir 37042
Manning Dr 37042
Manning Hts 37040
Manning Gate Rd 37042
Manorstone Ln 37042
Manscoe Pl 37043
Manson St 37040
Maple Ln 37040
Maple St 37042
Maple Park Dr 37040
Maple Tree Ln 37040
Maplemere Dr 37040
Maplewood Dr 37042
Marcie Ct 37042
Marcy Ct 37042
Margie Ct 37042
Margrave Dr 37042
Margret Dr 37042
Marianne Ln 37043
Marie Dr 37042
Marietta Pl 37043
Marigold Dr 37042
Marina Way 37040
Marion St 37042
Mark Ave 37043
Mark Spitz Dr 37042
Market St 37042
Markie Dr 37043
Marla Cir, Ct & Dr 37042
Marrast Dr 37043
Marshall Dr 37042
Martha Ln 37043
Martin Rd 37042
Martin St 37040
Mary Beth Ln 37042
Marymont Dr 37042
Marys Oak Dr 37042
Mason Ct & Way 37042
Matheson Dr 37043
Matlock Rd 37043
Matthew Ct & Dr 37042
Maureen Dr 37043
Max Ct 37043
Maxshire Ct 37043
Maxwell Dr 37043
May Apple Dr 37042
Mayflower St 37040
Mayhew Rd 37040
Mayo Rd 37043
Mcadoo Creek Rd 37043
Mcallister Dr 37042
Mccalls Way 37042
Mccan Dr 37042
Mcclain Dr 37040
Mcclardy Rd 37042
Mcclure Rd & St 37040
Mccormick Ln 37040
Mcdaniel Rd 37043

Mcgraw St 37040
Mcgregor Dr 37040
Mckinley Ct 37042
Mcmanus Cir 37042
Mcmurry Rd 37042
Meachem Dr 37042
Mead Ct 37043
E, S, N & W Meadow Cir, Ct & Dr 37043
Meadow Knoll Ct & Ln 37040
Meadow Ridge Ln 37040
Meadowbrook Dr 37042
Meadowgate Ln 37040
Meadowgreen Dr 37040
Meagan Ct 37042
Mearns Ct 37043
Med Park Dr 37043
Medical Ct 37043
Medical Center Ct 37043
Melanie Ln 37042
Melinda Dr 37042
Melissa Ln 37042
Mellon Rd 37040
Melodie Dr 37043
Melrose Dr 37042
Memorial Cir & Dr 37043
Memorial Drive Ext 37043
Mercantile Dr 37040
Merchants Blvd & Ct 37040
Meredith Ct & Way 37042
Merganser Dr 37042
Meriwether Rd 37040
Merritt Dr 37043
Merritt Lewis Ln 37042
Merrywood Dr 37043
Meshaw Trl 37040
Michael Dr 37043
Mickey Ct 37042
Mickle Ln 37043
Mile High Ct & Dr 37042
Miles Ct 37042
Mill Creek Rd 37042
Millenium Plz 37040
Miller Dr & Rd 37043
Millington Dr 37040
Mills Dr 37042
Millstone Cir 37042
Millswood Dr 37042
Mimi Rd 37040
Mimms Rd 37043
Minglewood Dr 37042
Minor Dr 37042
Mississippi Ave 37042
Misty Ct & Way 37042
Mitchell St 37042
Mobley Rd 37043
Mollie Webb Dr 37043
Monarch Ct & Ln 37042
Moncrest Dr 37042
E Monica Dr 37042
Monroe St 37040
Montana Ave 37042
Montclair Dr 37043
Montee Ln 37043
Monterey Pl 37043
Montgomery Pkwy 37043
Montrose Dr 37042
Moody Rd 37040
Moore Rd 37040
Mooreland Dr 37040
W Mor Dr 37043
Morgan Ct & Rd 37040
Morningside Dr 37042
Morris Rd 37040
Morrison Ct 37040
Morrison Dr 37042
Morrison Ln 37040
Morstead Dr 37042
Mosley Rd 37043
Moss Rd 37043
Moss Rose Rd 37040
Mossland Dr 37042
Mossy Oak Cir 37043
Mount Carmel Rd 37043
Mount Vernon Dr 37043
Mountain Way 37043

Mountain View Ct & Dr 37043
Mr C Dr 37040
Mt Pisgah Rd 37040
Muddy Branch Rd 37043
Mulberry Pl 37043
Mumford St 37040
Murff Rd 37043
Murfield Ct 37040
Mutual Dr 37042
Myrtle Dr 37040
Nadia Ct & Dr 37040
Nam St 37042
Nan Ln 37040
Nandina Ct 37043
Nantucket Dr 37040
S Naples Ct N 37040
Nashboro Rd 37042
Nat Hoosier Ln 37040
Nathaniel Ct 37042
Neal Ct 37042
Neblett Rd 37040
Ned Dr 37042
Needless Rd 37040
Needlewood Dr 37040
Needmore Ct 37040
Needmore Rd
100-1699 37040
1701-1759 37042
1761-2099 37042
Neely Aly 37040
Neena Ct 37042
Nelsons Way 37043
Nepsa Ct 37040
New Rd 37040
New Castle Rd 37043
New England Pl 37043
New Grange Cir & Ct 37040
New South Dr 37043
Newman Dr 37042
Nice Dr 37042
Nichols Dr 37042
Nick Dr 37042
Nicole Rd 37040
Noble Dr 37042
Nolen Rd 37040
Norfolk Ave 37043
Norma Ct 37043
Norman Dr & Ln 37040
Normandy St 37042
Norris Dr 37042
Northeast Dr 37040
Northfield Dr 37040
Northridge Ct & Dr 37042
Northway Dr 37042
Northwest Ct 37042
Northwind Dr 37042
Northwood Ter 37042
Norwood Trl 37043
Notgrass Rd 37042
Nottingham Pl 37042
Nussbaumer Rd 37042
Nuthatch Cir 37042
Oak Ln 37040
Oak St 37042
Oak Arbor Ct 37040
Oak Creek Dr 37040
Oak Glen Ln 37043
Oak Hill Dr & Rd 37040
Oak Lawn Dr 37042
Oak Park Ct, Dr & Ter 37042
Oak Plains Rd 37043
Oak Valley Dr 37042
Oakdale Dr 37040
Oakland Dr & Rd 37040
Oakmont Dr 37042
W Observatory Ct & Dr 37040
Oconner Ln 37042
Ogburn Chapel Rd 37042
Ogles Dr 37042
Old Ashland City Rd 37043
Old Bend Rd 37040
Old City Ferry Rd 37040
Old Clarksville Pike 37043
Old Dotsonville Rd 37042

Old Dover Ct & Rd 37042
Old Duke Dr 37043
Old Dunbar Cave Rd 37043
Old Excell Rd 37043
Old Farmers Rd 37043
Old Gratton Rd 37043
Old Highway 48 37040
Old Hopkinsville Hwy 37042
Old Mack Rd 37040
Old Mill Rd 37042
Old Russellville Pike
1903A-1903Z 37043
1300-2199 37043
2200-2699 37040
Old Sango Rd 37043
Old Seven Mile Ferry Rd 37040
Old Timber Ct & Rd 37042
Old Trenton Rd 37040
E Old Trenton Rd 37043
Old Tylertown Ln 37040
Oldham Dr 37043
Olive Cir 37043
Olive Branch Rd 37042
Oliver Loop 37040
Olney St 37040
Omalley Dr & Ln 37042
Ontario Ln 37043
Orchard Rd 37042
Orchard Hills Dr 37040
Oriole Cir 37043
Orleans Dr 37042
Orman Dr 37042
Ortex Dr 37040
Osage Ct 37042
Osprey Dr 37042
Otis Smith Dr 37043
Outfitters Dr 37040
Outlaw Field Rd 37042
Overlook Cir 37043
Overlook Pointe 37043
Overton Dr 37042
Owl Hollow Rd 37040
Oxford Ct 37043
Pace Dr, Pl & Rd 37043
Pachuta Trl 37040
Paddock Rd 37043
Paddy Run Rd 37042
Pageant Ln 37040
Palamino Dr 37042
Palmyra Rd 37040
Pam Dr 37043
Panorama Dr 37042
Parade Ct & Dr 37040
Paradise Hill Rd
1200-1399 37040
1400-1899 37043
Parchman Rd 37040
Pardue Ct & Dr 37043
Parham Dr 37040
Paris Dr 37042
W Park Dr 37043
Park Ln 37042
Parker Dr 37042
Parkland Cir 37043
Parkside Dr 37042
Parkview Ct & Dr 37042
Parkvue Village Way 37043
Parkway Pl 37042
Parrot Dr 37042
Parsons Way 37042
Partridge Ct 37043
Pashold Rd 37040
Pat Dr 37040
Patel Way 37043
Patricia Dr & Ln 37040
Patrick St 37040
Patriot Park Ct 37042
Patton Rd 37042
Paula Dr 37042
Pavilion Way 37043
Pea Ridge Rd 37040
Peabody Dr 37042
Peaceful Valley Rd 37040
Peach St 37042
Peachers Dr 37042

Peachers Mill Rd 37042
Peachers Ridge Rd 37042
Peartree Dr 37043
Pebble Ct 37042
Pebblecreek Ct 37040
Peggy Dr 37042
Pembroke Rd 37042
Pembrook Pl 37042
Pendleton Dr 37042
Pennridge Rd 37042
Pergola Ct 37043
Perigo Rd 37040
Periwinkle Pl 37040
Perkins Ave 37040
Persimmon Ct 37040
Persinger Ln 37042
Peterson Ln 37040
Phillip Long Rd 37043
Pickens Rd 37040
Pickering Ln 37040
Pickering Rd 37043
Pin Oak Dr 37040
Pine St 37042
E Pine Mountain Rd 37042
Pinetree Rd 37042
Piney Dr 37042
Pinnacle Pt 37043
Pinto Ct 37042
Piter Rd 37043
Pitt Ln 37043
Pitty Pat Rd 37042
Plantation Dr 37042
Plum St 37042
Plymouth Rd 37040
Poindexter Rd 37042
W Point Dr 37043
Pointer Ln 37042
Polk St 37040
Pollard Ct & Rd 37042
Polly Dr 37042
Pond Apple Rd 37043
Pontangs Dr 37042
Pony Ct 37042
Poole Rd 37043
Pope St 37040
Poplar Ct 37040
Poplar Hl 37043
Poplar St 37040
Poppy Dr 37042
Port Royal Rd
300-899 37040
900-2199 37043
3100-3198 37040
Porter Hills Dr 37043
E Porters Bluff Rd 37040
Post Ct & Rd 37043
Poston St 37040
Potomac Ct & Dr 37043
Potters Ct & Ln 37040
Powell Rd 37043
Power St 37042
Powers Rd 37043
Prescott Dr 37042
Press Grove Dr 37043
Pressler Way 37043
Preston Dr 37042
Preston Bagwell Rd 37043
Prewitt Ln & Rd 37040
Priest St 37040
Primrose Ct 37043
Prince Dr 37043
Princess Ct 37043
Princeton Cir, Ct & Dr 37042
Prissy Rd 37042
Proctor Dr 37043
Professional Park Dr 37040
Progress Dr 37040
Promontary Ln 37040
Prospect Cir 37043
Providence Blvd & Ct 37042
Provo Dr 37040
Public Sq 37040
Pueblo Trce 37040
Pullman Ct 37040
Pumping Station Rd 37040
Putnum Dr 37042

Quail Hollow Rd 37043
Quail Ridge Rd 37042
Quarry Rd 37042
Queens Ct 37043
Queens Bluff Way 37043
Queensbury Rd 37042
Quentin Dr 37042
Quicksilver Ct & Ln 37042
Quincy Ln 37043
Quiver Ln 37043
R S Bradley Blvd 37042
Rabbit Ct 37043
Rachel Ct 37043
Rafiki Dr 37042
Rainbow St 37042
Rainswood Ct 37043
Raintree Dr 37042
Raleigh Ct & Dr 37043
Ramblewood Dr 37040
Ramona Dr 37042
Ranch Hill Dr 37042
Randell Dr 37042
Randle Brothers Ln 37043
Randolph Ave 37042
Ranger Ln 37042
Rapids Ct 37040
Ratchford Dr 37042
Rattling Rd 37040
Raven Rd 37042
Ray Dr 37042
Reagan Ct 37042
Reasons Dr 37042
Rebecca Ln 37042
Rebecca Ann Ct 37043
Red Apple Ct 37040
Red Coat Run 37043
Red Fox Trl 37042
Red Paint Rdg 37043
Red River St 37040
Redbud Ln 37043
Redwood Ln 37042
Reeves Dr 37043
E & W Regent Dr 37043
Rembrandt Dr 37040
Remington Trce 37043
Renee Ct 37043
Renfro Ct 37043
Retriever Ct 37043
Revere Rd 37043
Reynolds St 37040
E & W Rhett Butler Rd 37042
Rhonda Ct 37040
Richards Dr 37043
Richardson Rd & St 37040
Richaven Rd 37043
Richmond Dr 37042
Richmond Pl 37040
S Richview Ct, Pl & Rd 37043
S Ridge Trl 37043
Ridge Meadow Dr 37042
Ridge Runner Ct 37042
Ridgecrest Dr 37040
Ridgeland Dr 37043
Ridgeline Dr 37042
Ridgepoint Ct 37040
Ridgepole Dr 37040
Ridgeway Dr 37040
Ridgewood Dr 37043
Riley Rd 37042
Ringgold Ct & Rd 37042
River Rd 37040
River Run 37043
River Ter 37043
River Bend Dr 37043
River Heights Dr 37040
River Hills Dr 37043
Rivermont Dr 37043
N & S Riverside Dr 37040
Riverview Dr 37040
Riverwood Pl 37040
Roan Dr 37042
Roanoke Rd & Sta 37043
Rob Rd 37040
Robb Ave 37040

Robercrest Rd 37043
Robert Ave 37042
Robert St 37040
Robert S Brown Dr 37043
Roberts Rd & St 37040
Robertson Ct 37042
Robin Dr 37042
Robin Pl 37043
Robin Ann Ave 37042
Robin Hill Rd 37043
Robin Hood Dr 37042
Robin Lynn Dr 37042
Rockwood Hts 37040
Rocky Ford Rd 37040
Rocky Hill Rd 37042
Rocky Top Ct 37040
Roedeer Dr 37042
Rolling Hills Ct 37043
Rolling Meadow Dr 37040
Rolling Rock Ct 37043
Rollins Dr 37040
Rollow Ln 37043
Roman St 37040
Rome Ln 37040
S Roscoe Dr 37042
Roscommon Way 37040
Rosebrook Dr 37042
Rosebury Ln 37043
Rosehill Dr 37042
Roselawn Dr 37042
Rosemary Dr 37042
S Rosewood Dr 37043
Ross Ln 37042
Rossview Rd 37043
W Rossview Rd 37040
Rotary Hills Ct 37043
Rotary Park Dr 37043
Rowand Ct 37042
Rowdy Trl 37042
Rowe Ln 37040
Roxbury Ln 37043
Roy Rd 37040
Royal Oaks Ct 37043
Royster Ln 37042
Rubel Rd 37040
Ruby Dr 37040
Rudolph Dr 37040
Rudolphtown Rd 37043
Rue Le Mans Dr 37042
Runnymeade Dr 37043
Rushton Ln 37043
Russell Dr 37040
Russet Dr 37040
Russet Ridge Dr 37040
Rustys Ln 37042
Ruth Dr 37040
Rutting Dr 37040
Ryan Dr 37040
Ryder Ave 37042
Rye Dr 37043
Sable Dr 37042
Sage Meadow Ln 37040
Saint Andrew Ct 37043
Saint John St 37040
Sale Rd 37043
Salem Ct 37042
Salem Rd 37040
Salem Ridge Rd 37040
Salisbury Way 37043
Sam Houston Cir 37040
Samantha Ln 37040
Sampson St 37040
Samuel Dr 37043
Sandburg Dr 37042
Sanders Rd 37043
Sandlewood Dr 37040
Sandpiper Dr 37042
Sandstream Ct 37042
Sandy Dr 37043
Sango Dr, Rd & Xing 37043
Sango Commons Way 37043
Sango Place Villa Dr 37043
Sarah Dr 37042
Sarah Beth Ct 37043
Sarah Elizabeth Dr 37042
Saratoga Dr 37042

Savannah Trace Dr 37043
Saxon Dr 37042
Scar Dr 37042
Scarborough Dr 37043
Scarlet Dr 37040
Scarlett Ohara Ct 37042
Scenic Dr 37043
Scott Dr 37042
Scott Rd 37043
Scottish Cir 37040
Scrub Oak Dr 37042
Seagull Dr 37042
Sealpoint Ct 37040
Seay Ct 37043
Secretariate Ct 37042
Sedgwick Ln 37043
Selph Ln 37042
Seminole Trl 37042
Senator Dr 37042
N & S Senseney Cir & Dr 37042
Sentinel Dr 37043
Sequoia Dr 37043
Sequoia Ln 37040
Setter Rd 37042
Settlers Trce 37043
Seven Mile Ferry Rd N 37040
Seven Springs Rd 37043
Sevier St 37042
Sewell Ct & Dr 37042
Shadeland Dr 37043
Shadow Ct 37043
Shadow Bluff Ct 37040
Shadowbend Cir & Ln 37043
N & S Shadowlawn Ct 37040
Shadowood Rd 37043
Shady Ln 37042
Shady Bluff Trl 37043
Shady Grove Rd 37043
Shady Hill Ct 37042
Shady Lawn Dr 37043
Shady Maple Dr 37043
Shadybrook Ln 37040
Shadyside Ln 37043
Shadytree Ct 37042
Shagbark Cir 37043
Shalimar Dr 37042
Shamrock Ct 37043
Shanee Ter 37042
Shannon St 37042
Sharp Trl 37042
Sharpie Dr 37040
Sharptail Trl 37042
Shasta Ct 37042
Shaub Ct 37042
Shaw Dr 37042
Shearon Ln 37040
Shearor St 37040
Sheffield Way 37043
Shelby Dr 37043
Shelby St 37042
Shellie Dr 37043
Shelton Cir 37042
Shelton Ct 37040
Shelton St 37040
Shenandoah St 37043
Sheriff Dr 37042
Sherman Ct 37042
Sherry Ct 37042
Sherwood Dr 37043
Sherwood Hills Ct & Dr 37042
Shetland Way 37043
Shield Dr 37042
Shiloh Rd 37042
Shivas Rd 37042
Shockey Dr 37042
Shorehaven Dr 37042
Short Ct & St 37042
Short A St 37042
Short Bluff Ct & Dr 37040
Short Stacker Dr 37040
Shortridge Dr 37042
Shoveler Ct & Way 37042
Sierra Ct 37040

Sikorsky Ln 37042
Silty Ct & Dr 37042
Silver Dr 37040
Silver Fox Ct & Ln 37040
Silver Leaf Dr 37043
Silver Star Dr 37043
Simba Dr 37042
Simpson Dr 37043
Simpson Ln 37042
Sinclair Dr 37042
Single Tree Dr 37040
Skelton Dr 37040
Skyline Ter 37040
Skyview Cir 37042
Slayden Cir 37040
Sloan Rd 37043
Sly Fox Dr 37040
Smith Ln 37043
Smith Branch Rd 37042
Smith Brothers Ln 37043
Smith Place Rd 37040
Smokestack Dr 37040
Smokey Ct 37042
Snoopy Dr 37040
Snowball Ln 37042
Snowshoe Ln 37040
Solar Way 37040
Solid Rock Ct 37042
Somerset Ln 37042
Sonja Dr 37042
Southern Dr 37042
Southern Pkwy 37040
Southgate Ln 37040
Southpoint Dr 37043
Southwood Ct & Dr 37042
Sparkleberry Dr 37042
Sparrow Dr 37040
Spees Dr 37042
Spencer Ln 37042
Sphinx Ct 37042
Spike Ct 37040
N & S Spring Aly & St 37040
Spring Creek Ct 37040
Spring Creek Village Rd 37040
Spring House Trl 37040
Spring Terrace Ct & Ln 37040
Spring Water Dr 37040
Springhaven Dr 37042
Springlot Rd 37043
Springs Inn Rd 37043
Springside Ct 37043
Spruce Dr 37042
St Ives Way 37042
Stacker Dr 37040
Stacy Ln 37043
Stafford St 37040
Stag Ct & Ln 37043
Starlight Ln 37043
State Garage Ln 37040
State Line Rd 37043
Steel Springs Rd 37040
Steel Stock Rd 37040
Steeple Ridge Way 37043
Steeplechase Ct 37043
Steffi St 37040
Stella Ct & Dr 37040
Stepford Dr 37043
Stephanie Dr 37042
Stephen Ct 37042
Stephen Dr 37043
Stillwood Dr 37042
Stokes Rd 37043
Stone Briar Dr 37043
Stone Container Dr 37040
Stone Hill Ct 37042
Stone Manor Way 37043
Stone Mountain Rd 37043
Stone Trail Dr 37043
Stone Valley Ct 37043
Stonebrook Dr 37042
Stonecrossing Dr 37042
Stonegate Dr 37043
Stonemeadow Rd 37043
Stonemill Ct 37043

Stones Manor Ct 37043
Stonewall Ct & Ln 37040
Stoney Creek Ct 37040
Storybook Dr 37042
Stowe Ct 37040
Strassbourg Rd 37043
Stratford Way 37043
Strawberry Aly 37040
Sturdivant Dr 37042
Sue Dr 37042
Suellen Way 37043
Sugar Tree Dr 37043
Sugarcane Way 37040
Sugarhill Ct 37040
Suiter Rd 37040
Sullivan St 37040
Sulphur Springs Rd 37043
Sumac Ct 37043
Summer St 37040
Summer Lawn Dr 37043
Summer Terrace Ln 37040
Summerfield Dr 37042
Summergrove Ln 37043
Summerhaven Rd 37042
Summertree Ln 37040
Summit Hts 37040
Summit View Cir 37043
Sun Valley Rd 37040
Sunbelt Dr 37042
Sunbrite Dr 37042
Sunfield Dr 37042
Sunny Slope Ct & Dr 37043
Sunnyview Dr 37043
Sunrise Dr 37042
Sunset Ct 37042
Sunset Dr 37040
Sunset Meadows Way 37042
Sunshine Dr 37042
Superior Ln 37043
Surrey Ridge Rd 37043
Susan St 37042
Swan Ln 37043
Swan Lake Dr 37042
Sweetbriar Dr 37043
Sweetwater Dr 37042
Swift Dr 37040
Sycamore Dr 37040
Sydney Louise Dr 37042
Syracuse Dr 37042
Tabby Dr 37042
Taft Dr 37042
Taits Station Dr 37042
Talley Dr 37043
Talton Ct & Dr 37040
Tamera Ln 37042
Tammy Dr 37042
Tana Way 37042
Tandy Dr 37042
Tanglewood Dr 37043
Tanglewood Rd 37040
Tannahill Ct & Way 37043
Tara Blvd 37042
Tate Ln 37043
Taylor Rd 37042
Teacher Dr 37042
Teakwood Dr 37040
Teal Dr 37042
Ted A Crozier Sr Blvd 37043
Tennessee Ave 37040
Tennyson Dr 37042
Terminal Rd 37040
Terrace Dr 37043
Terraceside Cir 37040
Terrier Way 37042
Thayer Ln 37043
Theresa Dr 37042
Thermal Ct 37042
Thistlewood Dr 37042
Thomas Ln 37040
N Thomas Rd 37043
Thomas St 37040
Thompkins Ln 37043
Thompson Ln 37040
Thornberry Dr 37043
Thornhurst Dr 37040
Thrush Dr 37040

Timber Court Dr 37043
Timber Lake Dr 37043
Timberdale Dr 37042
Timberline Pl & Way 37042
Timberridge Dr 37042
Timberwood Dr 37040
Timothy Ave 37042
Tiny Town Rd 37042
Titans Ln 37042
Tobacco Rd 37042
Todd Dr 37043
Todd Phillips Ct & Trl 37042
Tolliver Ct & Way 37040
Tom Dr 37043
Tom Moore Rd 37043
Tommy Oliver Rd 37042
Torrington Ln 37042
Tower Dr 37042
Towes Ln 37043
Townsend Ct & Way 37043
Trace Ct 37043
Traceview Pl 37040
Tracy Ln 37040
Tradewinds N 37040
Tradewinds Ter 37040
Trahern Cir, Ln & Ter 37040
Trainer Dr & Rd 37042
Tranquill Ln 37043
Travis Pl 37040
Treeland Ct & Dr 37040
Treemont Dr 37043
Trelawny Ct & Dr 37043
Trenton Rd 37040
Trevor Dr 37043
Trey Ct 37043
Trey Phillips Dr 37042
Trophy Trce 37040
Trough Springs Rd 37043
Troutbeck Ct 37040
Tuckaway Ct 37043
Tudor Ln 37042
Tulip Ct 37040
Tulip Poplar Ct 37043
Turn Row Dr 37043
Turnberry Cir 37043
Turner Ln 37040
Turner Reynolds Ct 37043
Turtle Creek Ct & Rd 37043
Tuscon Ct 37042
Twelve Oaks Blvd 37042
Twin Cedars Dr 37043
Twin Rivers Rd 37040
Tyler St 37040
Tyler Brown Dr 37040
Tylertown Rd 37040
Tynewood Dr 37042
Uffelman Dr 37043
E Union St 37040
Union Hall Rd 37040
University Ave 37040
Ussery Ln 37040
Ussery Rd 37043
Ussery Rd S 37040
Utopia Dr 37043
Valencia Dr 37043
Valley Rd 37043
Valley Crest Ln 37043
Valley View Cir 37040
Van Buren Ct 37042
Vanleer St 37040
Vannoak Dr 37043
Vantage Ct 37040
Variance Dr 37042
Vaughan Rd 37043
Velmas Way 37042
Venessa Dr 37042
Venison Ln 37042
Vera Dr 37040
Veranda Cir 37042
Verdun Dr 37042
Verisa Dr 37043
Verkler Dr 37042
Via Dr 37043
Victoria Ct 37043
Victory Rd 37042
Viewmont Dr 37040

Village Ct, Dr & Way 37043
Vine St 37040
Viola Ct 37043
Virginia Ct 37040
Virginia Dr 37040
Virginia Ter 37042
Vista Ln 37043
Vivian Dr 37042
Vogue Hill Rd 37040
Wagon Trail Rd 37042
Wakefield Dr 37043
Waldorf Dr 37042
Walkaway Ct 37043
Walker Cir & St 37042
Wall St 37040
Wallace Blvd 37042
Walnut Dr 37040
Walnut St 37040
Walnut Grove Rd 37042
Walter Rd 37043
Walter Head Rd 37043
Warfield Blvd & Dr 37043
Warfield Boulevard Ct 37043
Warner Rd 37042
Warren Cir & Dr 37040
W Washington Ct & St 37040
Water Wood Dr 37043
Waterfall Dr 37043
Waterford Cir & Ct 37040
Waterloo Dr 37043
Waters Edge Dr 37043
Watertown Pl 37043
Watts Ct 37043
Waylon Ct 37043
Wayne St 37042
Waywick Dr 37043
Weatherby Dr 37043
Weatherly Ct & Dr 37043
Webb Rd 37040
Wedgewood Ct 37042
Wedgewood Dr 37043
Weeping Willow Dr 37042
Welch Rd 37043
Welch St 37040
Welchwood Dr 37040
Wellington Dr 37043
Wells Ct 37043
Wellsford Ct 37043
Welsey Dr 37042
Wennona Dr 37042
West Ave, Ct, Dr & Rd 37040
Westchester Ct, Dr & Pl 37043
Westfield Ct 37040
Westwood Dr 37043
Weymouth Ct 37043
Wheatfield Ct & Ln 37040
Wheeler Rd & St 37040
Whetstone Ct 37042
Whirlaway Cir 37042
Whispering Heights Dr 37043
Whispering Hills Trl 37043
White Birch 37042
White Face Dr 37040
White Oak Rd 37040
Whitehall Dr 37042
Whitetail Dr 37043
Whitfield Dr 37042
Whitfield Rd 37040
N Whitfield Rd 37040
Whitland Dr 37043
Whitman Aly & Xing 37043
Whitt Ln 37042
Widgeon Dr 37042
Wilcox St 37040
Wild Fox Ct 37040
Wilderness Cir & Way 37042
Wildwood Dr 37040
Wiley Brown Rd 37043
Will Way 37043
Willard Rd 37042
William Suiters Ln 37042
Williams Ln 37040
Williams Rd 37043
Williamsburg Rd 37043

Willow Cir ... 37043
Willow Hts ... 37040
Willow Ter ... 37043
N Willow Bend Ct & Dr ... 37043
Willow Brook Dr ... 37043
Willow Hollow Rd ... 37043
Wilma Rudolph Blvd
2277A1-2277A1 ... 37040
1500-2032 ... 37040
2031-2031 ... 37041
2033-3199 ... 37040
2034-3198 ... 37040
Wilmac St ... 37040
Wilson Ct & Rd ... 37043
Wimbledon Ct ... 37043
Windchase Dr ... 37042
Windermere Dr ... 37043
Windham Dr ... 37043
Windhaven Ct & Dr ... 37040
Winding Bluff Way ... 37040
Winding Creek Ct ... 37043
Winding Way Rd ... 37043
Windmeade Cir & Dr ... 37042
Windmill Ct & Dr ... 37040
Windriver Rd ... 37042
Windroe Ct & Dr ... 37042
Windrush Dr ... 37042
Windsong Ct ... 37043
Windsor Dr ... 37043
Windwood Ct ... 37043
Winesap Rd ... 37040
Wingate Dr ... 37043
Winn Mor Dr ... 37043
Winston Ct ... 37042
Winterhaven Ct ... 37042
Winters Ct ... 37043
Wisdom St ... 37040
Wiser Dr ... 37042
Wisteria Ct ... 37040
Wofford Dr ... 37042
Wolfchase Ct & Dr ... 37042
Wonderboy Ct ... 37042
Woodale Dr ... 37042
Woodard St ... 37040
Woodbridge Dr ... 37042
Woodbury Dr ... 37042
Woodhaven Ct & Dr ... 37042
Woodland Dr ... 37043
Woodland St ... 37040
Woodlawn Dr ... 37040
Woodlawn Rd ... 37042
Woodmeadow Dr ... 37043
Woodmont Blvd ... 37040
Woods Aly ... 37040
Woods Rd ... 37043
N & S Woodson Rd ... 37043
Woodstock Ct ... 37040
N Woodstock Dr ... 37040
Woodstock Ln ... 37043
N Woodstock Way ... 37040
Woodtrace Dr ... 37042
Woody Ln ... 37043
Woody Hills Dr ... 37040
Wooten Rd ... 37042
Wren Dr ... 37040
Yankee Dr ... 37042
Yarbrough Ln & Rd ... 37040
Yeager Ct ... 37042
Yeager Dr ... 37040
York Rd ... 37042
York St ... 37040
York Meadows Rd ... 37042
Yorkbar Ct ... 37043
Yorkshire Dr ... 37043
Yorktown Rd ... 37042
Yvonne Dr ... 37042
Zachry Dr ... 37042
Zinc Plant Rd ... 37040
Zinnia Dr ... 37040
Zurich Ct & Dr ... 37040

NUMBERED STREETS

All Street Addresses ... 37040

CLEVELAND TN

General Delivery ... 37311

POST OFFICE BOXES MAIN OFFICE STATIONS AND BRANCHES

Box No.s
1 - 1524 ... 37364
2001 - 6110 ... 37320
4000 - 4000 ... 37364
8000 - 8081 ... 37320

NAMED STREETS

A St SE ... 37323
Abbey Cv NE ... 37312
Abby Glen Dr NE ... 37312
Abshire Ln NE ... 37323
Acorn Ln NE ... 37312
Adkisson Dr NW ... 37312
Airport Rd NW ... 37312
Albert Lawson Rd NE ... 37323
Alberta Peach St SE ... 37323
Alecia Ln SE ... 37323
Alexanders Cir NW ... 37312
Alexandria Ct NW ... 37312
Alexian Way NW ... 37312
Alice St NE ... 37323
Alley St NE ... 37311
Alma Ln SE ... 37323
Alpine Ct NW ... 37311
Alta Vista St NW ... 37312
Alton Ave SE ... 37323
Alvin Ct NW ... 37312
Amber Way SW ... 37311
American Dr NE ... 37323
Amherst Way NW ... 37312
Anatole Ct & Ln ... 37312
Anatole Pointe NW ... 37312
Anders Rd SE ... 37323
Andrew Dr NW ... 37311
Andrew Jackson Ln SE ... 37323
Angie Ct & Ln NE & NW ... 37312
Ann Ln NW ... 37312
Anna Belle Ln NW ... 37312
Annette Ln SE ... 37323
Apache Trl NW ... 37312
Apd 40
1700-2799 ... 37323
3201-3497 ... 37311
3499-4199 ... 37311
Appalachia Trl NE ... 37323
Apple Orchard Dr NW ... 37312
Archer Ln SE ... 37323
Arlena Dr NW ... 37312
Armstrong Ln & Rd ... 37323
Arnold Ave & St ... 37311
Arp St SE ... 37311
Arrow Dr NE ... 37312
Arrowhead Ln SE ... 37311
Ascalon Dr SE ... 37323
Ash Dr NW ... 37312
Ashford Ct NW ... 37312
Ashland Ter NE ... 37312
Ashley Ct NE ... 37312
Ashlin Meadow Ln NE ... 37312
Ashlin Ridge Dr NE ... 37312
Ashlin Woods Dr NE ... 37312
Ashwood Dr SE ... 37323
Aster Dr NW ... 37312
Asterwood Ln & Trl ... 37312
Aurora Ave SE ... 37311
Austin Ln SE ... 37323
Autumn Dr NE ... 37323
Autumn Ridge Dr NW ... 37312
Autumn Wind Dr SW ... 37311
Avenwood Cir NW ... 37312
Ayers Dr NE ... 37323
Azalea Ave & Dr ... 37312
Bailey Cir SW ... 37311
Baker Rd SW ... 37311
Bald Eagle Dr NW ... 37312
Baldwin St SE ... 37311
Ball Rd & St ... 37323
Balsm Ct NW ... 37312
Barberry Dr NW ... 37312
Barker Ln NW ... 37312
Barnes St NE ... 37311
Barneys Ln NE ... 37323
Barpen St NW ... 37312
Bartlett Cir NE ... 37312
Basswood Ct NW ... 37312
Basswood Pl SE ... 37323
Bates Pike SE
1200-2499 ... 37311
2500-6499 ... 37323
Bates St NE ... 37311
Baugh St NE ... 37311
Bayberry Ln NW ... 37312
Bea St SE ... 37323
Beard Cir SW ... 37311
Beaty Dr NW ... 37312
Beck St SE ... 37323
Beech Cir NW ... 37312
Beech Cove Dr NW ... 37312
Bell Rd & St ... 37323
Bell Chase Way NE ... 37312
Bell Crest Dr NW ... 37312
Bell Tower Ln NE ... 37312
Belleview Dr SE ... 37323
Bellfounte Rd NE ... 37312
Bellingham Dr NE ... 37312
Belmont Cir NW ... 37312
Ben Dr NW ... 37311
Benjamin Cir NW ... 37312
Bennett Ln SW ... 37311
Bent Oak Trl SE ... 37323
Bent Tree Dr NW ... 37312
Bentley Park Dr NW ... 37312
Benton Dr NW ... 37312
Benton Pike NE
600-1599 ... 37311
1700-6899 ... 37323
Bentridge Cv NW ... 37312
Benwood Trl NE ... 37323
Bernham Dr NW ... 37312
Berry St NE ... 37311
Berrywood Cir NE ... 37323
Berywood Trl NW ... 37312
Bettis Ave SW ... 37311
Bible St NE ... 37311
Big Pine Dr SE ... 37323
Bigsby Creek Rd NW ... 37312
Bimbo Trl SE ... 37323
Birdie Ct NW ... 37312
Blackburn Rd SE
2100-2399 ... 37311
2400-3099 ... 37323
Blackburn Hollow Rd NW ... 37312
Blackfox Rd SW ... 37311
Blair Rd NW ... 37312
Blairs Bnd NE ... 37323
Blake Ct NW ... 37312
Bland Dr NE ... 37312
Blossom Trl NE ... 37312
Blount Ave SW ... 37311
Blue Grass Cir SE ... 37323
Blue Springs Ln & Rd ... 37311
Blue Springs Church Rd SW ... 37311
Blueberry Hill Pl & Rd ... 37312
Blueberry Hills Rd NE ... 37312
Bluebird Nature Ln SE ... 37323
Bluff Dr NW ... 37312
Blythe Ave SE ... 37311
Blythe Rd SE ... 37323
Blythe Ferry Pl & Rd ... 37312
Blythewood Rd SW ... 37311
Bo St SE ... 37323
Boatwright Cir NW ... 37312
Bobby Taylor Ave ... 37311
Bobo Ave NW ... 37312
Bohannons Rd SE ... 37323
Bow Pl & St ... 37312
Bower Ln SE ... 37311
Bowman Ave NW ... 37311
Bowman Circle Dr NE ... 37312
Boyd St SW ... 37311
Brackin Rd SE ... 37323
Brad St NW ... 37312
Bradley St NW ... 37312
Bramblewood Trl NW ... 37311
Brandon Ln NE ... 37323
Brandy Oaks Dr NW ... 37312
Breckenridge Dr NW ... 37312
Brent Dr SW ... 37311
Brentwood Dr & Trl NW & SW ... 37311
Brian Ln & Rd NE & NW ... 37312
Briarcliff Ln NW ... 37312
Briarwood Pl NW ... 37312
Bridget Ln NW ... 37312
Brighton Blvd NW ... 37312
Broad St NW & SW ... 37311
Brock Rd NE ... 37323
Broken Arrow Ln SW ... 37311
Bromley Dr SE ... 37323
N Brook Dr NE & NW ... 37312
Brook Bryson Rd SE ... 37311
Brook Hollow Dr SE ... 37323
Brook Valley Dr NW ... 37311
Brookcrest Dr NE ... 37323
Brooke Ln NE ... 37323
Brookfield Ct NE ... 37312
Brookhill Ln NE ... 37323
Brooklawn Trl SE ... 37323
Brookside Dr NW ... 37312
Brookview Dr SE ... 37323
Brookview St NW ... 37312
Brookwood Dr NE ... 37323
Broomfield Rd SE ... 37323
Brown Ave NW ... 37311
Brown Dr SE ... 37323
Brown Rd SE ... 37323
Browning Rd SE ... 37323
Brownstone Cir NE ... 37323
Brownwood Dr SE ... 37323
Brushwood Ct NE ... 37312
Bryan Cir SE ... 37323
Bryant Dr SW ... 37311
Bryson Ln SE ... 37311
Buchanan Cir & Rd ... 37323
Buckeye Ln NW ... 37312
Bullington Rd SW ... 37311
E Bunt Dr SE ... 37323
Burke Rd SE ... 37323
Burkeridge Dr SE ... 37323
Burl Oaks Dr NE ... 37323
Burley Dr NW ... 37312
Burlington Dr NW ... 37312
Burning Tree Dr NW ... 37312
Burnt Hollow Trl SE ... 37323
Burris Ln NW ... 37312
Business Park Dr NE ... 37311
Byrd Rd NE ... 37323
C And C Ln ... 37323
Cabrera Ln SE ... 37323
Caldwell Rd SE ... 37323
Calfee Ln SE ... 37323
Calhoun Rd SE ... 37323
Calico Ave NE ... 37323
California Ln SW ... 37311
Callaway Ln NE ... 37323
Cambridge Ln NW ... 37312
Camellia Ave NW ... 37312
Campbell Dr NW ... 37312
Campbell Bridge Rd NW ... 37312
Canary Dr NW ... 37312
Candice Dr NE ... 37323
Candies Ln NW ... 37312
Candies Creek Ln NW ... 37312
Candies Creek Rd SW ... 37311
Candies Creek Ridge Rd NW ... 37312
Candlelight Cv NE ... 37312
Canterbury Ct NW ... 37312
Caperton Dr NE ... 37312
Cardinal Ln NW ... 37312
Cardinal Oaks NE ... 37323
Carl Whitworth Ln SE ... 37323
Carlos Way SE ... 37323
Carmen Ln SE ... 37323
Carnation Ave NW ... 37312
Carol Dr SE ... 37323
Carolina Ave NE ... 37311
Carolyn Ct SE ... 37323
Carriage Dr & Ln ... 37312
Carriage Hills Dr NE ... 37312
Carrie Dr NW ... 37312
Carrie St SE ... 37323
Carroll Ave & Ln ... 37323
Carrot Dr NE ... 37311
Carson Rd NE & SE ... 37323
Carter Rd SE ... 37323
Cascade Hills Dr NW ... 37312
Casteel Rd SE ... 37323
Castle Dr NW ... 37312
Cates Ln NE ... 37323
Catherine Cir NW ... 37312
Cayce Whaley Rd SE ... 37323
Caywood Dr NW ... 37311
Cedar Ave NW ... 37312
Cedar Dr SE ... 37323
Cedar Ln SW ... 37311
Cedar Creek Cir NW ... 37312
Cedar Creek Xing NE ... 37323
Cedar Hill Ln NW ... 37312
Cedar Springs Rd SE ... 37323
Cedar Springs Church Rd SE ... 37323
Cedarwood Trl NW ... 37312
Centenary Ave NW ... 37311
Centerview Ln SE ... 37323
Central Ave & St ... 37311
Century Ave SE ... 37311
Chambliss Ave NW ... 37311
Champion Dr NW ... 37312
Chapperell Trl NW ... 37312
Charles Cir SE ... 37323
Charles St NE ... 37311
Charleston Dr NE ... 37312
Charlotte Dr NE ... 37323
Charterwood Ln NE ... 37312
Charwood Trl NW ... 37312
Chase Ln NE ... 37323
Chatata Dr NE ... 37323
Chatata Valley Rd NE ... 37323
Chelsa Dr NE ... 37323
Cherokee Dr NE ... 37323
Cherokee Trl NW ... 37312
Cherry St NE ... 37311
Cherry St SE ... 37323
Cherry Laurel Trl NE ... 37323
Cherub Ct NE ... 37323
Chestnut Cir NW ... 37312
Chestnut Ln NW ... 37312
Chestnut St SE ... 37311
Chestnut Grove Ln NE ... 37323
Chestnut Oak Dr SW ... 37311
Chestuee Cir, Dr, Ln & Rd NE ... 37323
Chetola Dr NE ... 37323
Chilcutt Rd NE ... 37323
Chilhowee Cir NW ... 37312
Chip Dr NE ... 37323
Chippewa Ave SE ... 37311
Chippewah Circle Dr NE ... 37312
Christian Dr NW ... 37312
Church St NE & SE ... 37311
Cincinnati Ave SE ... 37311
Cindy Cir NW ... 37312
Circle Dr NE ... 37323
Circle Dr SW ... 37311
E Circle Dr NW ... 37312
City View St SE ... 37311
Clairmont Dr NE ... 37312
Clara Ln SE ... 37323
Clarence Dr SE ... 37323
Clay Baker Rd NW ... 37311
Clayton Ln & St ... 37323
Clearcreek Rd NE ... 37323
Clearview Cir NE ... 37312
Clearwater Dr NE ... 37312
Clemmer St NE ... 37311
Cliff Dr SE ... 37323
Cliffside Dr NE ... 37312
Climer Rd NE ... 37323
Clinch St NE ... 37311
Cline Rd NE ... 37312
Clingan Dr NW ... 37311
Clingan Ridge Dr NW ... 37312
Clint Dr NE ... 37312
Cloudview Pl NE ... 37312
Clover Dr NW ... 37312
Cloverleaf Cir SE ... 37311
Cloverleaf Ct NE ... 37323
Club Dr SW ... 37311
Cobblestone Creek Rd NW ... 37312
Cochise Dr & St ... 37323
Cody St NW ... 37312
Coffey Dr NE ... 37323
Cohulla Rd SE ... 37323
Collegeview Dr NW ... 37312
Collins Dr NW ... 37312
Colonial Ct SE ... 37323
Colony Ln NW ... 37312
Concord Pl NW ... 37312
Conner Rd NW ... 37311
Connie Ct NE ... 37312
Cook Rd SW ... 37311
Cookdale Trl NW ... 37312
Cooper St SE ... 37323
Copper Top Ln NE ... 37312
Cora Dr SE ... 37323
Corporate Dr SW ... 37311
Corvin Rd NE ... 37323
Cottage Grove Cir NW ... 37312
Cottage Stone Ln NE ... 37312
Cottonwood Bnd NW ... 37312
Country Club Dr SW ... 37311
Country Meadows Dr SE ... 37323
Country Place Dr NW ... 37312
Countrywood Dr SE ... 37323
Courtland Crest Dr SW ... 37311
Courtyard Ln NE ... 37312
Cove Lake Dr NW ... 37312
Covenant Ct, Cv & Dr ... 37323
Coventry Ct NW ... 37312
Covington Dr NE ... 37312
Covy Ct NE ... 37312
Cowan St NW ... 37312
Crab Apple Ln SE ... 37323
Craigmiles St NE ... 37311
Craven Ln NE ... 37312
Crawford Dr & Ln ... 37323
Cree Ln NW ... 37312
Creek Bend Cir & Ct ... 37312
Creek Side Ln NW ... 37312
Creekside Dr & Pl ... 37312
Crescent Dr SE ... 37323
Cress St NE ... 37311
Crest Dr & St ... 37311
Crestridge Ln NW ... 37312
Crestview Dr & Pl ... 37312
Crestwood Dr NW ... 37312
Cromwell Cir NW ... 37312
Cross Ln & St ... 37312
Crossing Pl NE ... 37323
Crossing Way NW ... 37312
Crosswinds Trl NE ... 37312
Crown St NW ... 37312
Crown Colony Dr NW ... 37312
Crystal Ct & Ter ... 37323
Crystal Spring Rd SE ... 37323
Crystal View Dr NW ... 37312
Cumberland Trce NW ... 37312
Cumberland Hills Cir NW ... 37312
Cunningham Cir NE ... 37323
Curtis Ln SE ... 37311
Curtis Rd SE ... 37323
Curtis St SE ... 37311
Cynthia Dr NE ... 37323
Daisy Ave NW ... 37312
Dakota Dr NE ... 37323
Dale Ln SE ... 37323
Dallas Ln NW ... 37312
Dalton Pike SE
1800-2299 ... 37311
2300-8599 ... 37323
Danberry Ln NE ... 37323
Daniel Ln SE ... 37323
Danview St SE ... 37323
Davis Cir, Dr, Ln, Rd & Trl NW ... 37312
Davy Crockett Rd NE ... 37323
Dawn Dr SE ... 37311
De Armond Ln NE ... 37323
Dean Pl NW ... 37312
Deer Trl NW ... 37312
Deer Run Ln & Trl ... 37311
Degree Trl NW ... 37312
Dellview Way SW ... 37311
Dellwood Ln NE ... 37312
Dempsey Cir SW ... 37311
Denham Dr SE ... 37323
Dennis Suits Rd SW ... 37323
Denton Hollow Rd NW ... 37312
Derby Ln ... 37312
Devon Pl SE ... 37323
Diamond Ridge Dr NE ... 37312
Diane Ave SE ... 37323
Diane St NE ... 37312
Dixie Dr NE & SE ... 37323
Dixie Court Dr SE ... 37323
Dixon Dr NE ... 37323
Dockery Ln & St ... 37323
Doe Meadow Ln NW ... 37312
Dogwood Cir NE ... 37323
Dogwood Pl NW ... 37312
Dogwood Trl NE ... 37323
Dogwood Trl NW ... 37312
Dooley St NE & SE ... 37311
Dorset Ln SE ... 37323
Doss Ln NE ... 37312
Douglas Cir NW ... 37311
Dowdy Rd SE ... 37323
Drake Dr NW ... 37312
Drema Ln NW ... 37312
Driftwood Trl NW ... 37312
Dry Valley Ln SW ... 37311
Dry Valley Rd NE ... 37312
Duckworth Ln SE ... 37323
Dunhill Pl NW ... 37311
Dunn Farm Rd SE ... 37323
Durham Dr SE ... 37323
Durkee Rd NE & SE ... 37323
Eagle Dr NW ... 37312
Eagle Park NE ... 37323
Eagle Creek Rd NW ... 37312
Eagle Head Ct NE ... 37312
Earls Ln NW ... 37312
East St NE & SE ... 37311
Easterly Dr SW ... 37311
Eastview Ave NW ... 37312
Eastview Cir NW ... 37311
Eastview Ln SE ... 37323
Eastview Ter SE ... 37323
Ed Cross Rd SE ... 37323
Eddie Wilson Ln NW ... 37312
Edgemon St SE ... 37323
Edgewater Dr NW ... 37311
Edgewood Cir & Dr ... 37312
Edwards St NE & SE ... 37311
Eggleston Dr SE ... 37323
Eisenhower St NE ... 37311
El Monte Cir NE ... 37323
Elaine Ln NW ... 37312
Eldredge Ave, Cir & Dr ... 37312
Eldridge Ln SW ... 37311
Eldridge Rd NW ... 37312
Eleanor Dr SW ... 37311
Elijah Way NW ... 37312
Elizabeth Way NE ... 37323
Elkmont Cir SE ... 37323
Elkmont Dr SE ... 37323
Elkmont Rd NW ... 37312
Ella Dr SE ... 37323
Ellis Cir NW ... 37312
Ellis Dr SE ... 37323
Ellisa Dr SE ... 37323
Elliston Dr SW ... 37311

Elliston Rd SE 37323
Elm Dr NE 37312
Elrod Ln SE 37323
Elrod Pl SE 37311
Elrod St SE 37311
Emerald Way SW 37311
Emerson Dr SE 37323
Emmett Ave NW 37311
Emmyllie Ct NE 37312
W End Dr NW 37311
English Ct SE 37323
English Oaks Cir & Dr 37323
Ensley Rd SE 37323
Enterprise Dr SW 37311
Ernest Longwith Rd NE 37312
Essex Dr SE 37323
Euclid Ave SE 37311
Eugenia Ave NW 37311
Eureka Rd NW 37312
Evans Rd NE 37323
Eveningside Dr NE & NW 37312
Everhart Dr NW 37311
Executive Park NW 37312
Fair St SE 37311
Fair Oaks Ct NE 37323
Fairfield Farm Rd NW 37312
Fairhill Dr NE 37323
Fairlawn Dr NE 37323
Fairmont Ave NW 37311
Fairoak Ln NW 37312
Fairview Dr SE 37323
Fairway Dr SW 37311
Falcon Dr & Ln 37323
Fall Ct NE 37312
Falling Leaf Cir NE 37312
Farmingdale Pl SE 37323
Farmway Dr SE 37323
Farrah Ct SE 37323
Farris Rd SE 37323
Farris St NE 37312
Farris St NW 37312
Faulk Ct & Dr 37312
Fawn Hill Ln NW 37312
Faye Dr SE 37323
Fern Dr SE 37323
Fernwood Dr NE 37323
Fernwood Pl NW 37312
Fetzer Rd SE 37323
Fieldstone Pl NE 37312
Fieldwood Ave & Dr 37323
Finnell Rd NW 37312
Fisher St SE 37311
Flagstone Ct NE 37323
Flagstone Dr NE 37323
Flagstone Pt NW 37312
Fleetwood Dr NE 37323
Fletcher Rd NW 37312
Flintsprings Rd SE 37323
Flora Ln 37323
Fore Dr SW 37311
Forest Dr SE 37323
Forest Ln NE 37312
Forest Ln SE 37323
Forest Ridge Cir & Dr 37311
Forestview Dr & Pl 37312
Forrest Ave NE 37311
Foster Ln SE 37311
Fox Trl NW 37312
Fox Crest Dr SW 37311
Fox Farm Trl SE 37323
Fox Hill Ln SW 37311
Fox Ridge Trl SW 37311
Fox Run Ln NE 37323
Foxfire Rd NE 37323
Frank Ln SE 37323
Franklin Ave NW 37312
Frazier Ln SE 37323
Frazier Park Dr NE 37323
Frederick St NW 37311
Freedom Pkwy NW 37312
Freewill Rd NW 37312
French Ave NW 37311
French Oaks Ln SE 37323
Fritz St SE 37323
Frontage Rd NW 37312
Frontier Ave NE 37323
Fulbright Rd NE 37312
Gable Dr NW 37312
Gale Dr NE & NW 37312
Gardenia Ave NW 37312
Gary St NW 37311
Gatlin Rd NE 37323
Gaut St NE & SE 37311
Gaye Dr SE 37323
Geneve Ln SW 37311
Gentle Mist Ct & Ln 37312
Gentry Ln SE 37311
George Ave NW 37312
George St NE 37311
Georgetown Cir NW 37312
Georgetown Dr NW 37312
Georgetown Rd NW
100-2699 37311
3300-7299 37312
Georgia Cir NW 37311
Georgia Bell Cir SE 37323
Geren Dr NE 37323
Gibson Dr NE 37312
Gibson Dr SE 37323
Gieger Rd NE 37312
Gilliland Dr SE 37323
Gilliland Rd SE 37311
Ginger Circle Dr SE 37323
Glen Oaks Trl NE 37312
Glenmore Dr NW 37312
Glenwood Dr NW 37311
Godfrey Ln & St 37311
Goins Rd NE 37323
Gold Pointe Dr NE 37312
Golden Ct NW 37312
Goldstar Dr SW 37311
Goldston Rd NE 37323
Golf Dr SE 37323
Golf Dr SW 37311
Golf View Ct & Dr 37312
Goode Rd SE 37323
Goode St SW 37311
Goodwill Rd SE 37323
Goodwin Rd NW 37312
Gordon St NE 37311
Grace St SW 37311
Grand Dr NE 37312
Grand View Dr SW 37311
Grayson Way SE 37323
Green Dr NW 37311
Green Hill Rd NE 37323
Green Shadow Rd SE 37323
Green Valley Dr SE 37323
Greenbriar Trl NE 37323
Greenbrier Dr NW 37312
Greenbrier Rd SE 37323
Greendale Dr & Pl 37323
Greenfield Ave NW 37312
Greenhills Ct, Cv, Dr, Ln & Ter SE 37323
Greenridge Dr NW 37312
Greenwood Ave NE 37311
Greenwood Dr NW 37312
Greenwood Trl NW 37312
Gregory Dr SE 37323
Gregory Ln NW 37312
Greystone Ln SE 37323
Griffith Dr SE 37323
Grove Ave NW 37311
Grove Ave SE 37323
Grove Ave SW 37311
Grove Cir NW 37312
Grovers Mill Ct SE 37323
Guthrie Ave NW 37311
Guthrie Dr NW 37311
Guthrie St NW
2501-2599 37311
2600-2699 37312
Hackberry Dr NW 37311
Hall Norwood Rd SE 37311
Ham Dr NE 37323
Hamilton Cir NW 37312
Hampton Dr SE 37311
Hancock Rd NE 37323
Hancock Oaks Trce NE 37323
Hannah Cir NW 37311
Hannah Dr SE 37323
Hannah Ln NW 37311
Hannah Rd NW 37311
Hardeman Ln NE 37312
Hardwick St NE & SE 37311
Hardwick Farms Pkwy NE 37312
Harle Ave NW & SW 37311
Harper St NW 37312
Harpo St NW 37312
Harris Cir NW
2200-2499 37311
2500-3099 37312
Harris Ln NE 37312
Harris Creek Rd & Trl 37311
Harrison Pike 37311
Harvest Glen Dr NW 37312
Harvest Hill Ct NE 37312
Harvey Rd NE 37312
Haun Dr SW 37311
Hawk St NE 37311
Hawk St SE 37323
Hawkins Rd SE 37323
Hawkins Hollow Rd SE 37323
Hawthorne Lndg NW 37312
Haywood Dr NW 37312
Headrick Ln SE 37323
Hearthstone Dr NE 37312
Heather Ln NW 37311
Heather Oaks Trl SE 37323
Heatherwood Ct NW 37312
Heaven Hill Ln NE 37323
Hedge Dr NE 37312
Hedgeview Way SW 37311
Helms Ln SE 37323
Helmshurst Ln SE 37323
Helton Rd SW 37311
Henderson Ave NW 37312
Hendricks Ln NE 37312
Hensley Rd NW 37312
Heritage Ln SE 37323
Heritage Hills Cir NE 37323
Heritage Place Dr NW 37312
Hewitt St SE 37323
Hickory Dr NW 37311
Hickory Crest Dr NE 37323
Hickory Hills Dr & Trl 37312
Hickory Oak Dr SE 37323
Hickory Top Rd SE 37311
Hickory View Pl NW 37311
Hicks Rd NE 37312
Hidden Forrest Dr NE 37323
Hidden Hills Dr SE 37323
Hidden Oaks Dr NE 37323
Hidden Oaks Trl NE 37323
Hidden Valley Rd NW 37312
High St NE & SE 37311
Highland Ave NW 37311
Highland Dr NE 37312
Highland Dr SW 37311
Highway Dr NW 37312
Highway 411 37323
Hill St SE 37311
Hilldale Dr NE 37312
Hillmont Pl NW 37312
Hillsdale Dr SE 37323
Hillside Dr & Pl 37312
Hilltop Dr NE & NW 37312
Hillview Dr NE 37323
Hillview Dr NW 37312
Hillwood Ln NE 37323
Hindman Pl NW 37312
Hiwassee Ave NE 37312
Holiday Inn Express Way NW 37312
Holliday Dr NW 37312
Hollow Rd NE 37323
Hollow View Dr SE 37323
Holloway Rd SW 37311
Holly Hl NW 37312
Holly Trl NW 37311
Holly Brook Cir NE 37323
Holly Ridge Dr NW 37311
Holmes Dr SE 37323
Holmes St NW 37311
Holt St SE 37311
Home Place Ct SE 37323
Homestead Cir & St 37323
Honor Ln NW 37312
Hoof Beat Trl 37311
Hooper Gap Rd NW 37312
Hopewell Dr & Pl 37312
Horiderm St NE 37311
Horton Ln & Rd 37323
Houston Ave NW 37312
Howard Cir SE 37311
Howard Rd NE 37323
Howard St SE 37311
Howell St SE 37323
Hudson Dr NW 37312
Huff Ave SW 37311
Hughes Ave NW 37312
Hughes Rd NW 37311
Hughes Rd SE 37323
Hughes Lake Rd SE 37323
Humbard Rd SE 37323
Hummingbird Dr NW 37312
Humphrey Bridge Rd SW 37311
Hungry Hollow Rd SE 37323
Hunt Rd SE 37323
Hunt Cliff Dr NW 37311
Hunter Trl NE 37312
Hunter Hills Pl NE 37312
Hunters Ct SE 37323
Hunters Cv NW 37312
Hunters Trce NW 37312
Hunters Run Cir, Pl & Trl 37312
Huntingdon Trce NE 37312
Huskey Dr SE 37323
Hysinger Dr NW 37312
Industrial Ct, Dr, Ln & Way SW 37311
Industrial Park Access Rd SW 37311
Inman St E & W 37311
Interlackin Cir NW 37312
Interstate Dr NW 37312
Inverness Dr NW 37312
Iris Ave NW 37312
Irongate Ct NE 37312
Ironwood Dr SE 37323
Ivy Way NW 37312
J Mack Cir SW 37311
Jackson Cir SE 37323
Jackson Dr NE 37312
Jackson St NW 37312
Jacobs Aly & Ave SE & SW 37311
James Ave NW 37311
James Ct NW 37311
James Pt NE 37312
James Asbury Dr NW 37312
Janes Way NE 37323
Janet St SE 37323
Jay Haven Ln NW 37312
Jenkins Rd NE 37323
Jensen Ave SE 37323
Jill St NE 37312
Jim Jones Rd SE 37323
Joe Stinnett Rd SE 37323
Joel Dr SW 37311
John Ct NW 37312
John Smith Rd SW 37311
Johnathon Dr SE 37323
Johnson Ave NW 37311
Johnson Blvd SE 37311
Johnson Rd SE 37323
Jones Ave SW 37311
Jones Dr SE 37323
Jonida Ct NE 37312
Jordan Ave NW 37311
Jordan Dr SE 37323
Joseph Thomas Dr SW 37311
Joshua Dr SE 37323
Joy St NE 37311
Juanita St NW 37312
Julian Dr NE 37312
Julian Rd NE 37323
Kansas Ln SE 37323
Kathy Dr SE 37311
Kay Mar Ct SE 37323
Kegan Ct NE 37323
Keith St NW
1-2499 37311
2500-4499 37312
Keith St SW 37311
Keith Valley Rd SE 37323
Keller Ln SW 37311
Kelley Ln SW 37311
Kelly St NW 37312
Kensington Vw NW 37312
Kensington Park Trl NW 37312
Keri Ln NE 37312
Kersey Rd NE 37323
Key St NW 37312
Keystone Dr NE 37312
Kile Ln SW 37311
Kile Lake Ln & Rd 37323
Kilgore Cir SW 37311
Kimberly Dr NW 37312
Kincaid Rd SE 37323
King Ct SE 37323
King St SE
800-1099 37311
1100-2399 37323
King Andrew Ct NW 37312
King Arthur Ct NW 37312
King Den Dr NW 37312
King Edward Ave SE 37311
King Ridge Dr NW 37312
Kingdom Dr NE 37323
Kinser Rd SE 37323
Kiowa Ln NW 37312
Kirby Dr SE 37323
Knighthood Trl NW 37312
Knights Ct NW 37312
Knobb Hill Dr NW 37312
Knollwood Ct & Dr 37311
Kyker Bonner Ave NW 37311
Kyle Ln NW 37312
Lacy Rd SE 37323
Ladd Springs Rd SE 37323
Lake Dr SE 37323
W Lake Dr NW 37312
Lake St NW 37312
Lake Circle Dr NE 37312
Lakeland Dr NE 37312
Lakeside Pl NW 37312
Lakeview Dr SE 37323
Lakewood Dr NW 37312
Lamar Lawson Rd NE 37323
Lancaster Ln SE 37323
Lancelot Ln NW 37312
Landmark Ct NE 37312
N Lane St SW 37311
Lang St NE & SE 37311
Lankford Dr NW 37311
Lauderback Rd SW 37311
Lauderdale Memorial Hwy NW 37312
Laurel Dr NW 37312
Laurel Bluff Rd SW 37311
Laurel Hills Dr NW 37311
Laurel Oaks Dr NW 37312
Laurel Springs Dr NW 37311
Lauren Dr & Way 37323
Lay St SE 37311
Lazy Acres Rd NE 37323
Lead Mine Valley Rd SW 37311
Leaf Dr NW 37312
Leamington Ln SE 37323
Leamon Rd NE 37312
Leatha Ln NW 37312
Lebannon Valley Church Rd SW 37311
Lebanon Dr & Rd 37323
Ledford Rd NE 37323
Ledford Calfee Rd SE 37323
Lee Dr NW 37312
N Lee Hwy 37312
S Lee Hwy 37311
S Lee Hwy SW 37311
Lee Ln SW 37311
Lee St SE 37311
Lee Ridge Rd SE 37323
Lenox Ct & Dr 37312
Lewis St NE 37311
Lewis Lane Rd NE 37312
Lexington Pl NW 37312
Life Bridges Ln SW 37311
Lightfoot Rd NE 37323
Lilac Dr NW 37312
Linda Cir NW 37312
Linda Dr SE 37323
Linden Ave SE 37311
Linden Dr SE 37323
Liner Rd NE 37312
Lisa St NE 37312
Litchfield Ln NW 37312
Little Falls Cir NW 37311
Little John Cir SE 37323
Live Oak Trl NE 37323
Loebner Ln NW 37312
Lofty View Ln NW 37312
Logan Rd NW 37312
Lois St SE
1400-2099 37311
2100-2299 37323
London Dr SE 37323
Lone Tree Dr NE 37312
Longview Dr SE 37323
Lou Dr SE 37323
Lou Manor Dr SE 37323
Loving Ln NE 37323
Low Brook Ct NE 37312
Lower Chestuee Rd 37323
Lower Woods Trl NE 37323
Lowery St NE & SE 37311
Luckyleaf Trl NE 37323
Luke Rd NE 37323
Lupton Ln SW 37311
Lyles Rd SE 37323
Lynch Cir NW 37312
Lynda Cir SE 37323
Lynn Dr SE 37323
Lynncrest Dr NE 37323
Mac St NW 37312
Macedonia Church Rd SE 37323
Macmillan Rd NE 37323
Maden Rd SE 37323
Magnolia Ave NE 37311
Magnolia Ct NW 37312
Malibu Dr SE 37323
Mallard Trl NW 37312
Manchester Trl NE 37312
Maney Dr NE 37323
Mansion Hill Cir & Ct 37312
Mantooth Rd SE 37323
Maple Dr NW 37312
Maple St NE 37311
Mapleleaf Dr NW 37312
Mapleton Ct & Dr 37312
Mapleton Forest Dr NW 37312
Mapleton Ridge Dr NW 37312
Marie Cir NW 37312
Marion Cir SE 37323
Marlie Cir NW 37312
Marshall Cir & Ln 37323
Martin Dr NW 37311
Maryland Cir SE 37323
Marylyn Ct NE 37323
Mason Rd SE 37323
Matt Cir SE 37323
Maynardsville Mnr NE 37323
Mccann Dr SE 37311
Mcclanahan Dr NW 37312
Mcclanahan Rd SE 37323
Mcclure Rd SE 37323
Mccrackin Dr & Rd 37323
Mccullough Rd NE 37323
Mcdaris Cir SE 37323
Mcdonald Ln SW 37311
Mcgrady Dr SE 37323
Mcguire Ln SW 37311
Mcintire Ave NE 37312
Mcintosh Ln NE 37323
Mckamy St NE 37311
Mclain Dr NW 37311
Mcnabb Dr NW 37312
Mcreynolds Ave SE 37323
S Meade Cir SW 37311
Meade Ct NE 37312
Meador Lake Rd NE 37323
Meadow Ave NW 37312
Meadow Ln SE 37323
Meadow Lane Rd SE 37323
Meadow View Dr NE 37323
Meadowbrook Dr SE 37323
Meadowbrook Ln NW 37312
W Meadows Ln NE 37312
Meadowwood Cir NE 37323
Medlin Rd NW 37312
Melrose Dr NW 37311
Michelle Dr & Pl 37323
Michigan Avenue Rd NE 37323
Michigan Avenue School Rd NE 37323
Midfield Cir & Ct 37323
Midway Dr SE 37323
Mikel Rd SE 37323
Mikel St NW 37312
Miles Ct NW 37312
Mill Creek Trl NE 37323
Mill Run Pl NE 37323
Mill Stone Ln NE 37323
Millard Dr NW 37312
Millbrook Cir SE 37323
Million Dr & Rd 37323
Milne Ave NW 37311
Mimosa Dr NW 37312
Minnis Rd NE 37323
Misty Ln SW 37311
Misty Meadows Cir SE 37323
Mitchell Rd NW 37312
Mitchell Rd SE 37323
Mohawk Ct NW 37311
Mohawk Dr NW 37312
Monte Carlo Dr NW 37312
Montgomery Ave NE 37311
Monza Ln NW 37312
Moore Cir & Pl NE & NW 37312
Moreland Dr NE 37312
Moreland Dr NW 37311
Morgan Dr NW 37312
Morgan Johnston Cir NE 37312
Morning Glory Ln NE 37323
Morningside Dr NE 37323
Morrison Ln NE 37312
Mount Bethel Rd SE 37323
Mount Vernon Dr NW 37311
Mountain Cv NW 37312
Mountain Cove Pl NW 37312
Mountain Pointe Dr NW 37312
Mountain View Dr SE 37323
Mouse Creek Rd NW 37312
Mowery Rd NW 37312
Mulberry Ln NE 37312
Mull Rd 37323
Mysinger Rd SW 37311
Nancy Cv & Dr 37323
Nantahala Dr SE 37323
Navaho Trl NW 37312
Neal Dr NW 37312
Needlewood Ln NW 37312
Neely Cir NE 37311
Nell Ave NW 37312
Nesting Ridge Rd NW 37312
Nevin Dr & Ln 37311
New St SE 37323
New Castle Dr NE 37312
New Friendship Ln NE 37323
New Hope Rd SE 37323
New Murraytown Rd NW 37312

Newby Rd SE 37323
Newman Dr SE 37323
Newton Dr SE.......... 37323
Newton Rd SE 37311
Neyman St SE 37311
Nicholson Dr SW 37311
Nicola Cir SE 37323
Niki Way NE 37312
Nina Dr NE 37323
Nipper Dr SE........... 37323
Norfolk Ct SE 37323
Noriverl Rd SE 37323
Norman Rd SE.......... 37323
Norman Chapel Rd
NW 37312
Norris Way NE 37323
North Dr, Ln & St 37312
Northcrest Cir NE 37312
Northeast Rd SE 37311
Northmont Dr NE 37312
Northview Dr NW 37312
Northwood Dr NW 37312
Norwood Dr SE 37323
Nottingham Cir SE 37323
Nuckolls Ave NW 37311
Nychole Dr SE 37323
Oak Cir & St 37311
Oak Grove Rd SE 37311
Oak Hill Ct NE 37323
Oak Tree Ln SE 37311
Oakcrest Ave NW 37312
Oakdale Ave NW 37312
Oakland Dr NW
2100-2499 37311
2500-3099 37312
Oakland Ln SE 37323
Oakland Trl SE 37323
Oakwood Cir NE 37312
Occonechee Cir NE 37323
Ocoee Pl NW 37312
Ocoee St N
3106A-3106B 37312
1-2499 37311
S Ocoee St 37311
Ocoee Trce NW 37312
Ocoee Xing NW 37312
Ocoee Hills Cir & Dr ... 37323
Officer St SE 37323
Ogle Dr SE 37311
Ohio Ave NW 37311
Old 25th St NE & NW .. 37311
Old Armstrong Cir SE .. 37323
Old Bates Pike NE 37311
Old Benton Pike NE 37323
Old Blue Springs Rd
SE 37311
Old Charleston Ln & Rd
NE & NW 37312
Old Chattanooga Pike
SW 37311
Old Chestuee Rd NE ... 37323
Old Federal Rd SE 37323
Old Frazier Rd SE 37323
Old Freewill Dr NW 37311
Old Freewill Rd NW 37312
Old Georgetown Rd, St
& Trl 37312
Old Goins Rd SW 37311
Old Harrison Cir, Ln &
Pike 37311
Old Horton Rd SE 37323
Old Johnson Rd NE 37323
Old Johnson Rd SW ... 37311
Old Kile Lake Rd SE ... 37323
Old Kinser Cir & Rd 37323
Old Lead Mine Valley Rd
SW 37311
Old Mcclure Rd SE..... 37323
Old Mcdonald Georgetow
Rd NW 37312
Old Mouse Creek Rd
NW 37312
Old Parksville Rd & Trl
NE & SE 37323
Old Pond Rd SE 37323
Old Powerline Ln NE ... 37323
Old Powerline Rd NE
200-699 37311
1000-1299 37323
Old Spring Place Rd
SE 37323
Old Stage Ln NE 37323
Old Stone Rd SE....... 37323
Old Tasso Pl & Rd 37312
Old Weatherly Switch Rd
SE 37323
Old York Rd NE 37323
Ollie St SE 37323
Ollie Jane Way NE 37312
Orchid Dr NW 37312
Oriole Dr NW 37312
Orlando Dr NE 37323
Orr Rd SE 37311
Orrie Moss Ct SE 37323
Osment Rd SE......... 37323
Otis St SE 37323
Outlet Rd SE 37323
Overbriar Dr NE 37312
Overbrook Cir NW 37312
Overdale Dr NW 37312
Overhead Bridge Rd
NE 37311
Overlook Dr NE 37312
Ownby Rd SE 37323
Oxford Pl NW 37312
Ozark St NW 37312
Par Ct NW 37312
Paradise Ln NW 37312
Paradise Park NE 37323
Paragon Pkwy & Pt 37312
Park Ave & St NE &
NW 37311
Park Creek Dr NW 37312
Parker Ave SW 37311
Parker Dr NE 37323
Parker St NE 37311
Parkside Pl NE 37311
Parkway Dr SE 37323
Parkwood Dr NE 37323
Parkwood Trl NW 37312
Partridge Rd NW 37312
Patricia Pl NE 37312
Patterson Ln & Rd 37323
Paul Huff Pkwy NW 37312
Pea St NE 37311
Peaceful Pt NE 37323
Peach Orchard Hill Rd
NE 37323
Peach Tree Cir NE 37323
Peachtree Ln NE 37323
Peachtree Pointe Pkwy
NE 37323
Pearl Dr SW 37311
Pebble Brook Cir NE ... 37312
Pebble Ridge Dr NW ... 37311
Pebble Ridge Dr SE ... 37323
Peerless Dr NW 37312
Peerless Rd NW
2100-2599 37311
2600-4199 37312
Peerless Xing NW 37312
Pell Rd & St 37323
Pembridge Cir NW 37312
People St NE 37311
Peppertree Dr NE 37323
Perimeter Dr SE........ 37323
Perry St SE 37311
Petty St SE 37311
Phillips Dr NE 37312
Phillips St SW 37311
Pickens St SE.......... 37323
Pin Oak Ct & Dr 37323
Pin Oaks Cir NE 37323
Pine Dr NE 37312
Pine Dr SE............. 37323
Pine Ridge Dr SE 37323
Pine Trail Dr NW 37312
Pinecrest Ave NW 37312
Pinecrest Dr SE 37323
Pineview Dr NW 37312
Pinewood Cv NW 37312
Pintail Way NW 37312
Pirkle Rd NE 37323
Plantation Dr SE 37323
Planters Ridge Dr NW .. 37312
Playland Rd NE 37312
Pleasant Grove Pl &
Trl 37311
Pleasant Grove Church
Rd SW 37311
Poindexter Dr SE 37323
Pointe South SE 37323
Polk County Ave NE 37311
Pond St SE 37311
Ponderosa Dr NW 37312
Poplar St NE 37311
Postoak Dr NW 37312
Poteet Rd SE 37323
Pounds St SE 37323
Powell Dr & St SW &
SE 37311
Powerline Dr NE 37323
Powhatan Dr NE 37323
Prairie St SE 37323
Preservation Dr NE..... 37323
Princess Ln NE 37312
Princeton Hill Cir & Dr .. 37312
Professional Park Dr
NW 37312
Prospect School Rd
NW 37312
Providence Ln NW 37312
Pryor Dr SW 37311
Pryor Rd NE 37312
Puente Dr NE 37323
Pugh St NE 37311
Quail Cv & Holw NE &
NW 37312
Quail Run Trce NE 37312
Quill Dr NW 37311
Rabbit Valley Rd NW ... 37312
Raben Dr NW 37312
Raider Dr NW 37312
Railroad St NE 37311
Raines Dr NW 37311
Ralph Buckner Blvd
NE 37311
Ramblewood Cir NW ... 37312
Ramor Dr NE 37323
Ramsey St NE & NW .. 37312
Ramsey Bridge Rd SE . 37323
Randolph Dr SW 37311
Randolph Samples Rd
SE 37323
Ravenwood Ln NE 37312
Reagan Rd SE 37323
Rebecca Dr SE 37323
Red Cardinal Dr NE 37312
Red Clay Rd SW 37311
Red Clay Park Rd SW . 37311
Red Hill Valley Rd SE .. 37323
Red Oak Dr NW 37312
Redbud Dr NW 37312
Redspire Way NE 37312
Redwood Dr NE 37312
Refreshment Ln SW 37311
Reuben Dr NW 37312
Rhondale Ave SE 37323
Richey St NE 37311
Ridge Dr SE 37323
Ridge Park Dr NE 37311
Ridge Point Dr NW 37311
Ridge Top Dr NW 37312
Ridgefield Ct SW 37311
Ridgestone Dr NW 37312
Ridgeview Ave NW 37312
Ridgeview Dr NE 37311
Ridgeview Dr NW 37312
Ridgeview St SE 37323
Ridgeway Ct, Dr & Pl .. 37312
River Birch Dr NW 37312
Riveria Dr SE 37323
Roadway Dr SE 37323
Robbie Ct NE 37312
Roberts Ln NE 37312
Robin Dr & Ln 37312
Robin Cove Rd NW 37312
Robin Hood Dr NW 37312
Robin Hood Dr SE 37323
Rock Hill Rd SW 37311
Rockdale Ct SE 37323
Rockland Ct NW 37311
Rodney Dr & Way 37323
Rogers Dr SE 37323
Rolling Brook Cir, Dr &
Pl 37323
Rolling Hills Dr NW 37312
Rolling Wood Trl NE ... 37312
Rollins Ridge Rd NW ... 37312
Rose Ave NW 37312
Rose Dr NE 37323
Rose Hill Ln NE 37311
Rosedale Dr SE 37323
Rosewood Dr NE 37312
Roxbury Ct NW 37312
Royal Dr NW 37312
Royal Oaks Dr NE 37323
Runway Dr NW 37312
Rustic Dr NW 37312
Ruth Ln SE 37323
Ruth Way SW 37311
Rutledge Dr NE 37323
Rymer Rd NE 37323
Rymer Rd NW 37312
Sabrina Dr SE 37323
Saddle Creek Dr NW ... 37312
Sagefield Dr SE 37323
Sahara Dr NW 37312
Sam Whaley Rd SE 37323
Samples Chapel Rd
SE 37323
Sandidge Rd SE 37323
Sandra Dr SE 37323
Sara Dr SE 37323
Saratoga Pl NW 37312
Savannah Ave NE 37312
Savannah Ridge Trl
NE 37323
Scarlet Oaks Dr NW 37312
Scenic Dr SE 37323
School St SW 37311
Schrader Dr NW 37312
Scotts Ln SW 37311
Sellers Ave SE 37311
Sells Ln NE 37312
Seminole Dr NW 37312
Sequoia Rd NW 37312
Serenity Dr SE 37323
Shadow Crest Trl NW .. 37312
Shadowood Dr SE 37323
Shady Ln NE 37323
Shady Hollow Cir SE ... 37323
Shady Lane Pl SW 37311
Sharon Dr NE 37312
Sharpe Ave SE 37323
Sharpe Rd SW 37311
Shawn Ct NE 37312
Sheeler St SE 37311
Sheep Ranch Rd SE ... 37323
Sheffield Ln NE 37323
Sheila Dr SE 37323
Shenandoah Ln NW 37312
Shepard St NE 37311
Sherry Dr SE 37323
Shingle Hollow Rd
NW 37312
Shipman Ln 37323
Shire Ln NW 37312
Shope Cir & Rd 37323
Short St NE 37311
Short Hill Ct SE 37323
Silver Trl NE 37323
Silver Maple Cir SW 37311
Silver Springs Trl NW .. 37312
Simrita Cir SE 37323
Singletree Dr NW 37312
Sioux Dr NW 37312
Sipes Rd & St NW &
SW 37311
Skylar Dr NE 37312
Smith Dr SW 37311
Somerset Ct & Dr 37323
Sourwood Trl NW 37312
Southern Ct NW 37312
Southern Heights Cir
SE 37311
Southern Oaks Dr SE .. 37323
Southforke Dr & Way ... 37311
Southgate Dr SW 37311
Sparrows Point Dr NE .. 37312
Spicer Rd SE 37323
Spring St NW & SW ... 37311
Spring Creek Blvd &
Dr 37311
Spring Hollow Rd SW .. 37311
Spring Meadow Ln SE . 37311
Spring Place Rd SE
200-299 37323
1200-1799 37311
1800-6699 37323
Spring Place Ter SE ... 37311
Spring Walk Dr NW 37312
Springdale Dr NE 37312
Springfield Ct NE 37323
Springhill Dr NE 37312
Springhouse Rd NE 37323
Stafford Ave NW 37312
Stanton Dr SE 37323
Star St SE 37323
Star Vue Dr SW 37311
Starlet Cir NE 37323
State Pl NW 37312
Stately Oaks Pl NW 37312
Steed Ave & St 37311
Steelwood Dr SE 37323
Steeple Cir NE 37312
Steeple Chase Ln NE .. 37323
Stellatta Cv NW 37312
Stephen Dr SE 37323
Stephens Rd NE 37312
Stepp Ln SE 37323
Sterling Pt NW 37312
Stiles Ave NW 37312
Stillwood Ct NW 37312
Stinnet Rd SE 37323
Stone Dr SE 37323
Stone Castle Dr NE 37312
Stone Crest Pl NW 37311
Stone Glen Trl NW 37312
Stone Reagan Rd SE .. 37323
Stonebriar Dr NE 37312
Stonebridge Ln NE &
NW 37323
Stonegate Cir NW 37312
Stonewood Ct & Dr 37311
Stoney Brook Dr NE 37323
Stratford Cir NW 37312
Strawberry Ln NE 37311
Strawhill Rd SE 37323
Strawhill Church Rd
SE 37323
Stuart Ave NW 37311
Stuart Rd NE 37312
Stuart Xing NE 37312
Stuckey Dr NW 37312
Suffolk Ct SE 37323
Sugar Creek Rd SE 37323
Summer Breeze Cir
NE 37323
Summerfield Ave NW ... 37311
Sun St SE 37323
Sun High Ct SE 37323
Sun Hill Rd SW 37311
Sunburst Ct & Ln 37312
Sunflower Cir NW 37312
Sunray Dr NW 37312
Sunrise Xing NE 37323
Sunset Ave NW 37311
Sunset Dr NW 37312
Sunset Ln NE 37312
Sunset Trl NE 37311
Surrey Ln NE 37312
Sussex Pl SE 37323
Sweet Bay Cir NW 37312
Sweet Gracie Ln NW ... 37312
Sweetbriar Ave NW 37311
Sycamore Dr NE &
NW 37312
Tacoma St NW 37312
Talley St NW 37312
Tallwood Trl NE 37312
Talons Ridge Rd NW ... 37312
Tam O Shanter Dr
NW 37312
Tamarac Trl SE 37323
Tanglewood Ct SE 37323
Tanglewood Dr NW 37312
Tasso Ln NE 37312
Tasso Rd NE 37323
Teague Rd SW 37311
Teakwood Ct SW 37311
Teakwood Trl SE 37323
Teal Dr NW 37312
Tennessee Nursery Rd
NW 37311
Terrace Ave NW 37312
Thomas Ave NW 37311
Thompson Ln & St NW
& SE 37311
Thompson Springs Rd
SE 37323
Thoredg Rd NW 37312
Thorne Cir SE 37323
Thornwood Dr NE 37312
Thoroughbred Dr NW ... 37312
Thurman Ln NW 37312
Tiffany Ln SE 37323
Tilley Dr SE 37323
Tillie Rd NE 37312
Timber Ct SE 37323
Timber Trl NW 37312
Timber Hill Dr & Ln 37323
Timber Lake Dr NW 37312
Timber Trace Cir & Pl .. 37311
Timberdale Trl SE 37323
Tippings Ct 37311
Tipton Dr SE 37323
Tl Rogers St NE 37312
Todd Rd SE 37323
Tomahawk Cir NW 37312
Tonia Dr SW 37311
Topaz Way SW 37311
Towering Oaks Ln SE .. 37323
Trailview Dr SE 37323
Travis St NW 37312
Treasury Dr SE 37323
Treemont Cir NE 37312
Tremolat Ln NW 37312
Trewhitt Dr & Rd 37323
Tri Cir NE 37312
Triplett Cir NW 37312
Trunk St NE 37311
Tulip Ave NW 37312
Tunnel Hill Rd SW 37311
Turner Ln NE 37323
Turner Brown Trl SE ... 37323
Turning Leaf Trl NE 37312
Twin Brook Dr SW 37311
Twin Creeks Cv & Dr ... 37312
Twin Oaks Ct & Dr 37323
Union Rd SE 37323
Unity Dr NE 37312
Urbane Rd NE 37312
Valley Dr SE 37323
N Valley Dr NW 37312
Valley Head Rd NW 37312
Valley Hills Dr, Ln &
Trl 37311
Valley View Rd SE 37323
Vance Dr & St 37312
Varnell Dr SW 37311
Varnell Ln SE 37323
Varnell Ln SW 37323
Varnell Rd SW 37311
Vermont Cir & Dr 37312
Victory St SE 37323
Victory St SW 37311
Victory Cove Ln SW 37311
N View St SW 37311
Villa Dr NW 37312
Village Ct & Way 37312
Village Green Dr NW ... 37312
Village Oak Cir NW 37312
Virgil Rymer Rd NE 37323
Virginia Ave SW 37311
Vista Dr NW 37312
Volunteer Dr SW 37311
Waddell Rd SW 37311
Wagner Cir NW 37311
Wahoo Cir SE 37323
Walker St NE 37311
Walker Brow Trl NW ... 37312
Walker Brow Ridge Rd
NW 37312
Walker Valley Rd NW .. 37312
Walnut Ave NW 37312
Walnut Dr NW 37311
Walnut Grove Ln NE ... 37323
Warren Turner Rd NE .. 37323
Washington Ave SE 37311
Water Oak Pl NW 37312
Waterlevel Hwy
1200-2299 37311
2600-7199 37323
Waterville Dr SE 37323
Watkins St SE 37323
Watson Rd NE 37323
Waverly Dr NE 37312
Wayfarer Dr SE 37323
Weatherford Dr NE 37312
Weatherly Switch Rd
SE 37323
Weatherly Switch Trl
SW 37311
Webb Ln NE 37323
Wedgewood Dr NW 37312
Weeks Cir & Dr 37312
Weeks Crest Cir NE 37312
Weeping Willow Trl
NW 37312
Weese Rd SE 37323
Wen Dell Ln SE 37323
Wesdell Ln NW 37312
Wesley Ct SE 37323
Wesley Hogan Rd NW . 37312
Wesley Ridge Ln SW ... 37311
Wesleyan Rd SW 37311
N West Cir NW 37312
Westbrook Cir & Dr 37312
Westhaven Pl NW 37312
Westland Dr SW 37311
Weston Ct & Pl 37312
Weston Hills Dr NW 37312
Westover Dr SW 37311
Westside Dr NW
200-2099 37311
2500-3499 37312
Westview Dr NE 37312
Westview Ln SE 37323
Westwood Ct NW 37311
Whaley Rd SE 37323
Whipporwill Dr NW 37312
Whispering Hills Dr
SE 37323
Whisperwood Trl NE ... 37312
White St SE 37311
White Oak Rd NW 37312
White Oak Valley Rd
NW 37312
White Pine Loop NE ... 37323
Whitecrest Cir & Dr 37311
Wiggins St SE 37311
Wilcox Cir SW 37311
Wild Oak Rd SE 37323
Wildwood Ave SE 37311
Wildwood Dr SE 37323
Wildwood Lake Rd SE . 37311
Wilhoit Dr SE 37323
Wilkinson Rd NE 37323
Will Lewis Dr SE 37323
Willbrook Cir NE 37323
William Way NW 37312
William Way SE 37323
Williams St NE 37311
Williamsburg Cir & Rd .. 37323
Willow St NW 37311
Willow Bend Trl NW 37312
Willow Creek Cv NE 37323
Willow Oak Cir NW 37312
Willow Springs Dr NE .. 37323
Wilson Ave SE 37311
Wilson Dr NW 37312

Wilson Ln NW 37312
Wilson Way NE 37312
S Wilson Heights Cir & Rd 37312
Wilton Ln NW 37312
Wimberly Dr SE 37323
Windcrest Dr & Pl 37312
Windermere Ln NE 37323
Winding Creek Cir NW .. 37312
Winding Glen Dr NW 37312
Windsor Cir NE 37312
Windswept Dr NE 37312
Windtrace Dr NW 37312
Windy Hill Ct SE 37323
Windy Ridge Dr NE 37312
Winesap Way SW 37311
Winnetawka Ave SE 37311
Winwood Trl NW 37312
Wisdom Way NE 37323
Wolfe Dr NW 37311
Woodberry Dr NW 37312
Woodbine Cir NW 37312
Woodchase Way NE 37311
Woodchase Close NE .. 37311
Woodcreek Dr NW 37311
Woodcrest Cir NW 37312
Woodcroft Ct NW 37312
Woodfrin Dr SE 37323
Woodgate Dr SE 37323
Woodhill Ln NE 37312
Woodland Dr NW 37312
Woodland Dr SE 37323
Woodland Cove Dr & Pl 37312
Woodlawn Ave NW 37312
Woodlawn St SE 37323
Woodmill Ct NE 37312
Woodmore Dr NW 37311
Woodmore Ln NW 37312
Woodridge Dr SE 37323
Woods Trl NE 37323
Woods Lake Way SE 37323
Woodstream Pl NE 37312
Woodvale St NW 37311
Woodvine Cir NW 37312
Woolen Cir & St 37311
Worth St NW & SW 37311
Wright Ln NE 37323
Wyatt Long Dr SE 37323
Wynwood Dr NW 37311
Yellowood Ct NW 37312
York Ln & Rd 37323
Young Rd SE 37323
Zale Dr SE 37323
Zion Dr NW 37312
Zion Hill Rd SE 37323
Zius Cir & Ct 37311
Zora Dr NW 37311

NUMBERED STREETS

1st St NE 37311
2nd St NE 37311
3rd St NW 37311
4th St NE 37311
5th NW & SE 37311
6th St NE 37311
7th St NE 37311
8th St NE 37311
9th St SE 37311
10th St NE 37311
11th NE & SE 37311
12th NE & SE 37311
13th St NE 37311
14th NW & SE 37311
15th St NE 37311
16th NE & SE 37311
17th St NE 37311
18th St NE 37311
19th St NE 37311
20th St NE
100-1799 37311
2100-3299 37323
20th St NW 37311
20th St SE 37311
21st St NE 37311
22nd St NE 37311
800-1899 37311
2600-3299 37312
23rd St NW 37311
24th St NW 37311
25th NE & NW 37311
26th NE & NW 37312
27th St SE 37323
28th St SE 37323
29th St SE 37323
30th St NE 37312
30th St SE 37323
31st St NE 37323
35th St NW 37312
35th St SE 37323
36th St SE 37323
37th St NE 37312
41st NE & NW 37312
49th St NW 37312
51st NE & NW 37312
56th St NW 37312

CLINTON TN

General Delivery 37716

POST OFFICE BOXES MAIN OFFICE STATIONS AND BRANCHES

Box No.s
All PO Boxes 37717

NAMED STREETS

All Street Addresses 37716

COLLIERVILLE TN

General Delivery 38017

POST OFFICE BOXES MAIN OFFICE STATIONS AND BRANCHES

Box No.s
All PO Boxes 38027

NAMED STREETS

Abbeville St 38017
Abbington Rd 38017
Ailene Rd 38017
Alan Cv 38017
Aldersgate St 38017
Aldis Cv 38017
Alexander Cv 38017
Alexandria Dr 38017
E Almadale Ct 38017
Almadale Farms Pkwy .. 38017
Almadale Lake Dr 38017
Almond Willow Cv 38017
Althea Ln 38017
Altona Cv 38017
Alydar Dr 38017
Amber Grove Cv & Ln .. 38017
Amber Hill Cv 38017
Amber Waves Ln 38017
Amelia Cv 38017
Amroth Cv & Dr 38017
Andrew Way Rd 38017
Andy Cv 38017
Aniston Way 38017
Anita Cv 38017
Ansley Cv 38017
Antebellum Cv & Way .. 38017
Arlie Cv 38017
Asbury Dr 38017
Ashana Dr 38017
Ashboro Dr 38017
Ashcraft Cir 38017
Ashfarm Way 38017
Ashglen Cir & Cv E, N, S & W 38017
Ashley Dr 38017
Ashley Hall Ct 38017
Ashton Woods Ct 38017
Aubrey Cv 38017
Auburn Oaks Dr 38017
Auburn Woods Cv & Dr 38017
Autumn Lake Dr 38017
Autumn Meadows Ln 38017
Autumn Oak Cv 38017
Autumn Oaks Cir 38017
Autumn Run Cv & Dr .. 38017
Autumn Trail Cv & Dr .. 38017
Autumn Winds Dr 38017
Avent Ridge Cv & Dr .. 38017
Bailey Creek Cv N & S 38017
Bailey Station Rd 38017
Bailey Woods Dr & Ln .. 38017
Ballard Cv & Rd 38017
Bancroft Ave 38017
Barbara Lynn Dr 38017
Barkley Dale Cv & Dr .. 38017
Barkley Estates Dr 38017
Barkley Gate Dr 38017
Barkley Glenn Dr 38017
Barkley Hall Dr 38017
Barkley Manor Cv & Dr 38017
Barn Hill Dr 38017
Barn Swallow Ln 38017
Barton Creek Dr 38017
Bayhill Woods Cv & Dr 38017
Beautiful Pl 38017
Beaver Run Cv & Dr 38017
Beaver Wood Cv 38017
Bechers Brook Cv 38017
Beckenhall Cv & St 38017
Beckett Ridge Cv 38017
Bee Jay Cv 38017
Belle Watley Cv & Ln .. 38017
Bellewood Cv 38017
Bent Creek Cv 38017
Bentwood Birch Cv 38017
Bentwood Creek Cv & Dr 38017
Bentwood Oak Dr 38017
Bentwood Peak Cv 38017
Bentwood Run Dr 38017
Bentwood Tree Cv 38017
Berryfield Cv 38017
Big Wood Cv N 38017
Big Woods Cv S 38017
Billy Bryant Rd 38017
Black Duke Cir E & W .. 38017
Black Wolf Dr 38017
Blackberry Cv & Dr 38017
Blue Gray Cir & Rd 38017
Bonnie Blue Cv 38017
Booth Ln 38017
Bouldincrest Ave 38017
Bowling Brooke Dr 38017
Brackenshire Cv & Ln .. 38017
Braddeck Dr 38017
Bradford Rdg & Trl 38017
Bradford Ridge Cv 38017
Bradford Trace Dr 38017
Bradford Trail Cv 38017
Bradley Cv 38017
Brado Dr 38017
Brandy Oak Cv 38017
Brangus Cv 38017
Braswell Way 38017
Bravo Rd 38017
Bray Park Dr E & W 38017
Bray Station Rd 38017
Braygood Dr 38017
Brayhill Cv 38017
Brayridge Cv 38017
Brayshore Dr 38017
Braystone Trl 38017
Braywind Dr 38017
Breakstone Cv 38017
Briamat Cv 38017
Briarbrook Cv 38017
Bridge Dr 38017
Bridgepointe Dr 38017
Brier Hills Dr 38017
Brierwood Cir 38017
Brinsley Cv & Dr 38017
Briston Ln 38017
Broken Arrow Cv 38017
Brook Follow Dr 38017
Brooke Edge Ln 38017
Brookmere Dr 38017
Brooks Bend Rd 38017
Brooks Bluff Cv 38017
Brookstone Cv 38017
Brotherwood Cv 38017
Buckland Bluff Cv 38017
Buckley Briar Ln 38017
Bull Creek Ln 38017
Burkman Dr 38017
Burley Cv & Rd 38017
Burrows Rd 38017
Burrows Oak Cv 38017
Burton Briar Cir 38017
Bushrod Cv 38017
S Byhalia Rd 38017
Calumet Farms Dr 38017
Cambrooke Cv & Dr 38017
Campden Dr 38017
Canal Loop Turn Dr 38017
Cannon Ave 38017
Canter Gait Ln 38017
Canterbury Rd 38017
Cardinal Dr 38017
Carianne Cv 38017
Carisbrooke Dr 38017
Carmel Cv 38017
Carmony Cv & St 38017
Carnegie Club Dr 38017
Caroline Cv 38017
Carolton Cv 38017
Carrington Elm Cir E & W 38017
Carrington Oak Ln E & S 38017
Carruthers Rd 38017
Casca Cv 38017
Cascade Falls Rd 38017
Cassidy Ln 38017
Castle Creek Cv 38017
Castle Pines Cir 38017
Catamount St 38017
Catesby Cv & Dr 38017
Cedar Brook Dr 38017
Cedar Post Cv 38017
N Center St 38017
S Center St
100-598 38017
131-559 38017
131-131 38027
Center Hill Rd 38017
Center Ridge Rd 38017
Center Springs Dr & Pl 38017
Chadwick Manor Cir 38017
Chalice Ln 38017
Chaney Cv & Dr 38017
Charles Hamilton Dr 38017
Charrington Ln 38017
Chestnut Hill Rd 38017
Chetopa Ln 38017
Chickadee Cv 38017
Chickasaw Land Cv & Way 38017
Chinquapin Dr 38017
N & S Chulahoma Rd .. 38017
Civic Center Dr 38017
Claverton Cv 38017
Clear Creek Rd 38017
Clearstone Cv 38017
Clermont Pl 38017
Clifton Pl 38017
Cloudy Cape Cv 38017
Clover Ridge Dr 38017
Cobbs Hall Cv 38017
Colbert Cv & St E, S & W 38017
Cold Creek Cv & Dr 38017
Coleherne Cv & Rd 38017
Coley Way 38017
College St 38017
Collierville Rd 38017
Collierville Arlington Rd 38017
Collingham Cv & Dr 38017
Commerce Pkwy & Rd .. 38017
Concordia Cv & Dr 38017
Conser St 38017
Constable Ct 38017
Cooper St 38017
Coors Creek Cv & Dr .. 38017
Copper Leaf Cv 38017
Cotham Dr 38017
Coton Hall Cv 38017
Cottage Grove Dr 38017
Cotton Creek Dr 38017
Cotton Hill Ln 38017
Cotton Row Cv 38017
Cottonwood Cir & Dr .. 38017
Country Way 38017
Country Forest Cv & Dr 38017
Country Place Dr E & W 38017
Country Springs Dr 38017
Countryridge Cir 38017
Courtfield Cv & Ln 38017
Courtney Cv 38017
Courts Meadow Cv 38017
Covered Bridge Cv 38017
Cox Hollow Cv 38017
Creek Valley Dr 38017
Creekview Cv 38017
Crenshaw Vw 38017
Crescent Dr 38017
Crestover Dr 38017
Crimson Oaks Ln 38017
Crimsonwood Dr 38017
Crisscross Ln 38017
Critton Dr 38017
Critz Cv 38017
Crooked Creek Cv & Rd 38017
Cross Point Cv & Dr 38017
N & S Crossberry Cv 38017
Crossview Ln 38017
Crosswinds Cv & Way .. 38017
Cruzenshire Cv 38017
Crystal Creek Cv E & W 38017
Culberson Cir 38017
Cypress Springs Ln 38017
Cypress Wells Dr 38017
Dalhoff Downs 38017
Dana Dr 38017
Danbrooke Dr 38017
Dannon Ln 38017
Dannon Springs Dr 38017
Daventry Cv & Dr 38017
Dean Rd 38017
Deans Cv 38017
Deans Creek Dr 38017
Deep Pond Dr 38017
Deep Woods Rd 38017
Dehaig Ln 38017
Deloach Ln 38017
Denali Park Cv & Dr 38017
Denham Cv & Rd 38017
Desert Pine Ln 38017
Dibrell Trail Dr 38017
Distribution Pkwy 38017
Dixon Pl 38017
Dogwood Cv & Vly 38017
N & W Dogwood Creek Ct & Dr 38017
Dogwood Lake Cv 38017
Doris Meadow Cv 38017
Douglas Dr 38017
Dove Valley Rd 38017
N & S Dubray Pl 38017
Dubray Bridge Dr 38017
Dubray Creek Cv 38017
Dubray Lake Cir 38017
Dubray Manor Cv & Dr 38017
Dudney Mead Cv 38017
N & S Duncan Woods Dr 38017
Dunn Ridge Cv 38017
Dunwick Cv 38017
Durwood Cv & Ln 38017
Duscoe Cv & St 38017
Dusk Ridge Rd 38017
Dymoke Dr 38017
Eagle Creek Cv 38017
Eagleton Nest Cv 38017
Early Earner Cv 38017
Easonwood Ave 38017
Eastley St 38017
Eastwood Ter 38017
Echo Cv 38017
Edenberg Dr 38017
Eider Cv 38017
Elk River Cv & Dr 38017
Ellas Pond Cv 38017
Ellawood Ln 38017
Ellie Cv & Pl 38017
Elm Creek Cv 38017
Elm Grove Cir 38017
Elm Spring Dr 38017
Emeriera Dr 38017
Empressor Cv 38017
Enjelica Cv 38017
Estanaula Rd 38017
Eulas Ridge Cv 38017
Evans View Cv & Ln 38017
Evergreen Ridge Cv E & W 38017
Fabert Cv 38017
Fair Oaks Cv & Dr 38017
N & S Fairmont Cir & Dr 38017
Fairway Glen Cv & Dr .. 38017
Fairwoods Dr 38017
Fall Springs Rd 38017
Fallen Oaks Dr 38017
Fallen Timbers Cv 38017
Fallen Woods Cv 38017
Farish Downs Ct 38017
Fed Ex Pkwy 38017
Federal Ridge Dr & Rd 38017
Federal Row Dr 38017
Fernhall Cv 38017
Fernleigh Cv 38017
Fireweek Ln 38017
Fisherville Rd 38017
Fitzgerald St 38017
Five Oaks Ln 38017
Flatrock Ln 38017
Fleming Rd 38017
Flemings Dr 38017
Fletcher Cv, Dr & Rd 38017
Fletcher Brook Cv 38017
Fletcher Hollow Rd 38017
Flickers Nest Cv 38017
Florencewood Cv & Dr .. 38017
Forest Trl 38017
Forest Bridge Dr 38017
Forest Chase Cv & Dr .. 38017
Forest Island Dr 38017
Forest Oaks Cv 38017
Forest Shadows Dr 38017
Forest Station Cv, Ln & Rd 38017
Forest Wind Cv & Dr 38017
Forest Wood Cv E & W 38017
Forestdale Dr 38017
Forrest Grove Cv & Dr .. 38017
Forsythe Trl 38017
Fort Rosalie Cv 38017
Fort Sumpter Cv & Ln .. 38017
Fossil Pl 38017
Four Oaks Ln 38017
Fox Chase Cv N & S 38017
Fox Lair Cv & Dr 38017
Fox Run Ln 38017
Fox Springs Dr 38017
Foxberry Cv 38017
Foxboro Cv 38017
Frank Rd 38017
Franklin Dale Cv 38017
Fredericksburg Cv 38017
Friendship Cv 38017
Furlong Cv 38017
Gable Cv & Ln 38017
Gallina Cir 38017
Garden Trail Cv & Ln .. 38017
Garden Wind Cv 38017
Garner Grove Cv 38017
Genevieve Ln 38017
Gettysburg Cv 38017
Ghost Creek Cv & Dr .. 38017
Ginny Ln 38017
Glacier Bay 38017
Glaze Ave & Cv 38017
Glen Allan Cv 38017
Glen Echo Rd 38017
Glenogle Ln 38017
Golden Miller Cv 38017
Goldfinch Cv 38017
Goldsmith Ct 38017
Gorgie Cv 38017
Gosnold Bluff Cv & Rd 38017
Grace Cv 38017
Grafton Cv 38017
Grainfield Cv 38017
Grand Central Cir E 38017
Grand Cypress Cv & Dr 38017
Grand Steeple Cv & Dr 38017
Grapevine Dr 38017
Gravetye Pl 38017
E & W Graycrest Ave .. 38017
Grayson Cv & St S 38017
Great Falls Rd 38017
Greely St 38017
Green Fairway Cv N & S 38017
Green Level Rd 38017
Green Oaks Ln 38017
Green Tree Cv 38017
Greenbank Dr 38017
Greenbrier Lakes Blvd & Cv 38017
Greenbrier Trace Cv 38017
Greencliff Rd 38017
Greenview Cv & Rd 38017
Greenway Dr 38017
Grey Wolf Dr 38017
Greystoke Ln 38017
Grove Rd 38017
Grove Park Rd 38017
Grove Ridge Ln 38017
Gunningham Way 38017
Gunnison Cv & Dr 38017
Gwynn Manor Ct 38017
Hackney Way 38017
Halle Pkwy 38017
Halle Park Cir & Dr 38017
Halle Ridge Cv 38017
Halley St 38017
Hallsworth Cv 38017
Hammerly Ct 38017
Handforth Cv 38017
Hardwick St 38017
Hardwood View Cv 38017
E & W Harpers Ferry Dr & Rd 38017
Harris Cv, St & Way 38017
Harris Estate Dr 38017
Harris Park Rd 38017
Harts Way 38017
Hartsway Cv 38017
Hartwell Mnr N & W 38017
Hartwell Manor Cv 38017
N Hartwell Ridge Dr 38017

Street	ZIP
Harvest Oaks Dr & Rd	38017
Hatcher Patch Cv	38017
Hatton Cv & St	38017
Hawk Inlet Dr	38017
Hawks Peaks Rd	38017
Hayslett Rd	38017
Heather Lake Cv & Dr	38017
Heather Ridge Cv	38017
Herb Parsons Way	38017
Hermitage Trail Dr	38017
Heyonka Cv	38017
Hibdon Way	38017
Hickory Nut Rd	38017
Hickory Oaks Cir	38017
Hickory Tree Cv	38017
Higginson Sq	38017
Highway 193	38017
Highway 196	38017
Highway 57	38017
Highway 72	38017
Hillwood Ln	38017
Hinton Cv	38017
Hollow Dr	38017
Holly Cv	38017
Holly Forest Dr	38017
Holly Leigh Cv	38017
Holmes Rd	38017
Holmes Oaks Dr	38017
Home Pl	38017
Homeville Rd	38017
Hope St	38017
Horseshoe Bend Trl	38017
Hound Hill Pl	38017
Hound Ridge Cv	38017
S Houston Levee Rd	38017
Howling Dr	38017
Hoyahka St	38017
Hughes Cv & Rd	38017
Hulsey Cir	38017
Hunter Cv	38017
Hunters Mill Cv & Trl	38017
Hunters Retreat Dr	38017
Hunters Way Ln	38017
Huntley Cv	38017
Hurdle St	38017
Ian Mercer Dr	38017
Indian Hollow Cv	38017
E Indian Wells Dr	38017
Industrial Park Ln	38017
Irby Glade Cv	38017
Iron Creek Ct & Cv N & S	38017
Irongate Ct & Dr	38017
Irwins Gate Dr	38017
Irwins Grove Ln	38017
Itawamba Cv & Rd	38017
Ivy Brook Cv & Ln	38017
Ivy Grove Ln	38017
Ivy Wood Cv & Ln	38017
Jack Straw Blvd	38017
Jaffrey Ave	38017
Jamerson Farm Cv & Rd	38017
James Cv	38017
Jasper Park Ln	38017
Jaybird Way	38017
Jeffrey Ln	38017
Jenniferlee Ln	38017
Jennings Mill Ln	38017
Jockey Cv	38017
Joe Ct & Dr	38017
Joe Wood Cv	38017
Joel Cv	38017
John Cv	38017
John Ridge Cv & Dr	38017
Johnash Ct	38017
Johnson Park Dr	38017
Jolly Way	38017
Juliana Cv	38017
Junco Cv	38017
Juneau Way	38017
Justana Dr	38017
Katelyn Cv & Way	38017
Kathy Cir	38017
Katie Cv	38017
Katz Pl	38017
Keisie Cv	38017
Kelsey St	38017
Kelsey Woods Ln	38017
Kenaw St	38017
Kenrose St	38017
Kensington Cir	38017
Keough Dr & Rd	38017
Kernstown Cv	38017
Key Rd	38017
Kimberly Cv	38017
King Oaks Cv	38017
King Ridge Cv & Dr	38017
Kirk Rd	38017
Klug Cv	38017
La Croix Dr	38017
Lago Ln	38017
N Lake Cv	38017
Lake Hollow Ln	38017
Lake Meadow Cv & Dr	38017
Lake Mist Dr	38017
Lake Page Dr	38017
E & W Lake Pointe Dr	38017
Lakefront Dr	38017
Lakes Edge Dr	38017
Lakeview Dr	38017
Lakewood Cv & Trl	38017
Lancelot Cir, Cv & Ln	38017
Landing Oaks Dr	38017
Landing Party Cv & Ln	38017
Lark Hill Cv	38017
Larson Bay Ln	38017
Laura Ann Dr	38017
Laurel Park Cv & Dr	38017
Laurel Pines Dr	38017
Laurelwood Pl	38017
Lawncrest Cv	38017
E & W Lawnwood Cv & Dr	38017
Leake Place Cv	38017
Lee Levee Cir	38017
Legacy Barn Dr & Trl	38017
Legacy Farm Ct & Pl	38017
Legacy Lake Cir, Ln & Trce	38017
Legends Dr	38017
Leighton Cv	38017
E, N, S & W Levee Oaks	38017
Liles Ln	38017
Lincoln Dr	38017
Lindi Dr	38017
Linkenholt Cv & Dr	38017
Lisson Cv & Ln	38017
Little Oak Ln	38017
Littles Way	38017
Logan Loop	38017
Logwood Briar Cv N & S	38017
Lonewood Way	38017
Lonhill Cv & Dr	38017
Loughridge Ln	38017
Lovejoy Ln	38017
Loves Landing Cv	38017
Lower Fields Ln	38017
Loyde Ln	38017
Macon Rd	38017
Macon Ridge Dr	38017
Madison Farms Ln	38017
N & S Madison Row Ct	38017
Magnolia Dr & Ln	38017
Magnolia Garden Cv	38017
N & S Main Ext & St	38017
Majestic Trl	38017
Mallard Lake Cv & Rd	38017
Mann Dr	38017
Manor Grove Cv	38017
Mansfield Mnr N & S	38017
Maple Valley Cv & Dr	38017
Marci Cv	38017
N Market Blvd	38017
Market Center Dr	38017
Marsh Creek Ln	38017
Marsh Springs Ln	38017
Martinsburg Cv	38017
Martway St	38017
Mayfield Rd S & W	38017
N & S Mccall Cv & Dr	38017
Mccool Forest Ln	38017
Mcdonald Glen Cv	38017
Mcferrin Ln	38017
Mcginnis Cir	38017
Meadow Glen Dr	38017
Meadow Ridge Dr	38017
Meadow Vale Dr	38017
Meadowbirch Ln	38017
Melbury Rd	38017
Memory Ln	38017
Mercersburg Cv	38017
Merchants Park Cir	38017
Merriweather Dr	38017
Metatero Cv	38017
Mid South Cv	38017
Midnight Sun Dr	38017
Milestone Cir & Dr	38017
Milford Cv	38017
Military Cv & Rd	38017
Mill Springs Cv	38017
Mills St	38017
Milton Dr	38017
Mindy Cir	38017
Mintmere Dr	38017
Miss Camryn Ln	38017
Miss Dylan Cv	38017
Mistwood Cv N & S	38017
Misty Brook Cv	38017
Misty Glen Dr	38017
Misty Hill Dr	38017
Mockingbird Ln	38017
Monterey Dr & Rd	38017
N & S Monterey Farms Cv	38017
Monterey Mills Cv & Rd	38017
Moore Ln	38017
Moorefield Cv & Rd	38017
Morganshire Dr	38017
Morning Mac Dr	38017
Morris Manor Dr	38017
Morton Rd	38017
Moss Creek Cv	38017
Mosswood Cv	38017
Mossy Oak Ln	38017
N & S Mount Pleasant Rd	38017
Mount Zion Rd	38017
Mountain Side Dr	38017
Muirfield Cv	38017
Muirhead Cv	38017
E & W Mulberry St	38017
Myrtlewood Cv	38017
Napier Woods Dr	38017
Natchez St	38017
National Club Dr	38017
Neely St	38017
Neshoba Nook Cir	38017
Nevil Ct	38017
New Ballard Rd	38017
New Byhalia Rd	38017
New Chulahoma Rd	38017
New Gale Cv	38017
New Point Cv	38017
Newington St	38017
Newton Nook	38017
Neyland Cv & Dr	38017
Nine Oaks	38017
E & W Nolley Cv & Dr	38017
Norfolk Southern Way	38017
Northcross Pl N	38017
Oak Cv	38017
Oak Arrow Cv	38017
Oak Bluff Ln	38017
Oak Club Ln	38017
Oak Creek Dr	38017
Oak Heights Ln	38017
Oak Lake Cir & Cv	38017
Oak Timber Cir	38017
Oak Tree Dr	38017
Oak Wild Cv	38017
Oak Wood Ln	38017
Oakleigh Dr	38017
Oakmont Ridge Cv	38017
Ogilie Cv & Ln	38017
Oilstone Cv	38017
Old Bray Cv	38017
Old Byhalia Rd	38017
Old Collierville Arlin Rd	38017
Old Course Cv & Dr	38017
E & W Old Hearthstone Cir	38017
Old Oak Ln	38017
E & W Old State Line Dr & Rd	38017
Ole Bob Dr	38017
Ollie St	38017
Open Woods Ln	38017
Orchard Cir E	38017
Osprey Creek Dr	38017
Ostlers Way	38017
Otter Creek Cv	38017
Owens Cv	38017
Page Manor Cv	38017
Panola Cv	38017
Park Hill Rd	38017
Park Manor Ln	38017
Park Ridge Pkwy	38017
Park Side Cir, Dr & Ln	38017
Parkview Cv & Dr	38017
Parnell Rd	38017
Patina Dr	38017
Patrick Dr	38017
Patton Place Cv	38017
Pear Valley Cv	38017
Pearson Oaks Dr	38017
Pebble Creek Cv	38017
Pebworth Ln	38017
Pecan Grove Cv	38017
Pecan Harvest Dr	38017
Pecan Ridge Dr	38017
E & W Pecan Valley St	38017
Penshurst Dr	38017
Percheron Pass	38017
Percy Pl	38017
Pete Dr	38017
Petersburg Cv	38017
Peterson Lake Cv & Rd	38017
Peyton Pkwy	38017
Peyton Path Cv	38017
Peyton Ridge Cv & Dr	38017
Pikes Peak Dr	38017
Pilgram Ridge Rd	38017
Pilot Rock Rd	38017
Pin Pointe Dr	38017
Pine Grove Cv & Dr	38017
Pinnacle Point Dr	38017
Piper St	38017
Plains Cv	38017
Plantation Vw	38017
Plantation Elm Cv	38017
Plantation Forest Cv	38017
Plantation Lake Cv & Rd	38017
Planters Ridge Cv & Dr	38017
Planters Trace Ln	38017
Polk Woods Cv	38017
Polo Dr	38017
Polo Run Cv & Dr	38017
E & W Poplar Ave	38017
Poplar Acres Rd	38017
Poplar Bluff Cv	38017
Poplar Leaf Rd	38017
Poplar View Ln & Pkwy E, N, S & W	38017
Poppy Hills Dr	38017
Port Natchez Cv & Dr	38017
E & W Porter Run Dr	38017
Poston Oak Cv	38017
Powder Springs Cv	38017
E & W Powell Cv & Rd	38017
Powell Run Cv	38017
Preakness Run Ln	38017
Prestworth Dr	38017
Progress Rd	38017
Purple Finch Cv	38017
Purple Mountain Cv	38017
Quail Chase Ln	38017
Quail Crest Dr	38017
Quail Forest Dr	38017
Queen Cv	38017
Queen Oak St	38017
Queens Bridge Rd	38017
Queensbury Ct	38017
Quiet Cv	38017
Quinn Rd	38017
Rain Drop Dr	38017
Rain Hollow Cir E	38017
Rain Lake Ln E	38017
Rainhill Dr	38017
Rainwater Dr	38017
Rainy Pass Rd	38017
Raleigh Lagrange Dr & Rd	38017
Ramport St	38017
Ravenna Cv	38017
Rebel Rd	38017
Red Bark Cv & Dr	38017
Red Bend Cv	38017
Red Sea Dr	38017
Red Stone Dr	38017
Red Wolf Dr	38017
Reston Ave	38017
Revell Cv & Pt	38017
Reynolds Rd	38017
Rhett Butler Dr	38017
Rhetts Way	38017
Ridge Peaks Dr	38017
Ridge Springs Rd	38017
Ridgewood Dr	38017
Riding Brook Dr & Way	38017
Rillbrook Dr	38017
River Bank Dr	38017
River Branch Cv & Dr	38017
River Pine Dr	38017
River Ridge Dr	38017
Robbins Nest Cv	38017
Rocky Joe Dr	38017
Roehampton Ct & Cv	38017
Rogers Wood Cv	38017
Rolling Oaks Ln	38017
Rose Trellis Rd	38017
Roseberry Cv	38017
Rowen Oak Cv & Rd	38017
N & S Rowlett St	38017
Roxburgh Cv & Dr	38017
Royal Aberdeen Cv	38017
Royal Crown Dr	38017
Royal Elm Dr	38017
Royal Forest Dr	38017
Royal Pecan Way	38017
Royal Troon Cv	38017
Russ Meadow Cv	38017
Russell Rd	38017
Russell Creek Cir	38017
Russell Farms Rd	38017
Russell Hill Cv	38017
Rutledge Cv & St	38017
Saddle Rock Ln	38017
Saffron Hill Cv	38017
Sagewood Dr	38017
Saintsbury Dr	38017
Saybrook Cv	38017
Scarlet Ohara Cv & Dr	38017
Scarlet Tanager Cv & Ln	38017
Scarletts Way	38017
Schilling Blvd	38017
Schilling Bend Cmn	38017
Schilling Farm Cir & Rd	38017
Schilling Oaks Ln	38017
Schilling Park Blvd	38017
School Cross Ln	38017
Schrader Ln	38017
Sea Biscuit Dr	38017
Seattle Slew Dr	38017
Serenbe Cv	38017
Seven Pines Rd	38017
Shadow Walk Cv & Ln	38017
Shady Forest Cv	38017
Shady Woods Cv	38017
Shallow Brook Ln	38017
Shallow Creek Cv & Ln	38017
Shanborne Cv	38017
S Shea Rd	38017
Shea Oaks Cv W	38017
Shea Woods Dr	38017
Sheffield Dr	38017
E Shelby Dr	38017
Shelby Post Dr & Rd	38017
Shelton Rd	38017
Shining Sea Cv	38017
Shively Ave	38017
Shoal Creek Ln	38017
Shrewsbury Run E & W	38017
Signature Farm Ln	38017
Signature Glen Cir E	38017
Signature Hill Dr	38017
Signature Lake Cir	38017
Silver Plum Cv	38017
Silver Wolf Dr	38017
Silverman Dr	38017
Simmonsridge Dr	38017
Six Crowns St	38017
Six Oaks Ln	38017
Skyline Trl	38017
Smoky Oaks Ln	38017
Snowden Farm Cv & Rd	38017
Songbird Rd	38017
Sontevillage Cv	38017
E & W South St	38017
Southern Belle Dr	38017
Southern Home Rd	38017
Southern Pride Dr	38017
Southwind Cv	38017
Spacious Sky Cv	38017
Spring Mill Rd	38017
Springmont Trl	38017
Spruce Valley Ln	38017
Squire Dudney Dr	38017
Staircase Dr	38017
Stanalone Way	38017
Standing Rock Ave & Cv	38017
Stanhope Cv & Rd	38017
Stanton Hall Rd	38017
Starlight Cv & Dr	38017
Starling Dr	38017
Statesboro Dr	38017
Statfield Dr	38017
Steeple Ridge Cv	38017
Sterling Oaks Cv & Ln	38017
Stillwind Ln	38017
Stone Creek Cv	38017
Stone Hedge Cv	38017
Stone Oaks Cv	38017
E & W Stonevillage Cv & Dr	38017
Stoney Brooke Rd	38017
Stotts Way	38017
Strong Dr	38017
Sugar Cv & Ln	38017
Sugarbush Cv N & S	38017
Summer Springs Rd	38017
Summit Cv	38017
Summit View Cv	38017
Sumpter Cv	38017
Sunflower Ln	38017
Sunnybrook Cir	38017
Sunriver Cv & Dr	38017
Surrey Oaks Cv & Dr	38017
Sweet Apple Cv	38017
N & W Sweet Rain Dr	38017
Sweetie Cv, Dr & Ln	38017
Swynford Ln	38017
Sycamore Rd	38017
Sycamore Farms Rd	38017
Sydney Bender Ln	38017
Sykes Grove Cv	38017
Talamore Cv	38017
Tall Forest Ln	38017
Tall Oaks Cv	38017
Tall Spruce Cv & Ln	38017
Tamburlaine Cv	38017
Tanglewood Way	38017
E & W Taplow Way	38017
Tara Oaks Cv & Dr	38017
Tara Woods Cv & Dr	38017
Tararidge Cv & Dr	38017
Taraview Rd	38017
Tarren Mill Cir E	38017
Tartan Ln	38017
Taylors Way	38017
Teal Valley Cv	38017
N & S Templeton Cir	38017
Ten Oaks Dr	38017
Tenby Cv	38017
Tender Oaks Cv	38017
Thornbuck Cv	38017
Timber Ridge Dr	38017
Tissington Dr	38017
Tom Ct	38017
Totty Cv & Ln	38017
Township Cv	38017
Tranquil Woods Cv	38017
Travelers Cv	38017
Treaty Rd	38017
W, N & S Tree Cv & Dr	38017
Tribal Land Cv	38017
Tribal Woods Cv & Rd	38017
Turnberry Cv	38017
Turtle Creek Cv & Dr	38017
Tuscarora Cv	38017
Tuscumbia Cv & Rd	38017
Twin Hawk Cv	38017
Twin Hill Way	38017
Twin Lakes Rd	38017
Twin Leaf Dr	38017
Twinnings Ct & Ln	38017
Upper Fields Ln	38017
Us Highway 72	38017
Valleyview Cv & Ln	38017
E & W Valleywood Cv & Dr	38017
Varanda Cv	38017
Venice Cv	38017
Verlington Cv & Dr	38017
Victoria Cv	38017
Village Cross Ln & Loop	38017
Village Ridge Pl & Rd	38017
Vista Ridge Dr	38017
Vivian Leigh Cv & Ln	38017
Von Hall Dr	38017
Wahkin Rd	38017
Wainwright Ct	38017
Wakehurst Dr	38017
Walnut St	38017
Walnut Grove Rd	38017
Walston Ln	38017
E & W Walton Lake Dr	38017
Warwick Oaks Ln E	38017
Warwick Willow Cv & Ln	38017
Washington St	38017
Waterford Cv & Rd	38017
N & S Waverton Cv	38017
Webb Cv	38017
Webbview Dr	38017
Welbeck Cv	38017
Wellington Way	38017
Wellington Way Cv	38017
West St	38017
Weston Dr	38017
Whealdon Way	38017
Wheatley Cv	38017
Whisper Trl	38017
Whisper Hill Cv & Dr	38017
Whisper Hollow Cv	38017
Whisper Run Dr	38017
Whisper Sage Dr	38017
Whisper Spring Dr	38017
Whisperwood Dr	38017
Whisperwoods Cv	38017

E & W White Rd 38017
White Pass Dr 38017
Whitecap Rd 38017
Whitney Way 38017
Whittenburg Dr 38017
Wild Chestnut Ln 38017
Wildbird Cv & Ln 38017
Wildcreek Cv & Dr 38017
Wildfox Dr 38017
Wilkes Cv 38017
William Rd 38017
Willow Bend Cv & Dr 38017
Willow Reade Cv 38017
Wilson St 38017
Win Cv 38017
Winburn Dr 38017
E Winchester Blvd & Rd 38017
Wincreek Cv & Dr 38017
Windbrook Cv & Dr 38017
Windebank Ct 38017
Windgrove Cv 38017
Winding Ridge Rd 38017
Winding Valley Cv & Ln 38017
Winding Wood Cir E 38017
Windover Cv & Rd 38017
Windsong Park Dr 38017
Windsor Hill Cir 38017
Windsor Park Cv & Ln 38017
Windy Knoll Cv 38017
Windy Oaks Dr 38017
Windy Ridge Cv 38017
Winford Dr 38017
Winhill Ln 38017
Winlawn Cv & Dr 38017
Winleaf Cv & Dr 38017
E & W Winoka Cv & Rd 38017
Winrose Dr 38017
Winsail Dr 38017
Winsley Way 38017
Wintree Ln 38017
Wolf Hunt Cv & Dr 38017
Wolf Lair Cv & Dr 38017
Wolf Pack Cv & Dr 38017
Wolf Ridge Cv & Dr 38017
Wolf River Blvd 38017
Wolf Run Rd 38017
Wolf Trap Rd 38017
Wood Cv 38017
Wood Valley Dr 38017
Woodfern Cv 38017
E & W Woodlawn Cir 38017
Wright Rd 38017
Wycliffe Blvd 38017
Wynbrooke Ln 38017
Wyncreek Dr 38017
Wynmanor Dr 38017
Wynmont Grove Cv 38017
Wynwood Cv & Dr 38017
Yancey Cir N & S 38017
Yankee Rd 38017
Yellowhammer St 38017
York Haven Dr 38017
Yorktown Cv & Rd 38017

COLUMBIA TN

General Delivery 38401

POST OFFICE BOXES MAIN OFFICE STATIONS AND BRANCHES

Box No.s
All PO Boxes 38402

NAMED STREETS

All Street Addresses 38401

NUMBERED STREETS

All Street Addresses 38401

COOKEVILLE TN

General Delivery 38501

POST OFFICE BOXES MAIN OFFICE STATIONS AND BRANCHES

Box No.s
1 - 1504 38503
2001 - 6004 38502
49001 - 49779 38506

NAMED STREETS

Abby Ct 38506
Abner Allen Rd 38501
Adams St 38506
Adams Acres Rd 38506
Albert Dr 38506
Albert Swift Ln 38501
Alberta Ave 38501
Alcorn St 38506
Alex Ln 38506
Alexander Rd 38506
Alfs Way 38506
Allen Ave 38501
Allen Dr 38501
Allen Ln 38501
N Allen Rd
900-1200 38501
1201-1219 38506
1202-1298 38501
1221-1299 38501
Allen Hollow Rd 38501
Alpine St 38501
Amanda Dr 38501
Amber Dr 38506
Amber Meadows Rd 38506
Amon Rd 38506
Anderson Ln 38501
Andover Ct 38501
Andy Haney Rd 38506
Anson Rd 38501
Anson Maxwell Rd 38506
Apple St 38506
Apple Valley Ct & Dr 38501
April Ln 38506
Arbor Pl 38506
Arlington Rd 38506
Armstrong Ave 38501
Arthur Dr 38501
Ash Ave 38501
Ashlyn Ln 38501
Ashwood Dr 38501
Aspen Dr 38501
Aspen Trl 38506
Audrey Pl 38506
Auguste Cir 38506
Autumn Ave 38501
Avery Pl 38501
Avey Cir 38506
Avondale Ct 38506
Aw Randolph Rd 38506
Baker St 38501
Baker Mountain Rd 38506
Ballard Ln 38501
E & W Bangham Rd 38501
Barlow Dr 38501
Barnes Dr 38501
Barnes Rd 38506
Baron Cir 38501
Bartlett Dr 38506
Bartlett Rd 38501
Bates Dr 38501
Battlefield Rd 38506
Bay View Dr 38506
Bayshore Dr 38506
Beachnut Dr 38506
Beacon Hill Rd 38506
Beam Ave 38501
Bear Trl 38506
Bear Creek Cir, Ln, Pt & Rd 38506
Bear Lake Rd 38506
Beckner Ln 38506
Becky Ln 38501
Beecher Blvd 38506
Belford Rd 38506
Bell Ln & Rd 38506
Belmont Dr 38506
Ben Jared Rd 38506
Ben Loftis Rd 38501
Ben Mason Rd 38506
Bend Spring Ln 38506
Benjy Cir 38501
Bennett Ln
100-148 38506
101-147 38501
149-150 38501
151-190 38506
152-188 38501
192-198 38506
Bennett Rd 38506
Bennie Dr 38501
Benson Rd 38506
Benton Young Rd 38501
Big Mac Dr 38506
Big Oak Dr 38501
Big Orange Dr 38501
Big Springs Cir 38501
Bilbrey Rd & St 38506
Bilbrey Park Dr 38501
Bilbrey Qualls Rd 38506
Bill Smith Rd 38501
Biltmore Cir & Dr 38501
Birch Cir 38501
Birchwood Ct 38501
Birdie Ct 38506
Bishop Trce 38501
Blackberry Ln 38506
Blackburn Way 38501
Blackburn Fork Rd 38501
Blackburn Hill Dr 38501
Blackwell Rd 38506
Blaine Ave 38501
Blake Cir 38501
N Blaylock Mountain Rd 38506
Blue Bird Ln 38501
Blue Ridge Ln 38501
Bluegrass Dr 38506
Boatman Ln 38506
Boatman Rd 38506
Boatman St 38501
Bob Bullock Rd 38506
Bob Gentry Rd 38506
Bob Johnson Ln 38501
Bob Lynn Rd 38501
Bob Pigg Ln 38501
Bob White Cir 38506
Bobar Ln 38501
Bobby Nichols Dr 38506
Bohannon Ave 38501
Bohannon Ln 38506
Boone Dr 38506
E & W Borden St 38501
Bouton Bnd & Dr 38501
Bowers Rd 38506
Bowman St 38506
Bowman Branch Rd 38501
Bowser Rd 38506
Boxwood Cir 38506
Boyd Ln 38506
Boyd St 38501
Boyd Farris Rd 38506
Bradford Trce 38501
Bradley Dr 38501
Bradshaw Blvd 38506
Brandi Ln 38506
Brandon Ave & Dr 38501
Brangus Ln 38506
Braswell Ave 38501
Bray Dr 38501
Breeding Ave 38501
Breeding Farm Rd 38506
Breen Ln 38506
Brewer Ave & St 38506
Brian Dr 38506
Briar Ln 38506
Briarcrest Ln 38501
Briargate Way 38501
Briarstone Ct & Dr 38506
Briarwood Dr 38501
Bridgeway Dr 38506
Bridle Path 38501
Briery Creek Rd 38501
E Broad St
1-9 38503
2-8 38501
10-1399 38501
W Broad St 38501
Brook Ln 38506
Brookdale Ave 38506
Brookfield Dr 38501
Brookland Ct 38506
Brookmeade Ct 38506
Brookshire Dr 38506
Brookside Dr 38506
Brookstone Ct & Dr 38506
Brookwood Ct & Dr 38501
Brotherton Dr 38506
Brotherton Mountain Rd 38506
Brotherton Pointe 38506
Brown Ave 38501
Brown Cir 38506
Brownie Nelson Ln 38506
Browns Mill Rd 38506
Bryant Ave 38501
Bryce Dr 38501
Buck Ave 38501
Buck Dr 38506
Buck Lake Rd 38506
Buck Mountain Rd & Trl 38506
Buckingham Pl 38501
Buena Vista Cir 38501
Buffalo Valley Rd 38501
Bullet Hole Rd 38501
Bunker Hill Rd
301-351 38501
353-1199 38501
1200-6999 38506
S Bunker Hill Rd 38506
Burgess Allen Rd 38506
Burgess Falls Rd 38506
Burgess Mill Rd 38506
Burgess School Rd 38506
Burks Ln 38506
Burton Ln 38506
Burton Branch Rd 38506
Burton Cove Rd 38506
Bush Rd 38501
Buzzard Ln 38506
Bybee Ave 38501
Byrne Ave 38501
Byrne Meadows Ln 38501
C C Camp Rd 38501
Cab Anderson Ln 38501
Calloway Ct 38501
Cambridge Ct 38506
Camden Ln 38501
Campbell Dr & Ln 38501
Camry Dr 38501
Canada Flatt Rd 38506
Candace Dr 38506
Candyland Cir & Dr 38506
Cane Creek Rd 38506
Canter Ln 38501
Canterbury Dr 38501
Capshaw Dr 38501
Cardinal St 38501
Carew Ln 38506
Carlen Ave 38501
Carlisle Rd 38501
Carmack Rd 38506
Carmel Dr 38506
Carol Ln 38501
Carolina Ave 38501
Carr Ave 38501
Carr Farm Rd 38506
Carriage Ln 38506
Carroll Dyer Rd 38501
Carson Cir 38506
Carter Rd 38506
Carver St 38501
Cass Ct 38501
Castle Dr 38501
Castlebrooke Ln 38501
Cavalier Dr 38501
N Cedar Ave 38501
S Cedar Ave 38501
Cedar St 38506
Cedar Branch Ln 38501
Cedar Creek Cir 38501
Cedar Hills Dr 38506
Cedar Springs Dr 38506
Celtic Dr 38501
W Cemetery Rd 38506
Center Ct 38501
Chad Ln 38501
Charles St 38506
Charles Haney Rd 38501
Charleston Dr 38501
Charleston Rd 38506
Charlie Maxwell Rd 38501
Charlie Peek Ln 38501
Charlotte Dr 38501
Charlton Sq 38501
Chatsworth Blvd 38501
Cherokee Dr 38506
Cherry Ave 38501
Cherry Creek Rd 38506
Chester King Rd 38501
Chestnut Ave 38501
Chilcut Rd 38506
Chimney Springs Rd 38506
Chitwood Cir 38506
Chloe Ln 38501
Choate Cemetery Rd 38501
Chocolate Dr 38501
Chote St 38501
Christian Community Rd 38506
Christie Cir 38501
Christmas Ln 38501
Church Ave 38501
Church Ct 38506
Church St 38501
E Church St 38506
W Church St 38506
Churchill Dr 38506
Cinderella Dr 38501
Cindy Dr 38506
Circle Dr
100-299 38506
1100-1299 38501
Circle Ln 38501
Clara Reid Ln 38506
Clara Williams Ln 38506
Clark Ave 38501
Clark Rd 38506
Clark Cemetery Rd 38501
Claude Green Rd 38506
Claude Loftis Rd 38501
Clay Ave 38501
Clay Cemetery Ln 38506
Claybrook Dr 38506
Clayton Dr 38506
Clear Valley Rd 38501
Clearfield Ln 38506
Clearview Dr 38506
Clearview Ln 38501
Cleghorn Creek Rd 38506
Clemmons Rd 38501
Cliff Ln 38501
Clifton Ln 38506
Clinton Ln 38501
Clinton Conley Rd 38506
Clouse Dr 38501
Clover Ave 38501
Clover Hill Dr 38501
Cloverdale Dr 38506
Cobble Ln 38506
Cobblestone Dr 38506
Coffelt Ave 38501
College St 38501
Colonial Dr 38506
Columbia St 38501
Conaster Ln 38506
Concord Dr 38501
Concord Ln 38506
Conner Rd 38506
Constitution Ct 38501
Contraband Ln 38501
Cooke Ln 38506
Cooke St 38501
N Cookeville Hwy & Ln 38506
Cooper Rd & Sq 38506
Copeland Ln 38506
Copperfield Dr 38501
Cora Rd 38501
Cottonwood Ct 38506
Cougar Ln 38501
Countess Trl 38501
Country Ln 38501
Country Club Ct, Pl & Rd 38501
Country Meadows Ln 38501
Country Wood Cir 38501
County Farm Rd 38501
County Services Dr 38501
Cove Rd 38506
Cove View Cir 38506
Cowan Rd 38506
Cozine Ln 38506
Crabtree Cir 38501
Craighead Dr 38501
Crawford Chapel Rd 38506
Crawford Mill Ln 38506
Creek Dr, Ln & Rd 38506
Creekside Ln 38506
Creekwood Dr 38501
Crescent Dr 38501
Crescent Spring Ln 38501
N Crestwood Dr 38501
Crockett Ave 38501
Crockett Trl 38506
Crowne Way 38501
Crystal Ct 38501
Crystal Springs Dr 38506
Cumber Ln 38501
Cumberland Ct 38506
Cumby Rd 38501
Cummins Ln 38501
Cummins Falls Ln 38501
Cummins Mill Rd 38501
Cunningham Rd 38506
Curtis Dr, Rd & Way 38506
Curtiswood Ct 38506
Cynthia St 38506
Cyphers Dr 38506
Cypress Ave 38501
Dacco Dr 38506
Dacco Quarry Rd 38506
Dakota Ave 38501
Dale Ln 38501
Dalton Ln 38501
Daniel Hill Ln 38501
Daniels Ln 38506
Darty Rd 38501
Darwin St 38501
Dave Dietz Rd 38506
Dave Huddleston Rd 38501
Davidson Ave 38501
Davis Ave 38501
E Davis Rd 38506
W Davis Rd 38506
Decatur Ln 38506
Deck Mountain Rd 38506
Deer Creek Dr 38501
Deer Run Rd 38506
Deerfield Dr 38501
Deerfield Ln 38506
Deerhaven Dr 38506
Deerwood Cir 38506
Deerwood Ct 38501
Deletta Dr 38506
Dellwood Ave 38506
Delman Dr 38501
Denny Rd 38506
Denton Ave 38501
Depot St 38501
Derby Ln 38501
Design Dr 38501
Dietz Dr 38506
Dishman Rd 38506
Ditty Rd 38506
N & S Dixie Ave 38501
Dixie Park Dr 38501
Dixie Plaza Dr 38501
Dixon Ln 38501
Dodson Branch Hwy & Rd 38501
Dodson Chapel Rd 38506
Dogwood Cir 38501
Dogwood Ct 38506
Dogwood Dr 38506
Dogwood Ln 38506
Donna Pl 38506
Doris Dr 38501
Double Springs Rd 38501
Douglas St 38501
Douglas Chapel Rd 38506
Dover Dr 38501
Dow Huddleston Rd 38506
Dowell St 38501
Downing St 38506
Dry Creek Rd 38501
S Dry Valley Rd 38506
Dubois Rd 38501
Duke Rd 38501
Duncans Chapel Rd 38506
Durant St 38506
Dustin Ln 38506
Dyer Ave & Ln 38501
Dyer Creek Rd 38501
Dyer Grimes Rd 38501
Dyer Long Rd 38501
Eagle Pt 38506
Eagle Landing Dr 38506
Eagles Landing Dr 38506
Early Ln 38501
East Rd 38501
Eastgate Cir 38506
Eastlake Dr 38506
Eastwood Dr 38506
Easy St 38506
Eaton Rd 38501
Echo Valley Dr 38501
Eckles Cemetery Rd 38506
Edgebrook Dr 38506
Edgefield Ct 38506
Edgerowe Ct 38506
Edgewood Dr 38501
Edmonds Ln 38506
Edwin St 38501
Eighteen Grand Pl 38506
Elbert Mackie Rd 38506
Elizabeth Ave 38501
Elk Dr 38506
Ellen Cir 38501
Eller Ridge Rd 38506
Ellis Ave 38501
N Elm Ave 38501
S Elm Ave 38501
Elm St 38506
Elrod Ave 38501
Elwin Dr 38506
Emerald Rd 38506
Emily Ct 38506
Emily Ln 38501
Enclave Cir & Pt 38506
W End St 38501
England Dr 38501
England Ln 38506
Ensor Dr 38501
Epperson Ave 38506
Essex Ct & Rd 38506
Evelyn Ct 38506
Evergreen Pl 38506
Ewell Dr 38506
Ezra Dr 38506
Fairbanks St 38501
Fairground Ln & St 38501
Fairview Rd 38501

Street	ZIP
Fairway Dr	38501
Falcon Trl	38506
Falling Water Rd	38506
Farley Ave	38501
Farley Rd	38506
Farmington Dr	38501
Fawn Dr	38501
Fawn Trl	38506
Faye Dr	38501
Fentress Dr	38501
N & S Ferguson Ave	38501
Fern Cir	38506
Ferrell Dr	38506
Fetterolf Ln	38506
Fiesta Dr	38501
Fire Fly Ln	38506
Fireside Dr	38501
Fisk Rd	
500-1499	38501
1900-3599	38506
Fisk Park Dr	38506
Fitz Ln	38501
Five Mile Ln	38501
Flatt Ave, Cir & Rd	38501
Flatt Hollow Rd	38501
Fleetguard Rd	38506
Fleming Ave	38501
Flintwood Ave	38506
Foreman Dr	38501
Forest Cir	38506
Forest Hill Rd	38506
Forest Hills Dr	38501
Forrest Rd	38501
Forrest Cove Ln	38501
Forrest Hill Rd	38506
Fortney Ln	38501
Foster Cir	38501
Fountain Cir	38506
Foutch Dr	38501
Fowler Montgomery Rd	38506
Fox Ln	38506
Fox Chase Ct & Ln	38506
Fox Den Ln	38506
Fox Knob Ln	38506
E Fox Ridge Rd	38501
N Franklin Ave	38501
S Franklin Ave	38501
Franklin Ct	38506
Freedom Ave	38501
Freehill Rd	38501
Freeze St	38501
Friar Tuck Ln	38501
Friendship Ln	38501
Frisbie Ln	38506
Front St	38501
Frosty Ln	38501
Gainesboro Grade	38501
Galermar Rd	38506
Garden Ln	38501
Garrett Ave	38506
Garrison Rd	38501
Garrison Cemetery Ln	38501
Gaw St	38501
Gayle Cir	38501
Geeseway Dr	38506
Genco Dr	38506
Gentry Ln	38501
Gentry School Ln	38501
Georgetown Rd	38501
Gibbons Rd	38506
Gibson Ave	38501
Gilliam Ln	38506
Gilmer Montgomery Rd	38501
Glenn Rd	38501
Glenrose Ave	38501
Glenrose Cir	38506
Glenwood Dr	38501
Golden Cir	38506
Golden View Ln	38506
Goodwin Rd	38501
Goodwin Cemetery Rd	38506
Goolsby Ave	38501
Goolsby Ln	38506
Gould Dr	38506
Gra Mar Dr	38506
Gracie Ln	38506
Grademere Dr	38501
Grady Pigg Ln	38501
Grand Ridge Dr	38501
Grandiose Dr	38501
Grandview Dr	38506
Green Gate Ln	38506
Green Meadow Rd	38506
Green Mountain Rd	38506
Green Springs Rd	38506
Greenbriar Ln	38501
Greene Ln	38506
Greenfield Dr	38501
Greenland Ave	38501
Gresham Dr	38506
Grider Rd	38506
Grimsley Rd	38501
Grundy Rd	38501
S Grundy Quarles Hwy	38501
H Warren Ln	38501
Hamlet Ave	38501
Hampton Cir	38501
N Hampton Cir	38506
E Hampton Ct	38501
N Hampton Dr	38506
Hampton Crossroads	38506
Haney Dr	38506
Harding Rd	38506
Hardscrabble Ln	38501
Hardys Chapel Rd	38506
Hargis Dr	38506
Hargis Ln	38506
Harley Dr	38501
Harp Ave	38506
Harris Ln	38501
Harve Allen Ln	38501
Harvie Mills Rd	38506
W Haven Dr	38501
Haven Ln	38506
Hawkins Crawford Rd	38501
Hawthorn Dr	38501
Hayes Dr	38506
Hearld Ct	38501
Heartland Ln	38506
Heather Ln	38506
Heathrow Dr	38506
Heathwood West Dr	38506
Helen Ct	38501
Helen Pl	38506
Henry Rice Rd	38506
Hensley Trl	38501
Herbert Garrett Rd	38506
Heritage Cir	38506
Heritage Green Way	38506
Hermitage Ave	38501
Hetzel Ln	38501
N Hickory Ave	38501
Hickory Cv	38506
Hickory Hill Dr	38506
Hidden Cove Rd	38506
Hidden Springs Ln	38501
E & W High St	38506
High Meadow Dr	38501
Highland Ave	38501
Highway 111	38501
Highway 111 N	38506
Highway 293	38506
Highway 70 E	38506
Hilham Rd	
2300-2499	38501
2500-9399	38506
Hill Ave, Cir & Rd	38501
Hillary Ct	38506
Hillsdale Dr	38506
Hillside Dr	38506
Hilltop Dr	38506
Hillwood Cir	38501
Hillwood Dr	38506
Hiram Brown Rd	38506
Hitchcock Dr	38506
Hobart Phillips Rd	38501
Hobert Rd	38501
Hodges Stockton Rd	38506
Holder Ave	38501
Holladay Rd	
600-1499	38501
1500-1699	38506
1700-1799	38501
Holland Ct & Dr	38506
Hollow Cir	38506
Holloway Ln	38501
Holly Ave & Ln	38501
Homer Carr Rd	38501
Homestead Cir	38506
Hooks Ln	38506
Hooper Burgess Rd	38506
Hoover Ave	38506
Hopper Ln	38506
Horace Lewis Rd	38506
Horner Rd	38501
Horseshoe Cir & Dr	38506
Howard Draper Rd	38501
Howell Ln	38506
Hub Cir	38506
Huddleston Dr	38501
E Hudgens St	38501
Hulon Dyer Rd	38501
Humble Dr	38501
Hummingbird Ln	38501
Hunter Ave	38501
Hunter Cove Rd	38506
Hunter Hills Ln	38506
Huntington Dr	38501
Huntland Rd	38506
Huntland Hills Rd	38506
Hutcheson Rd	38506
Hyder Mountain Rd	38506
Imperial Dr	38506
Independence Ct	38501
Indian Trl	38506
Indian Hills Rd	38506
Industrial Cir	38506
Inglewood Dr	38501
Interstate Dr	38501
Iris Ave	38506
Iris St	38501
Ironwood Rd	38501
Isaac Huddleston Rd	38506
Issacs Pass	38506
Ivy Ln	
200-299	38506
1300-1399	38501
J E Bartlett Rd	38506
E & W Jackson St	38501
Jager Dr	38506
Jake Dr	38501
Jake Davis Rd	38506
James Dr & St	38501
James Kinnard Ln	38501
James Ray Ln	38506
S Jamestown Ct & Rd	38501
Jamison Ln	38506
Janie Dr	38501
Jasper Dr & Ln	38506
Jb Pigg Ln	38506
Jean Ct	38501
N Jefferson Ave	38501
S Jefferson Ave	
1-97	38501
99-1099	38501
1100-5999	38506
Jeffrey Cir	38501
E & W Jere Whitson Rd	38501
Jeremiah Rd	38506
Jerry White Ln	38501
Jessica Ln	38506
Jill Cir	38506
Jim Anderson Rd	38501
Jim Robertson Rd	38506
Jim Smith Rd	38506
Joe Harris Ln	38506
Joe Martin Rd	38501
Joe Rawlings Rd	38506
Joel Holmes Ln	38501
Joff Dr	38501
John Clark Ln	38501
John Garrison Rd	38501
Johnnie Bud Ln	38501
Johnny Bilbrey Ln	38506
Johnny Stamps Rd	38506
Johnson Ave	38501
Johnson Dr	38506
Johnson Rd	38506
Joshua Rd	38501
Joy Dr	38501
Joy Ln	38506
Js Breedlove Dr	38506
Juanita Dr	38506
Judd Ln	38501
Julia Dr	38506
June Bug Rd	38506
June Chapel Rd	38506
Kacie Ave	38501
Karen Cir	38506
Kave Dr	38506
Kay Cir	38506
Kay Dr	38501
Kayla Ct	38506
Keller Rd	38506
Kello Rd	38501
Kelly Stockton Ln	38501
Kendall Dr	38506
Kenway St	38501
King St	38501
Kings Ct	38501
Kinnard Ln	38501
Kinniard Rd	38501
Kirby Ln	
1-99	38501
1700-1899	38506
Kirby Smith Rd	38506
Knight Church Rd	38501
Kuykendall Rd	38501
Kyle Dr	38501
Lacie Dr	38506
Lafever Rd	38506
Lafever Cemetery Rd	38506
Lake Ln	38506
Lake Crest Cir	38506
Lake Pointe Dr	38506
Lake Valley Dr	38506
Lake View Dr	38506
Lake Villa Cir	38506
Lakeland Dr	38506
Lakepark Ct	38506
Lakeshore Dr	38506
Lakewood Ct	38506
Lancaster Rd	38506
Landscape Rd	38506
Lane Ave	
100-235	38506
237-299	38506
300-399	38501
Lane Farm Rd	38501
Langford Ln	38501
Langford Hill Rd	38501
Lankford Rd	38506
Laura Pl	38506
Laurel Ave	38501
Laurel Park Cir	38501
Lee Ave & Rd	38501
Lee Seminary Rd	38506
Lemings St	38501
Lemon Farris Rd	38506
Leon Dr	38506
Leon Luke Rd	38506
Lester Fox Rd	38501
Levi Cir	38501
Lewis St	38501
Lewis Trce	38501
Lexington Ct	38501
Lexus Pl	38506
Liberty Ct	38501
Liberty Church Rd	38501
Lilac Ln	38506
Lilac Pt	38501
Lillian Cir	38501
Linda Ave	38506
Linden St	38501
Lindenwood Dr	38506
Lindsey Ln	38501
Linkwood Rd	38506
Linnaeus Ave	38501
Linwood Dr	38501
Little Ln	38506
W Little John Ln	38501
Littlebrook Rd	38501
Littleford Cv	38506
Llana Ln	38501
Locust Ave	38501
Locust Grove Rd	38501
Loftis Dr	38506
Loftis Ln	38501
Log Cabin Ln	38506
Lollipop Cir	38506
Lone Oak Dr & Ln	38501
Long Lane Rd	38506
Long Meadow Dr	38501
Longstreet Dr	38506
Looper Ln	38506
Louis Ave	38501
Louisiana Ave	38501
S Lovelady Rd	38506
Lovell Dr	38506
S Lowe Ave	38501
E Loweland Rd	38501
Lowhorn St	38506
Lucy Ln	38506
Luke Ln	38506
Lynn Chapel Rd	38501
Lynn Hill Rd	38501
Mabe Ln	38506
Mabry School Rd	38501
Macedonia Rd	38506
Macedonia Cemetery Rd	38506
Mack Phy Ln	38506
Mack Ray Rd	38506
Mackay Ln	38506
Mackie Rd	38506
Madden Ln	38506
Maddux Ave	38501
Maddux Ct	38506
Maddux Rd	38501
N & S Madison Ave & Pl	38501
Magnolia Ct	38501
Magnolia Dr	38506
Magura Dr	38501
Mahan Rd	38506
Mahler Ave	38501
E & W Main St	38506
Mal Allen Ln	38501
Malone Ln	38506
Manassas Rd	38506
Manhattan Pl	38501
Manning Pl	38501
Mansell Rd	38506
N Maple Ave	38501
S Maple Ave	
1-1199	38501
1200-1599	38506
Maple Trce	38501
Maple Point Dr	38501
Maple Shade Cir	38501
Maple Valley Ln	38506
Maplewood Dr	38501
Marie Dr	38506
Marigold Pl	38501
Markwater St	38506
Mary Dodson Ln	38501
Mason Pt	38506
Mason Rd	38501
Mason Valley Rd	38506
Massa Ave	38501
Masters Rd	38506
Mathison Cir	38506
Mattson St	38501
Maxwell St	
100-199	38506
500-699	38501
Mayberry Ln	38501
Mayfield Dr	38501
Maynard Hollow Rd	38501
N Mcbroom Chapel Rd	38501
Mccaskey Ct	38506
Mccauley St	38506
Mcclain Rd	38501
Mcclellan Ave & Ct	38501
Mccormick Cir	38506
Mcculley Rd	38506
Mcdonald Rd	38501
Mcduffee Ln	38501
Mcgee Ln	38501
Mcgregor Ln	38501
Mckinley St	38506
Meadow Cir	38506
Meadow Rd	38501
Meadow Wood Dr	38506
Meadowlark Ave	38501
Meadows Ln	38501
Medical Center Blvd	38501
Melanie Dr	38506
Melrose Dr	38501
Melton Rd	38506
Mercy Ln	38506
Mesa Ct	38501
Messenger Rd	38506
Middlebrook Rd	38506
Middleford Dr	38506
Midnight Ln	38506
Mike Maxwell Rd	38506
Mikonda Dr	38506
Milfred Ave	38501
Milk Barn Ln	38506
Mill Ave	38501
Mill Dr	38501
Mill Ln	38501
Mill St	38506
Mill Creek School Rd	38506
Miller Ave & Rd	38501
Mills Creek Ln	38501
Millstone Ct	38506
Mine Lick Creek Rd	
1700-3799	38501
3800-5599	38506
Minnear St	38501
Miracle Rd	38506
Miranda Ln	38501
Mirandy Rd	38506
Mississippi Ave & Ct	38501
Missouri Ave	38501
Mitchell Ave	38501
Mockingbird Ln	38506
Mockingbird Hill Cir	38501
Montgomery Ave	38501
Monticello Cir & Dr	38506
Moore Ln & Rd	38506
Morgan Haney Rd	38506
Morningside Dr	38501
Morris Ln	38501
Mount Herman Rd	38506
Mount Pleasant Rd	38506
E Mount Vernon Ct, Dr & Rd	38501
Mountain Top Ln	38506
Mountain View Dr	38506
Mulligan Ct	38506
Mullins St	38506
Murphy Rd	38506
Mustang Ln	38506
Myleigh Ave	38501
Nash Ave	38501
Nash Rd	38506
Neal Ln	38506
Neal St	38501
Neely Rd	38506
E & W Netherland Rd	38506
New Heritage Dr	38506
New Hope Dr	38506
New London Dr	38506
Newhall Cir	38501
Newman Dr	38501
Newt Rd	38506
Nicholas Ave	38506
Nichols Ave	38506
Nimrod Hill Ln	38501
Noel Dr	38506
Norfolk Dr	38506
Norman Mayberry Rd	38501
North Dr	38501
Northwind Dr	38506
Norton Dr	38506
Nottingham Dr	38506
Nova Cir	38501
Null Rd	38506
N Oak Ave	38501
S Oak Ave	38501
W Oak Dr	38501
Oak Trl	38506
Oak Haven Pl	38506
Oak Hill Dr	38501
Oak Park Cir & Dr	38506
Oak Trace Ln	38501
Oakdale Cir & Dr	38501
Oakhurst Cir	38506
Oaklawn Ct & Dr	38501
Oakley Cir & Dr	38506
Oakmont Cir	38506
Oakwood Ln	38506
Officers Chapel Rd	38506
Old 136 Rd	38506
Old Bridge Rd	38506
Old Cavalry Rd	38506
Old Dodson Branch Rd	38501
Old Gainesboro Hwy	38501
Old Hawthorne Ln	38506
Old Highway 42	38506
N & S Old Kentucky Rd	38501
Old Qualls Rd	38506
Old Salem Dr	38506
Old Sparta Rd	38506
Old Stewart Rd	38506
Old Thompson Ln	38506
Old Walton Cir	38506
Old Walton Rd	
700-1099	38501
2500-3199	38506
Olyvia Ct	38506
One Eleven Pl	38506
Opossum Rd	38506
Orchard St	38501
Oreilly Ln	38501
Overlook Cir & Pt	38506
Overstreet Dr	38506
Owen Farm Ln	38501
Oxford Pl	38506
P Brewington Rd	38501
Paine Rd	38501
Paleface Rd	38506
Palkway Dr	38501
Panther Ln	38506
Paran Rd	38506
Paran Pointe Dr	38506
W Paris St	38501
Park Dr	38501
Park West Dr	38501
Parker Ct	38501
Parker Pl	38506
Parkway Cir & Dr	38501
E & W Paron Rd	38506
Parragon Rd	38506
Pat Dillon Rd	38506
Patrick St	38501
Patton St	38506
Paxton Ct	
100-128	38501
129-199	38506
Peace Ln	38506
Peaceful Valley Ln	38501
W Peach Orchard Rd	38501
N Peachtree Ave	38501
Pearl Ave	38506
Pebblestone Way	38506
Peek Dr	38501
Pen Oak Dr	38501
Pennock St	38506
Penny Ln	38501
Penthouse Rd	38506
Peppermint Dr	38506
Perimeter Park Dr	38501
Petite Dr	38501
Pharris Rd	38501
Phifer Mountain Rd	38506
Phillips Dr	38501
Phillips Rd	38501
Phillips St	38506
Phillips Bend Ct	38506
Phillips Cemetery Rd	38506
Phillips Ridge Ln	38501

Phy Rd 38506
Phy Cemetery Rd 38506
N & S Pickard Ave 38501
Pigeon Rd 38506
Pigeon Roost Creek Rd 38506
Pilot Dr 38506
Pimlico Dr 38506
Pine Ave 38501
Pine Hill Rd 38506
N Pine Hill Rd 38501
Pine Valley Rd 38506
Pinewood Ct & Dr 38501
Pipkin Rd 38501
Pippin Ln & Rd 38501
Pitts Dr 38501
N & S Plantation Cir, Dr, Ln, Pt & Vw 38506
Pleasant Hill Dr 38501
Pleasant View Dr 38501
Plum Hollow Ln 38501
Plunk Whitson Rd 38501
S Pointe Rd 38506
N Pointe Cove Cir 38506
Polly Dr 38501
Pondview Cir 38506
Poplar Ave 38501
Poplar Grove Rd 38506
Poplar Springs Rd
  100-1599 38506
  1600-1799 38501
  2300-2899 38506
Porter Brown Ln 38506
Post Oak Cir & Rd 38506
Post Oak Bridge Rd 38506
Poston Ln 38506
Poston Andrews Ln 38506
Poston Whiteaker Rd 38506
Preakness Dr 38506
Presley Ln
  500-599 38501
  5700-5999 38506
Pritchard Pass 38506
E Proffitt St 38501
Proffitt Hill Dr 38501
Providence Rd 38506
Purple Martin Ln 38506
Putnam Dr 38501
Quail Dr & Ln 38506
Quail Hollow Cir 38501
Quarterhorse Ln 38501
N Quinland Lake Ct & Rd 38506
Rachel Ln 38501
Rader Ave 38506
Raider Dr 38501
Raines Cir 38506
Ramsey Ln & Rd 38501
Randolph Rd 38506
Randolph Mill Rd 38506
Randy Dr 38501
Raspberry Ln 38506
Ray Dr & Ln 38506
Rc Buck Dr 38506
Rd Anderson Rd 38506
Reagan St 38501
Rebecca Pl 38506
Rector Cir 38501
Reed Ln 38506
Reeser Ln 38501
Renea Cir 38506
Reserve Dr 38506
Rhea Ave 38501
Rice Cir 38501
Rickman Rd 38506
Rickman Monterey Hwy 38506
Ridgecrest Dr 38506
Ridgedale Dr 38501
Ridgetop Dr 38506
Ridgewood Rd 38501
Riley Ln 38506
Rileys Path 38506
River Bend Ct & Dr 38506
River Cross Ln 38506
N Riveroaks Dr 38506

E & W Riverside Dr 38506
Rl Hopkins Ln 38501
Robbins Ln 38506
Roberson Cemetery Rd 38506
Robert Ln 38506
Roberts Rd 38501
Roberts Hollow Ln 38501
Roberts Matthews Hwy 38506
Robin Ln 38501
Robinson Rd 38501
Robinson Hill Ln 38506
Robinwood Ln 38501
Rockwell Dr 38506
Rockwell Hollow Rd 38506
Rocky Point Rd 38506
Rodgers Rd 38506
Rolling Hills Rd 38506
Rose Garden Ln 38501
Rosebank Ave 38506
Rotary Centennial Dr 38501
Royal Cir 38506
Royal Oak Dr 38501
Ruby Ln 38501
Russell Strausse Rd 38501
Ryan Cir 38501
Saddle Ln 38501
Saint Charles Pl 38501
Saint James Pl 38501
N Salem Rd 38506
Salem Church Rd 38501
Sams St 38506
Samuel Dr 38501
Sandy Rd 38506
Sanford Rd 38506
Sarah Dial Ln 38506
Savannah Trce 38501
Scenic Dr 38501
Scenic Ln 38506
Scott Ave 38501
Scott And Jones Rd 38501
Security Pl 38506
Seven Springs Rd 38506
Shadow Ln 38501
Shady Ln
  800-999 38501
  2600-5599 38506
Shady Oak Cir 38501
Shady Oak Dr 38506
Shag Rag Rd 38506
Shanks Ave 38501
Shannon Dr 38506
Shannon Village Rd 38506
Sharon Ave 38501
Shawn Ln 38501
Sheep Bluff Rd 38506
Sheffield Ct 38506
Shelby Dr 38501
Shenandoah Ln 38506
Shepherd Hills Rd 38501
Sheraton Dr 38501
Sherman Dr 38506
Sherrill Dr 38501
Sherry Cir 38506
Sherwood Ln 38501
Shipley Rd & St 38501
Shipley Church Rd 38501
Shipley School Rd 38501
Short St
  100-199 38506
  300-499 38501
Simmons St 38506
Sims Ln 38501
Singleton Ln 38501
Skyline Dr 38506
Skymont Dr 38506
Skyview Dr 38501
Sliger Rd 38506
Slim Bray Rd 38506
Smith Ln 38501
S Smith Chapel Rd 38501
Solon Jared Rd 38506
Somerset Dr 38501
Songbird Ln 38501
South Dr 38501

Southern Woods Ct 38506
Southgate Dr 38501
Southmeade Ct & Dr 38506
Southside Dr 38506
Southwind Ct 38506
Southwood Dr 38501
Southwood Ln 38506
Sparkle Ln 38501
Sparks Dr 38506
Speck Rd 38501
W Speck Rd 38506
Spence Ln 38501
Spicer Rd 38506
Spring Dr 38506
E Spring St
  1-1399 38501
  1400-2299 38506
W Spring St 38501
Spring Creek Cir 38506
Spring Creek Rd
  100-3799 38501
  5000-10199 38506
Spring Park Dr 38501
Spring Valley Rd 38501
Springboro Rd 38506
Springdale Dr 38501
N Spruce Ave 38501
Spurgeon Dr 38501
Spurlock Dr 38506
Stafford Dr 38506
Staley Ave 38501
Stallion Rd 38506
Stamps Way 38506
Stamps Shady Grove Rd 38506
Standing Stone Hwy 38506
Stanley Carr Subdivision Rd 38506
Stargazer Dr 38501
Starlight Rd 38506
State St 38501
Steakley Dr 38501
Stella Smith Rd 38506
Step Rock Hill Rd 38506
Sterling Hitchcock Rd 38506
E & W Stevens St 38501
Steward Rd 38506
Steward Cemetery Rd 38506
Stewart Ln 38501
Stockton Ln 38506
Stone Cir 38501
Stone Creek Dr 38501
Stone Seminary Rd 38506
Stonebridge Cir 38501
Stonehenge Ct 38506
Stonewall Dr 38506
Stoney Creek Rd 38506
Stoneybrook Ct 38506
Stout St 38501
Stover Dr 38506
Stratford Dr 38506
Suffolk Dr 38506
Sugarhill Pl 38501
Sugarland Dr 38501
Sugartree Pl & Pt 38501
Sullivan Rd 38506
Sullivan St 38501
Sulphur Rd 38506
Summerfield Rd 38506
Summerhaven Ave 38501
Sumter Dr 38501
Sun Valley Cir & Rd 38501
Sunbright Cir 38506
Sunflower Ln 38501
Sunny Dr 38501
Sunny View Ln 38501
Sunnymeade Dr 38501
Sunset Dr 38501
Sutton Pl 38501
Swafford Rd 38501
Swallows Ln 38506
Swallows Chapel Rd 38506
Swann Rd 38506
Swift St 38506
Sycamore St 38501
Syracuse St 38501

T Short Ln 38501
Talley Ln 38501
Tanasi Trl 38506
Tanglewood Dr 38501
Tara Dr 38501
Taylor Cir 38506
Taylor Rd 38501
Tech Village Cir 38501
Tenn Tex Dr 38506
Terrace Hill Rd 38501
Terry Ave 38501
Texas Ave 38501
The Lane Rd 38506
Thelma Rd 38501
Thomas Cir 38506
Thomas Rd 38501
E Thomas Allen Rd
  100-299 38501
  300-1299 38506
W Thomas Allen Rd 38501
Thompson Ln & Rd 38506
Thompson Place Ln 38506
Thorne Ln 38506
Thorne Gap Rd 38506
Tiffany Pl 38506
Tiger Ct 38506
Timber Ln & Trl 38501
Timber Trail Ln 38501
Timber View Ln 38506
Timothy Dr 38506
Tolbert Dr 38506
Tom Allen Ln 38501
Tommy Dodson Hwy 38506
Top Rd 38506
Tornado Rd 38501
Transport Dr 38506
Treewood Dr 38501
Trent Ln 38506
Trinity Ln 38506
Tulip Ln 38501
Turkey Creek Rd 38506
Turnberry Pl 38506
Twin Creeks Dr 38506
Twin Gap Rd 38506
Tyler Dr 38501
Tyler Springs Ln 38506
Universal Dr 38506
Valley Forge Rd 38501
Valley View Rd 38506
Vance Dr 38506
Verble Sherrell Rd 38506
E Veterans Dr 38501
Vickers Ln & Pl 38501
E Victory View Dr 38506
Village Ct & Rd 38506
Vine Ridge Ave 38501
Vinson Ave 38501
Violet Ln 38506
Virgil Murphy Cir 38506
Virginia Ave 38501
Virginia St 38506
Vista Cir 38506
Vivian Dr 38501
Volunteer Dr 38506
Wade Ln 38501
Wade Conley Rd 38506
Wakefield Dr 38501
Walker Mountain Rd 38506
Walking Horse Ln 38501
Wall Ave 38501
E Wall St 38506
W Wall St 38506
N & S Walnut Ave & Trce 38501
Walnut Commons Ln 38501
Walnut Grove Rd 38506
Walter Ln 38501
Walter Reed Rd 38501
Walton Ln & Trl 38501
Warren Ave 38506
N Washington Ave 38501
S Washington Ave 38501
E Washington St 38506
W Washington St 38506
Wassom Cemetery Rd 38501
Watauga Dr 38501

Watauga Rd 38506
Waterloo Rd 38506
Watermill Rd 38501
Watson Rd 38506
Waynetta Rd 38501
Webb Ave 38506
Wedgewood St 38501
Welch Ave 38501
Welch Rd 38506
Wells Dr 38501
Wesley Dr 38506
West Cir 38501
Westgate Cir 38506
Westgate Rd 38501
Westmoreland Ct 38506
Weston Dr 38506
Westpoint Dr 38501
Whippoorwill Hill Dr 38506
White Rd 38506
White Cemetery Rd 38501
E & W White Oak Dr 38501
Whiteaker Springs Rd 38506
E & W Whitehall Ct & Rd 38501
Whites Point Dr 38506
N & S Whitney Ave 38501
Whitson Ave 38501
Whitson Chapel Rd 38506
Whittaker Rd 38506
Wildflower Ln 38506
Wildwood Ct & Rd 38501
Wilhite Ave 38501
Willard Brown Ln 38506
Willet Rd 38506
William Hawkins Ln 38501
Williams Cir, Ln & Sq 38506
Williams Enterprise Dr 38506
Williamsburg Cir 38506
Willis Martin Rd 38501
N Willow Ave 38501
S Willow Ave
  1-1116 38501
  1117-1147 38506
  1118-1148 38501
  1149-1299 38506
Willow Brook Dr 38501
Willow Industrial Ct 38501
Willow Valley Ct 38501
W Wilmouth Rd 38506
Wilshire Dr 38506
Wilson Ave 38501
Winchester Dr 38506
Windingbrook Ct 38506
Windle Community Rd 38506
Windrowe Dr 38506
Windsong Dr 38501
Windsor Dr 38506
Windsor St 38501
Winebarger Rd 38506
Wingfoot Ct 38506
Winston Dr 38506
Winterhill Dr 38501
Wj Robinson Rd 38506
Wolf Pond Rd 38506
Womack Ave 38501
Woodlake Trce 38501
Woodland Ave & Hts 38501
Woodlawn Dr 38501
Woodmont Cir 38501
Woodtrace Ct 38501
Woodview Cir 38506
Woodview Dr 38501
Woodwinds Dr 38501
Wright Ave 38506
Wyleswood Dr 38501
Wynd Walker Dr 38506
Wyndemere Ct 38506
Wyndwalker Ln 38506
Wynnwood Dr 38501
Yorktown Ct 38501
Young Rd 38501
Young Cemetery Ln 38501
Young Mill Ln 38501
Zeb Warren Rd 38506
Zenith Allen Ln 38501
Zion Rd 38501

Zion Hill Rd 38506

NUMBERED STREETS

1st Ave 38506
E 1st St 38501
W 1st St 38501
2nd Ave N 38506
2nd Ave S 38506
W 2nd St 38501
3rd Ave 38506
E 3rd St 38501
W 3rd St 38501
4th Ave 38506
4th Ave N 38506
E 4th St 38501
W 4th St 38501
5th Ave 38506
W 5th St 38501
E & W 6th 38501
E & W 7th 38501
E & W 8th 38501
E & W 9th 38501
E & W 10th 38501
E 11th St 38501
E & W 12th 38501
E & W 13th 38501
E & W 14th 38501
E 15th St 38501
E & W 16th 38501
E & W 17th 38501
E 18th St 38501
E 20th St 38501
E 21st St 38501
E 22nd St 38501

CORDOVA TN

General Delivery 38018

POST OFFICE BOXES MAIN OFFICE STATIONS AND BRANCHES

Box No.s
All PO Boxes 38088

NAMED STREETS

Abbey Grove Ln 38018
Abbotsbury Pl N & S 38016
Abbott Cv 38016
Aberlour Dr 38016
Acadia Pl 38018
Ada Cv & Ln 38016
Addison Park Cv 38016
Adikson Dr 38016
Admington Pl 38016
Adobe Ln 38016
Afterglow Cv 38018
Afton Grove Rd 38018
Alana Cv 38016
Albon Cv & Dr 38016
Alcove St 38016
Alidar Pl 38016
Allentown Cir & St 38016
Alliance Pl 38016
Almstead Cv 38018
Amber Springs Cv 38018
Ambergate Ln 38016
Amberly Rd S 38018
Amberly Grove Cv 38018
Amberly Village Dr 38018
Amberly Way Dr 38018
Amundsen Cv 38018
Angel Crest Cir 38016
Anise Cv 38016
Anisetree Dr 38018
Annes Cir 38018
Ansley Park Cv 38018
Antler Cv E & W 38016
Apple Grove Dr 38016

Apple Wood Cv 38018
Apple Yard Ln 38016
Applemill Cv & Dr 38016
Appling Rd
  1100-1199 38018
  1200-2099 38016
Appling Care Ln 38016
Appling Chase Cv 38016
Appling Club Cir 38016
Appling Hill Ln 38016
Appling Meadow Cv & Dr 38016
Appling Mist Dr 38016
Appling Oaks Cir & Dr 38016
Appling Rain Dr 38016
Appling Ridge Dr 38018
Appling Walk Ln 38016
Appling Wood Cv & Rd 38016
Apron Cv 38016
Apsley Pl 38016
Arbor Bend Ln 38018
Arbor Hollow Cir 38018
Arborgate Cv 38016
Arcaro Way 38018
Archstone Dr 38016
Arendal Cv 38018
Aristides Ct 38016
Armscote Pl 38016
Artis Alan Ln 38018
Ascott Pl 38016
Ashburton Pl N & S 38016
Ashbury Cv 38018
Ashbury Oak Cv & Dr 38018
Ashlee Farm Rd 38016
Ashley Creek Ln 38016
Ashley Glen Cir E 38018
Ashley Nicole Cv 38016
E & W Askersund Cv 38018
Aspen Glade Cv 38016
Aspen Green Cv 38016
Aspen Meadow Cv & Dr 38018
Aspen View Cv 38018
Atherstone Pl 38016
Autumn Bluff Cv 38018
Autumn Creek Dr
  7700-7855 38018
  7856-7858 38016
  7857-7899 38018
  7860-7998 38016
  8000-8099 38016
Autumn Glade Ln 38016
Autumn Grove Cv 38018
Autumn Hollow Dr 38016
Autumn Sage Cv 38018
Autumn Tree Cv 38016
Autumn View Cv 38018
Autumndale Cv & Dr 38016
Avalon Way 38016
Avanti Dr 38018
Averbury Cv & Dr 38016
Averett Cv & Ln 38016
Aylesbury Pl N & S 38016
B St 38018
Bakers Glenn Ln 38018
Bale Rd 38016
Ballarat Cv 38018
Banstead Cv & Dr 38016
Baptist Church Rd 38018
Barbie St 38016
Bardwell Cv 38016
Barge Dr 38016
Barnsbury Way 38016
N & S Barnwell Cv 38016
Baronsmede Cv 38016
Barrow Dr 38016
Barwyn Pl N & S 38016
Bay Orchard Cv & Ln 38018
Bayberry Hill Dr 38018
Bazeberry Rd 38018
S Bazemore Rd 38016
E Beaman Cir 38016
Bear Track Cv 38018
Beaver Trail Dr 38016

Beaver Valley Cv & Ln 38018
Becca Pt 38016
Beckenham Cv & Dr 38016
Becket Cv 38016
Bedlington Dr 38016
Beech Bend Trl 38018
Beecham Pl N & S 38016
Beechcroft Pl N & S 38016
Beechwood Cv 38018
Begall Cv 38018
Belfiore Ln 38018
Belgian Cv N & S 38016
Belgrade Pl 38016
Belle Trees Dr 38016
Belledeer Cv & Dr 38016
Bellehurst Cv & Dr 38016
Bellevue Pkwy & Trce 38016
Bellevue Grove Cv 38016
Bellingham Ln 38018
Bena Cv 38016
Benchmark Dr 38018
S Bend Dr 38016
Bendigo Dr 38018
Bending Elm Cv & Dr 38016
Bending Pine Ln 38018
Bentwood Cir 38018
Bergen Cv & Dr 38018
S Beringer Dr 38018
N & S Berkshire Cv 38018
Bernese Cv 38016
Berry Bush Ln 38018
Berry Garden Cir E 38016
Berry Hollow Cv 38016
Berryhill Rd 38016
Berwick Pl 38016
Big Orange Rd 38018
Birch Creek Cv 38016
Bird Stone Cv 38016
Bishop Dozier Dr 38016
Black Bear Cir E & W 38016
Blackalder Cv 38016
Blake Rd 38018
Bloomsbury Ave 38016
Blue Rapid Ln 38016
Bluff Ridge Cv 38018
Bluff View Cv 38018
Bluffside Cv & Pt 38018
Blufftop Cv 38018
Boathook Ln 38018
Bohemia Cv & Dr 38016
Bonnie Ln 38016
Bonniebrow Cv 38018
Boones Hollow Cv & Dr 38018
Bowmore Cv & Dr 38016
Box Turtle Cv 38016
Boxford Ln 38016
Brackenbury Cv & Ln 38016
Brady Creek Cv 38016
Brady Hill Dr 38018
Brady Hollow Cv & Ln 38016
Brancaster Dr 38016
Branchwood Ln 38016
Brancott Cv 38018
Branley Oak Dr 38016
Bredbury Cv E & W 38016
Breeze Way 38018
Breezehill Dr 38016
Breezy Gate Dr 38016
Breezy Oak Cv 38018
Breezy Ridge Cv & Trl 38016
Breezy Valley Cv & Dr 38018
Brent Cv & Ln 38016
Brentford Cv 38016
Brentlawn Dr 38016
Brentridge Dr 38018
Brer Bear Cv 38018
Brer Fox Cv 38018
Brer Rabbit Cv 38018
Briarwood Cv 38018
Briarwyck Rd 38016
Bridge Creek Dr 38016
Bridgefield Dr 38018
Bridgewater Cv 38016
Bridgewater Rd 38018
Bridgewater Church Rd 38018
Bridle Glen Cv & Ln 38016
Bridlewood Ln 38016
Brier Harbor Cv 38016
Brightleaf Pl 38016
Brightwood Dr 38016
Brigstock Cv 38016
Brimfield Cv & Dr 38016
Brimhill Cv & Ln 38016
Broadstone Cv & Ln 38016
Broken Rock Cv 38016
Brook Ridge Cir & Dr 38018
Brooklawn Dr 38018
Brookview Cv 38018
Brownsford Cv & Ln 38016
Brownstone Ln 38018
Bruins Trce 38018
Brussels Ln 38018
Bryan Station Rd 38016
Brynhurst Pl 38016
Buck Ridge Cv 38016
Buck Trail Cv 38018
Buckeye Rd 38018
Buckhurst Rd 38018
Buckingham Cv 38018
Buckstone Cv 38016
Burlingate Dr 38018
Burslem Cv 38016
Byre Hollow Cv 38018
Cairn Cv & Dr 38018
Cairn Creek Cv & Dr 38018
Cairn Drive Ext 38018
Calderdale Cv & Dr 38018
Calebs Ln 38018
Calebs Ridge Dr 38018
Caliber Dr
9400-9580 38016
9581-9599 38016
9582-9598 38016
Callaway Ct 38016
Camden Grove Cv 38018
Cameron Ridge Trl 38016
Camille Way 38016
Campaldino Ave 38018
Camron Dr 38016
Canberra Ln 38016
Candle Ridge Cv & Dr 38016
W Cannon Cv 38016
Canopy Ln 38016
Canterbury Court Cv 38016
Canterwood Dr 38016
Capas Cv 38016
Caper Tree Dr 38016
Carina Pass 38016
Carlsbad Rd 38016
Carlton Ridge Dr
1200-1279 38018
1280-1599 38016
Carlyn Cv 38016
Carriage Ct & Ln 38016
Carrol Ridge Ln 38016
Carrollwood Cv & Ln 38016
Casentino St 38018
Casey Ln 38018
Cassabella Cv 38016
Cates Cv 38016
Cathedral Ln 38018
Causey Ln 38018
Cedar Bend Cv 38016
Cedar Brake Dr 38016
Cedar Brook Cv 38016
Cedar Chase Cv 38016
Cedar Chest Dr 38016
Cedar Fall Cv 38016
Cedar Farms Cv & Dr 38016
Cedar Glade Cv 38016
Cedar Glen Cv 38016
Cedar Grove Cv 38016
Cedar Hollow Cv & Dr 38016
Cedar Mills Cir, Cv & Dr 38016
Cedar Mist Cv E & W 38016
Cedar Reach Cv 38016
Cedar Run Cv & Dr 38016
Cedar Trail Cv 38016
Cedar Trails Dr 38016
Center Rd 38018
Centerview Pkwy 38016
Century Oaks Dr 38016
Cerise Ave 38016
Chadwick Glen Rd 38016
Chalkwell Ave & Cv 38016
Chapel Creek Cv & Pkwy N & S 38016
Chapel Park Blvd 38016
Chapel Place Cv 38016
Chapel Ridge Cv & Dr 38016
Chariden Dr 38016
Charles Bryan Rd
1100-1699 38018
1700-1999 38016
Charlton Way 38018
Charly Hill Ln 38016
Charly View Ln 38016
Chartridge Cv & Dr 38016
Chase Farm Ln 38018
Chastain Pl 38018
Chatham Ln 38018
Chatman Cv & Way 38018
Chena Bay Ln 38016
Cherry Farms Rd 38016
Cherry Hollow Cv 38018
Cherry Leaf Cv 38018
Cherry Ridge Cv 38016
Cherry Spring Cv & Dr 38016
Cherry Tree Cv 38016
Cherrywood Cv 38018
Cheshunt Ln 38016
Chesterfield Pl 38016
Chickering Cv & Ln 38016
E Chimneyrock Blvd 38016
Chingford Cv 38016
Chippingham Dr & Pl 38016
Chivas Dr 38016
Chris Suzanne Cir 38016
Chrysalis Cv & Ln 38016
Chucker Valley Cv 38016
Churchill Gate Cv 38016
Cider House Cv & Ln 38016
Cinderhill Cv E & W 38016
Cirrus Cv 38018
Citico Dr 38016
Citrus Bend Cv & Dr 38016
Clair Harbor Cv 38016
Clarke Landing Cv & Dr 38016
Clear Sky Path & Way 38018
Cleek Cv 38016
Clinton Way Cv & Ln 38018
Clover Run Cv 38016
Cloverwood Ln 38016
Club Dr & Pkwy 38016
Club Center Dr 38016
Clumber Dr 38016
Clunan Cv 38016
Colefield Cv 38016
Colemont Dr 38016
Coleridge Cv 38016
Colie Stolz Cv 38016
Colonial Towers Dr 38016
Concord Green Cv 38016
Coolidge Cv 38016
Cooper Ridge Cv 38016
Coral Leaf Ln 38016
Coral Shell Ln 38016
Coral Tree Cv & Ln 38016
Cordova Rd 38016
Cordova Center Dr 38016
Cordova Club Dr E 38018
Cordova Green Dr 38018
Cordova Mills Cv 38016
Cordova Park Rd 38016
Cordova Ridge Pl 38018
Cordova Rose Cv 38016
Cordova Station Ave 38018
Coriander Ln 38018
E, N & W Cortona Cir & Pl 38018
Cosby Cv 38018
Cosby Mill Cv 38018
Cottage Farms Dr 38016
Cottage Oaks Cv & Dr 38016
Cotton Patch Dr 38016
Cotton Ridge Cv N & S 38018
Cotton Trail Cv 38018
Country Pl 38018
Country Air Cv 38018
Country Creek Cv 38016
Country Downs Cv & Ln 38016
Country Glade Cv & Dr 38016
Country Leaf Cv 38016
Country Maple Cv 38016
Country Mill Cv 38016
Country Pecan Cv 38016
Country Squire Ln & Pl 38018
Country Village Dr 38016
Country Walk Dr 38018
E & N Country Way Dr 38018
Countrywood Fwy & Pkwy 38016
Crayton Ridge Cv & Dr 38018
Creek Front Dr 38016
Creek Way Cv 38016
Creeks Edge Cv & Dr 38016
Creekside Cir N & S 38016
Crested Ln 38016
Crestmont Cv 38016
Crimson Creek Dr 38016
Crimson Mill Dr 38016
Crimson Ridge Ln & Rd 38016
Cross Breeze Dr 38016
Cross Hill Rd 38018
Cross Meadow Rd 38018
Cross Ridge Rd 38016
Cross Valley Cv & Dr 38018
Cross Wood Ln 38018
Crossmont Cv 38016
Crossvine Cv N & S 38016
Crown Cv 38016
Crystal Lake Dr 38016
Cullendale St 38016
Cully Rd 38018
Cypress Grove Ln 38016
Daeva Cv 38018
Daisy Grove Dr 38016
Dal Whinnie Trl 38016
Dalemore Ln 38016
Dalgety Cv 38018
Dalry Cv 38018
W Darren Loop 38018
Dartford Cv & Dr 38016
Davies Plantation Rd 38016
Davis Way 38018
Debbie Kay Ln 38018
Deer Meadow Cv & Dr 38016
Deer Run Cv 38016
Deer Valley Cv 38016
Delafield Ave 38016
Dena Cv E & W 38016
Derby Ln 38018
Destin Dr 38018
Dew Cv 38016
Dewars Cv N & S 38016
Dewberry Ln 38016
Dexter Ln, Rd & Run E & W 38016
N & S Dexter Chase Cir 38016
Dexter Creek Ln 38016
Dexter Grove Ct & Dr 38016
Dexter Hills Dr 38016
Dexter Hollow Dr 38016
Dexter Lake Dr 38016
Dexter Manor Dr 38016
Dexter Oaks Ct & Ln 38016
Dexter Park Dr 38016
Dexter Ridge Cv E & W 38016
Dexter Run Cir 38016
Dexter Springs Loop 38016
Dexter Woods Dr 38016
Dirks Cairn Cv & Rd 38016
Divi Ln 38018
Doe Trail Cv 38018
Dogwood Leaf Cv 38016
Dove Hollow Cir & Dr 38018
Doveland Dr 38018
Dry Well Cv 38016
Duck Call Cv 38016
Dulwich Rd 38016
Duncanshire Rd 38016
Dundee Cv 38016
Dunnan Cv 38016
Duomo Cv 38018
Durhamshire Cv & Dr 38016
Dusty Cv & Ln 38018
Duval Ave 38016
Eagle Brier Cv 38016
Eagle Glade Cv 38018
Eagle Shore Dr 38016
Eagle Spring Cv 38016
Eagle View Dr 38016
Eagleridge Ln 38016
Eagleridge Center Ln 38016
Eaglet Cv 38016
Eastmont Ln 38016
Easton Dr 38016
Eatonwick Dr 38016
Eckley Cv & Pl 38016
Ecklin Dr 38016
Ecklin St 38018
Eclipse Cv 38018
Eddystone Ln 38016
Eden Brook Ln 38016
Edgeburg Ln 38016
Edney Ridge Dr 38016
Elderberry Cv & Ln 38016
Elise Cv & Dr 38016
Elkhorn Dr 38016
Elmington Dr 38016
Emerald Creek Ln 38016
Emerald Greens Ct & Dr N 38016
Enclave Rd 38016
E & W End Row 38016
Englehart St 38016
English Mill Cv 38016
English Walnut Cv 38016
Enquirer Ct 38016
Ensworth Ct 38016
Equestrian Dr 38016
N Ericson Cv, Dr & Rd 38018
Esprit Pl 38016
Essex Court Cv 38016
Essexbriar Cv 38016
S Estacada Way 38018
Evening Grove Cv 38018
Eveninghill Cv & Dr 38016
Exbury Dr 38018
Exeter Pl 38016
Exocet Dr 38018
Eyrie Crest Cv 38016
Fairway Forest Dr E 38016
Fairway Gardens Dr 38016
Fairway Vista Ct 38016
Fallingwater Ln 38016
Falls Creek Cir 38016
Far Dr 38016
Fareham Cv 38016
Farkleberry Dr 38016
Farley Ave 38016
Farmyard Cv & Dr 38016
Farwoods Dr 38018
Fawn Ridge Cv 38016
Fay Rd 38018
Featherwind Cv N & S 38016
Fenmore Cv 38016
Fern Glade Cv 38016
Fern Meadow Cv 38016
Fern Valley Cv N 38018
Fieldstone Trl 38016
Finsbury Cv 38016
Fischer Steel Rd 38016
Flame Leaf Cv 38018
Fleets Hill Cv & Dr 38018
Fleets Run Dr 38016
Fletcher Cv 38016
Fletcher Creek Pkwy 38016
Fletcher Crest Cv 38016
Fletcher Park Cir & Cv E, N, S & W 38016
N Fletcher Run Cir 38016
Fletcher View Dr 38016
Fletcher Wood Dr 38016
Fletchers Fork Ct 38016
Floral Spring Dr 38016
Forest Breeze Dr 38018
Forest Hill Irene Rd N
1-200 38018
202-298 38018
2100-2399 38016
2401-2499 38016
Forest Hill Irene Rd S 38018
Forest Park Dr N & S 38018
Forest Run Cv 38016
Forest Village Pl 38018
Forrest Ridge Cv 38018
Fountain Brook Ln 38016
Fountainview Cv 38016
Fox Glade Cv & Ln 38016
Fox Green Cv 38016
Fox Heather Cv 38016
Fox Trace Cv 38018
Fox Trace Dr 38016
Foxmoor Ln 38016
Foxwood Cv 38016
Freedom Woods Cv 38018
Freeman Oaks Cv 38018
N & S Frence Creek Cv 38016
Friars Pl 38016
Friars Point Ln 38018
Fulton Cv & Ln 38016
Gallop Cv & Dr 38018
Garden Gate Dr 38016
Garden Park Cv & Dr 38016
Garden Willow Ln 38016
Garden Woods Cv & Dr 38016
Garmin Ln 38018
Garrett Ridge Rd 38016
Gateshead Ln 38018
George Brett Dr 38018
Gerald Ford Dr E & W 38016
German Creek Cv & Dr 38018
German Oak Dr 38018
German Park Cv 38016
Germantown Ct 38018
N Germantown Pkwy
300-1049 38018
1050-2549 38016
S Germantown Pkwy 38018
Germantown Bend Cv 38016
Gilden St 38016
Gimel Ln 38016
Glen Arbor Cir 38018
Glen Fiddich Ln 38016
Glen Gyle Cv 38018
Glen Park Dr 38016
Glen Rock Cv 38016
Glen Turret Dr 38016
E, S & W Glendale Ct & Cv 38018
Glendower Cv 38016
Glennmere Way 38018
Glenway Cv 38016
Golden Arrow Cv 38018
Golden Nugget Ln 38016
Goodlett Farms Pkwy 38016
N & S Goodlett Grove Cv 38018
Gooseberry Cv 38016
Goshawk Cv 38016
Grace Ann Ct 38016
Gracie Cv & Ln 38016
Grandbury Pl 38016
Grange Way Dr 38018
Grangewood Cv 38016
Grapetree Trl 38018
Grasmere Pl 38016
Grassmeade Cv 38018
Grays Hollow Cv & Dr 38018
Grays Lake Cv 38018
Grays Meadow Dr 38018
Grays Mill Cv 38018
Grays Park Cv & Dr 38018
Grays Song Dr 38018
Graystone Ct & Ln 38016
Green Arrow Cv 38018
Green Fern Cv 38018
Green Heron Ln 38018
Green Moss Cv & Dr 38018
Green Pine Cv 38018
Green Trail Cv 38018
Green Turtle Trl E 38018
Greenalder Cv N & S 38016
Greengate Cv 38018
Grendel Pl 38016
Grey Bair Cv 38018
Grey Heather Way 38018
Grey Hill Cv & Dr 38018
Grey Leaf Cv 38018
Grey Squirrel Cv 38018
Greywood Cv & Ln 38018
Griffin Ln 38016
Griffin Park Dr 38018
Griffon Cv & Dr 38018
Grigsby Ln 38018
Grouse Hollow Cv 38018
Grouse Meadows Dr 38018
Grove Rd 38016
Grove Creek Cv 38018
Grove Manor Dr & Way 38016
Grovewood Dr 38018
Guasco Cv 38018
Gum Tree Cv 38018
Gunner Hills Cv 38018
Hailsham Cv 38018
Hall Valley Cv 38018
Halls Hill Ln 38016
Hamburg Cv 38016
Hamilton Farms Dr 38016
Hamilton Hill Cv & Dr 38016
Hamilton View Dr 38016
Hammersmith Ln 38016
Hampton Court Rd E & N 38016
Hampton Oaks Cv 38016
Hampton Wood Cv 38016
Harbor Oak Cv 38016
Hardwood Cv & Trl 38016
Harley St 38016
Hatchie Cv & Dr 38016
Hathaway Pl E & W 38016
Havanese Ln 38016
Havenwood Dr 38016
Havishire Cv 38018
Hawk Glade Cv 38018
Hawkcrest Cv & Dr 38018
Hawksbury Cv 38018
Hawksmoor Pl 38016
Hawkview Dr 38018
Hay Loft Dr 38018
Haystack Cv 38018
Hazel Crest Ln 38018
Hazelnut Ln 38016
Headley Cv 38016
Hearth Stone Cv & Dr 38016
Heath Cv 38016
Heather Hill Dr 38016
Heather Leigh Cv & Ln 38018
Helmsley Cv & Dr 38016
Hemmingwood Rd 38016
Herbert Rd 38018
Herring Cv & Ln 38018
Herrington Cv 38018
Hertford Pl E & W 38018
Hervay Cv & Ln 38016
Hickory Path Dr 38016
Hickory Trail Dr 38018
Hidden Falls Cv & Dr 38016
Hidden Ridge Ln 38016
Hidden Springs Cv 38016

Higdon Cv 38016
High Cotton Cv 38018
Highland Glen Cir N & S 38016
Holly Grove Rd 38018
Holly Hall Cv 38018
Honey Dr 38016
Honey Dew Cv 38016
Hoska Cv 38018
Houston Birch Cv & Dr 38016
N Houston Levee Rd
  1-197 38018
  199-1279 38018
  1280-2899 38016
S Houston Levee Rd 38016
Humphrey Rd 38018
Humphreys Hill Dr 38016
Hunters Crossing Dr 38018
Hunters Green Cir & Cv 38018
Hunters Lake Dr 38018
Hunters Point Dr 38018
Hunters Rest Ln 38016
Huntgate Cv 38016
Huntington Fwy & Pl 38016
Huntington Oak Dr 38016
Indian Cv 38018
Indigo Cir 38016
Inglenook Dr 38018
Ireland Dr 38018
Iris Mdws Dr 38016
Ivy Laurel Cv 38018
Ivy League Ln 38018
Ivy Mist Cv E & W 38016
Jackson Pond Cir 38018
Jacob Dr 38016
Jared Michael Ln 38016
Javelin Cv 38018
Jessa Cv 38018
Jessica Lauren Cv & Dr 38018
Johnston Cv & St 38016
Judith Cv 38016
Julip Cv 38018
Juniper Cv E & W 38016
Juniper Valley Dr 38016
Kamali Ave 38018
Karen Mill Cv & Ln 38016
Karlstad Cv 38018
Kay Oak Cv 38016
Keaton Ave 38018
Keeli Cv 38016
Keely Dr 38018
Keighley Cv 38016
Kenbrook Cv 38018
Kenmont Cv & Dr 38016
Kenneland Ct 38018
Kentshire Cv 38018
Kentwood Estates Dr 38018
Kerry Dr 38018
Kerry Valley Ln 38018
Kettering Dr 38018
Kevin Cv 38016
Killdeer Cv & Ln 38016
Kimberly Rose Dr 38016
King William St 38016
Kings Cross Cv & Ln 38016
Kings Pond Cv 38016
Kings Trail Cv & Dr 38016
Kingsrow Pkwy 38016
Kristiandsund Cv 38018
Lacewing Trace Ct, Cv & Ln 38016
Lagrange Cir N & S 38018
Lagrange Belle 38018
Lagrange Crest Rd 38018
Lagrange Downs Rd 38018
Lagrange Grove Cv & Dr 38018
Lagrange Hill Dr & Rd 38018
Lagrange Pines Rd 38018
Lake Edge Cv & Dr 38016
Lake Hill Ct 38016
Lake Springs Cv & Ln 38016
Lakefield Cv 38016
Lakeside Cv 38016
Lanthorn Cv & Dr 38016
Lapel Cv 38016
Lathbury Pl N & S 38016
Latting Ln & Rd 38016
Latting Hills Cv 38016
Latting Woods Rd 38016
Lawson Dr 38016
Layton Rd 38016
Lazzini Cv 38016
Leaf Manor Cv 38018
Leaf Trail Ct, Cv & Ln 38018
Leafhaven Cv 38016
Leafhopper Cv 38016
Leconte Gap St 38018
Leconte Hill Cv 38018
Leda Cv 38018
Lee Side Cv & Dr 38016
Leery Cv 38016
Leif Cv E & W 38018
Leisure Crest Ct 38016
Lemasa Dr 38016
Lenoir Pl 38016
Lenow Rd 38016
Lenzi Marie Cv 38016
Lichfield Ct 38016
Lida Cv & Ln 38018
Lilac Pl 38016
Lillehammer Cv 38018
Linden Grove Cv 38018
Linden Hill Ln 38016
Lindsey Leaf Cv 38018
Lindstrom Cv & Dr 38016
Linell Cv & Ln 38016
Links View Ln E 38018
Linkwood Ln 38018
Linnean Cv 38016
Littlemore Dr & Fwy 38016
Locust Grove Dr 38016
Loften Cv 38016
Loganberry Ln 38016
Lomond Way 38016
Londonderry Ln 38016
Longshadow Cv & Ln 38016
Lorena Cv 38016
Lost Brook Dr 38016
Lost Grove Ln 38016
Lost Trail Dr 38016
Loxley Fwy & Pl 38016
Ludgate Pl E & W 38016
Lurry Ln 38016
Luxor Ln 38016
Lybrook Cv E & W 38016
Lycomedes Cv 38016
Lynham Cv & Dr 38016
Lynx Run Cv 38016
Lyric Ln 38016
Mabry Mill Cv & Rd 38016
Macklowe Cv 38016
Macon Rd
  6900-8300 38018
  8255-8255 38088
  8301-8999 38018
  8302-8998 38018
  9001-10599 38016
Macon Ter 38018
Macon Hall Rd 38016
Macon Hollow Rd 38018
Macon Oak Rd 38018
Macon Station Dr 38018
Macon View Dr 38018
Macon Wood Cv 38018
Magilbra St 38016
Magnolia Cv 38016
Magnolia Bloom Cv 38016
Magnolia Farms Cv 38016
Magnolia Glen Cv 38016
Magnolia Leaf Cv 38016
Manchester Cir 38016
Mandel Knoll Cv 38016
Mangrove Dr 38016
Manor View Cv 38016
Manslick Rd 38018
Maple Creek Dr 38016
Maple Hollow Loop 38016
Marbella Cv 38018
Marblehead Ln 38018
Marcross Cv 38016
Marhill Cv 38016
Marie Rd 38016
Market Plz 38016
Marsh Ln 38018
Martingale Xing 38016
Marysville Ave
  8500-8628 38018
  8501-8569 38018
  8571-8603 38018
  8605-8627 38018
  8629-8699 38018
May Apple Dr 38016
May Orchard Ln 38018
Mayhurst Ln 38018
Maythorn Cv 38018
Mcallen Cv 38016
Mccleskey Cv 38018
Mclaren Ln 38018
Meadow Bark Cv 38016
Meadow Green Dr 38016
Meadow Mill Cv 38016
Meadow Pines Cv 38016
Meadow Ridge Cv & Dr 38016
Meadow River Cv 38016
Meadow Trail Cv & Dr 38016
Meadow Way Cv 38016
Meadowbank Rd 38016
Meadowgrass Dr 38016
Meaghan Dr 38016
Medina Cv 38016
Meis Ln 38016
Meverett Cv 38016
Midas Cv 38018
Middle Essex Cv 38016
Midlands Cir 38018
Mikada Ln 38018
Mikayla Ln 38018
Milano Cv 38018
Milbrey St 38018
Mill Farm Cv & Dr 38016
Mill Glen Cv 38016
Mill Hill Ave 38016
Minda Path 38016
Minda Path Cv 38016
Mirage Ln 38018
Mirror Lake Ln 38016
Misty Birch Ln 38018
Misty Brook Cv & Ln 38016
Misty Elm Dr 38016
Misty Grove Cv 38016
Misty Knoll Dr 38016
Misty Point Cv 38016
Misty Ridge Cv 38016
Misty Shadow Dr 38016
Misty Woods Cv N & S 38016
Monarch Dr 38016
E & W Montebello Cir & Way 38018
Montego Dr & Pl 38016
Moriarty Rd 38018
Morning Garden Cv 38016
Morning Glow Cv & Dr 38016
Morning Grove Ct 38016
Morning Grove Cv
  8900-9099 38018
  9300-9399 38016
Morning Grove Cv S 38016
Morning Grove Dr 38016
Morning Hill Cv & Dr 38016
Morning Lake Dr 38016
Morning Park Cv & Dr 38016
Morning Ridge Rd 38016
Morning Shadow Dr 38016
Morning Sun Rd 38016
Morning Trace Dr 38016
Morning Walk Dr 38016
Morning Woods Cv & Dr 38016
Mossy Hill Cv 38018
Mossy Knoll Dr 38018
Mount Airy Dr 38016
Mount Badon Cv & Ln 38016
Mulligan Ln 38018
Myron Cv N & S 38016
Mysen Cir, Cv & Dr 38018
Naples Dr 38018
Napoli Dr 38018
Narvick Cv 38018
Nate Cv 38018
Needle Oak Dr 38016
Needle Pine Dr 38016
Nesting Dove Cv & Ln 38016
Nesting Wood Cir E & W 38018
New Appling Rd 38016
New Well Cv & Ter 38016
Niblik Cv & Pass 38016
Nolan Ln 38018
Nolton Cir 38018
Nordmore Cv 38018
Norseman Dr 38018
Northport Rd 38016
Northshore Ct 38016
Norwich Dr 38018
Notting Hill Rd 38016
Nottingham Cir 38018
Nova Cv 38016
Nutbush Pl 38016
Nutmeg Ln 38018
Oak Barn Ln 38016
Oak Bough Cv 38016
Oak Hedge Cv 38016
Oak Hollow Ln 38016
Oak Knoll Cv 38018
Oak Moss Cv 38016
Oak Springs Cv & Dr 38016
Oak Trail Ln 38018
Oak Vale Dr 38016
Oaken Bucket Dr 38016
Oakengate Cv 38016
Oasis Cv 38016
Oban Cv & Dr 38016
Ocoee Dr 38016
Odom Way 38016
Old Brook Cv 38016
Old Dexter Rd 38016
Old Mill Strm 38016
Old Post Rd 38018
Old River Cv & Rd 38016
Old Well Cv & Ter 38016
Oldham Cv & Dr 38016
Orchard Park Cv 38016
Orleans Grove Dr 38018
Oslo Cv 38018
Otterburn Cv 38016
Overcup Oaks Cv & Dr 38016
Overlea Cv 38016
Owls Roost Ln 38016
Paddle Wheel Dr 38016
Painted Desert Ln 38018
Palm Springs Dr 38016
Palmina Cv 38018
Pantherburn Cir & Trce 38018
Par View Cv 38016
Paradise Dr 38018
Park Crest Cv & Dr 38016
Parkbrook Ln 38018
Parson Dr 38016
Parson Forest Cv 38018
Partridge Woods Cv 38018
Patriot Cv & Ln 38018
Pearbrook Ct 38016
Pemberton Ln 38016
Penbrook Fwy & Pl 38016
Pendrell Cv & Ln 38016
Pepper Hollow Ct 38016
Pewter Ln 38016
Pheasant Acre Ln E & W 38016
Pheasant Hollow Dr 38016
Pine Arbor Ln 38016
Pinkerton Rd 38016
Pinscher Ln 38016
N Pisgah Rd 38016
Pisgah Forest Cv & Ln 38016
Plantation Gate Cv 38018
E & N Plantation Oaks Dr 38018
Plantation Place Cv 38018
Plantation Trail Cv 38018
Plantation Woods Cv 38018
Planters Grove Cv & Dr 38018
Pleasant Grove Fwy 38018
Plum Creek Dr 38016
Port Douglas Cv & Dr 38018
Portside Dr 38018
Presmond Rd 38016
Prestine Loop 38018
Prism Cv E & W 38018
Puddin Cv & Ln 38016
Purple Leaf Cv & Ln 38016
Quails Nest Cv 38018
Quailwood Cv 38018
Quick Fox Cv 38016
Quick River Cv 38016
Racquetball Ln 38016
Radiance Dr 38018
Radley Cv 38016
Radnor Cv 38016
Rain Dance Way 38018
Rainsong Cv 38016
Raleigh Lagrange Rd 38018
Ramsford Cv 38016
Randle Valley Dr 38018
Ranmar Dr 38016
Raspberry Ln 38016
Rathmore Dr 38016
Rayberry Ln 38016
Raybrad Dr 38016
Reading Cv 38016
Rebel Rd 38018
Recital Cv 38018
Red Barn Dr 38016
Red Creek Dr 38016
Red Fern Cir E & W 38018
Red Fox Cv 38018
Red Thorn Cv 38018
Red Tulip Cv 38018
Red Vintage Cv & Ln N 38016
Redalder Cv 38018
Redditt Rd 38018
Redmond Cir, Cv & Dr E, N & W 38016
Reflections Cv 38016
S Regatta Dr 38016
S & W Regis Cv & Pl 38018
Registry Ln 38016
Reksten Cv 38018
Rembrook Dr 38016
Reserve Dr 38016
Rhodesian Dr 38016
Rhonda Cir E 38018
Richards Way Dr 38016
Ridge Fall Cv & Dr 38018
Ridgeglen Rd 38016
River Creek Cv 38016
River End Cv 38016
River Farms Cv 38016
River Hollow Cv & Dr 38016
River Knoll Dr 38016
River Meadow Cv & Dr 38018
River Mill Cv 38016
River Pine Cv & Dr 38016
River Rise Dr 38016
River Sound Dr 38016
River Star Cv 38016
W Riveredge Cv & Dr 38018
Rivertrail Cv 38018
Riverwood Farms Pkwy 38016
Roby Cv 38016
Rochelle Ln 38016
N Rockcreek Cv, Pkwy & Pl 38016
Rocky Brook Cv & Dr 38018
Rocky Cannon Rd 38018
Rocky Field Cv & Dr 38018
Rocky Forest Cv N & S 38018
Rocky Glen Cv 38018
Rocky Hills Cv & Dr 38018
Rocky Meadows Trl 38016
Rocky Mill Cv 38018
Rocky Oaks Trl 38018
Rocky Point Rd 38018
Rocky Stream Dr 38016
Rocky Top Cv 38016
Rocky Valley Cv 38018
Rocky Woods Cv & Dr 38018
Rogers Rd 38018
Rogers Park Ave 38016
Roland Rd E 38016
Rolling Rock Cv 38018
W Rosemeade Cir, Crk & Cv E & W 38016
Rosewood Cv 38018
Rotherwood Pl 38016
Roundabout Ln 38018
Roundtree Ln & Pl 38016
Rowley Cv 38016
Royal Chartres Sq E 38018
Royal Commons Cv 38016
S Ryamar Cv N 38016
Ryan Cv 38016
Saddle Brook Trl 38016
Saddle Chase Cv 38016
Saddle Glen Cv 38016
Saddle Hill Cv 38016
Saddlewood Cv 38018
Safe Harbor Ln 38016
Sag Harbor Cir 38016
Sail Cv 38016
W San Gabriel Cv W 38016
Sanbyrn Dr 38018
Sand Creek Cv 38016
Sandy Hill Cv E & W 38018
Sandy Stone Ln 38016
Sanga Cir E 38018
Sanga Cir W 38018
N Sanga Rd
  1-1149 38018
  1150-1299 38016
S Sanga Rd 38018
Sanga Creek Rd 38018
Sanibelle Ln 38016
Santa Anita Cv W 38016
Sara Cv 38018
Sarsen Cv & Dr 38016
Sasha Cv 38016
Satinwood Pl 38016
Sawmill Creek Ln 38016
Saxony Cv 38016
Scarborough Ln 38016
Scarlet Oaks Cv 38016
Scofield Cv & Dr 38018
Seagull Dr 38016
Seahawk Cv 38016
Seaside Dr 38016
Secretariat Ct 38018
Secretariat Path 38018
Sedona Dr 38016
Shadow Glen Cv 38016
Shadow Grove Cv 38018
Shadow Point Cv E & W 38016
Shadow Ridge Cv 38016
Shady Elm Dr 38018
Shady Fern Cv 38018
Shady Leaf Cv 38018
Shady Meadow Ln 38016
Shady Morning Ln 38016
Shady Trail Cv 38016
Shady Well Ln 38016
Shallow Glen Trl 38016
Shallow Rock Cv 38016
Shelby Grove Ct & Dr 38016
Shelley Renee Cv & Ln 38018
Sherburne Cv 38018
Shetland Cv 38016
Shingle Oaks Cv & Dr 38016
Shippan Cv N & S 38016
Shorey Cv, Ln & Way 38018
Show Boat Cv & Ln 38018
Silver Hollow Cv 38016
Silver Sands Dr 38018
Siskin Cv & Dr 38016
Skylar Cv 38018
Skylar Mill Ave 38018
Smokehouse Dr 38016
Snow Drift Ln 38016
Solana St 38016
Sorghum Mill Dr 38016
Sorrento Pl 38018
Southall Cv & St 38016
Southern Woods Dr & Rd 38016
E & W Southfield Cir 38016
Spanish Trail Ln 38018
Speerberry Cir & Ln 38016
Speyburn Cv & Ln 38016
Spice Wood Ln 38018
Spillway Cir 38016
Spinnaker Ln 38018
Spirit Lake Cv 38016
Spoon Cv 38016
Spradlin Ct 38016
Spring Garden Cv 38016
Spring Grove Cv 38018
Spring Orchard Cv 38018
Springer Cir & Dr 38018
Spruce Ln 38016
Spruce Glen Cv & Dr 38018
Spruce Grove Ln 38016
Spruce Leaf Cv 38018
Spruce Tree Cv 38016
St Ives Cv 38016
Stable Cv 38018
Stable Park Ct 38016
Stable Run Cv 38016
Stable Run Dr
  1000-1259 38018
  1260-1699 38016
Stablemill Cv & Ln 38016
Stafford Cir 38018
Starboard Dr 38018
Starcross Ave 38016
Stavenger Cv 38018
Steadman Ln 38018
Steeplebrook Cv & Dr 38016
Stephen Dr 38016
Sterling Ridge Dr 38016
Stern Ln 38016
Still Forest Cv 38016
Still Oaks Cv 38016
Stixx Ln 38018
Stockbridge Ln 38016
Stoksund Cv 38018
Stone Stream Cv & Dr 38018
Stone Valley Cv 38016
Stone Wood Cv E & W 38018
Stonedale Cv & Dr 38016
Stoneleigh Rd 38016
Strait Cv 38016
Strawberry Ln 38016
Sturbridge Way 38018
Success Cv 38016
Sugarwood Dr 38016
Summer Grove Cv & Rd 38018
Summer Sweet Cv 38016
Summerfield Ln 38018
Sun Vista Dr E 38018
Sunnyvale St N & S 38018
Sunshine Cv & Dr 38016
Sunstar Dr 38018
Surrey Cv 38018
Surrey Hill Pl 38016
N & S Sussex Ct & Ln 38018
Sutters Mill Cv E & W 38016
Suttle Cv 38016
Sutton Meadow Ln 38016
Sutton Ridge Ln 38016
Swansea Cv 38016
Sweet Rose Dr 38016
Tailwater Ln 38016
Talisker Cv & Dr 38016

Tall Hickory Dr 38016
Talmadge Pl 38016
Tamarind Ln 38018
Tamhaven Ct & Dr 38016
Tanasi Cv & Dr 38016
Taylor Ridge Cv 38016
Teal Lake Cv 38016
Teal Wing Cv & Ln 38016
Tealwood Ln 38018
Tefall Cv E & W 38016
Tenacity Ct 38018
Tennis Court Dr 38016
Terindi Dr 38018
Tern Rest Cv 38016
Terra Wood Rd 38016
Thakeham Pl N & S 38016
Thor Rd 38018
Thorgenson Cv 38018
Thorn Tree Ln 38016
Thorncliff Dr & Fwy 38016
Thornton Cv 38016
Three Pines Cv 38016
Tidmington Dr 38016
Timber Creek Dr 38016
Timber Glen Dr E 38016
Timber Grove Dr 38018
Timber Hill Trl 38016
Timber Knoll Cv & Ln 38018
Timber Line Cv 38016
Timber Lodge Rd 38016
Timber Oaks Cv 38018
Timber Run Cv 38016
Timber Trace Dr 38018
Timber Trail Cv 38018
Timber View Cv 38018
Timber Walk Cv 38018
Timberlake Dr E & W 38018
Timberlane Dr 38018
Tivoli Ln 38018
Tonstad Cv 38018
Torrington Ct, Cv & Dr 38016
Toth Cv 38016
Town N Country Dr 38016
Tracewood Cv 38016
Traditional Pl 38016
Trail Hill Cv & Ln 38016
Trail Ridge Ln 38016
Trail Run Ln 38016
Trailmont Ln 38016
Tramway Pl 38016
Trappers Cv 38018
Travers Cv & Ln 38018
Tree Court Cv 38016
Tree Haven Cv 38016
Tree Top Cv 38018
Trinity Rd 38018
Trinity Creek Cv 38018
Trinity Mills Rd 38016
Trondheim Dr 38018
Tropicana Cv & Dr 38018
Trotters Stop Cv 38018
Tryon Cv 38018
Tucker Creek Cv & Ln 38018
Tugboat Ln 38016
Tunsberg Cv & Dr 38016
Turtle Hill Dr 38016
Twin Rivers Dr 38016
Twin Springs Cv 38018
Twisted Oak Cv N & S 38016
Tyler Pl 38018
Unbridle Way 38016
Us Highway 64 38016
Val Halla Cv 38018
Valley Edge Cv & Dr 38016
Valley Grove Cv 38018
Valley Ridge Trl 38016
Valley Run Cv, Dr & Ln 38016
Valley Sage Cv 38016
Valley Springs Cv 38018
Valmont Cir & Dr 38016
Vardon Ln 38016
Varnavas Dr 38016
Vauxhall Pl 38016
Vermeer Cv 38018
Versilia Ave & Cv 38018
Vesta St 38016
Vickery Ln 38016
W Viking Cv & Dr 38018
Vine Grove Ln 38018
Vintage Dr 38016
Volleyball Ln 38016
Vorlich Cv 38016
Waif Woods Cv & Ln 38018
Waldeck Cv 38016
Walden Pine Ct 38018
Walnut Ln 38018
N & S Walnut Bend Cv & Rd 38018
E Walnut Creek Rd 38018
Walnut Forest Cv 38018
Walnut Gardens Dr 38018
Walnut Grove Rd 38018
Walnut Hill Rd 38018
Walnut Hollow Cv 38018
Walnut Knoll Cv & Ln 38018
Walnut Leaf Cv & Dr 38018
Walnut Point Cv 38018
Walnut Ridge Cv, Ln & Loop 38018
Walnut Run Rd 38018
Walnut Trace Cv & Dr 38018
Walnut Trail Cv 38018
Walnut Tree Cv & Dr 38018
Walnut Valley Cv & Ln 38018
Walnut Woods Cv N & S 38018
Waterstone Pl 38016
Wayside Cv 38016
Weatherwood Ln 38018
Webbing Dr 38016
Weeping Cherry Ln 38016
Wellspring Ln 38016
Wenham Cv E & W 38016
Wentonwood Ln 38018
Wesley Woods Cir & Dr 38018
Westbriar Dr 38016
Wharfside Dr 38016
Whatling St 38016
Whisper Edge Cv 38016
Whistler Dr 38018
Whistler Valley Dr 38016
Whitcomb Ln 38016
Whitesmills Cv 38016
Wickwood Dr 38018
Widgeon Lake Cv 38016
Wigan Cv 38016
Wilderidge Ln 38016
N & S Wilderwood Ln 38016
William Keith Cv 38018
Williamswood Rd 38016
Willow Glen Ln 38016
Willow Tree Cir & Ln 38018
Willow Vista Ct 38016
Wilpat Dr 38018
Winburg Cv 38016
Wind River Cir E 38016
Windbreak Rd 38016
Windrush Cir 38016
Windstream Ln 38016
Windy Meadow Ln 38016
Wininger Cv 38016
Winrock Rd 38016
Winsford Ln 38018
Winship Dr 38016
Winter Gate Dr 38018
Winter Leaf Dr 38018
Winter Springs Ln 38016
Winterbrook Ln 38018
Winterfalls Trl 38018
Winterfields Dr 38018
Wintergreen Cv & Ln 38018
Wirily Ln 38016
Wolf Meadow Cv 38018
Wolf View Cv 38018
E & W Wolfchase Cir & Ln 38016
Wood Arbor Pkwy 38018
Wood Cade Cv 38018
Wood Cairn Cv 38018
Wood Farms Cv & Dr 38016
Wood Glen Cv 38016
Wood Grove Cv 38016
Wood Kirk Cv 38018
Wood Manor Cv 38016
Wood Mills Cv & Dr E & W 38016
Wood Moss Cv 38018
Wood Oak Cv & Dr 38016
Wood Run Cv 38016
Wood Sage Cv & Dr 38016
Wood Shadows Ln N 38018
Wood Trail Cir 38016
Wood Wren Cv 38018
Woodchase Cv & Dr 38016
Woodchase Glen Dr 38016
Woodcock Cv 38018
Woodland Bluff Ln 38018
Woodland Brook Ln 38018
Woodland Creek Cv & Ln 38018
Woodland Edge Cv & Ln 38018
Woodland Glade Cv N & S 38018
Woodland Glen Dr 38018
Woodland Green Ct 38016
Woodland Hills Dr 38018
Woodland Levee Way 38018
Woodland Manor Blvd & Cv 38018
Woodland Ridge Dr 38018
N & S Woodland Rose Cir N & S 38016
Woodland Run Ln 38018
Woodland Spruce Dr 38018
Woodland Trace Ln 38018
Woodland View Cv & Ln 38018
Woodland Vista Dr 38018
Woodlark Cv 38016
Woodlee Cv 38016
Woodmark Dr 38018
Woolrich Dr 38016
Worchester Cv 38018
Wren Hollow Cv 38016
Wrigley Dr 38018
Wynne Rd 38016
Wynne Grove Rd 38016
Wynne Ridge Rd N & S 38016
Yellow Stone Dr 38016
Zenith Cv N & S 38018
Zircon Cv 38016

NUMBERED STREETS

All Street Addresses 38018

CROSSVILLE TN

General Delivery 38555

POST OFFICE BOXES MAIN OFFICE STATIONS AND BRANCHES

Box No.s
1 - 1478 38557
1501 - 2018 38558
2501 - 7005 38557

NAMED STREETS

Abbey Cir 38555
Abbey Pl 38558
Abington Pl 38558
Ackia Dr 38572
Acoma Dr 38572
Acorn Ln 38571
E & W Adams Ct & St 38555
Adams Creek Rd 38571
Adelaide St 38555
Adler Ln 38558
Admiral Cir 38558
Airstream Cir & Dr 38572
Al Goss Rd 38571
Alandale Ct 38558
Alapattah Cir 38572
Albatross Cir 38555
Albemarle Cir, Ct, Ln, Pl & Ter 38558
Albert Frye Rd 38571
Albert Wood Rd 38572
Aldergate Ct & Ln 38558
Alderwood Ln 38558
Alisha Ln 38571
Allen Burgess Rd 38572
Alloway Ct 38558
Altakima Ct 38558
Altakima Ln 38572
Altanglen Ln 38558
Amanda Ln 38571
Amesbury Cir & Ct 38558
Amherst Dr & Ln 38558
Andover Ln 38558
Andrew Ln 38571
Andrews Ln 38555
Anglewood Dr 38558
Ann St 38555
Anselm Cir 38555
Antique Village Dr 38571
Apache Ct & Trl 38572
Apoka Ln 38572
Apoxsee Cir 38572
Apple Cir 38555
Apple Rd 38572
Apple Trace Ln 38555
Appleby Ct 38558
Aqum Cir 38572
Arapaho Dr 38572
Archie Tate Farm Rd 38571
Arden Pl 38558
Argona Pt 38558
Arkham Ln 38555
Arlis Holman Dr 38555
Arnold Smith Rd 38572
Arnolds Way 38571
Arrowhead Dr
1-199 38571
1000-1299 38572
Arrowhead Pt 38572
Artella Cir & Ct 38558
Ash Cir 38555
Ashdown Ln 38558
Ashford Dr 38572
Ashford Pl 38558
Aster St 38555
Atkins Rd 38571
Atlantic Ave 38555
Atoka Ln 38572
Augustine Ct & Ln 38558
Autumn Dr 38571
Autumn Trl 38572
Avon Ln 38558
Azalia Ave 38555
Aztec Trl 38572
Bacham Ct & Ln 38558
Backwoods Way 38555
Baier Rd 38571
Bainbridge Ct & Rd 38558
Baisley Ln 38572
Baker Ln 38555
Baker Farm Rd 38571
Baltusrol Cir, Ct & Rd 38558
Banbury Ln 38558
Bangor Ct 38558
Baragona Ln 38571
Barkley Pl 38558
Barnwell Ln 38571
Barnwell Loop 38572
Barringer Rd 38571
Barrington Ct 38558
Barton Ln 38571
Basses Creek Ln 38572
Basswood Cir 38555
Bateman Dr 38572
Bateman Rd 38571
Bay Ct 38558
Bay Colony Ter 38558
Bayberry Dr 38555
Beach Loop & Rd 38572
Beach Point Cir 38572
Beachwood Ct, Dr & Ln 38558
Beam Branch Rd 38571
Bean Ln 38555
Bean Pot Campground Loop & Rd 38571
Bear Ct 38571
Bear Creek Loop & Rd 38571
Bear Den 38571
Beasley Ln 38571
Beason Ln 38558
Beaty Rd 38571
Beaver Rd 38572
Bebe Rd 38571
Beck Ln 38572
Bee Cir 38555
Beech Cir & Dr 38555
Beechcroft Ln 38558
Beecher Ln 38572
Beehive Ln 38571
Begley Dr 38571
Bell Rd 38571
Bellingwood Plz 38558
Bellwood Rd 38558
Belvedere Ln 38558
Belvin Rd 38555
Ben Tollett Ln 38571
Benbigh Ln 38558
W Benefit Rd 38572
Benningham Ct & Ln 38558
Bent Oak Ln & Ter 38558
Bent Tree Dr 38555
Benton Dixon Rd 38571
Benwick Ct 38558
Benwick Dr 38555
Berkeley Sq 38558
Berkshire Ct & Loop 38558
Berlingwood Ct, Ln & Ter 38558
Bermond Cir 38558
Berry Ct 38558
Bethel Ln 38572
Beverly Hills Cir 38555
Bible Way 38555
Big Horn Cir, Ct, Dr & Loop 38572
Big Lick Rd 38572
Bilbrey Dr 38571
Bilbrey Ln 38571
Bilbrey Rd 38571
Bilbrey St 38555
Bill Barnwell Rd 38571
Bill Brown Rd 38571
Bill Hall Rd 38571
Billy Goat Rd 38571
Bingham Ln, Ter & Way 38558
Birch Cir 38555
Birchwood Dr & Ln 38555
Bird Walk Ln 38572
Bishop Ter 38558
Bishop Campbell Rd 38572
Black Bear Ct 38571
Black Cloud Dr 38572
Black Oak Cir 38558
Black Oak Ln 38555
Black Wolf Dr 38572
Blackburn Ct & Dr 38558
Blackfoot Dr 38572
Blalock Dr 38571
Blaylock Rd 38572
Bledsoe Park Rd 38572
Blue Spruce Dr 38571
Bluebird Cir 38555
Bluebird Ct 38571
Bluebird Dr 38571
Bluff Rd 38555
Bluff View Dr 38571
Bluff View Ter 38558
Boanna Cir & Ln 38572
Bob Austin Rd 38571
Bob Tollett Loop 38555
Bob White Dr 38555
Bolin Ln 38571
Bolin Rd 38572
Bonanza Dr 38571
Bond Ln 38558
Bow Rd 38572
Bowman Loop 38571
Boyd St 38555
Brackenridge Ln 38558
Bradbury Ln 38555
Braddock St 38571
Bradford Dr 38555
Bradford Ln 38558
Bradrock St 38571
Bradshaw Family Rd 38571
Brady Ln 38555
Brady Rd 38571
Braeswick Cir 38558
Bragg Cir 38555
Brambleton Ct, Dr & Ln 38558
Brandenburg N 38571
Brantenwood Cir 38558
Braun Cv & St 38555
Braun Hill Cir 38555
Brave Ln 38572
Breckenridge Dr 38572
Breeding Rd 38555
Brenda Ln 38555
Brendel Rd 38571
Brentwood Pl 38558
Brewer Rd 38572
Briar Ct 38558
Briarwood Dr & Loop 38558
Brighton Ct & Ln 38558
Bristol Ln 38558
Bristow Rd 38571
Brittanys Ln 38571
Britton Ln 38558
Brixton Ln 38558
Broadleaf Pl 38555
Brockhaven Ln 38558
Broken Arrow Ct & Dr 38572
Broken Bow Ln 38572
Brokenwood Ln 38558
Bromley Ln 38558
Brompton Ct 38558
Brook St 38555
Brookhaven Dr 38555
Brooks Ln 38558
Brookshire Ln 38558
Brookside Dr 38555
Brookstone Dr 38555
Brown Ave 38555
Brown Dr 38571
Brown Rd 38555
Browns Ln 38571
Browns Creek Dr 38571
Browns Gap Rd 38555
Browntown Rd 38572
Bruce Ln 38572
Bruceshire Ct 38558
Brummel Ln & Way 38558
Brunswick Pl 38558
Bryant Mill Rd 38572
Brylee Ln 38572
Bryon Ln 38558
Buchanan Sq & St 38555
Buck Cir 38555
Buck Ct 38571
Buck Ln 38571
Buck Rd 38571
Buck Creek Rd 38555
Buck Lewis Rd 38572
Buck Patton Rd 38555
Buck Run Rd 38571
Buckingham Ct & Dr 38558
Buckner Ter 38558
Buckridge Rd 38572
Bud Tanner Rd 38571
Buddys Trl 38571
Buena Vista Dr 38555
Buffalo Dr 38572
Bullard Ln
1-99 38571
2-98 38572
Bullock Ct 38571
Bullock Trailer Ct 38571
Burchette Dr 38572
Burgess Dr, Ln, Loop & Rd 38572
Burk Dr 38572
Burley Carr Rd 38571
Burnaby Ct 38558
Burnaloy Ct 38558
Burnett St 38555
Burnt Oak Ter 38558
Burrough Ln 38558
Burton Ct & Ter 38558
Butler Ct 38558
Butternut Ridge Rd 38571
Button Rd 38571
Buzzard Ln 38572
Byers Ln & Rd 38571
Byrds Creek Cv, Dr & Ln 38555
Byron Ln 38558
Cabin Ln 38572
Cactus Cir 38555
Cahita Ln 38572
Cal Kemmer Ln 38555
Calderwood Cir 38558
Calloway Dr 38555
Calusa Cir & Ln 38572
Calvin Kerley Rd 38572
Cambridge Ln 38558
Camden Ct 38558
Camelford Ter 38558
Camelia Dr 38555
Camelot Ln 38558
Camille Ln 38572
Camp Nakanawa Rd 38571
Campbell Dr 38572
Campbell St 38555
Canary Ct & Dr 38555
Caney Creek Dr 38571
Canterbury Cir 38558
Canterbury Dr 38558
Canterbury Ln 38555
Canyon Vw 38571
Cape Ct 38558
Cappshire Rd 38558
Cardinal Loop 38555
Carey Ct, Dr & Rd 38571
Carey Airport Rd 38571
Carl Nail Ln 38555
Carlow Dr 38572
Carnoustie Dr 38558
Carol Ln 38571
Carousel Dr 38555
Carriage Dr 38555
Carrie Dr 38572
Carson Ln & Rd 38571
Carson Pugh Rd 38571
Carter Rd 38555
Carter Town Rd 38571
Caryonah Rd 38571
Cas Cade Ln 38555
Cassady Pl 38555
Cassidy Ln 38572
Cassie Ln 38571
Castillo Ln 38555
Castle Cir 38555
Castlebar Ln 38558
Castlebridge Ln 38558
Casto Pugh Rd 38571
Cathedral Dr 38558
Catoosa Blvd 38558
W Catoosa Canyon Dr 38571
Cavalier Ln & Ter 38558
Cedar Cir 38555
Cedar Ct 38555
Cedar Dr 38555
Cedar Rd 38572
Cedar Ridge Cir 38558
Cedar Ridge Ct 38558
Cedar Ridge Ln 38555
Cedarbrush Ln 38558
E Center Town Dr 38555

Street	ZIP
Central Ave	38555
Chacoto Dr	38572
Chanhassen Pl	38558
Channing Ln	38555
Chanute Trl	38572
Chapel Hill Dr	38555
Charles Pl	38558
Charleston Ln	38555
Charlie Brown Rd	38572
Charlie Mccoy Rd	38571
Charlotte Ct	38558
Charlton Ln	38558
Chase Ln	38571
Chatham Ct, Ln & Ter	38558
Chelsea Dr	38555
Chelsea Ln	38558
Chelteham Ln	38558
Cherokee Ct	38572
Cherokee Dr	38572
Cherokee Ln	38571
Cherokee Pl	38572
Cherokee Rd E	38572
Cherokee Trl	38572
Cherry St	38572
S Cherry Branch Loop & Rd	38571
Cheshire Ct, Dr, Ln & Ter	38558
Chestnut Ct, Ln & St	38555
Chestnut Hill Rd	
1-1870	38555
1877-1929	38571
1931-10317	38571
10319-10547	38571
Chestnut Oak Dr & Rd	38571
Cheyenne Ct & Dr	38572
Chica Cir, Ct & Rd	38572
Chickasaw Dr	38572
Chief Daybreak Dr	38572
Chief Red Cloud Dr	38572
Chief White Eagle Ln	38572
Chinook Ln	38572
Chinswick Dr	38558
Chippewa Dr & Trl	38572
Choctaw Dr & Ln	38572
Chris Cir	38558
Christian Rd	38572
Christopher Ln	38558
Chuckles Pkwy	38555
Church Dr	38571
Church St	38555
Cinder Ln	38571
Cinnamon Cir	38571
Circle Dr & Rd	38572
Circle Drive Ct	38572
Citrus Ct	38555
City Lake Rd	38572
Claremont Cir, Ct & Dr	38558
Clarence Blaylock Rd	38572
Clarington Park Dr	38572
Clason Pt	38558
Clay Wyatt Rd	38572
Claysville Rd	38571
Claysville Access Rd	38571
Clear Creek Rd	38571
Clearview Ln	38571
Cleggan Dr	38572
Clerkenwell Pl	38558
Cleveland St	38555
Clifford Selby Rd	38572
Cliffside Cir, Ct & Dr	38558
Clifty Rd	38572
Cline Rd	38571
Clinebrook Dr	38558
Clint Lowe Rd	38572
Clinton Wright Ln	38572
Clover Ln	38555
Cloverdale Cir	38558
Cobb Rd	38571
Cochise Ct & Trl	38572
Cohise Dr	38572
Colby Cir	38571
Cold Springs Rd	38571
Cold Water Dr	38571
N Cole St	38572
Coleman St	38555
Collinwood Ct	38558
Color Ct	38571
Commanche Dr & Trl	38572
Commercial Dr	38555
Compostell Plz	38558
Confederate Rd	38571
Conley Rd	38571
Connely Dr	38572
Conrad Cir, Ct & Dr	38558
Cook Rd	
164-170	38555
172-1899	38555
2242-2398	38571
2400-3199	38571
Cool Breeze Blvd	38572
Coon Hollow Rd	38572
Cooper Ln	38555
Copper Pt	38555
Copperhead Ln	38571
Copperhead Rd	38572
Coppett Rd	38572
Corson Way	38555
Cother St	38555
Cottage Cir	38558
Cotton Patch Dr	38555
Cottonwood Dr	38555
Cottrell Ln	38571
S Country Dr	38572
Country Club Dr	38572
Country Meadow Ln	38572
Country Oaks Dr	38555
Country Side Dr	38555
Countryside Ct	38572
County Garage Rd	38555
County Line Rd	38572
County Seat Rd	38555
Courtenay Ct	38558
Cow Pen Rd	38571
Cowart Ln	38572
Coweta Dr	38572
Cox Ave	38555
Cox Ln	38571
Cox Valley Ln & Rd	38555
Coyote Ct & Dr	38572
Crab Apple Ln	38555
Crabtree Rd	38571
Cravens Dr	38572
Crazy Horse Dr	38572
Creek Cir	38558
Creek Ct	38558
W Creek Dr	38572
Creek Rd	38572
Creek Vale Dr	38555
Creek View Dr	38555
Creekside Ln & Trl	38571
Creekway Cir & Dr	38555
Creekwood Dr	38555
Creigmont Ct, Dr & Ln	38558
Crescent Pt	38555
Crest Cir, Dr & Ln	38555
W Creston Rd	38571
Creston Cemetery Rd	38571
Crestview Dr	38555
Crestview Ln	38555
Crestview Loop	38571
Critter Creek Rd	38572
Critter Crossing Rd	38572
Crockett Cir	38572
Crockett Lake Dr	38572
Cromwell Ln	38558
Crooked Way	38572
Cross Creek Pl	38555
Crossbow Cir & Dr	38555
Crossings Way	38555
Crossover Ln & Rd	38572
Crossroads Dr	38555
Crossville Medical Dr	38555
Crosswinds Blvd	38572
Crow Dr	38572
Crown Ct	38558
Crystal Ln	38571
Cumberland Dr, Plz & Sq	38555
Cumberland Apts Ln	38555
Cumberland View Dr	38571
Curt Rimmer Rd	38572
Custer Rd	38571
Cv Hale Ln	38572
Daddys Creek Ln & Trl	38555
Daisy Ave	38555
Dale Clingham Rd	38572
Dalefield Loop	38558
Dallas Smith Rd	38555
Dalmation Ln	38572
Dalton Ter	38558
Dane Dr	38572
Daniel Dr	38555
Daren Dr	38571
Darrell Ave	38555
Dartmoor Dr	38558
Darwin Ln	38558
Dave Garrett Rd	38571
Davenshire Dr	38558
David Crockett Rd	38572
Davidson Ct	
1-199	38555
200-599	38571
Davidson Ln	38571
Davidson Rd	38555
Davis Rd	38572
Dawn Ct & Ln	38555
Daybreak Ln	38571
Daymon Cir	38572
Dayton Ave, Ct & Dr	38555
Dayton Spur Rd	38555
Deathridge Rd	38555
Deck Ln & Rd	38572
Deep Draw Ct, Ln & Rd	38555
Deep Water Ln & Rd	38571
Deer Cir	38555
Deer Run	38571
E Deer Creek Dr	38571
Deer Run Cir	38572
Deer Track Ln	38571
Deerfield Rd	38555
Delaware Dr	38572
Delborne Ct	38558
Delbridge Ln	38558
Denny Oaks Rd	38571
Densbury Ct	38558
Derby Ct	38558
Derbyshire Ln	38558
Derry Dr	38572
Desoto Dr	38572
S Detour Rd	38555
Devon Loop & Rd	38558
Dewsbury Ter	38558
Diane Cir	38572
Diane St	38555
Dickens Ln	38558
Diden Loop	38571
Diego Ln	38572
Dillon St	38555
Dishman Ln	38572
Division Dr & St	38555
Dixie Dr	38572
Dixon Rd	38571
Dockside Ct & Dr	38558
Dodd Ct	38558
Dodson Ct	38571
Dodson Ln	38555
Dodson Rd	38571
Dogwood Ave	38555
Dogwood Cir	38571
Dogwood Trl	38572
Don Kerley Rd	38555
Doncaster Ct	38558
Donna Ln	38555
Donnbrook Dr	38558
Dooley Ct & St	38555
Dorchester Ct	38558
Doris Dr	38555
Dorton Rd & Way	38555
Dorton Access Rd	38555
Dosha Ct	38555
Dove Dr	38555
Dove Cote Ter	38558
Dovenshire Dr	38558
Dover Ln	38558
Doyle Ct	38558
Dream Catcher Ln	38571
Dreamland Ln	38555
Drew Howard Rd	38558
Driftwood Ct	38558
Drowning Creek Rd	38571
Druid Cir & Lndg	38558
Dublin Dr	38572
Dublin Ln	38558
Dublin Ter	38558
Duer Ct	38555
Dugger Branch Rd	38572
Dunbar Ave	38555
Dunbar Dr	38555
Dunbar Ln	38555
Dunbar Rd	38572
Dunfer Ter	38558
Dunhan Rd	38558
Dunrovin Dr	38555
Dunsby Ct	38558
Dunway Dr	38572
Dunwich Ct	38558
Durango Rd	38572
Dustin Ln	38571
Dwyer Dr	38572
Dykes Ln & Rd	38571
Dylan Ln	38558
Eagle Cir, Ct & Ln	38558
Eaglefeather Ln	38571
Earl Jones Rd	38555
East Ln & St	38555
Eastland Rd	38572
Easton Cir & Ct	38558
Ed Houston Rd	38571
Edgemere Ct & Dr	38558
Edinburgh Ter	38558
Edwards Ln	38555
Edwards Rd	38571
Effingham Ln	38558
Eldonwood Dr	38555
Eldridge Loop	38571
Eli Ford Ct & Rd	38571
Elijah Bilbrey Ln	38571
Elizabeth Dr	38558
Elmo Dr	38555
Elmore Ln & Rd	38555
England Ln	38571
England Loop	38571
England Rd	38571
England Ter	38558
Erin Rd	38572
Ernest Neal Rd	38571
Eroh Rd	38571
Essex Ln	38558
Estate Dr & Way	38555
Estate Loop Trl	38555
Estates Lake Dr	38571
Ethan Brooke Ln	38572
Eugene Ct	38555
Eureka Dr	38571
Evans St	38555
Evelyn Ave	38555
Evergreen Dr	38555
Ewa Dr	38572
Executive Dr	38555
Exeter Dr	38558
Experiment Station Rd	38571
Fair Oaks Rd	38572
Fairfax Ter	38558
Fairfield Blvd	38558
Fairhaven Dr	38558
Fairview Ct, Dr, Loop & Rd	38571
Fairway Ct	38571
Fairway Dr	38558
Fairway St	38571
Falling Trees Ln	38572
Fallingbrook Dr	38555
Farmer Rd	38571
Farmers Creek Ln	38572
Farmington Ln	38555
Farrington Rd	38558
Farrington Way	38555
Farris Rd	38571
Farthing Ct	38558
Fawn Ct	38571
Fawn Loop	38555
Feldwood Ct	38558
Felix Ct	38558
Fellowship Ln	38555
Fence Ln	38571
Fenway Ct	38558
Fern Creek Trl	38571
Ferndale Ln	38558
Ferry Bend Trl	38571
Fields Rd	38572
Fields Garrett Rd	38572
E & W Fifth St	38555
Filburn Ln	38571
Findley Dr	38555
Finley Rd	38571
Finsbury Ct & Ln	38558
Firetower Ln	38571
E & W First St	38555
Fish Rd	38555
Fitzgerald Ln	38571
Five Oaks Dr	38555
Flagstone Ln	38555
Flamburough Ct	38558
Flamingo Dr	38555
Flat Rock Rd	38572
Flathead Rd	38572
Florida Ave	38572
Flossmoor Cir	38558
Floyd Rd	38571
Flynn Dr	38572
Flynns Cove Rd	38572
Flynns Cove Cemetery Rd	38572
Folkstone Rd	38558
Fontis Ter	38558
Forbus Dr	38555
Ford Ln & St	38555
Forest Dr	38555
Forest Rd	38571
Forest Crossover	38555
Forest Haven Ln	38572
Forest Hill Ct, Dr & Ter	38558
Forest Park Ln	38571
Forest View Cir, Ct & Dr	38558
Forman Ct	38558
Fountain Sq	38555
Four H Center Dr	38572
E Fourth St	38555
Fox Trl	38571
Fox Creek Rd	38571
Fox Den Ct	38558
Fox Den Dr	38572
Fox Den Ln	38571
Fox Hollow Dr	38571
Fox Run Rd	38571
Foxfire Rd	38555
Foxwell Ln	38558
Foxwood Ct & Dr	38571
Frankie Ln	38555
Franklin St	38572
Franny Kerwin Way	38572
Frazier Ln & Rd	38572
Fred Ford Rd	38571
Fred Tollett Rd	38572
Fredonia Rd	38571
French Ln	38555
Friar Ln	38558
Frost Rd	38571
Frost Creek Dr	38571
Fuller Ln	38571
Funnel Creek Rd	38571
Gabriel Gentry Ln	38572
Gail Winds Ln	38572
Gardens View Dr	38555
Garfield Ct	38558
Garfield Dr	38555
Garfield Ln	38558
Garrett Ln	38555
Garrett Rd	38571
Garrison Loop	38555
Gate Rd	38571
Genesis Ave	38571
Genesis Rd	
1-2083	38555
2426-18099	38571
Genesis Sq	38555
Gentry Ln	38572
George Smith Rd	38571
George Walker Rd	38571
Georgia Ct	38555
Georgia Dr	38572
Geronimo Dr	38555
Geronimo Ln	38572
Gilford Ter	38558
Gislornes Cir	38555
Glad Acres Rd	
1-299	38555
301-499	38572
Glastonbury Ct	38558
Glen Phil Ct	38555
Glencove Ct	38558
Glenrock Ter	38558
Glenwood Cir	38555
Glenwood Dr	38558
Glenwood Pl	38555
Glory Loop	38572
Glouchestershire Ct & Ln	38558
Gluff Ave	38555
Godsey St	38555
Golden Ct	38558
Golden Brook Dr	38555
Golf Club Ln	38571
Golf Club Crossover	38571
Goodstock Rd	38555
Goodwin Cir	38555
Goose Pointe Cir	38571
Gordon Rd	
1-361	38555
400-612	38572
613-679	38555
614-680	38572
681-682	38555
683-703	38572
684-704	38555
705-731	38572
733-1599	38572
744-1298	38555
1462-1598	38572
Gore Dr	38571
Gore Rd	38555
Goss Rd	38571
Goti Dr	38572
Gower Ln	38558
Grace Dr	38571
Grace Ln	38555
Grace Hill Dr	38571
Graham Cir	38555
Graham Ct	38558
Graham Dr	38555
Graham Rd	38555
Grandview Dr	38555
Grandview Ln	38571
Grant Cir	38555
Grapevine Rd	38572
Grasmere Ct	38558
Grassland Rd	38572
Gray Eagle Dr	38572
Gray Fox Ct & Dr	38571
Green Ln	38571
Green Meadows Ln	38555
Greenbrier Loop	38558
Greendale Dr	38555
Greenleaf Ct	38558
Greenview Ln	38571
Greenwells Rd	38558
Greenwood Cir, Ct & Rd	38558
Gregory Ln	38572
Grenta Ct	38558
Greystone Ct	38558
Greystone Dr	38571
Greystone Ln	38571
Gridiron Ln	38555
Grouse Ct & Ter	38558
Gua Rd	38572
Guiness Dr	38572
Guinevere Ln	38555
H B Farmer Rd	38571
Hague Ct	38558
Hale Dr	38555
Hale Rd	38572
Hale St	38572
Halifax Ct	38558
Hall Dr	38572
Hall Rd	38571
Halstead Dr & Ln	38555
Hamby Dr	38571
Hamby Ln	38555
Hamels Ct & Ln	38558
Hamlet Cir & Dr	38558
Hammersmith Rd	38558
Hampshire Ln	38558
Hampstead Ct	38558
Hampton Ct	38558
Hampton Pt	38558
Hampton Sq	38558
Hanning Dr	38558
Harding Rd	38572
Harding St	38555
Harlech Ct & Ln	38558
Harless Wood Rd	38572
Harley Cir & Ct	38558
Harlton Ln	38558
Harper Ln	38555
Harrell Ln	38558
Harris Ln & Rd	38571
Harrison Ave & Rd	38555
Hartlepool Ct & Ter	38558
Harville Ln & Rd	38571
Hassler Ln & Rd	38555
Hasting Cross	38558
Hatler Rd	38555
Havenridge Cir, Ct, Dr & Pl	38558
Havenwood Ln	38571
Hawes Cir	38558
Hawthorn Cir & Loop	38555
Hayes Dr	38555
Hayes Ln	38571
Hayes Rd	38555
Hayes St	38555
Haywood Ct	38558
Hazel Ln	38555
Hazelwood Rd	38558
Heather Glen Cir, Ct & Dr	38558
Heather Ridge Cir	38555
Heather Ridge Ct	38558
Heatherhurst Cir, Ct & Dr	38558
Hedgewood Cir & Pt	38558
Heiskell Ct	38558
Hell Hole Rd	38572
Hemlock Ct	38558
Hemlock Dr	38555
Hemlock Ln	38571
Henline Rd	38571
Henry Ave	38555
Henry Dr	38571
Henry Cemetery Rd	38571
Henry Farm Rd	38571
Hensley Ln	38571
Herbert Houston Rd	38555
Heritage Cir & Loop	38571
Hermans Ln	38555
Hernandez Dr	38571
Hernando Cir & Trce	38572
Hershel Tabor Rd	38572
Hertford Dr & Ln	38558
Hickey Ln	38571
Hickory Cir	38555
Hickory Ct	38571
Hickory Dr	38571
Hickory Ln	38555
Hickory St	38555
Hickory Cove Ct & Ln	38558
Hickory Gap Ln	38572
Hickory Hollow Cir	38555
Hickory Hollow Dr	38555
Hickory Hollow Rd	38572
Hickory Lake Ln	38572
Hickory Ridge Ln	38558
Hickory View Ln	38572
Hidden Dr	38571

Hidden Hollow Cir & Dr ... 38571
Hidden Valley Dr ... 38572
Highgate Dr ... 38558
Highland Dr ... 38572
Highland Ln ... 38555
Highland Sq ... 38555
Highland St ... 38555
Highland Courtyard Loop ... 38555
Highland Ridge Dr ... 38555
Highway 127 N
3100-3916 ... 38571
Highway 127 N
3918-4389 ... 38571
4390-4399 ... 38572
4400-4402 ... 38571
4401-4403 ... 38572
4404-4745 ... 38571
4746-4986 ... 38572
4747-5835 ... 38571
4988-5440 ... 38571
5442-5498 ... 38572
5500-5836 ... 38571
5837-5839 ... 38572
5840-16499 ... 38571
Highway 127 S ... 38572
Highway 68 ... 38555
Highway 70 E ... 38555
Highway 70 N ... 38571
Hileah Dr ... 38572
Hill Rd ... 38572
Hillary Ln ... 38572
Hillbilly Hollow Rd ... 38555
Hillcrest Dr ... 38555
Hillendale Dr ... 38558
Hillendale Rd ... 38572
Hillendale Acres Ln ... 38572
Hills Dr & Ln ... 38555
Hillsway ... 38555
Hilltop Dr ... 38555
Hillwood Dr ... 38555
Hilton Ln ... 38558
Hinch Dr ... 38572
Hinch Mountain View Rd ... 38555
Hinds Rd ... 38571
Hinkle Ln ... 38555
Hipswell Ct ... 38558
Hiwassee Rd ... 38572
Hodden Cir ... 38555
Hodge Ave ... 38555
Hodgo Dr ... 38571
Holiday Ct, Dr & Ter ... 38555
Holiday Hills Dr ... 38555
Hollaran Ln ... 38572
Hollis Ln ... 38555
Hollow Dr & Ln ... 38571
Hollow Log Trl ... 38572
Holly Ct ... 38558
Holly Dr ... 38555
Holly Ln ... 38558
Holly Acres Dr ... 38571
Holopaw Ln ... 38572
Holstein Ln ... 38571
Homberg Ln ... 38558
Homestead Dr ... 38555
Hondo Ct & Dr ... 38572
Honeysuckle Dr ... 38571
Honeysuckle Ln ... 38572
Hood Dr ... 38555
Hoover Rd ... 38572
Hopi Dr ... 38572
Horizon Dr ... 38571
Horn St ... 38555
Horse Way ... 38572
Hoskins Ln & Rd ... 38571
Hospitality Dr ... 38555
Hounds Run ... 38571
Houston Dr ... 38555
Houston Ln ... 38572
Houston Rd ... 38555
Howard Ln ... 38555
Howard Ter ... 38558
Howard Springs Rd ... 38571
Hubbard Rd ... 38572

Hubert Conley Rd ... 38571
Hubo Cir ... 38555
Huckleberry Ln ... 38555
Huddleston Rd ... 38572
Hullet Ct ... 38558
Humberg Ct & Ln ... 38558
Hummingbird Cir ... 38572
Hummingbird Dr ... 38572
Hummingbird Ln ... 38571
Hunter Dr ... 38555
Hunters Ln ... 38571
Hunterwood Ct & Ln ... 38558
Huntington Dr ... 38558
Huron Dr & Trl ... 38572
Hurstwood Ct & Ln ... 38558
Hutoha Dr ... 38572
Hyder Cir & Loop ... 38571
Hyder Ridge Rd ... 38555
Idlewood Ter ... 38558
Ike Burgess Rd ... 38572
Impa Dr ... 38572
Indian Rock Loop ... 38572
Industrial Blvd ... 38555
Innisbrook Cir & Ter ... 38558
Interchange Dr ... 38571
Interstate Dr ... 38555
Interstate Ln ... 38571
Inwood Ct, Dr & Ter ... 38558
Iowa Dr ... 38572
Iris Cir & Ln ... 38555
Irish Ln ... 38572
Iron Wood Cir & Ct ... 38571
Iroquois Ln ... 38572
Irwin Ave ... 38555
Isabella Ln ... 38572
Isham St ... 38555
Ithaca Ln ... 38572
Iuka Ln ... 38572
Ivanhoe Ln ... 38555
Ivey Rd ... 38571
Ivy Ave ... 38555
Ivy Ln ... 38558
Ivy Brook Ln & Loop ... 38558
Ivydale Ln ... 38558
Jack Tollett Rd ... 38572
Jackie Dr ... 38571
Jacobs Xing ... 38555
Jada Dr ... 38555
Jade Ln ... 38571
Jake Wallace Rd ... 38571
James Russell Rd ... 38572
Jamestown Ct ... 38555
Jana Dr ... 38558
Jantel Dr ... 38555
Jarrow Ct & Ln ... 38558
Jasper Dr ... 38558
Jay Houston Rd ... 38572
Jedd Dr ... 38571
Jefferson St ... 38572
Jeffs Rd ... 38572
Jerry Edmonds Rd ... 38572
Jesse Loop ... 38555
Jim Garrett Rd ... 38571
Jk Bowman Ln ... 38571
Jody Lynn Ln ... 38572
Joe Tabor Rd ... 38571
John Myers Rd ... 38572
John Q Wyatt Rd ... 38571
John Taylor Rd ... 38572
John Turner Dr ... 38572
Johnson Rd ... 38572
Jones Ln ... 38572
Jones Rd ... 38571
Jonia Ln ... 38571
Joseph Ln ... 38572
Julien Ct ... 38558
Juniper Dr ... 38558
Justice St ... 38555
Justice Center Dr ... 38555
Justin Ln ... 38571
Kachina Ln ... 38572
Kanapolis Dr ... 38572
Kates Korner ... 38555
Katherine Dr ... 38555
Kato Dr ... 38572
Katta Trce ... 38572

Kaw Cir & Ct ... 38572
Kawa Ln ... 38572
Keagle Farm Rd ... 38571
Kearney Dr ... 38555
Keating Loop ... 38555
Keato Ct, Dr & Ln ... 38572
Keck Ln ... 38571
Kellet Dr ... 38555
Kelsie Ln ... 38572
Kemmer Rd ... 38555
Kendrick Ln ... 38571
Kenilworth Ln ... 38558
Kenneth St ... 38555
Kenny Carey Rd ... 38571
Keno Dr ... 38572
Kent Ct ... 38558
Kenwood Ct & Dr ... 38558
Kerrigan Rd ... 38555
Keswick Ln ... 38558
Keta Ln ... 38572
Kevins Way ... 38555
Keyes Rd ... 38571
Keyes St ... 38555
Kiddie Cir ... 38572
Kidwell Ln ... 38571
Kila Ct, Dr & Pl ... 38572
Kilby Farm Rd ... 38572
Killary Rd ... 38572
Killearn Ct ... 38558
Kima Rd ... 38572
King Arthur Ct ... 38558
King John Ln ... 38558
Kings Ln ... 38558
Kings Row ... 38571
Kingsboro Dr & Ln ... 38558
Kingsbridge Ln ... 38558
Kingsbury Cir ... 38558
Kingsdown Dr ... 38558
Kingsley Ct ... 38558
Kiowa Dr ... 38572
Kirby Rd ... 38572
Kirkland Dr & Rd ... 38555
Kiswick Ter ... 38558
Kittyann Dr ... 38555
Klamath Cir ... 38572
Knights St ... 38555
Knights Way ... 38571
Knights Horse Xing ... 38572
Knollwood Ln ... 38558
Knollwood Trl ... 38571
Knotts Ct ... 38558
Kusa Cir ... 38572
L Henry Rd ... 38571
L R Neal Rd ... 38571
Lafayette Pt & Ter ... 38558
Lake Ct ... 38555
Lake Dr ... 38572
Lake St ... 38572
Lake Catherine Cir, Ct & Ln ... 38558
Lake Forest Ln ... 38558
N Lake Frances Rd ... 38571
Lake Point Ct ... 38555
Lakeridge Ter ... 38558
Lakeshire Dr ... 38558
Lakeshore Cir, Ct, Ln & Ter ... 38558
Lakeside Cir, Dr & Ter ... 38558
Lakeview Dr ... 38558
Lakewood Cir & Dr ... 38558
Lakyn Dr ... 38571
Lambeth Ct ... 38558
Lancashire Rd ... 38558
Lancaster Ct, Dr & Ln ... 38558
Lancer Ct & Dr ... 38572
Land Ln ... 38571
Lantana Dr ... 38572
Lantana Rd
2-24 ... 38555
26-1648 ... 38555
1649-15699 ... 38572
15701-16137 ... 38572
Lantana Firetower Rd ... 38572
Larch Dr ... 38555
Larissa St ... 38555
Larry Lewis Rd ... 38571

Larson Rd ... 38572
Laswell Ln ... 38558
Lauras Ln ... 38555
Laurel Cir ... 38555
Laurel Ln ... 38555
Laurel Pt ... 38571
Laurel Rd ... 38555
Laurelton Ct & Ln ... 38555
Laurelwood Ln ... 38555
Lavender Ln ... 38555
Laver Ct ... 38558
Lawson Dr ... 38555
Lawson Rd ... 38571
Lawsontown Ln & Rd ... 38572
Layken Ln ... 38555
Layne Dr ... 38572
Leaf Cir & Ln ... 38558
Lechmere Cir, Dr & Ter ... 38558
Ledford Dr ... 38555
Lee Ave ... 38555
Lee Cir ... 38555
Lee Dr ... 38555
Lee Ln ... 38572
Lee St ... 38555
Lee June St ... 38555
Leeds Ter ... 38558
Leffle Webb Rd ... 38572
Legion Loop & Rd ... 38571
Leinster Ct, Ln & Ter ... 38558
Leisure Ln ... 38572
Leland Pryor Rd ... 38571
Lenix Ct ... 38558
Leven Links Ct ... 38558
Lewellen Ln ... 38558
Lewis Dr ... 38571
Lewis Ln ... 38572
Lewis Rd ... 38572
Lexham Ct ... 38558
Leyden Cir, Ct & Dr ... 38558
Liddle Ln ... 38558
Lifelike Ln ... 38572
Lige Rd ... 38555
Lillian Ct ... 38555
Limerick Dr ... 38572
Limestone Rd ... 38555
Lincoln St ... 38572
Lincolnshire Dr ... 38555
Linda St ... 38572
Linden Ct ... 38558
Linder Loop ... 38571
Lindsey Knoll Cir & Ct ... 38558
Linger Lake Dr, Ln & Trl ... 38571
Lisa Ct & Ln ... 38558
Little Blvd & Mdw ... 38555
Little Cove Rd ... 38555
Little Fox Dr ... 38572
Little Jim Garrett Rd ... 38571
Little John Loop ... 38555
Little Randolph Rd ... 38571
Little Rental Ln ... 38555
Little Shoe Dr & Ln ... 38571
Littlemore Ter ... 38558
Liverpool Cir ... 38558
Livesay St ... 38555
Livingston Rd
1-1299 ... 38555
1300-1499 ... 38571
Loch Loosa Dr ... 38572
Lochmor Ct ... 38558
Locksley Cir ... 38555
Locust Grove Dr ... 38555
Lon Barnwell Rd ... 38571
Londell Ct ... 38558
London Ct ... 38558
Londonderry Ct ... 38558
Lone Wolf Cir ... 38572
Long Dr ... 38555
Long Rd ... 38571
Looper Ln ... 38571
Lori Ln ... 38555
Loshbough Rd ... 38572
Louise St ... 38555
Lowe Dr ... 38571
Lowe Rd ... 38572

N Lowe Rd ... 38571
Loxley Ln ... 38558
Loyd Woody Rd ... 38571
Luckys Dr ... 38555
Luke Ln ... 38555
Lundy Ct ... 38558
Lupton Cir ... 38558
Luther Farley Ln ... 38555
Lynch Rd ... 38555
Lynhurst Cir & Dr ... 38558
Lynn Dr ... 38555
Lynnhaven Ln ... 38558
Lytham Way ... 38558
Madeline Ct ... 38558
Magnolia Ln & St ... 38555
E Main St ... 38571
N Main St ... 38555
S Main St ... 38555
Mallard Cir ... 38555
Mallard Ct ... 38572
Mallard Pt ... 38571
Malver Dr ... 38555
Malvern Ct & Rd ... 38558
Manchester Rd ... 38558
Manhato Ct & Rd ... 38572
Manitou Dr ... 38572
Maple Ln ... 38572
Maple St ... 38555
Maple Grove Dr ... 38555
Maplewood Ct ... 38558
Maranatha Ln ... 38555
Marian Cir ... 38555
Marie Ln ... 38555
Mariners Ct, Dr & Pt ... 38558
Mariners Pt Dr ... 38555
Markham Ct, Ln, Ter & Way ... 38558
Marlbond Ct ... 38558
Marmaduke Dr ... 38572
Marquette Ct & Ter ... 38558
Martha Dr ... 38571
Martin Ln ... 38571
Martin Rd ... 38555
Martin Burgess Rd ... 38572
Mary Carr Rd ... 38555
Maryetta St ... 38555
Marylebone Ln ... 38558
Marymont Dr ... 38555
Masonary Dr ... 38571
Mast Dr ... 38555
Matherly St ... 38555
Mathews Rd ... 38572
Mawila Ridge Rd ... 38555
Mayberry Ct & St ... 38555
Mayfair Dr ... 38571
Mayland Dr, Loop & Rd ... 38571
Mayland Ballfield Dr ... 38571
Maynard Rd ... 38571
Mccampbell Rd ... 38571
Mcclanahan Dr ... 38571
Mccormic Rd ... 38571
Mccormick Ln ... 38571
Mcelhaney Dr ... 38555
Mcginnis Rd ... 38571
Mcguire Stone Farm Ln ... 38555
Mcintire Dr ... 38571
Mckinley Ln ... 38572
Mclarty Ln ... 38555
Mcneices Ridge Rd ... 38572
Meadow Dr ... 38555
Meadow Creek Ct, Dr & Ln ... 38572
Meadowlark Cir ... 38558
Meadowood Ln ... 38558
Meadowview Dr ... 38558
Meadowview Ln ... 38555
Mecca Dr ... 38572
Melrose Pl ... 38558
Mena Ln ... 38572
Menasha Dr ... 38572
Meridian Rd ... 38555
Merrimac Trl ... 38572
Methodist Campground Loop ... 38555

Mica Cir ... 38572
Middlebrook Pl ... 38555
Midway Rd ... 38572
Mile Branch Rd ... 38555
Miller Ave ... 38555
Miller Ct ... 38571
Miller Rdg ... 38571
Miller Way ... 38555
Millstream Ln ... 38555
Milnor Cir, Ct & Ter ... 38558
Milo Webb Dr ... 38572
Milt Carey Ln ... 38555
Mimosa Ln ... 38572
Mineola Trl ... 38572
Minetta Ct & Dr ... 38558
Miracle Ln ... 38555
Mitchell Blvd ... 38555
Moccasin Ln ... 38572
Mockingbird Dr ... 38555
Modac Cir & Dr ... 38572
Mohave Dr ... 38572
Mohawk Dr ... 38572
Monks Ln ... 38558
Monticello Ln & Loop ... 38558
Moonbeam Trl ... 38572
Mooneyham Ln ... 38572
Moore Ln ... 38571
Morgan Cir ... 38572
Morgan Rd ... 38555
Morning Star Dr & Ln ... 38572
Morris Ln ... 38558
Motthaven Ct & Dr ... 38558
Mountain Creek Rd ... 38572
Mountain View Cir ... 38558
Mountain View Ct ... 38558
Mountain View Dr ... 38558
Mountain View Ln ... 38572
Mountain View Rd ... 38572
Mountain View Ter ... 38558
Mountain Village Ln ... 38555
Muddy Branch Ct, Ln & Rd ... 38571
Mulberry Cir ... 38555
Municipal Ave ... 38555
Muskogee Ln ... 38572
Mutts Rd ... 38572
My Yamaha Dr ... 38555
Myra Dr ... 38572
Myrtle Ave & Ct ... 38555
Myrtle Acres Dr & Ln ... 38555
Nameoki Cir ... 38572
Narcissus St ... 38555
Natchez Cir ... 38558
Natchez Trce ... 38572
Navajo Trl ... 38572
Neal Ave ... 38555
W Neecham St ... 38555
Needham Ter ... 38558
Nehasane Ln ... 38572
Nesbit Cross ... 38558
Netherton Ct & Ln ... 38555
New Ross Ct ... 38572
Newberry Ln ... 38572
Newberry Rd ... 38571
Newcastle Ct & Ln ... 38558
Newcom Ct ... 38558
Newgate Ct, Pl & Rd ... 38558
Newton Ln & Rd ... 38572
Nichols Rd ... 38571
Nicholson Dr ... 38572
Nickel Ln ... 38558
Niska Dr ... 38572
Nocatee Trce ... 38572
Norcross Rd ... 38558
Norman Dr ... 38571
Norris Ln ... 38571
Norris Rd ... 38571
Norris St ... 38572
North St ... 38555
Northfield Dr ... 38571
Northridge Dr & Ter ... 38558
Northside Dr
2-299 ... 38571
300-1099 ... 38555
Northwood Dr ... 38571
Norwich Dr & Ter ... 38558

Norwood Pl ... 38558
Nottaway Ter ... 38558
Nottingham Cir ... 38555
Nuneaton Ter ... 38558
O Camp Dr ... 38572
Oak Dr, Rd & St ... 38555
Oak Crest Dr & Ln ... 38555
Oak Grove St ... 38555
Oak Hill Dr ... 38572
Oak Park Cir ... 38572
Oakburn Ct ... 38558
Oakcrest Cir & Ct ... 38558
Oakes Rd ... 38571
Oaklett Dr ... 38558
Oakley Dr ... 38555
Oakmont Dr & Way ... 38555
Oakway ... 38555
Oakwood Ln ... 38572
Obed Ct ... 38555
Obed Plz ... 38555
Obed Pt ... 38571
Obed St ... 38555
Obed Pines Rd ... 38571
Obed River Rd ... 38555
Obrien Dr ... 38555
Ocalala Trl ... 38572
Ocan Cir ... 38572
Oceola Cir ... 38572
Office Dr ... 38555
Officers Knob ... 38572
Offutt Loop ... 38571
Ohara Ct ... 38572
Ojibwa Ln ... 38572
Oklahoma Ct ... 38572
Oklahoma Dr ... 38572
Oklahoma Rd ... 38555
Okmulgee Ln ... 38572
Ola Cir ... 38572
Old Baldwin Rd ... 38571
Old Bohannon Mine Rd ... 38571
Old Claysville Rd ... 38572
Old Dorton Rd ... 38555
Old Elmore Rd ... 38571
Old Flynns Cove Rd ... 38572
Old Genesis Rd ... 38571
Old Grapevine Rd ... 38572
Old Grassy Cove Rd ... 38555
Old Highway Cir ... 38555
Old Highway 28 ... 38555
Old Highway 70 ... 38572
Old Homestead Hwy ... 38555
Old Jamestown Hwy ... 38555
Old Kentucky Stock Rd ... 38571
Old Lantana Rd
1-1099 ... 38555
1100-1298 ... 38572
Old Mail Rd ... 38555
S Old Mail Rd ... 38572
Old Meadows Pl ... 38571
Old Mount Zion Rd ... 38571
Old Peavine Ct, Ln & Rd ... 38571
Old Pikeville Hwy ... 38555
Old Plow Rd ... 38571
Old Pomona Dr & Rd ... 38571
Old Ross Rd ... 38572
Old Stagecoach Pl ... 38571
Old Stagecoach Rd ... 38555
Old Tanner Cemetary Rd ... 38571
Old Us Highway 127 ... 38571
Old Watkins Rd ... 38555
Old West Adams St ... 38555
Old Winesap Rd ... 38572
Olinger Ln ... 38555
Ona Cir & Rd ... 38572
Oneida Ln ... 38572
Open Meadow Dr & Ln ... 38555
Open Range Rd ... 38555
Open Sky Dr ... 38572
Orange Cir ... 38555
Orange Dr ... 38555
Orange Rd ... 38572

Street	ZIP
Orchard Ln	38571
Orchid Cir	38558
Ormes Rd	38555
Osage Rd	38572
Oscar Elmore Ln	38555
Ostego Dr	38572
Oswego Cir, Ct & Rd	38572
Otomi Cir & Dr	38572
Ottawa Ct	38572
Otter Ln	38572
Otter Point Ln	38571
Otterburn Ct & Ln	38558
Otto Warner Rd	38571
Ottoma Dr	38555
Our Way Dr & Loop	38555
Overlook Cir	38558
Overlook Ct	38558
Overlook Cv	38558
Overlook Dr	38555
Overlook Ln	38558
Overlook Ter	38558
Overview Rd	38572
Owego Cir	38572
Owenby Dr	38572
Oxford Cir	38558
Oxford Dr	38555
Pace Ave	38555
Pahokee Ln	38572
Pahue Dr	38572
Palmer Ln	38571
Palmetto Dr	38555
Pamala Ln	38558
Panther Ct	38571
Paola Ct	38572
Paradise Valley Rd	38572
Park Ln	38571
Park St	38555
Park Ter	38558
Park Trce	38555
Park Lane Spur	38571
Park Place Ave	38555
Parker Ford Rd	38571
Parkside Pl	38555
Parkview Pl	38555
Parkway Ct, Dr & Ln	38572
Parliment Ter	38558
Parnell Rd	38572
Parsons Ridge Rd	38571
Passman Ln	38571
Patton Ln	38571
Patton Norris Rd	38572
Paul Gentry Rd	38572
Paul Turner Dr	38571
Pawnee Rd	38572
Peace Pipe Bnd	38572
Peachtree Dr & St	38555
Pear Cir	38555
Peavine Plz	38571
Peavine Rd	
100-299	38555
301-475	38571
477-3227	38571
3228-3292	38558
3229-6173	38571
3294-5244	38571
6601-6697	38558
6699-8399	38558
Peavine Firetower Rd	38571
Pedelty St	38572
Peebles Cir & Rd	38558
Peeples Ct & Ln	38558
Pelfrey Rd	38555
Penny Ln	38555
Pensouni Rd	38572
Penzance Ct	38558
Peoto Dr & Ln	38572
Pequot Dr	38572
Perry Creek Dr	38572
Pete Dixon Rd	38572
Peter Pan Ave	38572
Peterbilt Ln	38555
Phillips Dr	38555
Phipps Rd	38571
Phyllis St	38555
Piccadilly Ln	38558
Pigeon Ridge Rd	38555
Pima Ct, Dr & Pl	38572
Pin Oak Ln	38555
Pine Ct, Dr & Trce	38572
Pine Grove Rd	38571
Pine Ridge Cir	38555
Pine Ridge Rd	38572
Pine Tree Cir	38571
Pinehurst Ct	38558
Pineridge Ct & Loop	38558
Pineway	38555
Pinewood Dr	38555
Piney Wood Ln	38571
Pioneer Ct, Dr & Loop	38571
Piute Rd	38572
Plantation Dr	38572
Plantation Ln	38555
Plateau Rd	38571
Plateau Firetower Rd	38571
Plateau Paradise Ln	38572
Pleasant Hill Dr	38571
Plum Cir	38555
Pocahontas Ln	38572
Pocohontas Trl	38572
Point Rd	38571
Poke Patch Ln & Rd	38572
Pomeroy Ct & Dr	38558
Pomo Cir	38572
Pomona Ct, Dr & Rd	38571
Ponderosa Dr	38555
Ponderosa Ln	38571
Pontiac Ln	38572
Poore Dr	38555
Poplar Dr	38571
Poplar St	38555
Porcelain Tile Dr	38555
Potato Farm Rd	38571
Potter Rd	38571
Pottersville Ln	38571
Pow Camp Rd	38572
Premier Dr	38555
Prentice St	38555
Prescott Ln & Ter	38558
Prestonwood Cir, Ct, Dr, Ln & Ter	38558
Preswick Cir	38558
Primrose Ct	38555
Prior Cir	38555
Proffitt Ln	38571
Proffitt Rd	38571
Proffitt Sq	38555
Prospect Pl	38558
Pueblo Dr	38572
Pugh Rd	38555
Pugh Cemetery Rd	38571
Puncheon Camp Creek Rd	38572
Putney Ct	38558
Quail Pt	38571
Quail Hollow Ct & Dr	38555
Quail Ridge Dr	38555
Queensbury Ln	38558
Quill Ct	38558
Rabbit Hill Dr	38571
Rabbit Track Rd	38571
Raccoon Cir	38572
Raccoon Dr	38571
Raccoon Ln	38555
Raccoon Creek Rd	38572
Rachel Dr	38571
Rachel Rd	38572
Raines Rd	38571
Ralph Adams Rd	38571
Ralph Leach Rd	38571
Ramey Rd	38571
Ramsey Rd	38572
Randolph Rd	38571
Randy Rd	38572
Rankhorn Ln	38571
Raquet Club Dr & Ln	38571
Rattlesnake Dr	38571
Ray Hodgin Rd	38571
Rays Ln	38572
Reagan Dr	38555
Reagan Ln	38571
Real Mccoy Dr	38572
Rebecca Dr	38555
Rebel Run Dl & Rd	38558
Rector Ave	38555
Rector Ln	38555
Rector Rd	38571
Red Rd	38572
Red Brush Dr	38555
Red Dog Saloon Rd	38555
Red Fox Ct & Dr	38571
Red Gold Farm Ln	38571
Red Oak Dr	38555
Red Oak Ln	38572
Red Williams Rd	38571
Redmond Ln	38571
Redwine Rd	38555
Redwing Cir, Dr & Loop	38572
Redwood Cir	38571
Reed Rd	38572
Regency Pkwy	38555
Regina Dr	38571
Rena Cir	38572
Renwick Ct & Dr	38558
Reppert Ln	38571
Reservation Pl	38572
Retreat Dr	38572
Rhea Rd	38555
Rhodendron Cir	38555
Rickett Ct	38558
Rickie Ln	38555
E Ridge Dr	38555
Ridge Ln	38571
Ridge Rd	38572
Ridge Rd W	38572
Ridge Crest Cir & Ct	38558
Ridgeland Ct & Ter	38558
Ridgeline Dr	38571
Ridgemont Dr	38555
Ridgeview Ct & Trl	38571
Ridgeway	38555
Ridgewood Dr	38555
Ridley Dr	38572
Ridley St	38555
Rimmer Ln	38572
Ripswell Ct	38558
River Ln	38555
River Rd	38572
N River Rd	38572
River Bend Dr	38555
River Oaks Dr	38555
River Otter Dr	38571
River Run Dr	38555
Riverchase Dr	38571
Riverview Ct	38571
Riverview Dr	38555
Riverview Ln	38555
N Riverview Ln	38555
S Riverview Ln	38555
Robbins Dr	38572
Robbins Ln	38571
Robbins Rd	38572
Robbins Nest Dr	38571
Roberts Dr	38555
Robin Cir	38555
Robin Ct	38571
Robin Hood Ct	38558
Robin Hood Dr	38558
Robin Hood Ln	38558
Rochdale Ct & Ln	38558
Rock Quarry Rd	38555
Rock Ridge Cir & Ter	38558
Rockledge Dr	38558
Rockwood Ave	38555
Rocky Ln	38571
Rocky Creek Dr	38572
Rocky Top Dr	38571
Rocky Top Ter	38558
Rodgers Rd	38572
Rodman Ct & Ter E	38558
Rogers Rd	38571
Roland St	38555
Rolling Green Cir, Ct & Dr	38558
Rolling Hills Ln	38572
Roma Dr	38555
Rome Rd	38555
Romney Loop & Rd	38558
Rose St	38555
Rosebud Ln	38572
Rosemont Cir	38558
Rosewood Dr	38555
Rossmore Ct & Pl	38558
Rotherham Ct, Dr & Ln	38558
Roundstone Ter	38558
Rowewood Ln	38558
Roy Mccoy Rd	38571
Royal Cir, Pl & Ter	38558
Rugby Ct, Pl & Rd	38558
Running Creek Dr	38572
Runnymeade Rd	38558
Russell Ct	38571
Russell Ln	38555
Russell Rd	38571
Russell Ridge Rd	38555
Russett Ln	38572
Rusty Blue Dr	38555
Rutgers Cir	38558
Ryan Rd	38571
Ryder Rd	38572
Rye Woody Rd	38571
Saddle Brook Ln	38571
Saint Alphonsus Way	38555
Saint Andrews Cir	38558
Saint George Dr & Pl	38558
Saint James Pt	38555
Sam Marsh Rd	38572
Samaritan Way	38558
Sampson Rd	38572
Sandpiper Loop	38555
Sandra Ln	38555
Sandy Creek Rd	38571
Sanje Ct	38572
Santee Ct	38572
Saponac Dr	38572
Sarah Ln	38571
Saratoga Ct & Dr	38572
Sarvis Rd	38571
Satsuma Dr	38555
Sauk Cir	38572
Savannah Ln	38555
Sawmill Rd	38555
Scarlett Dr	38555
Scenic Dr	38555
School Ave & St	38555
Schuberts Ln	38571
Scott Ave	38555
Scott Creek Dr	38571
Scunthorpe Cir & Ln	38558
Sebald Cir	38555
Seca Dr	38572
E & W Second St	38555
Sedgemoor Ct & Ln	38558
Seminole Cir, Loop & Rd	38572
Seneca Cir, Ct & Trl	38572
Sequoia Dr	38572
Sequoyah Cir	38571
Shadberry Dr	38572
Shadow Ln	
1-139	38555
132-138	38571
140-198	38555
141-199	38555
Shadow Mountain Dr	38572
Shadowmont Ct	38572
Shadowwood Ln	38571
Shady Loop	38571
Shady Oak Ln	38572
Shalako Dr	38572
Shannondale Ln	38558
Sharon Cir	38572
Sharon Dr	38555
Shawnbury Pt	38558
Shawnee Cir & Rd	38572
Sheffield Dr & Ln	38558
Shelby Rd	38571
Shelley Ln	38558
Shepards Way	38555
Sherburne Ct	38558
Sheree St	38555
Sherman Dr	38555
Sherwood Cir	38558
Sherwood Dr	38555
Shield Cir	38555
Shoemake Rd	38571
Shopsmith Rd	38558
Shore Ln	38558
Shoreline Dr	38555
Short Rd	38555
Short Sawmill Rd	38555
Shorty Barnes Rd	38571
Shoshone Loop	38572
Shotgun Dr	38571
Shug Cir	38572
Siever Rd	38572
Silver Twigg Trl	38571
Silversmith Rd	38558
Simmons St	38572
Sinclair Ln	38572
Sinclair Ter	38558
Sioux Rd & Trl	38572
Sioux City Ln	38572
Sitting Bull Pt	38572
Sky Rd	38555
Skyline Ct & Dr	38572
Sleepy Hollow Ln	38571
Sligo St	38572
Small Ln	38571
Small Plz	38558
Smee Rd	38572
Smith Rd	38571
Smoky Mountain Ave	38572
Snead Ct & Dr	38558
Snow White Dr	38572
Snowdon Pt	38558
Sourwood Dr	38571
South Dr	38555
Southbend Dr	38555
Southerdown Pt	38558
Southgate Dr	38555
Southgate Ln	38558
Southridge Cir	38555
Southtower Rd	38572
Southview St	38555
Southwark Ct	38558
Southway	38555
Southwind Dr	38572
Southwood Dr	38572
Sparta Dr	38555
Sparta Hwy	38572
Spear Cir	38555
Spencer Ln	38571
Spiers Way	38555
Spiers Branch Rd	38555
Spikes Ln	
1-599	38572
2-598	38571
Spillway Cir	38558
Spokane Dr & Ln	38572
Spooner Dr	38571
Sportsman Club Rd	38555
Spotswood Pt	38558
Spring Gap Rd	38572
Spring Lake Dr	38558
Springdale Dr	38558
Springwater Cir	38572
Spruce Dr	38572
Spruce Loop	38555
Staffordshire Ct & Ln	38558
E Stanley St	38555
Stanley Hood Rd	38571
Star Dr	38571
Stat Dr	38572
Stave Mill Rd	38572
Steve Tabor Rd	38572
Stevens St	38555
Stillington Loop	38558
Stirlingshire Dr	38558
Stone Dr	38555
Stone Loop	38571
S Stone Rd	38571
Stone St	38572
Stonecrest Ave & Loop	38571
Stoned Trl	38571
Stonehenge Dr	38558
Stoneway	38555
Stonewood Cir, Ct & Dr	38558
Storie Ave	38555
Stout Dr	38555
Stover Ln	38571
Stowell Ln	38572
Stratford Dr	38558
Sugar Ln	38571
Sugarbush Cir & Ln	38558
Suggs Ln	38572
Sullivan Dr	38555
N & S Summerhaven Dr	38555
Summertime Ct & Ln	38558
Summerwind Ct & Dr	38571
Suncrest Cir	38558
Sunderland Cir & Pl	38558
Sundown Ln	38571
Sundrop Ln	38571
Sunny Acres Dr	38555
Sunset Dr	38555
Sunset Ln	38555
Sunset Pt	38571
Sunset Rd	38572
Sunset Ridge Dr	38571
Sunshine Rd	38555
Surles Dr	38571
Swallows Rd	38571
Swan Rd	38555
Sweeney Dr	38555
Sweetbriar Ct	38558
Sweetgum Dr	38555
Swicegood Rd	38571
Sycamore Dr	38555
N Sycamore Ln	38571
S Sycamore Ln	
1-99	38572
100-199	38571
200-399	38572
400-599	38571
501-599	38572
Sydney Ct	38555
Sylvester Davis Dr	38571
T O Smith Rd	38571
Tabernacle St	38555
Tabor Dr	38555
Tabor Loop	38571
Takesa Dr	38555
Talahatchie Dr	38572
Tammy Dr	38571
Tangerine Cir	38555
Tanglewood Trl	38571
Tanner Dr & Rd	38571
Tate Rd	38571
Tavistock Ct, Ln & Ter	38558
Tawas Loop	38572
Tawny Oak Ln & Loop	38558
Taylor Ave	38555
Taylor Rd	38572
Taylor St	38555
Taylor Hollow Rd	38572
Taylors Chapel Rd	38572
Tecumesh Ln	38572
Ted Davis Rd	38572
Teeple Ln	38571
Tekesta Ct & Rdg	38572
Telequat Dr	38572
Tennessee Ave	38555
Tennessee Rd	38572
Tennessee Lakes Dr	38571
Tennessee Outdoors Dr	38555
Tennessee Stone Ct & Rd	38555
Tenth St	38555
Thames Ct & Ter	38558
The Crossings	38555
The Gardens Dr	38555
Thistle Ct	38571
Thomas St	38555
Thomas Springs Rd	38572
Thompson Ln	38555
Thompson Rd	38571
Thornhill Ln	38558
Thrushwood Dr	38558
Thurman Ave	38555
Thurman Ln	38571
Tia Ln	38572
Tidewater Dr	38571
Tiffanie Ln	38571
Tiffany Ct	38558
Tiger Lilly Rd	38572
Timber Ln	38571
Timber Creek Rd	38571
Timber Wolf Ln	38572
Timberland Rd	38572
Timberline Rd	38571
Timothy Dr	38572
Tipton Rd	38571
Todd Rd	38571
Tom Smith Rd	38571
Tom Welch Rd	38571
Tomah Dr	38572
Tomahawk Dr	38572
Tomlon Rd	38555
Topez Dr	38572
Torrey Pines Ln	38558
Tottenham Cir	38558
Towering Trl	38555
Towers Lake Rd	38572
Town Loop	38555
Town Branch St	38555
Town Centre Dr & Way	38571
Trafalger Dr & Ln	38558
Trails End	38571
Trappers Run	38571
Tremont Dr	38558
Trentwood Ct, Dr & Ter	38558
Tres Cir	38572
Tresa St	38572
Triple R Ln	38571
Troy Cir	38571
Truman Sherrill Rd	38572
Trunton Ct	38558
Tsala Ct & Dr	38572
Tulip Ct & Dr	38555
Turkey Blind Rd	38572
Turkey Oak Rd	38555
Turner Rd	38555
Turner Cemetery Rd	38558
Turner Greenhouse Rd	38572
Turner Lake Trl	38571
Turtle Pt	38571
Tuttle Dr & Ln	38571
Twickenham Ter	38558
Twilight Dr	38572
Twin Oaks Ter	38558
Underwood St	38555
Uno Ln	38572
Usgiya Ln	38572
Ut Shop Rd	38571
Utah Trce	38572
Ute Ln	38572
Utility Dr	38572
Valarian Dr & Ter	38558
Valley Ln	38555
Valley Loop	38572
Valley View Rd	38572
Vandever Ln & Rd	38572
Vanwinkle Rd	38572
Vanwinkle Cemetery Rd	38572
Vaughn Dr & St	38555
Veho Cir & Ct	38572
Vfw Loop	38555
Vianinte Rd	38571
N & S Victor Way	38555
Victoria Ct & Way	38558
Village Ln	38555
Villageway	38555
Vinerist Dr	38555
Virgil Smith Ln & Rd	38571
Vista Ter	38558
Vista Trl	38571
Volunteer Ct & Dr	38555
Wabash Ln	38572
Wagner Ln	38571
Wahoo Dr	38572
Wakefield St	38555

Waldelle Dr ... 38558
Walden Ridge Cir, Dr & Ter ... 38558
Walker Rd ... 38572
Walker St ... 38555
Walker Hill Cir & St ... 38555
Walla Walla Trce ... 38572
Wallingford Ln ... 38558
Wallop Dr & Ln ... 38571
Walnut Dr ... 38555
Walnut Loop ... 38572
Walsingham Ct & Ln ... 38558
Walters Pl ... 38572
Walton Rd ... 38571
Wampum Dr ... 38572
War Club Dr ... 38572
War Eagle Cir & Dr ... 38572
Warehouse Rd ... 38558
Warpath Cir & Dr ... 38572
Warrington Rd ... 38558
Warwickshire Dr & Ter ... 38558
Washington St ... 38572
Waterview Dr ... 38555
Wattenbarger Rd ... 38571
Waukegan Ln & Rd ... 38571
Waukesha Dr ... 38555
Waweka Dr ... 38572
Wayfarer Ln ... 38572
Waylon Rd ... 38571
Wayne Ave ... 38555
Webb Ave ... 38555
S Webb Ave ... 38555
Webb Loop ... 38572
Weketa Cir & Dr ... 38572
Welch St ... 38555
Wellington Ct ... 38558
Wells Rd ... 38555
Welshpool Rd ... 38558
Werthwyle Dr ... 38555
Wessex Ct ... 38558
West Ave
- 2-38 ... 38555
- 40-2150 ... 38555
- 2151-2297 ... 38571
- 2152-2198 ... 38555
- 2299-2399 ... 38571
- 2401-2499 ... 38571

Westchester Dr ... 38558
Westheria Dr ... 38555
Westminster Ct ... 38558
Westridge Cir, Ct & Ter ... 38558
Westway ... 38555
Westwind Dr ... 38555
Westwind Way ... 38572
Westwood Blvd ... 38571
Wexford Ln ... 38558
White Oak Cir ... 38555
White Oak Ln ... 38571
White Oak Farm Rd ... 38572
White Pine Ct ... 38555
White Pine Ln ... 38571
White Pine Trl ... 38555
Whitecrest Dr ... 38571
Whitehead Dr ... 38555
Whitehorse Dr ... 38572
Whitetail Ln ... 38572
Whittenburg Rd ... 38571
Whitworth Cir & Ter ... 38558
Wichita Dr ... 38572
Wickham Ln ... 38558
Wicklow Dr ... 38572
Wightman Rd ... 38571
Wilbanks Rd ... 38571
Wilbourn Cir, Ct & Dr ... 38558
Wild Azalea Trl ... 38571
Wild Boar Ln ... 38571
Wild Horse Trl ... 38572
Wild Leaf Ct ... 38558
Wild Plum Dr ... 38555
Wild Plum Ln ... 38572
Wild Rose Dr ... 38555
Wildwood Ln ... 38571
Wiley Ford Rd ... 38555
Will Cir & Dr ... 38555
Will Wyatt Ct & Ln ... 38572
Willard Brown Rd ... 38572
William Reed Rd ... 38572
Williams Rd ... 38571
Willow Pt ... 38571
Willow St ... 38555
Willowood Dr ... 38571
Willowwood Loop ... 38555
Wilshire Heights Dr ... 38558
Wilson Dr ... 38555
Wilson Ln ... 38555
Wilson Rd ... 38571
Wilson Way ... 38572
Wimberly Rd ... 38558
Winchester Dr ... 38558
Wind Song Dr & Trl ... 38555
Windcrest Rd ... 38558
Windermere Ct ... 38558
Windermere Dr ... 38555
Windermere Ter ... 38558
Windsor Pt & Rd ... 38558
Windstone Ln ... 38558
Windswept Dr ... 38571
Windtree Trl ... 38555
Windy Acres Dr ... 38571
Winningham Rd ... 38572
Winslow Ln ... 38558
Winter Green Ct ... 38558
Wistarbrook Dr ... 38571
Witt Rd ... 38571
Wolf Ter ... 38558
Wolf Creek Dr ... 38571
Woodgate Dr & Ln ... 38571
Woodhaven Dr ... 38571
Woodland Ct
- 1-54 ... 38558
- 55-99 ... 38571
- 56-398 ... 38558
- 301-399 ... 38558

Woodland Dr ... 38572
Woodland Ter ... 38558
Woodland Townhomes ... 38558
Woodlands Cir & Ct ... 38571
Woodlawn Rd ... 38555
Woodlawn Commercial Rd ... 38555
Woodmere Mall ... 38555
Woodmere Mall Cir ... 38555
Woodridge Ln & Rd ... 38571
Woods Hollow Ln ... 38571
Woodsway ... 38555
Woodwind Ln ... 38555
Woody Ct ... 38555
Woody Cemetery Rd ... 38571
World Outreach Dr ... 38571
Wren Cir ... 38555
Wren Ct ... 38558
Wright Ln ... 38572
Wyandot Cir & Ct ... 38558
Wyatt Ct ... 38555
Wyatt Dr ... 38571
Wyatt Loop ... 38555
Wyatts Way ... 38572
Wycliff Ln ... 38558
Yakama Dr ... 38572
Yee Haw Ct ... 38572
Yeehaw Ln ... 38572
Yellow Dog Dr ... 38572
Yellow Knife Dr ... 38572
York Ct, Ln & Rd ... 38555
Yorkshire Ter E ... 38558
Youngs Ln ... 38571
Yucatan Cir ... 38572
Yuchi Dr ... 38572
Yuork Ct & Dr ... 38572
Yurch Dr ... 38572
Yvonne Ave ... 38555

DICKSON TN

General Delivery ... 37055

POST OFFICE BOXES MAIN OFFICE STATIONS AND BRANCHES

Box No.s
All PO Boxes ... 37056

NAMED STREETS

A G Myatt Dr ... 37055
Academy St ... 37055
Acorn Dr ... 37055
Adcock Cemetery Rd ... 37055
Adult Center Rd ... 37055
Anderson Rd ... 37055
Andrese St ... 37055
Annette Dr ... 37055
Annwood St ... 37055
Applegate Ln ... 37055
Archway Cir ... 37055
Aries Aly ... 37055
Arrington Dr ... 37055
Arvitt Rd ... 37055
Aspen Cir ... 37055
Autumn Way ... 37055
Baggett Ln ... 37055
Baker Rd ... 37055
Baker Cemetery Rd ... 37055
Balthrop Branch Rd ... 37055
Balthrop Hollow Rd ... 37055
Bar B Q Rd ... 37055
Barzandi Dr ... 37055
Batey Cir & Ct ... 37055
Bbq Rd ... 37055
S Bear Creek Rd ... 37055
Beasley Dr ... 37055
Bel Arbre Pl ... 37055
Belford Dr ... 37055
Bellwood Cir & Dr ... 37055
Belmont Dr ... 37055
Ben Rd ... 37055
Berry Rd ... 37055
Big Bartons Creek Rd ... 37055
Bills Ln ... 37055
Billy Wynn Rd ... 37055
Birch St ... 37055
Birdie Ct ... 37055
Bishop Ln ... 37055
Bitter Sweet Rd ... 37055
Bittersweet Bnd ... 37055
Black Rd ... 37055
Black Oak Dr ... 37055
Blakemore Rd ... 37055
Blakewood Dr ... 37055
Blaylock Rd ... 37055
Blue Rd ... 37055
Blue Moon Rd ... 37055
Bluebird Ln ... 37055
Blurton Dr ... 37055
Bobwhite Dr ... 37055
Bradford Dr ... 37055
Brady Dr ... 37055
Brannon Dr ... 37055
Branson Dr ... 37055
Brazzell Ave, Ln & Rd ... 37055
Brentwood Dr ... 37055
E & W Broad St ... 37055
Broadmore Dr ... 37055
Broadview Dr ... 37055
Broadway Dr ... 37055
Brook Dr ... 37055
Brookside Dr ... 37055
Brown Hollow Rd ... 37055
Brown Street Rd ... 37055
Browning Cir ... 37055
Bruce Dr, Rd & St ... 37055
Bryan Ave ... 37055
Bryant Ave ... 37055
Buck Spicer Rd ... 37055
Buckhorn Dr ... 37055
Bud Vineyard Rd ... 37055
Burgess Ln & Rd ... 37055
Burnett Ct, Ln & Rd ... 37055
Burnt Barn Rd ... 37055
C C C Rd ... 37055
Cage Cir ... 37055
Cage Baggett Rd ... 37055
Camber Ln ... 37055
Canary Dr & Way ... 37055
Candlewood Dr ... 37055
Capriole Dr ... 37055
Caps Rdg ... 37055
Caraway Ct ... 37055
Cardinal Cir & Rd ... 37055
Caroline Ln ... 37055
Castings Dr ... 37055
Cecil St ... 37055
E & W Cedar St ... 37055
Cedarview Dr ... 37055
Cemetary Dr ... 37055
Center Ave ... 37055
Central High St ... 37055
Chandler Rd ... 37055
Charles Ct ... 37055
N & S Charlotte St ... 37055
Chatfield Way ... 37055
Cherry St ... 37055
E & W Chestnut Dr & St ... 37055
Chilton Ln ... 37055
Chipmunk Dr ... 37055
S Choate Rd ... 37055
E & W Christi Dr ... 37055
Chuck Sanders Rd ... 37055
Church Rd & St ... 37055
Churchfield Dr ... 37055
Circle U Dr ... 37055
City Lake Dr ... 37055
Clairmont Dr ... 37055
Clement Aly, Dr & Pl ... 37055
Cliff Dr ... 37055
Clifton Rd ... 37055
Clifton Cemetery Rd ... 37055
Codie Dr ... 37055
E & W College Ct & St ... 37055
Colt Dr ... 37055
Columbia Rd ... 37055
Cook Dr ... 37055
Coon Creek Rd ... 37055
Cottonwood Dr ... 37055
Country Ln ... 37055
Country Club Dr ... 37055
Covington Ln ... 37055
Cowan Rd ... 37055
Crafton ... 37055
Creekside Dr ... 37055
Creekstone Ct ... 37055
Crestview Dr & Pl ... 37055
Crestview Park Dr ... 37055
Crosby Dr ... 37055
Cross Roads Village Dr ... 37055
Crossway Dr ... 37055
Crow Crutcher St ... 37055
Cullum Ave ... 37055
Dade Cir ... 37055
Deal Ct ... 37055
Deason Rd ... 37055
Debbie Dr ... 37055
Deerwood Ct & Rd ... 37055
Delaney Cir ... 37055
W Dell Rd ... 37055
Dell Way One ... 37055
Dell Way Three ... 37055
Dell Way Two ... 37055
Dennison Pl ... 37055
Denny Rd ... 37055
Dewey Dr ... 37055
Diana Dr ... 37055
Dickson Ave ... 37055
Dickson Plaza Dr ... 37055
Dillon Rd ... 37055
Doe Ln ... 37055
Dogwood Ct & Ln ... 37055
Donegan Rd ... 37055
Donegan Crossing Rd ... 37055
Double Branch Rd ... 37055
Dowdy Rd ... 37055
Dragon Dr ... 37055
Druid Hills Dr ... 37055
W Dry Hollow Rd ... 37055
Dudley Ln ... 37055
Dugan Cemetery Rd ... 37055
Duke Loop & Rd ... 37055
Dull St ... 37055
Dupree Rd ... 37055
Dykeman Rd ... 37055
Eagle Cir ... 37055
Eastdale Ln ... 37055
Eastwood Dr ... 37055
Echo Rd ... 37055
Edgefield Cir ... 37055
Edgewood Dr, Pl & Rd ... 37055
Edgewood Cemetery Rd ... 37055
Edwards Aly ... 37055
Edwin Rd ... 37055
Eleazer Dr ... 37055
Elkins Rd ... 37055
W & E End Ave & Dr ... 37055
England Dr & Rd ... 37055
English Oak Ct ... 37055
S Eno Rd ... 37055
Fabric Rd ... 37055
Fairview Rd ... 37055
Faith Rd ... 37055
Fannie Branch Rd ... 37055
Farrar Ln ... 37055
Federal Cir ... 37055
Ferbee Rd ... 37055
Few Ln & Rd ... 37055
Fielder Rd ... 37055
Fiesta Dr ... 37055
Fire Tower Rd ... 37055
Fisher Rd ... 37055
Flagstone Ct ... 37055
Fleet Town Rd ... 37055
Flowers St ... 37055
Flowwood Dr ... 37055
E Forest Park Dr ... 37055
Forrest Hills Cir & Dr ... 37055
Fortner Rd ... 37055
Fowlkes Dr ... 37055
Frame One Rd ... 37055
Frank Clement Pl ... 37055
Frazier Cemetery Rd ... 37055
Frederick Ln ... 37055
Freeman Ave ... 37055
Friar Tuck Dr ... 37055
Fuqua Aly ... 37055
Furnace Hollow Rd ... 37055
Fussell Aly & Rd ... 37055
Fussell Spur Rd ... 37055
Garden View Ct ... 37055
Garners Creek Rd ... 37055
Gaskins Rd ... 37055
Gentry Cir ... 37055
Gilliam Ln ... 37055
Gilliam Hollow Rd ... 37055
Glass Rdg ... 37055
Glendale Dr ... 37055
Glenn Baker Rd ... 37055
Goodson Rd ... 37055
Grab Creek Rd W ... 37055
Grandview Dr ... 37055
Greenbrier St ... 37055
Greenhaven Cir ... 37055
Greer Cir ... 37055
Grindstone Hollow Rd ... 37055
Grove Springs Rd ... 37055
Gum Branch Rd ... 37055
Guy Bishop Ln ... 37055
Haley Rd ... 37055
Haliburton Way ... 37055
Halliday Rd ... 37055
Hamilton Aly ... 37055
Hampton Rd ... 37055
Hannah Rd ... 37055
Hardin Ave ... 37055
Hargrove Rd ... 37055
Harmon Springs Rd ... 37055
Harrell Cemetery Rd ... 37055
Harrington Rd ... 37055
Harris Rd ... 37055
Hayes Cir ... 37055
Hayshed Rd ... 37055
Heather Ln ... 37055
Helberg St ... 37055
Henslee Dr ... 37055
Herbison Ln ... 37055
Herman Ave ... 37055
Hester Dr ... 37055
Hickory Dr, Ln & Run ... 37055
Hickory Hill Dr ... 37055
Hickory Hollow Dr ... 37055
Hickory Pointe ... 37055
Hicks Rd ... 37055
High St ... 37055
High Lake Dr ... 37055
Highland Dr ... 37055
Highway 46 S ... 37055
Highway 47 E ... 37055
Highway 48 N & S ... 37055
Highway 70 E & W ... 37055
Highway 96 ... 37055
Hill Rd ... 37055
Hillcrest Rd ... 37055
E & W Hills Ter ... 37055
Hillside Dr ... 37055
Hilltop Rd ... 37055
Hillview Dr, Rd & St ... 37055
Hillwood Dr ... 37055
Hogin Rd ... 37055
Holland Rd & Trl ... 37055
Home Place Rd ... 37055
Hopes Way ... 37055
Hortense Rd ... 37055
Hoyt Rd ... 37055
Hubert Dr ... 37055
Hubert Redden Rd ... 37055
Hudson Rd ... 37055
Hughes St ... 37055
N & S Hummingbird Ln ... 37055
Humphres Dr ... 37055
E Humphries County Line Rd ... 37055
E & W Hunt St ... 37055
Hunter Trl ... 37055
Hurt Ln ... 37055
Hyndman Ct & Rd ... 37055
Ille Greer Rd ... 37055
Iron Gate Ln ... 37055
W Iron Hill Rd ... 37055
Jackson Rd ... 37055
Jackson Bros Blvd ... 37055
Jason Chapel Rd ... 37055
Jerico Rd ... 37055
Jesse Work Rd ... 37055
Jessikas Pl ... 37055
Johnstone Dr ... 37055
Jones Concrete Dr ... 37055
Jones Creek Rd ... 37055
Js Redden Cemetery Rd ... 37055
Jump Off Rd ... 37055
June Dr ... 37055
Kaiser Cir & Rd ... 37055
Kennel Rd ... 37055
Kentucky St ... 37055
Kevin Dr ... 37055
Kimberly Dr & Way ... 37055
Kimbro Rd ... 37055
W & E Lake Cir & Dr ... 37055
Lake Circle Dr ... 37055
Lake Valley Rd ... 37055
Lake Villa Blvd & Ct ... 37055
Laken Ln ... 37055
Lakeview Cir & Dr ... 37055
Lakewood Dr ... 37055
Lane Rd ... 37055
Lankford Holw & Ln ... 37055
Larkwood Dr ... 37055
Laurel Ave & Ct ... 37055
Laurel Hills Dr ... 37055
Lecomte Rd ... 37055
Lee Dr & Rd ... 37055
Lee Ridge Rd ... 37055
Leeza Loop ... 37055
Lena Rd ... 37055
Lewis Hollow Rd ... 37055
Little John Rd ... 37055
Livestock Rd ... 37055
Lock Dr ... 37055
Locke Hollow Rd ... 37055
Lockhart St ... 37055
Log Wall Rd ... 37055
Lone Oak Dr ... 37055
Louise Dr ... 37055
Lovell Ave ... 37055
Lowes Rd ... 37055
Lucas Ln & Rd ... 37055
Luffman Rd ... 37055
Luther Ct & Rd ... 37055
Luther Hogin Rd ... 37055
Lyle Ln ... 37055
M And M Ln ... 37055
M Dickson Rd ... 37055
Mack St ... 37055
Madison Ridge Blvd ... 37055
Mae Cir ... 37055
Magnum Dr ... 37055
Maid Marion Ln ... 37055
N & S Main St ... 37055
Maley St ... 37055
Manley Ln & Loop ... 37055
Maple St ... 37055
Maple Grove Rd ... 37055
Maplewood Dr ... 37055
Marilyn Dr ... 37055
Marshall Stuart Dr ... 37055
Martha Ave ... 37055
Martin Luther King Jr Blvd ... 37055
Mason Ct ... 37055
Masonic St ... 37055
Mathis Dr ... 37055
Maysville Rd ... 37055
Mcclurkan Rd ... 37055
Mccreary Hts & St ... 37055
Mcdonald Dr & Loop ... 37055
Mcelhiney Rd ... 37055
Mcfarland Ln ... 37055
Mcintire Aly ... 37055
Mckenzie St ... 37055
Mclemore St ... 37055
Meadow Dr ... 37055
Meadow Green Way ... 37055
Meadow Haven Ln ... 37055
Meadowlark Ct & Dr ... 37055
Meadowood Ln ... 37055
Meadowview Ln ... 37055
Melrose Dr ... 37055
Midland Dr ... 37055
Mill Rd ... 37055
Miller St ... 37055
Milton Rd ... 37055
Minorcrest Dr ... 37055
Mockingbird Ln ... 37055
Moore Rd ... 37055
Moore Hollow Rd ... 37055
Moran Way ... 37055
Mount Lebanon Rd ... 37055
N & S Mount Sinai Rd ... 37055
N & S Mulberry St ... 37055
Murrell Rd & St ... 37055
Music Rdg ... 37055
Mustang Dr ... 37055
Myatt Ave & St ... 37055
Myatt Cemetery Rd ... 37055
Nails Creek Dr & Rd ... 37055
Nancy Shawl Rd ... 37055
Natchez Blvd ... 37055
Natchez Park Dr ... 37055
Nels Adams Rd ... 37055
Nelson Rd ... 37055
Nesbitt St ... 37055
Newsome Dr ... 37055
Nicks Ln ... 37055
Nols Adams Rd ... 37055
Noname Rd ... 37055
Nottingham Rd ... 37055
Nubbin Ridge Rd ... 37055
Oak Ave & Dr ... 37055
Oak Grove Rd ... 37055
Oak Leaf Dr ... 37055
Oak Park Dr ... 37055
Oakland Dr ... 37055
Oaktree Ln ... 37055
Oakview Dr ... 37055
Oakwood Cir & Dr ... 37055
Odell Rd ... 37055
Old Beaver Creek Rd ... 37055
Old Charlotte Pike ... 37055
Old Columbia Rd ... 37055

Old Garners Creek Rd 37055
Old Highway 46 S 37055
Old Jones Creek Rd 37055
Old Number One Rd 37055
Old Pond Ln 37055
Old Ruskin Rd 37055
Old Stage Rd 37055
Old Sylvia Rd 37055
Old Wynn Rd 37055
Olive St 37055
E Overhill Dr 37055
E & W Park Ave & Cir 37055
Park Circle Dr 37055
Parker Ln 37055
Parker Bridge Rd 37055
Parkway Dr W 37055
Pate Ln 37055
Patterson St 37055
Payne Springs Rd 37055
Peery Hl 37055
Pelham Rd 37055
Perleris Rd 37055
Pheasant Hollow Rd 37055
Pickett St 37055
Pigeon Hollow Rd 37055
Pin Oak Dr 37055
Pinewood Dr 37055
Piney Rd 37055
Piney River Rd 37055
Plantation Ct 37055
Pleasant Valley Dr 37055
E Plunders Creek Rd 37055
Polly Willey Rd 37055
Pomona Rd 37055
Pond Rd 37055
Pond Circle Rd 37055
Pond Rail Rd 37055
Pond Switch Rd 37055
Poplar Bnd & St 37055
Post Oak Ct & Dr 37055
Potter Rd 37055
Premdor Dr 37055
Pringle Dr 37055
Printwood Dr 37055
Pruett Rd 37055
Pruett Springs Rd 37055
Pumphill Rd 37055
Quail Ct 37055
E & W Quail Hollow Way 37055
E & W Railroad St 37055
Ramey Ln 37055
Ramsey Way 37055
Raney Hill Rd 37055
Ratliff Ln 37055
Ravenwood Cir 37055
E & W Ray St 37055
Raymond Rd 37055
Rays Loop 37055
Red Oak Cir 37055
Redbud Dr 37055
Redden Ln 37055
Redden Cemetery Rd 37055
Redden Hollow Rd 37055
Redwood Dr 37055
Reep Rd 37055
Reeves St 37055
Regency Ln 37055
Reliance Rd 37055
Remington 37055
Reserve Dr 37055
Reynolds Ln 37055
Rick St 37055
E & W Rickert Ave 37055
Rickert Camp Rd 37055
Ridge Rd 37055
Ridgecrest Cir & Dr 37055
Ridgemont Dr 37055
Riedland Dr 37055
Robert Ct 37055
Robert Porter Rd 37055
Robin Rd 37055
Robin Hood Rd 37055
Robinson Dr & Rd 37055
Rock Church Rd 37055
Rocky Dr 37055
Rocky Top Dr 37055
Rogers Dr 37055
Rosey Dr 37055
Rouse Rd 37055
Roy Donegan Rd 37055
Royal Oak Dr 37055
Ruby Ct 37055
Ruger Dr 37055
Russell Dr & Ln 37055
Russell Cemetery Rd 37055
Saddle Creek Cir 37055
Sam Hollow Rd 37055
Sam Vineyard Rd 37055
Sanders Ln 37055
Sanker Rd 37055
Sattway Dr 37055
Saw Mill Rd 37055
Scenic Dr 37055
Schrader Heights Dr 37055
Scott Dr & St 37055
Sendero Bad 37055
Shadow Cv 37055
Shady Hill Rd 37055
Shady Hollow Rd 37055
Shady Oak Dr 37055
Shadybrook Cir 37055
Shekinah Rd 37055
Sherron Dr 37055
Sherry Ln 37055
Shiloh Dr 37055
Short Rd & St 37055
Shorty Few Rd 37055
Silver Leaf Cir 37055
Singleton Rd 37055
Skyline Cir
100-207 37055
206-206 37056
208-298 37055
209-299 37055
Skyline Dr 37055
Southerland Rd 37055
Southwood Dr 37055
Spanish Ct 37055
Spindle Rd 37055
S Spradlin Rd 37055
Spring St 37055
Spring Branch Rd 37055
Springer Dr 37055
Springer Work Rd 37055
State St 37055
Stephen St 37055
Stephen Nicks Dr 37055
Sterling Spring Rd 37055
Stewart Rd 37055
Street Rd 37055
Suggs St 37055
Sullivan Rd 37055
Summerall Rd 37055
Sunny Brook Dr 37055
Sunny Ridge Cir & Ct 37055
Sunrise Ln 37055
Sunset Cir & Rd 37055
Suzanne Dr 37055
Sycamore Rd 37055
Sylvia Rd 37055
Sylvis Rd & St 37055
Tanglewood Dr 37055
Taylor Rd & St 37055
Teal Dr 37055
W Tennessee City Rd 37055
Tennsco Dr 37055
Texas Hollow Rd 37055
Thompson Rd 37055
Thompson Cemetery Rd 37055
Tices Spring Ct 37055
Tidwell Switch Rd 37055
Timberline Rd 37055
Travis Dr 37055
Treemont Rd 37055
Troy Donegan Rd 37055
Tucker Rd 37055
Turkey Creek Rd 37055
Turner Dr 37055
Turtlecreek Ln 37055
Twin Pine Rd 37055
Two Mile Rd 37055
Underhill Dr 37055
Union Rd 37055
Upper Lake Dr 37055
Valley Rd W 37055
Valley View Dr 37055
Valleywood Ct & Dr 37055
Villa Cir 37055
Village Cir, Holw & Ln E & W 37055
Virgil Bellar Rd 37055
Vondohlen Ln 37055
Wade Ave 37055
Walker Rd & St 37055
Walker Branch Rd 37055
E & W Walnut St 37055
Walnut Grove Rd 37055
Warren Pl 37055
Warren G Medlay Dr 37055
Water St 37055
Watson Ln 37055
Wayne F Mill Rd 37055
Weaver Dr 37055
Wells Rd 37055
Wells Cemetery Rd 37055
Wes Pine Acres 37055
Westfield Rd 37055
Westmeade Dr 37055
White Oak Dr 37055
Wildcat Rd 37055
Wiley Branch Rd 37055
Will Bell Rd 37055
Williams Ln 37055
Willow Bend Rd 37055
Willow Branch Rd 37055
Willow Creek Ln 37055
Willowwood Rd 37055
Wills Rd 37055
Wills Cemetery Rd 37055
Wilson Hollow Rd 37055
Winchester Cir 37055
Woodland Dr 37055
Woodlawn Dr 37055
Woodmont Dr 37055
Woodside Dr 37055
Woodycrest Rd 37055
Woodycrest Close 37055
Worley Furnace Rd 37055
Yates Ln 37055
Yellow Creek Rd 37055

NUMBERED STREETS

All Street Addresses 37055

DYERSBURG TN

General Delivery 38024

POST OFFICE BOXES MAIN OFFICE STATIONS AND BRANCHES

Box No.s
All PO Boxes 38025

NAMED STREETS

A St 38024
Acadian Blvd 38024
Agee Ln 38024
Airport Rd 38024
Allen Ave 38024
Allen Hines Rd 38024
Alvinwood Cir 38024
Amanda Ave 38024
Anchorage Ave 38024
Anderson Rd 38024
Andrea Dr 38024
Apache Cv 38024
Apple Dr 38024
Arahwana Ln 38024
Ashley Rd 38024
Aspen Cir 38024
Auburn Ave 38024
Augusta St 38024
Avery Ave 38024
Ayers St 38024
Azalea Ln 38024
Aztec Dr 38024
B St 38024
Baker St 38024
Bandelan Rd 38024
Barnes Rd 38024
Barney St 38024
Barry Rd 38024
Baxter St 38024
Bean Mill Rd 38024
Beaver Rd 38024
Beaver Creek Cv 38024
Beech Cir 38024
Bekaert Ln & Rd 38024
Bell Ave 38024
Bend Rd 38024
Benjamin Dr 38024
Beth Ave 38024
Beverly Dr 38024
Birch Ln 38024
Bishop Rd & St 38024
Blake Cv & Dr 38024
Bluff Dr 38024
Bonicord Rd 38024
Bonicord Road Ext 38024
Booths Point Rd 38024
Bose St 38024
Bowen Ln 38024
Brasfield St 38024
Bratton Ave 38024
Brayton Ave 38024
Brewer Rd 38024
Brickbat Rd 38024
Brigance Ave 38024
Broadway Ave 38024
Brookhollow Ln 38024
Brooks Ave 38024
Brown St 38024
Browning St 38024
Bruce Ave 38024
Bruceville Slab Rd 38024
Bunn Rd 38024
Burch Rd 38024
Burgies Chapel Rd 38024
Burkhead Rd 38024
Burks Pl 38024
Burnt Mill Rd 38024
Bush Rd & St 38024
Butterworth Ave 38024
Byars St 38024
Byron St 38024
Calcutt Ave 38024
Caleb Dr 38024
Calvin Moore Rd 38024
Cameron Cv 38024
Cane Creek Cv 38024
Cannon Cv 38024
Capps Dr 38024
Carol Ann Ave 38024
Carrie Dr & St 38024
Carrie Street Ext 38024
Carter Ln 38024
Cathey Rd 38024
Cecil Dr 38024
E & W Cedar St 38024
Central St 38024
Chandler Dr 38024
Charles St 38024
Charlie Ennis Rd 38024
Cheatham St 38024
Cherokee Trl 38024
Cherry Cir & St 38024
Chestnut Cir 38024
Chicago Ave 38024
Chickasaw Blf 38024
Chris Dr 38024
Christie Ext & St 38024
N Church Ave
100-400 38024
309-309 38025
401-499 38024
402-498 38024
S Church Ave 38024
Circle Dr 38024
Claiborne Dr 38024
Clanton Rd 38024
Clark St 38024
Clifton Dr & Rd 38024
Clubhouse Dr 38024
College St 38024
Commerce Ave & St 38024
Community Park Rd 38024
Compress St 38024
Concord Cv 38024
N & S Connell Ave & St 38024
Cook St 38024
Cooley Rd 38024
Coon Club Ln 38024
Cooper Dr & Ln 38024
Copeland Rd 38024
Cornelian Dr 38024
Cortez Cv 38024
Cottonwood Ln, Rd & St 38024
Council Rd 38024
Country Club Rd 38024
W Countryman St 38024
Countryview Ln 38024
E & W Court St 38024
Cow Ln 38024
Craig Rd 38024
Crawford Ave 38024
Cribbs Rd 38024
Criswell Rd 38024
Crossgate Rd 38024
Crossno St 38024
Cumberland St 38024
Curry St 38024
Custer Ave 38024
Cypress Cv 38024
Dana St 38024
Daniel Ln 38024
Daniel Boone Dr 38024
David Dr & Rd 38024
Davis Rd 38024
Davy Crockett Cv 38024
Dawn Dr 38024
Dawson St 38024
Deal Rd 38024
Dean Dr 38024
Deer Track Cv 38024
Defoe Rd 38024
Delta Pine Ave 38024
Dennis St 38024
Dianne Ct & Dr 38024
Dillon Dr 38024
Dixie Ave 38024
Dobbs St 38024
Dogwood Cir 38024
Don Hurley Rd 38024
Dove Dr 38024
Downing St 38024
Doyle St 38024
Dozier Ln 38024
Drew Rd & St 38024
Ducky Ln 38024
Dummy Line Rd 38024
Duncan Rd 38024
Dyer Ave 38024
Dyersburg Sq 38024
Eagle Cv 38024
Eaglewood Dr 38024
Eastlawn Dr 38024
Edmond Sorrell Rd 38024
Egbert St 38024
Elizabeth St 38024
Ellen Dr 38024
Elm Ave & Ln 38024
Emerson Ln 38024
Emerson Lane Ext 38024
Empire Ave 38024
Ennis Ln 38024
Everett Ave 38024
Evergreen Pl 38024
Ewell Ave 38024
Fair Rd & St 38024
Fairbanks Ave 38024
Fairfield Dr 38024
Fairway Dr 38024
Fakes Ave 38024
Federal Dr 38024
Ferguson Ave 38024
Ferrell Ave 38024
Field Rd 38024
Finch Rd 38024
Finley Cir & St 38024
Finley Cemetery Rd 38024
First Citizens Pl 38024
Fisher Cir 38024
Flicker Dr 38024
Flowering Dogwood Ln 38024
Flowers Rd 38024
Forcum St 38024
Ford St 38024
Forrest St 38024
Forshee St 38024
Fort Hudson Dr & Rd 38024
Fort Hudson Road Ext 38024
N & S Fowlkes Ave, Rd & St 38024
Foxridge Run 38024
Frank Maynard Dr 38024
Frankie Dr 38024
Franklin Ave 38024
Friendship Rd 38024
Fuller Ave & Rd 38024
N Fumbanks Ave 38024
Gail Cir 38024
Garhill Rd 38024
Garland St 38024
Gentry St 38024
George Weakley Rd 38024
Glen St 38024
Glen Oaks Ln 38024
Glenwood Rd 38024
Golf Course Rd 38024
Gordon Rd & St 38024
Granger Cir 38024
Grant St 38024
Greenburg Rd 38024
Greenway St 38024
Gurley Dr 38024
Habitat Cv 38024
Haddock Rd 38024
Hamer Rd 38024
Hampton Ln & Pl 38024
Hanks Ln 38024
Harness Rd 38024
Harrell Ave 38024
W Harris Rd & St 38024
Harrison Ln & Rd 38024
Hart St 38024
Harton Ave & Row 38024
Harts Cir & Ln 38024
Hatley Ln 38024
Hawthorne Ave & Ln 38024
Haynes Rd 38024
Hazel Cir 38024
Heathridge Dr 38024
Hendrix Dr 38024
Henry St 38024
Hickory Cir 38024
High Ave 38024
Highland Dr 38024
Highway 104 E & W 38024
Highway 210 N & S 38024
Highway 211 38024
Highway 51 Byp 38024
Highway 78 N 38024
Hike Ave 38024
Hillcrest Ave 38024
Hillside Cv 38024
Hobert Ave 38024
Hodge Ave 38024
Hoff Rd 38024
Hogwallow Rd 38024
Holden Ave 38024
Holly Ln 38024
Holly Springs Cemetery Rd 38024
Holmes Rd 38024
Holt St 38024
Honeysuckle Cv & Rd 38024
Hopper Ln 38024
Hornbrook St 38024
Horner Rd 38024
Hoss Everett Rd 38024
Huffine Rd 38024
Huish Rd 38024
Hull St 38024
Hunter Ln 38024
Hurricane Hill Rd 38024
Indian Trce 38024
Industrial Rd 38024
Ingram Rd 38024
Isaac Hayes Dr 38024
Jackson St 38024
Jackson Crossing Rd 38024
Jake Mallard Rd 38024
James H Rice Rd 38024
Jamestown Rd 38024
Janice Ln 38024
Jay Ave 38024
Jb Ave 38024
Jenkinsville Jamestown Rd 38024
Jim Bowie Rd 38024
Jo Cir 38024
Jo Circle Ext 38024
Joe G Baker Ave 38024
John Elliott Rd 38024
John Mark Dr 38024
Johnson St 38024
Jones Rd & St 38024
Jordan Ave 38024
Josh Dr 38024
Joshua Cir & Loop 38024
Joyce St 38024
Juniper Cir 38024
Kari Cir 38024
Katie Cv 38024
Keats St 38024
Kelly Rd 38024
Kendall Ln 38024
Kimbrell Ln 38024
N & S King Ave 38024
Kirk Cir 38024
Kist Ave 38024
Kit Carson Rd 38024
Klondike St 38024
Knapp Ave 38024
Kw Ave 38024
Laird St 38024
Lake Rd 38024
Lake Luanna Est 38024
Lakeview Cv 38024
Lakewood Dr & Est 38024
Lamar St 38024
Lannom Dr 38024
N Lattawoods Dr 38024
Laura Ln 38024
Lawson Ln 38024
Leake St 38024
Lee St 38024
Legends Cv 38024
Leggett Rd 38024
Leigh Dr 38024
Lela Rd 38024
Lennie Clark Rd 38024
Lenox Boothpoint Rd 38024
Lenox Nauvoo Rd 38024
Lewis Ave 38024
Lexie Cobb Rd 38024
Liberty Ave 38024
Light Dr & St 38024
Lincoln Ave 38024
Linden Rd 38024
Lipford Cir 38024
Little Ln 38024
Live Oak St 38024
Lloyd Ln 38024
Longfellow Ave 38024
Lovers Ln 38024
Lucretia Ln 38024
Luster Cir 38024
Lynn St 38024
Lyte Cir 38024

Mackey Rd ... 38024
Magazine St ... 38024
Magnolia Dr & Ln ... 38024
N, S, E & W Main Ave & St ... 38024
Mall Blvd ... 38024
Mall Loop Rd ... 38024
Maple Cir & St ... 38024
Maplewood Cv ... 38024
E, N, S & W Market St ... 38024
Marr Dr ... 38024
Martin Luther King Dr ... 38024
Mason Ave ... 38024
Masonic St ... 38024
Maxey Dr ... 38024
May St ... 38024
Mcarthur St ... 38024
Mcbride Rd ... 38024
Mccullough Chapel Rd ... 38024
Mcdearmon St ... 38024
Mcgaughey St ... 38024
Mcguire Rd ... 38024
Mckee Ave ... 38024
Mclean Ave ... 38024
Meacham Rd ... 38024
Meadowood Cv ... 38024
Meadowview Dr ... 38024
Meeks St ... 38024
Melinda Ln ... 38024
Melissa Ln ... 38024
Melody Acres Dr ... 38024
Melton Ave ... 38024
Memorial Dr ... 38024
Menzie Rd ... 38024
Merriman Ave ... 38024
Mesa Ln ... 38024
Metalwood Cv ... 38024
Michael Ln ... 38024
Michael Lynn Ln ... 38024
Mickey Cir ... 38024
N & S Mill Ave ... 38024
Miller St ... 38024
Millsfield Hwy ... 38024
Mitchell Ln ... 38024
Monroe St ... 38024
Moody Cir & Dr ... 38024
Morgan Rd ... 38024
Morning Rd ... 38024
Moss St ... 38024
Nathan Ln ... 38024
Nauvoo School Rd ... 38024
Navajo Cir ... 38024
Norman Ln ... 38024
Northview Cv ... 38024
Oak St ... 38024
Oak Ridge Rd ... 38024
Oak Ridge Road Ext ... 38024
Oakleigh Dr ... 38024
Oakmont Ave ... 38024
Oakview Ave ... 38024
Oakwood Cv ... 38024
Okeena Dr ... 38024
Old Fowlkes Rd ... 38024
Old Highway 20 ... 38024
Old Lenox Rd ... 38024
Old State Rt 20 ... 38024
Ozment Rd ... 38024
Palestine Cemetery Rd ... 38024
Palmer Rd & St ... 38024
Palmer Subdivision Rd ... 38024
Park Thurman Cir ... 38024
Parker Ave & Rd ... 38024
Parks St ... 38024
E & W Parkview St ... 38024
Parr Ave ... 38024
Pate Ave ... 38024
Peabody Ave ... 38024
Peach Ave & Rd ... 38024
Pease Ave ... 38024
Pecan Cv & Ln ... 38024
Peckerwood Point Rd ... 38024
Pennell Ln ... 38024
Pennell Lane Ext ... 38024
Perciful Rd ... 38024
Permenter Ln ... 38024
Perry Cir & Dr ... 38024
Phillips St ... 38024
Pierce Rd ... 38024
Pig Ln ... 38024
Pike Rd ... 38024
Pillow Ave ... 38024
Pin Oak Dr ... 38024
Pine Ln ... 38024
Pine Ridge Rd ... 38024
Pinehurst Cv ... 38024
Pioneer Rd ... 38024
Pioneer Road Ext ... 38024
Plantation Dr ... 38024
N & S Plum Rd ... 38024
Plummer Cir ... 38024
Polk Rd ... 38024
Polo Dr ... 38024
Ponder Rd ... 38024
Poplar Cir & St ... 38024
Porch Rd ... 38024
Pounder Rd ... 38024
Powell Rd ... 38024
Pressler Rd ... 38024
Price St ... 38024
Primrose Ln ... 38024
Prince Ave ... 38024
Pruitt Ln ... 38024
Pursell Ln ... 38024
Putter Ln ... 38024
Quail Hollow Dr ... 38024
Radio Rd ... 38024
Railroad St ... 38024
Rambo Rd ... 38024
Randall Rd ... 38024
Rawles Ave ... 38024
Reagan Rd ... 38024
Reaves St ... 38024
Recreation Dr ... 38024
Red Bell Rd ... 38024
Red Bud St ... 38024
Redbud Ln ... 38024
Redwood Ln ... 38024
Reelfoot Dr ... 38024
Reeves Rd ... 38024
Rehoboth Church Rd ... 38024
Resthome Rd ... 38024
Revell Cv & Rd ... 38024
Reynolds Ave ... 38024
Richardson Hill Rd ... 38024
Ricks St ... 38024
Ridge St ... 38024
Ridgeway St ... 38024
River St ... 38024
River Ridge Cv ... 38024
Roberts Ave ... 38024
Rock Springs Church Rd ... 38024
Roellen Newbern Rd ... 38024
Rogers Rd ... 38024
Rose Dr ... 38024
Rosemont Cv ... 38024
Ross Ave ... 38024
N & S Rucker Ave ... 38024
Saint Andrews Cv ... 38024
Saint George Ave ... 38024
Saint John Ave ... 38024
Saint Joseph Ave ... 38024
Salem Rd ... 38024
Salenfriend Cv ... 38024
Sam Davis Rd ... 38024
Sam Houston Dr ... 38024
Samaria Bend Rd ... 38024
N & S Sampson Ave ... 38024
Sandra St ... 38024
Sandwood Cv ... 38024
Sarah Cir ... 38024
Scarlet Cir ... 38024
W Schaffer St ... 38024
Scotsman Trce ... 38024
Scott St ... 38024
Sedonia Dr ... 38024
Sellars Dr ... 38024
Seratt Rd ... 38024
Shady Ln ... 38024
Shannon Ave & St ... 38024
Sharp St ... 38024
Sharpe St ... 38024
Shaw Ave ... 38024
Shelby Dr ... 38024
Shelly Ave ... 38024
Silver Rd ... 38024
Simpson Ln & Rd ... 38024
Simpson Hill Rd ... 38024
Sir James Ave ... 38024
Sir Lionel St ... 38024
Skyline Hts ... 38024
Slaughter Dr ... 38024
Slaughter Pen Rd ... 38024
Smith Ave & St ... 38024
Sorrell Chapel Loop & Rd ... 38024
Southern Ave ... 38024
Southview Dr ... 38024
Southwind Cv ... 38024
Speedway Ave ... 38024
Sq Rd ... 38024
Stadium Dr ... 38024
Star Cir ... 38024
Starlight Dr ... 38024
Steve Dr ... 38024
Stevens Ave ... 38024
Still Ave ... 38024
Stoneville Rd ... 38024
Sugg Pl ... 38024
Summers Dr ... 38024
Sun Rd ... 38024
Sunnybrae Ave ... 38024
Sunset Blvd ... 38024
Susan Ln ... 38024
Suzy Ave ... 38024
Sycamore Cir & Dr ... 38024
Sylvan Rd ... 38024
Tar Hill Rd ... 38024
Tarrant Ave ... 38024
Tate Rd ... 38024
Tatum Rd ... 38024
Taylor Rd ... 38024
Tc Lock Rd ... 38024
S Tennyson Ave ... 38024
Thomas Ave ... 38024
Thompson Ln ... 38024
Thorntree Dr ... 38024
Tibbs St ... 38024
E & W Tickle St ... 38024
Timothy Dr ... 38024
Tipton Ave ... 38024
Todd Ave ... 38024
Troy Ave & Cir ... 38024
Tucker Cir, Dr & St ... 38024
Tulip Ln & St ... 38024
Turner Ave ... 38024
Twilight Dr ... 38024
Twilla Ln ... 38024
Twin Oaks Ln ... 38024
Union St ... 38024
Unionville Rd ... 38024
Upper Finley Rd ... 38024
Us Highway 412 ... 38024
Us Highway 51 Byp S, E, N & W ... 38024
Valley Dr & Rd ... 38024
Vaughn Ave & St ... 38024
Vendall Rd ... 38024
Vernon St ... 38024
Viar Rd ... 38024
Vicki St ... 38024
Victory Ave ... 38024
Village St ... 38024
Volunteer Blvd ... 38024
Wabash Ave & Cir ... 38024
Wade Hampton Rd ... 38024
N & S Walker Ln ... 38024
Wallace St ... 38024
Walnut Ave, Cir, Dr, Ln & St ... 38024
Walnut Lane Ext ... 38024
Walton Rd ... 38024
Ward Dr ... 38024
Warren Clark Rd ... 38024
Watkins St ... 38024
Weaver Ln ... 38024
Wedgewood Cv ... 38024
Welch Rd ... 38024
Wells Rd ... 38024
Wendell Ave ... 38024
Wesley Dr ... 38024
Westlake Ave ... 38024
Westwood Cv ... 38024
E & W Wheeler St ... 38024
White Row ... 38024
White Oak Cir & Dr ... 38024
Whites Row ... 38024
Whitnel Rd ... 38024
Whitnell Rd ... 38024
Whitney Young Cv ... 38024
Wilkinson Dr ... 38024
Willard Ln ... 38024
William Cody Rd ... 38024
Williams Dr, Ln & St ... 38024
Willie Johnson Rd ... 38024
Willow Cir ... 38024
Wilson Cir & Dr ... 38024
Woodlawn Ave ... 38024
Woods Ave ... 38024
Woodside Ln ... 38024
Wren St ... 38024
Wright Ave ... 38024
Yarbro Rd ... 38024
Yellow Twig Ln ... 38024
Younger Ln ... 38024
Youth Home Rd ... 38024

NUMBERED STREETS

All Street Addresses ... 38024

ELIZABETHTON TN

General Delivery ... 37643

POST OFFICE BOXES MAIN OFFICE STATIONS AND BRANCHES

Box No.s
All PO Boxes ... 37644

NAMED STREETS

All Street Addresses ... 37643

NUMBERED STREETS

All Street Addresses ... 37643

FRANKLIN TN

General Delivery ... 37064

POST OFFICE BOXES MAIN OFFICE STATIONS AND BRANCHES

Box No.s
1 - 1889 ... 37065
680001 - 689500 ... 37068

NAMED STREETS

Abbey Ln ... 37067
Abbott Pl ... 37064
Abercairn Dr ... 37064
Abington Way ... 37069
Abington Ridge Ct & Ln ... 37067
Abram Ct ... 37064
Academy St ... 37064
Acadia Ave ... 37064
Acton St ... 37064
Adair Ct ... 37064
Adams Ct & St ... 37064
Addison Ave ... 37064
Adelynn Ct N & S ... 37064
Akin Ct ... 37064
Albany Ct & Dr ... 37067
Albert Cir ... 37064
Alcott Ct ... 37069
Aldwych Cir ... 37069
Alex Ct & Rd ... 37064
Alexander Dr & Plz ... 37064
Alfred Ladd Rd E ... 37064
Alicia Dr ... 37064
Allen Dr ... 37064
Allenhurst Cir ... 37067
Allyson Ln ... 37064
Alpha Dr ... 37064
Alpine Ct ... 37069
Althea Pl ... 37064
Alton Park Ln ... 37069
Ambelside Ct ... 37069
Ambergate Ct ... 37064
Amberleigh Ct ... 37067
Ambiance Way ... 37067
Amhearst Ct ... 37064
Amy Ct ... 37064
Andover Grn ... 37069
Andrews Ct ... 37069
Ann Ct ... 37064
Ann Crockett Ct ... 37064
Annfield Way ... 37064
Anni Watkins Ct ... 37064
Anston Park ... 37069
Antebellum Ct ... 37064
Apollo Dr ... 37069
Applecross Dr ... 37064
Appomattox Pl ... 37064
Arbor Dr ... 37069
Archers Way ... 37069
Arcola Ct ... 37067
Ardmore Pl ... 37064
Arklow Ct ... 37067
Arlington Pl ... 37064
Arno Rd
4000-6398 ... 37064
4001-4005 ... 37067
4007-6399 ... 37064
Arrowhead Rd ... 37069
Arsenal Ct & Dr ... 37064
Ascot Ln ... 37064
Ash Dr ... 37064
Ash Grove Ct ... 37069
Asheboro Pl ... 37064
Ashlawn Ct ... 37064
Ashton Park Blvd ... 37067
Ashwood Ct ... 37064
Aspen Grove Dr ... 37067
Astor Way ... 37064
Athena Ct ... 37069
Athey Ct ... 37064
Augusta National Ct ... 37069
Autumn Lake Trl ... 37067
Autumn Springs Ct ... 37067
Averwater Ct ... 37067
Avery Ct ... 37067
Avery Valley Dr ... 37067
Avon River Rd ... 37064
Avondale Dr ... 37064
Aylesford Ct & Ln ... 37069
Ayrshire Cir ... 37064
Azalea Ct & Ln ... 37064
Backbone Ridge Rd ... 37064
Baffin Ln ... 37067
Bagsby Ln ... 37064
Bailey Rd ... 37064
Baker Ln ... 37064
Bakers Bridge Ave & Rd ... 37067
Ballington Dr ... 37064
Baltusrol Rd ... 37069
Banbury Park Ln ... 37069
Bancroft Cv & Way ... 37064
Band Dr ... 37064
Bantry Ct ... 37067
Banwell Park ... 37069
Barclay Ln ... 37064
Barkleigh Ln ... 37064
Barlow Dr ... 37064
Barnes Ct ... 37069
Barnwood Ct ... 37064
Barrel Springs Hollow Rd ... 37069
Barrington Ct & Dr ... 37067
Basil Ct ... 37064
Bateman Ave ... 37067
Battery Ct ... 37064
Battle Ave ... 37064
Battlefield Dr ... 37064
Battlewood St ... 37069
Baxter Ln ... 37069
Bayhill Cir ... 37067
Beacon Hill Ct & Dr ... 37067
Bear Creek Rd ... 37064
Beard Rd ... 37064
Beasley Dr ... 37064
Beauchamp Cir ... 37067
Becky Ln ... 37064
Bedford Cmn & Way ... 37064
Bedford Creek Rd ... 37064
Beechlawn Dr ... 37064
Beechs Tavern Trl ... 37069
Bel Aire Dr ... 37064
Belle Brook Dr ... 37067
Belle Mina Ln ... 37064
Belle Vista Ct ... 37064
Bellegrove Ct ... 37069
Belmont Cir ... 37069
Bembridge Ln ... 37069
Ben Brush Cir ... 37069
Bending Chestnut Rd ... 37064
W & E Benjamin Ct & Dr ... 37067
Benmore Dr ... 37064
Bent Tree Rd ... 37067
Bentgrass Ct ... 37069
Bentley Ct ... 37069
Benton Ln ... 37067
Bernard Way ... 37067
Berry Cir ... 37064
N & S Berrys Chapel Ct & Rd ... 37069
Bertrand Dr ... 37064
N Berwick Ln ... 37069
Berwick Pl ... 37064
Beta Dr ... 37064
Bethlehem Loop Rd ... 37069
Bexley Park Dr ... 37069
Big Ben Ct ... 37067
Big East Fork Rd ... 37064
Big Sky Ln ... 37067
Billingsly Ct ... 37067
Biltmore Ct ... 37067
Binkley Dr ... 37069
Birchwood Cir ... 37064
Birkdale Ct ... 37064
Birken Cv ... 37064
Bishops Way ... 37064
Blackhorse Pkwy ... 37069
Blackjack Dr ... 37067
Blake Baskin Ct ... 37064
Blakely Ct ... 37064
Blarrelm Dr ... 37069
Blazer Rd ... 37064
Bledsoe Dr & Ln ... 37067
Blenheim Cir ... 37064
Blossom Ct ... 37064
Blue Grass Dr ... 37064
Blue Springs Ct & Rd ... 37069
Bluebell Way ... 37064
Bluelake Ct ... 37064
Bob O Link Dr ... 37069
Bobby Dr ... 37069
Bois D Arc Ln ... 37069
Bonnhaven Dr ... 37067
Bonnie Pl ... 37064
Bostic St ... 37064
Bowman Rd ... 37064
Boxley Valley Rd ... 37064
Boxley View Ln ... 37064
Boxwood Dr ... 37069
Boy Scout Rd ... 37064
Boyd Mill Ave & Pike ... 37064
Braden Cir ... 37067
Bradford Dr ... 37064
Bradley Ct ... 37067
Bradley Dr ... 37069
Brae Burn Ln ... 37069
Braemere Dr ... 37064
Braintree Rd ... 37069
Bramerton Ct ... 37069
Bramley Pl ... 37069
Bramley Close ... 37069
Branch Ct ... 37064
Brandon Dr ... 37064
Brandon Park Ct & Way ... 37064
Brandyleigh Ct ... 37069
Bratton Place Dr ... 37067
Braveheart Dr ... 37064
Braylon Cir ... 37064
Breckenridge Rd ... 37067
Breezway Ln ... 37067
Brennan Ln ... 37067
Brentwood Pointe ... 37067
Brevet Dr ... 37064
Brewster Dr ... 37067
Brick Path Ln ... 37064
Brickenhall Dr ... 37069
Brickston St ... 37067
Bridal Way Ct ... 37069
Bridge St ... 37064
Bridgeway Dr ... 37064
Bridlewood Trl ... 37067
Brienz Valley Dr ... 37064
Brigadoon Way ... 37064
Brighton Ct ... 37069
Briksbury Dr ... 37067
Brilliantine Cir ... 37064
Brimstead Dr ... 37064
Brink Pl ... 37064
Brittney Ct ... 37067
Brixham Park Dr ... 37069
Broadgate Dr ... 37067
Broadley Ct ... 37069
Broadmoor Cir ... 37067
Broadwell Cir ... 37067
Brockton Pl ... 37064
Bromley Park Ln ... 37069
Brookline Ct ... 37069
Brookside Dr ... 37069
Brookwood Ave ... 37064
Browning Way ... 37067
Broyles Ln ... 37069
Bruce Gardens Cir ... 37064
Bryana Ct & Dr ... 37064
Buchanan Ln ... 37064
Buckingham Cir ... 37064
Buckworth Ave ... 37064
Buddleia Ln ... 37067
Buds Farm Ln ... 37064
Buena Vista Dr ... 37069
Buford St ... 37064
Bunker Dr ... 37064
Burghley Ln ... 37064
Burlington Pass ... 37069
Burnside Dr ... 37067
Burton Dr ... 37067
Bush Dr ... 37064
Buttercup Cv ... 37064
Butterfly Ct ... 37069
Butternut Dr ... 37067
Byron Way ... 37064
Cabot Dr ... 37064
Cadet Cir, Ct & Ln ... 37064
Cain Hollow Ct ... 37067
Cairnview Dr ... 37064
Cakebread Ct ... 37067
Calderwood Ct ... 37067
Caldwell Ct ... 37064
Cale Ct ... 37064
Calgary Ct ... 37067
Calib Ct ... 37067
Calista Ct ... 37064
Callahan Pl ... 37067
Callie Way Dr ... 37064
Calloway Ct ... 37067
Calvin Ct ... 37064

Cambridge Pl 37067
Camellia Ct 37064
Cameron Ct 37067
Campbell Rd 37064
Canary Ct 37064
Candlewood Dr 37069
Candytuft Ct 37067
Cannon Dr 37069
Cannon St 37064
Cannonade Cir 37069
Canterbury Ln 37069
Canterbury Rise 37067
Canters Ct 37067
Canton Stone Dr 37067
Cape Breton Ct 37067
Captain Freeman Pkwy 37064
Carden Dr 37069
N & S Cardinal Ct 37067
Cardova Dr 37067
Carl Rd 37064
Carlisle Ln 37064
Carnousti Dr 37069
Carnton Ln 37064
Carolina Close Dr 37069
Caroline Cir 37064
Carolyn Ave 37064
Carothers Pkwy
- 3001-3099 37067
- 3400-3499 37064
- 3500-9299 37067

Carothers Rd 37067
N Carothers Rd 37067
S Carothers Rd
- 3800-4198 37067
- 4200-4299 37067
- 4300-4599 37064

Carphilly Cir 37069
Carr Ave 37064
Carriage Park Dr 37064
Carrington Ct 37064
Carrolton Dr 37064
Carronbridge Way 37067
Carter Ln & St 37064
Carters Creek Pike 37064
Carters Glen Pl 37064
Carver Ct 37064
Cascade Estates Blvd 37064
Cascade Falls Ct 37064
Caselton Ct 37069
Cassie Ct 37064
Casterline Ct 37069
Castle Ct & Dr 37067
Castlebury Ct 37064
Castlewood Dr 37064
Cattail Ln 37064
Cavalcade Cir & Dr 37069
Cavalry Dr 37064
Caysens Square Ln 37064
Cecil Lewis Dr 37067
Cedar Ct & Dr 37064
Cedar Creek Dr 37067
Cedarmont Dr 37067
Cedarview Ln 37067
Celebration Cir 37067
Celeste Ln 37064
Center Point Pl 37064
Century Ct 37064
Century Oak Dr 37069
Chad Ct 37067
Chadwell Ln 37069
Chalford Ct 37069
Chamberlain Park Ln 37069
Champions Cir 37064
Championship Blvd 37064
Chantilly Ln 37067
Chapel Ct 37069
N Chapel Rd 37067
Chapel Lake Cir 37069
Chapelwood Dr & Ln 37069
Chardonnay Trce 37067
Charing Cross Cir 37064
Charleston Ln 37067
Chase Ct 37064
Chase Point Dr 37067
Chatfield Way 37067
Chatsworth Ct 37064
Cheekwood Ct 37069
Chelsey Cv 37064
Cheltenham Ave 37064
Cherokee Pl 37064
Cherry Dr 37064
Cherry Grove Rd 37069
Cherry Hills Dr 37069
Cherrywood Pt 37064
Cheshire Cir 37069
Chester Stevens Ct & Rd 37067
Chesterfield Pl 37064
Chestnut Ln 37064
Cheswicke Ln 37067
Chickasaw Pl 37064
Chickering Dr 37064
Childs Ln 37067
Chippenham Ct 37069
E & W Chownings Ct 37064
Chrisman Dr 37064
Church St 37064
Churchill Pl 37067
Circle View Dr 37067
Circuit Rd 37064
Citadel Ct 37067
Citation Dr 37069
Claire Ct 37064
Clairmonte Cir, Dr & Ln 37064
Clapham St 37064
Clare Park Dr 37069
Clareece Park Pl 37069
Clarendon Cir 37069
Claret Ct 37067
Claridge Ct 37064
Claude Yates Dr 37064
Clayborne Ct 37064
Clearbrook Ct 37064
Cleburne St 37064
N & S Clematis Ct 37067
Cliffe Run 37067
Cline Ct 37067
Clocktower Dr 37067
Clouston Ct 37064
Clover Leaf Ln 37067
Clover Meadows Dr 37067
Cloverbrook Ln 37067
Clovercroft Rd 37067
Cloversprings Ln 37067
N & S Clubhouse Ct 37067
Clyde Cir 37064
Coachman Dr 37069
Cobbler Ridge Ct & Rd 37064
Cobert Ln 37064
Coburn Ln 37069
Cody Cir 37064
Coe Ln 37064
Coleman Rd 37064
Collier Dr 37064
Collinwood Pl 37069
Collinwood Close 37069
Colonial Ct 37064
Colt Ln 37069
Columbia Ave
- 500-599 37064
- 510-510 37065
- 600-3098 37064
- 601-3099 37064

Columbia Pike 37064
Compton Ln 37069
Comtide Blvd 37067
Confederate Dr 37064
Connelly Ct 37064
Conservatory Dr 37067
Cool Springs Blvd 37067
Cool Springs Ct 37064
Cooper Creek Ln 37064
Cooper Ledge Cir 37064
Copperfield Pl 37067
Coral Bell Ln 37067
Coreopsis Ct 37067
Corey Dr 37067
Corinne Ct 37064
Cormac St 37064
Cornelia Ct 37064
Cornerstone Cir, Ln & Way 37064
Coronation Ct 37064
Corporate Centre Dr 37067
Cothran Dr 37064
Cotswold Park Ct 37069
Cottage Ln 37064
Cottingham Dr 37067
Cotton Ln 37069
Cottonwood Cir, Ct & Dr 37069
Countess Nicole Ct 37067
Country Rd 37069
Country Club Pl 37069
Countryside Ct & Dr 37069
Countrywood Dr 37064
County Landfill Rd 37064
N & S Course Vw 37067
Covey Dr 37067
Crabtree Ct 37069
Crafton Ave 37064
Cranesville Ln 37064
Creekside Br, Ct & Ln 37064
Creekstone Blvd 37064
Creekwood Ct 37064
Crescent Centre Dr 37067
Crestfield Pl 37069
Crestlawn Pl 37064
Crestview Ct 37064
Crofton Park Ln 37069
Cromford Pl 37069
Crooked Oak Ct 37067
Cross Creek Ct & Dr 37067
Crossway Dr 37064
Crowder Rd 37064
Crown Dr 37064
Crowne Brook Cir 37067
Crystal Falls Cir 37064
Cullman Ct 37064
Culpepper Cir & Ln 37064
Cumberland Park Dr 37069
Cummins St 37064
Curry Ct 37064
Cynthiana Ln 37067
Cypress Ct 37069
Cypress Point Dr 37069
Dabney Dr 37064
Daffodil Ct 37064
Dale Ct 37067
Dale Ewing Rd 37064
Dallas Blvd 37064
Dandridge Dr 37067
Daniel Mcmahon Ln 37069
Daniels Dr 37064
Dark Woods Dr 37064
Darrell Ct 37064
Dartmoor Ln 37064
Davenport Blvd 37069
David Dr 37069
Davidson Dr 37064
Davis Hollow Rd 37064
Daylily Dr 37067
Deanna Ct 37067
Decatur Cir 37067
Deejay Dr 37064
Deer Haven Ct 37067
Deer Lake Rd 37069
Deer Park Ln 37069
Deer Park Close 37069
Deercrest Cir 37069
Deerfield Ct & Ln 37069
Del Rio Ct 37069
Del Rio Pike
- 100-999 37064
- 2900-3299 37069

Delacy Ct 37067
Delta Blvd 37067
Delta Springs Ln 37064
Denby Ct 37064
Dennis Ct 37067
Derby Ln 37069
Devonshire Dr 37064
Devrow Ct 37064
Diamond Ct & Dr 37064
Dickinson Ln 37069
Dodson Ct 37064
Doe Rdg 37067
Dogwood Ln 37064
Dominion Ct 37067
Donelson Creek Pkwy 37064
Dora Whitley Rd 37064
Doral Dr 37069
Dorris Ct 37069
Doug Thompson Rd 37064
Douglass Glen Ln 37064
Dover Pl 37067
Downs Blvd 37064
Downy Meade Ct & Dr 37064
Drake Ct 37064
Draper Ct 37064
Drayton Ct 37067
Drury Ln 37064
Duckhorn Ct 37067
Duke Dr 37067
Dunbar Ct 37064
Dunbrooke Ct 37064
Dundee Dr 37064
Dunkeld Ct 37069
Dunrobin Dr 37067
Dunwoody Ct 37069
Durham Manor Dr 37064
Dyke Bennett Rd 37064
Eagles Glen Ct & Dr 37067
Earlham Ct 37067
Eastcastle Ct 37069
Eastern Flank Cir 37064
Eastgate Ct 37067
Eastgate Crescent Pl 37069
Eastover Ct 37064
Eastview Cir 37064
Eastwind Ct 37064
Eaton Ct 37064
Echo Ln 37069
Eddy Ct & Ln 37064
Eden Park Dr 37067
Edgewater Ct 37069
Edgewood Blvd 37064
Edgewood Ct 37069
Edinboro Way 37064
Edmond Ct 37064
Edward Curd Ln 37067
Edwards Cir & Dr 37064
Egypt Hollow Rd 37064
Eiderdown Ct & Dr 37064
Eliot Rd 37064
Elk Hollow Ct 37069
Elk Springs Ct 37069
Ellington Dr 37064
Elm St 37064
Elmwood Ct 37064
Emerald Ct & Dr 37064
Emery Ln 37064
Emily Ct 37064
W End Cir 37064
Engle Ct 37069
Englishwood Ct 37067
Enterprise Ct 37067
Ericksen Ct 37064
Erin Ln 37064
Ernest Rice Ln 37069
Essex Ct 37067
Essex Park Cir 37069
Eton Ct 37064
Evan Ct 37064
Evans St 37064
Evelyn Ct 37064
Everal Ln 37064
Everbright St 37064
Ewingville Dr 37064
Excalibur Ct 37067
Fair St 37064
Fairbourne Grn 37069
Fairfax Pl 37064
Fairground St 37064
Fairmont Dr 37064
Falcon Creek Dr 37067
Falkirk Ct 37064
Falls Church Ct 37064
Fanchers Ct 37064
Fannich Ct 37064
Farmington Dr 37069
Farrier Ln 37064
Farrington Pl 37069
Fawn Cir & Ct 37067
Featherstone Dr 37069
Federal St 37067
Fenner Ct 37067
Fernvale Rd 37064
Ferris Ct 37067
Fieldcrest Cir 37064
Fielden Ct 37067
Fieldmont Rd 37067
Fieldstone Pkwy 37069
Figuers Dr 37064
Findon Ct 37064
Fine Ln 37067
Finnhorse Ln 37064
Fire Tower Rd 37064
Firefly Ct 37069
Firth Ct 37067
Fitzgerald St 37064
Flagstone Ct & Dr 37069
Flanders Ct 37067
Fleetwood Dr 37064
Flemings Ct 37067
Fletcher Ct 37067
Flintlock Ct & Dr 37064
Floyd Rd 37064
Fontaine Dr 37064
Ford Ln 37064
Forest Lake Ct 37064
Forest Ridge Ct 37069
Forrest Dr & St 37064
Forrest Crossing Blvd & Cir 37064
Forrest Park Cir 37064
Fort Granger Dr 37064
Founders Pointe Blvd 37064
Fountainwood Blvd 37064
Fowler Cir 37064
E & W Fowlkes St 37064
Fox Hill Ct 37069
Foxcroft Cir 37067
Foxhaven Dr 37069
Foxwood Ln 37069
Franintr Dr 37067
Franklin Rd
- 100-300 37064
- 301-301 37069
- 302-302 37064
- 303-599 37069
- 601-699 37069

Franklin Common Ct 37067
Franklin South Ct 37064
Frazier Dr 37067
Freedom Ct & Dr 37067
Freesia Ct 37064
French Town Ln 37067
Friars Bridge Pass 37064
Fristoe Ln 37064
Front St 37064
Fulton Greer Rd 37064
Fulwood Dr 37067
Gadsden Pl 37067
Gainsway Ct 37069
Gallagher Dr 37064
Gallant Ridge Dr 37064
Galleria Blvd 37067
Galloway Dr 37064
Gambrel St 37067
Garden Club Ct 37067
Gardendale Dr 37064
Gardengate Dr 37069
Gardenia Way 37064
Gardenridge Dr 37069
Gardenshire Ct 37069
Gardner Dr 37064
Garner Hall Ln 37064
Garrison Rd 37064
Gatewick Ct 37067
Gay Dr 37069
General George Patton Dr 37067
General J B Hood Dr 37069
General N B Forrest Dr 37069
Generals Retreat Pl 37064
Generals Way Ct 37064
Georgian Cir 37067
German Ln 37067
Gilbert Dr 37064
Gillespie Dr & Rd 37067
Gillette Ct & Dr 37069
Gilroy Cir 37067
Gist St 37064
Glade Ct & Dr 37069
Gladstone Ln 37064
Glass Ln & St 37064
Glass Springs Dr 37064
Glastonbury Dr 37069
Glen Haven Ln 37069
Glen Lakes Ct 37069
Glen Oaks Dr 37067
Glen View Cv 37064
Glenbeag Ct 37064
Glenbrook Dr 37064
Glencoe Ct 37064
Glendower Pl 37064
Gleneagle Ln 37067
Gloucester Ct & St 37064
Gold Hill Ct 37069
Golden Ct 37064
Golden Leaf Ct 37067
Golden Meadow Ln 37067
Golf Club Ln 37064
Good Neighbors Rd 37064
Goose Creek Byp & Dr 37064
Gosey Ln 37064
Gosey Hill Rd 37064
Gosling Dr 37064
Gothic Ct 37067
Governors Ridge Ct 37064
Grace Point Ct 37067
Grafton Dr 37069
Granbury St 37064
Granby Ct 37069
Grandview Mnr 37064
Grange Hill Ct 37067
Granger View Cir & Ct 37064
Grant Park Ct & Dr 37067
Granville Rd 37064
Grassmere Rd 37064
Gray Fox Ln 37069
Grayson Ct 37064
Green Rd 37069
Green St 37064
Green Acres Dr 37064
Green Chapel Rd 37064
Green Harbor Cir 37069
Green Hills Blvd 37067
Green Valley Blvd 37064
Greenbriar Dr & Rd 37064
Greenland Dr 37069
Greenleaf Way 37069
Greenmeadow Dr 37069
Greer Ct 37064
Greerview Cir 37064
Grenadier Dr 37064
Grey Cliff Ct & Dr 37064
Greystone Dr 37069
Grigsby Rd 37064
Grove Ln 37064
Guineveres Retreat 37067
Guy Ferrell Rd 37067
Habersham Way 37067
Haddon Ct 37067
Haislip Ct 37064
Halberton Dr 37069
Halfacre Dr 37064
Hamlet Dr 37064
Hamlets End Way 37067
Hampden Ct 37069
Hampsted Ln 37069
N Hampton Ct & Cv 37064
Hampton Height Ln 37064
Hanley Ln 37069
Hanson Dr 37067
Hardison Dr 37064
Hargrove Rd 37064
Hargrove Ridge Rd 37064
Harlinsdale Ct 37069
Harlinsdale Dr 37064
Harold Ct 37064
S & W Harpeth Dr & Rd 37064
Harpeth Hills Dr 37069
Harpeth Industrial Ct 37064
Harpeth Ridge Rd 37069
Harpeth School Rd 37064
Harris Ct 37064
Harris Patton Ct 37064
Harrow Ln 37064
Harrowden Ln 37064
Hartington Ct 37064
Hartland Rd 37069
Harts Landmark Dr 37069
Harve Ct 37067
Harvest Ct 37067
Harvington Dr 37069
Harwick Dr 37067
Hastings Ln 37069
Hatfield Dr 37064
Hattington Dr 37067
Hatton Pl 37067
Hawthorne Cir & Ct 37069
Hay Market Ct 37067
Heather Ct & Dr 37069
Heatherset Pl 37069
Heatherset Close 37069
Heathersett Dr 37064
Heathstone Cir 37069
Heaton Close 37069
Helmsdale Ln 37069
Helping Hands Dr 37064
Henpeck Ln 37064
Herbert Dr 37067
Heritage Ct 37067
Heritage Pointe Dr & Pl 37064
Hermitage Dr 37067
Hickory Dr & Ln 37064
Hickory Hills Dr 37067
Hickory Ridge Dr 37064
Hidden River Ln 37069
Hideaway Trl 37069
High Hopes Ct 37064
High Meadow Dr 37069
High Point Ridge Rd 37069
Highgrove Cir 37069
Highland Ave 37064
Highway 96 37064
Hill Dr 37064
Hillhaven Ln 37064
Hillsboro Rd
- 500-1154 37064
- 1155-1197 37069
- 1156-1198 37064
- 1199-2699 37069

Hillside Dr 37067
Hillview Dr 37069
Hillview Ln 37064
Hobbs Dr 37064
Hodges Ct 37067
Holcombe Ln 37064
Holder Rd 37067
Holiday Ct 37067
Holland Park Ln 37069
Hollow Ct 37067
Holly Hill Dr 37064
Hollyhock Way 37064
Holmes Cir 37064
Homestead Ln 37064
Homewood Ct 37067
Honey Suckle Valley Ln 37064
Honeysuckle Cir 37067
Hooper Ln 37064
Hope Ave 37067
Hopewell Ridge Rd 37064
Hopewood Ct 37064
Horthor Dr 37064
Horton Ct & Ln 37064
Hospitality Dr 37067
Houchin Dr 37064
Hourglass Ct 37067
Howell Dr 37069
Howland St 37064
Hudson Ln 37067

Huffine Manor Cir 37067
Huffine Ridge Dr 37067
Hughes Xing 37064
Hulme Ln 37064
Hunt Ct 37064
Hunter Rd 37064
Hunters Bnd & Ct 37069
Hunters Chase Dr 37064
Hunters Trail Dr 37069
Hunting Creek Rd 37069
Hunting Hills Dr 37067
Huntington Ct 37067
Huntsman Cir 37064
Hurstbourne Park Blvd 37067
Hyannis Ct 37064
Idlewild Ct 37069
Incinerator Rd 37064
Independence Dr E 37067
Independence Dr W 37067
Independence Sq 37064
Indian Creek Cir 37064
Indian Head Ct 37069
Indian Meadows Dr 37064
Indian Springs Dr 37064
Indian Valley Rd 37064
Inman Branch Rd 37064
Innovation Dr 37067
International Dr 37067
Inverness Dr 37069
Inwood Way 37064
Iris Pl 37064
Iron Gate Ct & Dr 37069
Irvine Ln 37064
Isaac Ln 37064
Ivan Creek Dr 37064
Jackson Hollow Rd 37064
Jackson Lake Dr 37069
Jackson White Rd 37064
Jaclyn Ct 37064
James Ave 37064
Jameson Dr 37064
Jamison Station Ln 37064
Janice Ct 37064
Jasmine Ct 37067
Jasper Ave 37064
Jaybee Ct 37064
Jeb Stuart Dr 37069
Jeff Holt Rd 37064
Jefferson Ct & Dr 37064
Jefferson Davis Dr 37069
Jennette Pl 37064
Jennifer Ct 37069
Jennings St 37064
Jensome Ln 37064
Jepson Ct 37067
Jessica Ln 37064
Jewell Ave 37064
Jill Ct 37064
Joel Cheek Blvd 37064
John Clark Ct 37067
John J Ct 37067
John Williams Rd 37067
Johnson Aly & Cir 37064
Joining St 37064
Jonathan Ct 37069
Jordan Rd 37067
Joseph St 37064
Jubilee Ridge Rd 37069
Julia Ct 37064
Julianna Cir 37064
Justin Dr 37064
Kaci Ln 37064
Kaitlyn Ct 37067
Karnes Dr 37064
Kathleen Ct N & S 37064
Keller Trl 37064
Kelly Ct 37064
Kemp Farm Ln 37064
Kendall Ct 37069
Kennedy Ct 37064
Kensington Pl 37067
Kentons Way 37067
Kerlind Ct 37067
Keswick Grove Ln 37067
Keystone Ct & Dr 37064
Kilburn Ct 37067

Kiln Hill Ct 37069
Kilrush Dr 37069
Kiltie Way 37069
Kimberleigh Ct 37069
King Ln 37064
King Arthur Cir & Dr 37067
King Davids Ct 37067
King Richards Ct 37067
King William Ct 37064
Kings Gate Ln 37064
Kings Mill Ct 37064
Kingsley Ct 37067
Kinnard Dr 37064
Kinnard Springs Rd 37064
Kinnie Rd 37069
Kirkwood Dr 37067
Kittrell Rd 37064
Knob Ct 37064
Knob Hill Dr 37069
Knoll View Dr 37067
Knowle Pl 37069
Kristen Ct 37064
Kylie Ln 37064
Ladd Rd 37067
Lagan Ct 37064
E & W Lake Ct 37067
Lake Ridge Ct & Way 37069
Lake Valley Ct & Dr 37069
Lakemont Cir 37067
Lakeview Dr 37067
Lancaster Dr 37064
Lancelot Ln 37064
Landon Ct 37064
Landrake Close 37069
Lanes End Dr 37067
Langford Ct 37067
Langley Dr 37064
Larkspur Cv 37064
Larkton Pl 37069
Lasalle Ct 37067
Lasata Dr 37067
Laurawood Ln 37067
Laurel Ct 37064
Laurelbrooke Ln 37069
Lawn View Ct & Ln 37064
Lawrence Rd 37069
Lawrin Park 37069
Leaf Ct 37067
Leanne Way 37069
Leaton Ct 37069
Ledgelawn Ct 37064
Lee Cir & Ct 37064
Lee Valley Trl 37064
Leeds Dr 37067
Leesburg Ct 37067
Legacy Hills Dr 37064
Legends Club Ln 37069
Legends Crest Dr 37069
Legends Glen Ct 37069
Legends Park Cir 37069
Legends Ridge Ct &
Dr 37069
Leicester Ct 37067
Leigh Valley Rd 37069
Leipers Creek Rd 37064
Leipers Valley Trl 37064
Lena Ln 37067
Les Waggoner Rd 37067
Les Watkins Rd 37064
Letitia Dr 37067
Levisa Ln 37064
Lewisburg Ave & Pike 37064
Lexington Pkwy 37069
Liberty Pike
300-899 37064
1000-1799 37067
Liberty Hills Dr 37067
N & S Lick Creek Rd &
Trl 37064
Lighthouse Ter 37064
Lilac Cir 37064
Lille Ct 37067
Lilly Valley Trl 37064
Limerick Ln 37067
Linden Ct 37069
Linden Isle Dr 37064

Lindisfarne Rd 37064
Lindsey Ct 37064
Link Dr 37064
Lionheart Ct 37067
Lipton Ct 37067
Lish Pewitt Rd 37064
Little East Fork Rd 37064
Little Teton Pass 37064
Lockwood Ridge Ln 37064
Log Valley Trl 37064
Logans Cir 37067
Loggers Run 37069
London Ln 37067
Lone Oak Trl 37064
Long Ln 37064
Longmont Ct 37067
Longwood Dr 37069
Loomis Ct 37069
Lorena Ct & Dr 37067
Loston Ct 37064
Lovell Ct 37069
Lucerne Ln 37064
Lucinda Ct 37064
Lula Ln 37064
Lumber Dr 37064
Lumsden Ln 37064
Luna Ct 37064
Lundy Pass 37069
Lyle Ct 37064
Lynn Ct 37064
Lynnwood Ct & Dr 37069
Lyon Ct 37067
Lyric Ln & Spgs 37064
Lysbeth Ct 37064
Mack Ln 37064
Mackenzie Way 37064
Maddux Way 37069
Madeira St 37064
Madeline Ct 37064
Madering St 37064
Madison Ct 37064
Magnolia Dr 37064
Main St 37064
Majestic Ln 37064
Malcolm Dr 37067
Mallard Ct & Dr 37064
Mallory Ln 37067
Mallory Station Rd 37067
Malvern Rd 37069
Manderly Trl 37069
Mandy Ct 37069
Manley Ct 37069
Manning Ln 37064
Mansfield Ct 37069
Maple Ct 37064
Maple Dr 37064
Maple Ln 37067
Maplegrove Ct & Dr 37064
Maplewood Dr 37064
N & S Margin St 37064
Marigold Dr 37064
Mark Ct 37067
Market St 37067
Market Exchange Ct 37067
Marlborough Pl 37064
Marrimans Ct 37067
Martin Ct 37069
Martingale Dr 37067
Mary Lindsay Polk Dr 37067
Marymount Dr 37067
Masters Ct & Dr 37064
Matherson Ct 37067
Matthew Pl 37064
Mauldin Woods Trl 37064
Mayberry Ct & Ln 37064
Mayfield Dr 37067
Mcarthur Ct 37064
Mccain Dr 37064
Mccallister Ct 37064
Mcewen Dr 37067
Mcgavock Cir 37064
Mcgeachy Ln 37067
Mcgregor Ct 37064
Mcintyre Ct 37069
Mclean Ct 37067

Mclemore Cir, Rd &
Way 37064
Mcmillan Rd 37064
Mcphail Ct 37064
Meacham Ln 37064
W Meade Blvd 37064
Meadowcrest Cir 37064
Meadowglade Ln 37064
Meadowgreen Ct & Dr 37069
Meadowlawn Dr 37064
Mealer St 37067
Meandering Way 37067
Medford Pl 37064
Meeks Rd 37064
Meeting St 37064
Megan Ct 37064
Melander Ct 37064
Melba Cir 37064
Melody Dr 37067
Mentelle Dr 37069
Mercury Dr 37064
Meredith Pl 37064
Meridian Blvd 37067
Meridian Ct 37069
Merion Dr 37069
Merlot Ct 37064
Merylinger Ct 37067
Middleboro Cir 37064
Midlothian Dr 37069
Midwood St 37067
Mile End Rd 37064
Milky Way Cir & Ln 37064
Mill Pond Cir 37069
Millbank Ln 37064
Millersprings Ct 37064
Millhouse Dr 37064
Milton Fox Rd 37064
Minga Cir 37064
Miranda Pl 37067
Mirrasou Ct 37067
Mission Ct 37067
Mistico Ln 37064
Misty Ct 37064
Misty Rivers Ln 37064
Misty Woods Ct 37067
Mockingbird Dr 37069
Moher Blvd 37069
Molly Bright Ln 37064
Monks Way 37064
Monte Bella Pl 37067
Montelena Dr 37067
Montgomery Way 37067
Monticello Rd 37064
Montpier Dr 37069
Montridge Ct 37067
Montrose Ct 37069
Montwood Ct 37064
Moore Rd 37064
Moran Rd 37069
Morning Mist Ln 37064
Morningside Dr 37069
Morrissey St 37064
Morriswood Ct & Dr 37064
Moss Ln 37064
Mount Hope St 37064
Mountbatten Dr 37067
Mt Hebron Ln 37064
Mt Laura Ln 37064
Muirfield Dr 37069
Mulberry St 37064
Murfreesboro Rd
400-1399 37064
1400-4725 37067
Murray Creek Ln 37069
Myles Manor Ct 37064
Nadine Ln 37064
Nancy Ct 37067
Nantucket Cir 37069
Narrow Ford Ln 37064
Natchez Rd 37069
Natchez St 37064
Natchez Trace Rd 37064
Natchez Valley Ln 37064
Nathan Tomlin Rd 37064
Neely Ct 37067
Nestledown Dr 37067

New Highway 96 W 37064
Newbary Ct 37069
Newcastle Dr 37067
Niblick Ct 37064
Nichol Mill Ln 37067
Nissan Way 37067
Noah Dr 37064
Noble Cir 37069
Noble King Rd 37064
Nolen Ln 37064
Norman Ct 37064
Norman Park Ct 37067
Norvich Ct 37069
Oak Cir & Dr 37064
Oak Meadow Dr
400-811 37064
810-810 37068
813-999 37064
Oakbranch Cir 37064
Oakland Hills Dr 37069
Oakleaf Ct & Dr 37064
Oakmont Dr 37069
Oakwood Ct, Dr & Rd E
& W 37064
Ober Brienz Ln 37064
Old 96 37064
Old Arno Rd 37064
Old Carters Creek
Pike 37064
Old Charlotte Pike
2400-2699 37064
3700-3899 37069
Old Charlotte Pike E 37064
Old Charlotte Pike W 37064
Old Coleman Rd 37064
Old Harding Pike &
Rd 37064
Old Hillsboro Rd
1200-1799 37069
1800-4349 37064
4351-4399 37064
Old Liberty Pike 37064
Old Natchez Trce 37069
Old Nathan Tomlin Rd 37064
Old Peytonsville Rd 37064
Old South Berrys Chapel
Rd 37069
Olde Cameron Ln 37067
Oleander St 37064
Olympia Pl 37067
Olympia Fields Dr 37069
Oneil Ln 37067
Orchid Trl 37064
Ormesby Pl 37064
Oscar Green Rd 37064
Overlook Dr 37069
Overview Ln 37064
Owen Watkins Ct 37067
Owl Hollow Rd 37064
Oxford Dr 37064
Oxford Gln 37067
Oxford Glen Dr 37067
Pace Hvn 37069
Padgett Ct 37067
Panther Ct 37064
Parham Rd 37064
Parish Pl 37067
Park St 37064
Park Run Dr 37067
Parker Branch Rd 37064
Parkview Dr 37064
Parkway Ct 37064
Parshot Ln 37064
Parsons Pl 37064
Partnership Cir 37064
Passage Ln 37064
Pate Rd 37064
Patricia Lee Ct 37069
Patrick Ave 37064
Patriot Ln 37067
Peaceful Haven Ln 37064
Peach Hollow Rd 37064
Pearl St 37064
Pearre Springs Way 37064
Pebble Beach Dr 37069
Pebble Creek Rd 37064

Pebble Glen Dr 37064
Pebble Springs Dr 37067
Pebble View Dr 37064
Pemberton Heights Dr 37067
Pembroake Ln 37064
Penbrook Dr & Pass 37069
Pendlebury Park Pl 37069
Pendragon Ct 37067
Penn Way Ct 37064
Pennystone Cir & Dr 37067
Periwinkle Cv 37064
Perkins Dr 37064
Perkins Ln 37069
Perrone Way 37069
Petes Pl 37064
N & S Petway St 37064
Pewitt Rd 37064
Peyton Ct 37064
Peytona Ln 37064
Peytonsville Rd 37064
Peytonsville Trinity Rd 37064
Phillips Dr 37067
Pickwick Park Ct 37067
Piedmont Cir 37064
Pigskin Ct 37064
Pilati Pl 37064
Pine Circle Dr 37069
Pinehurst Dr 37069
Pinewood Rd 37064
Pintail Ct 37067
Pioneer Ln 37064
Pishon Trl 37064
Players Mill Rd 37067
Plaza St 37064
Pleasant Hill Rd 37067
Ploughmans Bend Dr 37064
Plumleaf Ct 37069
Polk Place Dr 37064
Pond View Ct 37064
Ponder Dr 37069
Pontypool Pass 37069
Poor House Hollow
Rd 37064
Poplar Rd & St 37064
Porter St 37064
Poteat Pl 37064
Powder Mill Dr 37064
Powell Sullivan Rd 37064
Poydras St 37069
Prairie View Dr 37064
Pratt Ln 37064
Premier Ct S 37067
Prescott Pl 37069
Prestwick Ln 37069
Price Rd 37069
Priest Pl 37067
Primrose Ln 37064
Prince Charles Way 37064
Prince Of Wales Ct 37064
Prince Valiant Ct 37067
Prince William Ln 37064
Princess Cir 37064
Promenade Ct 37064
Prospect Ave 37064
Provence Ct 37067
Providence Trl 37064
Public Sq 37064
Quail Ct 37064
Quail Hollow Cir 37067
Queen Marys Ct 37064
Queens Ct 37064
Quest Ridge Rd 37064
Rafe Ct 37064
Ralston Ln 37064
Rand Pl 37064
Rathkeale Ln 37067
Ravens Trace Ln 37064
Ravenwood Ct 37064
Reams Pl 37064
Rebecca Ct 37064
Rebel Cir 37064
Red Fox Ct 37064
Redbud Ct 37064
Reddick St 37064
Redwing Ct 37064
Regiment Ct 37064

Reigh Ct 37069
Reliance Dr 37067
Resource Pkwy 37067
Reveille Ct 37064
Revere Ln 37064
Reynolds Rd 37064
Rich Cir 37064
Richards Glen Dr 37067
Richmond Pl 37064
Ridge View Ct 37067
Ridgecrest Dr 37069
Ridgemont Pl 37064
Ridgestone Dr 37064
Ridgetop Ct 37067
Ridgeway Dr 37067
Ridgewood Rd 37064
Ridley Ct & Dr 37064
Rigby Dr 37064
Ripley Ln 37064
Rising Sun Ln 37064
River Landing Dr 37069
River Ridge Pl 37064
Riverbend Dr 37064
Riverbend Nuss 37064
Rivergate Dr 37064
Rivermont Cir 37064
Riverside Dr 37064
Riverview Dr 37064
Riverwood Ct, Dr & Pl 37069
Rizer Point Dr 37069
Road Of The Round
Table 37067
Roanoke Pl 37064
Rob Roy Ct 37064
Roberts St 37064
Robin Hill Rd 37064
Rocking Chair Pl 37067
Rockymayne Ln 37064
Roderick Cir & Pl 37064
Rombauer Ct & Dr 37067
Ronald Dr 37064
Rosa Helm Way 37067
Rose Hill Ct 37069
Rosebud Cir 37064
Rothwell Pl 37069
Royal Xing 37064
Royal Oaks Blvd 37067
S Royal Oaks Blvd 37064
Royal Oaks Ct 37064
Rucker Ave 37064
Running Springs Ct 37064
Rural Plains Cir 37064
Rush St 37067
Russell Rd 37064
Russem Ln 37064
Ruth Ct 37064
Rutherford Ln 37064
Saddlebridge Ln 37069
Saddleview Ct, Dr &
Ter 37067
Sadler Way 37069
Saint Andrews Dr 37069
Saint Anne Way 37064
Saint Georges Way 37064
Saint Ignatius Ln 37064
Saint James Dr 37064
Saint John Pl 37064
Saint Michaels Ct 37064
Salem Ct 37064
Sam Houston Ct 37069
Sandcastle Cir & Rd 37069
Sanders Ct 37069
Sarah Anne Ct 37064
Sarah Davis Ln 37064
Sattui Ct 37064
Savage Pointe Dr 37064
Savannah Way 37067
Savannah Springs Dr 37064
Savoy Ct 37064
Sawyer Rd 37069
Sawyer Bend Cir, Ct &
Rd 37069
Scarlett Park Ct 37069
Scenic Hills Dr 37064
Scenic View Dr W 37064
Schoolpath Ln 37064

Scioto Ln 37069
Scotsman Ln 37064
Scott Dr 37067
Scottish Ct 37064
Scramblers Knob 37069
Scruggs Ave 37064
Scurlock Ct 37067
Seaboard Ln 37067
Seaton Park Pl 37069
Sebastiani Ct 37067
Sedberry Rd 37064
Sedgewick Pl 37067
Selinawood Pl 37067
Seminole Dr 37069
Seneca Ct 37067
Serene Valley Trl 37064
Serinas Way 37064
Settlers Ct 37064
Shade Tree Ln 37064
Shadow Cv 37069
Shadow Green Dr 37064
Shadowlawn Ct 37069
Shady Glen Ct 37069
Shadycrest Ln 37069
Shallow Stream Ln 37064
Shannon Ln 37064
Sharpe Dr 37064
Shawnee Dr 37064
Sheffield Pl 37067
Shelby Ln 37064
Shenandoah Trl 37069
Shepherd Dr 37069
Sherbourne Grn 37069
Sherwood Ter 37064
Shingle Way 37067
Short Ct 37064
Signature Ct 37064
Silverado Trce 37064
Silvercreek Ct 37069
Simmons Ln 37069
Sims Ln 37069
Sir John Ct 37064
Sir Winston Pl 37064
Skye Valley Rd 37064
Skyhawk Pl 37064
Skylark Ct 37064
Slade Ct 37067
Sliders Knob Ave 37067
Smith Ln 37069
Snapdragon Ct 37067
Sneed Rd W 37069
Sneed Glen Dr 37069
Snowbird Hollow Rd 37064
Snowden St W 37064
Solomon Dr 37064
Somerton Park 37069
Sontag Dr 37064
Southall Ln & Rd 37064
Southampton Ct 37064
Southern Valley Pass 37064
Southwinds Dr 37064
Spalding Ct 37069
Sparks Creek Ln 37064
Spears Grove Ln 37064
Spencer Creek Pass & Rd 37069
Spicer Farm Ln 37064
Spokane Ct 37069
Spring St 37064
Spring Cabin Ln 37064
Spring Creek Dr 37067
Spring View Dr 37064
Springcroft Dr 37067
Springdale Dr 37064
Springhouse Cir & Ct 37067
Springlake Dr 37064
S Springs Dr 37067
St Stephens Way 37064
Stable Ct, Dr & Rd 37069
Stableford Ln 37069
Stadium Ct 37064
Stafford Close 37069
Stagecoach Cir & Dr 37067
Stags Leap Way 37064
Stalcup Ct 37064
Stanford Dr 37067
Stanley Park Ln 37069
Stansberry Ln 37069
Stanton Hall Ln 37069
Stanwick Dr 37067
Stardust Ct 37069
Starlight Ln 37069
Starling Ln 37064
Starnes Mill Rd 37067
State Blvd 37064
E & W Statue Ct 37067
Stefan Ct 37064
Sterling Park Ter 37069
Stewart St 37064
Still House Hollow Rd 37064
Stillcreek Dr 37064
Stoddard Ct 37064
Stone Mill Ln 37064
Stonebridge Park Dr 37069
Stonegate Dr 37064
Stonehaven Cir 37064
Stonewall Jackson Dr 37069
Stonewater Blvd 37064
Stoney Point Ln 37067
Strahl St 37064
Stratford Ct 37069
Strathmore Dr 37064
Stream Valley Blvd 37064
Streamside Ln 37064
Sturbridge Dr 37064
Sugartree Ln 37064
Summer Haven Cir 37069
Summer Hill Cir & Rd 37064
Summerset Grn 37069
Sumter Ct 37067
Sun Valley Rd 37069
Sundance Ln 37064
Sundown Cir 37069
Sunflower Ct 37064
Sunrise Cir 37067
Sunset Dr 37064
Sunset Ridge Dr 37069
Sunwater Cv 37064
Surrey Ln 37067
Susan Ct 37064
Sussex Ct 37067
Sutters Way 37067
Swanson Ln 37064
Sweeney Hollow Rd 37064
Sweethaven Ct 37069
Sycamore Dr & St 37064
T J Pass 37064
Tabitha Dr 37064
Talbot Trl 37069
Talon Way 37069
Tam O Shanter Cir 37069
Tamara Cir 37069
Tarragon Ct 37064
Tarrington Ln 37069
Tattinger Ct 37064
Taylor Cemetery Rd 37064
Tee Lolly Ln 37064
Teil Dr 37064
Temple Rd 37069
Temple Crest Dr & Trl 37064
Tensaw Cir 37067
Terrapin St 37067
Terri Park Way 37067
Thatcher Way 37064
The Lady Of The Lake Ln 37067
Thomas Glen Cir 37069
Thompson Aly 37064
Thornbrook Ln 37064
Thornton Dr 37064
Thrushgill Ln 37067
Tiffany Ct 37064
Tiger Lily Ct 37064
Tilton Dr 37067
Timberline Ct & Dr 37069
Tinnan Ave 37067
Tippecanoe Dr 37067
Tippett Hollow Ct 37064
Toddington Ct 37067
Toliver Ct 37067
Toll House Cir 37064
Tom Anderson Rd 37064
Tom Robinson Rd 37064
Tonbridge Cir 37064
Tonya Ct 37064
Toon Creek Ln 37064
Towne Park Ln 37067
Townsend Blvd 37064
Trace End Dr 37069
Traceview Dr 37064
Trail Ridge Dr 37067
Tramore Ct 37067
Traviston Dr 37064
Treelawn Pl 37064
Treemont Ln 37069
Treeshore Ln 37069
Trent Park Pl 37069
Trenton Ln 37067
Trinity Rd 37067
Triple Lindy Ln 37067
Tristan Dr 37064
Troon Ct 37069
Trotter Dr 37067
Trotters Ct, Ln & Pl 37067
Truman Rd 37064
Tudor Ct 37067
Tulip Ln 37064
Tullamore Ct & Ln 37067
Tulloss Rd 37067
Turnberry Dr 37064
Turnbrook Ct & Ln 37064
Turndale Ct 37064
Turning Wheel Ln 37067
Twickenham Pl 37069
Twin Oaks Ct & Dr 37064
Twin Square Way 37067
Two Rivers Ln 37069
Tyne Dr 37064
Tynebrae Dr 37064
Tywater Crossing Blvd 37064
Unity Cir 37064
Upland Dr 37067
Valley Creek Ct 37064
Valley Ridge Rd 37064
Valleyview Dr 37064
Valor Ct 37064
Vantage Way 37067
Vaughn Rd 37069
Vaughn Crest Dr 37069
Vera Valley Rd 37064
Verandah Ln 37064
Verde Meadow Dr 37067
Vernon Rd 37067
Verona Dr 37064
Victoria Ct 37067
Victoria Dr 37064
Victorian Park Cir 37067
Vienna Ct 37067
Villinova Pl 37064
Vincent Dr 37067
Vineyard Green Ct 37069
Vinings Ct 37067
Vintage Cir 37064
Vintage Green Ln 37064
Vintage Grove Ln 37064
Violet Dr 37067
Virginia Ct 37064
Vista Cir 37067
Waddell Hollow Rd 37064
Wadestone Trl 37064
Wagon Ct 37064
Walden Dr 37064
Walesworth Dr 37069
Walker Hill Rd 37064
Walnut Dr 37064
Walnut Grove Dr 37069
Walter King Rd 37064
Walter Roberts St 37064
Walters Ave 37067
Walton Rd 37069
Wandering Cir & Trl 37067
Wardington Pass 37069
Warren Cir, Ct & Rd 37067
Warrior Dr 37064
Warwick Park Ln 37069
Waterbury Cir 37067
Watercress Dr 37064
Watermark Way 37064
Watermill Trce 37069
Waterstone Blvd, Ct & Dr 37069
Watkins Rd 37064
Watkins Creek Dr 37067
Watson Branch Dr 37064
Watson Glen Shopping Ctr 37064
Watson View Dr 37067
Waverly Pl 37067
Wayside Ct 37069
Wedgewood Ct & Dr 37069
Wellington Grn 37064
Welsh Ln 37064
Wembly Ct 37067
Wendron Ct 37069
Werthan Cir 37064
Westerly Dr 37067
Westfield Dr 37064
Westhaven Blvd & Cir 37064
Westminster Dr 37067
Westwind Ct 37064
Wexford Ct 37069
Whalley Ct 37069
Wheaton Hall Ln 37069
Whig Ct 37067
Whispering Hills Dr 37069
Whistler Cv 37067
White Ct 37064
White Crane Ln 37064
White Moss Pl 37064
Whitehall Dr 37069
Whitewater Way 37064
Whitley Ct 37069
Whitman St 37064
Wickliff Ct 37067
Widogen Ct 37064
Wilcot Way 37069
Wild Elm St 37064
Wild Timber Ct 37069
Wildflower Ct 37064
Wildwood Ct 37064
Wilhoite Rd 37064
Wilkins Branch Rd 37064
William Wallace Dr 37064
Williamsburg Dr 37069
Williamsburg Pl 37064
Williamson Sq 37064
Willowbrooke Cir 37069
Willowsprings Blvd 37064
Wilshire Dr 37064
Wilson Pike 37067
Wimbledon Cir 37069
Winberry Dr 37064
Winburn Ln 37069
Winchester Dr 37069
Windcrest Ct 37069
Windcross Ct 37067
Winder Cir & Dr 37064
Windmere Ct 37064
Windsor Dr 37064
Windsor Way 37069
Windward Ln 37064
Winged Foot Dr 37069
Winslow Rd 37064
Winter Hill Rd 37069
Wiregrass Ln 37064
Wise Rd 37064
Wisteria Dr 37064
Wolford Cir 37067
Wolverton Dr 37067
Wonderland Ct 37069
Woodcrest Ct & Ln 37067
Wooden Gate Dr 37064
Woodhaven Ct 37069
Woodland Ct 37064
Woods Ct 37064
Woodside Ct 37067
Woodview Ct 37064
Woolman Ct 37064
Worthy Dr 37064
Wren Ct 37064
Wrennewood Ln 37064
Wynbrook Ct 37064
Wyndchase Cir 37067
Wyndham Hill Ln 37069
Wynthrope Way 37067
Yarmouth Ct 37064
Yellow Lantern Ct 37064
Yorkshire Garden Cir & Ct 37067
Yorktown Rd 37064
Youngblood Ct 37067
Zinnia Ln 37064

NUMBERED STREETS

All Street Addresses 37064

GERMANTOWN TN

General Delivery 38138

POST OFFICE BOXES MAIN OFFICE STATIONS AND BRANCHES

Box No.s
All PO Boxes 38183

RURAL ROUTES

03 38138
01, 05 38139

NAMED STREETS

Acorn Landing Dr 38139
Adair Bridge Cv 38138
Adryon Cv 38139
Ainsworth Dr 38138
Akerswood Cv & Dr 38138
Alder Branch Ln 38139
Aldershot Dr 38139
Aldwych Dr 38138
Allen Court Dr 38139
Allenby Cv, Grn & Rd 38139
Allenby Lakes Dr 38139
Almadale Pl 38139
Andora Valley Cv 38139
Anniston Cv 38138
Anns Ln 38138
Apahon Ln 38138
Appaloosa Dr 38138
Apple Valley Cv & Rd 38138
Arden Landing Cv & Dr 38139
Arden Meadows Dr 38139
E & W Arden Oaks Dr 38139
Arden Walk Ln 38138
Armadale Dr 38139
Arthur Rd 38138
Ash Grove Cv 38139
Ashbrook Cv 38138
Ashmere Dr 38139
Ashmont Dr 38138
Ashstone Cv & St 38138
Ashworth Rd 38138
Aspen Pine Cv 38138
Autobahn Dr 38139
Barncliff Cv 38139
Barrentr Dr 38139
Bauxhall Dr 38138
Bavarian Dr 38138
Baynard Loop E & W 38139
Baytown Cv 38138
Beau Ridge Cv 38138
Beaufort Cv 38138
Beaux Bridge Cv 38138
Beaverwood Dr 38138
Bedford Cv & Ln 38139
Beekman Cv & Pl 38139
Bekah Rd 38138
Belfort Dr 38138
Belgrave Cv & Dr 38138
Bell Manor Cv & Dr 38138
Belle Fleurs Cv 38139
Bellville Dr 38138
Bensonwood Dr 38138
Bent Creek Dr 38138
Billy Cross Dr 38138
Birch Park Ln 38139
Birch Post Cv 38138
Birchton Dr 38139
Birchtree Cv & Dr 38138
Birkhill Cv 38139
Birnam Wood Cv & Dr 38138
Bixby Pl N & S 38138
Black Springs Dr 38138
Blackberry Cv 38138
Blackberry Farm Rd 38138
Blackberry Ridge Cv 38138
Blair Ln & Pl 38139
Blue Grass Cv & Ln 38138
Bobwood Dr 38138
Bolling Brook Cv 38138
Bonavis Ln 38139
Bonnybridge Dr 38139
Boulinwood Ln 38138
Brachton Ave 38139
Bradford Pl 38138
Brandemere Dr 38139
Brandon Hall Dr 38139
Branford Pl 38138
Brantwood Cv 38139
Breezy Creek Rd 38138
Brenley Cv 38138
Briar Creek Cv & Dr 38139
Briarbirch Cv 38139
E & N Bridge Dr 38139
Bridge Forest Dr 38138
Bridgetowne Cv 38139
W Brierbrook Rd 38138
Brigance Cv 38139
Broad Leaf Cv 38139
Brook Bridge Cv 38138
Brooke Cir 38139
Brookline Cv 38138
Brooksedge Cv & Dr 38138
Brookside Cv & Dr 38138
Brooxie Cv 38138
Brownleaf Cv 38138
Brush Creek Cv 38138
Bryn Manor Ln 38139
E Bryn Mawr Cir & Cv 38138
Bubbling Brook Dr 38139
Buck Ram Cir 38138
Buckingham Dr 38139
Buckthorn Cv & Dr 38139
Burfordi Ln 38139
Burntwood Cv 38138
Burrows Farm Cv 38138
Buttonwood Cv 38139
Cairn Ridge Cv & Dr 38139
Calkins Cv & Rd 38139
Calkins Hill Cv 38139
Calumet Cv 38138
Cambury Cv E & W 38138
Canale Tagg Cv 38138
Cane Creek Dr 38138
Canella Cv 38138
Canon Gate Cv 38138
Canterbury Cv 38139
Cape Charles Cv 38138
Capital Dr 38138
Cardross Cv 38139
Carnton Dr 38138
Carrick Dr 38139
Carters Grove Ln 38138
Cartwright Cv 38139
Cattail Cv 38138
Cavershamwood Ln 38138
Caylors Wood Cv 38138
Cd Smith Rd 38138
Cedar Dale Dr 38139
Cedar Lake Cv & Dr 38138
Cedar Lane Cv & Dr 38138
Cedar Ridge Cv & Dr 38138
Cedarcrest Cv 38138
Cedarville Dr 38138
Cedarwood Dr 38138
Centre Oak Way 38138
Charstone Dr 38138
Chatham Cv 38138
Chatsworth Dr 38138
Chelsea Park Cv & Dr 38138
Cherry Laurel Cv 38139
Cherryfield Ln 38138
Chertsy Cv & Dr 38138
Chesley Ln 38138
Chestwick Cv & Dr 38139
Chico Cv 38138
E & W Churchill Downs 38138
Cielo Dr 38138
Circle Gate Dr 38138
Circle Trees Cv 38138
Circleshade Dr 38138
Claiborne Dr 38138
Claiborne Farm Cv & Dr 38139
Clandon Cv 38138
Clarington Dr 38138
Clayton Pl 38139
Cliffrose Cv 38138
Cloverbrook Ln 38138
Coachmans Dr 38138
Coathbridge Dr 38139
Cobblestone Cv 38138
Colebrook Cv 38139
Colins Barre Cv 38139
Collection Cv 38138
Colthurst Cv 38139
Colton Cv 38138
Connor Cv 38138
Coppershire Cv N & S 38138
Corbin Cv & Rd 38139
Cordes Cir & Rd 38138
Cordie Lee Cv & Ln 38138
Cordova Cv & Rd 38138
Cornuta Ln 38139
Cornwall Cv & St 38138
Corporate Center Dr 38138
E & S Corporate Edge Dr 38138
Corporate Gardens Dr 38138
Corsica Cv & Dr 38138
Cottage Glen Cir E & W 38138
Cotton Boll Cv & Rd 38138
Cotton Cross Cv & Dr 38138
Cotton Plant Rd 38138
Country Rd 38138
Crail Cv 38139
Cranbrook Dr 38138
Creathwood Cv 38138
Creek Bridge Dr 38138
Creek Ridge Cv 38139
Crestwyn Cv & Dr 38138
Crooked Creek Ln 38138
Crooked Oak Dr 38138
Cross Country Dr 38138
Cross Pike Dr 38138
Cross Ridge Dr 38138
Cross Village Cv & Dr 38138
Crossbow Cv 38138
Crossflower Cv 38138
Crye Crest Cv 38139
Cumbernauld Cir N 38139
Currywood Cv 38138
Dalkeith Dr 38139
Danbury Cv 38138
Danforth Ln 38138
Darby Dan Cv & Ln 38138
Davenport Cv 38139
Deanwood Cv 38139
Deauville Cv 38138
Deep Valley Cv & Dr 38138
Deer Walk Cv 38139
Deerfield Ln 38138
Deerwoods Cv 38139
Dell Oak Cv 38139
Delmead Cv 38139
Deodara Cv 38138
Desmond Cv 38139
N Devonshire Cv & Way 38139
Dewhurst Cv 38138
Dian Cv 38138

Dickens Cv 38139
Doe Meadow Dr 38139
Dogwood Ct 38139
Dogwood Pl 38139
Dogwood Rd
  7500-8175 38138
  8176-9370 38139
Dogwood Rd S 38139
Dogwood Creek Cv & Rd 38139
Dogwood Crest Cir 38138
Dogwood Estates Cv & Dr 38139
Dogwood Garden Dr 38139
Dogwood Glenn Cv 38139
Dogwood Grove Cv 38139
Dogwood Grove Dr 38138
Dogwood Hollow Dr 38139
Dogwood Meadows Cv 38139
Dogwood Oaks Cv & Dr 38139
Dogwood Pass Cv 38139
Dogwood Trail Dr 38139
Dogwood Villa Dr 38138
Donegal Cv 38139
Donnington Cv & Dr 38138
Donnybrook Dr 38138
Doral Cv 38138
Dove Field Cv 38138
Dove Grove Cv 38139
Dove Meadow Cv E & W 38139
Dove Spring Cv 38138
Dovie Ln 38138
Dowden Cv 38139
Dr Martin Rd 38138
Dragonfly Cv 38138
Drayton Cv 38138
Drayton Hall Ln 38139
Drury Ln 38139
Duckhorn Dr 38138
Duke Cir 38139
Dumfries Cv 38139
Dunedin Cv 38138
Duntreath Mdws & Rd 38139
Duntreath Valley Dr 38139
Eagle Branch Cv 38138
Ealing Cir 38139
Eastern Ave 38138
Edenfield Cv 38138
Edmonton Park Ln 38138
Ednam Cv 38139
Edwards Mill Rd 38139
Effingham Dr 38138
Egerton Ln 38138
Elderslie Dr 38139
Eldor Rd 38138
Elm Leaf Dr 38138
Elm Ridge Cv 38138
Elm Row Dr 38138
Elmhurst Dr 38138
E Enclave Holw & Ln 38139
Enclave Green Cv & Ln E, N & W 38139
Enclave Hollow Ln & Loop 38139
Enterprise Ave 38138
Enton Cv 38139
Eversholt Ln 38138
Everwood Cv 38138
Exeter Rd 38138
Falling Leaf Cv & Dr 38139
Farindon Cv & Dr 38138
Farmingdale Rd 38138
Farmington Blvd
  7651-7775 38138
  7776-8244 38138
  7776-7776 38183
  7777-8243 38138
  8245-8799 38138
W Farmington Blvd 38138
Farmington Cv 38139
Farmington Bend Dr 38139
Farmoor Rd 38139
Farnifold Dr 38138
Farrah Ln 38139
Featherleigh Ln 38138
Fernspring Cv 38138
Fernwood Cv 38138
Fiddlers Elbow Dr 38138
Finney Cv 38139
Fireside Cv 38138
Flowers Oak Cv 38138
Fords Station Rd 38138
Forest Bend Ct & Cv 38138
Forest Centre Dr 38138
Forest Downs Rd 38138
Forest Estates Cv 38139
Forest Glade Cv 38138
Forest Hill Ln 38139
Forest Hill Way 38139
Forest Hill Irene Cv 38139
Forest Hill Irene Rd
  1900-2949 38139
  2950-3699 38138
Forest River Ln 38139
Forestwood Rd 38138
Foster Dale Cv 38139
Foster Grove Rd 38139
Foster Ridge Rd 38138
Fountainside Dr 38138
Fox Creek Dr 38138
Fox Fern Rd 38138
Fox Grape Cv 38138
Fox Hill Cir & Dr E, N & S 38139
Fox Ridge Rd 38139
Frank Rd 38139
Friarlynch Ln 38139
Gainesway Dr 38138
Gallery Ct 38138
Galway Cv 38139
Garden Pl 38139
Garden Arbor Dr 38138
Garner Woods Cv 38138
Gayle Ln 38138
Georgetown Pl 38139
S, N & W Germantown Rd & Sq 38138
Germantown Village Sq 38138
Germanwood Ln 38138
Glen Meadow Ln 38138
Glen Ridge Cv 38139
Glenalden Dr 38138
Glenbar Dr 38139
Glenbrae Cv 38139
Glenbuck Cv & St 38139
Glenda Rd 38139
Glenllyn Cv 38139
Golden Chance Cv 38138
Golden Fields Dr 38138
Goodview Dr 38139
Gorham Pl 38139
Goringwood Ln 38138
Goswell Ct 38138
Gotten Cv & Way 38139
Grabersbridge Cv 38139
Grand Oak Dr 38138
Grandbury Way 38139
Gray Ridge Cv 38138
Great Oaks Cv & Rd 38138
Green Clover Cv 38139
Green Downs Cv 38138
Green Forest Cv 38138
Green Holly Cv 38138
Green Knoll Dr 38138
Green Leaves Dr 38139
Green Orchard Cv 38138
Green Pastures Cv N & S 38138
Greenbrier Cv 38139
Greenfields Rd 38139
Greensprings Cv & Ln 38138
Grenville Dr 38138
Gresham Cv 38139
Grey Cliff Dr 38138
Grist Mill Cv 38139
Grove Ct & Rdg 38138
Grove Brook Ct 38138
Grove Forest Cv 38139
Grove Hollow Ln 38139
Grove Lake Ct 38138
Grove Meadow Ct 38138
Grove Mill Cv 38138
Grove Park Cv 38139
Grove Row Dr 38139
Grove Spring Dr 38139
Grove Trail Cv & Ln 38139
Grove View Cv 38139
Grovecrest Cv & Rd 38139
Grovelawn Cv & Dr 38139
Groveshire Ct 38138
Groveway Cv & Dr 38139
Grovewood Cv 38138
Guilford Cv 38139
Gumleaf Cv 38138
Guyboro Cv 38139
Gwynn Hollow Cv & Ln 38139
Gwynnbrook Cv 38139
Hacks Cross Rd 38138
Halleford Cir 38139
Hampstead Ln 38139
Hampton Grove Ln 38138
Hapano Dr 38138
Harding Cv 38138
Harlan Cv 38139
Harrod Cv 38139
Haseley Ln 38138
Havenhill Cv 38138
Havenhurst Dr 38138
Havershire Cv 38138
Hawksprings Cv 38138
Hawthorn Hill Cv & Dr 38139
Hayden Rd 38138
Hayley Cv 38138
Hazelton Dr 38138
Heatherbrook Ln 38138
Heatherglen Dr 38138
Heatherly Cv 38138
Heathmore Pl 38138
Heathstone Cv 38138
Hedgegrove Cv 38138
Hedgeview Ln 38139
Herron Walk Cv 38139
Hickory Glen Cv & Dr 38138
Hidden Oaks Cv & Dr 38138
Highgate Dr 38138
Hill Creek Cv 38138
Hobbits Glen Dr 38138
Hocking Cv 38139
Hocksett Cv 38139
Hollow Creek Cv & Rd 38138
Hollow Fork Cv & Rd 38138
Holly Heath Cv & Dr 38138
Holly Hill Cv & Dr 38138
Holly Spring Dr 38138
Hollybrook Ln N & S 38138
Hollyhock Cv & Dr 38138
Honey Hill Cv 38138
Honey Tree Cv & Dr 38138
Horsham Dr 38139
S & W Houston Cv, Pass & Way 38139
S Houston Levee Cv & Rd 38139
N & S Houston Oak Dr 38139
Houston Oaks Cv & Dr 38139
Howard Rd 38138
Hughes Creek Cv 38139
Hundred Oaks Cv & Dr 38139
Huntcliff Cv 38138
Hunters Dr 38138
Hunters Creek Dr 38138
Hunters Forest Cv & Dr 38138
Hunters Grove Ln 38138
Hunters Hill Cv & Dr 38138
Hunters Horn Cv 38138
Hunters Run Dr 38138
Huntleigh Way 38138
Idlewood Cv 38139
Ingleside Farm E 38139
Inglewood Cv 38138
Innsbruck Dr 38138
Inspiration Dr 38138
Ivy Leaf Cir & Dr 38138
Jenna Rd 38138
Jermyn Cv 38138
Johannesburg Dr 38139
Johnson Rd 38139
Johnson Road Ext 38139
Judicial Dr 38138
Kateland St 38139
Keasler Cir E & W 38139
Kelchner Cv 38138
Kempton Dr 38139
Kenney Dr E 38139
Kilbirnie Cv & Dr 38139
Kimbrook Cv & Dr 38138
Kimbrough Rd 38138
Kimbrough Green Dr 38138
Kimbrough Grove Rd 38138
Kimbrough Park Pl 38138
Kimbrough Woods Cv & Pl 38139
Kimdale Dr 38138
Kimforest Dr 38138
Kimridge Dr 38138
Kinderhill Cir & Ln 38138
Kingcastle Cv 38138
Kinlock Cv 38139
Kinross Cv 38139
Kintyre Pl 38139
Kirby Pkwy 38138
Knob Oak Cv 38138
Knoll Ln 38138
Knotting Hill Dr 38139
Kostka Ln 38139
L Anguille Ln 38139
Laird Cir 38139
Lakespur Cv 38139
Lancashire Cv 38138
Landfair Dr 38138
Lansdowne Ln 38139
Lansingwood Cv & Dr 38139
Latimer Cv & Dr 38138
Lauder Ln 38139
Laurel Ln 38139
E & W Laurel Hollow Cir & Ln 38139
Laurel Knoll Cir & Ln 38139
Laurel Ridge Cv 38138
Laurinburg Cir 38138
Lawton Trl 38138
Leeds Cv 38139
Leesburg Dr 38139
Legends Dr 38139
Leighton Creek Cv 38138
Lennox Cv & Dr 38138
Level Creek Dr 38139
Liggon Green Ln 38139
Lindell Cv 38139
Linton Cv 38139
Lipsey Cv 38139
Lockesley Cv N & S 38139
Londonderry Cv 38138
Long Oak Dr 38138
Longwood Ln 38138
Lower Woods Cv 38139
Ludlow Cv 38139
Lutonwood Cv 38139
Mac Cv 38138
Magnolia Ridge Cv & Dr 38138
Magnolia Tree Rd 38138
Maiden Cv 38138
Maize Cv 38138
Malabar Dr 38138
Malcolm Cv 38138
Mallard Ln 38138
Mandeville Xing 38138
Manor Oaks Cv 38139
Manor Woods Ct 38138
Maple Creek Cv 38139
Maple Grove Cv & Dr 38139
Maple Shadow Cv 38139
Mardite Cv 38138
Marthas Cv 38138
Martin Grove Ln 38138
Mary Hill Cv 38139
Masters Dr 38139
May Woods Ln 38138
Mcclellan Ln 38138
Mchenry Cir & Cv E, N & S 38138
Mcvay Cv & Rd 38138
Mcvay Manor Cv 38138
Mcvay Station Ct 38138
Meadow Run 38138
Meadow Creek Bridge Cv 38138
Meadow Glen Dr 38138
Meadow Hill Cv 38138
Meadow Run Cv 38138
Meadow Wood Cv 38138
Mer Rouge Dr 38138
Mercedes Blvd 38139
Merchants Row 38138
Mikeyair Dr 38138
Mill Run 38138
Miller Farms Rd 38138
Millstone Cv 38138
Mimosa Cv & Dr 38138
Mimosa Tree Dr 38138
Misty Creek Cv & Dr 38138
Misty Hollow Cv 38138
Mistywood Ln 38138
Mont Alban Cv 38139
Mont Blanc Dr 38139
Montavesta Dr 38139
Monte Carlo Cv & Dr 38139
Monte Vallo Cv 38138
Moore Rd 38138
Moss Tree Rd 38138
Mossy Creek Cv & Dr 38138
Mount Repose Dr 38139
Mourning Dove Cv 38139
Mulkins Ln 38139
Mustang Dr 38138
Myrtle Bend Dr 38139
Neshoba Cir, Cv & Rd 38138
Neshoba Trace Cv 38138
Netherhall Cv & Dr 38139
New Meadow Dr 38139
New Riverdale Rd 38139
Newfields Rd 38139
Newsum Dr 38138
Night Shade Dr 38139
Nikerton Dr 38138
Nohapa Cv 38138
Norcross Dr 38139
North St 38138
Oak Hill Cv & Rd 38138
Oak Manor Dr 38138
Oak Run Cv & Dr 38138
Oak Trail Dr 38139
Oakhurst Cv 38139
Oaklawn Ln 38138
Oakleigh Cv & Ln 38138
Oakleigh Manor Cv & Ln 38138
Oaksedge Cv 38138
Oakville Dr 38138
Old Bridge Ln 38138
Old Elm Cv & Ln 38138
Old Houston Levee Rd 38139
Old Mill Cv & Rd 38138
Old Plantation Cv 38139
Old Post Crk 38138
Old Towne Ln 38139
Old Village Cv & St 38138
Ole Pike Cv & Dr 38138
On The Hl 38139
On The Bluff Cv 38139
On The Glade Cv 38139
On The Hill Cv 38139
Orchard Grove Cv 38138
Orchard Hill Cv & Dr 38138
Orians Cv 38139
Orleans Walk Cv 38139
Otterburn Ln 38139
Overhill Cv 38138
Overlook Dr 38138
Oxford Cv 38139
Paddock Cv 38139
Padington Park Ln 38138
Paget Ct 38139
Pangbourne Cv 38138
Panoha Dr 38138
Park Creek Cv & Dr 38139
Park Ridge Dr 38138
W Park Trail Dr 38139
Parker Cir 38138
Parkgate Cv & Dr 38139
Pecan Trees Dr 38138
Penbrook Cv 38138
Penmont Dr 38138
Pepper Bush Ln 38139
Pete Mitchell Rd 38138
Pierpoint Cv 38138
Pike Wood Cv & Dr 38138
Pine Crk E & W 38138
Pine Needle Cv & Dr 38139
Pine Valley Cv 38138
Pine Valley Ln
  8100-8169 38138
  8170-8499 38139
Pinnacle Creek Dr 38138
Pittsfield Cv 38138
Plantation Cir & Rd 38138
Plantation Way Ln 38139
Poplar Ave
  6516-9449 38138
  9450-9598 38139
  9451-9529 38138
  9600-9899 38139
Poplar Pike 38138
Poplar Estates Pkwy 38138
Poplar Grove Cir & Ln 38139
E & S Poplar Lake Dr 38138
Poplar Woods Cir E 38138
Port Charlotte Dr 38138
Positano Ln 38138
Prestwick Dr 38139
Professional Plz 38138
Pyron Oaks Cv 38138
Queens Ct 38138
Radford Ridge Rd 38138
Ravencliff Cv 38138
E, S & W Ravenhill Dr 38138
Ravensdale Cv 38138
Red Maple Cv 38139
Redbud Trail Cv & Dr 38139
Redfield Dr 38138
Regents Walk 38138
Renfrew Ln 38138
Rhineland Dr 38138
Rich Hill Cv 38138
Richman Ln 38139
Rico Cv 38138
Ridgetown Ln 38138
Riggs Rd 38138
River Bend Dr 38138
River Glen Cv & Dr 38139
River Park Cv & Dr 38139
River Reach Rd 38138
River Valley Dr 38138
Riverain Cv 38138
Riverchase Cv & Dr 38139
Riverdale Cv & Rd 38138
Riverwind Cv 38138
Riverwood Cv & St 38138
Rochester Cv 38138
Rock Maple Cv 38139
Rocky Hollow Cv & Rd 38138
Rolling Valley Dr 38138
E Romano Way 38138
Rooksworth Cv 38139
Rosehaven St 38138
Rothchild Rd 38139
Round Hill Cv 38138
Rowan Ln 38138
Roxbury Cv 38138
Rubyshade Cv 38138
Rue Jordan Cv 38138
Rustleaf Cv 38138
Rye Rd 38139
Saddle Ridge Dr 38138
Saddlegait Cv 38138
San Augusta Cv 38139
San Augustine Ln 38138
Sanders Hill Cv 38138
Sanders Ridge Ln 38138
Sandpoint Dr 38139
Sandy Berry Cv 38138
Sandy Creek Dr 38138
Savannah Way S 38138
Saxton Green Ln 38139
Scarlet Rd 38139
Scruggs Dr 38138
Seesselshire Ln 38138
Selkirk Cv 38139
Seton Pl 38139
Shadeley Dr 38138
Shadowbrook Cv 38139
Shadowmoss Ln 38138
Shady Creek Dr 38138
Shallow Ford Cv 38139
Shannon Oaks Cv 38138
Shepards Bush Ln 38139
Shepherdwood Ln 38138
Sherman Oaks Dr 38139
Signature Cv 38138
Silkwood Dr 38138
Silver Shadows Ln 38138
Silverbark Dr 38138
Silverthorn Cv 38139
Siward Cv 38138
Sleepy Hollow Ln 38138
Somerset Ln 38138
Sonning Dr 38138
Sophie Ln 38138
Southern Ave 38138
Southmoore Cv 38138
Sparkling Lake Cv 38138
Splinter Oak Cv 38138
S Spring Hollow Cv & Ln 38139
Spring Loop Dr 38139
Spring Meade Cv & Ln 38139
Springmead Dr 38139
Stafford Park Ln 38139
Stags Leap Cir 38138
Stamford Cv & Dr 38138
Star Meadow Cv 38139
Station Hill Rd 38138
Steedham Ln 38139
E & S Steeplegate Cv & Dr 38138
Steinerbridge Ln 38139
Stillbrook Dr 38138
Stirling Ln 38139
Stockton Pl 38139
Stone Creek Dr 38138
Stone Farm Cir 38138
Stone Mill Cv 38138
Stone Walk Pl 38138
Stonegate Cv & Pass 38138
Stonewyck Rd 38138
Stout Rd 38138
Stratfield Cv & Dr 38139
Sundance Cv 38138
Sunny Creek Dr 38138
Sunset Cv, Pl & Rd 38138
Surrey Ln 38138
Sweet Maple Cv 38139
Sweet Oaks Cir & Cv 38138
Sweetwood Dr 38138
Sycamore Creek Cv 38139
Sycamore Trail Dr 38139
Tabor Ct 38139
Tagg Dr 38138
Tallwood Dr 38138
Talmage Cv 38139
Tamarack Ln 38138
Tamerlane Ln 38138
Tanoak Cv & Dr 38138
Tealstone Dr 38139
Teddington Dr 38138
Telluride Cv 38139
Terrene Ln 38139
Thornbrook Cv 38138
Thorncroft Dr 38138

Three Chimneys Dr E & W 38138
Tilden Ct 38139
Toro Cv 38138
Tottenham Cv 38139
Towering Pines Cv 38138
Trailwood Ln 38138
Triton Cv 38139
Troon Cv 38139
Trowbridge Cv 38138
Turpins Glen Dr 38138
Tuscany Way 38138
Us Highway 72 38138
Val Verde Dr 38138
Valley Crest Ln 38138
Vienna Way 38138
Village Shops Dr 38138
Vineyard Way 38138
Walden Woods Cv 38139
Walking Horse Cir 38138
Walters Woods Ln 38139
Walworth Ct 38138
Wargate Ln 38138
Washington Way 38139
Waterleaf Dr 38138
Watkins Rd 38138
Waverly Xing 38138
Waxlander Cir 38138
Weeping Willow Rd 38138
Wellesley Pine Cv 38138
Wellsley Dr 38139
Wellton Dr 38138
Wentworth Ln 38139
West St 38138
Westcott Dr 38138
Western Ave 38138
Westfair Cir & Dr 38139
Westminster Ln 38138
Weston Pass 38138
Westwood Manor Dr 38139
Wetherby Cv & Dr 38139
Wethersfield Cir & Dr 38138
Wheatland Dr 38139
Wheatley Dr 38138
Wheatstone Cv 38138
Whipper Ln 38138
Whispering Pines Cir & Dr 38139
Whitemarsh Dr 38138
Wickersham Cv & Ln 38139
E Wicklow Way 38139
Wickshire Cv E & W 38138
Widgeon Way Dr 38139
Wild Oak Cv 38138
Wilderness Cv & Dr 38139
Willey Cv & Rd 38138
William Brown Dr 38139
Williams Glen Cv 38139
Willinghurst Dr 38139
Willisshire Ln 38139
Willow Brook Rd 38138
Willow Oak Rd 38139
Willowbend Cv 38138
Winchester Rd 38138
Windham Pl 38138
Winding Way 38139
Winding Creek Dr 38138
Winding Oak Way 38138
Winding Way Cv 38139
Windstone Cv & Way 38138
Windy Oaks Cv & Dr 38139
Wine Leaf Cv & Dr 38139
Winged Foot Ln 38138
Winners Cir 38138
Winnton Cv 38138
Winterberry Cv 38138
Winthrop Ct 38139
Wishanger Cv 38139
Woffington Ln 38138
Wolf Bend Rd 38138
Wolf Park Dr & Rd 38138
Wolf River Blvd
7201-7397 38138
7399-8000 38138
8002-8098 38138
9380-9999 38139
Wolf River Cir 38138
Wolf Trail Cv 38138
Wood Briar Dr 38138
Wood Creek Cv & Dr 38138
Woodbend Cv & Rd 38138
Woodford Ln 38138
Woodgate Dr 38138
Woodhall Cv 38138
Woodhurst Cv 38139
Woodland Oaks Dr 38139
Woodlane Cv & Dr 38138
Woodleaf Dr 38138
Woodridge Cv & Ln 38138
Woodruff Cv & Dr 38138
Woods Chapel Cv 38139
Woodside Dr 38138
Woodsong Cv 38138
Wooduck Cv 38139
Wyndhurst Pl 38138
Wynterhall Dr 38138
Yester Oaks Dr 38139
Yorkchester Rd 38139
Zurich Dr 38138

NUMBERED STREETS

All Street Addresses 38138

GOODLETTSVILLE TN

General Delivery 37072

POST OFFICE BOXES MAIN OFFICE STATIONS AND BRANCHES

Box No.s
All PO Boxes 37070

NAMED STREETS

Abiding Pl 37072
Agee Rd 37072
Aintree Ct 37072
Alamert Rd 37072
Allen Rd 37072
Alta Loma Rd 37072
Amelia Ct 37072
Andover Ct 37072
Angela Cir 37072
Anna Dr 37072
Appalachain Dr 37072
Apple Valley Rd 37072
Apple View Ct & Rd 37072
Appletree Rd 37072
Asbee Ct 37072
Ashlea Ct 37072
Ashley Dr 37072
Ashtead Ct 37072
Bailey St 37072
Bailey View Ct 37072
Baker Rd 37072
Baker Station Rd 37072
Barnett Dr 37072
Bass St 37072
Baxter Ln 37072
Bell St 37072
Bella Vista Dr 37072
Bellar Dr 37072
Bennett Dr 37072
Benton Ct 37072
Bethel Rd 37072
Betts Rd 37072
Bingham Dr 37072
Birdwell Ct & Dr 37072
Bland Pass 37072
Blue Ridge Pkwy 37072
Bluebird Dr 37072
E & W Bobby Ct 37072
Braxton Park Ct & Ln 37072
Brenton Ct 37072
Brick Church Pike 37072
Brockhampton Ct 37072
Brookside Rd 37072
Brookview Cir & Ct 37072
Browns Lake Rd 37072
Bruce Ln 37072
Bryan House Dr 37072
Buck Hill Rd 37072
Buckingham Ct 37072
Buffalo Run 37072
Business Park Cir 37072
Butleigh Ct 37072
Butterfield Ct 37072
C Smith St 37072
Cafe Rd 37072
Caldwell Dr 37072
Calebs Walk 37072
Cambridge Ct 37072
W Campbell Rd 37072
Canton Ct 37072
Carlin Dr 37072
Carlton Pl 37072
Carol Ann Dr 37072
S Cartwright Cir, Ct, Pkwy & St N & S 37072
Cascade Ln 37072
E & W Cedar St 37072
Cerro Vista Dr 37072
Champney Ct 37072
Charleston Dr 37072
Chelsea Dr 37072
Cherokee Trl 37072
Cheshire Ct 37072
Cheyenne Trl 37072
Chickasaw Trl 37072
Chiswick Ct 37072
Christina Ct 37072
Church St 37072
Cima Dr 37072
Cimmaron Dr 37072
Cindy Pl 37072
Clifton Ct & Dr 37072
Cobb St 37072
Cobblestone Place Dr 37072
Conference Dr 37072
Connell St 37072
Connie Ave 37072
Connor Dr 37072
Copper Creek Dr 37072
Corbridge Ct 37072
Cove St 37072
Crawford Hill Rd 37072
Creek Trl 37072
Creek Trail Ct 37072
Creekside Dr 37072
Creekview Ln 37072
Crencor Dr 37072
Crief Dr 37072
Crocker Springs Rd 37072
Cunniff Ct & Pkwy 37072
Cycle Ln 37072
Cynthia Trl 37072
Darby Rd 37072
Debra Dr 37072
Deep Wood Dr 37072
Denson Ln 37072
Depot St 37072
Dickens Ln 37072
N & S Dickerson Pike & Rd 37072
Digby Ct 37072
S Dividing Ridge Rd 37072
Dogwood Ln 37072
Donald St 37072
Dora Dr 37072
Dorchester Ct 37072
Dorothy Dr 37072
Dorr Dr 37072
Dorris Ave 37072
Douglas Ln 37072
Dover Ct 37072
Drake St 37072
Draper Cir & Dr 37072
Dry Creek Ln & Rd 37072
Dry Creek Pointe Ct 37072
Dyer Ln & Rd 37072
East Ave & Ct 37072
Eastlawn Dr 37072
Echo Ln 37072
Echo Hill Blvd 37072
Edgar Dillard Rd 37072
Edgebrook Rd 37072
Edmondson Ct 37072
Elba Dr 37072
Elizabeth Ct 37072
Ellen Dr 37072
Ellis Ln 37072
Emily Ct & Dr 37072
E End Rd 37072
Engel Ave 37072
Eric Ct 37072
Essex Ct & Dr 37072
Fairbanks Rd 37072
Fannin Dr 37072
Finney Ct 37072
Fisher Rd 37072
Flat Ridge Rd 37072
Fonnic Dr 37072
Fontaine Dr 37072
Forest Oaks Dr 37072
Forks Rd 37072
Fox Chase Dr 37072
Frances St 37072
Freeman Hollow Ct & Rd 37072
French St 37072
Friendship Ct & Dr 37072
Frontier Ln 37072
Gallop Ln 37072
Garrett Dr 37072
Gates Rd 37072
Gaylemore Dr 37072
Genelle Dr 37072
Geneva Dr 37072
Glancy St 37072
Glendower Ct 37072
Glenwood Dr 37072
Goldie Ct & Dr 37072
Goodlettsville Plz 37072
Grace Dr 37072
Graceland Ct & Dr 37072
Graves Rd 37072
Green Acres Ct & Dr 37072
Green Valley Dr 37072
Greenleaf Cir 37072
Greens Cir 37072
Greer Rd 37072
Habersham Ct 37072
Hanover Ct 37072
Happy Hollow Ct & Rd 37072
Happy Valley Rd 37072
Hardaway Dr 37072
Hardwick Ct 37072
Harris St 37072
Hasty Dr 37072
Heathcote Ct 37072
Heather Dr 37072
Henry Rd 37072
Hickory Ct 37072
Hidden Trails Dr 37072
High Chaperal Dr 37072
High Mesa Ct 37072
S High Ridge Ct, Dr & Trl N 37072
Highland Ave 37072
Highland Heights Dr 37072
Highway 31 W 37072
Highway 41 S 37072
Hillcrest Rd 37072
Hills Hollow Rd 37072
Hinkle Ln 37072
Hitt Ln 37072
Hogans Branch Rd 37072
Hollis Ct 37072
Holloway Ct & Rd 37072
Hollywood St 37072
Huffman Rd 37072
Indian Hills Mound 37072
Iroquois Trl 37072
Isaac Dr 37072
Ivey Point Rd 37072
Ivy Hill Ln 37072
Jackson Rd & St 37072
Jackson Heights Rd 37072
Janette Ave & Ct 37072
Jarrett Rd 37072
Jesse Brown Dr 37072
John Wayne Dr 37072
Jones Ave & Dr 37072
Joshuas Run 37072
Judith Ct 37072
Justin Ct 37072
Kasper Way 37072
Katherine Ct & Dr 37072
Kathy Ave 37072
Katy Hill Dr 37072
Kayla Dr 37072
Kenwood Dr 37072
Kimberly Dr 37072
Knollwood Ct 37072
L-N Ct 37072
Lakeside Dr 37072
Lama Terra Ct & Dr 37072
Lampley Ct 37072
Lance Park Cir 37072
Langbrae Dr 37072
Lassiter Dr 37072
Laurel Ct 37072
Lenox Pl 37072
Lewis Dr 37072
Lick St 37072
Lickton Pike 37072
Lidgate Ter 37072
Liebengood Rd 37072
Lindberg St 37072
Lindsey Dr 37072
Lodge St 37072
Long Dr 37072
Long Hollow Ct & Pike 37072
Longview Dr 37072
Loretta Dr 37072
Louisville Hwy 37072
Lower Walkers Creek Rd 37072
Lowes Ln 37072
Lucien Dr 37072
Lura Ln 37072
Luster Rd 37072
Luton Pl 37072
Lynn Dr 37072
Madison Ct 37072
Madison Creek Rd 37072
N & S Main St 37072
Mansker Dr 37072
Manskers Acres Ln 37072
Maple Ct & Dr 37072
N & S Maple Ridge Ln 37072
Marcie Ann Dr 37072
Marita Ave 37072
Marshall Greene Cir 37072
Mason Cir, Ct & Ln 37072
Mathes Ct & Dr 37072
Mavella Ct 37072
Mccaw Ct 37072
Mccoin Dr 37072
Mcmahan Rd 37072
Mcmurtry Rd 37072
Meadow Ln 37072
Meadowcreek Cir 37072
Meadowlark Ln 37072
Melissa Ct & Dr 37072
Memorial Dr 37072
Millers Creek Rd 37072
Milwell Dr 37072
Mission Rdg 37072
Mitchell Ct 37072
Moncrief Ave 37072
Monica Ave 37072
Montgomery Rd 37072
W Monticello Ave 37072
Morning View Ct 37072
Moss Trl 37072
Myers Ave 37072
Mystic Hill Ct & Dr 37072
Natalie Dr 37072
Nathan Dr 37072
Navajo Ct 37072
Nella Dr 37072
New Brick Church Pike 37072
New Hitt Ln 37072
New Rader Rd 37072
Newberry Ct 37072
Newcastle Ct 37072
Norfolk Dr 37072
Normerle St 37072
Northbrook Rd 37072
Northchase Dr 37072
Northcreek Blvd
100-300 37072
301-301 37070
301-399 37072
302-398 37072
Northfork Ln 37072
Northgate Cir & Dr 37072
Northwind Ct & Dr 37072
Norwood Ct 37072
Oak Bluff Ln 37072
Oak Forest Dr 37072
Oakwood Ln 37072
Obryan St 37072
Old Baker Rd 37072
Old Brick Church Pike 37072
Old Dickerson Rd 37072
Old Hickory Ct 37072
Old Louisville Hwy 37072
Old Shiloh Rd 37072
Old Springfield Hwy & Pike 37072
Old Stone Bridge Rd 37072
Overlook Trl 37072
Oxford Ct 37072
Page Dr 37072
Paige Park Ln 37072
Park Ct, Dr & Pl 37072
Patton Branch Rd 37072
Payne St 37072
Pear Orchard Dr 37072
Peggy Ct 37072
Pendleton Hill Rd 37072
Pickeral Ln 37072
Pinnacle Ct 37072
Placid Grove Ln 37072
Plateau Ct 37072
Pleasant Green Dr 37072
Plemel Ln 37072
Pole Hill Rd 37072
Preston Run 37072
Professional Park Dr 37072
Rachel Dr 37072
Ragan Ct 37072
Ralph Holw 37072
Redwood Ln 37072
Ridge Rd & Trl 37072
Ridge Hill Rd 37072
Ridgecrest Dr 37072
Ridgerunner Ct 37072
Ridgewood Rd 37072
Rivergate Dr & Pkwy 37072
Rivergate Meadows Dr 37072
Roanoke Dr 37072
Robert Cartwright Dr 37072
Roberts Rd 37072
Rolling Meadows Dr 37072
Roscoe St 37072
Rose Garden Ln 37072
Rosehill Ct & Dr 37072
Ruby Ln 37072
Saddleback Dr 37072
Sadie Ln 37072
Safe Harbor Dr 37072
Salt Lick Trl 37072
Sampson Park Cir 37072
Sassafras Ct & Ln 37072
Seminole Ct 37072
Shaw Rd 37072
Shawnee Ct 37072
Sheffield Ct 37072
Shell Ln & Rd 37072
Shevel Dr 37072
Skyline Dr 37072
Slaters Creek Ln & Rd 37072
Slaters Creek Access Rd 37072
Smiley Hollow Rd 37072
Smokeys Ridge Trl 37072
Solitude Cir 37072
Southampton Ct 37072
Space Park N 37072
Spero Rd 37072
Spring Hollow Rd 37072
Springfield Hwy 37072
State Auto Blvd 37072
Station Dr 37072
Stephanie Pl 37072
Strawberry Hill Rd 37072
Strudwick Dr 37072
Summit Ct 37072
Sunnyslope Ct & Ln 37072
Swanton Ct 37072
S Swift Dr & Rd 37072
Swift Springs Ct 37072
Sydney Dr 37072
Tabor Dr 37072
Tamela Ct 37072
Tara Ln 37072
Ted Dorris Rd 37072
S Thompson Ln 37072
Thornberry Trce 37072
Timber Ct 37072
Timber Trail Rd 37072
Tinnin Rd 37072
Trace Dr 37072
Trailing Blossom Ln 37072
Trebor Dr 37072
Trellis Way 37072
Tudor Ct 37072
Turners Bnd 37072
W Twelve Stones Ct & Xing 37072
Two Mile Pike 37072
Union Hill Rd 37072
Utley Dr 37072
Valerie Ct 37072
Valley Dr 37072
Valley View Ct & Rd 37072
View Ridge Dr 37072
Vine Ln 37072
Virginia Ave 37072
Wade Cir 37072
Walker Rd 37072
Wallace Dr 37072
Walnut Ct & Dr 37072
Watts Rd 37072
Weeping Willow Way 37072
Welshwood Ct 37072
West Rd 37072
Westlawn Dr 37072
Williamson Rd 37072
Willis Branch Rd 37072
Willow Trl 37072
Willow Creek Dr 37072
Willow Crest Ct 37072
Wilshire Ct 37072
Wilson Ln 37072
Wilt Ct 37072
Winding Way 37072
Winding Creek Rd 37072
Winding Ridge Dr 37072
Windsor Trce 37072
Windsor Green Blvd 37072
Wingo Way 37072
Witham Ct 37072
Woodland Dr 37072
Woodshire Dr 37072
Woody Ln 37072
Wren Rd 37072
Wyndom Ct 37072
Wynlands Cir & Dr 37072
N & S Wynridge Way 37072
Yvonne Ct & Dr 37072

GREENEVILLE TN

General Delivery 37743

POST OFFICE BOXES MAIN OFFICE STATIONS AND BRANCHES

Box No.s
1 - 4807 37744

5000 - 5999 37743

NAMED STREETS

A St 37745
Ab St 37745
Academy St 37743
Acorn Cir 37745
Acton Ct 37743
Airport Rd 37745
Albany Rd 37743
Albany Acess 37743
Albert St 37743
Alderman Dr 37745
Alexander St 37745
Alexander Ferry Ln 37743
Alice St 37743
Alisha Dr E & W 37745
Allen Ln 37743
E Allens Bridge Rd 37743
Alpine Cir, Cv & Dr 37743
Amber Ln 37743
Amity Rd 37743
Anderson Loop & St 37743
Andes Cir 37743
Andrew Johnson Dr 37743
E Andrew Johnson Hwy 37745
W Andrew Johnson Hwy
1-1699 37745
1700-2398 37743
2400-6400 37743
6402-6598 37743
Angel Hl 37745
Ann St 37743
Appian Way 37745
Apple St 37745
Arbor View Ln 37743
Archcrest Ct 37743
Arlie Waddell Ln 37743
Armitage Dr 37745
Arnold Rd 37743
Arnold Palmer Dr 37743
Ash Meadow Dr 37743
Asheville Hwy 37743
Ashland Dr 37743
Ashley Cir 37743
Ashway Ter 37743
Aspen St 37743
Astor Bowers Rd 37743
Austin St 37745
Avery Ln 37745
Avondale Ln & Rd 37745
Aw Johnson Park 37743
Ayers Ln 37745
Babbs Mill Rd 37745
Bachman Dr 37745
Back Creek Rd 37743
Bailey Ln & St 37745
Baileyton Park & Rd 37745
Baileyton Access 37745
Baileyton Church St 37745
Baileyton College St 37745
Baileyton Main St 37745
Bainey Broyles St 37745
Ball Rd 37745
Bandy Rd 37743
Baneberry Rd 37745
Banks St 37745
Barkley Rd 37745
Barkwood Park 37743
Barnside Ln 37745
E Barton Ridge Rd 37745
W Barton Ridge Rd 37743
Baughard Hill Rd 37743
Baxter St 37745
Bayberry St 37743
N Bays Mountain Rd 37745
Bear Hollow Rd 37745
Becky Dr 37743
Bedford Cir 37743
Belle Arden Dr 37745
Belle Meade Ct 37745
Bellwood Ln 37743
Belmont Dr 37745
Benbow Rd 37743
E Bernard Ave 37745
W Bernard Ave 37743
Bernard Rd 37745
Berry Pick Ln 37745
Bethel Ln 37745
Bible Acres Ln 37743
Biddle St 37745
Big Valley Trl 37743
Bill Dobson Ln 37745
Billy Bible Rd 37745
Birchwood Ln 37745
Bird Cir 37743
Bird Dr 37745
Bird Rd 37743
Birds Bridge Rd 37743
Birdwell Cir 37743
Birdwell Mill Rd 37743
Bishop Loop 37743
Black Rd 37743
Black Bear Rd 37745
Black Oak St 37745
Blackhorn Ln 37745
Blake Rd 37743
Blazer Ln 37743
Blue Bell St 37743
Blue Jay Rd 37743
Blue Springs Pkwy 37743
Bluebonnet Ln 37743
Bob Smith Blvd 37745
Bobbie Ave 37743
Bohannon Ave 37745
Bolton Rd 37745
Bonita Way 37745
E & W Bonnie Johnson Ln 37743
Booker Ln 37745
Boone Dr 37745
Boulder Ln 37743
Boulder Loop 37745
Bowers Rd 37743
Bowman Rd 37743
Brad St 37743
Bradley Ave 37745
Braketree Ln 37745
Brentwood Dr 37745
Briar Patch Ln 37743
Briarbend Ln 37743
Briargate Ln 37745
Briarwood Ct 37743
Briarwood Dr 37745
Bright Hope Rd 37743
Britton Ave 37743
Britton Ln 37743
Britton St 37745
Broad St 37745
Brooks Dr & St 37743
Broom Factory Rd 37743
Brown Ave 37743
Brown Ln 37745
Brown Mountain Rd 37745
Brown Springs Rd 37745
Browns Cir 37743
Browns Bridge Rd 37745
Browns Hill Ln & Loop 37745
Browns Ridge Rd 37743
E & N Broyles St 37745
Bruce Collins Ln 37743
Brumley Dr N & S 37743
Brunner St 37745
Brush Creek Rd 37743
Brushwood Ln 37745
Bryant Ln 37743
Buckboard Rd 37743
Buckingham Ct & Rd 37743
Buffalo Creek Ln 37743
Bullfrog Ln 37743
Burkey Ln 37745
Burkey Rd 37743
Burnett Chapel Ln 37743
C St 37745
Cabe Ct 37745
Cal Dobson Trl 37743
Callie Vw 37743
Camelot Ln & Park 37745
Camp Creek Rd 37743
Camp Joshua Ln 37743
Campbell Dr 37745
Campbell Ln 37743
Campbell Rd 37745
Campbell Heights Rd 37743
Canary Rd 37743
Caney Creek Ln 37745
Canoe Way 37743
Capri Dr 37745
Cardinal Ln 37743
Carlton Ridge Ln 37745
Carmel Hl 37743
Carolina Dr 37743
Carriage Ln 37745
Carson St 37743
Carters Valley Rd 37745
Cartwheel Rd 37743
Ccu Blvd 37745
Cecil Davis Rd 37743
Cedar Ave & St 37743
Cedar Creek Rd 37743
Cedar Creek Cave Rd 37743
Cedar Creek School Rd 37743
Cedar Hill St 37743
Centennial Ln 37745
Center St E & W 37743
Central St 37745
Champion Cir 37743
Chandler Cir 37743
Chaney Rd 37743
Chapel St 37743
Chapman Dr 37745
Charles St 37743
Charlie Doty Rd 37745
N & S Chase Ct & Ln 37745
Chermann Rd 37745
Cherokee Blvd 37743
Cherokee Dr 37745
Cherokee Loop 37743
Cherry St 37745
Cherrydale Dr 37743
Chestnut St 37745
Chickasaw Dr 37743
Chickory Ln 37743
Chinaberry Ct 37745
Choctaw Ln 37743
Christman Way 37743
Christy Ct 37743
E & W Church St 37745
Church Hill Cir & Rd 37745
Cicero Ave 37743
Cindy Dr 37745
Circle Dr 37745
Circle Heights Dr 37745
Clay Way 37745
Claybrook Ln 37743
Clear Mountain Trl 37745
Clem St 37743
Club House Ln 37743
Cm Jones Rd 37745
Cobble Ln 37743
Cochran Ln 37743
Cocke County Rd 37743
Coile St 37743
N College St
100-199 37743
200-299 37743
S College St 37743
College Hills Dr 37745
College View Dr 37745
Collins Rd 37745
Colonial Cir 37745
Colricia Dr 37745
Colvert Rd 37743
Colyer Rd 37743
Connell Rd 37743
Coolidge St 37743
Cooter Way 37743
Cork Way 37743
Corncrib Valley Ln 37745
Cosley Ln 37743
Cottage Dr 37745
Cottonwood Dr 37745
Courthouse Aly 37743
Cove Creek Rd 37745
Cox Cir & Rd 37743
Cox Hill Rd 37743
Coyote Ln 37745
Craft Ln 37743
E & W Craft Springs Rd 37745
Cranberry Cir 37743
Crescent Dr 37743
Cress Aly 37745
Crest Dr 37745
Crestview Dr 37745
Crestwood Dr 37745
Crockett Ln 37745
Cross Anchor Park 37745
Crossover Dr 37743
Crowfoot Aly 37743
Crum Cir & St 37743
Crumley Rd 37745
Crystal Ln 37745
Culbertson Rd 37745
Cumberland Dr 37745
Curtis St 37745
E Cutler St 37743
N Cutler St
100-199 37743
200-299 37745
S Cutler St 37743
Cutshall Ave 37743
Cutshaw Ln 37743
Cutshaw Gap 37743
Cypress St 37745
Daisy St 37745
E & W Dale Ct 37745
Daniel Boone Ln 37745
Dark Hollow Ln 37745
Darnell Rd 37743
Davis Dr 37745
Davis St 37743
Davy Crockett Dr 37743
Davy Crockett M H Park 37743
Dead Wood Ln 37743
Dearstone Dr & Ln 37743
Debusk Park & Rd 37743
Decatur St 37743
Deerfoot Ln 37743
Deerwood Rd 37743
Delta Cir 37743
Delta Valley Rd 37745
Delwood Cir 37745
Denver Rd 37743
E & W Depot St 37743
Desormeaux Way 37743
Devault Dr 37745
Devonshire Ct 37745
Diane Ln 37743
Dixie Rd 37743
Doak Dr 37745
Dobson Dr 37745
Doc Hawkins Rd 37745
Dodd Branch Rd 37745
Dodson St 37745
Dogwalk Rd 37745
Dogwood Dr & Loop 37745
Dominique Ln 37743
Doolittle Rd 37745
Doty Ln 37745
Doty Chapel Rd 37745
Doughty Ave 37745
Doughtys Chapel Rd 37745
Dove Trl 37745
Doyle Davis Rd 37745
Driftwood Cir 37745
Dublin Ct 37745
Dulaney Rd 37743
Dyer Cir 37745
Dyer Rd 37743
Dyer St 37743
Dykes Hawkins Rd 37745
Eagle Roost 37743
Ealey Rd 37743
Earl St 37743
Earlington Dr 37743
Easterly Dr & Ln 37743
Eastview Ln 37743
Easy St 37745
Echo Dr 37743
Ed Crum Way 37745
Edens Rd 37745
Edgewood Dr 37743
Eldridge Ln 37743
Elgin St 37743
Elk St 37745
Ell St 37743
Ellenburg Ln 37745
Elliot Ln 37745
Elm St 37743
Emerald Dr 37745
Emmert St 37745
Emory Dr 37745
Enchanted Ln 37745
Enterprise Ln 37745
Erwin Hwy 37745
Everhart Dr 37745
Fairfield Dr 37745
Fairgrounds Cir, Ln & Rd 37745
Fairlawn Dr 37743
Fairmeadow Ln 37743
Fairway Dr & Ln 37743
Faith Ct 37745
Fallen Bridge Ln 37743
Fann Dr 37743
Fannin Rd 37743
Farmington Dr 37743
Farnsworth Ln 37743
Fernwood Dr 37745
Fiesta Ln 37743
Fillers Mill Rd 37743
Flag Branch Rd 37743
Flamingo Cir 37743
Flamingo Rd 37743
Flatwoods Rd 37743
W Floral St 37743
Florence St 37745
Flower Valley Rd 37745
Fodderstack Rd 37745
Fodderstack Mountain Loop 37745
Fodderstack Ridge Rd 37745
Foggy Bottom Ln 37745
Forest St 37743
Forest Hills Dr 37745
E Fork Rd 37743
Forked Deer Rd 37743
Fox Mays Rd 37743
Foxford Rd 37743
Francis Dr 37743
Frank Thacker Ln 37745
S Franklin St 37745
Frazier St 37743
Friendship Rd S 37745
Fry St 37743
Fullview Dr 37745
Gaby Cir 37743
Gaby Ln 37745
Gail Walker Cir 37743
Galbreath Dr 37743
Gallihar Ln 37743
Galway Ct 37745
Gap Mountain Rd 37745
Garden Cir 37745
Garden St 37743
Garden Oaks Ln 37745
Gardner Ln 37745
Garland Dr 37745
Garrett Hill Rd 37743
Gass Dr 37745
Gass Memorial Rd 37745
Gatewood Rd 37745
Gefellers Dr 37743
Genoa Dr 37745
Gentry Way 37743
George Bailey Ln 37745
George Malone Rd 37745
Gibson Rd 37743
Gilland Dr 37745
Gilland St 37745
Gilland Way 37743
Glenfield Trl 37745
Glenn Cir 37743
Glenn Mcamis Ln 37745
Glenn Renner Ln 37743
Glenwood Dr 37743
Goddard Dr 37745
Goldenrod Ln 37745
Golf Course Cir 37743
Golf Trace Dr 37743
Golf Villa Dr 37743
Gopher Rd 37743
Gosnell Rd 37743
Gott Dr 37745
Grace Dr 37745
Graham Ln 37743
Grandview Ave 37743
Granite Ln 37743
Grapevine Trl 37745
Grassy Creek Rd 37743
Gray Rd 37743
Green Lawn Ave 37743
S & W Greene Ctr & St 37743
Greene Mountain Rd 37743
Greeneville Pkwy 37745
Greenfield Ct 37745
Greenfield St 37745
Greenway St 37743
Greenwood Dr 37745
Gregg Mill Rd 37743
Gregory Ave 37745
Grey Ln 37743
Greybark Ln 37745
Greystone Rd 37743
Greystone St 37745
Greystone Mountain Rd 37743
E & W Grove St 37745
Guinn Dr & Rd 37743
Hackberry St 37743
Hal Henard Rd 37745
Hall St 37745
Hampton Ct 37745
Haney Aly & Park 37743
Haney Hill Rd 37743
Hankins St 37745
Hankins Spring Ln 37745
Hannah St 37745
E & N Hardin St 37745
Harlan St 37745
Harmon Dr 37745
Harmon Park 37743
Harmony Cir 37743
Harold Cemetery Rd 37745
Harrison Dr & Rd 37743
Hartman Ln & Rd 37743
Hartshaw Dr 37743
Hawk Hollow Rd 37743
Hawkins Ln 37745
E & W Hawthorne Ct 37745
Haynes Blvd 37743
Hazel Dr 37745
Hazel Shelton Ln 37743
Heart K Dr 37743
Heather Ln 37745
Heather Way 37743
Heatherwood Loop 37745
Heavens Gate Ln 37743
Hemlock Ln & Trl 37745
Henard Rd 37743
Henry St 37743
Hens Ln 37745
Herantow Rd 37743
Heritage Ct 37743
Heritage Hills Dr 37745
Hermitage Dr & St 37745
Heron Ln 37743
S Hickory Cir 37743
Hickory Dr 37745
Hickory Trl 37745
Hidden Hts 37743
Hidden Valley Ln 37745
High St 37745
High Court Hl 37745
N Highland Ave 37745
S Highland Ave 37743
N Highway 107 37745
Highway 70 Byp 37743
N & S Hill St 37745
Hillcrest Dr 37745
Hillcrest Park 37743
Hillcrest St 37743
W Hillcrest St 37743
Hillcut Rd 37743
Hilliard St 37745
Hillrise Dr 37745
Hillside Ct 37745
Hilltop Dr 37745
Hixon Ave & Cir 37743
W Hogan Ave & Ln 37743
Holiday Ln 37743
Holland Ln & Rd 37745
Hollow Rock Ln 37743
Hollow Tree Ct 37745
Holly Ln & Park 37745
Holly Bush Ln 37745
Holly Creek Rd 37745
Holly Leaf Ln 37745
Holston Dr 37743
Holt Ct 37743
Home St 37743
Honeydew Ln 37743
Honeys Hl 37743
Honeysuckle Ln 37743
Hoover Rd 37745
Hope Rd 37745
Hopeville Ave 37745
Horseshoe Cir 37745
Horton Hwy 37745
House Rd 37743
Housley Ave 37745
Houston Valley Rd 37743
Humboldt Ln 37745
Hummingbird Ln 37743
Humphreys Rd 37745
Hutton Rd 37743
Idletime Dr 37743
Indian Grove Ln 37745
Indian Hills Cir 37743
Indian Hills Dr 37743
Industrial Rd 37745
N Irish St
100-199 37743
200-699 37745
S Irish St 37743
W Irish St 37743
Isley Ln 37745
Ivy Ln 37745
J Mell Johnson Rd 37745
Jack Ln 37743
Jack Norton Rd 37743
Jackson Ln E & W 37745
Jay Brooks St 37745
Jaybird Ln 37743
Jays Ln 37743
Jearoldstown Rd 37745
Jearoldstown Church Ln 37745
Jefferson St 37745
Jennifer St 37745
Jennings Ln 37743
Jennings Creek Ln 37743
Jewell Sayler Ln 37745
Jim Fox Rd 37743
Jimmy Johnston Rd 37743
Joe Johnston Ln 37743
Joe Pye Ln 37743
John Deere Rd 37743
John Graham Rd 37745
Johnson Rd 37743
Johnson St 37745
Johnson Hollow Ln 37745
Jonathan Ln 37745
Jones Ln 37743
Jones St 37745
Jones Bridge Rd 37743
Jones Chapel Ln 37745
Jones Quarry Rd 37745
Joseph Dr 37743
Jr Gray Rd 37743
Jr Kenney Ln 37745
Jubliee Rd 37745
Judy Dr 37743
Jules Ct 37745
Juniper St 37745
Justice Ln 37745

Street	ZIP
Justis Dr	37745
K St	37745
Katherine Ln	37743
Kathy Ave	37743
Keeneland Cir	37743
Keith Dr	37745
Kelley Gap Rd	37743
Kelly Dr & Ln	37745
Kendall Dr	37745
Kennedy Cir	37743
Kennel Ln	37743
Kenney St	37745
Kenneytown Rd	37745
Kenwood Dr	37745
Keplar Ln	37745
Kesterson St	37743
Kevin Ln	37745
Key Ln	37745
Kidwell School Rd	37745
Kilday Ln & Park	37745
Kimbili Dr	37745
King Dr & St	37743
King Arthur Ln	37745
King Arthur Trl	37743
Kingsley Ave	37745
Kingsport Hwy	37745
Kinser Park Ln	37743
Kirk Dr	37743
Kiser Blvd	37745
Kiser Loop	37743
Kiser Blvd Access	37745
Kitchen Branch Rd	37743
Kite Rd	37745
Knight St	37745
Knob Rd	37745
Knollwood Dr	37745
La Shambra Ln	37743
Lady Marion Trl	37743
Lafayette St	37745
Lake Dr	37745
Lake St	37743
S Lake St	37743
Lakeshore Dr & Park	37743
Lakeview St	37743
Lancer Ln	37743
Landair Way	37743
Landon St	37743
Lariat Ln	37745
Larkspur Ln	37745
Lauderdale Rd	37743
Laughlin Rd	37743
Laughlin Sq	37745
Laurel St	37743
Laurel Gap Dr	37745
Lavada St	37745
Laws Rd	37743
Lee St	37745
Leming St	37743
Leonard St	37745
Lexington Ct	37745
Liberty Way	37745
Lick Hollow Rd	37745
Light Ln	37745
Light St	37743
Lincoln Dr	37745
Linda St	37743
Linden Ave	37745
Link Hills Cir	37743
Links Mill Cir & Rd	37743
Links View Dr	37743
Little Brook Ln	37745
Little Indian Creek Rd	37743
Little John Trl	37743
Little Meadow Creek Rd	37743
Live Oak Ln	37743
Lobo Loop	37745
Locust St	37745
Loftus Ln	37745
Lofty Hts	37743
Log Cabin Rd	37743
Logwood Ln	37745
Lone Star Rd	37745
Lonesome Pine Trl	37745
Long Creek Rd	37743
Longview Dr & Pl	37745
Lords Ln	37743
Loretta St	37743
N Loretta St	37745
Lorraine St	37743
Lost Mountain Pike	37745
Love St	37745
Lovers Ln	37743
Loves Ln	37743
Lower Paint Creek Rd	37743
Luster Ln & Park	37743
Luther Dr	37745
Luttrell St	37743
Lyle Cir	37745
Lynn Ave	37745
Lynn Smith Ln	37743
Magnolia Dr	37743
N Main Ext	37745
N Main St	
100-199	37743
200-1999	37745
S Main St	37743
W Main St	37743
Majestic Cir & Ln	37743
Maple Ave & Crst	37743
Marble Rd	37745
Marie St	37743
Marietta Dr	37745
Marley Dr	37743
Marshall Ln	37743
Martingale Dr	37743
Masengill Rd N	37743
Mason St	37745
Max Way	37743
Mayor Ave	37745
Mays St	37743
Mcabee Dr	37745
Mcamis Rd	37745
Mccall Ave	37745
Mccormick Cir	37743
Mccoy Rd	37745
E Mckee St	37743
S Mckee St	37743
W Mckee St	37743
Mckee Way	37745
Meadow Ln	37745
Meadow Landing Ln	37743
Meadow Wood	37745
Meadowlark Dr	37743
Melody Cir & Rd	37743
Memory Ln	37745
Mikes Ave	37745
Mill Dr	37745
S Mill Rd	37743
Millers Chapel Rd	37745
Milligan Dr	37743
Mimosa Dr	37745
Mimosa Ln	37745
Mingo Trl	37743
Misty Hill Ln	37743
Misty Woods Ln	37743
Moccasin Ln	37743
Mockingbird Ln	37743
Mohawk Trl	37743
Monaco Dr	37745
Monarch Pt	37745
Monroe St	37745
Monte Vista Rd	37745
Montford Ave	37745
Monument Ave	37743
Monument Turn	37743
Moon Creek Rd	37745
Moore Ave	37745
Moore St	37743
Morgan Loop	37743
Morgan Rd	37745
Morningside Dr	37745
Morrow Ln	37745
Morse Ln	37743
Moser St	37745
Mount Bethel Rd	37745
Mount Hebron Rd	37743
Mount Pleasant Cir, Ln & Rd	37743
Mount Pleasant Circle Ext	37743
Mountain Loop	37745
Mountain River Dr	37743
Mountain View Cir	37743
Mountain View Dr	37743
Mountain View Ln	37745
Mudd Hollow Ln	37745
Mulberry Rd	37745
Murdock Rd	37745
Myers St	37743
Myers Acres Ln	37743
Myrtle St	37743
Mysinger Rd	37743
Nadine Ave	37743
Nanci Ln	37743
Nanny Rd	37743
Naples Ln	37743
Navaho St	37743
N Nelson St	37743
Nevada Ave	37745
New Hope Rd	37745
Newcastle Dr	37745
Newport Hwy	37743
Newton Slagle Ln	37745
Noah Gass Ln	37745
Noellwood Dr	37743
Nolichuckey Rd	37745
Nolichuckey Overlook	37743
Norma Dr	37745
Northwood Ln	37745
Norton Rd	37743
Oak Grove Ave & Rd	37745
Oak Hills Pkwy	37745
Oakland Park	37745
Oakmont Ln	37743
Ocean Blvd E & W	37745
Odell Cir	37743
Old Asheville Hwy	37743
Old Baileyton Rd	37745
Old Brown Mountain School Rd	37745
Old Cemetery Rd	37745
Old Erwin Hwy	37743
Old Indian Hill Trl	37743
Old Kentucky Rd S & W	37743
Old Knoxville Hwy	37743
Old Mine Rd	37745
Old Mountain Rd	37745
Old Newport Hwy	37743
Old Orchard Dr	37745
Old Ridge Ln	37745
Old Shiloh Cir & Rd	37745
Old Stage Rd	37745
Old Tusculum Rd	37745
Old Wilson Hill Rd	37745
Oliphant Dr	37743
Olivet Hvn	37745
Olivet Mountain Rd	37745
Olympia Dr	37745
Orchard St	37745
Orebank Rd	37745
Oregon Trl	37743
Oriole Dr	37743
Orrick Ln	37743
Ostrich Rd	37743
Ottway Rd	37743
Outer Dr	37743
Oven Creek Ln	37743
Overbrook Ln	37745
Overlook Dr	37745
Owen Ln	37745
Oxford Ln	37745
Paint Mountain Rd	37743
Palmer St	37745
Pandora Ln	37743
Panoramic View Dr E & W	37743
Panther Ln	37743
Par Ln	37743
Paradise Cv	37745
Park Ave E	37745
Park Ave W	37743
Park Ln	37743
Park Pl	37743
Park St	37743
Parkwood Cir	37745
Parman Rd	37743
Parrish Dr	37743
Parton Loop	37745
Partridge Ln	37745
Pates Ln	37743
Patricia Ln	37743
Patriot Xing	37745
Paul St	37743
Paul Weems Rd	37743
Payne Hollow Ln	37745
Peach Orchard Rd	37745
Pearl Aly & St	37743
Peavine Way	37743
Pebblehill Park	37745
Pelican Ln	37743
Pennsylvania Ave	37743
Peppermint Ln	37743
Perry St	37745
Perry Davis Rd	37743
Persimmon Ln	37743
Pierce Way	37743
Pigeon Creek Rd	37745
Piggyback Ln	37745
Pike Rd	37745
Pilot Knob Rd	37745
Pine Loop & St	37745
Pine Straw Rdg	37745
Pinecrest Ct E	37745
Pinecrest Ct W	37745
Pinecrest Dr	37745
W Pines Rd	37745
Pinewood Cir	37745
Piney Grove Rd	37743
Pinto Rd	37745
Pioneer Ln	37745
Pisgah Rd	37745
Plainview Heights Cir	37745
Plantation Dr	37745
Planters Row	37745
Pleasant View Dr	37745
Pleasure Cir	37745
Plowshare Rd	37745
Plum Tree Ln	37743
Plymouth Hl	37743
E Point Trce	37745
Polk St	37745
Ponderosa Dr	37743
Pony Trl	37743
Poor Farm Rd	37745
Poplar Ct	37745
Poplar Springs Rd	37743
Possum Creek Rd	37743
Possum Creek Access Rd	37743
Powell St	37745
Prairie Ln	37745
Price Ln	37743
Price Cemetery Ln	37745
Pristine Pt	37745
Professional Plaza Dr	37745
Prospect Ave	37743
Pruitt Ln & Rd	37743
Pumpkin Bloom Ln	37743
Puppy Love Ln	37743
Pyburn Ln	37743
Quail Ridge Ln	37743
Quillen Shell Rd	37745
Rabbit Gap Rd	37745
Rader Ln	37743
Rader Union Ln	37745
Raders Sidetrack Rd	37743
Radford Dr	37745
Railroad Ln	37745
Railroad St	37745
Rainbow Cir	37743
Rambling Ct	37745
Rambo Rd	37743
Rankin Dr	37745
Rattlesnake Rdg	37745
Raven Ln	37743
Ray Casteel Rd	37745
Rayley Ct	37745
Raymond Rd	37745
Reaves Aly	37743
Reaves Hill Dr	37745
Reaves Mill Rd	37743
Rebel Rd	37743
Red Hill Rd	37743
Redbud Dr	37743
Redgate Rd	37743
Rednour St	37743
Reed Ave	37743
Reed Rd	37745
Regency Park	37745
Rehobeth Church Ln	37743
Remine Ave	37745
Remington Ct	37743
Revonda Cir	37743
Reynolds Hollow Rd	37745
Rhea Cir	37743
Richard Blake Rd	37743
Richland Rd	37743
Ricker Ave & Rd	37743
Ridgecrest Dr	37743
E & W Ridgefield Ct	37745
Ridgemont Dr	37745
Ridgeview Dr	37745
Riles Cir	37743
Ringdove Ln	37743
River Rd	37743
River Bend Rd	37743
River Bluff Cir	37743
River Pointe Dr	37743
River Trace Ln	37743
River Walk Ct	37743
Riverview Dr	37743
Roaring Fork Rd	37743
Robert Harmon Rd	37743
Robert Kilday Rd	37745
Roberts Cir	37743
Robin Hood Trl	37743
Robinhood Rd	37745
Robinson St	37745
Rockwell Dr	37745
Rockwood Dr	37743
Rocky Hill Dr	37743
Rocky Top	37743
Roller St	37743
Rolling Hills Ln & Rd	37743
E & W Rollins St	37743
Rollins Chapel Rd	37745
Rollins Ridge Rd	37743
Romans Dr	37743
Ronnie St	37743
Rooster Ln	37743
Rose Ln	37745
Ross Blvd	37743
Round Knob Ln & Rd	37743
Royal St	37745
Royce St	37743
N & S Rufe Taylor Rd	37745
Runion Way	37743
Rupert Ramsey Ln	37743
Russell Park	37745
Rustic Ct	37745
Saint James Rd	37743
Salem Rd	37743
Sam Doak St	37745
Sam Jenkins Ln	37745
Sanders Rd	37743
Sanford Cir	37743
Saunders Way	37743
E & W Savanna Ct	37745
Saville Way	37745
Sawyer Way	37743
Sayler Rd N & S	37745
Scenic Dr	37743
Schofield Dr	37745
Seaton Ave & Rd	37745
Sentelle Rd	37743
Sequoia Trl	37743
Serral Dr	37745
E & W Sevier Ave & Hts	37745
Shadow Wood Park	37745
Shady Ln	37743
Shady Rest Cir & Cv	37745
Shakerag Rd	37743
Shallow Creek Ln	37745
Shane St	37743
Shawnee Ln	37743
Shelton Ln	37745
Shelton Mission Rd	37743
Shepherd Dr	37743
Shiloh Rd	37745
Shiloh Shoals Dr	37745
Shipley Ln	37745
Shipley Rd	37743
Simpson St	37743
Single Tree Ln	37743
Sioux Trl	37743
Skippers Park	37745
Skyview Dr & Ln	37745
Skyway Ln	37745
Slate Creek Rd	37743
Sleepy Hl	37743
Sleepy Hollow Ln	37745
Smelcer Ln	37743
Smith Ln	37745
Smith St	37743
Smith Hollow Rd	37743
Smokehouse Ln	37745
Smokey View Dr	37745
Snake Hollow Rd	37743
Snapps Ferry Park & Rd	37745
Snyder Ln	37743
Songbird Dr	37743
Southridge Dr	37743
Southwind Cir	37743
Sparrow Ln	37743
Sparta St	37745
Spears Dykes Rd	37745
Speedway Dr	37743
Spencer St	37745
E Spencer St	37743
Spider Stines Rd	37745
Spring St	37743
Spring Creek Pl	37745
Springbrooke Park	37743
Spruce St	37745
St Wilhoit Dr	37745
E & W Stagecoach Rd	37745
Stanbery Cir	37745
Stanley Ln	37745
Stanton Ln	37743
Starlite Dr	37743
Starnes Ln	37745
Starnes Hollow Ln	37745
Starway Ln	37745
State St	37743
Stephen Brooks Rd	37745
Stills Rd	37743
Stomper Rd	37745
Stone Crest Park	37743
Stone Mountain Ln	37745
Storm Rd	37743
Stratford Dr	37743
Strong St	37743
Sugar Cane Ln	37745
Sulphur Springs Loop	37745
E & W Summer St	37743
Summer Hill Ln	37745
Summey Cir	37745
Summey Reynolds Park	37745
Summit Dr	37743
Sun Valley Dr & Vlg	37745
Sunburst Aly	37743
Sunny Meadow Ln	37743
Sunnydale Rd	37743
Sunnyside Loop & Rd	37743
Sunnyside Ridge Dr	37745
Sunnyslope Ln	37743
Sunnyview Rd	37743
Sunrise Ave	37745
Sunrise Cir	37743
Sunrise Dr	37743
Sunrise Ln	37743
N & S Sunset Blvd & St	37743
Surtout Rd	37745
Susong Dr	37745
Susong Ln	37743
Susong Rd	37743
Susong Memorial Rd	37743
Swan Acres Park	37745
Swanee Ln	37745
Swatsell Ln	37743
Sweetbriar Ln	37743
Swift Park	37743
Sycamore Ct & St	37745
Sylvan Cir	37743
T Elmer Cox Rd	37743
Tabor Ln & Rd	37743
Takeoff Ln	37745
Takoma Ave	37743
Tamara Ct & Ln	37743
Tanglewood Dr	37743
Tarlton Cir	37743
Tateho Rd	37745
Taylor Ln	37745
Ted Weems Rd	37745
Temple St	37743
Tennessee Dr	37743
Terry Leonard Dr	37745
Thistle Cv	37745
Thornwood Dr	37745
Tilson Ln	37745
Timber Ln & Trl	37743
Timber Ridge Rd	37743
Timbers Ln & Trl	37745
Tiny Ln	37743
Tob Cooter Ln	37745
Tomahawk Ln	37745
Trails End Ln	37743
Tristan Way	37743
Troy Morelock Ln	37743
Tucker Way	37745
Tunnel Ln	37745
Tunnell Rd	37743
Tusculum Blvd, Byp & Cir	37745
Tusculum Heights Dr	37745
Tweed Springs Rd	37743
Twin Barns Rd	37743
Twin Oaks Dr	37745
S Unaka Aly, Dr & St	37743
Underwood Way	37743
Union Rd	37743
Union St	37743
Upland Ave	37743
Vagabond Ln	37743
Valerie Ln	37743
Valiant Cir & Dr	37743
Valk Ln	37743
Valley View Dr	37743
Valleyview Rd	37743
Van Hill Est & Rd	37745
Vann Rd	37743
Vault Hl	37745
Venice Ln	37745
Veranda Ct	37745
Vestal Ct	37745
Vicky St	37743
Victory Blvd	37743
Viking Cir	37743
Viking Pl	37745
Viking Mountain Rd	37743
Villa Ct & Ln	37745
Village Dr	37743
Vintage Ln	37743
Virginia Dr	37745
Vista St	37745
Volunteer St	37745
Waddell Love Rd	37743
Waddell Mountain Rd	37743
Walker Dr	37745
Walkers Park	37745
Walkers Ford Rd	37743
Walnut St	37745
Walnut Grove Rd	37743
Walters Ln & Rd	37743
Ward Park	37743
Warrensburg Rd	37743
Warrensburg Road Access	37743
N & S Water Fork Rd	37743
Watercress Dr	37745
Waterstone Cir	37745
Wattenbarger Gap Rd	37745
Wayfair Cir & Dr	37743
Wayland Dr	37743
Waymar Ln	37745
Wayside Ln	37745

Wedgewood Ln 37745
Weemes St 37743
Weems Rd 37745
Wellington Dr 37743
Wesley Ave 37743
N & S Wesley Chapel Rd 37745
West St 37745
Westbrook Dr 37743
Whirlwind Rd 37743
Whispering Rd 37743
Whispering Oaks Ln 37745
Whispering Ridges Rd 37743
Whisperwood Dr 37743
White Rd 37745
White Sands Rd 37743
Whitehouse Rd 37745
Whittaker Dr 37745
Wi Bowman Rd 37743
Widow Hollow Rd 37745
Wilburn Ln 37745
Wild Turkey Ln 37743
Wildberry Ln 37745
Wildwood Ct 37745
Willis Dr & St 37745
Willow Creek Ct, Dr & Ln 37743
Wilson Dr 37743
Winchester Dr 37743
Windcrest Trl 37745
Windcrest Way 37743
Windover Park 37743
Windover Rd 37745
Windsong Rd 37745
Windswept Ln 37743
Windward Ln 37743
Windwood Dr 37745
Windy Hl 37745
Wines Rd 37745
Wintergreen Ave 37745
Woodbury Cir 37745
Woodcrest Cir & Dr 37745
Wooded Hts 37743
Woodfield Rd 37743
Woodhaven Cir & Ln 37745
Woodland Cir 37743
Woodlawn Dr & Rd 37745
Woodlyn St 37743
Woodmont Dr 37743
Woodridge Cir 37743
Woodside Dr 37745
Woolsey Rd 37745
Woolsey College Rd 37743
Worley Dr 37743
Wren St 37745
Wykle Rd 37743
Wynwood Ave 37743
Y St 37745
York Dr 37745
Young Cir 37743

NUMBERED STREETS

All Street Addresses 37743

HENDERSONVILLE TN

General Delivery 37075

POST OFFICE BOXES MAIN OFFICE STATIONS AND BRANCHES

Box No.s
All PO Boxes 37077

NAMED STREETS

Abberley Cir 37075
Aberdeen Dr & Pt 37075
Addington Rd 37075
Affirmed Dr 37075
Agee Cir & Ct 37075
Airfloat Dr 37075
Alderwood Dr 37075
Alexander Ct & Dr 37075
Alexandrea Ct & Pl 37075
E Allen Ct, Dr & Rd N & S 37075
Allison Dr 37075
Alred Cir 37075
Anchor Dr 37075
N Anderson Ln & Rd 37075
Andrew Ct 37075
Andrews Run 37075
Anglepointe 37075
Annapolis Bend Cir 37075
Annas Ct 37075
Antebellum Cir 37075
Antler Ln 37075
Apache Ct 37075
Applewood Ct 37075
Applewood Valley Dr 37075
Arrowhead Dr 37075
Ash Ct 37075
Ashford Ct 37075
Ashland Pt 37075
Aspen Ct 37075
Atchley Ct 37075
Atherton Ct 37075
Audubon Ln 37075
Augusta Ct 37075
Avery Trace Cir 37075
Avondale Rd 37075
Avondale Access Rd 37075
Bahia Mar Pt 37075
Ballentrae Ct & Dr 37075
Barbara Dr 37075
Bartlett Ln 37075
Bates Ct 37075
Bay Dr 37075
Bayshore Ct & Dr 37075
Bayview Ct & Dr 37075
Beacon Light Cv 37075
Beaumont Ct & Dr 37075
Bedford St 37075
Beechwood Ct 37075
Bellepointe 37075
Belmont Cir 37075
Benniel Dr 37075
Bennington Ct & Pl N 37075
Bent Creek Ct 37075
Bentree Ct & Dr 37075
Benwick Rd 37075
Berrington Ct 37075
Berry Hill Dr 37075
Berryfield Ct 37075
Berryview Ct 37075
Berrywood Ct & Dr 37075
Bethea Ct 37075
N & S Birchwood Dr 37075
Birnam Ct 37075
Bledsoe Dr 37075
Blue Ridge Ct, Dr & Trce N & S 37075
Bluegrass Cir, Cv, Dr & Pt 37075
Bluegrass Commons Blvd 37075
Bluewater Dr 37075
Bonita Pkwy 37075
Boone Holman Dr 37075
Bostring Dr 37075
Bradford Cir 37075
Brant Ln 37075
Bratton Ct 37075
E & W Braxton Ln 37075
Breakwater Dr N 37075
Breckinridge Ct 37075
Briarcrest Ct & Ln 37075
Bridle Ct 37075
Brierfield Way 37075
Brinkley Branch Rd 37075
Brittan St 37075
Brixton Blvd 37075
Brookside Ct & Dr 37075
Brunswick Dr 37075
Buchanan Cir & Pl 37075
Buckhaven Ct & Dr 37075
Buena Vista Dr 37075
Burlington Ct 37075
Burnham Cir & Dr S 37075
Burntash Ln 37075
Burrus Ave 37075
Busby Hollow Ln 37075
Business Ct 37075
Cabin Branch Cir 37075
Cages Rd 37075
Caldwell Dr 37075
Callender Ct & Ln 37075
Callis Rd 37075
Calloway Ln 37075
Camarado Ln 37075
Camden Ct N 37075
Camino Cir 37075
Camp Creek Cir & Ct 37075
Campus Dr 37075
Candle Pl 37075
Candle Wood Ct & Dr 37075
Candlewick Pl 37075
Candy Ln 37075
Canfield Pl 37075
Cannons Xing 37075
Canterbury Ln 37075
Capps Ln 37075
Captains Cir 37075
Carden St 37075
Cardinal Ln 37075
Carlton Dr 37075
Carly Close E & W 37075
Carlyle Ct 37075
Carol Dr 37075
Carolyn Cir 37075
Carriage Ln, Pl & Way 37075
Carriage Hill Dr 37075
Carrington Pl & Rd 37075
Castle Ct 37075
Castleview Dr 37075
Cattail Ln 37075
Caudill Dr 37075
Cavalier Dr 37075
Cedar Ct 37075
Cedar Ridge Ln & Way 37075
Cedar Springs Trl 37075
Cedar Valley Rd 37075
Cedarcrest Dr 37075
Cedarwood Dr 37075
Center Point Ct & Rd S 37075
Centerpoint Rd 37075
Chadwick Ct 37075
Chambliss Ct 37075
Chaparral Dr 37075
Chapel Ct N & S 37075
Charleston Ct 37075
Chasepointe Dr 37075
Chatsworth Ct 37075
Cherokee Pt & Rd 37075
Cherry Hill Dr 37075
Cheryl Ct & Dr 37075
Chesapeake Harbor Blvd 37075
Chesire Pl 37075
N & S Chestnut 37075
Cheviot Ct 37075
Cheyenne Dr 37075
Chickamauga Dr 37075
Chippendale Dr 37075
Chipwood Dr 37075
Chiroc Rd 37075
Chiswick Ct 37075
Choctaw Ct & Dr 37075
Cinema Dr 37075
Circle Dr 37075
Citation Cir 37075
Clairmonte Ln 37075
Clarendon Pl 37075
Clearview Cir 37075
Clifftop Dr 37075
Cline Ave & Ct 37075
Clovercrest Dr 37075
Cloverdale Ct 37075
Cloverfield Ct 37075
Coachlight Ct 37075
Coachman Pl 37075
Coarsey Blvd 37075
Cobbler Cir 37075
Coldwater Dr 37075
Cole Ct & Dr 37075
Colonial Ct & Dr 37075
Colony Dr 37075
Commerce Dr 37075
Connie Dr 37075
Cool Springs Ct 37075
Cornelia Dr 37075
Coulsons Ct 37075
N Country Club Dr 37075
Country Hills Dr 37075
Country View Dr 37075
Countryside Dr 37075
Countrywood Dr 37075
Courtside Pl 37075
Cranwill Dr 37075
Craven Ct 37075
Creekglen Ct & Dr 37075
Creekside Ct 37075
Creekwood Ln 37075
Cresthaven Ct 37075
Crestmont Dr 37075
Crestview Dr 37075
Crestwood Ct 37075
Crimson Way 37075
Crooked Creek Ct & Ln 37075
Crosby Dr 37075
Cross Bow Ct & Dr 37075
Cross Cove Ct 37075
Cross Creek Ct & Ln 37075
Crossfield Dr 37075
Crosspointe 37075
Crossroad Dr 37075
Crossroads Ct 37075
Crown Ct 37075
Cumberland Dr & Pl 37075
Cumberland Blue Trl 37075
Cumberland Hills Dr 37075
Cumberland Shores Dr 37075
Curtis Crossroads 37075
Curtiswood Dr 37075
Dale Ave 37075
Dalton Cir 37075
Dana Dr 37075
Daniel Dr 37075
Daniel Smith Dr 37075
Danwood Ct 37075
Darwood Ct 37075
Davidson Ct 37075
Deer Ridge Ln 37075
Deerfoot Ct 37075
Deerpoint Cir, Ct, Dr & Ln 37075
Deerwood Dr 37075
Del Ray Trl 37075
Delft Dr 37075
Dennis Rd 37075
Devon Ct 37075
Devonshire Trl 37075
Diddle Ct & Dr 37075
Dillon Dr 37075
Doe Valley Dr 37075
Dogwood Pl 37075
Dolphus Dr 37075
Donmond Dr 37075
Donna Ct & Dr 37075
Donnawood Ct 37075
Donovan Ct 37075
Doral Ln & Pl 37075
Dorcas Dr 37075
Dorris Ct & Dr 37075
Dorset Dr 37075
Dover Ct & Pt 37075
Downing Ct 37075
Drakes Creek Rd 37075
Drakes Hill Ct 37075
Dunn St 37075
Dwight Cherlyn Ct 37075
Earline Dr 37075
East Dr 37075
Eastridge Ct 37075
Edgehill Ln 37075
Edgeview Ct & Dr 37075
Edgewater Ct & Pl 37075
Edgewood Dr 37075
Elderberry Dr 37075
Eldorado Ct 37075
Elissa Dr 37075
Elizer Ct & St 37075
Elm Hill Cir 37075
Elmsford Ct 37075
Elnora Ct & Dr 37075
England Pl 37075
English Ct 37075
Erin Ct 37075
Ernest Wright Ln 37075
E Ervin Dr & St 37075
Eventide Dr 37075
Evergreen Cir & Ct 37075
Evian Springs Way 37075
Executive Park Dr 37075
Fairgrove Cir 37075
Fairlake Ct 37075
Fairways Dr 37075
Falling Leaf Ln 37075
Fawn Ct 37075
Fieldcrest Cir, Ct & Dr 37075
Flaxton St 37075
Flint Dr 37075
Forest Harbor Ct & Dr 37075
Forest Meadows Ct & Dr 37075
Forest Retreat Rd 37075
Forest View Dr 37075
Forestpointe 37075
Fortune Dr 37075
Fountain Brooke Dr 37075
Foxcross Dr 37075
Foxwood Trl 37075
Frazor Ln 37075
Free Hill Rd 37075
Freshrun Dr 37075
Frey Ln 37075
Fulman Rd 37075
Gadwall Cir 37075
Gail Dr 37075
Galway Lk N & S 37075
Gander Way 37075
Gannett Rd 37075
Garrett Ln 37075
Gates Ct & Dr 37075
Gateway Ln 37075
Gatire Dr 37075
Gatone Ct & Dr 37075
General Smith Pl 37075
Georgetown Dr 37075
Glance Ct 37075
Glen Leven Way 37075
Glen Oak Blvd & Ct 37075
Glenbrook Way 37075
Glencrest Dr 37075
Glenn Hill Dr 37075
Glenview Dr 37075
God Why Ct 37075
Golden Leaf Ln 37075
Golf Ct 37075
Golf Club Cir, Ct & Ln 37075
Golf View Dr 37075
Goshentown Rd 37075
N & S Governors Cv 37075
Governors Point Blvd 37075
Grand View Ct 37075
Grapevine Ct & Rd 37075
Green Meadows Dr 37075
Greenlawn Dr 37075
Greenyards Pl 37075
Grove Ln S 37075
Hacketts Ct 37075
Haddaway Dr 37075
Hamilton Ct 37075
Hampton Ct 37075
Hancedg Dr 37075
Hanover Ct 37075
E & W Harbor Ct & Dr 37075
Harbortowne Dr 37075
Harlan Ave 37075
Harlequin Blvd 37075
Harmony Ln 37075
Harrington Holw 37075
Hatcher Ln 37075
Hattie Ct 37075
Haven St 37075
Havenwood Ct 37075
Haverford Ct 37075
Hazel Path 37075
Hazel Path Ct 37075
Hazelwood Ct & Dr 37075
Hearthside Ct N & S 37075
Heathrow Ln 37075
Hedgelawn Dr 37075
Hemlock Ct 37075
Hepplewhite Dr 37075
Heritage Woods Dr 37075
Herman Harrison Dr 37075
Herons Nest Ln 37075
Hickory Trl & Way N 37075
Hickory Heights Dr 37075
Hickory Hill Dr 37075
Hickory Hills Dr 37075
Hidden Ct & Pt 37075
Hidden Lake Ct & Rd 37075
Hidden Way Ct 37075
High Cliff Dr 37075
High Point Anchorage 37075
Highland Rdg 37075
Highlander Dr 37075
Hill Ln 37075
Hillcrest Dr 37075
Hillsdale Dr 37075
Hillside Ct & Dr 37075
Hilltop Dr 37075
Hillview Dr 37075
Hillwood Ct & Dr 37075
Hogan Way 37075
Hogan Bridge Ln 37075
Hogans Branch Rd 37075
Holly Ct & Dr 37075
Holmes Dr 37075
Homestead Ct, Dr, Ln & Pl W 37075
Honeysuckle Dr 37075
Huckleberry Way 37075
Hull Ln 37075
Hunters Ln & Trl 37075
Huntington Pl 37075
Hunts Ln 37075
Hurt Rd 37075
Imperial Blvd
100-106 37075
105-105 37077
107-199 37075
108-198 37075
Imperial Pt 37075
Indian Dr 37075
Indian Lake Blvd, Ct & Rd 37075
Indian Lake Forest Ct 37075
Industrial Park Dr 37075
Ingrid Way 37075
Inlet Dr 37075
Inverness Ct 37075
Iris Ct & Dr 37075
Iroquois Ct 37075
Island Dr 37075
Island Brook Dr 37075
Ivy Dr 37075
Jackson Ln 37075
Jackstaff Dr 37075
Jameson Pl 37075
Jamestown Pl 37075
Jefferson Dr 37075
Jenkins Ct & Ln 37075
Jennings Dr 37075
Jensen Ln 37075
Jessica Lauren Ct 37075
John Henry Ln 37075
Jones Ct, Ln & Rd 37075
Judson Dr 37075
Karens Way 37075
Karens Pvt Way 37075
Keene Vly N & S 37075
Kellyn Ln 37075
Kemper Trl 37075
Kendall Farms Dr 37075
Kensington Ct 37075
Kenton Loop 37075
Keystone Ln 37075
Kidron Way 37075
Kimber Ln 37075
Kimberly Ct 37075
Kinwood Ct 37075
Kiser Ave 37075
Knights Bridge Sta 37075
Knob Cir 37075
Knoll Ln 37075
Knollwood Ct 37075
Knox Ct 37075
Koleberg Ct & Trl 37075
La Bar Ct & Dr 37075
La Greta Dr 37075
La Plaza Dr 37075
La Sabre Dr 37075
La Via Dr 37075
La View Rd 37075
La Vista Dr 37075
Lacebark Ln 37075
Lagrange Dr 37075
Lake Deville Dr 37075
Lake Forest Pt 37075
Lake Harbor Dr 37075
Lake Haven Ln 37075
Lake Park Dr 37075
Lake Ridge Dr 37075
Lake Terrace Ct & Dr 37075
Lake Valley Rd 37075
Lake Vista Dr 37075
Lakecrest Cir 37075
Lakeside Cir 37075
Lakeside Park Ct & Dr 37075
Lakeview Ct & Dr 37075
Lands End 37075
Latham Ct 37075
Latimer Ct & Ln 37075
Lauderdale Ct 37075
Laurel Ct & Ln 37075
N & S Laurens Way 37075
Lavergne Cir 37075
Lee Ct 37075
Leeward Pt 37075
Legends Dr 37075
Leota Dr 37075
Lesa Dr 37075
Lexington Sta 37075
Liberty Ct & Cv 37075
Lightberry Ln 37075
Lighthouse Cir 37075
Lincoln Ct 37075
Linda Dr 37075
Linden Dr 37075
Lisa Knutson Ln 37075
Loch Leven Way 37075
Lock Three Rd 37075
Long Hollow Ln, Pike & Way 37075
Longview Dr, Pl & Rdg 37075
Louann Ln 37075
Louise Ave 37075
Lucinda Ln 37075
Luke Ct 37075
Luna Ln 37075
Lynhurst Cir 37075
Lynn Dr 37075
Macy Dr 37075
E & W Main St 37075
Mallard Dr 37075
Manor Way 37075
Mansker Farm Blvd 37075
Mansker Park Dr 37075
Maple Dr, St & Way N & S 37075
Maple Forest Ct 37075
Maple Row Blvd 37075
Maple View Trl 37075
Margaret Dr 37075
Marseille Ct & Dr 37075
Marshall St 37075
Martin Dr 37075

Masters Ct & Way 37075
Maureen Dr 37075
Mayfield Ln 37075
Mayhaw Ln 37075
Mcbratney Dr 37075
Mckain Xing 37075
Mckee Ln 37075
Mcmurtry Rd 37075
Meadow Ct & Ln 37075
Meadow Circle Ct 37075
Meadow Creek Ct & Ln 37075
Meadow Crest Ct 37075
Meadow Lake Ct & Dr 37075
Meadowpointe E & W 37075
Meadowvue Dr 37075
Melanie Dr 37075
Melody Ln 37075
Merrick Rd 37075
Merrimac Dr 37075
Mid Town Ct 37075
Milburn Rd 37075
Mill Point Cir 37075
Millbrook Rd 37075
Mir Pkwy 37075
Mockingbird Hill Rd 37075
Molly Walton Dr 37075
Monitor Ln 37075
Monthaven Blvd 37075
Monthaven Park Pl 37075
Morchella Private Way 37075
Morningview Dr 37075
Morris St 37075
Moss Ct 37075
Mount Olivet Ct, Ln & Rd 37075
Mountainwood Dr 37075
Moyna Dr 37075
Mud Hollow Rd 37075
Music Village Blvd 37075
Myrtlewood Ln 37075
Nan Dr 37075
Narrow Ln 37075
Natchez Dr 37075
Nathan Forest Ct & Dr 37075
Nauta Ct 37075
Neptune Dr 37075
Neverbreak Dr 37075
New Hope Rd 37075
New Shackle Island Rd 37075
Newman St 37075
Newmans Trl 37075
Newport Cir & Ln 37075
Nokes Ct & Dr 37075
Northlake Ct & Dr 37075
Northlawn Cir 37075
Northview Ct & Dr 37075
Oak Ct & Pl 37075
Oak Hill Ct 37075
Oak Leaf Ct & Dr 37075
Oak Meadow Ct 37075
Oakvale Ct 37075
Oakwood Ct 37075
Old Shackle Island Ct & Rd 37075
Orange Blossom Ct 37075
Orchard Valley Cir & Rd 37075
Otter Cv 37075
Otter Glenn Dr 37075
Otterman Ct 37075
Overlook Cir & Dr 37075
Owen Ct 37075
Paducah Dr 37075
Pana Ct & Dr 37075
Paradise Dr 37075
Parisian Dr 37075
Park Cir & Ln 37075
Parkwood Ln 37075
Parsons Way 37075
Patmore Ln 37075
Patton Ln 37075
Paxton Ct & Dr 37075
Peachtree Ln 37075
Peartree Dr 37075
Pebble Creek Dr 37075
Pecanwood Ct 37075
Peck Pl 37075
Pembroke Ct & Dr 37075
Peninsula Park Dr 37075
Pico Ct 37075
Pilot Knob Ln & Rd 37075
Pin Oak Dr 37075
Pine Bark Cir 37075
Pine Branch Trl 37075
Pintail Pl 37075
Pioneer Ct 37075
Plaza Dr 37075
Pleasantview Dr 37075
Plumlee Ct & Dr 37075
Polk Ct 37075
Porter Ct 37075
Post Oak Rd 37075
Powell Dr 37075
Power Plant Rd 37075
Pres Blon Dr 37075
Private Dr 37075
Privett Ct 37075
Promontory Way 37075
Quartering Pl 37075
Rachels Ct 37075
Radcliff Ln 37075
Raindrop Ln 37075
Raintree Dr 37075
Raspberry Valley Ct 37075
Read Tavern 37075
Rebecca Ct & Dr 37075
Rebel Rd 37075
Red Maple Ct 37075
Redbud Dr 37075
Redondo Ct N & S 37075
Redwood Way 37075
Rhodes Ln 37075
Rice Ct & Rd 37075
W Ridge Ct & Dr N & S 37075
Ridgecrest Dr 37075
Ridgemar Trl 37075
Ridgemont Ct 37075
E Ridgeview Ct & Trce 37075
Riva Rdg 37075
River Rd 37075
River Bend Rd 37075
River Chase 37075
Riverbirch Ln 37075
Riverwood Ct & Dr 37075
Riviera Dr 37075
Robbieview Ct 37075
Roberta Dr 37075
Robinhood Cir 37075
Rock Castle Ct & Ln 37075
Rockland Hts & Rd 37075
Rockton Ct 37075
Rolling Hills Dr 37075
Ropers Ct 37075
Rosewood Ct 37075
Rowdy Dixie Ct 37075
Royal Ct 37075
Ruby Dr 37075
Ruland Cir 37075
Rushing Water Ct 37075
Rutherford Way 37075
Ryan Dr 37075
Saddle Dr 37075
Sagamore Trce 37075
Sain Ave 37075
Saint Andrews Dr 37075
Saltwood Pl 37075
Sanders Ferry Rd 37075
Sandpiper Cir 37075
Sandy Valley Rd 37075
Sandy Valley Farms Ln 37075
Saranac Trl 37075
Saratoga Blvd 37075
Saunders Ct 37075
Saundersville Rd 37075
Savannah Way 37075
Savely Ct & Dr 37075
Savo Bay 37075
Scarlet Ct 37075
Scarsdale Dr S 37075
Scenic View Dr 37075
Scotch Ct & St 37075
Secretariat Pl 37075
Sequoyah Dr & Trl 37075
Sessler Ct 37075
Settlers Way 37075
Shadow Ln 37075
N & S Shadowhaven Way 37075
Shady Dr 37075
Shady View Dr 37075
Shadydale Dr 37075
Shaw Ln 37075
Shawnee Dr 37075
Shell Ln & Rd 37075
Shelter Cv 37075
Shenandoah Dr 37075
Sherbrooke Ln 37075
Shiloh Rdg 37075
Shirley Dr 37075
Shivel Dr 37075
Shore Hill Ct 37075
Shorecrest Cir 37075
Shoreside Dr 37075
Shute Ln 37075
Silver Maple Ct 37075
Sioux Ct 37075
Skyview Ct & Dr 37075
Sleepy Hollow Ct 37075
Smoke Rise Ln 37075
Snug Harbor Dr 37075
Somerset Downs Blvd 37075
Sophie Ct 37075
Sorrel Ct 37075
Southburn Ct & Dr 37075
Southern Trce 37075
Southlawn Cir 37075
Spade Leaf Blvd 37075
Spearpoint Dr 37075
Spring Creek Trl 37075
Spring Haven Ct 37075
Spring Valley Rd 37075
Springhouse Ct 37075
Spruce Dr 37075
Spy Glass Way 37075
Stadium Dr 37075
Stafford Ct 37075
Stark Knob Rd 37075
Sterling Ct & Rd 37075
Stillhouse Rd 37075
Stillwater Ct & Trl 37075
E & W Stirling Ct 37075
Stirlingshire Ct & Dr 37075
Stirrup Ct 37075
Stonebrook Ln 37075
Stonehollow Way 37075
Stones Throw 37075
Stonewall Ct & Dr 37075
Stoneway 37075
Stoney Brook Way 37075
Stop 30 Rd 37075
Strathmore Ct & Way 37075
Stuart Dr 37075
Sugar Maple N & S 37075
Summerlake Pl 37075
Summerwood Ct 37075
Summit Ln 37075
Sumner Ct 37075
Sumner Meadows Ct & Ln 37075
Sunset Ct, Dr & Pl 37075
Surrey Hill Pt 37075
Susan Ct & Dr 37075
Sweet Oak Rdg 37075
Sycamore Ct 37075
Tamaras Ct & Way 37075
Taylor Industrial Blvd 37075
Ten Oaks Dr E & W 37075
Tennessee Way 37075
Terry Lynn Dr 37075
The Lndg 37075
The Hollows Ct 37075
Thicket Ln 37075
Thistle Ct 37075
Thomas Dr 37075
Thorn Hill Ct 37075
Thornwood Pl 37075
Tiffany Ln 37075
Timber Trl 37075
Timber Hills Rd 37075
Timberlake Dr 37075
Timberline Dr 37075
Tini Mae Ln 37075
Tioga Trl 37075
Tower Hill Ln 37075
Township Ct & Dr 37075
Trace Ct 37075
Trail East Dr 37075
Trail Ridge Dr & Way 37075
Travis St 37075
Treemont Ct 37075
Trenton Ln 37075
Trident Pl 37075
Troon Ct 37075
Trousdale Ct & Dr 37075
Trout Valley Dr 37075
Trucord Dr 37075
Turning Leaf Way 37075
Twin Bay Dr 37075
Twin Oaks Ct 37075
Two Valley Rd 37075
Tyne Bay Dr 37075
Tyree Ln 37075
Tyree Hollow Ln 37075
Tyree Springs Ct & Rd 37075
N & S Valley Dr & Rd 37075
Valley Brook Dr 37075
Valley View Ct 37075
Vandywood Ct 37075
Veebelt Dr 37075
Venetian Way 37075
Venlee Dr 37075
Ventura Ct 37075
Victoria Ct & Ln 37075
Villa Way 37075
Village Ct 37075
Vinewood Dr 37075
Vintage Cir 37075
Vista Ct 37075
Vollan Ct 37075
Volunteer Dr 37075
Vulco Dr 37075
Wagon Ct 37075
Walden Ct 37075
Wallingford Ct 37075
Walnut Ct, Dr & Trce 37075
Waltham Ct 37075
Walton Ct & Trce 37075
Walton Ferry Rd 37075
Walton Village Ct & Dr 37075
Ward Ln 37075
Warren Pl 37075
Waterford Way 37075
Waters Edge Ln 37075
Waterview Cir & Dr 37075
Wayne Ct 37075
Weeping Willow Rd 37075
Welcome Ln 37075
Werner Dr 37075
Wessex Ct 37075
N Wessington Ct & Pl 37075
Westbank Dr 37075
Wexford Hall 37075
Whirlaway Ct 37075
Whispering Way 37075
Whispering Wind Way 37075
White Oak Ct & Way 37075
Whitley Pl 37075
Wickham Ct 37075
William Shy Dr 37075
Williamsburg Dr 37075
Willis Dr 37075
Willow Park Cir 37075
Wilmington Ct 37075
Windham Cir, Cv & Dr 37075
Winding Way Dr 37075
Windmill Pointe Cir 37075
Windsor Park Ln 37075
Windstar Bay Blvd 37075
Windward Pt 37075
Winston Hills Pkwy 37075
Winton Ct 37075
Wonder Valley Rd 37075
Wood Duck Ln 37075
Woodhaven Way 37075
Woodland Ct 37075
Woodridge Dr 37075
Woodvale Ct & Dr 37075
Woodyside Dr 37075
Worcesters Pt 37075
Wynbrooke Trce 37075
Wyncrest Ct & Way 37075
Wyncrest Commons Ct 37075
Wyndermere 37075
Wyndsor Ct 37075
Yorkshire Ct 37075
Yorkside Ct & Pl 37075

JACKSON TN

General Delivery 38301

POST OFFICE BOXES MAIN OFFICE STATIONS AND BRANCHES

Box No.s
1 - 2996 38302
3001 - 3976 38303
7001 - 7980 38302
9001 - 9298 38314
10001 - 12588 38308

NAMED STREETS

A St 38301
Aaron Long Rd 38301
Abbey Pl 38305
Abby Chase 38305
Abigail Dr 38305
Abraham Dr 38305
Acornridge Cv 38305
N Acres Dr 38301
Ada Cv 38305
Adair Rd 38305
Adams St 38301
Addison Cv & Way 38305
Admirals Pt 38305
Airways Blvd 38301
Alberta Cv 38305
Alcaro Rd 38301
Alderbrook Ln 38305
Aldridge Ln 38305
Alexander St 38301
Alexis Cv 38305
Algie Neely Rd 38301
Alice St 38301
Allen Ave & St 38301
Almo Dr 38305
Alpine Cv 38301
Alta Vista Dr 38305
Altamont Dr 38301
Amanda Cv 38305
Amber Oaks Cv 38305
Amberwood Cv 38305
American Dr 38301
Amhurst Cv 38305
Amos Cv 38305
Amy Dr 38301
Anderson Dr 38301
Angela Cv 38305
Anglewood Dr 38305
Anglin Ln 38301
Ann Mckay Dr 38301
Apachie Cv 38305
Applestone Dr 38305
Applewood Cv 38305
Arbor Oak Dr 38305
Arbor Ridge Cv 38305
Arbor View Dr 38305
Arbuckle Cv 38305
Archie Rd 38305
Archwood Dr & St N 38301
Arlington Ave 38301
Armstrong Rd 38301
Arrow Dr 38305
Arrowhead St 38301
Ash St 38301
Ashland Cv 38305
Ashport Rd 38305
Ashton Cv 38305
Ashwood Cv 38305
Ashworth Cv 38305
Aspen Ave 38301
Auburndale Cv 38305
Auditorium St 38301
Audubon Lake Cir 38305
Augusta Cir 38305
Austin Cv 38305
Autumn Leaf Cv 38305
Autumn Valley Dr 38305
Autumnwood Cv 38305
Avalon Dr 38301
Avondale Cv 38305
Ayers Dr 38301
Aztec Dr 38305
B St 38301
Bagby Point Rd 38305
Bailey Ln 38305
Baker Dr 38305
E & W Baltimore St 38301
Bancorp South Pkwy 38305
Banks Aly 38301
Barfield Cv 38305
Barham St 38301
Barkley Ln 38305
Barksdale Cv 38305
Barkwood Cv 38305
Barr Ave 38301
Barrett Pl 38305
Barringer Ln 38305
Barrington Cv 38305
Barrymore Cv 38305
Barton St 38301
Bascom Rd 38305
Basswood Cv 38305
Bates St 38301
Battery Cv 38305
Battlefield Cv 38305
Batton Rd 38301
Bayberry Dr 38305
Baymeadows Dr 38305
Beacon Hill Dr 38305
Beasley St 38301
Beaumont Dr 38305
Beaver Cv 38305
Beckford Cv 38305
Bedford Farms Dr 38305
Bedford White Rd 38305
Beech Bluff Rd 38301
Beech Tree Cv 38305
Beechwood Dr 38301
Beinville St 38305
Belfield Cv 38305
Belgrove Cv 38305
Bell Camp Rd 38301
Bellcrest Cv 38305
Belle Haven Cv 38305
Belle Trace Cv 38305
Bellingham Dr 38301
Bellmeade Cv & Dr 38301
Bells Hwy 38305
Bellvue St 38301
Bellwood Cv 38305
Belmont Ave 38301
Bemis Ln 38301
Bemis Cemetery Rd & Spur 38301
Ben Lifsey Dr 38301
Benchmark Pl 38301
Benjamin Dr 38305
Bennett St 38301
Benson Ln 38301
Bent Brook Trl 38305
Bent Creek Ln 38305
Bent Oaks Dr 38305
Bent Tree Cv 38305
Bent Twig Dr 38305
Bentbrook Cv 38305
Bentmeade Cv 38305
Bentwillow Cv 38305
Berkshire Dr 38305
Bermuda Cv & Dr 38305
Berry St 38301
Berryhill Dr 38301
Bertha St 38301
Bess Ln 38305
Beth Pl 38305
Bethany Dr 38301
Bethel Park Cv 38305
Bettfield Dr 38305
Betty Dr 38305
Betty Holland Rd 38305
Beverly Hills Dr 38305
Biggs St 38301
Birch St 38301
Birch Hollow Ln 38305
Birchwood Ln 38305
Birdsong Cv 38305
Bishop Pl 38301
Black Oak Dr 38305
Black Thorne Cv 38305
Blackberry Trl 38305
Blair Dr 38305
Blairs Chapel Rd 38301
Blake St 38301
Bloomfield Cv 38305
Bloomington Cv 38305
Blossomwood Cv 38305
Blue Grass Cv 38305
Bluebird Cv 38305
Boardwalk Cv 38301
Bobrick Dr 38301
Bolivar Hwy 38301
Bon Air Cir 38305
Bond St 38301
Bonnedelle Cv 38305
Bonwood Dr 38301
Booker St 38301
Boone Ln & St 38301
Bordeaux Dr 38305
Bowling Dr 38305
Boyd Dr & Ln 38305
Boyd Farms Dr 38305
Brackenhouse Sq 38305
Braddock Pl 38305
Bradfield Cv 38305
Bradford Sq 38305
Bradmere Cv 38305
Braewood Cv 38305
Branch Cv 38305
Branch Creek Dr 38305
Branching Pine Cv 38305
Branson Pl 38305
Bray Ln & Rd 38301
Bree Cv 38305
Breezewood Cv 38305
Brenda Cv & Ln 38301
Brentmeade Cv 38305
Brentshire Sq 38305
Brentwood Dr 38301
Breuington Dr 38305
Brianfield Cv & Dr 38305
Briar Cv 38301
Briarcliff Dr 38301
Briarleaf Blvd 38301
Briarwood Cir & Ln 38301
Bridlepath Dr 38305
Bridlewood Cv 38305
Briggs St 38301
Brindlewick Dr 38305
Broadfield Dr 38301
Broadleaf Cv 38305
Broadmeadow Dr 38305
Broadmoor 38305
Broadview Dr 38305
Bronzewood Cv 38301
Brookhaven Dr 38305
Brookhollow Cv 38305
Brooks Dr 38301
Brooks Ln 38305
Brooksie Dr 38305

Brooksies Pond Cv 38305
Brookstone Pl 38305
Brookwood Dr 38305
Browns Church Rd 38305
Brownstone Cv 38305
Brownsville Hwy 38301
Bruce St 38301
Brushfield Ln 38305
Brushwood Cv 38305
Bryant St 38301
Bryce Dr 38305
Buck Ridge Cv 38305
Bucksnort Cv 38305
Buckthorn Cv 38305
Budde St 38301
Burkett St 38301
Burkett Switch Rd 38301
Burlington Cv 38305
Burning Tree Cv 38305
Burton St 38301
Butler St 38301
Butternut Cv 38305
Buttonwood Dr 38305
C St 38301
C E Boyd Rd 38305
Cabin Creek Dr 38305
Caitlin Ln 38301
Caldwell Pl 38305
Caldwell Rd 38301
Calumet Dr 38305
Calvin Dr 38301
Cambrian Way 38305
Cambrian Way Cv 38305
Cambridge Dr & Ln 38305
Camden St 38301
Camellia Dr 38301
Camelot Cv 38305
Campbell Aly 38301
Campbell Ln 38301
Campbell St
100-1399 38301
1400-2899 38305
Campbell Oaks Dr 38305
Candlewick Dr 38305
Candlewood Cv 38305
Cane Creek Rd & Spur 38301
Cannonhurst Cv 38305
Canvasback Cv 38305
Caradine Dr 38301
Carl Kirkland Dr 38301
Carlisle Dr 38301
Carlos St 38301
Carlton Pl 38305
Carnell St 38301
Carol Ann Dr 38301
Carolane Dr 38305
Carriage House Dr 38305
Carroll St 38301
Carruthers Dr 38301
Carson Aly & St 38301
Carter St 38301
Carters Grv 38305
Carthage Rd 38305
Cartmell St 38301
Carver Ave & Cv 38301
Cascade Cv 38305
Case Dr 38301
Casey Jones Ln 38305
Castle Heights Dr 38301
Castle Pines Dr 38305
Castlegate Dr 38305
Castlerock Cv 38305
Catalina Dr 38301
Cave House Rd 38305
Cedar St 38301
Cedar Crest Cv 38305
Cedar Ridge Cv 38305
Cedarbrook Pl 38305
Cedarlane Cv 38305
Cemetery Aly 38301
Centennial Dr 38301
Central Ave 38301
Central Ln 38305
Centre Plaza Dr 38305
Century St 38305

Cerro Gordo Rd 38301
Chancellor Pl 38305
Chandlers Cv 38305
Channel Creek Dr 38305
Channing Way 38305
Chapel Creek Dr 38305
Chapel Ridge Dr 38305
Charjean Dr 38305
Charles Latham Dr 38301
Charlesmeade Dr 38305
Charleston Pl & Sq 38305
Charlotte Dr 38301
Chatwick Cv 38305
Chatwood Cv 38305
Chelsea Ln 38301
Cherokee Dr 38301
Cherry Pl 38301
Cherry Blossom Cv 38305
Cherrywood Pl 38305
Chesswood Blvd 38305
E & W Chester St 38301
Chester Levee Rd 38301
Cheyenne Dr 38305
Chickasaw Dr 38305
Chickering Rd 38305
Chinaberry Cv 38305
Chippewa Cir 38305
Chipwood Dr 38301
Chloe Pl 38305
Christmasville Cv & Rd 38305
Chuck Cv 38301
N & S Church St 38301
Churchill Cv 38305
Cinnamon Cv & Dr 38305
Citrus Springs Cv 38305
Claiborne Dr 38305
Clairmont Dr 38301
Clairpointe Cv 38305
Clark Cv 38301
Clay St 38301
Clayton St 38301
Clearfield Dr 38305
Cliffwood Cv 38305
Clinical Center Dr 38305
Cloverdale St 38301
Coach Dr 38301
Coats Cv & Dr 38305
Coatsland Dr 38301
Cobb Rd 38305
Cobble Ridge Cv 38305
Coffman Dr 38301
Coleman Aly 38301
Coleman Cv 38305
E & W College St 38301
College Park Cv 38301
Collinwood Cv 38305
Colonial Cv 38305
Colony Ln 38305
Colorado St 38301
N Colorado Street Ext 38301
Commanche Cv & Trl 38305
Commerce St 38301
Commerce Center Blvd & Cir 38301
Commodore Cv 38305
Compass Dr 38301
N Conalco Dr 38301
Concord Dr 38305
Conger St 38301
Conrad Dr 38305
Constellation Cir 38305
Coolwood Dr 38301
Cooper Anderson Rd 38305
Copper Creek Dr 38305
Copper Ridge Cv 38305
Corporate Blvd 38305
Cottage Ln 38301
Cotton Blossom Cv 38305
Cotton Grove Rd 38305
Cotton Hill Ln 38305
Cotton Ridge Dr 38305
Cottonwood St 38301
Country Chase Dr 38305
Country Club Cv & Ln 38305
Country Hills Dr 38301

Countryside Dr 38305
Countryway Dr 38305
Countrywood Cv & Dr 38305
Courtland St 38301
Courtney Cv 38301
Craig St 38301
Craven Cv 38305
S Creek Dr 38301
Creekwood Dr 38305
Crescent Ave 38301
Crest St 38301
Crest Ridge Dr 38305
Crestwood Dr 38305
Crews Ln 38305
Crocker St 38301
Cross Brook Cv 38305
Cross Creek Cv & Dr 38305
Cross Pointe Dr 38305
Crossview Dr 38305
Crown Cv 38305
Crownfield Cv 38305
Crownpointe Cv 38305
Crystal Cv 38305
Crystal Lake Dr 38301
Culpepper Cv 38305
Culver Cv 38305
N Cumberland St 38301
Currie Ave 38301
Curry Ln 38301
Cynthia Cir 38305
Cypress Gardens Dr 38301
D St 38301
Dairy St 38301
Dakota Cv 38301
Dalewood Cv 38305
Dalton Dr 38305
Dancy St 38301
Daniel Rd 38305
Darlington Cv 38305
Daugherty St 38301
Davenport Cv 38305
David Dalton Dr 38301
Davidfield Cv 38305
Davidson St 38301
Davis St 38301
Dawn Pl 38305
Dawnwood Cv 38305
Dawson Cv 38301
Day St 38301
Dayton Cv 38305
E & W Deadrick St 38301
Dean Cv 38305
Dearborne Cv 38305
Dearmon Pl 38305
Deberry St 38301
Deborah Dr 38305
Deep Gap Rd 38301
Deepwood Dr 38305
Deer Creek Cv 38305
Deer Pointe 38305
Deere Ln 38305
Deerfield Cv 38305
Dellwood Dr 38301
Dempster St 38301
Denim Cv 38305
Denise Dr 38305
Denwood Dr 38305
Depot St 38301
Derbyshire Dr 38305
Derringer Cv 38305
Desha Dr 38301
Devonshire Sq 38305
Dinkins Ln 38301
Directors Row 38305
Division Ave 38301
S Dixie Ln 38301
Doak Mason Rd 38305
Dodson Cv 38305
Doe Meadow Cv 38305
Doe Run Cv 38305
Dogwood Cir & Dr 38305
Dominion Dr 38305
Donnet Cv 38305
Donovan St 38301
Doral Cv 38305
Dorothy Cv 38305

Double Creek Cv 38305
Doubletree Cv 38305
Douglas Cts 38301
Douglas Wood 38301
Dovecrest Cv 38305
Dr F E Wright Dr
1500-2011 38301
2012-2198 38305
2200-2599 38305
Dr Martin Luther King Jr Dr 38301
Dreamland Pl 38305
Driftwood Cv & Dr 38305
Duke Rd 38301
Duncan Dr 38305
Dunn Ridge Dr 38305
Dupree St 38301
Durley Dr 38305
Dustin Cv & Dr 38301
Dyer Creek Ln 38305
Eagle Cv 38305
Eaglecrest 38305
Eastmont Cv & Dr 38301
Eastview Ave 38301
Easy St 38301
Eden St 38301
Edenfield Dr 38305
Edenwood Dr 38301
Edgehill Dr 38301
Edgemont Cv & Dr 38305
Edgewater Cv 38305
Edgewood St 38301
Edwards Dr 38301
El Morgan Dr 38305
Elizabeth St 38301
Ellendale Cv & Pl 38305
Ellis Dr 38301
Elm Sq & St 38301
Elmfield Cv & Dr 38305
Elmhurst Dr 38305
Elmwood Cv & Dr 38305
Emerald Lake Dr 38305
Emerald Ridge Cv & Dr 38305
Emerson Dr 38305
Emmet St 38301
Emory Hill Dr 38301
Emporium Dr 38305
E End St 38301
Epperson Dr 38305
Erin Dr 38305
Ester Cv 38305
Eureka St 38301
Eutah St 38301
Everett St 38301
Evergreen St 38301
Executive Dr 38305
Express Dr 38305
Extension St 38301
Ezekial Dr 38305
Fair Acres Cv & Dr 38305
Fair Oaks Dr & Pl 38305
Fairchild Cv 38305
Fairfax Cv 38305
Fairfield Pl 38305
N & S Fairgrounds St 38301
Fairmeadow Cv 38305
Fairmont Ave 38301
Fairway Blvd & Cv 38305
Falconwood Cv 38301
Fall Creek Dr 38305
Farestone Cv 38305
Faris St 38301
Farmington Dr 38305
Farmwood Cv 38305
Farrar St 38301
Farwell St 38301
Fawn Ridge Dr 38305
Fawnwood Cv 38305
Federal Dr 38305
Fenner St 38301
Ferguson Dr 38305
Fern Dr 38305
Ferndale Cv 38305
Fernlawn St 38301
Fernwood Dr 38305

Fiberglass Rd 38301
Fieldbrook Cv 38305
Fieldcrest Dr 38305
Fielddale Dr 38305
Fields Chase 38305
Fieldview Cv 38305
Finch Cv 38301
Finnwick Cv 38305
First St 38301
Fite Ln 38301
Fitzgerald Rd 38301
Flagstone Dr 38305
Flaxen Cv & Dr 38305
Fleetwood Dr 38305
Fleming St 38301
Flex Dr 38301
Flint Dr 38305
Fly Rd 38305
E & W Forest Ave & Cv 38301
Forest Downs Dr 38305
Forest Edge Cv 38305
Forest Pointe Dr 38305
Forestry Rd 38301
Fountain Pl 38305
Fowler St 38301
Fox St 38301
Fox Den Cv 38305
Fox Pond Cv 38305
Fox Ridge Rd 38305
Fox Run Dr 38305
Foxboro Cv 38305
Foxlea Cv & Dr 38305
Foxworth Dr 38305
Franwood Cv & Dr 38301
Fredricksburg Cv & Dr 38305
Freeman St 38301
Friars Point Rd 38305
Fun Pl 38305
Galaxy Dr 38305
Garden Dr 38305
Gardencrest Cv 38305
Gardner St 38305
Garland Dr 38305
Garneal St 38301
Garner Rd 38305
Gates St 38301
Gateway Dr 38305
Gatewick Dr 38305
Georgetown Cv 38305
Georgian Cv 38305
Gerdau Ameristeel Rd 38305
N Gettysburg Dr 38305
Gideon Cv 38305
Gill St 38301
Gillman Ln 38301
Gin St 38301
Gladhill Cv 38305
Glass St 38301
Glen Acres Dr 38301
Glen Dillon Dr 38305
Glen Eagle Cv 38305
Glen Eagles Dr 38305
Glen Echo Dr 38305
Glen Eden Dr 38301
Glendale St 38301
Gleneice Cv 38305
Glenhurst Dr 38305
Glenwood Dr 38305
Godwin Dr 38305
Goldcrest Cv 38305
Golden Brooke Dr 38305
Golden Leaf Cv 38305
Golden Oak Cv 38305
Golden Pond Cv 38305
Goldfield Cv 38305
Goldmyth Cv 38305
Gooden Cv 38305
Gordon St 38301
Grace Cv 38305
Grace Ln 38301
Gracelyn Dr 38305
Grady Montgomery Dr 38305
E & W Grand St 38301
Grand Haven Dr 38305
Grandview Dr 38305

Grassland Cv & Dr 38305
Grassmeade Cv 38305
Grayson Ln 38305
Great Oaks Dr 38305
Green Acres Dr 38301
Green Coral Cv 38305
Greenbriar Cv & Ln 38305
Greencastle Dr 38305
Greendale Dr 38305
Greenfield Dr 38305
Greenhill Dr 38305
Greenpark Cv 38305
Greensborough Cv & Dr 38305
Greenvalley Dr 38305
Greenview Dr 38305
Greenway Dr 38305
Greenwich Cv 38305
Greenwood Ave 38301
Gregg St 38301
Gretchen Ln 38305
Grey Bark Cv 38305
Greystone Sq 38305
Griffin St 38301
Grove Ave 38301
Grove Hill Ln 38305
Grovemont Cv 38305
Gumwood Cv 38305
H O Forgy Dr 38301
Hackberry Ln 38301
Hale St 38301
Hall Rd 38301
Hallie Anderson Rd 38305
Hamilton Dr & St 38301
Hamlett Cv 38305
Hampstead Cv 38305
N Hampton Ln 38305
Hancock Cv 38305
Hannah Dr 38305
Hanover Cv & Dr 38305
Hansford Pl 38305
Harbert Pkwy 38301
Hardee St 38301
Harmony Ln 38301
Harper Cv 38305
Harpeth Dr 38305
Harris Ln 38305
Harris Rd 38301
Harris St 38301
Harrison St 38301
Hart Rd 38301
Hartford Sq 38305
Hartmus Ln 38305
Harts Bridge Rd W 38301
Hartsfield Dr 38305
Harvest Dr 38305
Harvey Johnson Rd 38301
Hastings Pl 38305
Hatchmor Dr 38305
Hatton St 38301
Haughton Aly 38301
Haverhill Dr 38305
Hawk Meadow Cv 38305
Hawthorne St 38301
Hayes Branch Trl 38301
Hayneshaven Dr 38301
N & S Hays Ave 38301
Hayworth Cv 38305
Hazelton Cv 38305
Hazelwood Cv 38305
Hc Walton Dr 38301
Hearthstone Cv 38305
Hearthwood Cv 38305
Heatherwood Cv & Dr 38305
Hedgefield Dr 38305
Hedgerow Pl 38305
Hedgewood Ln 38305
Hefley Cv 38305
Hemlock Cv 38305
Hemmingway Cv 38305
Henderson Rd 38305
Heritage Sq 38305
Hermitage Pl 38305
E Herron Ave & St 38301
Herron Grove Rd 38301
Hezekiah Cv 38305

Hiawatha Dr 38305
Hickory Ln 38305
Hickory Glen Dr 38305
Hickory Hills Dr 38305
Hickory Hollow Dr 38305
Hicks St 38301
Hidden Meadow Ln 38305
Hidden Springs Ln 38305
Hidden Valley Dr 38305
High St 38301
High Oaks Dr 38305
N Highland Ave
100-1814 38301
1815-1897 38305
1816-1898 38301
1899-3494 38305
S Highland Ave 38301
Highland Hills Cv 38305
Highland Ridge Cv 38305
Highleadon Dr 38305
Highpoint Rd 38305
Highview St 38301
Highway 45 N 38305
Highway 45 S 38301
Highway 45 Byp
1-1199 38301
1200-3999 38305
Highway 70 E 38305
Highway 70 Byp 38301
Hill Dr & St 38301
Hillard Ln 38301
Hillary Dr 38305
Hillcrest Circle Dr 38301
Hillmont Cv 38305
Hillsborough Cv 38305
Hillshire Cv & Dr 38305
Hillside Lndg 38305
Hillwood Cv 38305
Hiscox Rd 38305
Holiday Dr 38305
Holland Ave 38301
Holland Ln 38301
Hollinsworth Cv 38305
Holloway Dairy Rd 38301
Holly St 38301
Holly Hill Dr 38301
Holly Ridge Cv & Dr 38305
Hollywood Dr
100-1499 38301
1500-2256 38305
2258-2298 38305
Homeview Cv 38305
Homewood Cv 38305
Honey Bear Cv & Dr 38305
Honeysuckle Dr 38301
Hopkins St 38301
Hopper Barker Rd 38305
Horton Rd 38301
Hospital Blvd 38305
Howeston Mill Dr 38305
Howlett Cv 38305
Hudson Dr 38301
Hughes Dr & Rd 38305
Hull Cv 38305
Hulsey Cv 38305
Hummingbird Cv 38305
Humphrey Cv 38305
Hundley Ave 38301
Hunt Ave 38301
Hunter Hill Dr 38305
Hunters Creek Dr 38305
Hunters Green Cv 38305
Huntersville Providence Rd 38301
Huntington Pl 38305
Hurt St 38301
Hurtland Dr 38305
Hurts Chapel Rd 38301
Idlebrook Cv 38305
Idlehour Dr 38305
Idlewild St 38301
Impala Dr 38305
Inca Cv 38305
Independence Ln 38305
Indian Cv 38305
Industrial Dr 38301

Ingleside St 38301
Ingram St 38301
Innsdale Cv 38305
Institute St 38301
International Cv 38305
Irby St 38301
Iris Dr 38301
Ironwood Cv 38305
Iroquois Dr 38305
Isaac St 38305
Iselin St 38301
Ivy Hill Dr 38305
Ivybrook Cv & Dr 38305
J L Vickers Rd 38305
Jack Exum Ln 38305
Jackson Ave & St 38301
Jackson Country Club Ln 38305
Jackson Walk Plz 38301
Jacob Cv & St 38305
Jadewood Dr 38305
James St 38301
James Buchanan Dr 38301
James Lawrence Rd 38301
Jamestown Dr 38305
Jane Cv 38305
Janie Ln 38305
Jason Dr 38305
Jeff Dr 38305
Jefferson St 38301
Jeffrey Ct 38305
Jeremiah Dr 38305
Jeremy Dr 38305
Jill Cv 38301
Johanna Cv 38305
John Pope Rd 38305
John Smith Rd 38305
John Williams Rd 38301
Johnnie Hughes Rd 38301
Johnson St 38301
Johnston Loop Rd 38301
Joseph Cv 38305
Joy Ln 38305
Joyce Dr 38305
Judge Walter B Harris Dr 38305
Judson Cv 38305
Judson St 38301
Justiss Rd 38301
Kanewood Cv 38305
Kay Dr 38305
Keelange Cv 38305
Kemmons Dr 38305
Kemp St 38301
Kenny Mac Loop 38305
Kensington Cv & Pl 38305
N Kentucky St 38301
Kenwood Cir 38301
Kenworth Blvd 38305
Keswick Cv 38305
Key Senter Rd 38305
E & W King St 38301
King Arthur Dr 38305
King David Dr 38305
Kingsfield Dr 38301
Kingsley Cv 38305
Kingston Dr 38305
Kinnewick Cv 38305
Kipling Dr 38305
Kirbywood Cv 38305
Klein Dr 38305
Knollwood Dr 38305
Knottywood Cv 38305
Labelle St 38301
Laconte St 38301
E & W Lafayette St 38301
N Lake Ave, Cv, Dr & St 38301
Lake Pointe Dr 38305
Lakehaven Dr 38305
Lakeside Cv & Rd 38305
Lakeview Cv 38305
Lakewood Cir, Cv & Dr E 38305
Lamar Cir & Dr 38305
Lambuth Blvd 38301
Lancaster Cv 38305
Lancelot Dr 38305
Landmark Loop 38305
Lands End 38305
Lane Ave & Rd 38301
Lansbury Pl 38305
Lanway Cv 38305
Laplace Dr 38305
Larimer Dr 38301
Larkwood Dr 38305
Lashawte Cir 38301
Laticha Cv 38301
E Laurel Ln & Rd 38301
Laurel Creek Dr 38305
Laurelwood Cv 38305
Laurie Cir 38305
Law Rd 38305
Law Road Ext 38305
Lawnwood Dr 38305
Lawrence Aly 38301
Lawrence Switch Rd
  1-299 38301
  301-321 38301
  386-699 38305
Lazywood Cv 38305
Leafwood Cv 38305
Lealand Ln 38305
Leamon Phillips Rd 38305
Lebanon Church Rd 38305
Lee St 38301
Leebark Cv 38305
Leeper Ln 38301
Leewood Cv 38305
Legend Oaks Cv 38305
Leigh Ln 38305
Leisure Ln 38305
Lennon Cv 38305
Lennox Village Dr 38305
Lenoir Ave 38301
Leon Dr 38305
Lesa Dr 38305
Leslie Dr 38305
Lesters Chapel Rd 38301
Lewis T Brantley Dr 38301
Lewis Trailer Park 38305
Lexington Ave 38301
Libby Ln 38301
Liberty Rd 38305
N Liberty St 38301
S Liberty St 38301
Liddon St 38301
Lilac Ln 38301
Lillie Cv 38305
Lincoln Cir & St 38301
Linda Vista Dr 38301
Linden St 38301
N & S Lindsey St 38301
Link Dr 38305
Little Brook Ln 38305
Little Prarie Cv 38305
Littleberry Cv 38305
Live Oak Cv & Pl 38305
Livingston Way 38305
Lochlea Cv & Dr 38305
Lochridge Cv 38305
Lockwood Dr 38301
Locust Ln 38301
Lodenwood Cv 38305
Loftwood Cv 38305
Logan St 38301
Lohrig Rd 38301
London Park Pl 38305
Lone Oak Dr 38305
Long Meadow Dr 38305
Longleaf Dr 38305
Longview Cv 38305
Longworth Cv 38305
Loop Rd 38301
Lost Creek Dr 38305
Lost Treasure Cv 38305
Love Rd 38301
Lowell Thomas Dr 38301
Lower Brownsville Rd 38301
Loydell Cv 38305
Lucas Cv 38301
Lundy Ln 38301
Luter Cv 38301
Lynchburg Cv 38305
Lynley Cv 38305
Lynn St 38305
Lynn Haynes Rd 38301
Lynoak Cv 38305
Lynwood Dr 38301
Mack St 38305
Maddox Dr 38305
Madison St 38301
Magnolia Pl 38305
Magnolia St 38301
Magnolia Landing Ct 38305
E & W Main St 38301
Malesus Heights Dr 38301
Mallard Pt 38305
Mallard Creek Cv 38305
Mallory Dr 38305
Malone Rd 38305
Malone Park Cv 38305
Manchester Bay 38305
Manley Dr 38305
Manor Rd 38305
Maple St 38301
Maplemere Cv 38305
Maplewood Dr 38305
Marcon Pl 38301
Marianne St 38305
Marigold Dr 38301
Mark Cv 38301
Market St 38301
Markwest Cv 38305
Markwood Ln 38305
Marlene Dr 38301
Marlow Dr 38305
Martha St 38301
Martin St 38301
Maryland Dr 38301
Maryville Cv 38301
Mason St 38301
N & S Massachusetts St 38301
Matheny Rd 38305
Matrix Cv 38305
Max Lane Dr 38305
May Dr 38305
Mayberry Cv 38305
Mayfield Dr 38305
Maywood Dr 38305
Mcabee Rd 38301
Mccaslin Rd 38301
Mcclellan Rd 38305
Mccool Dr 38305
Mccorry St 38301
Mccowat St 38301
Mcdaniel Dr 38305
Mcgee Loop 38305
Mcintosh Dr 38305
Mckenzie Rd 38301
Mclean Cv 38305
Mcleary Rd 38305
Mcmaster Ln 38301
Mcminn Rd 38305
Mco Rd 38305
Mcree St 38301
Meadow St 38301
Meadowbrook Dr 38305
Meadowlands Cv 38305
Meadowood Dr 38305
Medical Center Dr 38301
Medical Park Ct 38305
Melissa Cv 38305
Melrose St 38301
Melwood St 38305
Menzies Ln 38301
Mercer Dr 38305
Meridian Dr 38301
Meridian Springs Dr 38301
Merrimack Dr 38305
Merry St 38301
Michelle Ln 38301
Middle Ave 38301
Middle School Rd 38305
Middleton St 38301
Mifflin Rd 38301
Mill Dr 38305
Mill St 38301
Mill Brook Ln 38305
Mill Creek Cv 38305
Mill Masters Dr 38305
Millennium Dr 38301
Miller Ave 38305
Miller Rd 38301
Millie Park Dr 38305
Millsap Dr 38305
Millstream Dr 38305
Millview Cv 38305
Mimosa Dr 38301
Minor Pope Way 38305
Miraway Cv 38305
N & S Missouri St 38301
Misty Meadow Cv 38305
Mitchell St 38301
Mobile St 38301
Mockingbird Cv 38305
Moize Cut Off Rd 38305
Mona Lisa Dr 38301
Monroe Ave & St 38301
Montclair Dr 38305
Monticello Cv 38305
Moore Rd 38301
Moorewood Dr 38305
Morgan St 38301
Morning Breeze Ln 38305
Morning Dew Cv 38305
Morning Grove Dr 38305
Morningside Dr 38301
Morrison Cv 38305
Morton St 38301
Moses Dr 38305
Moss Dr 38305
Moss Branch Cv 38305
Moss Woods Cv 38305
Mossy Oak Trl 38305
Moundview Dr 38301
Mount St 38301
Mt Pinson Rd 38301
Mulbury Cv 38305
Murphey Dr 38305
Murray Guard Dr 38305
Muse St 38301
Nance Aly 38301
Natchez Pl 38305
Navajo Cv 38305
Neff Cir & St 38301
Nehemiah Dr 38305
Nellie Cv 38301
Netherwood Dr 38305
New St 38301
New Deal Rd 38305
New Market St 38301
Newton St 38301
Nickelson Cv 38305
Normandy Pl 38305
North Ave & St 38301
Northern Cv 38305
Northfield Cv 38305
Northfork Cv 38305
Northhaven Dr 38305
Northland Dr 38301
Northpointe Dr 38305
Northshore Cv & Dr 38305
Northside Dr 38301
Northside Rd 38305
Northwind Dr 38305
Northwood Aly & Ave 38301
Northwyke Dr 38305
Norton Dr 38305
Norvel Dr 38301
Nottingham Dr 38305
Novy St 38301
Oak Aly & St 38301
Oak Grove Rd 38301
Oak Park Dr 38301
Oakbrook Dr 38305
Oakhaven Dr 38305
Oakmont Pl 38305
Oakmont Woods Cir & Dr 38305
Oakridge Dr 38305
Oakslea Pl 38301
Oakwood Dr 38301
Oconnor St 38301
Oddys Trl 38301
Odell Rd 38301
Ohara Ln 38305
Oil Well Rd 38305
Okeena Cv & Dr 38305
Old Bells Loop & Rd 38305
Old Boone Ln 38305
Old Denmark Rd 38301
Old Hickory Blvd & Cv 38305
Old Humboldt Rd 38305
Old Linen Cv 38305
Old Malesus Rd 38301
Old Medina Rd & Xing 38305
Old Oak Cir 38305
Old Pinson Rd 38301
Old Stage Rd 38305
Oldham Dr 38305
Omar Cir 38301
Oneal St 38301
Oneil Oak Way 38305
Orchard St 38301
E & W Orleans St 38301
Otis St 38301
Overhill Dr 38305
Overlook Cv 38305
Overpass Vw 38305
Overton Dr 38301
Oxford Dr 38305
Paddock Pl 38305
Palmer Dr 38305
Palmetto Cv 38305
Pammara Ln 38305
Panola St 38301
Parallel Dr 38305
Parchman Dr 38305
Park Ave 38301
Park Blvd 38301
W Park Pl 38301
E Park Sq 38305
Parkburg Rd 38301
Parker Dr 38305
Parkridge Dr 38301
Parkstone Pl 38305
Parkview Cir 38301
N Parkway
  1-1584 38305
N Parkway
  1585-2099 38301
  2101-3119 38301
  2100-2799 38301
Parkwood Trce 38301
Parrott Ln 38305
Partridge Cv 38301
Pascagoola Dr 38305
Passmore Ln 38305
Pattie Cv 38301
Paul Coffman Dr 38301
Payne St 38301
Peabody Ave 38301
Pearl Ave 38301
Pearson Dr & Ln 38305
Pecan Cir 38301
Pemberton Cv 38305
Pennington Pl 38305
Penny Cv & Ln 38305
Pepper Rdg 38305
Pepper Tree Rd 38305
Perrington Cv 38305
Perry Switch Rd 38301
Person St 38301
Phebus Ln 38305
Phillips Rd & St 38301
Phoenix Rd 38305
Physicians Dr 38305
Pickens Cv 38305
Pillow Rd 38305
Pimlico Cv 38305
Pin Oak Cv 38305
Pine St 38301
Pine Meadow Dr 38305
Pine Needles Ln 38301
Pine Tree Dr 38301
Pinecrest Dr 38305
Pinehurst Cv 38301
Pinewood Cv & Dr 38305
Pinnacle Dr 38301
Pipkin Rd 38305
Plainsbrook Pl 38305
Plainsfield Pl 38305
Plantation Rd 38305
Planters Ln & Row 38305
N Plaza St 38305
Pleasant St 38301
Pleasant Hill Church Rd 38301
Pleasant Plains Rd 38305
Pleasant Plains Ext Rd 38305
Plymouth Cv 38305
Plymouth Rock Dr 38305
Point O Woods Dr 38301
Polk St 38301
Pond View Cv 38305
Pony Cv 38305
Poolview St 38305
Poplar Ln 38305
Poplar Plains Dr 38305
Porter St 38301
Potts Chapel Rd
  1-299 38301
  300-999 38305
Powell Cv 38305
Powell Rd 38301
Premiere Dr 38301
Prescott 38305
Preston Aly & St 38301
Prestwick Dr 38305
Primrose Dr 38305
Prince Dr 38301
Prince Edward St 38301
Princeton Pl 38305
Princeton St 38301
Pritchard Cv 38305
Prospect Ave 38301
Providence Rd 38301
Pueblo Cv 38305
Quail Cv & Rdg 38305
Quail Creek Dr 38305
Quaker Oats Dr 38301
Quiet Dale Dr 38305
Quinn Dr 38301
Quinwood Dr 38305
R Deloach Rd 38305
Rachel Dr 38305
Radio Rd 38301
Radio Park Dr 38305
Ragland Rd 38305
Rahab Cv 38305
Railroad St 38301
Rainbow Cv 38305
Raindrop Cv 38305
Raines Springs Rd 38301
Raintree Cv 38305
Raleigh Pl 38305
Ramblewood Dr 38305
Rampart Dr 38305
Randi Dr 38305
Ranger Rd 38301
Raven Rst 38305
Ravenwood Dr 38305
Rawlingwood Cv 38305
Raymond Glade Cv 38305
Rebecca Greer Dr 38301
Rebel Cv & Rd 38301
Red Ln 38301
Red Deer Cv 38305
Red Hawk Dr 38305
Red Oak Cv 38305
Redbud St 38301
Reddick Cv 38305
Redfield Dr 38305
Redleaf Pl 38305
Redwood Cv 38305
Reeves Rd 38301
Reflection 38305
Regency Dr 38301
Reid Hollow Ln 38305
Renee Cv 38301
Revere Cir 38305
Reynolds Dr 38305
Rhea St 38301
Rhone St 38301
Rich St 38301
Rich Smith Way 38301
Richard Rd 38301
Richfield Cv 38305
Richland Cv 38305
Richmeade Cv 38305
Richmond St 38301
Richstone Cv 38305
Ridgecrest Rd 38305
Ridgecrest Road Ext 38305
Ridgedale Dr 38305
Ridgefield Pl 38305
Ridgemont Dr 38305
Ridgeoak Pl 38305
Ridgeview Dr 38301
Ridgewood Cv 38305
Riley Cv 38305
River Chase Dr 38305
River Oaks Dr 38305
Riverport Dr 38301
Rivers St 38301
Riverside Dr 38301
Roanoak Cv 38305
Roberts Ln & St 38301
Robin Ln 38305
Robinhood Ln 38305
Robins St 38301
Rochelle Rd 38301
Rochester Cv 38305
Rock Pointe Dr 38305
Rock Ridge Cv 38305
Rockwell Cv & Rd 38305
Rocky Springs Rd 38301
Rodger Dr 38305
Roland Ave 38301
Rolling Acres Dr 38305
Rolling Hills Dr 38305
Rolling Meadows Dr 38305
Romie Dr 38305
Ronald Dr 38301
Rooker Dr 38305
Roosevelt Pkwy 38301
Rose Hill Dr 38301
Rosedale St 38301
N & S Rosewood Cir 38301
Ross Rd 38301
Rossfield Cv 38305
Roxbury Dr 38305
Roxy Cv 38301
Royal Aly 38301
N Royal Ct 38301
N Royal St
  100-1728 38301
  1730-1744 38301
  1746-2283 38305
  2285-2299 38305
S Royal St 38301
Royal Oaks Pl 38305
Rugby Cv 38305
Running Brook Cv 38305
Rushmeade Rd 38305
Rushwood Dr 38305
Russell Rd
  1-699 38301
  700-899 38305
Rust Rd 38301
Rustic Bridge Dr 38305
Ruth Dr 38305
Rutherford Ave 38301
Rutledge Pl 38305
Saddlebrook Dr 38305
Sagefield Cv 38305
Sagewood Cv 38305
Saint Andrews Dr 38305
Saint James Cv 38305
Samuel Dr 38305
San Arbor Cv 38305
Sand Pebble Dr 38305
Sandalwood Cv 38305
Sandbourne Cv 38305
Sandhill Rd 38301
Sandhurst Cv 38305
Sandpiper Pl 38305
Sandra Ln 38301
Sandstone Cir 38305

Sandy Dr 38301
Sarah Cv 38305
Sarasota Cv 38305
Savoy Aly 38301
Scallion Dr 38301
Scarlet Oak Cv 38305
Scott St 38301
Scottland Dr 38301
Searcy Taylor Rd 38301
Seavers Rd 38301
Seay Cv 38305
Sebastian Dr 38305
Second St 38301
Security Dr 38305
Sedgefield Dr 38305
Sedgewick Cv 38305
Seminole Pl 38305
Seneca Pl 38301
Sequoia Dr 38305
Serenade Cv 38305
Seven Oaks Dr 38305
Seventeen Grn 38305
Shaded Brook Ln 38305
Shadow Cv 38305
Shadow Lake Dr 38301
Shadow Lawn Dr 38301
Shadow Ridge Dr 38305
Shady Ln 38305
Shady Meadows Dr 38305
Shady Oaks Dr 38301
N & S Shannon St 38301
Sharon Rd 38301
Sharpestone Cv 38305
Shaw Rd 38301
Shelby St 38301
Sherburn Dr 38301
Sherrell Dr 38301
Sherry Dr 38301
Sherwood Dr & Ln 38305
Shiloh Dr & Spgs 38305
Shirlee Dr 38301
E Shore Ln 38305
Short St 38301
Siesta Dr 38305
Silver Leaf Dr 38305
Silver Maple Ln 38305
Silvercrest Cv 38305
Silverdale Cv 38305
Silverhill Cv 38305
Silverthorne Dr 38305
Simms Aly & St 38301
Singing Tree Dr 38305
Single Oak Cv 38305
Sipes Cv 38305
Skyhaven Cv & Dr 38305
Skyline Dr 38301
Skyridge Dr 38305
Skyview Dr 38305
Sleepywood Cv 38305
Smallwood Dr 38305
Smith Ln 38301
Smithfield Dr 38305
Softwind Cv 38301
Sommersby Dr 38305
South St 38301
Southern St 38301
Southpointe Dr 38305
Southshore Cv & Dr 38305
Southside Dr 38301
Southwide Dr 38305
Southwind Dr 38305
Southwood Dr 38301
Spain Rd 38305
Speece Cv 38301
Spicewood Cv 38305
Spindrift Dr 38305
Spoke Aly 38301
N Spring Dr 38305
Spring Creek Law Rd 38305
Springbrook Dr 38305
Springfield Cv 38305
Springside Cv 38305
Springtime Cv 38305
Springview Dr 38305
Spruce Dr 38301
Sta Les Cv 38305
Standridge Cv 38305
Stanfill Ln 38301
Stanfill Rd 38305
Stanford Dr 38301
Stanworth Grv 38305
N Star Dr 38305
Starlight Cv 38305
Starwood Cv 38305
State St 38301
Station Oak Dr 38305
Steam Mill Ferry Loop, Rd & Spur 38301
Steeplechase Dr 38305
Stephens St 38301
Sterling St 38301
Sterling Farm Dr 38305
Stewart Rd 38305
Stoddert St 38301
Stokley Cv 38305
Stone Oak Cv 38305
Stone Ridge Dr 38301
Stone Spring Cir 38305
Stonebridge Blvd 38305
Stonebrook Pl 38305
Stonecreek Cir 38305
Stonecrest Dr 38305
Stonehaven Cir, Cv, Dr & Rd 38305
Stonehaven Woods 38305
Stonehenge Dr 38305
Stonehill Cv 38305
Stonewall St 38301
Stonewater Creek Dr 38305
Stoneygate Cv 38305
Stornaway Dr 38305
Stowecroft Cv 38305
Stratford Ln 38305
Sullivan St 38301
Summar Dr 38301
Summer Tree Dr 38305
Summerfield Dr 38305
Summerset Cv 38305
Summerview Dr 38305
Sunburst Cv 38305
Suncrest Dr 38305
Sundown Cv & Dr 38305
Sunhaven Dr 38305
Sunhurst Cv 38305
Sunnymeade Dr 38305
Sunnyside Dr 38301
Sunset Ave 38301
Sunvalley Dr 38305
Surrey Downs Cv 38305
Susan Cv 38301
Sutton Pl 38305
Swan Dr 38301
Sweetbay Cv & Dr 38301
Sweetbriar Cir 38301
Sweetwater Cv 38305
Sycamore St 38301
Sylvan Cv 38305
Syringa Cv 38305
Tahlequah Dr 38305
Talbot St 38301
Tall Oaks Dr 38305
Tall Pines Cv 38305
Tanger Lake Cv 38305
Tanglewood Ln 38301
Tannehill Cv 38305
Tanyard St 38301
Taten St 38301
Taylor St 38301
Taylor Cook Cv 38305
Teaberry Dr 38305
Technology Center Dr 38301
N Tennessee St 38301
Terilyn Dr 38305
Terrace Pl 38301
Thackery Pl 38305
Theus St 38301
Thistlewood Dr 38305
Thomas Cv 38305
Thomas St 38301
Thompson Ln 38301
Thornhill Cv 38305
Thornwood Cv 38305
Tige Hopper Rd 38305
Tigrett Pl 38301
Timberhill Dr 38301
Timberlake Cv & Dr 38305
Timbers North Cv 38305
Timmy Cv 38301
Tinker Hill Cv & Rd 38305
Tomlin St 38301
Tonya St 38305
Torrey Pines Dr 38305
Trace Dr 38305
Tracewood Cv 38305
Trafalgar Sq 38305
Trail Dr 38301
Trailwood Dr 38301
Tri Community Rd 38305
Tricia Cv 38301
Truck Center Dr 38305
Tuckahoe Cv & Rd 38305
Tucker St 38301
Turtle Creek Dr 38305
Tuscany Cv 38305
Twilight Cv 38305
Twin Oaks Pl 38305
Tyre Cv 38305
Ugn Pkwy 38305
Union Ave 38301
Union Fort Dr 38305
Union University Dr 38305
Unitech Dr 38301
United Dr 38305
University Cv 38305
E University Pkwy 38305
W University Pkwy
1-162 38305
161-161 38308
163-499 38305
164-498 38305
Upper Browns Church Rd 38305
Us Highway 412 E & W 38305
Us Highway 70 Byp 38301
Valentine Rd 38301
Valley Ave 38301
Valley Brook Dr 38301
Valley Oak Loop 38305
Valleydale Dr 38305
Valleyfield Cv 38305
Valleyview Cv 38305
Vance Ave 38301
Vanden St 38301
Vandenburg Cv 38305
Vann Dr 38305
Vaughn Rd 38305
Vega Dr 38305
Venture Pkwy 38305
Viewmont Cv 38305
Villa Dr 38301
Villagewood Dr 38305
Vincent St 38301
Vine Hill Rd 38301
Virgil Purham Ln 38305
Virginia St 38301
Vistaview Cv 38305
Volunteer Blvd 38305
Wakefield Cv 38305
Walden St 38301
Walerelm Dr 38305
Walker Ave 38301
Walker Rd 38305
Wallace Cv 38305
Wallace Rd
1-299 38301
300-1099 38305
Walnut St 38301
Walnut Creek Dr 38305
Walnut Grove Cv 38305
Walnut Trace Dr 38305
Walsh St 38301
Ward Grove Rd 38305
Warehouse Courtyard 38301
Warfield Cv 38305
Washington St 38301
Washington Douglas Cir 38301
Water Dance Cv 38305
Water Ridge Pl 38305
Waterford Dr 38305
Waterview Cv 38305
Watkins Cv 38305
Watlington Rd 38301
Watson Rd 38305
Waverly Dr 38301
Waynick Rd 38305
Weatherford Sq 38305
Weatheridge Cv & Dr 38305
Weatherstone Dr 38305
Weaver Cv 38305
Webb St 38301
Webber St 38301
Webster St 38301
Wedgewood Cv & Ter 38305
Weir St 38301
Wellington Cv & Dr 38305
Wells Aly & St 38301
Wells Lassiter Rd 38301
Wellwood Rd 38301
Wentworth Dr 38305
Weslake Cv 38305
Wesley Dr 38305
West Aly 38301
Westchester Ct 38305
Westmoreland Pl 38301
Weston Dr 38305
Westover Dr & Rd 38301
Westwind 38305
Westwood Ave 38301
Westwood Gardens Dr 38301
Whaler Way 38305
Whalley Dr 38301
Wheatfield Dr 38305
Wheatstone Dr 38301
Wheeling Dr 38305
Whisper Creek Dr 38305
Whispering Hills Dr 38305
Whispering Pines Trlr Park 38305
White St 38301
White Birch Cv 38305
White Oaks Dr 38305
White Plains Dr 38305
Whitehall St 38301
Whitfield Cv & Dr 38305
Whitney Cv 38305
Whitsitt Park 38301
Whittington Rd 38301
Wild Valley Dr & Ln 38305
Wildberry Cv 38305
Wilderness Cv 38305
Wildleaf Cv 38301
Wildwood Ln 38301
Wiley St 38301
Wiley Parker Rd 38305
Wilkinson St 38301
Will Mcknight Dr 38301
Willa Dr 38301
William Bailey Ln 38305
Williams St 38301
Williamsburg Cv 38305
Williamsburg Village Dr 38305
Willie Adams Rd 38305
Willow St 38301
Willow Branch Dr 38305
Willow Green Dr 38305
Willow Oak Ln 38305
Willowridge Cir 38305
Wilmington Cv 38305
Wilshire Dr 38301
Wilson St 38301
Winchester Cv 38305
Windale Dr 38305
Windcrest Dr 38305
Windemere Cir & Dr 38305
Windfield Cv 38305
Winding Creek Dr 38305
Winding Oaks Dr 38305
Windover Rd 38305
Windsong Cv 38305
Windsor Ln 38301
Windwood Cv & Dr 38305
Windy City Rd 38305
Windy Hill Cv & Rd 38305
Winfield Pl 38305
Winners Cir 38301
Winston Pl 38305
Winterwood Dr 38305
Wisdom St 38301
Wisteria St 38301
Wood Cemetery Ln 38305
Wood Duck Cv 38305
Wood Hill Rd 38305
Wood Thrush Cv 38305
Woodard Dr 38305
Woodberry Trl 38305
Woodbine Dr 38305
Woodcrest Dr 38305
Woodgate Cv 38305
Woodgrove Dr 38305
Woodhaven Dr 38301
Woodland Dr 38305
Woodmanor Pl 38305
Woodmere Dr 38301
Woodmont Dr 38305
Woodmoss Cv 38305
Woodrow St 38301
Woodruff St 38301
Woods Edge Dr 38301
Woodscreek Dr 38305
Woodshire Cv 38305
Woodwinds Cv 38305
Wright Dr 38305
Wright Industrial Cv 38301
Wrights Mill Dr 38305
Wyndchase Dr 38305
Wyndelake Cv 38305
Wyndhurst Dr 38305
York St 38301
Yorkshire Cv 38305
Yoshino Dr 38301
Young St 38301
Zachary Ln 38305

NUMBERED STREETS

All Street Addresses 38301

JOHNSON CITY TN

General Delivery 37601

POST OFFICE BOXES MAIN OFFICE STATIONS AND BRANCHES

Box No.s
1 - 2969 37605
3001 - 6196 37602
8001 - 9799 37615
10001 - 70734 37614

NAMED STREETS

Abbott Dr 37601
Acorn Ct 37601
Adair Dr 37601
Adams St 37615
E Adams St 37601
W Adams St 37604
Adobe Dr 37601
Afton St 37601
Air Products Dr 37615
Airport Rd 37615
Alexander Dr 37604
Alf Taylor Rd 37601
Allen St 37601
Allison Ct 37615
Allison Ln 37604
Almeda Dr 37604
Alpine Rd 37604
Alta Tree Blvd & Ct 37604
Althea St 37601
Amanda Dr 37615
Amber Dr 37601
Amesbury Ct 37615
Amherst Cir & Ct 37601
Amity Ln 37601
Amoyee Dr 37601
Anathoth Ln 37601
Anchor Ln 37615
Anderson Rd 37601
Anderson Chapel Cir & Rd 37601
Andi Brandon Ln 37601
Andrews Dr 37601
Angel Pl 37601
Angeline Dr 37615
Angus Ct 37615
Angus Hill Rd 37601
Anthurium Ave 37604
Antioch Rd 37604
Apache Dr 37604
Appaloosa Trl 37604
Appletree Ct 37615
Arber Ln 37601
Arbor Dr 37604
Arlington Dr 37601
Arrowhead Dr 37601
Arrowood Private Dr 37601
Arroyo Dr 37604
Ashe St 37604
Ashlee Rd 37601
Ashley Rd 37604
Ashwood Dr 37604
Ashworth Ct 37615
Aspen Dr 37601
Austin Ridge Ct 37615
S Austin Springs Rd 37601
Austin Village Blvd 37601
Autumn Dr 37615
Autumn Breeze Ln 37601
Autumn Chase Dr 37601
Autumn Creek Ct & Ln 37615
Autumn Hill Private Dr 37601
Avondale Cir & Dr 37604
Avonlea Pl 37604
Azalea Rdg 37601
Aztec Dr 37604
Bailey Ln 37601
Bairvette Ave 37604
Baker St 37601
Baldridge Dr 37604
Ballard Rd 37604
Bandera Ct 37604
Bank Saylor Rd 37604
Bank Saylors Rd 37604
Banks Rd 37601
Barberry Rd 37604
Barker Rd 37615
Barnes Ln 37601
Barnett Dr 37604
Baron Dr 37601
Bart Green Dr 37615
Bartlett St 37601
N & S Barton St 37604
Bashor Ln 37601
Bauchman Dr 37615
Baxter St 37601
Bayberry Ct 37615
Beacon Hill Ct 37604
Beadind Rd 37615
Beadindo Rd 37615
Beaujolais Sq 37604
Becca Cir 37601
Becky Dr 37601
Bedding Pl 37604
S Beech Dr & St 37604
Beech Tree Pt 37601
Beecham Ln 37604
Beechnut St 37601
Beechwood Cir, Ct & Dr 37604
Bell Ridge Rd 37601
Bellington Dr 37615
Bellview Ct & Dr 37601
Belmeade Cir 37601
Belmont St 37604
Belshire Ct 37615
Belvedere Dr 37604
Ben Jenkins Rd 37615
Ben Wood Rd 37601
Bend Ct 37615
Bent Oak Dr 37604
Bentley Parc 37615
Bentwood Ln 37615
Berea Dr 37604
Berkshire Cir 37604
E Bernie St 37601
Berry Ln 37604
Berry Patch Ln 37604
Bert St 37601
Bethesda Pl 37604
Bettie St 37601
Betty Ave 37601
Beverly Hill Rd 37604
Bh Graybeal Ln 37601
Big Ridge Rd 37601
Big Valley Dr 37601
Bill Bennett Rd 37604
Bill Booth Rd 37604
Bill Garland Rd 37604
Bingham Ct 37604
Birch St 37604
Birdie Dr 37601
Bishop Rd 37601
Black St 37601
Blackberry Ct 37604
Blackberry Rd 37601
Blackwood Way 37615
Blaine Ave 37601
Blakemore Cir 37604
Blazerview Rd 37615
Blevins Ln 37604
Blevins Rd 37601
Blue Bird Ct & Dr 37601
Blue Friday Rd 37615
Bluefield Dr 37601
Blunden Ln 37604
Boatdock Rd 37615
Boathouse Rd 37615
Bob Davis Rd 37615
Bob Fitz Rd 37615
Bob Jobe Rd 37615
Bob Scott Rd 37615
Bobby Hicks Hwy 37615
Boggs Ln 37604
Boles Dr 37604
Bondwood Cir 37604
Bonita Dr 37604
Boone Ave 37615
Boone Dr 37615
Boone Rd 37615
Boone St 37615
N Boone St 37604
S Boone St 37604
Boone Avenue Ext 37615
Boone Dock Ln 37615
Boone Hill Ct 37615
Boone Ridge Dr 37615
Boone View Dr 37615
Boones Creek Rd 37615
Boones Station Rd 37615
Boonesboro Rd 37615
Boring Chapel Rd 37615
Boring Ford Rd 37615
Borla Dr 37604
Bowers Ave & St 37601
Bowman Rd & Trl 37601
Boyd St 37604
Brackenwood Ct 37601
Bradford Ln 37601
Bradley Rd 37601
Bradley Gouge Rd 37604
Brandon Ct 37615
Brandonwood Dr 37604
Brantly Ln 37604
Breckenridge Dr 37604
Brentwood Dr 37601
Brethern Church Rd 37615
Briarcliff Rd 37604
Briarwood Ct 37604
Briarwood Dr 37615
Brice Ln 37604
Brickey Ln 37601

Bridgewater Ct 37615
Bridgewood Ct 37604
Brightridge Dr 37615
Bristol Ct 37604
Bristol Hwy 37601
Brittany Dr 37615
Broad Leaf Dr 37601
Broadmoor Rd 37604
N & S Broadway St 37601
Broadwood Cir 37604
E & W Brook Ln 37601
Brook Hollow Rd 37604
Brookdale Dr 37601
Brooke Green Dr 37604
Brookfield Dr 37601
Brookhaven Dr 37604
Brooklawn Ct 37604
Brookview Dr 37615
Brookwood Dr 37615
Browder Rd 37615
Brown Ave 37601
Brown Oaks Mnr 37604
Brownbark Ln 37615
Browns Rd 37615
Browns Mill Blvd 37615
Browns Mill Ct 37604
Browns Mill Rd
2300-3500 37604
3502-3598 37604
3700-3799 37615
Browns Mill Road Ext 37604
Broyles Dr 37601
Bryant Ln 37604
Bryclair Private Dr 37601
Brystone Dr 37615
Buccaneer Dr 37604
Buckingham Dr 37604
Buckingham Rd 37615
Buffalo Rd & St 37604
Buffalo Creek Rd 37601
Buffalo Ridge Rd 37615
Buffalo Road Ext 37604
Buffalo Valley Church Rd 37601
Buford Whitson Dr 37601
Bunton Rd 37604
Burbank Dr 37601
Burhl Chase Rd 37615
Burkley Ct 37604
Burnt Hickory Ln 37604
Burton France Rd 37604
Business Way 37615
Butler Rd 37604
Buttermilk Rd 37615
Byrd St 37601
C Denton Rd 37604
Cabindale Rd 37615
Cade Rd 37601
Cain Dr 37604
Cairo Dr 37615
Caitlin Ct 37604
Caleb Ct 37601
Calvin Phillips Dr 37601
Cambridge Ave 37604
Cambridgeshire Ct 37615
Camden Ln 37601
Camelot Cir 37604
Candle Knob Rd 37601
Candor Rd 37615
Canterbury Rd 37601
Captains Ln 37615
Car Mol Dr 37601
Cardinal Ct 37604
Care Ln 37601
Carl Hopkins Ct 37601
Carl Kelley Ln 37601
Carlotta Ln 37601
Carolina Cv 37615
Carolina St 37601
Carr Rd 37604
Carr St 37615
Carr Cemetery Rd 37601
Carriage Ave 37601
Carriage Ct 37604
Carriage Hills Pl 37604
Carroll Dr 37615
Carroll Creek Rd
100-1299 37601
1300-2999 37615
Carrville Ave 37601
Carson Dr 37601
Carter Ave 37604
Carter Dr 37601
Carter Sells Rd 37604
Cash Hollow Rd 37601
Casteel Rd 37601
Castleton Ct 37615
Castlewood Ct 37601
Cathedral Ct & Dr 37601
Catoosa Ct 37601
Cattail Pt 37601
Cedar Ln 37615
Cedar Park 37615
Cedar Pl
100-199 37615
1100-1199 37604
Cedar Pt 37615
Cedar St 37601
Cedar Creek Dr & Rd 37615
Cedar Grove Rd 37601
Cedar Point Pl 37601
Cedar Point Rd
100-286 37601
287-399 37615
Cedar Valley Blvd 37615
Celina Ct 37615
Cemetery Ln 37601
Center St 37615
N Center St 37604
S Center St 37604
Central Dr 37601
Central St 37604
Central Point Ln 37604
Centre Park Dr 37615
Century Ln 37604
Chadsworth Ln 37601
Chadwick Cir 37615
Chadwick Rd 37615
Chamber Dr 37601
Chapel St 37615
Chapman St 37604
Charla Ln 37601
Charles St 37601
Charleston Ct 37604
Charleston Sq 37601
Charter Ct & Row 37604
Charway Dr 37601
Chase Dr 37604
Chatham Dr 37604
Chaucer Ct 37615
Chelsea Ct & Ln 37601
Cherish Ct 37615
Cherokee Rd & St 37604
Cherokee Ridge Ct 37604
Cherry St
1-99 37601
100-108 37615
110-398 37615
115-125 37604
127-211 37615
221-299 37604
301-399 37615
Chesterfield Ct & Dr 37604
Chestnut Ln 37601
E Chestnut St 37601
W Chestnut St 37604
Chickasaw St 37604
Chickees St 37604
E Chilhowie Ave 37601
W Chilhowie Ave 37604
Chock Creek Rd 37601
Choctaw St 37604
Christa Dr 37601
Christian Ln 37601
Christian Church Rd 37615
Christine Ct 37601
Cimarron Dr 37601
Cindy Ct 37604
Cindy Dr 37601
Cindy Anne Dr 37615
Circle Ct 37601
Circle Dr 37615
Circleview Dr
100-299 37615
300-2599 37604
City Garage Rd 37601
Claibourne St 37601
Clairmont Rd 37601
Clamar St 37604
Clarendon Ln 37601
Clark Dr 37601
Clark St 37604
Clarks Ct 37604
Claude Gray Rd 37604
Claude Simmons Rd 37604
Clay Rd 37604
Clearview Dr 37604
Clearview St 37615
Clearwood Dr 37604
Clemson Ct 37601
Cleveland Rd 37615
Cliff Dr 37615
Cliffside Dr 37604
Cliffview Cir & Dr 37615
Clinchfield St 37604
Clinton Dr 37604
Cloudland Dr 37601
Clover Cir, Dr & St 37604
Cloverdale Ln 37604
Cloyd St 37601
Club Dr 37601
Clyde Harrison Rd 37615
Coach St 37615
Cobblestone Ct 37601
Coby Ln 37615
Coldwater Dr 37601
College Rd 37601
College Heights Dr & Rd 37604
Collins Dr 37604
Colonial Dr 37601
Colonial Ridge Rd 37604
Colony Ct & St 37615
Colony Park Dr 37604
Colorado St 37601
Colt Ln 37601
Comfort Ct 37615
N & S Commerce St 37604
Concord Ln 37601
Concord St 37604
Cooper Dr 37604
Copas Dr 37615
Copper Ct 37601
Copper Hill Dr & Ln 37601
Cornerstone Dr 37615
Corporate Dr 37604
Corum Rd 37615
Cory Dr 37604
Cotty Jones Dr 37604
Country Club Dr 37601
Country Garden Rd 37601
Countryside Dr 37604
Coventry Ct 37604
Coveview Ct 37601
Cox Cir & Rd 37615
Cox Farm Ct 37601
Coy Ct 37615
Cr Dr 37614
Cranberry St 37601
N Creek Cir 37615
Creek Dr 37604
N Creek Dr 37615
Creek View Ct 37615
Creekmore Dr 37601
Creekside Dr 37601
Creola Way 37601
Crescent St 37604
Crescent Lake Pl 37615
Cresland Dr 37601
Crest Ct 37601
Creston Ct 37615
Crestview Ct 37601
Crestview Dr 37604
Crestwood Dr 37601
Cretsinger Dr 37601
Crockett Ct 37615
Crocus St 37601
Cross Creek Ct 37615
N & S Crossbow Ln 37604
Crosstimber Ct 37601
Crouch Ct & Rd 37615
Crowell Ln 37601
Crown St 37601
Crystal Springs Cir 37615
Crystal Springs Dr 37601
Cumberland Ct 37615
Cuyler Willee Rd 37601
D Street Dr 37604
Dakota Pl 37601
Dalewood Dr & Rd 37601
Dallas Mccracken Dr 37601
Dalton Dr 37604
Daniels Way 37615
Daniels Trail Dr 37615
Darnell Dr 37601
Dave Buck Rd 37601
David Cir 37604
David Miller Rd 37604
Davis St 37604
Dawn Dr 37615
E & W Dawson Dr 37604
Dayton Dr 37615
Daytona Dr 37601
Dean St
1-99 37601
100-299 37615
900-1299 37601
Deepwood Dr 37601
Deer Run Ct 37601
Deerpark Ln 37604
Degrassee Ln 37601
Delaware St 37604
Dellwood Ln 37615
Delmer Salts Rd 37615
Delta St 37615
Dennis Dr 37601
Denny Mill Rd 37604
Devonshire Ave 37601
Dewberry Cir 37604
Dewey Dugger Rd 37601
Dillon Ct 37615
Division St 37601
Dogwood Ln 37604
Dogwood St 37615
Don May Rd 37615
Doodle Bug Ln 37601
Doolittle Rd 37615
Dorothy St 37604
Dorothy Keister Way 37601
Dosser Ln 37601
Dotson Dr 37601
Dotwood Ct 37615
Douglas Dr 37604
Douglas Shed Rd 37615
Dove Ln 37615
Downing Ct 37604
Downtown Sq 37604
Dresden Ave 37604
Drewtanner Ln 37604
Dru Ln 37601
Dry Creek Rd 37604
Dublin Rd 37615
Duchess Ct 37615
Dugger St 37604
Duke St 37601
Dunham Cir 37601
Durham Rd 37615
Dusty Dr 37604
Dutch St 37615
Dyer St 37601
Dykes Hill Ln 37601
Eagle Ct 37601
Eagle Nest Dr 37601
Earl Cir & St 37601
Earl South Rd 37601
Earnest St 37604
East Dr 37615
Eastern Star Rd 37615
Eastgate Cir 37604
Eastridge Ct 37601
Eastwood Dr 37604
Ebony Ln 37615
Echo Ln 37604
Ed Carpenter Rd 37601
Ed Gage Ln 37615
Ed Martin Rd 37615
Eddie Williams Rd 37601
Edgehill Cir 37601
Edgewater Ct 37615
Edgewood Dr
100-199 37615
700-799 37601
Edgewood St 37604
Edna Cir 37604
Edwards Ct & Dr 37601
Elizabeth Ave 37615
Elizabeth Ann Dr 37601
Elizabethton Hwy 37601
Elliott And Scott Cir 37604
Elm Ln 37604
Elm St 37601
Elm Heights St 37615
Elmer Good Rd 37615
Elmwood St 37604
Elvin Shirley Rd 37601
Embassy Row 37601
Embreeville Rd 37604
Emerald Ct 37604
Emerald Chase Cir 37615
Emmanuel Dr 37601
Emory Ln 37604
Empress Ct 37615
Enfield Ct 37604
Englewood Blvd 37601
Equius Via Private Dr 37601
Estate Ct & Dr 37604
Evan Ln 37615
Evergreen Dr 37604
Exum St 37601
Fagan Rd 37601
Fairfield Ct 37604
Fairhaven Rd 37601
Fairlawn Cir & Dr 37601
Fairridge Rd 37604
E Fairview Ave 37601
W Fairview Ave 37604
Fairway Ct 37601
Fairway Dr
100-199 37615
1600-1999 37601
Fairway Ln 37601
Faith Cir 37604
Falcon St 37604
Fall St
100-199 37615
500-799 37604
Fallen Leaf Dr 37601
Ferguson Rd 37604
Ferndale Rd 37604
Ferrell Dr 37601
Fieldcrest Cir 37604
Fieldstone Dr 37615
Fine Rd 37604
Fink Dr 37604
First St 37615
First Scott Dr 37601
Fish Ln 37615
Fitness Way 37604
Five Oaks Dr 37604
Flamingo Ct 37601
Fleetwood Ct 37604
Fleming Rd 37601
Fletcher Dr 37601
Flint Ct & Dr 37604
Flo Ct 37604
Flonter Rd 37601
Flora Ave 37604
Florida Ave 37601
Flourville Rd 37615
Forbes Rd 37601
Ford Ln & St 37615
Ford Creek Rd 37615
Forest Ave 37601
Forest Dr 37615
Forest St 37615
Forest Acres Dr 37604
Forest Dale Ln 37604
Forest Hill Dr 37604
Forest View Dr 37615
Fork Ln 37604
Foster Ct 37604
Fountain Ct, Pl & Sq 37604
Fox Rd 37601
Fox Den Ct 37604
Fox Run Ln 37604
Foxx St 37604
N & S Foxxborough Ln 37604
Foy Fitch Ln 37615
Frances St 37604
Frank Humphreys Ln 37601
Frank James Rd 37601
Frank Jones Rd 37601
Frank T Williams Ln 37601
Franklin St & Ter 37604
Franklin Square Ct 37604
Franklin Terrace Ct 37604
Freckles Ct 37601
Fredricksburg Rd 37604
Free Hill Ext & Rd 37615
Freeman Ln 37615
Fremont Dr 37601
Friar Tuck Rd 37604
Friars Path Ln 37601
Friendship Ct 37615
Frog Level Rd 37615
Frontage Rd 37604
Fulkerson Rd 37615
Fulton Dr 37601
Furches Dr 37615
Furnace Rd 37601
Galen Dr 37604
Galloway Dr 37601
Galway Ct 37615
Garden Dr & Way 37604
Gardner St 37604
Garland Way 37604
Garland Farm Blvd 37615
Gate Way Dr 37604
Gatewood Dr 37615
Gb Nelson Rd 37615
Gentry Carson Dr 37615
Gentry Hamilton Rd 37615
George Miller St 37615
Georgetown Row 37601
Georgia St 37601
Geraldine St 37615
Gibson Rd & St 37601
Gilbreath Dr 37614
Gilliam Ln 37615
E, N & W Gilmer Park & St 37604
Ginger Ct & Ln 37601
Glacier Rd 37604
Glass Rd 37615
Glaze Rd 37601
Glen Abbey Way 37615
Glen Ayre Dr 37615
Glen Echo Rd 37604
Glen Mize Way 37615
Glen Oaks Dr & Pl 37615
Glendale Dr 37604
Glenstone Ct 37601
Glyn Cir 37604
Glynridge St 37601
Gouge Ln 37601
Grace Dr 37604
Grace Meadows Ct 37615
Grady Dr 37604
Granbrook Dr 37601
E Grand Ave 37601
Grand Avenue Ext 37601
Grand Oaks Dr 37615
Grandview Rd 37601
Granite Ct & Dr 37604
Grassy Cir 37615
Grassy Valley Rd 37615
Gray St 37604
Gray Commons Cir 37615
Gray Ruritan Dr 37615
Gray Station Rd 37615
Gray Station Sulphur S Rd 37615
Grays Pointe Cir & Ct 37615
Great Oak Way 37615
Green Ln 37601
Green Leaf Ct 37604
Green Meadows Dr 37604
Green Pond Rd 37604
Green Valley Ct & Dr 37601
Greenbriar Cir 37601
Greenbriar Ln 37615
Greenbriar Rd 37604
Greendale Rd 37601
Greenfield Dr 37604
Greenlee Rd 37601
Greenline Rd 37604
Greenway Dr 37604
Greenwood Dr 37604
Gresham Ln 37604
Greyland Dr 37615
Grindstaff Ln 37601
Grist Mill Ct 37615
Grove St
1-99 37601
101-107 37615
109-399 37615
Grover St 37601
Guaranda Dr 37604
Guy St 37601
H And P Private Dr 37601
Hackney Rd 37615
Hale Dr 37615
Hale St 37601
Hale Meade Dr 37615
Hales Chapel Rd 37615
Haley Cir 37615
Halfway Ct 37604
Hall Ln 37615
Hallbrook Dr 37615
Hamilton Pl 37604
Hamilton St
100-199 37615
200-1099 37604
Hamm Rd 37601
Hammett Rd 37615
Hammock Ln 37615
Hamshire St 37601
Hankal Rd 37615
Hannah Ct 37615
Hannifan Dr 37615
Hanover Cir 37601
Hanover Rd 37604
Hanson Dr 37601
Happy Valley Rd 37601
Harber Ln 37601
Harbor Approach 37601
Harbor Light Dr 37601
Harbor Point Dr 37615
Harbour Dr 37601
Harbour View Dr 37615
Harding Ave 37604
Harmony Cir 37615
Harrell Rd 37604
W Harris Dr 37604
Harrison St 37604
Harry Gouge Dr 37601
Hart Ave 37604
Harvey Ln 37604
Harwood Rd 37615
Hastings Ct 37604
Haven Ln 37604
Havendale Rd 37601
Haver Hill Ct 37604
Hawk Ln 37615
Hawkins Hill Ln 37601
Hawthorne Dr 37601
Hawthorne Church Rd 37601
Hayfield Dr 37615
Haynes Dr 37604
Hays Farm Ct 37615
Hazel St 37604
Hazelwood Dr 37615
Hd Crumley Rd 37601
Headtown Rd 37604
Heath Ln 37601
Heather Ln 37601
Heatherly Ln 37604
Helen Ct 37604
Hemlock Ln 37604
Hendrix Dr 37601
Henry Ln 37615

Street	ZIP
Henry St	37601
Herb Hodge Rd	37601
Heritage Pl	37604
Heritage Rd	37615
Hermarad Dr	37604
Herrin Dr	37604
Hickory Blf & Ct	37601
Hickory Springs Rd	37604
Hicks Dr	37615
Hicks Rd	37604
Hicks Acres Dr	37615
Hidden Farm Dr	37601
Hidden Hollow Ct	37604
Hidden Oaks Dr	37601
Hidden Valley Rd	37601
Hiddenbrook Ln	37615
Hideaway Hills Rd	37615
High St	37604
High Point Dr	37601
Highland Ave	37604
Highland Dr	37601
E Highland Rd	37601
W Highland Rd	37604
Highland Church Rd	37615
Highland Falls Ct	37615
Highland Gate Dr	37615
Highland Glen Ct	37615
Highland Grove Ct & Dr	37615
Highland Hills Dr	37615
Highland Ridge Blvd, Ct & Ter	37615
Highridge Rd	37604
Hill Rd	37601
Hill St	
100-199	37615
1800-1999	37604
Hillcrest Dr	
100-700	37604
702-798	37604
2100-2199	37615
E Hillcrest Dr	37604
W Hillcrest Dr	37604
Hilldale Ave	37615
Hillendale Ln & Rd	37615
Hillmont Dr	37601
Hillmoor Dr	37601
Hillrise Blvd	37601
Hillrise Rd	37615
Hills Ave	37601
S Hills Cir	37601
N Hills Dr	37604
S Hills Dr	37601
Hillsboro Ave	37604
Hillside Dr & Rd	37601
Hilltop Cir	37615
Hilltop Dr	37604
Hilltop Rd	37601
Hillview Ct	37615
Hilo Dr	37604
Hilton Ln	37604
Hiwassee Heights Dr	37601
Hiwassee Hill Dr & Ext	37601
Hl Good Rd	37615
Hog Hollow Rd	37615
Hogans Aly	37604
Holland Ln	37604
Hollow Timbers Dr	37615
Hollow View Dr	37615
Holly Ln	37615
Holly St	37604
Hollyhill Rd	37604
Hollywood Ln	37604
E Holston Ave	37601
W Holston Ave	37604
Homestead Ln	37604
Honaker Ct	37615
Honey Hollow Rd	37604
Honey Locust Dr	37601
Honeycutt Private Dr	37601
Honeysuckle Ct	37615
Honeysuckle Ln	37604
Honeywood Dr	37604
Hoover St	37604
Hope And Pray Pvt Dr	37601
Hopper Rd	37604
Hopson Rd & St	37601
Horseshoe Bnd	37604
Horseshoe Cir	37615
Horseshoe Dr	37601
Howard Hyder Rd	37601
Howwen Cir & Dr	37604
Hr King Rd	37615
Huckleberry Ct	37604
Huffine Cir & Rd	37604
Huffman Hollow Rd	37601
Huffman Private Dr	37601
Hugh Cox Rd	37615
Hughes Ln, Rd & St	37601
Hummingbird Ln	37604
Humphreys Ln	37601
Hunters Ct E & W	37601
Hunters Lake Dr	37604
Hunters Ridge Rd	37604
Huntington Way	37604
Ian Dr	37604
Idlewild Dr	37601
Idlewilde Dr	37601
Idlewylde Cir & Ln	37601
Imperial Ct	37615
Indian Dr	37601
Indian Point Cir	37604
Indian Ridge Rd	37604
Industrial Dr	37604
Industrial Rd	37615
Ingleside Ter	37604
Innovation Dr	37604
Internet Plz	37604
Interstate Ln	37601
Irene St	37604
Iris Ave	37601
Iron St	37601
Isenberg Dr	37615
Iva Lee Ln	37615
Ivanhoe Dr	37601
Ivy Ct	37615
Ivy Ln	
100-199	37615
2000-2099	37604
Ivy Oak Cv	37601
J Walking Way	37615
Jack Martin Ln	37615
E Jackson Ave, Blvd & Ter	37604
Jackson Lane Private Dr	37601
James Kebbler Ln	37615
Jamestown Ct & Rd	37604
Jared Dr	37604
Jarrett Buck Loop	37601
Jax Dr	37615
Jay St	37601
Jaynes Rd	37601
Jays Dr	37615
Jd King Rd	37615
Jennifer Dr	37604
Jenniferbrook Ct	37615
Jerome St	37601
Jerry St	37615
Jessica Dr	37601
Jessicas Way	37615
Jewell St	37601
Jim Buck Rd	37601
Jim Elliot Rd	37601
Jim Ford Ln	37615
Jim Funkhouser Rd	37604
Jim Mcneese Rd	37604
Jim Richmond Rd	37615
Jingles Ln	37601
Jk Gray Ln	37615
Jl Seehorn Jr Rd	37614
Joe Carr Rd	37601
Joe Hale Dr	37615
John Cox Rd	37615
John Exum Pkwy	37604
Johnson Ave	37604
Johnson Ln	37601
Johnson City Plaza Dr	37601
Jonathon Ln	37601
Joshua Ln	37601
Joy Ct, Dr & St	37601
Judd Ln	37604
Judge Gresham Rd	37615
Judith Dr	37604
Judson Dr	37615
Julian Ln	37615
Julie Ct	37604
Julie Ln	37601
Justus Dr	37604
Katana Ln	37604
Kate St	37615
Kathy St	37601
Katies Way	37615
Kay Ct	37604
Kaywood Ct	37601
Ke Dr	37604
Keefauver Rd	37615
Keeland Dr & Ln	37615
Keene Rd	37601
Keeview Ct & Dr	37615
Keith Ln	37601
Kennedy St	37604
Kennesaw Dr	37615
Kensington Ct	37601
Kensington Pl	37615
Kentland Dr	37604
Kentucky St	37601
Kenwood Dr	37604
Ketron Ln	37601
Keyes Ln	37601
Kilby Rd	37604
Kimberly Ct & Ln	37604
Kimrod Dr	37601
King Dr	37615
E King St	37601
W King St	37604
King Richard Blvd	37604
King Springs Rd	37601
Kings Row	37604
Kings Mountain Ct	37604
Kingsley Cir	37601
Kingsport Hwy	37615
Kingston Ct	
100-199	37615
1000-1099	37601
Kinley Dr	37604
Kipping St	37601
Kirkpatrick Dr	37601
Kitzmiller Rd	37615
Klm Dr	37615
Knob Creek Rd	
1000-2950	37604
2951-2997	37615
2952-2998	37604
2999-3300	37615
3302-7298	37615
Knob Creek Dock Rd	37601
Knobb Hill Rd	37601
Knoll Dr	37604
Knollwood Cir	37604
Knox St	37604
Kram Ct	37615
Kwickway Ln	37615
Labconnect Ln	37615
Lacasa Dr	37601
Lacy St	37604
Ladonna Dr	37615
Lafe Cox Dr	37604
Lake Dr	
100-199	37615
900-999	37601
Lake St	37615
Lake Approach Dr	37601
Lake Drive Ext	37601
Lake Harbor Ct & Dr	37615
Lake Haven Dr & Ext	37615
Lake Meadow Dr	37615
Lake Park Dr	37615
Lake Ridge Sq	37601
Lake Village Ct	37601
Lakecrest Ln	37615
Lakeland Dr	37601
Lakeridge St	37615
Lakeside Dr	37615
E Lakeview Dr	37601
W Lakeview Dr	37601
Lakeview Ln	37615
Lakeview St	37615
Lakewood Dr	37601
Lamar Ave	37615
Lambert Rd	37601
Lambeth Ct & Dr	37601
Lamons Ct & Ln	37604
Lamont St	37604
Landis Dr	37601
Lara Ct	37604
Larchmont Ln	37604
Lark St	37604
Larkspur Dr	37604
Larkwood Ct	37604
Larry Ln	37604
Lauderdale Dr & Ln	37601
Laurel Ave	37604
Laurel Cyn	37615
Laurelbrook Ct	37615
Laurels Rd	37601
Laurens Glen Ln	37601
Lazy Ln	37615
Lazywood Dr	37601
Leach Rd	37601
Leanne Cir	37604
Ledford Ct	37615
Lee Cir	37604
Lee Dr	37615
Lee St	37604
Lee Carter Dr	37601
Leedham Ln	37601
Leeland Rd	37604
Legion St	37601
Lehigh St	37604
Leisure Ln	37604
Lester Rd	37615
Lester Harris Rd	37601
Lester Heights Rd	37615
Lewis Ct	37615
Lexington Ct	37615
Liberty Bell Blvd	37604
Liberty Church Rd	37615
Library Ln	37601
Lick Ln	37604
Lillers Chapel Rd	37601
Lilley Ln	37604
Lillian Ln	37601
Lilly Dr	37604
Limited Centre St	37604
Lin Snyder Rd	37615
Lincoln Ave	37604
Lincoln Avenue Ext	37604
Linden Ave	37601
Lindsay Ln	37615
Linkwood Dr	37601
Lita Dr	37604
Live Oak Ct	37615
Lizabeth Dr	37604
Lizzy Dr	37615
Llewellyn Wood	37601
Locklane Dr	37601
Locust Ln	37604
E Locust St	37601
W Locust St	37604
Log Cabin Ln & Rd	37615
Logans Run	37615
Loire Ct	37604
Loire Valley Rd	37604
Lois Dr	37615
Lone Oak Rd	37604
Lone Star Dr	37601
Long St	37601
Longview Dr	37604
Longwood Dr	37615
Lookout Pt	37601
Lori Ann Dr	37601
Louise St	37601
Love St	
100-199	37615
300-899	37604
Lovelace St	37604
Lowell St	37601
Lowridge Rd	37604
Lp Auer Rd	37604
Ltd Pkwy	37604
Luray Pl	37615
Lyle St	37604
Lyndall St	37601
Lynn Ln	37604
Lynn Rd	
100-399	37604
1000-1099	37601
S Lynn Rd	37604
Lynn Terrace Ct	37604
Lynnwood Dr	
1-199	37615
1300-1699	37601
E Lynwood Cir	37604
W Lynwood Cir	37604
Lynwood Ln	37615
Lyons Dr	37601
Machamer Ct	37604
Mack St	37604
Madelyn St	37615
Maden Ct & Dr	37615
Madison Ct	37601
Magnolia Ave & Ext	37604
E Main St	
100-299	37604
300-531	37601
530-530	37605
532-2198	37601
533-2199	37601
1127-1-1127-2	37601
W Main St	37604
Majestic Dr	37615
Majesty Ln	37601
Mallard St	37601
Manchester Ln	37601
Mannington Ct	37604
Maple Ct	37615
Maple Dr	37615
E Maple St	37601
W Maple St	37604
Marable Ln	37601
Maranatha Way	37604
Marbleton Rd	37601
Marboro Dr	37601
Margo Dr	37601
Marguerite Ln	37601
Marion Ct & Dr	37601
Mark Dr	37615
Mark Twain Ct	37604
E Market St	
100-199	37604
200-1299	37601
W Market St	37604
Marketplace Dr	37604
Marshall Ct	37601
Martin Ct	37601
Martin Ln	37604
Martin Farm Rd	37601
Martindale Dr	37601
Martins Glen Ct & Ln	37615
Mary St	
100-199	37615
1700-1899	37604
Mary Anne Keys Ln	37601
Mary Evelyn Cir	37601
Mary Key St	37601
Matherly Rd	37615
Matson Ct	37604
Max Jett Rd	37601
May Apple Ln	37615
Mayfield Dr	37604
Mayflower Rd	37601
Mcafee Blf	37615
Mcarthur St	37601
Mccall Cir	37604
Mccalmont Dr	37601
Mcclain Ct	37615
Mcclellan Dr	37604
Mcclure St	37604
Mccormick Ct	37604
Mccracken Dr	37615
Mccray Rd	37615
Mcgregor Pl	37604
Mcinturff Ln	37604
Mcintyre Ln	37601
Mckinley Rd	37604
Mckinley Church Rd	37604
Mckinney Cir	37615
Mcneil Ln	37601
Mcqueen Hollow Rd	37601
Meadow Ct	37615
Meadow Green Ct & Dr	37601
Meadowbrook Dr & Ln	37604
Meadowview Ave	37601
Meadowview Dr	37604
Med Tech Pkwy	37604
Mel Cir	37601
Melanie Way	37601
Melborne Dr	37601
Melinda Ln	37604
Melrose Ave & Cir	37601
Memory Gardens Rd	37615
Mercury Rd	37601
Meredith Cir	37615
Meridale Dr	37601
Meridith St	37604
Merritt Dr	37604
Merry St	37601
Merrywood Dr	37604
Mesa Dr	37615
Mia Gracie Ct	37615
Miami Dr	37601
Michael Dr	37604
Michaels Ridge Blvd	37615
Midland Cir	37601
Midway St	
100-199	37615
2200-2299	37601
Mikapea Dr	37601
E Millard St	37601
W Millard St	37604
Millbrook Dr	37604
Millenium Pl	37604
Miller Ave	37601
Miller Ln	37604
Miller St	37604
Miller Hill Rd	37601
Miller Private Dr	37601
Millercrest Dr	37604
Milligan Ave, Hwy, Ln & St	37601
Milligan View Rd	37601
Millstone Dr	37615
Millwheel Dr	37615
Millwood Dr	37615
Mimosa Ln	37604
Miner Cir	37604
Minga Dr	37604
Mint Hill Rd	37601
Misamore Ln	37615
Mission Way Rd	37601
Mistletoe Ct	37604
Misty Ln	37604
Mize Rd	37601
Mizpah Hills Dr	37604
Moccasin Ct	37604
Mockingbird Hl	37601
Mockingbird Ln	37604
Mohler Rd	37615
Molton Cir	37615
Monarch Ct	37601
Mont Tipton Rd	37601
Montclair Dr	37604
Monteray Ct	37604
Montgomery St	37604
Monument Ct	37601
Moody Ln	37615
Moorland Dr	37604
Morey Hyder Rd	37601
Morgan Ct	37604
Morningside Dr	37604
Morris Ln	37615
Mose St	37601
Mosier Rd	37601
Mosley Rd	37615
Moss Creek Dr	37604
Moss Creek Ii	37604
Mount Crest Dr	37601
Mountain Home Dr	37604
Mountain View Cir	37601
N Mountain View Cir	37601
S Mountain View Cir	37601
Mountain View Dr	
100-100	37601
102-300	37601
302-598	37601
2100-2299	37615
E Mountain View Rd	37601
W Mountain View Rd	37604
E Mountcastle Dr	37601
W Mountcastle Dr	37604
Mountcastle Pl	37601
Mulberry St	37601
Mullins St	37604
Muskett Dr	37604
Muskhogean Dr	37604
Mustang Gln	37604
E Myrtle Ave	37601
W Myrtle Ave	37604
Nantucket Dr	37604
Narrow Ln	37604
Nathan Lynn Ln	37601
Nathaniel Ct & Dr	37604
Navaho Dr	37604
Nave Dr	37601
Neece Ln	37601
Neth Dr	37601
New St	37601
New Haven Dr	37604
Newbern Dr	37604
Newton Ln & St	37604
Nick Dr	37615
Nightingale Ct	37601
Niles Ln	37604
Nix Rd	37601
Noah Dr	37615
Norris Jones Rd	37604
Norris Private Dr	37601
North Ln	37604
North Rd	37601
N North St	37604
S North St	37604
Northeast Dr	37601
Northgate Dr	37604
Northpark Dr	37604
Northridge Cir	37604
Northvale Ct	37604
Northwood Ave	37615
Northwood Ct	37601
Northwood Dr	37601
Northwood Pl	37615
Norwood Dr	37615
Nottingham Pl	37604
Nunley Dr	37604
Oak Ln	37604
Oak St	
200-1099	37601
2100-2499	37615
Oak Cliff Ct	37601
Oak Glen Cir	37604
Oak Grove Blvd	37601
Oak Grove Loop	37615
Oak Grove Rd	37615
Oak Grove Vlg	37615
Oak Leaf Cir & Ct	37601
Oak Street Ext	37601
Oakdell Ct	37604
E Oakland Ave	37601
W Oakland Ave	37604
W Oakland Ct	37604
Oakstone Dr	37601
Ocala Dr	37601
Odell Cir	37604
Odom Acres Dr	37601
Oglewood Cir	37604
Okeechobee Dr	37604
Okolona Rd	37601
Old Boones Creek Rd	37615
Old Buffalo Rd	37601
Old Gray Station Rd	37615
Old Grist Mill Blvd	37615
Old Lewis Rd	37601
Old Mill Rd	37615
Old Milligan Hwy	37601
Old Settlers Way	37615
Old Stage Rd	37615
Old Watson Rd	37604
Olde Oaks Dr	37615
Olgia Ln	37604
Oliver Ln	37601

Oliver Approach 37601
Omaha Ln 37601
One St 37615
Onion Ln 37601
Onnie Chase Rd 37615
Opal Ct 37604
Oracle Ct 37604
Orchard Dr 37604
Orchard St 37615
Oregon St 37601
Orlando Dr 37601
Orleans St 37601
Orr Ct 37615
Osborne Rd 37601
Osborne Private Dr 37601
Oscar Banks Rd 37601
Oscar Miller Rd 37604
Osceola St 37604
Osprey Pt 37604
Ovalwood Dr 37615
Overlook Ct 37604
Oxbow Ln 37604
Oxford Pl 37601
P Keefauver Rd 37615
Pactolas Rd 37604
Paddle Creek Rd 37601
Paduch Dr 37601
Paduch Ridge Rd 37601
Page Ave 37601
Pagel Ct 37604
Paige Ln 37601
Palisades Pt 37601
Palomino Pass 37604
Pansy St 37601
Par Ct 37601
Pardee St 37601
Park Ave & Ct 37601
Park Hill Rd 37601
Parkwood Ln 37604
Parton Cir 37604
Partridge Ln 37604
Parwood Ct 37601
Pat Simmons Cemetery Rd 37601
Patrick Dr 37601
N Patrick Dr 37615
S Patrick Dr 37615
Patrick Ln 37615
Patsy Ln 37601
Patton Cemetary Rd 37601
Paty Dr 37604
Pawnee St 37604
Payne Loop 37604
Peach Blossom Ct 37604
Peachtree St 37604
Peakes Pike 37615
Pearman Rd 37601
Pebble Creek Dr 37604
Peggy Ln 37601
Pendleton Cir 37601
Peninsula Dr 37615
Peoples St 37604
Peoples Farm Rd 37601
Pepper Ridge Ct 37615
Periwinkle Ct 37615
Perma R Rd 37604
Perry Cir 37604
Peterson Pl 37601
Pfeiffer Ridge Rd 37601
Pheasant Hollow Ln 37601
Phillip Ct 37604
Phillip Drew Ct & Dr 37604
Phillips Ln 37615
Phillips St 37601
Picadilly Ln 37615
Pickens Bridge Rd 37615
Pickle Rd 37601
Piedmont Rd 37601
Pierce Ln 37604
Pilgrim Ct 37601
Pine Ct 37601
Pine Ln 37601
E Pine St 37601
W Pine St 37604
Pine Forest Ln 37601
Pine Grove Ave 37601

Pine Hill Dr 37615
Pine Hill Rd 37601
Pine Knot Ln 37601
Pine Ridge Rd 37601
Pine Timbers Ct & Dr 37604
Pinecrest Ln 37601
Pinewood Rd 37601
Pinnacle Dr 37615
Pioneer Ave 37604
Piper Gln 37615
Plantation Dr 37604
Platinum Ct 37604
Plazz Ave 37601
Pleasant Ct 37615
Pleasant Dr 37601
Pleasant Hill Rd 37604
Pleasant View Dr 37604
Plum Tree Ct 37615
Plymouth Rd 37601
Point 21 37615
Polk Ave 37604
Poplar Rd 37615
E Poplar St 37601
W Poplar St 37604
Poplar Grove Rd 37601
Poplar Hill Dr & Ext 37604
Poplar Wood Ct 37604
Port Cir 37604
Possum Hollow Rd 37615
Post Oak Ct & Dr 37615
Powder Branch Rd 37601
Powell St 37604
Powers Ct 37615
Prescott Dr 37601
Preservation Cir 37601
Presnell Dr 37604
Presswood Rd 37604
Preston Rd 37601
Price Rd 37604
Primrose Ct 37601
Prince St 37601
Princeton Gdn, Ln & Rd 37601
Professional Park Dr 37604
Promise Land Dr 37615
Province Dr 37615
Purple Martin Rd 37615
Quail Dr & Run 37601
Quail Harbour Dr 37601
Quail Ridge Rd 37601
Quail Run Ct 37601
Quality Cir 37615
Quarry Dr 37615
Quary Rd 37601
Queens Ct 37604
Queensboro Cir 37601
Raccoon Ridge Ln 37601
Rachel Ct 37615
Railroad St 37601
Rainbow Dr 37601
Rambling Cir & Rd 37604
Ramsey Dr 37615
Ranch Rd 37601
Ranger Trl 37615
Raspberry Ridge Rd 37601
Ravenwood Dr 37604
Ravine Dr 37601
Rebeccas Ln 37615
Red Ln 37615
Red Fern Cir 37604
Red Oak Cir 37604
Red Row Rd 37601
Redbud St 37604
Redbush Ct 37601
Redman Ln 37615
Redskin Dr 37601
Redstone Rd 37604
Reed Cir 37601
Reeser Rd 37601
Regal Ct 37604
Regency Dr 37604
Regency Sq 37601
Renee Dr 37601
Reserve Pl 37615
Reston Ct 37601
Rhododendron Ln 37601

Rhody Dr 37615
Rich Acres Rd 37601
Richard St 37615
Richland Ct & Hts 37615
Riddell St 37604
E Ridge Dr 37601
Ridgecrest Dr 37601
Ridgecrest Rd 37604
Ridgefield Cir, Dr & Rd 37601
Ridgeheights Dr 37615
Ridgeland Cir 37601
Ridgeland Dr 37601
Ridgeland Rd 37604
Ridgemont Rd 37601
Ridgetop Dr 37615
Ridgeview Dr
100-299 37615
600-699 37604
Ridgeview Meadows Dr 37615
Ridgeway Rd 37601
Ridgewood Ct 37604
Ridgewood Ln 37604
Ridgewood Ter 37601
Rigsby Rd 37615
Rilke Ct 37604
River Rd 37601
Riverview Dr 37601
Rj Bowman Ln 37604
Rl Deakins Rd 37615
N Roan St
100-4299 37601
4300-5299 37615
5301-5325 37615
S Roan St 37601
Robert Ct 37601
Roberts Ln 37601
Robin Hood Ln 37604
Robinson Dr 37604
Rock Garden Rd 37604
Rockhouse Rd 37601
Rockingham Rd 37615
Rockingham Meadows Dr 37615
Rocky Ln 37601
Rocky Rd 37604
Rocky Ridge Rd 37601
Rocky Top Rd 37601
Roger Ln 37601
Rolling Acres Dr 37615
Rolling Hills Dr 37604
Ronald Ln 37601
Roosevelt St 37601
Roscoe Fitz Rd 37615
Rose Ave 37601
Rose Dr 37615
Roseberry Ln 37604
Rosebud Ln 37615
Roseview Dr 37615
Rosewood Cir & Ln 37615
Rotherwood Dr 37601
Roundtree Ct & Dr 37604
Rovan Cir & Dr 37601
Rowe Ln 37601
Roweland Dr 37601
Roxford Dr 37604
Roy Martin Rd 37615
Royal Cir & Ct 37604
Royal Troon 37604
Royston St 37604
Ruby Ln 37615
Russell Dr 37615
Russum Ave 37604
Rustic Rd 37604
Ruth Ct 37604
Saddlebrook Ln 37615
Sage Ct 37604
Sage Dr 37604
Sage Ln 37601
Saint Annes Ct 37604
Saint Louis St 37601
Saint Marys Ct 37601
Salem Dr 37615
Salvage Ln 37604
Sam Jenkins Rd 37615

Sam Slagle Ln 37604
Sanctuary Ct 37615
Sandy Ct 37604
Sandy Dr 37601
Sanford Dr 37601
Sarah St 37601
Sarah Annie Dr 37601
Sargent King Dr & Rd 37615
Savannah Dr 37604
Savannah Ter 37601
Savignon Ct 37604
Sawyers Pond Dr 37604
Saylor Rd 37615
Sb Snyder Dr 37615
Scenic Dr
100-199 37615
1700-1799 37604
Scenic Oak Dr 37615
Scenic View Dr 37601
Schumway Dr 37601
Scott Ct 37604
Scott Rd 37604
Scott St 37601
Sea Biscuit Ct 37604
Seaton Rd 37615
Sells Ave 37604
Seminole Dr 37604
Sequoyah Dr 37604
Service Merchandise Dr 37615
Settlers Way 37615
Sevier St 37604
Sewanee Rd 37601
Seward Dr 37604
Shadden Rd 37615
Shade Tree Way 37604
Shadow Ln 37615
Shadowood Dr 37604
Shady Ln 37601
Shadybrook Dr 37604
Shadyrest 37615
Shallowbrook Ln 37615
Shannon Ln 37601
Shannon View Rd 37615
Sharon Dr 37604
Sharondale Ct 37601
Sharpsburg Dr 37604
Shawnee Dr 37604
Sheets Hollow Rd 37601
Sheffield Cir 37615
Sheffield Ct 37604
Shel Kel Dr 37615
Shelby St 37604
Shelldrake Ct 37601
Shenandoah Dr 37601
Shephard Cir 37615
Shepherd Rd 37601
Sheri St 37615
Sherri Hill Rd 37601
Sherwood Dr 37601
Shipley Rd 37615
Shirley St 37615
Shoreline Dr 37615
Sid Martin Rd 37615
E Side Ave 37601
Signal Dr 37604
Silkwood Ct 37615
Silver Oak Dr 37615
Silverdale Dr 37601
Simmons Rdg 37604
Simms Rd 37601
Singletree Ct 37615
Sinking Creek Rd
100-500 37601
502-598 37601
1700-2599 37604
Sioux Dr 37604
Skyland Cir & Dr 37615
Skyline Dr 37604
Slagle Ln 37604
Sleepy Hollow Ln & Rd 37604
Sluder Rd 37615
Smalling Rd 37615
Smith Ct 37615
Smith St 37601

Snowden Ct 37615
Snowden Ter 37601
Snyder Dr & Rd 37615
Solomon Ln 37601
Somerset Dr 37604
Sourwood Ct 37604
Sourwood Dr 37615
South Ct 37601
Southview Dr 37601
Southwest Ave 37604
Sparks Rd 37601
Spencer Ln 37604
Spice Hollow Rd 37604
Spin To Win Ln 37601
Spratlin Park Dr 37615
Spring Dr 37601
Spring St
100-1399 37604
2100-2199 37615
Spring City Dr 37601
Spring Hill Rd 37604
Spring Knoll Ct 37601
E Springbrook Dr 37601
W Springbrook Dr 37604
Springview Dr 37615
Springwinds Loop 37601
Spruce St 37601
Spurgeon Ln 37615
Spurgeon Gap Rd 37615
Spurgeon Island Rd 37615
Squibb Dr 37601
St Clair St 37604
Staff Ln 37604
Stafford Ln & Rd 37615
Stanley Ave 37604
Stanley Rd 37615
Stanmoore Dr 37601
State Pl 37601
E State Of Franklin Rd 37601
N State Of Franklin Rd
300-1099 37604
1100-1100 37602
1100-1198 37604
1101-1199 37604
W State Of Franklin Rd 37604
Staunton Cir 37601
Steel St 37601
Steeple Cir 37601
Steeplechase Ct & Dr 37601
Stepp Ln 37601
Sterling Cir & Ct 37604
Sterling Springs Dr 37604
Steven Cir & Dr 37604
Stewart St 37601
Stinson Rd 37604
Stone Dr 37601
Stonebriar Ct 37615
Stonecrest Ct 37604
Stoneridge Dr 37604
Stoneybrook Dr 37601
Stoots Hl 37601
Story Rd 37615
Strait Dr 37615
Stratford Ct 37615
Straw Flower Pl 37604
Strawberry Ln 37604
Strawberry Field Dr 37604
Street Dr SW 37604
Suffolk Rd 37615
Sugar Maple Ln 37601
Sugar Mill Dr 37604
Sugartree Ct & Rd 37604
Summer Pl 37601
Summer Rose Ln 37601
Summit Ave 37604
Summitt Dr 37604
Sumpter Dr 37604
Sun St 37615
Sun Chase Ct 37615
Sun Valley Rd 37604
Suncrest Dr & St 37615
Suncrest Village Ln 37615
Sundale Cir & Rd 37604
Sunny Cliff Dr 37601

Sunnydew Cir 37604
Sunnyvale Dr 37601
Sunnyview Cir & Ct 37601
Sunrise Ave 37604
Sunrise Valley Dr 37604
Sunset Ct 37604
Sunset Dr 37604
Sunset Rd 37615
Sunset Meadows Ct 37615
Sunset Ridge Blvd & Ct 37615
Surcey Ln 37615
Surrey Ln 37604
Susannah St 37601
Sutphin Rd 37604
Swadley Rd 37601
Swanee Dr 37604
Sweetwater Ct 37601
Sweetwood Dr 37615
Sycamore St 37604
Sylvan Dr 37604
Tagor Dr 37604
Tall Oak Cir 37601
Tall Pines Ln 37601
Tallapoosa Rd 37604
Tamarack Dr 37604
Tamassee Dr 37601
Tami Dr 37601
Tammy St 37601
Tampa Ct 37601
Tangency Dr 37615
Tanglewood Ln 37604
Tannery Rd 37601
Tara Ct 37615
Tate Rd 37615
Taylor Ave 37601
Taylor Dr 37604
Taylor St 37604
Taylor Ridge Ct 37601
Taylortown Rd 37601
Technology Ln 37604
Tee Ct 37601
Teresa Rd 37615
Teresa Inez Ct 37601
Terrace Ct 37601
Terrace Dr 37604
Terrace Lake Dr 37601
Textile St 37604
Thomas Ct 37615
Thomas St 37604
Thomas And Webb Rd 37604
Thompson Rd 37615
Three St 37615
Thunder Bay Dr 37615
Timberlake Rd 37601
Tipton St 37604
Tittle Dr 37615
Todd Dr 37604
Toll Branch Ln, Rd & Spur 37601
Tom Mitchel Ln 37615
Tom Pate Rd 37604
Top Side Cir 37604
Topeka St 37601
Towne Sq 37601
Townsend Cir 37601
Townview Dr 37604
Trail Ln 37615
Treadway Dr 37601
Treadway Ln 37601
Treadway St 37604
Treasure Ln
101-199 37604
325-325 37614
Tree Top Ln 37601
Tremont Ln 37601
Trenton Dr 37604
Tri Cities Business Park Dr 37615
Triangle Rd 37604
Trillium Trl 37604
Trivette Concourse 37601
Tucker Ln 37601
Tulip St 37601
Tullioka St 37601

Tulsa Dr 37601
E & W Tunbridge 37604
Twin Falls Dr 37601
Twin Oaks Dr 37601
Two St 37615
E Unaka Ave 37601
W Unaka Ave 37604
Unaka Ct 37601
Unaka View Rd 37601
Unicoi Dr 37601
University Pkwy
100-806 37604
807-807 37614
808-1398 37604
809-1399 37604
University Pl 37604
Utah St 37601
Valley Bnd 37615
Valley Cir 37615
Valley Ln 37604
Valley Pt 37615
Valley St
100-199 37615
700-799 37601
Valley Place Dr 37615
Valley View Dr 37601
Valleyview St 37615
Vanderbilt Dr 37601
Vanleer Ave 37604
Vanover Rd 37601
Vernon Rd 37615
Vernon St 37604
Veterans Way 37604
Vicksburg Rd 37604
Victor Dr 37601
Victoria Ct 37604
Victory Ln 37615
View Bend St 37601
Villa Ct 37615
Villa View Pt 37604
Village Dr 37604
Village Ln 37615
Vincent Dr 37615
Vine Ln & St 37604
Vines St 37604
Vip Rd 37601
Virgil Green Rd 37601
Virginia St 37604
Voncannon Dr 37601
Wade St 37604
Walker Dr 37601
Walker St 37615
Walkers Bend Rd 37615
Walking Horse Rst 37604
Wall St 37601
E Walnut St 37601
W Walnut St 37604
W Walnut Street Ext 37604
Walter Way 37615
Wanee Ct 37601
Warren Rd 37604
Warrior Ct 37604
Warrior Ln 37601
Washington Ave & St 37604
E Watauga Ave 37601
W Watauga Ave 37604
Watauga Rd 37601
Watauga Flats Rd 37601
Water St & Way 37601
Water Oak Ct 37615
Water Tank Hill Rd 37604
Waterbrooke Ln 37604
Waterford Ct 37615
Waters Edge Dr 37604
Watertank Rd 37615
Watson Rd 37604
Wayfield Dr 37601
Wayland Blvd
3900-3999 37604
4200-4299 37615
Wayland Ct 37604
Wayne Oliver Dr 37601
Wb Yeats Dr 37604
Weaver Ave 37601
Weaver Hill Rd 37601
Weaver Hollow Rd 37601

Wedgewood Rd 37604
Welbourne St 37601
Welcome Ct 37615
Wellington Ct 37615
Wendover Dr 37604
Wentworth Ct 37604
Wesinpar Rd 37604
Wesley Ct & St 37601
West Dr & Rd 37615
Westin Parc 37615
Westminister Dr 37604
Westshore Pt 37601
Westview Cir 37604
Westwood St 37604
Wheeler St 37604
Whisper Bnd 37604
Whisper Ct 37601
Whispering Pines Rd 37601
Whisperwood Ln 37601
White St 37615
White Oak Ct SW 37604
White Way Dr 37601
Whitehall Dr 37604
Whitehead St 37601
Whitewood Blvd 37601
Whitney Ln 37601
Whitney St 37604
Whitson Rd 37615
Whittling Wood Dr 37601
Wichita St 37601
Widner Ln 37615
Wilcox Ln 37604
Wild Rose Ln 37601
Wildflower Ln 37604
Wildwood Ct 37615
Wildwood Dr 37601
Wiley Rd 37615
Will Lane Rd 37615
Willet Ln 37601
William Rd 37601
William Nelson Ln 37604
Williams St 37601
Williamsburg Sq 37604
Willmar Cir & St 37604
Willmary Rd 37601
Willocks Rd 37601
Willow Oak Dr 37601
Willow Springs Dr 37604
Willow Tree Ct 37604
Willowbrook Dr 37601
Willowood Ct & Dr 37604
Willows Ridge Ct 37601
Willows Trace Dr 37601
Wilson Ave 37604
Wiltshire Dr 37615
Winchester Ct 37601
Wind Tree Ln 37604
Windle Sham Ct 37604
Windridge Ct 37601
Windridge Colony 37601
Windrow Ct 37615
Windsong Dr 37615
Windsor Ct & Ln 37601
Windwood Dr 37604
Windyhill Dr 37615
Wine Rd 37615
Winter St 37604
Winter Haven Dr 37601
Wiseman Ln 37601
Wiseman Farm Rd 37601
Wm Savage Rd 37601
Wolfe Rdg 37601
Wolfe Spring Rd 37615
Woodbriar Dr 37604
Woodbury Dr 37615
Woodby Dr 37615
Woodcrest Dr & Ln 37601
Woodhaven Dr 37604
Woodhaven Rd 37601
Woodhill Rd 37604
Woodland Ave, Cir, Ct, Dr & Rd 37601
Woodlawn Dr 37604
Woodlyn Rd 37601
Woodmont Dr 37601
Woodridge Dr 37604
Woodside Ct 37615
Woodside Dr 37604
Woodstone Ct 37601
World Of Dolls 37601
Worth Cir 37601
Wren Way 37601
Wyndale Rd 37604
Wyndham Dr 37615
Wynn Dr 37604
Wyntuck Ln 37615
Xanadu Ct 37604
York Cir & St 37601
Young Rd 37604
Young St 37601
Young Saylor Rd 37604

NUMBERED STREETS

1st St 37604
E 7th Ave 37601
E 8th Ave 37601
W 8th Ave 37604
E 9th Ave 37601
W 9th Ave 37604
E 10th Ave 37601
W 10th Ave 37604
E 11th Ave 37601
W 11th Ave 37604
W 12th Ave 37604
4j Dairy Ln 37615

KINGSPORT TN

General Delivery 37664

POST OFFICE BOXES MAIN OFFICE STATIONS AND BRANCHES

Box No.s
1 - 2580 37662
3001 - 3996 37664
4002 - 4299 37665
5001 - 6856 37663
7001 - 7916 37664

NAMED STREETS

Aaron Way 37664
Abbey Rd 37663
Aberdeen Trl 37664
Abilene Dr 37664
Adair Ave 37665
Adair Ct 37663
Adaline St 37660
Adams Ave 37665
Adrian Dr 37664
Aesque St 37665
Aesque St Ext 37665
Afton St 37660
Airport Pkwy 37663
Akers Ave 37665
Alabama St 37660
Alameda Pl 37664
Alamo Pl 37660
Alcoa Dr 37660
Alden St 37664
Alderwood Dr 37664
Alice Private Dr 37663
Allandale Cir 37660
Allen Dr 37660
Allgood Dr, Ln & Rd 37665
Alpine Trl 37663
Alpine Xing 37660
Altamont Dr 37663
Alvin St 37660
Amber St 37660
Ambleside Rd 37660
Ambridge Dr 37664
Ambrosia Dr 37664
American Way 37660
Amersham Cir & Rd 37660
Ames St 37660
Amy Ave 37664
Anchor Pt 37664
Anco Dr & Pl 37664
Andover Ct 37663
Andrew St 37660
Aneta Ave 37660
Anngea Ln 37660
Ansley St 37660
Apache Dr 37664
Apple Ct 37660
Apple Grove Cir 37664
Appleberry Cir 37663
Appleton Ct 37664
April Private Dr 37660
Aqueduct Ct E & W 37660
Arapaho Dr 37664
Arbor Pl 37665
Arbor Ter 37660
Arbutus Ave 37660
Arcadia Dr 37660
Arch St 37660
Archcrest St 37664
Archdale Dr 37663
Arden Ln 37664
Ardmore Pl 37664
Argonne St 37664
Arley St 37664
Arlington Cir, Ct, Dr & Pl 37663
Armstrong Ave 37664
Armstrong Dr 37660
Arondale Ct 37664
Arrow Cir 37664
Arrowhead Dr & Trl 37664
Arrowood Dr 37664
Asbury St 37660
Ascot Dr 37663
Ash St 37664
Ashfield Dr 37664
Ashley St 37664
Ashley Oaks Private Dr 37663
Ashwood Ave 37664
Aspen St 37664
Aston Pl 37660
Astor St 37660
Atlee St 37660
Atoka Cir & Ln 37664
Audie St 37665
Aurawood Dr 37660
Aurora Rd 37663
Austin St 37665
Autumn Ln 37664
Autumn Knoll Ct 37664
Ava Dr 37663
Avalon St 37664
Azalea Pl 37660
Aztec Dr 37664
Babbling Brk 37664
Bacon Rd 37663
Bagwell St 37664
Bailey Ranch Rd 37660
Baines Ave & Rd 37660
Baker St 37665
Ball Orchard Private Dr 37660
Ball Village Private Dr 37664
Bancroft Chapel Rd
100-899 37660
6101-6199 37664
Bancroft Private Dr 37660
Bard Ln 37660
Barger Pl 37664
Barnes St 37660
Barnett Dr 37664
Barnsley Pl 37660
Barrington Ct 37663
Barton St 37660
Bay Meadow Pl 37660
Bayberry Dr 37663
Bays Cove Cir & Trl 37660
Bays Mountain Trl 37660
Bays Mountain Park Rd 37660
Bays View Ct & Rd 37660
Beartown Rd 37660
Beaver Ln 37660
Beechcliff Dr 37664
Beechnut Dr 37660
Beechwood Ct, Dr & Rd 37663
Bel Air Ln 37663
Belden Rd 37660
Bell Rd 37664
Bell Flower Ct 37663
Bell Hollow Rd 37664
Bell Ridge Dr 37665
Bell Ridge Rd
400-700 37665
701-1099 37660
Belle Forest Ct 37663
Bellingham Dr 37660
Bellvue Ave 37660
Belmeade Dr & Pl 37664
Belmont Cir 37664
Belmont Ct 37660
Belmont Dr 37664
Belsay Dr 37660
Belvedere Ln 37663
Belvoir Ct 37660
Belwood Trl 37664
Benmore Dr 37664
Benny Mowell Rd 37660
Bent Ct & St 37660
Bentley St 37660
Berkeley Rd 37660
Berkshire Ln 37660
Bermuda Dr 37660
Bernard Cir 37664
Berry St 37664
Bert St 37665
Bertha Greer St 37665
Bertsie Shipley Rd 37660
Bessie Morrison Rd 37660
Bethany St 37660
Bethel Ln 37660
Beulah Church Dr & Rd 37663
Beulah Park Dr 37663
Beverly Hill St 37664
Big Echo Ct 37663
Big Ridge Rd 37660
Birch St 37664
Birchfield Pvt Ct 37660
Birchwood Rd 37660
Birdwell St 37664
Biscayne Dr 37665
Bishop Rd 37664
Bishop St 37665
Black Oak Dr 37660
Blackberry Hl 37664
Blackburn Ave 37665
Blackfoot Dr 37664
Blackheath Rd 37660
Blackmore St 37665
Blairs Gap Rd 37660
Blakemore Dr 37664
Blakewood Ct 37660
Blakley Dr 37664
Blarney Pl & Rd 37664
Bloomingdale Dr, Pike & Rd 37660
Bloomington Dr 37660
Blue Bell Dr 37660
Blue Haven Dr 37663
Blue Sky Ln 37664
Bluegrass Dr 37660
Bluff Rd 37664
Blythewood Dr 37664
Bob Jobe Rd 37663
Bobby Dr 37660
Bomitch Dr 37664
Bonaire Rd 37660
Bond Dr & Ln 37664
Bonita St 37664
Bonnie Ln 37660
Bonnie Crawford Rd 37660
Booker St 37660
Boone St 37660
Boone Dam Rd 37663
Boone Ridge Dr 37663
Booth Ct 37663
Borden St 37664
Boss Rd 37664
Boulder Ct 37660
Bowater Dr 37660
Bowie Pl 37660
Bowlin Ln 37660
Boxwood Cir 37663
Boxwood Ln 37660
Boyd Path Ct 37660
Bradbury St 37660
Bradford Ln 37663
Bradley St 37664
Bragg Rd 37660
Bragg Private Dr 37660
Bramblewood Dr 37660
Bramere Dr 37664
Branch St 37660
Branding Pl 37660
Brandon Dr & Ln 37660
Brandonwood Rd 37660
Brandywine Rd 37660
Breckenridge Trce 37663
Breeding Ln 37660
Brentan Trl 37660
Brentford Ln 37664
Brentwood Dr 37660
Brianna Dr 37660
Briarcliff Rd 37660
Briarfield Dr 37660
Briarwood Rd 37664
Brickey St 37660
Bridge St 37660
Bridgeforth Xing 37664
Bridgewater Ln 37660
Bridle Ct 37663
Bridwell St 37664
Bridwell Heights Rd 37664
Bright Pvt Dr 37660
Brighton Ct 37660
Brightridge Dr 37664
Brightwood Ln 37663
Brittany Dr 37663
Broad St 37660
Broadview St 37665
Broadwood Dr 37660
Brockway Dr 37663
Brook St 37660
Brookfield Dr 37663
Brookfield Ln 37663
Brookfield Rd 37660
Brookhaven Dr 37660
Brookings Way 37664
Brooklawn Dr 37660
Brookridge Dr 37664
Brookside Cir, Dr & Ln 37660
Brookside School Ln 37660
Brookvalley Dr 37664
Brookwood Cir & Rd 37664
Brownlow Rd 37660
Bruce St 37664
Brumley St 37665
Brunswick St 37660
Bryan Ct 37660
Buchelew Dr 37663
Buckingham Ct 37660
Buckles Dr 37660
Bullis Rd 37663
Burgh Heath Dr 37660
Burke Dr 37660
Burleson St 37660
Burning Trl 37664
Burns St 37665
Burnside Dr 37663
Burwind Ct 37660
Busbee St 37664
Butchers Private Dr 37660
C St 37664
Cain St 37660
Caintuck Rd 37664
Caldwell St 37665
Callie Ct 37664
Calton Hl 37664
Calumet Cir & Ct 37660
Cambridge Ct 37660
Camby Dr 37664
Camden Dr 37660
Camelia Ave 37660
Campbell St 37660
E Campground Rd 37664
Caney Dr 37660
Cannon St 37664
Cannonero Ct 37660
Canongate Rd 37660
Canova Ct 37664
Canterbury Rd 37660
Canton Rd 37663
Capri St 37660
Cardinal St 37660
Caribbean Dr 37660
Carl Dykes Rd 37660
Carlisle Dr 37660
Carnegie Ct 37664
Carole St 37660
Carolina Ave 37664
Carousel Pvt Dr 37660
Carr St
1000-1099 37665
3000-3099 37663
Carrberry Ct 37663
Carrington Ct 37660
Carroll St 37664
Carrollwood Dr 37660
Carrollwood Heights Rd 37660
Carter St 37664
Carters Valley Gdns 37660
E Carters Valley Rd
100-172 37665
173-499 37660
457-1-457-2 37660
461-1-461-3 37660
W Carters Valley Rd
100-710 37665
712-712 37665
713-1400 37660
1402-2698 37660
Carters Valley Private Dr 37660
Carver St 37660
Cascade St 37664
Cascade Falls Ct 37664
Cassell Dr 37660
Cassidy Ct & Rd 37664
Castaway Dr 37663
Castle Oaks Dr 37663
Castleton Ct 37660
Catawba St 37660
Catlin Ct 37664
Cavern Dr 37664
Cedar Ave 37660
Cedar Ct 37663
Cedar Dr 37660
Cedar St 37660
Cedar Branch Rd 37664
Cedar Brook Ct 37664
Cedar Crest Dr 37663
Cedar Ridge Private Dr 37660
Cedarwood Ct 37663
Cedarwood Dr 37664
Celtic Ct 37660
Centenary Rd 37663
E Center St
100-1299 37660
1300-2999 37664
W Center St
100-399 37660
320-320 37662
320-320 37665
400-998 37660
401-999 37660
Centerbrook Cir 37663
Central St 37664
Chadwell Rd 37660
Chadwick Dr 37660
Chancery Ln 37663
Chandler St 37665
Chaney Dr 37660
Chapel Dr 37665
E & W Charlemont Ave 37660
Charles St 37660
Charles E Brooks Way 37660
Charlotte St 37660
Charlton Green Dr 37663
Charsley Rd 37660
Chase St 37663
Chase Private Dr 37660
Chateaugay Rd 37660
Cheekwood Dr 37660
Chelsea Cir 37664
Chelsea Ct 37663
Cherokee Hl 37664
Cherokee St 37660
Cherokee Village Dr NE 37660
Cherry St 37660
Chert Dr 37663
Chesapeake Ct 37660
Chesterfield Dr 37663
Chestnut St 37664
Chestnut Hills Dr 37664
Chestnut Ridge Rd 37664
Cheyenne Ln 37664
Chickasaw Rd 37664
Chico Dr 37660
Childress St 37660
Chio Way 37663
Chippendale Cir, Rd & Sq 37660
Chippendale Rd Ext 37660
Chippewa Ln 37664
Christy Dr 37660
Chucky Ave 37660
E & W Church Cir & Ln 37660
Church Hill Dr 37660
Church View Dr 37664
Church View Dr Ext 37664
Cimarron Dr 37664
Cindy Pl 37660
Circle Dr 37660
Circle Pl 37660
Circle St 37660
Circle Vw 37664
Citation Cir 37660
Clairmont Pl 37660
Clandon Dr 37660
Clara Dr 37660
Claremont Rd 37660
Clark Ave & Cir 37665
W Clay St 37660
Claybank Rd 37665
Clayman Rd 37664
Claymore Dr 37663
Clear Creek Cir 37660
Clearview St 37660
Clearwater Dr 37664
Clearwood Ave 37660
Cleek Rd 37660
Cliffside Dr 37660
Cliffside Rd 37664
Cliffside Private Dr 37663
Cliffview Dr 37663
Clinch St 37660
Clinchfield St 37660
Clinic Dr 37663
Clint St 37660
Clint Street Ext 37660
Clinton St 37660
Clipse Rd 37660
Cloister Ln 37660
Clonce Ave 37665
Clouds Ford Rd
1600-1799 37665
1800-1999 37660
Clover St 37664
Clover Bottom Dr 37660
Cloverdale Rd 37660
Cloverleaf Ct 37664
Clyce St 37660
Coal Pit Hollow Ln 37660
Cobblestone Pl 37660
Cochise Trl 37664
Cole Light Rd 37660
Coley St 37660
Colfax Ave 37660

Colonial Ct 37663
Colonial Heights Rd 37663
Colonial View Rd 37663
Columbine Rd 37660
Commanche Dr 37664
Commerce St 37660
Commission Dr 37660
Compton Ter 37660
Concord St 37664
Conway Dr 37664
Cooks Ct, Pt & Ter 37664
Cooks Arbor Ct 37664
Cooks Inlet Rd 37664
Cooks Landing Rd 37664
Cooks Valley Rd 37664
Cooper St 37665
Copas Rd 37663
Cope Rd 37663
Coralwood Ct & Dr 37663
Cork Ln 37664
Cornerstone Ct 37660
Cory Way 37663
Country Dr 37664
Country Hill Dr 37663
Countryshire Ct 37663
Courtland Cir 37663
Cove St 37660
Coventry Wynd Rd 37664
Cox Rd 37663
Cox Hollow Rd
200-499 37664
500-1099 37663
Cox Trail Pl 37660
Crabapple Ln 37663
Craighead Rd 37660
Cranshaw Dr 37660
Cranshaw Dr Ext 37660
Crawford Rd 37660
Cree St 37664
S Creek Ct 37663
Creekmore Dr 37663
Creekview Dr 37660
Crescent Dr 37664
Crest Rd 37664
Crestwood Ct & Dr 37663
Crockett Hill Rd 37660
Cross St 37660
Crown Cir 37660
Crystal View St 37660
Cumberland St 37660
Curtis Ct 37664
Cypress St 37664
D St 37664
Dahlia St 37660
Dakota Dr 37664
Dale St 37660
Dale Alley St 37660
Dallas Vaughn Private Dr 37664
Dalton St 37665
Danbury St 37665
Dancy Ln 37663
Daniel Way 37660
Darby Ct 37660
Darlington Dr 37660
Darnell Dr 37665
De Lee Dr 37663
Deadrick Dr 37663
Dean Rd 37664
Dean St 37665
Dean Private Dr 37664
Deck Ln & St 37663
Deer Ridge Ct 37663
Deerborn Ln 37660
Deercreek Private Dr 37660
Deerfield Ave 37660
Deerwood Ln 37663
Dehaven Pl 37660
Deland Dr 37664
Delawana St 37665
Delaware St 37665
Delivia St 37660
Dellwood St 37665
Delrose Dr 37660
Deneen Dr & Ln 37660
Dennison St 37665

Derby Dr 37660
Derting St 37660
Derwood Ct 37660
Desoto St 37664
Devault St 37660
Devens Ct 37664
Devine Cir 37664
Devonshire Ct 37660
Dewberry Cir 37663
Dewey Ave 37664
Dexter Rd 37660
Diana Ave, Cir & Rd 37660
Dickerson St 37665
Dickerson Private Dr 37660
Dickson Pl 37664
Dickson Rd 37660
Dillow Cir & Dr 37663
Dillwyn St 37665
Dinsmore St 37660
Dixieland Dr 37665
Dobyns Dr 37664
Dogwood Dr & Ln 37663
Dogwood Private Dr 37660
Donelson Dr 37660
Donna Ct & Pl 37660
Donnie Crawford Rd 37660
Dora St 37665
Dorothy St 37660
Douglas Private Dr 37663
Douglass St 37660
Dover Dr 37664
Downing Pl 37663
Drake Ave 37660
Droke Farm Private Dr 37663
Druid Hls 37663
Druid Hills Ct 37663
Drumcastle Ave 37660
Dublin Rd 37664
Duke St 37665
Dunbar St 37660
Dundee Cir 37660
Dunlap Rd 37663
Dupont Dr 37664
Dutchess Dr 37663
Dykes Rd 37660
E St 37664
Eagle St 37660
Eagle Pointe Dr 37664
Earl St 37665
Easley Dr 37664
Easley Rd 37660
East Ave 37660
Eastbrook Dr 37663
Eastern Private Dr 37663
Eastern Star Ext & Rd 37663
Eastern Star Road Ext 37663
Eastland Dr & Pl 37664
Eastley Ct & Rd 37660
Eastline Dr 37664
N Eastman Rd
100-199 37660
700-1900 37664
1901-2099 37660
1902-2098 37664
S Eastman Rd 37660
Eastwind Pl 37660
Eastwood Ave 37664
Easy St 37663
Eauclair St 37664
Echo Ave, Ct & Dr 37665
Eden Roc Rd 37664
Edens Way 37664
Edens Ridge Rd 37664
Edens View Rd 37664
Edgewood Cir 37663
Edinburgh Channel Rd 37664
Edison St 37665
Edith Rd 37664
Edmond Cir 37663
Edna Pvt Dr 37660
Edward St 37665
Elizabeth St 37660
Ellen St 37664
Elmhurst Dr 37663
Elmwood Ave 37660
Emerald Dr 37664

Emerson St 37660
Emmett St 37665
Emory Ln 37660
Emory Church Rd 37664
Enterprise Pl 37660
Epps Rd 37665
Ernie Dr 37660
Ervin Ct 37664
Erway Ct 37664
Essex Dr 37660
Esterville Rd 37660
Ethel Dr 37664
Euclid Rd 37660
Evergreen Dr 37663
Evergreen Rd 37663
Exchange Ct 37664
Executive Park Blvd 37660
Exeter Pl 37660
F St 37664
Fain Ave 37660
Fairbanks St 37660
Fairdale Rd 37664
Fairfax Rd 37660
Fairfield Ave 37664
Fairhaven Ave 37664
Fairhill Dr 37664
Fairidge Dr & Pl 37664
Fairlane Dr 37663
Fairlawn Dr 37663
Fairmont Ave 37660
Fairoaks Rd 37664
Fairview Ave
500-1599 37660
1600-2199 37665
Fairway Ave 37665
Fairwood St 37660
Fall Creek Rd 37664
Falling Leaf Dr 37664
Falling Water Ln 37664
Farragut Ave 37664
Farris Rd 37660
Faulk Ln 37660
Faye St 37660
Feathers Ct 37664
Fedderson St 37660
Federal St 37664
Fellowship Ln 37660
Ferguson St 37660
Ferncliff Dr 37660
Ferndale Ln 37660
Fernwood Dr 37663
Ferrell Ave 37663
Ferry Dr 37663
Fiddlers Way 37664
Fieldpond Dr 37664
Fieldstone Ct & Dr 37664
Finley Villa Private Ct 37660
Fish Ln 37663
Fisher Dr 37664
Flagship Dr 37663
Flanary St 37660
Flanders St 37665
Fleenor Ln 37660
Fleetwood Ct & Dr 37660
Fleming Rd 37660
Fletcher Ave 37665
Floraland Dr 37664
Floyd St 37660
Fondulac Dr 37663
Fontaine Ct 37660
Fontana St 37660
Foothills Rd 37663
Forbes St 37665
Ford Ave & Rd 37663
Fordtown Rd 37663
Forego Ct 37660
Forest Cir & St 37660
Forest Edge Ct 37663
Forest Hills Dr 37663
Forest View Dr & Rd 37660
Forestdale Rd 37660
Forrest Ridge Dr 37660
Fort Henry Dr
1500-3699 37664
3700-6299 37663
Fort Robinson Dr 37660

Fountain Ln 37664
Fox Chase Dr 37664
Fox Lair Pl 37664
Fox Path Ct 37663
Fox Run Ct 37664
Foxcroft Dr 37664
Foxfire Ln, Pl & Trl 37664
Foxport Rd 37664
Foxtail Ln 37660
Foxwood Ln 37664
Frady Rd 37664
Frank St 37665
Franklin Sq 37664
Franklin St 37665
Fredrick St 37660
Freeman Dr 37665
Freemont Dr 37663
Frontier Dr 37664
Fuller St 37664
Fulton Ave 37660
G St 37664
Gables Pl 37664
Gaines St 37664
Gale Ave & Ln 37660
Galemont Dr 37660
Galloway Rd 37664
Galloway St 37665
Gammon Rd 37663
Garden Dr 37664
Garfield Dr 37664
Garland Ave & St 37660
Garlands Private Dr 37664
Garmon Dr 37663
Garnett Dr 37660
Garwood Dr 37663
Gary St 37660
Gatewood Dr 37663
George Ct 37660
Georgia Private Dr 37660
Gibbs Rd 37660
E & W Gibson St 37660
Gibson Mill Rd 37660
Gilders Private Dr 37663
Gillenwater Dr 37665
Gillespie Ave & St 37665
Gilmer St 37665
Gilmore St 37664
Girls Club Pl 37660
Glademill Dr 37663
Glasgow Station Rd 37664
Gleason St 37665
Glen Ave 37665
Glen Alpine Rd 37660
Glen Eden Rd 37664
Glenbrook Dr 37664
Glenburn Rd 37660
Glencliff Dr 37663
Glendale Rd 37664
Glendora Dr 37663
Glenmont Ct 37660
Glenwood St 37664
Globe St 37660
Gloucester Ct 37660
Goal St 37665
Golden Oak Ln 37664
Goldie Crawford Rd 37660
Golf Ridge Dr 37664
Goods Dr 37660
Goodview Dr 37660
Goodview Private Dr 37660
Gordon St 37665
Gott St 37664
Grace Dr 37664
Gragg Ln 37660
Graham St 37660
Granada Ct 37660
Granada Pvt Ct 37660
Granby Rd
500-1799 37660
1800-2099 37665
Grandview Cir 37660
Grandview Ct 37664
Grandview Dr 37660
Grandview St 37665
Grant Pl 37660
Grassland Ct 37664

Gravely Rd
100-399 37665
400-1099 37660
Gray Ave 37660
Green Ct 37663
Green Ln 37664
Green Hills Dr 37663
Green Lake Dr 37663
Green Meadow Dr 37663
Green Private Dr 37663
Green Spring Cir 37664
Green Valley Dr 37664
Greenfield Ave & Pl 37664
Greengate Rd 37663
Greenleaf Dr 37663
Greenvine Pl 37660
Greenway St 37660
Greenwood Ln 37663
Gregory Rd 37665
Grey Fox Dr 37664
Grimes Cir 37663
Grimm Rd 37663
Grove Dr 37663
Grove Hill Rd 37660
Gum Springs Rd 37660
Gustavis Ave & Ct 37664
Haga Rd 37660
Halifax Dr 37660
Hall Cir 37663
Hall St 37660
Halo Dr 37664
Hamilton Pl, Rd & Way 37663
Hamlin St 37665
Hammond Ave 37660
Hampton Ave 37660
Hampton Grn 37663
Hanover Ct 37660
Happy Hill Rd 37660
Harbor Cir & Dr 37664
Harbor Chapel Rd 37664
Harbor Springs Rd 37664
Harding Rd 37663
Harkleroad St 37660
Harmony Ridge Dr 37665
Harold Hill Rd 37660
Harr Town Rd 37664
Harrell Private Rd 37660
Harris Ave 37664
Harrison Ave 37665
Harte St 37664
Harvey Brooks Cir 37660
Harwich Pl 37660
Hash Hollow Rd 37665
Haven Dr 37663
Havendale Rd 37660
Havenette Ct 37663
Hawaii St 37660
Hawk St 37664
Hawkins Ln 37663
Hawthorne St 37660
Hayes St 37660
Haynes Dr 37660
Haywood Dr 37660
Hazelnut Dr 37664
Hazelwood Ave 37664
Heather Ln 37664
Heather Glen Dr 37663
Heatherly Rd 37660
Heatherview Ct 37663
Heatherwood Ln 37663
Hedge Dr 37660
Hedgerow Ct 37663
Helmsdale Dr 37664
Hemlock Ln 37664
Hemlock Rd 37663
Hemlock Park Cir, Dr, Ln & Pl 37663
Henry Ln 37663
Henrys Private Dr 37663
Heritage Ln 37664
Hermitage Dr 37664
Herron Dr 37663
Hi Dr 37663
Hialeah Dr 37660
Hiara Dr 37660

Hickam St 37660
Hickam Orchard Rd 37660
Hickory St 37664
Hickory Hill Rd 37664
Hickory Tree Private Dr 37663
Hicks Ave 37660
Hicks Hollow Rd 37660
Hidden Acres Ct 37660
Hidden Acres Rd 37664
Hidden Pines Dr 37664
Hidden Valley Rd 37663
Hideaway St 37664
High Ridge Rd 37660
Highland St 37664
Highlea Dr 37663
Highpoint Ave & Cir 37665
Highridge Dr 37664
Highview Ave 37665
Highway 11 W 37660
Highway 75 37663
Hill Rd 37664
Hill St 37660
Hillandale Dr 37663
Hillcrest Dr 37664
Hillhurst Cir 37660
Hillmont Dr 37660
Hillsboro Cir 37660
Hillshire Ln 37660
Hilltop Dr 37664
Hillview Rd 37664
Hillvue Dr 37663
Hilton St 37663
Hilton Hill Rd 37663
Hinkle Rd 37660
Historic Hills Rd 37663
Hiwassee Cir & Dr 37664
Hobart St 37664
Hobbs St 37664
Holcomb St 37660
Holden Dr 37663
Holiday Dr 37664
Holiday Hills Rd 37664
Holland Dr 37663
Hollis St 37660
Holly St 37660
Hollydale Dr 37663
Hollywood Dr 37660
Holston St 37660
N Holston River Dr 37660
N Holston River Drive Ext 37660
Holyoke St 37664
Homestead Dr 37663
Honeycutt Dr 37660
Honeysuckle Dr 37663
Honeysuckle Ln 37660
Honeysuckle Pl 37663
Hood Rd W 37660
Hooven St 37664
Hopkins St 37664
Horse Creek Ln 37660
Horseshoe Bnd 37660
Horseshoe Dr 37663
Hospitality Pl 37663
Houston Ave 37664
Howard St 37660
Hughes Dr 37660
Hull Dr 37664
Hunter Ln 37664
Hunters Crossing Ln 37664
Huntington Ct & Pt 37660
Huntington Woods Cir 37660
Hurd Rd 37660
Huron Cir 37664
Hutchinson Dr 37660
Hydaway Pl 37664
Hyde Pl 37664
Hyder Ave 37660
Idle Hour Rd 37660
Idlewild Dr 37660
Impala Dr 37660
Imperial Cir 37660
Imperial Dr 37663
Inca Ln 37664

Independence Dr & Way E & W 37660
Indian Center Ct 37660
Indian Ridge Dr 37660
Indian Trail Dr 37660
Industry Dr 37660
Ingle St 37664
Inglewood Dr 37664
Ingram St 37664
Inwood Dr 37664
Iris Dr 37660
Iroquois Ln 37664
Isaac St 37660
Island Dr 37660
Island Rd 37664
Island St 37660
Issac Ave 37660
Ivanhoe St 37660
Ivory St 37660
Ivy Dl & Dr 37663
Jack White Dr 37664
Jackson Pl & St 37660
Jackson Hollow Rd 37663
Jade Ct 37664
James St 37660
James C White Dr 37660
Jan Way 37660
Jandon Ln 37663
Jared Dr 37660
Jasmine Pl 37664
Jayne Rd 37660
Jd White Private Dr 37660
Jean St 37663
Jefferson Ave 37664
Jennifer St 37660
Jennings Dr 37660
Jericho Dr 37663
Jerry Ln 37664
Jersey St 37660
Jessee St 37664
Jett Rd 37660
Joann Dr 37660
N John B Dennis Hwy
1700-1799 37664
2000-3099 37660
S John B Dennis Hwy
1000-1099 37664
1200-1799 37660
John Gaines Blvd 37664
John Phillips Rd 37660
Johnson St 37665
Jonathan Way 37660
Julip Dr 37663
June Dr 37664
Justin Dr 37663
Kallen Dr 37660
Kanan Dr 37664
Karen Rd 37660
Katherine St 37660
Keeneland Ct 37660
Keller St 37660
Kelly Ln 37664
Kelso Ct 37660
Kendleworth Dr 37660
Kendrick St 37663
Kendrick Creek Rd S 37663
Kenmore Dr 37664
Kennedy Dr 37663
Kennerly Addition Rd 37663
Kenridge St 37664
Kensington Ln 37664
Kent St 37664
Kentfield Dr 37660
Kenwood Rd 37664
Kerns St 37665
Kerry Ct 37660
Kestner St 37660
Kestner Private Dr 37660
Ketron Dr 37660
Keystone St 37660
Kilkenny Rd 37664
Kim Dr 37663
Kimbark Ln 37660
Kimberly Dr 37663
Kimberly Rd 37664
Kincaid St 37660

King St 37660
Kingfisher Ct 37663
Kings Rd 37664
Kings Bay Dr 37660
Kings Grant Rd 37663
Kings Meadow Private Dr 37664
Kings View Rd 37660
Kingsberry Ct 37663
Kingsland Ct 37660
Kingsley Ave 37660
Kingsport Hwy 37663
Kingston Ct 37660
Kinsler Ave 37665
Kinsler Pvt Ln 37665
Kinzer Ln 37660
Kiowa St 37664
Kirk St 37660
Kistner Rd 37664
Kite St 37664
Kitzmiller Rd 37663
Knights Bridge Cir 37664
Knollwood Ln 37660
Knox Pope Rd 37660
Konnarock Rd 37664
Kreh Private Dr 37664
Kyle St 37665
L Jack Dr 37664
L Jack Pvt Dr 37664
Lafayette Cir 37664
Lake St 37660
Lake Aire 37663
Lake Forest Dr 37663
Lake Park Ct & Dr 37664
Lake Valley Ct & Rd 37664
Lakecrest Dr 37663
Lakefield Cir 37663
Lakeland Dr 37664
Lakeridge Dr & St 37663
Lakeshore Dr 37663
Lakeside Dr 37664
Lakeside Ln 37663
Lakeside Dock Dr 37663
Lakeview Cir 37663
Lakewood Dr 37663
Lakewood Rd 37660
Lakota Pl 37660
Lamar Ct 37664
Lamasa Dr 37660
Lamberth Dr 37663
Lambeth Pl 37660
Lamont St 37664
Lana View Dr 37664
Lancaster Dr & Rd 37663
Lancer Rd 37660
Landon Ct 37664
Lane Dr 37664
Lane Rd 37664
Larkspur Dr 37660
Larry St 37664
Larry Neil Way 37660
Lasalle St 37665
Latimer St 37660
Laurel St 37664
Laurel Pond Ln 37660
Laurelwood Dr 37660
Laurelwood Pond 37660
Lawndale Cir 37664
Lawrence St 37665
Lawson Dr 37660
Lazy Ln 37663
Le Amron Dr 37665
Leaf Pt 37663
Leaning Pine Rd 37660
Leaside Dr 37664
Lebanon Rd 37663
Ledges Dr 37664
Lee St 37660
Leedy Rd 37664
Leeland Dr 37660
Legion Dr 37664
Lehigh St 37664
Lemay Dr 37664
Lenoir Rd 37660
Leslie Ct 37663
Lewis Ln 37660

Lexington Ln 37664
Liberty Dr & Ln 37663
Liberty Church Rd 37663
Light St 37663
Light Street Ext 37663
Lightwood St 37660
Lilac St 37660
Lincoln St
1400-1499 37660
1700-1899 37664
Lincolnshire Cir 37663
Linda Ct 37664
Linden Rd 37664
Lindenwood Dr 37663
Lindkaye Dr 37663
Linville St
1100-1399 37660
1400-1599 37664
Little St 37660
Little Echo Ct 37663
Little Horse Gap Private Dr 37660
Little Valley Rd 37660
Littleton Rd 37660
Live Oak Dr 37660
Livesay Dr 37665
Lochiel Ct 37664
Lochridge Bnd 37663
Lochwood Cir & Rd 37660
Lockport Cir 37664
Locust St 37664
Lodge Pine Walk 37660
Log Cabin Private Dr 37660
Lola Mere Dr 37660
Lomax St 37660
London Private Dr 37660
Lone Oak Dr 37663
Lone Star Rd 37660
Lone Star Road Ext 37660
Lonesome Pine Rd 37664
Lonewood Cir & Dr 37663
Long St 37665
Long Hollow Rd 37660
Longreen Rd 37660
Longview Ln & St 37660
Lookout Dr 37663
Louis St 37660
Louita Dr 37660
Lovedale Dr 37660
Lowell Dr 37660
Lowrance Dr 37660
Lucerne Ln 37663
Lucille Pl 37663
Lucinda Rd 37660
Lucy Pl & Rd 37660
Luray Pl 37665
Lydia Ln 37664
Lynch Rd 37660
Lynda Ln 37664
Lynn Ave & St 37665
Lynn Garden Dr
200-869 37660
870-1899 37665
Lynnbrook Ln 37664
Lynnwood Ct 37664
Lynnwood Rd 37660
Mack Ct 37663
Madison St 37665
Magic View Dr 37660
Magnolia Ave 37664
Mahlon Dr 37663
E & W Main St 37660
Malabar Dr 37660
Malcolm Ln 37660
Malvern Ct & Dr 37660
Manchester Pl 37663
Mandan Rd 37664
Manderley Rd 37660
W Manor Ct & Dr 37660
Maple St 37660
Maple Hill Private Dr 37663
Maple Oak Ln 37660
Maplewood St 37660
Marble St 37660
Marcum Ave 37665
Marcus St E 37663

Marietta St 37660
Marilee Way 37660
Marion St 37660
E & W Market St 37660
Martin St 37665
Martin Luther King Dr 37660
Martingale Sq 37663
Mary St 37660
Mary Jane Rd 37660
Mason Rd 37660
Massengill Dr 37660
Matilda Pl 37664
Maxwell Ave 37664
May Ave 37665
Mayfair Rd 37663
Mayfield Ave 37665
Maywood Dr 37660
Mcclain Rd 37660
Mcconnel Ln 37665
Mcconnell Rd 37660
Mcconnell St 37664
Mccoy St 37664
Mcculley Ln & Pl 37664
Mcfarland Dr 37664
Mcgee St 37660
Mcgregor Dr 37660
Mcintosh Dr 37663
Mckenzie Dr 37660
Mckinney Dr & St 37660
Mclean Rd 37660
Mcneil St 37665
Mcteer Dr 37663
Meade Trl 37663
Meadow Ln 37663
Meadow Rd 37664
Meadow Brook Dr 37663
Meadow Brook Ln 37660
Meadow Crest Dr 37663
Meadow Dale Cir 37663
Meadow Glade Cir 37663
Meadow Glen Cir 37663
Meadow Lane Ext 37663
Meadowview Ln & Pkwy 37660
Megan Ct 37664
Mellwood Dr 37660
Melody Ln 37665
Melrose Ave & Ln 37664
Melvin St 37665
Memorial Blvd & Ct 37664
Merman Rd 37663
Merry Oaks Dr 37663
Merrywood Ave 37664
Mesa Dr 37664
Michelham Dr 37660
Michelle Dr 37660
Middlebrook Dr 37660
Midfield Dr 37665
Midland Dr 37664
Midview Pl & St 37665
Milam St 37660
Milburn Ave 37660
Milhorn Rd 37663
Mill St 37660
Mill Creek Rd
100-341 37660
342-1499 37664
Miller St 37664
Millington Ct 37663
E & W Millpond St 37660
Millye St 37664
Milton Ct 37664
Mimi Ct 37660
Mimosa Dr 37660
Minga Rd 37663
Minga Store Rd 37663
Minnich Trl 37660
Minton Pl & St 37660
Misty Dr 37660
Mitchell Rd
200-1099 37663
4300-4699 37664
Mocassin St S 37660
Mockingbird Ln 37663
Mohawk Cir 37664
Mohawk St 37665

Mohican Ln 37664
Montana Ave 37660
Montclair Rd 37664
Monte Vista Dr 37660
Monterey Ave 37664
Montezuma Rd 37664
Montford Dr 37663
Monticello Pl 37665
Montrose Ave 37664
Montsweag Ct 37664
Moody Dr & Ln 37664
Moody Private Dr 37664
Moose Ln 37660
Moreland Dr
200-499 37660
600-1250 37664
1251-1999 37663
Morelock St 37660
Morelock Private Dr 37660
N & S Morgan St 37664
Morison Ave 37660
Morning Dove Dr 37663
Morning Star Ct & Dr 37664
Morningdale Dr 37664
Morningside Cir 37664
Morrell Ct 37664
Morrison Ave 37660
Morsby Ct 37660
Mosby Ln 37663
Mount Andrews Pvt Dr 37660
Mount Ida Pl 37660
Mount Vernon Dr 37664
Mount View Rd 37664
Mountain Dr 37664
Mountain Pine Ln 37660
Mountain View Ave 37664
Mowdy Ln 37664
Mt Vue 37663
Mull St 37665
Mullenix Private Dr 37660
Mullinex Ln 37660
Mullins St
100-399 37665
400-499 37660
Murrell Rd 37660
Musselman Private Dr 37663
Mustang Dr 37664
Myranda Ln 37660
Myron St 37660
Myrtle St 37660
Nall St 37664
Nankatie Dr 37663
Nassau Dr 37660
Natchez Ln 37664
Nathan St 37664
Navaho Ln 37664
Nave Dr 37663
Neal Ln 37660
Needham Dr 37664
Nelms Ln 37665
Nelson St 37660
Netherland Ln 37660
Netherland Inn Rd & Ter 37660
Nevermore Ln Pvt Dr 37664
E & W New St 37660
New Beason Well Rd 37660
New Moore Rd 37660
New Summerville Rd 37663
Newbern Rd 37664
Newland Ave 37660
Nickleby Ct & Dr 37663
Nicole Pl 37660
Noble St 37665
Nokomis Private Dr 37660
Nola Ln 37664
Norfolk Pl 37660
Norma Dr 37660
Norris Ave 37665
Northcott Cir, Dr & Ln 37660
Northwood Dr 37664
Northwood Pl 37665
Norwich Pl 37660
Norwood St 37660
Nottingham Ct & Rd 37663
Oak Ct 37663

Oak St 37660
Oak Drive Cir 37665
Oak Forest Pl 37664
Oak Glen Dr 37665
Oak Haven Dr 37664
Oak Tree Ln 37663
Oak View St 37664
Oakdale Rd 37664
Oakland St 37660
Oaklawn St 37660
Oakleaf Dr 37663
Oakley Pl 37664
Oakmont Dr 37663
Oakwood Dr 37664
Oasis Ln 37660
Odd Fellow Rd 37664
Odessa Rd 37664
Oglewood Rd 37664
Okey Mowell Rd 37660
Oklahoma Cir 37664
Old Beason Well Rd 37660
Old Bell Hollow Rd 37664
Old Blairs Gap Rd 37660
Old Castle Rd 37660
Old Cooks Valley Rd 37664
Old Dunlap Rd 37663
Old Fordtown Rd 37663
Old Gibson Mill Rd 37660
Old Island Trl 37664
Old Kinkead Rd 37660
Old Mill Ct 37664
Old Mill Creek Rd 37660
Old Moreland Dr 37663
Old Pactolus Rd 37663
Old Parker Private Dr 37664
Old Stage Rd 37664
Old Wilcox Dr 37660
Oldham Ct 37660
Olinger Dr 37660
Ollis Bowers Hill Rd 37664
Olterman Private Dr 37665
Olympian Way 37660
Olympus Cir & Dr 37663
Omar Dr 37664
Oneida Ct 37664
Opal St 37660
Orange St 37660
Orbin Dr 37660
Orchard Ct & Pl 37660
Orebank Rd 37664
Orleans Rd 37665
Ormond Dr 37664
Osage Dr 37660
Osceola Dr 37664
Otari Dr 37664
Overhill Dr 37660
Overlook Rd 37664
Overview Ct 37663
Oxford Ct
400-499 37663
2300-2399 37660
Pace St 37665
Packing House Rd 37660
Pactolus Rd 37663
Page Pl & St 37660
Palmer Rd 37660
Palmyra Dr 37663
Palomino Dr 37664
Panay Rd 37660
Pansy Dr 37664
Parham Pl 37660
Paris Ave 37665
E Park Dr 37660
W Park Dr 37665
Park St 37664
Park Place Dr 37663
Park Ridge Ct 37664
Park Ridge Dr 37660
Park Terrace Rd 37663
Parkcliff Dr 37664
Parker Dr 37660
Parker Ln 37660
Parker St 37664
Parker Hill Dr 37665
Parkerson Dr 37664
Parkway Dr 37663

Parson Dr 37660
Parton Dr 37660
Partridge Pl 37663
Patrick Ct 37660
Patrick Henry Cir 37663
Patterson Rd 37660
Patton St 37660
Pauline Rd 37660
Pavilion Dr 37660
Pawnee Ct 37664
Peach Orchard Dr 37665
Peachtree Dr 37664
Pear St 37664
Pearl St 37664
Peavler Dr 37660
Pebble Ct & Dr 37660
Peers St 37664
Peery St 37665
Pembroke St 37665
Pendleton Pl 37664
Pendleton St 37660
Pendragon Rd 37660
Pennsylvania Ave & Rd 37660
Peppertree Ct & Dr 37664
Periwinkle Pl 37660
Perry St 37660
Pettyjohn Rd 37664
Pheasant Ct 37663
Philon Dr 37660
Phoenix Ct 37663
Pickens Cir 37660
Pickens Ct 37663
Pickens Rd 37663
Pickwick Ct 37663
Piedmont St 37660
Pierce St 37664
Pine St 37664
Pine Cone Cir 37660
Pine Grove Ave 37660
Pine Needle Path 37660
Pine Ridge Ln 37663
Pinebrook Dr & Pl 37660
Pinecrest Rd 37660
Pinehurst Dr 37660
Pineola Ave 37664
Pinewood Pl 37664
Pinon Dr 37663
Pioneer Pl 37664
Pioneer Haven Ln 37663
Pitkin Dr 37664
Pitt Rd 37663
Plainview St 37664
Plantation Rd 37660
Pleasant Ave 37664
Pleasant Hill Dr 37664
Pleasley Rd 37660
Pocahontas Dr 37664
S Pointe Ct 37663
Polk St 37664
Polo Fields Pl 37663
Pond Springs Rd W 37664
Pondella Ave 37660
Poor Hollow Rd 37664
Poplar Ln 37663
Poplar St 37660
Poplar Grove Rd 37664
Porter Ave 37663
Portland Ave 37660
Post St 37664
Post Oak Dr 37663
Potato Hill Rd 37660
Pratt Rd 37660
Preakness Ct 37660
Prescott St 37660
Press St 37660
Preston Ct 37664
Preston Dr 37664
Preston Pl 37664
Preston Pl N 37660
Preston Park Dr 37664
Prestwick Ct 37660
Pridemore St 37660
Primrose St 37665
Prince Forest Private Dr 37664

Princess Grove Private Dr 37664
Princeton Rd 37660
Professional Park Pvt Dr 37663
Proffitt Ln 37663
Promise Ln 37660
Prospect Dr 37664
Providence Pt 37664
Pueblo Dr 37664
Pulitzer Pl 37660
Pulpit Ln 37660
Purr Lane Private Dr 37664
Putnam St 37660
Quail Pt 37663
Quail Heights Ct 37663
Quail Hill Cir 37663
Quail Pvt Dr 37663
Qualls Rd 37660
Queens Garden Private Dr 37664
Queensbury Ct 37660
Quillen St 37665
Quincy Ct 37664
Rabbit Run Trl 37660
Radcliffe Ave 37664
Ragsdale Rd & St 37660
Ragsdale Private Dr 37660
Ragsdale St Ext 37660
Rainbow Cir 37660
Raintree Dr 37665
Ramah Rd 37660
Rambling Rd 37663
Ramsey Ave 37665
Randall St 37660
Randich Dr 37660
Randolph St 37664
Ranier Dr 37660
Ransome Ln 37660
Raven Cir 37664
Raven St 37660
Raventree Dr 37664
Ravenwood Dr 37660
E & W Ravine Rd 37660
Rc Barrett Rd 37660
Reardon Ln 37660
Rector Dr 37665
Red Bud Cir & Dr 37664
Red Cedar Branch Rd 37664
Red Maple Rd 37664
Red Oak Ln 37663
Red Oak Plantation Dr 37663
Red Robin Ln 37664
Redwood Dr 37664
Reedy Pl & St 37660
Reedy Creek Rd 37664
Reese St 37660
Regency Dr 37663
Regional Park Dr 37660
Remington Ct 37663
Renaissance Sq 37664
Reservoir Rd 37660
Revere St 37660
Rich Dr 37660
Rich Dr Ext 37660
Richland Dr 37663
Rick Slaughter Ct 37660
Riddle St 37660
Ridge Rd 37660
Ridge Haven Dr 37660
Ridgecrest Ave
1100-1191 37665
1193-1199 37665
1200-1499 37660
Ridgecrest Cir 37665
Ridgefields Rd 37660
Ridgeline Dr 37664
Ridgemont Cir & Dr 37663
Ridgepine Rd 37660
Ridgetop Trl 37664
Ridgeview St 37664
Ridgeway Dr & Rd 37664
Ridgewood Dr 37660
Riggs Rd 37660
Riley James Private Dr 37663

Rim Rock Rd 37664
Ring St 37660
Rippling Br 37664
Rippling Run 37663
Ritter Ct 37663
S River Dr 37660
River Bridge Rd 37663
River Edge Ct, Dr & Pl 37660
Rivermont Cir, Ct & Dr 37660
Riverport Ln & Rd 37660
Riverside Ave 37660
Riverwatch Cir 37660
Riverwoods Pl 37660
Roan Ct & St 37665
Roanoke Hl 37665
Robalee St 37665
Roberts Ln 37660
Robertson St 37660
Robin Ct 37664
Robin Ln 37660
Robin St 37664
Robindale Ct & Ln 37663
Robinwood Rd 37663
Rock City Rd 37664
Rock Rose Cir 37664
Rock Springs Dr
  100-499 37660
  500-1199 37664
Rock Springs Rd
  100-499 37663
  500-2899 37664
Rock Springs Valley Rd 37664
Rock Valley Dr 37664
Rockford St 37664
Rockwell Pl 37664
Rockwood Pl & St 37664
Rocky Ln & Rd 37660
Rocky Hill Ln 37660
Roderick Ct 37663
Rogan St 37660
Rogers Ave 37660
Roller Dr 37663
Roller St 37660
Rolling Dr 37660
Rolling Hills Dr 37660
Rolling Pvt Dr 37660
Ronald Dr 37664
Rose St 37660
Rose Garden Cir 37660
Roseberry Rd 37660
Roseberry Road Ext 37660
Rosebrooke Ct 37664
Rosedale Dr 37665
Rosefield Dr 37660
Rosehaven Ct 37663
Rosemont St 37660
Rosetree Ln 37660
Rosewood Cir 37664
Rosewood Dr 37660
Rosewood Ln 37664
Ross St 37664
Rotherwood Dr 37660
Roxana Dr 37664
Roxbury Ln 37664
Royal Cir 37664
Royal Dr 37663
Royal Mile Dv 37664
Ruby Falls Ln 37664
Rufus Rd 37660
Running Deer Trl 37663
Rushmore Rd 37660
Russell St 37660
Rustic Way 37664
Rustic Hills Dr 37660
Rutledge Rd 37663
Ryan Rd 37660
Ryder Dr 37664
Saddle Ridge Dr 37664
Sail Makers Whip Ct 37664
Saint Andrews Dr 37664
Saint Charles Pl 37660
Saint Erics Ct 37660
Salem St 37660
Salley St 37660
Salvation Rd 37660
Sam Gammon Rd 37663
Samoset Dr 37660
Samuel St 37660
Sand St 37660
Sandpiper Cir 37663
Sandridge Dr 37663
Sandy Rd 37660
Sanford Dr 37664
Saratoga Rd 37660
Sasanoa Ct 37664
Sassafras Ct 37660
Satanta Rd 37664
Saxon Rd 37660
Scenic Ct 37663
Scotland Rd 37660
Scott Dr 37660
Scott St 37664
Scott County Rd 37660
Seaver Rd 37660
Sedgefield Rd 37660
Selena St 37664
Selena Street Ext 37664
Selkirk Dr 37664
Seminole Ln 37664
Seneca Rd 37664
Sequoyah Dr 37660
Serenity Ct 37665
Settlers Trl 37664
E Sevier Ave
  100-1134 37660
  1135-2199 37664
W Sevier Ave 37660
Sevier Terrace Dr 37660
Sewanee Ave 37664
Shadow Ln 37664
Shadow Wood Ln 37663
Shady Dr 37660
Shady View Rd
  100-299 37660
  300-1299 37660
Shadyside Dr 37663
Shamrock St 37664
Shannon St 37664
Sharondale Ave 37660
Sharron Rd 37660
Shaw St 37660
Shawnee Dr 37664
Sheffield St 37660
Shelby St 37660
Shepparton Ln 37660
Sheridan Sq 37660
Sheringham Ct 37660
Sherman Pl 37660
Sherrill Dr 37660
Sherry St 37660
Sherwood Pl & Rd 37664
Shipley St 37664
Shipley Ferry Rd 37663
Shipp St 37660
Shipp Springs Rd 37660
Shirley St 37660
Shoals Rd 37663
Shoemaker Ct E & W 37660
Short Ln 37663
Short St 37660
Short Hill Dr 37660
Shuler Dr 37664
Sierra Dr 37664
Signature Trl 37664
Siler Dr 37660
Silver Ct 37664
Silverdale Rd 37660
Silverleaf Ct 37660
Simpson St 37660
Sioux Dr 37664
Sir Echo Dr 37663
Skelton Bluff Rd 37660
Sky S 37660
Sky Dr 37665
Sky View Dr 37660
Sky Vista Ct 37664
Skyland Dr & Ln 37664
Skyland Falls Ct 37664
Skyline Ave 37664
Slaughter St 37664
Sleepy Hollow Rd 37663
Smith Dr 37664
Smith Rd 37663
Smith St 37660
Snapps Ferry Rd 37663
Sonnett Ct 37664
Sourmash Dr 37660
Southcote Dr 37660
Southgate Dr, Pl & Trl 37660
Southwood Dr 37660
Spardale St 37664
Spearhead Cir 37664
Spenlow Ct 37663
Spindletop Cir & Ct 37660
Spring Ln 37663
Spring St 37664
Spring Brook Dr 37663
Spring Creek Wynd 37664
Spring Hill Dr 37664
Spring Valley Dr 37660
Springdale Ln 37660
Springfield Ave 37664
Springleaf Ct 37663
Springview St 37664
Springwood Ln 37660
Spruce St 37664
Stadium Ct & Dr 37664
Stafford St 37660
Stage Rd 37664
Stagecoach Rd 37664
Stagshaw Ln 37660
Stallard St 37663
Stapleton Dr 37665
Stardust Rd W 37660
Starlight Rd 37660
Starling Dr 37663
Starnes St 37665
Steadman St 37664
Steeplechase Ct & Dr 37664
Stella St 37665
Sterling Ln 37664
Stevenson Hill Rd 37663
Stewball Cir 37660
Stillwater Ct 37664
Stillwood Ave & Ct 37664
Stinson Dr 37660
Stone Ct 37664
E Stone Dr 37660
W Stone Dr 37660
Stone Edge Cir & Dr 37660
Stonebrook Pl 37660
Stonegate Rd 37660
Stoneview St 37660
Stonewall St 37665
Stoney Point Rd 37664
Stratford Rd 37664
Stratton Pl 37663
Strickland Ct 37660
Striera Dr 37663
Strieral Dr 37663
Stuart Dr 37664
Stuffle St & Ter 37660
Sue St 37663
Suffolk Ct & St 37660
Sugarpine Dr 37660
Sugarwood Dr 37663
E Sullivan Ct 37664
E Sullivan St 37660
W Sullivan St 37660
Sullivan Gardens Dr & Pkwy 37660
Summer St 37664
Summer Hills Ct 37663
Summer Private Dr 37660
Summerview Ct 37663
Summerville Rd 37663
Summerville Farms Ct 37663
Summitt Dr 37664
Summitt Oaks Cir 37663
Sumpter Rd 37663
Sunbright Dr 37664
Sunbury Ct 37664
Suncrest Dr 37665
Sundale Ln 37665
Sundown Dr 37664
Sunningdale Rd 37660
Sunny Ln & Pl 37660
Sunnyside St 37664
Sunnyview Dr 37665
Sunpoint Dr 37665
Sunrise Ct 37665
Sunset Ave 37665
Sunset Dr 37660
Surmont Ct 37660
Surrey Dr 37664
Susan Cook Pl 37664
Sussex Dr 37660
Swannanoa Ave 37664
Sweetbriar Rd 37665
Sycamore St 37664
Sylvan Dr 37663
Tacoma Rd 37664
Taft Pt 37660
Talbert Cir 37664
Tall Oaks Ct 37663
Tall Tree Dr 37663
Tallwood Dr 37660
Tams Ln 37664
Tanglewood Dr 37664
Tanner Ct 37660
Tansey Ln 37660
Tarkington St 37660
Tate Dr 37660
Taylor Ln 37660
Teaberry Cir 37663
Teal Ct 37663
Teasel Dr 37660
Ted Dykes Rd 37660
Telstar Dr 37664
Temple Star Rd 37660
Temple Star Rd Ext 37660
Tennessee St 37660
Tenneva Pl & St 37665
Terry Dr 37660
Texas St 37665
Thackeray Ct 37663
Thistlewood Dr 37663
Thomas St 37660
Thomas Acres Rd 37664
Thompson St 37660
Thorngrove Dr 37660
Thornton Dr 37664
N & S Thornwood Pl 37660
Three Oaks Dr 37660
Tidewater Ct 37660
Tiffany Ct 37663
Tiffany St 37664
Tilson Rd 37660
Tilson Hill Rd 37660
Tilthammer Dr 37660
Timberidge Trl 37660
Timberlake Ct & Ln 37664
Timberland Cir & Ct 37664
Timbers Edge Ct & Trce 37660
Timbertree Branch Rd 37660
Timberwood Cir 37660
Timrick St 37664
Tinker Ln 37664
Tip Top Ave 37665
Tipton St 37660
Toddman St 37660
Todds Dr 37660
Tomahawk Dr 37664
Tompkins St 37660
Top Sail Ct 37664
Topper St 37660
Tory Ln 37660
Toy Crawford Rd 37660
Trace Ct 37664
Tranbarger Dr 37660
Travis Cir 37660
Treetop Private Dr 37664
Trevor Dr 37660
Tri Cities Xing 37663
Trials End St 37660
Triangle Cir 37664
Trinity Ln 37664
Truxton Dr 37660
Tulip Tree Rd 37663
Tuscany Way 37663
Twin Hill Private Dr 37660
Twin Hills Dr 37660
Tyler St 37660
Tyson Ln 37660
Underwood Ct 37660
Unicoi St 37660
Union St 37660
Union Way 37664
Union Hill St 37660
University Blvd 37660
Upland Dr 37663
Upper Ledges Dr 37664
W Valley Dr 37664
Valley St 37660
Valley Estates Ct 37663
Valley Falls Ct 37664
Valley High Private Dr 37660
N Valley View Cir 37664
Valleydale Dr 37664
Van Horn St 37660
Van Oaks Dr 37665
Vance St 37664
Vanderbilt Way 37664
Vanderpool Private Dr 37660
Velma St 37665
Venture Park 37660
Vermont Dr 37660
Vesta Ave 37660
Vfw Rd 37663
Victory Ln 37664
View St 37663
Viewforth Ct 37664
Vincent Ln 37660
Violet St 37663
Virgil Ave & Ln 37665
Virginia Ave 37664
W Virginia Ave 37660
Virginia Dr 37660
Virginia St 37665
Wabash St 37660
Waco Ct 37664
Wadlow Gap Rd 37660
Wagon Wheel Ln 37663
Wahoo Dr 37663
Wahoo Valley Rd 37663
Wakefield Ct 37663
Wakefield St 37660
Walker St 37665
Wall St 37665
Wallace Ct 37664
Wallace Alley St 37663
Walnut Ave 37660
Walton Ct & Rd 37663
Waltz Ln 37663
Wampler St 37665
Wandering Ct & Dr 37660
E & W Wanola Ave 37660
Ward Ave & Pl 37660
Warpath Dr 37664
Warrick Dr 37660
Warrior Dr 37663
Warrior Falls Dr 37664
Washington Ave 37664
Watauga St
  500-1399 37660
  1400-1699 37664
Wateree St 37660
Waterford Dr 37664
Waterman Private Rd 37660
Waterside Dr 37663
Waterside Private Dr 37663
Watterson St 37660
Waverly Rd 37664
Wayne St 37660
Wayne Construction Rd 37660
Weaver Ln 37664
Wedgewood Cir 37660
Weeks Ave 37660
Welch Rd 37660
Welk Rd 37660
Wellington Blvd 37660
Wembeck Dr 37664
Wendover Dr 37663
Wentworth St 37660
Wesley Rd 37664
Wessex Dr 37663
West Ave 37660
Westbrook Dr 37663
Westfield Dr
  200-499 37664
  600-799 37663
Westfield Pl 37664
Westminister Pl 37663
Westmoreland Ave 37664
Westwind Dr 37660
Wexler St 37660
Wheatley St 37660
Whipoorwill Ln 37660
Whirlaway Cir 37660
Whispering Way 37663
Whispering Hills Dr 37660
Whisperwood Cir & Dr 37660
Whitcomb St 37664
White St 37664
White Hawk Way 37663
White Oak Ln 37663
White Pine Ln 37660
Whitehaven Dr 37660
Whitehills Rd 37660
Whitley Dr 37660
Wicklow Dr 37664
Wide Oak Pvt Dr 37660
Widener Rd 37663
Wiembley Dr 37664
Wil Rho Cir 37660
Wilburn Dr 37664
N & S Wilcox Ct & Dr 37660
Wild Rose Ln 37660
Wildwood Dr 37660
Wildwood Rd 37663
Willard Dr 37663
Williams Rd 37660
Willmary Dr 37664
Willow St 37664
Willow Hollow Rd 37663
Willow View Dr 37660
Willowbend Ct, Dr, Ln & Pl 37660
Willowbrook Ct, Dr, Pl & Trce 37660
Willowcrest Pl 37660
Wilma St 37665
Wilmont Dr 37663
Wimberly Pl 37660
Wimbledon Ct 37664
Winchester Dr 37663
Winchester Ln 37660
S Wind Dr 37664
Windale Ave 37660
Windhaven Acres 37660
Windmere Pl 37664
Windridge Dr 37660
Windsor St 37660
Windsor Falls Ln 37664
Windsor Forest Dr 37663
Windy Pl 37660
Winegar Ave 37660
Winesap Rd 37663
Winfield Dr 37663
Wingate Rd 37660
Winston Cir 37664
Winston Dr 37665
Winterbrook Cir & Dr 37663
Witherspoon Dr 37663
Wohlford Pl 37664
Wolfe St 37660
Wonderland Dr 37660
Wood Ct 37663
Wood Eden Dr 37660
Wood View Ct 37664
Woodberry Cir 37663
Woodbine St 37660
Woodcliff Dr 37664
Woodcrest Dr 37663
Wooddale Cir 37664
Woodfern Pl 37660
Woodfield Dr 37660
Woodgreen Ln 37660
Woodhaven Dr
  4400-4499 37664
  6000-6099 37663
Woodland Ave 37665
Woodlark Ln 37660
Woodlawn Dr & Rd 37660
Woodleaf Ln 37663
Woodmere Dr 37663
Woodmont Ave 37660
Woodoak Dr 37664
Woodpond Ct 37664
Woodridge Ave 37664
Woodridge Cir 37663
Woods Way 37664
Woodside Dr 37664
Woodstock Pl 37663
Woodstone Dr 37663
Worthington Dr 37663
Wrenwood Ct 37663
Wynfield Ct 37663
Wynhaven Dr 37663
Yadkin St 37660
Yale Sq 37664
Yokley St 37660
York St 37664
Yorktown Rd 37663

KNOXVILLE TN

General Delivery 37950

POST OFFICE BOXES MAIN OFFICE STATIONS AND BRANCHES

Box No.s
1 - 2847 37901
3001 - 3954 37927
5001 - 5957 37928
6001 - 6924 37914
7001 - 7520 37921
8007 - 8007 37924
9001 - 9899 37940
10001 - 11914 37939
12001 - 12990 37912
13101 - 13199 37920
14001 - 14988 37914
15001 - 15994 37901
18001 - 18740 37928
19800 - 19820 37939
20001 - 20939 37940
22000 - 25276 37933
26001 - 26399 37912
27001 - 27909 37927
30001 - 36033 37930
50001 - 59100 37950
70001 - 71554 37938
80001 - 80146 37924

NAMED STREETS

Aaron Ln 37920
Abbey Rd 37917
Abbey Mist Ln 37931
Abbey Wood Ln 37922
Abbott Ln
  600-699 37923
  1600-1699 37914
Abelia Way 37931
Abercorn Rd 37921
Aberdeen Ln 37920
Abilene Pl 37917
Abington Ln 37909
Abner St 37921
Abner Cruze Rd 37920
Abners Ridge Dr 37934
Abraham Ln 37931
Abrams Dr 37922
Abrams Creek Way 37922
Academy Way 37923
Acapulco Ave 37921
Acco Rd 37924
Acker St 37917
Ackerman Ln 37920
Ackley Cir 37934
Acorn Dr 37918

Acorn Woods Way 37918
W Acres Dr 37919
Acuff St 37917
Ada Ln 37918
Adair Ave 37917
Adair Dr 37918
Adams Ave 37917
Adams Gate Rd 37931
Adcock Ave 37921
Addie Rd 37923
Addison Dr 37918
Addison St 37915
Adelene Ln 37918
Adelia Dr 37920
Adell Ree Park Ln 37909
Adenleigh Way 37922
Admiral Rd 37934
Admiral Bend Way 37934
Admirality Ln 37920
Adrian Rd 37918
Advantage Pl 37922
Aeronca Rd 37919
Affinity Way 37922
Afton Dr 37918
Agawela Ave 37919
Agnes Rd 37919
Agora Way 37920
Aiden Hollow Way 37920
E & W Aiken Ln 37922
Ailor Ave
1600-2499 37921
2500-2699 37919
Ailsie Dr 37920
Ainsworth Dr 37909
Airelack Rd 37914
Airport Hwy 37920
Airtree Ln 37931
Ala Dr 37920
Alameda Dr 37932
Alamo Ave 37920
Alan Springs Ln 37938
Alandale Dr 37920
Alanridge Ln 37932
Alarrana Ave 37921
Albany Rd 37923
Albemarle Ln 37923
Albert Ave 37917
Alberta Dr 37920
Albunda Dr 37919
Alco Cir 37923
Alcoa Hwy & Way 37920
Alcott Ln 37918
Alcott Manor Ln 37922
Alden Glen Way 37919
Aldenwood Ln 37919
Alder Dr 37919
Alder Tree Ln 37938
Aldergate Way 37922
Aldingham St 37912
Alex Ln 37922
Alexander St 37917
Alexander Cavet Dr 37909
Alexia Rd 37923
Alfredda Delaney St 37921
Alice St 37914
Alice Bell Rd
2300-2399 37914
2600-3599 37917
Alki Ln 37919
Alkison Ln 37931
Allee De Papillon Dr 37922
Alleen Rd 37920
Allegheny Rd 37914
Allen Ave 37920
Allen Dr 37912
Allen Rd 37920
Allen Kirby Rd 37934
Alliance Dr 37921
Allison Way 37918
Alma Ave 37914
Almanac Ln 37932
Almond Way 37912
Aloha Ave 37921
Alpha Ave 37921
Alpha Terrace Ln 37938
Alpine Dr 37920
Alps Way 37919
Alta Vista Way 37919
Altacrest Ln 37931
Altamira Dr 37934
Altamont Way 37923
Althea Dr 37920
Althrope Way 37923
Alvaros Ln 37934
Alvin Ln 37920
Alysha Vineyard Way 37931
Alysun Nikole Dr 37934
Am Luttrell Rd 37924
Amanda Cir 37922
Amanda Ct 37915
Amarillo Ln 37922
Ambassador Pl 37918
Amber St 37917
Amber Dawn Ln 37920
Amber Glades Ln 37922
Amber Jack Ln 37934
Amber Lantern Way 37932
Amber Meadows Cir 37932
Amber Ridge Way 37918
Amberfield Ln 37918
Amberleigh Dr 37922
Amberleigh Bluff Way 37922
Amberset Dr 37922
Amberwood Dr 37919
Amblecote Rd 37923
Ambleside Ct 37922
Amblewinds Ln 37922
Ambling Ln 37912
Ambrister St 37921
Ambrose St 37921
Amburn Ln 37923
Ambus Ln 37920
Amelia Rd 37917
American Glass Way 37932
Amerock Blvd 37914
Amesbury Rd 37934
Amherst Ave 37915
Amherst Rd
1400-1899 37909
1900-3199 37921
Amherst Woods Ln 37921
Amos Ln 37938
Amsterdam Ln 37938
Amston Dr 37938
Anchor Ct 37934
Anchor Villas Ln 37934
Anchorage Cir 37934
Ancient Oak Ln 37931
Andalusian Way 37922
Anderson Ave 37919
E Anderson Ave 37917
W Anderson Ave
100-199 37917
700-999 37921
Anderson Dr 37920
Anderson Ln 37918
Anderson Pl 37918
Anderson Rd 37918
Anderson View Way 37918
Andersonville Pike 37938
Andes Rd 37931
Andes St 37914
Andes Crossing Way 37931
Andoah Rd 37918
Andover Blvd 37934
Andover Dr 37914
Andover Green Way 37918
Andover View Ln 37922
Andover Village Way 37918
Andrea Ln 37921
Andrew Pl 37917
Andrew Brook Ln 37923
Andrew Johnson Hwy 37924
Andrews Crossing Rd 37931
Andrews Point Way 37931
Andy Holt Ave 37916
Angel Oak Ct 37922
Angeles Dr 37918
Angelia Dr 37921
Angola Rd 37921
Anita Dr 37920
Ankara Ct 37923
Ankara Dr 37921
Ann Baker Furrow Blvd 37916
Ann Marie Way 37931
Anna Rd 37920
Annalee Way 37921
Annandale Rd 37934
Annatole Ln 37938
Anniversary Ln 37914
Annona Dr 37918
Ansley Cir 37923
Ansley Ct 37934
Ansley Woods Way 37923
Anteelah Trl 37919
Anthem View Ln 37922
Antietam Rd 37917
Antiqua Ln 37921
Antler Ln 37931
Antrim Way 37919
Apache Rd 37924
Apache Trl 37920
Apex Dr 37919
Apollo Dr 37921
N & S Apopka Dr 37914
Appalachian Way 37918
Appaloosa Way 37922
Appian Way 37923
Apple Blossom Way 37920
Apple Grove Ln 37922
Apple Orchard Way 37923
Apple Valley Dr 37924
Appleby Ln 37920
Appleby Ridge Way 37920
Applegate Ln 37934
Appleton Way 37934
Applewood Dr 37921
Appomattox Ln 37922
April Dr 37919
April Springs Ln 37918
Aqua Ln 37931
Aquamarine Rd 37918
Aquoni Dr 37912
Aragon Ln 37923
Aralia Ln 37918
Arapahoe Ln 37918
Arbor Pl 37917
Arbor Branch Ln 37922
Arbor Gate Ln 37932
W & E Arbor Trace Dr & Ln 37909
Arbor Vitea Dr 37919
Arborbrooke Dr 37922
Arborcrest Way 37918
Arbutus Ln 37920
Arcadia Dr 37920
Archer Rd 37918
Archibald Way 37938
Archie Weigel Rd 37914
Archwood Ln 37918
Arden Rd 37919
Ardmore Dr 37923
Ardrock Dr 37914
Argonne Rd 37923
Argyle Dr 37914
Ariel Ln 37923
Arkansas Rd 37921
Arkwright Ln 37921
Arlie Dr 37918
Arline Dr 37938
Arlington Dr 37934
Armiger Ln 37932
Arms Rd 37924
Armstead Pl 37917
Armstrong Ave 37917
Armstrong Rd 37924
Army St 37920
Arnheim Way 37920
Arnold St 37920
Aromatic Aster Rd 37918
Aronimink Pt 37934
Arrow Dr 37914
Arrow Wood Rd 37919
Arrowhead Trl 37919
Artella Dr 37920
Arthur St 37921
Arthur Harmon Rd 37920
Artis Ln 37923
Artistry Rd 37918
Aruba Ln 37921
Asa Whitaker Way 37923
Asbury Rd 37914
Asbury Cemetery Rd 37914
Asbury School Rd 37914
Ascot Ct 37923
Ashbourne Way 37923
Ashbridge Ln 37932
Ashbrooke Way 37923
Ashburton Dr 37909
Ashby Rd 37923
Ashby Field Ln 37918
Asher Ln 37931
Asheville Hwy
3900-5499 37914
5500-9299 37924
Ashfield Cir 37922
Ashford Dr 37934
Ashford Glen Dr 37918
Ashgrove Pl 37919
Ashland Ave 37914
Ashland Springs Way 37922
Ashley Ct 37921
Ashley Michelle Ct 37934
Ashley Oak Way 37923
Ashmeade Rd 37922
Ashridge Rd 37931
Ashton Ct 37923
E Ashton Ct 37934
W Ashton Ct 37934
Ashton Pointe Ln 37931
Ashwood Pl 37917
Aspen Dr 37919
Aspen Grove Way 37931
Aspen Ridge Ln 37932
Aspenwood Dr 37934
Asrock Dr 37924
Aster Ln 37921
Aster Rd 37918
Aston Ct 37923
Astoria Dr 37918
Atchley St 37920
Atchley Hill Way 37920
Atchley Ridge Way 37919
Athens Rd 37923
Atherton Ln 37931
Atkins Rd 37918
Atlantic Ave 37917
Atlas Ln 37922
Atlearis Rd 37920
Atlee Summit Ln 37931
Atoka Ln 37917
Attwood Ct 37923
Aubrey Ln 37912
Audena Ln 37919
Audrianna Ln 37918
Audubon Dr 37918
Augusta Ave 37920
Augusta Hills Rd 37922
Augusta National Way 37934
Augustan Ln 37934
Auklet Ln 37922
Ault Rd & St 37914
Aultman Rd 37920
Aurora Ln 37912
Austin Park Ln 37920
Autry Way 37909
Autry Ridge Ln 37934
Autumn Ln 37912
Autumn Bluff Rd 37932
Autumn Creek Dr 37924
Autumn Glade Ln 37934
Autumn Hollow Ln 37932
Autumn Kayla Ln 37918
Autumn Knoll Dr 37920
Autumn Leaves Ln 37934
Autumn Oaks Ln 37921
Autumn Path Ln 37918
Autumn Ridge Dr 37922
Autumn Rose Ln 37918
Autumn Springs Dr 37938
Autumn Trace Dr 37919
Autumn Tree Ln 37922
Autumn Valley Ln 37922
Autumnwood Cir 37932
Avallon Pl 37934
Avalon Trl 37920
Avashire Ln 37931
Avebury Ln 37921
Avensong Ln 37909
Avenue A 37920
Avenue B 37920
Avenue C 37920
Avery Way 37922
Avery Village Way 37921
Avery Woods Ln 37921
Avice Lennon St 37921
Avis Ln 37914
Avocet Ln 37922
Avon Cir 37909
Avon Park Cir 37918
Avondale Ave 37917
Avonmouth Rd 37914
Award Winning Way 37932
Axton Dr 37934
Aylesbury Dr 37918
Azalea Dr 37909
Azrock Dr 37914
Aztec Ln 37931
Babelay Rd 37924
Babs Rd 37920
Badgett Dr 37921
Badgett Rd 37919
Bafford Pl 37920
Bagley Ln 37923
Bagwell Rd 37924
Bailey Bridge Way 37938
Bailey Cove Cir 37909
Bailey Park Ln 37922
Bajor Ln 37938
Baker Ave 37920
Bakersfield Way 37918
Bakertown Rd 37931
Bakertown Station Way 37931
Balcor Cir 37923
Bald Eagle Blvd 37922
Baldwin Ave 37920
Baldwin Station Ln 37922
Bales Ln 37914
Bales Rd 37914
Bales St 37917
Ball Rd 37931
Ball Camp Pike
4300-5899 37921
6600-8899 37931
Ball Camp Byington Rd 37931
Ball Camp School Rd 37931
Ball Park Ln 37920
Ballard Dr 37918
Balmoral Ln 37912
Balraj Ln 37921
Balsam Dr 37918
Baltusrol Rd 37934
Banbury Rd 37934
Bancroft Ln 37934
Banks Ave 37917
Bantry Ln 37934
Banyan Way 37914
Banyon Wood Ln 37920
Barbados Ln 37921
Barbara Dr 37918
Barbara Ln 37934
Barbee Ln 37923
Barber St 37920
Barber Hill Ln 37920
Barberry Dr 37912
Barbrow Ln 37932
Barbury Ln 37931
Barcelona Dr 37923
Barclay Dr 37920
Barclay Heights Ln 37920
Bardill Ln 37919
Bardon Rd 37919
Barger Pond Way 37912
Barharbor Way 37934
Barineau Hill Ln 37920
Barker Ave 37915
Barksdale Dr 37918
Barkwood Rd 37921
Barley Cir 37922
Barlow Cir 37923
Barn Valley Way 37921
Barnard Rd 37921
Barnbrook Ln 37918
Barnsley Rd 37934
Barnstable Ln 37922
Baron Dr 37923
Barrar Ave 37920
Barrington Blvd 37922
Barstow Way 37912
Bartlett Ln 37922
Barton St 37917
Barton Place Ln 37922
Basenger Dr 37938
Basil Ln 37923
Basilfield Dr 37920
Bass Ln 37922
Bassett Ln 37932
Basswood Rd 37921
Batavia Way 37923
Bateau Ln 37922
Bathurst Rd 37909
Batson Ln 37919
Battery St 37919
Battery Hill Cir 37934
Battle Front Trl 37934
Baum Dr 37919
Baverton Dr 37921
E Baxter Ave 37917
W Baxter Ave
100-299 37917
500-1499 37921
Bay St 37912
Bay Circle Dr 37918
Bay Garden Ln 37938
Bay Wood Cir 37922
Bayberry Dr 37921
Bayhill Ridge Ln 37922
Bayless Ave 37917
Baylor Cir 37923
Bayou Bend Way 37922
Bays Mountain Rd 37920
Bayshore Rd 37934
Baytree Ct 37934
Bayview Dr 37922
Bazemore Ln 37938
Beacon Hill Ln 37919
Beacon Light Way 37931
Beacontree Ln 37934
Beagle Chase Ln 37919
N & S Beaman St 37914
Beaman Lake Rd 37914
Bear Creek Ln 37922
Bear Cub Way 37912
Beard Dr 37921
Bearden Pl 37917
Bearden Rd 37919
Bearden Park Cir 37919
Bearden View Ln 37909
Beartooth Way 37924
Beasley Ln 37918
Beatrice Way 37931
Beauchamp Loop 37938
Beaumont Ave 37921
Beaver Branch Way 37918
Beaver Brook Dr 37918
E Beaver Creek Dr 37918
Beaver Dam Ln 37931
Beaver Glade Ln 37931
Beaver Hill Ln 37931
Beaver Ridge Rd 37931
Beaver Run Ln 37931
Beaver Trace Ln 37931
Beaverton Rd 37919
Beaverwood Dr 37918
Beck Pl 37915
Beckworth Ct 37919
Becky Ln 37920
Bedford Ave 37914
Bedloe Way 37920
Bedrock Way 37918
Beech St 37920
Beecher Mayfield Way 37922
Beechleaf Rd 37924
Beechmont Dr 37920
Beechvale Dr 37922
Beechwood Dr & Rd 37920
Beehive Ln 37923
Beeler Rd 37918
Beeler Ridge Way 37918
Begonia Way 37931
Belcaro Dr 37918
Belcourt Dr 37918
Belfast Ln 37931
Belgian Way 37922
Bell Ln 37914
Bell Rd
7100-7499 37918
7500-8399 37938
Bell St 37915
Bell Brook Ln 37923
Bell Valley Dr 37934
Bella Capri Ln 37918
Bella Vista Ln 37914
Bellamy Oaks Dr 37922
Bellcastle Ct 37938
Bellchase Ln 37918
Belle Glade Ln 37923
Belle Grove Rd 37934
Belle Mina Way 37923
Belle Terra Rd 37923
Belleaire Ave 37921
Belleaire Dr 37934
N Bellemeade Ave 37919
Bellerive Ave 37918
Bellevue St 37917
Bellfield Rd 37934
Bellflower Way 37932
Bellgreen Ln 37918
Bellingham Dr 37919
Bellview Rd 37917
Bellwood Ln 37918
Belmont Heights Ave 37921
Belmont Park Ln 37931
Belt Rd 37920
Belvedere Ave 37920
Belvoir Ave 37917
Ben Alder Ln 37931
Ben Hur Ave 37915
Benceney Rd 37931
Bend Way 37922
Bennett Pl 37909
Bennington Cir & Dr 37909
Benson Ln 37932
Bent Grass Ln 37922
Bent River Blvd 37919
Bent Tree Rd 37934
Bentbrook Way 37932
Bentley St 37914
Bentley Park Ln 37922
Benton Cir 37920
Benton Dr 37931
Benwick Ln 37934
Berbera Dr 37921
Berea Ave 37920
Berkford Rd 37918
Berkley Pl 37919
Berkley Walk Way 37931
Berlin Dr 37923
Bermuda Dr 37934
Bernard Ave
100-499 37917
500-699 37921
Bernhurst Dr 37918
Bernstein Ln 37938
Berringer Station Ln 37932
Berry Ln 37914
Berry Rd 37920
Berry Hill Dr 37931
Berry Patch Way 37914
Berrywood Dr 37932
Bert Newman Ln 37931
Bertelkamp Ln 37931
Bertie Rand St 37920
N Bertrand St 37917
S Bertrand St 37915
Berwick Ln 37934
Beryl Ln 37914
Beta Dr 37920
Betham Ln 37931

Bethany Way 37918
Bethany Hills Rd 37938
Bethel Ave 37915
Better Tomorrow Dr 37921
Betty Ln 37931
Beverly Pl & Rd 37918
Beverly Field Way 37918
Beverly Oaks Dr 37918
Beverly Park Cir 37918
Beverly Square Way 37918
Bexhill Dr 37922
Bexley Cove Ln 37922
Bickerstaff Blvd 37922
Biddle St 37914
Big Ben Way 37919
Big Fork Way 37924
Big Horn Ln 37934
Big Logan Way 37923
Big Oak Ln 37934
Bigtree Dr 37934
Bill Murray Ln 37912
Bill Williams Ave 37917
Billings Way 37924
Billy Neal Ln 37924
Biloxi Ln 37923
Bingham Dr 37922
Birch Grove Way 37922
Birch Hill Ln 37932
Birch Run Ln 37919
Birch Springs Dr 37932
Birchbrook Dr 37918
Birchwood Rd 37921
Birdie Ln 37918
Birdsnest Way 37931
Birdsong St 37915
Birdstone Ln 37919
Bisbee Ln 37931
Bisco Dr 37931
Bishop Rd 37938
Bishop St 37921
Bishop Knoll Ln 37938
Bishops Bridge Rd 37922
Bishops View Ln 37932
Bismark Trl 37909
Bison Dr 37920
Bitteroot Way 37932
Bittersweet Rd 37918
Black Rd 37932
Black Bear Rd 37923
Black Oak Dr 37912
Black Oak Ridge Ln 37918
Black Powder Dr 37934
Black Rock Cir 37934
Blackberry Ln 37909
Blackburn Dr 37934
Blackgum Cir 37918
Blackhawk Trl 37920
Blackheath Rd 37922
Blacks Ferry Rd 37931
Blacksburgh Ln 37922
Blacksferry Rd 37931
Blackstock Ave 37921
Blackstone Dr 37934
Blackwood Dr 37923
Blaine Ln 37920
Blaine St 37921
Blair Ln 37932
Blairwood Dr 37938
Blake Hill Way 37920
Blakely Ct 37924
Blakemore Rd 37914
Blakeney Dr 37909
Blakewood Dr 37922
Bland Ln 37920
Blankenship Ln 37924
Blarney Ln 37923
Blazing Star Ln 37918
Blessed Way 37923
Blinken St 37932
Block House Way 37923
Blooming Grove Way 37920
Blossom Rd 37912
E & W Blount Ave 37920
Blow Dr 37920
Blows Ferry Rd 37919
Blue Ash Ln 37931

Blue Crane Ln 37922
Blue Herron Rd 37934
Blue Jay Ln 37938
Blue Lake Cir 37918
Blue Max Way 37920
Blue Meadow Ln 37932
Blue Sage Ln 37924
Blue Spring Ln 37932
Blue Spruce Way 37912
Blue Star Dr 37914
Blue Teal Ln 37922
Blue Valley Ln 37922
Bluebell Ln 37931
Bluebird Dr 37918
Bluefield Rd 37921
Bluegrass Rd 37922
Blueridge Dr 37919
Bluestone Ln 37938
Bluet Dr 37918
Bluewood Ln 37921
Bluff Dr 37919
Bluff St 37917
Bluff Point Dr 37920
Bluff Shore Dr 37922
Bluff View Rd 37919
Blythewood Dr 37923
Boardwalk Blvd 37922
Bob Carnes Rd 37924
Bob Cummings Rd 37920
Bob Gilland Way 37920
Bob Gray Rd
9200-10199 37923
10200-10699 37932
Bob Kirby Rd
800-1199 37923
1200-1699 37931
Bob Smith Ln 37924
Bob Varner Rd 37918
Bob White Rd 37920
Bobby Dr 37921
Bobcat Ln 37921
Bobolink Rd 37934
Boden Ln 37914
Boggs Ave 37920
Bogie Ln 37918
Bold Meadows Ct 37938
Boles Rd 37931
Boling Ln 37920
Bolivar Cir 37922
Bolling Ln 37919
Bolton Ln 37922
Bombay Ln 37932
Bona Rd 37914
Bonair Rd 37918
Bond St 37917
Bonita Dr 37918
Bonneville Dr 37931
Bonnie Roach Ln 37922
Bonnie View Ave 37914
Bonny Kate Dr 37920
Bonnybridge Ln 37922
Bonnyman Dr 37921
Bonnywood Way 37912
Booker St 37921
Bookwalter Dr 37912
Boomerang Ln 37931
Boone St 37917
Boone Hall Ct 37932
Boones Creek Ln 37912
Booth St 37919
Bordeaux Cir 37919
Border St 37914
Boright Dr & Pl 37917
Boring Ln & Rd 37934
Boruff St 37917
Boss Rd 37931
Boston Ln 37932
Bosworth Rd 37919
Boteny Ln 37919
Botsford Dr 37922
Boulder Way 37918
Boulder Springs Ln 37932
Boundary Ln
100-199 37924
300-399 37934
Bounds Rd 37912

Bouquet Ln 37924
Bowers Rd 37914
Bowers Park Cir 37920
Bowling Ave 37921
Bowling Ln 37918
N Bowman Rd 37924
Bowman Valley Rd 37920
Bowstring Trl 37920
Boxwood Ln 37917
Boxwood Sq 37919
Boxwood Garden Way 37918
Boyd St 37921
Boyd Station Rd
10400-12799 37934
12800-13199 37922
Boyd Walters Ln 37931
Boyds Bridge Pike 37914
Boyington Dr 37932
Boys Run Way 37920
Brabson Dr 37918
Brackett Rd 37938
Brackfield Acres Way 37932
Braddocks Blvd 37922
Braden Ln 37914
Braden Dickey Ln 37932
Braden Oak Ct 37909
Bradford Ln 37919
Bradford St 37920
Bradford Pear Ct 37932
Bradley Ave 37917
Bradley Bell Dr 37938
Bradley Lake Ln 37921
Bradshaw Rd
3900-3999 37912
4700-4799 37921
4800-4898 37912
4900-4999 37912
Bradshaw Garden Dr & Rd 37912
Brady St 37920
Braelinn Dr 37918
Bragdon Ln 37919
Bragg St 37921
Braithwaite Ln 37922
Brakebill Rd 37924
Brakebill Cutoff 37924
Bramble Ln 37912
Bramblewood Ln 37922
Brampton Rd 37934
Branch Ln 37924
Branch Field Ln 37918
Branch Hill Ln 37931
Branchview Dr 37932
Brancroff Cir 37920
Brandau Dr 37920
Brandau St 37921
Brandon Rd 37922
Brandville Rd 37924
Brandywine Cir 37922
Branner St 37917
Brannigan Cir 37923
Branson Ave 37917
Brantham Cir 37923
Brantley Dr 37923
Branton Blvd 37922
Brasilia Ct 37923
Brass Ridge Ln 37921
Braveheart Way 37923
Brays Cir 37931
Brazelton Rd 37918
Breakers Pt 37922
Breakwater Dr 37922
Bream Dr 37922
Brechin Ln 37909
Breckenridge Ln 37938
Breda Dr 37918
Breeden Rd 37920
Breeden Lawson Way 37920
Breezeway Dr 37934
Breezewood Ln 37921
Breezy Point Ln 37938
Breezy Ridge Trl 37922
Brent Dr 37923
Brentway Cir 37909
Brentwood Rd 37917
Bretton Ridge Ln 37919

Bretton Wood Dr 37919
Briar Way 37923
Briar Creek Dr 37934
Briar Gate Ln 37934
Briar Patch Way 37921
Briar Rock Ln 37920
Briarfield Ln 37931
Briargate Ave 37919
Briarglen Dr 37919
Briarhill Ln 37921
Briarwood Blvd & Dr 37923
Brice St 37917
Brickchase Ln 37918
Brickey Ln 37918
Brickton Way 37919
Bridalwood Dr 37917
Bridge Ave 37916
Bridge Garden Rd 37912
Bridge Valley Ln 37932
Bridge View Rd 37914
Bridgemore Blvd 37934
Bridgeport Dr 37934
Bridgestone Pl 37919
Bridgette Cir 37920
Bridgewater Rd 37923
Bridle Ct 37921
Bridle Chase Way 37938
Bridlebrooke Dr 37938
Brierbrook Ln 37921
Briercliff Rd 37918
Brierley Dr 37921
Brierview Ln 37921
Brig Ln 37914
Bright Oak Way 37931
Bright Star Way 37912
Brightmoor Ct 37923
Brighton Ct 37934
Brighton Farms Blvd 37932
Brightwood Way 37923
N & S Briscoe Cir 37912
Bristol Cir 37923
Bristol Bay Way 37923
British Station Ln 37922
Britling Dr 37922
Brittany Dr 37931
Brittany Deanne Ln 37934
Brittany Hills Way 37938
Britton Dr 37912
Britton Hts 37920
Brixworth Blvd 37934
Broadleaf Way 37921
Broadmeadow Way 37912
Broadmoor Pt 37934
Broadview Dr 37912
N Broadway St
100-2601 37917
2600-2600 37927
2603-4599 37917
2606-4598 37917
4600-6199 37918
S Broadway St 37902
Broadwood Dr 37934
Brochardt Blvd 37934
Brock Ave 37919
Brock Rd 37938
Brogdon Place Way 37914
Broken Arrow Dr 37923
Broken Creek Ln 37920
Broken Ridge Way 37914
Broken Rock Ln 37924
Broken Saddle Rd 37934
Broken Shaft Ln 37922
Broken Wing Rd 37931
Bromfield Ln 37922
Bromley Ln 37923
Bronco Ln 37921
Brook Green Rd 37919
Brook Mist Cir 37931
Brook Run Way 37920
Brook Song Dr 37920
Brooke Valley Blvd 37922
Brooke Willow Blvd 37932
Brookfield Ln 37918
Brookfield Xing 37921
Brookglen Ln 37932
Brookhaven Dr 37931

Brookhill Ln 37917
Brooklawn St 37934
Brookline Pt 37934
Brookmeade Ct 37920
Brookmill Rd 37932
Brookmoor Ln 37920
Brookridge Cir 37920
Brooks Ave
2000-2399 37915
2400-3399 37914
Brookshire Way 37923
Brookside Ave 37921
Brookstone Dr 37934
Brooktree Rd 37919
Brookvale Ln 37919
Brookview Ln 37919
Brookview Centre Way 37919
Brookwood Rd 37917
Broome Rd
300-370 37923
371-397 37909
372-398 37923
399-899 37909
Brown Ave 37917
Brown Dr 37918
Brown Rd 37920
Brown Atkin Dr 37919
Brown Gap Rd 37918
Brown Mountain Loop 37920
Brown Vista Way 37920
Brownaire Ln 37920
Browning Ave 37921
Brownlow Rd 37938
Brownlow Newman Ln 37914
Brownstone Way 37924
Brownvale Rd 37931
Brownvue Rd 37931
Bruce Smith Rd 37922
Brucewood Ln 37923
Bruhin Rd
4000-4099 37918
4100-4799 37912
Bruhin St 37917
Bruhin Villas Way 37912
Brunswick St 37917
Bryan Ln 37921
Bryant Ln 37932
Buchanan Ave 37917
Buckboard Ln 37920
Buckeye Dr & Rd 37919
Buckhaven Ct 37923
Buckhead Trl 37919
Buckingham Dr
100-199 37919
200-299 37909
Buckley Rd 37934
Buckmill Ln 37934
Bucknell Dr 37938
Buckner Ave 37920
Buckshot Way 37918
Buckskin Trl 37920
Buckthorn Dr 37912
Bud King Rd 37920
Bud Mcmillan Rd 37924
Buddy J Ln 37918
Buena Rd 37919
Buena Vista Dr 37920
Buffalo Ave 37921
Buffat Mill Rd
2400-3499 37917
3500-5099 37914
Buford St 37920
Buick St 37921
Bull Run Dr 37938
Bunker Ln 37922
Bunker Hill Dr 37920
Bunting Dr 37934
Burbank Cir 37918
Burbury Ln 37921
Burch Cove Way 37922
Burchell Ln 37920
Burgandy Pl 37919
Burge Ave 37915
Burges Fall Ln 37931
Burgess Ave 37921
Burgess Dr 37934

Burkbrooks Ln 37914
Burkhart Rd 37918
Burleson Rd 37920
Burlwood Rd 37921
Burnell Ln 37920
Burnett Ln 37920
Burnett Creek Rd 37920
Burney Cir 37934
Burnheim Way 37920
Burning Trl 37909
Burning Tree Ln 37923
Burns Rd 37914
Burnside Pl 37934
Burnside St 37921
Buroak Cir 37934
Burris Rd 37924
Burton Rd 37919
E & W Burwell Ave 37917
Burwood Rd 37921
Busbee Rd 37920
Bush Ln 37920
Bushwood Dr 37918
Business Park Ln 37932
Butcher Rd 37938
Butler Dr 37918
Buttercup Cir 37921
Butterfield Ln 37934
Butterfly Way 37924
Buttermilk Rd 37932
Butternut Cir & Ln 37934
Buttonwood Ln 37934
Buxton Dr 37922
Byfield Ct 37934
Byington Beaver Ridge Rd 37931
Byington Solway Rd 37931
Byrd Ave 37917
Byron Ln 37934
C Dr 37924
Cabbage Dr & Ln 37938
Cabin Rd 37918
Cabot Dr 37934
Cabot Ridge Ln 37922
Cadbury Dr 37921
Cadence Ln 37918
Cades Cove Rd 37922
Cadet Dr 37922
Cadmium Ln 37938
Caesar Dr 37918
Cagney Ct 37922
Cahaba Ln 37914
W Cain Rd 37921
Cain Oak Pl 37909
Cairn Cir & Ct 37923
Caitlin Marie Ln 37924
Calaford Dr 37918
Calais Ct 37919
Calderwood Dr 37923
E Caldwell Ave 37917
Caleb Rd 37920
Caledonia Ave 37916
Calgary Falls Ln 37931
Calhoun St 37921
Calibur Ln 37918
Calico Ln 37932
California Rd 37921
Callahan Dr 37912
Callaway St 37921
Callie Oglesby Ln 37914
Callister Cir 37918
Calloway View Dr 37934
Calthorpe Ln 37912
Calumet Dr 37919
Calvert Ln 37918
Calypso Way 37923
Cambridge Cir 37923
Cambridge Dr 37924
Cambridge Rd 37920
Cambridge St 37920
Cambridge Crest Ln 37919
Cambridge Gables Ln 37938
Cambridge Reserve Dr 37924
Cambridge Shores Ln 37938
Cambridge Woods Ln 37923
Camby Ln 37931
Camdenbridge Dr 37934

Cameadwa Rd 37932
Camelia Rd NW 37912
Camelot Ct 37922
Camero Ln 37923
Camp Ave 37917
Camp Light Way 37923
Campbell Ln 37912
Campbell Rd 37914
Campbell Lakes Dr 37934
N Campbell Station Rd
1004A-1004B 37932
101-101 37934
103-799 37934
800-2599 37932
S Campbell Station Rd 37934
Campfire Dr 37931
Campo Way 37920
Campus Ln 37918
Camrose Ln 37931
Canary Ave 37920
Canberra Dr 37923
Canby Hills Rd 37923
Candace Cir 37921
Candle Pine Dr 37931
Candlenut Ln 37934
Candler Ln 37921
Candlewick Rd 37932
Candlewood Dr 37923
Candora Ave 37920
Candy Ln 37920
Caneel Dr 37931
Canfield Ln 37924
Canmore Ln 37919
Cannon Point Way 37922
Cannon Ridge Dr 37918
Cannondale Rd 37922
Cansler Ave 37921
Cantabrain Ct 37918
Canterbury Dr 37920
Canton Hollow Rd 37934
Canton Place Ln 37922
Canvas Back Ln 37922
Canyon Oak Pl 37909
Cape Brittany Way 37932
Capella St 37917
Capeside Ln 37931
Capistrano Dr 37922
Capital Dr 37922
Capitol Blvd 37931
Cappy Dr 37920
Capri Dr 37912
Captains Way 37922
Caracas Rd 37922
Caravel Ln 37922
Carbine Ln 37918
Carbury Rd 37921
Cardan Dr 37909
Carden Jennings Ln 37932
Cardinal Dr 37918
Cardindale Dr 37918
Cardwell Dr 37921
Cardwell Pl 37914
Caribou Ln 37931
Carl Valentine Cir 37931
Carls Ln 37920
Carlton Cir 37922
Carlyle Rd 37934
Carmel Rd 37922
Carmichael Rd 37932
Carnation Dr 37921
Carnegie Way 37922
Carnoustie Pt 37934
Carolina Way 37923
Carollwood Rd 37932
Carolyn Ln 37920
Caron Dr 37912
Carowinds Ln 37924
Carpenter Rd
1300-1599 37924
6300-7899 37931
Carpenter Run Ln 37932
Carr Ln 37938
Carr St 37919
Carraway Cir 37938
Carriage Ln 37920

Carriage House Way ... 37923
Carriage Station Ln ... 37934
Carrick St ... 37921
Carrie Belle Dr ... 37912
Carrie Reagan Ln ... 37931
Carrington Dr ... 37923
Carrington Rd ... 37909
Carroll Creek Ln ... 37912
Carry Back Ln ... 37923
Carson Ave ... 37917
Carta Rd ... 37914
Carter Rd ... 37918
Carter Grove Way ... 37923
Carter Mill Dr ... 37924
Carter Ridge Dr ... 37924
Carter View Ln ... 37924
Cartwright Ln ... 37923
Carus Rd ... 37918
Carver Rd ... 37918
Cary St ... 37919
Casa Bella Dr ... 37918
Casa Real Cv ... 37922
Cascade Ln ... 37923
Cascade Falls Ln ... 37931
Cascade Meadows Way ... 37918
Cascadia Ln ... 37918
Casey Dr ... 37909
Cash Rd ... 37924
Cashmere Ln ... 37934
Caspian Dr ... 37932
Cassell Dr ... 37912
Cassell Valley Way ... 37912
Cassidy Ln ... 37934
Castaic Ln ... 37932
Castalie Ln ... 37918
N & S Castle St ... 37914
Castle Oak Pl ... 37909
Castle Pines Ln ... 37920
Castlebridge Ct ... 37922
Castlegate Blvd ... 37918
Castleglen Ln ... 37922
Castleman Ln ... 37921
Castlerock Ct ... 37919
Castlestone Ln ... 37938
Castlewood Rd ... 37931
Caswell Ave ... 37917
Catalina Rd ... 37918
Catalpa Ave ... 37914
Cate Ave ... 37919
Cate Rd ... 37931
Cathedral Ln ... 37924
Catherine Mcauley Way ... 37919
Cathy Rd ... 37938
Catlett Rd
  100-399 ... 37920
  800-1199 ... 37932
Catoosa Ln ... 37914
Cavalcade Rd ... 37912
Cavalier Ave ... 37915
Cavalier Dr ... 37921
Cavenders Way ... 37932
Cavendish Ct ... 37923
Cavette Hill Ln ... 37934
Cavetton Rd ... 37923
Cawood Falls Ln ... 37931
Cayman Ln ... 37918
Cayuga Dr ... 37914
Cecil Ave ... 37917
Cecil Johnson Rd ... 37921
Cedar Ave
  100-599 ... 37917
  900-999 ... 37914
Cedar Ln
  100-1299 ... 37912
  1300-2699 ... 37918
Cedar Bark Ct ... 37934
Cedar Bend Rd ... 37918
Cedar Berry Way ... 37932
N Cedar Bluff Rd ... 37923
S Cedar Bluff Rd ... 37922
Cedar Branch Rd ... 37931
Cedar Cove Pt ... 37932
Cedar Croft Cir ... 37932
Cedar Crossing Rd ... 37938
Cedar Grove Rd ... 37923
Cedar Heights Rd ... 37912
Cedar Hurst Ln ... 37932
Cedar Point Way ... 37921
Cedar Ridge Dr ... 37934
Cedar Ridge Rd ... 37924
Cedar Springs Ln ... 37923
Cedar Valley Way ... 37931
Cedar View Way ... 37919
Cedarbreeze Rd ... 37918
Cedarbrook Ln ... 37922
Cedarchase Blvd ... 37918
Cedarcrest Rd ... 37938
Cedardale Ln ... 37932
Cedargreens Rd ... 37924
Cedarhill Rd ... 37919
Cedarpark Ln ... 37923
Cedartop Ln ... 37923
Cedarwood St ... 37914
Celebration Rd ... 37934
Cella Homma Ln ... 37909
Celtic Ln ... 37923
Cement Plant Rd ... 37924
Centennial Way ... 37923
Center Ave ... 37915
Center Court Way ... 37922
Center Cross Dr ... 37934
Center Park Dr ... 37922
Centerline Dr ... 37917
Centeroak Dr ... 37920
Centerpoint Blvd ... 37932
Centervue Crossing Way ... 37932
Centerwood Dr ... 37920
N Central St
  100-199 ... 37902
  200-3199 ... 37917
S Central St ... 37902
Central Avenue Pike
  4000-6799 ... 37912
  6800-7099 ... 37918
Central View Rd ... 37912
Century Ct ... 37919
Century St ... 37921
Cessna Rd ... 37919
Ceylon Rd ... 37909
Chad Tomlinson Cir ... 37931
Chadwick Dr ... 37909
Chaho Rd ... 37934
Chalkstone Way ... 37922
Chalmers Dr ... 37920
Chamberlain Blvd ... 37920
Chamberlain Manor Way ... 37920
Chambers Way ... 37920
Chambliss Ave ... 37919
Champions Pt ... 37934
Champions Trail Ln ... 37931
Chancellors Ln ... 37934
Chandler Rd ... 37922
Channel Point Dr ... 37922
Channing Ln ... 37934
Chantilly Dr ... 37917
Chanute Ln ... 37922
Chaparral Dr ... 37920
Chapel Ln ... 37920
Chapel Glen Ln ... 37934
Chapel Grove Ln ... 37934
Chapel Hill Ln ... 37938
Chapel Point Ln ... 37934
Chapes Ln ... 37932
Chapman Hwy ... 37920
Char Leen Ln ... 37920
Charing Rd ... 37922
Chariot Ln ... 37918
Charity Way ... 37938
Charlene Ln ... 37912
Charles Dr ... 37918
Charles Rd ... 37919
Charles Towne Ct ... 37923
Charlie Haun Dr ... 37917
Charlie Weaver Way ... 37912
Charlotte Dr ... 37924
Charlottesville Blvd ... 37922
Charlton Dr ... 37920
Charmwood Way ... 37938
Charter Oak Way ... 37922
Chartwell Rd ... 37931
Chase Hill Dr ... 37918
Chastity Way ... 37909
Chatam Ridge Ln ... 37932
Chateaugay Rd ... 37923
Chatham Cir ... 37909
Chaucer Ct ... 37921
Chelsea Rd ... 37922
Cheltenham Dr ... 37922
Cheney Rd ... 37922
Chenoweth Cir ... 37909
Chentinc Dr ... 37919
Cheowa Cir ... 37919
Cherahala Blvd ... 37932
Cherbourg Ln ... 37918
Cheri Dr ... 37923
Cherish Grace Way ... 37938
E & W Chermont Cir ... 37918
Cherokee Blvd ... 37919
Cherokee Cv ... 37920
Cherokee Trl ... 37920
Cherokee Bluff Dr ... 37920
Cherokee Peak Ln ... 37912
Cherokee Springs Way ... 37919
Cherokee Woods Way ... 37920
Cherry Dr
  6000-6199 ... 37924
  6500-6699 ... 37919
N Cherry St
  100-799 ... 37914
  900-2699 ... 37917
S Cherry St ... 37914
Cherry Arcade St ... 37917
Cherry Blossom Ln ... 37931
Cherry Branch Dr ... 37938
Cherry Grove Rd ... 37931
Cherry Hill Ave ... 37914
Cherry Hill Ln ... 37931
Cherry Laurel Ln ... 37919
Cherry Oak Pl ... 37909
Cherry Tree Ln ... 37919
Cherrybrook Dr ... 37912
Cherrylog Rd ... 37921
Cherrywood Rd ... 37921
Chert Pit Rd ... 37923
Chervue Blvd ... 37918
Chesapeake Way ... 37923
Cheshire Dr ... 37919
Chesney Rd ... 37931
Chesney Hill Ln ... 37931
Chesney Oaks Ln ... 37924
Chesswood Dr ... 37912
Chester Rd ... 37914
Chester St ... 37915
Chesterfield Dr ... 37909
Chestnut St ... 37920
N Chestnut St ... 37914
S Chestnut St ... 37914
Chestnut Grove Rd ... 37932
Chestnut Hill Ln ... 37924
Chestnut Oak Dr ... 37909
Chestnut View Dr ... 37921
Chevas Cir ... 37918
Chevy Dr ... 37922
Chevy Ln ... 37923
Chewasa Rd ... 37918
Cheyenne Dr & Rd ... 37920
Chicadee Dr ... 37919
Chicago Ave ... 37917
Chickamauga Ave ... 37917
Chickasaw Rd ... 37919
Chickering Way Ln ... 37923
Chicory Cir ... 37923
Chiefs Way ... 37924
Childrens Way ... 37922
Childress St ... 37920
Childress Glenn Ln ... 37920
Chilhowee Ave ... 37917
Chilhowee Ct ... 37914
Chilhowee Dr ... 37914
N Chilhowee Dr
  100-499 ... 37914
  500-799 ... 37924
S Chilhowee Dr ... 37914
Chillicothe St ... 37921
Chillingsworth Ln ... 37938
Chimney Point Dr ... 37922
Chimney Ridge Rd ... 37923
Chimney Rock Ln ... 37920
Chimney Sweep Dr ... 37923
Chinkapin Ln ... 37921
Chip Cove Ln ... 37938
Chipman St ... 37917
Chippewa Cir ... 37919
Chipwood Cir ... 37932
Chisholm Trl ... 37919
Chiswick Rd ... 37922
Chloe Dr ... 37918
Choto Rd ... 37922
Choto Farms Way ... 37922
Choto Highlands Way ... 37922
Choto Marina Way ... 37922
Choto Markets Way ... 37922
Choto Mill Ln ... 37922
Chowning Dr ... 37934
Christi Ridge Way ... 37931
Christin Lee Cir ... 37931
Christine Ave ... 37920
Christine Lynnac St ... 37938
Christus Way ... 37922
Chukar Rd ... 37923
E Church Ave ... 37915
W Church Ave ... 37902
Church St
  100-199 ... 37918
  1100-1199 ... 37934
Churchill Rd ... 37909
Churchland St ... 37920
E & W Churchwell Ave ... 37917
Cilla Rd ... 37920
Cimarron Trl ... 37919
Cinder Ln ... 37914
Cindy Ln ... 37912
Circle Dr ... 37920
Circle Ln ... 37919
Circle Hill Dr ... 37919
Circle Lake Ln ... 37920
Circle Oak Dr ... 37920
Circle Park Dr ... 37916
Circle Wood Ln ... 37920
Citadel Ln ... 37922
Citation Cir ... 37931
Citation Ln ... 37912
Citico St ... 37921
Citrus St ... 37917
City Lights Way ... 37914
Citydweller Way ... 37921
Cityview Ave ... 37915
Claiborne Ln ... 37938
Claiborne Pl ... 37917
Claire Stevens Cir ... 37931
Clairidge Rd ... 37918
Clairmont Dr ... 37918
Clairson Dr ... 37931
Clancy Ave ... 37920
Clarence Ln ... 37920
Clark Dr ... 37938
Clark Pl ... 37917
Clark St ... 37921
Clary Ln ... 37919
Claude St ... 37914
Claudius Rd ... 37918
Clay St
  1000-1199 ... 37934
  2000-2099 ... 37917
Clayberry Dr ... 37931
Claybrook Ct ... 37923
Clayfield Ln ... 37931
Clays Corner Way ... 37924
Clays Mill Ct ... 37938
Clayton Rd ... 37920
Cleage St ... 37920
Clear Crk ... 37938
Clear Brook Dr ... 37922
Clear Point Dr ... 37932
Clear Ridge Rd ... 37922
Clearbrook Dr ... 37918
Clearfield Rd ... 37922
Clearview St ... 37917
Clearwater Ct & Dr ... 37923
Clemente Ln ... 37922
Clemons Rd ... 37920
Clermont Rd ... 37921
Cletus Way ... 37938
W Cliff Dr ... 37909
Cliff Barnes Dr ... 37921
Cliffbranch Ln ... 37931
Clifford St ... 37915
Cliffrock Ln ... 37922
Cliffside Ln ... 37914
Cliffwood Rd ... 37921
Cliftgate Rd ... 37909
Clifton Rd
  100-499 ... 37921
  8200-8399 ... 37920
Climbing Rd ... 37912
Climbing Ivy Way ... 37918
Clinbrook Ave ... 37921
W Clinch Ave
  100-899 ... 37902
  900-2399 ... 37916
Clinch View Ln ... 37931
Cline Rd ... 37938
Cline St ... 37921
Clingman Dr ... 37922
Clingmans Dome Dr ... 37922
Clinton Hwy
  2400-6799 ... 37912
  6800-7099 ... 37921
Clinton Plaza Dr ... 37912
Clipper Ln ... 37922
Cloister Way ... 37912
Cloudbreak Ln ... 37938
Clove Ln ... 37921
Clovefield Ln ... 37920
Clover Rd ... 37912
Clover Blossom Way ... 37920
Clover Fields Ln ... 37932
Clover Fork Dr ... 37934
Clover Hill Ln ... 37922
Clover Ridge Ln ... 37931
Cloverdale Ln ... 37918
Cloverleaf Ln ... 37922
Clowers Dr ... 37924
Clubhouse Way ... 37909
Clubvue Way ... 37932
Cluster St ... 37914
Clyde St ... 37921
Coach Rd ... 37934
Coachman Ln ... 37919
Coatbridge Ln ... 37924
Coatney Rd ... 37920
Cobble Crk ... 37919
Cobblestone Cir ... 37938
Coburn Dr ... 37922
Cochise Dr ... 37918
Cody Ln ... 37938
Coesta Cir ... 37914
Coffey St ... 37920
Coffman Dr ... 37920
Cogdill Rd
  100-399 ... 37922
  9701-9797 ... 37932
  9799-10499 ... 37932
Coile Ln ... 37922
Coile Rd ... 37918
Coker Ave ... 37917
Colby Way ... 37914
Colby Station Ln ... 37922
Colchester Ct ... 37920
Colchester Ridge Rd ... 37922
Cold Creek Way ... 37918
Cold Stream Ln ... 37920
Cole Ln
  1900-1999 ... 37932
  8600-8899 ... 37938
Colebrook Ln ... 37922
Coleman Rd ... 37909
Coleridge Dr ... 37919
Coleville Way ... 37923
Colina Cir ... 37922
College St ... 37921
College Park Ln ... 37918
Collette Rd ... 37918
Collier Pass Ln ... 37922
Collingwood Rd ... 37922
Collins Ln ... 37918
Colonade Rd ... 37922
Colonial Ave ... 37917
Colonial Cir ... 37918
Colonial Dr ... 37920
Colonial Estates Way ... 37920
Colonial Forest Ln ... 37919
Colonial Ridge Ln ... 37934
Colony Park ... 37909
Colony Way ... 37919
Colony Village Way ... 37923
Colorado Rd ... 37921
Colt Dr ... 37918
Colter St ... 37920
Colts Foot Ln ... 37918
E & W Columbia Ave ... 37917
Columbine Cir ... 37919
Coluzzi Dr ... 37923
Comanche Dr ... 37914
Comblain Rd ... 37934
Comet Ln ... 37914
Comfort Ave ... 37920
Comice Way ... 37918
Commander Way ... 37934
Commodore Ln ... 37934
Commodore Pt ... 37922
Commons Point Dr ... 37932
Community Dr ... 37909
Compton Ln & St ... 37920
Comstock Rd ... 37923
Concord Rd ... 37934
N Concord St ... 37919
S Concord St ... 37919
Concord Crossing Ln ... 37934
Concord Farms Ln ... 37934
Concord Park Dr ... 37922
Concord Villas Way ... 37934
Concord Woods Dr ... 37934
Condridge Dr ... 37918
Conductor Way ... 37931
Confederacy Cir ... 37934
Confederate Dr ... 37922
Congress Ln ... 37918
Congressional Pt ... 37934
Conley Ln ... 37918
Connecticut Ave ... 37921
Conner Dr ... 37918
Conner Springs Ln ... 37932
Conners Creek Cir ... 37932
Connex St ... 37914
Connie Rd ... 37909
Conrad St ... 37917
Conridge Dr ... 37918
Constance Way ... 37923
Contentment Ln ... 37920
Continental Dr ... 37922
Conway Cir ... 37921
Cook Dr ... 37920
Cool Breeze Rd ... 37938
Cool Springs Blvd ... 37934
Cooler Ln ... 37914
Cooper Ln ... 37932
Cooper Rd ... 37914
Cooper St ... 37917
Cooper Meadows Ln ... 37938
Copeland St ... 37917
Copper Lantern Dr ... 37931
Copper Ridge Rd ... 37931
Copper Valley Rd ... 37938
Copperfield Dr ... 37934
Copperleaf Dr ... 37931
Copperstone Ln ... 37922
Copperwood Ln ... 37923
Coral Cir ... 37923
Coral Reef Cir ... 37922
Coral Sand Ln ... 37938
Coral Springs Ln ... 37922
Coram St ... 37917
Corbin Ln ... 37931
Corbitt Dr ... 37917
Corby Ln ... 37934
Cordoba Rd ... 37923
Corn Silk Dr ... 37918
Cornelia St ... 37917
Cornelia Cartwright Ave ... 37921
Cornell Ln ... 37938
Cornerbrook Ln ... 37918
Cornerid Rd ... 37924
Cornerstone Dr ... 37932
Corning Rd ... 37923
Cornview Ln ... 37938
Cornwall Rd ... 37931
Coronada Ln ... 37922
Corporate Dr ... 37923
Corporate Point Way ... 37932
Correll Rd ... 37917
Corridor Park Blvd ... 37932
Corsairs Dr ... 37922
Corteland Dr ... 37909
Cortez Dr ... 37923
Cortina Cir ... 37922
Corto Ln ... 37934
Corum Rd ... 37924
Coster Rd ... 37912
Cotesworth Ln ... 37922
Cotswold Ln ... 37922
Cottage Pl ... 37917
Cottage Creek Ln ... 37934
Cottage Row Ln ... 37922
Cottage Square Way ... 37918
Cottage Wood Way ... 37919
Cottington Ln ... 37922
Cotton Blossom Ln ... 37934
Cotton Briar Way ... 37923
Cottonwood Dr ... 37921
Cottrell St ... 37920
Couch Mill Rd
  11200-11599 ... 37931
  11600-12599 ... 37932
Cougar Dr ... 37921
Council Pl ... 37920
Council Fire Dr ... 37918
Counsellor Ln ... 37914
Country Ln ... 37938
Country Brook Ln ... 37921
Country Club Way ... 37923
Country Estates Way ... 37923
Country Meadow Dr ... 37918
Country Oak Cir ... 37909
Country Scene Rd ... 37938
Countryhill Ln ... 37923
Countryside Cir & Ln ... 37923
Countryside Center Ln ... 37931
Countryway Dr ... 37922
Countrywood Dr ... 37923
Court Dr ... 37919
Court Field Rd ... 37922
N & S Courtney Oak Ln ... 37938
Courtyard Way ... 37931
Cove Creek Ln ... 37919
Cove Field Rd ... 37919
Cove Island Rd ... 37919
Cove Point Ln ... 37922
Cove View Way ... 37919
Covebrook Ln ... 37919
Coventry Rd ... 37923
Coventry Creek Ln ... 37919
Coventry Park Blvd ... 37931
Covered Bridge Blvd ... 37932
Covey Rise Trl ... 37922
Covington Dr ... 37919
Cowan St ... 37921
Coward Mill Rd ... 37931
Cox Ln ... 37914
Cox St ... 37919
Coxboro Ct ... 37923
Coy Way ... 37912
Coyote Canyon Way ... 37932
Crabapple Ln ... 37923
Cracker Barrel Ln ... 37914
Cragfont Way ... 37923
Craghead Ln ... 37920
Craig Rd ... 37919
Craig Cove Rd ... 37919
Craig Leath Way ... 37918
Craigland Ct ... 37919
Cranberry Dr ... 37918
Cranston Dr ... 37922

Cranwood Dr 37923
Crawford Rd 37918
Creed Way 37938
S Creek Rd 37920
Creek Bank Dr 37920
Creek Rock Ln 37918
Creek Song Ct 37920
Creek Stone Ln 37924
Creekhead Dr 37909
Creekside Ln 37923
Creekview Ln 37923
Creekwood Dr 37918
Creekwood Ter 37934
Creighton Cir 37922
Crenshaw Ave & Rd 37920
Crepe Myrtle Ln 37931
Crescent Ave & Dr 37920
Crest Brook Dr 37923
Crest Forest Rd 37923
Crest Haven Blvd 37932
Crest Point Rd 37932
Crested Butte Ln 37922
Crested Springs Way 37923
Crestfield Rd 37921
Cresthill Dr 37919
Crestland Rd 37938
Crestline Dr 37922
Crestmont Rd 37917
Crestmore Cir 37919
Crestpark Rd 37912
Crestridge Rd 37919
Crestview Rd 37934
Crestview St 37915
Crestwicke Ln 37934
Crestwood Dr 37914
Crestwood Rd 37918
Creswell Ct & Dr 37919
Crimson Ln 37931
Crimson Tree Ln 37919
Crippen Rd 37918
Crippled Mule Pt 37934
Crisp Ln 37920
Cristata Cir 37918
Criswell Hill Ln 37922
Crockett St 37917
Crocus Ln 37909
Crofton Ln 37934
Cromwell Rd 37923
Crooked Oak Ln 37931
Crooked Pine Ln 37921
Crooked Springs Rd 37932
Crosby Dr 37909
Cross St 37918
Cross Bridge Cir 37934
Cross Creek Rd 37923
Cross Meadow Rd 37934
Cross Park Dr
8700-9040 37923
9039-9039 37930
9041-9199 37923
9042-9198 37923
Cross Valley Rd 37917
Crossfield Dr 37920
Crossgate Dr 37912
Crosslane Rd 37931
Crossroads Way 37918
Crosswind Dr 37934
Crosswind Landing Ln 37924
Crosswood Blvd 37924
Crouch Dr 37917
Crowfield Rd 37922
Crown Rd 37918
Crown Hill Dr 37918
Crown Point Dr 37934
Croydon Rd 37921
Crozier Ave 37921
Crumley Ln 37918
Crusero Ln 37924
Cruze Rd 37920
N Cruze St 37917
S Cruze St 37915
Cruze Farm Way 37918
Crystal Way 37918
Crystal Brook Ln 37934
Crystal Cove Way 37919
Crystal Lake Dr 37919
Crystal Point Dr 37938
Crystal View Way 37919
Cub Ln 37918
Cullen Pl 37917
Culpepper Rd 37917
Cumberland Ave
100-699 37902
1000-2299 37916
Cumberland Ridge Dr 37922
Cumberland View Cir 37912
Cumberland Wood Dr 37921
Cummins Ln 37921
Cunningham Ln 37920
Cunningham Rd 37918
Cupboard Dr 37918
Cupola Way 37918
Cureton Rd 37931
Curie Pl 37914
Currier Ln 37919
Curtis Ln 37918
Curtis Rd 37914
Curving Rd 37912
Custis Ln 37920
Cutlass Rd 37934
Cutters Run Ln 37932
Cynruss Dr 37918
Cynthia Ln 37922
Cypress Ln 37920
Cypress Pt 37938
Cypress Grove Ln 37922
Cypress Lake Dr E & W 37923
Cypress Tree Ln 37918
Cypresswood Ln 37932
Dabert Ln 37931
Dahlia Dr 37918
Daily St 37915
Dairy Ln 37938
Daisy Ave 37915
Daisy Pt 37920
Daisy Mae Ln 37938
Daisywood Dr 37932
Dakota Ave 37921
Dale Ave 37921
Dalemere Dr 37923
Dalen Ln 37932
Dalewood Rd 37921
Dallas St 37914
Dalton Ln 37923
Dalton Place Way 37912
Damas Rd 37921
Dameron Ave
100-299 37917
600-1199 37921
Dan Ln 37938
Dan Rose Rd 37920
Dana Ln 37923
Dana Point Way 37932
Danbury Rd 37919
Dance Ave 37919
Dancing Light Ln 37922
Dandridge Ave 37915
Dandyline Dr 37914
Daniel Rd 37920
Daniels Ave 37917
Daniels Rd 37938
Daniels Branch Ln 37924
Dansons Ln 37923
Dante Rd 37918
Dante School Rd 37918
Dantedale Rd 37918
Danville Cir 37923
Daphne Dr 37914
Darby Dr 37924
Daresa Ln 37914
Darien Ct 37922
Dark Creek Ln 37932
Dartford Rd 37919
Dartmoor Rd 37931
Dartmouth Rd 37914
Darwin Way 37918
Data Ln 37932
Davanna St 37917
Dave Rd 37938
Davenport Rd 37920
S David Ln 37922
David Everette Ln 37938
David Johnson Rd 37918
David Tippit Way 37931
Davida Rd 37912
Davinci Ln 37918
Davis Ln 37923
Davis Rd 37920
Davis St 37920
Davison Ave 37917
Davron Ln 37918
Dawn St 37921
Dawn Chase Way 37931
Dawn Oaks Ln 37918
Dawn Redwood Trl 37922
Dawn Ridge Ln 37918
Dawn Wood Way 37932
Dawns Pass 37919
Dawson St 37920
Dawson Creek Ln 37922
W Day Cir 37919
Daybreak Dr 37931
Dayflower Way 37932
Daylily Dr 37920
Daymark Ln 37922
Daystar Ln 37918
Dayton St 37921
Daytona Ln 37920
De Armond Ln 37920
De Paul Ln 37914
Deaderick Ave 37921
Deaderick Rd 37920
Deadwood Rd 37934
Deanbrook Rd 37920
Deane Hill Dr 37919
Deanvue Dr 37920
Deanwood Ln 37934
Dearing Way 37932
Deaton Hollow Rd 37914
Debbie Rd 37922
Debonair Dr 37912
Debra Dr 37938
Debusk Ln 37922
Decatur Dr 37920
Dee Ct 37931
Dee Peppers Dr 37931
Deep Cove Way 37922
Deep Hollow Ln 37923
Deep Springs Rd 37932
Deep Woods Ln 37934
Deer Creek Dr 37912
Deer Lake Dr 37912
Deer Ridge Ln 37912
Deer Run Dr 37912
Deer Trot Ln 37920
Deer Valley Way 37931
Deerborn Ln 37932
Deerbrook Dr 37922
Deerfield Rd 37921
Deerpath Ln 37918
Deerwood Rd 37923
Deery St 37917
Dekalb Dr 37920
Del Mabry Dr 37914
Delapp Dr 37912
Delaware Ave 37921
Delbourne Dr 37919
Delden Rd 37918
Delft Way 37923
Delle Meade Dr 37931
Dellwood Dr 37919
Delmonte Way 37932
Delray Rd 37923
Delrose Dr 37914
Delta Rd 37914
Delta Way 37919
Delverton Way 37912
Demarcus Ln 37918
Dempsey Rd 37932
Dempster St 37917
Denmark St 37931
Denning Ln 37931
Denson Ave 37921
Denton Ct 37923
Denwood Rd 37920
Dephine Ln 37920
E & W Depot Ave 37917
Derby Chase Blvd 37934
Derby Gate Rd 37920
Derby Run Dr 37934
Dereck Dr 37912
Derieux Dr 37917
Derris Dr 37919
Desoto Way 37921
Destin Cir 37934
Destiny Ridge Way 37932
Deva Dr 37920
Deventer Ridge Dr 37919
Devon Dr 37918
Devon Springs Way 37918
Devonbrook Way 37918
Devonshire Dr 37919
Devonwood Ct 37922
Dewdrop Ln 37914
Dewey Way 37912
Dewey Burnett Ln 37920
S Dewey Roberts Sr St 37915
Dewine Cir & Rd 37921
Dexter Ln 37920
Diamond Trace Way 37918
Diamondview Way 37931
Diana Ln 37923
Diane Dr 37922
Diane Gayle Dr 37924
E & W Dick Ford Ln 37920
Dick Lonas Rd 37909
Dickson St 37914
Diggs Rd 37932
Dill St 37917
Dillfield Ln 37920
Dillon St 37915
Dineen Dr 37934
Dinwiddie St 37921
Diplomat Cir 37918
Directors Dr 37923
Distant View Ln 37922
Distribution Dr 37914
Divide St 37921
Division St 37919
Dixie View Rd 37934
Dixon Rd 37934
Dixon Spring Ln 37918
Dobe Way 37932
Dobson Park Ln 37922
Dockside Ln 37922
Dodd St SE 37920
Dodge Rd 37912
Dodson Ave 37917
Dodson Rd 37920
Doe Creek Way 37918
Doe Wood Ln 37912
Dogwen Rd 37938
Dogwood Cv 37919
Dogwood Dr 37919
Dogwood Ln 37919
Dogwood Rd
5400-5999 37918
10600-10899 37931
Dogwood Cove Ln & Rd 37919
Dollar Dr 37921
Dolph Dr 37931
Dolphin Harbor Rd 37938
Dominick Pt 37934
Dominion Cir 37934
Donald Lee Derrickson Ave 37921
Donaldson St 37920
E Doncaster Dr 37932
Dongate Ln 37931
Doningham Dr 37918
Donna Ln 37920
Donna Lee Way 37918
Donnell St 37914
Donovan Ln 37922
Dooley St 37920
Dora St 37921
Dorado Dr 37912
Doral Cir 37938
Doral Pt 37934
Dorcee Ln 37934
Dorchester Dr 37909
Doris Cir 37918
Dorset Dr 37923
Dorset Hill Dr 37932
Double Eagle Ln 37922
Double Tree Rd 37932
Doublehead Ln 37909
Doughty Dr 37918
Douglas Ave 37921
Douglas Wood Ln 37920
Dove Ln 37918
Dove Nest Way 37918
Dove Wing Ln 37938
Dovefield Dr 37923
Dover St 37920
Dover Cliff Ln 37922
Dovewood Way 37918
Dovington Dr 37920
Dow Dr 37920
Dowell Springs Blvd 37909
Downing Dr 37909
Downing Creek Ln 37932
Downridge Rd 37912
Downtown West Blvd 37919
Dowry Ln 37919
Doyle Ln 37922
Doyle St 37920
Dozer Ln 37920
Drakewood Ln & Rd 37924
Draper Way 37914
Draper Cemetery Rd 37938
Dreager Rd 37920
Dreamview Ln 37922
Dresden Dr 37923
Dresser Rd 37920
Drew Way 37920
Drifting Dr 37912
Drinnen Ave 37920
Drinnen Rd 37914
Drive E 37920
Drive D 37920
Druid Dr 37920
Drummer Ln 37924
Dry Branch Way 37918
Dry Gap Pike
100-699 37912
700-1899 37918
Dry Hollow Rd 37920
Dryad St 37919
Drybrook Ln 37921
Dryden Ln 37934
Dublin Dr 37923
Duchess Way 37912
Duck Cove Dr 37922
Duck Pond Way 37924
Duck Springs Ln 37932
Dude Ln 37931
Dudley Way 37912
Dudley Station Ln 37922
Duke Rd 37918
Dukesbury Dr 37919
Dulaney Way 37919
Dunaire Dr 37923
Dunaway Rd 37931
Dunbar St 37921
Dunbarton Ct 37923
Duncan Rd 37919
Duncan Farms Way 37919
Duncan Ridge Way 37919
Duncan Woods Ln 37919
Duncans Glen Dr 37919
Dundee Rd 37934
Dunheith Dr 37934
Dunhill Way 37919
Dunlap Dr 37914
Dunlap Ln 37914
Dunlap Rd 37920
Dunn Rd & St 37920
Dunnview Ln 37934
Dunraven Dr 37922
Dunsford Dr 37919
Dunsten Dr 37931
Dunwoody Blvd 37919
Durbin Dr 37912
Durham Rd 37931
Durham Park Ln 37918
Durmast Dr 37914
Durwood Rd 37922
Dusty Way 37932
Dutch Valley Dr 37918
Dutchtown Rd
9200-10099 37923
10100-10799 37932
Dutchwood Ln 37921
Duxbury Ln 37931
Duzane Dr 37934
Dyer Ln 37920
Dyers Cove Way 37931
Dyestone Gap Rd 37931
E Dr 37924
Eagle Dr 37914
Eagle Brook Dr 37923
Eagle Creek Ln 37932
Eagle Crest Ln 37921
Eagle Glen Dr 37922
Eagle Nest Ln 37922
Eagle Pointe Dr 37931
Eagle Ridge Way 37938
Eagle Spring Ln 37932
Eaglepath Ln 37922
Eagles Landing Way 37923
Eagles View Dr 37922
Eagles Vista Ln 37924
Eaglewatch Way 37931
Eaglewood Ln 37921
Eakers Rd 37920
Earl Ave 37920
Earl Bryan St 37938
Early Rd 37922
Early Morning Ln 37922
Early Woods Ln 37922
Earnhardt Way 37938
Earvin Magic Johnson Dr 37921
East Rd 37920
Eastburn Dr 37914
Easterland St 37917
Eastern Dr 37919
Easton Rd 37920
Eastshire Ln 37922
Eastwood Dr 37920
Easy Way 37919
Ebenezer Rd
100-1299 37923
1300-1999 37922
Ebenezer Oaks Ln 37922
Echo Dr 37919
Echo Brook Ln 37932
Echo Springs Rd 37923
Echo Valley Rd 37923
Echodale Ln 37920
Ed Stallings Ln 37931
Edbury Dr 37922
Edds Rd 37914
Eden Ln 37938
Edenbridge Way 37923
Edenfield Dr & Ln 37938
Edenshire Dr 37922
Edford Ave 37918
Edgar St 37920
Edgebrook Way 37922
Edgefield Rd 37918
Edgeview Way 37918
Edgewood Ave 37917
Edgeworth Ln 37924
Edina Dr 37938
Edinburgh Pl 37919
Edington Rd 37920
Edison Dr 37932
Edith Keeler Ln 37938
Edmonds Ave 37920
Edmondson Ln 37918
Edna Dr 37920
Edonia Dr 37918
Edwards Dr 37920
Eiffel Ln 37938
El Camino Ln 37932
El Monte Cir 37922
El Pinar Dr 37922
El Prado Dr 37922
El Rancho Trl 37932
Elaine Ln 37918
Elder Rd 37912
Elderberry Dr 37919
Elderwood Rd 37921
Eldridge Rd 37918
Eleanor St 37917
Elegant Dr 37918
Elissa Ln 37918
Eliza Glynne Ln 37931
Eliza Pointe Way 37921
Elizabeth Ave
400-699 37920
4900-5099 37912
Elizabeth Downs Ln 37931
Elk Ln 37920
Elk Rd 37918
Elk Camp Ln 37918
Elk Hill Way 37912
Elk Horn Ln 37922
Elkhart Ln 37919
Elkins St 37917
Elkmont Cir & Rd 37922
Elkwood Dr 37921
Ellen Ave & St 37920
Ellery Ln 37918
Ellesmere Dr 37921
Ellington Way 37932
Elliott Rd 37920
Ellis Ln 37924
Ellis Rd 37920
Ellis St 37920
Ellison Ln 37919
Ellison Rd 37914
Ellistown Rd 37924
Ellisville Ln 37909
Elm St 37921
Elm Crest Ln 37932
Elm Grove Ln 37932
Elm Hill Cir 37919
Elm Ridge Way 37921
Elmbrook Ln 37918
Elmhurst Way 37923
Elmira Ln 37931
Elmore Ln 37934
Elmview Dr 37921
Elmwood Dr 37918
S Elmwood St 37914
Elmwood School Rd 37924
Elna Marie Dr 37924
Elsie Jean Way 37918
Ely Ave 37921
Ely Park Ln 37924
Elyria Dr 37912
Embarcadero Dr 37923
Ember Crest Trl 37938
E Emerald Ave 37917
W Emerald Ave
200-399 37917
700-927 37921
929-999 37921
Emerald Hills Ln 37912
Emerald Pointe Ln 37918
Emerald Ridge Ln 37938
Emerald Woods Way 37922
Emerson Park Dr 37922
Emerton Rd 37918
Emily Ave 37914
Emmett St 37919
Emoriland Blvd 37917
Emory Pl 37917
E Emory Rd 37938
W Emory Rd 37931
Emory Chase Ln 37918
Emory Church Rd 37922
Emory Cove Way 37938
Emory Oak Ct 37909
Emory Pointe Ln 37918
Ena Rd 37918
Enchanted Ln 37918
Enchanted Spring Way 37932
Enclave Way 37919
W End Ave 37934
W End Ln 37919
E End Rd 37920
Endecott Way 37918
Endicott Ridge Ln 37918
Engert Rd 37922
England Dr 37920

English Station Rd 37934
English Village Way 37919
Ensign Ln 37934
Ensley Dr 37920
Enterprise Dr 37909
Episcopal School Way 37932
Equestrian Way 37921
Erin Dr 37919
Erma Ln 37918
Ernestine Dr 37924
Essary Dr 37918
Essex Dr 37922
Estelle Cir 37920
Ester Way 37909
Estonia Dr 37918
Ethans Glen Dr 37923
Ethel Ln 37912
Etheld Reda Dr 37931
Eubanks Ave 37921
Euclid Ave 37921
Eutaw Pl 37919
Eva Marie Way 37931
Evan Spencer Way 37918
Evangeline Ln 37938
Evans Rd
100-299 37920
12400-12799 37934
Evans St 37921
Evelyn Dr 37909
Evelyn Mae Way 37923
Evening Breeze Way 37932
Evening Ridge Ln 37922
Evening Shade Ln 37919
Evening Star Ln 37918
Evening Sun Ln 37938
Everett Rd
100-899 37934
900-2299 37932
Evergreen Dr 37918
Everhart Ln 37921
Eversham Ln 37909
Everwood Oak Ln 37918
Evolve Way 37915
Excalibur Cir 37931
Executive Park Dr 37923
Exemouth Dr 37914
Exeter Ave 37921
Exford Ct 37934
Exodus Ln 37938
Explorer Ln 37912
Extine Ln 37920
Ezell St 37917
Faber St 37918
Faddis Ln 37918
Fair Dr
1000-1299 37912
1300-2599 37918
Fair Oaks Ln 37921
Fairbanks Way 37918
Faircrest Ln 37919
Fairdale Way 37938
Fairfax Ave 37917
Fairfield Rd 37919
Fairhaven Pl 37931
Fairhill Ln 37918
Fairlawn Ct 37920
Fairmont Blvd 37917
Fairview St 37917
Fairway Rd 37917
Fairway Oaks Ln 37922
Fairwinds Rd 37931
Fairwood Ave 37917
Faith Ln 37924
Faith Promise Ln 37931
Falcon Dr 37923
Falcon Crest Ln 37919
Falcon Pointe Dr 37922
Falcon Ridge Way 37921
Falconite Way 37921
Fall Branch Way 37938
Fall Creek Ln 37912
Fall Garden Ln 37932
Fall Haven Ln 37932
Fallen Oaks Dr 37932
Fallen Rock Dr 37923
Falling Leaves Cir 37909
Falling Waters Rd 37922
Fallkirk Way 37923
Family Inn Dr 37912
Fannie Webb Rd 37920
Fantasia Rd 37918
Fantasy Way 37932
Far Vista Ln 37914
Faranda Way 37931
Farland Dr 37909
Farlow Dr 37934
Farm Cottage Way 37921
Farmbrook Ln 37918
Farmgate Ln 37934
Farmhouse Dr 37934
Farmington Dr 37923
Farne Island Blvd 37923
Farr Dr 37934
Farragut Ave 37917
Farragut Dr 37914
Farragut Commons Dr 37934
Farragut Crossing Dr 37934
Farragut Farms Blvd 37934
Farragut Hills Blvd 37934
Farrell Park Ln 37922
Farrington Dr 37923
Farris Dr 37912
Faulkner Ln 37922
Fawnie Ln 37918
Fawnridge Ln 37938
Fawnwood Rd 37921
Fawver Ln 37914
Fay St 37921
Fayette Ln 37924
Feathers St 37920
Federal Blvd 37934
Federal Rd 37914
Feldspar Ln 37938
Felix Rd & St 37918
Fellowship Ln 37914
Felty Dr 37918
Fennel Rd 37912
Fenway Ln 37912
Fenwood Dr 37918
Ferd Hickey Rd 37909
Ferguson St 37917
Fern St 37914
Fern Meadow Way 37919
Fernbank Rd 37924
Ferncliff Way 37923
Ferndale Rd 37918
Fernway Dr 37923
Fernwood Rd 37923
Ferrell Ln 37932
Ferret Rd 37934
Ferry Rd 37920
Fieldcrest Ln 37918
Fielden Dr 37918
Fieldshire Dr 37918
Fieldstone Rd 37938
Fieldstone Farms Ln 37921
Fieldview Ln 37918
Fieldwood Dr 37918
Fig Tree Way 37931
Fillmore Ave 37921
Filter Plant Rd 37920
Fincastle Ln 37934
Finch Rd 37934
Finchwood Ln 37924
Fine Ave 37917
Finger Rd 37920
Finlaw Way 37922
Finley Cane Ln 37932
Firefly Way 37912
Firestone Pt 37934
Firethorne Way 37923
Firewood Ln 37922
First Ave 37924
Fiser Ln 37934
Fisher Ln 37924
Fisher Pl 37920
Fitzgerald Rd 37931
Flagg Ave 37917
Flagler Rd 37912
Flagstone Way 37923
Flamingo St 37920
Flanders Ln 37919
Flathead Way 37924
Flatwood Ln 37918
Fleenor Rd 37934
Fleetwood Cir & Dr 37921
Fleming St 37917
Fleming Valley Ln 37938
Flenniken Ave 37920
Flennwood Way 37920
Fleta Ln 37918
Flickenger Ln 37922
Flint Rd 37921
Flint Gap Rd 37914
Flint Hill Dr 37921
Flintlock Rd 37931
Flintrock Cir 37920
Flora St 37917
Florence Rd 37920
Florence Gardens Rd 37938
Florenza Ln 37918
Floret Way 37921
Floriade Way 37923
Flotilla Dr 37934
Floyd Ln 37923
Flyway Ln 37934
Foley Dr 37918
Folkstone Pl 37931
Folsom Ave 37917
Fontaine Rd 37920
Fontana St 37917
Fontis Dr 37918
Foolish Pleasure Ln 37931
Foote Mineral Ln 37923
Foothills Dr 37938
Forbes Ln 37931
Ford Ln, Pl & St 37920
E & W Ford Valley Rd 37920
Fordham Way 37934
Fords Cove Ln 37934
Fordtown Rd 37920
Forest Ave 37916
W Forest Blvd 37909
Forest Ct 37919
S Forest Dr 37920
Forest Ln 37918
N Forest Rd 37909
Forest St 37931
Forest Brook Rd 37919
Forest Crest Rd 37922
Forest Edge Way 37923
Forest Glen Dr 37919
Forest Grove Cir 37920
Forest Heights Rd 37919
Forest Hills Blvd 37919
Forest Landing Way 37918
Forest Oak Dr 37919
N & S Forest Park
Blvd 37919
Forest Ridge Cir 37932
Forest Valley Ln 37931
Forest View Rd 37919
Forest Village Way 37919
Forestal Dr 37918
Forestdale Ave 37917
Fork Station Way 37938
Forrelle Way 37918
Forrester Rd 37918
Forsythe St 37917
Fort Ave 37920
Fort Hill Rd 37920
Fort Promise Dr 37921
Fort Sanders West
Blvd 37922
Fort Sumter Rd 37938
Fort West Dr 37934
Fortner Ln 37938
Fortress Ln 37922
Foster Ln 37920
Fountain Dr
4300-4399 37912
5500-6299 37918
Fountain Rd 37918
Fountain Brook Ln 37923
Fountain City Rd 37918
Fountain Gate Rd 37918
Fountain Head Ln 37918
Fountain Park Blvd
2900-3499 37917
3500-3599 37914
Fountain Valley Dr 37918
Fountain View Way 37918
N & S Fountaincrest
Dr 37918
Four Seasons Ln 37934
Foust Dr 37924
Foust Hollow Rd 37938
Fowler Ln 37918
Fox Rd 37922
Fox St 37917
Fox Brook Ln 37932
W Fox Chase Cir 37934
Fox Chase Ln 37920
Fox Cove Rd 37922
Fox Crossing Blvd 37923
Fox Dale Ln 37934
E Fox Den Dr 37934
Fox Hollow Trl 37923
Fox Lake Dr 37923
Fox Landing Ln 37922
Fox Lonas Rd 37923
Fox Manor Blvd 37909
Fox Meadow Cir 37923
Fox Park Ln & Rd 37931
Fox River Way 37923
Fox Run Ln 37919
Fox Valley Ln 37938
Foxall Cir 37923
Foxboro Dr 37912
Foxbranch Cir 37918
Foxcroft Dr 37923
Foxfield Ln 37922
Foxfire Ct 37923
Foxford Dr 37934
Foxglen Blvd 37918
Foxglove Ln 37918
Foxhaven Rd 37918
Foxhound Rd 37918
Foxlair Rd 37918
Foxtrail Dr 37918
Foxvue Rd 37922
Foxwood Rd 37921
Fragrant Cloud Ln 37918
Fraker Rd 37918
Francis Cir 37909
Francis Rd 37909
Francis St
900-1099 37916
1500-7699 37924
Francis Station Dr 37909
Frank St 37919
Frank Gardner Ln 37932
Frank Herron Rd 37932
Frank Watt Rd 37909
Franklin Ln 37920
Franklin Creek Ln 37931
Franklin Hill Blvd 37922
Franklin Station Way 37916
Fraternity Park Dr 37916
Frazier Rd 37914
Frazier St 37917
Frederick Dr 37931
Frederick John St 37938
Fredericksburg Blvd 37922
Fredonia Rd 37912
Fredrickstein Dr 37918
Freels Ln 37922
Freels Bend Pt 37931
Freeman Ln 37918
Freemason St 37917
Freeway Heights Dr 37938
Fremont Pl 37917
French Rd 37920
French Broad Ln 37914
French Creek Dr 37920
French Lace Ln 37918
Fresh Garden Dr 37918
Fretz Rd
600-799 37934
900-1199 37932
Freund St 37920
Friars Way 37922
Friars Path Ln 37923
Friendly Way 37924
Friendship Ln 37912
Fringe Tree Dr 37938
Frisco Ln 37922
Frogpond Ln 37922
Fronda Ln 37920
Front Ave 37902
Front Royal Ln 37922
Frontier Trl 37920
Frostland Ln 37931
Frostwood Rd 37921
Frosty Way 37912
Fruitwood Ln 37934
Fry Rd 37931
Ft Hill Rd 37920
Fujii Farm Ln 37931
Fuller Ave 37915
Fulton Dr 37918
Furen Rd 37938
Furness Way 37920
Gable Run Dr 37931
Gaboury Ln 37918
Gaines Rd 37918
Gainesborough Dr 37909
Gaineswood Rd 37918
Gaiter Cir 37915
Galahad Rd 37931
Galba Rd 37918
Galbraith St 37921
Galbraith School Rd 37920
Galewood Rd 37919
Galileo Dr 37918
E & W Gallaher Ferry
Rd 37932
Gallaher Station Dr 37919
N Gallaher View Rd 37923
S Gallaher View Rd 37919
Gallant Ln 37918
Gallant Fox Way 37923
Gallerani Dr 37922
Gallery Way 37938
Gallows Point Dr 37931
Galveston Rd 37923
Galway St 37917
Galyon Ln 37920
Game Day Way 37902
Gammon Way 37922
Gander Grove Way 37932
Gap Rd
3300-3699 37921
3900-4199 37912
Garcia Way 37912
Garden Dr 37918
S Garden Rd 37919
Garden Cress Trl 37914
Garden Crossing Way 37932
Garden Meadow Dr 37912
Garden View Ln 37912
Garden Villa Way 37909
Garden Walk Ln 37931
Gardenia Dr 37914
Garfield Ave 37915
Garfield Terrace Dr 37938
Garland Rd 37922
Garnet Dr 37919
Garnett Woods Way 37922
Garrison Dr 37931
Garrison Ridge Blvd 37922
E & W Garwood Cir 37918
Gary Rd 37917
Gary Douglas Ln 37931
Gary Walker Ln 37918
Gaslight Ln 37931
Gaston Ave 37917
Gate Ln 37909
Gate Post Way 37931
Gatekeeper Way 37931
Gates Mill Dr 37934
Gateswalk Ln 37924
Gatewater Ln 37922
Gateway Ln 37920
Gatewood Ln 37919
Gatwick Dr 37922
N Gay St 37917
S Gay St
100-799 37902
800-800 37929
801-999 37902
900-998 37902
Gayle Rd 37922
Gayview Dr 37920
Gazebo Point Way 37920
Gem Apparel Ln 37921
Gemini Way 37918
Genesis Ln 37938
Geneva Ln 37923
Genny Lynn Dr 37918
Genoa Ln 37918
Gentian Ln 37922
Gentlewinds Dr 37931
Genuine Risk Rd 37931
George Bounds Rd 37924
George Light Rd 37931
George Lovelace Ln 37932
George Miller Ln 37932
George Walter Way 37912
George Whittaker Rd 37931
George Williams Rd
8900-8999 37923
9000-9999 37922
Georgetowne Dr 37934
Georgia Ln 37924
Georgia St
400-499 37915
500-599 37917
Georgia St NE 37917
Gerald R Ford St 37919
Geraldine St 37917
Germantown Ln 37920
Geronimo Rd 37934
Gerson Dr 37920
Gertrude Ave 37920
Geta Rd 37918
Gettysburg Rd 37921
Gettysvue Dr & Way 37922
Geyland Heights Rd 37920
Geyser Ln 37934
Ghiradelli Rd 37918
Gibbons St 37917
Gibbs Dr & Ln 37918
Giffin St 37921
Gila Trl 37919
Gilbert Dr 37932
Gilbert Ln 37920
W Gilbert Ln 37920
Gilbert Station Ln 37932
Gilian Ln 37934
Gill Ave 37917
Gillcrest Dr 37938
Gillenwater Dr 37917
Gillespie Ave 37917
Gillette Ln 37918
Gilson Ln 37922
Ginger Ln 37932
Gingerfield Rd 37921
Gingham Rd 37918
Ginn Dr 37920
Ginnbrooke Ln 37920
Gisele Way 37931
Giverny Cir 37922
Glacier Way 37924
Glade Hill Dr 37909
Gladstone Ln 37917
Glasgow Rd 37918
Glass Ln 37920
Glastonbury Rd 37931
Gleason Dr
8717A-8717B 37923
7500-8499 37919
8500-8899 37923
Glen Abbey Blvd 37934
Glen Arden Dr 37931
Glen Bean Ct 37919
Glen Clark Way 37920
Glen Cove Dr 37919
Glen Creek Rd 37924
Glen Eagle Ln 37921
Glen Echo Dr 37923
Glen Forest Ln 37919
Glen Iris Ln 37934
Glen Ives Way 37919
Glen Meadow Rd 37909
Glen Oaks Dr 37918
Glen Vale Dr 37919
Glen Willow Dr 37934
Glenbrook Cir & Dr 37919
Glencroft Dr 37922
Glenda Ln 37920
Glendale Rd 37917
Glendower Way 37923
Glenfield Dr 37919
Glengarry Ct 37921
Glenhaven Rd 37918
Glenhill Dr 37919
Glenhurst Rd 37920
Glenlake Blvd 37931
Glenleigh Ct 37934
Glenmary Rd 37919
Glenmay Dr 37921
Glenmora Grove Way 37923
Glenmore Cir 37919
Glenn Ave 37921
Glennifer Ln 37918
Glennshire Dr 37923
Glenoaks Dr 37912
Glenpark Rd 37921
Glenrothes Blvd 37909
Glensprings Dr 37922
Glenstone Ct 37934
Glenview Dr 37917
Glenwalker Ln 37938
E Glenwood Ave 37917
Glider Ave 37917
Global Way 37932
Globe Dr 37912
Glory Way 37923
Gloucester Cir 37918
Gnarled Pine Ln 37922
Goddard Ln & Rd 37920
Godfrey St 37917
Goff Rd 37920
Goforth Ave 37915
Goins Dr 37921
Golden Cloud Ln 37931
Golden Fox Ln 37934
Golden Gate Rd 37918
Golden Harvest Rd 37934
Golden Pond Way 37918
Golden Ridge Ln 37938
Golden Shore Way 37922
Goldenfern Ln 37931
Goldenrod Cir 37921
Goldenview Ln 37932
Goldfinch Ave 37920
Goldleaf Cir 37923
Goldsboro Cir 37922
Golf View Ln 37922
Golfclub Rd 37919
Gondola Dr 37920
Goodys Ln 37922
Gooseneck Dr 37920
Gorby Way 37923
Gordon Pl 37918
Gordon Smith Rd 37938
Gore Rd 37919
Gose Cove Ln 37931
Gossamer Way 37923
Gothic Manor Way 37923
Gouffon Rd 37918
Government Farm Rd 37920
E Governor John Sevier
Hwy
100-2299 37920
2300-5599 37914
5600-6199 37924
W Governor John Sevier
Hwy 37920
Governors Ln 37934
Grace Ln 37919
Grace St 37917
Grace Point Way 37938
Gracemont Blvd 37938
Gracewood Way 37934
Graham Way 37912
Grainger Ave 37917
Granada Ln 37923
Grand Ave 37916
Grand Rose Way 37924

Grand Valley Rd 37920
Granda Dr 37909
Grande Shores Way 37922
Grandeur Dr 37920
Grandin Rd 37920
Grandview Dr 37919
Grane Lefe St 37938
Granite Hill Ln 37923
Grant Rd 37924
Grantop Dr 37923
Granville Ter 37915
Grapevine Ln 37921
Grass Walk Ln 37924
Grassey Creek Way 37921
Grassy Meadow Blvd 37931
Grassy Pointe Ln 37931
Grata Rd 37914
Gratz St 37917
Graves Ln 37938
Graves Rd 37938
Graves St 37915
Gray Rd 37938
Gray Eagle Ln 37932
Gray Fox Ln 37920
Gray Gables Dr 37931
Gray Heights Way 37938
Gray Hendrix Rd 37931
Gray Leaf Cir 37918
Gray Oaks Ln 37932
Gray Squirrel Ln 37923
Graybeal Rd 37932
Graybrook Ln 37920
Graycreek Ln 37923
Graycroft Cir & Dr 37918
Grayland Dr 37923
Graystone Ln 37938
Great Meadows Dr 37920
Great Oaks Way 37909
Great Wood Way 37922
Greatcoat Ln 37922
Greeley Ln 37934
Greeley Ford Rd 37920
Green Rd 37931
Green Acre Dr 37924
Green Garden Dr 37934
Green Heron Blvd 37938
Green Hills Rd 37919
Green Meadow Ln 37917
Green Meadows Dr 37920
Green Oak Ln 37932
Green Pasture Dr 37924
Green Pine Dr 37920
Green Ridge Cir 37919
Green Spring Ln 37932
Green Summers Rd 37938
Green Valley Dr 37914
Greenberry Ln 37938
Greenbrier Dr 37919
Greenbrier Ridge Way 37909
Greenbrook Dr 37931
Greencrest Rd 37918
Greendale Rd 37918
Greene Ln 37920
Greenfern Way 37912
Greenfield Ln 37917
Greenland Way 37932
Greenleaf Ave 37919
Greens Crossing Rd 37909
Greensboro Way 37912
Greenscape Dr 37938
Greentree Ln 37931
Greenview Dr 37918
Greenway Dr 37918
Greenwell Dr & Rd 37938
Greenwich Ln 37932
Greenwood Ave 37920
Greenwood Rd 37918
Greer Pl 37917
Greer Rd 37918
Gregg Ruth Way 37909
Gregory Oaks Ln 37912
Grenada Blvd 37922
Grenoble Dr 37909
Gresham Rd 37918
Grey Pointe Dr 37922
Greylock Way 37931
Greywell Rd 37922
Greywolfe Dr 37921
Greywood Dr 37923
Griffins Gate Ln 37912
Griffith Dr 37914
Griffith Rd 37938
Grigsby Chapel Rd 37934
Grigsby Gate Way 37912
Grigsby Loop Cir 37934
Grinnell Cir 37924
Grinstead Rd 37934
Grist Mill Cir 37909
Groner Dr 37915
Grospoint Dr 37923
Gross Ave 37921
Ground Breaker Way 37919
Grousemoor Dr 37919
Grove Cir 37918
Grove Dr 37918
Grove Rd 37924
Grove St 37917
Grove Branch Ln 37922
Grove Hill Ln 37932
Grove Lake Way 37922
Grove Park Rd 37918
Grove Villas Way 37918
Grovedale Dr 37922
Guinn Rd 37931
Guinnview Way 37931
Guinnwood Ln 37922
Gulf Chase Ln 37923
Gulf Park Dr 37923
Gulf Stream Dr 37923
Gulfwood Rd 37923
Gull Ln 37919
Gumwood Ln 37921
Gunnison Way 37921
Guyot Dr 37922
Gwinfield Dr 37920
Gwinhurst Rd 37934
Gynevere Dr 37931
Hackberry Rd 37931
Hackman St 37920
Hackworth Rd 37931
Haggard Dr 37917
Hailes Abbey Ln 37922
Hale Rd 37917
Halesworth Ln 37922
Haley Glenn Ln 37920
Haleyford Ln 37922
Halifax Rd 37922
Hall Rd
7600-8199 37920
9800-10099 37923
Hall St 37920
Hall Acres Dr 37918
Hall Of Fame Dr 37915
N Hall Of Fame Dr 37917
Hallbrook Rd 37918
Halls Gap Rd 37938
Halls View Rd 37938
Hallsdale Cir & Rd 37938
Hamid Pl 37920
Hamilton Rd 37920
Hamilton Ridge Ln 37922
Hamlet Rd 37918
Hammer Rd
6100-6414 37914
6415-6497 37924
6416-6498 37914
6499-7599 37924
Hammerstone Ln 37922
Hammock Ln 37934
Hammond Ln 37912
Hampshire Dr 37909
Hampson Ln 37919
Hampton Ave 37914
Hampton Ct 37922
Hampton Roads Dr 37934
Hamstead Ct 37922
Hancock St 37917
Handence Rd 37938
Handley Ln 37921
Hankins Ln 37914
Hanna Pt 37923
Hannah Ave 37921
Hannah Brook Rd 37918
Hannah View Way 37921
Hannahs Park Ln 37921
Hanover Dr 37920
Hanover Pt 37922
Hansard Ln 37920
Hansmore Pl 37919
Hanson Ave 37915
Happy Acres Dr 37918
Haralson Ln 37938
Harbin Ln 37934
Harbin Ridge Ln 37909
Harbor Way 37934
Harbor Cove Dr 37938
Harbor Pointe Way 37922
Harbor View Way 37934
Harbor Walk Way 37918
Harbour Front Way 37922
Harbour Park Ln 37934
Harbour Shore Dr 37934
Hardin Farms Ln 37932
Hardin Hill Rd 37917
Hardin Ridge Way 37931
Hardin Valley Rd 37932
Harding Dr 37932
Hardwicke Dr 37923
Hardwood Rd 37918
Hardy Ln 37924
Harlaxton Ct 37923
Harley Dr 37919
Harmon Rd 37920
Harmony Ln & Rd 37912
Harmony Grove Way 37931
Harold Ave 37915
Harold Ln 37920
Harold Duncan Way 37931
Harpen Rd 37931
Harper Dr 37931
Harper Pl 37922
Harpers Ferry Ln 37922
Harrell Cir 37938
Harrell Ln 37938
Harrell Rd 37931
Harriet Tubman St 37915
Harriett Pl 37912
Harrington Dr 37922
Harris Ave 37909
Harris Ln 37920
Harris Rd
1300-3499 37924
3500-4399 37918
Harris St 37921
Harrisburg Ct 37909
Harrison Rd 37934
N Harrison St 37914
S Harrison St 37914
Harrison Forest Way 37921
Harrison Glen Ln 37922
Harrison Springs Ln 37932
Harrogate Dr 37923
Harrow Rd 37934
Harry St 37919
Harry Lane Blvd 37923
Harsch St 37920
Hart Rd 37922
Hartford Rd & St 37920
Hartland Ln 37938
Hartley Ln 37918
Harts View Dr 37922
Hartwinn Ln 37918
Harvest Ln 37931
Harvest Grove Ln 37918
Harvest Mill Way 37918
Harvey Rd
1100-1999 37922
3300-3499 37918
Harvey St 37917
Haskin Knoll Ln 37918
Hastings Ln 37909
Hatcher Dr 37921
Hatmaker Ln 37932
Hatteras Dr 37934
Hatton Ave 37921
Haun St 37917
S Haven Rd 37920
Havenbrooke Way 37922
Havenhill Ln 37914
Havenstone Ln 37918
Haverhill Dr 37909
Haversack Dr 37922
Haverty Dr 37931
Hawfinch Ln 37922
Hawick Ln 37924
Hawk Crest Ln 37921
Hawk Haven Ln 37931
Hawkdale Ln 37922
Hawkins St 37921
Hawks Landing Dr 37931
Hawks View Way 37922
Hawks Wing Way 37914
Hawkstowe Ln 37934
Haws Rd 37920
Hawthorne Ave 37920
Hawthorne Dr 37919
Hay Meadow Trl 37920
Hayden Dr 37919
Hayes Ln 37932
Hayes Rd 37912
Hayfield Rd 37922
Haynes Pl 37917
Haynes Sterchi Rd 37912
Haynesfield Ln 37918
Hayslope Dr 37919
Hayswood Rd 37914
Haywood Ave 37920
Hayworth Dr 37920
Hazel Pl 37917
Hazelbrook Way 37912
Hazelgreen Way 37912
Hazelnut Dr & Ln 37931
Hazelwood Rd 37921
Hazen St 37915
Headlands Way 37918
Hearthside Rd 37934
Hearthstone Ln 37923
Heartwell Way 37932
Heather Ct 37919
Heather Ln 37912
Heather Way 37919
Heather Glen Rd 37919
Heatherbrook Dr 37931
Heatherfield Ln 37909
Heathermoor Dr 37934
Heatherton Way 37920
Heatherwood Ct 37934
Heathgate Rd 37922
Heathland Dr 37934
Heathrow Dr 37919
Heathwood Bnd 37923
Hedge Ave 37916
Hedgeapple Ln 37920
Hedgewood Dr 37918
Heins Ct 37912
Heins Rd 37918
Heins St 37921
Heiskell Ave
100-299 37917
1000-1299 37921
Helen Dr 37918
Helix Ln 37920
Helmbolt Rd 37909
S Hembree St 37914
Heming Way 37912
Hemingway Grove Cir 37922
Hemlock Rd 37919
Hempshire Dr 37922
Hempstead Dr 37923
Henderson Ln 37922
Henderson Rd 37931
Henderson Bend Rd 37931
Henderson Hollow Rd 37931
Hendrix Ln 37921
Hendrix Rd 37920
E & W Hendron Chapel
Rd 37920
Henegar Rd 37917
Henge Point Ln 37922
Henley St 37902
Henrietta Ave 37915
Henrietta Dr 37912
Henry Ave 37920
Henry Frye Way 37922
Henry Haynes Dr 37920
Henry Hollow Way 37920
Henry Knox Way 37920
Hensley Dr 37909
Henson Rd 37921
Herbert Ln 37938
Herfordshire Ln 37922
E & W Heritage Dr 37934
Heritage Cove Way 37924
Heritage Lake Blvd 37922
Heritage Oaks Way 37923
Herman Ave 37914
Hermitage Dr 37920
Heron Perch Ln 37922
Herron Dr 37919
Herron Rd
400-799 37934
800-899 37932
Herron Cove Dr 37922
Heumsdale Dr 37924
Hewitt Ln 37932
Hialeah Dr 37920
Hiawassee Ave 37917
Hiawatha Dr 37919
Hibbert Rd 37932
Hibicus Rd 37914
Hicken Rd 37938
Hickey Rd 37932
Hickman St 37920
Hickory St 37912
Hickory Trl 37932
Hickory Creek Rd 37932
Hickory Glen Rd 37932
Hickory Grove Ct 37922
Hickory Haven Way 37921
Hickory Hill Ln 37922
Hickory Hills Dr 37919
Hickory Hollow Rd 37919
Hickory Knoll Ln 37931
Hickory Manor Way 37931
Hickory Nut Ln 37924
Hickory Orchard Way 37920
Hickory Path Way 37922
Hickory Ridge Cv 37923
Hickory Springs Dr 37932
Hickory Valley Way 37918
Hickory View Cir 37921
Hickory Way Ln 37918
Hickory Wind Ln 37938
Hickory Woods Rd 37934
Hickoryborough Ln 37922
Hickoryoak Ln 37919
Hidalgo Ct 37923
Hidden Ln 37920
Hidden Brook Ln 37938
Hidden Cove Ln 37922
Hidden Creek Cir 37934
Hidden Deer Ln 37922
Hidden Glen Ln 37922
Hidden Green Ln 37922
Hidden Grove Rd 37934
Hidden Hollow Ln 37922
Hidden Meadow Dr 37922
Hidden Oak Way 37922
Hidden Springs Rd 37914
Hidden Valley Rd 37923
Hidell Rd 37914
Higdon Dr 37931
Higgins Ave 37920
High Ave 37920
High Dr 37921
N High Dr 37924
High Alpine Ln 37918
High Bluff Ln 37918
High Forest Ln 37934
High Grove Ln 37918
High Heath 37919
High Lark Ln 37923
High Meadow Dr 37932
High Mesa Dr 37938
High Oak Rd 37934
High Point Way 37912
High School Rd 37912
High Springs Rd 37932
High View Ln 37931
High Vista Ln 37931
Highbank Ln 37938
Highbridge Dr 37922
Highcliff Dr 37934
Highfield Rd 37923
Highgate Cir 37931
Highgrove Garden
Way 37922
Highland Ave 37916
Highland Cir 37920
Highland Ct 37912
Highland Dr
400-1099 37912
1100-2699 37918
Highland Creek Ln 37931
Highland Crest Way 37920
Highland Garden Way 37938
Highland Hills Rd 37919
Highland Place Way 37919
Highland Point Dr 37919
Highland View Dr 37920
Highland View Rd 37938
Highlander Way 37922
Highlands Cove Ln 37922
Highstone Ln 37934
Hightop Rd 37914
Hightop Trl 37923
Highvue Dr 37932
Highwick Cir 37934
Highwood Ct & Dr 37920
Hilda Ln 37921
E Hill Ave 37915
W Hill Ave 37902
Hill Rd 37938
Hillard Ln 37920
Hillbrook Dr 37931
Hillcrest Ct 37920
Hillcrest Dr 37918
Hilldale Dr 37914
Hillman Rd 37932
Hillock Rd 37918
Hillridge Rd 37912
N Hills Blvd 37917
S Hills Dr 37920
W Hills Rd 37909
Hillsboro Hts 37920
Hillsboro Rd 37924
Hillshire Ln 37922
Hillside Ave 37914
Hillside Ln 37920
Hillside Terrace Ln 37924
Hilltop Rd 37920
Hillvale Cir 37919
E & W Hillvale Turn 37919
Hillview Ave 37914
Hillview Rd
600-699 37919
1300-1399 37920
4500-4599 37919
Hillwood Dr 37920
Hilton Rd 37921
Hilton Industrial Way 37921
Hinton Ave 37917
Hinton Rd 37921
Historic Ferry Way 37922
Hitchcock Way 37923
Hitching Post Dr 37931
Hobble Ln 37938
N & S Hobbs Rd 37934
Hobby Ln 37914
Hocotake Ln 37912
Hodge Rd 37931
Hodges Ferry Rd 37920
Hodges Landing Dr 37920
Hoff Ln 37938
Hogan Way 37912
Hoitt Ave 37917
Holbert Dr 37938
Holbert Ln 37914
Holbrook Dr 37918
Holder Ln 37922
Holderwood Ln 37922
Holiday Blvd 37921
Holirose Ln 37918
Holland Dr 37918
Hollander Ln 37931
Holles Ln 37922
Hollingsfield Dr 37922
Hollow Oak Ln 37921
Hollow Ridge Ln 37931
Hollow Tree Way 37912
Holloway Dr 37919
Holly St 37917
Holly Berry Dr 37938
Holly Crest Ln 37938
Holly Grove Way 37918
Holly Ridge Ln 37931
Hollyhock Ln 37918
Hollywood Rd
500-999 37919
1000-1699 37909
Holman Dr 37909
Holmouth Ln 37914
Holston Ct 37914
Holston Dr
3800-5699 37914
5700-6099 37924
Holston Ferry Dr 37924
Holston Heights Ln 37914
Holston Hills Rd 37914
Holston Park Rd 37914
Holston River Rd 37914
Holston View Ln 37914
Holt Ln
100-199 37931
6600-6699 37919
Homberg Dr 37919
Home St 37920
Homestead Dr 37918
Homewood Rd 37918
Honey Grove Ln 37923
Honey Ridge Way 37924
Honeydew Ln 37931
Honeytree Ln 37938
Honeywood Ln 37918
Honors Way 37922
Hooks Ln 37938
Hope Way 37909
Hope Springs Way 37932
Hopemont Way 37923
Hopewell Rd 37920
Hopkins Ave 37921
Hopper Ln 37932
Hopscotch Ln 37931
Horseshoe Dr 37920
Horseshoe Bend Ln 37931
Horsestall Dr 37918
Horton Rd 37918
Hosea Ln 37938
Hospitality Cir 37909
Hotel Rd 37918
Hound Ears Pt 37934
Houser Rd 37919
Houston St 37914
Houstonia Dr 37918
Howard Dr 37918
Howard St 37917
Howard Baker Ave 37915
Howard Baker Jr Blvd 37915
Howard Bennett Way 37931
Howell Ave 37920
Howell Ln 37924
Hoyle Beals Dr 37931
Hubbs Ln 37912
Hubbs Crossing Ln 37938
Hubert Bean Rd 37918
Huckleberry Ln 37924
Huckleberry Springs Rd
800-900 37924
902-998 37924
935-2399 37914
Huday Rd 37924
Huddersfield Way 37920
Hudson Terrace Way 37924
Huffaker Ferry Rd 37920
Hughes Ln 37932
Hughlan Dr 37934
Hull Ln 37931
Humes St 37917
Hummer Ln 37912
Humphrey Rd 37917
Hunt Crest Rd 37931
Huntcliff Ln 37922

Hunter Chase Ln 37923
Hunter Valley Ln 37922
Hunterhill Dr 37923
Hunters Trl 37921
Hunters Creek Ln 37922
Hunters Glen Dr 37921
Hunters Green Rd 37932
Hunters Hollow Way 37932
Hunters Ridge Way 37914
Hunters Run Ln 37932
Hunting Fox Ln 37934
Huntington Rd 37919
Huntland Dr 37919
Huntwood Ln 37923
Huray Ln 37917
Huron St 37917
Hurst Ln 37918
Hurstbourne Ct 37919
Hutchinson Ave 37917
Hutton Rd 37912
Huxley Rd 37922
Hyacinth Way 37923
Hyatt Rd 37918
Hyde Park Ln 37921
Hydrangea Way 37914
Ida Dr 37920
Ida Hertzler Ln 37934
Ideal Dr 37938
Idlewood Ln 37923
Ike Ln 37918
Ike Ammons Rd 37931
Ila Perdue Dr 37931
Ilex Cir 37919
Immanuel St 37920
Impala Way 37938
Imperial Dr 37918
Incline St 37920
Independence Ln 37914
Indian Rd 37914
Indian Hills Dr 37919
Indian Moccasin Ln 37918
Indian Springs Ln 37932
Indigo Ln 37921
Indigo Wood Ct 37920
Industrial Pkwy E & W 37921
Industrial Heights Dr 37909
Industry Ln 37921
Ingersoll Ave 37920
Inglecrest Ln 37934
Ingleside Ln 37918
Inglewood Dr 37914
Ingram Ln 37938
Inisbrook Way 37938
Inlet Dr 37922
Innovation Dr 37932
E & W Inskip Dr & Rd 37912
Intrigue Ln 37918
Inverness Pt 37934
Inverness Rd 37931
Inverrary Cir 37918
Investment Dr 37932
Inwood Rd 37921
Iona Way 37912
Iredell Ave 37921
Irene Ave 37920
Iris Ln 37920
Irola St 37924
Iron Duke Way 37919
Ironstone Ln 37938
Ironwood Rd 37921
Iroquois Dr 37914
Iroquois St 37915
Irwin St 37917
Isaac Ln 37938
Isabella Cir 37915
Isaih Ln 37938
Isherwood Ln 37922
Ishman Way 37931
Iskagna Dr 37919
Island Ct 37921
Island Bay Way 37931
Island Home Ave, Blvd & Pike 37920
Island River Dr 37914
Island View Ln 37924
Islandic St 37931

Islington Ave 37917
Ithaca Dr 37918
Iva Ln 37918
Ivan Scott Dr 37938
Iverson Ln 37932
Ivey Ln 37914
Ivey Glen Ct 37922
Ivey Green Way 37919
Ivory Gables Way 37912
Ivory Tower Dr 37931
Ivy Ave 37914
Ivy Bridge Rd 37931
Ivy Brook Way 37912
Ivy Chase Ln 37934
Ivy Falls Way 37923
Ivy Gate Ln 37934
Ivy Hollow Dr 37931
Ivy Lake Dr 37934
Ivy Mill Ct 37924
Ivy Point Ln 37922
Ivy Rock Way 37918
Ivy Rose Dr 37918
Ivy Stone Way 37918
Ivywood Ln 37931
Jack Dance St 37919
Jack Jones Rd 37920
Jackie Ln 37920
Jackie Jordon Way 37920
Jacksboro Pike 37918
E Jackson Ave 37915
W Jackson Ave 37902
Jackson Rd 37921
Jackson Oaks Way 37922
Jackson Ridge Ln 37924
Jacques Dr 37921
Jade Rd 37919
Jade Pasture Ln 37918
Jade Tree Ln 37938
Jadestone Way 37923
Jadewood Ln 37923
Jakes Walk Ln 37932
Jamaica Ln 37921
Jamber Way 37931
James Ave 37921
James Dr 37920
James Rd 37914
James Agee St 37916
Jamestowne Blvd 37934
Jamey St 37914
Jana Ln 37931
Jana Chris Ln 37918
Jane Bennett Way 37931
Janes Meadow Rd 37932
Janice Dr 37938
Janmer Ln 37909
Japonica Way 37931
Jarmann Rd 37934
Jarrett Ln 37923
Jason Dr 37938
Jasper Ln 37934
Java Way 37923
Jay Way 37909
Jayne Ln 37918
Jc White Rd 37920
Jeanie Ln 37938
Jefferson Ave
1500-2499 37917
2500-2899 37914
Jefferson Grove Way 37922
Jefferson Oaks Dr 37938
Jeffrey Ln 37934
Jenkins Ln
900-1299 37934
8300-8499 37938
Jenkins Rd
4800-5099 37918
7300-8999 37931
Jenkins St 37921
Jenkins Creek Dr 37931
Jennifer Dr 37938
Jennings Ave 37917
Jenny Cook Cir 37923
Jenso Dr 37912
Jerbeeler Dr 37931
Jerdan Rd 37919
Jericho Ln 37918

Jerry Ln 37920
Jersey Ave 37919
Jessamine St 37917
Jessica Lauren Way 37931
Jessica Taylor Dr 37931
Jessie Rd 37924
Jessilee Dr 37938
Jett Ln & Rd 37920
Jewel Way 37938
Jilson Rd 37920
Jim Armstrong Rd 37914
Jim Jones Ln 37931
Jim Luttrell Ln 37918
Jim Sterchi Rd 37918
Joan Rd 37924
Jockey Run Trl 37920
Joe Daniels Rd 37931
Joe Hinton Rd 37931
Joe Lewis Rd 37920
Joey Ln 37938
John Andrew Ln 37931
John Deere Dr 37917
John Hall Rd 37920
John May Dr 37921
John Norton Rd 37920
John Romines Way 37918
John Ross Ct 37921
John Sevier School Rd 37924
John Toole Rd 37920
Johnson Ln 37920
Johnson Rd 37931
Johnson Cemetery Rd 37938
Johnson Frazier Cem Rd 37914
Johnsons Corner Rd 37934
Johnston St 37921
Johnston Vista Way 37938
Joiner Way 37934
Jolly Ln 37931
Jomandowa Dr 37919
Jonah Ln 37918
Jonathan Ave & Way 37920
Jones Rd 37918
Jones St 37920
Jonesboro Rd 37920
Joneva Rd 37932
Jonquil Dr 37909
Jonteel Dr 37914
Jordan St 37921
Joseph Dr 37918
Joseph Gate Ln 37931
Josephine Rd 37918
Josepi Dr 37918
Joshua Rd 37938
Jourolman Ave 37921
Joy Rd 37914
Joyce Ave 37921
Jr Dr 37921
Js Davis Ln 37932
Juanita Cannon St 37914
Jubilee Ct 37918
Jubilee Center Way 37912
Judah Ln 37918
Judith Dr 37920
Judson Ln 37921
Judy Reagan Ln 37931
Julia Ct 37938
Julian Ln 37914
Julian St 37920
Julie Ln 37932
Junco Ln 37934
June St 37920
Juneau Ln 37931
Juneberry Way 37932
Juniper Dr 37912
Justin Dr 37918
Kaitlin Ln 37922
Kalispell Way 37924
Kalmia Rd 37909
Kantebury Dr 37917
Kanuga Dr 37912
Kara Ln 37919
Karen Dr 37918
Karla Dr 37920
Karnes Ave 37917

Karns Crossing Ln 37931
Karns Valley Dr 37931
Karnswood Dr 37918
Kashmir Way 37918
Kasson Rd 37920
Kate Brook Ln 37921
Kates Path Ln 37932
Katey Springs Way 37917
Katherine Ave 37921
Kathy Ln 37932
Katia Ln 37938
Katie Oak Dr 37932
Katrina Ln 37912
Kay St 37920
Kay Meg Way 37922
Kaydee Way 37918
Kays Ridge Ln 37914
Kaywood Rd 37920
Keats Ln 37934
Keck Rd 37912
Keeble Ave 37920
Keepesake Way 37919
Keith Ave 37921
Keithway Ln 37918
N Keller St 37917
S Keller St 37915
Keller Bend Rd 37922
Kelley Farm Way 37932
Kelly Pl 37919
Kellys Cove Ln 37931
Kelsey Ln 37922
Kelso Way 37923
Kemp Fain Ln 37932
Kemper Ln 37920
Kempfield Way 37920
Kempton Rd 37909
Ken Ln 37931
Kenbrook Ln 37921
Kencedg Ave 37917
Kendall Rd 37919
Kendallmac Ln 37931
Kenesaw Ave 37919
Kenilworth Dr 37919
Kenilworth Ln
2500-3499 37917
3500-4299 37914
Kennedy Ln 37920
Kennedy Rd 37914
Kenner Ave 37915
Kennington Rd 37917
Kennon Rd 37909
Kennon Park Ln 37909
Kennon Springs Ln 37909
Kenro Dr 37915
Kensi Dr 37912
Kensington Cir 37919
Kensington Dr 37922
Kent St 37914
Kentfield Dr 37919
Kenton Way 37922
Kentucky St 37915
Kentwell Rd 37932
Kentwood Rd 37912
Kenwood Ln 37938
Kenyon St 37917
Keowee Ave 37919
Kephard Cir 37922
Kermit Dr 37912
Kern Pl 37917
Kern Rd 37918
Kerri Way 37909
Keshia Way 37932
Kesterbrooke Blvd 37918
Kesterson Rd 37918
Kesterwood Ct, Dr & Rd 37918
Kettering Way 37923
Kettle Dr 37918
Kevin Rd 37923
Key Ln 37920
Key Hole Ln 37934
Keystone Ave 37917
Kidder Ln 37923
Kilbridge Dr 37924
Kildare Dr 37923
Killarney Rd 37923

Kilmer Dr 37922
Kilpatrick Way 37932
Kim Ln 37917
Kim Watt Dr 37909
Kimaron Ln 37938
Kimball Ln 37934
Kimbee Rd 37923
Kimberlin Heights Rd 37920
Kimbrough Dr 37922
Kincaid St 37917
Kincannon Ct 37918
Kincer Farms Dr 37922
King Rd 37920
King St 37917
King Arthur Way 37923
King Charles Way 37923
King George Way 37918
King Post Trl 37932
Kingdom Ln 37938
Kingfish Dr 37924
Kingland Ave 37920
Kinglet Dr 37919
Kingman Dr 37912
W Kings Way 37923
Kings Crossing Way 37918
E & W Kings Gate Rd 37934
Kings Mountain Ln 37920
Kings Point Rd 37931
Kingsbury Dr 37919
Kingsdale Dr 37919
Kingsford Way 37919
Kingsmore Dr 37921
Kingsridge Dr 37923
Kingston Ct 37919
Kingston Pike
2300-8599 37919
8600-9199 37923
9200-10699 37922
10700-13199 37934
Kingston Park Dr 37919
Kingstree Ln 37919
Kingwood Dr & Rd 37918
Kinlock Ln 37921
Kinnamon Rd 37920
Kinzalow Dr 37909
Kinzel Way 37924
Kinzell Ln 37924
Kinzer St 37920
Kipling Park Ln 37922
Kirbury Ln 37909
Kirby Rd 37909
Kirby Glen Dr 37923
Kirby Hills Cv 37923
Kirkstone Ln 37918
Kirkwall Ln 37909
Kirkwood St 37914
Kittredge Ct 37934
Kitts Rd 37924
Kitty Hawk Way 37912
Kituwah Trl 37919
Kiva Dunes Ln 37938
Klondike Way 37923
Knight Rd 37920
Knightsbridge Dr 37922
Knob Creek Ln 37912
Knoll Top Ct 37932
Knoll Tree Dr 37932
Knollcrest Ln 37920
Knolls View Dr 37920
Knollwood Cir 37919
Knott Ave 37919
Knott Rd 37921
Knottingwood Blvd 37923
Knotty Oak Way 37920
Knotty Pine Way 37920
Knowledge Ln 37938
Knox Ln 37917
Knox Rd 37918
Knoxville Center Dr 37924
Knoxville College Dr 37921
Knoxville Zoo Dr 37914
Knoxwood Dr 37921
Kodak Rd 37914
Kohlmier Rd 37912
Kohlston Rd 37918
Konda Dr 37920

Koon Ln 37931
Koto Wood Ct 37920
Kramer Way 37909
Kranbrook Ln 37921
Kristi Dr 37922
Kroger Park Dr 37922
Kurtzman St 37915
N Kyle St 37917
S Kyle St 37915
La Christa Way 37921
La Farve Ln 37931
La Paloma Dr 37923
La Villas Dr 37917
Labrusca Ln 37921
Lacy Rd 37912
Ladbrook Ln 37922
Ladera Cir 37922
Lady Slipper Ln 37934
Lafayette Rd 37921
Lagerfield Ln 37918
Lago Cir 37922
Lake Ave 37916
S Lake Blvd 37920
Lake Ln 37919
Lake Bluff Ct 37920
Lake Breeze Rd 37934
Lake Brook Blvd 37909
Lake Court Ln 37923
Lake Emerald Ln 37922
Lake Forest Cir & Dr 37920
Lake Glen Ln 37920
Lake Haven Rd 37934
Lake Heather Rd 37934
Lake Heritage Way 37922
Lake Hills Dr 37934
Lake Loudon Blvd 37916
Lake Mill Ln 37934
Lake Mountain Ln 37938
Lake Park Cir 37934
Lake Point Ct 37920
Lake Ridge Dr 37934
Lake Shore Dr 37920
Lake Springs Rd 37924
Lake View Dr
100-199 37920
3300-3499 37919
Lake Village Cir 37938
Lake Vista Ln 37934
Lakecove Way 37922
Lakecrest Dr 37920
Lakefront Dr 37922
Lakehurst Ln 37934
Lakeland Dr 37919
Lakeland View Way 37922
Lakelet Ct 37922
Lakemont Ln 37922
Lakemoor Dr 37920
Lakepoint Dr 37922
Lakeshire Dr 37922
Lakeside St 37914
Lakeside Centre Way 37922
Lakewood Dr 37920
Lakewood Ln 37921
Lakin Rd 37924
Lamar St 37917
Lambent Ln 37918
Lamesa Ln 37934
Lammie Branch Ln 37938
Lamons Quarry Ln 37932
Lamour Rd 37909
Lamp Dr 37912
Lampwick Ln 37912
Lamson Ct 37909
Lancaster Dr 37920
Lancaster Ridge Dr 37932
Lance Dr 37909
Lancelot Dr 37931
Lancer Dr 37921
Lancewood Dr 37920
Land Oak Rd 37922
Landbrook Dr 37921
Landing Ln 37934
Landings River Way 37915
Landmark Dr 37923
Landon Dr 37921
Lands End Ln 37931

Landstone Way 37923
Landview Dr 37914
Lanesborough Way 37934
Langford Ave 37920
Langland St 37915
Langley Pl 37922
Langston Dr 37918
Lani Ln 37932
Lanier Ln 37923
Lanntair Farm Ln 37922
Lansdowne Dr 37922
Lansing Ave 37914
Lantana Ln NW 37912
Lantern Ridge Ln 37921
Lapsley Pl 37915
Laramie Dr 37912
Larch Ln 37909
Larch St 37921
Large Oak Ln 37921
Largo Vista Rd 37922
Larigo Dr 37914
Larimer St 37921
Lark Ln 37919
Lark Meadow Dr 37934
Larkfield Way 37924
Larkwood Ln 37921
Larry Cir & Dr 37920
Larue Ln 37938
Larvik Ct 37918
Lasalle Ln 37921
Lassie Way 37909
Latham Ave 37920
Laura Lee Ln 37922
Laura Lynn Cir 37923
Laurans Ave 37915
Laurel Ave 37916
N Laurel Cir 37912
S Laurel Cir 37912
Laurel Brooke Ln 37934
Laurel Creek Way 37924
Laurel Falls Ln 37931
Laurel Grove Ln 37922
Laurel Hill Rd 37923
Laurel Lake Rd 37932
Laurel Oak Ln 37931
Laurel Pointe Ln 37931
Laurel Ridge Ln 37922
Laurel Valley Rd 37934
Laurel View Rd 37917
Laurel Woods Dr 37921
Laurelwood Rd 37918
Lauren Michelle Ln 37924
E & W Laurens Ln 37922
Laurens Glen Ln 37923
Laurinda Rd 37914
Lavendale Cir 37920
Lavender Ln 37921
Laverne Ln 37922
Lavesta Dr 37918
Lawford Rd 37919
Lawhorn Ln 37922
Lawnpark Dr 37923
Lawrence Rd 37912
Lawson Ave 37917
Lawton Blvd 37934
Lay Ave 37914
Layden Dr 37919
Layman St 37920
Layton Ln 37909
Lazy Ln 37912
Lazy Creek Way 37918
Leadenhall Gardens Way 37922
Leahbun Ln 37909
Leath Ln 37931
Leatherwood Ln 37934
Lebanon St 37919
Lebel Rd 37934
Lechmeres Pt 37922
Leclay Dr 37938
Leconte Dr 37915
Leconte Ln 37912
Leconte Rd 37914
Leconte View Ln 37920
Leconte Vista Way 37919
Ledgerwood Ave 37917

Ledgerwood Rd 37938
Lee Ln 37920
Lee Rd
1900-4599 37921
5500-5599 37918
Lee St 37917
Leeland Way 37919
Leenern St 37902
Leeper Ln 37921
Leeper Blake Cir 37924
Leeward Ln 37934
Leflore Ave 37921
Legacy Ln 37919
Legacy Park Rd 37922
Legacy Pointe Way 37921
Legacy View Way 37918
Legend Oaks Ln 37918
Legends Lake Ln 37922
Legg Ln 37924
Legion Dr 37920
Leigh Ln 37920
Leland St 37917
Leland Straw Way 37922
Lemon St 37917
Lemonwood Ln 37921
Lena Ln 37938
Lenbrook Ln 37918
Lenland Ave 37920
Lennox Dr 37909
Lennox View Way 37923
Leon Dr 37914
Leonard Pl 37917
Leonie Ln 37921
Leopard Way 37918
Leroy Ave 37921
Lesa Ln 37912
Lesley Marie Ln 37919
Leslie Ave 37921
Leslie Ann Ln 37931
Lester Rd 37920
Letsinger Rd 37932
Letterman Rd 37919
Levens Way 37922
Lewallen Ct 37914
Lewis Ave 37920
Lewis Rd 37914
Lewisbrooke Ln 37922
Lexann Ln 37917
Lexington Dr 37932
Leyton Dr 37923
Libby Way 37924
Liberty St
100-1199 37919
1200-1499 37909
1500-2099 37921
Liberty Station Ln 37920
Lichen Ln 37920
Lick Creek Way 37924
Light House St 37923
Lighted Path Way 37931
Lightfoot Way 37923
Lightspring Ln 37917
Lilac Ave 37914
Lillian Dr 37920
Lilly Way 37919
Lily Pond Ln 37922
Lilywood Ln 37921
Lima Ln 37923
Lina Ct 37931
Linberry Ln 37914
E Lincoln Cir 37918
W Lincoln Cir 37918
Lincoln Dr 37914
Lincoln St 37920
Lincolnshire Dr 37922
Linda Lou Way 37917
Lindal Rd 37931
Lindbergh Blvd 37917
Linden Ave
1300-2499 37917
2500-3999 37914
Lindenhall Cir 37934
Lindmont Rd 37918
Lindsay Pl 37919
Lindsey Ln 37934
Lindsey Blair Ln 37918
Lindy Dr 37920
Lindy View Ln 37920
Lineback Rd 37921
Linford Rd 37920
Lingburton Ave 37914
Link Pl 37921
Link Rd 37918
Linksvue Dr 37922
Linton Rose Ln 37918
Lion Heart Ln 37919
Lippencott St 37920
Lismore Ln 37922
Litch Field Way 37920
Little Creek Ln 37922
Little Field Way 37923
Little John Ln 37918
Little Madison Way 37923
Little Man Ln 37931
Little Ridge Way 37931
Little River Dr 37920
Little Switzerland Rd 37920
Little Valley Ln 37919
Littlewood Ter 37918
Live Oak Cir 37932
Liveoak Dr 37920
Liverpool Ln 37920
Livingston Dr 37919
Liz Vista Ln 37931
Llanerch Pt 37934
Lloyd Ave 37920
Lobelia Ln 37920
Lobetti Rd 37931
Loblolly Ln 37934
Locarno Dr 37914
Loch View Ct 37922
Lockett Rd 37919
Locklear Way 37931
Lockwood Dr 37918
Locust St 37902
Locust Grove Ln 37918
Locust Hill Ln 37920
Locustwood Way 37921
Lodgepole Ln 37934
Loflin Cir 37922
Loftis Ln 37924
Loftwood Dr 37920
Log Haven Dr 37920
Logan Ave 37921
Loganberry Ln 37934
Loice Ln 37924
Loki Ln 37914
Loma Dr 37922
Lombard Pl 37915
Lon Roberts Dr 37918
Lonas Dr 37909
Lonas Spring Dr 37909
London Cir 37917
Londonderry Rd 37923
Londontown Way 37909
Lone Star Way 37932
Lone Tree Way 37931
Lone Willow Dr 37934
Lonely Oak Ln 37932
Lonesome Pine Dr 37932
Long Ln 37924
Long Bow Rd 37934
Long Branch Dr 37922
Long Farm Way 37932
Long Hollow Rd 37938
Long Leaf Ln 37932
Long Meadow Dr 37920
Long Ridge Rd 37934
Long Shadow Way 37918
Long Shot Ln 37918
Longcreek Ln 37923
Longcress Dr 37918
Longfellow Way 37924
Longford Dr 37922
Longmeade Dr 37923
Longstreet Pl 37934
Longvale Dr 37920
Longview Rd 37919
Longwood Dr 37918
Lonor Dr 37918
Lonsdale Pike 37921
Looking Glass Ln 37919
Lookout Ct 37920
Lookout Pt 37934
Loop Rd 37934
Lora Ln 37914
Loraine St
1200-1399 37909
1400-1799 37921
Lorimar Pl 37919
Lost Tree Ln 37934
Loudoun Rd 37934
Louis Wise Ln 37920
Louise Ave
2300-2499 37915
2500-2799 37914
Louisiana Ave 37921
Louisville Dr 37921
Lourdes Ln 37934
Love Song Ln 37914
Lovelace Rd 37932
Lovell Rd
100-499 37934
500-2499 37932
Lovell Center Dr 37922
Lovell Crossing Way 37932
Lovell Heights Rd 37922
Lovell View Cir & Dr 37932
Lovenia Ave 37917
Loves Creek Rd 37924
Low Country Way 37938
Lowe Rd 37918
Lower Pond Way 37920
Lowland Ln 37920
Lowwood Dr 37920
Loyston Pike 37938
Lucado Way 37909
Lucerne Ln 37921
Lucile Ln 37921
Lucinda Dr 37918
Luck Ave 37917
Lucy Way 37912
Ludbury Ln 37921
Ludlow Ave 37917
Ludlow St 37918
Lufkin Ln 37918
Luger Rd 37918
Luke Valley Way 37938
Lukes Woods Ln 37922
Luna Vista Ln 37922
Lunaria Rd 37920
Lundy Rd 37920
Lupine Dr 37924
Luscombe Dr 37919
Lutie Rd 37912
Luttrell Rd 37918
W Luttrell Rd 37918
Luttrell St 37917
Luwana Ln 37917
Luxmore Dr 37919
Luz Ln 37923
Lyke Rd 37924
Lyle Ave 37919
Lyle Bend Ln 37918
Lyme Ln 37923
Lynbrulee Ln 37920
Lyndell Rd 37918
Lynette Rd 37918
Lynn Ave 37921
Lynn Chase Ln 37932
Lynnmont Rd 37921
Lynnview Dr 37918
Lynnwood Dr
100-128 37918
130-132 37918
131-131 37928
133-399 37918
134-398 37918
Lyons Way 37917
Lyons Bend Rd 37919
Lyons Head Dr 37919
Lyons Pointe Ln 37919
Lyons Ridge Rd 37919
Lyons View Pike 37919
E & W Lyttleton Ln 37922
Lytton Hall Ln 37922
Mable Couch Way 37931
Mabry Hood Rd
100-199 37922
200-200 37932
201-299 37922
202-298 37922
300-1199 37932
Mac Ln 37918
Mac Alice Dr 37918
Macarthur Ln 37934
Macbeth Way 37919
Mace Ln 37938
Macedonia Ln 37914
Macintosh Cir 37932
Mackin Ln 37931
Macqueen Ln 37909
Macy Blair Rd 37931
Madeira Rd 37918
Madison Ave 37932
Madison Ln 37922
Madison Rd 37912
Madison Grove Ln 37922
Madison Oaks Rd 37924
Madison Ridge Ln 37922
Madonna Cir 37918
Madrid Ct 37923
Magazine Rd 37920
Magic Lantern Dr 37918
Magness Rd 37920
Magnet Pl 37915
E Magnolia Ave
100-2499 37917
2500-4099 37914
W Magnolia Ave 37917
Magnolia Grove Way 37922
Magnolia Pointe Ln 37931
Magnum Ln 37918
Mahalia Dr 37921
Mahogany Ln 37938
Mahogany Wood Trl 37920
Main 37901
W Main St 37902
Maintenance Ln 37914
Maize Dr 37918
Majestic Ln 37918
Majestic Grove Rd 37920
Major Ave 37921
Major Reynolds Pl 37919
Majors Rd 37938
Makena Cove Way 37909
Malachi Cir 37918
Malibu Dr 37918
N Mall Rd 37924
S Mall Rd NE 37917
Mall St 37921
Mallard Ln 37923
Mallard Bay Dr 37922
Mallory Rd 37919
Mallow Dr 37922
Malmaison Way 37923
Malmsbury Rd 37921
Maloney Rd 37920
Maloneyville Rd 37918
Malta Rd 37921
Manchester Rd 37920
Mandalay Rd 37921
Manderly Way 37909
Mandrell Dr 37918
Mandy Ct 37921
Mango Dr 37918
Manis Ln 37923
Manis Rd 37924
Mannassas Ln 37917
Manning Ln
1700-1799 37912
12700-12799 37932
Manning Rd 37931
Mannington Dr 37917
Manor Dr 37914
Manor Rd 37920
Manor Crest Ln 37922
Manor Station Ln 37934
Manor View Dr 37923
E & W Mansfield Dr 37918
Mansion Ave 37914
Mantooth Ln 37932
Maple Dr 37918
Maple Ln 37920
Maple Rd 37912
Maple Branch Ln 37912
Maple Chase Way 37918
Maple Creek Way 37931
Maple Crest Ln 37921
Maple Grove Way 37921
Maple Hollow Ln 37931
Maple Knot Ln 37931
Maple Loop Rd 37920
Maple Ridge Ln 37923
Maple Run Ln 37919
Maple Seed Rd 37922
Maple Springs Ln 37931
Maple Sunset Way 37912
Maple Trace Blvd 37918
Maple Valley Ln 37931
Maple View Way 37918
Maplegreen Ln 37922
Maplehill Rd 37914
Maplehurst Ct 37902
Maples Rd 37920
Maples Glen Ln 37923
Maples Mountain Way 37921
Maplestone Ln 37918
Mapletree Dr 37934
Maplewood Dr 37920
Marashi Rd 37920
Marble Hill Blvd 37914
Marble Springs Rd 37920
Marchmont Rd 37923
Marco Ln 37924
Marconi Dr 37909
Mare Haven Ln 37920
Maremont Rd 37918
Margaret Ln 37920
Margaret Rachael Cir 37931
Marguerite Rd 37912
Maria Ave 37921
Marietta Ave 37917
Marietta Church Rd 37932
Marigold Ln 37909
Marilois Ln 37938
Marilyn Dr 37914
Marilyn Collins Way 37931
Marina View Ln 37920
Marine Rd 37920
Mariners Pt 37922
Marion Dr 37918
Marion St 37921
Maritime Way 37920
Marjorie Ln 37917
Mark Rd 37920
Mark Joseph Ln 37931
Market Sq & St 37902
Market Place Blvd 37922
Markham Rd 37922
Markirk Ln 37931
Marlboro Rd 37909
Marlee Park Blvd 37921
Marley Ln 37922
Marmor Dr 37920
Mars Hill Rd 37923
Marsala Ln 37938
Marsfield Rd 37934
Marsha Way 37938
Marshall Dr 37918
Marshall St 37920
Marshall Grove Ln 37922
Marshbird Ln 37922
Marshy Swamp Pt 37932
Marston Ln 37920
Martel Ln 37920
Martha Ave 37921
Martha Ln 37912
Martha Berry Dr 37918
Martha Knight Cir 37932
Martha Oak Ln 37918
Martin Ln 37914
Martin Rd 37938
Martin Luther King Jr Ave
1205-1297 37915
1299-2499 37915
2500-4099 37914
Martin Mill Pike 37920
N & S Martinwood Rd 37923
Marty Cir 37932
Marty Mcguiness Cir 37931
Marvel Ln 37938
Marvin Shafer Way 37931
N & S Mary St 37914
Mary Emily Ln 37924
Mary Sharp Way 37931
Mary Whitaker Way 37923
Maryland Ave 37920
Maryville Pike 37920
Mascarene Rd 37921
Mascot Rd 37924
Mash Ln 37918
Massachusetts Ave 37921
Masters Ln 37918
Masterson Rd 37920
Matalin Ln 37918
Matlock Dr 37921
Matterhorn Ct 37918
Matthew Ln 37923
Matthews Pl 37917
Matthews Cove Ln 37934
Mattox Ln 37922
Maud Booth Way 37917
Maupin Dr 37918
Mauser Pt 37934
Maxey St 37920
Maxwell St 37917
Maxwell Manor Ln 37932
May Ave 37921
May Apple Rd 37920
Mayfair Dr 37920
Mayfield Ave 37920
Mayfield Dr 37918
Mayflower Dr 37920
Maynard Ave 37917
Maynardville Pike
6200-7299 37918
7300-9199 37938
Mays Rd 37914
Mays Chapel Rd 37938
Maywood Rd 37921
Mcabe Ln 37919
Mcbride Ln 37932
Mccall Ln 37920
Mccalla Ave
1100-2299 37915
3900-4399 37914
Mccamey Rd 37918
Mccammon Rd 37920
Mccampbell Ave 37917
Mccampbell Dr
4700-5899 37918
7600-7699 37920
Mccampbell Ln 37918
Mccampbell Hill Ln 37918
Mccampbell Wells Way 37924
Mccarrell Ln 37920
Mccarty Ln & Rd 37914
Mcclain Dr 37912
Mcclellan St 37921
Mccloud Rd 37938
Mccloud Springs Ln 37938
Mcclroy Ave 37919
Mcclung Ave 37920
Mcclure Ln 37920
Mcconnell St 37915
Mccormick Pl 37923
Mccormick St 37920
Mccroskey Ave 37917
Mccubbins Ln & Rd 37924
Mccurry Rd 37924
Mcdaniel Ave 37920
Mcdaniel Rd 37924
Mcdonald Rd 37914
Mcelroy Ave 37919
Mcfall Ln 37918
Mcfee Rd 37934
Mcghee Ave 37921
Mcghee Tyson Airbase 37950
Mcgill Ln 37920
Mcguffeys Dr 37934
Mcintyre Rd 37914
Mckamey Rd 37921
Mckenzie Pl 37917
Mckenzie Meadows Way 37932
Mckinley St 37917
Mckinley Pointe Ln 37934
Mckinnon Ridge Ln 37918
Mcmillan Rd 37914
Mcmillan St 37917
Mcmillan Creek Dr 37924
Mcmillan Station Rd 37924
Mcmillian Rd 37924
Mcminn Ave 37917
Mcmurray St 37917
Mcnabb Ave 37920
Mcneil Mynatt Way 37938
Mcnutt Rd 37920
Mcnutt St 37917
Mcpeake Ln 37909
Mcpherson St 37921
Mcspadden St 37921
Mcteer St 37921
E & W Meadecrest Dr 37923
Meadow Ct 37920
Meadow Rd 37918
Meadow Breeze Way 37918
Meadow Chase Ln 37931
Meadow Cove Pt 37922
Meadow Creek Trl 37931
Meadow Falls Ln 37931
Meadow Glade Ln 37918
Meadow Glen Dr 37919
Meadow Oak Ln 37920
Meadow Pointe Ln 37934
Meadow Ridges Ln 37922
Meadow Rue Trl 37918
Meadow Stone Ln 37938
Meadow Top Ln 37931
Meadow Trace Way 37924
Meadow View Rd 37914
Meadow Vista Cir 37922
Meadow Wells Dr 37924
Meadowbrook Cir 37918
Meadowcrest Way 37918
Meadowfield Dr 37923
Meadowland Dr 37924
Meadowlark Ln 37918
Meadowood Ln 37919
Meadowrun Ln 37931
N Meadows Blvd 37938
Meadowview Ln 37932
Mechanics Way 37921
Mecklenburg Ct 37923
Medallion Ln 37934
Medaris Dr 37938
Medford Rd 37922
Media Dr 37914
Mediate Way 37912
Medical Center Way 37920
Medlin Heights Rd 37918
Mee St 37915
Meeting House Rd 37931
Meg Dr 37914
Meghans Ln 37931
Mehaffey Rd 37931
Melanie Ln 37918
Melbourne Ave 37917
Melford Ln 37934
Melinda Ln 37922
Mellaris 37934
Mellen Ave 37919
Mello Sweet Way 37914
Mellon Point Way 37924
Mellowood Cir 37920
Melody Ln 37912
Melrese Rd 37918
Melrose Ave & Pl 37916
Melstone Rd 37912
Melton Ct 37912
Melton Lake Way 37932
Melton View Ln 37931
Memory Ln 37914
Mendonhall Estates Blvd 37938
Mendosa Dr 37909
Mercedes Ln 37934
Mercer St 37921

Merchant Dr 37912
Merchants Center Blvd 37912
Mercury Dr 37932
Meredith Rd 37921
Merida Dr 37931
Meriwether Ln 37934
Merle Ln 37931
Merlin Cir 37931
Merrick Dr 37919
Merrimac Dr 37934
Merriman Ln 37914
Merrissa Way 37938
Merriwood Dr 37919
Merry Ln 37920
Mesa Verde Ln 37922
Mesquite Ln 37921
Metler Dr 37912
Metler St 37917
Metron Center Way 37919
Metroplex Ct 37917
Metropolitan Way 37921
Miami St 37917
Micah Dr 37938
Micah Ln 37921
Michael St 37914
Michaels Ln
1200-1499 37912
7501-7597 37920
7599-7699 37920
Michaels Ranch Way 37918
Micro Way 37912
Middle Creek Ln 37921
Middle Ridge Ln 37921
Middlebrook Pike
1700-5899 37921
5900-8199 37909
8200-9199 37923
9200-9899 37931
Middlebrook Pike S
4701-4707 37921
N Middlebrook Pike 37921
S Middlebrook Pike
5000-5098 37921
Middlebrook Ridge Ln 37931
Middlefield Ln 37931
Middleground Ln 37923
Middleton Pl 37923
Middleview Way 37909
Midhurst Dr 37934
Midlake Dr 37918
Midland Ave 37919
Midpark Rd 37921
Midshipman Ln 37934
Midsouth Rd 37919
Midview Ln 37938
Midway Rd 37914
Midway St 37921
Mike Campbell Dr 37918
Mikels Ln 37920
Miken Ln 37938
Milam Cir 37919
Milano Way 37923
Mildred Dr 37914
Miles Ct 37923
Mill Rd 37924
Mill Branch Ln 37938
Mill Cove Ln 37931
Mill Creek Ln 37921
Mill Pond Dr 37917
Mill Race Way 37924
Mill Ridge Dr 37919
Mill Run Dr 37922
Millard Beets Rd E &
W 37909
Miller Ave 37920
Miller Creek Rd 37931
Miller Main Cir 37919
Miller Place Way 37924
Millertown Pike
4500-5099 37917
5100-8899 37924
Millet Ln 37918
Milligan St 37914
Millington Park Way 37909
Mills Way 37909
Millsaps Way 37920

Millstone Ln 37922
Millstream Ln 37931
Millwood Rd 37920
Milroy Ln 37918
Milton St 37917
Milwaukee Way 37932
Mimosa Ave 37920
Mineral Springs Ave 37917
Minge Rd 37931
Mingle Ave 37921
Minglewood Rd 37918
Minnesota Ave 37921
Minnis Ave 37920
Mint Rd 37918
Mira Vista Ln 37922
Miracle Ln 37938
Mirkwood Dr 37922
Mishas Meadow Way 37932
Miss Ellie Dr 37921
Mission Rd 37920
Mission Bell Ln 37914
Mississippi Ave 37921
Missoula Way 37932
Missouri Ln 37909
Mistletoe Dr 37924
Misty Trce 37919
Misty Brook Ln 37922
Misty Creek Way 37918
Misty Glen Ln 37909
Misty Grove Ln 37922
Misty Hill Way 37917
Misty Meadow Pl 37919
Misty Mountain Cir 37932
Misty Point Way 37914
Misty Springs Rd 37932
Misty Valley Way 37932
Misty View Ln 37931
Misty Wood Rd 37938
Mitchell Dr 37912
Mitchell St 37917
Mobile Dr 37923
Moccasin Ln 37921
Mockingbird Dr 37919
Mockingbird Ln 37918
Modesto Ln 37934
Mohawk Ave 37915
Mohawk Dr 37914
Mohican St 37919
Mollianna Way 37918
N & S Molly Bright Rd 37924
Mona Ln 37914
Mona Lisa Ln 37918
Monaco Way 37914
Monarch Ct 37918
Mondale Rd 37912
Monday Ln 37914
Moneta Rd 37919
Money Pl 37917
Moneymaker Dr 37923
Monitor Ln 37934
Monmouth St 37917
Monroe Dr 37938
Monroe Ln 37938
Monroe St 37917
Monroe Senter St 37921
Mont Cove Blvd 37922
Mont Glen Dr 37920
Mont Richer Ave 37918
Montacres Ln 37919
Montague Dr 37923
Montalee Way 37924
Montbelle Dr 37918
Montbrook Ln 37919
Montclair Ave 37917
Montcrest Rd 37918
Monte Vista Rd 37914
Monterey Ln & Rd 37912
Montford Ln 37922
Montgenevere Dr 37918
Montgomery Ave 37921
N & S Monticello Dr 37934
Montina Rd 37912
Montlake Dr 37920
Montrose Rd 37918
Montserrat Ln 37921
Montview Rd 37914

Montvue Rd 37919
Montvue Center Way 37919
Montwood Dr 37921
Monument Blvd 37922
E & W Moody Ave 37920
Moody Hollow Rd 37931
Mooers St 37920
Moon Shores Dr 37938
Moonlight Way 37917
Moonlight Meadow
Way 37912
Moore Rd 37920
Moorgate Dr 37922
Moreland Ave 37917
Moreland Heights Rd 37920
E & W Morelia Ave 37917
Moreno Ln 37922
Moreview Ln 37934
Morgan Rd 37920
Morgan St 37917
Morgan Hill Cir 37916
Morgan Overlook Dr 37931
Morgan Path Ln 37934
Morgan Proctor Way 37920
Morgan Springs Way 37917
Morin Way 37920
Morning Breeze Ln 37931
Morning Crest Way 37920
Morning Dew Ln 37931
Morning Dove Cir 37918
Morning Glory Pl 37912
Morningbrooke Blvd 37918
Morningside Dr 37915
Morningstar Ln 37909
Morrell Rd 37919
Morris Ave 37909
Morris Rd 37938
Morrison Way 37919
Morrow Rd 37923
Morton Ln 37920
Morton Manor Way 37923
Morton Place Way 37912
Mortons Meadow Rd 37932
Mosaic Ln 37924
Mosby Cir 37922
Moser Ln 37934
Moses Ave 37921
Moshina Rd 37914
Moss Dr 37912
Moss Creek Rd 37912
Moss Grove Blvd 37922
Moss View Ln 37932
Mossy Hollow Way 37922
Mossy Oaks Ln 37921
Mossy Point Way 37922
Moulden Hollow Rd 37914
Mount Dr 37914
Mount David Dr 37920
Mount Forest Way 37921
Mount Holly Ln 37931
Mount Mabry Ln 37938
Mount Olive Rd 37920
Mount Pleasant Rd
2900-2999 37921
4900-4999 37918
Mount Royal Blvd 37918
Mount Vernon Dr 37920
Mount Vista Dr 37920
Mountain Breeze Ln 37934
Mountain Brook Rd 37938
Mountain Creek Ln 37923
Mountain Grove Dr 37920
Mountain Hill Ln 37931
Mountain Lake Ln 37922
Mountain Laurel Rd 37924
Mountain Mist Ln 37918
Mountain Park Dr 37918
Mountain Pass Ln 37923
Mountain Ridge Ln 37920
Mountain Rise Dr 37938
Mountain Shadow Dr 37918
Mountain Spring Way 37917
Mountain Terrace Rd 37932
Mountain View Rd 37934
Mountain Vista Rd 37931
Mountaincrest Dr 37918

Mountair Dr 37924
Mountcastle St 37916
Mountie Ln 37924
Mourfield Rd 37922
Mowbray Way 37923
Moyers Rd 37920
Mugho St 37912
Muhammed Cir & Dr 37921
Mulberry Rd 37918
Mulligan Way 37922
Mulvaney St 37915
Mundal Rd 37918
Mundy St 37917
Municipal Center Dr
11400-11408 37934
11409-11409 37922
11409-11409 37933
11410-11498 37934
11411-11499 37934
Murdock Dr 37932
Murphy Ave 37921
Murphy Rd 37918
Murray Dr 37912
Murry Dr 37912
Music Way 37920
Musket Trl 37920
Mustang Trl 37920
Mutton Hollow Rd 37920
Muzzle Ln 37918
Myart Ln 37919
Myers Ave 37921
Myloshane Ln 37931
Mynatt Ave 37919
Mynatt Rd 37918
Mynderse Ave 37921
Myrick Way 37931
Myrtle St 37917
Myrtlewood Dr 37921
Mystic St 37922
Mystic Ridge Rd 37922
Mystic River Way 37912
Mystical Way 37923
Nadine St 37917
Nall Dr 37918
Nancy Lynn Ln 37919
Nandina Dr 37912
Nantasket Rd 37922
Napa Valley Way 37931
Naples Rd 37923
Naraca Dr 37922
Nash Rd 37914
Nassau Dr 37934
Natalie Nehs Dr 37931
Natchez Ave & St 37915
Nathan Dr 37938
Nathaniel Rd 37918
N & S National Dr 37914
Nativity Ln 37924
Nature Ln 37912
Nature Trails Blvd 37931
Natures Pond Way 37923
Naueda Dr 37912
Nautical Dr 37934
Navaho Rd 37919
Navarre Dr 37919
Navigator Pt 37922
Navins Ln 37920
Navy Dr 37920
Naylor Ridge Ln 37922
Neal Dr 37918
Neal Chase Way 37918
Neals Commerce Lndg 37914
Neals Landing Rd 37924
Neartop Trl 37923
Needham Ln 37912
Needles Dr 37923
Neel St 37920
Neely Ln 37922
Nehemiah Ln 37938
Neilwoods Dr 37919
Nelson Cir & St 37915
Nerva Rd 37918
Netherland Dr 37918
Nettleton Dr 37917
Neubert Rd 37914
Neubert Quarry Rd 37920

Neubert Springs Rd 37920
Neville Ln 37923
E New St 37915
New Beaver Creek Dr 37931
New Beverly Church
Rd 37918
New Canaan Dr 37922
New Harvest Ln 37918
New Henderson Rd 37931
New York Ave 37921
Newberry Rd 37921
Newcastle Rd 37909
Newcom Ave 37919
Newcomb Ln 37932
Newcross Rd 37922
Newfane Cir 37922
Newgate Rd 37934
Newhill Ave 37920
Newington Ln 37912
Newport Rd 37934
News Sentinel Dr 37921
Newton St 37920
Neyland Dr
300-999 37902
1000-2799 37916
Nicholas Dr & Rd 37912
Nicholas View Ln 37931
Nichols Ave 37917
Nichols Ln
2200-2299 37914
7200-7599 37920
Nichols Rd 37918
Nichols St 37919
Nichols Quarry Rd 37920
Nicholson Ave 37920
Nickerson Ave 37917
Nickle Ln & Rd 37921
Nicks Rd 37918
Nicole Chase Ln 37924
Nighbert Ln 37922
Night Cap Ln 37919
Night Hawk Ln 37923
Night Heron Dr 37922
Nightingale Ln 37909
Nixon Rd 37920
Noah Ln 37932
Nobscot Rd 37919
Noce Dr 37934
Nocona Dr 37909
Nod St 37932
Noelton Dr 37919
E Nokomis Cir 37919
W Nokomis Cir 37919
Nokomis Dr 37914
Nolan Ave 37921
Nolichucky Ln 37920
Nolina Rd 37922
Nora Rd 37918
Nora Mae Ln 37932
Noragate Rd 37919
Noras Path Ln 37932
Norcross Dr 37923
Norcross Rd 37922
Norden Dr 37934
Noremac Rd 37924
Norfolk Dr 37922
Norlake Cir 37922
Norman Jack Ln 37938
Normandy Dr 37919
Norris Fwy
7200-7399 37918
7400-8799 37938
Norris Ln
2300-2599 37924
8500-8699 37938
North Ave 37917
Northampton Blvd 37931
Northboro Rd 37912
Northcrest Cir 37918
Northern Rd 37918
Northgate Dr 37938
Northshire Ln 37922
N Northshore Dr 37919
S Northshore Dr
100-8499 37919
8500-12999 37922

Northshore Hills Blvd 37922
Northshore Woods Dr 37919
Northside Dr 37912
Northview St 37919
Northwind Dr 37919
Northwood Dr 37923
Norton Rd 37920
Norvell Dr 37918
Norwalk Ave 37914
Norway St 37931
Norwind Ln 37912
Norwood Dr 37914
Noslen Rd 37924
Notting Hill Way 37923
Nottingham Rd 37918
Nova Ln 37914
Nubbin Ridge Dr 37919
Nubbin Ridge Rd 37923
Nuggett Rd 37938
Nutgrove Ln 37931
Nuthatcher Rd 37923
Nutmeg Cir 37938
Nutwood Cir 37934
O Barr Rd 37914
Oak Ave 37921
Oak Rd
4900-4999 37912
5600-5899 37918
5900-6099 37912
Oak Branch Cir 37917
Oak Chase Rd 37918
Oak Cove Ln 37922
Oak Creek Ln 37932
Oak Forest Rd 37920
Oak Glade Ln 37918
Oak Glen Way 37921
Oak Grove Ln 37919
Oak Grove St 37920
Oak Hampton Way 37919
Oak Harbor Ln 37921
Oak Haven Rd 37932
E Oak Hill Ave 37917
W Oak Hill Ave
101-111 37917
113-199 37917
700-999 37921
Oak Hollow Rd 37932
Oak Landing Ln 37934
Oak Leaf Rd 37918
Oak Meadow Way 37918
Oak Park Dr 37918
Oak Ridge Hwy
6500-6599 37921
6600-9099 37931
Oak Tree Ln 37938
Oak Valley Dr 37918
Oak Villa Way 37931
Oakbank Ln 37921
Oakborough Ln 37922
Oakbrook Ct 37918
Oakcrest Rd 37912
Oakdale Trl 37914
Oaken Dr 37938
Oakhill Dr 37912
Oakhurst Dr 37919
Oakland Dr 37918
Oakland St 37914
Oakland Hills Pt 37934
Oakleaf Cir 37924
Oakledge Way 37931
Oakleigh Way 37919
Oakleigh Township Dr 37921
Oaklett Dr 37912
Oakley Downs Rd 37934
Oakmont Cir 37934
Oaks Rd 37938
Oakshire Cir 37922
Oakside Dr 37920
Oakstone Ln 37918
Oakvale Dr 37920
Oakview Rd 37918
Oakwood Ln 37921
Oakwood Hills Ln 37931
Oasis Ln 37938
Obrien Rd 37918
Ocala Dr 37918

Ocencor Dr 37909
Ocoee Trl 37917
Oconee Ln 37920
Oconnell Dr 37934
October Ln 37931
Odell Rd 37920
Odessa Ln 37920
Odin St 37932
Office Park Cir 37909
Ogg Rd 37938
Ogle Ave 37920
Oglesby Rd 37914
Oglewood Ave 37917
Ohara Dr 37918
Ohio Ave 37921
Oil Baron Way 37921
Okey St 37920
E & W Oklahoma Ave 37917
Ola Mathis Dr 37912
Old Amherst Rd 37909
Old Andersonville Pike 37938
Old Andes Rd 37931
Old Blacks Ferry Ln 37931
Old Broadway St 37918
Old Callahan Dr 37912
Old Carriage Ct 37923
Old Cedar Bluff Rd 37923
Old Central Avenue
Pike 37912
Old Clinton Pike 37921
Old Cobbs Ferry Rd 37931
Old Colony Pkwy 37934
Old Dandridge Pike 37914
Old Dandridge Stage
Coach Rd 37914
Old French Rd 37920
Old Guinn Rd 37931
Old Henderson Rd 37931
Old Hollow Rd 37938
Old Jacksboro Pike 37938
Old Kent Dr 37919
Old Kingston Pike 37919
Old Maloneyville Ln 37918
Old Maryville Pike 37920
Old Maynardville Pike
6300-6699 37918
7400-9199 37938
Old Mcdonald Rd 37914
Old Millertown Pike 37924
Old Ruggles Ferry
Pike 37924
Old Rutledge Pike 37924
Old Settlers Trl 37920
Old Spanish Trl 37919
Old Stage Rd 37934
Old State Rd 37914
Old Tavern Cir 37934
Old Tazewell Pike 37918
Old Towne Ct 37923
Old Valley Rd 37920
Old Valley View Dr 37917
Old Vine Ave 37915
Old Washington Pike 37918
Old Weisgarber Rd 37909
Olde Colony Trl 37923
Olde Pioneer Trl 37923
Olde Timber Trl 37924
E Oldham Ave 37917
W Oldham Ave
100-499 37917
800-1799 37921
Oleander Way 37931
Oleary Rd 37918
Olive Rd 37934
Olive St 37917
N Olive St 37917
S Olive St 37915
Olive Branch Ln 37931
Olive Grove Ln 37934
Oliver Rd 37920
Olivia Carson Ln 37918
Ollie Davis Dr 37914
Olympic Dr 37934
Omari Ridge Way 37932
Omega Terrace Ln 37938
Omni Ln 37932

One Friday Ln 37922
Oneal St 37921
Ontario St 37914
Op Pickel Ln 37914
Opal Ave 37919
Opal Dr 37912
Orabella Rd 37921
Oran Rd 37934
Orange Ave 37921
Orange Blossom Ln 37931
Orangewood Rd 37921
Orchard Ave
  2900-3299 37917
  6400-6599 37919
Orchard Creek Ln 37918
Orchard Crossing Ln 37934
Orchard Meade Ln 37923
Orchid Dr 37912
Oregon Ave 37921
Oriole Dr 37918
Orkney Cir 37931
Orlando St 37917
Orleans Dr 37919
Ormand Ln 37923
Osage Dr 37921
Osborne Rd 37914
Oscar Armstrong Rd 37914
Osler Ln 37909
Osprey Ln 37922
Osprey Point Ln 37922
Oswald St 37917
Ottari Dr 37918
Ottinger Dr 37920
Outer Dr 37921
Outlet Dr 37932
Ovencene Ave 37916
Overbrook Dr 37920
Overhill Rd 37914
Overland Trl 37919
Overlook Cir 37909
Overton Ln 37923
Overton Pl 37917
Overview Dr 37922
Owana Dr 37914
Owens Rd 37920
Owl Hollow Rd 37923
Ownby Ln 37919
Oxbow Ln 37931
Oxford Dr 37922
Oxford Station Ln 37932
Oxmoor Rd 37931
N Ozark Cir & Rd 37912
Pace Ln 37912
Paces Mill Ln 37938
Pacific St 37917
Packard Ln 37934
Paddington Rd 37922
Paddock Ln 37921
Paige St 37917
Painter Ave 37919
Painter Farm Ln 37931
Palace Ln 37918
Palace Green Rd 37924
Paladin Ln 37934
Palermo Rd 37918
Palestine Ln 37934
Palm Dr 37914
Palm Beach Way 37922
Palmer Ln 37924
Palmer St 37920
Palmetto Rd 37921
Palmleaf Rd 37918
Palmstone Ln 37918
Palmwood Dr 37921
Palmyra Dr 37918
Palomino Way 37922
Pam Ct 37918
Pamela Ln 37920
Panama Dr 37923
Pandora Rd 37919
Panorama Dr 37920
Pansy Ave 37921
Papermill Dr
  3500-5199 37909
  6001-6097 37919
  6099-6899 37919
Papermill Sq 37909
Papermill Place Way 37919
Papermill Pointe Way 37909
Paramount Rd 37924
Parasol Ln 37924
Parham St 37915
Paris Rd 37912
Parish St 37914
N Park Blvd 37917
N Park Cir 37912
S Park Cir 37912
NW Park Dr 37921
W Park Dr 37909
Park St 37914
N Park 40 Blvd 37923
Park Edge Way 37923
Park Glen Rd 37919
Park Grove Ln 37921
Park Hill Cir 37909
Park Place Blvd 37934
Park Shadow Way 37924
Park Village Rd 37923
Park West Blvd 37923
Parkbrook Ln 37919
Parkdale Rd 37912
Parker Rd 37924
Parker Hill Ln 37924
Parkgate Ln 37934
Parklake Dr 37920
Parkman Dr 37918
Parkridge Cir & Dr 37924
Parkside Dr
  9500-10699 37922
  10700-11699 37934
Parkstone Ln 37924
Parktop Ln 37923
Parkview Ave
  2100-2499 37917
  2500-2799 37914
W Parkway Ave 37912
Parkway Dr 37918
Parkwood Rd 37921
Parliament Dr 37919
Parrish Rd 37923
Parrish Hill Ln 37938
Parsonage Ln 37920
Partners Pl 37921
Partridge Ln 37923
Partridge Run Ln 37919
Parva Dr 37914
Pasadena Ln 37922
Pascal Dr 37921
Pat Rd 37922
Patel Way 37909
Path Way 37931
Pathfinder Ln 37932
Patricia Cir 37914
Patriot Way 37931
Patsy Ave 37921
Patton St 37915
Patty Rd 37924
Paula Rd 37912
Pauline Way 37938
Pauly Brook Way 37932
Pavestone Way 37931
Pawnee Rd 37909
Paxton Dr 37918
Paxton Grove Ln 37922
Payne Rd 37914
Peach View Dr 37922
Peachtree St 37920
Peachwood Rd 37921
Peacock Way 37914
Peaks Landing Way 37918
Pear Leaf Cir 37934
Pearl Pl 37917
Pearson Ave 37920
Pebble Beach Pt 37934
Pebble Creek Rd 37918
Pebble Point Ln 37938
Pebble Run Way 37918
Pebble Shore Ln 37931
Pebblebrook Way 37921
Pebblestone Ln 37938
Pecanwood Way 37921
Pecos Rd 37934
Pedigo Rd 37938
Pedigo St 37920
Pelahatchia Way 37912
Pelham Rd 37914
Pell St 37920
Pellashore Way 37922
Pelleaux Rd 37938
Pellissippi Pkwy
  200-2499 37932
  2500-3499 37931
Pelsor Ln 37918
Peltier Rd 37912
Pembridge Rd 37912
Pembroke Ave 37917
Pemmbrooke Shire Ln 37909
Pendelton Dr 37924
Penelope Ln 37918
Penfield Ln 37918
Pennell Ln 37931
Pennington Way 37909
Penny Ln 37918
Pennyroyal Dr 37920
Penrod Ln 37918
Pensacola Rd 37923
Pentucket Way 37921
Penwood Dr 37922
Peony Dr 37918
W Pepper Ct 37923
Peppercorn Ln 37912
Pepperdine Way 37923
Pepperhill Rd 37921
Peppertree Ln 37923
Pepperwood Ln 37934
Pequoid St 37915
Perch Dr 37922
Percival Way 37919
Percy Way 37923
Peregrine Way 37922
Perennial Way 37914
Pergola Way 37914
Perimeter Park Rd 37922
Periwinkle Rd 37918
Perry Rd 37914
Pershing St 37917
Pershing Hill Ln 37919
Persimmon Ln 37922
Perth Cir 37922
Pertinax Dr 37918
N Peters Rd
  100-299 37923
  300-599 37922
S Peters Rd
  100-499 37923
  500-899 37922
Petersburg Rd 37921
Peterson Ln 37920
Peterson Rd 37934
Petsafe Way 37932
Pettway Ave 37920
Pewter Dr 37909
Peyton Pl 37918
Pheasant Ln 37923
Pheasant Ridge Trl 37922
Pheasants Glen Dr 37923
Phifer Ln 37918
Philips Dr 37914
Phillipi Ln 37917
Phillips Ave 37920
Phlox Ln 37919
Phyllis Ln 37938
Piccadilly Rd 37909
Pickel Ln 37914
Pickens Gap Rd 37920
Pickering St 37914
Picket Place Way 37923
Pickett Ave 37921
Pickle Ln 37914
Pickwick Rd 37914
Piedmont St 37921
Pierre Marques St 37938
Pike Pl 37920
Pilkay Rd 37919
Pilleaux Dr 37912
Pimbrook Ln 37923
Pin Oak Cir 37934
W Pine Ln 37909
Pine Bluff Blvd 37909
Pine Brook Dr 37922
Pine Cone Ln 37932
Pine Creek Rd 37932
Pine Garden Ln 37923
Pine Glen Way 37921
Pine Grove Rd 37914
Pine Harbor Ln 37938
Pine Hill Dr 37932
Pine Hill Ln 37920
Pine Knoll Ct 37920
Pine Marten Way 37909
Pine Meade Rd 37923
Pine Meadows Ln 37934
Pine Needle Ln 37921
Pine Ridge Rd 37938
Pine Springs Rd 37922
Pine Thicket Ln 37922
Pine Valley Rd 37923
Pinebark Dr 37931
Pinebrook Dr 37909
Pinecrest Dr 37918
Pinecrest Rd 37912
Pinecroft Ln 37914
Pinedale Dr 37922
Pinehurst Dr 37917
Pinehurst Rd 37920
Pinellas Dr 37919
Pinen Dr 37938
Pineola Ln 37919
Pinestraw Ln 37932
Pinetree Ln 37909
Pineview Rd 37918
Pineway Cir 37912
Pinewood Dr 37918
Pinex Ln 37921
Piney Grove Church Rd
  900-2399 37909
  2400-2599 37921
Pinnacle Dr 37914
Pinnacle Pointe Way 37922
Pinner Dr 37919
Pinoak Ct 37923
Pintail Rd 37934
Pioneer Trl 37924
Piper Rd 37919
Piper Grove Ln 37931
Piperton Ln 37931
Pipkin Ln 37922
Pitner Pl 37920
Pittman Dr 37932
Pitts Field Ln 37922
Plainfield Rd 37923
Planingt Rd 37912
Plantation Dr 37921
Plantation Pine Dr 37921
Plantation Trace Way 37912
Platinum Dr 37938
Playground Rd 37924
Plaza St 37920
Pleasant Forest Dr 37934
Pleasant Hill Rd 37924
Pleasant Knoll Ln 37915
Pleasant Ridge Rd
  3100-3899 37921
  3900-6299 37912
  6300-6899 37921
Pleasant Run Ln 37918
Pleasant Square Way 37921
Pleasant Trace Cir 37912
Pleasant View Ln 37914
Pleasantwood Dr 37921
Plum St 37920
Plum Creek Dr 37922
Plum Field Way 37920
Plum Rose Ln 37918
Plumb Branch Rd 37932
Plumb Creek Cir 37932
Plumb Ridge Rd 37932
Plumlee Ln
  100-199 37924
  5900-5999 37914
Plummer Dr 37918
Plumwood Dr 37921
Plyly St 37920
Plymouth Rd 37914
Pocahontas Dr 37914
Pocanno Rd 37919
Poets Corner Way 37919
W Point Dr 37934
S Point Rd 37920
Point Oaks Dr 37919
Point Wood Dr 37920
Polk St 37917
Polkwright Ln 37919
Pollock Ln 37914
Polo Club Ln 37922
Polte Ln 37922
Pompeii Ln 37918
Pond Run Way 37924
Pond View Way 37932
Ponder Cir & Rd 37923
Pondside Ln 37931
Pony Express Dr 37934
Popejoy Rd 37922
Popen Dr 37938
Poplar Pl 37918
Poplar Crest Way 37918
Poplar Glen Dr 37922
Poplar Hill Rd 37922
Poplar Ridge Rd 37932
Poplar Wood Trl 37920
Poppy Ln 37922
Poppywood Rd 37932
Porch Swing Rd 37938
Porchfield Ln 37934
E Port Dr 37922
Port Charles Dr 37934
Port Royal Ln 37938
Porter Ave 37914
Porterfield Gap Rd 37920
Portland St 37919
Portsmouth Rd 37909
Post Oak Dr 37920
Poston Way 37918
Potomac Rd 37920
Potter St 37917
Potterstone Dr 37922
Power Dr 37920
Powers St 37917
Prairie Clover 37918
Praise Ln 37918
Prater Ln 37922
Pratt Rd
  5300-5599 37912
  8300-8599 37920
Pratt St 37917
Pratts Chapel Ln 37924
Prentice Ave 37914
Presario Ln 37920
Prescott Way 37919
Presidential Ln 37931
Presidents Dr 37934
Pressnell Ln 37924
Preston Ln 37921
Preston Landing Way 37922
Prestonwood Ln 37921
Prestwick Ct 37923
Prestwick Ridge Way 37919
Price Ave 37920
Price Ln 37922
Prime Way 37918
Primrose Ave 37921
Primus Rd 37912
Prince Albert Way 37934
Prince George Parish Dr 37934
Princess Ln 37931
Princess Ann Ct 37918
Princeton Ct 37919
Princeton Falls Ln 37938
Prindend Ave 37915
Prism Ln 37921
Probus Rd 37918
Proctor St 37921
Proffitt Ln 37931
Prospect Pl 37915
Prospect Rd 37920
Prosperity Rd 37923
Prosser Rd 37914
Providence Way 37931
Providence Glen Ln 37934
Providence Grove Way 37919
Providence Ridge Way 37932
Provincial Dr 37909
Provision Cares Way 37909
Pruden Dr 37918
Pruett Pl 37917
Pryor Dr 37921
Pryse Farm Blvd 37934
Pueblo Pl 37921
Pugh Ave 37920
Pugh Hall Ln 37938
Pulaski Rd 37914
Pullman Way 37918
Pump House Way 37938
Purdue Dr 37921
Purple Martin Way 37922
Putters Way 37922
Quail Dr 37919
Quail Grove Ln 37920
Quail Hollow Rd 37923
Quail Pointe Rd 37934
Quail Ridge Ln 37920
Quail Run Rd 37938
Quails Bend Ln 37923
Quality Ln 37931
Quarry Rd 37938
Queen St 37917
Queen Anne Way 37916
Queen Victoria Way 37934
Queenborough Ln 37931
Queensbridge Dr 37922
Queensbury Dr 37919
Queensgate Dr 37918
Quicksilver Way 37922
Quiet Way 37918
Quiet Brook Ln 37914
Quiet Pond Way 37932
E & W Quincy Ave 37917
Raccoon Valley Dr 37938
Raceland Way 37934
Rachelle Ct 37923
Racing Run Rd 37920
Racquet Club Way 37923
Rader Pl 37917
Radford Pl 37917
Radiance Dr 37912
Radnor Rd 37918
Raeburn Ln 37934
Ragsdale Ave 37909
Railside Ave 37914
Rain Forest Dr 37923
Rain Tree Rd 37923
Rainbow Dr 37922
Rainbow Rd 37912
Rainbow Falls Rd 37922
Rainbow Hill Ln 37938
Rainbow Ridge Way 37919
Raindrop Rd 37923
Rainer Blvd 37918
Raines Ln 37920
Rainpointe Way 37931
Raj Rd 37921
Raleigh Ave 37917
Rambling Rd 37912
Rambling Brooks Ln 37918
Ramona Ct & St 37921
Ramsey Ln 37914
Ramsey St 37921
Ramsgate Dr 37919
Randall Park Dr 37922
Randolph St
  100-199 37915
  200-699 37917
Randonell Rd 37920
Ranger Ln 37924
Rangeview Way 37920
Rapids Rd 37914
Raposa Rd 37923
Rare Earth Dr 37938
Rather Rd 37931
Ratliff Ln 37914
Raven Ct 37922
Raven Rd 37918
Raven Grove Way 37918
Raven Hill Ct 37922
Ravenbrook Ln 37922
Ravenel Cir 37922
Ravenwood Cir 37922
Rawhide Trl 37920
Ray Gap Rd 37920
Ray Krebbs Ct 37921
Ray Mears Blvd 37919
Razell Way 37932
Reagan Ave 37919
Reagan Rd 37931
Reagan Woods Ln 37931
Reaves Rd 37912
Rebecca Ln 37920
Rebel Pass 37934
Recreation Ln 37918
Rector St 37921
Red Ashe Ln 37918
Red Bay Way 37919
E & W Red Bud Dr & Rd 37920
Red Canyon Rd 37934
Red Clover Ln 37918
Red Dog Ln 37914
Red Ellis Ln 37924
Red Fox Dr 37922
Red Hellard Ln 37923
Red Hill Ct 37924
Red Leaf Way 37923
Red Maple Ct 37931
Red Meadow Rd 37931
Red Mill Ln 37934
Red Saile Rd 37909
Red Valley Way 37918
Red Water Ln 37932
Reddege Rd 37918
Redeemer Ln 37919
Redgrave Rd 37922
Redmont Ln 37922
Redoak Ln 37919
Redrock Ln 37938
Redtail Hawk Way 37921
Redwen Rd 37938
Redwine St 37920
Redwing Ln 37931
Redwood Rd 37920
Redwood Burl Ln 37931
Ree Way 37909
Reece Way 37918
Reed Ln 37920
Reed St 37921
Reedsworth Ln 37922
Reflection Bay Dr 37938
Regal Ln 37918
Regality Way 37923
Regency Rd 37931
Regent Ln 37923
Regents Park Rd 37922
Region Ln 37914
Rehburg Way 37932
Reinhardt Ln 37924
Reliability Cir 37932
Reliant Ln 37914
Rellim Rd 37914
Remagen Ln 37920
Remington Rd 37923
Remington Way 37919
Remington Grove Ln 37909
Renaissance Ln 37934
Rendava Ln 37921
Renford Rd 37919
Rennboro Rd 37923
Rennoc Rd 37918
Reno Ln 37922
Repass Dr 37920
Representative Ln 37931
Research Dr 37932
Reserve Ln 37914
Resolute Rd 37918
Reston Ct 37923
Retreat Way 37920
Revere Ln 37923
Rex Rd 37924
Rexburg Dr 37921
Reynolds St 37921
Rhea Rd 37920
Rhealand Ln 37921

Rhett Ln 37922
Rhode Island Rd 37912
Rhodes Valley Way 37920
Rhododendron Ct 37931
Rhodora Ct & Rd 37923
Rhonda Ln 37920
Rhyne Ln 37918
Rhyne Cove Ln 37931
Richard Ln 37914
Richard Browning Way 37920
Richards St 37921
Richfield Ln 37924
Richland Colony Rd 37923
Richmond Ave 37921
Richwood Ln 37932
Rickard Dr NW 37912
Ricketts Ln 37932
Ridan Dr 37909
Rider Ave 37917
Ridge Ave 37917
S Ridge Rd 37920
Ridge Creek Ln 37938
Ridge Grove Rd 37918
Ridge Oak Ln 37922
Ridge Run Dr 37921
Ridgebrook Ln 37921
Ridgecrest Dr 37918
Ridgecross Way 37920
Ridgedale Rd 37921
Ridgefield Rd 37912
Ridgegate Ln 37931
Ridgeland Dr 37932
Ridgemont Dr 37918
Ridgepark Ln 37912
Ridgepath Ln 37922
Ridgerock Ln 37909
Ridges Meadow Ln 37931
Ridgetop Rd 37921
Ridgeview Rd 37918
Ridgewalk Ln 37931
Ridgeway Ln 37919
Ridgewood Rd 37918
Rifle Range Rd 37918
Riggs Ave 37920
Rim St 37917
Ring Rd 37924
Rio Vista Ln 37919
Ripon Cir 37923
Rippling Dr 37932
Rising Rd 37924
Rising Brooks Ln 37918
Rising Fawn Dr 37923
Rising Mist Ln 37922
Rising Ridge Way 37931
Rising View Ln 37922
Rival Ln 37918
Rivanna Ln 37922
Rivendell Way 37922
N & S River Trl 37922
River Bank Way 37922
River Berry Way 37914
River Birch Ct 37932
River Breeze Ln 37923
River Club Way 37922
River Crest Dr 37922
River Dale Ln 37932
River Haven Pt 37922
River Landing Way 37914
River Maple Way 37914
River Oak Dr 37920
River Oaks Pt 37922
River Place Dr 37914
River Point Cove Rd 37919
River Ridge Rd 37922
River Shores Dr 37914
River Sound Dr 37922
River Towne Way 37920
River Trace Blvd & Ln 37920
River Valley Way 37923
Riverbend Dr 37919
Riverbriar Rd 37919
Riverchase Dr 37920
Riveredge Cir 37920
Riverfront Way 37915
Rivergate Dr 37920
Riverlake Dr
7500-7599 37920
10600-10699 37922
Rivermist Ln 37922
Rivers Run Dr 37914
Riverside Dr
100-2499 37915
2500-3799 37914
Riverside Rd 37914
Riverside Forest Way 37915
Riverstone Ln 37918
Riverview Dr 37914
Riverview Crossing Dr 37924
Riverwalk Ln 37922
Riverwood Dr 37920
Riviera Way 37922
Roaming Dr 37912
Roane Dr 37934
Roanoke Cir 37920
Robert Huff Ln 37914
Robert Love Dr 37914
Roberts Dr 37918
Roberts Rd 37924
Robin Rd 37918
Robin Ben Ln 37924
Robin Heights Dr 37921
Robin Hood Rd 37919
Robindale Dr 37921
Robins Nest Ln 37919
Robinson Rd 37923
Robinson Ridge Ct 37923
Robinwood Ln 37922
Rochat Dr 37918
Rochdale Ln 37931
Rock Arbor Way 37922
Rock Bridge Ln 37921
Rock Springs Dr 37932
Rockbrook Dr 37931
Rockcrest Rd 37918
Rockford Ln 37922
Rockhaven Rd 37920
Rockingham Dr 37909
Rockley Rd 37932
Rockstone Ln 37938
Rockwell Rd 37920
Rockwell Farm Ln 37934
Rockwood Ln 37921
Rocky Ln 37918
Rocky Branch Way 37918
Rocky Creek Way 37918
Rocky Hill Ln & Rd 37919
Rocky Mountain High
Blvd 37918
Rocky Path Ln 37931
Rocky Ridge Way 37924
Rocky View Way 37918
Rodeo Dr 37934
Roderick Rd 37923
Roemeadow Ln 37922
Rogers Ln 37920
Rogers St 37917
Rogers Island Rd 37922
Rohar Rd 37921
Rojo Ln 37922
Roland Ln 37931
Rollen Rd 37920
Rolling Creek Rd 37934
Rolling Hills Ln 37931
Rolling Meadows Ln 37932
Rolling Ridge Dr 37921
Rollins Rd 37918
Romines Dr 37914
Romulus Ln 37931
Rondo Rd 37918
Ronnie Ln 37920
Roosevelt Rd 37914
Rosalyn Dr 37914
Rosann Ln 37918
Roscoe Ln 37914
Rose Dr 37918
Rose Briar Ct 37938
Rose Garden Way 37919
Rose Petal Ln 37938
Rose Wine Way 37931
Rosebay Rd 37918
Rosedale Ave 37915
Rosedown Ct 37918
Rosemont Blvd 37923
Rosewood Rd 37924
Ross Rd 37914
Ross Mccloud Way 37938
Roswell Rd 37923
Roth Way 37918
Rotherwood Dr 37919
Rothesay Ln 37909
Rothmoor Dr 37918
Round Hill Ln 37912
Round Table Way 37919
Roundlake Way 37918
Roundtree Rd 37923
Rouse Ln 37918
Rowan Cir & Rd 37912
Rowena Ln 37931
Roxbury Pt 37922
Roy Dr 37923
Roy Lowe Ln 37920
Royal Birkdale Rd 37934
Royal Crown Dr 37919
Royal Harbor Dr 37922
Royal Heights Dr 37920
Royal Mew Ct 37922
Royal Oaks Dr 37931
Royal Prince Way 37912
Royal River Dr 37914
Royal Springs Blvd 37918
Royal Way Ln 37934
Royalview Rd 37921
Rubicon Ln 37932
Rubin Reed Rd 37920
Ruble Rd 37920
Rucker Rd & St 37921
Rudder Ln 37919
Rudder Rd 37920
Rudder Falls Way 37919
Rudder Oaks Way 37919
Rudder Valley Ln 37919
Rudy St 37921
Ruffian Ln 37923
Rufford Ln 37922
Rufus Graham Rd 37924
Rugby Ave 37920
Ruggles Dr 37924
Ruggles Ferry Pike 37924
Ruh Rd 37918
Rule Rd 37920
Rum Hill Ln 37923
Runnymede Dr 37918
Rush Limbaugh Ln 37932
Rush Miller Rd 37914
Rushbrook Dr 37923
Rushing Wind Ln 37922
Rushland Park Blvd 37924
Rushmere Ln 37922
Rushmore Dr 37923
Ruskin Dr 37923
Russell Run Rd 37918
Russfield Dr 37934
Russgate Blvd 37934
Russwood Dr 37920
Rustic Ln 37938
Rustic Bridge Trl 37932
Rustic Oak Dr 37919
Rutgers Dr 37919
Rutland Cir 37934
Rutledge Pike
4000-5099 37914
5100-8899 37924
Ryan Pl 37919
Rye Ln 37918
Ryegate Dr 37922
Sable Point Ln 37924
Sabre Dr 37919
Saddle Way 37922
Saddle Creek Pass 37921
Saddle Path Ln 37931
Saddle Ridge Dr 37934
Saddlebrooke Dr 37938
Saddlecrest Ln 37923
Saddlegate Rd 37920
Saddlerack St 37914
Saga Ln 37931
Sage Ln 37931
Sagebrush Way 37932
Sagefield Dr 37920
Sagemont Ln 37934
Sagewood Dr 37932
Sailpointe Ln 37922
Sails Way 37932
Sailview Rd 37934
Saint Andrews Dr 37934
Saint Anselm Ln 37922
Saint Catherine Ct 37938
Saint Charles Ln 37934
Saint Croix Ln 37918
Saint Francis Way 37919
Saint Germaine Dr 37922
Saint Gregorys Ct 37931
Saint Ives Blvd 37922
Saint James Ave 37920
Saint John Ct 37934
Saint Lucia Ln 37921
Saint Mary St 37917
Saint Paul St 37920
Saint Petersburg Rd 37922
Saint Regence Ln 37922
Saint Simon Way 37912
Saint Thomas Ave 37923
Salem St 37919
Salem Church Rd 37938
Salford Way 37912
Salisbury Ln 37934
Sallee Ln 37918
Sallings Rd 37922
Salome Ln 37938
Saluda Rd 37922
Sam Cooper Ln 37918
Sam Crawford Ln 37931
Sam Cruze Rd 37920
Sam Houston St 37920
Sam Lee Rd 37932
Sam Tillery Ln 37918
Sam Walton Way 37938
Sammara Way 37920
Sams Ln 37920
Samuel Ln 37938
San Cristebal Ln 37921
San Jose Ln 37922
San Juan Ln 37914
San Lucki Way 37909
San Madre Dr 37922
San Marcos Dr 37938
San Martin Ln 37934
San Miguel Ln 37922
Sanborn Ave 37917
Sanctuary Ln 37932
Sand St 37914
Sand Hill Ln 37918
Sand Point Dr 37914
Sandalwood Rd 37921
Sanderling Ln 37922
Sanders Dr 37918
Sanders Ln 37915
Sanders Rd 37923
Sanderson Rd 37921
Sandhurst Dr 37923
Sandis Ln 37924
Sandpiper Ln 37922
Sandra Ave 37917
Sandra Dr 37918
Sandringham Ct 37934
Sands Rd 37931
Sandstone Rd 37931
Sandstone Loop Way 37920
Sandusky Rd 37912
Sandy Ln 37920
Sandy Knoll Way 37918
Sanford Pl 37917
Sanford Rd 37912
Sanford Day Rd 37919
Sanland Ave 37914
Sanquine Way 37917
Santa Fe Trl 37919
Santa Monica Rd 37918
Santala Dr 37909
Santeelah Ln 37918
Sanwood Rd 37923
Sapphire Rd 37919
Sarah Ln 37924
Sarasota Dr 37923
Saratoga Cir & Dr 37920
Sarvis Dr 37920
Saturn Ln 37932
Sauer Pt 37934
Savage Ln 37938
Savannah Ct 37923
Savoy St 37921
Sawgrass Rd 37922
Sawyer Ln 37924
Saxton Ave 37915
Saybrook Ln 37923
Saylor Ct 37917
Sayne Ln 37920
Scalybark Dr 37920
Scarborough Ln 37918
E & W Scarlett Ct &
Ln 37920
Scarlett Oak Ct 37909
Scenic Dr 37919
Scenic Hills Rd 37912
Scenic Oaks Rd 37938
Scenic Ridge Cv 37923
Scenic Ridge Rd 37912
Scenic Valley Ln 37922
Scenic View Cir & Dr 37938
Scenicwood Rd 37912
Scepter Way 37912
Schaad Rd
2700-4399 37921
4600-5399 37931
Schaeffer Rd 37932
Scheel Rd 37912
Schenley Rd 37923
Schofield St 37921
School View Way 37938
Schoolcraft Way 37919
Schooner Ln 37934
Schriver Rd 37919
Schubert Rd 37912
Scioto Pt 37934
Scots Pine Ln 37922
Scotsbury Cir 37919
Scotswood Cir 37919
E Scott Ave 37917
W Scott Ave
100-299 37917
500-1299 37921
Scott Ln 37922
Scottie Ln 37919
Scottish Pike 37920
Scottsdale Dr 37922
Sea Ray Dr 37914
Seabury Ct 37931
Seahorn Ave 37914
Seaman St 37919
Sean Grove Way 37921
Seasonal Way 37909
Seaton Ave 37920
Seattle Slew Ln 37931
Seaver Dr 37909
Secluded Way 37918
Secretariat Blvd 37931
Sedalia Trl 37920
Sedgefield Dr 37923
Sedgefield Rd 37934
Sedgewick Dr 37922
Sedgley Dr 37922
Seeber Dr 37918
Seekirk Ln 37931
Selby Ln 37922
Sellers Ln 37932
Selma Ave
2400-2499 37915
2500-4199 37914
Seminole Ave 37915
Seminole Ln 37914
Seminole Rd
100-499 37914
4600-4899 37918
Senate Ln 37931
Senators Trl 37920
Seneca Rd 37914
Sentry Ln 37919
Sepal Way 37921
September Ln 37924
Sequoyah Ave & Sq 37919
Sequoyah Gardens
Way 37919
Serena Cir 37919
Serene Cove Way 37920
Serenity Ln 37934
Serlio Way 37920
E & W Sesame Ln 37938
Settlers Trl 37924
Settlers Cove Ln 37922
Settlers Path Ln 37920
Settlers Pond Way 37923
Settlers Ridge Ln 37931
Seve Ln 37909
Seven Islands Rd 37920
N Seven Oaks Dr 37922
Sevenoaks Trl 37922
Sevier Ave 37920
Sevier Heights Rd 37920
Sevierville Pike 37920
Sexton Ln 37932
Seymour Ave 37917
Shade Tree Ln 37922
Shade Weaver Rd 37938
Shadewell Dr 37938
Shadow Ln 37922
Shadow Brook Dr 37922
Shadow Creek Rd 37918
Shadow Ridge Dr 37918
Shadowfax Rd 37934
Shadowood Dr 37938
Shady Ln 37918
Shady Bend Ln 37922
Shady Dell Trl 37914
Shady Glen Way 37922
Shady Grove Ln 37921
Shady Hollow Ln 37922
Shady Knoll Ln 37919
Shady Meadow Ln 37932
Shady Mill Ln 37922
Shady Oak Ln 37931
Shady Pines Rd 37919
Shady Ridge Ln 37934
Shady Slope Way 37932
Shady Springs Ln 37923
Shady View Ln 37922
Shadybrook Cove Ln 37922
Shadycrest Dr 37909
Shadyland Dr 37919
Shadywood Ln 37923
Shaftsbury Dr 37921
Shaker Dr 37931
Shaler Ln 37920
Shalidar Dr 37921
Shalimar Rd 37914
Shalimar Point Way 37918
Shallow Brook Cir 37931
Shallow Cove Way 37938
Shallowford Rd 37923
Shamrock Ave 37917
Shamrock Dr 37918
Shamus Way 37918
Shane Ln 37921
Shangri La Dr 37914
Shanianc Dr 37918
Shanks Ln 37938
Shannon Ln
4900-5099 37918
6601-6699 37920
Shannon Run Dr 37918
Shannon Valley Dr 37918
Shannon Valley Farms
Blvd 37918
Shannondale Rd 37918
Sharae Dr 37924
Sharon Rd 37919
Sharon View Dr 37938
Sharp Ln 37912
Sharps Ridge Mem Park
Dr 37917
Sharpsburg Rd 37917
Shasta Dr 37912
Shaunessy Way 37932
Shaw Dr 37917
Shawn Rd 37923
Shawnee Ln 37919
Shea St 37921
Shearwater Ln 37922
Sheffield Dr 37909
Shelbourne Rd 37917
Shelbyville Rd 37922
Sheldon Chase Ln 37932
Shell Ln 37918
Shelley Dr 37909
Shenandoah Dr 37909
Shepard St 37917
Sheraton Ln 37920
Sherbourne Dr 37919
Sheretz Dr 37923
Sheridan St 37921
Sherlake Ln 37922
Sherman St 37921
Sherrill Blvd 37932
Sherrod Dr 37924
Sherrod Rd 37920
Sherry Dr 37918
Sherway Rd 37922
Sherwin Rd 37931
Sherwood Dr 37919
Shetland Dr 37920
Shields Ave 37914
Shielingworth Ct 37921
Shiloh Dr 37909
Shimla Way 37922
Shimmering Brooks Ln 37918
Shinnecock Ln 37918
Shipe Rd 37924
Shipman Dr 37918
Shipwatch Ln 37920
Shirecliffe Ln 37934
Shirland Ct 37922
Shirley Way 37909
Shirley Couch Way 37931
Shoaf Ln 37914
Shoffner Ln 37938
Shoppers Ln 37921
Shore Line Rd 37932
Shorecove Way 37922
Shoregate Ln 37938
Shoreham Blvd & Cir 37922
Shorewood Ln 37932
Short Rd 37921
Shorthorn Dr 37931
Shotsman Ln 37918
Shrewsbury Dr 37921
Shumaker Rd 37924
Shumard Ave 37914
Side Board Rd 37918
Sidebrook Ave 37921
Siena Ln 37934
Sierra Rd 37912
Sierra Vista Ln 37922
Signal Point Rd 37922
Signal Station Rd 37920
Signature Ln 37922
Silent Brook Ln 37921
Silent Springs Ln 37931
Silicon Valley Way 37931
Silkwood Rd 37920
Silo Way 37923
Silva Dr 37914
Silver Pl 37917
Silver Birch Ct 37931
Silver Charm Way 37938
Silver Cloud Ln 37909
Silver Creek Rd 37924
Silver Fox Ln 37909
Silver Grass Ln 37931
Silver Grove Ln 37931
Silver Leaf Way 37931
Silver Maple Ln 37919
Silver Springs Dr 37932
Silverbell Cir 37921
Silverbrook Dr 37923
Silverdale Ln 37922
Silveredge Rd & Way 37918
Silverglen Ln 37921
Silverhawk Way 37923
Silverhill Dr 37921
Silverstone Ln 37932
Silverwood Rd 37921

Street	ZIP
Simmons Rd	
300-499	37922
500-699	37932
Simona Rd	37918
Simpson Rd & St	37920
Sims Rd	37920
Sinclair Dr	37914
Singing Hills Pt	37934
Singletree Ln	37922
Sinking Springs Rd	37914
Sioux Ln	37914
Sir Arthur Way	37919
Sir Keegan Way	37916
Sir Walter Way	37919
Sisk Rd	37921
Siske Ave	37931
Sky Dr	
200-299	37920
300-399	37912
Sky Blue Dr	37923
Sky Song Ln	37914
Skylark Rd	37938
Skyline Dr	37914
Skyview Dr	37917
Slade Dr	37931
Slate Valley Ln	37923
Slater Mill Ln	37921
Sleepy Fox Ln	37922
Sleepy Hollow Way	37924
Slippery Rock Ln	37931
Sloping Hill Ln	37931
Smallman Rd	37920
Smallwood Dr	37920
Smelser Rd	37920
Smith Ln	37920
Smith Rd	37934
Smith Evans Ln	37920
Smith School Rd	37914
Smithland Ln	37931
Smithwood Rd	37918
Smoke Creek Rd	37934
Smoke Rise Ln	37922
Smoke Tree Rd	37938
Smokey Falls Way	37924
Smokey Ridge Way	37931
Smoky Trl	37909
Smoky River Rd	37931
Smoky View Rd	37920
Snapdragon Way	37931
Snowbird Dr	37922
Snowdon Dr	37912
Snowmass Dr	37918
Snowood Dr	37918
Snowypointe Way	37931
Snyder Rd	37932
Snyder Ridge Ln	37932
Snyder School Rd	37932
Soapberry Cir	37938
Soaring Hawk Way	37932
Socony Ln	37909
Solar Dr	37921
Solitude Way	37932
Solomon Dr	37938
Solway Rd	37931
Solway Ferry Rd	37931
Solway School Rd	37931
Somersby Ln	37922
Somerset Rd	
100-299	37915
7300-7499	37909
Somersworth Dr	37934
Son Light Way	37918
Sonesta Dr	37938
Sonja Dr	37934
Sony Ln	37923
Sood Rd	37921
Sorority Village Cir	37916
Sorrenta Rd	37918
Sourwood Ln	37921
South Cir	37920
Southbend Cir	37922
Southbreeze Cir	37919
Southbrook Dr	37920
Southdale Rd	37920
Southern Shade Blvd	37932
Southfield Dr	37920
Southfork Dr	37921
Southgate Rd	37919
Southshire Ln	37922
Southside Rd	37920
Southwick Cir	37934
Southwood Dr	37920
Spangler Rd	37920
Spanish Moss Way	37918
Spanish Oak Dr	37932
Spar Dr	37918
Sparkle Ln	37931
Sparkling Star Ln	37931
Sparks Rd	37931
Sparrow Dr	37914
Sparta Ln	37934
Sparwood Ln	37932
Speedway Cir	37914
Spelling Way	37909
Spence Pl	37920
Spencer St	37917
Spice Ln	37921
Spice Tree Way	37931
Spicewood Ln	37921
Spindletop Ct	37938
Spindlewood Ln	37924
Spinnaker Rd	37934
Splendor Dr	37918
Split Oak Dr	37920
Split Ridge Rd	37922
Sportster Way	37920
Sprankle Dr	37919
Sprawls Pt	37932
Spring Dr	37920
Spring St	
1000-1199	37934
1200-1299	37920
Spring Bluff Way	37932
Spring Branch Ln	37934
Spring Creek Rd	37920
Spring Garden Way	37918
Spring Glen Way	37919
Spring Haven Ln	37919
Spring Hill Rd	
1000-2599	37914
2600-2799	37917
Spring Hollow Dr	37932
Spring Meadow Ln	37914
Spring Park Rd	37914
Spring Pass Way	37919
Spring Petal Way	37912
Spring Valley Dr	37917
Spring View Ln	37918
Spring Water Ln	37934
Springbrook Rd	37921
Springcrest Dr	37914
E & W Springdale Ave	37917
Springer Dr	37918
Springfield Dr	37923
Springhouse Way	37931
Springlake Dr	37920
Springplace Blvd & Cir	37924
Springpointe Way	37931
Springridge Ln	37931
W Springs Dr	37922
Springside Ln	37922
Springtime Way	37912
Springvale Ln	37918
Springwood Cir	37931
Spruce Dr	37920
Spruce St	37917
Spruce Ridge Way	37920
Sprucewood Rd	37921
Spur Rd	37934
Spurlin Rd	37918
Spy Glass Way	37922
Stable Ln	37938
Stadium Dr	37916
Staffwood Rd	37922
Stagecoach Trl	37909
Stahl Dr	37934
Stair Ave	37921
Stanfort Ln	37918
Stanley Ave	37914
Stanley Rd	37938
Stanton Rd	37918
Staplehurst Ln	37932
Star Gazing Ln	37938
Star Ray Ln	37931
Starboard Way	37932
Starbuck Ln	37914
Starhurst Dr	37921
Starkey Ln	37932
Starlite Ln	37920
Starmont Trl	37909
Stars Cove Ln	37931
Starview Way	37917
State St	37902
State Wood Ct	37920
Stately Cir	37923
Staten Ln	37918
States View Dr	37922
Station View Rd	37919
Station West Dr	37934
Statley Oaks Ln	37938
Staub St	37919
Steedsfort Ln	37922
Steele Rd	37932
Steeple Shadow Way	37918
Steeplechase Dr	37922
Steinbeck Ln	37922
Stekoia Ln	37912
Stephanie Ln	37918
Stephens Landing Way	37932
Stephenson Dr	37916
Sterchi St	37921
Sterchi Park Way	37912
Sterchi Village Blvd	37918
Sterling Ave	37924
Sterling Rd	37918
Stetson Way	37922
Steven Dr	37938
Stevens St	37920
Stevie Ln	37924
Stewart St	37917
Stewart Ridge Rd	37938
Still Meadow Ln	37918
Still Oak Way	37919
Still Water Ln	37922
Stillbrook Ln	37938
Stillglen Ln	37921
Stillmeadow Ln	37931
Stillwell Dr	37912
Stillwood Dr	37919
Stock Creek Blvd & Rd	37920
Stockbridge Ln	37909
Stockton Dr	37909
Stokely Ln	37918
Stolman Way	37918
Stone Ln	37917
Stone Rd	37920
Stone Bluff Ct	37924
Stone Canyon Ln	37922
Stone Creek Dr	37918
Stone Cutter Way	37918
Stone Harbor Way	37922
Stone Hedge Dr	37909
Stone Henge Ln	37922
Stone Hollow Dr	37924
Stone Mill Dr	37919
Stone Tower Rd	37922
Stone Villa Ln	37934
Stone Vista Ln	37934
Stonebranch Way	37922
Stonebriar Ln	37932
Stonebrook Dr	37923
Stonebury Way	37922
Stonecress Ln	37920
Stonehaven Dr	37938
Stonehills Pl	37938
Stoneleigh Rd	37912
Stonemont Ct	37931
Stoneoak Ln	37920
Stoneridge Dr	37931
Stonewall Dr	37920
Stonewall St	37921
Stonewood Dr	37921
Stonington Ln	37931
Stony Point Rd	37914
Stonycroft Ln	37918
Stonyhill Rd	37918
Stooksbury St	37914
Stormer Rd	37918
Stout Ln	37920
Strafford Cir	37923
Strasbourg Ct	37923
Stratfield Way	37919
Stratford Rd	37920
Stratford Park Blvd	37912
Strathmore Rd	37922
Stratton Dr	37919
Stratton Wood Cir	37919
Straw Flower Dr	37922
Strawberry Farms Way	37914
Strawberry Hills Ln	37914
Strawberry Plains Pike	
4000-7399	37914
7400-9199	37924
Strolling Dr	37912
Stubbs Bluff Rd	37932
Sturbridge Ct	37931
Sturbridge Ln	37919
Suburban Rd	37923
Sudberry Ln	37922
Sue Ellen Dr	37921
Suffolk Dr	37922
Sugar Creek Ln	37920
Sugarmaple Ln	37914
Sugarwood Dr	37934
Sullins St	37919
Sullivan Rd	37921
Sully Cir	37921
Sultan Ln	37923
Sumac Dr	37919
Summer Dr	37924
Summer Grove Ln	37931
Summer Line Way	37919
Summer Oak Ln	37918
Summer Rose Blvd	37918
Summer Spring Blvd	37931
Summer Wood Dr	37923
Summercrest Way	37918
Summerdale Dr	37934
Summerfield Dr	37921
Summerhill Dr	37922
Summerhouse Way	37931
Summers Rd	37938
Summershade Ln	37922
Summertime Ln	37938
E & W Summit Cir	37919
Summit Forest Ct	37922
E Summit Hill Dr	37915
W Summit Hill Dr	37902
Summit Lake Ct	37922
Summit Mountain Ct	37922
Summit Station Ln	37932
Summit View Rd	37920
Summit Vista Way	37922
Summitridge Ln	37921
Summitt Ave	37917
Sun Valley Rd	37921
Sunbeam Ln	37920
Sundancer Rd	37934
Sunday Silence Dr	37918
Sundew Rd	37914
Sundown Rd	37934
Sundrop Dr	37921
Sunflower Rd	37909
Sunlit Terrace Rd	37938
Sunny Ln	37912
Sunny Cove Way	37922
Sunny Creek Way	37918
Sunny Hill Ln	37938
Sunny Ridge Ln	37920
Sunny Springs Ln	37922
Sunnybrook Ln	37919
Sunnydale Rd	37923
Sunnyside Ln	37931
Sunnyslope Dr	37931
Sunnyview Dr	37914
Sunnywood Ln	37912
Sunpoint Rd	37923
Sunray Ln	37921
Sunrise Dr	37919
Sunrise Ln	37921
Sunrise St	37921
Sunrose Rd	37914
Sunset Ave, Ct & Rd	37914
Sunset Heights Dr	37914
Sunset Ridge Ln	37920
Sunshine Cir	37923
Sunshine Ln	37921
Sunsplash Ln	37918
Sunstone Way	37922
Sunstrand Dr	37924
Sunview Cir	37934
Sunwood Dr	37924
Superior St	37914
Surfside Shores Ln	37938
Surrey Rd	37915
Susan Renee Ln	37924
Susanne Ave	37920
Susong Dr	37912
Sussex Cir	37919
Sutherland Ave	
1701-1897	37921
1899-2099	37921
2100-4435	37919
4434-4434	37939
4437-4499	37919
Sutherland View Way	37919
Sutters Mill Ln	37909
Sutton Ln	37909
Suwannee Rd	37923
Suzu Way	37923
Swafford Rd	
2600-3099	37932
3101-3109	37931
3111-3399	37931
Swaggerty Rd	37920
Swan Falls Way	37922
Swan Pond Ln	37914
Swanner Rd	37918
Swanson Ln	37932
Swaps Ln	37923
Swathmore Ct	37919
Sway Branch Ln	37922
Sweet Ln	37938
Sweet Bay Ln	37918
Sweet Clover Way	37932
Sweet Gate Ln	37922
Sweet Kathleen Ln	37918
Sweet Pine Way	37921
Sweet View Way	37931
Sweet William Way	37938
Sweetbrier Dr	37918
Sweetgum Dr	37934
Sweetwater Ln	37920
Sweetwood Ln	37932
Swinford Ct	37922
Switch Yard Ln	37920
Sycamore Cir	37934
Sycamore Dr	37921
Sycamore Grove Way	37921
Sycamore View Ct	37921
Sydney Bean Way	37918
Sylvan Ln	37919
Sylvan St	37914
Sylvania Ave	37920
Sylvia Dr	37912
Taggart Ln	37938
Tahoe Ln	37918
Tailwind Ln	37924
Tain Rd	37919
Talahi Dr	37919
Taliluna Ave	37919
Taliwa Ct & Dr	37920
Taliwa Garden Dr	37920
Tall Cedars Rd	37922
Tall Oaks Dr	37920
Tall Pine Ln	37920
Tall Timber Dr	37931
Tallahassee Dr & Ln	37923
Tallent Rd	37912
Tally Ho Dr	37920
Tallywood Cir	37918
Tamarack Rd	37919
Tambark Dr	37917
Tamerlane Cir	37931
Tamiami Trl	37924
Tampa Rd	37923
Tamworth Ln	37921
Tan Rara Dr	37922
Tanager Ln	37919
Tanforan Dr	37923
Tanglewood Dr	37922
Tanglewood Rd	37912
Tania Ln	37920
Tannahill Dr	37909
Tanner Ln	37919
Tansy Ln	37918
Tappie Torrie Ln	37922
Tara Cir	37918
Tara Hill Dr	37919
Tarklin Valley Rd	37920
Tarleton Ave	37914
Tarwater Rd	37920
Tate Pt	37923
Taunton Ln	37918
Tavistock Way	37918
Tay Cir	37922
Taylor Rd	37920
Taylor Ford Rd	37920
Taylor Morgan Way	37924
Taylors Landing Dr	37934
Taylors View Ln	37921
Tazewell Pike	37918
Tazewell Pointe Way	37918
Teaberry Ln	37919
Teague Way	37938
Teakwood Rd	37919
Teal Creek Ln	37931
Tech Center Dr	37912
Technology Dr	37932
Tecoma Dr	37917
Tecoy Ln	37921
Tecumseh Dr	37912
Tedford Rd	37922
Tedlo Ln	37920
Tee Ln	37918
Teeple St	37917
Tekoa St	37921
Tekoa Quarry Rd	37921
Tell Mynatt Rd	37938
Tempest Ln	37931
Temple Ln	37938
Temple Acres Dr	37938
Templeton Rd	37918
Ten Mile Rd	37923
Ten Oak Way	37914
Tenbury Ln	37921
Tennessee Ave	37921
Tennyson Dr	37909
Tenwood Dr	37921
Tera Springs Way	37917
Teranes Way	37920
Teras Point Way	37918
Terra Rosa Dr	37932
Terrace Ave	
1800-2299	37916
4200-4299	37912
Terrace View Dr	37918
Terrace Woods Way	37919
Terrapin Station Ln	37932
Terri Cir	37923
Terry Dr	37924
Tervada Dr	37931
Testerman Dr	37921
Teton Ln	37922
Tewksbury Dr	37921
Texas Ave	37921
Texas Valley Rd	37938
Thalia St	37917
Thayer Cir	37923
Thimble Fields Dr	37922
Third Creek Rd	37921
Thistle Ln	37919
Thistledown Ln	37922
Thistlewood Way	37919
Thomas Ln	37918
Thomas Rd	37920
Thomas St	37921
Thomas Henry Way	37938
Thomas Hill Way	37917
Thomas Weaver Rd	37938
Thompson Pl	37917
Thompson Rd	37932
Thoreau Ln	37922
Thornapple Dr	37938
Thornbird Way	37932
Thornbury Ct	37919
Thornbush Ln	37934
Thorngrove Pike	37914
Thorngrove Estate Way	37914
Thornhill Way	37931
Thornton Dr	37934
Thornwood Dr	37921
Thorpe Rd	37920
Thrall Rd	37918
Threadstone Ln	37932
Three Points Rd	37924
Thrush Ln	37918
Thunder Bay Way	37938
Thunderbolt Way	37923
Thunderhead Rd	37922
Thurman Ln	37920
Thurmer Dr	37914
Tiberius Rd	37918
Tiburon Way	37918
Tice Ln	37918
Ticonderoga Ln	37920
Tidewater Ct	37923
Tierra Verde Dr	37922
Tiffany Ln	37912
Tiffany Ann Ct	37938
Tiger Way	37918
Tigris Pointe Ln	37924
Tilbury Way	37921
Tillery Ave	37917
Tillery Ln	37918
Tillery Rd	37912
Tillery Square Ln	37912
Tillman Rd	37912
Tilson St	37920
Tim Bennett Ln	37918
Timber Cir	37920
Timber Pass	37909
Timber Glow Trl	37938
Timber Green Ln	37921
Timber Oaks Ct	37922
Timber Run Ln	37918
Timberbrook Ln	37938
Timbercreek Way	37924
Timbercrest Trl	37909
Timbergrove Cir & Dr	37919
Timberhill Ct	37934
Timberlake Dr	37920
Timberlane Cir	37924
Timberview Ln	37919
Timothy Ave	37914
Tims Ln	37912
Tina Ln	37920
Tindell Ave	37920
Tindell Ln	37918
Tingley Ln	37934
Tinley Dr	37931
Tinover Ct	37938
Tinsmith Way	37931
Tippens Ln	37920
Tipton Ave	37920
Tipton Ln	37918
Tipton Overlook Way	37920
Tipton Station Rd	37920
Tiptop Dr	37923
Titanium Ln	37918
Titus Way	37918
Tobago Ln	37921
Tobby Hollow Ln & Rd	37931
Tobe Ln	37938
Tobias Ln	37922
Tobler Ln & Rd	37919
Todd Ln	37921
Todd Helton Way	37916
Todwick Ln	37934
Tokalon Dr	37932
Tolson Ln	37921
Tolson Rd	37938
Tom Pat Way	37924
Tomache Dr	37909
Tomahawk Trl	37920
Tomar Ln	37938
Tomassee Dr	37920
Tomlinson St	37920
Tompkins Valley Way	37918

Toms Ln 37914
Tonalea Rd 37909
Tonti Ln 37909
Toole Dr 37919
Tooles Bend Rd 37922
Top O Knox Dr 37918
Topaz St 37917
Topeka St 37917
Topoco Dr 37922
Topsail Way 37918
Topside Rd 37920
Topview Ln 37934
Torch Light Ln 37921
Toressa Ln 37922
Tori Rd 37923
Tori Court Ln 37938
Torrey Pines Pt 37934
Torrington Ct 37934
Tortola Way 37922
Totanka Ln 37931
Touraine Pl 37919
Towanda Trl 37919
Tower Dr 37912
Town And Country Cir 37923
Town Center Blvd 37922
Towne Rd 37934
E Towne Mall Cir 37924
Townhouse Way 37921
Townview Dr 37915
Toxaway Dr 37909
Trace Ct 37912
Trace Chain Ln 37917
Trace Manor Ln 37912
Tracer Ln 37924
Tracy Way 37931
Traditional Dr 37909
Trailhead Cir 37920
Trails End Rd 37931
Train Station Way 37931
Trane Dr 37919
Tranquilla Dr 37919
Transport Ln 37924
Trapper Ln 37931
Travis Dr 37921
Trebor Ln 37914
Tree Ridge Rd 37922
Tree Top Way 37920
Tree Trunk Rd 37934
Treemont Rd 37912
Treetop Ridge Ln 37919
Trehaven Dr 37912
Trellis Way 37914
Trent Ln 37922
Trent Valley Ln 37938
Trenton Rd 37920
Trentville Way 37924
Tres Bien Ln 37920
Trescott Dr 37921
Trestle Way 37918
Trevi Rd 37918
Trey Oaks Ln 37918
Treybrooke Ln 37918
Treyburn Dr 37934
Treymour Way 37922
Treywood Ln 37922
Trigg St 37915
Trillium Ln 37920
Trinity Dr 37918
Triple Crown Blvd 37934
Triplett Ln 37922
Tristan Rd 37931
Trophy Run Ln 37920
Tropicana Dr 37918
Trossachs Ln 37922
Trotter Ave & Rd 37920
Trousdale Rd 37921
Troutman Ln
1100-1199 37924
8500-8799 37931
Trowbridge Ln 37934
Troy Cir 37919
Truan Ridge Way 37918
Truman Ave 37921
Trump Way 37923
Trumpet Vine Ln 37918
Trundle Rd 37920
Truslow St 37915
Tsawasi Rd 37931
Tuberose Ln 37920
Tucson Ln 37922
Tugaloo Dr 37919
Tulane Rd 37914
Tulip Ave 37921
Tulip Poplar Ln 37931
Tully Rd 37919
Tumbled Stone Way 37931
Tumbleweed Trl 37920
Tunbridge Ln 37922
Tunnel Rd 37931
Tupelo Way 37912
Turf Rd 37923
Turkey Dr 37934
Turkey Cove Ln 37934
Turkey Creek Rd 37934
Turkey Run Ln 37931
Turnberry Dr 37923
Turnborrow Ln 37918
Turnbrook Way 37919
Turner St 37917
Turning Leaf Ln 37922
Turpin Ln 37932
Turtle Creek Dr 37934
Turtle Dove Way 37932
Turtle Point Ln 37919
Tuxford Ln 37912
Twelve Trees Ln 37922
Twin Branch Dr 37922
Twin Brooks Blvd 37918
Twin Creek Rd 37920
Twin Harbour Dr 37934
Twin Hill Ln 37932
Twin Maple Dr 37938
Twin Pines Dr 37921
Twin Springs Rd 37920
Twin View Dr 37932
Twining Dr 37919
Twinleaf Ln 37920
Two Notch Dr 37920
Tyler Jacob Way 37931
Tylers Garden Way 37918
Tynemouth Dr 37914
Tyrone Dr 37922
Tyson St 37917
Ulster Ave 37915
Ultra Way 37909
Umber Dr 37918
Unaka St 37921
Underhill Ln 37921
Underwood Pl 37917
Underwood Rd 37914
Unicorn Dr 37923
Union Ave 37902
Union Rd 37934
Union Camp Ln 37934
Union School Rd
500-910 37924
912-928 37924
921-927 37914
929-2299 37914
Unity Dr 37918
University Ave 37921
Upchurch Rd 37912
Upland Ave 37917
Upper Ridge Way 37932
Uppingham Dr 37918
Urban Way 37921
Vada Cir 37912
Vahid Rd 37920
Val St 37921
Valdena Dr 37914
Valdosta Rd 37921
Vale Rd 37918
Vale View Rd 37922
Valencia Pt 37934
Valencia Rd 37919
Valerie Ln 37938
Valgro Rd 37920
Valley Ave 37920
Valley Dr 37920
Valley Trl 37934
Valley Brook Dr 37934
Valley Creek Way 37918
Valley Crossing Way 37932
Valley Dale Rd 37923
Valley Estates Dr 37920
Valley Forge Dr 37920
Valley Grove Ln 37931
Valley Hill Ln 37922
Valley Park Ln 37909
Valley Stream Way 37917
Valley View Dr 37917
Valley View Ln 37931
Valley View Rd 37924
Valley View Landing Ln 37932
Valley Vista Rd 37932
Valley Woods Ln 37922
Valleybrook Dr 37931
Van St 37921
Van Dyke Dr 37919
N Van Gilder Pl 37917
S Van Gilder Pl 37915
Van Horn Rd 37918
Van Huss Ave 37917
Vanardo Way 37912
Vance Rd 37921
Vancurry Ln 37934
Vandemere Dr 37921
Vander Ridge Ln 37919
Vandeventer Ave 37919
Vanosdale Rd 37909
Varner St 37919
Vasco Humphrey Way 37938
Vassar Ln 37938
Vaughn Ln 37914
Vaughn St 37920
Vee Ln 37914
Velma Dr 37918
E & W Velmetta Cir 37920
Venetian Way 37912
Venice Rd 37923
Venido Dr 37932
Ventura Dr 37938
Vera Dr 37917
Verbena St 37914
Vercelli Ln 37938
Verdi Ln 37922
Vermilion Rd 37922
Vermont Ave 37921
Vestine Dr 37918
Veterans Way 37931
Vicar Ln 37919
Vice Mayor Jack Sharp Rd 37914
Vickie Karen Dr 37938
Vicksburg Ln 37921
Vickys Way 37920
Victor Dr 37912
Victoria Dr 37922
Victoria St 37915
Victorian Way 37916
Victory St 37919
Vie St 37918
Vienna Dr 37912
S View Cir 37920
View Rd 37917
View Harbour Rd 37934
View Park Dr 37920
View Point Ln 37922
Viewcrest Ln 37932
Viking Dr 37932
Villa Rd 37918
Villa Crest Cir & Dr 37923
Villa Forest Way 37919
Villa Garden Way 37932
Villa Grande Ln 37938
Villa Haven Way 37912
Villa Ridge Way 37932
Village Dr 37919
Village Crest Way 37924
Village Green Pkwy 37934
Villaview Way 37919
Vincent St 37917
Vincinda Cir 37924
E Vine Ave 37915
W Vine Ave 37902
Vinings Way 37919
Vinson Ln 37923
Vintage Dr 37921
Virgil Ln 37920
Virgil Rushing Way 37914
Virginia Ave 37921
Virginia Lee Ln 37918
Virginia Pine Way 37932
Virtue Rd 37934
Vista Ln 37921
Vista Trl 37934
Vista Brook Ln 37934
Vista Delmar Way 37919
Vista Glen Way 37919
Vista Oaks Ln 37919
Vista Ridge Way 37909
Vista View Ln 37924
Vitex St 37918
Vixen Ln 37918
Volena Pl 37920
Voltz Ln 37914
Volunteer Blvd 37916
Volunteer Landing Ln 37915
Volunteer Village Way 37931
Volwood Ln 37922
Vucrest Ave 37920
Vultee Ln 37923
Wachese Ln 37912
Waco Rd 37919
Waconda Dr 37920
Wade Ln 37912
Wade Green Way 37931
Wadsworth Dr 37921
Wager Ln 37931
Wagon Rd 37920
Wagon Tongue Ln 37931
Wagon Wheel Cir 37934
Wagon Wheel Ln 37920
Wahli Dr 37918
Waits Field Way 37920
Wake Robin Rd 37918
Wakefield Rd 37922
Wakerly Place Ln 37931
Walbrook Dr 37923
Walcot Ln 37909
Waldave Ln 37920
Walden Dr 37919
Walden Legacy Way 37931
Walden View Ln 37932
Walden Woods Ct 37921
Walfred Dr 37912
Walker Blvd
3700-4599 37917
4600-4699 37918
Walker Rd 37938
Walker St 37919
Walker Springs Ln & Rd 37923
Walkercrest Ln 37918
Walking Dr 37912
Walkup Dr 37918
Wall Ave 37902
Wall Flower Ln 37924
Wallace Ave 37920
Wallace Dr 37920
Wallace Rd 37919
Wallace St 37921
Wallerton Ct 37938
Walleye Dr 37922
Wallingford Rd 37923
Wallwood Rd 37912
Walmar Dr 37920
Walnoaks Rd 37921
Walnut Cv 37932
Walnut St 37902
Walnut Branch Ln 37922
Walnut Breeze Ln 37918
Walnut Creek Ln 37932
E & W Walnut Grove Dr & Rd 37918
Walnut Hills Dr 37920
Walnut Ridge Ln 37921
Walnut Springs Ln 37920
Walnut Valley Dr 37919
Walnut View Way 37922
Walpine Ln 37921
Walridge Rd 37921
Walrock Ln 37921
Walter Reed Ln 37920
Walton Cir 37934
Wandering Rd 37912
Warbler Rd 37918
Ward Rd 37918
Wardley Rd 37934
Warehouse Park Ln 37932
Warlex Rd 37918
Warm Springs Way 37923
Warmstone Way 37931
Warner Dr 37912
Warren Ave 37917
Warrenpark Ln 37912
Warrior Trl 37922
Washburn St 37919
Washington Ave 37917
Washington Ct 37917
Washington Pike
1400-5299 37917
5300-7000 37918
7002-7198 37918
Washington Grove Way 37922
Washington Ridge Way 37917
Washington Valley Ln 37918
Wassman Rd 37912
Watauga Ave 37917
Watauga Dr 37918
Water Hill Dr 37922
Water Lilly Way 37918
Water Mill Trl 37922
Water Oak Ct 37909
Water Place Way 37922
Water Plant Rd 37914
Water Tower Rd 37920
Water Valley Way 37932
Waterbury Ln 37912
Watercress Dr 37918
Waterford Dr 37934
Watergrove Dr 37922
Watering Pl 37931
Watermour Way 37912
Waters Edge Ln 37919
Waterside Ln 37922
Watersong Ln 37922
Waterview Trl 37922
Waterwheel Way 37919
Watson Pl 37920
Watt Rd 37932
N Watt Rd 37934
S Watt Rd 37934
Waverly St 37921
Wavetree Dr 37931
Way Station Trl 37934
Wayland Ave & Rd 37914
Wayne Dr 37914
Waynesboro Ln 37923
Waynewood Rd 37912
Wayside Rd 37931
Weatherly Hills Blvd 37934
Weatherstone Dr 37922
Weathervane Dr 37934
Weaver Rd 37931
Weaver St 37917
Weaver Cemetery Rd 37938
Web View Ln 37938
Webb Ln 37921
Webb School Ln 37923
Webber Rd 37920
Webster Ave 37921
Webster Dr 37938
Webster Groves Ln 37909
Wedgewood Dr 37914
Weems Rd 37918
Weeping Willow Ct 37931
Weisbrook Ln 37909
E Weisgarber Rd
900-1236 37909
1237-1237 37950
1238-1498 37909
1239-1499 37909
N Weisgarber Rd
200-699 37919
800-999 37909
S Weisgarber Rd 37919
Welch Rd 37938
Wellesley Ln 37934
Wellhelm Dr 37932
Wellington Dr 37919
Wellington Chase Ln 37932
Wellington Pt Ln 37938
Wellington West Dr 37932
Wells Ave 37917
Wells Rd 37920
Wells Fargo Dr 37934
Wells Scenic View Ln 37938
Wells Station Rd 37931
Wellsburg Way 37931
Wellsley Manor Way 37919
Wellswood Ln 37909
Wembley Ct 37922
Wembley Hills Rd 37922
Wendi Ann Dr 37924
Wendover Rd 37932
Wenlock Rd 37922
Wentworth Dr 37917
Wenwood Dr 37921
Werkbund Way 37920
Werndl Dr 37934
Wesley Pl 37922
Wesley Rd 37909
Wesley Ridge Ln 37921
Wessex Dr 37923
West St 37919
Westavia Dr 37909
Westborough Rd 37909
Westbridge Dr 37919
Westbrook Rd 37919
Westbury Rd 37922
Westchase Dr 37919
Westchester Dr 37918
Westcott Blvd 37931
Westcourt Dr 37919
Westdale Dr 37909
Westerly Winds Rd 37931
Western Ave 37921
Western Rd 37938
Westerwood Dr 37919
Westfield Rd 37919
Westford Dr 37919
Westgate Dr 37921
Westgrove Dr 37919
Westhampton Pl 37919
Westin Pl 37922
Westland Dr
6200-8299 37919
8300-8899 37923
8900-10899 37922
Westland Bay Dr 37922
Westland Crossing Way 37922
Westland Lakes Way 37922
Westmeade Rd 37921
Westmere Dr 37909
Westminster Ln 37909
Westminster Rd 37919
Westmont Cir 37919
Westmoreland Blvd 37919
Weston Rd 37918
Westop Trl 37923
Westover Dr 37919
Westover Ter 37914
Westport Rd 37922
Westridge Dr 37909
Westside Dr 37909
Westview Ave 37921
Westway Cir 37919
Westwood Rd 37919
Wethersfield Ln 37934
Wexford Ln 37921
Wexgate Rd 37931
Wexton Ln 37934
Weybridge Ln 37919
Weymouth Ln 37914
Whaley Ln & St 37920
Whately Way 37923
Wheatfield Pl 37919
Wheatland Dr 37931
Wheaton Pl 37919
Whedbee Dr 37921
Wheeler St 37917
Whelahan Farm Rd 37924
Whinchen 37950
Whirlaway Cir 37923
Whisper Trace Ln 37919
Whisper Wood Rd 37918
Whispering Cove Dr 37922
Whispering Hills Ln 37934
Whispering Oaks Dr 37938
Whispering Wind Ln 37922
Whistler Woods Way 37922
Whistlers Way 37918
White Ave 37916
White Ln 37920
White Arum Ln 37922
White Ash Ln 37919
White Birch Ct 37932
White Bossom Way 37918
White Cedar Way 37938
White Chapel Ln 37914
White Creek Dr 37920
White Frye Ln 37922
White Lightning Way 37938
White Oak Dr 37920
White Oak Ln 37917
White Petal Way 37912
White Pine Cir 37909
White Poplar Way 37912
White School Rd 37920
Whitehall Rd 37909
Whitehorse Rd 37919
Whites Pond Way 37923
Whitesburg Dr 37918
Whitestone Rd 37938
Whitetail Ln 37932
Whithorn Ln 37909
Whitlock Ln 37924
Whitlow Ave 37919
Whitman Dr 37909
Whitmont Ln & Rd 37931
Whitney Pl 37917
Whitower Dr 37919
Whittaker Dr 37919
Whittbier Dr 37932
Whitten Ln 37922
Whittington Dr 37923
Whittington Creek Blvd 37922
Whittle Springs Rd 37917
Whittmore Ln 37918
Whitworth Dr 37938
Wichita Dr 37921
Wickam Rd 37931
Wickersham Dr 37922
Wickford Way 37931
Widener Rd 37920
Widgeon Ln 37934
Widow French Ln 37920
Widow Newman Ln 37924
Wiebelo Dr 37931
Wil Loyd Dr 37912
Wilani Rd 37919
Wilbanks Rd 37912
Wild Cherry Ln 37918
Wild Fern Ln 37931
Wild Geese Rd 37934
Wild Oak Dr 37918
Wild Plum Way 37932
Wild Rose Ln 37932
Wildacres Way 37920
Wildberry Ct 37932
Wildcat Way 37918
Wilder Pl 37915
Wildercliff Ln 37918
Wilderness Rd 37917
Wildflower Way 37922
Wildtree Ln 37923
Wildview Way 37920
Wildwood Ct 37920
Wildwood Ln 37918
Wildwood Garden Dr 37920
Wiley Ln 37920
Wilford Rd 37912
Wilkerson Rd
2000-2099 37922
5200-6199 37912
Wilkesboro Ln 37912
Wilkins St 37921

Wilkinson Rd ... 37923
Wilkshire Dr ... 37921
Will Dr ... 37938
Willette Ct ... 37909
William Stephen Way ... 37931
Williams Rd ... 37932
Williams St ... 37917
Williams Bend Rd ... 37932
N & S Williamsburg Dr ... 37934
Williamson Dr ... 37938
Willingham Dr ... 37934
Willis Pl ... 37920
Willmann Ln ... 37919
Willoughby Rd ... 37920
Willow Ave ... 37915
Willow Bend Way ... 37931
Willow Bluff Cir ... 37914
Willow Branch Ln ... 37931
Willow Cove Way ... 37934
Willow Creek Ln ... 37909
Willow Crossing Dr ... 37922
Willow Falls Way ... 37917
Willow Field Ln ... 37931
Willow Fork Ln ... 37938
Willow Grove Dr ... 37932
Willow Hill Ct ... 37934
Willow Loop Way ... 37922
Willow Oak Dr
2900-3099 ... 37909
5400-5499 ... 37914
Willow Point Way ... 37931
Willow Ridge Way ... 37934
Willow Spring Dr ... 37938
Willow Trace Ln ... 37938
Willow View Ln ... 37922
Willow Walk Ln ... 37922
Willoway Dr ... 37912
Willowbrook Ln ... 37918
Willowcreek Pointe Ln ... 37931
Willowcrest Ln ... 37934
Willowdale Dr ... 37921
Willowood Rd ... 37922
Wilmington Dr ... 37919
Wilmouth Run Rd ... 37918
Wilnoty Dr ... 37931
Wilona Ln ... 37922
Wilshire Rd ... 37919
Wilson Ave
2300-2499 ... 37915
2500-3499 ... 37914
Wilson Dr ... 37924
Wilson Rd ... 37912
Wilton Ln ... 37922
Wimbledon Dr ... 37923
Wimpole Ave ... 37914
Winbrook Cir ... 37922
Winchester Dr ... 37919
Wind Chime Cir ... 37918
Wind Creek Way ... 37922
Wind Hill Cir ... 37909
Windamere Rd ... 37923
Windancer Ln ... 37922
Windbrook Rd ... 37923
Windcastle Ln ... 37923
Windcliff Ln ... 37931
Windcrest Rd ... 37931
Windflower Way ... 37932
Windgate St ... 37919
Windgrove Ln ... 37912
Windham Hill Rd ... 37934
Winding Hill Ln ... 37931
Winding Oak Dr ... 37918
Winding Ridge Trl ... 37922
Winding Way Dr ... 37923
Windingbrooke Ln ... 37918
Windlass Rd ... 37934
Windpointe Way ... 37931
Windsock Ln ... 37924
Windsor Ave ... 37919
Windsor Springs Ln ... 37914
Windswept Ln ... 37922
Windtrace Ln ... 37914
Windtree Ln ... 37921
Windtree Oaks Way ... 37920
Windview Way ... 37919
Windward Dr ... 37934
Windwhisper Blvd ... 37924
Windy Knoll Dr ... 37938
Windy Ridge Pt ... 37922
Windy Way Dr ... 37932
Winfield Ln ... 37921
Winford Rd ... 37920
Winged Foot Pt ... 37934
Winglet Ln ... 37922
Winkle Ln ... 37920
Winmont Turn ... 37922
Winners Dr ... 37920
Winona St ... 37917
Winslow Dr ... 37920
Winstead St ... 37920
Winston Rd ... 37919
N Winston Rd
100-399 ... 37919
400-499 ... 37909
1900-1999 ... 37919
Winter Garden Way ... 37912
Winter Oaks Way ... 37918
Winter Sun Ln ... 37922
Winter Winds Ln ... 37909
Winterberry Ln ... 37932
Wintergreen Cir & Dr ... 37912
Winterset Dr ... 37912
Winterwood Ln ... 37923
Winthrope Way ... 37923
Wisdom Ln ... 37938
Wise Ln ... 37920
Wise Hills Rd ... 37920
Wise Springs Rd ... 37918
Wishing Well Ln ... 37918
Wisteria Way ... 37931
Wisteria View Way ... 37914
Witherspoon Ln ... 37934
Withlow Dr ... 37912
Witt Pl ... 37915
Wittenham Dr ... 37921
Wolf Den Ln ... 37932
Wolf Valley Ln ... 37938
Wolfenbarger Ln ... 37938
Wolverine Ln ... 37931
Wonder View Ln ... 37938
Wonderland Ln ... 37914
Wood Duck Ln ... 37912
Wood Field Cir ... 37922
Wood Harbour Rd ... 37934
Wood Oak Ct ... 37922
Wood Song Ln ... 37914
Woodbark Trce ... 37921
Woodbend Trl ... 37919
Woodberry Dr ... 37912
Woodbine Ave
1400-2499 ... 37917
2500-3399 ... 37914
Woodbridge Ln ... 37921
Woodbrier Rd ... 37923
Woodbrook Dr ... 37919
Woodburn Dr ... 37919
Woodbury Ct ... 37922
Woodby Ln ... 37914
W Woodchase Dr &
Rd ... 37934
Woodcliff Dr ... 37934
Woodcock Cir ... 37923
Woodcove Ln ... 37922
Woodcreek View Ln ... 37931
Woodcrest Dr ... 37918
Woodcroft Dr ... 37938
Wooddale Dr ... 37912
N Wooddale Rd ... 37924
S Wooddale Rd ... 37924
Wooddale Church Rd ... 37924
Wooddale Woods Way ... 37924
Wooded Ln ... 37922
Wooded Acres Dr ... 37921
Woodedge Ln ... 37934
Woodfern Rd ... 37918
Woodford Bend Way ... 37934
Woodglen Dr ... 37921
Woodhaven Dr ... 37914
Woodhill Pl ... 37919
Woodhollow Ln ... 37932
Woodington Ct ... 37921
Woodlake Dr ... 37918
E Woodland Ave ... 37917
W Woodland Ave
100-299 ... 37917
700-999 ... 37921
Woodland Ct ... 37919
Woodland Dr ... 37919
Woodland Ln ... 37919
Woodland Brae ... 37919
Woodland Reserve Ln ... 37919
Woodland Ridge Ln ... 37919
Woodland Trace Dr ... 37934
Woodlawn Dr ... 37912
Woodlawn Pike ... 37920
Woodlawn Gardens
Way ... 37920
Woodlawn School Rd ... 37920
Woodleaf Dr ... 37912
Woodmere Ln ... 37920
Woodmont Rd ... 37917
Woodpark Ln ... 37923
Woodpointe Dr ... 37931
Woodridge Dr ... 37919
Woodrose Ct ... 37934
Woodrow Dr ... 37918
Woodrush Dr ... 37918
Woods Creek Rd ... 37924
Woods End Dr ... 37918
Woods Smith Rd ... 37921
Woodsboro Rd ... 37922
Woodsedge Rd ... 37924
E & W Woodshire Dr ... 37922
Woodside St ... 37919
Woodslope Cir ... 37912
Woodsmoke Cir ... 37934
Woodson Dr ... 37920
Woodsprings Dr ... 37923
Woodthrush Ln ... 37920
Woodvale Dr ... 37918
Woodview Dr
700-999 ... 37912
6800-6899 ... 37920
Woodview Ln ... 37909
Woodville Ln ... 37921
Woody Dr ... 37934
Worcester Rd ... 37934
Workman Rd ... 37921
Worlds Fair Park Dr
700-899 ... 37902
900-1099 ... 37916
Worth St ... 37917
Worthington Dr ... 37938
Worthington Ln
6700-6999 ... 37918
8800-8899 ... 37914
Wray St ... 37917
Wren Rd ... 37918
Wren Valley Way ... 37918
Wrens Creek Ln ... 37918
Wrens Nest Ln ... 37932
Wrenwood Way ... 37918
Wright Rd
6000-6199 ... 37938
6800-7199 ... 37931
Wright St ... 37917
Wrights Ferry Rd ... 37919
Wrinkle Ave ... 37920
Wycliffe Ct ... 37921
Wye Way Ln ... 37920
Wyndcroft Dr ... 37914
Wyndham Way ... 37923
Wyndham Hall Ln ... 37934
Wyndham Pointe Ln ... 37931
Wynmoor Cir ... 37931
Wynn Ave ... 37920
Wynrush Cir ... 37923
Wyoming Ln ... 37932
Yacht Haven Ln ... 37934
Yachtsman Way ... 37922
Yankee St ... 37914
Yarber Way ... 37918
Yarnell Ave ... 37920
Yarnell Rd ... 37932
Yarnell Station Blvd ... 37932
Yates Ln ... 37912
Yellow Birch Way ... 37931
Yellow Leaf Way ... 37912
Yellow Oak Ln ... 37931
Yellow Pine Ln ... 37932
Yellow Rose Way ... 37918
Yellowbrick Way ... 37938
Yellowjacket Rd ... 37920
Yellowstone Rd ... 37914
York Rd ... 37938
Yorkcrest Dr ... 37912
Yorkland Way ... 37923
Yorkshire Dr ... 37909
Yorktown Rd ... 37920
Yosemite Trl ... 37909
Young Ave ... 37920
E Young High Pike
100-138 ... 37920
137-137 ... 37940
140-298 ... 37920
201-299 ... 37920
W Young High Pike ... 37920
Yount Rd ... 37931
Yuma Dr ... 37931
Zachary Taylor Rd ... 37922
Zenia St ... 37914
Zesta Ln ... 37924
Zimmerman Way ... 37922
Zinc Rd ... 37938
Zion Ln ... 37931
Zirkle Dr ... 37918
Zoe Way ... 37909
Zoee Springs Ln ... 37918
Zola Ln ... 37922

NUMBERED STREETS

1st Rd ... 37914
2nd Dr ... 37934
2nd Ln
5800-5899 ... 37912
7700-7799 ... 37924
3rd Ave ... 37917
3rd Dr ... 37934
3rd Ln ... 37912
3rd Rd ... 37914
E 4th Ave ... 37917
N 4th Ave ... 37917
W 4th Ave ... 37921
E 5th Ave
100-2499 ... 37917
2500-3299 ... 37914
W 5th Ave
1-599 ... 37917
700-1499 ... 37921
5th St ... 37918
N 6th ... 37917
7th Ave ... 37917
8th Ave ... 37917
9th Ave ... 37917
11th St ... 37916
12th St ... 37916
13th St ... 37916
14th St ... 37916
16th St ... 37916
17th St ... 37916
17th St SW ... 37916
N 17th St ... 37921
18th St ... 37916
19th St ... 37916
20th St ... 37916
21st St SW ... 37916
N 21st St ... 37921
22nd St ... 37916
23rd St SW ... 37916
N 23rd St ... 37921

LEBANON TN

General Delivery ... 37087

POST OFFICE BOXES MAIN OFFICE STATIONS AND BRANCHES

Box No.s
All PO Boxes ... 37088

NAMED STREETS

Abbey Rd ... 37090
Abney Ln ... 37090
Acacia Grove Ln ... 37087
Academy Rd ... 37087
E & W Adams Ave &
St ... 37087
Africa Rd ... 37087
Alan John Way ... 37087
Alden Ln ... 37087
Alexander Dr ... 37087
Alhambra Dr ... 37087
Allen Ln ... 37087
Alligood Way ... 37090
Allison Ct & Dr ... 37087
Alsup Mill Ln ... 37090
Amana Dr ... 37087
Amarillo Dr ... 37087
Amberjack Way ... 37087
Amberwood Way ... 37090
Amburn Ln ... 37090
Amelia Pl ... 37090
Anderson Ave ... 37087
Andy Cir & Dr ... 37087
Angel Cv ... 37087
Antietam Ct & Dr ... 37087
Applevalley Rd ... 37087
Appomattox Dr ... 37087
Arcadia Pass ... 37087
Arctic Dr ... 37090
Arlington Rd ... 37087
Armstrong Ct ... 37087
Armstrong Pl ... 37090
Arrowhead Dr ... 37087
Asbury Hawn Dr ... 37087
Athens Rd ... 37087
Atkinson Rd ... 37090
Atwood Ct ... 37087
Auntie M Ln ... 37087
Autumn Crk ... 37087
Autumn Ridge Ct ... 37087
Averitts Ferry Ln ... 37087
Babb Ct & Dr ... 37087
E & W Baddour Pkwy ... 37087
Bainbridge Rd ... 37087
Baird Ct & St ... 37087
Baird Park Cir ... 37087
Bairds Ml E & W ... 37090
Baker Ct ... 37087
Baldy Ford Rd ... 37090
Ballentrace Blvd ... 37087
Bansonda Rd ... 37090
Barnes Dr ... 37087
Barton Brook Ln ... 37087
Barton Ferry Ct ... 37087
Barton Shore Ct ... 37087
Bartons Cv ... 37087
Bartons Creek Rd ... 37090
Bartonwood Dr ... 37087
Bassett Hall Ct ... 37087
Bates Rd ... 37087
Bay Ct ... 37087
Beard Ave ... 37087
Beasleys Bend Rd ... 37087
Beech Log Rd ... 37090
Bel Air Dr ... 37087
Belcher Dr ... 37090
Bellvue Dr ... 37090
Bellwood Rd ... 37087
Belmont Way ... 37087
Belotes Ferry Rd ... 37087
Ben Green Rd ... 37090
Bending Chestnut Dr ... 37087
Benita Way ... 37087
Bent Tree Ct ... 37087
Benton Clay Ct ... 37087
Berea Church Rd ... 37087
Berry Ave ... 37090
Bethany Ln ... 37087
Bethlehem Rd ... 37087
Bettis Rd ... 37090
Bettye Blvd & Ct ... 37087
Big Springs Rd
1-2999 ... 37087
3000-5899 ... 37090
Birchwood Dr ... 37087
Birmingham Rd ... 37090
Bishop Ln ... 37087
Blackberry Ln ... 37087
Blair Ln & Rd ... 37087
E Blairmont Ct & Dr ... 37087
Blairwood Ct ... 37087
Blevin Rd ... 37087
Bloodworth Rd ... 37087
Blue Devil Blvd ... 37087
Blue Ribbon Downs ... 37087
Blue Well Rd ... 37090
Bluebird Ext ... 37087
Bluebird Rd
700-3599 ... 37087
3600-10599 ... 37090
Bluefield Ln ... 37087
Bluegrass Cir, Ct &
Pkwy ... 37090
Bluewater Dr ... 37087
Bluff Dr ... 37087
Bobwood Dr ... 37087
Bond Rd ... 37090
Bonnie Blue Way ... 37087
Bonnie Oaks Ct & Dr ... 37087
Bonnie Valley Dr ... 37087
Borck Ln ... 37090
Bordeaux Ct ... 37090
Braden Ave ... 37087
Bradley Ct ... 37087
Bradshaw Rd ... 37087
Branchside Dr ... 37087
Brandy Ln ... 37090
Brewington Ln ... 37087
Breyerton Way ... 37087
Brian St ... 37087
Briana Rd ... 37087
Briarcliff Dr ... 37087
Briarhill Ct & Rd ... 37087
Bridgestone Pkwy ... 37090
Briskin Ln ... 37087
Brockten St ... 37087
Bronson Pt ... 37087
Brookside Cv ... 37087
Brookwood Ln ... 37087
Brown Rd ... 37087
Brunswick Dr ... 37087
Buck Run Ct ... 37087
Buckeye Pl ... 37087
Buckingham Ct ... 37090
Buckingham Ln ... 37087
Buckshot Ct & Dr ... 37087
Burchett Dr ... 37087
Burdock St ... 37087
Burford Rd ... 37087
Burnt House Anx &
Rd ... 37090
Business Park Dr ... 37090
Butler Cv ... 37087
C L Manier St ... 37087
C P Stewart Blvd ... 37087
Cadet Ct ... 37087
Cages Ferry Rd ... 37087
Cainsville Ct ... 37087
Cainsville Rd
200-1199 ... 37087
1200-14999 ... 37090
Cairo Bend Rd ... 37087
Callie Ln ... 37090
Callis Ln & Rd ... 37090
Cambridge Rd ... 37087
Camilla Ln ... 37087
Campbell St ... 37087
Canal St ... 37087
Canoe Branch Rd ... 37087
Canyon Creek Dr ... 37087
Capitol Dr ... 37087
Caplenor Ln ... 37090
Carson Dr ... 37087
Cartel Ct & Dr ... 37087
Carter Grove Ct ... 37087
Carthage Hwy ... 37087
Caruthers Ave ... 37087
Carver Ln ... 37087
Cassidy Dr ... 37087
N Castle Heights Ave &
Ct ... 37087
Castleview Dr ... 37087
Castlewood Ln ... 37087
Cave Springs Rd ... 37087
Cedar St ... 37087
Cedar Bluff Rd ... 37087
Cedar Forest Rd ... 37090
Cedar Grove Ln & Rd ... 37087
Cedar Knob Ln ... 37087
Cedar Way Dr ... 37087
Cedarwood Dr ... 37087
Center St ... 37087
Center Hill Rd ... 37087
Centerville Rd ... 37087
Central Pike ... 37090
Chalford Pl ... 37087
Chaparral Dr ... 37087
Chapman Dr ... 37087
Charity Ln ... 37087
Charleston St ... 37087
Chateau Dr ... 37087
Chelsea Ln ... 37090
Cherokee Dr ... 37087
Cherokee Dock Rd ... 37087
Cherry St ... 37087
Cherry Blossom Way ... 37087
Cherry Dale Dr ... 37087
Cherry Hill Ln ... 37090
Cherry Point Ct ... 37087
Chesapeake Ct & Pt ... 37087
Chestnut Dr & Ln ... 37087
Chicken Rd ... 37090
Chrissa Ln ... 37087
Christine Dr ... 37087
Christy Dr ... 37087
Churchill Downs ... 37087
Circle Dr ... 37087
Classic View Dr ... 37087
Clay Dr & Pl ... 37087
Clearview Dr ... 37087
Clemmons Ln ... 37090
Cleveland Ave & St ... 37087
Clover Dr ... 37087
Cloverhill Ln ... 37090
Cody Dr ... 37087
Coe Ln ... 37087
Colchester Cir ... 37087
Cole Ave ... 37087
Coles Ferry Pike ... 37087
Colgate Ave ... 37087
N & S College St ... 37087
Colonial Dr ... 37087
Colorado Cir ... 37087
Comer Ln ... 37087
Commerce Rd & Way ... 37090
Conatser Rd ... 37087
Concord Rd ... 37087
Cook Dr ... 37087
Corey Ln ... 37090
Cotton Cloud Ln ... 37090
Countrywood Dr ... 37087
Creekwood Xing ... 37087
Creighton Ln ... 37087
Crest Dr ... 37087
Crosswinds Dr ... 37090
Crowell Ln
499-599 ... 37087
600-699 ... 37090
N & S Cumberland Dr,
Sq & St ... 37087
S Cumberland Center
Blvd ... 37087
Curtis Dr ... 37087
Cypress Ct ... 37087
Cypress Hill Dr ... 37087
Dahlia Dr ... 37087
Dakota Dr ... 37087
Dana Dr ... 37087
Danby Cir ... 37090
Dandelion Dr ... 37087
Darlenes Way ... 37087
Davidson Ct ... 37087
Davis Ln ... 37090
Davis Ln N ... 37087
Davis Rd ... 37087

Street	ZIP
Dawn Pl	37087
Dawson Ln	37087
Debate Ln	37087
Dedmon St	37087
Deer Ridge Ln	37087
Deer Trace Dr	37087
Deermeadow Ln	37090
Dellwood Dr	37087
Delmar Cir	37087
Denny Ln	37090
E Denny Rd	37090
N Denny Rd	37087
E Depot St	37087
Derby Downs	37087
N & S Dickerson Chapel Rd	37087
Dillard Ln	37087
E Division St	37090
Dixie Ave	37090
Doe Trl	37087
Doe Ridge Ct	37087
Dogwood Dr	37087
Dogwood Ln	37090
Donnell Ct	37087
Dorchester Dr	37090
Double Log Cabin Rd	37087
Dr James Fisher Cir	37087
Drakes Dr	37087
Draper Ln	37087
Drifting Cir W	37087
Droste Ln	37087
Dude Trl	37090
Dudley Ln	37087
Duke Dr	37090
Dump Rd	37087
Dunaway Rd	37090
Dunstan Ct	37087
Dyer Ln	37087
Earheart Pl	37090
S Eastgate Blvd & Ct	37090
Eastland Ave	37087
Eastland Ln	37090
Eastover Rd	37090
Easy St	37087
Eatherly Dr	37087
Eatherly Ln	37090
Eddie Hill Dr	37090
Eddins Rd	37090
Edgehill Dr	37087
Edgewood Dr	37087
Edwards Ave	37087
Edwards Rd	37090
Elenburg Ln	37087
Eliza Way	37087
Elkins Dr	37087
Ellis Park	37087
Elm Ct & St	37087
Elmwood Dr	37087
W End Hts	37087
Estes Rd	37087
Et Acres	37087
Ewing Ct & Dr	37087
Fairfield Dr & Pl	37087
Fairgrounds Ct	37087
Fairview Ave	37087
Fairways	37087
Faith Ln	37087
Falcon Crk	37087
Fall Creek Rd	37090
Falling Leaf Ln	37087
Falls Blvd	37090
Farmington Dr	37087
Fay St	37087
Fernwood Ln	37087
Fields Ln	37087
Fire Tower Rd	37090
Fisher Ln	37087
Fite Dr	37090
Five Oaks Blvd & Cir	37087
Flat Woods Rd	37090
Flatt Rock Rd	37090
Flippin Rd	37087
Floral St	37087
Fontenay Dr	37090
Ford Rd	37087
E & W Forrest Ave	37087
Forrest Park Dr	37087
Fox Hunt Ln	37087
Fox Run Rd	37087
Franklin Rd	
1-899	37087
900-7899	37090
Franklin Ter	37087
Freedom Dr	37087
Freetown Ln N	37087
Friendship Dr	37087
Gail Ct	37087
Gaston Park Dr	37087
E Gay St	
100-227	37087
226-226	37088
228-298	37087
229-299	37087
W Gay St	37087
Geers Ct & Dr	37087
Genesco Pkwy	37090
Georgia Ct	37087
Geris Way	37087
Gibson Dr	37087
Gilbert Valley Dr	37090
Gilmore Hill Rd	37087
Glen Haven Ct	37087
Glenn Cir	37090
Glenway Cv & Pt	37087
Glidepath Way	37087
Gloucester Dr	37087
Glover St	37087
Gordon Dr	37087
Goshen Rd	37087
Grant Hwy	37090
Grassland Dr	37087
Green Rd & St	37087
Greene Dr	37087
Greenlawn Dr	37087
Greensward Ave	37087
Greentree Cir	37087
Greentree Point Cir	37087
Greenwood Dr	37090
N Greenwood Ext	37087
Greenwood Rd	37090
N Greenwood St	37087
S Greenwood St	37087
Grenoble Dr	37090
Griffin Landing Ln	37087
Gulf Ave	37087
Gwendolyn Dr	37087
Gwynn Ct	37087
Gwynn Ln	37087
Gwynn Rd	37090
Hale Ct	37087
Haley Ln	37087
Hamilton Chambers Rd	37087
Hamilton Springs Blvd	37087
Hamilton Station Xing	37087
Hammond Ave	37087
Hampton Dr	37087
Hancock Ln	37087
Hankins Dr	37087
Happy St	37087
Harbor Dr & Pt	37087
Harding Dr	37087
Hartman Dr	37087
Hartman Plantation Cir & Ct	37090
S Hartmann Dr	
101-103	37087
105-699	37087
900-1299	37090
Hartsville Pike	37087
Hartwell Ct	37087
Harvest Ct	37087
Harvest Land Dr	37090
N & S Hatton Ave	37087
Haynes St	37087
Head Ct	37087
Head Homes	37087
Hebron Rd	37090
Hellums St	37087
Henderson Rd	37090
Henley Dr	37087
Heritage Rd	37087
Heydel Cir	37087
Hiawatha Dr	37087
Hickory Cir & Ct	37087
Hickory Point Dr	37087
Hickory Point Ln	37090
Hickory Ridge Rd	
1-5299	37087
5300-7099	37090
Hickory Valley Rd	37087
Hicks Hollow Rd	37087
Hidden Acres	37087
E & W High St	37087
High Country Rd	37087
High School Dr	37090
Highland Ct & Park	37087
Highway 109 N	
100-3599	37090
Highway 109 N	
3600-10899	37087
Highway 141 S	37087
Hill St	37087
Hillakes Ln	37090
Hillcreek Dr	37087
Hillcrest Ct & Dr	37087
Hillock Trce	37087
Hiwassee Rd	37087
Hobbs Ave	37087
Hobbs Ln	37090
Holland Ln	37087
Hollow Oak Dr	37087
Holloway Cir	37090
Holloway Dr	37087
Holloway Rd	37090
Holt Rd	37087
Honeysuckle Ln	37087
Horn Dr	37087
Horn Springs Rd	37087
Hosier Ct	37087
Hunt Ln	37090
Hunter Dr	37087
Hunters Ln	37087
Hunters Creek Blvd	37087
Hunters Point Pike	37087
Hurd Ct	37087
Hurricane Creek Rd	37090
Hutchinson Pl	37090
Idlewild Dr	37087
Indian Hills Rd	37087
Ingram Ct	37087
Inman Ct	37087
Innovative Way	37090
J Branham Dr	37087
Jacky Gammons Ln	37087
Jacquelin Dr	37087
James Pl	37090
Jameston Dr	37087
Jarod Way	37087
Jarrell Rd	37087
Jasmine St	37087
Jay St	37087
Jenkins Rd	37087
Jennings Ave	37087
Jennings Pond Rd	37090
Jennings View Dr	37090
Jessica Dr	37087
Jim Draper Dr	37087
Jodie Ct	37087
John Galt Dr	37087
Johnson Rd	37087
Jonathan Dr	37087
Jones Rd	37090
Jonquil Way	37090
Joseph St	37087
Joy Dr	37087
Joyce Ct	37087
June Dr	37087
Justice Ln	37087
Karlee Ct, Dr & Est	37087
Keaton St	37087
Kelly Cir, Dr & Ln	37087
Kelly Lynn Ct	37090
Kelsie Cir & Dr	37087
Kemp Ln	37087
Ken Cir	37087
Kent Dr	37087
Kimber Ln	37087
Kinderhill Way	37090
Kirkpatrick Lake Rd	37087
Knob Rd	37087
Knoll Ln	37087
Knollwood Lndg	37087
Knowles Rd	37090
Knox Crest Ln	37090
Knoxville Ave	37087
Koble Dr	37087
Kristopher Dr	37087
Kyle Cir	37087
Lago Vista Dr	37087
Lake Dr & St	37087
Lake Wood Rd	37087
Lakeshore Dr	37087
N Lakeview Dr	37087
Lane Rd	37087
Largo Vista Dr	37087
Larkspur Ave	37090
Latta Cir	37087
Laura Ln	37087
Laura Thompson Trl	37090
Lawrence Rose Rd	37087
Lea Cir	37087
Leah Ct	37087
Lealand Ln	37087
Lebanon Hwy & Rd	37087
Ledgewood Dr	37087
Lee Ct & Rd	37087
Leeanna Ln	37090
Leeville Pike	
100-799	37087
800-6399	37090
Leeville Rd	37090
Leftwich Ct	37087
Legends Ct	37090
Legends Dr	37087
Legends Ln	37090
Legends Pt	37090
Legends Trl	37090
Legends Vw	37090
Legends Way	37090
Legends Crest Dr	37090
Legends Ridge Dr & Rd	37090
Lei Lani Dr	37087
Lena Way	37087
E & W Lester Ave	37087
Letcher Ave	37087
Leviton Dr	37090
Lewis Ct	37087
Lexington Dr	37087
NE Liberty Ln	37087
Ligon Dr	37087
Ligon Rd	37090
W Lilac Dr	37087
Lillard Pl	37087
Lily Dr	37087
Lindbergh Dr	37090
Lindsley Rd	37090
Linger Ln	37087
Linwood Dr	37087
Linwood Rd	37090
Lisa Cir	37087
Lock 5 Rd	37087
Locust Grove Rd	37090
Lone Pine Dr	37087
Louise Ln	37087
Lovers Ln	37087
S Lovers Ln	37090
Lucas Ct	37087
Luchan Dr	37087
Lucille St	37087
Lyle St	37087
Mabry Ct	37087
Maddox Simpson Pkwy	37090
Madrid Dr	37087
Magnolia Dr	37087
E & W Main St	37087
Maize Ln	37087
Manchester Blvd	37090
Mann Rd	37087
Manners Rd	37087
E, N & S Maple Dr & St	37087
Maple Crest Dr	37090
Maple Hill Rd	37087
Marion St	37087
E & W Market St	37087
Marks Cir	37087
Martha Cir	37090
Martha Leeville Rd	37090
Martin Ave	37087
Mary Kay Cir	37087
Maryland St	37087
Mayfair Dr	37087
Mayflower Way	37087
Mcclain Ave	37087
Mccowan Dr	37087
Mccreary Pl & Rd	37090
Mccrory Dr	37087
Mcfadden Ct	37087
Mcgregor St	37087
Meade Dr & Pt	37087
Meadow Crest Way	37090
Meadowlane Dr	37087
Meadowlook Dr	37087
Meadows Dr	37087
Meandering Dr	37090
Medical Center Dr	37087
Melanie Dr	37087
Melody Dr	37090
Melrose St	37087
Merriweather Ln	37087
Mill Rd	37090
Mimosa Ct	37087
Mini Ct & Dr	37087
Misty Lake Dr	37087
Mitchell Ln & Rd	37087
Moccasin Rd	37090
Mockingbird Ln	37087
Monument Ln	37087
Moody Ct	37087
Moore Rd	37090
Moore Haven Dr	37087
Moriah Dr	37090
Morris Ln	37087
Moss Ct	37087
Moss Glen Rd	37090
Mulberry Ln	37090
Mulberry St	37087
Murfreesboro Rd	37090
Murphy Dr	37087
Murphy Ln	37090
Murphys Place Ln	37087
Murray Ct	37087
Nathan St	37087
Neal St	37087
Neighborly Ct	37087
New Market Ave	37087
Newby Rd	37090
Newby St	37087
Nickolas Cir & Dr	37087
Nina Cir	37087
Nixon Dr	37090
Noah Ct	37087
Noahs Ark Cir	37087
Nokes Rd	37090
Norene Rd	37090
North St	37087
Northlynn Dr	37087
Northview Cir	37087
O Hara Cv	37087
Oak St	37087
Oak Grove Rd	37090
Oak Hill Cir & Dr	37087
E Oakdale Dr	37087
Oakmont Pl	37087
Odum Ln	37090
Oil Springs Dr	37087
Old Bluebird Rd	37087
Old Hartsville Pike	37087
Old Horn Springs Rd	37087
Old Hunters Point Pike N	37087
Old Laguardo Rd E & W	37087
Old Murfreesboro Rd E	37090
Old Pecan Ln	37087
Old Road Ln	37087
Old Rome Pike	37087
Old Shannon Rd	37090
Old Trammel Ln & Rd	37090
Olive Cir	37087
Orchard Dr	37087
Orchard Hill Ln	37087
Orian Ln	37087
Oriole Dr	37087
Outlet Village Blvd	37090
Overlook Ln	37087
Owen St	37087
Owl Cir & Dr	37087
Pace Dr	37090
Page Ave	37087
Palani Cir	37087
Palmer Cir & Rd	37090
Palmer Place Dr	37090
Paradise Hills Ln	37090
Paris Ct	37090
Park Ave & Dr	37087
Parkside Cir	37087
Parkview Homes Ct	37087
Patrick Ct & St	37087
Payton Farms Rd	37087
Peace Ave	37087
Pebble Cove Rd	37087
Pebble Point Rd	37087
Pemberton Dr	37087
Pennsylvania Anx & Ave	37087
Pershing Hl	37087
Petersburg Ct	37087
Peyton Cir, Ct & Rd	37087
Pharoah Dr	37087
Phelan Dr	37090
Philadelphia Rd	37087
Phillips Ct & Rd	37087
Phoenix Pl	37087
Physicians Way	37090
Piedmont Dr	37087
Piercy Ct	37087
Pine St	37087
Pinewood Dr	37087
Pinhook Rd	37090
Plantation Blvd	37087
Plaza Cir	37087
Pleasant View Dr	37087
Plymouth Dr	37087
Pocahontas Trl	37087
Pointe Ct	37087
Pointe Barton Dr	37087
Ponderosa Trl	37087
Pooh Bear Ln	37087
Poplar Hill Rd	37090
Poraltow Rd	37087
Powell Grove Cir & Rd	37090
Powells Chapel Rd	37090
Preakness Pl	37087
Prichard St	37087
Primrose Ln	37087
Princeton Ct & Dr	37087
Prosperity Way	37090
Providence Dr & Rd	37087
Prowell Lake Rd	37087
Pryor Creek Rd N	37090
Public Sq	37087
Purnell Rd	37090
Quail Meadow Dr	37090
Qualls Ln	37090
Quarles Dr	37087
Quita Cir	37087
Raden Dr	37087
Railroad Ave	37087
Ramsey Ln	
1-499	37087
500-899	37090
Ramsey Rd	37087
Raspberry Ln	37087
Red Cedar Ln	37090
Red Fox Ct	37087
Redbud Ave	37090
Redbud Dr	37087
Remington Rd	37090
Rhett Pl	37087
Riceland Rd	37090
E & W Richmond Shop Rd	37090
Ridgecreek Xing	37087
Ridgecrest Ln	37087
River Dr	37087
Roanoke Dr	37087
Roberts Ln	37087
Rock Castle Dr	37087
Rock Island Way	37087
Rocky Ln & Rd	37087
Rocky Valley Rd	37090
Rogers Ln & St	37087
Rollingwood Dr & Xing	37087
Rome Pike	37087
Rome First St	37087
Rosa Dr	37087
Rutledge Ln	37087
Ryan Ct	37087
Saddlebrook Dr	37087
Saddlestone Dr	37090
Safari Camp Rd	37090
Sagamore Dr	37087
Salem Rd	37090
Sam Houston Dr	37087
Sanders Ave	37087
Sanford Ln	37087
Santa Anna Dr	37087
Sara Cir	37090
Saratoga Dr	37087
W Saulsbury Rd	37090
Scarlett Pl	37087
Scotts Dr	37087
Serenity Way	37090
Shady Cir & Trl	37087
Shady Crest Dr	37087
Shady Stone Way	37090
Shady Valley Dr	37087
Sheath Cir & Ct	37087
Shema Ln	37087
Shenandoah Trl	37087
Sherwood Ln	37090
Shipper Rd	37087
Shirley Dr	37087
Short St	37087
Shorter Rd	37090
Shoulders Ln S	37090
Signature Pl	37087
Silver Meadow Dr	37090
Simmons Bluff Rd	37090
Slaters Dr	37087
Sloan St	37087
Smart Park Dr	37090
Smith Dr & Rd	37087
Sneed Ln	37087
Somerset Dr	37090
Southfork Ct & Dr	37087
Southside Park Dr	37090
Spar Mine Rd	37087
Sparta Pike	
800-1199	37087
1200-3099	37090
Spearhead Dr	37090
Speck Rd	37087
Speedwell Ln	37087
Spickard Rd	37090
Sportshaven Rd	37087
E & W Spring St	37087
Spring Creek Ln	37090
Spring Creek Rd	37087
Spring Hill Cir	37087
Spring Meadow Ln	37087
Springdale Dr	37087
Springfield Dr	37087
Spruce Dr	37087
Stallings Ct	37087
Standish Dr	37087
Steeplechase Ct & Dr	37090
Sterling Oak Ct	37087
Stewart Rd	37087
Stewarts Ferry Pike	37090
Still Creek Way	37087
Stokes St	37087
Stone St	37087
Stone Edge Dr	37087
Stone Hollow Ln	37087
Stonebridge Dr	37090

Stonebrook Dr & Pt 37087
Stonegate Dr 37090
Stonehenge Dr 37090
Stonewall Ct 37087
Stoneway Dr 37087
Stroud Dr 37087
Stumpy Ln 37090
Suanne Dr 37087
Sugar Flat Rd 37087
Suggs Dr 37087
Sullins St 37087
Summercrest Dr 37087
Summerfield Dr 37087
Summerplace Cir, Dr & Ln 37087
Sunnyview Dr 37090
E & W Sunset Dr 37087
Surprise Ln 37087
Surrey Pl 37090
Swindell Hollow Rd 37090
Sycamore Ln & St 37087
Talley Dr 37087
Tanager Ct 37087
N & S Tarver Ave 37087
Taryton Dr 37087
Tater Peeler Rd 37087
SE Tater Peeler Rd
1-99 37087
1000-7999 37090
Taylorsville Rd 37087
Ten Oaks Dr 37087
Ten Throw Dr 37087
Tenear Dr 37087
Tennessee Blvd 37087
Terry Ln 37087
Thany Ct 37087
Thomas Rd & Ter 37087
Thomas Vance Ct 37087
Thorne Ct & Dr 37087
Timber Trail Dr 37090
Tims Way Dr 37087
Tirzah St 37087
Tomlinson Ln, Pl & Rd 37087
Tomlinson Hills Dr 37087
Toshiba Dr 37087
Tott St 37087
Trace Dr 37090
Trammel Ln & Rd 37090
Travelers Ct 37087
Treasury Ln 37087
Tribble Ln 37087
Trice Pl & Rd 37087
Trinity Cir, Dr & Ln 37087
Trousdale Ferry Pike
1-6000 37087
6001-6013 37090
6002-6014 37087
6015-10699 37090
Troy Rd 37087
Trusty Rd 37090
Tuck Ln 37087
Tucker Trice Blvd 37087
Tuckers Gap Rd 37090
Tulip Ave 37090
Turnberry Rd 37090
Twelve Oaks Ct & Ln 37087
Twin Cove Dr 37087
Twyla Ct & Dr 37087
Tyler Ct 37087
Tyree Access Rd 37087
Union Rd 37087
University Ave 37087
Upton Hts 37087
Valleyview Cir & Ct 37087
Vance Ln 37087
Vanhook Dr 37087
Vanview Dr 37087
Vesta Rd 37090
Vicksburg Ct & Ln 37087
Victor Ave 37087
Villa Cir 37090
Village Cir 37087
Vincent Cason Ave 37087
Vine Ct & Way 37087
Vineyard Way 37087
Virginia Ave 37087
Vosswood Dr 37087
Wade Hampton Dr 37087
Wagoner St 37087
Walker Ln 37087
Walleye Pike 37087
Walnut Way 37087
Walnut Grove Rd 37090
Walnut Hill Rd 37090
Walter Morris Rd 37087
Ward St 37087
Ward Hill Rd 37087
Washington Dr 37087
Waters Hill Cir 37087
NE Watson Cir, Rd & St 37087
Watson Cir Ext 37087
Waverly Pl 37087
Weatherly Dr 37087
Weaver Rd 37090
Webster St 37087
Wesley Way 37087
West St 37087
Western Ave 37087
Westfield Dr 37090
Westhill Dr 37087
Westhill Drive Ext 37090
Westland Dr 37087
Westlynn Dr 37087
Westview Dr 37087
Westwood Dr 37087
Wheeler St 37087
Whippoorwill Rd 37090
White Oaks Dr 37087
Whitepine Dr 37087
Whitmore St 37087
Wildberry Dr 37087
Wildcat Way 37090
Wildwood Ave 37087
Wilkes Pt 37087
Wilkins Run 37087
Willard Hagan Dr 37090
Williams Rd & St 37087
Wilson Ave & Rd 37087
Wilson Boat Dock Rd 37087
Winchester Ct 37090
Windham Ct & Trl 37090
Windmere Dr 37090
Windmill Dr 37087
Winston Ave 37087
Winter Dr 37087
Winwood Dr 37087
Wjb Pride Ln 37087
Woodall Rd 37090
Woodhaven Ct 37087
Woodland Dr 37087
Woodmont Ave 37087
Woods Edge Dr 37090
Woods Ferry Rd 37087
Woodside Dr 37087
Woolard St 37087
Woolen Mill St 37087
Wooten Ct 37087
Wrightford Dr 37087
Yeager Pl 37090
Yelton Rd 37087
York St 37087
Yorktown Dr 37087
Young Rd 37090
NE Young Rd 37087
Zachary Rd 37090

LENOIR CITY TN

General Delivery 37771

POST OFFICE BOXES MAIN OFFICE STATIONS AND BRANCHES

Box No.s
All PO Boxes 37771

NAMED STREETS

N & S A St 37771
Abbie Dr 37772
Abbott Rd 37771
Acadia Cir 37771
Adessa Pkwy 37771
Alex Smith Ln 37771
Alexander Rd 37772
Alexis Ln 37772
Allen Rd 37772
Allen Shore Dr 37772
Allison Ln 37771
Alpine Dr 37771
Amberly Ct 37772
Anchor Dr 37771
Anglewood Dr 37772
Antioch Church Rd E & W 37772
Antique Ln 37771
Arrowhead Ct 37772
Ashe Ave 37771
Ashford Ln 37772
Augusta Ln 37772
Avery Cir & St 37772
N & S B St 37771
Babbs Rd 37771
Bank St 37771
Barclay Ct 37772
Barger Ln 37772
Barkmoor Dr 37771
Battlecreek Way 37772
Beacon Ct 37772
Beals Lndg 37772
Beals Chapel Rd 37772
Bell Ave
800-1100 37771
1101-1197 37772
1102-1198 37771
1199-1299 37772
Benjamin Dr 37771
Bethel Dr 37772
Big Hill Rd 37772
Bill Smith Rd 37772
Birchwood Ln 37771
Bird Rd 37771
Biscayne Dr 37772
Blackberry Ridge Dr 37772
Blackburn Ln 37771
Blackfoot Way 37772
Blair Rd 37771
Blue Herron Dr 37772
Blue Tick Ln 37771
Bob Young Ln 37772
Bon St 37771
Bona Vista Ln 37771
Brandon Dr 37771
Brandywine Dr 37772
Breazale Rd 37771
Brentwood Pl 37772
Brewster Rd 37771
Brittni Ln 37771
Britts Dr 37772
Broadway St E
1100-1299 37772
100-1099 37771
W Broadway St 37771
Brooksview Rd 37771
Browder Hollow Rd 37771
Browder School Rd 37771
Bussell Ferry Rd 37771
Buster Blvd 37772
Buttermilk Rd W 37771
N & S C St 37771
C And C Rd 37771
Calloway Cir & Dr 37772
Cameron Ln 37772
Candlenook Ln 37771
Cardinal View Ct 37772
Cardwell Chapel Rd 37771
Careen Ct 37772
Carrington Blvd 37771
Carter Rd 37772
Carters Chapel Rd 37771
Casa Del Lago Way 37772
Casey Ln 37772
Cassidy Ct 37772
Castaway Ln 37772
Cattlemans Dr 37772
Caulderwood Ln 37771
Cedar Cir 37772
Cedar Park Dr 37772
Chelsea Cir 37772
N & S Cherry St 37771
Chestnut Ridge Dr 37771
Cheyenne Blvd 37772
Chimney Rock Dr 37771
Chrisman Rd 37772
Church Dr 37771
City Park Dr 37772
Clarke Rd 37771
Clear Cove Ct 37772
Clinchview Dr 37771
Cobblestone Dr 37772
Coffey Cir 37771
Coley Ln 37771
Columbus Dr 37771
Commodore Dr 37772
Conkinnon Dr 37772
Copenhaver Rd 37771
Cordova Ln 37771
Cornett Rd 37771
Cory Dr 37771
Coulter Shoals Cir 37772
Country Ln 37771
Cove View Ln 37772
Covenant Cir 37772
Cranfield Ln 37772
Creekwood Ct 37772
Creekwood Cove Blvd & Ln 37772
Crescent Oaks Ln 37772
Cress Ln 37772
Crestfield Ln 37771
Crestview Cir & Dr 37772
Crestwood Dr 37771
Crisp Rd 37771
Crooked Oak Dr 37771
Cross Creek Private Ln 37771
Cruze Rd 37772
Cusick Cir & Ln 37772
Cypress Point Dr 37772
N D St 37771
Dairy Ln 37772
Davis Dr 37772
Davis Ln 37771
Davis Ridge Rd 37771
Dead End Rd 37771
Deaton Rd 37772
Deep Cove Ln 37772
Deerfield Ct & Ln 37772
Del Rio Ln 37771
E & W Depot St 37771
Devyn Ln 37772
Dewitt Dr 37772
Dixie Lee Cir & Ln 37772
Dixie Meadows Dr 37772
Dixon Rd 37772
Dogwood Ln 37772
Dogwood Ln E 37772
Dogwood Ter 37771
Donaldson Light Ln 37772
Donna Dr 37771
Downing Ct 37772
Doyle St 37771
Driftwood Ct 37772
Duff Rd 37771
Duggan Rd 37771
Duncan Rd 37772
Dunridge Ln 37772
Dunsmore Rd 37771
Dynasty Dr 37771
N E St 37771
Easter Ridge Rd 37772
Eaton Village Trce 37771
Eblen Ln 37771
Eblen Cave Rd 37771
Echo Hollow Rd 37771
Eden Way 37772
Edge Ln 37771
Edgefield Ln 37771
Edgewater Way 37772
Edinburgh Ln 37771
Edith Ln 37771
El Camino Ln 37771
El Grande Ln 37771
Elizabeth Way 37772
Ellis Rd 37771
Elm Hill Rd 37771
Emerald Court Pl 37771
Essex Ct 37772
Evans Ln 37771
Evergreen Cir 37772
Evern Rogers Rd 37771
Executive Meadows Dr 37771
N & S F St 37771
Fairview Dr & Rd 37771
Falcon Fire Ct 37772
Falcon Head Ct 37772
Fallon Ln 37771
Fawnwood Way 37772
Fieldstone Dr 37772
Fine Rd 37772
Finley Dr 37771
Flagstone Blvd 37772
Flanagan Ln 37771
Flora Dr 37771
Fog Hill Ln 37771
Foothills Rd 37771
Ford Rd 37772
Forest Heights Cir 37772
Forest Hills Dr 37772
Fort Loudoun Medical Center Dr 37772
Foster Dr 37772
Foster Rd 37772
Fountainhead Ct 37772
Foute Town Rd 37772
Fox Hunters Rd 37772
Frances Dr 37771
Friendship Rd 37772
Friendsville Rd 37772
N G St 37771
Gallery Ct 37772
Galyon Dr 37771
Garnet Hill Dr 37772
Gaston Rd 37771
Gayle Ave 37771
Gentry Rd 37771
Giles Rd 37772
Gladstone Rd 37771
Glen Mar Dr 37772
W Glenbrook Dr 37771
Glencroft Ln 37771
W Glenfield Dr 37771
Glenridge Ln 37771
Glenshire Ln 37771
E & W Glenview Cir & Dr 37771
Golf Club Ln 37771
Grallark Rd 37771
Granada Dr 37772
Grand St 37771
Grandview Dr 37772
Grayson Freedman Ln 37771
Green Meadows Ln 37771
Greenleaf Ln 37771
Grubb Ln & Rd 37771
Gunter Dr 37772
N H St 37771
Hackney Chapel Rd 37772
Hair Ln 37771
Hall St 37771
Halls Ferry Rd 37771
Hamilton Ave 37771
Hank Way 37772
Happy Hollow Rd 37771
Harbor Pl 37772
Harbor Point Ct 37772
Harbour Point Cv 37772
Harbour View Dr 37772
Hardin Dr 37772
Hardwick Ln 37771
Harmon Ln 37771
Harrison Ave 37771
Harrison Ln 37771
Harrison Rd 37771
Harvey Rd 37772
Hatteras Cir & Way 37772
Hattley Rd 37771
Heape Rd 37771
Heather Ln 37771
Helm Rd 37772
Hendrix Way 37771
Henline Rd 37771
Hewins Rd 37772
Hickman St 37772
Hickory Creek Rd 37771
Hidden Oaks Ln 37772
Hidden Valley Ln & Rd 37772
Highland Ave 37771
Highland Cir 37772
Highland Park Dr 37771
Hightower Ln 37771
Highway 11 E 37772
Highway 11 W 37771
Highway 321 N 37771
Highway 321 S 37772
Highway 70 E
100-130 37771
Highway 70 E
131-16999 37772
Highway 70 W 37771
Highway 95 N 37772
N Hill St 37771
Hillcrest Dr 37772
W Hills Dr 37771
Hillsborough Ln 37772
Hillside Ln 37771
Hilltop Dr 37772
Hines Ct 37771
Hines Valley Rd 37771
Hirst Cir 37772
Hoffman Dr & Ln 37771
Holbrook Ave 37771
Holland Trl 37772
Holly Leaf Ln 37772
N Holston Dr 37772
Hope Creek Rd 37772
Hotchkiss Valley Rd E 37771
Houston St 37771
Hubbard Rd 37771
Huntsville Hollow Rd 37771
Hw Slaton Way 37772
N I St 37771
Industrial Park Dr 37771
Interchange Park Dr 37772
Ivy Ave 37771
Jackson Bend Rd 37772
Jacksonian Way 37772
James Dr 37772
Jan Way 37771
Jessie Ln 37771
Jim Conner Rd 37771
Jim Hartsook Dr 37771
Johnson Cir & Dr 37771
Jones Rd 37771
Judson Way 37772
Julie Ln 37771
N K St 37771
Kagley Dr 37772
Karmadale Dr 37772
Kash Rd 37771
Keaton Rd 37772
Keener Ln 37772
Kelly Ln 37772
Kelsey Ln 37772
Kennedy Dr 37772
Kennesaw Ln 37771
Kerr St 37771
Kevin Ln 37772
Kimbrell Rd 37772
Kimerson Ct 37772
Kingston Hwy & St 37772
Kirk Ave 37771
Krystle Ct 37771
La Casa Ln 37771
Lake Cove Dr 37772
Lake Crest Dr 37772
Lake Forest Dr 37772
Lake Harbor Dr 37772
Lakeland Dr 37772
Lakeland Estates Dr 37771
Lakeland Farms Rd 37772
Lakeside Dr 37772
Lakeview Rd 37772
W Lamar Alexander Pkwy 37772
Lancaster Dr 37771
Lane Rd 37772
E Lee Dr & Hwy 37771
Lee Hi Ln & St 37772
Leeper Pkwy 37772
Leeward Way 37772
Leland Way 37771
Lennox Ct 37772
Lenoir City Plz 37771
Leona Dr 37772
Letterman Rd 37772
Lewis Ln 37771
Lighthouse Point Dr 37772
Liles Rd 37771
Lina Way 37772
Linden Ln 37772
Linder Ln 37772
Linginfelter Ln 37772
Little Mountain Ln 37771
Lloyd Ln 37771
Locomotive Dr 37771
Locust St 37771
Long Rd 37772
Long Cove Ct 37772
Loudon Ridge Rd 37771
Lucy Ln 37772
M St 37771
Maclaren Way 37772
Magnolia Cir 37772
Malone Rd 37771
Manis Dr & Rd 37771
Manning Ln 37772
Maple St 37771
Mapletree Ln 37772
Marina Way 37772
Market Dr 37771
Martel Rd 37772
Martin Dr 37771
Mashburn Dr 37772
Matlock Rd 37771
Mcbride Way 37771
Mcdaniel Ln 37772
Mcfalls Ln 37771
Mcghee Blvd 37771
Mckamie Ln 37772
Mckinney Ave 37771
Mcnew Rd 37771
Meadow Dr & Rd W 37772
Meadow Walk Ln 37772
Mealer Rd 37771
Medical Park Dr 37772
Melissa Way 37772
Midway Rd 37772
Miller Rd 37772
Mimosa St 37772
Mincey St 37771
Misty Ridge Dr & Way 37772
Misty View Ln 37772
Moats Dr 37771
Montcrest Dr 37771
Monticello Dr 37771
Montview Rd 37771
Monument St 37772
Moore Ridge Rd 37771
Morning Point Dr 37772
Morton Ln & Rd 37772
Mountain Dr 37772
Mountain View Rd 37771
Muddy Creek Rd 37772
Myers Rd 37771
N St 37771
Neeley Rd 37772
Nelson St 37771
Newberry Dr 37772
Newton Rd 37771
Nichols Rd 37772
Nicolosi Ln 37771
Northshore Dr 37772
Northside Dr 37772
Northview Dr 37771

Norwood St 37771
O St 37771
N & S Oak St 37772
Oak Chase Blvd 37772
Oak Grove Rd 37771
Oak Hills Dr 37771
Oakland Ave 37771
Oakley Glen Ln 37772
Oakum Ct 37772
Oakwood Dr 37771
Oakwood Estates Dr 37772
Old Bailey Rd 37772
Old Eblen Rd 37771
Old Farm Rd 37771
Old Greenback Rd 37772
Old Hickory Ln 37772
Old Highway 95 37771
Old Loudon Pike 37771
Old Midway Rd 37772
Old Spears Rd 37772
Old Stage Rd 37772
Old Waller Ferry Dr & Rd 37771
Olympic Dr 37771
Orchard Dr 37772
Oren White Rd 37771
Osprey Cove Ct E & W 37772
Otter Ln 37772
Outer Dr 37771
Overlook Rd 37771
Palmer Dr 37772
Panther Dr 37771
Pardue Ln 37772
Parkway Dr 37771
Parris Dr 37772
Pate Rd 37772
Pauls Ln 37771
Paw Paw Plains Rd 37771
Pawnook Farm Rd 37771
Pearl Dr 37772
Pebble Ct 37772
Pembrook Point Ct 37772
Perkle Rd 37772
Phelps Rd 37772
Phillips Rd 37771
Pike St 37771
Pine Ridge Dr 37771
Pine Top St 37772
Pinecrest Cir 37772
Pinewood Dr 37771
Point Harbor Dr 37772
Poplar St 37771
E Port Dr 37772
Porter Ln 37772
Portland Dr 37771
Prestwick Ln 37771
Price Rd 37771
Proffitt Hill Dr 37772
Q St 37771
Ranchero Dr 37772
Rawhide Trl 37772
Red Grouse Dr 37772
Redbud Ct 37771
Redwolf Way 37772
Reeves St 37771
Rest Camp Rd 37772
Ridgebark Ln 37772
Ridgeview Dr 37771
Riley Dr 37771
River Chase Rd 37772
River Point Dr 37772
Riverview Rd 37771
Roberts Cir 37772
Robinson Cir & Dr 37772
Rock Springs Anx & Rd 37771
Rocky Top Rd 37771
Rodney Rd 37772
Rogers Cir & Dr 37771
Rosa Way 37772
N & S Rose St 37771
Roundup Ln 37772
Ruritan Rd 37771
Rushbrook Ln 37771
Russell Ln 37772
Sable Ct 37771
Saint Thomas Way 37772
Sam Ray Burn Pkwy 37771
Sandy Shore Dr 37772
Scenic Dr 37772
Scenic Hill Ln 37771
Scenic View Ln 37771
Selma St 37771
Shadowbay Ln 37772
Shady Ln 37771
Sharp Dr 37771
Shaw Ferry Ln 37772
Shaw Ferry Rd 37772
Shaw Ferry Rd N 37772
Shenandoah Dr 37771
Shipley Ln 37772
Silo Dr 37772
Silver Leaf Dr 37772
Silver Oaks Ln 37772
Simpson Rd 37771
Simpson Rd E 37772
Simpson Rd W 37771
Skyview Dr 37772
Smith Valley Rd 37772
Smith Waller Ln 37771
Snodderly Rd 37771
Snow Rd 37772
Southern Way 37772
Spring Pl & Rd 37771
Spring Oak Ln 37772
Spring View Dr 37772
Stevens Ln 37771
Stillwater Cir 37772
Stinnett Rd 37772
Stone Harbor Blvd 37772
Stonebrook Ln 37772
Strange Rd 37772
Sugarlimb Rd 37771
Sutton Ln 37771
Sweeten Rd 37771
Taffrail Dr 37772
Taft Packett Rd 37772
Tate Coley Rd 37771
Taylor Dr 37772
Tee Ln 37771
The Oaks Ct 37771
Thomas Wood Way 37772
Thompson Rd 37772
Thornton Dr 37772
Thurmer Cir 37772
Timber Cir 37772
Timber Ridge Dr 37771
Timberline Dr 37772
Tinnel Ln & Rd 37772
Tom Lee Rd 37771
Town Creek Cir 37771
Town Creek Pkwy 37771
Town Creek Rd E 37772
Town Creek Rd W 37771
Tracy Ln 37771
Trades Dr 37771
Tristan Ct 37771
Tristan Way 37772
Tucker Ln 37771
Turkey Pen Ln 37772
Turman Dr 37772
Turn Lane Rd 37771
Turnberry Cir 37772
Turner Ln 37771
Turtle Cove Ct 37772
Twin Coves Cir & Dr 37772
Twin Lakes Rd 37772
Unitia Rd 37772
Upper Jones Rd 37771
Valley Dale Dr 37771
Valleyview Dr 37772
Vaughn Rd 37772
Vaughns Chapel Rd 37771
Viking Way 37772
Vincil St 37771
Vineyard Rd 37772
Virginia Ln 37771
Virtue Rd 37772
Waller St 37771
Waller Ferry Rd 37771
N & S Walnut St 37771
Wampler Dr 37772
Ward Rd 37771
Warren Cove Ln 37772
Waterford Cir 37772
Waters Edge Way 37771
Watterri Rd 37772
Webb Cir 37771
Wedgewood Dr 37772
Wesley Rd 37772
West Ln 37771
Westchester Ct 37772
Wheat Rd 37771
Wheeler Dr 37772
Whispering Oaks Dr 37771
White Wing Rd 37771
Whitney Dr 37772
Wilkerson Ln 37772
Williams Ferry Rd 37771
Williamsburg Dr 37772
Willingham Dr 37771
Willow Ridge Rd 37771
Wilson Ln 37772
Wilson Rd 37772
Wilson St 37771
Winchester Dr 37772
Windlass Dr 37772
Windswept Dr 37772
Windward Pt 37772
Windy Oaks Ct 37772
S Wingate Way 37771
Wipp Rd 37771
Woodlawn Rd 37771
Woodlawn Church Rd 37771
Yale Ave 37771
Yarberry Rd 37772
Yedear Rd 37772
Yellowstone Ln 37771
Yosemite Dr 37771
Yvonne Way 37771
Zane Ln 37772

NUMBERED STREETS

E 1st Ave
100-1099 37771
1104-1399 37772
W 1st Ave 37771
E 2nd Ave
100-1101 37771
1102-1399 37772
W 2nd Ave 37771
E 3rd Ave
100-1199 37771
1200-1399 37772
W 3rd Ave 37771
E & W 4th 37771
E & W 5th 37771
E & W 6th 37771
W 7th Ave 37771
W 8th Ave 37771
E & W 9th 37771
W 10th Ave 37771
11 Estates Dr 37772

MADISON TN

General Delivery 37115

POST OFFICE BOXES MAIN OFFICE STATIONS AND BRANCHES

Box No.s
All PO Boxes 37116

NAMED STREETS

All Street Addresses 37115

NUMBERED STREETS

All Street Addresses 37115

MANCHESTER TN

General Delivery 37355

POST OFFICE BOXES MAIN OFFICE STATIONS AND BRANCHES

Box No.s
All PO Boxes 37349

NAMED STREETS

All Street Addresses 37355

NUMBERED STREETS

All Street Addresses 37355

MARYVILLE TN

General Delivery 37804

POST OFFICE BOXES MAIN OFFICE STATIONS AND BRANCHES

Box No.s
2001 - 2900 37804
4001 - 9840 37802

NAMED STREETS

Abbott Rd 37803
Acorn Way 37801
Adas Way 37803
Advent St 37801
Agate Cir 37804
Aggie Dr 37803
Air Bag Way 37801
Akers St 37804
Alcoa Trl 37804
Aldersgate Rd 37804
Alex Way 37801
Alexander St 37804
Alfred Mccammon Rd 37804
Alisha Way 37801
Allegheny Cove Way 37803
Allegheny Loop Rd 37803
Allen Ct 37804
Allen Dr 37803
Allison Ave 37804
Alnwick Blvd 37801
E Alpine Dr 37804
Aluminum Ave 37804
Alvin York St 37801
Amanda Dr 37801
Amberland Ln 37804
Amburn Dr 37803
Amburn Meadows Ln 37801
Amerine Rd 37804
Amhurst Dr 37801
Amity Crest Ln 37803
Amy Dr 37801
Amy Renee Way 37801
Andera Dr 37801
Anderson Ave 37803
Andrea Dr 37804
Andrew Way 37801
Andrew Boyd Dr 37804
Andy Ln 37803
Angus Blvd 37803
Apache Ct 37801
Apache Dr 37801
Apache Rd 37804
Appalachia Dr 37803
Applewood Way 37803
Arabian Ln 37801
Arbor Dr 37804
Archer Ave 37804
Ardennes Dr 37801
Ardmore Cir 37804
Argo Dr 37801
Argonne Dr 37804
Argyle Way 37801
Armona Rd 37801
Arnhem Cir 37801
Arnold St 37804
Arrowhead Blvd & Dr 37801
Arthur Ave 37804
Arthur Walker Rd 37803
Asbury Dr & Way 37804
Ashbrook Ln 37801
Asher Way 37803
Aster Pl 37804
Atchley Dr 37801
Atchley Apartments 37801
Atlantic Ave 37801
Auburn Dr 37801
Aud Orr Dr 37801
Augusta Ave 37804
Auto Dr 37801
Autumn Dr 37804
Autumn Brook Dr 37801
Autumn Oak Cir 37801
Autumn View Dr 37803
Avalon Bay Ln 37804
Azalea Dr 37804
Bailey Way 37803
Baker Ridge Way 37803
Bannockburn Cir 37803
Barbara Ln 37803
Barberry Ct 37804
Barclay Ct 37803
Barker Ln 37803
Barkshed Rd 37803
Barnes Ave 37803
Barney Patton Cir 37804
Barrington Blvd 37803
Barsha Fields Ln 37804
Bart Trl 37803
Bart Giffin Rd 37803
Bartlett St 37804
Bass Aly 37803
Bastogne Dr 37801
Baumgardner Rd 37803
Baxter View Dr 37804
Bay Cir 37801
Bayberry Ter 37804
Beaumont Ave 37803
Beaver Dr 37801
Beaver Creek Xing 37804
Beck St 37801
Beckford Dr 37801
Bedford Ct 37803
Beech Grove Trl 37803
Belfair Ln 37804
Belfast St 37801
Belgradia Ct 37803
Belle St 37803
Belle Meade Dr 37803
Belleau Dr 37804
Belleville Ave 37803
Bellwood Dr 37803
S Belmont Ave & Dr 37804
Belvedere Ct 37803
Ben Abbott Rd 37803
Benjamin Dr 37804
Benny Delozier Dr 37804
Bens View Ct 37803
Berea Cir 37803
Berryhill Dr 37801
Berrywood Dr 37801
Bert Garner Ln 37803
Berwyn Dr 37803
Best Rd & St 37803
Bethany Ct 37803
Bexley Dr 37803
Big Bend Dr 37803
Big Dee Ln 37801
Big Elm Rd 37801
Big Gully Rd 37801
Big Springs Rd 37801
Big Z Dr 37801
Bill Everett Rd 37803
Biltmore Dr 37801
Binfield Rd 37801
Bingham Ln 37801
Birdwell Dr 37804
Bishop Hollow Rd 37803
Bittle Ave & Rd 37804
Black Forest Dr 37801
Black Sulfer Way 37803
Blackberry Way 37803
Blacksmith Ln 37803
Blackstock Dr 37801
Blair Ln 37804
Blake Dr 37801
Blankenship Rd 37803
Blockhouse Rd 37803
Bloomfield Cir 37803
Blount Ave 37804
Blue Beech Dr 37803
Blue Forest Ct & Ln 37803
Blue Holly Cir 37803
Blue Phlox Ln 37803
Blue Sky Dr 37801
Bluebell Cir 37804
Bluebird Ln 37803
Bmh Cancer Ctr 37804
Bmh Physicians Office Bldg 37804
Boardman Ave 37803
Bob Baribeau Dr 37801
Bob Irwin Rd 37803
Bob Thompson Rd 37803
Bob Wilson Pl 37804
Bobwhite Cir & Dr 37803
Bogart Ln 37804
Bogle St 37804
Bolinger Rd 37801
Bonnie Brae Dr 37801
Bonnie Vista Dr 37804
Borghild Dr 37801
Boulder St 37804
Boyd Ave 37803
Bradford Way 37803
Bradley St 37804
Brae Ct 37801
Bramblewood Dr 37801
Brandi Ln 37804
Brandon Lee Dr 37804
Brandon Park Dr 37804
Brannon Dr 37803
Brantley Park Blvd 37804
Breedlove Ln 37804
Brentwood Dr 37804
Brewer Rd 37801
Briar Hill Way 37803
N & S Briarcliff Cir 37803
Brick Mill Rd 37801
Brickmill Commercial Dr 37801
Bridger Ln 37801
Bridgewater Xing 37804
Bridgeway Dr 37801
Brighton Dr 37803
Brighton Meadows Dr 37803
Brittingham Dr 37801
Broad Run Dr 37803
Broaderick Blvd 37801
Broadmoor Dr 37803
E Broadway Ave 37804
W Broadway Ave 37801
Broadway Church St 37804
Broadway Towers 37801
Broady Ln 37803
Brook Ave 37801
Brookdale Rd 37801
Brookfield Ln 37803
Brookhollow Trl 37804
Brooklyn Ln 37804
Brookmeade Ave 37804
Brookshire Blvd 37803
Brookside Ave 37804
E Brown School Rd 37804
Brownlee St 37801
Browns Ct 37804
Broyles Ave 37801
Brunswick Dr 37803
Bryan Ln 37803
Bryant Hollow Rd 37803
Buchanan Rd 37803
Buck Hollow Rd 37803
Buckhaven Ct 37803
Buckingham Cir 37803
Bunberry Ln 37801
Bungalow St 37801
S Burchfield Ln 37803
Burchfield St 37804
Burlingame Dr 37801
Burnside Dr 37801
Burwood St 37801
Butler Rd 37804
Butler Mill Rd 37803
Butterfly Gap Loop & Rd 37803
Butterfly Hollow Rd 37803
Butternut Dr 37804
Buttonwood Ct 37803
Byerley Ave 37804
Cable Rd 37803
Calderwood Ave & Hwy 37801
Calumet Ct 37801
Camden Dr 37803
Camellia Trce 37801
Camelot Dr 37803
Camley Ct 37801
Candlewood Ct 37804
Candora Rd & Xrd 37804
Cannon Rd 37801
Cansler Ct & Dr 37801
Canterbury Cir 37803
Cape Dr 37801
Cardin Ln 37804
Cardinal St 37803
Carlton Ct 37804
Carolyn Ln 37801
Carowinds Cir 37803
Carpenters Campground Rd 37803
Carpenters Grade Rd 37803
Carpenters School Rd 37803
Carpenters View Dr 37801
Carter Ave 37803
Carter Dr 37801
Carter Springs Dr 37801
S Carver Rd 37801
Cascade Ln 37803
Casey Ln 37801
Cates St
200-399 37801
400-899 37803
Caughron Way 37803
Cavalier Dr 37803
Cave Mill Rd 37804
Cavet Dr 37803
Cayugas Ln 37801
Cecelia Ave 37804
N Cedar St 37801
S Cedar St 37803
Cedar Park Dr 37803
Cedar Pointe Ln 37801
Cedargate Dr 37803
Cedarlawn Blvd 37801
Cedarwood Ln 37803
Celtic Rd 37801
Centenary Rd 37803
Centenary Church Rd 37803
Centennial Church Rd 37804
Century Dr 37803
Champions Dr 37801
Chancellors Ct 37801
Chantay Dr 37803
Chantilly Ln 37803
Chapel Meadows Way 37801
Chapelwood Cir 37804
Charles St 37804
Charles Earl Ln 37803
Charleston Ln 37803
Chas Way Blvd 37803
Chase Dr 37804
Chasewood Ln 37803
Chaucer Cir 37803
Chelsea Ln 37803
Cheltenham Rd 37804
Cherbourg Dr & St 37801

Street	ZIP
Cherokee Ct	37801
Cherokee Dr	37801
Cherokee St	37804
Cherokee Heights Dr	37801
Cherokee Professional Park	37804
Cherry Dr	37804
Chessingham Dr	37801
Chester Cir	37804
Chesterfield Dr	37803
Chesterhill Ct	37804
Chestnut Ln	37801
Chesty Puller Cir	37803
Chevelle Way	37801
Cheyenne Ct	37801
Chickadee Cir	37801
Chicory	37801
Chilhowee Ave	37801
Chilhowee Trl	37803
Chilhowee Heights Rd	37803
Chilhowee Medical Park	37804
Chilhowee Mountain Trl	37803
Chilhowee View Rd	37803
Chilly Springs Rd	37803
Chilton Dr	37803
Chinaberry Dr	37804
Chippendale Dr	37803
Chippewa Rd	37804
Chota Rd	37803
Choto Ct	37801
Chris Lail Way	37801
Christenberry Dr	37801
Christi Lynn Ct	37804
Christie Hill Rd	37803
E Church Ave	37804
W Church Ave	37801
Churchill Dr	37803
Cimarron St	37801
Cinema Dr	37804
Circle Dr	37803
Claremont Dr	37803
Clarion Ave	37803
E Clark Ave	37804
Clark St	37803
N Clark St	37803
S Clark St	37803
Claymore Ct	37801
Clayton Ct & Rd	37804
Clayton Homes Dr	37804
Clearview Rd	37801
Clendenen Rd	37801
Cliff Ct	37803
Clifford Russell Rd	37801
Clifton Way	37803
Clover Hill Rd	37801
Clover Hill Mill Rd	37801
N Clover Hill Ridge Rd	37801
Clyde Cir	37804
Clydesdale St	37801
Coada Ln	37801
Cobble Way	37803
Cochran Pl & Rd	37803
Coffey Way	37801
Coker Rd	37801
Cokesbury Cir	37804
Colby Cv	37801
Colby Dr	37803
N Coleman Dr	37803
S Coleman Dr	37803
Coleman St	37804
Colleen Ct	37801
College St	37804
College Woods Ln	37803
Collin Way	37804
Colonel Jim Dr	37804
Colonial Cir	37803
Colonial Ct	37801
Colony Dr	37803
Columbia Rd	37801
Columbus St	37804
Comanche Trl	37804
Comfort Ave	37801
Commercial Dr	37801
Compton Dr	37804
Comstock Dr	37803
Conde Linsday Cir	37801
Condry Ln	37803
Coning Rd	37803
Continental Dr	37804
Cooks Hollow Rd	37801
Cooper St	37803
Coral Cir	37801
Cordell Ave	37804
Cornell Rd	37801
Coronado Crest Rd	37804
Cottage Glen Ln	37801
Coulter Rd	37804
Country Meadows Ln	37803
Countryside Ct	37804
County Farm Rd	37801
Court Cir	37804
Court St	37804
N Court St	37804
S Court St	37803
Court Christopher Way	37801
Courtyard Cir	37804
Cove Cir	37801
Coventry Ct	37803
Covington Ln	37804
Cowan St	37804
Coyote Way	37801
Cracker Jack Way	37801
Cranberry Dr	37804
Cranfield Dr	37801
Crawford St	37804
Crazy Horse Dr	37801
Creason Dr	37801
Creekstone Cir	37804
Creekwood Dr	37804
Creole Dr	37801
Crescent Ridge Ct	37804
Crest Rd	37804
Crestfield Ct	37804
Crestline Dr	37803
Crestridge Dr	37804
Crestview Dr	37803
Cripple Creek Ln	37801
Crisp Cir	37801
Crooked Creek Way	37803
Crooked Stick Dr	37801
SW Cross Rd	37803
Cross Creek Dr	37803
Crye Rd	37801
Crystal Ln	37804
Cullen St	37804
Culverts Cv	37801
N & S Cumberland St	37804
Cunningham St	37803
Cupp Ave	37804
Cureton Ave	37804
Currie Ave	37804
N & S Cusick Rd & St	37804
Custer Rd	37804
Cutshaw Rd	37803
Cypress Dr	37803
Cyrus Way	37801
Daisy Cir	37804
Dakota Ct & Dr	37801
Danbury Ct	37804
Daniel Way	37803
Danielle Ct	37803
Dante Cir	37803
Darby Cir	37804
Darwick Cir	37803
Dave Ln	37801
Dave Cooper Rd	37803
Davenport Rd	37801
Daventry Dr	37804
David Ln	37803
Davis Dr	37803
Davis Acres Dr	37804
Davis Ford Rd	37804
Dawn Hill Ln	37801
Dawnybrook Dr	37804
Daybreak Dr	37801
De Armond Ln	37804
Deer Run Dr	37803
Deerfield Cir	37804
Deerstone Dr	37801
Defoe Cir & Ct	37804
Dell Cir & Rd	37804
Delozier Ln	37804
Deltas Way	37803
Denton Hayes Rd	37803
Desimone Dr	37801
Destiny Ln	37804
Devictor Dr	37801
Devon Cir	37804
Dewberry Dr	37804
Diamond Branch Rd	37801
Disney Ln	37803
Dixie Way	37803
Dixon Rd	37801
Doc Hannah Rd	37803
Doc Norton Rd	37804
Dockery Dr	37804
S Dogwood Dr	37804
Dogwood Hill Ln	37803
Doll Ave	37801
Dominion Dr	37803
Doral Dr	37801
Doris Ln	37803
Dorothy Dr	37804
Dotson Memorial Rd	37801
Douglas Ave	37804
Downey Dr	37801
Downing Cir	37803
Dragonfly Way	37803
Dreia Dr	37801
Druid Hill Cir & Dr	37804
Dryden Ln	37804
Dublin Dr	37803
Duke Rd	37803
Dunbarton Dr	37803
Duncan Dr & Rd	37803
Dundee Dr	37803
Dunkirk Dr	37801
Dunlap St	37801
Dunn Ave	37804
Dusjane Way	37801
Dusty Ln	37801
Duward Ct	37803
Eagle Dr	37803
Eagle Crossing Dr	37801
Eagle Ridge Rd	37803
Eagleton Rd	37804
East St	37804
Eastover Dr	37803
Eastwood Dr	37803
Eau Clair Dr	37803
Echo Hill Way	37801
Eckles Dr	37804
Ed Davis Rd	37801
Edinburgh Dr	37803
Edna Garland Rd	37801
Ednas Way	37803
Effie Henderson Dr	37803
Effler Rd	37803
Eggers Ln	37803
Elderberry Rd	37801
Eleanor Dr	37803
Eleanor Davis Dr	37804
Elizabeth St	37804
Elkmont Cir	37801
Ellington Dr	37804
Ellis Ave	37804
Elm Dr	37804
Elmer Lambert Rd	37803
Elmira Ln	37804
Elsborn Ridge Rd	37801
Emert Williams Rd	37803
Emma Ln	37803
Emma Ross Ln	37803
Emory Ave	37804
English Ave	37804
Enterprise Way	37801
Epworth Rd	37804
Erin Dr	37803
Esponge Meadow Way	37803
Esquire Dr	37801
Essex Ct	37803
Estonia Way	37803
Ethan Ln	37803
Eva Jean Dr	37804
Evan Cir	37804
Evelyn Ave	37801
Everett Ave	37804
N & S Everett High Rd	37804
Everett Pointe Ln	37804
Excellence Way	37801
Exeter Ct	37803
Eyers Way	37803
Fairfield Dr	37804
Fairlawn Cir	37801
Fairoaks Dr	37803
Fairview Blvd & Dr	37803
Fairview School Cir	37803
Falcon Dr	37803
Fallen Oak Cir	37803
Farmington Way	37801
Farmview Dr	37804
Farris Rd	37803
W Faye Dr	37803
Faye St	37804
Feist Way	37803
Feldspar Ln	37804
Felix Ct	37803
Field Crest Ln	37801
Fielding Dr	37804
Fieldview Rd	37804
Finch Dr	37801
Fir Ct	37804
Firefly Ln	37803
Firewood Ln	37803
E First St	37804
Five Oaks Ln	37801
Flanders Ln	37803
Fletcher Ct & St	37804
Flintstone Ct	37803
Floyd Dr	37804
Floyd Lambert Rd	37803
Floyd Porter Rd	37803
Floyd Walker Rd	37801
Foch St	37801
Fontana Ave	37804
Foothills Mall & Plz	37801
Foothills Mall Dr	37801
S Foothills Plaza Dr	37801
Foothills Village Cir	37801
Forest Ave	37804
Forest Hill Rd	37803
Forest Lake Way	37803
Forestwood Cir	37803
Forster St	37803
Foss Rd	37801
Fossil Ln	37804
Foster Ct	37804
Fowler Dr	37803
Fox Cv	37803
Fox St	37801
Foxdale Dr	37803
Foxglove Ln	37801
France Ct & Ln	37803
Francis St	37804
Franklin Dr	37801
Franklin Hill Blvd	37804
Fred Lawson Rd	37801
Freds Ct	37801
Freedom Dr	37801
Freemont Cir	37804
French St	37804
Friendship Way	37803
Front St	37804
Ft Overlook	37801
Gadwall Ln	37801
Galax Way	37804
Galyon Rd	37803
Gamble Ave	37801
Gamble Ln	37804
Gap Creek Rd	37803
Garden Vale Apts	37803
Garden View Dr	37803
Garland Rd	37801
Garner Cir	37803
Garner Hills Way	37803
Garrett Ln	37804
Garwood Ln	37803
Gary Jarvis Dr	37801
Gateway Rd	37804
Gaudio Way	37801
Gayle Ln	37803
Gee Tipton Dr	37801
Genesis St	37804
Genie Davis Dr	37801
Geno Cir	37803
George St	37804
Georgetown Ct	37803
Gethsemane Rd	37803
Gilbert Ave	37804
Gillenwater Ct & Rd	37801
Gilliland Ln	37804
Ginger Way	37804
Glade Dr	37803
Gladstone Cir	37804
Glasow St	37801
Glen Echo Dr	37801
Glen Oaks Dr	37804
Glenfield Cir	37804
Glenwood Dr	37803
Gloucester Ct	37803
E & W Goddard Ave	37803
Golden Rose Dr	37803
Goldleaf St	37801
Golf View Dr	37801
Gossett Ridge Way	37803
Governors Ct	37801
Grace Ct & St	37804
Grand Vista Dr	37803
Grandview Dr	37803
Grange Way	37804
Grant Ct	37804
Grant Townhouse Dr	37804
Grassland Dr	37804
Grassmere Pt	37803
Graves Rd	37803
Green Rd	37804
Green Briar Cir	37803
Greenbelt Dr	37804
Greencrest Dr	37803
Greeneforest Dr	37803
Greenfield Cir	37804
Greenfield Dr	37803
Greenhill Dr	37804
Greenway Dr	37803
Greenwich Dr	37803
Greenwood Dr	37803
Grey Ridge Rd	37801
Greyson Woods Dr	37803
Gribble Rd	37803
Griffin Ave	37804
Griffitt St	37804
Griffitts Mill Cir	37803
Griselda Dr	37803
Grove St	37804
Guadal Canal Dr	37803
Gulf Cir	37801
Habitat Cir	37801
Hackamoor Ln	37803
Hackberry Ln	37801
Hackney Ln	37801
Haig St	37801
Hale St	37801
Haley Way	37801
Hallerins Ct	37801
Hammontree Ln	37801
Hampshire Dr	37801
S Hampton Way	37803
Hampton Park Dr	37801
Hanna Ave	37804
Harainso Rd	37804
Harbor Town Dr	37801
Harbor View Ln	37801
Hardwick Dr	37803
Harkleroad Cir	37801
Harmon Rd	37804
Harold Dr	37803
E Harper Ave	37804
W Harper Ave	37801
Harrell St	37804
Harrington Ct	37803
Harris Hill Rd	37804
Harrisdale St	37801
Harrison Carver Rd	37801
Hartford Ave	37803
Harvard St	37801
Harvest Ln	37801
Harvey St	37804
Harville St	37804
Hastings Ct	37803
Hatcher Ln	37803
Havenwood Ct & Dr	37804
Haverford Ln	37804
Hawk Hill Way	37801
Hawks Ridge Dr	37801
Hawthorne Dr	37803
Hayden Ct	37804
Headrick Dr	37803
Headrickview Dr	37804
Heartland Dr	37801
Heather Glen Dr	37801
Heathmoore Ct	37803
Heathrow Dr	37801
Helens Ct	37803
Helmsley Ct	37803
Helton Rd	37804
Henderson St	37804
Henry G Lane St	37801
Hepatica Dr	37804
N & S Heritage Dr	37801
Heritage Crossing Dr	37804
Heritage Square Ct	37803
Heritage View Dr	37804
Heron Ave	37803
Hi View Ln	37801
Hickory Dr	37804
Hickory Ln	37801
Hickory Corner Cir & Dr	37804
Hickory Nut Way	37801
Hidden Cove Ct	37803
Hiddenbrook Ln	37804
High St	37804
High Park Cir	37803
High Rose Blvd	37801
High Tower Rd	37804
Highland Ave	
200-399	37801
400-699	37803
Highland Rd	37801
Highway 72	37801
Hill Ct	37803
Hill Run Dr	37803
Hillcrest Ave	37801
W Hills Dr	37803
Hillside Ave	37804
Hilltop Dr	37804
Hillview Dr	37801
Hillwood Dr	37804
Himeswood Way	37803
Hitch Rd	37804
Hitchhike Trl	37803
Hitson Rd	37801
Hodges Ln	37803
Hoegridge Pt	37803
Holder Rd	37801
Holliday Dr	37804
Holly St	37804
Holton Rd	37803
Holyrood Way	37803
Home Ave	37801
Homer Byerly Ct	37804
Homestead Ct	37804
Honeysuckle Rd	37801
Hood St	37803
Hooklot Rd	37803
Hoover St	37801
Hope St	37801
Hopewell Rd	37801
Hopi Dr	37804
Horace Taylor Ct & Rd	37803
Hotel Ave	37804
Houston Ave	37804
N Houston St	37801
Houston Town St	37801
Howard St	37804
Howard Cupp Way	37803
Howard Jones Rd	37801
Howard School Rd	37801
Howell Cir	37803
Hubbard Dr	37804
Hubbard School Rd	37803
Hudson St	37801
Huffstetler Rd	37803
Hughes Loop	37803
Hummingbird Dr	37803
Hunnicut Ave	37804
E Hunt Rd	37804
W Hunt Rd	37801
Hunter Ln	37803
Hunters Rdg	37803
Hunters Hill Blvd & Way	37803
Hunters Way Ct	37803
Huntington Ct & Pl	37803
Huntington Farms Rd	37803
Hurstbourne Ln	37803
Hutsell Hill Way	37803
Hutton Ridge Rd	37801
Impalla Way	37801
Incline Ln	37804
Independence Dr	37803
Indian Shadows Dr	37801
Indian Warpath Rd	37803
Indian Wells Dr	37801
Indiana Ave	37803
Ingrid Dr	37801
Innisbrook Cir	37801
Inverness Dr	37801
Ironwood Cir	37804
Irwin Ave	37804
Island Dr	37801
Issac Ct	37804
Ivey Vine Dr	37801
Ivy Log Ln	37804
Ivy Ridge Ln	37801
Jackson Ave	37801
Jackson Hills Dr	37804
Jade Ln	37804
Jama Way	37803
James Ave	37803
James Mcmillian Dr	37803
Jameson Way	37801
Jamestown Way	37803
Jameswood Dr	37804
Jamie Dr	37804
Janes Rd	37803
Janet Ln	37804
Janeway Rd	37801
Jasmine Ln	37801
Jeania Ln	37801
Jefferson Ave	37803
Jennings Rd	37801
Jericho Rd	37803
Jericho Valley Way	37803
Jersey Way	37803
Jeseph Ct	37803
Jess Cir	37801
Jessicas Way	37801
Jett Rd	37804
Jewell Weed Way	37803
Jodi Ln	37801
John Anthony Ln	37804
John Bouldin Dr	37801
John Helton Rd	37804
John Mill Way	37801
John Noah Myers Rd	37803
Johnson Rd	37804
Jones Ave	37804
Jordon Way	37801
Jos Way	37803
Joshua Dr	37804
Jubilee Cir	37801
June Bug Way	37803
Juneau Way	37801
Justin Dr	37801
Kagley Chapel Rd	37803
Kagley View Rd	37803
Karch Dr	37803
Karenwood Dr	37804
Karina Cir	37804
Karrow St	37803
Kathryn Ct	37804
Katie Ct	37801
Katie Brook Ln	37803
Kayla Dr	37803
Keeble Rd & St	37804

Keeneland Dr 37803
Keeper Way 37803
Keith Rd 37801
Keller Dr 37803
Keller Ln 37801
Kelton Ln 37803
Kenilworth Cir 37804
Kenmark Dr 37803
Kennedy St 37801
Kennesaw Ct 37801
Kensington Blvd 37803
Kerr Rd 37803
Kerrway Ln 37804
Kessler Way 37801
Keylee Ln 37804
Keystone Dr 37804
Kian Ct 37801
Kidd Ave & St 37804
Kiefer Ln 37804
Kimberly Way 37803
Kin Ridge Rd 37803
King Cir 37801
King St 37804
Kings Grant Rd 37804
Kingstown Colony Dr 37803
Kinzel Ave 37804
Kirk Patrick Ln 37801
Kirkland Blvd 37803
Kittrell Ave 37804
Klair Ct 37801
Knecia Ln 37801
Knights Bridge Rd 37803
Knob Rd 37803
Knoll Ln 37804
Knouff Dr 37803
La Blancos Rd 37803
Lacy Ln 37801
Lady Bug Ln 37803
Lafayette Ln 37803
Lafollette Dr 37801
Lager Dr 37801
Lagrange Dr 37804
Lamar St 37804
E Lamar Alexander Pkwy 37804
W Lamar Alexander Pkwy
200-1022 37801
1024-2498 37803
1047-1047 37804
1101-2499 37801
Lamb Rd 37803
W Lambert Ln 37803
Lancaster Ln 37803
Landau Dr 37801
Landon Ln 37801
Lanier Rd 37801
Lanier Cross Rd 37801
Lansdale Dr 37803
Lansdowne Ln 37804
Larkspur Ln 37803
Larry Rd 37803
Laurel Ln 37801
Laurel Ridge Dr 37801
Laurie St 37803
Lavista Dr & Xrd 37804
Lawrence Ave 37803
Laws Chapel Rd 37803
Leah Ln 37803
Leatherwood Dr 37803
Leconte Dr 37803
Lee Ave 37801
Lee St 37804
Lee Lambert Loop & Rd 37803
Lee Shirley Rd 37801
Lee Thompson Ln 37801
Leeds Ct 37803
Legacy Ln 37803
Legends Way 37801
Lejeune Dr 37804
Leniz Dr 37803
Lennox Cir 37803
Lenore Ln 37804
Lenox View Way 37804
Level Dr 37801

Levi St 37804
Lexy Dr 37803
Leyte Dr 37801
Liberty Church Rd 37803
Lighthouse Way 37801
Lilac Ln 37801
Lili Marlene Way 37801
Lillie Dr 37804
Lima Ct 37803
Lin Ln 37801
Lina St 37804
Lincoln Rd 37804
Lincolnshire Dr 37803
Linda Ln 37803
Lindbrook Way 37803
Lindell Way 37801
Lindrick Ln 37801
Linebarger Dr 37801
Linwood Ln 37804
Lisa Dr 37803
Liscom Dr 37804
Little Best Rd 37803
Little Doubles Rd 37803
Little Tn School Rd 37801
Lively Rd 37801
Liverpool Ln 37803
Livia Dr 37803
Liz Vista Ct 37803
Llama St 37801
Loch Leigh Way 37801
Locha Poka Dr 37803
Logan Dr 37803
Logans Chapel Loop 37804
Lonas Dr 37803
Londonderry Ln 37803
S Long Hollow Rd 37801
Look Rock Crest Dr 37803
Lora Dr 37803
Lord Ave 37801
Lorena Ln 37804
Lori Lea Dr 37803
Lorraine Way 37801
Lou Ln 37804
Loudon Ave 37804
Louella Dr 37803
Louisville Loop & Rd 37801
Louniank Rd 37801
Lovecrest Dr 37801
Lovingood Way 37801
Lowe Ln 37803
Lucy Ln 37803
Ludgate Hill Cir 37803
Ludlow Dr 37803
Ludwick Dr 37803
Lunar Way 37801
Luther Rd 37804
Luther Jackson Dr 37804
Luther Mac Ln 37801
Lydia Ln 37804
Lynn Cir 37803
Lynn Dr 37804
Macard St 37801
Mackenzie Dr 37804
Macon St 37803
Madison Ave 37804
Maggie St 37803
Magill Ave 37804
N Magnolia St 37801
S Magnolia St 37803
Main Rd 37804
Majestic Dr 37801
Malaby Dr 37801
Mallard Ln 37803
Malvern Cir 37804
Manassas Dr 37804
Manchester Dr 37803
Manheim Cir 37804
Manning Ln 37804
N Maple St 37801
S Maple St 37803
Maple Oak Dr 37801
Marcaro Ln 37801
Marina Harbour Dr 37801
Marion St 37804
Mark Ln 37803
Market Place Dr 37801

Marlboro Ct 37803
Marlin Rd 37801
Marshall St 37804
Martha Neoma St 37804
Martin Rd 37801
Martin St 37804
Martingale Way 37801
Marvin Cir 37803
Mary Way 37801
Mary Charles Dr 37801
Mary Frances Dr 37804
Maryville Mhp 37804
Maryville Towers 37801
Mason Ct 37801
Masters Dr 37801
Matlock Rd 37803
Matthews Rd 37801
Mavis Ln 37804
Maxwell Ln 37803
May Ave 37804
Mayapple Dr 37801
Mayfair E 37803
Mayflower Dr 37801
Mayfly Way 37803
Mcadams Ave 37804
Mcarthur Park & Rd 37804
Mcbrayer Ln 37801
Mccall Rd 37804
Mccammon Ave
100-199 37804
200-2799 37801
E Mccammon Ct 37804
W Mccammon Ct 37804
Mcculley Ln 37801
Mcculloch Ave 37801
Mcghee Rd 37803
Mcghee St 37801
Mcghee Springs Rd 37803
Mcginley St 37804
Mcilvaine Dr 37803
Mcmasters Pl 37801
Mcnabb Pl 37801
Mcneilly Cir 37803
Mcnutt Ave 37803
Mcspadden Rd 37803
Meade St 37804
Meadow Breeze Dr 37803
Meadow Oaks Dr 37803
Meadside Dr 37804
Medinah Cir 37801
Mel Hall Rd 37803
Melanie Ct & Dr 37803
Melbourne Dr 37804
Melissa Ln 37801
Melody Ln 37804
Melrose St 37803
Melvin Ave 37803
Memorial Dr 37803
Mercer Dr 37801
Meredith Ct 37803
Merganser Ln 37801
Merritt Rd
100-199 37803
200-599 37804
Mesa Rd 37804
Micah St 37804
Michaels Ct 37803
Michelle Pl 37801
Middle St 37804
Middlesettlements Rd 37801
Middlewood Dr 37803
Mildred Meadows Dr 37804
Miles Rd 37804
Milford Ave 37804
Miller Ave 37803
Milligan Rd 37803
Millstone Dr 37803
Milton Cir 37803
Mimosa Cir 37801
Mini Huskey Rd 37801
Mint Rd 37803
Mint Meadows Dr 37803
Miracle Landing Dr 37803
Miranda Way 37803
Mishas Way 37803
Mistletoe Dr 37804

Misty Mountain Dr 37803
Misty View Dr 37804
Mitchell Ave 37804
Mize Ln 37803
Mize Farm Ct 37803
Mo Dell Way 37801
Mockingbird Dr 37803
Mogridge Way 37803
Monroe Ave 37804
Montclair Cir 37803
Monte Vista Dr 37803
Montgomery Ct & Ln 37803
Monticello Dr 37803
Montvale Rd
100-299 37801
300-4999 37803
Montvale Air Park Rd 37803
Montvale Station Rd 37803
Morganton Rd 37801
Morganton Square Dr 37801
Morningside Ave 37804
Morton Cir 37804
Mossy Grove Ln 37801
Mount Carmel Ln 37801
Mount Lebanon Rd 37804
Mount Tabor Rd 37801
Mountain Breeze Ct 37803
Mountain Shadow Ln 37803
Mountain View Ave 37803
Mountain View Cir 37801
Mountainside Ct 37804
Muirfield Dr 37801
Mulberry Dr 37804
Mullendore St 37804
Mullins Way 37801
Murphy Rd 37801
Murphy Myers Rd 37803
Muscadine Dr 37803
Muscoday Rd 37803
Muscovy Way 37801
Mustang Dr 37801
Mutton Hollow Rd 37803
Mynders Ave 37801
Mystery Way 37803
Nails Creek Rd 37804
Nandina Dr 37801
Nantucket Way 37804
Naomi Dr 37804
Narrow Gate Rd 37801
Nathan Hills Cir & Dr 37801
National Dr 37804
Navajo Rd 37804
Navarone Cir 37804
Nean Ln 37804
Neff St 37804
Neighbors Way 37803
New Blockhouse Rd 37803
New Providence Dr 37803
Newbury Ln 37803
Newcastle Way 37803
Niagara Way 37803
Nickel Point Dr 37803
Nicole Ct 37801
Nina Delozier Rd 37804
Nola View Dr 37804
Nolan Dr 37801
Norcross Rd 37803
Norris Ave 37804
Northfield Dr 37804
Northlake Dr 37801
Northwood Dr 37803
Norton Pond Dr 37803
Norwich Ct 37803
Norwood St 37804
Norwood Village Ln 37801
Nottingham Ct 37801
Nova St 37804
Nuchols Rd 37804
W O Hearon Ln 37801
Oak St 37804
Oak Glen Cir 37803
Oak Hill Dr 37804
Oak Landing Ln 37801
Oak Leaf Cir 37804
Oak Park Ave 37803
Oakburne Ln 37803

Oakdale St 37801
Oakwood Dr 37803
Ocean Dr 37801
Ocoee Dr 37801
Oconnor Rd 37801
October Ln 37804
S & W Odell Ln & Rd 37801
Old Clover Hill Rd 37803
S Old Glory Rd 37801
N Old Grey Ridge Rd 37801
Old Highway 72 37801
Old Knoxville Hwy & Pike 37804
Old Laws Chapel Rd 37803
Old Mcginley Dr 37803
Old Middlesettlements Rd 37801
Old Mount Tabor Rd 37801
Old Niles Ferry Dr 37803
Old Niles Ferry Rd
1400-3599 37803
3600-5599 37801
Old Piney Rd 37803
Old Plantation Way 37804
Old Railroad Bed Rd 37801
Old Reservoir Rd 37804
Old Sam Houston School Rd 37804
Old Smoky Mountain Rd 37801
Old Whetzell Rd 37803
Old Whites Mill Rd 37803
Oleary Ln 37803
Olivia Ln 37804
Olympia Dr 37804
Onyx Ln 37804
Ora Mae Way 37803
Orangewood Dr 37803
Oriole Ln 37803
Oris Miller Rd 37801
Orr Cir 37801
Orton Dr 37804
Ostenbarker St 37804
Ova Broady Ln 37803
Overland Dr 37801
Oxbow Way 37804
Oxford Dr 37803
Oxford Hills Dr 37803
Ozark St 37801
Ozone Ln 37803
Painter St 37801
Palma Way 37803
Panorama Dr 37801
Panoramic View Dr 37804
N & S Panoscenic Dr 37803
Par Dr 37801
Paradise Ln 37801
Paradise Hills Dr 37804
Paramount Cir 37804
Park Dr 37804
Park Lane Ct 37803
Parkside Dr 37803
Parkview Ct & Dr 37803
Parliament Dr 37804
Parrott Rd 37804
Partnership Pkwy 37801
Partridge Way 37801
W Patrick Ave 37804
Patterson Rd 37804
Patty Rd 37803
Paul Lankford Dr 37801
Pea Ridge Rd 37804
Peabody Dr 37803
Peach Orchard Rd 37803
Peachtree Dr 37801
Peak Way 37801
Pearle Dr 37801
Pearly Anthony Rd 37803
Pearson Ave 37804
Pearson Springs Rd 37803
Pearson Springs Park Ln 37803
Pebble Ln 37804
Pebbletree Apts 37801
Peery Rd 37804
Pellissippi Pl 37804

Pembroke Pl 37803
Penn Dr 37803
Penn Marydel Way 37803
Pennington Cir 37803
Pennsylvania Ave 37804
Peppermint Rd 37804
Peppermint Hills Dr 37804
Percheron St 37801
Periwinkle Ln 37804
Perry Pexton Dr 37804
Pershing St 37801
Persimmon Way 37803
Peters Rd 37801
Peterson Ln 37803
Pflanze St 37804
Phoebe Dr 37801
Pickering Cir 37803
Piedmont Cir 37803
Pierce Ln 37804
S Pine St 37804
Pine Grove Way 37801
Pinebark Dr 37801
Pinecrest Cir 37803
Pinedale St 37801
Pineoak Dr 37803
Pineview Rd 37803
Pinewood Dr 37803
Piney Level Rd 37803
Piney Level Church Rd 37803
Pink Dogwood Ln 37803
Pleasant Hill Rd 37803
Pleasant View Ave 37803
Ploesti Cir 37801
Plott Way 37803
Plymouth Dr 37801
Pocono Way 37803
Point Cir 37801
Pollard Valley Dr 37803
Pollys Way 37801
Ponderosa Ln 37803
Poplar Grove Rd 37804
Poplar Mills Ln 37803
Port Pl 37801
Porter Cir 37804
Porter St 37801
Porter Bridge Rd 37803
Portland Dr 37803
Portsmouth Cir 37803
Post Oak Ln 37801
Potter Rd 37803
Prestwick Dr 37803
Primrose Cir 37804
Princeton Rd 37801
Priscilla Dr 37803
Pritchard Ct 37804
Proffitt Springs Rd 37801
Providence Rd 37804
Pryor Rd 37804
Pueblo Ct 37803
Putters Green Ln 37801
Pyott Dr 37803
Quail Run Dr 37804
Quantico Dr 37804
Queen Cir 37801
Queen Anne Ct 37803
Queen Ridge Way 37804
Quinn Dr 37803
N & S Rachaels Cir 37804
Radnor Rd 37804
Rafer Ave 37803
Rahn Ave 37804
Railroad St 37804
Raintree Dr 37804
Rambling Rd 37801
Rampart Dr 37804
Ramsey Rd 37801
Rankin Dr 37804
Rapids Way 37804
Raulston Rd 37803
Raulston View Dr 37803
Ravencrest Dr 37801
Ravenwood Dr 37801
Ray Ave 37803
W Ray Ave 37803
Ray Ln 37801

Raylee Dr 37803
Reagan Rd 37801
Reagan Mill Rd 37803
Red Rd 37803
Red Hawk Dr 37803
Red Oak Rd 37803
Red Wing Way 37801
Redbud Dr 37804
Redbud Valley Dr 37801
Redwood Ave 37803
Regal Tower 37804
Regent Cir & Ct 37803
Reiley Dr 37801
Reise Ln 37801
Remagen Ln 37801
Remington Park Dr 37803
Reservoir Rd 37804
Rhodwin Ave 37803
Rice St 37804
Richard B Way 37804
Richardson Ln 37801
Richwood Dr 37803
Riden Dr 37804
Ridge Rd 37803
Ridge View Rd 37801
Ridgecrest Dr 37803
Ridgefield Dr 37804
Ridgestone Path 37801
Ridgeview Dr 37801
Ridgeway Trl 37801
Rile View Rd 37801
Ripley Dr 37803
River Ford Rd 37804
River Run Dr 37804
Riverside Dr 37804
Riverview Dr 37804
Robert Ave 37803
Robert C Jackson Dr 37801
Robin Rd 37803
Robin Ridge Dr 37801
Rock Hill Rd 37804
Rockdale Ln 37801
Rockingham Dr 37803
Rogtremar Way 37801
Rolling Acres Way 37801
Rommel Dr 37804
Ronjo Dr 37803
Roosevelt Dr 37801
Rosebud Dr 37803
Rosecrest Dr 37803
Ross Dr 37801
Ross Springs Dr 37801
Rouen Ct 37801
Roy Ave 37804
Roy Hancock Rd 37803
Royal Dr 37801
Royal Oaks Dr 37801
Royal View Dr 37801
Ruby Dr 37803
Ruby Tuesday Dr 37803
Rugby Pl 37804
Rule St 37804
Runnymede Cir 37804
Ruscello Dr 37801
Ruskin Cir 37803
Russell Dr 37804
Russell Hollow Rd 37801
Rusty Way 37801
N Ruth St 37801
S Ruth St 37803
Ruth Riggs Way 37801
Saddle Horn Trl 37803
Sagebrush Way 37801
Saint Andrews Way 37801
Saint Johns Dr 37801
Sam Houston School Rd 37804
Sam James Rd 37803
Sam Moses Ln 37804
Samuel Cir 37804
Sandidge Rd 37804
Sandy Ct 37803
Sandy Crossing Dr 37803
Sandy Springs Rd 37803
Santeetlah St 37801
Sarah Way 37803

Saratoga Dr ... 37804
Sassafras Way ... 37803
Savannah Park Dr ... 37803
Savannah Village Dr ... 37803
Sawgrass Way ... 37803
Scarlet Dr ... 37804
Scarlet Rose Ct ... 37801
Scarlett Oaks Rd ... 37801
Scenic Dr ... 37803
Seals Crossing Way ... 37803
Selkirk Dr ... 37803
Seminole Dr ... 37804
Seneca Cir ... 37804
Sentell Cir & Dr ... 37803
Sequoia Ct & Dr ... 37801
Sequoyah Ave ... 37804
Settlers Pointe Cir ... 37804
Seven Oaks Ln ... 37801
Sevier Ave ... 37804
Sevierville Rd ... 37804
Shadow Ridge Rd ... 37803
Shadowbrook Dr ... 37803
Shadowood Dr ... 37803
Shady Ln ... 37803
Shady Creek Rd ... 37801
Shane Dr ... 37804
Shannondale Way ... 37803
Shasta Rd ... 37801
Shawn Dr ... 37803
Shawnee Dr ... 37804
Sheffield Dr ... 37804
Shelba Way ... 37801
Shelby Dr ... 37804
Sheldon Pl ... 37803
Shepherds Grove Rd ... 37804
Sherwood Dr ... 37801
Sherwood Place Way ... 37801
Shetland Pl ... 37804
Shields Rd ... 37803
Shiloh Ct ... 37804
Shintank Rd ... 37803
Shird Franklin Rd ... 37803
Shirley Ct ... 37803
Short St ... 37804
Short Mountain Way ... 37803
Shugs Way ... 37801
Sienna Way ... 37803
Silver Brook Ln ... 37803
Silver Creek Ln ... 37804
Silverbell Dr ... 37804
Simerly St ... 37804
Simmons St ... 37801
Simpson Dr ... 37801
Sims Rd ... 37804
Sims Place Rd ... 37804
Singleton St ... 37804
Singletree Cir ... 37801
Sir Edward Ln ... 37803
Sky Ln ... 37803
Skyline Dr ... 37801
Skyview Dr ... 37803
Smedely D Butler Dr ... 37803
Smith Rd ... 37803
Smithview Dr ... 37803
Smokemont Cir & Dr ... 37801
Smokey Rd ... 37801
Smokey Mountain Dr ... 37801
Smoky View Cir ... 37801
Smoky View Estates Dr ... 37801
Snowshill Way ... 37803
Soft Rush Way ... 37803
Solomon Seal Way ... 37803
Somerset Dr ... 37803
Songbird Dr ... 37801
Sourwood Ct ... 37803
Southcliff Dr ... 37803
Southdowne Dr ... 37801
Southern Oaks Dr & Ln ... 37801
Southfork Pl ... 37801
Southside Dr ... 37801
Southview Dr ... 37803
Southwind Rd ... 37803
Southwood Dr ... 37803
Spalding Dr ... 37803
Sparks Dr ... 37803
Sparrow Dr ... 37801
Spence Cir ... 37804
Spence Field Dr ... 37803
Spencer Dr ... 37801
Springdale St ... 37801
Springfield Rd ... 37804
N & S Springview Rd ... 37801
Spurgeon Ln ... 37804
Spyglass Dr ... 37801
Squirrel Run Rd ... 37801
St Clair Ln ... 37804
Stable Xing ... 37803
Stafford Rd ... 37804
Staffordshire Ct ... 37803
Stanley Ave ... 37803
Station Dr ... 37804
Stephens Rd ... 37803
Sterling Ave ... 37803
Stetson Dr ... 37801
Stilwell Cir ... 37804
Stone Dr ... 37803
Stonecrest Ct, Dr & Pl ... 37804
Stonehaven Ct ... 37803
Stonehenge Dr ... 37803
Stoneleigh Ln ... 37803
Stonetree Dr ... 37801
Stratford Blvd & Pl ... 37803
Strawberry Patch Rd ... 37803
Stump Rd ... 37803
Sugarpine Way ... 37801
Sugarwood Dr ... 37803
Summerfield Dr ... 37801
Summitt Dr ... 37804
Sun Valley Dr ... 37801
Sundance Rd ... 37803
Sunnyside St ... 37804
Sunrise Dr ... 37803
N Sunset Dr ... 37801
Sunset Ridge Ct ... 37804
Sunset View Loop ... 37801
Suzane Dr ... 37803
Swanee Dr ... 37804
Swarthmore Ln ... 37804
Sweet Briar Dr ... 37803
Sweetpea Dr ... 37804
Sycamore Dr ... 37803
Sylvan Cir ... 37803
Tackwood Trl ... 37803
Taconic Way ... 37804
Tainan Dr ... 37804
Talbott Ln ... 37804
Tallent Way ... 37801
Tamjo Dr ... 37801
Tanasee Ct ... 37801
Tannehill Dr ... 37801
Tapoco Ave ... 37801
Tarawa Ln ... 37804
Tarbett Ct & Rd ... 37804
Tarpley St ... 37803
Taylor Rd ... 37803
Teaberry Dr ... 37804
Teal Dr ... 37801
Tech Dr ... 37803
Tedford Ave ... 37801
Tee Delozier Rd ... 37803
Teffeteller Ln ... 37803
Tekoa Way ... 37804
Tellico St ... 37803
Temple Rd ... 37804
Tennessee St ... 37804
Tessa Dr ... 37801
Teton Way ... 37803
Thistle Way ... 37801
Thomas Ave & Dr ... 37804
Thompson Bridge Rd ... 37801
Thornhill Dr ... 37804
Thunder Creek Dr ... 37801
Tiffany Way ... 37803
Tilley Rd ... 37803
Timber Wood Rd ... 37801
Timbercreek Dr ... 37803
Timberline Dr ... 37801
Timberview Ct ... 37803
Tips Way ... 37804
Tipton Dr ... 37803
Tipton Ln ... 37804
Tipton Loop Rd ... 37803
Tipton Myers Dr ... 37804
Tipton Shop Rd ... 37803
Tom Mccall Rd ... 37801
Tomahawk Dr ... 37803
Tomahawk Trl ... 37801
Tommy Baker Rd ... 37801
Tomotley Rd ... 37801
Topside View Dr ... 37803
Tory Dr ... 37801
Touchstone Dr ... 37801
Tower View Way ... 37803
Towhee Dr ... 37801
Tradewinds Dr ... 37803
Trail Ridge Dr ... 37803
Tranquility Ln ... 37803
Travis Cir ... 37804
Tremont Cir ... 37803
Trenton Blvd ... 37803
Trey Lee Way ... 37801
Treyvista Ct ... 37803
Triad Way ... 37803
Triangle Park Dr ... 37801
Trigonia Rd ... 37801
Trillium Cir ... 37804
Trinity Way ... 37803
Triple Oak St ... 37804
Tristan Ln ... 37803
Troy Ave ... 37804
Tuckaleechee Pike
1400-3599 ... 37803
3600-4099 ... 37804
Tuckaleechee Trl ... 37803
Tudor Cir ... 37803
Tulip Ln ... 37801
Turkey Pen Rd ... 37803
Turkey Pen Branch Rd ... 37803
Turnberry Ln ... 37803
Turner St ... 37801
Tuscany Ln ... 37803
Twin Falls Dr ... 37803
Twin Island Dr ... 37804
Twin Ridges Dr ... 37803
Twins Way ... 37803
Tyler Dr ... 37801
Tyler Crossing Way ... 37801
Tyvola Ct ... 37801
Unaka Ave ... 37801
Us Highway 411 S ... 37801
Utah Beach Dr ... 37801
Vaden Rd ... 37801
Valemont Dr ... 37803
Valencia Cir ... 37801
Valentine Rd ... 37804
Valley Breeze Cir ... 37803
Valleyview Dr ... 37803
Vanderbilt Cir ... 37801
Varden Rd ... 37801
Vaughn Rd ... 37803
Venice Ave ... 37801
Verdant Ln ... 37804
Vicuna St ... 37801
View Dr ... 37801
Villa Ct ... 37801
Vineyard St ... 37804
Vineyard Hill Way ... 37803
Vintage Ct ... 37801
Violet Way ... 37804
Virginia Dr ... 37803
Vista Grande Dr ... 37804
Volunteer Dr ... 37801
Wade Cir ... 37803
Wadsworth Dr ... 37801
Wagon Wheel Rd ... 37803
Wakefield Cir ... 37803
Walden Cir ... 37803
Wales Ave ... 37804
Walker Blvd ... 37803
Walker Cir ... 37803
Walker Rd ... 37801
Walker School Rd ... 37803
Wallace Harris Ave ... 37801
Wallace Hitch Dr ... 37801
Wallace Taylor Rd ... 37803
Walland Gap Dr ... 37804
Waller Ave ... 37803
Walnut St ... 37804
Walton Way ... 37801
Warbler Way ... 37803
Ward Dr ... 37801
Warren St ... 37801
Warrior Path ... 37803
Warwick Cir ... 37803
N & S Washington St ... 37804
Watauga Dr ... 37803
Water Lily Ln ... 37801
Waterloo Rd ... 37803
Waters Rd ... 37803
Waters Way ... 37804
Waters Place Dr ... 37803
Watkins Rd ... 37801
Watson Dr ... 37801
Waycross Ave ... 37804
Wayne Cir ... 37804
Weaver Hill Dr ... 37803
Webster Ct ... 37804
Wedgewood Estates Dr ... 37801
Weldon Dr ... 37801
Well St ... 37804
Wells Rd ... 37801
Wells Valley Dr ... 37801
Wentworth Ct ... 37801
Wesley Ln ... 37804
Westchester Ct ... 37803
Westcliff Dr ... 37803
Westcove Ct ... 37803
Western Springs Dr ... 37804
Westfield Dr ... 37804
Westland Sta ... 37801
Westminster Dr ... 37801
Westmoreland Dr ... 37803
Westover Dr ... 37803
Westridge Cir ... 37803
Westside Dr ... 37801
Westside Park Dr ... 37801
E Westwood Dr ... 37803
Weyburn Ln ... 37803
Wheatgrass Point Dr ... 37804
Wheatmoor Dr ... 37804
White Ave ... 37803
White Elm Cir ... 37801
White Oak Ave ... 37803
White Rose Ave ... 37803
Whitecrest Dr ... 37801
Whitefield Ln ... 37804
Whitehall St ... 37803
Whites Mill Rd ... 37803
Whitman Ct ... 37803
Whittenburg Dr ... 37804
Whittington Blvd ... 37803
Wilaway Rd ... 37801
Wilcox St ... 37804
Wilder Chapel Ln ... 37804
Wildflower Way ... 37803
N Wildwood Rd ... 37804
Wildwood Hills Dr ... 37804
Wildwood Springs Rd ... 37804
Wilkinson Pike ... 37803
Willard St ... 37803
William Blount Dr ... 37801
Williams St ... 37803
Williams Mill Rd ... 37804
Williamson Chapel Rd ... 37801
Willie Boring Cir ... 37803
Willingham Ln ... 37803
Willis Rd ... 37803
Willocks Ave ... 37804
Willow Dr ... 37803
Willow Bend Dr ... 37804
Willow Branch Cir ... 37803
Willow Creek Cir ... 37804
Willow Pond Dr ... 37803
Wilshire Pl ... 37803
Wilson Ave ... 37803
Wilson Rd ... 37801
Wimbledon Blvd ... 37803
Winchester Cv ... 37803
Windemere Cir ... 37804
Windlau Ct ... 37804
Windridge Dr & Pl ... 37803
Windsor Dr ... 37803
Windtree Pl ... 37803
N & S Wingate Way ... 37803
Winged Foot Dr ... 37801
Winona Cir ... 37801
Winter St ... 37801
Withers Dr ... 37804
Wolfe Dr ... 37801
E & W Woodbine Ct & Dr ... 37803
Woodbury Ct ... 37803
Woodcove Cir ... 37801
Woodcrest Dr ... 37804
Wooddale St ... 37801
Woodfield Cir ... 37803
Woodgate Dr ... 37804
Woodglen Ct ... 37804
Woodgrove Ln ... 37803
Woodland Dr & Trce ... 37803
Woodland Acres Rd ... 37804
Woodlawn Ave ... 37804
Woodmont Dr ... 37804
Woodsboro Ln ... 37804
Woodside Park Dr ... 37801
Woodthrush Dr ... 37803
Woodward Ct ... 37803
Worthington Blvd ... 37801
Wright Rd ... 37804
Wynberry Ct ... 37804
E Yale Cir ... 37803
Yale St ... 37801
Yearling Ln ... 37803
Yellow Rose Ln ... 37803
York Cir ... 37803
Yorkshire Ct ... 37803
Young Ave ... 37801
Zelmer Ln ... 37801
Zenith Dr ... 37803
Zina Ln ... 37801

NUMBERED STREETS

N 3rd St ... 37804
4 Mile Rd ... 37803
N & S 4th ... 37804
N & S 5th ... 37804
6 Mile Rd ... 37803
6 Mile Cemetery Rd ... 37803
N & S 6th ... 37804
7th St ... 37804
8th St ... 37804
9 Mile Rd ... 37801

MCMINNVILLE TN

General Delivery ... 37110

POST OFFICE BOXES MAIN OFFICE STATIONS AND BRANCHES

Box No.s
All PO Boxes ... 37111

RURAL ROUTES

02, 06 ... 37110

NAMED STREETS

All Street Addresses ... 37110

MEMPHIS TN

General Delivery ... 38101

POST OFFICE BOXES MAIN OFFICE STATIONS AND BRANCHES

Box No.s
1 - 2930 ... 38101
3001 - 3999 ... 38173
5000 - 6008 ... 38101
9001 - 9998 ... 38190
11001 - 11992 ... 38111
13001 - 13492 ... 38113
16001 - 16999 ... 38186
17000 - 17992 ... 38187
18001 - 18999 ... 38181
22001 - 22999 ... 38122
26001 - 26645 ... 38126
27001 - 27810 ... 38167
30001 - 30997 ... 38130
34001 - 34997 ... 38184
40001 - 42259 ... 38174
70001 - 71060 ... 38107
80001 - 80740 ... 38108
111001 - 111630 ... 38111
140001 - 141074 ... 38114
161000 - 163001 ... 38186
171111 - 172354 ... 38187
181000 - 182758 ... 38181
221001 - 221196 ... 38122
240001 - 242210 ... 38124
271001 - 271600 ... 38167
280001 - 281780 ... 38168
300005 - 309012 ... 38130
341001 - 343418 ... 38184
613101 - 613707 ... 38101
750000 - 757810 ... 38175
770001 - 775000 ... 38177
820001 - 821016 ... 38182
901001 - 902430 ... 38190

RURAL ROUTES

04, 09, 12 ... 38109
14, 17, 31, 37, 41, 42, 43 ... 38125
02 ... 38127
30, 34 ... 38141

NAMED STREETS

A Rd ... 38109
A Duncan Dr ... 38118
Aaron Cv ... 38135
Aaron Rd ... 38109
Aaron Brenner Dr ... 38120
Abbey Cv ... 38141
Abbey Ln ... 38134
Abbeycrest Dr ... 38109
Abbie Woods Cv ... 38120
Abbottsford Ave ... 38128
Abel St ... 38126
Abelia Hill Cv & Dr ... 38135
Abercorn Cv ... 38119
Abercrombie Ln ... 38119
Aberdeen Ave ... 38127
Aberfoyle Cv ... 38119
Abergeldie Dr ... 38119
Abernathy Rd ... 38116
Abigail Bluffs Cv & Dr ... 38135
Abingdon Cv ... 38119
Acacia St ... 38116
Achaean Ave ... 38127
Ackerman Ave & Cv ... 38134
Acklen Rd ... 38109
Acme Cv ... 38128
Acorn Dr
4900-5099 ... 38122
6100-6399 ... 38134
Acorn Ridge Cv ... 38125
Acree St ... 38134
Acro Cv ... 38127
Adair Dr ... 38127
Adams Ave
1-599 ... 38103
600-839 ... 38105
840-999 ... 38103
Addah Dr ... 38133
Adderley Rd ... 38127
Addington Dr ... 38128
Addison Rd ... 38108
Adelaide St ... 38106
Adeline St ... 38118
Aden St ... 38127
Adina Cv & Dr ... 38135
Adney Gap Cv & Dr ... 38134
Adolphus Ave ... 38106
Adrian Dr ... 38122
Adrianne Pl ... 38133
Adrick Cv & Rd ... 38128
Advantage Cv ... 38141
N & S Advantage Way Dr ... 38128
Ae Beaty Dr ... 38133
Afternoon Ln ... 38141
Afton Villa Dr ... 38103
Agape Rd ... 38128
Agate Cv ... 38127
Aggie Dr ... 38109
Agnes Pl ... 38104
Ainsworth St ... 38134
Air Center Cv ... 38118
Air Park Cv & St ... 38118
Air Trans Rd ... 38118
Airport Interchange Ave ... 38132
Airview Rd ... 38109
Airways Blvd
1150-2499 ... 38114
2500-2929 ... 38132
2930-5698 ... 38116
2931-3249 ... 38131
3251-5699 ... 38116
Ajanders Cv & Dr ... 38127
Alabama Ave ... 38105
Alameda Ave & Cv ... 38108
Alamo St ... 38114
Alaska St ... 38107
Albany Ave ... 38108
Albatross Cv ... 38128
Albemarle Dr ... 38135
Albercorn Cv ... 38125
Albright Dr ... 38135
Alcorn Ave ... 38112
Alcott Cv ... 38125
E Alcy Rd
800-1529 ... 38106
1530-2799 ... 38114
Alcy Manor Ln ... 38114
Alcy Park Ln ... 38114
Alden Rd ... 38116
Aldersgate Rd ... 38117
Aldridge Cv & Dr ... 38109
Alex Cv ... 38128
Alex Dickson Cv ... 38133
Alexa Dr ... 38116
Alexander St ... 38111
Alexandrite Cv ... 38109
Alfaree St ... 38134
Alford St ... 38109
Alfred Dr ... 38133
Algiers Dr ... 38116
Alibi Ct & Dr ... 38115
Alice Ave ... 38106
Alice Dr ... 38109
Alice Ann Dr ... 38128
N & S Alicia Dr ... 38112
Alida Ave ... 38106
Aline Rd ... 38127
Alixs Dr ... 38125
All Spice Dr ... 38117
Alladin Ave ... 38120
Allandale Rd ... 38111
Allard Cv ... 38119
Allbright Cv ... 38133
Allen Pkwy ... 38128
Allen Pl ... 38126
Allen Rd ... 38128
Allenbrooke Cv ... 38118
Allencrest Cv ... 38128
Allendale Cv & Dr ... 38128
Allison Ave
3000-3299 ... 38112
3850-4099 ... 38122
Allison Cv ... 38122
Allrand Rd ... 38118
Allshore St ... 38118
Alma Dr ... 38127
Alma St ... 38107

Almo Ave 38118
Almond Cv
3100-3199 38111
3900-4099 38115
Aloha Ave 38118
Alpena Ave 38127
Alpine Ave
3900-4049 38108
4050-4099 38128
Alps Rd 38128
Alrose Ave 38117
E Alston Ave 38126
W Alston Ave 38106
Alta Rd 38109
Alta Vista Ave 38127
Althorne Rd 38134
Alton Ave 38106
Altruria Rd
2400-3339 38134
3340-4200 38135
4202-4298 38135
Altruria Creek Ct 38135
Alumni Ave 38111
Alvin Ave 38114
E Amanda Cir 38128
N Amanda Cir 38128
S Amanda Cir 38128
Amanda St 38117
Amanda Oaks Cir N 38141
Amarillo St 38114
Amber Ln 38111
Amber Leaf Ln 38115
Amber Rebecca Cv 38133
Amberly Rd 38119
Amberview Cv 38141
Amberwood Cv & Dr 38141
Amboy Rd 38117
Ambrose Rd 38116
American Way
3400-4999 38118
5000-5299 38115
Amersham Dr 38119
Ames Cv 38134
Amesbury St 38135
Amethyst Cv 38127
Amey Rd 38109
Amherst Cv & St 38106
Amido Ave 38114
Amity Ave 38108
Amsden Ave 38112
Amselle Cir 38127
Amstel Cv 38133
Amy Ln 38128
Anchor Cv 38117
Ancroft Cv 38128
Andaman Cv 38135
Anderson Rd 38109
Anderson St 38104
Anderton Springs Cv & Dr 38133
Andorra Ct 38118
Andover Cv & Dr 38109
Andrea Bluff Cv 38135
Andreas Dr 38128
Andrew Crossing Dr 38128
Andrews Rd 38135
Andy Rd 38109
Andy Way Ln 38128
Angarath Dr 38125
Angel Ave 38122
N Angela Rd
5000-5199 38117
5300-5799 38120
S Angela Rd
5000-5229 38117
5230-5599 38120
Angelace Cv & Dr 38135
Angelin Dr 38135
Angelina Pl 38122
Angelus St
1-189 38104
190-499 38112
Angola Cv 38109
Anita Rd 38134
Ann Ct 38128

Ann Arbor Ct, Cv & Ln E & S 38128
Ann Welting Cv 38133
Anna Dr 38109
Anna Calla Way 38133
Annandale Cv & Dr 38125
Annarose Dr 38133
Annesdale St 38104
Annette Ln 38127
Annie St 38107
Ansnow Ln 38118
Antigua Cv & Dr 38119
Antilles 38141
Antona Pl 38106
Antwerp Ave E & W 38135
Apollo St 38116
Appian Cv & Dr S 38128
Apple Crk 38125
Apple Cv 38109
Apple Blossom Dr 38115
Apple Tree Dr 38115
Applebrook Ln 38134
Applegate Rd 38109
Applestone Cv & St 38109
Appleton Ave 38109
Appleville Cv & St 38109
Applewhite Ln 38109
Applewood Cv & Dr 38118
Appling Rd
2200-3769 38133
3770-3999 38135
Appling Way 38133
Appling Center Cv & Dr 38133
Appling City Cv 38133
Appling Crest Dr 38133
Appling Estate Dr 38133
Appling Farms Pkwy 38133
Appling Glen Cv & Dr 38133
Appling Green Cv & Dr 38133
Appling Lake Dr 38133
Appling Mill Way 38133
Apricot Cv 38115
April Cv 38109
April Forest Cv & Dr 38141
April Woods Cir 38107
Aqua Cv 38127
Aquarius Ave 38118
Arawata Ln 38111
Arbor Ct 38128
Arbor Pl N 38115
Arbor Pl S 38115
Arbor Commons Cir 38120
Arbor Creek Trl 38115
Arbor Grove Way 38119
Arbor Lake Cv & Dr 38141
Arbor Lane Cv & Dr 38133
Arbor View Ct 38134
Arborgreen Cv 38133
Arborvalley Ln 38119
Arborwood Dr 38115
Arcadia St 38119
N & S Arcadian Cir 38103
Archer Cv & Dr 38109
Archie Dr 38127
Archwood Dr 38128
Arden Ave 38112
Ardent Cv & Rd 38118
Ardmore Cv & St 38127
Ardmore View Ct 38127
Ardvale Rd 38128
Ardwick Ct & Dr 38119
Areka Hill Cv & Dr 38135
Argo Ave 38109
Argonne St 38127
Argosy Dr 38116
Argot Ave 38118
Argyle Ave 38107
Arkansas St
900-1099 38106
1450-1699 38109
2400-2499 38104
Arlene Ave 38127
Arlington Ave 38114
Armand Dr 38103

Armistead Ave 38114
Arms Ave 38128
Armstrong Ave 38115
E Armstrong Rd 38109
W Armstrong Rd 38109
Arnold Cv 38118
Arnold Pl 38126
Arnold Rd 38118
Arose Ln 38118
Arrendale St 38118
Arrington Ave 38107
Arrow Cv & Rd 38109
Arrowbrook Ln 38134
Arrowhead Ct & Rd 38118
Arrowood Ave 38118
Arroyo Rd 38128
Arsenal Cv & St 38128
Art Cv & Dr 38118
Artesian Aly 38105
Arwine Rd 38128
Asa Dr 38109
Ascot Park Common Dr 38120
Ascroft Ln 38119
Ash St 38108
Ash Creek Cv 38141
Ash Hill Ln 38135
Ash Park Dr 38141
Ashaway Cv 38119
Ashbriar Ave 38120
Ashbridge Cv 38120
Ashburn St 38109
Ashby Ave & Ct 38106
Ashcroft Cv & Dr 38125
Ashford Rd 38109
Ashinsou Rd 38109
Ashland St
200-499 38105
3200-3399 38127
Ashlar Ln 38118
N & S Ashlawn Cv & Rd 38112
Ashley Sq N & S 38120
Ashley Oaks Dr 38125
Ashleyhurst Ln 38116
Ashridge Cv & Pl 38141
Ashton Rd 38134
Ashton Manor Ln 38125
Ashview Cv 38118
Ashville Dr 38127
Ashwood Cv & St 38118
Ashworth Cv 38118
Aspen Ave 38128
Aspenbrook Ln 38134
Aspenhill Dr 38135
Aspenway Dr 38115
Asphodel Dr 38103
Aspire Ln 38111
Asquith Pl 38115
Aste St 38106
Asteroid Dr 38109
Astro Cv 38134
Atherton Cv 38119
Atkins Cv & Dr 38109
Atkinson Cv 38133
Atlantic St 38112
Atlantic Way Dr 38118
Atlas St 38108
Atmore St 38118
Atoll Ln 38118
Atwater Ln 38119
Atwood Ave 38111
Auber Rd 38116
Aubra Rd 38111
Auburn Rd 38116
Auburn Tree Cv 38134
N Auburndale St
1-184 38104
185-299 38112
600-999 38107
S Auburndale St 38104
Audie Dr 38109
Audrey Cv 38127
Audubon Dr 38117
Audubon Ridge Bnd 38135
Audubon View Cir 38117

August Cv 38109
August Dr 38133
August Moon Cv & Ln 38135
Aureen Dr 38109
Aurora Cir 38111
Auster Cv 38125
Austin Cv 38134
Austin St 38108
Austin Forest Cv 38125
Austin Green Bay 38133
Austin Peay Hwy
2700-2798 38128
2800-3730 38128
3711-3711 38168
3731-4299 38128
3732-4298 38128
4300-4899 38135
Austin Way Dr 38141
Austinwood Dr 38118
Autry Cv 38135
Autumn Ave
1100-1179 38105
1180-1399 38104
1600-2500 38112
2502-2628 38112
3400-3799 38122
Autumn Cir 38115
Autumn Branch Ln 38109
Autumn Brook Cv & Dr 38141
Autumn Crest Cv 38125
Autumn Evening Ln 38125
Autumn Forrest Dr 38125
Autumn Glen Cv & Dr 38134
Autumn Gold Ln 38119
Autumn Harvest Ln 38125
Autumn Leaf Ct & Dr 38116
Autumn Morning Cv & Ln 38125
Autumn Ridge Ct 38115
Autumn Song Dr 38125
Autumn Springs Cv 38125
Autumn Valley Dr 38135
Autumn Wood Cv 38141
Autumnhill Dr & Ln 38135
Autumnwood Ave 38115
Autumnwood Dr 38116
Aux Arms Dr 38128
N Avalon St
1-189 38104
190-599 38112
600-1099 38107
S Avalon St 38104
N & S Avant Ln 38105
N & S Avenel Cv 38125
Avenue Of Pnes 38119
Avenue Of Commerce 38125
Avery Ave 38112
Aviva Dr 38120
Avon Cv 38117
Avon Rd
1-499 38117
650-1099 38122
Avon Woods Cv 38117
Avondale Ave 38122
Aw Willis Ave 38105
Ayers St
100-599 38105
600-1199 38107
Aynsley Cv 38117
Ayrshire Cv 38119
Azalea Garden Way 38111
Azalea Hill Cv 38135
Azalea Terrace Cir 38117
Azalia St 38106
Babs Rd 38116
Backbay Cv 38141
Bacon St 38128
Baggett Dr 38127
Bainbridge Dr 38119
Baine Ave 38111
Baintree Cv 38119
Baird Cv 38135
Baird Dr 38119
Baird Ln 38135
Baja Dr 38127

Baja Valley Dr 38133
Balboa Cir 38116
Bald Cypress Cv 38141
Bald Eagle Dr 38115
Bald Oak Dr 38141
Baldwin Ave 38127
Baldwin Sq 38117
Balfour St 38127
Ball Rd
1400-1569 38106
1570-2399 38114
N Ball Rd 38106
W Ball Rd 38106
Ballantrace Ct & Dr 38134
Ballard Cv & Dr 38133
Ballard Brook Cv 38135
Ballenmoor Dr 38141
Ballenshire Ct & Dr 38134
Balsam Cv 38127
Baltic St 38112
Baltimore St
400-599 38111
600-1699 38114
Bammel Ave 38107
Banbury Ave & Cv 38135
Bandye Ln 38133
Bangalore Ct 38119
Bankside Dr 38118
Bankston Cv 38127
Banneker Cv 38109
Bannock St 38116
Bannockburn Rd 38128
Banyan Cv & Ln 38133
E Barbara Cir 38128
W Barbara Cir 38128
Barbara Dr 38108
Barbaro Dr 38134
Barberry Cv & St 38128
Barboro Aly 38103
Barbour St 38106
Barbourville Dr 38127
Barbwood Dr 38118
Barclay Ave 38111
Barcrest Dr 38134
Bardstown Rd 38134
Bare Oak Dr 38141
Barfield Cir 38120
Barfield Rd
4000-5039 38117
5500-5709 38120
5711-5799 38120
Bargin Pl 38107
Barkley Cv 38134
Barksdale Ct 38104
Barksdale Cv 38114
N Barksdale St
1-189 38104
600-1099 38107
S Barksdale St
1-789 38104
790-1999 38114
Barkshire Cv & Dr 38141
Barkwood Dr 38109
Barley Cv 38141
Barnes Ct 38106
Barnett Pl 38111
Barnstable Cv & Rd 38125
Baroness Dr 38116
Baronne Pl & Way 38117
Barr Ave 38111
Barren Brook Dr 38125
Barrentine Dr 38134
Barrett Pl 38107
Barrington Cv 38125
Barris Dr 38132
Barron Ave
2400-3029 38114
3030-4199 38111
Barron Cir E 38111
Barron Cir S 38111
Barron Cir W 38111
Barron Ct 38114
Barry Rd 38117
Barry Meadows Cv 38125
Barrycrest Dr 38134
Barrymor Dr 38125

Barsanti St 38122
Barta Dr 38127
Bartlett Blvd
2300-3399 38134
3400-3499 38135
Bartlett Rd
700-999 38122
1300-2899 38134
Bartlett Center Dr 38134
Bartlett Corporate Cv & Dr 38133
Bartlett Country Rd 38135
Bartlett Crest Cv & Dr 38134
Bartlett Gap Cv, Dr & Ln 38133
Bartlett Grove Cv & Rd 38134
Bartlett Heights Cv & Dr 38134
Bartlett Oaks Dr 38134
Bartlett Park Dr 38133
Bartlett Stage Cv 38134
Bartlett View Ln 38134
Bartlett Woods Dr 38134
Bartley Rdg 38135
Barton Dr 38116
Barton St 38106
Bartonwood Cv & Dr 38141
Barwick Dr 38134
Barwood Cir 38122
Basil Rd 38109
Baskel Dr 38116
Baskin St 38127
Bassett Hall Dr 38125
Bassfield Cv & Dr 38133
Basswood St 38118
Batchelor Rd 38109
E Battle Creek Cv 38134
W Battle Creek Cv 38134
Battle Creek Dr
2600-2799 38128
5000-5299 38134
Battle Forest Cv 38128
Battleboro Dr 38134
Battlefield Cv 38128
Battlefield Dr 38128
Battlefield Pl 38125
Baudette Cv & Ln 38135
Bauman Dr 38108
Baxter Ave 38127
Baxter Cv 38133
Bay Cv 38118
N Bay Cv 38125
Bay Ln 38118
Bay Hollow Cv 38125
Bay Leaf Cv & Dr 38118
Bay Magnolia Cir 38115
Bay Meadow Cir N & S 38125
Bay Park Dr 38141
Bay Pointe Cir E 38128
Bay View Cv 38125
Bayberry Cv 38120
Bayberry Dr 38128
Baybrook Ln 38134
Bayhill Dr 38125
Bayliss Ave
3300-4049 38122
4050-4499 38108
Bayou Bend Cv 38125
Bayshore Dr 38115
Bayside Cv 38109
Baysweet Dr 38125
Bayview Cv & Dr 38127
Baywind Cv & Dr 38109
Baywood Dr 38134
Beach St 38126
Beach Shore Cv 38125
Beacon Rd 38109
Beacon Hill Cv & Dr 38127
Beacon Hills Dr 38127
Beacon Park Dr 38134
Beacon Point Rd 38125
Beaconfield Cv 38141
Beagle Cv & Dr 38118
Beale St 38103

Bear Dr 38118
Bear Creek Cv & Ln 38141
Bear Mountain Dr 38119
Bear River Rd 38118
Beard Pl 38112
Bearfield Pl 38112
Bears Paw Cir 38120
Beartown Cv 38133
Beasley St 38111
Beatrice Cv 38133
Beatrice St 38122
Beatty Cv 38116
Beau Pre N & S 38120
Beauchamp Cv & Dr 38118
Beaumont Ave 38114
Beauregard Ave 38104
Beauregard Cv 38125
Beauvior Pl 38127
Beaver Aly 38126
Beaver Creek Ln 38125
Beaver Creek Rd 38128
Beaverbrook Rd 38127
Beaverlodge Dr 38141
Beaverton Dr 38127
Becker Way 38116
Beckman Dr 38135
Becky Cv 38119
Bede Rd 38128
Bedford Cv 38135
Bedford Ln 38118
Bedford Rd 38135
Bedford Valley Ln 38135
Beebee Ave 38104
Beech Grove Rd 38118
Beech Row Ln 38128
Beechcliff Ln 38128
Beechdale Cv 38128
Beechill Dr 38135
Beechmont St 38127
Beechollow Dr 38128
Beechpark Rd 38128
Beechridge Cv 38128
Beechrun Cv & Dr 38128
Beechwood Ave 38106
Behnke Ave 38114
Belfast Dr 38127
Belgrave Dr 38119
Belhaven St 38117
Belin Dr 38133
Bell Ave 38108
Bella Pl 38106
Bellbranch Dr 38116
Bellbrook Dr 38116
Bellbrook Center Dr 38116
Belle Forest Dr 38115
Belle Grove Cv & Rd 38115
E & W Belle Haven Rd 38109
Belle Meade Cv & Ln 38117
Belle Oak Rd 38115
Belle Tower Rd 38115
Belleair Dr 38104
Belleau St 38127
N Bellevue Blvd
1-189 38104
190-599 38105
600-1999 38107
S Bellevue Blvd
1-929 38104
930-1349 38106
Bellmont Cv 38134
Bellwood Cv & Dr 38128
Belmar St 38106
E Belmont Cir 38108
W Belmont Cir 38108
Belmont Cv 38135
Belmont Dr 38135
Belmont Run Cv 38125
Belover Dr 38127
Belsfield Cv & Rd 38119
Belt Line Cv & St 38111
N Belvedere Blvd
2-12 38104
14-199 38104
600-1099 38107
1100-1199 38108

S Belvedere Blvd 38104
Belvedere Ct 38104
E & W Belz Blvd 38109
Ben Avon Way 38111
Ben Venue Cv 38118
Benadine Pl 38115
Benbow Dr 38116
S & W Bendel Cir 38117
Bender Rd 38116
Bending Oaks Cv E & W 38128
Bending River Cv & Rd 38135
Benford St 38109
Benham Ave 38127
Benjestown Rd 38127
Benna Cv 38119
Bennett Ave 38114
Bennett Ln 38116
Benning St 38106
Bennington Cir 38141
Benoit Dr 38141
Bensford Ln 38125
Benson Rd 38109
Bent Ct 38128
Bent Birch Cv 38115
Bent Grass Cir & Cv 38125
Bent Oak Ln 38115
Bent Tree Ave 38134
Bentley Cv 38118
Bentley Pl 38120
Benton St 38106
Berclair Rd 38122
Berea Rd 38109
Beretta Rd 38133
Berkeley Ave 38108
Berkeley Sq 38120
Berkely Woods Dr 38125
Berkshire Ave
1600-4099 38108
4100-4399 38128
N & S Berlinwood Cv & Dr 38133
Bermuda Run 38116
Bernadine Dr 38116
Berry Ln 38128
Berry Rd 38117
Berry Hill Cv 38141
Berrybrook Cv & Rd 38115
Berrydale Ave 38118
Berryman Dr 38125
Berrypick Ln S 38141
Berrywood Ave 38118
Berta Cv & Rd 38109
Bertha Ave 38106
Bertram Cv 38118
Berwind Rd 38116
Bestway Dr 38118
Bethan Cv 38125
Bethay Dr 38125
Bethel Ave 38107
Bethlehem Ave 38127
Bethune Cv 38109
Betty Jo Ln 38117
Bevel Rd 38109
Beverly St 38114
Beverly Hills Rd 38128
Beverly Terrace Dr 38109
Bevy Ridge Cv & Ln 38125
Bey St 38114
Bf Goodrich Blvd 38118
Bickford Ave 38107
Biddlesdon Ln 38125
N & W Big Bend Dr 38116
Big Chimney Dr 38141
Big Creek Cv 38135
Big Springs Ln 38133
Big Tree Cv 38128
Bigelow St 38127
Biggs St 38108
Billco Rd 38109
Billigan Aly 38106
Billion Rd 38127
Billway Dr 38118
Billy Maher Rd 38135
Biltmore St 38122

N Bingham St
1-849 38112
850-1099 38108
S Bingham St 38112
Birch St 38108
N Birch Bend Rd & Sq 38116
Birch Fork Dr 38115
Birch Glen Dr 38115
Birch Hollow Dr 38115
Birch Lake Dr 38119
Birch Mill Cv & Rd 38135
Birch Run Cv & Ln 38115
Birch Walk Dr 38115
Birchbark Ln 38120
Birchbrook Ln 38134
Birchdale Dr 38127
Birchfield Dr & Ter 38127
Birchleaf Rd 38116
Birchmeadow Cv 38115
Birchshade Cv 38115
Birchvale Dr 38125
Birdie Cv 38115
Birdsong Ave 38106
Birdsong Ferry Cv & Rd 38118
Birdwood Dr 38125
Birken Dr 38134
Birkenhead Rd 38134
Birmingham Ln 38125
Birthstone Ave & Cv 38109
E & W Biscayne Rd 38109
Biscoe Ave 38122
Bishop Way 38135
Bishop Dale Cv & Dr 38141
Bishop Hills Dr 38128
Bishop Morton Way 38111
Bishop Row Dr 38126
Bishops Ct 38111
Bishops Cv 38135
Bishops Bridge Rd 38118
Bishops Gate Dr 38115
Bishops Knoll Cv 38135
Bishops Valley Cv & Ln 38135
Bismark St 38109
Bison St 38109
Bitter Creek Cv & Dr 38127
Bittersweet Dr 38125
Black Rd 38117
Black Bass Cv 38109
Black Bay Cv 38128
Black Birch Cv 38125
Black Diamond Cv 38127
Black Forest Dr 38128
Black Grove Dr 38125
Black Mountain Dr 38119
Black Mtn Dr 38119
Black Oak Dr 38119
Black Thorne Cv 38119
Black Walnut Dr 38135
Black Water Trl 38119
Blackberry Bush Rd 38115
Blackbird Dr 38115
Blackburg Dr 38135
Blackhawk Rd 38109
Blackheath Dr 38135
Blackiston Cv 38109
Blackraven Dr 38115
Blackrock Ln 38141
Blacksmith Cv 38125
Blacksmith Dr 38127
Blackstone Ln 38127
Blackwell Cv & Rd 38134
Blackwing Ct & Dr 38115
Blair Hunt Dr 38109
Blairmore Ave 38109
Blaisdell Cv 38133
Blakely Dr 38120
Blakemore Rd 38106
Blakeview Pl 38134
Blakewood Pl 38106
Blanchard Rd 38116
Blanche Rd 38109
Bland Ln 38133
Blandford Dr 38141

Blanding Ave & Cv 38118
Bledsoe Aly 38126
Bledsoe Rd 38141
Blenheim Ave 38134
Blenheim Ln 38125
Blimey Cv 38116
Bloomfield Cv & Dr 38125
Blossom Cv 38133
Blossom Ln 38115
Blue Rd 38108
Blue Bonnet Rd 38118
Blue Crane Ln 38114
Blue Diamond Cv & St 38109
Blue Grouse Cv & Ln 38125
Blue Gum Dr 38118
Blue Heron Cv 38120
Blue Jay Rd 38116
Blue Lake Ln 38141
Blue Pearl Cv 38109
Blue Plum Cv 38125
Blue Ridge Cv & Pkwy 38134
Blue River Cv & Dr 38128
Blue Sky Cv 38133
Blue Springs Ave 38134
Blue Stone Dr 38125
Blue Willow Cv & Rd 38141
Blue Wing St 38141
Bluebell Cv & St 38109
Blueberry Dr & Hl 38116
Bluebill Cv 38141
Bluebird Rd 38116
Bluefield St 38128
Bluemont Dr 38134
Blueridge Dr 38134
Blues Blvd 38115
Blueslate Cv 38133
N Bluff Pt 38135
S Bluff Pt 38135
Bluff Rd 38117
Bluff Wood Cv & Dr 38128
Bluffdale St 38118
Blythe St 38104
Bobbitt Dr 38134
Bobby Jones Rd 38125
Bobo Ln 38118
Bobo Rd 38125
Bobolink Cv & Trl 38134
Bobwhite Cv 38128
Bocage Cv 38103
E Bodley Ave
2-198 38109
200-459 38109
460-999 38106
W Bodley Ave 38109
Boeingshire Cv & Dr 38116
Bogart St 38116
Bogey Dr 38125
Bolen Huse Rd 38128
Bon Air St 38112
Bon Lin Cv & Dr 38133
Bona Terra St 38109
Bond Ave 38106
Bondale Ave 38118
Bonita Dr 38109
Bonnell Ave 38109
Bonnie Dr 38116
Bonnie St 38122
Bontura Dr 38128
Bonwood Ave 38109
Boone St 38127
Boone Manor Dr 38125
Booth Forrest Cv & Dr 38135
Boothbay Cv 38141
Boothes Ridge Dr 38125
Bordeaux Cir E 38125
Bordeaux Cir S 38125
Bordeaux Cir W 38125
Bordeaux Ln 38141
Bordeaux Creek Cv N & S 38125
Bordeaux Ridge Cv N & S 38125
Borden Dr 38116
Bostick Rd 38133

Boston St
300-599 38111
600-1099 38114
Boswell Rd
4900-4999 38117
5200-5399 38120
Boulder Creek Cv 38134
Bourbon Pl 38106
Bovay Rd 38127
Bow St 38109
Bowdoin Dr 38127
Bowdre Pl 38126
Bowen Ave, Cir & Cv 38122
Bowers Rd 38109
Bowie Rd 38109
Bowman Ave 38128
Bowmar Cv 38128
Box Elder Cv 38115
Boxberry Ln 38116
Boxborough Cv 38119
Boxdale Cv & St 38118
E Boxtown Rd 38109
Boxwood St 38108
Boxwood Green Ln 38117
Boyce Ave 38111
Boyce Rd 38117
Boyd Ln 38134
Boyd St 38126
Boyle Ave 38114
Boylston Dr 38141
Boysenberry St 38134
Boyte Cv 38134
Brackendale Way 38125
Brad Dr 38127
Brad Forrest Cv 38125
Bradbury Cv & Dr 38122
Bradcliff Cv & St 38109
Bradcrest Cv & Dr 38128
Braden Dr 38127
Bradfield Run 38125
Bradford Dr 38109
Bradley St 38114
Bradley Ridge Cv & Ln 38125
Bradwood Ave 38109
Brady Ct & Dr 38116
Braemar Dr 38128
Bragg Ln 38134
Braidwood Cv 38134
Brakebill Ave & Cv 38116
Bramble Cv 38119
Bramblewood Ln 38109
Branch St 38127
Branchway Dr 38116
Brandale St 38118
Branderham Dr 38134
Brandon Cir 38114
Brandon Ln 38133
Brandy Ave 38128
Brandy Station Rd 38118
Brandye Lynne Cv 38133
Brandywine Blvd 38127
Brandywine Cv 38115
Brannick Dr 38134
Branson Dr 38133
Brantford Ave 38120
Brantley Rd 38109
Branwood Cv 38134
Braxton Ct & Ln 38115
Braycliff Ave & Cv 38109
Braycrest Cv 38128
Breamhaven Cv 38109
Breckenwood Dr 38127
Breedlove St 38107
Breeds Hill Dr 38125
Breenwood Ln 38119
Breeze Wood Cv & Ln 38125
Breezy Meadows Ln 38135
Bremington Pl 38111
Brenmar Ave 38122
Brenmarda Ln 38116
Brennan Dr 38122
Brenners Pl 38134
Brenrich Cv N & S 38117
Brentdale Ave 38118
Brenton Ave 38120

Brentway Dr 38118
Brentwood Cir E 38111
Brentwood Cir S 38111
Brentwood Cir W 38111
Brentwood Pl 38134
Brett Dr 38127
Brevard Dr 38116
Brewer Ave 38114
Brewers Lndg 38104
Brewster Ave 38127
Brian Cv 38114
Brian Casey Cv 38133
Brianway Dr 38118
Briar Cv 38116
Briar Pl 38115
Briar Patch Ln 38115
Briar Rose Rd 38111
Briar Trail Cv 38135
Briarbend Ln 38141
Briarberry Ln 38109
Briarcliff Ave 38117
Briarcrest Ave 38120
Briarfield Cv & Ln 38135
Briarhill Dr 38135
Briarly Ln 38135
Briarmeadows Dr 38120
E & W Briarpark Dr 38116
Briarpark Loop Dr 38116
Briarway Cv & Rd 38115
Briarwood Rd 38111
Brick Cottage Ln 38105
Brickmont Rd 38135
Bricknell Cv 38128
Brickwood Ln 38128
Bridelwreath Dr 38125
Bridge Meadow Cv & Ln 38125
Bridge Mill Ln 38125
Bridge Way Dr 38118
Bridge Wood Cv 38125
Bridgedale Ave 38118
Bridgeport Dr 38114
Bridgers Dr 38128
Bridgestone Cir 38135
Bridgewalk Ln 38119
Bridle Path Dr 38134
Briercrest Ln 38127
Brierdale Ave 38120
Brierfield Ave 38120
Briergate Dr 38134
Brierglen Ave 38120
Brierhaven Ave 38120
Brierhedge Ave 38120
Brierich Dr 38135
Brierview St 38120
Bright Cv 38134
Bright Ridge Cv 38115
Bright Star Cv & Ln 38134
S Brighton Cv & Rd 38128
Brighton Place Dr 38117
Brightwood Cv & Dr 38134
Brigidier St 38116
Brindley Dr 38128
Bringlewood Cv 38118
Briona Cv & St 38125
Brisdane St 38118
Brister Cv & St 38111
Bristerwood Dr 38111
Bristol Dr 38119
Bristol Glen Dr 38135
Bristol Meadow Cv & Ln 38125
Bristol Oaks Ln 38133
Bristol Park Cir & Dr 38133
Bristol Pine Ln 38133
Britt Way 38125
Brittain Cv 38135
Brittany Rd 38127
Britton St 38108
Broad Ave 38112
Broad Creek Cv 38141
Broad Oaks Ave 38116
Broadford Dr 38125
Broadmoor St 38111
Broadway Rd 38135
Broadway St 38133

Brockcliff Cv 38128
Brockcrest Cv & St 38128
Brockwood Ave & Cv 38109
Broken Oak Cv & Dr 38127
Bromley Ln 38134
Brompton Rd 38118
Bronte Ave 38134
Bronze Dr 38125
Brook Creek Cv 38141
Brook Hollow Cv 38119
Brook Meadow Rd 38133
Brook Mill Cv, Dr & Ln 38125
Brook Shade Ln 38125
Brook Trail Cv & Ln 38135
Brook Tree Cir 38119
Brookbriar Cv 38125
Brookbury Cv 38125
Brookdale St 38118
Brookfield Rd 38119
Brookgreen Dr 38116
E & W Brookhaven Cir 38117
Brookhill Ln 38135
Brookins St 38108
Brookleaf Cv 38125
Brookline Rd 38128
Brooklyn Ave 38114
Brookmeade St 38127
E Brooks Rd
1-449 38109
500-2199 38116
2200-2399 38132
W Brooks Rd 38109
Brooks Manor Cv 38119
Brooksbank Cv N & S 38141
Brooksvalley St 38119
Brooksville Dr 38127
Brookview Cv 38127
Brookwater Cv & Ln 38125
Brookway St 38109
Brookwood Cv 38117
N Brother Blvd 38133
Brower St 38111
Browley Rd 38109
Brown Ave
1100-1899 38107
2100-2399 38108
Brown Ln 38109
Brownbark Cv & Dr 38115
Browning Ave & Cir 38114
Brownlee Rd 38116
Brownwood Ave 38116
Bruce St
900-1099 38104
1100-1599 38114
Bruins Dr 38116
Brunswick Rd 38133
Brunswick Forest Cir & Dr S & W 38133
Brunswick Park Cv 38133
Brunswick View Cv 38133
Bruntsfield Cv 38135
Brush Everhard St 38134
Brushwood Cv & Dr 38109
Bruton Ave, Cv & Pl 38135
Bruton Parish Cv & Dr 38133
Brutonwood Cv 38118
Bryan St 38108
Brydon Dr 38134
Bryndale Ave 38118
Bryson Cv 38128
Bubbling Wells Rd 38127
Buchanan Ave 38122
Buck St 38111
Buckles Cv 38133
Buckley Cv 38133
Buckner St 38122
Bucksport Ln 38118
Buena Vista Pl 38112
Buffalo Rd 38109
Buffalo Springs Ln 38135
Buffer Dr 38128
N Buford Ellington Dr 38111
Builders Way 38109
Bullington Ave 38106
Bunker Hill Dr 38125

Buntyn St
200-599 38111
600-1699 38114
Buoy St 38109
Bur Oak Dr 38118
Burbank Rd 38118
Burdan Cv 38118
Burdette Ave 38127
E Burdock Ave 38106
W Burdock Ave 38109
Burgess Cv & Dr 38118
Burgundy Rd 38111
Burkehill Dr 38135
Burkett Rd 38127
Burkson Cv 38119
Burlingame Dr 38141
Burlington Cir 38127
Burloe Cv & Ln 38133
Burma Rd 38106
E Burnette Cv & Pl 38141
Burnham Ave & Cv 38127
Burning Tree Cv & Ln 38125
Burns Ave 38114
Burnstown Ln 38133
Burnt Pines Dr 38125
Burr Rd 38108
Burris St 38106
Burrow Ave 38128
Burt Cv 38119
Burton Church Cv 38134
Burwood Dr 38109
Busby Ave & Cv 38127
Business Dr 38125
Business Center Dr 38134
Business Park Dr 38118
Busy Cv & St 38125
Butler Ave 38126
E Butler Ave
1-219 38103
220-359 38126
361-499 38126
W Butler Ave 38103
N & S Butler Woods Cv 38126
Butterfly Dr 38133
Butterfly View Cv 38133
Buttermilk Cv & Dr 38125
Butternut Cv & Dr 38133
Butterworth Rd 38116
Buxbriar Ave 38120
Buxton Rd 38116
Buxway Dr 38118
E & W Byfield Dr 38109
Byrd Ave 38114
Byrn Rd 38132
Byron Dr 38109
Byron Rd 38122
E Cabana Cir 38107
Cabernet Cv E & W 38141
Cable Ave 38114
Cabot Ct 38103
Cades Cv 38125
Cadraca Dr 38122
Calais Rd 38120
Caldwell Ave 38107
Caledon Cv 38119
Caledonian Rd 38119
Calgary Cv & Pl 38125
Calgene St 38120
E Calhoun Ave 38106
W Calhoun Ave 38103
W California Ave 38106
California Terrace Dr 38122
Calla Cv & Dr 38135
Callahan Dr 38127
Callaway Hills Cv & Dr 38125
Callie Rd 38127
Callie Powell Cv 38135
Callis St 38114
Callis Creek Dr 38119
Callis Cut Off Rd 38119
Calvary Crk 38128
Calvary Colony Rd 38127
Calvert Ave 38108
Calvin Rd 38109

Street	ZIP
Calypso Ct	38118
E & W Camberley Cir & Ct	38119
Cambrain Cv & Dr	38134
Cambridge Ave	38106
Cambridge Dr	38116
Cambridge Station Ct & Dr	38115
Camden St	38118
Camelia Cv	38115
Camelia Ln	38134
Camelot Ave, Cv & Ln	38118
Cameo Ave	38128
Cameron St	38106
N & S Camilla St	38104
Camphor Tree Cv	38133
Camrose Cv	38119
Camry Ln	38119
Cana Rd	38109
Canal St	38115
Canary Cv & Ln	38109
Candace Dr	38116
Candi Cv	38125
Candlelight Dr E & W	38109
Candlewood Cv	38119
Candlewyck Cir	38114
Candy Apple Cv	38119
Cane Rd	38106
Cane Meadow Cir	38106
Cane Ridge Dr	38109
Canehill Cv & Ln	38135
Canewood Ave	38134
Canfield Ave	38127
Canisbay Rd	38128
Canna Hill Ct, Cv & Dr	38135
Canning Cv	38119
Cannon St	38106
Cannondale Cv	38119
Canterbury Dr	38122
Canton Dr	38116
Cantor Ave	38114
Canyon Rd	38134
Cap Dr	38118
Capaha Dr	38118
Cape Henry Dr	38128
Capen Ave	38118
Capewood Dr	38127
Capilano Dr	38125
Capital Ave	38107
Capri St	
1600-1999	38117
2800-3099	38118
Caprice Dr	38135
Capricorn Cv & Dr	38128
Caradine St	38112
Carahills Ln	38133
Carat Cir	38133
Caravel Dr	38115
Caraway Cv	38117
Carbon Cv & Rd	38109
Carbondale Dr	38114
Cardiff Cv	38125
Cardigan Dr	38119
Cardinal Ave	38111
Cardinal Hill Cv	38135
Carebi Way	38135
Carey Dr & Rd	38109
Cargo Cir	38118
Caribou Dr	38115
Carissa Holly Ct	38115
Carla Ln	38135
Carlock Cv	38118
E & W Carlos Rd	38117
Carlton Rd	38106
Carlyle Ave	38127
Carmen Cv & Sq	38125
Carmi Cv	38116
Carnegie St	38106
Carnes Ave	
2000-2899	38114
2900-3899	38111
4800-4999	38117
Carney St	38127
Carnival Cv	38125
Carnoustie Cv & Rd	38128
Carol Dr	38116
Carol Ann Cv	38127
Carol Elaine Cir	38133
Carol Trace Walk	38115
E Carolina Ave	
1-99	38103
100-499	38126
W Carolina Ave	38103
Carolot Cv & Ln	38135
Carolyn Dr	38111
Carpenter St	
200-799	38112
1500-1699	38108
Carr Ave	38104
Carraway Cv	38135
Carriage Dr	38134
Carriage Glen Dr	38135
Carrick Ct	38134
Carrie Brook Cv	38135
Carrier St	38116
Carrington Rd	
2900-3029	38114
3030-3799	38111
Carroll Ave	38105
Carrolton Ave	38127
Carrozza Cv	38116
Carruthers Pl	38112
Carson St	38111
Cart Path	38125
Carter Ave	38122
Carter Creek Cv	38125
Carterville Pl	38127
Carthage Cv	38125
Carvel St	38118
Carver Ave	38114
Cary Hill Cv & Dr	38141
Carya Dr	38135
Carysbrook Cv	38120
Casann Ave & Cv	38128
Cascade St	38127
Cascade Hill Cv	38135
Cash Cv	38125
Cashmere Cv	38125
Cassie Ave	38127
Castalia St	38114
Castaway Dr	38115
Castex St	38109
Castile St	38135
Castle Ave	38122
Castle St	38107
Castle Creek Ln	38115
Castle Heights Cv & Dr	38141
Castle Oak Cv	38141
Castle Ridge Cv	38141
Castle View Cv	38141
Castlebay Rd	38128
Castlegate Cv & Ln	38141
Castleman Cv & St	38118
Castlewood Ave	38109
Catalina Rd	38111
Catalpa Hill Cv & Dr	38135
Catawba Ln	38111
Catbird Ct	38119
Catherine St	38111
Cato Ct	38109
Catoosa Cv	38135
Cavalier Dr	38109
Cavern Cv & Dr	38128
Caversham Cv	38119
Cazassa Rd	38116
Cecil Ave	38108
Cecil Dr	38116
Cecilia Dr	38117
Cedar Ave	38107
Cedar Rd	38135
N & S Cedar Bark Cv	38128
Cedar Bluff Dr	38127
Cedar Branch Cir	38128
Cedar Creek Cv	38141
Cedar Forrest Dr	38119
Cedar Glenn Dr	38128
Cedar Hills Rd	38135
Cedar Leaf Cv	38128
Cedar Meadow Dr	38128
Cedar Oak Cv	38134
Cedar Park Dr	38141
Cedar Path Dr	38115
Cedar Pine Dr	38128
Cedar Ridge Cv E	38128
N Cedar Ridge Dr	38118
Cedar Ridge Ln	38128
Cedar Springs Dr	38128
Cedar Trace Cv	38125
Cedar Valley Dr	38116
Cedar View Rd	38118
Cedar Way Ct	38116
Cedarbrook Ln	38134
Cedarcrest Ct	38141
Cedargreen Cv	38128
Cedarhurst Ave	38127
Cedarshade Cv	38135
Cedartown Dr	38127
Cedartree Dr	38141
Cedarwood Cv	38118
Cedell Dr	38127
Cedric Cv	38118
Cedrick Ave	38118
Cela Rd	38128
Celeste Dr	38127
Cella St	38114
Celt Cv & Dr	38118
Celtic Cv	38134
Centennial Dr	38125
Center Dr	38112
N Center Ln	
1-439	38103
440-599	38105
600-999	38107
S Center Ln	38103
S Center Rd	38109
Central Ave	
1000-2649	38104
2650-4099	38111
Central Cv	38111
Central Ln	38117
Central Ter	38111
N Central Park St	38111
Centralia Rd	38135
N & S Century St	38111
Century Arbor Ln & Pl	38134
Century Center Cv & Pkwy	38134
Cessna Rd	38109
Ceylon Ct	38119
Chablis Cv	38115
Chadwick Cir	38114
Chairman Dr	38131
Chalfonte Cv	38141
Chalgrove Cv	38134
Chalkshire Cv	38125
Challenge Dr	38115
Chalmers Rd	38120
Chamberlain Dr	38119
Chamberlain Ln	38128
Chambliss Cv & Rd	38116
Champa Ave	38109
Champaign St	38134
Champale Ave	38135
Champion Hills Dr	38125
Championship Dr	38125
Chancellor Cv & St	38118
Chancery St	38116
Chandler St	38127
Chaney Ln	38133
Chanlone Way	38115
Channel 3 Dr	38103
Channing Cv	38125
Chantilly Dr	38127
W Chantrey St	38128
Chanwil Pl	38117
Chapel Rd	38128
Chapelle Cir E & W	38120
Chapman Ave	38119
Charbon Cv & Ln	38133
Chardonnay Cv E & W	38141
Charing Cross St	38116
Charity Glen Cv & Dr	38135
Charjean Cv & Rd	38114
Charlene Rd	38135
Charles Dr	38116
Charles Pl	38112
Charles Brown Cv	38133
Charles Bryan Cv	38134
Charles Bryan Rd	
2000-2199	38133
2300-3199	38134
Charleston Ct	38103
Charleston Rd	38128
Charleston Sq	38122
Charleston Run Cv	38125
Charlestowne Pl	38115
Charleswood Ave	
3500-3799	38122
4200-4599	38117
Charlotte Cir N	38117
Charlotte Cir S	38117
E Charlotte Cir	38117
Charlotte Rd	38109
Charrin Cv	38118
Charter Ave	38109
Charter Oak Dr	38109
Chartres Pl	38106
Chartwell Cv & Ln	38120
Charwell Ln	38116
Chase Wood Dr	38125
Chateau Rhodes Cir	38111
Chatfield Dr	38116
Chatham Pond Cir & Ln	38135
Chattering Ln	38127
Chatwood Cv & St	38122
Chatworth St	38127
Chaucer Ln	38134
Chauncey	38141
Cheekwood Ave	38134
Chelmsford Cv	38134
Chelsea Ave	
1-1399	38107
1400-3699	38108
Chelsea Avenue Ext	38108
Chelsea Hill Dr	38128
Chelsea Nicole Cv	38135
Chelwood Dr	38141
Chemberry Pl	38120
Chenches Ave	38126
Cherbourg Ln & Pl	38120
Cherokee Ave	38106
Cherokee Blvd	38111
Cherokee Dr	38111
Cherokee Rose Ln	38125
Cheron Cv	38118
Cherry Cir E	38117
Cherry Cir W	38117
E Cherry Dr	38117
Cherry Ln	38117
W Cherry Ln	38117
Cherry Rd	
1-1999	38117
2600-3799	38118
Cherry Bark Cv & Dr	38141
Cherry Blossom Dr	38133
Cherry Blossom Ln	38120
Cherry Breeze Cv & Dr	38133
Cherry Center Dr	38118
N Cherry Creek Ln	38141
Cherry Hall Pl	38117
Cherry Hill Dr & Ln	38135
Cherry Park Dr	38120
W Cherry Place Dr	38117
Cherry Valley Ln	38116
Cherrydale Cv	38111
Cherrydale Rd	
4000-4379	38111
4380-4499	38117
Cherryhill Pkwy & Rdg	38120
Cherrywood Cv	38128
Cheryl Dr	38116
Cheryl Crest Ln	38115
Chesapeake Dr	38141
Chesapeake Way	38125
Cheshire Cv	38134
Cheshire Dr	38116
Chessway Dr	38116
Chester Cv	38134
Chester Ln	38119
Chesterfield Cv	38134
Chesterton Cv & Dr	38127
Chesterwood Ct & Dr	38118
Chestnut Ave	38106
Cheston Ave	38118
Cheval Dr	38125
Chevron Cv & Rd	38118
Chevy Chase	38125
Chicago Ave	38107
Chichester Ln	38119
Chickamauga Ave	38109
Chickasaw Cv	38117
E Chickasaw Cv	38111
E Chickasaw Pkwy	38111
W Chickasaw Pkwy	38111
Chickasaw Rd	
4100-5099	38117
5300-5399	38120
Chickasaw Oaks Dr	38111
Childers Ave & Cv	38127
Childress Rd	38132
Childs Cv & Dr	38116
Chilligan Dr	38109
Chinaberry Cv & Dr	38115
Chinkapin Oak Cv	38141
Chip Rd	38117
Chippewa Ct & Rd	38118
Chisca Ave	38111
Chism Rd	38109
Chiswick Ln & Pl	38128
Chiswood Cv & St	38134
Choctaw Ave	
2800-2899	38114
3030-3299	38111
Choctaw Ln	38119
Chowning Rd	38135
Christina Wood Dr	38135
Christine Cir & Rd	38118
Christine Gardens Rd E	38118
Christopher Ave	38118
Christopher Cv	38134
Christoval Cv & St	38133
Christy Cv	38111
Christy Ln	38135
Christyshire Dr	38128
Chrysler Dr	38118
Chuck Ave	38118
Chuckwood Rd	38117
Chumbler Dr	38128
Chumley Dr	38119
Churchill Cv & St	38118
Churchill Downs Dr	38135
Churnak Cv	38118
Cicalla Ave	38122
Cimino Cv	38135
Cimmaron Cv & Dr	38109
Cincinnati Rd	38106
Cinderella Dr & St	38109
Cinders Rd	38133
Cindy Ln	38127
Cindy Lynn Ln	38141
Cinnamon Cv & Dr	38117
Circle Ave	38112
E Circle Rd	38127
N Circle Rd	38127
S Circle Rd	38127
Citadel Cv	38134
Citation Dr	38118
City House Ct	38103
Clack Pl	38126
Clair Douwie Cv	38133
Claire Ave	38127
Clairice Cv	38133
Clancy St	38106
Clanden St	38116
E Clanlo Dr	38104
Clara Cv	38116
Claredale Dr	38133
Claree Dr	38116
Claremont Cir	38114
Clarendon Rd	38118
Clarice Dr	38109
Clarion Dr	38135
Clarion Ln	38119
Clark Aly	38117
Clark Pl	38104
Clarke Cv	38115
Clarke Rd	
2700-4199	38115
4200-4699	38141
Clarke Address	38115
Clarksdale Ave	38108
Classic Cir & Dr	38125
Claudette Cv & Rd	38118
Claudine Cv	38127
Clawson Cv	38117
Claybrook Cv	38107
N Claybrook St	
1-599	38104
600-1399	38107
S Claybrook St	38104
Claycreek Rd	38120
Claymore Dr	38116
Clayphil Ave	38111
Clayton Ave	38108
Cleaborn St	38126
Clear Water Dr	38128
Clearbrook Cv & St	38118
Clearfield Dr	38127
Clearpark Cv & Dr	38127
Clearpoint Dr	38141
Clearpool Pt N & S	38141
Clearpool Circle Rd	38118
Clearview Cv	38134
Clearwater Cv	38141
Clearwood Cv & Rd	38134
Cleary Dr	38141
Clement Rd	38109
Clementine Rd	
1200-1599	38106
1600-1799	38114
Clemmer Dr	38125
Cleo Ave	38122
Cleoford Ave	38127
Cleopatra Cv & Dr S	38128
N & S Cleveland St	38104
Cliffdale Cv & St	38127
Clifford Ave	38106
Clifton Ave	38127
Climping Rd	38119
Clinchport Cir	38127
Clinchstone Cir	38128
Clingmans Cv	38135
Clinton Pl	38126
Clinton Rd	38109
Cloar Cv	38111
Cloister Ave & Cv	38118
Cloister Green Cv & Ln	38120
Cloudburst Cv & Rd	38141
Cloudland Dr	38118
Clove Dr	38117
N & W Clover Dr	38120
Clover Hill Cv & Dr	38135
Cloverdale Dr	38114
Clovia Ln	38114
Clovis Cv	38125
Clower Rd	38109
Cloyce Cv	38128
Club Lk	38125
Club Ln	38115
Club Walk	38111
Club At Southwind	38125
Club Breeze Dr	38125
Club Bridge Dr	38118
Club Green Dr	38116
Club House Dr	38115
Club Ridge Cir	38115
Club Tower Cv & Dr	38111
Clubhill Dr	38125
Clubview Dr	38125
Clyde Ave	38107
Clydes Place Cv	38133
Clydesdale Dr	38109
Coach Dr	38128
Coachouse Cv	38134
Coahoma Pl	38126
Cobalt Cv	38128
Cobalt Bay Loop	38103
Cobblestone Dr	38125
Cochese Cv & Rd	38118
Cochran St	38105
Cody Dr	38115
Coffee Dr	38118
Coffeeville Cv	38133
Cognac Cv	38141
Cohasset Cv	38125
Cohay Ave	38134
Coke Cv	38127
Coker St	38107
Colby St	38107
Cole Rd	
4600-5219	38117
5220-5399	38120
Colebrook Ave	38116
Coleen Rd	38111
Colegrove St	38120
Coleman Ave	
3000-3289	38112
3290-3699	38122
Coleman Rd	38128
Colewood Ave	38118
Colfax Ave	38116
Colgate Rd	38106
College St	38106
College Park Dr	38126
Collier Rd & St	38127
Collingwood Cv	38120
Collingwood Rd	38117
Collins Cir	38105
Collins St	38112
Collins Chapel Cir	38105
Collins Way Cv & Dr	38141
Collins Wood Cv	38125
Colonial Cv & Rd	38117
Colonial Green Pl	38117
Colonial Oak Ln	38116
Colony Ln	38119
Colony Park Dr	38118
Colonyhill Dr	38135
E Colorado Ave	
1-99	38106
220-499	38126
W Colorado Ave	38106
Colson Cv	38125
Columbia St	38112
Columbine Ct	38118
Colwell Aly	38106
Comanche Ct & Rd	38118
Combs St	38108
Comet Cv	38118
Command Dr	38118
Commerce Cir	38118
Commercial Pkwy	38116
Common Oaks Ct	38120
Commonwealth Dr	38116
Community Dr	38118
Como St	38126
Compress Dr	38106
Compton Ave	38106
Comstock Cv	38125
Concord View Dr	38125
Concorde Rd	38118
Confederate Cir E	38125
Conifer Cv	38119
Conlee Pl	38111
Connahbrook Dr	38116
Connemara Ave	38109
Connie Ct	38109
Conrad Cv	38127
Conridge Dr	38125
Constance Ave	38134
Conti Cv	38127
Contract Dr	38118
Contractors Pl	38115
Convair Rd	38132
Conway Dr	38127
Conwell Rd	38120
Cook Rd	38109
Cookie Cv	38118
Cooper Rd	38133
Cooper St	38103
N Cooper St	38104
S Cooper St	
1-1099	38104
1100-1699	38114
Copiah Cv	38119

Copper Hill Cv 38134
Copper Leaf Cv & Dr 38141
Copper Ridge Cv N & S 38134
Copper Valley Cv & Dr E, S & W 38141
Copperfield Dr 38119
Coppock St 38107
Coral Dr 38127
Coral Creek Ln 38125
Coral Hill Dr 38135
Corban Cv 38135
Cordell Cv & St 38118
Coredalm Rd 38120
Corkwood Dr 38127
Cornelia Ln 38117
Cornell St 38127
Corner St 38127
Corner Oak Dr 38141
Corning Ave 38127
Cornstalk Cv 38127
Coro Cv & Rd 38109
Corporate Ave E 38132
Corrine Ave 38107
Corry Rd 38106
Corsica Dr 38120
Cortez Cv 38115
Cortina Ct 38115
Coscia St 38127
Cosgrave Cv 38125
Cosgrove Cv 38117
Cosheco Cv 38125
Cosmic Cir & Dr 38115
Cosmos Cv & Dr 38118
Cossitt Pl 38126
Coteswood Rd 38134
Cotswold Cv 38128
Cotswold Ln 38125
Cottage Ln 38125
Cottingham Pl 38120
Cotton Dr 38118
Cotton Bale Cv & Ln 38119
Cotton Gin Pl 38106
Cotton Grove Ct, Cv & Ln 38119
Cotton Plant Cv & Rd 38119
Cotton Ridge Dr 38133
Cottonlane Ave 38118
Cottonway St 38118
Cottonwood Cv 38118
Cottonwood Rd
4000-5329 38118
5330-5699 38115
Cotulla Cv 38133
Coughlin Dr 38116
Coulter Ln 38133
Count Basie Ct 38115
Country Birch Cv 38115
Country Bluff Dr 38135
Country Brook Dr 38141
Country Club Ln 38111
Country Green Rd 38133
Country Haven Dr 38133
Country Knoll Ct 38135
Country Lake Dr 38133
Country Lane Cv & Dr 38133
Country Lawn Cv 38133
Country Manor Dr 38133
Country Meadow Ln 38133
N Country Oaks Cir 38115
S Country Oaks Cir 38115
Country Oaks Cv 38125
Country Oaks Dr 38125
Country Park Dr 38133
Country Side Rd 38133
Country Squire Cv 38128
Country Trail Dr 38133
Country View Ln 38134
Countryhill Cv & Dr 38135
County Gate Rd 38119
Course View Cv & Dr 38135
Court Ave
83-137 38103
139-499 38103
600-769 38105
770-999 38103
1000-2399 38104
N Court Ave 38103
S Court Ave 38103
Court St 38134
Courtland Pl 38104
Courtney Dr 38128
Courtney Ln 38141
Courtney Ridge Cv 38125
Courtyard Plz 38119
Coventry Dr 38127
Coventry Mall 38118
Covington Cv 38134
Covington Pike
1100-1198 38122
1700-3709 38128
3710-4899 38135
Covington Way
4900-4999 38128
5000-5199 38134
Coward Pl 38104
Cowden Ave
1820-2299 38104
3000-3699 38111
Cowdrie Cv 38119
Coweta Pl 38107
N & S Cox St 38104
Crab Orchard Cv 38125
Crabapple Ln 38117
Cracklerose Dr 38127
Craft Rd
300-499 38109
600-1299 38116
Crafton Ave 38108
Crafton Ln 38125
Craig St 38118
Craigmont Cv 38128
Craigmont Dr
4500-5059 38128
5060-5499 38134
Craigwood Dr 38116
Crain Cv & Rd 38128
Cranberry Dr 38134
Cranbury Park Cv & Dr 38141
Cranford Rd 38117
Cranleigh Cv 38141
Crawford Ct 38116
Crawford Pl 38107
Crawford Way 38116
Crazyhorse Dr 38118
Creek Bend Dr 38125
Creek Laurel Way 38125
Creek Manor Cv & Ln 38125
Creek Mist Cv 38141
Creek View Cir & Dr 38128
Creekbed Cv 38141
Creekside Dr 38117
Creekstone Cir 38127
Creekwood Dr 38128
Creighton Ave & Cv 38118
Crepe Myrtle Dr 38115
Crescent Ln 38120
Crescent Rd 38116
Crescent Bluff Ct 38106
Crescent Glen Cir 38133
Crescent Hill Dr 38133
Crescent Park Dr 38141
Crescent Ridge Cv 38133
Crescent River Dr 38133
Cresser St 38116
Crest Ave 38112
Crest Cv 38135
Crested Oak Cv 38141
Crested Pine Cv 38135
Cresthaven Rd 38119
Crestmere Pl 38112
Creston Ave 38127
Crestridge Cv & Rd 38119
Crestview Dr 38134
Crestway Dr 38134
E & W Crestwood Dr 38119
Crestwyn Hills Dr 38125
Crete Ave 38111
Crewe St 38119
Cricket Glen Cv 38134
Crider Cv & St 38111
Crievewood Dr 38135
Crillion Dr 38109
Crimmins Cv 38119
Crimson Cir 38116
Crimson Cv 38115
Crimson Rd 38116
Crimson Leaf Cv 38125
Crimson Tree Cv 38141
Cristil St 38118
Crockett Cv 38141
Crockett Pl 38107
Croft Oaks Cv 38134
Croley Dr 38118
Crompton Pl 38134
Cromwell Ave & Cv 38118
Cross Dr 38112
Cross Creek Ct & Cv 38125
Cross Oak Cv & Dr 38141
Cross Timber Ln 38125
Crossbrook Ln 38134
Crossfield Cv & Rd 38109
Crossing Cv 38134
Crossover Ln 38117
Crosswater Ln 38125
Crosswood Cv 38127
Crow Rd 38108
Crowell Cv & St 38133
Crowfarn Dr 38118
Crown Imperial Dr 38115
Crowther Cv 38119
Croydon Ave 38116
Croydon Cv 38141
Crump Ave
1700-1999 38107
3000-3299 38112
Crump Rd 38141
Crumpler Rd 38141
Crutchfield Cv 38133
Crystal Ave 38112
Crystal Brook Cv 38133
Crystal Hill Dr 38141
E & W Crystal Oak Cv & Dr 38141
Crystal Springs Dr 38128
Crystal View Cv 38141
Cuffeywood Cv & Dr 38135
Cullen Cv 38119
Cullenwood Rd 38116
Culloden Cv 38119
Culpepper Cv 38141
Cumberland St 38112
Cumbrian Ct 38134
Cummings St 38106
Cupwood Cv 38134
Curbertson Cv & St 38134
Curbstone Cv 38135
Curleybark Cv 38135
Curry Ave 38108
Curtis St 38118
Curzon Ave 38118
Cushman Rd 38134
Custer St 38114
Cutter Mill Rd 38141
Cynthia Pl 38126
Cypress Cir 38112
Cypress Dr 38112
Cypress Rd 38128
Cypress Bend Cv 38125
Cypress Lake Dr 38119
Cypress Point Dr 38115
Cypresswood Ave & Cv 38109
Dabbs Ave 38127
Dabler Pl 38134
Daffodil Cv 38128
Dagan Cv & St 38109
Daggett Rd 38109
Dagmar St 38128
Dahlia Dr 38127
Daisy Ellen Cv 38133
Daisywood Ln 38118
Dakar Ave 38127
Dakota Pl 38106
Dale Lavern Rd 38116
Dalebranch Dr 38116
Dalebrook Cv & St 38127
Dalewood Ave 38127
Dallas St 38114
Dalron Dr 38135
Dalton Rd 38109
Dalton Downs Dr 38135
Damascus Rd 38118
Damone Ave 38109
Dan Kuykendall Cv 38111
Dana Dr 38108
Dana Cheryl Ln 38135
Danberry Ave 38116
Dandelion Ct 38118
Daneman Dr 38133
Daniel Riggs Cv 38125
Danielson Pl 38114
Danita Cv & St 38122
Danner Ct 38103
Danny Ave 38111
N Danny Thomas Blvd
1-189 38103
190-499 38105
S Danny Thomas Blvd
1-179 38103
180-839 38126
Danny Thomas Pl 38105
Dante Ave & Cv 38128
Danube Ln 38119
E Danville Cir 38118
W Danville Cir 38118
Danville Cv 38118
Danville Rd
1700-1999 38117
2900-3179 38118
Daphne Cv & Rd 38118
Darby St 38128
Dardon Ave 38116
Dare Ave 38134
Dargen Ave 38118
Darlene St 38106
Darlington Cv & Dr 38118
Darlow St 38122
Darm Ave 38127
Darnell Dr 38116
Darolyn St 38134
Darrow St 38118
Dartmoor Cv 38119
Dartmouth Dr 38119
Dashwood Dr 38119
Datsun Dr 38116
Dattel St 38122
Dauphin Ave 38127
E Davant Ave
1-199 38109
450-899 38106
W Davant Ave 38109
Daverins Ave 38107
Davey Cv & Dr 38127
David Dr 38116
David St 38114
Davidcrest Dr 38128
Davidson Cv 38119
Davidson Dr 38116
Davidson Rd 38118
Davies Manor Dr 38133
Davies Plantation Rd 38133
Davieshire Cv & Dr 38133
Davis Cir 38128
Davis Cv 38116
Davis St 38108
Dawes Ave 38108
Dawn Cv & Dr 38127
Dawn Oaks Cv 38125
Dawnhill Rd 38135
Dawnridge Cv 38135
Dawnridge Dr 38118
Dawnwood Cv 38114
Dawson Ln 38134
Daybreak Cv & Dr 38135
Days Rd 38116
Days Creek Blvd 38116
Daysland Cv 38125
Dayton St 38122
Daytona Rd 38108
Daywood Ave 38127
Deadrick Ave 38114
Dearborn St 38109
Dearing Cv 38118
Dearing Rd
1000-1999 38117
2900-3099 38118
E Dearing Rd 38117
Deb Dr 38127
Debbidan Cv 38108
Debbie Crest Dr 38115
Debby Cv, Dr & St 38127
Deborah Ave 38108
Debra Cv E & W 38133
Decatur Cv 38107
Decatur St
100-599 38105
600-1499 38107
December St 38109
Decker St 38134
Dedo Cir & Cv 38135
Dee Cv 38119
Dee Rd 38117
Dee Ann Dr 38119
Deen Ave 38116
Deep Brook Dr 38128
Deer Cv 38133
Deer Ln 38118
Deer Xing 38115
Deer Creek Rd 38128
Deer Crest Ln 38134
Deer Forest Dr 38115
Deer Glade Ln 38133
Deer Park Dr 38115
Deer Ridge Dr & Ln 38134
Deer Run Ct 38116
Deer Trail Cv 38109
Deer Trail Ln
1100-1299 38109
7600-7999 38133
Deer Valley Rd 38109
Deerfield Cv 38135
Deerfield Dr 38134
Deerfield Rd 38135
Deerfield Trce 38133
Deergrove Rd 38141
Deerland St 38109
Deermont Dr 38134
Deerskin Cv & Dr 38109
Deerstone Dr 38135
Deerwood Ave & Cv 38111
Del Norte St 38116
Delaney Cv 38116
Delano Ave 38127
Delaware St 38106
Delgate Cv 38125
Dell Ave 38112
Dell Glade Dr 38111
Dellrose Dr 38116
Dells Ave 38127
Dellwood Ave 38127
Delmar Ave 38105
Delmonico Cv 38135
Delmont Rd 38117
Deloach St 38111
Delp St 38118
Delray Ave 38127
Delsa Cir 38116
Delta Cv 38103
Delta Rd 38109
Deluth Ave 38118
Demeter Cv 38118
Demetra Cv 38133
Demo Ave 38116
Democrat Rd
2100-2399 38132
2400-3699 38118
E Dempster Ave
1-199 38109
500-1599 38106
W Dempster Ave 38109
Dena Dr 38127
Deneen Dr 38109
Denimwood Dr 38109
Denison St 38111
Denmark Dr 38103
Denson Dr 38116
Denton Cv N & S 38125
Denver Cv & St 38127
Denwood Ave 38120
Depanne Rd 38116
Depass Rd
1400-1499 38122
1500-1699 38108
Derbyshire Ave 38127
Derma Cv 38133
Derron Ave
5200-5329 38118
5330-5599 38115
Des Arc Dr 38109
Desert Rose Cv 38133
Desha St 38117
E & W Desoto Ave 38106
Dessa Dr 38127
Detroiter Dr 38127
Deumaine Pl 38106
Devel St 38118
Devenshire Ln 38141
Deventer Cv 38133
Devereux Dr 38128
Devine St 38133
Devon Dr 38116
Devon Way 38111
Devonshire Ave 38117
Devoy Ave 38108
Dew Mist Cv 38141
Dewees Dr 38116
Dewitt Cv 38118
Dexter Ave 38108
Diamond Way 38109
Diana St 38104
E Dianne Cir 38114
N Dianne Cir 38114
S Dianne Cir 38114
W Dianne Cir 38114
Dianne Dr 38116
Dickinson St
300-599 38112
600-999 38107
Dickmann Ave
3000-3169 38114
3170-3299 38111
Dietz Cv 38135
Dillard Rd 38128
Dille Pl 38111
Dillworth St 38122
Dimwood Cv & St 38134
Diplomat Pl 38134
Directors Cv, Dr & Row 38131
Discover Dr 38141
E Dison Ave 38106
W Dison Ave 38109
Distribution Dr 38141
Distriplex Cv & Dr 38118
Distriplex Farms Dr 38141
Dividend Dr 38132
Dixie Rd 38109
Dobbin Ferry Ave 38118
Doberman Cv & Dr 38134
W Dodd Rd 38109
Dodge Dr 38128
Doe Run Ln 38134
Doe Run Lane Cv 38134
Doe Valley Cv 38135
Doefield Trl 38135
Dogwood Dr 38111
Dogwood Ln 38116
Dokkum Cv & Dr 38133
Dolan Dr & Rd 38116
Domar St 38118
Don St 38109
E & W Don Krag Cir 38106
Don Valley Cv & Dr 38133
Donald Rd 38106
Doncaster Ln 38125
Donerles Ave 38108
Dongourney Cv 38125
Donleigh Dr 38135
Donna Ave 38114
Donna Cv 38114
Donna Dr 38127
Donnegan Cv 38125
Dora Cv & St 38122
Dorado Ave & Cv 38128
Dorchester St 38118
Dorff Dr 38116
Dorian Ave 38107
Doris Ave 38106
Dorothy Pl 38104
Dorrie Ln 38117
Dorrington Cv 38133
Dorset Dr 38117
Dorsey Ave 38120
Dotberry Cv 38109
Dothan St 38118
Dottie Ave 38106
Double Springs Cv 38125
Double Tree Cv & Rd 38109
Doubleton Dr 38116
Douglas Pkwy 38106
Douglass Ave
2300-2899 38114
2900-4099 38111
Dove Ave 38106
Dove St 38127
Dove Call Cv 38128
E & W Dove Creek Cir & Dr 38128
Dove Flight Ln 38116
Dove Glen Cv 38133
Dove Ridge Cv 38135
Dove Roost Cv 38119
Dovecote Ln 38120
Dovecrest Rd 38134
Dovefield Ln 38135
Dovehill Cv 38135
Dover Ave 38106
Dovewood Rd 38134
Dow Pl 38106
Dowel St 38128
Dowling Cv 38118
Down River Dr 38103
Downing St 38117
Downs Dr 38135
Dr Ml King Jr Ave
200-398 38126
400-799 38126
801-899 38126
1001-1099 38104
Drake Cv & St 38106
Drake Manor Cv 38117
Drayon Cv 38128
Drayton Woods Dr 38134
Dreger Rd 38109
Drew Rd 38109
Drew Valley Cv & Dr 38133
Drexel Ave 38135
Driftwood Ave 38127
Driscoll St 38125
Driver St
180-1009 38126
1150-1499 38106
Driving Park Ct 38107
Dromedary Dr 38133
Drowsy Ln 38127
Druid Hill Dr 38128
Drury Way Ln 38128
Dry Fern Cv 38135
Duane Cv 38118
Dublin Ave & Way 38114
Dubois Dr 38109
Ducan Ln 38133
Duchess Dr N & S 38116
Duck River Rd 38135
Duckling Cv 38141
Dudley St 38103
S Dudley St 38104
Duelling Oaks 38116
E & W Dugan Cir 38116
Duke Rd
1400-1499 38122
1500-1699 38108
Duke Ellington Ave 38115
Dumaine Way 38117
Dumas St 38127
Dumbarton Rd 38128
Dumbarton Oaks Dr 38127
Dumbeath Cv & Rd 38128
E & W Dunbar Rd 38109
Duncan Williams Rd 38119

Dungreen St 38118
Dunlap Cv 38107
Dunlap St 38105
N Dunlap St
1-50 38103
51-99 38105
52-148 38103
119-149 38103
150-599 38105
600-1199 38107
S Dunlap St
1-189 38103
190-399 38126
Dunleith Dr 38103
S Dunmoor St 38114
Dunn Ave
700-1719 38106
1720-3169 38114
4400-4799 38117
Dunn Cv 38114
Dunn Rd 38111
Dunnavant St 38106
Dunnellon Ave 38134
Dunnhaven St 38106
Dunscomb Pl 38105
Dunsford Way 38119
Dunstan Cv 38119
Dunwoody Ave 38120
Dupont Ave 38127
Dupre St 38115
Durango Cv & Ln 38109
Durant St 38116
Durbin Ave 38122
Durby Cir & St 38114
Durford Wood Cv 38128
Durham Ave 38127
Duron Ln 38119
Durrand Dr 38118
Dusty Rose Cv 38125
Dusty Trail Ln 38133
Dutro Pl
200-299 38106
300-599 38126
Dutton Pl 38115
Dutwiler Rd 38135
Dwain Cv 38134
Dwight Cv & Rd 38114
Dwyer St 38122
Dycus Cv & St 38116
Dyer Pl 38122
Dylan Valley Cv & Dr 38135
Eads Ave 38106
Eagan Cv 38134
Eagle Dr 38115
Eagle Trce 38125
Eagle Bead Cv 38125
Eagle Crest Dr 38117
Eagle Nest Trl 38128
Eagle Ridge Ln 38135
Eagle River Rd 38118
Eagle Valley Cv 38135
Eaglewood Dr 38115
S & W Earhart Dr 38134
Earl Dr 38128
Earls Court Cv & Rd 38118
Early St 38127
Early Maxwell Blvd 38104
Earlynn Dr 38133
Earnett St 38128
E & W Easeaway Cv 38135
Eason Ave 38116
East Dr
600-799 38112
840-999 38108
East Rd 38128
East St
70-179 38103
180-389 38126
390-899 38104
N & S East Yates Rd 38120
Eastbourne Pl 38117
Eastbrier Dr 38135
Eastbrook Ln 38134
Eastdale Ln 38134
Eastend Dr 38104
Easterly Ln 38125
Eastern Cv & Dr 38122
Eastfield Cv 38118
Easthampton Cv 38134
Eastland Dr 38111
Eastlawn St 38111
Eastline Dr 38128
Eastman Rd 38109
Eastmoreland Ave 38104
Eastover Cv, Dr & Pl 38119
Eastport Cv 38118
Eastridge Cv & Dr 38120
Eastview Cv 38111
Eastview Dr 38111
Eastview St 38112
Eastwind Cv 38125
Eastwind Dr 38116
Eastwood Ave 38112
Eaton Cv & St 38120
Ebbtide St 38109
Echles Ct & St 38111
Echo Hills Ln 38125
Eddie Ln 38109
Eddington Cv 38125
Eden St 38127
Eden Park Dr 38111
Edenburg Dr 38127
Edenshire Ave 38117
Edenshire Cv 38119
Edgar St 38127
Edgefield Cv & Dr 38128
Edgehill St 38128
Edgemont Ave 38128
Edgeware Cv & Rd 38118
Edgewater Cv 38134
Edgewater Dr 38115
N & S Edgewood Cv & St 38104
Edgewood Park Cv 38104
Edgeworth Ln 38119
Edison Cv & Rd 38118
Edith Ave
200-329 38106
330-939 38126
1250-1399 38106
Edmondshire Ct & Dr 38134
Edmondson Ave 38114
W Edsel Ave 38109
Educators Ln 38133
Edward Ave & Cv 38107
Edwards Rd 38133
E Edwin Cir 38104
Edwin Forest Rd 38141
Effie Rd 38106
Egan Dr 38115
Egerton Cir 38119
Eggleston Rd 38125
Eglesfield Dr 38116
Egypt Central Rd
2900-5199 38128
5200-6999 38135
Egypt Church Rd 38128
Egyptian Cv 38128
E Eh Crump Blvd
1-219 38106
220-919 38126
920-1059 38104
W Eh Crump Blvd 38106
Einat Cv 38134
El Camino Ave 38116
El Rincon Dr 38125
Elaine Ave 38122
Elba Cv 38133
Elbert Cv & Dr 38127
Elcar Dr 38127
Elder Cv & Rd 38109
Elders Row Dr 38126
Eldorado St 38128
Eldridge Ave
900-1099 38107
1600-2499 38108
Elgin Dr 38115
Elizabeth Cv 38141
Elizabeth Ln 38122
Elizabeth Grace Cv 38134
Elk Grove Cv & Rd 38115
Elk Point Dr 38128
Elk Run Ct 38116
Elkfield Cv 38135
Elkgate 38141
Elkins St 38114
Elkmont Rd 38116
W Elkwood Cv & St 38111
Ellearee Dr 38133
Ellen Ln 38109
Ellen Davies Cv & Dr 38133
Ellendale Rd 38135
Ellenview Cv N & W 38133
Ellenwood Cv 38133
Ellington St 38108
Elliott Rd 38108
Ellis Rd 38133
Elliston Rd
1100-1599 38106
3600-4349 38111
Ellsworth St 38111
Elm Ave 38106
Elm Park Rd 38118
Elm River Cv 38127
Elmer Ave & Cv 38109
Elmfield Cv 38127
Elmhill Dr 38135
Elmhurst Ave 38115
Elmore Cv 38134
Elmore Rd
4800-4999 38128
5000-6799 38134
Elmore Park Cv 38134
Elmore Park Rd
2300-2999 38134
2966-2966 38184
3000-3398 38134
3001-3399 38134
Elmore Ridge Cv & Ln 38134
Elmore Woods Cv & Ln 38134
Elmridge St 38118
Elms Court Dr 38128
Elmview Ln 38116
Elmwood Cv 38141
Elmwood Park St 38104
Eloise Rd 38106
Elton Cv 38109
Elvis Cv 38116
Elvis Presley Blvd
1350-3099 38106
3100-5699 38116
Elwood Ln 38117
Ely St 38106
Elysian Cv & Dr 38128
Elzey Ave 38104
Embassy Dr 38108
Emerald St 38115
Emerald Hills Dr 38115
Emerald View Way 38109
Emerson Ave & Cv 38128
Emily Ave 38122
Emily Pl 38115
Emily Elizabeth Dr 38118
Emmason St 38106
Emmet St 38115
Emmie St 38114
Emmons Dr 38128
E & W Emory Rd 38109
Empire Ave 38107
Encanto Rd 38109
Enchanted Oak Pl 38120
Encino Cv 38115
Enfield Rd 38116
Engineer Rd 38109
England St 38127
Engleside Cv 38125
Englewood Cv 38127
Englewood St 38106
English Cv & Dr 38125
English Pecan Cv 38128
English Towne Dr 38128
Englishill Dr 38135
Enid Ave 38115
Enterprise Ave 38114
Epping Way Dr 38128
Epworth Cv & Dr 38135
Eric Dr 38134
Eric Ln 38115
Erie Ave 38114
Erin Dr
500-520 38117
521-599 38117
521-521 38177
522-598 38117
Ernest Cv 38141
Ernie Dr 38116
E & S Erwin Dr 38117
Escape Aly 38103
Escrow St 38128
Espalier Cir & Cv 38119
Esperance St 38135
Espie Cv 38125
Esplanade Pl 38106
E Essex Ave 38106
W Essex Ave 38109
Essex Ct 38119
Essex Dr 38119
Essex Pl 38120
Essexshire Ave 38117
Estate Dr 38119
Estate Pl 38120
Estate Office Dr 38119
Estes St 38115
Estill St 38109
Estival Pl 38126
Estridge Cv & Dr 38122
Ethel Rd 38135
Ethel St 38114
Ethlyn Ave
1000-1699 38106
2100-2199 38114
Euclid Ave 38114
Eugene Rd 38116
Eupora Cv 38119
Eva St 38112
Eva Webb Cv 38133
Evadne Ave 38108
Evelyn Ave
1600-1909 38114
1910-2399 38104
Even Mist Cv 38120
Evenches Ave 38103
Evening Light Dr 38135
Evening Shade Cv 38125
Evening Star Cv 38125
Evening Wind Cv 38141
Eveningview Dr 38134
Evensong Cv 38120
Eventide Dr 38120
Everest St 38127
Everett Ave 38112
Everett Ln 38115
Everetts Folly St 38134
N Evergreen St
1-184 38104
185-599 38112
600-1119 38107
1120-1299 38108
S Evergreen St 38104
Exchange Ave
140-699 38105
1300-1399 38104
Executive Dr 38115
Executive Centre Dr 38134
Executive Court Dr 38131
Expedition Pl 38103
Explorer Ave 38134
Eyers Rd 38109
Eyrie Dr 38115
Ezell St 38111
Fair Cv 38115
Fair Elms Cv 38118
Fair Fall Dr 38116
Fairbanks St 38128
Fairborn Dr 38115
Fairbrook Ave & Cv 38118
Fairchild Cv 38120
Fairfax St 38108
Fairfield Cir 38117
Fairfield Rd 38116
Fairhaven Ln 38128
Fairhill Ln 38135
Fairhope Rd 38109
Fairlane Cv 38115
Fairlane Dr 38128
Fairley Cv & Rd 38109
Fairmeade Ave 38114
Fairmeadow Rd 38117
Fairmont Ave
3500-3999 38122
4100-4299 38108
Fairmont Cv 38108
Fairoaks Ave 38122
Fairview Dr 38109
Fairview St 38106
E, W, N & S Fairway Ave & Cv 38109
Fairway Heights Cv 38135
Fairway Hill Cv 38135
Fairway Meadow Cir E 38109
Fairway Oaks Dr 38134
Fairway View Cir & Cv 38135
Fairway Wood Cv 38135
Fairwind Cv 38125
Fairwood Cv 38125
Fairwood Ln 38120
Faith Cv 38109
Falcon Cv & Dr 38109
Falcon Ridge Cv 38135
Falkirk Rd 38128
Falkland Dr 38125
Fall Leaf Cv 38125
Fall River Dr 38115
Falling Acorn Ln 38125
Falling Bark Dr 38134
Falling Mist Ln 38141
Falling Oak Cv 38125
Falling Oak Way 38134
Falling Star Cv 38134
Falling Stream Cv & Dr 38127
Falling Tree Dr 38141
Falls Dr 38116
E Falls Rd 38109
W Falls Rd 38109
Falls Hollow Cv 38125
Fallstone Rd 38125
Falmouth Rd 38134
Fann Rd 38115
Fannie St 38109
Fannin Ave 38115
Far View Cv 38128
Fargo Rd 38128
Farm Rd 38134
Farm Hill Dr 38141
Farm Ridge Dr 38141
Farm View Dr 38141
Farmer Ave 38114
Farmhill Cv 38135
Farmhouse Dr 38125
Farmstone Cv 38135
Farmville Rd 38122
Farmwood Dr 38116
Farnell Ave 38134
E, N, S & W Faronia Dr, Rd & Sq 38116
Farrington St 38109
Farris Cir & Rd 38109
Farrisview Blvd 38118
Farrow Ave 38106
Farrow Rd 38116
Faulkner Rd 38118
Faulkner Rdg 38134
Favell Dr 38116
Fawn Cv 38111
N, S & W Fawn Hollow Cir & Cv 38141
Fawn Valley Cv & Dr 38125
Faxon Ave
800-1199 38105
1200-1599 38104
1600-3289 38112
3290-4199 38122
E & W Fay Ave 38109
Fayette Rd 38128
February Rd 38109
Federal Ave 38118
Feldspar Cv 38118
Felipe St 38127
Felix Ave
1400-1909 38114
1910-2139 38104
2500-2999 38111
Fellowship Loop 38118
Fellsway Cv 38119
Felton Rd 38128
Felts Station Rd 38127
Fenway Dr 38141
N & S Fenwick Rd 38111
Ferber Ave 38114
Ferdie Cv 38127
Ferguson Rd
1200-1499 38106
5500-5899 38134
Ferlerle Dr 38128
Fern Creek Dr 38115
Fern Hollow Rd 38125
Fern Ridge Rd 38115
Fern Valley Dr 38125
Fernbank Cv & Ln 38125
Fernbrook Dr 38118
Ferncliff Cv 38127
Ferncrest Dr 38135
Ferndale Rd 38122
Fernglen St 38141
Fernhill Cv 38127
Fernleaf Ave 38134
N & S Fernway Cv & Dr 38117
Fernwood Ave 38106
E Fernwood Ave 38109
Ferrell Dr 38134
Ferrell Park Cv & Dr 38116
Ferry Ct 38126
Fescue Ln 38115
Fiat Cv 38127
Fiber Rd 38109
Field Flower Ct 38118
Fieldbrook St 38127
Fieldcrest Ave 38134
Fieldlark Dr 38109
Fields Ave & Rd 38109
Fiesta Dr 38120
Fig Leaf Cir & Cv 38109
Filmore Ave & Cir 38114
Fincastle Cv 38134
Finch Cv 38127
Finch Dr 38127
Finch Rd 38141
Finchwood Ave & Cv 38115
S Finlay St 38112
Finley Rd 38116
Fir Ln 38115
Firefly Cv 38119
Firenze Ln 38106
Firerock Cir 38118
Firestone Ave 38107
Firethorne Dr 38115
Firewood Ln 38118
First Green Dr 38116
Fisher Ave 38112
Fiske Rd 38135
Fiske Ridge Cv 38135
Fiske Valley Cv & Dr 38135
Fite Rd 38127
Fitzgerald Dr 38109
Five Colonies Ln 38119
Fizer Ave 38111
Fizer Cv 38117
Fizer Rd 38114
Flagstaff Ln 38119
Flaherty Pl 38133
Flairwood Cv & Dr 38118
Flamingo Cv & Rd 38117
Flanders Ave 38118
Flatwood Cv 38134
Flaut St 38122
Fleda Rd 38120
Fleece Pl 38104
Fleet Pl 38126
Fleetbrook Dr 38116
Fleetgrove Ave 38117
Fleets Harbor Dr 38103
Fleets Island Dr 38103
Fleetview Ave 38117
Fleetway Ave 38115
Fleetwood Pl 38114
Fletcher Creek Cv & Dr 38133
Fletcher Glen Dr 38133
Fletcher Ridge Ln 38133
Fleur De Lis Cv 38117
Flicker St 38104
Flint Dr 38115
Flintlock Dr 38135
Flodden Cv & Dr 38119
Flora Ave 38114
Florence St 38104
Florette Dr 38116
Florian St 38109
Florida St
600-759 38103
760-1449 38106
1450-2499 38109
Florida Park Cir 38106
Flower Hill Dr E & W 38135
Flower Valley Ave 38128
Flowering Cherry Ln 38115
Flowering Peach Cv & Dr 38115
N & S Flowering Tree Cv & Dr 38134
Flowers St 38122
Flowerwood Rd 38134
Floyd Ave 38127
N & S Fluss Cv & Rd 38135
Flynn Rd 38109
Flynthill Cv & Dr 38135
Fog Hollow Ln 38125
Foggy Ridge Cv 38115
Foggy River Ln 38135
Fontaine Rd
2400-2699 38106
3000-3499 38116
Fontana Ave 38115
Foote Park Cir, Cv, Ln & Pl 38126
Foothill Dr 38133
Forbury Cv 38119
Ford Cv 38109
Ford Pl 38126
Ford Rd 38109
Forenney Dr 38115
Forest Bend Ct 38125
Forest Brook Dr 38118
Forest Creek Cv 38141
Forest Crest Cv 38125
Forest Glen Cv & St 38118
Forest Grove Cv & Dr 38119
Forest Hill Ct 38134
Forest Hill Irene Rd 38125
Forest Hills Dr 38134
Forest Lake Dr
700-799 38117
4000-4098 38128
Forest Lakes Cv 38128
Forest Meadow Dr 38125
Forest Mist Dr 38125
Forest Oak Way 38118
Forest Oasis Cv & Ln 38135
Forest Valley Cv & Dr 38141
Forest View Dr 38118
Forest View Sq 38115
Foriew Dr 38125
E & W Forked River Cv 38135
Formosa Rd 38109
Forrest Ave
900-1199 38105
1200-1299 38104
1500-2999 38112
3400-3700 38122
3702-3944 38122
Forrest Cir 38135
Forrest Dr 38122
Forrester Rd 38109
Forsyth Dr 38115
Fortner Dr 38128
Fortune Ave 38127
Fossil Creek Rd 38120
Foster Ave
1500-1719 38106

1720-1999 38114
Fosterwood Dr & Sq 38115
Fostoria Rd 38109
Found St 38125
Founders Ln 38103
Fountain Ct 38106
Fountain Bay Dr 38120
Fountain Creek Dr 38120
Fountain Crest Cv & Dr 38120
Fountain Gate St 38109
Fountain Lake Dr 38120
Fountain River Dr 38120
Four Seasons Dr 38133
Fox St 38111
E & W Fox Bend Ave & Cv 38115
Fox Bridge Cv 38125
Fox Chase Dr 38115
Fox Den 38141
Fox Gap Cv 38141
Fox Hedge 38141
Fox Hollow Dr 38115
E & W Fox Horse Cv 38141
Fox Hound 38141
Fox Hunt Dr 38115
Fox Hunt Ln 38134
Fox Lair Ave 38115
Fox Lake Ln 38115
Fox Leigh Dr 38115
Fox Meadows Cv & Rd 38115
Fox Plaza Dr 38115
Fox Race Cv 38141
Fox Ridge Dr 38115
Fox Run Cv 38119
Fox Valley Dr 38127
Foxbriar Dr 38115
E Foxburrow Cir 38115
Foxcroft St 38111
Foxdale Rd 38115
Foxfield Cv & Trl 38135
Foxgate Dr 38115
Foxhall Cv & Dr 38118
E & N Foxhill Dr 38135
Foxwood Dr 38115
N & W Foy Cir 38122
Foyle Cv & Way 38125
Frances Pl 38111
Frances Wood Cv & Dr 38135
Francisco Blvd & St 38116
E Frank Ave
1-199 38109
450-799 38106
W Frank Ave 38109
Frankfort St 38122
Frankie Ln 38109
Frankie Carolyn Dr 38118
Franklin St 38112
Fransol Cv 38108
Frayser Blvd
800-2950 38127
3100-3198 38128
Frayser Cir 38127
Frayser Dr 38127
Frayser Manor Dr 38127
Frayser Raleigh Rd 38128
Frayser School Dr 38127
Frayser View Dr 38127
Fred St 38107
Fredericks Ave 38111
Fredonia St 38127
Freehold Cv, Dr & Ln 38125
Freelark Ln 38115
Freeman Cv 38134
Freeman St 38122
Freemile Ave 38111
Freemont Rd 38114
Freeport Ave 38141
Freland Dr 38118
French Cv 38134
French Bend Ln 38127
French Broad Cv & Ln 38135
French Market Cir E 38141
Frentriv Dr 38116
Freshwater Dr 38115
Fresno Ave 38115
Friar Tuck Rd 38111
Friddell Cv 38133
Frieden Trl 38125
Friendly Way 38115
Friendship Cv & Ln 38115
Frisco Ave 38114
N Front St
1-439 38103
440-599 38105
600-999 38107
S Front St 38103
Frost Dr 38125
Frost Hill Cv 38135
Frosty Leaf Dr 38141
Frosty Meadow Cv & Dr 38125
Fulham Pl 38128
Fuller Rd 38118
Fun Valley Dr 38125
Furry Cv 38125
Gabay St 38106
Gadwall Dr N & W 38141
E Gage Ave
1-399 38109
400-899 38106
W Gage Ave 38109
Gail Dr 38133
Gail Bluff Cv 38135
Gailwood Ave 38122
Gailwood Dr 38134
Gailyn Cv & Dr 38135
Gaines Aly 38106
Gainsville Ave 38109
Gaiters Park Ln 38126
Gaither Cv, Pkwy & St 38106
Galahad Cv 38134
Galaxie St 38134
Galileo Cv 38134
Gallan Ct & Dr 38134
Gallery Dr 38125
Galloway Ave
500-1099 38105
1400-1499 38104
1500-2099 38112
3300-3699 38122
E Galloway Dr 38111
N Galloway Dr 38111
S Galloway Dr 38111
W Galloway Dr 38111
Galloway Oaks Cv 38111
Galveston St 38114
Galvin Cv 38134
Gamewell Rd 38111
Gandy Cv & Dr 38133
Ganymede Cv 38115
Gap Knoll Cv 38133
Garden Cv 38134
Garden Ln 38111
Garden Rd 38134
Garden Birch Cv 38115
Garden Gap Dr 38134
Garden Grove Cir & Cv 38128
Garden Leaf Dr 38134
E, N, S & W Garden Manor Dr 38125
Garden Oak Cv 38120
Garden Oaks Dr
4600-4699 38116
6600-6899 38120
Garden Oaks Way 38116
Garden Reach Cv 38120
Garden River Cv 38120
Garden Row Dr 38126
Garden Walk Ln 38128
Gardenbrook Dr 38134
Gardendale St 38141
Gardener Cv 38135
Gardenia Cv & Dr 38117
Gardens Way 38111
Gardenview Dr 38116
Gardenwood Dr 38116
Gardners Rd 38134
Garfield St 38114
Garland St
100-599 38104
700-1199 38107
Garner Pl 38135
Garnett Rd 38117
Garrick Dr 38119
Garrison Ave 38128
Garrison Park Cir 38119
Garver Rd 38128
Gary St 38122
Gascony Dr 38115
Gaston Ave
100-329 38106
330-499 38126
Gatehouse Dr 38134
Gates Cv 38115
Gateway Dr 38116
Gateway Pl 38122
Gateway Inlet Cv 38119
Gatewood Dr 38134
Gattling Cv & St 38127
Gausco Rd 38106
Gavick Cv & Dr 38125
Gawco Dr 38108
Gayle Ave 38127
Gaylord Ln 38118
Gaylyn Ct 38114
Gayoso Ave 38103
Gaywinds Ave & Cv 38115
Gazebo Cv 38115
E Ge Patterson Ave
1-229 38103
231-247 38126
249-399 38126
W Ge Patterson Ave 38103
E & W Geeter Rd 38109
E Gemini Cv 38134
W Gemini Cv 38134
Gemini Dr 38109
Gemstone Way 38109
Gendark 38101
Genesis Cir 38106
Gentry Ave 38108
Genyth Ave 38128
George Cv 38134
George Rd 38109
George Wythe Cv 38134
Georgetown Dr 38118
E Georgia Ave
1-99 38103
100-899 38126
W Georgia Ave 38103
Georgian Dr 38127
Gerald Rd 38122
Geraldus Ave 38111
Gerard Pl 38107
German Creek Park 38125
German Hollow Cv 38125
German Leaf Cv 38125
Germanshire Cv & Ln 38125
Germanshire Oaks Cv 38125
N Germantown Pkwy 38133
N Germantown Rd 38133
S Germantown Rd
3050-3649 38119
3650-4610 38125
4612-4688 38125
4690-5299 38141
Germantown Trl
6900-7019 38141
7020-7399 38125
Germantown Road Ext 38115
N Germanwood Ct 38125
Geronimo Ct 38118
Gertrude Dr 38125
Getwell Cv 38118
Getwell Rd
800-1999 38111
2000-5699 38118
Gherald St
1200-1299 38122
1300-1499 38108
Giacosa Pl 38133
Giaroli St 38122
Gibbons Ave & Pl 38127
Gibbs Cv & Pkwy 38128
Gigem Dr 38109
Gila Dr & Ln 38135
Gilbert Ave 38106
Gilbert Rd 38116
Gilford Dr 38141
Gill Ave 38106
Gill Rd 38109
Gilleas Rd 38109
Gillespie Cir & Rd 38134
Gillette Cv 38135
Gillham Cv & Dr 38134
Gillia Cir E 38135
Gillie Cv 38133
Gillie St 38127
Gilliland Ave 38127
Gilmore Rd 38109
Gilson Rd 38117
Gin Wade Cv 38125
Gina Dr 38118
Ginger Cir 38118
Ginger Snap Cv 38125
Gingerhill Ln 38133
Ginkgo Ln 38125
Ginners Dr 38134
Girvan Ct & Dr 38134
Given Ave
3000-3289 38112
3290-5099 38122
Given Cv 38122
Givenchy Pl 38104
Glade View Dr 38120
Gladeside Dr 38117
Gladeview Pl 38120
Gladney Dr 38114
Gladstone Cv & St 38128
Glankler St 38112
Glasgow St 38127
Glastonburg Ln 38134
Gleason Ave 38106
Glen Grn 38125
Glen Creek Ln 38125
Glen Echo Dr 38115
Glen Eden Dr 38125
Glen Laurel Way 38115
Glen Logan Rd 38134
Glen Oaks Dr 38119
Glen Trace Cv 38135
Glenalp St 38127
Glenarm Ave & Cv 38109
Glenbriar Dr 38119
Glenbrook St 38109
Glenburee Cv & St 38109
Glenchase Dr 38135
Glencliff St 38119
Glencoe Dr 38115
Glencoe Rd 38109
Glencrest Ln 38117
Glendale Dr 38128
Gleneagles Dr 38141
Glenfield Cv 38133
Glenfinnan Rd 38128
E & S Glengarry Cv & Rd 38128
E & N Glenhome Dr 38134
Glenlivet Dr 38119
Glenmeade Cv & Dr 38116
Glenn Ave 38127
Glenn Dr 38134
Glenn St 38106
Glenover Dr 38134
Glenroy Dr 38125
Glenshade Dr 38116
Glenshaw Dr 38128
Glenview Ave
1500-1719 38106
1720-1899 38114
Glenwick Dr 38141
Glenwild Ave & Cv 38119
Glenwood Pl 38104
Global Dr 38141
W Gloria Rd 38116
Glory Cir 38114
Gloucester Ave & Cv 38135
Gloucester Way Dr 38125
Glyn Carroll Cv 38133
Glynbourne Pl 38117
Glynn Vale Cv N & S 38125
Glynn Ville Dr 38125
Goff Ave 38114
Goforth Way 38134
Gold Ave 38106
Gold Leaf Ln 38125
Gold Run Cv 38128
Gold Stream Cv & Ln 38125
Goldbrier Ln 38134
Golden Ave 38108
Golden Eagle Dr 38115
Golden Oaks Cv & Dr 38118
Golden Park Dr 38141
Golden Star Cv 38134
Golden Valley Ln 38133
Goldeneye Dr 38141
Goldie Ave 38122
Golf Hl 38125
Golf Club Cir 38109
Golf View Cv 38135
Golf Walk Cir S 38125
Golightly Dr 38128
Gooch Rd 38109
Good Fortune Cv & Ln 38135
Goodbar Ave 38104
Goodhaven Dr 38116
Goodland Cir & St 38111
Goodlett Cv 38111
Goodlett Pl 38117
N Goodlett St 38117
S Goodlett St
1-559 38117
560-1999 38111
2800-3699 38118
Goodloe Ave 38106
S & W Goodman Cir & St 38111
Goodway Ln 38117
Goodwick Dr 38125
Goodwill Ln 38108
Goodwill Rd 38109
E & W Goodwyn Cir, Cv & St 38111
Goodwyn Green Cir 38111
Gookin Pl 38111
Gopher Ridge Cv 38135
Gordon St 38122
Gordon Bernard Cv 38133
Gosbrook Ln 38125
Gothard Rd 38128
Gotten Pl & St 38111
Gouverneur St 38135
Gowan Dr 38127
Gower St 38122
Grace Ave 38106
Grace View Ln 38135
Graceland Cv & Dr 38116
Graceland Pines St 38116
Gracewood St 38112
Gracious Way Cv 38135
Grady Ln 38127
Gragg Ave 38108
Graggland Cir 38108
Gragson Dr 38106
Graham Cv 38108
N Graham St
1-399 38117
400-1399 38122
1400-1999 38108
S Graham St 38111
Graham Oaks Ct 38122
Grahamdale Cir 38122
Grahamwood Cv & Dr 38122
Gramont Cv 38119
Granada Rd 38109
Grand St 38114
Grand Bay Cv 38125
N Grand Cedar Ln 38128
Grand Fields Ln 38119
E & W Grand Heights Dr 38109
Grand Island Dr 38103
Grand Opera Cv & Rd 38106
Grand Pines Dr 38125
Grand Pyramid Dr 38128
Grand Slam Dr 38125
Grandview Ave
3900-3938 38111
3940-4099 38111
4100-4299 38117
Grandview St 38111
Granehampton Ln 38111
Granite Creek Rd 38125
Grant Ave 38107
Grantham Rd 38109
Grants Aly 38105
Granville Ave 38109
Granville Ln 38104
Grapevine Cv 38133
Grapewood Cv 38134
Grassy Knoll Cv 38135
Grassy Point Cv 38135
Grassy Valley Dr 38141
Gratton Ln 38119
Graves Rd 38116
Gray Duck Dr 38109
Gray Fox Cv 38141
Gray Oak Ave 38115
Grayce Dr 38134
Grecco Dr 38128
Greeff Ln 38111
Green Crk 38125
Green Dr 38115
Green Rd 38109
Green Acres Rd 38117
Green Ash Cv 38125
Green Belt Dr 38125
Green Bush Pl 38111
Green Crest Dr 38133
Green Dolphin St 38111
Green Glade Rd 38120
Green Glen Dr 38133
Green Grove Dr 38141
Green Hall Way 38128
Green Hollow Cv & Ln 38133
Green Ivy Dr 38133
Green Meadows Rd 38120
Green Oaks Dr 38117
Green Park Ave 38126
Green River Rd 38128
Green Shadows Cv & Ln 38119
Green Stone Cv 38125
Green Terrace Dr 38127
Green Valley Rd 38115
Green View Dr 38135
Green Willow 38125
Greenbark Dr 38115
Greenberry Hill Cv 38141
Greenbranch Cv & Dr 38118
Greenbriar Dr 38117
Greenbrook Bnd & Pkwy 38134
Greencedar Ln 38135
Greendale Ave & Cir 38127
Greenfield Rd 38117
Greengrass Cv 38116
Greenland Rd 38134
Greenlaw Aly 38105
Greenlaw Ave 38105
Greenlaw Pl 38107
Greenleaf Cv, Rd & St 38135
Greenlodge Ln 38119
Greenmill Dr 38119
Greenmount Ave 38122
Greenridge Cv 38115
Greenside Dr 38125
Greentree Dr 38128
Greentree Valley Ct 38119
Greenvale St 38120
Greenview Cir 38108
Greenway Ave, Cv, Pl & Rd 38117
Greenwood Dr 38115
Greenwood St 38106
N & S Greer St 38111
Gregory Ave 38127
Grenadier Cv 38127
Grenoble Ln 38115
Grey Rd 38108
Grey Bark Cv & Dr 38118
Grey Oaks Dr 38103
Greybriar Dr 38125
Greylock Cv 38141
Greythorne Dr 38125
Griffith Ave 38107
Griggs Ave 38108
Grimes Pl & St 38106
Grinstead Cv 38141
Grosvenor Ave 38119
Grouse Ln 38141
Grove Ave
500-879 38126
880-1099 38104
W Grove Dr 38135
Grove Creek Pl 38117
Grove Dale St 38120
Grove Hill Pl 38120
N & S Grove Park Cir & Rd 38117
Grove Run Pl 38111
Grovehaven Cir & Dr 38116
Gruber Cv & Dr 38127
Guernsey Ave
3000-3289 38112
3290-3999 38122
Guffin Cv & Rd 38135
Guilder Cv 38133
Guildhall Dr 38128
Guillory St 38134
Guinevere Ln 38135
Gulf Ave & Cv 38114
Gull Rd 38109
Gunsmoke Ave 38128
Gunther Cv 38133
Guthrie Ave 38107
Guthrie Ln 38133
Gwendolyn Dr 38125
Gwyllim Cv 38125
Gwynne Cv 38120
Gwynne Rd
4000-5299 38117
5300-5599 38120
Gypsy Cv 38133
Haas Ave 38109
Hackberry Cv 38120
Hackberry Ln 38109
Hackmar Cv 38125
Hacks Cv 38119
Hacks Cross Rd 38125
Hackworth Cv 38127
Hacton Cv 38119
Hadden St 38126
Haddington Cv & Dr 38119
Hadley Dr 38133
Hadley Rd 38111
Haisch Rd 38127
Halcomb Ln 38127
Hale Ave 38112
Hale Rd 38116
Haledale Rd 38116
Haleville Rd 38116
Haley Rd 38134
Half Moon Cv 38125
Haliburton St 38128
Hallbrook St 38127
Hallett Ln 38119
Hallshire Cv & Dr 38115
Hallview Dr 38128
Hallwood Dr 38107
Hally Pl 38106
Halstead St 38134
Hamilton Dr 38125
Hamilton St 38114
Hamlin Pl 38105
Hammett Dr 38109
Hammond Rd 38128
Hampshire Ave 38117
Hampstead Cv 38115
Hampton Pl 38126
Hampton Hill Cv & Dr 38134
Hampton Manor Cv & Ln 38128
Hamstead Cv 38128
Hanauer St 38109
Hancock Cv & Dr 38116
Hangar Rd 38118

Street	ZIP
Hanley St	38114
Hanna Dr	38128
Hannibal Cv	38103
Hanover Dr	38119
Hansberry Dr	38125
Hanson Rd	38108
Hanwood Ave	38108
Happiland Pl	38106
Happy Trl	38116
Happy Hollow Ln	38135
Happy Trail Ct	38116
Harahan Rd	38109
Haraway St	38118
Harbert Ave	
1227-2349	38104
2700-2799	38111
Harbins Pl	38109
Harbor Bend Cir & Rd	38103
Harbor Club Cir E	38103
Harbor Common Dr	38103
Harbor Creek Dr	38103
Harbor Crest Dr	38103
Harbor Edge Cir & Dr	38103
Harbor Isle Cir E	38103
Harbor Park Dr	38103
Harbor Point Ln	38103
Harbor Ridge Ln N & S	38103
Harbor River Cv & Dr	38103
Harbor Station Rd	38115
Harbor Town Blvd & Sq	38103
Harbor View Dr	38103
Harbor Village Dr	38103
Harcourt Way	38119
Hardgreaves Ln	38125
Hardin Ave	
3100-3289	38112
3290-3499	38122
Hargrove Ave	38127
Harlem St	38114
Harley Wind Dr	38134
Harlingen Dr	38133
Harmen St	38108
Harmon Cv	38135
Harmon Crest Dr & Sq	38115
Harmon Wood Ln	38115
Harmony Ct	38122
Harmony Woods Dr	38122
Harpeth Cv & Dr	38134
Harpy Dr	38125
Harrell St	38112
Harriet Rd	38128
Harrington Ave	38118
Harris Ave	
2970-3169	38114
3170-3399	38111
N Harris Cir	38114
W Harris Cir	38114
Harrison St	38108
Harrow Ln	38114
Harry Ave	38106
Harsh Cv	38127
Hart Cv	38115
Hartford Dr	38134
Hartford Pl	38114
Hartland St	
1600-1799	38108
1800-1999	38128
Hartz Dr	38116
Harvard Ave	38112
Harvest Ln	38133
Harvest Fields Cir	38125
Harvest Hill Cv & Rd	38141
Harvest Knoll Cv & Ln	38125
Harvest Moon Cv	38141
Harvest Park Cv & Dr	38125
Harvest Run Cv	38141
Harvest Valley Dr	38128
Harvester Ln E	38127
Harvey Cv	38122
Harvey Hill Dr	38141
Harvey Pointe Ln	38125
Harville St	38111
Harwick Dr	38119
Harwood Cv & Rd	38120
Hastings Cir E	38107
Hastings Cir W	38107
Hastings St	
500-599	38105
600-799	38107
Hatcher Cir	38118
Hatchfield Ln	38115
Hathaway Ln	38117
Haughton Ln & Pl	38128
Havana St	38106
Haven Cir	38106
Haven Ct	38109
Haver Cv	38116
Haverford Cv	38119
Haverhill Rd	38111
Haversham Way	38119
Haverwood Ave	38116
Hawk Dr	38118
Hawkeye Cv & St	38109
Hawkhurst St	38119
Hawkins Mill Rd	
2100-2699	38127
2950-4099	38128
Hawks Call Ln	38135
Hawks Hollow Cv	38135
Hawthorne Rd	38134
E Hawthorne Rd	38134
Hawthorne St	
190-599	38112
600-1099	38107
Hayden Pl	38111
Hayfield Cv & Ln	38141
Hayling Cv	38135
Haymarket Cv & Rd	38120
N, S & W Hayne Cir & Rd	38119
Haynes Rd	38133
Haynes St	
300-889	38111
890-1399	38114
Hays Rd	38114
Haywood Ave	38127
Hazards Cv	38115
Hazel Cv	38128
Hazelhedge Dr	38116
Hazelwood Ave	38122
Hazelwood Rd	38109
Healey Rd	38111
Heard Ave	38108
Hearst Ave	38114
Hearthside Cv	38119
Heartland Ln	38109
Heartwood Dr	38135
Heathcliff Cv & Dr	38134
Heather Cv	38119
Heather Dr	38119
Heather Ln	38111
Heather Row	38141
Heather Knoll Cv	38125
Heather Ridge Dr	38115
Heather View Dr	38125
E & N Heatherhill Dr	38135
Heatherton Cv	38125
Heatherway Dr	38117
Heatherwood Cv	38119
Heatherwood Dr	38141
Heatherwood Ln	38117
Heathrow Cv	38115
Heber Ave	38114
Hebron Dr	38116
Heckle Ave	38111
Hedge Hills Ave	38117
Hedge Park Dr	38141
Hedgegrove Dr	38117
Hedgemore Cv	38135
Hedgerow Dr	38109
Hedges Dr	38128
N Hedgewall Cir	38141
Hedgewood Ave	38116
Hedgewood Cv	38135
Hedgewood Ln	38135
Hedgewyck Ct	38117
Hedgington Dr	38125
Hedman Ave	38127
Heiskell Pl	38126
Heistan Pl	38104
Helen Ann Dr	38127
Helene Cv & Rd	38117
Helmwood St	38127
Helsley Rd	38108
Hemingway Ave	38128
Hemlock Ln	38117
Hemlock St	38106
Hemsley Ave	38109
Henderson Pl	38126
Henderson St	38127
Hendricks Ave & Cv	38111
Henley Dr	38114
Hennington Ave	38109
Henredon Dr	38141
Henrietta Rd	38134
Henry Ave	
1-1799	38107
2200-2399	38108
3000-3289	38112
3290-3499	38122
Henry Cir	38112
Herald Sq	38120
Heritage Ave	38115
Heritage Lake Cv & Dr	38109
Heritage Oak Dr	38125
Hermitage Dr	38116
Hernando Pl	38126
Hernando Rd	38106
Hernando St	
1-189	38103
270-799	38126
Heron Oaks Cv	38120
Heronswood Cv & Dr	38119
Herron Aly	38117
Herzl St	38117
Hester Ave	38111
Hester Rd	38116
Hewlett Rd	38109
Heyde Ave	38114
Hiawatha St	38117
E Hibiscus Ln	38127
Hichiney Dr	38135
Hickman St	38116
Hickory Ave	38107
E Hickory Blf	38128
W Hickory Blf	38128
Hickory Cv	38141
Hickory Way	38119
Hickory Bark Dr	38141
Hickory Bend Rd	38115
Hickory Branch Cv & Dr	38141
Hickory Commons	38141
Hickory Creek Dr	
3200-3299	38115
4400-4599	38135
Hickory Crest Cv & Dr	38119
Hickory Farms Cir & Dr	38115
Hickory Forest Dr	38119
Hickory Greene Cv & Dr	38141
Hickory Grove Dr	38141
Hickory Grove Ln	38134
Hickory Hill Rd	
2800-3734	38115
3735-4179	38115
3735-3735	38175
3736-3998	38115
4180-5599	38141
Hickory Hill Sq	38115
Hickory Hollow Dr	38133
Hickory Hollow Ln	38115
Hickory Jack Ave	38134
Hickory Lake Cv	38119
Hickory Leaf Cv & Dr	38141
Hickory Meadow Ln	38115
Hickory Mill Sq	38115
Hickory Nutt Ln	38141
Hickory Point Cv & Ln	38115
Hickory Ridge Cv	38116
Hickory Ridge Dr	38116
Hickory Ridge Mall	38115
S Hickory Ridge Mall	38115
Hickory Ridge Trl	38115
Hickory Shadow Ln	38141
Hickory Station Ct & Dr	38115
Hickory Trace Cv	38141
Hickory Valley Cv	38116
Hickory View Pl	38115
Hickory Villas Dr	38115
Hickory Wood Cv	38116
Hicks Rd	38109
Hicky Cv & St	38109
Hidden Arbor Ct	38128
Hidden Creek Cv	38134
Hidden Fern Ct & Ln	38135
Hidden Forest Cv	38135
Hidden Grotto Rd	38125
Hidden Lake Dr	38128
Hidden Valley Ln	38109
Hidden Water Dr	38134
Hidden Woods Cv	38128
Higbee Ave	
1900-2139	38104
2700-2799	38111
High Rd	38128
High St	38105
High Bridge Ct & Dr	38118
High Meadow Dr	38128
High Plains Rd	38135
High Point Cv	38109
High Point Dr	38122
High Point Ter	
1-359	38111
360-639	38122
High Ridge Pt	38125
High Ridge Rd	38135
High Tree St	38134
Highgrove Dr	38125
Highland Cv	38111
N Highland Rd	38128
N Highland St	
1-309	38111
310-1449	38122
1450-1999	38108
S Highland St	38111
Highland Court Dr	38111
Highland Oaks Cv & Dr	38125
Highland Park Pl	38111
Highmans Aly	38105
Hightor Ln	38125
Hilda St	38109
Hill Dr	
3900-4099	38115
5000-5199	38109
Hill Gail Dr	38141
Hill Lake Dr	38135
Hillbrook St	38109
Hillcrest St	38112
Hilldale Ave	38117
Hillgate Cv & St	38118
Hillindale Dr	38133
Hillis St	38127
Hillman Way Dr	38133
Hillmont Ave	38122
Hillridge St	38109
Hillsboro Cv	38127
Hillshire Cir, Cv & Dr	38133
Hillside Ave	38127
Hilltop Rd	38135
Hillview Ave	38109
E Hillview Cv	38114
E Hillview Dr	38114
W Hillview Dr	38114
Hillwood Dr	38128
Hillyglen Cv	38135
Hilton St	38114
Hilyard Ln	38126
Hindman Ave	38127
Hinton Ave, Cv & Pl	38119
Hitchcock Dr	38128
Hix Pl	38107
Hobart Pl	38126
Hobbits Roost St	38134
Hobbs Cv	38135
Hobbs Dr	38111
Hobson Cv & Rd	38128
Hocker Hedge Cv	38128
Hodge Cv & Rd	38109
Hodges St	38111
Hofburg Cv & St	38127
Hogan Cv & Dr	38118
Holeman Rd	38118
Holiday Dr	38109
Holland Ave	38109
Holland Dr	38127
Holliday St	
1200-1299	38122
1300-1499	38108
Hollins Ave	38112
Hollis F Price St	38126
Hollister Cv & Ln	38135
Hollorn Ln	38125
Hollow Gap Cv	38133
Hollow Valley Cv	38141
Hollowell Ave	38109
Holly St	38112
Holly Berry Cv & Dr	38118
Holly Glen Cv	38133
Holly Grove Dr	38119
Holly Hearth Cv	38135
Holly Heath Dr	38119
Holly Hedge Dr	38128
Holly Park Dr	38141
Holly Ridge Cv & Dr	38118
Hollydale Cv	38127
W Hollyford Rd	38114
Hollyoke Ln	38117
Hollyview Dr	38125
N Hollywood St	
101-167	38112
169-839	38112
840-1999	38108
2000-3700	38127
3702-3948	38127
S Hollywood St	
100-199	38112
200-399	38104
400-599	38111
Holman Pl	
1700-1799	38114
3400-3499	38118
Holmes Cir	38111
E Holmes Rd	
1-799	38109
800-2229	38116
2230-5599	38118
5600-7010	38141
7011-9099	38125
W Holmes Rd	38109
N Holmes St	
1-289	38111
290-599	38112
600-1299	38122
1300-1799	38108
S Holmes St	38111
Holmes Crest Ln	38118
Holsten Creek Cv	38135
Holt Dr	38116
Homedale Ave	38116
Homer St	38122
Hometown Dr	38133
Homewood Cv	38128
Homewood Dr	38128
Homewood Rd	38118
Honduras Cv & Rd	38109
Honey Bee Ln	38134
Honey Locust Cv	38119
Honeybrook Rd	38134
Honeysuckle Ln	38109
Honeywood Ave	38118
Honor Park Dr & Loop	38118
Hood Ave	38134
Hood St	38108
Hooker St	38134
Hoover Dr	38128
Hope St	38111
Hopewell Rd	38117
Hopkins Ave	38112
Horace St	38106
Horizon Cv	38133
Horizon Center Blvd	38133
Horizon Lake Dr	38133
W Horn Lake Cv & Rd	38109
Hornbeam Rd	38127
Hornsby Cv & Dr	38116
Horse Shoe Cv	38109
Horseshoe Trl	38115
Horton Rd	38127
Hoskins Dr	38114
Hoskins Rd	
2900-3029	38114
3030-3199	38111
Hoskins Road Ext	38111
Hotchkiss Ln	38104
Houck Ave	38108
Houghton Cv	38128
Houston St	38111
Houston Levee Rd	38125
Howard Aly	38106
Howard Dr	38109
Howardcrest Dr	38128
Howell Ave	38108
Hubbard Ave	38108
N & S Hubert Ave & Cir	38108
Huckleberry Cv	38109
Huckleberry St	38116
Huckleberry Ridge Dr	38116
Hudgins Rd	38116
Hudson St	38112
Hugenot St	38114
Hughes Glen Cv	38125
Hughes Meadow Cv & Dr	38125
Huling Ave	38103
Hull Ave	38112
Hulon St	38134
Humber St	38106
N & S Humes St	38111
Hummingbird Ln	38117
Humphrey Oaks Cir	38120
N Humphreys Blvd	38120
Humphreys Center Dr	38120
Humphreys Farm Cv	38120
Hungerford Rd	38118
Hunt Ln	38115
Hunt Cliff Trce	38128
Hunter Ave	38108
Hunter Rdg	38125
Hunter Trail Cv	38125
Hunterfield Trl	38135
Hunters Trl	38120
Hunters Bluff Dr	38120
E, S & W Hunters Glen Cv & St	38128
Hunters Oak Dr	38120
Hunters Place Dr	38115
Hunters Trace Dr	38120
Hunters Tree Cv & Dr	38125
Hunters Way Dr	38115
Hunters Woods Sq	38115
Huntingdon Ln	38111
Huntington Trail Dr	38115
Huntley Dr	38132
Huntridge Cv	38128
Huntsman Cv & Ln	38120
Huron Ave	38107
Hurst Ct	38135
Hutson Rd	38116
Hutton Way	38116
Hy Crop Row	38120
Hyacinth Cv & Dr	38115
Hyde Park Blvd	38108
Hyman Dr	38133
I A C Dr	38116
Ida Pl	38126
N Idlewild St	
1-99	38104
600-1099	38107
S Idlewild St	38104
Ila Ct & Ln	38109
E & W Illinois Ave	38106
Imagination Dr	38118
Imogene St	38114
Imperial Ave	38107
Imperial Oak Cv & Dr	38115
Ina Cv	38133
Independent Dr	38118
Indian Dr	38122
Indian Bend Ln	38109
Indian Brook Cv	38125
Indian Ridge Ln	38115
Indian Trail Dr	38141
Indian Village Dr	38109
E & W Industrial Ave	38109
Inez St	38111
Ingle Ave	38109
Ingleside Dr	38134
Inkberry Ln	38117
Inman Cv & Rd	38111
Inniswood Cv & Dr	38135
Innsbrock Ln	38115
Innsbrook Cv & Dr	38115
Interfaith Pl	38109
International Dr	38120
Interstate Dr	38116
Inverary Cv & Dr	38119
Invergarry Rd	38128
Inverness Dr	38125
Inverness Parkway Dr	38115
Inwood Dr	38109
Ioka Ave	38126
Irene Blvd	38125
Iris Cv	38125
Irma St	38127
Iron Ivy Ln	38105
Ironwood Cv	38125
Ironwood Dr	38115
Iroquois Rd	38111
E & S Irvin Dr	38119
Irvin Calvin Dr	38106
Irvin Park Cv	38119
Isabelle St	38122
Isherwood Cv & Rd	38125
Isis Cv	38128
N Island Dr & Pl E	38103
Island Bluff Dr	38103
Island Crest Cir	38103
Island Forty Rd	38127
Island Harbor Dr	38103
Island Mist Cir	38103
Island Park Cir & Dr	38103
Island Point Dr	38103
Island Ridge Dr	38103
Island Shore Dr	38103
Island Town Cv & Dr	38103
Island Village Dr	38103
Isle Bay Dr	38103
Isle Creek Dr	38103
Isle Pointe Dr	38103
Isle View Dr	38103
Isleworth Dr	38125
Ivan Rd	38109
Ivanhoe Cv & Rd	38134
Ivanhoe Forest Cv	38141
Ivawood Dr	38134
Ivory Ave	38107
Ivy Rd	38117
Ivy Bend Cv	38125
Ivy Chase Cv	38117
Ivy Hollow Dr	38133
Ivy Lake Cv & Ln	38133
Ivy Meadows Dr	38115
J Alan Dr	38135
Jack Kramer Dr	38117
Jacklyn Ave	38106
Jackson Ave	
1-139	38103
140-759	38105
760-1999	38107
2000-2329	38112
2330-2799	38108
2800-3199	38112
3200-3599	38122
3600-3799	38108
3800-4799	38128
Jackson Pit Rd	38118
Jacoby Ave	38106
Jade Ln	38111
Jadewood Cv	38125
Jalna Cv	38125
Jamaica Ave	38117
Jamaica Dr	38108
Jamerson Rd	38122

James Ln 38128
James Rd
1700-2949 38127
2950-4299 38128
James St 38106
James Kent Ct 38118
Jamestown Ave 38115
Jameswood Dr 38128
Jamie Cv & Dr 38116
Jan Dr 38127
Jane Eyre St 38134
Jane Marie Cv 38135
Janelle Cv 38133
N, S & W Janice Ave & Cir 38122
Janis Dr 38116
Janssen Dr 38128
Jardin Pl 38141
Jardin Place Cv 38141
Jasmine Cv & Dr 38115
Jason Dr 38120
Jasper Ave 38128
Jay Cv 38127
Jayne Lewis Cv 38133
Jean Dr 38118
Jeanne Dr 38109
Jeannine St 38111
Jeff Cv & Dr 38109
Jefferson Ave
1-499 38103
500-839 38105
840-909 38103
910-999 38105
1000-2399 38104
N Jefferson Pl 38105
S Jefferson Pl 38105
Jeffrey Ave 38114
Jeffries Cv 38133
Jehl Pl 38107
Jenkins St 38118
Jennette Pl 38126
Jenny Ln 38135
Jenson Cv & Rd 38109
Jenwood St 38134
Jerelyn Cv 38128
Jermyn Ct 38119
Jernigan Cv 38128
Jerusalem St 38109
Jessamine Ave 38126
Jessica Dr 38135
Jessie Lee Ln 38118
Jet Cv 38118
Jewell Rd 38128
Jib Cv 38119
Jills Creek Cv & Dr 38133
Jireh Cv & Dr 38128
Joanne St 38111
Jody Cv 38135
Joe Brooks Dr 38134
Joel Ave 38127
Joest Dr 38127
Joffre Ave 38111
Johanna Dr 38114
John A Denie Rd 38134
John Edwards Ln 38128
John Paul St 38114
E & W John Ronza Cir 38106
John Sikes Dr 38115
John Thomas Cv 38133
Johns River Rd 38116
Johnson Ave
3000-3299 38112
4600-4799 38117
E Johnson Cir 38112
N Johnson Cir 38112
W Johnson Cir 38112
Johnson Cv 38117
Johnwood Dr 38122
Jolly Dr 38109
Jolson Ave 38114
Jonathan Cv 38133
Jones Rd 38128
Jones St 38105
Jonetta St 38109
Jonquil Dr 38133
Jonquil Ln 38109
Jonsey Ln 38125
Jordan Dr 38116
Josee Ln 38135
Joseph Pl 38107
Josephine St
300-599 38111
600-899 38114
Joshua Cv 38133
E & W Josibpet Cir & Ln 38116
Joslyn Cv & St 38128
Joubert Ave 38109
Jowood Cv 38134
Joy Ln 38114
Joy Pl 38104
Joyce Ln 38116
Juanita Cir & Cv N, S & W 38133
Juca Cv & Ln 38116
Judith Ave & Cv 38114
Judson St 38114
Judy Cv 38111
Judy Lynn Ave & Cv 38118
Julann Dr 38115
Julia St 38127
Julian Ct 38119
Juliet Ave 38127
Julius Lewis Dr 38118
Jumper Ln 38134
June Rd 38119
Juneway Dr 38134
Juniper Ave 38117
Juniper Ridge Cv & Dr 38125
Jupiter Ave 38134
Justine St 38127
Jw Williams Ln 38105
Kalamath Cv 38128
Kallaher Ave 38122
Kalty Ct 38125
Kamali Ave 38134
Kamali Ct 38128
E Kamali Cv 38134
W Kamali Cv 38134
Kamin Ln 38125
Kanawha Cv 38118
N & S Kanita Cv 38125
Kansas St
660-759 38103
760-1469 38106
1470-2399 38109
Kant St 38106
Karen Cv 38128
Karen Manor Ln 38127
Kassel Cv & Rd 38116
Kate Bond Rd 38133
Katherine Ln 38141
Kathy Cv & Rd 38118
Katie Cv 38125
Kaye Rd 38117
Kayla Cv 38141
Kearney Ave 38111
Keating St 38114
Keats Rd
3000-3389 38134
3390-3599 38135
Keatswood Cir, Cv & Dr 38120
Kedvale Dr 38109
Keel Ave 38107
Keen Rd 38106
Keeneland Cv 38135
Keeshond Cv 38134
Keith Cv 38133
Kel Creek Cv 38122
Kelli Nicole Cv 38135
Kellogg Ave 38114
Kelly Cir & Rd E, N & S 38111
Kelmscott Cv & Dr 38119
Keltner Cir 38114
Kemel Ln 38134
Kemper Cv & Dr 38115
Kenbridge Dr 38134
Kendale Ave
1500-1719 38106
1720-1999 38114
Kendall Ln 38133
Kendall Pl 38128
Kendall Rd 38122
Kendrick Rd 38108
Kenie Ave & Cv 38118
Kenilworth Pl 38112
Kenland Dr 38118
Kenmar Cv 38128
Kennedy St 38106
Kenner Ave 38114
Kenner Cv 38135
Kennet Ct 38141
Kenneth Cv & St 38128
Kennibec Cv 38125
Kennings Dr 38125
Kenny Crest Dr 38115
Kenosha Rd 38118
Kensett Dr 38127
Kensington Pl 38107
Kent Rd 38116
Kent St 38111
Kental Dr 38119
Kentucky Dr 38106
Kentucky St
530-759 38103
760-1400 38106
1402-1498 38106
2000-2399 38109
Kentwood Ln 38118
Kenwick Way 38119
Kenwood Ave 38122
Kenwood Cv 38134
Kenwood Ln 38134
Kenwood Rd 38134
Kenyon Cv 38125
Keokee Cv 38128
Kerfield Dr 38128
Kerr Ave
760-1719 38106
1720-2299 38114
Kerston Dr 38128
Kerwin Dr 38128
Kerwood Ave 38128
Kesswood Ct 38119
Kestrel Ln 38125
Keswick Cv & Dr 38119
Ketchum Cv & Rd 38114
Kettle Creek Dr 38128
Kettlebrook Cv 38128
Kevin Dr 38135
Kevinridge Cv E & W 38125
Keyes Dr 38116
Keynon Cv & Dr 38125
Keystone Ave 38128
Keystone Cv 38115
Keystone Dr 38115
Kicker Cv 38128
Kieferwoods Cv 38135
Kilarney Ave & Cv 38116
Kilday Cv 38125
Kildee Cv 38128
Kilgore Cv 38133
Killdeer St 38109
Kilock Ct 38134
Kimball Ave
1300-1499 38106
2350-3169 38114
3170-4349 38111
4350-4999 38117
Kimball Cv 38114
Kimbark Forest Cv 38134
Kimbark Woods Cv & Dr 38134
Kimberly Rd 38127
Kimberly Dawn Cv 38133
Kimberly Elise Dr 38135
Kimbrough Pl 38104
Kimner St 38127
Kin Cv 38119
Kinard Cv & Dr 38128
Kinbrook Cv 38141
Kindle Creek Dr 38141
Kindle Hill Cv & St 38141
Kindle Ridge Cv & Dr 38141
Kindle Station Cv 38141
Kindle Woods Dr 38141
Kindness Cv 38115
Kinforest Cv N & S 38141
King Rd 38109
King Arthur Cv 38135
King George Cv 38118
King Henry Cv 38118
King James Cv & Dr 38118
King John Cv 38118
Kingfisher Dr 38128
Kingham Cv & Dr 38119
Kings Cv 38135
Kings Pt 38120
Kings Arms Cv & St 38115
Kings Bay Dr 38128
Kings Bench Dr 38118
Kings Crown Dr 38125
Kings Deer Dr 38128
Kings Forest Dr 38135
Kings Fox Cv 38125
Kings Glade Dr 38128
Kings Grant Cv & Dr 38125
Kings Horn Dr 38128
Kings Lynn Cv 38128
Kings Meadow Dr 38135
Kings Oasis Way 38135
Kings Park Rd 38117
Kings Port Dr 38128
Kings Valley Cv E & W 38128
Kingsbrook Rd 38117
S Kingsbury Rd 38122
Kingscrest Cv & Ln 38115
Kingsgate Ave 38118
Kingsgate Cv 38117
Kingsgate Dr 38116
Kingsgate Pl N 38117
Kingsgate Pl S 38117
Kingsland Cv & Dr 38125
Kingsley Ave & Cv 38127
Kingsmen Cv 38128
Kingston Pl & St 38127
Kingsview Dr 38114
Kingsway Dr 38127
Kingswood Cir & Cv 38134
Kinilwood St 38134
Kinsman Rd 38120
Kinston Park Dr 38141
Kipling Ave 38128
Kippley St 38112
Kirby Ave 38111
Kirby Pkwy
1240-1308 38120
1310-1759 38120
1950-2416 38119
2418-2628 38119
3026-4159 38115
4160-4699 38141
Kirby Rd
1901-1927 38119
1929-3025 38119
3026-3699 38115
Kirby Arms Dr 38115
Kirby Brooks Dr 38115
Kirby Center Cv 38115
Kirby Downs Cv & Dr 38115
Kirby Forest Cv 38119
Kirby Gate Cv 38119
Kirby Lakes Dr 38135
Kirby Lawn Cv 38119
Kirby Meadows Cv & Dr 38115
Kirby Mills Cv 38115
Kirby Mliss Cv 38115
Kirby Oaks Cv, Dr & Ln N & S 38119
Kirby Ridge Cv 38119
Kirby Terrace Dr 38115
Kirby Trace Cv & Ln 38119
Kirby Trees Dr & Pl 38115
Kirby Valley Dr 38115
Kirby Whitten Pkwy 38135
Kirby Whitten Rd
2400-2749 38133
2750-3399 38134
Kirby Woods Cv & Dr 38119
Kirbywills Cv 38119
Kirk Ave 38109
Kirkcaldy Rd 38128
Kirkland Ave 38106
Kirkside Cv 38117
Kirkwall Rd 38128
Kirkwood Cv & Rd 38116
Kittie Lee Ln 38118
Kitty Cv & Dr 38128
Kiwanis Rd 38128
Kline Ln 38119
Klinke Ave 38127
Kney St 38107
Knight Cv 38118
Knight Ln 38115
Knight Pl 38126
Knight Rd 38118
Knight Arnold Rd
3200-5329 38118
5330-5909 38115
7100-7199 38119
Knight Arnold Road Ext 38115
Knight Trails Cir 38115
Knightsbridge Cir & Dr 38115
Knightway Cv & Rd 38118
Knob Cv & Dr 38127
Knollfield Dr 38134
Knollwood Cv & Dr 38119
Knotty Oaks Dr 38141
Knox Ave 38127
Kolmar Dr 38109
Kostka Dr 38116
Kostner Cv 38109
Kozar Ave 38108
Krayer St 38106
Kristy Cv & Dr 38118
Kristywood Cv 38133
Kriter Ln 38117
Kroel Cv 38135
Kruger Rd 38108
Krystal Lake Dr 38119
Kylan Dr 38125
Kyle St
980-1099 38114
1100-1499 38106
La Casa Dr 38133
Labelle St 38114
Labonte Dr 38127
Labrador Ln 38116
Lace Bark Cv 38128
Lacewood Cv & Dr 38115
Lacey Cv 38135
Laclede Ave 38126
Laconia Ln 38118
Lacosta Dr 38134
Ladbrook Rd 38118
Ladue St 38127
Ladurl Cv 38133
Lady Slipper Ln 38141
Lafarge Dr 38128
E, N, S & W Lafayette Cir & St 38111
Lagena St 38106
Lagrange Ave 38107
Lagrange Park Cv 38111
Laguna Ln 38119
Laird Dr 38141
Lake Dr 38117
N Lake Dr 38116
Lake Pl 38112
Lake Arbor Dr & Pl 38115
Lake Branch Cv & Dr 38109
Lake Country Cv 38133
Lake Cross Dr E & W 38125
N Lake Forest Dr 38128
Lake Garden Dr 38134
Lake Grove St 38108
Lake Hickory Dr 38115
Lake Miguel Rd 38109
E, N, S & W Lake Oaks Dr 38134
Lake Park Cv & Rd 38127
Lake Point Cir 38141
Lake Pointe 38125
N & W Lake Shore Dr 38127
Lake Tide Cv 38120
Lake Valley Cv & Dr 38141
Lake Vernell Dr 38109
Lake View Cv 38135
Lake View Trl 38115
Lake Villa Cv 38125
Lake Village Dr 38125
Lake Vista Dr 38128
Lakebrook Dr 38116
Lakecrest Cir 38127
Lakehurst Dr 38128
E & W Lakeland Dr 38127
Lakemont Cv & Dr 38128
Lakeridge Dr 38109
Lakerun Cir 38119
Lakeside Dr 38133
Lakeview Rd
2800-3899 38116
3900-5299 38109
Lakewin Ct 38118
N, S & W Lakewood Cv & Dr 38128
Lamar Ave
1060-1519 38104
1520-3199 38114
3200-5799 38118
Lamar Cir 38114
Lamar Cv 38114
Lamb Pl 38118
Lamb Woods Cv & Dr 38135
Lambert St 38108
Lamesa Ln 38133
Lammermuir Rd 38128
Lamont Cv 38119
Lamphier Ave
3100-3289 38112
3290-3499 38122
Lanark Ct 38134
Lancaster Dr 38120
Lancaster Sq 38117
Lancelot Dream Cv 38135
Lancer Dr 38115
N & S Landing Way 38115
Landis St 38104
Landmark Cv 38134
Landon Ln 38119
Lands End Dr 38128
Landview Cv & St 38118
Landy Ln 38128
Lane Ave 38105
Lanette Rd 38109
Langdale Cv 38119
Langston Cv 38117
Langston St 38122
Lanier Ln 38117
Lanlee Dr 38125
Lanrick Cv 38119
Lansdowne Dr 38128
Lansford Dr 38128
Lansing Dr 38115
Lantrip Dr 38109
Lapaloma Cir & St 38114
Laramie St 38106
Larch Ln 38119
Larch Trail Dr 38134
N & S Larchmont Cir & Dr 38111
Laredo St 38127
Largeo Cv 38125
Lark Rd 38108
Lark Creek Cv 38125
Lark Hill Cv 38135
Lark Valley Ln 38135
Larkin Ave 38104
Larkspur Dr 38111
Larkwood Cv & Dr 38118
Larose Ave 38114
Larry Ln 38122
Larue St 38122
Lasalle Pl 38104
Laser Ln 38119
Lastrada St 38116
Latham St
840-1009 38126
1010-1999 38106
2000-2399 38109
Latrobe Dr 38109
Laudeen Dr 38116
N Lauderdale St
1-189 38103
190-399 38105
S Lauderdale St
1-179 38103
180-1149 38126
1150-2399 38106
Lauderdale Oak Cv 38126
Lauderdale Woods Cv 38126
Laughlin Rd 38118
Laura Cir E 38133
Laura Cir N 38133
Laura Cir S 38133
Laura St 38114
Laura Jo Cv 38109
Laura Springs Dr 38128
Laurel St 38114
Laurel Trce 38128
Laurel Bend Dr 38125
Laurel Bluff Ct E & S 38135
Laurel Brook Cv 38125
Laurel Creek Rd 38134
Laurel Downs Rd 38128
Laurel Forest Cv 38125
Laurel Green Dr 38125
Laurel Home Cv 38125
E Laurel Lake Cv & Dr 38125
Laurel Landing Cv 38125
Laurel Leaf Cv 38128
Laurel Manor Cv 38125
Laurel Oaks 38117
Laurel Run Dr 38125
Laurel Springs Dr 38125
Laurel Tree Dr 38125
Laurel Valley Dr 38135
Laurelcrest Cv & Dr 38133
Laurelfield Ln 38125
Laurelhill Ln 38135
Laurelwood Dr 38117
Lauren Dr & Ln 38133
Lauren Ashley Cv 38133
Lauren Beth Cv 38135
Laurencekirk Rd 38128
Lauretta Ave 38127
Laurie Ln 38120
Lausanne St 38117
Laverne Ln 38117
Lavita Cv 38133
Lawn Ln 38133
Lawndale Dr 38109
Lawnhill Dr 38135
Lawnview St 38109
Lawrence Ave 38112
Lawrence Rd 38122
Lawrenceton Cv 38115
Lazy Hollow Cv 38125
Lazybrook Cv 38118
Le Chateau Cv 38125
Leacrest Ave & Cv 38109
Leafy Hollow Dr 38127
Leaning Oak Dr 38141
Leaning Trees Ln 38109
Leash Ln 38141
Leath St
100-599 38105
600-1099 38107
Leatherwood Ave
4200-4349 38111
4350-4799 38117
Leavert Ave 38127
Leawood St 38122
Lebarrett Cv 38120
Leclaire Ln 38109
Leconte Cir 38127
Ledbetter Ave & Cv 38109
Ledell Cv 38116
Ledger Rd 38106
Ledgestone Cmns 38133
Ledgewood Ln 38135
Lee Ave 38107
Lee Cv 38127
Lee Pl 38104
Lee Oaks Cv 38133

Leech Cv & Rd 38109
Leeridge Dr 38134
Leeward Cv 38125
Lefleur Pl 38120
Leflore Pl 38106
Legacy Dr 38119
Legend Dr 38118
Lehi Cv & Dr 38128
Lehr Dr 38116
Leichester Ln 38134
Leigh Dr 38116
Leisure Ct 38118
Leisure Ln 38134
Leland St 38106
Lema Pl 38105
Lemac Dr 38109
Lemans Ln 38119
Lemaster St 38104
Lemoyne Park Dr 38126
Lenden Wood Rd 38120
Lenow Pl 38126
Lenow Park Dr 38126
Lenox Ct 38116
Lenox Pl 38104
Lenox Center Ct 38115
Lenox Park Blvd & Dr 38115
Lenta Cv 38127
Leon Pl 38107
Leona Ave 38117
Leonard Rd 38109
Leonora Dr 38117
Leroy Ave 38108
Leschallas Dr 38128
Leslie Cv 38111
Lessa Ln 38134
Lester St 38112
Leta Cv 38119
Letrec Cv 38127
Levee Rd
600-1299 38107
1300-1499 38108
1500-1599 38107
Leven Cv & Rd 38118
W Levi Rd 38109
Leweir St 38127
Lewellen Rd 38116
Lewis St 38107
Lexie Cv, Dr & St 38116
Lexington Cir 38120
N Lexington Cir 38107
S Lexington Cir 38107
W Lexington Cir 38107
Lexington Rd 38120
Lexington Club Ct & Cv 38117
Lexington Park Cir E & N 38120
Lexus Ln 38119
Leyland Cv 38119
Leyton Ave & Cv 38127
Libby Ln 38127
Liberty Ave 38108
Liberty Ridge Cv 38125
Lichen Dr 38134
Life Ave 38107
Lightsfoot Ln 38109
Lightwood Cv 38134
Ligon Ct 38116
Lillian Cv & Dr 38109
Lilly Woods Cv 38134
Lily Ln 38111
Limestone Ln 38141
Limewood Ave 38134
Lin Cv 38119
Lincoln St 38114
Linda Dr 38118
Linda Ln 38117
Linda Joyce Dr 38133
Lindawood Cv 38118
Lindawood Ln 38128
Lindbergh Rd 38114
Linden Ave
1-199 38103
200-398 38126
400-719 38126
721-891 38126
921-963 38104
965-2199 38104
Linden Yard Dr 38126
Lindsey St 38104
Lindseywood Cv 38117
Links Dr E & S 38125
Linwood Rd 38116
Lion Ct & St 38107
E, N, S & W Lions Gate Cv & Dr 38116
Lipford St 38112
Lipscomb Cv & Dr 38125
Lisa Ave 38127
Lisa Cv 38127
Lisa Ln 38141
Lisa Marie Cv 38133
Litcherman St 38115
Little Brook Cir N & S 38115
Little John Rd 38111
Little Weaver Ln 38109
Littlefield Cv 38119
Litty Ct 38103
Live Oak Cv & St 38115
Liverpool Dr 38116
Livewell Cir 38114
Llano Ave & Cv 38134
N Lloyd Cir 38108
S Lloyd Cir 38108
W Lloyd Cir 38108
Lloyd St 38114
Lloydminster Cv 38141
Ln Ave 38108
Loch Lomond Rd 38116
Loch Neil Cv 38141
Lochearn Rd 38116
Lochinvar Rd 38116
Lochlevin Cv & Dr 38119
Lochmoor Ave 38115
Lochober Cv 38119
Lock Bay Ln 38135
Lockesburgh Cv 38128
Lockett Pl 38104
Lockhart St 38116
Lockhaven Ave 38106
Lockmeade Dr 38127
Lockwood Cv & St 38128
Locust St 38108
Locust Bend Rd 38125
Locust Ridge Sq 38115
Loddon Cv 38119
Lodestone Loop & Way 38109
Loeb St 38111
Lofts Rd 38118
Lofty Oak Rd 38115
Logancrest Cv & Ln 38119
Logistics Dr 38118
Lola Ave 38114
Lombardy Ave, Pl & Rd 38111
London Cv 38141
London Dr 38120
London Bridge Dr 38127
Lone Oak Cv 38109
Lone Rock Cv & Dr 38128
Lone Star Cv 38134
Long St 38114
Long Blade Ave 38128
Long Bow Dr 38116
Long Branch Dr 38109
Long Creek Rd 38125
Long Leaf Dr 38117
Longacre Ave & Cv 38134
Longate Dr 38132
Longbrook Ln 38134
Longcrest Rd 38109
Longfellow Rd 38108
Longhollow Cv & Dr 38128
Longlane Cv & Dr 38133
Longline Rd 38134
Longmeadow Cv & Dr 38134
Longmont Cv & Dr 38128
Longreen Dr 38120
Longsneck Ave & Cv 38128
Longstreet Dr 38114
Longtree Ave & Cv 38128
Longview Dr 38106
Longwood Dr 38134
Lookout Ave 38127
Looney Ave 38107
Lora Will Ln 38109
Loraine Rd 38109
Loral Cv 38109
Lord Dunmore Cv 38134
Lorece Ave & Ln 38117
Loree Cv 38109
Lorne Cv 38119
Lorraine Cv & St 38122
Los Angeles St 38112
Los Gatos Ct & Dr 38115
Lost Oak Dr & Pl 38115
Lost Shadows Cv 38128
Lotus Rd 38109
Louis Carruthers Dr
4100-4198 38118
4200-4240 38118
4233-4233 38130
4242-4598 38118
Louisa St 38126
Louise Rd 38109
Louisiana St
660-699 38103
900-1399 38106
Louisville Ave
1000-1299 38107
1400-1599 38108
Lounette St 38114
Love Aly 38107
Lovestone Cv 38109
Lovitt Dr 38119
Lowbranch Dr 38116
Lowe Cv 38127
Lowell Ave 38114
Lowin Cv 38128
Lowndes Cv 38115
Lowrance Rd 38125
Lowry Rd 38115
Lt Geo W Lee Ave 38103
Lucas Aly & St 38104
Lucca Ave 38109
Lucerne Dr 38115
Lucerne Pl 38126
Lucibill Rd 38116
Lucille Ave 38106
Lucinda Cv 38125
Lucky Trail Dr 38128
Lucy Ave 38106
Lucy Crest Cv 38115
Lucy Gage Cv 38133
Lugarda Ln 38125
Lunar Dr 38109
Lundee Pl & St 38111
Lunsford Dr 38125
Luther Rd 38135
Luverne St 38108
Luxury Cv 38135
Luzon Cv & Dr 38118
Lyceum Ln
400-599 38105
600-1099 38107
Lyceum Rd 38106
Lydgate Ave 38109
Lydgate Cv 38116
Lydgate Dr 38116
Lydgate Rd 38116
Lydia St 38106
Lyford Ave & Cv 38119
Lygon Cv 38119
Lyle Dr 38116
Lyman Ave 38107
Lynbar Ave 38117
Lynchburg Cv 38134
Lynchburg St
2700-3494 38134
3495-3799 38135
Lyndale Ave
1300-1999 38107
2500-3299 38112
Lynmouth St 38118
Lynn Ave 38122
Lynn Manor Dr 38127
Lynnbrier Ave 38120
Lynnbrook Pl 38116
Lynncrest St 38122
Lynnfield Cv 38119
Lynnfield Rd 38119
Lynnfield St 38120
Lynngate Dr 38141
Lynwood Ave 38127
Lyon Ave 38108
Lytle Cir & St 38122
Mable Dr 38109
Macaulay Ave & Cv 38127
Macgruder Cv 38119
Macinness Dr 38119
Mackham Ave & Cv 38118
Mackinnon Dr 38119
Macleod Dr 38119
Maclin Ln 38128
Macon Cv 38134
Macon Rd
3200-5099 38122
6100-6899 38134
Macy Rd 38109
Maddox Ave 38128
Madeline Cir 38127
Madewell Cv & St 38127
Madewood Dr 38103
Madison Ave
1-57 38103
59-949 38103
950-2349 38104
2350-2729 38112
2730-2899 38111
Madras Pl 38115
Madrid Ave 38112
Magazine Sq 38103
Magee Cv & Dr 38128
Magevney St 38128
Maggie Dr 38109
Maggie Oaks Cv & Dr 38135
Magnolia Dr 38117
Magnolia Grv 38120
Magnolia Ln 38125
Magnolia Manor Cir 38117
Magnolia Mound Dr 38103
Magnolia Woods Dr 38134
Mahannah Ave 38107
Maher Cv & Trl 38135
Maher Lake Ln 38135
Maher Ridge Ln 38135
Maher Valley Cv 38135
Maher View Ln 38135
Mahue Dr 38127
Maid Marian Ln 38111
Maiden Ln 38120
Maiden Grass Dr 38135
Maids Morton Ln 38125
N Main St
1-439 38103
440-599 38105
600-1099 38107
S Main St
1-759 38103
760-1699 38106
2000-2399 38109
Maison Privee Cv 38120
Majestic Ave 38107
Majestic Oak Pl 38120
Majuba Ave 38109
Mal Cv 38135
Malboro Rd 38120
Malco Way & Xing 38125
Malcomb St 38112
Malej Rd 38141
Mall Of Memphis 38118
Mallard Nest Cv & Dr 38141
Mallard Point Cv 38109
Mallard Point Dr 38128
E Mallard Ridge Dr 38141
Malloch Dr 38119
E Mallory Ave
1-439 38109
440-1599 38106
3500-4349 38111
4350-4799 38117
W Mallory Ave 38109
Mallory Depot Dr 38122
Mallory Heights Dr 38109
Malone Ave 38114
Malone Rd 38118
Maltan Ave 38115
Malvern St 38104
Mamie Rd 38128
N Manassas St
1-599 38105
600-1299 38107
S Manassas St 38103
Manchester Rd 38114
Mandalay Dr 38111
Mandy Smith Ln 38135
Mangum Rd 38134
Manhattan Ave 38112
Manigan Aly 38126
Manila Ave 38114
Manito St 38117
Manley Rd 38120
Mann Cir E 38103
Manndale Dr 38127
Manning Dr
3200-3299 38133
3300-3499 38128
W Manor Cir 38116
Manor Cv 38120
Manor Ln 38127
Manor Brier Dr 38125
Manor Haven Dr 38128
N Mansfield St 38107
S Mansfield St 38104
Manson Rd 38109
Maple Dr 38108
Maple Hill Dr 38118
Maple Hill Farms Cv 38135
Maple Lawn Dr 38116
Maple Leaf Cv 38115
Maple Ridge Cv & Rd 38134
Maple Tree Dr 38115
Maplebrook Ln 38134
Maplecrest Cv & Rd 38116
Maplehurst Dr 38127
Mapletree Cv 38141
Maplewood St 38108
Marble Ave
1-1059 38107
1060-2399 38108
Marble Hill Ln 38135
Marbro Dr 38114
Marbry Cv & Dr 38134
Marcel Ave & Cv 38122
Marcia Rd 38117
Marconi Cv 38118
Marcus Cv 38134
Marechalneil St 38114
Margaret Rd 38109
Margaretta Rd 38128
Margaux Cv E & W 38141
Margie Dr 38127
Margo Ln 38122
Margot St 38118
Marguerite Dr 38109
Maria St 38122
Marianna St
300-599 38111
600-1699 38114
Marianne Ln 38117
Marietta Blvd & Cv 38135
W Marigold Ln 38109
Marina Cv 38115
Marina Cottage Dr 38103
Marina Point Ln 38103
Mariner Cv 38133
Mario St 38127
Marion Ave
3500-4099 38111
4800-4999 38117
Marissa Cv 38125
Maritavia Dr 38127
Marjorie Cv & St 38106
Mark Ave 38107
Mark Adams Cv 38133
Mark Twain St 38127
Market St 38105
Market Square Dr 38125
W & N Markham Cir, Dr & Pl 38118
Markim Dr 38133
Markley St 38127
Marksman St 38106
Marlboro Ct 38125
Marlene St 38118
Marlin Ave 38117
Marlin Cv 38117
Marlin Rd 38116
Marlowe Ave 38109
Marne St 38111
Marquis Dr 38125
Marr Cv 38134
Marrakesh Cir 38103
Mars Ave 38134
Marsh Ave 38127
Marsh Point Cv 38125
Marsha Woods Cv & Dr 38125
Marshall Ave 38103
Marsonne St 38109
Marston Rd 38118
W Mart Rd 38109
Martha Cv 38122
Martha Dr 38127
Martha Cole Ln 38118
Marthagene Dr 38116
Marthas Pt 38141
Martin Cir 38106
Martin Edwards Pl 38116
Martindale Ave 38128
Marty Cv & St 38109
Marvin St 38127
Marwood St 38127
Mary Cv & Dr 38111
Mary Angela Rd 38109
Mary Ann Dr 38117
Mary Beth Cv 38134
Mary Elizabeth Cv & Dr 38134
Mary Jane Ave & Cv 38116
Mary Lee Cv & Dr 38116
Mary Nancy Cv 38134
Mary Oaks Dr 38133
Mary Starnes Dr 38117
Mary Tucker Cv 38133
Marygene Dr 38116
Maryland Ave 38126
Maryland Cir E 38133
Maryland Cir S 38133
Maryland Cir W 38133
Maryland Ct 38133
Marynelle Cv & St 38116
Marywood St 38106
Mason Ave 38122
Mason Cv 38120
Mason Rd
5000-5229 38117
5230-5799 38120
Mason St 38126
Masonwood Ln 38116
Massey Cv 38120
Massey Ln 38120
Massey Rd 38119
E Massey Rd 38120
W Massey Rd 38120
Massey Estates Cv 38120
N & S Massey Hill Dr 38120
Massey Manor Cv & Ln 38120
Massey Oaks Cv 38120
Massey Pointe Cv & Ln 38120
Massey Station Rd 38134
Massey Wood Cv 38120
Masters Dr 38115
Masterson Cv & St 38109
Matilda St 38117
Matt Cv 38128
Matthews Ave 38108
Maude Cv 38133
Maulden Dr 38116
Maumee Cv 38125
Maumee St 38109
Maurine Dr 38116
Maury St 38107
Maverick Ave 38127
Maxey Rd 38111
E & W Maxima Cv 38120
Maxine St 38111
Maxwell Dr 38109
May St 38108
May Creek Cv 38119
May Hollow Cv 38119
May Springs Dr 38141
Maybelle St 38122
Mayfair Ave 38122
Mayflower Ave 38122
Mayhill Dr 38116
Maynard Dr 38109
Mayo Ave 38128
Maywood St 38114
Mcadams St 38108
Mcadoo Ave 38112
Mcalister Dr 38116
Mcarthur Dr 38128
Mccain Rd 38109
Mcclure Rd 38116
Mccomb Ave 38107
Mcconnell St 38112
Mccool Ave 38114
Mccorkle Rd 38116
Mccrory Ave 38122
Mcculley St 38134
Mcdavitt Pl
500-599 38105
600-699 38107
Mcdermitt Rd 38120
Mcduff Ave 38111
Mcduff Rd 38128
Mcelrie Cv 38133
Mcelroy Cv & Rd 38120
Mcevers Cir & Rd 38111
Mcewen Pl 38126
Mcfarland Cv & Dr 38109
Mcgee Cv 38128
Mcgehee Cv 38133
Mcgill Rd 38120
Mcgowan Dr 38127
Mcgregor Ave 38127
Mcintosh Cv 38111
Mckans Cv 38120
Mckayla Cv 38135
Mckee Rd 38109
Mckell Dr 38127
Mckellar Ave 38106
E Mckellar Ave
1-199 38109
350-1299 38106
W Mckellar Ave 38109
Mckellar Hills Ave 38116
Mckellar Park Ct 38116
Mckellar Woods Ct & Dr 38116
Mckenzie Cv & St 38118
Mckinley St 38126
Mckyle Cv 38120
N Mclean Blvd
2-12 38104
14-189 38104
190-599 38112
600-1119 38107
1120-1299 38108
S Mclean Blvd
1-789 38104
790-1699 38114
Mclean Grove Dr 38112
E Mclemore Ave
1-1699 38106
1800-2199 38114
W Mclemore Ave 38106
Mcmillan St 38106
Mcmurray St 38118
Mcnair St 38108
N Mcneil St
1-189 38104
190-599 38112
700-1199 38107
1200-1499 38108
S Mcneil St 38104
Mcpherson Cv & Rd 38116

Mcqueen Cv & Dr 38119
Mcrae Rd 38114
Mcree St 38134
Mcvay Rd 38119
Mcvay Place Dr 38119
Mcvay Trail Dr 38119
Mcweeny Ave 38128
Mcwhirter Ave 38127
Meade Ave & Cir 38122
Meadow Dr 38111
Meadow Bend Dr 38141
Meadow Chase Cv & Ln 38115
Meadow Cliff Dr 38125
Meadow Court Dr 38135
Meadow Creek Rd 38115
Meadow Cross Cv & Dr 38141
Meadow Glade Ln 38134
Meadow Heath Ln 38115
Meadow Mist Cv 38133
Meadow Oak Pl 38120
Meadow Park Cv 38115
Meadow Ridge Trl 38141
Meadow Rise Cv & Dr 38119
Meadow Top Cv 38141
Meadow Vale Dr 38125
Meadow Valley Dr E 38141
Meadowbriar Trl 38125
Meadowbrook Rd 38109
Meadowbrook St 38122
Meadowcrest Cir & Cv 38117
Meadowfair Rd 38118
Meadowfield Ln 38135
Meadowgrove Cv & Ln 38120
Meadowhill Cv & St 38106
Meadowick Ave 38115
Meadowlake Dr E 38115
Meadowland Dr 38133
Meadowlands Pl 38135
Meadowlark Ln 38116
Meadowlark Pl 38133
Meadowmoor Cv 38125
Meadowood Ave 38109
Meadows Ln 38118
Meadows End Ln 38141
Meadowside Cv 38125
Meadowview Ln 38116
Meadvale Rd 38120
Meagher St 38108
Meda St
700-1099 38104
1100-1299 38114
Medford Cv & St 38127
Mediterranean Dr 38118
Medley Ln 38118
Medora Cv 38118
Meegan Dr 38135
Meggie Ln 38135
Megwood Dr 38133
Meier Cv & Dr 38118
Melakenc Rd 38118
Melanie Ave 38118
Melanie June Dr 38135
Melbourne St 38127
Melinda Ave 38108
Melissa Dr 38127
Melissa Woods Dr 38135
Melita Rd 38120
Melody Ln 38120
Melodywood Dr 38118
Melrose Cv 38106
Melrose St
500-799 38104
900-1099 38114
1100-1199 38106
Meltech Blvd 38118
Melton Ave 38109
Melvin Rd 38120
Melwood St 38109
Memphis Arlington Rd
5800-7809 38135
7810-8699 38133
Memphis Depot Pkwy 38114
Memphis Oaks Dr 38118
Menager Rd 38106
Menawa Cir 38118
Mendel Dr 38135
Mendenhall Cv 38122
Mendenhall Mall 38115
Mendenhall Pl 38117
N Mendenhall Rd
1-599 38117
600-999 38122
S Mendenhall Rd
1-899 38117
2600-4199 38115
4200-4999 38141
Mendenhall Park Pl 38115
E Mendenview Dr 38117
Mendota Cv 38133
Mensi St 38127
Mercer Dr 38127
Merchant St 38108
Mercury Cv & St 38134
Merimac Cv & Dr 38134
Merker Rd 38108
Merlcrest Cv 38128
Merle St 38118
Merlin Ave 38106
Merlins Woods Dr 38135
Merlot Cv 38125
Merrideth St 38109
Merritt Cv & St 38128
Merriwether Ave 38105
Merrycrest Dr 38111
Merryville St 38128
Merrywind Cv & Rd 38115
Merrywood Gln 38117
N Merton St
1-839 38112
1300-1699 38108
S Merton St 38112
Mesa Dr 38133
Mesquite Cv & Rd 38120
Messick Cv & Rd 38119
Metal Museum Dr 38106
Metcalf Ln 38125
Metcalf Pl 38104
Metrie Dr 38114
E & W Metropolitan Cir, Cv & Ln 38118
Mew Cv 38119
Meyers Rd 38108
Miac Cv & Dr 38118
Miami Cv & Rd 38111
E & W Mich Will Cir 38109
Michael Cv 38116
Michael Rd 38116
Michael St 38111
Michael Barton Cv 38134
E Michelle Cir 38107
Michigan St 38106
Mickey Dr 38116
Middle Ct 38119
Middle Dr 38106
Middlebrooke Cv 38141
Middlesex Ave 38118
Middleton Pl 38103
Midhurst Rd 38119
Midland Ave 38111
Midnight Cv 38125
Midsummer Way 38115
Midway Rd 38108
Migaldi Dr 38125
Mignon Ave 38107
Mike Dr 38127
Mikewood Cv & Dr 38128
Milam Rd 38120
Miles Dr 38111
Milford Rd 38120
Milkyway Cv & Dr 38134
Mill Aly 38105
Mill Ave
1-329 38105
330-399 38107
Mill Ln 38128
Mill Branch Park Dr S 38116
Mill Creek Cv
1200-1399 38134
6500-6699 38135
Mill Creek Rd 38134
Mill Gate Cv 38116
Mill Landing Cv 38116
Mill Port Cv N & S 38116
Mill Stream Cv & Dr 38116
Millard Rd 38109
Millbranch Rd 38116
Millbridge Cv & Ln 38120
Millbrook Ave 38127
Millen Dr 38119
Miller Rd 38118
Miller St 38106
Miller Creek Ln 38125
Millers Cv 38125
Millers Bend Dr 38126
Millers Glen Cv, Ln & Way 38125
Millers Grove Ln 38125
Millers Meadow Dr 38125
Millers Pond Cir & Dr 38119
Millgrove Park Dr 38135
Millicent Ct 38125
Millie Dr 38135
Millikan Cv 38133
Millington Rd 38127
Millview Ct & Dr 38116
Millwalk Dr 38116
Millwood Rd 38109
N & S Milnor Dr 38128
Milstead Rd 38122
Milton Ave 38111
Mimi Cv 38118
Mimosa Ave
2800-3299 38112
3500-3899 38111
Mimosa Rd 38128
Mimosa Hill Ln 38135
Mina Ave 38103
Minden Rd
3800-3999 38111
4000-5099 38117
Mineral Rd 38120
Mineral Crest Cir N & S 38125
Mineral Wells Rd 38141
Mingle Cv & Dr 38115
Mink Cir & St 38111
Minna Pl 38104
Minnehaha St 38117
Minnie St 38107
Minor Cv & Rd 38111
Mint Dr 38117
Mintane Cv 38125
Miracle Pt 38120
Miramichee Dr 38111
Mirror Ave 38127
Mission Hills Dr 38125
Mission Ridge Rd 38115
Mississippi Blvd
400-544 38126
546-1149 38126
1150-1699 38106
Mist Hollow Dr 38133
Mistic Lake Dr 38128
Mistletoe Cv 38141
Misty Crest Cv 38141
Misty Fields Cv 38125
Misty Forest Cv 38125
Misty Isle Dr 38103
Misty Lake Cv 38135
Misty Meadows Ln 38125
Misty Moor Ln 38141
Misty Morning Dr 38141
Misty Oak Dr 38125
Misty River Rd 38135
Misty Springs Dr 38125
Mitch St 38115
E & W Mitchell Ln & Rd 38109
Moccasin Cv & Dr 38109
Mockingbird Ln 38117
Modder Ave 38109
Modena Cv 38119
Mohawk Ave 38109
Mojave Pl 38115
Moline Rd 38109
Molly Cv 38122
Molsonwood Cv & Dr 38135
Mon Cheri Ln 38119
Mona Dr 38116
Monaco Rd 38117
Monan Cv 38119
Monessen Dr 38128
Monette Ave & Cv 38127
W Monica Dr 38134
Monmouth Dr 38120
Monroe Ave
1-949 38103
950-2349 38104
2350-2499 38112
Monroe Avenue Ext 38103
Monroes Dr 38134
Monsarrat St 38109
Montague Ave & Cv 38114
Montana St 38109
S Montclair Dr 38111
Monteagle Dr 38109
Montee Rd 38109
Monteigne Blvd 38103
Montelo Rd 38120
Monterey Dr 38128
Monterrey Sq 38111
N Montgomery St
1-599 38104
600-1099 38107
S Montgomery St 38106
E Monticello Cir 38115
W Monticello Cir 38115
Monticello Dr 38107
Monticello Ln 38115
Montpelier Dr 38134
Montreat Dr 38134
Montridge Cv 38115
Montrose Dr 38117
Moon St 38111
Moonfall Way 38141
Moonstone Cv 38125
Moorquake Cv 38119
Moray Cv 38119
Morehead St 38107
Morgan Rd 38128
Morgan House Dr 38125
Morgan Tree Ln 38125
Morgantown Cv 38141
Moriah Ln, Run, Trl & Way 38115
Moriah Woods Blvd 38117
Morlye Pl & St 38111
Morning Dew Ct 38118
Morning Dew Ln 38133
Morning Flower Cv & Dr 38135
Morning Glory Ct 38118
Morning Light Cv & Dr 38135
Morning Mist Ln 38133
Morning Star Cv 38134
Morning Vista Dr 38134
Morningbell Cv 38135
Morningrise Cv 38135
Morningsgate Cv 38135
Morningside Pl 38104
Morningside St 38127
Morningview Cv & Dr 38118
Morris Rd 38118
N & S Morrison St 38104
Mosby Ave 38105
Mosby Rd 38116
Mosel St 38109
Moses Cv 38133
Mosley Aly 38117
Moss Rd 38117
Moss Bank Cv 38135
Moss Hollow Cv 38134
Moss Rose Cv & Dr 38115
Moss Valley Dr 38133
Mossbrook Ln 38134
Mossville St 38109
Mossy Rock Cv 38133
Mound St 38114
Mount Hickory Dr 38115
Mount Hood St 38118
Mount Hope Dr 38103
Mount Moriah Pkwy 38115
Mount Moriah Rd
600-1699 38117
2000-6015 38115
Mount Moriah Ter 38115
Mount Moriah Vw 38115
Mount Moriah Road Ext 38115
Mount Olive Rd 38108
Mount Palomar Cv & Dr 38134
Mount Pisgah Rd 38109
Mount Vernon Rd 38111
Mountain Ash 38125
Mountain Park Dr 38141
Mountain Terrace St 38127
Mourfield St 38114
Mowrey Cv 38135
Mozelle St 38128
N & S Mud Island Rd 38103
Muirfield Dr 38125
Mulberry St 38103
Mullen Rd 38114
Mullins Station Cv & Rd 38134
Munford Ave 38106
Munson Rd 38134
Murff Ave & Cv 38119
Murley Ave 38114
Murphy Dr 38106
Murray Ave 38119
S Murray Hill Ln 38120
Murrell Pl 38106
Muskerry Cv 38125
Myers Rd 38115
Mynders Ave 38111
Myrlen Way 38118
Myrna Ln 38117
Myrtle St 38103
Nabors Way 38105
Nadine Ave 38127
Nakomis Ave 38117
Nam Ni Dr 38128
Namur Cv 38109
Nancy Ln 38134
Nancy Rd 38118
Nanjack Cir 38115
Nantucket Dr 38109
Naomi Cv 38141
Napoleon Pl 38106
Naragansett Cv 38125
Narcissus Cv & Dr 38135
Nash Cv & Dr 38125
Nassau St 38117
Natalie St 38128
Natchez Ln 38111
Natchez Pt 38103
W Natchez Pt 38103
Nathan Ave 38112
Nathaniel Cir E & W 38134
National St
600-1549 38122
1550-1799 38108
Nautical Cv 38125
Navaho Ave 38118
Navajo Ln 38119
Naylor Cv, Dr & Rd 38128
Nebraska Ave 38106
Nedra Ave 38108
Needle Ridge Rd 38135
Neely Cv 38109
Neely Rd 38109
Neely St 38105
Nefler Ave 38106
Nehemiah Way 38109
Neil Dr 38134
Neil St 38112
Nelia Cv 38116
Nellie Rd 38116
Nellwood Ln 38117
Nelson Ave
1600-1909 38114
1910-2399 38104
2700-2799 38111
Nelson Way Dr 38141
Nelson Wood Cv 38125
Neptune St
500-819 38104
820-1149 38126
1150-1299 38106
Neshoba Rd 38120
Nester Cv 38109
Netherwood Ave
1400-1719 38106
1720-1999 38114
Nettleton Ave 38103
Neva Ln 38114
Nevis Dr 38125
New Allen Rd 38128
New Britain Dr 38125
New Brownsville Rd 38135
New Brunswick Rd 38133
New Castle Rd 38117
New Covington Pike 38128
New Found Gap Rd 38125
New Frayser Blvd 38128
New Gate Dr S 38116
New Getwell Rd 38118
New Horn Lake Rd 38109
New Leaf Ln 38141
New London 38115
New Oak Ct 38116
New Raleigh Rd 38128
New Raleigh Lagrange Rd 38128
New Tchulahoma Rd 38118
New Willow Rd 38111
New York St 38104
Newark Ave 38106
E, N & S Newberry Ave & Ln 38115
Newell St 38111
Newgate Dr 38118
Newhaven Ave 38117
Newling Ln 38125
Newman Ct 38126
Newmarket Dr 38134
Newstone Dr 38135
Newton Dr 38109
Newton Rd
3800-3899 38128
4900-5099 38109
Newton Oak Cir & Cv E, S & W 38117
Neyland Valley Dr 38135
Niagara Cv 38125
Nicholas Cv 38134
Nicholas Ln 38125
Nicholas St 38107
Nicole Cv 38135
Nicolet Dr 38109
Niese St 38106
Night Sail Dr N & S 38103
Nightingale Dr 38127
Nike Way 38128
Nile Cv 38128
Nina Dr 38127
Nipoma Cv 38125
Nix Cv 38127
Nixon Aly 38126
Nixon Dr 38134
Noah Ln 38133
Nob Cv 38119
Noble Ave 38127
Noel Mission Dr 38125
Nonconnah Blvd 38132
Nonconnah Rd 38109
Nonconnah View Cv 38119
Nora Rd 38109
Nora Lee Ln 38118
Norbrook Dr 38116
Nordstrom Cv 38135
Norfield Dr 38115
Norfleet Ave 38109
Norfolk St 38106
Norhan Cv 38119
Norich Ave 38117
Norma Aly & Rd 38109
Normal Cir 38111
Norman Ave 38108
Normandy Ave
4300-4779 38117
5240-5499 38120
Normandy Cir 38111
Normandy Ln 38117
Normandy Pl 38120
Normandy Rd 38120
Norris Ave 38111
Norris Cir 38106
Norris Rd 38106
Norriswood Ave 38111
North Dr
1300-1399 38109
2100-2399 38112
North St 38134
Northampton Dr 38134
Northaven Cv & Dr 38127
Northbridge Ave 38118
Northcliffe Dr 38128
Northdale Dr 38128
Northfield Cir 38128
Northgate St 38127
Northhill Cv 38127
Northmeade Ave 38127
Northmoor Ave 38128
Northside Dr 38127
Northumberland Ln 38128
Northwind Cv 38125
Northwind Dr 38128
E Northwood Cv & Dr 38111
Northwood Glen St 38128
Northwood Hills Cv & Dr 38128
Norton Ln 38135
Norton Rd 38109
Norwal Rd 38117
E Norwood Ave
1-199 38109
400-499 38106
W Norwood Ave 38109
Nottingham Rd 38111
Nottoway Blvd 38103
Novarese St 38122
N November 6th St
1-599 38103
600-1199 38107
S November 6th St 38103
Noyes Ct 38119
Nunn Cv 38125
Nunnelee Ave 38127
Nutall Oak Cv 38141
Oak Cv 38135
Oak Mnr 38119
Oak Rd 38135
Oak St 38106
Oak Acres Cv & Ln 38135
Oak Allee St 38115
Oak Bark Dr 38116
Oak Bark Ln 38135
Oak Branch Cir & Cv E, N, S & W 38135
Oak Chase Cv & Ln 38125
Oak Cliff Rd 38111
Oak Court Cv N 38141
Oak Court Cv S 38141
Oak Court Dr 38117
Oak Creek Cv 38115
Oak Estates Dr 38119
Oak Forest Dr 38135
Oak Forest Way 38118
N & S Oak Grove Rd 38120
Oak Hollow Cir & Dr 38116
Oak Hurst Cv & Dr 38141
Oak Lake Cv & Ln 38118
Oak Limb Cv 38135
Oak Meadow Ave 38134
Oak Park Cv & Dr 38134
Oak Post Ave 38116
Oak Ridge Dr 38111
Oak River Rd 38120
Oak Royal Dr 38128
Oak Shade Cv 38118
E, N, S & W Oak Shadows Cir 38119
E Oak Side Cv & Dr 38118
Oak Trace Cv & Dr 38135
Oak Tree Cv 38118
Oak Valley Dr 38141

Oak Walk Cv & Ln 38135
Oak Wind Dr 38141
Oakbend Dr 38115
Oakbridge Cv 38120
Oakbrook Ct 38117
Oakbrook Cv 38134
Oakcrest Ave 38128
Oakdale St 38112
Oakden Cv, Ln & Rd 38125
Oakfield Dr 38133
Oakhaven Rd 38119
Oakland Ave 38106
Oakland Chase 38125
Oakland Hills Cv & Ln 38115
Oaklawn St 38114
Oakleaf Ave & Cv 38134
Oakleaf Office Ln 38117
Oakley Ave 38111
Oakmont Pl 38107
Oakmoor Cir & Ct E, N, S & W 38135
Oaksedge Dr 38117
Oakshire Cv & St 38109
Oakvalley Rd 38116
Oakview St 38114
Oakville Dr 38118
Oakway Ln 38118
Oakwood Dr 38116
Oakwood St 38108
Oberle Ave & Rd 38127
Obion Dr 38127
October Rose Cv & Dr 38119
Ogden Ave 38112
Ogunquit Ln 38118
Ok Robertson Rd 38127
Olathe Dr 38128
Old Allen Rd 38128
Old Austin Peay Hwy 38128
Old Bailey Ct 38116
Old Brompton Cir 38115
Old Brownsville Rd
2900-3489 38134
3490-6599 38135
Old Cedar Cv 38119
Old Creek Cv 38135
Old Creek Rd 38125
Old Cuba Benjestown Rd 38127
Old Dominion Ct 38125
Old Dominion Dr 38118
Old Dutch Way 38133
E Old Farm Rd 38125
Old Forest Cv & Rd 38125
Old Getwell Rd 38118
Old Hernando Rd 38116
Old Hickory Rd 38116
Old Ivy Cv 38119
Old Lake Cv & Pike 38119
Old Lamar Ave 38118
Old North Dr 38125
Old North Bridge Dr 38125
Old Oak Dr 38119
Old Orchard Cv 38119
Old Quarry Rd 38118
Old Raleigh Lagrange Rd 38128
Old Raleigh Millington Rd 38128
Old Squaw Cv 38141
Old Stone Cv 38125
Old Street Ct 38118
Old Summer Rd 38122
Old Us Highway 78 38118
Old Village Ln 38125
Old Waverly Cv & Dr 38125
Oldfield Dr 38134
Olds Ave 38128
Ole Bartlett Ct 38134
E Olive Ave 38106
W Olive Ave 38106
Olive Rd 38135
Olive Bark Cv & Dr 38134
Oliver Ave
1800-1909 38114
1910-2399 38104
Olivia Forest Cv & Rd 38141

Olivia Hill Dr 38133
Olmstead Ave 38106
Olympic St 38107
Omega Ave 38106
One Pl 38116
Ontario Ave 38127
Onyx Cv 38127
Opal Cv 38109
Opportunity Rd 38109
Ora Mae Ln 38134
Orange Ave 38106
Orange Blossom Ct 38118
Orange Leaf Ct 38115
Orange Tulip Cv & Dr 38135
Orangegrove Dr 38109
Orangewood Rd 38134
Orchard Ave 38127
Orchi Rd 38108
N Orchid Dr 38114
Oregon Dr 38115
Orenda Ave 38107
Orgill Ave 38106
Orgill Rd 38133
Oriole Cv 38134
Oriole St 38108
Orion Cv 38134
Orland St 38127
Orleans Rd 38116
N Orleans St 38105
S Orleans St
1-69 38103
70-1149 38126
1150-2299 38106
Orman Ave 38127
Ormand Dr 38125
Orphanage Ave 38107
Orr St 38108
Ortie Dr 38109
Osborn Dr 38127
Osceola Rd 38109
Otis Ct 38106
Otsego Dr 38109
Otter Dr 38128
Outer Pkwy 38109
Outland Rd 38118
Outland Center Dr 38118
Outlet Rd 38109
Outlook Cv 38134
Overbrook Cv & Dr 38128
Overcreek Ln 38133
Overland Pl 38111
Overlook Cir 38119
Overton Ave
1-139 38103
140-299 38105
Overton Crossing St 38127
Overton Park Ave
1000-1099 38105
1200-1499 38104
1500-1999 38112
Overton Park Ln 38127
Overton Square Ln 38104
Overview Rdg 38141
Overview Ridge Cv 38141
Owen Rd 38122
Owl Hollow Dr 38114
Owlswick Ln 38125
Oxbow Cv 38128
Oxford Ave 38112
Oxford Lake Ct 38116
Oxford Park Dr 38116
Oxford Square Ct & Dr 38116
Ozan St 38108
Ozark St 38108
Pace Rd 38116
Pacific Ave 38112
Paddington Cv 38128
Page Cv 38119
Pagely Pl 38134
Painted Oak Cv & Dr 38116
Palace Grn 38115
Palace View Ln 38134
Palermo Ave 38106
Palgrave Ln 38125
Palisade St 38111

Pallwood Rd 38122
Palm Ave 38128
Palm Cv 38127
Palm St 38127
Palm Jackson Rd 38128
Palmer Aly 38106
Palmer Rd 38116
Palmetto Ave 38107
Palo Alto Dr 38119
Palo Verde Dr 38115
Pamela Dr 38127
Pamela Ann Dr E 38135
Pamsijo Ln 38116
Panama St
1100-1199 38122
1500-1699 38108
Panbrook Cv 38128
Panda Ln 38120
Pandora St 38117
Paper Birch Cv & Ln 38119
Par Ave 38127
Par 3 Dr 38115
Paragon Pl 38132
Parakeet Rd 38109
Paramount Cv 38135
Pardue Dr 38125
Parfet Cv 38128
Parham St 38127
Park Ave
2200-3029 38114
3030-4119 38111
4120-5149 38117
5150-5830 38119
5821-5821 38187
5831-6299 38119
5832-6298 38119
Park Ln 38103
Park Castle Cv 38108
Park Court Dr 38119
Park Forest Dr 38141
Park Lake Cir & Dr 38118
Park Mill Cv 38125
Park Place Ctr 38119
Park Town Pl 38104
Park Valley Rd 38119
Parkchester Ave 38118
Parkdale Dr
100-699 38109
700-799 38116
Parker Ave 38111
Parker Rd 38109
Parkhaven Ln 38111
Parkhurst Ct 38116
Parkland Rd 38111
Parkline Dr 38125
Parkmont Dr 38125
Parkrose Rd 38109
Parkside Ave 38117
Parktree Cv 38141
Parkview Cv 38104
Parkview Dr 38128
E Parkway N
1-179 38104
E Parkway N
180-599 38112
E Parkway S
1-1099 38104
1100-1299 38114
N Parkway
1-139 38103
140-1199 38105
1200-1419 38104
1420-2299 38112
S Parkway E
1-1719 38106
1720-2399 38114
S Parkway W 38109
Parkway Pl 38112
Parkway Ter 38114
E Parkway South Pkwy 38104
Parkway View Cir 38106
Parkwin Dr & Pl 38118
Parkwood Rd 38128
Parnassus St 38108
Parnell Ave 38108

Parr Bonner Cv 38133
Parrot Cv 38109
Partee Cv 38111
Partridge Ct 38141
Partridge Cv 38128
Pasadena Pl 38104
Pasherli Ave 38114
Pat Dr 38127
Patches Cv & Dr 38133
Pate Rd 38133
Pathway Cir 38115
Patmore Rd 38134
Patricia Cv 38133
Patricia Dr 38112
Patricia Ellen Cv & Dr 38133
Patricia Leigh Cv 38134
Patrick Rd 38114
Patrick Henry Dr 38134
Patsy Cir E 38125
Patte Ann Dr 38116
Patterson Cv & St 38111
Patton St
900-1009 38126
1010-1699 38106
Patty Hill Cv 38133
Paul Pl 38117
Paul Crossing Dr 38128
Paul R Lowry Rd 38109
Paula Cv & Dr 38116
N Pauline St 38105
S Pauline St 38104
Paullus Ave & Cv 38127
Pavilion Dr 38109
Pavilion Grn N 38119
Pavilion Grn S 38119
Pavilion Grn W 38119
Pawnee Ave 38109
E & W Paxton Ln 38109
Peabody Ave 38104
Peabody Pl
1-101 38103
100-100 38173
102-298 38103
103-299 38103
Peabody Sq 38104
Peabody Green Cv & Dr 38104
Peace St 38109
Peace River Dr 38141
Peach Ave
900-1099 38105
1200-1499 38104
1650-1799 38112
Peach Blossom Cv 38125
Peach Valley Dr 38141
Peachtree Cv 38135
Peachtree Ln 38135
Peachtree St 38122
Peacock Ridge Pl 38114
Pear Ave 38107
Pearce St 38107
Pearl Pl 38126
Pearson Rd 38118
Peartree Cv 38125
Peastria Dr 38141
Pebble Beach Ave & Cv 38115
Pebble Creek Ln 38120
Pebblehill Dr 38135
Pebblerock Cv 38141
Pebblewood Cv 38141
Pecan Cir 38114
Pecan Trce 38135
Pecan Acres Cv 38135
Pecan Creek Cir N & S 38128
Pecan Forest Ct 38128
Pecan Gardens Cir E & W 38122
Pecan Grove Ln 38120
Pecan Lake Cir & Dr 38115
Pecan Mill Ln 38128
Pecan Orchard Dr 38128
Pecan Park Cv & Dr 38128
Pecan Trace Cv 38135
Pecanhill Dr 38135

Pecanville Cv 38135
E & W Peebles Rd 38109
Peg Ln 38117
Peggy Rd 38128
Peggy Jo Ct & Dr 38116
Pelham Cir 38120
Pelican Ln 38109
Pelican Bay Dr 38125
Pembine Cv & Dr 38128
Pembroke Rd 38128
Pembroke Ellis Cv & Dr 38133
Pendleton St 38114
Penguin Cv 38128
Penn Gap Cv 38134
Pennel Cv & Rd 38116
Pennington Gap Cv & Dr 38134
Pennsylvania St
900-1449 38106
1450-2499 38109
Penwood Cv 38118
Pepper Xing 38135
Pepper Tree Rd 38109
Peppermill Ln 38125
Peppertree Ln 38117
Pepperwood St 38134
Pera Ave 38127
Percy Rd 38109
Peregrine Cv & Ln 38125
Perennial Gap Dr 38133
Peres Ave 38108
W Perimeter Dr 38118
Periwinkle St 38127
Perkins Cv 38117
Perkins Ext 38117
N Perkins Rd
1-539 38117
540-1099 38122
S Perkins Rd
1-1999 38117
2600-3999 38118
W Perkins Rd 38117
Perkins Ter 38117
S Perkins Cutoff Rd 38118
Perkins Grove Cv 38122
Perkins Manor Cv 38117
Perry Cv & Rd 38106
Pershing Ave 38112
Pershing Park Dr 38127
Persimmon Trl 38125
Persimmon Hill Cv 38135
Persimmon View Cv & Dr 38135
E Person Ave
1-1719 38106
1720-2299 38114
W Person Ave 38109
Perth Cv 38119
Perthshire Cv 38119
Peter Cv 38133
Peterson Ridge Ln 38135
Peterson Valley Ln 38135
Petosky St 38118
Petten Cv & Dr 38133
Pettite Cv 38109
Petworth Rd 38119
Peyton Cir 38107
Peyton Randolph Cv & St 38134
Pharaoh Dr 38128
Pheasant Dr 38116
Pheasant Place Cv 38141
Pheasant Ridge Cv 38141
Pheasant Run Ln 38141
Pheasant Walk Cv 38141
Phelan Ave 38126
Philadelphia St
600-1099 38104
1100-1399 38114
Philgrove Way 38125
Phillips Pl 38106
Phillips Rd 38134
Phillipson Way 38125
Philsar St 38106
Philsdale Ave 38111

Philwood Ave & Cv 38122
Phipps Dr 38125
Phyllis Cv & Ln 38118
Picardy St 38111
Pickering Dr 38115
Pickett Cv & Rd 38109
Pidgeon Rd 38117
Pidgeon Hall 38119
Pidgeon Perch Ln 38116
Pidgeon Roost Rd 38118
Pidgeon Woods Cv 38119
Piedmont Ave 38108
Piedmont Cv 38115
Piermont St 38135
Pikes Peak Ave
3800-4099 38108
4100-4199 38128
Pilgrim Rd 38116
Pillow St 38106
Pillsbury Pl 38133
Pilot Dr 38118
Pin Oak Ave 38128
Pin Oak Cv 38125
Pinbranch Ct 38115
Pine Cir 38115
Pine St 38104
Pine Allee Cv 38115
Pine Bark Cv 38120
Pine Cone Cv 38141
Pine Forrest Dr 38125
Pine Hill Pl 38106
Pine Hollow Dr 38116
N Pine Lake Dr 38134
Pine Oak Cv & Ln 38135
Pine Ridge Cv & Ln 38118
Pine Shadows Dr 38120
Pine Top Cir E 38141
Pine Tree Ct & Dr 38115
Pinebrake Cv 38125
Pinebrook Dr 38116
Pinecrest Dr 38111
Pinedale Ave 38127
Pinefrost Cv & Ln 38125
Pinegate Dr 38125
Pinehill Park Dr 38141
Pinehurst St 38117
Pineview Rd 38125
Pinewood St 38117
Piney Bluff Rd 38135
Piney Point Dr 38125
Piney River Rd 38135
Piney Woods Ave 38118
Pinkie Rd 38109
Pinnacle Pt 38134
Pinnacle Farms Dr 38125
Pinnacle Oaks Dr 38125
Pinola Ave 38134
Pintail Cv 38141
Piomingo Ave 38103
Pioneer St 38106
Piper Glen Cv 38125
Pipers Gap Cv & Dr 38134
Pipers Green Ln 38135
Piping Rock Dr 38116
Pippin St 38128
Pips Ridge Ln 38133
Pitney Ln 38127
Pittman Rd 38109
Plainview St 38111
Plant Rd 38109
Plantation Cv 38119
Planters View Cv & Rd 38133
Planters Wood Cv 38133
Plato Ave 38128
Players Cir, Fwy & Ln 38125
Players Club Cir 38125
Players Club Pkwy 38125
Players Club Pkwy W 38119
Players Forest Dr 38119
Plaza Ave 38111
S Plaza Dr 38116
Pleasant Cv 38122
Pleasant Rd 38109
Pleasant Hill Rd 38118

Pleasant Hollow Ct & Dr 38115
Pleasant Run Rd 38118
Pleasant View Rd 38134
Pleasantville Dr 38125
Pleasantwood Rd 38141
Pleasure Dr 38118
Plover Dr 38127
Plum Ave 38107
Plum Rd 38128
Plum Hill Dr 38135
Plum Orchid Cv 38133
Plum Valley Cv & Dr 38141
Plumblee Cv E & W 38141
Plymouth Ave 38128
Podesta Cv 38134
Podesta St 38120
Poe Ave 38114
Poinciana Rd 38120
Point Cv & Dr 38115
Point Church Ave 38127
Point Church Rd
3800-4059 38127
4060-4999 38128
Point Hill Cv 38125
Point Pleasant Ave 38118
Point West Cv 38134
Pointe S 38125
Pointe North Cv 38125
Pointe South Cv 38125
Pojest Dr 38127
Polder Dr 38133
N & S Pole Cv 38125
Polk Ave
600-879 38126
880-999 38104
Polly Dr 38133
Polo Grounds Blvd 38125
Pomona Ave & Cv 38116
Pompano Cir 38103
Ponca St 38109
Pond St 38106
Ponderosa Ave 38116
Ponderosa Pine Trl 38115
S Pondside Cir & Dr 38119
Pondview Cv 38119
E Pontotoc Ave
1-189 38103
200-799 38126
W Pontotoc Ave 38103
Pool St 38127
Poolside Dr 38116
Pope St
300-1069 38112
1100-1198 38108
1200-1799 38108
Popinjay Dr 38116
Poplar Ave
1-329 38103
330-1199 38105
1200-2348 38104
2349-2759 38112
2760-4089 38111
4090-5049 38117
5050-5050 38157
5051-5209 38117
5052-5098 38117
5100-5100 38137
5102-5208 38117
5210-6515 38119
Poplar Pike 38119
Poplar Crest Cv 38119
Poplar Oaks Cir 38120
Poplar Pines Dr 38119
Poplar Ridge Cv & Dr 38120
Poplar Tree Cv 38119
Poppen Dr 38111
Poppenheimer Way 38125
Poppy Ln
100-199 38111
3800-3999 38135
Port Albert Ln 38133
Port Oak Pl 38120
Port Royal Cv 38125
Porter Rd 38109
N Porter Sq 38134

Street	ZIP
S Porter Sq	38134
Porter St	38126
Portia St	38118
Portland Ave	38127
Portree Dr	38125
Portsmouth Cv	38125
Post Creek Cv	38125
Post Elm Ln	38133
Post Oak Cv	38119
Post Oak Ln	38125
Potomac Dr	38128
Potters Cross Dr	38125
Powder Mill Cv & Rd	38125
Powell Ave	
3000-3289	38112
3290-4499	38122
Powers Rd	38128
Prado Ave	38116
Prairie View Dr	38134
Praline Dr	38135
Pratt St	38106
Precious Stone Cv	38109
Premier Ave & Cv	38118
Prentiss Cv	38119
Prentiss Pl	38112
E Prescott Cir	38111
S Prescott Cir	38111
Prescott Cv	38111
Prescott Rd	38118
S Prescott Rd	38111
N Prescott St	38111
Prestancia Cv S	38125
Preston St	38106
Pretoria Ave	38109
Price Dr	38134
Pride Cv	38118
Primacy Pkwy	38119
Prime Minister St	38116
Primrose Cv	38117
Prince Cv	38115
Prince Andrew Cv	38135
Prince Charles Cv	38135
Prince Edward Pl	38120
Prince George Cv & St	38115
Prince John Cv	38135
Prince Philip Cv	38135
Prince Rupert Ln	38128
Princeton Ave	38112
Princeton Cv	38117
Princeton Rd	38117
Princeton Forest Cv	38117
Princeton Grove Cv	38117
Princeton Oaks Cv	38117
Princeton Road Ext	38120
Princeton Wood Cv	38117
Print Ave	38108
Priscilla Ave	38128
E & N Proctor Dr	38118
Profit Dr	38132
Progress Ave	38114
Prospect St	38106
Prosperity Way	38135
Proud Land Cv & Dr	38119
Providence Dr	38116
Provine Ave	38126
Pruett Ct	38111
Pryor St	38127
Ptarmigan Cv & Trl	38134
Pueblo Ave	38127
Punkin Park	38125
Puryear Rd	38116
Putting Green Cv	38115
Pyramid Ln	38128
Pyramid Pl	38132
Quail Ave	38112
Quail Covey Dr	38141
Quail Creek Cv	38119
Quail Crest Ln	38141
N & S Quail Flight Cv	38141
Quail Glen Ct	38135
N Quail Hollow Ct & Rd	38120
Quail Landing Dr	38135
Quail Meadow Cv & Xing	38135
Quail Park Cir	38134
Quail Path Cv	38134
Quail Pointe Cir E	38120
Quail Ridge Cv	38135
Quail Ridge Dr	38135
Quail Ridge Ln	38116
Quail Ridge Trl	38141
Quail Thicket Dr	38134
Quail Valley Cv	38134
E & W Quailbrook Cv & Dr	38134
Quailfield Ln	38135
Quailrun Ln	38109
Quality Dr	38118
Quarry Rd	38125
Quartz Dr	38109
Queen Anne Dr	38135
Queen Elizabeth Fwy	38116
Queen Fairway St	38116
Queens Dr	38128
Queens Crown Ct	38125
Queens Lace Ct	38118
Queens Ring Cv	38125
Queensbury Ave	38108
Queensbury Cir	38122
Queensgate Ave	38118
Queenshead Dr	38128
Queensland Dr	38116
Quest Way	38115
Quicksilver Cv	38125
Quill Dr	38116
Quinby Dr	38127
Quince Cv	38119
Quince Rd	
4350-5319	38117
5320-7399	38119
Quinn Ave	
1200-1719	38106
1900-2099	38114
Quintell Ave	38128
Rabb Rd	38119
Rabbit Run	38115
Race St	38106
Rachael Rd	38127
Racine St	38111
Racquet Club Dr	38119
E Racquet Club Pl	38117
N Racquet Club Pl	38117
W Racquet Club Pl	38117
Radar Rd	38109
Radford Rd	38111
N Radford Rd	38114
S Radford Rd	38114
Ragan St	38106
Ragan Farm Dr	38141
Ragan Ridge Dr	38141
Railton Rd	38111
E Rainbow Dr	38107
Rainbranch Dr	38116
Rainbrook Ln	38134
Raine Pl	38104
E Raines Rd	
1-669	38109
670-2299	38116
3000-5399	38118
5400-6949	38115
W Raines Rd	38109
Raines Oak Cv & Dr	38109
Rainey Cv & Dr	38127
Rainey Woods Cv & Dr	38125
Rainford Cv & Dr	38128
Rainier Dr	38127
Raintree Cv & Dr	38115
Rainwater Cv	38115
Rainwood Dr	38116
Raja Dr	38127
Raleigh Common Dr	38128
Raleigh Lagrange Rd	
4200-4268	38128
4270-5029	38128
5030-6884	38134
6886-6918	38134
Raleigh Millington Rd	38128
Raleigh Ridge Cv & Dr	38128
Raleigh Springs Mall	38128
Raleigh Woods Dr	38128
Ralston Rd	38106
Rambling Brook Dr	38133
Ramill Rd	38128
Rammesses Ave	38127
Ramona St	38108
Rampart Pl	38106
Rampole Ave	38127
Ramsey Rd	38127
Rand Ave	38127
Randall Dr	38116
Randle St	38107
Randolph Pl	38120
Randolph St	38127
Randy Cv & Ln	38118
Raner Creek Dr	38135
W Range Cv	38125
W Range Hills Dr	38127
Range Line Rd	38127
Range View Cir	38128
Ranger Ave	38109
Ransdorp Dr	38133
Ransom Ln	38120
Rappahannock Dr	38134
Ratliff Ln	38126
Raven Ave	38106
Ravencrest Cv N & S	38135
Ravendale Ave	38134
Ravenden Rd	38116
Ravenoak Ct & Dr	38115
Ravens Nest Dr	38115
Ravensworth Dr	38109
Ravenwood Dr	38134
Rawdon Ave	38128
Rawlings Pl	38107
Ray Blanton Cv	38111
Ray Charles Dr	38115
Rayben Cir	38115
Rayburn St	38106
Raymond St	38114
Raymond Skinner Dr	38104
Raymore Rd	38117
Rayner St	
830-1099	38114
1100-2199	38106
Read St	38122
Reata Pass	38109
Rebecca St	38111
Rebeh Cv & Rd	38109
Red Dr	38106
Red Row	38107
Red Acres Pl	38111
Red Birch Dr	38115
Red Bird Ln	38111
Red Gum Cv	38119
Red Hill Dr	38119
Red Leaf Cv	38141
Red Leaf Ln	38109
E & W Red Oak Dr & St	38112
Red Oaks Cir	38115
Red Osier Dr	38125
Red River Cv & Dr	38125
Red Rock Cv	38109
W Red Sox Ln	38105
N Redbud Cir	38114
W Redbud Cir	38114
Redbud Rd	38109
Redbud St	38114
Redcliff Dr	38128
Redcoat Rd	38128
Redding Ave	38120
Reddoch Cv	38119
Reddoch St	38120
Redenbacher Ln	38125
Redfearn Cir N	38133
Redfearn Cir S	38133
Redfearn Cv	38120
Redfearn Ln	38133
Redford Ave & Cv	38135
Redvers Ave	38127
Redwing Rd	38118
Redwood Ave	38108
Redwood Ct	38115
Reed Ave	38108
Reenie Ave	38128
Reese Rd	38133
N Reese St	38111
S Reese St	38111
E Reese Grove Ct	38133
Reese Lake Cir & Cv	38133
Reese Point Cv & Dr	38133
Regal Blvd	38118
Regal Plaza Dr	38116
Regan Cv	38133
Regency Oaks Cv & Dr	38135
E & N Regency Park Cir	38115
Regent Pl	38106
Regents Cv	38135
Regents Park Dr	38104
Reindeer Ave	38115
Rembert Pl	38104
N Rembert St	38104
S Rembert St	
1-1099	38104
1100-1199	38114
Remington Trce	38119
Remla St	38116
Remsen Ave & Cv	38135
Renault St	38118
Rendezvous Ln	38118
Renners Cv & Rd	38128
Reno Ave	38107
E Renshaw Dr	38122
Rensslaer Dr	38135
Rental Rd	38118
Renwal St	38127
Republic Dr	38118
Republican Dr	38118
Resources Dr	38134
Restbrook Ave	38127
Restington Ln	38119
Retreat Cv	38133
Retreat Ln	38114
Revere Cv	38125
Revere Rd	38120
S & W Rex Rd	38119
Reynard Rd	38128
Reynell Cv	38119
Rhea Ave	38122
Rhiannon Dr	38125
Rhine Ln	38119
Rhode Island Ave	38106
Rhodes Ave & Cv	38111
Rhythm Ct	38115
Rialto Cv	38125
Rice St	38108
Rich Cv	38120
Rich Rd	
5000-5239	38117
5240-5799	38120
Rich Creek Cv	38125
Richbriar St	38120
Richbrook Dr	38135
Richburg Ave & Cv	38135
Richdale Ln	38135
Riche Rd	38128
Richert St	38108
Richfield Dr	38134
Richland Dr	38116
Richland Lake Dr	38133
Richland Ridge Dr	38133
Richland Valley Dr	38133
Richland View Ln	38133
Richmond Ave	38106
Richmond Cir N	38125
Richmond Cir S	38125
Richmond Cv	38125
Richmond Rd	38125
Richmond Hills Dr	38125
Richmond Oaks Cv & Dr	38125
Richway Cv	38135
Richwood Cv	38134
Richwood Pl	38125
Richwood St	38134
Rickard Rd	38116
Rickey Rd	38128
Ricky Bell Cv	38133
N Ridge Ave	38128
S Ridge Ave	38128
Ridge Dr	38115
Ridge Rd	38109
Ridge Trl	38109
Ridge Bend Rd	38120
Ridge Cap Dr	38115
Ridge Creek Cv & Dr	38128
Ridge Grove Ln	38115
Ridge Lake Blvd	38120
Ridge Lake Dr	38119
Ridge Manor Dr	38115
Ridge Meadow Cv	38128
Ridge Meadow Pkwy	38115
Ridge Oak Pl	38120
Ridge Park Dr	38128
Ridge Run Cv	38128
Ridge Top Cv	38115
Ridge Top Pl	38141
Ridge Tree Dr	38128
Ridge Valley Trl	38141
Ridge Walk Dr	38125
Ridgebrook Ln	38134
Ridgecrest St	38127
Ridgedale St	38127
Ridgefield Rd	38111
Ridgehill Dr	38141
Ridgeland St	38119
Ridgelaurel Ter	38125
Ridgeline Cv & Dr	38115
Ridgemont Ave	38128
Ridgemoor Ave	38118
Ridgepoint Dr	38134
Ridgestone Dr	38128
Ridgevale Ave	38119
Ridgeview Rd	38127
Ridgeway Blvd	38115
Ridgeway Rd	
1171-1197	38119
1199-2799	38119
2900-4199	38115
Ridgeway Sq	38115
Ridgeway St	38106
Ridgeway Center Pkwy	38120
Ridgeway Loop Rd	38120
Ridgewood Dr & Rd	38116
Ridgewood Park Rd	38116
Ridgewyck Dr	38115
Rienel Rd	38111
Rienzi Dr	38103
Rigeland Dr	38115
Riggory Cv	38125
Rile St	38109
Riley Aly & Ave	38114
Rim Creek Ln	38135
Riney St	38127
Rio Lobo Dr	38128
Ripley St	38127
Ripplebrook Rd	38120
Ripplechase Dr	38133
Rippling Brook Cv	38125
Rippling Creek Cv & Ln	38135
Rising Mist Cv	38133
River Birch Rd	38119
River Boat Cir	38103
River Breeze Dr	38103
River Bridge Cir & Ln	38103
River Commons Cir S & W	38120
River Currents Dr	38103
River Estates Dr	38103
River Fall Cv & Dr	38120
River Green Cv & Dr	38120
River Grove Cir	38128
River Grove Cv	38120
River Heights Dr	38103
River Isle Cv & Dr	38103
River Landing Dr	38103
River Lights Ln	38103
River Look Cir	38103
River Manor Dr	38103
River Mist Dr	38125
River Mist Ln	38103
River Oak View Cv & Dr	38120
River Oaks Cv, Pl & Rd	38120
River Oaks Place Cv	38120
River Park Dr	38103
River Ridge Cv	38120
River Rock Pl	38103
River Run Ln	38119
River Spring Cv	38120
River Tide Cv & Dr	38120
E & W River Trace Dr	38134
River Trail Rd	38120
River Valley Ln	38119
River View Cv & Rd	38120
Riverbluff Pl	38103
Riverbrook Dr	38116
Rivercrest Ave	38119
Rivercrest Ln	38135
Riverdale Rd	
3034-3399	38119
3401-3497	38115
3499-4179	38115
4180-5699	38141
Riverdale Bend Rd	38125
Rivergate Dr	38109
Riverhead Ave	38135
Riverport Rd	38109
Riverset Ln	38103
Riverside Blvd	
800-1279	38106
1280-2199	38109
Riverside Dr	38103
N Riverside Dr	38103
Riverstone Dr	38125
Riverview Dr E & W	38103
E Riverwalk Dr	38120
W Riverwalk Dr	38120
Riverwalk Pl	38103
Riverwood Cv	38119
Riviera Dr	38108
Rks Commercial Cv	38114
Roane Rd	38117
Roanoke Ave	38106
Robbiedon St	38128
Robbins Ridge Ln	38119
Robert Ln	38114
Robert Dell Cv	38117
Robert Everett Cv	38111
Roberta Dr	38112
Roberts Rd	38106
Robertson Rd	38127
Robeson Ave	38105
Robin Rd	38111
Robin Crest Cv	38125
Robin Hill Dr	38135
Robin Hood Ln	38111
Robin Hop Ln	38134
Robin Park Cir	38111
Robin Perch Cv	38119
Robindale Ln	38117
Robins Roost	38134
Robinsoncrest Dr	38128
Robinwood Cv	38111
Rochester Rd	38109
Rock Rd	38122
Rock Bass Dr	38127
Rock Garden Cv	38135
Rock Point Dr	38116
S Rock Ridge Cv & Rd	38134
Rock Springs Rd	38125
Rockbridge Cv	38134
Rockbrook Dr	38141
Rockdale Ave	38116
Rocket Dr	38127
Rockingham Rd	
6700-6949	38141
6950-7099	38125
Rockledge Dr	38135
Rockwood Ave	38122
Rocky Crk	38125
Rocky Knob Dr	38116
Rocky Park Dr	38141
Rocky Ridge Dr	38141
Rodi Cv	38109
Rodney Rd	38116
Rogers Ave	38114
Roland Pl	38104
Roland St	
600-819	38104
820-1099	38114
Rolling Fields Dr	
4800-4899	38128
5000-5199	38134
Rolling Glen Cv	38134
Rolling Green Dr	38125
Rolling Hills Dr	38127
Rolling Meadows Dr	
4700-4899	38128
5100-5299	38134
E & N Rolling Oaks Dr	38119
Rolling Ridge Cv	38141
Rolling Ridge Sq	38115
E & N Rolling Woods Dr	38128
Rollingbrook Ln	38134
E Rollins Rd	38109
W Rollins Rd	38109
Rollins St	38106
Roman Ct	38109
Romford Ln	38119
Ronald Rd	38120
Ronda St	38108
Ronhart St	38109
Ronnie Ave	38128
Roosevelt Ave	38127
Roper Rd	38128
Rosa St	38109
Rosamond Ave	38122
N & S Rose Rd	38117
Rose Creek Cv	38118
Rose Garden Cv	38133
Rose Heather St	38109
Rose Trail Dr	38133
Rosebanks Rd	38116
Rosebay Ln	38134
Rosebud Ln	38107
Rosebury Dr	38125
Rosecliff Ave	38116
Rosecrest Rd	38109
Rosedale Dr	38111
Rosefield Cv & Rd	38118
Rosehaven Ave	38127
Roseland Pl	38111
Roselawn Dr	38119
Roseleigh Ln	38119
Rosemary Ln	38104
Rosemont Ave	38116
Roseside Cv	38118
Rosewell Cv	38111
Rosewind Cir & Cv	38141
Rosewood Ave	38106
E & W Rosita Cir	38116
Ross Cv	38141
Ross Rd	
3600-4159	38115
4160-5599	38141
5601-5699	38141
Ross Creek Cv & Dr	38141
Ross M Lynn Dr	38111
Ross Manor Dr	38141
Ross Ridge Dr	38141
Rosser Rd	38120
Rossi Cv	38118
E Rossiland Cir	38122
Rossmore Cv	38128
Rosswood Dr	38128
Roswell Dr	38141
Rouge Bluff Rd	38127
Round Rock Cv & Ln	38125
Roundleaf Dr	38125
Rourke Cir & Cv	38125
Rover Ave	38108
Rowe Ave	38106
Roxbury Ct & Dr	38119
Roxee Run Cv	38133
Roxshire Cv	38125
Royal Ave	38107
Royal Arms Ct & Dr	38115
Royal Elm Cv	38128

Royal Hills Cv ... 38128
Royal King Dr ... 38135
Royal Knight Cv & Dr ... 38118
Royal Oaks Cv & Dr ... 38116
Royal Palace Cv ... 38128
Royal Pine Dr ... 38128
Royal Ridge Dr ... 38128
Royal Run Dr ... 38128
Royal Valley Cv & Dr ... 38135
Royal View Cv & Dr ... 38128
Royal Wood Dr ... 38128
Royalcrest Dr & Pl ... 38115
Royce Cv ... 38125
Royston Ln & Loop ... 38125
Rozelle Cv ... 38114
Rozelle St
100-819 ... 38104
820-1099 ... 38114
1100-1999 ... 38106
2300-2599 ... 38114
Ruby Cv & Ln ... 38111
Ruby Creek Cv ... 38109
Ruby Oaks Dr ... 38106
Rudder Rd ... 38118
Rue Beaumonde Dr ... 38120
Ruffle Cv & Dr ... 38134
Rugby Pl ... 38127
Running Bird Ln ... 38135
Running River Pl ... 38103
Runningbrook Cir &
Cv ... 38141
Runway Rd ... 38118
Rushmeade Cir N & S ... 38125
Rushmore Rd ... 38116
Ruskin Cv ... 38134
Ruskin Rd
1500-1699 ... 38108
2900-3299 ... 38134
Russell Cir ... 38108
Russell Ct ... 38135
Russell Hurst Dr E &
W ... 38135
Russelwood Dr ... 38128
Russwood Rd
1100-1299 ... 38122
1300-1799 ... 38108
Rust Ave & Rd ... 38127
Rustic Dr ... 38133
Rustling Oaks Cir &
Dr ... 38117
Rutgers Rd ... 38106
Ruth Dr ... 38109
Ruth Rd ... 38106
Ruthie Cv ... 38127
Rutland Rd ... 38114
Ryan St ... 38127
Ryans Run Rd ... 38141
Ryanwood Ave ... 38116
Ryder Ave ... 38106
Sabal Hill Dr ... 38135
Sabine St ... 38117
Sable Dr ... 38128
Sable Pl ... 38134
Saddleback Cir ... 38141
Saddlehorn Cv ... 38125
Safari Dr ... 38111
Saffarans Ave ... 38107
Sagamore Cv ... 38127
Sage Rd ... 38114
Sage Grass Cv ... 38128
Sage Meadow Dr ... 38133
Sagebrush Ln ... 38115
Sagewood Dr ... 38116
Saginaw Rd ... 38134
Sailors St ... 38108
Saint Agnes Dr ... 38112
Saint Albans Fwy ... 38111
Saint Andrews Fwy &
Grn ... 38111
Saint Augustine Sq ... 38104
Saint Charles Ave ... 38107
Saint Charles Cv ... 38127
Saint Charles Dr ... 38127
Saint Clair Pl ... 38127
Saint Cloud Pl ... 38127
Saint Croix Pl ... 38127
Saint Denis Pl ... 38127
Saint Elmo Ave
1600-2949 ... 38127
3600-4799 ... 38128
Saint Elmo Rd ... 38135
Saint Henrys Pl ... 38116
Saint Johns Pl ... 38116
Saint Josephs Pl ... 38116
Saint Margarets Pl ... 38116
Saint Marks Cv ... 38125
Saint Nick Dr ... 38117
Saint Paul Ave ... 38126
Saint Phillips Pl ... 38116
Saint Pierre Blvd ... 38122
Saint Remy Pl ... 38120
Salem St ... 38122
Salisbury Pl ... 38119
Sally Lou Cv ... 38133
Sallyemac Cv ... 38118
Salmon Dr ... 38115
Salter Rd ... 38109
Sam Cooper Blvd ... 38112
Sample St ... 38114
Samuels St ... 38114
San Bernardo Ave ... 38116
San Mateo Cv ... 38115
Sancongs Ave ... 38111
Sand Crossing Cv ... 38125
Sand Fox Cv ... 38141
Sandbrook St ... 38116
Sandburg St ... 38128
Sanderlin Ave ... 38117
Sanders Ave ... 38108
Sanderwood Dr ... 38118
Sandhurst Ave ... 38119
Sandpiper Ave ... 38127
Sandra St ... 38122
Sandray Dr ... 38128
Sandridge St ... 38122
Sandstone Cv ... 38134
Sandwick Rd ... 38128
Sandwood St ... 38127
Sandy Cv ... 38122
Sandy Brook Cv ... 38125
Sandy Park Cv & Dr ... 38141
Sandy Springs Dr ... 38128
Sandyslate Cv ... 38133
Sandywood Ln ... 38133
Sanford Rd ... 38109
Santa Cv ... 38116
Santa Barbara St ... 38116
Santa Clara Ave ... 38116
Santa Cruz Cv & Dr ... 38133
Santa Monica Cv & St ... 38116
Santa Valley St ... 38133
Santaolina Dr ... 38134
Sapphire Ave ... 38109
Sara Jane Ln ... 38133
Sara Woods Dr ... 38133
Sarabee Ln ... 38118
Saranac Ave ... 38135
Saratoga Ave ... 38114
W Sarazens Cir ... 38125
Sardis St ... 38106
Sassafras River Dr ... 38125
Satellite St ... 38134
Satin Oak Cv ... 38141
Satinwood Cv & Dr ... 38119
Saturn Dr ... 38109
Saulsbury Pl ... 38104
Saunders Ave ... 38127
Saunderton Way ... 38125
Sauterne Cv ... 38115
Sauvignon Cv ... 38141
Savoy Ave ... 38106
Sawgrass Dr ... 38125
Sawmill Dr ... 38128
Sawyer Cir ... 38103
Sax Rd ... 38109
Saxon Ave
600-939 ... 38126
940-1299 ... 38106
Scaife Rd ... 38116
Scaper St ... 38114
Scarlet Leaf Cv & Dr ... 38141
Scarletcrest Ln ... 38115
Scenic Hwy & Ter ... 38128
Scenic Pines Ct ... 38116
Scenicwood Cv ... 38118
Scepter Cv & Dr ... 38135
Schanna Dr ... 38135
Scheibler Rd ... 38128
Schilling Cv E & W ... 38125
School Ave ... 38112
Schoolfield Cv & Rd ... 38127
Schutt Rd ... 38116
Scotland Rd ... 38128
Scott St ... 38112
Scott Crossing Dr ... 38128
Scottie Dr ... 38116
Scottscraig Cv ... 38135
Scottsdale Ave
4500-5329 ... 38118
5330-5999 ... 38115
Scottsdale Cv ... 38115
Scottsway Rd ... 38115
Scottwood Cv ... 38115
Scrivener Dr ... 38134
Sea Horse Dr ... 38141
Sea Isle Rd
1400-5319 ... 38117
5320-5499 ... 38119
Sea Shore Rd ... 38109
Seaforth Cv & Dr ... 38127
Sealy Ave ... 38118
Seattle St ... 38114
Seawind Cv ... 38115
Sebring Dr ... 38119
Second Green Dr ... 38116
Sedgwick St ... 38109
Selden Cv ... 38128
Select Ave ... 38114
Selfridge Cv ... 38125
Selinda Cv ... 38127
Selkirk Dr ... 38115
Sellers St ... 38127
Selman Ave ... 38112
Seminary Cv & Dr ... 38115
Seminole Ln ... 38119
Seminole Rd ... 38111
Semmes St
600-1349 ... 38111
1351-1397 ... 38114
1399-3099 ... 38114
Semple Ave ... 38127
Senator St ... 38118
Seneca Ave ... 38117
September Ave ... 38116
Sequoia Cv ... 38117
Sequoia Rd
4000-5199 ... 38117
5200-5399 ... 38120
Serenade Ln ... 38118
Sesame St ... 38134
N & S Session Ct ... 38119
Seth Cv ... 38133
Sevella Rd ... 38128
Seven Oaks Dr ... 38116
Seven Valley Cv & Dr ... 38141
Severson Ave ... 38106
Sevier St
1-99 ... 38111
300-799 ... 38122
Seville Ln ... 38141
Sewanee Rd ... 38109
Sexton St ... 38107
Seymour St ... 38108
Shadcrest Cv & Rd ... 38128
Shade Cv ... 38125
Shade Tree Cv & Dr ... 38134
Shades Spring Cv ... 38125
Shades Valley Cv ... 38125
Shadow Bark Cv ... 38128
Shadow Creek St ... 38141
Shadow Crest Cv &
Rd ... 38125
Shadow Lace Cv ... 38119
Shadow Leaf Cv N &
S ... 38128
Shadow Oaks Cv &
Dr ... 38125
Shadowfall Cv & Dr ... 38141
Shadowland Cv & Dr ... 38125
Shadowlawn Blvd ... 38106
Shadowline Cv & Dr ... 38109
Shadowood Cv & Ln ... 38119
Shady Ln ... 38106
Shady Birch Rd ... 38116
Shady Courts Pl ... 38105
Shady Forest Cv ... 38125
Shady Glen Rd ... 38120
Shady Grove Ln ... 38120
Shady Grove Rd
4500-5219 ... 38117
5220-6099 ... 38120
E Shady Grove Rd ... 38120
S Shady Grove Rd ... 38120
Shady Grove Ter ... 38120
Shady Hall Ct ... 38117
Shady Hollow Ln ... 38116
Shady Mill Cv ... 38135
Shady Oak Ave ... 38112
Shady Oaks Cv ... 38133
Shady Oaks Dr ... 38133
Shady Oaks Ln ... 38117
Shady Park Ln ... 38120
Shady Pines St ... 38120
Shady Ridge Cv
5300-5399 ... 38141
6600-6799 ... 38135
Shady Ridge Dr ... 38141
Shady Rose Cv ... 38119
Shady Valley Cv ... 38128
Shady Vista Dr ... 38127
Shady Woods Cv ... 38120
Shadybrook Cv ... 38119
Shadyside Cv ... 38133
Shagbark Ct ... 38115
Shaker Cv & Ln ... 38141
Shakespeare Dr ... 38125
Shallow Wood Ct ... 38115
N Shallowhill Dr ... 38135
Shamrock Aly ... 38106
Shandy Dr ... 38125
E & W Shankman Cir ... 38108
Shannon Ave ... 38108
Shannon Cir ... 38118
Sharon Cv ... 38122
Sharon Dr ... 38122
Sharon Ln ... 38127
Sharp Plaza Blvd ... 38115
Sharpe Ave
3000-3119 ... 38114
3120-3699 ... 38111
Shasta Ave ... 38108
Shaw Pl ... 38126
Shawnee Ave & Cir ... 38106
Shayne Cv & Ln ... 38109
Sheffield Ave & Cv ... 38118
Shelborne Cir ... 38134
Shelbourne Dr ... 38108
E Shelby Dr
1-749 ... 38109
750-2229 ... 38116
2230-5449 ... 38118
5450-6969 ... 38141
6970-6972 ... 38125
6971-6973 ... 38141
6974-9099 ... 38125
W Shelby Dr ... 38109
Shelby St
2000-2299 ... 38109
2700-3399 ... 38134
Shelby Air Dr ... 38118
Shelby Briar Dr ... 38134
Shelby Commons Ct ... 38116
Shelby Cross Cir & Cv ... 38125
Shelby Forest Cv ... 38125
Shelby Oaks Cir & Dr ... 38134
Shelby Springs Rd ... 38134
Shelby Trace Cv ... 38125
Shelby Trail Rd ... 38127
Shelby View Dr ... 38134
Shelby Wood Cv ... 38125
Shell Lane Ave, Cv &
Pl ... 38109
Shelley Cv ... 38115
Shelley St ... 38114
Shelly Lyn Dr ... 38134
Shelter Cv ... 38118
Shelter Run Ln ... 38135
Shemwell Ave ... 38118
Shenandoah Dr ... 38134
Shepherd Ln ... 38117
Shepherds Tree St ... 38116
Sheridan St ... 38107
Sherlyn Cv ... 38135
Sherrie Cv & St ... 38114
Sherrycrest Cv & Dr ... 38128
Sherwood Ave ... 38106
Shifri Ave ... 38117
Shillingford Dr ... 38119
Shiloh Dr ... 38127
Shinault Ln ... 38125
Shindent Ave ... 38127
Shire Oaks Cv ... 38125
E Shirley Cir ... 38127
W Shirley Cir ... 38127
Shirley Cv ... 38122
Shirley Dr ... 38109
Shirlington Ave ... 38115
Shirlwood Ave ... 38122
Shoemaker Ct ... 38103
Shofner Ave ... 38109
Shop Rd ... 38109
Shore Cv & Dr ... 38109
Shoreham Dr ... 38118
Shoreline Cir ... 38141
Shoriank St ... 38106
Short St ... 38108
Shortside Ln ... 38118
Shotwell St ... 38111
Showcase Blvd ... 38118
Shubert Cv ... 38109
Shuler Dr ... 38119
Shulman Cv ... 38118
Shultz Ave ... 38114
Shuster Cv ... 38118
Sidney Rd ... 38116
Sienna Rd ... 38134
Sierra St ... 38128
Siesta Cv ... 38120
Signal St ... 38127
Silas Rd ... 38109
Silhouette Ave ... 38115
Silky Cv ... 38134
E & W Silver Cv, Pl &
St ... 38106
Silver Chalice Dr ... 38115
Silver Hill Dr & Ln ... 38135
Silver Lake Ln ... 38119
Silver Maple Ave ... 38109
Silver Maple Cv ... 38119
Silver Oak Cv ... 38141
Silver Oak Pl ... 38120
Silver Peak Ln ... 38125
Silver Stone Cv & Dr ... 38125
Silverage Ave ... 38109
Silverbriar Ct ... 38135
Silvercreek Ct & Dr ... 38134
Silverland Cv ... 38115
Silverleaf Cv ... 38115
Silverleaf Dr ... 38134
Silverleaf Rd ... 38115
Silverwind Cv & Dr ... 38125
Silverwood Cv & Dr ... 38133
Simmental Hill St ... 38128
Simmons Pl ... 38126
Simpson Ave ... 38106
Sims Ave ... 38106
Simsbury Cv & Dr ... 38118
Sinclair St ... 38127
Singing Trees Dr ... 38116
Singingwood Dr ... 38127
Singleton Pkwy ... 38128
Sioux St ... 38111
Sipes Ave ... 38127
Sir Galahad Ln ... 38135
Sir Ians Cv ... 38135
Sitler St ... 38114
Skidmore Cv ... 38119
Skipping Stone Trce ... 38125
Skippy St ... 38116
Sky Harbor Cv ... 38118
Sky Ridge Dr ... 38127
Sky Way Dr ... 38127
Skycastle Cv ... 38127
Skye Dr ... 38125
Skylake Cv & Dr ... 38127
Skylark Dr ... 38109
Skylight Dr E ... 38135
E Skyline Cir ... 38127
Skylonda Ct & Cv ... 38127
Skyview Cir ... 38135
Skyward Cv ... 38118
Slash Pine Cv ... 38119
Slate Rd ... 38116
Sledge Ave ... 38104
Sleepy Bend Cv ... 38133
Sleepy Hollow Rd ... 38134
Sleepy Oak Cv & Dr ... 38141
Sleepy Woods Cv ... 38134
Sloan St ... 38118
Slocum Ave ... 38127
Slumber Cv & Ln ... 38127
Smith Ave ... 38107
Smith Haven Dr ... 38114
Smith Mill Cv ... 38125
Smith Ridge Cv & Rd ... 38127
Smithfield Cv ... 38125
Smokey Ln ... 38141
Smythe Ave ... 38114
Smythe Farm Rd ... 38120
Snow Fire Cv ... 38119
Snow Frost Cv ... 38125
Snow Park Ln E & W ... 38119
Snow Ridge Cv ... 38115
Snowden Ave
1100-1999 ... 38107
2500-2699 ... 38112
E Snowden Cir ... 38104
W Snowden Cir ... 38104
Snowmass Ln ... 38141
Snowshill Cv ... 38120
Snyder Rd
6800-6949 ... 38141
6950-7299 ... 38125
Soapstone Cv & Dr ... 38109
Sobota Cir ... 38109
Socorro Cv, Dr & St ... 38128
Sofamor Danek Dr ... 38132
Soft Wood Cv ... 38134
Solar Ln ... 38118
Solitaire Cv & Way ... 38109
Solway Dr ... 38119
Somerset Ave ... 38104
Somerset Cv ... 38119
N Somerville St ... 38104
S Somerville St
200-799 ... 38104
900-1199 ... 38106
Somerville Mall St ... 38104
Sonic Dr ... 38125
Sonnet Cv ... 38134
Sonoma Cv ... 38118
Sonora Dr ... 38115
Sophia St ... 38118
South Ave ... 38106
Southaire Dr ... 38118
Southampton Dr ... 38119
Southaven Rd ... 38109
Southbridge St ... 38118
Southbrook Mall ... 38116
Southern Ave
1000-1299 ... 38104
1300-2139 ... 38114
2140-2399 ... 38104
2400-4099 ... 38111
4100-4800 ... 38117
4695-4695 ... 38124
4801-5099 ... 38117
4802-5098 ... 38117
Southern Cv ... 38117
Southern Pl ... 38111
Southern Way ... 38133
Southern Hill Dr ... 38125
Southern Oaks Pl ... 38111
Southern Peaks Rd ... 38109
Southhill Ave ... 38109
Southington Ave ... 38118
Southland Mall ... 38116
Southland St ... 38109
Southlawn Ave ... 38111
Southlinks Cv ... 38125
Southmeade Ave ... 38127
Southpoint Dr ... 38118
Southport Dr ... 38116
Southridge Blvd ... 38141
Southview Ave ... 38109
Southwall Cv & St ... 38114
Southway Dr ... 38118
Southwide Dr ... 38118
Southwind Cv ... 38125
Southwind Dr
1300-1399 ... 38116
8500-8799 ... 38125
Southwind Park Cv ... 38125
Southwood Ave ... 38111
Southwood Dr ... 38120
Southworth Ct ... 38118
Southwyck Ln ... 38116
Spainwood Ave & Cv ... 38120
Spaniel Cv ... 38141
Sparks Cv & St ... 38106
W Sparrow Springs
Loop ... 38135
Sparrow Wood Ln ... 38115
Sparta Dr ... 38119
Sparton Dr ... 38127
Speck Dr ... 38108
Speed St ... 38107
Spence Cv ... 38125
Spencer Dr ... 38115
Spencer Forest Cv E &
W ... 38141
Spences Bridge Dr ... 38141
Spey Cv & Dr ... 38119
Sphinx Cv ... 38128
Spice Cv ... 38118
Spicer Cv ... 38134
Spiegel Dr ... 38116
Spindlewood Ave ... 38109
Spinners Cv ... 38134
Spinola Cv & Ln ... 38133
Spirit Of 76 Dr ... 38116
Split Oak Cv ... 38141
Split Oak Dr ... 38115
Split Rail Cv ... 38125
Split Rail Dr ... 38133
Spoon Hollow Cv ... 38125
Spoonbill Dr ... 38109
Sportsway Ct ... 38118
Spotted Fawn Cv & Dr ... 38133
Spottswood Ave
2300-2785 ... 38114
2786-4099 ... 38111
4600-5199 ... 38117
Spottswood Manor Dr ... 38111
Sprankle Ave ... 38118
Spring Rd ... 38128
Spring St ... 38112
Spring Glen Dr ... 38128
Spring Grove Cir ... 38119
Spring Hill Cv & Dr ... 38127
Spring Hollow Dr ... 38115
Spring Lake Rd ... 38135
Spring Leaf Ln ... 38141
Spring Morning Ct ... 38125
Spring Oak Cv ... 38125
Spring Park Dr ... 38141
Spring Ridge Dr ... 38127
Spring River Rd ... 38141
Spring Shadow Dr ... 38118
Spring Valley Cv & Dr ... 38128
Spring View Dr ... 38127
Spring Water Cv ... 38128
Springbranch Cv ... 38115
Springbrook Ave ... 38116
Springdale Cir ... 38127
Springdale St
800-939 ... 38112
940-1499 ... 38108
Springdale Run Dr ... 38108
Springfield Rd ... 38128
Springland St ... 38134
Springwind Cv & Rd ... 38141

Spruce Hollow Cv ... 38134
Spruce Lake Ln ... 38119
Sprucehill Dr ... 38135
Spumante ... 38115
Sputnik Dr ... 38118
Squire Ct ... 38115
E Squire Ln ... 38116
N Squire Ln ... 38116
S Squire Ln ... 38116
St Ann Cir ... 38117
St Honore Dr ... 38116
St James Dr ... 38116
St Joseph Fwy ... 38120
St Jude Pl ... 38105
St Kitts Pl ... 38127
St Lawrence Ln ... 38119
St Martin St ... 38103
St Paul Ave ... 38126
St Philip Dr ... 38133
St Regis Cv ... 38119
St Vincent Pl ... 38120
Stacey Rd ... 38109
Stacey St ... 38108
Stacy Diane Cv ... 38135
Stafford Ave ... 38106
Staffordshire Rd ... 38134
Stage Ave ... 38127
E Stage Plz ... 38134
N Stage Plz ... 38134
Stage Rd
4200-5091 ... 38128
5093-5099 ... 38128
5096-5098 ... 38134
5100-6859 ... 38134
6346-6448 ... 38134
6860-7300 ... 38133
7302-7398 ... 38133
Stage Center Cv & Dr ... 38134
Stage Coach Dr ... 38134
Stage Hills Blvd ... 38133
Stage James Rd ... 38128
Stage Oaks Dr ... 38134
Stage Park Dr & Pl ... 38134
Stage Post Dr ... 38133
Stage Village Cv ... 38134
Stallion St ... 38116
Stanbrook Ave ... 38128
Standard Dr ... 38111
Standridge St ... 38108
Stanley Cv & Dr ... 38122
Stansell Ct ... 38125
Stanton Rd ... 38108
Staples Cv ... 38135
Star Cv & Dr ... 38134
Star Crest Dr ... 38134
Star Garden Cv ... 38134
Star Gaze Cv ... 38134
Star Line Rd ... 38109
Star Ridge Dr ... 38134
Star Valley Dr ... 38134
Stardust Cv & Dr ... 38134
Starfire Cv ... 38125
Starkenburg Ln ... 38115
Starling Pl ... 38108
Starnes Cv ... 38116
Starr Ave ... 38106
Starsdale St ... 38118
Startouch Cv ... 38141
Starway Dr ... 38135
Starwood Dr ... 38115
State Rd ... 38134
State St ... 38114
State Line Rd
6400-6965 ... 38141
6966-7999 ... 38125
Stately Way ... 38135
Staten Ave ... 38108
Station Way ... 38115
Steamboat Bnd ... 38127
Steele St ... 38127
Steele Manor Dr ... 38127
Steeple Chase Cir ... 38141
Steeplechase Dr ... 38134
Steffan Woods Cv ... 38135
Stella St ... 38127
Stellar Ln ... 38125
Stephan Ridge Cv & Dr ... 38135
Stephanie Ave ... 38127
Stephanie Cv ... 38133
Stephanie Ln ... 38128
Stephen Forest Cv & Rd ... 38141
Stephens Pl ... 38126
Stepherson Rd ... 38118
Sterling Dr
1500-1699 ... 38119
8701-8799 ... 38133
Steuben Dr ... 38134
Steve Cv & Rd ... 38111
Steve Ann Cir ... 38111
Steve Way Dr ... 38111
Steven Franklin Dr ... 38133
Steven View Dr ... 38115
E & N Stevens Cir ... 38116
Stevenson St ... 38106
Stevenwoods Ave & Cv ... 38141
Stewart Forest Cv E & W ... 38141
Stiles Dr ... 38127
Still Meadow St ... 38116
Stillwater Cv ... 38125
Stillwood Dr ... 38128
Stirrup Dr ... 38125
Stock Bridge Ct ... 38118
Stockport Cv & Dr ... 38141
Stone St ... 38118
Stone Break Cv ... 38135
Stone Bridge Dr ... 38134
Stone Chase Cv ... 38135
Stone Gap Cv ... 38141
Stone Garden Dr ... 38134
Stone Gate Dr ... 38128
Stone Hill Dr ... 38135
Stone Hollow Cv ... 38135
Stone Lake Dr ... 38135
Stone Manor Rd ... 38125
Stone Park Cv ... 38141
Stone Ridge Dr & Ln ... 38115
Stone Shadows Dr ... 38125
Stone Way Ln ... 38128
Stonebrook Ave & Cir ... 38116
Stoneham Rd ... 38109
Stonehenge Cv N & S ... 38135
Stonehurst Ave ... 38127
Stonetrace Cir, Cv & Dr ... 38135
Stonewall St
1-189 ... 38104
190-599 ... 38112
600-1099 ... 38107
1200-1499 ... 38108
Stoney Cv ... 38134
Stoney Creek Cv ... 38141
Stoney Hill Dr ... 38141
Stonington Dr ... 38125
Stony Glen Dr ... 38133
Stony Point Dr ... 38141
Stormy St ... 38128
Stornaway Dr ... 38119
Storr Dr ... 38125
Storz Rd ... 38122
Stout Cv & Rd ... 38119
Stovall Ave ... 38108
Stowe St ... 38128
Strahorn Ave ... 38109
Stratford Rd ... 38122
E Strathmore Cir ... 38112
Strathspey Cv & Dr ... 38119
Strauss Ct & Way ... 38116
Strawbridge Cv & Dr ... 38135
Stribling St ... 38111
Stuart Rd ... 38111
Studdard Cv ... 38128
Students St ... 38127
Sturbridge Ln ... 38141
Sturgeon Ave ... 38111
Successful Ln ... 38135
Sudbury Ln ... 38115
Suesand Cv & Dr ... 38128
Suffolk Ct ... 38119
Sugar Creek Rd ... 38118
Sugar Maple Cv ... 38119
Sugar Pecan Cv ... 38128
Sugar Tree Ave ... 38134
Sugar Tree Ln ... 38135
Sugarcrest Ln ... 38135
Sugarloaf St ... 38108
N & W Suggs Cv & Dr ... 38120
Sulgrave Cv & Dr ... 38119
Sulky Ln ... 38128
Sullivan Cv & Dr ... 38109
Sullivan Woods Cv ... 38117
Summer Ave
2300-3289 ... 38112
3290-5349 ... 38122
5350-6860 ... 38134
Summer Crk E ... 38141
Summer Crk N ... 38141
Summer Trl ... 38115
Summer Breeze Cv ... 38125
Summer Creek Cv ... 38141
Summer Gale Dr ... 38134
Summer Glen Dr ... 38135
Summer Hills Cir ... 38134
Summer Knoll Cir & Cv ... 38134
Summer Oaks Cv & Dr ... 38134
Summer Place Ln ... 38115
Summer Ridge Dr ... 38115
Summer Shade Cv & Ln ... 38116
Summer Sun Sq ... 38115
Summer Trace Dr ... 38134
Summer Trees Dr ... 38134
Summerbrook Ln ... 38134
Summerdale Cv & Dr ... 38133
Summerhill Dr ... 38134
Summerhurst St ... 38118
Summerlane Ave ... 38118
Summerlin Cv ... 38125
Summernite Dr ... 38133
Summerset Cv ... 38135
Summerview Ave ... 38118
Summerwood Ave ... 38109
Summit Arbors Cir ... 38128
Summitridge Dr ... 38128
Summitt St ... 38104
Sumners Wells Rd ... 38118
Sumter Cv & St ... 38122
Sun Cv ... 38134
Sun Mist Cv ... 38128
Sun Ridge Cv & Dr ... 38128
Sunburst Cv ... 38119
Sunbury Cir ... 38133
Suncrest Dr ... 38127
Sundale Cv & Way ... 38135
Sundown Cv ... 38109
Sundown Ln
4500-4699 ... 38109
7900-8099 ... 38133
Sundust Cv ... 38119
Sungate Cir & Dr ... 38135
Sungrove Cir E & N ... 38135
Sunny Cv ... 38127
Sunny Autumn Ln ... 38125
Sunny Glade Cv ... 38133
Sunny Haven Dr ... 38135
Sunny Hill Dr ... 38127
Sunny Hollow Cv ... 38133
Sunny Meadows Rd ... 38135
Sunny Morning Cv & Dr ... 38141
Sunny Trail Cv & Dr ... 38135
Sunny View Dr ... 38127
Sunnybrook St ... 38127
Sunnyfield Cv ... 38118
Sunnymeade Cv ... 38135
Sunnyside Cv & St ... 38135
Sunnyslope Cv & Dr ... 38141
Sunray Cv ... 38135
Sunray Dr ... 38118
Sunrise Ln ... 38133
Sunrise St ... 38127
Sunrise Ridge Cir & Dr ... 38135
E Sunset Pt ... 38135
N Sunset Pt ... 38135
Sunset St ... 38108
Sunset Haze Dr ... 38103
Sunset Lake Cv & Ln ... 38135
Sunstone Ave & Cv ... 38109
Sunswept Dr ... 38133
Sunvalley Cv & Dr ... 38109
Supreme Ave ... 38114
Surrey Hollow Cv ... 38134
Surrey Park Dr ... 38134
Surrey Wood Dr ... 38134
Sussex Ave ... 38116
Sutherland Dr ... 38119
S Sutton Dr ... 38127
W Sutton Dr ... 38127
Sutton Pl ... 38120
Suzanne Dr ... 38127
Suzette St ... 38126
Swallow Ln ... 38116
Swan Aly ... 38106
Swan Lake Dr ... 38119
Swan Nest Cv ... 38120
E, N & S Swan Ridge Cir & Cv ... 38122
Swanbrook St ... 38109
Swanson Cv & St ... 38118
Swarthmore Dr ... 38119
Swaying Pine Ln ... 38115
Sweet Berry Cv ... 38120
Sweet Cherry Cv ... 38125
Sweet Gum Dr ... 38134
Sweet Oak Cv ... 38134
Sweet Springs Dr ... 38128
Sweet Tree Dr ... 38128
Sweet Whisper Cv & Ln ... 38125
Sweetbriar Cv & Rd ... 38120
Sweetwater Cv & Ln ... 38135
Sweetwood Cv ... 38125
Swift St ... 38109
Swinnea Rd ... 38118
Swoosh Dr ... 38128
Sybil Rd ... 38118
Sybil St ... 38127
Sycamore Ave ... 38105
Sycamore Bnd ... 38119
Sycamore Bark Dr ... 38134
Sycamore Grove Ln ... 38120
Sycamore Heights Ln ... 38134
Sycamore Hill Dr ... 38135
Sycamore Manor Cv ... 38134
Sycamore Ridge Rd ... 38134
Sycamore Square Ln & Mall ... 38134
Sycamore View Rd ... 38134
Sycamore Woods Dr ... 38134
Sydney St ... 38108
Sylben Cv ... 38120
Sylva Rena Dr ... 38134
Sylvan St ... 38107
Sylvan Hills Cv ... 38128
Syon Cv & Dr ... 38119
T And B Blvd ... 38125
Tacoma Ave ... 38116
Tagen Ct, Cv & Dr ... 38133
Tahiti Ln ... 38117
Tahoe Rd ... 38109
Talbot Ave ... 38103
Talisman Cv ... 38119
Talisman Dr ... 38127
Tall Birch Cv ... 38115
Tall Meadow Cv ... 38135
Tall Oaks Cir ... 38118
Tall Trees Cir & Dr ... 38117
Tall Willow Dr ... 38141
Talley Pl ... 38106
Tallyho Rd ... 38128
Talon Dr ... 38115
Tam Oshanter Ave ... 38115
Tamara Cv & Dr ... 38135
Tamarron Cir & Ct ... 38125
Taminsou Dr ... 38119
Tammwood Dr ... 38116
Tammy Cv & Ln ... 38116
Tampa Ave & Cv ... 38106
Tamsway Cir ... 38116
Tanbark Ave ... 38128
Tangbourne Dr ... 38119
Tangle Oaks Dr ... 38134
Tangleberry Cv & Ln ... 38119
Tanglewood St
650-1099 ... 38104
1100-1299 ... 38114
Tankard Dr ... 38125
Tankerston Cv & Dr ... 38125
Tant Cv & Rd ... 38128
Tantallon Ln ... 38125
Tapton Pl ... 38126
Tara Ln ... 38111
Taransay Rd ... 38128
Tarbet Cv & Dr ... 38119
Tarbora Ave ... 38114
Tarkington Dr ... 38128
Tarleton Dr ... 38128
Tarry Park & Way ... 38118
Tarrytown Dr ... 38117
Tarrywood Dr ... 38118
Tarus Dr ... 38135
Tate Ave ... 38126
Tatewood Cv ... 38141
Tatum Rd ... 38122
Tawny Cv ... 38115
Taylor St ... 38106
Tayner St ... 38108
Tchula Tech Rd ... 38118
Tchulahoma Rd ... 38118
Teaberry Ln ... 38134
Teakrock Ln ... 38118
Teal Ave ... 38118
Techno Cv & Ln ... 38105
Teekwood Cv ... 38134
Tellico Dr ... 38128
Temple Ave ... 38109
Tempo Dr ... 38127
Tena Dr ... 38128
Tena Rea Cv ... 38118
Tena Ruth Cv ... 38118
Tennessee St
330-759 ... 38103
900-1199 ... 38106
Tennyson Cv & Rd ... 38108
Teresa Cv ... 38128
Terlearb Rd ... 38132
Terminal St ... 38106
Terrace Dr ... 38127
Terrace Ln ... 38116
Terrell Pl ... 38111
Terri Crest Dr ... 38115
Terri Lynn Cv ... 38141
Terry Cir ... 38107
Terry Franklin Dr ... 38133
Tessland Rd ... 38128
Tetlow Dr ... 38116
Teton View Dr ... 38125
Texas Ct, Dr & St ... 38106
Texel Cv ... 38133
Thackery Dr ... 38128
Thames Rd ... 38114
The Is ... 38125
The Elms Ave ... 38127
The Forest Gate Rd ... 38120
The Oaks Ave ... 38127
The Place St ... 38128
The Ridge Cv ... 38125
The Springs Ct ... 38128
The Willows Cv & Pl ... 38119
Theda Ave ... 38127
Thelma Cv ... 38109
Theodore St ... 38122
Thigpen Dr ... 38134
Third Green Dr ... 38116
Thirteen Colony Mall ... 38115
Thistle Cv & Pt ... 38135
Thistle Down Cv ... 38115
Thistle Knoll Cv ... 38135
Thistle Point Cv ... 38135
Thistle Ridge Ln ... 38135
Thistle Valley Ln ... 38135
Thistlebrook Dr ... 38115
Thistledown Dr ... 38117
Thistleway Dr ... 38141
Thomas Rd ... 38134
Thomas St
500-1999 ... 38107
2000-4199 ... 38127
Thoreau Cv ... 38125
Thorn Ridge Cv ... 38117
Thornbury Blvd ... 38125
Thornfield Dr ... 38134
Thornwood Ln ... 38119
Thousand Oaks Blvd ... 38118
Thread Needle Ct ... 38118
Threave Ln & Pl ... 38125
Three Pl ... 38116
Three Doves Cv ... 38133
Thrift Ave ... 38127
E & W Thriveaway Cv ... 38135
Thrush Rd ... 38108
Thrushcross Cv & Dr ... 38134
Thrushoaks Cv ... 38134
Thunderhead Cv ... 38125
Thunderstone Cir E ... 38125
Tickle Dr ... 38134
Tide Cir ... 38134
Tides Ridge Cv ... 38120
Tiergarten St ... 38109
Tiffany Rd ... 38134
Tiffany Oaks Cv & Ln ... 38135
Tifton Ave ... 38135
Tigrett Cv ... 38119
Tikamthi Cv ... 38109
Tillman Cv ... 38112
Tillman St
1-199 ... 38111
200-1099 ... 38112
Tilton St ... 38111
Tim Tam Ave ... 38127
Timber Ln ... 38112
Timber Trl ... 38115
Timber Jump Cv ... 38141
Timber Ridge Cv ... 38128
Timber Ridge Dr ... 38141
Timber Rise Cv & Rd ... 38125
Timber Run Dr ... 38135
Timber Valley Cv ... 38125
Timberbrook Ln ... 38134
Timberdale Ave ... 38135
Timberley Cv ... 38119
Timberline Dr ... 38128
Timberwood Dr ... 38128
Time St ... 38128
Timmeron Cv ... 38135
Timmons Ave ... 38119
Timothy Cv ... 38114
Timothy Dr ... 38116
Tina Cv ... 38133
Tippah Cv ... 38119
Tipton Cv ... 38125
Tishomingo Cv & Ln ... 38111
Titan Dr ... 38109
Titus Rd ... 38111
Tm Henderson Ave ... 38107
Tobin Dr ... 38133
Toby Ln ... 38111
Todd Dr ... 38109
Todds Creek Cv ... 38127
Toehill Cv ... 38128
Tomahawk St ... 38109
Tomco Cv ... 38109
Tonawanda Cv & St ... 38109
Tonto Rd ... 38109
N & S Tonya Marie Cv & Ln ... 38135
Tooley Cv ... 38133
Top Notch Loop ... 38125
Topaz Cv ... 38125
Tori Dr ... 38114
Torrey Pines Cir ... 38125
Tory Hill Ln ... 38133
Toscana Park Ct ... 38117
Toulouse St ... 38103
Tour Cir ... 38125
Tournament Dr S ... 38125
Towering Oaks Dr ... 38117
Towhee Cv ... 38134
Townes Ave ... 38122
Townhall Ln ... 38128
Townhouse Way ... 38118
Townley Dr ... 38127
Townsend Ave ... 38127
Toyota Plz ... 38103
Trace Valley Cv ... 38135
Tracer Ln ... 38119
Tracy Lynn Dr ... 38125
Tradeport Dr ... 38141
Tradewind Cv & Ter ... 38118
Trafalgar Rd ... 38134
Trail Creek Ln ... 38135
W Trail Lake Dr ... 38125
Tranquil Crk ... 38125
Tranquil Ln ... 38116
Tranquility Dr ... 38116
Transport Ave ... 38116
Trask St ... 38106
Travelo Dr ... 38127
Travis Rd ... 38109
Treadway Trl ... 38141
Treadwell St ... 38122
Treasure Hills Cv ... 38128
Treasure Island Dr E & W ... 38115
Treasurer Dr ... 38131
Tree Breeze Cv ... 38135
Tree Line Cv ... 38133
Tree Spring Cv ... 38135
Tree Top Ln ... 38133
Treebrook Way ... 38119
Treemont Cv & Dr ... 38127
Trenton Dr ... 38135
Treva Dr ... 38127
Trevathan Cir & Rd ... 38109
Trey Hobbs Cv ... 38135
Treys Cv ... 38133
N Trezevant St
500-819 ... 38112
820-1699 ... 38108
2900-4099 ... 38127
S Trezevant St ... 38114
Trezevant View Pl ... 38111
Tricia Dr ... 38127
E & W Trigg Ave ... 38106
Trillium Trl ... 38141
Trimble Pl ... 38104
Trinity Park Dr ... 38118
Trinsons Ave ... 38104
Tristri Dr ... 38131
Troon Dr ... 38125
Troost Dr ... 38128
E & W Trophy Way ... 38125
Trout Valley Cv & Dr ... 38141
Troy Ave ... 38108
Troyer Ave ... 38114
Trudy Cv & St ... 38128
Trufant Ave ... 38128
Truffle Cv ... 38128
Truitt St ... 38114
Truman Ave & Cv ... 38108
Truse Pkwy & Rd ... 38117
Trysting Oak Dr ... 38141
Tuckahoe Cv, Ln & Rd ... 38117
N & S Tucker St ... 38104
Tudor Ct ... 38125
Tudor St ... 38127
Tuggle Rd
3800-3999 ... 38111
4600-5199 ... 38118
Tulane Cv N ... 38109
Tulane Cv S ... 38109
Tulane Rd
3100-3799 ... 38116
4100-5379 ... 38109
Tulip Rd ... 38109
Tulip Bend Dr ... 38135
Tulip Creek Dr ... 38135
Tulip Grove Dr ... 38135
Tulip Hill Dr ... 38135
Tulip Poplar Dr ... 38115
Tulip Rose Dr ... 38125
Tulip Run Dr ... 38135
Tulip Trail Cv & Dr ... 38133

Tulip Tree Cv & Dr 38115
Tully Rd 38109
Tully St 38107
Tully Farms Cv 38119
Tulsa Ave 38127
Tumberland Dr 38106
Tumbler Ridge Ln 38125
Tumbridge Cv 38128
Tunbridge Pl 38141
Tunica St
1100-1300 38108
1283-1283 38182
1301-1499 38108
1302-1498 38108
Tunis Ave & Cv 38104
Tunstall St 38114
Tupelo St 38108
Turco Dr 38128
Turkey Run Ln 38116
Turnage Valley Dr 38133
E & W Turnberry Pl 38125
Turner Ave 38114
Turtle Cv 38141
Turweston Cv 38125
Tuscany Dr 38115
Tut Cv 38128
Tuton Cv 38109
Tutwiler Ave
1100-1999 38107
2500-3289 38112
3290-4899 38122
Twain Ave 38114
Twelve Oaks Cir 38117
Twilight Ave & Cv 38128
Twiller Cv 38133
Twin Angel Cv 38125
Twin Eagles Cir E &
W 38125
Twin Lakes Dr 38128
Twin Valley Cv & Ln ... 38135
Twin Woods Ave & Cv . 38134
Twine Rd 38134
Twinkletown Cv & Rd .. 38116
Twinmeadows Cv &
Dr 38134
Twinmont Cv & St 38128
Twisting Ridge Cv 38141
Two Pl 38116
Tyla Dr 38127
Tyler Cv 38133
Tylertown Ave & Cv ... 38134
Tyndale Dr 38125
Tyne St 38111
Tyrol Ct 38115
Tyron Cv 38135
Ultima Cv 38125
Uncle Remus Rd 38115
Union Ave
1-899 38103
901-919 38103
920-1569 38104
1520-1520 38174
1570-2348 38104
1571-2349 38104
2350-2629 38112
2740-2899 38111
Union Avenue Ext 38112
United Dr 38118
Universal Dr 38118
University Cir 38112
University Cv 38127
University St
500-599 38112
600-1119 38107
1120-1399 38108
2900-4399 38127
Upland Ct 38115
Upton Cv 38128
Uptown St 38107
Uptown Village Cir 38107
Urbana Rd 38109
Us Highway 51 N 38127
Us Highway 64 38133
Us Highway 70 38133
E & W Utah Ave 38106
Utility Rd 38116

Vaal Ave 38109
Vagabond Dr 38127
Val Marie Ln 38133
Valdaz Rd 38109
Valene Cir 38141
Valeta Cv 38125
Vallendar Cv & Dr 38135
Valley Blvd 38106
W Valley Cir 38109
Valley Cv 38141
Valley Rd 38109
Valley Bend Dr 38141
Valley Chase Ln 38133
Valley Glen Dr 38133
Valley Glynn Dr 38125
Valley Hill Cv 38125
Valley Lake Dr 38135
Valley Mist Cv & Dr ... 38133
Valley Oak Dr 38141
Valley Park Cv & Dr ... 38115
Valley Stream Cv &
Dr 38128
Valley Trace Cv 38141
Valley View Dr 38133
Valleybrook Cv & Dr ... 38120
Valleydale Cv & Dr 38141
Valse Rd 38106
Van Der Veer Dr 38133
Van Eaton Ln 38133
Van Hersh Dr 38133
Van Horn Ave 38112
E & W Van Huesen
Dr 38109
Van Leer Dr 38133
Vance Ave
1-189 38103
190-919 38126
920-1699 38104
Vance Park Pl 38126
Vancouver Cv 38141
Vandale Ave 38108
Vandalia St 38112
Vander Oak Dr 38116
Vanderbilt Rd 38106
Vandergreen Dr 38116
Vanderhorn Dr 38134
Vanderschaaf Dr 38133
Vanderwood Dr 38128
Vanguard Dr 38131
Vann Ave 38111
Vantage Dr 38131
Vantage Pt 38120
Vantech Dr 38115
Vanuys Rd 38111
Vassar Dr 38119
Vaughn Cv 38133
Vaughn Rd 38122
Vayu Ct & Dr 38127
Vega Ct 38116
Velma St 38104
Velmagi St 38128
Venable Rd 38118
Venetian Cswy 38115
Venson Dr
3100-3389 38134
3390-3599 38135
Venture Dr 38131
Venus Ave 38134
Vera Cruz St 38117
Vera Louise Cir 38133
Verbena Dr 38108
Verdun Cv & St 38114
Verne Rd 38117
Vernelle Ave 38109
Vernon Ave & Cv 38122
Verosa Ave 38117
Verse Cv 38127
Vescovi Ln 38141
Vescovo Dr 38117
Vesey Ave 38114
Via Lopez Dr 38133
Via Roma Dr 38127
Vickie Cv & Dr 38109
Vicksburg Cv 38103
Vicky Ln 38127
Vicoscia Ave 38127

Victor Dr 38122
Victor St 38106
Victoria Rd 38116
Victoria Park Cv & Ln .. 38127
Victorian Pl 38104
E Victory Heights Ln ... 38118
Villa Rd 38108
Villa Del Rey Dr 38116
Village Ln 38103
Village Rd 38117
Village Green Ln 38133
E & W Village Grove Dr
& Pl 38115
Village Oak Cv
900-999 38120
3600-3799 38118
5300-5399 38141
Village Park Cv & Rd ... 38141
Village Pines Cir 38116
Village Woods Ct & Dr . 38116
Villagreen Dr 38118
Villawood Dr 38118
Vince Cv 38119
Vine Ave 38127
Vinewood Ln 38109
Vineyard Haven Pl 38128
Vinings Creek Cv E &
W 38119
Vinton Ave & Sq 38104
Violet Ave & Cv 38122
Virgil Rd 38134
E Virginia Ave 38106
W Virginia Ave
1-199 38106
200-299 38103
Virginia Dr 38106
Virginia Run Cv 38122
Viscount Ave 38118
Vista Dr 38114
Vista Grande St 38127
Vistaview Cv & St 38127
Vivia Ave 38122
Volendam Cv 38133
Vollintine Ave
900-2099 38107
2100-2499 38108
Vollintine Cv 38108
Voltaire Ave 38128
Volunteer Ave 38109
Vondel Cv 38133
Votive Dr 38127
Wabash Ave
1300-1599 38106
1900-2199 38114
Waco St 38114
Wade St 38128
Waders Ridge Dr 38141
Wagner Pl 38103
Wagnon Cv 38125
Wagon Road Gap 38134
Wagon Trail Cv & Ln ... 38109
Wagon Wheel Cv 38133
Wagon Wheel Dr 38127
Wakefield Cv 38134
Wakefield Dr 38117
Walcott Cv 38125
Walden Cv 38125
Walden Glen Cv & St ... 38128
Walden Meadow Dr 38135
Walden Ridge Dr 38135
Walden Valley Cv &
Dr 38135
E Waldorf Ave 38106
W Waldorf Ave 38109
N Waldran Blvd
1-189 38104
190-599 38105
600-699 38107
S Waldran Blvd 38104
Waldrup St 38116
Walearth Rd 38117
Wales Ave
3900-4049 38108
4050-4299 38128
Walk Pl 38106
Walk Rd 38109

Walker Ave
100-219 38106
220-830 38126
832-868 38126
870-1299 38106
1400-1909 38114
1910-2399 38104
2500-3699 38111
Wall St 38134
Wallace Rd 38117
Wallingford St 38118
Walloon St 38118
Walnut Rd 38128
Walnut St
100-179 38103
180-899 38126
Walnut Court Ln 38111
Walnut Creek Cv 38118
N Walnut Grove Cir 38117
S Walnut Grove Cir 38117
W Walnut Grove Cir ... 38117
Walnut Grove Ct 38117
Walnut Grove Pl 38120
Walnut Grove Rd
2800-3989 38111
3990-5239 38117
5240-7989 38120
Walnut Hall Ct 38119
Walnut Hill Dr 38109
Walpole Ave 38118
Walsingham Cv & Dr ... 38128
Walter St 38108
Walter Forest Cv 38141
E & W Walthal Cir 38111
Walton Lk 38118
Walton Rd 38117
Walton Hill Cv & Dr 38125
Walts Aly 38126
Wanatah St 38109
Wanda St 38111
Wandering Way 38115
War Memorial Dr 38104
Warbonnet St 38109
Ward Ave 38108
Warden Rd 38122
Warfield Dr 38117
Warford Pl 38108
Warford St
1000-1899 38108
2700-3499 38128
Waring Cv 38122
Waring Rd
1-469 38117
470-1199 38122
Warner Ave 38127
E Warren St 38106
Warrington Cv & Rd ... 38118
Warwick Ave 38117
Washburn Cv & Dr 38109
Washington Ave
1-329 38103
330-999 38105
1200-2399 38104
Washington Square Dr . 38114
Waskom Dr 38116
Wasser Cv 38135
Watauga Ave 38111
Water Rd 38128
Water Fowl Ln 38141
Water Lily Trl 38127
Water Mill Cv & Dr 38116
Water Oak Cv 38125
Water Oak Dr 38127
Water Point Cv & Dr ... 38141
Water Tree Dr 38118
Waterbury Cv 38119
Waterdance Dr 38135
Waterfall Dr 38133
Waterford Cir & Pl 38125
Waterfowl Way 38120
Waterfront Oak Dr 38128
S Watergrove Dr 38119
Waters Bend Cv 38141
Waters Edge Cv N 38141
Waters Edge Cv S 38141
Waters Edge Dr 38127

Waterscape Cv 38119
Waterside Cv 38125
Waterside Dr 38119
Waterstone Oak Way ... 38115
Watertown Ln 38114
Waterview Cir & Cv 38119
Waterway Cir 38119
Waterworks Ave 38107
N Watkins St
1-599 38104
600-1199 38107
1200-1599 38108
2000-5849 38127
S Watkins St 38104
Watman Ave 38118
Watson St
500-1999 38111
2700-3099 38118
Watteker Rd 38128
Watts Ave 38108
Waverly Ave
1500-1699 38106
1800-2799 38114
2900-3099 38111
Wax Myrtle Dr 38115
Wax Wing Ln 38134
Way Wood Cv 38135
Wayfarer Cir 38115
Waymar Dr 38117
Wayne Ave 38122
Wayne Pl 38133
Waynoka Ave
2900-3899 38111
4000-4099 38117
N Waynoka Cir 38111
S Waynoka Cir 38111
Waynoka Cv 38111
Waynoka Ln 38111
We Freeman Dr 38114
Weakley Ave 38107
Weathers Dr 38126
Weatherwood Cv 38141
Weaver Ave 38106
Weaver Cv 38109
Weaver Rd 38109
Weaver Fields Ln 38109
Weaver Glenn Ln 38109
Weaver Meadows Ln ... 38109
Webb St 38106
Webb Utility Rd 38118
Webbway Dr 38116
Webster Ave 38126
Wedge Cv 38115
Wedge Hill Cv 38125
Wedgewick Cv 38134
Wedgewood Cv 38141
Wedgewood St 38111
Wehmeir Dr 38109
Weiner Cv 38122
Weiner Rd
1100-1299 38122
1300-1799 38108
Weizman St 38117
Welancot Ave 38105
Welchlawn Cv & St 38134
Welchshire Ave & Pl ... 38117
Weldon Pl 38117
Welford Dr 38133
Wellington Cv 38117
S Wellington St
840-1149 38126
1150-2299 38106
Wellons Ave & Cv 38127
Wells Ave 38107
Wells Farms Cv 38135
Wells Fields Cv 38135
Wells Grove Cv & Dr ... 38135
Wells Station Rd
1100-1299 38122
1300-1899 38108
Wellsgate Cv & Pt 38135
Wellsville Rd 38117
Wellwick Dr 38133
Wellwood St 38109
Welsh Rd 38117
Wemberley Cv & Dr 38125

Wendt Ave 38128
Wendy Dr 38114
Wendy St 38133
Wentworth Cv & Dr 38125
Wesfield Cv & Dr 38115
Wesgate Trl 38141
Wesley Ct 38119
S Wesley Ct 38119
Wesley Dr 38116
Wesley Forest Cir, Cv
& Dr N & S 38109
N & S Wesley Oaks Cir
& Dr 38109
Wesley Park Dr 38135
Wesleyan Pl 38119
Wesselly Ave 38112
Wessex Dr 38116
Wesson Cv 38133
West Dr 38112
S West Park Loop 38111
Westbrook Rd 38135
Westbury Dr 38141
Westchester Cir & Dr ... 38134
Westcliff Cv 38115
Westelle St 38128
Western Dr 38122
Western Park Dr 38109
Westlake Dr 38115
Westlawn Dr 38114
Westley Rd 38109
Westline Dr 38128
Westmeade St 38118
Westminster Rd 38120
Westmont Cv & Rd 38109
Westmore Cv & St 38106
Westover Ave 38108
Westridge Cv & Dr 38135
Westview Rd 38109
Westwood Cv 38128
Wetherburn Cv 38125
Wetherburns Cir 38134
Weymouth Cv & St 38108
Wharf St 38106
Wheat Springs Cv 38133
Wheatfield Dr 38133
Wheaton Cv & St 38117
Wheel Cv 38119
Wheelers Cv & Pl 38135
Wheelers Run Cv 38135
Wheeling Cv 38119
Wheelis Dr 38117
Whipporwill Cv 38109
Whisper Valley Dr 38141
Whispering Ct, Ln & Pl E
& S 38115
Whispering Bend Cv &
Dr 38125
Whispering Elm Dr 38125
Whispering Oak Pl 38120
Whispering View Dr ... 38125
Whispering Wind Cv ... 38135
Whisperwind Cv 38125
Whistling Duck Dr 38109
Whitaker Cv & Dr 38116
White Ash Cv 38119
White Birch Dr 38115
White Cliff Dr 38117
White Clover Ln 38109
White Diamond St 38109
White Fox Cv & St 38109
White Lake Cv 38125
White Manor Ct 38125
White Oak Dr 38116
White Oaks Rd 38117
White Owl Ln & Sq 38128
White Pearl Ln 38109
White Sands St 38118
N White Station Rd
1-659 38117
660-1099 38122
S White Station Rd 38117
Whitebark Dr 38133
Whitebridge Cv & Rd ... 38135
Whitebrook Dr & Plz ... 38118
Whitehall Ave & Cv 38117

Whitehaven Ln
600-769 38109
770-1199 38116
E & S Whitehaven Park
Cir 38116
Whitehead Way 38141
Whitehill Dr 38135
Whitehorn Cv 38135
Whiteley Cv 38141
Whitepine Cv & St 38109
Whiteplains Cv & Rd ... 38116
Whitepoint Ave 38109
Whiterock Ave 38109
Whitesboro Ave & Cv .. 38109
Whiteside Cv & St 38109
Whitestone Ave 38109
Whitetail Ln 38115
Whiteville Ave & Cv 38109
Whitewater Cv & Rd ... 38117
Whiteway Cv & Dr 38117
Whitewood Cv 38109
Whitfall Cv N & S 38125
Whitfield Ave 38107
Whitford Pl 38106
Whiting St 38117
Whitman Ave 38112
Whitman Rd 38116
Whitmar Pl E 38120
Whitmore Rd 38106
Whitney Ave
500-2899 38127
2950-3299 38128
Whitten Pl 38133
Whitten Rd
900-1799 38134
1800-2849 38133
2850-2999 38134
3701-3797 38135
3799-4099 38135
4101-4299 38135
Whitten Grove Cv &
Dr 38134
Whitten Pine Dr 38134
Whitten View Ln 38134
Whittier Rd
3700-3899 38108
6200-6299 38134
Whittington St 38114
Whitworth Rd 38116
Wichita Ave 38106
Wickcliff Ln 38118
Wickerwood Cv 38119
Wickett Ln 38125
Wickham Dr 38118
Wicklow Dr & Ln 38141
Wicks Ave 38126
Wil Linda Ln 38109
Wil Mar Dr 38109
Wilbec Rd 38117
Wilburn Ave 38117
Wilchester Ln 38116
Wilcox Ave 38111
Wilcrest Dr 38134
Wild Cv & Dr 38135
Wild Apple Cv 38125
Wild Bloom Dr 38133
Wild Briar Ct 38118
Wild Cherry Cv 38117
Wild Elm Cv 38120
Wild Fern Dr 38135
Wild Holly Cv 38125
Wild Maple Ct & Cv 38120
Wild Oaks Dr 38120
Wild Plum Ct 38118
Wild Plum Cv 38125
Wild Ridge Cir 38120
Wild Rye Ln 38115
Wild Violet Dr 38133
Wildberry Ct 38135
Wildberry Ln 38119
Wildbrook Cv 38120
Wilde Fall Rd 38134
Wildflower Cv 38109
Wildflower Ln 38125
Wildleaf Cv & Dr 38116
Wildrose St 38114

Wildwind Cv & Dr 38115
Wildwood Dr 38111
Wildwood Ln 38135
Wildwood Rd 38135
N Wildwood Rd 38135
W Wildwood Rd 38135
Wilfong Rd 38134
Wilkinson Pl 38111
Will Cv 38125
Will Scarlet Rd 38111
Willard Dr 38118
N Willett St
1-189 38104
190-499 38112
600-1099 38107
1200-1499 38108
S Willett St
1-829 38104
830-1099 38114
1100-1599 38106
Willey St 38119
William Arnold Rd 38117
William Cary Dr 38127
William Little Dr 38133
William Tell Cv & Dr 38127
Williams Ave
400-899 38126
1200-1399 38104
Williams Cv 38134
Williamsburg Ln 38117
Williford St 38112
Willis St 38108
Willoughby St
800-1099 38126
1100-1199 38106
Willoughby Oak Ln 38135
Willow Cv 38111
Willow Pl 38107
Willow Rd
4200-4349 38111
4350-4999 38117
Willow Break Dr 38135
Willow Creek Ct & Dr 38118
Willow Hill Cv & Ln 38128
Willow Lake Blvd 38118
Willow Lake Rd E 38127
Willow Oaks Dr 38128
Willow Park Cv & Dr 38141
Willow Pond Cv 38125
Willow Rest Dr 38133
Willow Run Ln 38116
Willow Way Cv & Ln 38141
Willow Wood Ave 38127
N Willow Wyck Dr 38118
Willowgrove Cv 38116
Willowview Ave 38111
Wills St 38111
Wilmette Ave 38108
Wilmore Rd 38117
Wilsford Cv 38125
Wilshire Rd 38111
Wilson Cv 38134
Wilson Rd
600-799 38109
1500-2172 38116
Wilson St 38106
Witham Trl 38119
Wilton Ave 38120
Wilton Cv 38117
Wimble Rd 38134
Winbranch Dr 38116
Winbrook Dr 38116
Winchest Ct 38118
Winchest Cv 38115
Winchest Pl 38118
Winchester Ave 38105
E Winchester Pl 38116
W Winchester Pl 38116
Winchester Rd
200-499 38109
500-2769 38116
2770-3716 38118
3701-3799 38181
3717-5305 38118
3718-5328 38118
5330-6989 38115
6990-9999 38125
N Winchester Sq 38118
S Winchester Sq 38118
W Winchester Sq 38118
Winchester Hills Dr 38119
Winchester Park Cir, Ct & Dr 38118
Winchester Pointe Cv 38115
Wincross Dr 38119
Wind Breeze Dr 38109
Wind Hill Dr 38135
Wind Meadow Ln 38115
Wind Passage Way 38135
Wind Ridge Cv 38141
Wind Shadow Cv 38125
Wind Tree Cv & Dr 38135
Wind Valley Cv & Dr 38125
Windchime Cv 38128
Windcrest Rd 38116
Winddrift Cir 38125
E Windemere Cir & Ln 38125
Winder Dr 38128
Winder Gap Cv 38133
Winderly Cv 38125
Winderly Pine Cv 38125
Windermere Rd 38128
Windersville Dr 38133
Winderwood Cir 38128
Windflower Ln 38134
Windgarden Cv 38125
Windham Rd 38116
Winding Ln 38133
Winding Birch Dr 38115
Winding Brook Ln 38116
Winding Hill Cv & Dr 38128
Winding Hollow Way 38125
Winding Path Cv & Dr 38133
Winding River Cir & Way 38120
Winding Wind Cv 38135
Winding Wolf Pl 38120
Windmill Ln 38120
Windolyn Cir & Way 38133
Windover Rd 38111
Windover Grove Dr 38111
Window Dr 38135
Windrush 38125
Windsong Dr 38125
Windsor Pkwy 38127
E Windsor Rd 38109
W Windsor Rd 38109
Windsor Park Rd 38133
Windward Cv
4600-4699 38109
7200-7299 38125
Windward Dr 38109
Windy Ave 38128
Windy Gap Cv 38135
Windy Haven Cv 38133
Windy Hollow Cir & Cv 38118
Windy Lou Ct & Dr 38116
Windy Scape Dr 38135
Windy Trail Cv 38135
Windy Willow Cv & Rd 38125
Windyke Cv & Dr 38125
Winestone Cv 38120
Winfield Rd 38116
Winfred Cir 38127
Wingate Cv 38118
Wingate St 38127
Wingate Park Cv 38119
Wingdale Rd 38117
Wingfield Rd 38122
Wingood Cir 38118
Winhoma Dr 38118
Winker Dr 38128
Winner St 38118
Winnie Ave 38127
Winnona Ave 38108
Winoak Ln 38119
Winpark Ct & Ln 38118
Winplace Rd 38118
Winrow St 38117
Winslow Rd 38109
Winston Dr 38127
Winter Cv 38128
Winter Flower Dr 38115
Winter Harbor Ln 38125
Winter Oak Ln 38120
Winter Run Cv 38125
Winter Tree Dr 38115
Winterpark Cv & Dr 38141
S Winton Pl & Rd 38117
Winward Ln 38119
Winway Dr 38116
Winwood Dr 38128
Wisbey Ct 38125
Wisconsin Ave 38106
Wishing Star Cv 38134
Wisteria Cv & Dr 38116
Wisterwood Cv 38116
Withers St 38104
Wittenham Cv 38119
Wolf Hollow Dr 38133
Wolf Lake Dr 38133
Wolf Pine Ln 38133
Wolf River Pkwy 38120
Wolf Shadow Ln 38133
Wolf Spring Ln 38133
Wolf Trace Ln 38133
Wolf Trail Dr 38128
Wolf Valley Ln 38133
Wolf Willow Ln 38133
Wolfcreek Pkwy 38133
Wolfden Cir 38133
Wolstenholme Cv & Dr 38133
Wood St 38126
Wood Berry Ct 38135
Wood Birch Cv 38115
Wood Bridge Cv & Rd 38119
Wood Fox Cv 38125
Wood Glade Ln 38116
Wood Grove Rd 38117
Wood Hearth Ct & Cv 38135
Wood Meadow Cv 38141
Wood Park Dr 38141
Wood Rail Cv 38119
Wood Thrush Cv & Dr 38134
Wood Trail Dr 38120
Woodberry Cv S 38141
Woodbine Rd 38116
Woodbine St 38106
Woodbourne Ct 38115
Woodbranch Ct 38116
Woodbriar Cv 38120
Woodburn Dr 38127
Woodbury Rd 38111
Woodcliff Dr 38127
Woodcock Ct 38116
Woodcrest Dr 38111
Wooddale Ave
4300-5599 38118
5600-5699 38115
Wooddale Cv 38118
Wooden Heart Ct 38116
Woodfield Dr 38116
Woodfield Park Rd 38134
Woodhaven Rd 38128
Woodhills Dr 38128
Woodhollow Cv 38135
Woodhollow Dr 38118
Woodhue Ave 38109
N Woodlake Cir 38118
S Woodlake Cir 38118
Woodlake Dr 38119
Woodland Ave 38106
Woodland Dr 38111
Woodland Hills Cv 38127
Woodlark Ave 38117
Woodlawn St
600-1299 38107
5400-5899 38134
Woodlawn Ter 38127
Woodlawn Terrace Cir 38127
Woodmere Cv & Ln 38117
Woodmont Dr & Pl 38117
Woodpark Cv & Ln 38135
Woodridge Dr 38116
Woodrow St 38127
Woods Edge Dr 38134
Woods Landing Rd 38125
Woods Run Ln 38115
Woodshire Rd 38125
Woodsman Ln 38135
Woodston Rd 38117
Woodstone Cir 38116
Woodstone Mnr 38115
Woodvale Cv & Dr 38127
Woodview Dr 38117
Woodward St
600-749 38104
1200-1499 38106
Woodway Dr 38120
Woodwind Dr 38128
Woody Ln 38115
Woody Creek Cv & Rd 38141
Woody Hollow Cv 38125
Wooley Cv 38133
Worchester Ln 38134
Worden Cv 38125
Wordsworth Ave 38128
Wortham Ave 38107
Worthing Ln 38119
Worthington Cir & St 38114
Wren Cv 38134
Wren Rd 38108
Wrens Roost Cir 38119
Wrenwood St 38122
Wright Rd 38122
Wright St 38126
Wrister Cv 38135
Write Pl 38128
Wunderlich Cv 38111
Wyatt Dr 38109
Wychemere Dr 38128
Wychewood Dr 38117
Wyndance Cir, Cv & Dr 38135
Wyndham Cv 38120
Wynfrey Pl 38120
Wynslow Ct & Cv 38117
Wynton St 38106
Wyntuck Pl 38117
Wytham Cv & Dr 38119
Wythe Cv 38135
Wythe Rd
3100-3499 38134
3500-3699 38135
Wythe House Cv 38134
Y M V Rd 38109
Yale Ave 38112
Yale Cv 38128
Yale Rd
4000-5069 38128
5070-6800 38134
6802-6898 38134
7300-7499 38133
Yalewood Dr 38134
Yates Cv 38120
N Yates Rd 38120
S Yates Rd
1-949 38120
950-1099 38119
Yates St 38134
Yazoo Aly, Ct & St 38106
Yellow Birch Dr 38128
Yellowood Cv & Rd 38134
Yokefellow Cir 38125
Yokley Cv & Rd 38109
Yoriance Rd 38134
York Ave 38104
Yorkhill Dr 38135
Yorkshire Cv & Dr 38119
Yosemite Ct 38116
Young Ave
1800-1909 38114
1910-2399 38104
2500-2999 38111
Yvonne Cv 38135
Zachariah Cv 38133
Zaio Ave 38122
Zane Rd 38128
E & W Zanola Cir 38114
Zanone Ave 38114
Zelda Ln 38122
Zelin St 38108
Zilphia Pl 38107
Zodiac Rd 38118
Zorro Cv 38133
Zoysia Dr 38115

NUMBERED STREETS

1st Ave 38109
1st Cv 38134
1st Northside Dr 38127
2nd Cv 38134
N 2nd St
2-189 38103
190-599 38105
600-1999 38107
2300-2899 38127
S 2nd St
4-8 38103
580-613 38126
614-700 38101
615-799 38126
2nd Northside Dr 38127
3rd Cv 38134
3rd Rd 38135
N 3rd St
1-189 38103
190-599 38105
600-1099 38107
S 3rd St
1-329 38103
330-554 38126
555-555 38101
556-748 38126
750-1679 38106
1680-5699 38109
4th Ave 38135
N 4th St
1-189 38103
190-599 38105
600-799 38107
S 4th St
1-189 38103
190-1199 38126
4th Crompton Ct 38134
N 5th St
440-599 38105
600-608 38107
S 5th St 38126
N 6th St
450-599 38105
600-1199 38107
6th Crompton Sq 38134
7th Rd 38135
N 7th St
400-599 38105
600-1399 38107
7th Crompton Ct 38134
8th Rd
4500-5299 38109
6900-7199 38135
9th Rd 38109
11th Rd 38109
12th Rd 38109

MILLINGTON TN

General Delivery 38053

POST OFFICE BOXES MAIN OFFICE STATIONS AND BRANCHES

Box No.s
1 - 2000 38083
54001 - 54480 38054

NAMED STREETS

A St 38053
Abston Rd 38053
Adirondack Cv 38053
Admiral Rd 38053
Alder Wood Dr S 38053
Alexander Hill Dr 38053
Allegheny Cv 38053
Almond Creek Cv 38053
Amherst Rd 38053
Amy Ann Dr 38053
Anaconda Cv 38053
Anchuca Cv 38053
Angie St 38053
Annie Mae Cv & Dr 38053
Annielee St 38053
Apache Cv 38053
Arapaho St 38053
Arctic Cv 38053
Armour Cv & Rd 38053
Arnette Pl 38053
Ash Rene Dr 38053
Aspen Cv 38053
Astoria Rd 38053
Attu Ext & St 38053
Augusta Cv 38053
Austin Peay Hwy 38053
Autumn Sun Rd 38053
Aycock Rd 38053
B St 38053
Babe Howard Ave 38053
Baileys Creek Cv & Dr 38053
Baker St 38053
Balsa Glenn Dr 38053
Bannest Rd 38053
Barbara Ln 38053
Barclay St 38053
Barney Cv 38053
Barnsley Cv 38053
Barret Rd 38053
Bass Rd 38053
Bateman Rd 38053
N Bay Dr 38053
Baywood Cv & Dr 38053
Beauvoir Dr 38053
Benjestown Rd 38053
Bennett Wood Dr 38053
Bethuel Rd 38053
Bette Lu Dr 38053
Big Creek Church Rd 38053
Bigcreek View Cir E 38053
Bill Knight Ct & Rd 38053
Biloxi Cv & St 38053
Bilrae Cir & Pl 38053
Black Gum Dr 38053
Black Springs Rd 38053
Blacksprings Cv 38053
Blake View Ln 38053
Bland Ave 38053
Blue Creek Cir 38053
Blue Hills St 38053
Blue Sky Dr 38053
Bluff Cv & Rd 38053
Bobo Blvd 38053
Bolton Bottom Rd 38053
Bolton Estates Rd 38053
Bonhome Richard Dr 38053
Bonnie Brae Dr 38053
Boone Wood Cv 38053
Boskey Dr 38053
Bougainville St 38053
Boulder Cv 38053
Boxer Dr 38053
Braeswood Dr 38053
Brinkley St 38053
Broad Meadows Dr 38053
Brockman Dr 38053
Brooks Meadow Rd 38053
Brunswick Rd 38053
Brushy Mill Cv 38053
Bubbling Creek Ln 38053
Bucknell Rd 38053
Buford Ave 38053
C St 38053
Cades Brook Cv & Dr 38053
Camp John Rd 38053
Campbell Rd 38053
Canney Creek Cv 38053
Captain Rd 38053
Carter Rd 38053
Cassell Dr 38053
Catalina Dr 38053
Cates Dr 38053
Catskill Cv 38053
Cedar Bay Dr 38053
Cedar Hills Dr 38053
Cedar Ridge Dr 38053
Cedar Rose Dr 38053
Center College Rd 38053
Chadwell Cv & Rd 38053
Chambers Rd & St 38053
Chandeleur Cv & Dr 38053
Charles Bartlett Rd 38053
Chase Rd 38053
Chaser Rd 38053
Cherokee Rd 38053
Chestnut Oak Cv 38053
Cheyenne Rd 38053
Chickasaw Bluff Cv 38053
Childress Rd 38053
Church St 38053
Clancy Rd 38053
Clear Creek Dr 38053
Cloverhaven Dr 38053
Cloverland Cv 38053
Cold Springs Ln 38053
Colorday Cv 38053
Columbia Woods Ln 38053
Comanche Dr 38053
Commander Rd 38053
Commodore Rd 38053
Constellation Dr 38053
N & S Cooper Dr 38053
Copper Creek Blvd 38053
Corona Cv 38053
Coronado Rd 38053
Corsair Dr 38053
Cortney Cv 38053
Corvus Loop 38053
Cottage Hill Cv & Dr 38053
Covington Pike Rd 38053
Craig Rd 38053
Creek Mill Ct 38053
Crenshaw Rd 38053
Crestfield Rd 38053
Crigger Rd 38053
Cross Creek Dr 38053
Cuba Millington Rd 38053
Currie Rd 38053
Cuspidon Cv 38053
Dakar St 38053
Dale St 38053
Dawn Haven Dr 38053
Dawson Ridge Dr 38053
Deadfall Rd 38053
Deer Lake Dr 38053
Delashmit Rd 38053
Densford Cir W 38053
Division Ln 38053
Dixon Rd 38053
Dodson Rd 38053
Donnell Rd 38053
Doris Cir N & S 38053
Douglas Oaks Dr 38053
Dower Rd 38053
Duncan Rd 38053
Eagle St 38053
Eagles Hunt Rd 38053
Easley St 38053
Eckois Cv 38053
Eleanor Cv 38053
Eli St 38053
Elk Cv 38053
Ellen St 38053
Elrod Dr & Loop 38053
Emmitt St 38053
Endahwin Cv 38053
Eniwetok 38053
Ensign Rd 38053
Enterprise St 38053
Epperson Mill Rd 38053
Epperson Wood Dr 38053
Essex St 38053
Etta Rd 38053
Evander Rd 38053
Faith Rd 38053

Faulk Rd 38053
Fawn Lake Dr 38053
Fellowship Baptist Chur Rd 38053
Fern Rd 38053
Ferrin Cv 38053
Field Oak Rd 38053
Finnie Rd 38053
Fite Rd 38053
Fleetwood Dr 38053
Forbess Ln 38053
Forrestal Dr 38053
Franklin Dr 38053
Freudenberg Dr 38053
Friendship Church Rd 38053
Fulcher Rd 38053
Fullerton Pl 38053
Funa Futti 38053
G St 38053
Garden Ridge Cv & Dr 38053
Garnet Rd 38053
Gin Rd 38053
Glenmore Ln 38053
Glenn Cv 38053
Godwin Rd 38053
Goldsby Pl 38053
Gore Rd 38053
E & N Gragg Rd 38053
Grannys Path 38053
Grassy Lake Rd 38053
Gravesmont Trl 38053
Greenhill Rd 38053
Greenlawn Cv 38053
Greenside Rd 38053
Gunlock Dr 38053
Gunn Rd 38053
Hallbrook Dr 38053
Hamlet Rd 38053
Harkness Cv 38053
Harrold Cv & St 38053
N & S Helene Cv & Dr 38053
Herring Hill Rd 38053
Hickory Cv & Ln 38053
Hickory Meadow Rd 38053
High Seas Dr 38053
High Tide Dr 38053
Hill St 38053
Hilldale Cv & Ln 38053
Hilltop Ln 38053
Hines Rd 38053
Holly Heights Cv 38053
Home Acres Cv & Rd 38053
S & W Honeysuckle Ln 38053
Hood St 38053
Hope Rd 38053
Hornet Ave 38053
Howard Pl 38053
Hunter Bay Dr 38053
Ic Rd 38053
Independence Rd 38053
Integrity Ave 38053
Integrity Dr
5700-5719 38053
5720-5722 38054
5721-5799 38053
5730-5798 38053
Intrepid Dr 38053
Isom Cv 38053
J Lynn Ln 38053
Jack Cv 38053
Jackie Cv 38053
Jamestown Dr 38053
Janie Ave & Cv 38053
Jaybird Ln 38053
Jean Cv 38053
Jeffery St 38053
Jericho Rd 38053
Joe Dr 38053
Joe Ervin Ln 38053
John Paul Jones Ave 38053
John Sunderland Dr 38053
Jones Rd 38053
Juana Cv & Dr 38053
Julia Cv 38053
Julie Cv 38053
Karista St 38053
Kay Cv 38053
Kelly Cir 38053
Kelsey Lauren Cv 38053
Kerr Rd 38053
Kerrville Rosemark Rd 38053
King Lake Ln 38053
King Station Rd 38053
Kiowa St 38053
Knollview Dr 38053
Krosp Rd 38053
Kyllie Dr 38053
Lake Port Dr 38053
Langley Dr 38053
Laraine Dr 38053
Leamont Dr 38053
Leggett Vw 38053
Leighton Ln 38053
Lelah Ln 38053
Leo Holland Dr 38053
Lightning Dr 38053
Little John Rd 38053
Locke Rd 38053
Locke Cuba Rd 38053
Logans Path Rd 38053
Lorianti 38054
Louise Dr 38053
Lucy Rd 38053
Mahoney Rd 38053
Main Rd 38053
Mariner Rd 38053
Marshall Cv 38053
Martha Rd 38053
Martin Rd 38053
Martinwest Dr 38053
Martinwood Dr 38053
Marvin Rd 38053
Mary Lynn Cv & Dr 38053
Matthews Rd 38053
Max Dr 38053
Mccain St 38053
Mccalla Rd 38053
Mcclarin Dr 38053
Mccreight Dr 38053
Mcdaniel Dr 38053
Mcmullen Cir 38053
Meade Lake Rd 38053
Meadowview Dr 38053
Memphis St 38053
Merrel Dr 38053
Merrill Rd 38053
Micro Dr 38053
Midway St 38053
Miller Rd 38053
Millington Arlington Rd 38053
Milton Rd 38053
Misslow Cv 38053
Missy Ln 38053
Mitscher Dr & St 38053
Monasco Rd 38053
Montgomery Rd 38053
Moonbeam Rd 38053
Moonlight Ln 38053
Moonview Rd 38053
Moose Rd 38053
Moton Cir 38053
Mudville Rd 38053
Muncey Dr 38053
Myrel Rd 38053
Nancy Dr 38053
Nautilus Ave 38053
Navaho Cv 38053
Naval Support Activity 38054
E & W Navy Cir & Rd 38053
Nelson Rd 38053
Neptune Pl 38053
New Bethel Rd 38053
Newport Blvd & Rd 38053
Nichols Cv 38053
Nimitz Rd 38053
North Ave 38053
Northend Cv & Rd 38053
Northknoll Ave 38053
Northland Dr 38053
Oak Glen Cv 38053
Oak Harbour Trce 38053
Oak Pebble Cv & Ln 38053
Oak Spring Cv & Dr 38053
Oakhurst Ave 38053
Oates Cir 38053
Obie Brown Rd 38053
Oconner St 38053
Oglesby Rd 38053
Old Glory Dr 38053
Old Millington Rd 38053
Old Raleigh Millington Rd 38053
Old Tipton Rd 38053
Oneill Dr 38053
Ophelia Rd 38053
Organized Camp Rd 38053
Osprey Dr 38053
Painted Sea Dr 38053
Palmwood Cv 38053
Pam Dr 38053
Pannell Dr 38053
Parkington Rd 38053
Parkland Dr 38053
Patricia Ln 38053
Patrol St 38053
Paula Cv 38053
Payton Rd 38053
Penny Ln 38053
Perry Ln 38053
Petty Rd 38053
Phantom Dr 38053
Pilot Rd 38053
Pitts St 38053
Pleasant Ridge Rd 38053
Polaris Dr 38053
Port Harbor Dr 38053
Port Haven Cv & Rd 38053
Port Royal Dr 38053
Powder Plant Dr 38053
Prairie Cv 38053
Prather St 38053
Pruitt St 38053
Pryor Pl 38053
Quay Hill Dr 38053
Queen Sinclair Cir 38053
Quinn Cir 38053
Quito Cv & Rd 38053
Quito Drummonds Rd 38053
Quito Memorial Cemetery Rd 38053
Raible Dr 38053
Raleigh Millington Rd 38053
Rams Horn Cv & Dr 38053
Rankin Branch Rd 38053
Rast Rd 38053
Ray Bluff Rd 38053
Redwood Rd 38053
Regulus St 38053
Renda St 38053
Renter St 38053
Rhino Dr 38053
Richard Wilson Dr 38053
Riddick Rd 38053
Ridge Bay Cv 38053
Ridgeway Ln 38053
River Bluff Rd 38053
Riverchase Dr 38053
Robena Ln 38053
Robin Hood Cir 38053
Rockford Rd 38053
Roger Ln 38053
Rosalind Way 38053
Rosedown Rd 38053
Rosemark Rd 38053
Royal Mews Dr 38053
Rushing Creek Ln 38053
Russell Dr 38053
Russell Bond Rd 38053
Rust Ave & Rd 38053
Ryan Hill Rd 38053
Ryburn Dr 38053
Saddlebrook Dr 38053
Saint Paul Rd 38053
Sallie Rd 38053
Sandy Hollow Ln 38053
Saratoga Rd 38053
Sartori Dr 38053
Sassy Tree Cv & Ln 38053
Savitz Dr 38053
School Ave & Rd 38053
Sea Board Dr 38053
Sea Breeze Dr 38053
Sea Weed Dr 38053
Seawolf Dr 38053
Second Ave 38053
Shady Dell Cv 38053
Shakerag Rd 38053
Shamrock Rd 38053
Shane Rd 38053
Shangrila Dr 38053
Sheila Cv & St 38053
Shelby Rd 38053
Sherman Rd 38053
Shipp Rd 38053
Sigler Ln 38053
Silent Brook Dr 38053
Singleton Ave & Pkwy 38053
Skyhawk Loop 38053
Slayden Pl 38053
Sledge Rd 38053
Smith Rd 38053
Snoal Cv 38053
Snowy Creek Ln 38053
Soderlund Cv & Dr 38053
South St 38053
Southknoll Ave 38053
Southworth St 38053
Sparrow St 38053
Spring Harbor Dr 38053
Spring Port Dr 38053
Springton Ave 38053
Squirrel Cv 38053
Sullivan Rd 38053
Sunshine Dr 38053
Susan Rd 38053
Susie Cv 38053
Sweet Bark Rd 38053
Sykes Rd 38053
Sylvan Rd 38053
Sylvanshire Cv 38053
Talley Rd 38053
Talos Dr 38053
Tamarack Dr 38053
Tartar Dr 38053
Tecumseh St 38053
Terrell Ln 38053
Terrier Dr 38053
Thal Cv 38053
The Holly Ln 38053
The Ketta Ln 38053
Theda Cv 38053
Thompson St 38053
Thornhill Dr 38053
Thunder Ridge Dr 38053
Tickle View Dr 38053
Tippy Dr 38053
Tipton Lake Cir E & W 38053
Tom Cat Dr 38053
Tommie Ln 38053
Tompkins Ln 38053
Townwood Dr 38053
Tracy Rd 38053
Trading Post Ln 38053
Tumblebrook Cv 38053
Tumbling Creek Dr 38053
Turkey Cv 38053
Turnbridge Dr 38053
Twin Oaks Dr 38053
Typhon St 38053
Tywalp Cv 38053
Union Cir & Rd 38053
Us Highway 51 N & S 38053
Ventura Rd 38053
Veterans Pkwy 38053
Victory Ln 38053
Viewcrest Dr 38053
Vincent Cv & Rd 38053
Wages Dr 38053
E & W Wagon Hill Rd 38053
Walker Rd 38053
Walnut Cv 38053
Walsh Cv & Rd 38053
Wampum Rd 38053
Wanda Dr 38053
Ward Rd 38053
Water Briar Rd 38053
Watercrest Dr 38053
N Watkins Rd 38053
Waverly Farms Rd 38053
Waycross Ave 38053
Wells Ext & Rd 38053
West St 38053
Westknoll Dr 38053
Whippoorwill Cir 38053
Wilkinsville Rd 38053
William L Osteen Dr 38053
Willow Brook St 38053
Willow Springs Cv & Dr 38053
Windbrook Dr 38053
Woodglen Dr 38053
Woodgreen Dr 38053
Woodstock Cuba Rd 38053
Woodstock Hills Dr 38053
Woodstock View Dr 38053
Wortham Rd 38053
Zachary St 38053

NUMBERED STREETS

All Street Addresses 38053

MORRISTOWN TN

General Delivery 37813

POST OFFICE BOXES MAIN OFFICE STATIONS AND BRANCHES

Box No.s
1 - 792 37815
1001 - 2380 37816
3001 - 6007 37815
14001 - 14358 37814

NAMED STREETS

Acacia Cir 37813
Academy Dr 37814
Acorn Ln 37814
Adams St 37814
Ailshie Rd 37813
Air Park Blvd
5000-5099 37813
5700-5799 37814
N Air Park Blvd 37814
S Air Park Blvd 37813
Alexander Rd 37813
Algonquin Dr 37813
Alkazar St 37814
Allegiance Way 37813
Allen Rd 37813
Allison St 37814
Alpha Dr 37814
Alpha Valley Home Rd 37813
Alpine St 37814
Amanda Ave 37813
Amanda Harrison Ct 37814
Amesbury Dr 37814
Anderson St 37814
E & W Andrew Johnson Hwy 37814
Andy St 37814
Anne Cir 37814
Annie Ln 37813
Apostle Rd 37814
Appalachian Trce 37814
Apple Blossom Ln 37814
Apple Tree Cir 37814
Appley Dr 37814
Arden Ln 37813
Arnold Ave 37813
Arrow Dr 37814
Arthur Dr 37813
Ash St 37813
Ashburne Dr 37814
Ashford Dr 37813
Ashland Oaks Dr 37813
Ashley Ct 37814
Aspen Ave 37813
Audrey Ln 37813
S Austin Rd 37813
Autumn Ln 37814
Avery Ln 37813
Azalea Ct 37814
Bacon Ln & Rd 37813
Baird Ave 37813
Baker St 37813
Balch St 37813
Bales Dr 37814
Baltic Dr 37814
Barker Rd 37814
Barkley Landing Dr 37813
Barton Dr 37814
Barton Springs Dr 37813
Bay View Way 37813
Bayberry Dr 37813
Baylor Ave 37814
Bear Springs Rd 37814
Beatrice Dr 37814
Beaudelaire Dr 37814
Beaumont Ln 37814
Beaver Rd 37814
Bebber St 37814
Beech St 37813
Beechurst Ave 37813
Beechwood Cir 37814
Beets Cir 37814
Bell Rd 37813
Belle Meade Cir 37814
N Bellwood Rd 37814
S Bellwood Rd
100-299 37814
300-1099 37813
Belmont Dr 37814
Benjamin Blvd 37814
Benton Hale Rd 37813
Berg Ln 37813
Berkeley Dr 37814
Berkline Dr 37813
Berkshire Dr 37814
Bertie Cir 37814
Bethel Rd 37813
Bethesda Rd 37814
Betsy Ln 37814
Beulah St 37813
Bewley Rd 37813
Big Elm Dr 37814
Big Woods Dr 37813
Birch Ave 37814
Birchwood Cir 37814
Bireley St 37814
Blackberry Ln 37814
Blackburn Dr 37814
Blair St 37814
Blue Grass Dr 37814
Blue Ridge Dr 37814
Bluebird Cir 37814
Boardwalk Cir 37814
Boat Launch Rd 37814
Boatmans Mountain Rd 37814
Boatmans Ridge Rd 37814
Bobbie Ct 37814
Boddington Ct 37814
Bohanan Rd 37813
Bond Cir 37814
Bonneville Dr 37814
Bonnie Ln 37813
Bounds Dr 37813
Bowman St 37813
Boyd School Rd 37813
Brad Dr 37814
Bradford Sq 37814
Bradley St 37813
Brady Dr 37814
Branch Way 37813
Brandywine Cir 37814
Branner St 37814
Breeding Pike Rd 37813
E Brentwood Dr 37814
Briarcliff Cir 37814
Brice Cir 37814
Bridle Path 37814
Brighton Ln 37813
Brights Pike 37814
Brights View Ln 37814
Brimer Rd 37813
Britt Ln 37814
Britton Ct 37814
Brockland Dr 37813
Brockwood Dr 37813
Brogan Rd 37813
Brookfield Dr 37814
Brookside Dr 37813
Broughton Ct 37814
Brown Ave 37813
Broyles Ln 37814
Bruce St 37814
Buell Chapel Rd 37813
Buffalo Trl 37814
Buggy Rd 37814
Bullard Dr 37814
Burl Ln 37814
Burns Dr 37814
Bushong Ave 37814
Butler St 37813
Buxton Rd 37813
Cain Ave 37813
Calderstone Ct 37814
Call St 37814
Callaway Cir & Dr 37814
Calvary Dr 37813
Calvin Rd 37814
Cambridge Dr 37814
Camellia Ct 37814
Cameron Rd 37814
Camilla Ave 37814
Campbell St 37814
Canary Ln 37814
Cannon Cir 37814
Canter Dr 37813
Canter King Rd 37813
Canterbury Dr 37814
Cardinal Dr 37814
Carlyle Pl 37814
Carmel Dr 37813
Carmichael St 37814
Carnation Dr 37814
Carolyn Dr 37814
Carriger St 37814
Carroll Rd 37813
Carter Cemetery Rd 37813
Castain Dr 37813
Castile Ave 37814
Catalonia Ave 37814
Catawba Ln 37814
Catron Ln 37814
Cave St 37813
Cedar St 37814
Cedar Cove Dr 37814
Cedar Trace Ln 37814
Cedarwood Ln 37814
Celeste Ave 37814
Centennial Ct 37813
Center St 37813
Central Church Rd 37814
Chan Ln 37814
Chapman St 37813
W Charles St 37813
Charleston Ct 37813
Charlotte St 37814
Cherokee Dr 37814
Cherokee Park Rd 37814
Cherry Ave 37814
Chestnut Ave 37814
Chestnut Oak Dr 37814
Chickasaw Dr 37814
Choctaw St 37813
Chris Cir 37814
Christian Valley Rd 37814
Christmas Dr 37814
Christopher Ct 37814

Street	ZIP
Christopher Ln	37813
Chucky River Rd	37813
N Church St	37814
N Circle Dr	37813
Citrus Ln	37814
Claire Ln	37814
Clancy Ave	37814
Clarence Ln	37814
Claude Collins Rd	37813
Clear Springs Rd	37814
Clear View Rd	37814
Cleveland Ave	37813
Clinch Dr	37814
Clinchview Rd	37814
Cline Ave	37814
Clint Cir	37813
Clover Dale Ln	37813
Clover Leaf Dr	37813
Clyde Thomas Rd	37813
Cobble Ln	37813
N Coffey Rd	37813
Cole Rd	37814
College Park Dr	37813
Collegewood Dr	37813
Collins St	37814
Collinson Ford Rd	37814
Colonial Dr	37814
Colony Cir	37813
Combs Ln	37814
Commerce Blvd	37814
Connie St	37814
Conrad Dr	37814
E & W Converse St	37814
Cooper Dr	37813
Copeland Cir	37814
Copper Ridge Rd	37814
Corbin Dr	37814
Cordell Hull Dr	37814
Cotton Tail Ln	37814
Cotton Wood Ln	37814
Country Rd	37814
Country Club Dr	37814
Court Dr	37814
Cove Rd	37813
Covington Dr	37814
Cowan Ln	37814
Cox Rd	37814
Cracker Rd	37813
Creechwood Dr	37813
Creek View Ln	37814
Crescent St	37813
Crest View Cir	37814
Crest Way Dr	37814
Crestwood Dr	37814
Crigger Rd	37813
Crockett Ridge Rd	37814
Crocus Ct	37813
Cross Dr	37814
Crossroads Blvd	37813
Crown Cir	37814
E & W Croxdale Rd	37813
Crystal Brook Dr	37814
Cub Cir	37814
N Cumberland St	37814
S Cumberland St	
100-199	37814
200-804	37813
803-803	37815
806-1898	37813
829-1899	37813
Custer Dr	37813
D Accord Ct	37814
D Short Dr	37814
Dailey Gazette Rd	37814
N Daisy St	37814
S Daisy St	
100-199	37814
200-499	37813
Dalton Cir	37814
Dalton Ford Rd	37814
Dan Dr	37814
Danbury Dr	37813
Dandelion Cir	37814
Daniel Boone Dr	37814
Daniels Dr	37813
Darbee Dr	37814
Darnell Rd	37814
David Ave	37814
Davis Ave	37814
N Davy Crockett Pkwy	37814
S Davy Crockett Pkwy	37813
De Vault St	37814
Deanna Ct	37814
Dearing Rd	37813
Debi Cir	37813
Dedra St	37814
Deena Cir	37814
Deer Ridge Dr	37814
Deerfield Dr	37813
Dehart Dr	37813
Delana Dr	37814
Deleonardo Dr	37813
Delta Dr	37814
Deneen Ln	37814
Depew Cir	37814
Derbyshire Ct	37814
Desota Ave	37813
Dewberry Dr	37814
Diane Ave	37814
Dice St	37813
Dogwood St	37814
E & W Donaldson Dr	37814
Donna St	37814
Dontinch Dr	37814
Dougherty Dr	37814
Douglas Ave	37813
Douglas Cir	37814
Dove St	37814
Dover Rd	37813
Doyal Dr	37814
Dr M L King Pkwy	37813
Drew Dr	37813
Driftwood Dr	37814
Drinnon Dr	37814
Dublin Ln	37814
Duggan Dr	37813
Dunn St	37814
Durham Dr	37813
Dylan Ln	37813
Eagle Trl	37813
Eagle Heights Dr	37813
Eagles Nest Dr	37813
Eagles View Ct	37813
Early Bird Hl	37813
N & S Easley Ct	37814
Eastern Ave	37813
Eastpoint Ln	37814
Eastwood Cir	37814
E Economy Rd	37814
N Economy Rd	37814
S Economy Rd	37813
W Economy Rd	37814
Eddie Price Blvd	37813
Elgerlotte Ln	37814
Elgin Dr	37814
Elk Dr	37814
Ellaree Dr	37813
Ellen Dr	37814
Eller Rd	37813
Elm St	37814
Elm Way Cir	37814
Eloise Dr	37814
Elwood Dr	37814
Embassy Dr	37814
Emerald Ave	37814
Emerson St	37813
Emily Ln	37814
English St	37813
Enka Hwy	37813
Erie Ct	37814
Essex Ln	37814
Ethel Ave	37813
Euclid Ave	37813
Evans Ave	37814
Everett Rd	37813
Evergreen Dr	37814
Fairfax Cir	37813
N Fairmont Ave	37814
S Fairmont Ave	37813
Fairview Rd	37814
Falcon Rd	37814
Farm Rd	37813
Faulkner Rd	37814
Fawn Ln	37814
Federal Blvd	37814
Fern Cir	37814
Fernwood Rd	37813
Fernwood Church Rd	37813
Fir St	37813
Fish Hatchery Rd	37813
Fisher Rd	37814
Flemings Dr	37813
Fletcher Rd	37814
Floyd Hall Rd	37814
Foard Dr	37814
Forest Dr	37814
Forgey Ave	37813
Fort Hill Rd	37814
Fowler Dr	37814
Fox Dr	37814
Fox Trott Ln	37814
Foxcreek Ct	37814
Foxglove Ln	37814
Frank Rd	37814
Franklin Ln	37814
Fred Rd	37814
Freshour St	37813
Frontier Way	37814
Fuller Dr	37813
Fuller Estate Cir	37813
Fulton Rd	37814
Gaby Cir	37814
Gammon Ave	37814
Garretson St	37814
Gary St	37813
Gaston St	37813
Gateway Service Park Rd	37813
Geneva Cir	37813
George St	37814
George Beets Cir	37814
George Byrd Rd	37813
George Ellis Rd	37813
Gilbert St	37814
N Glenn St	37814
Godwin St	37813
Golden Dr	37814
Goodson Ave	37814
Granby Dr	37813
Grand Dr	37814
Grandview St & Trce	37814
Grant St	37814
Gray St	37814
Grazeland Dr	37814
Green Hill Dr	37814
Green Way Dr	37813
Greene Dr & Rd	37814
Gregg Rd	37814
Gretchen Dr	37813
Grigsby Rd	37813
Grove Dale Dr	37814
Guy Collins Rd	37813
Hale Ave	
100-199	37814
200-599	37813
Halifax Cir	37813
Hall Dr	37813
Hamblen Ave	37813
Hamblen Dock Rd	37814
Hamilton Ave & Pl	37814
Hampshire Ln	37813
E Hampton Blvd	37813
Hampton Cir	37814
Hampton West Blvd	37814
Hansford Pl	37814
Harbin Cir	37814
Harbor Dr	37814
Harbor View Dr & Rd	37814
Hardy Rd	37813
Harley Rd	37813
Harrell St	37814
Harrison St	37813
Hartman Rd	37814
Harville St	37813
N Haun Dr	37814
S Haun Dr	37813
Hayden Ct	37814
Hayter Dr	37813
Hazelwood Cir	37814
Heathcliff Rd	37813
Hedrick St	37813
Helton Ln	37813
Helton Gaby Rd	37814
Hemlock Cir	37814
Henrietta Dr	37814
N Henry St	
100-135	37814
134-134	37816
137-1499	37814
138-1498	37814
S Henry St	37813
Herbert Harville Dr	37813
Herron Dr	37813
Heykoop Dr	37814
Hiawatha Rd	37814
Hibiscus Dr	37814
Hickey St	37814
Hickory Ln	37813
Hickory Shadow Dr	37814
Hickory View Dr	37814
N High St	37814
S High St	37813
High Oak Dr	37814
Highland Dr	37813
Highview Dr	37813
N Hill St	37814
S Hill St	
100-199	37814
200-599	37813
Hill Trail Dr	37814
E & W Hillcrest Dr	37813
Hillside Cir	37814
Hilltop Dr	37814
Hillvale Dr	37813
Hindley Rd	37813
Hinkle Dr	37814
Hite Rd	37814
Hodge Ct & Dr	37814
Holder Dr	37814
Holdway St	37813
Holiday Dr	37814
Holland Cir	37814
Holly Ave	37814
Holly Tree Ln	37814
Holston Dr	37814
Holston Crest Dr	37814
Holston Valley Rd	37814
Holts Church Rd	37814
Hoover Dr	37814
Horner Dr	37814
Horseshoe Trl	37814
Housley Cir & St	37814
Houston St	37813
Howard Allen Rd	37813
Howell Rd	
100-299	37814
300-1299	37813
Howerton Dr	37814
Hubble St	37814
Hugh Dr	37813
Hundred Oaks Dr	37813
Hunter Rd	37814
Huntington Park	37814
Hurricane Ln	37813
Ida Moyers Rd	37814
Indian Path	37813
Indian Trl	37814
Industrial Ave	37813
Inman St	37813
Inman Bend Rd	37814
Interplast Dr	37814
Interstate View Dr	37814
Iris St	37813
Iroquois Ave	37813
Isaac Ave	37814
Ivanhoe Rd	37814
Ivy Ln & St	37814
E Jackson Cir	37813
N Jackson St	37814
S Jackson St	37813
Jacobs Rd	37813
Jacqulin St	37814
N James St	37814
S James St	37813
Jarnigan Ave	37813
Jay St	37814
Jaybird Rd	37814
Jefferson St	37814
Jefferson Diamond Rd	37814
Jeffrey Ln	37813
Jellicorse Rd	37814
Jennifer Dr	37814
Jenny Ln	37814
Jesse Bean Cir	37814
Jessica Dr	37814
Jinks Ct	37814
Joanne Cir	37814
Joe Hall Rd	37813
Joe Stephens Rd	37814
John Sevier Dr	37814
Johns Dr	37814
Johnson Dr	37814
Jolley Ct	37814
Jonathan Dr	37814
Jones St	37813
Jones Franklin Rd	37813
Josh Ln	37813
Judy Dr	37814
Julian Ave	37814
Junction Ln	37813
Juniper Ln	37813
Kandenna Dr	37814
Kasey St	37814
Katerina Dr	37814
Katie Ln	37814
Keith Ln	37813
Keller Rd	37813
Kelly St	37813
Keltic Dr	37814
Kennedy Cir	37813
Kensington Ct & Dr	37814
Keystone Dr	37814
Kidwell Church Rd	37814
Kidwell Ridge Rd	37814
Kimberly Dr	37814
King Ave	37814
Kingswood Dr	37813
Knollwood Dr	37814
Lacefield Dr	37814
Ladysmith Ln	37813
Lake Dr	37814
Lake Forest Dr	37814
Lake Front Dr	37814
Lake Meadow Ln	37814
Lake Park Cir	37814
Lake Point Dr	37814
Lakemont Cir	37814
Lakemoore Dr	37814
Lakeview Cir & Dr	37814
Lakeway Rd	37814
Lakewood Dr	37814
Lakins Dr	37813
Laminite Dr	37813
Lampkin Dr	37814
Lancaster Ct	37814
Landmark Dr	37814
Langdon Rd	37813
Lanter Dr	37814
Larch Cir	37814
Larry Baker Dr	37813
Laterre Ln	37814
Laura Dr	37814
Laurel St	37813
Lawrence St	37814
Lawson Rd	37814
Le Conte St	37814
Ledean Dr	37814
Ledford Ave	37813
Lee Dr	37814
Lee Ridge Rd	37814
Leepers Ferry Rd	37813
Leewood Dr	37814
Leia Dr	37814
Leming Rd	37814
Lennie Ave	37813
Leslie Dr	37814
Levant Dr	37813
Lewis St	37813
Libby Ln	37813
Liberty Downs Dr	37814
Liberty Hall Dr	37813
Liberty Hill Rd	37813
N Liberty Hill Rd	37814
S Liberty Hill Rd	37813
Liddington Ln	37814
Lila St	37814
Lilac St	37814
Lilly Ln	37814
Lincoln Ave	37813
Linda St	37813
Line St	37814
Linwood Ln	37814
Litz Dr	37813
Lloyd St	37814
Lochmere Dr	37814
Lochmere Greene Dr	37814
Lockley Ct	37813
Locust Ave	37813
Locust Grove Ct	37814
Lon Cir	37813
Lone Oak Dr	37814
Long Ave	37814
Long Creek Rd	37813
Long Ferry Rd	37814
Longstreet Rd	37813
Lonnie Cir	37813
Lookout Dr	37814
Lori Ln	37814
Lorino Ln	37813
Lorino Park Rd	37813
E & W Louise Ave	37813
Lowland Pike	37813
Ludlow Ct	37814
Luke Dr	37814
Lumbardy Dr	37814
Lyman Rd	37814
Macarthur St	37814
Macedonia Rd	37814
Maden Dr	37813
Madison St	37814
Mae Collins Rd	37813
Magnolia Ave	37814
E & W Main St	37814
Majestic Magnolia Ln	37814
Mall Dr	37814
Manchester Ave	37813
E Manley Court Cir	37814
Maple Ave	37814
Maple Leaf Dr	37814
Maple Valley Rd	37813
Marcum Dr	37814
Marguerite St	37814
Marion St	37814
Mark Ln	37814
Mars St	37814
Marsh Ave	37814
Marshall Ave	37814
Marthas Vineyard	37814
Martindale Dr	37814
Marty Dr	37814
Masengill Ave	37814
Matthew Trce	37813
Maupin Cir	37814
Maxey Rd	37813
Mayes Rd	37813
Mayo Dr	37813
Mcanally Cir	37814
Mcbride Rd	37814
Mcclanahan Rd	37813
Mcclister Rd	37813
Mcconnell St	37814
Mccrary Dr	37814
Mcdaniel St	37814
Mcfarland St	37814
Mcghee Ave	37814
Mcginnis Rd	37814
Meadow Lane Cir	37813
Meadow Run Dr	37814
Meadowland Dr	37814
Meadowlark Dr	37814
Meadowview Ln	37814
Medlin Rd	37814
Melrose Ave	37814
Memorial Ave	37814
Merchants Green Dr	37814
Merwin St	37813
Michael St	37814
Midridge Dr	37814
Mike Dr	37813
Milburn St	37814
S Mill St	
100-198	37814
300-498	37813
301-399	37814
401-499	37813
Mill Race Rd	37814
Mill Wheel Rd	37814
Miller Ave	37814
Millers Landing Blvd	37813
Millers Point Dr	37813
Millsap Rd	37813
Mimosa Dr	37814
Mineral Hills Rd	37813
Misty Hill Ln	37814
Misty Wood Dr	37813
Ml King Blvd	37813
Mohawk St	37813
Monroe St	37814
Montcastle Dr	37814
Monteverdi Ct	37814
Montrose Ave	37813
Montvue Ave	37813
N Morelock Rd	37814
Morgan Rd	37813
Morningside Dr	37814
E Morris Blvd	37813
W Morris Blvd	
100-1931	37813
1932-1999	37814
Morton St	37814
Mountain Laurel Rd	37814
Mountain View Dr	37814
Moyer Ln	37814
Murray St	37814
Murrell Rd	37814
Musick Rd	37814
Musser Rd	37813
Nancy Cir	37814
Naomi Dr	37814
Nathan Dr	37813
Neblett Rd	37813
Neikirk Dr	37813
Neil Cir	37814
Nelson School Rd	37813
Nena Cir	37814
Neuhoff Rd	37813
New Cut Rd	37814
New Line Rd	
100-299	37814
300-499	37813
Nightingale St	37814
Noes Chapel Rd	37814
Nolen Rd	37814
Norland Dr	37813
Norman St	37814
Northbrook Dr	37814
Northview Dr	37814
Northwind Dr	37814
Norton Dr	37814
O Donoghue Rd	37813
Oak St	37813
Oak Trace Dr	37813
Oakcrest Dr	37814
Oakdale Ln	37814
Oakwood Cir	37814
Old Andrew Johnson Hwy	37814
Old Colony Ln	37814
Old Enka Hwy	37813
Old Ford Rd	37814
Old Highway 11e	37814
Old Highway 160	37813
Old Highway 25e	37813
Old Hollow Rd	37813
Old Kentucky Rd	37814
Old Liberty Hill Rd	37814
Old Lowland Rd	37814
Old Oak Ln	37814
Old Stage Rd	37814
Old West Main St	37813
Old White Pine Rd	37813
Old Witt Rd	37813

Ontario Cir 37814
Orchard St 37814
Orchard Grove Ln 37814
Oriole Ct 37814
Osprey Dr 37814
Otto Way 37814
E, N, S & W Outer Dr .. 37814
Overlook Dr 37813
Overview Dr 37814
Ozark Dr 37814
Page Dr 37813
Palomino Rd 37813
Panda Dr 37814
Panorama Dr 37814
Panther Creek Ct & Rd 37814
Panther Creek Park Rd 37814
Panther Springs Rd 37814
Paper Mill Dr 37814
N Park Ave 37814
S Park Ave 37813
Park Place Dr 37814
Park View Dr 37814
Parker Rd 37813
Parkside Ave 37814
Parkway Dr 37814
Parkway Church Rd 37814
Parrish Cir 37814
Patricia Cir 37814
Paul St 37814
Pauline Ave 37813
Paw Paw Ct 37813
Peace Dr 37814
Peachtree St 37814
Pearce Dr
1-199 37814
200-399 37813
Pearl Dr 37814
Peck Ave 37813
Pembrook Dr 37813
Pendleton Ave 37813
Pennell Cir 37814
Perry Ave 37814
Piedmont Cir 37814
Pilgrim Rd 37814
Pin Oak Dr 37814
Pine Barren Dr 37814
Pine Brooke Rd 37813
Pine Cone Dr 37814
Pine Haven Dr 37814
Pinecrest Ln 37813
Pinewood Cir 37814
Piper St 37814
Pleasant Ave 37813
Polk St 37814
Pope Rd 37813
Poplar St 37813
Porter St 37814
Portrum Dr 37814
Potter Rd 37813
Prado Dr 37814
Praleari Rd 37813
Prater Dr 37814
Price Dr 37813
Primrose Ct 37813
Priscilla St 37814
Pritchard Dr 37813
Progress Pkwy 37813
Providence Cir 37814
Pryors Passing 37813
Purkey St 37814
Quail Ln 37814
Quail Hollow Rd 37814
Quentin Cir 37814
Quillen Dr 37814
Rader St 37814
Railroad Ave 37814
Rainbow Cir 37814
Rambling Rd 37814
Ramona Cir 37813
Randolph Dr 37813
Raritan Dr 37813
Raun Rd 37814
Raven Rd 37814
Ravenwood Dr 37814

Ray St 37814
Rayburn Dr 37814
Rebel St 37814
Red Dr 37814
Red Bird St 37814
Red Bud Dr 37814
Red Fox Ave 37813
Red Oak Dr 37814
Redwood St 37813
Reed St 37813
Reeds Chapel Rd 37814
Reese St 37814
Regency Cir 37814
Reggie Dr 37813
Reno Dr 37814
Resource Dr 37813
Reynolds Rd 37814
Rhett Cir 37814
Rich Cir 37814
Richardson St 37814
Richie St 37814
Ricker St 37814
Ridge St 37813
Ridgecrest St 37814
Ridgelawn Ave 37814
Ridgemont Dr 37814
Rippetoe Ave 37813
River Rd 37813
River View Dr 37813
Robin Cir 37813
Robinson Creek Rd 37813
Roblee Rd 37813
Rock Church Rd 37813
Rockwell Dr 37813
Roddy Dr 37814
Roe Junction Rd 37813
Rogers Rd 37813
Rolling Springs Dr 37814
Romar St 37814
Romona Cir 37813
Roosevelt Dr 37813
Rosa Cir 37814
E & W Rose St 37814
Rosedale Ave 37813
Rosella St 37814
Rosemeade Dr 37814
Rotherfield Ct 37814
Rouse Rd 37814
Rugel Dr 37814
Russell Cir & St 37813
Rustic Cir 37814
Ruthena Cir 37813
Rutledge Ave 37813
Ryder Ln 37813
Saddle Ridge Ln 37814
Sagewood Dr 37813
Saint Johns Rd 37814
Saint Paul Rd 37813
Sakura Dr 37813
Salinas Ln 37813
Sam Adams Rd 37813
Sam King Ln 37813
San Francisco Dr 37814
Sanoria Ln 37813
Sawyers Rd 37813
Scarlett Dr 37814
Scarlett Oak Dr 37813
Scenic Dr 37813
Scenic Lake Cir 37814
School St 37813
Seagle Ln 37813
Seal Brooks Rd 37814
Seals Ln 37813
Secretariat Dr 37814
Seminole St 37813
Sequoyah Dr 37813
Seven Oaks Dr 37814
Seville Rd 37813
Seymour St 37813
Shadow Ln 37813
Shadow Wood Ln 37814
Shadowland Way 37814
Shady Ln 37814
Shady Creek Ct 37814
Shady Grove Rd 37814
Shady Woods Rd 37814

Shandee Ln 37814
Shannon Rd 37814
Shannons Little Mtn Rd 37814
Shareef Dr 37814
Shea Ct 37814
Sherwood Dr 37814
Shields Dr 37814
Shields Ferry Rd 37814
Shirley Ln 37813
Shockley Ave 37814
Short St 37814
Sigmon St 37814
Silver Fox Trl 37814
Sisson Dr 37814
Skeen Rd 37813
E & W Skyline Dr 37813
Smithview Dr 37814
Smokey View Dr 37814
Snowflake Dr 37814
Snyder Rd 37813
Solod Dr 37814
Soloman Ridge Way 37814
Southern Dr 37814
Southern Ter 37813
Southfork Cir 37814
Spangle Rd 37814
Spencer Dr 37814
Spencer Hale Rd 37813
Spoone Ave & Cir 37814
Spout Springs Rd 37814
Spring St 37814
Spring Creek Dr 37814
Spring Hollow Dr 37814
Springvale Rd 37813
Spruce St 37813
St Ives Ct 37814
Stacy Ave 37814
Standifer Ln 37814
Stansberry Rd 37813
Stapleton Rd 37813
Starboard Crest Rd & Way 37814
State St 37814
Statem Gap Rd 37813
Stetzer Cir & Cv 37814
Stillwell Ave 37814
Stonebrook Ln 37814
Stream View Ln 37814
Stuffel Rd 37814
Sublett Rd 37814
Suburban Dr 37814
N Sugar Hollow Rd 37814
S Sugar Hollow Rd 37813
Sugar Maples St 37813
Sulphur Ln 37813
Sulphur Springs Rd 37813
Summit Ln 37813
Summit Ridge Dr 37814
Sunflower Ct 37814
Sunrise Ave 37813
E & W Sunset Hls 37814
Sunset Strip 37814
Superior Ct & Dr 37814
Susong Dr 37814
Sussex Ln 37814
Sycamore St 37813
Sykes Rd 37813
Taft St 37813
Tagen Ln 37813
Talbott Rd 37813
Talley Rd 37813
Tanasi Trl 37814
Taylor Rd 37814
Tazewell Cir 37814
Technology Way 37813
Tennessee Ave 37813
Tennessee Hills Dr 37814
Teresas Way 37814
Terrace Ln 37813
Terrace View Dr 37814
Terrell Cir 37814
Terri St 37814
Testerman Dr 37814
Thomas Dr 37814
Thomas R James Dr 37813

Thompson Creek Rd 37813
Throughbred Run 37814
Thurbread Run 37813
Timber Creek Ln 37814
Timbercrest Dr 37814
Tip Top Cir 37814
Tom Treece Rd 37814
Tomahawk Hill Rd 37814
Toni Ave 37813
Tornado Trl 37813
Tracy St 37814
Trade St 37813
Treece St 37813
Tretower Ct 37814
Trojan Trl 37813
Truman St 37814
Tulip St 37813
Turkey St 37814
Turley Bridge Rd 37814
Turley Mill Rd 37814
Turner St 37814
Tyler Cir & Rd 37814
Union Ave 37813
Urban Dr 37813
Utility St 37814
Valley St 37813
Valley Home Rd 37813
Valley View Dr 37813
Van Buren St 37814
Vantage View Dr 37814
Vennie Cir 37814
Veterans Pkwy 37813
Vicki St 37814
Victor Rd 37814
Vifan Dr 37814
Vine Rd 37813
Vineyard Rd 37813
Violet St 37814
Virgie Rd 37813
Virginia Ave 37814
Volunteer Dr 37814
Waddell Rd 37813
Wagon Rd 37813
Wagon Wheel Dr 37814
Walden Dr 37814
Waldo Dr 37813
Walker Dr 37814
Wallace Farm Rd 37813
Walnut Dr 37813
Walnut Hill Dr 37814
Walters Dr 37814
Wanda Ter 37814
Warren Dr 37814
Warwick Ct 37814
Washington Ave 37814
Watercrest St 37814
Waters Edge Dr 37814
Watkins Chapel Rd 37813
Wayman St 37814
Wayne Johnson Rd 37814
Webb Dr & Rd 37813
Wedgewood Dr 37814
Weesner St 37814
Wellington Blvd 37814
Wendy Cir & St 37814
Wentworth Sq 37813
Western Ave 37814
Westover Pl 37813
Whitaker Ln 37814
White Ave 37814
White Oak Cir 37814
White Oak Church Rd 37813
White Oak Grove Rd 37813
White Wood Cir 37814
Whitecliff St 37813
Whiteside Dr 37814
Wide View Dr 37814
Wilder St 37813
Wildflower Ct 37813
Wildlife Way 37813
W Wildwood Dr 37814
Wiley Blount Dr 37814
Wilkie Ave 37814
Williams St 37813
Willow St & Way 37814
Willow Greene Dr 37814

Willow Springs Dr 37814
Willow Tree Ln 37814
Wilshire Blvd 37814
Wilson Ave 37814
Wilson Hale Rd 37813
Wind Cir 37814
Wind Crest Dr 37814
Windfield Dr 37813
Windhaven Ct 37813
Windridge Ln 37814
Windsong Ln 37813
Windsor Rd 37813
Windswept Way 37814
Wintergreen Rd 37814
Wisteria Dr 37814
Witt Rd 37813
Witt Acres Cir 37813
Witt View Dr 37813
Woodbine St 37813
Woodbury Ct 37813
Woodchuck Dell 37814
Woodcrest Dr 37814
Wooddale Rd 37814
Wooddawn Dr 37814
Woodhaven Dr 37813
Woodland Dr 37813
Woods Dr 37814
Woodview Dr 37814
Woodway Dr 37814
Wright Ln 37814
Wylie Miller Rd 37813
Wynn St 37814
Yankee St 37814
York St 37813
Yorkshire Ct 37814
Yorkshire Ln 37813
Zimmerman Dr 37814

NUMBERED STREETS

E & W 1st North 37814
E 1st South St 37813
E & W 2nd North 37814
W 2nd South St 37813
E & W 3rd North 37814
E & W 3rd South 37813
E & W 4th North 37814
E & W 4th South 37813
E & W 5th North 37814
E & W 6th North 37814
W 7th North St 37814
W 8th North St 37814
W 9th North St 37814
W 10th North St 37814
W 11th North St 37814
E & W 13th North 37814

MOUNT JULIET TN

General Delivery 37122

POST OFFICE BOXES MAIN OFFICE STATIONS AND BRANCHES

Box No.s
All PO Boxes 37121

NAMED STREETS

Abernathy Pt & Way 37122
Abston Ct 37122
Acadia Ln 37122
Acorn Way 37122
Adams Ln 37122
Adelaide Ct 37122
Adeles Gdns 37122
Adelmont Ct 37122
Affirmed Dr 37122
Aidan Ln 37122
Aldi Blvd 37122
Alex Ct & Way 37122

Alexis Ct & St 37122
Alice Springs Ct 37122
Allison Ct & Way 37122
Alsdale Rd 37122
Alvin Sperry Pass & Rd 37122
Amber Dr 37122
Amy Ct 37122
Andrew Ct 37122
Antebellum Ln 37122
Anthony Way 37122
Anthony Branch Dr 37122
Arbor Springs Dr 37122
Archwood Vly 37122
Arden Ct 37122
Arrow Pt 37122
Asbury Pl 37122
Ashcroft Way 37122
Ashmore Ct 37122
Ashwood Dr 37122
Assault Ct 37122
Athens Dr 37122
Audrey Rd 37122
Augusta Dr & Ln 37122
Austins Way 37122
Autumn Ridge Dr 37122
Avalon Isle 37122
Aventura Dr 37122
Avery Park Ln 37122
Baker Pl 37122
Bar Dr 37122
Barnett Rd 37122
Barrett Dr 37122
N & S Bass Dr & Ln 37122
Bastion Cir S 37122
Battalion Way 37122
Battle Flag Ln 37122
Bayou Dr 37122
Beach Ln 37122
Beacon Hill Ct, Dr & Ln 37122
Beagle Run 37122
Beckwith Rd 37122
Bedford Bnd 37122
Belinda Pkwy 37122
Bellwood Dr 37122
Bench Ln 37122
Benders Ferry Rd 37122
Benton Harbor Blvd 37122
Benton Hill Dr 37122
Berkshire Blvd 37122
Beth Dr 37122
Betsy Ross Ct & Dr 37122
Bicycle Ln 37122
Billingsham Ct 37122
Biltmore Ct 37122
Blackbird Rd 37122
Bland Dr 37122
Blockade Ln 37122
Blossom Valley Ct 37122
Bluebird Ct 37122
Bob White Ct & Ln 37122
Bobbye Ct 37122
Bobwood Dr 37122
Boulder Creek Ct 37122
Boxcroft Cir & Ct 37122
Bradford Park Rd 37122
Braid Dr 37122
Brandon Ct 37122
Breckenridge Dr 37122
Brenlan Ct 37122
Brenthaven Dr 37122
Bridge Mill Dr 37122
Brigadier St 37122
Brisbane Ct, Dr & Ln 37122
Brooks Xing 37122
Brookstone Blvd, Cir, Ct, Dr & Pl 37122
Brookvalley Cir, Ct & Pl 37122
Buckhead Trl 37122
Buffalo Trl 37122
Bugler Rd 37122
Burgess Rd 37122
Burgunda Ln 37122
Burnett Rd 37122

Burris Ct & Rd 37122
Burton Ct, Pl & Rd 37122
Burton Point Rd 37122
Cactus Trl 37122
Cahaba Ct 37122
Cairns Dr E & W 37122
Cajawa Dr 37122
E & W Caldwell St 37122
Calibre Ln 37122
Camden Cir & Ct 37122
Camelot Bay 37122
Cami Ct 37122
Camille Victoria Ct 37122
Campbell Dr & Rd 37122
Canberra Way 37122
Candlelit Cv 37122
Cannon Ln 37122
Canter Ct 37122
Canterbury Cir & Trl 37122
Cape York Ct 37122
Cardiff Ln 37122
Cardinal Ln 37122
Carole Ln 37122
Caroline Ct 37122
Carphilly Ct 37122
Carriage Trl 37122
Carrick Ct 37122
Carter Ln 37122
Carver Ln 37122
Cascabel Pl 37122
Castleman Rd 37122
Castlewood Dr 37122
Catalpa Ct & Dr 37122
Cedar Creek Dr 37122
Cedar Creek Village Rd 37122
Cedar Grove Church Rd 37122
Cedar Tree Ln 37122
Cedarbend Ct & Dr 37122
Cedardale Ct & Rd 37122
Cedarhill Ct 37122
Cedarwood Ct 37122
Celeste Ct 37122
Central Pike 37122
Chadwick Ct 37122
Chamblee Ct 37122
E & W Chandler Ct, Rd & Way 37122
Charleston Way 37122
Charlie Daniels Pkwy 37122
Chateau Ct 37122
Chesapeake Way 37122
Chris Ln 37122
Christina Dr 37122
Christine Ct 37122
Cindi Ct 37122
Citadel Dr 37122
Citation Ct, Dr & Way 37122
Clark Ct & Dr 37122
NW Clearview Dr 37122
Clearwater Ct 37122
Clemmons Rd 37122
Clifford Ct 37122
Clinton Pl 37122
Clovercroft Trl 37122
Clyde Cir 37122
Cobblestone Lndg & Way 37122
Colony Ct E & W 37122
Commodore Pl 37122
Concord Ter 37122
Connelly Ct 37122
SW Cook Rd 37122
Cooks Ln & Rd 37122
Cooks Hill Ct & Rd 37122
Cooks Road Ext 37122
Copperfield Ct 37122
Cora Ct 37122
Corinth Rd 37122
Cornerstone Ct 37122
Cottonwood Crk & Dr 37122
Couchville Pike 37122
Count Fleet Ct 37122
Country Haven Ct & Trl 37122

Creek Pt 37122
Creek Landing Cir 37122
Creekbend Cir 37122
Creekfront Dr 37122
Creekview Dr 37122
Creekwood Ct & Dr 37122
Creole Way 37122
Crestmark Dr 37122
Crestview Ct, Cv & Dr 37122
N & S Cromwell Ct 37122
Cross Dr 37122
Crossings Cir & Ln 37122
Crosswinds Dr 37122
Crystal Ct 37122
Curd Rd 37122
Cynthia Ct 37122
Cypress Ct 37122
Cypress Glen Dr 37122
Dahlgren Dr 37122
Dallas Dr 37122
Danbury Ln 37122
Dani Ct 37122
Darwin Way 37122
Davis Dr 37122
Davis Corner Rd 37122
Dawn Dr 37122
Deerfield Dr 37122
Deervale Ct 37122
Del Web Blvd 37122
Dell Dr 37122
Denny Dr 37122
Devan Kishan Way 37122
Dexters Run 37122
Dickens Dr 37122
Dinah Ct 37122
E & W Division St 37122
Dogwood Dr & Trl 37122
Dogwood Hills Ct & Dr 37122
Donna Kaye Ct 37122
Doral Pointe 37122
Douglas Robert Dr 37122
Due West Dr 37122
S Dunnwood Ct, Ln & Loop 37122
Eagle Trace Dr 37122
Eakes Dr 37122
Eakes Thompson Rd 37122
Earhart Rd 37122
Earl Pearce Cir 37122
Eastgate Blvd 37122
Eastwood Pl 37122
Edgewater Dr 37122
Elise Ct 37122
Elizabeth Dr 37122
English Woods 37122
Erin Ln 37122
Escalade Dr 37122
W Essex Ln 37122
Estate Dr 37122
Eugenia Ct 37122
Evan Ct 37122
Evergreen Pl 37122
Fair Meadow Ct & Trl 37122
Fairview Dr 37122
Fairview Knoll Dr 37122
Falcon Ct 37122
Farmstead Ln 37122
Faulkner Ln 37122
Fawns Creek Xing 37122
Fellowship Rd 37122
Ferrelli Cv 37122
Fescue Dr 37122
Fiberglass Dr 37122
Fieldcrest Dr 37122
Fieldstone Ct 37122
Forest Bend Ct & Dr 37122
Forrest Lawn Cir, Ct & Dr 37122
Foster Ln 37122
Foxglove Pl 37122
Foxhaven Ct 37122
Francis Cir 37122
Fredricksburg Rd 37122
Freemantle Ct 37122
Gailynn Marie Dr 37122
Gaines Park 37122
Gallant Fox Ct 37122
Gallop Dr 37122
Gambill Cove Tubbs Rd 37122
Garden Dr 37122
Gardendale Ct 37122
Garrett Way 37122
Gateway Cir 37122
Gay Winds Dr 37122
George Ct 37122
Georgian Way 37122
Gilley Rd 37122
Gina Ct 37122
Ginger Ct 37122
Glade Dr 37122
Gladeville Cir, Ct, Dr & Rd 37122
Gleaves Glen Dr 37122
Glen Ct 37122
Glen Oaks Dr 37122
Glen Trail Dr 37122
Glenwood Dr 37122
Gloucester Ln 37122
Gold Ct 37122
Golden Grv 37122
Golden Bear Gtwy 37122
Graceland Ct 37122
Green Forest Ct & Dr 37122
Green Valley Rd 37122
N & S Greenhill Rd 37122
Greenlawn Ct 37122
Greenstone Ln 37122
Greer Ct 37122
Grey Pl 37122
Greystone Rd 37122
Guardino Dr 37122
Guethlein Rd 37122
Guill Rd 37122
Guinevere Pt 37122
Gwin Pl 37122
Hampshire Ct 37122
Hannah Ct 37122
Harkreader Rd 37122
Harrisburg Ln 37122
Hartford Ln 37122
Hatcher Rd 37122
Hatfield Ln 37122
Hawthorne Vly 37122
Hayes Ln 37122
Heather Ct 37122
Henley Rd 37122
Heritage Dr & Pl 37122
Herschel Dr 37122
Hessey Pass & Rd 37122
Hickory Trce 37122
Hickory Ridge Rd 37122
Hickorydale Ct 37122
Hidden Cove Rd 37122
Hidden Creek Dr 37122
Hidden Harbour Dr 37122
Hidden Ridge Cir & Ct 37122
Highlands Ridge Dr 37122
Highpoint Ct 37122
E Hill Dr 37122
Hillbrook Dr 37122
Hilldale Dr 37122
Hillside Dr 37122
Hilltop Dr 37122
Hillview Dr 37122
Hillwood Ct & Dr 37122
Hobart Way 37122
Holly Hills Dr 37122
Hood Dr 37122
Hope Dr 37122
Horseshoe Ct & Cv 37122
Hunter Dr 37122
Hunters Pl 37122
Hunters Run Ln 37122
Hunting Hills Dr 37122
Idlewood Ct & Dr 37122
Inaugural Dr 37122
Independence St 37122
Industrial Dr 37122
Infantry Run 37122
Irene Dr 37122
Jackson Rd & Trl 37122
Jackson Hollow Rd 37122
James Matthew Ln 37122
Jamies Way 37122
Jarod Ct 37122
Jaywood Ln 37122
Jefferson Dr 37122
Jernigan Dr 37122
Jewel Pl 37122
Jim Joe Aly 37122
Jo Anne Pt 37122
John Hager Rd 37122
John Wright Rd 37122
Jones Ln 37122
Joseph Hayes Ct 37122
Joshua Dr 37122
Julie Dr 37122
Juliet Dr 37122
Juno Ct 37122
Kailey Hayes Ct 37122
Kalye Ct 37122
Karen Ct & Dr 37122
Kathryn Rd 37122
Kebu Rd 37122
Keeling Dr 37122
Keenan Ln 37122
Kelly June Dr 37122
Kelsey Glen Dr 37122
Kendall Cove Ln 37122
Killian Way 37122
Kimberly Ct & Dr 37122
Kimwood Dr 37122
King Arthurs Pl 37122
Kings Rd 37122
Kingston Cir & Ct 37122
Kirkland Cir 37122
Kirkwood Dr 37122
Krisen Ct 37122
Lacie Ct 37122
Lady Joslin Ct 37122
Lake Forest Dr 37122
Lake Haven Dr 37122
Lake Meadow Trl 37122
Lakeshore Rd 37122
Lakeside Ct 37122
Lakeside Meadows Cir & Dr 37122
W Lakeview Cir & Dr 37122
N Lamar Rd 37122
Lamar Hill Rd 37122
Lance Ct & Way 37122
Lancelot Dr 37122
Landings Way 37122
Lane Dr 37122
Largo Vista Pass 37122
Larkin Ct 37122
Larson Dr 37122
Laurel Hills Dr 37122
Lavonne Pl 37122
Lawnview Pt 37122
Laycrest Dr 37122
Leah Ct 37122
Lebanon Rd 37122
Leeville Rd 37122
Legacy Park Rd 37122
Lenora Ln 37122
Lenox Ct 37122
Leslie Way 37122
Lexie Ct & Ln 37122
Liberty Chapel Rd 37122
Line Dr 37122
Lineberry Blvd 37122
Loch Lorne Ct 37122
Logue Rd 37122
Lohman Rd 37122
Lone Oak Rd 37122
Longview Ct & Dr 37122
Lori Ln 37122
Lost Cove Ct 37122
Lovell Dr 37122
Lucy Dr 37122
Luvon Ct 37122
Lynnhaven Ct 37122
Maddox Rd 37122
Madeline Ct 37122
Magnolia Estates Blvd 37122
Main St 37122
Maple Ct, Ln & Way 37122
March Pl 37122
Market Pl 37122
Martha Leeville Rd 37122
Marvin Layne Rd 37122
Masters Way 37122
Mayfield Ln 37122
Mays Chapel Rd 37122
Mcintosh Dr 37122
Mckinnon Ct 37122
Meadow Ct, Gln, Park & Pt 37122
Meadowbrook Ct 37122
Meadowglen Cir 37122
E Meadows Dr 37122
Meadowview Ct, Dr & Ln 37122
Meb Ct 37122
Melbourne Ct & Ter E 37122
Michael Cir 37122
Michael Lee Dr 37122
Midgett Rd 37122
Midtown Loop & Trl 37122
Millpond Ct 37122
Millwood Ln 37122
Minette Ct 37122
Mires Rd 37122
Monthemer Cv 37122
Monticello Dr 37122
Moonlite Trl 37122
Moreland Dr 37122
Moreland Hills Dr 37122
Morningside Dr 37122
Morningview Dr 37122
Morriswood Dr 37122
Moss Dr 37122
Mossy Pt 37122
N Mount Juliet Rd
1-2490 37122
2491-2491 37121
2491-4299 37122
2492-4198 37122
S Mount Juliet Rd 37122
Mount Vernon Ct & Ln 37122
Mountview Dr 37122
Mundy Memorial Dr 37122
Muscogee Way 37122
Mystic Pt 37122
Mystic Streams Dr 37122
Naomi Dr 37122
Napoli Dr 37122
Nathan Ct 37122
Navy Cir 37122
Nero Ct 37122
Newberry Ct & Ln 37122
Nice Rd 37122
Nicholas Ct 37122
Nighthawk Ct & Ln 37122
Noel Dr 37122
Nonaville Rd 37122
Norfolk Ct 37122
Normandy Dr & Hts 37122
Northern Rd 37122
Norwood Ct 37122
Nottingham Cir 37122
Oak Ct 37122
Oak Branch Ln 37122
Oak Cove Ct 37122
Oak Knoll Cir 37122
Oak Meadow Ln 37122
Oak Point Ln & Ter 37122
Oak Valley Dr 37122
Oakforest Way 37122
Oakhall Ct, Dr, Ln & Trce 37122
Oakland Run 37122
Oaklawn Ct 37122
Oakmont Dr 37122
Oakridge Ct 37122
Oaksprings Pl 37122
Oakwood Ct & Ter 37122
Old Corinth Church Rd 37122
Old Lebanon Dirt Rd 37122
Old Mount Juliet Rd 37122
Old Pleasant Grove Rd 37122
Old Towne Dr 37122
Olivia Ct 37122
Omaha Ct 37122
Opus Industrial Blvd 37122
Orleans Ave 37122
Orlinger Ct & Pl 37122
Oslo Rd 37122
Overlook Dr 37122
Oxford Dr 37122
Paddock Ct & Pl 37122
Paddock Place Dr 37122
Page Cir, Dr & Pl 37122
Paixham Pl 37122
Palisade Dr 37122
Paradise Dr 37122
Parallel Pl 37122
Park Crest Ct 37122
Park Glen Dr 37122
Park Knoll Dr 37122
Parkwood Ct & Dr 37122
Parrish Cres, Hl, Pl, Pt & Way 37122
Parrish Woods 37122
Partridge Cir, Ct & Dr 37122
Pascal Dr 37122
Patriotic Way 37122
Patton Dr 37122
Paul Dr 37122
Pebble Pass & Pt 37122
Pebble Beach Cir & Cv 37122
Pebblebrook Dr 37122
Pebblestone Ct & Dr 37122
Pemberton Ct 37122
Pembrook Pt 37122
Perth Ct 37122
Pheasant Run Ct & Dr 37122
Pin Oak Pl 37122
Pine Crest Ct 37122
Pine Grove Rd 37122
Pinehurst Pt 37122
Pinewood Ct 37122
Plaza Dr 37122
Pleasant Grove Pl & Rd 37122
Pointview Cir 37122
Polecat Rd 37122
Polly Ann Dr 37122
Ponty Pool Dr 37122
Pope Rd 37122
Poplar Dr & Pl 37122
Port Andreas 37122
Port Kembla Dr 37122
Port Stewart Ct 37122
Port William Ct 37122
Posey Hill Rd 37122
Post Oak Pt 37122
Potomac Ct 37122
Pratston Ct 37122
Primrose Trl 37122
Privateer Ln 37122
Providence Pkwy & Trl 37122
Providence West Blvd 37122
Pruitt Ct 37122
Putnam Ln 37122
Quad Oak Dr 37122
Quarry Rd 37122
Quarry Loop Ext & Rd 37122
Queens Dr 37122
Queensland Way 37122
Rachel Ln 37122
Rankin Dr 37122
Raven Xing 37122
Reagan Ln & Rd 37122
Red Ink Dr 37122
Reed Ct 37122
Regent Ct 37122
Regent Park Dr 37122
Reserve Pl 37122
Ridgecrest Dr 37122
Ridgetop Dr 37122
Ridgeview Dr 37122
Ridgeview Preserve Dr 37122
Ridgewater Way 37122
River Dr 37122
River Branch Ct 37122
River Heights Dr 37122
Riverside Dr 37122
Riverview Rd 37122
Rockdale Fellowship Rd 37122
Rockytop Trl 37122
Rodney Way 37122
Rolling Creek Dr 37122
Rolling Meadow Ct & Dr 37122
Ronda Dr 37122
Rookwood Ct 37122
Rosewood Trl 37122
Rothman Blvd 37122
Royal Dr 37122
Royal Oaks Dr 37122
Rue Joey 37122
NW & S Rutland Dr & Rd 37122
Saddle Brk, Crst & Vw 37122
Saddle Creek Dr 37122
Saddle Horn 37122
Saddle Ridge Dr 37122
Saddle Wood Dr 37122
Salient Ln 37122
Samantha Ct 37122
Sanders Ln 37122
Sandy Dr 37122
Sanford Dr 37122
Santa Fe Trl 37122
Saundersville Rd 37122
Saundersville Ferry Rd 37122
Saw Ct 37122
Schooner Ln 37122
Scotland Trce 37122
Scout Dr 37122
Searcy Rd 37122
Second St 37122
Secretariat Dr 37122
Seven Springs Ct, Dr, Ter & Way 37122
Sewell Ct 37122
Shadow Ln 37122
Shadow Creek Cv 37122
Shady Hollow Dr 37122
Sheila Ann Ct & Dr 37122
Shelby Trce 37122
Shelley Dr 37122
Shelton Ct 37122
Shoreline Dr 37122
Short Dr & St 37122
Silver Oak Ct 37122
Silver Springs Dr & Ln 37122
Singing Springs Ct & Rd 37122
Sir Barton Ct 37122
Skyler Xing 37122
Sleepyhollow Way 37122
Somerset Pl & Trce 37122
Sondra Ct 37122
Sophia Ct 37122
Sports Rd 37122
Spring Hill Rd 37122
Spring Valley Dr 37122
SE Springdale Dr 37122
St Charles Pl 37122
Stacey Ct 37122
Stafford Dr 37122
Stanley Dr 37122
Starlite Trl 37122
Starr Dr 37122
Station Cir 37122
Sterling Ct 37122
Sterling Woods Dr 37122
Stewarts Ferry Pike 37122
Stirrup Ct 37122
Stockbridge Way 37122
Stone Hill Ct & Rd 37122
Stonebrook Cir 37122
Stonefield Ct & Dr 37122
Stonegate Dr 37122
Stonehenge Ct & Dr 37122
Stonehollow Way 37122
Stonehurst Ct 37122
Stonemeade Ct 37122
Stoner Creek Ct 37122
Stoneridge Ct 37122
Stonewall Ct & Dr 37122
Stoneway Ct 37122
Stoney Creek Rd 37122
Streamside Dr 37122
Sullivan Bend Rd 37122
Summer Lk & Pl 37122
Summit Pt & Way 37122
Sun Valley Rd 37122
Sunny Acre Ct & Dr 37122
Sunnymeade Dr 37122
Sunrise Cir & Ct 37122
Sunset Cir, Ct, Dr, Pt & Trl 37122
Sutler Pl 37122
Suzanne Ct 37122
Swallow Cv 37122
Sword Ln 37122
Sycamore Dr 37122
Sydney Ter 37122
Sylvan Park Ct 37122
Tall Oak Trl 37122
Tanglewood Dr 37122
Tanya Ct 37122
Tararack Ct 37122
Tasmania Ct 37122
Tate Ln 37122
Teddys Pl 37122
Terrace Ct 37122
Terrace Hill Rd 37122
Thelma Dr 37122
Thomas Lndg 37122
Thoreau Ct & Pl 37122
Thorntree Ct 37122
Thornwood Ct 37122
Thrush Ct & Dr 37122
Thurman Dr & St 37122
Tillman Dr 37122
Timber Trl 37122
Timber Cove Dr 37122
Timber Lake Dr 37122
Timber Oak Dr 37122
Timber Ridge Ct 37122
Timber Trail Dr 37122
Tinnell Rd 37122
Toby Ct & Trl 37122
Toliver Trce 37122
Toulouse St 37122
Traci Ct 37122
Trailridge Cir 37122
Tumbleweed Trl 37122
Turner Trce E & W 37122
Twilight Bay 37122
Tyrone Dr 37122
Underwood Rd 37122
Utah Ct 37122
Vail Run 37122
Valley Vw 37122
Valley Brook Dr 37122
Valley Forge Ct & Dr 37122
Valley Spring Dr 37122
Valleyview Dr 37122
Vanderbilt Rd 37122
Veneta View Dr 37122
Vickie Ct 37122
Victoria Pl 37122
Victory Rd 37122
Village Dr 37122
Virginia Hill Dr 37122
Vivrett Ln 37122
Walden Ct & Pl 37122
Wallaby Pl 37122
War Admiral Ct 37122
Warren Hill Dr 37122
Water View Ter 37122
Waterbrook Dr 37122
Watercress Ct 37122
N & S Waterford Ct 37122
Waters Edge Cir & Dr 37122
Watson Ct 37122
Wax Wing Ct 37122
Wayfield Ln 37122
Weakley Ln 37122
Weeping Elm Rd 37122

Wembly Ln 37122
Wentworth Ct 37122
Weston Ct & Dr 37122
Weybridge Dr 37122
Whirlaway Dr 37122
Whispering Breeze 37122
Whitnel Dr 37122
Will Ct 37122
Williamsburg Rd 37122
Willis Pass 37122
Willoughby Station Blvd 37122
Willow Brook Pass & Pt 37122
Willow Creek Dr 37122
Willowpond Ct 37122
Wilson Blvd & Dr 37122
Windgrove Ter 37122
Windhaven Bay 37122
Winding Way 37122
Windrush Rd 37122
Windsor Pl 37122
Windtree Ct, Pass & Trce 37122
Windward Dr 37122
Windy Rd 37122
Wintergreen Way 37122
Woodcrest Cir 37122
Woodland Ct 37122
Woodlawn Dr 37122
Woodlea Dr 37122
Woodridge Ct & Pl 37122
Woods Ct & Run 37122
Woodsong Pt 37122
Woodsway Ct 37122
Woodvale Dr 37122
Woodwind Pt 37122
Wrencrest Dr 37122
Wrenwood Way 37122
Wright Meadow Ct 37122
Wyndham Hill Ct 37122
Wynfair Ct 37122
Yachts Lndg 37122
York Rd 37122
Young Dr 37122
Yvonne Ct 37122

NUMBERED STREETS

All Street Addresses 37122

MURFREESBORO TN

General Delivery 37130

POST OFFICE BOXES MAIN OFFICE STATIONS AND BRANCHES

Box No.s
1 - 3393 37133
4007 - 4282 37129
5016 - 8196 37133
10001 - 20732 37129
330001 - 338806 37133

NAMED STREETS

Aaron Ct 37129
Abbie Rd 37128
Abby Ct 37129
Aberdeen Cir 37130
Abigail Ave 37129
Abrams Ct 37130
N & S Academy St 37130
Acorn Ave 37129
Adams Cir 37129
Adams Dr 37129
Adams Ln 37130
Adams Rd 37130
Adcock Rd 37128
Adonis Dr 37128
Adwell 37129
Agate Dr 37128
Agripark Dr 37128
Aire Ct 37128
Airport Ave 37130
Alamo Ave 37129
Albany Ct 37129
Alchemy Ct 37128
Alcove Ct 37128
Alexander Blvd 37130
Alexandria Dr 37129
Alford Rd 37129
Allegra Ct 37128
Allen Ave & Rd 37129
Allen Barrett Rd 37129
Allenby Trl 37128
Allgrin Ct 37128
Allison Pl 37127
Allston Dr 37128
Almar Knot Dr 37128
Almaville Rd 37128
Alpine Way 37129
Alsup Rd 37129
Alsup Mill Rd 37130
Altoga Ct 37129
Alydar Run 37127
Alysheba Run 37128
Amal Dr 37128
Amanda Way 37129
Amber Dr 37129
Amber Glen Ct & Dr 37128
Amberly St 37129
Amberwood Cir 37128
American Ave 37129
American Horse Trl 37127
Amerson Ct 37127
Amherst Dr 37128
Amsterdam Ct 37130
Anatole Ct 37130
Anchor St 37130
Andrea Brook Ct 37129
Andrew Ct 37129
Andrew Jackson Blvd 37129
Andy Peach Dr 37128
Angelyn Dr 37129
Anglo Ct 37129
Anita Ct 37130
Annadel Ct & St 37128
Annapolis Ct 37128
Annelle Rd 37127
Annex Ct 37127
Anniston Dr 37130
Antebellum Dr 37128
Anthem Way 37128
Antietam Ct & Ln 37130
Antler Dr 37130
Apache Trl 37129
Apache Moon Ter 37127
Apollo Dr 37130
Apostle Ln 37129
Apple Cross Ct 37127
Appletree Ct 37129
Applewood Ln 37127
Appomattox Ct & Dr 37130
Apricot Ln 37129
April Ln 37130
Arapaho Dr 37128
Arcadia Ct 37130
Archer Ave 37129
Aretha Ct & Dr 37128
Argyle Ave 37127
Aristocrate Dr 37128
Ark Ln 37128
Arkansas Ct 37129
Arkow Ln 37128
Armadale Dr 37128
Armor Pl 37128
Armory Dr 37129
Armstrong Valley Rd 37128
Arnette St 37130
Arnold Dr 37129
Arnold Ln 37127
Arrow Ct 37127
Arrowhead Ct 37127
Arrowhead Pl 37129
Art Ct 37130
Arthur Dr 37127
Asbury Ct, Ln & Rd 37127
Ascot Close 37130
Ash St 37130
Ashers Fork Dr 37128
Ashford Ct 37129
Ashington Ct 37128
Ashland Ct 37128
Ashlawn Dr 37129
Ashley Dr 37128
Aspen Ave 37130
Aster Ct 37128
Athens Ave 37128
Atlas St 37130
Auburn Ct 37128
Audubon Ln 37128
August Cir 37129
Aurora Cir 37127
Aurora Dr 37129
Autumn Ct 37129
Autumn Glen Dr 37129
Autumn Oakes Ct 37129
Autumn Wood Dr 37129
Auxbury Pl 37129
Avalon Pl 37128
Avellino Cir 37130
Avenal Ct 37129
Avenue Way 37129
Averwater Run 37128
Avington Ct & Way 37128
Avon Rd 37129
Axelwood Dr 37128
Azalea Ct 37128
Azeri Ave 37128
Aztec Dr 37128
Azure Way 37128
N & S Baird Ln 37130
Bairdscorner Ct & Dr 37130
Baker Rd 37129
Bakerview St 37129
Ballater Dr 37128
Balmoral Way 37130
Balson Dr 37128
Baltimore Rd 37128
Bancroft Ct 37129
Banks St 37129
Banner Dr 37129
Banyon Dr 37128
Barbara Ct 37129
Barclay Ct 37128
Barfield Rd 37128
Barfield Church Rd 37128
Barfield Crescent Rd 37128
Barfield Farm Rd 37128
Bark Pl 37130
Barker St 37130
Barnsley Dr 37128
Barnstable Ct 37127
Baron Ct 37129
Barretts Ridge Dr 37130
Barrow Ct 37130
Bartway Dr 37130
Barwood Dr 37128
Basil Ct 37128
Baskinbrook Ct 37130
Bass Ave & Rd 37129
Bastogne Way 37129
Batey Cir 37129
Battle Ave 37129
Battlefield Pkwy 37129
Battleground Dr 37129
Battleview Pl 37128
Baulcom Ct 37128
Baxter Rd 37130
Bayard Ave 37130
Bayberry Ct 37130
Baywood Ave 37129
Beaconcrest Cir 37128
Bear Branch Cv 37130
Bear Paw Ln 37130
Beasley Ct 37130
Beaufort St 37127
Beaulah Ct & Dr 37128
Beaumont Dr 37129
Beck Ct 37128
Bedford Ct 37129
Bedrock Dr 37130
Beechwood Cir 37128
Beesley Rd 37128
Belfast Ct 37129
Belfort Ct 37130
Belinda Dr 37130
Belize Ct 37127
Bell Rd 37129
E Bell St 37130
Bella Vida Pl 37129
N & S Bellah Ct 37127
Belle Chase Dr 37130
Belle Haven Dr 37128
Belle Oaks Dr 37130
Belle Rive Dr 37128
Bellwood Dr 37130
Belmont Ct 37129
Belvidere Ct 37127
Bendview Ct 37129
Benjamin Dr 37128
Benley St 37130
Bennett St 37129
Bennington Dr 37129
Benson Pl 37129
Berkeley St 37129
Berkshire Ln 37129
Berry Pl 37130
Berryfield Dr 37127
Berryhill Dr 37127
Berryside Dr 37128
Berwick Dr 37128
Beryl Dr 37128
Bethany Cir 37128
Betsy Ann Ave 37129
Betsy Ross Dr 37129
Betty Ford Rd 37130
Beverly Randolph Dr 37129
Big Eagle Trl 37127
Big Oak Dr 37129
Big Sandia Dr 37128
Bigbee Ct 37128
Bilbrey Dr 37128
N & S Bilbro Ave 37130
Bill Rice Ranch Rd 37128
Bill Smith Dr 37129
Billingham Dr 37128
Billy Blvd 37127
Billy St 37130
Biltmore Cir 37128
Bimelech Ln 37128
Binder Ln 37127
Binford Ct 37130
Bingham St 37129
Birch Dr 37129
Birchwood Cir 37128
Birdsong Ave 37129
Bishop Ave 37127
Bishop St 37129
Black Bear Trl 37127
Black Fox Ct & Xing 37127
Black Hawk Way 37127
Black Stallion Ct 37130
Blackberry Ln 37130
Blackfoot Trl 37128
Blackjack Way 37129
Blackman Rd
1800-2499 37128
2500-5399 37129
Blackpool Ct 37128
Blackwater Dr 37128
Blade Ct 37127
Blair St 37129
Blake Ct 37130
Blakely Dr 37128
Blanchard Ln 37128
Blansett Dr 37129
Blanton Dr 37129
Blantons Pt 37129
Blaze Dr 37128
Blooming Oak Pl 37130
Blossoms Ct 37129
Blue Fox Trl 37129
Bluebell Ave 37129
Bluecreek Cir 37129
Blueridge Dr 37129
Bluespruce Way 37128
Bluewing St 37130
Bluff Ave 37129
Bold Ruler Ct 37127
Bolden Dr 37127
Bonaventure Ct 37127
Bond Ct 37129
Bonwood Dr 37128
Boone Ct 37130
Bowers Ln 37129
Bowlin Rd 37130
Boxelder Way 37128
Boxwood Ln 37127
Boyd Dr 37129
Boyle Ct 37128
Bradberry Dr 37130
Bradford Pl 37130
Bradworth Dr 37130
Bradyville Pike
600-798 37130
800-2153 37130
2154-9399 37127
Braley Ct 37129
Bramble Trl 37129
Branch Pl 37130
Brandies Cir 37128
Brandywine Dr 37129
Brandywood Dr 37130
Bravo St 37129
Braxton Dr 37130
Braxton Bragg Dr 37129
Bray Ct 37128
Breckenridge Dr 37129
Breeze Dr 37129
Breezing Ct 37128
Brentmeade Dr 37130
Brewster Ct 37130
Brian Ct 37130
Briar Ct 37129
Briar Bend Dr 37128
Briarwood Dr 37130
Brick Way 37130
Brickle Ct & Dr 37128
Bridge Ave 37129
Bridget Dr 37129
Bridgeway St 37128
Bridle Ct & Dr 37129
Brigade Loop 37128
Brighton Dr 37130
Brink Bend Ct 37130
Brinkley Ave 37129
Brinkley Rd 37128
Brinxton Run 37128
Briston Ct 37127
Briton Ct 37130
Brittany Trce 37127
NW Broad St
100-699 37130
700-732 37129
734-5699 37129
SE Broad St
100-2099 37130
2100-2299 37127
Broadlands Dr 37130
Broadmor St 37129
Brockway Dr 37127
Broken Creek Ln 37129
Brook Highland 37128
Brookfield Dr 37130
Brookhill Dr 37128
Brooklet Ct 37128
Brookrun Rd 37129
Brookside Path 37128
Brookwood Ln 37129
Brown Dr 37130
Brownlee Cv 37129
Browns Chapel Rd 37129
Bruce Dr 37129
N & S Brunswick Ct 37127
Bryson Trl 37129
Buck Ln 37129
Buck Cherry Way 37128
E & W Buckeye Bottom Rd 37129
Buckeye Valley Rd 37129
Buckingham Dr 37129
Buckle St 37129
Buckskin Ct 37128
Buckthorne Way 37128
Bud Ct 37130
Buffalo River Ct 37129
Bumblebee Dr 37129
Bundy Ct 37129
Bunny Ct 37130
Burgess St 37128
Burleson Ln 37129
Burlington Ct 37128
Burns Ct 37130
Burns Pl 37127
Burnside Dr 37128
Burnt Knob Rd 37129
Burr Ct 37129
E & W Burton St 37130
Bushman Ct 37130
Bushnell Dr 37130
Business Campus Dr 37130
Butler Dr & St 37127
Butterfly Bnd 37129
Byrd Ave 37129
Byron Ave 37129
Cabot Ct 37129
Cain Ct 37130
Calabash Cir 37129
Calais Ct 37127
Calderwood Ct 37130
Caleb Ct 37129
E & W Calgary 37129
Calico Ct 37129
California Ct & Dr 37129
Callaway Ct 37127
Cally St 37128
Calumet Trce 37127
Calydon Ct 37128
Camborne Cir 37129
Cambridge Ct 37128
Cambridge Dr 37129
Camden Ct 37128
Cameron Ct 37130
Camilla Ln 37129
Camp Site Ct 37127
Campbell Ct 37130
Campfire Dr
200-299 37128
300-599 37129
Camptrail Rd 37128
Cancun Ln 37128
Candlewick Ct 37127
Candy Cane Ct 37129
Caney River Ct 37129
Cannock Ct 37129
S Cannon Ave 37129
Cannon Hill Dr 37129
Cannonsgate Ln 37128
Cannonwood Ct 37129
Canterbury Ct 37129
Canterbury Ln 37130
Canterbury Chase 37128
Canvasback Ct 37130
Cap Davis Ct 37129
Caraway Dr 37130
Carbon Copy Ct 37130
Cardinal Dr 37130
Caribou Trl 37129
Carl Adams Dr 37129
Carlow Ct 37127
Carly Ct 37128
Carlyle Ct 37130
Carmel Dr 37128
Carnegie Way 37130
Carnes Ct 37129
Carnton Ct 37130
Carol Dr 37128
Caroline Dr 37128
Carolyn Ct 37130
Carpet St 37130
Carriage Dr 37128
Carrick Dr 37128
Carver Ave 37130
Casbah Run 37128
Cascade Ct 37127
Cascade Falls Dr 37129
Cason Ct, Ln & Trl 37128
Cason Square Blvd 37128
Casper Ct 37128
Castle Ct 37129
E Castle St 37130
W Castle St 37129
Castleford Dr 37128
Castlegate Ct 37129
Castlemere Ct 37130
Castlerea Dr 37128
Castleton Dr 37128
Castleview Ct 37130
Castlewood Ct 37128
Castlewood Dr 37129
Catalina Ct 37128
Cataract Dr 37129
Catawba Way 37130
Catherine St 37129
Cathy Ct 37130
Cavalier Dr 37129
Cavalry Ct 37128
Cavendish Dr 37128
Cayuga Dr 37130
Cedar Rd 37127
N Cedar Grove Rd 37127
Cedar View Dr 37130
Celtic Ct 37129
Center Pointe Dr 37130
Centertree Dr 37128
Central Blvd 37130
Central Park Dr 37130
Central Valley Rd 37129
Chad Ct 37129
Chadwick Dr 37129
Chaffin Pl 37129
Chalice Dr 37127
Chamberlain Dr 37129
Chancel Ct 37129
Chanda Ln 37129
Chandler Ct 37129
Chandler Pl 37130
Chapel Brook Way 37129
Chapel Hills Dr 37129
Chariot Dr 37130
Charles Ct 37130
Charleston Blvd & Ct 37130
Charter Ct 37129
Chartwell Ct 37130
Chase Ln 37130
Chasteen Ct 37130
Chatham Ct 37129
Chato Ct 37127
Chaucer Dr 37129
Chelanie Cir 37129
Chelmsford Ct 37128
Cherokee Ct 37130
Cherry Ln
100-199 37130
200-1499 37129
Cherry Blossom Ln 37129
Chersidg Dr 37130
Chertsey Ct 37127
Chesapeake Cir & Trl 37129
Cheshire Pl 37129
Chester Ct 37128
Chesterfield Ct 37129
Chesterfield Dr 37127
E & W Chestnut St 37130
Chickamauga Dr 37128
Chickasaw Rd 37130
Chinoe Dr 37129
Chipara Dr 37128
Chippen Ct 37128
Chippendale Dr 37129
Chippewa Pl 37128
Chisholm Rd 37129
Choctaw Trce 37129
Choir Ct 37129
Chopin Ct N & S 37128
Christopher Ln 37127
Christy Ct 37130
N Church St 37130
S Church St
100-824 37130
825-2399 37130
825-825 37133
826-2398 37130
2400-3199 37127

Churchill Farms Dr 37127
Cicada Cir 37129
Cider Dr 37129
Cimarron Trl 37129
Cinch Ct 37128
Citation Ln 37129
City View Dr 37130
Claire Ct 37129
Clairmont Dr 37129
Clarence Ct 37130
E Clark Blvd 37130
W Clark Blvd 37129
Claude Jones Rd 37129
Clay Ct 37128
Claymore Run 37130
Clays Mill Dr 37129
Clearview Ct 37129
N Clearview Dr 37129
W Clearview Dr 37128
Clearwater Ct 37129
Clemente Way 37129
Clifdon Ct 37128
Clifford Dr 37129
Cliffview Ct 37128
Cloister Dr 37128
Clover Ave 37130
Clovercroft Dr 37130
Cloverdale Way 37129
Cloverfield Ct 37130
Cloverhill Dr 37128
Clubridge Ct 37129
Clydeway Dr 37130
Cobalt Ct 37128
Cobble Ct 37129
Cobblefield Ave 37129
Cobia Dr 37128
Cochise Ct 37127
Coffee Ave 37129
Colchester Ct 37128
Coldstream Rd 37127
Coleman Rd 37127
Colfax Dr 37129
Colgate Ct 37128
E College St 37130
W College St
100-799 37130
800-2399 37129
College Heights St 37130
College View Dr 37130
Colonial Cir 37129
Columbia Ct 37129
Colyn Ave 37128
Comanche Way 37128
Comer Cir & Dr 37128
Comet Ct 37127
Commerce Park 37130
Commercial Ct 37129
Community Cir 37128
Compassion Ln 37128
E Compton Rd 37130
Concord Cir 37129
Concord Ct 37130
Confederate Rd 37128
Conference Center Blvd 37129
Conhocken Ct 37128
Conquer Dr 37128
Conquest Rd 37128
Contessa Dr 37128
Conway Ct 37130
Cooks Ave & Ct 37129
Cool Springs Dr 37127
Coolidge Ct 37128
Coontree Ct 37129
Cooper Dr 37129
Cooper Rd 37127
Copper Hollow Dr 37130
Copperas Ct 37128
Coral Dr 37127
Corinth Ct 37129
Cornelius Dr 37129
Cornell Pl 37129
Corner Ct & Dr 37129
Cornerstone Dr 37128
Cornwall Ct 37129
Corsica Ct 37130
Cortez Dr 37128
Cotswold Ln 37128
Cottingham Dr 37128
Cotton Ct 37129
Cotton Mill Dr 37129
Cottonfield Ln 37128
Cottonwood Dr 37128
Couch Rd 37127
Coulter Ct 37129
Council Bluff Pkwy 37127
Country Almond Way 37128
Country Park Ln 37128
Countryside Rd 37127
County Farm Rd 37127
Couples Ct 37128
Court Dr 37128
Courthouse 37130
Courtland St 37130
Covenant Blvd 37128
Coventry Ln 37128
Cozumel Ct 37128
Cpt Joe Fulghum Dr 37129
Crab Apple Ln 37127
Craig Ct 37130
Cranberry Dr 37129
Cranor Rd 37130
Crape Cir 37129
Craythorne Dr 37129
Crazy Horse 37127
Cree Ct 37129
Creek Oak Dr 37128
Creekhill Ave 37130
Creekmont Dr 37129
Creekpoint Ln 37129
Creekround Ct 37130
Creekside Dr 37128
Creekview Dr 37128
Creekwalk Dr 37130
Creekwood Ct 37128
Crenshaw Dr 37128
Crescent Ln & Rd 37128
Crescent Meadows Ct 37128
Crescent Ridge Rd 37128
Crest Ct 37129
Crestland Ave 37130
Crestmount Dr 37129
Crestwood Dr 37128
Crickett Ln 37129
Crimson Ct 37127
Crocus Ct 37128
Cromwell Dr 37128
Cross Dr 37129
Cross Creek Ct 37129
Cross Creek Dr 37127
Cross Meadow Dr 37130
Cross Valley Way 37129
Crossfield Dr 37127
Crosspark Dr 37129
Crossway Ave 37130
Crosswood Ct 37127
Crosswoods Dr 37129
Crown Ct 37129
Crown Hill Dr 37129
Crowne Pointe Dr 37130
Crusade Rd 37129
Crystal Ct 37129
Crystal Bear Trl 37128
Cumulus Ct 37127
Curve Ct 37129
Cushing Ave 37130
Cusick Ct 37128
Cutoff Rd 37129
Cynthia Ln 37127
Cypress Dr 37130
Cypress Gardens Dr 37130
D Ann Dr 37129
Dahlia Dr 37128
Daisy Ct 37128
Dakota Dr 37129
Dakota Way 37130
Dallas Ct 37130
Dalmally Dr 37128
Daly Dr 37128
Damascus Rd 37128
Damsel Ct 37129
Dancing Wolf 37128
Dandelion Dr 37129
Danoher Walk 37128
Dashiel St 37129
Davey Dr 37127
David Ave 37130
Davy Crockett Dr 37129
Dawson Pl 37129
Dayclear Dr 37129
Debonair Ln 37128
Debra Dr 37129
Deer Run Rd 37128
Deerfield Dr 37129
Deerrun Rd 37129
Deerskin Ct 37128
Deerview Dr 37128
Deerwood Ave 37130
Dejarnette Ln 37130
Delano Ct 37130
Delbridge Rd 37127
Delmar Ave 37130
Derby Ct 37130
Destiny Dr 37130
Dewsbury Dr 37128
Diamond Ct 37127
Diana St 37130
Diane St 37129
Diawa Ct 37128
Dibrell Ct 37130
Dickens Ct 37129
Dill Ln 37130
Dilton Way 37127
Dilton Mankin Rd 37127
Dimaggio Way 37129
Dinky Ln 37129
Division St 37130
Dixie Ln 37129
Dixon Ct 37128
Dodd Trl 37128
Doe Dr 37129
Dogwood Dr 37129
Dominic Cir 37130
Dominion Dr 37129
Donald Bradley Ct 37130
Donard Ct 37128
Doncaster Ct 37130
Donnell St 37130
Dora Elizabeth Ct 37129
Dorian Blvd 37130
Dorothy Dr 37127
Dorset St 37130
Dosie St 37129
Dothan Dr 37128
Double Springs Rd 37127
Doug Taylor Rd 37130
Douglas Ave 37129
Dove Ln 37128
Dover St 37130
Dow St 37130
Downing Ct 37129
Dragonfly Ln 37130
Drake Rd 37130
Drayton Dr 37130
Dreamwood Ct 37129
Drema Ct 37127
Drexel Ct 37128
Drucker Ln 37128
Drum Ct 37129
Dublin Ct 37128
Duchess Cir 37129
Dudley St 37130
Duffield Dr 37129
Dugan Ct 37130
Duke Ct 37129
Dumas Ct 37127
Duncan Ct 37129
Dunlop Dr 37129
Dunmire Dr 37129
Dunraven Dr 37128
Dunroe Ct 37128
Durham Ct 37128
Dusan Blvd 37129
Dutton Ct 37130
Dynasty Dr 37128
Eagle St 37130
Eaglecliff Ct 37128
Earl Ct 37130
East St 37130
Eastland Ave 37130
Eastridge Dr 37130
Eastview Dr 37128
Eastwoods Dr 37130
Eaton St 37130
Ebb Ct 37128
Eclipse Dr 37129
Ed Todd Ct 37128
Edgewater Fls 37129
Edgewood Ct 37130
Edinburgh Ln 37130
Edmondson Ct 37129
Edward Ct 37129
Effie Seward Dr 37129
Eiffel Ct 37128
Elaina Ln 37128
Elam Rd 37127
Elam Farms Pkwy 37127
Elderberry Way 37128
Elijah Dr 37129
Elizabeth Dr 37128
Elk River Dr 37129
Elliott Dr 37129
Ellis Pl 37129
Ellis Rd 37130
Elliston Pl 37129
Elm St 37130
Elmhurst Dr 37129
Elmwood Dr 37128
Elora Ct 37127
Elrod St 37130
Els Ct 37128
Elton Ct 37130
Embassy Dr 37128
Emerald Dr 37130
Emery Ct & Rd 37130
Emma Ct 37128
Empire Blvd 37130
Empire Maker Way 37128
Empress Dr 37130
Enfield Dr 37128
English Hill Dr 37130
Ennismore Ct 37128
Epps Wood Ct N & S 37129
Esquire Ct & Dr 37130
Essex Ct 37130
Estes Run 37130
Estes St 37129
Esther Ln 37129
Estill Ct 37127
Evanback Ct 37130
Evans St 37129
Eventide Dr 37130
Evergreen Dr 37128
Evergreen St 37130
Everton Dr 37128
Evreux Dr 37129
Ewing Blvd 37130
Exeter Dr 37130
Factors Walk 37128
Factory Rd 37130
Fair Oak Ct 37130
Fairfax Ave 37130
Fairhaven Ln 37128
Fairmont Dr 37129
Fairview Ave 37130
Faithway Dr 37128
Falcon Dr 37130
Faldo Dr 37128
Fall Pkwy 37129
Fall Creek Dr & Pass 37129
Fall View Ct 37129
Fallacy Ct 37129
Fallen Acorn Ct 37129
Falling Branch Ct 37129
Falling Leaf Ct 37130
Falling Tree Ct 37130
Falsetto Ln 37128
Fann Rd 37128
Fantasia Ct 37129
Faran David Ct 37129
N & S Farm Ct 37128
Farmwood Dr 37128
Farrar St 37129
N & S Fawn Ct 37129
Fawnfield Cir 37129
Fawnwood Dr 37129
Faxon Ct 37128
Feather Ct 37130
February St 37129
Federal Ct 37129
Felicity Ct 37128
Fens Way 37129
Fenwick Close 37130
Feranins Dr 37129
Fern Dr 37130
Field Rd 37130
Fieldcrest Dr 37128
Fieldstone Dr 37127
Fieldview Dr 37128
Fire Oak Ct 37129
Firerock Dr 37128
First Pl 37129
Flag Ct 37127
Flat Rock Rd 37130
Fleming Farms Dr 37128
Fletz Cir 37129
Floraton Rd 37127
Florence Rd 37129
Flower Park Dr 37130
Flowers Ct 37130
Floyd Ave 37127
Folcroft Dr 37130
Folger Ct 37130
Fontana Ct 37128
Foothills Ct & Dr 37129
Forest Glen Cir & Ct 37128
E Fork Dr 37129
Forrest Ln 37129
Forrest St 37130
Forrest Pointe Dr 37130
Forsman Ct 37128
Forsyth St 37127
Fortress Blvd 37128
Foundry Cir 37128
Four Season Dr 37129
Fowler St 37130
Fox Camp Ct 37127
Fox Creek Dr 37127
Fox Den Way 37130
Fox Hill Dr 37130
Fox Point Ct 37129
Fox Ridge Dr 37128
Fox Spring Ct 37127
Foxcroft Rd 37128
Foxdale Dr 37130
Foxfire Ct 37129
Foxmoor Ct 37129
Foxside Ln 37128
Foxview Ct 37129
Foxworth Ct 37127
Frank Robinson Dr 37130
Franklin Ln 37130
Franklin Rd 37128
Franklin Heights Dr 37128
Freedom Ave 37129
Freedom Ct 37129
Freedom Dr 37127
Fresca Ct 37129
Friendship Cir 37130
Frisco St 37130
N Front St 37130
S Front St
100-199 37130
300-499 37129
Fruition Ct 37128
Fulwood Ct 37130
Furman Dr 37129
Future Valley Dr 37130
Gaitherhill Dr 37130
Galahad Dr 37127
Galaxy Ct 37129
Galloway Ct 37130
Galston Ct 37128
Garcia Blvd 37128
Garden Ct 37129
Garden City Dr 37127
Gardendale Dr 37130
Gardenia Way 37130
Gardenwood Ct 37129
Gardner Dr 37130
Garrison Cv 37130
Garrison Dr 37129
Gary Ct 37128
Gary Bowman Ct 37130
Gaston Ct 37128
Gateland Dr 37127
Gateway Blvd 37129
Gateway Ct 37127
Gateway Dr 37127
Gatewood Dr 37129
Gayle Ln 37130
Gaylord Ct 37130
Gazebo Park Dr 37129
Gehrig Ct 37129
General Ct 37129
General Bradley Ave 37129
General Cabot Ct 37129
General Eisenhower Dr 37129
General Kirk Dr 37129
General Marshall Ct 37129
General Mills Way 37127
General Patton Ave 37129
General Raines Dr 37129
General Westmoreland Ct 37129
Geneva Dr 37128
Genoa Dr 37128
Gentry Ter 37130
George Patterson Dr 37127
Georgetown Ct & Ln 37129
Ghee Rd 37127
Giacomo Dr 37128
Gilbert St 37129
Gill Ct 37129
Ginger Ct 37129
Givan Ct 37130
Glad Ct 37128
Gladys Ct 37128
Glasgow Dr 37130
Glastonbury Way 37129
Glaze Ct 37130
Glen Brook Dr 37128
Glenda Dr 37128
Glenhaven Dr 37130
Glenis Dr 37129
Glenridge Dr 37128
Glenside Ct 37128
Glenview Dr 37129
Glenwood Dr 37129
Gloria St 37129
Goddard Ct 37127
Gold Valley Dr 37130
Golden Bear Ct 37128
Golden Creek Ct 37129
Goldenrod Cir 37128
Golf Ln 37129
Golfield Ct 37127
Golfview Ct 37127
Gordon Ct 37129
Gordon Ter 37130
Graduate Ln 37130
Grail Ct 37128
Grand Ct 37129
Grandview Dr 37130
Grange Pl 37129
Granite Springs Way 37130
Granny Smith Dr 37127
Grantland Ave 37129
Grantown Dr 37128
Grass Creek Ct 37127
Grassland Dr 37129
Grassmere Ct 37129
Gravett St 37129
Graybar Ln 37129
Great Sun Ct 37127
Green Acres Ln 37129
Green Valley Rd 37130
Greenbrier Dr 37130
Greenfield Ct 37128
Greenhill St 37129
Greenland Dr 37130
Greenock Dr 37128
Greenview Dr 37128
Greenway Ct 37130
Greenway Dr
1600-1699 37129
7300-7699 37130
Greenwing Ct 37130
Greerson Ct & Dr 37130
Gresham Ln 37129
Greyrock Cir 37130
Grigg Ave 37129
Grimes Ct 37127
Grindstone Way 37129
Gritton Ct 37129
Grove Cir 37128
Grove Ct 37129
Grovewood Dr 37129
Guinevere Ct 37127
E & W Gum Rd 37127
Gum Puckett Rd 37127
Gunnerson Ave 37130
Guy James Rd 37130
Gweneth Cir 37128
Gwynn Ave 37130
Haddington Cir 37130
Hale Ave 37130
Haley Rd 37129
Halifax Ct 37130
Hall St 37129
Halleys Dr 37127
Halligen Ct 37127
Hallmark Dr 37129
Halls Hill Pike 37130
Halverson Dr 37128
Hamberton Cir 37128
Hamblen Ct 37130
Hamilton Dr 37129
Hamlet Dr 37128
Hammock Dr 37128
Hampton Dr 37129
Hamstead Ln 37129
Hanby Dr 37130
S Hancock St 37130
Handley St 37127
Haney Ct 37128
Hannah Dr 37128
Hanover St 37130
Hanson Ct 37129
Harding Pl 37129
Hardwick St 37130
Hardwood Dr 37129
Harley Way 37129
Harmony Ct 37129
Harpering Ln 37128
Harpeth River Ct 37129
Harrell Ct 37130
Harris St 37130
Harrison Ave 37130
Harrison Rd 37128
Hartford Dr 37129
Hartlepool Dr 37128
Harvest Grove Blvd 37129
Harwell Ln 37128
Hastings St 37130
Haven Dr 37130
Haverford Ct 37128
Havering Dr 37128
Haviland Way 37128
Hawk Eye Ct 37128
Hawkins Ave 37130
Hawksbeard Ct 37128
Hawksridge Dr 37130
Hawthorn Pl 37130
Hayden Ct 37129
E & W Hayes St 37130
Haynes Dr 37129
Haynes Haven Ln 37129
Hazelwood Dr & St 37130
Headwater Ct 37128
Heartland Ln 37127
Heather Ct & Pl 37128
Heatherwood Ct & Dr 37129
Heathrow Dr 37129
Hedgeapple Ln 37130
Helen Dr 37128
E & W Hembree St 37130
Hemlock Dr 37128
Henderson Ln 37130
Henry Ln 37129

Henry Hall Dr 37129
Hensfield Dr 37128
Herald Ln 37130
Hereford Ct 37129
Heritage Park Dr &
Plz 37129
Heroes Ln 37129
Herring Xing 37130
Herron St 37130
Hibiscus Ct 37128
Hickerson Dr 37129
Hickman Ave 37129
Hickory Ct, Ln & Rdg 37129
Hickory Grove Rd 37129
Hickory Hills Dr 37128
Hidden Cove Ct 37128
Higdon Dr 37128
Higgins Ln 37130
High Meadow Dr 37129
Highfield Dr 37128
Highgate Rd 37129
N Highland Ave 37130
S Highland Ave 37130
Highland Ct 37129
Highland Ter 37130
Highland Oaks Dr 37130
Highland Park Dr 37129
Highpointe Ct 37129
Highship Rd 37130
Highway 99 37128
Hillard Dr 37129
Hillcrest Dr 37129
Hilldale Dr 37129
Hillingdon Dr 37127
Hillmont Dr 37129
Hillside Ct 37130
Hillview Dr 37127
Hillwood Blvd 37128
Hiwassee Ct 37127
Hixon Ct 37129
Hoch Ct 37128
Hodge Dr 37130
Hogan Dr 37128
Holbeach Dr 37130
Holden Ct 37128
Holderwood Dr 37128
Holgate Ct 37129
Holiday Dr 37129
Hollicom Dr 37129
Hollow Tree Way 37129
Holloway Cir 37127
Hollyhock Ct 37130
Hollyridge Ct 37130
Holsted Dr 37128
Holts Ct 37128
Homewood Dr 37127
Honeybee Dr 37129
Honeysuckle Ct 37129
Honeysuckle Breeze
Ln 37128
Honeywood Pl 37130
Honor Ct 37127
Hooper St 37129
Hope Way 37129
Hopewell Ct 37127
Horander Rd 37127
Hord Rd 37129
Horncastle Dr 37130
Hornsby Ln 37129
Horseshoe Bend Trl 37129
Houk Ct 37129
Houston Dr 37130
Howard Rd 37127
Howell Dr 37130
Huddleston Ave 37129
Hughes Rd 37127
Hunt St 37130
Huntington Dr 37130
Huntwood Dr 37129
Huntwood St 37130
Hutchinson Ln 37128
Hutchinson Rd 37130
Hyacinth Ct 37128
Hyle Ave 37128
Idlewood Dr
1600-1699 37129
3600-3799 37130
Imperial Ct 37129
Independence Way 37129
Indian Pl 37129
Indian Camp Ct 37129
Indian Creek Blvd 37128
Indian Park Dr 37128
Industrial Dr 37129
Inglewood Ct 37127
Innsbrooke Blvd 37128
Inverness Dr 37129
Iona Ct 37127
Irby Ln 37127
Iris Ave 37128
Iron Horse Ct 37128
Irongate Blvd 37129
Ironwood Ct 37129
Iroquois Ct 37127
Isaiah Dr 37130
Isis Ct 37128
Islington Dr 37128
Ithaca St 37130
Ivanhoe Ct 37127
Ivy Ct 37130
Ivy Glen Dr 37128
J D Todd Rd 37129
Jackie Ln 37129
Jackson Rd 37130
Jackson St 37130
Jackson Trl 37129
Jackson Alan Dr 37130
Jacobs Rd 37127
Jakes Ave 37130
Jakes Rd 37127
James Dr 37129
James B Ward Rd 37129
James Edmon Ct 37129
James Luscinski Dr 37129
Jamestown Dr 37129
Jamie Cir 37130
Jamison Pl 37129
Jamison Downs Dr 37129
Janell Trl 37128
Janice Dr 37128
January Ct & St 37129
Janzen Ct 37128
Jared Obrien Ct 37128
Jarvis Dr 37129
Jasmond Ct 37128
Jasper Rd 37127
Jasper Johnson Rd 37127
Jay Ct 37129
Jayhawk Ct 37128
E Jefferson Pike 37130
W Jefferson Pike 37129
Jefferson Valley Dr 37129
Jen Ct 37130
Jenkins Dr 37128
Jennifer Ct 37129
Jerickia Ct 37129
Jerico Rd 37130
Jernigan Ln 37129
Jerry Anderson Dr 37128
Jessica St 37130
Jester Ct 37129
Jeter Way 37129
Jetton Dr 37130
Jillson Ct 37129
Jim Cedar Dr 37128
Jim Houston Ct 37129
Joben Dr 37128
Joe B Jackson Pkwy 37127
Joe Bond Trl 37129
Joe Brown Rd 37129
John Bragg Hwy 37127
John Deere Dr 37128
John Lee Ln 37129
John Locke Ln 37129
John R Rice Blvd 37129
Johnny Ruth Ct 37127
Johnson Rd 37127
Johnson St 37130
Jon Paul Ct 37128
Jonah Dr 37129
Jonathan Way 37127
Jones Blvd 37129
Jones Dr 37129
Jones Ln 37127
Jonquil Ct 37128
Joplin Ct 37130
Jordan Ave 37130
Jose Way 37130
Joseph Ct & Ln 37128
Joshua Ct 37129
Josiah Ct 37128
Josie Ct 37130
Journey Dr 37130
Jubilee Ct 37128
Judson Close 37130
Juliet Ave 37130
Jumper Ct 37128
Juneberry Way 37128
Juniper Dr 37129
Jupiter Pl 37130
Justice Rd 37129
Kadyday Way 37128
Kanatak Ln 37128
Kansas Dr 37129
Kari Dr 37129
Karin Ln 37129
Karleigh Ct 37130
Katelyn Ct 37128
Kathleen Ct 37127
Katie Ct 37128
Katydid Xing 37129
Kay St 37130
Kaylee Cir 37128
Kedzie Dr 37130
Keegan Dr 37130
Keeneland Ct 37127
Keenland Dr 37127
Keenland Commercial
Blvd 37127
Keepsake Diamond Ln 37128
Kelly Close 37130
Kendell Ct 37129
Kenmare Ct 37127
Kennedy Dr 37129
Kenneth Ave 37129
Kensington Dr
1400-1699 37130
1700-1999 37127
Kensington Square Ct 37130
Kenslo Ave 37129
Kent Pl 37130
Kentucky Derby Ln 37127
Kerr Ave 37130
Kerry Ln 37128
Kerrybrook Dr 37129
Kevin Dr 37129
Keystone Ct & Dr 37129
Kicking Bear Ct 37127
Kildare Ct 37129
Kilkenny Ct 37130
Killarney Dr 37128
Kimberly Dr 37129
Kimbro Rd 37128
Kindred Cv 37129
King Tucks Rd 37129
Kingman Ave 37129
N & S Kings Ct &
Hwy 37129
Kings Point Dr 37130
Kings Ridge Dr 37129
Kingsgate Dr 37130
Kingston Ct 37127
Kingwood Dr 37129
E Kingwood Dr 37130
Kinnard Ct 37130
Kinsale Ave 37128
Kirkwood Ave 37130
Kirtley Ct 37130
Kite Ct 37128
Kittrell Halls Hill Rd 37130
Kitty Ct 37130
Knight Cir 37129
Knight Dr 37128
Knollwood Pl 37130
Knox St 37129
Kody Ct 37128
Kristen Dr 37128
Kristi Charline St 37128
Kubota Dr 37128
Kuchar Ct 37128
Kyle Ct 37129
Lakebrook Dr 37130
Lakehill Cir 37130
Lakes Edge Dr 37130
N Lakeshore Dr 37130
Lakeview St 37130
Lambeth Dr 37128
Lancaster Ct 37129
Lancaster Gate Pl 37128
Lancelot Ct & Dr 37127
Landfill Rd 37130
Landmark Ln 37128
Landview Dr 37128
Langston Ct 37128
Langtry Ct 37129
Lansdan Dr 37128
Laramie Ct 37128
Lark Ct 37129
Larkway Dr 37129
Larry Ct 37130
Lascassas Pike 37130
Lasseter Dr 37130
Laura Ct 37129
Laura Jeanne Blvd 37129
Laurel Ct
1500-1599 37130
3500-3599 37129
Laurel Ln 37127
Laurel Grove Ct 37129
Laurel Hill Ct 37129
Laurel Mountain Rd 37129
Lauren Ln 37130
Laurie Pl 37128
Lavender Trl 37127
Lawncrest Cv 37129
Lawndale Dr 37129
Lawrence Rd 37128
Lazarus Way 37128
Leaf Ave 37130
Leanna Rd 37129
Leanna Central Valley
Rd 37129
Leanna Swamp Rd 37129
Lear Ct 37129
Leatherwood Dr 37128
Lebanon Rd 37129
Leconte Ct 37128
Lee Ave 37129
Lee Ln 37127
Lee St 37130
Leeds Ct 37129
Legare Ct 37128
Lehigh Dr 37128
Lehman Trl 37128
Leland Ct E & W 37128
Lenox Cv 37130
Lentil Dr 37128
Leonard Hudson Rd 37129
Leslie Ln 37128
Lester Fleming Dr 37128
Lewis Cir 37129
Lews Ct 37128
Lexham Ct 37128
Lexington Ct 37129
Lexington Trce 37130
Lexmark Cir 37128
Libby St 37129
Liberty Ct
400-499 37127
2100-2299 37129
Liberty Dr 37129
Lila Ct & Dr 37128
Lilac Ct 37128
Lillard Rd 37130
Lilly Ln 37128
Limerick St 37129
Lincoya Dr 37127
Linden Ln 37128
Lindsey Ln 37129
Lisburn Dr 37128
Lismore Dr 37127
Little Adams Run 37129
Little Hope Rd 37129
Little Turtle Way 37127
Liza Jane Ct 37129
Loblolly Dr 37128
Locerbie Dr 37128
Lockwood Ct 37128
E Lokey Ave 37130
W Lokey Ave
100-399 37130
900-1199 37129
Lolita Dr 37130
Lomond Dr 37127
London Ave 37129
London View Dr 37128
Londonderry Dr 37129
Lone Eagle Dr 37128
Lone Oak Dr 37128
Lonestar Ct 37129
Long Meadow Dr 37129
Long Shadow Ct 37129
Longford Dr 37129
Longview Dr 37129
Look Rock Ct 37130
Lou Ct 37129
Louise St 37130
Louvre Ct 37128
Love Ct 37129
Lovelace Ln 37130
Lowe Rd 37127
Loxley Ln 37127
Loyd St 37129
Lucille Ln 37129
Lucky Cir & Ct 37130
Luge Ct 37129
Lunar Dr 37129
Lynch Dr 37130
Lynn St 37129
Lynnford Dr 37128
Lynnwood Cir 37130
Lytle Ct 37127
E Lytle St 37130
W Lytle St 37130
Lytle Creek Dr & Rd 37127
Mabry Dr 37127
Mac Duff Dr 37128
Macarthur Ave 37129
Maceddnia Dr 37130
Mack Ct 37130
Mackintosh Dr 37128
Maddie Ct 37130
Madison Ave 37130
Magnolia Ct & Dr 37128
Magnolia Grove Ct 37130
Mahogany Trl 37130
E Main St
100-2311 37130
2313-2315 37130
2317-2397 37127
2399-2999 37127
W Main St
200-499 37130
500-1200 37129
1202-1298 37129
Maitland Dr 37129
Majesty Dr 37129
Major Dr 37129
Mall Circle Dr 37129
Mallard Ct 37130
Malone Dr 37129
Malvern Dr 37129
Manchester Pike 37127
Mandella Way 37127
Manderlay Way 37130
Mandy Ln 37129
N & S Maney Ave 37130
Mankin Cir 37127
Mankin Mcknight Rd 37127
Mannon Ct 37127
Manor Dr 37130
Manor Farm Dr 37129
Manson Ct & Pike 37129
Mantes St 37129
Mantle Way 37129
Manus Rd 37127
Maple Ln 37129
Maple St 37129
N Maple St 37130
S Maple St 37130
Maple Valley Dr 37130
Mapleside Ln 37128
Maplewood Ct 37129
Marathon Dr 37129
Marauder Ct 37127
Marcus Cir 37130
Margaret Close 37130
Marian Ln 37130
Maricopa Dr 37128
Marietta Ave 37129
Marigold Dr 37130
Marilyn Ct 37129
Marion Davis Dr 37129
Mark Ln 37130
Mark Allen Ln 37129
Marlow Ave 37127
Mars St 37130
Mary Ave 37127
Mary Beth Ct 37130
Mary Lake Way 37128
Marylebone St 37129
Marymont Dr 37129
Marymont Springs
Blvd 37128
Maryweather Ln 37128
Mason Ct 37130
Masterpiece Ave 37130
Matheus Ct & Dr 37128
Mathis Ct 37129
Matterhorn Run 37130
Matthews Rd 37130
Mattingly Way 37129
Maxfli Dr 37129
Maximillion Cir 37128
Maxwell St 37130
May Ln 37130
Maya Dr 37128
Maybrook Ct 37128
Mayfair Ave 37130
Mayfield Dr 37128
Maylon Dr 37128
Maymont Dr 37130
Mcclaran Pl 37129
Mccord Cir 37129
E & W Mccoury Ln 37130
Mccreary Rd 37129
Mcdaniel Ct 37130
Mcfadden Ave 37129
Mcfarlin Rd 37130
Mckaig Rd 37127
Mckenzie Ct 37129
Mckinley Pl 37130
E Mcknight Dr 37130
W Mcknight Dr
100-199 37130
300-599 37129
Mcniel Dr 37128
Mcrae Ct 37129
Meadow Ct 37129
Meadow Ln
200-399 37128
3100-3399 37130
Meadow Lark Dr 37128
Meadowbrook Rd 37129
Meadowcrest Cv & Dr 37129
Meadowgreen Dr 37130
Meadowhill Dr 37130
Meadowland Dr 37127
Meadowridge Ct 37130
Meadowwood Dr 37128
Medford Campbell
Blvd 37127
Medical Center Pkwy 37129
Medora Ct 37130
Meigs Dr 37128
Melstone Ct 37127
Melvin Dr 37128
Memorial Blvd 37129
Merchants Walk 37128
Mercury Blvd
500-2300 37130
2301-2315 37127
2302-2398 37130
2317-2399 37130
Mercy Ct 37128
Meridia Dr 37129
Merlin Dr 37127
Merrywood Ct 37129
Mershon Dr 37128
Merton Dr 37128
Messick Ct 37130
Mi Tech Dr 37130
Michalean Dr 37128
Michelle St 37128
Middle Tennessee Blvd
100-899 37129
900-2999 37130
Middleborough Ct 37130
Middlebury Ct & Dr 37128
Middleton Ln 37130
Miles Dr 37129
Milky Way 37129
Mill St 37129
Millbrook Ct 37128
Millwood Ct & Dr 37127
Milwalkee Ct 37130
Mimosa Ct 37127
Minerva Dr 37130
Minor St 37130
Mirabella Way 37130
Miranda Dr 37129
Mission Ridge Dr 37130
Missionary Way 37129
Misty Ln 37129
Mitchell Dr 37129
Moccasin Trl 37129
Mockingbird Ln 37130
Mohawk Trl 37129
Mohican Ct 37127
Molloy Ln 37129
Molly Trl 37128
Mona Rd 37129
Monarch Dr 37129
Monet Ct 37129
Monroe St 37130
Monrovia Dr 37128
Montcalm Ln 37129
Montclair Ave 37129
Monte Hale Dr 37129
E & W Monterey Ct 37127
Monticello Ct 37129
Monty Ct 37127
Moonlite Ct 37128
Mooreland Ln 37128
Moray Ct 37130
Morgan Rd 37129
Morgan Taylor Dr 37129
Moriah St 37128
Morning Mist Ct &
Way 37128
Morris Dr 37130
Morris Close 37130
Morton Rd 37128
Mosaic Trl 37130
Mosey Ln 37127
Moss Trl 37128
Mount Ayre Way 37129
Mount Herman Rd 37127
Mount Tabor Rd 37127
Mountain Maple Ct 37128
E Mtcs Dr & Rd 37129
Muirwood Blvd 37128
Mulberry Grove Rd 37127
Mullberry Ct 37130
Mullins Ct 37129
Mural Ln 37127
Murfree Ave 37129
Murfreesboro St 37127
Myers Dr 37129
Myers Parsons Way 37127
Nahanee Ct 37130
Nancy Dr 37129
Nancy Seward Dr 37129
Nandina Ct 37129
Nashua Ct 37128
Natchez Trace Ct 37127
Nathan Ct 37130
National Dr 37128
Navajo Ct 37127
Naylor Ave 37130
Neilson Ct 37129
Nelson Ln 37129

Nesbitt Dr 37130
Nestledown Dr 37129
Netherland Dr 37130
Neutrino Dr 37129
New Eanes Dr 37128
New Holland Cir 37128
New Hope Baptist Cir 37130
New Nashville Hwy 37129
New Salem Hwy
300-1499 37129
1600-2799 37128
Newark Ct 37127
Newberry Dr 37130
Newcastle Dr 37129
Newport Ct 37129
Newton Ave 37129
Neyland Way 37129
Niagra Ct, Ln & Way 37129
Nick Price Dr 37129
Nickajack Trl 37127
Nickens Rd 37129
Nicklaus Way 37128
Nightwalk Ct 37130
Nimbus Ln 37127
Nimitz Ct 37129
Nina Marie Ave 37129
Ninebark Ct 37128
Noble Ct 37128
Norman Ave 37130
Norris Ln 37130
North Cv 37129
North Rd 37128
Northboro Ct 37129
Northbrook Ct 37130
E Northfield Blvd 37130
W Northfield Blvd 37129
Northwoods Cv & Dr 37130
Norton Ct 37127
Nottaway Ct 37129
Nugget Ct 37130
Nyu Pl 37128
O Green Cv 37129
Oak Dr 37128
E Oak St 37130
W Oak St 37130
Oak Crest Ct 37127
Oak Hill Dr 37130
Oak Knoll Ct 37127
Oak Point St 37130
Oak Tree Ct 37130
Oakhaven Dr 37129
Oakleaf Dr 37130
Oakleigh Cv & Dr 37129
Oakside Ct 37128
Oaktown Burrows Dr 37129
Oakview Dr 37130
Oakwood Cir 37128
Obrien Dr 37130
Ocala Rd 37128
Octavia St 37129
Odessa Ave 37128
Oggi Ct 37129
Ohio Ct 37127
Old Almaville Rd 37128
Old Castle Dr 37127
Old Fort Pkwy
200-2300 37129
2302-2350 37129
2352-2398 37128
2400-3099 37128
Old Glory Ct 37129
Old Gresham Ln 37129
Old Halls Hill Pike 37130
Old Lascassas Rd 37130
Old Lebanon Pike & Rd 37129
Old Lodge Ln 37129
Old Main Cir 37130
Old Murfreesboro Rd S 37129
Old Nashville Hwy 37129
Old Pitts Ln 37130
Old Salem Rd
500-1399 37129
3000-3199 37128
Old Shores Rd 37128
Old South Rd 37128
Old Stewart Creek Rd 37129
Oldham Dr 37130
Oleander Ln 37129
Olin Taylor St 37129
W Olive St 37130
Olivet Dr 37128
Olmstead Ct & Dr 37128
Olympia Pl 37130
Oneida Ct 37128
Orange Ct 37130
Orchard Park Dr 37128
Ordway St 37129
Ormond St 37130
Orwell St 37129
Osborne Ln 37130
Oscar Ct 37128
Ossabaw Dr 37128
Ottawa Pl 37129
Oval Hesson Ln 37128
Overall St 37129
Overcast Ct 37129
Overhill Ct 37130
Overlook Pl 37130
Owasa Trl 37130
Oxford Dr 37129
Oxford Hall Ave 37128
Oxmoor Valley Ct 37130
Ozark Ct 37127
Pacific Pl 37128
Paddock Ct 37130
Paddock Dr 37128
Pagosa Ct 37130
Painted Pony Dr 37128
Palace Pl 37129
Palisade Dr 37129
Palm Ct 37130
Palmer Dr 37130
Palomar Dr 37129
Pantera Dr 37128
Paradigm Ct 37130
Paradise Dr 37127
Park Ave 37129
Park Cir 37130
W Park Dr 37129
Park Hill Rd 37129
Parklawn Dr 37130
Parkview Ter 37130
Parkwood Ct 37130
Parkwood Dr 37128
Parsons Ct 37129
Parsons St 37127
Paschal Dr 37128
Passage Dr 37130
Patcole Ct 37129
Patricia Cir 37128
Patriot Dr 37130
Patterson Ave 37129
Paul Norman Dr 37127
Paulownia Cir 37129
Pavilion Pl 37129
Pavillion Ct 37127
Pavin Ct 37128
Pawnee Trl 37128
Peace Pl 37130
Peachtree St 37129
Peacock Ave 37129
Pearcy St 37129
Pearlknob Ct 37130
Peartree Ct 37128
Pebble Brook Dr 37127
Pebblecreek Ln 37130
Pecan Ct 37130
Pecan Ridge Dr 37128
Peconic Pl 37130
Pellas Pl 37127
Pendarvis Ln 37130
Pender Ct 37129
Penn Ct 37128
Pennant Ct 37129
Pennington Dr 37127
Pennsauken Ct 37128
Penny Ln & Plz 37130
Pepperdine Dr 37128
Peralto Pl 37128
Perlino Dr 37128
Perlou Ln 37128
Persimmon Cir 37129
Peters Ct 37128
Pheasant Run Trl 37130
Philistia Ct 37127
Phillips Rd 37130
Phillips Faith Chapel Church Rd 37130
Piccadilly Dr 37128
Pillar Dr 37128
Pine Ct 37130
Pine Hill Ct 37129
Piney River Ct 37129
Pinnacle Hills Dr 37128
Pintail Ct 37130
Pippin Ct 37127
Pisa Cir 37129
E Pitts Ln 37130
Plantation Dr 37128
Planter Ct 37128
Player Dr 37128
Plum St 37129
Plymouth Ct 37127
Polk Dr 37129
Polo Ct 37129
Poplar Ave
700-899 37130
1000-1499 37129
Porter St 37127
Portree Ct 37128
Portside Ct 37128
Post Dr 37128
Potters Ct 37128
Potts Rd 37129
Powells Chapel Rd 37129
Power Ave 37129
Prairieview Dr 37127
Praise Ct 37129
Prater Ct 37128
Precept Dr 37129
Precious Ave 37128
Premier Dr 37128
Prescott Ct 37128
Presley Dr 37128
Prestige Ct 37128
Prestwick Dr 37130
Pretoria Run 37128
Primm Ln 37129
Prince Ln 37129
Prince Edward Ct 37130
Princess Cir & Ct 37129
Princeton Ln 37129
Princeton Oaks Ln 37129
Pritchett Dr 37129
Progress Ct 37130
Psalm Pl 37129
Public Dr 37127
Public Sq 37130
N Public Sq 37130
S Public Sq 37130
Puckett Rd 37128
Puckett Creek Xing 37128
Pulley Dr 37129
Quail Chase Cv 37129
Quaker Ct 37128
Quanah Parker Trl 37127
Quantum Ct 37128
Queens Ct 37129
Quest Ave 37130
Rabbit Rd 37129
Rachel Ct 37129
Rack Ct 37129
Racquet Club Dr 37128
Ragland Ave 37130
Ragland Ln 37128
Raider Dr 37130
Raleigh Ct 37130
Ramblewood Dr 37129
Rambush Dr 37128
Rampart Ln 37128
Ramsey Rd 37127
Ran Harris Ct 37129
N & S Ranch Rd 37129
Randolph St 37129
Ransom Ct & Dr 37130
Ravenel Ct 37130
Ravenwood Dr 37129
Reach Ln 37129
Reagan Dr 37129
Red Bank Ln 37128
Red Cloud Ct 37128
Red Feather Trl 37128
Red Fox Ct 37129
Red Jacket Trce 37127
Red Mile Rd 37127
Red Oak Ct & Trl 37130
Red Top Ct 37128
Red Willow Ct 37128
Redbud Dr 37128
Redfield Dr 37129
Redland Ct 37128
Redmont Dr 37128
Redmoon Run 37128
Redwood Dr 37127
Reed Downs Dr 37129
Reedwood Dr 37128
Reelfoot Ct 37129
Regal Ct & Dr 37129
Regency Ct 37129
Regency Park Dr 37129
Regenwood Dr 37129
Regina Ct 37128
Reid Aly & Ave 37130
Reidhurst Dr 37127
Remenham Ln 37129
Renaissance Ave 37129
Republic Ave 37129
Retreat Ct 37129
Rexland Pl 37129
Reynolds Dr 37129
Rice St 37129
Richard Rd 37129
Richardson Ave 37130
Richland Pl 37130
Richland Richardson Rd 37130
Richmond Ave 37130
Richpine Ct & Dr 37128
Ricky Ct 37127
Riddick Ct 37127
Rideout Ln 37128
Ridgebend Dr 37128
Ridgecrest Dr 37130
Ridgefield Dr 37129
Ridgely Rd
300-399 37130
500-598 37129
600-999 37129
Ridgepark Ct 37130
Ridgeview Ct 37129
Ridings Ct 37128
Rigsby Ave 37129
Riley Rd 37130
Rincon Ct 37127
Rindle Ct 37129
Ringwald Rd 37130
Ripken Ct 37129
Risen Star Dr 37128
Ritz Ln 37130
Riven Ct 37129
River Rd 37129
River Barfield Rd 37128
River Birch Farms Dr 37130
River Chase Dr 37128
River Downs Blvd 37128
River Oaks Dr 37129
River Road Rd 37129
River Rock Blvd, Ct & Xing 37128
River Terrace Dr 37129
Riverbend Dr 37129
Rivercrest Dr 37129
Riveredge Ct 37128
Riverside Dr 37129
Riverstone Dr 37128
Riverview Dr 37129
Riverwalk Blvd 37130
Riviera Dr 37130
Roanoke Dr 37129
Rob Cir 37129
Robert Haston Rd 37129
Robert Rose Dr 37129
Roberts Ct 37129
Roberts St 37130
Robinson Rd 37130
Robinwood Dr 37128
Rochester Dr 37130
Rock Haven Rd 37127
Rocking Horse Ln 37130
Rockingham Dr 37129
Rocky Ln 37130
Rocky River Ct 37129
Rocky Top Rd 37127
Roellen Rd 37130
Rogers St 37130
Rolling Creek Dr 37128
Rolling Oaks Ct 37129
Rome Ct 37127
Ronald Dr 37129
Roscommon Dr 37128
Rose Ave 37130
Rose Cir 37128
Rose Garden Ct 37127
Rosebank Dr 37129
Rosebud Ct 37129
Rosie Mae Ct 37127
Roslyn Ct 37128
Round Rock Dr 37128
Round Table Ct 37129
Roundtree Ave 37129
Rowland Rd 37128
Rowland Way 37129
Rowlette Cir 37127
Roxburghe Ct 37128
Roxbury Ct & Dr 37128
Roxie Ct 37128
Roy Arnold Rd 37130
Royal Dr 37129
Royal Garden Dr 37130
Royal Glen Blvd 37128
Royal Oak Ave 37129
Rt Johnson Dr 37129
Ruark Ln 37128
Ruby Dr 37129
Rucker Ln 37128
Rucker Rd 37127
Ruland Pl 37128
Running Wolf Ct 37128
Runnymeade Dr 37127
Rushmore Dr 37129
Rushwood Dr 37130
Russell Ct & Dr 37130
Ruston Ct 37128
Ruth Ave 37129
N, S & W Rutherford Blvd & St 37130
N Rutherland Blvd 37130
Rutledge Way 37129
E & W Rye Ct 37128
Saber Ct 37128
Sabin Ct 37128
Saddle Dr 37130
Saddlebrook Dr 37129
Saddlewood Ct 37128
Sadler Ct 37130
Sagewood Ct 37128
Saint Andrews Dr 37128
Saint Charles Pl 37129
Saint Clair St 37130
Saint Ives Ct & Dr 37128
Saint James St 37128
Saint Johns Dr 37129
Saint Patrick Ct 37128
Salem Cove Ln 37128
Salem Creek Blvd 37128
Salem Glen Xing 37128
Salem Park Ct 37129
Sallee Dr 37129
Sally Ann St 37129
Saltlick Pl 37129
Sam Houston Ave 37129
Sam Jared Dr 37130
Samantha Ct 37130
Samsonite Blvd 37129
Sanbym Dr 37130
Sanctuary Pl 37128
Sanders Ct 37129
Sandra Dr 37130
Sandstone Dr 37130
Sanford Dr 37130
Santana St 37129
Sapelo Way 37128
Sapphire Dr 37128
Sara Dilton Rd 37127
Sarah Ct 37129
Saratoga Ct & Dr 37130
Sassafras Dr 37128
Satinwood Dr 37129
Satterfield Ct 37128
Savannah Rdg 37127
Savely Ct 37129
Savoy Dr 37130
Sawmill St 37128
Sawyer Dr 37129
Saxony Ct 37129
Sayre Ln 37127
Scales St 37130
Scarlett Dr 37130
Scenic Dr 37129
Scepter Dr 37129
Schoolside St 37128
Schroer Dr 37128
Scotchase Ct 37130
Scott St 37129
Scottish Dr 37128
Scottland Dr 37130
Sculling St 37129
Seals Ave & Way 37129
Searcy St 37129
Seascape Ln 37128
Sedgeridge Ave 37129
Seminole St 37127
Sentry Ct 37130
Sequoya Trce 37127
Serena Ct 37129
Sergio Ave 37128
Serviceberry Dr 37128
Settlers Rd 37129
E & W Sevier St 37130
Sewanee Pl 37128
Seward Xing 37129
Shacklett Rd 37129
Shade Ct 37127
Shadeland Ct 37129
Shadow Ct 37129
Shady Ln 37130
Shady Forest Dr 37128
Shady Glen Cir 37128
Shady Grove Cv & Dr 37128
Shadywood Ln 37130
Shafer Dr 37128
Shagbark Trl 37130
Shallow Water Way 37127
Shaman Xing 37128
Shamrock Ct 37130
Shannon Dr 37129
Sharondale Dr 37129
Sharpsville Rd 37130
Shawnee Dr 37130
Shaylin Xing 37128
Shea St 37128
Shearron Ct 37130
Sheffield Dr 37128
Sheila Ct 37129
Shelby St 37127
Shelbyville Hwy 37127
Shelley St 37129
Shellsford Cir 37128
Shelly Plum Dr 37128
Sherborne Ct 37128
Sherrill Blvd 37130
Sherrington Rd 37128
Sherwood Ln 37129
Shield Ct 37129
Shinnecock Ct 37127
Shoreham St 37130
Shores Ct & Rd 37128
Short Pl 37129
Shoshone Pl 37129
Shoteka Dr 37128
Showtime Dr 37128
Shrewsbury Dr 37129
Siegel Rd 37129
Sierra Dr 37129
Silver Ct 37130
Silver Lakes Ct 37130
Silver Point Dr 37130
Silver Springs Ct 37128
Silverado Way 37130
Silverhill Dr 37129
Silverstone Dr 37130
Singer Rd 37129
Singer Sewing Co 37129
Sioux Pl 37129
Sirtim Ct 37128
Sitting Bull Xing 37128
Skipton Dr 37128
Sky Harbor Dr 37129
Skylark Dr 37129
Skyview Dr 37128
Slater Dr 37128
Slippery Rock Dr 37129
Sloan St 37130
Slover Ct 37128
Smith St 37129
Smith Hall Rd 37130
Smiths Xing 37129
Smitty Dr 37128
Smotherman Ct 37129
Snead Dr 37128
Snell Ct & Rd 37127
Snyder Ct 37129
Soaring Eagle Ct 37127
Solar Ct 37129
Soloman Ct 37130
Solona Ct 37128
Somerset Dr 37129
Sorrell Ct & Dr 37128
Southbend Dr 37128
Southern Pl 37129
Southgate Blvd 37128
Southpark Dr 37128
Southpointe Ct & Way 37130
Southridge Blvd 37128
Sovereign St 37128
Sparco Cir 37128
Spartacus Way 37129
Spartan Ct 37128
Spaulding Cir 37128
Spectrum Ct 37128
Spence Creek Ln 37128
Spencer Dr 37129
Spike Trl 37129
Spire St 37129
Splash Pl 37130
Splinter Ct 37130
Split Rail Rd 37128
Spoonbill Ct 37130
Spottswood Cir 37128
N & S Spring St 37130
Spring Cove Dr 37128
Spring Creek Dr 37129
Springhouse Dr 37128
Springleaf Ct 37130
Spruce Ct 37128
Spruce Haven Ct 37130
Spur St 37129
Squire Ct 37129
Staley Ct 37128
Staley St 37129
Standing Bear Way 37127
Stanford Ct 37130
Stanianc Dr 37128
Starbuck Ct 37130
Starhurst Dr 37128
Starnes Ct & Dr 37128
E State St 37130
Steaford Ct 37127
Steel Horse Ct 37128
Steelson Ct & Way 37128
Stepfields Cv 37130
Stephenson Dr 37127
Sterling St 37127
Sterlingshire Dr 37128
Stetson Ct 37128
Stevens Bnd 37127
Stewart Creek Rd 37129
Stewarts Bend Dr 37129
Stillwell Ct 37130
Stockton Dr 37128

Stockwell Dr 37128
Stokesly Dr 37128
Stone Mill Cir 37130
Stone River Ct 37129
Stonebrook Dr 37128
Stonehedge Dr 37128
Stones River Ln 37128
Stones River Mall Blvd 37129
Stones Throw Dr 37129
Stonetrace Dr 37128
Stonewall Blvd 37130
Stoney Meadow Dr 37128
Stormello Ln 37128
Stow Xing 37128
Stratford Rd 37129
Stratford Hall Cir 37130
Stratus Dr 37127
Strickland Dr 37127
Stroop Ln 37129
Stub St 37129
Sugar Maple Ct 37130
Sugarbush Ct 37127
Sugartree Dr 37129
Sulphur Springs Rd 37129
Summertime Dr 37129
Summit Ct 37130
Sun Cir 37130
Sun King Ct 37130
Sunday Silence Way 37128
Sunland Ct 37128
N & S Sunny Ridge Ct 37130
Sunnycrest Ct & Dr 37129
Sunnyside Ct & Dr 37129
Sunnyview Dr 37128
Sunray Dr 37127
Sunrise St 37130
Sunset Ave & Cir 37129
Surevue Dr 37127
Surrey Ct & Dr 37129
Susan Dr 37129
Sutton Pl 37129
Suzanne Dr 37128
Swamp Leanna Rd 37129
Swanholme Dr 37128
Swarthmore Ct 37128
Sweet Bay Ct 37128
Sweetbriar Ave 37128
Sweetspire Dr 37128
Swilly Ct 37128
Swindon Close 37130
Swiss Air Dr 37129
Sycamore Cir 37130
Sycamore Dr 37128
Sydney Pl 37130
Sykes Dr 37129
Tabasco Way 37128
Tabitha St 37129
Taborwood Trl 37127
Tahoma Trl 37128
Tamarac Dr 37128
Tambark Cir 37128
Tanglefoot Cv 37129
Tanglewood Ct & Trl 37130
Tanima Ct 37130
Tanya Ct 37130
Tara Ct & Trce 37128
Tartan Ct 37130
Tasha Ln 37128
Taunton Ct 37127
Taylor Pl 37129
Taylor Close 37130
Teakwood Ct 37130
Teal Ct 37128
Teaside Ln 37128
Tedder Blvd 37129
Telescope Trce 37127
Tellico Ave 37129
Telluride Ln 37129
Tellyman Ave 37130
Temple Ct 37130
Templeton Ln 37130
Ten Bears Way 37128
Tenby Dr 37127
Tennerton Ln 37129
N & S Tennessee Blvd 37130
Teresa Ln 37128
Terragreen Ct 37130
Terrapin Ct 37128
Tessa Ct 37128
Tetanka Ct 37128
Texas Way 37129
Thad Ct 37128
Thames Ct 37129
Thatcher Ct, Pl & Trce 37129
Thetahill Rd 37130
Thistle Bend Ct 37130
Thistle Rock Ct 37130
Thomas Ct 37127
N Thompson Ln 37129
W Thompson Ln 37129
Thompson Rd 37128
Thoroughbred Ln 37127
Throne St 37129
Thrush Pl 37130
Thunder Gulch Way 37128
Thurston Dr 37129
Ticonderoga Ave 37129
Tidesridge Ct & Cv 37128
Tiffany Ct 37128
Tiffin Ct 37128
Tiger Woods Way 37129
Timber Pl 37130
Timber Creek Dr 37128
Timberlake Dr 37129
Timberwoods Pl 37130
Tinnell Ct 37129
Tioga Ct 37129
Tiree Dr 37128
Titans Cir 37127
Titus Ln 37128
Todd Ct 37130
Toddington Dr 37130
Tomahawk Trce 37129
Tombee Ct 37128
Tommy Martin Dr 37130
Torre Ct 37129
Tortuga Ct 37127
Tour Dr 37130
Tourmaline Dr 37128
Towbridge Dr 37129
Tower Dr 37129
Tracy Cir 37130
Tradewinds Trl 37128
Trafalgar Ct 37128
Trailside Dr 37130
Trailstar Ct 37130
Tralee Ct 37128
Travis Ct 37130
Tremont Dr 37130
Trenton Ct 37130
Trevino Ct 37128
Trevor Trl 37128
Tricia Pl 37129
Trinity Dr 37129
Triple Crown Dr 37127
Trish St 37128
Trundle St 37130
Tuckahoe Ct 37129
Tudor Ct 37129
Tulane Ct 37128
Tulip Hill Dr 37127
Tullock Trl 37128
Tune Ave 37129
Turfland Ct & Dr 37127
Turnberry Ct 37130
Turner Ave 37127
Turnstone Ct 37128
Turquoise Ln 37129
Turret Way 37129
Turtle Trce 37127
Turtle Rock Ct 37129
Tweedle Ct 37130
Twelve Oaks Ln 37127
Twin Feather Dr 37129
Twin Oak Dr 37130
Twin View Dr 37128
Twisted Oak Dr 37129
Two Deer Trl 37129
Tybarber Ave 37129
Tybee Trl 37127
Tyler Ct 37130
Tyne Ave 37130
Ulster Ct 37129
Unbridled Dr 37128
United Dr 37128
N & S University St 37130
Upland Ct 37129
Upperglade Ct 37130
Uptown Sq 37129
Uriah Pl 37129
Urlacher Dr 37129
Usa Today Way 37129
Valley Bend Rd 37129
Valley Grove Dr 37128
Valleywood Cv 37129
Van Cleve Ln 37129
Vance Dr 37127
Vanessa Ct 37130
Vapor Trl 37127
Vassar Ct 37129
Vaughn Rd 37128
Vaughn St 37130
Veals Pl & Rd 37127
Velma Ln 37129
Velvet Ct 37128
Venada Trl 37128
Venetian Way 37129
Ventura Ct 37129
Venus Pl 37130
Veranda Cir & Pl 37130
Verde Ct 37128
Vermont Ct 37130
Verona Pl 37130
Vestry Ave 37129
Veterans Pkwy 37128
Victoria Dr 37129
Victory Gallop Ln 37128
Vicwood Dr 37128
Villa St 37129
Village Ct 37130
Village Green Cir 37128
Villanova Pl 37128
Vince Ct 37128
Vincion Rd 37130
E & W Vine St 37130
Vinemont Dr 37130
Vintage Ct 37130
Vintage Grove Pkwy 37130
Violet Ct 37128
Virginia Ave 37130
Visor Ct 37129
Vista Ct 37128
Volunteer Rd 37128
Wachovia Way 37129
Wade Rd 37130
Wade Springs Rd 37130
N Wagon Trl 37128
Wakonda Ct 37130
Waldorf Ct 37130
Waldron View Dr 37130
Wales Ct 37129
Walking Dr 37130
Wall St 37130
Walla Ct 37128
Wallace Ct & Dr 37129
Walnut Ln 37129
N Walnut St 37130
S Walnut St
100-199 37130
500-599 37129
Walt Rd 37129
Walter Hale Ct 37129
Walton Dr & Ln 37130
War Emblem Ln 37128
War Paint Ct 37127
Ward Dr 37129
Wargo Ct 37128
Warmingfield Dr 37127
Warren St 37129
Warrior Dr 37128
Washington Blvd 37129
Watauga Way 37129
Waterford Rd 37129
Waters Edge Ct 37130
Watson Ct 37128
Watsonwood Ct 37129
Watts Ln 37127
Wayne St 37129
Waywood Dr 37128
Wears Dr 37128
Webb Ln 37129
Webb Rd 37128
Webster St 37129
Wedgewood St 37129
Weeks Rd 37127
Welchance Rd 37127
Wellhurst Dr 37129
Wellington Dr 37129
Wellington Pl 37128
Wellspring Ct 37130
Wenlon Dr 37130
Wentworth Ct 37127
Wessex Dr 37129
West St
600-799 37130
8800-8899 37129
Westbrook Dr 37130
Westchester Ct 37129
Westerland Dr 37130
Westerwald Dr 37127
Westfield Dr 37129
Westgate Blvd 37128
Westhaven Dr 37128
Weston Blvd 37128
Westridge Dr 37128
Westside Ct 37130
Westview Dr 37128
Westwick Ct 37128
Westwood Dr 37130
Wexford Dr 37129
Weybridge Dr 37128
Wheatley Cv 37130
Whimsical Dr 37128
Whirlaway Dr 37127
White Blvd 37129
White Cloud Trl 37127
White Dove Ct 37128
White Oak Dr 37128
White Oak Ln 37130
Whiteamore Run 37128
Whitebud Ln 37128
Whitehall Rd 37130
Whitehaven Dr 37128
Whitewater Ln 37129
Whitson Ct 37129
Whitt Dr 37129
Whittle Ct 37128
Whitus Rd 37128
Whitworth Cv 37130
Wickham Ct 37129
Wicklow Dr 37128
Wigan Dr 37130
Wilbur St 37129
Wildflower Way 37129
Wildmaple Ct 37129
Wiles Ct 37130
Wilkinson Pike 37129
Will Drew Dr 37128
Williams Dr 37129
Williamson Ct 37128
Willow Cv 37128
Willow Dr 37127
Willow Cove Dr 37128
Willow Hill Cir 37127
Willowbend Dr 37128
Willowbrook Dr 37130
Wilmington Ct 37127
Wilson Ave 37130
Wilson Meadow Ct 37127
Wilson Overall Rd 37127
Wilton Ct 37129
Wiltshire Dr 37129
Wimbledon Rd 37127
Wind Copen Ct 37130
Windemere Dr 37128
Windover St 37129
Windsong Ct & Pl 37129
Windsor St 37130
Windsor Green Dr 37129
Windwalker Ct 37128
Windy Cove Dr 37130
Winesap Ct 37127
Winfield Ct 37129
Winfrey Dr 37130
Wingate St 37130
Winsford Ct 37130
Winslow Ct 37128
Winston Pl 37130
Winter Way 37129
Winter Wood Dr N & S 37129
Winterberry Dr 37130
Winthorne Ct & Ln 37129
Wiseman Pl 37130
Wismar Ct 37130
Wisp Ct 37128
Wolves Trl 37127
Wolves Den Pl 37128
Womack Ln
200-299 37130
301-1899 37130
3500-3599 37127
Wood Ridge St 37128
Wood Valley Dr 37130
Woodbridge Dr 37129
Woodbury Pike & St 37127
Woodcraft Dr 37127
Woodfin Ct 37130
Woodgreen Rd 37130
Woodhill Dr 37129
Woodland Dr 37130
Woodland St 37129
Woodline Cir 37128
Woodmont Dr 37129
Woodmore Dr 37130
Woodridge Trl 37130
Woodruff Ct 37128
Woods Ct 37130
Woods Edge Dr 37130
Woods Green Rd 37130
Woods View Dr 37130
Woodside Ct 37130
Worchester Ct 37129
Wrather Pl 37130
Wren St 37130
Wright Haven Ct 37130
Wycheck Ln 37127
Wyndham Cv 37129
Wynell Way 37129
Wynthrope Hall Dr 37129
Wythe Close 37130
Yeargan Rd 37128
Yearwood Ave 37130
York Ct 37129
Yorkshire Ct 37130
Yorktown Ct 37129
Youree Rd 37127
Yukon Ct 37129
Yuma Ct 37129
Zephyr Ct 37128
Ziffell Dr 37128
Zoe Ct 37129

NUMBERED STREETS

All Street Addresses 37130

NASHVILLE TN

General Delivery 37202

POST OFFICE BOXES MAIN OFFICE STATIONS AND BRANCHES

Box No.s
1 - 50 37202
6 - 6 37224
98 - 98 37222
101 - 593 37202
566 - 566 37222
650 - 650 37202
656 - 656 37222
664 - 664 37219
671 - 850 37202
888 - 888 37219
941 - 5226 37202
17001 - 17999 37217
20000 - 28100 37202
40001 - 42116 37204
50001 - 59652 37205
60001 - 68580 37206
70001 - 78820 37207
90001 - 92594 37209
100001 - 101642 37224
110001 - 112088 37222
120001 - 129020 37212
140000 - 149376 37214
150001 - 159360 37215
160001 - 160980 37216
171000 - 178230 37217
190001 - 198999 37219
210001 - 219009 37221
222222 - 222222 37222
280100 - 282512 37228
290001 - 293390 37229
305001 - 305309 37230
305200 - 305200 37229
305341 - 308025 37230
330001 - 333229 37203
333333 - 333333 37222
340001 - 340032 37203
440001 - 440585 37244
500000 - 500000 37230

NAMED STREETS

Abbay Dr 37211
Abbeywood Ct & Dr 37215
Abbott Ct & Dr 37211
Abbott Glenn Ct 37215
Abbott Martin Rd 37215
Abbottsford 37215
Aberdeen Rd 37205
Abernathy Rd 37218
Academy Pl & Sq 37210
Achievement Dr 37209
Ackerman Ct 37204
Acklen Ave
801-897 37203
899-1199 37203
1200-3399 37212
Acklen Park Dr
100-299 37203
400-599 37205
Acorn Dr 37210
Adair Rd 37214
Adallart Ave N 37219
Adams Park 37205
Adams St 37208
Adams Mill Ct 37211
N & S Adamwood Ct & Dr 37211
Adara Ln 37211
Addine St 37216
Adelicia St 37212
Adkisson Ln 37205
Adlai St 37207
Aimes Ct 37221
Ainlay Dr 37217
Air Freight Blvd 37217
Air Lane Dr 37210
Airpark Dr 37206
Airpark Center Dr E 37217
Airpark Commerce Dr 37217
Airport Center Dr 37214
Airport Service Rd
900-920 37214
922-998 37214
935-937 37227
939-999 37214
Airways Blvd 37217
Airways Cir 37214
Airwood Dr 37214
Alabama Ave 37209
Aladdin Dr 37217
Alameda St
2100-2799 37208
3100-4099 37209
Alamo Pl 37209
Alandee St 37214
Alarkern Dr 37217
Albar Dr 37221
Albert Ct & Dr 37204
Albion St
1800-2699 37208
2801-2997 37209
2999-4399 37209
Alcott Dr 37215
Alden Ct 37209
Alder Ct
300-399 37217
800-899 37220
Alder Dr 37220
Aldrich Ln 37207
Alexander Cir 37208
Alfred Dr 37205
Alhambra Cir 37207
Alice Ave 37211
Alice St 37218
Aline Ave 37207
Alison Ct 37217
Allen Pl 37205
Allen Rd 37214
Allendale Dr 37205
Allens Ln 37221
Allenwood Dr 37207
Allied Dr 37211
Allison Pl 37203
Alloway St 37203
Almond St 37201
Almonte Ct 37215
Alpine Ave & Ter 37218
Alpine Park Ave 37218
Altentann 37215
Alteras Cir & Dr 37211
Althorp Way 37211
Alto Vista Dr 37205
Alton Rd 37205
Alvinwood Dr 37214
Amalie Ct & Dr 37211
Amanda Ave 37215
Amber Ct 37221
Amber Hills Ln 37221
Amberwood Cir & Pl 37221
Ambrose Ave 37207
American Ct & Rd 37209
Ames Ct & Dr 37218
Amherst Ct 37214
Amherst Dr 37214
Amherst Way 37221
Amy Lynn Dr 37218
Anchorage Ct & Dr 37220
Anderson Pl 37216
Anderson Rd 37217
Andover Dr 37215
Andover Way 37221
Andrew Pl 37216
Andrew Rucker Ln 37211
Andrew T Whitmore St 37210
Andy St 37216
Angel Ct 37214
Anisha Pl 37207
Ann St 37216
Anna Ct 37207
Annandale 37215
Annesway Dr 37205
Annex Ave & Ct 37209
Anson Ln 37211
Anthes Dr 37210
Antioch Pike 37211
Antler Ridge Cir 37214
Anton Ct & Dr 37211
Apex St 37206
Apple Ct & Dr 37211
Apple Ridge Cir 37211
Apple Valley Cir 37207
Applecross Dr 37220
Appleton Dr 37210
Appleton Pl 37203
April Ln 37211
Aquatic Rd 37211
Ararat Ave 37210
Arbor Dr 37221

- Arbor Creek Blvd, Ln & Way ... 37217
- Arcade Aly ... 37219
- Archer St ... 37203
- Ardee Ave ... 37216
- Arden Dr ... 37211
- Ardenwood Ct ... 37215
- Ardsley Pl ... 37215
- Arena Ave ... 37203
- Argo Ln & Pl ... 37211
- Argyle Ave ... 37203
- Arkland Pl ... 37215
- Arlington Ave ... 37210
- Arlington Pl ... 37221
- Armistead Pl ... 37215
- Armory Dr ... 37204
- Armory Oaks Dr ... 37204
- Arrington St ... 37207
- Arrowhead Dr ... 37216
- Arrowood Dr
  - 400-499 ... 37211
  - 500-599 ... 37220
- Arthur Ave ... 37208
- Artic Ave ... 37207
- Artisan Ln ... 37204
- Arundel Ct ... 37215
- Asberry Ct & Dr ... 37221
- Ash St
  - 300-399 ... 37210
  - 500-598 ... 37203
  - 600-899 ... 37203
- Ash Briar Cir ... 37211
- Ash Grove Ct & Dr ... 37211
- Ash Valley Dr ... 37215
- Ashcroft Pl ... 37215
- Ashfield Ct ... 37211
- N & S Ashford Ct ... 37214
- E Ashland Dr ... 37215
- Ashland City Hwy ... 37218
- Ashlar Cir ... 37211
- Ashlawn Cir ... 37211
- Ashlawn Ct
  - 100-512 ... 37215
  - 600-699 ... 37211
- Ashlawn Dr ... 37211
- Ashlawn Pl ... 37211
- Ashley Ct & Dr ... 37211
- Ashley Park Dr ... 37205
- Ashmont Cir, Ct & Dr ... 37211
- Ashmore Dr ... 37211
- Ashton Ave ... 37218
- Ashwood Ave ... 37212
- Ashworth Cir ... 37211
- Aslan Ct ... 37221
- Aspen Dr ... 37208
- Aspenwood Ln ... 37221
- Aster Dr ... 37211
- Athens Way ... 37228
- Atkins Dr ... 37211
- Atlas Dr ... 37211
- Atrium Way ... 37214
- Atwell Dr ... 37207
- Atwood Dr ... 37220
- Aubrey Ct & Dr ... 37214
- Auburn Ln ... 37215
- Auction Way ... 37207
- Audubon Rd ... 37204
- Augusta Dr ... 37207
- Austin Ave ... 37210
- Austin Ln ... 37207
- Autumn Ct ... 37221
- Autumn Chase Dr ... 37214
- Autumn Leaves Ln ... 37221
- Autumn Ridge Dr ... 37207
- Autumnwood Ct & Dr ... 37221
- Avalon Dr
  - 1-99 ... 37207
  - 1900-2199 ... 37216
- Avenal Ave ... 37211
- Averitt Express Dr ... 37211
- Avery Park Dr ... 37211
- Aviemore Dr ... 37220
- Aviemore Close ... 37220
- Avoca Ave ... 37203
- Avondale Cir ... 37207
- N Avondale Cir ... 37207
- Avondale Dr ... 37206
- Avondale Park Blvd ... 37221
- Ayleworth Ln ... 37221
- Azalea Pl ... 37204
- Bagleyshop Dr ... 37209
- Bailey St ... 37206
- Bainbridge Dr ... 37211
- Baird Ct ... 37214
- Bakertown Rd ... 37211
- Balbade Dr ... 37215
- Baldwin Ct ... 37207
- Baldwin Arbor ... 37215
- Ballow Ln ... 37221
- Balmoral Dr ... 37220
- Balmy Ave ... 37209
- Banbury Dr ... 37207
- Bancroft Ct & Pl ... 37215
- Bandywood Dr ... 37215
- Baptist World Center Dr ... 37207
- Barbara Lynn Way ... 37207
- Barclay Dr ... 37206
- Barker Rd ... 37214
- Barksdale Harbor Dr ... 37214
- Barlin Ct & Dr ... 37221
- Barlow Dr ... 37211
- Barnes Cove Dr ... 37211
- Barnett Dr ... 37207
- Barrett Rd ... 37211
- Barrywood Dr
  - 300-499 ... 37211
  - 500-699 ... 37220
- Barton Ave ... 37212
- Barton Ln ... 37214
- Barton Vale Ct & Dr ... 37211
- Baskin Dr ... 37205
- Bass Ave ... 37211
- Bass St ... 37203
- Basswood Dr ... 37209
- Batavia St
  - 1900-2799 ... 37208
  - 2800-2998 ... 37209
  - 3000-3799 ... 37209
- Bate Ave ... 37204
- Batey Ct ... 37221
- Batey Dr ... 37204
- Battery Dr & Ln ... 37220
- Battlefield Dr
  - 817-925 ... 37204
  - 927-1099 ... 37204
  - 1200-1599 ... 37215
- Baugh Rd ... 37221
- Baxter Ave ... 37216
- Baxter Ln ... 37220
- Bay Cove Ct & Trl ... 37221
- Bayview Dr ... 37217
- Beacon Dr ... 37215
- Beacon Ln ... 37209
- Beals Ln ... 37218
- Bear Rd ... 37215
- Bear Trak ... 37221
- Beauregard Dr ... 37215
- Beautiful Valley Ct & Dr ... 37221
- Beddington Park ... 37215
- Bedford Ave ... 37215
- Bedfordshire Ct ... 37221
- Beech Ave
  - 2017A-2017C ... 37204
  - 1800-1999 ... 37203
  - 2000-2099 ... 37204
- Beech Bend Ct & Dr ... 37221
- Beech Brook Ct ... 37214
- Beech Grove Way ... 37211
- Beech Hollow Ct & Dr ... 37211
- Beech Ridge Rd ... 37221
- Beechmont Pl ... 37206
- Beechwood Ave ... 37212
- Beekman Dr ... 37215
- Bel Air Dr ... 37217
- Belair Way ... 37215
- Belcaro Cir ... 37215
- Belclaire Pl ... 37205
- Belcourt Ave ... 37212
- Belden Way ... 37221
- Belding Dr ... 37214
- Belgrave Park ... 37215
- Bell Rd
  - 100-499 ... 37217
  - 1400-1699 ... 37211
  - 2900-2999 ... 37217
  - 3100-3699 ... 37214
  - 3701-3799 ... 37214
- Bell Arbor Dr ... 37207
- Bell Grimes Ln ... 37207
- Bella Ct ... 37207
- Bellafonte Ct ... 37221
- Bellavista Blvd ... 37207
- Belle Chasse Ct & Dr ... 37221
- Belle Forest Cir ... 37221
- Belle Forrest Ave ... 37206
- Belle Glen Dr ... 37221
- Belle Lake Dr ... 37221
- Belle Meade Blvd ... 37205
- Belle Park Cir ... 37205
- Belle Pointe Ct & Dr ... 37221
- Belle Valley Dr ... 37209
- Bellebrook Cir ... 37205
- Bellefield Ave ... 37218
- Bellevue Dr S ... 37205
- Bellevue Dr W ... 37205
- Bellevue Rd ... 37221
- Bellevue Rd N ... 37221
- Bellevue Manor Dr ... 37221
- Bellingrath Dr ... 37211
- Bellmore Ave & Pl ... 37209
- Bellshire Ct & Dr ... 37207
- Bellshire Terrace Ct & Dr ... 37207
- Bellwood Ave ... 37205
- Belmont Blvd
  - 3901A-3901B ... 37215
  - 1900-3299 ... 37212
  - 3300-4299 ... 37215
- Belmont Cir E ... 37212
- Belmont Park Ct & Ter ... 37215
- Belton Dr ... 37205
- Belvidere Dr ... 37204
- Belwood St ... 37203
- Ben Allen Rd
  - 100-399 ... 37207
  - 500-599 ... 37216
  - 601-899 ... 37216
- Benay Rd ... 37214
- E & W Bend Dr ... 37209
- Bending River Dr ... 37221
- Benedict Ct ... 37214
- Benham Ave ... 37215
- Benita Dr ... 37211
- Benjamin St ... 37206
- Bennett Pl ... 37207
- Benson Rd ... 37214
- Benson St ... 37206
- Bent Tree Dr ... 37221
- Benton Ave ... 37204
- Benton Smith Rd ... 37215
- Berkshire Dr ... 37216
- Bermuda Dr ... 37214
- Bernard Ave & Cir ... 37212
- Berrien St ... 37210
- Berry Rd ... 37204
- Berry St ... 37207
- Berry Hill Dr ... 37204
- Berrywood Dr ... 37204
- Berrywood Rd ... 37216
- Berrywood Way ... 37207
- Bessie Ave ... 37207
- Beth Dr ... 37206
- Bethany Blvd & Ct ... 37221
- Bethwood Dr ... 37207
- Bevendean Dr ... 37211
- Bienville Dr ... 37211
- Big Oak Dr ... 37207
- Biggs Rd ... 37209
- Biloxi Ave ... 37204
- Biltmore Dr ... 37204
- Binkley Dr ... 37211
- Birch Bark Dr ... 37221
- Birch Glen Ct ... 37221
- Bircham Ct ... 37221
- Birkdale Pl ... 37221
- Bismark Dr ... 37210
- Black Cherry Ct ... 37215
- Blackberry Hl ... 37221
- Blackberry Rd ... 37215
- Blackburn Ave ... 37205
- Blackman Ct & Rd ... 37211
- Blackstone Pl ... 37210
- Blackwater Dr ... 37221
- Blackwood Dr ... 37214
- Blair Blvd ... 37212
- Blake Dr ... 37211
- Blakemore Ave ... 37212
- Blanchard Pl ... 37214
- Blank St ... 37208
- Blanton Ave ... 37210
- Blevins Dr ... 37204
- Blue Brick Dr ... 37214
- Blue Heron Rd ... 37221
- Blue Hills Ct & Dr ... 37214
- Blue Mist Ct ... 37217
- Blue Ridge Dr ... 37207
- Blue Springs Dr ... 37211
- Bluebell Ct ... 37218
- Blueberry Hill Rd ... 37218
- Bluefield Ave & Sq ... 37214
- Bluestem Ct ... 37221
- Bluewater Cir, Dr, Trce & Way ... 37217
- Blythe Ct E & W ... 37221
- Bna Dr ... 37217
- Boatner Dr ... 37207
- Boaz Ln ... 37211
- Bob White Ct & Dr ... 37218
- Bobby Ave ... 37216
- Bolster Ct ... 37211
- Bomar Blvd ... 37209
- Bon Air Cir ... 37209
- Bonaventure Pl ... 37205
- Bonerwood Ct & Dr ... 37211
- Bonner Ave ... 37215
- Bonnie Briar Ln ... 37212
- Bontemps Dr ... 37207
- Booker St
  - 2300-2799 ... 37208
  - 2900-2999 ... 37209
- Boone Trce ... 37221
- Bordeaux Pl ... 37207
- Borowood Dr ... 37217
- Boscobel St
  - 100-299 ... 37213
  - 600-1999 ... 37206
- Bosley Oaks ... 37205
- Bosley Springs Rd ... 37205
- Boulder Park Dr ... 37214
- Boundary Run ... 37221
- Bounty Dr ... 37210
- Bowling Ave
  - 602A-602B ... 37215
  - 100-500 ... 37205
  - 502-598 ... 37205
  - 600-800 ... 37215
  - 802-3498 ... 37215
- Bowlingate Ln ... 37215
- Bowring Park ... 37215
- Bowwood Dr ... 37217
- Boxcroft Pl ... 37205
- Boxmere Pl ... 37215
- Boxwood Dr ... 37211
- Boyce Ct ... 37218
- Boyd Dr ... 37218
- Bracken Trl ... 37214
- Bradfield Ct & Dr ... 37220
- Bradford Ave ... 37204
- Bradford Grn ... 37221
- Bradford Hills Ct, Cv, Dr & Pl ... 37211
- Bradongt Ave ... 37206
- Braebury Cir ... 37211
- Braidwood Dr ... 37214
- Bramblewood Dr
  - 300-499 ... 37211
  - 500-599 ... 37220
- Brancaster Ln ... 37211
- Branch Ct ... 37216
- Branch St
  - 1500-1599 ... 37206
  - 1600-2499 ... 37216
- Branch Creek Rd ... 37209
- Branch Oak Trl ... 37214
- Brandau Ave N ... 37203
- Bransford Ave ... 37204
- Branwood Dr ... 37214
- Brasher Ave ... 37206
- Brattlesboro Dr & Pl ... 37204
- Braxton Hill Ct ... 37204
- Bray Dr ... 37218
- Breckenridge ... 37215
- Breckston Ln ... 37221
- Brelinto Dr ... 37207
- Brendale Ct ... 37214
- Brenner Ct & Dr ... 37221
- Brent Glen Pl & Pt ... 37211
- Brentlawn Ct, Dr & Rd ... 37220
- Brentview Ct & Dr ... 37220
- Brentview Hills Ct & Dr ... 37220
- Brentwood Pl, Sq & Ter ... 37211
- Brentwood East Dr ... 37211
- Brentwood Highlands Dr ... 37211
- Brentwood Knoll Ct ... 37211
- Brentwood Oaks Dr ... 37211
- Bresslyn Ct & Rd ... 37205
- Brevard Ct ... 37211
- Brevity Ln ... 37220
- Brewbock Ct ... 37221
- Brewer Ct & Dr ... 37211
- Briarcliff Ct ... 37211
- Briarwick Dr ... 37218
- Briarwood Crst ... 37221
- Briarwood Dr ... 37211
- Brick Ct & Dr ... 37207
- Brick Church Pike ... 37207
- Brick Church Park Dr ... 37207
- Brickdale Ln ... 37207
- Brickmont Ct & Dr ... 37207
- Bridgedale Ct ... 37207
- Bridgepoint Dr ... 37207
- Bridgeport Dr ... 37221
- Bridgestone Park ... 37214
- Bridgeview Ln ... 37221
- Bridgewalk Pl ... 37209
- Bridgewater Ct & Dr ... 37221
- Bridgeway Cir & Dr ... 37211
- Bridle Dr ... 37221
- Bridleway Trl ... 37215
- Briggs Ave ... 37211
- Brighton Pl & Rd ... 37205
- Brighton Close ... 37205
- Brighton Village Dr ... 37211
- Brightwood Ave ... 37212
- Briksberry Ct ... 37221
- Briley Pkwy ... 37217
- Briley Park Blvd N & S ... 37207
- Brindley Dr ... 37220
- British Woods Dr ... 37217
- Britt Pl ... 37208
- Brittany Ct & Dr ... 37206
- Brixworth Ln ... 37205
- Broadmoor Dr
  - 100-299 ... 37207
  - 300-1099 ... 37216
- Broadview Dr ... 37217
- Broadway
  - 100-399 ... 37201
- Broadway
  - 400-900 ... 37203
  - 901-903 ... 37202
  - 902-2098 ... 37203
  - 905-2099 ... 37203
- Broadwell Dr ... 37220
- Brome Ct & Ln ... 37218
- Bronte Ave ... 37216
- Brook Glen Cv & Way ... 37221
- Brook Hollow Rd ... 37205
- Brookdale Dr ... 37207
- E & W Brookfield Ave & Dr ... 37205
- Brookhaven Dr ... 37204
- Brookhill Cir ... 37215
- Brooklyn Ave ... 37207
- Brookmeade Dr ... 37204
- Brookmont Ter ... 37205
- Brookridge Trl ... 37211
- Brooksboro Ter ... 37217
- Brookshire Dr ... 37211
- Brookside Court Anx ... 37209
- Brookvale Ter ... 37209
- Brookview Dr ... 37214
- Brookview Forest Ct, Dr & Pl ... 37211
- Brookway Dr ... 37207
- Brookwood Ln ... 37220
- Brookwood Pl ... 37205
- Brookwood Ter ... 37205
- Broomfield Dr ... 37216
- Brown St ... 37203
- Browndale Ct ... 37207
- Browning Rd ... 37211
- Brownlee Dr ... 37205
- Brownwood Dr ... 37214
- Brucewood Dr ... 37211
- Bruner Ct ... 37211
- Brunswick Dr ... 37207
- Brunswick Pl ... 37221
- Brush Hill Ct & Rd ... 37216
- Brushy Creek Ln ... 37211
- Bryce Cir, Ct, Cv & Rd ... 37211
- Buchanan Ct & St ... 37208
- Buchi Ct ... 37204
- Buck Run Dr ... 37214
- Buckland Abbey ... 37215
- Buckskin Ct ... 37221
- Buena Vista Ct & Pike ... 37218
- Buenaview Blvd & Ct ... 37218
- Buffalo Rd ... 37221
- Buford Pl ... 37204
- Bullock Ave ... 37207
- Bunkerhill Dr ... 37217
- Bunny Dr ... 37211
- Burbank Ave & St ... 37210
- Burch Ave ... 37203
- Burch St ... 37208
- Burchwood Ave ... 37216
- Burgandy Hill Ct, Rd & Trl ... 37211
- Burges Dr ... 37209
- Burgess Ave ... 37209
- Burleigh Ct ... 37221
- Burlington Ct & Pl ... 37215
- Burlwood Ct ... 37207
- Burns Ave ... 37203
- Burns St ... 37216
- Burrus St ... 37216
- Burton Ave ... 37215
- Burton Hills Blvd ... 37215
- Burton Valley Rd ... 37215
- Bush Rd ... 37217
- Bushnell St ... 37206
- Buthento Dr ... 37220
- Butler Cir & Rd ... 37217
- Buttercup Dr ... 37221
- Byrne Dr ... 37211
- Byron Ave ... 37205
- Byrum Ave ... 37203
- Cabana Cir, Ct & Dr ... 37214
- Cabin Hill Rd ... 37214
- Cabot Dr ... 37209
- Cabot Pl ... 37221
- Caden Dr ... 37210
- Cadillac Ave ... 37204
- Cahal Ave ... 37206
- Cain Harbor Dr ... 37214
- Caldwell Ave
  - 1000-1199 ... 37204
  - 1200-1499 ... 37212
- Caldwell Ct ... 37204
- Caldwell Ln ... 37204
- Caledonian Ct ... 37211
- Calhoun Ave ... 37210
- California Ave ... 37209
- Call Hill Pl & Rd ... 37211
- Calloway Ct ... 37221
- Callywood Ct ... 37217
- Calvert St ... 37216
- Calvin Ave ... 37206
- Cambridge Ave ... 37205
- Cambron Dr ... 37221
- Camden Dr ... 37211
- Camellia Pl ... 37216
- Camelot Dr ... 37221
- Cameo Dr ... 37211
- Camilla Caldwell Ln ... 37218
- Cammack Ct ... 37205
- Campa Cir ... 37211
- Campbell Cir, Dr & St ... 37206
- Campton Rd ... 37211
- Cana Cir ... 37205
- Canady Ave ... 37211
- Candlestick Dr ... 37211
- Candy Ln ... 37211
- Cane Ct ... 37217
- Canebrake Dr ... 37209
- Caningt Ave ... 37212
- Cannery Row ... 37203
- Cannon St ... 37210
- Canoe Ct ... 37221
- Canterbury Dr ... 37205
- Cantrell Ave
  - 200-299 ... 37205
  - 600-999 ... 37215
- Cantrell Sq ... 37215
- Canyon Ct ... 37221
- Capella Ct ... 37214
- Capers Ave ... 37212
- Capital Funds Ct ... 37217
- Capitol Blvd ... 37219
- Capitol Pt ... 37203
- Capitol View Dr ... 37207
- Capps Dr ... 37207
- Capri Ct & Dr ... 37209
- Carden Ave ... 37205
- Cardiff Dr ... 37211
- Cardinal Ave ... 37216
- Cargile Ln & Rd ... 37205
- Carillon Dr ... 37217
- Carl Pl ... 37209
- Carla Ct ... 37217
- Carlisle Ct N & S ... 37214
- Carloss Dr ... 37210
- Carlton Dr ... 37215
- Carlyle Pl ... 37211
- Carnahan Ct ... 37214
- Carnavon Pkwy ... 37205
- Carney Ave ... 37210
- Carolyn Ave ... 37216
- Carriage Dr ... 37221
- Carriage Hl ... 37205
- Carrington Ct & Pl ... 37218
- Carroll St ... 37210
- Carson St ... 37211
- Carson Trl ... 37218
- Carter Ave ... 37206
- Carter St
  - 301-399 ... 37210
  - 800-899 ... 37206
- Carters Glen Dr ... 37221
- Carterwood Ct & Dr ... 37207
- Cartwright St ... 37203
- Caruthers Ave ... 37204
- Carvell Dr ... 37203
- Casa Ct & Dr ... 37214
- Cass St ... 37208
- Castaway Ct ... 37217
- Castle Rising ... 37215
- Castlegate Cir & Dr ... 37217
- Castleman Ct & Dr ... 37215
- Castlewood Ct ... 37215
- Castlewood Dr ... 37214
- Catalina Dr ... 37217
- Catamaran Ct ... 37217
- Catamont Pass ... 37214
- Cates Pl ... 37217
- Cather Ct ... 37214
- Catherine Johnson Pkwy ... 37209
- Cathy Jo Cir, Ct & Dr ... 37211
- Catina Dr ... 37217
- Cato Rd ... 37218
- Cato Ridge Ct, Dr & Ln ... 37218

Cauley St 37210
Cavalier Ct & Rd 37221
Cave Rd 37210
Caylor Dr 37215
Cecil Ct S 37207
Cecilia Ave 37208
Cedar Cir 37218
Cedar Ct 37211
Cedar Cv 37209
Cedar Dr 37211
Cedar Ln 37212
Cedar Crest Dr 37209
Cedar Forest Ct & Dr 37221
Cedar Hill Rd 37211
Cedar Knob 37221
Cedar Ridge Rd 37214
Cedar Rock Dr 37211
Cedar Springs Dr 37217
Cedarcreek Cir, Ct, Dr, Pl & Trl 37211
Cedarmont Cir, Ct & Dr 37211
Cedarstone Way 37214
Cedarvalley Ct & Dr 37211
Cedarview Dr 37211
Cedarway Ln 37211
Cedarwood Dr 37216
Celebration Way 37211
Celina Dr 37207
Cement Plant Rd 37208
Centennial Blvd, Cir & Pl 37209
Centerpoint Ln 37209
Centerview Dr 37214
Central Ave
3512A-3512C 37205
500-599 37211
3500-3899 37205
Century Blvd 37214
Century St 37208
Century Oak Ct & Dr 37211
Cephas St 37208
Chaffin Dr 37221
Chaleang St 37213
Chalmers Dr 37215
Chalmette Ct 37215
Chamberlin St 37209
Chambers Dr 37211
Champions Ct & Dr 37211
Chancery Ln 37205
Chancery Ln S 37215
Channelkirk Ln 37215
Chapel Ave 37206
Chapman Dr 37206
Charles Ct 37218
Charles E Davis Blvd 37210
Charlesgate Ct & Pl 37215
Charleston Park 37205
Charleston Place Cir 37215
Charlie Pl 37207
Charlotte Ave
300-399 37201
400-400 37219
402-499 37219
900-2499 37203
2500-5499 37209
Charlotte Pike
6399A-6399B 37209
4600-7799 37209
7800-8299 37221
Charlotte Road Cir 37209
Chartwell Mnr 37215
Chase Ave 37206
E Chase Ct 37221
W Chase Ct 37221
Chase St 37216
Chaseview Ct & Rd 37221
Chateau Ln 37215
Chateau Glen Pl 37215
Chateau Valley Ct, Dr & Ln 37207
Chathum Ct 37215
Chatsworth Dr 37215
Chatsworth Pl 37205
Cheatham Pl 37208
Cheek Rd 37205
Cheekwood Ter 37205
Chelmsford Pl 37215
Chepstow Dr 37211
Cherbron Dr 37207
Cherokee Ave 37207
Cherokee Rd 37205
Cherokee Station Dr 37209
Cherry Ave 37203
Cherry Blossom Trl 37215
Cherry Blossum Ct 37215
Cherry Glen Cir 37215
Cherry Laurel Ct 37215
Cherry Plum Ct 37215
Cherrywood Dr 37211
Chesapeake Cir, Ct, Dr & Pl 37207
Cheshire Dr 37207
Chessington Ct & Dr 37221
Chester Ave 37206
Chesterfield Ave & Way 37212
Chestnut St
100-198 37210
200-399 37210
400-799 37203
Chestnut Hill Dr 37215
Cheswick Ct 37215
Chet Atkins Pl 37212
Chicamauga Ave 37206
Chickasaw Ave 37207
Chickering Cir, Ct, Ln, Mdws & Rd 37215
Chickering Park Dr 37215
Chickering Woods Dr 37215
Childrens Way 37212
Childress Xing 37218
Chilton St 37211
Chimney Hl 37221
Chipmunk Ln 37221
Chippewa Cir 37221
Chovanec Dr 37211
Chris St 37207
Christiansted Ln 37211
Christopher Pl 37205
Church St
2-98 37201
100-399 37201
400-699 37219
700-2111 37203
2113-2199 37203
Church Street Aly 37203
Churchill Ct 37205
Churchill Dr 37211
Churchwood Dr 37220
Cinnamon Pl 37211
Cisco St 37204
Citation Ct & Dr 37217
Citrus Dr 37211
Claiborne St 37210
Clairmont Pl 37215
Clairton Ct 37215
Clare Ave 37209
Clarendon Ave 37205
Claridge Dr 37214
Clarksville Pike
1800-2899 37208
2900-4799 37218
Claxton Ct 37221
Clay St 37208
Clayborne Ct 37215
Claymille Blvd, Ct & Pl 37207
Claypool St 37216
Claytie Cir & Ct 37221
Clayton Ave
800-1099 37204
1101-1199 37204
1200-1599 37212
Clearbrook Ct & Dr 37205
Clearlake Dr E & W 37217
Clearview Ave 37206
Clearview Dr 37205
Clearwater Ct & Dr 37217
Cleeces Ferry Rd
1000-1099 37209
4400-4999 37218
Cleghorn Ave 37215
Clematis Dr 37205
Clemmons St 37210
Clendenin Rd 37220
Cleveland Ave 37210
Cleveland St
317A-317B 37207
1-699 37207
801-899 37206
Cliff Dr 37218
Cliffdale Rd 37214
Clifton Ave
2000-2299 37203
2300-4199 37209
Clifton Ln
900-998 37204
1000-1199 37204
1200-1298 37215
1300-1599 37215
Clifton Pl 37215
Cline Ave 37206
Clinton St 37203
Clintondale Dr 37218
Clipper Ct 37211
Clofton Dr 37221
Cloister Dr 37205
Clonmel Rd 37220
Close Cir & Ln 37205
Cloudland Dr 37205
Clover St 37209
Cloverdale Ct & Rd 37214
Cloverland Dr 37211
Cloverleaf Dr 37216
Clovernook Dr 37210
Cloverwood Dr 37214
Club Dr 37215
Club Pkwy 37221
Clydelan Ct 37205
Coarsey Dr 37217
Coastal Ct E & W 37217
Cobble Ct, Cv, Pl & St 37211
Cobbler Ct 37221
Cochran Dr 37220
Cockrill St 37208
Cockrill Bend Blvd & Cir 37209
Cocoa Dr 37218
Cody Hill Ct, Cv, Pl & Rd 37211
Coffee St 37208
Colbert Dr 37206
Colby Dr 37211
Cold Creek Trl 37211
Cold Spring Ct 37221
Cold Stream Ct, Dr & Pl 37221
Coldered Dr 37218
Cole Ave 37210
Colewood Dr 37215
Coley Davis Ct & Rd 37221
Colfax Dr 37214
Colice Jeanne Rd 37221
College Ave 37209
Collier Ave 37211
Collins Rd 37221
Collins Trace Ct 37221
Collinscrest Ct 37221
Collinswood Dr 37221
Colonial Cir 37214
Colonial Heritage Ct & Dr 37217
Colony Ct 37204
E Colony Ct 37221
S Colony Ct 37221
E Colony Dr 37221
S Colony Dr 37221
E Colony Pl 37221
Colony Pt E 37217
Colony Pt W 37217
Colorado Ave 37209
Colt Ct & Dr 37221
Columbia Ave 37209
Columbine Pl 37204
Combs Dr & Ter 37207
Comet Dr 37209
Commerce St
200-336 37201
338-398 37201
400-499 37219
500-598 37203
600-799 37203
801-999 37203
Commonwealth Cir & Ct 37221
Compton Ave 37212
Compton Rd 37215
Compton Trce 37215
Comroe Rd 37211
Concord Park E & W 37205
Concord Mill Ln 37211
Coney St 37216
Confederate Dr 37215
Conifer Pl 37214
Connelly Dr 37217
Conrad Dr 37206
Constitution Ave 37207
Continental Dr 37209
Convair Cir 37217
Convent Pl 37212
Conviser Dr 37207
Conway St 37209
Cooper Ln & Ter 37216
Copeland Dr 37215
Copley Ln 37204
Coral Rd & Way 37204
Corbett Ln 37209
Cordell Dr 37214
Corder Dr 37206
Cornelia Ct & St 37217
Cornerstone Ct 37221
Cornet Dr 37217
Corning Dr 37211
Cornish Dr 37207
Cornwall Ave, Ct & Dr 37205
Coronado Ct 37221
Cottage Ln & Pl 37214
Cotton Ln 37211
Cotton Blossom Ct & Ln 37221
Cottonwood Dr 37214
Couch Dr 37209
Couchville Pike 37217
Cougar Dr 37209
Country Dr 37211
Country Club Ln 37205
Country Wood Cir 37214
County Hospital Rd 37218
Courtland Dr 37204
Courtney Ave & Ct 37218
Coventry Ct & Dr 37211
Cowan Ct 37207
Cowan St
201-299 37213
300-999 37207
Cowden Ave 37209
Cozy Creek Ln 37211
Craig Ave 37204
Craighead Ave 37205
Craighead St 37204
Craigmeade Cir & Dr 37214
Cranapple Cv 37207
Crater Hill Dr 37215
Cravath Dr 37207
Crealewood Dr 37214
Creek St 37210
Creek Valley Ct 37221
Creek View Ct 37221
Creekbend Dr 37207
Creekland Ct 37218
Creekside Ct & Dr 37211
Creekstone Cir 37214
Creekview Dr 37217
Creekway Ct 37218
Creekwood N 37218
Creekwood Cir 37218
Creekwood Dr 37207
Creighton Ave 37206
Crescent Rd 37205
Crescent Hill Pl & Rd 37206
Crest Hollow Ct 37211
Crest Ridge Ct 37221
Crestdale Dr 37214
Crestfield Ct & Dr 37211
Crestline Dr 37214
Crestmeade Dr 37221
Crestmont Ct 37207
Crestmoor Rd 37215
Crestridge Dr 37204
Crestview Dr 37215
Crestwood Dr
800-899 37204
2600-2699 37214
Criddle St 37219
Crieve Rd 37220
Crislynndale Dr 37207
Crockett Ct & St 37207
Croley Ct & Dr 37209
Cromwell Dr 37215
Crosby Ln 37211
Cross St 37207
Cross Creek Rd 37215
Cross Timbers Dr 37221
Crossbrooke Dr 37221
Crossfield Dr 37214
Crosswind Dr & Pl 37211
Crosswood Ct & Dr 37214
Crouch Dr 37207
Crowder Ct 37211
Crowe Dr 37218
Crown Point Pl 37211
Crownhill Dr 37217
Crump Dr 37214
Crutcher St
300-600 37213
601-699 37206
602-698 37213
Crutchfield Ave 37210
Cruzen St 37211
Crystal Ct 37207
Crystal Dr 37210
Csx Dr 37204
Cub Creek Rd 37209
Culvert St 37210
Cumberland Bnd 37228
Cumberland Cir 37214
Cumberland Pl 37215
Cumberland Trce 37214
Cumberland Cove Dr 37207
Cummins Dr 37217
Cummins Sta 37203
Curdwood Blvd 37216
Currey Rd 37217
Currywood Dr 37205
Curtis Ct 37207
Curtis Dr 37207
Curtis St 37218
Curtis Hill Ct 37218
N & S Curtiswood Cir & Ln 37204
Cynthia Ln 37207
Cypress Dr 37211
D Ville Dr 37217
Dabbs Ave
1800-1899 37210
1900-2399 37217
Dabbs Ct 37217
Dade Dr 37211
Dahlia Cir & Dr 37210
Dakota Ave 37209
Dale Ave & Ln 37204
Dalebrook Ct & Ln 37206
Dalemere Ct & Dr 37207
Dallas Ave 37212
Dan Kestner Ct & Dr 37221
Danbury Ct 37214
Danby Dr 37211
Dandint Dr 37221
Danestone Ct & Dr 37220
Daniel Ct & Trce 37221
Danyacrest Dr 37214
Darbi Trace Ct 37221
Darbytown Dr 37207
Darden Pl 37205
Darlington Ct, Dr & Pl 37211
Darold Ct 37211
Dartmouth Ave 37215
Davenport Dr 37217
Daventry Ct 37221
Daverlet St 37203
David Ct & Dr 37214
Davidson Dr 37205
Davidson Rd 37205
Davidson St
200-700 37213
702-1398 37213
1001-1397 37206
1399-1600 37206
1602-1998 37206
Davidwood Ct 37214
Davis St 37216
Dawn Dr 37211
Day St 37218
Dayton Ave 37210
Deacons Ln 37211
Deaderick St
300-398 37201
315-315 37238
Deal Ave 37209
Dearborn Dr 37214
Decatur St 37210
Dedham Dr 37214
Deep Woods Cir, Ct & Trl 37214
Deer Pt 37209
Deer Trce 37211
Deer Estates Dr 37221
Deer Foot Ct 37221
Deer Lake Dr 37221
Deer Park Cir & Dr 37205
Deer Pointe Ct 37221
Deer Ridge Ln 37221
Deer Way Dr 37211
Deerbrook Dr 37221
Deercreek Trl N & S 37217
Deercrossing 37220
Deerfield Dr 37208
Deerhurst Ct 37221
Deerpath Dr 37217
Deervale Dr 37217
Deerwood Ct & Dr 37214
Del Crest Dr 37217
Delaney Dr 37214
Delaware Ave 37209
Delk Ave 37208
Dell Pkwy 37217
Dellrose Dr 37214
Dellway Dr 37207
Dellway Villa Rd 37207
Delmar Ave 37212
Delmas Ave 37216
Delray Ct & Dr 37209
Delta Ave 37208
Delta Queen Dr 37214
Delvin Dr 37211
Demarius Dr 37216
Demetros Ct & Pl 37217
Demonbreun St
201-297 37201
299-399 37201
400-1599 37203
Demoss Rd 37209
Dempsey Dr 37217
Dennis Dr 37207
Dennywood Dr 37214
Derby Trce 37211
Desmond Dr 37211
Desoto Dr 37210
Desplane Dr 37217
Devon Dr 37220
Devon Ln 37211
Devon Valley Dr 37221
Devon Way Ct 37221
Devonshire Dr 37207
Dew St 37206
Dewain Dr 37211
Dewees Ave 37204
Dickerson Pike 37207
Dillard Ct 37220
Dillehay Ct 37211
Dinah Ct 37214
Disspayne Dr 37214
Division St 37203
Dixon Dr 37206
Doak Ave 37218
Dobbs Ave 37211
Doctor Richard G Adams Dr 37207
Dodge Dr 37210
Doe Ridge Ct 37214
Doge Ct & Pl 37204
Dogwood Pl 37204
Dogwood Trl 37209
Dolan Rd 37218
Dolphin Dr 37211
Dominican Dr 37228
Don Allen Rd 37205
Donald St 37207
Doncaster Ln 37221
Donelson Pike
100-799 37214
801-999 37214
1200-1499 37217
1501-2999 37217
Donelson St 37210
Donelson Hills Dr 37214
Donelsonwood Dr 37214
Donna Hill Ct & Dr 37214
Donna Kay Dr 37211
Doral Ct 37221
Doral Country Dr 37221
Dorcas Ct & Dr 37215
Dorchester Ave 37216
Dorincha Dr 37211
Dorman Dr 37215
Dorris Ave 37204
Dorshire Ln 37221
Dortch Ave 37210
Dothan Ln 37211
Doubletree Ln 37217
Douglas Ave
906A-906C 37206
100-799 37207
800-1699 37206
E Douglas Ave 37206
S Douglas Ave 37204
W Douglas Ave 37206
Dove Pl 37218
Dove Ridge Cir 37221
Dove Valley Ct & Dr 37221
Dovecote Dr 37220
Dover Rd 37211
Doverside Ct & Dr 37207
Dovewood Ct 37211
Dowlan St 37208
Downey Dr 37205
Downeymeade Ct & Dr 37214
Downwind Ct 37217
Dozier Pl 37216
Dr Db Todd Jr Blvd
400-799 37203
900-2010 37208
2012-2098 37208
Dr Walter S Davis Blvd 37209
Dracut Ln 37211
Drake Ave 37211
Drakes Ct 37218
Drakes Branch Rd 37218
Drakes Hill Dr 37218
Drakewood Ln 37218
Draughon Ave 37204
Dresden Cir 37215
Drew Pl 37205
Drexel St 37203
Driftwood St 37210
Druid Dr 37210
Drummond Ct & Dr 37211
Dubois Dr 37207
Dudley Ave 37212
Dugger Dr 37206
Duke St 37207
Duluth Ave 37209
Dumas Dr 37211
Dumbarton Dr 37207
Dunailie Ct & Dr 37217
Dunaway Dr 37221
Dunbar Dr 37207
Duncan St 37210
Duncanwood Ct & Dr 37204
Dundee Ln 37214

Dundonnell Pl 37220
Dunham Springs Ln & Rd 37205
Dunmore Dr 37214
Dunn Ave 37211
Dunston Dr 37211
Duquaine Ct 37205
W Durrett Dr 37211
Dusk Ct 37221
Dustin Ln 37220
Duxbury Ct 37215
Dyer Ct 37218
Dyne Ct 37207
Eades Ct 37221
Eaglewood Ln 37207
Earlene Dr 37216
Earlington Dr 37215
Early Ave 37206
Earps Ct 37221
East Ln 37218
Eastboro Dr 37209
Eastdale Ave & Pl 37216
Easthagen Dr 37217
W Eastland Ave & Ct 37206
Eastmoreland St 37207
Easton Ct 37214
Eastside Ave 37206
Eastview Ct & Dr 37211
Eastwood Ave 37212
Eatherly Dr 37220
Eaton Ct 37218
Eatons Creek Rd 37218
Ebenway Dr 37205
Ebony Dr 37214
Echo Ln 37218
Echo Hill Rd 37215
Eckhart Dr 37211
Ed Temple Blvd 37208
Eddings Ln 37214
Eddystone Ct 37207
Eden Ave 37215
Eden St 37208
Edenbridge Way 37215
Edgar St 37210
Edge Moor Dr 37217
Edge O Lake Dr 37217
Edgehill Ave
800-1199 37203
1200-2099 37212
Edgemont Dr 37214
Edgeview Dr 37211
Edgewater Dr 37217
Edgewood Ave 37207
Edgewood Pl 37206
Edinburgh Dr 37221
Edison St 37211
Edith Ave 37207
Edmondson Pike 37211
Edmonson Cir 37211
Edsel Dr 37209
Edwards Ave 37216
Edwin St 37207
Edwin Warner Dr 37205
Eisenhower Dr 37211
Elaine Ave 37209
Elaine Dr 37211
Elanor Dr 37217
Elberta St 37210
Elder Pl 37215
Elderberry Ct 37217
Eldon Ct 37214
Electric Ave 37206
Elgin St 37211
Elissa Dr 37217
Elizabeth Rd 37218
Elizabeth St 37211
Elizabeth Jordan St 37209
Elizabethan Dr 37205
Elkins Ave 37209
Elkmont Dr 37211
Ellendale Ave 37205
Ellenwood Dr 37211
Eller Ct, Dr & Ln 37221
Ellery Ct
200-229 37214
230-230 37229
231-299 37214
232-298 37214
Ellesmere Rd 37205
Ellington Cir 37211
Elliott Ave
1800-1899 37203
1900-2399 37204
2401-2499 37204
Elliston Pl 37203
Ellwood Ct 37205
Elm Ct 37214
Elm Run 37214
Elm St 37203
Elm Hill Pike
800-2199 37210
2200-2398 37214
2400-3599 37214
Elm Run Ct & Way 37214
Elm Tree Dr 37210
Elmhurst Ave 37207
Elmington Ave 37205
Elmont Cv & Ter 37211
Elmshade Ct & Ln 37211
Elmwood Ave 37212
Elvira Ave 37216
Elwood Ct 37214
Elysian Fields Ct 37211
Elysian Fields Rd
200-699 37211
700-799 37204
Ember Lake Dr 37214
Emerald Ct & Dr 37218
Emerson St 37216
Emery Dr 37214
Emma Neuhoff Ct 37205
Emmett Ave 37206
Empire Dr 37211
Enchanted Cir, Ct & Way 37218
Enclave Cir 37211
W End Ave
1600-3499 37203
3500-3522 37205
3524-4100 37205
4102-4208 37205
W End Cir 37203
W End Pl 37205
W End Close 37205
English Ivy Dr 37211
English Village Dr 37211
Enloe St 37207
Ennis Rd 37210
Enoch Dr 37211
Enoch Jones St 37208
Enos Reed Dr 37210
Enquirer Ave 37205
Ensley Blvd 37210
Ensworth Ave & Pl 37205
Envious Ln 37217
Eric Dr 37207
Erica Pl 37204
Erin Ln 37221
Ermac Dr 37214
Errol Ln 37209
Erwin Ct 37205
Essex Ave 37216
Essex Pl 37212
Estbury Ct 37215
Esterbrook Dr 37221
Estes Rd 37215
Esteswood Dr 37215
Esther Ave 37218
Ethel St 37209
Eugenia Ave 37211
Eulala Cir, Ct & Dr 37211
Eutopia Ave 37211
Evander St 37206
Evans Rd 37204
Evansdale Dr 37220
Evanston Ave 37207
Eve Cir 37218
Evelyn Ave
200-299 37205
1600-1799 37216
Evelyn Dr 37210
Everett Dr 37215
Evergreen Ridge Pt 37217
Ewing Ave 37203
Ewing Dr 37207
Ewing Ln 37207
Ewing Creek Dr 37207
Ewing Valley Rd 37207
Ewingdale Dr 37207
Ewingwood Dr 37207
Executive Way 37207
Explorer Trl 37221
W Express Dr 37210
W Expressway Park Dr 37210
Ezell Pike
200-699 37217
3200-3200 37211
3202-3299 37211
Ezell Rd 37211
Factory St 37210
Fain St 37210
Fair Meadows Ct & Dr 37211
Fairbrook Dr 37214
Fairfax Ave 37212
Fairfield Ave 37210
Fairground Ct 37211
Fairhaven Ct & Dr 37211
Fairlane Dr 37211
Fairmeade Ct & Dr 37218
Fairmont Ct, Dr & Pl 37203
E Fairview Dr 37218
Fairway Dr 37214
Fairwin Ave 37216
Fairwood Dr 37209
Falkirk Ct 37221
Fall Dr 37207
Fall St 37206
Falling Leaf Ln 37207
Falling Water Ct 37221
Falls Creek Dr 37214
Fallview Trl 37211
Fannie Williams St 37210
Farley Pl 37210
Farmington Ct & Pl 37221
Farmview Dr 37218
Farrar Ave 37215
Farrell Pkwy & Rd 37220
Farriswood Dr 37204
Fatherland St
1-299 37213
400-2099 37206
Faulkner Dr & Pl 37211
Fawn Creek Pass 37214
Fawnwood Ct & Pl 37207
Felicia St 37209
Felts Ave 37211
Ferenchi Dr 37205
Ferguson Ave 37212
Fern Ave 37207
Fernbrook Ln 37214
Fernco Dr 37207
Ferndale Ave 37215
Fernwood Dr 37216
Ferringdon Ct 37221
Fessey Ct 37204
Fessey Park Rd 37204
Fesslers Ln
1-715 37210
714-714 37224
716-1298 37210
717-1299 37210
Fesslers Pkwy 37210
Fiber Glass Rd 37210
Fieldcrest Dr 37211
Finland St 37208
Finley Dr 37217
Finn St 37206
Finnland Dr 37207
Fire Tower Rd 37221
Firestone Ct 37209
Fisher Ct 37221
Fisher Dr 37214
Fisk St 37203
Fitzgerald Dr 37214
Fitzpatrick Ct, Pl & Rd 37214
Five Oaks Dr 37217
Flamingo Dr 37207
Fleetwood Dr
6400-6699 37209
6700-6899 37205
Flicker Dr 37218
Flintlock Ct & Pl 37217
Flora Maxwell Rd 37211
Floral Dr 37211
Flushing Dr 37211
Fogg St 37203
Fogle St 37211
Foley Dr 37211
Fonnic Dr 37207
Fontana Ave 37204
Foothill Ct & Dr 37217
Footpath Ter 37221
Fordomatic Dr 37209
Forest Acres Ct & Dr 37220
Forest Hills Dr 37220
Forest Lake Dr 37211
Forest Place Cir 37215
Forest Side Ct 37221
Forest Trace Dr 37217
Forestwood Dr 37209
Forge Ridge Cir & Ct 37217
Forges Dr 37217
W Fork Ct 37220
Formosa St 37208
Forrest Ave 37206
Forrest Green Dr 37216
Forrest Oaks Ct, Dr & Pl N & S 37221
Forrest Park Ave 37215
Forrest Park Dr 37205
Forrest Valley Cir, Ct & Dr 37209
Forrester Dr 37217
Forsythe Pl 37205
Fort Negley Blvd & Ct 37203
Fortland Dr 37206
Foster Ave 37210
Foster Ct 37210
Foster Hl 37215
Foster Pl 37207
Foster St 37207
Foster Creighton Dr 37204
Foundation Ct 37209
Foundry Dr 37209
Four Forty Blvd 37204
Fox Ave 37210
Fox Trl 37221
Fox Hollow Rd 37205
Fox Hunt Pt 37221
Fox Vale Ln 37221
Fox Way Pt 37221
Foxglove Dr 37211
Foxhall Rd 37215
Foxhall Close 37215
Foxwood Dr 37215
Foxwood Ln 37210
Frances Ave 37204
Frandiso Ave N 37201
Franklin Ave 37206
Franklin Dr 37209
Franklin Pike
2300-4500 37204
4502-4598 37204
4600-5559 37220
Franklin St
1-100 37201
102-198 37201
400-599 37203
Franklin Limestone Ct & Rd 37217
Fransworth Dr 37205
Fredricksburg Dr 37215
Free Silver Rd 37207
Freedom Ct, Dr & Pl 37209
Freeland Station Rd 37228
Freightliner Dr 37210
Fremont Ave 37216
French Landing Dr 37228
Freno Ln 37214
Frisco Ave 37209
Frith Dr 37206
Frontier Ct & Ln 37211
Frost St 37214
Fulton St 37206
Futura Ct & Dr 37209
Fyffe Ln 37211
Gailwood Ln 37214
Gains St 37207
Galaxie Dr 37209
Galbraith Dr 37215
Gale Ln
800-1199 37204
1400-1799 37212
Gale Park Ln 37204
Galesburg Ct & Dr 37217
Gallatin Ave 37206
Gallatin Pike 37216
Gann Dr 37210
Garden St 37210
Gardendale Dr 37215
Gardner Ln 37207
Garfield St 37208
Garland Ave 37212
Garrett Dr 37211
Garrison Dr 37207
Garry Dr 37211
Gartland Ave 37206
Garwood Dr 37210
Gateway Ln 37220
Gatewood Ave 37207
Gatlin Dr 37210
Gauphin Pl 37211
Gay St
200-399 37201
401-497 37219
499-500 37219
502-598 37219
1000-1199 37203
Gayland Ct 37210
Gaylord Dr 37214
Gaywinds Ct 37214
Gaywood Dr 37211
Gear St 37216
Geneiva Dr 37216
General Bate Dr 37204
General Forrest Ct 37215
General George Patton Rd 37221
General Hood Trl 37204
General Lowrey Dr 37215
Generosity Way 37211
Geneva Cir 37209
Gentry Ave 37206
George E Horn Rd 37221
George Gaines Rd 37221
George L Davis Blvd 37203
Georgetown Ct 37215
Georgetown Dr 37205
Georgia Ave & Ct 37209
Georgian Pl 37215
Gerald Pl 37205
Gerald St 37207
Geyser St 37210
Giant Oak Dr 37217
Gillespie Ave 37205
Gillette Rd 37211
Gillock St 37216
Gilman Ave 37205
Gilmore Ave 37204
Gilmore Crossing Ln 37218
Glade St 37207
Gladstone Ave 37211
Glastonbury Rd 37217
Gleaves St 37203
Glen Ave 37204
Glen Echo Pl & Rd 37215
Glen Eden Dr 37205
Glen Leven Dr 37204
Glen West Dr 37215
Glenavon Ct 37220
Glencarron Dr 37220
Glencliff Ct & Rd 37211
Glendale Ln 37204
Glendale Pl 37215
Glendale Sq 37204
Glendale Garden Dr 37204
Glendower Ct 37204
Glengarry Dr 37217
Glengoyne Pl 37220
Gleniris Ct 37221
S Glenleigh Ct 37221
Glenmary Ct 37205
Glenmeade Dr 37216
Glenmont Ct & Dr 37210
Glenmore Pl 37220
Glenn Ct 37217
Glenn Abbey 37215
Glenoaks Dr 37214
Glenpark Ct & Dr 37217
Glenridge Ct, Dr & Ln 37221
Glenridge Close 37221
Glenrose Ave, Cir & Ct 37210
Glenvale Dr 37221
Glenview Dr 37206
Glenway Ct & Dr 37221
Glenwood Ave 37204
Gloucester Ln 37221
Glynda Dr 37216
Goff St 37208
Goins Rd 37211
Golden Hill Ct 37218
Golden Hills Dr 37218
Goldenrod Ct 37221
Goldstone Ct 37215
Golf St 37216
Golf Club Ln 37215
Gooch St 37207
Good Day Ct 37207
Goodbar Dr 37217
Goode Ct 37216
Goodland Rd 37211
Goodloe Dr 37215
Goodmorning Dr 37207
Goodnight Ct 37207
Goodpasture Ter 37221
Goodrich Ave 37218
Goodwin Ct & Dr 37217
Gordon Ter 37207
Gower Rd 37209
Gra Mar Dr 37216
Grace St 37207
Grace Crest Pt 37217
Graeme Dr 37214
N & S Grafton Ct 37217
Granada Ave & Ct 37206
Grand Ave
1300-1599 37212
1600-1699 37203
1700-2099 37212
Grandview Ave 37211
Grandview Dr
1000-1199 37204
1200-1599 37215
Grandville Blvd & Ct 37207
Granny White Ct 37204
Granny White Pike
4410A-4410B 37204
4418A-4418C 37204
4508A-4508B 37204
4518A-4518B 37204
3000-3098 37204
3100-4599 37204
4600-5299 37220
Granny White Trce 37220
Grantland Ave 37204
Grapevine Ln 37221
Grassland Ln 37220
Grassmere Park 37211
Gray St 37203
Gray Oaks Dr 37204
Graybar Ln
900-1199 37204
1200-2061 37215
2063-2099 37215
Graycroft Ave 37216
Graylynn Dr 37214
Grayson Ct & Dr 37205
Grayswood Ave 37215
Great Circle Rd 37228
Greeley Dr 37205
W Green Ln 37207
Green Park 37215
Green St 37210
Green Vw 37205
Green Hills Dr 37215
Green Hills Village Dr 37215
Green Meadows Ln 37221
Green Ridge Dr 37214
Green Valley Ct & Dr 37220
Greenbranch Ct 37207
Greenbriar Trce 37214
Greenfield Ave 37216
Greenland Ave 37216
Greenleaf Dr 37211
Greenside Pl 37206
Greentree Dr 37211
Greenvale Ct & Dr 37221
Greenway Ave 37205
Greenway Glen Way 37209
Greenwich Park 37215
W Greenwood Ave, Cir & Ct 37206
Greerland Dr 37204
Gregg Ct 37217
Greggwood Dr 37207
Gregory Dr 37216
Greymont Dr 37217
Greystone Rd 37204
E & W Griffin Ct 37221
Griffith Rd 37221
Griggs Pl 37217
Grinstead Pl 37216
Grissom Dr 37204
Grizzard Ave 37207
Groadela Ave 37216
Groome Dr 37205
Grosse Point Ct 37209
W Grove Ave 37203
Grove Creek Ave 37214
Grover St 37207
Groves Park Rd 37206
Grubbs Rd 37211
Grundy St 37203
Guaranty Dr 37214
Guest Dr 37216
Guill Ct 37214
Gulf Coast Ct 37217
Gun Club Rd 37205
Gupton Ct 37218
Gwen Dr 37207
Gwendolyn Ct 37218
Gwynn Dr 37216
Gwynnwood Dr 37207
Habersham Ave 37214
Hackberry Ln 37206
Hackworth St 37210
Haden Ct 37215
Hagan St 37203
Hailey Ave 37218
Halcyon Ave 37204
Haleys Hope Ct 37209
Hall Ct 37211
Hallmark Rd 37218
Hallows Dr 37221
Hamden Dr 37211
Hamilton Ave 37203
W Hamilton Ave 37218
W Hamilton Ct 37218
S Hamilton Rd 37218
W Hamilton Rd 37218
Hammack Ct & Dr 37214
Hammersmith Ct 37211
Hammond Dr 37208
Hampshire Pl 37221
Hampton Ave 37215
Hampton Pl 37215
Hampton St 37207
Hancock St 37207
Hangar Ct & Ln 37217
Hanover Rd 37216
Hanover Sq 37215
Hansrote Ct & Cv 37221
Happy Hollow Rd 37216
Hapwood Dr 37205
Harbor Way 37214
Harbor Hill Ct & Pl 37214
Harbor Lights Dr 37217
Harbor Valley Ct 37214
Harborwood Cir, Dr & Pt 37214

Street	ZIP
Harbour View Dr	37217
Harcourt Cir	37205
Harding Pike	37205
Harding Pl	
100-200	37205
202-298	37205
300-308	37211
310-721	37211
723-749	37211
751-799	37204
1200-4099	37215
4300-4499	37205
5000-5199	37211
5200-5299	37217
Harding Hill Ln	37215
Harding Industrial Dr	37211
Harding Mall Dr	37211
Harding Road Ct	37205
Harding Trace Ct	37221
Hardingwoods Pl	37205
Harlin Dr	37211
Harness Dr	37221
Harold Dr	37217
Harold Prewett Dr	37218
Harpeth Ct, Ln, Pkwy & Rd E & W	37221
Harpeth Bend Dr	37221
Harpeth Crest Dr	37221
Harpeth Glen Trce	37221
Harpeth Hills Dr	37215
Harpeth Knoll Ct & Rd	37221
Harpeth Lake Ct	37221
Harpeth Mill Ct	37221
Harpeth Oaks Ct	37221
Harpeth Ridge Dr	37221
Harpeth Run Dr	37221
Harpeth Springs Dr	37221
Harpeth Trace Ct, Dr & Pl	37221
Harpeth Valley Ct, Pl & Rd	37221
Harpeth View Cir, Ct, Dr & Pl	37221
Harpeth Wood Dr	37221
Harrell Ct	37214
Harriette Ct	37206
Harrison St	
200-329	37211
330-799	37219
800-1199	37203
Harriswood Dr	37205
Harrow Ct & Dr	37221
Hart Ave	37206
Hart Ct	37207
Hart Ln	
100-399	37207
400-800	37216
802-1098	37216
Hart St	
27A-27C	37210
1-64	37210
66-298	37210
2500-2699	37207
Hartford Dr	37210
Harvard Ave	37205
Harvest Ln	37218
Harwich Ct	37211
Harwood Dr	37206
Haselton Rd	37221
Hastings Rd	37214
Hasty Dr	37211
Hathaway Ct	37205
Hatteras Way	37221
N Haven Ct	37211
Havendale Dr	37207
Havenhill Dr	37217
Haverford Ave & Dr	37205
Haverhill Ct	37215
Havering Chase	37215
Hawk View Ct	37207
Hawkdale Dr	37211
Hawkins St	37203
Hawkwood Ln	37207
Hawthorn Dr	37214
Hawthorne Pl	37212
Hayden Dr	
1500-1599	37206
1800-1899	37216
Haydenberry Ct & Cv	37221
Hayes St	37203
Haynes St	37207
Haynes Meade Cir	37207
Haynes Park Ct & Dr	37218
Haynie Ave	37207
Haysboro Ave	37216
Haywood Ct & Ln	37211
Hazelwood Cir	37220
Hazelwood Dr	37212
Heady Dr	37205
Healy Ct & Dr	37207
Heartland Dr	37214
Heath Rd	37221
Heathcote Ave	37210
Heather Ct	37211
Heather Pl	37204
Heaton Way	37211
Hedgewood Dr	37216
Hedrick St	37203
Heidi Ct	37211
W Heiman St	37208
Helen Dr	37217
Helms Ln	37214
Helmwood Dr	37216
Hemingway Dr	37215
Hemlock Ave	37216
Hemstead St	37209
Henderson Dr	37221
Heney Dr	37214
Henry Pl	37203
Henry Ford Dr	37209
Henry Hale Pl	37203
Herbert Pl	37215
Herman St	37208
Hermitage Ave	37210
Hermitage Plz	37209
Hermosa St	37208
Herron Dr	37210
Hester Ave	37210
Hester Beasley Rd	37221
Hewlett Ct & Dr	37211
Hiawatha Ct	37221
Hibbitts Ct & Rd	37214
Hickory Pl	37214
Hickory Plz	37211
Hickory Run	37211
Hickory Ter	37207
Hickory Bark Ct & Ln	37211
Hickory Bend Dr	37214
Hickory Hill Ct	37214
Hickory Hollow Rd	37221
Hickory Lake Dr	37209
Hickory Plaza Dr	37211
Hickory Run Ct	37211
Hickory Trace Dr	37211
Hickory Trace Pl	37221
Hickory Trail Dr	37209
Hickory Valley Rd	37205
Hickory Villa Dr	37211
Hickorydale Dr	37210
Hickoryview Dr	37211
Hicks Rd	37221
Hidden Springs Dr	37207
Hidden Terrace Ct	37216
Hide A Way Ct	37217
Higgins Rd	37211
High St	37211
High Estes	37215
High Forrest Ct	37221
High Point Trace Ct	37221
High Rigger Ct & Dr	37217
Highcrest Dr	37211
Highland Ave	37212
Highland Dr	37207
Highland Way	37211
Highland Crest Dr	37205
Highland Park Ct & Dr	37205
Highland Trace Cv & Dr	37207
Highland Villa Cir & Dr	37211
N & S Highlands Ct & Dr	37221
Highview Dr	37206
Highway 100	
6598A-6598B	37205
Highway 100	
5409-5997	37205
5999-6699	37205
6701-6799	37205
6800-9599	37221
Highway 70 S	37221
Highway 96	37221
Hildreth Dr	37215
Hill Ave	37210
Hill Ct	37220
N Hill Dr	37207
Hill Rd	37220
N Hill St	37210
Hill Circle Dr	37209
Hill Creek Dr	37211
Hill Place Dr	37205
Hill Road Cir	37220
Hillbrook Ct & Dr	37211
Hillcott Dr	37215
Hillcrest Ave	37204
Hillcrest Pl	37203
Hilldale Dr	37215
Hillenglade Dr	37207
Hillhaven Ct	37220
Hillhurst Dr	37207
Hillmeade Ct & Dr	37221
Hillmont Ct	37221
Hillmont Dr	37215
Hillmore Dr	37218
Hills Chapel Rd	37211
Hillsboro Cir	37215
Hillsboro Dr	37215
Hillsboro Pike	
2600-2603	37212
2911-2997	37215
2999-6399	37215
Hillsboro Pl	37215
Hillsdale Ave	37205
Hillside Ave	37203
Hillside Dr	37212
Hillside Rd	37207
Hilltop Ave	37216
Hillview Hts	37204
Hillwood Blvd	
100-799	37205
800-899	37209
W Hillwood Dr	37205
N Hilson Ct, Dr & Rd	37211
Himes Dr	37206
Hinkle Dr	37218
Hitching Post Ln	37211
Hite St	37209
Hobbit Ln	37211
Hobbs Ct & Rd	37215
Hockett Dr	37218
Hodge Cir & Ct	37218
Hody Dr	37206
Hogan Rd	37220
Holbrook Dr	37211
Holder Ct & Dr	37217
Holgate Ct	37221
Holland Ln	37218
Holleare Ave	37204
Hollis Hill Dr	37211
Hollow Tree Ct	37221
Holly Frst	37221
Holly St	37206
Holly Hill Ct	37221
Holly Springs Rd	37221
Holly Trace Ct & Way	37221
Hollybrook Cres	37221
Hollydale Dr	37217
Holman Ave	37203
Holt Br & Rd	37211
Holt Briar Ct	37211
Holt Creek Ct	37211
Holt Grove Ct	37211
Holt Hills Ct, Pl & Rd	37211
Holt Run Ct & Dr	37211
Holt Valley Rd	37221
Home Rd	37216
Home Haven Dr	37218
Homeland Dr	37218
Homestead Rd	37207
Honey Creek Ln	37211
Honeyhill Ct & Dr	37217
Honeysuckle Dr & Rd	37204
Honeywood Dr	37205
Hood Ave	37215
Hoods Hill Rd	37215
Hooper Ct	37211
Hooten Hows Rd	37221
Hope Cv	37217
Hope Hill Ct	37211
Hopedale Dr	37211
Hopewood Ct & Dr	37211
Hopkins St	37215
Horace Mann Dr	37218
Hornbuckle Ln	37218
Horner Ave	37204
Horseshoe Dr	37216
Horseshoe Ln	37221
Horton Ave	
1101-1199	37203
1200-1699	37212
Hospital Ln	37218
Houston St	37203
Howard Ave	37216
Howell Pl	37205
Howerton Ave	37213
Howerton St	37206
Hubbard St	37210
Huckleberry Rd	37205
Huckleberry Trl	37221
Huffine St	37216
Hughes St	37208
Humber Dr	37211
Hume St	37208
Hummingbird Dr	37218
Humphreys St	37203
Hunley Dr	37207
Hunt Pl	37215
Hunt Club Rd	37221
Hunters Ln	37207
Hunters Rdg	37211
Hunters Run	37209
Hunters Trl	37209
Hunters Bow Cir	37211
Hunters Hill Rd	37214
Hunters Meadow Ln	37216
Huntington Cir	37215
Huntington Pkwy	37211
Huntington Ridge Dr	37211
Huntleigh Dr	37206
Huntmaster Cir	37211
Huntwick Trl	37221
Huntwood Pl	37221
Hurdwood Dr	37211
Hutson Ave	37216
Hutton Dr	37210
Hyde Park	37215
Hyde St	37208
N Hydes Ferry Rd	37218
Hydesdale Ln	37218
Hynes St	37203
Idaho Ave	37209
Ilawood Ct & Dr	37211
Illinois Ave	37209
Ilolo St	37207
Imperial Dr	37210
Incline Dr	37211
Indian Creek Rd	37209
Indian Hills Dr	37221
Indian Ridge Dr	37221
Indian Springs Dr	37221
Indian Summer Ct & Dr	37207
Indiana Ave	37209
Industrial Pkwy	37218
Industry St	37210
Inga Ave	37216
Inga St	37206
Ingleside Dr	37214
Inglewood Cir, Ct & Dr N & S	37216
International Plz	37217
Interstate Blvd S	37210
Interstate Dr	37213
Inveraray	37215
Inverness Ave	37204
Inwood Dr	37211
Ireland St	37208
E & W Iris Dr	37204
Iron Gate Ct	37221
Ironwood Dr	37214
Iroquois Ave & Ct	37205
Irving Ln	37214
Island View Ct	37214
Islandia Ct & Dr	37217
Islay Ct	37209
Iverson Ave	37216
Ivy Dr	37216
Ivy St	37209
Ivywood Dr	37210
J J Watson Ave	37211
Jackson Blvd	37205
Jackson St	
1010A-1010B	37208
200-399	37201
400-700	37219
702-798	37219
900-1799	37208
Jackson Downs Blvd	37214
Jackson Way Ct	37214
Jacqulyn Dr	37211
Jade Dr	37210
Jakes Ave	37216
James Ave & Ct	37209
James Milton Ct	37221
James Robertson Pkwy	
100-399	37201
400-498	37219
500-600	37219
602-798	37219
900-998	37203
Jamesborough Ct & Pl	37215
Jamestown Park	37205
Jamestown Green Ct	37215
Jane St	37208
Janie Ave	37216
Jansing Dr	37211
Jasmin Dr	37211
Jay Ct, Dr & St	37210
Jc Napier Ct & St	37210
Jeans Ct	37216
Jefferson Sq	37215
Jefferson St	37208
Jeffery Dr	37211
Jenkins Ct & St	37208
Jennings St	37208
Jenry Ct & Dr	37214
Jess Neely Dr	37212
Jessamin Rd	37204
Jessie Dr	37211
Jetway Dr	37217
Jewell St	37207
Jo Johnston Ave N	37203
Joann Ct	37211
Jobee Creek Cv	37214
Jocelyn Hills Dr	37205
Jocelyn Hollow Cir, Ct & Rd	37205
John St	37210
John A Merritt Blvd	37209
John L Copeland Blvd	37207
John L Driver Ave	37209
John Mallette Dr	37218
Johnakin Dr	37211
Johnstone Ct	37215
Jonell Dr	37210
Jones Ave, Cir & Pl	37207
Jones Park Ct	37207
Jones View Dr	37207
Jonesboro Ct & Dr	37214
Jonquil Dr	37211
Joplin Ct & Dr	37210
Jordan Dr	37218
Jordan Ridge Dr	37218
Jordonia Station Rd	37218
Josam Dr	37211
Joseph Ave	37207
Joy Cir	37207
Joya Dr	37214
Joyce Ln	37216
Joyner Ave	37210
Jr Pro Football Dr	37211
Judd Ct & Dr	37218
June Dr	37214
Kable Cir	37211
Karen Dr	37217
Kassia St	37207
Katherine St	37216
Katie St	37207
Kay Ct	37211
Keeley Ct & Dr	37211
Keeling Ave & St	37216
Keith St	37210
Keller Ave	37216
Kellow St	37208
Kenaum Ct	37209
Kendall Dr	37209
Kendall Park Dr	37217
Kenesaw Dr	37215
Kenilwood Dr	37204
Kenilworth	37215
Kenmore Ct & Pl	37216
Kennedy Ave	37216
Kenner Ave	37205
Kennington N & S	37214
Kennith Dr	37207
Kensington Park	37215
Kensington Pl	37212
Kent Rd	37214
Kenton Pl	37217
Kentucky Ave	37209
Kenway Rd	37215
Kenwick Ct W	37221
Kenwood Dr	
1100-1399	37216
6000-6099	37215
Kermit Dr	37217
Kern Dr	37211
Kevin Ct	37211
Keystone Ave	37211
Keyway Dr	37205
Killean Ct	37209
Kimbark Dr	37215
Kimberly Dr	37214
Kimpalong Dr	37205
Kincannon Dr	37220
Kingfisher Pt	37221
Kings Cir, Ct & Ln	37218
Kingsbury Dr	37215
Kingston St	37207
Kingsview Ct	37220
Kingswood Ave	37216
Kingview Ct & Dr	37218
Kinhawk Ct & Dr	37211
Kinley Ct	37221
Kinross Ave	37211
Kinsdale Dr	37211
Kinsington Dr	37216
Kipling Dr	37217
Kirby Dr	37217
Kirk Ave	37218
Kirkbrook	37221
Kirkfield Dr	37211
Kirkland Ave	37216
W Kirkland Ave	37216
Kirkland Pl	37212
Kirkman Ln	37220
Kirkwood Ave	
800-1000	37204
1002-1198	37204
1200-1599	37212
W Kirkwood Ave	37204
Kirtland Rd	37215
Kittrell Rd	37221
Kline Ave	37211
Knapp Blvd	37217
Knight Dr	37207
Knob Rd	37209
Knobdale Rd	37214
Knobview Dr	37214
Knolls Pl	37211
Knollwood Rd	37215
Knowles Ave	37204
Knowles St	37208
Knox Ave	37204
Korean Veterans Blvd	
301-399	37201
600-700	37203
702-798	37203
Kottas Pl	37217
Kraft Dr	37204
Kreitner Dr	37221
La Vista Dr	37215
Laboldi Ave	37207
Lacy St	37208
Lady Ct	37214
Ladybird Ct & Dr	37217
Lafayette Ct	37205
Lafayette St	
1-299	37210
400-699	37203
701-799	37203
Lagrange Dr	37218
Laird Rd	37205
Lake Ct & Dr	37214
Lake Aire Ct & Dr	37217
Lake Forest Ct & Dr	37217
Lake Park Dr	37211
Lake Point Ct	37214
Lake Terrace Cir & Dr	37217
Lakebrink Ct, Dr & Way	37214
Lakeford Dr	37214
Lakehurst Dr	37206
Lakeland Dr	37214
Lakemont Ct & Dr	37220
N & S Lakeridge Pass, Pl, Run & Way	37214
Lakeside Ct	37217
Lakeview Dr	
5000-5099	37220
7400-7699	37209
Lakevilla Dr	37217
Lallemand Ct & Dr	37211
Lamar Dr	37205
Lambert Dr	37220
Lamearad	37229
Lanawood Ct & Dr	37217
Lancaster Ave & Way	37212
Landau Dr	37209
Landers Ave	37211
Landmark Ct	37211
Landon Dr	37220
Lane Ct & Dr	37207
Lanewood Ct	37211
Langston Dr	37211
Lansing Dr	37209
Laramie Ave	37209
Larchwood Dr	37214
Laredo Ave	37209
Largo Dr	37211
Larimore Dr	37214
Larkspur Dr	37207
Larkway Ct & Dr	37211
Larmon Dr	37204
Lasalle Ct	37205
Lathan Ct	37207
Lauderdale Rd	37205
Lauer Dr	37214
Laurel St	37203
Laurel Forest Dr	37214
Laurel Park Dr	37205
Laurel Ridge Dr	37215
Lauren Ct	37217
Lauren Evelyn Way	37207
Laurent St	37206
Laurinda Dr	37217
Lausanne Dr	37211
Lavergne Ct	37210
Lawing Dr	37207
Lawncrest Dr	37210
Lawndale Dr	
200-299	37211
301-307	37217
309-399	37217
Lawrence Ave	37204
Lazenby Dr	37206
Lazy Creek Ln	37211
Le Bon Rd	37211
Lea Ave	
1-99	37210
101-127	37210
400-999	37203
Leafland Ave	37210

Leake Ave 37205
Lealand Ct 37204
Lealand Ln
3000-4499 37204
4501-4597 37220
4599-4999 37220
Lealto Ct 37214
Learning Ln 37221
Leath Dr 37211
Leatherwood Dr 37214
Leawood Dr 37218
Lebanon Pike
1911A-1911B 37210
700-2199 37210
2200-3199 37214
Lebanon Pike Cir 37210
Leblanc Ct 37221
Ledford Dr 37207
Lee Davis Rd 37216
Leeanne Dr 37211
Legate Ct 37211
Legend Hall Dr 37215
Leland Ave 37216
Lelawood Cir 37209
Lellyett Ave 37209
Lemont Ct & Dr 37216
Lemuel Rd 37207
Lena St 37208
Lenora Ct 37217
Lenore St 37206
Lenox Ave 37209
Lenox Village Dr 37211
Leo Ct & Ln 37211
Leon St 37221
Leonard Ave 37205
Leonard Ridge Ct 37221
Leondale Ter 37207
Leopole Rd 37211
Leslie Ave
2300-2398 37203
5600-5899 37209
Leslie Ct 37206
Lester Ave 37210
Leswood Ln 37207
Lethia Dr 37206
Leveson Way 37211
Levy Ln 37207
Lewis Rd 37221
Lewis St 37210
Lewisdale Ct 37211
Lexington Ct 37215
Lexington Dr 37211
Lexington Grn 37215
Lexington Point Dr 37221
Libble Rd 37218
Liberia St 37207
Liberty Sq 37215
Ligon Ave 37207
Ligon Dr 37204
Lila Ln 37218
Lillian St 37206
Lillywood Rd 37205
Linbar Dr 37211
Lincoln Ave 37218
Lincoln Ct 37205
Lincoln St 37210
Lincoya Ct & Dr 37214
Lincoya Bay Dr 37214
Lincoya Creek Dr 37214
Lindawood Dr 37215
Lindell Ave
1900-2099 37203
2101-2197 37204
2199-2399 37204
Lindell St 37216
Linden Ave 37212
W Linden Ave 37212
Linden Sq 37215
Linder Industrial Dr 37209
Lindsay Meadow Ct 37207
Lindsley Ave 37210
Lindsley Park Dr 37206
Linmar Ave 37215
Lipscomb Dr 37204
Lisa Ln 37210
Lischey Ave & Pl 37207
Lishwood Dr 37214
Litchfield Way 37215
Little Ave 37206
Little Bridge Pl 37221
Little Green St 37210
Little Hamilton Ave 37203
Litton Ave 37216
Littonwood Dr 37216
Live Oak Rd 37210
Lloyd Ave 37218
Lock Rd 37207
Lock Two Rd 37214
Lockland Dr 37206
Locklayer St 37208
Lockwood Ct & Dr 37214
Locust St 37207
Locustwood Dr 37211
Log Cabin Rd 37216
Logan St 37211
Lombardy Ave 37215
London Way 37221
Londonberry Rd 37221
Lone Oak Cir & Rd 37215
Lone Oak Village Way 37215
Loney Dr 37210
Long Ave 37206
Long Blvd 37203
Long Meadow Rd 37205
E & W Longdale Dr 37211
Longfellow Dr 37214
Longfield Ave 37206
Longhunter Cir, Ct & Ln 37217
Longleaf Ct 37207
Longview Ave 37211
Longwood Ct & Pl 37215
Looby Cir 37208
Lookout Dr 37209
Lords Chapel Dr 37211
Loring Ct 37220
Lorna Dr 37214
Lorraine Ave 37207
Lotta Ave 37207
Louanne Dr 37217
Louise Ave 37203
Louise Dr 37211
Louisiana Ave 37209
Love Cir 37212
Love Joy Ct 37216
Lovell Ave 37209
Lovewood Dr 37216
Loxley Dr 37211
Loyola Dr 37205
Lozier St 37209
Lucas Ln 37207
Lucile St 37207
Lucky Dr 37211
Lumar Ln 37214
Lumberjack Rd 37214
Luna Cir, Ct & Dr 37211
Lunn Cir, Ct & Dr 37218
Lutie Ct, Dr & St 37210
Luton St 37207
Lyle Ave 37203
Lyle Ct 37210
Lyle Ln 37210
S Lyle Ln 37210
Lyman Ln 37211
Lyncrest Dr 37214
Lyndale Ct & Dr 37207
Lyndeboro Ct 37221
Lyndon Parks Dr 37217
Lynmeade Ct & Dr 37210
Lynmont Dr 37215
Lynn Ct & Dr 37211
Lynnbrook Ct & Rd 37215
Lynnwood Blvd
804A-804B 37205
100-999 37205
1000-1199 37215
Lynnwood Ln 37205
Lynnwood Ter 37205
Lynwood Ave 37203
Lyric Ln 37207
Lytle Dr 37218
Mackie Pl & St 37209
Maclaurin Ct 37207
Madeline Dr 37211
Madia Vale Dr 37221
Madison St 37208
Magazine St 37203
Magnolia Blvd 37212
Magnolia Cir 37203
Magnolia Ct E 37221
Magnolia Ct W 37221
Magnolia Ln 37211
Magnolia Pl 37211
Magnolia Rd 37204
Magnolia Trl 37221
Magnolia Hills Ct & Dr 37221
Mailan Dr 37206
Main St
1-399 37213
400-1099 37206
Mainstream Dr 37228
Malden Dr 37210
Mallard Dr 37218
Mallory St 37203
Malone Ave 37205
Malquin Dr 37216
Malta Dr 37207
Manchester Ave
198A-198B 37206
100-399 37206
1800-2099 37218
Manila St 37206
Manley Dr 37220
Manor Dr 37205
Manorwood Ct 37211
Mansfield Ave & Ct 37206
Manuel Dr 37211
Maple Ave 37210
Maple Pl 37216
Maple Dale Ct 37221
Maple Grove Ln 37211
Maple Valley Ct 37211
Maplecrest Dr 37214
Maplehurst Ln 37204
Mapleleaf Dr 37210
Maplemere Dr 37215
Maplesong Ct & Dr 37211
Maplewood Ln 37216
W Maplewood Ln 37207
Maplewood Pl 37216
Maplewood Trce 37207
Marauder Dr 37209
Marc Ct & Dr 37211
Marcella Dr 37217
Marchant Dr 37211
Marcia Ave 37209
Marcus Dr 37211
Marengo Ln 37204
Margo Ln 37211
Marie St 37207
Marigold Dr 37211
Marilyn Rd 37209
Marina St
400-499 37207
800-999 37206
Marion Ave 37216
Mark Dr 37216
Marlborough Ave 37212
Marler Rd 37221
Marlin Ave 37215
Marquette Dr 37205
Marriott Dr 37214
Mars Dr 37217
Marsden Ave 37216
Marshall Ct 37212
Marshall St 37207
Marswen Dr 37216
Martha Ave 37216
Martin St 37203
Marwood Ct & Ln 37210
Mary St 37208
Mary Anton Ct 37211
Mary Evelyn Ct 37217
Mary Helen Dr 37220
Marydale Ct & Dr 37207
Mashburn Ct 37210
Mashburn Dr 37211
Mashburn Rd 37210
Mason Ave 37203
Masonwood Dr 37207
Massman Dr
600-799 37210
801-899 37210
900-1328 37217
1330-1334 37217
Massman Manor Dr 37217
Masterpiece Ct 37211
Matilda St 37207
Matthew Ln 37215
Matthews Ave 37216
Matthews Ct 37207
Matthews Pl 37206
Mattie St 37218
Maudina Ave 37209
Maury St 37210
Mavert Dr 37211
Maxey Ln 37216
Maxon Ave 37209
Maxwell Ave 37206
Maxwell Ct 37220
Maybelle Ln 37205
Mayer Ln 37218
Mayfair Ave 37215
Mayfair Rd 37205
Mayflower Pl 37204
Maymanor Cir 37205
Maynard Ct 37218
Maynor St 37216
Mays St 37211
Maywood Dr 37211
Mcadoo Ave 37205
Mcalpine Ave 37216
Mcarthur Ridge Ct 37220
Mccain Dr 37211
Mccall St 37211
Mccampbell Ave & Rd 37214
Mccann St 37210
Mccarn St 37206
Mccarthy Park Ln 37207
Mcchesney Ave 37216
Mcclellan Ave 37211
Mcclurkin Ave 37206
Mccombs Ave 37211
Mcconnell St 37204
Mccool Ct & Rd 37218
Mccrory Ln 37221
Mccrory Creek Rd 37214
Mcdaniel St 37208
Mcdonald Ct & Dr 37217
Mcdowell Dr 37218
Mcewen Ave 37206
Mcferrin Ave 37206
Mcgavock Pike
1420A-1420Z 37216
100-299 37214
300-599 37217
600-799 37214
800-899 37217
1100-2399 37216
2400-3299 37214
3400-3599 37217
Mcgavock St 37203
Mcginnis Dr 37216
Mcgrace Ln 37220
Mciver St 37211
Mckeand Ave 37204
Mckeige Ct & Dr 37214
Mckennell Dr 37206
W Mckennie Ave 37206
Mckinley St 37207
Mckinney Ave 37208
Mcknight Ln 37221
Mclemore Ave 37203
Mcmahan Ave 37216
Mcmillan Ct 37211
Mcmillan St 37203
Mcmurray Cir, Ct & Dr 37211
Mcnairy Ln 37204
Mcnally Dr 37211
Mcpherson Cir, Ct, Dr & Ln S 37221
Meade Ave
500-1899 37207
3001-3097 37211
3099-3299 37211
W Meade Dr 37205
Meadow Ct 37207
Meadow Dr 37215
N Meadow Ln 37221
Meadow Rd 37218
Meadow Cliff Dr 37210
Meadow Glen Ct 37221
Meadow Hill Dr 37218
Meadow Lane Dr 37221
Meadow Ridge Cir & Ct 37221
Meadow Rose Dr 37206
Meadow Trace Ct 37221
Meadow View Dr 37221
Meadowbrook Ave 37205
Meadowcrest Ln 37209
Meadowlake Ter 37217
Meadowood Dr 37214
Meadowside Ln 37207
Meadowwood Dr 37205
Mecca Dr 37214
Media St 37209
Medial Ave 37215
Medical Dr 37214
Medora Ave 37216
Meharry Blvd 37208
Melbourne Dr
2400-2499 37214
6100-6299 37215
Melinda Dr 37205
Melmack Dr 37211
Melody Ln 37214
Melpar Dr 37211
Melpark Dr 37204
Melrose Ave 37211
Melva Dr 37211
Melville Dr 37204
Melvin Jones Dr 37217
Menzler Rd 37210
Mercomatic Ct & Dr 37209
Mercury Dr 37217
Meredith Ave 37210
Meridian Ct & St 37207
Merlyn Ln 37214
Merrill Ln 37211
Merrimac Ct 37215
Merritt Ave 37203
Merry St 37208
Merry Oaks Dr 37214
Merrylodge Ct 37207
Merrymount Dr 37221
Mesa Dr 37217
Meta Cir, Ct & Dr 37211
Metro Center Blvd 37228
Metroplex Dr 37211
Mexico Dr 37218
Miami Ave 37214
Michael Dr 37214
Michigan Ave 37209
Middle St 37208
Middleboro Ct 37215
Middlebrook Cir 37221
Middleton Ave 37203
Middleton Cir 37215
Middleton Ct 37215
Middleton St 37210
Middleton Park Ln 37215
Midland Ave 37209
Midnight Sun Cir 37211
Midvale Dr 37214
Mike Shields Ct 37218
Mildred Ct 37211
Mildred Shute Ave 37210
Miles Ct 37205
Milesdale Ct & Dr 37204
Milford Rd 37218
Mill Run Cir 37221
Mill Station Ct & Dr 37207
Millbrook Cir & Dr 37221
Miller St 37210
Millerwood Dr 37211
Millrace Ln 37205
Millstone Ln 37205
Millwood Dr 37217
Milner Ct & Dr 37211
Milson Ave 37203
Milton Dr 37216
Mimosa Dr 37211
W Minister Dr 37221
Minnette Ct 37207
Mint Leaf Dr 37211
Misty Ct 37214
Misty Pines Cir 37211
Mitchell Rd 37206
Mock Orange Cir 37217
Mockingbird Rd 37205
Modena Ct & Dr 37214
Mohawk Dr 37205
Molloy St 37201
Monetta Ave 37216
Money Tree Way 37217
Monroe St 37208
Montcastle Ct & Dr 37221
Montclair Dr 37211
Montcrest Dr 37215
Montelle Ln 37211
Monterey Dr 37220
Montgomery Ave 37207
Monticello Dr & St 37207
Montrose Ave 37204
Moonlight Dr 37207
Moore Ave
2-98 37210
400-699 37203
Moorewood Ct & Dr 37207
Moormans Arm Rd 37207
Moran Ave 37216
Morena St 37208
Morgan Trace Ct 37221
Morganmeade Ct & Dr 37216
Morningside 37215
Morningside Dr 37207
Morrisey Ct 37221
Morrison St 37208
Morriswood Ct & Dr 37204
Morrow Ave 37204
Morrow Rd 37209
Morton Ave 37211
Morton Mill Cir, Ct & Rd 37221
Moss Rd 37221
Moss Creek Ct 37221
Moss Rose Ct & Dr 37216
Mossdale Dr 37217
Moultrie Park 37205
Mound Ct 37207
Mount Carmel Pl 37205
Mount Pisgah Ct & Rd 37211
Mountain Valley Bnd, Dr & Ln 37209
Mountain View Dr 37215
Mountainside Dr 37215
Mulberry St 37203
Mulberry Way 37207
Mullen Cir 37217
Mulloy Aly 37203
Munn Ln & Rd 37214
Murfreesboro Pike
1218A-1218B 37217
Murphy Ave 37203
Murphy Ct 37203
Murphy Rd
3400-3499 37203
3500-3599 37205
3600-4699 37209
Murray Cir & Pl 37216
Music Cir & Sq E, N, S & W 37203
Music City Cir 37214
Music Valley Dr 37214
Musket Trl 37217
Myhr Dr & Grn 37221
Myrick Dr 37214
Myrtle St 37206
Myrtlewood Dr 37211
Nall Ave 37209
Nance Ln 37210
Nanearle Pl 37220
Naples Ave 37207
Napoleon Ave 37211
Nashboro Blvd & Grns 37217
Nashboro Greens Ct & Way 37217
Nashua Ave, Ct & Ln 37209
Nassau St 37208
Natchez Ct 37211
N Natchez Ct 37211
Natchez Trce 37212
Natchez Bend Rd 37221
Nautilus Dr 37217
Navaho Cir 37211
Navaho Ct 37207
Navaho Trl 37211
Neal Ter 37203
Neartop Dr 37205
Nebraska Ave 37209
Ned Shelton Rd 37217
Needles Ct 37214
Neese Dr 37211
Neighborly Ave 37209
Neil Ave 37206
Neill Ave 37206
Neilwood Dr 37205
Neilworth Ln 37214
Neldia Ct 37206
Nelson Pl 37214
Nelson Merry St 37203
Nesbitt Ct & Dr 37207
Nestor St 37210
Neuhoff Ln 37205
Nevada Ave 37209
New Haven Ct 37214
New Natchez Trce 37215
New Sawyer Brown Rd 37221
New York Ave 37209
Newberry Rd 37205
Newhall Dr 37206
Newman Ave 37216
Newman Pl 37204
Newsom Grn 37221
Newsom Station Rd 37221
Newsome St 37211
Newton Ct & St 37209
Niagara Ct & Dr 37214
Nichol Ln 37205
Nichol Rd 37209
Nichols Ct 37205
Noble Valley Dr 37214
E & W Nocturne Dr 37207
Nocturne Forest Ct & Dr 37207
Nodyne Dr 37214
Noel Green Ct 37204
Noelton Ave
900-1099 37204
1200-1299 37215
Nolensville Pike
4504A-4504Z 37211
1900-4113 37211
4112-4112 37222
4114-6398 37211
4115-6399 37211
Nolensville Rd 37210
Noonan Ct & Dr 37206
Norcross Dr 37217
Norfleet Dr 37220
Norma Dr 37211
Normandy Cir & Pl 37209
Norris Ave 37204
Northbrook Dr 37207
Northcrest Ct & Dr 37211
Northcrest Commons Cir 37211
Northoak Dr 37211
Northridge Cir, Ct & Dr 37221
Northumberland 37215
Northview Ave 37216
Norton Ave 37207
Norvel Ave 37216
Norwalk Ct & Dr 37214
Norway Ct & Ter 37211
Norwood Dr 37204
Nottingham Pl 37221
Novak Ln 37211
Nubell St 37208

Nunahi Trl 37221
Nunley Dr 37211
Nunnery Ln 37221
O Neal Dr 37208
Oak Ct 37206
Oak St
400-599 37203
800-999 37216
Oak Cliff Dr 37214
Oak Grove Dr 37217
Oak Haven Ct & Trce 37209
Oak Meadows Ln 37215
Oak Park Dr 37207
Oak Ridge Dr 37207
Oak Valley Dr 37207
Oak Valley Ln 37220
Oakhill Dr 37206
Oakhurst Dr 37216
Oakland Ave 37212
Oakland St 37210
Oaklawn Ave 37215
Oakleigh Hl 37215
Oakley Dr
300-399 37211
400-699 37220
Oakmont Cir 37209
Oakview Dr 37207
Oakway Ct 37214
Oakwood Ave 37207
Obrien Ave 37209
N & S Observatory Ct & Dr 37215
Ocala Cir, Ct & Dr N & S 37211
Oceanside Dr 37204
Oceola Ave 37209
Ogden Dr 37218
Ohio Ave 37209
Old Buena Vista Pike 37218
Old Charlotte Pike 37209
Old Club Ct & Ln 37215
Old Elm Hill Pike 37214
Old Ezell Rd
600-698 37217
700-899 37217
3200-3299 37211
Old Glenrose Ave 37210
Old Goins Rd 37211
Old Harding Ct 37221
Old Harding Ln 37221
Old Harding Pike
5701-5897 37205
5899-5999 37205
7000-8799 37221
Old Hermitage Ave 37210
Old Hickory Blvd
1199A-1199C 37207
101-197 37221
199-399 37221
400-741 37209
743-799 37209
1101-1109 37207
1111-1599 37207
2100-2299 37215
2301-2399 37215
2400-2999 37221
3800-5899 37218
5901-5999 37218
14800-15699 37211
Old Hydes Ferry Pike 37218
Old Lebanon Rd 37214
Old Matthews Rd 37207
Old Murfreesboro Pike 37217
Old Paragon Mills Rd 37211
Old Smith Springs Rd 37217
Old Trail Ct 37207
Old Tree Ct 37210
Old Trinity Ln 37207
Old Village Rd 37211
Old Williamsburg Ct 37215
Oldfield Dr 37214
Oldham St 37213
Olen Taylor Dr 37217
Olga Ave 37216
Olive Cir 37217
Olive Branch Rd 37205
Olmsted Dr 37221
Olsen Ln 37218
Olympic St 37203
Oman St 37203
Omandale Dr 37204
Omohundro Ct, Dr & Pl 37210
Oneida Ave 37207
Onslow Way 37221
Opry Aly 37219
Opry Mills Dr 37214
Opryland Dr 37214
Ordway Pl 37206
Oriel Ave 37210
Oriole Pl 37215
Orlando Ave 37209
Orleans Dr 37212
Ormond Dr 37205
Ortega Rd 37214
Osage St 37208
Osprey Ct 37211
Osprey Ln 37221
Otay St 37216
Otter Ln 37211
Otter Creek Rd
800-1199 37220
1200-2099 37215
Otter Valley Ln 37215
Outer Dr 37204
Ovendens Dr 37228
Overbrook Ct & Dr 37204
Overby Rd 37207
Overcreek Ct & Dr 37217
Overcrest Ct & Dr 37211
Overhill Cir 37214
Overhill Dr 37215
Overlook Dr 37212
Overton Ct 37220
Overton Ln 37220
Overton Park 37215
Overton Rd 37220
Overton St 37203
Overton Lea Rd 37220
Owen St 37208
Owsley Ct 37214
Oxbow Dr 37207
Oxford Rd 37215
Oxford St 37216
Oxton Hill Ln 37215
Ozark St 37206
Paces Ferry Dr 37214
Packard Dr 37211
Paddle Wheel Ct & Dr 37214
Paddock Ln 37205
Paddock Park 37220
Paden Dr 37206
Pafford Dr 37206
Page Rd 37205
Paige Cir & Ct 37207
Palmer Pl 37203
Palomar Ct 37211
Pamela Dr 37217
Panorama Dr 37218
Pappus Ct 37207
Paragon Dr 37211
Paragon Mills Rd 37211
Paris Ave
1000-1199 37204
1200-1599 37212
Parishwood Ct 37211
Park Ave 37209
Park Cir 37205
Park Ct 37211
Park Dr 37214
Park Gln 37204
Park Ln
900-999 37221
6300-6399 37205
Park Mdws 37215
Park Plz 37203
Park St 37209
Park Center Ave 37209
Park Crescent Cir 37215
Park Dale Dr 37217
Park Hill Dr 37205
Park Ridge Dr 37215
Park South Ct 37210
Park Terrace Dr 37204
Parkview Cir 37204
Parkway Dr 37207
Parkwood Ter 37220
Parman Pl 37203
Parmer Ave 37205
Parmley Ln 37207
Parris Ave 37210
Parry Dr 37217
Parthenon Ave 37203
Partner Way 37211
Pasadena Dr 37204
Pascal Ct 37207
Pasquo Rd 37221
Patina Cir 37209
Patio Ct & Dr 37214
Patomic Dr 37221
Patricia Dr 37217
Patriot Way 37214
Patten Ln 37221
Patterson St
400-599 37211
1600-2499 37203
Patton Ave 37209
Patton Hill Rd 37207
Paulawood Dr 37207
Pavilion Blvd 37217
Payson Ct 37211
Peabody St
1-313 37210
315-325 37210
600-699 37203
Peach Blossom Sq 37205
Peach Creek Cres 37214
Peach Orchard Dr 37204
Peachtree St 37210
Peak Hill Cir & Cv 37211
Pear Ct 37221
Pearl St
1600-1999 37203
2400-2499 37208
Pearson Pl 37211
Pebble Brk 37221
Pecan St 37208
Pecan Valley Rd 37218
Peerman Dr 37206
Pegram St 37209
Pembroke Ave 37205
Penfield Dr 37211
Peninsula Ct 37217
Penn Meade Dr & Way 37214
Pennington Ave
100-1099 37206
2200-2299 37216
2301-2399 37216
2500-2599 37206
2600-2699 37216
Pennington Bend Rd 37214
Pennock Ave 37207
Pennsylvania Ave 37209
Pennywell Dr 37205
Percy Dr 37205
Percy Priest Dr 37214
Percy Warner Blvd 37205
Perimeter Rd 37217
Perimeter Hill Dr 37211
S Perimeter Park Dr 37211
Perimeter Place Dr 37214
Perkins St 37210
Perlen Dr 37206
Persia Way 37211
Petrie Ct 37211
Petway Ave 37206
Pewitt Rd 37218
Pheasant Dr 37218
Philfre Ct 37217
Phillips St 37208
Philwood Dr 37214
Phipps Dr 37218
Piccadilly Pl 37215
Pickell Dr 37210
Picture Ridge Ter 37216
Piedmont Ave 37216
Pierce Ave 37212
Pierpoint Dr 37207
Pilcher Ave 37209
Pillow St 37203
Pine St 37203
Pine Forest Dr 37221
Pine Hill Ln & Rd 37221
Pine Meadow Ct 37221
Pine Ridge Dr & Rd 37207
Pinecrest Dr 37211
Pinehurst Dr
1900-1999 37216
6100-6199 37215
Pineview Dr 37207
Pineview Ln 37211
Pineway Dr 37217
Pinewood Rd 37216
Pinnacle Pl 37221
Pioneer Ln 37206
Pittswood Dr 37214
Pittway Dr 37207
Plantation Ct 37221
Plateau Pkwy 37205
Players Ct 37211
Pleasant Green Rd 37214
Pleasant Hill Rd 37214
Pleasant Valley Rd 37204
Pleasant View Dr 37214
Plum St 37207
Plus Park Blvd 37217
Plymouth Ave 37216
Point East Dr 37216
Polk Ave
1-200 37210
202-220 37210
222-299 37203
300-1200 37210
1202-1298 37210
Polk Forest Cir & Ct 37207
Polo Ct & Pl 37211
Polo Club Rd 37221
Ponder Pl 37228
Pontotoc Ave 37206
Poplar Ave 37210
Poplar Ct 37216
Poplar Ln 37210
Poplar Pl 37216
Poplar St 37210
Poplar Creek Rd & Trce 37221
Poplar Creek Trace Ct 37221
Poplar Hill Ct 37214
Poplar Ridge Ct & Dr 37221
Poplar Valley Ct 37221
Poplarwood Ln & Rd 37221
Porter 37203
Porter Ave 37206
Porter Rd 37206
Porter Ter 37206
Porter House Dr 37211
Portland Ave 37212
Portman Dr 37214
Portview Dr 37217
Post Pl & Rd 37205
Post Creek Rd 37221
Poston Ave 37203
Postwood Pl 37205
Potter Ln 37206
Powder Mill Rd 37205
Powell Ave & Pl 37204
Powers Ave 37206
Precious Ct 37214
Premier Dr 37209
Prentice Ave 37204
Prescott Ct 37204
Prescott Pl 37211
Prescott Rd 37204
Preston Dr 37206
Preston Taylor Pl 37209
Prestwick Ct 37205
Price Circle Rd 37205
Priest Rd 37215
Priest Lake Dr 37217
Priest Woods Ct & Dr 37214
Primrose Ave & Cir 37212
Prince Ave 37207
Princess Ln 37218
Princeton Ave 37205
Printers Aly 37201
Pritchett Dr 37220
Prospect Hl 37205
Providence Hts 37211
Providence Park Ln 37211
Public Sq 37201
Pullen Ave 37207
Pulley Rd 37214
Pumping Station Rd 37210
Purnell Dr 37211
Putnam Ct & Dr 37218
Quail Ct, Rd & Run E & W 37214
Quail Creek Rd 37221
Quail Ridge Dr 37207
Quail Run Ct 37214
Quail Valley Rd 37214
Quail View Dr 37214
Quality Way 37207
Qualynn Dr 37207
Queen Ave 37207
Queens Ln 37218
Queens Lane Ct 37218
Quimby Ct 37211
Quinn Cir & Ct 37210
Rachel Dr & Rd 37214
Radcliff Dr 37221
Radford Dr 37217
Radnor St 37211
Ragland Dr 37220
Ragsdale Ct 37214
Rainbow Pl 37204
Rains Ave 37203
Rainwood Ct & Dr 37207
Ramble Hill Cir & Ct 37211
Ramble Wood Cir 37221
Rambling Rd 37217
Rambling Brook Rd 37218
Ramblingwood Ct 37217
Ramsey St 37206
Ranchero Dr 37209
Randall Dr 37211
Randolph Pl 37215
Rannoch Pl 37220
Ransom Pl & Way 37217
Rascoe Rd 37210
Ravens Gln 37211
Ravenwood Dr 37216
Ravenwood Hills Cir 37215
Ravine Dr 37217
Raymond St 37211
Raymond Roberts Dr 37221
Raywood Ct & Ln 37211
Reasonover Grn 37221
Rebecca Ave 37216
Recovery Rd 37211
Red Cedar Ct 37214
Red Maple Dr 37221
Red Oak Dr 37205
Red Rose Ct 37218
Red Tanager Ct 37221
Redbud Dr 37215
Redcastle Rdg 37211
Redd Ct 37211
Redleaf Ridge Cir 37211
Redmon St 37209
Redmond Ct & Ln 37211
Redwood Dr 37220
Reelfoot Cir, Ct & Dr 37214
Regency Dr 37221
Regent Dr 37220
Reid Ave 37203
Reidhurst Ave 37203
Reischa Ct & Dr 37211
Reischa Sue Cir & Ln 37211
Renee Dr 37214
Reservoir Ct 37203
Resha Ln 37218
Restover Ct 37214
Rev Dr Enoch Jones Blvd 37208
Revels Dr 37207
Revere Park 37205
Revere Pl 37214
Rexdale Dr 37217
Reynolds Rd 37217
Rhett Dr 37211
Rhonda Ln 37205
Rice Ave 37217
Rich Ct 37211
Rich Acres Dr 37207
Richard Irwin Ct 37211
Richard Jones Rd 37215
Richards St 37215
Richardson Ave
1-999 37207
3500-3599 37205
Richbriar Cir, Ct & Rd 37211
Richfield Dr 37205
Richland Ave 37205
Richmar Ct & Dr 37211
Richmond Dr 37216
W Richmond Hill Dr 37207
E Ridge Dr 37211
Ridge Top Dr 37207
Ridgecrest Dr 37216
Ridgefield Ct, Dr & Way 37205
Ridgelake Pkwy 37209
Ridgeland Dr 37214
Ridgemont Dr 37207
Ridgeside Dr 37207
S Ridgeview Dr 37220
Ridgeway Dr 37214
Ridgewood Dr 37215
Ridley Blvd 37203
Ries Ave 37209
Rigden Mill Dr 37211
Rigger Ct 37217
Ringgold Dr 37207
Ritchie Dr 37220
River Ct
100-199 37221
2900-2999 37218
River Dr 37218
River Rd 37209
River Trce 37218
River Bend Cir 37221
River Bend Dr 37214
River Bend Rd 37221
River Bend Way 37221
River Fork Dr 37221
River Hills Dr 37210
River Junction Dr 37221
River Meade Way 37214
River Oaks Cv 37214
River Park Ct & Dr 37221
River Ridge Ct, Dr & Ter 37221
River Road Pike 37209
River Rouge Ct & Dr 37209
River View Dr 37209
River Walk Ct & Dr 37214
Riverbend Ct, Dr, Ln & Rd 37221
Riverbranch Ct 37221
Rivercliff Dr 37218
Rivercrest Ct, Cv, Pass & Way 37214
Riverfront Dr 37221
Riverland Dr 37221
Riverplace Dr 37221
Riverpoint Ct & Pass 37214
Rivers Edge Ct & Dr 37214
Riverside Dr
2123A-2123B 37216
200-1599 37206
1600-2399 37216
Riverspring Dr 37221
Riverstone Blvd, Ct & Dr 37214
Rivervalley Dr 37221
Riverview Dr 37214
Riverview Bend Dr 37221
E Riverwood Cir & Dr 37216
Robbie Ct 37214
Robert Burns Dr 37217
Robert E Lee Ct & Dr 37215
Roberta St 37206
Roberts Ave 37206
Robertson Ave 37209
Robertson St 37210
Robertson Academy Rd 37220
Robin Rd 37204
Robin Hill Rd 37205
Robin Springs Rd 37220
Robwood Dr 37207
Rochelle Dr 37220
Rock St 37207
Rock City St 37216
Rock Harbour Ct 37221
Rock Wall Rd 37221
Rockdale Ave 37204
Rockeford Dr 37221
Rocky Ln 37209
Rodney Ct & Dr 37205
Roger Ave 37207
Roger Williams Ave 37207
Roleeson Ln 37207
Rolland Rd 37205
Rollett Ct 37211
Rolling Fork Ct & Dr 37205
Rolling Hills Dr 37221
Rolling River Ct & Pkwy 37221
Rollingwood Ln 37217
Rolynn Dr 37210
Roma Ct 37211
Roman Dr 37207
Rome Ave 37209
Rosa L Parks Ave 37203
Rosa L Parks Blvd
100-799 37203
900-1899 37208
2000-2599 37228
Rose St 37210
Rose Cliff Dr 37206
Rose Hall 37212
Rose Park Dr 37206
Rosebank Ave
315A-315B 37206
100-1599 37206
1800-1999 37216
Rosebank Ct 37206
Rosedale Ave
536A-536B 37211
1511A-1511B 37207
300-599 37211
1300-1599 37207
Rosedale Ct 37207
Rosedale Pl 37211
Rosehaven Dr 37211
Roselawn Cir 37215
Rosemary Ln 37210
Rosemont Ave 37215
Roseview Dr 37206
Rosewood Ave 37212
Roslyn Ct 37221
Roundhill Ct, Cv, Dr & Pl 37211
Rowan Ct & Dr 37207
Roy St 37207
Roy Acuff Pl 37203
Royal Pkwy
400-524 37214
525-525 37229
526-898 37214
527-899 37214
Royal Crest Ave 37214
Royal Oaks Dr & Pl 37205
Roycroft Pl 37203
Rs Gass Blvd 37216
Rucker Ave 37210
Rudolph Ave 37206
Rudy Cir 37214
Rugby Dr 37207
Ruland Pl 37215
Runabout Dr 37217
Rundle Ave 37210
W Running Brook Rd 37209
Running Deer 37221
Rural Ave 37209
Rural Hill Cir, Ct & Rd 37217
Rushing Brook Cir 37221
Ruskin Ave 37216
Russell Rd 37221

Russell St
1-197 37213
199-299 37213
400-2099 37206
Russellwood Dr 37204
Russleo Dr 37209
Rustic Ct 37214
Rutledge St 37210
Ryan Ct 37221
Rychen Dr 37217
Sable Ridge Ct 37221
Sabre Dr 37211
Saddle Dr 37221
Saddle Ridge Ct &
Trce 37221
Sadler Ave & Ct 37210
Sailboat Ct & Dr 37217
Saindon St 37211
Saint Andrews Pl 37204
Saint Charles Pl 37212
Saint Danasus Dr 37211
Saint Edwards Dr 37211
Saint Francis Ave 37205
Saint Henry Dr 37205
Saint James Park & Pl 37215
Saint Joseph Dr 37218
Saint Jules Ln 37211
Saint Louis St 37208
Saint Luke Dr 37205
Saint Marys Ln 37218
Saint Mellion 37215
Saint Thomas Dr 37205
Salem Dr 37211
Salem Mason Dr 37208
Salyer Dr 37205
Sam Boney Dr 37211
San Marcos Dr 37220
Sanborn Dr 37210
Sandalwood Ct 37221
Sandburg Ct & Pl 37214
Sandpiper Cir 37221
Sandra Dr 37210
Sandy Dr 37216
Sandy Creek Rd 37221
Sanford Ave 37211
Santi Ave 37208
Saratoga Dr 37205
Saturn Dr 37217
Saunders Ave & Ct 37216
Saussy Ct & Pl 37205
Savannah Pl 37204
Savoy Cir 37205
Sawyer Brown Ct 37221
Sawyer Brown Rd
7400-7499 37209
7500-9399 37221
Saxon Ct 37205
Saxon Dr 37215
Saxon Mist Ct & Dr 37217
Say Brook Cir 37221
Saylor Ct 37209
Scarcroft Ln 37221
Scarritt Pl 37203
Scarsdale Rd 37215
Scenic Dr 37204
Scenic River Ln 37221
Scenic View Dr 37221
Scholarship Dr 37209
School Ln 37217
Schrader Ln 37208
Schrader Acres Dr 37208
Scobey Dr 37210
Scomangt St 37208
Scotland Pl 37205
Scott Ave
1-2099 37206
2100-2999 37216
Scott Valley Dr 37217
Scotwood Dr 37211
Scout Dr 37211
Scovel St 37208
Seaboard Dr 37211
Sedberry Rd 37205
Seesaw Ct & Rd 37211
Seifried St 37208
Selena Dr 37211

Selma Ave 37214
Seminary St 37207
Seminole Ave 37211
Seneca Ct & Dr 37214
Seneca Forest Ct &
Dr 37217
Sennadale Ln 37207
Sentinel Dr 37209
Sequoyah Ln 37221
Setliff Pl 37206
Setter Ct 37207
Setters Rd 37218
Settlers Ct & Way 37221
Seven Hills Pl 37215
Seven Mile Cir & Ct 37211
Sevier Ct & St 37206
Sewanee Rd 37220
Seymour Ave 37206
Shackleford Ct & Rd 37215
Shacklett Dr 37214
Shadescrest Dr 37211
Shadetree Ct 37207
Shadow Ln
900-1199 37206
2300-2999 37216
Shadow Glen Dr 37211
Shadowood Ct 37217
Shadowood Dr 37205
Shadowstone Pl 37220
Shady Ln 37206
Shady Creek Ln 37211
Shady Dale Rd 37218
Shady Grove Dr 37214
Shady Oak Dr 37217
Shane Point Pl 37211
Sharkenc St 37210
Sharon Hill Cir 37215
Sharondale Ct & Dr 37215
Sharonwood Dr 37215
Sharpe Ave 37206
Shasta Dr 37211
Shauna Ct & Dr 37214
Shawn Dr 37211
Shawnee Dr 37205
Shawnwood Cir 37218
Sheffield Ct 37215
Sheffield Dr 37211
Sheffield Pl 37215
Sheffield Sq 37221
Shelby Ave
100-299 37213
400-1999 37206
Shelton Ave 37216
Shenandoah Ct 37220
Shepard St 37210
Shepards Sq 37211
Sheppard Pl 37205
Sherbourne Ave 37204
Sherbrooke Ct, Cv &
Ln 37211
Sheridan Rd 37206
Sherman Ct 37214
Sherman Oaks Dr 37211
Sherwood Ct 37215
Sherwood Dr 37215
Sherwood Ln 37216
Shetland Ct 37211
Shiaway Ct 37217
Shiloh Dr 37205
Shipp Ln 37207
Shirley St 37203
Shirmar Dr 37211
Shreeve Ln 37207
Shumate Ln 37217
Shys Hill Rd 37215
Sidco Dr 37204
Siena Dr 37205
Sigler St 37203
Signal Hill Dr 37205
Silas Dr 37207
Silkwood Cir & Dr 37221
Sills Ct 37220
Silo Ct 37221
Silverbrook Ct 37221
Silverdene Pl 37206
Silverleaf Ct & Ter 37221

Simmons Ave 37211
Simpkins St 37208
Simpson Ct 37211
Sinbad Dr 37214
Sitting Mill Ct 37211
Sky Valley Grv 37217
Skyline Dr 37215
Skymont Dr 37215
Skyview Dr 37206
Slate Dr 37216
Slaydon Dr 37207
Sleepy Hollow Dr 37217
Sloan Rd 37209
Smartt Dr 37220
Smiley St 37206
Smith Springs Ct &
Rd 37217
Smithwood Dr 37214
Smokewood Way 37221
Sneed Rd
500-599 37221
4000-4399 37215
Sneed Ter 37215
Snell Blvd 37218
Snook Dr 37210
Snowden Rd 37204
Snyder Ave 37209
Solley Dr 37216
Solness Ave 37218
Solon Dr 37206
Solway Ct 37209
Somerhill Ct 37221
Somerset Ct 37217
Somerset Dr 37217
Somerset Pl 37221
Somerset Farms Cir, Ct
& Dr 37221
Sommersby Ct 37221
Sonar St 37214
Songwriter Cir 37220
Sonya Dr 37209
Soper Ave 37204
South St
800-1199 37203
1300-1599 37212
Southcrest Dr 37211
Southerland Dr 37207
Southern Turf Dr 37211
Southgate Ave 37203
Southlake Ct & Dr 37211
Southmeade Pkwy 37204
Southoak Dr 37211
Southridge Dr 37207
Southside Ave 37203
Southside Cir 37212
Southside Ct 37203
Southside Pl 37203
Southview Dr 37218
Southwind Dr 37217
Southwood Dr 37217
Southwood Park Pl 37217
Space Park S 37211
Spain Ave 37216
Sparrow Ct 37221
Sparta Rd 37205
Spartan Dr 37211
Spears Rd 37207
Spence Cir 37210
Spence Ct 37210
Spence Ln
100-599 37210
600-999 37217
Spence Enclave Ct, Ln &
Way 37210
Spencer St 37209
Sperry Ave 37215
Spicewood Cir & Ln 37211
Spickard Ct 37218
Splitwood Ct 37211
Spring Ct 37207
Spring Pl 37221
Spring St 37207
Spring Creek Dr 37209
Spring Place Dr 37214
Spring Ridge Ct, Dr &
Ln 37221

Spring Valley Ln & Rd 37214
Springbrook Dr 37204
Springdale Dr 37215
Springhaven Ct 37221
Springhouse Ln 37214
Springlake Ct 37221
Springview Dr 37214
Springwater Dr 37221
Sprint Dr 37209
Spruce St 37203
Stacy Dr 37221
Stacy Square Ct &
Ter 37221
Stafford Dr 37214
Staffordshire Dr 37221
Stainback Ave 37207
Stallion Ct & Dr 37221
Stallworth Dr 37220
Stammer Pl 37215
Standing Stone Ct &
Dr 37207
Stanford Ct & Dr 37215
Stanley St 37210
Stanvid Dr 37216
Stanwyck Dr 37207
Starboard Ct & Dr 37217
Starlight Dr 37207
Starliner Ct & Dr 37209
Starlit Rd 37205
State St 37203
Stateline Rd 37210
Steamboat Ct & Dr 37214
Steele Ct 37214
Steeplechase Ct & Ln 37221
Steffisburg Dr 37211
Sterling Rd 37215
Sterling St 37209
Sterling Boone Dr 37210
Sterling Cross 37211
Stevens Ln 37218
Stevenson St 37209
Stewart Pl 37203
E Stewarts Ln 37218
Stewarts Ferry Pike &
Pkwy 37214
Still Hollow Rd 37215
Still Spring Hollow Ct &
Dr 37221
Still Water Cir 37221
Stillmeadow Dr 37211
Stillwood Dr 37220
Stilton Dr 37207
Stinson Rd 37214
Stirrup Ct & Dr 37221
Stirton Rd 37210
Stivers St 37218
Stockdale Ln 37207
Stockell St 37207
Stockett Dr 37221
Stockyard St 37201
Stokers Ln 37218
Stokers Ln N 37207
Stokers Ln S 37207
Stokes Ln 37215
Stokesboro Ct 37215
Stokesmont Rd 37215
Stokeswood Pl 37215
Stone Ln 37211
Stone Briar Ct 37211
Stone Chimney Ct 37214
Stone Creek Ct & Rd 37221
Stone Heath Ct 37211
Stone Mountain Ct 37211
Stone Ridge Ct & Dr 37211
Stone Run Dr 37211
Stonecrest Dr & Way 37209
Stonehaven Ct & Dr 37215
Stonehindge Way 37221
Stonehurst Dr 37215
Stonemeade Dr 37221
Stones River Ct, Cv &
Rd 37214
Stonewall Dr 37220
Stonewall Jackson Ct 37220
Stoneway Trl 37209
Stoneway Close 37209

Stonewood Ct 37217
Stonybrook Dr 37221
Stormlight Ct N & S 37217
Straightway Ave & Cir 37206
Strasser Dr 37211
Stratford Ave 37216
Stratton Ave 37206
Strawberry Cv 37207
Strawberry Hl 37215
Strickland Dr
700-2198 37206
2200-2299 37206
3000-3099 37221
Stringfellow Rd 37209
Strouse Ave 37206
Stuart Glen Dr 37215
Student Center Ln 37203
Sturbridge Ct 37215
Sugar Creek Cir 37214
Sugar Hill Dr 37211
Sugar Maple Ln 37221
Sugar Mill Dr & Trl 37211
Sugar Tree Rd 37215
Sugar Valley Dr 37211
Sugarberry Ct 37211
Sugarbush Ct 37211
Sugarloaf Ct & Dr 37211
Sugarplum Rd 37211
Sugartree Pl 37215
Sulphur Creek Rd 37218
Sultana Ave 37207
Sumatra Dr 37218
Summer Pl 37206
Summerlake Dr 37214
Summerly Dr 37209
Summertime Dr 37207
Summerview Ct & Cv 37221
Summerwind Cir 37215
Summerwood Ln 37221
Summit Oaks Ct, Dr &
Pl 37221
Summit Ridge Cir, Ct, Dr
& Pl 37215
Summitt Ave
900-999 37203
1001-1199 37203
2100-2299 37218
Sumner Ave 37206
Sunbar Ln 37211
Sunderland Cir 37221
Sunlight Dr 37211
Sunliner Dr 37209
Sunnett Pl 37211
Sunnybrook Dr 37205
Sunnymeade Dr 37216
Sunnyside Dr 37205
Sunnyview Ct & Dr 37218
Sunnywood Dr 37211
Sunrise Ave 37211
Sunrise Ct 37221
Sunset Cir 37207
Sunset Dr 37207
Sunset Pl 37212
Sunset Hills Ter 37215
Sunvalley W 37221
Surf Dr 37207
Surrey Rd 37214
Susan Dr 37214
Susannah Ct & Dr 37209
Sussex Cir 37205
Sussex Ct 37207
Sussex Dr 37207
Suter Ct & Dr 37211
Sutherland Ave 37205
Sutton Hill Rd 37204
Swallow Pt 37221
Sweeney Ave 37217
Sweet Bay Cir 37221
Sweet Cherry Ct 37215
Sweetberry Ct & Dr 37211
Sweetbriar Ave 37212
Sweetgum Cir, Ct &
Ln 37221
Sweetwood Rd 37214
Swiss Ave 37211
Sycamore Ln 37215

Sycamore Rd 37204
Sycamore Ridge Cir 37214
Syfert Ln 37211
Sylvan St
200-299 37213
500-598 37206
600-899 37206
Sylvan Glen Ct 37209
Sylvan Park Ln 37209
Sylvania Dr 37207
Symphony Pl 37201
Taggart Ave 37205
Taigans Ct 37218
Tall Trees Ln 37209
Tallwood Dr 37211
Tally Green Ct 37214
Tammany Dr
1500-1799 37206
1800-2099 37216
Tampa Dr 37211
Tamworth Dr 37214
Tanglewood Ct 37211
Tanglewood Dr 37216
Tanksley Ave 37211
Tara Dr 37215
Tara Ann Ct 37217
Tarmac Way 37211
Tarrywood Ln 37217
Tate Ct 37214
Taylor Rd 37211
Taylor St 37208
Taylor Merritt Ct 37209
Taz Hyde Rd 37218
Teakwood Dr 37214
Tempany Ct 37207
Temple Ave 37215
Temple Rd 37221
Temple Hollow Cir 37221
Temple Ridge Ct & Dr 37221
Templegate Dr 37221
Templeton Dr 37205
Templewood Ct & Dr 37214
Tennessee Ave 37209
Teradwa Dr 37215
Terminal Ct 37210
Terminal Dr 37214
Tern Ct 37221
Terrace Pl 37203
Terry Dr 37209
Terry Trce 37205
Thackery Dr 37207
The Commons Dr 37215
Theodore Rd 37214
Theresa Ave 37205
Thistlewood Dr 37216
Thomas Ave 37216
Thomas St 37210
Thompson Ave 37204
Thompson Ln
2-60 37211
62-537 37211
539-599 37211
600-799 37204
900-999 37211
E Thompson Ln 37211
W Thompson Ln 37211
Thompson Pl 37217
Thorncrest Rd 37211
Thorndale Ct 37215
Thrasher Way 37221
Thrible Springs Ct &
Dr 37211
Thunderbird Ct & Dr 37209
Thurman St 37204
Thuss Ave 37211
Tibbs Ct & Dr 37211
Tidwell Rd 37209
Tidwell Hollow Rd 37218
Tiffany Dr 37206
Tiger Cir 37207
Tigerbelle Dr 37209
Tillman Ln 37206
N Timber Dr 37214
S Timber Dr 37214
Timber Grv 37214
Timber Ln 37215

Timber Pt 37214
Timber Run 37214
Timber Gap Dr 37221
Timber Ridge Cir 37211
Timber Ridge Dr 37217
Timber Valley Dr 37214
Timberdale Ct & Dr 37211
Timberhill Ct & Dr 37211
Timberland Dr 37217
Timberline Ct 37207
Timberline Dr 37221
Timberway Cir & Dr 37214
Timberwood Dr & Pl 37215
Timmons St 37211
Timothy Dr
4000-4199 37218
5900-5999 37215
Timwood Dr 37214
Tinney Cir & Pl 37217
Tintern Abbott Ct 37211
Titans Way 37213
Tobylynn Cir, Ct & Dr 37211
Todd Preis Dr 37221
Toddington Dr 37215
Toddway Ct 37214
Tolbert Rd 37209
Tolkien Ln 37211
Toney Rd 37207
Toomer Ct 37217
Torbay Dr 37211
Torbett St 37209
Torrington Ct & Rd 37205
Toshas Ct 37218
Tote Ln 37211
Tower Pl 37204
Town Park Dr 37217
Townes Ct & Dr 37211
Townsend Dr 37203
Townview Pl 37217
Towry Dr 37211
Trace Ct 37221
Trace Creek Ct & Dr 37221
Trace Glen Ct 37221
Trace Park Cir & Ct 37221
Trace Ridge Ln 37221
Traceside Dr 37221
Traceway Dr 37221
Trade Winds Ct 37214
Trading Post Ct 37221
Traemoor Village Ct, Dr,
Pl & Way 37209
Trails Cir 37214
Trails End Ln 37214
Trailway Cir & Dr 37207
Trailwood Cir 37207
Trailwood Ct 37214
Trailwood Pl 37207
Transit Ave 37210
Traughber Dr 37206
Travelers Ct 37220
Travelers Ridge Dr 37220
Travis Dr 37211
Tredco Dr 37210
Treeline Ct 37221
Treemont Ct 37220
Tremont Ave 37212
Treutland Ave & Pl 37207
Trevecca Ave 37206
Trevor St 37209
Treyburn Ct 37221
Trice Dr 37209
Trimble Ct 37215
Trimble Rd 37215
Trimble St 37210
E Trinity Ln 37207
Trinity Hills Pkwy 37207
Trousdale Dr
3600-4699 37204
4700-5399 37220
Troy Ct & Dr 37207
Truett Ave 37206
Trumpet Cir 37218
Truxton Ct 37214
Truxton Dr 37214
Truxton Pl 37205
Ts Jackson Ave 37209

Tuckahoe Ct, Dr & Sq E & W 37207
Tuckaway Ct 37205
Tucker Rd 37218
Tudor Ln 37211
Tuggle Ave 37211
Tuia Ln 37211
Tulane Ct 37215
Tulip Way 37221
Tulip Hill Dr 37210
Tuliptree Ct & Ln 37221
Tune Airport Dr 37209
Turley Dr 37211
Tusculum Ct & Rd 37211
Tusculum Square Dr 37211
Twin St 37209
Twin Circle Dr 37217
Twin Elms Ct 37210
Twin Lawn Dr 37214
Twin Oaks Cir, Ct & Dr 37211
Twinmont Ct 37215
Two Rivers Ct 37214
Tyne Blvd
  800-1199 37220
  1200-4499 37215
W Tyne Dr 37205
Tyne Ridge Ct 37220
Tyne Valley Blvd & Ct 37220
Tynewood Dr 37215
Una Recreation Rd 37217
Underwood St 37208
Union Ct 37207
Union St
  1-399 37201
  400-499 37219
  501-799 37219
University Ct & St 37210
University Park Dr 37204
Upland Dr 37216
Upshaw Dr 37214
N & S Upton Ct & Ln 37209
Upwind Ct 37217
Urban Pl 37206
Urbandale Ave 37209
Utah Ave 37209
Utopia Ave 37211
Vaden Dr 37211
Vail Ct 37215
E & W Vailview Ct & Dr 37207
Vailwood Dr 37215
Vale Ln 37214
Valeria Ct & St 37210
Valhalla 37215
Valley Ave 37218
E Valley Ct 37205
W Valley Dr 37211
Valley Frg 37205
Valley Rd
  2800-2898 37215
  3900-4000 37205
  4002-4098 37205
E Valley Rd 37205
Valley Bend Dr 37214
Valley Brook Pl & Rd 37215
Valley Cove Ct 37221
Valley Creek Ln 37207
Valley Park Dr 37216
Valley Ridge Dr 37211
Valley Trace Ct & Dr 37221
Valley Vista Rd 37205
Valleypark Dr 37221
Valleywood Dr 37211
Van Buren St 37208
Van Leer Dr 37220
Vance Ave 37208
Vanderbilt Pl 37212
Vanderhorst Dr 37207
Vantage Way 37228
Vantage Way Ct 37228
Vashti St 37207
Vaughn Rd 37221
Vaughn St 37207
Vaughns Gap Ct & Rd 37205
Vaught Dr 37209
Vaulx Ln 37204
Vauxhall Dr 37221
Venture Cir 37228
Venus Dr 37217
Verbena Dr 37211
Verielan Dr 37214
Veritas St 37211
Vernon Ave
  600-799 37209
  900-999 37203
Vernon Winfrey Ave 37207
Vester Ave 37207
Vesters Ln 37218
Vicar Dr 37211
Vickey Ct 37211
Victoria Park 37205
Victory Ave 37213
Viking Rd 37218
Villa Pl 37212
Villa Crest Dr 37220
Villa Green Dr 37215
Village Ct 37206
Village Pl
  200-299 37211
  1000-1099 37207
Village Trce 37211
Village Trl 37207
Village Way 37211
Village At Vanderbilt 37212
Village Green Dr 37217
Village Hall Pl 37215
Village Hills Dr 37217
Village Spring Dr 37207
Village Trace Ct 37211
Vine Ct 37205
Vine St 37203
Vine Hill Rd 37204
Vine Ridge Dr 37205
Vinewood Ct 37217
Vinson Dr 37217
Vintage Pl 37215
Virginia Ave 37216
Visco Ct & Dr 37210
Vista Ct 37207
Vista Cv 37207
Vista Dr 37218
Vista Ln 37207
Vista Pl 37207
Vistavalley Ct 37218
Vistaview Dr 37218
Vivelle Ave 37210
Vivian Dr 37211
Vossland Dr 37205
Vosswood Dr 37205
Vulcan Dr 37211
Vultee Blvd 37217
Wa Weka Cir 37221
Wabash Pl 37221
Waco Dr 37209
Wade Ave
  901-997 37203
  999-1199 37203
  1300-1499 37212
Waggoner Ct & Dr 37214
Wagon Ct & Dr 37221
Wakefield Dr 37220
Walcott Dr 37214
Waldkirch Ave 37204
Wales Ct, Dr & Pt 37211
Walker Ct & Ln 37207
Walking Horse Ct & Hl 37211
Wallace Ln 37215
Wallace Rd 37211
Wallingford Sq 37211
Walnut Dr 37205
Walnut Grove Cir 37215
Walnut Hill Dr 37214
Walsh St 37208
Walters Ct 37218
Walton Ln 37216
Wanda Dr
  400-499 37214
  500-599 37210
Warbler Way 37221
Ward Ave 37206
Ward St 37207
Warden Dr 37216
Warfield Dr & Ln 37215
Warmstone Ct 37209
Warner Pl 37205
Warner St 37203
Warren St 37208
Warwick Ln 37205
Washington Ave 37206
Washington Park 37205
Waterbury Pt 37221
Watercress Dr 37214
Waterford Cir 37221
Waterloo Ct 37209
Waters Ave 37206
Waters View Dr 37217
Waterswood Dr 37220
Watervale Dr 37221
Waterway Ct 37221
Watsonwood Dr 37211
Watts Cir, Ln & Ter 37209
Wauford Dr 37211
Waverly Ave 37203
Waverunner Ct & Dr 37217
Waxhaw Dr 37214
Waycross Dr 37211
Wayland Ct & Dr 37215
Wayne Dr 37206
Wayside Ct 37205
Weakley Ave 37207
Weatherside Ct 37209
Weaver Dr 37217
Webster Dr 37207
Webster Ln 37205
Wedgewood Ave
  500-1199 37203
  1200-1398 37212
  1400-1900 37212
  1902-2098 37212
Wedgewood Park 37203
Welch Rd 37211
Welcome Ln 37216
Wellesley Trce 37215
Wellington Ave 37212
Wellington Sq 37214
Wellington Park Ct 37215
Wellman Dr 37214
Wellmoor Ct 37209
Welshwood Dr 37211
Welton Ct 37221
Wemberton Dr & Pl 37214
Wendell Ave 37206
Wentworth Ave, Cir & Ct 37215
Weona Dr 37214
Wesley Ave 37207
Wesley Ct 37209
Wesleyville St 37217
Wesleywood Dr 37205
Wessex Ct & Dr 37211
West Ave 37206
Westbelt Dr 37209
Westboro Dr 37209
Westbrook Ave 37205
Westchase Dr 37205
Westchester Dr 37207
Westcott Dr 37221
Westcrest Dr 37211
Westerly Dr 37221
Western Hills Dr 37214
Western Shore Dr 37214
Westfall Dr 37221
Westfield Dr 37221
Westgate Ct 37221
Westhampton Pl 37205
Westhaven Dr 37221
Westlake Dr 37205
Westlawn Ct, Dr & Pl 37209
Westminster Pl 37205
Westmont Ave 37215
Westmoreland Dr 37212
Weston Way Dr 37221
Westover Dr 37205
Westover Park Ct 37215
Westport Dr 37218
Westvale Dr 37221
Westview Ave 37205
Westview Dr 37212
Westward Winds Dr 37221
Westwood Ave 37212
Westwood Dr 37204
Westwood Trce 37212
Wexford Pt 37221
Wexford Downs Ln 37211
Wf Rust Ct 37221
Wh Davis Dr 37208
Wharf Ave 37210
Wharton Dr 37211
Wheatfield Ct & Way 37209
Wheaton Ct 37214
Wheeler Ave 37211
Wheless St 37208
Whetstone Ct 37209
Whipple Pl 37214
Whispering Hills Ct & Dr 37211
Whispering Oaks Pl 37211
Whispering Pines Ct 37209
Whispering Trace Ct 37221
Whispering Valley Dr 37211
Whitaker Dr 37211
White Ave 37204
White Ct 37211
White Bridge Pike 37209
White Bridge Pl 37209
White Bridge Rd 37205
White Oak Ct 37216
White Oak Dr 37215
White Oak Ln 37221
White Pine Ct & Dr 37214
Whiteheath Ct 37221
Whites Creek Pike 37207
Whitland Ave 37205
Whitland Crossing Dr 37214
Whitney Ave 37210
Whitney Park Dr 37207
Whitney Place Ct 37215
Whitsett Rd 37210
Whitworth Blvd & Way 37205
Whorley Ct & Dr 37217
Wickson Ave 37210
Widewater Ct 37221
Wilbur Pl 37204
Wilburn St 37207
Wilclay Dr 37209
Wild Iris Dr 37221
Wildberry Ln 37209
Wildflower Ln 37217
Wildview Dr 37211
Wildwind Ct 37209
Wildwood Ave 37212
Wildwood Dr 37217
Wilford Dr 37214
Wilhagan Rd 37217
Wilhugh Pl 37209
Wilkerson Dr 37211
Willard Dr 37211
William Bailey Dr 37207
William Edmondson St 37203
William Howard Ct & Pl 37209
Williamette Dr 37221
Williams Ct 37209
Williamsburg Dr 37214
Williamsburg West Ct & Dr 37221
Williamsport Ct 37221
Willis St 37207
Willoughby Way 37221
Willow Ct 37211
Willow Ln 37211
Willow St 37210
Willow Brook Dr 37211
Willow Creek Ct 37207
Willow Creek Dr 37221
Willow Creek Rd 37207
Willow Oak Ct & Dr 37221
Willow Springs Dr 37216
Willowbranch Dr 37217
Willowdale Ct 37220
Willshire Dr 37215
Wilmar Dr 37220
Wilmoth Ct & Rd 37207
Wilowen Dr 37210
Wilson Blvd 37215
N Wilson Blvd 37205
S Wilson Blvd 37205
Wilsonia Ave 37205
Wilsonwood Pl 37206
Wimbledon Rd 37215
Wimpole Dr 37211
Windemere Cir, Ct & Dr 37214
Windemere Woods Dr 37215
Winding Way Rd 37216
Windover Dr 37218
Windrowe Dr 37205
Windsor Ave 37216
Windsor Ct 37211
Windsor Dr 37205
Windsor Park Ln 37205
Windsor Terrace Dr 37221
Windwood Cir & Ln 37214
Windypine Dr 37211
Winfield Dr 37211
Winford Ave 37211
Winfrey St 37210
Wingate Ave 37211
Wingrove Ave 37203
Winn Ave 37209
Winston Ave W 37211
Winston Dr 37218
Winston Pl 37204
Winter Ct 37211
Winter Pl 37207
Winter Breeze Ct 37221
Winterbrook Rd 37207
Winthorne Ct & Dr 37217
Winward Ct 37217
Winwood Pl 37214
Wolfeboro Ln 37221
Wood Trl 37207
Wood Bridge Ct & Dr 37217
Wood Duck Ct 37214
Woodale Ln 37207
Woodard Ave 37210
Woodberry Ct & Dr 37214
Woodbine St 37211
Woodbury Falls Ct & Dr 37221
Woodcraft Ct & Dr 37214
Wooddale Ln 37214
Woodett Dr 37211
Woodfield Ct, Cv & Dr 37211
Woodfolk Ave 37207
Woodford Pl 37215
Woodhaven Dr 37204
Woodhurst Dr 37220
Woodlake Ct 37214
Woodland St
  100-299 37213
  301-303 37213
  305-397 37206
  399-1899 37206
Woodland Way 37209
Woodland Hills Dr 37211
Woodland Pointe Dr 37214
E Woodlands Ave, Trce & Trl 37211
Woodlark Ct 37214
Woodlawn Dr
  2100-2598 37212
  2600-2799 37212
  2800-3899 37215
  3900-4099 37205
  4101-4199 37205
Woodleigh Dr 37215
Woodmaker Ct 37214
Woodmere Ct 37221
Woodmere Dr 37217
Woodmont Blvd
  145A-145B 37205
  998A-998B 37204
  100-102 37205
  104-199 37205
  800-1099 37204
  1400-3999 37215
  4000-4099 37205
Woodmont Cir 37205
Woodmont Ln 37215
Woodmont Hall Pl 37205
Woodpoint Dr 37207
Woodridge Dr 37207
Woodsman Ct 37214
Woodson Ln 37211
Woodspring Ct 37211
Woodstock Dr 37207
N & S Woodstone Ln 37211
Woodstream Dr 37221
Woodvale Dr 37204
Woodward Dr 37207
Woodwind Ct 37214
Woodycrest Ave 37210
Woodyhill Dr 37207
Worchester Dr 37221
Work Dr 37207
Wortham Ave 37215
Wrenwood Ave 37205
Wwcr Ave 37218
Wyatt Park 37221
Wyn Oak Cir 37205
Wynbrook Ct 37221
Wyndham Pl 37215
Wynfall Ln 37211
Wynfield Ct 37211
Wynham Pl 37221
Wynstone 37215
Wyoming Ave 37209
Yancey Dr 37215
Yeaman Pl 37206
Yearling Way 37221
Yellow Wood Ct 37221
Yelton Ct & Dr 37211
Yoest Dr 37207
Yokley Dr 37207
Yoradert Ave 37209
Yorkshire Cir, Ct & Rd 37211
Yorktown Rd 37211
Youngs Ln
  600-999 37207
  1200-1299 37218
Zermatt Ave 37211
Zimmerlee St 37203
Zophi St 37216
Zuric Ct 37221

NUMBERED STREETS

1st Ave N
  100-1089 37201
  1091-1099 37201
  1100-1199 37208
1st Ave S
  1011A-1011B 37210
  100-499 37201
  900-1399 37210
N 1st St
  100-299 37213
  300-499 37207
S 1st St 37213
2nd Ave N
  100-1099 37201
  1100-1799 37208
2nd Ave S
  1045A-1045B 37210
  100-465 37201
  500-1599 37210
N 2nd St
  619A-619B 37207
  100-298 37213
  300-1299 37207
S 2nd St 37213
3rd Ave N
  101-137 37201
  1100-2099 37208
3rd Ave S
  100-399 37201
  501-515 37210
N 3rd St 37207
S 3rd St 37213
4th Ave N 37219
  417-419 37201
  418-1098 37219
  421-1099 37219
  1100-2099 37208
4th Ave S
  100-499 37201
  500-1599 37210
  1601-1699 37210
S 4th St 37206
5th Ave N 37219
  1100-2099 37208
5th Ave S 37203
N 5th Ct 37207
N 5th St 37207
S 5th St
  100-198 37206
  200-899 37206
  900-999 37213
6th Ave N
  100-199 37203
  200-1000 37219
  1100-1900 37208
6th Ave S 37203
N 6th St
  100-299 37206
  800-1400 37207
S 6th St
  1-899 37206
  900-1099 37213
7th Ave N
  100-199 37203
  201-399 37219
  401-699 37219
  1100-1899 37208
7th Ave S 37203
N 7th St
  100-299 37206
  1000-1098 37207
  1100-1299 37207
S 7th St 37206
8th Ave N
  100-311 37203
  313-399 37203
  900-1899 37208
8th Ave S
  100-1999 37203
  2000-2299 37204
S 8th Ct 37206
N 8th St
  100-499 37206
  1100-1299 37207
S 8th St 37206
9th Ave N
  100-198 37203
  900-2299 37208
9th Ave S
  100-298 37203
  2101-2197 37204
9th Cir S 37203
N 9th St 37206
S 9th St 37206
10th Ave N
  100-899 37203
  900-2399 37208
10th Ave S
  100-1999 37203
  2000-2999 37204
10th Cir N 37203
N 10th St 37206
S 10th St 37206
11th Ave N
  200-899 37203
  900-2399 37208
11th Ave S
  100-1400 37203
  1402-1898 37203
  2100-2299 37204
N 11th St 37206
S 11th St 37206
12th Ave N
  100-599 37203
  901-1497 37208
12th Ave S
  2907A-2907D 37204
  100-1999 37203
  2000-3000 37204
N 12th St 37206
S 12th St 37206
13th Ave N 37203
13th Ave S
  800-899 37203

900-1199 37212
S 13th Ct 37206
S 13th St 37206
13th Avenue Cir 37212
14th Ave N 37208
101-397 37203
399-899 37203
900-2499 37208
14th Ave S
601-697 37203
699-899 37203
900-1899 37212
N 14th St 37206
S 14th St 37206
15th Ave N
100-399 37203
1800-2299 37208
15th Ave S 37212
N 15th St 37206
S 15th St 37206
16th Ave N
100-899 37203
900-1999 37208
16th Ave S
100-199 37203
1000-1699 37212
N 16th St 37206
S 16th St 37206
17th Ave N
100-899 37203
900-1799 37208
17th Ave S
100-199 37203
1000-1699 37212
1701-1799 37212
N 17th St 37206
S 17th St 37206
18th Ave N
100-811 37203
2000-2008 37208
18th Ave S
1028A-1028B 37212
700-899 37203
900-2321 37212
18th Ct N 37208
N 18th St 37206
S 18th St 37206
19th Ave N
100-799 37203
800-999 37208
19th Ave S
1908A-1908B 37212
100-899 37203
900-2199 37212
S 19th St 37206
20th Ave N 37203
20th Ave S
100-199 37203
900-2399 37212
S 20th St 37206
21st Ave N
100-699 37203
800-1799 37208
21st Ave S
100-128 37203
130-420 37203
422-1210 37203
1201-1297 37212
1299-2599 37212
22nd Ave N
200-400 37203
402-498 37203
700-1799 37208
22nd Ave S
1200-1498 37212
1500-1599 37212
2701-2797 37215
2799-2999 37215
22nd Ct N 37208
23rd Ave N
101-197 37203
199-400 37203
402-498 37203
1300-2399 37208
23rd Ave S
1600-1699 37212
2900-3099 37215

23rd St 37209
24th Ave N
2200A-2200B 37208
200-399 37203
500-599 37209
700-2499 37208
24th Ave S 37212
24th St 37209
25th Ave N
200-399 37203
500-699 37209
700-2599 37208
25th Ave S 37212
25th Avenue Ct N 37208
26th Ave N 37209
700-2599 37208
26th Ave S 37212
27th Ave N
101-199 37203
400-699 37209
700-1199 37208
27th Ave S 37212
28th Ave N
605A-605D 37209
100-329 37203
330-699 37209
700-2099 37208
28th Ave S 37212
29th Ave N
100-399 37203
700-999 37209
29th Ave S 37212
30th Ave N
100-299 37203
900-999 37209
30th Ave S 37212
31st Ave N
100-399 37203
400-1099 37209
31st Ave S 37212
32nd Ave N 37209
32nd Ave S 37212
32nd Ct N 37209
33rd Ave N 37209
33rd Ave S 37212
34th Ave N 37209
35th Ave N 37209
36th Ave N 37209
37th Ave N 37209
38th Ave N 37209
39th Ave N 37209
40th Ave N 37209
41st Ave N 37209
42nd Ave N 37209
43rd Ave N 37209
44th Ave N 37209
45th Ave N 37209
46th Ave N 37209
47th Ave N 37209
48th Ave N 37209
49th Ave N 37209
50th Ave N 37209
51st Ave N 37209
52nd Ave N 37209
53rd Ave N 37209
54th Ave N 37209
55th Ave N 37209
56th Ave N 37209
57th Ave N 37209
60th Ave N 37209
61st Ave N 37209
62nd Ave N 37209
63rd Ave N 37209
100 Oaks Shopping Ctr 37204

NEW TAZEWELL TN

General Delivery 37825

POST OFFICE BOXES MAIN OFFICE STATIONS AND BRANCHES

Box No.s
All PO Boxes 37824

NAMED STREETS

All Street Addresses 37825

NEWPORT TN

General Delivery 37821

POST OFFICE BOXES MAIN OFFICE STATIONS AND BRANCHES

Box No.s
All PO Boxes 37822

NAMED STREETS

All Street Addresses 37821

NUMBERED STREETS

All Street Addresses 37821

OAK RIDGE TN

General Delivery 37830

POST OFFICE BOXES MAIN OFFICE STATIONS AND BRANCHES

Box No.s
All PO Boxes 37831

NAMED STREETS

Adams Ln 37830
Adelphi Rd 37830
Administration Rd
100-109 37830
108-108 37831
111-299 37830
112-298 37830
N & S Alabama Rd 37830
Albany Rd 37830
Albion Rd 37830
Albright Rd 37830
Alder Ln 37830
Alger Rd 37830
Alhambra Rd 37830
Alvin Weinberg Dr 37830
Amanda Dr & Pl 37830
Amherst Ln 37830
Andover Cir 37830
Anna Rd 37830
Antioch Dr 37830
Apple Ln 37830
Arcadia Ln 37830
Arizona Rd 37830
Arkansas Ave 37830
E & W Arrowwood Rd .. 37830
Artesia Dr 37830
Asbury Ln 37830
Ashland Ln 37830
Aspen Ln 37830
Athens Rd 37830
Atlanta Rd 37830
Audubon Rd 37830
Badger Rd 37830
Baker Ln 37830
Balboa Cir 37830
Balsam Rd 37830
Baltimore Dr 37830
Barrington Dr 37830
Baylor Dr 37830
Baypath Dr 37830
Beechwood Ln 37830
Belgrade Rd 37830
Belle Creek Dr 37830
Bellhaven Ln 37830
Belmont Ct 37830
S Benedict Ave 37830
Bennett Ln 37830
Berea Rd 37830
Berkley Rd 37830
Bermuda Rd 37830
Berwick Dr 37830
Bethel Valley Rd 37830
Bethune Cir 37830
Bettis Ln 37830
Beverly Cir 37830
Blue Mountain Ct 37830
Blue Ridge Ct 37830
Boeing Rd 37830
Bogola Rd 37830
Bradford Cir 37830
Bradley Ave 37830
Brandeis Ln 37830
Brentwood Dr 37830
Brewster Ln 37830
Briar Rd 37830
Briarcliff Ave 37830
Briarwood Dr 37830
Bridgewater Ln 37830
Brisbane Rd 37830
Broadberry Ave 37830
Broadway Ave 37830
Brockton Ln 37830
Brookside Dr 37830
Brussels Rd 37830
E & W Bryn Mawr Cir .. 37830
Bunchberry Rd 37830
Bunker Ln 37830
Burchfield Dr 37830
Burgess Ln 37830
Bus Terminal Rd 37830
Butler Rd 37830
Byron Ln 37830
Cahill Ln 37830
Cairo Rd 37830
Caldwell Dr 37830
California Ave 37830
Calvin Ln 37830
Camden Dr 37830
Canterbury Rd 37830
Capital Cir 37830
Cardinal Ln 37830
Carleton Ln 37830
Carlisle Ln 37830
Carnegie Dr 37830
Carson Ln 37830
Carver Ave 37830
Cascade Ln 37830
Case Ln 37830
Cedar Ln & Rd 37830
Centennial Blvd 37830
Centennial Bluff Blvd 37830
Center Park Ln 37830
Central Ave 37830
Centrifuge Way 37830
Chatham Ln 37830
Chester Ln 37830
Chestnut Hill Rd 37830
Chincen Rd 37830
Claremont Rd 37830
Clarion Rd 37830
Clark Ln & Pl 37830
N Claymore Ln 37830
Clayton Way 37830
Clearview Ct 37830
Clemson Dr 37830
Clifton Cir 37830
Coalyard Rd 37830
Cobblestone Ct 37830
Coe Rd 37830
Colby Rd 37830
Colgate Rd 37830
N & S Columbia Dr 37830
Comet Ln 37830
Commerce Park Dr 37830
Compton Ln 37830
Concord Rd 37830
Connors Cir, Dr & Pl 37830
Converse Ln 37830
Cooper Cir & Ln 37830
Copper Ridge Ct 37830
Cornell Ln 37830
Cottage Ct 37830
Cove Pointe Ln 37830
Crane Ln 37830
Creek View Ct 37830
Crescent View Ln 37830
Crest Pointe Ln 37830
Crestview Ln 37830
Cross Creek Pl 37830
Crossroads Blvd 37830
Crystal Cove Ln 37830
Culver Rd 37830
Cumberland View Dr 37830
Curie Ln 37830
Cypress Ln 37830
Dallas Ln 37830
E & W Dalton Rd 37830
E & W Damascus Rd .. 37830
Dana Dr 37830
Danbury Dr & Ln 37830
Dancer Ln 37830
Daniel Ln 37830
Dansworth Ln 37830
Dartmouth Cir 37830
Darwin Ln & Rd 37830
Dasher Ln 37830
Davidson Ln 37830
Davis Ln 37830
Dayton Rd 37830
Decatur Rd 37830
Deerfield Ln 37830
Delaware Ave 37830
Delmar Cir 37830
Devanshire Ct 37830
Devon Ln 37830
Dewey Rd 37830
S Dillard Ave 37830
Disston Rd 37830
Ditman Ln 37830
E Division Rd 37830
Dixie Ln 37830
Donner Ct & Dr 37830
Dover Ln 37830
Downing Dr 37830
Dresden Rd 37830
East Dr 37830
Eastburn Ln 37830
Eastridge Dr 37830
Eaton Ln 37830
Edgehill Ln 37830
Edgemoor Rd 37830
Edinboro Ln 37830
Edison Ln 37830
Elliott Cir 37830
Elmhurst Dr 37830
Elza Dr 37830
Emerson Cir & Pl 37830
Emory Ln 37830
Emory Valley Rd 37830
Endicott Ln 37830
Enfield Ln 37830
Englewood Ln 37830
English Ct 37830
Erskine Ln 37830
Esquire Ct 37830
Essex Ln 37830
Euclid Cir & Pl 37830
Europia Ave 37830
Evans Ln 37830
Everest Cir 37830
Fairbanks Rd 37830
E & W Fairview Rd 37830
Fallberry St 37830
E & W Farragut Rd 37830
E & W Faunce Ln & Rd 37830
E & W Fernhill Ln & Rd 37830
Firestone Rd 37830
Fisk Ave 37830
Flanagan Loop 37830
Flint Rd 37830
Florida Ave 37830
Floyd Culler Ct 37830
Fordham Rd 37830
E & W Forest Ln 37830
Forestberry St 37830
Fortenberry St 37830
Franklin Rd 37830
Fulton Ln 37830
Galeberry Ave 37830
Garnet Ln 37830
Gates Dr 37830
E & W Geneva Ln 37830
Georgia Ave 37830
W Gettysburg Ave 37830
Glassboro Dr 37830
Glendale Ln 37830
Goldengate Ln 37830
Goldenview Ln 37830
Golfcrest Ln 37830
Gordon Rd 37830
Gorgas Ln 37830
Goucher Cir 37830
Graceland Rd 37830
Graham Pl 37830
Grandcove Ln 37830
Greenbriar Ln 37830
Greenwood Ln 37830
Greystone Dr 37830
Greywood Pl 37830
Groves Park Blvd E 37830
Gum Hollow Rd 37830
Hackberry St 37830
Halsted Ct 37830
Hamilton Cir 37830
Hampshire Cir & Ct 37830
Hampton Rd 37830
Handel Ln 37830
Hanover Pl 37830
Happy Ln 37830
Hardinberry St 37830
Hardwick Pl 37830
Harland Ct 37830
Harper Ln 37830
Hartford Pl 37830
Hatleyberry St 37830
Haven Hill Ln 37830
Hawthorne Ct 37830
Hazleton Ln 37830
Heath Ln 37830
Henderson Ln 37830
Hendrix Dr 37830
Henley Pl & Rd 37830
Heritage Dr 37830
Hermitage Blvd 37830
N & S Hickory Ln & Pl 37830
Hickory Hollow Dr 37830
High Point Ln 37830
Highland Ave 37830
Highway 58 37830
Hillside Rd 37830
Hollbrook Ln 37830
N & S Hollywood Cir 37830
E & W Holston Ln 37830
Honeysuckle Ln 37830
Hooper Ct 37830
Houseboat Row 37830
Houston Ave 37830
Howard Ln 37830
Hoyt Ln 37830
Hubbell Pl 37830
Hugh Ln 37830
Humbolt Ct 37830
E & W Hunter Cir & Pl 37830
E & W Hutchinson Cir & Pl 37830
Hutton Ln 37830
S Illinois Ave 37830
Inca Cir 37830
Independence Ln 37830
Indian Ln & Pl 37830
Inn Ln 37830
Insologic Way 37830
Iona Cir 37830
Irene St 37830
Iris Cir 37830
Iroquois Rd 37830
E & W Irving Ln 37830
Ithaca Ln 37830
Ivanhoe Rd 37830
Ivy Ln 37830
Jackson Sq 37830
Jade Ln 37830
Jarrett Ln 37830
Jasper Ln 37830
Jay Ln 37830
N & S Jefferson Ave, Cir & Ct 37830
Jefferson Terminal Rd .. 37830
Jellico Ln 37830
Jersey Ln 37830
Joel Ln 37830
Johnson Rd 37830
Jonathan Ln & Pl 37830
Joy Ln 37830
Judd Ln 37830
Kelvin Ln 37830
Kentucky Ave 37830
Kenwyn Rd 37830
Keystone Ln 37830
Kimball Ln 37830
Kingfisher Ln 37830
Kingsley Rd 37830
Knoll Ln 37830
Laboratory Rd 37830
Lafayette Dr 37830
Lake Hills Dr 37830
Lakecrest Ln 37830
Lakeview Ln 37830
Lancaster Rd 37830
S Lansing Rd 37830
Larson Dr 37830
Lasalle Rd 37830
Latimer Rd 37830
Lawrence Ln 37830
Lawton Rd 37830
Lea Way 37830
Lehigh Ln 37830
Lewis Ln 37830
Liberty Ct 37830
E, N & W Lincoln Cir & Rd 37830
Lind Pl 37830
Lindale Ln 37830
Littonberry St 37830
Livingston Rd 37830
Locust Ln 37830
Louisiana Ave 37830
Loyola Ln 37830
Lullaby Ln 37830
Lynwood Ln 37830
Macaw Ln 37830
Macon Ln 37830
W & E Madison Ln & Rd 37830
E & W Magnolia Ln 37830
E & W Maiden Ln 37830
Main St 37830
Mallard Ln 37830
E & W Malta Rd 37830
Maltese Ln 37830
Malvern Rd 37830
Manchester Rd 37830
Manhattan Ave 37830
Maple Ln 37830
Marietta Cir 37830
Marion Rd 37830
Marquette Rd 37830
Marshall Cir 37830
Maryville Cir 37830
Marywater Ln 37830
Marywood Ct 37830
Mason Ln 37830
Mayfair Ln 37830
Maywood Rd 37830
Mead Ln 37830
Meadow Rd 37830
Meadowlark Ln 37830
Meco Ln 37830
E & W Melbourne Rd .. 37830
Melton Lake Dr 37830
Melton Lake Peninsula . 37830
Michigan Ave 37830

Middlebury Rd 37830
Midland Rd 37830
Midway Ln 37830
Milan Way 37830
Milton Ln 37830
Miramar Cir 37830
Mississippi Ave 37830
Mistletoeberry Rd 37830
Mitchell Rd 37830
Mockingbird Ln 37830
Mohawk Rd 37830
Monaco Ln 37830
Montana Ave 37830
Montclair Rd 37830
Monticello Rd 37830
Montreal Ln 37830
Moore Ln 37830
Morgan Rd 37830
E Morningside Dr 37830
Morris Ln 37830
Moss Rd 37830
Mountain View Ln 37830
Moylan Ln 37830
Nantucket Way 37830
Naples Ln 37830
Nasson Ln 37830
Nathan Ln 37830
Nebraska Ave 37830
Nesper Rd 37830
Netherlands Rd 37830
Nevada Cir 37830
Neville Ln 37830
New Bedford Ln 37830
New York Ave 37830
Newark Ln 37830
Newberry Cir 37830
Newcastle Ln 37830
E & W Newcomb Rd 37830
Newcrest Ln 37830
Newell Ln 37830
Newhaven Rd 37830
Newhope Ln 37830
E & W Newkirk Ln 37830
Newport Dr 37830
Newridge Rd 37830
Newton Ln 37830
Niagara Ln 37830
Nixon Rd 37830
Nolan Rd 37830
Norman Ln 37830
Normandy Rd 37830
Norris Ln 37830
Northberry West Rd 37830
Northwestern Ave 37830
Norton Rd 37830
Norway Ln 37830
Norwood Ln 37830
Oak Ln 37830
Oak Ridge Hwy & Tpke 37830
Ogden Cir & Ln 37830
Oglethorpe Pl 37830
Ogontz Ln 37830
Oklahoma Ave 37830
Old Edgemoor Rd 37830
Old Forest Trl 37830
Old Hickory Ct 37830
Olean Rd 37830
Olmstead Ln 37830
Olney Ln 37830
Oneida Ln 37830
Ontario Ln 37830
Oppenhfimer Way 37830
Orange Ln 37830
Orau Way 37830
Orchard Cir & Ln 37830
Orkney Rd 37830
Osage Rd 37830
W Outer Dr 37830
Oxford Rd 37830
Pacific Rd 37830
Packer Rd 37830
Paine Ln 37830
Palisades Pkwy 37830
Palladium Way 37830
Pallas Rd 37830
Palmer Rd 37830
Palmetto Ln 37830
Panama Rd 37830
Paoli Ln 37830
Paris Ln 37830
Park Ln 37830
Park Meade Dr & Pl 37830
Parkberry Rd 37830
Parker Rd 37830
Parma Rd 37830
Parsons Rd 37830
W & E Pasadena Ln & Rd 37830
E & W Passmore Ln & Rd 37830
Patriot Ln 37830
Pavillion Dr 37830
E & W Pawley Ln & Rd 37830
Peach Rd 37830
Pearl Rd 37830
Pelham Rd 37830
Pembroke Rd 37830
Pennsylvania Ave 37830
Phillips Ln 37830
Pickwick Ln 37830
Piedmont Rd 37830
Pine Ln 37830
Pineberry East Rd 37830
E Pinnacle Way 37830
Pleasant Rd 37830
Plumberry Ave 37830
Plymouth Cir 37830
Pocono Ln 37830
Pomona Rd 37830
Poplar Rd 37830
Porter Rd 37830
Potomac Cir 37830
Powell Rd 37830
Pratt Ln 37830
Presidential Dr 37830
W & E Price Ln & Rd 37830
Princeton Ave 37830
Providence Rd 37830
N & S Purdue Ave 37830
Queens Rd 37830
Quincy Ave 37830
Raccoon Rd 37830
Radcliff Ter 37830
Radisson Cv 37830
Raintree Pl & Xing 37830
Raleigh Rd 37830
Rand Cir 37830
Randolph Rd 37830
Ravenwood Xing 37830
Regent Cir 37830
Renovare Blvd 37830
Revere Cir 37830
Rice Rd 37830
Rider Rd 37830
Ridgeway Ctr 37830
River Dr 37830
Rivers Ct 37830
Rivers Run Blvd & Way 37830
Riverside Dr 37830
Riverview Dr 37830
Robertsville Rd 37830
Robin Ln 37830
Rockbridge Greens Blvd 37830
Rockingham Ln 37830
Rolling Links Blvd 37830
Round Hill Pt 37830
Royal Troon Cir 37830
Royce Cir 37830
N & S Rutgers Ave 37830
Salem Rd 37830
Sanford Ln 37830
Scarboro Ln & Rd 37830
Scenic Dr 37830
Scott Ln 37830
Second St 37830
N & S Seneca Rd 37830
Sequoia Ln 37830
Seymour Ln 37830
Shagbark Ln 37830
E & W Sheridan Cir & Pl 37830
Skyline View Dr 37830
Solway Ferry Rd 37830
E & W Southwood Ln 37830
Spelman Ave 37830
Stanton Ln 37830
Stonebridge Way 37830
Summit Pl 37830
Sweet Gum Ln 37830
Tabor Rd 37830
Tacoma Rd 37830
Talmeda Rd 37830
Tamara Ln 37830
N & S Tampa Ln 37830
Tansi Ln 37830
Targa Ln 37830
S Taube Ln 37830
Taylor Rd 37830
Teejay Dr 37830
Telemann Ln 37830
Teller Village Ln 37830
Temple Rd 37830
Tempura Dr 37830
E & W Tennessee Ave 37830
Tennyson Rd 37830
Terri Ln 37830
Thayer Ln 37830
Thelma Rd 37830
Thornton Rd 37830
Tidewater Ln 37830
Tiffany Pl 37830
Tiffin Dr 37830
Tilden Rd 37830
Timbercrest Dr 37830
Tomlinson Rd 37830
Towne Rd 37830
Townsend Rd 37830
Tracy Ln 37830
Trenton Dr 37830
Trevecca Ln 37830
Trevose Ln 37830
Tucker Rd 37830
N & S Tulane Ave 37830
E Tulsa Rd 37830
Turner Rd 37830
Tusculum Dr 37830
Tuskegee Dr 37830
Tyler Rd 37830
E & W Tyrone Rd 37830
Tyson Rd 37830
Udall Ln 37830
Ulena Ln 37830
Ulysses Ln 37830
Umbria Ln 37830
Underwood Rd 37830
Union Rd 37830
Union Valley Rd 37830
Upsal Rd 37830
Utah Ave 37830
Utica Cir 37830
Uvalde Ln 37830
Valetta Ln 37830
Valley Ct 37830
Valley Forge Dr 37830
Valparaiso Rd 37830
Van Hicks Pl & Rd 37830
E & W Vance Rd 37830
E & W Vanderbilt Dr 37830
Vassar Rd 37830
Venus Rd 37830
Verbena Rd 37830
Vermont Ave 37830
Vernon Rd 37830
Victoria Rd 37830
Victorious Blvd E & W 37830
Vienna Rd 37830
Viking Rd 37830
Villanova Rd 37830
Viola Rd 37830
Virginia Rd 37830
Vista Rd 37830
Wabash Ln 37830
Waddell Cir & Pl 37830
Wade Ln 37830
E & W Wadsworth Cir & Pl 37830
Wainwright Rd 37830
Wakefield Rd 37830
Wakeman Ln 37830
N & S Walker Ln 37830
Wallace Rd 37830
Wallberry Rd 37830
Walnut Ln 37830
Walpole Ln 37830
Walsh Ln 37830
Waltham Ln & Pl 37830
Walton Ln 37830
Warehouse Rd 37830
Warrior Cir & Ln 37830
Warwick Ln 37830
Washburn Cir 37830
Waterview Dr 37830
Wayne Pl & Rd 37830
Wayside Rd 37830
Wedgewood Rd 37830
Weldon Ln 37830
Wellington Cir 37830
Wendover Cir 37830
Wesley Ln 37830
Westlook Cir & Dr 37830
Westover Dr 37830
Westoverlook Dr 37830
Westview Ln 37830
Westwind Dr 37830
Whippoorwill Dr 37830
Wilberforce Ave 37830
Wildcat Ln 37830
Wilderness Ln 37830
Wildwood Dr 37830
Willard Ln 37830
William Ln 37830
Willow Ln 37830
Wilson St 37830
Wiltshire Dr 37830
Wimberly Ln 37830
Winchester Cir 37830
Windgate Pl & Rd 37830
Windham Rd 37830
Windhaven Ln 37830
Windsong Ln 37830
Winston Ln 37830
Wolf Creek Way 37830
Wood Ridge Ln 37830
Woodbury Ln 37830
Woodland Trce E 37830

PIGEON FORGE TN

POST OFFICE BOXES MAIN OFFICE STATIONS AND BRANCHES

Box No.s
All PO Boxes 37868

NAMED STREETS

Aerie Way 37863
Alexander Pl 37863
Alpine Mountain Way 37863
Alpine Village Way 37863
Alps Way 37863
Americana Dr 37863
Appalachia Dr 37863
Arrow Wood Way 37863
N & S Asbury Dr & Rd 37863
Ashe Way 37863
Ashley Ave 37863
Autumn Ln 37863
Barefoot Pass Way 37863
Battle Ground Dr 37863
Battle Hill Rd 37863
Bear Cove Way 37863
Bellwood Ave 37863
Big Bear Way 37863
Black Hawk Way 37863
Black Oak St 37863
Blue Dunn Ct 37863
Bohanan Dr 37863
Boone Acres Way 37863
Bradford Way 37863
Briar Way 37863
Briarcliff Way 37863
Brook Stone Way 37863
Brooklin Way 37863
Brookwood Dr 37863
Bruce Ogle Way 37863
Bud Ln 37863
Bud Reid Way 37863
Butler St 37863
Cain Hollow Rd 37863
Caney Creek Rd 37863
Carlstown Dr 37863
Carolina Rd 37863
Carolina Cove Way 37863
Cates Ln 37863
Cedar Rd 37863
Cedar Top Ln 37863
S Center Rd & St 37863
Chapel Way 37863
Chapel View Cir 37863
Charlotte Ct 37863
Cherry Dr 37863
Cherry Laurel Dr 37863
Cherry Ridge Way 37863
Chickasaw Gap Way 37863
Choctaw Hill Way 37863
Christmas Tree Ln 37863
Christopher Ave 37863
Circle Dr NE 37863
City Park Dr 37863
Clabough Way 37863
Clear Point Ln 37863
Clintwood Way 37863
Cobbler Way 37863
Cobblestone Dr 37863
Cole Dr & St 37863
Colonial Dr 37863
Community Center Dr 37863
Conner Dr 37863
Conner Heights Rd 37863
Conrad Way 37863
Cook St 37863
Cool Hollow Ave 37863
Country Oaks Dr 37863
Creekwalk Blvd 37863
Crestview Dr 37863
Cross Ave 37863
Cross View Dr 37863
Daisy Trl 37863
David Lewelling Dr 37863
Day Springs Rd 37863
Dellinger Hollow Rd 37863
Dew Drop Ln 37863
Dixie Ave 37863
Dogwood Cir & Pl 37863
Dollywood Ln 37863
Dollywood Parks Blvd 37863
Dorminey Dr 37863
Duggan St 37863
Eagle Pointe Way 37863
Eagles Boulevard Way 37863
Eagles Claw Way 37863
Eagles Ridge Way 37863
Emert St 37863
Evans Rd 37863
Falcons Nest Way 37863
Falling Leaf Way 37863
Fenway Dr 37863
Florence Dr 37863
Forest Dr & St 37863
Forest Ridge Way 37863
Forest Vista Way 37863
Forge Ave & St 37863
Forge Hideaway Loop & Rd 37863
Forrest Way 37863
Garden Way 37863
Garland St 37863
Garland Harmon Dr 37863
Georgianne Ct 37863
Gloryland Way 37863
W Gold Dust Dr 37863
Golden Circle Dr 37863
Golden Eagle Way 37863
Goldrush Rd 37863
Golf Dr & Rd 37863
Golf View Blvd 37863
Golingto Rd 37863
Gray Hawk Way 37863
Greenwood Way 37863
Grindstone Ridge Rd 37863
Harrier Court Way 37863
Hatcher Cir 37863
Hazelwood Ln 37863
Henderson Rd 37863
Henderson Chapel Rd 37863
Henderson Springs Blvd & Rd 37863
Heritage Hills Dr 37863
Hickory Dr & Ln 37863
High Valley Dr & Ln 37863
Highland Park Dr 37863
Hill Ave 37863
Hillis Dr 37863
Hilltop Dr 37863
Hitching Post Rd 37863
Honey Bee Cove Way 37863
Householder St 37863
Houser Ridge Rd 37863
Hunter Hawk Way 37863
Huskey St 37863
Indian Knob Cir 37863
Indiana Ave 37863
Iron Circle Dr 37863
Iron Mountain Rd 37863
Island Dr 37863
Jake Thomas Rd 37863
Jamesena Miller Dr 37863
Jess Wilson Rd 37863
John Myers Dr 37863
Joshua Ln 37863
Junior Mccarter Dr 37863
Keegan Dr 37863
Kerrys View Way 37863
Kidwell Way 37863
Kings Hills Blvd 37863
Kittyhawk Way 37863
Lafollette Cir 37863
Laurel Dr 37863
Laurel Crest Ln 37863
Laurel Lick Rd 37863
Laurelwood Dr 37863
Lazy Ln 37863
Lee Cardwell Cir 37863
Leonard Huskey Ln 37863
Lester Ct 37863
Lethco Way 37863
Library Dr 37863
Little Cove Rd 37863
Lloyd Huskey Rd 37863
Loraine St 37863
Maple Ln 37863
Marshall Acres 37863
Mayes Rd 37863
Mayes Loop Rd 37863
Mcgill St 37863
Mcmahan Rd 37863
Mcmahan Hollow Rd 37863
Meadow View Ln 37863
Meadowbrook Dr 37863
Meriwether Way 37863
Methodists St 37863
Middle Creek Rd 37863
Midvalley Dr 37863
Mill St 37863
Mill Creek Rd 37863
Mill View Dr 37863
Monte Wood Cir 37863
Moose Ridge Way 37863
Mossy Stone Way 37863
Mount Zion St 37863
Mountain Laurel Way 37863
Mountain View Ln & St 37863
Mountain Vista Dr 37863
Mr Marshall Dr 37863
Mullendore Ln 37863
Music Rd 37863
Music Mountain Dr 37863
Myers St 37863
Nancy St 37863
Nellie St 37863
New Pioneer Trl 37863
Nighthawk Way 37863
Noland Dr 37863
Oak Pt & Rd 37863
Oak Ridge St 37863
Oaks View Ct 37863
Ogle Dr 37863
Old Gate Rd 37863
Old Mill Ave, Ln & St 37863
Oldham St 37863
Only Way 37863
Osprey Way 37863
Park View Cir 37863
Parkway 37863
Parlin Dr 37863
Parton Sutton Ln 37863
Pebble Stone Way 37863
Pee Dee Dr 37863
Peggy Ln 37863
Peppercorn Way 37863
Peregrine Way 37863
Pickel Dr & St 37863
Pin Oak View Dr 37863
Pine Dr, Rd & Way 37863
Pine Knob Rd 37863
Pine Mountain Rd 37863
Pinemont Dr 37863
Pinyon Cir 37863
Plantation Dr 37863
Plaza Dr & Way 37863
Progress Hill Blvd 37863
Quill Gordon Ct 37863
Ranmoor Way 37863
Reagan Dr 37863
Reagan Hollow Rd 37863
Red Oak Dr 37863
Rena St
3000-3236 37863
3235-3235 37868
3237-3499 37863
3238-3498 37863
Ridge Rd 37863
Ridgetop Resort Way 37863
Ridgewood Way 37863
E River Rd 37863
River Bank Rd 37863
River Port Way 37863
Riverbend Loop 37863
Rocky Creek Way 37863
Rolen Hollow Rd 37863
Rolling Hills Dr 37863
Round Top Rd 37863
Royal Coachman Dr 37863
Rush Branch Rd 37863
Ruth Hall Rd 37863
Saint Charles Pl 37863
Sand Pike Blvd 37863
Sand Ridge Way 37863
Scenic Hills Rd 37863
Scenic Loop Rd 37863
Scenic View Ln 37863
Sequoia Rd 37863
Seth Rd 37863
Sevier Ave 37863
Sharon Dr 37863
Shiloh Rd 37863
Shirley Ave 37863
Showplace Blvd 37863
Silver Stone Way 37863
Singing Pines Rd 37863
Sleepy Hollow Ct 37863
Smelcer Dr 37863
Smith Ln 37863
Smoky Dr 37863
Spring Stone Way 37863
Spring Valley Rd 37863
Starkeytown Rd 37863
Steven Ct 37863
Stirrup Ln 37863

Stone Ridge Way 37863
Stonebrook Dr 37863
Sugar Hollow Rd 37863
Sugar Mountain Way 37863
Sugarfoot Way 37863
Suncrest Rd 37863
Sunnyview Dr 37863
Sunset Dr & St 37863
Sycamore St 37863
Sylvan Glen Way 37863
Tammy King Rd 37863
Tanasi Trl 37863
Teaster Ln 37863
Tiger Dr 37863
Timber Way 37863
Tinker Hollow Rd 37863
Town Overlook St 37863
Travis Ln 37863
Tree Top Way 37863
Trentham Way 37863
Trotter Way 37863
Troy Dr 37863
Twin City Way 37863
Twin Mountain Way 37863
Valley Dr 37863
Valley Heights Dr 37863
Valley View Dr 37863
Veterans Blvd 37863
Vickwood Ln 37863
Village Way 37863
Waldens Main St 37863
Waterfall Way 37863
Watson Ct 37863
Wear Ln 37863
E Wears Valley Rd 37863
Whaley Dr 37863
Whistling Wind Way 37863
White Cap Ln 37863
White Falcon Way 37863
White Oak Ln 37863
Wier Farm Way 37863
Wild Fern Way 37863
Wilderness Plateau 37863
Willa View Dr 37863
Willow St 37863
Wilson St 37863
Winston St 37863
Woodridge Way 37863
Wright Way 37863

NUMBERED STREETS

All Street Addresses 37863

SEVIERVILLE TN

General Delivery 37862

POST OFFICE BOXES MAIN OFFICE STATIONS AND BRANCHES

Box No.s
All PO Boxes 37864

NAMED STREETS

Aaron Ct & St 37876
Aaron Branch Way 37876
Abbey Lane Way 37862
Abbie Rae Dr 37876
Abbott Rd 37862
Abiding Love Way 37862
Acorn Way 37876
Adella Ave 37862
Ailey Church Ln 37876
Aintree Dr 37876
Air Museum Way 37862
Airport Rd 37862
Alden Glenn Ct 37876
E Alder Branch Rd 37876
Alderman Rd 37862
Alexanderia St 37862
Alf Ownby Dr 37862
Allen Rd 37876
Allen Way 37862
Allendale Ln 37876
Allenridge Dr 37876
Allensville Rd & Rdg 37876
Allensville Acres Rd 37876
Alliene Way 37876
Ally Ln 37876
Alpine Dr 37876
Alpine Ridge Way 37876
Alum Cave Cv 37862
Alvins Ridge Dr 37876
Am King Way 37876
Amanda Ln 37876
Amanda Jane Way 37862
Amanda View Way 37876
Amarlee Way 37876
Amber Ln 37862
Ambrose Paine Ln 37862
Amis Way 37876
Amolee Ln 37876
Amy Lea 37862
Anderson Way 37876
Angela Dr 37876
Angela Starr Dr 37876
Angels Attic Way 37862
Angler Way 37876
Anna Faye Way 37876
Anthony Ln 37876
Apache Trail Way 37876
Appaloosa Way 37876
Apple Ln 37876
Apple Ridge Way 37862
Apple Valley Rd 37862
Apple View Way 37862
Applewood Rd 37862
Arabian Way 37876
S Arch Rock Dr 37876
Arden Ln 37876
Ariell Lea 37862
Arnold Park Way 37876
Arron Way 37876
Arrow Way 37876
Arrowhead Dr 37876
Arrowhead Mountain Way 37876
Arthur Ln 37876
Aryel Overlook Way 37862
Asa St 37876
Ash Dr 37876
Ashley Lea 37862
Ashton Ln 37876
Aspen Ct 37876
Aster Ct 37862
Atchley Dr & Rd 37876
Audley Dr 37876
Audley Moore Rd 37876
Audrey Jo Ln 37876
Austin View Way 37876
Autumn Path Way 37862
Autumn Ridge Way 37876
Autumn Valley Way 37862
Autumn View Way 37862
Autumn Woods Ln 37862
Autumns Peak Way 37876
Avenue A 37876
Avenue B 37876
Avenue C 37876
Avenue D 37876
Avery Ln 37862
Avon Cir 37876
Azalea Cir & Trl 37876
Backhome Ln 37876
Bacon Ct 37876
Badger Rd 37876
Baker Rd & Way 37876
Bales Way 37876
Bales Island Way 37876
N Ball Hollow Rd 37876
Balsam Cir 37876
Balsam Slopes Rd 37862
Barbara Way 37862
Barbara Lynn Way 37876
Barber Way 37862
Barbwire Way 37862
Barkenhowl Way 37862
Barkley Dr 37862
Barnes Blvd 37876
Barnes Dr 37862
Barron Way 37876
Barry View Way 37862
Barton Fields Dr 37862
Bass Ln 37876
Bassett Way 37876
Basswood Ct 37876
Bates Gibson Rd 37876
Bativa Garden Ct 37876
Battle Top Rd 37876
Bay Meadows Way 37876
Bayfront Dr 37876
Beach Way 37876
Beach Front Dr 37876
Beach Hollow Ct 37876
Beach View Ln 37876
Beal Ct 37862
Beal Woods Dr 37862
Bear Camp Way 37862
Bear Claw Way 37876
Bear Country Way 37876
Bear Creek Way 37862
Bear Crossing Way 37862
Bear Hollow Way 37876
Bear Mountain Ln 37876
Bear Path Way 37876
Bear Paw Ridge Way 37862
Bear Paw Trail Way 37876
Bear Pen Gap Rd 37876
Bear Run Way 37862
Bear Springs Way 37862
Bear Valley Rd 37876
Bear View Rd 37876
Bears Den Way 37876
Bearwallow Way 37876
Beaver Run Way 37862
Beech Ct 37876
Beech Rd 37862
Beechview Dr 37862
Begonia Way 37876
Bell Rd 37862
Bell Field Way 37862
Belle Ave 37862
Belle Meadows Blvd 37862
Bench Mountain Way 37862
Bend View Ln 37876
Benjamin Blvd 37876
Bent Tree Ln 37862
Benton Way 37876
Berry Trail Dr 37876
Bertie St 37862
Bethel Church Rd 37876
Beverly Hills Dr 37862
Big Buck Ln 37876
Big Chiefs Skyview Dr 37862
Big Cove Ct 37862
Big Dogwood Rd 37876
Big River Overlook Dr 37876
Big Rock Way 37862
Bill Flagle Way 37876
Billard Way 37876
Binginham Is 37876
Birch Dr 37876
Birchwood Ln 37862
Bird Hill Rd 37876
Bird Nest Way 37862
Bird Ridge Rd 37876
Bird View Ln 37862
Birds Creek Rd 37876
Birdsong Way 37876
Bj Belk Way 37876
Black Bear Ln 37876
Black Bear Cub Way 37862
Black Bear Ridge Way 37862
Black Oak Dr 37876
Black Oak Way 37862
Black Oak Ridge Rd 37876
Black Powder Ln 37876
Black Walnut Flats Rd 37862
Blackberry Way 37876
Blaine Way 37876
Blake Lea 37862
Blalock Dr 37862
Blalock Way 37876
Blalock Hollow Rd 37876
Blanket Mountain Way 37862
Blanton Dr 37862
Blossom Way 37876
Blossom Hollow Way 37876
Blowing Cave Rd 37876
Blue Bonnet Dr 37862
Blue Iris Way 37876
Blue Mist Rd 37876
Blue Ridge Dr 37862
Blue Ridge Rd 37876
Blue Ridge Way 37862
Blue Springs Way 37862
Blue Spruce Way 37876
Blue Tick Way 37876
Bluebird Cove Ln 37862
Bluebird Ridge Way 37876
Bluegrass Rd 37862
Bluff Heights Rd 37876
Bluff Mountain Rd 37876
Bluff Ridge Rd 37876
Bluff View Way 37876
Bluffside View Way 37876
Boardly Hills Blvd 37876
Boat Launch Rd 37876
Bob Hollow Rd 37876
Bobcat Way 37862
Bobcat Trail Way 37862
Bobs Pass 37876
Bobwhite Trl 37876
Bogart Dr 37862
Bogle Spring Loop 37862
Bohanan Hollow Rd 37876
Bohanan Top Rd 37876
Bonnie Ln 37876
Boo Boo Way 37862
S Boogertown Rd 37876
Boulders Crest Ln 37876
Boundary Way 37876
Bourne Way 37876
Bow Ct 37876
Boxwood Ln 37862
Boyds Creek Hwy 37876
Boyds Creek Church Rd 37876
Brackins Hollow Rd 37876
Bradley Ln, Rd & Trl 37876
Bramblebrook Way 37876
Branch Way 37876
Brandon Ln 37876
Brandy Way 37876
Breeden Branch Rd 37876
Breezy Rd 37876
Breezy Ridge Dr 37876
Brianna Leigh Ln 37862
Briar Lea 37862
Briarwood Dr 37862
Brice Hollow Way 37876
Brightstone Way 37876
Briley Way 37862
Broad Ave 37862
Broad River Ln 37876
Broadview Cir 37876
Broadview Dr 37862
Bronte Way 37876
Brooke Hollow Ln 37862
Brothers Way 37862
Brown Way 37876
Bruce St 37862
Bryan Rd 37862
Bryan View Rd 37876
Bryant Hollow Way 37876
Bryce View Ln 37862
Bryson Ct 37876
Buck Way 37876
Buck Board Ln 37862
Buck Hill Dr 37876
Buck Horn Rd 37876
Buckeye Knob Way 37862
Buckeye View Way 37876
Buds Ridge Way 37862
Buena Dr 37862
Buena Vista Dr & Way 37876
Bull Hill Rd 37876
Burchfiel Way 37876
Burchfiel View Way 37862
Burden Hill Rd 37862
Burgess Ln 37876
Burke Ave 37876
Burning Oaks Dr 37876
Burning Tree Ln 37862
Burns Rd 37862
Burridge Dr
400-699 37862
700-999 37876
Bush Hollow Way 37876
Business Center Cir 37876
Butterfly Hill Way 37876
Butternut Ln 37876
Byrd Hollow Rd 37876
Byrds Cross Rd 37876
Cabin Mountain Way 37876
Cabin Village Way 37862
Camborne Dr 37862
Camden Way 37876
Cameron Ln 37862
Camp Hollow Rd 37876
Camp Smoky Ln 37876
Campbell Hollow Rd 37876
Canaway Way 37876
Candy Tuft Dr 37862
Canterbury Ln 37862
Canterbury Downs Rd 37862
Canupp Dr 37876
Car Donna Dr 37862
Carl St 37862
Carpel Way 37876
Carroll Hill Ln 37876
Carvers Ln 37876
Cascades Ct 37862
Cascading Falls Ln 37876
E & W Casey Dr 37862
Castle Rise Way 37862
Catawba Rd 37876
Cate Rd 37862
Catlett Dr 37876
Catlett Rd 37862
Catlettsburg Rd 37876
Caton Ave & Rd 37862
Caton Branch Rd 37876
Catons Chapel Rd 37876
Cats Paw Ln 37862
Cattail Trl 37862
Caughron Dr 37876
Caughron Mountain Rd 37876
Cecil Ln 37876
Cedar Dr 37862
Cedar Ln 37862
Cedar Pass 37876
Cedar St 37862
Cedar Ter 37862
Cedar Bend Loop 37862
Cedar Bluff Rd 37876
Cedar Falls Way 37862
Cedar Hill Dr 37862
Cedar Hills Rd 37862
Cedar Point Rd 37876
Cedar Springs Valley Rd 37876
Cedar Top Dr 37862
Cedarwood Dr 37876
Cee Cee Way 37876
Center St 37862
Center View Rd 37862
Central Ave 37862
Chamberlain Ln 37862
Chambers Way 37876
Chance Way 37876
Chances Ridge Dr 37876
Chaney Rd 37876
Channel View Way 37876
Chapel Rd 37876
Chapel View Ct 37876
Chapman Hwy 37876
Charles Way 37876
Charles Lewis Way 37876
Charleston Ct 37862
Chelan Way 37876
Chelsea Jo Ln 37876
Cherokee Cir & Dr 37862
Cherokee Circle Dr 37862
Cherokee Conner Dr 37862
Cherokee Path Way 37876
Cherokee Ridge Way 37862
Cherokee Valley Dr 37862
Cherry St 37862
Cherry View Ln 37876
Chester Mountain Rd 37876
Chestnut Ct 37876
Chestnut Ln 37862
Chestnut Oak Way 37876
Chestnut Ridge Ct 37876
Chestnut Springs Way 37876
Chicory Way 37876
Chilhowee Dr 37862
Chinquapin Dr 37876
Chipmunk Way 37862
Chris Way 37876
Christy Way 37876
Chucky Burl Rd 37876
Church St 37862
Churchill Downs Way 37876
Cinnamon Way 37862
N & S Circle Dr 37862
Circle C Way 37876
Clabo Ln 37876
Clabo Rd 37862
Clabo Hollow Rd 37876
Clabo Mountain Ln 37862
Claud Way 37876
Claude Maples Cir 37876
Claude Shields Way 37876
Clayton Way 37876
N & S Clear Fork Rd 37862
Clear Springs Gulch Rd 37862
Clear Valley Dr 37862
Clearview Cir & Rd 37862
Clearwater Way 37876
Cliffside Way 37876
Climbing Bear Way 37876
Clingmans Vw 37876
Cloud Way 37876
Cloud View Dr 37862
Clover Cir 37876
Cloverdale Ct 37862
Cloverleaf Ln 37862
Club Dr 37862
Cluster Oak Way 37876
Clyde Way 37876
Clyde Mitchell Ln 37876
Cody Dr 37862
Cody View Way 37876
Cold Springs Rd 37876
Cole Rd 37876
Collier Dr 37862
Colton Cir 37862
Columbine Lea 37862
Commerce St 37862
Commission Dr 37862
Compton Ct 37862
Conley Dr 37876
Connatser Ln & Rd 37862
Connely St 37862
Conner Ct 37862
Conner View Ct 37862
Connie Houston Dr 37862
Conrad Way 37862
Cool Brook Ct 37876
Cool Creek Rd 37862
Cool Water Ln 37862
Copeland Rd 37876
Cornus Ave 37862
Cotter Cir & Way 37862
Cottontail Cove Way 37876
Counselor Dr 37862
Country Ln & Way 37862
Country Colonial St 37862
Country Creek Ln 37862
Country Dreams Way 37862
Country Meadows Dr 37862
Country Path Way 37876
Country Pines Way 37876
Country Place Way 37862
Country Store Rd 37876
County Garage Rd 37876
Court Ave 37862
Courtney Ln 37876
Cove Rd 37876
Cove Creek Dr & Way 37862
Cove Crest Dr 37862
Cove Meadows Dr 37862
Cove Mountain Ln & Rd 37862
Cove Ridge Way 37862
Cove Spring Way 37876
Cove View Ln 37862
Cove View Way 37876
Covemont Ln & Rd 37862
Covenant Dr 37876
Covered Bridge Way 37862
Covered Wagon Rd 37862
Coveside Way 37876
Covington Cir 37876
Cowden Spring Way 37876
Coy Rhea Way 37876
Coyote Peak Way 37862
Cozy Way 37876
Cp Howard Dr 37876
Cp Wilson Dr 37862
Crabapple Way 37876
Crawfish Way 37862
Creative Way 37876
Creek Ave & Way 37862
Creek Falls Way 37862
Creek Hollow Way 37876
Creek Overlook Way 37862
Creek Path Way 37876
N Creek Side Dr & Ln 37876
Creekview St 37862
Crescent Dr 37862
Crescent Way 37876
Crestview Ct 37862
Cricket Wood Way 37862
Cristobal Way 37862
Crocket Way 37876
Crockett Hill Ln 37862
Crofford St 37862
Cross St 37862
Cross Over Rd 37876
Cross Park Ln 37876
E & W Crosscut Way 37876
Crossridge Rd 37876
Crown Cir 37862
Crystal View Dr 37876
Cub Cir 37862
Cub Run Way 37862
W Cummings Chapel Ct & Rd 37876
Cupid Way 37876
Cypress Ln 37876
Cypress Cove Way 37876
Cypress View Ct 37862
Daffodil Way 37862
Dahlgren Way 37876
Daisy Ct 37876
Dalton Dr 37876
Dandelion Ct 37862
Dartmoor Way 37862
Darvan Way 37876
Daryl Way 37876
Davis Ln 37876
Dawn Ln 37876
Daxa Way 37876
Day Lilly Way 37876
Dayne Dr 37876
Dead Oak Ct 37876
Deane Hill Dr 37862
Debras Way 37876
Dee Jay Way 37876
Deep River Dr 37876
Deer Browse Way 37876
Deer Field Cir 37862
Deer Foot Way 37876
Deer Haven Rd 37876
Deer Meadows Rd 37862
Deer Ridge Ln 37876
Deer Run Way 37862
Deer Stand Dr 37876
Deer Valley Way 37876
Deerskin Rd 37862

Delight Ln 37876
Dellwood Dr 37876
Delta Way 37862
Delta Dawn Dr 37862
Denison Way 37876
Denton Ct & Rd 37862
Derby Way 37876
Destiny Way 37876
Dewberry Ln 37862
Dickey Dr 37862
Dishers Mountain Rd 37876
Ditney Ln & Way 37876
Dixon Branch Rd 37876
Dixon Farm Rd 37876
Dockery Ct 37876
Dockery Branch Rd 37876
Dockery Hollow Rd 37876
Dodgen Way 37862
Dogwood Ct 37876
Dogwood Dr 37876
Dogwood Ln 37862
E Dogwood Ln 37862
N Dogwood Ln 37876
Dogwood St 37876
Dogwood Cove Way 37862
Dogwood Loop Dr 37876
Dogwood Ridge Way 37862
Dolly Parton Pkwy
500-712 37862
711-711 37864
713-1599 37862
714-1598 37862
Dollys Dr 37876
Donegal Way 37862
Donnie Lee Way 37876
S Dorset Ln 37862
Double D Dr 37876
Double Oaks Way 37862
Douglas Bay Way 37876
Douglas Dam Rd 37876
Douglass Ln 37876
Dove Dr 37876
Dove View Rd 37862
Dove Wing Way 37862
Downing Ln 37876
Doyle Ct 37876
Dream Way 37876
Driftwood Cir 37876
Drue Fox Way 37862
Dry Hollow Ct 37876
Duck Pond Ln 37876
Dudley Dr 37876
Duncan Spring Rd 37876
Dunn Way 37876
Dunn Hollow Rd 37862
Dupont Springs Rd 37876
Durham Ln 37862
Dwight Ln 37876
Dyke Rd 37876
Dyke 9 Rd 37876
Eagle Pt 37876
Eagle Cloud Way 37862
Eagle Crest Way 37876
Eagle Eye Rd 37876
Eagle Feather Dr 37876
Eagle Springs Rd 37876
East Ave 37862
Eastgate Rd 37862
Eastgate Homes 37862
Eastline Way 37876
Easy St 37862
Echota Way 37876
Ed Huff Cir 37876
Edens Way 37876
Edge Park Dr 37862
Edgewater Dr 37862
Eds Ln 37876
Edward Dr 37876
Eight Point Ln 37876
Eledge Ln 37876
Eledge Farm Rd 37876
Eledge View Ln 37876
Elk Hound Way 37876
Ella Dr 37862
Ella Way 37876
Ellendale Cv 37862

Ellis Ln 37862
Ellis Rd 37862
Ellis Lead Way 37876
Ellis Woods Loop 37876
Ellison Ct 37876
Elm Cir 37876
Elm Ct 37876
Elm Ln 37862
Elm St 37862
Elm Way 37876
Elvin Branch Rd 37876
Emerald Way 37876
Emerald Point Way 37876
Emerald Springs Loop 37862
Emert Ave 37862
Emerts Cove Rd 37876
Emhouse Way 37876
Emily Dr 37876
Enchanted Forest Ln 37876
E End Rd 37876
Engle Town Rd 37862
English Hills Dr 37876
English Valley Ln 37876
Eric Ct 37876
Ernest Mcmahan Rd 37862
Estate Dr 37862
Estele Dr 37876
Eternity Way 37876
Ethan Rd 37876
Etherton Rd 37876
Evans Chapel Rd 37876
Evergreen Dr 37862
Fain Rd 37876
Fair Valley Ln 37876
Fairgarden Cir & Rd 37876
Faiths Way 37876
Falcon View Way 37862
Falin Way 37876
Fall Lea 37876
Fantasy Way 37876
Fawn View Dr 37876
Faye Way 37876
Feld Wynde Close
Way 37862
Ferguson Ln 37876
Fern Brook Way 37862
Fiddlers Way 37876
Fiesta Blvd & Way 37876
Finchum Ln 37876
Finchum Hollow Rd &
Way 37876
Fine Ln 37862
Fine Glen Dr 37862
Fini Way 37876
E Fir St 37876
Firefly Ln 37862
Firefly Trail Way 37862
Fishermans Way 37876
Flat Branch Rd 37876
S & W Flat Creek Rd &
Way 37876
Flat Creek East Blvd 37876
Flatwood Rd 37862
Fleming Ln & Way 37876
Floyd Ln 37862
Floyd Rd 37876
Flying Squirrel Way 37862
Foggy Way 37876
Foothills Forest Way 37876
Ford Ave 37862
Forest Breeze Way 37876
Forest Court Ln 37876
Forest Hills Dr 37876
Forest Trail Dr 37876
S Fork Dr 37862
Forks Of The River
Pkwy 37862
Four Point Ln 37876
Four Seasons Ln 37862
Fox Ln & Rd 37862
Fox Bar Way 37862
Fox Berry Way 37862
Fox Cemetery Rd 37876
Fox Church Rd 37876
Fox Crossing Rd 37862
Fox Den Rd 37876

Fox Hunters Ln 37876
Fox Meadows Blvd 37862
Fox Ridge Way
1900-1999 37862
4000-4099 37876
Fox View Ln 37876
Fox Vista Dr 37876
Foxfire Way 37876
Foxwell Way 37876
Foxwood Dr 37862
Franke Hollow Rd 37876
Frankie Ln 37876
Franklin Dr 37862
Franklin Ln 37876
Fred King Ln 37876
Fred Ramsey Rd 37876
Fred Sales Pl 37876
Fredrick Ln 37876
Freedom Way 37876
French Broad Cir 37876
Friar Wood Ln 37876
Frontier Vw & Way 37876
Frost Valley Ct 37876
Furniture Your Way 37862
Gallahad Ct 37876
Gann Dr 37862
Garden Hill Ct 37862
Gary Wade Blvd 37862
Gatewood Ct 37862
Gator Point Rd 37876
Gay St 37862
Gear Dr 37876
Gentlemens Way 37876
George Davis Ave 37862
S Georgia Ct & Way 37876
Georgian Ln 37862
Gibson Cir 37876
Gibson Hollow Ln 37862
Gibson Hollow Rd 37876
Gilbert Ln 37876
Gilland Dr 37862
Gimlet Dr 37876
Ginas Way 37862
Ginnys Trl 37876
Ginseng Way 37862
Gists Creek Rd 37876
Gladys Breeden Cir 37876
Glasgow St 37876
Glen Eden Way 37862
Glen Ray Ln 37876
Glenda Ln 37862
Glenn Huskey Rd 37862
Glennhill Ln 37862
Glenns Lea 37876
Glenview Way 37862
Gliding Crane Way 37876
Gnatty Trl 37876
Gnatty Branch Rd 37876
Gneiss Ct 37862
Goingback Cir 37876
Golden Circle Dr 37862
Golden Pond Way 37862
Golf Club Dr 37876
Goose Way 37862
Goose Gap Rd 37876
Gospel Ln 37876
Gossett Rd 37876
Grace Ave & Way 37862
Graduate Dr 37862
Grady Lee Way 37862
Grand Vista Dr 37876
Grannys Nob Way 37862
Grant Ln & Rd 37876
Grant Valley Ln 37876
Grassy Branch Loop &
Rd 37876
Grassy Meadow Ln 37862
Gray Slate Cir 37876
Gray Wolf Dr 37862
Greater Kendra Way 37862
Green Ct 37876
Green Acres Cir 37862
Green Bay Dr 37876
Green Pasture Ln 37876
Green Pine Ln 37862
Green Top Rd 37876

Green Tree Way 37876
Green Valley Rd 37862
Greenway Dr 37862
Gregg Ct 37876
Gregory Valley Dr 37876
Grey Fox Run 37862
Greystone Ridge Dr 37876
Grinders Way 37862
Grist Mill Ln 37862
Grotto Ln 37876
Grouse Ridge Rd 37862
Grove Way 37876
Guffy Hollow Rd 37876
Gulf Stream Way 37876
Gum Stand Rd 37876
Gurrhawk Way 37862
Hackberry Dr 37862
Haggard Dr & Rd 37876
Hailey Way 37862
Haley Lynn Rd 37862
Half High St 37876
Haney Rd 37876
Hansels Lea 37876
Happy Creek Rd 37876
Happy Hollow Ln 37876
Happy Hollow Rd 37862
Happy Trails Way 37862
Harbor Point Dr 37876
Hardin Ln 37876
E Hardin Ln 37862
Hardin Rd 37876
Hardin Hills Rd 37876
Hardwork Rd 37862
Harmony Hill Ln 37862
Harrell Hills Way 37862
Harris Mountain Way 37876
Harrisburg Rd 37876
Harrisburg Mill Rd 37876
Harrison Creek Rd 37876
Harvest Way 37862
Harvest Moon Ln 37862
Hatcher Mountain Rd 37862
Hatcher Top Rd 37862
Hatcher View Way 37862
Hattie Branch Rd 37876
Haven Ln 37876
Hawk Hollow Dr 37862
Hawkeye Vw 37862
Hawks Nest Way 37862
Hawks Point Way 37862
Hawks View Trl 37876
Hazel Dr 37862
Headrick Dr 37862
Headrick Lead 37862
Heartwood Way 37876
Heather Ln & Rd 37876
Heather Lane Way 37862
Heather Lea Dr 37862
Heather Mccarter Ln 37862
Heatley Ln 37862
Heavens Way 37876
Heavens Path Way 37862
Heavens View Ln 37876
Helen Ct 37876
Helicopter Ride Blvd 37862
Helton Rd 37876
S Helton Rd 37862
Helton Way 37876
Helton End Way 37876
Hemlock Ct 37862
Hemlock Ln 37876
N Henderson Ave 37862
Henry Branch Way 37876
Henry Huskey Ln 37862
Henry Town Rd 37876
Herb Ownby Way 37862
Herendon Way 37876
Heritage Ln & Way 37876
Herman Large Ln 37876
Hh Rogers Way 37876
Hialeah Way 37876
Hickey Rd 37876
Hickory St 37862
Hickory Hill Dr 37876
Hickory Hills Rd 37862
Hickory Hollow Way 37862

Hickory Knoll Way 37862
Hickory Manor Rd 37862
Hickory Nut Way 37876
Hickory Patch Way 37862
Hickory Ridge Way 37862
Hickory Tree St 37876
Hickory Tree Hollow
Rd 37876
Hicks Dr 37862
Hidden Cir 37876
Hidden Cove Way 37876
Hidden Harbor Ln 37876
Hidden Hollow Way 37862
Hidden Mountain Rd 37876
Hidden Springs Way 37862
Hideaway Way 37876
Hideaway Hills Cir 37862
Hideaway Ridge Cir 37862
High Dr & St 37862
High Forest Way 37862
High Ridge Way 37862
High Rock Way 37862
High Top Loop 37862
High View Ct & Rd 37876
Highpoint Ln 37876
Hikers Path Way 37862
Hiley Dr 37862
Hill Hollow Dr 37876
Hillcrest Dr & Rd 37862
Hills Creek Rd 37876
Hillside Dr 37876
Hilltop Cir, Rd & Way 37876
Hobe Maples Way 37876
Hodge Rd 37876
Hodges Ln 37876
Hodges Bend Rd 37862
Hodges Farm Way 37862
Hodges Ferry Rd 37876
Holbert Cemetery Rd 37876
Holiday Ln 37876
Hollow Branch Way 37862
Holly Ct 37862
Holly Dr 37876
Holly Ln 37862
Holly Pass 37862
Holly Tree Way 37876
Hollyberry Ct 37876
Hollywood Cir 37862
Home Place Way 37876
Honey Ln 37876
Honey Do Way 37876
Honey Oaks Way 37876
Honeymoon Hollow
Way 37876
Honeysuckle Ln 37876
Honeysuckle Way 37862
Honeysuckle Ridge
Way 37876
Hook Rd 37876
Hopson St 37862
Hornbuckle Ln 37876
Horse Gap Rd 37876
Hoss Ridge Way 37862
Howard Dr 37862
Huckleberry Way 37862
Huckleberry Hill Rd 37862
Huff Ct & Ln 37876
Hummingbird Ln 37862
Hummingbird Hill Way 37876
Hunter Hills Way 37876
Hurlbut Way 37862
Hurley Dr 37876
Hurst Way 37876
Hurst Hollow Rd 37876
Huskey Dr & Ln 37862
Huskey Grove Rd 37862
Illa Clyde Lane Way 37862
Indian Ct & Ln 37862
Indian Gap Cir & Rd 37876
Indian Ridge Way 37876
Indian Springs Rd 37862
Indian Warpath Rd 37876
Indigo Ln 37862
Industrial Park Dr 37862
Industry Dr 37862
Infinity Ln 37876

Ingle Hollow Rd 37876
Ingram Inn 37876
Inn Of The Clouds Dr 37862
Instrumental Ave 37876
Iris Ct 37876
Irvine Ln 37876
Isaac Thomas Ln 37862
Island Blvd 37876
Island View Rd 37876
Ivy Way 37876
Jack Delozier Dr 37876
Jackie Dr 37876
Jacks Pass 37876
Jackson St 37862
Jada Ln 37876
Jaguar Dr 37876
Jakes Ridge Way 37862
Jama Dr 37876
James Rd 37876
James Phillips Way 37876
Jared Rd 37876
Jasmine Trl 37862
Jason Pl 37876
Jayell Rd 37862
Jays Lead Way 37876
Jeans Way 37876
Jed Trl 37862
Jenkins Rd 37876
Jensen Ridge Ln 37876
Jersey Dr 37862
Jessica Lea 37862
Jessie Rd 37876
Jetta View Ln 37876
Jf Shular Way 37876
Jh Headrick Dr 37862
Jim Fain Rd 37876
Jim Parton Way 37876
Jims Way 37876
Jj Cir 37862
Jl Myers Rd 37862
Jobey Green Hollow
Rd 37876
Joel Ave 37876
John Boy Trl 37862
John L Marshall Dr 37862
John Sevier Dr 37876
John Spears Way 37876
Johns Ct 37876
Jones Cove Rd &
Way 37876
Jonola Rd 37876
Jorden Creek Way 37876
Joshua Way 37876
Joy St 37862
Joyner Hills Ln 37876
Judy Top Ln 37876
Julia Way 37876
Julia Allison Dr 37876
Junaluska Way 37876
June Bug Way 37862
Junior Way 37876
Juniper Way 37862
Justus Way 37876
Kandy Way 37876
Kanuga Ct 37876
Karsons Ct 37876
Katelyns Ln 37876
Katherine Lea 37862
Kathern St 37862
Katie Ln 37862
Katy Hollar Rd 37862
Kay View Dr 37876
Keats Way 37876
Keener Ln 37862
Kellum Creek Rd 37876
Kelly Hills Rd 37876
Kerr Rd 37876
Kettle Creek Way 37876
Key Way 37876
S Kilby St 37862
Kildee Ln 37862
Killam Way 37862
Kim Allen Way 37862
Kim Lane Way 37862
Kimberly Ln 37862
Kimberly Heights Rd 37876

Kimsey Way 37876
Kindred Way 37876
Kinfolks Ridge Way 37876
King St 37862
S King Branch Rd 37876
King Estates Rd 37876
King Hollow Rd 37876
Kingdom Ct 37876
Kingfisher Ave 37862
Kings Row 37862
Kingsbrook Way 37876
Kingsview Ct 37862
Kirby Ln 37862
Kirkwood Way 37876
Kissing Way 37862
Klaver Rd 37862
Knife Works Ln 37876
Knight Hollow Rd 37876
Knights Way 37862
Knoll Ct 37876
Knoll Run Ct 37876
Knoll Top Way 37876
Ko Way 37876
Ko Mcmahan Way 37876
Korey Blvd 37876
Kristina Way 37862
Kulpan Way 37862
Kyker Rd 37876
Kyker Ferry Rd 37876
La Croix Way 37862
Lafollette Way 37876
Lafollette Cemetery Ln 37876
Lake Dr 37876
Lake Meadows Way 37876
Lake Oaks Way 37876
Lake Smoky Rd 37876
Lake View Cir, Ln, Loop
& Rd 37876
Lakeshore Ave & Dr 37876
Lakeside Ct 37876
Lakeside Dr 37862
Lakeside Pl 37876
Lakeside Way 37876
Lakeview Dr 37876
Lamon Hollow Rd 37876
Lamons Loop 37876
Landmark Blvd 37862
Lane Hollow Rd 37876
Laney Way 37876
Lariat Ln 37862
Larix Way 37876
Laughing Bear Way 37862
Laughing Pine Ln 37862
Laura Ln 37862
Laurel Ln 37876
Laurel Cove Trl 37862
Laurel Creek Rd 37876
Laurel Falls Ln 37862
Laurel Lick Rd 37862
Laurel Path Way 37862
Laurel Ridge Way 37862
Laurel Valley Way 37862
Laurelwood Ave & Ln 37862
Lawson Ln 37862
Lawyer Ln 37862
Lazy River Ln 37876
Leamar Dr 37876
Leatherwood Ln 37862
Leatherwood Rd 37876
Leconte Dr 37876
Leconte Landing Ln 37862
Ledo Rd 37862
Lee Cir 37862
Lee Proffitt Way 37876
Lees Path 37876
Legacy Dr 37876
Legacy Vista Dr 37876
Legend Dr 37876
Legend View Ct 37862
Legion Way 37876
Leisure Ct & Ln 37876
Lena Acres Way 37876
Lennis Way 37876
Leo Sharp Rd 37862
Lera Ct 37862
Leslie Way 37876

Street	ZIP
Levee Way	37876
Lewelling Rd	37862
Lexington Pl	37862
Lexington Park Ave	37862
Lexy Ln	37862
Licking Spring Way	37876
Licklog Hollow Rd	37876
Lightfoot Way	37862
Lighthouse Way	37876
Lillard Allen Ln	37876
Lillie Blvd	37876
Lily Ct	37876
Lin Creek Dr & Rd	37876
Lindder Dr	37876
Lindsey Dr & Way	37876
Line Springs Ln	37862
Linwood Ct	37876
Lisa Dr	37876
Little Bluff Way	37876
Little Branch Rd	37876
Little Brook Way	37876
Little Cabin Loop	37862
Little Cove Rd	37862
Little Cove Church Rd	37862
Little Cove Springs Way	37862
Little Creek Way	37862
Little Cub Way	37862
Little Fall Ct	37876
Little Island Way	37876
Little Kaycee Dr	37876
Little Kelsey Way	37876
Little Lamb Way	37862
Little Laurel Rd	37862
Little Pigeon Dr	37862
Little Valley Rd	37862
Live Oak Ln	37862
Livingston Way	37876
Lizi Loop Way	37862
Llama Ln	37862
Locust Ridge Rd & Way	37876
Lodge Pole Way	37876
Logan Ridge Dr	37876
Lohman Rd	37876
Lona Dr	37862
London Ln	37862
Lone Eagle Dr	37876
Lone Pine Way	37876
Lone Ridge Dr	37862
Lones Branch Ln	37876
Lonesome Pine Way	37862
Lonesome Valley Rd	37862
Long Branch Rd	37876
Long Hollow Rd	37876
Long Oak Ct	37876
Long Rifle Rd	37862
Long Springs Rd	37876
Longspur Trl	37876
Longvale Ln	37862
Longview Dr	37862
Look Afar View Dr	37876
Look Out Way	37862
Loop Rd	37876
E Loop Rd	37862
W Loop Rd	37862
Lords Way	37876
Lori Ellen Ct	37876
Lorre Way	37862
Lost Branch Rd	37862
Lost Valley Dr	37862
Love Rd	37862
Loveday Ln	37876
Low Sunset Dr	37876
Lowe Valley Dr	37862
Lower Bluff Way	37862
Lower Peach Orchard Way	37876
Lower Powdermill Rd	37876
Luke Lea	37862
Lum Way	37876
Lumber Jack Way	37876
Luther Way	37876
Luther Catlett Cir	37876
Lyema St	37862
Lynn Ct	37876
Lynn Dr	37862
Lyon Springs Ln & Rd	37862
Mabels Ln	37876
Mac Way	37862
E & W Madison Dr & Rdg	37876
Madron Dr	37862
Mae Ln	37862
Maggie Mack Ln	37862
Magic Kingdom Ln	37876
E & W Main St	37862
Majestic Oak Way	37876
Majestic Prince Way	37876
Majestic View Way	37862
Malibu Ct	37876
Mallard Way	37876
Manis Rd	37862
Manker Way	37862
Manning Ct & Way	37876
Manning Hollow Rd	37876
Manning Ridge Dr	37876
Manoah Way	37876
Maple Leaf Way	37862
Maplecrest Ln	37876
Maples Dr	37876
Maples Branch Rd	37876
Maples Hollow Rd	37876
Maplewood Cir & Way	37876
Maranohe Way	37862
Margaret Hollow Way	37862
Margretta Way	37862
Marian Lake Way	37862
Marigold Ct	37862
Mark Ann Dr & Ln	37862
Markhill Dr	37862
Marshall Cir, Ln & St	37862
Marshall Springs Way	37862
Martin Ln	37876
Mary Kay Dr	37862
Mary Lee Way	37862
Mary Lona Circle Way	37862
Mary Ridge Farm Rd	37862
Mary Rose Way	37876
Mason Ln	37862
Massey Rd	37862
Matt Rd	37876
Matthew Ln	37876
Matthews Way	37876
Matthews Hollow Rd	37876
Mattie Jane Way	37862
Mattox Cemetery Rd	37862
Maurice Rd	37876
Max Ln	37862
Maxie Ct	37876
Maxwell Ln	37876
Mayberry Ln	37862
Mayors Dr	37862
Mays Ln	37862
Mccam Cir	37862
Mccarter Cir	37876
Mccarter Dr	37862
Mccarter Ln	37876
Mccarter St	37876
Mccarter Way	37862
Mccarter Hollow Rd	37876
Mccarter Sisters Way	37876
Mccleary Rd	37876
Mccleary Bend Rd	37876
Mcclure Ln	37862
Mcclure Rd	37876
Mccoig Rd	37876
Mccroskey Ln	37862
Mccroskey Island Rd	37876
Mcdonald Way	37876
Mcfalls Way	37862
Mcgill Rd	37862
Mcinturf Way	37862
Mckenzie Way	37876
Mckinley St	37876
Mckinley View Blvd	37862
Mckinney Dr	37876
Mcmahan Ave	37862
Mcmahan Sawmill Rd	37862
Mcpherson Ln	37862
Mcqueen Way	37876
Meadow Ct & Ln	37862
Meadow Crest Ln	37876
Meadow Ridge Cir	37862
Meadow View Dr & Rd	37862
Meadowbrook Ln	37862
Meadowlands Cir	37876
Meadowlark Ln	37862
Meadowlark Cove Rd	37876
Meadows Dr	37876
Mechanics Way	37862
Medical Park Ct	37862
Megan Ridge Dr	37876
Megan View Ln	37876
Melanie Way	37862
Melodey Ln	37862
Memory Way	37876
Meredith Way	37876
Meridan Way	37876
Merritt Way	37876
Middle Ct	37862
Middle Way	37876
Middle Creek Rd	37862
Middle Ridge Rd	37862
Middlebrook Ct	37862
Mikey St	37876
Milford Haven Dr	37862
Mill Dam Way	37876
Miller Creek Way	37862
Millers Way	37876
Millers Ridge Way	37862
Millican Grove Rd	37876
Millwood Dr	37862
Mindy Jo Way	37862
Mini Home Ct	37876
Mistletoe Loop	37876
Misty Ct	37862
Misty Ln	37876
Misty Blue Mountain Dr	37876
Misty Bluff Trl	37862
Misty Mead Dr	37876
Misty Meadow Ln	37876
Misty Morning Way	37862
Misty Mountain Way	37876
Misty Shadows Dr	37862
Mitchell Dr	37876
Mitchell Farm Rd	37876
Mize Ln	37862
Mockingbird Way	37862
Monarch Cir	37876
Monhollen Dr	37862
Monte Vista Dr	37862
Montevallo Rd	37876
Montgomery Rd	37876
Moon Ct	37876
Moon Hollow Rd	37876
Moonside Ln	37876
Moore St	37876
Morgan Way	37876
Morning Eagle Ln	37876
Morning Glory Ct	37862
Morning Star Way	37862
Morning View Ln	37876
Morningside Dr	37862
Mortar Rd	37876
Mossy Trl	37876
Mossy Cove Way	37876
Mossy Creek Ln	37862
Mount Dr	37876
Mountain Blvd	37876
Mountain Dr	37876
Mountain Way	37876
Mountain Ash Way	37876
Mountain Berry Dr	37862
Mountain Folks Way	37876
Mountain Glenn Way	37862
Mountain Glory Trl	37876
Mountain High Trl	37876
Mountain Holly Way	37876
Mountain Lakes Way	37862
Mountain Lodge Way	37862
Mountain Meadows Way	37862
Mountain Memories Way	37876
Mountain Overlook Way	37876
Mountain Peak Way	37862
Mountain Rest Way	37876
Mountain Scenic Way	37876
Mountain Spring Way	37876
Mountain Top Ln	37876
Mountain Trail Way	37876
Mountain Tyme Way	37862
Mountain Valley Ln	37862
Mountain View Cir	37862
Mountain View Ct	37876
Mountain View Dr	37862
Mountain View Rd	37862
S Mountain View Rd	37876
Mountain Vista Rd	37876
Muddy Hollow Rd	37876
Mullinax Ln	37876
Muncey Ct	37862
Murphy Cir & Rd	37862
Murphy Denton Rd	37876
Murphys Chapel Dr	37876
Murray Ridge Rd	37876
Murrell Ln	37862
Murrell Meadows Dr	37876
Muscadine Ct	37876
Mustang Way	37876
My Pl	37862
Myers Rd	37862
Mystical Mountain Way	37876
Nan Way	37876
Nascar Dr	37862
Nathan Way	37862
National Way	37876
Native Dancer Way	37876
Natures Ln	37862
Neal Dr	37876
Needles Way	37876
Neighbor Way	37876
Nellie Dr	37876
Nevils Way	37876
New Center Dr & Rd	37876
New Era Rd	37862
S New Era Rd	
600-999	37862
1000-1399	37876
W New Era Rd	37876
New Mountain Way	37876
New Riverside Dr	37862
Newcomb Dr	37876
Newland Circle Ln	37876
Newman Town Rd	37862
Newport Hwy	37876
Newsome Rd	37876
Newt Huff Ln	37876
Newt Reagan Rd	37876
Niagra Ln	37862
Nicholas Ridge Way	37862
Nicholas View Way	37876
Nichols St	37862
Nichols Branch Way	37876
Nicoha Blvd	37876
Nikki Way	37876
No Business Way	37876
Noel Hill Way	37876
Norlil Rd	37876
North Pkwy	37876
North St	37862
Northstar Way	37876
Norton St	37862
Norwell Way	37876
Nucum Hollow Rd	37862
Nuns Cove Rd	37876
O Shields Way	37876
N Oak Ct	37876
Oak Dr	37862
Oak St	37862
Oak Cluster Dr	37862
Oak Crest Dr	37862
Oak Haven Ct & Way	37876
Oak Hill Rd	37862
Oak Lake Dr	37876
Oak Sky Way	37876
Oak View Dr	37876
Oak Vista Ct	37876
Oakley Manor Ct	37862
Oakmont Dr	37876
Oakridge Way	37876
Oakview Ln	37876
Oakville Ln	37862
Oakwood Dr	37876
Obes Way	37876
Obes Branch Rd	37876
Ogle Ct	37876
Ogle Ln	37862
Ogle Rd	37876
Ogle St	37862
Ogles View Rd	37862
Ola View Pt	37876
Old Barn Cir	37876
Old Birds Creek Rd	37876
Old Country Way	37862
Old Covered Bridge Rd	37876
Old Crow Rd	37876
Old Douglas Dam Rd	37876
Old Engle Town Rd	37862
Old Hag Hollow Way	37876
Old Happy Hollow Rd	37876
Old Harrisburg Rd	37876
Old Jayell Rd	37862
Old Knoxville Hwy	
400-1299	37862
1300-2099	37876
Old Laurel Ln	37876
Old Mill Rd	37876
Old Mountain Rd & Way	37876
Old Newport Hwy	
1100-1699	37862
1700-3499	37876
Old Powder Springs Way	37876
Old Red Ln	37876
Old Sharp Hollow Way	37862
Old Thomas Byrd Rd	37876
Old Thomas Cross Rd	37876
W Old Valley Rd	37862
Old Wilhite Rd	37862
Olde Tyme Way	37862
Oldham Creek Rd	37876
Oldham Springs Way	37876
Ole Smoky Way	37862
Oliver Way	37876
Ollie St	37876
Olympia Ct	37862
Oma Lee Dr	37876
One Mule Ln	37876
Orchard Dr	37876
Orchard Trail Way	37862
Orchard Valley Way	37876
Overhill Way	37876
Overholt Trl	37862
Overlook Ct, Dr & Way	37876
Owens Way	37876
Owenwood Dr	37876
Owls Cove Way	37862
Ownby Cir, Dr & Rd	37862
Ownby View Way	37862
W Paine St	37862
Paine Lake Dr	37862
Paint Horse Way	37876
Painter Mountain Way	37876
Palomino Way	37876
Pamela Cir	37862
Panorama Dr	37862
Panther Way	37876
N Panther Creek Rd	37876
Paradise Way	37876
Paradise Falls Way	37862
Paradise Ridge Dr	37862
Paradise View Way	37876
Parish Way	37876
Park Ln	37876
E Park Ln	37876
Park Rd	37862
Park Place Ave	37862
Parkside Village Way	37862
N Parkway	37862
Parkway View Ct	37876
Parrott Way	37876
Parrotts Chapel Rd	37876
Parrotts Landing Way	37876
Parton Ave	37862
Parton Ln	37876
Parton Hollow Rd	37876
Parton Woodcraft Rd	37876
Pasofino Way	37876
Patricia Holt Blvd	37862
Patrick Way	37862
Patriot Way	37862
Patterson Rd	37876
Patterson Lead Way	37876
Pattons Way	37876
Patty Ave	37862
Patty View Way	37862
Paulas Huskey Cir	37876
Pawnee Ct	37876
Payne School Dr	37876
Peaceful Way	37876
Peach Orchard Rd & Way	37876
Peach Tree St	37862
Peak Loop	37862
Pearl Valley Rd & Way	37876
Pebbles Mountain Way	37862
Pecan Ln	37862
Pembroke Dr	37876
Penelope Ln	37876
Peninsula Rd	37876
Penny Way	37862
Penzance Dr	37862
Perry Way	37876
Perry Catlett Dr	37876
Perry Circle Ln	37862
Persimmon Ridge Way	37876
Pheasant Ridge Rd	37876
Phillips Rd & Way	37876
Pigeon St	37862
Pigeon River Rd & Way	37862
Pigeon View Way	37876
Pikes Peak Way	37862
Pilgrims Way	37876
Pin Oak Dr	37862
Pine Trl	37876
Pine Crest Ln	37862
Pine Grove Rd	37876
Pine Haven Dr	37862
Pine Hollow Way	37876
Pine Mountain Rd & Way	37862
Pine Peak Way	37876
Pine Valley Way	37876
Pinebark Way	37876
Pinecrest Way	37862
Pinehurst Dr	37862
Pineridge Way	37876
Pinetree Way	37876
Pinewood Way	37862
Piney Dr	37876
Piney Cove Way	37862
Piney Overlook Ln	37862
Piney Ridge Way	37862
Pioneer Trl & Way	37876
Pittman Center Rd	37876
Placid Dr	37862
Pleasant Vw	37862
Pleasant Hill Rd	37876
Pleasant Oaks Rd	37876
Pleasant Valley Dr	37876
Pleasant View Ln	37862
Pleasure Rd	37876
Plum Creek Way	37862
Pond Ct	37876
Pool St	37862
Pope Way	37876
Poplar Ct & St	37862
Poplar Ridge Way	37876
Poplar View Ln	37876
Possum Cove Way	37862
Possum Hide A Way	37876
Possum Ridge Way	37876
Posty Way	37862
Powder Springs Rd	37876
Powdermill Estates Rd	37876
Preakness Way	37876
Present Way	37876
Preserve Way	37876
Prey Ct	37876
Price Way	37876
Price Cove Rd	37876
Price Mccarter Way	37876
Primrose Ct	37862
Prince St	37862
Priscilla Ln	37862
Priscilla Heights Ln	37862
Promise Way	37862
Providence Rd	37876
Providence Hills Rd	37876
Pullen Rd	37862
Pumpkin Path Way	37862
Quail Way	37862
Quail Hollow Way	37876
Quail Run Way	37876
Quarter Horse Way	37876
Quartz Ct	37876
Quiet Way	37876
Quiet Valley Way	37862
Rabbit Point Way	37876
Raccoon Den Way	37862
Raccoon Hollow Way	37862
Rachel St	37876
Railroad St	37862
Rainbow Rd	37862
Rainbow Falls Ln	37862
Rainbow Ridge Rd	37862
Ralph Conner Way	37862
Ramsey Way	37876
Ranch Way	37862
Rand Rd	37876
Randys Loop Dr	37876
Rauhuff Hollow Rd	37876
Raven Way	37862
Raven Fork Cir	37876
Raven View Way	37876
Ravens Den Way	37862
Ravens Ford Way	37876
Rayfield Ln	37876
Rayfield Hollow Way	37862
Raymond Hollow Rd	37876
Rays Gap Rd	37876
Reba Way	37876
Rebel Hill Dr	37876
Red Bank Cir & Rd	37876
Red Bone Way	37876
Red Bud Ln & Rd	37876
Red Cedar Ln	37876
Red Cedar Ridge Rd	37876
Red Fox Ridge Way	37862
Red Maple Ln	37876
Red Rooster Way	37876
Red Sky Dr	37862
Red Wolfe Rd	37862
Redbird Ridge Way	37876
Redbud View Rd	37876
Redmond Way	37876
Redtail Rd	37862
Reed Howard Ln	37876
Reed Schoolhouse Rd	37876
Reese Rd	37862
Regal Ct	37876
Regans Ridge Way	37876
Regency Ct	37862
Reid Ln	37876
Renatta Way	37876
Renee Rd	37862
Restful Way	37876
Retirement Way	37862
Retreat St	37862
Retreat Way	37876
Revenuer Rd	37862
Revetta Cir	37862
Rex Way	37876
Reynolds Ln	37876
Rhododendron Ln	37876
Rhubarb Ln	37876
Riceland Dr	37862
Rich Mountain Way	37876
Richard Rd	37876

Richardson Cove Rd ... 37876
Ricks Hollow Way ... 37876
N Ridge Cir ... 37862
N Ridge Ct ... 37862
S Ridge Ct ... 37862
Ridge Ln ... 37876
N Ridge Pl ... 37876
S Ridge Pl ... 37876
Ridge Rd ... 37862
E Ridge Rd ... 37862
N Ridge Rd ... 37876
Ridge Creek Cir ... 37876
Ridge View Dr ... 37876
Ridgeback Ln ... 37862
Ridgecrest Dr ... 37876
Ridgecrest Trl ... 37862
Ridgecrest Way ... 37862
Ridgecrest Loop Ln ... 37876
Ridgefield Dr ... 37876
Ridgehigh Pass ... 37876
Ridgeland Cir ... 37862
Ridgetop Way ... 37876
Ridgeway Trl ... 37862
Rimmel Rd ... 37862
Rippling Waters Cir ... 37876
Risen Star Way ... 37876
Rising Fawn Way ... 37876
N River Blvd ... 37876
River Ln ... 37876
River Pl ... 37862
River Rd ... 37862
River Bend Dr & Rd ... 37876
River Bluff Way ... 37876
River Bottom Dr ... 37862
River Breeze Dr ... 37876
River Colony Ct ... 37862
River Dance Ln ... 37876
River Divide Rd
500-1199 ... 37876
1200-1799 ... 37862
River Garden Ct ... 37862
River Meadows Dr ... 37876
River Mist Ln ... 37876
River Path Way ... 37876
River Place Way ... 37862
River Run Cir ... 37862
River Sounds Dr ... 37862
River Valley Cir ... 37862
River View Ter ... 37876
River Vista Cir ... 37876
Riverbrook Dr ... 37862
Riverdale Dr ... 37862
Rivergate Dr ... 37862
Rivergate Ridge Ct ... 37862
Riverpark Way ... 37862
Rivers Edge Ln ... 37862
Rivershore Ln ... 37876
Riverside Dr ... 37862
Riversong Way ... 37876
Riversong Ridge Way ... 37876
Rivertrail Ln ... 37862
N Riverview Cir & Dr ... 37862
Riverwalk Dr ... 37862
Rl Williams Way ... 37876
Roadway Inn Ln ... 37876
Roaring Creek Way ... 37862
Robert Green Way ... 37876
Robert Henderson Rd ... 37862
Robert Ridge Rd ... 37862
Roberts Ct & Rd ... 37862
Robertson View Pt ... 37876
Robeson Rd ... 37862
Robin Hood Dr ... 37876
Robinson Gap Rd ... 37876
Robinwing Ct ... 37876
Rock Garden Ct ... 37876
Rockgarden Way ... 37876
Rocking Chair Ln ... 37862
Rocky Flats Rd ... 37876
Rocky Top Rd ... 37876
Rocky Top Way ... 37862
Rocky Top Ridge Way ... 37876
Rogers Ln, Pl & Way ... 37876
Rolen Rd & Way ... 37876
Rolling Meadows Dr ... 37876
Romance Ridge Way ... 37876

Romines Ln ... 37876
Ronnies Ln ... 37876
Rose Ct & Pass ... 37876
Rosencrans Ln ... 37862
Ross Way ... 37876
Roth Rd ... 37876
Round Top Way ... 37862
Roundtop Dr ... 37862
Roy Way ... 37876
Royal Chase Ct ... 37862
Royal Heights Dr ... 37876
Royal View Way ... 37862
Rubye Rd ... 37876
Rugh Ridge Way ... 37876
Rule Way ... 37876
Rule Hollow Rd ... 37876
Runt Rd ... 37876
Runyan Cir & Ln ... 37862
Rushing River Rd ... 37876
Russell Hollow Rd ... 37876
Russie Gap Rd ... 37862
Rustic Way ... 37876
Ruth Ln ... 37862
Saddle Way ... 37876
Saddle Brook Way ... 37862
Saddleback Way ... 37876
Sage Ct ... 37876
Sage Grass Way ... 37862
Saint Ives Ct & Dr ... 37862
Saint Johns Ct ... 37862
Sallys Ct ... 37876
Sam Brown Rd ... 37876
Sam Ellis Way ... 37876
Sam Houston Ln ... 37862
Sam Mccarter Way ... 37876
Sams Rd ... 37876
Samuel Wear Dr ... 37862
Sand Ct ... 37876
Sand Plant Rd ... 37876
Sanders Ln ... 37876
Sanders Ridge Way ... 37876
Sandstone Way ... 37862
Sandy Bottom Cir ... 37862
Sandy Point Ln ... 37876
Santa Anita Way ... 37862
Santella Way ... 37862
Sapwood Way ... 37876
Sarek Ave ... 37876
Sassafras Trl ... 37876
Savannah Ln ... 37862
Sawmill Ln ... 37862
Sawmill Branch Dr ... 37862
Sb Ogle Ln ... 37876
Scarlett Meadows Dr ... 37876
Scenic Dr ... 37862
Scenic Mountain Dr &
Loop ... 37876
Scenic Woods Way ... 37876
Schneider Ln ... 37862
N School House Gap
Rd ... 37876
S Schrader Rd ... 37876
Scott St ... 37876
Scott Way ... 37862
Scottish Highland Way ... 37862
Seagle Hollow Rd ... 37876
Seaton Springs Rd ... 37862
Seaton View Pt ... 37876
Seattle Slew Way ... 37876
Secona Way ... 37876
Second Ln ... 37876
Secretariat Way ... 37876
Seldon Ogle Dr ... 37862
Sencebaugh Dr ... 37876
Sequoya Way ... 37876
Serene View Dr ... 37876
Serenity Brook Way ... 37862
Settle Way ... 37862
Settlers View Ln &
Way ... 37862
Sevier St ... 37862
Shaconage Trl ... 37876
Shade Tree Ln ... 37862
Shadow Ridge Dr ... 37862
Shady Dr ... 37862
Shady Ln ... 37876

Shady Way ... 37876
Shady Creek Way ... 37862
Shady Grove Ct & Rd ... 37876
Shady Oaks Way ... 37876
Shady Shores Dr ... 37876
Shagbark Hickory Rdg ... 37862
Shamrock Way ... 37876
Shannon Cir ... 37862
Sharon Ct ... 37876
Sharp Rd ... 37876
Sharp Hollow Rd ... 37862
Sharpes Ridge Way ... 37862
Shelby Way ... 37862
Shell Mountain Rd ... 37876
Shelnutt Way ... 37862
Sherwood Frst ... 37876
Shields Dr ... 37862
Shields Ln ... 37876
Shields Ter ... 37876
Shinbone Rd ... 37876
Shirley Myers Ln ... 37862
Shooting Star Way ... 37862
Short St ... 37876
Shular Hollow Way ... 37876
Sierra Ln ... 37862
Sierra Way ... 37876
Silver Way ... 37862
Silver Charm Way ... 37876
Silver Poplar Ln ... 37876
Silverado Ct ... 37876
Silverbell Dr ... 37876
Silvercrest Ct ... 37862
Sims Rd ... 37876
Sims Cemetery Rd ... 37876
Singing Bird Way ... 37876
Sinkhole Springs Way ... 37862
Six Point Ln ... 37876
Ski View Dr & Ln ... 37876
Sky View Dr ... 37876
Skyhawk Ln ... 37876
Slate Gap Way ... 37876
Slip Ofa Rd ... 37876
Slippery Rock Cir ... 37862
Smelcer Ln ... 37876
Smelcer Hollow Rd ... 37876
Smith Cir ... 37862
Smithwood Rd ... 37862
Smokey Bluff Trl ... 37862
Smokey Mountain Queen
Rd ... 37876
Smokies Edge Rd ... 37862
Smoky Cove Rd ... 37876
Smoky High Ln ... 37876
Smoky Mountain Way ... 37876
Smoky Mountain View
Dr ... 37876
Smoky Ridge Way ... 37862
Smoky Vista Way ... 37862
Smokyview Dr ... 37862
Snapdragon Rd ... 37876
Snapp Rd & St ... 37862
Snappwood Dr ... 37862
Snoopy Way ... 37862
Snowbank Way ... 37862
Somerset Ln ... 37862
Songbird Way ... 37876
Soul Mate Way ... 37862
Sourwood Ct ... 37876
Sourwood Way ... 37862
Sourwood Honey Dr ... 37876
South Blvd ... 37862
South Dr ... 37862
South Way ... 37876
Sparks Ln ... 37862
Sparrow Ln ... 37862
Spear Point Ln ... 37876
Spence Way ... 37862
Spence Mountain
Loop ... 37876
Spencer Clack Ln ... 37862
Spicer Ln ... 37862
Sportsman Way ... 37876
Spotted Fawn Way ... 37876
Spotted Owl Way ... 37862
Spring Ct ... 37876
Spring Dr ... 37876

Spring St ... 37862
Spring Branch Rd ... 37862
Spring Cove Way ... 37862
Spring Creek Way ... 37876
Spring Hill Dr ... 37876
N & S Spring Hollow
Rd ... 37876
Spring Lea ... 37862
Spring View Dr ... 37862
Springer Rd ... 37862
Spruce Ct ... 37862
Spruce Dr ... 37862
Spurgeon Hollow Rd ... 37876
Spurling Way ... 37862
Spurling Hill Way ... 37862
Stackstone Rd ... 37862
Stardust Mountain
Way ... 37862
Starr St ... 37876
Starr Crest Dr ... 37876
Starr Ridge Dr ... 37876
Starr View Dr ... 37876
Starrbright Ln ... 37876
Starwood Way ... 37862
Stepping Stone Dr ... 37862
Sterling Ct ... 37876
Stetson Ln ... 37876
Stewart St ... 37876
Stiles Rd ... 37876
Still Rest Rd ... 37876
Stinnett Dr ... 37862
Stinnett Rd ... 37876
Stockton Dr ... 37876
Stone Trl ... 37876
Stone Creek Way ... 37876
Stone Mill Ct ... 37862
Stone Wood Way ... 37862
Stoner Rd ... 37876
Stones Throw Ln ... 37876
Storm Cloud Way ... 37862
Storm Lee Ct ... 37876
Sugar Camp Cir & Vw ... 37862
Sugar Loaf Rd ... 37876
Sugar Maple Loop Rd ... 37862
Sugar Tree Dr ... 37862
Sugar View Dr ... 37876
Sugarland Cir ... 37862
Sulfur Springs Way ... 37862
Sumac Ct ... 37876
Summer Ln ... 37876
Summerfield Ln ... 37876
Summit Trails Dr ... 37862
Summit View Way ... 37862
Sunflower Way ... 37876
Sunnydale Dr ... 37862
Sunnydell Ln ... 37876
Sunnyside Ave ... 37862
Sunrise Blvd, Cir, Dr &
Ln ... 37862
Sunset Cir & Rd ... 37862
Sunset View Rd ... 37876
Sunshine Way ... 37862
Surries High Top Way ... 37862
Sutton Way ... 37862
Suttons Rd ... 37876
Swadis Dr ... 37876
Swan Saddle ... 37876
Swann Saddle Rd ... 37876
Swans Pt ... 37876
Swans Ferry Rd ... 37876
Swaying Pines Dr ... 37876
Swearingen Way ... 37862
Sweden Furnace Way ... 37876
Sweetbriar Way ... 37876
Sweetheart Way ... 37862
Sybill Lee Ln ... 37876
Sycamore Dr ... 37876
Sycamore Ln ... 37862
Sylvia Ln ... 37876
Tahoe Trl ... 37876
Tan Bark Way ... 37876
Tanager St ... 37862
Tanglewood Dr ... 37876
Tara Ln ... 37862
Tarwater Ln ... 37862
Tarwater Rd ... 37876

Tatem Marr Way ... 37876
Tattle Branch Rd ... 37876
Taylor Way ... 37876
Teaberry Hill Way ... 37862
Teaberry Mountain Ln ... 37862
Teague Ln ... 37862
Tekoa Mountain Way ... 37876
Temple Ln ... 37862
Ten Point Ln ... 37876
Terry Rd ... 37876
Thad Trl ... 37876
Thayer Ln ... 37862
Thomas Ln & Rd ... 37876
Thomas Cross Rd ... 37876
Thomas Headrick Rd ... 37862
Thomas Loop Rd ... 37876
Thomaswood Trl ... 37876
Thumper Ln ... 37876
Thunder Mountain Rd ... 37862
Thunder Ridge Rd ... 37876
Thurman Cir ... 37876
Tiffany Way ... 37862
Tiffany Cove Way ... 37862
Timber Way ... 37876
Timber Grove Rd ... 37862
Timber Ridge Way ... 37876
Timber View Way ... 37876
Timberlake Cir ... 37876
Timberlake Dr ... 37862
Timberlodge Ln ... 37862
Timbertop Way ... 37876
Tirres Hl ... 37862
Tomahawk Way ... 37862
Tomahawk View Dr ... 37876
Top Rd ... 37876
Top Of The World Dr ... 37876
Top View Cir ... 37876
Topland Way ... 37876
Topsfield Way ... 37876
Topside Dr & Rd ... 37862
Torri Dr ... 37876
Torri Top Way ... 37876
Tower Rd ... 37876
Towering Hemlock Dr ... 37876
Towering Oaks Dr ... 37876
Town View Ct ... 37862
Trace Way ... 37862
Tracy Ln ... 37876
Tradition Ln ... 37862
Trail Dr & Way ... 37862
Trailer Park Ln ... 37876
Trails End Ln & Way ... 37876
Tramel Rd ... 37862
Tranquil Way ... 37876
Tranquility Ln ... 37876
Trapper John Way ... 37862
Trappers Ridge Ln ... 37862
Travel Way ... 37862
Tread Way ... 37862
Treebeard Way ... 37876
Treehouse Ln ... 37876
Trentham Ln ... 37862
Triple Crown Way ... 37876
Trout Way ... 37862
Tsali Dr & Way ... 37862
Tulip Cir ... 37862
Tunis Rd ... 37876
Tunnel Ridge Dr ... 37876
Turf Way ... 37876
Turkey Ct ... 37876
Turkey Hollow Ln ... 37876
Turkey Pen Way ... 37876
Turkey Trot Way ... 37862
Turkey Valley Ln ... 37876
Turtle Dove Trl ... 37862
Tweety Bird Way ... 37862
Twelve Point Ln ... 37876
Twin Hollow Way ... 37876
Twin Lake Dr ... 37876
Twin Oaks Rd & Way ... 37876
Twin Pines Way ... 37876
Twin Point Way ... 37876
Twin Rock Dr ... 37862
Twin Springs Ln ... 37876
Two Rivers Blvd ... 37876
Tyler Way ... 37876

U St ... 37862
Unbridled Way ... 37876
Uncle Harvey Rd ... 37862
Union Crest Ct ... 37876
Union Dell Ct ... 37876
Union Hill Dr ... 37876
United Blvd ... 37876
Upper Middle Creek
Rd ... 37876
Upper Ridge Ct ... 37862
Valentine Branch Rd ... 37876
Valley Ln, Rd & Way ... 37862
Valley Cove Way ... 37862
Valley Creek Way ... 37862
Valley Farms Ln ... 37876
Valley High Rd ... 37862
Valley Home Rd ... 37862
Valley Mountain Way ... 37862
Valley Springs Way ... 37862
Valley View Cir ... 37876
Valley View Rd ... 37862
Valley Woods Dr ... 37862
Valleydale Way ... 37862
Verless Ogle Rd ... 37876
Verna Way ... 37876
Veterans Blvd ... 37862
Vic King Way ... 37862
Vickers Ln ... 37876
Victoria Cir ... 37862
Victorias Lndg ... 37862
Victory Ln ... 37876
View Dr ... 37862
E View Dr ... 37876
E View St ... 37862
W View St ... 37862
View Seeker Way ... 37876
Villa Loop Cir ... 37862
Villa Ridge Pl ... 37862
Villa View Dr ... 37862
Village Cir, Dr & Ln ... 37862
Village Hollow Dr ... 37862
Village Summit Dr ... 37862
Vine Ct ... 37876
Violet Ct ... 37876
Virginia Ave & Ln ... 37876
Vista Cir ... 37862
Vista Dr ... 37862
Vista Way ... 37876
Vista Meadows Ln ... 37876
Von Way ... 37876
Von Cannon Ln ... 37876
Vonnie View Way ... 37876
Wade Ln ... 37876
Wagner Dr ... 37862
Wagon Wheel Ln ... 37876
Walden Ct ... 37862
Walden Cove Way ... 37862
Walden Ridge Rd ... 37862
Waldens Creek Rd ... 37862
Waldroup Springs Way ... 37862
Walini Way ... 37876
Walker Ln ... 37862
Walker Trl ... 37876
N Walker Way ... 37876
Walking Horse Ln ... 37876
Walkingstick Ct ... 37876
Wall St ... 37862
Walnut Ct ... 37876
Walnut Ln ... 37876
Walnut Rd ... 37862
Walnut Way ... 37862
Walnut Church Way ... 37876
Walnut Flats Rd ... 37862
E Walnut Grove Rd ... 37876
Walnut Hill Ln ... 37876
Walnut Ridge Way ... 37862
Walnut Vista Way ... 37876
Walt King Way ... 37876
Walt Price Rd ... 37876
Walter Webb Dr ... 37862
Walters Way ... 37876
War Paint Trl ... 37876
Warbler Pt ... 37876
Watauga St ... 37862
Water Oak Way ... 37876
Waterfall View Ln ... 37876

Watson Ln & Rd ... 37862
Watson Hollow Way ... 37876
Wears Dr ... 37862
Wears Cove Rd ... 37862
Wears Mountain Ln ... 37862
Wears Overlook Ln ... 37862
Wears Valley Rd ... 37862
E Wearwood Dr ... 37862
Webb Rd ... 37876
Webb Creek Rd ... 37876
Webb Lane Way ... 37862
Webbs Overlook Way ... 37876
Wendell Dr ... 37876
Wendell Burnett Rd ... 37876
Wendron Moors Dr ... 37862
Wesley Ln & Way ... 37876
Westin Way ... 37876
Westland Dr ... 37862
Westover Dr ... 37862
Westside Hills Rd ... 37876
Westwood Dr ... 37862
Whaley Rd & Way ... 37876
Whaley Hollow Rd ... 37876
Whaleys Trail Ln ... 37862
Whetstone Rd ... 37862
Which A Way ... 37862
Whimsical Way ... 37876
Whipoorwill Hill Way ... 37862
Whisper Creek Ln ... 37862
Whispering Pines Way ... 37876
White Halo Ct ... 37876
White Oak Dr ... 37862
White Oak Ridge Ln ... 37862
White Oak Tree Ln ... 37876
White Pine Way ... 37876
White Tail Ln ... 37876
White Timberlake Dr ... 37876
Whites School Rd ... 37876
Whitetail Ridge Way ... 37862
Wichert Ln ... 37876
Wickcliffe Ct ... 37876
Wicks Way ... 37876
Wild Flower Way ... 37876
Wild Heron Way ... 37862
Wild Iris Way ... 37862
Wild Pine Way ... 37876
Wild Plum Way ... 37876
Wild Turkey Way ... 37876
Wildcat Rd ... 37862
Wildcat Ridge Rd ... 37862
Wilderness Way ... 37876
Wildflower Ln ... 37876
Wildwind Dr ... 37862
Wildwood Way ... 37876
Wiley King Way ... 37876
Wiley Noland Rd ... 37876
Wilhite Rd ... 37876
Wilhite Creek Rd ... 37876
Will Bryan Ln ... 37862
Willard Way ... 37876
William Holt Blvd ... 37862
Williams Rd ... 37876
Williams Hollow Rd ... 37876
Willow Ln & Trce ... 37862
Willow Creek Ln ... 37876
Willow Heights Way ... 37876
Willow Tree Rd ... 37862
Willow Wood Dr ... 37876
Wills Crest Way ... 37876
Wilma Way ... 37876
Wilson Rd ... 37876
Wilson Hollow Way ... 37876
Windfall Estates Dr ... 37876
Winding Dr ... 37876
Windmere Way ... 37862
Windrush Cir ... 37862
Windsong Way ... 37876
Windsor Rd ... 37862
Windswept View Way ... 37876
Windy Ln ... 37876
Windy Cove Way ... 37876
Windy Meadows Ln ... 37876
Winfield Dunn Pkwy ... 37876
Wingspan Dr ... 37876
Winter Wonder Ln ... 37876
Wisteria Ln ... 37862

Witt Hollow Rd 37862
Wolf Way 37862
Wolf Ridge Way 37862
Wonderland Ln 37862
Woodcock Trl 37876
Wooddale Way 37876
Woodhaven Dr 37862
Woodland Dr 37862
Woods Dr 37862
Woods Way 37876
Woodside Ln 37862
Woodstock Dr 37862
Woodvale Ln 37876
Worth Rd 37876
Woullard Way 37876
Y Rd 37862
Yellow Pine Ct 37876
Yellow Spring Park Rd 37876
Yellowwood Dr 37876
Zachary Thomas Rd 37876
Zelig Ln 37876
Zenith Way 37876
Zeta Way 37876
Zion Dr 37862
Zion Hill Rd 37876
Zion Hill Church Rd 37876

NUMBERED STREETS

1 Way St 37862
1st Ln 37876
1st St 37862

SHELBYVILLE TN

General Delivery 37160

POST OFFICE BOXES MAIN OFFICE STATIONS AND BRANCHES

Box No.s
All PO Boxes 37162

NAMED STREETS

All Street Addresses 37160

SODDY DAISY TN

General Delivery 37379

POST OFFICE BOXES MAIN OFFICE STATIONS AND BRANCHES

Box No.s
All PO Boxes 37384

RURAL ROUTES

03 37379

NAMED STREETS

Alex Ln 37379
Angler Dr 37379
Ann Marie Ln 37379
Apollo Dr 37379
Apple St 37379
Arapaho Dr 37379
Armstrong Rd 37379
Arnat Dr 37379
Arrivel Pt 37379
Ashes Ave 37379
Ashley Dr 37379
Autumn Breeze Ln 37379
Autumn Glen Dr 37379
Autumn Terrace Ln 37379
Autumn View Cir 37379
Back Valley Rd 37379
Bailey Farms Rd 37379
Banner Elk Rd 37379
Baptist View Dr 37379
Barbara Dr & Ln 37379
Barbee Rd 37379
Bass Bay Ln 37379
Battleground Cir 37379
Bayfront Dr 37379
Bayview Rd 37379
Baywood Dr 37379
Bean St 37379
Bear Trail Dr 37379
Beene St 37379
Bell St 37379
Bellacoola Rd 37379
S Bend Rd 37379
Bent Tree Ct 37379
Benton Ln 37379
Berry Ln 37379
Berry Meadow Way 37379
Beverly Ln 37379
Bice Rd 37379
Big Cedar Rd 37379
Big Pine Ln 37379
Billingsley Rd 37379
Birdsong Way 37379
Black Powder Ln 37379
Blackshear Ct 37379
Blakeslee Dr 37379
Blanchard Rd 37379
Blue Ridge Dr 37379
Bonnelia Cir 37379
Boulder View Dr 37379
N Bowman Rd 37379
Bowman Cemetery Rd 37379
Boxwood Ln 37379
Boyd St 37379
Brandy Way 37379
Branford Dr 37379
Bream Ln 37379
Bream Hollow Ln 37379
Breeze Dr 37379
Breeze Hill Ln 37379
Brett Daniel Way 37379
Bretton Dr 37379
Briar Rd 37379
Briar Ridge Ln 37379
Brickhill Ln 37379
Bridgestone Dr 37379
Brimstone Trl 37379
Britt Lauren Way 37379
Broad Leaf Ln 37379
Broadway 37379
Broken Rock Trl 37379
Brooke Stone Dr 37379
Brow Lake Rd 37379
Brown Rd 37379
Brumlow Hollow Rd 37379
Bryclee Ln 37379
Buckthorne Dr 37379
Buffalo Ln 37379
Bunker Ridge Trl 37379
Burchard Rd 37379
Burnett Rd 37379
Burns St 37379
Burroughs Ln 37379
Callie Marie Dr 37379
Calypso Ln 37379
Canyon Cir 37379
Canyon Rim Dr 37379
Captains Cove Dr 37379
Card Rd 37379
Carden St 37379
Carey Rd 37379
Casey Holw 37379
Catawba Trl 37379
Celica Dr 37379
Cemetery St 37379
Cera Club Rd 37379
Channel Front Ct 37379
Chariot Dr 37379
Chelle Dr 37379
Chestnutview Dr 37379
Chimney Hills Dr 37379
Chimney Lake Cir 37379
Chip Dr 37379
Church St 37379
Cindy Dr 37379
Cinnamon Trl 37379
Civic Club Dr 37379
Claire Cir 37379
Classic Dr 37379
Clay Hill Dr 37379
Clayton St 37379
Clift Rd 37379
Clift Cave Rd 37379
Clift Eldridge Ln & Rd 37379
Clift Mill Rd 37379
Clipper Bay Dr 37379
Cody Ln 37379
Coffee Tree Ln 37379
Coke Bowman Rd 37379
Coke Oven Rd 37379
Coleman Rd 37379
Coleman Cemetery Rd 37379
College Park Ln 37379
College Station Ln 37379
Collins Ln & Rd 37379
Colony Park Ln 37379
Consolidated Dr 37379
Cool Way 37379
Copeland Cemetery Rd 37379
Corbett Dr 37379
Country Brook Ln 37379
Country Mill Ln 37379
Cowboy Way 37379
Cox Ln 37379
Cozy Trl 37379
Crappie Cir 37379
Crawley Rd 37379
Creasman Hill Ln 37379
Creek Hollow Ln 37379
Criswell Ct 37379
Crowe Cir 37379
Crystal Ln 37379
Daffodil Cir 37379
Daisy Ave 37379
Daisy Dallas Rd 37379
Dallas Bay Rd 37379
Dallas Hollow Rd 37379
Dallas Lake Rd 37379
Dallas Place Rd 37379
Dallas Point Rd 37379
Dalton Ln 37379
Davenport Rd 37379
Dayton Pike
8300-10576 37379
10575-10575 37384
10578-13498 37379
10601-13499 37379
Dell Dr 37379
Demetra Ln 37379
Denali Trl 37379
Dendia Rd 37379
Depot St 37379
Dividing Ridge Rd 37379
Dividing Ridge Cemetery Rd 37379
Divot Ct 37379
Dockside Dr 37379
Dodd Cemetery Rd 37379
Dogwood Ln & Ter 37379
Donna Dr 37379
Douglas Rd 37379
Dreamfield Dr 37379
Driftwood Rd 37379
Duckett Ln 37379
Ducktown St 37379
Durban Point Dr 37379
Durham St 37379
Eastwind Dr 37379
Echo Ln 37379
Edd Clift Ln 37379
Eickhoff Ln 37379
Eldridge Rd 37379
Ell Rd 37379
Ell Dee Ln 37379
Elliott St 37379
Elsea Dr 37379
Emerald Bay Dr 37379
Emerald Creek Cir 37379
Emerald Pointe Dr 37379
Emery Rd 37379
Emperor Ct 37379
Eric Brian Ln 37379
Essie Ln 37379
Eustice Rd 37379
Evans Rd 37379
Eveningside Dr 37379
Fairway Ln 37379
Fairwind Ln 37379
Falcon Run Dr 37379
Fallen Leaf Dr 37379
Family Pl 37379
Fineout Dr 37379
Flat Top Rd 37379
Flintshire Ln 37379
Floyd Brown Rd 37379
N Fork Dr 37379
Fortress Pass 37379
Francis St 37379
Frankie Ln 37379
Freedom Bay Dr & Loop 37379
Freeport Dr 37379
Friendship Ln 37379
Fritts Rd 37379
Frizzell Ln 37379
Frontage Rd 37379
Gaddis Ln 37379
Gann Rd 37379
Gannaway St 37379
Geneva Trl 37379
Glenda Ln 37379
Glengerrie Dr 37379
Gordon St 37379
Graham Rd 37379
Granny Walker Cemetery Rd 37379
Grant Rd 37379
Graves Rd 37379
Gravitt Rd 37379
Green Ln 37379
Green Pond Rd 37379
Green Valley Rd 37379
Greene St 37379
Greenfield Rd 37379
Gretchen Cir 37379
Gross Rd 37379
Grove Place Rd 37379
Gulf View Dr 37379
Gunpowder Ln 37379
Guth Rd 37379
Hackberry Ln 37379
Hair St 37379
Haleigh Ter 37379
Hallett St 37379
Hamby Rd 37379
Hamilton Ave 37379
Hankins Rd 37379
Harbor Rd 37379
Harbor Crest Dr 37379
Harbor Landing Dr 37379
Harbor Point Dr 37379
Hardwood Ln 37379
Harmony Ln 37379
Harris St 37379
Harrison Ln 37379
Harvest Ct 37379
Harvest Knoll Ln 37379
Hatch Trl 37379
Hatlin Dr 37379
Haven Bay Ln 37379
Hazel Alder Ln 37379
Heiss Mountain Rd 37379
Hemlock St 37379
Hendon Rd 37379
Henson Gap Rd 37379
Heron Cove Ln 37379
Hickman St 37379
Hicks Ln 37379
Hidden Cove Rd 37379
Hidden Ridge Dr 37379
Hideaway Ln 37379
Higdon St 37379
E Highwater Rd 37379
Hill Top Crst 37379
Hixson Pike & St 37379
Hogue St 37379
Holly Cir 37379
Holly Hill Rd 37379
Hood Cir 37379
Horseshoe Dr 37379
Hotwater Rd 37379
Housley Rd 37379
Huckleberry Ln 37379
Hughes Rd 37379
Hughs Trail Rd 37379
Hunt St 37379
Hunt Heights Dr 37379
Hunter Trace Dr 37379
Hunters Hollow Dr 37379
Hunters Ridge Rd 37379
Huron Ln 37379
Hyatte Rd 37379
Igou Ferry Rd 37379
Incline St 37379
Indian Ridge Ln 37379
Industrial Park Dr 37379
Iroquois Ln 37379
Jacarilla Dr 37379
Jacob Dr 37379
Jacquelin Dr 37379
Jane Manor Cir 37379
Jays Ct 37379
Jeneva Ln 37379
Jenkins Cir & Rd 37379
Jirah Ct 37379
Jonas Dr 37379
Jones Gap Rd 37379
Jones Valley Rd 37379
Karen Dr 37379
Kashaya Ln 37379
Kerry Ln 37379
Kingsboro St 37379
Ladino Ln 37379
Lake Carolyn Ln 37379
Lake Haven Rd 37379
Lakesite Dr 37379
Lakeview Cir 37379
Lakewood Ave & Cir 37379
Lasley Ln 37379
Laurbrow Rd 37379
Layne Rd 37379
Ledford Rd 37379
Lee Pike 37379
Leeward Ln 37379
Leighton Dr 37379
Lena Ln 37379
Lenora Dr 37379
Lewis Dr, Rd & St 37379
Lightning Dr 37379
Lillard Rd 37379
Limited Dr 37379
Linwood Cir 37379
Lisa Ln 37379
Little Dr 37379
Little Creek Trl 37379
Lloyd Springs Rd 37379
Log Cabin Ln 37379
Logstone Ln 37379
Lombardi Rd 37379
Lonesome Trl 37379
Longo Dr 37379
Loop Rd 37379
Lou Ln 37379
Love Ln 37379
Lovelady Rd 37379
Lovelady Lewis Rd 37379
Lovell Rd 37379
Lower Ridge Trl 37379
Lure Ln 37379
Luttrell Dr 37379
Lyons Ln 37379
M Kaddesh Way 37379
Macon Way 37379
Madison Ave 37379
Magnum Ln 37379
Main St 37379
Majesty Dr & Ln 37379
Mandy Ln 37379
Maple Pl & St 37379
Marina Cir, Dr & Ln 37379
Marrick Dr, Ln & Way 37379
Matthew Rd 37379
May Rd 37379
Mayflower Rd 37379
Mcafee Rd 37379
Mccallie Ferry Rd 37379
Mcgill Rd 37379
Meadowlark Trl 37379
Meadowview Ln 37379
Midway Church Rd 37379
Millard Rd 37379
Miller Rd 37379
Miller Country Rd 37379
Millsap Rd 37379
Millsaps St 37379
Millsaps Coal Rd 37379
Millwoode Ln 37379
Mimosa Dr 37379
Mohawk Ln 37379
Montlake Cir & Rd 37379
Moore Ln 37379
Morgan Ln 37379
Morningside Dr 37379
Mount Annie Church Rd 37379
Mount Tabor Rd 37379
Mountain Rd 37379
Mountain View Dr 37379
Mowbray Pike 37379
Nale Dr 37379
Native Trl 37379
Natural Way 37379
Nature Trl 37379
Nee Cee Dr 37379
Neighbors Dr 37379
Nelson Rd 37379
Newman Rd 37379
Newman Green Rd 37379
Nissi Way 37379
Norman St 37379
Northern Trails Dr 37379
N & S Oak St 37379
Oak Cove Dr & Ln 37379
Oakwood Dr 37379
Old Back Valley Rd 37379
Old Dallas Hollow Rd 37379
Old Dayton Pike 37379
Old Hixson Pike 37379
Old Hotwater Rd 37379
Old Montlake Rd 37379
Old Thatcher Rd 37379
Olivia Ln 37379
Orval Dr 37379
Osage Dr 37379
Ottawa Dr 37379
Owen Ln 37379
Partridge Ln 37379
Peach St 37379
Pear Tree Ln 37379
Pebblestone Dr 37379
Pelfrey Ln 37379
Pendall Ln 37379
Pendergrass Rd 37379
Penny Ln 37379
Penobscot Dr 37379
Perkins Pt 37379
Peters Rd 37379
Pickett St 37379
Pima Trl N 37379
Pine St 37379
Pine Cove Dr 37379
Pineway Trl 37379
Plainview Dr 37379
Ples Ln 37379
Plow Ln 37379
Plum St 37379
Poe Rd 37379
Point Place Rd 37379
Polan Ln 37379
Poling Cir 37379
Ponderosa Dr 37379
Poplar St 37379
Port Royal Dr 37379
Porter St 37379
Posey Hollow Rd 37379
Pottery Ln 37379
Prairie Schooner Cir 37379
Pruett St 37379
Putter Pl 37379
Quiet Trl 37379
Railroad St 37379
Ratledge Rd 37379
Rattisseau Ln 37379
Reaching Way 37379
Reco Dr 37379
Red Bird Ct & Ln 37379
Red Bud Rd 37379
Red Leaf Ln 37379
Reed Ln 37379
Reynolds Rd 37379
Ribbonwood Dr 37379
Ricole Trl 37379
E & W Ridge Trail Rd 37379
Ritchie Rd 37379
Ritchie Ridge Ln 37379
Ritz Way 37379
River Landing Dr 37379
Rivergate Ter 37379
Rivergate Bay Ln 37379
Robert Garland Vw 37379
Rock Quarry Rd 37379
Rocky Point Rd 37379
Rocky Point Club Trl 37379
Rolling Shores Cir 37379
Rolling Wind Dr 37379
Rophe Dr 37379
Rose Rd 37379
Rose Marie Ct 37379
Royal View Ln 37379
Ryan Rdg 37379
Saddle Horse Trl 37379
Sage Grass Ln 37379
Sanderling Ct 37379
Sandstone Ter 37379
Santa Barbara Cir 37379
Sassafras Ln 37379
School St 37379
Scribner Rd 37379
Seneca Ln 37379
Sequoyah Rd 37379
Sequoyah Access Rd 37379
Shearer St 37379
Shelter Ln 37379
Sheri Place Ln 37379
Shingle Oak Dr 37379
Shipley Rd 37379
Shirestone Ct 37379
Shirley Loretta Ln 37379
Shooting Star Cir 37379
Shore Dr 37379
N & S Shore Acres Rd 37379
Shoreline Dr 37379
Shoreline Heights Dr 37379
Short Leaf Dr 37379
Sims Rd 37379
Sir Carlos Dr 37379
Skip Ln 37379
Skyridge Trl 37379
Slippery Elm Ln 37379
Sluder Ln 37379
Smith Rd & St 37379
Smith Cemetery Cir & Rd 37379
Smith Morgan Rd 37379
Sneed Rd 37379
Snowy Ln 37379
Soddy Bluff Vw 37379
Soddy View Ln 37379
Sour Mash Ln 37379
Sovereign Pointe Dr 37379
Sparrowfield Way 37379
Spitzy Ln 37379
Spotted Fawn Trl 37379
Spradling Rd 37379
Spring St 37379
Springfield Rd & St 37379
Staghorn Dr 37379

Standard Dr 37379
Standifer Rd 37379
Standifer Grant Rd 37379
Starry Way 37379
Stonesage Rd 37379
Stonesthrow Way 37379
Stormer Rd 37379
Stormy Ridge Dr 37379
Sugar Maple Ln 37379
Sugar Pine Dr 37379
Summercrest Vw 37379
Summers Dr 37379
Summers Park Ln 37379
Sunderland Ln 37379
Sunset Valley Dr 37379
Susan Ln 37379
Swafford Rd 37379
Sweet Gum Ln & Rd ... 37379
T Crowe Rd 37379
Tadpole Ln 37379
Tanoka Ct 37379
Taylor Ln 37379
Telgado Ln 37379
Terrace Falls Dr 37379
Thad Ln 37379
Thatcher Rd 37379
Thatcher Crest Dr 37379
Thicket Rd 37379
Thomas St 37379
Thrasher Pike & Trl 37379
Thunder Dr 37379
Timberline Cir 37379
Tobacco Rd 37379
Tommie Ln 37379
Tonja Ln N & S 37379
Tractor Trl 37379
Trojan Hill Dr 37379
Trojan Run Dr 37379
Trojan View Dr 37379
Trout Trl 37379
Tsati Ter 37379
Turner Rd 37379
Turnstone Dr 37379
Twilight Dr 37379
Union Fork Rd 37379
Upper Ridge Trl 37379
Uren Ln 37379
Valley St 37379
Viewmont Ln 37379
Vine St 37379
Violette Dr 37379
Virgil Ln 37379
E & W Walden Cir & St 37379
Walker Rd 37379
Walking Horse Ln 37379
Wall St 37379
Wallace St 37379
Walmart Dr 37379
Walnut Cir & St 37379
Ward Rd 37379
Warwickshire Dr 37379
Waterfall Trl 37379
Watershore Dr 37379
Waterside Way 37379
Weathersby Rd 37379
Wedgeway Millsaps Rd 37379
Weeks Rd 37379
Welch Rd 37379
Wellthor Cir 37379
Wendy Cir 37379
West Pkwy 37379
Westbrook Ave 37379
Westwind Dr 37379
Whippersnapper Way ... 37379
Whirling Wind Ln 37379
Whisper Willow Rd 37379
Whispering Bend Dr 37379
White Dr 37379
Wild Life Pl 37379
Wild Turkey Ln 37379
Wildlife Pl 37379
Wilkes Ave 37379
William Cody Ln 37379
Williams St 37379
Willow Creek Dr 37379
Wilson St 37379
Winding Bluff Ln 37379
Windjammer Dr 37379
Windtop Ln 37379
Windward Ln 37379
Windy Hollow Ln 37379
Windy Ridge Dr 37379
N & S Winer Dr 37379
Winterhawk Trl 37379
Wood Ln 37379
Woodoak Rd 37379
Woodsage Ct & Dr 37379
Woodstream Ln 37379
Worley Rd 37379
Wren St 37379
Wright Dr 37379
Wyatts Ln 37379
Wynn Ln 37379
Yaphank Rd 37379
Yogi Ln 37379
Young Rd 37379
Zeus Ct 37379
Zion Ln 37379

UNION CITY TN

General Delivery 38261

POST OFFICE BOXES MAIN OFFICE STATIONS AND BRANCHES

Box No.s
All PO Boxes 38281

NAMED STREETS

All Street Addresses 38261

NUMBERED STREETS

All Street Addresses 38261

Texas

People QuickFacts	Texas	USA
Population, 2013 estimate	26,448,193	316,128,839
Population, 2010 (April 1) estimates base	25,145,561	308,747,716
Population, percent change, April 1, 2010 to July 1, 2013	5.2%	2.4%
Population, 2010	25,145,561	308,745,538
Persons under 5 years, percent, 2013	7.3%	6.3%
Persons under 18 years, percent, 2013	26.6%	23.3%
Persons 65 years and over, percent, 2013	11.2%	14.1%
Female persons, percent, 2013	50.3%	50.8%
White alone, percent, 2013 (a)	80.3%	77.7%
Black or African American alone, percent, 2013 (a)	12.4%	13.2%
American Indian and Alaska Native alone, percent, 2013 (a)	1.0%	1.2%
Asian alone, percent, 2013 (a)	4.3%	5.3%
Native Hawaiian and Other Pacific Islander alone, percent, 2013 (a)	0.1%	0.2%
Two or More Races, percent, 2013	1.8%	2.4%
Hispanic or Latino, percent, 2013 (b)	38.4%	17.1%
White alone, not Hispanic or Latino, percent, 2013	44.0%	62.6%
Living in same house 1 year & over, percent, 2008-2012	82.6%	84.8%
Foreign born persons, percent, 2008-2012	16.3%	12.9%
Language other than English spoken at home, pct age 5+, 2008-2012	34.6%	20.5%
High school graduate or higher, percent of persons age 25+, 2008-2012	80.8%	85.7%
Bachelor's degree or higher, percent of persons age 25+, 2008-2012	26.3%	28.5%
Veterans, 2008-2012	1,611,660	21,853,912
Mean travel time to work (minutes), workers age 16+, 2008-2012	24.9	25.4
Housing units, 2013	10,255,642	132,802,859
Homeownership rate, 2008-2012	63.9%	65.5%
Housing units in multi-unit structures, percent, 2008-2012	24.1%	25.9%
Median value of owner-occupied housing units, 2008-2012	$128,000	$181,400
Households, 2008-2012	8,782,598	115,226,802
Persons per household, 2008-2012	2.8	2.61
Per capita money income in past 12 months (2012 dollars), 2008-2012	$25,809	$28,051
Median household income, 2008-2012	$51,563	$53,046
Persons below poverty level, percent, 2008-2012	17.4%	14.9%

Business QuickFacts	Texas	USA
Private nonfarm establishments, 2012	537,839	7,431,808
Private nonfarm employment, 2012	9,350,829	115,938,468
Private nonfarm employment, percent change, 2011-2012	4.0%	2.2%
Nonemployer establishments, 2012	2,014,124	22,735,915
Total number of firms, 2007	2,164,852	27,092,908
Black-owned firms, percent, 2007	7.1%	7.1%
American Indian- and Alaska Native-owned firms, percent, 2007	0.9%	0.9%
Asian-owned firms, percent, 2007	5.3%	5.7%
Native Hawaiian and Other Pacific Islander-owned firms, percent, 2007	0.1%	0.1%
Hispanic-owned firms, percent, 2007	20.7%	8.3%
Women-owned firms, percent, 2007	28.2%	28.8%
Manufacturers shipments, 2007 ($1000)	593,541,502	5,319,456,312
Merchant wholesaler sales, 2007 ($1000)	424,238,194	4,174,286,516
Retail sales, 2007 ($1000)	311,334,781	3,917,663,456
Retail sales per capita, 2007	$13,061	$12,990
Accommodation and food services sales, 2007 ($1000)	42,054,592	613,795,732
Building permits, 2012	135,514	829,658

Geography QuickFacts	Texas	USA
Land area in square miles, 2010	261,231.71	3,531,905.43
Persons per square mile, 2010	96.3	87.4
FIPS Code	48	

(a) Includes persons reporting only one race.
(b) Hispanics may be of any race, so also are included in applicable race categories.
FN: Footnote on this item for this area in place of data
NA: Not available
D: Suppressed to avoid disclosure of confidential information
X: Not applicable
S: Suppressed; does not meet publication standards
Z: Value greater than zero but less than half unit of measure shown
F: Fewer than 100 firms
Source: US Census Bureau State & County QuickFacts

3 DIGIT ZIP CODE MAP

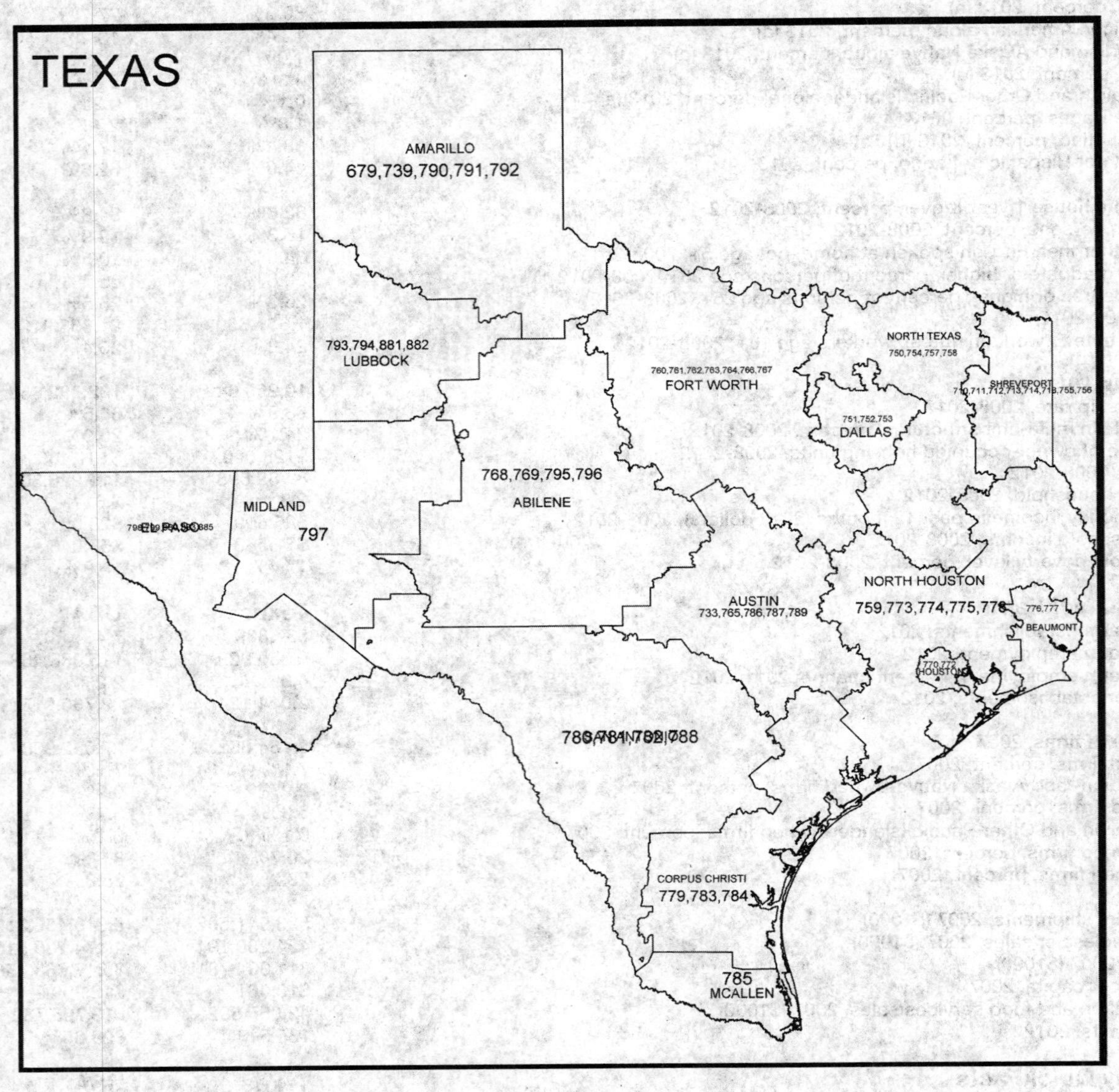

Texas

(Abbreviation: TX)

Places with more than one ZIP code are listed in capital letters, See pages indicated.

Post Office, County	ZIP Code
Abbott, Hill	76621
Abernathy, Hale	79311
ABILENE, Taylor (See Page 3587)	
Ace, Polk	77326
Ackerly, Martin	79713
Acton, Hood	76049
Addison, Dallas	75001
Adkins, Bexar	78101
Adrian, Oldham	79001
Afton, Dickens	79220
Agua Dulce, Nueces	78330
Aiken, Floyd	79221
Alamo, Hidalgo	78516
Alamo Heights, Bexar	78209
Alanreed, Gray	79002
Alba, Wood	75410
Albany, Shackelford	76430
Albert, Gillespie	78671
Aledo, Parker	76008
ALICE, Jim Wells (See Page 3590)	
Alief, Harris	77411
ALLEN, Collin (See Page 3590)	
Alleyton, Colorado	78935
Allison, Wheeler	79003
ALPINE, Brewster (See Page 3592)	
Alta Loma, Galveston	77510
Altair, Colorado	77412
Alto, Cherokee	75925
Alton, Hidalgo	78573
Alvarado, Johnson	76009
ALVIN, Brazoria (See Page 3592)	
Alvord, Wise	76225
AMARILLO, Potter (See Page 3592)	
Ames, Liberty	77575
Amherst, Lamb	79312
Anahuac, Chambers	77514
Anderson, Grimes	77830
Anderson, Grimes	77875
Andice, Williamson	78628
Andrews, Andrews	79714
ANGLETON, Brazoria (See Page 3598)	
Anna, Collin	75409
Annetta, Parker	76008
Annetta N, Parker	76008
Annetta S, Parker	76008
Annona, Red River	75550
Anson, Jones	79501
Anthony, El Paso	79821
Anton, Hockley	79313
Apple Springs, Trinity	75926
Aquilla, Hill	76622
ARANSAS PASS, San Patricio (See Page 3598)	
Arcadia, Galveston	77517
Archer City, Archer	76351
Arcola, Brazoria	77583
Argyle, Denton	76226
ARLINGTON, Tarrant (See Page 3598)	
Armstrong, Kenedy	78338
Arp, Smith	75750
Art, Mason	76820
Artesia Wells, La Salle	78001
Arthur City, Lamar	75411
Asherton, Dimmit	78827
Aspermont, Stonewall	79502
Atascocita, Harris	77346
Atascosa, Bexar	78002
ATHENS, Henderson (See Page 3606)	
Atlanta, Cass	75551
Aubrey, Denton	76227
Aurora, Wise	76078
AUSTIN, Travis (See Page 3607)	
Austwell, Refugio	77950
Avalon, Ellis	76623
Avery, Red River	75554
Avinger, Cass	75630
Avoca, Jones	79503
Axtell, Mclennan	76624
AZLE, Tarrant (See Page 3626)	
Bacliff, Galveston	77518
Bagwell, Red River	75412
Bailey, Fannin	75413
Baird, Callahan	79504
Balch Springs, Dallas	75180
Balch Springs, Dallas	75181
Balcones Heights, Bexar	78201
Ballinger, Runnels	76821
Balmorhea, Reeves	79718
Bandera, Bandera	78003
Bangs, Brown	76823
Banquete, Nueces	78339
Bardwell, Ellis	75101
Barker, Harris	77413
Barksdale, Edwards	78828
Barnhart, Irion	76930
Barnum, Polk	75939
Barry, Navarro	75102
Barstow, Ward	79719
Bartlett, Bell	76511
Bartonville, Denton	76226
Bastrop, Bastrop	78602
Batesville, Zavala	78829
Batson, Hardin	77519
BAY CITY, Matagorda (See Page 3626)	
Bayou Vista, Galveston	77563
Bayside, Refugio	78340
BAYTOWN, Harris (See Page 3626)	
Bayview, Cameron	78566
Beach City (See Baytown)	
Beasley, Fort Bend	77417
BEAUMONT, Jefferson (See Page 3629)	
Bebe, Gonzales	78614
Beckville, Panola	75631
BEDFORD, Tarrant (See Page 3633)	
Bedias, Grimes	77831
Bee Cave (See Austin)	
Bee Caves (See Austin)	
Bee House, Coryell	76525
BEEVILLE, Bee (See Page 3634)	
BELLAIRE, Harris (See Page 3635)	
Bellevue, Clay	76228
Bellmead (See Waco)	
Bells, Grayson	75414
Bellville, Austin	77418
Belmont, Gonzales	78604
Belton, Bell	76513
Ben Arnold, Milam	76519
Ben Bolt, Jim Wells	78342
Ben Franklin, Delta	75415
Ben Wheeler, Van Zandt	75754
Benavides, Duval	78341
Benbrook (See Fort Worth)	
Bend, San Saba	76824
Benjamin, Knox	79505
Berclair, Goliad	78107
Bergheim, Kendall	78004
Bertram, Burnet	78605
Best, Reagan	76932
Beverly Hills, Mclennan	76711
Bevil Oaks, Jefferson	77713
Big Bend National Park, Brewster	79834
Big Lake, Reagan	76932
Big Sandy, Upshur	75755
BIG SPRING, Howard (See Page 3635)	
Big Wells, Dimmit	78830
Bigfoot, Frio	78005
Biggs Field, El Paso	79908
Birome, Hill	76673
Bishop, Nueces	78343
Bishop Hills, Potter	79124
Bivins, Cass	75555
Black, Parmer	79035
Blackwell, Nolan	79506
Blanco, Blanco	78606
Blanket, Brown	76432
Bledsoe, Cochran	79314
Bleiblerville, Austin	78931
Blessing, Matagorda	77419
Bloomburg, Cass	75556
Blooming Grove, Navarro	76626
Bloomington, Victoria	77951
Blossom, Lamar	75416
Blue Mound, Tarrant	76131
Blue Ridge, Collin	75424
Bluegrove, Clay	76352
Bluff Dale, Erath	76433
Bluffton, Llano	78607
Blum, Hill	76627
BOERNE, Kendall (See Page 3635)	
Bogata, Red River	75417
Boling, Wharton	77420
Bon Ami, Jasper	75956
Bon Wier, Newton	75928
Bonham, Fannin	75418
Booker, Lipscomb	79005
Booth, Fort Bend	77469
BORGER, Hutchinson (See Page 3637)	
Boston, Bowie	75570
Bovina, Parmer	79009
Bowie, Montague	76230
Boyd, Wise	76023
Boys Ranch, Oldham	79010
Brackettville, Kinney	78832
Brady, Mcculloch	76825
Brandon, Hill	76628
Brashear, Hopkins	75420
Brazoria, Brazoria	77422
Brazos Bend, Hood	76048
Breckenridge, Stephens	76424
Bremond, Robertson	76629
BRENHAM, Washington (See Page 3637)	
Briarcliff, Travis	78669
Briaroaks, Johnson	76028
Bridge City, Orange	77611
Bridgeport, Wise	76426
Briggs, Burnet	78608
Briscoe, Wheeler	79011
Broaddus, San Augustine	75929
Brock, Parker	76087
Bronson, Sabine	75930
Bronte, Coke	76933
Brookeland, Jasper	75931
Brookesmith, Brown	76827
Brooks City Base, Bexar	78235
Brookshire, Waller	77423
Brookside Village, Brazoria	77581
Brookston, Lamar	75421
Brownfield, Terry	79316
Brownsboro, Henderson	75756
BROWNSVILLE, Cameron (See Page 3639)	
BROWNWOOD, Brown (See Page 3642)	
Bruceville, Mclennan	76630
Bruni, Webb	78344
BRYAN, Brazos (See Page 3643)	
Bryson, Jack	76427
Buchanan Dam, Llano	78609
Buckholts, Milam	76518
Buda, Hays	78610
Buffalo, Leon	75831
Buffalo Gap, Taylor	79508
Buffalo Springs, Lubbock	79404
Bullard, Smith	75757
Bulverde, Comal	78163
Buna, Jasper	77612
Burkburnett, Wichita	76354
Burke, Angelina	75941
Burkett, Coleman	76828
Burkeville, Newton	75932
BURLESON, Johnson (See Page 3646)	
Burlington, Milam	76519
Burnet, Burnet	78611
Burton, Washington	77835
Bushland, Potter	79012
Byers, Clay	76357
Bynum, Hill	76631
Cactus, Moore	79013
Caddo, Stephens	76429
Caddo Mills, Hunt	75135
Caldwell, Burleson	77836
Call, Newton	75933
Calliham, Mcmullen	78007
Callisburg, Cooke	76240
Calvert, Robertson	77837
Camden, Polk	75934
Cameron, Milam	76520
Camp Verde, Kerr	78010
Camp Wood, Real	78833
Campbell, Hunt	75422
Campbellton, Atascosa	78008
Canadian, Hemphill	79014
Canton, Van Zandt	75103
Canutillo, El Paso	79835
Canyon, Randall	79015
Canyon Lake, Comal	78130
Canyon Lake, Comal	78132
Carbon, Eastland	76435
Carlsbad, Tom Green	76934
Carlton, Hamilton	76436
Carmine, Fayette	78932
Carrizo Springs, Dimmit	78834
CARROLLTON, Dallas (See Page 3648)	
Carthage, Panola	75633
Cashion Community, Wichita	76305
Cason, Morris	75636
Castell, Llano	76831
Castle Hills, Bexar	78213
Castroville, Medina	78009
Castroville, Medina	78056
Cat Spring, Austin	78933
Catarina, Dimmit	78836
Cayuga, Anderson	75832
Cedar Creek, Bastrop	78612
CEDAR HILL, Dallas (See Page 3650)	
Cedar Lane, Matagorda	77415
CEDAR PARK, Williamson (See Page 3651)	
Cee Vee, Cottle	79223
Celeste, Hunt	75423
Celina, Collin	75009
Center, Shelby	75935
Center Point, Kerr	78010
Centerville, Leon	75833
Centralia, Trinity	75834
Chandler, Henderson	75758
Channelview, Harris	77530
Channing, Hartley	79018
Chapman Ranch, Nueces	78347
Chappell Hill, Washington	77426
Charlotte, Atascosa	78011
Chatfield, Navarro	75105
Cherokee, San Saba	76832
Chester, Tyler	75936
Chico, Wise	76431
Chicota, Lamar	75425
Childress, Childress	79201
Chillicothe, Hardeman	79225
Chilton, Falls	76632
China, Jefferson	77613
China Grove, Bexar	78263
China Spring, Mclennan	76633
Chireno, Nacogdoches	75937
Chriesman, Burleson	77838
Christine, Atascosa	78012
Christoval, Tom Green	76935
Cibolo, Guadalupe	78108
Cisco, Eastland	76437
City By The Sea, San Patricio	78336
Clarendon, Donley	79226
Clarksville, Red River	75426
Clarksville City, Gregg	75693
Claude, Armstrong	79019
Clayton, Panola	75637
Clear Lake Shores, Galveston	77565
CLEBURNE, Johnson (See Page 3653)	
Clemville, Matagorda	77414
CLEVELAND, Liberty (See Page 3654)	
Clifton, Bosque	76634
Clifton, Bosque	76644
Clint, El Paso	79836
Clodine, Fort Bend	77469
Clutch City, Harris	77002
Clute, Brazoria	77531
Clyde, Callahan	79510
Coahoma, Howard	79511
Coffee City, Anderson	75763
Coldspring, San Jacinto	77331
Coleman, Coleman	76834
COLLEGE STATION, Brazos (See Page 3656)	
Collegeport, Matagorda	77428
Colleyville, Tarrant	76034
Collinsville, Grayson	76233
Colmesneil, Tyler	75938
Colorado City, Mitchell	79512
Columbus, Colorado	78934
Comanche, Comanche	76442
Combes, Cameron	78535
Combine, Dallas	75159
Comfort, Kendall	78013
COMMERCE, Hunt (See Page 3659)	
Como, Hopkins	75431
Comstock, Val Verde	78837
Concan, Uvalde	78838
Concepcion, Duval	78349
Concord, Leon	77850
Cone, Crosby	79357
CONROE, Montgomery (See Page 3659)	
Converse, Bexar	78109
Cookville, Titus	75558
Cool, Parker	76066
Coolidge, Limestone	76635
Cooper, Delta	75432
Copeville, Collin	75121
Coppell, Dallas	75019
Copper Canyon, Denton	75077
Copperas Cove, Coryell	76522
Corinth (See Denton)	
CORPUS CHRISTI, Nueces (See Page 3663)	
Corrigan, Polk	75939
CORSICANA, Navarro (See Page 3670)	
Cost, Gonzales	78614
Cotton Center, Hale	79021
Cottonwood Shores, Llano	78657
Cotulla, La Salle	78014
Coupland, Williamson	78615
Cove (See Baytown)	
Covington, Hill	76636
Coyanosa, Pecos	79730
Crandall, Kaufman	75114
Crane, Crane	79731
Cranfills Gap, Bosque	76637
Crawford, Mclennan	76638
Creedmoor, Hays	78610
Cresson, Hood	76035
Crockett, Houston	75835
Crosby, Harris	77532
Crosbyton, Crosby	79322
Cross Plains, Callahan	76443
Cross Timber, Johnson	76028
Crossroads, Denton	76227
Crowell, Foard	79227
Crowley, Tarrant	76036
Crystal Beach, Galveston	77650
Crystal City, Zavala	78839
Cuero, De Witt	77954
Cumby, Hopkins	75433
Cuney, Cherokee	75759
Cunningham, Lamar	75434
Cushing, Nacogdoches	75760
Cut And Shoot (See Conroe)	
CYPRESS, Harris (See Page 3671)	
Cypress Mill, Blanco	78663
D Hanis, Medina	78850
Daingerfield, Morris	75638
Daisetta, Liberty	77533
Dale, Caldwell	78616
Dalhart, Dallam	79022
Dallardsville, Polk	77332
DALLAS, Dallas (See Page 3675)	
Dalworthington Gardens, Tarrant	76013
Damon, Brazoria	77430
Danbury, Brazoria	77534
Danciger, Brazoria	77431
Danevang, Wharton	77432
Darrouzett, Lipscomb	79024
Davilla, Milam	76523
Dawn, Deaf Smith	79025
Dawson, Navarro	76639
Dayton, Liberty	77535
Dayton Lakes, Liberty	77535
De Berry, Panola	75639
De Kalb, Bowie	75559
De Leon, Comanche	76444
Dean, Wichita	76305
Deanville, Burleson	77852
Decatur, Wise	76234
Decker Prairie (See Magnolia)	
Decordova, Hood	76049
Deer Park, Harris	77536
DEL RIO, Val Verde (See Page 3692)	
Del Valle, Travis	78617
Dell City, Hudspeth	79837
Dell City, Hudspeth	79847
Delmita, Starr	78536
DENISON, Grayson (See Page 3694)	
Dennis, Parker	76439
DENTON, Denton (See Page 3695)	
Denver City, Yoakum	79323
Deport, Lamar	75435
Dermott, Scurry	79549
Desdemona, Eastland	76445
DESOTO, Dallas (See Page 3698)	
Detroit, Red River	75436
Devers, Liberty	77538
Devine, Medina	78016
Deweyville, Newton	77614
Dfw, Dallas	75261
Dfw Airport, Dallas	75261
Dialville, Cherokee	75785
Diana, Upshur	75640
Diboll, Angelina	75941
Dickens, Dickens	79229
Dickinson, Galveston	77539
Dike, Hopkins	75437
Dilley, Frio	78017
Dime Box, Lee	77853
Dimmitt, Castro	79027
Dinero, Live Oak	78350
Dobbin, Montgomery	77333
Dodd City, Fannin	75438
Dodge, Walker	77334
Dodson, Collingsworth	79230

Donie, Freestone 75838
Donna, Hidalgo 78537
Doole, Mcculloch 76836
Dorchester, Grayson 75459
Doss, Gillespie 78618
Double Oak, Denton 75077
Doucette, Tyler 75942
Dougherty, Floyd 79231
Douglass, Nacogdoches 75943
Douglassville, Cass 75560
Driftwood, Hays 78619
Dripping Springs, Hays 78620
Driscoll, Nueces 78351
Dryden, Terrell 78851
Dublin, Erath 76446
Dumas, Moore 79029
Dumont, Cottle 79248
DUNCANVILLE, Dallas
(See Page 3699)
Dunlay, Medina 78861
Dunn, Scurry 79516
Dyess Afb, Taylor 79607
Eagle Lake, Colorado 77434
EAGLE PASS, Maverick
(See Page 3700)
EARLY, Brown
(See Page 3701)
Earth, Lamb 79031
East Bernard, Wharton 77435
East Tawakoni, Rains 75472
Eastland, Eastland 76448
Easton, Gregg 75641
Ecleto, Karnes 78111
Ector, Fannin 75439
Edcouch, Hidalgo 78538
Eddy, Mclennan 76524
Eden, Concho 76837
Edgecliff Village, Tarrant 76134
Edgewood, Van Zandt 75117
EDINBURG, Hidalgo
(See Page 3702)
Edmonson, Hale 79032
Edna, Jackson 77957
Edom, Van Zandt 75754
Edroy, San Patricio 78352
Egypt, Wharton 77436
El Campo, Wharton 77437
El Cenizo, Webb 78046
El Indio, Maverick 78860
El Lago, Harris 77586
EL PASO, El Paso
(See Page 3705)
Elbert, Young 76372
Eldorado, Schleicher 76936
Eldorado Afs, Schleicher 76936
Electra, Wichita 76360
Elgin, Bastrop 78621
Eliasville, Young 76481
Elkhart, Anderson 75839
Ellinger, Fayette 78938
Elm Mott, Mclennan 76640
Elmaton, Matagorda 77440
Elmendorf, Bexar 78112
Elmo, Kaufman 75118
Elsa, Hidalgo 78543
Elysian Fields, Harrison 75642
Emory, Rains 75440
Enchanted Oaks, Henderson 75156
Encinal, La Salle 78019
Encino, Brooks 78353
Energy, Comanche 76452
Enloe, Delta 75441
ENNIS, Ellis
(See Page 3718)
Enochs, Bailey 79324
Eola, Concho 76937
Era, Cooke 76238
Estelline, Hall 79233
Etoile, Nacogdoches 75944
EULESS, Tarrant
(See Page 3718)
Eustace, Henderson 75124
Evadale, Jasper 77615
Evant, Coryell 76525
Everman, Tarrant 76140
Fabens, El Paso 79838

Fair Oaks Ranch
(See Boerne)
Fairfield, Freestone 75840
Fairview, Collin 75069
Falcon, Zapata 78564
Falcon Heights, Starr 78545
Falfurrias, Brooks 78355
Falls City, Karnes 78113
Fannin, Goliad 77960
Farmers Branch
(See Dallas)
Farmersville, Collin 75442
Farnsworth, Ochiltree 79033
Farwell, Parmer 79325
Fate, Rockwall 75132
Fayetteville, Fayette 78940
Fentress, Caldwell 78622
Ferris, Ellis 75125
Fieldton, Lamb 79326
Fife, Mcculloch 76825
Fischer, Comal 78623
Flat, Coryell 76526
Flatonia, Fayette 78941
Flint, Smith 75762
Flomot, Motley 79234
Florence, Williamson 76527
Floresville, Wilson 78114
FLOWER MOUND, Denton
(See Page 3719)
Flowermound
(See Flower Mound)
Floydada, Floyd 79235
Fluvanna, Scurry 79517
Flynn, Leon 77855
Follett, Lipscomb 79034
Forest, Cherokee 75925
Forest Hill
(See Fort Worth)
Forestburg, Montague 76239
Forney, Kaufman 75126
Forreston, Ellis 76041
Forsan, Howard 79733
Fort Bliss, El Paso 79906
Fort Davis, Jeff Davis 79734
Fort Hancock, Hudspeth 79839
Fort Hood, Bell 76544
Fort Mc Kavett, Menard 76841
Fort Sam Houston, Bexar 78234
Fort Stockton, Pecos 79735
FORT WORTH, Tarrant
(See Page 3722)
Fowlerton, La Salle 78021
Francitas, Jackson 77961
Franklin, Robertson 77856
Frankston, Anderson 75763
Fred, Tyler 77616
Fredericksburg, Gillespie 78624
Fredonia, Mason 76842
FREEPORT, Brazoria
(See Page 3741)
Freer, Duval 78357
Fresno, Fort Bend 77545
FRIENDSWOOD, Galveston
(See Page 3741)
Friona, Parmer 79035
FRISCO, Denton
(See Page 3742)
Fritch, Hutchinson 79036
Frost, Navarro 76641
Fruitvale, Van Zandt 75127
Ft Worth, Tarrant 76101
Fulshear, Fort Bend 77441
Fulton, Aransas 78358
Gail, Borden 79738
GAINESVILLE, Cooke
(See Page 3746)
Galena Park, Harris 77547
Gallatin, Cherokee 75764
GALVESTON, Galveston
(See Page 3747)
Ganado, Jackson 77962
Garciasville, Starr 78547
Garden City, Glasscock 79739
Garden Ridge, Comal 78266
Garden Valley, Smith 75771
Gardendale, Ector 79758

GARLAND, Dallas
(See Page 3749)
Garrison, Nacogdoches 75946
Garwood, Colorado 77442
Gary, Panola 75643
Gatesville, Coryell 76528
Gause, Milam 77857
Geneva, Sabine 75959
George West, Live Oak 78022
GEORGETOWN, Williamson
(See Page 3752)
Geronimo, Guadalupe 78115
Giddings, Lee 78942
Gilchrist, Galveston 77617
Gillett, Karnes 78111
Gillett, Karnes 78116
GILMER, Upshur
(See Page 3755)
Girard, Kent 79518
Girvin, Pecos 79740
Gladewater, Gregg 75647
Glazier, Hemphill 79014
Glen Flora, Wharton 77443
Glen Rose, Somervell 76043
Glenn Heights, Ellis 75154
Glidden, Colorado 78943
Gober, Fannin 75443
Godley, Johnson 76044
Golden, Wood 75444
Goldsboro, Coleman 79519
Goldsmith, Ector 79741
Goldthwaite, Mills 76844
Goliad, Goliad 77963
Gonzales, Gonzales 78629
Goodfellow Afb, Tom Green 76908
Goodrich, Polk 77335
Gordon, Palo Pinto 76453
Gordonville, Grayson 76245
Goree, Knox 76363
Gorman, Eastland 76454
Gouldbusk, Coleman 76845
Graford, Palo Pinto 76449
Graham, Young 76450
GRANBURY, Hood
(See Page 3756)
GRAND PRAIRIE, Dallas
(See Page 3759)
Grand Saline, Van Zandt 75140
Grandfalls, Ward 79742
Grandview, Johnson 76050
Granger, Williamson 76530
Grangerland, Montgomery 77302
Granite Shoals, Burnet 78654
Grape Creek, Tom Green 76901
Grapeland, Houston 75844
GRAPEVINE, Tarrant
(See Page 3762)
GREENVILLE, Hunt
(See Page 3763)
Greenwood, Wise 76246
Gregory, San Patricio 78359
Gridiron, Harris 77054
Groesbeck, Limestone 76642
Groom, Carson 79039
Groves, Jefferson 77619
Groveton, Trinity 75845
Grulla, Starr 78548
Gruver, Hansford 79040
Guerra, Jim Hogg 78360
Gun Barrel City
(See Mabank)
Gunter, Grayson 75058
Gustine, Comanche 76455
Guthrie, King 79236
Guy, Fort Bend 77444
Hale Center, Hale 79041
Hallettsville, Lavaca 77964
Hallsville, Harrison 75650
Haltom City, Tarrant 76111
Hamilton, Hamilton 76531
Hamlin, Jones 79520
Hamshire, Jefferson 77622
Hankamer, Chambers 77560
Happy, Swisher 79042
Hardin, Liberty 77561
Hargill, Hidalgo 78549

Harker Heights, Bell 76548
Harleton, Harrison 75651
HARLINGEN, Cameron
(See Page 3765)
Harper, Gillespie 78631
Harrold, Wilbarger 76364
Hart, Castro 79043
Hartley, Hartley 79044
Harwood, Gonzales 78632
Haskell, Haskell 79521
Haslet, Tarrant 76052
Hasse, Comanche 76442
Hawkins, Wood 75765
Hawley, Jones 79525
Hays, Hays 78610
Hearne, Robertson 77859
Heartland, Kaufman 75126
Heath, Rockwall 75032
Heathridge, Kaufman 75126
Hebbronville, Jim Hogg 78361
Hedley, Donley 79237
Heidenheimer, Bell 76533
Helotes, Bexar 78023
Hemphill, Sabine 75948
Hempstead, Waller 77445
HENDERSON, Rusk
(See Page 3767)
Henrietta, Clay 76365
Hereford, Deaf Smith 79045
Hermleigh, Scurry 79526
Hewitt, Mclennan 76643
Hext, Menard 76848
Hickory Creek, Denton 75065
Hico, Hamilton 76457
Hidalgo, Hidalgo 78557
Hide A Way, Smith 75771
Hideaway, Smith 75771
Higgins, Lipscomb 79046
High Island, Galveston 77623
Highland Haven, Burnet 78654
Highland Village, Denton 75077
Highlands, Harris 77562
Hill Country Village, Bexar 78232
Hillister, Tyler 77624
Hillsboro, Hill 76645
Hilltop Lakes, Leon 77871
Hitchcock, Galveston 77563
Hobson, Karnes 78117
Hochheim, De Witt 77967
Hockley, Harris 77447
Holiday Lakes, Brazoria 77515
Holland, Bell 76534
Holliday, Archer 76366
Holly Lake Ranch, Upshur 75755
Hollywood Park, Bexar 78232
Hondo, Medina 78861
Honey Grove, Fannin 75446
Hooks, Bowie 75561
Horizon City
(See El Paso)
Horseshoe Bay, Llano 78657
HOUSTON, Harris
(See Page 3768)
Howardwick, Donley 79226
Howe, Grayson 75459
Hubbard, Hill 76648
Hudson Oaks, Parker 76087
Huffman, Harris 77336
Hufsmith, Harris 77337
Hughes Springs, Cass 75656
Hull, Liberty 77564
HUMBLE, Harris
(See Page 3808)
Hungerford, Wharton 77448
Hunt, Kerr 78024
Huntington, Angelina 75949
HUNTSVILLE, Walker
(See Page 3811)
HURST, Tarrant
(See Page 3813)
Hutchins, Dallas 75141
Hutto, Williamson 78634
Hye, Blanco 78635
Idalou, Lubbock 79329
Imperial, Pecos 79743
Indian Lake, Cameron 78566

Industry, Austin 78944
Inez, Victoria 77968
Ingleside, San Patricio 78362
Ingram, Kerr 78025
Iola, Grimes 77861
Iowa Park, Wichita 76367
Ira, Scurry 79527
Iraan, Pecos 79744
Iredell, Bosque 76649
Irene, Hill 76650
IRVING, Dallas
(See Page 3813)
Italy, Ellis 76651
Itasca, Hill 76055
Ivanhoe, Fannin 75447
Izoro, Coryell 76528
Jacinto City, Harris 77029
Jacksboro, Jack 76458
Jacksonville, Cherokee 75766
Jamaica Beach, Galveston 77554
Jarrell, Williamson 76537
Jasper, Jasper 75951
Jayton, Kent 79528
Jbsa Ft Sam Houston,
Bexar 78234
Jbsa Lackland, Bexar 78236
Jbsa Randolph, Bexar 78150
Jefferson, Marion 75657
Jermyn, Jack 76459
Jersey Village
(See Houston)
Jewett, Leon 75846
Joaquin, Shelby 75954
Johnson City, Blanco 78636
Joinerville, Rusk 75658
Jolly, Wichita 76305
Jones Creek, Brazoria 77541
Jonesboro, Coryell 76538
Jonestown, Travis 78645
Jonesville, Harrison 75659
Josephine, Collin 75164
Joshua, Johnson 76058
Jourdanton, Atascosa 78026
Judson, Gregg 75660
Junction, Kimble 76849
Justiceburg, Garza 79330
Justin, Denton 76247
Kamay, Wichita 76369
Karnack, Harrison 75661
Karnes City, Karnes 78118
KATY, Harris
(See Page 3816)
Kaufman, Kaufman 75142
Keechi, Leon 75831
Keene, Johnson 76059
KELLER, Tarrant
(See Page 3824)
Kemah, Galveston 77565
Kemp, Kaufman 75143
Kempner, Lampasas 76539
Kendalia, Kendall 78027
Kendleton, Fort Bend 77451
Kenedy, Karnes 78119
Kenedy, Bee 78125
Kennard, Houston 75847
Kennedale, Tarrant 76060
Kenney, Austin 77452
Kent, Culberson 79855
Kerens, Navarro 75144
Kermit, Winkler 79745
Kerrick, Dallam 79051
KERRVILLE, Kerr
(See Page 3825)
Kildare, Cass 75562
KILGORE, Gregg
(See Page 3827)
KILLEEN, Bell
(See Page 3828)
Kingsbury, Guadalupe 78638
Kingsland, Llano 78639
KINGSVILLE, Kleberg
(See Page 3831)
Kingsville Naval Air Station,
Kleberg 78363
Kingsvl Naval, Kleberg 78363

KINGWOOD, Harris
(See Page 3831)
Kirby, Bexar 78219
Kirbyville, Jasper 75956
Kirvin, Freestone 75848
Klein
(See Spring)
Klondike, Delta 75448
Knickerbocker, Tom Green 76939
Knippa, Uvalde 78870
Knollwood, Grayson 75092
Knott, Howard 79748
Knox City, Knox 79529
Kopperl, Bosque 76652
Kosse, Limestone 76653
Kountze, Hardin 77625
Kress, Swisher 79052
Krugerville, Denton 76227
Krum, Denton 76249
Kurten, Brazos 77862
Kyle, Hays 78640
La Blanca, Hidalgo 78558
La Coste, Medina 78039
La Feria, Cameron 78559
La Grange, Fayette 78945
La Grulla, Starr 78548
La Joya, Hidalgo 78560
La Marque, Galveston 77568
La Mesa, Dawson 79331
LA PORTE, Harris
(See Page 3832)
La Pryor, Zavala 78872
La Salle, Jackson 77969
La Vernia, Wilson 78121
La Villa, Hidalgo 78562
La Ward, Jackson 77970
Lackland Afb, Bexar 78236
Lacy Lakeview, Mclennan 76705
Ladonia, Fannin 75449
Lago Vista, Travis 78645
Laguna Heights, Cameron 78578
Laguna Park, Bosque 76634
Laguna Park, Bosque 76644
Laguna Vista, Cameron 78578
Laird Hill, Rusk 75666
Lajitas, Brewster 79852
Lake City, San Patricio 78368
Lake Creek, Delta 75450
Lake Dallas, Denton 75065
Lake Jackson, Brazoria 77566
Lake Kiowa, Cooke 76240
Lake Limestone, Limestone 76642
Lake Worth
(See Fort Worth)
Lakehills, Bandera 78063
Lakeside
(See Fort Worth)
Lakeview, Hall 79239
Lakeway
(See Austin)
Lakewood Village, Denton 75068
Lamesa, Dawson 79331
Lampasas, Lampasas 76550
LANCASTER, Dallas
(See Page 3833)
Lane City, Wharton 77453
Laneville, Rusk 75667
Langtry, Val Verde 78871
Lantana, Denton 76226
LAREDO, Webb
(See Page 3834)
Larue, Henderson 75770
Lasara, Willacy 78561
Latexo, Houston 75849
Laughlin Afb, Val Verde 78840
Laughlin Afb, Val Verde 78843
Lavernia, Wilson 78121
Lavon, Collin 75166
Lawn, Taylor 79530
Lazbuddie, Parmer 79053
Leaday, Coleman 76888
LEAGUE CITY, Galveston
(See Page 3838)
Leakey, Real 78873
LEANDER, Williamson
(See Page 3840)

Ledbetter, Fayette 78946
Leesburg, Camp 75451
Leesville, Gonzales 78122
Lefors, Gray 79054
Leggett, Polk 77350
Lelia Lake, Donley 79240
Leming, Atascosa 78050
Lenorah, Martin 79749
Leon Junction, Coryell 76528
Leon Valley
(See San Antonio)
Leona, Leon 75850
Leonard, Fannin 75452
Leroy, Mclennan 76654
LEVELLAND, Hockley
(See Page 3843)
LEWISVILLE, Denton
(See Page 3843)
Lexington, Lee 78947
Liberty, Liberty 77575
Liberty Hill, Williamson 78642
Lillian, Johnson 76061
Lincoln, Lee 78948
Lindale, Smith 75706
Lindale, Smith 75771
Linden, Cass 75563
Lindsay, Cooke 76250
Lingleville, Erath 76446
Lingleville, Erath 76461
Linn, Hidalgo 78563
Lipan, Hood 76462
Lipscomb, Lipscomb 79056
Lissie, Wharton 77454
Little Elm, Denton 75068
Little River Academy, Bell 76554
Littlefield, Lamb 79339
Live Oak, Bexar 78233
Liverpool, Brazoria 77577
Livingston, Polk 77351
Llano, Llano 78643
Lockhart, Caldwell 78644
Lockney, Floyd 79241
Lodi, Marion 75564
Log Cabin, Henderson 75148
Lohn, Mcculloch 76852
Lolita, Jackson 77971
Lometa, Lampasas 76853
London, Kimble 76854
Lone Oak, Hunt 75453
Lone Star, Morris 75668
Long Branch, Panola 75669
Long Mott, Calhoun 77979
LONGVIEW, Gregg
(See Page 3845)
Loop, Gaines 79342
Lopeno, Zapata 78564
Loraine, Mitchell 79532
Lorena, Mclennan 76655
Lorenzo, Crosby 79343
Los Ebanos, Hidalgo 78565
Los Fresnos, Cameron 78566
Los Indios, Cameron 78567
Lost Pines, Bastrop 78612
Lott, Falls 76656
Louise, Wharton 77455
Lovelady, Houston 75851
Loving, Young 76460
Lowake, Concho 76855
Lozano, Cameron 78568
LUBBOCK, Lubbock
(See Page 3849)
Lucas, Collin 75002
Lueders, Jones 79533
LUFKIN, Angelina
(See Page 3853)
Luling, Caldwell 78648
Lumberton, Hardin 77657
Lyford, Willacy 78569
Lyons, Burleson 77863
Lytle, Atascosa 78052
MABANK, Kaufman
(See Page 3855)
Macdona, Bexar 78054
Madisonville, Madison 77864
MAGNOLIA, Montgomery
(See Page 3857)
Magnolia Springs, Jasper 75956
Malakoff, Henderson 75148
Malone, Hill 76660
Manchaca, Travis 78652
Manor, Travis 78653
Mansfield, Tarrant 76063
Manvel, Brazoria 77578
Maple, Bailey 79344
Marathon, Brewster 79842
Marble Falls, Burnet 78654
Marble Falls, Llano 78657
Marfa, Presidio 79843
Marietta, Cass 75566
Marion, Guadalupe 78124
Markham, Matagorda 77456
Marlin, Falls 76661
Marquez, Leon 77865
MARSHALL, Harrison
(See Page 3859)
Mart, Mclennan 76664
Martindale, Caldwell 78655
Martinsville, Nacogdoches 75958
Maryneal, Nolan 79535
Mason, Mason 76856
Masterson, Moore 79058
Matador, Motley 79244
Matagorda, Matagorda 77457
Mathis, San Patricio 78368
Maud, Bowie 75567
Mauriceville, Orange 77626
Maxwell, Caldwell 78656
May, Brown 76857
Maydelle, Cherokee 75772
Maypearl, Ellis 76064
Maysfield, Milam 76520
Mc Camey, Upton 79752
Mc Caulley, Fisher 79534
Mc Dade, Bastrop 78650
Mc Gregor, Mclennan 76657
Mc Kinney
(See Mckinney)
Mc Leod, Cass 75565
Mc Neil, Travis 78651
Mc Queeney, Guadalupe 78123
Mcadoo, Dickens 79243
MCALLEN, Hidalgo
(See Page 3861)
Mccamey, Upton 79752
Mccoy, Karnes 78113
Mcdade, Bastrop 78650
Mcdonald Observatory, Jeff Davis 79734
Mcfaddin, Victoria 77973
MCKINNEY, Collin
(See Page 3862)
Mclean, Gray 79057
Mcmahan, Caldwell 78616
Mcneil, Travis 78651
Mcqueeney, Guadalupe 78123
Meadow, Terry 79345
Meadowlakes, Burnet 78654
Meadows Place, Fort Bend 77477
Medina, Bandera 78055
Megargel, Archer 76370
Melissa, Collin 75454
Melvin, Mcculloch 76858
Memphis, Hall 79245
Menard, Menard 76859
Mentone, Loving 79754
Mercedes, Hidalgo 78570
Mereta, Tom Green 76940
Meridian, Bosque 76665
Merit, Hunt 75458
Merkel, Taylor 79536
Mertens, Hill 76666
Mertzon, Irion 76941
MESQUITE, Dallas
(See Page 3867)
Mexia, Limestone 76667
Meyersville, De Witt 77974
Miami, Roberts 79059
Mico, Medina 78056
Midfield, Matagorda 77458
Midkiff, Upton 79755
MIDLAND, Midland
(See Page 3869)
Midlothian, Ellis 76065
Midway, Leon 75850
Midway, Madison 75852
Milam, Sabine 75959
Milano, Milam 76556
Miles, Runnels 76861
Milford, Ellis 76670
Millersview, Concho 76862
Millican, Brazos 77866
Millsap, Parker 76066
Minden, Rusk 75680
Mineola, Wood 75773
Mineral, Bee 78125
MINERAL WELLS, Palo Pinto
(See Page 3872)
Mingus, Palo Pinto 76463
Mirando City, Webb 78369
MISSION, Hidalgo
(See Page 3872)
MISSOURI CITY, Fort Bend
(See Page 3876)
Mobeetie, Wheeler 79061
Monahans, Ward 79756
Monroe City, Chambers 77514
Mont Belvieu, Harris 77520
Montague, Montague 76251
Montalba, Anderson 75853
Monte Alto, Hidalgo 78538
MONTGOMERY, Montgomery
(See Page 3878)
Moody, Mclennan 76557
Moore, Frio 78057
Moran, Shackelford 76464
Morgan, Bosque 76671
Morgan Mill, Erath 76465
Morgans Point Resort, Bell 76513
Morse, Hansford 79062
Morton, Cochran 79346
Moscow, Polk 75960
Moulton, Lavaca 77975
Mound, Coryell 76558
Mount Calm, Hill 76673
Mount Enterprise, Rusk 75681
MOUNT PLEASANT, Titus
(See Page 3881)
Mount Selman, Smith 75757
Mount Vernon, Franklin 75457
Mountain City, Hays 78610
Mountain Home, Kerr 78058
Mt Sylvan, Smith 75771
Mt Vernon, Franklin 75457
Muenster, Cooke 76252
Muldoon, Fayette 78949
Muleshoe, Bailey 79347
Mullin, Mills 76864
Mumford, Brazos 77807
Mumford, Robertson 77867
Munday, Knox 76371
Murchison, Henderson 75778
Murphy, Collin 75094
Mustang Ridge, Hays 78610
Myra, Cooke 76253
N Richland Hills, Tarrant 76117
N Richland Hills, Tarrant 76118
NACOGDOCHES, Nacogdoches
(See Page 3882)
Nada, Colorado 77460
Naples, Morris 75568
Nash, Bowie 75569
Natalia, Medina 78059
Naval Air Station/ Jrb, Tarrant 76127
Navasota, Grimes 77868
Nazareth, Castro 79063
Neches, Anderson 75779
Nederland, Jefferson 77627
Needville, Fort Bend 77461
Nemo, Somervell 76070
Nevada, Collin 75173
New Baden, Robertson 77870
New Berlin, Guadalupe 78155
New Boston, Bowie 75570
NEW BRAUNFELS, Comal
(See Page 3884)
New Caney, Montgomery 77357
New Deal, Lubbock 79350
New Diana, Upshur 75640
New Home, Lynn 79381
New Home, Lynn 79383
New London, Rusk 75682
New Summerfield, Cherokee 75780
New Ulm, Austin 78950
New Waverly, Walker 77358
Newark, Wise 76071
Newcastle, Young 76372
Newton, Newton 75966
Niederwald, Hays 78640
Nixon, Gonzales 78140
Nocona, Montague 76255
Nolan, Nolan 79537
Nolanville, Bell 76559
Nome, Jefferson 77629
Nordheim, De Witt 78141
Normangee, Leon 77871
Normanna, Bee 78142
North Branch, Dallas 75244
North Houston, Harris 77315
NORTH RICHLAND HILLS, Tarrant
(See Page 3888)
North Zulch, Madison 77872
Northfield, Childress 79201
Northlake, Denton 76226
Norton, Runnels 76865
Notrees, Ector 79759
Novice, Coleman 79538
Nursery, Victoria 77976
O Brien, Haskell 79539
Oak Leaf, Ellis 75154
Oak Point, Denton 75068
Oak Ridge, Cooke 76240
Oak Ridge North, Montgomery 77385
Oak Ridge North, Montgomery 77386
Oakalla, Burnet 78608
Oakhurst, San Jacinto 77359
Oakland, Colorado 78951
Oakville, Live Oak 78060
Oakwood, Leon 75855
Odell, Wilbarger 79247
Odem, San Patricio 78370
ODESSA, Ector
(See Page 3890)
Odonnell, Lynn 79351
Oglesby, Coryell 76561
Oilton, Webb 78371
Oklaunion, Wilbarger 76373
Old Glory, Stonewall 79540
Old Ocean, Brazoria 77463
Old River Winfree, Harris 77520
Old River Winfree, Harris 77520
Olden, Eastland 76466
Olmito, Cameron 78575
Olmos Park, Bexar 78212
Olney, Young 76374
Olton, Lamb 79064
Omaha, Morris 75571
Onalaska, Polk 77360
ORANGE, Orange
(See Page 3893)
Orange Grove, Jim Wells 78372
Orangefield, Orange 77639
Orchard, Fort Bend 77464
Ore City, Upshur 75683
Orla, Reeves 79770
Ottine, Gonzales 78658
Otto, Mclennan 76682
Ovalo, Taylor 79541
Overton, Rusk 75684
Ovilla, Ellis 75154
Oyster Creek, Brazoria 77541
Ozona, Crockett 76943
Paducah, Cottle 79248
Paige, Bastrop 78659
Paint Rock, Concho 76866
Palacios, Matagorda 77465
PALESTINE, Anderson
(See Page 3895)
Palisades, Randall 79118
Palm Valley, Cameron 78552
Palmer, Ellis 75152
Palmhurst
(See Mission)
Palmview
(See Mission)
Palo Pinto, Palo Pinto 76484
Paluxy, Hood 76467
PAMPA, Gray
(See Page 3897)
Pandora, Wilson 78143
Panhandle, Carson 79068
Panna Maria, Karnes 78144
Panola, Panola 75685
Panorama Village, Montgomery 77304
Pantego
(See Arlington)
Paradise, Wise 76073
PARIS, Lamar
(See Page 3897)
Park Row
(See Katy)
Parker, Collin 75002
PASADENA, Harris
(See Page 3899)
Pattison, Waller 77423
Pattison, Waller 77466
Patton Village, Montgomery 77372
Pattonville, Lamar 75468
Pawnee, Bee 78145
Pear Valley, Mcculloch 76852
PEARLAND, Brazoria
(See Page 3901)
Pearsall, Frio 78061
Peaster, Parker 76485
Pecan Gap, Delta 75469
Pecos, Reeves 79772
Peggy, Atascosa 78062
Pendleton, Bell 76564
Penelope, Hill 76676
Penitas, Hidalgo 78576
Pennington, Trinity 75856
Penwell, Ector 79776
Pep, Hockley 79353
Perrin, Jack 76486
Perry, Mclennan 76682
Perryton, Ochiltree 79070
Petersburg, Hale 79250
Petrolia, Clay 76377
Pettus, Bee 78146
Petty, Lamar 75470
PFLUGERVILLE, Travis
(See Page 3904)
Pharr, Hidalgo 78577
Phillips, Hutchinson 79007
Pickton, Hopkins 75471
Pierce, Wharton 77467
Pilot Point, Denton 76258
Pine Island, Waller 77445
Pinehurst, Montgomery 77362
Pineland, Sabine 75968
Piney Point Village, Harris 77024
Pipe Creek, Bandera 78063
Pittsburg, Camp 75686
Placedo, Victoria 77977
Plains, Yoakum 79355
PLAINVIEW, Hale
(See Page 3905)
PLANO, Collin
(See Page 3906)
Plantersville, Grimes 77363
Pleasant Valley, Wichita 76305
Pleasanton, Atascosa 78064
Pledger, Matagorda 77468
Plum, Fayette 78952
Point, Rains 75472
Point Comfort, Calhoun 77978
Point Venture, Travis 78645
Pointblank, San Jacinto 77364
Pollok, Angelina 75969
Ponder, Denton 76259
Pontotoc, Mason 76869
Poolville, Parker 76487
Port Acres, Jefferson 77640
Port Aransas, Nueces 78373
PORT ARTHUR, Jefferson
(See Page 3912)
Port Bolivar, Galveston 77650
Port Isabel, Cameron 78578
Port Lavaca, Calhoun 77979
Port Mansfield, Willacy 78598
Port Neches, Jefferson 77651
Port O Connor, Calhoun 77982
Porter, Montgomery 77365
Portland, San Patricio 78374
Post, Garza 79356
Poteet, Atascosa 78065
Poth, Wilson 78147
Pottsboro, Grayson 75076
Pottsville, Hamilton 76565
Powderly, Lamar 75473
Powell, Navarro 75153
Poynor, Henderson 75782
Prairie Hill, Limestone 76678
Prairie Lea, Caldwell 78661
Prairie View, Waller 77445
Premont, Jim Wells 78375
Presidio, Presidio 79845
Presidio, Presidio 79846
Price, Rusk 75687
Priddy, Mills 76870
Princeton, Collin 75407
Proctor, Comanche 76468
Progreso, Hidalgo 78579
Progreso Lakes, Hidalgo 78596
Prosper, Collin 75078
Providence Village, Denton 76227
Purdon, Navarro 76679
Purmela, Coryell 76566
Putnam, Callahan 76469
Pyote, Ward 79777
Quail, Collingsworth 79251
Quanah, Hardeman 79252
Queen City, Cass 75572
Quemado, Maverick 78877
Quinlan, Hunt 75474
Quintana, Brazoria 77541
Quitaque, Briscoe 79255
Quitman, Wood 75783
Rainbow, Somervell 76077
Raisin, Victoria 77905
Ralls, Crosby 79357
Rancho Viejo, Cameron 78575
Randolph, Fannin 75475
Randolph Air, Bexar 78150
Randolph Air Force Base, Bexar 78150
Ranger, Eastland 76470
Rankin, Upton 79778
Ransom Canyon, Lubbock 79364
Ransom Canyon, Lubbock 79366
Ratcliff, Houston 75858
Ravenna, Fannin 75476
Raymondville, Willacy 78580
Raymondville, Willacy 78598
Raywood, Liberty 77582
Reagan, Falls 76680
Realitos, Duval 78376
Red Oak, Ellis 75154
Red Rock, Bastrop 78662
Red Springs, Baylor 76380
Redford, Presidio 79846
Redwater, Bowie 75573
Refugio, Refugio 78377
Reklaw, Cherokee 75784
Reno, Lamar 75462
Rhome, Wise 76078
Rice, Navarro 75155
Richards, Grimes 77873
RICHARDSON, Dallas
(See Page 3913)
Richland, Navarro 76681
Richland Hills, Tarrant 76118
Richland Springs, San Saba 76871
RICHMOND, Fort Bend
(See Page 3915)
Richwood, Brazoria 77515
Ridge, Robertson 77856
Riesel, Mclennan 76682
Ringgold, Montague 76261
Rio Bravo, Webb 78043
Rio Frio, Real 78879
Rio Grande City, Starr 78582

Rio Hondo, Cameron 78583
Rio Medina, Medina 78066
Rio Vista, Johnson 76093
Rising Star, Eastland 76471
River Oaks, Tarrant 76114
Riverside, Walker 77367
Riviera, Kleberg 78379
Roanoke, Denton 76262
Roans Prairie, Grimes 77875
Roaring Springs, Motley 79256
Robert Lee, Coke 76945
Robinson, Mclennan 76706
Robstown, Nueces 78380
Roby, Fisher 79543
Rochelle, Mcculloch 76872
Rochester, Haskell 79544
Rock Island, Colorado 77470
Rockdale, Milam 76567
Rockland, Tyler 75938
ROCKPORT, Aransas
(See Page 3919)
Rocksprings, Edwards 78880
ROCKWALL, Rockwall
(See Page 3920)
Rockwood, Coleman 76873
Roganville, Jasper 75956
Rogers, Bell 76569
Rollingwood, Travis 78746
Roma, Starr 78584
Roman Forest, Montgomery 77357
Romayor, Liberty 77368
Roosevelt, Kimble 76874
Ropesville, Hockley 79358
Rosanky, Bastrop 78953
Roscoe, Nolan 79545
Rose Hill Acres, Hardin 77657
Rosebud, Falls 76570
Rosenberg, Harris 77469
Rosenberg, Fort Bend 77471
Rosharon, Brazoria 77583
Ross, Mclennan 76684
Rosser, Kaufman 75157
Rosston, Cooke 76263
Rotan, Fisher 79546
Round Mountain, Blanco 78663
ROUND ROCK, Williamson
(See Page 3922)
Round Top, Fayette 78954
Round Top, Fayette 78961
Rowena, Runnels 76875
ROWLETT, Dallas
(See Page 3925)
Roxton, Lamar 75477
Royse City, Rockwall 75189
RULE, Haskell
(See Page 3926)
Runaway Bay, Wise 76426
Runge, Karnes 78151
Rusk, Cherokee 75785
Rye, Liberty 77369
S Padre Isl E, Cameron 78597
Sabinal, Uvalde 78881
Sabine Pass, Jefferson 77655
Sachse, Dallas 75048
Sacul, Nacogdoches 75788
Sadler, Grayson 76264
Sagerton, Haskell 79548
Saginaw
(See Fort Worth)
Saint Hedwig, Bexar 78152
Saint Jo, Montague 76265
Salado, Bell 76571
Salineno, Starr 78585
Salt Flat, Hudspeth 79847
Saltillo, Hopkins 75478
Sam Norwood, Collingsworth 79077
SAN ANGELO, Tom Green
(See Page 3927)
SAN ANTONIO, Bexar
(See Page 3929)
San Augustine, San Augustine 75972
San Benito, Cameron 78586
San Diego, Duval 78384
San Elizario, El Paso 79849
San Felipe, Austin 77473
San Isidro, Starr 78588
San Juan, Hidalgo 78589
San Leon, Galveston 77539
SAN MARCOS, Hays
(See Page 3961)
San Perlita, Willacy 78590
San Saba, San Saba 76877
San Ygnacio, Zapata 78067
Sanctuary, Tarrant 76020
Sanderson, Terrell 79848
Sandia, Jim Wells 78383
Sanford, Hutchinson 79078
Sanger, Denton 76266
Santa Anna, Coleman 76878
Santa Clara, Guadalupe 78124
Santa Elena, Starr 78591
SANTA FE, Galveston
(See Page 3962)
Santa Maria, Cameron 78592
Santa Rosa, Cameron 78593
Santo, Palo Pinto 76472
Saragosa, Reeves 79780
Saratoga, Hardin 77585
Sargent
(See Bay City)
Sarita, Kenedy 78385
Satin, Falls 76685
Savannah, Denton 76227
Savoy, Fannin 75479
Schertz, Guadalupe 78108
Schertz, Guadalupe 78154
Schulenburg, Fayette 78956
Schwertner, Williamson 76573
Scotland, Archer 76379
Scottsville, Harrison 75688
Scroggins, Franklin 75480
Scurry, Kaufman 75158
Seabrook, Harris 77586
Seadrift, Calhoun 77983
Seagoville, Dallas 75159
Seagraves, Gaines 79359
Sealy, Austin 77474
Sebastian, Willacy 78594
Security Services, Bexar 78236
Segno, Polk 77351
SEGUIN, Guadalupe
(See Page 3963)
Selma, Guadalupe 78154
Selman City, Rusk 75689
Seminole, Gaines 79360
Seven Points, Kaufman 75143
Seymour, Baylor 76380
Shady Shores, Denton 76208
Shafter, Presidio 79843
Shallowater, Lubbock 79363
Shamrock, Wheeler 79079
Shavano Park
(See San Antonio)
Sheffield, Pecos 79781
Shelbyville, Shelby 75973
Shenandoah, Montgomery 77380
Shepherd, San Jacinto 77371
Sheppard Afb, Wichita 76311
Sheridan, Colorado 77475
SHERMAN, Grayson
(See Page 3964)
Shiner, Lavaca 77984
Shiro, Grimes 77876
Shoreacres, Harris 77571
Sidney, Comanche 76474
Sienna Plantation, Fort Bend 77459
Sierra Blanca, Hudspeth 79851
Silsbee, Hardin 77656
Silver, Coke 76945
Silver, Coke 76949
Silverton, Briscoe 79257
Simms, Bowie 75574
Simonton, Fort Bend 77476
Singleton, Grimes 77831
Sinton, San Patricio 78387
Skellytown, Carson 79080
Skidmore, Bee 78389
Slaton, Lubbock 79364
Slidell, Wise 76267
Slocum, Anderson 75839
Smiley, Gonzales 78159
Smithland, Marion 75657
Smithville, Bastrop 78957
Smyer, Hockley 79367
Snook, Burleson 77878
SNYDER, Scurry
(See Page 3966)
Socorro
(See El Paso)
Somerset, Bexar 78069
Somerville, Burleson 77879
Sonora, Sutton 76950
Sour Lake, Hardin 77659
South Bend, Young 76481
South Houston, Harris 77587
South Lake, Tarrant 76092
South Mountain, Coryell 76528
South Padre Island, Cameron 78597
South Plains, Floyd 79258
South Texarkana, Bowie 75501
Southlake, Tarrant 76092
Southland, Lubbock 79364
Southmayd, Grayson 76268
Spade, Lamb 79369
Speaks, Lavaca 77964
Spearman, Hansford 79081
Spicewood, Travis 78669
Splendora, Montgomery 77372
Spofford, Maverick 78877
SPRING, Harris
(See Page 3966)
Spring Branch, Comal 78070
Springlake, Lamb 79082
Springtown, Parker 76082
Spur, Dickens 79370
Spurger, Tyler 77660
St Paul, Collin 75098
STAFFORD, Fort Bend
(See Page 3976)
Stagecoach, Montgomery 77355
Stamford, Jones 79553
Stanton, Martin 79782
Staples, Guadalupe 78670
Star, Mills 76880
Stephenville, Erath 76401
Sterling City, Sterling 76951
Stinnett, Hutchinson 79083
Stockdale, Wilson 78160
Stonewall, Gillespie 78671
Stowell, Chambers 77661
Stratford, Sherman 79084
Strawn, Palo Pinto 76475
Streetman, Freestone 75859
Sublime, Lavaca 77986
Sudan, Lamb 79371
SUGAR LAND, Fort Bend
(See Page 3976)
Sullivan City, Hidalgo 78595
Sulphur Bluff, Hopkins 75481
SULPHUR SPRINGS, Hopkins
(See Page 3981)
Summerfield, Castro 79085
Sumner, Lamar 75486
Sun City, Williamson 78628
Sundown, Hockley 79372
Sunnyvale, Dallas 75182
Sunray, Moore 79086
Sunrise Beach, Llano 78643
Sunset, Montague 76270
Sunset Valley
(See Austin)
Surfside Beach, Brazoria 77541
Sutherland Springs, Wilson 78161
Sweeny, Brazoria 77480
Sweet Home, Lavaca 77987
Sweetwater, Nolan 79556
Swinney Switch, San Patricio 78368
Sylvester, Fisher 79560
Taft, San Patricio 78390
Tahoka, Lynn 79373
Talco, Franklin 75487
Talpa, Coleman 76882
Tarpley, Bandera 78883
Tarzan, Martin 79783
Tatum, Rusk 75691
Taylor, Williamson 76574
Taylor Lake Village, Harris 77586
Taylor Landing, Jefferson 77705
Teague, Freestone 75860
Tehuacana, Limestone 76686
Telegraph, Edwards 76883
Telephone, Fannin 75488
Telferner, Victoria 77988
Tell, Childress 79259
TEMPLE, Bell
(See Page 3981)
Tenaha, Shelby 75974
Tennessee Colony, Anderson 75861
Tennyson, Coke 76953
Terlingua, Brewster 79852
TERRELL, Kaufman
(See Page 3983)
Terrell Hills, Bexar 78209
TEXARKANA, Bowie
(See Page 3984)
TEXAS CITY, Galveston
(See Page 3986)
Texhoma, Sherman 73960
Texline, Dallam 79087
Texon, Reagan 76932
The Colony, Denton 75056
The Hills, Travis 78738
The Woodlands, Montgomery 77354
Thicket, Hardin 77374
Thomaston, De Witt 77989
Thompsons, Fort Bend 77481
Thorndale, Milam 76577
Thornton, Limestone 76687
Thorntonville, Ward 79756
Thrall, Williamson 76578
Three Rivers, Live Oak 78071
Throckmorton, Throckmorton 76483
Tiki Island, Galveston 77554
Tilden, Mcmullen 78072
Timbercreek Canyon, Randall 79118
Timpson, Shelby 75975
Tioga, Grayson 76271
Tivoli, Refugio 77990
Todd Mission, Grimes 77363
Tokio, Yoakum 79376
Tolar, Hood 76476
Tom Bean, Grayson 75090
TOMBALL, Harris
(See Page 3987)
Tool, Kaufman 75143
Tornillo, El Paso 79853
Tow, Llano 78672
Toyah, Reeves 79785
Toyahvale, Reeves 79786
Trent, Taylor 79561
Trenton, Fannin 75490
Trinidad, Henderson 75163
Trinity, Trinity 75862
Trophy Club, Denton 76262
Troup, Smith 75789
Troy, Bell 76579
Truscott, Foard 79227
Tuleta, Bee 78162
Tulia, Swisher 79088
Turkey, Hall 79261
Turnertown, Rusk 75689
Tuscola, Taylor 79562
Twitty, Wheeler 79079
Tye, Taylor 79563
TYLER, Smith
(See Page 3989)
Tynan, Bee 78391
Uhland, Hays 78640
Umbarger, Randall 79091
Universal City, Bexar 78148
Utopia, Uvalde 78884
UVALDE, Uvalde
(See Page 3994)
Va Hospital, Harris 77030
Valentine, Presidio 79854
Valera, Coleman 76884
Valle De Oro, Oldham 79010
Valley Mills, Bosque 76689
Valley Spring, Llano 76885
Valley View, Cooke 76272
Van, Van Zandt 75790
Van Alstyne, Grayson 75495
Van Horn, Culberson 79855
Van Vleck, Matagorda 77482
Vancourt, Tom Green 76955
Vanderbilt, Jackson 77991
Vanderpool, Bandera 78885
Vealmoor, Howard 79720
Vega, Oldham 79092
Venus, Johnson 76084
Vera, Baylor 76380
Verhalen, Reeves 79772
Veribest, Tom Green 76886
VERNON, Wilbarger
(See Page 3994)
VICTORIA, Victoria
(See Page 3994)
VIDOR, Orange
(See Page 3997)
Vigo Park, Swisher 79088
Village Mills, Hardin 77663
Village Of The Hills, Travis 78738
Vinton, El Paso 79821
Voca, Mcculloch 76887
Volente, Williamson 78641
Von Ormy, Bexar 78073
Voss, Coleman 76888
Votaw, Hardin 77376
WACO, Mclennan
(See Page 3997)
Wadsworth, Matagorda 77483
Waelder, Gonzales 78959
Waka, Ochiltree 79093
Wake Village, Bowie 75501
Walburg, Williamson 78673
Wall, Tom Green 76957
Waller, Harris 77484
Wallis, Austin 77485
Wallisville, Chambers 77597
Walnut Springs, Bosque 76690
Warda, Fayette 78960
Waring, Kendall 78074
Warren, Tyler 77664
Warrenton, Fayette 78961
Washington, Washington 77880
Waskom, Harrison 75692
Watauga
(See Fort Worth)
Water Valley, Tom Green 76958
WAXAHACHIE, Ellis
(See Page 4000)
Wayside, Armstrong 79094
WEATHERFORD, Parker
(See Page 4002)
Webberville, Bastrop 78621
Webster, Harris 77598
Weesatche, Goliad 77993
Weimar, Colorado 78962
Weinert, Haskell 76388
Weir, Williamson 78674
Welch, Dawson 79377
Wellborn, Brazos 77881
Wellington, Collingsworth 79095
Wellman, Terry 79378
Wells, Cherokee 75976
WESLACO, Hidalgo
(See Page 4004)
West, Mclennan 76691
West Columbia, Brazoria 77486
West Lake Hills, Travis 78746
West Lake Hls, Travis 78746
West Orange, Orange 77630
West Point, Fayette 78963
West Tawakoni, Hunt 75474
West University Place, Harris 77005
Westbrook, Mitchell 79565
Westhoff, De Witt 77994
Westlake, Denton 76262
Westminster, Collin 75485
Weston, Collin 75097
Weston Lakes, Fort Bend 77441
Westworth Village, Tarrant 76114
Wetmore
(See San Antonio)
Wharton, Wharton 77488
Wheeler, Wheeler 79096
Wheelock, Robertson 77882
White Deer, Carson 79097
White Oak, Gregg 75693
White Settlement, Tarrant 76108
Whiteface, Cochran 79379
Whitehouse, Smith 75791
Whitesboro, Grayson 76273
Whitewright, Grayson 75491
Whitharral, Hockley 79380
Whitney, Hill 76692
Whitsett, Live Oak 78075
Whitt, Parker 76490
Whon, Coleman 76878
WICHITA FALLS, Wichita
(See Page 4006)
Wickett, Ward 79788
Wiergate, Newton 75977
Wildorado, Oldham 79098
Wilford Hall Usaf Hosp, Bexar 78236
WILLIS, Montgomery
(See Page 4009)
Willow City, Gillespie 78675
Willow Park, Parker 76008
Wills Point, Van Zandt 75169
Wilmer, Dallas 75172
Wilson, Lynn 79381
Wimberley, Hays 78676
Winchester, Fayette 78945
Windcrest
(See San Antonio)
Windom, Fannin 75492
Windthorst, Archer 76389
Winfield, Titus 75493
Wingate, Runnels 79566
Wink, Winkler 79789
Winnie, Chambers 77665
Winnsboro, Wood 75494
Winona, Smith 75792
Winters, Runnels 79567
Wixon Valley, Brazos 77808
Woden, Nacogdoches 75978
Wolfe City, Hunt 75496
Wolfforth, Lubbock 79382
Woodcreek, Hays 78676
Woodlake, Trinity 75865
Woodlawn, Harrison 75694
Woodloch, Montgomery 77302
Woodsboro, Refugio 78393
Woodson, Throckmorton 76491
Woodville, Tyler 75979
Woodway, Mclennan 76712
Wortham, Freestone 76693
Wrightsboro, Gonzales 78677
Wylie, Collin 75098
Yancey, Medina 78886
Yantis, Wood 75497
Yoakum, Lavaca 77995
Yorktown, De Witt 78164
Ysleta Del Sur Pueblo
(See El Paso)
Zapata, Zapata 78076
Zavalla, Angelina 75980
Zephyr, Brown 76890

ABILENE TX

General Delivery 79604

POST OFFICE BOXES MAIN OFFICE STATIONS AND BRANCHES

Box No.s
1 - 3968 79604
4011 - 7736 79608
9998 - 9998 79604
9998 - 9998 79608

RURAL ROUTES

01, 06, 08, 12 79601
02, 05, 10, 14, 17, 20, 21 79602
04 79603
09 79605
03, 07, 11, 15, 22 79606

NAMED STREETS

W Access Dr 79602
Ackers Rd 79601
Adam Ave 79602
Airport Blvd 79602
Airport Parking Cir 79602
Alameda Rd 79605
N Alameda Rd 79603
Alamo Dr 79605
Albany St 79605
Alex Way 79602
Alisons Way 79602
Allen Acres 79602
Almond St 79601
Amanda 79601
Amarillo Ct & St 79602
Ambler Ave
100-198 79601
200-1699 79601
1700-3999 79603
E Ambler Ave 79601
Ambrocio Flores Jr Rd 79603
American Dr 79606
Amherst Dr 79603
Amy Cir 79606
Amy Lynn Ave 79603
Anderson St 79603
Andy St 79605
Angels Breath Rd 79601
Angie Ln 79602
Ann Arbor Ln 79603
Annette Ln 79606
Anson Ave
300-1699 79601
1700-2299 79603
Anthony St 79603
Antilley Rd 79606
Apache Ln 79601
Apple Blossom Dr 79602
Arapaho Trl 79606
Arlington Ave 79606
Arnold Blvd 79605
N Arnold Blvd 79603
Arrington Rd 79606
Arrow Pt 79601
Arrowhead Dr 79606
Arthurs Cir 79606
Ash St 79601
Aspen Dr 79601
Atlantic Dr 79606
Auburn Dr 79602
Augusta Dr 79606
Austin St 79601
Autumn Sage Ln 79606
Avenida Cortez 79602
Avenida De Baca 79602
Avenida De Coronada 79602
Avenida De Leon 79602
Avenida De Silva 79602
Avenue E 79601
Avenue D 79601
Avenue F 79601
Aviator Dr 79606
Avondale St 79605
Aztec Dr 79605
Aztec Rd 79602
Bacacita Farms Rd 79602
Bacon Dr 79601
Baird St 79602
Baize Rd 79602
Baker St 79605
Balboa Bch 79606
Bald Eagle St 79605
Ballinger St 79605
Bandana Ln 79602
Bar B Trl 79602
Barrow St 79605
Bay Bridge Cir 79602
Bay Hill Dr 79606
Bay Shore Ct 79602
Bay Water Dr 79602
Baylor St 79602
Beacon Hill Rd 79601
Beall Blvd 79606
Beck Ave 79606
Beckham St 79603
Beech St 79601
Beechwood Ln 79603
Bel Air Dr 79603
Bell Plains Rd 79606
Belmont Blvd 79602
Belton St 79605
Beltway N 79601
Beltway S
901-1097 79602
Beltway S
1099-1499 79602
1700-5299 79606
E Beltway S 79602
Ben Richey Dr 79602
Benbrook St 79605
Benelli Dr 79602
Bennett Dr 79605
Bent Tree Dr 79602
Benz Dr 79602
Beretta Dr 79602
Berry Ln 79602
Bettes Ln 79606
Bickley St 79605
Big Bend Trl 79602
Big Sky Dr 79606
Big Water Trl 79602
Biltmore Ct 79606
Birch Dr 79606
Birchwood St 79603
Bird Blvd 79601
Bishop Rd 79606
Black St 79602
Blackburn Rd 79602
Blackfoot Rd 79601
Blackhawk Rd 79602
Blair St 79605
Bledsoe Rd 79606
Blue Jay Ct 79605
Blue Quail Dr 79605
Bluebird Ln 79602
Bluebonnet Ct 79606
Blueridge Dr 79605
Bluff Crest Ln 79601
Bob O Link Dr 79606
Bob White Ct 79605
Bobby St 79602
Bois Darc St 79601
Bonanza Dr 79602
Bonnie Cir 79606
Boogaloo Ln 79602
Booth St 79605
Boston Rd 79601
N Bowie Dr 79603
S Bowie Dr 79605
Boynton Rd 79606
Boys Ranch Rd 79602
Bramlett Trl 79601
Brantley Cir 79606
Bratton Ct 79601
Braune Rd
200-498 79603
500-1299 79603
1300-2499 79606
Brenda Ln 79606
Brentwood Dr
2000-2899 79605
3100-3299 79606
Briar Cliff Path 79602
Briarwood St 79603
Brick Rd 79601
Bridge Ave 79603
Bridle Path Ct & Ln 79606
Bristol Ct 79606
Broadway St 79605
Broken Bough Trl 79606
Bronco Dr 79602
Brook Dr 79602
Brookhaven St 79605
Brookhollow Dr 79605
Bruce Dr 79606
Bruce Way 79601
Buccaneer Dr 79605
Buckshot Rd 79602
Buckskin Rd 79602
Buffalo Gap Rd
2400-2502 79605
2501-2501 79608
2503-4199 79605
2504-4198 79605
4200-8299 79606
Bumpergate Rd 79603
Bunker Hill Dr 79601
Burbank Dr 79605
Burger St 79603
Burl Harris Dr 79602
Buttercup Dr 79606
Butterfield Trl 79606
Butterfield School Rd 79606
Butternut St 79602
Button Willow Ave & Pkwy 79606
Bynum Ln & St 79602
Byrd Dr 79601
Byron Pl 79601
Caballo Dr 79602
Cactus Ln 79602
Cactus Trl 79605
Cactus Rose Trl 79602
Caddo Dr 79602
Caldwell Rd 79601
Caldwell St 79603
Cambridge Ct 79603
Campbell Dr 79602
Campus Ct 79601
Camri Ln 79602
Canterbury Dr 79602
Canyon Ct 79601
Canyon Ln S 79606
Canyon Rock Ct & Rd 79606
Capitol Ave 79603
Caprock Rd 79606
Cardinal Ln 79602
Carl St 79605
Carnation Ct 79606
Carrera Ln 79602
Carriage Rd 79605
Carrie Ann Ln 79606
Carter Ln 79602
N Carver St 79601
Castle Dr 79602
Castle Rd 79606
Castle St 79602
Castle Rock Cv 79602
Catalina Ct & Dr 79606
Catclaw Dr 79606
Caton Pl 79605
Cecil St 79603
Cedar Bnd 79602
Cedar St 79601
Cedar Branch Ct 79606
Cedar Crest Dr 79601
Cedar Lake Dr 79606
Cedar Run Rd 79606
Central St 79605
Central Park Blvd 79606
Cerromar St 79606
Cessna Dr 79601
Chachalaca Ln 79605
Champions Dr 79606
Chanticleers Ln 79602
Chaparral Cir 79605
Chapel Hill Rd 79605
Chariot Cir 79602
Charles Ln 79606
Charter House Dr 79606
Chateau Dr 79603
Chaucer Dr 79602
Cherokee Cir 79601
Cherokee Hills Ln 79606
Cherry St 79602
Cherry Bark St 79606
Cherry Blossom Dr 79602
Cherry Hills St 79606
Cheshire Dr 79601
Chestnut St 79602
Cheyenne Cir 79601
Chickasaw Rd 79601
Chiggers Trl 79602
Chimney Cir 79606
Chimney Rock Ct & Rd 79606
Chimneywood Ct 79602
China St 79602
Choctaw Pt 79601
Chris Dr 79606
Christopher Dr 79602
Chriswood Dr 79601
Chucker Ct 79605
Church St 79601
Cicily Ln 79606
Cinch Trl 79606
Cinderella Ln 79602
Cindy Kay Trl 79602
Circle Dr 79602
Circle Nineteen 79606
Circle Of Holly 79605
Circle One 79606
Circle Twenty 79606
N Clack St
100-2499 79603
3200-3998 79601
4000-4100 79601
4102-4798 79601
S Clack St
104-1998 79605
2000-3298 79606
3300-6000 79606
6002-7998 79606
Clairmont St 79605
Clariece Dr 79606
Clark Rd 79602
Clarks Dr 79602
Clearlake Ct 79606
Clearwater Ct 79602
Clinton St 79603
Clipper Ct & Dr 79606
Clover Ln 79606
Cloverleaf Ln 79601
Clyde St 79605
Coachlight Rd 79603
Cobblestone Ln 79606
Cockerell Dr 79601
Cocopah Trl 79606
Codybug Rd 79602
Cole Dr 79606
College Dr 79601
College St
1900-2099 79602
2200-3299 79605
Collett Rd 79601
Collins Ave 79603
Collins Dock Cir 79601
Colonial Dr 79603
Colony Hill Rd 79602
Colt Ct & Rd 79606
Columbia Dr 79605
Comanche Trl 79601
Commerce Dr 79603
Compere Blvd 79601
Concord Ct & Dr 79603
Conestoga Dr 79606
Congress Ave & Ct 79603
Connally St 79602
Constitution Ave 79601
Contera Ct 79602
Continental Ave 79601
Contour Dr 79606
Cooke St 79605
Cool Breeze Cir 79601
Cooper Ct 79602
Cornell Dr 79602
Cornerstone Ct 79602
Coronado Ct 79605
Corsicana Ave
200-1799 79605
2200-2399 79606
Cotton Candy Rd 79602
Cottonwood St 79601
Cougar Way 79606
Country Pl S 79606
Countryside Cir & Dr 79606
County Road 100 79601
County Road 101 79601
County Road 102 79601
County Road 103 N & W 79601
County Road 105 79601
County Road 107 79601
County Road 108 N & W 79601
County Road 109 S 79602
County Road 110 79602
County Road 114 79601
County Road 115 79602
County Road 123 79601
County Road 137 79601
County Road 141 79602
County Road 150 79601
County Road 151 79601
County Road 152 79601
County Road 153 79601
County Road 154 79601
County Road 155 79601
County Road 156 79601
County Road 203 79602
County Road 207 79601
County Road 215 79602
County Road 218 79602
County Road 219 79601
County Road 220 79602
County Road 222 79602
County Road 224 79602
County Road 226 79602
County Road 227 79602
County Road 228 79602
County Road 229 79601
County Road 232 79602
County Road 238 79602
County Road 239 79601
County Road 242 79602
County Road 256 79606
County Road 257 79606
County Road 258 79602
County Road 264 79602
County Road 270 79601
County Road 289 79606
County Road 290 79606
County Road 291 79606
County Road 297
300-599 79603
County Road 297
700-1399 79606
County Road 298 79603
County Road 300
200-699 79603
12000-12299 79601
County Road 301
100-1099 79603
13401-13597 79601
13599-16199 79601
County Road 302 79601
County Road 303
5400-5499 79602
9500-12100 79601
12102-12898 79601
County Road 304 79601
County Road 306 79601
County Road 307 79601
County Road 309 79601
County Road 310 79601
County Road 311 79601
County Road 313
101-199 79606
9900-11699 79601
County Road 314 79606
County Road 315
100-199 79606
13200-14199 79601
County Road 316 79606
County Road 318
101-197 79606
199-1599 79606
10001-10099 79601
County Road 319
200-400 79606
402-698 79606
4300-7299 79601
County Road 320 79601
County Road 321
100-399 79606
7001-7059 79601
7061-7199 79601
County Road 325 79601
County Road 327 79601
County Road 329 79601
County Road 331
100-199 79606
7200-7599 79601
County Road 332 79606
County Road 334 79601
County Road 335 79606
County Road 337 79606
County Road 339 79601
County Road 341 79601
County Road 347 79601
County Road 348 79601
County Road 353 79601
County Road 355 79601
County Road 356 79601
County Road 370 79601
County Road 406 79601
County Road 408 79601
County Road 412 79601
County Road 494 79603
County Road 503 79601
County Road 504 79601
County Road 505 79601
County Road 511 79601
County Road 522 79601
County Road 583 79606
County Road 584 79606
County Road 587 79606
County Road 660
100-198 79601
200-299 79603
County Road 661 79606
Courtyard Ln 79606
Cove Rd
100-200 79601
201-239 79602
202-298 79601
241-299 79601
300-599 79602
9300-9899 79601
Covenant Dr 79606
Coventry Cir 79602
Covey Ln 79605
Coyote Run 79602
Craig Dr 79606
Crawford Dr 79602
Creek Bend Ct 79602
Crescent Dr 79605
Crest Way 79606
Crestline Dr 79602
Crestwood Dr 79603
S Crockett Dr 79605
N Crockett St 79603
Crooked Branch Cir 79602
Crooked Creek Rd 79602
Crooked Trail Dr 79602
Crossroads Dr 79605
Crown Pl 79606
Crows Nest Rd 79601
Crystal Crk 79606
Cullar Dr 79602
Curry Ln
2900-3399 79605
3400-5399 79606
Cynthia Ct 79602
Cypress St 79601
Cypress Point St 79606
Daisy Ct 79606
Dana Ct 79606
N Danville Dr
800-2499 79603
2501-2599 79603
3601-4399 79601
4800-4898 79601
S Danville Dr
100-4499 79605
4500-5099 79602
Darrell Dr 79606
Davids Ct 79602
Davis Dr 79605
Dawn Ct 79605
Dayton Dr 79605
Deborah Dr 79601
Dee Ann Ct 79606
Deer Trl 79602
Deer Field Trl 79602
Deer Run Dr 79601
Deerwood Ln 79606
Delano St 79601
Delaware Rd
400-498 79605
401-2997 79606
2999-3199 79606
Delwood Dr 79603
Denton St 79605
Derby Rd 79606
Derrick Dr 79601
Diamond Lake Dr 79601
Dillingham St 79603
Dimmitt St 79602
Directors Pkwy 79606
Dixon Rd 79601
Dollar Bill Dr 79602
Dominion Ct 79606
Don Juan St 79605
Dove Cir 79605
Dove Creek Path 79602
Driftwood Ct 79602
Drovers Ln 79602
Drummond Rd 79606
Dub Wright Blvd
1400-1499 79605
3500-3599 79606
3601-3699 79606
Duchess Ave 79606
Duke Ln 79602
Dundee St 79606
Dunnam Dr 79602
Durango Dr 79605
Durham Cir 79606
Dusty Ct 79606
Dutton Cir 79601
Dyess Farms Ln 79606
Eagle Dr 79605
Eagle Pass Rd 79602
Earls Cv 79606
N East St 79606
Eastover Dr 79601
Echo Ct 79602
Edge Cliff Ct 79606
Edgemont Ct 79605
Edgemont Dr
1300-2099 79602
2100-3499 79605
4200-4899 79606
Edgewater Rd 79602
Edgewood Dr 79605
Edna St 79602
Edward Ct 79601
Elijah Ln 79605
Elm St 79602
Elm Cove Cir & Dr 79605
Elm Creek Rd 79601
Elmdale Rd 79601
Elmdale Rd N 79601

Elmdale Rd S 79602
Elmwood Dr 79605
Enchanted Rock Rd 79606
Encino Rd 79605
Energy Dr 79602
Eplens Ct 79605
Erie Cir & St 79605
Esman Ct 79606
Estates Dr 79602
Estes St 79602
Evergreen St 79601
Expo Dr 79602
Ezra St 79602
Fair Dr 79601
Fairfield Pl 79606
Fairmont St 79605
Fairmount St 79605
Fairway Oaks Blvd 79606
Falcon Dr 79606
Fannin St 79603
Fawn Ln 79602
Fieldstone Rd 79602
Filly Ct & Rd 79606
Firedog Rd 79606
Fishing Village Cir 79601
Five Oaks Rd 79606
Five Points Pkwy 79603
Flat Water Dr 79602
Flintrock Dr 79606
Fm 1082 79601
Fm 1178 S 79602
Fm 1235 79606
N Fm 1235 79603
Fm 1750 79602
Fm 18 79602
Fm 2404 79601
Fm 2833 79601
Fm 3034 79601
Fm 3308 79601
Fm 3522 79601
S Fm 600 79601
Fm 603 79602
Fm 604 N 79601
Fm 707 S
8200-8399 79602
S Fm 707
3800-5499 79606
Fm 89 79606
Foothill Rd 79602
Foothills Rd 79601
Formosa St 79602
Forrest Ave 79603
Forrest Hill Rd 79606
Fortune Ave 79601
Foster Ln 79601
Founders Pl 79601
Foxfire Dr 79606
Foxmoor Ct 79605
Fradinto St 79601
Franklin St 79601
Frenchmans Creek Rd 79605
Friars St 79602
Fulton St
1900-2099 79602
2300-3199 79605
Fulwiler Rd 79603
Gann St 79601
Garden Grove Ln 79606
Gardenia Cir 79605
Garfield Ave 79601
Gary Ln 79601
Gateway 79602
Gathright Dr 79606
Gays Way 79606
Georgetown Dr 79602
Gibson St 79603
Gill Dr 79601
Gilmer Ave 79606
Glen Abbey Ct & St 79606
Glen Eagles Ct 79601
Glendale Dr 79603
Glenhaven Dr 79603
Glenna Dr 79606
Glenwood Dr 79605
Golden Eagle St 79605
Goliad Dr 79601
Graham St 79603
Grand Ave
100-299 79606
300-316 79605
301-317 79606
318-3699 79605
Granite Cir 79606
Grape St 79601
Green St 79603
Green Acres Rd 79605
Green Bay Cir 79602
Green Meadows Cir 79605
Green Valley Dr 79601
Greenbriar Dr 79605
Greenfield Rd 79602
Greenridge Ct 79602
Greenslope Dr 79606
Greenthread St 79606
Griffith Rd 79601
Griggs St 79602
Grouse Ct 79605
Grove St 79605
Hacienda Ranch Dr 79602
Hailey St 79602
Hamilton St 79602
Hampton Hills St 79606
Handsome Jack Rd 79602
Harbour Town St 79606
Hardison Ln 79602
Hardwick Rd 79606
Hardy St 79601
Harmony Dr 79603
Harrisburg Rd 79602
Harrison Ave 79601
Hartford St 79605
Harvard Pl 79603
Harwell St 79601
Harwood St 79605
Hawk Cir 79605
Hawn Cir 79605
Hawthorne St 79605
Hayter Rd 79601
Healing Water Trl 79602
Health Center Dr 79606
Hearne Dr 79606
Hearthstone Ct 79606
Heartland Ct 79606
Hedges Rd 79605
Helena Cir 79606
Hendrick Dr 79602
Hendricks Cir & Dr 79602
Henson St 79603
Heritage Cir & Ln 79606
Hi Vu Dr 79606
Hialeah Ct & Dr 79606
Hickory St 79601
Hidden Valley Dr 79603
High St 79603
High Life Cir 79606
High Meadows Dr 79605
High Sierra 79606
Highland Ave 79605
Hill St 79602
Hill Country Dr 79606
Hill Haven Dr 79601
Hillcrest Dr 79601
Hilliard Cir 79601
Hillside Rd
201-297 79606
299-399 79606
700-2000 79603
2002-2198 79603
Hilltop Rd 79601
Hillview Rd 79601
Hilton Head 79606
Hohertz St 79603
Holbron St 79603
Holiday St 79605
Hollis Dr 79605
Holly Way 79606
Hollywood Dr 79602
Homestead Pl 79601
Honey Bee Rd 79601
Honeysuckle Ct 79606
Honor Roll Ct 79606
Hope St 79603
Horintri Dr 79606
Horseshoe Cir 79602
Hospital Dr & Pl 79606
Houston St 79601
Hoylake Dr 79606
Huckleberry Ln
700-1699 79601
1700-2399 79603
Hummingbird Cir 79606
Hunt St 79605
Hunters Cir 79606
Hunters Glen Rd 79605
Huntington Pl 79606
Huron Dr 79603
Ians Ct 79606
Iberis Rd S 79606
Ida Ln 79602
Idle Creek Trl 79602
Idlewild St
1700-1999 79602
2100-2599 79605
Impact Dr 79603
Independence Blvd 79601
Indian Trl 79602
Industrial Blvd
200-2299 79602
2300-2799 79605
4200-4298 79602
E Industrial Blvd 79602
Ingram Ln 79602
Innisbrook Dr 79606
Interlachon St 79606
Interstate 20 W
11800-11899 79601
E Interstate 20 79601
W Interstate 20
4100-5598 79603
Inverness St 79606
Inverrary Dr 79606
Inwood Ln 79605
Iris St 79603
Iron Eagle Rd 79602
Ivanhoe Ln 79605
Ivy Ln 79603
Jachintr St 79602
Jackson St 79602
Jamaica St 79601
James Ct 79606
Jameson St 79603
Jamestown Rd 79602
Janice Ln 79603
Janna Dr 79606
Jarman St 79601
Jeanette St 79602
Jefferies St 79603
S Jefferson Dr 79605
N Jefferson St 79603
Jennifer Cir & Ln 79606
Jennings Dr 79606
Jeremy Ln 79602
Jerome St 79602
Jester Cir 79606
Jet St 79606
John C Stevens St 79601
John Carroll Dr 79606
John Knox Dr 79606
Johnson Rd 79601
Jolly Rogers Rd 79601
Joseph Cir 79602
N Judge Ely Blvd 79601
S Judge Ely Blvd 79602
Juniper Cir 79605
Justice Way 79602
Kala Dr 79606
Kallies Cv 79606
Kansas St 79603
Karen Dr 79606
Kellye Ct 79606
Kenny Cir 79606
Kensington Dr 79605
Kenwood Dr 79601
Kerry Ln 79606
Kevin Ct 79606
Key Ln 79602
Killough Cv 79601
Kimble St 79605
Kings Ct 79605
Kings Cross St 79602
Kingsbury Rd 79602
Kingston Ct 79605
Kingwood Cir 79602
Kirkman St 79602
Kirkwood St 79603
Knights Ct 79606
Knollwood Ct & Dr 79606
Kristi Path 79602
Kyla Row 79605
La Cantera Ct 79606
La Hacienda Dr 79602
La Jolla Bch 79606
N La Salle Dr 79603
S La Salle Dr 79605
Laguna Dr 79605
S Lake Dr 79602
E Lake Rd 79601
W Lake Rd 79601
Lake Trl 79606
Lake Point Cir 79606
Lakeshore Dr 79602
Lakeside Dr 79602
Lakeview Rd 79602
Lakeway Dr 79602
Lakewood Dr 79601
Lamar Cir 79601
Lamesa Ave 79605
Lancaster Dr 79601
Lance Dr & Ln 79602
Lancelot Rd 79602
Lane Ave 79601
Lantana Ave 79606
Lariat Trl 79605
Lark Ct 79605
Larkin St 79603
Larned Ln 79602
Latigo Trl 79606
Laurel Ct 79606
Laurel Dr 79603
Lawrence Cir 79605
Lawyers Ln 79602
Legacy Dr 79606
Legends Trl 79601
N Leggett Dr 79603
S Leggett Dr 79605
Lewis Ln 79601
Lewis And Clark Trl 79602
Lexington Ave 79605
Liberty Blvd 79601
Lido Ct 79606
Ligustrum Dr 79605
Lilac Cir 79605
Lillius St 79603
Lily Ct 79606
Lincoln Dr 79601
Lincolnshire Way 79606
Linda Vis 79606
Link Belt Dr 79606
Lisa Ln 79601
S Litatte St 79605
Live Oak Trl 79606
Llano St 79605
Locust St 79602
Lollipop Trl 79602
Loma Vis 79601
Lone Star Dr 79602
Lonesome Dove Trl 79602
Long Shadows Ln 79606
Longbotham St 79602
Loop 322
400-499 79601
1400-4999 79602
N Loop 322 79601
Lost Tree Cir 79606
Lowden St
700-1699 79601
1700-2399 79603
E Lowden St 79601
Luzon St 79601
Lynbrook Dr 79606
Lynwood Ln 79605
Lytle Trl & Way 79602
Lytle Acres Dr 79602
Lytle Cove Rd 79602
Lytle Creek Dr 79602
Lytle Place Dr 79602
Lytle Shores Dr 79602
Lytle Way Cir 79602
Mabray Ln 79606
Madera Way 79602
Madison Ave 79601
Magnolia St 79603
Main St 79606
S Main St 79605
Majestic Sky 79606
Mallon Way 79606
Manciples Way 79602
Mandevilla Dr 79606
Manly Rd 79601
Many Waters Dr 79602
Maple St 79602
Marathon Ct & Rd 79601
Marauder Ct & Dr 79606
Margaritas Way 79606
Mariah 79602
Mark Ct 79606
Marlboro Dr 79606
Marlin Dr 79602
Marsalis Dr 79603
Marshall St 79605
Mary Lou Ln 79606
Matador St 79605
Matthew Ct 79602
Maxwell Dr 79602
Mccracken St 79602
Mcgee Dr 79602
Mcgeehee Rd 79606
Mcleod Dr 79602
Mcmahan St 79601
Meadow Dr 79606
Meadow Ln 79602
Meadow Lake Dr 79606
Meadowbrook Dr 79603
Meadowick Ln 79606
Meadowlark Dr 79601
Meander St 79602
Medical Dr 79601
Medina St 79606
Melinda Ln 79603
Melissa Ln 79606
Melrose St 79605
Memorial Dr 79606
Merchant St 79603
Merion St 79606
Mesa Bnd & Rdg 79606
Mesa Springs Blvd & Cir 79606
Mesquite Ln & St 79601
Michael Ct 79606
Mid Pines Cir 79606
Midway St 79602
Mikes Way 79602
Milestone Dr 79606
Milford St 79601
Military Dr 79605
Mill Ct 79603
Miller Ln 79602
Miller St 79605
Millie Ct 79606
Milliorn Ranch Rd 79606
Mimosa Dr 79603
Minda St 79602
Minter Ln 79603
Miss Ellie Ln 79602
Mission Hls 79606
Mistletoe Ct 79606
Mobile Dr 79601
N Mockingbird Ln 79603
S Mockingbird Ln 79605
Mohawk Rd 79601
Mohegan Rd 79601
Monroe St 79601
Monterrey Cir 79605
Monticello Cir & St 79605
Moonlight Dr 79606
Moore Dr & St 79605
Moore Park Rd 79601
Morning Side 79606
Morris St 79605
Morrow Ln 79601
Mossy Oak Dr 79602
Mourning Dove Ln 79606
Muirfield St 79606
Mulberry St 79601
E Musgrave Blvd 79601
Musgrave Trl 79606
Musken Rd 79601
Myrtle St 79601
Nandina Cir 79605
Navajo Cir 79602
Neas Rd 79601
Nelson St 79601
Nesmith Rd 79602
Newcastle Dr 79601
Newman Rd 79601
Nichols Rd 79602
Ninth Hole St 79603
Nonesuch Rd 79606
Nora Rd 79601
Nora Miller Rd 79602
North Dr 79605
North St 79603
E North 10th St 79601
E North 11th St 79601
E North 12th St 79601
E North 13th St 79601
E North 14th St 79601
E North 15th St 79601
E North 16th St 79601
E North 17th St 79601
E North 18th St 79601
E North 19th St 79601
E North 1st St 79601
E North 20th St 79601
E North 21st St 79601
E North 22nd St 79601
E North 23rd St 79601
E North 7th St 79601
Northland Ct 79601
Northshore Dr 79601
Northway Dr 79601
Notre Dame Cir & St 79602
Nottingham Rd 79602
Nugent Rd 79601
Nun Ct 79602
Oak St 79602
Oak Knoll St 79606
Oak Ridge Ct 79606
Oakland Dr 79603
Oaklawn Dr 79606
Oakmont St 79606
Oakwood Ln 79605
Ohlhausen Rd 79606
Oil Belt Ln 79605
Oil Center Dr 79601
Old Andy St 79605
Old Anson Rd
2200-3699 79603
3701-3897 79601
3899-4200 79601
4202-4498 79601
Old Coleman Hwy 79602
Old Elmdale Rd 79602
Old Forrest Hill Rd 79606
Old Ironsides Rd 79601
Old Key Ln 79602
Old Orchard Rd 79605
Oldham Ct & Ln W 79602
Olsen Blvd 79601
Olympic Cir 79606
Orange St 79601
Orange Blossom Dr 79602
Osage Rd 79601
Oscar St 79602
Over St
1900-2099 79602
2100-3199 79605
E Overland Trl 79601
W Overland Trl
300-1698 79601
1700-3198 79603
4100-4198 79601
8400-8498 79603
Oxford St 79605
Pack Saddle Pass 79602
Pack Saddle Farms Rd 79602
Paint Brush Dr 79606
Palm St 79602
Palomino Rd 79602
Pamela Dr 79606
Pardoners Rd 79602
Park Ave 79603
Parkcrest Dr 79605
Parker Dr 79602
Parramore St
1400-1699 79601
2000-2299 79603
Parsons Rd 79602
Partridge Pl 79605
Pasadena Dr 79601
Patricia Ln 79606
Patriot Dr 79606
Patriot Commons Rd 79601
Patsye Ann Cv 79606
Patty Lynn 79606
Peach St 79602
Peach Blossom Dr 79602
Peake St 79603
Pebble Beach St 79606
Pebblebrook Ct 79606
Pebbles Pl 79606
Pecan St 79602
Peeble Beach St 79606
Pemelton Dr 79601
Penney Ln 79606
Pennington Dr 79606
Pennington Rd 79602
Penrose Dr 79601
Pensacola Dr 79606
Peppergrass Ln 79606
Peppermill Ln 79606
Periwinkle Trl 79602
Petroleum Dr 79602
Pewter Ln 79601
Pheasant Dr 79606
Picadilly St 79606
Piedmont Dr 79601
Pilgrim Rd 79602
Pilot St 79606
Pin Oak Ct 79606
Pine St
100-400 79601
341-341 79604
401-5499 79601
402-5498 79601
Pinehurst St 79606
N Pioneer Dr 79603
S Pioneer Dr 79605
Piper Way 79601
Piping Rock Dr 79606
Plachenw St 79603
Play St 79602
Plaza St 79603
Pleasant Hill Dr 79601
Plover Ln 79606
Plum St 79601
Plymouth Rock Rd 79601
Pollard Rd 79602
Ponderosa Cir 79605
Poplar St 79602
Port Rd 79602
Portland Ave 79605
Post Oak Rd
2000-2699 79605
2700-3299 79606
Potomac Ave 79605
Potosi Rd 79602
Poverty Point Cir 79601
Pradera Cir 79606
Prado Verde Dr 79602
Prairie Creek Way 79602
Prairie Harvest Rd 79602
Prairie Moon Rd 79602
Prairie Star Rd 79602
Prairie View Ave 79606
Preakness Cir 79606
Presidio Ct & Dr 79605
Preston Trl 79606
Primrose Cir & Dr 79606
Princess Ln 79606

Princeton St 79602
Private Road 1031 79601
Private Road 1071 79601
Private Road 1080 79601
Private Road 2031 79602
Private Road 2180 79602
Private Road 2181 79602
Private Road 2201 79602
Private Road 2221 79602
Private Road 2222 79602
Private Road 2224 79602
Private Road 2225 79602
Private Road 2226 79602
Private Road 2227 79602
Private Road 2242 79602
Private Road 2243 79602
Private Road 2244 79602
Private Road 2246 79602
Private Road 2247 79602
Private Road 2282 79602
Private Road 2284 79602
Private Road 2286 79602
Private Road 2287 79602
Private Road 2309 79602
Private Road 2311 79602
Private Road 2371 79601
Private Road 2507 79602
Private Road 2545 79602
Private Road 3102 79601
Private Road 311 79601
Private Road 314 79601
Private Road 3141 79601
Private Road 320 79601
Private Road 3201 79601
Private Road 3203 79601
Private Road 322 79601
Private Road 324 79601
Private Road 325 79601
Private Road 326 79601
Private Road 327 79601
Private Road 333 79601
Private Road 340 79601
Private Road 341 79601
Private Road 3411 79601
Private Road 343 79601
Private Road 3481 79601
Private Road 355 79601
Proctor Dr 79603
Prominent Way 79606
Prosperity Rd 79602
Pueblo Dr 79605
Purdue Ln 79602
Purple Sage Rd 79602
Pyracanthia Cir 79605
Quail Ter 79606
Quail Nest Ln 79601
Quail Run St 79605
Quaker Rd 79602
Queen Anns Lace 79606
Queens Ct 79602
Questa Dr 79605
Quicksilver Rd 79602
Radcliff Rd 79602
Radford Dr 79601
Rain Dance Cir 79601
Rainey Rd 79601
Rainey Creek Ranch Rd 79602
Rainey Ridge Ln 79602
Raintree Cir 79605
Ranch Rd 79602
Randy Ave 79606
Raymonds Way 79602
Reading St 79603
Reagan Cir 79605
Rebecca Ln 79606
Red Hawk Cir & Ct 79605
Red Oak Cir 79606
Redbird Ln 79605
Redbud Cir 79605
Redwood Dr 79603
Reeves St 79602
Regent Dr 79605
Regional Plz 79606
Remington Rd 79602
Remuda Dr 79602
Republic Ave 79601
Revelie St 79605
Revere Ct 79601
Rex Allen Dr 79606
Rexie Cir 79606
Rhodes St
1600-1699 79601
2000-2099 79603
Rhonni Ct 79602
Riata Rd 79602
Richland Ct & Dr 79603
Richmond St 79605
Ricsan Rd 79605
Ridgecrest Dr 79602
Ridgeline Dr 79606
Ridgemont Dr 79606
Ridgmar Ln 79606
Ridgway Cir & Rd 79606
Rim Rock Rd 79606
Rio Mesa Dr 79606
Riomar Ct 79606
River Bend St 79603
River Oaks Cir & Rd ... 79605
Rivercrest Dr 79605
Riverside Blvd & Park .. 79605
Riviera Cir 79606
Roadrunner Ct 79601
Roanoak Dr 79603
Roberts St 79605
Robertson Dr 79606
Robin Rd 79605
Rocky Point Rd 79601
Rodeo Dr 79602
Rodgers St 79605
Rolling Green Dr 79606
Roma Ln 79603
Roosevelt St
1400-1699 79601
1700-2099 79603
Rosa St 79605
Rose St 79602
Rosedale Dr 79605
Rosewood Dr 79603
Ross Ave 79605
Rountree Dr 79601
Royal Court Cir 79606
Royal Crest Dr 79606
Ruby St 79605
Ruby Esther Cir 79606
Rucker St 79603
Rue Maison St 79605
Ruidosa Ave 79605
Running Water Trl 79602
Russell Ave 79605
Rusty Trl 79606
Ruswood Cir & Dr 79601
Ryan Cir 79606
Sable Cir 79606
Saddle Creek Rd 79602
Saddle Lake Spur 79602
S Saddle Lakes Dr 79602
Saddlewood Dr 79605
Sage Cir 79606
Sagehen Rdg 79605
Saint Andrews St 79606
Salinas Dr 79605
Sally Ct 79606
Sammons St 79605
San Jacinto Dr 79601
N San Jose Dr 79603
S San Jose Dr 79605
San Miguel Dr 79605
Sandefer St
700-1699 79601
1700-3299 79603
Sandpiper St 79602
Sandy St 79601
Sanford Ln 79602
Santa Barbara Dr 79601
Santa Fe St 79605
Santa Monica Dr 79605
Santos St 79605
Sawbuck Trl 79602
Saxon St 79605
Sayles Blvd 79605
Scenic Way 79602
Scoobie Trl 79602
Scooter Ct 79606
Scotland Ct 79601
Scott Pl 79601
Scottish Rd 79601
Scouts Cv 79606
Scranton Ln 79602
Seamans Way 79602
Sears Blvd 79603
Seminole Rd 79601
Sera Dr 79606
Serrot Ct 79602
Seth Ct 79606
Seville Cir 79606
Sewell St 79605
Shadow Way 79606
Shadow Wood Dr 79601
Shady Brook Cir 79605
Shady Glen Ln 79606
Shallow Water Trl 79602
Shanna 79601
Sharon Rd 79606
Shelton St 79603
Shenandoah Dr 79605
Shepherd St 79605
Shepherds Cv 79605
Sherbrooke Ln 79606
Shere Lynne Dr 79606
Sherman Dr 79605
Sherry Ln 79603
Sherwood Dr 79606
Shirley Rd
2300-2399 79603
2501-2897 79601
2899-6399 79601
Shoreline Cir & Dr 79602
Short St 79602
Shotgun N & S 79603
Sierra Sunset 79606
Silo View Rd 79601
Silver Oaks Dr 79606
Silver Shadow Dr 79602
Silver Spur Ln 79606
Simmons St 79601
Sioux Trl 79606
Sir Thopas Ct 79602
Skyline Dr 79606
Smith Dr 79601
Snipe Ln 79605
Somerset Pl 79601
E South 11th St 79602
E South 21st St 79602
E South 24th St 79602
E South 27th St 79602
E South 5th St 79602
E South 7th St 79602
Southern Cross Rd 79606
Southlake Dr 79602
Southmoor Dr 79606
Southwest Dr
2700-3499 79605
4100-5199 79606
Southwind Cir 79602
Spanish Trl 79603
Spanish Oak Ct 79606
Spears Cir 79601
Spindletop Dr 79602
Spinks Rd
100-698 79603
700-799 79603
801-3199 79603
5400-5598 79601
5600-6399 79601
6500-8999 79603
Spring Creek Rd
100-499 79601
4700-5199 79602
Springbrook St 79605
Springer Cir 79603
Springwater Ave 79606
Spur Trl 79606
E Spur 707 79602
Spyglass Hill Ct 79606
Spykes Rd 79601
Squires Rd 79602
Stafford St 79601
Stallion Rd 79606
E Stamford St 79601
W Stamford St
201-1699 79601
1701-5999 79603
Starlight Dr 79606
State St
800-1599 79601
1700-4899 79603
State Highway 351 79601
E State Highway 36 S & W 79602
Stephen St 79606
Sterling St 79606
Stevenson Dr 79601
Stewart Rd 79606
Stonecrest Ct & Dr 79606
Stonegate Rd 79606
Stonehedge Rd 79606
Stowe St 79605
Stratford St 79605
Sue Ellen Dr 79601
Sue Lookout 79606
Sugar Biscuit Ln 79602
Sugarberry Ave 79602
Sugarloaf Ave 79602
Summerhill Rd 79601
Summers St 79603
Summit Rd 79601
Summoner Ln 79602
Sunburst Rd 79602
Suncrest Dr 79606
Sundance Rd 79602
Sunflower Cir 79606
Sunlake Dr 79601
Sunnibrook Ct 79601
Sunrise Ave 79602
Sunset Dr 79605
Surrey Sq 79606
Susan St 79606
Sutherland St 79606
Swenson St 79603
Swift Water Dr 79602
Sycamore St 79602
Sylvan Dr 79605
T And P Ln 79602
Tabard Trl 79602
Tamarisk Cir 79606
Tamy Ct 79602
Tanglewood Rd 79605
Tannehill Dr 79602
Taos Dr 79605
Teakwood St 79601
Teel Dr 79606
Tempest Ln 79602
Teresa Ln 79606
Terri Ann Cir 79606
Texas Ave 79605
Texas St 79603
Thompson Pkwy 79606
Tierra Ct 79602
Timbercat Ct & Dr 79606
Timothy Ln 79602
Tiquewood Cir 79605
Titan St 79606
Todd Run 79606
Todd Trl 79602
Tom Roberts Dr 79602
Township Ct 79601
Tracy Lynn St 79601
Tradition Dr 79606
Trafalgar Sq 79605
Trail Blazer Dr 79602
Trail Creek Dr 79602
Trailend Dr 79601
Trails End Rd 79602
Trailway Dr 79601
Trainrider Way 79602
Transformer Trl 79602
Travis Ct 79605
N Treadaway Blvd 79601
S Treadaway Blvd 79602
Treanor Dr 79602
Trinity Ln 79602
Truman St 79601
Tulane Dr 79602
Turkey Run 79602
Turkey Creek Ln 79602
Turkey Trot Rd 79601
Turnberry Cir 79606
Turner Plz 79606
Turtle Cv 79601
Tuscany Dr 79606
Tweetie Pie Ln 79602
Twin Crk 79606
Twin Oaks Dr 79606
Twylight Trl 79606
Uinsoal Rd 79602
Union Ln 79601
University Blvd
700-1699 79601
1700-2799 79603
Us Highway 277 79601
Us Highway 277 S
5000-5299 79605
Us Highway 277 S
5400-11799 79606
11801-11999 79606
15201-15997 79601
15999-16899 79601
Us Highway 80 E
200-2499 79601
Us Highway 80 W
6600-6899 79605
E Us Highway 80
2500-5099 79601
W Us Highway 80
7700-8399 79603
Us Highway 83
6000-6299 79606
6500-8199 79602
Us Highway 83 N 79601
S Us Highway 83 79602
Valholla Ct 79606
Valley Forge Rd 79601
Varsity Ln 79602
Vegas Rd 79605
Velta Ln 79606
Venice Dr 79606
Ventura Dr 79605
Verbena St 79606
Veterans Dr 79605
Vicki Dr 79606
Victoria St 79603
Victory Dr 79606
S View Trl 79602
Village Dr 79606
Vine St 79602
Vinson Rd N & S 79602
Virgil St 79602
Vision Dr 79602
Vista Ln 79601
Vista Rdg 79606
Vista Del Sol 79606
Vista Grande 79606
Vita Ct 79606
Vogel St
800-1699 79601
1700-3499 79603
Wackadoo Dr 79602
Wagner St 79603
Wagon Wheel Ave 79606
Wake Forrest Ln 79602
Waldemar St 79605
Waldrop Dr 79606
Wall St 79603
Walnut St 79601
Walsh Ln 79603
War Paint Rd 79601
Ward Dr 79605
Warren Dr 79603
E Washington Blvd & St 79601
Waters Edge Dr 79602
Waterside Ct 79606
Waterway Ln 79606
Waverly Ave & Cir 79602
Weatherman Ln 79602
Weavers Way 79602
Weehunt Ct 79606
Wende Rd 79602
Wenwood Rd 79606
West Trl 79605
Westchester Dr 79606
Western Hills Dr 79605
Western Plains Ave 79606
Westheimer Rd 79601
Westminster Dr 79602
Westmoreland St 79603
Westridge Dr 79605
Westview Dr 79603
Westway Dr 79602
Westwood Dr & Mall ... 79603
Whispering Oaks Ct 79606
White Blvd 79606
White Dove Cir 79602
White Mines Rd 79603
White Oaks Dr 79606
Whiterock Dr 79602
Whitewing Way 79606
Whittier St 79605
Wild West Cir 79602
Wildlife Trails Pkwy 79601
N Willis St 79603
S Willis St 79605
Willow Dr & St 79602
Willow Pond Rd 79602
Willow Ridge Rd 79606
Willow View Rd 79606
Willow Wood Dr 79606
Willow Wren 79602
Wilshire Ct & Dr 79603
Wilson St 79601
E & N Wind Rd 79601
Windmill Cir 79606
Windsor Rd 79605
Winged Foot Cir 79606
Winners Cir 79606
Winterhawk Dr 79606
Wishbone Dr 79603
Wisteria Cir & Way 79605
Wits End 79601
Wolfe Rd 79602
Woodard St 79605
Woodcock Cir 79605
Woodglenn Cv 79606
Woodhaven Cir 79605
Woodhollow Cir 79606
Woodlake Dr 79606
Woodland Trl 79605
Woodlawn Dr 79603
Woodridge Dr 79605
Woods Pl 79602
Woodway Cir 79606
Wychwood Dr 79605
Wyndham Ct 79606
Wyndrock Dr 79606
Wynrush Cir 79606
Yale Ave 79603
Yaw Rd 79601
Yellow Brick Rd 79602
Yellowstone Trl 79602
Yeomans Rd 79602
Yorktown Dr 79603
Young Ave 79601
Zachry Cv 79606
Zoo Ln 79602

NUMBERED STREETS

N 1st St
600-1699 79601
1700-5699 79603
S 1st St
701-1197 79602
1199-1399 79602
1401-2099 79602
2101-2897 79605
2899-6600 79605
6602-6698 79605
N 2nd St
201-497 79601
499-1699 79601
1700-4999 79603
S 2nd St
400-798 79602
800-1599 79602
2100-3399 79605
N 3rd St
500-1699 79601
1700-5599 79603
S 3rd St
300-398 79602
400-2099 79602
2100-6699 79605
N 4th St 79601
400-1799 79602
2900-3499 79605
N 5th St
300-1699 79601
1700-2499 79603
S 5th St
400-2099 79602
2100-4999 79605
N 6th St
300-1699 79601
1700-3699 79603
S 6th St
400-498 79602
500-2099 79602
2200-4999 79605
N 7th St
300-1699 79601
1700-4899 79603
S 7th St
200-1999 79602
2100-6299 79605
N 8th St
400-1699 79601
1700-2399 79603
S 8th St
100-2099 79602
2100-3499 79605
N 9th St
500-1399 79601
1700-5599 79603
S 9th St
1100-2099 79602
2500-3499 79605
N 10th St
500-1699 79601
1700-5599 79603
S 10th St
900-1899 79602
2100-3499 79605
N 11th St
400-1699 79601
1700-3999 79603
S 11th St
200-2099 79602
2200-3499 79605
N 12th St
700-1699 79601
1700-5199 79603
S 12th St
300-1999 79602
2100-3699 79605
N 13th St 79601
300-2099 79602
2200-3299 79605
N 14th Ct 79603
N 14th St
200-1699 79601
1900-4599 79603
S 14th St
100-2099 79602
2100-4999 79605
N 15th St
1000-1699 79601
1700-2099 79603
S 15th St
1000-2099 79602
2500-3399 79605
N 16th St
600-1699 79601
1700-2099 79603
S 16th St
800-2099 79602
2600-3199 79605
N 17th St
1000-1699 79601
1700-2199 79603
S 17th St 79602
N 18th St
700-1699 79601

1700-4199 79603
S 18th St
300-2099 79602
2100-3199 79605
N 19th St
600-638 79601
640-1699 79601
1700-2299 79603
S 19th St
900-2099 79602
2100-3199 79605
N 20th St
1500-1699 79601
1700-2599 79603
S 20th St
900-2099 79602
2100-4499 79605
N 21st St
700-1699 79601
1700-1999 79603
S 21st St
900-2099 79602
2100-2198 79605
2200-3399 79605
S 22nd St
200-1799 79602
2100-3299 79605
S 23rd St
200-1799 79602
2100-3499 79605
S 24th St 79605
S 25th St
200-1399 79602
2100-2899 79605
N 26th St 79601
S 26th St 79602
S 27th St
100-2099 79602
2100-3499 79605
S 28th St 79605
S 29th St
2000-2099 79602
2100-2199 79605
S 30th St 79602
N 31st St 79601
S 31st St 79602
S 32nd St
1000-2099 79602
2300-3499 79605
S 33rd St 79605
S 34th St 79605
S 35th St 79605
S 36th St 79602
S 38th St 79605
S 39th St
1600-1799 79602
2300-2899 79605
S 40th St 79605
S 41st St
2000-2299 79602
2300-2899 79605

ALICE TX

General Delivery 78332

POST OFFICE BOXES MAIN OFFICE STATIONS AND BRANCHES

Box No.s
All PO Boxes 78333

NAMED STREETS

All Street Addresses 78332

NUMBERED STREETS

All Street Addresses 78332

ALLEN TX

General Delivery 75002

POST OFFICE BOXES MAIN OFFICE STATIONS AND BRANCHES

Box No.s
All PO Boxes 75013

RURAL ROUTES

01, 03, 04, 05, 07, 09, 15, 22, 23, 24, 27, 28 .. 75002
08, 10, 11, 13, 14, 16, 17, 18, 19, 20, 25, 29 .. 75013

NAMED STREETS

Abbott Ln 75013
Abby Ln 75002
Abby Way 75013
Aberdeen Dr 75002
Abilene Ct 75013
Acadia Dr 75002
Acton Dr 75013
Alameda Ct 75013
Alamosa Dr 75013
Albrook Dr 75002
Aldenwood St 75002
N & S Alder Dr 75002
Alexander Ct 75002
N & S Allen Dr & Plz 75013
Allen Central Dr 75013
N & S Allen Heights Dr 75002
Allentown Pkwy 75002
Allenwood Dr 75002
N & S Alma Dr 75013
Alpine Dr 75013
Alyssa Ct 75013
Amber Ct 75002
Amblewood Dr 75002
Ambrose Dr 75002
Amhurst Ct 75002
Amy Dr 75013
Anacostia Ln 75002
Anderson Ct 75013
Andover Dr 75002
Andrews Pkwy 75002
Andys Ln 75002
S Angel Pkwy 75002
N & S Anna Dr 75013
Annalea Brook Dr 75002
Anns Ln 75002
Anns Way 75013
Apollo Ct 75002
Appalachian Dr 75002
Apple Creek Cir 75002
Apple Hill Dr 75013
April Rain Dr 75002
Arbor Park Dr 75013
N Arbor Ridge Dr 75002
Arches Park Ct & Dr 75013
Arezzo Ln 75013
Arizona Dr 75013
Armstrong Dr 75002
Arrowhead Dr 75002
Artemis Ct 75013
Arthur Ct 75002
Asbury Ln 75002
Ascot Ct 75002
N & S Ash Dr 75002
Ashby Ct, Dr & Pl 75002
Ashcrest Ct 75002
Ashford Ln 75002
Ashland Ct 75013
Ashley Ln 75002
Ashwood Dr 75002
Aspen Ct 75002
Astor Dr 75002
Astoria Dr 75013
Athens Ct 75013
Audrey Way 75013
Audubon Dr 75002
Audubon Pond Way 75013
N & S Austin Dr 75013
Autumn Lake Dr 75002
Autumn Oaks Dr 75002
Autumnmist Dr 75002
Avalon Ct 75013
Aylesbury Dr 75002
Azalea Dr 75002
Balboa Ln 75002
Baldwin Ct 75013
Ballantrae Dr 75013
Balleybrook Ln 75002
Ballinger Way 75013
Balmorhea Dr 75013
Baltimore Dr 75002
Bandelier Dr 75013
Bandera Ct & Dr 75013
Bandy Ln 75002
Barclay Dr 75013
Bardwell Dr 75002
Barrymore Ln 75013
Barton Creek Ct 75002
Barton Springs Ct 75002
Basil Ct 75002
Bastrop Dr 75013
Bastrop Rd 75002
Bauer Ct 75002
Bayshore St 75002
Beacon Hill Dr 75013
Bear Creek Dr 75013
Bear Crossing Dr 75013
Beaumont Ct & Dr 75013
Bedell Ln 75002
Bee Caves Ct & Rd 75002
Beechwood Ct 75002
Begonia Dr 75002
Bel Air Ct & Dr 75013
Belhaven Dr 75013
Bell Dr 75002
Bella Rae 75002
Bellevue Ct & Dr 75002
Bellmeade Ct 75013
Bellnap Dr 75013
Belmont Ct 75002
E Belmont Dr 75002
W Belmont Dr 75013
Belvedere Ct & Dr 75013
Bending Branch Way 75013
Bent Creek Dr 75002
Bentley Dr 75013
Benton Dr 75013
Berkley Rd 75002
Berkshire Ct 75002
E Bethany Dr 75002
W Bethany Dr 75013
W Bethany Rd 75013
Bethany Creek Blvd 75002
Bethany Lake Blvd 75002
Bethlehem Rd 75002
Betsy Ln 75002
Beverly Cir 75002
Beverly Ln 75013
Big Bend Dr 75013
Big Horn Ct 75002
Big Spring Dr 75013
Big Valley Cir 75013
Biltmore Ct 75013
Birdsong Dr 75013
Biscayne Ct 75013
Bishop Gate 75002
Blackberry Ln 75013
Blackenhurst Ln 75002
Blackstone Dr 75002
Blackwell Dr 75002
Blackwood Dr 75013
Blair Ct 75002
Blanco Dr 75013
E & W Blondy Jhune Rd 75002
Bloom St 75002
Blossom Ct 75013
Blue Ridge Ct 75013
Bluebonnet Dr 75002
Bluffs Ln 75002
N & S Bluffview Dr 75002
Boerne Ct 75002
Bois D Arc Ln 75002
Bolin Rd 75002
N & S Bonham Dr 75013
Bonnie Ct 75002
Bordeaux Ct 75002
Bossy Boots Dr 75013
Boulder Dr 75002
Bowie Ct
200-399 75002
1600-1699 75013
Boxwood Dr 75013
Boyd Dr & Pl 75013
Boyle Pkwy 75013
Bozeman Dr 75002
Bracknell Dr 75002
Bradford Trace Dr 75002
Brae Burn Way 75002
Branch Creek Dr 75002
Brandon Ct 75013
Brandywine Dr 75002
Bray Central Dr 75013
Brazoria Dr 75013
Brazos Ct 75002
Brenda Ln 75002
Brenham Ct & Dr 75013
Brentwood Ct 75013
Brewster Ct 75002
Briarbrook Ln 75002
Briarcliff Dr 75013
Briardale Dr 75002
Briarhollow Ct & Dr 75002
Bridgewater Dr 75013
Bridgeway Ln 75013
Bridle Trl 75002
Bright Leaf Dr 75013
Bristol Dr 75013
Broad Brook Ln 75013
Broadmoor Dr 75002
Brockdale Park 75002
Brockhurst Ln 75013
Brook Dr 75002
Brook Ridge Ave 75002
Brookcrest Ct 75002
Brookhaven Dr 75002
Brookhollow Dr 75002
Brookside Dr 75002
Brookview Dr 75002
Brookwood Dr 75002
Brunello Ct 75013
Brushy Creek Dr 75002
Bryan Blvd 75013
Bryce Canyon Ln 75002
Buchanan Pl 75002
Buckeye Dr 75013
Buckingham Ln 75002
Buckthorne Dr 75002
Buffalo Springs Dr 75013
Bullingham Ln 75002
Buoy Bay Ct 75013
Bur Oak Dr 75002
Burberry Dr 75002
Burke Dr 75002
Burnet Dr 75002
Burnside Dr 75013
Bush Cir & Dr 75013
N & S Butler Cir & Dr 75013
Byrn Dr 75013
Caballero Dr 75013
Cabela Dr 75002
Cabernet Dr 75002
Cactus Ct 75013
Caddo Lake Dr 75002
Caledonia Ct 75002
Caliche Trl 75013
Calisto Dr & Way 75013
Calstone Dr 75013
Caman Park Dr 75002
Cambridge Dr 75002
Camden Dr 75002
Camelot Dr 75013
Cameron Ln 75002
Candlewood Dr 75002
Candlewyck Xing 75013
Canterbury Ct & Dr 75013
Canton Ct 75013
Canyon Ct 75013
Canyon Springs Dr 75002
Capital Dr 75013
Caprock Rd 75002
Capstan Dr 75013
Cardinal Dr 75013
Carey Ln 75002
Carlisle Dr 75002
Carlsbad Dr 75002
Carnation Dr 75002
Carnegie Ct 75002
Carolyn Ln 75002
Carson Dr 75002
Carter Ct 75002
Cartier Xing 75013
Cascades Dr 75002
Cassandra Ln 75002
Castleford Dr 75013
Cayman Dr 75013
N & S Cedar Dr 75002
Cedar Bend Cir & Trl 75002
Cedar Brook Ct 75002
Cedar Crest Ln 75002
Cedar Elm Cir & Ln 75002
Cedar Grove Ct 75002
Cedar Springs Dr 75002
Centennary Dr 75002
Central Expy N & S 75013
Century Pkwy 75013
Chadwick Dr 75013
Chambers Dr 75013
Chandler Ct 75002
Channel Islands Dr 75013
Chaparral Rd 75002
Chapel Ct 75002
Chardonnay Dr 75002
Charles River Ct 75013
Charleston Dr 75002
Charter Oak St 75002
Chatfield Ln 75002
Chelsea Blvd 75013
Cherokee Ct 75013
Cherry Blossom Ln 75002
Cherrywood Ct 75002
Chestnut Hill Dr 75013
Cheyenne Dr 75002
Childress Ln 75013
Chimney Rock Dr 75002
Chisholm Trl
1-99 75002
1600-1699 75013
Chittamwood Ln 75002
Chloe Dr 75013
Choice Ln 75002
Christian Ln 75002
Christine Dr 75002
Church Ln 75002
Cibolo Dr 75013
Cimarron Trl 75002
Cimmaron Cir 75002
Cinnamon Ct 75013
Circle Cove Dr 75002
Cisco Ct 75013
Citrus Way 75002
City Road 150 75013
Claire Ln 75013
Claremont Dr 75002
Clarke Springs Dr 75002
Clear Creek Dr 75002
Clear Springs Dr 75002
Clear Water Dr 75013
Clearbrook Dr 75002
Clearcrest Dr 75002
Clearlake Dr 75002
Clearmeadow Dr 75002
Clearview Dr 75002
Clearwood Ct 75002
Cliff Creek Dr 75002
Clove Glen Ct 75002
Clover Ct & Dr 75002
E Coats Dr 75002
W Coats Dr 75013
Cobblestone Dr 75002
Cold Springs Ct 75002
Colgate Dr 75013
Collin Dr 75002
Colony Dr 75013
Colorado Dr 75013
Comal Dr 75013
Comanche Dr 75013
Combine Dr 75002
Compton Ct 75013
Concho Dr 75013
E & W Concord Ln 75002
Conifer Dr & Ln 75013
Connell Ln 75002
Connor Ln 75002
Conroe Dr 75013
Constellation Dr 75013
Cool Springs Dr 75013
Cooper Ct 75002
Copano Dr 75013
Copperas Cove Ct 75013
Copperhill Cir 75002
Cordilleran Ct & Dr 75013
Cordova Dr 75013
Corinth Ct 75013
Corinth Chapel Rd 75002
Corkwood Dr 75002
Cornell Ln 75002
Coronado St 75013
Corsham Dr 75002
Cottonwood Dr 75002
Cottonwood Bend Dr 75002
Cotulla Dr 75013
Cougar Dr 75013
Country Bnd, Ln & Pl 75002
Country Brook Ln 75002
Country Club Rd 75002
Countryside Dr 75002
County Road 1034 75002
County Road 149 75013
County Road 321 75002
County Road 391 75002
County Road 887 75002
County Road 888 75002
County Road 889 75002
County Road 890 75002
County Road 891 75002
Coventry Ct & Ln 75002
Covina Ct 75013
Cox Farm Ests 75002
Coyote Run 75002
Crabapple Ct 75002
Crater Lake Ct 75002
Creek Bend Ln 75002
Creek Springs Dr 75002
Creek Valley Ct 75002
Creek View Ln 75002
Creekcrest Ct 75002
Creekside Ct 75094
Creekside Ln 75002
Creekway Dr 75013
Creekwood Ct 75002
Crepe Myrtle Hl 75002
Crescent Dr 75002
Crestland Dr 75002
Crestmoor Dr 75013
Crestview Cir & Dr 75002
Crestwood Ct 75002
Crockett Ct 75002
Cross Creek Ct 75013
Cross Plains Dr 75013
N Crossing Dr 75013
Crystal Pass 75002
Crystal Springs Dr 75013
Cumberland Dr 75002
Cupressess Ct 75013
Curtis Rd 75002
N & S Custer Rd 75013
Cutter Ln 75013
Cypress Dr 75002
Daisy Dr 75013
Dalhart Dr 75013
Danbury Ct 75002
Daniel Dr 75002
Dartmouth Ln 75002
Darton Dr 75002
Darwin Cir 75002
Dearborn Rd 75002
Deep Well Dr 75002
Deer Brooke Dr 75002
Deercreek Dr 75013
Deerfield Rd 75013
Deerlake Ct & Dr 75002
Defford Ln 75002
Del Cano Dr 75002
Del Rio Ct 75013
Denali Dr 75013
Desert Ct 75013
Desoto Ct 75002
Dickens Ln 75002
Dillehay Dr 75002
Donihoo Ln 75002
Donna Ln 75002
Doris Dr 75002
Douglas Ave 75013
Dove Brook Ct & Dr 75002
Dove Cove Cir 75002
Dove Creek Ln 75013
Downing St 75013
Draycot Ct 75002
Drexel Ct 75013
Driftwood Ct 75013
Droinwich Cir 75002
Dublin Rd 75002
Dublin Creek Cir & Ln 75002
Dublin Park Dr 75094
Duchess Dr 75013
Duke Ct 75013
Dumont Ct 75002
Dunlay Ct 75013
Dunleer Dr 75013
Dunnaway Xing 75002
Dustin Dr 75002
Eagle Lake Ct 75002
Eagle Nest Ln 75013
Eagle Pass Way 75013
Earlham Dr 75002
Earls Ct 75002
Eastgate Ln 75002
Easton Ln 75002
Edelweiss Dr 75002
Edgefield Ln 75002
Edgehill Dr 75013
Edgemont Ct 75013
Edgewater Ct 75094
Edgewater Dr 75002
Edgewood Ln 75013
Edinburg Ct 75013
Edison Ln 75002
Edmonson Dr 75002
Elisa Ln 75002
Elizabeth Ct 75002
Ellis Cir & St 75002
Elm Brook Ct 75002
Elm Grove Dr 75002
Elm Spring Ct 75002
Elmsted Dr 75013
Elyza Ct 75002
Emerson Dr 75002
Emery Down Dr 75013
Enchanted Rock Dr 75013
Enchantment Ln 75013
Enclave Dr 75002
Englenook Dr 75002
English Oak Dr 75002
Enterprise Blvd 75013
Erin Ct 75002
Esmond Ct 75013
Esparanza Ct 75013
Estacado Dr 75013
Estados Dr 75002
Estate Ln 75094
Estates Pkwy & Rd 75002
Estelle Ln 75002
Estes Park Ct & Dr 75013
Eton Dr 75013
Euclid Dr 75013
Evangeline Way 75002
Evanvale Dr 75013
Everglades Dr 75013
Evergreen Dr 75002
Ewing Ct 75002
Exall St 75013
Exchange Pkwy 75002
E Exchange Pkwy 75002

Street	ZIP
W Exchange Pkwy	75013
Exchange Pl	75013
Experian Pkwy	75013
Fair Hill Dr	75013
Fairbrook Dr	75002
Fairfax Dr	75013
Fairfield Ln	75013
Fairhaven Dr	75002
Fairlawn St	75002
Fairwood Dr	75002
Falcon Dr	75013
Falcon Trace Dr	75013
Fall Dr	75002
Fallcreek Ct	75002
Falling Leaf Dr	75002
Fannin Ct	75013
Farm Dl	75002
Farmington Dr	75002
Farmoor Ct	75002
Fawn Hollow Ct	75002
Fawn Valley Dr	75002
Featherbrook Ct	75002
N & S Federal Dr	75013
Field Dr	75013
Fieldstone Dr	75002
Fir Harbor Ct	75002
Fireside Dr	75002
Fisher Dr	75002
Flagler Ct	75013
Flameleaf Dr	75002
Flint Ridge Dr	75002
Florence Ct	75013
Fm 3286	75002
Fontana Ct	75013
Ford Cir & Ln	75002
Forest Bend Dr	75002
E, N & W Forest Grove Ln & Rd	75002
Forest Grove Estates Rd	75002
Forestview Dr	75002
S Fountain Gate Cir & Dr	75002
Fountain Park Dr	75002
Fountain View Ct	75013
Fox Trl	75002
Fox Glen Dr & Pl	75013
Fox Trail Dr	75002
Foxworth Ct	75013
Francie Way	75013
Franklin Dr	75013
Freestone Dr	75002
Furman Ct	75013
Garden Brook Way	75013
Garden Park Dr	75013
Gardenia Dr	75002
Georgetown Dr	75013
Giddings Ct	75002
Gillespie Dr	75002
Ginny Ct	75002
Glacier Dr	75002
Gladewater Dr	75013
Glasgow Ln	75013
Glen Ellen Ct	75002
Glen Meadows Dr	75002
Glen Rose Ct & Dr	75013
Glenbrook Cir	75002
Glencove Cir	75002
Glendale Ct	75013
Glendover Dr	75013
Glenmere Dr	75013
Glenmont Ct	75013
Glenmore Dr	75002
Glenville Dr	75013
Glenwick Pl	75013
Gold Dust Trl	75002
Golden Pond Cir	75002
Goliad Dr	75002
Goodman Dr	75002
Goodnight Ln	75002
Graham Ln	75002
Granbury Dr	75013
Grand Canyon Way	75002
Grand Teton Dr	75002
Granger Dr	75013
Grapevine Dr	75002
Grasmere Pl	75002
Grassland Dr	75013
Grassy Creek Dr	75002
Grassy Glen Dr	75002
Grassy Shore Ct	75013
Great Basin Ct	75013
Great Meadow Dr	75013
Green Brook Dr	75002
Green Meadow Cir	75002
Green Valley Ln	75002
Greenbriar Dr	75013
Greenfield Ln	75013
Greenhill Ct	75002
Greenleaf Ct	75002
N & S Greenville Ave	75002
Greenway Dr	75013
Greenwich Dr	75013
Greeting Gate Ln	75002
Gregory Ln	75002
Grey Ln	75002
Greystone Dr	75013
Grimsworth Ct & Ln	75002
Grosvenor Pl	75013
Gruene Trl	75002
Guadalupe Dr	75002
Hackberry Ln	75002
Hackberry Branch Dr	75002
Haley Ct	75002
Halyard Dr	75013
Hamilton Dr	75002
Hamilton Grn	75013
Hampton Dr	75013
Hanover Ct & Dr	75002
Hansberry Dr	75002
Happy Trails Ct	75002
Hardeman Ct	75002
Hardwick Ct	75013
Harlequin Pl	75002
Harper Dr	75002
Harrison Dr	75002
Hart Ln	75002
Harvard Ln	75002
Harvest Glen Dr	75002
Harvest Mountain Ct	75002
Harvest Run Dr	75002
Hathaway Dr	75002
Haven Pl	75002
Haverford Dr	75013
Hawkwood Way	75013
Hawthorne Cir & Dr	75002
Hayden Ln	75002
Hazelwood Dr	75002
Hearthstone Ct	75002
Heartland Dr	75002
Heather Brook Dr	75002
Heather Glen Cir	75002
Heatherwood Dr	75002
Hebron Dr	75013
Hedgcoxe Rd	75013
Hedgewood Ln	75013
Hefner Dr	75013
Hemingway Ct	75002
Henderson Ct	75013
Hennessey Dr	75013
Herefordshire Ln	75002
Heritage Cir, Ct, Pkwy, Pl & Way S	75002
Heritage Woods Pl	75002
Hermitage Dr	75013
Hickory Trl	75002
Hickory Bend Dr	75002
Hickory Hill St	75002
Hidden Cove Ct	75002
Hidden Creek Dr	75002
Hidden Pass Ln	75002
Hidden Spring Dr	75002
High Country Ln	75002
High Meadow Dr	75002
Highland Cir, Ct & Dr	75002
Highpoint Dr	75002
Hightrail Dr	75002
Hill Haven Dr	75002
Hillcrest Cir & Dr	75002
Hobb Hill Ln	75002
Hockley Ct	75013
Hogge Dr	75002
Hollow Ridge Dr	75002
Holly Cir & Ln	75002
Holmes Ct	75002
Holyoak Ln	75002
Home Park Dr	75002
Homestead Trl	75002
Honey Creek Ln	75002
Honeysuckle Ln	75002
Hopewell Dr	75013
Hopkins Dr	75002
Horseman Dr	75002
Hot Springs Dr	75013
Humbolt Dr	75002
Hunt Dr	75002
Huntcliffe Ct	75013
Hunters Creek Ct	75013
Huntington Ln	75002
Idlewood Dr	75002
Imperial Dr	75013
Indian Trl	75002
Ingram Ln	75002
Inverness Ln	75002
Ireland Ct	75002
Ironwood Dr	75002
Irvine Dr	75013
Italy Dr	75013
Jamison Dr	75013
Janna Way	75002
Jasmine Ct	75002
Jennifer Ct	75002
Jeremy Ct	75002
Jessica Ln	75002
Jordan Ct	75002
Joshua Ct & Pl	75002
Juliet Dr	75013
Junction Dr	75013
Juniper Dr	75002
N & S Jupiter Rd	75002
Kansas Ct	75013
Kara Ln	75002
Katey Mae Ct	75002
Keith Dr	75002
Kenilworth St	75013
Kennedy Dr	75002
Kenshire Ct	75013
Kensington Ct	75002
Kenwood Ct	75002
Kenya Dr	75002
Kerrville Dr	75013
Keystone Dr	75002
Kilgore Ct	75013
Kingsbury Ct	75013
Kingsley Ct & Dr	75013
Kingswood Dr	75002
Kinkade Ln	75013
Kipling Dr	75002
Kirby Ln	75013
Kirkwood Dr	75002
E & W Kittyhawk Dr	75013
Klondike Ln	75002
Knights Ct	75013
Knoll Ct	75002
Knott Ct	75013
Krum Ct	75013
La Cantera Dr	75002
Laguna Ct	75013
Lairds Ln	75013
Lake Falcon Dr	75002
Lake Highlands Dr	75002
Lake Meade Dr	75002
Lake Ridge Dr	75002
Lake Tawakoni Dr	75002
Lake Texoma Cir	75002
Lake Travis Dr	75002
Lake Whitney Ln	75002
Lakeside Dr	75002
Lakeview Dr	75002
Lakeway Dr	75013
Lakewood Dr	75002
Lamar Ln & Rd	75002
Lampasas Dr	75013
Lamplight Way	75013
Lancaster Gate	75013
Landon Ln	75013
Landridge Dr	75013
Lands End Dr	75013
Landsford Dr	75013
Laredo Cir	75013
Larkspur Dr	75002
Laura Ct	75002
Laurel Hl	75002
Lauren Way	75002
Lawn Meadow Cv & Dr	75002
Leading Ln	75002
Leading Lane Cir	75002
Leameadow Dr	75002
Leander Ct	75002
Ledgemont Ct	75013
Lee Dr	75002
Legend Ct	75002
Lehigh Ln	75013
Lemon Cv	75002
Lewis Ln	75002
Lexington Ave	75013
Lighthouse Ln	75013
Lily Ct	75002
Lime Cv	75002
Limestone Ct	75013
Lincoln Ct	75013
Linda Ct	75002
Lindsey Ln	75002
Linford Dr	75013
Live Oak Ln	75002
Livingston Dr	75002
Llano Dr	75013
Lochness Dr	75013
Lombardy Way	75002
Lomond Ct	75013
Londonderry Dr	75013
Lone Star Ct	75013
Long Rd	75002
Long Cove Ct	75002
Long Prairie Ct & Rd	75002
Longwood Ct & Dr	75013
Lorelle Ct	75013
Loring Dr	75013
Lorraine Ave	75002
N Lost Vly	75002
Lost Creek Ct & Dr	75002
Lost Hollow Ct	75002
E & W Lucas Rd	75002
Lucas Creek Dr	75002
Luckenbach Dr	75013
Lucy Ln	75013
Lunenburg Dr	75013
Lynge Dr	75013
Lynn Ln	75002
Macrae Ct	75013
Macrocarpa Rd	75013
Madera Ct	75013
Magnolia Dr	75002
Mahogany Dr	75002
E Main St	75002
W Main St	75013
Mainsail Dr	75013
Majesty Dr	75013
Mala Ct	75002
S Malone Rd	75002
Mammoth Dr	75002
Mandarin Cv	75002
Manor Cir & Ln	75002
Maple Creek Ave	75002
Mapleleaf Fall Dr	75002
Maplewood Ln	75002
Marble Falls Ct & Dr	75013
Marchmont Dr	75002
Margaux Dr	75002
Marigold Dr	75002
Mark Twain Dr	75002
Market St	75013
Marshad Dr	75002
Marshall Dr	75013
Marwood Ct & Dr	75013
Mary Ct	75094
Mary Lee Ln	75002
Mason Dr	75013
Matagorda Dr	75002
Maxwell Creek Dr	75002
Mayflower Dr	75002
Mccallum Dr	75013
Mcclure Dr	75013
Mccoy Ct	75002
Mccreary Rd	75002
E Mcdermott Dr	75002
W Mcdermott Dr	75013
Mcgarity Ln	75002
Mckamy Dr	75013
Mckenzie Ct & Dr	75013
Mcmillen Rd	75002
Mcwhirter	75002
Meadow Ln	75002
Meadow Creek Dr	75002
Meadow Glen Dr	75002
Meadow Mead Dr	75002
Meadow Park Ct & Dr	75002
Meadowbend Ct	75002
Meadowbrook St	75002
Meadowgate Dr	75002
Meadowridge	75002
Medical Dr	75013
Medina Ln	75013
Mefford Ln	75013
Meg Dr	75013
Meghan Ct	75013
Melgrave Ct	75002
Melinda Dr	75002
Melody Mall Dr	75002
Meredith Dr	75002
Merino Dr	75013
Merribrook Ln	75002
Merrimac Dr	75002
Mesa Verde	75002
Michelson Ln	75002
Middle Town Ct	75013
Midhurst Dr	75013
Mill Run Dr	75002
Millenium Dr	75013
Mills Ct	75013
Millwood Ln	75002
Mineral Springs Dr	75002
Misty Meadow Dr	75013
Mistywood Ln	75002
Monaco Dr	75002
Monahans Dr	75013
Monica Dr	75013
Monroe Ct & St	75002
Montclair Dr	75013
Monterrey St	75013
Montgomery Pl	75002
Monticello Cir	75002
Moonlight Trl	75002
Morel Dr	75002
Morideli Dr	75002
Morning Dew Ct	75013
Morningside Ct & Ln	75002
Morrow Ln	75002
Moss Glen Ln	75013
Moss Ridge Cir & Rd	75002
Mossbrook Ln	75002
Mountain Laurel Ln	75002
Mountain Side Dr	75002
Muir Woods Dr	75002
Murdoch Ln	75002
Mustang Dr	75002
Mystic Cove Ct	75013
Nandina Dr	75002
Napa Dr	75013
Naples Dr	75013
Natalie Ct	75013
Natchez Trce	75013
Natha Ct	75002
Navarro Ct & Dr	75013
Neches Dr	75013
Needham Dr	75013
Nestledown Dr	75002
New Bedford Ln	75002
New England Ct	75002
Newberry Dr	75013
Newport Dr	75013
Nick Cir	75013
Nightingale Dr	75013
Noah Trl	75013
Nob Hill Pl	75013
Noblewood Dr	75002
Nocona Dr	75013
Norfolk Ct	75002
Normandy Ln	75002
Northaven Dr	75002
Northbrook Ct	75013
Northfork Ln	75002
Northridge Dr & Pkwy	75002
Norwich St	75013
Nottingham Pl	75013
Nueces Dr	75013
Oak Brook Dr & Ln	75002
Oak Forest Ln	75002
Oak Hollow Dr	75002
Oak Point Dr	75013
Oak Tree Rd	75002
Oakmont Dr	75002
Oakwood Dr	75013
Ohara Dr	75002
Ola Ln	75013
Old Bethany Rd	75013
Old Country Dr	75013
Old Custer Rd	75013
Old Gate Ln	75002
Oldbridge Dr	75002
Olney Dr	75013
Olympia Dr	75002
Open Sky Ct	75013
Orange Cv	75002
Orchard Ln & Rd	75002
Orchard Gap Ln	75002
Orr Rd	75002
Outerbridge Dr	75002
Overbrook Dr	75002
Overhill Dr	75013
Overton Dr	75002
Oxford Cir, Pl & Way	75002
Ozark Dr	75002
Padre Cir	75013
Palace Way	75013
Palazzo Ln	75013
Palisade Ct & Dr	75013
Palmetto Dr	75013
Palo Duro Dr	75013
Palo Pinto Dr	75013
Palomino Dr	75002
Pampa Dr	75013
Pantego Ln	75013
Panther Ln	75013
Paradise Cir	75013
Paris Ct	75013
Park Ln	75002
Park Place Dr	75002
Park Ridge Dr	75013
E Parker Rd	75002
Parker Village Dr	75002
Parkhurst Ln	75013
Parkside Cir	75013
Parkview Cir	75002
Parrant Ct	75094
Patagonian Pl	75013
Patricia Dr	75002
Peach Tree Ct	75002
Pebble Run Dr	75002
Pebblebrook Dr	75002
Pebblestone Ct	75002
Pecan Bnd & Ct	75002
Pecan Creek Ln	75002
Pecan Grove Cir	75002
Pecan Orchard Dr	75002
Pecos Ct	75013
Pedernales Way	75013
Pelican Dr	75013
Pembroke Ct	75002
Pembrook Ln	75013
Pennington Dr	75002
Periwinkle Dr	75002
Pershore Ln	75002
Persimmon Ct	75002
Petersburgh Pl	75013
Petunia Dr	75002
Pheasant Dr	75013
Philip Dr	75013
Phoebe Dr	75013
Pilot Point Dr	75013
Pin Oak Ln	75002
Pine Bluff Dr	75002
Pine Burst Dr	75013
Pine Trail Dr	75002
Pinkerton Ln	75002
Pioneer Dr	75013
Placer Dr	75013
Plateau Dr	75002
Pleasant Run	75002
Plum Ct	75002
Plumas Dr	75013
Poco Dr	75002
Poets Way	75002
Polo Ln	75013
Ponderosa Dr	75002
Ponds Edge Dr	75013
Pool Ln	75002
Port Isabel Dr	75013
Post Oak Ln	75002
Potomac Ln	75013
Prado Verde Dr	75002
Prairie View Dr	75002
Preakness Park	75002
Prescott Rd	75002
Presidio Ct	75013
Prestige Cir	75002
Princeton Ln	75002
Private Road 5211	75002
Private Road 5252	75002
Private Road 5449	75002
Providence Dr	75002
Pulitzer Ln	75002
Purdue Dr	75002
Putnam Ln	75013
Quail Run Dr	75002
Quanah Ct	75013
Quinlan Dr	75013
Rachels Ct	75013
Rainforest Cir, Ct & Ln	75013
Rainier Ct	75002
Raintree Cir	75013
Ramsay Dr	75002
Ramsey Ct	
1218-1299	75002
1800-1899	75094
Ranchview Ct	75002
Rathbone Dr	75002
Ravenhurst Dr	75013
Ravensthorpe Dr	75002
Red Oak Cir & St	75002
Red River Ln	75002
Red Star Rd	75002
Red Store Ct	75002
Red Tip Dr	75002
Redbird Ln	75013
Redbud Dr	75002
Redeemer Rd	75002
Redwood Dr	75002
Regal Dr & Way	75002
Regency Dr	75002
Regina Dr	75013
Reserve Ct	75002
Reynolds Ct	75002
Rice Ct	75013
Richardson Ct	75002
Richmond Ln	75013
Ricks Ct	75094
E Ridge St	75002
Ridgemont Dr	75002
Ridgemore Dr	75002
Ridgeview Dr	
901-1897	75013
1899-1999	75013
4800-5099	75002
Rio Grande Ct & Dr	75013
Rising Star Dr	75013
Rising Sun Rd	75002
River Oaks Dr	75002
Rivercrest Blvd & Ct	75002
Riverdale Dr	75013
Rivergrove Rd	75002
Riverside Ct	75013
Roaming Road Dr	75002
Roanoke Dr	75013
Roaring Springs Dr	75002
Robert Sender Ct	75002
Rock Creek Estates Ln	75002
Rock Ridge Cir, Ct & Rd	75002

Rockcrossing Ln 75002
Rockefeller Ln 75002
Rockford Ct 75013
Rockland Trl 75002
Rockport Ln 75013
Rocky Creek Ln 75002
Rogers Ct 75013
Rolling Brook Dr 75002
Rolling Hills Dr 75002
Rolling Knolls Dr 75002
Rolling Meadows Ct 75013
Rolling Ridge Dr 75002
Rollingwood Cir & Dr 75002
Rollins Dr 75013
Roma Ct & Ln 75013
Rose Dr 75002
Rosemoor Dr 75013
Rosewood Ln 75002
Rotan Ct 75013
Roundrock Dr 75002
Rush Creek Dr 75002
Rushmore Dr 75002
Rusk Dr 75002
Rustic Trl 75002
Rutgers Ct 75002
Rutledge Ln 75002
Sabine Ct 75013
Saddle Trl 75002
Saddlebrook Dr 75002
Sadie Ct 75002
Sagebrush Ln 75002
Saginaw Ct 75013
Saint Andrews Dr 75002
Saint Anne Dr 75013
Saint Ives Dr 75013
Saint James Dr 75002
Saint Johns Ave 75002
Saint Lawrence Ct 75094
Salado Dr 75013
Salvia Springs Dr 75002
Sam Rayburn Tollway 75013
San Carlos Ave 75002
San Jacinto Dr 75013
San Leanna Dr 75013
San Mateo Ct & Dr 75013
San Saba Ct 75013
Sanderlain Ln 75002
Sanderson Ln 75002
Sandlewood Dr 75002
Sandstone Dr 75002
Sandy Ln 75013
Sandy Creek Dr 75002
Sandy Trail Dr 75002
Santa Fe Trl 75002
Sara Ct 75002
Saratoga Dr 75013
Sarita Dr 75013
Savannah Cir 75002
Sawmill Dr 75002
Saxon Way 75013
Scarlet Oak Dr 75002
Scarlett Dr 75002
Scotia Dr 75013
Scotts Bluff Dr 75002
Scottsman Dr 75013
Seeport Dr 75013
Seguin Ct 75013
Seminole Trl 75002
Serenity Ct 75002
Settlers Ct 75002
Shaddock Park Ln 75013
Shadetree Ln 75013
Shadow Lakes Blvd 75002
Shady Ln 75002
Shady Brook Dr 75002
Shady Creek Cir 75002
Shady Knolls Dr 75002
Shady Oaks Ct 75002
Shady Valley Dr 75002
Shadyglen Dr 75002
Shadywood Dr 75002
Shallowater Dr 75013
Shannon Ct & Dr 75002
Shawnee Trl 75002
Shelborn Dr 75002
Shelby Dr 75013

Shenandoah Dr 75002
Shepherds Creek Dr 75002
Sherman Ct 75013
Shetland Dr 75013
Shiloh Dr 75002
Shiner Dr 75013
Shumard St 75002
Sierra Ct 75013
Sierra Vis 75002
Silver Creek Cir 75002
Silver Spur Dr 75002
Silver Trace Ln 75013
Silverleaf Ln 75002
Silverton Dr 75002
Skyline Ct 75002
Skyview Dr 75002
Sleepy Hollow Dr 75002
Sloan Dr 75013
Sminters Dr 75013
Smith Rd 75094
Snider Ct & Ln 75002
Snowberry Dr 75013
Soapberry Dr 75002
Solano Dr 75013
Solaro Ct 75013
Solitude Ct 75002
Sonoma Dr 75002
Sonora Dr 75013
Sophia St 75013
Southfork Dr 75013
Southpoint Ct 75002
Southridge Pkwy 75002
Southview Dr 75002
Southwestern Dr 75013
Southwick Ln 75013
Spicewood Dr 75013
Spinnaker Dr 75013
Spring St 75002
Spring Air Dr 75002
Spring Brook Dr 75002
Spring Creek Dr 75002
Spring Leaf Ct 75002
Spring Valley Rd 75002
Spring Willow Dr 75002
Springcrest Ct 75002
Springdale Ct 75002
Springfield Ln 75002
Springhill Estates Dr 75002
Springmeadow Dr 75002
Springview Dr 75002
Spur Dr 75013
Spurgin Rd 75002
Spyglass Dr 75002
Squire Ct 75002
St Mary Dr 75002
Stablerun Dr 75002
Stacy Rd 75002
E Stacy Rd 75002
W Stacy Rd 75013
Stallion Dr 75002
Stanford Dr 75002
Stansted Manor Dr 75002
N Star Rd 75002
Starcreek Pkwy 75013
S State Dr 75002
Sterling Ct 75002
Sterling Brown Ln 75002
Stillforest Dr 75002
Stinson Rd 75002
Stone Creek Dr 75002
Stonebridge Cir 75013
Stonehill Ct 75002
Stonemont Ct 75013
Stoneport Ln 75002
Stonewick Dr 75002
Stony Oak Ct 75002
Strain Ln 75002
Stratton Mill Dr 75002
Streams Way 75002
Stretford Ln 75002
Stubbs Dr 75002
Sugar Bush Trl 75002
Sul Ross Dr 75002
Summer Glen Ct & Dr 75002
Summer Oaks Dr 75013
Summer Place Dr 75002

Summerfield Dr 75002
Summerside Dr 75002
Sun Meadow Rd 75013
Suncreek Dr & Pl 75013
Sunderland Ct & Dr 75013
Sundown Ln 75002
Sunflower Dr 75002
Sunny Slope Dr 75002
Sunridge Way 75002
Sunrise Dr 75002
Sunset Ct 75013
Sunshine Dr 75002
Surrey Ln 75013
Susan Cir 75002
Sussex Ln 75013
Sutter Dr 75002
Suzanne Dr 75002
Swan Landing Ln 75013
Sweet Gum Dr 75002
Sweet Peach Dr 75002
Sweetbay Dr 75002
Sweetbriar Dr 75002
Sweetwater Ln 75013
Sycamore Ln 75002
Sycamore Creek Rd 75002
Tamsworth Ct 75002
Tanglewood Dr 75002
Tarrytown Ln 75013
Tartan Dr 75013
Tascosa Ct 75013
Tatum Dr 75013
Taylor Ln 75002
Taylor Rd 75013
Teasbend Ln 75002
Tehama Ct 75013
Temperate Dr 75013
Tenbury Ct 75002
Terlingua Ct 75013
Terrace Ln 75002
Terracotta Dr 75013
Terrell Dr 75002
Texas Hills Ct 75002
Thistle Cir 75002
Thoreau Ln 75002
Thornbury Ct & Ln 75013
Tiburon Ct 75013
Tiffany Ct 75013
Timber Trl 75002
Timber Ridge Dr 75002
Timberbend Trl 75002
Timbercreek Ct & Dr 75002
Timberlake Cir 75013
Timberline Ln 75002
Timberview Dr 75002
Timmaron Dr 75013
Tokalaun Ct 75013
Toole Dr 75013
Toulouse Ct 75013
Tractor Trl 75002
Trails End 75002
Trailwood Dr 75002
Travis Ct & Dr 75002
Travis Ranch Rd 75002
Tree Row Dr 75002
Trenton Way 75013
Trinidad Ln 75013
Trinity Dr & Park 75002
Truscott Ln 75013
Tudor Dr 75013
Tulane Ct 75013
Tulare Dr 75002
Turnberry Ct & Ln 75002
Tuscany Ct 75013
Tustin Ct 75013
Twilight Rd 75013
Twin Creeks Dr 75002
Tyler Ct 75013
University Dr 75013
Uvalde Ct 75013
Valencia Dr 75013
Valley View Dr 75002
Valleycrest Ct 75002
Vaquero St 75013
Vashon Dr 75013
Veneto Dr 75013
Venice Ct 75013

Ventura Ct 75013
Venture Dr 75013
Verde Ct 75013
Vermont Ct 75013
Versailles Ave 75002
Victorian Cir & Dr 75002
Villa Dr 75013
Village Green Dr 75013
Villanova Ct 75013
Vinecrest Ln 75002
Vinehill Ct 75002
Vineland Ct 75002
Vineyard Dr 75002
Violet Dr 75002
Virginia Pl 75094
Vista Bend Dr 75002
Vista Ridge Pkwy 75002
Wagon Wheel Dr 75002
Wakefield Ln 75013
Walden Ct 75002
Wales Ct 75013
Walker Ln 75002
Wallace Dr 75013
Walnut Dr 75002
Walnut Springs Dr 75013
Wandering Way Dr 75002
Warm Springs Dr 75002
Washington Dr 75002
Water Oak Dr 75002
Waterdown Dr 75013
Waterford Way 75013
Waterrock Dr 75013
Watson Dr 75002
N & S Watters Rd 75013
Watters Crossing Ct 75013
Way Cir & Dr 75002
Webb Ln 75002
Wedgewood Way 75002
Weeping Willow Ct 75002
Welborn Ln 75002
Wendy Ln 75002
Wentwood Dr 75002
Wesley Dr 75013
Wessex Ct 75002
Westbury Ln 75013
Westchase Dr 75002
Westchester Dr 75002
Westfield Way 75002
Westford Dr 75013
Westminister Ave 75002
Westmont Dr 75013
Westmore Ln 75002
Weston Ct 75002
Westwind Dr 75002
Westwood Ct 75013
Wheat Ridge Rd 75002
Wheatberry Ct & Ln 75002
Wheaton Ct 75013
Whisenant Cir & Dr 75013
Whispering Acres Ln 75002
Whispering Glen Dr 75002
Whistle Brook Dr 75013
White Oak St 75002
White River Dr 75013
White Rock Ct & Trl 75002
Whitman Cir, Dr & Pl 75002
Whitney Ct 75013
Wilderness Way 75002
Wildwood Pl 75013
Wilkes Dr 75002
William B Yeats Cir 75002
Williams Dr 75013
Willingham Dr 75013
Willoughby Dr 75002
Willow Dr 75002
Willow Bend Ct 75002
Willow Brook Dr 75002
Willow Creek Cir 75002
Willow Oak Dr 75002
Willow Point Cir 75002
Willow Ridge Dr 75002
Willow Winds St 75013
Wills Point Ct & Dr 75013
Wilshire Ct 75002
Wiltshire Ct 75002
Wimberly Ct 75013

Wimbledon Dr 75013
Wind Elm Ct & Dr 75002
Windgate Way 75002
Windham Ln 75013
Winding Trail Dr 75002
Winding Way Ln 75002
Windmere Way 75013
Windmill Ct 75002
Windmill Creek Dr 75002
Windream Ln 75002
Windsong Way 75002
Windsor Dr & Pl 75002
Winecreek Ct 75002
Winecup Ct 75002
Wingsong Ln 75013
E & N Winningkoff Rd 75002
Winnsboro Ct 75013
Winslow Dr 75002
Winterbrook Ct 75002
Winterwood Dr 75002
Winthrop Dr 75013
Winton Dr 75013
Wolf Creek Dr 75002
Wolverley Ln 75002
Wood Creek Ln 75002
Wood Duck Ln 75013
Woodbridge Ct & Dr 75013
Woodcreek Cir 75002
Wooded Ln 75013
Woodhaven Ct 75002
Woodlake Dr 75013
Woodland Ct 75002
Woodland Pond Dr 75013
Woodmont Dr 75002
Woodmoor Cir 75002
Woodmoor Dr 75013
Woodrose Ct 75013
Woodsboro Ct 75013
Woodson Dr 75002
Woodstream Ln 75002
Woodview Cir & Ct 75002
Worchester Ln 75002
Wrotham Ln 75013
Wyndham Way 75013
Xavier Dr 75002
Yale Dr 75002
Yellowstone Dr 75002
Yopont Ln 75002
Yorkshire Dr 75002
Yosemite Dr 75002
Young Dr 75002
Youpon Dr 75002
Yukon Ct 75013
Zavala Dr 75002
Zilker Ct 75002

ALPINE TX

General Delivery 79830

POST OFFICE BOXES MAIN OFFICE STATIONS AND BRANCHES

Box No.s
All PO Boxes 79831

HIGHWAY CONTRACTS

65 79830

NAMED STREETS

All Street Addresses 79830

NUMBERED STREETS

All Street Addresses 79830

ALVIN TX

General Delivery 77511

POST OFFICE BOXES MAIN OFFICE STATIONS AND BRANCHES

Box No.s
All PO Boxes 77512

NAMED STREETS

All Street Addresses 77511

NUMBERED STREETS

All Street Addresses 77511

AMARILLO TX

General Delivery 79105

POST OFFICE BOXES MAIN OFFICE STATIONS AND BRANCHES

Box No.s
1 - 2974 79105
200 - 200 79120
751 - 2171 79189
3001 - 4180 79116
5000 - 6289 79117
7001 - 8999 79114
9000 - 9982 79105
10001 - 10274 79116
15000 - 15956 79105
19001 - 21216 79114
30001 - 37000 79120
50001 - 54680 79159
90501 - 90503 79105
91405 - 91406 79114
92001 - 92004 79120
95901 - 95901 79159

RURAL ROUTES

03, 09, 16 79108
02, 05, 07, 08, 10, 11, 13, 14, 19, 25 79118
04, 12, 15, 18, 21, 24, 26, 27 79119
01, 06, 17, 20 79124

NAMED STREETS

A Ave 79111
Aberdeen Dr & Pkwy 79119
Acacia Ln 79124
Academy Dr 79119
Achieve Dr 79119
N Acres Dr 79108
Adair Dr 79108
N Adams St 79107
S Adams St 79101
Adams Way 79118
Addelyn Ave 79119
Addison Dr 79119
Adirondack Trl 79106
Admiral Ct 79124
Adobe Dr 79111
Advance Pl 79119
Air Park St 79103
Aires Dr 79108
Airport Blvd
1700-1798 79118
10000-14499 79111
Airway Blvd 79118
N Alabama St 79106
S Alabama St
100-999 79106
1000-1599 79102
Alamo Rd 79110
Albany Dr 79118
Albert Ave 79106
N Aldredge St 79107
S Aldredge St
200-298 79102
300-399 79102
2200-2899 79103
3600-4599 79118
Alexandra 79118
Alexandria Ave 79118
Alice St 79106
Alicia Dr 79109
Allen St 79110
Allison Ln 79118
Almond Ave 79107
Alpha St 79110
Alpine Ln 79109
Alta Vista St 79106
Alvarado Rd 79106
E Amarillo Blvd
101-197 79107
199-8199 79107
8201-8399 79107
8500-8598 79108
8600-10500 79108
10502-15398 79108
W Amarillo Blvd
100-298 79107
300-2099 79107
2300-7099 79106
7101-7499 79106
8200-8302 79124
8301-8301 79159
8303-8399 79124
8304-8398 79124
Amarillo St 79108
Amarillo Creek Rd 79124
Amberwood Ln 79106
American Dr 79111
Amherst Dr 79109
Amy St 79118
Anaheim Pl 79118
Andover Dr
5600-7099 79109
7300-7400 79119
7402-7498 79119
Andretti Dr 79118
Andrews Ave 79106
Angel Ln 79118
Angelus Dr
2900-3200 79107
3202-3598 79107
4000-4899 79108
Angus Trl 79124
Anna St 79106
Antelope Dr 79108
Antigua Pl 79118
Antoine Ln 79119
Anton Pl 79109
N Apache St 79107
S Apache St 79103
Apollo Trl 79118
Appaloosa Rd 79108
Applewood Dr 79108
Appomattox Rd 79118
N Arapahoe St 79107
Arbor St 79110
Arcadia St 79109
Arch Ter 79106
Arden Rd
3701-3897 79118
3899-3999 79118
4200-5299 79110
5900-6398 79109
6400-6800 79109
6802-7298 79109
Arena Dr 79119
Arielle Ave 79118
Arkansas Trl 79108
Arlie Rd 79108
Arlington St 79106
Armand St 79110
Armstrong St 79106

Arnold Pl 79107
Arnot Rd 79124
Arp Pl 79109
Arroyo Dr 79108
Arroyo Vista Pl 79124
N Arthur St 79107
S Arthur St
200-1799 79102
2000-2899 79103
Ascension Pkwy 79119
Asher Ln 79119
Ashland Dr 79119
Ashley Ln 79118
Ashton Rd 79119
Ashville Pl 79119
Aspen St 79106
Aspire Pl 79119
Aster St 79107
Astoria St 79109
Atkinsen St
2300-2399 79106
3600-3699 79109
Attebury Dr 79118
Audrey Ln 79118
Ault Dr 79121
Aussie Dr 79118
N Austin St 79106
S Austin St
100-799 79106
900-1699 79102
1800-3699 79109
4200-4899 79110
4901-5299 79110
Autumn Pl 79109
Avent St 79118
Avenue L 79108
Aviation Pl 79118
N & S Avondale St 79106
Azalea Ave 79110
Azalea Dr 79118
B Ave 79111
Baccus 79124
Back Acres Rd 79119
Badger St 79118
Bagarry St
1000-1499 79104
2800-3299 79103
Bailey Ln 79118
Baker St 79111
Ballybunion Ct 79124
Balsam Ln 79107
Baltus Pl 79121
Baltusrol Dr 79124
Bandera Dr 79111
Banks Dr 79124
Barbara Ln 79109
Barber Pl 79124
Barclay Dr 79109
Barn Rd 79118
Barrett Pl 79121
Barrington Ct 79119
Barstow Dr 79118
Barton St 79108
Basswood Ln 79124
Baughman Dr 79121
Baxter Dr 79119
Bay Rock Cir 79118
Bayberry Ln 79124
Baylor Ct 79119
Bayshore Dr 79118
Bayswater Rd
6200-7399 79109
7400-7900 79119
7902-7998 79119
Beacon Rd 79118
Bear Trl 79118
Beau Brummel Pl 79121
Beaver Dr 79107
Bedford Rd 79106
Bedwell Pl 79121
Beech St 79106
Beefco Rd 79118
Beeson St 79119
Bell Park 79109
Bell St
1100-3399 79106
3400-7299 79109
7900-8098 79110
8401-8499 79110
11801-12197 79118
12199-16100 79118
16102-16198 79118
Bella Rosa Ln 79124
Bellaire St 79106
N & S Belleview St 79106
Belpree Rd 79106
Benchmark St 79108
N Bend Dr 79108
Bengal Ct 79124
Benge Dr 79108
Bennett St 79119
Bennington Dr 79119
Bent Oak Dr 79124
Bent Tree Dr 79121
Benton Dr 79110
Benwood Sq 79109
Berget Dr 79106
Berkley Ct 79118
Bernard Ave 79107
Bernay St 79119
Berry Rd & St 79108
Bertrand Rd 79108
Besetzney Ln 79119
Beta Ln 79110
N & S Beverly Dr 79106
Big Boulder Rd 79118
Big Horn Trl 79108
Big Sky Dr 79124
Biggs St 79106
Binder St 79118
Birch St 79107
Birdsong Ln 79118
Birkshire Dr 79109
N Birmingham St 79107
S Birmingham St
300-398 79104
400-999 79104
1901-2897 79103
2899-3399 79103
Bismarck Ave 79118
N Bivins St 79107
S Bivins St
300-999 79104
2200-3199 79103
Black Oak Dr 79110
Blackburn St 79109
Blackfoot Trl 79118
Blackhawk Rd 79119
Blacksmith Ln 79109
Blackwing Rd 79108
Blake Ave 79119
Blanca Dr 79108
Blanton St 79119
Blenheim Dr 79119
S Blessen Rd
2601-2697 79124
2699-2700 79124
2702-2798 79124
3600-5198 79119
5200-10800 79119
10802-11098 79119
Blissful Ln 79107
Blossom Ct 79124
Blossom Trl 79118
Blossom Way 79124
Blue Eyes Trl 79108
Blue Quail Dr 79124
Blue Sage Cir 79124
Blue Sky Dr 79118
Bluebell St 79107
Bluebird St 79109
Bluebonnet Dr 79108
Blueridge Ct 79109
Bob White Trl 79124
Bobcat Rd 79118
N Bolton St 79107
S Bolton St
600-899 79104
901-1499 79104
1801-2197 79103
2199-2599 79103
N Bonham St
2-98 79106
1300-2099 79107
S Bonham St
101-197 79106
199-699 79106
900-1699 79102
1900-2899 79109
4001-4097 79110
4099-5199 79110
5800-6399 79118
E & W Bonita Ave 79108
Bonnie Dr 79108
Bordeaux Ln 79119
Bosque Ave 79118
Boston Pl 79107
Bourgeois St 79108
Bowie St
100-599 79106
800-898 79102
900-1699 79102
1900-1998 79109
2000-3599 79109
3800-5199 79110
S Bowie St 79118
N & S Bowyer St 79106
Box Canyon Ln 79118
Boxwood Ln 79109
Boyd St 79108
Bradford Dr 79109
Brandon Rd 79109
Brandywine Ct 79119
Brazos St 79102
Bremond Dr 79109
Brennan Blvd, Ct, Gdns, Park & Ter 79121
Brentwood Dr 79106
Brentwood Rd 79118
Brett St 79118
Breuk Ln 79119
Brianna Dr 79119
Briar St 79109
Briarwood Dr 79124
Brickplant Rd 79124
Bridle Trails Dr 79119
Brighton Pl 79119
Brinkman Dr 79106
Bristol Rd 79109
Britain Dr 79109
Brixton Dr 79108
Broadcast Ctr 79101
Broadmoor St 79106
Broadway Dr 79108
Broken Arrow Trl 79118
Bronco Dr 79108
Brook Ave 79107
Brook Hollow Dr 79108
Brookfield Dr 79124
Brooklyn Pl 79106
Brooks Cir 79124
Brookview Way 79124
Brookwater Cir & Pl 79124
Brown Ave 79108
Browning St
1-297 79104
299-999 79104
2500-3199 79103
N Bryan St 79106
S Bryan St
100-298 79106
300-899 79106
900-1599 79102
1601-1699 79102
3500-3699 79109
4600-4799 79110
Buccola Ave 79119
N Buchanan St 79107
S Buchanan St
100-1599 79101
1600-1799 79102
1801-1899 79102
1901-2097 79109
2099-2699 79109
2701-2899 79109
Buck St 79108
Buckskin Rd 79124
Buena Vista St 79106
Buffalo Trl 79109
Buffalo Airport Rd 79118
Buffalo Springs Trl 79119
Buntin St 79107
Burlington Rd 79118
Burrell St 79119
Burrus Pl 79121
Bush Dr 79106
Busher Ln 79108
Bushland Blvd 79106
Bushland Rd 79119
E Business 40 79108
Business Interstate 40 79124
Business Park Dr 79110
Butte Cir 79124
Byrd Dr 79108
Cactus Dr 79118
E Cactus St 79108
W Cactus St 79108
Caddell St 79119
Caddo Rd 79108
Callahan St 79106
Calumet Pl 79121
Calumet Rd 79106
Cambridge Rd 79124
Camden Ln 79109
Camino Alto Dr 79118
Camp Ln 79110
Campus Dr 79109
Canadian St 79108
Candletree Ct 79119
Canode Dr 79121
Canterbury Pl 79109
Canyon Cir 79118
Canyon Dr
1500-1598 79101
1600-1698 79102
2100-2198 79109
2200-3000 79109
3002-7498 79109
3301-8699 79110
8200-9198 79119
16001-16099 79119
Canyon Bend Rd 79118
Canyon Creek Dr 79118
Canyon Crest Dr 79124
Canyon Pass Rd 79118
Canyon Rim Rd 79118
Cape Colony Dr 79119
Cape Verde Ct 79119
Caprock Ln 79118
Capulin Ln 79110
Care Cir 79124
Carl St 79108
Carlton Dr 79109
Carmel Ave 79110
Carnegie Pl 79107
Carnoustie Ln 79124
Carole Ln 79110
S Carolina 79102
N Carolina St 79106
S Carolina St
100-1099 79106
1100-1999 79102
Carolyn St 79107
Carson Dr 79109
Carter St
1000-1499 79104
2800-3299 79103
Casa Ave 79108
Casa Dr 79111
Casa Grande St 79118
Casey Rd 79118
Casino Dr 79118
Cason Dr 79119
Casper Pl 79124
Cassidy Dr 79119
Cat Creek Ln 79108
Catalpa Ln
3601-3697 79110
3699-5199 79110
5201-6899 79110
5300-5398 79109
6700-6898 79110
Catskill Ave 79121
Cavin Rd 79119
Cayman Ct 79124
Cedar Ln 79118
Cedar St 79106
Cedar Creek Dr 79124
Cedar Hollow Dr 79124
Cedar Meadow Cir 79124
Cedar Springs Trl 79119
Cedarwood Dr 79118
Celia St 79121
Center Ave 79106
Centerport Blvd 79108
E & W Central Ave 79108
Century Dr 79110
Cervin Dr 79121
Chalet Ct 79124
Challenge Dr 79119
Chama St 79102
Champions Cir 79124
Chandler Dr 79109
N Channing St 79107
S Channing St
800-1098 79104
1101-1199 79104
2800-3299 79103
Chapman Dr 79118
Charlene Ave 79106
Charles St 79106
Charleston Rd 79118
Charlotte St 79107
Charnetta Trl 79108
Charolais Trl 79124
Chasity Cir 79124
Chatham Rd 79119
Chattanooga Rd 79118
Chelsea Dr 79109
S & W Chenot Dr 79109
Cherokee Dr 79108
Cherokee Trl 79109
E Cherry Ave 79108
W Cherry Ave 79108
Cherry St 79106
Chesapeake Pl 79119
Cheshire Dr 79109
Chestnut St 79107
Chevy Chase Dr 79118
Cheyenne Ter 79106
Chicago Ave 79104
Chico Pl 79107
Chief Joseph Trl 79108
Chisholm Cir & Trl 79109
Chloe Cir 79119
Choctaw Trl 79118
Christina Ave 79121
Chucker St 79124
Church Rd 79124
Church St 79109
Cimarron Ave 79102
Cinderella Ln 79121
Cindy Ln 79118
Cinema Dr 79124
Circle Dr 79110
Circle C Trl 79118
Circle J Rd 79118
Circle View Dr 79118
Cisco Dr 79111
Citadel Dr 79124
City Lake Rd 79119
City View Dr 79118
Civic Cir 79109
Clabern Dr 79121
Clara Ln 79108
Clara Allen Trl 79118
Claremont Dr 79109
Clarence St 79110
Claret St 79110
Clarke St 79108
Claude Rd 79118
Clearmeadow Dr 79119
Clearwater Ct 79110
Clearwell St 79109
Clema St 79107
Cleon Ct 79109
N Cleveland St 79107
S Cleveland St
100-198 79102
200-1799 79102
2000-2899 79103
E Cliffside Ave 79108
W Cliffside Ave 79108
Cliffside Cir 79124
Cliffside Dr 79118
Cliffside Rd 79124
Clifton Ave 79106
Climer Cir 79124
Cline Rd 79110
Clint Ave 79119
Cloister Pkwy 79121
Cloud Crest Dr 79124
Clover Dr 79102
Club Meadows Dr 79124
Clubview Dr 79124
Clyde St 79106
Cobblestone Dr 79119
Cochise Pl 79118
Cody Dr 79119
Coke Ln 79108
Colchester Pl 79121
Cole St 79106
Colgate St 79109
Colida Ln 79108
College Ave 79109
Collin Wade Rd 79124
Colonial Dr 79124
Colony Rd 79118
E & W Colorado Ave 79108
Colton St 79118
Columbia Ln 79109
Columbine St 79107
Columbus 79118
Comanche Dr 79108
Comanche St 79109
Commerce St 79109
Compton Ln 79118
Concho Ave 79104
Concord Rd 79109
Contented Ln 79109
Continental Pkwy 79119
Copper Dr 79108
Coral Cir 79110
Cord St 79108
Cornell St 79109
Coronado Trl 79110
Cortona Dr 79119
E Costley Rd 79118
W Costley Rd 79119
Cottonwood Cir 79118
Cottonwood Ln 79108
E Cottonwood St 79108
W Cottonwood St 79108
Cougar Dr 79109
N Coulter St 79124
S Coulter St
1000-1198 79106
1200-3399 79106
3400-4499 79109
4500-4698 79119
4700-12600 79119
12602-12798 79119
Country Ln 79118
Country Club Dr 79124
Countryside Dr 79119
County Road 1 79118
E County Road 34 79118
W County Road 34 79124
E County Road 46 79118
County Road 58 79118
W County Road 58 79119
County Road A 79108
Coury Ln 79124
Covenant Ln 79109
Covington Pkwy 79121
Coyote Blf 79124
Coyote Spgs E 79119
Coyote Spgs N 79119
Coyote Trl 79124
Cpt Augustus Mccrae Trl 79118
Cpt Woodrow Call Trl 79118
Craft Center Rd 79118
Craig Dr 79106
Crain Pl 79121
Crawford Rd 79108
Creekside Dr 79124
Crenshaw St 79124
Crestview Ave 79124
Crestway Ter 79106
Criss Dr 79110
Crist St 79118
Crockett St
100-699 79106
701-797 79102
799-1699 79102
1900-3599 79109
4000-5199 79110
S Crockett St 79118
Cromwell Dr 79109
Cross St 79118
Crouch St 79106
Cruse Cir & Ln 79118
Crystal Ave 79108
Currie Ln 79107
Curtis Dr 79109
Cutter Ln 79118
Cypress Pt 79124
D Ave 79111
Dahlia St 79107
Dakota Trl 79118
Dalana St 79124
Dale St 79107
N Dalinerl St 79107
Dallam Rd 79119
N Dallas St 79107
S Dallas St
500-1699 79104
1800-3399 79103
Dallington Dr 79119
Damon Dr 79124
Dan Dr 79119
Dana Ln 79118
Danbury Dr 79109
Daniel Dr 79109
Danvers Dr 79106
Darden St 79107
Darrell Ave 79110
Dartmouth St 79109
David Dr & St 79108
Daws Dr 79124
De Shazo Pl 79121
Deann Cir & Dr 79121
Decamp Ave 79118
Deer Trl 79118
Deer Haven Trl 79118
Deer Park Dr 79124
Delta St 79110
Denton St 79108
Derrick Pl 79121
Desert Rose Pl 79106
Destiny Pl 79119
Detroit St 79103
Devon Dr 79109
Devonshire Rd 79109
Dewey Ave 79124
Diamond Ct 79124
Diaz Ranch Rd 79108
Didrickson Ln 79124
Digby Ln 79119
Distant Dr 79118
Dixie St
1000-1098 79106
1201-1299 79102
Dixon Ave 79109
Dixon St 79118
Dobie St 79118
Dodson Dr 79110
Dolphin Ter 79118
Dominion St 79119
Domino Ln 79108
Don Dr 79107
Donda St 79118
Donde Dr 79108
Donnelly Dr 79118
Doral Dr 79124
Doris Dr 79109
Dorothy St 79118
Double D Rd 79118
Double Tree Pl 79124
Douglas Dr 79110
Dove St 79124
Dover Rd 79109
Dowell Rd 79119

N Dowell Rd 79124
S Dowell Rd
2000-2098 79124
14800-14899 79119
14901-16099 79119
Downtown Dr 79118
Drake Elm Pl 79124
Drexel Ln & Rd 79109
Dreyfuss Dr 79121
Dreyfuss Rd 79106
Dripping Springs Trl 79124
Dryden Ct 79119
Dukes Pl 79109
Duling Ln 79110
Dumas Dr
1301-1497 79107
1499-2699 79107
4001-4797 79108
4799-7799 79108
7801-8099 79108
Dunaway St
1000-1499 79104
2800-3299 79103
Duncan Dr 79109
Dunhill Rd 79108
Duniven Cir 79109
Durango Dr 79111
Durham Dr 79118
Durrett Dr 79124
Durrett Pl 79109
Dusty Dr 79108
Dusty Trl 79118
E Ave 79111
S Eagerenc St 79103
Eagle Ln 79118
Eagle Crest Dr 79103
Eagle Point Dr 79103
Easely Pl 79119
S Eashersi St 79102
East St 79107
N Eastern St
600-799 79107
801-1199 79107
2501-3497 79108
3499-8000 79108
8002-8098 79108
S Eastern St
1000-1799 79104
1801-2097 79118
2099-8399 79118
Eaton Dr 79109
Echo Dr
2400-3499 79107
4000-5299 79108
Eddy St
2900-3000 79106
3002-3198 79106
3300-3699 79109
Edenbridge Dr 79119
Edenburg Dr 79106
Edgeware Pl 79109
Edgewater Dr 79106
Edgewood Dr 79109
El Paso Dr 79118
El Rancho Rd 79108
Elaine St 79119
Eldon Ln 79108
Eldorado Dr 79111
Elena St 79119
Elk Rd 79118
Ellsworth Pl 79109
Elm St 79107
Elmhurst Dr 79121
Elmhurst Rd 79106
Elmwood Dr 79109
Emerald Ct 79124
Emil Ave 79106
Emily Pl 79118
Emory Ct & Dr 79110
Empire Pl 79119
Endicott Dr 79119
Englewood Dr 79108
English Rd 79108
English Bay Pkwy 79119
Enterprise Cir 79106
Erik Ave 79106
Ernest Lee Dr 79124
Escondido Pl 79118
Essex Ct 79121
Estacado Ln 79109
Estates Dr 79124
Estes St 79107
Estrella Pl 79124
Ethan Ln 79109
Euclid St 79110
Eula St 79107
Euston Dr 79109
Evans St 79106
Evelyn St 79109
Everett Ave 79106
Evergreen St 79107
Exmoor Rd 79118
Explorer Trl 79118
F Ave 79111
N Fairfield St 79107
S Fairfield St
1100-1598 79104
1900-3199 79103
Fairlane St 79108
N & S Fairmont St 79106
Fairview Blvd 79104
Fairway Dr 79124
Falcon Rd 79109
Falcon Club Dr 79119
Fanchun St 79119
N Fannin St
1-99 79106
800-2099 79107
S Fannin St
100-198 79106
200-600 79106
602-798 79106
900-1699 79102
1900-2299 79109
4200-5799 79110
5800-6399 79118
Fargo Dr 79118
E Farmers Ave 79118
W Farmers Ave
301-1797 79118
1799-2000 79118
2002-3098 79118
4200-5199 79118
5800-5898 79109
Farrell Dr 79121
Farwell Dr 79109
Fegal Rd 79119
Fenley Dr 79121
Ferrin Park 79124
Fescue Ave 79118
Fewell Trl 79119
Fieldlark Dr 79118
Fieldstone Dr 79124
N Fillmore St 79107
S Fillmore St
1-1400 79101
1402-1598 79101
3001-3097 79110
3099-3599 79110
First United Bank
Pkwy 79119
Fisk St 79106
Five J Trl 79118
S Flachara St 79101
Fleetwood Dr 79109
Fleming Ave 79106
Flint St 79118
N Florida St 79106
S Florida St
100-999 79106
1000-1299 79102
Flower St 79110
Floyd Ave 79106
Flying A Trl 79118
Flying W Trl 79118
E & W Fm 1151 79118
Fm 11870 79119
Fm 11910 79119
S Fm 1258 79118
S Fm 1541 79118
E Fm 1912 79108
N Fm 1912
600-781 79118
N Fm 1912
783-799 79118
1400-3799 79108
3801-5599 79108
S Fm 1912 79118
Fm 2186 79119
Fm 2219 79119
Fm 245 79108
Fm 2575 79108
Fm 2590 79119
Folsom Rd 79108
Foothill Dr 79124
Ford Ave 79108
Fordham Dr 79109
N & S Forest St 79106
S Fork Ave 79118
Fountain Ter 79106
Four D Trl 79118
Four Elms Dr 79119
Four Sixes Trl 79118
Fouts Pl 79121
Fox St
600-699 79111
10900-11599 79118
11601-12499 79118
Fox Hollow Ave 79108
Fox Hunt Ave 79108
Fox Ridge Rd 79118
Fox Terrier Ave 79108
Foxcroft Dr 79109
Foxglove St 79107
Foxtail St 79118
Foxtail Pine Pl 79124
Freddie Rd 79118
S Freliso St 79110
Fremont Pl 79107
Frenerso Dr 79121
Fresno Dr 79118
Fringe Tree Pl 79124
Fritch Hwy 79108
Frog Leap Ln 79118
Front Blvd 79106
Fulham Dr 79109
Fulton Dr 79109
Gables St 79110
Gainsborough Dr 79121
Gainsborough Rd 79106
Gallardia St 79108
Gamma Ln 79110
Garden Ln 79106
Garden Oaks Dr 79119
Garden Way Dr 79119
Gardenia St 79107
N Garfield St 79107
S Garfield St
301-397 79102
399-1199 79102
1201-1799 79102
2000-2899 79103
Garland St 79106
Garrett St 79108
Garwood Rd 79109
Gary Dr 79118
Gary Ln 79110
Gaston Ave & Ct 79119
Gatewood St 79109
Gem Lake Rd 79106
Genevie Rd 79118
Gentry Dr 79124
George Ter 79106
Georgetown Dr 79119
N Georgia St
1-499 79106
501-1099 79106
8101-8499 79108
S Georgia St
100-198 79106
200-899 79106
900-1699 79102
1800-1898 79109
1900-3700 79109
3702-4098 79109
4100-4999 79110
5001-5299 79110
6000-9098 79118
9100-15600 79118
15602-17098 79118
Gerald Dr 79121
Geronimo Rd 79108
Gettysburg Rd 79118
Ghost Dance Trl 79124
Gina Ln 79118
N & S Girl Scout Rd 79124
Givens Ave 79108
Gladstone Ln 79121
Glen Eagle Trl 79118
Glenn St 79108
Glenoak Ln 79109
Glenrosa Ln 79124
Glenview Ct 79124
Glenwood Dr 79119
Gloria St 79108
Goal Pl 79119
Golden Dr 79111
Golden Chestnut Ln 79124
Golden Pond Pl 79121
Goldenrod St 79107
N & S Goliad St 79106
Goodbar Trl 79108
Goodfellow Ln 79121
Goodnight Trl
4500-5399 79109
7600-8499 79110
Gordon St 79104
Grace Ln 79124
Graham St 79108
Gramercy Pkwy 79106
Granada Dr 79109
Granapple Ave 79118
N Grand St 79107
S Grand St
100-198 79104
200-1610 79104
1612-1698 79104
1800-3300 79103
3302-4298 79103
6201-7399 79118
8600-8698 79118
Grand Oak Ave 79118
Grande Dr 79108
N Grant St 79107
S Grant St
100-999 79101
1001-1199 79101
2600-2698 79103
Grantham Dr 79109
Green Haven Rd 79110
Greenbriar Dr 79119
Greentree Ct 79119
Greenway Pl 79109
Greenways Dr 79119
Greenwich Pl 79119
Greenwood Ln 79109
Greg St 79118
Gregory Dr 79106
Grenoble St 79110
Gresham Dr 79110
Greyhawk Rd 79119
Grimes Cir 79118
Grisham Ln 79118
Gunn Ct 79106
Gypsyman Ln 79108
H Ave 79111
Hacienda Dr 79111
Hackberry Dr 79118
Haddock Ln 79118
Hadley Dr 79118
Hagy Blvd 79106
Haimes St 79118
Hall Ave 79109
Hallmark Ave 79119
Halsey Trl 79118
Halstead St 79106
Hamilton Dr 79119
Hammon St 79118
Hamner Dr 79107
Hampton Dr 79109
Hamstead Dr 79109
Hancock Rd 79119
Hancock St
2300-2399 79106
2401-3399 79106
3400-3899 79109
Hansford Cir & Dr 79106
Hanson Rd 79106
Hardin Dr 79110
Hardwick Dr 79109
Hardy St 79106
Harmony St
2300-3299 79106
3400-4399 79109
Harper St 79107
Harrington Cir 79121
Harris Dr 79103
N Harrison St 79107
S Harrison St
100-1599 79101
1600-1899 79102
1900-3500 79109
3502-3598 79109
3600-4299 79110
Harvard St 79109
E Hastings Ave 79108
W Hastings Ave
100-998 79108
3600-4198 79124
Hatfield Cir 79109
Hatton Rd 79110
Havenville Dr 79118
Hawk Ln 79118
Hawthorne Dr 79109
N Hayden St 79107
S Hayden St
100-399 79106
400-698 79101
700-1099 79101
1100-1799 79102
1900-3499 79109
3600-4699 79110
Hayes Rd 79124
N Hayes St 79107
S Hayes St 79103
Hazel Ave 79107
Headquarters Rd 79124
Heather St 79107
Heidi Ln 79108
Helium Rd
1-100 79124
102-1998 79124
9001-9497 79119
9499-11699 79119
11701-16299 79119
Hemlock Pl 79124
Henning St 79106
Herlerli Dr 79111
Herman St 79102
Hermosa Dr 79108
Herring Ln 79118
Herring Park Dr 79119
Hesperus Dr 79118
Hester Dr 79124
Hetrick Dr 79108
Hickory St 79107
Higgins Pl 79121
High Point Dr 79124
N Highland St 79107
S Highland St
400-899 79104
901-1099 79104
1700-2999 79103
E Highway 60 79108
E Highway 66 79108
Hill Dr 79118
Hill Rd 79119
N Hill St 79107
S Hill St
500-1499 79104
1501-1799 79104
2700-3500 79103
3502-3698 79103
Hill View Dr 79124
Hillcrest St 79106
Hillside Rd
4100-4199 79110
4800-4898 79109
4900-7299 79109
7300-7799 79119
Hilltop Dr 79108
Hines Rd 79108
Hinsdale Dr 79109
Hinsey Dr 79108
Hobbs Rd 79109
Hodges St
1000-1499 79104
2800-3299 79103
Hogan Dr 79124
Holbrook St 79118
Holiday Dr 79109
Holly St 79108
Hollywood Rd
1200-1698 79118
1700-5800 79118
5802-6398 79118
6700-6800 79119
6802-7198 79119
E Hollywood Rd 79118
Holyoke Trl 79121
Hombre Ln 79108
Homestead Trl 79118
Hondo St 79102
Hope Rd
1601-1797 79124
1799-3099 79124
3101-3399 79124
3400-3698 79119
3700-7699 79119
7701-10899 79119
Horizon Rd 79118
N Houston St 79107
S Houston St
1-99 79101
101-197 79102
199-1799 79102
2000-2899 79103
Hoving Pl 79121
Howard Dr 79106
Hubbard St 79118
Hud Dr 79124
Hudson Ave 79108
Huey Pl 79121
N Hughes St 79107
S Hughes St
1-99 79106
1400-1800 79102
1802-1898 79102
2000-3499 79109
3600-4699 79110
Hunter Dr 79119
Huntington Dr 79109
Hurst St 79109
Hyde Pkwy 79109
Hyman St 79108
I Ave 79111
Ian Dr 79119
Ida Louise Ct 79110
Imperial Dr 79121
Imperial Trl 79106
N & S Independence
St 79106
Indian Trl 79110
Indian Hill Rd 79124
Indian Lake Rd 79118
Industrial St 79104
Ingram Dr 79108
Inman Dr 79104
Interstate 27 79119
E Interstate 40
900-5698 79103
E Interstate 40
1501-2199 79102
2301-5499 79104
5601-5699 79103
6000-11400 79118
11402-14298 79118
W Interstate 40
400-3898 79102
1101-3897 79109
3899-3999 79109
4000-4198 79102
4001-4199 79109
4200-7400 79106
7402-8598 79106
7701-8599 79121
8700-19199 79124
Irene Dr 79107
Iris St 79107
Iroquois Ave 79107
Irving Ln 79121
Irvington Ct 79119
Irwin Rd 79108
Ivanhoe Dr 79108
J Ave 79111
Ja Trl 79118
Jacksnhole 79118
N Jackson St 79107
S Jackson St
100-1599 79101
1600-1799 79102
1900-3499 79109
3501-3599 79109
3600-4599 79110
Jacoda Ave 79118
Jake Spoon Trl 79118
Jamaica St 79118
James Ave 79106
James Louis Dr 79110
Jameson Dr 79121
Jameson Rd 79106
Jamie Ln 79118
Jamie Trl 79110
Janae St 79118
Janet Dr
100-199 79118
3100-3599 79109
Jared Pl 79109
Jasmine St 79107
Jason Ave 79107
Jean Ave 79109
Jean Ln 79118
N Jefferson St 79107
S Jefferson St 79101
Jennie Ave 79106
Jennifer St 79107
Jennings Dr 79118
Jenny Ln 79118
Jersey Elm Pl 79124
Jessie Ln 79119
Jewell Dr 79109
Jill Ct 79119
Jim Dr 79124
Johanna St 79119
John Dr 79110
John David Cir 79124
Johnny Ave 79124
Johns Way Blvd 79118
N Johnson St 79107
S Johnson St
101-697 79101
699-1599 79101
1600-1799 79102
1801-1999 79102
Jonathan St 79118
Jordan St 79106
Joseph Rd 79119
Josephine Cir 79118
Joshua Deets 79118
Journey St 79110
Juaquin Ln 79108
Judd Blvd 79124
Judy St 79106
Juett Attebury Rd 79118
Julian Blvd 79102
Julie Dr 79109
Juniper Dr 79109
Justin Dr 79109
Kachina Dr 79124
Kalee Dr 79109
Kansas St 79106
Karen St 79106
Katie Ln 79118
Keith St 79110
Kelly Pl 79108
Kendall Rd 79124
Kensington Pl 79121
N Kentucky St 79106
S Kentucky St
100-999 79106
1000-1699 79102
2401-2499 79109
2600-2698 79109
Kerr Pl 79121
Ketler St 79104

Street	ZIP
Keystone Dr	79108
Kileen Dr	79109
Killgore Dr	79106
Kimberly Rd	79111
Kinderhook Ct	79119
King Ave	79106
King Hill Dr	79124
Kingery Pl	79107
Kings Pl	79109
Kingsbury Dr	79109
Kingsgate Dr	79119
Kingston Rd	
3200-3399	79106
3400-4499	79109
Kingswood Cir	79109
Kirk Dr	79110
Kirkland Dr	79106
Klinke Rd	79108
Knight St	79107
Knoll Dr	
3400-3799	79118
3800-4199	79110
Knoxville Dr	79118
Kodiak Ave	79118
Koetting Ln	79118
Kukihalo Rd	79124
Kuykendall Ln	79119
La Costa Dr	79124
La Fiesta Ln	79118
La Gloria Trl	79108
La Mesa Ave	79107
La Paloma St	79106
La Reata Ln	79124
La Ruth St	79108
N & S La Salle St	79106
Lacona Dr	79119
Lafayette Ln	79118
Lago Dr	79108
Lago Vista St	79118
Laguna Dr	79110
Laguna Vista Rd	79119
Lair Rd	79118
N Lake St	79107
S Lake St	79104
Lake Front Ln	79121
Lake Tanglewood Dr	79118
N Lakeside Dr	
2-598	79118
701-799	79107
2300-9099	79108
S Lakeside Dr	79118
Lakeview Dr	79109
E Lakeview Rd	79118
W Lakeview Rd	79118
akwood Dr	79118
N Lamar St	79106
S Lamar St	
100-900	79106
902-910	79106
911-1600	79102
1602-1698	79102
3400-3699	79109
4400-4598	79110
4600-4799	79110
amount Dr	79110
ancaster Rd	79124
andon Dr	79119
ane View Dr	79124
angtry Ct & Dr	79109
aredo Trl	79110
ariat Dr	79111
ark St	79124
arkspur Pl	79106
arry St	79106
as Colinas Ct	79124
as Tecovas Trl	79124
auder St	79119
aurel St	79109
auren Ln	79108
aurie Ln	79119
awndale Dr	79103
awrence Blvd	79106
awson Ln	79106
awton Dr	79110
azy B Rd	79118
azy Two Rd	79118
Leah Trl	79110
Learning Tree Ln	79119
Ledgestone Dr	79119
Legend Ave	79121
Leigh Ave	79110
S Leigh St	79118
Leland Dr	79110
Lemon St	79107
Lenwood Dr	79109
Leo Ln	79110
Leroy Way	79108
Lesly Dr	79118
Letha Ln	79118
Lewis Ln	79109
Lexington Sq	79119
Lexis St	79119
Liberty Cir S	79119
Lightfoot Dr	79108
Lilac Ln	79106
Limestone Dr	79119
N Lincoln St	79107
S Lincoln St	
100-698	79101
700-1599	79101
1600-1800	79102
1802-1898	79102
1900-2000	79109
2002-2798	79109
Linda Cir & Dr	79109
Lindberg St	79107
Linden Ln	79106
Lindsey Ln	79121
Line Ave	
1401-1497	79101
1499-1600	79101
1602-1798	79101
1900-1998	79102
2201-2297	79106
2299-3999	79106
Lion Rd	79118
N Lipscomb St	79107
S Lipscomb St	
100-399	79106
500-698	79101
700-1099	79101
1100-1699	79102
1701-1799	79102
1900-1998	79109
2000-3500	79109
3502-3598	79109
3600-4699	79110
Lisa Ln	79118
Lisbon St	79118
Little Fox Rd	79118
Littlerock Dr	79118
Live Oak Dr	79110
Livingwater Dr	79118
Lloyd Dr	79110
Lobo Trl	79124
Locke Pl	79124
Lockney St	79106
Locust St	79109
Logan Pl	79119
Loma Linda Ln	79118
Loma Vista Dr	79108
Lombard Rd	79106
Lometa Dr	79109
London Ct	79119
Lone Star Rd	79119
Long Dr	79108
Longleaf Ln	79124
Longoria Rd	79119
Looby Ln	79124
E Loop 335 N	79108
E Loop 335 S	79118
N Loop 335 E	79108
N Loop 335 W	79124
S Loop 335 E	79118
S Loop 335 W	79119
W Loop 335 N	
2801-3199	79108
W Loop 335 N	
7800-7899	79124
W Loop 335 S	
301-399	79118
6700-8499	79119
Lost Canyon Dr	79124
Lost Creek Trl	79124
N & S Louisiana St	79106
Love Ave	79108
Lowes Ln	79106
Loyce Ave	79109
Ls Trl	79118
Lufrank St	79118
Lundy Ln	79119
Lyles St	79106
Lyndale Dr	79109
Lynette Dr	79109
Lynnlee Cir & Pl	79121
Lytham Ct	79124
Macarthur Trl	79118
Mack Rd	79118
Mackenzie Trl	79124
Madera Pl	79124
N Madison St	79107
S Madison St	
200-1599	79101
1600-1699	79102
1701-1799	79102
1900-2099	79109
Madrid St	79118
Mager Dr	79108
Magnolia St	79107
Main St	79118
Makenna Ct	79119
Malibu Way	79124
Mammoth Ln	79110
Manchester Rd	79124
N Manhattan St	79107
S Manhattan St	
100-1000	79104
1002-1198	79104
1701-1797	79103
1799-3000	79103
3002-3198	79103
Manor Cir	79109
Manor Haven Ct	79119
Manzella St	79108
Maple St	79107
Margarita Ln	79118
Maria Ln	79118
Marika Cir	79124
Marion St	
3300-3399	79106
3400-3499	79109
Mariposa Dr	79124
Mark Rd	79118
Marlboro Rd	79118
Marlowe Rd	79108
Marni Trl	79110
N Marrs St	79107
S Marrs St	
300-1098	79104
1700-2999	79103
Marsh Pl	79121
Marshall Dr	79108
Martin Rd	
800-840	79107
841-841	79117
842-3498	79107
1001-3499	79107
Mary Dell Dr	79109
Mary Jon Dr	79119
Mary Rose Ave	79118
N & S Maryland St	79106
Massie Dr	79108
N Masterson Rd	79108
S Masterson Rd	79118
Matador Trl	79109
Mathis Dr	79118
Mattie Rd	79118
Maverick St	79109
Maynor Pl	79121
Mays St	79109
Mcafee Ln	79118
Mccall Pl	79121
Mccarty Blvd	79110
Mcclary St	79108
E Mccormick Rd	79118
W Mccormick Rd	
1101-1397	79118
1399-7200	79118
7202-7298	79118
7301-7597	79119
7599-8600	79119
8602-18898	79119
Mccoy Dr	79109
Mckay Ct	79118
Mckenzie Rd	79118
Mckinley Ln	79110
Mclemore Ln	79108
N Mcmasters St	
1-999	79106
1001-1299	79106
1301-1499	79107
S Mcmasters St	79106
Meadow Dr	79109
Meadowgreen Dr	79110
Meadowland Dr	79124
Meadowlark Dr	79118
Medi Park Dr	79106
Medical Dr	79106
Meister St	79119
Melfrank Dr	79124
Melody Dr	79118
Melody Ln	79108
Memory Ln & Pl	79109
Memphis Ave	79118
Merchant Dr	79121
Mercy Ct	79118
Meredith Ln	79118
Merion Pl	79124
Meritta Ln	79118
Mesa Cir	79109
Mesa Verde Dr	79107
Mescalero Trl	79118
Mesilla Ave	79108
Mesquite Ave	79108
Mesquite Dr	79118
Mesquite Springs Trl	79119
Mia Dai Dr	79118
Michael Ln	79118
Michaela Ct & Dr	79119
Michelle Dr	79109
Middleboro Dr	79109
Midsummer Ct	79109
Midwick Dr	79118
N Milam St	79106
S Milam St	
100-600	79106
602-798	79106
900-1699	79102
1800-1898	79109
1900-3699	79109
4700-5799	79110
5800-5999	79118
W Mile View Dr	79124
Milford Dr	79109
Miller Rd	79108
Millie Pl	79119
Milligan Pl	79119
Mills Ln	79118
Mimosa Ln	79107
N Mirror St	79107
S Mirror St	
300-798	79102
2000-2899	79103
3500-4599	79118
N Mississippi St	79106
S Mississippi St	
100-198	79106
200-1019	79106
1020-1199	79102
Missy Dr	79119
Mitcham Dr	79121
Moberly Dr	79111
Mobilhomestead Dr	79107
E & W Mobley St	79108
Mockingbird Ln	79109
Mohawk Dr	79109
Mollie Dr	79110
Monet Rue	79121
Monk St	79108
N Monroe St	79107
S Monroe St	
101-197	79101
199-1599	79101
1600-1799	79102
1900-3500	79109
3502-3598	79109
3600-4399	79110
Montague Dr	79109
Montana Way	79118
Montclair Ct & Dr	79124
Montcrest Way	79124
Monterey Dr	79110
Monticello Ct	79119
Montview Dr	79124
Moore St	79107
Mooregate Dr	79109
Morgan St	79118
Morning Dr	79108
Moser Dr	79110
Mosley St	79119
Moss Ln	79109
Mountain Dr	79108
Muirfield Ln	79124
Mulberry Trl	79124
Mule Deer Rd	79124
Mustang St	79102
Myatt Dr	79119
Myrtle Dr	79118
N Nance St	79107
S Nance St	79104
Nancy Ellen St	79119
Napa Pl	79118
Naples Ct	79119
Nashville	79118
Nassau Trl	79118
Navajo Rd	79108
Navajo Trl	79110
Navasota Dr	79109
Neal St	79118
Nebhut Rd	79108
Nebraska St	
2700-3399	79106
3400-3699	79109
N Nelson St	79107
S Nelson St	
300-498	79104
500-999	79104
1001-1599	79104
1700-3199	79103
Nena Ln	79119
Neuches Ave	79104
Nevermind Pl	79109
New England Dr & Pkwy	79119
Newlin Cir	79109
Newport Dr	79124
Newt Dobbs Trl	79118
Nez Perce Trl	79108
Nicholas Cir & Dr	79109
Nick St	79119
Nimbus Ln	79110
Nix St	79107
Noah St	79118
Nogo St	79119
Norahs Ln	79119
Norfolk Dr	79119
Northridge Dr	79108
Norwich Dr	79109
Norwood Dr	79119
Notre Dame Dr	79109
Nottingham Rd	79124
Nova Scotia Ct	79119
Oak Dr	79107
Oakcrest Ln	79109
Oakdale Dr	79103
Oakhurst Dr	79109
Oakman Dr	79109
Oakmont Ln	79118
Oakridge Ln	79124
Oakview Dr	79119
Office Park Dr	79110
Old Kent Rd	79109
Old Mill Rd	79124
Oldham Cir	79109
Oleta Dr	79110
Olive St	79103
Oliver Pl	79106
Olsen Blvd	
3300-4199	79109
4200-4899	79106
Olsen Cir	79106
Olympia Dr	79110
Olympic Ct	79124
Omaha Ave	79106
One O One Trl	79118
Oneill Dr	79109
N Ong St	79107
S Ong St	
100-299	79106
701-799	79101
1300-1398	79102
1400-1799	79102
1900-3499	79109
3600-4699	79110
Onwetsia Rd	79118
Opal Ct	79124
Orange St	79107
Oregon Trl	79109
Orry Ave	79119
Ortega Rd	79118
N Osage St	79107
S Osage St	
301-897	79104
899-999	79104
2600-2899	79103
3500-13699	79118
13701-13999	79118
Otsego Dr	79106
Ottawa Trl	79118
Ottobahn	79119
Outback Trl	79118
Overland Ave	79108
Overlook Cir	79118
Overlook Dr	79109
Oxbow Trl	79106
Oxford Dr	79119
Ozark Trl	79109
Pace St	79118
Packard Ave	79108
Padron Ave	79108
Pagoda Dr	79110
Painted Daisy Pl	79106
Pajaretta Dr	79110
Palacio Cir & Dr	79109
Paladin Dr	79111
Palermo Rd	79118
Palm St	79107
Palmer Dr	
3300-3399	79106
3400-3499	79109
Palmetto Trl	79106
N & S Palo Duro St	79106
Palo Pinto St	79118
Paloma Dr	79108
Palomino Dr	79118
Palomino St	79106
Panhandle Ave	79108
Pans St	79118
Paradise St	79107
Paragon Dr	79119
Paramount Blvd	79109
Park Ave & Cir E, N, S & W	79108
Park Place Ave	79101
Park Ridge Dr	79109
Park Village Cir	79109
Parker St	
100-599	79106
600-698	79101
700-1000	79101
1002-1098	79101
1300-1699	79102
1900-3299	79109
3600-5399	79110
Parkside Dr	79109
Parkview Dr	79106
Parkway Dr	79119
Parkwood Pl	79119
Parr St	79106
N Parsley Rd	79108
S Parsley Rd	79118
Partridge Dr	79124
Paseo Ave	79108
Patrick Pass	79124
Patriot Dr	79119
Patterson Dr	79109
Patton Ave	79118
Patton Ter	79106
Pavillard Dr	79108
Pawnee Dr	79109
Peach Tree St	79109
Peantind Dr	79124
Pebble Beach Ct	79124
Pebblebrook Dr	79119
Pecan St	79107
Pecos St	79102
Pelman Pl	79109
Pembroke Ave	79108
Pennsylvania Dr	79119
Pepper Tree Pl	79124
Percell St	79118
Perry Ave	79119
Perry Ct	79124
Perry Ln	79119
Persimmon Ln	79124
Peterson Rd	79118
Pettitt St	79108
Pheasant Ln	79118
Phil Langen Blvd	79106
N Philadelphia St	79107
S Philadelphia St	
100-999	79104
1900-3200	79103
3202-3398	79103
Phillips Dr	79109
Picassico Dr	79108
Pichon Dr	79108
Pico Blvd	79110
N Pierce St	79107
S Pierce St	
1-97	79101
99-1599	79101
1600-1699	79102
1701-1799	79102
2100-2999	79109
3000-3199	79110
Pikes Peak Dr	79110
Pilgrim Dr	79119
Pin Oak Dr	79110
Pine St	
2700-2899	79103
3600-4599	79118
Pine Hurst Pl	79119
Pine Valley Ln	79124
Pinecrest Dr	79124
Pinehurst Dr	79109
Pineridge Dr	79119
Pinnacle Dr	79119
Pinon Ave	79107
Pinon Dr	79118
Pinto Dr	79118
Pinto Ln	79106
Pioneer Ln	79118
Pitaya Pl	79118
Pitt Rd	79118
Pittsburg St	
201-297	79104
299-999	79104
1900-3199	79103
Plains Blvd	
3000-3199	79102
3201-3999	79102
4101-6099	79106
E & W Plantation Rd	79118
Plateau Ln	79106
Plaudit Trl	79108
Player Pl	79124
Plaza St	79109
Pleasant Ct	79110
Plum Ln	79121
Plum Creek Dr	79124
Plymouth Dr	79119
Podzemny Rd	79118
Pohnert Ln	79118
W Point Dr	79121
Point West Pkwy	79124
Pokaman Ln	79108
N Polk St	
1-99	79101
100-1700	79107
1702-2498	79107
S Polk St	
1-1599	79101

1600-1799 79102
1801-1899 79102
1900-1998 79109
2000-3299 79109
3400-4399 79110
Pomona Dr 79110
Pond Dr 79118
Ponderosa Ln 79107
Pony Dr 79108
Pony Rd 79118
Poplar St
200-299 79118
300-2599 79107
Poppin Ln 79121
Porielli Rd 79119
Port Ln 79106
Port O Call Dr 79118
Porter Dr 79110
Portland Ave 79118
Portrush Ct 79124
Potomac Dr 79108
Potter Dr 79108
Potter Rd 79118
Potts Dr 79118
Prairie Ave 79109
Prairie Edge Rd 79118
Prairie Garden Rd 79119
Prairie View St 79124
Precision Pl 79119
Prentrad Dr 79109
Prescott St 79118
Preston St 79110
Prestwick Ln 79124
Prestwick St 79118
N & S Primrose Pl 79106
Princeton St 79109
Progress Dr 79119
N & S Prospect St 79106
Prosper Dr 79119
Providence 79118
Provo Pl 79118
Pryor St
1000-1499 79104
1501-1799 79104
2900-3299 79103
Puckett Dr 79109
Pueblo Trl 79118
Pullman Rd 79111
S Pullman Rd 79118
Purdue St 79109
Purple Sage Cir 79124
Quadrille Park & St 79106
Quail Blvd & Trl 79124
Quail Creek Dr 79124
Quail Ridge Rd 79118
Quail Springs Trl 79119
Quarry St 79124
Quarter Horse Dr 79104
Quedito Dr 79108
Queens Pl 79109
Quiet Cir 79109
Quincy Dr 79108
Quinlin Ct 79118
Rabbit Run 79124
Rachel Rd 79118
Racine Trl 79108
Radiant Ln 79109
Raef Rd 79108
Raindrop Ln 79110
Raintree Ct 79119
Rally Rd 79119
Ramada Trl 79108
Ramage Dr 79118
Ranch Rd 79124
Ranch Trl 79118
W Ranch View Rd 79124
Rancho Trl 79108
Ranchview Dr 79124
Randall St 79109
Randolph Rd 79106
Randy St 79124
Range Trl 79108
Ranier Dr 79110
Ransome Dr 79107
Rapstine Cir 79124
Raton Trl 79108

Ravine Trl 79108
Raymond Rd 79119
Reagan Ct 79124
Reba Cir 79109
Rebecca Dr 79109
Rebel Rd 79102
Red Lake Cir 79108
Red Oak Dr 79110
Red Rock Rd 79118
Red Wing Rd 79119
Reding Rd 79108
Redondo Dr 79107
Redwood St 79107
Reeder Dr 79121
Reeves Dr 79124
Relatta Ave 79110
Remuda Pl 79124
Rendezvous Trl 79108
Renegade Trl 79108
Reno Trl 79108
Republic Ave 79109
Reserve Ct 79124
Revere Dr 79119
Reward Pl 79119
Rhine Ave 79110
Rhonda Ave 79118
Ricardo Dr 79109
Richard Ave 79106
Richmond Rd 79118
Ricks St
1000-1499 79104
2800-3299 79103
Ridgecrest Cir 79109
Ridgemere Blvd 79107
Ridgewood Dr 79109
Ries Ln 79118
Rietman St 79108
Rigdon St 79121
Riker Ln 79108
Riley Ln 79108
Riley Elizabeth Pl 79119
Rim Ranch Dr 79124
Rimrock Dr 79118
Rimrock Trl 79108
Rimsite Dr 79118
Rincon Ave 79110
Rio Trl 79108
Rio Grande St 79104
Rio Lobo St 79110
Rita Blanca Trl 79108
River Rd
3400-3599 79107
4000-10299 79108
River Birch Pl 79124
Rivercrest Dr 79108
Riveria Trl 79108
Rj Dr 79119
Rm 1061 79124
Roach Dr
8000-8099 79121
9000-9099 79124
Road Runner 79118
Roadrunner Ct 79119
Roaring Trl 79108
Robbie Rd 79118
Robbie St 79119
Roberta Dr 79108
Roberts Dr 79118
N Roberts St 79107
S Roberts St
300-398 79102
400-1599 79102
1601-1699 79102
2000-2899 79103
3600-4599 79118
Rochelle Ln 79109
Rochester 79118
Rocker K Rd 79118
Rockwell Rd 79118
W Rockwell Rd
4000-7298 79118
8800-12298 79119
Rocky Rd 79118
Rogers St 79106
Rolling Trl 79108
Rolling Prairie Dr 79118

Ron Dr 79107
Rondo Ave 79110
N Roosevelt St 79107
S Roosevelt St 79103
Rose Dr 79108
Rosebud 79118
Rosemary Ln 79119
N & S Rosemont St 79106
Rosenda Ln 79124
Rosewood Ave 79118
Ross St
100-298 79102
300-1799 79102
1801-1999 79102
2300-2898 79103
2301-2301 79120
2303-2899 79103
3600-4600 79118
4602-4698 79118
Ross Osage St 79103
Roxton Dr 79109
Royal Rd
2600-2899 79106
3400-3699 79109
Royce Dr 79110
Ruidoso Trl 79108
Rule St 79107
Running M Trl 79118
Running W Trl 79118
Rushmore Dr 79110
N Rusk St
1-399 79106
1400-1499 79107
S Rusk St
100-899 79106
900-1599 79102
1601-1699 79102
3200-3699 79109
4600-4799 79110
4801-4899 79110
5800-5999 79118
Russell Dr 79118
Russell St 79104
Rustic Trl 79108
Rutgers St 79109
Rutson Dr 79109
Ryan Palmer Ln 79124
Sabre Trl 79124
Saddleback Rd 79119
Saddlehorn Rd 79119
Sage St 79118
Sage Meadow Dr 79124
Sagebrush Ave 79108
Saint Andrews Dr 79124
Saint Andrews Rd 79118
E & W Saint Francis
Ave 79108
Saint Louis Dr 79118
Saint Paul St 79106
Salem Dr 79110
S Sallerel St 79106
San Angelo Ave 79118
San Antonio Dr 79118
San Jacinto Ave 79106
San Jose Dr 79118
San Saba St 79118
Sanborn St 79107
Sandench St 79118
Sanders Ave 79108
Sandhills Ln 79124
Sandie Ct & Dr 79109
Sandlewood Ave 79118
Sanford St 79108
Sangria Ln 79118
Santa Fe Trl 79110
Sarah Ln 79108
Saratoga Dr 79108
Sarazen Pl 79124
Savannah Rd 79118
Savoy Dr 79118
Scotswood Dr
3900-4098 79118
4100-4199 79118
4200-4699 79110
Scotty Dr 79110
N Seminole St 79107

S Seminole St
301-1599 79104
1700-2999 79103
3001-3199 79103
Sequoia St 79107
Seth Ln 79108
Seven S Trl 79118
Seville Dr 79121
Shadow Ct 79110
Shady Ln 79109
Shady Brook Dr 79124
Shadywood Dr 79119
Shannon Dr 79118
Sharman Loop 79124
Sharon Dr 79118
Shasta Dr 79110
Shawnee Trl 79109
Sheffield Rd 79124
Shelby Dr 79109
Sheldon Rd
6501-6997 79109
6999-7099 79109
7500-8199 79119
Shenandoah Rd 79118
Shepherd Ave 79108
Sheri Cir 79124
Sherman Trl 79124
Sherrill Dr 79108
Sherwood Ln 79110
Shield Ct & Dr 79110
Shiloh Rd 79118
Shinnecock Dr 79124
Shiraz Blvd 79124
N & S Shore Dr 79118
Shores Ct 79110
Short St 79102
Short Oaks 79124
Shreveport Dr 79118
Shylana Ave 79119
N Side Dr 79108
Sideoats Ave 79118
Sierra Ct 79109
Sierra Pl 79118
Sierra Hills Rd 79124
Siesta Ln 79118
Silver Hill Cir 79108
Silverbell Ln 79124
Simmons Cir 79108
Simpson Dr 79121
Sinclair St 79119
Skipper Trl 79108
Skokie Rd 79118
Skylark Dr 79118
Skyline Dr 79108
Slater Cir 79110
Sleepy Hollow Blvd 79121
Slope Dr 79108
Smiley St 79106
Smith Ave 79108
Smoketree Dr 79124
Snead Ln 79124
Snowball Trl 79108
Soaring Eagle Dr 79103
Sombrero Dr 79108
Somerset Dr 79109
N Soncy Rd 79124
S Soncy Rd
2000-2098 79124
2100-3399 79124
3400-8800 79119
8802-9098 79119
Sophia Ln 79108
Southbend Dr 79119
Southlawn Cir 79110
Southpark Dr 79109
Southridge Dr 79118
Southside Dr 79109
Southwood Dr 79119
Spade Dr 79104
Spanky Ln 79110
Spark St 79108
Spartanburg Dr 79119
Speer Rd 79124
Spencer St 79109
Spirit Ln 79119
Spokane Ave 79118

N Spring St 79107
S Spring St
500-1599 79104
2500-3299 79103
Spring Cherry Ln 79124
Springfield Ave 79118
Springwood Dr 79119
Spruce St 79103
Spur 228
900-999 79111
Spur 228
1100-1298 79118
Spur 591 79107
Spurlock Ln 79118
Squaw Springs Trl 79124
Stacy Cir 79121
Stagecoach Trl 79124
Stanley St 79109
Stapleton St 79109
Star Ln 79109
Star Bright Ln 79108
Stardust Ln 79118
State Highway 136 79108
Steeplechase Dr 79106
Steffi Ct 79110
Stepp Ave 79110
Sterling Dr 79110
Steves Way 79118
Stewart Dr 79118
Stinnett Rd 79108
Stockton Dr 79118
Stone Dr 79109
Stone View Dr 79124
Stonebridge Gate 79124
Stoneham Dr 79109
Stoneridge Ct 79119
Stoneridge Dr 79124
Stony Pt 79121
Storage Dr 79110
Strader Rd 79119
Strawman Trl 79108
Stray Horse Trl 79124
Streit Dr 79106
Stromberg Pl 79121
Stuart Dr 79104
Stubbs St 79106
E & W Studebaker
Ave 79108
Stuyvesant Ave 79121
Success Pl 79119
Sue Ter 79107
Sugarloaf Dr 79110
Sumac Pl 79124
Summit Cir 79109
Sunburst St 79110
Suncrest Way 79124
Sundance Ln 79119
E Sundown Ln 79118
W Sundown Ln
1201-2697 79118
2699-4199 79118
4201-4799 79118
7601-8997 79119
8999-11299 79119
11301-14799 79119
Sundown Trl 79118
Sunflower Dr 79118
Sunflower Pl 79106
Sunlake Dr 79124
Sunlite St
2701-3097 79106
3099-3399 79106
3400-3699 79109
Sunrise Dr 79104
Sunset Ter 79106
Surf Dr 79110
Susan Dr 79110
Susan Ln 79118
Susie Rd 79118
Sutton Pl 79124
Suzanna St 79119
Sweet St 79118
Sweetbay Ln 79124
Sweetgum Ln 79124
Sweetwater Trl 79124
Sycamore St 79107

Syracuse Dr 79109
T Bar Trl 79118
T O Rd 79118
Tacoma Dr 79118
Tallahassee Dr 79118
Tammy Ave 79108
Tangier Ave 79118
Tangle Aire Ln & Pt 79118
Tanglewood Dr & Rd 79118
Tank Ln 79118
Taos Dr 79118
Tappan Zee St 79121
Tara Rd 79118
Tarrington Dr 79109
Tarrytown Ave 79121
Tarter Ave
7800-7999 79121
8800-8899 79119
Tartugo St 79108
Tascocita Cir 79124
Tascosa Rd 79124
Tawney Ave 79106
Taylor Rd 79119
N Taylor St 79107
S Taylor St
97-97 79101
99-1599 79101
1600-1799 79102
2000-2098 79109
2100-3100 79109
3102-3198 79109
3201-3297 79110
3299-3899 79110
Teakwood St 79107
Teal Ct 79106
Teckla Blvd
2000-3399 79106
3400-4499 79109
Tee Anchor Blvd 79104
Tejas Trl 79110
Tempe St 79118
Temple Dr 79110
Tennant St 79104
N & S Tennessee St 79106
Tennis Ct 79118
E Terielaw Ave 79104
Terrace Dr 79109
Terry St 79107
Terryville Dr 79109
Theda Dr 79109
Theresa Ave 79108
Thornberry Ave 79118
Thorne Dr 79107
Thornton Dr 79109
Thunder Rd 79119
Thurman St
2900-2999 79106
3400-3699 79109
Tierra Dr 79108
Tiffani Dr 79109
Tilden Ct 79124
Tiltrotor Dr 79111
Timber Dr 79121
N, E, S & W
Timbercreek Cir & Dr 79118
Timothy Ln 79118
Tipton St 79108
Tivis St 79119
Tj Dr 79119
Toby St 79110
Tomahawk Trl 79124
Tonja Ave 79108
Topeka Dr 79118
Torre Dr 79109
Tower Dr 79104
Tower Rd 79108
Tradewind St 79118
Trail View St 79124
Trammell Ave 79118
Tranquil Cir 79109
Tranquility Cir & Rd 79118
N Travis St 79107
S Travis St
100-399 79106
601-897 79101
899-1099 79101

1101-1197 79102
1199-1699 79102
2000-3299 79109
3600-5299 79110
5800-5898 79118
5900-6399 79118
Trevino Ave 79124
Triangle Dr
7800-8098 79107
8100-8199 79107
8500-8598 79108
8600-10399 79108
Trigg St
1000-1499 79104
1501-1799 79104
2800-3299 79103
Trinchera Dr 79110
Trinidad St 79118
Tripp Ave 79121
Triumph Pl 79119
Troon Ct 79124
Troveta Dr 79110
Troy Dr 79121
Truman St 79118
Tucker Rd 79118
Tucson Dr 79109
Tudor Dr 79104
Tulane Dr 79109
Tularosa St 79102
Tule Dr 79108
Tulia Dr 79109
Tulip Ave 79110
Tumbleweed Dr 79110
Turtle Creek Dr 79118
Tuscany Vlg 79119
Tutbury Ct 79119
Twin Lakes Rd 79118
Twin View Dr 79124
Two Deer Trl 79124
N Tyler St
1-5 79101
7-99 79101
101-297 79107
299-1599 79107
S Tyler St
96-98 79101
100-1599 79101
1600-1800 79102
1802-1898 79102
1900-1998 79109
2000-3499 79109
3500-4400 79110
4402-4498 79110
Tyndale Ln 79118
Underwood Dr 79121
Union Rd 79119
Upman Rd 79108
Upton Rd 79119
Us Highway 287 79118
N Us Highway 287 79108
S Us Highway 287 79118
E Us Highway 66 79108
Ute Trl 79119
Vail Dr 79118
Val Verde Ave 79118
Valcour Dr 79119
E & W Valencia Dr 79118
Valhalla Ln 79124
Valley Ave 79108
Valleyview Dr
8600-8699 7911
8800-9098 79118
N Van Buren St 7910
S Van Buren St
100-198 7910
200-1599 7910
1600-1799 7910
1801-1899 7910
1900-3599 7910
3600-4399 7911
Van Kriston Dr 7912
Van Tassel St 7912
Van Winkle Dr
3500-4499 7912
4500-4799 7911
Van Zandt St 7911
Vance Ave 7911

Vantage Ln ... 79109
Venetia Rd ... 79118
Venice Dr ... 79110
Ventura Dr ... 79110
N Vernon St ... 79107
S Vernon St
500-900 ... 79104
902-1698 ... 79104
2500-3299 ... 79103
Versailles Dr ... 79121
Veterans St ... 79106
Victoria St ... 79106
Victory Dr ... 79119
E, N, S & W View Dr & Ln ... 79124
Viewpoint Ave ... 79124
Viewpoint Dr ... 79118
Villa Pl ... 79109
Vinewood St ... 79108
Virginia Cir ... 79109
N Virginia St ... 79106
S Virginia St
100-999 ... 79106
1000-1900 ... 79102
1902-1998 ... 79102
3400-4799 ... 79109
Vision Dr ... 79119
Vista Dr ... 79124
Voyager Trl ... 79118
Wabash St ... 79109
Wagon Trl ... 79118
Wagon Wheel Rd ... 79124
Wajo Ln ... 79108
Walden Ave ... 79107
Walesa Ct ... 79119
Walker Dr ... 79107
Walking H Trl ... 79118
Wallace Ave ... 79108
Wallace Blvd
901-1197 ... 79106
1199-7499 ... 79106
7500-7999 ... 79124
Walls Rd ... 79118
Walnut St ... 79107
Walpole Pl ... 79109
Walters St ... 79106
Wandering ... 79118
Wapiti Ln ... 79108
Ward St ... 79110
Warehouse Road 3 ... 79111
Warehouse Road 4 ... 79111
N Washington St ... 79107
S Washington St
601-699 ... 79101
1100-1298 ... 79102
1300-1700 ... 79102
1702-1898 ... 79102
1900-3500 ... 79109
3502-3598 ... 79109
3600-5499 ... 79110
5501-5699 ... 79110
Washington Park Pl ... 79118
Watford Cir ... 79109
Watson Pl ... 79110
Wayne St
3300-3399 ... 79106
3400-3799 ... 79109
Wayside Dr ... 79106
Wc Trl ... 79118
Webb Rd ... 79108
Wells St ... 79106
Wentworth Dr ... 79109
Wesley Rd ... 79119
Wesley St ... 79121
Westbrook ... 79118
Westbury Dr ... 79109
Westcliff Cir & Pkwy ... 79124
N Western St
1-500 ... 79106
502-1098 ... 79106
1200-8399 ... 79124
8401-8599 ... 79124
9300-9398 ... 79108
9400-10599 ... 79108
10601-12699 ... 79108
S Western St
100-306 ... 79106
307-307 ... 79116
308-2098 ... 79106
309-2099 ... 79106
2100-5001 ... 79109
5000-5000 ... 79114
5002-5298 ... 79109
5003-5199 ... 79109
5800-8200 ... 79110
8202-8798 ... 79110
9901-11797 ... 79118
11799-15299 ... 79118
Western Grove Dr ... 79108
Western Plaza Dr ... 79109
Westgate Dr ... 79106
Westgate Pkwy ... 79121
Westhaven Cir, Dr & Vlg ... 79109
Westhills Trl ... 79106
Westlawn St ... 79102
Westminster Cir ... 79119
Westover Pl ... 79119
Westway Trl ... 79109
Westwind Ave ... 79106
Westwood Dr ... 79124
Wheatstraw Rd ... 79118
Wheeler Ln
1500-1698 ... 79118
1700-2599 ... 79118
5300-5399 ... 79110
While A Way Rd ... 79109
Whippoorwill Ln ... 79121
N Whitaker Rd ... 79108
S Whitaker Rd ... 79118
White Plns ... 79118
White Bluff Trl ... 79118
White Buffalo Rd ... 79124
White Hills Trl ... 79124
White Oak Dr ... 79110
White Plains Ave ... 79121
White Tail Ave ... 79124
Whitecotton Pl ... 79121
Whitewing Dr ... 79108
Whitney Ln ... 79110
Whittier Dr ... 79110
Wichita Ave ... 79107
Wilbur Dr ... 79110
Wild Horse Trl ... 79118
Wild Plum Dr ... 79118
Wild Primrose ... 79118
Wildflower Dr ... 79118
Wilkerson St ... 79119
Will Ave ... 79119
N Williams St ... 79107
S Williams St
100-1200 ... 79102
1202-1598 ... 79102
2200-2899 ... 79103
3600-4599 ... 79118
Williamsburg Pl ... 79119
Williamson Trl ... 79118
Willis Knight St ... 79108
Willow St
900-999 ... 79102
2700-2899 ... 79103
3600-4799 ... 79118
Willow Bridge Dr ... 79106
E & W Willow Creek Dr ... 79108
Willow Oak Pl ... 79124
Willow Way Ave ... 79118
Wilshire Dr ... 79110
N Wilson St ... 79107
S Wilson St
2000-2899 ... 79103
3600-4599 ... 79118
Wimberly Rd ... 79109
Winchester Rd ... 79102
Wind Song Dr ... 79103
Windham Dr ... 79109
Winding River Rd ... 79119
Windmill Ln ... 79124
Windridge Pl ... 79109
Windrock St ... 79118
Windsor Rd ... 79124
Windtree Park ... 79121
Windwood Ave ... 79118
Wineinger Rd ... 79118
Winery Rd ... 79118
Wingate Cir ... 79109
Winifred Rd ... 79119
Winkler Dr ... 79109
Winners Cir ... 79110
Winslow Cir & St ... 79109
Winton Dr ... 79121
Wisdom Dr ... 79106
Withers Ave ... 79108
Wolflin Ave
1100-3299 ... 79109
3501-4097 ... 79102
4099-4199 ... 79102
4200-6999 ... 79106
7001-7103 ... 79106
Wolflin Vlg ... 79109
Woodbury Pl ... 79124
Woodfield St ... 79109
N Woodland St ... 79107
S Woodland St
1001-1097 ... 79104
1099-1599 ... 79104
1900-3199 ... 79103
Woodmont Dr ... 79119
Woodridge Cir ... 79109
Woodside Dr ... 79124
Woodstone St ... 79106
Woodward St ... 79106
Worley Dr ... 79108
Wrangler Trl ... 79110
Wren St ... 79124
Xavier Pl ... 79107
Xit Trl ... 79118
Xl Trl ... 79118
Yaeger Ln ... 79108
Yale St ... 79109
Yaupon Pl ... 79124
Yorinewo Dr ... 79108
Yorkshire Ct ... 79121
Yucca Ave ... 79118
Yucca Dr ... 79108
W Yucca Dr ... 79124
Yucca Ln ... 79118
Yuma Pl ... 79118
Zachary Pl ... 79119
Zane Pl ... 79119
Zapata Ln ... 79109
Zelma St ... 79109
Zillie Rd ... 79118
Zita Rd ... 79118
Zuni Trl ... 79119

NUMBERED STREETS

NW 1st Ave
700-898 ... 79107
2000-4199 ... 79106
SE 1st Ave
200-204 ... 79101
8401-8497 ... 79118
SW 1st Ave
300-599 ... 79101
900-4699 ... 79106
NE 2nd Ave ... 79107
NW 2nd Ave
100-298 ... 79107
300-900 ... 79107
902-1098 ... 79107
2100-4199 ... 79106
SE 2nd Ave ... 79101
SW 2nd Ave
300-699 ... 79101
1600-4699 ... 79106
NE 3rd Ave ... 79107
NW 3rd Ave
101-697 ... 79107
2100-3900 ... 79106
SE 3rd Ave
100-299 ... 79101
1001-1197 ... 79102
2200-3400 ... 79104
8200-11298 ... 79118
SW 3rd Ave
100-899 ... 79101
1000-4599 ... 79106
NE 4th Ave ... 79107
NW 4th Ave
700-898 ... 79107
2700-4799 ... 79106
SE 4th Ave
201-397 ... 79101
1100-1198 ... 79102
SW 4th Ave
201-297 ... 79101
1400-4199 ... 79106
NE 5th Ave ... 79107
NW 5th Ave
100-198 ... 79107
2300-2398 ... 79106
SE 5th Ave
201-397 ... 79101
1000-1098 ... 79102
2501-2597 ... 79104
SW 5th Ave
100-1299 ... 79101
1500-4199 ... 79106
NE 6th Ave ... 79107
NW 6th Ave ... 79107
SE 6th Ave
200-299 ... 79101
1000-1298 ... 79102
2400-3598 ... 79104
SW 6th Ave
100-298 ... 79101
1600-4000 ... 79106
NE 7th Ave ... 79107
NW 7th Ave ... 79107
SE 7th Ave
100-198 ... 79101
1200-1298 ... 79102
SW 7th Ave
201-297 ... 79101
1900-4199 ... 79106
NE 8th Ave ... 79111
SE 8th Ave
100-598 ... 79101
1100-1298 ... 79102
2200-2698 ... 79104
SW 8th Ave
100-1899 ... 79101
2200-2398 ... 79106
E 9th Ave ... 79105
NE 9th Ave ... 79107
NW 9th Ave
100-198 ... 79107
2400-2500 ... 79106
SE 9th Ave
100-199 ... 79101
1001-1197 ... 79102
2400-2498 ... 79104
SW 9th Ave
200-1599 ... 79101
2400-5600 ... 79106
NE 10th Ave
101-197 ... 79107
9701-9707 ... 79111
NW 10th Ave
100-1700 ... 79107
2400-4199 ... 79106
SE 10th Ave
101-297 ... 79101
1000-2199 ... 79102
2200-4400 ... 79104
SW 10th Ave
101-197 ... 79101
1800-2498 ... 79102
3000-4899 ... 79106
NE 11th Ave
100-498 ... 79107
12901-12999 ... 79111
NW 11th Ave
100-2399 ... 79107
2400-2699 ... 79106
SE 11th Ave
101-597 ... 79101
1000-1599 ... 79102
2601-3397 ... 79104
SW 11th Ave
300-1599 ... 79101
3100-3499 ... 79102
3500-5399 ... 79106
NE 12th Ave ... 79107
NW 12th Ave
100-398 ... 79107
2601-3897 ... 79106
SE 12th Ave
100-498 ... 79101
1300-1399 ... 79102
3001-3297 ... 79104
SW 12th Ave
400-499 ... 79101
1000-1398 ... 79102
4200-4299 ... 79106
NE 13th Ave
100-398 ... 79107
13100-13199 ... 79111
NW 13th Ave ... 79107
SE 13th Ave
400-600 ... 79101
1200-1298 ... 79102
3300-4399 ... 79104
SW 13th Ave
1000-1599 ... 79102
4200-4299 ... 79106
NE 14th Ave
201-2997 ... 79107
13300-13399 ... 79111
NW 14th Ave ... 79107
SE 14th Ave
201-397 ... 79101
1200-1298 ... 79102
3300-5999 ... 79104
SW 14th Ave
301-397 ... 79101
1000-1300 ... 79102
4200-4299 ... 79106
NE 15th Ave ... 79107
NW 15th Ave ... 79107
SE 15th Ave
300-398 ... 79101
1300-1799 ... 79102
3300-4399 ... 79104
SW 15th Ave
101-297 ... 79101
1000-3499 ... 79102
4200-5800 ... 79106
NE 16th Ave ... 79107
NW 16th Ave ... 79107
SE 16th Ave
100-198 ... 79101
1201-1497 ... 79102
3401-3497 ... 79104
SW 16th Ave
100-198 ... 79101
4200-5199 ... 79106
W 16th Ave ... 79102
NE 17th Ave
3600-6799 ... 79107
12301-12399 ... 79111
NW 17th Ave ... 79107
SE 17th Ave
100-500 ... 79102
502-598 ... 79102
3601-3797 ... 79104
3799-5399 ... 79104
SW 17th Ave
200-1299 ... 79102
4300-4399 ... 79106
NE 18th Ave
1301-1397 ... 79107
1399-6799 ... 79107
13100-13399 ... 79111
NW 18th Ave ... 79107
SE 18th Ave ... 79102
SW 18th Ave ... 79102
NE 19th Ave ... 79107
NW 19th Ave ... 79107
SE 19th Ave ... 79103
NE 20th Ave ... 79107
NW 20th Ave ... 79107
SE 20th Ave ... 79103
SW 20th Ave
1000-1699 ... 79109
5001-5099 ... 79106
NE 21st Ave
3500-5899 ... 79107
13100-13299 ... 79111
NW 21st Ave ... 79107
SE 21st Ave
100-298 ... 79109
901-997 ... 79103
SW 21st Ave
200-298 ... 79109
4201-5297 ... 79106
NE 22nd Ave ... 79107
SE 22nd Ave
100-198 ... 79109
200-500 ... 79109
502-598 ... 79109
1700-2198 ... 79103
2200-4800 ... 79103
4802-4898 ... 79103
SW 22nd Ave ... 79109
NE 23rd Ave ... 79107
SE 23rd Ave
300-399 ... 79109
800-2299 ... 79103
NE 24th Ave
800-998 ... 79107
5200-5299 ... 79108
5400-5498 ... 79107
8800-8898 ... 79108
NW 24th Ave ... 79107
SE 24th Ave
201-297 ... 79109
800-898 ... 79103
SW 24th Ave ... 79109
NE 25th Ave ... 79107
SE 25th Ave
200-299 ... 79109
900-4900 ... 79103
NE 26th Ave
3000-4099 ... 79107
9800-9899 ... 79108
SE 26th Ave
501-599 ... 79109
900-2199 ... 79103
SW 26th Ave ... 79109
NE 27th Ave
3000-3099 ... 79107
9800-9899 ... 79108
12200-12298 ... 79111
SE 27th Ave
401-499 ... 79109
700-3799 ... 79103
3801-4199 ... 79103
SW 27th Ave ... 79109
NE 28th Ave ... 79108
SE 28th Ave
100-198 ... 79109
2000-2598 ... 79103
2600-4899 ... 79103
SW 28th Ave ... 79109
NE 29th Ave ... 79111
SE 29th Ave
101-299 ... 79109
901-3397 ... 79103
3399-4899 ... 79103
SW 29th Ave ... 79109
SE 30th Ave ... 79103
SW 30th Ave ... 79109
SE 31st Ave
101-199 ... 79109
3600-4299 ... 79103
SW 31st Ave ... 79109
NE 32nd Ave ... 79107
SE 32nd Ave ... 79103
SW 32nd Ave ... 79109
NE 33rd Ave ... 79107
SE 33rd Ave ... 79103
SW 33rd Ave
101-3997 ... 79109
3999-4199 ... 79109
6000-6099 ... 79106
NE 34th Ave ... 79107
SE 34th Ave
301-399 ... 79110
400-500 ... 79103
1500-2000 ... 79118
2101-2197 ... 79103
SW 34th Ave
101-197 ... 79109
7300-8699 ... 79121
8900-9999 ... 79124
19200-19699 ... 79119
NE 35th Ave ... 79107
SE 35th Ave
101-199 ... 79110
3600-3899 ... 79103
SW 35th Ave ... 79109
SE 36th Ave
100-299 ... 79110
1601-1997 ... 79118
3600-3899 ... 79103
SW 36th Ave
100-198 ... 79110
201-399 ... 79110
4700-7299 ... 79109
SE 37th Ave ... 79110
SW 37th Ave
100-398 ... 79110
4200-7299 ... 79109
SE 38th Ave ... 79118
SW 38th Ave
200-400 ... 79110
4200-7299 ... 79109
SE 39th Ave
100-199 ... 79110
2100-2199 ... 79118
SW 39th Ave
101-199 ... 79110
5600-7299 ... 79109
SE 40th Ave
101-199 ... 79110
2100-2199 ... 79118
SW 40th Ave
201-399 ... 79110
1800-1898 ... 79110
5600-5699 ... 79109
SE 41st Ave ... 79118
SW 41st Ave
101-197 ... 79110
199-1200 ... 79110
1202-1298 ... 79110
5600-5699 ... 79109
SE 42nd Ave ... 79118
SW 42nd Ave
300-1098 ... 79110
1100-2599 ... 79110
5300-5399 ... 79109
5401-7099 ... 79109
SE 43rd Ave ... 79118
100-399 ... 79110
5600-5699 ... 79109
SE 44th Ave ... 79118
SW 44th Ave ... 79110
SE 45th Ave ... 79118
SW 45th Ave
300-2899 ... 79110
3100-3398 ... 79109
3400-6900 ... 79109
6902-7298 ... 79109
7301-7397 ... 79119
7399-8699 ... 79119
SE 46th Ave ... 79118
SW 46th Ave ... 79110
SW 47th Ave ... 79110
SW 48th Ave ... 79110
SW 48th Ave ... 79110
SW 48th Ave ... 79110
5700-6099 ... 79109
SW 49th Ave
2400-2499 ... 79110
4001-4097 ... 79109
SW 50th Ave
2400-2499 ... 79110
4000-5899 ... 79109
SW 51st Ave ... 79109
SW 52nd Ave ... 79110
SW 53rd Ave ... 79109
SW 54th Ave ... 79109
SW 55th Ave ... 79109
SW 57th Ave ... 79109
SE 58th Ave ... 79118
SW 58th Ave ... 79110
SW 59th Ave ... 79118
SW 60th Ave ... 79118
SW 61st Ave ... 79118
SW 62nd Ave ... 79118
SW 76th Ave ... 79118
SW 77th Ave ... 79119
SW 81st Ave ... 79119
SW 83rd Ave ... 79119

SE 114th Ave 79118

ANGLETON TX

General Delivery 77515

POST OFFICE BOXES MAIN OFFICE STATIONS AND BRANCHES

Box No.s
All PO Boxes 77516

RURAL ROUTES

04 77515

NAMED STREETS

All Street Addresses 77515

NUMBERED STREETS

All Street Addresses 77515

ARANSAS PASS TX

General Delivery 78336

POST OFFICE BOXES MAIN OFFICE STATIONS AND BRANCHES

Box No.s
All PO Boxes 78335

RURAL ROUTES

01, 01 78336

HIGHWAY CONTRACTS

01, 01 78336
01, 01 78336

NAMED STREETS

A1 Hill Rd 78336
Adolfo Rd 78336
Allen Blvd 78336
Amberjack Dr 78336
Angelfish Ct 78336
Angelita Dr 78336
N & S Arch St 78336
Arena Rd 78336
Armstrong Rd 78336
N & S Atlantic St 78336
N & S Avenue A 78336
Banty Ln 78336
N & S Bay Ct & St 78336
Bay Harbor Dr 78336
Bayside Pl 78336
Bayview Dr 78336
E & W Beasley Ave 78336
Benoit Ln 78336
Bentwood Ln 78336
Bigelow St 78336
W Blossom Ave 78336
Bluefish Ct 78336
N Business Highway 35 78336
W Chastain Ave 78336
Chrisden Ln 78336
W Cleveland Blvd 78336
Collins Ln 78336
N Commercial St 78336
S Commercial St
100-699 78336
634-634 78335
701-2299 78336
702-2298 78336
W Compton Ave 78336
County Road 102 78336
County Road 114 78336
County Road 114a 78336
County Road 126 78336
County Road 126a 78336
County Road 128a 78336
County Road 130 78336
County Road 132 78336
County Road 134a 78336
County Road 1402 78336
County Road 1428 78336
County Road 1432 78336
County Road 1740 78336
County Road 1794 78336
County Road 1810 78336
County Road 1838 78336
County Road 1866 78336
County Road 1894 78336
County Road 1916 78336
County Road 1942 78336
County Road 1944 78336
County Road 1960 78336
County Road 1974 78336
County Road 1986 78336
County Road 1996 78336
County Road 2010 78336
County Road 2028 78336
County Road 2048 78336
County Road 2127 78336
County Road 2170 78336
County Road 2192 78336
County Road 2212 78336
County Road 4287 78336
County Road 431 78336
County Road 4343 78336
County Road 4351 78336
County Road 4373 78336
County Road 4439 78336
County Road 4491 78336
County Road 4641 78336
County Road 4673 78336
County Road 4691 78336
County Road 4705 78336
County Road 4755 78336
County Road 4783 78336
County Road 747 78336
County Road 93 78336
County Road 93a 78336
County Road 93b 78336
County Road 95 78336
County Road 97 78336
County Road 99 78336
E Danforth Ave 78336
E & W Deberry Ave 78336
Demory Ln 78336
Denipat Ln 78336
Dolphin Ct 78336
Dominguez Rd 78336
Donnan Ct 78336
Driftwood Dr 78336
Durham Rd 78336
W Ebert 78336
Ester Dr 78336
S Euclid St 78336
N & S Fm 1069 N 78336
Fm 1848 78336
Fm 2725 78336
Fm 3512 78336
Foggy Hill Rd 78336
Freedom Way 78336
Freeman St 78336
Gator Cir 78336
Gena Ln 78336
W Gile Ave & Pl 78336
Gillespie Ln 78336
E & W Goodnight Ave 78336
E & W Greenwood Ave 78336
Gulf Gate Blvd 78336
W Harrison Blvd 78336
W Hazlett Ave 78336
E & W Highland Ave 78336
Highway 1069 78336
Highway 35 Byp 78336
E Highway 361 78336
Holden Rd 78336
N & S Houston St 78336
Huff St 78336
W Ireland Ave 78336
Jackson Pl 78336
Jacoby Ln 78336
Jocelyn Rd 78336
E & W Johnson Ave & Rd 78336
Kays Rd & St 78336
Keller Ln 78336
Kenwood Dr 78336
Kirby Rd 78336
Kring Rd 78336
La Buena Vida Dr 78336
N & S Lamont St 78336
Lee Rd 78336
W Lenoir Ave 78336
Lisa Ann Dr 78336
Live Oak St 78336
Longoria Rd 78336
W Lott Ave 78336
Mack Rd 78336
Mackerel Ct 78336
E & W Maddox Ave 78336
E & W Magnolia Ave 78336
Mallard Dr 78336
Maria Rd 78336
Marshall Ln 78336
W Matlock Ave 78336
Maverick Trl 78336
N & S Mccampbell St 78336
N Mccann Ave 78336
E & W Mcclung Ave 78336
Mcmullen Ln 78336
Mesquite Cir 78336
Michigan Ave 78336
Millsville Rd 78336
Misty Ln 78336
W Moore Ave 78336
Morrow St 78336
Mundine Rd 78336
Munson Dr 78336
Murphy Rd 78336
Myrtle Ave 78336
Nelson Ave 78336
Oak Ln & Lndg 78336
Oak Glen Dr 78336
Oak Harbor Dr 78336
Oak Haven Dr 78336
Oak Park Dr 78336
Owens Ln 78336
N & S Pacific St 78336
W Palm Dr 78336
Payne Ave 78336
Pelican Ave 78336
Pelican Nest Dr 78336
Pompano Dr 78336
Porpoise Dr 78336
Port Royal 78336
Port Saint Claire 78336
Private Durham Rd 78336
Private Road 129 78336
Private Road 4615 78336
Private Road 93b 78336
E & W Pryor Ave 78336
Rabbit Run Rd 78336
N & S Railroad St 78336
E Ransom Rd 78336
Red Oak St 78336
Redfish Ct 78336
Resendez Rd 78336
W Rhodes Ave 78336
N & S Rife St 78336
Rodeo Dr 78336
Sailfish Ct 78336
N & S Saunders Ln & St 78336
Sawyer Ln 78336
Sea Breeze Dr 78336
Sea Mist Dr 78336
Sea View Dr 78336
Shaver Rd 78336
Sherwood Frst 78336
Smith Rd 78336
E & W Spencer Ave 78336
Spoonbill Ave 78336
E & W Stapp Ave 78336
State Highway 188 78336
N State Highway 35 78336
E & W Stoddard Ave 78336
Stone St 78336
Tarpon Ct 78336
Teal Cir 78336
Tinsley Ln 78336
Tropical Breeze Ln 78336
Turnbough St 78336
S Verineral St 78336
S Verinerl St 78336
S Walker 78336
Wehring Ln 78336
Wendi Ln 78336
E & W Wheeler Ave 78336
Whispering Wind 78336
N & S Whitney St 78336
Williams Rd 78336
E & W Wilson Ave 78336
Windy Oaks Dr 78336
E & W Yoakum Ave 78336
W Young Ave 78336

NUMBERED STREETS

All Street Addresses 78336

ARLINGTON TX

General Delivery 76004

POST OFFICE BOXES MAIN OFFICE STATIONS AND BRANCHES

Box No.s
1 - 2620 76004
3261 - 3844 76007
5003 - 7553 76005
9998 - 9998 76003
13001 - 14661 76094
90020 - 90487 76004
90601 - 90613 76006
91201 - 91201 76012
91507 - 91588 76015
95019 - 95080 76005
99604 - 99630 76096
120001 - 124240 76012
150001 - 153238 76015
170001 - 175939 76003
180001 - 183940 76096
200001 - 203080 76006
300001 - 301318 76007

RURAL ROUTES

101, 113, 20, 22, 34, 55, 64, 68, 69, 71, 76, 79, 87, 89, 93, 95, 96 76001
100, 102, 104, 106, 109, 110, 111, 48, 78, 81, 88, 92, 98, 99 76002
112 76005
01, 04, 07, 08, 10, 11, 12, 16, 18, 21, 23, 27, 32, 36, 37, 38, 42, 52, 67, 83 76016
06, 09, 14, 15, 17, 19, 24, 26, 39, 44, 45, 46, 49, 53, 56, 58, 60, 62, 65, 72, 74, 82, 85, 86, 76017
03, 25, 35, 41, 47, 50, 54, 57, 63, 70, 73, 80, 84 76018

NAMED STREETS

A E Petsche Ct 76012
Aaron Ave 76012
Abbermare Ct & Dr 76001
Abbey Ln 76012
Abbey Glen Ct 76002
Abbott Ave 76018
Abe Lincoln Ct 76011
Abelia Ct 76017
Aberdeen Dr 76015
Abigail Dr 76002
E Abram St 76010
W Abram St
100-699 76010
700-2499 76013
Acacia Dr 76006
Academy Cir, Ct, Dr & Pl 76013
Acapulco Ln 76017
Ackers Dr 76001
Acorn Ct 76012
Adams Ct & Dr 76011
Adamstown Pl 76017
Adirondack Trl 76002
Adrian Ct 76016
Ainsworth Ct 76016
Aires Dr 76001
Airport Cir 76010
Alameda Ct 76016
Alamo Dr 76012
Alan A Dale Rd 76013
Alaska St 76011
Albany Ln 76002
Alcott Dr 76001
Alcove Ct 76002
Alder Dr 76012
Aldergate Dr 76012
Aleta St 76010
Alexandria Dr 76015
Alexis Ave 76006
Algonquin Ave 76017
Alicante Dr 76017
Alice St 76010
Allegheny Dr 76012
Allen Ave & Ct 76014
Allencrest Dr 76001
Allison Ct 76015
Almandora Dr 76002
Almond Dr 76006
Aloe Ct 76017
Alpaca Ct 76001
Alpine Dr 76016
Alps Ct 76012
Alston St 76013
Alta Verde Cir & Ct 76017
Alta Vista Ln 76017
Altersgate Ln 76001
Altman Cir & Dr 76011
Alvey Dr 76017
Ambarella St 76002
Ambassador Row 76013
Amber Ridge Dr 76002
Ambercrest Dr 76002
Ambers Cir 76010
Amberway Dr 76014
Amberwood Ct 76016
Amerada Cir 76017
Amesbury Dr 76011
Amhurst Dr 76014
Amicable Ct & Dr 76016
Ammonite Ct 76002
Amsterdam Ln 76002
Amy Ct 76016
Anchorage Dr 76016
Andalusia Ct & Trl 76017
Andover Ct 76010
Andrea Dr 76014
Andrews St 76011
Andromeda Way 76013
Anemone Ct 76002
Angel Fire Ln 76001
Angelina Dr 76018
Anglican Dr 76002
Angora Trl 76002
Anita Dr 76012
Ann Dr 76016
Annapolis Dr 76017
Annies Ln 76016
Annondale Ct 76017
Anson Ct 76006
Antares Way 76016
Antelope Run 76002
Antero Dr 76006
Antony Ct 76017
Anvil Creek Dr 76001
Apache St 76012
Apaloosa Trl 76015
Appian Way 76013
Apple Blossom Ln 76014
Appletree Ln 76014
Apricot Glen Dr 76006
April Dr 76016
Arabian Ct 76017
Aramic Ct 76001
Aramis Dr 76016
Arapaho Dr 76018
Arbor Ln 76010
Arbor Chase Cir 76011
Arbor Oaks Dr 76006
Arbor Town Cir 76011
Arbor Valley Dr 76016
Arborcrest Dr 76012
Arborgate Dr 76017
E Arbrook Blvd 76014
W Arbrook Blvd
100-699 76014
700-2499 76015
Arcadia Dr 76017
Arch Dr 76015
Arch Bridge Ct 76017
Archbishop Ct 76017
S Archbridge Ct 76017
Archway Ct 76016
Archwood Ln 76017
Ardmore Dr 76018
E Arkansas Ln
400-2598 76014
401-3399 76010
W Arkansas Ln
100-698 76014
101-699 76010
700-1926 76013
1927-2097 76013
1928-2498 76013
2099-2199 76013
2201-2499 76013
2500-6399 76016
Arlena Dr 76012
Arlington Downs Rd 76011
Arlington Highlands Blvd 76018
Arlington Webb Rd 76018
Armstrong Dr 76014
Arnold Ave 76010
Arrowhead Dr 76013
Arrowwood Dr 76001
Artesia Ct 76016
Arthur Dr 76013
Ascension Blvd 76006
Ascension Bluff Dr 76006
Ascension Point Dr 76006
Ascott Ct 76012
Ashbury Ct & Dr 76015
Ashcreek Ct 76018
Ashcroft Ln 76006
Asher Ct 76006
Ashfield Ct 76012
Ashford Ln 76006
Ashgrove Dr & Pl 76006
Ashland St 76012
Ashley St 76016
Ashmede Ct 76013
Ashmount Ln 76017
Ashton Ct 76015
Ashwood Dr 76016
Ashworth Ct 76017
Aspen Ct & Dr 76013
Astoria Dr 76013
Astro Ct 76012
At T Way 76011
Atherton St 76002
Atlantis Ter 76016
Atlas Dr 76002
Atlee Ct 76006
Auburn Ct & Dr 76012
Audubon Dr 76018
August Run 76017
Augusta Ln 76012
Aurora Ct 76017
Austin St 76012
Autry Ct 76017
Autumn Ln 76012
Autumn Trl 76016
Autumn Glen Ct 76016
Autumn Mist Way 76005
Autumn Oaks Trl 76006
Autumn Ridge Ct 76016
Autumn Springs Ct & Dr 76001
Autumn Wheat Trl 76017
Autumncrest Dr 76002
Autumnwood Dr 76016
Avalon Ln 76014
Avanti Dr 76001
Avenue D 76011
Avenue E E 76011
Avenue F 76011
Avenue G 76011
Avenue H E 76011
Avenue J 76006
Avery Dr 76006
Avila Dr 76017
Avington Ct 76015
Avon Dr 76015
Avondale Ct 76011
Avonhill Dr 76015
Axis Deer Rd 76002
Azalea Dr 76013
Bacara Ln 76001
Bacury Rd 76002
Badger Vine Ln 76005
Bagpiper Way 76018
Bahar Ct & Dr 76010
Bailey Ct 76017
Bainbridge Dr 76018
Bainwood Trl 76015
Baird Farm Cir 76006
Baird Farm Rd
1100-1199 76011
1800-2399 76006
Baird Hollow Ln 76011
Balboa Ct 76016
Balconies Ln 76017
Baldwin Dr 76012
Baldwin Acres Ct 76001
Ballesteros Ct 76014
Ballpark Way
1000-1198 76011
1200-1599 76011
1800-1974 76006
1975-1975 76005
1975-2499 76006
1976-2498 76006
Ballweg Rd 76002
Ballycastle Dr 76017
Balsam Dr 76006
Baltic Ave 76011
Bama Dr 76017
Bamboo Dr 76006
Bancroft Ct 76017
Bandera Dr 76018
Bannack Dr 76001
Bantry Ln 76002
Barbados Dr 76012
Barbara Ln 76018
Barberry Dr 76018
Barcelona Dr 76016
Barclay Dr 76018
E Bardin Rd
100-198 76018
200-1302 76018
1301-1301 76096
1303-1899 76018
1304-1898 76018
W Bardin Rd 76017
Bardin Greene Dr 76018
Barker St 76012

Barnes Dr 76013
Barnett Blvd 76017
Barnhill Ct 76016
Barnsley Ct 76016
Baroncrest Dr 76017
Barred Owl Rd 76002
Barrington Ct & Pl 76014
Barry Dr 76013
Barton Dr 76010
Basil Dr 76006
Bassett Dr 76018
Basswood Ct 76016
Bastrop Dr 76002
Bateman Way 76017
Bates Ct 76011
Bay Chase Dr 76016
Bay Club Dr 76013
Bay Cove Ct & Dr 76013
Bay Hill Dr 76018
Bay Lakes Ct 76016
Bay Oaks Dr 76012
Bay Point Dr 76016
Bay Springs Ct 76016
Bayberry Dr 76017
Baybridge Dr 76002
Baybrooke Ln 76017
Baylor Dr 76010
Baymeadows Ln 76017
Bayonne Ct 76016
Bayou Dr 76018
Bayshore Dr 76016
Bayside Ct 76016
Baywood Ln 76014
Beach Ln 76014
Beacham St 76011
Beachplum Way 76002
Beachview Dr 76016
Beacon Ct 76017
Beaconsfield Ln 76011
E Beady Rd 76006
Beagle Dr 76018
Bear Creek Ln 76006
Bear Run Rd 76001
Beastere Dr 76011
Beaufort Ct 76018
Beckett Dr 76017
Beckwith Dr 76018
Becky Dr 76001
Bedford Ct 76017
Bedrock Ln 76006
Bee Dr 76017
Beechgrove Dr 76018
Beechwood Dr 76006
Beef Creek Dr 76001
Beeman Dr 76002
Belchase Way 76001
Belemeade St 76014
Belfry Ct 76011
Bell St 76001
Bellaire Ct 76013
Bellcrest Dr 76002
Belle Point Ct 76017
Bellefontaine Ct & Dr 76017
Bellevue Ln 76012
Bellglen Ct 76016
Bellingham Pl 76001
Belmont St 76012
Belmont Park Dr 76017
Belton Ct & Dr 76018
Beltway Pl 76018
Belvedere Dr 76010
Benedict Ln 76002
Benge Dr 76013
Benjamin Ln 76002
Bennett Dr 76013
Bennington Dr 76018
Bent Creek Dr 76013
Bent Haven Dr 76013
Bent Oaks Dr 76001
Bent Tree Ln 76016
Bentfield Pl 76016
Bering Dr 76013
Berkeley Ln 76015
Berlinetta Dr 76001
Bermuda Ct 76011
Berrigan Dr 76002
Berry Down 76010
Berryhill Dr 76017
Bert Dr 76012
Berwick Ct 76017
Beryl Ct & Dr 76002
Beth Ln 76010
Betsy Ross Dr 76002
Betty Ln 76006
Bever Blvd 76013
Beverly Ln 76015
Big Bear Lake Ct & Dr 76016
Big Bend Ln 76002
Big Buck Trl 76002
Big Oak Ct 76001
Big Springs Dr 76001
Big Sur Dr 76006
Bigfork Dr 76001
Biggs Cir & Ter 76010
Bighorn Rdg 76002
Billings St 76010
Billy B Ave 76010
Biondi Trl 76001
Birch St 76012
Birchwood Dr 76006
Bird Dr 76010
Birkhill Trl 76001
Birmingham Dr 76012
Biscay Dr 76016
Bise Pl 76006
Bishop Dr 76010
Bishop Creek Ct 76016
Bittersweet Dr 76001
Black Oak Ln 76012
Black Spruce Ct 76001
Black Willow Ln 76002
Blackberry Dr 76016
Blackhaw Ct 76015
Blackhill Ct 76012
Blackstone Ter 76017
Blacktail Trl 76002
Blackwood Dr 76013
Bladensburg Way 76017
Blair Ln 76014
Blake Dr 76001
Blake Ashton Dr 76001
Blanca Dr 76016
Blanco Ct 76001
Bland Dr 76010
Blaney Dr 76001
Bloomfield Dr 76012
Blossom Trl 76016
Blossom Park Ct 76016
Blossomwood Ct & Dr 76017
Blue Creek Ln 76006
Blue Danube St 76015
Blue Duck Trl 76002
Blue Feather Ct 76016
Blue Forest Dr 76001
Blue Lake Blvd 76005
Blue Meadow Trl 76017
Blue Mesa Dr 76017
Blue Quail Dr 76017
Blue Sage Ln 76014
Blue Sky Dr 76002
Blue Spruce Dr 76018
Blue Water Dr 76010
Bluebird Dr 76001
Bluebonnet Trl 76013
Bluegrass Ct 76017
Blueleaf Dr 76018
Blueridge Ct 76016
Bluffcreek Ln 76006
Bluffview Ct 76011
Boardwalk Ct & St 76011
Bobwhite Dr 76014
Boggs Dr 76013
Bois D Arc Dr 76013
Boise Dr 76017
Bolivar Dr 76002
Bonanza Ct & Dr 76001
Bonaparte Dr 76006
Bonito Dr 76002
Bonner Ln 76014
Bonneville Dr 76016
Bordeaux Ct 76016
Borden Dr 76017
Border Pl 76013
E Border St 76010
Boronia Rd 76002
Bosque Ln 76006
Botts Dr 76012
Bowen Ct 76012
N Bowen Rd 76012
S Bowen Rd
100-199 76012
300-1115 76013
1114-1114 76094
1116-2298 76013
1117-2199 76013
1500-2199 76013
2201-2299 76013
2300-3399 76015
3400-4399 76016
4400-5499 76017
Bowie St 76012
Bowman Springs Rd 76016
Boxelder Dr 76018
Boxwood Ct 76017
Boyd Ct & Trl 76017
Bracken Pl 76017
Brad Dr 76013
Bradbury Ct 76014
Braddock Ct 76017
Braden Ln 76016
Bradford Dr 76010
Bradley Ct & Ln 76017
Bradwood Ct 76011
Brady Ct 76018
Bralisou Dr 76016
Bramble Creek Ct 76001
Bramblewood Ct 76017
S Branch Dr 76001
Branch Hollow Ln 76001
Branchview Ct & Dr 76017
Branchwood Dr 76001
Brandy Wood Trl 76018
Brannon Rd 76016
Bratcher Dr 76002
Brazoswood Cir & Ct 76017
Breckenridge Dr 76011
Breezewood Dr 76017
Brenhaven Rd 76017
Brenner Ct 76017
Brent Dr 76012
Brentcove Dr 76001
Brentford Pl 76006
Brentgate Ct & Dr 76017
Brentwood Cir 76013
Bretts Ct 76017
Brianna Ln 76001
Briar Glenn Ln 76006
Briar Knoll Dr 76006
Briar Meadow Dr 76014
Briarbrook Ct 76006
Briarcliff Ct & Dr 76012
Briarcreek Dr 76012
Briarcrest Ln 76012
Briardale Ct 76013
Briarhill Ct 76016
Briaroaks Ct 76011
Briarpath Ln 76018
Briarwood Blvd 76013
Bricken Ct 76018
Bridges Dr 76012
Bridgeton Dr 76018
Bridgeview Dr 76010
Bridgewater Dr 76017
Bridle Oaks Dr 76001
Bridle Path Ln 76016
Bridlegate Dr 76016
Bridlewood Dr 76002
Brigadoon Ct 76013
Brigalow St 76002
Bright Meadow Ct 76016
Bright Star Trl 76017
Brighton Dr 76012
Brim Ct 76012
Brinker Ct 76011
Brisbane Dr 76018
Bristlecone Ct & Dr 76018
Bristol Dr 76013
British Ct & Ln 76002
Britt Dr 76013
Brittany Ln 76013
Broadacres Ln 76016
Broadleaf Dr 76001
Broadmoor Ave 76010
Brockgreen Ct 76014
Brockton Ct 76018
Broken Arrow Ct 76002
Broken Bough Ln 76001
Broken Kettle Rd 76002
Brook Canyon Dr 76018
Brook Creek Ct 76018
Brook Forest Dr 76018
Brook Hill Ct & Ln 76014
Brook Shadows Ct 76016
Brookarbor Ct 76018
Brookbriar Ct 76018
Brookcrest Dr 76018
Brookdale Dr 76014
Brookfall Dr 76018
Brookfield Dr 76001
Brookgate Ct & Dr 76016
Brookglen Dr 76018
Brookgrove Ct 76018
Brookhaven Trl 76001
Brookhollow Ct 76013
Brookhollow Plaza Dr 76006
Brookhurst Ln 76014
Brookknoll Dr 76018
Brooklawn Dr 76018
Brookleaf Dr 76018
Brookline Ct 76006
Brookmeadow Ct 76018
Brookmont Ct & Dr 76018
Brookmoor Dr 76016
Brookneal Ct 76018
Brookridge Dr 76015
Brooks Dr 76012
Brookshire St 76010
Brookside Dr 76012
Brookstone Dr 76001
Brookvalley Dr 76018
Brookview Dr 76010
Brookway Ln 76006
Brookwood Ln 76001
Brown Blvd
800-899 76011
1700-2599 76006
Brown Oaks Dr 76011
Browning Dr
100-2299 76010
2300-2499 76014
Brownlee Ln 76018
Brownwood Ln 76017
Brunson Ct 76012
Brunswick Way 76018
Brushfire Ct 76001
Bryan Dr 76011
Bryce Ln 76013
Brynmawr Ct 76014
Buccaneer Cir 76016
Buchanan Dr 76011
Buckboard Rd 76017
Buckeye Ct 76017
Buckingham Dr 76015
Bucknell Dr 76012
Buckskin Trl 76015
Buena Vista Dr 76010
Buffalo Ct & Dr 76013
Bull Valley Way 76005
Bunker Hill Dr 76011
Bunny Run Ln 76006
Burdekin Way 76002
Burgess Ct 76015
Burgundy Ct 76016
Burlwood Dr 76016
Burney Rd 76006
Burney Oaks Ln 76006
Burning Springs Ct & Dr 76017
Burningtree Ct 76014
Burnwood Ct 76016
Burr Oak St 76012
Burton Dr 76011
Busch Dr 76014
Bushdale Dr 76002
Business Pl 76001
Butler Dr 76012
Buttercup Ln 76002
Butterfield Rd 76017
Buttermilk Dr 76006
Byron Ln 76012
Cabernet Ln 76001
Cabin Ct 76002
Cabot Ct 76006
Cabotwood Ct 76015
Cactus Ct 76017
Caddo Village Rd 76001
Cadillac Blvd 76016
Calais Way 76006
Calcutta Ct 76016
Calender Rd
3000-3799 76017
6000-8199 76001
Calender Park Ct 76001
Calerelm Dr 76010
Cales Dr 76013
Calgaroo Pl 76002
Calgary Ln 76001
Calico Ln 76011
Caliente Ct & Dr 76017
California Ln
1100-2899 76015
3000-3299 76016
Calmont Dr 76001
Calumet Dr 76017
Cambridge Dr 76013
Camden Ct 76013
Camellia Dr 76013
Cameron Dr 76017
Camino Real Ln 76002
Camino Verdes Blvd 76017
Camp Creek Dr 76002
Campeche Dr 76015
Campfire Creek Dr 76018
Canal Ct 76016
Canalview Dr 76016
Canary St 76013
Canberra Ln 76017
Candice Ln 76013
Candler Dr 76011
Candlewick St 76014
Candlewood Dr 76012
Canis Dr 76001
Canongate Dr 76015
Canterbury Ct 76013
Canton Jade Way 76005
Cantor Dr 76011
Canyon Way 76018
Canyon Creek Dr 76001
Canyon Crest Ct 76006
Canyon Oaks Dr 76011
Canyon Ridge Ct 76006
Canyonwood Dr 76012
Cape Cod Ct 76017
Cape Hatteras Ln 76015
N Capistrano Ct S 76015
Capitol Hill Dr 76017
Caplin Dr 76018
Capri Ln 76015
Caprock Dr 76018
Capstan Dr 76002
Cara Ln 76012
Carallia Ct 76002
Cardamon Dr 76010
Cardinal St 76010
Cardinal Oaks Ct 76017
Caribou Dr 76002
Carina Ct & Dr 76013
Carl Rd 76015
Carla Ave & Ct 76014
Carlisle Dr 76017
Carlsbad Dr 76018
Carlton Dr 76015
Carlyle Ct 76014
Carmel Ct 76012
Carnation Dr 76016
Carnoustie Trl 76001
Carol Ln 76017
Carpenter Dr 76017
Carriage Pl 76014
Carriage Creek Dr 76001
Carriage House Cir 76011
Carrington Dr 76001
Carson Ct 76017
Carswell Ter 76010
Carter Dr
400-2299 76010
2300-3399 76014
Carthage Way 76017
Cartwright Pl 76014
Casa Bella Dr 76010
N Casa Blanca Ct S 76015
Casa Grandes Dr 76002
Cascade Ln 76014
Cascade Sky Dr 76005
Casey Ct 76013
Cassia Way 76002
Castanada Dr 76018
Castelon Ct 76016
Castle Ct & Rd 76014
Castle Creek Rd 76017
Castle Gardens Dr 76013
Castle Oak Ct 76012
Castle Oaks Dr 76012
Castle Rock Rd 76006
Castlegate Ct 76001
Castlehill Ct 76016
Castleview Dr 76001
Castlewick Ct 76018
Castlewood Ln 76012
Catalo Ln 76010
Catamaran Ln 76012
Cattail Dr 76001
Causley Ave 76010
Cavalier Dr & Pl 76017
Cavalry Post Dr 76017
Cavendish Dr 76014
Cecile Ct 76013
Cedar Ln 76013
E Cedar St 76011
W Cedar St
300-699 76011
700-1399 76012
Cedar Brush Trl 76014
Cedar Cove Ct 76016
Cedar Creek Ct 76016
E & W Cedar Elm Dr 76012
Cedar Hill Ln 76014
Cedar Point Dr 76010
Cedar Ridge Dr 76017
Cedar Springs Ter 76010
Cedar View Ct & Dr 76006
Cedarbrook Dr 76006
Cedarland Blvd 76011
Cedarland Plaza Dr 76011
Cedarwood Ct 76017
Celeste Ct 76012
Celtic Ct & Dr 76017
Centennial Dr 76011
N Center St 76011
S Center St
100-2299 76010
2300-3699 76014
Central Park Dr 76014
Centreway Pl 76018
Ceran Dr 76016
Chad Dr 76017
Chaffee Ct & Dr 76006
Chalice Rd 76014
Chalkstone St 76002
Chamberland Ct & Dr 76014
Chambers Creek Ct & Ln 76002
Chamblee Ct 76014
Champion Ct 76017
Chancel Ct 76017
Chandler Ln 76014
Channing Park Dr 76013
Chantilly Ct 76015
Chaparral Ln 76012
Chapel Downs Ct & Dr 76017
Chapel Hill Ln 76014
Chapel Springs Ct & Dr 76017
Chaperito Trl 76016
Charles Ct 76013
Charles City Dr 76018
Charleston Ct 76014
Charlotte Ct 76002
Charolais Way 76017
Charred Wood Dr 76016
Charter Oak Ct 76012
Chase Ct 76013
Chasemore Ln 76018
Chasewood Cir 76011
Chatam Cir 76014
Chateau Trl 76012
Chatfield Pl 76017
Chatham Green Ln 76014
Chatham Village Rd 76014
Chatsworth Ct 76018
Chaucer Dr 76018
Chaumont Ct & Trl 76013
Cheddar Ct 76017
Chelmsford Trl 76018
Chelsea Dr 76016
Cheney Dr 76018
Cherokee St 76012
Cherry Dr 76013
Cherry Laurel Ln 76012
Cherry Point Dr 76010
Cherry Sage Ct & Dr 76001
Cherryhill Ct 76016
Cherrytree Dr 76001
Cherrywood Ln 76016
Cheryl Ct & Ln 76013
Chesapeake Dr 76014
Cheshire Dr 76016
Chesterfield Pl 76017
Chestnut Dr 76012
Cheycastle Ct 76001
Cheyenne Ct 76013
Chicory Ln 76010
Chimney Ct 76016
Chimney Hill Ct & Dr 76012
Chimney Rock Dr 76017
Chinaberry Dr 76018
Chincenw Dr 76006
Chinook Dr 76014
Chinquapin Oak Ln 76012
Chip N Dale Dr 76012
Chipwood Ct 76017
Chisholm Trl 76013
Chuckwagon Ct 76002
Chukka Dr 76012
Church St 76016
Churchill Ct 76017
Churchill Downs Dr 76017
Churchview Ct 76016
Churchwood Dr 76016
Cimarron Ln 76014
Cindy Ct 76012
Cinnamon Park Cir 76016
S Circle Dr 76010
Citadel Dr 76012
Citation Dr 76017
Citrus Ln 76014
Claire Ct 76012
Claireisa Ct 76015
Clareton Dr 76018
Claridge Dr 76018
Clarion Trl 76017
Clark Ct 76015
Clarksburg Ct 76017
Classen Trl 76002
Claudia St 76010
Clay Court Ln 76017
Clay Hill Ct 76014
Clayborn Ct 76014
Claysford Ct 76015
Clear Creek Dr 76001
Clear Fork Trl 76002
Clear Lake Ct 76017
Clear Pool Dr 76018
Clearbrook Ct 76013
Clearhaven Ct & Dr 76014
Clearwater Dr 76001
Clearwood Ct & Dr 76014
Cleburn Dr 76012
Clemson Ct & Dr 76012
Cliffmere Dr 76002
Cliffside Ct 76017

Cliffside Dr 76018
Cliffwood Ct 76016
Clint Ct 76014
Cloisters Dr 76011
Cloud Ct 76017
Cloudcrest Ct 76017
Cloudcroft Dr 76014
Cloudridge Ct 76016
Cloudveil Dr 76002
Clover Ln 76015
Clover Hill Rd 76012
Clover Park Dr 76013
Cloverdale Cir & St 76010
Clovis Ct 76016
Cloyne Dr 76002
Clubview Ct 76013
Coach Ln 76017
Cobble Ct 76013
Cobblestone Ln 76001
Cochise Dr 76012
Cody Dr 76018
Cohoke Dr 76018
Coke Dr 76010
Colbi Hill Ct & Dr 76014
Cold Creek Dr 76002
Cold Springs Dr 76017
Coldsworth Ct 76018
Coldwater Ln 76006
Colebrook Ct & Trl 76017
Colgate Ct 76014
Colima Ct 76006
Collard Rd 76017
Colleen Dr 76016
College St 76010
College Oaks Dr 76010
N Collins St
100-2399 76011
2400-2899 76006
3100-4098 76005
S Collins St
100-2299 76010
2300-4199 76014
4201-4297 76018
4299-6000 76018
6002-6498 76018
Colonial Ct 76013
Colonnade Dr 76018
Colony Dr 76002
W Colony Dr 76001
Colony Club Ct 76016
Colorado Cir & Ln 76015
Colson Dr 76002
Colt Dr 76017
Columbia Dr 76016
Columbine Ct 76013
Colwick Ln 76002
Comanche Ct 76012
Commander Ct 76017
Commerce Dr 76011
Commercial Blvd E 76001
Companion Way 76006
Comstock Dr 76001
Conchos Trl 76017
Concord Dr 76014
Condor Ct 76001
Conestoga Ct 76016
Congressional Dr 76018
Conley Dr 76013
Connally Ter 76010
Connecticut Ln 76001
Conquest Dr 76006
Convention Center Dr 76011
Cooks Ct 76002
Cool Springs Dr 76001
Coolidge Dr 76011
Cooper Ct 76011
N Cooper St
100-198 76013
200-2399 76011
2400-2699 76006
S Cooper St
100-498 76013
101-797 76010
799-899 76010
901-2199 76010
1100-2198 76013
2200-2299 76013
2300-4300 76015
4302-4398 76015
4400-5999 76017
6000-8199 76001
Cooper Corner Cir 76010
Cooper North Cir 76011
Cooper Square Cir 76013
E Copeland Rd 76011
Coping Ln 76001
Copper Canyon Dr 76002
Copper Chase Dr 76006
Copper Creek Dr 76006
Copper Ridge Rd 76006
Copperfield Dr 76001
Copperwood Ct 76001
Cora St 76011
Coral Dr 76010
Coralberry Ct 76014
Coralwood Dr 76012
Corbin Ct & Dr 76002
Cordoba Ct 76014
Corinthian Ct 76016
Cork Oak Ct 76012
Corkwood Trl 76001
Cornell Dr 76015
Cornerstone Ln 76013
Cornfield Dr 76017
Cornflower Dr 76018
Cornish Oak Ct 76012
Cornvalley Dr 76017
Corona Ct 76002
Coronado St 76014
Coronation Ct & Dr 76017
Coronet Ct & Ln 76017
Corporate Dr E & W 76006
Corriander Trl 76010
Corsair Ct 76016
Cortez Dr 76001
Corvallis Ct & Trl 76006
Corvette Ct 76016
Cory Ct 76017
Cory Lee Ct 76015
Corzine Dr 76013
Costa De Oro Ct 76017
Cotillion Ct & Dr 76017
Cottage Park Ct 76013
Cottie Ln 76010
Cotton Valley Ln 76002
Cottoncreek Cir & Dr 76011
Cottonwood St 76014
Cottonwood Club Rd 76010
Coulter Ct & Ln 76016
Count Fleet Dr 76011
Country Ln 76018
Country Club Ct 76013
Country Club Dr 76002
Country Club Rd 76013
Country Creek Dr 76001
Country Green Ln 76011
Country Place Cir 76016
Country Ridge Ln 76006
Country Wood Ct 76011
Countryside Dr 76014
Courtland Dr 76017
Courtney Ct 76015
Courtney Ln 76006
Courtside Dr 76002
Cousins Ct & Ln 76012
Cove Hollow Dr 76002
Covebrook Ct 76012
Covemeadow Ct & Dr 76012
Coventry Ct & Ln 76017
Covey Dr 76014
Covina Ct 76001
Coyote Ln 76018
Craig Hanking Dr 76010
Craighton Ct 76012
Cranbrook Dr 76016
Cranford Ct 76001
Crater Lake Dr 76016
Cravens Park Dr 76018
Creede Ave 76018
Creek Bank Ln 76014
Creek Crossing Ct &
Ln 76018
Creek Dale Dr 76015
Creek Point Ln 76002
Creek Run Rd 76001
Creek Valley Dr 76018
Creek Walk Pl 76015
Creek Wood Dr 76006
Creekbend Ct & Dr 76001
Creekford Dr 76012
Creekfront Ct 76018
Creekhollow Dr 76018
Creekmeer Ct 76011
Creekpark Ct & Trl 76018
Creekridge Dr 76018
Creekside Ct & Dr 76013
Creekview Dr 76016
Creekway Ln 76017
Crepe Myrtle Dr 76017
Crescent Dr 76006
Cresswell Ct & Dr 76001
Crest Dr 76017
Crest Creek Dr 76010
Crest Glen Dr 76002
Crest Grove Dr 76012
Crest Lake Ct 76016
Crest Line Dr 76012
Crest Oak Ct 76012
Crest Park Dr 76006
Crest Point Dr 76012
Crested Butte Cir 76017
Crestfield Dr 76016
Cresthaven Dr 76013
Crestmont Ct 76017
Crestmoor Ct 76016
Crestover Ct 76016
Crestridge Ct & Dr 76013
Crestview Dr 76018
Crestwood Dr 76011
Cricket Ct 76016
Crimson Ct 76018
Cripple Creek Dr 76014
Cristopher Ct 76015
Crockett Dr 76014
Cromwell Dr 76018
Crooked Creek Ln 76006
Crooked Oak Ct 76012
Cross Bend Ct & Dr 76016
Cross Country Trl 76001
Cross Creek Ct 76017
Cross Cut Dr 76018
Cross Hill Ct 76016
Cross Timbers Trl 76006
Crossbow Ln 76001
Crossgate Ct 76016
Crowley Ct & Rd 76012
Crown Ln 76010
Crown Colony Dr
500-699 76006
2300-2499 76011
Crownhill Ct & Dr 76012
Crownpoint Ct & Ln 76002
Crystal Cir 76006
Crystal Creek Ln 76001
Crystal Oak Ln 76005
Cuchara Ln 76018
Cumberland Ct 76014
Cunningham Dr 76002
Curry Rd 76001
Curt Dr 76016
Curtis Ct & Dr 76012
Curtis Mathes Way 76018
Custer St 76014
Cutlass Ct 76016
Cydnie Ann Ct 76014
Cypress Ct 76014
Cypress Chase Dr 76011
Cypress Club Dr 76010
Cypress Creek Ln 76010
Cypress Hills Ct 76006
Cypress Point Dr 76010
Cypress Springs Ct &
Dr 76001
Cypresswood Trl 76014
Daffodil Ct 76018
Daisy Dr 76017
Dakota Dr 76002
Dale Ct & Dr 76010
Dalworth St 76011
Dan Gould Dr 76001
Dana Point Dr 76017
Danbury Ct & Dr 76016
Danforth Ct & Pl 76017
Dangerfield Ct 76017
Daniel Dr
1500-2299 76010
2300-3699 76014
Danuers Ln 76002
Darby Dr 76010
Darcy Ln 76001
Darlene Ln 76010
Darrow Ln 76017
Dartmouth Ct & Dr 76015
Daryl Dr 76010
Dauphine Ct 76016
David Ln 76013
N Davis Dr
100-198 76013
201-697 76012
699-2499 76012
S Davis Dr 76013
Dawn Dr 76010
Dawn Light Dr 76001
Dawnview St 76014
Dawnwood Ct 76017
Daytona Dr 76014
De Pauw Dr 76012
Debbie Ln
600-1400 76002
1402-1498 76002
2701-2799 76010
Debra Dr 76010
Declaration Dr 76002
Decoy Ct & Dr 76002
Dee Ln 76011
Deer Creek Dr 76010
Deer Crossing Dr 76002
Deer Hollow Dr 76002
Deer Lodge Ct 76017
Deer Path Dr 76012
Deer Valley Ln 76001
Deerfield Cir 76015
Deerwood Park Dr 76017
Del Mar Ln 76012
Del Norte Dr 76016
Del Ray Ct 76013
Del Rio Dr 76015
Delaford Dr 76002
Delaney Ter 76018
Delia Ct 76012
Delk Dr 76013
Dellwood St 76013
Delta Dr 76012
Denali Dr 76002
Denham Dr 76001
Denise Ct 76001
Derek St 76016
Desert Rose Ct 76002
Design Rd 76014
Deuce Dr 76017
Devine Dr 76001
Devonshire Ct & Dr 76015
Dewey Dr 76018
Diamond Oaks Cir &
Ct 76018
Diamond Point Dr 76017
Diana Dr 76011
Dickens Ct 76015
Dickerson Dr 76013
Dimes St 76002
Dipert Ct 76012
Diplomacy Dr 76011
Directors Dr 76011
Dirt Rd 76017
Ditto Ave 76010
Divanna Ct 76002
Dividend Ct 76012
E Division St 76011
W Division St
100-699 76011
700-4499 76012
Dixon Ln 76012
Dockside Ct 76002
Dodd Ct 76016
Dodson Lake Dr 76012
Dogwood Dr 76012
Donald Ter 76010
Donna St 76013
Donnell Dr 76012
Doolittle Dr 76014
Doral Ct 76013
Dorcas Ln 76013
Dorchester Dr 76014
Dorset Ct 76001
Doskocil Dr 76017
Doss Cir 76013
Doty Ln 76001
Double Oak Ct 76001
Doubles Dr 76017
Doug Russell Rd 76010
Douglas Ct 76012
Dove Trl 76002
Dove Hollow Way 76016
Dove Meadows Dr 76002
Dovecreek Dr 76016
Dover Ln 76010
Dover Gardens Dr 76017
Downing Ct 76017
Downsview Ct 76016
Drake Elm Way 76005
Drawbridge Dr 76012
Drew Ct & Ln 76017
Driftwood Ct 76016
Drummond Dr 76012
Dry Creek Ln 76017
Dublin Ct 76002
Duckview Ct 76016
Dudley Cir 76010
Duff Dr 76013
Dufferin St 76016
Dugan St 76010
Duluth Dr 76013
Dumont Dr 76006
Duncan Ct 76013
Duncan Perry Rd 76011
Dundee Dr 76002
Dunkirk Ln 76017
Durango Ln 76014
Durham Dr 76014
Duster Cir 76018
Dustin Trl 76016
Dusty Ridge Trl 76002
Duther Dr 76015
Duval Dr 76002
Duxbury Ct 76015
Dye Dr 76013
Eagle Lake Ct 76016
Eagle Nest Dr 76017
Eagle Park Ln 76011
Eagle Point Trl 76002
Eagle Ridge Dr 76016
Eagle Rock Rd 76017
Eagle Trace Dr 76018
Earle St 76016
Early Bird Dr 76001
Easom Cir 76006
N East St 76011
S East St 76010
Eastcreek Dr 76018
Eastpointe Ave 76018
Eastwick Dr 76002
Easy St 76013
Echo Hill Ct 76001
Echo Lake Ct 76001
Echo Summit Ln 76017
Echols St 76011
Eden Ln 76010
Eden Rd 76001
E Eden Rd 76002
Eden Green Dr 76001
Edenbrook Dr 76001
Edendale Dr 76018
Edenwood Dr 76001
Edgar St 76013
Edge Creek Ln 76017
Edgebrook Ct 76015
Edgehill Dr 76014
Edgemont Dr & Pl 76017
Edgestone Pl 76006
Edgewater Ct 76016
Edgewood Ct 76013
Edinboro Dr 76012
Edinburgh St 76018
Edmundson Ct & Dr 76002
Edna St 76010
Edwards Dr 76017
El Brevo Ct 76017
El Caballero Ct 76017
El Capitan Ct 76017
El Rancho Ct & Dr 76017
El Salvador Ct 76017
Elaine Ct 76010
Elbe Dr 76001
Elder Dr 76010
Elderberry Dr 76001
Elderwood Dr 76006
Eldorado Dr 76001
Eldoro Dr 76006
Electra Dr 76001
Elgenwood Trl 76015
Elite Cir 76010
Elizabeth St 76013
Elk Trl 76002
Elkhart Ct 76016
Elkins Dr 76016
Elkwood Ln 76016
Elliott St 76013
Elliott Oaks Dr 76017
Ellis Rd 76012
Ellsworth Ln 76006
N Elm St 76011
S Elm St 76010
Elm Branch Dr 76017
Elm Crest Dr 76012
Elm Forest Cir 76006
Elm Point Dr 76010
Elm Springs Dr 76001
Elm Tree Ct 76017
Elmgrove Ct 76015
Elmhurst Ct & Dr 76012
Elmridge Dr 76012
Elmview Dr 76018
Elmwood Dr 76010
Elrod Dr 76017
Embarcadero Dr 76014
Embassy Ct 76013
Ember Ct & Dr 76016
Ember Glen Dr 76018
E Embercrest Dr 76018
W Embercrest Dr 76017
Emearank Dr 76001
Emerald Pl 76011
Emerald Isle Dr 76012
Emerald Lake Dr 76013
Emerald Oaks Ct 76017
Emerald Park Blvd &
Ct 76017
Emerson Ct 76016
N & S Emma Dr 76002
Empery Ct 76017
Empire Cir 76002
Enamor Dr 76016
Enchanted Cir 76016
Enchanted Bay Blvd 76016
Enchanted Isle Ct &
Dr 76016
Enchanted Lakes Blvd 76016
Enchanted Oaks Dr 76016
Encino Dr 76001
Enclave Cir, Dr & Way 76011
Endicott Dr 76018
Enfilar Ln 76017
England Ct & Rd 76013
Engleford Dr 76015
Engleside Dr 76018
English Chase Ct 76016
Englishoak Dr 76016
Englishtown Dr 76016
Ensenada Ct 76002
Ensign Ct 76017
Enterprise Pl 76001
Enterprise Life Pkwy 76011
Eric Ave 76012
Ericville Dr 76001
Escondido Dr 76016
Espanola Dr 76017
Esquire Dr 76018
Essex Ct 76016
Estates Dr 76016
Eucalyptus Dr 76006
Euclid Dr 76013
Eunice St 76010
Evening Dr 76001
Evening Shade Ln 76002
Eveningcrest Ct 76002
Everest Ln 76001
Everglades Ct 76002
Evergreen Cir 76011
Everton Dr 76001
Evie Ct 76016
Exchange Dr 76011
Exeter Ct 76017
Express St 76001
Fab Four Ln 76016
Fair Meadow Dr 76012
Fair Oaks Dr 76011
Fairbanks Dr 76011
Fairbrook Ave 76010
Faircrest Dr 76018
Faireast Ct 76018
Fairfax Ct 76015
Fairfield Ct 76017
Fairglen Dr 76002
Fairhaven Ct 76018
Fairlane Dr 76001
Fairmount Dr 76017
Fairview St 76010
Fairway Ct 76013
Faithful Trl 76018
Falcon Lake Dr 76016
Falcon Mill Rd 76001
Falcon Perch Cir 76001
Falcon Reach Way 76005
Falcon River Way 76001
Falcon Wood Ct 76016
Falconcrest Ct & Dr 76017
Falconer Cir 76006
Fall River Dr 76006
Fallcreek St 76014
Fallen Antler Pl 76002
Fallwood Dr 76014
Fannin Dr 76001
Fannin Farm Way 76001
Farmhill Dr 76018
Farmingdale Dr 76001
Farragut Dr 76018
Farris Dr 76017
Fawn Meadow Trl 76017
Fawn Valley Ct 76017
Fawnhollow Ct 76001
Featherstone Ct 76001
Felicia Ln 76017
Fence Line Rd 76001
Fennel Ln 76010
Fenwick Ln 76018
Fern Meadow Rd 76017
Ferncreek Ct 76017
Ferndale Ln 76006
Fernwood Dr 76001
Ficus Ct 76017
Field St 76010
Field Crest Ct 76012
Field Lark Dr 76002
N Fielder Rd 76012
S Fielder Rd
200-298 76013
300-2299 76013
2300-3599 76015
3601-3699 76015
Fielder North Plz 76012
Fielders Glen Dr 76015
Fieldgate Ct & Dr 76016
Fieldstone Ct 76018
Fiero Dr 76001
Fig Tree Ln 76014
Fiji Dr 76015
Fillmore Dr 76011
Findlay Ct & Dr 76012
Firebird Ct 76002
Fireside Dr 76016
Firethorn Dr 76017
Firewood Dr 76016

Firglen Dr 76006
Fish Creek Dr 76018
Fisher Ct 76001
Fitzgerald Ct 76012
Five Points Dr 76018
Flagstone Ct & Dr 76017
Flamewood Dr 76001
Flamingo Dr 76012
Flat Wood Ln 76018
Flaxford Trl 76001
Fleet Cir 76010
Fleetwood Ct 76014
Fleur De Lis Ct 76012
Flintridge Ct & Dr 76017
Flintshire Ct 76017
Flintwood Ln 76002
Flooded Gum St 76002
Flora Vista Ct 76002
Florence St 76010
Florida Dr 76015
Flower Dr 76017
Flower Garden Dr 76016
Flowerwood Ct 76017
Flushing Quail Dr 76002
Flyers Ln 76018
Foley Dr 76013
Fonda Dr 76017
Fondren Dr 76001
Ford St 76013
Forest Dr 76013
Forest Bend Dr 76017
Forest Brook Ln 76006
Forest Dale Ln 76006
Forest Edge Dr 76013
Forest Glade Ln 76006
Forest Glen Ct 76013
Forest Hills Dr 76011
Forest Hollow Ln 76006
Forest Mist Dr 76001
Forest Oaks Cir & Ln 76006
Forest Park Dr 76001
Forest Point Dr 76006
Forest Ridge Ct 76016
Forest Valley Dr 76018
Forestburg Dr 76001
Forestcreek Ct 76016
Forester Cir 76006
Forestgate Cir & Dr 76017
Forestlake Ct 76017
Forestshire Ct 76001
Forestview Dr 76016
Forestway Ct 76001
Forestwind Ct 76001
Forestwood Dr 76006
W Fork Dr 76012
Forrest Dr 76012
Forrest Green Ct 76016
Forrestal Dr 76010
Fort Branch Dr 76016
Fort Edward Dr 76002
Fort Hunt Dr 76016
Fort Stockton Dr 76017
N Forty Cir 76006
Forum Dr 76010
Fossil Creek Dr 76002
Fossil Garden Dr 76002
Fossil Hill Dr 76002
Fossil Lake Ct & Dr 76002
Fossil Rim Trl 76002
Foster Dr 76012
Foster Creek Ln 76017
Founders Trl 76015
Fountainwood Dr 76012
Four Winds Dr 76018
Fox Ct 76001
Fox Chase Dr 76001
Fox Creek Trl 76017
Fox Glen Dr 76001
Fox Hill Ct & Dr 76015
Fox Hollow Ct & Dr 76016
Fox Hunt Dr
5600-5899 76017
6000-6399 76001
Fox Rio Trl 76017
Fox River Trl 76017
Fox Run Rd 76016

Foxborough Trl 76001
Foxcroft Ln 76014
Foxfire Dr 76017
Foxford Trl 76014
Foxgrove Ct 76017
Foxhaven Ct 76017
Foxmeadow Trl 76017
Foxmoor Ct 76016
Foxpoint Ct & Trl 76017
Foxridge Dr 76017
Foxwood Ct 76012
Franciscan Dr 76015
Franklin Cir, Ct & Dr 76011
Freedom Ct & Ln 76002
Freeman Ct 76013
Freestone Ct & Dr 76017
Frelara Dr 76014
French Wood Dr 76016
Freshwood Ct 76017
Friar Tuck Dr 76013
Friendly Dr 76011
Friendly Vlg 76006
Friendswood Dr 76013
Frio River Rd 76001
E & W Front St 76011
Frontier Dr 76012
Fuller St
300-699 76011
700-899 76012
Fulton Ct 76015
Fuqua St 76012
Furrs St 76006
Gable Ct 76012
Galahad Ln 76014
Galaxy Dr 76001
Galleria Dr 76011
Galveston Dr 76002
Galway Glen Ct 76016
Gambrel Rd 76014
Garden Dr 76001
Garden Ln
1-99 76016
2300-2499 76015
Garden Corner Rd 76017
Garden Creek Dr 76018
Garden Green Dr 76001
Garden Grove Dr 76013
Garden Oaks Dr 76012
Garden Park Ct 76013
Garden Ridge Ln 76006
Garden Shadow Ln 76011
Garden View Dr 76018
Gardenia Dr 76016
Gardiner St 76012
Garner Blvd 76013
Garrison St 76018
Gary Ln 76016
Gate Pointe Way 76018
Gateway Ln 76017
Gatewood Dr 76016
Gatwick Ln 76016
Gay St 76010
Gaye Ln 76012
Gaylewood Ct 76017
Gemini Ct 76011
Gemstone Trl 76002
Gene Ln 76010
General Ln 76018
Geneseo Ln 76002
Geneva Ln 76017
Gentle Springs Dr 76001
Gentle Wind Dr 76018
Gentry Dr 76018
George Finger Rd 76002
Georgetown St 76015
Georgia St 76012
Gerald Ln 76001
Geraldine Ln 76010
Gessner Ct 76018
Gettysburg Dr 76002
Gibbins Ct & Rd 76011
Gilbert Cir 76010
Gilday Dr 76002
Gillon Dr 76001
Giltin Ct & Dr 76006
Gina Dr 76013

Gittiban Pl 76013
Glacier Lake Dr 76013
Glade Dr 76001
Gladstone Dr 76018
Gladwynne Way 76012
Glasgow Ct, Dr & Ter 76015
Glassboro Cir 76015
Glen Creek Ct 76015
Glen Dale Dr 76017
Glen Eagle Dr 76001
Glen Echo Ln 76001
Glen Falls Dr 76001
Glen Field Ct 76015
Glen Garden Dr 76016
Glen Hollow Cir 76016
Glen Knoll Ct 76016
Glen Pines Ct & Dr 76016
Glen Rapids Ct 76015
Glen Ridge Ct & Dr 76016
Glen Rock Pl 76014
Glen Springs Dr 76016
Glen Valley Dr 76018
Glenbrook Dr 76015
Glenbury Ct 76006
Glencrest Cir 76010
Glengate Ct & Dr 76016
Glenhaven St 76010
Glenlawn Ct 76016
Glenmoor Dr 76001
Glenn Crossett Ct & St 76010
Glenshire Dr 76002
Glenview Ln 76014
Glenwick Ln 76012
Glenwillow Dr 76018
Glenwood Dr 76017
Gloucester Ct 76018
Glynn Oaks Dr 76010
Golden Creek Ln 76006
Golden View Ct 76001
Goldenrain Dr 76018
Goldenrod Ln 76013
Goldmark Dr 76006
Golf Club Dr 76001
Golf Green Dr 76001
Goliad Ct & Dr 76012
Goodwin Dr 76006
Gordon Cir 76010
Grace Cir & St 76010
Grace Garden Ct 76013
Grady Ln 76016
N & S Graham Dr 76013
Grammercy Park Dr 76015
Granada Dr 76014
Grand Ave 76010
Grand Ct 76013
Grand Canyon Ct 76002
Grand Lake Ct 76016
Grandview Dr 76012
Granite Dr 76013
Grant Pl 76013
Grantmont Dr 76016
Grants Pkwy 76014
Grapevine Ln 76014
Grasswood Ct & Dr 76017
Graves Blvd 76013
Graybell Dr 76018
N Great Southwest Pkwy 76011
Greek Row Dr 76013
Green St 76014
Green Acres Cir, Ct & St 76017
Green Apple Ln 76014
Green Creek Dr 76001
Green Forest Ct 76012
Green Gate Dr 76012
Green Hill Dr 76014
Green Hollow Dr 76017
Green Meadow Ct 76013
Green Mere Dr 76001
Green Mountain Ln 76018
NE Green Oaks Blvd 76006
NW Green Oaks Blvd
701-799 76006
1200-2899 76012

SE Green Oaks Blvd 76018
SW Green Oaks Blvd
700-1698 76017
1700-4107 76017
4108-4108 76003
4108-5798 76017
4109-5799 76017
W Green Oaks Blvd
1200-2299 76013
2300-4499 76016
Green Oaks Cir 76006
Green Oaks Ct 76006
Green Park Dr 76017
Green Stone Dr 76001
Green Tee Ct & Dr 76013
Green Valley Ln 76014
Green Willow Ct 76001
Greenbelt Rd 76012
Greenbend Dr 76018
Greenbriar Ln 76013
Greenbrook Dr 76016
Greencove Dr 76012
Greencrest Dr 76016
Greenfield Dr 76016
Greenleaf Dr 76017
Greenridge Dr 76017
Greensborough Ln 76001
E & W Greenspoint Ct & Dr 76001
Greenspring Dr 76016
Greenway St 76010
Greenway Glen Dr 76012
Greenwich Dr 76018
Greenwood Ln 76013
Gregory Ct 76013
Grenoble Dr 76006
Grey Dawn Dr 76017
Grey Goose Trl 76002
Grey Willow Ct & Ln 76002
Greystoke Dr 76011
Griffin Ln 76001
Grindstone Ct 76002
Grissom Dr 76016
Grove St 76014
Grovecrest Ct & Dr 76018
Grovewood Ln 76014
Guadalupe Ct & Rd 76002
Guerin Dr 76012
Guildwood Dr 76017
Guinevere St 76014
Gulf Stream Ln 76001
Gumwood Dr 76014
Gunnison Ct & Dr 76006
Gunston Ln 76017
Gwinnett Cir 76017
Hacienda Dr 76017
Hack Wood Trl 76018
Hackberry Dr 76013
Haddonstone Dr 76017
Hadley Dr 76011
Half Moon Dr 76001
Halifax Ct & Dr 76013
Hallmark Dr 76011
Hambendo Dr 76012
Hamilton Cir 76013
Hamlet Ave 76001
Hampshire Dr 76013
Hampstead Ct 76013
Hampton Rd 76017
Hancock St 76013
Handenne Dr 76015
Hannah Dr 76014
Hanover Ct & Dr 76014
Hanrahan Ct 76002
Harbor Way 76006
Harbor Town Dr 76018
Harder Dr 76016
Hardin Dr 76018
Hardisty Dr 76001
Hardy Pl 76010
Harmon Ter 76010
Harmony Ct 76015
Harriett St 76010
E Harris Rd 76002
W Harris Rd 76001
Harris Hawk Way 76005

Harris Meadows Dr 76002
Harris Ridge Dr 76002
Harrison Ave 76011
Harry Ct 76012
Hartman Ct 76006
Harvard Dr 76015
Harvest Hill Ln 76014
Harwell Dr 76011
Harwood Rd 76018
Harwood Crossing Dr 76018
Hastings Ct & Dr 76013
Hat Creek Ct 76002
Havenbrook Dr 76001
Havenwood Dr 76018
Haverford Dr 76016
Hawaii Ln 76016
Hawkins Cemetery Rd 76017
Hawthorne Dr 76012
Hayes Dr 76011
Haywood Ct 76010
Hazelwood Ct 76015
Headwater Dr 76015
Hearthwood Ct 76016
Heather Trl 76011
Heather Brook Ln 76006
Heather Hill Ct 76006
Heather Way Dr 76012
Heather Wood Ln 76006
Heatherbrook Dr 76001
Heathercrest Dr 76018
Heatherglen Dr 76017
Heathrow Ct 76016
Hedgeapple Ct & Dr 76001
Hedgerow St 76010
Hedgeway Dr 76016
Helen Cir & Dr 76011
Helmsford Dr 76016
Hemingsford Ct 76016
Hemingway Ct & Dr 76006
Hemlock Dr 76018
Hems Ln 76001
Henderson Dr 76010
Hendricks Dr 76011
Henry Ct 76017
Hensley St 76010
Hereford Dr 76014
Heritage Ct 76016
Heritage Oaks Ct 76001
Hermisillo Ct 76002
Hermitage Pl 76015
Herrington Ct 76018
Herschel St 76010
Hester St 76011
Hialeah Dr 76017
Hibiscus Dr 76018
Hickory St 76012
Hickory Hill Dr 76014
Hickory Valley Ct 76006
Hickory Wood Trl 76018
Hidalgo Ln 76014
Hidden Bluff Trl 76006
Hidden Creek Dr 76016
Hidden Isle Ct 76016
Hidden Meadow Dr 76006
Hidden Oaks Ct & Ln 76017
Hidden Pines Ct 76016
Hidden Ridge Dr 76006
Hidden Springs Dr 76001
Hidden Trails Dr 76017
Hidden Woods Ct 76006
Hideaway Ct & Dr 76017
Hideout Trl 76016
Hiett Ave 76010
High Country Trl 76016
High Creek Dr 76017
High Eagle Dr 76001
High Island Dr 76017
High Meadows Dr 76014
High Mesa Ct & Dr 76016
High Oak Dr 76012
High Plains Ct 76014
High Point Rd 76015
High Springs Ct 76016
High Trail Ct 76017
Highbank Dr 76018
Highbrooke Dr 76001

Highcrest Ct & Dr 76017
Highgate Dr 76016
Highgrove Dr 76001
Highland Dr 76010
Highland Villa Ln 76012
Highlander Blvd
300-399 76018
700-999 76015
Highridge Dr 76014
Highview St 76013
Highway 287 76017
Hill Ct 76010
Hill Country Ct & Dr 76012
Hill Haven Ln 76014
Hillary Ln 76012
Hillbrooke Dr 76001
Hillcrest Dr 76010
Hillcroft Ave 76018
Hilldale Blvd 76016
Hillgreen Dr 76002
Hillridge Ct 76012
Hillside Dr 76013
Hilltop Ln 76013
Hillvalley Dr 76013
Hillview Dr 76011
Hillwood Ct 76017
Hinsdale Dr 76006
Hogan Ln 76014
Holiday Dr 76010
Hollandale Cir 76010
Hollis St 76013
Hollow Creek Rd 76001
Hollow Tree Ct & Dr 76018
Hollowridge Ln 76006
Holly Trl 76016
Holly Brook Ln 76006
Holly Hill Ct 76014
Holly Hock Ct & Dr 76001
Holly Hollows Dr 76016
Holly Oak St 76012
Holly Park Dr 76014
Holly Spring Ct & Dr 76018
Hollyleaf Dr 76017
Hollypoint Ct 76015
Hollyridge Ct 76015
Hollywood Dr 76013
Holm Oak St 76012
Holt Rd 76006
Home Place Ct 76016
Homemaker Hills Dr 76010
Homestead Ct & Rd 76017
Homewood Trl 76015
Honey Dr 76001
Honey Creek Ln 76006
Honey Hollow Dr 76002
Honey Locust Trl 76017
Honeysuckle Way 76011
Honeytree Dr 76016
Hontley Dr 76001
Hoover Dr 76011
Hopewell Ct 76016
Horizon Trl 76011
Horseway Dr 76012
Hosack St 76010
Hott Springs Dr 76001
Houston St
500-699 76011
700-1099 76012
Howell St 76010
Hoya Dr 76015
Hudson Dr 76015
Hudson Falls Dr 76002
Hudsonwood Dr 76001
Hunter Cove Dr 76001
Hunter Glade Ln 76012
Hunter Hill Dr 76012
Hunter Park Ct 76017
N Hunter Place Ct & Ln 76006
Hunter Ridge Dr 76013
Hunter View Ct 76013
Hunters Ct 76016
Hunters Glen Cir 76015
Hunters Point Dr 76006
Hunterwood Ln 76017
Huntington Dr 76010

Huntwick Blvd 76016
Hyannis Ct & Dr 76018
Hyde Park Ct & Ln 76015
Hyden Dr 76001
Iberis Ct & Dr 76018
Ichabod Cir 76013
Ida St 76010
Idlecreek Dr 76016
Idlewood Dr 76014
Ijaz Dr 76017
Impala Dr 76001
Independence Ave 76017
Indian Trl 76016
Indian Creek Dr 76010
Indian Hill Dr 76018
Indian Oaks Trl 76017
Indian Springs Trl 76016
Indian Summer Ln 76016
Indian Wells Ct & Dr 76017
Indiana St 76011
Indigo Ln 76015
Industrial Ct 76011
Inez Dr 76013
Inglewood Ln 76016
Inks Lake Dr 76018
Inniswood Cir 76015
Innsbrooke Dr 76016
Inspiration Pt 76016
International Pkwy 76011
E Interstate 20 76018
W Interstate 20 76017
Interway Pl 76018
Inverness Dr 76012
Inverray Ct 76017
E Inwood Dr 76010
W Inwood Dr
500-699 76010
700-1199 76013
Iris Ln 76016
Irish Glen Dr 76014
Iron Horse Ct 76017
Iron Stone Ct 76006
Ironbark Dr 76018
Irongate Dr 76012
Ironwood Ct 76016
Island Bay Dr 76016
Island View Dr 76016
Ithaca Ct & Dr 76002
Ivanhoe Ln 76016
Ivy Ln 76011
Ivy Brook Ct 76006
Ivy Charm Way 76005
Ivy Glen Dr 76017
Ivy Hill Dr 76016
Ivycrest Trl 76017
Ivygreen Ct 76013
Ivywild Ct 76016
Ivywood Ct 76016
Jabez Ct 76002
Jacaranda Way 76002
Jackson Dr 76013
Jackson Square Dr 76010
Jagera Way 76002
Jakes Dr 76014
James St 76013
James River Dr 76018
Jamestown Ct 76013
Jana Ln 76001
Janann Ave 76014
Jane Ln 76001
Janet Cir 76013
Jasmine Trl 76017
Jasmine Fox Ln 76005
Jason Dr 76016
Jasper Dr 76017
Jasper Dove Way 76005
Jay Cir 76012
Jaywood Ct 76017
Jeanell Ln 76001
Jeannette Ct 76010
Jefferson St 76012
Jefferson Cliffs Way 76006
Jefferson Court Ln 76006
Jefferson Point Dr 76006
Jennie Ln 76002
Jennifer Ln 76002

Jerry Ln 76017
Jerry Crocker St 76011
Jersey Ln 76018
Jessie Ct 76002
Jessup Trl 76006
Jewell Dr 76016
Jimat Dr 76013
Jo Lyn Ln 76014
Joanna Ct & Ln 76014
Jocyle St 76010
Joey Ln 76010
Johns Ct 76016
Johnson Ave 76011
Jonathan Ln 76010
Jones Dr 76013
Jordan Ln 76012
Josephine Dr 76017
Joshua Ct 76016
Joshua Tree Ct 76002
Joyce St 76010
Juanita Dr 76013
Jubilee Trl 76014
Judy Lynn Dr 76014
Julias Ln 76006
Juliette Run 76002
June Evening Dr 76001
Juniper Dr 76018
Jurassic Ct & Dr 76002
Justin Lyn St 76012
Justiss Dr 76011
Kalmia Ct & Dr 76018
Karalyn Ct 76016
Karen Ct 76014
Kasmier Ct 76001
Katey Ln 76017
Katherine Ct 76016
Kathey Dr 76017
Kathryn Ct 76018
Kathy Ann Ct 76001
Katydid Ct & Ln 76002
Kay Lynn Ln 76016
Kayla Ct 76010
Kee Brook Dr 76017
Keeler Dr 76001
Keith Willow Ct 76018
Kelham Ct 76015
Kelleemac Ct 76018
Kelly Ter 76010
Kelly Elliott Rd
4200-4399 76016
4400-5999 76017
6000-6699 76001
Kelly Glenn Ln 76017
Kelly Hill Dr 76017
Kelly Perkins Rd 76016
Kelsey Ln 76017
Kemp Dr 76018
Kempton Dr 76001
Ken Ave 76001
Kendall Dr 76001
Kenilworth Dr 76001
Kennedy Dr 76011
Kennington Dr 76012
Kenosha Ln 76002
Kensington Ct 76016
Kent Dr 76010
Kenwood Ter 76013
Kerby St 76013
Kerry Dr 76013
Kesler Dr 76017
Kevin Ln 76014
Keymar Way 76014
Keystone Dr 76006
Kidd Dr 76013
Kilkenny Dr 76002
Killala Ct 76014
Killian Dr 76013
Kilrush Dr 76014
Kimberly Dr 76010
Kindling Ct 76016
King Richard Ct 76012
King William Dr 76018
Kingfisher Ln 76002
Kingly Ln 76017
Kings Row St 76010
Kingsborough Dr 76015

Kingsbridge Rd 76014
Kingscote Ct 76010
Kingsferry Ct & Dr 76016
Kingsford Ct 76017
Kingston St 76015
Kingstree Ct 76017
Kingsway Dr 76012
Kingswick Dr 76016
Kingswood Ct & Dr 76001
Kinross Dr 76002
Kiowa Dr 76012
Kipling Ct 76014
Kippers Ct 76016
Kira Ct 76006
Kircaldy Ct 76015
Kissimmee Dr 76002
Kite Ct 76014
Kittery Ln 76002
Kitty Hawk Dr 76014
Klinger Rd 76016
Knight St 76015
Knightsbridge Rd 76014
Knoll Ln 76010
Knoll Crest Dr 76014
Knollwood Ct 76006
Knotted Oaks Trl 76006
Knottingham Dr 76001
Knox Dr 76010
Kodiak Ct 76013
Kraft St 76010
Kramar Ct & Dr 76016
Kristin Ct & Ln 76012
Kristinwood Dr 76014
Kuykendall Dr 76001
Kyle Dr 76011
N L Robinson Dr 76011
La Costa Ct 76013
La Frontera Trl 76002
La Reja Cir 76006
La Viva Ln 76017
Labrador Dr 76002
Lace Bark Way 76005
Lachelle Ln 76010
Lackland St 76010
Lacy Ct 76017
Laguna Ln 76012
Lagustrum Ct 76017
Lake Champlain Dr 76016
Lake Country Dr 76012
Lake Fork Ln 76002
Lake Front Trl 76002
Lake Havasu Ct 76016
Lake Hawkins Dr 76002
Lake Jackson Dr 76002
Lake Louise Dr 76016
Lake Mead Blvd 76016
Lake Oak Dr 76017
Lake Park Ct & Dr 76016
Lake Point Dr 76016
Lake Pontchartrain Dr 76016
Lake Powell Dr 76016
Lake Roberts Way 76002
Lake Tahoe Dr 76016
Lake Whitney Dr 76002
Lakehill Ct 76016
Lakehurst Ct & Dr 76016
Lakemont Ct & Dr 76013
Lakeridge Rd 76016
Lakeshore Ct & Dr 76013
Lakeside Dr 76013
Lakeview Cir 76013
Lakeway Ct & Dr 76018
Lakewood Dr 76013
Lakey Dr 76018
E Lamar Blvd
400-1699 76011
1700-2599 76006
W Lamar Blvd 76012
Lamar Cir 76011
Lampe St 76010
Lamplighter Cir 76012
Lancelot Ln 76014
Land Rush Dr 76012
Landers Ln 76014
Landhope Cir 76016
Landmark Ct 76013

Landover Hills Ln 76017
Landrun Ln 76017
Lands End Dr 76016
Landshire Dr 76014
Lanette Ln 76010
Langford Dr 76018
Lansdowne Dr 76012
Lansingford Trl 76017
Lantana Dr 76018
Larchmont Dr 76006
Laredo Ct 76015
Largo Ln 76015
Lariat Ln 76015
Larimore Dr 76015
Larkspur Dr 76013
Larry Ln 76017
Las Brisas Dr 76006
Las Jardines Ct 76013
Las Luna Ln 76012
Las Palmas Ln 76012
Lasalle Dr 76016
Lasso Rd 76017
Latham Ct 76001
Latigo Dr 76001
Latrium Pl 76010
Laughlin Ct 76012
Laura Ln 76010
Laurel Dr 76012
Laurel Oak Ct & Ln 76001
Laurel Valley Ct & Ln 76006
Laurelhill Ct 76015
Laurelwood Dr 76010
Lavaca Dr 76018
E Lavender Ln 76010
W Lavender Ln
100-199 76010
1200-2499 76013
Lavern St 76013
Lavon Creek Ln 76006
Lawndale Dr 76017
Lawrence Rd 76006
Layla Rd 76016
Lazy Bayou Dr 76002
Le Mans Ct 76016
Leacrest St 76010
Leadville Dr 76001
Leagrove Ct 76016
Leaning Oak Ct 76002
Leatherleaf Ln 76015
Ledbetter Ct & Rd 76001
Lee Dr 76016
Leedsfield Ct 76017
Leesburg Ct 76017
Leffler Ln 76017
Legacy Point Dr 76006
Legend Rd 76014
Legget St 76018
Leigh Ann Ln 76010
Leighsford Ln 76006
Leighton Dr 76015
Lejuan Ct 76010
Lemesa Ct 76016
Lemon Dr 76018
Lemondrop Ct 76017
Lemontree Ct & Dr 76017
Lennon Ave 76016
Lennox Ln 76018
Leonard Ct 76015
Leslie Ct & Dr 76012
Lester Dr 76016
Levelland Dr 76017
Lexington Dr 76014
Liberty Trl 76002
Lido Ln 76015
Lieschen Ct 76012
Lighthouse Rd 76002
Lilac Dr 76018
Lillard Rd 76012
Lillian Ave 76013
E Lilly Ln 76010
W Lilly Ln
100-199 76010
1200-1299 76013
Lime Tree Ln 76014
Limestone Dr 76014
Lincoln Ct 76006

Lincoln Dr
500-699 76006
1700-2099 76011
2101-2299 76011
2400-2718 76006
2720-2798 76006
Lincoln Sq 76011
Lincoln Green Cir & Dr 76011
Lincrest Ct 76012
Linda Vista Ave 76013
Lindberg Dr 76016
Lindblad Ct
2100-2299 76013
2300-2499 76016
Linden Dr 76017
Lindsey Ct 76015
Lions Gate Ct 76001
Lisa Ln 76013
Little Rd
2300-4599 76016
4600-5499 76017
Little Brook Ln 76010
Little Creek Ct 76017
Little Hollow Ct 76016
Little John Ct 76012
Little Pond Ct 76016
N Little School Rd 76017
Littlestone Dr 76014
Live Oak Ct & Ln 76012
Livermore Dr 76017
Llano Trl 76015
Loblolly Pine Dr 76012
Loch Chalet Ct 76012
Loch Lomond Ct & Dr 76012
Lochngreen Trl 76012
Lockhart Dr 76002
Lodgecreek Ct 76016
Lombardy Ln 76013
Lomita Ln 76010
London Ln 76017
Londonderry Ct 76018
Lone Elm Ct 76018
Lone Ivory Trl 76005
Lone Oak Dr 76017
Lone Wolf Ct 76002
Lonesome Dove Trl 76002
W Lonesome Dove Trl 76001
Long Beach Dr 76001
Long Island Ln 76017
Long Ridge Ln 76014
Longacres Ct 76016
Longbow Ln 76002
Longbranch Ct 76012
Longhorn Ln 76017
Longhurst Ct 76013
Longmeadow Dr 76015
Longshadow Dr 76017
Lookout Trl 76017
Lora King Ct 76006
Lordsburg Ct & Trl 76017
Lori Cir 76010
Lorraine Dr 76017
Los Altos Ct 76006
Los Cabos Ln 76012
Los Colinas Ct 76013
Los Prados Trl 76006
Los Robles St 76006
Lost Canyon Trl 76002
Lost Creek Dr 76006
Lost Crossing Trl 76002
Lost Forest Dr 76011
Lost Springs Ct 76012
Lost Trail Ct 76002
Lotus Dr 76001
Louise Way Dr 76017
Love Wood Ln 76013
Loveland Dr 76018
Lovell Ct & Dr 76012
E Lovers Ln 76010
W Lovers Ln
500-699 76010
900-1799 76013
Lovingham Ct & Dr 76017
Loyd Dr 76002
Lucas Dr 76015

Lucern Ct 76012
Lucy Ln 76016
Luna Linda Dr 76010
Lupin Pl 76016
Luttrell St 76010
Lynbrook Ln 76015
Lynda Ln
300-699 76010
700-1199 76013
Lyndale Dr 76013
E Lynn Creek Dr 76002
W Lynn Creek Dr 76001
Lynnfield Ct & Dr 76014
Lynnwood Ct & Dr 76013
Lyra Ct & Ln 76013
Macgregor Dr 76002
Madeline Ct 76001
Madinah Dr 76010
Madison Ct & Dr 76011
Madrid Ct 76013
Magic Mile St 76011
Magnolia St 76012
Magnum Dr 76018
Mahogany Dr 76018
Mahonia Ct 76017
Mahonia Way 76014
Maid Marian Ct 76012
E Main St 76010
W Main St
100-699 76010
700-1199 76013
Mainsail Ln 76002
Majesty Dr 76011
Malibu Ct 76017
Malletwood Rd 76002
Maluck Ln 76011
Mammoth Cave Dr 76002
Manassas Dr 76017
Manchester Ct & Dr 76012
Mancuso Dr 76001
Mandalay Dr 76016
Mandy Way 76017
Mango Ct 76018
Manhassett Dr 76018
Manor Way 76018
Manorwood Ct 76016
Mansanillo Ct 76002
Mansfield Rd 76017
Mansfield Webb Rd 76002
Maple St 76011
Maple Canyon Ct & Dr 76002
Maple Leaf Dr 76017
Maple Springs Dr 76001
Mapleside Ln 76017
Mapleton Ct 76018
Mapleview Dr 76018
Maplewood St 76018
Mar Brook Ln 76017
Marathon St 76013
Marble Dr 76013
Marble Arch Ln 76015
Marble Falls Ct & Dr 76002
Marcellus Ct 76011
Mardell Dr 76016
Margaret Dr 76012
Marie Ter 76010
Marie Weldon Ct & Ln 76001
Marietta Dr 76017
Marigold Ct 76017
Marilyn Ln 76010
Marina Bay Ct 76013
Marina Shores Ct 76016
Marine Ct 76016
Mariposa Ln 76010
Mark Dr 76013
Mark Twain Ct 76006
Marlee Ln 76014
Marlow Pl 76014
Marquette St 76018
Marquis Cir E & W 76016
Marseille Dr 76013
Marshalldale Dr 76013
Marshfield Ct 76016
Marsland Ln 76001
Martha Ct 76001

Marthas Vineyard Dr 76001
Martin Luther Dr 76010
Martinique Ct & Dr 76012
Martinsburg Sq 76017
Martsy Ct 76014
Marvin Pl 76010
Marvin Gardens St 76011
Mary St 76010
Marydale Dr 76013
Mashburn Ln 76010
Mason Ave 76012
Mason Dells Dr 76001
Massachusetts Bay Dr 76001
Matlock Rd
2101-2199 76010
2400-4199 76015
4200-5999 76018
6001-6199 76018
6200-8199 76002
Matlock Centre Cir 76015
Matlock Meadow Ct & Dr 76002
Matt Ln 76012
Matthews Ct & Dr 76012
Maxwell Ct 76015
Maybrook Ct 76014
E Mayfield Rd 76014
W Mayfield Rd
500-600 76014
602-698 76014
700-2299 76015
3900-5599 76016
Mayfield Villa Dr 76014
Mayflower Ct 76014
Mayhill Ct 76014
Mayhugh Ct 76015
Maywood Dr 76017
Mazatlan Ct & Dr 76002
Mazourka Dr 76001
Mcbride St 76013
Mccartney Ct 76012
Mcdeavitt Dr 76011
Mckamy Oaks Trl 76017
Mckay Ct & St 76010
Mckenzie Pl 76018
Mckinney St 76012
Mcmillian Ct 76016
Mcmurtry Dr 76002
Mcqueary St 76012
Meadow Ln 76010
Meadow Bend Dr 76002
Meadow Glen Ct & Dr 76018
Meadow Green Dr 76017
Meadow Hill Ln 76006
Meadow Oaks Dr 76010
Meadow Park Dr 76017
Meadow Vista Dr 76002
N & S Meadow Way Cir 76015
Meadowbrook Blvd 76012
Meadowbrook Dr 76010
Meadowcreek Ct 76001
Meadowcrest Dr 76002
Meadowdale Rd 76017
Meadowedge Rd 76001
Meadowlake Ct 76013
Meadowlark Dr 76017
Meadowmere Ct & Ln 76001
Meadowside Trl 76017
Meadowview Dr 76016
Meadowwood Trl 76014
Meandering Way 76011
Median Way 76017
Medical Centre Dr 76012
Medicine Pass 76010
Medina Dr 76017
Mediterranean Ave 76011
Medlin Dr 76015
Megan Way 76016
Melbourne Ct 76013
Melbourne Dr
700-799 76012
1900-2699 76013
Melear Dr 76015
Melissa St 76010
Melody Dr 76001

Melody Pond Way 76005
Melrose St 76010
Melstone Dr 76016
Melville Dr 76015
Memorial 76017
Memory Ln 76011
Menefee St 76010
Menlo Park Dr 76002
Mentor Dr 76002
Mercedes Dr 76001
Merchants Row 76018
Meredith Dr 76014
Meridian St 76011
Merlot Ln 76002
Merrilee Dr 76011
Merritt Way 76018
Merritt Way Ct 76018
Mertis Dr 76002
Mesa Dr 76014
Mesa Glen Dr 76001
Mesa Ridge Ct 76002
Mesa Verde Trl 76017
N Mesquite St 76011
S Mesquite St 76010
Mesquite Hill Dr 76002
Michael Ct 76010
Michelle Dr 76016
Michener Dr 76011
Michigan Ave 76013
Michigan Ct 76016
Mid Pines Ct 76012
Midbury Ct 76015
Middlebrook Dr 76016
Midhurst Dr 76013
Midway Rd 76011
Mignon Dr 76017
Miguel Ln 76016
Mikasa Dr 76001
Milam Ln 76002
Milby Rd 76013
Milby Oaks Cir 76013
Mill Creek Dr 76010
Mill Crossing Pl 76006
Mill Height Dr 76014
Mill Lake Dr 76006
Mill Ridge Dr 76018
Mill Run Dr 76006
Millbrook Ct & Dr 76012
Miller Ct 76013
Miller Ln 76013
Miller Rd 76006
Millikin Dr 76012
Millington Trl 76017
Millpond Dr 76002
Millsprings Ct & Dr 76017
Millview Dr 76012
Millwood Ct & Dr 76016
Milton Dr 76002
W Milton Dr 76001
Mimosa Dr 76012
Mineral Springs Rd 76001
Minnie Dr 76012
Minot Ct 76001
Mintwood Pl 76016
Minuteman Ln 76002
Mira Lago Ln 76017
Mirabell Ct 76015
Miramar Dr 76002
Miriam Ln 76010
Miron Ct 76001
Mission Hills Dr 76018
Mission Ridge Dr 76016
Mistletoe Ct & Ln 76013
Misty Brook Dr 76013
Misty Cove Dr 76013
Misty Creek Dr 7601
Misty Crest Dr 7601
Misty Glen Trl 7601
Misty Meadow Ln 7600
Misty Oak Ln 7601
Misty Ridge Cir 7601
Misty Wood Ct & Dr 7601
W Mitchell Cir 7601
Mitchell Ct 7601
Mitchell Pkwy 7600
E Mitchell St 7601

W Mitchell St
100-699 76010
702-798 76013
800-1399 76013
Mobile Ave 76017
Mockingbird Ln 76013
Modesto Dr 76001
Mohawk Dr 76012
Monaco Ct & Dr 76010
Monarch Dr 76006
Moneta Ct 76001
Monroe St 76013
Montana Dr 76002
Montclair Ct & St 76015
Monte Carlo Dr 76015
Montego Ct & Dr 76002
Monterra Ct 76014
Monterrey Ct & St 76015
Monthaven Dr 76001
Monticello Ct 76012
Monties Ln 76015
Montpelier Ct 76017
Montreau Ct 76012
Montridge Ct 76016
Moody Ct 76012
Moon Dance Ct 76001
Moon River Ct & Dr 76002
Moonlight Ct 76016
Moonrise Dr 76002
Moore Ter 76010
Moorewood Ct & Dr 76017
Moorhead Ct 76014
Morgan Pl 76010
Morgan Woodward Way 76006
Morning Elm Way 76005
Morningcrest Ct 76002
Morningstar Ln 76001
Morris Ln 76016
Morris Heights Dr 76016
Moselle Dr 76016
Moss Dr 76016
Moss Glen Trl 76002
Moss Hill Dr 76018
Mossberg Dr 76002
Mossridge Ct 76016
Mosstree Dr 76001
Mosswood Ct 76015
Mossy Oak St 76012
Mount Carmel Dr 76017
Mountain Lake Ct 76016
Mountainwood Dr 76016
Mourning Dove Dr 76002
Mt Vernon Ct 76017
Mt Zion Dr 76018
Muirfield Dr 76001
Mulder Dr 76001
Mule Deer Dr 76002
Mullins Dr 76014
Munser Ct 76010
Murphy Ct 76016
Murray St 76011
Murwick Dr 76016
Musket Ln 76002
Mustang Dr 76001
Myers Rd 76017
Myna Dr 76002
Myrtle Dr 76018
Nancy Cir 76013
Nandina Dr 76014
Nantucket Ln 76001
Naomi Ln 76011
Napier Dr 76016
Nassau Ct 76012
Natches Dr 76014
E Nathan Lowe Rd 76002
W Nathan Lowe Rd 76017
National Ct 76017
Navaho St 76012
S Nedderman Dr 76010
W Nedderman Dr 76013
Neils Ct 76002
Nellie Dr 76002
Nelson Ter 76011
Nelwin Pl 76016
Nemo Ct 76010
Netherland Dr & Pl 76017
Nettletree St 76018
New Castle Ct 76013
New Haven St 76011
New Mill Ln 76012
New York Ave
200-2299 76010
2300-4099 76014
4100-4198 76018
4200-6499 76018
6500-7599 76002
Newbury Dr 76014
Newforest Ct 76017
Newington Ln 76018
Newport Ct 76015
Newsom Ct 76013
Newton St 76010
Niagara Falls Ct 76002
Nichols Dr 76012
Nicki Ln 76014
Nicole Ct & Way 76002
Nighthawk Trl 76002
Nightshade Dr 76018
Nikos Pl 76006
Nocona Ln 76018
Nolan Ryan Expy 76011
Nolen Ct 76012
Nora Ct & Dr 76013
Norfolk Dr 76015
Norman Cir 76014
E & W North St 76011
Northaven Ct 76012
Northbend Cir 76011
Northbrook Ct 76012
Northcrest Dr 76012
Northglen Ct & Dr 76012
Northlake Ct 76012
Northmeadow Ct & Dr 76011
Northpointe Ave 76018
Northridge Dr 76012
Northstar Ln 76017
Northwood Ct 76012
Norton Ct 76016
Norway Pine St 76012
Norwich Ct 76015
Norwood Cir, Ln & Pl E & W 76013
Nottinghill Gate St 76014
November Ct 76016
Nueces Trl 76012
Nut Pine Dr 76012
O Henry Ct 76006
Oak Ln 76017
Oak Mnr 76012
N Oak St 76011
S Oak St 76010
Oak Bend Dr 76016
Oak Bluff Dr 76006
Oak Bourne Dr 76016
Oak Branch Ct & Dr 76016
Oak Brook Ct & Rd 76016
Oak Cliff Ln 76012
Oak Club Dr 76017
Oak Country Dr 76017
Oak Cove Rd 76017
Oak Creek Dr 76017
Oak Forest Ct 76012
Oak Gate Ct 76016
Oak Glen Ct & Trl 76012
Oak Grove Dr 76013
Oak Hill Dr 76006
Oak Hollow Dr 76001
Oak Knoll Ct 76016
Oak Leaf Dr 76006
Oak Manor Ct 76012
Oak Moor 76010
Oak Point Dr 76010
Oak Shadow Ct 76017
Oak Springs Ct & Dr 76016
Oak Trail Ct 76016
Oak Tree Ln 76013
Oak Valley Dr 76016
Oak View Ct 76012
Oak Village Blvd 76017
Oakcrest Dr 76012
Oakhaven Ct 76016
Oakhurst Dr 76013
Oakland Hills Dr 76018
Oaklawn Ct 76001
Oakmead Dr 76011
Oakmont Ct 76013
Oakridge Dr 76013
Oakside Ct & Dr 76016
Oakwood Ct & Ln 76012
Oates Ln 76006
Ocho Rios Ct 76012
Oconnor St 76002
Office Park Dr 76016
Ogden Dr 76001
Old Barn Dr 76016
Old Dominion Ct & Dr 76016
Old London Ln 76017
Old Mill Dr 76011
Old Oak Dr 76012
Old Place Rd 76016
Old Pond Dr 76011
Old Spanish Ct 76002
Oldfield Dr 76016
Oldgate Ln 76002
Oleander St 76010
Olen Ct 76001
Olive Tree Ln 76014
Olivewood Dr 76001
Olivia Ln 76012
Olivia Way 76002
Olivia Meadow Dr 76002
Olympia Ct & Dr 76013
Omega Dr 76014
On Point Ct 76002
Onyx Ct 76017
Opus Dr 76001
Oram St 76010
Orange St 76012
Orange Blossom Ln 76014
Orangegrove Cir 76006
Orangewood Ln 76001
Orchard Dr 76012
Orchard Hill Ct & Dr 76016
Orchid Ct & Ln 76016
Oregon Trl 76002
Oriental Ave 76011
Oriole Dr 76010
Orthopedic Way 76015
Ortiz Dr 76010
Osage Ct & Dr 76018
Osler Dr 76010
Ottawa Ln 76017
Overbrook Ct & Dr 76014
Overhill Dr 76010
Overland Ln 76014
Overlook Ct 76012
Overridge Ct & Dr 76017
Overton Dr 76018
Overview Dr 76017
Owl Creek Dr 76018
Ox Bow Ct 76006
Oxen Ct 76017
Oxford St 76013
Ozark Dr 76014
Pacer Ln 76018
Paces Trl 76017
Pacific Dr 76001
Packard Dr 76001
Paddington Ct 76017
Paddockview Dr 76017
Pagoda Dr 76017
Painted Desert Ct 76001
Paisley Dr 76015
Palencia Ct 76006
Paleon Dr 76002
Palmer Ct 76014
Palmwood Trl 76014
Palo Alto Dr 76015
Palo Duro Ct 76017
Paloma Way 76006
Palomino Ct & Dr 76017
Palos Verdes Blvd 76017
Pamela Ln 76010
Pampas Ct 76018
Panorama Ct 76016
Pantego Dr 76013
Paradise Dr 76001
Park Ave N 76010
Park Ave S 76010
Park Dr 76016
Park Ln 76012
Park St 76011
Park Chase Ave 76011
Park Flower Ct 76017
Park Green Dr 76001
Park Grove Ct 76015
Park Highland Way 76012
Park Hill Dr 76012
Park Hurst Dr 76001
Park Manor Ct 76017
Park Place Ct 76016
Park Ridge Ct & Ter 76012
Park Row Ct 76013
E Park Row Dr 76010
W Park Row Dr
100-699 76010
700-2199 76013
2200-2218 76013
2201-4099 76013
2220-2500 76013
2502-3398 76013
Park Run Dr 76016
Park Springs Blvd
1600-2299 76013
4200-4299 76016
4400-5999 76017
6400-6499 76001
Park Springs Cir 76013
Park Springs Ct 76013
Park Square Dr 76013
Park Valley Ct 76017
Park Village Dr 76014
Park Vista Dr 76012
Park Willow Ln 76011
Parkchester Dr 76015
Parkcrest Ter 76012
Parkdale Ct 76013
Parker Rd 76012
Parker Trl 76016
Parker Oaks Ct & Dr 76016
Parkford Ln 76001
Parkland Point Blvd 76017
Parkmead Ct & Dr 76014
Parkmeadow Dr 76018
Parkmont Dr 76001
Parkside Ct 76016
Parkside Dr 76001
Parktree Dr 76001
Parkview Dr 76010
Parkway Ct & Ln 76010
Parkwood Ave 76013
Parliament Ct & Dr 76017
Partridge Ave & Ct 76017
Pasadena Ln 76015
Pathway Ct 76016
Patio Ter 76010
Patricia St 76012
Patrick Dr 76010
Patriotic Ct 76002
Patsy Ct 76016
Patterson Pl 76012
Paula Dr 76012
Pavia Ct 76006
Pax Ct 76002
Paxton Ave 76013
Paxton Run Ct 76002
Peach St 76011
Peachtree Ln 76013
Peachwood Ct & Dr 76016
Pear Tree Ln 76014
Peargrove Cir 76006
Pebble Way 76006
Pebblebeach Ct 76013
Pebblebrook St 76014
Pebblewood Dr 76006
N Pecan St 76011
S Pecan St 76010
Pecan Acres Ct 76013
Pecan Chase Cir 76012
Pecan Creek Dr 76001
Pecan Park Dr 76012
Pecan Square Dr 76012
Pecandale Dr 76013
Pecanwood Dr 76001
Peebles Ct 76013
Pegasus Dr 76013
Pelham Mnr 76016
Pelican Ct 76016
Penbrook Dr 76015
Pennant Dr 76011
Pennie Ct 76013
Pennington Dr 76014
Pennridge Ln 76017
Pennsylvania Ave 76017
Penny Belle Ln 76002
Penny Royal Ct 76002
Pepperidge Ct & Dr 76014
Peppermill Cir 76013
Peppertree Ct 76014
Peregrine Trl 76001
Periwinkle Dr 76002
Perkins Pl & Rd 76016
Perrin St 76010
Perryland Dr 76013
Petalwood Dr 76017
Petersburg Dr 76014
Petra Ct & Dr 76017
Peyco Dr N & S 76001
Peyton Pl 76010
Pheasant Trl 76016
Phillips Ct 76010
Pickford Ct 76001
Piedmont Dr 76016
Pier Nine Dr 76016
Pierce Dr 76011
Pierce Arrow Dr 76001
Pierron Dr 76002
Pikes Peak Way 76002
Pikeview Ter 76011
Pilant St 76010
Pilgrim Ln 76002
Pimlico Dr 76017
Pin Oak Ct & Ln 76012
Pine St 76011
Pine Cone Cir 76011
Pine Hollow Ct 76006
Pine Meadow Ct 76012
Pine Needle Ln 76011
Pineglen Ct 76016
Pinegrove Cir 76006
Pinehurst Dr 76012
Pineridge Dr 76016
Pinevalley Dr 76001
Pinewood Dr 76010
Pinion Dr 76017
Pinto Ct 76017
Pinwood Cir 76001
E Pioneer Pkwy 76010
W Pioneer Pkwy
100-699 76010
700-7399 76013
1922-1922 76013
1924-3700 76013
3702-3798 76013
Pirate Point Cir 76016
Pitcairn Ln 76015
Pitkin Dr 76006
Pittsford Ln 76002
Placid Cir 76012
Plainview Ct 76002
Plainview Dr 76018
Plantain Ct 76002
Plantation Dr 76014
Plaza St 76010
N & S Pleasant Cir & Pl 76015
E, S & W Pleasant Forest Ct & St 76015
Pleasant Hill Ct & Dr 76016
Pleasant Oaks Ct 76016
W Pleasant Ridge Rd
1700-2399 76015
2401-2499 76015
2500-6499 76016
Pleasant Valley Ln 76015
Pleasant Villa Dr 76016
Pleasant Wood Ct & Trl 76016
Pleasantview Dr
4200-4299 76016
4300-4599 76017
Plover Ln 76015
Plum Ln 76010
Plum Tree Ct 76016
Plum Vista Pl 76005
Plumeria Dr 76002
Plumgrove Cir 76006
Plumwood Dr 76016
Plymouth Ct 76013
Pocassett Dr 76018
Poinsetta Ln & Pl 76006
Point Trl 76015
Point Star Dr 76001
Pointclear Ct 76017
Pointer Pl 76002
Polk Cir & Dr 76011
Polo Club Ct & Dr 76017
W Poly Webb Rd 76016
Pompano Ct 76013
Pomponessett Dr 76001
Ponderosa St 76014
Ponselle Dr 76001
Pontiac Ct & Dr 76013
Pony Express Trl 76002
Poplar Dr 76006
Poplar Vista Ln 76002
Poppyseed Dr 76018
Port Au Prince Dr 76012
Port Phillip Dr 76002
Port Richmond Way 76018
Portales Ct & Dr 76016
Porters Ln 76012
Portland Dr 76018
Porto Bello Ct 76012
Portofino Ct & Dr 76012
Portsmouth Dr 76018
Post Oak Ct & Dr 76002
Post Wood Ln 76018
Postbridge Ct 76012
Potomac Pkwy 76017
Powder Horn Ln 76018
Powder Wood Ln 76018
Powell Dr 76013
Prado Real Dr 76017
Prairie St 76011
Prairie Fire Rd 76002
Prairie Hill Ln 76010
Prairie Oaks Dr 76010
Prairie Vista Dr 76001
Prairie Wood Ct 76018
N Prairieview Ct S 76017
Prather Ct 76017
Preakness Ct 76017
Prentice St 76018
Prescott Dr 76018
Presidents Corner Dr 76011
Preston Bend Dr 76016
Preston Hollow Ct 76012
Preston Trail Ct 76013
Prestonlake Ct 76012
Prestonwood Ct & Dr 76012
Prestwick Dr 76001
Primavera Dr 76002
Primrose Ct & Ln 76014
Prince Charles Ct 76017
Prince Of Wales 76017
Princess Pl 76014
Princess Anne 76017
Princeton Dr 76015
Princewood Ct 76016
Proctor Pl 76013
Promise Creek Dr 76002
Providence Ct 76015
Pryor Dr 76001
Pueblo Ct 76012
Purdue Dr 76012
Purpletop Dr 76002
Pyracantha Dr 76017
Quail Ct & Ln 76016
Quail Briar Ln 76002
Quail Brook Dr 76001
Quail Creek Dr 76017
Quail Crest Ct & Dr 76014
Quail Field Dr 76001
Quail Meadows Ln 76002
Quail Point Ln 76002
Quail Ridge Dr 76002
Quail Roost Ln 76002
Quail Run Rd 76014
Quail Springs Dr 76002
Quail Trail Ln 76002
Quail Valley Ln 76011
Quartz St 76002
Queen Ann Ct 76001
Queen Elizabeth 76017
Queenlily Ct 76018
E & W Queens Ct 76014
Queensborough Dr 76015
Quiet Waters Dr 76016
Quince Orchard Ct 76017
Quincy Ct 76013
Quinlan Ct 76018
Rachel Ct 76017
Racquet Club Ct & Dr 76017
Radcliffe Dr 76012
Rafael Ct 76002
Ragland Rd 76002
Ragwood Rd 76002
Rain Forest Dr 76017
Rainbow Dr 76011
Rainbow Creek Ct 76012
Rainer Dr 76016
Raines St 76010
Rainland Ct & Dr 76002
Raintree Ct 76012
Rainwater Dr 76001
Rainwood Ct 76017
Raleigh Cir 76010
Rall Ct 76015
Rambler Ct & Rd 76014
Ramblewood Cir 76014
Rambling Creek Ct & Dr 76016
Ramey Dr 76014
Ramos Dr 76015
Ramsgate Ct 76013
Ran Ln 76013
Rana Dr 76013
Ranch Dr 76018
Ranchero Ct 76017
Ranchogrande Dr 76017
Ranchvale Ln 76002
Randalito Dr 76010
E Randol Mill Rd 76011
W Randol Mill Rd
100-699 76011
701-797 76012
799-2999 76012
Randolph St 76010
Randy Dr 76013
Randy Snow Rd 76011
Ranger Run Cir 76006
Raper Blvd 76013
Ratliff Ridge Ct 76012
Raton Dr 76018
Raton Ridge Ln 76002
Rattlers Ct 76002
Raven Meadow Dr 76002
Ravenhill Ln 76016
Ravens Ct 76001
Ravenwood Dr 76013
Ravinia Cir & Dr 76012
Rawhide Dr 76017
Ray St 76010
Rayborn Dr 76010
Raydon Dr 76013
Raynorwood Ct 76015
Reading Rd 76011
Rebecca Ln 76014
Red Birch Dr 76018
Red Cactus Ct 76017
Red Cedar Ln 76011
Red Coat Ln 76002
Red Cypress Ct 76012
Red Deer Way 76002
Red Fern Dr 76001
Red Fox Ct 76006
Red Maple Ct 76001
Red Oak Ln 76012
Red River Dr 76017

Red Rock Dr 76017
Red Stag St 76002
Redarlet Dr 76018
Redbrook Ct & Dr 76014
Redbud Ct & Dr 76012
Redding Ct 76001
Redheart St 76002
Redleaf Dr 76017
Redmont Dr 76001
Redondo Dr 76006
Redstone Ct & Dr 76001
Redwater Dr 76018
Redwood St 76014
Reedway Ct 76018
Reever St 76010
Reflection Bay Dr 76013
Regal Dr 76016
Regal Oaks Dr 76001
Regency Ct 76010
Regency Place Ct 76006
Regent Dr 76001
Regents Park Ct 76017
Regulus Ct 76013
Remington Dr 76010
Remynse Dr
2200-2299 76010
2300-2399 76014
Renee Dr 76001
Reseda Dr 76015
Retail Connection Way 76018
Retriever Dr 76002
Reverchon Dr 76017
Revolution Ln 76002
Rhinevalley Dr 76012
Rice Ct 76012
Richard Dr 76010
Richbrooke Dr 76016
Richmond Dr 76014
Rickey Ln 76001
Ridge Dr 76016
Ridge Estates Ct 76001
Ridge Haven Dr 76011
Ridge Oak Ln 76006
Ridge Pointe Dr 76017
Ridge Run Rd 76014
Ridge Springs Ct 76017
Ridge Top Ln 76006
Ridgebrook Dr 76015
Ridgecrest Dr 76017
Ridgedale Dr 76013
Ridgefield Ct 76017
Ridgeglen Dr 76011
Ridgeline Dr 76017
Ridgemont Ct 76012
Ridgemoor Ct 76016
Ridgeside Ct & Dr 76013
Ridgetree Ln 76017
Ridgeview Ct & Dr 76012
Ridgeway St 76010
Ridgewood Ter 76012
Ridings Pl 76011
Riesling Way 76001
Rifleman Trl 76002
Rimcrest Dr 76017
Rimrock Ct 76017
Rio Ct 76017
Rio Altos Dr 76017
Rio Bravo Dr 76017
Rio Vista Ln 76017
Ripplesprings Ct 76016
Rising Meadow Dr 76018
Rising Sun Ct 76017
Rita Ln 76014
River Bend Rd 76014
River Bluffs Dr 76002
River Hills Cir, Ct &
Dr 76006
River Legacy Dr 76006
River Park Dr 76006
River Ridge Rd 76017
River Rock Cir 76006
Riverbrook Ct 76001
Riverchase Ln 76011
Rivercrest Dr 76006
Riverforest Ct & Dr 76017
Riverhead Dr 76015
Riveroaks Dr 76006
Riverplace Dr 76006
Rivervalley Ct 76006
Riverview Dr 76012
Riviera Ct 76012
Road Runner Dr 76002
Road To Six Flags W 76012
Road To Six Flags St
E 76011
Road To Six Flags St
W 76011
Roanoke St 76014
Roberts Cir 76010
Robin Ln 76010
Robin Rd 76013
Robins Lair Ct 76012
Robinwood Ct & Dr 76017
Roby Dr 76001
Rochelle Dr 76016
Rochester Ln 76002
Rock Creek Ct 76010
Rock Haven St 76018
Rock Inlet Ct 76016
Rock Meadow Trl 76017
Rock Ridge Ct 76017
Rock Springs Dr 76001
Rockbrook Ct & Dr 76006
Rockby Ct 76001
Rockcliff Ct 76012
Rockcreek Dr 76010
Rockdale Dr 76018
Rockfield Ct 76012
Rockford Ct 76017
Rockgate Ct 76011
Rockhampton Dr 76016
Rockhill Ct 76016
Rockland Dr 76016
Rockwall Ct 76017
Rockwood Trl 76016
Rocky Branch Ct & Dr 76013
Rocky Canyon Ct 76011
Rocky Canyon Rd 76012
Rocky Point Ct & Dr 76018
Rogers Ct 76013
E Rogers St 76011
W Rogers St 76011
Rolling Green Rd 76017
Rolling Hills Trl 76011
Rolling Meadows Dr 76015
Romack Ct 76012
Roman Ct 76013
Rome Ct 76017
Ron Mcandrew Dr 76013
Roosevelt Ct 76013
Roosevelt Dr
1900-2099 76013
2100-2199 76013
2300-3799 76016
Roosevelt St 76011
Rosarita Rd 76002
Rose St 76010
Rose Spirit St 76005
Rosebud Ct & Dr 76016
Rosedale Ln 76006
Roselle Ct 76018
Rosemary Dr 76014
Rosemead Dr 76014
Rosemont Ct 76017
Rosetree Ct 76016
Rosewood Ln 76010
Rosita St 76002
Ross Trl 76012
Rosslyn Chapel Ct 76012
Roswell Ct & Ln 76002
Roundup Trl 76017
Rovato Dr 76001
Rowcrop Dr 76017
Roy Bean Ct 76002
Royal Cir 76017
Royal Arch East Ct 76012
Royal Arch West Ct 76012
Royal Club Ct & Dr 76017
Royal Colonnade 76011
Royal Dominion Ct 76006
Royal Field Dr 76011
Royal Gate Dr 76016
Royal Glen Ct & Dr 76012
Royal Hill Ln 76014
Royal Meadow Ln 76017
Royal Mile Ct & Dr 76015
Royal Springs Dr 76001
Royalcrest Dr 76017
Royaloak Dr 76016
Royalwood Dr 76006
Royce Dr 76016
Ruby St 76010
Ruger Dr 76006
Ruidosa Ct S 76002
Ruidoso Ct & Dr 76017
Rumford Trl 76017
Rumson Dr 76006
Running Brook Dr 76010
Running Creek Dr 76001
Runnymede Ct 76016
Rush Ct 76017
Rush Creek Dr 76017
Rush Springs Ct & Dr 76016
Rush Valley Ct 76016
Rushing Meadow Ct 76016
Rushing Wind Ct 76001
Rushmoor Dr 76016
Rushview Dr 76016
Russell Rd 76001
Russell Curry Rd 76001
Russwood Dr 76012
Rustic Forest Trl 76016
Rustic Ridge Ct 76017
Rustle Leaf Dr 76017
Rutgers Ct 76015
Ruth St 76010
Ruthella Dr 76010
Rutherford Ln 76014
Rutland Dr 76002
Ryan Ct 76001
Ryan Plaza Dr 76011
Ryder Dr 76013
Rye Glen Dr 76017
Sabinas Ct 76002
Sabine Pass Ln 76006
Saddle Creek Cir 76015
Saddle Oak Dr 76001
Saddle Ridge Ct & Rd 76016
Saddleback Rd 76017
Saddlehorn Dr 76017
Safari Trl 76018
Safe Harbour Dr 76016
Saffron Ln 76010
Sage Cir 76016
Sage Bloom Dr 76017
Sagebrush Ct & Trl 76017
Sagecanyon Ct 76016
Sahara Dr 76012
N & S Saint Andrews
Ct 76011
Saint Carlos St 76010
Saint Claire Dr 76012
Saint George Pl 76015
Saint Michaels Dr 76011
Salem Dr 76014
Salida Dr 76001
Salsbury Cir 76014
Salt Flats Trl 76002
Saltillo Ln 76015
Salton Ln 76001
Sam Houston Dr 76014
Sammons Davis Ct 76015
Samuels Ln 76010
San Clemente Dr 76017
San Diego Dr 76015
San Francisco Ct 76012
San Frando Dr 76010
San Jacinto Dr 76012
San Jose Ct & St 76002
San Juan Ct 76012
San Luis Ct 76016
San Marcos Dr 76012
San Martin Dr 76010
San Mateo Ct 76017
San Miguel Ct 76016
San Paulo Ct 76012
San Rafael Dr 76013
San Ramon Ct & Dr 76013
San Saba Ln 76006
Sand Creek Ct 76006
Sand Hill Ct 76014
Sand Springs Ct 76017
Sandalwood Ln 76017
Sandberry St 76002
Sandcastle Trl 76012
Sandgate Dr 76002
Sandhurst Dr 76001
Sandpiper Dr 76013
Sandra Kay Ln 76015
Sandstone Ct & Dr 76001
Sandusky Ct 76017
Sandy Ct 76012
Sandy Hook Ln 76018
Sandy Oak Ct 76016
Sandy Point Ct & Dr 76018
Sandybrook Dr 76001
Sanford Ct 76012
E Sanford St 76011
W Sanford St
101-197 76011
199-620 76011
622-698 76011
700-2499 76012
Sangre Ct & Trl 76016
Sanibel Ln 76018
Sansome Dr 76018
Santa Anna Dr 76001
Santa Fe Cir 76016
Santa Fe Ct 76017
Santa Fe Dr 76017
Sapphire Ct & Dr 76017
Saquaro Lake Ct 76016
Sarah Ct & Dr 76013
Sarasota Dr 76017
Saratoga Ln 76017
Sassafras Rd 76002
Satinwood Ct 76001
Sausalito Dr 76016
Savannah Ct 76014
Savannah Club Dr 76017
Savoy Dr 76006
Sayles Ave 76018
Scarlett Ct 76012
Scenic Dr 76013
Scenic Bay Ct & Dr 76013
Scenic Forest Trl 76016
Scenic Point Trl 76006
Schenectady Rd 76017
School Hill Cir 76017
Schoolside Ct 76016
Scientific Dr 76014
Scots Legacy Dr 76015
Scots Wood Dr 76015
Scotsbluff Ct 76001
Scotsview Ct 76015
Scott Dr 76012
Scottsdale Dr 76018
Scouts Vis 76006
Sea Island Trl 76001
Sea Rim Dr 76018
Seaboard Dr 76014
Seachest Ln 76016
Seaford Rd 76001
Seasons Rd 76014
Secret Ct 76006
Secretary Dr 76015
Sedalia Dr 76018
Seegers Dr 76018
Seely St 76018
Seese Dr 76018
Segram Ct 76017
Selfridge Dr 76014
Selina Ct 76016
Seminole Dr 76010
Sendero Ct & Dr 76002
Seneca Dr 76017
Senior Circle Dr 76010
Senior Creek Dr 76010
September Ct 76001
Sequoia Ln 76010
Serenade Ct 76015
Serenity Ct 76016
Sesame Dr 76010
Sesco St 76013
Setting Sun Ln 76012
Settlement Dr 76001
Settlers Glen Trl 76002
Seven Hills Rd 76002
Seville Ct 76013
Sexton Dr 76015
Shadow Ct & Dr W 76006
Shadow Crest Dr 76018
Shadow Ridge Ct &
Dr 76006
Shadow Wood Ct &
Dr 76006
Shadowfax Dr 76002
Shady Ln 76013
S Shady Ln 76001
Shady Brook Dr 76002
Shady Forge Trl 76005
Shady Glen Dr 76015
Shady Hill Ln 76016
Shady Hollow Dr 76013
Shady Meadow Ct 76013
Shady Oaks Ct 76012
Shady Park Dr 76013
Shady Path Ln 76010
Shady Point Dr 76013
Shady Springs Ct &
Dr 76017
Shady Valley Ct & Dr 76013
Shady View Ct 76013
N & S Shadycreek Ct &
Dr 76013
Shadydale Dr 76012
Shadyway Dr 76018
Shadywood Ct 76012
Shale Ct 76002
Shamrock Dr 76016
Shamrock Bend Ln 76012
Shana Ct 76014
Sharon St 76010
Sharon Lee Dr 76001
Sharpshire Ln 76014
Shavano Ct 76006
Shawn Ct 76014
Shea Ct 76014
Sheehan Ct 76012
Sheerwater Rd 76002
Sheffield Ct & Dr 76013
Sheila Dr 76010
Shellbrook Ct 76016
Shelley Ct & Dr 76012
Shelmar Ct & Dr 76014
Shelterwood Ln 76016
Shelton St 76013
Shelton Home Ct 76017
Shenandoah Dr 76014
Shepherds Glen Ln 76010
Sherburne Dr 76018
Sheridan Cir & Ct 76017
Sherman St 76012
Sherri Oak Ln 76012
Sherry St
100-2099 76010
2101-2199 76010
2300-2349 76014
2350-2350 76010
2351-3699 76014
2400-3698 76014
5000-5499 76018
Sherwood Dr 76013
Sherwood Forest Ct 76012
Shining Waters Ln 76002
Shoal Creek Dr 76001
Shore Breeze Ct 76016
Shorecrest Cir 76010
Shores Ct 76016
Shorewood Ct & Dr 76016
Shortleaf Pine Dr 76012
Shoshoni Dr 76002
Sibley Dr 76015
Sidney St 76010
Sieber Dr 76016
Sienna Dr 76002
Sierra Ct & Ln 76016
Sierra Vista Ct 76017
Sigh Ct 76006
Sigmond Dr 76017
Signal Peak Dr 76017
Silber Rd 76017
Silent Dr 76017
Silkcrest Trl 76017
Silkwood Trl 76016
Silo Rd
5700-6199 76018
6300-6798 76002
6800-7399 76002
Silver Bow Trl 76017
Silver Cliff Ct 76016
Silver Creek Dr 76006
Silver Leaf Dr 76013
Silver Maple Dr 76018
Silver Oak Ln 76017
Silver Spruce Dr 76001
Silver Spur Dr 76001
Silver Wind Ct 76016
Silverbrook Ln 76006
Silvercrest Dr 76002
Silverpoint Ct 76017
Silverton Dr 76001
Silvertop Rd 76002
Silverwood Dr 76006
Simi Dr 76001
Sinclair Ct 76002
Sipes Ct 76018
Six Flags Dr 76011
Skipper Ct 76015
Sky Lake Ct 76018
Skylark Dr 76010
Skyline Dr 76011
Slaughter St 76011
Sleepy Hollow Dr 76006
Sleepy Oaks Cir 76011
Smallwood Dr 76001
Smintann Dr 76002
Smith Ln 76013
Smith Barry Rd 76013
Smoke Tree Dr 76018
Smokerise Ct & Dr 76016
Smokey Ct 76014
Smouldering Wood Ct &
Dr 76016
Smugglers Cv 76016
Snapdragon Ln 76002
Snead Ct 76014
Snow Mass Dr 76016
Snow Ridge Ct 76018
Snowdon Dr 76018
Snowivy Ct 76001
Snowy Owl St 76002
Solano Ct & Dr 76017
Soledad St 76002
Solitude Ct 76017
Somerset Dr 76013
Sommerville Ct 76013
Sonora Ct & Dr 76012
Sophie Ln 76010
Sounder Dr 76001
E South St
100-299 76010
300-398 76004
301-799 76010
400-798 76010
W South St 76010
Southbridge Ln 76002
Southbrook Ct 76006
Southcrest Dr
2200-2299 76013
2300-2899 76016
4200-4299 76013
Southdale Dr 76010
Southeast Pkwy 76018
Southern Charm Ct 76016
Southern Hills Blvd 76006
Southern Oak Dr 76011
Southern Pine Ct 76018
Southgate St 76013
Southmoor Dr 76010
Southpark Cir & Dr 76013
Southpoint Dr 76017
Southridge Ct & Dr 76010
Southseas Ln 76015
Southwest Plz 76016
Southwind Dr 76002
Southwood Blvd 76013
Sovereign Ct 76012
Spanish Cir 76016
Spanish Trl
2201-2299 76013
2400-2422 76016
2424-2799 76016
Spanish Moss Dr 76018
Spanish Oak Ct 76002
Sparkford Ct 76013
Spartan Dr 76001
Speer St 76010
Spencer Dr 76002
Spencer Lakes Dr 76001
Spice Island Dr 76002
Spicewood Ln 76017
Spies Springs Ct 76006
Spillway Ln 76006
Spinnaker Dr 76016
Spitfire Dr 76001
Splendor Ct 76010
Splitbranch Ln 76017
Splitrail Ct 76002
Spoonbill Ct 76002
Spring Dr 76012
Spring Brook Dr 76001
Spring Creek Ct & Rd 76017
Spring Garden Dr 76016
Spring Hill Ct & Ln 76016
Spring Lake Dr 76012
Spring Meadows Dr 76014
Spring Miller Ct 76002
Spring Mist Dr 76011
Spring Oak Pl 76017
Spring Walk Ln 76010
Spring Willow Dr 76018
Springbranch Dr 76006
Springcrest Dr 76010
Springdale Ct 76006
Springfield Dr 76016
Springleaf Ln 76018
Springmere Dr 76012
Springmont Ct 76012
Springpark Dr 76014
Springridge Dr 76014
Springsong Ln 76017
Springtime Ct 76017
Springwood Dr 76001
Sprocket Dr 76015
Spruce Dr 76018
Spruce Forest Ct 76001
Spruce Point Dr 76010
Sprucewood Ln 76017
Spur Ridge Ct 76002
Spyglass Hill Dr 76018
Squaw Creek Ct 76018
Squirrel Run Ct 76002
St Alban Ct 76001
St Charles Ct & Dr 76013
St Croix Ct 76012
St Germain Dr 76016
St Gregory St 76013
St Ives Ct 76017
St James Pl 76011
St Joseph Way 76002
St Lawrence Way 76002
St Leonard Dr 76001
St Maria Ct 76013
St Paul Dr 76013
St Tropez Ln 76013
St Vincent Ct 76013
Stacey Ct 76013
Stacey Renee Ct 76002
Stadium Dr
100-199 76010
300-598 76011
600-699 76011
701-899 76011
Stadium Dr W 76011
Stadium Pl 76006
Stadium Oaks Ct 76011
Stafford Dr 76012
Stage Line Ct & Dr 76017
Stage West Dr 76017
Stagecoach Dr 76013
Stagetrail Dr 76017

Stampede Dr 76010
Stanhope Ln 76001
Starke Ct 76006
Starlight Ct 76016
Starlinda Ct 76012
Starmont Ln 76017
Starr Ln 76016
Station Dr 76015
Steamboat Cir & Ct 76006
Steeplechase Ct & Trl 76016
Steeplewood Ct & Trl 76016
Stefani Ct 76013
Stella Ct 76017
Stennett Dr 76006
E Stephens St 76018
W Stephens St 76017
Stephie Ann Ct 76002
Sterling Ct 76012
Sterling Forest Dr 76010
Sterling Green Trl 76017
Stetter Dr 76001
Stevedore St 76016
Stewart Dr 76013
Stiles Dr 76002
Stillmeadow Dr 76014
Stinson Dr 76001
Stockbridge Ct 76015
Stockton Dr 76006
Stolper Dr 76013
Stone Bluff Ct 76017
Stone Branch Dr 76001
Stone Bridge Dr 76006
Stone Canyon Ct 76012
Stone Haven Ct 76012
Stone Meadow Ct 76017
Stone Mesa Ct 76001
Stonebriar Ct 76001
Stonebrook Dr 76012
Stonecreek Dr 76014
Stonecrest Ln 76011
Stonedale Dr 76002
Stoneford Ct 76001
Stonegate St 76010
Stonehenge Dr 76014
Stonehill Ct 76012
Stonehurst Ct 76014
Stoneleigh Ct 76011
Stoneridge Ct 76014
Stoneriver Rd 76006
Stonetrail Cir & Rd 76006
Stoneway Dr 76011
Stonewick Dr 76016
Stonewood Ct 76017
Storie Rd 76001
Stornoway Trl 76012
Stowe Springs Ln 76002
Strait Ln 76013
Stratford Ct 76015
Stratton Ln 76006
Strawberry Ln 76011
Streambed Ct 76006
Streamside Dr 76018
Sturgeon Ct 76001
E Sublett Rd 76018
W Sublett Rd
700-4899 76017
4900-5198 76001
Sudbury Way 76018
Suffolk Dr 76001
Sugar Maple Dr 76001
Sugar Plum Ln 76015
Sugar Tree Ct 76017
Sugarmill Ct 76014
Sullivan Ct 76016
Sumac Ct 76017
Summer Ct 76001
Summer Bay Cir 76011
Summer Breeze Ct 76001
Summer Brook Cir 76011
Summer Creek Ct & Dr 76018
Summer Day Dr 76014
Summer Glen Ct & Dr 76001
Summer Oaks Ct 76011
Summer Place Dr 76014
Summer Trail Ct 76016
Summer Tree Cir & Ln 76006
Summerfield Dr 76018
Summergrove Dr 76001
Summerleaf Dr 76001
Summerwood Dr 76017
Summit Ave 76013
Summit Peak Ct & Dr 76017
Summit Ridge Trl 76017
Sun Glow Dr 76006
Sun Grace Dr 76001
Sun View Ct 76001
Suncrest Ct 76002
Sundance Dr 76006
Sunday Hill Dr 76016
Sunflower Dr 76014
Sunlight Ct & Dr 76006
Sunny Meadow Ct 76016
Sunnybrook Ln 76014
Sunnypark Dr 76014
Sunnyvale Dr 76010
Sunray Valley Ct 76012
Sunrise Ct & Dr 76006
Sunset Ct 76013
Sunset Ln
2300-2398 76015
2500-3900 76016
3902-3998 76016
Sunset Hills Ct 76012
Sunset Oaks St 76016
Sunshine Valley Dr 76016
Suntree Ct 76014
Superior Dr 76013
Surfside Ct 76016
Surrey Cir 76014
Surrey Oaks Ct & Dr 76006
Susan Dr 76010
Sussex Dr 76014
Sutherland Ct 76017
Sutton Ct & Dr 76018
Swafford St 76015
Swaim Ct 76001
Swainson Trl 76002
Swan Ct 76015
Swan Lake Dr 76017
Sweetbriar Dr 76011
Sweetgum Trl 76014
Sweetpea Ln 76006
Swiss St 76010
Switchgrass Rd 76002
Sycamore Dr 76013
Sylvan Ct & Dr 76012
Syracuse Ct 76002
Tabasco Trl 76002
Table Rock Ct 76006
Tabor Dr 76002
Tacoma Dr 76017
Tads Ln 76014
Taft Dr 76011
Tall Tree Ct 76018
Taluca St 76010
Tamanaco Ct 76017
Tamarack Ct 76018
Tamarron Ln 76017
Tampa Bay Way 76002
Tampico St 76010
Tan Oak Ln 76010
Tanbark Ln 76001
Tangerine Ct 76011
Tanglewood Ln 76012
Tanner Ct 76018
Tarpley St 76013
Tate Springs Rd 76016
Tatum Dr 76012
Taunton Ct 76018
Tave Ct 76016
Taylor St 76011
Teakwood Dr 76014
Teal Hill Dr 76017
Teal Ridge Dr 76017
Tealcove Dr 76017
Tealpond Dr 76017
Team Ct 76018
Tech Centre Pkwy 76014
Telluride Dr 76001
Tempest Dr 76001
Templeton Dr 76006
Ten Wood Ct 76018
Tennessee Trl 76017
Tennis Villa Dr 76017
Tennyson Dr 76013
Teresa Ct 76001
Terlingua Ln 76010
Terra Dr 76017
Terrace St 76012
Terrace Glen Dr 76002
Terrebonne Ct 76014
Terrell Cir 76011
Terry Dr 76010
Terry Lewis St 76011
Terrycroft Dr 76016
Texas Dr 76015
Thackery Dr 76018
Thames Dr 76017
Thannisch Ct & Dr 76011
Tharp St 76010
Thistle Ridge Ct & Ln 76017
Thomas Pl 76010
Thomas Chapel Dr 76014
Thomason Cir 76006
Thoreau Ln 76016
Thorn Hill Dr 76001
Thornbird Ln 76001
N & S Thornbush Cir 76013
Thorncliffe Dr 76016
Thornton St 76013
Thorntree Ct 76016
Thoroughbred Dr 76017
Thousand Oaks Dr 76017
Three Oaks Dr 76016
Thunderbird Dr 76002
Tiara Ct 76017
Ticino Valley Ct & Dr 76016
Tidal Trce 76016
Tidewater Dr 76018
Tierce Blvd 76013
Tierra Del Sol Rd 76002
Tiffany Ct 76016
Tiffany Oaks Ln 76016
Tiffany Park Ct 76016
Tillman Dr 76006
Timber Ter 76013
Timber Cove Ct 76017
Timber Gardens Ct 76016
Timber Green Dr 76016
Timber Oaks Ct & Ln 76010
Timber Run Dr 76001
Timber Trail Ct & Dr 76016
Timberbrook Ct 76015
Timbercreek Dr 76017
Timbercrest Dr 76017
Timberfalls Trl 76015
Timberlake Cir, Ct & Dr 76010
Timberline Ct 76006
Timbersedge Trl 76015
E & W Timberview Ln 76014
Timberwood Cir 76015
Tin Cup Dr 76001
Tina Marie Rd 76012
Tinsley Dr 76017
Tioga Dr 76002
Tippler Dr 76002
Tish Cir 76006
Tiverton Ct 76001
Toby Ct 76001
Tofftrees Dr 76016
Tokalon Ln 76002
Toltec Ct 76002
Tombstone Dr 76001
Tomlin Ln 76012
Tomlinson Ct 76017
Topaz Dr 76001
Torch Dr 76015
Torrey Ln 76017
Torrington Dr 76012
Tottenham Ct 76016
Toulouse Dr 76016
Tournament Trl 76017
Tower Dr 76010
Towerwood Dr 76001
Town North Dr 76011
Townlake Cir 76016
Trace Mills Dr 76014
Trail Brush Dr 76014
Trail Crest Dr 76017
Trail Dust Ln 76017
Trail Glen Ct 76013
Trail Lake Dr 76016
Trail Oak Ct 76016
Trailblazer Ct 76002
Trailhead Dr 76013
Trailridge Dr 76012
Trails Edge Ct & Dr 76017
Trailview Dr 76018
Trailwood Ct 76014
Tranquility Ct & Dr 76016
Trapper Ct 76001
Travis Ct 76014
Travis Ranch Trl 76002
Treasure Island Trl 76016
Treecrest Dr 76017
Treehaven Ct & Dr 76016
Treehollow Ln 76017
Treepoint Dr 76017
Treetop Trl 76015
Treeview Dr 76016
Tremont Ct 76015
Trent Dr 76010
Tretorn Ct 76017
Trevino Dr 76014
Trevor Way 76001
Trinity Cir 76006
Trinity Bend Cir 76006
Trinity Height Dr 76014
Trinity Knoll Cir 76006
Trinity Mills Dr 76014
Trinity Oaks Ct & Dr 76006
Triple S Rd 76017
Trisha Val Ct 76016
Triumph Trl 76002
Trowbridge Dr 76013
Troy Ln 76016
Truman St 76011
Truver Ln 76001
E Tucker Blvd 76010
W Tucker Blvd 76013
Tudor Ct 76017
Tulane Dr 76012
Tulip Dr 76013
Tumbleweed Ct 76017
Turf Club Dr 76017
Turnberry Dr 76006
Turner Way 76001
Turner Warnell Rd 76001
Turnstone Dr 76018
Turpin Dr 76013
Turtle Cove Ct 76018
Turtle Creek Dr 76010
Tuscany Ct & Ln 76016
Tuscany Oaks Dr 76016
Tuscany Park Dr 76016
Tuscola Dr 76018
Twelve Oaks Ct 76012
Twin Cedar Ct 76018
Twin Creek Dr 76015
Twin Elms Dr 76012
Twin Lakes Ct 76016
Twin Maple Ct & Dr 76018
Twin Oaks Ct 76006
Twin Parks Ct & Dr 76001
Twin Pine Ct 76018
Twin Post Ct & Dr 76014
Twin Springs Dr 76016
Twin Spruce Ct 76018
Twin Timbers Dr 76018
Twin Willows Dr 76017
Twinhill Ct & Dr 76016
Two Jacks Ct 76017
Tyler St 76012
Umbrella Pine Ct 76018
Underhill Dr 76012
Union Dr 76002
Unique Dr 76015
University Dr 76013
Us 287 Hwy 76001
Uta Blvd
100-699 76010
719-1097 76013
1099-1199 76013
Ute Dr 76012
Vail Ct & Dr 76012
Valcasi Dr 76001
Valencia Dr 76002
Valerie Ct 76013
Valley Ct & Ln 76013
Valley Branch Dr 76001
Valley Forge Ct & Ln 76002
Valley Meadow Dr 76016
Valley Mills Dr 76018
Valley Oaks Ct & Ln 76012
Valley Ridge Ct 76017
Valley Spring Dr 76018
Valley View Dr 76010
Valley Vista Rd 76006
Valleybrooke Ct & Dr 76001
Valleycreek Ln 76017
Valleycrest Dr 76013
Valleydale Ct & Dr 76013
Valleygreen Dr 76017
Valleywood Dr 76013
Valparaiso Trl 76017
Van Cir 76011
Van Buren Cir & Dr 76011
Van Hook Ct 76013
Vancil Ct & Dr 76018
Vancouver Dr 76012
Vandalia Trl 76017
Vanderbilt Dr 76014
Vanessa Cir 76013
Vaquero Ct & Dr 76017
Varacruz Dr 76010
Varsity Cir 76013
Vassar Ct 76015
Vela Dr 76014
Velvet Antler Trl 76002
Venetian Cir 76013
Ventnor Ct 76011
Ventura Dr 76015
Verandah Ln 76006
Vermillion Trl 76002
Vermont Ct 76001
Vernon Dr 76015
Verona Ct 76012
Versailles Dr 76006
Vestavia Ct 76018
Via Cortez St 76017
Via Nautla St 76017
Via Oro St 76017
Via Playa St 76017
Via Real St 76017
Via Tortuga St 76017
Vicksburg Dr 76017
Victor Ct 76013
Victoria Dr 76012
Victoria Sta 76017
Victory Crest Dr 76002
Vidalia Dr 76016
Vienna Ct 76010
Viewside Cir 76011
Viewtop Ln 76012
Viking Trl 76001
Villa Ln 76017
Villa Brook Ln 76017
Villa Del Mar Ave 76017
Villa Mar Dr 76017
Villa Park Dr 76017
Villa Vera Dr 76017
Village Cir 76012
Village Glen Trl 76016
Village Green Ct 76012
Village Oak Dr 76017
Village Wood Ct 76012
Villanova St 76018
Vincennes Ct 76017
Vine St 76011
Vine Ridge Ct 76017
Vinetree Dr 76002
Vineyard Dr 76015
Vinson St 76010
Vintage Dr 76001
Vintage Lake Dr 76016
Violet Ln 76006
Virburnum Ct 76018
Virginia Ln 76010
Virginia Sq 76017
Viridian Park Ln 76005
Viscount Dr 76016
Vista Trl 76002
Vista Chase Ct 76001
Vista Creek Ct 76016
Vista Ridge Ct 76013
Vista Verde Dr 76017
Vista Wood Dr 76017
Vistaview Ct 76016
Viveca Dr 76014
Volunteer Dr 76014
Vonner Ct 76011
Voyagers Dr 76012
Wabash Ct 76014
Waggoner Dr 76013
Wagon Wheel Trl 76013
Wakefield Cir, Ct & Dr 76015
Wakeforest Ct 76012
Walden Trl 76016
N Waldrop Dr 76012
Wall St 76018
Wallace Meadows Ct 76001
Wallingford Dr 76018
Walnut Dr 76012
Walnut Hill Cir 76006
Walnut Springs Dr 76001
Walters Ln 76012
Waltham Ct 76012
Wamsetta Dr 76018
Wanda Way 76001
Warancom Dr 76017
Wareham Ct & Dr 76017
Warnell Walsh Rd 76002
Warnford Pl 76015
Warren Dr 76002
Warrington Ct 76014
Warwick Dr 76015
Washington Cir & Dr 76011
Watch Hill Ct 76002
Water Bend Dr 76002
Water Fowl Trl 76002
Water Oak Dr 76002
Water Ridge Dr 76016
Waterbury Pl 76013
Watercress Cir 76012
Waterdance Cir & Ln 76010
Waterford Cir 76014
Waterhill Ln 76017
Waterlilly Dr 76002
Waterside Dr 76012
Watertown Ln 76002
Waterview Dr 76016
Waterwalk Ct 76002
Waterway Ct 76012
Waterwood Dr 76012
N Watson Rd
400-1199 76011
1201-1699 76006
S Watson Rd
100-1499 76010
1501-2299 76010
2500-3598 76014
4200-5999 76018
7401-7499 76002
7600-7798 76002
Waverly Ct & Dr 76015
Waxwing Ct & Dr 76018
Waycross Ct & Dr 76016
Wayland Dr 76012
Weatherby Dr 76006
Weaver Dr 76001
Web St 76011
Webb Ferrell Rd 76002
Webb Lynn Rd 76002
Wedge Dr 76013
Wedgewood Ct 76013
Weeks Ave 76010
Weeping Willow Ln 76002
Welleado Dr 76013
Wellington Ct 76013
Wellridge Dr 76017
Wellston Ct & Dr 76018
Wembley Rd 76014
Wembley Downs Dr 76017
Wentworth Ct & Dr 76001
Wesley Dr 76012
Wesson Rd 76002
N West St 76011
S West St 76010
N & S Westador Ct & Dr 76015
Westbain Dr 76015
Westbrook Dr 76002
Westbury Ct 76013
Westchester Dr 76015
Westcliff Ct 76016
Westcrest Dr 76013
Westen Club Way 76017
Wester Way Dr 76013
Western Blvd 76013
Westfield Ct 76001
Westgate Dr 76015
Westgrove Dr 76001
Westhaven Rd 76017
Westkendal Ln 76015
Westlake Ct 76013
Westminister Ct 76015
Westmoor Pl 76015
Westover Ct & Dr 76015
Westpointe Way 76018
Westridge Dr 76012
Westview Ter 76013
Westway Pl 76018
Westwind Dr 76017
Westwood Dr 76012
Westyork Dr 76015
Wet N Wild Way 76011
Weyborn Dr 76018
Weyhill Dr 76013
Weymouth Ct 76013
Wharton Ct 76001
Wheatfield Ct 76001
Wheeler Dr 76018
Whippoorwill Ct 76014
Whisper Crest Dr 76002
Whisper Glen Dr 76017
Whisper Meadow Ln 76006
Whisper Ridge Ln 76006
Whispering Creek Dr 76018
Whispering Oak Ct 76012
Whispering Trail Cir 76013
Whisperton Dr 76016
Whisperwood Trl 76016
Whistler Dr 76006
White Dove Dr 76017
White Fawn Rd 76002
White Fields Way 76002
White Hall Rd 76001
White Oak Ct & Ln 76012
White Spruce Dr 76018
White Swan Dr 76002
White Tail Ln 76002
White Way Dr 76013
White Willow Ln 76002
White Wing Dr 76014
Whitlit Dr 76002
Whitney Ln 76013
Wickersham Dr 76014
Wickford Dr 76018
Wicklow St 76002
Wilcrest Dr 76010
Wild Deer Way 76002
Wild Goose Way 76016
Wild Holly Ln 76017
Wild Horse Ct 76017
Wild Ivy Ct 76016
Wild Oak Ct 76016
Wild Prairie Dr 76002
Wild River Dr 76002
Wild Rose Ct 76006
Wild Turkey Trl 76016
Wild West Dr 76017
Wildbriar Dr 76014
Wilder Ln 76006
Wilderness Ct 76001
Wildflower Ln 76006
Wildgrove Ct 76016
Wildplum Dr 76015
Wildrock Ct & Dr 76001
Wildview Ct 76017

Wildwood Dr 76011
Wilhitte Dr 76001
Wilkes Ct 76017
Will Scarlet Rd 76013
Williams St 76010
E & W Williamsburg Mnr 76014
Willington Dr 76018
Willis Ave 76010
Willoughby Ln 76011
Willow Run 76013
Willow Bend Ct & Dr 76017
Willow Branch Dr 76017
Willow Creek Ct 76011
Willow Crest Dr 76017
Willow Elm Ct & Dr 76017
Willow Oak Ln 76001
Willow Park Ct & Dr 76017
Willow Point Dr 76010
Willow Ridge Dr 76017
Willow Springs Dr 76001
Willow Tree Dr 76017
Willow Valley Dr 76017
Willow View Dr 76017
Willow Wind Ct 76017
Willowbrook Ct & St 76011
Willowdale Dr 76016
Willowglen Ln 76006
Willowood Cir 76015
Willowstone Trl 76018
Wilma Ln 76012
Wilmette Dr 76018
Wilmor Ct 76018
Wilshire Blvd & Ct 76012
Wilson Dr 76011
Wimbledon Ct & Dr 76017
Wimbledon Oaks Ln 76017
Winchester Ct 76013
Wind Brooke Dr 76001
Wind Drift Trl 76017
Wind Elm Ct 76002
Wind Rock Ct 76017
Windcastle Dr 76018
Winderemere Dr 76014
Windgate Ct 76012
Windhurst Dr 76015
Winding Rd 76016
Winding Creek Ct 76016
Winding Hollow Ln 76006
Winding Oaks Ct & Dr 76016
Windmill Ct 76013
Windshift Dr 76014
Windsong Dr 76001
Windsor Ct & Dr 76012
Windsor Place Ct 76015
Windsor Wood Dr 76015
Windsprint Way 76014
Windstone Dr 76018
Windswept Ct & Pl 76012
Windy Gap Dr 76002
Windy Hills Ct 76017
Windy Meadow Ct & Dr 76017
Windy Pine Ln 76015
Winewood Ln 76013
Wingfield Dr 76017
Wingren Ln 76014
Wingrove Dr 76015
Winnsboro Ct 76015
Winslow Ct & Dr 76015
Winston Ter 76014
Winter Fire Way 76005
Winter Park Ln 76018
Winter Pass Trl 76002
Winter Sunday Way 76012
Winterberry Ct 76018
Wintercrest Ct 76017
Wintergreen Ct 76014
Winterset Trl 76016
Wintersmith Dr 76014
Winterwood Ct 76017
Winthorp Dr 76001
Wiscasset Dr 76010
Wisteria Ct 76014
Wolf Creek Ct & Dr 76018
Wolff Dr 76015

Wood Ln 76001
Wood Cliff Ct 76012
Wood Springs Ct 76017
Wood Wind Dr 76013
Woodard Way 76011
Woodbine Ct & St 76012
Woodbrook St 76011
Woodbury Ct 76017
Woodcastle Ct 76016
Woodcreek Dr 76016
Woodcrest Ln
- 400-699 76010
- 1000-1299 76013

Wooded Acres Ct & Dr 76016
Wooded Creek Cir 76016
Wooded Edge Ct 76001
Wooded Glen Ct 76013
Woodfern Dr 76018
Woodfield Dr 76016
Woodford Dr 76013
Woodhaven Dr 76010
Woodhill Dr 76016
Woodhollow Dr 76016
Woodlake Dr 76016
Woodland Dr 76012
Woodland Oaks Dr 76013
Woodland Park Blvd & Ct 76013
Woodland West Dr 76013
Woodmeadow Ct & Dr 76016
Woodmont Ct & Dr 76017
Woodridge Cir, Ct & Dr 76013
Woodrow St 76012
Woodruff Ct 76017
Woods Dr 76010
Woods Edge Dr 76016
Woodsetter Ct & Ln 76017
Woodshire Dr 76016
Woodside Ct 76013
Woodside Dr
- 1800-2299 76013
- 2300-4199 76016
- 4500-4799 76013

Woodsong Trl 76016
Woodstock Blvd 76006
Woodstone Ct 76016
Woodview Ct & St 76013
Woodville Ct 76017
Woodway Dr 76017
Woolwich Dr 76001
Worcester Ct 76001
Worth St 76014
Worth Forest Ct & Dr 76016
Worthing Pl 76017
Wren Ct & Dr 76013
Wrentham Dr 76016
Wrexgate Ct 76016
Wright St 76012
Wyndham Pl 76017
Wynn Ter 76010
Wynncrest Cir & Ln 76006
Wyrick Ct 76012
Xavier Dr 76001
Yachtclub Ct & Dr 76016
Yale Dr 76015
Yates St 76010
Yaupon Dr 76018
Yearling Way 76002
Yellowstone Dr 76013
York Beach Pl 76002
York Minster Ct 76006
York River Dr 76018
Yorkfield Ct 76001
Yorkford Dr 76001
Yorkhill Dr 76001
Yorkmeadow Dr 76001
Yorkshire Dr 76013
Yorktown Dr 76014
Yosemite Dr 76002
Young Ct 76002
Yucatan Ct 76002
Yucca Ct & Dr 76017
Zachary Dr 76002
Zachum Dr 76002
Zapata Dr 76015
Zephyr Ct 76002
Zinfandel Ln 76001
Zoeller Ct 76014
Zuefeldt Dr 76002
Zuma Dr 76006

NUMBERED STREETS

E & W 1st 76010
E 2nd St 76010
- 100-399 76010
- 1200-1999 76013

E & W 3rd 76010
E 4th St 76010
- 200-399 76010
- 900-1199 76013

W 6th St 76010
106th St 76011
107th St 76011
108th St 76011
109th St 76011
110th St 76011
111th St 76011
112th St 76011
113th St 76011

ATHENS TX

General Delivery 75751

POST OFFICE BOXES MAIN OFFICE STATIONS AND BRANCHES

Box No.s
All PO Boxes 75751

RURAL ROUTES

01, 07, 08, 10 75751
02, 03, 04, 09 75752

NAMED STREETS

Aaron St 75751
Airport Rd 75752
Allen St 75751
Alma Lena Ct 75752
An County Road 404 75752
An County Road 4043 75752
An County Road 476 75751
An County Road 491 75751
An County Road 4910 75751
An County Road 4915 75751
An County Road 492 75751
An County Road 493 75751
An County Road 494 75751
An County Road 497 75751
An County Road 498 75751
An County Road 499 75751
An County Road 4990 75751
An County Road 4991 75751
Angelina Dr 75752
Angie Ln 75751
Anglin St 75751
Arrowhead Dr 75751
Ashley Ct 75752
Athens Brick Rd 75751
Athens Fish And Game 75752
E & W Baker St 75751
Bandera Ct & St 75752
Barbara St 75751
Barker St 75751
Basher St 75751
Bayshore Dr 75752
Bear Creek Cir 75752
Bel Air Dr 75751
Belmont St 75751
Ben Belt Dr 75751
Beverly Dr 75752
Birch St 75751
Blackmon St 75751
Blaine Rd 75751
Blake St 75751
Blossom Ln 75751
Blue Bird Ln 75752
Blythe View Rd 75752
Bob St 75751
Bogota St 75752
Bonham Rd 75752
Bradley Dr 75751
Brentwood Cir & Dr 75751
Bridle View Ct 75752
Broadmore St 75751
Broken Spoke Trl 75751
Brown Rd 75752
Bryson Ave 75751
Buggy Hub Trl 75751
Bunny Rabbit Rd 75751
Buster St 75751
Butler Rd 75752
Cardinal St 75751
Caroline Cir 75752
Carroll Dr 75752
N Carroll St 75751
S Carroll St 75751
Cary Cir 75751
Cason St 75751
E & W Cayuga Dr 75751
Cecil Ln 75752
Cedar Ln 75751
Champion Ranch Rd 75752
N & S Charles St 75751
E Charlie St 75751
Charlya Cir & Dr 75752
E Chase St 75751
Chelsa Ct 75752
Cherokee Trce 75751
Cherry Ln 75751
Cheryl Ln 75751
Christina Ct 75752
Church St 75751
W Circle St 75752
Claudia Dr 75751
Clear View Ct 75752
Clifford St 75751
Clint Ct 75752
E & W Clinton Ave 75751
Coleman Aly 75751
E & W College St 75751
Colonial Cir & Dr 75751
Colorado St 75751
Commanche St 75751
Commercial St 75751
E & W Corsicana St 75751
Cottonwood St 75751
Country Ln 75752
Country Club Cir 75751
County Road 1102 75751
County Road 1103 75751
County Road 1104 75751
County Road 1105 75751
County Road 1106 75751
County Road 1108 75751
County Road 1111 75751
County Road 1113 75751
County Road 1114 75751
County Road 1115 75751
County Road 1116 75751
County Road 1117 75751
County Road 1118 75751
County Road 1119 75751
County Road 1120 75751
County Road 1121 75751
County Road 1122 75751
County Road 1123 75751
County Road 1124 75751
County Road 1125 75751
County Road 1127 75751
County Road 1200 75751
County Road 1205 75751
County Road 1208 75751
County Road 1209 75751
County Road 1213 75751
County Road 1214 75751
County Road 1215 75751
County Road 1216 75751
County Road 1404 75751
County Road 1405 75751
County Road 1406 75751
County Road 1407 75751
County Road 1408 75751
County Road 1436 75751
County Road 1500 75751
County Road 1502 75751
County Road 1503 75751
County Road 1504 75751
County Road 1505 75751
County Road 1507 75751
County Road 1508 75751
County Road 1509 75751
County Road 2800 75751
County Road 2803
- 8700-8799 75751
- 8801-8997 75752
- 8999-9999 75752
- 10001-10699 75752

County Road 2805 75751
County Road 2806 75751
County Road 3700 75752
County Road 3703 75752
County Road 3704 75752
County Road 3705 75752
County Road 3707 75752
County Road 3710 75752
County Road 3711 75752
County Road 3713 75752
County Road 3714 75752
County Road 3715 75752
County Road 3717 75752
County Road 3718 75752
County Road 3721 75752
County Road 3722 75751
County Road 3800 75752
County Road 3801 75752
County Road 3804 75752
County Road 3810 75752
County Road 3811 75752
County Road 3814 75752
County Road 3815 75752
County Road 3816 75752
County Road 3817 75752
County Road 3818 75752
County Road 3819 75752
County Road 3821 75752
County Road 3822 75752
County Road 3824 75752
County Road 3825 75752
County Road 3826 75752
County Road 3900 75752
County Road 3901 75752
County Road 3902 75752
County Road 3903 75752
County Road 3904 75752
County Road 3907 75752
County Road 3909 75752
County Road 3910 75752
County Road 3911 75752
County Road 3912 75752
County Road 3913 75752
County Road 3914 75752
County Road 3918 75752
County Road 3919 75752
County Road 3920 75752
County Road 3921 75752
County Road 3922 75752
County Road 3923 75752
County Road 3924 75752
County Road 3925 75752
County Road 41126 75751
County Road 41511 75751
County Road 41512 75751
County Road 41513 75751
County Road 41514 75751
County Road 41515 75751
County Road 41516 75751
County Road 41518 75751
County Road 4503 75752
County Road 4504 75752
County Road 4506 75752
County Road 4507 75752
County Road 4508 75752
County Road 4509 75752
County Road 4510 75752
County Road 4511 75752
County Road 4512 75752
County Road 4513 75752
County Road 4517 75752
County Road 4518 75752
County Road 4520 75752
County Road 4522 75752
County Road 4523 75752
County Road 4524 75752
County Road 4600 75752
County Road 4601 75752
County Road 4602 75752
County Road 4603 75752
County Road 4604 75752
County Road 4607 75752
County Road 4608 75752
County Road 4609 75752
County Road 4610 75752
County Road 4612 75752
County Road 4613 75752
County Road 4614 75752
County Road 4615 75752
County Road 4616 75752
County Road 4618 75752
County Road 4619 75752
County Road 4621 75751
County Road 4622 75751
County Road 4628 75752
County Road 4700 75752
County Road 4702 75752
County Road 4704 75752
County Road 4705 75752
County Road 4706 75752
County Road 4709 75751
County Road 4800 75752
County Road 4801 75752
County Road 4802 75752
County Road 4803 75752
County Road 4804 75752
County Road 4805 75752
County Road 4806 75752
County Road 4807 75752
County Road 4812 75752
County Road 4816 75752
County Road 4817 75752
County Road 4819 75752
County Road 4825 75752
County Road 4900 75752
County Road 4908 75752
County Road 4910 75752
County Road 7704 75752
Craig Dr 75751
Cream Level Rd
- 800-1199 75751
- 1300-1398 75752
- 1400-1499 75752

Creekside Cir & Dr 75752
Crestview 75751
Crestview Dr 75752
Crestway Dr & St 75751
Crown Pointe Dr 75752
Crystal Dr 75752
Davis Dr 75751
Davis Ln 75752
Dean St 75751
Deer Park Est 75751
Deer Run Rd 75752
Delete 75751
Dickens 75751
Dogwood Trl 75751
Dorsey Cir, Dr & Ln 75752
Double Oaks Rd 75752
Doubletree Trl 75751
Douglas Rd 75751
Dove Creek Dr 75751
Dull Averiette St 75751
Dusty Rd 75752
Early Morning Dr 75752
Eastridge 75752
Edmonson Ave 75751
Edna St 75751
Elaine Dr 75751
Elizabeth 75752
Elizabeth Ln 75751
Elizabeth St 75751
Elm St 75751
Emily Ln 75751
Emma St 75751
England St 75751
Enterprise St 75751
N Erwin St 75751
Estate Dr 75751
Etna St 75751
Fairway Dr 75751
N Faulk St 75751
Flaralde 75752
Flat Creek Rd 75751
S Fly In Lake Rd 75752
Fm 1615 75752
Fm 1616
- 1100-1198 75751

Fm 1616
- 1200-1799 75751
- 1801-1899 75751
- 5901-6097 75752
- 6099-8699 75752
- 8701-8999 75752

Fm 1803 75752
Fm 1861 75752
Fm 2329 75751
Fm 2339 75752
Fm 2494 75751
Fm 2495
- 1300-2800 75751
- 2802-2898 75751
- 2901-2997 75752
- 2999-5800 75752
- 5802-6498 75752

Fm 2709 75752
Fm 2752 75752
Fm 2892 75752
Fm 2961 75751
Fm 2970 75751
Fm 317 75752
Fm 3273 75751
Fm 59 75751
Fm 753 75751
Fm 804 75752
Fm 858 75752
E Foggle St 75751
Ford St 75751
Foreman Dr 75751
Frank St 75751
Freeman Dr 75751
Frizzell St 75751
Garrett St 75751
N & S Gauntt St 75751
Gibson Rd 75751
Grand View Dr 75752
Green Ct 75751
Green Gate Rd 75752
Guadalupe Cir & Dr 75751
Haggard Ln 75752
N Hamlett St 75751
Hawn St 75751
High Point Ct 75752
Highland Dr 75751
Hillcrest Dr 75751
Hillside Dr 75751
Hodge Ct & St 75751
Hollytree 75751
Hopson Dr 75752
Horseshoe Dr 75752
Humphrey St 75751
Icon Ranch Rd 75752
Impala Point Cir & Dr 75752
Impala South Rd 75752
Impala South Ii 75752
Industrial Dr 75751
James St 75751
Jamie Ct 75752
Jenny Ln 75751
Joe Prince Dr 75751
Jonathan St 75751
Karen Ct 75751
Kaufman Rd 75751
Kim Ln 75752
Kirkwood 75751
Kyle St 75751

La Acres ... 75752
La Jolla Dr ... 75751
Lacosta St ... 75751
Lago Vista Dr ... 75752
Laird Ln ... 75751
Lake Estate Dr ... 75751
Lakefront Shores Rd ... 75752
Lakeside Dr ... 75751
Lana Ln ... 75751
Land Grant Trl ... 75751
E & N Lane Ave ... 75751
Lantana ... 75751
E & W Larkin St ... 75751
Larue St ... 75751
Laster Rd ... 75752
Laurel Rd ... 75751
Laurie Dr ... 75751
E Lee St ... 75751
Legacy Ln ... 75751
Leland Dr ... 75751
Lewis Ct ... 75752
Lila Ln ... 75751
Linda Ln ... 75751
Linden Dr & Ln ... 75751
Lindsey Ln ... 75751
Little Red Rd ... 75752
Live Oak St ... 75751
Loise Ln ... 75752
Loland Dr ... 75751
Loma Linda Dr ... 75752
Lonnie Dr ... 75751
NE Loop 317 ... 75752
NW Loop 317
1000-1094 ... 75752
1096-1099 ... 75752
2200-2999 ... 75751
Loop 7 ... 75751
NE Loop 7 ... 75752
SW Loop 7 ... 75751
Louise Ln ... 75751
Lovers Ln ... 75751
Loyola Dr ... 75751
Lucas Dr ... 75751
Madole St ... 75751
Magnolia Rd & St ... 75751
N Maple St ... 75751
Martin St ... 75751
Martin Luther King Jr Blvd & Cir ... 75751
Mary Beth Ln ... 75751
Maryland Dr ... 75751
E Massey St ... 75751
Matthews St ... 75751
Maxine Dr ... 75751
Mcarthur St ... 75751
Mccaleb St ... 75751
Mccarley St ... 75751
Mcdonald Dr & St ... 75751
S Mcgee St ... 75751
Meadow Dr & Pl ... 75751
Meadowview St
500-598 ... 75751
1600-1999 ... 75752
Medical Cir ... 75751
Mill Run Pl & Rd ... 75751
Miramar Ct ... 75752
Mission Ave ... 75751
Mitchell St ... 75751
Mockingbird Ln ... 75751
Montgomery St ... 75751
Moody St ... 75751
N Morrison St ... 75751
Mosley Dr ... 75751
Mulberry Dr ... 75751
N & S Murchison St ... 75751
Neches St ... 75752
N Needmore St ... 75751
Nicole Dr ... 75751
Oak Ridge Estates Rd ... 75751
Oak Tree Dr ... 75751
Oak Wood Place Dr ... 75751
Old Kaufman Rd ... 75751
Old Tyler Hwy ... 75751
Open Gate Ranch Rd ... 75752
Oval Dr ... 75751
Over Look Pt ... 75752
Owen St ... 75751
Pace Ranch Rd ... 75751
N & S Palestine St ... 75751
Palmetto St ... 75751
Palomino Ct ... 75752
S Palomita Cir ... 75751
Park Dr ... 75751
Park Place Dr ... 75751
Parrish Ct ... 75752
Parsons Pkwy ... 75751
Patterson Rd ... 75751
Peach St ... 75751
Pearl St ... 75751
Pecan Cir ... 75751
Pedernales Ct E, N, S & W ... 75752
Peninsula Cir ... 75752
Peninsula Point Dr ... 75752
Penny Ln ... 75751
Persouth ... 75751
Pine Ln ... 75751
Pine Oak Dr ... 75751
Pine Ridge Ct ... 75752
Pine View Ct ... 75752
N & S Pinkerton St ... 75751
E Pinkie St ... 75751
Plantation Point Dr ... 75752
Pleasant Run Cir ... 75752
Pool St ... 75751
Powderhorn Dr ... 75751
N & S Prairieville St ... 75751
Prince St ... 75751
Private Road 5101 ... 75751
Private Road 5102 ... 75751
Private Road 5103 ... 75751
Private Road 5104 ... 75751
Private Road 5105 ... 75751
Private Road 5106 ... 75751
Private Road 5201 ... 75751
Private Road 5202 ... 75751
Private Road 5203 ... 75751
Private Road 5204 ... 75751
Private Road 5205 ... 75751
Private Road 6801 ... 75751
Private Road 6802 ... 75751
Private Road 6804 ... 75751
Private Road 7091 ... 75752
Private Road 7404 ... 75752
Private Road 7703 ... 75752
Private Road 7704 ... 75752
Private Road 7705 ... 75752
Private Road 7803 ... 75752
Private Road 7901 ... 75752
Private Road 7903 ... 75752
Private Road 7904 ... 75752
Private Road 7905 ... 75752
Private Road 8501 ... 75752
Private Road 8502 ... 75752
Private Road 8801 ... 75752
Private Road 8802 ... 75752
Private Road 8858 ... 75752
Private Road 8859 ... 75752
Private Road 8901 ... 75752
Progress Way ... 75751
Ranch Rd
600-699 ... 75752
2700-7899 ... 75751
Ravenwood Dr ... 75751
Red Oak Cir ... 75752
Redbud Cir & Ct ... 75751
Reierson Ave ... 75751
Reserve Dr ... 75752
Reynolds Rd ... 75751
Richardson Rd ... 75752
Richardson St ... 75751
Rico Dr ... 75751
Risko ... 75752
Robbins Rd ... 75751
Rocky Ridge Rd ... 75751
Rolling Dr ... 75751
Rolling Hills Ct ... 75752
Romans Rd ... 75751
Roosevelt St ... 75751
Rose Garden Cir ... 75751
Rose Point Ln ... 75752
Rosedale Dr ... 75751
Royal St ... 75751
Royal Crest Dr ... 75751
Royal Mountain Rd ... 75751
Rusko Vlg ... 75752
Ruth St
700-799 ... 75751
4800-4899 ... 75752
Sabine St ... 75752
Saddle Ridge Ct ... 75752
Saint Joseph St ... 75751
Saint Thomas Dr ... 75751
San Saba St ... 75752
Sand Springs Rd ... 75751
Sawyer St ... 75751
E & W Scott St ... 75751
Seneca Dr ... 75751
Settlers Loop ... 75751
Shady Trl ... 75751
Shelby Ln ... 75751
Sherwood Dr ... 75752
Shore Crest Ct & Way ... 75752
Short St ... 75751
Singletree Trl ... 75751
Slagle St ... 75751
Southoak Dr ... 75751
Southpark Cir ... 75752
Southwood Dr ... 75752
Sportsman Ranch Rd ... 75752
Stallion Lake Ct ... 75752
State Highway 19 N ... 75752
State Highway 19 S ... 75751
State Highway 31 E
1800-2399 ... 75751
State Highway 31 E
2900-4500 ... 75752
4502-4698 ... 75752
State Highway 31 W ... 75751
E & W Stephens Ct ... 75751
Stirman St ... 75751
Stonebridge ... 75751
Stoneleigh St ... 75751
Suncrest Dr ... 75752
Sunny Ln ... 75751
Sunrise ... 75752
Sunset Ct ... 75752
Sycamore St ... 75751
Tamara St ... 75751
Tanglewood Dr ... 75752
Tanglewood St ... 75751
Tannellhill Way ... 75751
Teresa Ln ... 75751
Terry Dr ... 75751
Thunderbird Dr ... 75751
Tillison St ... 75751
Timber Hill Dr ... 75751
Torribrooke Ln ... 75751
Trail Ridge Rd ... 75751
Trey Cir ... 75752
Two Mile Cir ... 75752
E & W Tyler St ... 75751
N Underwood St ... 75751
Us Highway 175 E
1100-1198 ... 75751
1200-2599 ... 75751
2601-2699 ... 75751
2700-2898 ... 75752
2900-6200 ... 75752
6202-6598 ... 75752
Us Highway 175 W ... 75751
Us Highway 287 ... 75751
Valle Vista Dr ... 75751
Valley View Dr ... 75752
Van Winkle Cir ... 75751
Viewpoint Dr ... 75752
Vz County Road 2918 ... 75752
Vz County Road 2922 ... 75752
Vz County Road 4206 ... 75752
Vz County Road 4210 ... 75752
Vz County Road 4215 ... 75752
Vz County Road 4218 ... 75752
Vz County Road 4220 ... 75752
Vz County Road 4222 ... 75752
Vz County Road 4223 ... 75752
Wagontree Trl ... 75751
N Walker St ... 75751
Wallace St ... 75751
Walnut Cir ... 75751
Ward Ln ... 75751
Water View Ct ... 75752
Waterford Est ... 75752
Waverly Way ... 75752
Webster Way ... 75751
Wellington Ln ... 75751
Wildflower Ln ... 75751
Wildlife Way ... 75752
Williams St ... 75751
Willowbrook Cir & Dr ... 75751
Wilson St ... 75751
Windmill Ln ... 75751
N & S Wofford St ... 75751
Wood St ... 75751
Woodcrest Dr ... 75752
Wooded Creek Dr ... 75751
Woodland Dr ... 75752
Woodland St ... 75751
York St ... 75751

NUMBERED STREETS

1st St ... 75751
3rd St ... 75751
6th St ... 75751
4d Cir ... 75752

AUSTIN TX

General Delivery ... 78701

POST OFFICE BOXES MAIN OFFICE STATIONS AND BRANCHES

Box No.s
A - Z ... 78713
AA - AA ... 78713
TEA - TEA ... 78711
1 - 1992 ... 78767
2001 - 2776 ... 78768
2903 - 2986 ... 78769
2903 - 2986 ... 78768
3001 - 3976 ... 78764
4001 - 4999 ... 78765
5001 - 5999 ... 78763
6000 - 6625 ... 78762
6357 - 6357 ... 78703
6701 - 6960 ... 78762
6907 - 6907 ... 78716
7001 - 8770 ... 78713
9001 - 10994 ... 78766
9998 - 9998 ... 78714
9998 - 13942 ... 78711
14001 - 16777 ... 78761
17001 - 19820 ... 78760
26001 - 30580 ... 78755
33003 - 33556 ... 78764
40001 - 43533 ... 78704
49001 - 49999 ... 78765
50001 - 50594 ... 78763
66001 - 66996 ... 78766
78774 - 78774 ... 78711
80001 - 85800 ... 78708
90001 - 99091 ... 78709
140001 - 149997 ... 78714
150001 - 159099 ... 78715
160001 - 165001 ... 78716
170001 - 172000 ... 78717
180001 - 181258 ... 78718
200001 - 209270 ... 78720
270001 - 270276 ... 78727
300001 - 303534 ... 78703
340001 - 343000 ... 78734
400010 - 400500 ... 78704
500001 - 500276 ... 78750
551000 - 559017 ... 78755
650001 - 650120 ... 78765
660001 - 660438 ... 78766
679000 - 679099 ... 78767
684001 - 689008 ... 78768

RURAL ROUTES

02 ... 78719

HIGHWAY CONTRACTS

02 ... 78736

NAMED STREETS

A Ln ... 78703
Abbate Cir ... 78721
Abbey Cir ... 78727
Abbey Dr ... 78737
Abbey Glen Ln ... 78753
Abbott Dr ... 78737
Abby Ann Ln ... 78747
Abelia Dr ... 78727
Aberdeen Cir ... 78745
Aberdeen Ct ... 78737
Aberdeen Dr ... 78745
Aberdeen Way ... 78753
Abervil Trl ... 78717
Abilene Cv & Trl ... 78749
Abingdon Pl ... 78723
Abney Dr ... 78729
Above Stratford Pl ... 78746
Acacia Bud Dr ... 78733
Academy Dr ... 78704
Acadia Ct ... 78737
Acadian Trl ... 78727
Acapulco Ct & Dr ... 78734
Accomac Dr ... 78748
Acers Ln ... 78725
Acorn Cv ... 78744
Acorn Creek Trl ... 78750
Acorn Grove Ct ... 78744
Acorn Oaks Dr ... 78745
Acropolis Ct ... 78759
Acton Dr ... 78736
Ada Ct ... 78744
Adair Cv & Dr ... 78754
Adak Cv ... 78729
Adalee Ave ... 78723
Adam L Chapa Sr St ... 78702
Adams Ave ... 78756
Addie Roy Rd ... 78746
Addison Ave ... 78757
Adel Cv ... 78749
Adelaide Dr ... 78739
Adelanto Ct ... 78738
Adelphi Cv & Ln ... 78727
Aden Ct & Ln ... 78739
Adina St ... 78721
Adirondack Cv & Trl ... 78759
Adirondack Summit Dr ... 78738
Adobe Trl ... 78737
Adonis Dr ... 78729
Adriane Dr ... 78721
Adventurer ... 78734
Aemilian Way ... 78730
Aerie Cv ... 78759
Afton Ln ... 78744
Aftonshire Way ... 78748
Agape Ln ... 78735
Agarita Cv ... 78734
Agarita Dr ... 78737
Agarita Rd ... 78734
Agatha Cir ... 78724
Agave Cv ... 78750
Agave Bloom Cv ... 78738
Aggie Ln ... 78757
Agua Vis ... 78734
Agua Caliente Cv ... 78744
Aguila Cir ... 78734
Aguja Ct ... 78738
Ainez Dr ... 78744
Ainsworth St ... 78745
Aire Libre Dr ... 78726
Airline Ter ... 78719
Airole Way ... 78704
Airoso Cv ... 78745
Airport Blvd
700-1199 ... 78702
1201-1899 ... 78702
1901-2197 ... 78722
2199-4499 ... 78722
4501-5197 ... 78751
5199-5499 ... 78751
5501-5699 ... 78751
5700-6999 ... 78752
Airport Commerce Dr ... 78741
Aitne Ln ... 78725
Ajuga Ct ... 78734
Akron Cv ... 78723
Alabama Dr ... 78745
Alaina Ct ... 78737
Alameda Dr ... 78704
Alameda Trace Cir ... 78727
Alamo St
1100-1399 ... 78702
1401-1699 ... 78702
2000-2199 ... 78722
2201-2299 ... 78722
Alamosa Dr ... 78759
Alasan Cv ... 78730
Alata Cv ... 78759
Alazan Cir ... 78734
Albania Way ... 78729
Albata Ave ... 78757
Albert Rd ... 78745
Alberta Cv & Dr ... 78739
Alberta Ridge Trl ... 78726
Albury Cv ... 78758
Alcanza Dr ... 78739
Alcorn Cir ... 78748
Alcott Cv & Ln ... 78748
Alcove Ct ... 78757
Aldama Dr ... 78739
Aldea Dr ... 78745
Alden Dr ... 78758
Aldenburgh Ct ... 78737
Alder Cv ... 78750
Alderbrook Dr ... 78758
Alderwood Cv ... 78717
Alderwood Dr ... 78745
Aldford Cir & Dr ... 78745
Aldridge Dr ... 78754
Aldwyche Dr ... 78704
Alegre Pass ... 78744
Alegria Rd ... 78757
Aletha Ln ... 78745
Alex Ave ... 78728
Alex Ln ... 78748
Alexander Ave
1201-1399 ... 78702
1700-1798 ... 78702
1900-2098 ... 78722
2100-2299 ... 78722
Alexandria Dr ... 78749
Alexis Cv ... 78741
Alexs Ln ... 78748
Alf Ave ... 78721
Alfred ... 78748
Algarita Ave ... 78704
Alguno Rd ... 78757
Alhambra Dr ... 78759
Ali Cv ... 78724
Alimony Cv ... 78727
Alison Park Trl ... 78750
Allamanda Dr ... 78739
Allandale Rd ... 78756
Alleghany Dr ... 78741
Allegro Ln ... 78746
Allegro Lugar St ... 78749
Allen Rd ... 78746
Allen St ... 78702
Allenwood Dr ... 78734
Alleyton Cv & Dr ... 78725
Allison Cv & Dr ... 78741
Allium Dr ... 78733
Allred Dr ... 78748
Allston Ln ... 78746
Allwood Path ... 78748
Allyson Ct ... 78744
Alma Dr ... 78753
Almaden Dr ... 78717
Almarion Dr & Way ... 78746
Almirante Cv ... 78738
Almond Cv ... 78750
Almondsbury Ln ... 78748
Aloe Cv ... 78750
Aloe Vera Cv & Trl ... 78750
Along Creek Cv ... 78717
Alophia Dr ... 78739
Aloysia Dr ... 78748
Alpha Collier Dr ... 78728
Alpheus Ave ... 78759
E & W Alpine Cir & Rd ... 78704
Alsace Trl ... 78724
Alsatia Dr ... 78748
Alta Ct ... 78731
Alta Loma Dr ... 78749
Alta Mesa ... 78759
Alta Verde Dr ... 78759
Alta Vista Ave ... 78704
Althea Ct ... 78753
Altoga Dr ... 78724
Altona Way ... 78717
Altum St ... 78721
Altus Cv ... 78759
Alum Rock Cv & Dr ... 78747
Alverstone Way ... 78759
Alvin Devane Blvd ... 78741
Alvin High Ln ... 78729
Aly May Dr ... 78748
Amalfi Cv ... 78759
Amanda Dr ... 78729
Amanda Ellis Ct & Way ... 78749
Amaranth Ln ... 78754
Amarillo Ave ... 78729
Amarra Dr ... 78735
Amasia Cv & Dr ... 78729
Amber Pass ... 78745
Amber Oak Cv & Dr ... 78748
Amberglen Blvd ... 78729
Amberly Pl ... 78759
Amberwood Cv ... 78759
Ambleside Dr ... 78759
Amblewood Way ... 78753
Ambrosia Dr ... 78738
Amelia Cv ... 78750
Amelia Way ... 78730
Ameno Dr ... 78734
American Kestrel Dr ... 78738
Ames Ct & Ln ... 78739
Amesbury Ln ... 78752
Amesite Trl ... 78726
Amesley Cv ... 78727
Ameswood Dr ... 78723
Amethyst Trl ... 78750
Amherst Dr ... 78727
Amiata Ave ... 78734
Amis Ave & Ct ... 78734
Ammunition Dr ... 78748
Ampezo Trl ... 78749
Amur Dr ... 78745
Amwell Cv ... 78733
Amy Cir ... 78759
Amy Donovan Plz ... 78758
Amy Francis St ... 78725
Anacapo Cv ... 78727
Anaconda Ln ... 78730
Anahuac Trl ... 78747
Anaqua Dr ... 78750
Anarosa Loop ... 78727
Anatole Ct ... 78748
Anchor Ln ... 78723
Anchusa Trl ... 78736
Andalusia Dr ... 78759
Andenwood Dr ... 78726
E Anderson Ln ... 78752
W Anderson Ln
100-451 ... 78752
453-599 ... 78752
900-3100 ... 78757
3102-3398 ... 78757
Anderson Sq ... 78757
Anderson Mill Rd
8400-9500 ... 78729
9502-9598 ... 78729
9700-11700 ... 78750
11702-11798 ... 78750
11800-11898 ... 78726
11900-12599 ... 78726

12601-12699 78726
Anderson Village Dr 78729
Andes Cv 78759
Andora Dr 78717
Andover Pl 78723
Andrea Ridge Cv 78738
Andrea Woods Cv 78744
Andreas Cv 78759
Andrew Zilker Rd 78746
Andrews Ln 78759
Andromeda Cv 78727
Andtree Blvd 78724
Anemone Cv 78759
Angel Oak St 78748
Angelfire Ln 78746
Angelina St 78702
Angelwylde Dr 78733
Angleton Cv 78748
Anglin Ln 78737
Angus Rd 78759
Anikawi Dr 78746
Anise Dr 78741
Anita Dr 78704
Anita Marie Ln 78728
Ankara Ct 78730
Anken Dr 78741
Ann Pl 78728
Ann Arbor Ave 78704
Ann Jene Ct 78744
Ann Taylor Dr 78745
Anna St 78748
Annette Cv 78724
E & W Annie St 78704
Annie Oakley Trl 78753
Anselm Ct 78739
Antelope Cir 78745
Antelope Run 78748
Antero Dr 78759
Anthony St 78702
Antigo Ln 78739
Antigua Dr 78759
Antigua Way 78738
Antler Dr 78741
Antler Ln 78726
Antler Bend Rd 78737
Antoine Cir 78744
Antoinette Pl 78727
Antone St 78723
Antonio Way 78734
Aoudad Trl 78749
Apache Pass 78745
Apache Creek Cv 78735
Apache Forest Dr 78739
Apache Springs Cir 78737
Aplomado Falcon 78738
Apollo Dr 78758
Appalachian Dr 78759
Appaloosa Run 78737
Appaloosa Chase Dr 78732
Apple Carrie Cv 78745
Apple Orchard Ln 78744
Apple Valley Cir 78747
E & W Applegate Dr 78753
Applegreen Ct & Ln 78738
Appletree Ln 78726
Applewood Ct 78738
Applewood Dr 78758
Appomattox Dr 78745
Apricot Glen Dr 78746
April Dr 78753
Aqua Azul Ct 78733
Aqua Azul Path 78734
Aqua Verde Ct 78733
Aqua Verde Dr 78746
Aquifer Cv 78746
Arabian Trl 78759
Aragon Dr 78759
Aralia Dr 78750
Aralia Ridge Dr 78739
Arapahoe Pass & Trl 78745
Arax Cv 78731
Arbole Cv 78739
Arboleda Cv 78745
Arboles Cir 78737
Arbor Cir & Ln 78745
Arbor Ash Ct 78744
Arbor Downs Rd 78748
Arbor Glen Way 78731
Arbor Lake Cv 78732
Arbor Oaks Cv 78759
Arbor Pavillion Ln 78744
Arbor Ridge Ct 78744
Arboretum Blvd 78759
Arbroath Ln 78754
Arbutus Cv 78746
Arcadia Ave 78757
Arcana Cv 78730
Arch Ter 78750
Arch Hill Cir & Dr 78750
Archdale Dr 78748
Archipelago Trl 78717
Archstone Dr 78739
Arctic Ct 78724
Ardash Ln 78759
Ardath St 78757
Arden Dr 78745
Ardenwood Rd 78722
Ardmore Cir 78744
Argentia Rd 78757
Argonne Forest Cv & Trl 78759
Argos Ln 78759
Argyle Dr 78749
Ari Ct 78741
Aria Dr 78738
Aria Loop 78736
Aria Rdg 78738
Aries Ln 78724
Arikara River Dr 78748
Ariock Cv & Ln 78739
Arion Cir 78730
Aristocrat Dr 78725
Arizona Oak Ln 78724
Arla Cv 78717
Armadillo Cv 78734
Armadillo Rd 78745
Armaga Cv 78727
Armaga Springs Rd 78727
Armstrong Ave 78724
Arnold Dr 78723
Arnold Ln 78748
Arona Cv 78730
Arpdale St 78704
Arronimink Cir 78746
Arrow Dr 78749
Arroweye Trl 78733
Arrowhead Dr 78731
Arrowhead Pass 78729
Arrowpoint Cv 78759
Arrowwood Dr 78727
Arroyo Cyn 78736
Arroyo Rd 78734
Arroyo Blanco Cv & Dr 78748
Arroyo Claro 78734
Arroyo Seco
5600-5698 78756
Arroyo Seco
5700-5799 78756
6300-6698 78757
6700-6800 78757
6802-7298 78757
Artesian Cir 78758
Arthur Ln 78704
Arthur Stiles Rd 78721
Aruba Ct 78733
Arvin Dr 78738
Asa Dr 78744
Asbury Dr 78724
Ascot Cv 78746
Ash Cv 78753
Ashberry Dr 78723
Ashbrook Pl 78738
Ashby Ave 78704
Ashcroft Ct 78749
Ashdale Dr 78757
Ashen Ln 78747
Ashenche Dr 78758
Asherton Cv 78750
Asheville Pl 78749
Ashland Cir & Dr 78723
Ashleaf Cv 78759
Ashley Way 78744
Ashley Dawn Ln 78704
E & W Ashley Rose Ln 78717
Ashley Worth Blvd 78738
Ashprington Cv & Ln 78754
Ashton Cv & Rdg 78750
Ashton Woods Cir 78727
Ashwood Rd 78722
Ashworth Dr 78746
Asmara Ct & Dr 78750
Aspen Dr 78737
Aspen St 78758
Aspen Brook Dr 78744
Aspen Creek Pkwy 78749
Aspen Highlands Dr 78746
Aspendale Cv & Dr 78727
Astor Pl 78721
Astoria Dr 78738
Astro View Dr 78724
Atascosa Dr 78744
Athens Trl 78729
Atkinson Rd 78752
Atlanta St 78703
Atlantic St 78734
Atlantis Dr 78725
Atlas Cv 78730
Attar Cv 78759
Attayac St 78702
Atterbury Ln 78753
Atwater Cv
100-199 78737
9000-9199 78733
Atwood St 78741
Auburn Dr 78723
Auburndale St 78723
Auburnhill St 78723
Auckland Ct & Dr 78749
Auction Oak Dr 78748
Audane Dr 78727
Audrey Ct & Dr 78704
Audubon Pl 78741
August Dr 78753
Augusta Ave 78703
Augusta National Cv & Dr 78746
Aurora Cir 78757
Aurora Dr
5300-5499 78756
5900-6099 78757
Austin Center Blvd 78731
Austin Center St 78726
Austin Highlands Blvd 78745
Austin Park Ln 78758
Austin Woods Dr 78759
Austins Colony Blvd 78725
Austral Cv & Loop 78739
Australis Cv 78732
Austrina Pass 78732
Autumn Bay Dr 78744
Autumn Oaks Dr & Pl 78738
Autumn Ridge Dr 78759
Autumnleaf Holw 78731
Ava Ln 78724
Ava Marie Ln 78717
Avalon Ave 78744
Avebury Cir 78753
Avella Dr 78729
Avenal Dr 78738
Avendale Dr 78738
Avenue N 78727
Avenue A 78751
Avenue B 78751
Avenue C
3900-4699 78751
Avenue C
5700-5799 78752
Avenue D
3900-4699 78751
5700-5799 78752
Avenue F
3800-5599 78751
5601-5699 78751
5700-5899 78752
Avenue G
3800-5599 78751
5700-5899 78752
Avenue H 78751
Avenue K 78728
Avering Ln 78754
Avery Club Dr 78717
Avery Island Ave 78727
Avery Ranch Blvd 78717
Avery Station Loop 78717
Avery Trestle Ln 78717
Avian St 78748
Aviara Dr 78735
Aviary Cv 78744
Avispa Way 78738
Avocet Dr 78745
Avon Pl 78723
Avondale Rd 78704
Awalt Dr 78734
Axel Ln 78721
Axis Dr 78749
Axtellon Ct 78749
Ayala Dr 78725
Aylesbury Ln 78745
Aylford Ct 78739
Ayres Dr 78746
Azalea Trl 78759
Azalea Blossom Dr 78748
Azimuth Dr 78717
Aztec Dr 78703
Aztec Fall Cv 78746
Azure Shores Ct 78732
Babbling Brook Dr 78728
Back Ct 78731
Back Bay Ct & Ln 78739
Back Of The Moon St 78734
Backtrail Dr 78731
Badger Bnd 78749
Bagby Dr 78724
Baggins Cv 78739
Bahama Rd 78733
Bahia Cir 78741
Bailey Ln 78756
Bainbridge Ln 78750
Baja Cv 78759
Baker St 78721
Bal Harbor Rd 78733
Balamos Dr 78729
Balboa Ln 78727
Balboa Rd 78733
Balcones Dr 78731
Balcones Way 78750
W Balcones Center Dr 78759
Balcones Club Dr 78750
Balcones Woods Cir, Cv & Dr 78759
Baldridge Dr 78748
Baldwin Dr 78724
Balfour Falls Ln 78748
Ballenton Ct & Ln 78739
Ballimamore Dr 78717
Ballybunion Pl 78747
Ballycastle Trl 78717
Ballyclarc Dr 78717
Balsam Holw 78731
Baltus Dr 78758
Baltusrol Dr 78747
Bamford Dr 78731
Banbridge Trl 78717
Banbury Bnd 78745
W Bancendo St 78703
Bancroft Trl 78729
Bancroft Woods Cv & Dr 78729
Banda 78725
Bandera Rd 78721
Bandera Creek Trl 78735
Bandera Ranch Trl 78750
Bandon Dr 78717
Bangor Bnd 78758
Banianso Dr 78747
Banister Ln
800-1098 78704
1100-4100 78704
4102-4198 78704
4300-4700 78745
4702-4798 78745
Banks Ct 78739
Bankside St 78748
Banning Ln 78724
Bannock Ln 78747
Bannockburn Dr 78749
Banpass Ln 78736
Bantom Woods Bnd 78724
Banton Rd 78722
Banyon St 78757
Bar X Dr 78727
Barasinga Trl 78749
Barbara St 78757
Barbara Jordan Blvd 78723
Barbie Ct 78734
Barbrook Cv & Dr 78726
Barbuda Dr 78734
Barcelona Cv & Dr 78752
Barchetta Dr 78758
Barclay Dr 78746
Barclay Heights Ct 78746
Barefoot Cv 78730
Bargamin Dr 78736
Barge St 78745
Barhill Dr 78704
Barkbridge Trl 78744
Barkdale Ct 78744
Barker Hollow Cv & Pass 78739
Barker Ridge Cv & Dr 78759
Barker Vista Cv 78759
Barkley Dr 78727
Barksdale Dr 78725
Barkwood Dr 78748
Barley Cv 78750
Barn Owl Dr 78754
Barn Swallow Dr 78746
Barney Dr 78734
Barnhill Dr 78758
Barns Trl 78754
Barnsdale Way 78745
Barnsley Dr 78745
Barolo Cv 78738
Baronets Trl 78753
Barons Ct 78754
Barr Ln 78754
Barranca Cir 78731
Barras Branch Dr 78748
Barrel Bnd 78748
Barrett Ln 78733
Barrhead Cv 78717
Barricks Cv 78727
Barrie Dr 78734
Barrington Cv 78753
Barrington Dr 78753
Barrington Way 78759
Barrow Ave 78751
Barrow Glen Loop 78749
Barryknoll St 78729
Barsana Ave & Rd 78737
Barstow Ave & Ct 78749
Bart Hollow Dr 78750
Barteny Cv 78724
Bartholdi St 78753
Bartlett St 78704
Barton Blvd 78704
Barton Pkwy 78704
Barton Skwy
2200-2598 78704
2600-2799 78704
2800-2898 78746
2900-2999 78746
Barton Club Dr 78735
Barton Creek Blvd
600-1098 78746
1200-4700 78735
4702-5398 78735
Barton Hills Dr 78704
Barton Point Cir & Dr 78733
Barton Springs Rd
200-1999 78704
2200-2299 78746
Barton View Dr 78735
Barton Village Cir 78704
Bartoncliff Dr 78704
Bartons Bluff Ct & Ln 78746
Barwood Park 78753
Basford Rd 78722
Basil Cv & Dr 78750
E Basin Ledge 78746
Bass Cv 78737
Basswood Ln 78723
Bastian Cv 78739
Bastogne Loop 78739
Bastrop Hwy 78741
Bat Falcon Dr 78738
Bat Hawk Cir 78738
Batak Ln 78749
Baton Rouge Dr 78727
Battle Bend Blvd 78745
Battle Bridge Dr 78748
Bauerle Ave 78704
Bavaria Ln 78749
Baxter Cir 78736
Baxter Dr 78745
Baxter Ln 78736
Baxter Springs Rd 78745
S Bay Ln 78739
Bay City Bnd 78725
Bay Hill Cv & Dr 78746
Bay Laurel Trl 78750
Bayberry Dr 78759
Bayfield Dr 78727
E & W Baylee Love Ln 78717
Baylor St 78703
Bayou Bnd 78759
Bayridge Cv & Ter 78759
Bayside Dr 78744
Bayswater Gdns 78729
Baythorne Dr 78747
Bayton Dr 78738
Bayton Loop 78745
Baywood Dr 78759
Beach Cir & Rd 78734
Beacham Ct 78739
Beachmont Ct & Ln 78739
Beacon Dr 78734
Beaconcrest Dr 78748
Beaconsdale Cir & Dr 78727
Beaman Ct 78750
Beanna St 78705
Bear Creek Dr & Pass 78737
Bear Hollow Cv 78739
Bear Springs Trl 78748
Beard Ave 78748
Beardsley Cv & Ln 78746
Bearing Cv 78717
Bears Den Ct 78739
Beartrap Ln 78729
Beartree Cir 78730
Beatty Ct & Dr 78749
Beauchamp Sq 78729
Beauford Dr 78750
Beaumont St 78734
Beauregard Cir 78745
Beaver St 78753
Beaver Trl 78746
Beaver Brook Ln 78748
Beaver Creek Dr 78759
Beaver Pelt Cv 78754
Beck Cir 78758
Becker Ave 78751
Beckett Cir 78749
Beckett Rd 78749
Beckett St 78757
Beckwood Dr 78726
Bedford St 78702
Bedrock Trl 78727
Bee Cave Pkwy 78738
Bee Cave Rd
3201-3201 78716
5900-6098 78746
6100-8999 78746
9000-9899 78733
Bee Caves Rd 78746
Bee Tree Cir 78746
Beebrush Ln 78748
Beecave Woods Dr 78746
Beech Dr 78758
Beecher Ln 78746
Beechmoor Dr 78723
Beechnut Dr 78748
Beechwood Holw 78731
Begonia Cir & Ter 78741
Beinville Cv 78749
Bel Fay Ln 78749
Bel Lago Cv 78734
Belafonte Blvd 78724
Belcara Pl 78732
Belclaire Cir & Ln 78748
Belfast Dr 78723
Belfield Ln 78725
Belfin Dr 78717
Belford Dr 78757
Belforte Ave 78734
Belgrave Falls Ln 78748
Bell Ave
11501-11597 78759
11599-11999 78759
12001-12097 78727
12099-12299 78727
Bell Haven Ct 78744
Bell Mountain Dr 78730
Bella Cima Dr 78734
Bella Colinas Dr 78738
Bella Montagna Cir 78734
Bella Riva Dr 78734
Bella Strada Cv 78734
Bella Vista Cv 78734
Bella Vista Trl 78737
Bellagio Dr 78734
Bellaire Dr 78741
Bellancia Dr 78738
Belle Star Ct 78753
Bellevue Pl 78705
Bellflower Cv 78759
Bellows Falls Ave 78748
Bellvue Ave 78756
Bellwood Cv 78738
Belmont Cir & Pkwy 78703
Belmont Park Dr 78746
Belmont Stables Ln 78728
Belmoor Dr 78723
Belo Horizonte Cir 78731
Belterra Dr 78737
Belvedere St 78731
Ben Crenshaw Way 78746
Ben Garza Ln 78749
Ben Howell Dr 78704
E Ben White Blvd
100-799 78704
801-1099 78704
1901-1997 78741
1999-7323 78741
7325-7699 78741
7701-7899 78744
7901-7999 78741
W Ben White Blvd 78704
Benbrook Dr 78757
Bench Mark Dr 78728
S Bend Ave 78736
Bend Cv 78704
N Bend Dr 78758
Bend Of The River Dr 78746
Bender Dr 78749
Bending Trl 78744
Bending Bough Trl 78758
Bending Oak Rd 78749
Bendridge Trl 78744
Benecia Ct 78738
Benelva Dr 78705
Bengston St 78702
Bennedict Ln 78746
Bennett Ave
4400-5699 78751
6900-7699 78752
Bennington Ln 78753
Bent Cedar Cv 78750
Bent Oak Cir 78749
Bent Tree Ct 78746
Bent Tree Rd 78759
Bentley Dr 78748
Bentley Garner Ln 78748
Bentsen Ln 78723
Bentwood Rd 78722
Benwick Cir 78723
Berene Ave 78721
Berenson Ln 78746
Berger St 78721

Bergfield Dr	78744
Bergstrom Dr	78719
Bering Cv	78759
Berkeley Ave & Cv	78745
Berkett Cv & Dr	78745
Berkman Dr	
3801-3897	78723
3899-6800	78723
6802-6898	78723
7100-7298	78752
7300-7599	78752
Berkshire Dr	78723
Bermuda	78734
Bernardino Cv	78728
Bernoulli Dr	78748
Berry Hill Cir & Dr	78745
Berrycone Cv	78750
Berryessa Pass	78732
Berryhill Way	78731
Berrylawn Cir	78723
Berryline Cv & Way	78724
Berrywood Dr	78753
Bert Ave	78704
Berthound Dr	78758
Berwyn Cir & Ln	78745
Beryl Oak Dr	78744
Bescott Dr	78728
Bess Ln	78748
Best Way	78725
Bethune Ave	78752
Bettis Blvd	78746
Bettis Trophy Dr	78739
Betty Cook Dr	78723
Betty Jo Dr	78704
Betula Dr	78734
Beverly Rd	78703
Beverly Hills Dr	78731
Beverly Skyline	78731
Beverly Villas Ct	78732
Bevin Cv	78744
Bexley Ct & Ln	78739
Bexton Cir	78745
Bickler Rd	78704
Bidens Pl	78733
Bidwell Dr	78729
Bienville St	78727
Bierce St	78701
Big Trl	78759
Big Bend Dr	78731
Big Bill Ct	78734
Big Boggy Trl	78747
Big Canyon Dr	78746
Big Cat Cv	78750
Big Hollow Dr	78728
Big Horn Cir	78735
Big Horn Dr	78734
Big Meadow Rd	78737
Big Oak Holw	78750
Big Sky Cv	78737
Big Thicket Dr	78747
Big Timber Dr	78735
Big Trail Cir & Cv	78759
Big View Dr	78730
Bigelow Dr	78724
Biggs Dr	78741
Bilboa Dr	78759
Bilbrook Pl	78748
Bill Baker Dr	78748
Bill Hickcock Pass	78748
Bill Hughes Rd	78745
Billiem Dr	78727
Billingham Trl	78717
Billings Ln	78733
Billy Bonney Ct & Pass	78749
Billy Fiske Ln	78748
Billy Mills Ln	78748
Bing Cherry Ln	78750
Birch Creek Rd	78744
Birchbark Trl	78750
Birchleaf Trl	78748
Birchover Ln	78754
Birchwood Ct	78745
Bird Brook Ln	78747
Bird Call Pass	78754
Bird Creek Dr	78758
Birdie Dr	78738
Birdlip Cir	78733
Birdwood Cir	78704
Birmingham Dr	78748
Birnam Wood Ct	78746
Bisbee Ct	78745
Biscay Dr	78759
Biscayne Cv	78734
Biscuit Dr	78754
Bismark Cv	78745
Bismark Dr	78748
Bissel Cir & Ln	78745
Bissett Ct	78738
Bissonet Ln	78752
Bitter Creek Dr	78744
Bittern Holw	78758
Bitternut Cv	78759
Bitteroot Cir	78726
Bitteroot Trl	78744
Bitterwood Dr	78724
Bivins Ct	78724
Bixler Dr	78744
Black Angus Cv & Dr	78727
Black Canyon Dr	78729
Black Gap Pass	78724
Black Hills Dr	78748
Black Mesa Cv & Holw	78739
Black Mountain Dr	78736
Black Oak St	78729
Black Wolf Run	78738
Blackacre Trl	78746
Blackberry Dr	78745
Blackfoot Trl	78729
Blackhawk Dr	78759
Blackjack Cv	78744
Blackmoor Dr	78759
Blacksmith Ln	78748
Blackson Ave	
300-899	78752
900-998	78752
900-900	78761
901-1099	78752
Blackvireo Dr	78729
Bladen Springs Cv	78717
Blaine Rd	78753
Blair Way	78704
Blairview Ln	78748
Blake St	78748
Blakeney Ln	78753
Blalock Dr	78758
Blanchard Dr	78734
Blanco St	78703
Blanco River Pass	78749
Bland St	78703
Blantran Dr	78738
Blarwood Dr	78745
Blazewood Dr	78724
Blazing Star Dr	78737
Blazyk Dr	78737
Bleich Ln	78754
Blessing Ave	78752
Blinn Cir	78723
Blissfield Cv & Dr	78739
Blocker Ln	78719
Bloomfield Dr	78745
Bloomfield Hills Ln & Pass	78732
Blossom Bell Dr	78758
Blossomwood Dr	78727
Blue Cv	78745
Blue Beach Cv	78759
Blue Bird Ln	78745
Blue Bluff Rd	78724
Blue Cat Ln	78734
Blue Creek Ln	78758
Blue Crest Dr	78704
Blue Dawn Trl	78744
Blue Fox Dr	78753
Blue Hill Ct & Dr	78736
Blue Jay Dr	78734
Blue Jay Ln	78732
Blue Jay Pt	78734
Blue Lake Ct & Cv	78734
Blue Lilly Dr	78759
Blue Martin Cir	78750
Blue Meadow Dr	78744
Blue Quail Dr	78758
Blue Ridge Dr	78753
Blue Ridge Trl	78746
Blue Spring Way	78753
Blue Spruce Cir	78723
Blue Stem Trl	78735
Blue Valley Dr	78748
Blue Water Cir & Dr	78758
Bluebell Cir	78741
Blueberry Hl	78745
Blueberry Trl	78723
Bluebonnet Ln	78704
Bluecreek Cv	78735
Bluegrass Dr	78759
Blueridge Ct	78731
Bluesky Way	78745
Bluestar Cv & Dr	78739
Bluestein Dr	78721
Bluestem Ct	78737
Bluestone Cir	78758
Bluestone St	78744
Bluewood Ln	78748
N Bluff Dr	78745
Bluff St	78704
Bluff Trl	78737
Bluff Bend Dr	78753
Bluff Canyon Dr	78754
Bluff Park Cir	78746
Bluff Springs Rd	78744
Bluffridge Cir & Dr	78759
Bluffside Dr	78759
Bluffstone Cv	78759
Bluffton Cv	78730
Bluffview Dr	78704
Blumie St	78745
Bluntleaf Cv	78750
Blythewood Dr	78745
Boardman Ln	78746
Boardwalk Dr	78729
Boatwright Cv	78725
Bob Cat Run	78731
Bob Harrison St	78702
Bob White Dr	78758
Bobby Ln	78745
Bobcat Trl	78750
Bobtail Cv	78739
Boca Raton Dr	78747
Bodark Ln	78745
Bodgers Dr	78753
Boffi Cir	78758
Bogey Ct	78744
Boggy Ridge Dr	78748
Bold Ruler Way	78746
Boleynwood Dr	78745
Boling Dr	78736
Bolivia Dr	78729
Bolles Cir	78753
Bolm Rd	
4601-4697	78702
4699-4700	78702
4702-4998	78702
5000-5298	78721
5300-6100	78721
6102-6598	78721
Bolton Dr	78737
Bolton St	78748
Bon Air Dr	78757
Bon Terra Dr	78731
Bonaire Ct	78738
Bonaparte Bnd	78750
Bonaventure Dr	78730
Bond Dr	78741
Boneta Cv & Trl	78729
Bonham Ln	78736
Bonham Ter	78704
Boniface Ln	78729
Bonita St	78703
Bonnell Ct & Dr	78731
Bonnell Vista Cv & St	78731
Bonnett St	78741
Bonnie Rd	78703
Bonnie Brae St	78753
Bonniebrook Dr	78735
Bonnieview St	78704
Bonsonti	78712
Booker Ave	78752
Boomer Ln	78729
Boon Cv	78732
Boothill Dr	78748
Boquillas Canyon Dr	78717
Borage Dr	78744
Bordeaux Ln	78750
Borden Rd	78757
Borden Springs Cv	78717
Bordley Ct & Dr	78748
Borello Dr	78738
Bosque Ln	78754
Bosswood Dr	78727
Boston Ln	78735
Bottlebrush Dr	78750
Boulder Crk	78724
Boulder Hts	78738
Boulder Ln	78726
Bouldin Ave	78704
Bouleware Dr	78744
Boundless Valley Dr	78754
Bounty Trl	78749
Bourbon St	78727
Bourg Cv	78744
Bouvet Ct	78727
Bow Ct	78748
Bowditch Dr	78730
Bowerton Dr	78754
Bowery Pl & Trl	78753
Bowhill Dr	78731
Bowie Rd	78733
Bowie St	78703
Bowling Ln	78734
Bowling Green Dr	78757
Bowman Ave	78703
Bowstring Cv	78735
Boxcar Run	78745
Boxdale Dr	78757
Boxelder Cv	78735
Boxwood Ct	78745
Boyce Ln	78754
Boyd Ln	78732
Boyds Way	78748
Boyer Blvd	78758
Boyle Ln	78724
Bracken Ct	78731
Brackenridge St	78704
Bradbury Ln	78753
Bradel Cv	78726
Bradenton Ct	78738
Bradford Dr	78758
Bradford Edward Cv	78759
Bradford Pear Ln	78744
Bradley Dr	78723
Bradner Dr	78748
Bradshaw Dr	78737
Bradshaw Rd	78747
Bradsher Dr	78745
Bradwood Rd	78722
Brady Ln	78746
Braeburn Gln	78729
Braemar Cv & Dr	78747
Braes Ridge Dr	78723
Braes Valley St	78729
Braesgate Cv & Dr	78717
Braeswood Rd	78704
Braewood Dr	78758
Braided Rope Dr	78727
E Braker Ln	78753
W Braker Ln	
101-397	78753
399-499	78753
501-699	78753
800-898	78758
900-1899	78758
1822-1822	78708
1900-3398	78758
1901-2699	78758
3900-4399	78759
4401-4999	78759
Bramber Ln	78754
Bramble Dr	78745
Bramble Bush Dr	78747
Bramblecrest Dr	78726
Bramblewood Cir	78731
Bramhall Dr	78717
Branch St	78702
Branching Oak Ct	78759
Branchwood Dr	78744
Branden Ct	78750
Brandi Ct	78759
Branding Chase St	78727
Branding Iron Pass	78734
Brandon Way	78733
Brandon Parke Trl	78750
Brandt Dr	78742
Brandt Rd	78744
Brandts Wood St	78744
Brandywine Cir	78750
Brandywine Ct	78727
Brandywine Ln	78727
Branigan Ln	78759
Brannon Cv	78759
Bransford Cv	78753
Branston Dr	78753
Brantley Bnd & Cv	78748
Brasher Dr	78748
Brass St	78702
Brass Buttons Trl	78734
Brassie St	78741
Brassiewood Dr	78744
Bratton Ln	78728
Bratton Heights Dr	78728
Bratton Ridge Xing	78728
Braxton Cv	78741
Braxton Valley Cv	78754
Braylen Cv	78748
Brayton Park Dr	78717
Brazos St	78701
Brecon Ln	78748
Brecourt Manor Way	78739
Breedlove Ct	78721
Breeze Holw	78741
Breeze Ter	78722
Breeze Way	78723
Breeze Point Cv	78759
Breezeknoll Cir	78746
Breezewood Dr	78745
Breezy Pass	78749
Breezy Hill Dr	78724
Breezy Pass Cv	78749
Bremen St	78703
Bremner Dr	78749
Brenda St	78728
Brents Elm Dr	78744
Brentwood St	
300-799	78752
800-2099	78757
Bret Ln	78721
Brett Cv	78746
Brettonwoods Ln	78753
Brewster St	78704
Briana Shay Dr	78727
Brianna Maribela Ct	78717
Brians Meadow Cv	78746
Briar St	78704
Briar Hill Dr	78741
Briar Hollow Dr	78729
Briar Ridge Dr	78748
Briarcliff Blvd	78723
Briarcrest Dr	78704
Briardale Dr	78758
Briargate Dr	78753
Briargrove Dr	78704
Briarpatch Ct	78737
Briarton Dr	78747
Briarwick Dr	78729
Briarwood Ln	78757
Briarwood Trl	78746
Brickford Cv	78745
Bricklebush Cv	78750
Bridge Hill Cv	78746
Bridge Point Pkwy	78730
Bridgeport Dr	78758
Bridgetown Dr	78753
Bridgewater Cv & Dr	78723
Bridgeway Ct & Dr	78704
Bridgewood Trl	78729
Bridle Path	78703
Bridlewood Dr	78727
Bridlington Cir	78745
Brigadoon Cv	78750
Brigadoon Ln	78727
Brigham Ct & Dr	78732
Bright Leaf Ter	78748
Bright Sky Overlook	78732
Bright Star Ln	78736
Brightling Ln	78750
Brightman Ln	78733
Brighton Cir	78753
Brighton Ln	
100-299	78737
1400-1499	78753
Brighton Rd	78745
Brightside St	78729
Brightwood Dr	78746
Brimfield Ct & Dr	78726
Brimstone Ln	78717
Brinwood Ave	78704
Brisbane Rd	78745
Brista Way	78726
Bristle Oak Trl	78750
Bristlecone Ln	78759
Bristlewood Cv	78732
Bristol Dr	78723
Bristol Ridge Ct	78726
Brittany Blvd	78745
Brittany Point Ln	78738
Brittlyns Ct	78730
Brixey Cv & Ln	78754
Brixham Cv	78753
Broad Brook Dr	78747
Broad Leaf Cv	78750
Broad Oaks Dr	78759
Broadbay Cv & Dr	78717
Broadhill Dr	78723
Broadmeade Ave	78729
Broadmoor Dr	78723
Broadview St	78723
Broadway St	78702
Broadwinged Hawk Cv & Dr	78738
Brock Cir	78745
Brockman Ln	78744
Brockman St	78757
Brockton Dr	78758
Brodick Dr	78717
Brodie Ln	
5201-5397	78745
5399-5499	78745
5401-5797	78745
5501-6499	78745
5799-8600	78745
8602-8798	78745
9000-12099	78748
12101-12399	78748
Brodie St	78704
Brodie Springs Trl	78748
Broken Arrow Ln	78745
Broken Bow Pass	78745
Broken Bow Trl	78734
Broken Brook Cv	78726
Broken Lance Dr	78737
Broken Oak Dr	78745
Broken Shoe Trl	78750
Broken Spoke Trl	78744
Brompton Cir	78745
Bromsgrove Dr	78717
Bronc Dr	78759
Bronco Bend Loop	78744
Bronte Dr	78752
Bronzewood Dr	78736
S Brook Dr	78736
Brook Creek Cv	78744
Brook Crest Rd	78744
Brook Valley Cir & Dr	78724
Brookdale Ln	78723
Brookfield Dr	78758
Brookhaven Dr	78704
Brookhaven Trl	78746
Brookhill Dr	78745
Brookhollow Cv & Dr	78752
Brookhurst Cv	78733
Brooklyn St	78704
Brooks Hollow Rd	78734
Brookside Dr	78723
Brookswood Ave	78721
Brookview Rd	78722
Brookwood Cir, Cv & Rd	78750
Broomflower Dr	78739
Broomweed Cv	78738
Broten St	78748
Brougham Way	78754
Broughton Ct & Way	78727
Brown Ln	78754
Brown Bark Pl	78727
Brown Rock Trl	78749
Brownie Dr	78753
Browning Dr	78752
Brownlee Cir	78703
Brownwood Ct	78731
Brownwood Dr	78759
Bruce Dr	78735
Bruce Jenner Ln	78748
Bruning St	78751
Brunswick Dr	78723
Brunt Dr	78758
Brush Country Rd	78749
Brushy Holw	78750
Brushy St	78702
Brushy Glen Dr	78754
Brushy Ridge Cv & Dr	78744
Brushy View Cv	78754
Brushygate Cv	78717
Bruton Springs Rd	78733
Bryan St	78702
Brycen Ct	78750
Bryer Creek Trl	78717
Bryker Dr	78703
Bryn Mawr Cv & Dr	78723
Bryonhall Dr	78745
Bryonwood Dr	78724
Bryony Dr	78739
Bubbling Springs Trl	78729
Buccaneer Trl	78729
Buchanan Draw Rd	78738
Buck Race St	78748
Buckeye Ct	78758
Buckeye Trl	78746
Buckingham Cir	78704
Buckingham Pl	78745
Buckingham Rd	78759
Buckingham Gate Rd & Ter	78748
Buckman Mountain Rd	78746
Buckminster Ct	78746
Bucknell Dr	78723
Buckner Rd	78726
Buckpasser Cv	78746
Bucks Run	78744
Buckshot Trl	78729
Buckskin Pass	78745
Buckskin Trl	78737
Buckthorn Dr	78759
Budley S Degroot Ln	78748
Buell Ave	78757
Buena Suerte Dr	78749
Buena Vista Cir	78746
Buffalo Pass	78745
Buffalo Trl	78734
Buffalo Gap Rd	78734
Buffalo Grove Cv	78739
Buffalo Lake Ln	78747
Buffalo Tundra Dr	78754
Buggy Whip Trl	78750
Bulian Ln	78746
Bull Run	78727
Bull Creek Rd	
3601-3797	78731
3799-4799	78731
4801-5099	78731
5600-5899	78756
5900-6299	78757
Bull Hollow Dr	78750
Bull Mountain Cv	78746
Bull Ridge Dr	78759
Bull Run Cir	78727
Bullace St	78724
Bullard Dr	78757
Bullbrier Rd	78724
Bullick Holw	78732
Bullick Hollow Rd	78726
Bully Hill Cv	78759

Bumpstead Dr 78747
Bunche Rd 78721
Bundoran Dr 78717
Bundy Crest Cir 78723
Bundyhill Cir & Dr 78723
Bungalow Ln 78749
Bunker Hill Cv 78717
Bunny Run 78746
Bunny Hop Trl 78734
Bunting Dr 78759
Buoy Ln 78717
Burbank St 78757
Burford Pl 78704
Burgess Cv & Ln 78738
Burgundy Cv 78727
Burgundy Dr 78724
Burk Burnett Ct 78749
Burks Cv & Ln 78732
Burkwood Cv 78735
Burleson Ct 78741
Burleson Rd
2301-2397 78741
2399-3500 78741
3502-3598 78741
4401-4497 78744
4499-4599 78744
4516-4516 78760
4600-8298 78744
4601-7999 78744
8501-8599 78719
Burley Bnd & Cv 78745
Burliegh Cv 78745
Burlington Ct 78727
Burly Oak Cir & Dr 78745
Burlywood Trl 78750
Burmaster Ln 78750
Burnell Dr 78723
Burnet Ln 78757
Burnet Rd
11900A-11998A 78758
4000-5899 78756
5901-6297 78757
6299-8899 78757
8901-8999 78757
9100-11999 78758
12701-12799 78727
12801-12899 78727
12901-13899 78727
15201-15299 78728
Burney Dr 78731
Burnhill Dr 78745
Burning Oak Dr 78704
Burning Tree Cv 78734
Burns St 78752
Burnt Cir 78736
Burnt Oak Dr 78737
Burnwood Dr 78758
Burr Oak Ln 78727
Burr Ridge Dr 78729
Burrell Dr 78757
Burris Cir 78704
Burrough Cv & Dr 78745
Burton Dr 78741
Bush Coat Ln 78754
Bushnell Dr 78745
Business Dr 78758
Business Center Dr 78744
Business Park Dr 78759
Buster Crabbe Dr 78748
Butler Cir 78737
Butte Blvd 78731
Butterfly Pl 78738
Button Bend Cir & Rd 78744
Button Quail Cv & Dr 78758
Buttonbush Dr 78744
Buttonwood Dr 78759
Buvana Dr 78739
Buzz Schneider Ln 78748
Byers Cv & Ln 78753
Byrds Nest Dr 78738
Byron Dr 78704
Caballero Cv 78727
Cabana Ln 78727
Cabin Rd 78746
Cabinwood Cv 78746
Cabo Del Sol Ct & Cv 78738
Cabob St 78744
Cache Dr 78749
Cactus Bnd 78727
Cactus Ln 78745
Cactus Xing 78737
Cactus Wren Way 78746
Caddie St 78741
E & W Caddo St 78753
Cade Cir 78726
Cadillac Dr 78724
Cadiz Cir 78741
Cadoz Ct & Dr 78728
Cahill Dr 78729
Cahone Trl 78729
Caicos Cv 78734
Cain Harvest Cv & Dr 78754
Cainwood Ln 78729
Caira Cv 78750
Caisson Cir 78745
Cal Cv 78723
Cal Rodgers St 78723
Calabash Cv 78745
Calabria Ct 78738
Caladendra Dr 78741
Caladium Cir 78748
Calais Ct 78745
Calavar Dr 78726
Calaveras Dr 78717
Calaw Cv 78746
Calcite Trl 78750
Caldwell Dr 78750
Caleb Dr 78725
Caledonia Dr 78717
Calera Dr 78735
Calf Roping Trl 78727
Calhoun Canyon Loop 78735
Caliche Ln 78734
Calico Dr 78748
California Cv 78739
Calistoga Ct & Way 78732
Calithea Rd 78746
Callanish Park Dr 78750
Callbram Ln 78736
Calle Caliche 78733
Calle Limon 78702
Calle Verde Cv & Dr 78759
Calles St 78702
Callingwood Dr 78754
Callisto Ter 78727
Calloway Cv 78717
Calmar Cv 78721
Calumet Cv 78745
Calypso Dr 78734
Cama Valley Cv 78739
Camacho St 78723
Camas Dr 78728
Cambray Dr 78724
Cambria Cv & Dr 78717
Cambria Coast Run 78717
Cambridge Ct 78723
Camden Dr 78757
Camelback Dr 78733
Camelia Ln 78759
Camelot Cir 78745
Cameo Ln 78747
Cameron Loop 78745
Cameron Rd
5101-5297 78723
5299-6299 78723
6301-6399 78723
6701-6897 78752
6899-7651 78752
7653-7799 78752
7900-11200 78754
11202-11698 78754
Camillia Blossom Ln 78748
Caminita Cv 78739
Camino Alto 78746
Camino Arbolago 78734
Camino La Costa 78752
Camino Real 78757
Camino Seco 78731
Camino Viejo 78758
Camp Cv 78749
Camp Craft Rd 78746
Camp Fire Trl 78749
Camp Mabry 78703
Campden Dr 78745
Camperdown Elm Dr 78748
Campesina Dr 78727
Campfield Pkwy 78745
Campo Verde Ct & Dr 78749
Campo Viejo Cv 78746
Campos Dr 78727
Camwood Trl 78738
Cana Cv 78749
Canal St 78741
Canard Cir 78734
Canary St 78734
Candelaria Dr 78737
Candle Ridge Cv & Dr 78731
Candleleaf Ct 78738
Candlelight Ct 78757
Candlestick Pl 78727
Candletree Ln 78744
Candlewood Ct 78741
Cando Ct 78734
Cane Pace 78746
Canella Dr 78744
Canera Ct 78748
Caney St 78702
Caney Creek Rd 78732
Canfield Dr 78739
Canion St 78752
Canna Cv 78759
Cannes Cir 78745
Cannon Mark Way 78717
Cannon Mountain Dr & Pl 78749
Cannonade Ct 78746
Cannonleague Dr 78745
Cannonwood Ln 78745
N & S Canoa Hills Trl 78717
Canoas Dr 78730
Canoe Brook Dr 78746
Canoga Ave 78724
Canola Bnd 78729
Canon Wren Dr 78746
Canon Yeomans Ct & Trl 78748
Canonade 78737
Canonero Dr 78746
Canopy Creek Way 78748
Canteen Cir 78749
Canter Ln 78759
Canterbury Dr 78737
Canterbury St 78702
Canterbury Tales Ln 78748
Cantle Trl 78727
Canton Jack Rd 78717
Canus Cv & Dr 78748
E Canyon Cir 78746
W Canyon Cir 78746
Canyon Trl 78717
Canyon Vw 78746
Canyon Bluff Ct 78734
Canyon Creek Dr 78746
Canyon Crest Ct 78735
Canyon Edge Dr 78733
Canyon Glen Cir & Dr 78732
Canyon Parke Ct 78726
Canyon Ridge Dr 78753
Canyon Rim Dr 78746
Canyon Turn Trl 78734
Canyon Vista Way 78726
Canyonbend Cir 78735
Canyonside Trl 78731
Canyonwood Dr 78735
Cap Rock Dr 78735
Cap Stone Dr 78739
Capadocia Cv 78727
Cape Coral Dr 78746
Cape May Ln 78750
Cape Verde Cv 78744
Capehart Cv 78733
Capella Trl 78732
Capistrano Trl 78739
Capital Pkwy 78746
N Capital Of Texas Hwy
500-4799 78746
4801-4899 78746
6201-6697 78731
6699-7900 78731
7902-8398 78731
8501-8797 78759
8799-10100 78759
10102-10198 78759
S Capital Of Texas Hwy
501-597 78746
599-1299 78746
1301-1399 78746
1501-2999 78746
3701-4199 78704
Capitol Ct 78756
Capitol Dr 78753
Capitol Saddlery Trl 78732
Capitol View Dr 78747
Capri 78734
Capri Isle Ln 78717
Caprice Dr 78731
Capriola Dr 78745
Capsicum Cv 78748
Captain Bailys Ct 78753
Captain Hopkins Cv 78753
Caracara Dr 78750
Caracas Dr 78733
Caravan Cir 78746
Carbine Cir 78738
Carbondale Ave 78744
Cardiff Dr 78745
Cardin Dr 78759
Cardinal Hl 78737
Cardinal Ln 78704
Cardinal Flower Dr 78739
Cardinal Hill Cir & Dr 78758
Carefree Cir 78734
Carew Cv 78759
Cargo Ave 78719
Caribou Trl 78735
Caribou Parke Cv 78726
Carisbrooke Ln 78754
Carismatic Ln 78748
Carissa Cv 78759
Carla Dr 78754
Carleen Dr 78757
Carlisle Dr 78757
Carlotta Cv & Ln 78733
Carlow Dr 78745
Carlsbad Dr 78738
Carlson Dr 78741
Carlton Rd 78703
Carlton Ridge Cv 78738
Carlwood Dr 78759
Carmel Dr 78721
Carmel Park Ln 78727
Carmen Ct 78752
Carnarvon Ln 78704
Carnation Ter 78741
Carnelian Dr 78739
Carnforth Dr 78753
Carol Ann Dr
1-499 78737
3101-3499 78723
Caroline Ln 78724
Carolyn Ave 78705
Carovilli Dr 78748
Carpenter Ave 78753
Carranzo Dr 78735
Carrara 78746
Carrera Dr 78727
Carriage Dr 78752
Carriage House Ln 78737
Carriage Park Ln 78727
Carrington Dr 78749
Carrizo Ter 78758
Carry Back Ln 78746
Carshalton Dr 78758
Carson Rdg 78741
Carsonhill Dr 78723
Carter Ln 78744
Cartwright Cv 78731
Carver Ave 78752
Carwill Dr 78724
Cary Dr 78757
Casa Grande Dr 78733
Casa Verde 78734
Casablanca Ln 78734
Cascada Dr 78750
Cascade Blf 78738
Cascade Dr 78757
Cascade Caverns Trl 78739
Cascade Falls Dr 78738
Cascadera Dr 78731
Casey St 78745
Casimir Cv 78739
Casitas Dr 78717
Caslano Cv 78732
Caspian Dr 78749
Cass Ct 78754
Cassady Dr 78727
Cassandra Dr 78717
Cassat Cv 78753
Cassava Dr 78746
Cassia Cv & Dr 78759
Cassiopeia Way 78732
Cassye Cv 78759
Castana Bnd 78738
Castile Rd 78733
Castle Ct 78703
Castle Arch Ct 78749
Castle Hill St 78703
Castle Peake Trl 78726
Castle Pines Dr 78717
Castle Ridge Rd 78746
Castle Rock Ct 78750
Castle View Dr 78728
Castledale Dr 78748
Castlekeep Way 78745
Castleman Dr 78725
Castletroy Dr 78717
Castlewood Dr 78748
Castro St 78702
Caswell Ave 78751
Cat Creek Run & Trl 78731
Cat Hollow Dr 78731
Cat Mountain Cv & Dr 78731
Cat Tail Cv 78750
Catalina Dr 78741
Catalina Ln 78737
Catalonia Dr 78759
Catalpa St 78702
Catclaw Ct 78744
Cater Dr 78704
Catherine Dr 78724
Cats Eye Ln 78747
Catsby Ct 78724
Catskill Trl 78726
Catthorn Cv 78759
Cattle Cv 78748
Cattle Dr 78749
Cattle Trl 78748
Caudill Ln 78738
Cava Pl 78735
Cavalcade Ct 78746
Cavalier Ln 78757
Cavalier Canyon Dr 78734
Cavalry Ct 78731
Cavalry Ride Trl 78732
Cave Holw 78750
Caven Rd 78744
Cavern Mist Ln 78739
Cavern Springs Rd 78727
Caves Valley Dr 78717
Cavileer Ave 78757
Cayenne Ln 78741
Cayman Ln 78750
Caymen Pl 78749
Cayuga Dr 78749
Cayuse Cv 78748
Ceberry Dr 78759
Cebo Cv 78745
Cecil Dr 78744
Cedar Ave
1200-1899 78702
1900-2198 78722
Cedar Cv 78737
Cedar Gln 78745
Cedar St
3000-3799 78705
6401-6499 78746
12100-12899 78732
Cedar Bend Cv & Dr 78758
Cedar Branch Dr 78727
Cedar Cliff Dr 78759
Cedar Crest Cv & Dr 78750
Cedar Edge Dr 78744
Cedar Elm Trl 78735
Cedar Forest Dr 78750
Cedar Glen Cv 78734
Cedar Hurst Ln 78734
Cedar Ledge St 78734
Cedar Oak Dr 78746
Cedar Park Dr 78746
Cedar Paw Ln 78737
Cedar Point Dr 78723
Cedar Ridge Dr 78741
Cedar Rock Ct 78734
Cedar Springs Cir 78737
Cedar Stand Pass 78748
Cedar Valley Cv 78753
Cedarbrook Ct 78753
Cedarcliffe Dr 78750
Cedardale Dr 78745
Cedargrove Dr 78744
Cedarhurst Cir 78729
Cedarlawn Cir 78723
Cedarspur Rd 78758
Cedarview Dr 78704
Cedrick Cv 78748
Cedro Cv & Trl 78731
Celanova Ct 78738
Celery Loop 78748
Celeste Cir 78721
Celeta Ln 78759
Celtic Ct 78754
Cenewo Dr 78735
Centennial Trl 78726
Centennial Olympic Park 78732
S Center St 78704
Center Lake Dr 78753
Center Point Ln 78734
Center Ridge Dr 78753
Centimeter Cir 78758
Central Park Ct 78745
Central Park Dr 78732
Centralia Cv 78745
Centre Creek Dr 78754
Centre Park Dr 78754
Centrum Dr 78754
Century Oaks Ter 78758
Century Park Blvd 78727
Cerca Viejo Way 78746
Cercis Cv 78759
Cerro Cv 78731
Cerro Alto Cv 78733
Cervin Blvd & Cv 78728
Cervinus Run 78735
E Cesar Chavez St
101-197 78701
199-599 78701
601-799 78701
900-5099 78702
5101-5299 78702
W Cesar Chavez St
200-898 78701
1100-1198 78703
1501-2299 78703
Cessal Ave 78721
Cessna Ln 78717
Cetona Ct 78746
Ceylon Ct 78749
Cezanne St 78726
Chadbury Cv 78727
Chadwood Ct 78717
Chadwyck Dr 78723
Chainfire Cv 78729
Chalinso 78710
Chalk Hill Dr 78759
Chalk Knoll Cv & Dr 78735
Chalk Rock Cv 78735
Chalkstone Cv 78730
Challenger Cv 78734
Chalmers Ave 78702
Chama Cir 78750
Chamberlain Ct 78724
Chambly Cv 78730
Chameleon Ct 78738
Chamisa Dr 78730
Champ Ct 78750
Champion Dr
100-198 78734
200-399 78734
11500-11599 78750
Champion Grandview Way 78750
Champions Ln
1-99 78734
11001-11097 78747
11099-11199 78747
Championship Dr 78738
Chancellroy Dr 78759
Chancery Ct 78737
Chandon Ln 78734
Channel Rd 78746
Channel Island Dr 78747
Channing Cir 78745
Channing Dr 78748
Chantsong Ct 78724
Chaparral Rd 78745
Chaparral Trl 78744
Chapel Ln 78748
Chapel Down St 78729
Chapin Ln 78746
Chapman Ln 78744
Chappell Ln 78748
Chardon Ct 78738
Chardonnay Cv 78750
Charette Cv 78759
Charing Cross Rd 78759
Charis Ct 78735
Charla Cir 78728
Charlemagne Ct 78727
Charles Ave 78746
Charles St 78702
Charles Schreiner Trl 78749
Charleston Pl 78731
Charlesworth Dr 78745
Charlies Ln 78750
Charlotte St 78703
Charlotte Estates Dr 78744
Charlotte Rose Dr 78704
Charlton Dr 78723
Charlwood Dr 78757
Charm Cir 78727
Charnwood Ct 78729
Charolais Cv & Dr 78758
Charred Oak Dr 78759
Charthouse Cv 78730
Chartwell Dr 78723
Chase Cir 78721
Chasewood Cv & Dr 78727
Chasewych Dr 78745
Chaska Cv 78739
Chasm Lake Dr 78724
Chatam Berry Ln 78748
Chateau Ave 78734
Chateau Hl 78750
Chateau Village Way 78744
Chatelaine Cv & Dr 78746
Chatham Ave & Pl 78723
Chatham Wood Dr 78717
Chatsworth Cir 78704
Chatterton Ct 78729
Checotah Dr 78734
Cheddar Loop 78728
Cheerful Ct 78734
Chelmsford Dr 78736
Chelsea Ln 78704
Chelsea Glen Pl 78753
Chelsea Moor Cv 78759
Cheney Cv 78745
Cheno Cortina Cv & Trl 78749
Cheremoya Dr 78724
Cherico St 78702
Cherie Dr 78758
Cherisse Dr 78739
Cherokee St 78753
Cherokee Draw Rd 78738
Cherry Cv 78745
Cherry Ln 78703
Cherry Loop 78745
Cherry Park 78745
Cherry Creek Dr 78745
Cherry Hearst Ct 78750

Cherry Hill Dr 78704
Cherry Laurel Ter 78738
Cherry Meadow Cir & Dr 78745
Cherry Orchard Dr 78745
Cherry Tree Cir 78731
Cherrydale Dr 78745
Cherrylawn Cir 78723
Cherrywood Rd 78722
Chervil Dr 78759
Cheryl Lynn Rd 78747
Chesapeake Dr 78758
Chesapeake Bay Ln N & S 78717
Cheshire Dr 78723
Chesney Ridge Dr 78749
Chessington Dr 78750
Chester Cv & Ln 78750
Chester Forest St 78729
Chesterfield Ave
5301-5499 78751
5700-6599 78752
Chesterwood Cv 78746
Chestle Ct 78753
Chestnut Ave
1100-1899 78702
1900-2299 78722
Chestnut Holw 78750
Chestnut Hill Cv 78734
Chestnut Ridge Rd 78726
Cheswick Ct 78746
Cheverly Ct 78738
Chevy Cir 78723
Chevy Chase Dr 78752
Cheyenne Cir 78745
Chiappero Trl 78731
Chick Pea Ln 78748
Chickadee Ln 78734
Chickasaw Ct 78749
Chico St 78721
Chicon St
1-1899 78702
1900-2199 78722
Chicory Cv 78746
Chictora Cv 78759
Chihuahua Trl 78745
Childress Dr 78753
Chillip Cv 78753
Chiltern Forest Dr 78717
Chimayo Cv 78729
Chimney Cors 78731
Chimney Creek Cir 78723
Chimney Hill Blvd 78754
Chimney Rock Dr 78758
China Grv 78745
China Berry Rd 78744
China Garden Cv & Dr 78730
China Rose Dr 78724
Chinese Elm Ct 78748
Chinook Dr 78736
Chipmunk Rd 78734
Chippendale Ave 78745
Chippenhook Ct 78748
Chippeway Ln 78745
Chisholm Ln 78748
Chisholm Trl 78734
S Chisholm Trl 78748
Chisos Pass 78724
Chisos Trl 78717
Chiswick Dr 78753
Chittim Cir 78732
Choctaw Trl 78745
Choquette Dr 78757
Chote Ave 78702
Chris Cv 78746
Chrissys Cv 78733
Christensen Cv 78739
Christie Dr 78721
Christoff Loop 78748
Christopher Dr 78746
Christopher St 78704
Chromite St 78727
Chuck Wagon Trl 78749
Chukar Bnd & Cir 78758
Church Canyon Dr 78754

Churchill Dr 78703
Churchill Downs Dr 78746
Churchwood Cv 78746
Cicero Ln 78746
Cielo Azul Pass 78732
Cilantro Way 78741
Cima Cir 78737
Cima Oak Ln 78759
Cima Serena Ct & Dr 78759
Cimarron Trl 78745
Cinca Terra Dr 78738
Cinchring Ln 78727
Cinderella Dr 78752
Cindy Ln 78727
Cinnabar Trl 78726
Cinnamon Path 78704
Circle Cv 78741
Circle Dr
8800-11199 78736
11300-11699 78748
Circle Hvn 78741
Circle Bend Dr 78758
Circle G Ranch Rd 78737
Circle Oak Cv 78749
Circle Ridge Dr 78746
Circle S Rd 78745
Circletree Loop 78731
Circleview Dr 78733
Circulo De Amistad 78741
Cissus Cv 78759
Citadel Cv 78723
Citation Ave 78719
Citrus Cv 78750
City Park Rd 78730
Claburn Dr 78759
Claire Ave 78703
Clairmont Cv & Dr 78749
Clara St 78702
Clara Marie Cv 78749
Clara Rose Ct 78717
Clara Van St 78734
Clarendon Ln 78746
Claret Cv 78748
Clarewood Cir & Dr 78758
Clarice Ct 78757
Clarion Ct 78749
Clarion Cv 78746
Clarion Dr 78749
Clarkdale Ln 78757
Clarke St 78745
Clarksburg Dr 78745
Clarkson Ave
3400-3798 78722
4800-5298 78751
Clarno Dr 78749
Claro Vista Cv 78739
Claude Ct 78747
Claudia June Ave 78728
Clawson Rd
3001-3097 78704
3099-4399 78704
4400-4799 78745
Claxton Dr 78736
Clay Ave 78756
Clay Allison Pass 78749
Clayera Cv 78748
Claymoor Dr 78723
Claystone Cv 78744
Clayton Ln 78723
Claywood Dr 78753
Clear Cv 78704
Clear Pond Cv 78737
Clear Stream Xing 78753
Clear View Dr 78725
Clearbrook Trl 78729
Clearday Dr 78745
Clearfield Dr 78758
Clearock Dr 78750
Clearsky Cir 78745
Clearview Dr 78703
Clearwater Cir 78753
Cleese Dr 78741
Clematis Cv 78750
Clemente Cir 78737
Clementine Ln 78744
Clendenin Ct 78732

Clermont Ave 78702
Click Cv 78758
Clickett Cv 78753
Cliff Dr 78704
Cliff St 78705
Cliff Creek Dr 78726
Cliffbrook Ct 78738
Cliffbrook Dr 78747
Clifford Ave 78702
Clifford Dr 78745
Cliffs Edge Dr 78733
Cliffsage Ave 78759
Cliffside Dr 78704
Cliffstone Cv 78735
Cliffview Dr 78759
Cliffwood Cir 78759
Cliffwood Cv 78759
Cliffwood Dr 78733
Clifton Ln 78746
Clifton St 78704
Clipper Ct 78745
Clithea Cv 78759
Clivden Cir 78759
Clock Tower Dr 78753
Cloud Mountain Xing 78726
Cloudberry Cir 78745
Cloudcroft Dr 78749
Cloudview Dr 78745
Cloudy Ridge Rd 78734
Clove Cv 78750
Clover Ct 78745
Cloverbrook Ct 78738
Cloverdale Ln 78723
Cloverleaf Dr 78723
Clovis St 78741
Club Ct 78759
Club Ter 78741
Club Estates Pkwy 78738
Club Ridge Cv & Dr 78735
Clubhouse Dr 78734
Clubhouse Turn 78748
Clubview Ave 78741
Clubway Ln 78745
Clumpgrass Cv 78735
Clyde Ln 78754
Clyde Littlefield Dr 78712
Clydesdale Dr 78745
Coach House Rd 78737
Coachwhip Holw 78750
Coalwood Cv & Ln 78739
Coastal Dr 78749
Coatbridge Dr 78745
Coats Cir & Cv 78748
Cobbler Cv 78744
Cobblestone 78735
Cobblestone Ln 78750
Cocao Cir & Ln 78744
Cochise Trl
2000-2199 78733
14300-14499 78734
Cochrane Cv 78757
Cockburn Dr 78745
Cockney Dr 78748
Cockrell Ct 78749
Cody Ct 78704
Coffee Bean Cv 78728
Coffee Cup Cv 78744
Cog Hill Ct 78738
Cogbill St 78745
Cognac Cv 78724
Cohoba Dr 78748
Colberg Ct & Dr 78749
Colby Cv 78723
Cold Water Ln 78734
Coldstream Dr 78748
Coldwater Cyn 78730
Coldwater Mountain Cv 78730
Cole St
101-197 78737
199-499 78737
2700-2998 78705
Colebrook St 78749
Coleman St 78704
Coleridge Ln 78746

Coleto St
1100-1399 78702
1401-1499 78702
1900-2099 78722
2101-2299 78722
Coleto Creek Trl 78732
Coleus Cv 78750
Colfax Ave 78757
Colfax Dr 78724
Colgate Ln 78723
Colina Ln 78759
Colina Vista Loop 78750
Colinton Ave 78754
Collazo Way 78749
College Ave 78704
College Row 78702
Colleyville Dr 78738
Collier St 78704
Collindale Cv & Dr 78753
Collinfield Dr 78758
Collingsworth Dr 78753
Collingwood Dr 78748
Collins St 78745
Collins Creek Dr 78741
Collinwood West Dr 78753
Colmenero Cir 78741
Cologne Ln 78727
Colonel Winn Loop 78748
Colonial Dr 78758
Colonial Affair 78737
Colonial Club Dr 78747
Colonial Park Blvd 78745
Colony Rd 78737
Colony Creek Dr 78758
Colony Loop Dr 78724
Colony North Dr 78758
Colony Park Cv & Dr 78724
Colorado St 78701
Colorado Xing 78731
Colquitt Cv 78748
Colt Dr 78734
Colton Rd
5501-5597 78719
5599-5800 78719
5802-5898 78719
6201-6299 78744
Colton Bluff Springs Rd 78744
Columbia Cv & Dr 78723
Columbia Oaks Ct 78759
Columbine Dr 78727
Columbus Dr 78746
Columbus St 78704
Colusa Ct 78749
Comal St
1-1399 78702
1901-1999 78722
2001-2003 78712
2100-2102 78712
2101-2197 78722
2199-2299 78722
Comanche Trl 78732
Comanche Creek Dr 78735
Comanche Divide Cv 78738
Comburg Dr 78748
Comburg Castle Way 78748
Comet Cv 78734
Cometa St 78721
Comfort 78748
Comfort Cv 78731
Comiso Pala Path 78726
Commanders Point Dr 78734
Commerce St 78721
Commercial Center Dr 78744
Commercial Park Dr 78724
N & S Commons Ford Rd 78733
Commonwealth Way 78759
Companeros Way 78749
Compass Dr 78724
Comsouth Dr 78744
Conann Ct 78753
Concho St
1100-1399 78702
2100-2199 78722
Concho Creek Bnd 78735

Conchos Cv & Trl 78726
Conchos River Trl 78717
Concord Cir 78737
Concordia Ave 78722
Concordia University Dr 78726
Cone Cir 78731
Conejo Dr 78734
Conestoga Trl 78744
Confederate Ave 78703
Conference Cv 78730
Confidence Cv 78734
Congress Ave
100-900 78701
823-823 78767
823-823 78768
901-1799 78701
902-1898 78701
S Congress Ave
200-298 78704
300-3999 78704
3903-3903 78764
4100-8500 78745
8502-9098 78745
Congressional Cir 78746
Conifer Cv 78736
Connally Ln 78723
Connecticut Dr 78758
Connelly St 78751
Connie St 78728
Conrad Rd 78727
Conrad St 78758
Constant Springs Dr 78746
Constantino Cir 78745
Contessa Ct 78749
Conti Ct 78744
Contour Dr 78757
Convict Hill Rd 78749
Conway Springs Ct 78717
Cooing Ct 78744
Cookstown Dr 78759
Cookwood Cv 78736
Cool Spring Way 78737
Cool Water Dr 78748
Coolbrook Dr 78724
Cooper Dr 78753
Cooper Ln 78745
Cooper Hill Dr 78758
Coopers Crown Ln 78738
Coopers Hawk Cv 78738
Copano Ct & Dr 78749
Copeland St 78704
Copper Basin Cv 78717
Copper Cliff Ave 78727
Copper Creek Dr 78729
Copper Ellis Trce 78728
Copper Mount Cv 78746
Copper Ridge Ct 78734
Copper Ridge Cv 78747
Copper Ridge Ln 78734
Copperas Dr 78749
Copperbend Blvd 78744
Copperfield Dr 78753
Copperleaf Rd 78734
Copperlily Cv 78759
Coppermead Ln 78754
Copse Ct 78744
Coquina Ln 78746
Coral Gables Ct 78747
Coral Ridge Cir 78747
Coralberry Cv 78732
Coralvine Cv 78735
Corbe Dr 78726
Corbett Cv 78736
Corbin Ln 78704
Corbin Creek Cv 78717
Cordell Ln 78723
Cordero Dr 78717
Cordoba Dr 78724
Cordova Dr 78759
Coreopsis Dr 78733
Coriander Cv 78729
Coriander Dr
1300-1799 78741
12900-13199 78729
Coridan Dr 78727

Corinthian 78734
Cork Ln 78737
Cork Path 78745
Cormorant Cv 78730
Cornell St 78702
Corner Brook Cv & Pass 78739
Cornerwood Ct & Dr 78717
Cornflower Dr 78739
Cornish Cir 78745
Cornish Hen Cv & Ln 78747
Cornwall Dr 78748
Corona Dr 78723
Coronado Cir 78752
Coronado St 78702
Coronado Hills Dr 78752
Coronet St 78727
Corpus Christi Dr 78729
Corral Ln 78745
Corran Ferry Dr & Loop 78749
Corrie Cv 78749
Corrientes Cv 78739
Corsaire St 78734
Corsica Pl 78724
Corta St 78702
Cortaro Cv 78729
Cortina Dr 78749
Corto Ln 78733
Corto St 78744
Cortona Cv & Dr 78746
Corum Cv 78746
Cory Cactus Dr 78738
Costa Bella Cv & Dr 78734
Costakes Dr 78750
Costas Cv 78759
Cottage Grove Pass 78717
Cottesmore Ct 78717
Cottingham Dr 78725
Cottle Dr 78753
Cotton St 78702
Cottondale Rd 78738
Cottonmouth School Rd 78744
Cottonwood Cir 78723
Cottonwood St 78744
Cottonwood Shores Dr 78725
Cotulla Dr 78739
Coturnix Dr 78758
Cougar Cv 78745
Cougar Dr 78745
Cougar Run 78731
Coulver Rd 78747
Council Bluff Dr 78727
Counselor Dr 78749
Country Knls 78750
Country Trl 78732
Country Canyon Cv 78759
Country Creek Rd 78737
Country Lake Ct & Dr 78732
Country Trails Ln 78732
Country White Ln 78749
Counts Cv 78749
County Down Ct & Dr 78747
Couri Pass 78738
Court Of St James 78730
Courtland Cir 78737
Courtland Ln 78703
Courtleigh Cir 78759
Courtney St 78745
Courtyard Cv 78731
Courtyard Dr 78731
W Courtyard Dr 78730
Cousteau Ln 78746
Cove Creek Ln 78738
Covenant Canyon Trl 78734
Coventry Ln 78723
Covered Bridge Dr 78736
Covered Wagon Pass 78744
Covey Ct 78758
Covey Ridge Ln 78758
E Covington Dr 78753
W Covington Dr 78753
Covington Trl 78727
W Cow Path 78727
Cowden Dr 78732

Cowdray Park 78729
Cowher Ct 78739
Coyote Ct
3100-3199 78734
10900-10999 78748
Coyote Rdg 78737
Crabapple Ct 78738
Crabtree Cv & Dr 78750
Crackling Creek Dr 78736
Cradiank Dr 78726
Cradle Rock Trl 78748
Crafton Pl 78749
Crafty Cv 78749
Craggy Pt 78731
Craig Dr 78727
Craig Patrick Way 78748
Craigmont Dr 78745
Craigwood Cir & Dr 78725
Crampton Cv 78737
Cranbrook Cv 78748
Crandall Rd 78739
Crane St 78734
Cranford Ct 78726
Crater Lake Pass 78747
Crawford St 78731
Craybrough Cir 78724
Crazy Horse Dr 78737
Crazy Well Dr 78717
Crazyhorse Pass 78734
Credo Ln 78725
Cree Cir & Ln 78734
Creede Dr 78744
Creedmoor Dr 78719
Creek Btm 78731
N Creek Dr 78753
Creek Holw 78754
Creek Mdws 78731
Creek Mtn 78731
Creek Rdg 78735
Creek Bend Dr 78744
Creek Ledge 78731
Creek View Dr 78748
Creekbluff Dr 78750
Creekbranch Cv 78744
Creekline Dr 78745
Creekmere Ln 78748
Creekmont Cv 78748
Creeks Edge Cir & Pkwy 78733
Creekside Dr 78752
W Creekview Dr 78736
Creekwood Rd 78723
Creighton Ln 78723
Crenata Cv 78759
Crendenw Dr 78728
Creole Cv & Dr 78727
Crepe Myrtle Dr 78744
Crescent Blf 78734
Crescent Dr 78722
Crescent Heights Trl 78717
Crest Ave 78702
W Crest Ln 78724
Crest Meadow Ln 78748
Crest Oak Rd 78744
Crest Ridge Cir 78750
Crest View Dr 78734
Crest View Rd 78737
Crested Butte Dr 78746
Cresthaven Dr 78704
Cresthill Dr 78731
E & W Crestland Dr 78752
Crestmont Dr 78756
Creston Ln 78752
Crestone Rd 78744
Crestone Stream Dr 78738
Crestvale Dr 78704
Crestway Dr 78731
Crestwood Ct 78746
Crestwood Rd 78722
Cretys Cv 78745
Crewler Cv 78753
Cricket Hollow Dr 78758
Crinium Cv 78759
Cripple Creek Cv & Dr 78758
Crissom Ln 78728
Criswell 78754

Street	ZIP
Criswood Pl	78748
Critter Cyn	78746
Crockett St	78704
Crofford Ln	78724
Croftwood Dr	78749
Cromarty Cv & Ln	78754
Cromwell Cir	78741
Cromwell Hl	78703
Crooked Ln	78741
Crooked Oak Cv	78749
Crosby Cir	78746
Crosbyton Ln	78717
E & W Croslin St	78752
Crosne St	78754
Cross Crk	78734
Cross St	78702
Cross Park Dr	
8100-8198	78754
8200-8224	78754
8225-8299	78710
8225-8225	78714
8226-8798	78754
8301-8799	78754
Cross Valley Run	78731
Crosscreek	78737
Crosscreek Dr	78757
Crossdraw Dr	78731
Crossing Pl	78741
Crossland Dr	78726
Crossmeadow Dr	78750
Crosstimber Dr	78750
Crosswood Dr	78745
Croton Cv	78759
Crow Ln	78745
Crow Wing Cv	78730
Crowheart Cv	78746
Crowley Trl	78729
Crown Ct	
8800-8899	78729
10000-10099	78724
Crown Dr	78745
Crown Colony Dr	78747
Crown Oaks Dr	78753
Crown Ridge Dr & Path	78753
Crowncrest Cv & Dr	78759
Crownover St	78725
Crownspoint Cir & Dr	78748
Croydon Loop	78748
Crumley Ln	78741
Crumley Ranch Rd	78738
Crupp Ct	78753
Cruz St	78741
Crystal Ct	78728
Crystal Ter	78733
Crystal Way	78737
Crystal Caves Rd	78737
Crystal Creek Cir	78746
Crystal Creek Dr	78746
Crystal Creek Trl	78737
Crystal Downs Cv	78717
Crystal Hills Dr	78737
Crystal Mountain Dr	78733
Crystal Shore Dr	78728
Crystal Springs Ct	78738
Crystal Water Cv & Dr	78735
Crystalbrook Cv & Dr	78724
N & S Cuernavaca Dr	78733
Cuesta Ct & Trl	78730
Cuesta Verde	78746
Cueva Dr	78738
Cueva De Oro Cv	78746
Culberson Dr	78748
Culebra Cir	78734
Cullen Ave	78757
Cullen Ln	78748
Cullers Cv	78745
Culp St	78741
Culpepper Cv	78730
Culzean Dr	78754
Cumberland Rd	78704
Cumbria Ln	78727
Cupid Dr	78735
Curacao Ct	78738
Curameng Cv	78748
Cureton Cv	78747
Curlew Cv & Dr	78748
Curley Mesquite Cv	78745
Curly Leaf Cv	78750
Curpin Cv	78754
Current Cir	78736
Currier Cv	78717
Currin Ln	78748
Currywood Cir & Dr	78759
Curtis Ave	78722
Curve St	78702
Cusseta Cv & Ln	78739
Custer Ct	78734
Cutlass	78734
Cutler Ridge Pl	78749
Cutter Rd	78738
Cutting Horse Ln	78727
Cutty Trl	78734
Cy Ln	78753
Cypress Bnd	78744
Cypress Pt E	78746
Cypress Pt N	78746
Cypress Pt W	78746
Cypress Knee Ln	78734
Cypress Landing Cv	78717
Cypress Point Cv	78746
Cyrilla Dr	78759
Cyrus Cv	78739
D K Ranch Ct & Rd	78759
D Morgan Rd	78736
Dadiva Ct	78735
Daffan Ln	78724
Daffodil Dr	78744
Dagon Dr	78754
Dahlgreen Ave	78739
Dailey St	78703
Daisy Dr	78727
Daisy Path	78737
Dakota Ln	78729
Dale Dr	78757
Dalea Vista Ct	78739
Daleview Dr	78757
Dalewood Dr	78729
Dali Ln	78703
Dallas Dr	78729
Dallum Dr	78753
Dalmahoy Dr	78717
Dalton Ln	78742
Dalton St	78745
Damon Rd	78745
Dan Pass	78744
Dan Jean Dr	78745
Dana Cv	78746
Danbrook Cv	78753
Danbury Sq	78723
Dancy St	78722
Dandelion Trl	78745
Danforth Cv	78746
Daniel Dr	78704
Daniel Boone Dr	78737
Danli Ln	78749
Danny Dr	78759
Dante Ct	78748
Danvers Ct	78739
Danville Dr	78753
Danwood Dr	78759
Danz Blvd	78724
Daphne Ct	78704
Dapplegrey Ln	78727
Darby St	78721
Darcus Cv	78759
Darden Hills Rd	78737
Dark Ln	78717
Dark Ridge Cv	78737
Dark Shadow Cv	78749
Dark Star Ter	78726
Dark Valley Cv	78737
Darlington Cv & Ln	78723
Darnell Dr	78745
Darter Ln	78746
Dartmoor Dr	78746
Dartmouth Ave	78757
Darvone Cir	78745
Darwin Cv & Ln	78729
Daryl Cv	78758
Dasher Dr	78734
Dashwood Ct	78738
Datura Ct	78733
Daugherty St	78757
Dauphine Cv, Dr & St	78727
Dave Dr	78734
Dave Silk Dr	78748
Davenport Dv	78738
David St	78705
David Moore Dr	78748
David Thomas Rd	78746
Davis Ln	
2101-2597	78745
2599-2700	78745
2702-3398	78745
3101-3199	78748
3301-3399	78745
4801-4897	78749
4899-4999	78749
5001-6299	78749
Davis St	78701
Davis Mountain Cv & Pass	78726
Davis Oaks Trl	78748
Davy Crockett Dr	78737
Dawn Flower Cv	78738
Dawn Hill Cir	78736
Dawn River Cv	78732
Dawn Song Dr	78735
Dawning Ct	78736
Dawnridge Cir	78757
Dawson Rd	78704
Day Camp Ln	78754
Day Star Cv	78746
Daybreak Cv	78738
Daytona Dr	78733
De Paul Cv	78723
De Peer Ave & Cv	78717
De Soto Cir & Dr	78733
De Vaca Dr	78733
De Verne St	78704
Deadoak Ln	78759
Deadwood Dr	78744
Deaf Smith Blvd	78725
E Dean Keaton Rd	78722
E Dean Keeton St	
100-206	78712
301-305	78712
700-800	78705
802-998	78705
W Dean Keeton St	78712
Deatonhill Dr	78745
Debarr Dr	78729
Debba Dr	78734
Debcoe Dr	78749
Deborah Dr	78752
Deck Cv	78738
Decker Ln	78724
Decker Lake Rd	78724
Decker Prairie Dr	78748
Decoy Cv	78729
Dedham Ct & Ln	78739
Dee St	78745
Dee Gabriel Collins Rd	78744
Deen Ave	78753
Deep Cir & Ln	78744
Deep Brook Dr	78726
Deep Eddy Ave	78703
Deep Spring Cv	78730
Deep Well Dr	78738
Deepwoods Dr	78731
Deer Ln	78749
Deer Pass	78746
Deer Trak	78727
Deer Chase Trl	78747
Deer Falls Dr	78729
Deer Haven Rd	78737
Deer Hollow Ln	78750
Deer Ridge Cir	78731
Deer Run Dr	78744
Deer Shadow Pass	78733
Deerbrook Trl	78750
Deercreek Cir	78703
Deerfield Cv	78734
Deerfield Dr	78741
Deerfoot Trl	
2400-2699	78704
13200-13299	78737
Deerhorn Ct	78734
Deerhurst Ct	78734
Deeringhill Dr	78745
Deerwood Ct & Ln	78730
Deja Ave	78747
Del Carmen Cv	78759
Del Curto Rd	78704
Del Mesa Ln	78759
Del Monte Rd	78741
Del Rio Dr	78733
Del Robles Dr	78727
Delafield Ln	78752
Delano St	78721
Delarlet St	78701
N & S Delavan Ave & Cv	78717
Delaware Ct	78758
Delcrest Dr	78704
Deleon Ct	78733
Delfino Cir	78734
Delgado Way	78733
Della Torre Dr	78750
Dellana Ln	78746
Dellrey Dr	78758
Delmar Ave	78752
Delmonico Dr	78759
Deloney St	78721
Delores Ave	78721
Delores Ct	78734
Delphinus Walk	78732
Delsie Dr	78734
Delta Dr	78758
Delta Post Dr	78724
Delvin Ln	78728
Delwau Ln	78725
Delwood Ct	78723
Delwood Dr	78723
Delwood Pl	78703
Demona Cv & Dr	78733
Dempsey Ln	78748
Denali Pkwy	78726
Denbar Ct	78739
Denehoe Cv	78725
Denell Cir	78753
Denfield St	78721
Denim Trl	78739
Denise Cv	78737
Denise Dr	78717
Denson Dr	78752
Denton Dr	78758
Denver Ave	78723
Denwood Dr	78759
Depew Ave	78751
Deputy Dr	78748
Derby Cv	78723
Derby Downs Dr	78747
Derecho Bnd & Dr	78737
Deridder Ct	78744
Derringer Trl	78753
Descartes Cv	78753
Desco Dr	78748
Desert Flower	78746
Desert Forest Ct	78738
Desert Highlands Ct	78738
Desert Mountain Ct	78738
Desert Oak Cir	78749
Desert Primrose Dr	78748
Desert Quail Ln	78758
Desert Rose Cv	78750
Desert Willow Cv	78735
Desert Willow Loop	78748
Desert Willow Way	78737
Desirable Dr	78721
Dessau Rd	78754
Dessau Ridge Ln	78754
Destiny Cv	78738
Destiny Hills Dr	78738
Destinys Gate Dr	78727
Deupree Dr	78753
Devereux Dr	78733
Devine Ln	78748
Devon Cir	78723
Devonshire Cv & Dr	78723
Dewdrop Cv	78738
Dewey St	78721
Dexford Dr	78753
Dexler Dr	78734
Dexmoor Dr	78723
Dexter St	78704
Diamond Head Cir & Dr	78746
Diamondback Trl	78753
Diane Dr	78745
Dianella Ln	78759
Diaz St	78702
Dickson Dr	78704
Dillard Cir	78752
Dillion Hill Dr	78745
Dillman St	78703
Dime Cir	78744
Dime Box Trl	78729
Dimmit Ct	78732
Dinah Dr	78748
Dink Pearson Ln	78717
Dinsdale Ln	78741
Dionysus Dr	78753
Dip Cv	78704
Directors Blvd	78744
Distant View Dr	78736
W Dittmar Rd	78745
Dittmar Oaks Cv & Dr	78748
Dixie Dr	78744
Dixon Dr	78745
Dobbin Dr	78748
Dobie Dr	78753
Doc Holliday Trl	78753
Dodge Cattle Cv & Dr	78717
Doe Run	78748
Doe Trl	78746
Doe Meadow Dr	78749
Doe Valley Ln	78759
Doering Ln	78750
Dog Leg Dr	78717
Dogwood Holw	78750
Dogwood Creek Cv & Dr	78746
Dolce Vista Dr	78747
Dolcetto Ct	78738
Doliver Dr	78748
Dolphin Cv & Dr	78704
Domain Dr	78758
Dominic Dr	78745
Dominion Cv	78759
Dominion Hl	78733
Dominique Dr	78753
Don Ann St	78721
Dona Villa Dr & Pl	78726
Donahue Ln	78744
Donald Dr	78728
Doncaster Dr	78745
Dondale Cir	78746
Donegal Rd	78749
Donington Dr	78753
Donley Dr	78758
Donna Gail Dr	78757
Donner Cv & Ln	78749
Donovan Cir	78753
Dooley Trl	78724
Doolin Dr	78704
Doone Valley Ct	78731
Doonesbury Cv & Dr	78758
Doral Dr	78746
Dorchester Dr	78723
Dorchester Heights Ln	78754
Dorella Ln	78736
Doria Dr	78728
Doris Dr	78757
W Dorman Cv & Dr	78717
Dormarion Ln	78703
Dorotha Ct	78759
Dorothy Dr	78734
Dorset Dr	78753
Dorset Ln	78737
Dorsett Rd	78727
Dorsett Oaks Cir	78727
Dos Cabezas Dr	78749
Doss Rd	78734
Dosshills Dr	78750
Doswell Cv & Ln	78739
Dot Dr	78727
Double Bend Back Rd	78746
Double Dome Rd	78734
Double Eagle Dr	
100-199	78738
15800-16399	78717
Double Eagle Pass	78717
Double Fork Rd	78746
Double Spur Loop	78759
Double Tree Cv & Ln	78750
Doubloon Cv	78759
Douglas St	78741
Dove Ct & Dr	78744
Dove Creek Cv	78744
Dove Haven Dr	78753
Dove Springs Cir & Dr	78744
Dove Valley Cv & Trl	78729
Dovedale Cv	78738
Dovehill Dr	78744
Dovemeadow Dr	78744
Dover Pl	78757
Dover Ferry Xing	78728
Dovercliff Cv	78754
Dovewood Dr	78744
Dowd Ln	78728
Dowling Cv	78745
Down Cv	78704
Down Valley Ct	78731
Downie Pl	78746
Downing St	78759
Downridge Cv & Dr	78731
Downs Dr	78721
Doyal Dr	78747
Doyle Overton Rd	78719
Dragline Dr	78728
Dragon	78734
Dragonfly Ct	78744
Drake Ave	78704
Drawbridge Rd	78746
Drayton Dr	78758
Dresden Cv	78723
Drew Ln	78748
Drexel Dr	78723
Drift Dr	78736
Drifting Wind Run	78738
Driftwood Dr	78731
Dringenberg Dr	78729
Drip Rock Ln	78730
Driskill St	78701
Drossett Dr	78744
Drumellan St	78754
Drummond Dr	78754
Drury Ln	78737
Dry Bend Cv	78731
Dry Cliff Cv	78731
Dry Creek Dr	78731
Dry Creek Rd	78737
Dry Ledge Cv	78731
Dry Oak Trl	78749
Dry Run Cir	78737
Dry Season Trl	78754
Dry Tortugas Trl	78747
Dry Wells Rd	78749
Dryden St	78748
Dryfield Dr	78758
Dub Dr	78748
Duber Ln	78747
Dublin Dr	78745
Dubuque Ln	78723
Duchess Dr	78724
Duck Lake Ct & Dr	78734
Duckcreek Ct	78729
Dudley Dr	78735
Dudmar Dr	78735
Dueling Oak Cir	78750
Duffy Ln	78738
Duke Ave	78757
Duke Rd	78724
Dulac Cv & Dr	78729
Dulce Ln	78704
Dulcet Dr	78745
Dull Knife Dr	78759
Dulles Ave & Cv	78729
Dulwich St	78748
Dumaine Cir	78727
Dunbarton Dr	78723
Dunblane Way	78754
Dunbury Dr	78723
Duncan Ln	78705
Dundee Dr	78759
Dunfries Ln	78754
Dungan Ln	78754
Dungan St	78753
Dunham Forest Rd	78717
Dunkirk Dr	78736
N Dunlap Rd	78725
S Dunlap Rd	78725
Dunlap St	78704
Dunliegh Dr	78745
Dunn St	78745
Dunning Ln	78746
Dunsmere Ct & Dr	78749
Dunstan Dr	78745
Dupoint Cv	78748
Dupree Cir & Ln	78748
Duquesne Dr	78723
Duranta Cv	78759
Durham Dr	78753
Durwood St	78704
Dusik Ln	78746
Dusk Terrace Cv	78737
Dusky Thrush Trl	78746
Dusty Trail Cv	78749
Duval Rd	
3200-4100	78759
4102-4398	78759
4400-4698	78727
4700-5399	78727
Duval St	
2900-3599	78705
3601-3799	78705
3800-5599	78751
5700-5900	78752
5902-7598	78752
Dwyce Dr	78757
Dymalor Cir	78745
Dywer Ave	78704
Eagle	78734
Eagle Clfs	78731
Eagle Cv	78734
W Eagle Dr	78738
Eagle Knl	78717
Eagle Pt	78734
Eagle Feather Dr	78735
Eagle Lookout Dr	78733
Eagle Rising Cv	78730
Eagle Rock Cv	78750
Eagle Trace Trl	78730
Eagles Ct	78734
Eagles Lndg	78735
Eagles Glen Cv & Dr	78732
Eagles Landing Cv	78735
Eanes Cir	78746
Eanes School Rd	78746
Eaneswood Dr	78746
Earlyway Dr	78749
Earp Way	78729
Eashere Ln	78742
Eason St	78703
East Ave	78701
East Ct	78759
East Dr	78753
East Ln	78732
Eastcrest Dr	78752
Eastdale Dr	78723
Easter Cv	78757
Eastfield Ave	78721
Eastham Cv	78704
Eastledge Dr	78731
Eastman Cv	78750
Eastwend Dr	78753
Easy St	
1500-1699	78746
11500-11899	78748
Easy Day Cv	78745
Easy Wind Dr	
7000-7098	78752
7100-7299	78752
7300-7599	78757
Eaton Ln	
100-199	78737
2000-2099	78723
Eberhart Ln	78745
Ebert Ave	78721

Ebony St 78704
Ebony Hollow Cv & Pass 78739
Eby Ln 78731
Echo Blf 78737
Echo Ln
900-1299 78745
14000-14099 78732
Echo Bluff Cv 78754
Echo Hills Ct & Dr 78717
Echo Point Cv 78759
Echoridge Dr 78750
Eck Cv & Ln 78734
Eckert St 78722
Eclipse Ln 78739
Ecorio Ct & Dr 78728
Ed Bluestein Blvd
800-998 78721
1000-4199 78721
4201-4299 78721
5300-7200 78723
7202-7798 78723
Eddie Egan Ln 78748
Eddy Cv 78735
Eddystone St 78729
Edenbourgh Ln 78754
Edendale Ct 78756
Edenderry Dr 78717
Edens Dr 78704
Edenvale Path 78732
Edenwood Dr 78745
Edge Creek Dr 78744
Edge Park Cir 78744
Edgecliff Ter 78704
Edgecomb Cv 78737
Edgedale Dr 78723
Edgefield Ct & Dr 78731
Edgemont Dr 78731
Edgemoor Pl 78749
Edgerock Dr 78731
Edgerton Cv 78730
Edgeware Dr 78704
Edgewater Cv 78734
Edgewater Dr 78733
Edgewood Ave 78722
Edinburgh Cv 78749
Edinburgh Isle Ct 78738
Edmund Ct 78749
Edmundsbury Dr 78747
Eds Cv 78744
Edwards Dr 78734
Edwards Hollow Cv & Run 78739
Edwards Mountain Cv & Dr 78731
Edwardson Cv & Ln 78749
Edwin Ln 78742
Effingham St 78729
Eganhill Dr 78745
Egret Cir 78750
Ehrlich Rd 78746
Eiger Rd 78735
Eiler Rd 78719
Eilers Ave 78751
Ektom Dr 78745
El Camino Rd 78727
N El Dorado 78734
S El Dorado 78734
El Dorado Dr 78737
El Greco Cv 78703
El Mirando St 78741
El Norte Ct 78734
El Paso St 78704
El Reno Cv 78734
El Rey Blvd 78737
El Rio Dr 78734
El Salido Pkwy 78750
El Socorro Ln 78732
El Toro Cv 78746
El Viejo Camino 78733
Elana Ct 78741
Elander Dr 78750
Elara Dr 78725
Elder Cir 78733
Elderberry Cv 78745
Elderberry Dr 78745
Elderberry Rd 78737
Eldorado Trl
3300-3399 78748
3400-3599 78739
3601-3699 78739
Eleanor St 78721
Electra 78734
Eleos Cir 78735
Elfcroft Dr 78758
Elfen Cv & Way 78724
Elfland Dr 78746
Elijah St 78745
E & W Elizabeth St 78704
Elizabeth Jane Ct 78730
Elk Xing 78724
Elk Park Cir & Trl 78759
Elk Pass Dr 78744
Elkhart St 78702
Elkhorn Mountain Trl 78729
Elkwater Cv 78746
Ellaview Ln 78759
Ellen Ct 78750
Ellie Ln 78750
Ellingson Ln 78751
Ellington Cir 78724
W Elliott St 78753
Ellise Ave 78757
Elm Dr 78734
Elm St 78703
Elm Brook Dr 78758
Elm Creek Cv 78736
Elm Creek Dr 78744
Elm Forest Rd 78745
Elm Grove Cir 78736
Elm Ridge Ln 78727
Elmglen Dr 78704
Elmhurst Dr 78741
Elmira Rd 78721
Elmont Dr 78741
Elmsgrove Dr 78721
Elmwood Pl 78705
Elohi Dr 78746
Elton Ln 78703
Elvas Way 78758
Elwood Rd 78722
Elysian Flds 78727
Elysian Fields Cv 78727
Ember Glen Dr 78726
Emberwood Dr 78757
Emerald St 78745
Emerald Falls Dr 78738
Emerald Forest Cir, Cv & Dr 78745
Emerald Hill Dr 78759
Emerald Meadow Dr 78745
Emerald Oaks Dr 78739
Emerald Ridge Dr 78732
Emerald Wood Dr 78745
Emery Oaks Rd 78758
Emilie Ln 78731
Emma Loop 78737
Emma Browning Ave 78719
Emma Lee Ave 78727
Emma Long St 78723
Emma Sophia Ln 78717
Emma Thompson Way 78747
Emmett Pkwy 78728
Emmitt Run 78721
Emory Ln 78723
Emory Oak Ln 78738
Empire Ct 78737
Employee Ave 78719
Empress Blvd 78745
Encanto Trl 78744
Enchanted Cv 78737
Enchanted Ln 78745
Enchanted Forest Dr 78727
Enchanted Hilltop Way 78738
Enchanted Rock Cv 78726
Encinal Cv 78744
Encinas Rojas St 78746
Encinitas Ln 78749
Encino Cir 78723
Encino Verde St 78730
Enclave Cv 78731
Enclave Mesa Cir 78731
Enclave Vista Cv 78730
End Of The Trl 78734
Endcliffe Dr 78731
Endeavor Cir 78726
Ender Cv 78727
Endicott Dr 78728
Energy Dr 78758
Enfield Rd 78703
Englewood Dr 78745
English Ave 78724
English Glade Dr 78724
English Oak Dr 78748
Enid Dr 78734
Ennis Trl 78717
Entrada Cv 78730
Ephraim Rd 78717
Epic Ct 78726
Epperson Trl 78732
Epping Ln 78745
Epping Forest Cv 78730
Equestrian Cv & Trl 78727
Eric Cir 78744
Eric Heiden Ct 78748
Erica Leigh Ct 78726
Erin Ln 78756
Eruzione Dr 78748
Escabosa Dr 78748
Escala Dr 78735
Escarpment Blvd
6900-7098 78749
7100-8800 78749
8802-9698 78749
11401-11499 78739
Escavera 78738
Escondido Cv 78703
Eskew Dr 78749
Espanola Trl 78737
Esperanza Dr 78739
Esperanza Xing 78758
Espina Dr 78739
Espino Cv 78744
Espinosa Dr 78744
Esplanade Cir & St 78727
Esquel Cv 78739
Estana Ln 78739
Estancia Ln 78739
Estate Cir 78737
Estates Cv 78745
Estencia Rey Dr 78717
Estes Ave 78721
Esther Dr 78752
Estrada Ct 78732
Ethel St 78704
Etheredge Dr 78725
Ethridge Ave 78703
Etienne Cv 78759
Etna Dr 78738
Eton Ln 78727
Etta Ln 78748
Etta Pl 78753
Eubank Dr 78758
Euclid Ave 78704
Eudora Cv & Ln 78747
Eureka Dr 78745
Europa Ln 78727
Eva St 78704
Evadean Cir 78745
Evaline Ln 78745
Evangeline Trl 78727
Evans Ave 78751
Evanston Ln 78745
Evelina Trl 78737
Evelyn Rd 78747
Evening Primrose Path 78750
Evening Sky Cir 78735
Eveningstar Dr 78739
Eventide Ln 78748
Everest Ln 78727
Everglade Dr 78745
Evergreen Ave 78704
Evergreen Ct 78731
Evergreen Cv 78737
Evergreen Way 78737
Evolutions Path 78734
Ewing Cir 78746
Exchange Dr 78754
Executive Center Dr 78731
Exeter Dr 78723
Exmoor Dr 78757
Explorer Cv 78734
Exposition Blvd 78703
Exton Cv 78733
Faber Valley Cv 78754
Fabion Dr 78759
Faincout Dr 78748
Fainwood Ln 78749
Fair Oaks Dr 78745
Fair Valley Trl 78749
Fairbanks Dr 78752
Fairchild Dr 78748
Faircrest Dr 78753
Fairfax Walk 78705
Fairfax Ridge Pl 78738
Fairfield Dr
800-1499 78758
1500-1599 78757
Fairfield Ln 78751
Fairhill Dr 78745
Fairlake Cir 78734
Fairlane Dr 78757
Fairlawn Ln 78704
Fairmont Cir 78745
Fairmount Ave 78704
Fairplay Ct 78721
Fairview Dr 78731
Fairway Cv 78732
Fairway St 78741
Fairway Hill Dr 78750
Fairwood Rd 78722
Faith And Trust Cv 78717
Falcata Cv 78750
Falcon Cv 78745
Falcon Dr 78734
Falcon Head Blvd 78738
Falcon Head Nest Dr 78738
Falcon Hill Dr 78745
Falcon Ledge Dr 78746
Falcon Ridge Dr 78733
Falconhead Grove Loop 78738
Faldelaw Dr 78704
Faleantr Ln 78754
Fall Trl 78731
Fall Creek Dr 78753
Fall Meadow Ln 78747
Fallbrook Ct 78734
Fallen Timber Dr 78734
Fallen Tower Ln 78753
Fallenash Dr 78725
Falleste Dr 78727
Falling Brook Cv 78746
Falling Leaf Ln 78744
Falling Oaks Cv & Trl 78738
Falling Tree Cv 78759
Fallon Cv 78717
Falmouth Dr 78757
Fancy Gap Ln 78745
Fannin Falls Pl 78735
Fantail Loop 78734
Far Gallant Dr 78746
Far Vela Ln 78734
Far View Cv & Dr 78730
Far West Blvd
3400-3498 78731
3500-3600 78731
3575-3575 78755
3601-4699 78731
3602-4598 78731
Fareast Dr 78724
Farhills Dr 78731
Faridare Dr 78724
Farley Dr 78753
Farley Trl 78746
Farmdale Cv & Ln 78749
Farmers Cir 78728
Farmhaven Rd 78754
Farmington Ct 78736
Farnish Cv 78753
Farnswood Cir 78704
Faro Dr 78741
Farrah 78748
Farris Dr 78734
Fast Fox Trl 78746
Fast Horse Dr 78759
Fathom Cir 78750
Faubian Ln 78717
Fauntleroy Trl 78758
Fawn Dr 78741
Fawn Run 78735
Fawn Trl 78746
Fawn Creek Path 78746
Fawnhollow Cv 78750
E & W Fawnridge Dr 78753
Fawnwood Cv 78735
Faylin Dr 78753
Feather Hill Rd 78737
Feather Rock Trl 78734
Feathercrest Dr 78728
Feathergrass Ct 78758
February Dr 78753
Federal Cir 78744
Felicity Ln 78725
Felipe Dr 78747
Felix Ave 78741
Felspar Dr 78739
Felter Ln 78744
Fence Row 78744
Fence Line Dr 78749
Fence Post Trl 78750
Fenelon Dr 78753
Fennimore Cv 78717
Fenton Cv & Dr 78736
Fentonridge Dr 78745
Fenway Ct 78734
Ferdinand St 78702
Ferguson Dr 78753
Ferguson Ln 78754
Ferguson Cut Off 78724
Feritti Dr 78734
Fern Cv 78750
Fern Holw 78731
Fern Spring Cv 78730
Ferndale Cir & Cv 78745
Fernhill Dr 78717
Fernview Rd 78745
Fernwood Rd 78722
Ferret Path 78744
Fescue Ln 78738
Festus Dr 78748
Ficke Cv 78717
Fieldcrest Dr 78704
Fieldgate Dr 78753
Fieldstone Dr 78735
Fieldstone Loop 78737
Fieldwood Dr 78758
Fierro Cv 78729
Fiesta St 78702
Fig Vine Cv 78750
Fighter Dr 78719
Filbert Cv 78750
Filey Cv 78721
Fincastle Dr 78717
Finch Trl 78745
Finklea Cv 78730
Finley Dr 78731
Finn St 78734
Finnel Cv 78737
Finsbury Dr 78748
Fire Cv 78749
Firebird Cv & St 78734
Firecrest Dr 78748
Firefall Ln 78737
Firefly Dr 78744
Fireoak Dr 78759
Fireside Dr 78757
Firethorn Ct 78732
Firethorn Ln 78750
Firewheel Holw 78750
Firstview Dr 78731
Firwood Ct 78738
Firwood Dr 78757
Fiset Dr 78731
Fish Ln 78753
Fisher Island Dr 78717
Fitchwood Ln 78749
Fitzgibbon Dr 78725
Fitzhugh Rd 78736
Fitzroy Ave 78748
Five Acre Wood St 78746
Flagler Dr 78738
Flagstaff Cir & Dr 78759
Flagstone Dr 78757
Flamevine Cv 78735
Flaming Oak Cv 78749
N & S Flamingo Blvd, Cv & Dr 78734
Flamingsworth Holw 78750
Flanagan Cv 78704
Flashpan Cv 78729
Flashpoint Cv 78736
Flat Rock Dr 78737
Flat Top Ranch Rd 78732
Flatrock Ln 78735
Flaxen Dr 78747
Fleece Flower Cv 78735
Fleet Dr 78748
Fleetwood Dr 78704
Fleischer Dr 78728
Fleming Ct 78744
Fletcher St 78704
Fletcher Hall Ln 78717
Flicker Cv & Ln 78744
Flight Ln 78742
Flinders Reef Ln 78728
Flinnwood Cir 78750
Flint Ct 78734
Flintridge Rd 78746
Flintrock Cir 78737
Flintrock Rd 78738
Flintrock Trce 78738
Flintstone Cv 78736
Flora Cv 78746
Floradale Dr 78753
Floral Park Dr 78759
Florence Dr 78753
Florencia Ln 78724
Flores St 78702
Flournoy Dr 78745
Flower Scent Ct 78750
Floyd Dr 78753
Flushwing Dr 78754
Flycatcher Ct 78738
Flying Jib Ct 78734
Flying Scot St 78734
Flynn Cir 78736
Fm 1325 78728
Fm 1327 78747
Fm 1625
7500-7699 78744
Fm 1625
8300-11499 78747
E & W Fm 1626 78748
Fm 1826 78737
Fm 2244 78733
Fm 2244 Rd 78738
Fm 2769 78726
N Fm 620 78726
Fm 812 78719
Fm 969 78724
N Fm 973
2500-3699 78725
5100-8299 78724
S Fm 973
1300-2899 78725
7700-9299 78719
Foggy Glen Cv 78733
Foggy Mountain Dr 78736
Folkstone Cv 78750
Folts Ave 78704
Fonso Ln 78748
Fontaine Ave & Ct 78734
Fontana Dr 78704
Fontenay Dr 78744
Foothill Dr, Pkwy & Ter 78731
Fora Cir 78750
Forbes Dr 78754
Forbsdale Dr 78747
Ford St 78704
Fordham Cv & Ln 78723
Foremost Dr 78745
Forest Ave 78704
Forest Cv 78734
S Forest Dr 78745
Forest Trl 78703
Forest Way 78734
Forest Bend Dr 78704
Forest Heights Ln 78749
Forest Hill Dr 78745
Forest Hills Dr 78746
Forest Mesa Dr 78759
Forest View Dr
701-797 78746
799-999 78746
1000-1098 78746
7900-8199 78737
Forest Wood Rd 78745
Forestglade Dr 78745
Forsam Bnd 78725
Forsythe Dr 78759
Fort Benton Dr 78735
Fort Branch Blvd 78721
Fort Chadbourne Dr 78748
Fort Clark Cv & Dr 78745
Fort Davis Cv 78731
Fort Drum Dr 78745
Fort Hill Ct 78757
Fort Mason Dr 78745
Fort Mcgruder Ln 78704
Fort Moultrie Ln 78754
Fort Smith Trl 78734
Fort Sumter Cir & Rd 78745
Fort Worth Trl 78748
Fortuna Cv & Dr 78738
Fortune Dr 78704
Fortview Rd 78704
Fosseway Dr 78717
Fossil Rim Rd 78746
Fossmoor St 78717
Foster Ln 78757
Foster Ranch Rd 78735
Foundation Rd 78726
Fountainbleu Cir 78750
Four Iron Dr 78750
Four Oaks Ln 78704
Four Points Dr 78726
Four Star Blvd 78737
Fowler Dr 78738
Fowler Mill Cv 78717
Fox Chapel Dr 78746
Fox Chase Cir 78750
Fox Hollow Ct 78729
Fox Run Dr 78737
Foxboro Ct 78717
Foxcroft Pl 78746
Foxfield Cv & Ln 78738
Foxfire Dr 78746
Foxglen Dr 78704
Foxglove Ct 78739
Foxhound Cv & Trl 78729
Foxtail Cv 78704
Foxton Cv 78748
Foxtree Cv 78750
Foxtrot Ln 78738
Foxwood Cv 78704
Foy Cir 78744
Foy Dr 78734
Frances Dr 78746
W Frances Pl 78731
Francia Trl 78748
Francis Ave 78703
Francisco St 78702
Franklin Blvd 78751
Franklin Park Dr 78744
Franklins Tale Loop 78748
Franwood Ln 78757
Fraser Cv 78738
Frate Barker Rd 78748
Frazier Ave 78704
Fred Morse Dr 78723
Frederick St 78704
Freesia Ct 78739
Freewater Ln 78704
Freidrich Ln 78744
Freight Ln 78719
Fremont Cv 78727
French Pl 78722
French Harbour Ct 78734
N & W Fresco Dr 78731
Friar Tuck Ln 78704

Friar Villa Dr 78737
Friars Tale Ln 78748
Friendship Dr 78754
Friendswood Dr 78723
Friendswood Ln 78737
Frijolita St 78730
Frio Cv 78733
Fritsch Cv & Dr 78717
Fritz Hughes Park Rd 78732
Frock Ct 78748
Frodo Cv 78739
Froke Cedar Trl 78750
Front Royal Dr 78746
Frontera Ln & Trl 78741
Frontier Trl 78745
Frontier Valley Dr 78741
Frostwood Trl 78729
Fruitwood Pl 78758
Fruth St 78705
Frye Rye 78747
Fuente Cv 78745
Fulbright Ln 78749
Funston St 78703
Furlong Dr 78746
Furness Cv & Dr 78753
Furrow Cv 78753
Furrow Hill Dr 78754
Future Dr 78754
Fuzz Fairway 78728
Gabion Dr 78749
Gable Dr 78759
Gabriela Elyana Ct 78717
Gadwall Cv 78748
Gaelic Ct & Dr 78754
Gail Rd 78748
Gaillardia 78733
Gaines Ct 78735
Gaines Mill Cv & Ln 78745
Gaines Ranch Loop 78735
Galacia Dr 78759
Galahad Dr 78746
Galapagos Dr 78749
Galaxy St 78734
Galbraith Cv 78725
Galeana Trace Cv 78733
Galen Ct 78744
Galena Dr 78717
Galesburg Dr 78745
Galewood Dr 78758
Galewood Pl 78703
Galindo St 78741
Gallant Fox Rd 78737
Gallatin Dr 78736
Gallego Cir 78738
Galleria Cir 78738
Galleria Cv 78759
Galleria Pkwy 78738
Gallia Dr 78734
Galliano Cir 78749
Gallo Cir 78734
Gallop Cv 78745
Galloway Ln 78737
Galsworthy Ct & Ln 78739
Galveston Ln 78745
Galway St 78758
Gambels Quail Dr 78758
Gamez Cv 78704
Gandara Bnd 78738
Gannet Cv 78734
Ganttcrest Dr 78749
Ganymede Ct & Dr 78727
Garbacz Dr 78748
Garcreek Cir 78724
Garden St 78702
Garden Gate Dr 78725
Garden Grove Dr 78725
Garden Meadow Rd 78725
Garden Oaks Dr 78745
Garden Ranch Rd 78749
Garden Rose Path 78754
Garden View Cv & Dr 78724
Garden Villa Ct & Ln 78704
Gardenia Dr 78727
Gardenridge Holw 78750
Gardner Cv & Rd 78721
Garfield Ln 78727

Garland Ave 78721
Garnaas Dr 78758
Garner Ave 78704
Garnett St 78745
E Garrett Run 78753
W Garrett Run 78753
Garrett St 78737
Garrettson Dr 78748
Garrison Cir 78717
Garvey Cv 78748
Garwood St 78702
Gaston Ave 78703
Gaston Place Dr 78723
W Gate Blvd
4401-4497 78745
4499-8899 78745
9800-9898 78748
Gate Way 78727
Gate Ridge Dr 78748
Gate Tree Ln 78745
Gatehouse Dr 78753
Gates Ln 78750
Gateshead Cir & Dr 78745
Gatewood Trl 78729
Gathright Cv 78704
Gatling Gun Ln
11300-11599 78748
12200-12499 78739
Gato Path 78731
Gault St 78757
Gaur Ct & Dr 78749
Gavilan Cir 78734
Gaylor St 78752
Gaylord Dr 78728
Gazley Ln 78732
Gebron Dr 78734
Gee St 78745
Gem Cir 78704
Gemini Dr 78758
Gemstone Rd 78749
Gena Ct 78757
Genard St 78751
Gene Allan Rd 78727
Gene Johnson St 78751
General Williamson Dr 78734
Genesee Trl 78717
Geneva Cir & Dr 78723
Geniveive Ln 78741
Gent Dr 78729
Gentilly Cir 78727
Gentle Breeze Ter 78731
Gentle Oak Dr 78749
Gentlebrook Bnd 78738
Gentry Dr 78746
Geode Dr 78750
Geoffs Dr 78748
George St 78744
Georgia Coleman Bnd 78748
Georgia Landing Cv 78746
Georgia Lee Dr 78704
Georgian Dr 78753
Georgian St 78756
Georgian Oaks Dr 78739
Georgie Trace Ave 78747
Geoscience Dr 78726
Geraghty Ave 78757
Gerald Allen Loop 78748
Geranium Cv 78738
Gerona Dr 78759
Geronimo Trl 78734
Gessner Dr 78753
Gettysburg Dr 78745
Gibbs Hollow Cv 78730
Giblin Bnd 78728
E & W Gibson St 78704
Gidleigh Ct 78754
Gila Pass 78734
Gilbert Rd 78724
Gilbert St 78703
Giles Ln 78754
Giles St 78722
Gilia Dr 78733
Gillespie Pl 78704
Gillians Walk 78738
Gillis St 78745
Ginger St 78728

Gingerlily Cv 78745
Gingers Cv 78759
Ginita Ln 78739
Ginkgo Cv 78750
Ginre Cv 78759
Givens Ave 78722
Glacier Falls Ct 78727
Glacier Parke Cv 78726
Glade Line Dr 78744
Gladeview Dr 78745
Gladstone Dr 78723
Glasgow Dr 78749
Glass Mountain Trl 78750
Glazier Cir 78753
Glearadw Dr 78723
Glebe Path 78754
Glen Rd 78753
Glen Allen St 78704
Glen Echo Dr 78717
Glen Falloch Ct 78754
Glen Heather Ct & Dr 78734
Glen Meadow Dr 78745
Glen Oak Dr 78745
Glen Oaks Ct & Dr 78702
Glen Ora St 78704
Glen Rae St 78702
Glen Ridge Dr 78731
Glen Rock Dr 78738
Glen Rose Dr 78731
Glen Springs Way 78741
Glen Summer Cv 78753
Glencarrie Ln 78750
Glencliff Dr 78704
Glencoe Cir 78745
Glencrest Dr 78723
Glenda Ct 78753
Glendale Pl 78704
Glendora Ct 78738
Glenfiddich Ln 78738
Glengarry Dr 78731
Glenhaven Cir 78745
Glenhaven Path 78737
Glenhill Cv & Rd 78752
Glenhollow Path 78745
Glenlake Dr 78730
Glenn Cv 78746
Glenn Ln 78753
S Glenn St 78744
Glenvalley Dr 78723
Glenview Ave 78703
Glenville Cv 78738
Glenway Ct & Dr 78738
Glenwood Dr 78723
Glissman Rd 78702
Glomar Ave 78721
Gloucester Ln 78723
Glowing Star Trl 78724
Glowworm Cir 78744
Gnarl Dr 78731
Gnarled Oak Cv 78744
Gobi Dr 78745
Gochman St 78723
Goddard Bluff Dr 78754
Goeth Cir 78746
Gold Cave Dr 78717
Gold Crest Ct 78730
Gold Fish Pond Ave 78728
Gold Flower Holw 78731
Gold Moss Cv 78745
Gold Yarrow Dr 78730
Goldbridge Dr 78745
Golden Bear Cv & Dr 78738
Golden Gate Park 78732
Golden Hills Cir 78759
Golden Maize Dr 78746
Golden Meadow Dr 78758
Golden Oaks Ln 78737
Golden Palomino Ct 78732
Golden Pheasant Dr 78758
Golden Quail Dr 78758
Golden Rain Cv 78735
Goldenrod Cv 78750
Goldenwood Way 78737
Goldfinch Ct 78758
Goleta Ct 78749
Golf Crest Cv & Ln 78734

Golf Vista Dr 78730
Golfcourse Rd 78719
Goliad Ln 78745
Gonzales St 78702
Good Wood Dr 78744
Goodall Ct 78739
Goodard Bluff Cv 78754
Goodnight Ln 78757
Goodrich Ave 78704
Goodwater Ct 78737
Goodwin Ave
2801-3197 78702
3199-3599 78702
3601-3699 78702
3700-3711 78721
3713-3799 78721
Gordon Ct 78753
Gorham St 78758
Gorham Glen Ct & Ln 78739
Gorman Spgs 78737
Gossamer Dr 78754
Gouldville Ct 78739
Govalle Ave 78702
Governor Of Texas 78711
Governors Row 78744
Grace Ln 78746
Graceland Trl 78717
Graciosa Cv 78746
Gracy Dr 78758
Gracy Farms Ln 78758
E & W Grady Dr 78753
Grafton Ln 78737
Graham Pl 78705
Graham St 78702
Grallora Dr 78757
Grama Cv 78738
Grampian Cv 78754
Granada Dr 78741
Granada Hills Dr 78737
Granberry Dr 78745
Grand Avenue Pkwy 78728
Grand Canyon Dr 78752
Grand Champion Dr 78732
Grand Cypress Dr 78747
Grand Oak Cir, Cv & Dr 78750
Grand Teton Ct 78759
Grand View School 78726
Grande Ct 78723
Grandview St 78705
Granger Dr 78744
Granite Ln 78737
Granite Trl 78735
Granite Bay Pl 78732
Grant St 78721
Grant Cannon Ln 78738
Grant Forest Dr 78744
Granton Cv 78754
Grape Cv 78717
Grapevine Ct 78737
Grapevine Ln 78759
Grapewood Ct 78738
Grass Cv 78759
Grass Holw 78750
Grasshopper Dr 78748
Grassmere Ct 78739
Grassy Field Rd 78737
Graveyard Point Rd 78734
Gray Blvd 78758
Gray Camlet Way 78748
Gray Fox Dr 78759
Graybuck Rd 78748
Grayford Dr 78704
Grayledge Dr 78753
Grayson Ln 78722
Graywood Cv 78704
Grazing Deer Trl 78735
Great Britain Blvd 78748
Great Circle Cv 78717
Great Divide Dr 78738
Great Eagle Trl 78734
Great Hills Trl 78759
Great Northern Blvd 78757
Great Oaks Pkwy 78756
Great Plains Dr 78735
Great Willow Dr 78728

Green Ln 78703
Green Trl N 78731
Green Trl S 78731
Green Vly 78759
Green Acres St 78727
Green Cliffs Rd 78746
Green Emerald Ter 78739
Green Falls Ct 78746
Green Forest Dr 78745
Green Grass Trl 78744
Green Grove Dr 78725
N & S Green Hills Loop 78737
Green Leaf Dr 78725
Green Oaks Dr 78746
Green Pastures Cv & Dr 78725
Green River Trl 78729
Green Terrace Cv 78734
Greenbriar Ct 78756
Greenbrook Pkwy 78723
Greenfield Pkwy 78741
Greenflint Ln 78759
Greenhaven Dr 78757
Greenheart Dr 78745
Greenhill Pl 78759
Greenland Ln 78745
Greenlawn Pkwy 78757
Greenledge Cv 78759
Greenlee Dr 78703
Greenmeer Ln 78758
Greenmountain Ln 78759
Greenock St 78749
Greenridge Pl 78759
Greenridge Ter 78745
Greensboro Dr 78723
Greenshores Dr 78730
Greenslope Dr 78759
Greentree Ln 78745
Greenway St 78705
Greenwich Dr 78753
Greenwich Meridian 78759
Greenwood Ave
1100-1699 78721
1900-2299 78723
Gregg Ward Ln 78744
Gregory Pl 78746
Gregory St 78702
Grelle Ln 78744
Grennock Dr 78745
Grey Fawn Path 78750
Grey Fox Trl 78746
Grey Rock Ln 78750
Greybull Trl 78729
Greycloud Dr 78745
Greyfeather Dr 78759
Greymere Ct 78739
Greystone Dr 78731
Grider Pass 78749
Grierson Trl 78732
Griffin Ct 78731
Griffith St 78705
Grigsby Dr 78745
Grimes Ranch Ct & Rd 78732
Grimsley Dr 78759
Grissom Ct 78753
Gristmill Cv 78750
Griswold Ln 78703
Grizzly Oak Dr 78748
Grooms St 78705
Grosvener Ct 78746
Grouse Meadow Ln 78758
Grove Blvd 78741
Grove Ct 78746
Grove Ln 78724
Grove Crest Cir & Dr 78736
Grovedale Trl 78729
Grover Ave
4700-5500 78756
5502-5798 78756
5900-7599 78757
7601-7699 78757
Groveton Cv 78746
Grubstake Gulch St 78738
Grunt Ln 78734

Guadalupe St
100-298 78701
300-599 78701
510-510 78767
510-510 78768
600-1898 78701
601-1899 78701
1900-2499 78705
2500-2502 78712
2501-3799 78705
2508-3798 78705
3801-4097 78751
4099-5499 78751
5501-5599 78751
5800-7650 78752
7652-7698 78752
8201-8297 78753
8299-8699 78753
W Guadalupe St 78751
Guajolote Cir 78734
Guava Cv 78750
Guernsey Dr 78758
Guerrero Dr 78747
Guffey Dr 78725
Guidepost Trl 78748
Guildford Cv 78730
Guinevere St 78746
Gullett St 78702
Gun Bow Ct 78746
Gun Fight Ln 78748
Gun Metal Dr 78739
Gun Powder Ct 78748
Gungrove Cir & Dr 78750
Gunnison Pass 78724
Gunnison Rd 78738
Gunnison Turn Cv & Rd 78738
Gunsmoke Cir 78750
Gunter St
600-1135 78702
1136-1199 78721
Gustine Cv 78717
Gutherie Dr 78750
Gwendolyn Ln 78748
Gypsy Cv 78727
Gyrfalcon Cv 78738
Haas Ln 78728
Hachita Dr 78749
Hacienda Dr 78748
Hacienda Rdg 78738
Hackamore Dr 78748
Hackberry Ln 78753
Hackberry St 78702
Hackney Cv 78727
Haddick Cir 78745
Hadle Cv 78730
Haggans Ln 78739
Hainsworth Park Dr 78717
Halbert Dr 78750
Halder Cv 78717
Hale Dr 78749
Halendis Dr 78730
Haleralm Dr 78752
Haley Holw 78728
Half Moon Cv 78746
Half Penny Rd 78722
Halifax Dr 78753
Hall St 78757
Halliday Ave 78725
Hallshire Ct 78748
Halmark Dr 78723
Halsell Ct & Dr 78732
Halsey Ct 78739
Halwill Pl 78723
Hambletonian 78746
Hamden Cir 78717
Hamilton Ave 78702
Hamilton Rd 78759
Hamilton Pool Rd 78738
Hammack Dr 78752
Hammermill Run 78744
Hampshire Dr 78753
Hampsted Ct 78746
N Hampton Dr 78723
Hampton Rd 78705
Hampton Bliss Trce 78728

Hamrich Ct 78759
Hanbridge Ln 78736
Hanchal Dr 78717
Hancock Dr
2100-2499 78756
2501-2599 78756
2600-3499 78731
Haney Dr 78723
Hanger Dr 78719
Hanging Cliff Cv 78759
Hanging Oak Cir 78749
Hanging Valley Dr 78726
Hank Ave 78745
Hanna Cv 78729
Hanover Ln 78723
Hansa Cv, Dr & Loop 78739
Hansford Dr 78753
Happy Trl 78754
Happy Hollow Ln 78703
Harbor Hill Ct & Dr 78734
Harbor Light Cv 78731
Harbor View Rd 78746
Harcourt Dr 78727
Hard Rock Rd 78750
Hardeman St 78704
Hardin Ct 78753
Hardouin Ave 78703
Hardwood Trl 78750
Hardy Cir & Dr 78757
Hare Trl 78726
Hargis St 78723
Hargis Creek Trl 78717
Hargrave St 78702
Harley Ave 78748
Harleyhill Dr 78745
Harliquin Run 78758
Harlow Dr 78739
Harlyn Bay Rd 78754
Harmon Ave
3400-3498 78705
3500-3799 78705
3801-4297 78751
4299-5499 78751
Harold Ct 78721
Harold Green Dr 78725
Harper Lynn Ct 78717
Harpers Ferry Ln
3100-3499 78745
3500-3799 78749
Harpster Bnd 78717
Harrier Dr 78729
Harrier Marsh Dr 78738
Harriet Ct 78756
Harrington Cv 78731
Harris Ave 78705
Harris Blvd 78703
Harris Dr 78737
Harris Branch Pkwy 78754
Harris Park Ave 78705
Harrisglenn Dr 78753
Harrison Ln 78742
Harrogate Dr 78759
Harrowden Dr 78727
Hart Ln 78731
Hartford Rd 78703
Harthan St 78703
Hartley Cv 78748
Hartnell Dr 78723
Hartsmith Dr 78725
Hartwick Pl 78723
Harvard St 78702
Harvest Cir & Ln 78745
Harvest Meadow Ct 78738
Harvest Time Cv & Dr 78754
Harvest Trail Dr 78736
Harvestman Cv 78731
Harvey St 78702
Harway Ct 78745
Harwick Dr 78745
Harwill Cir 78723
Harwin Ln 78745
Harwood Pl 78704
Haskel Dr 78736
Haskell St 78702
Hastings Ln 78750
Haswell Ln 78749

Hathaway Dr 78757
Hatley Dr 78746
Hatteras Dr 78753
Hattery Ln 78717
Hatton Hill Ct 78725
Havana St 78704
Havelock Dr 78759
Havenbrook Cv 78759
Havenside Dr 78704
Havenwood Dr 78759
Haverford Dr 78753
Haversham Ct 78729
Havre Lafitte Dr 78746
Hawk Cv 78745
Hawk St 78734
Hawkeye Dr 78749
Hawkhaven Ln 78727
Hawks Canyon Cir 78732
Hawkshead Dr 78727
Hawthorne Heights Trl 78728
Hayden Bnd & Rdg 78738
Haydens Cv 78730
Hayes Ln 78759
Hayride Ln 78744
Hazelhurst Dr 78729
Hazeltine Ct 78734
Hazeltine Dr 78734
Hazeltine Ln 78747
Hazen Ln 78745
Headly Dr 78745
Headwater Ln 78746
Headway Cir 78754
Heanchil Ave 78756
Hearn St
300-398 78712
500-799 78703
N & S Hearsey Dr 78744
Hearthside Dr 78757
Hearthstone Dr 78757
Heartwood Dr 78745
Heatherbloom Ln 78738
Heathercrest Cir 78731
Heatherglen Ln 78758
Heatherwood Dr 78748
Heathrow Dr 78759
Heaton Park Cv 78717
Hedge Ln 78746
Hedgebrook Cv & Way 78738
Hedgefield Ct 78738
Hedgewood Dr 78745
Heflin Ln 78721
Heiden Ln 78749
Heights Dr 78746
Heinemann Dr 78727
Helecho Ct 78745
Helen St 78751
Heliotrope Ct 78733
Helms St 78705
Helms Deep Dr 78754
Hemingway St 78752
Hemlock Ave 78722
Hemphill Park 78705
Hendeney St 78702
Henderson St 78703
Hendon St 78748
Hendricks Dr 78729
Henge Dr 78759
Hennig Dr 78738
Henninger St 78702
Henry Kinney Row 78749
Henry Marx Ln 78735
Hensley Cir & Dr 78738
Herb Cv 78750
Herb Brooks Dr 78748
Hereford Way 78727
Hergotz Ln 78742
Heritage Dr 78737
Heritage Way 78703
Heritage Oaks Dr 78737
Heritage Village Dr 78724
Hermalinda St 78723
Hermes Dr 78725
Hermitage Dr 78753
Herndon Ln 78704
Hero Ct & Dr 78735

Heron Cv 78759
Heron Dr
400-599 78734
6201-6297 78759
6299-6599 78759
Heron Bay 78738
Herrera St 78742
Hess Dr 78748
Hester Rd 78725
Hether St 78704
Hewitt Ln 78748
Heyerdahl 78753
Hibbetts Rd 78725
Hibiscus Cv 78739
Hibiscus Dr 78724
Hibiscus Valley Dr 78739
Hickman Ave 78723
Hickok Ct 78753
Hickory Dr 78744
Hickory Holw 78731
Hickory Creek Cv & Dr 78735
Hickory Grove Dr 78753
Hickorystick Cv 78750
Hidalgo St 78702
Hidatas Cv 78748
Hidden Cv 78746
Hidden Holw 78731
Hidden Bluff Dr 78754
Hidden Brook Ct 78744
Hidden Canyon Cv 78746
Hidden Estates Dr 78727
Hidden Hill Cir 78745
Hidden Meadow Dr 78750
Hidden Oaks Dr 78745
Hidden Quail Dr 78758
Hidden Springs Ln 78737
Hidden Valley Trl 78744
Hidden View Cir & Pl 78724
Hidden West Blvd 78724
Hideaway Cv 78737
Hideaway Holw 78750
Higgins St 78722
High Canyon Pass 78738
High Gate Dr 78730
High Hollow Cv & Dr 78750
High Oak Dr 78759
High Sierra 78737
High Summit Ln 78737
High Valley Rd 78737
High Vista Cir 78737
Highgrove Ter 78703
Highland Ave 78703
Highland Ct 78731
Highland Dr 78734
Highland Pass 78731
Highland Ter 78731
Highland Ter W 78731
Highland Bluff Cv 78735
Highland Crest Dr 78731
Highland Haven Dr 78725
Highland Hills Cir, Dr, Ter & Trl 78731
Highland Horizon 78717
E Highland Mall Blvd 78752
Highland Oaks Trl 78759
Highland View Dr 78731
Highlandale Dr 78731
Highlander Cv & St 78734
Highpoint Cv & Dr 78723
Highsmith St 78725
Hightrail Way 78738
Highview Dr 78750
N Highway 183
12800-13899 78750
N Highway 183
13901-13997 78717
13999-14099 78717
Highway 290 W
7100-7598 78736
E Highway 290
6100-7399 78723
7401-7599 78723
7900-8598 78724
8600-9799 78724
9801-9899 78724

W Highway 290
4800-4898 78735
4801-4897 78735
4899-6499 78735
4901-4999 78735
6501-7099 78735
10900-11098 78737
11100-13999 78737
14001-14199 78737
E Highway 71 78742
W Highway 71
7000-7098 78735
7100-11599 78735
11700-11798 78738
11800-15599 78738
12301-12397 78738
12399-13699 78738
13701-13799 78738
15601-16799 78738
Hilcroft Cv 78717
Hiline Rd 78734
E Hill Dr 78731
Hill Country Blvd 78738
Hill Forest Dr 78749
Hill Meadow Cir & Dr 78736
Hill Oaks Ct 78703
Hill Oaks Dr 78749
Hill Wood Dr 78745
Hillbilly Ln 78746
Hillbrook Cir & Dr 78731
Hillcrest Ct 78746
Hillcrest Dr 78723
Hillcrest Ln 78721
Hillcroft Dr 78724
Hilldale Dr 78723
Hillhaven Dr 78748
Hillmont St 78704
Hillmoore Dr 78719
Hillrise Dr 78759
N Hills Dr 78731
Hillside N 78736
Hillside Ave 78704
Hillside Ct 78746
Hillside Dr
10900-11099 78736
16200-16599 78728
Hillside Hollow Dr 78750
Hillside Oak Ln 78750
Hillside Oaks Dr 78745
Hillside Terrace Cv & Dr 78749
Hillspring Cir 78721
Hillston Dr 78745
Hilltop St 78753
Hillview Rd 78703
Hillview Green Ln 78703
Hilwin Cir 78756
Hindon Ct & Ln 78748
Hiridge Hollow Dr 78750
Hispania Ct 78727
Hitcher Bnd 78749
Hitching Post Cir 78749
Hobbiton Trl 78739
Hobbs Cv 78749
Hobby Horse Ct 78758
Hoeke Ln 78744
Hoffman Cv & Dr 78749
Hog Eye Rd 78724
Hogan Ave 78741
Hogg Pecan Pass 78748
Holiday Hills Cv 78732
Holland Ave 78704
Hollar Sq 78754
Holliday Ct 78753
Hollister Dr 78739
Hollonge Dr 78745
Hollow Creek Dr 78704
Hollow Hook 78724
Hollow Oak Ct 78759
Holly Ct 78737
Holly Ln 78734
Holly St 78702
Holly Fern Cv 78750
Holly Hill Dr 78746
Holly Oak Cir 78744
Holly Springs Ct & Dr 78748

Hollybluff St 78753
Hollywood Ave 78722
Holme Lacey Ln 78750
Holmes Ct 78702
Holstein Dr 78758
Holster Ct 78748
Holt Dr 78749
Holton St 78702
Home Ln 78705
E Home Pl 78753
Home Depot Rd 78745
Homedale Cir & Dr 78704
Homestead Trl 78735
Homestead Village Cir 78717
Hondo Bnd 78729
Honey Bee Ln 78737
Honey Dew Ct & Ter 78749
Honey Tree Ln 78746
Honeybee Bnd 78744
Honeycomb Dr 78737
Honeycomb Rdg 78746
Honeycomb Rock Cir 78731
Honeysuckle Trl 78759
Hood Cir 78745
Hood Holw 78731
Hookbilled Kite 78738
Hopeland Dr 78749
Hopi Trl 78703
Hopkins Dr 78734
Horace Dr 78753
Horizon Ln 78719
Horn Ln 78703
Hornet Dr 78749
Hornsby St 78753
Hornsby Hill Rd 78734
Horse Mountain Cv 78759
Horse Wagon Dr 78754
Horseback Holw 78732
Horseback Hollow Ct 78732
Horseshoe Bnd 78731
Horseshoe Bend Cv 78704
Horseshoe Ledge 78730
Horton Trl 78749
Hosta Cv 78750
Hot Springs Ct & Dr 78749
Hotel Dr 78719
House Of Lancaster 78730
House Of York 78730
Houston St
800-1799 78756
3700-3798 78734
E & W Hove Loop 78749
Hovenweep Ave 78744
Howard Ln 78728
E Howard Ln 78753
W Howard Ln
100-198 78753
200-1100 78753
1102-1298 78753
4600-4898 78728
Howden Cir 78723
Howellwood Way 78748
Howerington Cir 78724
Hub Cv 78759
Hubach Ln 78748
Hubbard Cir 78746
Huckleberry Cv 78746
Huckleberry Ln 78748
Huddleston Ln
7700-7899 78745
8000-8098 78748
8100-8199 78748
Hudson Cir 78726
Hudson Holw 78759
Hudson Loop 78736
Hudson St 78721
Hudson Bend Rd 78734
Huebinger Pass 78745
Huerta St 78704
Hughes St 78732
Huisache St 78751
Hull Circle Dr 78746
Humble Cv 78730
Humboldt Ln 78746
Humington Dr 78758
Humming Bird Ln 78745

Hummingbird Ln
400-599 78734
13900-13999 78732
14001-14099 78732
Humphrey Dr 78729
Hundred Oaks Cir 78750
Hunnicut Ct 78748
Hunt Trl 78757
Huntcliff Dr 78731
Hunters Gln 78745
Hunters Ln 78753
Hunters Pass 78734
Hunters Trce 78758
Hunters Trce E 78758
Hunters Bend Rd 78725
Hunters Chase Dr 78729
Hunters Green Ct & Trl 78732
Hunterwood Pt 78746
Hunting Creek Ln 78748
Huntingdon Pl 78745
E & W Huntland Dr 78752
Huntleigh Way 78725
Huntridge Cir & Dr 78758
Huntwick Dr 78741
Huntwood Cv 78729
Hupa Cir 78729
Hurley Cv 78759
Hurlock Dr 78731
Huron Club Ct 78738
Hurst Holw, Pl & Vw 78734
Hurst Creek Cir & Rd 78734
Hutchinson Dr 78723
Huxley St 78748
Hyacinth Dr 78758
Hyclimb Cir 78723
Hycreek Dr 78723
Hycrest Dr 78759
Hyde Park Ct & Pl 78748
Hydro Dr 78728
Hyland Cir 78744
Hylawn Dr 78723
Hyman Ln 78742
Hymeadow Cir 78729
Hymeadow Dr
12300-12499 78750
12501-12599 78750
12600-13099 78729
Hyridge Dr 78759
Hyside Dr 78723
Ibis Cv 78745
Icarus Ct 78726
Icon St 78744
Idalia Dr 78749
Idle Hour Cv 78734
Idlewild Rd 78731
Idlewilde Run Dr 78744
Idlewood Cv 78745
Iguana Cir 78735
Image Cv 78750
Imagine Way 78738
Imes Ln 78725
Imperial Ct 78724
Imperial Dr 78725
N Imperial Dr 78724
Imperial Jade Dr 78728
Inca Ln 78733
Inca Dove Dr 78729
Independence Dr 78745
Independence Loop 78748
Indian Smt 78737
Indian Trl 78703
Indian Bend Dr 78734
Indian Canyon Cv & Dr 78746
Indian Creek Rd 78734
Indian Mound Dr 78758
Indian Point Dr 78739
Indian Quail Cir 78758
Indian Ridge Dr 78737
Indian Scout Trl 78736
Indian Tree Trl 78748
Indian Wells Dr 78747
Indiana Dunes Dr 78747
Indianhead Dr 78753
Indianwood Dr 78738

Indica Cv 78759
Indigo Cv 78732
Indigo Broom Loop 78733
Indigo Brush Dr 78726
Indigo Run Cv 78738
Indigo Sky Dr 78724
Indigo Waters Dr 78732
Indina Hills Cv & Dr 78717
Indio Cir, Cv & Dr 78745
Indus Cv 78730
Industrial Blvd 78745
S Industrial Dr 78744
Industrial Ter 78758
Industrial Oaks Blvd 78735
Inglewood St 78741
Inks Ave 78702
Inland Grn 78758
Inner Campus Dr
100-310 78712
2200-2299 78712
2200-2200 78713
Innes View Rd 78754
Innisbrook Dr 78747
Inridge Dr 78745
Inshore Cv & Dr 78730
Inspiration Dr 78724
Inter Council Cv 78731
Interchange Blvd 78721
Interlachen Dr 78717
Interlachen Ln 78747
N Interstate 35
1-1699 78702
N Interstate 35
2-1498 78701
2800-3798 78705
2901-4799 78722
3800-5898 78751
5301-6099 78723
6000-6098 78752
6100-7699 78752
7800-13699 78753
13700-13998 78728
14000-15300 78728
15302-16998 78728
S Interstate 35
1100-4098 78704
1201-3819 78741
4100-8398 78745
4301-9899 78744
9300-11498 78748
10001-11299 78747
11900-11998 78747
Intervail Dr 78746
Inverness Blvd 78745
Inverrary Cir 78747
Inwood Cir 78746
Inwood Cv 78746
Inwood Pl 78703
Inwood Rd 78746
Iola Cv 78717
Ionian Cv 78730
Iowa St 78734
Ipswich Bay Dr 78747
Ira Ingram Dr 78749
Irby Pass 78729
Iriona Bnd 78749
Irish Bend Dr 78745
Irma Dr 78752
Iron Bluff Pl 78738
Iron Horse Cv 78732
Iron Musket Cv 78748
Iron Oak Trl 78750
Irondale Dr 78717
Irongate Ave & Cir 78727
Ironwood Cir & Cv 78759
Iroquois Ln 78741
Irving Ln 78752
Isaac Pryor Dr 78749
Isabella Grace Ct 78717
Isabelle Dr 78752
Isernia Dr 78748
Island Ave 78731
Island Cv 78731
Island Way 78746
Island Knoll Dr 78746
Island Ledge Cv 78746

Island Oak Dr 78748
Island Wood Rd 78733
Islander Dr 78749
Isle Royale Way 78747
Ito Cv 78729
Iva Ln 78704
Ivalenes Hope Dr 78717
Ivanhoe Trl 78748
Ivory Key Ct 78745
Ivy Hills Dr 78759
Ivywood Cv 78729
J F K Dr 78724
J Gregg Cv 78759
J J Seabrook Dr 78721
J M Holloway Ln 78724
Jaborandi Dr 78739
Jacaranda Dr 78744
Jack Cook Dr 78723
Jack Nicklaus Dr 78738
Jack Rabbit Trl 78750
Jack Ryan Ln 78748
Jackie Robinson St 78721
Jacks Pass 78734
Jacks Pond Rd 78728
Jackson Ave 78731
Jackson Hole Cv 78746
Jacky St 78748
Jacob Gln 78727
Jacobs Creek Ct 78749
Jacqueline Ln 78724
Jadewood Ct 78748
Jaffna Cv 78749
Jain Ln 78721
Jaired Dr 78724
Jamaica Ct 78757
Jamboree Ct 78731
James Ln 78734
James St 78704
James Ander St 78745
James B Connolly Ln 78748
James Bausch Ln 78748
James Casey St 78745
James Haller Dr 78748
James Ryan Way 78730
James Vincent Dr 78725
Jamesborough St 78703
Jamestown Dr 78758
Jamie Glen Way 78753
Jamieson Dr 78750
Jan Ct 78753
Janabyrd Cv & Ln 78749
Jancy Dr 78750
Janey Dr 78757
Janice Dr 78703
January Dr 78753
Japonica Ct 78748
Jarratt Ave 78703
Jarrett Way 78728
Jarrod Lee Cv 78724
Jasmine Creek Dr 78726
Jasperwood Ct 78738
Javelin Dr 78734
Javelina Cir 78734
Jayne Cv 78737
Jays Ln 78749
Jean Dr 78753
Jeanette Ct 78745
Jeanne Marie Ct 78745
Jeff Davis Ave 78756
Jeffburn Cv 78745
Jefferson St
2600-2798 78703
2800-3499 78703
3500-4199 78731
Jeffery Cv & Pl 78746
W Jeffrey David Ln 78717
Jekel Cir 78727
Jekins Cv 78730
Jen Ln 78750
Jenaro Ct 78726
Jenibeth Ln 78744
Jennave Ln 78728
Jenner Cv & Ln 78729
Jennie Ave 78703
Jennifer Ln 78753
Jennings Dr 78727

Jennys Jump Dr 78733
Jentsch Ct 78745
Jeremiah 78747
Jersey Dr 78758
Jess Dr 78737
Jessamine Holw 78731
Jesse E Segovia St 78702
Jesse James Dr 78748
Jesse Owens Dr 78748
Jessica Ln 78727
Jessie St 78704
Jester Blvd 78750
Jester Dr 78745
Jester Wild Dr 78750
Jet Ln 78742
Jetta Ct 78753
Jewelfish Cv 78728
Jewell St 78704
Jill Sue Ct 78750
Jim Bridger Dr 78737
Jim Craig Ct 78748
Jim Davis Pl 78736
Jim Hogg Ave 78756
Jim Ryun Ln 78748
Jim Thorpe Ln 78748
Jimmy Clay Dr 78744
Jinx Ave 78745
Joachim Ln 78717
Jockey Bluff Cv & Dr 78748
Joe Sayers Ave 78756
W Johanna St 78704
Johanne Ct 78750
John Blocker Ct & Dr 78749
John Campbells Trl 78735
John Chisum Ln 78749
John Nance Garner Cir 78753
John Simpson Ct & Trl 78732
Johnny Miller Trl 78746
Johnny Morris Cv & Rd 78724
Johnny Weismuller Ln 78748
Johns Light Dr 78727
Johnson St 78703
Jolena Cir 78721
Jolly Hollow Dr 78750
Jollyville Rd
9000-11899 78759
11900-11900 78720
11900-12198 78759
11901-12099 78759
Jones Rd 78745
Jonquil Ct 78750
Jonwood Way 78753
Jordan Ln 78758
Jorge Dr 78731
Jorwoods Dr 78745
Joseph Dr 78734
Joseph Clayton Dr 78753
Josephine St 78704
Josh Ln 78730
Joshua Ct 78744
Jourdan Crossing Blvd 78753
Journeyville Ct & Dr 78735
Jousting Pl 78746
Joy Ln 78757
Joy St 78748
Joyce St 78757
Juanita St 78704
Jubilee Trl 78748
Judson Rd 78744
Judy Dr 78744
Julian Alps 78738
Julie Ln 78734
Juliet St 78704
Julius St 78702
July Dr 78753
Jumano Ln 78749
June Dr 78753
Juneberry Cv 78750
Juniper Rd 78746
Juniper St 78702
Juniper Trce 78738
Juniper Berry Way 78734
Juniper Junction Ln 78744

Juniper Ridge Dr 78759
Juno Cir 78724
Jupiter Hills Dr 78747
Justin Ln 78757
E K Ln 78754
Kabar Trl 78759
Kabaye Cv 78749
Kachina Dr 78735
Kaden Way 78738
Kaelan Cv 78730
Kaiser Cv & Dr 78748
Kalama Dr 78749
Kale Dr 78725
Kali Cv 78737
Kalindi Rd 78737
Kamar Dr 78757
Kammey Cv 78747
Kandy Dr 78749
Kangaroo Ln 78748
Kansas River Dr 78745
Kapok Ln 78759
Karankawa Cv 78731
Karen Ave 78757
Karen Ann Ct 78747
Kariba Cv 78726
Karling Dr 78724
Kasper St 78741
Kassarine Pass 78704
Kate Ln 78750
Kathy Cv 78704
Kathy Lynn Ct 78758
Katsura Ln 78746
Katter Ct 78734
Katy Ln 78748
Katydid Ln 78744
Katzman Dr 78728
Kavanagh Dr 78748
Kawnee Dr 78752
Kay Ln 78736
Kay St 78702
Kayden Ln 78738
Kayview Dr 78749
Kaywood Ct 78738
Kearsarge Cv & Dr 78745
Keasbey St 78751
Keating Ln 78703
Keats Dr 78704
Kedington St 78747
Keene Cv 78730
Keepsake Dr 78745
Keilbar Ln 78745
Keith Ln 78705
Keli Ct 78735
Kellies Farm Ln 78727
Kellog Ct 78745
Kellywood Dr 78739
Kelsing Cv 78735
Kelton Dr 78754
Kemah Dr 78748
Kemp St 78741
Kemp Hills Dr 78737
Kemper Cv 78746
Kempler Dr 78748
Kempson Dr 78735
Kempwood Dr 78750
Ken St 78758
Ken Aaron Ct 78717
Ken Caryl Dr 78747
Kenbridge Dr 78757
Kendal Dr 78753
Kendalia St 78748
Kendra Cv 78757
Keneshaw Dr 78745
Kenilworth Dr 78723
Kenmore Ct 78703
Kennan Rd 78746
Kennelwood Rd 78703
Kenneth Ave 78741
Kenniston Dr 78752
Kenora Ct 78738
Kenosha Pass 78749
Kensington Ln 78737
Kenspur Ln 78738
Kenswick Dr 78753
Kent Ln 78703
Kenter Xing 78728

Kentfield Rd 78759
Kentish Cv & Dr 78748
Kentshire Cir 78704
Kentucky Derby 78746
Kenwood Ave 78704
Kenyon Dr 78745
Keota Dr 78749
Kepler Cv 78729
Kerbey Ln
2900-3400 78703
3402-3498 78703
3500-3799 78731
Kern Ramble St 78722
Kerr Ave 78704
Kerri Strug Cv 78748
Kerrville Folkway 78729
Kerry Ct 78734
Kerrybrook Ln 78757
Kestrel Dr 78745
Keswick Dr 78745
Ketch Ct 78730
Ketona Cv 78759
Kettleman Ln N & S 78717
Kevin Ln 78734
Kevin Kelly Pl 78727
Kevin Taylor Dr 78745
Key West Cv 78746
Keynes Ln 78747
Keystone Bnd 78750
Kiana Dr 78729
Kiawah Island Cv & Dr 78717
Kidd Ln 78734
Kidneywood Trl 78735
Kids Cv 78737
Kieffer Ct 78750
Kiev Cv 78739
Kildare Cv 78724
Kildrummy Ln 78738
Kilgore Ln 78727
Kilkee Cv 78717
Killdeer St 78734
Kilmarnock Dr 78726
Kilmartin Ln 78754
Kilt Ct 78754
Kim Ln 78705
Kim Zmeskal Pl 78748
Kimberly Dr 78745
Kimberlyn Ln 78727
Kimble Cv 78757
Kimble Ln 78742
Kimmerling Ln 78758
Kimono Ridge Dr 78748
Kincaid Ct 78727
Kincheloe St 78725
Kincheon Ct 78749
Kincraig Ct 78754
Kind Way 78725
Kinder Pass 78727
King St 78705
King Albert St 78745
King Arthur Ct 78746
King Charles Dr 78724
King Edward Pl 78745
King George Dr 78745
King Henry Dr 78724
Kingfisher Creek Dr 78748
Kingman Dr 78729
Kings Ct 78725
Kings Hwy 78745
Kings Ln 78705
Kings Pt 78723
Kings Pt W 78723
Kings Row 78746
Kings View Ct 78750
Kingsbury St 78703
Kingsgate Dr 78748
Kingsland Ct & Way 78725
Kingwood Cv 78757
Kinloch Ct 78737
Kinney Ave & Rd 78704
Kinney Oaks Ct 78704
Kinnikinik Loop 78737
Kinser Ln 78736
Kinsey Ct 78734
Kiowa Pass 78745

Kiowa Draw Cv 78738
Kippling Dr 78752
Kiras Ct 78737
Kirby Cv 78759
Kirk Ave 78702
Kirkglen Dr 78727
Kirkham Dr 78736
Kirkland Ct 78738
Kirkland Hill Path 78754
Kirksey Dr 78741
Kirkwall Cv 78749
Kirkwood Rd 78722
Kirkwynd Dr 78754
Kirschner Pl 78758
Kisoba Ter 78749
Kissing Oak Dr 78748
Kissman Dr 78728
Kistler Cv 78759
Kit Carson Dr 78737
Kite St 78734
Kite Tail Dr 78730
Kittansett Cv 78746
Kittowa Cv 78746
Kitty Ave 78721
Kittyhawk Cv 78745
Kiva Dr 78749
Klattenhoff Dr 78728
Kleberg Ln 78723
Kleberg Trl 78747
Klondike Rush Pt 78726
Knap Holw 78731
Knarr St 78734
Knight Cir 78723
Knighten Ln 78725
Knights Brg 78759
Knipp Cv 78739
Knob Oak Ln 78735
Knoll Cv 78737
Knoll Crest Loop 78759
Knoll Pines Pass 78724
Knoll Ridge Dr 78758
Knollpark Cir & Dr 78758
Knollwood Cir 78746
Knollwood Cv 78731
Knollwood Dr
700-899 78746
3800-4099 78731
Knoreli Dr 78753
Knottingwood Ct 78744
Knotty Trl 78727
Knotty Pine Cv 78750
Knox Ln 78731
E Koenig Ln 78751
W Koenig Ln
101-399 78751
901-997 78756
999-2099 78756
Koerner Ln 78721
Kohlers Trl 78734
Kolache Cv 78750
Kollmeyer Cir & Dr 78734
Konstanty Cir 78746
Korth Dr 78749
Kramer Ln 78758
Krause Ln 78738
Krebs Ln 78704
Krinan Ct 78754
Kristi Dr 78746
Krizan Ave 78727
Krollton Dr 78745
Kromer St 78757
Krueger Ln 78723
Kuhlman Ave 78702
Kumquat Ct 78744
La Bahia Rd 78745
La Barzola Bnd 78738
La Calma Dr 78752
La Carman Ln 78749
La Casa Dr 78704
La Concha Cv & Pass 78749
La Costa Ct & Dr 78747
La Cresada Dr 78749
La Crosse Ave 78739
La Estrella Cv 78739
La Fauna Path & Vw 78737
La Frontera Blvd 78728

La Hacienda Dr 78734
La Jolla Dr 78733
La Llorona Ln 78717
La Mesa Dr 78704
La Naranja Cv & Ln 78749
La Plata Cv & Loop 78737
La Posada Dr 78752
La Posada St 78744
La Puente Dr 78749
La Roca Cv 78739
La Ronde St 78731
La Rosa Dr 78738
La Salle Dr
6700-6999 78723
12700-12799 78727
La Siesta Bnd & Ct 78749
La Strada Cir 78734
La Tosca Dr 78737
La Vista St 78704
Labrador Cv 78729
Labrador Bay Ct 78732
Laceback Ter 78738
Lacevine Ln 78735
Lacey Ave 78746
Lachlan Dr 78717
Ladera Blvd 78738
Ladera Norte 78731
Ladera Verde Dr 78739
Ladera Vista Dr 78759
Ladin Ln 78734
Ladle Ln 78749
Ladrido Ln 78727
Lady Suzannes Ct 78729
Ladybug St 78744
Ladywell Ln 78754
Lafayette Ave 78722
Lafitte Ln 78739
Lagerway Cv 78748
Lago Sol Ct 78732
Lago Verde Rd 78734
Lago Viento 78734
Lago Vista Dr 78734
Lagood Dr 78730
Laguna Dr 78741
Laguna Ln 78746
Laguna Cliff Ln 78734
Laguna Grande 78734
Laguna Loma Cv 78746
Laguna Vista Cv & Dr 78746
Laguna Woods Dr 78717
Laird Dr 78757
Lake Dr 78748
N Lake Dr 78724
Lake Loop 78734
Lake Trl 78746
Lake Austin Blvd 78703
Lake Champlain Ln 78754
Lake Charles Dr 78744
Lake Clark Ln 78747
Lake Cliff Ct & Trl 78746
Lake Como Dr 78734
Lake Creek Pkwy
10001-10199 78729
10109-10109 78717
10200-10299 78729
10301-10397 78750
10399-10499 78750
10501-10799 78750
N Lake Creek Pkwy 78717
Lake Estates Dr 78734
Lake George Ln 78754
N & S Lake Hills Dr 78733
Lake Mist 78734
Lake Ridge Dr 78733
E Lake Shore Dr 78734
Lake Stone Cv & Dr 78738
Lake Travis Dr 78734
Lake View Dr
4600-4699 78731
4900-13098 78732
13100-14099 78732
Lakecliff Hills Ln 78732
Lakehurst Dr 78744
Lakeland Dr 78731
E Lakeland Dr 78732
N Lakeland Dr 78732

W Lakeland Dr 78732
Lakeline Blvd 78717
Lakeline Mall Blvd & Dr 78717
Lakemoore Dr 78731
Lakeplace Ln 78746
S Lakeshore Blvd 78741
Lakeshore Dr 78746
Lakeside Dr 78723
Lakeside Trl 78734
Lakeview Cir 78731
Lakeview Dr 78734
Lakeway Blvd & Dr 78734
Lakeway Centre Ct 78734
Lakeway Hills Cv 78734
Lakewood Dr
6301-6599 78731
6700-6798 78731
7200-7899 78750
Lakewood Holw 78750
Lakewood Hills Ter 78732
Lakewood Point Cv 78750
Lakota Cv & Pass 78738
Lalew Cv 78747
Lamantilla Cv 78746
N Lamar Blvd
200-398 78703
400-1299 78703
1801-1899 78701
1901-2997 78705
2999-3508 78705
3507-3507 78703
3509-3799 78705
3510-3798 78705
3800-4500 78756
4502-4898 78756
4601-4897 78751
4899-5699 78751
5700-5798 78752
5800-7799 78752
7801-7829 78752
8001-8097 78753
8099-12800 78753
12802-13298 78753
S Lamar Blvd
200-4299 78704
4401-4497 78745
4499-4600 78745
4602-4798 78745
4701-4799 78745
Lamar Pl 78752
Lamar Square Dr 78704
Lambert Cir 78758
Lambert Ln 78719
Lambeth Ln 78748
Lambie St 78702
Lambs Ln 78744
Lamplight Ln 78731
Lamplight Village Ave
12301-12499 78758
12500-13599 78727
Lamplight Village Cir 78727
Lamppost Ln 78727
Lampwick Cir 78727
Lancaster Ct 78723
Lancaster Dr
2300-2599 78748
4901-4999 78723
Lance Rd 78734
Lance Way 78758
Lancelot Way 78746
Lancer Ln 78733
Lancret Hill Dr 78745
Land Creek Cv 78746
Landon Ln 78705
Lands End St 78734
Landscape Dr 78735
Landsman Dr 78736
Lane City Dr 78725
Langford Cv 78723
Langham St 78741
Langhoff Cv 78729
Langston Dr 78723
Langtry Ln 78749
Langwood Dr 78754
Lanier Dr 78757
Lanna Bluff Loop 78749

Lansbury Dr 78723
Lansdowne Rd 78754
Lanshire Dr 78758
Lansing Dr 78745
Lantana Holw 78731
Lantana Way 78749
Lantana Ridge Ct & Dr 78732
Laona Cv 78717
Lapin Cv 78739
Laramie Trl 78745
Laramie Parke Cv 78726
Larch Ter 78741
Larch Valley Dr 78754
Larchbrook Dr 78724
Larchmont Cv & Dr 78704
Laredo Dr 78748
Lareina Dr 78745
Largo Cv 78734
Lariat Trl 78734
Larical Trl 78724
Lariope Ln 78734
Lark Ct 78758
Lark Cv 78745
Lark Creek Cv & Dr 78744
Lark Glen Ln 78748
Larkins Ln 78753
Larkspur Rd 78758
Larkwood Ct & Dr 78723
Larlenta Dr 78729
Larry Ln 78722
Larson Cv 78748
Larue Belle Cv & Ln 78739
Las Brisas Dr 78746
Las Cimas Pkwy 78746
Las Colinas Dr 78731
Las Flores Dr 78732
Las Lomas Ct & Dr 78746
Las Palmas Dr 78759
Las Ventanas Dr 78731
Lassant Cv 78749
Lasso Path 78745
Latchwood Ln 78753
Lathe Cv 78727
Latigo Pass 78749
Latimer Dr 78732
Lating Stream Ln 78746
Latitude Ln 78717
Latta Dr 78749
Latteridge Dr 78748
Laura Ln 78746
Lauralan Dr 78736
Lauranne Ln 78733
Laurel Cir 78731
Laurel Hl 78737
Laurel Ln 78705
Laurel Canyon Dr 78731
Laurel Creek Cir & Dr 78726
Laurel Grove Dr 78758
Laurel Hill Cv 78730
Laurel Ledge Ln 78731
Laurel Ridge Cv 78732
Laurel Valley Dr 78731
Laurel Valley Rd 78746
Laurelwood Dr 78731
N Laurelwood Dr 78733
S Laurelwood Dr 78733
Laurelwood Trl 78746
Laurinburg Dr 78717
Lava Ln 78747
Lava Hill Rd 78744
Lavaca St 78701
Lavendale Ct 78748
Lavera Dr 78726
Laverty Pl 78753
Lavinia Ln 78753
Lawless St 78723
Lawndale Dr 78759
Lawnmont Ave 78756
Lawrence Dr 78734
Lawrence St 78741
Lawson Ln 78702
Lawton Ave 78731
Layton Loop 78727
Lazy Brk 78723
Lazy Ln 78757

Lazy Brook Cir 78723
Lazy Creek Dr 78724
Lazy Oaks Dr 78745
Lazy River Cv 78730
Lazyfield Trl 78727
Le Conte Cv 78749
Le Grande Ave 78704
Lea Cv 78731
Leadville Dr 78749
Leaf Cir & Ln 78759
Leafdale Pt 78738
Leafield Dr 78749
Leafwood Ln 78750
Leah Cv 78748
Leaning Oak Cir 78704
Leaning Rock Cir 78730
Leaning Willow Dr 78758
Leapwood Pl 78759
Lear Ln 78745
Leather Cv 78750
Leatherleaf Trl 78744
Leatherwood Cv 78759
Leberman Ln 78703
Leckrone Cv 78735
Lecompte Rd 78717
Leda Ln 78725
Ledesma Rd 78721
Ledge Dr 78750
Ledge Mountain Dr 78731
Ledgerock Cir 78746
Ledgestone Dr
200-799 78737
3401-3499 78731
Ledgestone Ter 78737
Ledgeway St 78746
Ledgewood Dr 78758
Lee Barton Dr 78704
Lee Hill Dr 78744
Lee Park Ln 78732
Leeann Dr 78758
Leeds Cv 78745
Leeds Mountain Cv 78747
Leesburg Cir 78758
Leeward Ct 78731
Legendary Dr 78727
Legends Ln 78747
Lehigh Dr 78723
Leigh St 78703
Leisure Dr 78754
Leisure Run Cv & Rd 78745
Leland St 78704
Lemens Spice Cv & Trl 78750
Lemens Sugar Cv 78750
Lemon Dr 78744
Lemon Mint Ct 78733
Lemonwood Dr 78731
Lemos Dr 78728
Lemuel Ln 78717
Lenape Cv & Trl 78736
Lendall Ln 78744
Lennox Dr 78745
Lenora St 78745
Lenwood Ct 78738
Leo St 78745
Leon St 78705
Leon Grande Cv 78759
Leona St
1100-1299 78702
1301-1899 78702
1901-2097 78722
2099-2299 78722
Leonard St 78705
Leopold Ln 78746
Leppke Cv 78744
Leprechaun Dr 78746
Leralynn St 78751
E Leslie Ave & Cir 78721
Lessin Ln 78704
Levander Loop 78702
Levata Dr 78739
Levenwood Ln 78724
Levering St 78725
Lewis Ln 78756
Lewis Mountain Dr 78737
Lewood Cir & Dr 78745

Lexington Dr 78737
Lexington Rd 78757
Leyton St 78729
Liberton Ln 78754
Liberty St 78705
Liberty Farms Dr 78754
Liberty Park Dr 78746
Libyan Cir & Dr 78745
Licorice Ln 78728
Lido Cir & St 78734
Lifford Ct 78753
Lightfoot Trl 78745
Lighthouse Way 78734
Lightsey Rd 78704
Lightwood Cv & Loop 78748
Ligustrum Cv 78750
Lilac Ln 78745
Lilley Brook Cv 78717
Lillian Ln 78749
Lily Ter 78741
Lily Lake Loop 78724
Lime Stone Cir 78731
Limerick Ave
12300-12499 78758
12500-12699 78727
Limerick Ln 78746
Limerock Holw 78744
Limestone Trl 78737
Limewood Ct 78727
Limon Ln 78704
Limoncillo Ct & Dr 78750
Linaria Cv & Ln 78759
Lincoln St 78702
Lincolnshire Dr 78758
Linda Ln 78723
Lindell Ave 78704
Linden St 78702
Lindenwood Cir 78731
Lindsey Cv 78748
Lindshire Ln 78748
Linford Dr 78753
Linger Ln 78721
Link Ave
5300-5499 78751
5501-5599 78751
5700-5899 78752
Linkmeadow Dr 78748
Links Ct 78738
Linnet Dr 78745
Linscomb Ave 78704
Linscomb Dr 78734
Linton Dr 78748
Lipan Trl 78733
Lipan Apache Bnd & Cv 78738
Lipanes Trl 78733
Lipizzan Ct & Dr 78732
Lipscomb St 78705
Liriope Cv 78750
Lisa Cv 78733
Lisa Dr 78733
E Lisa Dr 78752
W Lisa Dr 78752
Lishill Cv 78745
Lisi Anne Dr 78717
Little Barton Ln 78738
Little Beaver Trl 78734
Little Bend Dr 78746
Little Blue Stem Cv 78738
Little Bull Cv 78731
Little Creek Trl 78744
Little Deer Xing 78736
Little Dipper Path 78732
Little Elm Park 78758
Little Emily Way 78753
Little Fatima Ln 78753
Little Fox Trl 78734
Little Gull Dr 78729
Little Hill Cir 78725
Little John Ln 78704
Little Laura Dr 78757
Little Oak Dr 78753
Little Pebble Dr 78758
Little Spring Ln 78737
Little Texas Ln 78745
Little Thicket Rd 78736

Little Valley Cv 78741
Little Walnut Dr 78753
Little Walnut Pkwy 78758
Little Wind Cv 78730
Littlefield St 78723
Littleton Dr 78737
Live Oak Cir
800-1000 78746
1002-1098 78746
3300-3399 78731
E Live Oak St 78704
W Live Oak St 78704
Live Oak Ridge Rd 78746
Liveoak Dr 78746
Liverpool Dr 78745
Llano St 78702
Llano Estacado Ln 78759
Loadstone Cv 78724
Loasa Cv 78735
Lob Cv 78730
Lobelia Dr 78729
Loblolly Ln 78744
Loch Lommond St 78749
Loch Ness Cv 78750
Lochridge Dr 78758
Lochwood Bend Ct 78738
Locke Ln 78704
Lockerbie Ct & Dr 78750
Lockhart Dr 78704
Lockleven Cv & Loop 78750
Lockwood Cv 78723
Lodge Ct 78758
Lodge View Ln 78731
Loganberry Ct & Dr 78745
Logans Ln 78746
Logans Hollow Dr 78746
Logwood Dr 78757
Lohmans Spur 78734
Lohmans Crossing Rd 78734
Loire Ct 78744
Lois Ln 78750
E & W Lola Dr 78753
Loleta Way 78717
Loma Dr 78741
Loma Linda Dr 78746
Lomax Cv 78732
Lombardia Dr 78734
Lomita Dr 78738
Lomita Verde Cir & Ct 78749
London Dr 78745
Londonshire Ln 78739
Lone Cedar Ct 78734
Lone Deer Run 78737
Lone Mesa 78759
Lone Oak Dr 78704
Lone Oak Trl 78745
Lone Pine Ln 78747
Lone Rider Trl 78738
Lone Star Ln 78734
Lonerlet Dr 78731
Lonesome Dove Cv 78729
Lonesome Valley Ct & Trl 78731
Long Ct 78730
Long Arrow Cyn 78738
Long Bay Cv 78732
Long Bow Ln 78704
Long Bow Trl 78734
Long Branch Dr 78736
Long Canyon Dr 78730
Long Champ Ct & Dr 78746
Long Creek Rd 78737
Long Day Cv & Dr 78754
Long Point Dr 78731
Long Rifle Cv & Dr 78754
Long Summer Dr 78754
Long Vista Dr 78728
Long Voyage Dr 78754
Long Winter Dr 78754
Long Wood Ave & Cv 78734
Longbranch Dr 78734
Longhorn Blvd 78758
Longhorn Lndg 78734
Longhorn Pkwy 78732
Longitude Trl 78717
Longmont Ln 78737

E & W Longspur Blvd 78753
Longvale Dr 78729
Longview Rd 78745
Longview St 78705
Longwood Rd 78737
Lonsdale Dr 78729
Lonsonti Dr 78732
Lookout Ln 78746
Lookout Bluff Ter 78735
Lookout Cliff Pass 78737
Lookout Mountain Cv & Dr 78731
Loomis Dr 78738
W Loop 78758
Loralinda Dr 78753
Lord Derby Dr 78748
Loreto Dr 78721
Lorieriv Dr 78737
Loring Dr 78750
Lorrain St 78703
Lorraine Loop 78758
Los Altos Dr 78734
Los Arcos Cv 78739
Los Comancheros Rd 78717
Los Indios Cv & Trl 78729
Los Ranchos Dr 78749
Lost Cv 78746
Lost Cyn 78746
Lost Vly 78745
Lost Cavern Cv 78739
Lost Creek Blvd
1100-2500 78746
2502-2698 78746
3500-3799 78735
Lost Creek Cir 78746
Lost Horizon Dr 78759
Lost Maples Trl 78748
Lost Meadow Cv & Trl 78738
Lost Oasis Holw 78739
Lost Pine Cv 78739
Lost Trail Cv 78730
Lostridge Dr 78731
Lostwood Cir 78748
Lott Ave 78721
Lotus Cir 78737
Lotus Ln 78721
Lou John St 78727
Louis Ave 78721
W Louis Henna Blvd 78728
Louise Ln 78757
Louise Lee Dr 78725
Lounsbury Pl 78717
Lovage Dr 78727
Love Bird Cv & Ln 78730
Lovegrass Ln 78745
Loveland Cv 78746
Lovell Dr 78723
Lovely Ln 78744
Lovingood Dr 78721
Lovridge Ct 78739
Low Bridge Ln 78750
Lowdes Dr 78745
N & S Lowell Ln 78733
Loweswater Ln 78754
Loxley Ln 78717
Loyola Ln
2300-2398 78723
2400-5199 78723
5501-5599 78724
6200-6798 78724
Lubbock Ln 78729
Lucas Dr & Ln 78731
Lucayan Cv 78734
Lucia Cir 78734
Lucian St 78725
Luckenbach Ln 78729
Lucksinger Ln 78745
Lucy Cv 78724
Ludlow Ter 78723
Luke Ct 78750
Luling Ln 78729
Lullwood Rd 78722
Luna St 78721
Luna Montana Way N & S 78732
Luna Vista Dr 78738

Lunar Dr 78745
Lund St 78704
Lundie Cv 78726
Lupine Ln 78741
Lurlyne Ct 78744
Luton Cv 78745
Luvora Cv 78739
Lux St 78721
Lyckman Ln 78737
Lydia St 78702
Lyman Pl 78756
Lymko Dr 78728
Lynch Ln 78741
Lynchburg Dr 78738
Lyndhurst St 78729
Lyndon Dr 78732
Lyndon Ln 78729
Lynn St 78702
W Lynn St 78703
Lynnbrook Dr 78748
Lynncrest Cv 78726
Lynndale Dr 78756
Lynnhaven St 78749
Lynnville Trl 78727
Lynnwood St 78756
Lynridge Dr 78723
Lyon Club Ct 78738
Lyons Rd 78702
Lyra Cir 78744
Lyric Dr 78745
E M Franklin Ave
1100-1899 78721
1900-2199 78723
2201-2299 78723
Mabry Ct 78749
Machete Trl 78729
Maciver Dr 78754
Macken St 78703
Macmora Rd 78758
Maddy Way 78738
Madera Dr 78741
Madison Ave 78757
Madison Fork Dr 78738
Madrid Cv & Dr 78759
Madrona Dr
1-99 78744
4600-4699 78731
Madrone Cir 78737
Madrone Rd 78746
N Madrone Trl 78737
S Madrone Trl 78737
Madrone Mountain Way 78737
Madrone Ranch Trl 78738
Madrone Vista Dr 78738
Maelin Cv & Dr 78739
Maeves Way 78737
Magazine Cv & St 78727
Magdelena Dr 78735
Magee Bnd 78749
Magellan Dr 78733
Magenta Ln 78739
Magenta Sky Trl 78732
Magin Meadow Dr 78744
Magna Ct 78739
Magna Carta Loop 78754
Magnolia Mist Ln 78744
Magnolia Mound Cv & Trl 78727
Magnolia Ridge Cv 78738
Magnus St 78754
Magpie Cv 78746
Maguire Cv 78732
Maha Cir 78747.
Maha Rd 78719
Maha Loop Rd 78719
Mahan Dr 78721
Mahone Ave 78757
Maiden Ln 78705
Maidenhair Ln 78738
Maidenstone Dr 78759
Maine Dr 78758
Mairo St 78748
Maize Bend Dr 78727
Majestic Dr 78745
Majestic Arroyo Way 78738

Majestic Oaks Dr & Pass 78732
Majestic Ridge Rd 78738
Majorca Dr 78717
Malabar St 78734
Malaga Dr 78759
Malaquita Br 78738
Malbec Ct 78738
Malcom Trl 78754
Maldon Pl 78722
Malibu Cv 78730
Malish Ct 78746
Mallard Cv 78737
Mallard Ln 78729
Mallard Green Cv & Ln 78728
Mallet Ct 78737
Malone Ct & Dr 78749
Maltese Cross Dr 78748
Malus Ct 78734
Malvern Hill Ct & Dr 78745
Malvinas Cv 78739
Man O War Ave 78719
Manana St 78730
Manassas Dr 78745
Manchaca Rd
2800-4300 78704
4302-4398 78704
4400-7399 78745
7310-7310 78715
7401-8499 78745
8500-8598 78745
8600-8798 78748
8800-12199 78748
Manchester Cir 78745
Manchester Ln 78737
Mandeville Cir 78750
Manford Hill Dr 78753
Mango Ct 78734
Manipari Ln 78749
Manitou 78734
Manitou Springs Ct & Ln 78717
Mankato Dr 78748
Mankins Way 78728
Manlove St 78741
Manor Cir 78723
Manor Rd
1300-1598 78722
1600-2999 78722
3100-6800 78723
6802-6998 78723
Manor Ridge Ct 78746
Manorwood Rd 78723
Mansell Ave
600-999 78702
1001-1099 78702
1100-1199 78721
Mansfield Cir & Dr 78732
Mansfield Dam Ct 78734
Mansfield View Ct 78732
Mantle Dr 78746
Manzanillo Dr 78749
Manzanita St 78759
Map Cir & St 78721
Maple Ave
1200-1899 78702
1900-2199 78722
Maple Hollow Trl 78728
Maple Marsh Ct 78744
Maplelawn Cir 78723
Mapleleaf Dr 78723
Maplewood Ave 78722
Marathon Blvd 78756
Marathon Rd 78717
Maravillas Cv & Loop 78735
Marble Rd 78750
Marble Creek Loop 78747
Marble Crest Dr 78747
Marble Falls Cv 78729
Marble Ridge Dr 78747
Marblehead Dr 78727
Marblewood Dr 78731
Marbrys Ridge Cv 78731
Marbury Ct 78726
Marc Taylor Dr 78745

Marcae Ct 78704
Marcell St 78752
March Dr 78753
Marchmont Ln 78749
Marcus Pl 78721
Marcus Abrams Blvd 78748
Marcy St 78745
Marden Ln 78739
Marejada Dr 78724
Marfa Dr 78748
Margalene Way 78728
Margaret Cir 78737
Margaret St 78704
Margit Dr 78729
Margra Ln 78748
Margranita Cres 78703
Maria Anna Rd 78703
Mariachi Ct 78732
Mariah Cv 78717
Marias River Dr 78748
Maricopa Cv 78749
Marietta Dr 78748
Marigold Ter 78741
Marilyn Dr 78757
Marimba Trl 78729
Marin Ct 78738
Marina View Way 78734
Marina Village Cv 78734
Mariner 78734
Mariposa Dr
900-1200 78704
1202-1398 78704
1700-1799 78741
Mariscal Canyon Dr 78759
Maritime Way 78717
Maritime Alps Way 78738
Mark St 78721
Mark Rae St 78727
W Market Dr 78731
Market St 78738
Market Garden Ln 78745
Markham Ln 78753
Marks Cir 78721
Marl Ct 78747
Marlborough Cir & Dr 78753
Marlin Cv 78744
Marlo Dr 78723
Marlton Dr 78703
Marly Cv & Way 78733
Marogot Run 78758
Marquesa Dr 78731
Marquette Ln 78723
Marr Cv 78724
Marrero Dr 78729
Marseilles Dr 78750
Marsh Dr 78748
Marsh Creek Dr 78759
Marsha St 78728
Marshall Ln 78703
Marshall Ford Rd 78732
Marshitas Way 78748
Marston Cir & Ln 78753
Marthas Cv & Dr 78717
Martin Ave 78751
Martin Ct 78758
E Martin Luther King Jr Blvd
701-799 78701
1500-1698 78702
1700-2999 78702
3001-3099 78702
3200-5800 78721
5802-5898 78721
W Martin Luther King Jr Blvd 78701
Martindale Dr 78759
Martinique Pass 78734
E & W Mary St 78704
Mary Hargrove Ln 78748
Mary Lou Retton Ln 78748
S Mary Moore Searight Dr 78748
Maryanna Dr 78746
Marybank Dr 78750
Maryland Dr 78758
Marymount Dr 78723

Marywood Cir 78723
Mashie Cv 78744
Mason Ave 78721
Masterson Pass 78753
Matador Cir 78746
Matador Dr 78741
Matador Ln 78746
Matagorda St 78741
Matchlock Cv 78729
Mateo Cv 78717
Matisse Trl 78726
Matoca Way 78726
Matterhorn Ln 78704
Matthews Dr 78703
Matthews Ln 78745
Mattie St 78723
Mauai Cv & Dr 78749
Maude St 78702
Maufrais Ln 78744
Maufrais St 78703
Maulding Pass 78749
Mauna Kea Dr 78746
Maury Holw 78750
Maurys Trl 78730
Maverick Dr 78727
Maxwell Ln 78741
May Dr 78753
Mayan Way 78733
Maybelle Ave 78756
Maydelle Dr 78748
Maye Pl 78728
Mayhall Dr 78721
Mayleaf Cv 78738
Mayo St 78748
Mayview Dr 78724
Maywood Ave & Cir 78703
Mc Bee St 78723
Mcaloon Way 78728
Mcbrine Pl 78746
Mccall Ln 78744
Mccall Rd 78703
Mccallen Pass 78753
Mccallum Dr 78703
Mccandless St 78756
Mccann Dr 78757
Mccarthy Cir 78756
Mccarty Ln 78749
Mcclannahan Dr 78748
Mccloskey St 78723
Mcconnell Dr 78746
Mccormick Mountain Dr 78734
Mccullough St 78703
Mccurdy Cv 78732
Mcdade Dr 78735
Mcdonald Way 78754
Mcdows Hole Ln 78717
Mcelroy Dr 78757
Mcfarlie Cv 78750
Mcgregor Dr 78745
Mchale Ct 78758
Mcintyre Cir 78734
Mckalla Pl 78758
Mckenzie Dr 78719
Mckie Cv & Dr 78752
Mckinley Ave 78702
Mckinney Falls Pkwy 78744
Mckinney Springs Dr 78717
Mckittrick Canyon Dr 78759
Mcloughlin Pt 78726
Mcmeans Trl 78737
Mcmillian Dr 78753
Mcneil Dr
  3500-4000 78727
  4002-4398 78727
  5501-5697 78729
  5699-7400 78729
  7402-7498 78729
  9401-9497 78750
  9499-9999 78750
Mcneil Rd
  9301-9397 78758
  9399-9599 78758
  9601-9699 78758
  14000-14099 78728
Mcneil Merriltown 78727

Mcnelly Trl 78732
Mcphaul St 78758
Meacham Way 78749
Mead Parke Cv 78726
Meadgreen Cir, Ct & Dr 78758
Meador Ave 78752
Meadow Cir 78745
Meadow Crst 78744
Meadow Run 78745
E Meadow Bend Dr 78724
Meadow Creek Cir, Cv & Dr 78745
Meadow Green Ct 78736
Meadow Lake Blvd 78744
Meadow Lark Ave 78753
Meadow Lea Dr 78745
E Meadow Vale 78758
Meadowbank Dr 78703
Meadowbrook Dr 78703
Meadowfire Dr 78758
Meadowheath Cv & Dr 78729
Meadowland Dr 78738
Meadowlark St
  201-297 78734
  299-599 78734
  900-998 78758
Meadowlark St N 78734
Meadowlark St S 78734
Meadowmear Dr 78753
E & W Meadowmere Ln 78758
Meadowood Cv & Dr 78723
Meadowridge Dr 78704
S Meadows Blvd 78745
N Meadows Dr 78758
S Meadows Dr 78758
Meadowsouth Ln 78748
Meadowview Dr 78737
Meadowview Ln 78752
Meander Dr 78721
Meandering Way 78759
Meandering Creek Cv 78746
Meandering River Ct 78746
Mearns Meadow Blvd & Cv 78758
Mecca Cir & Rd 78733
Medalist St 78734
Medallion Ln 78750
Medfield Ct 78739
Medford Dr 78723
Median Rd 78734
Medical Dr 78734
Medical Pkwy
  100-299 78738
  3201-3799 78705
  3800-4499 78756
Medical Arts St 78705
Medici Ave 78734
Medicine Creek Dr 78735
Medina St 78702
Medina River Way 78732
Medinah Greens Dr 78717
Medio Calle 78733
Mediterra Pl & Pt 78732
Meehan Dr 78727
Meg Brauer Way 78749
Meghan Ln 78704
Meinardus Dr 78744
Mek Dr 78731
Melava Ct 78749
Melcher Ct 78739
Melibee Trl 78748
Melissa Ln 78704
Melissa Oaks Ln 78744
Mellow Ln 78759
Mellow Mdws 78750
Mellow Hollow Dr 78744
Mellow Meadow Dr 78750
Melody Ln 78724
Melody St 78734
Meloncon Cv 78735
Melridge Pl 78704
Melrose Cv & Trl 78727
Melshire Dr 78757
Melville Cv 78749

Melwood Dr 78724
Memorial Park 78732
Mendez St 78723
Mendocino Dr 78735
Mendota Cv 78717
Mendoza Dr 78721
Menifee St 78725
Menler Dr 78735
Menodora Dr 78748
Mercedes Bnd 78759
Merchants Tale Ln 78748
Mercury Ln 78727
Meredith Dr 78748
Meredith St 78703
Merenco Ln 78739
Meriden Ln 78703
Meridian Oak Ln 78744
Meridian Park Blvd 78739
Merimac 78731
Merion Cir 78754
Merion Dr 78737
Merion Cricket Ct & Dr 78747
Merle Dr 78745
Merlene Dr 78732
Mermaids Cv 78734
Merrie Lynn Ave 78722
Merriltown Rd 78728
Merritt Cir & Dr 78744
Merriwood Dr 78745
Merrybrook Cir 78731
Merrywing Cir & Cv 78730
Mesa Ct 78731
Mesa Cv 78731
Mesa Dr
  5701-5797 78731
  5799-8099 78731
  8100-8999 78759
Mesa Doble Ln 78759
Mesa Grande 78749
Mesa Hollow Dr 78750
Mesa Oaks Cir 78735
Mesa Ridge Ln 78735
Mesa Trails Cir 78731
Mesa Verde Cir 78749
Mesa Verde Ct 78749
Mesa Verde Dr 78737
Mesa Village Dr 78735
Mescalero Cv & Dr 78736
Mesquite Cv 78745
Mesquite Grove Rd 78744
Mesquite Spring Cv 78735
Messenger Stake 78746
Mestina Trl 78733
Metairie Cir 78727
Metcalfe Rd 78741
Meteor Dr 78745
Metric Blvd
  9101-9297 78758
  9299-12499 78758
  12500-12598 78727
  13401-13499 78727
Metro Center Dr 78744
Metropolis Dr 78744
Metropolitan Dr 78758
Mettle Dr 78734
Meuse Cv 78727
Meyrick Park Trl 78717
Mia Dr 78738
Mia Tia Cir 78731
Miami Dr 78733
Mica Cv 78749
Michael Dl 78736
Michael St 78704
Michael Angelo Way 78728
Michael Neill Dr 78730
Michael Wayne Dr 78728
Michaels Cv 78746
Michele Cir 78746
Michelle Ct 78744
Mickey Dr 78717
Midbury Ct 78748
Middale Ln 78723
Middle Ct 78759
Middle Ln 78753
Middle Earth Trl 78739

Middle Fiskville Rd
  5300-5498 78751
  5900-5998 78752
  6000-6100 78752
  6102-6898 78752
  9401-9497 78753
  9499-10100 78753
  10102-11298 78753
Middle Ground Cv 78748
Middlebie Dr 78750
Middlebury Cv 78723
Middlefield Ct 78748
Middleham Pl 78745
Midland Walk 78727
Midmorning Dr 78737
Midnight Ct 78750
Midoak Cir 78749
Midpark Ct 78750
Midwood Pkwy 78736
Mifflin Kenedy Ct & Ter 78749
Milagro Dr 78733
Milam Pl 78704
Milburn Ln 78702
Mildred St 78702
Miles Ave 78745
Milfoil Cv 78704
Milford Way 78745
Milky Way 78730
Mill Holw 78750
Mill St 78702
Mill Reef Cv 78746
Mill Springs Dr 78746
Mill Stone Dr 78729
Milla Cir 78748
Millay Dr 78752
Miller Ln 78737
Millikin Cv 78723
Millrace Dr 78724
Mills Ave 78731
Millway Dr 78757
Millwright Pkwy 78750
Milo Rd 78725
E & W Milton St 78704
Milton Lease Dr 78747
Mimebark Way 78724
Mimosa Dr 78745
Mims Cv 78725
Minch Rd 78754
Minda Cir & Dr 78758
Mineola Ct 78734
Minerva St 78753
Mini Cir 78745
Minikahda Cv 78746
Minnesota Ln 78745
Minnie Dr 78732
Minnie St 78745
Minnoch Ln 78754
Minot Cir 78748
Mint Julep Dr 78748
Minter Ct 78750
Minturn Ln 78748
Mira Loma Ln 78723
Mira Mesa Dr 78732
Mira Vista Dr 78732
Mira Vista Way 78726
Mirabeau St 78727
Mirador Dr 78735
Mirafield Ln 78737
Mirage Cv 78717
Miramar Dr 78726
Miramonte Cv & Dr 78759
Miranda Dr 78752
Miriam Ave
  1600-1700 78702
  1702-1898 78702
  1900-1998 78722
Mirror Lake Ln 78724
Miss Ashley St 78737
Miss Julie Ln 78727
Missel Thrush Ct & Dr 78750
Mission Rdg 78704
Mission Creek Cv & Dr 78735
Mission Hill Cir & Dr 78741
Mission Oaks Blvd 78735

Misting Falls Trl 78759
Mistletoe Heights Dr 78717
Misty Cv 78754
Misty Brook Cv & Dr 78727
Misty Creek Dr 78735
Misty Hill Cv 78759
Misty Hollow Cv 78759
Misty Slope Ln 78744
Misty White Dr 78717
Mistyglen Cir 78746
Mistywood Cir & Dr 78746
Mitchell Ln 78748
Mitra Dr 78739
Mixson Dr 78732
Mlk 78712
Mo Pac Cir 78746
N Mo Pac Expy
  5700-7598 78731
  12000-12499 78758
  12501-12503 78758
  12505-12897 78727
  12899-13199 78727
  13201-13899 78727
  13901-14797 78728
  14799-14899 78728
  14901-14999 78728
S Mo Pac Expy
  900-1799 78746
  1801-3799 78746
  4400-4499 78735
  5300-5398 78749
  5400-6699 78749
  6701-7199 78749
Moat Cv 78745
Moccasin Path 78736
Mocha Trl 78728
Mock Cherry Cv 78748
E & W Mockingbird Ln 78745
Modena Trl 78729
Modesto St 78757
Moeta Dr 78734
Mohawk Rd 78757
Mohle Dr 78703
Mojave Dr 78745
Molera Dr 78749
Molokai Dr 78749
Monaghan Trl 78727
Monahans Ln 78748
Monarch Dr 78748
Monarch Ln
  100-399 78737
  9700-9899 78724
Monarch Oaks Ln 78738
Mondonedo Cv 78738
Monet Dr 78726
Monica St 78758
Monitor Dr 78745
Monks Mountain Dr 78734
Monks Tale Ct 78748
Monmouth Cir 78753
Monona Ave & Cv 78717
E & W Monroe St 78704
Monsanto Dr 78741
Mont Blanc Dr 78738
Montagna Cv 78734
Montalcino Blvd 78734
Montana St 78741
Montana Norte 78731
Montana Sky Dr 78727
Montaque Cv & Dr 78729
Montclair Bnd 78732
Montclaire St 78704
Monte Carmelo Pl 78738
Monte Castillo Pkwy 78732
Monte Vista Dr 78731
Montebello Ct & Rd 78746
Monterey Path 78732
Monterey Oaks Blvd 78749
Monterrey Pl 78753
Montesa Dr 78726
Montevilla Dr 78726
Montezuma St 78744
Monticello Cir 78721
Montopolis Dr
  200-298 78741
  300-3099 78741

  3100-3498 78744
  3500-3599 78744
Montoro Dr 78728
Montour Dr 78717
Montoya Cir & Cv 78717
Montrose St 78705
Montview Dr 78732
Montview St 78756
Montwood Trl 78748
Moon Lark Ct 78746
Moon River Rd 78746
Moon Rock Rd 78739
Moon Shadow Cv & Dr 78735
Moonflower Dr 78750
Moonglow Dr 78724
Moonlight Bnd 78703
Moonmont Dr 78745
Moonseed Cv 78728
Moonview Dr 78741
Moorberry St 78729
Moorcroft Ln 78729
Moore Blvd 78705
Moore Rd 78719
Mooreland Dr 78748
Mooring Cir 78734
Moose Cv & Dr 78749
N Mopac Expy 78759
Morado Cir & Cv 78759
Moravian Cv 78759
Mordor Cv 78739
Mordred Ct & Ln 78739
Morelos St 78702
Morgan Ln 78704
Morgan Creek Ct & Dr 78717
Morgan Hill Trl 78717
Moritz Ln 78731
Morley Dr 78752
Morning Ct 78759
Morning Cloud Cv & St 78734
Morning Dew Dr 78749
Morning Glory Trl 78750
Morning Primrose Ct 78748
Morning Quail Dr 78758
Morning Sunrise Cv 78735
Morninghill Dr 78737
Morningstar Cir 78737
Morningsun Dr 78737
Morris Rd 78729
Morrow St
  600-698 78752
  701-799 78752
  800-1999 78757
Moscow Trl 78729
Mosley Ln 78727
Mosquero Cir 78748
Moss St 78722
Moss Rose Cv 78750
Mossback Cv & Ln 78739
Mossbrook Cv 78750
Mosshead Cv 78730
Mossrock Dr 78757
Mosswood Cir 78748
Mossy Bark Trl 78750
Mossycup Ln 78724
Motheral Dr 78753
Mount Barker Dr 78731
Mount Bartlett Dr 78759
Mount Bonnell Cir, Cv, Dr, Holw & Rd 78731
Mount Carrell Dr 78745
Mount Emory Cv 78759
Mount Larson Rd 78746
Mount Rainier Dr 78747
Mount Vernon Dr 78745
Mountain Trl 78732
Mountain Cedar Cv 78731
Mountain Crest Dr 78735
Mountain Lake Cir 78750
Mountain Laurel Dr 78703
Mountain Laurel Ln 78703
Mountain Laurel Way 78737
Mountain Oaks Dr 78733
Mountain Park Cv 78731

Mountain Path Cir & Dr 78759
Mountain Quail Rd 78758
Mountain Ridge Cir & Dr 78759
Mountain Shadows Cv & Dr 78735
Mountain Terrace Cv 78734
Mountain Top Cir 78731
Mountain View Ave 78734
Mountain View Dr 78704
Mountain View Rd 78703
Mountain Villa Cir, Cv & Dr 78731
Mountainclimb Dr 78731
Mountainwood Cir 78759
Mountbatten Cir 78730
Mourning Dove Cir & Dr 78750
Mowinkle Cv & Dr 78736
Mowsbury Dr 78717
Mozelle Ln 78744
Muckender Ln 78754
Muddler Cv 78733
Mueller Blvd 78723
Muffin Dr 78724
Muhly Cv 78738
Muir Ln 78746
Muirfield Cir 78747
Muirfield Greens Cv & Ln 78738
Muirlands Dr 78744
Mulberry Dr 78745
Mulberry Ln 78746
Mulberry Creek Ct & Dr 78732
Mulberry Mist Ct 78744
Muldoon Dr 78729
Muley Dr 78759
Mulford Cv 78741
Mullen Dr 78757
Mulligan Glen Ct 78753
Mumruffin Ln 78754
Munson St 78721
Murcia Dr 78759
Murfin Rd 78734
Murillo Cir 78703
Murmuring Creek Dr 78736
Muroc St 78757
Murray Ln 78703
Murron Dr 78754
Music Ln 78704
Muskberry Cv 78717
Muskdeer Dr 78749
Musket Cv 78738
Musket Rdg 78759
Musket Rim St 78738
Musket Valley Trl 78754
Mussett St 78754
Mustang Chase 78727
Muster Ct 78731
Myra Ct 78749
Myrick Dr 78731
Myrtle St 78702
Myrtle Beach Dr 78738
Mystic Forest Ln 78739
Mystic Oaks Cir & Trl 78750
Nachez Trl 78734
Nairn Dr 78749
Nakoma Dr 78734
Nalide St 78745
Nancy Dr 78745
Nancy Gale Dr 78735
Nandas Trl 78736
Nandina Cv 78726
Napa Dr 78738
Napier Trl 78729
Naples Cv 78739
Naples Ln 78737
Narrow Glen Pkwy 78744
Narrow Oak Trl 78759
Narrow Ridge Dr 78730
Nasco Dr
  5701-5899 78756
  5900-6699 78757
Nash Ave 78704

Nash Hernandez Sr Rd 78702
Nashua Ct 78746
Nasoni Cv 78749
Nassau Dr 78723
Natali St 78748
Nater Ln 78747
Nathan Dr 78728
Natick Ln 78739
National Park Blvd 78747
Native Dancer Cv 78746
Native Texan Trl 78735
Natrona Cv & Dr 78759
Natural Spring Way 78728
Nature Center Dr 78746
Natures Bnd 78753
Nautilus Ave 78738
Navajo Path 78745
Navarro Pl 78749
Navasota St 78702
Navidad Cv & Dr 78735
Navigator Dr 78717
Neal St 78702
Neans Dr 78758
Neches St 78701
Needham Ct & Ln 78739
Needle Nook Ct 78744
Needles Dr 78746
Neely Dr 78759
Neenah Ave & Cv 78717
Neenah Oak Loop 78717
Neider Dr 78749
Neidhardt Dr 78734
Neils Thompson Dr 78758
Nellie St 78704
Nelms Dr 78744
Nelray Blvd 78751
Nelson Cv 78724
Nelson St 78703
Nelson Oaks Dr 78724
Nene Dr 78750
Nepal Cv 78717
Nesbit Dr 78748
Nesting Way 78744
Nestlewood Dr 78754
Netleaf Rd 78724
Nevada Dr 78738
Nevada Path 78745
Never Bend Cv 78746
Neville Wood Ct 78738
New Airport Dr 78719
New Boston Bnd 78729
New Hampshire Dr 78758
New Haven Ct 78756
New Iberia Ct 78727
New Lido Dr 78734
New York Ave & Dr 78702
Newberry Dr 78729
Newcastle Ct 78737
Newcastle Dr 78745
Newfield Ln 78703
Newfoundland Cir 78758
Newhall Cv & Ln 78746
Newman Dr 78703
Newmont Rd 78758
Newning Ave 78704
Newport Ave 78753
Newport Ln 78754
Newton St 78704
Niagra Dr 78733
Nickerson St 78704
Nicklaus Pl 78746
Nickols Ave 78721
Nicola Trl 78745
Nicole Cv 78753
Nicolet Way 78717
Niemann Cv & Dr 78748
Night Camp Dr 78754
Night Heron Dr 78729
Nighthawk Ct 78758
Nightingale Ln 78734
Nightjar Dr 78748
Nile St 78702
Niles Cv 78737
Niles Rd 78703
Nine Oaks Cv 78759
Nivea Cv 78748
Nixon Dr 78746
Nixon Ln 78725
No Mor Cv 78758
Noack Dr 78734
Nob Hill Cir 78746
Noble Hill Ct 78730
Nobleman Dr 78754
Nocturne Cv 78750
Nogales Trl 78744
Nolina Cv 78759
Norchester Ct 78729
Norco Dr 78738
Nordham Dr 78745
Nordyke Ln 78725
Norfolk Dr 78745
Norman Trl 78749
Normandy St 78745
Normandy Ridge Ln 78738
Norris Dr 78704
Norseman Ter 78758
North Dr 78753
North Path 78759
North Plz 78753
North St 78756
North Way 78732
E North Loop Blvd 78751
W North Loop Blvd
100-198 78751
200-799 78751
800-2399 78756
Northcape Dr 78753
Northcrest Blvd & Cir 78752
Northcross Dr
7601-7799 78757
7700-7898 78757
7700-7700 78766
Northdale Dr 78723
Northeast Dr 78723
Northern Dancer Dr 78746
Northfield Rd 78727
Northforest Dr 78759
Northgate Blvd 78758
Northgrove Rd 78731
Northland Dr
2100-2799 78756
2801-3099 78757
3300-3500 78731
3502-3598 78731
Northledge Dr 78731
Northridge Dr 78723
Northridge Rd 78728
Northumberland Rd 78703
Northview Cv & Ln 78724
Northway Dr 78752
Northwest Dr 78757
Northwestern Ave 78702
Northwood Cir & Rd 78703
Norwalk Ln 78703
Norwegian Wood Dr 78758
Norwich Cv 78723
Norwich Castle 78747
Norwood Ln 78744
Norwood Rd 78722
Norwood Hill Rd 78723
Norwood Park Blvd 78753
Notches Dr 78748
Notre Dame Dr 78723
Nottaway Cv 78745
Nottingham Ln 78704
Nova Ct 78732
Nowotny Ln 78702
Noya Dr 78728
Noyes Ln 78732
Nubian Cv & Ln 78739
Nuckols Crossing Rd 78744
Nueces Ln 78737
Nueces St
200-598 78701
600-1899 78701
1900-2800 78705
2802-2898 78705
Nusser Ln 78739
Nutmeg Cv 78750
Nuttall Dr 78724
Nutty Brown Rd 78737
Nutwood Cv 78726
O K Corral 78748
Oak Aly 78745
Oak Blvd 78735
Oak Ct 78717
S Oak Dr 78704
Oak Plz 78753
Oak Trl 78753
Oak Bend Cv & Dr 78727
Oak Branch Dr 78737
N & S Oak Canyon Rd 78746
Oak Cliff Dr 78721
Oak Creek Cir, Cv & Dr 78727
Oak Crest Ave 78704
Oak Forest Ln 78736
Oak Glen Cv 78734
Oak Grove Blvd 78734
Oak Grove Cir 78736
Oak Haven Cv & Rd 78753
Oak Hedge Pl 78745
Oak Heights Dr 78741
Oak Hill Ln 78744
Oak Hollow Cir & Dr 78758
Oak Hurst Rd 78734
Oak Knoll Dr 78759
Oak Ledge Dr 78748
Oak Meadow Cir & Dr 78736
Oak Motte Ln 78744
Oak Park Dr 78704
Oak Ridge Dr 78746
Oak Run Dr 78758
Oak Shadows Cir 78758
Oak Shores Dr 78730
Oak Springs Dr
2700-2998 78702
3000-3099 78702
3101-3199 78702
3300-3699 78721
Oak Valley Ct 78736
Oak Valley Dr 78748
Oak Valley Rd 78737
Oak Valley Trl 78736
Oak View Cv & Dr 78759
Oakbluff Cv 78734
Oakbrook Dr 78753
Oakclaire Dr & Ln 78735
Oakdale Ct 78703
Oakdale Dr 78745
Oakglen Dr 78745
Oakgrove Ave 78702
Oakhaven Cir & Dr 78704
Oakhurst Ave 78703
Oakland Ave 78703
Oaklane Dr 78704
Oaklawn Ave 78722
Oakleaf Cir 78723
Oakley Ct 78753
Oakmont Blvd
2800-3499 78703
3500-3598 78731
3600-4799 78731
Oakmountain Cir 78759
SW Oaks 78737
N Oaks Dr 78753
Oakwood Cv 78731
Oakwood Dr 78753
Oasis Dr 78749
Oasis Pass 78732
Ocallahan Dr 78748
Oceanna Ct 78728
Ochiltree Dr 78753
Oconnor Dr 78717
Oconto Dr 78717
E & W Odell St 78752
Odessa Ln 78731
Odie Ln 78727
Oertli Ln 78753
Oestrick Ln 78733
Ogden Dr 78733
Ogier Dr 78724
Ohenry Cv 78731
Ohlen Rd
1600-1699 78758
1700-1999 78757
2001-2399 78757
Ohmfield Ct 78739
Oklahoma St 78734
Okner Ln 78745
Olander St 78702
Old 19th St 78705
Old Baldy Dr 78717
Old Baldy Trl 78737
Old Bastrop Hwy 78742
Old Bee Caves Rd 78735
Old Castle Rd 78745
Old Cedar Ln 78758
Old Corral Cv 78737
Old Course Dr 78732
Old Fredericksburg Rd
5600-5898 78749
5900-6100 78749
6102-6198 78749
6104-6104 78709
Old Harbor Ln 78739
Old Hickory Cv 78732
Old Koenig Ln 78756
Old Lampasas Trl 78750
Old Lockhart Rd 78747
Old Manchaca Rd 78748
Old Manor Rd
4900-5398 78723
7800-8698 78724
8700-9100 78724
9102-9698 78724
Old Post Loop 78744
Old Quarry Ln 78731
Old Quarry Rd 78717
E Old Riverside Dr 78741
Old Salt Trl 78732
Old San Antonio Rd 78748
Old Spicewood Springs Rd 78731
Old Stable Ln 78746
Old Stage Cv & Trl 78750
Old Stone Rd 78745
Old Stonehedge St 78746
Old Wagon Rd 78746
Old Walsh Tarlton 78746
Old West 38th St 78731
Oldfort Hill Dr 78723
Oleander Trl 78735
Oliphant St 78725
Olive St 78702
Olive Hill Dr 78717
Oliver Cir 78736
Oliver Dr
9900-9999 78736
10100-10299 78737
Oliver Cemetary Rd 78736
Oliver Loving Trl 78749
Olmos Dr 78744
Olson Dr 78750
Oltons Bluff Cv & Dr 78754
E Oltorf St
100-1300 78704
1302-1398 78704
1600-5599 78741
5601-6299 78741
W Oltorf St 78704
Olympia Fields Loop 78747
Olympiad Dr 78729
Olympic Overlook 78746
Olympus Dr 78733
Omega St 78721
Omro Cv 78717
On The Lake Rd 78732
One American Ctr 78701
One Oak Rd 78749
Oneal Ln 78759
Onion St 78702
Onion Creek Ct 78747
Onion Creek Dr 78744
Onion Creek Pkwy
1700-1898 78748
1900-1999 78748
2200-2300 78747
2302-2598 78747
Onion Crossing Dr 78744
Onion Hollow Cv & Run 78739
Onslow Dr 78748
Onyx Cv 78750
Opal Trl 78750
Opal Fire Dr 78728
Open Gate Dr 78726
Open Range Trl 78749
Open Sky Rd 78737
Ophelia Dr 78752
Orainers Dr 78736
Orange Blossom Way 78744
Orangewood Cir 78757
Orbit Rd 78758
Orchard St 78703
Orchard Hill Dr 78739
Orchid Ln 78727
Oregon Flats Trl 78727
Oreilly Ct 78734
Origins Ln 78734
Oriole Cv 78732
Oriole Dr 78753
Orion St 78734
Orisha Dr 78739
Orkney Ln 78754
Orland Blvd 78745
Orlando Rd 78733
Orleans Ct 78745
Orleans Dr 78744
Oro Valley Cv & Trl 78729
Orourk Ln 78739
Orr Dr 78748
Orrell Ct 78731
Orrick Dr 78749
Orsini Pl 78750
Orson Ct 78750
Osage Pt 78734
Osborne Dr 78729
Osprey Ct 78750
Osseo Cv 78717
Oteka Cv 78735
Othello Cv 78735
Ottawa Dr 78733
Ottenhome Dr 78738
Otter Creek Ct 78734
Ouida Dr 78728
Outcrop View Ln 78738
Outfitter Dr 78744
Outwood Mill Ln 78744
Ovalla Cv & Dr 78749
E Overaire St 78751
Overbrook Dr 78723
Overcup Oak Dr 78704
Overdale Rd 78723
Overhill Dr 78721
Overland Pass 78738
Overland Hills Cir 78746
Overlook Dr 78731
Overlook Pass 78738
Overton Pass 78729
Owen Ave 78705
Owen Tech Blvd 78728
Owl Cv 78750
Ox Eye Trl 78746
Oxaus Ln 78759
Oxen Ct & Way 78732
Oxford Ave 78704
Oxford Ct 78737
Oxsheer Dr 78732
Oystercatcher Dr 78729
Ozark Trl 78750
Ozarks Path 78738
Ozona Dr 78748
Ozone Pl 78728
Paces Mill Ln 78744
Pachea Trl 78726
Pack Saddle Pass 78745
Padbrook Park Cv 78717
Paddington Cir 78729
Padina Cv & Dr 78733
Padre Cv 78731
Padron Ln 78748
Page St 78723
Pagosa Ct 78737
Pagosa Springs Ct 78717
Paint Rock Dr 78731
Paintbrush Holw 78750
Painted Bunting Dr 78726
Painted Horse Cv 78738
Painted Pony Cv 78735
Painted Shield Dr 78735
Painted Valley Cv & Dr 78759
Pairnoy Ln 78739
Paisano Cir 78737
Paisano Rd 78746
Paisano Trl
3101-3297 78745
3299-3399 78745
13300-13399 78737
13401-13699 78737
Palace Pkwy 78748
Palacios Cv & Dr 78749
Palazza Alto Dr 78734
Palcheff Ct 78734
Paleface Ct 78734
Palfrey Dr 78727
Palgrave Ct 78739
Palinchi Dr 78733
Palisade Ct 78731
Palisade Dr
100-399 78737
4600-4899 78731
Palisades Cv & Pkwy 78732
Palisades Pointe Cv & Ln 78738
Pall Mall Dr 78748
Palladio Dr 78731
Palm Cir 78741
Palm Way 78758
Palma Cir 78744
Palma Plz 78703
Palmbrook Dr 78717
Palmdale Ct 78738
Palmer Path 78737
Palmera Cv 78744
Palmetto Cir 78749
Palmwood Cv 78757
Palo Alto Way 78732
Palo Blanco Ct & Ln 78744
Palo Duro Rd 78757
Palo Pinto Dr 78723
Palo Verde Dr 78744
Paloma Cir 78734
Palomar Ln 78727
Palomino Dr 78733
Palomino Trl 78744
Palomino Ridge Dr 78733
Palos Verdes Dr 78734
Pamela Dr 78728
Pamella Ct 78734
Pamona Dr 78727
Pampa Dr 78752
Pampas Cv 78750
Pamplona Vista Cv 78739
Panadero Cv & Dr 78747
Pandora St 78702
Pannell St 78722
Pannier Ln 78748
Panorama Dr 78732
Panorama Vista Dr 78735
Pansy Trl 78727
Pantera Rdg 78759
Panther Trl 78704
Panther Junction Trl 78717
Papa Leo Ct 78750
Pappys Way 78730
Par Cv 78744
Parade Rdg 78731
Paragon Ct 78734
Paraiso Pkwy 78738
Parakeet St 78734
Paralee Cv 78717
Paramount Ave 78704
Pardoners Tale Ln 78748
Parell Path 78744
Parismina Ln 78735
Pariva Trl 78726
Park Blvd 78751
Park Dr 78732
N Park Dr 78757
S Park Dr 78704
W Park Dr 78731
Park Ln
200-400 78704
402-498 78704
4800-4899 78732
Park Pl 78705
Park Plz 78753
Park At Woodlands Dr 78724
Park Bend Dr 78758
Park Center Dr 78753
Park Hills Dr 78746
Park Hollow Ct & Ln 78746
Park Thirty Five Cir 78753
Park View Dr 78757
Park Village Cv & Dr 78758
Parkcrest Dr 78731
Parkdale Cv 78757
Parkdale Dr 78757
Parkdale Pl 78745
Parker Bnd 78734
Parker Dr 78728
Parker Ln 78741
Parkfield Dr 78758
Parkinson Dr 78704
Parkland Dr 78729
Parkside Ln 78745
Parkside Rd 78738
Parkstone Heights Dr 78746
Parkview Cir 78731
Parkview Dr 78728
Parkview Pl 78731
Parkview Trl 78734
Parkway 78703
Parkwood Ct 78746
Parkwood Dr 78735
Parkwood Rd 78722
Parliament Cv 78724
Parliament Dr 78724
Parliament Pl 78759
Parliament House Rd 78729
E Parmer Ln
200-1299 78753
1301-1699 78753
1700-1800 78754
1802-1998 78754
W Parmer Ln
1100-1598 78727
1600-1624 78727
1625-1699 78754
1626-6098 78727
1701-6099 78727
6101-7697 78729
7699-7799 78729
7801-8799 78729
9200-15000 78717
15002-15098 78717
Parralena Ln 78728
Parrish Ln 78725
Parsons Dr 78758
Partage Cir 78747
Partridge Cir 78758
Partridge Bend Cv & Dr 78729
Pasadena Dr 78757
Pasaguarda Dr 78746
Pasatiempo Ct & Dr 78717
Pascal Ct & Ln 78746
Paseo Dr 78739
Paseo Del Toro Cv 78731
Pastanso Dr 78734
Pastel Pl 78745
Patagonia Pass 78738
Patchway Ln 78748
S Path 78759
Pathfinder Dr 78759
Patio Cir 78730
Patrica St 78728
Patrice Dr 78750
Patricia Ct 78750
Patron Dr 78758
Patsy Pkwy 78744
Patterson Ave 78703
Patterson Rd 78733
Patton Ave 78742
Patton Ln 78723
Patton Ranch Rd 78735
Paul E Anderson Dr 78748

Paul Jones Pass 78748
Paul Teresa Saldana ... 78702
Paul Thomas Dr 78717
Paulines Way 78717
Pauls Valley Rd 78737
Pavelich Pass 78748
Pavilion Blvd 78759
Pawnee Pass S 78738
Pawnee Pathway 78745
Pax Dr 78736
Paxton St 78752
Payne Ave 78757
Payton Falls Dr 78754
Payton Gin Rd
900-1198 78758
1200-1700 78758
1702-1898 78758
1901-1999 78757
Peabody Dr 78729
Peace Pipe Path 78746
Peacedale Ln 78723
Peaceful Hill Ln 78748
Peach Ct 78744
Peach Grove Ct & Rd .. 78744
Peach Tree St 78704
Peacock Ln 78704
Peadontr Rd 78722
N & S Peak Rd 78746
Peak Lookout Dr 78738
Peakridge Dr 78737
Peale Ct 78726
Pearce Rd 78730
Pearl St
1600-1899 78701
1900-2999 78705
Pearlstone Cv 78717
Pearson Brothers Dr 78717
Pearson Ranch Rd 78717
Pearwood Pl 78758
Pease Rd 78703
Peavy Dr 78725
Pebble Cv 78752
Pebble Path 78731
Pebble Beach Cv & Dr 78747
Pebble Brook Cv & Dr .. 78752
Pebble Garden Ct & Ln 78739
Pebblestone Cir 78735
Pecan Cir 78723
Pecan Dr
200-399 78753
13200-13899 78734
Pecan St 78727
Pecan Brook Dr 78724
Pecan Chase 78738
Pecan Creek Pkwy 78750
Pecan Grove Rd 78704
Pecan Park Blvd 78750
Pecan Springs Rd 78723
Pecanwood Ln 78749
Peck Ave 78751
Pecos St 78703
Pectoral Dr 78748
Peddle Path 78759
Pedernales St 78702
Pedernales Summit Pkwy 78738
Pedigree Cv & Dr 78748
Peekston Dr 78726
Pegasus St 78727
Peggotty Pl 78753
Peggy St 78723
Pegram Ave 78757
Pelham Dr 78727
Pelican Pt 78730
Pelican Bay Cv 78732
Pemberton Pkwy 78703
Pemberton Pl 78703
Pemberton Way 78737
Pembrook Trl 78731
Pencewood Ct & Dr 78750
Pendleton Ln 78723
Penelope Cir 78759
Penertho Dr 78744
Penick Dr 78741
Penion Dr 78748
Pennsylvania Ave
1500-1598 78702
1600-2299 78702
3300-3699 78721
Pennwood Ln 78745
Penny Ln 78757
Penny St 78721
Penny Creek Dr 78759
Penny Kathleen Ct 78717
Pentriso Dr 78746
Peonia Ct 78733
Peony Cv 78750
Peoples St 78702
Pepper Ln 78744
Pepper Grass Cv 78745
Pepper Mill Holw 78750
Pepper Rock Dr 78717
Pepperbark Ln 78748
Pepperell Ct 78753
Pepperidge Dr 78739
Pepperrock Cv 78717
Peppertree Ct & Pkwy .. 78744
Peppervine Cv 78750
Pequeno St 78757
Peralta Ln 78735
Peralto Cv 78730
Perceval Ln 78748
Perch Cv 78717
Peregrine Falcon Dr 78746
Perennial Ct 78748
Perez St 78721
Periwinkle Path 78745
Perkins Dr 78744
Perlita Dr 78724
Perpetuation Dr 78734
Perry Ave 78704
Perry Ln 78731
Perry Rd 78721
Perryton Dr 78732
Pershing Dr 78723
Persimmon Grv 78737
Persimmon Trl 78745
Persimmon Gap Dr 78717
Persimmon Ridge Ct 78732
Persimmon Valley Trl ... 78732
Perthshire St 78729
Pescadero Cv 78746
Pescado Cir 78734
Petaca Cv & Trl 78729
Peterson Ave 78756
Peterson Ct 78734
Peterson Ln 78734
Petes Path 78731
Petite I Cv 78750
Petite Ii Cv 78750
Petra Path 78731
Petrified Forest Dr 78747
Petticoat Ln 78746
Pevensey Dr 78745
Pevetoe St 78725
Pewter Ln 78744
Phantom Canyon Dr 78726
E Pheasant Dr 78753
W Pheasant Dr 78753
Pheasant Ln 78734
Pheasant Rock Rd 78729
Pheasant Roost 78758
Philco Dr 78745
Phillip Ct 78733
Phillips Cir 78734
Philomena St 78723
Phlox Dr 78734
Phoebe Ct 78727
Phoenix Pass 78737
Piazza Vetta Dr 78734
Picea Dr 78734
Pickard Ln 78748
Picket Rope Ln 78727
Pickfair Cv & Dr 78750
Pickle Dr 78702
Pickle Rd 78704
Pickwick Ln 78746
Piedmont Ave 78757
Piedmont Hills Pass 78732
Piedras Blanco Dr 78747
Pierce Range Rd 78738
Pieriere Dr 78759
Pike Rd 78734
Pilgrimage Dr 78754
Pilgrims Pl 78759
Pillow Rd 78745
Pima Trl 78734
Pin Oak Ct 78704
Pin Oak Path 78745
Pinckney St 78723
Pincushion Daisy Dr 78739
Pine Pl 78744
Pine Barrens Ct 78738
Pine Bluffs Trl 78729
Pine Knoll Dr 78758
Pine Meadow Dr 78745
Pine Warbler Dr 78729
Pinecrest Dr 78757
Pinedale Cv 78757
Pinehurst Cv & Dr 78747
Pineleaf Pl 78757
Pineridge Dr 78729
Pinevalley Dr 78747
Pinewood Ter 78757
Piney Creek Bnd 78745
Piney Point Dr 78729
Pinkney Ln 78739
Pinnacle Rd 78746
Pinnacle Crest Loop 78747
Pino Ln 78744
Pinon Vista Dr 78724
Pintail Cv 78729
Pinto Cv & Path 78736
Pinto Chase Ct 78732
Pioneer Pl 78757
Pioneer Farms Dr 78754
Pioneer Forest Dr 78744
Piper Ct 78750
Piper Glen Dr 78738
Pipers Field Dr 78758
Piping Plover Dr 78729
Piping Rock Trl 78748
Pirun Ct 78735
Pistachio Ct 78738
Pither Ln 78741
Pitter Pat Ln 78736
Piute Trl 78739
Pixie Cv 78746
Pizarro Cv 78749
Pizer St 78724
Placid Pl 78731
Plain Rock Pass 78728
Plain View Dr 78725
N Plains Ave 78757
Plains Trl 78758
Planeview Dr 78719
Plantain Cv 78730
Plantation Rd 78745
Planters Woods Dr 78730
Plateau Cir 78745
Platt Ln 78725
N Platt River Dr 78748
Platte Pass 78734
N Plaza Ct 78753
Plaza On The Lk 78746
Pleasant Cv
1-99 78746
1600-1699 78754
Pleasant Dr 78746
Pleasant Ln 78754
Pleasant Hill Ct 78738
Pleasant Meadow Cir ... 78731
Pleasant Panorama Vw 78738
Pleasant Run Pl 78703
N Pleasant Valley Rd 78702
S Pleasant Valley Rd
501-1297 78741
1299-3399 78741
5001-5097 78744
5099-7500 78744
7502-7598 78744
Plover Dr 78753
Ploverville Ln 78728
Plow Horse Cv 78754
Pluchea Cv 78733
Plum Cv & Dr 78734
Plum Hollow Overlook .. 78746
Plumas Ln 78745
Plumbrook Dr 78746
Plumcreek Cir 78703
Plumewood Dr 78750
Plumpton Dr 78745
Pluto Ln 78727
Plymouth Dr 78758
Pocmont Trl 78719
Pocono Cv & Dr 78717
Poinsetta Ln 78744
Point Bluff Dr 78746
Point Clear Ct 78747
Point North Dr 78724
Point O Woods 78735
Point Vista Pl 78753
Point West Dr 78759
W Pointer Ln 78758
Pointeview Dr 78738
Polar Dr 78757
Polaris Ave 78757
Polk 78748
Pollard Dr 78727
Pollo Dr 78725
Pollyanna Ave 78753
Polo Rd 78703
Polo Club Dr 78737
Pommel Cv & Dr 78759
Pompano Cv 78717
Pompey Ct 78739
Pompton Dr 78757
Ponca St 78702
Poncha Pass 78749
Poncho Springs Ln 78717
Ponciana Dr & Loop 78744
Pond Springs Rd 78729
Pond View Cir 78753
Pond Woods Rd 78729
Ponder Ln 78719
Ponderosa Pkwy 78727
Pondsdale Ln 78724
Ponoma Trl 78749
Pontevedra Pl 78738
Pontic Pass 78738
Ponton Pl 78731
Pony Ln 78727
Pony Chase 78727
Pool Canyon Cv & Rd .. 78734
Popano Cv 78746
Poplar Cv 78753
Poplar St 78705
Poppy Mallow Dr 78738
Poppy Seed Ln 78741
Poppy Wood Cv 78748
Poquito St
1100-1900 78702
1904-1998 78722
2000-2100 78722
2102-2298 78722
Poquonock Rd 78703
Poquoson Dr 78727
Porian Dr 78750
Porpoise St 78734
Porsche Ln 78749
Port Royal Dr 78746
Portage Cv 78717
Porter St 78741
Porterfield Dr 78753
Portland Trl 78729
Portmarnock Ct 78747
Porto Cima Ct 78738
Portobella Dr 78732
Portofino Ct & Dr 78732
Portofino Ridge Dr 78735
Portola Ct 78738
Portrush Ct 78747
Possum Hollow Dr 78729
Possum Trot St 78703
Post Rd 78704
Post Oak Gln 78737
Post Oak St 78704
Post Road Dr 78704
Posten Ln 78744
Postvine Dr 78724
Postwood Rd 78738
Poteau Cir 78734
Potomac Path 78753
E & W Potosi Cv 78717
Potters Trl 78729
Powder Mill Trl 78750
Powder River Rd 78759
Powderhorn St 78727
Powell Cir 78704
E Powell Ln 78753
W Powell Ln 78753
Powell St 78703
Poynette Pl 78717
Pozito Ct 78745
Pradera Dr 78759
Prado St 78702
Prairie Ln 78728
Prairie Trl 78758
Prairie Clover Path 78732
Prairie Dell 78752
Prairie Dog Trl 78750
Prairie Dove Cir 78758
Prairie Dunes Dr 78747
Prairie Hen Cv & Ln 78758
Prairie Knoll Ct 78758
Pranav Ln 78750
Prather Ln 78704
Pratolina Dr 78739
Pratt Ln 78748
Precipice Cv 78731
Preece Dr 78729
Premier Park St 78747
Prentice Ln 78746
Presa Dr 78753
Presa Arriba Rd 78733
Prescott Dr 78749
Preservation Cv 78746
Preserve Vista Ter 78738
Presidential Blvd 78719
Presidio Rd 78745
Preslar Cir 78736
Presque Cv 78726
Pressler St 78703
Prestancia Dr 78717
Preston Ave 78703
Preston Trails Cv & Dr . 78747
Prestonwood Cir 78734
Prestwood Pl 78746
Preswyck Dr 78723
Prezia Dr 78733
Prickly Pear Dr 78731
Prickly Poppy Cv 78733
Primrose Ln 78757
Primrose St 78753
Prince Dr 78752
Prince Andrew Ln 78730
Prince Am Dr 78745
Prince Charles 78730
Prince Valiant Dr 78745
Prince William 78730
Princes Ct 78738
Princeton Ave 78757
Princeton Dr 78741
Pringle Cir 78742
Priscilla Dr 78752
Prism Dr 78726
Prock Ln 78721
Promontory Point Dr 78744
Prospect Ave 78702
Provencial Cv & Dr 78724
Providence Ave 78752
Provines Dr 78753
Pruett St 78703
Pryor Ln 78734
Ptarmigan Cv & Dr 78758
Puccoon Cv 78759
Puckett Ct 78749
Puddleby Cv 78746
Puerta Vis 78759
Puma Trl 78731
Pumpkin Ridge Ct & Dr 78717
Pure Brook Way 78737
Purnell Dr 78753
Purnima Cv 78739
Purple Heron Dr 78746
Purple Sage Dr 78724
Purs Ln 78733
Purslane Cv 78733
Purslane Meadow Trl ... 78728
Pusch Ridge Loop 78749
Putnam Dr 78757
Putters Cv 78744
Pyegrave Pl 78753
Pyramid Dr 78734
Pyrenees Pass 78738
Pyreneese Dr 78759
Q Ranch Rd 78759
Quadros Pass 78729
Quail Blvd 78758
Quail Ct 78758
Quail Cv 78758
Quail Holw 78750
Quail Run 78746
Quail Cover Cir 78758
Quail Creek Dr 78758
Quail Crest Dr 78758
Quail Field Dr 78758
Quail Forest Cv 78758
Quail Hill Cir 78758
Quail Hutch Dr 78758
Quail Meadow Dr 78758
Quail Park Dr 78758
Quail Ridge Dr 78758
Quail Rock Cir 78758
Quail Valley Blvd & Dr . 78758
Quail Village Ln 78758
Quail Wood Dr 78758
Quailfield Cir 78758
Quaker Ridge Dr 78746
Quanah Parker Trl 78734
Quarry Rd 78703
Quarry Oaks Trl 78717
Quarter Boot Cv 78727
Quarter Horse Trl 78750
Quartz Cir 78750
Quassia Dr 78739
Queen Ct 78724
Queens Way 78759
Queens Park Cv 78717
Queensbury Cv 78726
Queensland Dr 78729
Queenswood Dr 78748
Quernus Cv 78735
Quick Hill Rd 78728
Quick Stream Dr 78724
Quick Water Cv 78735
Quicksilver Blvd & Cir .. 78744
Quiet Pond Ct 78728
Quiet Wood Dr 78728
Quiette Dr 78754
Quilberry Dr 78729
Quill Leaf Cv 78750
Quimper Ln 78749
Quincy Cv 78739
N & S Quinlan Park Rd 78732
Quinley Dr 78728
Quinn Trl 78727
Quintana Cv 78739
Quinton Cv & Dr 78747
Quitman Pass 78728
Quivira Rd 78745
Rabb Rd 78704
Rabb Glen St 78704
Rabbit Run Cir 78734
Raccoon Run 78736
Racebrook Ct 78734
Racetrack Dr 78748
Rachael Ct 78748
Racine Cv & Trl 78717
Radam Cir & Ln 78745
Radcliff Dr 78752
Radnor Dr 78738
Rae Dell Ave 78704
Raffee Cv 78731
Raging River Dr 78728
Rail Dr 78734
Rail Fence Cv 78748
Rain Creek Pkwy 78759
Rain Dance Cv 78746
Rain Forest Cv 78759
Rain Forest Dr 78746
Rain Lily Cir 78737
Rain Water Dr 78734
Rainbow Bnd 78703
Rainbow Ct 78729
Rainbow Cv 78746
Rainbow One St 78734
Rainbow Ridge Cir 78721
Rainbow Two St 78734
Raindance Cv 78737
Raindrop Cv 78759
Rainey St 78701
Raining Oak Cv 78759
Rainlilly Ln 78759
Raintree Blvd 78745
Raintree Pl 78759
Rainy Meadows Dr 78758
Raleigh Ave 78703
Raleigh Cir 78744
Ralph Ablanedo Dr 78748
Ralph C Craig Ln 78748
Ralph Cox Rd 78748
Ramble Ln 78745
Ramble Three St 78737
Ramblewood Dr 78748
Rambling Range 78727
Ramies Run 78749
Ramirez Ln 78742
Ramona St 78704
Ramos St 78702
Rampart Cir & St 78727
Ramsey Ave 78756
Ranch Rd 78745
Ranch Creek Dr 78730
Ranch Road 2222
3500-3798 78731
Ranch Road 2222
3800-5299 78731
5301-5699 78731
6700-6998 78730
7000-11500 78730
11502-11598 78730
Ranch Road 620 N
101-1097 78734
1099-1799 78734
1801-2199 78734
2201-2297 78734
2299-4199 78734
4400-4498 78732
4500-7000 78732
7002-7098 78732
11600-12399 78750
12401-12999 78750
13200-16299 78717
Ranch Road 620 S
101-897 78734
899-2399 78734
2400-3999 78738
3400-3498 78738
4001-4099 78738
Rancho Alto Rd 78748
Ranchview Ct 78732
Randall Dr 78753
Randlett Ct 78732
Randolph Pl 78746
Randolph Rd 78722
Randolph Ridge Trl 78746
Random Cv 78738
Randy Cir 78745
Randy Rd 78726
Range Oak Cir 78749
Range View Cv & Dr ... 78730
Rankin Trl 78729
E & W Rapid Springs Cv 78746
Rapture Cv 78749
Rare Eagle Ct 78734
Raritan Cv 78734
Raspberry Cv & Rd 78748
Rathdowney Cv 78717
Rathervue Pl 78705
Raton Pass 78724
Rattlebush Cv 78750
Ravello Pass 78749
Ravello Ridge Cv & Dr 78735
Raven Dr 78752

Ravenscroft Dr 78748
Ravensdale Ln 78723
Ravenwood Cv 78750
Ravey St 78704
Ravine Dr 78704
Ravine Ridge Cv & Trl . 78746
Rawhide Trl 78736
Ray Ave 78758
Ray Wood Dr 78704
Rayburn Ln 78723
Raymond C Ewry Ln ... 78748
Rayner Pl 78738
Raynham Hill Dr 78738
Rayo De Luna Ln 78732
Razil Ct 78748
Reaburn St 78749
Readvill Ct & Ln 78739
Reagan Ter 78704
Reagan Hill Dr 78752
Real St 78722
Real Catorce Dr 78746
Real Quiet Cv & Dr 78748
Real Wind Cv 78746
Rearden Rd 78745
Rebecca Dr 78758
Rebel Rd 78704
Recreation Ct 78717
Red Bird Ct 78726
Red Bird Ln 78745
Red Bluff Rd 78702
Red Bud Ridge Ln 78744
Red Cliff Dr 78758
Red Cloud Dr 78759
Red Clover Ln 78727
Red Deer Pass 78729
Red Egret Dr 78729
Red Feather Trl 78734
Red Fox Rd 78734
Red Gate Ln 78737
Red Hawk Cv 78739
Red Maple Cv 78759
Red Mesa Holw 78739
Red Oak Cir 78753
S Red Oak Cir 78753
Red Oak Cv 78737
Red Oak Valley Ct &
Ln 78732
Red Pebble Rd 78739
Red River Cv 78737
Red River St
1-1400 78701
1402-1898 78701
1601-1699 78712
1701-1899 78701
1900-2302 78712
2301-2313 78705
2315-2603 78712
3100-3198 78705
3200-3599 78705
3601-3799 78705
3801-4097 78751
4099-4999 78751
Red Rock Cv 78749
Red Stone Ct 78735
Red Stone Ln 78727
Red Tails St 78725
Red Willow Dr 78736
Redbud Trl
1-1499 78746
500-699 78748
Redd St 78745
Redfield Ln 78758
Redgate Ct & Ln 78739
Redlands St 78757
Redleaf Ln 78745
Redmond Cv & Rd 78739
N & S Redondo Dr 78721
Redrick Dr 78747
Redwater Dr 78748
Reeda Ln 78757
Reeders Dr 78725
Reese Dr 78745
Reese Ln 78757
Reeves Cir 78741
Reflection Bay Ct 78738
Refugio Ct 78732
Regal Ct 78725
Regal Row 78748
Regal Oaks Dr 78737
Regal Park Ln 78748
Regatta Ct 78734
Regency Cv & Dr 78724
Regents Park 78746
Regents Walk 78728
Regiene Rd 78725
Regolizia Cv 78739
Reicher Dr 78723
Reid Dr 78758
Reims Ct 78738
Reinli St
901-999 78751
1000-1151 78723
1153-1199 78723
Reliance Creek Dr 78754
Remington Ln 78758
Remington Reserve
Way 78728
Remmington Rd 78734
Remuda Trl 78745
Renaissance Ct 78728
Renel Dr 78758
Renfert Way 78758
Rennalee Loop 78753
Reno Dr 78745
Rental Car Ln 78719
Renton Dr 78757
Republic Of Texas
Blvd 78735
Resaca Blvd 78738
Research Blvd
7900-8098 78758
8100-8600 78758
8557-8557 78718
8601-9299 78758
8602-9298 78758
9300-12799 78759
Reservoir Ct 78754
Retama St 78704
Reunion Blvd 78737
Reveille Rd 78746
Revere Rd 78744
Rexford Dr 78723
Reyes St 78721
Reynolds Ct 78734
Reynolds Rd 78749
Reynosa Dr 78739
Rhea Ct 78727
Rhett Pl 78744
Rhett Butler Dr 78739
Rhodes Rd 78721
Rhonda Ct 78745
Rialto Blvd 78735
Rias Way 78717
Riata Park Ct 78727
Riata Trace Pkwy 78727
Riata Vista Cir 78727
Ribbecke Ave 78721
Ribbon Reef Ln 78728
Ribelin Ranch Rd 78750
Richard Ln 78703
Richard Carlton Blvd 78727
Richard King Ct & Trl .. 78749
Richard Walker Blvd 78728
Richardine Ave 78721
Richardson Ln 78741
Richcreek Rd 78757
Richelieu Rd 78750
Richerson Dr 78734
Richmond Ave 78745
Richwood Dr 78757
Rick Whinery Dr 78728
Rickem Cv 78758
Rickerhill Ct & Ln 78739
Rickey Dr 78757
Rico Cv 78731
Riddle Rd 78748
Riddlewood Dr 78753
Riders Trl 78733
Ridge Dr
1100-1199 78721
11400-11599 78748
Ridge Holw 78750
S Ridge Ln 78734
Ridge Line Dr 78737
Ridge Oak Dr 78731
Ridge Oak Rd 78749
Ridgeback Dr 78731
Ridgecrest Dr 78746
Ridgehaven Dr 78723
Ridgehill Dr 78759
Ridgelea Dr 78731
Ridgeline Dr & Trl 78731
Ridgemont Ct 78746
Ridgemont Dr 78723
Ridgemoor Dr 78731
Ridgepoint Dr 78754
Ridgeside Ct 78731
Ridgestone Dr 78731
Ridgetop Ter 78732
Ridgeview St 78704
Ridgeway Dr 78702
Ridgewell Pl 78749
Ridgewell Rd 78747
Ridgewood Rd 78746
Rifle Bnd 78736
Rigsbee Ct 78739
Riker Ridge Trl 78748
Riley Rd 78746
W & N Rim Cv & Dr ... 78731
Rim Rock Path 78745
Rim Rock Trl 78737
Rimcrest Cv 78735
Rimdale Dr 78731
Rimini Trl 78729
Rimner Cv 78759
Rimrock Dr 78738
Rimrock Trl 78723
Rimstone Trl 78736
Ringsby Cv & Rd 78747
Ringtail Rdg 78746
Rio Pass 78724
Rio Bravo Ln 78737
Rio Chama Ln 78738
Rio Grande St
400-498 78701
500-1899 78701
1900-2999 78705
Rio Mesa Dr 78732
Rio Robles Dr 78746
Rio Vista Dr 78726
Rip Ford Dr 78732
Ripon Cv 78717
Ripple Run 78744
Ripple Creek Rd 78746
Ripplewood Dr 78757
Rippling Creek Ct 78732
Rising Hills Cir & Dr 78759
Rising Smoke Loop 78736
Ritchie Dr 78724
Rittenhouse Shore Dr .. 78734
Riva Ridge Rd 78746
Rivalto Cir 78734
Rivendell Ln 78737
River Bnd 78732
River Rd
500-999 78734
3300-3799 78703
River St 78701
River Crossing Cir 78741
River Downs Cv 78746
River Garden Trl 78746
N River Hills Rd 78733
River Oaks Dr
400-799 78748
800-898 78753
900-999 78753
River Oaks Trl 78753
River Place Blvd
3800-6699 78730
6800-7799 78726
River Plantation Dr 78747
River Ridge Dr 78732
River Rock Ct 78739
River Terrace Cir 78733
River Wood Ct 78731
Rivercrest Dr 78746
Rivers Edge Way 78741
E Riverside Dr
100-699 78704
701-1199 78704
1300-1398 78741
1400-7399 78741
7401-7411 78741
7700-7898 78744
7900-7999 78744
8001-8299 78744
W Riverside Dr 78704
Riverside Farms Rd 78741
Riverstone Dr 78724
Riverton Dr 78729
Riverview St 78702
Riviera Rd 78733
Rivina Dr 78733
Rivka Cv 78741
Rivulet Ln 78738
Roadrunner Ln 78749
Roadrunner Rd 78746
Roan Ln 78736
Roanoke Dr 78723
Roaring Springs Dr 78736
Rob Roy Rd 78746
Rob Scott St 78721
Robalo Rd 78757
Robbie Dr 78759
Robbie Creek Cv 78750
Robbins Pl 78705
Robbins Rd 78730
Robbs Run 78703
Robert Browning St 78723
Robert Burns Dr 78749
Robert Dedman Dr 78712
Robert Dixon Dr 78749
Robert E Lee Rd 78704
Robert I Walker Blvd ... 78728
Robert Kleburg Ln 78749
Robert T Martinez Jr
St 78702
Robert Weaver Ave 78702
Robert Wooding Dr 78748
Roberto 78734
Roberts Ave 78704
Robertson St 78703
Robin Ct
8300-8399 78758
15000-15099 78734
Robin Dale Ct & Dr 78734
Robin Ridge Ln 78750
Robinhood Trl 78703
Robins Run 78737
Robins Nest Ln 78729
Robinsdale Ln 78723
Robinson Ave 78722
Robinson Family Rd 78738
Robinwood Cir 78758
Rochelle Dr 78748
Rochester Ln 78753
Rock Crk 78734
Rock Way 78746
Rock Bluff Dr 78734
Rock Castle Cv 78749
Rock Cliff Ct 78737
Rock Creek Dr 78746
W Rock Hollow Ln 78753
Rock Park Dr 78746
Rock Pigeon Dr 78729
Rock Springs Cv 78729
Rock Terrace Cir & Dr . 78704
Rock Vista Run 78737
Rock Way Cv 78746
Rock Way Dr 78736
Rockberry Cv 78750
Rockbridge Ter 78741
Rockcliff Rd 78746
Rockcrest Cir & Dr 78759
Rockdale Cir 78704
Rocket St 78734
Rockford Ln 78759
Rockgate Dr 78717
Rockhurst Ln 78723
Rockies Run Smt 78738
Rocking Chair Rd 78744
Rocking Horse Rd 78748
Rockingham Cir & Dr ... 78704
Rockland Dr 78748
Rockledge Cv & Dr 78731
Rockmoor Ave 78703
Rockpoint Cir & Dr 78731
Rockridge Ct & Dr 78744
Rockwell Ct & Pl 78726
Rockwood Cir 78736
Rockwood Ln 78757
Rocky Dr 78732
Rocky Bluff Ln 78737
Rocky Coast Dr 78738
Rocky Creek Blvd 78738
Rocky Ford Dr 78749
Rocky Ledge Rd 78746
Rocky Ridge Rd 78734
Rocky River Cv & Rd .. 78746
Rocky Spot Dr 78737
Rocky Spring Rd 78753
Rod Rd 78736
Rodeo Cv & Dr 78727
Roderick Lawson Ln 78754
Rodriguez Rd 78747
Roehampton Dr 78745
Rogers Ave 78722
Rogers Ln 78724
Rogers Ln W 78724
Rogers Rd 78758
Rogge Ln 78723
Rogues Roost Dr 78734
Roller Xing 78728
Rolling Green Dr 78734
Rolling Hill Dr 78758
Rolling Meadow Rd 78749
Rolling Oaks Trl 78750
Rolling Stone Cv 78739
Rollingwood Dr 78746
Rolston Pl 78726
Roma St 78704
Romayne Ln 78748
Romeria Dr 78757
Romford Dr 78704
Romney Rd 78748
Ronwood Dr 78750
Rooney Cv 78739
Roosevelt Ave 78756
Rooster Springs Rd 78737
Rosario Cv 78739
Rose St 78703
Rose Hill Cir 78745
Rose Mallow Way 78748
Rose Pavonia Pl 78728
Roseborough Dr 78747
Rosedale Ave 78756
Rosedale Ter 78704
Rosefinch Trl 78746
Rosemary Ln 78753
Rosemont St 78723
Rosenberry Dr 78747
Rosethorn Dr 78758
Rosetti Dr 78752
Rosewood Ave 78702
Rosita Ct 78748
Rosseau St 78725
Rossello Dr 78729
Rosson Rd 78736
Rotan Dr 78749
Rotherham Dr 78753
Rotunda Vw 78747
Rough Hollow Cv 78734
N & S Round Mountain
Dr 78734
Round Table Cv & Rd .. 78746
Roundtop Cir 78738
Roundup Trl 78745
Rountree Dr 78722
Rountree Ranch Ln 78717
Rowel Dr 78759
Rowena Ave 78751
Rowland Dr 78745
Rowlands Sayle Rd 78744
Rowood Rd 78722
Roxanna Dr 78748
Roxborough St 78729
Roxbury Ln 78739
Roxie Dr 78729
Roxmoor Dr 78723
Roy Butler Dr 78717
Royal Ct 78724
Royal Way 78737
Royal Ashdown Dr 78717
Royal Birkdale
Overlook 78746
Royal Crest Dr 78741
Royal Dublin Dr 78717
Royal Hill Dr 78741
Royal Lytham Dr 78747
Royal New Kent Dr 78717
Royal Oak Cv & Ln 78734
Royal Palms Dr 78744
Royal Tara Cv 78717
Royalwood Dr 78750
Ruby Dr 78753
Ruby Red Dr 78728
Rudder Dr 78738
Ruddington Dr 78748
Rudi Cv 78759
Rue St 78731
Rue De St Germaine ... 78746
Rue De St Raphael 78746
Rue De St Tropez 78746
Rue Le Fleur 78744
Rue St Raphael 78746
Ruel Cv 78717
Ruffed Grouse Dr 78758
Rufus Dr 78752
Rugged Earth Dr 78737
Ruidosa St 78719
Ruiz St 78723
Rum Runner Rd 78734
Rumfeldt St 78725
Run Of The Oaks St ... 78704
E Rundberg Ln 78753
W Rundberg Ln
100-398 78753
801-997 78758
999-2299 78758
2301-2399 78758
Rundell Pl 78704
Runnels Ct 78732
Running Bird Ln 78758
Running Brook Dr 78723
Running Brush Cv &
Ln 78717
Running Buck Ln 78750
Running Deer Dr 78759
Running Deer Trl 78734
Running Fox Trl 78759
Running Rope Cir 78731
Running Water Dr
7300-7499 78744
7500-8099 78747
Running Water Way 78737
Rupen Ct & Dr 78734
Rush Rd 78732
Rush Creek Ln 78732
Rush Pea Cir 78738
Rusk Ct 78723
Ruskin Pass 78717
Russell Dr
4301-4399 78704
4400-4599 78745
Russet Hill Dr 78723
Rust Rd 78750
Rusted Nail Cv 78750
Rustic Cv & Ln 78717
Rustic Manor Ct & Ln .. 78750
Rustic Oak Ln 78748
Rustic River Cv 78746
Rustic Rock Dr 78750
Rustle Ln 78750
Rustling Cir, Cv & Rd .. 78731
Rustling Oaks Trl 78759
Rustown Dr 78727
Rusty Dr 78744
Rusty Fig Dr 78750
Rusty Ridge Dr 78731
Rutgers Ave 78757
Ruth Ave 78757
Rutherford Ln
1000-1198 78753
1301-1399 78753
1601-1697 78754
1699-1799 78754
1801-1899 78754
Rutherford Pl 78704
Rutherglen Dr 78749
E & W Rutland Dr &
Vlg 78758
Rutledge Ln 78745
Rutledge Spur 78717
Rutter Ln 78736
Ruxton Cv & Ln 78749
Ryan Dr 78757
Ryan Matthew Dr 78727
Rydalwater Ln 78754
Ryoaks Cv 78717
Sabal Palm Rd 78724
Saber Trl 78750
Saber Creek Cv & Trl .. 78759
Sabinal Mesa Dr 78739
Sabine St 78701
Sabrina Cv & Dr 78747
Sacahuista Ct 78750
Sacbe Cv 78745
Sacramento Dr 78704
Sacred Arrow Dr 78735
Sacred Moon Cv 78746
Saddle Cir & Dr 78727
Saddle Back Pass 78738
Saddle Mountain Trl 78739
Saddleback Rd 78737
Saddlebrook Trl 78729
Saddlehorn Cv 78748
Saddler Ln 78724
Saddleridge Cv 78759
Saddlestring Trl 78739
Saffron St 78749
Sage Ct 78737
Sage Dr 78759
Sage Creek Loop 78704
Sage Grouse Dr 78729
Sage Hen Cir, Ct, Cv &
Dr 78727
Sage Hollow Cir & Dr .. 78758
Sage Mountain Trl 78736
Sage Oak Cv & Trl 78759
Sagebrush Cir 78745
Sagebrush Dr 78758
Sagebrush Trl 78745
Sager Dr 78741
Saguaro Rd 78744
Sahara Ave 78745
Sahm St 78723
Sailfish St 78734
Sailing Breeze Trl 78744
Sailmaster St 78734
Sailors Run 78734
Saint Albans Blvd 78745
Saint Amant Pl 78749
Saint Andrews Way 78746
Saint Anthony St 78703
Saint Cecelia St 78757
Saint Edwards Cir &
Dr 78704
Saint Elias St 78738
Saint Elmo Cir 78745
E Saint Elmo Rd
101-197 78745
199-799 78745
801-1099 78745
1601-2017 78744
2019-4699 78744
4701-4999 78744
W Saint Elmo Rd 78745
Saint Georges Grn 78745
E Saint Johns Ave 78752
W Saint Johns Ave
100-899 78752
1000-1999 78757
Saint Johns Cir 78757
Saint Joseph Blvd 78757
Saint Louis St 78757
Saint Phillip St 78757
Saint Richie Ln 78737
Saint Stephens Cv &
Dr 78746
Saint Stephens School
Rd S 78746

Sairenne St 78705
Salado St 78705
Salcon Cliff Dr 78749
Salem Ln 78753
Salem Hill Dr 78745
Salem House Way 78753
Salem Meadow Cir 78745
Salem Oak Cv 78748
Salem Park Ct 78745
Salem Walk Dr 78745
Sales St 78757
Salida Dr 78749
Salida Del Sol Pass 78732
Salina St
1-1899 78702
1900-1998 78722
2000-2199 78722
2201-2299 78722
Salinas Cv 78738
Salmon Dr 78749
Saloma Pl 78749
Salt Block Cir 78750
Salt Cedar Trl 78750
Salt Mill Holw 78750
Salt Springs Dr 78744
Saltillo Ct 78734
Salton Dr 78759
Salvia Cv 78759
Sam Carter Dr 78736
Sam Houston Cir 78731
Sam Maverick Pass 78749
Sam Rayburn Dr 78753
Sambuca Cir & Ct 78728
Samsung Blvd 78754
Samuel Bishop Dr 78736
Samuel Huston Ave 78721
San Antonio St
201-297 78701
299-1799 78701
1901-1905 78705
1907-2599 78705
3500-3799 78734
San Augustine Dr 78733
San Benito Ct 78738
San Bernard St 78702
San Carlos Dr 78757
San Diego Rd 78737
San Felipe Blvd 78729
San Gabriel St
1700-1899 78701
1900-2999 78705
San Giovani Ct 78738
San Jacinto Blvd
2-98 78701
100-1800 78701
1802-1898 78701
1923-2107 78712
2109-2199 78712
2201-2303 78712
2500-2598 78705
2801-2999 78705
San Jose St 78753
San Juan Dr 78733
San Juan Pass 78737
San Leanna Dr 78748
San Lucas 78737
San Luis Trl 78733
San Marcos St 78702
San Mateo Ct & Dr 78738
San Miguel Ln 78746
San Paublo Ct 78749
San Pedro St 78705
San Remo Blvd 78734
San Saba St 78702
San Savio Ct 78738
San Simeon Dr 78749
Sanceney Dr 78749
Sanchez St 78702
Sand Dollar Ct & Dr 78728
Sand Dunes Ave 78744
Sand Hill Dr 78744
Sand Hills Ln 78737
Sandalwood Cv 78757
Sandalwood Holw 78731
Sandberg Dr 78752
Sanderling Trl 78746

Sanders Ln 78748
Sanderson Ave 78749
Sandhurst Cir 78723
Sandia Loop 78735
Sandifer St 78725
Sandoval Ct 78732
Sandpiper Ave 78753
Sandpiper Cv 78737
Sandpoint Cv 78717
Sandra St 78745
Sandra Muraida Way 78703
Sandringham Cir 78704
Sandshof Cir & Dr 78724
Sandstone St 78737
Sandstone Trl 78750
Sandust Way 78719
Sandy Acre Ln 78746
Sandy Loam Trl 78750
Sandy Side Dr 78728
Sanford Dr 78748
Sanger Dr 78748
Sangiacomo Cv 78759
Sanostee Cv 78733
Sans Souci Cv & Pl 78759
Sansivera Cv 78750
Sansom Rd 78754
Santa Anna St 78721
Santa Clara St 78757
Santa Cruz Dr 78759
Santa Fe Dr 78741
Santa Maria St 78702
Santa Monica Dr 78741
Santa Rita St 78702
Santa Rosa St 78702
Santaluz Ln & Path 78732
Santee Dr 78738
Santiago St 78745
Santolina Cv 78731
Santos St 78741
Sapling Cv 78735
Sapote Ct 78744
Sara Dr 78721
Saracen Rd 78733
Sarah Ct 78757
Sarah Ann Dr 78725
Sarah Christine Ln 78717
Saralee Trl 78729
Sarasota Dr 78749
Saratoga Cv 78746
Saratoga Dr 78733
Sarducci Ln 78748
Sarong Way 78748
Saskatchewan Dr 78734
Sasparilla Cv 78748
Sassman Rd 78747
Satchel Dr 78754
Satellite Rd 78758
Saticoy Dr 78724
Satsuma Cv 78759
Saucedo St 78721
Saugus Ln 78733
Sauls Dr 78728
Saunders Ln 78758
Sausalito Dr 78759
Sautelle Ln 78749
Savage Springs Dr 78754
Savannah Ct 78739
Savannah Heights Dr 78717
Savannah Ridge Dr 78726
Saville Loop 78741
Savin Hill Ct & Ln 78739
Savorey Ln 78744
Savoy Ct 78738
Savoy Pl 78757
Sawatch Cir 78726
Sawdust Ct 78732
Sawgrass Cv 78746
Sawmill Dr 78749
Sawtooth Ln 78729
Sawyer Fay Ln 78748
Sawyer Ranch Rd 78737
Saxby Ct 78729
Saxon Ln 78741
Saxony Ln 78727
Sayan Cv 78738
Scales St 78723

Scamper Cv 78734
Scarlet Cir 78737
Scarlet Rdg 78737
Scarlet St 78728
Scarsdale Dr 78744
Scates Ct 78732
Scenic Cv 78739
Scenic Dr 78703
Scenic Bluff Dr 78733
Scenic Brook Dr 78736
Scenic Hills Dr 78703
Scenic Oaks Cir 78745
Scenic Oaks Dr 78737
Scenic Overlook Trl 78734
Scenic Ridge Cv 78735
Scenic View Dr 78746
Sceptre Cv 78727
Scheider Dr 78754
Schick Rd 78729
Schieffer Ave 78722
Schirra Pl 78753
Schleicher Trl 78732
School House Ct & Ln 78750
Schooner Cv 78734
Schooner Dr 78738
Schreiner Ct 78732
Schriber Rd 78719
Schriber St 78704
Schug Cv 78759
Schulle Ave 78703
Scioto Ct 78747
Scissortail Dr 78750
Scofield Ln 78727
Scofield Farms Dr
12400-12499 78758
12600-13099 78727
Scofield Ridge Pkwy 78727
Scorpion Dr 78734
Scotia Bluff Loop 78748
Scotland Well Cv & Dr 78750
Scotland Yard 78759
Scotsman Dr 78750
Scott Cres 78703
Scott Dr 78734
Scott Ln 78734
Scottish Pastures Cv &
Dr 78750
Scottish Thistle Dr 78739
Scottish Woods Cv &
Trl 78746
Scottsdale Rd 78721
Scout Blf 78731
N & S Scout Island Cir &
Cv 78731
Scribe Dr 78759
Scrub Oak Ln 78759
Scull Creek Dr 78730
Scurry St 78753
Sea Eagle Cv & Vw 78738
Sea Hero Ct & Ln 78748
Sea Jay Dr 78745
Seashell 78734
Seawind 78734
Seay St 78754
Sebastapol Cv 78726
Sebastians Run 78738
Sebrite Dr 78726
Secluded Holw 78727
Secrest Dr 78759
Secretariat Dr 78737
Secure Ln 78725
Sedgefield Dr 78746
Sedgemoor Trl 78748
Sedona Dr 78759
Seeling Dr 78744
Seiders Ave 78756
Seldalia Trl 78732
Selma Dr 78758
Selma Hughes Park
Rd 78732
Selway Dr 78736
Seminary Ridge Dr 78745
Seminole Dr 78745
Senda Ln 78725
Sendera Bonita 78734
Sendera Mesa Dr 78749

Sendero Dr 78735
Sendero Hills Pkwy 78724
Seneca Cir 78736
Seneca Falls Ln &
Loop 78739
Senecio Cv 78759
Senia 78738
Senna Hills Dr 78733
Senora Creek Ct 78735
Sentenal Dr 78748
Sentinel Hl 78737
September Dr 78753
Sequoia Dr 78758
Serafy Ct 78753
Serena Cv 78730
Serena Woods Ct 78759
Serene Hills Ct, Dr &
Pass 78738
Serene Hilltop Cir 78738
Serenity Ct 78737
Serrano Trl 78734
Service Ave 78719
Sesbania Dr 78748
Seton Ave 78705
Seton Center Pkwy 78759
Settlers Trl 78750
Sevan Cv 78731
Seven Oaks Cv 78759
Seven Wins Ct & Dr 78733
Sevilla Dr 78752
Seville Dr 78724
Shackelford Dr 78748
Shade Tree Cv 78759
Shade Tree Dr 78748
Shaded Cottage Ct 78744
Shadestone Ter 78732
Shadow Bnd 78745
Shadow Ln 78731
Shadow Bend Cv 78745
Shadow Hill Dr 78731
Shadow Mountain Cv &
Dr 78731
Shadow Oak Ln 78746
Shadow Valley Cv &
Dr 78731
Shadowood Dr 78757
Shadowridge Run 78749
Shadowview Dr 78758
Shady Ln
100-999 78702
1100-1199 78721
15300-15499 78717
Shady Cedar Dr 78744
Shady Creek Cv 78746
Shady Glade Ct 78756
Shady Hollow Dr 78748
Shady Oak Ct 78756
Shady Oaks Dr & Ter 78729
Shady Park Dr 78723
Shady Springs Rd 78758
Shady Valley Dr
3300-3499 78748
3500-3799 78739
Shadybrook Cv 78746
Shadyrock Dr 78731
Shadyview Dr 78758
Shadywood Dr 78745
Shag Bark Trl 78758
Shaker Trl 78754
Shakespearean Way 78759
Shale St 78749
Shallot Way 78748
Shallow Stream Cv 78735
Shallow Water Cv &
Rd 78717
Shallowbrook Trl 78744
Shallowford Dr 78736
Shane Landon Ct 78738
Shanghai Pierce Rd 78749
Shannon Dr 78724
Shannon Oaks Trl 78746
Shant St 78748
Shantivana Trl 78737
Sharl Cv 78737
Sharon Ln 78703
Sharper Mews Ln 78741

Sharps Rd 78734
Sharpshinned Hawk
Cv 78738
Sharpstone Trl 78717
Shasta Cv 78759
Shasta Ln 78729
Shattuck Cv 78717
Shavano Cv & Dr 78749
Shaw Ln 78744
Shawn Lee Cv 78753
Shawna Dnay Dr 78727
Shawnee Cir 78734
Sheba Cv 78759
Sheffield Dr 78745
Shelbourne Dr 78752
Shelby Ln 78745
Shelby Oak Ln 78748
Shelf Lake Ln 78724
Shelley Ave 78703
Shelter Cv 78730
Shelton Rd 78725
Shemya Cv 78729
Shenandoah Dr 78753
Shep St 78748
Shepard Dr 78753
Shepherd Mountain Cv 78730
Sheraton Ave 78745
Sherbourne St 78729
Sherbrooke St 78729
Sheri Oak Ln 78748
Sheridan Ave 78723
Sheriff Ct 78748
Sherman Ct 78734
Sherman Rd 78742
Sherry Lee Cv 78753
Sherwood Frst 78759
Sherwood Ln 78704
Sherwood Rd 78745
Sherwyn Dr 78725
Shetland Chase 78727
N Shields Dr 78727
Shier Cv 78745
Shiloh Ct & Dr 78745
Shimmering Cv 78731
Shiner St 78729
Shinnecock Hills Dr 78747
Shinoak Dr 78731
Shiny Rock Dr 78748
Shire Ridge Dr 78732
Shirley Ave 78752
Shively 78747
Shoal Cliff Ct 78705
Shoal Creek Blvd
1101-1699 78701
2300-2399 78705
2401-3299 78705
3900-5599 78756
5601-5699 78756
5700-8999 78757
Shoal Creek Dr W 78757
Shoal Crest Ave 78705
Shoal Edge Ct 78756
Shoalmont Dr 78756
Shoalwood Ave
4200-5899 78756
5900-6199 78757
6201-6299 78757
Shoot Out Ct 78748
Shops Pkwy 78738
Shore District Dr 78741
Shore Oaks Ct 78738
Shore Vista Cv & Dr 78732
Shoreline Dr
1300-1399 78741
3000-3599 78728
Shoreview Cv 78732
Shoreview Overlook 78732
Short Hackberry St 78702
Short Kemp St 78741
Short Springs Dr 78754
Short Summer Dr 78754
Shoshone Dr 78759
Shoshoni Trl 78737
Shotgun Ln 78748
Show Barn Cv 78750
Show Low Ct 78734

Showboat Cv 78730
Showdown Ln 78717
Shreveport Dr 78727
Shropshire Blvd 78753
Shuberg St 78721
Shumard Cir 78759
Shumard Oak Trl 78735
E Side Cv & Dr 78704
Side Oak Dr 78738
Side Oats Dr 78738
Side Saddle St 78745
Sidehill Path 78731
Sidereal Dr 78727
Siepel Dr 78724
Sierra Dr 78731
Sierra Arbor Ct 78759
Sierra Blanca St 78726
Sierra Colorado 78759
Sierra Grande Dr 78759
Sierra Leon 78759
Sierra Madre 78759
Sierra Montana 78759
Sierra Nevada 78759
Sierra Oaks 78759
Sierra Ridge Ct 78739
Sierra Tahoe 78759
Sierra Verde Trl 78759
Signal Pt 78724
Signal Hill Dr, Rd &
Vw 78737
Sika Way 78749
Silbury Dr 78758
Silcantu Dr 78748
Silent Trl 78746
Silk Oak Cv & Dr 78748
Silkgrass Bnd 78748
Silktail Cv 78730
Silkwood Cv 78739
Silmarillion Trl 78739
Silo Valley Dr 78754
Silver Cir 78734
Silver Spur 78727
Silver Charm 78737
Silver Creek Dr 78727
Silver Dale Cir & Dr 78736
Silver Dollar Cir 78744
Silver Hill Cir & Dr 78746
Silver Lake Ct 78732
Silver Mountain Cv &
Dr 78737
Silver Pine Cv 78733
Silver Quail Ln 78758
Silver Ridge Dr 78759
Silver Screen Dr 78747
Silver Wing Ct 78725
Silverado Cir 78746
Silverarrow Cir & Ct 78759
Silvercrest Cir & Dr 78757
Silverhill Cv & Ln 78759
Silverleaf Cir & Dr 78757
Silvermine Dr 78736
Silverplume Cir 78757
Silverspring Dr 78759
Silverstone Dr 78744
Silverton Ct 78753
Silverway Dr 78757
Silverwood Ct 78759
Simmons Rd 78759
Simon Pl 78759
Simond Ave 78723
Simonetti Dr 78748
Simpson Ln 78747
Sinclair Ave 78756
Singing Brk 78723
Singing Quail Dr 78758
Single Trce 78728
Single Oak Cv 78746
Single Shot Cir 78723
Single Trace Ct 78728
Singlefoot Ln 78744
Singleton Ave 78702
Singletree Ave 78727
Sinton Ln 78729
Sioux Ln 78734
N Sioux Trl 78729
S Sioux Trl 78729

Sir Christophers Cv 78729
Sir Gawain Dr 78745
Sir Ivor Cv 78746
Sir Thopas Trl 78748
Siringo Pass 78749
Sirius Cv 78732
Sirocco Dr 78745
Siskin Cv & Dr 78745
Sissinghurst Dr 78745
Sitio Del Rio Blvd 78730
Six Gun Trl 78748
Skahan Ln 78739
Ski Shores Ter 78730
Ski Slope Dr 78733
Skinner Cv 78759
Skipton Dr 78727
Sky Mountain Dr 78735
Sky Rock Dr 78739
Sky West Dr 78758
Skycrest Dr 78745
Skye Cv 78750
Skyflower Cv & Dr 78759
Skylark Dr 78757
Skyline Dr
100-499 78746
13800-14099 78732
Skyloop Dr 78745
Skynook Dr 78745
E & W Skyview Rd 78752
Skyway Cir 78704
Sl Davis Ave 78702
Slant Oak Dr 78729
Slate Creek Ct & Trl 78717
Slaughter Ln W
7400-7499 78739
E Slaughter Ln
301-797 78744
799-800 78744
802-898 78744
1101-1699 78747
W Slaughter Ln
100-3499 78748
3500-3598 78749
3600-7499 78749
Slaughter Creek Dr 78748
Slayton Dr 78753
Sledge Dr 78734
Sleepy Hollow Rd 78736
Slickrock Cv 78747
Slidell Ct 78727
Slingshot Rd 78717
Slippery Elm Trl 78750
Slow Poke Dr 78727
Slow Turtle Cv 78746
Sly Pass 78748
Sly Beaver Dr 78754
Small Dr 78731
Smith Rd 78721
Smith Oak Trl 78749
Smith School Rd 78744
Smoketree Cv 78735
Smokey Vly 78731
Smokey Hill Rd 78736
Smokey Mountain Dr 78727
Smoky Rdg 78730
Smooth Oak Dr 78759
Snake Eagle Cv 78738
Snapdragon Dr 78739
Snapper 78734
Sneed Cv 78744
Snipe Ct 78734
Snook Hook Trl 78729
Snow Finch Rd 78758
Snow Goose Rd 78758
Snowbird Pass 78749
Snowden Cv 78729
Snowdonia Cv 78738
Snowfall 78727
Snowmass Cv 78749
Snowmass Hts 78738
Snowy Owl Ct 78746
Soaring Eagle 78746
Socorro Cir 78739
Socorro Dr 78734
Socorro Trl 78739
Soft Cloud Cv 78717

Soft Wind Cir 78745
Softwood Dr 78744
Soho Dr 78748
Sojourner St 78725
Sol Wilson Ave 78702
Solana Vista Loop 78750
Solano Dr 78750
Soledad Ct 78732
Soleil Ct 78734
Solera Dr 78717
Solis Pl 78747
Solitary Fawn Trl 78735
Sombra Cv 78744
Sombrero Dr 78748
Somerset Ave 78753
Sommerland Way 78749
Songbird Cv 78750
Sonnet Ave 78759
Sonoma Cv & Dr 78738
Sonora Ct 78756
Sonora Cv 78759
Sooner St 78734
Sophie Dr 78734
Sophora Cv 78759
Sordello Dr 78752
Sorghum Hill Cv & Dr 78754
Sorrel Cv 78730
Sorrento Ct 78759
Sorret Tree Ct 78744
Soter Pkwy 78735
Sotol Cv 78759
Southcrest Dr 78746
Southeast Dr 78744
Southern Cross Dr 78717
Southern Hills Pl 78746
Southern Oaks Dr 78745
Southgate Cir 78704
Southgate Ln 78744
Southhill Cir 78703
Southland Dr 78704
Southport Dr 78704
Southridge Dr 78704
Southview St 78745
Southview Hills Cv 78719
Southward Cv 78733
Southway Dr 78704
Southwest Dr 78744
Southwest Pkwy 78735
Southwick Dr 78724
Southwind Dr 78745
Southwood Rd 78704
Sovran Ln 78750
Space Ln 78758
Spancreek Cir 78731
Spandera Cv 78759
Spaniel Dr 78759
Spanish Bay Cv 78732
Spanish Camp Cv 78725
Spanish Oak Cir 78737
Spanish Oak Dr 78731
Spanish Oak Ter 78731
Spanish Oak Trl 78731
Spanish Oaks Club Blvd & Dr 78738
Spanish Wells Dr 78717
Sparkling Brook Ln 78746
Sparkling Creek Cir & Dr 78729
Sparks Ave 78705
Sparrow Ln 78734
Sparrowglen Ln 78738
Sparta Ln 78729
Spartan Cv 78759
Spartanburg Cv 78730
Spear Oak Cv 78759
Spearhead Cv 78717
Spearman Dr 78757
Spearson Ln 78745
Spectrum Dr 78717
Speedway
1900-2098 78712
Speedway
2100-2511 78712
2513-2799 78712
3000-3799 78705
3800-4299 78751
4300-4300 78705
4300-4300 78765
4301-4699 78751
4302-4698 78751
Speer Ln 78745
Spellbrook Ln 78734
Spence St 78702
Speyside Dr 78754
Spice Berry Cv 78728
Spicebrush Cv & Dr 78759
Spiceland Cir 78724
Spicewood Ln 78759
Spicewood Pkwy 78750
Spicewood Club Dr 78750
Spicewood Mesa Cv 78759
Spicewood Springs Cv & Rd 78759
Spiderling Ct 78733
Spiller Ln 78746
Spillman St 78704
Spillman Ranch Loop 78738
Spillway Dr 78729
Spinnaker Cv 78731
Spinning Leaf Cv 78735
Spirea Cv 78749
Spirit Lake Cv 78746
Spirit Of Texas Dr 78719
Spivey Dr 78749
Splendor Pass 78738
Split Cedar Cv 78735
Split Oak Cir 78759
Split Rail Cv 78750
Split Rail Pkwy 78750
Split Rail Trl 78746
Split Rock Trl
3300-3399 78748
3400-3499 78739
Split Stone Way 78739
Splitarrow Dr 78717
Spofford St 78704
Spoke Ct 78744
Spotted Fawn Cir 78733
Spotted Horse Dr 78759
Spotted Horse Trl
3300-3399 78748
3400-3699 78739
Spotted Oak Cv 78759
Spotted Wolf Trl 78734
Sprague Ln 78746
Spring Cir
2900-2999 78723
10200-10300 78736
10302-10398 78736
W Spring Dr 78746
Spring Ln
2400-2499 78703
2418-2418 78763
2500-2698 78703
2501-2699 78703
Spring Branch Trl 78734
Spring Creek Dr 78704
Spring Fever Trl 78744
Spring Garden Rd 78746
Spring Hill Dr 78753
Spring Hollow Dr 78750
Spring Lake Dr 78750
Spring Meadow Cv & Rd 78744
Spring Valley Dr 78736
Spring Valley Rd 78737
Spring Wagon Ln 78728
Springdale Rd
100-198 78702
200-999 78702
1000-1899 78721
4301-4597 78723
4599-6500 78723
6502-6598 78723
7700-7898 78724
7900-8299 78724
8301-8399 78724
8501-8697 78754
8699-9500 78754
9502-10498 78754
Springer Ln 78758
Springmail Cir 78729
Springs Edge Dr 78717
Springs Head Loop 78717
Springtime Trl
7400-7499 78744
7500-7599 78747
Springvale Dr 78729
Springville Ln 78744
Springwater Cir 78753
Springwood Dr 78750
Sprinkle Rd 78754
Sprinkle Cutoff Rd 78754
Spruce Cv & Ln 78744
Spruce Gum Ln 78744
Spruceleaf Cir 78757
Sprucewood Cv & Dr 78731
Spur St 78721
Spurflower Cv & Dr 78759
Spurlock Dr 78731
Spurlock Vly 78746
Spyglass Cv 78737
Spyglass Dr 78746
Squaw Valley Ln 78717
Squires Dr 78734
Squirrel Holw 78748
Squirrel Oak Cir 78749
St Lucia 78734
St Stanislaws Dr 78748
Stacy Ln 78704
Stafford St 78722
Staffordshire Ln 78717
Stage Coach Trl 78745
Stage Stop Cir 78738
Staggerbrush Rd 78749
Staghorn Cv 78759
Stahl Cv 78731
Staked Plains Dr & Loop 78717
Stallion Dr 78733
Stambourne St 78747
Stamford Ln 78703
Standfield Ct 78732
Standing Oaks Ln 78746
Standing Rock Dr 78730
Standish Dr 78745
Stanley Ave 78745
Stanwich Dr 78717
Stanwood Dr 78757
Stanzel Dr 78729
Stapp Ct 78732
Star Dr 78745
Star St 78734
Star Grass Cir 78745
Star Light Ter 78721
Star View Trl 78750
Starboard Ct 78717
Starbright Dr 78745
Starcrest Ln 78724
Stardust Dr 78757
Stark St 78756
Starline Dr 78759
E & W Starling Dr 78753
Starstreak Dr 78745
E Stassney Ln
500-699 78745
701-799 78745
1800-1898 78744
1900-5299 78744
5301-6399 78744
W Stassney Ln 78745
State Highway 130 S 78747
N State Highway 130 78724
S State Highway 130 Serivce Nb Rd 78719
State Highway 45 78739
Staton Dr 78727
Staunton Dr 78758
Stave Oak Ln 78724
Steamboat Dr 78749
Steamboat Springs Cv 78746
Steamline Cir 78745
Stearns Ln 78735
Steck Ave
2500-3400 78757
3402-3498 78757
3601-3697 78759
3699-3899 78759
3901-4199 78759
Steed Dr 78749
Steele Run 78749
Steeple Chase Dr 78729
Steer Trl 78749
Stegner Ln 78746
Steiner Ranch Blvd 78732
Stellar Cv 78739
Stepdown Cv 78731
Stephanie Ln 78738
Stephanie Lee Ln 78753
Stephanie St John St 78727
Stephanne Creek Cv 78744
Stephany Taylor Dr 78745
Stepping Stone Cv 78727
Sterling Panorama Ct & Ter 78738
Sterlinghill Dr 78758
Sterzing St 78704
Steve Scarbrough Dr 78759
Steven Creek Way 78721
Stevens Cv 78723
Stevenson Ave 78703
Stewart Cv & Rd 78734
Stiles Cv 78721
Stillforest St 78729
Stillmeadow Ct & Dr 78738
Stillwater Ln 78729
Stillwood Ln 78757
Stobaugh St 78757
Stock Dr 78741
Stock Tank Cv 78717
Stokes Dr 78702
Stone Pass 78745
Stone Canyon Dr 78746
Stone Gate Cir & Dr 78721
Stone Ledge Cir 78736
Stone Ridge Cir 78746
Stone Ridge Dr 78734
Stone River Dr
100-399 78737
2100-2499 78745
Stone Shadow Cv 78734
Stone Terrace Dr 78734
Stone View Trl 78737
Stonebridge Dr 78758
Stonecliff Cir, Cv & Dr 78731
Stonecroft Dr 78749
Stonehaven Cir 78731
Stonehollow Dr 78758
Stonelake Blvd 78759
Stoneoak Ln 78745
Stoneridge Rd & Ter 78746
Stonethrow Dr 78748
Stonewall Ln 78746
Stonewall Ridge Ln 78746
Stoneway Dr 78757
Stoney Creek Cv 78734
Stoney Point Rd 78737
Stoneywood Dr 78731
Stonleigh Pl 78744
Stony Dr 78759
Stony Meadow Ln 78731
Storm Dr 78734
Stormy Ridge Rd 78739
Stout Oak Trl 78750
Stoutwood Cir 78745
Stowaway Cv 78734
Strader Cir 78734
Strand St 78748
Strandtman Cv 78702
Strass Dr 78731
Stratford Dr 78746
Stratford Hills Ln 78746
Stratford Reserve Pl 78746
Strathern Dr 78724
Stratton Ct 78737
Straw Flower Dr 78733
Strawberry Cv 78745
Streamside Dr 78736
Strickland Dr 78748
Strobel Ln 78748
Stroup Cir 78734
Struie Ln 78749
Strutton Cv 78759
Stuart Cir & Ct 78721
Stubble Quail Cir & Dr 78758
Sturgis Ln 78748
Sturmer St 78747
Suburban Dr 78745
Sudbury Cv 78748
Sue Ann Rose Dr 78717
Suena Dr 78741
Suffolk Dr 78723
Sugar Creek Dr 78746
Sugar Hill Dr 78748
Sugar Leaf Pl 78748
Sugar Maple Ct 78744
Sugar Shack Dr 78746
Sugarberry Ln 78748
Sugaree Ave 78757
Sugarloaf Dr 78738
Sully Creek Dr 78748
Sumac Dr 78731
Summer Cir & Dr 78741
Summer Alcove Way 78732
Summer Canyon Dr 78732
Summer Creek Ct & Dr 78704
Summer Oak Dr 78704
Summer Place Dr 78759
Summer Side Dr 78759
Summer Sky Dr 78736
Summer Stone Dr 78704
Summer Tree Ct 78759
Summer Wind Cir 78744
Summerhill Cv 78759
Summerset Trl 78749
Summersweet Cv 78729
Summervale Dr 78737
Summerwood Dr 78759
Summit Bnd 78759
Summit Dr 78728
Summit Pass 78737
Summit St 78741
Summit Edge Dr 78732
Summit View Pl 78703
Summoners Tale Ct 78748
Sumner Ct 78733
Sun Bird Ln 78734
Sun Drenched Path 78732
Sun Hill Dr 78758
Sun Shower Bnd 78724
Sun Spirit Dr 78735
Sun Tree Cv 78730
Sun Valley Ct 78734
Sun Vista Dr 78749
Sunbonnet Cv 78719
Sundara Dr 78739
Sunderland Dr 78753
Sunderland Trl 78747
Sundial Cv 78748
Sundown Dr 78738
Sundown Pkwy 78746
Sundown Rdg 78737
Sundown Trl 78739
Sunfish St 78734
Sunflower Dr 78719
Sunflower Trl 78745
Sungate Dr 78731
Sunhillow Bnd 78758
Sunkist Ln 78749
Sunland Dr 78748
Sunningdale Cv & St 78717
Sunny Ln
500-599 78704
3200-3299 78731
Sunny Brook Dr 78723
Sunny Hills Dr 78744
Sunny Slope Dr 78703
Sunny Vista Dr 78749
Sunnylawn Cir 78723
Sunnysky Way 78745
Sunnyvale St 78741
Sunridge Ct & Dr 78741
Sunrise Cir 78704
Sunrise Ridge Cv & Loop 78738
Sunset Cir 78704
Sunset Dr 78748
Sunset Ln 78704
Sunset Rdg 78735
Sunset Trl 78745
Sunset Vw 78704
Sunset Heights Cir 78735
Sunset Park Cv 78734
Sunshine Dr
4800-5298 78756
5300-5699 78756
5900-5999 78757
Sunstrip Dr 78745
Sunterro 78727
Sunview Rd 78738
Surrender Ave 78728
Surrey Dr 78745
Surrey Hill Dr 78746
Susan Dr 78734
Susie Ct 78757
Susie St 78748
Susquehanna Ln 78723
Sussex Dr 78745
Sussex Gardens Ln 78748
Sussman Ct 78728
Suter St 78748
Sutherlin Rd 78723
Sutter Creek Trl 78717
Sutterville Cv 78717
Sutton Dr 78734
Swallow Ct 78758
Swallow Dr 78750
Swallow Tailed Kite 78738
Swallowtail Dr 78737
Swan Dr 78750
Swan Valley Ln 78759
Swanee Dr 78752
Swanson Cv & Ln 78748
Swansons Ranch Rd 78748
Swearingen Dr 78758
Sweeney Cir & Ln 78723
Sweet Autumn Cv 78735
Sweet Basil Ct 78726
Sweet Cherry Dr 78750
Sweet Clover Dr 78745
Sweet Grass Ln 78738
Sweet Gum Cv 78735
Sweetbriar Ave 78723
Sweetbrush Dr 78703
Sweetgum Ct & Dr 78748
Sweetness Ln 78750
Sweetshade Ln 78759
Sweetwater Cv & Trl 78750
Sweetwater River Cv & Dr 78748
Sweetwood Trl 78737
Swelfling Ter 78737
Swenson Ave 78702
Swift Current Rd 78746
Swiftwater Trl 78738
Swindon Ln 78745
Swinley Forest Cv 78717
Swirling Wind Cv 78735
Swisher St 78705
Swiss Alps Ct 78738
Switch Willo 78727
Switchgrass Cv 78750
Sycamore Dr 78722
Sycamore Hills Rd 78717
Sydney Dr 78728
Sydney Marilyn Ln 78748
Sylvan Dr 78741
Sylvan Glade 78745
Sylvandale Dr 78745
Syracuse Cv 78723
Syrah Cir 78738
T Bar Trl 78759
Table Top Trl 78744
Tablerock Dr 78731
Tabor Ct 78748
Tabor Oaks Dr 78739
Taebaek Dr 78754
Taffy Ct 78704
Tahoe Trl 78745
Tahoe Parke Cir 78726
Tahoma Pl 78759
Talbot Cv & Ln 78746
Taline Cir 78748
Tall Oak Trl 78750
Tall Oaks Trl 78737
Tall Sky Trce 78724
Tall Withers Cv 78754
Talleyran Cv & Dr 78750
Tallison Ter 78704
Tallow Ct 78744
Tallow Field Way 78758
Tallow Tree Dr 78744
Tallowood Dr 78731
Tallstar Dr 78734
Tallwood Dr 78759
Tallyho Trl 78729
Taloga Ct 78749
Talyne Chaise Cir 78729
Tam Ct 78754
Tamango Way 78749
Tamar Ct & Ln 78727
Tamarac Ct 78734
Tamarack Trl 78727
Tamarisk Cir 78744
Tamarisk Cv 78747
Tamarron Blvd 78746
Tamayo Dr 78729
Tambre Bnd 78738
Tamil St 78749
Tampa Cv 78723
Tamranae Ct 78746
Tamworth Ave 78745
Tanager Cir 78737
Tanak Cv & Ln 78749
Tanaqua Cv & Ln 78739
Tanbark Cv 78759
Tandem Blvd 78728
Tanglebriar Cv & Trl 78750
Tangleridge Cir 78736
Tanglevine Dr 78748
Tanglewild Dr 78758
Tanglewood Trl 78703
Tannehill Ln
4000-4600 78721
4602-4698 78721
4800-4998 78723
Tanney St 78721
Tantallon Ct 78734
Tantara Ct & Dr 78729
Tantivy Dr 78729
Tanya Trl 78726
Taos Blvd 78745
Tapadera Trace Ln 78727
Tapadero Ct & Dr 78727
Tapo Ln 78724
Tara Dr
6100-6399 78744
6400-6799 78747
Tara Ln 78737
Taranto Dr 78729
Targa Ct 78749
Tarlton Cv & Ln 78746
Tarragona Ln 78727
Tarraza Ct 78732
Tarry Trl 78703
Tarryhill Pl 78703
Tarryhollow Dr 78703
Tartan Ln 78753
Tartan St 78734
Tartar Way 78733
Tasajillo Cv & Trl 78739
Taterwood Dr 78750
Tattershall Ln 78727
Taulbee Ln 78757
Taurus Walk 78738
Tavares Cv 78733
Tavia Cv 78733
Tavish Trl 78738
Tavistock Dr 78748
Tawny Cir & Dr 78745
Tawny Farms Rd 78748
Tay Ter 78754
Taylor Rd 78733
Taylor St 78702
Taylor Draper Cv & Ln 78759
Taylor Gaines St 78741
Taylor Ranch Rd 78717
Taylor Simonetti Ave 78728
Taylorcrest Cv & Dr 78749
Taylors Dr 78703
Taza Trl 78724
Tea Rose Trl 78748

Teaberry Cir & Dr 78745
Teagle Dr 78741
Teague Trl 78729
Teak Cv 78750
Teak Hawk Cv 78746
Teakwood Dr 78757
Teal 78734
Tealwood Trl 78731
Teasdale Ter 78753
Tecate Trl 78739
Tech Ridge Blvd 78753
Techni Center Dr 78721
Technology Blvd 78727
Teck Cir 78734
Tecumseh Dr 78753
Tedford St 78753
Tee Dr
7800-8099 78747
9400-9499 78750
Tehama Ct 78738
Tejas Trl 78745
Tejon Cir 78734
Tekoa Cv N & S 78746
Tello Path 78749
Telluride Trl 78749
Tellus St 78734
Temecula Pass 78717
Temple Dr 78721
Templemore Cv 78717
Tempranillo Way 78738
Ten Oaks Cir 78744
Tenava Ct 78726
Tenison Ct 78731
Tennison Hill Dr 78738
Tensley Trl 78748
Teresina Dr 78749
Teri Rd 78744
Terisu Cv & Ln 78728
Terjo Ln 78732
Tern Cir 78744
Terra Nova Ln 78727
Terra Oak Cir 78749
Terra Verde Dr 78717
Terrace Ct 78737
Terrace Dr
300-599 78704
16200-16599 78728
W Terrace Dr 78757
Terrace Bluff Dr 78754
Terrace Mountain Cv & Dr 78746
Terrace Parke Trl 78750
Terrain Ln 78731
Terranova Cv 78739
Terrapin Ct 78746
Terravista Dr 78735
Terraza Cir 78726
Terrell Hill Dr 78704
Terrilance Dr 78741
Terrina St 78759
Terry Dr 78721
Terry O Ln 78745
Tesoro Trl 78729
Tetbury Cv & Ln 78748
Tether Trl 78704
Teton Dr 78757
Teton Ridge Cv 78727
Tetons Ct 78738
Texas Ave 78705
Texas St 78734
Texas Trl 78737
Texas Oaks Cv & Dr 78748
Texas Plume Rd 78759
Texas Sage Ct 78732
Texas Star Ln 78746
Texas Sun Dr 78748
Texas Topaz Dr 78728
Texas Wildlife Trl 78735
Teya Ct 78749
Thackery Ct 78734
Thaddeus Cv 78746
Thames Cir & Dr 78723
Thannas Way 78744
Thatcher Dr 78717
Thaxton Rd
7800-7898 78744
7900-11399 78747
The Cir 78704
The High Rd 78746
The Hills Dr 78738
The Living End 78746
Theckla Ter 78756
Thelma Dr 78745
Theo Dr 78723
Theodora Cv 78753
Theresa Ave 78703
Theresa Blanchard Ln 78748
Theriot Trl 78727
Thermal Dr 78728
Thicket Trl 78750
Thickwoods 78735
Thinleaf Cv 78759
Thirlmare Ct 78754
Thistle Ct & Rdg 78733
Thistle Hill Way 78754
Thistle Moss Cv 78739
Thistlewood Dr 78745
Thomas Dr 78703
Thomas St 78732
Thomas Kincheon St 78745
Thomas Sinclair Blvd 78728
Thomas Springs Rd 78736
Thomaswood Ln 78736
Thompkins Dr 78753
Thompson Ln 78742
Thompson St 78702
Thoreau Ln 78746
Thoriv Dr 78725
Thorncliffe Dr 78731
Thornridge Rd 78758
Thornton Rd 78704
Thornwild Pass 78758
Thornwood Ct & Dr 78744
Thorny Brook Trl 78750
Thoroughbred Dr 78748
Thousand Oaks Cir, Cv & Dr 78746
Thrasher Ln 78741
Threadgill St 78723
Three Oaks Cir & Trl 78759
Three Points Rd 78728
Three Rivers Dr 78746
Thrush Ave 78753
Thrushwood Dr 78757
Thunder Trl 78734
Thunder Creek Rd 78759
Thunderbird Cv & Rd 78736
Thundercloud Cv 78717
Thunderhead Rd 78734
Thurgood Ave & Cir 78721
Thurmond St 78758
Thyone Dr 78725
Tibee Dr 78726
Tiber Cir 78733
Tiburon Ct & Dr 78738
Ti[illegible]ester Ct 78729
Tideland Cv 78730
Tidewater Cv 78717
Tierra Dr 78727
Tierra Grande Ct & Trl 78732
Tierra Linda Ln 78739
Tiffany Dr 78749
Tiffany Trl 78719
Tiffer Ln 78728
Tiger Eye Cv 78749
Tiger Lily Way 78739
Tilbury Ln 78745
Tilder Dr 78729
Tilghman Trl 78729
Tillerfield 78748
Tillery Sq 78702
Tillery St
101-497 78702
499-1199 78702
1300-1798 78721
1900-2299 78723
Tillotson Ave 78702
Timarou Ter 78754
Timber Trl 78731
Timber Brush Trl 78741
Timber Heights Dr 78754
Timber Ridge Cv 78733
Timber Ridge Dr 78741
Timber Ridge Pass 78733
Timber Ridge Rd 78741
Timber Wolf Cir & Trl 78727
Timbercrest Ln 78750
Timberline Dr 78746
Timberline Rdg 78746
Timberline Trl 78737
Timberside Dr 78727
Timberwood Cir 78703
Timberwood Dr 78741
Timbrook Trl 78750
Timothy Cir 78734
Timpanagos Dr 78734
Timson Ct 78731
Tin Can Dr 78754
Tin Cup Dr 78750
Tina Ct 78758
Tiner Trl 78724
Tinita Ct 78739
Tinmouth St 78748
Tinnin Ford Rd 78741
Tiombe Bnd 78749
Tip Cv 78704
Tipperary Cv 78759
Tipton Dr 78723
Tirado St 78752
Tisdale Dr 78757
Tishomingo Trl 78734
Titian Dr 78758
Titus Ct 78732
Tobago Cv 78749
Tobler Trl 78753
Tobrina Ln 78759
Tockington Way 78748
Todd Ln 78744
Toledo Dr 78759
Tollesboro Cv 78739
Tom Adams Dr 78753
Tom Green St 78705
Tom Kite Cir 78746
Tom Miller St 78723
Tom Sassman Rd 78747
Tom Wooten Cv & Dr 78731
Tomah Dr 78717
Tomahawk Trl 78745
Tomanet Trl
12300-12400 78758
12402-12498 78758
12500-12899 78727
12901-12999 78727
Tonkawa Trl 78756
Tonkawa Trl E 78738
Tonkawa Trl W 78738
Tonkowa Draw Rd 78738
Tonopa Ln 78724
Tonto Ln 78733
Toolwrich Ln 78739
Toomey Rd 78704
Top Cv 78704
Top O The Lake Dr 78734
Top Of Texas Trl 78735
Top Of The Trails Cv 78734
Topanga Ln 78724
Topawa Cv 78729
Toppel Cv 78730
Topperwein Dr 78758
Topridge Dr 78750
Tordera Dr 78738
Toreador Dr 78746
Tornasol Ln 78739
Toro Canyon Rd 78746
Toro Creek Cv 78759
Toro Ring St 78746
Torran Cv 78749
Torrance Ct 78738
Torres St 78741
Torrey Pines Cv 78746
Torrington Ct 78738
Torrington Dr 78737
Torrington Ln 78738
Tortosa Path 78729
Tortuga Cv, Pl & Trl 78731
Toscana Ave 78724
Tossa Ln 78729
Tottenham Ct 78729
Touchstone St 78723
Toulouse Dr 78748
Tour De France Cv 78733
Tournament Cv & Way 78738
Tourney Cv & Ln 78738
Tournus Trl 78744
Tovar Dr 78729
Towana Cir & Trl 78736
Towbridge Cir 78723
Tower Dr 78703
Tower Trl 78723
Tower View Ct 78723
Towering Oaks Dr 78745
Town Bluff Dr 78732
Town Creek Dr 78741
Town Hill Dr 78728
Town Lake Cir 78741
Towne Park Trl 78751
Townes Ln 78703
Townesouth Cir 78741
Townsborough Dr 78724
Township Cv & Trl 78759
Towser Ct 78744
Toyath St 78703
Trabadora Cv 78759
S Trace Dr 78745
Trace Chain Dr 78749
Trace Creek Pass 78724
Tracor Ln 78725
Tracton Ct & Ln 78739
Tracy Trl 78728
Tracy Lynn Ln 78721
Trade Center Dr 78744
Trading Bnd 78735
Trafalgar Dr 78723
Trail Cv 78746
Trail Crest Cir 78735
Trail Driver St 78737
Trail Of The Madrones 78746
Trail Of The Woods 78734
Trail View Cv 78734
Trail Weary Dr 78754
Trail West Dr 78735
Trailmaster Dr 78737
Trailridge Cir & Dr 78731
Trails End 78737
Trailside Dr 78704
Trailside Est 78724
Trailview Mesa Cv, Dr & Ter 78746
Trailwood Rd 78727
Tramson Dr 78741
Tranquil Ln 78728
Tranquilo Trl 78744
Transit Cir & Cv 78727
Trautwein Rd 78737
Travertine Cv 78735
Travesia Way 78728
Travis Cook Rd 78735
Travis Country Cir 78735
Travis Green Ln 78735
Travis Heights Blvd 78704
Travis Hills Dr 78735
Travis View Ct & Loop 78732
Travis Vista Dr 78738
Travis Woods Cv 78734
Trawood Path 78748
Treadsoft Cv 78748
Treadwell Blvd 78757
Treadwell St 78704
Treasure Cv 78745
Treasure Island Dr 78730
Treaty Oak Cir 78749
Treble Ln 78704
Trede Cv & Dr 78745
Tree Bend Cv & Dr 78750
Tree Fern Ln 78750
Tree Line Dr 78729
Treehaven Ct & Ln 78738
Treehouse Ln 78749
Treemont Dr 78746
Trelawney Ln 78739
Trendal Ln 78744
Trent Dr 78759
Trenton Dr 78736
Trevino Dr 78746
Trevone Path 78754
Treys Way 78745
Triangle Ave 78751
Trianon Ln 78727
Triboro Trl 78749
Tributary Ridge Ct & Dr 78759
Tridens Ct 78750
Trierli Dr 78741
Trillium Cv 78733
Trinity St
1-699 78701
701-1199 78701
1701-2297 78712
2299-2400 78712
2402-2498 78712
Trinity Hill Dr 78753
Trinity Hills Dr 78737
Triple Crown 78746
Tripod Dr 78747
Tripshaw Ln 78741
Triton Ct 78734
Trogon Ct 78750
Troll Hvn 78746
Trone Cir 78758
Tronewood Dr 78758
Troon Dr 78738
Troops Trl 78727
Trophy Cv 78748
Trophy Dr 78738
Trophy Pass 78748
Trotwood Dr 78753
Trout Cv & Dr 78749
Trowbridge Cv 78717
True Cv 78748
Truman Cv 78729
Truman Oak Cv 78724
Trumpet St 78724
Tucumcari Trl 78734
Tudor Blvd 78759
Tuffit Ln 78753
Tulane Dr 78723
Tulare Dr 78738
Tularosa Pass 78726
Tule Cv 78749
Tulloch Way 78754
Tulsa Cv 78723
Tumbleweed Dr 78724
N Tumbleweed Trl 78733
S Tumbleweed Trl 78733
Tumbling Cir 78731
Tumbling Creek Trl 78748
Tupelo Dr 78744
Tura Ln 78721
Turbine Dr 78728
Turf Cv 78748
Turkey Holw 78750
Turkey Run 78727
Turkey Creek Dr 78730
Turkey Hollow Trl 78717
Turkey Ridge Ct 78729
Turks Cap Cv 78750
Turks Cap Pass 78737
Turman Cv 78730
Turnabout Ln 78731
Turnbuoy Dr 78730
Turner Dr 78753
Turner Ln 78723
Turning Trl 78737
Turnstone Ct & Dr 78744
Turquoise Cv & Trl 78749
Turtle Ln 78726
Turtle Creek Blvd 78745
Turtle Dove Dr 78744
Turtle Mountain Bnd 78748
Turtle Point Dr 78746
Turtle Rock Rd 78729
Turtleback Ln 78727
Tuscany Way
8201-8299 78724
8300-8700 78754
8702-9198 78754
9001-9003 78710
9005-9199 78754
Tuscarora Trl 78729
Tuscola Cir 78734
Tusman Dr 78735
Tuxford Cv 78753
Tweed Ct 78727
Tweed Berwick Dr 78750
Tweedsmuir Dr 78750
Twelve Oaks Ln 78704
Twiggy Ln 78747
Twilight Trl 78748
Twilight Vis 78736
Twilight Mesa Dr 78737
Twilight Ridge Dr 78746
Twilight Shadow Dr 78749
Twilight Terrace Dr 78737
Twin Acres Dr 78738
Twin Creek Holw 78750
Twin Crest Dr 78752
Twin Hills Ct 78734
Twin Ledge Cir, Cv & Dr 78731
Twin Oaks Dr 78757
Twin Valley Cir, Cv & Dr 78731
Twinberry Cv 78746
Twisted Briar Ln 78729
Twisted Oaks Dr 78745
Twisted Tree Cv & Dr 78735
Two Coves Dr 78730
Two Iron St 78744
Two Rivers Cv 78717
Tydings Cv 78730
Tyhurst Dr 78749
Tyler St 78756
Tyndale Cv 78733
Tyrone Dr 78759
Tyson Cv 78758
Ulit Ave 78702
Ullman Dr 78734
Ullrich Ave 78756
Ullswater Cv & Ln 78750
Unbridled 78737
Underhill Rd 78734
Unincore Rd 78721
Unintank Rd 78719
Union Cir 78744
United Dr 78758
United Kingdom Dr 78748
University Ave
1900-2100 78705
2102-3098 78705
2401-2699 78712
3001-3099 78705
University Sta 78712
University Club Dr 78732
Uphill Ln 78741
Upland Dr 78741
Uplands Ridge Dr 78738
Upper Rivercrest Dr 78746
Upper Woods Cv 78734
Upson St 78703
Upvalley Ct & Run 78731
Uray Dr 78724
Ursa Major Path 78732
Us Highway 183 S
201-397 78741
Us Highway 183 S
399-800 78741
802-998 78741
2400-4798 78744
4800-7400 78744
7402-7498 78744
7901-8497 78747
8499-11100 78747
11102-11898 78747
Utah Flats Dr 78727
N & S Ute Trl 78729
Utica Cv 78739
Utopia Ct 78723
Uttimer Ln 78753
Uvalde Cv 78739
Uvalde Creek Dr 78732
V F W Rd 78753
Vail Dv 78738
Vail Valley Dr 78749
Vailco Ln 78738
Vailview Cv 78750
Val Dr 78723
Val Verde 78732
Valburn Cir, Ct & Dr 78731
Valcour Bay Ln 78754
Valderrama Ct & Dr 78717
Valdez St 78741
Vale St 78746
Valencia Cir 78759
Valeria St 78704
Valerio Ln 78735
Valerres 78711
Valhalla Ct 78738
Valiant Cir & Cv 78749
Vallarta Ln 78733
Vallecito Cv & Dr 78759
Vallejo St 78757
Valley Cir 78731
Valley Dale Dr 78731
Valley Forge Dr 78753
Valley High Cir 78744
Valley Hill Cir 78741
Valley Oak Dr 78731
Valley Ridge Ct 78746
Valley Springs Rd 78746
Valley View Dr 78733
Valley View Rd 78704
Valley Vista Rd 78737
Valleydale Cv 78757
Valleyfield Dr 78724
Valleyridge Cir & Dr 78704
Valleyside Rd 78731
Valona Dr 78717
Van Dyke Dr 78729
Van Winkle Ct & Ln 78739
Vance Cir 78701
Vance Ln 78746
Vanderbilt Cir & Ln 78723
Vandever St 78725
Vanguard St 78734
Vanshire Dr 78738
Vantage Point Dr 78737
Vaquero Cv & Trl 78759
Vara Dr 78754
Varcella Trl 78729
Varco Dr 78738
Vargas Rd 78741
Varner Ct 78732
Varrelman St 78725
Vasey 78724
Vasquez St 78741
Vassal Dr 78748
Vassar Dr 78723
Vaughan Cv 78732
Vaught Ranch Rd 78730
Velarde Cv 78729
Velasco Pl 78749
Velasquez Dr 78703
Veletta Pl 78735
Venado Dr
4200-4299 78731
15401-15499 78734
Vendrell Dr 78729
Veneer Dr 78748
Venetian Cv 78748
Venice Ln 78750
Venita Cv 78733
Ventura Dr 78741
Ventus St 78721
Vera Ln 78741
Vera Cruz 78737
Verandah Ct 78726
Verano Dr 78735
Verbank Villa Dr 78747
Verbena Dr 78750
Verchota Dr 78748
Verdant Way 78746
Verde Vis 78703
Verde Mesa Cv 78738
Verdebank Cir 78703
Verdi Pl 78746
Verela Dr 78725
Vermont Rd 78702
Vernon Ave 78723
Verona Cv & Trl 78749
Versante Cir 78726
Versilia Cir 78734

Versiua 78734
Vertex Blvd 78744
Vervain Ct 78733
Vestavio Ct 78747
Veterans Dr 78703
Vetters Ct 78750
Via Dr 78735
Via Cordova Ct 78732
Via Correto Dr 78749
Via Dono Dr 78749
Via Fortuna 78746
Via Grande Dr 78739
Via Media 78746
Via Ricco Dr 78749
Via Verde Dr 78739
Viamonte Ln 78739
Victor St 78753
Victoria Ct 78737
Victoria Dr 78721
Victory Dr 78704
View W 78735
S View Rd 78737
W View Rd 78737
View Ridge Ct 78737
View Ridge Dr 78724
Viewing Pl 78719
Viewpoint Dr 78744
Vigen Cir 78748
Viking Dr 78758
Vikki Ter 78736
Villa Ct 78704
Villa Maria Ct, Cv & Ln 78759
Villa Montana Way 78732
Villa Norte Dr 78726
Villa Oaks Cir 78745
Villa Park Dr 78729
Villacliff Cir 78759
Village Cir 78745
E Village Ct 78744
W Village Ct 78744
Village Cv 78744
Village Dr 78731
Village Ln 78744
E Village Ln 78758
W Village Ln 78758
Village Path 78744
Village Trl 78744
Village Walk 78744
Village Center Dr 78731
Village Creek Cir 78744
Village Green Dr 78753
Village Oak Ct 78704
Village Oak Loop 78717
Village Square Dr 78744
Village Trail Cir 78744
Village Way Ct & Dr 78745
Village West Dr 78733
Villanova Dr 78757
Villita Cv 78741
Villita Avenida St 78741
Vinalopo Dr 78738
Vinca Cir 78744
Vinca Dr 78734
Vine St 78757
Vine Hill Dr 78744
Vineland Dr 78722
Vinewood Cv & Ln 78757
Vinson Dr 78745
Vintage Hills Cv & Dr 78723
Vintage Stave Rd 78748
Vioitha Dr 78723
Vireo Cv 78746
Virginia Ave 78704
Virginia Dare Ln 78754
Virgo Ln 78724
Viridian Ln & Way 78739
Visa Rose Dr 78748
Visalia Ln 78727
Vista Ln 78703
Vista Rdg 78738
Vista Del Sol 78733
Vista Mountain Dr 78731
Vista Ridge Cv 78754
Vista Verde Cv & Dr 78732
Vista View Cir & Dr 78750

Vista West Cv 78731
Vitex Dr 78734
Vivas Ln 78735
Vixen Ct 78734
Vol Walker Cv & Dr 78749
Voltaire Dr 78752
Von Herff Ct 78732
Von Quintus Rd 78719
Vougeot Dr 78744
Voyageurs Ln 78747
Wade Ave 78703
Wadford St 78704
Wading Pool Path 78748
Wadley Pl 78728
Wadsworth Way 78748
Wafer Ash Way 78750
Wagon Bnd 78744
Wagon Rd W 78736
Wagon Trl 78758
Wagon Crossing Path 78744
Wagon Gap Dr 78750
Wagon Hitch Cv 78749
Wagon Train Cv & Rd 78749
Wagtail Cv & Dr 78748
Wake Forest Ln 78723
Wakefield Dr 78749
Walcott Dr 78725
Walden Cir 78723
Waldon Dr & Holw 78750
Waldorf Ave 78721
Waldrop Cv 78748
Walebridge Ct & Ln 78739
Wales Way 78748
Walhill Cv & Ln 78759
Walker Ln 78741
Walkingstick Ln 78744
Walkup Ln 78747
Wall St 78754
Wallace Cv 78750
Waller St 78702
Walling Dr 78705
Walling Forge Dr 78727
Wallingstone Ln 78750
Wallingwood Dr 78746
Wallis Dr 78746
Wally Ave 78721
Walnut Ave
1200-1899 78702
2100-2198 78722
2200-3299 78722
E Walnut Dr 78753
W Walnut Dr 78753
Walnut Bend Dr 78753
Walnut Clay Dr 78731
Walnut Creek Dr 78753
Walnut Grove Ct & Dr 78744
Walnut Hills Dr 78723
Walnut Hollow Cv 78744
Walnut Park Xing 78753
Walnut Ridge Dr 78753
Walpole Ln 78739
Walsall Cv & Loop 78749
Walser Cv 78735
Walsh St 78703
Walsh Tarlton Ln 78746
Walter St 78702
Walton Ln 78721
Walton Heath Cir 78747
Walworth St 78723
Wampton Way 78749
Wanakah Ct 78734
Wander Ln 78750
Wandering Mdws 78746
Wandering Way
10800-10898 78754
10900-11121 78754
11123-11199 78754
11140-11198 78753
Wandering Oak Rd 78749
War Path 78727
War Bonnet Dr 78733
Warbler Ct 78758
Warbler Dr 78734
Warbler Way 78735
Warbler Ledge 78738
Wardour Ln 78748

Ware Rd 78741
Wareham Ct & Ln 78739
Warehouse Row 78704
Warely Ln 78741
Warfield Way 78728
Warm Breeze Cv 78717
Warm Mist Cv 78717
Warm Moon Cv 78717
Warren St 78703
Warrington Cv & Dr 78753
Warwick Way 78748
Washington Sq 78705
Washita Dr 78749
Washoe Cir 78734
Wassail St 78744
Wasson Rd 78745
Watchful Fox Dr 78748
Watchhill Rd 78703
Watchwood Dr 78745
Water Ln 78732
Water Front Ave 78734
Water Mill Cv 78729
Water Oak Ln 78729
Water Race Ct 78729
Water Well Ln 78728
Water Wheel Cv 78729
Waterbank Cv 78746
Waterbrook Dr 78723
Watercrest Ct & Dr 78738
Waterfall Dr 78738
Waterfall Way 78753
Waterford Pl 78731
Waterford Centre Blvd 78758
Watering Rock Ln 78759
Waterline Rd 78731
Waterloo Trl 78704
Waterloo City Ln 78741
Watermelon Way 78725
Waters Way 78737
Waters Edge Cv & Dr 78731
Waters Park Rd 78759
Waterside Trl 78750
Waterston Ave 78703
Waterton Parke Cir & Cv 78726
Waterway Bnd & Cv 78728
Wathen Ave 78703
Watson St 78757
Watumba Rd 78734
Wavecrest Blvd 78728
Waverly Ct 78729
Waverly Spire Ct 78738
Wavertree Ct 78745
Waxberry Ln 78748
Waxler Ct 78754
Waxwing Cir 78750
Waxwing Ct 78758
Way Ln 78739
Wayborne Hill Dr 78723
Waycross Dr 78745
Waymaker Cv & Way 78746
Wayneroy Dr 78721
Waynesborough Dr 78724
Waynesburg Cv 78723
Wayside Blvd 78724
Wayside Dr 78703
Wayward Sun Dr 78754
Waywood Dr 78724
Weatherford Dr 78753
Weatherhill Cv 78730
Weathers Ln 78704
Weatherwood Cv 78746
Webb Ln 78734
Webberville Rd
1100-1999 78721
2200-3699 78702
Webbwood Way 78724
Weber Ave 78722
Wedgewood Dr 78753
Wee Scot Cv 78734
Weeks Cv 78727
Weeping Willow Dr 78753
Weidemar Ln 78745
Weiser Dr 78729
Welcome Gln 78759
Weldon Ln 78728

Weldon Springs Ct 78726
Weletka Dr 78734
Welland Cir 78759
Weller Dr 78750
Wellesley Ct 78737
Wellesley Dr 78754
Wellington Dr
100-399 78737
5300-5899 78723
5901-5999 78723
Wells Branch Pkwy 78728
Wells Fargo St 78737
Wells Port Cv & Dr 78728
Wellspring Dr 78738
Welshpool Ct 78737
Wendel Cv 78731
Wendts Way 78750
Wentworth Dr 78724
Werner Ave 78722
Werner Hill Dr 78753
Wesal Dr 78747
Wessex Way 78748
West Ave
200-1899 78701
2900-3599 78705
West Ct 78759
West Ln 78732
N West Pl 78731
Westall 78725
Westbank Dr 78746
Westbluff Cir 78759
Westbrook Dr W 78746
Westbury Trl 78758
Westchester Ave 78759
Westcreek Dr 78749
Wester Ross Ln 78738
Westerkirk Dr 78750
Western Dr 78745
Western Hills Dr 78731
Western Oaks Blvd 78749
Western Trails Blvd 78745
Westfalian Trl 78732
Westfield Dr 78731
Westforest Dr 78704
Westgate Cir 78746
Westhaven Dr 78746
Westheimer Dr 78752
Westhill Dr 78704
Westlake Cv, Dr & Pass 78746
Westland Dr 78704
Westledge Cir 78731
Westminster Dr 78723
Westminster Glen Ave 78730
Westmont Dr 78731
Westmoor Dr 78723
Westmorland Dr 78745
Westoak Dr 78704
N & S Weston Ln 78733
Westover Rd 78703
Westover Club Dr 78759
Westridge Dr 78704
Westrock Dr 78704
Westside Cv & Dr 78731
Westslope Cir, Cv & Dr 78731
Westview Dr 78731
Westview Rd 78749
Westview Trl 78737
Westward Cv & Dr 78733
Westward Ho Trl 78734
Westway Cir 78704
Westwood Ter 78746
Westworth Cir 78704
Wet Season Dr 78754
Wethersby Way 78753
Wethersfield Rd 78703
Wexford Dr 78759
Weyburn Dr 78757
Weyford Dr 78757
Wharton Ct 78732
Wharton Park Trl 78717
Wheatfall Ln 78748
Wheatley Ave 78752
Wheel Rim Cir 78749
Wheeler St 78705

Wheeler Branch Cir & Trl 78749
Wheeless St 78702
Wheless Cv & Ln 78723
Whifflewind Way 78754
Whipple Way 78745
N Whippoorwill St 78734
Whippoorwill Trl 78746
Whirlaway 78737
Whiskey River Dr 78748
Whispering Trl 78737
Whispering Creek Cir, Ct & Dr 78736
Whispering Oaks Dr 78745
Whispering Valley Dr 78727
Whispering Wind Way 78737
Whispering Winds Dr 78745
Whistlestop Cv & Dr 78749
Whistling Straits Dr 78717
White Cliff Dr 78759
White Creek Cv & Dr 78717
White Dove Pass 78734
White Eagle Rd 78748
White Elm Ct & Dr 78749
White Hawk Cir 78737
White Horse Trl 78757
White Ibis Dr 78729
White Magnolia Cir 78734
White Oak Dr 78753
White Rock Dr 78757
White Sands Dr 78734
White Tail Trl 78736
Whitebead Trl 78734
Whitebrook Dr 78724
Whitebrush Loop 78717
Whitecrowe Trl 78735
Whitefaulds Dr 78754
Whitehall Cv 78730
Whitemarsh Valley Walk 78746
Whitepine Dr 78757
Whites Dr 78735
Whitestone Dr 78745
Whitetail Run 78737
Whitethorn Ct 78746
Whiteway Dr 78757
Whitewing Ave 78753
Whiteworth Loop 78749
Whitis Ave
2000-2099 78705
2101-3199 78705
2300-2608 78712
2610-3198 78705
Whitley Dr 78738
Whitley Bay Dr 78717
Whitney Way 78741
Whitsun Dr 78749
Whitt Loop 78749
Whittman Cv 78757
Wichita St 78712
Wickersham Ln 78741
Wickfield Ln 78753
Wickford Cir 78704
Wickham Ln 78725
Wideleaf Cv & Dr 78724
Widge Dr 78727
Wier Hills Rd 78735
Wier Loop Cir & Rd 78736
Wight Cv 78723
Wightman Dr 78754
Wiginton Dr 78758
Wilbur Dr 78757
Wilcab Rd 78721
Wilcott Ct 78745
Wilcrest Dr 78748
Wild St 78757
Wild Basin Ldg, Rd & St 78746
Wild Briar Pass 78746
Wild Canyon Loop 78732
Wild Cat Holw 78746
Wild Cherry 78738
Wild Dunes Ct & Dr 78747
Wild Iris Ln 78727
Wild Oak Cir 78759
Wild Onion Dr 78744

Wild Plum Ct 78731
Wild Plum Way 78737
Wild Rice Cv 78738
Wild Rock Cv 78732
Wild Rose Dr 78737
Wild Turkey Cv 78737
Wild Turkey Pass 78734
Wilder Rdg 78759
Wilderness Cv & Dr 78746
Wildflower Ln 78733
Wildgrove Dr 78704
Wildleaf Dr 78724
Wildridge Cir & Dr 78759
Wildrose Dr 78721
Wildrye Dr 78738
Wildwind Pt 78746
Wildwood Cir 78737
Wildwood Rd 78722
Wildwood Trl 78734
Wildwood Hills Ln 78737
Wiley Way 78747
Wilke Dr 78704
Wilks Ave 78752
Will Rogers Ln 78727
Willamette Dr 78723
Willbert Rd 78751
Willers Way 78748
Willet Trl 78745
Willfield Dr 78753
Willheather Gln 78750
E William Cannon Dr
100-198 78745
200-899 78745
1700-5300 78744
5302-6998 78744
W William Cannon Dr
100-3499 78745
3601-4197 78749
4199-6300 78749
6302-6398 78749
6501-6597 78735
6599-6600 78735
6602-7098 78735
William Kennedy Dr 78727
William Wallace Way 78754
Williams St 78752
Williams Ridge Way 78731
Williamsburg Cir 78731
Williamson Creek Dr 78736
Williston Loop 78748
Willow St
500-599 78701
900-2799 78702
Willow Way 78744
Willow Bend Dr 78758
Willow Creek Dr 78741
Willow Springs Rd
3400-3499 78704
3501-3699 78704
4200-4399 78745
Willow Tank Dr 78717
Willow Walk Cv 78737
Willow Wild Dr 78758
Willowbridge Cir 78703
Willowbrook Dr 78722
Willowick Dr 78759
Willowood Cir 78703
Willowrun Cv & Dr 78704
Wilma Rudolph Rd 78748
Wilmes Dr 78752
Wilmont Cv 78717
Wilshire Blvd & Pkwy 78722
Wilson St 78704
Wilson Heights Dr 78746
Wilson Parke Ave 78726
Wilton Cir 78745
Wimberly Cv & Ln 78735
Winchell Ln 78725
Winchelsea Ct & Dr 78750
Winchester Ct 78745
Winchester Rd 78733
W Wind Trl 78745
Wind Cave Trl 78747
Wind River Rd 78759
Wind Song Cv 78750
Windcliff Way 78748

Windermere Mdws 78759
Winding Trl 78745
Winding Walk 78757
Winding Brook Dr 78748
Winding Creek Cv 78735
Winding Creek Dr 78735
Winding Creek Rd 78736
Winding Oak Cir & Trl 78750
Windledge Dr 78745
Windoak Dr 78741
Windridge Cv & Dr 78759
Windrift Way 78745
Windrush Dr 78729
Windshill Cir 78703
Windslow Ct 78723
Windsong Trl 78746
E Windsor Rd 78703
Windswept Cv 78745
Windswept Dr 78738
Windward Dr 78723
Windwood Ct 78738
Windy Trl 78758
Windy Brook Dr 78723
Windy Harbor Dr 78734
Windy Ridge Rd 78726
Windy Trail Cir 78758
Winecup Holw 78750
Winecup Way 78737
Winedale Dr 78759
Winfield Cv & Dr 78704
Winflo Dr 78703
Wing Rd 78749
Wing Feather Dr 78744
Wingate Way 78727
Winged Foot Cv 78747
Wingreen Loop 78738
Winnebago Ln 78744
Winning Colors 78737
Winnipeg Cv 78759
Winsome Ct 78731
Winsted Ln 78703
Winston Ct 78731
Winter Haven Rd 78747
Winter Park Rd 78746
Winterberry Dr 78750
Winterborne Ct 78754
Wintercreeper Cv 78735
Wintergreen Hl 78750
Winterstein Dr 78745
Winwick Way 78727
Wipple Tree Cv 78750
Wirth Rd 78748
Wirtz Ave 78704
Wishek Cv 78730
Wishing Well Dr 78745
Wisteria Cir & Trl 78753
Wisteria Valley Dr 78739
Wisterwood St 78729
Wistful Cv 78729
Witham Ln 78745
Withers Way 78727
Witsome Loop 78741
Wittmer Dr 78729
Wolf Ct 78731
Wolf Run 78749
Wolf Jaw Cv 78729
Wolfcreek Pass 78749
Wolftrap Dr 78749
Wolverine St 78757
Wolverton Dr 78745
Wommack Rd 78748
E & W Wonsley Dr 78753
Wood St 78703
Wood Trl 78746
Wood Acre Ln 78733
Wood Bine Dr 78745
Wood Chase Trl 78728
Wood Cliff Dr 78745
Wood Hollow Dr 78731
Wood Ibis Cir 78750
Wood Stork Dr 78729
Woodbriar Ln 78723
Woodbrook Cir 78759
Woodbury Dr 78704
Woodchester Ln 78727
Woodcreek Rd 78749

Woodcrest Dr ... 78759
Woodcroft Dr ... 78749
Woodcutters Way ... 78746
Wooded Lake Ct ... 78732
Woodfield Dr ... 78758
Woodglen Cv & Dr ... 78753
Woodgreen Cv ... 78745
Woodhall Cv ... 78717
Woodhaven Dr ... 78753
Woodhue Ct & Dr ... 78745
Woodlake Cir & Cv ... 78733
Woodland Ave
700-1300 ... 78704
1302-1398 ... 78704
1601-1697 ... 78741
1699-1912 ... 78741
1914-2298 ... 78741
Woodland Hills Cv & Trl ... 78732
Woodland Oaks Ct ... 78744
Woodland Village Dr ... 78750
Woodlands Ct ... 78738
Woodlawn Blvd ... 78703
Woodleigh St ... 78704
Woodmere St ... 78729
Woodmont Ave ... 78703
Woodmoor Cir & Dr ... 78721
Woodrow Ave
4900-5899 ... 78756
6000-6098 ... 78757
6100-7899 ... 78757
Woodrow St ... 78705
Woodshire Dr ... 78748
Woodside Dr ... 78735
Woodside Ter ... 78738
Woodstock Dr ... 78753
Woodstone Cv ... 78749
Woodstone Dr ... 78757
Woodstone Sq ... 78703
Woodthorpe St ... 78729
Woodvale Dr ... 78729
Woodview Ave
4701-4797 ... 78756
4799-5899 ... 78756
5900-6299 ... 78757
Woodview Ct ... 78746
Woodward St
101-497 ... 78704
499-599 ... 78704
601-899 ... 78704
1601-1697 ... 78741
1699-2009 ... 78741
2011-2099 ... 78741
2090-2098 ... 78744
2100-2299 ... 78744
Woodway Dr ... 78731
Woodwind Ln ... 78758
Woody Ridge Vw ... 78730
Wooldridge Dr ... 78703
Wooten Dr ... 78757
Wooten Park Dr ... 78757
Worcester Cv ... 78750
Worchester Cv ... 78746
Wordham Dr ... 78749
Wordsworth Dr ... 78704
World Of Tennis Sq ... 78738
Worn Sole Dr ... 78754
Wren Ave ... 78753
Wren Valley Cv ... 78746
Wright St ... 78704
Wrightwood Rd ... 78722
Wychwood Dr ... 78746
Wycliff Ln ... 78727
Wycombe Dr ... 78749
Wye Oak St ... 78748
Wykeham Dr ... 78749
Wyldwood Rd ... 78739
Wylie Dr ... 78748
Wynden Cv ... 78748
Wynne Ln ... 78745
Wynona Ave
5700-5899 ... 78756
5900-6198 ... 78757
6200-6299 ... 78757
Wynstone Ln ... 78717
Wyola Bnd ... 78717
Wyoming Valley Dr ... 78727
Yabers Ct ... 78725
Yacht Ct ... 78734
Yacht Club Cv ... 78734
E Yager Ln
301-997 ... 78753
999-1599 ... 78753
2000-2198 ... 78754
2201-2299 ... 78754
W Yager Ln ... 78753
Yandall Dr ... 78748
Yarborough Ave ... 78744
Yarbrough Dr ... 78748
Yarmont Way ... 78753
Yarrow Ct ... 78733
Yarsa Blvd ... 78748
Yates Ave ... 78757
Yaupon Cir ... 78734
Yaupon Crk ... 78734
Yaupon Dr ... 78759
Yaupon Holly Ln ... 78738
Yaupon Springs Cir ... 78737
Yaupon Valley Rd ... 78746
Yeadon Way ... 78717
Yearling Cv ... 78727
Yellow Bird Trl ... 78734
Yellow Jacket Ln ... 78741
Yellow Oak St ... 78729
Yellow Rose Cv & Trl ... 78749
Yellow Tail Cv ... 78745
Yellowleaf Trl ... 78728
Yellowpine Ter ... 78757
Yellowstar Dr ... 78738
Yellowstone Dr ... 78747
Yoakum St ... 78748
Yora Dr ... 78728
York Bridge Cir ... 78749
York Hill Dr ... 78723
Yorkshire Dr ... 78723
Yorktown Cv & Trl ... 78726
Yosemite Dr ... 78733
Young Ln ... 78737
Younger Ct ... 78753
Yucatan Ln ... 78727
Yucca Cv ... 78737
Yucca Dr
1-99 ... 78744
10300-11399 ... 78759
Yucca Hill Dr ... 78744
Yucca Mountain Rd ... 78759
Yvette Cv ... 78748
Zach Scott St ... 78723
Zachary Scott St ... 78747
Zacharys Way ... 78748
Zadock Woods Dr ... 78749
Zagros Way ... 78738
Zaragosa St ... 78702
Zebecca Creek Dr ... 78732
Zeke Bnd ... 78745
Zeller Ln ... 78753
Zen Gardens Ter & Way ... 78732
Zenith Cv ... 78759
Zennia St ... 78751
Zephyr St ... 78734
Zequiel Dr ... 78744
Zeus Cv ... 78759
Ziller Cv ... 78725
Zimmerman Ln ... 78726
Zion Way ... 78733
Zopilote Cir ... 78734
Zuni Dr ... 78759
Zuniga Dr ... 78749
Zyle Ln & Rd ... 78737

NUMBERED STREETS

S 1st St
101-597 ... 78704
599-3899 ... 78704
4001-4097 ... 78745
4099-7899 ... 78745
7900-7998 ... 78748
8000-8399 ... 78748
8401-11099 ... 78748
E 2nd St
201-297 ... 78701
299-599 ... 78701
900-3000 ... 78702
3002-3098 ... 78702
S 2nd St
901-997 ... 78704
999-3899 ... 78704
4400-4699 ... 78745
W 2nd St ... 78701
E 2nd 1/2 St ... 78702
E 3rd St
201-297 ... 78701
700-3099 ... 78702
S 3rd St
600-2700 ... 78704
4400-4599 ... 78745
W 3rd St
201-297 ... 78701
1401-1599 ... 78703
E 4th St
100-198 ... 78701
801-997 ... 78702
S 4th St ... 78704
W 4th St
101-197 ... 78701
1200-1298 ... 78703
E 5th St
101-397 ... 78701
900-1098 ... 78702
S 5th St ... 78704
W 5th St
100-700 ... 78701
800-1699 ... 78703
E 6th St
100-799 ... 78701
801-897 ... 78702
1914-1914 ... 78762
2000-2698 ... 78702
S 6th St ... 78704
W 6th St
101-197 ... 78701
801-825 ... 78703
802-802 ... 78701
827-1800 ... 78703
W 6th 1/2 St ... 78703
E 7th St
100-799 ... 78701
900-5199 ... 78702
S 7th St ... 78704
W 7th St
100-198 ... 78701
200-799 ... 78701
1100-1200 ... 78703
1202-2698 ... 78703
E 8th St
100-799 ... 78701
801-997 ... 78702
999-2799 ... 78702
S 8th St ... 78704
W 8th St
100-799 ... 78701
1200-2699 ... 78703
E 9th St
100-198 ... 78701
801-997 ... 78702
W 9th St
201-597 ... 78701
901-997 ... 78703
W 9th 1/2 St ... 78703
E 10th St
101-197 ... 78701
199-399 ... 78701
401-799 ... 78701
1000-2599 ... 78702
W 10th St
101-497 ... 78701
499-899 ... 78701
900-998 ... 78703
1000-2699 ... 78703
E 11th St
100-799 ... 78701
800-2599 ... 78702
W 11th St
300-498 ... 78701
500-899 ... 78701
1000-2399 ... 78703
E 12th St
301-497 ... 78701
900-3199 ... 78702
3301-3397 ... 78721
W 12th St
300-899 ... 78701
900-2500 ... 78703
E 13th St
200-298 ... 78701
800-3199 ... 78702
W 13th St
200-298 ... 78701
300-699 ... 78701
1200-1298 ... 78703
1300-1599 ... 78703
E 14th St
201-399 ... 78701
801-897 ... 78702
899-3199 ... 78702
W 14th St
200-799 ... 78701
1600-1699 ... 78703
E 14th 1/2 St
3000-3199 ... 78702
3200-3299 ... 78721
E 15th St
101-197 ... 78701
199-299 ... 78701
301-699 ... 78701
900-1099 ... 78702
W 15th St ... 78701
E 16th St
801-1697 ... 78702
1699-3199 ... 78702
3200-3300 ... 78721
3302-3998 ... 78721
W 16th St ... 78701
E 17th St
100-199 ... 78701
111-111 ... 78711
1700-3099 ... 78702
3200-3599 ... 78721
W 17th St ... 78701
E 18th St
200-598 ... 78701
1700-3099 ... 78702
3201-3299 ... 78721
W 18th St ... 78701
E 18th 1/2 St ... 78702
E 20th St ... 78722
W 20th St ... 78705
E 21st St
101-103 ... 78712
200-207 ... 78705
210-212 ... 78712
1600-1698 ... 78722
W 21st St
100-204 ... 78712
700-999 ... 78705
E 22nd St ... 78722
W 22nd St ... 78705
W 22nd 1/2 St ... 78705
E 23rd St ... 78712
W 23rd St ... 78705
E 24th St ... 78712
W 24th St
103-197 ... 78712
199-208 ... 78712
210-304 ... 78712
401-497 ... 78705
499-1300 ... 78705
1302-1398 ... 78705
1500-1598 ... 78703
W 24th 1/2 St ... 78705
W 25th St ... 78705
W 25th 1/2 St ... 78705
W 26th St ... 78705
E 27th St
100-198 ... 78705
101-103 ... 78712
W 27th St ... 78705
E 28th St ... 78722
W 28th St ... 78705
W 28th 1/2 St ... 78705
E 29th St
400-498 ... 78705
1200-1298 ... 78722
1300-1399 ... 78722
W 29th St
300-999 ... 78705
1100-1298 ... 78703
1300-1899 ... 78703
W 29th 1/2 St ... 78705
E 30th St
100-900 ... 78705
902-1098 ... 78705
1100-1198 ... 78722
1200-1399 ... 78722
W 30th St
101-397 ... 78705
399-999 ... 78705
1400-1999 ... 78703
W 30th 1/2 St ... 78705
E 31st St
100-899 ... 78705
1100-1299 ... 78722
W 31st St
101-197 ... 78705
199-1200 ... 78705
1202-1298 ... 78705
1500-1799 ... 78703
W 31st 1/2 St ... 78705
E 32nd St
100-298 ... 78705
300-999 ... 78705
1001-1099 ... 78705
1100-1799 ... 78722
W 32nd St
100-899 ... 78705
1400-1899 ... 78703
1901-1999 ... 78703
E 32nd 1/2 St ... 78705
E 33rd St ... 78705
W 33rd St
100-599 ... 78705
1700-1999 ... 78703
E 34th St
101-197 ... 78705
199-499 ... 78705
1400-1799 ... 78722
W 34th St
100-1399 ... 78705
1500-1698 ... 78703
1700-1999 ... 78703
E 35th St ... 78705
100-799 ... 78705
1500-3899 ... 78703
W 35th St Cutoff ... 78731
W 36th St ... 78731
E 37th St
100-798 ... 78705
800-999 ... 78705
1400-1500 ... 78722
1502-1598 ... 78722
W 37th St
300-699 ... 78705
701-899 ... 78705
1800-1999 ... 78731
E 38th St
100-1099 ... 78705
1700-1799 ... 78722
1901-1999 ... 78723
W 38th St
100-1299 ... 78705
1301-1399 ... 78705
1500-1598 ... 78731
1600-1999 ... 78731
E 38th 1/2 St
500-1013 ... 78751
1015-1099 ... 78751
1200-1298 ... 78722
1201-1899 ... 78722
1300-1800 ... 78722
1802-1898 ... 78722
1900-1999 ... 78723
W 38th 1/2 St ... 78751
E 39th St
201-497 ... 78751
499-1099 ... 78751
1800-1899 ... 78722
W 39th St
101-197 ... 78751
199-399 ... 78751
401-599 ... 78751
1000-1298 ... 78756
1801-1803 ... 78731
1805-1999 ... 78731
W 39th 1/2 St ... 78756
E 40th St
300-1099 ... 78751
1700-1899 ... 78722
W 40th St
200-298 ... 78751
300-400 ... 78751
402-498 ... 78751
1000-1599 ... 78756
1601-1699 ... 78756
1900-1999 ... 78731
E 41st St ... 78751
W 41st St
100-198 ... 78751
200-499 ... 78751
501-599 ... 78751
1000-1799 ... 78756
1900-1999 ... 78731
4100-4199 ... 78756
E 42nd St ... 78751
W 42nd St
201-297 ... 78751
299-500 ... 78751
502-598 ... 78751
1001-1497 ... 78756
1499-1699 ... 78756
1701-1799 ... 78756
1900-1999 ... 78731
E 43rd St ... 78751
W 43rd St
100-298 ... 78751
300-599 ... 78751
1000-1098 ... 78756
1100-1299 ... 78756
1301-1599 ... 78756
E 44th St ... 78751
W 44th St
200-499 ... 78751
501-599 ... 78751
1001-1197 ... 78756
1199-1799 ... 78756
2800-2998 ... 78731
E 45th St ... 78751
W 45th St
100-999 ... 78751
1100-1699 ... 78756
1701-2599 ... 78756
2600-2999 ... 78731
E 45th 1/2 St ... 78751
E 46th St ... 78751
W 46th St
100-300 ... 78751
302-398 ... 78751
1401-1497 ... 78756
1499-1899 ... 78756
E 47th St ... 78751
W 47th St
801-899 ... 78751
1400-1499 ... 78756
E 48th St ... 78751
2101-2199 ... 78756
2600-2699 ... 78731
E 48th 1/2 St ... 78751
E 49th St ... 78751
W 49th St
1100-1198 ... 78756
1200-2399 ... 78756
2401-2499 ... 78756
2600-2799 ... 78731
E 49th 1/2 St ... 78751
1200-1299 ... 78756
2600-2799 ... 78731
E 50th St ... 78751
W 50th St
100-198 ... 78751
2800-2899 ... 78731
E 51st St
100-198 ... 78751
1100-1798 ... 78723
1800-5200 ... 78723
5202-5698 ... 78723
W 51st St
100-699 ... 78751
701-799 ... 78751
1200-1499 ... 78756
E 52nd St
100-999 ... 78751
1001-1099 ... 78751
1100-1399 ... 78723
E 53rd St
200-1099 ... 78751
1100-1198 ... 78723
E 53rd 1/2 St ... 78751
E 54th St ... 78751
E & W 55th ... 78751
E & W 55th 1/2 ... 78751
E 56th St ... 78751
E 56th 1/2 St ... 78751

AZLE TX

General Delivery ... 76098

POST OFFICE BOXES MAIN OFFICE STATIONS AND BRANCHES

Box No.s
All PO Boxes ... 76098

RURAL ROUTES

01, 02, 03, 04, 05, 06, 07, 08, 09, 10 ... 76020

NAMED STREETS

All Street Addresses ... 76020

BAY CITY TX

General Delivery ... 77414

POST OFFICE BOXES MAIN OFFICE STATIONS AND BRANCHES

Box No.s
All PO Boxes ... 77404

RURAL ROUTES

01, 01, 01, 02, 02, 02, 03, 04 ... 77414

HIGHWAY CONTRACTS

01, 01, 02, 02, 02 ... 77414
01, 01, 02, 02, 02 ... 77414
01, 01, 02, 02, 02 ... 77414
01, 01, 02, 02, 02 ... 77414
01, 01, 02, 02, 02 ... 77414

NAMED STREETS

All Street Addresses ... 77414

NUMBERED STREETS

All Street Addresses ... 77414

BAYTOWN TX

General Delivery ... 77520

POST OFFICE BOXES MAIN OFFICE STATIONS AND BRANCHES

Box No.s
All PO Boxes ... 77522

NAMED STREETS

Abbott St 77520
Acacia Ln 77521
Adams St 77520
Adler Dr 77523
Adobe Ln 77521
Adonis Ave 77521
E & W Adoue St 77520
Agate Ln 77523
N & S Airhart Dr 77520
Alabama St 77520
Alamance St 77521
Alamo St 77521
Albatross Rd 77523
N & S Alexander Dr 77520
Alford St 77520
Allen Ln 77521
Allenbrook Dr 77521
Allman St 77520
Almond Dr 77520
Almond St 77521
Aloe Ave 77521
Alum Ln 77521
Alva St 77520
Amaryllis Ave & Rd 77521
Ambrosia Ln 77521
Amelia St 77520
American St 77520
Ammons St 77521
Amy Dr 77520
Anderson Rd 77521
Angelfish Cove Dr 77523
Annatto Dr 77521
Anne Dr 77521
Apache Ct & Trl 77521
Apache Meadows Dr 77521
Applerock Dr 77521
Arapajo St 77521
Arbor St 77520
E & W Archer Rd 77521
Arizona St 77520
Arkansas St 77520
Arnica St 77521
Arnold 77523
Aron St 77520
Arrowhead Dr 77521
Arroyo Cir 77521
Arthur Ct 77521
Ash St 77520
N & S Ashbel Ct & St 77520
Ashby St 77520
Ashley Ln 77521
Ashleyville Rd 77521
Ashwood Dr 77521
Aspen Ct 77523
S Atlantic St 77520
Atlantic Pipe Line Rd 77523
Augusta St 77523
Austin St 77520
Autumn Ln 77521
Autumn Fall St 77523
Autumn Oaks Dr 77521
Avalon Ln 77521
Avenue A 77523
Avenue J 77520
Avenue K 77520
Avenue L 77520
Avon St 77520
Azalea Dr 77520
E Baker Rd 77521
W Baker Rd
100-4299 77521
4301-4399 77521
4400-6099 77520
Bannock St 77521
Barberry Ln 77520
Barbers Loop 77523
Barbers Hill Rd 77521
Barcelona Cir & Way 77520
Barkaloo Rd 77521
Barnes St 77520
Baron Rd 77521
Baron Ridge Dr 77521
Barrymore Blvd 77520
Basalt Dr 77521
Basil Dr 77521
Battlebell Rd 77521
Bay Plz 77520
W Bay Rd 77523
Bay Habor Cir 77523
Bay Harbor Cir 77523
Bay Hill Dr 77523
Bay Hill Ln 77521
Bay Island Blvd 77523
Bay Leaf Dr 77521
Bay Oaks Dr 77523
Bay Oaks Harbor Dr 77523
Bay Place Dr 77523
Bay Ridge Dr 77523
Bay Run Ave 77521
Bay Wind Ct 77523
Bayless St 77520
Baylor St 77520
Bayou Blvd 77521
Bayou Bnd 77521
Bayou Dr 77520
Bayou Rd 77520
N & S Bayou Bend Dr 77521
Bayou Breeze Dr 77523
Bayou Vista Dr 77521
Bayou Woods Dr 77521
Bayside Dr 77523
Baytown Central Blvd 77521
Bayview Dr 77523
Bayvilla St 77520
Bayway Dr 77520
Beach Haven Rd 77523
Bear Creek Cir & Trce 77521
Beasley Reef Dr 77523
Beaumont Rd 77520
Beaver St 77523
Beaver Bend Ct 77521
Beech St 77520
Beecher St 77520
Belmont Cir 77523
Belvedere Dr 77520
Belview St 77521
Ben Mar Overlook 77523
Bentonite Blvd 77521
Berdley Ct 77521
Berkely Ct 77521
Bermuda Ave 77523
Betty Jane Ln 77521
Bienville Ave 77521
Bighorn St 77521
Birch Cir 77523
Birdsong Dr 77521
Bit Pl 77523
Black Bird Ln 77523
Black Horse Rd 77523
Black Pool St 77521
Black Rock St 77521
Black Stone St 77523
Blackcherry Ln 77523
Blossom Ln 77521
Blue Jay St 77523
Blueberry Rd 77523
Bluebill Bay 77523
Bluebird Cir 77523
Bob Smith Rd 77521
Bois D Arc Ln 77521
Bolster St 77520
Bonita Way 77520
Booker St 77523
Bookertee St 77520
Bowie St 77520
Boxwood Dr 77520
Boykin Ln 77523
Breda Dr 77521
Brentwood Dr 77520
Briar Ct 77521
Briar Oaks Ln 77523
Briar Patch St 77523
Briarclift Ln 77521
Briarcreek Dr 77521
Briarwood Dr 77520
Bridgette Ln 77523
Bridle Pl 77523
Britton St 77520
Broad St 77521
Broadleaf Ave 77521
Broadmoor Dr 77523
Broken Arrow St 77521
Brookfield St 77523
Brooks Crossing Dr 77521
Brownwood Dr 77520
Bruce Dr 77520
Buchanan Dr 77520
Buckeye St 77523
Bud Ln 77521
Buffalo Trl 77521
Burbank St 77520
N & S Burnett Ave & Dr 77520
Burning Tree Dr 77521
Busch Rd 77520
Bush Rd 77521
Caballito Ln 77521
Caballo St 77521
Cabaniss Ave 77520
Cactus St 77521
Cadbury Cir 77521
Caddo Ct & St 77521
Cajun Way 77523
Calamus Cir 77521
Caldwell St 77520
California St 77520
Camelia Cir 77520
Camelot St 77521
Camino Real St 77521
Canal St 77523
Canna Ct 77523
Canterbury Dr 77521
Canvasback Cay St N & S 77523
Caraway Cir 77521
Caraway Lake Cir & Dr 77521
Cardamon Ln 77521
Caribou Ct 77523
Carlisle Ct 77521
Carlswood St 77523
Carlton St 77520
Carnation Ct 77521
Carnegie St 77520
Carole Ln 77521
Carolina St 77520
Caroline Ave 77523
Carousel Cir 77521
Carriage Ln 77521
Carriage Trails Dr 77523
Carroll Rd 77523
Carver St
100-199 77523
800-1299 77520
Cary Ln 77521
Cary Creek Dr 77521
Casey St 77520
Castleview Cir & Dr 77521
Cayenne Ln 77521
Cedar Ave 77520
Cedar Blvd 77523
Cedar St 77520
Cedar Bayou Rd 77520
E & W Cedar Bayou Lynchburg Rd 77521
Cedar Bluff Dr 77521
Cedar Brake St 77520
Cedar Branch Dr 77521
Cedar Cove Dr 77521
Cedar Creek Dr 77520
Cedar Gully Rd 77523
Cedar Hill Dr 77521
Cedar Hollow St 77521
Cedar Landing Dr 77521
Cedar Point Rd 77523
Cedar View Dr 77521
Cedar View St 77523
Center St 77520
Chad 77521
Chance Ln 77521
Chandler Dr 77521
Chaparral Dr 77521
E Chaparral Dr 77523
W Chaparral Dr 77523
Charles Ave 77520
Charles Pl 77521
Charlotte Dr 77520
Chartrese Ave 77521
E Chase St 77521
Cherokee St 77521
Cherry St 77520
Chervil Ln 77521
Chesapeake St 77520
Chestnut 77520
Chetco Ln 77521
Cheyenne Ct 77521
Cheyenne St 77523
Chickasaw St 77521
Chicory Dr 77521
Chilton Dr 77520
Chinook St 77521
Chippewa St 77521
Choctaw St 77523
S Choctaw St 77523
Christopher 77521
Cielito Ln 77521
Cilantro Ln 77521
Cindy Ln 77523
Cinnamon Ln & St 77521
Cinnamon Lake Dr 77521
E Circle Dr 77521
N Circle Dr 77520
S Circle Dr
100-399 77521
400-1000 77520
1002-1098 77520
W Circle Dr 77521
Circle Back Rd 77523
Citrus Ct 77523
Clark Rd 77523
Clayton Dr 77520
Clear Sea Cir 77521
Clearwater Dr 77523
E & W Cleveland St 77520
Cline Rd 77521
Clyde Dr 77520
Coachlight Ln 77521
Coachman Dr 77521
Coastline St 77521
Cobblestone Ln 77521
Coburn St 77520
Colby Dr 77520
Coleus Ln 77521
Colonial Dr 77520
Colorado St 77520
Colson Ln 77521
Columbia St 77521
Comanche St 77521
N & S Commerce St 77520
Connelly Rd 77521
Connor Dr 77521
Cook Dr 77520
Copper Crk 77521
Coriander Ln 77521
Cotton Bnd, Ct, Ln, Run & Way 77523
Cotton Bayou Cir 77523
Cotton Creek Dr 77523
Cotton Lake Rd 77523
Cotton Wood Dr 77523
Cottonwood Dr 77521
Country Club Dr & Vw 77521
Country Club Cove Dr 77521
Country Squire Blvd 77523
Courtyard Blvd 77520
Cove Crk & Loop 77523
Coyote Ln 77521
Crabapple Dr 77520
Craig St 77521
Craigmont St 77521
Crawley Ln 77523
Creekbend Dr 77521
Creekside Ave 77523
Creekview Dr 77523
Crestbriar Ct 77521
Crestmont St 77521
Crestway St 77520
Crestwood Dr 77523
Crosby Cedar Bayou Rd
2600-2699 77521
3100-3199 77520
3200-6899 77521
5616-2-5616-5 77521
Crossvine Ave 77521
Crow Rd 77520
Crowell Ln 77521
Crown Ln 77521
Crystal Blvd 77521
Curry St 77521
Cynda Brooke Dr 77521
Cypress St 77520
Cypress Point Dr 77523
Dahlia Rd 77521
Dailey St 77520
Daisy Ln 77523
N Dakota St 77520
Dale St 77520
Dallas St
1500-1598 77520
7100-7299 77521
Dancing Sun Ct 77521
Daniel St 77520
Danna St 77523
Danubina St 77520
Date Palm Ct 77523
Daystar St 77523
De La Luna Ct 77521
Deanne St 77520
Deborah Ln 77521
Decatur Ave 77521
Decker Dr 77520
Deerwood Cir 77521
E & W Defee Ave 77520
Del Norte Dr 77521
Del Oro Ct & St 77521
Del Sol Ct 77521
Del Sur St 77521
Delta Pkwy & St 77523
Delynn St 77521
Demi Ln 77523
Denby St 77520
Dent St 77521
Derek Dr 77521
Devinwood Dr 77523
Dewberry Ln 77523
Diamond Way 77523
Dixie Ln 77523
Dogwood Ct 77523
Dogwood Ln 77521
Dogwood Trl 77521
Dolphin Hbr N 77523
Dolphin Hbr S 77523
Dolphin Ln 77520
Don Q Ln 77523
Donovan St 77520
Doral Ct & Dr 77521
Dorris St 77520
Douglas St 77520
Dow Reef Dr 77523
Dozent Ln 77523
Driftwood Dr 77521
Dripping Spring Ave 77523
Duke St 77520
Durrain Ferry Rd 77520
Dwinnell St 77520
Dyer St 77520
Dylan Dr 77521
Eagle Ct & Dr 77523
Eagle Creek Dr 77523
East Fwy 77521
East Rd 77521
East St
200-399 77520
7100-7399 77521
Eastpoint Blvd 77521
Eaves Dr 77520
Echinacea Cir & Dr 77521
Echols Dr 77520
Edgebrook Dr 77521
Edgewood St 77520
Edison Cts & St 77520
Edna St 77520
Egret Bay Dr 77523
Egret Canal N & S 77523
El Chaco St 77521
El Rancho Dr 77521
El Tigre Ln 77521
Ellen St 77521
Ellis School Rd 77521
Elm St 77520
Elmwood Ct
4900-4999 77521
8000-8099 77523
Elmwood Dr 77520
Elton St 77520
Elvinta St 77520
Emerald Bay Cir 77523
Emmett Hutto Blvd 77521
Erie St 77521
Espuela Ln 77521
Estate Dr 77521
Eugenio Santana Dr 77520
Evangeline Way 77523
Evergreen Rd
100-199 77520
1500-1599 77523
Evergreen St 77523
Fairtide Dr 77521
Fairway Dr 77521
Fan Palm Dr 77523
Fanestiel St 77520
Fawndale Way 77521
E Fayle St
1-2199 77520
2300-2599 77521
N Felton St 77520
Fennel Dr 77521
Ferguson St 77520
Feristre Rd 77521
Fern Cove Dr 77521
Fernwood Ct 77523
Ferry Rd
2700-3199 77520
4000-4099 77523
4500-4599 77520
Firebrush Ln 77521
Fisher Dr & Rd 77523
Fisher Reef Dr 77523
Fitzgerald Rd 77521
Flamingo Bay Cir 77523
Flamingo Bight N & S 77523
Fleetwood St 77520
Fleming Dr 77521
Florida St 77520
Fm 1405 Rd 77523
Fm 1409 Rd 77523
Fm 1942 Rd 77521
Fm 2354 Rd 77523
Fm 3180 Rd 77523
N & S Fm 565 Rd 77523
Fm2354 Rd 77523
Forest Ct & Trl 77521
Forest Gate Dr 77521
Forest Hollow Dr 77521
Forest Stone St 77523
Forestay Ln 77521
Forrest St 77520
Fort Worth St 77520
Fortinberry St 77520
Fortner St 77520
Fortune Dr 77520
Foster St 77520
Fox Dr 77521
Fox St 77523
Fox Hollow St 77521
E & W Francis St 77520
Frank Ln 77523
Frank Rd 77521
Freesia Ct 77521
French Pl 77520
Friars Ln 77521
Gail Rd 77521
N & S Gaillard St 77520
Gant St 77521
Garth Rd
1200-2499 77520
2800-2998 77521
3000-10299 77521
Gayla Ln 77521
Gem Stone Ct 77521
George St 77523
Georgia St 77520
Gillette St 77520
Ginger Park Dr 77521
Ginseng Dr 77521
Gladiola Ave 77521
Glenhaven Dr 77521
Gloria Ln 77521
Godfrey St 77521
Going Ln 77521
Gold Finch Rd 77523
Golden Rd 77521
Gomez St 77521
Goose Creek Dr 77521
Goss Rd 77521
Gou Hole Rd 77523
Graham St 77520
Grand Isle Ln 77523
Grantham Rd 77521
Granville St 77520
Green St 77520
Green Tee Dr 77521
Greenbriar St 77520
Greenleaf St 77523
Greenway Dr 77521
Greenwood Dr 77520
Gresham St 77520
E & W Gulf St 77520
Gulf Wind Cir 77523
Gulfway Dr 77521
Gulls Cut N & S 77523
Gwenn Ln 77521
Hackberry St 77520
Hadden Rd 77521
Hafer St 77520
Haider Ave 77521
Halcyon Ln 77521
Hampton Bay Dr 77523
Happy Valley Dr 77520
Harbor St 77520
Harbor Mist 77521
Harbour Ln 77523
Hardin Rd 77521
Harding St 77520
Harlem St 77521
Harlin 77523
Harmon Rd 77523
Harold Ln 77523
Harris St 77521
Harrison Ave 77520
Harrison St 77521
Hartman Dr 77521
Hartrick Ln 77521
Hartt St 77520
Harvard St 77520
Harvest Ln 77521
Harvey Blvd & St 77520
Hatcherville Rd 77521
Hawthorne Cir 77523
Hawthorne St 77520
Hazel St 77521
Hazelnut Ln 77523
Heather Ln 77521
Heatherwood Dr 77521
Hemlock Dr 77521
Heron Inlt N & S 77523
Hiawatha St 77521
Hickory Ln 77521
Hidalgo St 77521
Hidden Ln 77523
High St 77520
High Meadow Ln 77523
Highway Blvd 77520
N Highway 146
9032-1A-9032-1C 77523
N Highway 146
300-898 77520
900-4999 77520
5000-10899 77523
6236-1-6236-10 77523
9223-1-9223-14 77523
S Highway 146 77520
Highway 201 77520
Hildago St 77521
Hill St 77520
Hillcrest St 77520
Hillhurst Dr 77521
Hines St 77520
Hodges St 77521
N Holly Dr 77520

Holly Spring Ln 77523
E & W Homan St 77520
Homewood Ln 77521
Honey Crk 77523
Honeysuckle Dr 77520
Hopi St 77521
Horn Ct 77523
Houston St 77520
Houston Point Dr 77523
Huggins St 77520
Hugh Echols Blvd 77521
E & W Humble St 77520
Hummingbird St 77523
E & W Hunnicutt St 77520
Hunt Rd 77521
Hunter St 77520
Hunters Trl 77521
Hunters Canyon Rd 77521
Hunters Creek Ln 77521
Hunters Peak Ln 77523
Hunters Ridge Dr 77521
Hunters Trace Ln 77521
Hunters Way Ln 77521
Huntington Ln 77521
Huron Ct 77521
Hurst Rd 77523
Idaho St 77520
Idlewood Dr 77520
Ilfrey St 77520
Illinois St 77520
Independence Blvd 77521
Independence Pkwy N 77520
Indian Trl
3200-4899 77521
9600-9799 77523
Indiana St 77520
Interlachen St 77521
Interstate 10 E 77523
Inverness Dr 77523
Inwood Cir 77523
Inwood Dr 77521
Iowa St 77520
Iris Ct 77521
Iris Bay Ln 77521
Ironwood Dr & Ln 77521
Isabelle St 77521
Ivie Lee St 77520
E & W Jack St 77520
Jacktree Ln 77521
E & W James St 77520
James Bowie Dr 77520
Jasmine Dr 77520
Jeanie Ln 77521
Jefferson St 77520
Jennische St 77520
Jerusalem Ct 77521
Joe Patch Rd 77523
John A St 77520
John Martin Rd 77521
Johnson Rd 77521
Johnson St 77520
Jones Rd
1500-1599 77520
1800-3199 77521
N Jones St 77520
S Jones St 77520
Jordan Rd 77523
Joseph Ln 77523
Juarez St 77521
Judy 77523
Judy Ln 77521
Juniper Dr 77521
Juniper Bay Ln 77521
Kai Dr 77523
Kaitlyn Ln 77521
Kansas St 77520
Katherine St 77520
Kathleen Dr 77523
Katies Creek Ave 77523
Keeneland Cir 77523
Kelly Ln 77521
Kendall Rd 77523
Kentucky St 77520
Kern St 77520
Kettering Dr 77521
Kilgore Ave 77520

Kilgore Pkwy 77523
Kilgore Rd 77520
King St 77520
King Edwards Pl 77521
Kings Dr 77521
Kingsway Dr 77521
Kiowa Cir 77521
Kipling St 77520
Kirby Dr 77521
Knight Ln 77521
Knights Ct 77521
Knowlton Rd 77520
Krystal Ct 77521
Krystine Dr 77523
La Reforma Blvd 77521
Lacey Dr 77520
Lafayette Ln 77523
Lafayette St 77520
Lake Pointe Ln 77523
Lakeside Ave 77523
Lakeview Dr
1700-2099 77520
15000-15999 77523
15002-1-15002-2 77523
Lakewood Dr & Vlg 77520
Lanai Dr 77523
Lancelot 77521
Land Breeze St 77523
Landmark Dr 77521
Landon Ln 77523
Lanes End St 77520
Langston Dr 77523
Lantana 77523
Lantern Ln 77521
Larch Cir & Dr 77521
Laredo St 77520
Largo St 77520
Lariat Dr 77521
Lariat Pl 77523
E, N, S & W Laura Cir 77521
Laurel Ln 77523
Laurel St 77520
Lauren Ln 77521
Lauren Creek Dr 77523
Lavage Ln 77521
Lavender Ln 77521
Lawrence Rd 77523
Layton St 77520
Lazy Ln 77520
Lazy River Ln 77523
Leavins St 77520
Lee Dr 77520
Legends Bay Dr 77523
Leland Dr 77521
Lemongrass Ave 77521
Lennie Ln 77523
Leon St 77523
Lilac Dr 77521
Lilac Ln 77520
Lilac Rd 77521
Lillian St 77521
Lilly Ln 77523
Lincoln Cts & St 77520
Lincoln Cedar Dr 77523
Linda Ln
5300-5499 77521
8800-8899 77523
Lindberg St 77520
E Lindbergh Ct 77521
Lindenwood Dr 77520
Little Rd 77521
Little Oak Dr 77523
Littlehip Hawthorn Dr 77523
Littlewood St 77521
Live Oak St 77520
Lloyd Ln 77521
E & W Lobit St 77520
Lone Oak Ct & Dr 77521
Lonely Pine Dr 77521
Long Dr 77521
Long Leaf Ln 77521
Long Meadow Dr 77521
Longhorn Dr 77521
Longwood Dr 77523
Loreli Ln 77521

Lorraine Dr 77521
Lost Lake Dr 77523
Lost Pine Dr 77521
Lotebush Ln 77523
Louise St 77521
Louisiana St 77520
Lynn Brook Ln 77523
Lynnwood Dr 77521
Mable St 77520
Mabry Rd 77520
Macarthur St 77520
Mackrell St 77523
Madison Ave 77523
Madison St 77520
Magnolia Bnd 77523
Magnolia Bnd W 77523
Magnolia St 77520
Magnolia Cove Dr 77521
Main St 77523
N Main St
100-2599 77520
2700-9799 77521
9801-9999 77521
5790-1-5790-3 77521
7411-1-7411-3 77521
7619-1-7619-3 77521
S Main St 77520
W Main St 77520
Majestic Dr 77523
Majestic Ln 77521
Makah Cir 77521
Maley Rd 77523
Mallard Byu & Dr 77523
Mallards Way 77521
Mandalay Bay Dr 77523
Manor Dr 77521
Maple Dr & Ln 77521
Maplewood St 77520
Marian St 77520
Marigold Rd 77521
N Market Loop 77521
Market St 77520
Marlin Ln 77520
Marquis Ave 77521
Martin Luther King St 77520
Martinique Ln 77523
Marvin Rd 77521
Mary Ln 77523
Mary Ethel Rd 77521
Mary Wilbanks Ave 77520
Maryland St 77520
Maryon St 77523
Massey St 77520
Massey Tompkins Rd
100-3999 77521
4000-4099 77520
Mastic Dr 77521
May Apple St 77523
Mayhaw Dr 77520
Mayo St 77520
Mccollum Park Rd 77523
Mccullough St 77521
Mccune Ln 77523
Mcdaniels St 77521
Mcfarland St 77520
Mckinney Rd
100-199 77523
2700-2999 77520
3200-3699 77521
E Mckinney Rd 77523
Mclean Rd 77521
Mcphail Rd 77521
Meador Ln 77520
Meadowbrook Dr 77521
Meadowglen Dr 77521
Meadowick Dr 77521
Meadowlark Dr 77523
Meadowlark Ln 77521
Meadowood Cir & Dr 77521
Memorial Dr 77520
Memory Ln 77521
Meridian Blvd 77521
Merrilane St 77520
Mesa Ct 77521
Mescalero St 77521
Mesquite St 77521

Michaelis Ln 77521
Michigan St 77520
Middleton St 77520
Midway Dr 77521
Mill Creek Dr 77521
Miller Rd 77523
Minnesota St 77520
Minnie Ln 77523
Miriam St 77520
Mission Viejo St 77521
Mississippi St 77520
Missouri St 77520
Mocker Nut St 77523
Mockingbird St 77520
Mohave Cir 77521
Mohawk St 77521
Mohegan Ct 77521
Monroe St 77520
Montana St 77520
Montego Dr 77521
Montego Bay Dr 77523
Montezuma St 77521
Morelos Rd 77521
Moridarb St 77520
Morning Dr 77520
Morrell St 77520
Morris St 77520
Morrison St 77523
Mossey Oak Dr 77520
Mount Olive Ln 77523
Mourning Dr 77521
Mulberry Ln 77521
E & W Murrill St 77520
Musclewood Rd 77521
Myers St 77520
Myrtle Dr 77520
Mystery Ln 77523
Narcille St 77520
Natchez St 77520
Natchez Trce 77523
Nautilus Ln 77521
Navajo Trl 77521
E & W Nazro St 77520
Neal St 77520
Nebraska St 77520
Needlepoint Rd
7000-9999 77521
17900-20199 77523
Nevada St 77520
New Jersey St 77520
New Meadow Dr 77521
New Mexico St 77520
New York St 77520
Newcastle Dr 77521
Newman Dr 77521
Noble Ct 77521
Nolan Rd 77520
North Rd 77521
North St 77520
Northbend Dr 77521
Northridge Dr 77521
Northwood Dr 77521
Nowlin Dr 77521
Oak Haven St 77520
Oak Hollow St 77521
Oak Leaf St 77521
Oak Ridge Dr 77523
Oak Shadows St 77520
Oakland St 77520
Oaks Grande Rd 77523
Oakwood St 77520
Oakwood Court Dr 77521
Ocean Dr 77523
Ohio St 77520
Oklahoma St 77520
Old Irish Farm Rd 77523
Old Needlepoint Rd
9600-9999 77521
10700-11300 77523
11302-19798 77523
Old Oaks Dr 77521
Old River Dr 77523
Oleander Dr 77523
Oleander St 77521
Olive Cir & St 77520
Oliver Ln 77523

Omaha Dr 77521
Ontario St 77520
Orchard Cir 77521
Orchid St 77521
Oregano Dr 77521
Oregon St 77520
Osage Dr 77521
W Osage Dr 77523
E Osage St 77523
Oscar Nelson Jr Dr 77523
Otter Cir 77523
Owl Ln 77523
Packsaddle Ln 77521
Palm Cir 77523
Palm Dr
7300-7999 77521
8300-10199 77523
N Palm Dr 77521
Palmetto Ln 77521
Palomar St 77520
Pamela Dr 77521
Paprika Ln 77521
Paradise Rd 77521
Park St 77520
Park Bend Dr 77521
Park Creek Rd 77523
Park Grove Dr 77521
Park Lane Dr 77521
Park Shadow Dr 77521
Parkbriar Cir 77521
Parker Place Dr 77523
Parkleaf Dr 77521
Parkview Ct 77523
Parkway St 77520
Parkwood Dr 77521
Parsley St 77521
Patsy Dr 77520
Pawnee St 77521
E & W Pearce St 77520
Pearl St 77520
Pebble Brook St 77521
Pecan Dr 77520
Pecan Ln 77523
Pecan Forest Ln 77521
Pecan Grove Dr 77521
Pecan Loop Dr 77523
Pecan Manor St 77520
Peggy St 77520
Pelican Dr & Ln 77523
Pelican Bay Ln 77523
Pepper Mill St 77521
Peppercorn Dr 77521
Peppermint Dr 77521
Perch St 77523
Perry Rd 77523
Perry St 77521
N Perry St 77521
Pershing St 77520
Persimmon Dr 77520
Pickling Ln 77521
Pimlico Dr 77523
Pin Oak Dr
100-599 77520
4000-4199 77523
W Pin Oak Dr 77523
Pine St 77520
Pine Lake Ln 77521
Pine Meadows Blvd 77523
Pine Oak Ln 77521
Pine Ridge St 77523
Pine Shadows Blvd 77523
Pine Shadows Ln 77521
Pine Wind Ct 77521
Pine Wood Ct 77521
Pinebrook Ln 77523
Pinehurst St 77521
Pinemont St 77520
Pineville Dr 77521
Pinewood Court Dr 77521
Piping Rock St 77523
Pirates Run 77523
Plantation Dr 77523
Pleasant Dr 77520
Plumeria Ave 77521
Pocahontas Dr 77521
N Point Dr 77523

Point Barrow Rd 77523
Polly St 77520
Poncho Pl 77523
Ponderosa Dr 77521
Ponderosa Pine Dr 77523
Poplar Ct 77523
Post Oak Dr 77520
Price St 77520
Primrose Rd 77521
Prince St 77521
Procter Rd 77521
N Pruett St
200-2499 77520
3000-3099 77521
S Pruett St 77520
Pueblo St & Trl 77521
Purvis Ln 77521
Quail Hollow Cir & Dr 77521
Quailwood Dr 77521
Queens Ct 77520
Queenswood St 77521
Quiet Bay Dr 77523
Rabbit Hollow Dr 77521
Raccoon Dr 77521
Railroad Ave 77521
Railway St 77521
Railwood St 77521
Raintree St 77520
Ramsey Dr 77520
Range Ln 77523
Ravens Way 77523
Red Bud Ln 77520
Red Cedar Bnd, Dr & Trl 77521
Red Oak Ln 77523
Redberry Hill St 77521
N Redell Rd 77521
Redfish Run 77523
Redfish Reef Dr 77523
Redwood Dr 77523
Regal Dr 77521
E & W Republic St 77520
Rey Ave 77521
Rice Farm Rd 77523
Riceflower St 77523
Richard St 77520
Richards St 77521
Richardson Ln 77520
Ridge Canyon Rd 77521
Riggs St 77520
Rio Dr 77521
Ripple Creek Cir & Dr 77521
River Bend Dr 77523
River Circle Dr 77523
River Oaks Dr 77523
River Ridge St 77523
River Run Dr 77523
Rivera Rd 77521
Riverbend St 77521
Robert St 77521
N Robert Lanier Dr 77521
Roberts Blvd 77521
Robin Rd 77520
Rock Creek Rd 77523
Rocky River St 77523
Rodney Ln 77520
Rollingbrook Dr & St 77521
Rollingcreek Dr 77521
Rollingwood Cir & St 77520
Ronnie Dr 77523
Ronson Ln 77521
Rose Meadow Blvd 77521
Rosebay Rd 77521
Roseland Dr 77520
Rosemary Cir & Dr 77521
Roseshire Ln 77521
Rosewood Dr 77520
Rosille St 77520
Roy Ave 77520
Royal St 77521
Royal Palm Dr 77523
Rue Orleans St 77520
Running Creek Ct 77521
Running Deer 77523
Russell Ln 77521
Rusty Blackhaw Ln 77523

Ruth Ln 77523
Ruth St 77520
Sable Palm Dr 77523
Saddle Pl 77523
Saddlewood Dr 77523
Safflower Dr 77521
Saffron Ln 77521
Sage Cir & St 77521
Sagebrush Trl 77521
Saint Andrews Dr 77521
Salmon St 77523
San Jacinto Cir & Mall 77521
San Juan Pl 77523
Sand Plum Ln 77523
Sandalwood Cir 77521
Sandpiper Cir & Dr 77521
Sandy Ln 77520
Sandy Creek Dr 77523
Sanford St 77521
Santee Cir & Dr 77521
Sarah Ln
4500-4599 77523
6500-8199 77521
Sarsaparilla Dr 77521
Sativa Cir 77521
Savell Dr 77521
Sawgrass Cir & Dr 77521
Scarlet Cir 77521
Scarlett St 77520
Scenic Dr 77521
Schaffer St 77523
Schilling St 77520
Schoppa Ln 77521
Scott St 77520
Scottwood Dr 77521
Sea Crest Park Rd 77523
Seabird St 77521
Seminole St 77521
Seneca Ct 77521
Seneca Dr 77523
September Dr 77521
Sequoia St 77521
Sesame St 77521
Shadow Creek Ct 77523
Shady Ln 77520
Shady Grove St 77523
Shady Hill Dr 77521
Shale Dr 77521
Shana Ln 77523
Shannon Bnd 77521
Sharon Ln 77521
Shawnee St 77521
E Shawnee St 77523
W Shawnee St 77523
Shearer Ln 77521
Sheila Dr 77521
Shell Dock Rd 77523
Shelldrake Way 77521
N & S Shepherd Dr 77520
Sheppard Rd 77521
Sheri Ln 77521
Sheridan Dr 77520
Sherwood St 77520
Shirley St 77521
Short St 77521
Shoshone Dr 77521
Shoshoni St 77521
E & W Shreck St 77520
Sierra Dr 77521
Silner Fir Ln 77523
Silver Fir Ln 77523
Simms Rd 77523
Singleton Rd 77521
Sioux St 77521
Sjolander Cir & Rd 77521
Skyhawk Ln 77523
Skylane Rd 77523
Sleepy Crk 77523
Snomac Ct 77521
Sombrero St 77521
Somerset Dr 77521
Sonny Ln 77523
Sonora St 77521
Sorrel Cir 77521
South Rd 77521
South St 77520

Southwind Ct ... 77523
Southwood Cir & Dr ... 77520
Sparks Ct ... 77523
Sprangletop Ave ... 77521
Spring Crk ... 77523
Spring Ln ... 77521
Spring Branch Dr ... 77523
Spring Creek Cir ... 77521
Spruce Ln ... 77523
Spur Cir ... 77523
Spur 55 ... 77523
Squire Dr ... 77521
St Augustine Rd ... 77521
St Croix Way ... 77523
St Thomas St ... 77523
Stablebrook Dr ... 77523
Stacey Ln ... 77520
Staples Dr ... 77523
Starflower Ln ... 77521
Starr Ln ... 77521
Steinman St ... 77520
Stella St ... 77520
Sterling Dr ... 77523
E Sterling St ... 77520
W Sterling St ... 77520
Stewart St ... 77520
Still Water St ... 77521
Stimpson St ... 77520
Stockbridge St ... 77521
Stone Bridge St ... 77521
Stonehedge Dr ... 77521
Stoneybrook St ... 77521
Stowe St ... 77520
Strawn St ... 77520
Strickland St ... 77520
Sugar Bush ... 77523
Sugar Cane Dr ... 77523
Sugar Pine Ln ... 77523
Sumal Cir ... 77521
Summer Ln ... 77521
Sundance Ct ... 77521
Sundown Ln ... 77523
Sundowner Dr ... 77523
Sunny Dr & Ln ... 77521
Sunnybrook Ln ... 77521
Sunnyside Dr ... 77523
Sunrise Rd ... 77523
Sunset Dr ... 77520
Superior Dr ... 77521
Superior St ... 77520
Surrey St ... 77521
Swalm Center Dr ... 77520
Swan Ln ... 77523
Sweet Bay Cir & St ... 77523
Sweet Gum Ln ... 77521
Sycamore Ln ... 77523
Sylvan Ln ... 77521
Sylvia Ln ... 77523
Taft Cir & Dr ... 77520
Taino Dr ... 77521
Tallant St ... 77520
Tallow Cove Dr ... 77521
Tallow Wood Ct ... 77523
Tamarach Dr ... 77521
Tameyoza Ln ... 77521
Tammy Ln ... 77523
Tanglewood Dr ... 77523
Tanglewood St ... 77520
Taro Ln ... 77521
Tarpon Run ... 77523
Tarragon Ln ... 77521
Taylor Dr ... 77521
Teal Way ... 77523
Tejas St ... 77521
Tennessee St ... 77520
Terrace Dr ... 77521
Terrace Ln ... 77520
Terry Ln ... 77521
Texana ... 77523
E & W Texas Ave ... 77520
Texoma St ... 77520
Thibodeaux St ... 77520
Thomas Rd ... 77521
Thompson Rd ... 77521
Thompson St ... 77520
Thunder Bay ... 77523
Thunderbird Cir ... 77521
Thyme Cir & Ln ... 77521
Tilton Landing Dr ... 77523
Timber Ln ... 77520
Timber Creek Ave ... 77523
Timber Ridge St ... 77521
Tobago Ct ... 77523
Tobosa St ... 77521
Tompkins Dr ... 77521
Tonkawa St ... 77521
Toulouse Ave ... 77521
Town Cir ... 77520
Trailwood Dr ... 77521
Transport Dr ... 77523
Travis Ln ... 77523
Travis St ... 77520
Treasure Ct ... 77521
Tremont Dr ... 77523
Trenton Ln ... 77520
Trestletree Way ... 77521
Tri City Beach Rd
300-399 ... 77520
1700-17499 ... 77523
11010-1-11010-5 ... 77523
12322-1-12322-2 ... 77523
12618-1-12618-4 ... 77523
17201-1-17201-3 ... 77523
6102-1-6102-2 ... 77523
8830-1-8830-2 ... 77523
9128-1-9128-2 ... 77523
9344-1-9344-8 ... 77523
Trinidad Dr ... 77523
Trinity St ... 77520
Tucker Rd ... 77521
Tulip Ln ... 77521
Tumbleweed Ln ... 77521
Tumblewood Dr ... 77523
Turmeric Dr ... 77521
Turnberry Cir ... 77523
Turner St ... 77520
Tuscan Ln ... 77520
W Twisted Oak St ... 77521
Ulysses Ln ... 77521
Upland Way ... 77523
Utah St ... 77520
Vae Dr ... 77521
Venice St ... 77523
Veranda Dr ... 77523
Verdinell St ... 77521
Vermont St ... 77520
Victoria ... 77523
Viking Ln ... 77520
Village Ln ... 77521
Vine St ... 77520
Virginia St ... 77520
Vista Ave ... 77520
Waco St ... 77521
Wade Rd ... 77521
Walker Rd ... 77521
Walker St ... 77523
Wallace Rd ... 77523
Wallflower Ave ... 77521
E Wallisville Rd ... 77521
Ward Rd ... 77520
Warren Rd ... 77521
Wasabi Ln ... 77521
Washington St
1900-2099 ... 77520
7400-7699 ... 77521
Water Canyon Rd ... 77521
Water Oak St & Trl ... 77523
Water Point Dr ... 77523
Water Ridge Ln ... 77521
Waterwood Dr ... 77521
Weaver St ... 77520
Wellington Park ... 77520
Welton Ln ... 77523
West Rd ... 77521
Western St ... 77523
Westwood St ... 77520
Wheat Ln ... 77521
Wheatley St ... 77520
Whispering Pines St ... 77521
Whispering Winds Ct ... 77521
White Ash Ln ... 77521
White Pine Ln ... 77523
White Willow Ln ... 77523
Whitetail Dr ... 77521
N & S Whiting St ... 77520
Whiting Rock St ... 77521
Wichita Cir ... 77521
Wilburn Dr ... 77520
Wilburn Ranch Dr ... 77523
Wild Dunes Ct ... 77523
Wildlife Way ... 77523
Wildrose St ... 77520
Wildwood St ... 77520
William Ave ... 77520
William Trce ... 77523
Williams Ln ... 77523
Willow Ln & St ... 77520
Willow Glen Ln ... 77521
Willow Oak Dr ... 77521
Willowview Dr ... 77521
Wilma Ln ... 77523
Wilshire Ln ... 77521
Wilson Rd ... 77521
Wimberly Ln ... 77523
Wincrest Dr ... 77523
Windy Ln ... 77520
Windy Oaks St ... 77523
Winfree St ... 77523
Winkler St ... 77520
Winter Ln ... 77521
Winter Haven Dr ... 77521
Wisconsin St ... 77520
Wolfberry Ln ... 77521
Wood Ave ... 77520
Wood Duck Ln ... 77523
Wood Hollow Dr ... 77521
Wood Leaf Ct ... 77521
Woodall Ln ... 77523
Woodcrest Dr ... 77521
Wooded Trl ... 77521
Woodford St ... 77521
Woodlawn St ... 77520
Woodridge Ln ... 77523
Woodside Dr ... 77520
Woodstone Dr ... 77521
Wooster St ... 77520
E Wright Ave ... 77520
W Wright Ave ... 77520
Wright Blvd ... 77520
Wright Ln ... 77523
E & W Wye Dr ... 77521
Wyoming St ... 77520
Yaupon Dr ... 77520
S Yoradins Inlt S ... 77523
Yuma Dr ... 77521
Yupon St ... 77520
Zaragosa St ... 77521
Zavalla St ... 77521
Zeenat Blvd ... 77521

NUMBERED STREETS

1st St ... 77523
N 1st St ... 77520
S 1st St ... 77520
2nd St ... 77523
N 2nd St ... 77520
S 2nd St ... 77520
3rd St ... 77523
N 3rd St
2-198 ... 77520
200-999 ... 77520
1300-1499 ... 77523
S 3rd St ... 77520
N & S 4th ... 77520
N 5th St ... 77520
N 6th St ... 77520
N & S 7th ... 77520
N 8th St ... 77520
N 10th St ... 77520
N 11th St ... 77520

BEAUMONT TX

General Delivery ... 77704

POST OFFICE BOXES MAIN OFFICE STATIONS AND BRANCHES

Box No.s
1 - 2122 ... 77704
1983 - 1983 ... 77710
2161 - 4956 ... 77704
5001 - 5979 ... 77726
6001 - 6800 ... 77725
7001 - 7978 ... 77726
9998 - 9998 ... 77704
10001 - 12166 ... 77710
12001 - 18004 ... 77726
20001 - 26756 ... 77720
41001 - 50003 ... 77725

RURAL ROUTES

01, 03, 05, 07, 09, 11, 13 ... 77713

NAMED STREETS

A And M ... 77705
Abigail Ct ... 77705
Abilene St ... 77703
Abraham St ... 77705
Academy Dr ... 77706
Acadia Ln ... 77708
Acadiana Ct ... 77706
Acorn Circuit ... 77703
Ada St ... 77708
Adams St ... 77705
Adilade St ... 77705
Adsit St ... 77707
Afton Ln
4100-4499 ... 77705
6000-6299 ... 77706
Aggie Dr ... 77713
Agnes St ... 77703
Airline Dr ... 77705
Alabama St ... 77705
Alancom St ... 77703
Alaskan Dr ... 77713
Albany St ... 77703
Alece Ln ... 77713
Alford St ... 77713
Alford Oaks Dr & St ... 77713
Allen Dr ... 77708
Allison Way ... 77707
E Alma St ... 77705
Alpine Cir ... 77708
Alvoid St ... 77703
Amarillo St ... 77701
Amberwood Dr ... 77713
Amelia St ... 77707
Ammie St ... 77705
Amoco Rd ... 77705
Amos Ln ... 77713
Anastasia Ave ... 77705
Anchor St ... 77705
Anderson St ... 77703
Andrus St ... 77701
Angelina St
1900-2299 ... 77701
2300-2600 ... 77702
2602-2998 ... 77702
Anita St ... 77705
Anna Ln ... 77707
Annie St ... 77705
Annie Lou Dr ... 77705
Apremont Cir ... 77707
Arabella St ... 77701
Arbor Ln ... 77706
Arbor Wood ... 77705
Arbor Wood Ln ... 77706
Archie St ... 77701
Arkansas St ... 77707
Armstrong Dr ... 77707
Arrowhead Dr ... 77707
Arthur Ln
2801-2899 ... 77703
4001-4097 ... 77706
4099-4899 ... 77706
Ascot Cir ... 77706
Ashdown St ... 77706
Ashland Ln ... 77706
Ashleigh Pl ... 77705
Ashley St
1000-2299 ... 77701
2300-2699 ... 77702
Ashwood St ... 77703
Aspen Ln ... 77713
Astor St ... 77703
Atlanta St ... 77701
Aubey Rd ... 77705
Auburn St ... 77705
Audree St ... 77708
Audubon Pl ... 77706
Augusta Dr ... 77707
Augusta St ... 77705
Austin St ... 77706
Autumn Dr ... 77706
Avalon St ... 77707
Avenue E
600-2999 ... 77701
Avenue E
3300-3499 ... 77705
Avenue A
1-2999 ... 77701
3000-7099 ... 77705
Avenue B
500-2999 ... 77701
3100-3398 ... 77705
3400-7199 ... 77705
Avenue C
200-2999 ... 77701
3000-3098 ... 77705
3100-7299 ... 77705
Avenue D ... 77701
Avenue F ... 77701
Avenue G ... 77701
Avenue H ... 77701
Avenue I ... 77701
Avenue Of The Oaks ... 77707
Averill St ... 77703
Averrill St ... 77701
Avie Ln ... 77708
Azalea Dr
5600-5698 ... 77706
17800-18199 ... 77705
Babe Zaharias Dr ... 77705
Baker Rd ... 77707
Baldwin St ... 77703
Ballard Rd ... 77705
Balsa Ln ... 77713
Baltimore Rd ... 77705
Bamboo Ln ... 77708
Bancroft Dr ... 77706
Bandera Dr ... 77706
Bankston Ln ... 77706
Bankston Rd ... 77713
Barbara Ln ... 77705
Barnett Rd ... 77713
Barrett Rd ... 77708
Barrington Ave ... 77706
Bart Ln ... 77705
Barton Ln ... 77706
Barton St ... 77705
Basin St ... 77705
Bass Rd ... 77705
Basswood Ln ... 77713
Bay Hill Cir ... 77707
Baylor Cir & Ln ... 77705
Bayou Dr ... 77705
Bayou Ln ... 77713
Bayou Rd
1000-1399 ... 77705
3700-4200 ... 77707
4202-4298 ... 77707
Bayou Trce ... 77705
Bayou Bend Pl ... 77706
Bayou Brandt ... 77706
Bayou Din Dr ... 77705
Bayou Willow Dr ... 77705
Baywood Ln ... 77706
Beale St ... 77705
Bean Cts ... 77703
Beard St ... 77703
Beatrice St ... 77703
Beaumont Dr ... 77708
Beauview Dr ... 77713
Beauxart Garden Rd ... 77705
Beck St ... 77708
Bedford Dr ... 77708
Beech St
700-799 ... 77703
1100-1299 ... 77701
2401-2699 ... 77702
Bell Pointe ... 77706
Bellaire Ln ... 77706
Bellchase Dr ... 77706
Bellchase Gardens Dr ... 77706
Bellgreen Pl ... 77707
Belmont St ... 77707
Belvedere Dr ... 77706
Belvedere Pkwy ... 77707
W Bend ... 77706
Bender St ... 77705
Bennett Rd ... 77708
Benton Ln ... 77706
Berard Cir ... 77705
Berkley St ... 77703
Berkshire Ln ... 77707
Berry Dr ... 77705
Berry Rd ... 77706
Bertrand Rd ... 77713
Berwick Dr ... 77706
Bessemer Ave ... 77703
Best Rd ... 77713
Bethlehem Ave ... 77703
Bettes Ln ... 77708
Betty Ln ... 77703
Beverly Ave ... 77703
Bicentennial Ln & Pl ... 77706
Bienville Dr ... 77706
Big Hill Rd ... 77705
Big Oaks ... 77713
Bigner Rd ... 77708
Bingman St ... 77705
Birch Dr ... 77708
Birch Ln ... 77713
Birmingham St ... 77703
Black Ln ... 77713
Blackgum St ... 77713
Blackmon Ln
3000-3399 ... 77703
3500-3799 ... 77706
Blackwell Ln ... 77713
Blanch Rd ... 77713
Blanch St ... 77703
Blanchette St ... 77701
Blanco Rd ... 77705
Blanton Pl ... 77707
Blarney St ... 77706
Blaylock Ln ... 77707
Blewett Rd ... 77705
Blossom Dr ... 77705
Blossom St ... 77713
Blue Bonnet Ln
7700-8099 ... 77713
10900-11499 ... 77705
E & N Blue Stem ... 77713
Blueberry Ln ... 77708
Bluebird Way ... 77713
Bob St ... 77705
Bobbie Cir & Dr ... 77705
Bobolink Ln ... 77713
Bogan Rd ... 77713
Bolivar St
1100-3199 ... 77701
4600-4899 ... 77707
Bonham St ... 77701
Bonner Dr ... 77713
Bonney Briar Pl ... 77707
Bonnie Lee St ... 77705
Booker St ... 77705
Boondocks Rd ... 77705
Bordages Rd ... 77705
Borden Rd ... 77705
Bourbon St ... 77705
Boutwell Rd ... 77713
Bowen Dr ... 77708
Bowers Dr ... 77705
Bowie St ... 77701
Bowling Rd ... 77705
Boyd St ... 77705
Boyt Rd
4400-9899 ... 77713
10600-10999 ... 77705
Brace St ... 77708
Bradford Dr ... 77707
Bradley Aly & St ... 77701
Braeburn St ... 77707
Bragg Cir ... 77705
Brahma St ... 77703
Brandon St ... 77705
Brandywine St ... 77706
Brazos Ln ... 77705
Breeana Ct ... 77705
Brenda St ... 77713
Brenham St ... 77701
Brentwood Dr ... 77706
Brett Ln ... 77713
Brewton Cir ... 77706
Briar Ct ... 77706
Briar Rd ... 77708
Briar Way ... 77706
E Briar Bend Loop ... 77708
Briar Creek Dr ... 77706
Briarcliff Dr ... 77706
Briarmeadow Dr ... 77706
Brickyard Rd ... 77703
Brigance Rd ... 77705
Briggs St ... 77707
Brighton Ct ... 77706
Brighton Dr ... 77707
Bristol Dr ... 77707
Brittini Ct ... 77708
Broadleaf Dr ... 77708
Broadmoor Dr ... 77707
Broadoak St ... 77713
N Broadway ... 77713
Broadway St
200-2299 ... 77701
2300-2699 ... 77702
W Broadway St ... 77707
Brock St ... 77707
Brockman St ... 77705
Brooklyn St ... 77701
Brooks Rd
200-499 ... 77713
5100-5199 ... 77705
9700-12499 ... 77713
Broun St ... 77707
Broussard Rd ... 77713
Broussard St ... 77705
Browning Dr ... 77706
Brownstone Dr & Pl ... 77706
Bruce Dr ... 77708
Bryan Dr ... 77707
Bryant Way ... 77706
Buchanan St ... 77703
Buckingham Row ... 77706
Buena Vista Ln ... 77707
Buffalo Cir ... 77703
Buffalo St
3800-4899 ... 77703
8600-8899 ... 77713
Buffington Ln ... 77705
Buford St ... 77701
Bun St ... 77705
Burbank St ... 77707
Burgundy Pl ... 77705
Burlington Dr ... 77706
Burrell Ln & Loop ... 77705
Burrell Cemetery Rd ... 77705
Burrell Wingate Rd ... 77705
Burt St ... 77701
Burton St ... 77705
Butlin St ... 77705
Buttercup Ln ... 77713
Byrd St ... 77707
Bythewood Rd ... 77713
C D S Dr ... 77703
Cable Ave ... 77703
Cable St ... 77701

Street	ZIP
Cactus Ave & St	77705
Cadillac Ln	77705
Caffin Dr	77706
Calder Ave	77706
Calder St	
600-2299	77701
2300-3199	77702
Caldwell Ave	77703
E, N, S & W Caldwood Dr	77707
Calhoun Ave	77707
California St	77701
Callais Rd	77713
Callaway Dr	77706
Calumet Dr	77708
Calvin St	77707
Cambridge Dr	77707
Camelia Dr	77705
Camellia Dr	77706
Campbell St	77703
Campus St	77705
Canal St	77701
Candlelite Dr	77713
Candlestick Cir	77706
Candy Ln	77713
Canterbury Dr	77707
Canyon Cir	77707
Canyon Ln	77713
Capital Dr	77713
Capo Ln	77705
Captain Dr	77706
Captain Kidd Way	77713
Cara Ln	77706
Carabin St	77701
Cardinal Ct	77713
E Cardinal Dr	77705
W Cardinal Dr	77705
Carmel Cir	77707
Carnahan Pl	77707
Carnation Dr	77706
Carnegie St	77703
Caroline St	77703
Carpenter Rd	77713
Carrie Ln	77713
Carroll Ln	77713
Carroll St	77701
Carson Dr	77706
Cartwright St	
700-3299	77701
4200-4899	77707
Carver St	77705
Case St	77703
Casey Dr	
8800-8999	77707
9200-9399	77705
Casey St	77713
Cash Cir	77705
Cash Lee Ct	77713
E Caston St	77705
Caswell Rd	77708
Catalpa St	77703
Cathedral Sq	77701
Catherine Ln	77708
Cathryn Ln	77705
Cecil Dr	77706
Cedar St	77701
W Cedar St	77702
Celia Dr	77705
Cement St	77701
Center St	77701
Central Dr	
601-697	77706
699-2399	77706
8800-9199	77705
Central Caldwood Dr	77707
Central Pointe Dr	77706
Chadwick St	77706
Chaison St	77705
Chamberlin Dr & Rd	77707
Chambers St	77705
Chambless Dr	77705
Champions Dr	77707
Chandler Dr	77705
Chapel Ln	77705
E & W Chapin St	77705
Charles St	77703
Charleston Ln	77706
Charlie Richard Ln	77705
Charlotte Dr	77705
Charlton Wood	77705
Chase	77708
Chateau Cir & Ln	77707
Chatom Trce	77706
Chatwood Dr	77706
Cheek St	77705
Chelsea Pl	77706
Chemical Rd	77705
Cherokee Ln	77702
Cherry Dr	77703
Cherrywood Dr	77706
Cheryl St	77713
Cheska Holw	77706
Chestnut Ln	77713
Chevy Chase Ln	77706
Chimney Rock St	77713
N & S China Rd	77713
Chinn Ln	77708
Chinquapin Ln	77708
Chisholm Trl	77708
Christina Ct & Ln	77706
Christopher Ln	77705
Christopher St	77708
Christy Ln	77705
Church Rd	
10400-10699	77705
11100-11299	77713
Church St	77705
E Church St	77705
E Circuit Dr	77706
Clara St	77703
Clark St	77705
Clay Cir	77713
Claybourn Dr	77706
Clearview St	77701
Clearwater Ct	77705
Clemmons St	77707
Cleo St	77701
Cleveland St	77703
Click Dr	77708
Clifton St	77708
Clint Ln	77713
Clinton Dr	77713
Clinton St	77706
Clover Cir	77708
Cloverdale St	77703
Club Oaks Rd	77713
E Clubb Rd	77705
W Clubb Rd	77713
Coast St	77703
Coatsville St	77703
Cobblestone Ct	77713
Coburn Dr	77707
Cochran St	77705
Coffey Dr	77706
Cole Dr	77705
Cole Rd	
5400-5699	77708
5700-5999	77706
Coleman St	77703
College St	
100-3899	77701
3900-9799	77707
Collier Rd & St	77706
Collier Ranch Rd	77713
Collis St	77701
Colonial Dr	77707
Colorado St	77705
Colton Ln	77706
Columbia St	77701
Combs Dr	77705
W Commerce Pkwy	77707
Commerce St	77703
Comstock Rd	77708
Concord Rd	
1400-4899	77703
4900-7699	77708
Concord St	77701
Condon St	77701
Congress St	77705
Conrad St	77701
Conroe St	77705
Continental St	77706
Cooke St	77703
Coolidge St	77706
Coral Creek St	77707
Cordova St	77703
Corkwood Ln	77706
Corley St	
700-3799	77701
4200-4899	77707
Cornell Dr	77705
Cornerstone Ct	77706
Coronado Cir	77706
Cottage Grove Ct	77713
Cotton Ct	77701
E Cottonwood St	77703
Country Ln & Rd	77705
Country Club Blvd	77703
Country Club Dr	77705
Cousins St	77703
Covington Ct	77706
Cowart St	77708
Cox St	77703
Craig Ln	77713
Craig St	77701
Craigen Rd	77705
Crawford St	77706
Crescent Dr	77706
Crestland Loop	77705
Crestview Cir & Ln	77707
Crestwood Dr	77706
W Crockett St	77701
Crossmeadow Dr	77706
Crosstimbers	77705
Crow Rd	77706
Crystal Lakes Dr	77705
Cuchia St	77705
Cumberland Dr	77708
Cuniff Rd	77705
Cuniff St	77701
Cunningham St	77705
Curtis Ct	77708
Cypress Ln	77705
Cypress Point Dr	77707
Dairy Ridge Dr	77705
Daisy Dr	77706
Dakota St	77708
Dallas St	77703
Daniel Dr	77705
Dante Ln	77706
Dauphine Pl	77705
Davida Dr	77713
Davidson Rd	77705
Dawn Dr	
5000-5399	77706
7900-8199	77705
Deerchase Dr	77713
Del Pl	77705
Delaware St	
501-519	77703
521-3399	77703
3401-3497	77706
3499-6899	77706
E Delaware St	77703
Dellwood Ln	77706
Delmar Dr	77707
Delta Ln	77701
Denley	77713
Denton St	77707
Denver St	77703
Derby Ln	77706
Deshotel Rd	77713
Detroit St	77703
Devers Dr	77705
Devilleneuve St	77701
Devon St	77707
Dewberry Ln	77708
Dewey St	77703
Dexter St	77703
Diamond St	77705
Diamond D Dr	77713
Diane Dr	77706
Dickinson St	77703
Directors Row	77705
Dishman Rd	77713
Dixie Dr	77707
Dobson Rd	77708
Dogwood Dr	77705
Dogwood Ln	77703
Dollinger Rd	77703
Dolores St	77705
Donald Dr	77705
Donna Ln	77708
Donohue St	77705
Doral Dr	77707
Doris Ln	77708
Dorothy St	77705
Doty St	77707
Doucet St	77705
Doucette St	77701
Douglas St	77703
Dove Mdws	77705
Dover Dr	77708
Dowlen Pl	77706
Dowlen Rd	
100-4599	77706
4800-4899	77708
N Dowlen Rd	
3900-3949	77706
3910-3910	77726
3951-3999	77706
S Dowlen Rd	77707
Downs Rd	77705
Drexell St	77713
Driftwood Ln	77703
Driskill St	77706
Drummond St	77706
Dubois Rd	77705
Ducote St	77707
Duff St	77706
Dugat Rd	77705
Duke St	77703
Duncan Rd	77713
Duncan St	77707
Dunleith St	77706
Duperier St	77702
Durango Cir & Dr	77708
Durden St	77703
Durwood Dr	77706
Dusty Ln	77713
Dylan Dr	77707
Eagle Ave	77713
Eagle Ln	77705
Eagleson Ln & Rd	77705
Eaheart Cir	77706
Earl St	77703
Easley Dr	77713
East Dr	77706
East Ln	
1400-1444	77713
1446-2099	77713
11000-11299	77705
Eastex Fwy	
6480A1-6480A1	77708
700-800	77703
802-3998	77703
2701-7099	77706
4000-7098	77708
7100-11499	77708
Eastex Plaza Dr	77708
Eastlake Ave	77705
Easy St	77701
Ebonwood Ln	77706
Ector St	77705
Edgemore Dr	77707
Edgewater Dr	77713
Edgewood Ln	77706
Edmonds St	77705
Edson Dr	77706
Edwin St	77705
El Paso St	77703
Elaine Dr	77706
Elba St	77705
Elder St	77703
Eldridge Dr	77707
E Elgie St	77705
Elie Rd	77713
Elinor St	77705
Elizabeth Dr	77705
Elizabeth St	77701
Elk Run Cir	77707
Ellen Ln	77708
Ellington Ln	77706
Elm St	77703
Elmhurst Dr	77706
Elmira St	77705
Elmwood Ln	77706
Eloise St	77707
Elsie St	77713
Ember Ln	77707
Emerald Dr	77705
Emile St	77701
Emily Ln	77713
Emma St	77701
Emmett St	77701
Empire Row	77706
Enchanted Ave	77708
Enfield Ln	77707
Erie St	77705
Ernestine St	77703
Espar St	77705
Esplanade	77707
Essex St	77705
W Estate Dr	77706
Estates Of Montclaire	77706
Estelle St	77705
Ethel St	77705
Ethel Ann St	77713
Etta Ln	77708
Euclid St	77705
Evalon Ave	77706
Evalon St	
1000-2299	77701
2300-2699	77702
W Evangeline Dr, Ln & St	77706
Evans St	77703
Eveningview Ln	77707
Evergreen Ln	77706
Ewing St	77701
Executive Blvd	77705
Faggard Rd	77707
Fairfield St	77713
Fairmeadow St	77707
Fairmont Dr	77706
Fairview Ave	77705
Fairway Dr	77705
Fairway St	77703
Faith Rd	77713
Falcon Ln	77708
Falls Rd	77705
Falsworth Dr	77707
Fang Cir	77706
Fannett Rd	77705
Fannin St	
200-3599	77701
4900-5199	77707
Fatima St	77705
Fay St	77701
Fenway Park	77706
Fenwick Cir	77706
Ferndale Ln	77707
Fieldwood Ln	77706
Fillmore St	77703
Fir Ln	77713
Firethorn Dr	77708
Fisher Rd	77705
Flamingo Ln	77705
Fleetwood Ln	77706
Fleming Dr	77713
Fletcher St	77703
E & W Florida Ave & St	77705
Flowers St	77701
Flynn Dr	77713
Fm 3514	77705
Fm 365 Rd	77705
Foard Rd	77705
Foch St	77701
Folsom Dr	77706
Fonville Ave	77705
Ford St	77706
Forest Gln	77713
Forest Glade St	77713
Forest Park Dr	77707
Forest Trail Cir	77713
Forrest St	
100-1499	77701
1500-2799	77703
Forsythe St	
200-2899	77701
4401-4897	77707
4899-5199	77707
Fort St	77703
Fortune Ln	77705
Fox Cv	77713
Foxbriar Ln	
3300-3399	77706
11000-11099	77705
Frances Pl	77701
Francis	77705
Francis Ln	77713
Franklin St	77701
Frazier Dr	77707
Frederick St	77701
French Rd	
2500-3199	77706
3200-3599	77703
French Survey Rd	77705
Friartuck Ln	77707
Frint Dr	77705
Frio Dr	77713
Frontage Rd	77705
Frost St	77706
Fulbright St	77713
Fullbright Rd	77713
Fulton St	77701
Futura St	77706
Gage Rd	77713
Gager St	77708
Gail Dr	77708
Galewood Ln	77706
Gallier Rd	77713
Galveston St	77703
Galway Dr	77706
N & S Garden Dr & St	77705
Garden Oaks Dr	77706
Garden Villas	77713
Gardner St	77707
Garland St	77705
Garner Rd	
5400-6199	77708
12000-14999	77705
Garth St	77705
Garwood Ln	77706
Garza Rd	77705
Gateway St	77701
Gaulding Rd	77705
General Dr	77703
Geneva Est	77706
Genevieve St	77707
Genoa St	77705
Gentry Rd	77713
George St	77705
Georgetown St	77707
Georgia St	77705
Gerald St	77707
Gilbert Dr	77705
Gilbert Rd	77705
Gilbert St	77701
Giles St	77705
E Gill St	77703
Girolamo St	77703
Gladys Ave	77706
Gladys St	
800-2299	77701
2300-2699	77702
Glasgow Ln	77706
Glasshouse St	77703
Glen Dr	77705
Glen Meadow Ln	77706
Glen Oaks Cir	77708
Glen Oaks St	77705
Glen Rose Cir	77713
Glen Willow Dr	77706
Glenbrook Dr	77705
Glenbrook St	77713
Glendale St	77707
Gleneagles Dr	77707
Glenmeadow Dr	77706
Glenross Dr	77705
Glenwood St	77705
Glerendi Rd	77705
Glover St	77705
Glynn Ln	77707
Gober Rd	77708
Goldsborough Dr	77707
Goliad St	
401-697	77701
699-2999	77701
3000-4599	77705
Goodhue Rd	77706
Gorman Rd	77705
Grace Cir N & S	77705
Gracemount Ln	77706
Grand St	
701-797	77701
799-1399	77701
1401-1499	77701
1500-3899	77703
Grandberry St	77705
Grant St	77701
Gray Rd	77705
Gray St	77701
Grayson Ln	77713
Green Ave	77705
Green Meadow St	77706
Greenbriar Ln	77706
Greenfield Dr	77713
Greenmoor Ln	77705
Greenridge Ln	77707
Greenway Dr	77705
Greenwood Dr	
100-299	77705
6700-6799	77706
Greenwood Pl	77705
Greeves St	77707
Gregg Rd	77705
Grey Hawk	77707
Griffing Blvd & Rd	77708
Griffith Rd	77705
Grimes Rd	77705
Gross St	77707
Groves St	77701
Guess Rd	77708
Guffy St	77701
Guillory Rd	77705
Gulf St	
100-1499	77701
1600-3299	77703
Gulf States Rd	77701
Gums St	77713
Gunter St	77705
Guthrie Rd	77705
Guy Cir	77707
Hackberry Ln	77705
Hackberry St	77708
Haden Rd	77708
Hagner Rd	77705
Hale Ln & St	77703
Half Circle Rnch	77705
Hall St	77703
Halliday St	77706
Hamilton Dr	77708
Hampton Ln	77707
Hangar Dr	77705
Hanover Cir	77706
Happ St	77703
Happy Hollow Ln	77705
Harbor Oaks Dr	77706
Harding Dr	77703
Hardwood Ln	77706
Hargraves Ln	77705
Harmony Ln	77708
Harriot St	77705
Harris Rd	77705
Harrison Ave	77706
Harrison St	
600-2299	77701
2300-3199	77702
Hartel St	77705
Hatcher Ln	77705
Hawkins Aly	77701
Hayes Ln	77703
Haywood Dr	77708
Hazel St	
600-2299	77701
2300-2699	77702
Heartfield Ln	77706
Heather Ln	77706

Heatherwood Dr 77706
Hebert Aly, Rd & St 77705
Hegele St 77705
Heights Ave & Blvd 77706
Heisig St 77705
Helbig Rd 77708
Hemlock St 77701
Hensley Rd 77713
Heritage Ln 77706
Herring Aly & St 77701
Herrington Rd 77705
Hester St 77703
Hialeah Dr 77706
Hibiscus Cir 77706
Hickory Ln 77705
Hidden Valley Dr 77708
Higgins Cir 77706
W Highland Ave & Dr 77705
Highpoint Ave 77708
Highway 105
1200-3499 77713
Highway 105
5300-7099 77708
7100-13599 77713
Highway 124 77705
Highway 125 77705
Highway 347 S 77705
Highway 69 N & S 77705
Highway 73 77705
Highway 90 77713
Hill St 77703
Hillary Rd 77713
Hillcrest Dr 77713
Hillebrandt Rd & St 77705
Hillebrandt Acres 77705
Hodge Rd 77713
Holiday St 77713
Holland Dr 77707
Holly Ave 77705
Holly Ln 77705
Holly Rd 77713
Holly St 77701
Hollywood St 77701
Holmes St 77701
Holst St 77708
Holton Rd 77707
Homer Dr 77708
Honey Due Ln 77713
Honeysuckle Dr 77706
Hood Loop 77705
Hooks Ave 77706
Hoover Rd 77703
Horn St 77703
Hospital Dr 77701
Houston St
1100-2999 77701
3000-4299 77705
Howard St 77705
Howell Ct & St 77706
Humble Rd 77707
Humble Camp Rd 77705
Hummingbird Ln & St 77713
Humphries Rd 77705
Hunt Rd 77705
Hunter St 77705
Hurley Dr 77708
Hybrook Ln 77703
Hyde Ct 77706
Hyde Park Row 77706
Idylwood St 77703
Ih 10 77705
Imes Rd 77713
Indian Trl 77713
Indian Blanket 77713
Indindow Rd 77713
Industrial Rd 77705
Inez St 77705
Infinity Ln 77706
Innisbrook Dr 77707
Interstate 10 77705
Interstate 10 E
700-3198 77703
Interstate 10 E
1001-2195 77701
2201-3199 77702

Interstate 10 N
1-499 77707
2-1298 77702
577-1163 77706
Interstate 10 S
101-313 77702
102-2298 77707
401-2199 77701
2201-2297 77705
2299-7399 77705
Inverness Dr 77707
Inwood Dr 77713
Iola St 77705
Iowa St 77705
E & W Irby St 77705
Irene St 77705
Irion St 77705
Iris Ln 77706
Irma St 77701
Iron Oaks Dr 77713
Ironton St 77703
Irving St
1500-2499 77701
3000-5199 77705
Isla St 77703
Ivanhoe Ln 77706
Ives St 77703
Ivy Ln 77706
J Hood St 77707
Jackie Ln 77713
Jackson Rd 77706
Jackson St 77701
Jacob Ct 77705
Jacobs St 77701
Jagneaux 77713
Jaguar Dr 77702
James Ln 77705
Jancar Dr 77708
Japonica Dr 77708
Jasmine Dr 77706
Jason Ct 77705
Jay Dr 77706
Jean Dr 77707
Jeanette St 77703
Jefferson Aly & St 77701
Jenard 77708
Jennifer St 77707
Jeny Ln 77707
Jerry Dr 77703
Jerry Ware Dr 77705
Jett Ln 77708
Jill Ln
7800-7899 77713
11000-11099 77705
Jim Gilligan Way 77705
Jirou St
1100-1499 77701
2400-3299 77703
Joachimi St 77701
Jody Ln 77708
Joesam St 77713
Johns St 77701
Johnson Rd 77705
Johnson St 77703
Johnstown St 77703
Jonathan Ct 77705
Jordan Ave 77713
Joseph St 77705
Josey St 77707
Joshua Ct 77705
Joyce Ln 77713
Judy Ct 77705
Judy Ln 77708
Julie St 77713
Junker Rd 77707
Karen Ln 77706
Karlette Ln 77708
Karnes Rd 77705
Katherine Dr 77713
Kathy Ln 77713
Katy Dr 77707
N Keith Ln & Rd 77713
Kelice Rd 77705
Kelly Dr 77707
Kelly Camp Rd 77705
Kemper Cir 77707

Kenchalt St 77702
Kenmore St 77707
Kennedy Dr 77706
Kenner Rd 77705
Kenneth Ave 77705
Kent Rd 77705
Kent St 77703
Kenwood Dr 77706
Kidd Rd 77713
N & S Kilarney Dr 77705
Killarney Dr 77706
Killian Ln 77706
Kimberly Dr 77707
Kings Row 77706
Kings Court St 77701
Kingsley Dr 77705
Kingswood Dr 77708
Kipling Dr 77706
Kitchner St 77703
Knollwood Dr 77706
Koawood Ln 77713
Koelemay Dr 77705
Kohler St 77706
Kolander Rd 77713
Kolbs Cor 77705
Kristin Ln 77713
La Belle Rd 77705
E La Salle St 77703
Labelle Rd 77705
Labrie Rd 77713
Lackner St 77705
Lafayette Ln 77706
Lafin Dr 77705
Lake Rd 77705
E Lakeside Dr 77707
Lakeview Cir 77703
Lamar St 77701
Lampassas St 77703
Lampman Dr 77706
Lanark Ln 77706
Lancaster Ln 77708
Land St 77701
Landis Dr 77707
Landry Ln 77708
Landry Rd 77713
Langham Rd 77707
Langham St 77701
Lansing Dr 77706
Lantana Ln 77713
Lantern Dr & Ln 77713
Larch Ln 77713
Laredo St 77703
Larkspur Ln 77706
Larry St 77708
Latta Rd 77705
Laura Ln 77707
Laurel St
700-2299 77701
2300-3199 77702
3301-3397 77707
3399-5399 77707
Laurelwood St 77707
E Lavaca St 77705
Laverna Dr 77705
Lawhon Rd 77713
Lawrence Dr 77708
Lawson St 77701
Lazy Ln 77706
Le Bleu St 77707
Leaning Oaks Dr 77713
Leblanc Rd 77708
Lebonnet Dr 77705
Ledet Rd 77708
Lee Dr 77713
Lee St 77701
Lee Ann Ln 77707
Legion St 77705
Leight St 77703
Leiper St 77701
Lela St 77705
Lena Dr 77713
Lene Ln 77705
Leonard St 77701
Lethia St 77703
Lettie Ln 77705
Levingston Ranch Rd 77705

Levy St 77701
Lewis Dr 77708
Lexington Ct & Dr 77706
Libby Ln 77708
Liberty St
200-2299 77701
2300-3199 77702
Lilac Ln 77706
Limerick Dr 77706
Lincoln Dr 77705
Lincoln St 77701
Linda Ln 77708
Lindbergh Dr 77707
Lindsey St 77713
Linkwood St 77706
Linns Way 77706
Linson St 77703
Linzay St 77713
Lisa Ln 77713
Little Acres Rd 77705
Littlechase St 77706
Littlefield St 77706
Littlejohn Dr 77707
Littlewood Dr 77706
Liveoak St 77703
Livingston Rd 77705
Lockwood Dr 77706
Lola Ln 77707
Loma Ln 77707
Lombard St 77707
Lombardo Dr 77705
Long Ave 77706
Long Rd 77707
Long St
800-998 77701
1000-2299 77701
2300-2699 77702
Longfellow Dr 77706
Longhorn Rd 77705
Longmeadow St 77707
Longwood St 77707
Loop Rd 77713
Lorelock Ln 77703
Lori Ln
5600-5799 77713
10900-10999 77705
Lorilee St 77708
Lou St 77705
Louis Dr 77705
Louisiana St
800-2199 77701
2201-2299 77701
2301-2397 77702
2399-2999 77702
Lowrance Pl 77705
E Lucas Dr
300-3399 77703
3500-4399 77708
W Lucas Dr 77706
Lucille St 77705
Lufkin St 77703
Lulu Ln 77705
Lydia St 77705
Lyle St 77701
E Lynwood Dr 77703
M L King Jr Pkwy 77703
N M L King Jr Pkwy 77701
S M L King Jr Pkwy
100-2899 77701
3000-7599 77705
Mack Rd 77713
Maddox Cir & St 77705
Madera Ln 77706
Madison Ave 77701
Madison Ct 77705
Madison Rdg 77706
Magazine St 77701
Magnolia Dr 77705
Magnolia St
100-1499 77701
1500-4799 77703
1725-1-1725-4 77703
Mahan Rd 77707
Mahogony Run Dr 77707
Mahon Ln 77705
Maida Rd 77708

Maime St 77703
Main Ln 77713
Main St 77701
N Main St 77701
Maitland St 77707
E Major Dr 77713
N Major Dr
1-199 77707
200-1599 77706
1600-9999 77713
S Major Dr
77-79 77707
81-4214 77707
4216-4298 77707
6600-7099 77705
Mallett St 77705
Mallot Rd 77713
Manceda Dr 77706
Manchester Ct 77706
Mandy Ln 77705
Maness Rd 77713
Manion Ct & Dr 77706
Manning St 77703
Manor St 77706
Mapes St 77707
Maple St 77703
Maplewood Ln 77703
Marceline Blvd 77707
Marcus Dr 77708
Margaret Ln 77708
Margo Ln 77708
Marie St 77705
Marigold St 77705
Marina St 77703
Mariposa St 77703
Mark Cir 77705
Marshall Place Dr 77706
Marshall Woods Dr 77706
Martel Dr 77713
Martha Ln 77713
Martin St 77703
Martin Luther King Rd 77713
Martingale Way 77713
Mary St 77701
Mashed O St 77703
Masterson Dr 77707
Matthew Rd 77706
Maxwell Dr 77707
May St 77705
Mayhaw Dr 77708
Mazie Dr 77713
Mazzu St 77705
Mcanelly Dr 77708
Mcfaddin St
800-2299 77701
2300-3199 77702
3300-3399 77706
Mcgee Ln 77705
Mcgovern St 77701
Mchale St 77708
Mckesson Dr 77705
Mclean St 77707
Mcmoore Ln & Rd 77713
Meadow Ln 77705
Meadow Run 77713
Meadow Way 77707
Meadowbend Dr 77706
Meadowbrook Dr 77706
Meadowcreek Dr 77706
Meadowick Dr 77706
Meadowland Dr 77706
Meadowridge Dr 77706
Meadowvale Dr 77706
Meadowview Rd 77708
Medical Center Dr 77701
Medinah Dr 77707
N & S Meeker Rd 77713
Mel Sha Ln 77705
Melrose St 77708
Mercantile St 77705
Merilee Ln 77707
Merion Dr 77707
Merlot Dr 77706
Merrick Ln 77706
Metropolitan Ct & Dr 77706
Metz St 77705

Michael Ln 77705
Michael Rd 77713
Michelle Cv 77706
Midford Dr 77707
Milam St
100-3899 77701
4000-4899 77707
Milky Way Ln 77705
Miller St 77701
Milo Dr 77705
Milton Dr 77706
Mimosa Ln 77706
Minglewood Dr 77703
Minner Dr 77708
Minnie Dr 77708
Minor St 77702
Mintwood Dr 77713
Mississippi St 77707
Mistletoe Dr 77707
Mitchell Rd 77713
Mockingbird Ln 77707
Monica St 77707
Monroe St 77703
Montana St 77707
Montclair Dr 77707
Monterrey Dr 77706
Monticello St 77706
Montrose St 77707
Moonglow Dr 77713
Moonmist Dr 77706
Moore Rd 77713
Morgan Ln 77707
Morningside St 77703
Morningstar Pl 77705
Morrison St 77701
Morrogh Dr 77707
Moses St 77707
Moss St 77705
Moss Hill Dr 77713
Moss Lake Rd 77705
Mouton St 77705
Mueller St 77703
Mulberry St 77701
Municipal Dr 77705
Munsterman Pl 77707
Myrna Loy Dr 77705
Myrtle Beach Dr 77707
Nantucket Dr 77706
Natalie St 77705
Natchez Pl 77713
Natchez Trce 77706
Nathan St 77708
Navajo Trl 77708
Neches St 77701
Neicy St 77701
Nelkin Ln 77708
Nelson St 77705
Neuman Ln 77713
E & N Nevada St 77707
New York St 77707
Newfield Ln 77707
Niagara St 77713
Nichols Dr 77706
Nicole Ln 77713
Nissi St 77705
No Name 1 77705
No Name 2 77705
No Name 3 77705
Nobles And Geheb Rd 77713
Nolan St 77705
Nolia Rd 77713
Nona Dr 77705
Nora St 77705
Normandy St 77703
Norris St 77707
North St
600-2299 77701
2300-3199 77702
3300-3999 77706
Northmeadow Dr 77706
Norvell St 77707
Norwalk Ln 77707
Norwood Dr 77706
Nottingham Ln 77706
Oak Ln 77705
Oak Brook Dr 77706

Oak Grove Pl 77708
Oak Meadow Dr 77706
Oak Pointe 77707
Oak Ridge St 77713
Oakcrest Cir 77706
Oakcrest Dr 77713
Oakdale Dr 77705
Oakland St
1-97 77701
99-1499 77701
2000-2099 77703
Oakleigh Blvd 77706
Oakley Ln 77706
Oakmont Dr 77706
S Oaks Dr 77706
Oaks Ln 77708
Oaktrace St 77706
Oakwood Ln 77703
Ocean Dr 77707
Octavia St 77705
Odom Rd 77706
Office Park Dr 77707
Ogden Ave 77705
Ohio St 77705
Oklahoma St 77707
Old Big Hill Rd 77705
Old Dowlen Rd 77706
Old Fannett Rd 77705
Old Gilbert Rd 77705
Old Oak Ranch Rd 77705
Old Sour Lake Rd 77713
Old Viterbo Rd 77705
Old Voth Rd 77708
Oleander Ave 77705
Oleander Dr 77706
Olin Rd 77705
Oliver Dr 77705
Ollie St 77705
Omaha St 77703
Opal St 77705
Orange St 77701
Orchid Ln 77713
Oregon Ave 77705
Orgain St 77707
Oriole Dr 77707
Orleans St 77701
Osborne St 77703
Overbrook Ln 77703
Overhill Ln 77707
Oxford Ct 77706
Oxford St 77702
Paige 77705
Palermo Dr & Ln 77705
Palestine St 77701
Palm St 77705
Palmetto Dr 77708
Palmetto Dunes Cir 77707
Pampas St 77713
Pan St 77706
Pansy Dr 77706
Paris St 77703
Park Ln 77706
Park Loop 77705
Park St
300-2900 77701
2902-2998 77701
3000-5099 77705
Park Meadow Dr 77706
Park North Dr 77708
Park West Dr 77706
Parker Dr 77705
Parkview Dr 77705
E Parkway Dr 77705
Parrish St 77705
Parry St 77703
Parson Dr 77706
Patillo Rd 77705
Patna Dr 77713
Patricia Dr 77713
Patterson Rd 77705
Pauline St 77703
Peach St 77703
Pear St
2000-2399 77701
8600-9899 77713
N Pearl St 77701

Pebble Beach Dr ... 77707
Pecan Dr ... 77713
Pecan St ... 77701
Pecos St
1800-2299 ... 77701
2300-2999 ... 77702
Peggy Ann Ln ... 77705
Pennock St ... 77703
Pennsylvania St ... 77701
Pepperwood Ln ... 77708
Perl Rd ... 77713
Pershing St ... 77705
Perth Pl ... 77708
Pevitot Rd ... 77707
Peyton Dr ... 77706
Phelan Blvd
3400-4499 ... 77707
5801-5997 ... 77706
5999-9899 ... 77706
9900-10499 ... 77713
Phelps Rd ... 77705
Phillips St ... 77713
Phyllis Ln ... 77713
Picadilly Ln ... 77708
Pickwick Ln ... 77706
Pierce St ... 77703
Pierre Dr ... 77705
Pin Oak St ... 77708
Pinchback Rd ... 77707
Pindo Cir ... 77708
Pine St
300-1299 ... 77701
1500-5399 ... 77703
Pine Burr Blvd ... 77708
Pine Cove St ... 77713
Pine Haven St ... 77713
S Pine Island Rd ... 77713
Pine Island Levee Rd ... 77713
Pinehurst Dr ... 77707
Pineridge ... 77713
Pinetree Rd ... 77705
Piney Point Ln ... 77708
Pinkstaff Ln ... 77706
Pinkston St ... 77703
E Pipkin St ... 77705
Pittsburg St ... 77703
Plant Rd ... 77708
Plaza Dr ... 77706
Plaza 10 Dr ... 77707
Pleasant Dr ... 77713
Pleasant Bend Dr ... 77708
E Plum St ... 77703
E & W Pointe Dr &
Pkwy ... 77706
Pointe Park Dr ... 77706
Pollard St ... 77703
Pond Cir ... 77707
Pope St ... 77703
Poplar St ... 77701
Port St ... 77701
W Port Arthur Rd ... 77705
Porter St ... 77701
Posey St ... 77705
Post Oak Ln ... 77705
Potter Dr ... 77707
Potts St ... 77705
Powell St ... 77701
Pradice St ... 77705
Prairie St
700-3199 ... 77701
4600-4699 ... 77707
Prescott Dr ... 77706
Preston St ... 77705
Prestwick Cir ... 77707
Primer St ... 77703
Primrose St ... 77703
Prince St ... 77703
Priscilla St ... 77703
Proadons St ... 77701
Proctor St ... 77705
Prutzman Rd ... 77706
Quad Ln ... 77705
Quail Ct ... 77713
Quail Run ... 77705
Quail Hollow Dr ... 77707
Queens Row ... 77706
Quincy St ... 77701
Quinn St ... 77703
Quitman St ... 77708
R Daniel Dr ... 77705
Rafes Way ... 77706
Raleigh Dr ... 77706
Rampart St ... 77705
Randolph Cir ... 77706
Ranier St ... 77701
Rankin Dr ... 77706
Rapha St ... 77705
Ratcliff St ... 77703
Raton Cir ... 77708
Raven St ... 77705
Reagan St ... 77706
Rebecca Ln ... 77708
Red Oak Ln ... 77705
Redbird Ln ... 77705
Redwood Dr ... 77703
Reed St ... 77705
Reese ... 77708
Regent ... 77703
Regina Ln ... 77706
Reins Rd ... 77713
Rena St ... 77705
Renaud St ... 77703
Reno Cir ... 77708
Reynolds Rd ... 77707
Rfd Rd ... 77708
Rhone St ... 77703
Rice Cir & Ln ... 77705
Rice Field Rd ... 77713
Richard Dr ... 77708
Ricki Ln ... 77708
Ridgecrest Dr ... 77705
Ridgeland Ave & St ... 77706
Ridgeline Cir ... 77707
Ridgemont Dr ... 77706
Ridgeoak St ... 77713
Ridgewood St ... 77708
Riggs St ... 77707
Rikisha Ln ... 77706
Riksan Cv ... 77706
Rita Ln ... 77713
N River Bnd ... 77713
River Rd
3300-3499 ... 77708
7700-7799 ... 77713
N River Bend Dr ... 77713
River Oaks Blvd ... 77713
Rivercrest St ... 77703
Riviera Ct ... 77707
Roadrunner St ... 77708
Roberts Ave ... 77707
Roberts Ln ... 77713
Roberts Rd ... 77705
Roberts St ... 77701
Robinhood Ln ... 77703
Robinson St ... 77708
Rockwell St ... 77701
Rogers Ave ... 77705
Rohi St ... 77705
Roland Rd ... 77708
Rolfe Christopher Dr ... 77705
Roll Rd ... 77713
Rolling Hills Dr ... 77713
Rollingbrook Ln ... 77706
Roman St ... 77703
Romeda Rd ... 77705
Ronnie Ave ... 77705
Rose Ln
1400-1899 ... 77713
5100-5399 ... 77708
Rosedale Dr
5600-5799 ... 77708
5801-5999 ... 77706
Rosemary Dr ... 77708
Rosewood Dr & St ... 77713
Rosine St ... 77707
Roslyn Ct ... 77708
Rothwell St ... 77705
Roxton Ln ... 77707
Royal St ... 77701
Rue Dr ... 77708
Rusk St
2100-2299 ... 77701
2300-3199 ... 77702
Russell Dr ... 77703
Ruth St
1-199 ... 77707
3300-3399 ... 77705
Sabine Pass ... 77705
Sabine Consolidated
Rd ... 77705
Sabine Pass Ave ... 77701
Saddlewood Ct & St ... 77713
N & W Sage ... 77713
Saint Andrews Dr ... 77707
Saint Anthony St ... 77701
Saint Charles St ... 77703
Saint Helena St ... 77703
Saint James Blvd ... 77705
Saint Louis St ... 77705
Salem Cir ... 77706
Salida Dr ... 77708
Sallie St ... 77706
Sams Way ... 77706
San Anselmo St ... 77708
San Antonio St ... 77701
San Bruno St ... 77708
San Carlos St ... 77708
San Diego St ... 77708
San Jacinto St ... 77701
Sandelwood Trl ... 77706
Sandlin St ... 77707
Sandringham ... 77713
Sandwood Ln ... 77706
Sandy Ln ... 77705
Santa Fe St ... 77703
Sarah St ... 77705
Saratoga Cir ... 77706
Sassafras St ... 77708
Satinwood Ln ... 77713
Savannah ... 77707
Savannah Trce ... 77706
Sawgrass Cir ... 77707
Sawyer St ... 77702
Saxe St ... 77705
Scantilly Dr ... 77706
Scenic Dr ... 77713
Schwarner St ... 77701
Scotts Dr ... 77708
Scranton St ... 77703
Seagull Ln ... 77708
Seale Rd ... 77705
Seminole Dr ... 77707
Sensat Ln ... 77705
Sequoia Ln ... 77713
Serene Dr ... 77706
Shadow Ln ... 77706
Shadow Bend Dr ... 77706
Shadow Creek Dr ... 77707
Shady Ln
1900-2099 ... 77706
2101-2299 ... 77706
7100-7999 ... 77713
7331-1-7331-26 ... 77713
Shady Hollow Ln ... 77706
Shady Oaks ... 77705
Shaffer Dr ... 77705
Shakespeare Dr ... 77706
Shalom ... 77705
Shamrock Aly & St ... 77701
Shanahan Dr ... 77706
Shannon Ave ... 77705
Sharon Cir ... 77706
Sheffield St ... 77703
Sheila Ln ... 77713
Shelby St ... 77707
Shelia ... 77705
Shell St ... 77705
Shelley Dr ... 77705
Shennandoah Dr ... 77706
Shepherd Dr ... 77707
Sheridan Ln & Pl ... 77706
Sheridan Oaks Dr ... 77706
Sherman Rd ... 77713
Sherman St ... 77701
Sherwood Dr ... 77713
Shiloh Dr ... 77706
Shipley St ... 77713
Shire Ln ... 77706
Shirley Cir ... 77707
Shivers Dr ... 77708
Short St ... 77701
Sienna Trl ... 77708
Sierra Cir ... 77708
Signora St ... 77708
Silver St ... 77703
Silverleaf St ... 77707
Silverwood St ... 77708
E Simmons St ... 77703
Simon Dr ... 77705
Simpson Dr ... 77705
Singleton Rd ... 77708
Skipwith St ... 77701
Skyview Dr ... 77707
Sleepy Ln ... 77706
Smart St
2300-2999 ... 77702
4300-4499 ... 77713
Smelker St ... 77707
Smith Rd
3500-7599 ... 77713
8100-8399 ... 77705
Smokey Ln ... 77705
Smythe St ... 77705
Somerset St ... 77707
Somerville Cir ... 77713
South Dr ... 77705
South St
1100-2299 ... 77701
2300-2999 ... 77702
Southerland St ... 77705
Southern Pacific Rd
2600-2698 ... 77701
2700-2999 ... 77701
3000-4399 ... 77705
Southmeadow St ... 77706
Space St ... 77703
Sparks St ... 77705
Sparrow Way ... 77707
Speer Rd ... 77708
Spencer Dr ... 77708
Spindletop Ave, Dr &
Rd ... 77705
Springdale Ln ... 77708
Springmeadow Dr ... 77706
Spruce St ... 77703
Spurlock Rd ... 77713
Stacewood Dr ... 77706
Stacy ... 77705
Stacy St ... 77707
Stagg Dr ... 77701
Stanford St ... 77708
Stanton St ... 77701
Stardust Dr ... 77706
Starlite Dr ... 77713
Steelton St ... 77703
Steinhagen Rd ... 77705
Stephen Ln ... 77706
Stephenson St ... 77701
Sterling Ln ... 77706
Steve Dr ... 77703
Stewart St ... 77701
Stillwater Dr ... 77705
Stivers Dr ... 77705
Stone Cir ... 77706
Stone Oak Dr ... 77705
Stonebrook Ct ... 77706
Stonetown St ... 77713
Stratton Cir & Ln ... 77707
Sturrock Rd ... 77713
Sue Ln ... 77706
Sul Ross Ln ... 77706
Sullivan St ... 77705
Sulphur Dr ... 77705
Summer Wind Dr ... 77713
Summerwood St ... 77706
Sunbird Ln ... 77708
Sunburst Dr ... 77706
Sunbury Dr ... 77707
Sunflower Ln
2400-2599 ... 77713
8500-8599 ... 77705
Sunflower St ... 77713
Sunmeadow Dr ... 77706
Sunnydale Ln ... 77708
Sunnyside Dr ... 77707
Sunset Ct ... 77701
Sunset Dr ... 77705
Sunset St ... 77705
Sunshine Dr ... 77705
Surry Cir ... 77708
Sutherland St ... 77703
Suzanne Ct ... 77706
Swallow Dr ... 77707
Swarner Dr ... 77705
Sweetbay St ... 77707
Sweetgum Ln
2500-2699 ... 77703
11200-11699 ... 77705
Sweetgum Rd ... 77713
Swift Dr ... 77703
Swing Dr ... 77703
Sycamore St ... 77701
Taft St
2200-2499 ... 77703
4200-4899 ... 77706
Tagore St ... 77701
Tahoe Dr ... 77708
Taliaferro St ... 77703
Tall Pine St ... 77713
Tallamar Dr & Ln ... 77713
Tallow Cir & Dr ... 77713
Tangledahl Ln ... 77706
Tannis St ... 77703
Tanoak Dr ... 77713
Taylor St ... 77703
Taylors Cv ... 77705
Taylors Bayou Rd ... 77705
Teakwood Ln ... 77706
Tedroll Ln ... 77713
Tena Ln ... 77707
Tenaha St ... 77703
Tennyson Dr ... 77706
Terainda St ... 77707
Terrace Dr ... 77706
Terrell St ... 77701
Terry Rd ... 77705
Terry St ... 77707
Test St ... 77705
Texas St ... 77703
Thad Ln ... 77706
Thames Dr ... 77708
Thelisma Ln ... 77713
Theresa St ... 77705
Thomas Ct, Gln, Ln,
Park
& Rd ... 77706
Thoreau St ... 77707
Thornton Dr ... 77705
Thousand Oaks Dr ... 77713
E Threadneedle Aly &
St ... 77705
Tibbets Ln ... 77707
Tilson St ... 77701
Timber Creek Loop ... 77708
Timberline Ln ... 77706
Timberridge Ln ... 77713
Timberwood Ln ... 77703
Timms Ln ... 77705
Toccoa St ... 77703
Todd St ... 77707
Toledo St ... 77703
Tolivar Rd ... 77713
Tolivar Canal Rd ... 77713
Torrey Pines Cir ... 77707
Townhouse Ln ... 77707
Tracy St ... 77703
Trahan Rd ... 77713
Tram Rd ... 77713
Travis Dr ... 77703
Treadway Rd
3701-3897 ... 77706
3899-4299 ... 77706
4300-4499 ... 77708
Trinidad St ... 77703
Trinity St ... 77701
Trojan Dr ... 77707
Trontrie Rd ... 77708
Troon Dr ... 77707
Trotman Rd ... 77708
Truxton Ln ... 77706
Tulane St ... 77703
Tulip Dr ... 77706
Tupelo St ... 77708
Turnberry Cir ... 77707
Turner Rd ... 77713
Turningleaf Dr ... 77706
Turon St ... 77701
Twilight Dr ... 77706
Twin Circle Dr ... 77706
Twin Pines Ln ... 77705
Tyler St ... 77703
Tyrrell Park Rd ... 77705
Underhill St ... 77701
University Dr ... 77705
Unterbrink Ln ... 77713
Usan St ... 77705
Utica St ... 77703
Valmont Ave ... 77706
Van Buren St ... 77701
Vance St ... 77706
Vans Way ... 77706
Veatch St ... 77705
Vegas ... 77708
Ventura Ln ... 77706
Veo David Cormier Jr
Rd ... 77713
Vermejo Cir ... 77708
Vermont St ... 77705
Vernall Ln ... 77713
Verone St ... 77701
Verrett Dr ... 77705
Vestal St ... 77703
Veterans Cir ... 77707
Victoria Ct ... 77701
Victoria St
100-2999 ... 77701
3000-3199 ... 77705
Victory Ln ... 77705
Viking Dr ... 77706
W Villa Ln ... 77713
Village Dr & Ln ... 77713
Villiva Ln ... 77705
Vinson St ... 77713
Virgil St ... 77703
E & W Virginia St ... 77705
Viterbo Rd ... 77705
Voth Rd
7900-10399 ... 77708
10500-11799 ... 77713
Waco St
2700-2999 ... 77701
3000-3899 ... 77705
Wade St ... 77706
Walden Rd
5200-5499 ... 77705
5700-5900 ... 77707
5815-5815 ... 77720
5901-9999 ... 77707
5902-9998 ... 77707
12400-12999 ... 77713
Wales Dr ... 77708
Walker Rd ... 77713
Wall St
400-2899 ... 77701
4900-7199 ... 77707
Walnut St ... 77701
Walton St ... 77703
Ward St ... 77705
Warren St ... 77705
Washington Blvd
500-4299 ... 77705
4400-9999 ... 77707
Washington Village
Pkwy ... 77707
Water Edge ... 77707
Waters Rd ... 77706
Waverly St ... 77705
Wayside Dr ... 77713
Wayside St ... 77707
Weatherford Pl ... 77707
Weaver Dr ... 77706
Webb Ln ... 77706
Wedgewood Dr ... 77706
Wellington Cir & Pl ... 77706
Wellington Oaks St ... 77706
Wells Dr ... 77713
Wellspring Dr ... 77705
Wescalder Rd ... 77707
Wespark Cir ... 77705
West Ave ... 77703
West Ln ... 77713
West Rd ... 77713
Westbury Rd ... 77713
Westchase Dr ... 77707
Westchester Ln ... 77713
Western Trl ... 77713
Westgate Dr ... 77706
Westhaven Dr ... 77713
Westmeadow Dr ... 77706
Westmont Dr ... 77706
Westmoreland St ... 77705
Weston Ct ... 77706
Westpark Ave ... 77705
Westpine Rd ... 77713
Westridge Ln ... 77706
Westville Ln ... 77713
Westwood Blvd ... 77707
Wheat Dr ... 77706
Wheat Ln ... 77705
Whisper Wind Dr ... 77713
White Rd ... 77706
White Oak Ln
6000-6099 ... 77708
10400-10599 ... 77705
White Perch Ln ... 77705
Whittaker Ln ... 77706
Wickersham Pl ... 77706
Wier Dr ... 77706
Wiess St ... 77703
Wiggins Rd ... 77705
Wilbur Blvd ... 77705
Wilchester Cir & Ln ... 77706
Wilcox Ln ... 77706
Wildemeadow Dr ... 77706
Wilder Dr ... 77706
Wildflower Ln ... 77713
Wildwood Dr ... 77708
Wilford Rd ... 77705
Willard St ... 77703
Williamsburg Ln ... 77706
Willie Mae St ... 77703
Willis Ln ... 77708
Willow Pl ... 77707
Willow St
200-299 ... 77701
300-698 ... 77701
300-300 ... 77704
301-1299 ... 77701
Willow Way ... 77707
Willow Bend Ct & Dr ... 77707
Willow Creek Dr ... 77707
Willowglen Dr ... 77707
N & S Willowood Dr &
Ln ... 77703
Wilshire St ... 77703
Wilson St ... 77703
Winchester Cv ... 77706
Windcastle St ... 77713
Windchase Dr ... 77713
N, S & W Windemere Dr
& St ... 77713
Windhaven St ... 77713
Windmeadow St ... 77713
Windrose Dr ... 77706
Windsong St ... 77713
Windsor Pkwy ... 77706
Windswept St ... 77713
Windwood Ln ... 77706
Winfree St ... 77705
Wingate St ... 77713
Winged Foot Dr ... 77707
Winnsboro Cir ... 77713
Winston Dr ... 77705
Winter Ln ... 77707
Winterberry St ... 77707
Winzer Rd ... 77705
Wirt St ... 77703
Wisteria Dr ... 77706
Withers Ln ... 77703
Wood Park St ... 77706
Woodcrest Dr ... 77703
Wooded Creek Dr ... 77708

Woodhollow 77705
Woodland 77705
Woodland Park 77708
Woodlawn St 77703
Woodridge St 77706
E Woodrow St 77705
Woodsfield 77706
Woodside Dr 77707
Woodway Dr 77707
Wooten Rd 77707
Worcester St 77705
Wren Way 77707
Wright Ln 77713
Wyatt St 77705
Wynden Way 77706
Yarbrough Ln 77713
Yasmine Dior St 77705
Yaupon Dr 77708
Yellowstone Dr 77713
Yorkshire Cir & Dr 77713
Yorktown Ln 77707
Youngstown St 77703
Yount St 77706
Yucca Dr 77708
Zavalla St 77705
Zenith St 77706

NUMBERED STREETS

1st St 77705
N 1st St 77701
2nd St 77705
N 2nd St 77701
3rd St 77705
N 3rd St 77701
4th St 77705
N 4th St 77701
S 4th St
100-174 77701
176-2999 77701
3000-4799 77705
5th St 77705
N 5th St 77701
S 5th St
2300-2698 77701
2700-2999 77701
3000-4599 77705
6th St 77705
N 6th St 77701
S 6th St
100-2999 77701
3000-3098 77705
3100-3400 77705
3402-3598 77705
7th St 77705
N 7th St
1-1499 77702
1500-2299 77703
S 7th St 77701
8th St 77705
N 8th St 77702
S 8th St 77701
9th St 77705
N 9th St
200-1199 77702
2200-2799 77703
S 9th St 77701
10th St 77705
N 10th St
100-1199 77702
1201-1299 77702
2200-3299 77703
S 10th St
1-289 77702
291-299 77702
400-499 77701
11th St 77705
N 11th St
1-1400 77702
1402-1498 77702
2000-2994 77703
2996-2998 77703
S 11th St
1-149 77702
151-153 77702
300-2999 77701
3000-4199 77705
12th St 77705
200-399 77702
2500-2899 77701
13th St 77705
N 13th St 77702
S 13th St 77702
N & S 14th 77702
N & S 15th 77702
N 16th St 77703
18th St 77706
N 18th St 77707
19th St 77706
20th St 77706
21st St 77706
N 21st St 77707
N 22nd 77706
N 23rd St 77707
N 23rd St 77707
500-2399 77706
S 23rd St
427-601 77707
603-1699 77707
4700-4799 77705
24th St 77706
25th St 77706
N 27th St 77707
N 29th St 77707
88th Cir 77707

BEDFORD TX

General Delivery 76095

POST OFFICE BOXES MAIN OFFICE STATIONS AND BRANCHES

Box No.s
All PO Boxes 76095

NAMED STREETS

Aberdeen Dr 76021
Acorn St 76022
Airport Fwy
200-2998 76022
401-4299 76021
Amherst Cir & Dr 76021
Andover Ct & Dr 76021
Andrew Ct 76021
Ann St 76022
Annette Dr 76022
Apache Dr 76021
April Sound 76021
Aquaduct Ct & Dr 76022
Arbor Ct 76021
Arbor Crest Dr 76021
Arbor Mill Cir 76021
Arthurs Cir 76021
Ashbury Ct & Ln 76021
Ashford Dr 76021
Ashland Dr 76021
Ashwood Ln 76021
Aspen Dr 76021
Aspenwood Dr 76021
Atlanta Dr 76022
Audubon Ct 76021
Autumn Ln 76021
Autumn Chase Sq 76022
Autumn Shade Ct 76021
Autumnwood Ct 76021
Avinell Dr 76022
Barons Ct 76022
Barr Dr 76021
Baylor Dr 76021
Beachtree Ln 76021
Bedford Cir 76021
Bedford Ct E 76022
Bedford Rd
100-1199 76022
1200-4299 76021
Bedford Oaks Ct & Dr 76021
Bedfordshire 76021
Belle St 76022
Bellmont Ct 76022
Bent Oak Dr 76021
Bent Tree Ct & Ln 76021
Berkshire Ct & Ln 76021
Berwichshire Ct 76021
Berwick Ln 76021
Beverly Ct 76022
Birdsong 76021
Blessing Ct 76021
Blue Jay Ct 76021
Blue Quail Ct & Ln 76021
Bluebonnet Ln 76021
Bobwhite Dr 76021
Boston Blvd 76022
Bramble Oaks Ct 76021
Brandywine Dr 76021
Brasher Ln 76021
Brestol Ct E & W 76021
Briar Dr 76022
Briarhaven Dr 76021
Bridgeton Ln 76021
Brighton Ct 76021
Brightwood Ct & Dr 76021
Britany Cir 76022
Brookgreen Ct 76021
Brookhaven Cir 76022
Brookline Trl 76021
Brookshire Dr 76021
Brookside Ct & Dr 76021
Brookwood Blvd 76021
Brown Trl
800-1513 76022
1514-1798 76021
1800-3600 76021
3602-3998 76021
Bryan Cir, Ct & Dr 76022
Buckingham Ct 76021
Buckner Ct 76021
Burr Oak Ct 76021
Cachelle Ct 76021
Caldwell Dr 76021
Cambridge Cir E & W 76021
Candlewick Ct 76021
Canterbury Dr 76021
Cardinal Cir 76022
Carlisle St 76022
Carolyn Ct & Dr 76021
Carousel Dr 76022
Cedar Ln & Park 76021
Cedar Grove Ln 76021
Cedar Ridge Dr 76021
Cedar Springs Ct 76021
Central Dr
800-1849 76022
1850-3999 76021
Central Park Blvd 76022
Channing Ln 76021
Chaparral Ct 76022
Charleston Ct & Dr 76022
Chateau Valee Cir 76022
Chattanooga Dr 76022
Chaucer Ln 76021
Cheek Sparger Rd 76021
Cherokee Dr 76021
Cherry Blossom Ln 76021
Cheryl Ave 76022
Chestnut Ct & Way 76022
Chinaberry Dr 76021
Chittam Ln 76021
Cindy Ln 76021
Circle Ln 76022
Classic Ct E & W 76021
Clear View Dr E 76021
Clearmeadow Ct & St 76021
Cobblestone Ct 76021
Coble Ct 76021
Coffee Tavern Rd 76022
Columbus Ct 76022
Comanche Trl 76021
Commerce Pl 76021
Cottonwood Ln 76021
Country Pl 76021
Country Meadows Dr 76021
Countryside Dr 76021
Courtney Ln 76021
Coventry Dr 76021
Creek Villas Dr 76022
Creekside Ct 76021
Creekwood Ct 76021
Creighton Ln 76021
Crescent Ct 76021
Crest St 76021
Crestview Dr 76021
Cripple Creek Ct 76021
Crown Ct 76021
Crown Colony Ct 76021
Crystal Spgs 76021
Cumberland Dr 76022
Cummings Ct & Dr 76021
Cunningham Ct 76021
Cypress Ct 76021
Cypress Creek Ln 76021
Dalewood Ct & Ln 76022
Danielle Dr 76021
Dartmouth Ct 76022
Dee Ln 76022
Derby Cir & Ct 76021
Deuce Dr 76022
Devon Ct 76021
Devonshire Dr 76021
Dewberry Ct 76021
Diamond St 76021
Dogwood Ct 76021
Donna Ln 76022
Dora St 76022
Dorchester Dr 76021
Double Oak Ct & Dr 76021
Dover Ln 76021
Downing Ct 76021
Durango Pl 76021
Durango Ridge Dr 76021
Eagle Ct & Dr 76021
Eagles Nest Dr 76021
Edgecliff Dr 76022
Edgefield Ln 76021
Edgewater Ct & Dr 76021
Edgewood Ln 76021
El Campo 76021
Elaine Ct 76021
Elisha Ct & Dr 76021
Elizabeth Dr 76022
Ellison Ct 76021
Elm St 76021
Elm Branch Ct 76021
Em Bilger Jr Blvd 76021
Emerald St 76021
Evandale Dr 76022
Everest Dr 76021
Fairfax Dr 76021
Fairmont Ct 76021
Falcon Trl 76021
Field Ln 76021
Fieldcrest Ln 76021
Fieldstone Ct & Dr 76022
Folkstone Way 76021
Forest Dr 76021
Forest Glen Dr 76021
Forest Meadows Ct 76021
Forest Oak Ct 76021
Forest Park Cir 76021
Forest Ridge Dr
800-1899 76022
1900-3899 76021
Forum Pkwy 76021
Fox Glenn Cir 76021
Fox Hollow Dr 76021
S Gate 76021
Gettysburg Pl 76022
Glenbrook Ct 76021
Glenda Dr 76022
Glenoaks Ct & St 76021
Glenwood Ct 76021
Gold Hawk Ln 76022
Golden Gate Cir 76022
Golden Oak Dr 76021
Golden Rod Ct 76021
Granite Dr 76021
Green Country Ct 76021
Greendale Ct & Dr 76022
N Greentree Ln 76021
Greenway Dr 76021
Greenwood Ct 76021
Greg Dr 76021
Gregory Ave 76022
Hackberry Ln 76021
Halertho Dr 76022
Hampton Ct & Dr 76021
Harber Dr 76021
Hardisty Rd 76021
Harwood Ct 76021
Harwood Rd
201-237 76021
239-1301 76021
1300-1300 76095
1302-4298 76021
1303-4299 76021
Harwood Ter 76021
Hastings Ct & Pl 76021
Haven Dr 76022
Hayes Ln 76022
Hazlewood Ct 76021
Heather Brook Ct 76021
Helen Dr 76022
Hialeah Path 76022
Hickory Ct 76021
Hickory Crest St 76021
Hidden Oaks Dr 76022
Highbury Ct 76021
Highcrest Dr 76022
Highgate Ln 76021
Highland Dr 76021
Highpoint Rd 76022
Highway 121 76021
Hillandale Ct 76021
Hillside Ct 76022
Hillwood Way 76021
Holly Brook Ct 76021
Hollybush Ln 76021
Homecraft Ct, Dr & Ln 76021
Honor Oak Ln 76022
Horizon Dr 76021
Hospital Pkwy 76022
Hunters Glen Ct 76021
Huntington Ln 76021
Huntwich Dr 76021
Hurst Dr 76022
Indian Oaks Ct 76021
N Industrial Blvd 76021
James Ln 76022
Jasmine Ct 76021
Jennifer Ln 76021
Jerry Ln 76022
Jones Ct 76021
Joseph Ct 76021
Joshua Ct 76022
Juniper Ct 76021
Karen Dr 76021
Kathryn Ct 76021
Kensington Ct 76021
Kentwood Cir 76021
King Dr 76022
Kingston Ct 76022
Knoxville Dr 76022
L Don Dodson Dr
1800-2125 76021
2124-2124 76095
2126-2998 76021
2127-2999 76021
Lacebark Ln 76021
Ladera Dr 76021
Lakeview Ct & Dr 76021
Lancashire Ct 76021
Lancelot Ct 76021
Laurel Ct & Ln 76021
Lawana Dr 76022
Leafy Glen Ct 76022
Lee Dr 76022
Lexington Pl 76022
Lincolnshire Cir & Dr 76021
Linderhof Cir 76022
Live Oak Ln 76021
Loma Alta Dr 76021
Loma Verde Dr 76021
Lone Oak Ln 76021
Magnolia Ct & Ln 76021
Manchester Cir & Ct 76021
Maple Dr 76021
Maple Brook Ct 76021
Maplewood Ct 76021
Marble Dr 76021
Marshfield Dr 76021
Martha Dr 76022
Martin Dr 76021
Matterhorn Dr 76021
Mayfair Hill Ct 76021
Mccurry Ave 76022
Mclain Rd 76021
W Meadow Crk, Ct, Grn, Ln, Pl & Vw 76021
Meadow Creek Dr 76021
Meadow Park Cir & Dr 76021
Meadow Wood Ct & Ln 76021
Meadowlark Ln 76021
Meadowside Dr 76021
Meandering Way 76021
Medford Ct & Dr 76021
Memphis Dr 76022
Merrill Dr 76022
Mesquite Ct E & W 76021
Michael Ct & Dr 76022
Michael Sean Ct & Dr 76021
Miles Way 76021
Millridge St 76021
Mimosa Ct 76021
Minnie Ln 76022
Miranda Ter 76021
Misty Ct 76021
Misty Glen Ct 76021
Misty Woods Ct 76021
Monette Dr 76022
Monterrey St 76022
Morning Glory Ln 76021
Morningside Dr 76021
Morrow Dr 76021
Mossburg Dr 76022
Mossy Oak Ct & Ln 76021
Mountain Laurel Ln 76021
Mountain View Ct & Dr 76021
Mulberry Ln 76021
Municipal Ct 76021
Murphy Dr 76021
Nantucket Ct 76022
Natchez Ave 76022
Navajo Ln 76021
Nelson Ter 76022
New Bedford Ct 76022
New Haven Ct 76022
Norfolk Ct & Dr 76021
Norman Ln 76021
Northridge Dr 76021
Norwood Dr 76022
Nottingham Dr 76022
Oak Ln & St 76021
Oak Brook Dr 76021
Oak Cove Ln 76021
Oak Creek Ln 76022
Oak Hill Dr 76021
Oak Hollow Dr 76021
Oak Leaf Ln 76021
Oak Manor Ct & Dr 76021
Oak Park Dr 76021
Oak Shadow Cir 76021
Oak Timber Dr 76021
Oak Valley Dr 76021
Oakgrove Ln 76021
Oakhurst Dr 76022
Oaklawn Ct 76022
Oakmeadow Ct, Pl & St 76021
Oakmont Ct & Dr 76022
Oakridge Ct & Dr 76021
Oakwood Dr 76021
Old Kirk Rd 76022
Old Orchard Ct & Ln 76021
Oleander Ct 76021
Olen Ln 76022
Orchard Breeze 76021
Overbrook Ln 76021
Overhill Dr 76022
Oxford Ct 76021
Paint Brush Ln 76021
Park Ave & Ln 76021
Park Place Ave 76022
Park Place Blvd 76021
Parkview Ct 76021
Parkview Ln 76022
Parkwood Dr 76021
Patricia Ln 76022
Patti Dr 76022
Peach Blossom Ct 76021
Peadinso Dr 76021
Pearl St 76021
Pebblebrook Ln 76021
Pebblestone Ln 76021
Pecan Cir 76021
Pecan Bend Dr 76022
Pembroke Pl 76021
Periwinkle Ct & St 76021
Pheasant Ct 76021
Pilgrim Pl 76021
Pin Oak Ln 76021
Pine Creek Ct 76021
Pine Ridge Dr 76021
Pine Thicket Ct & Ln 76021
Pinewood St 76021
Pipeline Rd E 76022
Plaza Dr & Pkwy 76021
Pleasant Valley Cir 76021
Pleasantview Dr 76021
Plymouth Ct 76022
Poplar St 76021
Post Oak Ct & Dr 76021
Prescott Ct 76021
Prestwick St 76022
Primrose Ln 76021
Prince Ct 76021
Princess St 76021
Prudence Ct 76021
Quail Crest Dr 76021
Queens Ct & Way 76021
R D Hurt Pkwy 76021
Racquet Club Blvd 76022
Raintree Ct 76021
Rankin Dr 76022
Ravenswood Dr N 76022
Realistic Ct & Dr 76021
Red Oak Ln 76021
Redondo Rd 76021
Redwood St 76021
Regency St 76021
Regents Park 76022
Reliance Pkwy 76021
Renee St 76021
Richmond Dr 76022
Richwood Cir 76021
Ridge Ct & Dr 76021
Ridge Haven Cir 76021
Ridgewood Blvd 76021
River Forest Ct 76021
Robindale Ct & Dr 76022
Robinhood Ct & Ln 76021
Rochester Ct 76022
Rockwood Cir 76021
Rolling Meadows Dr 76021
Rollingshire Ct & Dr 76021
Rollingwood Ct 76021
Rose Pl 76021
Rosemary Ct 76021
Royal Ct 76021
Royal Crescent Dr 76021
Royal Oak Dr 76021
Ruby St 76021
Russell Ln 76022
Rustic Meadows Dr 76021
Rustic Woods Ct & Dr 76021
Rustling Leaves Ln 76021
Saddlebrook Dr N & S 76021
N, S & W Sage Ct & Ln 76021
San Fernando St 76021
San Marcos Ln 76021
Sanders Ct 76021
Sandlin Dr 76021
Sandshell St 76021
Sandy Way 76021

Sapphire St ... 76021
Savannah Way ... 76022
Saxon Dr ... 76021
Scenic Hills Ct & Dr ... 76021
School Ln ... 76021
Schumac Ln ... 76022
Sequoia Ct & Ln ... 76021
Serrano St ... 76021
Shady Ln ... 76021
Shady Brook Ct & Dr ... 76021
Shady Creek Ln ... 76021
Shady Elm Ct ... 76021
Shady Glen Ln ... 76021
Shady Grove Dr ... 76021
Shady Knoll Ln ... 76021
Shady Lake Dr ... 76021
Shady Meadow Dr ... 76021
Shady Nook Ct ... 76021
Shady Oak Ct ... 76021
Shady Pine Ct ... 76021
Shady Rest Ct ... 76021
Shady Ridge Dr ... 76021
Shady Turf Ct & Dr ... 76022
Shady View Dr ... 76021
Shady Willow Ct ... 76021
Shady Wood Ct & Dr ... 76021
Shannon Ln ... 76022
Shell Ct ... 76022
Shenandoah Ct & Dr ... 76021
Sherwood Dr ... 76022
Shirley Way ... 76022
Sierra Springs Dr ... 76021
Silverio Trl ... 76021
Silverwood Ct & Ln ... 76021
Simpson Ter ... 76021
Smith Ter ... 76021
Somerset Cir & Ter ... 76022
Sovereign Dr ... 76021
Spargercrest Dr ... 76021
Spicewood Rd ... 76021
Spring Brook Dr ... 76021
Spring Forest Dr ... 76021
Spring Garden Dr ... 76021
Spring Grove Dr ... 76021
Spring Lake Dr ... 76021
Spring Oaks Ct ... 76021
Spring Valley Dr ... 76021
Springdale Rd ... 76021
Springhaven Ct ... 76021
Stableway Ln ... 76022
Staffordshire Ct ... 76021
Stanford Ct & Dr ... 76021
Stanton St ... 76022
Steeplechase Dr ... 76021
Steeplewood Ct ... 76021
Stephenson Dr ... 76021
Stone Hollow Dr ... 76021
Stonecourt Dr ... 76021
Stonegate Ct ... 76022
Stonegate Dr ... 76022
Stonegate Dr N ... 76021
Storm Ct & Dr ... 76022
Story Ln ... 76021
Stratford Dr ... 76021
Sugar St ... 76021
Sugar Tree Ct ... 76021
Summer Hl ... 76021
Summit View Dr ... 76021
Sundance Ct ... 76021
Sunnybrook Ct ... 76021
Sunnyvale Ter ... 76022
Sunrise Ct ... 76021
Sunset Ln ... 76021
Sunshine Ct ... 76021
Susan Ct & Dr ... 76021
Sweet Wood ... 76021
Sylvia Dr ... 76021
Talisman Ct ... 76021
Tall Meadow Ct ... 76021
Tamworth Ct ... 76021
Tangle Oaks Ct ... 76021
Tanya Ct ... 76021
Teakwood Dr ... 76021
Teal Ln ... 76021
Tennis Dr ... 76022
Tibbets Dr ... 76022
Tiffany Glenn Ct ... 76021
Timber Glen Dr ... 76022
Timber Grove Dr ... 76021
Timber View Cir & Dr ... 76021
Timbergreen ... 76021
Timberline Dr ... 76021
Tranquilla Ter ... 76021
Trinity Ct ... 76022
Turtlerock Dr ... 76021
Uptown Blvd ... 76022
Versante Dr ... 76021
Vicksburg Dr ... 76022
Victoria Ct ... 76021
Village Cir ... 76022
Vine Rdg ... 76021
Vintage Way ... 76021
Vista Way ... 76021
Wade Dr ... 76022
Walnut Dr ... 76021
Walter St ... 76022
Warbler Ct & Dr ... 76021
Warwick Ct & St ... 76022
Warwickshire Ct E & W ... 76021
Wayfarer Rd ... 76021
Wayne Ct ... 76021
Wayside Ct & Dr ... 76021
Wedglea Ct & Dr ... 76021
Wellington Ct ... 76021
Welwyn Way Dr ... 76021
Wembley Wood Ln ... 76022
Wendover Ct ... 76021
Westmont Ct ... 76021
Westview Dr ... 76021
Wheaton Ct & Dr ... 76021
Whisperwood Ct & Ln ... 76021
White Oak Ln ... 76021
Whitebirch Ct ... 76021
Wildflower Ct ... 76021
Wildwood Cir ... 76021
Wilemon Dr ... 76022
Willomet Ct ... 76021
Willow Bnd ... 76021
Willow Ln ... 76021
Willow Way ... 76022
Willow Bend Ct ... 76021
Willow Creek Ct & Way ... 76021
Willow Crest Ct ... 76021
Wiltshire St ... 76021
Wimberly Ct & Dr ... 76021
Wimbleton Ct & Dr ... 76021
Winchester Way ... 76022
Windmill Ct ... 76021
Windomere Dr ... 76021
Windsong Ct & Ln ... 76021
Windsor Ct & St ... 76022
Windstone Ct ... 76021
Wingate Dr ... 76021
Wisteria Ln ... 76021
Woodbridge Dr ... 76021
Woodfield Way ... 76021
Woodhaven Ct ... 76021
Woodhill Ct & Ln ... 76021
Woodland Dr ... 76022
Woodmeadow St ... 76021
Woodmont Ct ... 76021
Woodpark Ln ... 76021
Woodpath Ln ... 76021
Woodrill Ct ... 76021
Woodson Cir & Dr ... 76021
Woodvale Dr ... 76021
Woodview Ter ... 76022
Wren Ct ... 76021
Yorkshire ... 76021

NUMBERED STREETS

All Street Addresses ... 76021

BEEVILLE TX

General Delivery ... 78102

POST OFFICE BOXES MAIN OFFICE STATIONS AND BRANCHES

Box No.s
All PO Boxes ... 78104

RURAL ROUTES

01, 03, 04 ... 78102

HIGHWAY CONTRACTS

02 ... 78102

NAMED STREETS

N & S Adams St ... 78102
N Airport Rd ... 78102
Alaniz Cir ... 78102
S Alta Vista St ... 78102
Aman Rd ... 78102
Anaqua St ... 78102
E Anderson St ... 78102
N & S Archer St ... 78102
Arnold Rd ... 78102
N Avenue E ... 78102
N Avenue B ... 78102
N Avenue C ... 78102
N Avenue D ... 78102
S Ballard St ... 78102
Bataan Rd ... 78102
E & W Bates St ... 78102
W Bell St ... 78102
Bennington Dr ... 78102
N Berry St ... 78102
Big Bend Dr ... 78102
Black Jack Rd ... 78102
Bluecrest Ln ... 78102
Bobwhite Trl ... 78102
E & W Bowie St ... 78102
Bronco Ln ... 78102
Brown Ranch Ln ... 78102
Bruff ... 78102
N & S Buchanan St ... 78102
N & S Burke St ... 78102
E & W Burr St ... 78102
Business 181 N & S ... 78102
SE Bypass 181 ... 78102
Byrd St ... 78102
Cagle Ln ... 78102
Cambria Dr ... 78102
N Cantu St ... 78102
S Canyon Dr ... 78102
Carr Rd ... 78102
Carrol Ln ... 78102
E & W Carter St ... 78102
E Catherine St ... 78102
W Cato St ... 78102
Central Ln ... 78102
Chaparral Trl ... 78102
Charco Rd ... 78102
Chartwell Dr ... 78102
Chase Rd ... 78102
Cherry Ln ... 78102
Chester Ln ... 78102
Chukar Dr ... 78102
Cisneros St ... 78102
N Claiborne St ... 78102
E & W Clare St ... 78102
E & W Cleveland St ... 78102
Cobb Webb Rd ... 78102
Coley Ln ... 78102
Colony Dr ... 78102
Comanche St ... 78102
N & S Comitas St ... 78102
Constellation Dr ... 78102
Cook Rd ... 78102
Coral Sea Dr ... 78102
E & W Corpus Christi St ... 78102
Country Club Dr & Pl ... 78102
County Road 201 ... 78102
County Road 204 ... 78102
County Road 301 ... 78102
County Road 302 ... 78102
County Road 304 ... 78102
County Road 305 ... 78102
County Road 306 ... 78102
County Road 307 ... 78102
County Road 308 ... 78102
County Road 310 ... 78102
County Road 312 ... 78102
County Road 314 ... 78102
County Road 317 ... 78102
County Road 318 ... 78102
County Road 321 ... 78102
County Road 322 ... 78102
County Road 323 ... 78102
County Road 324 ... 78102
County Road 325 ... 78102
County Road 326 ... 78102
County Road 327 ... 78102
County Road 328 ... 78102
County Road 329 ... 78102
County Road 331 ... 78102
County Road 332 ... 78102
County Road 333 ... 78102
County Road 334 ... 78102
County Road 335 ... 78102
County Road 337 ... 78102
County Road 338 ... 78102
County Road 340 ... 78102
County Road 342 ... 78102
County Road 343 ... 78102
County Road 344 ... 78102
County Road 345 ... 78102
County Road 346 ... 78102
County Road 347 ... 78102
County Road 348 ... 78102
County Road 4011 ... 78102
County Road 402 ... 78102
County Road 403 ... 78102
County Road 404 ... 78102
County Road 405 ... 78102
County Road 406 ... 78102
County Road 407 ... 78102
County Road 408 ... 78102
County Road 409 ... 78102
County Road 412 ... 78102
County Road 416 ... 78102
County Road 417 ... 78102
County Road 418 ... 78102
County Road 419 ... 78102
County Road 420 ... 78102
County Road 421 ... 78102
County Road 422 ... 78102
County Road 424 ... 78102
County Road 425 ... 78102
County Road 426 ... 78102
County Road 502 ... 78102
County Road 503 ... 78102
County Road 505 ... 78102
County Road 602 ... 78102
Cox St ... 78102
E & W Crockett St ... 78102
E Curvier St ... 78102
W Dagmar St ... 78102
Daisy Ln ... 78102
Deaf Smith Rd ... 78102
Deborah Perez Ln ... 78102
Dewey Dr ... 78102
Dial Dr ... 78102
W Diaz St ... 78102
Dickerson Rd ... 78102
Dodd Ln ... 78102
E Dolan St ... 78102
Donna Cir ... 78102
Donnacia Espinoza ... 78102
Dugat Dr ... 78102
Earls Trl ... 78102
E Elliott St ... 78102
Ellis Rd ... 78102
Elm Dr ... 78102
Emily Dr ... 78102
Encino Loma ... 78102
Enterprise St ... 78102
Essex St ... 78102
Everett Cir ... 78102
Everglades St ... 78102
Fairview Dr ... 78102
Fairway Rdg ... 78102
E & W Fannin St ... 78102
N & S Fenner St ... 78102
N & S Filmore St ... 78102
First Rd ... 78102
Fish Ln ... 78102
E Flakeral St ... 78102
E & W Flournoy St ... 78102
Fm 1203 ... 78102
Fm 1349 ... 78102
Fm 2441 N & S ... 78102
Fm 2816 ... 78102
Fm 2824 ... 78102
Fm 3355 ... 78102
E, S & W Fm 351 ... 78102
Fm 673 ... 78102
Fm 796 ... 78102
Fm 799 ... 78102
Fm 888 ... 78102
Forrestal Dr ... 78102
N Fowler St ... 78102
N Frontage Rd ... 78102
Gaitan Rd ... 78102
N Garfield St ... 78102
Garner St ... 78102
Gill Ranch Rd ... 78102
Glendale Dr ... 78102
E Gramman St ... 78102
Grenadier Dr ... 78102
Gulf St ... 78102
N Hackberry Dr & St ... 78102
N & S Hall St ... 78102
E Hancock St ... 78102
N & S Harrison Rd & St ... 78102
E & W Harwood Ave ... 78102
Haws Cir ... 78102
E Hayes St ... 78102
E & W Hefferman St ... 78102
Henry Ln ... 78102
Hereford Dr ... 78102
N Hidalgo St ... 78102
Hidden Acres ... 78102
S Highway 181 Byp N & S ... 78102
Highway 181 Frontage N ... 78102
Highway 202 ... 78102
Highway 59 E & W ... 78102
S Hillside Dr ... 78102
Hilltop Rd ... 78102
Hollis Ln ... 78102
Houlihon St ... 78102
E & W Houston St ... 78102
Hudson Rd ... 78102
Hudson Marshall Rd ... 78102
N Hugosota St ... 78102
E & W Huntington St ... 78102
E & W Hutchinson St ... 78102
Independence St ... 78102
E & SE Industrial Park Blvd ... 78102
E & W Inez St ... 78102
W Ireland St ... 78102
N & S Jackson St ... 78102
N & S Jefferson St ... 78102
E & W Jones Rd & St ... 78102
N Juarez St ... 78102
Kai Ln ... 78102
N & S Kathleen St ... 78102
E & W Kennedy St ... 78102
Kessler Ln ... 78102
S King St ... 78102
Kingfisher Dr ... 78102
Kingrea Ln ... 78102
Kinkler Ln ... 78102
Kitty Hawk Rd ... 78102
Kopplin Rd ... 78102
La Para Rd ... 78102
La Para Rio ... 78102
W Lamar ... 78102
Las Palmas Cir ... 78102
S Lassen Dr ... 78102
N & S Laurel St ... 78102
Lehman Dr ... 78102
Leland Cir ... 78102
Lexington Rd ... 78102
N & S Lightburne St ... 78102
Lilac ... 78102
Linney Ln ... 78102
N & S Live Oak Rd & St ... 78102
Lohse Rd ... 78102
Loma Linda ... 78102
Lonesome Oak Dr ... 78102
Lost Crk ... 78102
E Lott St ... 78102
E Louise Dr ... 78102
Lucy Ln ... 78102
N & S Madison Ave ... 78102
Magnolia Ave ... 78102
Mari Gail Rd ... 78102
Marie Pl ... 78102
Marshall Ln ... 78102
N Matamoras St ... 78102
Mayfair Dr ... 78102
N Mccoun Dr ... 78102
N Mckinley St ... 78102
Mesquite Ave, Cir & Rd ... 78102
Michelson Rd ... 78102
Midway St ... 78102
E & W Milam St ... 78102
Mineral Cemetery Rd ... 78102
N & S Minneapolis St ... 78102
N & S Minnesota St ... 78102
Mockingbird Ln ... 78102
N & S Monroe St ... 78102
Moore St ... 78102
W Morales St ... 78102
N Morris St ... 78102
S Mussett ... 78102
Newhall St ... 78102
Nimitz St ... 78102
Nogueira St ... 78102
Nopal Dr ... 78102
Oak Dr & Ln ... 78102
Oak Bend Rd ... 78102
Oak Grove Rd ... 78102
Oak Hill Dr ... 78102
Odemac Dr ... 78102
Ofstie ... 78102
Old Beeville St Marys Rd ... 78102
Old Highway 181 S ... 78102
Old Houston Hwy ... 78102
Old Saint Marys Rd ... 78102
Olympic Dr ... 78102
Orange Ln ... 78102
Oriole Ln ... 78102
Oriskany Dr ... 78102
Palo Blanco Cir ... 78102
Papaya St ... 78102
Parker Hollow Ln ... 78102
Patricio Trevino Ln ... 78102
Patton Rd ... 78102
Paul Pl ... 78102
Pfeil Ln ... 78102
Pieper Rd ... 78102
Pipit Ln ... 78102
N & S Polk St ... 78102
Post Oak Dr ... 78102
W Powell St ... 78102
Presa St ... 78102
Private Algea Ranch Rd ... 78102
Private Barrientes Ln ... 78102
Private Beasley Rd ... 78102
Private Benito Dr ... 78102
Private Brown Ranch Ln ... 78102
Private Buckskin Rd ... 78102
Private Byrd St ... 78102
Private Coffey Rd ... 78102
Private Country Ln ... 78102
Private Country Village Cir ... 78102
Private Daisy Ln ... 78102
Private Donna Cir ... 78102
Private Dunn Rd ... 78102
Private Eralio St ... 78102
Private Eugene Ln ... 78102
Private Hilltop Ranch Rd ... 78102
Private Jemison Ln ... 78102
Private Keilmann Rd ... 78102
Private Kelsey Ln ... 78102
Private Knandel Ln ... 78102
Private Lacey Ln ... 78102
Private Oxford Ln ... 78102
Private Paint Rd ... 78102
Private Palomino Rd ... 78102
Private Quiroga St ... 78102
Private River Oaks Dr ... 78102
Private Road 2002 ... 78102
Private Road 2014 ... 78102
Private Road 3002 ... 78102
Private Road 3003 ... 78102
Private Road 3004 ... 78102
Private Road 3005 ... 78102
Private Road 3006 ... 78102
Private Road 3007 ... 78102
Private Road 3011 ... 78102
Private Road 3012 ... 78102
Private Road 3013 ... 78102
Private Road 3016 ... 78102
Private Road 3017 ... 78102
Private Road 4001 ... 78102
Private Road 4002 ... 78102
Private Road 4003 ... 78102
Private Road 4004 ... 78102
Private Road 4005 ... 78102
Private Road 4010 ... 78102
Private Road 4012 ... 78102
Private Road 4013 ... 78102
Private Road 4014 ... 78102
Private Road 4016 ... 78102
Private Road 4018 ... 78102
Private Road 4020 ... 78102
Private Road 4021 ... 78102
Private Road 4080 ... 78102
Private Road 5002 ... 78102
Private Roan Rd ... 78102
Private Rodriguez Ln ... 78102
Private Rosie ... 78102
Private Salazar Dr ... 78102
Private Sorrel Rd ... 78102
Private Sugarek Ranch Ln ... 78102
Private Walters Ln ... 78102
Private Zimmer Ln ... 78102
Quail Trl ... 78102
Quail Ridge Dr ... 78102
Quarter Horse Dr ... 78102
S Quinn St ... 78102
E Rachal St ... 78102
Ramirez Rd ... 78102
E & W Randall St ... 78102
Ranger Rd ... 78102
Ranier Dr ... 78102
Ray Ln ... 78102
E & W Reagan Rd ... 78102
Red Bird Rdg ... 78102
Retama St ... 78102
W Reyes Rd & St ... 78102
Ridgeway Ln ... 78102
River Oaks Dr ... 78102
E Roberts St ... 78102
Robin Ln ... 78102
E Rosewood St ... 78102
Rudeloff St ... 78102
N Saint Marys St
- 100-200 ... 78102
- 111-111 ... 78104
- 201-4999 ... 78102
- 202-4998 ... 78102

S Saint Marys St ... 78102
Saltzman St ... 78102
N San Antonio Ave ... 78102
Sandoval St ... 78102
E Sarah St ... 78102

Saratoga St 78102
Second Rd 78102
Sequoia Dr 78102
Shady Ln 78102
Siboney St 78102
Skyline Dr 78102
Slay St 78102
Slayton Dr 78102
Smith Ln 78102
Southgate St 78102
W Springer St 78102
E & W Stamper St 78102
Star Trek Dr 78102
E Steiner St 78102
S Stephenson St 78102
Sugarek Rd 78102
Sunkist Dr 78102
W Sylvia St 78102
Tammy Ln 78102
Tammy Lynn Trl 78102
Taxiway Bravo 78102
Taylor Dr & St 78102
Third Rd 78102
Tigre 78102
E Toledo St 78102
Tonya Ln 78102
Towhee Cir 78102
Treptow St 78102
Tripoli St 78102
N & S Tyler St 78102
Valley Oaks Dr 78102
Veltri St 78102
Viggo Rd 78102
W Walton St 78102
N Washington St 78102
West Rd 78102
White Ln 78102
E Widhelm St 78102
E Wildcat Dr 78102
Windridge Dr 78102
Windsor Dr 78102
Wofford Ln 78102
Wren Ln 78102
Yahr Dr 78102
Yellowstone Dr 78102
Yorktown St 78102
Yosemite Dr 78102
W Youst St 78102
Yucca Trl 78102
Zowarka Menn Rd 78102

NUMBERED STREETS

All Street Addresses 78102

BELLAIRE TX

General Delivery 77401

POST OFFICE BOXES MAIN OFFICE STATIONS AND BRANCHES

Box No.s
All PO Boxes 77402

NAMED STREETS

Acacia St 77401
Allendale St 77401
Alpine Ct 77401
Anderson St 77401
Aspen St 77401
Atwell St 77401
Avenue B 77401
Azalea Trail Ln 77401
Basswood Ln 77401
Beech St 77401
Begonia St 77401
Bellaire Blvd
4300-5399 77401
5350-5350 77402
5352-5498 77401
5401-5499 77401
Bellaire Ct 77401
Bellaire Triangle Arc 77401
Bellview St 77401
Berkshire St 77401
Betty St 77401
Beverly Ln 77401
Birch St 77401
Bissonnet St 77401
Bolivar St 77401
Boulevard Grn 77401
Braeburn Dr 77401
Calvi Ct 77401
Camellia Ln 77401
Carol St 77401
Cascade St 77401
Cedar St 77401
Cedar Oaks Ln 77401
Chelsea St 77401
Cherrywood St 77401
Chestnut St 77401
Chimney Rock Rd 77401
Circle Dr 77401
College St 77401
Colonial St 77401
Compton Cir 77401
Cynthia St 77401
Darsey St 77401
Dashwood St 77401
Datonia St 77401
Dorothy St 77401
Edith St 77401
Effie St 77401
Elm Ct & St 77401
Englewood St 77401
Evergreen St 77401
Fern St 77401
Ferndale St 77401
Ferris St 77401
Florence St 77401
Fournace Pl 77401
Fournace Gardens Dr 77401
Gambier Ln 77401
Glenmont St 77401
Grand Lake St 77401
Haminced St 77401
Holly St 77401
Holt St 77401
Holton St 77401
Howard Ln 77401
Huisache St 77401
Imperial St 77401
Innsbruck St 77401
Ione St 77401
Jane St 77401
Jaquet Dr 77401
Jessamine St 77401
Jim West St 77401
Jolen Ct 77401
Jonathan St 77401
Kenyon Ln 77401
Lafayette St 77401
Lamont Cir 77401
Lampton Cir 77401
Larch Ln 77401
Laurel St 77401
Lehigh St 77401
Lennette Ct 77401
Linden St 77401
Little Lake St 77401
Live Oak St 77401
Locust St 77401
Lucerne St 77401
Lula St 77401
Lupin St 77401
Magnolia St 77401
Maple St 77401
Mapleridge St 77401
Marrakech Ct 77401
Mayfair St 77401
Mctighe Dr 77401
Medinah Pl 77401
Meredith Dr 77401
Merrie Ln 77401
Mildred St 77401
Mimosa Dr 77401
Mulberry Ln 77401
Nancy St 77401
Newcastle St 77401
Oakdale St 77401
Oleander St 77401
Otto Ct 77401
Palm St 77401
Palmetto St 77401
Pamellia Dr 77401
Park Ct 77401
Patrick Henry St 77401
Pauline Ave 77401
Pembrook Ct 77401
Phantum Ln 77401
Phil St 77401
Pin Oak Ln 77401
Pin Oak Estates Ct & Dr 77401
Pine Cir & St 77401
Pocahontas St 77401
Prospect Pl 77401
S Rice Ave 77401
Saint Moritz St 77401
Saint Paul St 77401
Saxon St 77401
Serenity Ln 77401
Sheffield St 77401
Spruce St 77401
Sunburst Ct & St 77401
Tamarisk St 77401
Teas St 77401
Terminal St 77401
Town Oaks Pl 77401
Townhouse Ct 77401
Valerie St 77401
Verone St 77401
Vivian St 77401
Wedgewood Dr 77401
Welford Dr 77401
Wendell St 77401
West Loop S 77401
Whipple Dr 77401
White Dr 77401
Whitehaven St 77401
Wildwood Ln 77401
Willow St 77401
Wilmington Dr 77401
Winslow Ln 77401
Wisteria St 77401
Woodlawn Pl 77401
Woodstock St 77401

NUMBERED STREETS

All Street Addresses 77401

BIG SPRING TX

General Delivery 79720

POST OFFICE BOXES MAIN OFFICE STATIONS AND BRANCHES

Box No.s
All PO Boxes 79721

NAMED STREETS

All Street Addresses 79720

NUMBERED STREETS

All Street Addresses 79720

BOERNE TX

General Delivery 78006

POST OFFICE BOXES MAIN OFFICE STATIONS AND BRANCHES

Box No.s
All PO Boxes 78006

NAMED STREETS

Adler St 78006
E & W Advogt St 78006
Affirmed Dr 78015
Agarita Cir & Ct 78006
Alatera Grv 78015
Alta Dr 78006
Alydar Cir 78015
Ammann Rd 78015
Anaqua Spgs 78006
Angel Fire Dr 78015
Antelope Hl 78006
Antlers Way 78006
Anza Run 78015
Apache Trl 78006
Apple Rock 78006
April Ln 78006
April Dawn 78006
Aqua Dr 78006
Aqueduct Ln 78015
Aransas Pass 78006
Arboleda Cir 78006
Arbor Vlg 78015
Arrowhead Dr & Ln 78006
Arroyo 78006
Ashfield Way 78015
Ashton Cir 78015
Auburn Xing 78006
August Ln 78006
Augusta 78006
Austin Dr S 78006
Autumn Gln 78006
Autumn Hl 78006
Autumn Hvn 78015
Autumn Rdg 78006
Autumn Spg 78006
Autumn Ter 78006
Autumn Sound 78006
Autumn Wind 78006
Avator Cir 78015
Axis Cir 78006
Axis Dr 78006
Axis Run 78015
Axis Deer Run 78006
Axton Dr 78015
Azalea Trl 78006
Balcones Bnd 78006
Bambi Dr 78006
E & W Bandera Rd 78006
Baseball Dr 78006
Battle Intense 78015
Baywind Pass 78015
Bearcat 78006
Becker Ln & St 78006
Belindin Dr 78006
Bella Springs Rd 78006
Belmont Rd 78006
Bent Trl 78006
Bentley Run 78015
Benton Dr 78006
Bentwood Dr 78006
Bergmann Rd 78006
Berlin Ln 78006
Bess St 78006
Bethany Way 78006
Biedenharn Rd 78006
Big Horn 78006
Big Springs Blvd 78006
Bird Song 78006
Bitter Spgs 78006
E & W Blanco Rd 78006
Blue Diamond 78006
Blue Heron Blvd & Trl 78006
Blue Jay Ct 78006
Blueberry Dr 78006
Bluebonnet Cir 78006
Bluebonnet Dr 78015
Bluestem Ln 78006
Bluff Vis 78006
Boerne Frst, Gln & Spg 78006
Boerne Cave 78006
Boerne Cliff Dr 78006
Boerne Haze 78006
Boerne Mist 78006
Boerne Stage Rd 78006
Boerne Stage Airfield 78006
Bold Forbes Cir 78015
Bonn Dr 78006
Bowmans Ln 78015
S Brackenridge 78006
Brandenburg Ct 78006
Branding Iron Rd 78006
Brandt Rd 78006
Breeze Way 78006
Bridle Path 78006
Bridlewood Trl 78006
Brilliance 78006
Brimhall Rd 78006
Bristow Way 78006
Britts Ln 78006
Brook Rdg 78015
Brooks Xing 78006
Brookside Ln 78006
Brookview Dr 78006
Brown Hawk 78006
Bruce Welkin 78006
Brunswick Dr 78006
Buckhorn Ln 78006
Buckskin Dr 78006
Burnt Cedar E & W 78015
Busby Rd 78006
Byron Dr 78006
Cabin Spgs 78006
Cactus Pear 78006
Caliza Blf, Crst, Cv & Ter 78006
Calk Ln 78006
Callaway Run 78015
Camden Chase 78015
Camino Hvn & Mnr 78015
Camino Cantera 78006
Camino Tower 78015
Camp Alzafar Rd 78006
Campo Viejo 78006
Candy Ln 78006
E Cantor Cir 78015
Canyon Blf 78006
Canyon Cir 78015
Canyon Loop 78006
Canyon Spgs 78006
Canyon Trl 78006
Canyon Crest Dr 78006
Canyon Ridge Dr 78006
Caprock Cir 78006
Carmel Vly 78015
Carol Ln 78006
Carolyn Ln 78006
Carriage Row 78006
Carrizo 78006
Cascade Caverns Rd 78015
Castle Rock 78006
Cat Spgs 78006
Cavalry Dr 78015
Cave Cir 78006
Cazneau Ln 78006
Cedar Ln, Pl, St & Trl 78006
Cedar Break Trl 78006
Cedar Ridge Rd 78006
Chaparral Hl 78006
Chaparral Creek Dr 78006
Chapel Hl 78006
Charger Blvd 78006
Chartwell Cir & Ln 78015
Chase Cir 78006
Cherry St 78006
Chesterna Dr 78006
Chinkapin Pass 78006
Chisholm Dr 78006
Christen Ct 78006
Churchill Rd 78006
Cibolo Ave 78006
Cibolo Ct 78015
Cibolo Dr 78006
Cibolo Holw N 78015
Cibolo Holw S 78015
Cibolo Pass 78015
Cibolo Path 78015
Cibolo Run 78015
Cibolo Trce 78015
Cibolo Vly 78015
Cibolo Vw 78006
Cibolo Basin Dr 78006
Cibolo Branch Dr 78006
Cibolo Bridge Dr 78006
Cibolo Creek Dr 78006
Cibolo Crossing Dr 78006
Cibolo Gap 78015
Cibolo Oak Ln 78006
Cibolo Ridge Trl 78015
Cielo Cv 78015
Cimarron Crst 78006
Cinco Ln 78006
Cindy Ln 78006
City Park Rd 78006
Clear Creek Cir 78006
Clear Sky 78015
Clear Spring Dr 78006
Clear Water 78006
Clearance 78006
E & W Cleo Ln 78006
Cliffdwellers Path 78006
Cloud Croft Ln 78015
Cloudy Dr 78015
Clubs Dr 78006
Clyde Rock 78006
Clydesdale Cir 78015
Cojak Cir 78015
Cold Riv 78006
Coldmotion Pkwy 78006
Colin Chase 78015
Colonial Oak 78015
Colonial Woods 78015
Colts Foot 78006
Comanche Trl 78006
Commerce Ave 78006
Concho Ln 78006
Connemara Dr 78015
Cool Ridge Cir 78006
Copperleaf 78015
Cordillera Rdg & Trce 78006
Corley Rd 78006
Cornerstone 78006
Coterie Pl 78006
Cottontail Cir 78006
Cottonwood Ave 78006
Coughran Rd 78006
Country Cor & Mdw 78006
Coveney Trl 78006
Covey Roost 78015
Coyote Cir 78006
Cozy Pass 78015
Cravey Rd 78006
Creek Spgs 78006
Creekside Cv, Dr & Ter 78006
Crested Butte 78006
Crosspoint 78006
Crow Rnch 78006
Crown Ter 78015
Crown Jewel 78006
Crystal Cir 78015
Curres Cir 78015
Cypress Ln & Pt 78006
Cypress Bend Dr 78006
Dailey St 78006
Daisy Ln 78006
Daly Rd 78006
Damascus Dr 78015
Dana Creek Dr 78015
Dana Top Dr 78015
Danube Pass 78006
Dapper Dan Dr 78015
Dawn Cir & Dr 78006
Dawnridge 78006
December Ln 78006
Deep Hollow Dr 78006
Deer Path 78006
Deer Smt 78015
Deer Trl 78006
Deer Creek Dr 78006
Deer Hollow Dr 78006
Deer Lake Dr & Spur 78006
Deer Leap 78015
Deer Meadow Dr 78006
Deer Ridge Dr 78006
Deer View Dr 78006
Deerwood Oaks 78006
Del Mar Rd 78006
Delta Dawn Ln 78015
Der Flugplatz 78006
Derby Dr 78006
Desert Flower 78006
Desert Gold 78006
Desert Rainbow 78006
Devonshire Rd 78006
Dew Rdg 78015
Dew Wood 78015
Dewberry Path 78006
Di Lusso Dr 78006
Diamond Dr 78006
Diamondridge 78006
Dietert Ave 78006
Dietz Elkhorn Rd 78015
Dixon Rd 78006
Dobie Spgs 78006
Dodge Rd 78006
Doe Dr 78006
Doe Meadow Dr 78006
Doeskin Dr 78006
Don Dr 78006
Dos Cerros Cir, Dr & Loop 78006
Double Eagle Cir 78015
Dove Ct & Mdw 78006
Dove Crest Dr 78006
Dove Mountain Dr 78006
Dower Ln 78006
Dresden Wood Dr 78006
Driftwood 78006
Drury Pass 78015
Duberry Rdg 78015
Dulling 78006
Dusty Corral 78006
Eagle Ct & Dr 78006
Ebensberger Ave 78006
Ebner St 78006
Ed Ln 78006
Edge Crk 78006
Edge Falls Rd 78006
El Maida 78006
Elbe St 78006
Elkhorn Knl 78015
Elm St 78006
Elm Bottom Trl 78006
Elm Springs Dr 78006
Emerald Hl 78006
Emery Ln 78006
Enchanted Gln 78015
Enchanted Ln 78006
Enchanted Park 78015
Enchanted Elm 78015
English Oaks Cir 78006
Enterprise Pkwy 78006
Equestrian 78015
Ernst Rd 78006
N & S Esser Rd 78006
Estancia Ln 78006
Eufaula 78006
E & W Evergreen St 78006
Eyhorn Dr 78006
E & W Fabra Ln & St 78006
Fabra Oaks Rd 78006
Fair Spgs 78006
Fair Oaks Pkwy 78015
Fairview Pl 78015
Fairway Run 78015
Fairway Ash 78015
Fairway Bend Dr 78015
Fairway Bluff Dr 78015

Street	ZIP
Fairway Green Dr	78015
Fairway Point Dr	78015
Fairway Spring Dr	78015
Fairway Trace Dr	78015
Fairway Trail Dr	78015
Fairway Valley Dr	78015
Fairway Vista Dr	78015
Falcon Crst & Pt	78006
Fall Spgs	78006
Fallow Pl	78015
Falls Ct	78006
Falls Ter	78015
Falls Vw	78015
Fawn Dr	78006
Fawn Ln	78006
Fawn Mtn	78015
Fawn Chase	78015
Fawn Valley Dr	78006
Fence Post	78006
Fire Dance	78006
Firebird Ln	78015
Fischer Dr	78006
Flagstone Hill Dr	78015
Flat Rock Dr	78006
Flemingfeld	78006
Flint Rock Dr	78006
Fm 1376 Rd	78006
Fm 289	78006
Fm 3351 N & S	78006
Fm 473	78006
Fm 474	78006
Forest Ridge Ln	78006
Fossil Rdg	78006
Foster Ln & Rd	78006
Fox Briar Ln	78006
Francis Ave	78006
E & W Frederick St	78006
Frey St	78006
Fritz Grosser Rd	78006
Front Gate	78015
Furtoso Way	78015
Garden St	78006
Gate Frst	78015
Gelvani Grv	78015
Gemstone	78006
Gil Pfeiffer	78015
Gilbert Ln	78006
Glade Dr	78006
Glenn Oaks Dr	78006
Gordon Cir	78006
Graham St	78006
Granadilla	78006
Grand Blvd & Loop	78006
Grand Coteau Dr	78015
Grand Turf	78015
Grand Valley Vw	78006
Green Mdws	78006
Green Cedar Rd	78006
Greenfield St	78006
Greg Dr	78006
Greyhound Cir & Ln	78006
Greystone Cir, Pt & Trl	78006
Grimm Ln	78006
Guadalupe Bnd	78006
Guthrie Rd	78006
Haag Rd	78006
Habenicht Fischer Rd	78006
Hagen Dr	78006
Hampton Bnd, Cv, Run & Way E & W	78006
Hannah Ln	78006
Hansel Dr	78015
Hardy Run	78015
Hardy Trl	78006
Harris Rd	78006
Harvest Gdn	78006
Harvest Creek Ln	78006
Heartstone	78006
Heartway	78006
Hein Rd	78006
Herff Rd & St	78006
Herff Ranch Blvd	78006
Heritage Pass	78006
Heritage Trl	78015
Hickman St	78006
Hidden Lk & Trl	78006
Hidden Gate	78015
Hidden Haven Dr	78006
Hidden Oaks Cir	78006
Hide Away Ln	78006
E & W High Bluff Cir	78006
High Cliff Dr	78015
High Eschelon	78015
High Sierra Dr	78006
High View Dr	78006
E & W Highland Dr	78006
Highland Woods	78006
Highlands Cv	78006
N & S Hill Top Dr	78006
Hill View Ln	78006
Hilltop Dr	78006
Hillview Loop	78006
Hitching Post	78006
Hollow Spgs	78006
Honey Hl	78006
Honey Bee Ln	78006
Honeycomb Dr	78006
Honeycomb Rock	78015
Horizon Crst	78006
Horse Hl	78006
Horseshoe Bnd	78006
E & W Hosack St	78006
Hoskins Trl	78006
Hughs St	78006
Hummingbird Hill Dr	78006
Hunters Clf & Crk	78006
Hunters View Cir	78006
Hyacinth Trce	78015
Indian Blf	78006
Indian Hills Ln	78006
Indian Knoll Dr	78006
Indian Springs Trl	78006
Industrial Dr	78006
Interstate 10 W	78006
Intrepid Dr	78015
Irons St	78006
Irving Hl	78006
Ivy Brk	78015
Ivy Ln	78006
N & S J Dr	78006
J Williams Rd	78006
Jackies Cv	78006
Jackrabbit Cir	78006
Jacob Dr	78006
James St	78006
Jamestown Sq	78015
Jamison Rd	78006
January Ln	78006
Jason Rd	78006
Jeep St	78006
Jennifer Dr	78006
Jim Dandy Cir	78015
Jodhpur	78015
Joe Klar Rd	78006
Joey Dr	78006
Johns Rd	78006
Jordan Pl	78006
July Ln	78006
Juniper Ln	78006
Kahilan Dr	78015
Kaitlin Ln	78006
Kalkallo Dr	78015
Karsch Rd	78006
Kasper Dr	78006
Kassel Dr	78006
Kasten Rd	78006
Katie Ct W	78006
Keeneland Dr	78015
Kemmer Trl	78006
Kempton Cir	78015
Kendall Ln, Pkwy & Rdg	78015
Kendall Oaks Dr	78006
Kendall Pointe Dr	78015
Kendall View Dr	78006
Kendall Woods Dr	78006
Kenwood Ave	78006
Kings Gate	78015
Kirschke Ranch Rd	78015
Kitty Kat Ln	78006
Knoll Spgs	78006
Knotty Grv	78015
Kreutzberg Rd	78006
Krieg Dr	78006
E & W Kronkosky St	78006
La Cancion Dr	78006
Lacey Ln	78006
Lake Blvd	78006
Lake Front Dr	78006
Lake Run Dr	78006
Lake Side Cir & Dr	78006
Lake Spur Dr	78006
Lake View Dr	78006
Lammtarra Cir	78015
Lamplighter	78015
Landa St	78006
Langbein Rd	78006
Lantana Holw	78006
Lariat Dr	78006
Lasso Fls	78006
Latigo Ln	78006
Lauren Ln	78006
Laurens Ln	78006
Lawrence Way	78015
Leather Leaf	78006
Ledge Dr	78015
Ledge Spgs	78006
Lee Mdws	78006
Legacy Pointe	78006
Legacy Woods	78015
Legend Holw	78006
Lehmann St	78006
Leslie Pfeiffer Dr	78015
Lewis Rd	78006
Liberty Park	78015
Lilly Crk	78006
Limestone Pass	78006
Little Hill Rd	78006
Little Joshua Creek Rd	78006
Live Oak Ln, Pass & St	78006
Llano Ct	78006
Lodge Spgs	78006
Lohmann St	78006
Lone Star	78006
Lone Tree	78006
Lonesome Ln	78006
Lonesome Dove	78006
Los Indios Rd	78006
Los Indios Ranch Rd	78006
Lost Vly	78006
Lost Creek Way	78015
Lost Creek Gap	78006
Lost Oaks	78006
Lost Pilot Ln	78006
Lott St	78006
Ludwig Dr	78006
N & S Main Plz & St	78006
Majestic Oaks Dr	78006
Mallard Dr	78006
Man O War Dr	78015
Mandetta Dr	78015
E & W March Ln	78006
Mark Twain Dr	78006
Market Ave	78006
Marlin Dr	78006
Marquardt Rd	78006
Marquise	78006
Marvil Lee Dr	78006
Maskat	78006
Mattick Ln	78006
May Ln	78006
Mayacama Pt & Rdg	78006
Maytum Pass	78006
Meadow Creek Trl	78015
Medical Dr	78006
Mellow Cir, Ct & Rdg	78015
Mellow Wind Dr	78015
Melodia Pl	78006
Menger Spgs	78006
Mesa Verde	78006
Mesquite St & Trl	78006
Michelle Ln	78006
Midnight Sun	78015
Miller Spgs	78006
Millstone Cv	78015
Miranda Rdg	78006
Mission Blf, Hvn, Pt & Smt	78015
Mission Ledge	78015
Mission Tower	78015
Misty Grv & Trl	78006
Misty Waters	78006
Monument Oak	78015
Moonlite Rdg	78006
Morning Cir	78006
Morningside Dr	78006
Morningview Cir	78006
Morro Hl	78015
Moss Rose	78006
Mosswood	78006
Mountain Trl	78015
Mountain Vw	78006
Mountain Creek Trl	78006
Mountain Spring Dr	78006
E & W Mountain Top Dr & Trl	78006
Mountain Views Dr	78006
Mountainview Trl	78006
Muirfield	78006
Mulberry Ln	78006
Mustang Run	78006
Mystic Chase	78015
Napa Lndg	78015
Nelson Hl & Rd	78006
Newton Aly	78006
Nichols Crk & Pass	78015
Nichols Rim	78015
Nixon Dr	78006
No Le Hace Dr	78015
Noble Lark Dr	78015
Noel Ct	78015
Noll Rd	78015
Nollkamper Rd	78006
Norris Ln	78006
North St	78006
Northview Dr	78006
Northview Pass	78015
Northwind	78006
Nottingham Ln	78006
November Ln	78006
Nueces Ct	78006
Oak Ln, Trl & Vly	78006
Oak Acres Ln	78006
Oak Bluff Blvd	78006
Oak Brook Way	78015
Oak Dell	78006
Oak Forest Dr	78006
Oak Grove Dr	78006
Oak Haven Ln	78006
Oak Hills Ln	78006
Oak Knoll Cir	78006
Oak Meadow Ln	78006
Oak Park Dr	78006
Oak Ridge Dr	78006
Oak View Dr	78006
Oakland Hls	78006
Oakview Bnd, Pass & Rdg	78015
Oakwood Ln	78015
October Ln	78006
Ogrady St	78006
Old Fredericksburg Rd	78015
Old San Antonio Rd	78006
Olde Nantucket	78015
Olivia Cir	78015
Orchid Trl	78006
Outlook Pt	78006
Ovaro Cir	78015
Overlook Rdg	78006
Paddock Ln	78015
Palo Alto	78006
Paradise Path	78006
Paradise Point Dr	78006
Paraiso Blf	78006
Paraiso Cir	78015
Paraiso Hvn	78015
Paraiso Mnr	78015
Paraiso Pt	78015
Park Dr	78006
Park Ln	78015
Park Pl	78006
Park Rdg	78006
Parkway	78006
Pasadera	78006
Peace Cir	78006
Peach Spgs	78006
Pebble Crk	78006
Pecan Pkwy & St	78006
Percheron Cir	78015
Persimmon	78006
Pfeiffer Rd	78006
Phil Wilson	78006
Phillip Rd	78006
Pilsen Dr	78006
Pimlico Ln	78015
Pine View Dr	78006
Pintado	78015
N & S Plant Ave	78006
Plantation Path	78006
Plantinum Ct	78015
Platten Creek Rd	78006
N Pleasant Valley Dr	78006
Pocono Rd	78006
Poehnert Rd	78006
Point Given Cir	78015
Pompano Dr	78006
Poppy Hls	78015
Post Oak Trl	78015
Poste Robles	78006
Prado Xing	78006
Prairie Falcon	78006
Preakness Ln	78015
Presidio Aly, Blf, Bnd, Clf, Crk, Crst, Cv & Hvn	78015
Presidio Ledge	78015
Presidio Mesa	78015
Presidio Sands	78015
Preston Trl	78006
Privilege Pass	78006
Proximity Dr	78015
Pyrite	78006
Quadrille Ln	78015
Quail Ct	78006
Quail Grove Ln	78006
Quiet Pt	78006
Raintree Hl, Rdg & Spur	78015
Raintree Woods Dr	78015
Ralph Fair Rd	78015
Ranch Blf	78006
Ranch Brk	78015
Ranch Crk	78006
Ranch Crst	78006
Ranch Dr	78015
Ranch Ln	78006
Ranch Pass	78015
Ranch Pt	78015
Ranch Ter	78015
Ranch Vw	78006
Ranch Oaks	78006
Ranchland Vw	78006
Ranger Dr	78006
Ranger Creek Rd	78006
Rattlesnake Blf	78006
Red Bird Ln	78006
Red Bud	78006
Red Bud Hl	78015
Red Oak Dr	78006
Redbird Ct	78006
Redfish	78006
Reed Rd	78006
Reserve Dr	78006
Resort Way	78006
Retama Rd	78006
Reunion Oak	78015
Rexon Cir	78015
Rhine St	78006
Richter Ave	78006
Ridge Pl & Trl	78006
Ridge Crest Dr	78006
Ridge Oaks Dr	78006
Ridge View Dr	78006
Ridges End Dr	78006
Ridgeview Trl	78015
Rio Cv & Pass	78015
Rio Bank	78015
Rio Brazos	78006
Rio Colorado	78006
Rio Cordillera	78006
Rio Frio Ct	78006
Riva Ridge Dr	78015
River Pt, Rd, Rdg, Trl, Vw & Xing	78006
River Bluff Dr	78006
River Forest Dr	78006
River Mountain Dr	78006
River Ranch Rd	78006
Riverwalk	78006
Riverwood	78006
Roadrunner Cir & Trl	78006
Roaring Crk	78006
Roberta Cir	78006
Robin Ct	78006
Robin Dale Dr	78015
Robins Way	78015
Rock Frst	78015
Rock St	78006
Rock Canyon Dr	78006
Rock Creek Cir	78006
Rock Oak Cir	78015
Rocking Horse Ln	78015
Rocky Blf, Path & St	78006
Rocky Top Rd	78006
Rodalyn Dr	78006
Rodeo Dr	78006
Roeder St	78006
Rolling Acres Rd	78006
Rolling Acres Trl	78015
Rolling View Dr	78006
Ronco Dr	78006
Roosevelt Ave	78006
Roseben Cir	78015
Rosebud St	78006
Rosewood Ave	78006
Roundup Dr	78006
Royal Ascot Dr	78015
Royal Mustang Cir	78015
Royal Turf Cir	78015
Royal Valance	78015
Rue Parker	78006
Ruffian Dr	78015
Rust Ln	78006
Rustic Chase	78015
Rusty Ln & Run	78006
Ryan St	78006
Sabine Rd	78006
Sable Run	78015
Saddle Pass	78015
Saddle Club Cir	78006
Saddle Horn	78006
Saddle Mountain Dr	78006
Saddle Side	78015
Saddle Song	78015
Saddle Star	78015
Saddle Tan	78015
Saddle View Dr	78006
Saddleback Cir	78015
Sage Cyn	78006
Sage Brush	78006
Sage Oaks Trl	78006
Sailfish Dr	78006
E & W San Antonio Ave	78006
San Saba	78006
Sandy Shl	78006
Sandy Oaks Dr	78015
Sansom Dr	78006
Santa Anita Rd	78006
Santa Fe Trl	78006
Saratoga Ln	78015
N & S Saunders St	78006
Savanah Jon Blvd	78015
Saxet Dr	78006
Scarlett Ridge Dr	78006
Scarteen	78015
Scenic Vw	78006
Scenic Bluffs Dr	78006
Scenic Chase	78015
Scenic Loop Rd	78006
Scheele Rd	78015
Schleicher St	78006
Schmidt Ln	78006
N & S School St	78006
Schryver St	78006
Schweppe St	78006
Scintilla Ln	78015
Scissor Tail Trl	78006
Scottie Dr	78006
Seabiscuit Dr	78015
Seattle Slew	78015
Secretariat Ln	78015
Seewald Rd	78006
Sendero Pt	78015
Sendero Rdg	78006
Sendero Ridge Dr	78015
Sendero Woods	78015
September Ln	78006
Serenity Dr	78006
Setterfeld Cir	78015
Settlers Peak	78015
Seven Sisters Dr	78006
Shade Tree	78015
Shadow Knls	78006
Shadow Valley Dr	78006
Shady Run	78006
Shady Meadow Dr	78006
Shady Oaks Dr	78006
Shady Ridge Dr	78006
Shadywood	78006
Shane Ln	78006
Sharon Dr	78006
Shooting Club Rd	78006
Short St	78006
Sidewinder	78006
Siebenicher Rd	78006
Silent Spg	78006
Silver Hills Dr	78006
Silver Spur Trl	78015
Sisterdale Rd	78006
Sisterdale Lindendale Rd	78006
Sky Blue Rdg	78015
Skyland Dr	78006
Skylight Trl	78006
Skyview Dr	78006
Slumberwood	78015
Smiser Smith Rd	78006
Smokey Riv N	78006
Smokey Riv S	78006
Smokey Vw	78015
Smokey Chase	78015
Softwind Cir	78015
Someday Dr	78006
Sonoma Ambre	78015
Sophia Cir	78006
Southfield	78006
Spanish Pass Rd	78006
Sparkling Springs Dr	78006
Sparkman Dr	78006
Sparrow Hawk Trl	78006
Spencer Rd	78006
Spider Rock	78006
Spotted Deer Trl	78006
Spring Rdg	78006
Spring Creek Rd	78006
Spring Hill Dr	78006
Spring Valley Cv & Dr	78006
Staffel St	78006
Stage Spgs	78006
Stahl St	78006
N Star Ct	78006
Star Dr	78015
N Star Rd	78015
Star Mica	78006
Star View Ct	78006
Starr Rnch	78015
Starwood	78006
State Highway 46 E & W	78006
Staudt St	78006
Steel Valley Dr	78006
Steeplechase Ln	78015
Stendebach Pl	78015
Stephanie Dr	78006
Stephanie Way	78015
Stetson Dr	78006
Stone Cyn	78006
Stone Ter	78015

Stone Creek Cir & Dr .. 78006
Stone Wall Dr 78006
Stonegate Dr & Rd N & S 78006
Strawberry 78006
Summer Gln 78006
Summer Song Cir 78015
Summer Sweet 78015
Summit Pass, Pt & Trl .. 78006
Summit Ridge Dr 78015
Sumpter Dr 78015
Sunglo 78015
Sunland 78015
Sunrise Dr 78006
Sunriver 78006
Sunset Dr 78006
Surrey Dr 78006
Sutter Mls 78006
Swede Cyn & Spgs 78006
Swedecreek 78006
Sweetridge Cir 78015
Sweetwind Cir 78015
Tapatio Dr E & W 78006
Tarpon Dr 78006
Tawny Way 78015
Teepee Ln 78006
Tempe Wilke Ln 78006
Terra Mnr & Vis 78015
Terra Bella 78015
Terrace Pt 78015
Terrace Trl 78006
Terret Cir 78015
Tessara Cir 78015
Texas Cedar Trl 78006
E & W Theissen St 78006
Thomas Dr & Rd E 78006
Thunder Hl, Rd, Rdg & Xing 78006
Thunder Creek Rd 78006
Thunder Valley Rd 78006
Tiffany Dr 78006
Timber Trl 78006
Timber Mountain Dr 78006
Timber Top Dr 78015
Timber View Dr 78006
Timberland Trl 78015
Tiptop Ln 78006
Tivoli Way 78015
Toepperwein Rd 78006
Toponga 78006
Torrie Trl 78006
Toutant Beauregard Rd 78006
Tower Rd 78006
Towering Vis 78006
Towne View Cir 78006
Trade Ave 78006
Tradition Trl 78015
Tradition Oak 78015
Trails End Rd 78006
Travis Ln 78006
Trillion Ct 78006
Triple Crown 78015
Turf Paradise Ln 78015
Turkey Run 78006
Turkey Knob 78006
Turner Ave 78006
Turning Leaf 78015
Twin Canyon Dr 78006
Twin Valley Dr 78006
Upper Balcones Rd 78006
Upper Cibolo Creek Rd 78006
Upper Sisterdale Rd 78006
Us Highway 87 N 78006
Valle Blf 78015
Valle Verde 78015
Vallerie Ln 78006
Valley Knl & Vw 78006
Valley View Spur 78006
Veneda Pl 78006
Venturer 78015
Verde Pt 78006
Versant Blf 78015
Victoria Ln 78006
View Ln 78006
View Point Ct & Dr E, N & W 78006
Village Cir, Cv & Dr 78006
Village Park Dr 78006
Vine Clf 78015
Vinerens Dr 78015
Violet Pass 78006
Vista Real Ave 78006
Vista Verde 78006
Vittoria Rdg 78006
N & S Wagon Wheel Dr 78015
N Walnut Way 78006
Walnut Grove Rd N 78006
Walters Rd 78006
Wanda St 78006
Waring Welfare Rd 78006
Wasp Creek Rd 78006
Wasp Creek Ranch Rd 78006
Water St 78006
Water Stone Pkwy 78006
Waterfall Ct 78006
Waterview Dr & Pkwy .. 78006
Well Spgs 78006
Wembley 78015
Whippoorwill Ct 78006
Whirlaway Cir 78015
Whisper Way 78006
Whisper Gate 78015
White Oak Trl 78006
White Tail Dr 78006
White Water Rd 78006
Whitworth Dr & Rd 78006
Wild Cherry Ln 78006
Wild Fire Dr 78015
Wild Horse Dr 78006
Wild Oak Hl 78015
Wild Rose 78006
Wild Sage 78006
Wild Turkey Blvd 78006
Willoughby Way 78006
Willow Bark 78006
Willow Wind Dr 78015
Willowbrook 78006
Wind Song 78006
Windchime Hl & Way ... 78015
Windermere Dr 78015
E & W Winding Loop, Path & Riv 78006
Windmill Cir 78015
Windridge Dr 78006
Windsor Dr 78006
Windview Dr 78006
Windwick 78006
Windwood Dr E 78006
Winged Foot 78006
Wingglen 78006
Winsbrook Dr 78006
Wollschlaeger Dr 78006
Wood Crst 78006
Wood Gln 78006
Wood Trl 78015
Wood Berry Ln 78015
Wood Bine Way 78015
Woodbridge 78015
Woodland Blvd 78006
Woodland Cir 78006
Woodland Grn 78015
Woodland Pass 78006
Woodland Pkwy 78015
Woodland Trce 78006
Woodland Vw 78015
Woodland Ranch Rd ... 78015
Woodway Bnd 78006
Woody Way 78006
Wyatt Trl 78015
Yoalana St 78006
Zoeller Ln 78006

NUMBERED STREETS

All Street Addresses 78006

BORGER TX

General Delivery 79007

POST OFFICE BOXES MAIN OFFICE STATIONS AND BRANCHES

Box No.s
All PO Boxes 79008

HIGHWAY CONTRACTS

01 79007

NAMED STREETS

Abilene St 79007
E & W Adams St 79007
Adobe Trl 79007
Airport Rd 79007
Alabama St 79007
Allred St 79007
Alpine St 79007
Alstar 79007
Altamira St 79007
Amaryllis St 79007
Andress St 79007
Antelope St 79007
Apache St 79007
Arline St 79007
Ash St 79007
Aspen St 79007
Augusta St 79007
Austin St 79007
Avalon St 79007
Bagwell St 79007
Baird St 79007
Baker St 79007
Balin St 79007
Bartush St 79007
Baylor St 79007
Bedivere St 79007
Beech St 79007
Beverly Dr 79007
Birdie Ave 79007
Blommaert St 79007
Bluebonnet St 79007
E Boeing Dr 79007
Bogey Cir 79007
Bois D Arc 79007
Borger Shopping Plz ... 79007
Bowie St 79007
Bowman Dr 79007
Boyd St 79007
Bradley St 79007
Brain St 79007
Brandon Dr 79007
Brier St 79007
Brierwood St 79007
Broadmoor St 79007
Brookshire St 79007
Brown St 79007
Brush St 79007
N & S Bryan St 79007
Buckner St 79007
Bulldog Blvd 79007
Bunavista St 79007
Bunton St 79007
Burch St 79007
Butadieno St 79007
Cable St 79007
Cactus Rd 79007
Caddo St 79007
Caliche St 79007
California St 79007
Cambridge Pl 79007
Campus Pl 79007
Canady St 79007
Canyon Dr 79007
Caprock St 79007
Carbon Rd & St 79007
Carbon Camp Rd 79007
Carolina St 79007
Carpenter St 79007
Carson St 79007
Castle Dr 79007
N & S Cedar St 79007
Chamisa St 79007
Chaparral St 79007
Chapman St 79007
Cheatham St 79007
Cherokee St 79007
Chickasaw St 79007
Cholla Ln 79007
Cimarron St 79007
Circle Dr 79007
Clayton St 79007
Clements St 79007
Cleveland St 79007
Clubhouse Dr 79007
Cobblestone Ln 79007
Coble Dr & St 79007
Coffee Cp & Dr 79007
College Ave 79007
Concord St 79007
Cooley Dr 79007
E & W Coolidge St 79007
Coronado Cir 79007
Cottonwood St 79007
Cottonwood Springs Trl 79007
Country Club Rd 79007
Creek St 79007
Creekview St 79007
Crockett St 79007
Cypress St 79007
Dallas St 79007
Danube St 79007
Davenport St 79007
Davis St 79007
Deahl St 79007
Deason St 79007
Del Coronado Way 79007
Del Rancho Rd 79007
Delaware St 79007
Deletore St 79007
Derr St 79007
Dillard St 79007
Dixon St 79007
Dogwood St 79007
Dolomita St 79007
Eagle Ln 79007
Elise St 79007
Elizabeth St 79007
Elm St 79007
Elmore St 79007
Empire St 79007
Estireno St 79007
Everest St 79007
Evergreen St 79007
Fairlanes Blvd 79007
Fairview St 79007
Fairway Dr 79007
Ferguson St 79007
Finger St 79007
Firewheel St 79007
Flarral St 79007
N & S Florida St 79007
Fm 1319 79007
Fm 1551 79007
Fm 1559 79007
Fm 2277 79007
Francis St 79007
Franklin St 79007
Fritch Hwy 79007
Froma St 79007
Frontera St 79007
Galahad St 79007
Gardner St 79007
Garrett St 79007
Gasoline St 79007
Gateway Cir 79007
Gawain St 79007
Geromino St 79007
Glenbrook Dr 79007
Golf Rd 79007
Golf Course Rd 79007
Gough St 79007
E & W Grand St 79007
Gravel Pit Rd 79007
Green St 79007
Hackberry St 79007
Haggard St 79007
Harrington St 79007
Harrison St 79007
N & S Harvey St 79007
Haven Holw 79007
Hazelwood St 79007
Hector St 79007
N & S Hedgecoke Dr & St 79007
Hemlock St 79007
Herbst St 79007
Hickory St 79007
Highway 136 79007
N Highway 207 79007
Hill St 79007
Hillshire St 79007
Hobby St 79007
Home Rd 79007
Hood St 79007
E House St 79007
Houston St 79007
Huber Ave 79007
Hwy 36 79007
Illinois St 79007
Ina St 79007
Indiana St 79007
Industrial Blvd 79007
Inglewood St 79007
Inverness St 79007
Jackson St 79007
E & W Jefferson St 79007
Jennie Ln 79007
Jennings St 79007
Jim Hall St 79007
Johnson St 79007
Johnson Plant St 79007
Jolly St 79007
Juanita Ln 79007
Juniper St 79007
Kafir St 79007
Kaye St 79007
Keikbusch St 79007
Keith St 79007
Lakeview St 79007
Lancelot St 79007
Laramie St 79007
Latimer St 79007
Lee St 79007
Linden St 79007
Lindsey St 79007
S Line Ave 79007
Linkshire Dr 79007
Linwood St 79007
Lister St 79007
Locust St 79007
Loma Linda Ln 79007
Madison St 79007
N & S Main St 79007
Maple St 79007
Marcy Dr 79007
Marigold St 79007
Martinez Pl 79007
Mary St 79007
Mccarthy St 79007
N Mcgee St 79007
S Mcgee St
100-501 79007
500-500 79008
503-1199 79007
600-1198 79007
Mcpherson St 79007
Meadowbrook Dr 79007
Medical Dr & Plz 79007
Megert Ctr 79007
Memre Ln 79007
Meredith St 79007
Mesquite St 79007
Michigan St 79007
Miller St 79007
Milner Rd 79007
Mimosa St 79007
Minnesota St 79007
Mississippi St 79007
Missouri St 79007
Mitchell St 79007
Mockingbird St 79007
Mohawk St 79007
Monroe St 79007
Montana St 79007
Moody St 79007
Moreland St 79007
Navajo St 79007
Nelson St 79007
Nonken St 79007
Oak St 79007
E & W Ocla St 79007
Odaniel St 79007
Ohio St 79007
Old Hwy 79007
Opal St 79007
Osage St 79007
Overlook St 79007
Ozmer St 79007
Paintbrush St 79007
Pantex St 79007
Par Ave 79007
N Park Pl & St 79007
Parkway St 79007
Patton Cir 79007
Pecan St 79007
Peiffer St 79007
Pellinore St 79007
Penn St 79007
Philview St 79007
Pine St 79007
Pinehurst St 79007
Pinon St 79007
Plains St 79007
Platt St 79007
Plum St 79007
Potter St 79007
Prairie St 79007
Premier Rd 79007
Primrose Ln 79007
Production St 79007
Quail Holw & Rdg 79007
Rigdon St 79007
Riverview Cp & St 79007
Roberts St 79007
Rocky Ridge Rd 79007
Roosevelt St 79007
Rotary St 79007
Sage St 79007
Saint James St 79007
Saint Johns Rd 79007
Salina St 79007
San Juan Way 79007
Sandstone Dr 79007
Sandtrap St 79007
Santa Fe St 79007
Sarasota St 79007
Scott Aly & St 79007
Seminole St 79007
N & S Shelton St 79007
Shilo Rd 79007
Short St 79007
Skycrest St 79007
Skyline Dr 79007
Smith St 79007
Snider Ln 79007
Somerset St 79007
Spruce St 79007
W Stephens Dr 79007
Sterling St 79007
Stevenson St 79007
Stinnett Hwy 79007
Takewell St 79007
Tansy St 79007
Taylor St 79007
Teague St 79007
Tech St 79007
Tejas Dr 79007
Texas St 79007
Thistle St 79007
Thompson St 79007
Thrams St 79007
Tierra Alto 79007
Timberlake Ct 79007
Tranquility Ln 79007
Tristram St 79007
Tumbleweed St 79007
Turner St 79007
Tyler St 79007
Union St 79007
University Pl 79007
Valley Dr 79007
Veta St 79007
Wade St 79007
Warner St 79007
Warwick St 79007
Weatherly St 79007
West Dr 79007
Western Ave 79007
Westhaven Dr 79007
Westridge St 79007
White St 79007
Whitlow St 79007
Whitney St 79007
Whittenburg St 79007
Wilbanks St 79007
Wilkinson Ave 79007
Williams Way 79007
Willowick St 79007
Wilshire St 79007
E & W Wilson St 79007
Wisconsin St 79007
Womack St 79007
Young St 79007
Yows St 79007
Yucca St 79007

NUMBERED STREETS

All Street Addresses 79007

BRENHAM TX

General Delivery 77833

POST OFFICE BOXES MAIN OFFICE STATIONS AND BRANCHES

Box No.s
All PO Boxes 77834

NAMED STREETS

A H Ehrig Dr 77833
E Academy St 77833
Adamek Rd 77833
Affleck Rd 77833
Ahrens Ave 77833
E Airline Dr 77833
Airport Rd 77833
E & W Alamo Dr & St .. 77833
All Jersey Rd 77833
Allen Rd 77833
Allison St 77833
Allyne Ln 77833
Alma Ln 77833
Alois Ln 77833
Anderson Ln 77833
Antique Ln 77833
Antler Ln 77833
Apache Dr 77833
Apperson Rd 77833
Arlen Ave 77833
Armbrister St 77833
Artesian Park Ln 77833
Asa Hoxie Rd 77833
Aspen Cir 77833
Atlow Dr 77833
N & S Austin Pkwy & St 77833
Autumn Rain Dr 77833
Ava Dr 77833
Aviation Way 77833
Axer St 77833
Azalea St 77833
Baber St 77833

Baranowski Rd 77833
Barbee St 77833
Barnhill St 77833
Batdorf Ln 77833
N & S Baylor St 77833
Beaver Rd 77833
Beazley St 77833
Beckendorf Ln 77833
Becker Dr 77833
Beckermann Rd 77833
Ben Dr 77833
Bent Tree Ln 77833
Benton Dr 77833
N & S Berlin Rd 77833
Betty Ln 77833
Big Bird Ln 77833
Bilski Ln 77833
Black Forest Ln 77833
Blake Dr 77833
Bleiblerville Rd 77833
Blinn Blvd 77833
E, N, S & W Blue Bell Ln & Rd 77833
Blue Jay St 77833
Bluebonnet Blvd 77833
Bluehaven Hl 77833
Bluehaven Hill Cir 77833
Bluff Rd 77833
Boehm Cir 77833
Boehnemann Rd 77833
Boggy Creek Rd 77833
Booth Ln 77833
Bormann St 77833
Botts St 77833
Bradley Ln 77833
Brandenburg Ln 77833
Brauner Ln 77833
Briar Creek Rd 77833
Briar Point Ln 77833
N & W Briarwood Dr 77833
Bridge St 77833
Bridle Creek Ln 77833
Brookbend Dr 77833
Brooke Cv 77833
Brooks Ln 77833
Brookside Dr 77833
Brown St 77833
E & W Bryan St 77833
Buchannan St 77833
Burch St 77833
Burleson St 77833
Buttercup Ln N 77833
Caddo Rd 77833
Campbell St 77833
Candlelight Cir 77833
Cantey St 77833
Captain Scott Rd 77833
Carlee Dr 77833
Carlinda Ln 77833
Carolyn St 77833
Carriage Ln 77833
Carrington Ln 77833
Cedar Cir & St 77833
Cedar Hill Rd 77833
Cedar Oaks Dr 77833
Cena Dr 77833
Center St 77833
Century Cir 77833
Champion Dr 77833
N & S Chappell Hill St 77833
Charles Lewis St 77833
Chase St 77833
E & W Chauncy St 77833
E Cheri Ln 77833
Cheyenne Dr 77833
Chriesman Rd 77833
Christmas Rd 77833
Church Rd & St 77833
Clay Ln & St 77833
Clay Creek Rd 77833
Clayton Dr 77833
Clearspring Dr 77833
Clem Ln 77833
Clinton St 77833
Clover Rd 77833
Club Rd 77833

Clyde Ln 77833
Cobble Gate Dr 77833
Cocks Crow Rd 77833
Coles Rd 77833
College Ave 77833
E & W Commerce St 77833
Confederate Ln 77833
Copelyn Springs Rd 77833
Corey St 77833
Cornish Dr 77833
Cottontail Ln 77833
Cottonwood St 77833
Country Club Rd 77833
Country Meadows Ln 77833
Country Place West Dr 77833
County Farm Ln 77833
County Road 30 77833
Crane Ln 77833
Crazy Horse Trl 77833
Creamery St 77833
Creekside Dr 77833
Creekwood Ln 77833
Crestview Ln 77833
Crockett St 77833
Cyndi Cir 77833
Cypress Cir 77833
Dabney Rd 77833
Daisy Dr 77833
Dallas St 77833
Dannheim Rd 77833
Dark St 77833
David Ln 77833
Dawson St 77833
S Day St 77833
Deer Ln & Rd 77833
Dempsey St 77833
Derrick Ln 77833
Desirable Cir 77833
Devault Ln 77833
Dierking Rd 77833
Dillard Rd 77833
Dillon St 77833
N & S Dixie Rd & St 77833
Dixon Ln 77833
Doe Run Ln 77833
Dogwood Rd 77833
N & S Douglas St 77833
N & S Drumm St 77833
Duprie Dr 77833
Durden St 77833
Earlywine Rd 77833
Edward Ln 77833
Eldon St 77833
Eleanor St 77833
Eledra St 77833
Elhart Ln 77833
Ellen St 77833
Ellermann Rd 77833
Elm Dr 77833
Emile St 77833
Emshoff Rd 77833
Everest Ln 77833
Ewing St 77833
Fairview Ave 77833
Farewell St 77833
Farmers Rd 77833
Faulkner St 77833
Fawn Rd 77833
Ferguson Ln 77833
W Fifth St 77833
W First St 77833
Five Oaks Ln 77833
Flewellen Rd 77833
Floral Ln 77833
Fm 109 77833
Fm 1155 E & N 77833
Fm 1935 77833
Fm 1948 N & W 77833
Fm 2193 77833
N Fm 2502 77833
Fm 2621 77833
Fm 2679 77833
Fm 2754 77833
Fm 2935 77833
Fm 332 77833

Fm 3456 77833
Fm 389 77833
Fm 390 E 77833
Fm 50 77833
Fm1935 77833
Forrest Ln 77833
Franklin St 77833
Fritz Rd 77833
Fuelburg Pease Ln 77833
Garlin Rd 77833
Garrett St 77833
Gay Hill St 77833
Geers Rd 77833
Geick Ln 77833
Genes Ln 77833
Geney St 77833
Gerke Rd 77833
E & W Germania St 77833
Giddings Ln & St 77833
Gilder St 77833
Gilmore Rd 77833
Glenblythe Rd 77833
Glenda Blvd 77833
Glenn Dr 77833
Goeke Rd 77833
Goessler St 77833
Grace Ln 77833
Grand Oaks Ln 77833
Granny Ln 77833
Graves Rd 77833
Grebe Rd 77833
Green St 77833
Green Meadows Ln 77833
Green Oaks Ln 77833
Greenvine Rd 77833
Greenway Dr 77833
Griffin Loesch Ln 77833
Grote Rd 77833
Gun And Rod Cir & Rd 77833
Haack Ln 77833
Hackberry Ln 77833
Hale Branch Ln 77833
Hall 77833
Hampshire Dr 77833
Hanath Ln 77833
Handley St 77833
Happy Hollow Rd 77833
Harrell Rd 77833
Harrington St 77833
Harris Spring Ln 77833
Harrisburg Rd 77833
Harrison Rd 77833
Hasskarl Dr 77833
Haynes St 77833
Heather Glen St 77833
Heights Cir 77833
Helm Rd 77833
Helmer Rd 77833
Heritage Dr 77833
Herrmann Ln 77833
Hickory Ln 77833
Hickory Bend Rd 77833
Hickory Hollow Ln 77833
Hidden Creek Ln 77833
Hidden Valley Ln 77833
Higgins St 77833
High St 77833
Highline Ln 77833
Highview Cir 77833
Highway 105 77833
Highway 290 E & W 77833
Highway 36 N & S 77833
Hill St 77833
Hillcrest Ln 77833
S Hillside Dr & Ln 77833
Hilltop Acres Ln 77833
Hoddeville School Rd 77833
Hogan Cir 77833
Hohenwalde School Rd 77833
Hollis Dr 77833
Holstein Ln 77833
Homeland Ln 77833
Hood Hotel Rd 77833
Hopmann Rd 77833

Hoppers Ln 77833
Horak Rd 77833
Horizon Ln 77833
Horstmann Rd 77833
Hosea St 77833
Houston St 77833
Hudson St 77833
Hueske Ln 77833
Huisache St 77833
Hummingbird Rd 77833
Husemann Rd 77833
Ike Ln 77833
Independence St 77833
Indian Creek Ln 77833
Indian Hill Ln 77833
Indian Paint Brush Rd 77833
Industrial Blvd 77833
S Jackson St 77833
Jackson Creek Ln 77833
Jackson League Cir 77833
Jamie Ln 77833
Jane Ln 77833
Janes Ln 77833
Janet St 77833
Janner Kuecker Ln 77833
Jasmine St 77833
Jason Ln 77833
W Jefferson St 77833
Jeffries St 77833
Jerry Ln 77833
Jersey Ln 77833
Jeske Rd 77833
Jo Ann St 77833
Joel St 77833
Johnson St 77833
Joseph St 77833
Josephine Ln 77833
Jungle Ln 77833
Kamas Rd 77833
Karen Ln 77833
Katherine St 77833
Kathryn Cir 77833
Kelly Ln 77833
Kelm Rd 77833
Kenjura Ln 77833
Kenney Hwy 77833
Kenney Hall Rd 77833
Kerr St 77833
Kessel Ln 77833
Kettler Rd 77833
Kevin Ln 77833
Key St 77833
Kimberly Ln 77833
Kirk Dr 77833
Knipstein Ln 77833
Kori Ln 77833
Kratz Rd 77833
Kuhn Ln 77833
Kurt Dr 77833
Kuykendall Rd 77833
L B J Dr 77833
L J St 77833
Lacy Ln 77833
Lake Forest Cir & Est 77833
Lakeview Cir, Dr & Rd 77833
Lakewood Cir 77833
Landua Dr 77833
Laney St 77833
Lange Lake Rd 77833
Lauraine Ln & St 77833
Lawndale Ave 77833
Lazy F Ln 77833
Leaning Oak Ln 77833
Ledbetter Ln 77833
Lee St 77833
Leghorn Dr 77833
Lehde Ln 77833
Lehmann Ln 77833
Leisure Rd 77833
Leslie D Ln 77833
Liberty St 77833
Lillie Lange Rd 77833
Limit St 77833
Linda Ln 77833
Little Rocky Rd 77833
Live Oak Dr & Ln 77833

Lockett St 77833
Loesch St 77833
Lois Wright Cir 77833
Lola Ln 77833
Longhofer St 77833
Longhorn Ln 77833
Longwood Dr 77833
N Loop Rd 77833
S Loop 497 Rd 77833
Lott Ln 77833
Louise Ln 77833
Lounge Rd 77833
E Lubbock St 77833
Lucky Ln 77833
Lueckemeyer Rd 77833
Luedemann Ln 77833
Lusk Ln 77833
Lynne Way 77833
Maass Rd 77833
Machemehl Rd 77833
Mae Way 77833
Magnolia Ln 77833
E & W Main St 77833
Main View St 77833
Mangrum St 77833
E & W Mansfield St 77833
Marcus Rd 77833
Marie St 77833
Mariposa Ln 77833
Marjorie St 77833
Mark T Dr 77833
N Market St
101-197 77833
199-400 77833
309-309 77834
401-799 77833
402-798 77833
S Market St 77833
Martin St 77833
Martin Luther King Jr Pkwy 77833
Mary Gene St 77833
Mary Vince Ln 77833
Matchett St 77833
Matilda St 77833
Mayfair Ln 77833
Mccrocklin Rd 77833
Mcintyre St 77833
Mcknight Rd 77833
Mcneese St 77833
Meadow Ln 77833
Meadow Brook Ln 77833
Medical Ct & Pkwy 77833
Meier Ln 77833
Melcher Ln 77833
Mertins Creek Rd 77833
Meyer Ln 77833
N Meyersville Rd 77833
Mill Creek Dr 77833
Mill House Ln 77833
Mills St 77833
Milroy Dr 77833
Miranda Ln 77833
Miss Lucy Ln 77833
Mockingbird Rd 77833
Mohawk Rd 77833
Moonbeam Ct 77833
Morgan St 77833
Mound Hill Rd 77833
Mount Olive St 77833
Mount Vernon Rd 77833
Mount Zion Rd 77833
Muellersville Ln 77833
Muery Rd 77833
Mulberry St 77833
Munz St 77833
Muse St 77833
Mustang Rd 77833
Navratil Dr 77833
Nelson St 77833
Neumann Rd 77833
New Wehdem Rd 77833
New Years Creek Ln 77833
Newman Ln 77833
Newman League Rd 77833
Niebuhr St 77833

Norris St 77833
Northview Circle Dr 77833
Nostalgia Ct 77833
O Malley Rd 77833
Oak Dr & St 77833
Oak Bend Cir 77833
Oak Hill Dr 77833
Oakcreek Ln 77833
Oakridge St 77833
Oakwood Dr 77833
Oil Field Rd 77833
N Oilfield Rd 77833
Old Baylor College Rd 77833
Old Burton Rd 77833
Old Chappell Hill Rd 77833
Old Gay Hill Rd 77833
Old Independence Rd 77833
Old Masonic Rd 77833
Old Mill Creek Rd 77833
Old N Market St 77833
Old Navasota Rd 77833
Old Phillipsburg Rd 77833
Our Ln 77833
Pahl St 77833
Palestine Rd 77833
N & S Park St 77833
Parker Ct 77833
Parkisons Ln 77833
Parkview St 77833
Paterenn Rd 77833
Peabody St 77833
Peach Creek Ln 77833
Peachtree Dr 77833
Pebble Ln 77833
Pecan St 77833
Pecan Circle Dr 77833
Pecan Glen Rd 77833
Pecan Meadows Est 77833
Pecan Mill Ln 77833
Pelkemeyer Ln 77833
Perkins Ln 77833
Peters Ln 77833
Petty St 77833
Phillips Ln 77833
Phillipsburg Church Rd 77833
Phillipsburg Mhp 77833
Pieper Rd 77833
Pin Oak Dr 77833
Pine Dr 77833
Pitchers Ln 77833
Pleasant Hill School Rd 77833
Pleasantview Ave 77833
Pledger Rd 77833
Plum Ln 77833
Plymouth Ln 77833
Poor Boys Ln 77833
Possum Trot St 77833
Post Oak Dr & Ln 77833
Prairie Hill Rd 77833
Prairie Lea St 77833
Progress Dr 77833
Putting Green Cir 77833
Quail Run Rd 77833
Quarry Rd 77833
Quebe Rd 77833
Ralston Creek Ct 77833
Rancho De Pancho Ln 77833
Randermann Rd 77833
Randle Hill Rd 77833
Rau Rd 77833
Ray Ln 77833
Reagan Beth Ln 77833
Rebecca Cir 77833
Red Oak Cir 77833
Red Tip Ln 77833
Reese Lockett St 77833
Rehburg Rd 77833
Reimer St 77833
Rhames Ave 77833
Rhapsody Rd 77833
Riata Ln 77833
Richardson Ln 77833
Riggs St 77833
Rink St 77833
Rippetoe St 77833

Rivers St 77833
Roadrunner Ln 77833
Robert C Appel Dr 77833
Robinhood Rd 77833
Rock Pit Ln 77833
S Rocky Rd 77833
Rocky Hill School Rd 77833
Rodney St 77833
Roger Rd 77833
Rolling Hills Ln 77833
Rolling Oaks Ln 77833
Rolling Ridge Ln 77833
Rolling Valley Ln 77833
E & S Rosedale Dr 77833
Rosenbaum Dr 77833
S Ross St 77833
Roxie Ln 77833
Royce Rd 77833
Rucker St 77833
Rudy Cir 77833
Ruth Cir 77833
Ryan Rd & St 77833
Sabine St 77833
N & S Saeger St 77833
Saint Peters School Rd 77833
Salem Rd 77833
Salem Cemetery Ln 77833
Sam Houston Rd 77833
Sander Rd 77833
Sandra Dr 77833
Sandy Creek Est & Ln 77833
Sandy Hill Rd 77833
Sawmill Rd 77833
E Sayles St 77833
Scattered Oaks Cir 77833
Scenic Dr 77833
Scenic Brook St 77833
Schlottman Rd 77833
Schoenau Rd 77833
Schomburg St 77833
Schroeder Rd 77833
Schroeder Mhp 77833
Schuerenberg St 77833
Schulte Blvd 77833
Schultz Rd N 77833
Schumacher St 77833
Schwartz Rd 77833
Scott Ct, Dr & Rd 77833
E & W Second St 77833
Seeker Rd 77833
Seelhorst St 77833
Selma Ln 77833
Seven Oaks Mhp 77833
Seven Vee Ln 77833
Seward Plantation Rd 77833
Shadow Lawn St 77833
Shadow Oak Cir 77833
Shady Ln 77833
Shady Acres Ln 77833
Shea St 77833
Shed Johnson Ln 77833
Sheely St 77833
Shelby Rd 77833
Shepard Ln & St 77833
Sherwood Rd 77833
Shirttail Rd 77833
Shoenau Rd 77833
Sierra Rd 77833
Simon Ave 77833
Sioux Cir 77833
E & W Sixth St 77833
Smoky Rd 77833
Spanish Oaks Dr 77833
Spencer St 77833
Spinn St 77833
Sportsman Cir 77833
Spreen Rd 77833
Spring Creek Rd 77833
Springfield Ln 77833
Springwood Dr 77833
N & S St Charles 77833
Steinfeld Ln 77833
Stephanie St 77833
Sternberg Ln 77833
E & W Stone St 77833

Stone Hill Dr 77833
Stone Hollow Dr 77833
Strangmeier Rd 77833
Stringer St 77833
Stuart Rd 77833
Success Ct 77833
Summer Ct 77833
Summit Rd 77833
Sun Oil Rd 77833
Sunset Rd 77833
Swain St 77833
Sweed St 77833
Sycamore St 77833
Sycamore Hill Ln 77833
T S Saul Rd 77833
Taft St 77833
Tamy Ln 77833
Tanglewood Dr 77833
Tappe Rd 77833
Tarver St 77833
Tass Ln 77833
Tegeler Rd 77833
Tequila Ln 77833
Terrier Hill Ln 77833
Texas St 77833
Thiel St 77833
Thielemann Ln 77833
W Third St 77833
Three Oaks Ln 77833
Tiaden Ln 77833
Tielke Ln 77833
Tigerpoint Rd 77833
Timberline Ct 77833
Tina Ln 77833
Tison St 77833
Toliver Rd 77833
Tom Dee St 77833
E & W Tom Green St 77833
Tom Willie Rd 77833
Tommelson Creek Rd 77833
Tommy Ln 77833
Tonckawa Hills Ln 77833
Top Hill Dr 77833
Tracye Lee Dr 77833
Trails End Ln 77833
Travis St 77833
Trey Ln 77833
Triangle Z Ln 77833
Tricia Ln 77833
Trinity St 77833
Turkey Creek Ln 77833
Turnbow Rd 77833
Twisted Oak Dr 77833
W Uekert Rd 77833
Union Ln 77833
N Valley Dr & St 77833
Valley Forge Ln 77833
Valley View Ln 77833
Valmont Dr 77833
E & W Valverde St 77833
Victoria St 77833
Victory Ln 77833
Vogler Ln 77833
E & W Vulcan St 77833
Wagon Yard Mhp 77833
Walker League Ln 77833
Walnut Bnd & St 77833
Walnut Hill Dr 77833
Walsch Ln 77833
Washington St 77833
Waters Rd 77833
Watts Rd 77833
Wauls Legion Rd 77833
Wayside Dr 77833
Weaver St 77833
Weeping Willow Cir 77833
Wehmeyers Mhp 77833
Weiss Ln 77833
Weldon Trace St 77833
Wellmanns Mhp 77833
Wernecke Ln 77833
Wesley Church Ln 77833
West Cir 77833
Westbrooke Cv 77833
Westerfeld Rd 77833
Westridge Rd & St 77833
Westwind Dr 77833
Westwood Ln 77833
Whisper Ln 77833
Whispering Oak Cir 77833
White Ct 77833
Whitfield St 77833
Whitley Ranch Ln 77833
Whitman Rd 77833
Wiedeville Church Rd 77833
Wieghat Ln 77833
Wiesepape Rd 77833
Wilder Rd 77833
Wilder Crest Ln 77833
Wildflower Rd 77833
W Wilkins St 77833
Will St 77833
Williams St 77833
Williams Creek Rd 77833
Willow Cir 77833
Windchime Ln 77833
Windswept Dr 77833
Windy Dr 77833
Windy Acres Rd 77833
Wintersong Dr 77833
Wm B Travis Ln 77833
Wolf Creek Rd 77833
Wonder Hill Rd 77833
Wood Creek Est & Rd 77833
Wood Glen Mdws 77833
Wood Ridge Blvd 77833
Woodlands Rd 77833
Woodside Dr 77833
Woodson Ln 77833
Woodward Springs Rd 77833
Wyandotte Ln 77833
Yager Dr 77833
Yegua Ln 77833
Yellow Rose Rd 77833
Zetter Rd 77833
Zibilski Rd 77833
Zientek Ln 77833
Zoo Ln 77833

NUMBERED STREETS

All Street Addresses 77833

BROWNSVILLE TX

General Delivery 78520

POST OFFICE BOXES MAIN OFFICE STATIONS AND BRANCHES

Box No.s
1 - 2324 78522
3001 - 6416 78523
8001 - 9138 78526
9000 - 9006 78520
9000 - 9006 78523

RURAL ROUTES

02, 08, 10, 15, 27, 28, 31, 37 78520
01, 06, 09, 11, 12, 14, 19, 21, 23, 24, 30 78521

HIGHWAY CONTRACTS

70 78521

NAMED STREETS

A Longoria 78520
Abbey 78526
Aberdeen Dr 78526
Abrahamson Dr 78526
Acacia Dr 78520
Acacia Lake Dr 78521
Acapulco Ave 78521
Achievement 78526
E & W Adams St 78520
Agave Ave 78526
Agua Bravo Dr 78526
Agua Clara Ct 78521
Agua Dulce Dr 78521
Agua Viva Ln 78521
Aguila Dr 78521
Ala Blanca 78521
Alabama Ave 78521
Alabama Pine St 78526
Alameda Dr 78521
Alamo Ave 78521
Alamo St 78520
Alamo Trl 78520
Alamosa Dr 78520
Alan A Dale St 78521
Alaska Rd 78521
Albans Dr 78526
Alberta Dr 78526
Aldridge Dr 78520
E & W Aldrin Ct 78521
Alex Ln 78520
Alexandra Ct 78521
Alice Cir 78520
Alicia 78526
Allende St
1-99 78520
200-298 78521
Alta Mesa Blvd 78526
Altamira 78520
Altas Palmas 78521
E Alton Gloor Blvd 78526
W Alton Gloor Blvd 78520
Amatista Dr 78521
Amelia Earhart Dr 78521
America Dr 78526
Amira Dr 78521
Ana Laura Ct 78521
W Anchor Dr & Rd 78521
Ancira Dr 78521
Andorra St 78520
Andrea Ct 78521
Anei Cir 78521
Angel Dr 78521
Angelas Ct 78526
Anglers Place Rd 78521
Anita Ct 78521
Anna 78526
Anthony Ct 78521
Antigua Ln 78520
Apollo Ave & Cir 78521
Applewind Way 78526
Applewood St 78520
Arboleda 78521
Arbor Park 78526
Arien Ct 78521
Arkansas Ave 78521
Arkansas River Dr 78520
Armadillo Cir 78526
E & W Armstrong Ct 78521
Arroyo Blvd 78520
Artemisa Ave 78526
Arthur St 78521
Aruba 78520
Ascension Dr 78526
Ash St 78521
Atascosa Dr 78526
Athens St 78520
Atlantic Ave 78521
Aubuck Pl 78521
Audrey 78526
Augusta Rd 78521
Aurora St 78526
Austin Rd 78521
Austrian Pne 78526
Autumn Mist 78526
Autumn Sage Dr 78526
Avalon Dr 78520
Avenida De La Plata 78521
Avenida Del Oro 78521
Avenida Del Palacio 78520
Avenida Del Sol 78526
Avenida Estrella 78526
Avenue A 78520
Avenue B 78520
Avila St 78520
Avy 78520
Azalea Trl 78520
Azteca Cir & Dr 78521
Azucena Ave 78521
Bahamas 78520
Bahia Cir 78521
Banburg Dr 78526
Bandon Ct 78526
Barbwire Ln 78526
Barcelona Ave & Dr 78526
Barnard Rd 78520
Barness St 78521
Barton Ln 78521
Basque Dr 78520
Bates Cir & St 78520
Bayou Ct 78521
Beachway Ave 78521
Beatric Isabel 78520
Beaudry Ct 78526
Beaver Lk 78520
Beaver Pond Dr 78520
Becky Cir 78521
Belinda Cir 78521
Belthair St 78520
Belvedere Dr 78520
Benden Cir 78521
Bengal 78521
Bennett Dr 78521
Benson 78521
N & S Bernal Dr 78521
Bertha St 78521
Bess Ct 78521
Betty Ct 78521
Bilbao Ct 78526
Billings Rd 78521
Billy Mitchell Blvd 78521
Billys Ct 78526
Birders Cv 78526
Bismark Blvd 78521
Bismark Ct 78526
Blanca Aurora 78520
Blanche St 78521
Blanco River St 78526
Blue Sage 78520
Blue Sky Dr 78520
Blue Spruce St 78526
Bluebonnet Dr 78521
Bluewing Cir 78520
Boardwalk 78526
Boca Chica Blvd
1-1799 78520
1801-1899 78520
2000-9799 78521
W Boca Chica Blvd 78520
Bogota 78526
Boise Ct 78526
Bon Aire Ln 78521
Bonham Rd 78521
Bonita Dr 78526
Bordeaux 78526
Border St 78520
Bouganvillia Dr 78520
Boulevard Of Champions 78520
Bowie Dr & Rd 78521
Box Car Rd 78521
Boxwood Ct 78521
Brasilia 78526
Bravo St
1-99 78520
101-199 78521
Brazos St 78521
Brazos River Cir 78520
Briar Ct 78521
Briarwyck Dr 78520
Broadmoor Rd 78521
E & W Broadway St 78520
Broken Spoke 78526
Brookshire Dr 78521
N Browne Ave 78521
S Browne Ave 78521
S Browne Rd 78521
Browne St 78520
Brownfield Rd 78520
Bryan Ct 78521
Buckeye Ct 78526
N & S Buckingham Ct 78526
Buena Vis 78520
Bueno Dr 78520
Burgos Ct 78526
Burgundy Dr 78526
Burnett Rd 78521
Burton Dr 78521
Business Dr 78521
Butler Rd 78520
C St 78520
Cablas Cir 78526
Caddell Rd 78526
Cadereyta St 78521
Cadiz Ct 78526
Cairo 78520
Cajun Ct 78521
Calder Ln 78520
Calgary Ct 78526
California Rd 78521
Calle Amistosa 78520
Calle Anacua 78520
Calle Argentina 78526
Calle Bolivia 78526
Calle Buenos Aires 78526
Calle Calmada 78526
Calle Cenizo 78520
Calle Chachalaca 78520
Calle Chiquita 78521
Calle Cielo 78520
Calle Columbia 78526
Calle Concordia 78526
Calle Condesa 78520
Calle Costa Rica 78526
Calle Deliciosa 78526
Calle Duquesa 78520
Calle Escondida 78526
Calle Espacio 78520
Calle Esplendida 78521
Calle Fresnal 78521
Calle Galaxia 78520
Calle Jacaranda 78520
Calle La Mansion 78521
Calle Maravillosa 78526
Calle Milagros 78526
Calle Monarca 78520
Calle Nortenia 78526
Calle Planeta 78520
Calle Pluton 78520
Calle Princesa 78520
Calle Real 78520
Calle Retama 78520
Calle Reyna 78520
Calle Roble 78521
Calle Sevillanas 78526
Calle Terrestre 78520
Calle Uruguay 78526
Calle Venezuela 78526
Calvin St 78521
Camaguey Ave 78526
Camargo St 78526
Camellia Dr 78521
Cameron Ave 78526
Camino Bronce 78521
Camino Cobre 78521
Camino De La Tierra 78526
N & S Camino Del Rey 78520
Camino Del Sol 78526
Camino Nikel 78521
Camino Verde Dr 78526
Campeche Ct 78526
Camper Dr 78521
Campo Real Cir 78520
Camwood Pl 78520
Cancun 78526
Candlewick Ct 78521
Canterbury Ct 78526
Cantu Rd 78521
Canyon Cir 78521
Canyon Lake Ct 78520
Capistrano Dr 78526
E Caplanto St 78520
Capri St 78520
Captain Basler Ave 78520
Caramia Ln 78520
Cardinal Ln 78521
Caribbean Dr 78520
Caribia Cir 78520
Carlis Run 78526
Carlos Ave 78526
Carlton Dr 78521
Carmen Blvd 78520
Carnation Dr 78526
Carnesi Dr 78521
Carolina Pne 78526
Carolina St 78521
Carranza St 78526
Carrizo Ln 78520
Carter Ct 78526
Carthage Ct 78520
Casa Blanca Dr 78521
Casa De Amigos 78521
Casa De Oro 78521
Casa De Palmas 78521
Casa Grande 78521
Casa Linda 78521
Cascabel Ct 78526
Castellano Cir 78526
E & W Catherine Cir & Ln 78520
Cattadori Ct 78521
Cavazos Rd 78526
Cayman 78520
Cedar Ave 78526
Cedar St 78521
Cedar Elm Xing 78520
Cedar Ridge Dr 78520
Cedar Trail Dr 78526
Ceiba Cir 78521
Cela Ave 78520
Cemetary Dr 78520
Center Dr 78520
Centerline Dr 78526
N Central Ave
1-2299 78521
2301-2399 78521
2801-3097 78526
3099-4700 78526
4702-4798 78526
S Central Ave 78521
Central Blvd 78520
Central Cir 78521
Central Park Dr 78520
Ceresa 78521
E & W Cernan Ct 78521
Cerro De Oro Dr 78526
Cesar 78526
Chablis Dr 78526
Chadwick Pl 78520
Champagne 78526
Champions Dr 78520
Champlain Dr 78526
Chapala Ct 78526
Chaparral St 78521
Chardonay Dr 78526
Charing Cross Cir 78521
Charmaine Ln 78526
Cheers St 78521
Chemical Rd 78521
Cheryl Ln 78521
Chestnut Oak Ln 78526
Chet Ave 78526
Chetumal Ct 78526
Cheyenne Ct 78526
Chiapas Ct 78526
Chicago Ave 78521
Chihuahua Ct 78526
Chilton St 78521
China St 78521
Chipinque St 78526
Choza Dr 78521
Christian 78521
Cibolo St 78521
Cielo Grande Dr 78526
Cienfuegos St 78526
Cifuentes St 78526
Cimarron St 78520
Cindy Nerea Ct 78526
Cirrus Dr 78526
Ciruela Ln 78521
Clarissa Dr 78521
Clavel St 78521
Clearview Dr 78526
Cleveland St 78521
Cliff Rose Cir 78521
Clover Dr 78521
N & S Clubhouse Rd 78521
Coach Cir 78521
Coahuila Ct 78526
Cobblestone Cir 78521
Coca Beach Ct 78526
Coconut Grv 78521
Codorniz Dr 78526
Coffee Port Rd 78521
Colibri Cir 78521
Colonial Dr 78520
Colony Trl 78526
Colorado North St 78520
Colorado River Dr 78520
Columbus Dr 78521
Coma St 78521
Commerce Dr 78521
Commercial Dr 78521
Concord Pl 78520
Conquistador St 78520
Continental Dr 78520
Coolidge St 78521
Coral Ct 78520
Cordoba Dr 78521
N & S Coria St 78520
Corine Cir 78521
Coronado 78521
Correa Rd 78520
Corto St 78520
Costa Brava 78520
Costa Del Sol 78520
Cottage Dr 78521
Cottontail St 78526
Cottonwood Dr 78520
Country Club Cir & Rd 78520
Courage Blvd 78521
Court St 78521
Cove Cir 78521
Coveway St 78521
E & W Cowan Ter 78521
Cowboy Rose Ln 78520
Cream Rose Ct 78520
Creek Ct 78520
Creek Wood 78526
Creekbend Dr 78521
Crepe Myrtle 78520
Crestview Dr 78520
Crestwood Dr 78526
Crockett Ave 78521
Cross St 78520
Cross Vine Dr 78526
Crosswind Way 78526
Crownridge Dr 78521
Cuba St 78526
Cummings Pl 78520
Cumulus Dr 78526
Cute Rose Ct 78520
Cynthia St 78521
Cypress Dr 78521
D St 78520
Daffodil Dr 78526
Dahlia Cir 78520
Daisy Dr 78521
N & S Dakota Ave 78521
Dale Ct 78520
Daleiden Dr 78526
Dalita Ct 78521
Dan St 78521
Dana Ave 78526
Dana St 78521
Danubio 78526
Darla Rd 78520
Date 78521
Date Palm St 78521
David Shor Rd 78521
Dawley St 78520
De Soto St 78521
Dean Porter Dr 78520
Dee Ann Ct 78521
Deep Spring St 78520
Deer Trl 78521

Deer Field Blvd 78521
Deer Haven Ct 78520
Deer Run Cir 78521
Dei Gratia Dr 78521
Del Mar Ct 78520
Del Prado Dr 78521
Del Rio Rd 78521
Del Sol St 78520
Del Valle Blvd 78520
Delia Ave 78526
Delia Ln 78520
Dellwood Dr 78526
Delpha Ln 78521
Delta Ct & Dr 78521
Dennet Rd 78526
Dennett Rd 78526
Dennis Ave 78526
Denver Ave 78526
Deo Juvante Dr 78521
Deo Volente Dr 78521
Devon Blvd 78526
Dew St 78520
Diamante Dr 78521
Diamondback 78526
Diego Ln 78521
Divina Dr 78526
Divisadero Rd 78520
Dix Dr 78520
Dockberry Cir & Rd 78521
Dolores Ave 78521
Dominica 78520
Don Quixote St 78521
Donna Dr 78526
Donnie Dr 78521
Dorris Rd 78526
Downs Dr 78521
Dragonwick 78526
Draper Dr 78521
Dreamway 78526
Druscilla Cir 78521
Dry Dock Ct 78521
Duck Pond Dr 78526
Dukie Dr 78521
Dulce 78520
Dulcinea St 78521
Duluth Rd 78520
Duncan Rd 78526
Dunlap St 78521
Durango Ct 78526
Duranta Ln 78520
Durazno St 78521
Dusk Dr 78520
Duval St 78526
E St 78520
Ea Cir 78521
W Eagle Dr 78521
East Ave 78521
East Dr 78520
Eastern Blvd 78521
Eastwood Dr 78521
Ebony Ave
1-299 78520
301-399 78520
8201-8299 78526
W Ebony Ave 78520
Ebony St 78520
Eddie Ct 78520
Edgewater Pl 78521
Edmonton Ct 78526
Eduardo Ave 78526
Egido St 78521
El Agua 78520
El Aire St 78520
El Arbol 78521
El Arca Dr 78520
El Arco St 78520
El Arroyo St 78520
El Astro 78521
El Brillo St 78520
El Camino St 78520
El Campo Dr 78521
El Cauce St 78520
El Cielo 78520
El Cruse 78520
El Dorado St 78520
El Encanto St 78520
El Fruto 78520
El Granero St 78520
El Gusto St 78520
El Jardin Heights Rd 78526
El Lago Dr 78526
El Litro 78520
El Mar St 78520
El Matador Dr 78521
El Metro 78520
El Paraiso 78520
El Parque St 78520
El Paso Rd 78520
El Pinal St 78520
El Portal St 78520
El Puente St 78520
El Retiro Cir 78520
El Rio St 78520
El Sol St 78520
El Valle Dr 78521
El Verde Ln 78520
Elca Ln 78521
Elda Ct & Dr 78521
Eleanor Ct 78521
Elena St 78521
Elizabeth St 78522
E Elizabeth St 78520
W Elizabeth St 78520
Elliott Cir 78521
Elm St 78521
Elm Ridge Ln 78520
Elma St 78521
Eloy St 78521
Elsa Ave 78521
Elston Ln 78520
Elyt Dr 78521
Emerald Ln 78520
Emerald Valley Blvd 78526
Emery Watts St 78521
Emilia Ln 78526
Ems Ln 78521
Enchanted Path 78526
Encino St 78520
English St 78521
Epi St 78521
Ericka Cir 78521
Escobedo St 78521
Espada Grande Ave 78526
Esperanza Ln 78520
Esperanza Rd 78521
Esperson St 78521
Espinosa 78526
Estero Dr 78521
Event Ctr 78526
Everglades Rd 78521
Evergreen Dr 78520
Evie Ave 78526
N Expressway
1-99 78526
N Expressway
100-2398 78521
101-3799 78520
2500-3798 78526
3800-3900 78526
3901-6799 78520
3902-7098 78526
S Expressway 78520
S Expressway 83
2-98 78520
100-200 78520
202-898 78520
3300-3399 78521
F St 78520
Fairfax St 78520
Fairfield Dr 78526
Fairway Dr 78520
Fairwind Dr 78521
Falcon Dr 78526
Fannin Ave 78521
Fargo Ave 78521
Farwest Trl 78526
Fay St 78520
Fern Dr 78521
Fiesta Dr 78521
Figueroa Ct 78521
E Filmore St 78520
Firefly Pl 78526
Firenze St 78520
Fireside Dr 78521
Firewheel Ln 78520
Fish Hatchery Rd 78520
Fishermans Place Rd 78521
Fjrm Ave 78520
Flamingo Dr 78520
Fleet St 78521
Flor De Mayo 78520
Flor De Valle Dr 78520
Florence Ln 78520
Florencia Ave 78526
Florida Rd 78521
Florida Pine St 78526
Fm 1421 78520
Fm 1732 78520
Fm 511 78526
Fm 802
101-1073 78520
1000-1072 78521
1074-1699 78521
1701-1899 78521
2000-2698 78526
2700-9099 78526
9101-9899 78526
E Fm 802 78521
Fonsi Dr 78521
Forest Blvd 78526
Fort Brown St 78520
Foust Rd 78521
Fox Run 78520
Frambuesa 78521
Franke Ave 78521
Frankfurt St 78520
Franklin Dr 78520
French Riv 78520
French St 78521
Fresa 78521
Fresnillo Dr 78526
Fresno St 78521
Frio River St 78526
N Frontage Rd 78521
S Frontage Rd
1000-1798 78520
1001-1799 78521
Frontera St 78521
Frontier Trl 78526
E & W Fronton St 78520
Fruitdale Dr & Ter 78521
Gabriel 78526
Galonsky St 78521
Galveston Rd 78521
Garcia Ln 78521
Garden St 78520
Garden Breeze 78526
Garden Grove Rd 78520
Garden View Ct 78526
Garden Woods Ave 78526
Gardenia St 78521
Garfield St 78521
Gastin Dr 78520
Gator Ct 78521
Gazelle St 78521
George Saenz Ln 78521
George Wilson St 78520
Georgia Pne 78526
Geraldine Ln 78526
German St 78521
Gibralter St 78520
Gila River Cir 78520
Gilson Rd 78520
Glenbrook Dr 78521
Glenn Ct 78521
Glerless Dr 78521
Gloria St 78521
Glynwood Dr 78526
Golfo Cir 78521
Goodwin Ct 78521
Gorgas Dr 78520
Grace Ave 78526
Granada Dr 78521
Grand Rpds 78520
Grande Blvd 78521
Granjeno Ave 78520
Grant St 78521
Grapefruit St 78521
Green Ct 78520
Greenbriar Ave 78520
Greenfield Dr 78521
Greenhaven 78521
Greenway Dr 78520
Greenwood Dr 78526
Gregory Ave 78526
Grey Fox Cir 78520
Greystone Dr 78521
Grotto Dr 78526
Gruta St 78521
Guadalajara Ave 78526
Guadalupe Cir 78526
Guadalupe River St 78526
Guanajay Ct 78526
Guayava Ln 78521
Guaymas St 78521
Guerrero St 78520
Guillien St 78521
Gulfwind Way 78526
Gutierrez Rd 78520
Habana St 78526
Hacienda Ln 78520
Hackberry Ct 78520
Hackberry Ln 78521
Haggar Dr 78521
Halo Dr 78520
Hamburg St 78520
Hamilton Ct 78526
Hannah Dr 78520
Harding St 78521
E Harrison St 78520
Harvard Ave 78520
Harvey Ave 78526
Harwell Dr 78521
Hauff Ln 78521
Haven Way 78521
Hawser Bend Rd 78521
E & W Hawthorne St 78520
Hayes St 78521
Haynes Ln 78521
Heart Dr 78520
Heather Ln 78521
Heavenly Gate 78520
Helen Ln 78520
Henrietta Ln 78521
Heritage Cir 78520
Heritage Trl 78526
Herlinda St 78520
Hermosa Ave 78526
Hermosillo Ct 78526
Heron Cv 78526
Hibiscus Ct 78520
Hidden Acres 78526
Hidden Hideaway 78526
Hidden Meadows Blvd 78520
Hidden Oaks 78526
Hidden Valley Dr 78521
Higgins Dr 78521
Highland Dr 78520
Highland Ter 78521
Highland Pine St 78526
Hill St 78521
Hillcrest Dr 78521
Hipp Ave 78521
Hitching Post 78526
Hockaday St 78521
Holly Ln 78521
Honey Dr 78520
Honey Bee Ln 78520
Honeydale Rd 78520
Hope Riv 78520
Hope King Cir & St 78521
Horizon Ln 78520
Horseshoe Lake Ct 78520
Hortencia Blvd 78521
Houston Rd 78521
Hubert Dr 78526
Hudson Blvd 78526
Hugo Dr 78521
Huisache St 78520
Hunters Break Dr 78526
Hunters Quest Cir 78520
Huntington Ct 78526
Ibc Cir 78526
S Illinois Ave & Rd N 78521
Impala Ct & Dr 78521
Imperial Ave 78520
Indian Shr 78526
N Indiana Ave
101-197 78521
199-1899 78521
1901-1999 78521
2000-2298 78526
2300-3199 78526
S Indiana Ave 78521
Industrial Dr 78521
Inspiration Pt 78526
International Blvd
600-1799 78520
1801-1997 78521
1999-3899 78521
N & S Iowa Ave 78521
Irapuato Ct 78526
Iris Dr 78526
Ironwood Ave 78526
Isabella Ct 78526
Isbell Dr 78521
S Isla De Palmas 78521
Iturbide St
1-99 78520
100-198 78521
Ivy Ln 78521
J C S Industrial Dr 78526
E & W Jackson St 78520
Jade Dr 78520
Jaguar St 78521
Jaime Cir 78521
Jaime J Zapata Ave 78521
Jalapa Ct 78526
Jalisco Ct 78526
Jane Ave 78521
Janet Ln 78526
Jaqou Rd 78521
Jasmine St 78521
Jason 78521
E & W Jefferson St 78520
Jeffery Ave 78521
Jenika Ave & Cir 78521
Jenkins Ave 78520
Jennifer Ave 78521
Jenny Cir 78521
Jessica St 78521
Jimenez St 78521
Jo Ann Ln 78520
Joanna St 78521
Joey Ct 78521
John Ave 78521
John Gibson Rd 78521
Johns Ave 78521
Johnson St 78521
Jonathan Ct 78526
Jose Colunga Jr St 78521
Jose Garza Rd 78521
Jose Marti Blvd 78526
Joseph 78526
Jovan Cir 78521
Juan Diego St 78526
Juarez St 78521
Juniper St 78526
Kana Dr 78526
Kansas Rd 78521
Kansas River Dr 78520
Katarina Ave 78526
Katy Ln 78526
Kee St 78521
Keith Ln 78521
Kelsey Dr 78521
Kennedy Ave 78520
Kensington Ln 78526
Kevin 78521
Key West Ct 78526
Killian Ave 78526
King Dr & St 78520
Kings Hwy 78521
Kingsway Dr 78526
Kiwi 78521
Kleberg Ave 78526
Knobhill Dr 78520
Kumquat St 78520
La Cantera Rd 78520
La Carreta Trl 78526
La Entrada Dr 78526
La Feria Rd 78520
La Granja Dr 78521
La Mancha St 78521
La Paz Ct 78526
La Pesca St 78520
La Plaza Dr 78521
La Posada Cir & Dr 78521
La Quinta Dr 78521
La Salida Dr 78520
La Silla Dr 78520
La Villita St 78521
Lago Rd 78520
Lago Escondido 78520
Lago Viejo 78520
Lago Vista Blvd 78520
Laguna Dr 78521
Laguna Azuel Dr 78520
Laguna Azul Dr 78526
Laguna De Palmas Dr 78526
Laguna Del Rey Dr 78526
Laguna Escondida 78520
Laguna Madre Dr 78526
Laguna Seca 78520
Laguna Verde Dr 78526
W Lake Ave 78520
Lake View Dr 78520
Lakeshore Dr 78521
Lakeside Blvd 78520
Lakeview Ln 78521
Lakeway Dr 78520
Lampasas St 78521
Lamplight 78526
Lance Ln 78520
Lancer Lake Dr 78521
Land O Lakes Dr 78521
Langan St 78521
Lantana Ln 78520
Laredo Rd 78520
Larkspur Dr 78526
Las Brisas Blvd 78520
Las Canas Cir 78526
Las Casas St
1800-1898 78520
2101-2197 78521
2199-2499 78521
Las Cruces Ct 78526
Las Lomas 78526
Las Mananitas 78520
Las Mitras Ln 78521
Las Nubes 78520
Las Palmas Cir 78521
Las Palomas St 78526
Las Villas Ave 78526
Laura Ln 78521
Laurel Ave & Ln 78526
Lawndale Ln 78521
Lazy Acres 78521
Lazy Creek Ln 78520
Lbj Blvd 78521
Lee Dr 78521
Lee Roy Cir 78521
Leece Dr 78521
Lemon St 78521
Leopard St 78521
Les Mauldin Rd 78521
Lester Dr 78521
E & W Levee St 78520
Lewis St 78520
Lexington Pl 78520
Lilac Ct 78520
Lily Ln 78520
Lima St 78521
Limon Ln 78521
Linares St 78521
Lincoln St 78521
Linda Ln 78521
Lindale Ct & Dr 78521
Lindsey Ln 78520
Lisa Ave 78526
Lisbon 78520
Lissa Dr 78521
Little Grove St 78521
Live Oak Cir 78520
Liveoak Rd 78521
Llama St 78521
Logo Vista Blvd 78520
Lohr St 78521
Lois Ln 78520
Loma Alta St 78520
Loma Linda Ave 78520
Loma Verde Dr 78526
London Ct 78526
E Loop 78520
Lorenaly Dr 78526
Los Altos St 78520
Los Angeles Ct 78521
Los Arboles 78521
Los Arboles Ave 78520
E Los Ebanos Blvd
200-1600 78520
1535-1535 78523
1601-1699 78520
1602-1698 78520
1901-2097 78521
2099-2599 78521
W Los Ebanos Blvd 78520
Los Lobos 78521
Los Mesquite Ln 78520
Los Portales 78526
Los Sabales Dr 78520
Los Tres Amigos Cir 78521
Louis Ave 78526
Lourdes Blvd 78521
Love Rose St 78520
E & W Lovell Ct 78521
Lovers Ln 78526
Lucy Cir 78521
Lucylle Ln 78520
Luz Ave 78520
Lynn Dr 78521
Lynx 78521
Mackintosh Dr 78521
Madeire Beach Ln 78526
Madero Dr 78526
E & W Madison St 78520
Madrid Ave 78520
Magali Cir 78521
Magdalena Ave 78526
Magnetek Dr 78521
Magnolia Ct 78520
Maguey 78521
Main St 78526
Maine Ave 78521
Malaga Ct 78526
Malta St 78520
Mamie Dr 78521
Mandarine Ln 78521
Mango Ln 78521
Mangrove Cir 78521
Mano Dr 78520
Mante Ct 78526
Mantua St 78526
Manzano St 78521
E & W Maple Cir 78521
Mar St 78521
Maravillas River St 78526
Marbella St 78520
Marfil Dr 78521
Margaret Ct 78521
Margarita St 78521
Maria Elena St 78521
Marian Pl 78520
Marina Ct 78521
Marine Dr 78520
Marine Way Dr 78521
Mariposa Cir 78521
Market Square St 78520
Marquette Ave 78520
Marrs Ave 78521
Marsella Blvd 78521
Martinal Rd 78526
Martinez Cir 78521
Marvis Dr 78521
Mary Lee Ct 78520
Maryland Ave 78521
Mason Ave 78520
Massey Way 78521
Matamoros 78521
Matanzas Ct 78526
Matehuala Ct 78526
Maverick Rd 78521

May St 78520
May Field St 78521
Mayorca Ave 78526
Mayorca St 78520
Mcallen Rd 78520
Mcdavitt Blvd 78521
Mcfadden Hut Dr 78520
Mckenzie Rd 78521
Mckinley St 78521
Mclelland Blvd 78520
Mead Lake Ct 78520
Meadow Brk 78526
Meadow Crk 78526
Meadow Ln 78521
Meadow Rdg 78526
Meadow Vw 78526
Meadow Glen Dr 78521
Mebec Ct 78521
N Medford Ave & Rd 78521
Media Luna Rd 78521
Media Luna St 78520
Medical Dr 78520
Medina St 78521
Megan St 78520
Melissa Dr 78521
Melva Ct 78520
Memorial Trl 78520
Mercedes Rd 78520
Merida Cir 78521
Merida Ct 78526
Merryman Rd 78520
Mesa Ave 78526
Mesquital Ave 78521
Mesquite Br 78520
Mesquite Grv 78520
Mesquite St 78520
Mesquite Trl 78526
Mesquite Wood Ct 78526
Mexico Blvd 78520
Michael Cir 78521
Michaelwood Dr 78526
Michelle Dr 78526
Michoacan Ct 78526
Midway Dr 78520
Milam Ave & Rd 78521
Mildred St 78521
Military Hwy & Rd 78520
Milo Rd 78521
Milpa Verde 78521
Mineral Loop 78521
N Minnesota Ave
100-798 78521
800-2299 78521
2301-2399 78521
2401-2599 78526
S Minnesota Ave 78521
Minot Ave 78521
Miraflores St 78520
Miramar 78520
Miramar Dr 78521
Mirandy Cir 78520
Mirasol St 78520
Mission Bend Dr 78526
Mississippi River Blvd 78520
Missouri River Dr 78520
Mitchell Ave 78521
Mobile Home Blvd 78521
Mockingbird Ln 78521
Molino De Viento 78521
Mona Dr 78526
Monaco Dr 78521
Monclova Dr 78521
Monica Dr & St 78521
E & W Monroe St 78520
Monsees Rd 78521
Montana Ave 78526
Monte Bello 78521
Monte Bonito 78521
Monte Cristo 78526
Monterrey Dr 78521
Montevideo 78526
Montreal Ct 78526
Montrose Cir 78526
Mora Rd 78521
Morelia Cir 78526
Morelos St
1-99 78520
100-199 78521
Morning Dr 78520
Morningside Rd 78521
Morrison Rd 78526
E Morrison Rd 78526
W Morrison Rd 78520
Morton St 78521
Mulberry Ln 78520
Mulberry St 78526
Munich St 78520
Mystic Bnd 78526
Nafta Pkwy 78526
Nahessi 78521
Nannette Ave 78526
Nansa Dr 78526
Naples St 78520
Naranjal 78521
Naranjo St 78521
Nasa Dr 78521
Navarra St 78526
Navidad River St 78526
Nayarit Ct 78526
Neale Dr 78520
Nectarin 78521
Nell Palmer 78520
Nevada Ave 78526
New Mexico Way 78521
Newfield Ln 78526
Nicholas Ct 78521
Nicholstone St 78526
Niki Ln 78520
Nimbus Dr 78526
Nina Ave 78526
Nispero Ln 78521
Noble Dr & Pne 78526
Nogalitos St 78526
Nolana Dr 78526
Nopal St 78520
Norfolk 78526
Norma Ln 78521
Norma Pechero Ln 78526
Normandy St 78520
North Dr 78520
North St 78521
Northridge Dr 78526
Northwood Dr 78520
Nottingham Ct 78526
Nueces St 78526
Nuevo Amanecer 78520
Nuevo Leon Dr 78521
Oak St 78521
Oakland 78520
Oakland St 78521
Oasis Dr 78521
Oaxaca Ct 78526
Obsidian 78526
Oceano Cir 78521
Ofelia Ave 78526
Ofelia Cir 78521
Oil Dock Rd 78521
N & S Oklahoma Ave 78521
Old Alice Rd
1-597 78520
599-2199 78520
2600-3100 78521
3102-3898 78521
6000-6299 78526
S Old Alice Rd 78520
Old Creek Ct 78521
Old Ebony St 78520
Old Highway 48 78521
Old Highway 77 78520
Old Military Hwy & Rd 78520
Old Oak Trl 78520
Old Port Isabel Rd
1-297 78521
299-2399 78521
2400-2498 78526
2500-4799 78526
4801-4999 78526
Old Spanish Trl 78520
Oliva 78521
Olivia Ave 78526
Olivia Ln 78520
Olmito St 78521
Orange St 78521
Orangewood Dr 78521
Orchid Dr 78526
Orchid Path 78520
Oriente Dr 78526
Oriole Ln 78521
Oro Cir 78521
Oslo 78520
Otila Rd 78521
Ottawa Ct 78526
Oviedo 78520
Owens Rd 78521
Pablo Garcia Dr 78520
Pablo Kisel Blvd 78526
Padre Island Hwy 78521
Pagosa St 78520
Palacio Real Cir & Dr 78521
Palm Blvd 78520
Palm Hvn 78521
Palm Vlg 78520
Palm Grove Dr 78521
Palma Areca Dr 78521
Palma Blanca Dr 78521
Palma Caribe Dr 78521
Palma De Micharos 78521
Palma Tejana Dr 78521
Palmae 78521
Palmas Ln 78520
Palmas Verdes Ct 78521
Palmera Dr 78521
Palmetto Cir & Ct 78521
Palmira Ct 78526
Palmito Hill Rd 78521
Palo Alto Dr 78521
Palo Azul Dr 78526
Palo Blanco St 78521
Palo Grande Dr 78521
Palo Verde Dr 78521
Paloma Blanca Dr 78521
Palomar St 78520
Palomino Ct 78526
Pamplona Ct 78526
Pandana St 78520
Panther 78521
Papaya Cir 78521
Pardo Ln 78520
Paredes Ave 78521
Paredes Line Rd
2-98 78521
100-2199 78521
2401-3797 78526
3799-6799 78526
6801-7299 78526
Paris St 78520
E Park Dr 78520
N Park Dr 78520
W Park Dr 78520
N Park Plz 78521
Park St 78520
Parkland Dr 78521
Parkview Ln 78526
Parkwood Pl 78520
Parliament Ct 78521
Parral Ct & St 78520
Pasadero Dr 78526
Paseo Plz 78521
Paseo Del Rey Dr 78526
Paseo Del Sol Dr 78526
Paseo Reforma 78520
Paso Del Rio Dr 78526
N & S Paso Doble Cir 78526
Paso Fino Ln 78520
Paso Real Dr 78521
Patricia Sofia 78520
Peach Rose Ct 78520
Peacock 78526
Pearl Dr 78521
Pecan 78520
Pecan Ave 78526
Pecos Dr 78526
Pecos River St 78526
Pedernales Cir 78521
Pelon Rd 78520
Peninsula Ln 78521
Penjamo St 78521
Pepper Tree Cir 78520
Peppermill Run 78526
Pera Ave 78521
Persimmon Dr 78526
Pheasant St 78526
Picadilly Cir 78521
Picasso Ln 78520
Pierce St 78520
Pierre Ave 78521
Pinar Del Rio Ave 78526
Pine Ln 78521
Pine Creek Ave 78526
Pine Falls Dr 78526
Pine Hearst Dr 78521
Pine Lake Dr 78526
Pine More Dr 78526
Pinebluff 78526
Pinion Dr 78526
Pink Rose St 78520
Pino St 78521
Pino Azul 78526
Pino Blanco 78526
Pino Verde 78526
Pinto Ct 78526
Pita Ct 78526
Plantation St 78526
Platano 78521
Plaza Santa Rosa 78520
Poinciana Dr 78521
Poinsettia Pl 78520
Polk St 78521
Pomelos St 78526
Pompeii St 78520
Poplar Cv 78521
Poplar Dr 78520
Porter St 78520
Portofino Blvd 78526
Portway Dr & St 78521
Post Oak Cir 78526
Power Plant Dr 78520
E Price Rd 78521
S Price Rd 78521
W Price Rd 78520
Primrose Ln 78521
Princess Palm 78521
Pristine Ln 78520
Professional Dr 78520
Provincia 78526
Puebla Dr 78521
Pueblo Ct 78526
Puerta De Cielo 78520
Purdue St 78520
Quail Trl 78520
Quail Glenn Trl 78526
Quail Hollow Dr 78520
Quality Ln 78526
Queensway Dr 78526
Quemado De Guines
St 78526
Quest Rd 78526
Queta St 78521
Quintana Roo Ct 78526
Rabbit Run Dr 78526
Rachel Cir 78526
Rainbow Dr 78520
Raintree Path 78520
Ramada Dr 78521
Ramireno Ln 78520
Ramirez Ln 78521
Rancho Viejo Ave &
Blvd 78526
Randy Lee Rd 78526
Raquel Ct 78520
Raul Cavazos Rd 78520
Rawhide Dr 78526
Ray Ave 78521
Real 78521
Reba St 78521
Rebecca Ln 78520
Red Pine 78526
Red Bay Cir 78521
Red Bud Dr 78526
Red Cedar 78526
Red Fox St 78520
Red Rose St 78520
Redwood Dr 78521
Regal Rd 78521
Regency 78526
Rego Rd 78520
Reina Esther Dr 78521
Rene Rd 78521
Rentfro Blvd 78521
Res St 78526
Resaca Blvd 78520
Resaca Dr 78520
Resaca Ln 78521
Resaca Vlg
1601-1699 78521
1619-1619 78526
Resaca Point Rd 78526
Resaca Vista Dr 78526
Retama Dr 78521
Rey Carlos Dr 78521
Rey David Dr 78521
Rey Enrique Dr 78521
Rey Fausto Dr 78521
Rey Jaime St 78521
Rey Jorge St 78521
Rey Juan Carlos St 78521
Rey Salomon St 78521
Ricky Rd 78521
Ridge Trl 78520
Ridgeline Dr 78526
Ridgely Rd 78520
Ridgemott Ct 78521
Ridgewood St 78520
Rincon St 78521
E Ringgold Rd & St 78520
Rio Ct 78526
Rio Bravo Dr 78520
Rio De Janiero 78526
Rio Grande Ave 78520
Rio Grande Dr 78521
Rio Sena 78526
Rio Vista Ave 78520
Ripple Creek Cir 78521
Ripplewind Way 78526
Riverbend Dr 78520
Riverside Blvd 78520
Riverwind Way 78526
Riviera St 78520
Rl Ostos Rd 78521
Roberto Ave 78526
Robindale Rd
101-197 78521
199-1100 78521
1102-2398 78521
2701-3197 78526
3199-5499 78526
Robinhood St 78521
Robins Ln 78520
Rockwell Cir & Dr 78521
Rocky Cir 78526
Roosevelt St 78521
Rosalee Ave 78521
Rose Ct 78521
Rose Briar Ct 78521
Rosedal Dr 78521
Rosemond Ct 78520
Rosewood Cir 78526
Rosinante St 78521
Rosita St 78520
Roslyn Ct 78521
Royal Oak St 78520
Royal Palm 78521
W Ruben M Torres
Blvd 78520
Ruben Torres Blvd
1000-1098 78521
1100-1699 78521
1701-1999 78521
2101-2199 78526
E Ruben Torres Blvd
1301-1399 78521
3401-3599 78526
Ruby Cir 78521
Ruby Red Ln 78521
Ruidoso Dr 78521
Ruiz Rd & St 78521
Russell Dr 78520
Rustic Manor Dr 78526
Rusty Nail Dr 78526
Sabal Palm Rd 78521
Sabinas St 78521
Sabine River Dr 78520
Sable Palm Cir 78521
Sacramento River Dr 78520
Sage Valley Trl 78520
Sagua Ct 78526
Sagua La Grande Ave 78526
Sahara Dr 78521
Saint Andrews Ln 78520
E & W Saint Charles
St 78520
E & W Saint Francis
St 78520
Saint James Dr 78521
Saint John Dr 78521
Saint Joseph Dr 78520
Saint Louis St 78521
Saint Michael St 78526
Saint Thomas Dr 78521
Saldivar Rd 78521
Salida De Luna 78526
Salida Del Sol 78526
Salisbury Ct 78526
Sally Ln 78526
Saltillo Ct 78526
Salvatierra St 78526
Sam Perl Blvd 78520
San Antonio Rd 78521
San Augustin Dr 78521
San Bernardino 78520
San Bernardo St 78521
San Cristobal St 78521
San Diego Ave 78526
San Eugenio St 78521
San Felipe Dr 78520
San Francisco Dr 78526
San Gabriel River Dr 78520
San Jacinto Dr 78521
San Joaquin St 78521
San Jose Ln 78521
San Juan Dr 78526
San Lorenzo St 78521
San Luis Dr 78521
San Manuel Ln 78521
E, N, S & W San
Marcelo Blvd 78526
San Marcos Dr 78521
San Marino Dr 78526
San Martin Dr 78521
San Mateo Dr 78521
San Miguel Cir & Dr 78521
San Pablo Ln 78521
San Patricio Dr 78521
San Pedro Ln 78521
San Rafael St 78521
San Ysidro 78520
Sancho Panza St 78521
Sancti Spiritus St 78526
Sandia St 78521
Sandy Ln 78521
Sandy Hill Dr 78520
Santa Anita Dr 78521
Santa Clara St 78526
Santa Cruz St 78521
Santa Elena St 78521
Santa Fe Dr & St 78521
Santa Isabel St 78521
Santa Lucia Dr 78521
Santa Paula Dr 78521
Santa Rosa Dr 78521
Santander Dr 78520
Santiago 78526
Santiago Ln 78521
Saphire Ct 78521
Sarita Dr 78521
Sasha Cir 78521
Savannah Dr 78526
Sawmill Draw 78526
Schaefer Ln 78526
Scott St 78521
Security Dr 78521
Segovia St 78520
Seneca 78526
Sequoia Dr 78521
Serenity Cir 78520
Sevilla Dr 78521
Seville Blvd 78526
Shadowbrook Ln 78521
Shaldenw Ave 78526
Shary Ave 78521
Shelly Ct 78521
Shenandoah River Dr 78520
Shepard Cts 78521
Shidler Dr 78521
N Shore Trl 78520
Shoreline Dr 78521
Short St 78521
Sicamoro Dr 78521
Sidekick Ave 78526
Siene Riv 78520
Sierra Grande Dr 78526
Sierra Madre Dr 78521
Sierra Valley Cir 78526
Siesta Dr 78521
Silver Oak Rd 78520
Silverado 78520
Simcoe Ct 78526
Simon Pl 78526
Simpson St 78521
Sinaloa Dr 78521
Sioux Fls 78521
Skyline Ln 78526
Skyview Dr 78521
Sleepy Hollow Dr 78526
Smith Rd 78526
Sol Rd 78526
Solerno 78526
Solid Dr 78526
Somerset Ln 78526
Sonny Dr 78521
Sonora Ct 78526
Soroa St 78526
Sorrento Dr 78520
Soto Dr 78520
South Dr 78520
Southern Dr 78520
Southmost Rd 78521
Spanish Ct 78520
Sports Park Blvd 78526
Springmart Blvd 78526
Squaw Valley Dr 78520
Stagecoach Dr 78526
Stanford Ave 78520
Stanolind Ave 78521
Staples Cir 78521
Star Ave 78520
Star Ruby Ln 78521
Starcrest Dr 78521
State Highway 4 78521
State Highway 48 78521
Staunton St 78520
Sterling Moon 78526
Stevens Dr 78526
Stillinger Dr 78521
Stillman Rd 78526
Stillwell Bend Rd 78520
Stone Oak 78526
Stoval Rd 78520
Stream Ct 78520
Sugar Grove Ln 78520
Sugar Mill Rd 78526
Sugar Tree Ln 78520
Summit Dr 78521
Sunbeam 78521
Sunburst Ln 78520
Sundown Dr 78520
Sunflower Dr 78521
Sunny Skies 78521
Sunnyside Ln 78520
Sunrise Blvd 78526
Sunrise Ln 78521
Sunset Dr 78520
Sunset Lake Dr 78520
Sunshine Rd & St 78521
Susan Cir 78520
Sweet St 78521
Sweet Rose Ct 78520
Sweetgum Ct 78526
Sybil Dr 78520
Sycamore Dr 78520
Sydney St 78520

Sylvia St 78521
Tabasco Ct 78526
Tabitha Cir 78521
Taft St 78521
Tahoe Lake Dr 78520
Tallowood Cir 78521
Tamarack Dr 78520
Tamarindo 78521
Tamaulipas Ct 78526
Tampico St 78521
Tan Oak Cir 78521
W Tandy Rd 78520
Tangelo St 78521
Tangerine Blvd 78521
Tanglewood Rd 78521
Tanya Cir 78521
Tapachula Dr 78521
Tapia Rd 78520
Tara Pl 78520
Taxco Dr 78521
Taylor St 78520
Teapa Dr 78521
Tecate Dr 78521
Tecuan Dr 78521
Ted Hunt Blvd 78521
Tenaza Dr 78526
Tepepan Dr 78521
Tepeyac Cir 78521
Tepic Dr 78521
Terrace Dr 78521
Texan Palmetto 78521
Texas Ave 78521
Texas Palm Cir 78521
Texcoco 78526
Thomas St 78521
Thornhill Trl 78521
Thors Hammer 78526
Ticonderoga Dr 78526
Tiffany Dr 78520
Tiger 78521
Tijuana Blvd 78521
Timber Dr 78521
Tito Ct 78521
Toledo Dr & St 78526
Toluca Dr 78526
Tonila Dr 78521
Tony Gonzalez 78521
Tonys Rd 78526
Topaz Cir 78521
Topo Chico Cir 78526
Tordesillas St 78526
Toronja Ave 78521
Toronto Ave 78526
Torreon Dr 78526
Torres Rd 78520
Tortuga Trl 78520
Towerwood Dr 78521
Toya Ln 78520
Tradition Cir 78526
Trailer Dr 78521
Trailwind Way 78526
Tranquil Trl 78521
Trappers Cv 78520
Trappers Chase 78526
Travis Rd 78521
Travis Lake Ct 78520
Treeline St 78526
Trinidad St 78520
Trinity Trl 78520
Tropical Dr 78520
Truman Dr 78521
Tudela St 78526
Tula Ct 78526
Tulane Ave 78520
Tulipan St 78521
N & S Tupelo Cir 78521
Turqueza Dr 78521
Turquia 78520
Turtle Creek Dr 78520
E Tyler St 78520
W University Blvd 78520
Uptown Ave 78520
Uruapan Ct 78526
Us Highway 281 78520
Us Military Hwy 281 Rd 78520

Utah Rd 78521
Uzman 78521
Valencia Ln 78521
Valladolid 78520
Valladolid St 78526
Vallarta St 78521
Valle Escondido Cir 78521
Valle Hermosa 78521
Valles Ct 78526
Valletta St 78520
Valley Riv 78520
Valor St 78521
Vamonos Dr 78526
E & W Van Buren St 78520
Vanessa Dr 78526
Varadero St 78526
Varela Ct 78526
Vasquez Rd 78520
Velma St 78521
Venice 78520
Ventura Dr 78526
Vera Ave 78521
Vera Cruz Ave 78521
Verbena Ln 78520
N Vermillion Ave
300-1800 78521
1802-1998 78521
2300-2498 78526
2500-2999 78526
S Vermillion Ave 78521
Vermont Ave 78521
Veterans Blvd 78521
Victoria Ct & Dr 78521
Victory St 78521
Vidos Dr 78520
Vienna St 78520
Viking Ln 78520
Villa Bonita St 78521
Villa De Puente 78521
Villa Del Angeles 78521
Villa Del Mar Cir 78521
Villa Del Rey Blvd 78521
Villa Del Sol 78526
Villa Del Sur 78526
Villa Franca St 78526
Villa Madrid Ave 78521
Villa Maria Blvd 78520
Villa Pancho Dr 78521
Villa Real Ct 78521
Villa Verde Dr 78521
Villa Vista Dr 78520
Village Dr 78521
Village Center Dr 78526
Villanova Ave 78520
Villas Soleadas 78526
Vineyard Dr 78526
Violet Dr 78526
Virtudes Ct & St 78526
Vista Ct 78521
Vista Del Golf 78526
Vista Del Sol Dr 78526
Vista Jardin Cir 78521
Vivero Dr 78526
Vivian Dr 78521
Wabash River Dr 78520
Waco Rd 78521
Wales Dr 78520
Walnut Cv 78521
Warren Ave 78520
Warwick Glen Dr 78526
E & W Washington St 78520
Water St 78520
Waterfront Dr 78520
Waterside Dr 78521
Weems St 78521
Wellington Ct 78526
Wendy Lue Ct 78526
Werbiski Dr 78521
Weslaco Rd 78520
Westchester Cir 78521
Western Blvd 78520
Westland Dr 78521
Westlawn Park 78520
Westminster Cir & Rd 78521
Westwind Dr 78526
Whisperwind 78526

White Oak Ln 78521
White Pine St 78526
Whitewing Dr 78521
Wild Bird Ln 78526
Wild Flower 78526
Wild Horse Trl & Vly 78520
Wild Olive Ct 78520
Wild Olive Dr 78526
Wild Olive Ln 78520
Wilderness Dr 78526
Wildrose Ln 78520
Willacy Ave 78526
Williams Ave 78520
Willow Bnd 78526
Willow Ct 78520
Willow Dr 78520
Willow Ln 78521
Wilson Dr & St 78521
Windcrest Dr 78521
Windhaus Rd 78521
Windsor Pl 78520
Windwood Way 78526
Winnipeg Ave 78526
Winterhaven Ln 78526
Wishingwell 78526
Wood Ave 78520
Wood Hollow Dr 78521
Woodhaven Dr 78521
Woodlands Ave 78526
Woodmere St 78521
Woodruff Ave 78520
Woodside 78526
Woodstone Dr 78526
Woodway Dr 78521
Yale Ave 78520
Yard Rd 78526
Yellow Pine St 78526
Yera St 78521
Yolanda St 78521
Yolanda Del Rio 78521
Yoli 78521
York Dr 78520
Young Dr 78521
Yucatan Ct 78526
Yukon River Dr 78520
Yvonne Dr 78521
Zacatecas Ct 78526
Zafiro Dr 78521
Zamora Dr 78526
Zaragosa St 78520
Zena Dr 78521
Zinnia St 78521

NUMBERED STREETS

E & W 1st 78520
E & W 2nd 78520
E & W 3rd 78520
E & W 4th 78520
5th Ave 78521
E 5th St 78520
SW 5th St 78520
W 5th St 78520
E & W 6th 78520
E & W 7th 78520
E & W 8th 78520
E & W 9th 78520
E & W 10th 78520
E 11th St
101-497 78520
499-1100 78520
1102-1198 78520
5400-5599 78521
W 11th St 78520
E 12th St
201-297 78520
299-1799 78520
2000-2599 78521
2601-5599 78521
W 12th St 78520
E 13th St
400-1799 78520
1900-1998 78521
2000-3000 78521
3002-3098 78521
W 13th St 78520

E 14th St
501-597 78520
599-1499 78520
1501-1799 78520
1900-4499 78521
W 14th St 78520
E 15th St
800-1399 78520
2001-2097 78521
W 15th St 78520
16th St 78521
E 16th St
1000-1500 78520
1502-1698 78520
2201-2397 78521
2399-2999 78521
W 16th St 78520
E 17th St
1000-1198 78520
1200-1599 78520
2001-2899 78521
2901-3400 78521
3402-3498 78521
W 17th St 78520
E & W 18th 78520
E 19th St
1000-1198 78520
1200-1599 78520
2000-3200 78521
3202-3298 78521
W 19th St 78520
E 20th St
1600-1698 78520
2000-3300 78521
W 20th St 78520
E 21st St
1200-1699 78520
2000-3299 78521
E 22nd St
1100-1198 78520
1201-1299 78520
1901-2997 78521
2999-3299 78521
E 23rd St 78521
E 24th St
1401-1497 78520
1499-1500 78520
1502-1598 78520
3000-3299 78521
E 25th St 78521
E 26th St
1500-1598 78520
3000-3699 78521
E 27th St 78521
E 28th St 78521
E 29th St 78521
E 30th St 78521
E 31st St 78521
E 32nd St 78521
370th Tc 78526

BROWNWOOD TX

General Delivery 76801

POST OFFICE BOXES MAIN OFFICE STATIONS AND BRANCHES

Box No.s
All PO Boxes 76804

RURAL ROUTES

01, 03, 05, 09 76801

HIGHWAY CONTRACTS

30 76801

NAMED STREETS

Aaron Rd 76801
Abilene St 76801
E & W Adams St 76801
Agan Ln 76801
Alamo Ct & Dr 76801
Almond St 76801
Alpine Ct 76801
Anchor Ln 76801
E & W Anderson St 76801
Ann Ln 76801
Apache Ct & Rd 76801
Aran St 76801
Arapaho Rd 76801
Ardee Dr 76801
Arrowhead Dr 76801
Asbury Ct & St 76801
Ash St 76801
W Austin Ave 76801
Avalon Ct 76801
Avenue E 76801
Avenue A 76801
Avenue B 76801
Avenue C 76801
Avenue D 76801
Avenue G 76801
Avenue H 76801
Avenue I 76801
Avenue J 76801
Avenue K 76801
Avenue L 76801
Avenue M 76801
Avenue X 76801
Avolyn Dr 76801
Azalea Dr 76801
Bailey St 76801
E & W Baker St 76801
Bally Castle Dr 76801
Bally Shannon Dr 76801
Bay Oaks Dr 76801
Baylie Dr 76801
Beach Club Rd 76801
Beaver St 76801
Beck Rd 76801
Belfast Dr 76801
Belle Plain St 76801
Belmeade St 76801
Ben Ave 76801
Berkley St 76801
Berryman Ln 76801
Big Hill Dr 76801
Big Rocky Creek Rd 76801
Blackbird Ln 76801
Blarney Dr 76801
Bluebonnet Ln 76801
Bluffview Dr 76801
Bond St 76801
Bonita St 76801
Bonnie Pl 76801
N Booker St 76801
Borden St 76801
Bowie Cir 76801
Boyett Dr 76801
Brady Ave & Ln 76801
Bray Dr 76801
Brazos St 76801
Brentwood Cir & Dr 76801
Brewster St 76801
Brick St 76801
Brin St 76801
Britney Ln 76801
Broadmoor Cir & Dr 76801
N & S Broadway St 76801
Brook Ln 76801
Brook Hollow St 76801
Brookdale Dr 76801
Brooks Ave 76801
Brown St & Trl 76801
Brownstone Ct 76801
Bryan Dr 76801
Buck View Rd 76801
Buckhorn Rd 76801
Burkett St 76801
Burnet Rd & St 76801
Burney Dr 76801
C And E Ln 76801
C C Woodson Rd 76801
Caballo Trl 76801

Calvert Rd 76801
Campa Dr 76801
Campus Dr 76801
Cana Cir 76801
Canoe Loop 76801
Canyon Creek Dr 76801
Carey St 76801
Carnegie St 76801
Carriage Ln 76801
Carrie Ln 76801
Cashell Dr 76801
Cedar St 76801
Center Ave
1-97 76801
99-601 76801
600-600 76804
603-2599 76801
800-2398 76801
N Center Ave 76801
Center Dr 76801
E & W Chandler St 76801
Chaparral Dr 76801
Cherry St 76801
Chestnut St 76801
China St 76801
Cindy Cove St 76801
Circle P Heights Rd 76801
Clark St 76801
Claudett Dr 76801
Cleburne St 76801
Clements 76801
Clifden Dr 76801
Cliff Dr 76801
Clover Leaf Dr 76801
Coggin Ave 76801
Coleman St 76801
Comanche Rd & St 76801
E & W Commerce St 76801
Congress St 76801
Coppic Ranch Rd 76801
Cordell St 76801
Cork Dr 76801
Corrigan Ave 76801
Cottage St 76801
Cottontail Ln 76801
Country Club Dr 76801
Country Oaks Ln 76801
Country Place Ln 76801
Countryside Dr 76801
County Road 100 76801
County Road 101 76801
County Road 102 76801
County Road 103 76801
County Road 104 76801
County Road 105 76801
County Road 106 76801
County Road 107 76801
County Road 108 76801
County Road 110 76801
County Road 112 76801
County Road 115 76801
County Road 116 76801
County Road 118 76801
County Road 120 76801
County Road 121 76801
County Road 129 76801
County Road 130 76801
County Road 131 76801
County Road 132 76801
County Road 133 76801
County Road 134 76801
County Road 135 76801
County Road 136 76801
County Road 137 76801
County Road 141 76801
County Road 145 76801
County Road 146 76801
County Road 147 76801
County Road 148 76801
County Road 149 76801
County Road 151 76801
County Road 152 76801
County Road 153 76801
County Road 174 76801
County Road 180 76801
County Road 189 76801

County Road 190 76801
County Road 198 76801
County Road 199 76801
County Road 200 76801
County Road 201 76801
County Road 202 76801
County Road 203 76801
County Road 215 76801
County Road 225 76801
County Road 226 76801
County Road 228 76801
County Road 229 76801
County Road 232 76801
County Road 233 76801
County Road 234 76801
County Road 235 76801
County Road 236 76801
County Road 237 76801
County Road 239 76801
County Road 264 76801
County Road 265 76801
County Road 411 W 76801
County Road 420 76801
County Road 424 76801
County Road 429 76801
County Road 439 76801
County Road 440 76801
County Road 441 76801
County Road 445 76801
County Road 454 76801
County Road 455 76801
County Road 456 76801
County Road 460 76801
County Road 461 76801
County Road 463 76801
County Road 464 76801
County Road 467 76801
County Road 469 76801
County Road 470 76801
County Road 471 76801
County Road 472 76801
County Road 473 76801
County Road 474 76801
County Road 475 76801
County Road 486 76801
County Road 497 76801
County Road 498 76801
County Road 499 76801
County Road 536 76801
County Road 537 76801
County Road 538 76801
County Road 541 76801
County Road 542 76801
County Road 543 76801
County Road 544 76801
County Road 546 76801
County Road 547 76801
County Road 550 76801
County Road 551 76801
County Road 553 76801
County Road 554 76801
County Road 557 Ln 76801
County Road 558 76801
County Road 559 76801
County Road 562 76801
County Road 563 76801
County Road 564 76801
County Road 568 76801
County Road 569 76801
County Road 572 76801
County Road 574 76801
County Road 588 76801
County Road 594 76801
County Road 599 76801
County Road 600 76801
County Road 601 76801
County Road 602 76801
County Road 603 76801
County Road 604 76801
County Road 605 76801
County Road 606 76801
County Road 607 76801
County Road 608 76801
County Road 609 76801
County Road 611 76801
Cove Cir 76801

Coventry Cir 76801
Crayton St 76801
Creekwood Cir 76801
Creel Dr 76801
Crestridge Dr 76801
Crestview Ct 76801
Crockett Dr 76801
Crothers St 76801
Custer Rd 76801
Dallas St 76801
Danhil Dr 76801
Dartmore St 76801
David St 76801
Davis Ln 76801
Days Trl 76801
Deepwater Rd 76801
Deer Trl & Xing 76801
Delwood Dr 76801
E & W Depot St 76801
Dickman Dr 76801
Dillard Dr 76801
Divine Ln 76801
Dixie Ct 76801
Doe Trl 76801
Donegal Dr 76801
Dorothy Ln 76801
Drisco Dr 76801
Dublin Dr & St 76801
Duckhorn Dr 76801
Duke St 76801
Durango Ct 76801
Durham Ave 76801
Eagle Point St 76801
Eason Dr 76801
Easter Ln 76801
Edgewood Dr 76801
Edwards St 76801
El Paso St 76801
Elizabeth Dr 76801
Elm St 76801
Elm Oak Dr 76801
Emerald Dr 76801
Englewood Ave 76801
English Ave 76801
Ennis Dr 76801
Epley St 76801
Ez Does It 76801
Fairway Dr 76801
Feather Bay Blvd 76801
Field Dr 76801
Fishook Dr 76801
N Fisk Ave 76801
Flatrock Rd 76801
Fm 1176 76801
Fm 1849 76801
Fm 1850 76801
Fm 2125 76801
Fm 2126 76801
Fm 2492 76801
Fm 2559 76801
Fm 2632 76801
Fm 3021 76801
Fm 3254 76801
Fm 45 E 76801
Fm 585 N 76801
Fm 586 E & W 76801
Forbess Dr 76801
Forest Hill Dr 76801
Fort Worth Ave 76801
Franke St 76801
Franklin Dr 76801
Frans Way 76801
Gifford St 76801
Gill St 76801
Gilligans Trl 76801
Glade St 76801
Glen Cv 76801
Glenwood Dr 76801
Gobbler Holw 76801
Goldie Ln 76801
Golding Rd 76801
Good Shepherd Dr 76801
Gordon Rd 76801
Graham St 76801
Grand View Dr 76801
Green River Rd 76801

N & S Greenleaf St 76801
Greenway Dr 76801
Grey Fox Trl 76801
Gustin Rd 76801
Hackberry St 76801
Hall St 76801
Hammer Dr 76801
Happy Camper Trl 76801
Harris St 76801
Harriss Ln 76801
Hawk Ln 76801
Hawkins St 76801
Healer Ln 76801
Hemphill St 76801
Hendricks St 76801
Hetzel St 76801
Hickory St 76801
Hidden Valley Dr 76801
High Meadows Dr 76801
High Mesa Cv & Dr 76801
High Top St 76801
Highland Dr 76801
Highway 279 76801
Highway 377 S 76801
Highway 45 E 76801
Highway 84 W 76801
Hill St 76801
Hill Crest Dr 76801
Hillcrest Dr 76801
Hillsboro St 76801
Hillside Dr 76801
Hillview Cir 76801
Hiroms Ln 76801
Hobbs Ln 76801
Hogg Creek Rd 76801
Holcomb St 76801
Home St 76801
Houston St 76801
Hunters Run 76801
Hutchins Trl 76801
Idlewild Dr 76801
Indian Creek Dr 76801
Ireland Dr 76801
Irma St 76801
Ivanhoe Ln 76801
J T Ln 76801
Jackson Ln 76801
Jane Ellen St 76801
Joes End 76801
Johnson St 76801
Jordon Ln 76801
Kay Dr 76801
Kelli Ln 76801
Killarney Dr 76801
Kirkland Dr 76801
Kitten Ln 76801
La Monte Dr 76801
Lackey St 76801
Lake Dr 76801
Lake Bridge Ln 76801
Lakehaven Dr 76801
Lakeside Dr 76801
Lakeview Ct 76801
Lakeway Dr 76801
Lakewood Dr & Ln 76801
Lamar Ter 76801
Lane St 76801
Lariat Ln 76801
E & W Lee St 76801
Leo Ln 76801
Lewis Ln & St 76801
Lexington Ln 76801
Lillie Kimble St 76801
Limerick Dr 76801
Limestone Ct 76801
Lipscomb St 76801
Longhorn Ln 76801
Looney St 76801
Lori Ln 76801
Lough Ree Dr 76801
Lovers Ln 76801
Luker Cir 76801
Magnolia St 76801
N & W Main Ave, Blvd & St 76801
Malone St 76801

Maple St 76801
Margaret Dr 76801
Market Place Blvd 76801
Matthew Trey Ln 76801
E & W Mayes St 76801
Mcarthur Cir 76801
Mccombs Blvd 76801
Meadow Ln 76801
Megillas Run 76801
Melwood Ave 76801
Memorial Park Dr 76801
Mesa View Rd 76801
Milam Dr 76801
Miller Dr 76801
Milton Ave 76801
Mimosa Dr 76801
Minton Ln 76801
Mintons Draw 76801
Monaghan Dr 76801
Monterrey Dr 76801
Monticello St 76801
Morelock Ln 76801
Morris St 76801
Morris Sheppard Dr 76801
Morriss Ln 76801
Mountain Valley Ranch Rd 76801
Mountain View Ln 76801
Mulberry St 76801
Neal Dr 76801
Neumann St 76801
New Castle Dr 76801
Norwood St 76801
Oak St & Trl 76801
Oak Hill Cir 76801
Oak Ridge Dr 76801
Oakdale Dr 76801
Oakland Dr & Ter 76801
Oakpark Dr 76801
Old Ln 76801
Orange St 76801
Park Dr & St 76801
Park Road 15 76801
Parkside Dr 76801
Parkview Ter 76801
Parkway Dr 76801
Patricia Ln 76801
Peach St 76801
Pebblebrook Ct 76801
Pecan St 76801
Pecan Bayou Ln 76801
Pecos Dr & St 76801
Pency Dr 76801
Penn St 76801
Pennsula Dr 76801
Petty St 76801
Pheasant Grove Ln 76801
Phillips Dr 76801
Poindexter St 76801
Poplar St 76801
Porter St 76801
Post 10 76801
Post 100 76801
Post 101 76801
Post 11 76801
Post 127 76801
Post 133 76801
Post 134 76801
Post 135 76801
Post 136 76801
Post 137 76801
Post 14 76801
Post 15 76801
Post 160 76801
Post 161 76801
Post 171 76801
Post 176 76801
Post 178 76801
Post 179 76801
Post 18 76801
Post 19 76801
Post 20 76801
Post 22 76801
Post 23 76801
Post 24 76801
Post 26 76801

Post 27 76801
Post 28 76801
Post 29 76801
Post 34 76801
Post 37 76801
Post 38 76801
Post 39 76801
Post 41 76801
Post 43 76801
Post 53 76801
Post 58 76801
Post 63 76801
Post 64 76801
Post 70 76801
Post 75 76801
Post 76 76801
Post 78 76801
Post 81 76801
Post 91 76801
Post 94 76801
Post 98 76801
Post 99 76801
Prater St 76801
Private Road 440 76801
Private Road 444 76801
Pruett Ln 76801
Quail Run 76801
Quail Creek Rd 76801
Red Fox Trl 76801
Redbird Dr 76801
Redstone Ct 76801
Regent Dr 76801
Retreat Rd 76801
Reynolds Ln 76801
Rhodes Rd 76801
Riggs Ln 76801
River Oaks Cir & Dr 76801
River Run Dr 76801
Riverbend Rd 76801
Riverside Dr 76801
N Riverside Park Dr 76801
Roanoke Ave 76801
Robertson Pt 76801
Robin Ln 76801
Rocky Ln 76801
Rocky Hill Rd 76801
Rocky Top Rd 76801
Rogan St 76801
Rolling Hills Rd 76801
Romero St 76801
Rose Cir & Ln 76801
Roselawn St 76801
Rosemary Ln 76801
Rosewood Dr 76801
Round Rock Ct 76801
Rush St 76801
Safe Haven Ln 76801
Sage Ln 76801
Saint Patrick Dr 76801
Sam Houston Dr 76801
San Benito Dr 76801
Sandy Beach Dr 76801
Santa Clara Dr 76801
Savoy Dr 76801
Schroeder Ln 76801
Secret Meadow Ln 76801
Shady Oaks Dr 76801
Shamrock Dr 76801
Shannon Dr 76801
Sharon St 76801
Sharp St 76801
Shaw Dr 76801
Shelbi Ln 76801
Sheridan Rd 76801
Sherman Dr 76801
Sherwood Dr 76801
Shore Crest Dr 76801
Sierra Dr 76801
Simmons St 76801
Skyview Ct 76801
Slayden St 76801
Smith Ln 76801
Song Bird Cir 76801
Southgate Dr 76801
Spillway Rd 76801
Sportsman Dr 76801

Spring Holw 76801
Springlake W 76801
Spruce St 76801
Stage Coach Rd 76801
Stanley Ln 76801
Starr Ln 76801
State Park Road 15 76801
Stephen F Austin Dr 76801
Stewart St 76801
Stonebridge Cir 76801
Stonebrook Ct 76801
Stonecreek Cir 76801
Stonegate Ct 76801
Streckert Dr 76801
Sunset Rd 76801
Sunset Beach Rd 76801
Surrey Ln 76801
Swiss St 76801
Tacos Trl 76801
Tangle Briar Dr 76801
Tannehill St 76801
Temple Ave 76801
Terrace Dr 76801
Texas St 76801
Thomas Dr 76801
Thrifty Ln 76801
Tipperary Rd 76801
Torres Ln 76801
Travis St 76801
Tres Colinas Ln 76801
Trigg St 76801
Triple K Ln 76801
Tulane Dr 76801
Turner Dr 76801
Turner Ranch Rd 76801
Valley View Dr & St 76801
Verde Dr 76801
Vick Dr 76801
Vickies Park Ln & Rd 76801
Victoria St 76801
Vincent St 76801
Vine St 76801
Virgil Gray Dr 76801
Waco St 76801
Wagon Wheel Ln 76801
Walnut St 76801
Ward St 76801
N & S Washington Ave 76801
Water St 76801
Waterford Dr 76801
Waterfront Rd 76801
Watson Ln 76801
Weedons Way 76801
Wesley St 76801
Western Hills Ln 76801
Western Oaks Ln 76801
Westridge Dr 76801
Whaley St 76801
Whitaker Ln 76801
Whitetail Ln 76801
Wildwood Trl 76801
Williams Ave 76801
Willis St 76801
Willowbend Rd 76801
Wilson St 76801
Winston Dr 76801
Wm Baugh Ln 76801
Wood Ave & St 76801
Woodland Park Dr 76801
Woodmans Ln 76801
Woodridge St 76801
Yale St 76801

NUMBERED STREETS

All Street Addresses 76801

BRYAN TX

General Delivery 77803

POST OFFICE BOXES MAIN OFFICE STATIONS AND BRANCHES

Box No.s
1 - 2380 77806
913 - 8625 77805

RURAL ROUTES

01, 02, 03, 07, 09 77808

NAMED STREETS

Academy St 77803
Acheson St 77803
Adams St 77801
Agape Way 77803
Agee Ct 77808
Aggie Way 77803
Alabama St 77803
N & S Alamo Ave 77803
Alani Dr 77801
Alba Ct 77808
Aldine Dr 77802
Alexander Rd 77808
Alexander Cemetery Rd 77808
Alice Ln 77807
Alice St 77803
Allen Cir 77803
Allen Rd 77807
Allen St 77803
Allen Forest Dr 77803
Allen Ridge Dr 77802
Althea Ct 77808
Altura Ct 77802
Amberglow Pl 77801
Ambrose Ct & Dr 77808
Anderson St 77803
Andert Rd 77808
Anita St 77803
Antone St 77803
Apache Ct 77802
Apple St 77803
Apple Creek Cir 77802
Arbor Dr 77802
Arizona Ave 77803
Arnold Ln 77808
Arrowhead Rd 77807
Ascot Ct 77808
Ash St 77803
Ashford Hills Dr 77801
Aspen St 77801
Atkins St 77801
Atlas Pear Dr 77807
Augusta Ct & Dr 77803
Austin St 77803
Austins Lndg & Xing 77808
Austins Colony Pkwy
1900-1999 77802
2300-3299 77808
Austins Creek Dr 77808
Austins Estates Dr 77808
Autry Ln 77803
Autumn Cir 77802
Autumn Lake Dr 77807
Avenue E 77803
Avenue A 77803
Avenue B 77803
Avenue C 77803
Avenue D 77803
Avon St 77802
Avondale Ave 77802
Baker Ave 77803
Bamboo St 77803
Banks Ave 77803
Bankside Ct 77802
Bar P Ranch Rd 77808
Barak Cir & Ln 77802
Barbara St 77803
Barnes Rd 77807
Barnhill Ln 77808
Barnsley Ct 77802
Barronwood Dr 77807
Bart Rd 77807
Barwick Cir 77802
Bassett Ct 77802
Bastrop Cir 77808
Batts St 77803
Bayberry Ct 77807

N & S Baylor Ave 77803
Beason St 77801
Beaver Pond Ct 77807
Beck St 77803
Bedford Ct & Dr 77802
Beentann Rd 77807
Bellview Cir 77803
Benbow Ln 77808
Bench Ln 77807
Benchley Dr 77807
Bennett St 77802
Bentley Ct 77802
Berger Dr 77802
Berka Ln 77803
Berleadi St 77801
Beth Ln 77807
Bethany 77807
Bethany Dr 77803
Bethel Ln 77802
Bexar Grass Ct & Dr 77802
Bickham Cemetery Rd 77808
Big Bend Dr 77803
Big Horn Dr 77803
Bina St 77803
Birch St 77803
Birchcrest Ln 77802
Bishops Gate Cir 77807
Bittle Ln
1000-1199 77803
1200-1399 77801
Bittle St 77803
Bizzell St 77801
Blanco Ln 77801
Blazing Trl 77808
Blinn Blvd 77802
Bloomsbury Way 77802
Blossie Cir 77807
Blossom St 77803
Blue Belle Dr 77807
Blue Heron Rd 77807
Bluebonnet St 77803
Bluegrass St 77803
Bluejay Ln 77803
Bluffton Dr 77808
Boatcallie Rd 77808
Boatwright St 77803
Bob White St 77802
Bois D Arc St 77803
Bomber Dr 77801
Bonham Dr 77803
Bonifazi Ln 77808
Bonneville St 77803
Boone St 77803
Boonville Rd
2200-2799 77808
3100-5699 77802
Borderbrook Dr 77801
Boulevard St 77803
Bourrone Ct 77802
Bowery St 77803
Bowman Ln 77808
Bowser St 77803
Box S Ranch Rd 77808
Boyd Ln 77807
Boyett St 77801
Bradley St 77803
Braeburn 77802
Braeswood Cir & Dr 77803
Brandywine Cir 77807
Bravo Ct 77808
N & S Brazos Ave 77803
N & S Brewer Dr 77802
Briar Ln 77803
Briar Bend Ct 77802
Briar Cliff Dr 77802
Briar Grove Cir 77802
Briar Oaks Dr 77802
Briarcreek Ct 77802
Briarcrest Dr 77802
E & W Briargate Dr 77802
Briarparc Ct 77802
Briarwood Cir 77802
Bridge Meadow Ln 77803
Brighton Dr 77802
Bristol St 77802
Briton Dr 77802

Britten Rd 77807
Broach Rd 77808
Broad Oak Cir 77802
Broadmoor Dr 77802
Brockhampton Dr 77802
Brogdon St 77803
Broken Arrow Cir 77807
Brompton Ln 77802
W Bronze Ln 77807
Brook Ln 77802
Brook Hollow Ct, Dr & Way 77802
Brookhaven St 77803
Brookside Dr E & W 77801
Brown Ln 77807
N Brown St 77802
S Brown St 77802
Bruce St 77803
Bruin Trce 77803
N & S Bryan Ave 77803
Bryant St 77803
Bullinger Creek Dr 77808
Burch Ln 77808
N & S Burleson Dr 77802
Burnett St 77803
Burning Tree Ct 77802
Burr Oaks Cir 77802
Burt Rd 77807
Burt St
  1000-1299 77803
  1300-1699 77802
Burton Dr 77802
Bush Ln 77807
C6 Ranch Rd 77808
Cabot Cir 77803
Cache Cv 77802
Cade Ave 77803
Caleb Ct 77803
Calhoun Rd 77808
California St 77803
Calvert Cir 77803
Calvin Cir 77803
Cambridge Dr 77802
Camelot Dr 77802
Campus Dr 77802
Candy Ln 77803
Candy Hill St 77803
Caney Ct 77808
Canterbury Dr 77802
Capitol Pkwy 77807
Cardiff Ct 77808
Cargill Dr 77808
Carley Ln 77807
Caroline Dr 77807
Carrabba Rd 77808
Carrabba St 77803
Carrier Ln 77807
Carroll Cir 77803
E & W Carson St 77801
Carter Ln 77808
Carter Creek Pkwy 77802
Carver St 77803
Cary Cir 77803
Cash Ln 77807
Casita Ct 77807
Cassandra Ct 77807
Cassib St 77803
Castellon Ct 77808
Castenson Rd 77808
Castle Ave 77808
Cavitt Ave
  1322-1324 77803
  1400-4099 77801
Cedar Cir & St 77803
Cedar Bend Cir 77807
Cedar Oak Cir 77802
Cedar Oaks Dr 77808
Cedarcrest Ln 77803
Cedarwood Dr 77807
Celias Dream 77803
Center St 77803
Chadley Ct 77803
Chakett Ct 77801
Chamberlain Cir 77802
Chaparral Cir 77802
Chapel Ct 77803
Charles Ave 77808
Charlotte Ln 77807
Chase Cir 77803
Chaucer Ct 77802
Chelsea Cir 77802
Cherry Bend Cir 77807
Cherry Creek Cir 77802
Cheshire Ct 77802
Cheshire Dr 77803
Chevy Chase 77802
Cheyenne Cir 77802
Chicago St 77803
Chick Ln 77807
Chigger St 77803
Chinaberry Dr 77803
Chinon Ct 77802
Chinquapin Ct 77807
Chisholm Trl 77803
Choctaw St 77802
Christopher Cir 77803
Churchill Dr 77801
Cids Ln 77807
Cindy Ln 77801
Clare Ct 77802
Clark St 77808
Clarks Ln 77808
Clay St 77801
Clay Hill Rd 77808
Clear Lake Rd 77808
Clearleaf Dr 77803
Cliff Rd 77808
Cliff St 77801
Clover Ln 77808
Club Dr 77807
Cnp Rd 77808
Cobb Rd 77808
Cobblestone Ln 77807
Cole St 77803
Coleman St 77808
S College Ave
  1200-1299 77803
  1300-4499 77801
College Main St 77801
College View Dr 77801
Collette Ln 77808
Collins St 77803
Colony Cir 77808
Colony Chase Dr 77808
Colony Creek Dr 77808
Colony Glen Dr 77808
Colony Hills Dr 77808
Colony Leaf Dr 77808
Colony Place Dr 77808
Colony Village Dr 77808
Colony Vista Dr 77808
Colson Rd
  2900-3199 77803
  3200-3699 77808
Columbus Ave 77803
Colwell Ct 77807
Comanche St 77802
Commerce St 77803
Concordia Dr 77802
Congo St 77803
N & S Congress St 77803
Conlee St 77803
Conner Ln & St 77808
Conquest Cir 77803
Conquistador Cir 77807
Conroy St 77808
Copper Falls Dr 77803
Coppercrest Dr 77802
Copperfield Dr 77802
Copperhead Rd 77808
Corporate Center Dr 77802
Cotrone Rd 77807
Cotrone Dix Ln 77807
Cottage Grove Cir 77801
Cottonwood St 77803
Cougar Trl 77807
N & S Coulter Dr 77803
Country Ct & Dr 77808
Country Club Dr 77802
Courtlandt Pl 77802
Courtney Cir 77802
Coventry Ct 77802
Coyote Run 77808
Craftwood Pl 77801
Craig St 77802
Crane Ave 77801
Creek Cir 77807
Creek Shadows Dr 77808
Creekside Dr 77807
Creekwood Dr 77803
Crenshaw St 77803
Crescent Dr 77801
E Crest Dr 77802
Creston Ln 77802
Crestwood Dr 77801
Cromwell Ct 77802
Cross Park Dr 77802
Crosswind Dr 77808
Crosswood 77808
Crystal Brook Dr 77803
Culpepper Dr 77801
Cunningham Ln 77803
Curtis St 77802
Cypress Cir
  2600-2699 77803
  6300-6399 77807
Cypress Rd 77807
Cypress Bend Cir 77801
Daflyn Ln 77807
Dale St 77803
Dansby St 77803
Darling Ln 77803
Darwin Ave 77803
Darwood Ct 77807
Davis St 77801
Dawn Ct 77802
Day Ave 77801
De Lee St 77802
Dean St 77803
Debbie Dr 77802
Deep Well Rd 77808
Deer Trl 77807
Deer Crossing Ct & Dr 77807
Deer Hill Dr 77807
Deer Trail Ct & Dr 77807
Degelia St 77803
Della Love Rd 77808
Dellwood St
  100-599 77801
  600-999 77802
Delma Dr 77802
Democrat Rd 77808
Denise St 77803
Devonshire St 77802
Dewberry Ln 77807
Diamondleaf Trce 77807
Dick Elliott Rd 77808
N & S Dillard St 77803
Dillon Ave 77803
Dilly Shaw Tap Rd 77808
Dimrill Dale Cir 77807
Dixie St 77803
Dobrovolny Rd 77807
E Dodge St 77803
W Dodge St 77801
Doerge St 77801
Dogwood Dr 77807
Dogwood Ln 77802
Dona Dr 77802
Dorchester Ct 77802
Double Deuce Ln 77807
Douglas St 77808
Draycott Ct 77802
Driftwood Dr 77803
Drillers Dr 77808
Dumas Dr 77803
Dunbar Dr 77803
E & W Duncan St 77801
Dunn St 77801
Durant Ct 77802
Dyer Ave 77803
Eagle Hill Ct 77807
Eagle Pass St 77803
N Earl Rudder Fwy
  100-1100 77802
  1101-2899 77803
  1102-1298 77802
  1300-2898 77808
East Dr 77803
Eastchester Dr 77802
Easterling Dr 77808
Eastshire Ct 77802
Eaton Ln 77807
Echo Glen Cir 77803
Echols St 77801
Eden Ln 77803
Edge St 77801
Edge Cut Off Rd 77808
Edge School House Rd 77808
Edgemore Dr 77802
Edgewood Dr 77802
Ehlinger Dr 77801
Eisenhower Ave 77803
Elaine Dr 77808
Elise Ln 77802
Elizabeth Cir 77802
Elkhorn Trl 77803
Ella Ln 77802
Ellehue Ln 77808
Ellen Lee Ct 77802
Elliott St 77802
Elm Ave 77801
Elm Cir 77807
Elm Creek Ct 77807
Elmo Weedon Rd 77808
Elmwood Dr 77802
Elvenking Ct 77807
Elvis Rd 77808
Emerald Dr 77803
Emils Ct 77803
Emily Dr 77807
Emmett St 77802
Emory Oak Dr 77807
Enfield St 77802
Enloe Ct 77802
Enloe Dr 77807
N & S Ennis St 77803
Esquire Ct 77808
Esther Blvd 77802
Ethan Ln 77808
Ethel Blvd 77802
Ettle St 77803
Eureka St 77803
Evergreen Cir 77801
Fairchild Dr 77803
Fairfield Ct 77802
Fairview St 77803
Fairway Dr 77801
Faith Cir 77803
Falcon Crest Dr 77808
Falling Water 77808
Fannin St 77803
Fawn Lake Dr 77808
Fawnwood Dr 77801
Fazzino Ln & Rd 77807
Feather Gln 77808
Feather Trl 77807
Ferrill Creek Rd 77808
Fickey Rd 77808
Field Creek Estates Dr 77808
Fig St 77803
Finfeather Cir 77801
Finfeather Rd
  1906A-1906C 77801
  700-898 77803
  900-1000 77803
  1002-1498 77803
  1500-3799 77801
Fisher Ranch Rd 77808
Five Points Rd 77808
Flanigan St 77801
Fleetwood St 77801
Florida St 77803
Fm 1179 77808
Fm 158 77808
N & S Fm 2038 77808
Fm 2223 77808
Fm 2549 77808
Fm 2776 77808
Fm 50 77807
Fm 974 77808
Foch St 77801
Forest Bnd 77801
Forest Cir 77803
Forest Ln 77803
Forest Glen Ct 77803
Forest Hills Ct 77803
Forestwood Dr 77801
Forge Hill Rd 77801
Forsthoff Rd 77808
Foster Rd 77807
Foundation Place Dr 77807
Founders Dr 77807
Fountain Ave 77801
Fountain Switch Rd 77807
Fourwinds Dr 77808
Fowler Dr 77807
Fox Dr 77801
Foxwood Dr 77803
Francis Rd 77808
Franciscan Dr 77802
Frankfort St 77808
Franklin Dr 77801
Fred Hall Rd 77807
Freedom Blvd 77802
Freeman Ave 77803
Frieda Ln 77808
Frio Cir 77801
Frontier Dr 77803
Fulton Ln 77808
Gabbard Rd 77807
Gainer St 77803
Galindo Way 77807
Galleart Dr 77802
Garden Ln 77802
Garden Acres Blvd 77802
Gateshead Rd 77801
Gato Ln 77807
Gaytha Cir 77801
Gemstone Dr 77808
George St 77808
Georgia Ave 77803
Gettysburg Ln 77802
Gholson St 77803
Gilbert St 77801
Glacier Dr 77803
Gleneagles Ct 77802
Glenn Oaks Dr 77802
Glenwood St 77801
Glockzin Ranch Rd 77808
Goessler Rd 77802
Goldberry Cir 77807
Golden Eagle Dr 77808
Goodson Bend Rd 77807
Gooseneck Dr 77808
Gopher Ln 77808
Gordon Ln 77808
N Gordon St 77802
S Gordon St 77802
Graham Dr 77803
Gramercy Park Dr 77802
Granite Ridge Pl 77801
Grant St 77803
Grapevine Dr 77807
Grassbur Rd 77808
Gray Stone Dr 77807
Green St 77801
Green Branch Loop & Trl 77808
Green Hill Dr 77808
Green Hill Tap Rd 77808
Green Oaks Dr 77802
Green Ridge Cir 77802
Green Valley Dr 77802
Greenfield Plz 77802
Greenleaf Ln 77808
Greenway Dr 77801
Griffith St 77803
Groesbeck St 77803
Grove Dr 77808
Hall St 77803
Halliwell Lyda Rd 77808
Hammond St 77803
Hampton Ct 77802
S Hampton Ct 77801
Hanus St 77803
Harbert Rd 77808
Hard Rock Cir 77807
Harding Rd 77807
Hardwood Dr 77803
Hardy St 77801
Hare Ln 77808
Harlem Ln 77803
Harman St 77803
Harris Ln & Rd 77808
Harrow Ct 77802
Harvey St 77803
N Harvey Mitchell Pkwy
  100-899 77807
  900-1799 77803
  1800-2899 77807
N & S Haswell Dr 77803
Hawks St 77808
Hazel St 77803
Hearne Rd 77808
Heath Ln 77807
Heather Ln 77808
Heatherwood Dr 77801
Hefti Cir 77803
Heights Ave 77808
Helena St 77801
Helms Gate Cir 77807
Henderson St 77803
Henry St 77803
Hensarling Ln 77808
Hensel Ave 77801
Hernandez Ln 77803
Heron Lakes Cir 77802
Hickory Ct 77808
Hickory St 77803
Hickory Ridge Cir 77807
Hidden Trl 77808
Hidden Hollow Cir 77807
Hidden Pond 77808
Higgs Dr 77807
High St 77808
High Country Dr 77808
Highland Dr 77801
Highway 21 E
  1800-3399 77803
Highway 21 E
  3400-5499 77808
Highway 21 W 77803
Highwood Ln 77803
Hill St 77803
Hillcrest Cir 77802
Hillside Dr 77802
Hilltop Dr 77801
Hilton Rd 77807
Holick Ln 77801
Holligan Trl 77808
Hollow Heights Dr 77808
Hollow Oak Cir 77802
Hollowhill Dr 77802
Holly Cir 77807
Holly Dr 77802
Hollydale St 77801
Holt St 77803
Homer Rice Rd 77807
Homestead St 77803
Homola Rd 77807
Honeysuckle Ln 77808
Hooper St 77808
Hopkins Ln 77808
Hoppess St 77802
Hoston Rd 77807
House Cemetery Rd 77808
N & S Houston Ave 77803
Howard St 77801
Howell Ave 77803
Hsc Pkwy 77807
Hudson St 77803
Hudspeth Rd 77808
Hummingbird Cir 77807
Hunington Dr 77802
Hunters Ln 77803
Hurta Ln 77808
N & S Hutchins St 77803
Hyde Park Ln 77802
Ibis Ct 77807
Imperial Valley Dr 77803
Independence Ave 77803
Indian Trl 77803
Indiana Ave 77803
Industrial Blvd 77803
Inlow Blvd 77801
Inverness Dr 77802
Inwood Dr 77802
Iverson Dr 77803
Ivory Ridge Dr 77803
J C Long Dr 77807
J M Moore Schoolhouse Rd 77808
J O Bailey Dr 77807
Jack Creek Rd 77808
Jackrabbit Ln 77808
Jackson Ave 77803
Jaguar Ct & Dr 77807
Jane Ln 77802
Jenkins St 77803
Jenna Ct 77802
Jim Mathis Rd 77808
Johnson St 77803
Jones Ln 77808
Jones Rd 77807
Jordan Loop 77803
Joseph Dr 77802
Joyce Rd 77808
Judythe Ct 77803
Julie Cir 77807
June St 77802
Juniper St 77803
Justin Ln 77807
Justine St 77803
Kasserman St 77802
Kazmeier Plz 77802
Kelli Ln 77802
Kendall Way 77803
Kensington Rd 77802
Kent St 77802
Kenwood Dr 77802
Kermitt St 77803
Kerry Ln 77803
Keystone Cir 77803
Keystone Dr 77807
Kim St 77803
Kimmy Dr 77807
Kingsdale Dr 77802
Kingsgate Dr 77807
Kingston Cir 77802
Kinnard Ave 77803
Kirkwood Dr 77802
Knight Dr 77802
Knightsbridge Ln 77802
Koch St 77802
Koenig St 77801
Konecny St 77803
Kopetsky Ln 77808
Kosarek St 77803
Krc Ln 77807
Kubin St 77803
Kuder Rd 77807
Kurten Ln 77808
Kurten Cemetery Rd 77808
Kuykendall Cir 77808
Labrisa Dr 77807
Lafayette Ln 77807
Lafountain Ln 77808
Lake Dr 77807
Lake St 77801
Lakeside Dr 77807
Lakeside St 77801
Lakeview St 77801
Lakeway Dr 77807
Lakewood Dr 77807
Lakewood St 77803
Lamar Dr 77802
Laura Ln 77803
Laurel St 77801
Laurel Trace Ct 77807
Lawrence St
  400-599 77801
  600-799 77802
Lazy Ln 77802
Lazy Oaks Ln 77802
Lee Ave 77803
Lee Hollow Dr 77802
Lee Morrison Ln 77807
Legacy Ct 77802
Legion Ct 77803
Leila Ct 77802

Leon St 77801
Leonard Dr 77803
Leonard Rd
1000-3199 77803
3700-7599 77807
Leslie Dr 77802
Lewisburg Ct 77808
Liberty Dr 77807
Lightfoot Ln 77803
Limestone Ct 77808
Lincoln St 77808
Linda Ln 77807
Link St 77801
Lis Ln 77807
Lisa Cir 77801
Littleton Ct 77802
Live Oak Cir 77807
Live Oak St 77803
Lloyd Ln 77808
Lobo Dr 77807
Lochinvar Ln 77802
Lock Ln 77803
Locke Rd 77808
Lockett Hall Cir 77808
Locksford Dr 77802
Log Cabin Ln 77807
Log Hollow Dr 77803
N & S Logan Ave 77803
London Cir 77802
Lone Oak Dr 77808
Long Dr 77802
Long Trussel Rd 77808
Longview Dr 77808
Lopez St 77803
Lorita Cir 77807
Lost Pine Dr 77807
Lottie Roth Rd 77808
Louis St 77803
Louisa Ct 77802
Louisiana Ave 77803
Lowery St 77803
Lucky St 77803
Lucy Ellen Pkwy 77807
Luedecke Ln 77807
Luza Ln 77807
Luza St 77802
Lyndhurst Dr 77802
Lynette Cir 77807
Lynn Dr 77801
Lynnwood Ct 77807
M And M Ranch Rd 77808
Macey Rd 77808
Madeline Dr 77802
Madison Ave 77803
Maglothin Ct 77802
Magnolia Dr 77807
Mahan St 77802
N & S Main St 77803
Major St 77802
Mallard Dr 77807
Maloney Ave 77801
Malvern St 77803
Manchester Dr 77802
Mancuso Rd 77808
Manning Way 77803
Manor Dr 77802
Manorwood Dr 77801
Maple Dr
1400-1599 77803
2100-2499 77807
Marcia Ln 77807
Margaret St 77803
Marino Rd 77808
Marsh St 77803
Marshall Ave 77803
Martell Ct 77808
E & W Martin Luther King Jr St 77803
Mary Lake Dr
600-699 77801
700-899 77802
Mary Payne Ln 77808
Mason St 77808
Matous Dr 77802
Matthews Way 77807
Maulice Ave 77801
Maurine St 77802
May St 77802
Maywood Dr 77801
Mcarthur Ave 77803
Mcashan St 77803
Mccarver Ln 77808
S Mcculloch St 77803
Mcdonald Ave 77807
Mcgill Ln 77808
Mchaney Dr 77803
Mckinney St 77801
Meadow Ln 77802
Meadow Briar 77802
Meadow Lark Cir 77808
Meadow Oaks Ln 77802
Meadowbrook Dr 77802
Meadowwood Dr 77802
Meg Ln 77807
Megan Dr 77808
Melba Cir 77802
Memorial Dr 77802
Mensik Rd 77808
E & W Mercers Lndg 77808
Merka Rd 77808
Mervins Run 77803
Mesa Dr 77802
Mesco Dr 77808
Mesquite Dr 77807
Mesquite St 77803
Mesquite Meadow Ln 77808
Miana Ct 77807
Michael Ln 77801
Michelle Cir 77807
Middle St 77803
Middlebury Dr 77802
Midway Ave 77801
Midwest Dr 77802
Milam St 77801
Military Dr 77803
Miller Ave 77801
Mills Ct 77808
Mills St 77802
Milton St 77803
Milwaukee St 77803
Mimosa Cir 77807
Mimosa Dr 77802
Minh St 77807
Minnesota Ave 77803
Miramont Blvd & Cir 77802
Miravista Ct 77802
Mirkwood Ct 77807
Mirrormere Cir 77807
Missouri Ave 77803
Mistywood Ct 77801
Mitchell St
400-599 77801
600-999 77802
Mize Rd 77808
Mobile Ave 77801
Mockingbird Rd 77803
Mohawk St 77802
Monito Way 77807
Montana Ave 77803
Montauk Ct 77801
Monterrey St 77803
Moonlight Dr 77808
Mooring Ln 77807
Moran St 77801
Morgan Rd 77808
Morning Star 77808
Morningside Dr 77802
Morris Ln 77802
Moss St 77803
Moss Hill Rd 77808
Mount Hope 77807
Mountain Wind Ct & Loop 77807
Muckleroy St 77803
Muirwood Ct 77807
Mumford Rd 77807
Mumford Benchley Rd 77807
Murphy Ln 77803
Muscatel 77807
Nagle St 77801
Nancy St 77808
Nash St 77802
Natalie St 77801
Navidad St 77801
Neel St 77803
Nemec Ln 77807
Nevada St 77803
New York St 77803
Newcastle Ct 77802
Newton St 77803
Nicole Ct 77802
Nighthawk Ct 77808
Noble Oaks Ln 77807
Nonie Dr 77807
North Ave 77802
North Ave E 77801
North Ave W 77801
Northcrest Dr 77801
Northside Dr 77803
Northtown Ln 77808
Northwood Dr 77803
Nottingham Ln 77802
Nubin Rd 77808
Nuches Ln 77803
Oak Cir 77802
Oak Ln 77802
Oak St
400-499 77801
500-899 77802
Oak Trl 77807
Oak Bend Dr 77802
Oak Bluff Cir 77802
Oak Cliff Cir 77802
Oak Forest Dr
7100-7299 77808
12100-13299 77807
Oak Grove Ln 77802
Oak Hill Dr 77802
Oak Hollow Cir 77808
Oak Hollow Dr 77802
Oak Knoll Pl 77802
Oak Lake Rd 77808
Oak Ridge Dr 77802
Oak Valley Cir 77802
N & S Oakland Ln 77808
Oaklawn St 77801
Oakridge Dr 77808
Oakside Dr 77802
Oakview St 77802
Oakwood St 77801
Oklahoma Ave 77803
Old College Rd 77801
Old Goodson Bend Rd 77807
Old Hearne Rd
1900-4599 77803
10500-17099 77807
Old Kurten Rd
1400-3399 77803
3400-4199 77808
Old Mumford Cir 77807
Old Oaks Dr 77802
Old Railroad Rd 77807
Old Reliance Rd 77808
Old Spanish Trl 77807
Olive St 77801
Oliver Ave 77803
Open Range Ct 77808
Opersteny Ln & Rd 77808
Oran Cir 77801
Orange Cv 77808
Oregon Trl 77803
Orlan Dr 77803
Orlean St 77803
Orman St 77801
Osborn Ln 77803
Osler Blvd 77802
E Osr 77808
W Osr 77807
Overcrest Dr 77808
Owen St 77808
Oxford St 77802
Palasota Dr 77803
Palermo Ln 77808
Palmetto Ln & Trl 77807
Pantera Dr 77807
Par Dr 77802
Paris St 77803
Park Ln 77802
Park Rdg 77802
Park St 77803
Park Crest Dr 77802
Park Glen Dr 77802
Park Hampton Dr 77802
Park Haven Cir 77802
Park Hollow Cir 77802
Park Hurst 77802
Park Land Dr 77802
Park Meadow Ln 77802
Park Oak Dr 77802
Park Row Pl 77802
Park Stone 77802
Park Village Ct 77802
Park Wood Ct 77802
N & S Parker Ave 77803
Parkway 77801
Parkway Ter 77802
Partridge Cir 77802
Pate Ln 77808
Patsys Gln 77803
Patton Ave 77803
Pauline St 77803
Peach St 77803
Peach Tree Dr 77808
Peale St 77803
Pear St 77803
E & W Pease St 77803
Pebblebrook Ln 77807
Pecan Cir 77807
Pecan St 77803
Pecan Knoll St 77802
Pecan Ridge Dr 77802
Pecos St 77801
Pelham Ct 77802
Pembrook Ln 77802
Pendleton Dr 77802
Peppertree Dr 77801
Persimmon Ridge Ct 77807
Peterson Way 77802
Peyton Rd 77807
Phil Gramm Blvd 77807
Phillips Dr 77808
Pierce St 77803
Piereens St 77803
Pin Oak St 77803
Pine Cir 77807
Pine St 77803
Pine Tree Dr 77802
Pinehurst Cir 77802
Pinewood Dr 77807
Pinon Ct 77802
Pinyon Creek Dr 77807
N & S Pioneer Cir & Trl 77808
Pitts Rd 77807
Plagens Rd 77808
Plainsman Ln 77802
Planters Loop 77808
Plaza Centre Ct 77802
Pleasant St 77801
Pleasant Hill Rd 77807
Pleasant Rose Cir 77808
Plum St 77803
N & S Polk Ave 77803
Poplar Cir 77801
Portofino Dr 77802
Positano Loop 77808
Post Oak Ln 77807
Post Office St 77801
Prairie Ct 77808
Prairie Dr
1300-1399 77803
1400-1899 77802
Prairie Flower Cir 77802
N & S Preston Ave 77803
Primrose St 77803
Priscilla Ct 77802
Prospect Ln 77808
Providence Ave 77803
E & W Pruitt St 77803
Puma Dr 77807
Quail Hollow Dr 77802
Quality Park Ln 77803
Queenslock Cir 77802
R W Schram Ln 77808
Rabbit Ln 77808
Ramona Cir 77807
Ranchette Ct 77808
N & S Randolph Ave 77803
Ranger Dr 77801
Raven Dr 77808
Ravens Nest 77808
Ravens Perch 77808
Ravenwood Dr 77802
Ravine Ave 77803
Rayna Cir 77807
Rebecca St 77801
Red Angus Rd 77808
Red Apple Ln 77808
Red Cedar Ct 77807
Red Oak St 77803
Red River Dr 77802
Red Robin Loop 77802
Red Rock Rd 77808
Red Slough Rd 77807
Redbud Dr 77807
Redbud St 77801
Redwood Cir 77807
N Reed Ave 77803
S Reed Ave 77803
Reed Ln 77808
Reese Ave 77801
Regent Ave 77803
Regmond Ln 77807
Reliance Church Rd 77808
Reno St 77803
Renwick Dr 77802
Restmeyer St 77803
Reynolds St 77803
Rhapsody Ct 77802
Riata Ct 77808
Richard St 77803
Richmond Ave 77802
Ridgedale St 77803
Ridgewood St 77801
Riley Rd 77808
Rio Grande Ln 77801
Risinger Ln 77801
Rivendell Ct 77807
River Bend Ct 77808
River Fern Ct 77808
River Forest Dr 77802
River Garden Ct 77808
River Hollow Ct 77808
River Lake Rd 77808
River Oaks Cir 77802
River Rock Dr 77808
River Valley Dr 77808
River Wood Ct 77808
Riverstone Dr 77808
Roberta Ct 77802
Roberts St 77803
Robertson St 77803
Robeson St 77803
Robinhood Cir 77803
Rochester St 77803
Rock Hollow Loop 77807
Rockwood Cir & Dr 77807
Rolling Glen Dr 77807
Rollins Ave 77803
Roosevelt St 77801
Rose St 77802
Rosedale St 77803
N & S Rosemary Dr 77802
Ross St 77801
Roughneck Dr 77808
Rountree Dr 77801
Roy Ball Rd 77808
Roy Rod Rd 77808
Royal St 77801
Ruby Cir 77807
Ruskin Dr 77802
Russell Dr 77803
Russell Ln 77807
Rust Ln 77808
Rustic Oaks Dr 77808
Rustling Oaks Dr 77802
Ruth Cir 77807
Rye Loop 77807
Rye School Rd 77807
Sadberry Rd 77807
Sage Ave 77803
Sagebriar Dr 77802
Sagebrush Dr 77808
Saint Louis St 77803
San Antonio St 77803
San Jacinto Ln 77803
Sand Creek Rd 77808
Sandalwood Ln 77807
Sandia Plz 77802
Sandpiper Cir 77802
Sandra Dr 77801
Sandy Ln 77801
Sandy Cove Dr 77807
Sandy Creek Dr 77807
Sandy Oaks Dr 77807
Sandy Point Rd
1200-1398 77803
1400-1600 77803
1602-1798 77803
1800-12799 77807
Sandy Shore Dr 77807
Santa Fe Trl 77803
Sarah Ln 77807
Saunders St 77803
Saxon Rd 77808
Sbisa Way 77807
Scanlin St 77803
Scasta Rd 77808
Scott Ln 77808
Scott St 77803
Seashera Rd 77808
Seminole Ct 77802
Serrano Ct 77802
Seth Ct 77807
Settlers Way 77808
Shadowood Dr 77803
Shady Ln
700-799 77802
7800-8599 77808
Shady Creek Dr 77808
Shady Park Ct 77802
Shannon Cir 77802
Sharon Dr 77802
Shawnee Cir 77802
Sheffield Terrace Ln 77802
Shelly Ln 77802
Sherwood Dr 77803
Shiloh Ave 77803
Shirewood Dr 77807
Shirley Dr & Rd 77808
Short Ave 77803
Short Stuff 77808
Sierra Ct & Dr 77802
Silkwood Dr 77803
Silver Hill Rd 77807
Silver Maple Dr 77803
Silver Oak Dr 77808
Silver Spur Cir 77801
N Sims Ave 77803
S Sims Ave 77803
Sims Ln 77807
Sims Lane Cut Off 77807
Sioux Cir 77802
Sisco Ln 77808
Skrivanek Dr 77802
Skylark Blvd 77808
Sleepy Hollow Ln 77807
Slippery Rock 77808
Smetana Rd 77807
Smith Ln 77807
Smith Rd 77808
Snowy Brook Trl 77807
Somerford Ln 77802
South Dr 77803
Southern Ln 77802
Southside Dr 77803
Southview Cir 77802
Spanish Hl 77807
Spring Holw & Ln 77802
Spring Creek Ranch Rd 77807
Spring Leaf Ct 77807
Spruce Ave 77801
Spruce Dr 77807
Sprucewood St 77801
Spur 231 77807
Staci Ln 77808
Stadium St 77803
Stafford Pt 77808
Stampede Dr 77808
Standing Rock Rd 77808
Stanfield Cir 77802
Stanley Trl 77807
Star St 77803
Starlight Dr 77808
E State Highway 21 77808
W State Highway 21 77807
State Highway 47 77807
N & S State Highway 6 77807
Staunton Dr 77803
Steamboat Run 77807
Steel Store Rd 77807
Steep Hollow Cir & Rd 77808
Stefanie Dr 77807
Stella Cir 77808
N & S Sterling Ave 77803
Stevener Dr 77808
Stevens Dr
1900-3099 77803
3400-3799 77808
Stevenson St 77808
Stillmeadow Dr 77802
Stone City Dr 77803
Stone Creek Dr 77808
Stone Haven Dr 77803
Stone Meadow Cir 77803
Stone View Ct 77803
Stratford Cir 77802
Strawser Ln 77807
Streamside Way 77807
Stretch Ln 77808
Strickland Ln 77808
Stuart St 77801
Sugar Hill Ln 77808
Sul Ross Dr 77802
Sulphur Springs Rd 77801
Summerwood Loop 77807
Suncrest St 77803
Sundown St 77803
Sunny Ln 77802
Sunnybrook Ln 77802
Sunnydell St 77807
Sunrise St 77803
Sunset St 77803
Sunup Dr 77808
Sutton Ct 77802
Sweet Gum Dr 77803
Sweetbriar Dr 77802
Sycamore Cir & Trl 77807
Symphony Park Dr 77802
N Tabor Ave 77803
S Tabor Ave 77803
Tabor Rd
3798B-3798C 77808
1600-2999 77803
3400-4099 77808
Taft Ct & Dr 77802
Taliaferro St 77803
Talon Cir 77808
Tanglewood Dr 77802
S Tatum St 77803
Tauber Ranch Rd 77808
Taylor Rd 77808
Tee Dr 77801
Tejas Ranch Loop 77808
Telluride Way 77807
Tennessee Ave 77803
Tercel Way 77808
Terrace Dr 77802
Tesori Dr 77802
Teton Dr 77803
N Texas Ave 77803
S Texas Ave
4101A-4101H 77802
100-1399 77803
1400-4613 77802
That Way 77807
This Way 77807
Thompson St 77803
Thornberry Dr 77808
Thurman Rd 77808

Tia Maria Cir 77807
Tidwell Ave 77803
Tiffany Park Cir & Dr ... 77802
Timber Ln 77801
Timberlake Dr 77801
Timberline Ct & Dr 77803
Timberton Dr 77802
Timberwilde Dr 77808
Tisdale St 77808
Todd St 77802
Toro Ln 77807
Towering Oaks Dr 77802
Towne Centre Way 77802
Townsend Ln 77808
Trace Bnd 77807
Tracy Ct 77802
N & S Traditions Blvd &
Dr 77807
Trails End 77808
Trailwood Dr 77808
Trant St 77803
Travis St 77803
Treadgold Ln 77802
Treebrook Ln 77808
Trellick Ct 77802
Trent Cir 77802
Trophy Dr 77802
Truman St 77801
Turkey Ave 77803
Turkey Creek Rd
900-1098 77801
1100-1499 77801
1500-3299 77807
Turning Leaf Dr 77807
Turtle Grove Cir 77807
Tuscany Ct 77802
Twin Creek Cir 77808
Twin Hill Dr 77807
Twin Oaks 77808
Twisted Oaks Dr 77802
Twisting Trl 77808
Una Ave 77803
Union St 77801
University Dr E 77802
Ursuline Ave 77803
Vail Ln 77807
Valley Rd 77807
Valley Oaks Dr 77802
Valley View Dr 77802
Vaquero Dr 77808
Varisco Ln 77807
Velma St 77803
Venice Dr 77808
Verde Dr 77801
Viceroy Dr 77802
Vicks Ln 77808
Victory St 77803
E Villa Maria Rd
100-112 77801
114-499 77801
500-598 77802
600-2899 77802
2901-3199 77803
W Villa Maria Rd
100-1499 77801
1500-3999 77807
Village Dr 77802
Vincent St 77803
Vine St 77802
Vinewood Dr 77802
Vintage Hills Dr 77808
W Virginia St 77803
Waco St 77803
Wagon Trail Ct 77808
Wagonwheel Rd 77808
Waldham Grove Ln 77802
Walker St 77802
Wallace St 77803
Wallin Rd 77807
Wallis Rd 77808
Walnut St 77803
Walnut Creek Ct 77807
Walter Banks Rd 77807
Wannabe Rd 77808
Warren Cir 77802
Warren Ranch Rd 77808

Warwick Ln 77802
N & S Washington
Ave 77803
Water Locust Dr 77803
Water Oak St 77803
Water Oaks Ln 77808
Water Well Rd 77807
Waterwood Ln 77803
Watson St 77801
Waverly Dr 77801
Wayside Dr 77802
Weatherly Dr 77803
Weaver St 77803
Weber Rd 77808
Webhollow Cir 77801
Wedgewood Cir 77801
Weedon Loop 77808
Wehrman Ln 77807
Welch Rd 77808
Wellborn Rd 77801
Wellhead Ln 77808
Wellington Ave 77803
Werlinger Rd 77808
Wessex Ct 77802
West St 77803
Western St 77802
Western Oaks Ct 77807
Westminster Dr 77802
Weston Ln 77807
Westridge Cir & Ct 77801
Westview St 77802
Westway 77807
Westwood Main Dr 77807
Wheeler St 77803
Wheelock Hall Rd 77808
Which Way 77807
Whispering Frst 77808
Whispering Oaks Cir ... 77802
White Oak St 77803
White Stone Dr 77807
Whitetail Ln 77808
Wickson Ct & Cv 77808
Wickson Lake Rd 77808
Wickson Ridge Dr 77808
Wilcox Ln 77808
Wild Dogwood Ln 77807
Wilde Oak Cir 77802
Wilderland Cir 77807
Wilderness Rd 77807
Wildflower Dr 77802
Wildlife Cir 77808
Wilhelm Dr 77803
Wilkes St 77803
Williams Bnd & Way 77808
Williams Glen Dr 77808
Williams Trace Dr 77808
Williamsburg Dr 77802
Williamson Dr 77801
Willow Ave 77801
Willow Cir 77807
Willow Bend Dr 77802
Willow Oak St 77802
Willow Ridge Dr 77807
Willowick Dr 77807
Wilson St 77803
Wilson Oaks Dr 77802
Wilson Pasture Rd 77808
Wimberly Pl 77802
Winchester Dr 77802
Windowmere St 77802
Windridge Dr 77802
Windsor Ct & Dr 77802
Windwood Cir 77802
Winfield Ct 77802
Winter St 77803
Wixon Rd 77808
Wixon Oaks Dr 77808
E Wm J Bryan Pkwy
2114A-2114E 77802
219A-219D 77803
101-1999 77803
2000-2098 77802
2100-2114 77802
2116-2298 77802
2119-2121 77801
2121-2121 77805

2123-2299 77802
W Wm J Bryan Pkwy
100-122 77803
124-299 77803
210-210 77806
300-1798 77803
301-1799 77803
Wood Ct 77808
Wood Oaks Dr 77808
Woodbend Dr 77803
Woodbine Ct 77802
Woodbriar Dr 77802
Woodcrest Dr 77802
Wooddale Cir 77807
Woodglen Cir 77808
Woodknoll Dr 77803
Woodland Dr 77802
Woodmeadow Dr 77802
Woodmere Dr 77802
Woodson Dr 77801
Woodville Rd
3104A-3104D 77803
Woodward Dr 77803
Woody Ln
3800-4399 77803
11300-11999 77807
Wrong Rd 77808
Yegua St 77801
Yellowstone Dr 77803
Yosemite Dr 77803
Young Pl 77807
Zak Rd 77808
Zweifel Rd 77808

NUMBERED STREETS

1st St 77801
2nd St 77801
4th St 77801
5th St 77801
W 14th St 77803
E & W 15th 77803
E & W 16th 77803
E & W 17th 77803
E & W 18th 77803
E & W 21st 77803
E & W 22nd 77803
E & W 23rd 77803
E & W 24th 77803
E 25th St 77803
1500-1899 77802
E 26th St
200A-200C 77803
1400-1899 77802
W 26th St 77803
E 27th St
100-1215 77803
1217-1221 77803
1300-1799 77802
W 27th St 77803
E 28th St
702A-702B 77803
1300-1799 77802
W 28th St 77803
E 29th St
100-198 77803
200-1199 77803
1200-4699 77802
W 29th St 77803
E 30th St 77803
E 30th St 77803
1100-1399 77802
W 30th St 77803
E 31st St
401-407 77803
1000-1699 77802
W 31st St 77803
E & W 32nd 77803
E & W 33rd 77803

BURLESON TX

General Delivery 76097

POST OFFICE BOXES
MAIN OFFICE STATIONS
AND BRANCHES

Box No.s
All PO Boxes 76097

RURAL ROUTES

01, 02, 03, 04, 05, 06,
07, 08, 09, 10, 11, 12,
13, 14, 15, 16, 17, 18,
19, 20, 21, 22, 24, 25,
26 76028

NAMED STREETS

Aaron Dr 76028
Acorn Ln 76028
Adams Dr 76028
Akers Ln 76028
Alan Ct & Dr 76028
Alda Ct 76028
Allen Trl 76028
Allison Ct 76028
E, NE & SW Alsbury
Blvd & Ct 76028
Alta Vista Ct 76028
Alydar Dr 76028
Amanda Ct 76028
Amber Ct 76028
NE Amy Ct & St 76028
NE & SW Anderson
St 76028
Andrew St 76028
Angel Dr 76028
Angela Dr 76028
Angus Dr 76028
NW Ann Lois Ln 76028
Anna Grace Dr 76028
Anna Lea Ln 76028
Antonios Ct 76028
E & W Apache Ct 76028
Applewood Ct 76028
Arbor Ln 76028
Arbor Lawn Dr 76028
Archdale Ct 76028
Arnold Ave 76028
Arrowhead Dr & Ln 76028
Ash St 76028
Aspen Ct & Ln 76028
Azalea Ct 76028
Bairds Ln 76028
N Baker Rd & St 76028
Baldridge Rd 76028
NW Barbara Ln 76028
Barbara Jean Ct & Ln .. 76028
Barberry Dr 76028
Barkridge Ct & Trl 76028
Baslow Ln 76028
Bear Plz 76028
Bear Mesa Ct 76028
Beard Dr 76028
Beaver Creek Dr 76028
Beechwood Ln 76028
Beeley Ln 76028
Belaire Dr 76028
Belle Meade Way 76028
Bellegrove Rd 76028
Ben Dr & St 76028
W Bend Blvd 76028
Benjamin Dr 76028
Bent Oaks Dr 76028
Bent Tree Ct & Trl 76028
Berkeley Dr 76028
Berkshire Ct & Dr 76028
Bernice Ct 76028
Berry Rd 76028
Bethany Ct 76028
E & W Bethesda Rd 76028
Betty L Ln 76028
Beverly Dr 76028
Bexley Dr 76028
Bicole Dr 76028
Bill Levey Rd 76028
Birch Ln 76028
Black Hills Dr 76028
Black Jack Ln 76028
Black Oak Ln 76028
Blackbird Ct 76028
Blackhawk Rd 76028
Blayke St 76028
Blazing Star Trl 76028

Blue Daze Ct 76028
Blue Marlin Dr 76028
Blue Ridge Dr 76028
Blue Star Ct 76028
Bluebird Ct 76028
Bluebonnet Ct & Dr 76028
Blythe Ct 76028
Bob White Ct & Trl 76028
Bond St 76028
Bonnards Peak Rd 76028
Bonniebrae Ct 76028
Boone Rd 76028
Boulder Ct 76028
Bowden Cir 76028
Boxwood Ln 76028
Brandon Ln 76028
Bransom St 76028
Breanne Ct 76028
Brenda St 76028
Bretts Way 76028
E Brian St 76028
Briar Haven Ct 76028
Briar Patch Ln 76028
Briarcrest Dr 76028
N & S Briaroaks Rd 76028
Bridle Path 76028
Brighton Way 76028
Broad Valley Ct & Dr ... 76028
Broadmoor Dr 76028
Brookhollow Dr 76028
Brooks Rd 76028
Brookside Ct 76028
Brown St 76028
Brown Crest Rd 76028
Brownfield Dr 76028
Brownford Dr 76028
Brownstone Dr 76028
NE & SW Brushy Mound
Rd 76028
Bryan Dr, Ln & St 76028
Buckenwo Dr 76028
Buffalo Run 76028
E & W Bufford St 76028
Bur Oak Dr 76028
N & S Burleson Blvd ... 76028
Burleson Oaks Dr 76028
Burleson Retta Rd 76028
C C Chandler Rd 76028
C Evans Dr 76028
Cains Meadow Ct 76028
Caleb St 76028
Camden Yard Dr 76028
Canadian Ln 76028
Candlelite Ct 76028
Canyon Cove Dr 76028
Canyon Pass Trl 76028
Cardinal Ct 76028
Cardinal Ridge Rd 76028
Carlin Ln 76028
Carol Ln 76028
Carols Cir & Ct 76028
Carter Ct 76028
Castle Rd 76028
Castle Hill Ct & Dr 76028
Castle Pines Dr 76028
Catherine Ln 76028
Cathy Dr 76028
Cedar Ln 76028
Cedar Ridge Ln 76028
Celeste Ln 76028
S Central Dr 76028
Centre Dr 76028
Chaparral Dr 76028
Charles Ave & Ct 76028
NW Charlyne Dr 76028
Charolais St 76028
S Chase Ct 76028
Chase Hill Ln 76028
Chase Landing Dr 76028
Cherokee Rose Ln 76028
Cherry Hills Ln 76028
Chestnut Ave 76028
Chisenhall Park Ln 76028
NW Chisholm Ct & Rd . 76028
Chloie St 76028
Christopher Ln 76028

Cimmaron Ct 76028
NE & SW Cindy Ct &
Ln 76028
Circle Dr 76028
Cirrus Dr 76028
Claire Ct 76028
Clairemont Ln 76028
N & S Clark St 76028
Clear View Ct 76028
Cliffside Dr N & S 76028
NE Clinton St 76028
Cliveden Blvd 76028
Clover Ln 76028
Clubhouse Cir 76028
Cochise Ct 76028
Cole Rd 76028
Coleman Rd 76028
Collett St 76028
Collins Cir, Ct, Dr &
Rd 76028
Colonial Cir & Pkwy 76028
Colorado Ct & Dr 76028
N & S Commerce St ... 76028
Connie St 76028
Conveyor Dr 76028
Cook Hills Rd 76028
Copperfield Dr 76028
Coral Vine Ln 76028
Cottonwood Way 76028
Country Squire Ln 76028
Country Vista Cir & Dr . 76028
County Road 1016 76028
County Road 1016a 76028
County Road 1016b 76028
County Road 1019 76028
County Road 1020 76028
County Road 1021 76028
County Road 518 76028
County Road 519 76028
County Road 523 76028
County Road 527 76028
County Road 528 76028
County Road 529 76028
County Road 529a 76028
County Road 530b 76028
County Road 531 76028
County Road 602 76028
County Road 603 76028
County Road 603a 76028
County Road 603c 76028
County Road 604 76028
County Road 605 76028
County Road 605a 76028
County Road 605b 76028
County Road 606 76028
County Road 608 76028
E & W County Road
714 76028
County Road 715 76028
County Road 802 76028
County Road 802a 76028
County Road 803 76028
County Road 804 76028
County Road 804a 76028
County Road 913 76028
County Road 914 76028
County Road 914a 76028
County Road 919 76028
County Road 920 76028
County Road 921 76028
Courtney Ln 76028
Cozby Ln 76028
NE Craig St 76028
Crawford Dr 76028
Crazy Horse Trl 76028
Creekside Ct 76028
Creekview Dr 76028
Crestline Trl 76028
Crestmont Ct & Dr 76028
Crestview Dr 76028
Crestwood Ct & Dr 76028
Crockett Dr 76028
Cross Creek Ct 76028
Cross Timber Rd 76028
Crown Ct 76028
Crystal Dr 76028

Cumberland Dr 76028
Curtis Ct & Rd 76028
Cypress Ln 76028
Daisy Ln 76028
Dandelion Trl 76028
Daniel 76028
Darla Ct 76028
Darren Dr 76028
Date Ct 76028
Daughters Dr 76028
Dave Angel Rd 76028
S David St 76028
Dawnridge Ct 76028
Day Break Trl 76028
Deborah Ct & Dr 76028
Deer Creek Dr 76028
Deerwood Dr 76028
Delaware St 76028
Delynn Ct 76028
Dema Ln 76028
Deniese Dr 76028
Destrehan Dr 76028
Diablo Dr 76028
Diamond Ln N 76028
Diamond Rose Ct &
Dr 76028
SE & SW Dian St 76028
Dillan Dr 76028
N & S Dobson St 76028
Doe Meadow Dr 76028
Dogwood Dr 76028
Donald Rd 76028
Donna Ct 76028
Donnybrook Dr 76028
Doris Walker Trl 76028
Dorothy Dr 76028
Dorsey St 76028
Doss Rd 76028
NW Douglas St 76028
Downwood Dr 76028
Drury Cross Rd 76028
Dudley Ln 76028
Dustin St 76028
Dylan Ct 76028
Eagles Nest Trl 76028
S East Dr 76028
Eden St 76028
Edgehill Rd 76028
Egan Way Ct 76028
Eldorado Dr 76028
E & W Eldred St 76028
Elizabeth Dr 76028
Elk Dr 76028
E Ellison St 76028
Elm Hill Blvd 76028
Embry Ln 76028
Emerald Ct 76028
Emerald Forest Dr 76028
Emerson Dr 76028
Emily Ct 76028
Enchanted Ct N & S ... 76028
Enchanted Acres Dr 76028
Eric Ln 76028
Erin Ct & Dr 76028
Esperanza Ln 76028
Etta Ln 76028
Eureka Ct 76028
Evandale Rd 76028
Evelyn Ln 76028
Evergreen Ct & Ln 76028
Exchange St 76028
Fairhaven Ct 76028
Fairway View Dr 76028
Faith Ct 76028
Fallow Deer Ct & Dr ... 76028
Falls Creek Ct 76028
Farris Rd 76028
Fenway Ct 76028
N Field St 76028
Firethorn Ct 76028
Firewheel Rd 76028
Firewood Dr 76028
Flagstone Dr 76028
Flamingo Cir 76028
Flatrock Rd 76028
Flora St 76028

Flounder Dr 76028
E Fm 1187 76028
Fm 1902 76028
Fm 2738 76028
Fm 731 76028
Forest Ct & Dr 76028
Forest Edge St 76028
Forest Green St 76028
Forest Hill Everman Rd 76028
Forgotten Ln 76028
S Fox Ln 76028
Fox Willow Ct 76028
Foxglove Ln 76028
Francine Ct 76028
SE & SW Gamble St 76028
Garden Ridge Dr 76028
Gardenia Ct 76028
SE Gardens Blvd 76028
Garrett St 76028
Gatewood Cir E & W 76028
Gayle St 76028
Geddes Ct 76028
Gehrig Cir 76028
Georgia Ave 76028
Glen Oak Dr 76028
Glen Ranch Dr 76028
Glencove St 76028
Glendale St 76028
Glenhaven Ct 76028
Glenn Ct 76028
Glenwick Ct 76028
Glenwood Dr 76028
Gold Creek Ct 76028
Golden Aster Ct 76028
Golden Valley Ct 76028
Golfing Green Ct 76028
SW Gordon St 76028
Gracie Ln 76028
Graham Dr 76028
Grant St 76028
Graystone Rd 76028
Green Mountain Rd 76028
Green Valley Cir E & W 76028
Greenhaven Dr 76028
Greenway Dr 76028
Greenwood Dr 76028
SE & SW Gregory St 76028
Grove Ct 76028
Hackberry Ct 76028
Haley Ln 76028
Hampshire Dr 76028
Hampton Pl 76028
Hannah St 76028
Hanover St 76028
Hanson Hl 76028
SE & SW Harris St 76028
NE & SW Haskew St 76028
Hassop Ln 76028
Headwaters Rd 76028
Hearthstone Dr 76028
Heather St 76028
Heberle Dr 76028
Heights St 76028
Hemphill St 76028
Hennessy Ct 76028
Hereford St 76028
Heritage Ct & Dr 76028
Hewitt St 76028
Hickory Ln & St 76028
Hidden Cove Ct 76028
Hidden Creek Pkwy 76028
Hidden Glen Ct 76028
Hidden Knoll Dr 76028
Hidden Lake Ct & Dr 76028
Hidden Meadow Dr 76028
Hidden Oaks Dr 76028
Hidden Ridge Dr 76028
Hidden Springs Dr 76028
Hidden Trail Ct 76028
Hidden View Ct 76028
Hiddenglen St 76028
Hiddenview Ln 76028
Higgins St 76028
Highcrest Dr 76028
Highpoint Pkwy & Rd 76028
Hill Top Cir 76028
Hillcrest Dr 76028
NW Hillery St 76028
SW Hillside Ct & Dr E & W 76028
Hollow Creek Rd 76028
Holly Dr 76028
Hondo Trl 76028
Hoover Rd 76028
Hopper Rd 76028
Houston Rd 76028
Hudson Ln 76028
Huebner Way 76028
Hughs Ln 76028
Huguley Blvd 76028
SW Hulen St 76028
Hunter Ln 76028
Hunters Cabin Ct 76028
Hunters Crossing Ln 76028
Hunters Field Blvd 76028
Hunters Knoll Dr 76028
Hunters Mill Trl 76028
Hunting Brook Ct 76028
N & S Hurst Rd 76028
Indian Blanket Dr 76028
Industrial Park Blvd 76028
S Interstate 35 W 76028
Irene St 76028
Ironstone Rd 76028
J Rendon Rd 76028
Jacie Ct 76028
Jackie Dr 76028
Jackson Crest St 76028
Jacobs Crossing Ct 76028
Jake Ct 76028
Jakes Mdw 76028
NE & NW James Cir 76028
Jana Ln 76028
NW Janie Ln 76028
Jasmine Ct 76028
Jay Ln 76028
Jayellen Ave & Ct 76028
Jayme Ct 76028
Jean Ln 76028
Jeffdale Dr 76028
Jennifer Ct, Dr & Ln 76028
Jessica Dr 76028
Jewett Rd 76028
NW Jill Ann Dr 76028
Jimmy Ct 76028
Joalene Ct 76028
Joey Ct 76028
John Ct 76028
John Charles Dr 76028
John Henry Dr 76028
NW & SE John Jones Dr 76028
NE Johnson Ave 76028
SW Johnson Ave
100-231 76028
232-232 76097
233-699 76028
234-698 76028
Joni Ct 76028
Joshua Dr 76028
Judith St 76028
Juniper Ln 76028
Keith Ct 76028
Kenneth Ln 76028
Ketron Ct & Rd 76028
E King St 76028
Kingfish Dr 76028
Kinglet Ct 76028
Kings Ct 76028
Kingswood Ct & Dr 76028
Kirk Ln 76028
Kramer Ct 76028
Krista Dr 76028
Kyle Cir 76028
Lace Ln 76028
Ladonna Ave & Ct 76028
Lakeside Dr 76028
Lakeview Cir 76028
Lambert Ln 76028
Landview Dr 76028
Lantana Ln 76028
Laredo Rd 76028
Lariat Ln 76028
Larkspur Ct 76028
Larkwood Ln 76028
Latta Pl E 76028
Laura Dr & Ln 76028
Laurelwood Rd 76028
Lauren Dr 76028
N & S Lawson St 76028
Legacy Estates Dr 76028
Lena Ln 76028
Lester St 76028
Lett Ln 76028
Levy Acres Cir E 76028
Levy County Line Rd 76028
Lightcatcher Way 76028
Lillian Rd 76028
Lime Ct 76028
Lincoln Oaks Ct & Dr 76028
Linda Dr 76028
Linden Dr 76028
Lisa St 76028
Litchfield Cir & Ln 76028
Little Ridge Ct 76028
Little Stone Ln 76028
Live Oak Ln 76028
Lone Cottonwood Ct 76028
Lone Oak Ct 76028
Longbranch Rd 76028
Longstone Dr 76028
Lorene St 76028
NW Lorna St 76028
Lovie Thomas Ln 76028
Loy St 76028
Lucy Trimble Rd 76028
Lunar Ln 76028
Lunday Ln 76028
Lynne Ln 76028
Lynnewood Ave 76028
Lytham Ct 76028
Madeline Ln 76028
Madera Dr 76028
Madison St 76028
NW Magnolia St 76028
N & S Main St 76028
Man O War Ct 76028
Mantle Ct 76028
Maple Ave 76028
Marc St 76028
Marcia Ln 76028
Margie St 76028
Marion Ln 76028
Maris Ct 76028
Mark Dr 76028
Markedstone Rd 76028
Market St 76028
Marquise Ct 76028
Marti Dr 76028
Mary Ann Ln 76028
Mary Kay Ct 76028
Marybeth Dr 76028
Masters Ct N & S 76028
Matthew Ct & St 76028
Maxwell Rd 76028
NE Mcalister Rd 76028
Mccullar Rd 76028
Mckavett Dr 76028
Mckinley Dr 76028
Meador Ln 76028
Meadow Dr & Ln 76028
Meadow Beauty Ct 76028
Meadow Breeze Ct 76028
Meadow Creek Ln 76028
Meadow Oaks Dr 76028
Meadow Ridge Dr 76028
Meadow Rose Trl 76028
Meadowbrook Dr 76028
Meadowcrest Dr 76028
Meadowview Ct 76028
Meandering Ln 76028
Medpark Cir & Dr 76028
Melrose Dr 76028
Memorial Plz 76028
Merced St 76028
Merion Dr 76028
Merrill Ct 76028
Merry Ct E & W 76028
Mesquite Dr 76028
Micah Rd 76028
NE Michael Dr 76028
Michelle St 76028
Miles Ave 76028
Military 76028
Mill Creek Ct 76028
E & W Miller St 76028
Mimosa Ct 76028
Mint Dr 76028
Mistflower Ave 76028
Misty Oak Trl 76028
Mitchell Ln 76028
Mockingbird Ln, Mdws & Rd 76028
Molly Ln 76028
Monticello Dr 76028
NE & SW Moody St 76028
Moonway Ln 76028
Moore Rd 76028
Morgan Dr 76028
NW Mound St 76028
Mourning Dove Dr 76028
Murphy Rd 76028
Muscadine Ct 76028
Naomi Ct 76028
Nash Ln 76028
Nathan St 76028
Nelson Pl 76028
NW & SE Newton Dr 76028
Nicole Dr & Way 76028
Noe Ln 76028
Northern Dancer Dr 76028
Northview Ter 76028
Norwood Ct 76028
Nutmeg 76028
Oak Ln, Pkwy, St & Trl 76028
Oak Branch Dr 76028
Oak Crest Ct & Rd 76028
Oak Grove Ln & Rd 76028
Oak Grove Rendon Rd 76028
Oak Hill Ct 76028
Oak Hollow Dr 76028
Oak Leaf Dr 76028
Oak Meadow Dr 76028
Oak Parkway Ct 76028
Oak Ridge Dr 76028
Oak Trail Dr 76028
Oak Valley Rd 76028
Oakbrook Dr 76028
Oakdale Ct & Dr 76028
Oakmont Dr 76028
Oakridge Ct & Rd 76028
Oakview Ct 76028
Oakwood Dr 76028
Oatlands Pl 76028
Old Highway 1187 76028
Old Oaks Ct & Dr 76028
Olive Ct 76028
Olivia Ct 76028
Overland Dr 76028
Oxbow Ct 76028
Oxford St 76028
Ozark Ave 76028
Paint Brush Ct & Trl 76028
Paloma Way 76028
Panorama Dr 76028
Park Pl 76028
NE & NW Park Meadow Ct & Ln 76028
Parker Dr E 76028
Parkridge Blvd 76028
Parkview Ct & Dr 76028
Patnoe Dr 76028
Patty B Ln 76028
Paula Ter 76028
Peaceful Valley Dr 76028
Peach Ln 76028
Peacock Ln 76028
Pebblecreek Dr 76028
Pecan Dr & St 76028
Pecan Hollow Ln 76028
Pecantree Ct 76028
Pecos Ct & Dr 76028
Penny Ln 76028
Pepperfield Ct 76028
Pheasant Run 76028
Phlox Ln 76028
Piccadilly Cir 76028
Pickett Ln 76028
Pin Cushion Trl 76028
Pine St 76028
Pine Mountain Dr 76028
Pineview Ct 76028
Pinnacle Dr 76028
Plainsview Dr 76028
Plantation Ct & Dr E & N 76028
Pleasant Manor Ave 76028
Pleasant Valley Dr 76028
Pleasant View Ct 76028
Plum Ct & Dr 76028
Plum Creek Trl 76028
Ponderosa Ln 76028
Post Ln 76028
Post Oak Ct, Dr & Ln 76028
Potomac Dr 76028
Prairie Grove Ln 76028
Prairie Timber Rd 76028
Preserve Oaks Ct & Dr 76028
Quail Ln 76028
Quails Path 76028
Queen Annes Dr 76028
Rachel St 76028
Raenae Dr 76028
Rail Ln 76028
Rainbow Crest St 76028
Ranch Country Ct 76028
Ranchouse Rd 76028
Ranchview Ct & Dr 76028
Ranchway Dr 76028
SW Rand Ct & Dr 76028
Randy Ln 76028
Raven Ct 76028
Reagan Ln 76028
Red Cedar Way 76028
Red Cloud Dr 76028
Red Oak Ct, Dr & Ln 76028
Redbird Ln 76028
Redbud Rd 76028
Redfish Dr 76028
Redhaw Ct 76028
Redstone Rd 76028
Redwing Ct 76028
Redwood Cir 76028
Remington Cir 76028
Rendon Rd 76028
E & W Rendon Crowley Rd 76028
Rendon Estates Way 76028
Rendon Oaks Dr 76028
E Renfro St 76028
Retta Mansfield Rd 76028
Ricky Ln 76028
Ridge Crest Dr 76028
Ridge Top Dr 76028
Ridgehill Ct & Dr 76028
Ridgeview Dr 76028
Rigney Way 76028
E & W Riviera Dr 76028
Robby Rd 76028
SE Robert St 76028
Roberts Rd 76028
Robin Ct & Dr 76028
Robindale Ln 76028
Rock Ridge Dr 76028
Rock Springs Dr 76028
Rock Tank Trl 76028
Roland St 76028
Rolling Meadows Dr 76028
Rolling Ridge Dr 76028
NE Rosamond St 76028
Rose Creek Ct 76028
Rose Meadow Ct 76028
Rose Rael Ct 76028
Rosemary Ct 76028
Rowsley Ln 76028
Royal Ct 76028
Royal Oak Ct & Ln 76028
Roys Ln 76028
Ruby Ct 76028
N Rudd St 76028
Russell Ln 76028
Rustling Elm St 76028
Ryan Ave & Ct 76028
Ryanfield Ct 76028
Saddle Hills Rd 76028
Sage Cir 76028
Saint Andrews Dr 76028
Sally Ann St 76028
Sanctuary Way 76028
Sandgate Dr 76028
Sandlewood Ln 76028
NW Sandra Ln 76028
Sandstone Ct & Rd 76028
Sandy Hl 76028
Scandia Ln 76028
Scarlet Sage Pkwy 76028
Schumacher Dr 76028
N & S Scott St 76028
Selman Ln 76028
Senter Ct 76028
Serenity Ln 76028
Seven Eagles Ln 76028
Shaded Ln 76028
Shaded Lane Cir 76028
Shadow Creek Ln 76028
Shadow Ridge Dr 76028
Shadow Valley Ct & Dr 76028
Shadow Wood Trl 76028
Shadowoak Cir, Ct & Dr 76028
Shadowridge Dr 76028
Shady Ct 76028
Shady Hill Ln 76028
Shady Hills Ln 76028
Shady Oaks Dr & Trl 76028
Shady Tree Ct 76028
Shaffstall Rd 76028
Shamrock Dr 76028
Shane Ln 76028
Shannon Ct 76028
Sheila Ln 76028
Shelby Dr 76028
Shelley Dr 76028
Shenandoah Ct & Dr 76028
Sherman Oaks 76028
Sherry Ln 76028
Sherwood Ct 76028
Sheryn Dr 76028
Shoreline Dr 76028
Short St 76028
Shorthorn St 76028
Sienna Ct 76028
Sierra Cir & Dr 76028
Sierra Blanca Dr 76028
Sierra Vista Ct & Dr 76028
Silver Mist Trl 76028
Silver Ridge Ct 76028
Silver Rose Blvd 76028
Silverthorne Dr 76028
Sky View Ct 76028
Skylark Dr 76028
Skyview Ct 76028
Smallwood Dr 76028
Smith St 76028
Snapdragon Ct 76028
Snapper Dr 76028
South Dr & Fwy 76028
Southern Oaks Ct & Dr 76028
SW Southridge Dr 76028
Southwood Dr 76028
Spanish Bay 76028
Spanish Moss Dr 76028
Spring Meadows Dr 76028
Spring Oaks Rd 76028
Springhill Ct & Dr 76028
NW Springtide Dr 76028
Springwillow Rd 76028
Spyglass Ct 76028
St Croix St 76028
Starling Ct 76028
Stefanie St 76028
Stella St 76028
Stella Mae Dr 76028
Stephenson Levy Rd 76028
Steven St 76028
Stillglen Trl 76028
Stockton Dr 76028
Stone Rd 76028
Stone Rose Ct 76028
Stonebrooke Dr 76028
Storm Cat Ln 76028
Storm Creek Ln 76028
Stribling Dr 76028
Stuckert Dr 76028
Sue Ann Ln 76028
NW Summercrest Blvd 76028
Summerwood Dr 76028
Summit Ct & Dr 76028
SW Sundown Ct & Trl 76028
Sunflower Ct 76028
Sunny Ln 76028
Sunny Meadows Dr 76028
SW Sunnybrook Dr 76028
SW Sunset Ln 76028
Sunspike Ct 76028
Surrey Ln 76028
NW Suzanne Pl & Ter 76028
Swale Ct 76028
Sweetwater Dr 76028
Syble Jean Ct & Dr 76028
Sycamore St 76028
Sydney Ln 76028
Sylvanglen St 76028
Tabasco Ln 76028
E Tabb St 76028
Tanglewood Dr 76028
Tantarra Dr 76028
Tara Dr 76028
Tarpon Ct 76028
NW & SE Tarrant Ave 76028
W Tarver Rd 76028
NE & SW Taylor St 76028
Taylor Bridge Ct 76028
Tejas Trl 76028
Tena Ct 76028
Teton Dr 76028
Thistle Meade Cir 76028
SW Thomas St 76028
Thomas Crossing Dr 76028
Thousand Oaks Dr 76028
Timber Ct & Rd 76028
Timber Creek Dr 76028
Timber Meadow Dr 76028
NE Timber Ridge Cir, Ct & Dr 76028
Timbercrest Dr E 76028
Timberview Ct 76028
Timothy Dr 76028
Tinker Trl 76028
Tioga St 76028
NE Todd Ct & St 76028
Towering Oaks Ct 76028
Tracy Lee Ct 76028
Tradition Dr 76028
Trail Tree Cir & Ct 76028
Trails End Rd & St 76028
Trailwood Ct & Dr E & W 76028
Triple H Dr 76028
Tumbling Trl 76028
Twin Oaks Ct 76028
Tye Crossing Ct 76028
Tye Oak Ct 76028
Tyler Ct 76028
Tyler James Dr 76028
Unger St 76028
Ute Creek Ct 76028
Vaden Ave 76028
Valderama Ct 76028
Valley Crest Ct & Dr 76028
Valley Green Ct 76028
Valley Ridge Ct & Rd 76028
E & W Valley Terrace Cir & Rd 76028
Valley View Ct & Dr 76028

Valley Vista Dr ... 76028
Vaughn Dr ... 76028
Vera Dr ... 76028
Verde Ct & Dr ... 76028
Vicksburg Ln ... 76028
Viewpoint Ln ... 76028
Village Oak Dr ... 76028
Village Park Ct & Trl ... 76028
Vineridge Ln ... 76028
Vinewood Ave & Ct ... 76028
Vineyard Ct ... 76028
Vista North Dr ... 76028
Vista Oak Blvd ... 76028
Vista View Dr ... 76028
Wagon Bow Dr ... 76028
Walnut St ... 76028
NW Wanda Way ... 76028
Warbler Ct ... 76028
Ward Ln ... 76028
N & S Warren St ... 76028
Weatherby Rd ... 76028
Weeping Willow St ... 76028
S West Dr ... 76028
Whispering Creek Ln ... 76028
Whispering Oaks St ... 76028
Whispering Spring Ct ... 76028
White Clover Ct ... 76028
White Marlin Dr ... 76028
White Oak Dr & Ln ... 76028
Wicker Way ... 76028
Wicker Hill Rd ... 76028
Wickham Dr ... 76028
Wild Goose Ct ... 76028
Wild Oaks Ct ... 76028
Wildcat Way N ... 76028
Wildwood Ln ... 76028
William Wallace Dr ... 76028
Willow Cir & Ln N, S & W ... 76028
Willow Chase Dr ... 76028
Willow Creek Dr ... 76028
Willow Oak Ln ... 76028
Willowbrowse Ct ... 76028
Willowood Dr ... 76028
NE & SW Wilshire Blvd ... 76028
N & S Wilson St ... 76028
Winding Oak Ln E & N ... 76028
Windridge Ln & Trl ... 76028
Windy Hill Ln ... 76028
Windy Meadows Dr ... 76028
Winepress Rd ... 76028
Wing Way ... 76028
Winnett Rd ... 76028
NW Wintercrest Rd ... 76028
NW Wood St ... 76028
Wood Dale Dr ... 76028
Wood Duck Ct ... 76028
Wood Hollow Ln ... 76028
Woodbine Ct & Dr ... 76028
N Woodcrest Dr ... 76028
Woodland Cir & Dr ... 76028
Woodlawn Ave ... 76028
Woodview Ct ... 76028
Wren Ct ... 76028
Wrigley Dr ... 76028
Wyche Ct ... 76028
Wysteria Ln ... 76028
Yaupon Ct ... 76028
Yosemite Way ... 76028
Yucca Ct ... 76028
Yukon Dr ... 76028

CARROLLTON TX

General Delivery ... 75006

POST OFFICE BOXES MAIN OFFICE STATIONS AND BRANCHES

Box No.s
All PO Boxes ... 75011

RURAL ROUTES

01, 05, 10 ... 75007
02, 04, 06, 07, 08, 09, 11 ... 75010

NAMED STREETS

Abbey Cv & Rd ... 75007
Aberdeen Bnd, Cir & Pl ... 75007
Adams Dr ... 75010
Addington Dr ... 75007
Afton Dr ... 75007
Alameda Dr ... 75007
E & W Alan Ave ... 75006
Albert Rd ... 75007
Alpine Dr ... 75007
Alsace Dr ... 75007
Alto Ave ... 75007
Alyssa Ln ... 75006
Amanda Cir ... 75007
Amber Ln ... 75007
Amberglow Ct ... 75007
Amesbury Ct ... 75007
Andress Dr ... 75010
Andrew Ln ... 75007
Angleridge Cv ... 75006
Ann Ave ... 75006
Antibes Dr ... 75006
Antioch Cir ... 75007
Apache Lake Dr ... 75010
Apollo Cir ... 75006
Apple Dr ... 75010
Applecross Ct ... 75007
Appletree Ln ... 75006
Aquatic Dr ... 75007
Arapaho Dr ... 75010
Arbor Ln ... 75010
Arbor Creek Dr
1801-1897 ... 75010
1899-2300 ... 75010
2302-4298 ... 75010
4101-4199 ... 75007
4201-4299 ... 75010
Arbor Crest Dr ... 75007
Arcadia Ln ... 75007
Argonne Dr ... 75007
Arledge ... 75007
Arles Ln ... 75007
Arrowhead Ln ... 75007
Artherfield Dr ... 75006
Arundel Dr ... 75007
Ash Hill Rd ... 75007
Ashleaf Dr ... 75007
Ashwood Ct & Ln ... 75006
Aspen ... 75007
Astaire Dr ... 75007
Auburn Dr ... 75007
Audrey Dr ... 75007
Audubon Ct ... 75010
Austin Dr ... 75006
Austin Waters ... 75010
Autumn Dr ... 75006
Avenida Cir ... 75006
Avignon Ct & Dr ... 75007
Bach Blvd ... 75007
Balfour Pl ... 75007
Balmoral Dr ... 75006
Banbury Ln ... 75006
Bandera Dr ... 75010
Barclay Dr ... 75007
Barona Dr ... 75010
Barton Rd ... 75007
Bastrop Dr ... 75010
Baxley Cir, Dr & St ... 75006
Bay Shr ... 75006
Beechwood Ct ... 75007
Bel Air Dr ... 75007
Belclaire Dr ... 75006
Bellflower Ct, Dr & Ln ... 75007
Belmeade Dr ... 75006
E & W Belt Line Rd ... 75006
Belton Dr ... 75007
Belvedere ... 75006
Benbrook Dr ... 75007
Bennington Dr ... 75007
Bentley Dr ... 75006
Berkshire Dr ... 75007
Beverly Dr ... 75010
Big Bend Dr ... 75007
Big Canyon Trl ... 75007
Big Sur Dr ... 75007
Birch Dr ... 75007
Bishop Hill Dr ... 75007
Black Duck Ter ... 75010
Black Oak Dr ... 75007
Blackfoot St ... 75010
Blackstone Dr ... 75007
Blair Ct ... 75010
Blanton Dr ... 75006
Blue Mesa Rd ... 75007
Bluebonnet Way ... 75007
Bluestem Ln ... 75007
Bluffview Ln ... 75007
Booth Dr ... 75006
Bordeaux Dr ... 75007
Bosque Dr ... 75010
Bowie Dr ... 75006
Bowin Ct ... 75010
Boyd Ct ... 75010
Boyington Dr ... 75006
Bradbury Dr ... 75007
Braddons Rd ... 75007
Bradley Ln ... 75007
Brake Dr ... 75006
Branch Trl ... 75007
E & W Branch Hollow Cir, Dr & Pl E ... 75007
Brandywyne Dr ... 75007
Brazos Dr ... 75007
Breamar Dr ... 75007
Brentwood Dr & Ln ... 75006
Bresee Dr ... 75010
Brewster Dr ... 75010
Briar Cv ... 75006
Briar Hill Dr ... 75007
Briarcrest Cv ... 75006
Briardale Dr ... 75006
Briarwood Ln ... 75006
Briarwyck Ct ... 75006
Briercroft Ct ... 75006
Brighton Dr ... 75007
Brisbane Dr ... 75007
Bristol Dr ... 75006
Britain Ct ... 75006
Brittainy Ct, Dr & Pl ... 75006
N & S Broadway St ... 75006
Broken Arrow Trl ... 75007
Broken Bow Trl ... 75007
Broken Gate Rd ... 75010
Bronco Blvd ... 75010
Brook Mount Ct ... 75006
Brooke Ct & Trl ... 75006
Brookshire Dr ... 75007
Brookside Dr ... 75007
Brookview Dr ... 75007
Brownwood Dr ... 75006
Buckskin Cir ... 75006
Buena Vista Ct ... 75007
Bunker Hill Dr ... 75006
Burgundy Dr ... 75006
Burning Tree Ln ... 75006
Bush Cir ... 75007
Buttonwood Dr ... 75006
Caddo Dr ... 75010
Caldwell Cir ... 75010
Cambridge Dr ... 75007
Cambridgeshire Dr ... 75007
Camden Way ... 75007
Camero Dr ... 75006
Camp Ave ... 75006
Cannes Ct, Dr & Pl ... 75006
Canoe Way ... 75010
Canon Gate Cir ... 75007
Canterbury Ct, Dr & Pl ... 75006
Canyon Trl ... 75007
Canyon Oaks Dr ... 75007
Capital Dr & Pkwy ... 75006
Capstone Dr ... 75010
Caraway St ... 75010
Cardinal Blvd ... 75010
Carillon Ln ... 75007
Carlton Rd ... 75007
Carmel Cir, Dr & Pl ... 75006
Carol Good Ln ... 75006
Caroline Pl ... 75006
Carriage Ct & Ln ... 75006
Carroll Ave ... 75006
Carrollton Pkwy ... 75010
Carter Dr ... 75006
Carver Dr ... 75010
Castille Dr ... 75007
Castle Rock Rd ... 75007
Catawba Ave ... 75010
Cattail Ct & Ln ... 75006
Cecil Ct & Dr ... 75006
Cedar Cir ... 75006
Cedar Elm Dr ... 75010
Cedar Ridge Ln ... 75007
Cedarbrush Dr ... 75006
Cedarcrest Dr ... 75007
Cedarwood Dr ... 75007
Cemetery Hill Rd ... 75007
Century Dr ... 75006
Chalfont Dr ... 75007
Chamberlain Dr ... 75007
Champion Cir & Dr ... 75006
Chapman Dr ... 75010
Charles Rd & St ... 75010
Charlotte Way ... 75007
Chatsworth Rd ... 75007
Chenault Dr ... 75006
Cherokee Path ... 75010
Cherrywood Ln ... 75006
Chesham Dr ... 75007
Cheshire Cir ... 75007
Chesterfield Dr ... 75007
Chestnut Rd ... 75007
Chevy Chase Dr ... 75006
Cheyenne Dr ... 75010
Chickasaw Dr ... 75010
Chief Dr ... 75007
Chimney Rock Dr ... 75007
Chippewa Ct ... 75010
Choctaw Dr ... 75010
Christie Ln ... 75007
Cibola Trl ... 75007
Cimarron Dr ... 75007
Clark Dr ... 75010
Clear Creek Ln ... 75007
Clearview Ct ... 75010
Clearwater Trl ... 75010
Clermont Ct ... 75007
N Cliff Dr ... 75010
Cliffbrook Dr ... 75007
Clint St ... 75006
Clinton St ... 75007
Clover Hill Ln ... 75007
Clubridge Dr ... 75006
Clubview Dr ... 75006
Clydesdale Way ... 75010
Cobblestone Dr ... 75007
Cochran Dr ... 75010
Colleen Ct ... 75007
W College Ave ... 75006
Cologne Dr ... 75007
Colonial Dr & Pl ... 75007
Colony Cv ... 75007
Colt Rd ... 75010
Colton Dr ... 75010
Columbian Club Dr ... 75006
Comanche Dr ... 75010
Commander Dr ... 75006
Commodore Dr ... 75007
Concord Dr & Pl ... 75007
Conrad Cir ... 75007
Copper Creek Ln ... 75006
Cordoba Dr ... 75006
Cornell Dr ... 75007
Corral Dr ... 75007
Cotton St ... 75006
Cottonwood Rd ... 75006
Country Pl ... 75006
Country Club Dr ... 75006
Country Lake Dr ... 75006
Country Place Cir & Ct ... 75006
Country Square Dr ... 75006
Country Villa Cir & Dr ... 75006
Countryside ... 75007
Courtland Cir ... 75007
Coventry Ln ... 75007
Cox St ... 75006
Coyote Rdg ... 75010
Crater Lake Ct ... 75006
Crawford Dr ... 75010
Creek Bnd ... 75007
Creek Valley Blvd & Cir ... 75010
Creek Wood Ct ... 75006
Creekbluff Dr ... 75010
Creekdale Ct ... 75006
Creekhollow Dr ... 75010
Creekmeadow Dr ... 75010
Creekridge Dr ... 75007
Creekside Ct ... 75007
Creekside Ln ... 75010
Creekstone Dr ... 75010
Creektree Dr ... 75010
Creekview ... 75006
Creekway Dr ... 75010
Creel Ln ... 75010
Crescent Cir & Dr ... 75006
N Crest ... 75006
Crest View Dr ... 75006
Crestedge Ln ... 75010
Crestover Cir ... 75007
Crestside Cir & Dr ... 75007
Crestwood Dr ... 75007
Cristina Cir ... 75006
Crockett Cir & Dr ... 75006
Croft Rd ... 75007
Cromwell Dr ... 75007
Crooked Creek Dr ... 75007
E & W Crosby Rd ... 75006
Crosson Dr ... 75010
Crowley Cir & Dr ... 75006
Crown Ct ... 75006
Crystal Ln ... 75007
Cutler Pl ... 75007
Dakota St ... 75010
Dale Cv ... 75006
Dallas Dr ... 75006
Dallshan Dr ... 75007
Daniel Way ... 75006
Davin Dr ... 75006
Day Dr ... 75010
Deep Valley Trl ... 75007
Deerfield Dr ... 75007
Degas Dr ... 75006
Del Ray Ct ... 75007
Delaford Cir, Ct, Dr & Pl ... 75007
Delaware Dr ... 75010
Denton Dr ... 75006
Dentonshire Dr ... 75007
Derby Run ... 75007
Derbyshire Ln & Pl ... 75007
Devon Dr ... 75007
Devonshire Dr ... 75007
Dew Valley Dr ... 75010
Dexter Ln ... 75010
Diamond Cluster ... 75010
Diamond Creek Ct ... 75010
Diamond Ridge Cir, Ct & Dr ... 75010
Dickens Ln ... 75010
Dickerson Pkwy
2401-2497 ... 75006
2499-2500 ... 75006
2502-2598 ... 75006
2629-2899 ... 75007
Dimmit Dr ... 75010
Diplomat Dr ... 75006
Dogwood Dr ... 75007
Donald Ave ... 75006
Donna Dr ... 75006
Dorchester Dr ... 75007
Dove Creek Ln ... 75006
Dover Dr ... 75006
Dozier Rd ... 75010
Dublin Dr ... 75006
Dudley Dr ... 75007
Duncan Way ... 75006
Dundee Pl ... 75007
Dunn Dr ... 75006
Dusk Meadow Dr ... 75010
Duval Dr ... 75010
Eaglepoint Dr ... 75007
Earhart Dr ... 75006
Earlshire Ln ... 75007
Eastgate Dr ... 75006
Eastwood Dr ... 75010
Echo Ct ... 75007
Echoridge Dr ... 75007
Ector Dr ... 75010
Edgecliff Cv ... 75006
Edgewood Ct ... 75007
Edinboro Ln ... 75006
Egret Ln ... 75007
Eisenhower St ... 75007
El Dorado Way ... 75006
Elder ... 75007
Electronics Dr ... 75006
Elizabeth Dr ... 75007
Elk Trl ... 75007
Elk Grove Rd ... 75007
S Elm St ... 75006
Elmbrook Dr ... 75010
Elmwood Ln ... 75006
Embassy Way ... 75006
Emerald Dr ... 75010
Emerson Ln ... 75010
Emily Ln ... 75010
Emory Oak Dr ... 75007
English Ln ... 75006
Erath Dr ... 75010
Ericksen Dr ... 75010
Erie St ... 75006
Espinosa Dr ... 75010
Estates Way ... 75006
Everglade Ct ... 75006
Evergreen St ... 75006
Fairfax Ln ... 75006
Fairfield Dr ... 75007
Fairgate Dr ... 75007
Fairway Dr ... 75010
Fairwind Ct ... 75007
Fairwood Ave ... 75006
Falcon Ridge Dr ... 75010
Falconet Ct ... 75010
Falkland Rd ... 75007
Fallcreek Cir & Dr ... 75006
Fallview Ln ... 75007
Fannidella Dr ... 75006
Fannin Dr ... 75006
Fawn Ridge Trl ... 75010
Feldman Dr ... 75010
Fens Dr ... 75007
Fernwood Cir ... 75006
Field Stone Dr ... 75007
Fieldview Cir ... 75007
Fisk Ln ... 75010
Flagstone Dr ... 75007
Flowers Dr ... 75007
Forms Dr ... 75006
Fort Point Ln ... 75007
Fountain Cv ... 75006
Fox Hollow Dr ... 75007
Foxboro Ln ... 75007
Foxcrost Ln ... 75006
Francis St ... 75006
E & W Frankford Rd ... 75007
Freshwater Dr ... 75007
Frosted Hill Dr ... 75010
Furneaux Ln ... 75007
Fyke Rd ... 75006
Gaines Ct ... 75010
Gallante Dr ... 75007
Galloway Ln ... 75007
Gardanne Ln ... 75007
Garden Dell Dr ... 75010
Garrett Dr ... 75010
Gaston Ct ... 75010
Gateway Ave ... 75006
Gatsby Way ... 75010
Gentle Glen Dr ... 75010
Georgetown Dr ... 75006
Geronimo Arrow ... 75006
Gillespie Dr ... 75010
Ginger Dr ... 75007
Glacier Ct ... 75006
Glascow Ct ... 75007
Glen Helen Cir ... 75007
Glen Hill Dr ... 75007
Glen Morris Rd ... 75007
Glenbrook Dr ... 75007
Glengarry Dr ... 75006
Glenhollow Cir ... 75007
Glenmere Ct ... 75007
Glenrose Ln ... 75007
Glenview ... 75007
Glenwood Ct ... 75006
Gold Rush Ln ... 75007
Golden Trl ... 75010
Golden Bear Ct & Dr ... 75006
Golden Gate Ct & Dr ... 75007
Golden Mew Dr ... 75010
Golden Trail Ct ... 75010
Grand Canyon Ct ... 75006
Grandview Dr ... 75007
Grapevine Ln ... 75007
Grasmere Dr ... 75007
Gravley Dr ... 75006
Green Oak Dr ... 75010
Green Ridge Ct & Dr ... 75007
Greenbrook Dr ... 75006
Greenglen Cir & Dr ... 75007
Greenhill Dr ... 75006
Greenmeadow Dr ... 75006
Greenstone Trl ... 75010
Greenvalley Dr ... 75007
Greenview Dr ... 75010
Greenway Park Dr ... 75007
Greenwich Dr ... 75006
Greenwood Cir & Rd ... 75006
Grenoble Dr ... 75007
Greystone Trl ... 75007
Grimes Dr ... 75010
Guerrero Dr ... 75006
Hackberry Ct ... 75007
Haley Cir ... 75006
Halifax Dr ... 75006
Halsey Way ... 75007
Hamilton Dr ... 75010
Hampshire Ln ... 75007
Hampton Ct ... 75006
Harbin Ct ... 75010
Harmony Ln ... 75006
Harper Ln ... 75010
Harrison Ct & Dr ... 75010
Hartford Dr ... 75007
Harvest Hill Ct & Rd ... 75010
Harvest Point Dr ... 75010
Haskell Dr ... 75010
Hawkins Ct ... 75010
Hawthorne Dr ... 75006
Hayden Dr ... 75006
Haymeadow ... 75007
Heads Ln ... 75006
Hearthstone Dr ... 75010
Heartside Pl ... 75006
Heather Ln ... 75010
Heather Glen Ct ... 75006
Heatherwoods Way ... 75007
E Hebron Pkwy
1000-1899 ... 75010
1900-2000 ... 75007
2002-2098 ... 75007
2200-3000 ... 75010
3002-3498 ... 75010
W Hebron Pkwy ... 75010
Hemingway Ln ... 75010
Hemphill Dr ... 75010
Heritage Cir ... 75006
Hersey Dr ... 75006
Hickory Dr ... 75006
Hidalgo Dr ... 75010
Hidden Valley Dr ... 75010
High Country Dr ... 75007
High Point Cir & Dr ... 75007
High Sierra Dr ... 75007
High Vista Dr ... 75007
Highbury Rd ... 75007
Highgate Ln ... 75007

Street	ZIP
Highland Dr	75006
Highland Heights Ln	75007
Highlander Way	75006
Highlands Creek Rd	75007
Highmeadow Cv	75006
Highridge Cv	75006
Hightrail Dr	75006
Hill Cv	75006
N Hill Dr	75010
Hilldale Cv	75006
Hillpark Ln	75007
Hillside Ln	75006
Hilltop Dr	75006
Hollow Way	75007
Hollow Ridge Dr	75007
Holly Dr	75010
Holly Hill Ln	75007
Homestead Ct & Ln	75007
Honeydew Dr	75007
Honors Club Dr	75006
Hood Cir & St	75006
Hopi Dr	75010
Hudspeth Dr	75010
Huffines Blvd	75010
Hunt Dr	75010
Hunters Rdg	75006
Hunters Trl	75007
Hunters Creek Dr	75007
Hunters Point Ln	75007
Hunting Brook Ct	75007
Hutton Dr	75006
Hyde Ct	75007
Illinois St	75010
Imperial Dr	75007
Incline Dr	75006
Indian Spgs	75007
Indian Lake Trl	75007
Indian Oaks Ln	75010
Indian Run Dr	75010
Indigo Ct	75007
Inspiration Cir	75010
International Pkwy	75007
N Interstate 35e	
1001-1097	75006
N Interstate 35e	
1099-2200	75006
2202-2598	75006
2600-2798	75007
2800-3302	75007
3304-3598	75007
S Interstate 35e	75006
Inverness Dr	75007
Iroquois Cir	75007
Irvine Dr	75007
Island Ct & Dr	75007
Ismaili Center Cir	75006
Ivy Ln	75007
Jackson Cir	75006
E Jackson Rd	
1001-1197	75006
1199-2031	75006
2030-2030	75011
2033-2099	75006
W Jackson Rd	75006
Jackson St	75006
Jahvani Ct	75007
Jamestown Ct & Ln	75006
Janna Way	75006
Janus Dr	75007
Jeanette Way	75006
Jennifer Ct	75007
Jessica Ln	75010
Jester Pl	75006
John Connally Dr	75006
Johnson Dr	75010
Joseph St	75010
N Josey Ln	
1100-1202	75006
1204-2599	75006
2601-2611	75007
2613-3756	75007
3755-3755	75011
3758-4198	75007
3901-4199	75007
4200-4799	75010
S Josey Ln	75006
Juniper Ln	75010
Kathy Dr	75006
Keller Way	75006
Keller Springs Ct, Pl & Rd	75006
Kellway Dr	75006
Kelly Blvd	
1401-1597	75006
1599-2599	75006
2600-3698	75007
3700-3899	75007
Kelly Pl	75007
Kenbob Cir	75007
Keneipp Rd	75006
Kensington Dr	75007
Kentwood Ln	75007
Kerr Ct	75010
Kestrel Way	75010
Keystone Ct	75007
Kickapoo Trl	75010
Kimberly Dr	75007
Kimble Dr	75010
King Arthur Blvd	75010
Kings Rd	75007
Kings Gate Dr	75006
Kingspoint Dr	75007
Kiowa Dr	75010
Kirby Rd	75006
Kirkwood Cir	75006
Kleber Dr	75010
Knollview Ln	75007
Knollwood Ln	75006
Kyan Ln	75006
Lacy Ln	75006
Laguna Ct & Pl	75006
Lake Bend Ter	75006
Lakecrest Cir & Ct	75006
Lakehill Ln	75006
Lakeland Dr & Pl	75006
Lakeridge Ln	75006
Lakeshore Ln	75006
Lakeside Ln	75006
Lakeview Ln	75006
Lakewood Ln	75006
Lakota Pl	75010
Lamar Dr	75006
Landover Dr	75007
Lands End Dr	75006
Lansdown Ct, Dr & Pl	75010
Lantern Trl	75007
Larkspur Dr	75010
Larner Rd	75006
Laura Ln	75007
Lavaca Ct & Trl	75010
Lawndale Dr	75006
Lawnview Dr	75006
Le Mans Ct & Dr	75006
Lee St	75010
Legacy Trl	75010
Legacy Trail Cir	75010
Leicester Ct & Dr	75006
Leisure Ln	75006
Lemay Dr	75007
Leon Dr	75010
Lincoln Dr & Pl	75006
Livingston Ln	75007
Lockwood Cir & Dr	75007
Lomar Dr	75007
Lone Star Dr	75010
Lone Wolf Trl	75007
Longwood Dr	75010
Lookout Pl	75007
Lorient Dr	75007
Lorraine Ct, Dr & Pl	75006
Luallen Dr	75007
Lucerne Cir	75007
Luke Ln	75007
Luna Rd	75006
Lymington Rd	75007
Lyon Ct	75007
Mac Arthur Dr	75007
Mackie Dr	75007
Mae Dr	75007
Magnolia Dr	75007
N Main St	75006
Malibu Dr	75006
Mallard Cv & Ln	75006
Manchester Ct & Dr	75006
Mangrove Dr	75007
Mann Ct	75010
Maple Ct	75007
Mapleview Dr	75007
Marble Falls Dr	75007
Marchant Blvd	75010
Marin	75006
Marken Ct	75007
Marseilles Ct	75007
Marsh Ln	
1201-1597	75006
1599-2541	75006
2543-2599	75006
2601-3697	75007
3699-3799	75007
3801-4299	75007
Marsh Ridge Rd	
4000-4098	75007
4200-4300	75010
4302-4398	75010
Mary Ln & St	75006
N & S Maryland St	75006
Mateo Cir	75007
Matthew Ln	75007
Maumee Dr	75010
Maverick Way	75010
Maxfield Ln	75006
Mayes Rd	75006
Mayfair Dr	75007
Mayflower Dr	75007
Maywood Ct & Dr	75007
Mccoy Ct, Pl & Rd	75006
Mcdaniel Dr	75006
Mcgee Ln	75010
Mcgreg Ln	75010
Mciver Ln	75006
Mckamy Dr	75006
Mckenzie Dr	75006
Mcparland Ct	75006
Meadfoot Rd	75007
Meadow Dr	75007
Meadow Cove Ct & Dr	75007
Meadow Creek Dr	75006
Meadow Ridge Dr	75010
Meadow Vista Dr	75007
Meadowbrook Cv	75006
Meadowdale Dr	75010
Meadowstone Ct & Dr	75006
Meadowview Ct	75010
Medical Pkwy	75007
Medina Dr	75007
Melbourne Rd	75006
Melissa Ct & Ln	75006
Melody Ln	75006
Melton Dr	75010
Memorial Ct	75010
Menard Dr	75010
Menlo Park Ln	75010
Menton Dr & Pl	75006
Mesa Dr	75010
Mesquite Dr	75007
Metrocrest Dr	75006
Miami Dr	75010
Midcourt Rd	75006
Middle Glen Dr	75007
Midway Rd	
2001-2497	75006
2499-2699	75006
4000-4299	75007
Milam Cir & Way	75006
Mill Trce & Trl	75007
Millcroft Cv & Ln	75006
Miller Ct	75006
Millview Pl	75006
Milsop Dr	75010
Miramar Dr	75007
Mission Ridge Trl	75007
Misty Ln	75006
Mistymeadow Ct	75006
Monetary Ln	75006
Montclair Cir, Dr & Pl	75007
Monterrey Pl	75006
Moonbeam Ln	75006
Morian Cir	75007
Morning Dove Ct	75007
Morning Glory	75007
Mossvine Dr	75007
Mosswood Dr	75010
Mountview Ct & Dr	75006
Muirfield Dr	75007
Mulberry Dr	75010
Muscogee Trl	75010
Myerwood	75007
Nature Bend Ln	75006
Navajo Cir	75007
Nazerene Dr	75010
Newcastle Dr	75007
Newport Dr	75006
Nimitz Dr	75007
Nob Hl	75006
Noble Ave	75006
Nolan Dr	75006
Normandy Ct & Dr	75006
North Cir	75006
Northland St	75006
Northmoor Dr & Way	75006
Northridge Ct, Dr & Pl	75006
Northshore Dr	75006
Northside Dr	75006
Northview	75007
Norwich Dr & Pl	75006
Nottingham Dr	75007
Oak Trl	75007
Oak Creek Dr	75007
Oak Grove Dr	75010
Oak Hill Cv & Rd	75007
Oak Hollow Ct	75010
Oak Mount Dr	75010
Oak Tree Dr	75006
Oakbluff Cir & Dr	75007
Oakwood Dr	75006
Odell Dr	75010
Old Denton Rd	
1900-2500	75006
2502-2598	75006
2600-4099	75007
4100-4200	75010
4202-4598	75010
Old Mill Rd	75007
Old Orchard Ct	75007
Oneida Dr	75010
Onyx Dr	75010
Orchard Ln	75007
Osceola Trl	75006
Overture Way	75006
Oxford Ln	75006
Oxfordshire Dr	75007
Pacifica St	75007
Pagosa Pl & Trl	75007
Paige Ct	75006
Palisades Dr	75007
Palm St	75006
Palo Alto Dr	75006
Palo Duro Dr	75007
Palomino Ct	75007
Palos Verdes Pl	75006
Panorama Dr	75007
Paradise Cv	75006
W Park Ave & Dr	75006
Park Heights Cir	75006
Parker Rd	75010
Parkside Dr	75006
Parkview	75006
Parkwood Dr	75007
Partridge Pl	75006
Pat Ln	75006
Patton Pl	75007
Pawnee Ct & Trl	75007
Paxton Dr	75007
Peach Tree Dr	75006
Pear St	75006
Pearl St	75006
Pecan Grv	75007
Pecan St	75010
Peninsula Way	75007
Penny Ln	75007
Peppertree Dr	75007
Peregrine Way	75010
N & S Perry Rd	75006
Peters Cv	75007
E & W Peters Colony Rd	75007
Phoenix Dr	75010
Piedmont Pl	75007
Pinecrest Dr	75010
Pinewood Cir	75007
Placid Dr	75007
Plano Pkwy	75010
Pleasant Run Rd	75006
Plumdale Dr	75006
Pocosin Dr	75007
W Point Dr	75007
Polser Rd	75010
Ponderosa Pine Ln	75007
Pontiac Dr	75006
Pony Ave	75010
Poplar Ct	75007
Post Oak Ln	75007
Prairie Dr	75007
Prescott Dr	75006
Presidio Cir	75007
Prestonwood Dr	75010
Primrose Ln	75007
Princess Ct	75006
Proctor Dr	75007
Province Ct & Dr	75007
Pueblo Dr	75006
Quail Glen Rd	75006
Quail Ridge Dr	75006
Queens Ct	75006
Quincy St	75007
Quivera Cir	75007
Rachel Ct	75006
Rafe St	75006
Raiford Rd	75007
Railhead Pl	75007
Raintree Cir, Ct & Dr	75006
Raleigh Dr	75007
Ramblewood Dr	75006
Rambling Ridge Ln	75007
Ramona St	75010
Ranchview Ct & Ln	75007
Randall Ln	75007
Randolph St	75006
Random Rd	75006
Ravine Cir & Trl	75007
Rayswood Cir & Dr	75007
Reagan Blvd	75006
Realty Dr	75006
Reata Dr	75010
Red Bluff Dr	75007
Red Maple Dr	75007
Red Oak Ln	75007
Red River Ct	75007
Red Spruce Ln	75010
Redbud Cir	75006
Reddenson Ct & Dr	75010
Redwood Dr	75007
Reeder Dr	75010
Regency	75007
Remington Dr	75007
Renwick Dr	75007
Reunion Cir	75007
Rheims Dr	75006
Rice Ln	75010
Ridge Rd	75006
Ridgecrest Trl	75007
Ridgedale Dr	75006
Ridgemeadow Cv	75006
Ridgeview Cir	75007
Ridgewood	75007
Riley Dr	75007
Rio Grande Ct	75007
River Birch Ln	75007
Riverside Dr	75007
Riverview Dr	75010
Robbins Dr	75010
Robin Hill Ln	75007
Robin Meadow Cir & Dr	75007
Rochelle Ln	75007
Rock Springs Ct	75007
Rockbrook Dr	75007
Rockett Dr	75007
Rockwood Dr	75007
Rodin Ln	75006
Rolling Mdw	75010
Rolling Hills Cir & Dr	75007
Rolling Oaks Dr	
3900-3998	75007
4000-4099	75007
4200-4298	75010
Rooney Ln	75007
Rose Cliff Ln	75007
Rose Hill Rd	75007
Rosebud Cir & Ct	75006
E & W Rosemeade Cir & Pkwy	75007
Rosemon Ave	75006
Rosewood Pl	75006
Ross Ave	75006
Roundrock Cir & Dr	75007
Roussillon Dr	75007
Royal Palm Ln	75007
Rubery Dr	75010
Running Duke Dr	75006
E & W Russell Ave	75006
Rustic Ln	75007
Ryan Ave	75006
Saddlebrook Dr	75010
Sage Hill Dr	75010
Sagemont Dr	75010
Saginaw Ln	75010
Sahara Ct	75010
Saint Albans Dr	75007
Saint James Dr	75007
Saint Johns Cir	75010
Saint Pierre Dr	75006
Saint Tropez Dr	75006
Salem Dr	75006
Sam Houston Blvd & Cir	75006
Sam Rayburn Run	75007
San Francisco St	75007
San Michael Dr	75006
San Saba Dr	75007
San Sebastian Dr	75006
San Simeon Pl	75006
Sancerre Ln	75007
Sandpiper Ln	75007
Sandy Lake Rd	75006
Sandy Ridge Ct	75007
Santa Fe Trl	75007
Sausalito Dr	75007
Savoy Dr	75006
Saxony Pl	75007
Scarborough Ln	75006
School Rd	75006
Scott Mill Cir	75006
Scott Mill Rd	
2300-2498	75006
2500-2599	75006
2800-3099	75007
Seabiscuit St	75010
Sedgeway Ln	75006
Selene Dr	75006
E Seminole Cir, Ct, Pl & Trl	75007
Senlac Dr	75006
Sequoyah Way	75006
Serenity Ct	75010
Shadow Moss Way	75007
Shady Lake Cir	75006
Shadygrove Ln	75006
Shadyview Cv	75006
Shakespeare St	75010
Shannon Cir, Ct & Pl	75006
Shawnee Trl	75007
Sheffield Sq	75007
Shenandoah Dr	75007
Shepherd Ln	75007
Sheraton Dr	75007
Sheridan Dr	75010
Sherwood Ln & Pl	75006
Shonka Dr	75007
Sierra Dr	75007
Silver Maple Dr	75007
Silverado Dr	75007
Silverleaf Dr	75007
Silverspring Rd	75006
Silverway Ln	75010
Silverwood Dr	75007
Simmons Pkwy	75006
Simpson Ln	75006
Sinclair St	75010
Sioux St	75010
Skylane Dr	75006
N Slope	75007
Smoky Hill Rd	75006
Snow Owl Ct	75010
Sojourn Dr	75006
Somerville Ln	75007
Sonata Ln	75007
Southampton Dr	75007
Southern Cir, Ct & Pl	75006
Southern Oaks	75007
Southmoor Dr	75006
Sparling Way Dr	75006
Spicewood Ln	75006
Spring Ave & Cir	75006
Spring Hollow Dr	75007
Spring Leaf Dr	75006
Spring Run Dr	75006
Springdale Dr	75006
Springwood Pl	75006
Spurwood Dr	75010
Spyglass Ct & Dr	75007
Squireswood Dr	75006
Staffordshire Dr	75007
Stain Glass Ct	75007
Standridge Dr	75007
Stanford Ct	75006
Starr Ct	75007
State Highway 121	75010
Station Pl	75007
Statler Dr & Pl	75007
Steenson Dr	75007
Stefani Ct & Pl	75007
Stein Way	75007
Steinbeck St	75010
Stewart Dr	75010
Stillwater Trl	75007
Stockton Dr	75010
Stone Dr	75010
Stone Glen Ln	75007
Stone Mill Cv	75006
Stonebrook Cir & Dr	75007
Stonecreek Ct, Dr & Pl	75006
Stonegate Dr	75010
Stonehenge Ln	75006
Stonewood Dr	75006
Stradivarius Ln	75007
Strait Ln	75010
Study Ln	75006
Sugar Creek Dr	75007
Sugarbush Dr & Ln	75007
Summer Lake Trl	75007
Summerhill Dr	75007
Summertree Dr	75006
Summit Cir & Dr	75006
Sumners Ct	75007
Sundance Cir	75007
Sunflower Cir	75007
Sunnyslope Dr	75007
Sunridge Rd	75006
Sunrise Ln	75006
Sunset Point Ln	75007
Sunstone Dr	75006
N & S Surrey Dr	75006
Surveyor Blvd	75006
Susan Ln	75007
Sussex Dr	75007
Sutters Mill Dr	75007
Sutton Dr	75006
Swan Forest Dr	75010
Sweetspring Dr	75007
Sycamore Dr	75007
Tahlequah Trl	75007
Tampico Dr	75006
Taos Trl	75007
Tappan Cir	75006
Tarpley Rd	75006
Tarrytown Dr & Pl	75007
Tartan Dr	75006
Taxco Dr	75006
Teakwood Trl	75006
Tecumseh Trce	75006

Telegraph Hill Trl 75007
Terrace Trl 75006
Terry Way 75006
Teton Pl 75006
Thomas Ln 75010
Thompson Dr 75010
Tiburon 75006
Tidal Dr 75007
Tierra Calle 75006
Timberleaf Cir, Dr & Pl 75006
Timberline Dr 75007
Timberwood 75006
Toews Ln 75007
Toluca Dr 75006
Topaz Dr 75010
Toulon Ln 75007
Towerwood Dr 75006
Trade Ctr 75007
N Trail Dr 75006
Trailview Dr 75007
Travis Dr 75006
Tree Line Dr 75007
Trend Dr 75006
E & W Trinity Mills Rd 75006
Trinity Springs Dr 75007
Trinity Square Dr 75006
Trinity Valley Dr 75006
Troutt Dr 75010
Turtle Rock Ct 75007
Upfield Dr 75006
Valez Dr 75007
Valley Ml 75006
Valley Glen Ct & Dr 75010
Valleycrest Ln 75006
Valleywood Dr 75006
Valwood Pkwy 75006
Van Winkle Dr 75007
E Vandergriff Dr 75006
Vantage Dr 75006
Venture Ct 75006
Vera Cruz Dr 75010
Verlaine Dr 75007
Versailles Dr 75007
Vestal Ln 75007
Via Vis 75006
Via Avenida 75006
Via Balboa 75006
Via Ballena 75006
Via Barcelona 75006
Via Blanca 75006
Via Bonita 75006
Via Bravo 75006
Via Catalina 75006
Via Cordova 75006
Via Corona 75006
Via Del Mar 75006
Via Del Norte Cir 75006
Via Del Oro 75006
Via Del Plata 75006
Via Del Sur 75006
Via Estrada 75006
Via La Paloma 75006
Via Los Altos 75006
Via Madonna 75006
Via Miramonte 75006
Via Sevilla 75006
Via Sonoma 75006
Via Valencia 75006
Via Ventura Cir 75006
Victoria Cv & Rd 75007
Viewmont Dr 75007
Villa Pl 75006
Vinylex Dr 75006
Virginia Pine Cir & Dr 75007
Vista Crest Dr 75007
Vista Glen Ln 75007
Vista Oaks Dr 75007
Vista Verde Cir 75006
Vista Woods Cir & Dr 75007
Wagonwheel Cir, Ct & Dr 75006
Wainwright Way 75007
Walker Dr & Pl 75007
Wallace Dr 75006
Walnut Ave, Plz & St 75006
Walnut Grove Ln 75007
Warberry Rd 75007
Warner St 75006
Waterford Way 75006
Watermill Ct 75006
Waynoka Dr 75007
Waypoint Dr 75006
Webb Chapel Rd 75006
Wedgewood Ln 75006
Wellington Rd 75007
E & W Wentwood Dr 75007
Westbrook Dr 75007
Westgate Dr 75006
Westgrove Dr 75006
Westminster Dr & Pl 75007
Westridge Ave 75006
Westway Cir 75006
Westwind Dr 75006
Westwood Cir 75006
Whippoorwill Ln 75006
White Ash Rd 75007
White Rose Ln 75007
Whitehurst Ln 75007
Whitlock Ln 75006
Whitman Ln 75010
Whitney Ln 75007
Wichita Dr 75010
Wickham Cir 75007
Wild Cherry Dr 75010
Wild Plum Dr 75010
Wilderness Way 75007
Wildrose 75007
Wiley Post Rd 75006
William Ln 75006
Williamson Ln 75010
Willow Pl & Rd 75006
Willow Ridge Cir & Trl 75007
Willow Wood Dr 75010
Willowbrook Trl 75006
Willowdale Dr 75006
Willowgate Ln 75006
Wilson Ln 75010
Wiltshire Dr 75007
Wimbledon Ct 75006
Winding Creek Dr 75007
Windsor Rd 75007
Windy Crest Cir & Dr 75007
Wingate Dr 75007
Winterberry Dr 75007
Wintergreen Rd 75006
Winterlake Dr 75006
Woodbury 75007
Woodcreek 75006
Woodcrest Ln 75006
Woodcroft Cir 75006
Woodhaven 75007
Woodland Trl 75007
Woodside Rd 75007
Wyandotte St 75010
Yellowstone Ln 75006
Yewpon Ct & Dr 75007
York Ct & Dr 75006
Yorkshire Dr 75007
Yosemite Ct 75006
Young Dr 75010
Zavala Ct 75010

NUMBERED STREETS

1st St 75010
4th Ave 75006
5th Ave 75006

CEDAR HILL TX

General Delivery 75104

POST OFFICE BOXES MAIN OFFICE STATIONS AND BRANCHES

Box No.s
All PO Boxes 75106

RURAL ROUTES

01, 02, 03, 05, 06, 07, 08, 09, 10, 11, 12, 13, 14, 15, 16, 17 75104

NAMED STREETS

Acres St 75104
Alabaster Pl 75104
Alden Dr 75104
Allen Ct & Dr 75104
Amberleaf Ct 75104
American Way 75104
Anderson Rd 75104
Angel St 75104
Angela Ct & Dr 75104
Antoine St 75104
Applewood Dr 75104
Aquarius Cir & Dr 75104
Arbor Dr 75104
Aries Ct & St 75104
Armadillo Ct 75104
Armstrong Dr 75104
Ash Ln 75104
Astoria Dr 75104
Atkins St 75104
Autumn Run Ct 75104
Azalea Ln 75104
Bailey Dr 75104
Baker Dr 75104
N Balfour Dr 75104
Ballard St 75104
Ballpark Way 75104
Bear Creek Rd 75104
Beard Dr 75104
Beatty Dr 75104
Becky Ln 75104
Bee Creek Dr 75104
Bee Hive Dr 75104
Beechwood Ln 75104
Belclaire Cir 75104
E & W Belt Line Rd 75104
Bending Oak Dr 75104
Bennett St 75104
Bent Creek Ct 75104
Bentgrass Cir 75104
Bentle St 75104
Bentle Branch Ln 75104
Bentwater Pkwy 75104
Berry Ln 75104
Beverly Cir 75104
Birchwood Ln 75104
Birdie Holw 75104
Birkshire Ln 75104
Biscayne Dr 75104
Bishop St 75104
Bistineau Dr 75104
Black Walnut Trl 75104
Blewitt Dr 75104
Blue Ridge Dr 75104
Bluebonnet Dr 75104
Bluechalk Dr 75104
Bluff Ct 75104
Bluff Ridge Dr 75104
Bosher Dr 75104
Boyd St 75104
Bradshaw St 75104
Brandenburg St 75104
Braswell St 75104
Bray St 75104
Breezeway Ct 75104
Breseman St 75104
Brewer Dr 75104
Briarglen Dr 75104
Briarwood Cv 75104
Briggs St 75104
Bristol Dr 75104
N & S Broad St 75104
Brooks Ct & Dr 75104
Brookside Dr 75104
Bryan Pl 75104
Bryant Ln 75104
Burleson St 75104
Burney Ct 75104
Busby Dr 75104
Caddy Ct 75104
Cain Ct & Dr 75104
Calvert Dr 75104
Cambridge Dr 75104
N & S Cannady Cir, Ct & Dr 75104
Canterbury Ct 75104
Canyon Rdg 75104
Canyon View Ct 75104
Capricorn Dr & St 75104
Carberry St 75104
Carolyn T Hunt Dr 75104
Carr St 75104
Cartwright Dr 75104
Castleman Dr 75104
Cathey St 75104
Cecile Cir 75104
Cedar Cir, St & Ter 75104
Cedar Bend Dr 75104
Cedar Cove Cir 75104
N & S Cedar Hill Rd 75104
Cedar Ridge Dr 75104
Cedar Trail Dr 75104
Cedar Valley Ln 75104
Cedarview Dr & St 75104
Cedarwood Dr 75104
Chadwick Ct & Dr 75104
Chambers St 75104
Chamblin Ct & Dr 75104
Chancellor Dr 75104
Chaparral Trl 75104
Chapel Pl 75104
Chapman St 75104
Charlotte Dr 75104
Charming Ave 75104
Chauvin Dr 75104
Cherlynne Dr 75104
Cherrytree Ln 75104
Chestnut Ln 75104
Christine Dr 75104
Christopher Dr 75104
Cindy Dr 75104
City View Ct 75104
Clancy Nolan Dr 75104
N & S Clark Cir & Rd 75104
Clear Creek Ct 75104
Clement Ct & Dr 75104
Cliffside 75104
Clover Hill Ln 75104
Cobblestone Ct 75104
Collins Blvd 75104
Cooper St 75104
Copeland Dr 75104
Couch Ln 75104
Countryside Dr 75104
County Line Rd 75104
Cove Hollow Dr 75104
Cove Meadow Ct 75104
Cox St 75104
Cozy Ln 75104
Crabtree Ct 75104
Crancord Dr 75104
Creekstone Ct & Dr 75104
Creekwood Dr 75104
Crenshaw Dr 75104
Cresthaven Dr 75104
Cresthill Dr 75104
Crestpark Dr 75104
Crestridge Dr 75104
Crestview Dr 75104
Crestway Dr 75104
Crestwood Dr 75104
Cross Creek Dr 75104
Crystal Cv 75104
Cumberland Dr 75104
Curtis Ln 75104
Cypress Bend Dr 75104
Daisy Ct 75104
Dandelion Dr 75104
Daniel Ln 75104
Dawson St 75104
Deerfield Ct 75104
Deloach Dr 75104
Delta Dr 75104
Dennis Dr 75104
Diamond Point Dr 75104
Dillard Cir 75104
Dogwood Dr 75104
Dollins St 75104
Donice Ct 75104
Donna Dr 75104
Dorcheat Dr 75104
Douglas Dr 75104
Driftwood 75104
N & S Duncanville Rd 75104
Dunwick Dr 75104
Eagle Pl 75104
Eagle Creek Dr 75104
Eden Dr 75104
Edgefield Way 75104
Elise 75104
Elk Pass 75104
Elliott Dr 75104
Elm Springs Ct 75104
Emerald Sound Dr 75104
Essex Dr 75104
Euless Dr 75104
Everest Ct & Dr 75104
Evergreen Trl 75104
Fairway Dr 75104
Falcon Holw & Trl 75104
Fieldstone Dr 75104
Finley St 75104
Flagstone 75104
Flameleaf Ln 75104
Flower Dr 75104
E Fm 1382
100-476 75104
475-475 75106
477-499 75104
478-498 75104
W Fm 1382 75104
Forbus St 75104
Ford Dr 75104
Forest Creek Dr 75104
Forest Hill Ct 75104
Fossil Ridge Dr 75104
Foster St 75104
Fountain View Blvd 75104
Fox Glenn 75104
Freedom Way 75104
Fuller Dr 75104
Gannon Way 75104
Garner Cir 75104
Garrett Ct 75104
Gemini Dr 75104
Germany Dr 75104
Gibson St 75104
Glacier Ln 75104
Glade Forest Ct 75104
Glencrest Cv & Dr 75104
Golden Pond Dr 75104
Grady Ln 75104
Grand Teton St 75104
Grand View Ct 75104
Graves Ct 75104
Green Pastures Dr 75104
Greenbriar Trl 75104
Greenleaf Ct 75104
Grigsby Way 75104
Grounds Rd 75104
Grove Mnr 75104
Grover Ct 75104
Hageman 75104
Halifax Ct & Dr 75104
Hall St 75104
Hamilton Ct & Dr 75104
Hampshire Ln 75104
Hannah Cir 75104
Harbor Lights Dr 75104
Hardwick Ln 75104
Hardy St 75104
Harrington Dr 75104
Hartin Dr 75104
Harvell Ct & Dr 75104
Harvest Glen Dr 75104
Hastings Ct & Dr 75104
Haswell St 75104
Hawthorn Dr 75104
Hayes St 75104
Heath Cir 75104
Heather Cir 75104
W Hendricks St 75104
Hickerson St 75104
Hickman St 75104
Hickory Knob Cir 75104
Hidden Canyon Loop 75104
Hidden Creek Ct 75104
Hidden Lakes Ct & Dr 75104
Hideaway 75104
High Dr 75104
High Meadows Way 75104
High Pointe Cir & Ln 75104
High Valley Ln 75104
S Highland Dr 75104
Highview Dr 75104
N & S Highway 67 75104
Hillcrest Ct 75104
Hillside Dr 75104
Hilltop Dr 75104
Hines Dr 75104
Hollow Creek Dr 75104
Holly Ln 75104
Holly Ridge Ct 75104
Holveck Dr 75104
Honeysuckle Ln 75104
Hood St 75104
Horton Dr 75104
Houston St 75104
Hunter Dr 75104
Imperial Pl 75104
Indian Trl 75104
Indigo Ct 75104
Industrial Way 75104
Iris Ln 75104
Ironwood Ln 75104
Ivy Ct 75104
Jack St 75104
James St 75104
Janet Ct 75104
Jasmine Cir 75104
Jealouse Way 75104
Jefferson St 75104
Jesse Ramsey Blvd 75104
N & S Joe Wilson Rd 75104
Johnston Ln 75104
Jones St 75104
Jorgenson Rd 75104
Juniper Ridge Rd 75104
Justice St 75104
Karen Dr 75104
Kari Ann Ct & Dr 75104
Kathrine Ct 75104
Kck Way 75104
Keessee Dr 75104
Kenya St 75104
Kimmel Dr 75104
King St 75104
King James Ct 75104
Kingswood Dr 75104
Kirk Ln 75104
Knight St 75104
Knob Hill Ct 75104
Knoll Manor Ct 75104
Koscher Ln 75104
Kristi Ln 75104
L Thompson St 75104
La Reata Ct 75104
Lake Cv 75104
Lake Ridge Pkwy 75104
Lake Vista Ct 75104
S Lakeview Dr 75104
Langston St 75104
Larue Dr 75104
Laurel St 75104
Laurel Hills Ct 75104
Lavender Dr 75104
Lay St 75104
Layman Dr 75104
Lazy Grove Ct 75104
Lee St 75104
Legend Ct 75104
Leisure Dr 75104
Lemons St 75104
Levee Ln 75104
Libra Dr 75104
Lighthouse Ct 75104
Linda Ln 75104
Lisa Ln 75104
E & W Little Creek Rd 75104
Lofton St 75104
Lois Ln 75104
Long Ct 75104
Longhorn Blvd 75104
Longleaf Dr 75104
Lookout Ct 75104
N & S Loop Dr 75104
Lovern Ct & St 75104
Lowe Dr 75104
Madison Dr 75104
Madlynne Dr 75104
Magic Valley Ln 75104
Magnolia Ln 75104
N & S Main St 75104
Majestic Park Ln 75104
Mallard Pointe Dr 75104
Mandy Ct 75104
Mansfield Rd 75104
Maplegrove Rd 75104
Marigold Dr 75104
Marker Dr 75104
Mars Dr 75104
Marshall Dr 75104
Mason Ln 75104
Massey Ln 75104
Masters 75104
Matterhorn St 75104
Mayes St 75104
Mayfield Dr 75104
Mcalister St 75104
Mccary St 75104
Mccomb Ln 75104
Mcgehee Ave 75104
Mckinley St 75104
Mcmackin St 75104
Mcmillan Dr 75104
Meadow Ridge Dr 75104
Meadow Vista Dr 75104
Meadowbend Dr 75104
Meadowbrooke Dr 75104
Meadowglen Dr 75104
Meandering Dr 75104
Melissa Ct 75104
Melody Cir 75104
Merrifield St 75104
Mid Lake Dr 75104
Middleton Dr 75104
Miles Ln 75104
E Miller Dr 75104
Mimosa Trl 75104
Mobley Rd 75104
Molly 75104
Molton Ct 75104
Monique 75104
Moonlight Bay Dr 75104
Moore St 75104
Morgan Cir 75104
Mosley Ct 75104
Moss Dr 75104
Mount Lebanon Rd 75104
Mount Mckinley Pl 75104
Mountain Lakes Dr 75104
Mountain View Ct 75104
Muirfield 75104
Mulberry Ct 75104
Mustang Ct 75104
Mystic Trl 75104
Mystic Shore Dr 75104
Nafus St 75104
Nance Dr 75104
Natchez Dr 75104
Nelson Dr 75104
Neptune Ct & Dr 75104
Newton Dr 75104
Nikki Dr 75104
Northwood Trl 75104
Nottingham Dr 75104
Nutting St 75104
Oak Ln 75104
Oak Creek Dr 75104
Oak Meadow Ln 75104
Oak Shadow Ct 75104
Oak Tree Cv 75104
Oakhill Ln 75104

Old Clark Rd ... 75104
Old Oak Dr ... 75104
Old Straus Rd ... 75104
Olympus St ... 75104
Orchard Hill Dr ... 75104
Overland Trl ... 75104
Overlook Cir ... 75104
Oxbow Dr ... 75104
Pagewood Ct ... 75104
Paintbrush Ct ... 75104
Paradise Ct ... 75104
Park Xing ... 75104
Park Garden Ct ... 75104
Parker Ct ... 75104
E & W Parkerville Rd ... 75104
Parkside Dr ... 75104
Parkway Ter ... 75104
Parkwood Dr ... 75104
E & W Parview Cir & Ct ... 75104
Passive Dr ... 75104
Patrick Ct ... 75104
Patton Dr ... 75104
Paul Dr ... 75104
Payne St ... 75104
Peak ... 75104
Pebble Beach Ln ... 75104
Pebblestone Ct ... 75104
Pecan Trl ... 75104
Pecan Ridge Ct ... 75104
Pemberton Pl ... 75104
Penn Pl ... 75104
Perry Ct ... 75104
Pettigrew Ct ... 75104
Phillip Dr ... 75104
Pickard Dr ... 75104
Pico St ... 75104
Pikes Peak ... 75104
Pine Tree Ln ... 75104
Pinehurst Ln ... 75104
Pinnacle Dr ... 75104
Plateau St ... 75104
E & W Pleasant Run Rd ... 75104
Plume Ct ... 75104
Plummer Dr ... 75104
Pogue St ... 75104
Poinsetta Ln ... 75104
Point Vw ... 75104
Ponds Ct & Way ... 75104
Pondview Dr ... 75104
Pool St ... 75104
N & S Potter St ... 75104
Prairie Acres Cv ... 75104
Preston Trl ... 75104
Prince St ... 75104
Promontory Dr ... 75104
Quail Ridge Dr ... 75104
Rabbit Rdg ... 75104
Ragland Dr ... 75104
Rainbow Ct & Ln ... 75104
Rainier St ... 75104
Rainsong Dr ... 75104
Ramsey St ... 75104
Ranch Ct ... 75104
Randy Rd ... 75104
Ravine Trl ... 75104
Rebecca Dr ... 75104
Red Oak Trl ... 75104
Redbud Ct ... 75104
Redding Dr ... 75104
Reeves Ln ... 75104
Reitz Dr ... 75104
Renaissance Pl ... 75104
Richards Dr ... 75104
Ridgecrest Dr ... 75104
Ridgeview Dr ... 75104
Right Field Ct ... 75104
River Mountain Ct ... 75104
N Roberts Rd ... 75104
Robin Rd ... 75104
Rock Ridge Dr ... 75104
Rockett Ln ... 75104
Rockies Ln ... 75104
Rocky Acres Rd ... 75104
Rocky Brook Dr ... 75104
Rocky Creek Cir & Dr ... 75104
Rohne Dr ... 75104
Rolling Oaks Rdg ... 75104
Rosebud Ct ... 75104
Rosehill Ln ... 75104
Rosewood Ln ... 75104
Round Rock Rd ... 75104
Royal Lytham Ct ... 75104
Royal Vista Dr ... 75104
Runyan St ... 75104
Ruth ... 75104
Saddlewood Ct ... 75104
Sagittarius Dr ... 75104
Samuel St ... 75104
Sanctuary Dr ... 75104
Sand Dollar Ct ... 75104
Sandlewood Ln ... 75104
Saturn Dr ... 75104
Scenic Ct ... 75104
Scott Dr ... 75104
Sebring Dr ... 75104
Serenity Dr ... 75104
Shady Brook Ln ... 75104
Shadyridge Dr ... 75104
Shadywood Dr ... 75104
Shakleford Cir ... 75104
Sharon Dr ... 75104
Sharp Dr ... 75104
Sheffield Dr ... 75104
Shell St ... 75104
Shenandoah ... 75104
Sherman Dr ... 75104
Sherwood Ct ... 75104
Shields Ave ... 75104
Shore Crest Dr ... 75104
Short St ... 75104
Sierra Way ... 75104
Simmons Way ... 75104
Simon Dr ... 75104
Sims Dr ... 75104
Singletree Cv ... 75104
Sink St ... 75104
Skyline Ct ... 75104
Sleepy Hollow Dr ... 75104
Smith Dr ... 75104
Somerset Dr ... 75104
Sonterra Dr ... 75104
Southern Oaks Dr ... 75104
Southwestern Dr ... 75104
Southwick Dr ... 75104
Spring Hollow Dr ... 75104
Springfield Dr ... 75104
Springtime Dr ... 75104
Stafford Ct & St ... 75104
Starlight Ct ... 75104
Steadman Dr ... 75104
Stewart St ... 75104
Stone Oak Ct ... 75104
Stone Trail Dr ... 75104
Stonefield Ln ... 75104
Stonewall Dr ... 75104
Stonewood Dr ... 75104
Stoney Creek Dr ... 75104
Stoney Hills Dr ... 75104
Straus Rd ... 75104
Streamside Dr ... 75104
Stringer Dr ... 75104
Suburban St ... 75104
Suffolk Ln ... 75104
Sugar Mill Rd ... 75104
Sullivan Dr ... 75104
Summer Brook Ct ... 75104
Summers Dr ... 75104
Summerwood Ln ... 75104
Summit Pl ... 75104
Sunflower Ln ... 75104
Sunrise Ct ... 75104
Sunset Xing ... 75104
Sunset Ridge Cir ... 75104
Sweeping Meadows Ln ... 75104
Sweetgum Dr ... 75104
Switzer Ct & Ln ... 75104
Tamaron Cv ... 75104
Tangle Way Ct ... 75104
Tanglewood Dr ... 75104
Tar Rd ... 75104
Taurus Dr ... 75104
Taylor St ... 75104
Teakwood Ln ... 75104
Tee Box Pl ... 75104
Ten Mile Dr ... 75104
Terrace Ln ... 75104
Texas St ... 75104
Texas Plume Rd ... 75104
Thorton Ct & Dr ... 75104
Tidwell St ... 75104
Tiger Trl ... 75104
Timber Creek Ct ... 75104
Timber Ridge Ct & Dr ... 75104
Timberline Dr ... 75104
Tindle St ... 75104
Topper Dr ... 75104
Tower Dr ... 75104
Town Square Blvd ... 75104
Town View Dr ... 75104
Trail Ridge Dr ... 75104
Trailwood Ct ... 75104
Tranquility Ln ... 75104
Trees Ct & Dr ... 75104
Tuley St ... 75104
Tulip Ct & Ln ... 75104
Tunnel St ... 75104
Turner Ct & Way ... 75104
Twilight Dr ... 75104
Twin Hills St ... 75104
Uptown Blvd ... 75104
Valerie Dr ... 75104
Valley View Dr ... 75104
Vance St ... 75104
Vedral Pl ... 75104
Venus Ct & St ... 75104
Vicki Ln ... 75104
Vincent St ... 75104
Vines Dr ... 75104
Vista Blvd ... 75104
Walnut Ridge Ct ... 75104
Walters Dr ... 75104
Wand Dr ... 75104
Watercourse Way ... 75104
N & S Waterford Oaks Cir & Dr ... 75104
Waters Edge Dr ... 75104
Waterstone Dr ... 75104
Waterview Dr ... 75104
Weaver St ... 75104
Webb Pl ... 75104
Wedgewood Ln ... 75104
Welcome ... 75104
Wells Ct ... 75104
Wentwood Dr ... 75104
Westar Ln ... 75104
Whispering Trl ... 75104
Whispering Oaks Cv ... 75104
White Ct & Dr ... 75104
White Oak ... 75104
White Tail Rdg ... 75104
Whitley St ... 75104
Whitney St ... 75104
Wilderness Pass ... 75104
Wildwood Ridge Ct ... 75104
Willacy Cir ... 75104
Williams St ... 75104
Willis Dr ... 75104
Willow Ln ... 75104
Willow Wood Dr ... 75104
Wilshire Ct ... 75104
Wilson St ... 75104
Wind Haven Ct ... 75104
Winding Crk ... 75104
Windmill Ct ... 75104
Windmill Hill Ln ... 75104
Windswept Dr ... 75104
Windy Ln ... 75104
Windy Meadow Dr ... 75104
E & W Wintergreen Rd ... 75104
Wisdom Dr ... 75104
Wishing Well Ct ... 75104
Witherspoon Ct & Rd ... 75104
Wolfe St ... 75104
Wood Ln ... 75104
Wood Dale Cir ... 75104
Wood Lake Dr ... 75104
Wood Ridge Dr ... 75104
Woodall Dr ... 75104
Wooded Creek Dr ... 75104
Woodland Manor Dr ... 75104
Worden Dr ... 75104
Wylie St ... 75104
Yorkshire Dr ... 75104
Young Dr ... 75104

CEDAR PARK TX

General Delivery ... 78613

POST OFFICE BOXES MAIN OFFICE STATIONS AND BRANCHES

Box No.s
All PO Boxes ... 78630

NAMED STREETS

Abbey Ln ... 78613
Abbotsbury Dr ... 78613
Acorn Ct ... 78613
Adventure Ln ... 78613
Alamo Plaza Dr ... 78613
Aldworth Dr ... 78613
Alexandra Ln ... 78613
Allerford Ct ... 78613
Allison Way ... 78613
Alta Monte Dr ... 78613
Amaryllis Ave ... 78613
Ambling Trl ... 78613
Amelia Dr ... 78613
Amy Lynn Ln ... 78613
Anderson Xing ... 78613
Anderson Mill Rd ... 78613
Andrew Cv ... 78613
Angus Dr ... 78613
Anna Ct ... 78613
Annadale Dr ... 78613
Antelope Cv & Rdg ... 78613
Anthony Ct ... 78613
Apache Cv & Dr ... 78613
Apollo Ln ... 78613
Appennini Cv & Way ... 78613
Argento Pl ... 78613
Ariella Dr ... 78613
Armatrading Dr ... 78613
Arrow Point Dr ... 78613
Arrow Wood Rd ... 78613
Arrowhead Trl ... 78613
Ascot Ln ... 78613
Ashbaugh St ... 78613
Aspen Cv ... 78613
Aster Pass ... 78613
Audra St ... 78613
Autumn Bend Ln ... 78613
Autumn Fire Cv & Dr ... 78613
Avante Dr ... 78613
Avenue Of The Stars ... 78613
Avery Elissa Ln ... 78613
Avery Ranch Blvd ... 78613
Avery Woods Ln ... 78613
Avondale Dr ... 78613
Ayes Ct ... 78613
Azalea Dr ... 78613
Azzuro Way ... 78613
Bagdad Rd ... 78613
Bakers Way ... 78613
Bald Cypress Cv ... 78613
Bamboo Trl ... 78613
Bandstand Ln ... 78613
Banyon Cv ... 78613
Barnett Dr ... 78613
Baron Ln ... 78613
Barrilla St ... 78613
Barsham Ct ... 78613
Barzona Bnd ... 78613
Basie Bnd ... 78613
Bayberry Ct ... 78613
Bedrock Ct ... 78613
Beechnut Cv & Trce ... 78613
Beeleigh Ct ... 78613
Belgian Bnd ... 78613
N & S Bell Blvd ... 78613
Bellamy Cir ... 78613
Ben Doran Ct ... 78613
Benevento Way ... 78613
Bent Bow Cv & Dr ... 78613
Berkshire Way ... 78613
Big Bend Dr ... 78613
Big Meadow Dr ... 78613
Big Spring Dr ... 78613
Big Sur Dr ... 78613
Big Thicket Dr ... 78613
Bindon Dr ... 78613
Birch Dr ... 78613
Birchington Dr ... 78613
Bird Dog Ln ... 78613
Birdie Cv ... 78613
Birds Nest Ct ... 78613
Bison Bnd ... 78613
Bit Ln ... 78613
Black Cherry Dr ... 78613
Blackbird Ct ... 78613
Blackjack Pass ... 78613
Blazing Star Trl ... 78613
Blue Bell Dr ... 78613
Blue Oak Cir ... 78613
N & S Blue Ridge Dr & Pkwy ... 78613
Blue Sage Dr ... 78613
Bluebonnet Dr ... 78613
Bluejack Pl ... 78613
Bluejay Dr ... 78613
Bluff Point Bnd ... 78613
Bluff View Rd ... 78613
Bmc Dr ... 78613
Boca Chica Dr ... 78613
Boerne Dr ... 78613
Bogart Rd ... 78613
Bohica Way ... 78613
Bois D Arc Ln ... 78613
Bondick Rd ... 78613
Bonnyrigg Ct ... 78613
Bow Ridge Cv & Dr ... 78613
Bower Dr ... 78613
Bowling Ct ... 78613
Bowstring Bnd ... 78613
Brahman Rd ... 78613
Bramble Dr ... 78613
Brangus Rd ... 78613
Branum Cv & Dr ... 78613
Brashear Ln ... 78613
Brazil Dr ... 78613
Brazos Bend Dr ... 78613
Breakaway Rd ... 78613
Brettonwoods Dr ... 78613
Brian Wood Ct & Dr ... 78613
Brianna Ct ... 78613
Briar Cv ... 78613
Briarwood Dr ... 78613
Bridal Path ... 78613
Bridal Path Cv ... 78613
Brighton Bend Ln ... 78613
Brindisi Way ... 78613
Brinkley Dr ... 78613
Briona Wood Ln ... 78613
Bristlewood Cv ... 78613
Brittway Ln ... 78613
Broken Arrow Dr ... 78613
Brook Bnd, Holw & Way ... 78613
Brook Meadow Trl ... 78613
Brookfield Cv ... 78613
Brookside Cv & Pass ... 78613
Brownstone Ln ... 78613
Brubeck Bnd ... 78613
Brushy Creek Loop & Rd ... 78613
Bryant Cv ... 78613
Bryce Canyon Dr ... 78613
Buck Ridge Rd ... 78613
Buckeye Trl ... 78613
Buckhaven Cv ... 78613
Buckshot Way ... 78613
Buckskin Rd ... 78613
N & S Buffalo Ave ... 78613
Bufflehead Ln ... 78613
Bull Creek Pkwy ... 78613
Bullhill Cv ... 78613
Bur Oak Cv ... 78613
Burnie Bishop Pl ... 78613
Burnt Oak Cir ... 78613
Butch Gap Cv ... 78613
Buttercup Creek Blvd ... 78613
Butternut Pl ... 78613
Byfield Dr ... 78613
C W Ranch Rd ... 78613
C-Bar Ranch Trl ... 78613
Cactus Flower Dr ... 78613
Cadillac Cv ... 78613
Camden Cv ... 78613
Cameron Cv ... 78613
Campfire Dr ... 78613
N & S Cannes Dr ... 78613
Canterbury Cv ... 78613
Canterfield Ln ... 78613
Canvasback Trl ... 78613
Canyon Springs Dr ... 78613
Caparzo Dr ... 78613
Caprock Ln ... 78613
Capulin Mtn ... 78613
Cardigan St ... 78613
Cardinal Ln ... 78613
Carol Michelle Cv ... 78613
Carriage Club Dr ... 78613
Carriage Hills Cv & Trl ... 78613
Casey Cv ... 78613
Cashell Wood Cv & Dr ... 78613
Cashew Ln ... 78613
Castellano Way ... 78613
Castleguard Way ... 78613
Cat Claw Cv ... 78613
Catamaran Cv ... 78613
Catchfly Cv ... 78613
Catherine Dr ... 78613
Cattle Dr ... 78613
Cedar Cv ... 78613
Cedar Brook Dr ... 78613
Cedar Crest Dr ... 78613
Cedar Hills Blvd ... 78613
Cedar Mound Pass ... 78613
Cedar Oaks Dr ... 78613
Cedar Park Dr ... 78613
N & S Celia Dr ... 78613
Cenizo Path ... 78613
Central Dr ... 78613
Century Ln ... 78613
Chaco Cyn ... 78613
Chalk Cv & Ln ... 78613
Challa Dr ... 78613
Chance Cv ... 78613
Charbray Ct ... 78613
Checker Dr ... 78613
Cherry Ln ... 78613
Cherry Creek Dr ... 78613
Cherry Laurel Dr ... 78613
Chestnut Xing ... 78613
Cheyenne Ln ... 78613
Chimney Swift Trl ... 78613
Chinaberry Ct ... 78613
Chinati St ... 78613
Chitina Ct ... 78613
Chula Vista Dr ... 78613
Church Park Rd ... 78613
Churchill Cv ... 78613
Cisco Cv ... 78613
Clarksville Ln ... 78613
Clay Ln ... 78613
Clayton Way ... 78613
Clear Creek Cv ... 78613
Clear Shadow Cv ... 78613
Clegg Dr ... 78613
Cloudview Cv & Ln ... 78613
Clover Ln ... 78613
Clover Flat Rd ... 78613
Clover Ridge Dr ... 78613
Cluck Creek Trl ... 78613
Clydesdale Dr ... 78613
Coachlamp Cv & Dr ... 78613
Colby Ln ... 78613
Colonial Pkwy ... 78613
Colorado Dr ... 78613
Colorado Bend Dr ... 78613
Colt St ... 78613
Colton Way ... 78613
Columbine Ave ... 78613
Comfort St ... 78613
Commercial Pkwy ... 78613
Conn Creek Rd ... 78613
Connor Mason Cv ... 78613
Connors Cv ... 78613
Continental Pass ... 78613
Coomes Pl ... 78613
Copford Ln ... 78613
Copper Breaks Ln ... 78613
Copper Lake Rd ... 78613
Copperlilly Cv ... 78613
Cora Cv ... 78613
Corabella Pl ... 78613
Coral Dr ... 78613
Corbin Way ... 78613
Cordova Cv ... 78613
Cortez Dr ... 78613
Costello Ct ... 78613
Cotton Pickin Ln ... 78613
Cottonweed Trl ... 78613
Cottonwood Cv ... 78613
Cottonwood Creek Trl ... 78613
N & S Cougar Ave ... 78613
Cougar Country ... 78613
Country Squire Dr ... 78613
Country View Way ... 78613
County Road 178 ... 78613
County Road 181 ... 78613
County Road 185 ... 78613
County Road 272 ... 78613
Courtney Ln ... 78613
Covala Dr ... 78613
Cox Cv ... 78613
Cranberry Cv ... 78613
Creekside Cv ... 78613
Creekstone Dr ... 78613
Creekwood Cv ... 78613
Crestview Dr ... 78613
Cricket Cv ... 78613
Cripple Creek Rd ... 78613
Crockett Rd ... 78613
Crocus Cv & Dr ... 78613
Crosswind Ct ... 78613
Crystal Hill Dr ... 78613
Culpepper Ln ... 78613
Culver Cliff Ln ... 78613
Cumberland Gap ... 78613
Cupolla Mtn ... 78613
Cypress Ln ... 78613
E Cypress Creek Rd ... 78613
Cypress Mill Cir ... 78613
Daffodil Dr ... 78613
Dagama Ct & Dr ... 78613
Dakota Dr ... 78613
Danciger Ln ... 78613
Dandridge Dr ... 78613
Danville Dr ... 78613
Darkwoods Ct & Dr ... 78613
Darless Dr ... 78613
Darnell Dr ... 78613
Dartford Bnd ... 78613
Dasher Dr ... 78613
David Cv ... 78613
Davis Mountain Loop ... 78613
Dayflower Trce ... 78613
Deepbrook Path ... 78613
Deer Grove Dr ... 78613
Deer Horn Cv & Dr ... 78613
Deer Ledge Trl ... 78613
Deer Run St ... 78613
Deer Trace Cv & Dr ... 78613
Deerfield Park Dr ... 78613
Del Norte Dr ... 78613
Del Roy Dr ... 78613
Denali Pass ... 78613
Derek Dr ... 78613
Dervingham Dr ... 78613

Desert Willow Pl 78613
Devil Rdg 78613
Dewberry Dr 78613
Diddley Cv 78613
Dijon Dr 78613
Diner Dr 78613
Dior Dr 78613
Disantis Pl 78613
Discovery Blvd 78613
Doefield Dr 78613
Dogwood Trl 78613
Doris Ln 78613
Dove Cir 78613
Dove Haven Loop 78613
Dove Hill Dr 78613
Dover Cv & Pass 78613
Drifting Leaf Dr 78613
Driftwood Dr 78613
Drop Tine Dr 78613
Drue Ln 78613
Dry Bean Cv 78613
Dry Creek Cv 78613
Dry Gulch Bnd 78613
Dunbar Ct 78613
Duncan Dr 78613
Durlston Ct 78613
Duster Cv 78613
Eagle Wing Dr 78613
Ebbsfleet Dr 78613
Ebony Ln 78613
Echo Ridge Ln 78613
Eclipse Cv 78613
Edelweiss Dr 78613
Edgewood Cir 78613
Edwards Walk Dr 78613
El Salido Pkwy 78613
El Sol Dr 78613
Eleanor Way 78613
Elkins Ln 78613
Elm Ct 78613
Elm Forest Dr 78613
Elmwood Cv & Trl 78613
Ely Ct 78613
Emily Cv 78613
Enchanted Rock Dr 78613
Erica Kaitlin Ln 78613
Etta James Cv 78613
Ezra Ct 78613
Fairhill Cv 78613
Fairweather Way 78613
Fall Creek Dr & Loop 78613
Fallen Oaks Dr 78613
Falling Leaves Ct 78613
Falmer Ct 78613
Farleigh Ln 78613
Farrington Ct 78613
Fawn Valley Dr 78613
Fawnfield Dr 78613
Feather Nest Dr 78613
Feathergrass Ct 78613
Fence Post Pass 78613
Fern Ct 78613
Fernglade 78613
Feta Ct 78613
Fieldstone St 78613
Fiorellino Pl 78613
Fire Ln 78613
Fire Glow Cv 78613
Flagstone Ct 78613
Flaming Tree Ct 78613
Flyway Ln 78613
Forest Trl 78613
Forest Oaks Path 78613
Foster Dr 78613
Founder Dr 78613
Fox Sparrow Trl 78613
Foxboro Ln 78613
Franklin Mountain Dr 78613
Friesian Ln 78613
N & S Frontier Ln 78613
Frostdale Dr 78613
S Gadwall Ln 78613
Galiceno 78613
Galloway Dr 78613
E Gann Hill Dr 78613
Gardenia Cir 78613
Garner Dr 78613
Garrett Cv 78613
Gaspar Bnd 78613
Gatepost Ct 78613
Gator Creek Dr 78613
Gholson Dr 78613
Giacomo Cv 78613
Giddens Dr 78613
Gillintr Dr 78613
Glacial Stream Ln 78613
Glacier Dr & Pass 78613
Glen Burnie Dr 78613
Glen Field Dr 78613
Glen Hollow St 78613
Glenwood Trl 78613
Gloucester Dr 78613
Gold Rush Dr 78613
Gold Star Dr 78613
Golden Arrow Ave 78613
Goldfinch Cv & Dr 78613
Gouda Ct 78613
Grand Falls Dr 78613
Grand Oaks Loop 78613
Grandridge Trl 78613
Granger Ln 78613
Granite Basin Ct 78613
Grapevine Dr 78613
Grayson Cv 78613
Great Valley Dr 78613
Greater Scaup Ln 78613
Green Field Dr 78613
Greer Dr 78613
Gretchen Dr 78613
Grist Ln 78613
Guara Dr 78613
Haleys Way 78613
Hall St 78613
Halter Ln 78613
Hangtree Cv 78613
Hannah Kay Ln 78613
Happy Cow Ln 78613
Harvest Cv 78613
Harvest Bend Ln 78613
Harvest Moon Dr & Pl 78613
Hatch Rd 78613
Hawk Dr 78613
Hawks Nest Cv 78613
Hawksbury Way 78613
Hawthorn Cv 78613
Heather Dr 78613
Heathmount Dr 78613
Hegarty Dr 78613
Henry Rifle Rd 78613
Heppner Dr 78613
Heritage Hill Cv 78613
Heritage Park Dr 78613
Hickory Dr 78613
Hickory Run Dr 78613
Highland Ct & Dr 78613
Hill Country Dr 78613
Hillcrest Dr 78613
Hillery Cv 78613
Hilltree Ln 78613
Hobart Dr 78613
Hoffman Ct 78613
Hollis Ln 78613
Hollow Ridge Dr 78613
Holly Trl 78613
Hollybrook Cv 78613
Honey Creek Ln 78613
Honey Springs Ln 78613
Honeysuckle Dr 78613
Honeyweed St 78613
Horizon Trl 78613
Horne Dr 78613
Howell Mountain Dr 78613
Hughes Dr 78613
Hummingbird Cir 78613
Hunter Ace Way 78613
Hunters Creek Cv & Dr 78613
Hur Industrial Blvd 78613
Indian Blanket Dr 78613
Indian Chief Dr 78613
Indian Lodge Dr 78613
Indian Springs Ct 78613
Industrial Blvd 78613
Inks Cv 78613
Irene Dr 78613
Iris Ln 78613
Ironwood Ct 78613
Izoro Bnd 78613
Jackson Dr 78613
Jacob Trl 78613
Jagged Rock 78613
Jane Cv 78613
Jasper Ln 78613
Jeffrey Dr 78613
Jenna Ln 78613
Jerry Ln 78613
John Tee Dr 78613
Jojoba Dr 78613
Jolie Ln 78613
Julianas Way 78613
Juneau Dr 78613
Juniper Trl 78613
Juniper Hills St 78613
Juniper Ridge Loop 78613
Kai Dr 78613
Kane Cv 78613
Kasdan Pass 78613
Kati Ln 78613
Katie Ln 78613
Keegans Way 78613
Kenai Dr 78613
Kendall Ct 78613
Kerr Trl 78613
Kettering Dr 78613
Killians Cv & Way 78613
Kimra Ln 78613
Kinclaven Ct 78613
King Eider Ln 78613
N & S Kings Canyon Dr 78613
Kinloch Dr 78613
Kittiwake Ln 78613
Knob Creek Ln 78613
Knoll Ridge Dr 78613
Kodiak Cv & Trl 78613
Kopperl Ct 78613
Kristen Ln 78613
Krupa Ct 78613
Kuskokwim Rd 78613
La Jaita Dr 78613
La Rochelle Dr 78613
Lady Day Cv 78613
N & S Lakeline Blvd 78613
Lakeline Mall Dr 78613
Lakeline Oaks Dr 78613
Laminar Creek Rd 78613
Lantana Ln 78613
Larkspur Way 78613
Larston Ln 78613
Lauren Trl 78613
Lauretta Wood Dr 78613
Lazy River Bnd 78613
Le Ann Ln 78613
Legend Oaks Ln 78613
Lexfield Ln 78613
Liberty Oaks Blvd 78613
Lilac Ln 78613
Limestone Ln 78613
Linden Loop 78613
Lion Heart Dr 78613
Little Creek Cv 78613
E Little Elm Trl 78613
Little Tree Bnd 78613
Live Oak Dr 78613
Livorno Cv 78613
Lloydminister Way 78613
Lobelia Dr 78613
Lobo St 78613
Locust Cv 78613
Lodestone Cir 78613
Lodosa Dr 78613
Loeffler Dr 78613
Lollipop Ln 78613
Lombardi Way 78613
London Ln 78613
Lone Buck Pass 78613
Lone Star Dr 78613
Lone Tree Ct 78613
Longhorn Cir 78613
Longhorn Acres St 78613
Longhorn Ridge Rd 78613
Lost Maples Loop 78613
Lost Pines Ln 78613
Lothian Dr 78613
Lou Hollow Pl 78613
Lovett Ln 78613
Lunday Dr 78613
Luray Dr 78613
N & S Lynnwood Trl 78613
Lynsenko Dr 78613
Macaw Dr 78613
Machado Rd 78613
Mackenzie Ln 78613
Macon Dr 78613
Madeline Loop 78613
Madisons Way 78613
Magnolia Ct 78613
Mahogany Ln 78613
Main St 78613
Mancini Cv 78613
Mancuso Bnd 78613
Mandarin Flyway 78613
Manley Way 78613
Mansfield Ln 78613
Maple Ln & Trl 78613
Marigold Ln 78613
Marquis Ln 78613
Martin Dr 78613
Martins Cv 78613
Marysol Trl 78613
Mathias St 78613
Maurice Cv & Dr 78613
Mayfield Way 78613
Mcbride Ln 78613
Mcgregor Ln 78613
Mcillwain Cv 78613
Mckendrick Dr 78613
Meadow Lark Cir & Dr 78613
Medical Pkwy 78613
Meghan Dr 78613
Melba Pass 78613
Melekhin Bnd 78613
Menteer Dr 78613
Merganser Ln 78613
Mertz Ln 78613
Mesa Verde St 78613
Mesquite Rd 78613
Mexican Hat Dr 78613
Mexican Plum Trl 78613
Michael Robert Way 78613
Midnight Star Dr 78613
Milan Dr 78613
Mill Stream Dr 78613
Mimosa Pass 78613
Mingus Dr 78613
Misty Morn Ln 78613
Mistywood Cir 78613
Monaco Dr 78613
Monarch Cv & Dr 78613
Monte Carlo Dr 78613
Moonlight Trl 78613
Moore Ln 78613
Moray Ln 78613
Mossy Grove Ct 78613
N & S Mount Rushmore Dr 78613
Mountain Laurel Dr 78613
Mulberry Way 78613
Muscovy Ln 78613
N & S Mustang Ave 78613
Mystic Summit Dr 78613
Nan Cv & Ln 78613
Nancy Jean Cv 78613
Nandina Dr 78613
Narrow Valley Dr 78613
Natalie Cv 78613
Nelson Ranch Loop & Rd 78613
E & W New Hope Dr & Spur 78613
Ney Cv 78613
Nicholas Zane Dr 78613
Nightingale Dr 78613
Nightshade Dr 78613
Oak Dale Dr 78613
Oak Grove Dr 78613
Oak Tree Ln 78613
Oakcrest Cir & Dr 78613
Oakland Dr 78613
Oakmont Ln 78613
Oakmont Forest Dr 78613
Oakridge Pass 78613
Oakshire Cv 78613
Oakwood Glen Cv & Dr 78613
Old Highway 183 78613
Old Mill Rd 78613
Old Sterling Rd 78613
Oldenburg Ln 78613
Oliver Loving Cv 78613
Orchard St 78613
Orchard Falls Dr 78613
Orchid Cir 78613
Orleans Dr 78613
Oro Viejo Cv 78613
Orsobello Cv & Pl 78613
Outpost Cv & Dr 78613
Paden Cir & Dr 78613
Pagedale Cv & Dr 78613
Paige Cv 78613
Paint Brush Cv & Trl 78613
Paintrock Cv 78613
Palmetto Dr 78613
Palo Alto Ln 78613
Palo Duro Dr 78613
Palomino Bnd 78613
Paper Moon Dr 78613
E, N & W Park Cir & St 78613
Parker Pl 78613
Parksville Way 78613
Parkway Dr 78613
Parkwest Dr 78613
W Parmer Ln 78613
Paseo Corto Dr 78613
Paseo Grand Dr 78613
Paso Fino Cv & Trl 78613
Passion Flower 78613
Peach Tree Ln 78613
Pebble Brook Rd 78613
Pebblestone Walk Dr 78613
Pecan Pass & St 78613
Pecan Park Blvd 78613
Pena Blanca Dr 78613
Pendleton Dr 78613
Penny Ln 78613
Pepper Grass Trl 78613
Persimmon Rd 78613
Petaluma Dr 78613
Peterson Dr 78613
Petrove Pass 78613
Petunia St 78613
Peyton Pl 78613
Pheasant Ridge Dr 78613
Piney Creek Ln 78613
Pipit Ct 78613
Plateau Rdg 78613
Plum Creek Rd 78613
Polar Ln 78613
Pomegranate Pass 78613
Poplar Ln 78613
Portwood Bend Cv 78613
Post Oak Cir 78613
Post River Rd 78613
Potomac Cir 78613
Powderham Ln 78613
Power Ln 78613
Prairie Mist Ct 78613
Preserve Trl 78613
Primrose Ln 78613
Primwood Path 78613
S Prize Oaks Dr 78613
Purdue Cv 78613
Purple Sage Dr 78613
Quail Cir 78613
Quail Creek Trl 78613
Quartz Ct 78613
Quest Pkwy 78613
Quicksilver Dr 78613
Quiet Creek Dr 78613
Quiet Moon Trl 78613
Rachel Rdg 78613
Raging River Rd 78613
N & S Rainbow Bridge Dr 78613
Rainfall Trl 78613
Rainy Creek Ln 78613
Raley Rd 78613
Rambler Valley Dr 78613
Rambling Cv & Trl 78613
Rathlin Dr 78613
Rattling Horn Cv 78613
Ravens Cv 78613
Ravensbrook Bnd 78613
Rawhide Trl 78613
Red Bay Dr 78613
Red Bird Dr 78613
Red Bud Dr 78613
Red Oak St 78613
Red Ranch Cir & Cv 78613
Redden Cv 78613
Remington Rd 78613
Retama Dr 78613
Reynaldo St 78613
Rhapsody Ridge Dr 78613
Rhondstat Run 78613
Rice Ave 78613
Richmond St 78613
Ridgeline Blvd 78613
Ridgetop Bnd 78613
Ridgewood Dr 78613
Riley Trl 78613
Rimstone Dr 78613
Ripperton Run 78613
Ripple Creek Ct 78613
Ritter Dr 78613
Riverine Way 78613
Riverwood Dr 78613
N, S, E & W Riviera Cir & Dr 78613
Roadrunner Dr 78613
Roanoke Dr 78613
Robby Ln 78613
Rockwood Ln 78613
Rocky Mound Ln 78613
Rocky Top Ln 78613
Rolling Brook Ln 78613
Rolling Plains Ct 78613
Romeo Dr 78613
Roseglen Dr 78613
Rosie Ln 78613
Rowley Dr 78613
Royal Ln 78613
Royce Ln 78613
Rummel Ranch Run 78613
Running Doe Ln 78613
Russet Valley Dr 78613
Ruthie Run 78613
Ryan Jordan Ln 78613
Saba Cv 78613
Sabinal Trl 78613
N Saddle Ridge Dr 78613
Saddlebrook Cir 78613
Sage Canyon Dr 78613
Saint Marys Ln 78613
Salerno Pl 78613
Saline Creek Dr 78613
San Mateo Ter 78613
Sand Creek Rd 78613
Sandhills Dr 78613
Sandra Cv & Dr 78613
Sang Saloon Rd 78613
Santana St 78613
Sapling Cv 78613
Sapphire Cv 78613
Savanna Ln 78613
Scarlet Maple Dr 78613
Sedalia St 78613
Sedbury Way 78613
Serene Oak Dr 78613
Serenity Springs Cv 78613
Settlement Cv & St 78613
Settlers Dr 78613
Settlers Home Dr 78613
Shadow Valley Cv 78613
Shady Brook Ln 78613
Shady Creek Trl 78613
Shady Grove Path 78613
Shady Trails Pass 78613
Shannon Meadow Cv & Trl 78613
Sharon Dr & Pl 78613
Shaun Dr 78613
Shea Cv & Dr 78613
Sheila Dr 78613
Shenandoah Dr 78613
Sheridan Trl 78613
Shetland Ln 78613
Shiloh St 78613
Shire 78613
Shooting Star Cv 78613
Shorthorn St 78613
Sienna Dr 78613
Silent Spring Dr 78613
Silver Maple Trl 78613
Silver Oak Trl 78613
Silverado Trl 78613
Silverstone Ln 78613
Simbrah Cv & Dr 78613
Simmons Dr 78613
Simon Ridge Ct 78613
Skip Tyler Dr 78613
Sky Ridge Ln 78613
Skyview St 78613
Slate Creek Dr 78613
Somerset Canyon Ln 78613
Sophora Pl 78613
Spanish Gold Ln 78613
Spanish Mustang Dr 78613
Spanish Oak St 78613
Sparkswood 78613
Spiderlily Vw 78613
Spoonbill Ct 78613
Sport Horse 78613
Spotted Fawn Cv 78613
Spring Arbor Ln 78613
Stallion Dr 78613
Stapleford Dr 78613
Star Light Cir & Cv 78613
Stardust Dr 78613
Starwood Dr 78613
Steer Acres Ct 78613
Steer Creek Ct 78613
Stenson Dr 78613
Stepp Bnd & Cv 78613
Sterling Heights Ct 78613
Stiles Cv & Ln 78613
Stillwell Rdg 78613
Stonehenge Cv 78613
Suffolk Ct 78613
Sugar Maple Ct 78613
Sugarberry Dr 78613
Sumac Ln 78613
Summer Rain Dr 78613
Summer Vista Cv 78613
Summerwood Ct 78613
Sunchase Blvd 78613
Sunny Ln 78613
Sunrise Ter 78613
Sunset Ter 78613
Sweetgum Trce 78613
Sweetwater Ln 78613
Sycamore Dr & St 78613
Tahoka Daisy Dr 78613
Taku Rd 78613
Talkeetna Ln 78613
Tall Cedars Rd 78613
Tallow Trl 78613
Tasha Ct 78613
Tattler Dr 78613
Teal Trl 78613
Terlingua Dr 78613
Terrace View Dr 78613
Territory Cv & Trl 78613
Texan Dr 78613
Texas Oak Way 78613
Theresa Cv 78613
Thistle Cir & Trl 78613
Thompson St 78613
Thoroughbred 78613
Three Arrows Ct 78613
Tierra Blanco Cv & Trl 78613

Tiger Horse Trl 78613
Tillman Dr 78613
Timber Trl 78613
Timber Ridge Dr 78613
Timbergrove 78613
Timberwood Dr 78613
Tivoli Dr 78613
Todd Ln 78613
Toro Grande Blvd & Dr 78613
Tosca Cv 78613
Townsman Trl 78613
Tracy Miller Ln 78613
Trafalger Cv 78613
Trail Dust Dr 78613
Trailhead Ct 78613
Trailridge Dr 78613
Treeline Dr 78613
Tremont Dr 78613
Tristan Way 78613
Truman Ln 78613
Trumpet Vine Trl 78613
Tulip Trail Bnd 78613
Turkey Path Bnd 78613
Turnbow Trl 78613
Twin Branch Dr 78613
Twin Creeks Club Dr 78613
Twin Oak Trl 78613
Tyree Rd 78613
Valk St 78613
Valley Pike Rd 78613
Valorie Ct 78613
Van Horn Cv & Way 78613
Vanderhill Cv 78613
Vaughter Ln 78613
Versailles Dr 78613
Vestavia Ridge Ln 78613
Victoria Cv & Dr 78613
N & S Vista Ridge Blvd & Pkwy 78613
Wagon Way 78613
Walking Horse Way 78613
Walnut Cv 78613
Walnut Creek Dr 78613
Walsh Glen Dr 78613
Walsh Hill Trl 78613
Walton Way 78613
Wanakah Ridge Cv & Dr 78613
Warren Cv 78613
Warwick Cv & Way 78613
Water Hole Trl 78613
Water Oak Dr 78613
Welch Way 78613
Welton Cliff Dr 78613
Wesson Cv 78613
Westminster Way 78613
Wheaton Trl 78613
Whippoorwill Dr 78613
Whistlers Walk 78613
Whistlers Walk Trl 78613
White Cir 78613
White Dove Cv 78613
White Elm Cv 78613
White Post Rd 78613
Whitechapel Ct 78613
E Whitestone Blvd
100-398 78613
400-499 78613
500-4398 78613
500-500 78630
501-4299 78613
W Whitestone Blvd 78613
Whitetail Pass 78613
Whitewing Dr 78613
Wickett Way 78613
Wicklow Mountain Trl 78613
Wide Antler Cv 78613
Wigeon Cv 78613
Wild Basin Ln 78613
Wild Rose Trl 78613
Wildbriar Ct 78613
Wilderness Path Bnd 78613
Wildlife Run 78613
Wiley Post Ln 78613
Williams Way 78613
Willow Ln 78613
Willowbrook Dr 78613
Wilson Ranch Pl 78613
Winchester Dr 78613
Windy Ter 78613
Windy Oaks Cv 78613
N Winecup Trl 78613
Winged Elm Dr 78613
Wood Creek Dr 78613
Woodall Dr 78613
Woodford Dr 78613
Woodhollow Cv & Ln 78613
Woodland Dr 78613
Woodridge Cv & Ln 78613
Woods Ln 78613
Woodstone Ct 78613
Wooten St 78613
Wren Cir 78613
Yalding Dr 78613
Yaupon Cv & Trl 78613
Yazoo Creek Ln 78613
Yellow Rose Trl 78613
Yorkshire Ln 78613
Yucca Ln 78613
Yukon Cir 78613
Zach Russell Dr 78613
Zacharys Run 78613
Zambia Dr 78613
Zappa Dr 78613
Zennor Ct 78613
Zeppelin Dr 78613
Zilker Dr 78613
Zoa Dr 78613

NUMBERED STREETS

All Street Addresses 78613

CLEBURNE TX

General Delivery 76033

POST OFFICE BOXES MAIN OFFICE STATIONS AND BRANCHES

Box No.s
All PO Boxes 76033

RURAL ROUTES

01, 04, 05, 06, 07, 08, 12 76031
02, 03, 09, 10, 11, 13, 15 76033

NAMED STREETS

N & S Aberdeen Dr 76033
Ada St 76031
Adams St 76033
Airport Dr 76033
Alvarado St 76031
Amanda Ln 76033
Angel Ct 76033
N & S Anglin St 76031
Annanhill St 76033
Apple Ct 76031
Arbor Spring Ct 76033
Armstrong St 76033
Arrowhead Rd 76031
Ascot Dr 76033
Ashwood Ct 76033
Atlantic St 76031
Austin Ave 76031
Avalon Ct 76033
Bailey Ct 76031
Baird St 76033
Bales St 76033
Barber Ave 76031
Barnes Rd 76031
E Barnett Dr 76033
Barry Ln 76031
Batterson St 76031
Baystone Rd 76033
Becca Ct 76031
Beech St 76031
Belle Plain Ct & Dr 76033
Bellevue Dr 76033
Belmont Rd 76033
Belvon Pl 76033
Ben Dr 76031
Bent Creek Dr 76033
Bent Wood Ln 76033
Berkley Ct & Dr 76033
Berry Ct & Dr 76033
W Bethesda Rd 76031
Betty Ln 76031
Black Oak Dr 76031
Blackfoot Dr 76033
Blair Dr 76031
Blakeley St 76031
Blakney St 76031
Blue Jay Dr 76033
Bluebonnet 76031
Bluestem Ct E 76033
Bluewater Dr 76033
Bob White Ct 76033
Bono Rd 76033
Boone Ct & St 76031
N Border St 76031
Boyd St 76031
Bozoki Rd 76031
Bradley Ct & Dr 76033
Bramblett Rd 76031
Brandon Dr 76033
N & S Brazos Ave 76031
S Briaroaks Rd 76031
Briarwood Dr 76033
Brook Ct & Ln 76033
Brookhaven St 76033
E Brown St 76031
W Brown St 76033
Browning Ln 76033
Bruntsfield Loop Dr 76033
Bryan St 76031
N Buffalo Ave 76033
S Buffalo Ave 76033
S Buffalo Ln 76033
Burgess Rd 76031
Burnham Dr 76033
Buthoriv 76031
Cactus Flower Ct 76033
N & S Caddo St 76031
Canton Rd 76033
Canyon Ct & Dr 76033
Carmela Ct 76031
Carnegie Ct & St 76033
Carnoustie Dr 76033
Carroll Dr 76033
Castle Royal Dr 76033
Cedar Ln & St 76031
Cedar Break Ct 76033
Cedar Grove Dr 76033
Cedar Ridge Ct 76033
Celeste Rd 76033
Center Ct & St 76033
Century Dr 76033
Chad Ct & St 76033
E Chambers St 76031
W Chambers St 76033
Chapel Ln 76031
Chase Ave 76031
Chaucer Dr 76033
E & W Cherry Ct 76031
Cherrywood Ct & Dr 76033
Chester St 76033
Chestnut Grove Dr 76033
Chickering Rd 76031
Chisholm Trl 76033
Christine St 76031
Cindy Ct & Ln 76033
Circle Dr 76033
Clara St 76031
Claude Ave 76031
Clear Creek Dr 76033
Clearfield Dr 76033
Cleburne St 76031
Cleveland St 76031
Cliffstone Ct 76033
Clubhouse Dr 76033
Coach Line Rd 76031
Cobblestone Ct & Ln 76033
Coleman St 76031
College St 76033
N & S Colonial Dr 76033
Colorado St 76031
Columbia St 76031
Commerce Blvd 76033
Complete Ct 76033
Concord St 76033
Conger St 76033
Conveyor Dr 76031
Corson St 76033
Cottonwood Ct 76033
W Country Rd 76033
Country Club Rd 76033
County Road 1018 76033
County Road 1022 76033
County Road 1102 76031
County Road 1104 76031
County Road 1104b 76031
County Road 1104c 76031
County Road 1107a 76031
County Road 1107b 76031
County Road 1107c 76031
County Road 1108 76033
County Road 1110a 76031
County Road 1112 76033
County Road 1114 76033
County Road 1115 76033
County Road 1116 76033
County Road 1117 76033
County Road 1117a 76033
County Road 1120 76033
County Road 1123 76033
County Road 1125 76033
County Road 1125b 76033
County Road 1126 76033
County Road 1200 76031
County Road 1202 76031
County Road 1204 76031
County Road 1205 76031
County Road 1210 76033
County Road 1217 76033
County Road 1218 76033
County Road 1219 76033
County Road 1224 76033
County Road 1224a 76033
County Road 1225 76033
N & S County Road 1226 76033
County Road 1226a 76033
County Road 1227 76033
County Road 1235 76033
County Road 1235b 76033
County Road 1236 76033
County Road 1237 76033
County Road 1238 76033
County Road 1239 76033
County Road 1240 76033
County Road 1240a 76033
County Road 1241 76033
County Road 1242 76033
County Road 1243 76033
County Road 1250 76033
County Road 307 76033
County Road 308
1700-2699 76033
5900-5998 76031
6000-6299 76031
County Road 309
1001-2197 76033
2199-2299 76033
4300-5799 76031
County Road 310 76031
County Road 310a 76031
County Road 312 76031
County Road 312b 76031
County Road 314 76031
County Road 314a 76031
County Road 314b 76031
County Road 316b 76031
County Road 316c 76031
County Road 316d 76031
County Road 317 76031
County Road 317a 76031
County Road 319 76033
County Road 325 76033
County Road 326 76033
County Road 414 76031
County Road 415 76031
County Road 417 76031
County Road 417a 76031
County Road 423 76031
County Road 424 76031
County Road 425 76031
County Road 425a 76031
County Road 425b 76031
County Road 425c 76031
County Road 426 76031
County Road 427a 76031
County Road 429 76031
County Road 700 76031
County Road 701 76031
County Road 701a 76031
County Road 702 76031
County Road 704a 76031
County Road 704c 76031
County Road 704d 76031
County Road 707 76031
County Road 711 76031
County Road 711c 76031
County Road 711d 76031
County Road 801 76031
County Road 801b 76031
County Road 801c 76031
County Road 805 76031
County Road 805a 76031
County Road 805b 76031
County Road 805c 76031
County Road 805f 76031
County Road 806 76031
County Road 807 76031
County Road 808 76031
County Road 809 76031
County Road 903 76033
Courtney Pl 76033
Crane Ave 76031
Crestridge Dr 76033
Crestview Dr 76033
Crestwood Dr 76033
Crichton Ct 76033
Cross Timber Rd W 76031
E Dabney St 76031
W Dabney St 76033
Dale St 76031
Dallas Ave 76031
Danny Ray Dr 76033
Darley Ct N & S 76033
Davis St 76033
Deerpark St 76033
Del Rio Ct 76033
Dewey St 76031
Dixon St 76033
Dogwood Ct 76033
Dorothy Dr 76031
Doty Rd 76033
N & S Douglas Ave 76033
Dove Ln 76031
Dove Creek Rd 76031
Downing Ln 76031
E Earl St 76031
W Earl St 76033
S Eastern 76031
Eastland St 76031
Edgebrook Ct 76033
Edgewood Ln 76033
Elizabeth St 76031
Elm St 76031
Elmira St 76031
Elmo St 76031
Emerson Dr 76033
English St 76033
Erie St 76031
Euclid St 76033
Evans St 76031
Faircrest Dr 76033
Fall Creek Rd 76033
Featherston St 76033
Fergason Rd 76031
N & S Field St 76033
Fir St 76031
Fm 1434 76033
N Fm 199 76033
Fm 200 76033
Fm 2135 76031
Fm 2174 76033
Fm 2280 76031
Fm 2331 76033
Fm 2415 76031
Fm 3048 76031
Fm 3136 76031
E Fm 4 76031
W Fm 4 76033
E Fm 916 76031
Forres Ct 76033
Forrest Ave 76033
Fort Worth Ave 76031
Fox Ct 76033
Fox Hollow Est 76033
Fox Run Rd 76033
Franklin St 76033
Front St 76031
Fuller Ave 76031
Fullerton Dr 76033
Futrell Ct 76031
Gage Rd 76031
Gardega Rd 76031
Gardendale Dr 76031
Gary St 76031
Gatewood Hill Dr 76033
Gatrix Ave 76033
George St 76031
Gleason Ave 76033
Glen Ct 76031
Glen Rose Ave 76033
Gleneagles Dr 76033
Glenhaven Dr 76033
Glenwood Dr 76033
Gold Cup Dr 76033
Graham St 76033
Granbury St 76033
Grand Ave 76033
Grandview Hwy & St 76031
Green River Trl 76033
Greenbriar Ln 76033
Gregory Ct 76033
Gresham Ave 76031
Hagler Rd 76033
Hal Ave 76031
Hanson Ln 76033
Harlin Dr 76033
Harmon St 76033
W Harrell St 76033
Harriette Cir 76033
Harvest Hill Rd 76033
Hawthorne St 76033
E Heard St 76031
W Heard St 76033
Heath St 76031
Heather Ct 76033
Helena Ct 76031
Hemphill Ct & Dr 76033
E Henderson St 76031
W Henderson St 76033
Herb Dr 76031
Hickory St 76033
Hidden Springs Ct 76033
High Mesa Dr 76033
Highland Dr & Rd 76033
N Highway 171 76033
S Highway 171 76031
S Highway 174 76033
E Highway 67
2100-4300 76031
4302-4398 76031
7001-7697 76033
7699-7799 76033
W Highway 67 76033
Hilandale Ct 76033
S Hill Dr 76033
Hill Ln
700-799 76033
2700-2799 76031
N Hill Ter 76031
Hill Terrace Pl 76033
Hillcrest Dr 76033
Hillsboro St 76033
Hilltop Ct & Dr 76033
Hines Rd 76031
Hix Rd 76031
Hodge St 76033
Hollingsworth St 76031
Hollow Point Ct 76033
N & S Holloway St 76033
Holly St 76033
Honeysuckle Ct & Dr 76033
Hopewell Rd 76031
Hull Rd 76031
Hummingbird Ln 76033
Huron St 76031
N Hyde Park Blvd & Ct 76033
Hyline Dr 76031
E Industrial Blvd 76031
W Industrial Blvd 76033
Island Grove Rd 76031
Ivanhoe St 76033
Ivy Ct 76033
J O Junge Rd 76033
Jack Burton Dr 76031
Jacob St 76033
E James St 76031
Janehaven Lks 76033
Jennifer Ct 76033
Jenny Dr 76031
Johnson Ln 76031
Joslin St 76033
Karen Ct 76033
W Katherine P Raines Rd 76033
E Katherine P Rains Rd 76031
Katy St 76031
Kendal Wood Ct 76033
Kilpatrick Ct 76033
E Kilpatrick St 76031
W Kilpatrick St 76033
Kim Ct 76031
Kimberly Dr 76031
N & S Kouns St 76031
Kristi Ct 76033
Ladybank Ct & St 76033
Lakecrest Ct 76033
Lakeshore Dr 76033
Lakeview Ct & Dr 76033
Lakeway Dr 76033
Lanark Ct 76033
Lane Ave 76033
Lane Prairie Rd 76031
Laurel Ln 76033
Leaning Oak Ln 76033
Lena St 76033
Leven Link Ct & St 76033
Lewis St 76031
Liberty St 76031
Lilly St 76033
Lincoln Park Dr 76033
Linda Ct & Ln 76033
Lindsey Ln W 76033
Lipscomb St 76031
Lisa St 76031
Live Oak Ct & Dr 76033
Locust St 76031
Loma Alta Pl 76033
E Lone Star Ave 76031
W Lone Star Ave 76033
Longfellow Ln 76033
Looney Ln 76031
Lovelady St 76033
Lundin Ct 76033
Luther Ln 76031
Lynn Ct 76033
Lynnwood Ct & Dr 76033
Madison St 76033
N & S Main St 76031
Malone Rd 76031
Mann Ct 76033
Manor Dr 76033
Mansfield Rd 76031

Maple St 76033
Marengo St 76033
Marie St 76033
Marti Dr 76033
Martin Dr 76031
Matthew Dr 76031
Maxie St 76033
May Ave 76031
Mayfield Pkwy 76033
Mcanear Ct & St 76033
Mcarthur Ln 76031
Mccoy St 76031
Meadow Ct 76033
Meadow Creek Ct 76033
Meadow View Dr 76033
Meadowlark Dr 76033
Mechanic St 76031
Melissa Ln 76031
Melissa St 76033
Meridith St 76031
Mesa St 76033
Milam Ct 76033
N & S Mill St 76033
Mimosa St 76033
Miracle Ln 76033
Mirimar Ct 76033
Miss Mary Rd 76031
Mitchell Ave 76033
Mockingbird Cir 76031
Monroe St 76033
N & S Monticello Dr 76033
Montrose Ct & St 76033
Moon St 76033
Moore Rd 76031
Morey Rd 76031
Morgan St 76031
Morningside Dr 76033
Mount Carmel Rd 76033
Muirfield Dr 76033
Mulberry St 76031
Murry Dr N 76033
Myers Ave 76033
Nairn Ct 76033
Natchez Ct 76033
Nicole Ln 76033
Nolan Ridge Dr 76033
N & S Nolan River Rd 76033
Northcrest Dr 76031
Northridge Dr 76033
Northside Dr 76033
Nottaway Dr 76033
Oak St 76031
Oak Hill Rd 76033
Oak Leaf Trl 76031
Oak Ridge Dr 76033
Odell St 76033
Old Betsy Rd 76031
Old Bridge Rd 76033
Old Foamy Rd 76033
Olive St 76031
N & S Oran Ave 76031
Overhill Dr 76033
Overland Dr 76033
Overlook Ct & Dr 76033
Pacific St 76031
Park Blvd 76033
Park St 76031
Park Ridge Dr 76033
Park Road 21 76033
Parkview Ct 76033
Peach Ln 76031
Peacock St 76031
Pear Ct 76031
Pearce St 76031
Pearl St 76031
Pebblecreek Dr 76033
Pecan Dr 76033
Pecan Vly 76031
Pecan Springs Rd 76031
Pecan Valley Ct 76031
N & S Pendell Ave 76033
Pennington Xing 76033
Phillips St 76033
Pine Bluff St 76031
Pipeline Rd 76033
Pittman St 76031
Pleasant View Ct 76033
E & W Plum Ct 76031
Poe Dr 76033
Poindexter Ave 76033
Polk Ln 76031
Ponderosa Cir 76031
Post Oak St 76031
Prairie Ave 76033
Prairie Ridge Ct E & W 76033
Preakness Ct 76033
Presidential Dr 76031
Preston Ct & Dr 76033
Prestwick Dr 76033
Princeton Pl 76033
Quail Holw 76033
Quail Run 76031
Quail Walk 76033
Quail Park Ln 76031
Raintree Ln 76033
Ramsey Ave 76031
Raylene Dr 76033
Rebecca St 76033
E Red Deer Rd 76031
Red Oak Dr 76033
Redwood Dr 76033
Remington Dr 76033
Retreat Blvd 76033
Retreat Clubhouse Dr 76033
Ridge Ct & Dr 76033
Ridge Run St 76033
Ridge View Dr 76033
Ridgecrest Dr 76033
Ridgemar Dr 76031
N & S Ridgeway Dr 76033
River Bend Rd 76033
Riverview Dr 76033
Riverway Dr 76033
Riverwood Trl 76033
Robbins St 76031
Roberts Ave 76033
Roberts Ct 76033
Roberts Ln 76031
Robin Pl 76033
N & S Robinson St 76031
Rockcrest Dr 76033
Rockdale Rd 76033
Rolling Hill Dr 76033
Rolling Oaks Ct & Dr 76031
Rose Ave 76033
Rosedown Ct 76033
Ross St 76031
Rough Rd 76033
Royal St 76031
Royal Birkdale Dr 76033
Royal Perth Dr 76033
Royal Winchester Dr 76033
Ruby Ln 76031
Rutledge Rd 76031
Sabine Ave 76031
Saint Augustine Dr 76033
Saint Leger Dr 76033
Sally Ln 76033
Sanders Rd 76031
Sandstone Dr 76033
Sandy St 76031
Santa Fe St 76031
Sarah Ln 76031
Savannah Ct 76033
Scudder St 76033
Scurlock Ave 76031
Security Dr 76033
Selkirk Ct 76033
Service Dr 76033
Shady Creek Ct & Dr 76033
E Shaffer St 76031
W Shaffer St 76033
Shale Cir 76033
Shannon Dr 76031
Sharron Ct 76033
Shaw St 76031
Shawnee Dr 76033
Shelley Ln 76033
Shelly Dr 76031
Sheridan Ln 76033
Shoreview Dr 76033
Short St 76033
Skyview St 76033
Slayton Rd 76031
Smiling Hills Ct 76031
W Smith St 76033
Smooth Stone Dr 76033
Snowberry St 76031
Som County Road 314 76033
Southern Blvd 76033
Southern Oaks Rd 76031
Sparks Dr 76033
Spell Ave 76033
Spencer Ln 76033
Spring Branch Dr 76033
Spring Creek St 76031
Spruce St 76031
Stanwood Ave 76033
Starling Ct 76033
Steinway Ln 76031
Stonegate Dr 76033
Stonelake Ct & Dr 76033
Stoneridge Ct 76033
Stonerway 76031
Stoney Creek Dr 76033
Strenerm St 76033
Stroud St 76033
Sugar Hill Ave 76033
Summer Wheat St 76031
Summercrest Dr 76033
Summerhill Ln 76033
Summit Ct E & W 76033
Sun Valley Dr 76033
Sunset Dr 76033
Surry Place Dr 76033
Susan St 76031
Taggart Ln 76031
Tanglewood Dr 76033
Tanya Ct 76031
Tennyson Ln 76033
Tepar Ln 76031
Terrace Ct 76031
Thurman St 76033
Tina St 76031
Topaz Dr 76031
Torrey Pine Ln 76033
Towne North Dr 76033
Trace Rd 76033
Tremont St 76031
Trinity St 76031
Troon Ct 76033
True Ln 76031
Turnberry Cir & Dr 76033
Turner St 76033
Turtledove Dr 76033
Twin Creeks Dr 76031
Twin Oaks Ct & Dr 76033
Valley View Ct & Dr 76033
Vantage Dr 76031
Vaughn Rd N 76033
E Vaughn Rd 76031
W Vaughn Rd 76033
Vics Ln 76031
Virginia Pl 76033
Walls Dr 76033
N & S Walnut St 76033
Walter Holiday Dr 76033
E Wardville St 76031
W Wardville St 76033
Warren St 76033
N & S Washington St 76031
Waters St 76031
Watersridge Cir 76031
Weatherford Hwy 76033
Wedgewood Dr 76033
Weeks Rd 76031
Wendell Ave 76031
Westcourt Dr 76033
E Westhill Dr 76031
W Westhill Dr 76033
Westhill Ter 76033
Westhill Terrace Ct 76033
Westlake Rd 76033
S Westmeadow Dr 76033
Westridge Dr 76033
Westvale Dr 76033
Whitefish Dr 76033
Whitenack St 76031
Whiterock St 76033
N & S Wilhite St 76031
Willana Ct 76033
Williams Ave 76033
E Willingham St 76031
W Willingham St 76033
Willow Bend St 76031
Willowcreek Ct & Rd 76033
Willowwood Dr 76033
E Wilson St 76031
W Wilson St 76033
Winding Creek Dr 76033
Windmill Ct & Rd E 76033
Windsor Oaks Ln 76031
Wolf Crk 76033
N & S Wood St 76033
Wood Haven Rd 76031
Woodard Ave 76033
Woodbine St 76031
Woodruff Rd 76033
Woodside Ln E 76033
Wordsworth Dr 76033
Wren Ct
100-199 76033
2100-2199 76031
Yellow Jacket Dr 76033

NUMBERED STREETS

W 1st St 76033
E 2nd St 76031
W 2nd St 76033
E 3rd St 76031
W 3rd St 76033
W 4th St 76033
W 5th St 76033

CLEVELAND TX

General Delivery 77327

POST OFFICE BOXES MAIN OFFICE STATIONS AND BRANCHES

Box No.s
All PO Boxes 77328

HIGHWAY CONTRACTS

01 77327

NAMED STREETS

A J Meekins Rd 77328
A J Murry Rd 77328
Aaron Ln 77328
Abb 77327
Acorn Pl 77328
Adams St 77327
Adelaide Dr 77327
Adrian Dr 77328
Adrian Hall Dr 77328
Adrilyn Rd 77328
Airie Ln 77328
Akin Ave 77327
Albright Ln 77328
Alder 77328
Allen Ave
100-399 77328
500-599 77327
Almeda St 77327
Alsobrooks Rd 77328
Angel St 77327
Anglin St
400-599 77327
600-699 77328
Angus Ct, Dr & Way 77328
Anmar Dr 77328
Anthony Rd 77328
Aranda Ln 77328
Artesian Ave 77327
Arvon St 77327
Ash Ln 77327
Ashley Cir 77328
Aspen St 77328
Austin St 77327
Autumn Ln
1-99 77327
10800-11599 77328
Avenue E 77327
B Lilley Rd 77328
B Roberts Ln 77328
B Trahan Rd 77328
Baker Ln 77328
Bambi Ct 77328
Barbara Dr 77327
Bardash St 77327
Barkley Ln 77328
Barrett Dr 77327
Bartlett Rd 77328
Bay St 77328
Bayou Bend Ln 77328
Bayou Oaks 77328
Bdy Ln 77328
Beach St 77327
Bear Ln 77328
Bedias Dr 77328
Belcher St 77327
Betty Dr 77327
Bettye Dr 77328
Beulah Land Dr 77327
Big Beaver 77328
Big Buck Dr 77328
Big Pine Loop 77327
Birch Ln 77328
Birch St
100-199 77328
200-309 77327
310-699 77328
Bird Creek Ln 77328
Blackburn 77327
N Blair Ave
700-1899 77327
1900-2499 77328
Blossom Ln 77328
Blue St 77327
Blue Teal 77328
Boars Run 77328
Boles Ln 77327
N & S Bonham Ave 77327
E & W Boothe Sq & St 77327
Boston Cir & St 77327
Boulevard St 77327
Bowen Loop 77328
Boyd Dr 77327
Bradley St 77327
Brandon Dr 77328
Brazewell Rd 77328
Brenda Ln 77328
Briar Bend Ct 77327
Brittany Ln 77328
Brown Rd 77328
Brown Bear 77328
Bryan Ave 77327
Bryant 77327
Burkett Ln 77327
Burr Oak 77328
S Butch Arthur Rd 77327
Butler Dr 77328
C Everitt Rd 77328
California Ave 77328
Calvarys Way 77327
Campbell St 77327
Campbell Acres Rd 77328
Cardinal Xing 77327
Carla Dr 77327
Carlotta Ln 77327
Carter St 77327
Cathy Ct 77327
Cearley St 77328
Cedar St
400-499 77327
500-11099 77328
Center Ave & Dr 77327
Chain O Lakes Resort 77327
Charity Blvd 77327
Charles St 77327
Charles Barker Ave 77327
Cherryhill Dr 77327
Chisolm Ct 77328
Church Ave 77327
Circle Dr 77327
Clay St 77327
N & S Cleveland Ave & Sq 77327
Cleveland Mhp 77328
Cliffbrook Cir & Ln 77327
Coach Whip Bnd 77327
Coburn Rd 77328
Coker Loop 77328
Coldsprings Rd 77328
Cole Dr 77328
N & S College Ave 77327
Cook St 77327
Corley Ln 77328
County Road 2109 77327
County Road 2113 77327
County Road 2114 77327
County Road 2115 77327
County Road 2116 N 77327
County Road 2117 77327
County Road 2119 77327
County Road 2120 W 77327
County Road 2121 E 77327
County Road 2122 77327
County Road 2122 A 77327
County Road 2122a 77327
County Road 2123 77327
County Road 2125 77327
County Road 2126 77327
County Road 2131 77327
County Road 2135 77327
County Road 2142 77327
County Road 2145 77327
County Road 2146 77327
County Road 2147 77327
County Road 2148 77327
County Road 2149 77327
County Road 2150 77327
County Road 2151 77327
County Road 2164 77327
County Road 2164a 77327
County Road 2164b 77327
County Road 2165 77327
County Road 2166 77327
County Road 2167 77327
County Road 2167a 77327
County Road 2167b 77327
County Road 2167c 77327
County Road 2168 77327
County Road 21681 77327
County Road 2169 77327
County Road 2170 77327
County Road 21705 77327
County Road 2171 77327
County Road 2172 77327
County Road 2173 77327
County Road 2174 77327
County Road 2176 77327
County Road 2176b 77327
County Road 2177 77327
County Road 2178 77327
County Road 2179 Anx 77327
County Road 2180 77327
County Road 2181 E 77327
County Road 2182 77327
County Road 2183 77327
County Road 2184 77327
County Road 2185 77327
County Road 2186 77327
County Road 2186a 77327
County Road 2187 77327
County Road 2188 77327
County Road 2189 77327
County Road 2190 77327
County Road 2191 77327
County Road 2192 77327
County Road 2193 77327
County Road 2194 77327
County Road 2195 77327
County Road 2196 77327
County Road 2197 77327
County Road 2198 77327
County Road 2199 77327
County Road 2200 77327
County Road 2201 77327
County Road 2202 77327
County Road 2203 77327
County Road 2205 77327
County Road 2206 77327
County Road 2208 77327
County Road 2208 1 77327
County Road 2208 2 77327
County Road 2208 3 77327
County Road 2209 N & S 77327
County Road 2212 77327
County Road 2213 77327
County Road 2215 77327
County Road 2216 77327
County Road 2217 77327
County Road 2218 77327
County Road 2219 77327
County Road 2220 77327
County Road 2221 77327
County Road 2222 77327
County Road 2223 77327
County Road 22235 Anx 77327
County Road 22236 Anx 77327
County Road 2224 77327
County Road 2224a 77327
County Road 2225 77327
County Road 2226 77327
County Road 2227 77327
County Road 2228 77327
County Road 2228a 77327
County Road 2229 77327
County Road 2230 77327
County Road 2231 77327
County Road 2232 77327
County Road 2233 77327
County Road 2234 77327
County Road 2234 1 77327
County Road 2234 2 77327
County Road 2235 77327
County Road 2236 77327
County Road 2237 77327
County Road 2238 77327
County Road 2239 77327
County Road 2239a 77327
County Road 2240 77327
County Road 2241 77327
County Road 2242 77327
County Road 2243 77327
County Road 2244 77327
County Road 2245 77327
County Road 2246 77327
County Road 2247 77327
County Road 2247a 77327
County Road 2248 77327
County Road 2249 77327
County Road 2250 77327
County Road 2251 77327
County Road 2252 77327
County Road 2253 77327
County Road 2254 77327
County Road 2255 77327
County Road 2256 77327
County Road 2257 77327
County Road 2258 77327
County Road 2259 77327
County Road 2260 77327
County Road 2261 77327
County Road 2265 77327
County Road 2266 77327
County Road 2267 77327
County Road 2268 77327
County Road 2269 77327
County Road 2270 77327
County Road 2271 77327
County Road 2272 77327
County Road 2273 77327

County Road 2274 77327
County Road 2275 77327
County Road 2276 77327
County Road 2277 77327
County Road 2278 77327
County Road 2279 77327
County Road 2280 77327
County Road 2281 77327
County Road 2282 77327
County Road 2283 77327
County Road 2284 77327
County Road 2284 1 ... 77327
County Road 2285 77327
County Road 2286 77327
County Road 2287 77327
County Road 2288 77327
County Road 2289 77327
County Road 2290 77327
County Road 2291 77327
County Road 2292 77327
County Road 2293 77327
County Road 2294 77327
County Road 2295 77327
County Road 2296 77327
County Road 2297 77327
County Road 2298 77327
County Road 2299 77327
County Road 22991 77327
County Road 2300 N ... 77327
County Road 2301 77327
County Road 2302 77327
County Road 2303 77327
County Road 2304 77327
County Road 2305 S ... 77327
County Road 2306 77327
County Road 2307 77327
County Road 2308 77327
County Road 2309 77327
County Road 2550 77327
County Road 2551 77327
County Road 2552 77327
County Road 2553 77327
County Road 2554 77327
County Road 2555 77327
County Road 2557 77327
County Road 2558 77327
County Road 2573 77327
County Road 2574 77327
County Road 2600 77327
County Road 2601 77327
County Road 2602 77327
County Road 2603 77327
County Road 2604 77327
County Road 2605 77327
County Road 2606 77327
County Road 2607 77327
County Road 2608 77327
County Road 2609 77327
County Road 2610 77327
County Road 2611 77327
County Road 2612 77327
County Road 2613 77327
County Road 2615 77327
County Road 2701 77327
County Road 2705 77327
County Road 2710 77327
County Road 2726 77327
County Road 2727 77327
County Road 2748 77327
County Road 2800 77327
County Road 2801 77327
County Road 2802 77327
County Road 2803 77327
County Road 2804 77327
County Road 2850 77327
County Road 2854 77327
County Road 2859 77327
County Road 2860 77327
County Road 2862 Dr .. 77327
County Road 2863 77327
County Road 2865 77327
County Road 2866 77327
County Road 2867 77327
County Road 2868 77327
County Road 2869 77327
County Road 2870 77327
County Road 2873 77327
County Road 2876 77327
County Road 2907 77327
County Road 2936 77327
County Road 304 77327
County Road 306 77327
County Road 308 77327
County Road 309 77327
County Road 310 77327
County Road 312 77327
County Road 3141 E & W 77327
County Road 3142 77327
County Road 316 77327
County Road 3160 77327
County Road 318 77327
County Road 3180 77327
County Road 3181 77327
County Road 3181a 77327
County Road 3182 77327
County Road 3182a 77327
County Road 3183 77327
County Road 3184 77327
County Road 3184a 77327
County Road 3185 77327
County Road 3186 77327
County Road 3187 77327
County Road 3188 77327
County Road 3189 77327
County Road 3189a 77327
County Road 3189b 77327
County Road 3189c 77327
County Road 319 77327
County Road 320 77327
County Road 3201 77327
County Road 322 77327
County Road 325 77327
County Road 3251 W ... 77327
County Road 3252 77327
County Road 3253 E ... 77327
County Road 327 77327
County Road 328 N & S 77327
County Road 3280 77327
County Road 329 77327
County Road 3290 77327
County Road 3291 77327
County Road 3292 77327
County Road 3293 77327
County Road 3294 77327
County Road 330 77327
County Road 331 77327
County Road 3310 77327
County Road 3310a 77327
County Road 3310b 77327
County Road 3310c 77327
County Road 3310d 77327
County Road 3311 77327
County Road 3311a 77327
County Road 3312 77327
County Road 3313 77327
County Road 3313a 77327
County Road 3314 77327
County Road 3314a 77327
County Road 3314b 77327
County Road 3315 77327
County Road 3316 77327
County Road 3316a 77327
County Road 3316b 77327
County Road 3317 77327
County Road 3317a 77327
County Road 3317b 77327
County Road 332 77327
County Road 337 77327
County Road 3370 77327
County Road 3370a 77327
County Road 3371 77327
County Road 3372 77327
County Road 3373 77327
County Road 3373a 77327
County Road 3374 77327
County Road 3375 77327
County Road 3376 77327
County Road 3377 77327
County Road 3378 77327
County Road 3379 77327
County Road 339 77327
County Road 3390 77327
County Road 342 77327
County Road 343 77327
County Road 3430 77327
County Road 3431 E, S & W 77327
County Road 3432 77327
County Road 3433 77327
County Road 3434 N & S 77327
County Road 3435 77327
County Road 345 77327
County Road 347 N & S 77327
County Road 3470 N & S 77327
County Road 3470a 77327
County Road 3471 77327
County Road 3472 N ... 77327
County Road 3473 77327
County Road 3474 77327
County Road 3475 77327
County Road 3476 77327
County Road 3477 77327
County Road 3478 77327
County Road 3479 77327
County Road 34791 77327
County Road 34792 77327
County Road 3479a 77327
County Road 3479b 77327
County Road 3479c 77327
County Road 3479d 77327
County Road 3479f 77327
County Road 3479g 77327
County Road 3479h 77327
County Road 3479i 77327
County Road 3479j 77327
County Road 348 77327
County Road 349 77327
County Road 3490 77327
County Road 351 77327
County Road 352 77327
County Road 353 77327
County Road 354 77327
County Road 3662 77327
County Road 3740 77327
County Road 3749 77327
County Road 37491 77327
County Road 37492 77327
County Road 37493 77327
County Road 375 77328
County Road 3750 N & S 77328
County Road 3751 77328
County Road 3752 77328
County Road 3753 77328
County Road 3755 77328
County Road 377 77327
County Road 3770 77327
County Road 379 77328
County Road 3790 77328
County Road 3791 77328
County Road 3792 77328
County Road 3793 77328
County Road 3794 77328
County Road 3794a 77328
County Road 3794b 77328
County Road 3795 77328
County Road 3796 77328
County Road 3796a 77328
County Road 3797 77328
County Road 3798 77328
County Road 3799 77328
County Road 3800 77328
County Road 3801 77328
County Road 381 S 77328
County Road 3810 77328
County Road 3812 77328
County Road 3813 77328
County Road 3815 77328
County Road 3818 77328
County Road 3819 77328
County Road 383 77327
County Road 385 77328
County Road 386 77328
County Road 388 77328
County Road 3880 77328
County Road 389 77328
County Road 3890 77328
County Road 3891 N & S 77328
County Road 3892 E & W 77328
County Road 3893 E & W 77328
County Road 38b 77328
County Road 390
  100-399 77328
County Road 390
  1000-1099 77327
County Road 392 77328
County Road 394 77328
County Road 395 77328
County Road 396 77328
County Road 3961 77328
County Road 3990 77328
County Road 3991 77328
County Road 3992 77328
County Road 3993 77328
County Road 3994 77328
County Road 3995 77328
County Road 3996 77328
County Road 3997 77328
County Road 3998 77328
Craig St 77327
Creek Dr 77328
Creek View Dr 77328
Creekwood Dr 77328
Crescent Blvd 77327
E & W Crockett St 77327
Croley Ctr 77327
Cross Cut 77328
Crossno Dr 77328
Crysel Rd 77328
Culberson St 77327
Cummins Ave 77327
Cunningham Rd 77327
Cypress Ln 77328
Cypress Creek Loop 77327
Cypress Lakes Cir 77327
Dabney Bottom Rd 77328
E & W Dallas St 77327
Daniel St 77327
Davis Hl 77327
Davis Reed Ln 77328
Daw Collins Rd 77328
Dayton Dr & St 77327
Deer Rdg 77327
Deer Creek Run 77328
Denison Ave 77327
Denson Reed Rd 77328
Derk Small Rd 77328
Desert Star 77327
Devin Rd 77328
Dodd Rd 77328
Dogwood Ln & Rd 77328
Dominy Dr 77327
Donna Ct 77327
Dora St 77328
Doris St 77327
Doru Dr 77327
N & S Dove Creek Dr 77328
Dr Rick Kelley St 77327
N & S Duck Creek Rd 77328
Dudley St 77327
Duncan Ave 77327
Dunnam Ave 77327
Dupree 77327
Duroc Ct 77328
Dusty Rd 77327
Duval Ln 77328
Eagle Creek Dr 77328
Eagle Nest 77327
East Ave 77327
Easy St 77327
Edgewood Ave 77327
Eichelberger Ln 77328
Eldridge Rd 77328
Elendor Dr 77328
Elephant Walk Ln 77327
Elizabeth St 77327
Elk St 77327
Ella Ln 77327
Elm St 77327
Elmira Ln 77327
Elwood Ave 77327
Enis Owens Rd 77328
Enloe Mcconnel Rd 77327
Ernest Ln 77328
Etyel 77328
Everitt Rd 77328
Fain St 77327
Faith Dr, Ln & Loop 77327
Falcon Crest Ln 77328
Falvey Ln 77328
Fannin St 77328
Farrow Ln 77327
Faulkner Rd 77328
N & S Fenner Ave 77327
Ferguson Dr 77327
Field Ave 77327
Fisher Ave 77327
Flancenw Rd 77328
Fletcher Rd 77328
Flora Ct 77328
Fm 1010 Rd 77327
Fm 163 Rd 77327
Fm 1725 Rd 77328
Fm 2025 Rd 77328
Fm 2090 Rd 77327
Fm 223 Rd 77327
Fm 2518 Rd 77327
Fm 2610 Rd 77327
Fm 787 Rd E & W 77327
Fm 945 Rd S 77328
Forest Dr 77328
Forest Ln 77328
Forest Park N 77327
Forest Reserve St 77328
Forest Service Rd 77328
Forest Service 276 Rd 77328
Forest Valley Dr 77328
E Fork Dr 77328
E Fort Worth St 77327
Fosters Bnd 77328
Fostoria Rd 77328
N Fostoria Rd 77328
Fostoria St 77327
Fostoria Tram Rd 77328
Four Pines St 77328
Fox Trot 77327
Foxmeadows Ln 77327
Frances Rd & St 77328
N & S Franklin Ave 77327
Friar Tuck 77327
Garden Ln 77328
Garner St 77327
Garret Rd 77327
Gary Dr 77328
S & W Geronimo Trl 77328
Gill Rd 77328
Gilmore Rd 77328
Ginger Meadow Ln 77328
Gingles Rd 77328
Gladstell Rd 77327
Glenda Ln 77327
Glory Way 77327
Goode Ct & Rd 77328
Goode City Ln 77328
Grace Ave & Way 77327
Grant St 77327
Grant Lake Cir 77327
Gray Dr 77328
Green Ave 77327
Green Tree Ln 77328
Greenbelt Dr 77328
Greenwood Dr 77328
Grey Goose 77328
Grimes Rd 77328
Griswold Rd 77328
Guinn St 77327
Gum St 77327
Guthrie Ln 77328
Guyler Ave 77327
H D Mettz Rd 77327
H Enloe Ln 77328
H Noble Rd 77328
Hales Rd 77328
Halleluja Blvd 77327
Haltom 77327
Hancock Ave 77327
Hanks St 77327
Hanna Belle Dr 77328
E & W Hanson St 77327
Harding Ave 77327
Hargrove Lilley Ln 77328
Harvey Ln 77327
Hays St 77327
Heavens Gate 77327
Helen St 77328
Hemlock Ln 77328
Hereford Way 77328
Heron Hvn 77327
Hickman Creek Dr 77328
Hickory Ct 77328
Hickory St
  100-399 77327
  400-499 77328
Hickory Hill Rd 77328
Hickory Knoll Ct 77328
Hicks Loop & Rd E, S & W 77328
Hidden Acres Dr 77328
Highway 105
  1-16399 77327
Highway 105
  18000-25799 77328
Highway 105 E
  1-16399 77327
  18000-25799 77328
Highway 105 W 77328
Highway 146 N 77327
Highway 321 77327
Highway 59 S 77327
Highway 59 North Byp 77327
Hill Rd 77328
Hilltop Sq 77327
Hoagland Dr 77327
N & S Holly Ave 77327
Holstein Dr 77328
Honey Suckle Dr 77327
Hope Ave & Loop 77327
Hopson Rd 77328
Horseshoe Bend Dr 77327
Horseshoe Way Loop 77328
Hortense St 77328
E & W Houston St 77327
Howard 77327
Hubert St 77327
Hudgins Ln 77327
Hull St 77327
Hulon Dr 77328
Hulon Hall Ct 77328
Humbird 77328
Hunt St 77327
Inglewood St 77327
Inwood St 77328
Issacks St 77327
Ivy Ln 77328
J A Morgan Rd 77328
J J Estates Rd 77328
J Johnson 77327
Jack Spera Way 77328
Jack Turner Rd 77328
N James Ave 77328
James Edny Dr 77327
Jammye Dr 77328
Jayhawker Rd 77328
Jefferson Ave 77327
Jenney St 77328
Jennifer Ln 77328
Joe Ln 77328
Jones Rd 77327
Jordan Ave 77327
Joyce Rd 77328
Joyful Way 77327
Junction Ave 77327
Kalmia 77327
Kennel Ln 77328
Kinsman Rd 77328
Kirby Ln 77328
Kirbywood Ct & Dr 77327
L Green Rd 77328
L R Outlaw Ln 77328
Ladner Stockton Rd 77328
Lake St N 77327
Lake Park Dr 77328
Lakeshore Dr 77327
Lakewood Ln 77327
Lamar St 77327
Larkin Ln 77327
Laurel Ct 77327
Lawrence Creek Rd 77328
Leaf Ln 77328
League St 77327
Lee Ave
  1-799 77328
  800-899 77327
Lee Ln 77327
Lee Turner Rd 77328
Lena Ln 77328
Lewis Rd 77328
Libby Dr 77328
Liberty Rd 77327
Liberty St
  300-999 77327
  1000-1099 77328
Liberty Creek Dr 77328
Lilley Ave 77327
Lilley Gilbert Rd 77328
Lilley Yeager Loop N & S 77328
E & W Lincoln St 77327
Lindley St 77327
Lindley Woods St 77328
Lisa Ln 77328
Longhorn Dr 77328
Loop 573 S 77327
Love Ave 77327
Lovett Ave 77327
Lucille Dr 77328
Lyle West Ave 77327
Lynch Rd 77328
M Kelley Rd 77328
Macie Ln 77328
Mae Plaster Dr 77328
Magnolia Ave 77327
Magnolia Dr 77328
N Magnolia Dr 77328
S Magnolia Dr 77328
Magnolia Rd 77328
Magnolia St 77328
Magnolia Trl 77328
Magnolia Way 77328
Magruder Ave 77327
Main St 77328
Major Rd 77328
Mandell Rd 77328
N & S Manthey Ave 77327
Maple Ave 77327
Maple St 77328
Margie St 77327
Marie Ln 77327
Martha Ave 77328
Martin Creek Dr 77328
Martin Luther King Dr 77327
Mary Loop 77328
Mary Jo St 77328
N & S Mason Ave 77327
Masters Trl 77327
Matthews St 77327
Maurine Ln 77328
Maxine Ln 77328
May Cox Rd 77328
Mayo St 77327
Mcadams Vann Rd 77328
Mcbee Rd 77328
Mcbride Rd 77328
Mcguinnis Rd 77328
Mckeller Ave 77327
Meadow Ct 77327
Meadow Lake Rd 77328
Meadows St 77328
Meekins Rd 77328
Megan Ln 77328
Memory Ln 77328
Merrell Rd 77328
Meryce Ln 77328
Metts Rd 77328

Michael St ... 77328
Midline Rd
25700-26999 ... 77328
27400-27499 ... 77327
Midway Rd ... 77328
Mildred St ... 77328
Mill St
400-599 ... 77327
600-699 ... 77328
Miller Dr ... 77327
Miller Rd ... 77328
Mimosa Ln ... 77327
Mimosa St ... 77328
Miracle Dr ... 77327
Miranda Dr ... 77328
W Mizell Ln ... 77328
Mockingbird Ln ... 77327
N & S Moody Ln & Rd ... 77328
Morgan Ln ... 77328
Morgan Cemetery Rd ... 77328
Morrell Rd ... 77328
Mosley Ln ... 77328
Moss Cir ... 77328
Moss Hill Dr ... 77327
Murphy Addition Rd ... 77328
Mustang Rd ... 77328
National Forest Rd ... 77328
Nebraska Rd ... 77328
Nevell St ... 77327
Newman St ... 77327
N Noble Rd ... 77328
Norma Ln ... 77328
Nottingham Is ... 77327
O Turner Rd ... 77328
Oak Cir ... 77328
S Oak Dr ... 77328
Oak Holw ... 77328
Oak St ... 77327
Oak Bend Ct & Loop ... 77327
Oak Crest Ln ... 77328
Oak Forest Blvd ... 77328
Oak High St E & W ... 77327
Oak Knoll Rd ... 77328
Oak Ridge Dr & St ... 77328
Oak Shadows Rd ... 77327
Oak Wood Dr ... 77328
Oakridge Dr ... 77328
Oakview Ln ... 77328
Ola Ln ... 77328
Old Coldsprings Rd ... 77327
Old Highway 105 ... 77328
Oliver Ln ... 77328
Orange St ... 77327
Orr Ln ... 77327
Owl Creek Ln ... 77328
Oxbo ... 77328
Palmetto Ave ... 77327
Pam Ln ... 77328
Park Ct ... 77327
Park Ln ... 77327
Park St ... 77328
Parker Rd ... 77328
Parkhurst Ave ... 77327
Pate St
400-499 ... 77327
500-699 ... 77328
Pauline Rd ... 77328
Peaceful Valley Dr ... 77327
Peach Ave ... 77327
Peach Bnd ... 77328
Peach Creek Valley Dr ... 77328
Peach Wood ... 77328
Peacock Ln ... 77328
Pearl St ... 77327
Pebble Springs Ln ... 77327
Pecan Grv ... 77328
Penny Rd ... 77328
Perry Ln ... 77328
Perry St ... 77327
Pickering Rd ... 77328
Pine Ct ... 77327
N Pine Ct ... 77328
S Pine Ct ... 77328
Pine Ln ... 77328
Pine Mdw ... 77327
Pine Rd ... 77328
Pine St ... 77327
Pine Bend Ct ... 77327
Pine Burr Ct ... 77327
Pine Knob Dr ... 77328
Pine Knott Rd ... 77328
Pine Ridge Dr ... 77327
Pine Shadows Rd ... 77328
Pine Valley Rd ... 77328
Pinemont Rd ... 77328
Pioneer Ln ... 77328
Plum Grove Rd ... 77327
Plumwood Est ... 77327
Preacher Denson Rd ... 77328
Presswood Dr ... 77327
Price Dr ... 77328
Private Road 2222a ... 77327
Private Road 22244 ... 77327
Private Road 2238 ... 77327
Purkerson Rd ... 77328
Quail Creek Dr ... 77328
Raccoon Ramble ... 77327
Rachel B Scott St ... 77327
Rainbow Mobile Home Park ... 77328
Rajak Rd ... 77328
Ramey Ave ... 77327
Ranchito Allegro ... 77327
Raquel Ln ... 77328
Rawlins Rd ... 77328
Rayburn Ave ... 77327
Rayburn Ln ... 77328
Reaves Rd ... 77328
Rebel Rd ... 77327
Red Man Rd ... 77328
Red Maple Vlg ... 77327
Red Oak Ct & Dr ... 77328
Redwood Ln ... 77328
Reed Rd ... 77328
Reese St ... 77327
Resurrection Pl ... 77327
Rice Rd ... 77328
Rice St ... 77327
Richards Rd ... 77328
Rickey St ... 77327
Ridley Ln ... 77328
E River Est ... 77327
River Rd ... 77328
River St ... 77327
River Creek Rd ... 77328
Road 2114 ... 77327
Road 2126 ... 77327
Road 2210 ... 77327
Road 2211 ... 77327
Road 2244 ... 77327
Road 22705 ... 77327
Road 2550 ... 77327
Road 2552 ... 77327
Road 2553 ... 77327
Road 2554 ... 77327
Road 2555 ... 77327
Road 2557 ... 77327
Road 2571 ... 77327
Road 2573 ... 77327
Road 2574 ... 77327
Road 2601 ... 77327
Road 2602 ... 77327
Road 2605 ... 77327
Road 2606 ... 77327
Road 2607 ... 77327
Road 2608 ... 77327
Road 2609 ... 77327
Road 2610 ... 77327
Road 2611 ... 77327
Road 2613 ... 77327
Road 2614 ... 77327
Road 2708 ... 77327
Road 2710 ... 77327
Road 2722 ... 77327
Road 2724 ... 77327
Road 2725 ... 77327
Road 2726 ... 77327
Road 2746 ... 77327
Road 2751 ... 77327
Road 2764 ... 77327
Road 2766 ... 77327
Road 2858 ... 77327
Road 2859 ... 77327
Road 2900 ... 77327
Road 2901 S ... 77327
Road 29015 ... 77327
Road 2902 ... 77327
Road 2903 ... 77327
Road 2905 ... 77327
Road 2906 ... 77327
Road 2907 ... 77327
Road 2908 ... 77327
Road 2909 ... 77327
Road 2910 ... 77327
Road 2911 ... 77327
Road 2915 ... 77327
Road 2917 ... 77327
Road 2923 ... 77327
Road 2927 ... 77327
Road 2930 ... 77327
Road 2932 ... 77327
Road 2935 ... 77327
Road 2936 ... 77327
Road 2937 ... 77327
Road 2939 ... 77327
Road 2941 ... 77327
Road 311 ... 77327
Road 312 ... 77327
Road 315 ... 77327
Road 333a ... 77327
Road 333b ... 77327
Road 334 ... 77327
Road 336 ... 77327
Road 342 ... 77327
Road 3430 ... 77327
Road 3431 ... 77327
Road 3432 ... 77327
Road 3433 ... 77327
Road 3434 N ... 77327
Road 3435 ... 77327
Road 3774 ... 77327
Road 3800 N & S ... 77328
Road 3801 ... 77328
Road 3802 ... 77328
Road 381 S ... 77328
Road 3810 ... 77328
Road 3817 ... 77328
Road 3818 ... 77328
Road 3819 ... 77328
Road 3860 ... 77328
Road 3861 ... 77328
Road 3961 ... 77328
Robin Hood ... 77327
Rock Pigeon ... 77327
Rogers Ave ... 77327
N & S Roosevelt Ave ... 77327
Ross Ave ... 77327
Roy Hall Dr ... 77328
Royal Cir ... 77328
Ruby Rd ... 77328
Rutherford Cir & Rd ... 77328
Rye Dr ... 77327
Sabine Dr ... 77327
Sam Houston Lake Est ... 77327
Sam Wiley Dr ... 77327
N & S San Jacinto Ave ... 77327
Sandy Pt ... 77327
Santa Fe St ... 77327
Scott Rd ... 77328
Sean Ct ... 77327
Security Way ... 77328
Security Cemetery Rd ... 77328
Security Forest Dr ... 77328
Sequoia Ln ... 77328
Seth Blvd ... 77328
Shade Crest Cir & Ln ... 77327
Shady Ln ... 77327
Shaw Rd ... 77328
Sheila St ... 77328
Shell Ave ... 77327
Shell Oil Rd ... 77328
Shelton Ln ... 77328
Shelton Mizell Rd ... 77328
Sherwood Dr ... 77328
Sherwood St ... 77327
Shirley Loop ... 77328
Shoreline Dr ... 77327
Short St ... 77327
Silcox Ln ... 77328
Simmons Dr ... 77328
Sims ... 77328
Sky Ln ... 77328
Slaughter Rd ... 77328
Sleepy Hollow Dr ... 77327
Smith Ln ... 77328
Smith Loop E ... 77327
Smith Loop N ... 77327
Smith Loop S ... 77327
Smith Rd ... 77327
Smith St ... 77327
Solomon St ... 77328
N & S Solon Trl ... 77328
Sour Lake Cir ... 77327
Southline St ... 77327
S Southline St ... 77327
W Southline St
100-599 ... 77327
600-603 ... 77328
605-613 ... 77328
N & S Southwind Trl ... 77328
Sparks Ln ... 77328
Spears Rd ... 77328
Spring Ln ... 77328
Spring Creek Rd ... 77328
Spring Grove Dr ... 77328
Spruce Ln ... 77328
Squire Rd ... 77328
Stacy Ct ... 77328
Stanford Ln ... 77327
Starkey Ln ... 77328
State St ... 77328
Stephanie Ct ... 77328
Stephens Rd ... 77328
Stillwood Rd ... 77328
Streen Plz ... 77327
Strickland Ln ... 77328
Strothers Ln ... 77327
Susan Dr ... 77327
Sweet Clover Ln ... 77328
Swick Trl ... 77327
Tabernacle Ct ... 77327
Taft Ave ... 77327
Talita Ave ... 77327
Tallow Vis ... 77328
Tammy Trl ... 77327
Tanner Ave ... 77327
Tarkington Mhp 1 ... 77327
Tarkington Mhp 2 ... 77327
Tarkington Mhp 3 ... 77327
Teaberry Ln ... 77327
Teepee Trl ... 77328
Teresa Ln ... 77327
Terry Dr ... 77327
Texas St ... 77328
Thomas Dr ... 77328
Thomas Ln ... 77327
Thomas St ... 77328
Thomas Creek Rd ... 77328
Thomas T Trl ... 77328
Tidwell Ln ... 77328
Timber Rd ... 77328
Timber Switch Rd ... 77328
Timm Ln ... 77327
Tom Carter Ln ... 77328
Tommy Sallas Rd ... 77327
Tony Tap Rd ... 77328
Trails End Dr ... 77328
Tranquility Trl ... 77327
N & S Travis Ave ... 77327
Tree Ct ... 77327
Trey Cir ... 77328
Truly Plz ... 77327
Truman St ... 77327
Tupelo Ln ... 77328
Turner Ln & Rd ... 77328
Twin Oaks Dr ... 77328
Tyler Rd ... 77328
Tymel Ln ... 77328
Us Highway 59 N & S ... 77327
Vann Beil Rd ... 77328
Victory Blvd ... 77327
Village Ln ... 77327
Vine Cir ... 77328
Vine St ... 77327
E & W Waco St ... 77327
Walker Ave ... 77327
Walker Dr ... 77328
N Walker Rd ... 77328
S Walker Rd ... 77328
Wall St ... 77327
Walls Mhp ... 77327
Walnut Ln ... 77328
Walnut Burl ... 77328
Walter Dr ... 77328
Walters Rd ... 77328
Ward Rd ... 77328
Ware Rd ... 77328
Warner Rd ... 77328
Washburn Ln ... 77328
N Washington Ave ... 77327
S Washington Ave ... 77327
Washington Rd ... 77328
Watson St ... 77327
Weir Rd ... 77328
Wells Ave ... 77328
Wells Rd ... 77327
Whiskey Branch Trl ... 77328
Whiskey Creek Ln ... 77328
Whisper Rd ... 77328
Whispering Bell ... 77327
White Buck Ct ... 77328
White Doe Ct ... 77328
White Heather ... 77327
White Oak Ct ... 77328
White Oak Dr ... 77327
N White Oak Dr ... 77327
S White Oak Dr ... 77327
White Rock Rd ... 77328
Whitmire Ln ... 77328
N & S William Barnett Ave ... 77327
Williams St ... 77327
Willow Ave ... 77327
Willow St ... 77328
Wilson St ... 77327
Winding Way ... 77327
Windwood ... 77327
N & S Winter Crk ... 77328
Wood Rd ... 77328
Wood Fern Dr ... 77327
Woodman Dr ... 77328
Woodpeckers Grv ... 77328
Woods Ln ... 77328
Yale St ... 77328
Yellowstone Rd ... 77328
Young Ln ... 77327
Youpon Ct ... 77327
Youpon St ... 77328

NUMBERED STREETS

All Street Addresses ... 77327

COLLEGE STATION TX

General Delivery ... 77840

POST OFFICE BOXES MAIN OFFICE STATIONS AND BRANCHES

Box No.s
A - T ... 77841
BA - BP ... 77841
CA - CR ... 77841
DB - DU ... 77841
FB - FS ... 77841
GK - GK ... 77841
HG - HG ... 77841
JB - JG ... 77841
1 - 3450 ... 77841
9001 - 12450 ... 77842
9998 - 15954 ... 77841
30012 - 40016 ... 77842

NAMED STREETS

A And R Dr E ... 77845
Abbate Rd ... 77845
Abbey Ln ... 77845
Aberdeen Pl ... 77840
Acorn Ln ... 77845
Addison Ct ... 77845
Adrienne Cir & Dr ... 77845
Afton Oaks Dr ... 77845
Ag Dr ... 77845
Agate Dr ... 77845
Airline Dr ... 77845
Alacia Ct ... 77845
Alexander Valley Ct ... 77845
Alexandria Ave ... 77845
Alexis Ct ... 77845
Alison Ave ... 77845
Alnwick Ct ... 77845
Alpine Cir ... 77840
Amanda Ln ... 77845
Amber Hill Ct ... 77845
Amber Ridge Dr ... 77845
Amber Stone Ct ... 77845
Ambergate Dr ... 77845
Amberley Pl ... 77845
Amberwood Ct ... 77845
Amethyst Ct ... 77845
Amherst Cir ... 77840
Amy Ct ... 77845
Anasazi Bluff Dr ... 77845
Anderson St ... 77840
Andover Ct ... 77845
Angel Fire Ct ... 77845
Angelina Cir ... 77840
Angus Ave ... 77840
Anna St ... 77840
Antelope Ln ... 77845
Antietam Dr ... 77845
Antler Cir ... 77845
Antone Ct ... 77840
Appaloosa Rd ... 77845
Apple Valley Ct ... 77845
Appleby Pl ... 77845
Appomattox Dr ... 77845
Apricot Gln ... 77845
April Bloom ... 77840
Arapaho Ridge Dr ... 77845
Arboleda Dr ... 77845
Arboles Cir ... 77840
Arctic Cir ... 77840
Ardenne Ct ... 77845
Arguello Dr ... 77840
Arhopulos Rd ... 77845
Arizona St ... 77840
Armistead St ... 77840
Arnold Rd ... 77845
Arrington Rd ... 77845
Arrowhead Ct ... 77845
Arroyo Ct N & S ... 77845
Arthur Ln ... 77845
Arundel Ct ... 77845
Ash St ... 77840
Ashburn Ave ... 77840
Ashford Dr ... 77840
Ashford West Dr ... 77840
Ashley Ct & Ln ... 77845
Ashley Stone Ct ... 77845
Aspen Heights Blvd ... 77845
Aster Dr ... 77845
Athens Dr ... 77840
Auburn Ct ... 77840
Augsburg Ct & Ln ... 77845
Augusta Cir ... 77845
Augustine Ct ... 77840
Aurora Ct ... 77840
Austin Ave ... 77845
Australia Ln ... 77845
Autumn Cir ... 77840
Autumn Chase Loop ... 77840
Autumnwood Dr ... 77845
Avenue A ... 77840
Avenue B ... 77840
Axis Ct ... 77845
Ayrshire St ... 77840
Azalea Ct ... 77840
Aztec Ct & St ... 77845
Bahia Dr ... 77845
Baker Meadow Loop ... 77845
Balcones Dr ... 77845
Ball Cir ... 77845
Ball St ... 77840
Ballybunion Ct & Ln ... 77845
Ballylough Ln ... 77845
Bandera Dr ... 77845
Banks St ... 77840
Barchetta Dr ... 77845
N Bardell Ct ... 77840
Barnstable Hbr ... 77845
Barnwood Dr ... 77845
Barron Rd ... 77845
Barron Cut Off Rd ... 77845
Barrow Ct ... 77845
Barthelow Dr ... 77840
Batts Ferry Rd ... 77845
Bay Oaks Ct ... 77845
Bayou Woods Dr ... 77840
Baywood Ct & Ln ... 77845
Beacon Ct ... 77845
Beatriz Ln ... 77845
Beckley Ct ... 77845
Bee Creek Dr ... 77840
Beeler Ln ... 77845
Bell St ... 77840
Bella Lago Ct ... 77845
Bellerive Bend Dr ... 77845
Belmont Cir ... 77845
Belsay Ave ... 77845
Belvoir Ct ... 77845
Benchmark Dr ... 77845
Bendwood ... 77845
Bent Oak St ... 77845
Bent Tree Dr ... 77845
Bentwood Dr ... 77845
Berkeley St ... 77840
Bermuda Ct ... 77845
Bernburg Ct & Ln ... 77845
Berry Crk ... 77845
Berwick Pl ... 77845
Bethpage Ct ... 77845
Bird Pond Rd ... 77845
Birdie Ct ... 77845
Birmingham Dr ... 77845
Bittern Dr ... 77845
Blackhawk Ln ... 77845
Blackjack Dr ... 77845
Blanco Dr ... 77845
Bloomfield Ln ... 77845
Blue Jay Ct ... 77845
Blue Quail Ln ... 77845
Blue Ridge Dr ... 77845
N & S Bluebonnet Cir & Dr ... 77845
Bluefield Ct ... 77845
Bluestem Cir & Dr ... 77845
Boardwalk Ct ... 77840
Bogey Ct ... 77845
Bolero Ct & St ... 77845
Bolton Ave ... 77840
Bonnie Ln ... 77845
Bosque Dr ... 77845
Boswell St ... 77840
Bougainvillea St ... 77845
Boulder Ct ... 77845
Boxley Bnd ... 77845
Boyett St ... 77840
Bracey Ct ... 77845
Bradley Rd ... 77845
Branding Iron Ct ... 77845
Brazos Dr ... 77845
Brazoswood Dr ... 77840
Breckenridge Ct ... 77845
Brentwood Dr E ... 77840
Briar Rose Ct ... 77845
Bridgeberry Ct ... 77845
Bridle Ct ... 77845
Bridle Trails Ct ... 77845
Bright Cir ... 77840

Bright Water Ln 77845
Brittain Ct 77845
Brittany Dr 77845
Brooks Ave 77840
Brookwater Cir 77845
Brookway Ct & Dr 77845
Brookwood Ln 77845
Brothers Blvd 77845
Brougham Pl 77845
Brussels Dr 77845
Buckingham Cir 77845
Bucknell Ct 77840
Buena Vis 77845
Buffalo Creek Loop 77845
Buggy Ln 77845
Bunker Hill Ct 77845
Bunny Ln 77845
Burgess Ln 77845
Burkhalter Ln 77845
Butler Ridge Dr 77845
Butte Dr 77845
Buttercup Cir 77845
Caddie Ct 77845
Caddo Cv 77845
Cain Rd 77845
Calico Ct 77845
Callie Cir 77845
Calumet Trl 77845
Calusa Springs Dr 77845
Camargo Ct 77845
Camber Ct 77845
Camellia Ct 77840
Camille Dr 77845
Camp Ct 77840
Campbell Ct 77845
Candace Ct 77845
Candle Stone Ct 77845
Canterbury Dr 77845
Cantle Ct 77845
Canyon Creek Cir 77840
Capistrano Ct 77845
Capps Dr 77845
Capstone Dr 77845
Cardinal Ln 77845
Carisbrooke Loop 77845
Carlisle Ct 77845
Carll Ln 77845
Carmel Ct & Pl 77845
Carnation Ct 77840
Carnes Ct S 77845
Carolina St 77840
Carriage Way 77845
Carriker Ct 77845
Carter Lake Dr 77845
Carters Cv 77845
Cascades Ct & Dr 77845
Castle Rock Pkwy 77845
Castlebrook Dr 77845
Castlegate Dr 77845
Caterina Ln 77845
Caudill St 77840
Cecilia Ct & Loop 77845
Cedar Cir 77845
Cedar Run 77840
Cedar Bend Rd 77845
Cedar Creek Ct 77845
Cedar Ridge Dr 77845
Cedar Rock Ct 77845
Cedar Springs Ct 77845
Celinda Cir 77845
Central Park Ln 77840
Chaco Canyon Dr 77845
Chadwick Ln 77845
Chalet Ct 77840
Chantal Cir 77845
Chappel St 77840
Charles Ct 77840
Charles Haltom Ave 77840
Charleston Ct 77845
Chenault Ln 77845
Chenoa Cv 77845
Cherokee Dr 77845
Cherry St 77840
Cherry Hills Ct 77845
Chesapeake Ct & Ln 77845
Chestnut Oak Cir 77845
Cheyenne Dr 77845
Chimney Hill Cir & Dr 77840
Chippendale St 77845
Church Ave 77840
Church St 77845
Churchill St 77840
Cimarron Ct 77845
Circle Dr 77840
Citation Cir 77845
Clan Vlg 77845
Clay Pit Rd 77845
Clayton Ln 77845
Clear Meadow Creek
Ave 77845
Clearview Trl 77845
Clearwood Ct 77845
Clement Ct 77840
Clipstone Pl 77845
Cloisters Dr 77845
Close Quarters Cir 77845
Cloud Ln 77845
Cloverdale Ct 77840
Clovis Ct 77845
Coachlight Ct 77845
Coastal Dr 77845
Cochise Ct 77845
Cody Dr 77845
Coeburn Ct & Dr 77845
Colchester Ct 77845
Cold Spring Dr 77845
Cole Ln 77845
Colgate Cir & Dr 77840
College Ave 77840
College Main 77840
Colonial Cir 77845
Colorado Ct 77845
Colton Pl 77845
Columbia Ct 77840
Columbus St 77840
Comal Cir 77840
Commando Trl 77845
Commons Lobby 77840
Commonwealth Ct 77845
Concho Pl 77845
Concord Cir 77845
Congressional Ct & Dr 77845
Connie Ln 77845
Conway Ct 77845
Cooner St 77840
Copper River Dr 77845
Copperfield Pkwy 77845
Coral Rdg E & W 77845
Cornell Dr 77840
Coronado Dr 77845
Corporal Rd 77845
Corregidor Dr 77840
Cortez Ct & St 77845
Cottage Ln 77845
Cougar Ct 77840
Country Meadows Ln 77845
Coventry Pl 77845
Cranberry Dr 77845
Crayke Pl 77845
Creagor Ln 77845
W Creek Ln & Xing 77845
Creek Meadow Blvd N 77845
Creekside Cir 77845
Creekview Ct 77845
Crenshaw Cir 77845
Crepe Myrtle Ct & St 77845
Crescent Pt 77845
Crescent Pointe Pkwy 77845
Crescent Ridge Dr 77845
Crest St 77840
Crested Point Ct & Dr 77845
Cricket Pass 77845
Cripple Creek Ct 77845
Crooked Stick 77845
Cross Crk 77845
Cross St 77840
Cross Timbers Dr 77840
Crosswater Dr 77845
Crown Ct 77845
Crown Ridge Ct 77845
Crystal Dove Ave 77845
Crystal Downs Ct 77845
Cullen Trl 77845
Culpepper Dr 77840
Culture Ln 77845
Cumberland Ct 77845
Cynthia Dr 77845
Cypress Dr 77840
Dairy Center Rd 77845
Daisy Ln 77845
Dakota Ridge Dr 77845
Dallis Dr 77845
Dan Williams Ln 77845
Danby Ct 77845
Dansby Ln 77845
Danville Ct & Ln 77845
Dartmouth St 77840
Davenport Dr 77845
Davids Ln 77845
Davidson Dr 77845
Dawn Lynn Dr 77845
Day Rd 77845
Dayton Ct 77845
Deacon Dr W 77845
Decatur Dr 77845
Deep Stone Ct 77845
Deer Run 77845
Deer Creek Dr 77845
Deer Park Dr 77845
Deerfield Dr 77845
Delrey Dr 77845
Derby Cir 77845
Detroit St 77840
Devrne Dr 77845
Dew Rd 77845
Dexter Dr 77840
Diamond Ct 77845
Dickson Rd 77845
Discovery Dr 77845
Doe Cir 77845
Dogwood St 77840
Dogwood Trl 77845
Dominik Dr 77840
Dott 77845
Double Eagle Ct 77845
Dove Trl 77845
Dove Chase Ln 77845
Dove Crossing Ln 77845
Dove Hollow Ln 77845
Dove Landing Ave 77845
Dove Run Trl 77845
Dover Dr 77845
Dowling Rd 77845
N Dowling Rd
1-299 77840
9600-12899 77845
S Dowling Rd 77845
Drake Dr 77845
Dresden Ln 77845
Driftwood Dr 77845
Driver Ct 77845
Drogo Ct 77845
Drummer Cir 77845
Durango Ct & St 77845
Durban Ct 77845
Durrand St 77845
Dusty Rd 77845
Dyess Rd 77845
Dymple Ln 77845
Eagle Ave 77845
Eagle Nest 77845
Eagle Pass Dr 77845
Earl Rudder Fwy S
500-2598 77840
901-2597 77840
2599-3299 77845
3301-8999 77845
Early Amber 77845
East Byp
1001-8999 77845
1100-2598 77840
2600-2798 77845
East Cir 77840
Eastmark Dr 77840
Ebbtide Cv 77845
Edinburgh Pl 77845
Edward St 77840
Egremont Ct 77845
Eisenhower St 77840
El Campo Trl 77845
Elbrich Ln 77845
Eleanor St 77840
Elkton Ct 77845
Elmo Weedon Rd 77845
Emberglow Cir 77840
Emerald Pkwy & Plz 77845
Emerald Dove Ave 77845
Enchanted Oaks Dr 77845
Encinas Pl 77845
Escondido Ln 77845
Essen Loop 77845
Essex Grn 77845
Ethic Ln 77845
F And B Rd 77845
F Ken Nicolas Ave 77840
Fable Ln 77845
Faimes Ct 77845
Faircrest Ct & Dr 77845
Fairfax 77845
Fairhaven Cv 77845
Fairview Ave 77840
Falcon Cir 77845
Fall Cir 77840
Fallbrook Loop 77845
Falling Leaf Ct 77845
Farah Dr 77845
Faraway Island Dr 77845
Farley 77845
Faulkner Dr 77845
Favor Rd 77845
Fawn Ct & Ln 77845
Feather Run 77845
Feather Run Cir 77845
Ferber Cir 77845
Ferguson 77845
Fern Ct 77845
Fernhaven Cir 77840
Festus Ln 77845
Fidelity St 77840
Field Stone Ln 77845
Fields 77845
Fieldstone Pl 77845
Fincastle Loop 77845
Finney 77845
Fireside Cir 77840
Firestone Dr 77845
First American Blvd 77845
Fitzgerald Cir 77845
Flagstone Ct 77845
Flint Cir 77845
Flying Ace Cir 77845
Flyway Rd 77845
Fm 158 Rd 77845
Fm 2154 Rd 77845
Fm 2347 77845
Fontaine Dr 77845
Foralens Rd 77845
Fore Ct 77845
Forest Dr
23A-23B 77840
1-599 77840
10600-13099 77845
Forest Oaks Dr 77845
Forrest Ln 77845
Foster Ave 77840
Foster Ln 77845
Fox Cir 77845
Foxfire Dr 77845
Francis Cir & Dr 77840
Fraternity Row 77845
Fredrick Ct 77845
Freestone Dr 77845
Freneau Dr 77845
Friar 77845
Frierson Rd 77845
Front St 77840
Front Royal Dr 77845
Frost Dr 77845
G H Alani Rd 77845
Gail Pl 77845
Gandy Rd 77845
Ganton Ct 77845
Gardenia St 77845
Gary Rd 77845
Gateway Blvd 77845
General Pkwy 77845
George Bush Dr 77840
George Bush Dr E 77840
George Bush Dr W
100-399 77840
1000-1899 77845
Georgia St 77840
Gettysburg Ct 77845
Gibbs Cir 77845
Gilbert St 77840
Gilchrist Ave 77840
Ginger Ct 77845
Glade St 77840
Gleeson Ct 77845
Glenhaven Dr 77840
Glenna Ct 77845
Gloria Allen Dr 77845
Gold Finch Cir 77845
Gold Nugget 77845
Golden Trl 77845
Golden Mist 77845
Goode Dr 77840
N Graham Rd 77845
Gramma Ct 77845
Grand Oaks Cir 77840
Gray Wolf Trl 77845
Graz Dr 77845
Great Oaks Dr 77845
Greenberry Cir & Ct 77845
Greenleaf Dr 77845
Greens Prairie Rd &
Trl 77845
Greentree Cir 77845
Greenwood Dr 77845
Greer Ln 77845
Greta Ct 77845
Gridiron Dr 77840
Grove St 77840
Guadalupe Dr 77845
Guernsey St 77840
Gunner Trl 77845
Gunoak Dr 77845
Gunsmith St 77840
Gus Roy Rd 77845
Haddox Ct 77845
Hadleigh Ln 77845
Hailes Ln 77845
Haines Dr 77840
Haley Pl 77845
Halifax Dr 77845
Hallaran Rd 77845
Hanna Ct 77845
Harbour Town Ct 77845
Hardwood Ln 77840
Hardy Weedon Rd 77845
Harper Valley Dr 77845
Harpers Ferry Rd 77845
Harrington Ave 77840
Harris Dr 77845
Harrisonburg Ln 77845
Hartford Dr 77845
Harvard Ct 77840
Harvest Dr 77845
Harvey Rd
100-1599 77840
1601-1699 77840
2600-4699 77845
Harvey Mitchell Pkwy S
400-499 77845
1200-1699 77840
1700-1898 77840
1701-2199 77840
2100-2130 77840
2130-2130 77842
2132-2298 77845
2300-2399 77845
Hasselt St 77845
Haupt Rd 77845
Haverford Rd 77845
Hawk Owl Cv 77845
Hawk Tree Dr 77845
Hawthorn St 77840
Hayesville Ct 77845
Haywood Dr 77845
Hazeltine Ct 77845
Hazy Meadow Ct 77845
Headwater Ln 77845
Hearst Ct 77845
Hearthstone Cir 77840
Heath Dr 77845
Heather Ln 77845
Hemingway Dr 77845
Henry Ct 77845
Hensel Dr 77840
Hereford St 77840
Heritage Ln 77845
Hickory Dr 77840
Hickory Ln 77845
Hickory Rd 77845
Hickory Nut Ln 77845
Hicks Ln 77845
Hidden Acres Dr 77845
Hidden Springs Way 77845
High Lonesome 77845
High Meadow Trl 77845
High Prairie Rd 77845
Highlands St 77840
Hill Cir & Rd 77845
Hillside Dr 77845
Hogan Aly 77845
Holik Dr & St 77840
Holleman Dr 77840
Holleman Dr E 77840
Holleman Dr S 77845
Holleman Dr W 77840
Hollow Stone Dr 77845
Hollyhock St 77845
Holston Hills Dr 77845
Holt St 77840
Hondo Dr 77840
Honeysuckle Ln 77845
Hook Ct 77845
Hope Ln 77845
Hopes Cv 77845
Hopes Creek Rd 77845
Hopes Creek Meadow
Cir 77845
Hopewell Ct 77845
Horse Haven Ln 77845
Horse Shoe Dr 77845
Horseback Ct & Dr 77845
Horseshoe Ln 77845
N Houston St 77841
Howe Dr 77845
Hunter Creek Dr 77845
Hunters Cv, Holw, Run &
Way 77845
Hunters Creek Rd 77845
Huntington Dr 77845
I And Gn Rd 77845
Imperial Loop 77845
Ina Mae Allen Rd 77845
Incourt Ln 77845
Indian Trl 77845
Indian Lakes Dr 77845
Inglewood Ct 77845
Inlow Blvd 77840
Innsbruck Cir 77845
Iris Ln 77845
Ironwood Dr 77845
Ivy Cv 77845
Jade Dr 77845
James Pkwy 77840
Jane St 77840
Jasmine Ct 77845
Jennifer Cir & Dr 77845
Joe Routt Blvd 77844
Joe Varisco Dr 77845
Johnny Bars Cir 77845
Johnson Creek Loop 77845
Jones Rd 77845
Jones Butler Rd
1100-1199 77840
11700-11799 77845
11801-12199 77845
Jordan Place Rd 77845
Joseph Creek Ct 77845
Jupiter Hills Ct 77845
Justin Ave 77845
Kalanchoe Ct 77840
Karten Ln 77845
Keefer Loop 77845
Kemp Rd 77845
Kendal Green Cir 77845
Kenyon Dr 77845
Kernstown Ln 77845
Kerry St 77840
Kimbolton Dr 77845
King Arthur Cir 77840
Kingsmill Ct 77845
Kinnersly Ln 77845
Kiowa Cv 77845
Kleine Ln 77845
Koppe Bridge Rd 77845
Korshea Way 77845
Krenek Tap Rd 77840
Kristi Ln 77845
Kyle Ave 77840
L And R Rd 77845
La Granja Ct 77845
La Posada Cir 77845
La Venta Way 77845
Lacy Well Rd 77845
Ladove Dr 77845
Lake Forest Ct N & S 77845
Lakefront Dr 77845
Lakeland 77845
Lakeshore Cir & Ct 77845
Lakeside Ct 77845
Lakeway Dr 77845
Lambermont Dr 77845
Lampwick Cir 77840
Lancaster Ct 77845
Lancelot Cir 77840
Landsburg Ct & Ln 77845
Langford St 77840
Lansing Ct 77840
Lapis Ct 77845
Laredo Ct 77845
Lariat Ln 77845
Larkspur Cir 77845
Latigo Ct 77845
Latinne Ct & Ln 77845
Laura Ln 77840
Laurel Valley Ct 77845
Lauren Dr 77845
Lavaca St 77840
Lavada Ln 77845
Lawyer Pl & St 77840
N & S Lazy Crk 77845
Leacrest Dr 77840
Ledgestone Trl 77845
Lee Ave 77840
Legacy Ln 77840
Lemon Tree Ln 77840
Lenert Cir 77845
Leona Dr 77840
Leopard Ln 77840
Leyla Ln 77845
Lienz Ln 77845
Liesl Ct 77845
Lieutenant Ave 77845
Lightsey Ln 77845
Lincoln Ave 77840
Linda Ln 77845
Linsey Ln 77845
Lister Ln 77845
Little Rock Ct 77845
Live Oak St
100-499 77840
14800-15099 77845
Llano Pl 77840
Lochbury Ct 77845
Lodgepole Cir & Dr 77845
Lone Star Ln 77845
Lonetree Dr 77845
Longleaf Cir & Dr 77845
Longmire Ct 77840
Longmire Dr
2100-2198 77840
2200-3999 77845
Longthorpe Ct 77845
Lori Ln 77845
Lorikeet Ct 77845
Los Robles Dr 77845
Lost Trl 77845
Louise Ave 77840

Street	ZIP
Lovett Ln	77845
Ludlow Ln	77845
Luther St W	77840
Lyceum Ct	77840
Lynn Elliott Ln	77845
Lynx Cv	77840
Macarthur St	77840
Mack Cooner Ln	77845
Madera Cir	77840
Magnolia Dr	77840
Maidstone Ct	77845
Mallory Ct	77845
Manassas Ct	77845
Mandarin Way	77845
Mandi Ct	77845
Manuel Dr	77840
Manzano Ct	77845
Maple Ave	77840
Maplewood Ct	77845
Marcy Ln	77845
Marielene Cir	77845
Marigold Ct & St	77845
Mariner Dr	77845
Mariners Cv	77845
Marion Pugh Dr	77840
Mark	77845
Markham Ct & Ln	77845
Marshall Ln	77845
Marsteller Ave	77840
Marta St	77845
Martingale Ct	77845
Martinsville Ln	77845
Maryem St	77840
Matoska Rdg	77845
Mcallester Ln	77845
Mccullough Rd	77845
Mcfarland Dr	77845
Mckenzie Terminal Blvd	77845
Mclaren Dr	77845
Mclister Dr	77845
Meadow Pass	77845
Meadow View Ct & Dr	77845
Meadowbrook Ct	77845
Meadowhill Dr	77845
Meadowland St	77840
Medina Dr	77840
Meir Ln	77845
Meredith Ln	77845
Merion Ct	77845
Merlemont Ct	77845
Merlin Dr	77845
Merrimac Ct	77845
Merry Oaks Dr	77840
Mesa Verde Dr	77845
Mescalero Ct	77845
Mickthea Ln	77845
Middleham Ave	77845
Midsummer Ln	77845
Milam Ave	77840
Mildonhall Ct	77845
Mile Dr	77845
Millcreek Ct	77845
Milner Dr	77840
Minter Spring Rd	77845
Mirror Pond Ct	77845
Mission Hills Ct & Dr	77845
Misty Ln	77845
Mojave Canyon Dr	77845
Momentum Blvd	77845
Monitor Ct	77845
Montclair Ave	77840
Monte Carlo	77840
Morgans Ln	77845
Morning Dove Cir	77845
Mortier Dr	77845
Moses Creek Ct	77845
Moss St	77840
Mossglenn Cir	77840
Muirfield Vlg	77845
Mullins Ct & Loop E, N & S	77845
Muncaster Ln	77845
Munson Ave	77840
Mustang Ln	77845
Myrtle Dr	77845
Myth Ln	77845
Nagle St	77840
Nantucket Dr	77845
Narrow Way	77845
Navajo Ridge Dr	77845
Navarro Dr	77845
Neal Pickett Dr	77840
Nelson Ln	77840
Neuburg Ct	77845
Nevada St	77840
Newark Cir	77845
Newton Rd	77840
Night Rain Dr	77845
Nimitz St	77840
Noel Ct	77845
Noirmont Ct	77845
Norfolk Ct	77845
Norham Dr	77845
Normand Cir & Dr	77845
Norton Ln	77845
Norwich Dr	77845
Nottingham Dr	77845
Nueces Dr	77840
Nunn St	77840
Nunn Jones Rd	77845
Nursery Rd	77845
Oak Crk, Crst, Run, Ter, Trl & Vw	77845
Oak Hills Cir	77845
Oak Lake Dr	77845
Oak Leaf	77845
Oakbrook Ct	77845
Oakdale Cir	77840
Oakhaven Cir	77840
Oakmont Cir	77845
Oaks Dr & St	77845
Oakwood Trl	77845
Odell Ln	77840
Old Barker Ranch Rd	77845
Old Ironsides Dr	77845
Old Jersey St	77840
Old Jones Rd	77845
Old May Ct	77845
Old Rock Prairie Rd	77845
Old Wellborn Rd	77845
Olden Ln	77845
Oldenburg Ct & Ln	77845
Olympia Way	77840
Olympia Buddy Rd	77845
Olympic Ct	77845
Oney Hervey Dr	77840
Onyx Dr	77845
Orchid St	77845
Oriole Ct	77845
Orr St	77840
Osage Trail Cv & Dr	77845
Paint Trl	77845
Paintbrush Cir	77845
Painted Sunset Ct	77845
Paleo Pt	77845
Palm Ct	77845
Palo Duro Cyn	77845
Paloma Ridge Dr	77845
Palomino Rd	77845
Pamela Ln	77845
Pamplin Ct	77845
Panther Ln	77840
Papa Bear Dr	77845
Park Pl & Rd	77840
Parker Ln	77845
Parkland Dr	77845
Parkview Dr	77845
Parnell Dr	77845
Parrot Cv	77845
Pasler St	77840
Passendale Ln	77845
Pate Rd	77845
Patricia St	77840
Pawnee Xing	77845
Pawnee Creek Ct	77845
Peach Creek Rd	77845
Peach Creek Cut Off	77845
Peach Crossing Dr	77845
Pearce St	77840
Pebble Creek Pkwy	77845
Pebblestone Ct	77845
Pecan Grove Ct	77845
Pedernales Dr	77845
Pelicans Point Cv	77845
Perry Ln	77845
Pershing Ave & Dr	77840
Petersburg Ct	77845
Peyton St	77840
Pheasant Ln	77845
Phoenix St	77840
Picadilly Cir	77845
Pickering Pl	77845
Pidmont Ln	77845
Pierre Pl	77845
Pikes Peak Ct	77845
Pine Ridge Dr	77840
Pine Valley Dr	77845
Pinon Dr	77845
Pintail Ln & Loop	77845
Pinto Run	77845
Pipeline Rd	77845
Piper Ln	77845
Piping Rock Ct	77845
E & W Placid Dr	77845
Plainfield Ct	77845
Plano Dr	77845
Pleasant Forest Dr	77845
Pleasant Grove Dr	77845
Plum Hollow Ct & Dr	77845
Polo Rd	77845
Pomel Cir & Dr	77845
Ponderosa Dr	77845
Poplar St	77840
Portsmouth Ct	77845
Post Oak Bnd	77845
Post Oak Cir	
1400-1499	77840
1900-2299	77845
Potomac Pl	77840
Potter Ln	77845
Prairie Dawn Ct & Trl	77845
Pratt Rd	77845
Preakness Cir	77845
Preston St	77840
Prestwick Ct	77845
Princeton Cir	77840
Pro Ct	77845
Pronghorn Ln & Loop	77845
Pueblo Ct N & S	77845
Puffin Way	77845
Purple Martin Cv	77845
Puryear Dr	77840
Putter Ct	77845
Quail Run	77845
Quails Nest Cir	77845
Quaker Ridge Ct & Dr	77845
Quality Cir	77845
Queens Ct	77845
Rainbow Trl	77845
Raintree Dr	77845
Ranch House Ct & Rd	77845
Ranchero Rd	77845
Ransberg Ct	77845
Ravenstone Loop	77845
Rayado Ct N & S	77845
Rayburn Ct	77840
Raymond Stotzer Pkwy	77845
Reatta Ln	77845
Red Hvn	77845
Red Hill Dr	77845
Redman Ln	77845
Redmond Dr	77840
Redwood St	77845
Reed Dr	77840
Regal Row	77845
Regal Oaks Dr	77845
Regensburg Ln	77845
Rehel Dr	77845
Remington Ct	77845
Renee Ln	77845
Rescue Ct	77845
Research Pkwy	77845
Retriever Run	77845
Reveille Rd	77845
Richards St	77840
Richland Ct N & S	77845
Rickey	77845
W Ridge Bnd, Crk, Ct, Cv, Dr, Grv, Loop, Run & Walk	77845
Ridge Bluff Dr	77845
Ridge Oak	77845
Ridgecraft	77845
Ridgecrest Dr	77845
N & S Ridgefield Cir	77840
Ridgeline Dr	77845
Ridgeview	77845
Ridgeway Dr	77845
Ridgewood St	77845
Rio Bravo Ct	77845
Rio Grande Blvd	77845
Ripplewood Ct	77845
Riskys Ranch Dr	77845
Ritchey Rd	77845
Riva Ridge Rd	77845
River Rd	77845
River Oaks Dr	77845
River Place Ct	77845
River Ridge Dr	77845
Rivers End Dr	77845
Riverstone Ct	77845
Riviera Ct	77845
Roanoke Ct	77845
Roans Chapel Rd	77845
Robelmount Dr	77845
Robin Dr & Trl	77845
Rock Bend Dr	77845
Rock Prairie Rd W	77845
Rock Spring Ct	77845
Rockcliffe Loop	77845
Rockingham Loop	77845
Rocky Briar Ct	77845
Rocky Creek Trl	77845
Rocky Meadows Dr	77845
Rocky Mountain Ct	77845
Rocky Oak Ct	77845
Rocky Rhodes Dr	77845
Rocky Vista Dr	77845
Rolling Rdg	77845
Rolling Hill Trl	77845
Rolling Rock Pl	77845
Rose Cir	77840
Rosebud Ct	77845
Rosemary Ln	77840
Rosewood Dr	77845
Roucourt Loop	77845
Roxborough Pl	77845
Royal Adelade Dr & Loop	77845
Royal Oaks	77845
Royder Rd	77845
Ruddy Duck Dr	77845
Rugen Ln	77845
Runaway Rd	77845
Running Brook Ct	77845
Sabine Ct	77840
Saddle Ln	77845
Saddle Creek Dr	77845
Sagewood Dr	77845
Saint Andrews Dr	77845
Salem Ct	77845
Sallie Ln	77845
Salzburg Ct	77845
San Benito Ct & Dr	77845
San Felipe Dr	77845
San Mario Ct	77845
San Pedro Dr	77845
San Saba Cir, Ct & Dr	77845
Sanctuary Ct	77840
Sandlewood Ct	77845
Sandpiper Cv	77845
Sandstone Dr	77845
Sandy Cir	77845
Santa Rita Ct	77845
Santour Ct	77845
Sapphire Ct & Dr	77845
Sara Dr & Ln	77845
Savannah Ct	77845
Scarborough Dr	77845
Schehin Rd	77845
Scoffield Dr	77845
Sconset Ct	77845
Sconterm St	77840
Scotney Ct	77845
Scott And White Dr	77845
Scrimshaw Ln	77845
Seamist Ln	77845
Sebesta Ln & Rd	77845
Seminole Pt	77845
Sendera Ct	77845
Seneca Spgs	77845
Serenity Cir	77845
Sergeant Dr	77845
Serval Ln	77840
Settlement Dr	77845
Shadow Bend Ct	77845
Shadow Oaks	77845
Shadowbrook Cir	77845
Shadowcrest Dr	77845
Shadowwood Dr	77840
Shady Dr	77840
Shaffer Rd	77845
Shallow Creek Loop	77845
Shellbournes Hl	77845
Shenandoah Dr	77845
Sherman Ct	77845
Shiloh Ct	77845
Shire Dr	77845
Shoal Creek Dr	77845
Short Rd	77845
Shoshoni Ct	77845
Silver Brook Ct	77845
Silver Oak Dr	77845
Silver Springs Ct	77845
Silverthorne Ln	77845
Simi Dr	77845
Sioux Springs Dr	77845
Skrivanek Ct	77840
Skyline Ct	77845
Slice Ct	77845
Smith Ln	77845
Smugglers Rd	77845
Snowdance Ct	77845
Snug Harbor Dr	77845
Socorro Ct	77845
Somerset Hills Ct	77845
Song Sparrow Ln	77845
Sonoma Cir	77845
Sophia Ln	77845
Southern Hills Ct	77845
Southern Plantation Dr	77845
Southern Trace Ct & Dr	77845
Southern Way Dr	77845
Southland St	77840
Southwest Pkwy E	77840
Southwood Dr	
1800-2199	77840
2200-2699	77845
Spanish Bay Ct	77845
Spartanburg Ct	77845
Spearman Dr	77845
Spicewood Ct	77845
Spring Crk	77845
Spring Loop	77845
Spring Branch Ct & Dr	77845
Spring Garden Dr	77845
Spring Hill Dr	77845
Spring Meadows Ct & Dr	77845
Springbrook Estates Dr	77845
Springfield Dr	77845
Springhaven Cir	77840
Springmist Dr	77845
Springwood Ct	77845
Spruce St	77840
Spyglass Ct	77845
Stagecoach Rd	77845
Stallings Dr	77840
Stallion Rdg	77845
Stanford Cir	77840
Starling Dr	77845
Stasney St	77840
State Highway 30	77845
State Highway 47	77845
State Highway 6 S	77845
Stauffer Cir	77845
Sterling St	77840
Stetson Dr	77845
Stevens Creek Ct	77845
Stewart Dr	77845
Stewarts Mdws	77845
Stillforest Cir	77845
Stillwater Rd	77845
Stirrup Dr	77845
Stockton Dr	77845
Stokes Cir	77845
Stone Castle Cir	77845
Stone Chase Ct	77845
Stone Cove Ct	77845
Stonebriar Cir	77845
Stonebridge Ct & Dr	77845
Stonebrook Dr	77845
Stonewall Ct	77845
Stonewater Loop	77845
Stoney Hills Ct	77845
Stony Brk	77845
Stony Creek Ln	77845
Stousland Rd	77845
Strand Ln	77845
Strasburg Cir	77845
Straub Rd	77845
Stuttgart Cir	77845
Suffolk Ave	77840
Sulphur Springs Rd	77845
Summer Ct	77840
Summer Court Cir	77840
Summerglen Dr	77840
Summit St	77845
Sumter Dr	77845
Sun Creek Cir	77845
Sun Meadow Ct & St	77845
Sundance Dr	77845
Sunflower Trl	77845
Sunlake Ct	77845
Sunny Ct	77840
Sunny Meadow Brook Ct	77845
Sunset Cv, Dr, Hl, Loop, Mdws, Rdg, Trl, Vly, Vw, Walk & Way	77845
Sussex Dr	77845
Suzanne Pl	77845
Sweetwater Dr	77845
Swiss Ct	77840
Sycamore Hills Ct & Dr	77845
Tahoma Trl	77845
Tall Timber Dr	77845
Tallulah Trl	77845
Tara Ct	77840
Tarrow St	77840
Tarset Ct	77845
Tauber St	77840
Taurus Ave & Cir	77840
Taylor Rd	77845
Teakwood Ct	77845
Teal Dr	77840
Technology Loop, Pkwy & Way	77845
Texas Ave S	
100-298	77840
300-2799	77840
2800-3299	77845
Thomas St	77840
Thompson St	77840
Thornton Ct	77840
Thoroughbred Rdg	77845
Thousand Oaks Rd	77845
Throckmorton St	77840
Tiffany Trl	77845
Timber Dr	77845
Timber St	77840
Timber Creek Ln	77845
Timber Knoll Dr	77845
Timberidge Dr	77845
Timberline Dr	77845
Timberwood Dr	77845
Time Dr	77845
Timm Dr	77840
Todd Trl	77845
Toddington Ln	77845
Toltec Trl	77845
Tonerbridge Dr	77845
Toni Ct	77845
Tonkaway Lake Rd	77845
Topaz Ct	77845
Tournay Ln	77845
Townplace Dr	77840
Trace Mdws	77845
Tranquil Path Dr	77845
Tranquillity Cir	77845
Treehouse Trl	77845
Treeline Dr	77845
Trellis Gate Ct	77845
Trigger St	77840
Trinity Pl	77840
Triple Rdg	77845
Triple Bend Cir & Rd	77845
Triumph Ct	77845
Trotter Ln	77845
Trumpeter Swan Ct & Dr	77845
Tucker Nuck	77845
Turk Ranch Rd	77845
Turkey Creek Rd	77845
Turkey Meadow Ct	77845
Turnberry Cir	77845
Turner St	77840
Turtle Dove Trl	77845
Turtle Rock Loop	77845
Tuscany Trce	77845
Twelve Oaks	77845
Twin Lakes Cir	77845
Twin Pond Cir	77845
Tyler Ct	77845
Tyree	77845
University Dr	77840
University Dr E	
100-1799	77840
1800-3398	77845
University Oaks Blvd	77840
Val Verde Dr	77845
Valley Cir	77845
Valley Brook Cir	77845
Valley View Dr	
1500-1899	77840
9500-10099	77845
Van Horn Dr	77845
Vassar Ct	77840
Velencia Ct	77845
Venture Dr	77845
Vicksburg Ct	77845
Victoria Ave	77845
Vienna Dr	77845
Village Dr	77840
Vincent Rd	77845
Vintage Oaks Ct & Dr	77845
Vinyard Ct	77840
Vista Ln	77845
Von Trapp Ln	77845
Wade Rd	77845
Wagner Ln	77845
Walcourt Loop	77845
Walnut Bnd & Rd	77845
Walnut Grove Ct	77845
Walton Dr	77840
Warkworth Rd	77845
Waterford Dr	77845
Waterway Dr	77845
Wayfarer Ln	77845
Wayne Ct	77845
Waynesboro Ct	77845
Weedon Loop	77845
Welcome Ln	77845
Wellborn Rd N	77840
Wellesley Ct	77840
Welsh Ave	
300-1900	77840
1902-2198	77840
2300-3499	77845
Weslayan Ct	77845
Westchester Ave	77845
Westfield Dr	77845
Westover St	77840
Wheaton Ct	77845
Whippoorwill Dr	77845
Whispering Rdg	77845

Whispering Creek Ct & Dr 77845
Whispering Oaks Dr 77845
Whistling Straits Ct, Dr & Loop 77845
White Creek Rd 77845
White Dove Trl 77845
White Fawn Cir 77845
White Rock Rd 77845
Whiterose Ct 77845
Whites Creek Ln & Rd 77845
Whitewing Ln 77845
Whitney Ct & Ln 77845
Whitwick Pl 77845
Wigeon Trail Dr 77845
Wild Burro Ln 77845
Wild Horse Run 77845
Wild Horse Creek Ct 77845
Wild Plum St 77845
Wild Rose Ct 77845
Wilderness Dr 77845
Wildewood Cir 77845
Wildrye Dr 77845
William D Fitch Pkwy 77845
Williams St 77840
Williams Creek Dr 77845
Williams Ridge Ct 77845
Willow Loop 77845
Willow Brook Dr 77845
Willow Pond Ct & St 77845
Wilshire Ct 77845
Wimbledon Cir 77845
Windfree Dr 77845
Windham Ranch Rd 77845
Winding Crk 77845
Winding Rd 77840
N & S Windjammer Ct 77845
Windmeadows Dr 77845
Windmill Ct 77845
Windrift Cv 77845
Windswept Dr 77845
Windwood Dr 77845
Windy Ryon Rd 77845
Winecup Cir 77845
Wingate Cir & Ct 77845
Winged Foot Dr 77845
Winter Park 77840
Wolf Run 77840
Wolf Pen Ct 77840
Wood Brook Ln 77845
Woodall Ct 77845
Woodcliff Ct 77845
Woodcreek Dr 77845
Wooded Dr 77845
Woodhaven Cir 77840
Woodlake Dr 77845
Woodland Pkwy 77840
Woodland Ridge Ct & Dr 77845
Woodland Springs Dr 77845
Woodlands Dr 77845
Woods Ln 77845
Woodsman Dr 77840
Woodview Dr 77845
Worthington Ct 77845
Yale Cir 77840
Yaupon Ln 77845
Yegua Creek Ct 77845
Yellowhouse Cir 77840
Yorkshire Dr 77845
Yorktown Ct 77845

NUMBERED STREETS

1st St 77840
2nd St 77840
12th Man Cir 77845

COMMERCE TX

General Delivery 75428

POST OFFICE BOXES MAIN OFFICE STATIONS AND BRANCHES

Box No.s
All PO Boxes 75429

RURAL ROUTES

01, 03 75428

NAMED STREETS

All Street Addresses 75428

NUMBERED STREETS

All Street Addresses 75428

CONROE TX

General Delivery 77301

POST OFFICE BOXES MAIN OFFICE STATIONS AND BRANCHES

Box No.s
1 - 3712 77305
7001 - 7411 77306
8001 - 8745 77302

NAMED STREETS

Aaron Pasternak Dr 77304
Abercrombie Pl 77384
Academy Dr 77301
Academy Way 77384
Acapulco Rd 77306
Accolade Way 77385
Acorn Hill Dr 77302
Acreman Rd 77306
Adams Rd 77306
Adams St 77301
Adcock Acres Dr 77303
Adkins St 77301
Airline Dr 77301
Airport Pkwy 77303
Airport Rd
600-898 77301
900-2299 77301
8900-10599 77303
Alabama Park 77302
Albert Moorehead Rd 77302
Alden Woods 77384
Aldine Westfield Rd 77385
Aldrich St 77302
Alexandria Dr 77302
Allen Dr 77304
Allen St 77301
Allendale Ln 77302
Alley Ln 77302
Allison St 77303
Alma St 77301
Alto Dr 77301
Amanda St 77304
Amber Park Dr 77303
Amherst Ct 77304
Amy Lee Dr 77304
Andershire Dr 77304
Anderson Rd 77304
Andrew Ridge Ln 77384
Angela Faye Way 77304
Angelina Ct, Dr & Ln 77302
Angler Park 77385
Anmar Dr 77303
Ann Ct 77385
Annie Belle 77304
Antilles Ln 77304
Antiqua Estates Ct 77385
Apache Cir 77304
Apple Orchard Trl 77301
Apple Valley Dr 77304
Appomattox Park 77302
N & S April Mist Cir 77385
Aquarius Rd 77306
Arbor Gln 77303
Arbor Strm 77384
Arbor Way 77303
Arbor Xing 77303
Arbor Hill Ct 77384
Arbor Ridge Ct & Ln 77384
Arbor Trail Ln 77384
Arbor Valley Trl 77384
Arcadia Way 77384
Archer Park 77385
Ardmore St 77302
Argo Rd 77301
Argonne Stone Ln 77302
Arkansas Park 77302
Arlington St 77301
Arnold St 77301
Arrowhead Pl 77304
Artesia 77304
Artesian Forest Dr 77304
Artesian Oaks Dr 77304
Artic Cir 77306
Ashland Dr 77385
Ashmore Estates Ct 77385
Ashway St 77385
Ashworth Ct 77385
Aspen Star Ct 77302
Atkinson Ln 77384
Atlanta Park 77302
Augusta Park 77302
Aurora Business Park Dr 77301
W Austin Rd & St 77301
Autumn Ash Dr 77302
Autumn Bend Dr 77303
Autumn Forest Ln 77384
Autumn Mist Ln 77302
Autumn Ridge Dr 77304
Autumn Run Ln 77304
Avebury Ct 77384
Avenue E 77301
Avenue A 77301
Avenue F 77301
E & W Avenue G 77301
Avenue H 77301
Avenue I 77301
Avenue J Pl 77301
Avenue L 77301
E Avenue M Ext 77301
Avery St 77302
Axleridge Dr 77384
Baccara Pl 77384
Bagpipe Way 77384
Ballard Cir 77304
Balsam Spruce Cir 77301
Barbara Ln 77301
Barber Ln 77303
Barbican Ct 77304
Baretta Dr 77301
Bark Bend Pl 77385
Barkley Park Ct 77384
Barkwood Cir 77304
Barons Pl 77304
Bart Lake Rd 77303
Bartle St 77301
S Barton Woods Blvd 77301
Baxter Rd 77306
Bay Ave 77301
Bay Ct 77304
Bay Bend Dr 77304
Bay Chapel Ct 77385
Bay Hill Ln 77304
Bay Laurel Ln 77304
Baylor Dr 77303
Bayou Dr 77304
Bayou St John 77304
Bayou Teche Ct 77302
Bayou Tisch 77304
Beach Rd 77304
Beach Airport Rd 77301
Beach Walk Blvd 77304
Beasley Rd 77301
Beau Rivage 77304
Beauregard Dr 77302
Becky St 77301
Bedford Ln
200-399 77303
15400-15599 77384
Beech Dr 77385
Beeson Rd 77306
Bell Ct 77302
Bella Vita Dr 77304
Bellingrath Park 77302
Bellisima Ct 77384
Bellshire Dr 77301
Belmont Ct 77304
Belton Shores Dr 77304
Belvedere Dr 77301
Ben Wiggins Rd 77303
Bending Oak Dr 77306
Bending Oaks 77385
N & S Bendrook Loop 77384
Bennette Woods Rd 77302
Bent Pine Dr 77302
Bergman Ct 77384
Berry Ct 77302
Berry Ln 77302
Berry Rd 77304
Bert Brown Rd 77302
Bertrand St 77301
Bethesda Dr 77384
Bettes St 77301
Betty St 77301
Big Holly Ln & St 77385
Big Oak Dr
1800-1899 77301
19000-19499 77302
Big Oaks Dr 77385
Biggs Ct 77302
Bihms Rd 77385
Bill Smith Rd 77384
Billandrea Ln 77304
Billie Bess Ln 77301
Biloxi Ct 77302
Bimbo Ln 77302
Bimms Dr 77385
Birch Cluster Ct 77301
Birdie Rd 77303
Black Bass Dr 77384
Black Bear St 77385
Black Buck Ln 77303
Black Forest Ct 77385
Black Percher St 77385
Blackberry Rd 77306
Blackberry Lily Ln 77385
Blair Rd & Xing 77385
Blake Rd 77304
Blanks Rd 77306
Bloomsbury Ct 77384
Blue Gill Rd 77384
Blue Grass Way 77304
Blue Jay Dr & St 77385
Blueberry Hill Dr 77385
Bluebird Pl 77385
Blush Hill Dr 77304
Bo Wood 77302
Board Xing 77304
Bob White Dr & St 77385
Bobolink Dr 77385
Boca Raton Dr 77304
Bodie Perry Rd 77306
Bois D Arc Dr 77301
Bond Ln 77303
Boney Rd 77385
Bonney 77385
Booker T Washington St 77301
Borthwick Ln 77301
Boulder Park Ct 77385
Boulder Ridge Dr 77304
Bounds Rd 77302
Bowie Bend Ct 77385
Bowles Rd 77304
Bowling Green Dr 77385
Bowman St 77301
Boyd Ln & Rd 77306
Brabner Way 77301
Brad Park 77304
Brady Ct 77302
Braley Park Ln 77385
Bramlet Dr 77304
Brampton Ct 77304
Branch Creek Ct 77304
Brandon Rd 77302
Branns Fern 77304
Brass Nail 77384
Braxton Bragg Ln 77302
Brenda Ln 77385
Brendan Woods Ln 77384
Brentwood Ct 77303
Brewster St 77301
Briac Ln 77301
Briar Ct 77304
Briar Pass 77301
Briar Cliff St 77385
Briar Cut Off 77301
Briar Glenn Dr 77301
Briar Grove Ct & Dr 77301
Briar Net 77301
Briarwood Dr E 77301
Bridlewood 77384
Brighton Way 77304
Brittany Way 77306
Brittney Ln 77303
Broad Oaks 77301
Broadmoor Ct 77304
Broadway Ave & St 77385
Brodie Ln 77301
Broken Bough Ln 77304
Broken Pine Ct 77304
Broken Ridge Dr 77304
Brook Forest Ct & Dr 77385
Brook Haven Dr 77385
Brook Hollow Dr 77385
Brookfield Ln 77302
Brooks Rd 77302
Brookwood Cir 77304
Browder St 77301
Browder Traylor Rd 77303
Brown Rd
300-399 77304
17500-17999 77306
Brown Oak Dr 77304
Bryant Rd 77303
Bryants Cir 77306
Buckingham Ct 77304
Buckingham Pl 77306
Buggy Ln 77302
Bull Run Ct 77302
Bulldog Ln 77306
Bullfrog Ln 77384
Bunny Hill Ct 77302
E & W Burberry Cir 77384
Burgandy Vine Ct 77384
Burnt Wood Ct 77385
Burton Forest Ct 77384
Bush Buck Ln 77303
Butler Dr 77303
Butler Rd 77301
Butler Road Ext 77301
Butlers Ct 77385
Butlers Dr 77306
Butlers Island St 77302
Bybee Dr 77301
Byrdsong Ct 77301
Cabbage Palm Ct 77385
Cabin Creek Ct 77385
Cable St 77301
Cactus Dr 77385
Cafe Dumonde 77304
Calais Ct 77304
Calfee Rd 77304
Calhoun Rd 77302
Callahan Ave 77301
Camborn Pl 77384
Cambridge Cir 77304
Camden Park Dr 77385
Camelback Ct 77304
Camelot St 77304
Cameo Way 77384
Canary Ct & St 77385
Cancun 77306
Candice Ct 77304
Candy Oak Ln 77306
Cane River Ln 77302
Canter Ct & Ln 77384
Canterbury Ct 77304
Canterbury Dr 77303
Cantrell Blvd 77301
Canyon Ct & Xing 77385
Canyon Creek Ln 77304
Canyon Crest Ln 77302
Canyon Cross 77385
Canyon Lake Creek Dr 77304
Canyon Ridge Ln 77304
Capshaw Ct 77385
Cardinal Trl 77302
Carissa Holly Dr 77384
Carl Pickering Dr 77303
Carla Ct 77302
Carlton St 77301
Carmen Blvd 77306
Carmita St 77385
Carnes St 77301
Carol Lee Ln 77301
N & S Carolina Park 77302
Carpenter Rd 77302
Carriage Ln
100-199 77385
8100-12499 77304
Carriage Run E 77384
Carriage Run W 77384
Carriage Hills Blvd 77384
Carriage House Way 77384
Carriage Lamp Ln 77384
Carriage Ridge Ln 77384
Carter Ln 77302
Carters Grv 77302
Cartwright Rd 77301
Casper Ct 77302
Cassowary Dr 77385
Castlewood Dr 77306
Catfish Ln 77384
Cattail Park Ct 77385
Cayman Est 77385
Cedar Cir 77302
Cedar Ln
100-199 77303
2000-2099 77301
11600-12299 77303
Cedar Creek Dr 77301
Cedar Forest Dr 77384
Cedar Hill Ln 77303
Cedar Knoll Ct & Dr 77301
Cedar Lake Ct 77384
Cedar Springs Dr 77384
Centennial Dr 77384
S Center St 77301
Centerline Rd 77384
Central Pkwy 77303
Chambers St 77301
Champion Ln 77304
Champion Forest Loop & Rd 77303
Champion Village Dr & Rd 77303
Chancellorsville Park 77302
Chandler Ln 77302
Chantilly Ln 77384
Chanty Way 77301
Chapel Hill Dr 77302
Chappel Wood Ln 77302
Chapperal Pipeline Rd 77302
Charles Ray Ln 77302
Charleston Park 77302
Charter Ln 77301
Charter Club Dr 77384
Charter Oaks Ct & Dr 77302
Chase Ct 77301
E Chase Ct 77304
W Chase Ct 77304
Chasewood Blvd 77304
Chasewood Ct 77303
Chateau Ln 77385
Chateau Woods Parkway Dr 77385
Chattanooga Park 77302
Chauncey Ct 77384
Chelsea Rd 77304
Cherokee Dr 77304
Cherry Hill Dr 77304
Chestnut Glen Ct 77301
Chestnut Meadow Dr 77384
Cheswood St 77301
Cheyenne Ct 77304
Chicadee Ln 77306
Chicora Wood Ct 77302
Chimney Swift Ln 77385
Chorale Grove Ct 77384
Chris Carrie Ln 77303
Christi Lyn Ln 77304
Christmas Tree Ln 77304
Cindy Ln
1700-1799 77304
18000-18999 77302
Circle Dr 77301
Circle Six Dr 77306
Clanton Rd 77301
Clarewood Ct 77385
Claridge Ct 77304
Claridge Oak Ct 77384
Clark Dr 77301
Clark Ln 77385
Clark St 77302
Clatt Way 77301
Clearbend Pl 77384
Cleveland Rd 77304
Cliff Manor Dr 77304
Climbing Rose Ct 77385
Climbing Tree St 77385
Clint Parker Rd 77303
Clinton St 77301
Coachlight Ln 77384
Coachman Dr 77384
Coaster Ln 77306
Cobblecreek Ct & Dr 77384
Cochise Ct 77304
Cochran St 77301
Coker Rd 77306
Cole Brook Ln 77304
Coleman St 77301
College St 77301
College Park Dr 77384
Collins St 77301
Colonial Ct 77304
Columbia St 77301
Columnberry Ct 77384
Commerce Oaks Dr 77385
Commercial Cir 77304
Compass Ct 77301
Conastoga Ct 77384
Concord Dr 77385
Condor Ct 77304
Condor Dr 77385
Condra Rd 77306
Conroe Dr
100-399 77301
15200-15499 77384
S Conroe Medical Dr 77304
N & W Conroe Park Dr 77303
Conti Ct 77304
Coon Hollow Rd 77306
Coon Massey Rd 77306
Cooper Ln 77303
Cooper Rd 77302
Copper Cv 77304
Copperhead Rd 77303
Coral Ct 77304
Coral Cove Pass Ln 77304
Cornflower Dr 77384
Corona Way 77306
Cory St 77301
Cotton Ln 77304
Cottonwood Dr 77302
Cottonwood Ln 77306
Cougar Creek St 77385
Country Ln 77384
Country Vlg 77302
Country Club Dr 77302
N Country Gate Cir 77384
Country Hill Ln 77304
Country Place Dr 77302
Country West Dr 77302
Courtyard Cir 77304
Cowan Ave 77301
Cox Rd 77385
Cozumel 77306
Crag Ct 77301
Crane Ct 77385
Crannog Way 77301
Crappie Trl 77384

N Creek Dr 77301
W Creek Dr 77304
Creek Forest Ln 77384
Creek Gate Rd 77385
Creek View Ln 77385
N & S Creekmist Pl 77385
Creekside St 77304
Creekwood Ln 77306
Creighton Rd 77302
Creighton Ridge Rd 77302
Cresent Mill Ln 77304
Crest Hill Dr 77301
Crestview Ln 77304
Crestwood Park 77385
Cricket Ln 77303
Crighton Crossing Dr ... 77302
Crighton Ridge Cir 77302
Criminal Justice Dr 77301
Cripple Crk 77304
Crockett Xing 77303
Crockett Bend Dr 77303
Crockett Forest Dr 77306
Crockett Martin N 77303
Crockett Martin Rd 77306
Crockett Trace Dr 77303
Crooke St 77301
Crooked Pine Ct 77304
Cross Creek Rd 77304
Cross Spring Park Ln .. 77385
Crowley Rd 77306
Crystal Crk 77303
Crystal Ct 77303
Crystal Ln 77303
N Crystal Rd 77302
Crystal Trl 77306
Crystal Creek Frst 77303
Crystal Forest Cir, Ct &
Dr 77306
N & S Crystal Springs
Cir & Dr 77303
Crysti Ct 77304
Cumberland Ct 77302
Cumberland Pkwy 77384
Cumberland Trl 77302
Curry Rd 77385
Curtis Creek Ct 77304
Custers Ct 77304
Cypress Cir 77302
Cypress Dr
200-499 77304
14700-14999 77302
Cypress Ln 77301
Daisy View Ct 77302
E Dallas St 77301
W Dallas St
100-900 77301
809-809 77305
901-1199 77301
902-1198 77301
Dam Site Rd 77304
Damico Ln 77306
Danika Oak Dr 77306
Dans Ln 77302
Danville Crossing Ct 77385
Darby Loop 77385
Dardenelle Ct 77384
Darlinghurst Dr 77384
Darnell St 77301
David Forest Ln 77384
E Davis St 77301
W Davis St
100-1199 77301
1200-6099 77304
Davis Cottage Ct 77385
Dawn Brook Ln 77384
Day Dr 77303
Dean Ct 77302
Decatur Ct 77384
Decker St 77301
Dee St 77301
Deep Dale Ln 77304
Deep Forest Dr 77306
Deep Woods Trl 77302
Deer Trce 77384
Deer Trl 77302
Deer Way 77303
Deer Crossing Ct 77384
Deer Glen Dr & Ln 77302
Deer Glen West Dr 77302
Deer Ridge Dr 77306
Deer Run Rd 77306
Deer Trail Dr 77306
Deerchase Dr 77384
Deerfield Meadow Dr ... 77384
Deerpath Dr 77303
Deerwood Dr & Rd 77306
Defor Rd 77301
N & S Delmont Dr E &
W 77301
Delores Ln 77384
Delores St 77301
Delta St 77301
N & S Delta Mill Cir &
Ct 77385
Denise Rd 77306
Derby Dr 77303
Deschner Rd 77303
Desert Star Ct & Dr 77302
Devon Mill Ct 77384
Devonshire Dr 77304
Dewberry Ln 77302
Diane St 77301
Dillon Dr 77303
Discovery Ln 77301
Dobbin Dr 77384
Dobyns Dr 77306
Dogwood Dr 77303
Dogwood Ln
9600-10199 77306
15000-15499 77303
Dogwood Trl 77304
Dogwood Cluster Ct 77301
Doire Dr 77301
Doncaster St 77303
Donna Rd 77306
Donwick Dr 77385
Doolan Dr 77301
Dorbandt Rd 77303
Dorrington Estates Ln .. 77385
Doty Dr 77303
Douget Rd 77303
Dove Ct 77385
Dove Meadow Dr 77384
Dover Dr 77304
Dr Martin Luther King
Jr Pl N & S 77301
Dragonfly Dr 77301
Drew Ln 77304
W Drifting Shadows Cir
& Ct 77385
Drowsy Pnes 77306
Druid Cir 77302
Duer Ln 77301
Duffy Rd 77302
Dumaine Ct 77304
Duncan Ln 77302
Dundee Dr 77301
Durham Dr 77302
Dusty Ln 77306
N & S Dylanshire Cir ... 77384
Eagle Post Dr 77304
Earls Row 77304
Easley St 77385
East Dr 77302
Eastwood Cir & Dr 77301
Eastwood Hills Dr 77385
Ed Kharbat Dr 77301
Edgar St 77301
Edgefield Ln 77302
Edinburgh Ct 77384
Edith Ln 77385
Ehlers Rd 77302
El Dorado St 77304
Elder Rd 77385
Elizabeth Rdg 77304
Elk Run Ct & Dr 77384
Ella Haynes Rd 77304
Elliotts Ct 77304
Ellis Park Ct & Ln 77304
Ellzey Ln 77302
Elm St 77301
Elmo Ct 77302
Elmore Ln 77385
Elmside Ct 77301
Eloise St 77301
Elrod St 77303
Ember Pines Ct 77384
Emerales Rd 77303
E, N, S & W Emerson
Cir 77306
Emery Mill Pl 77384
Emily Way 77302
Enchanted Oaks Ln 77304
Enchanted Stream Dr .. 77304
Endicott Ln 77302
Enterprise Row 77301
Eric Cir 77302
Erickson St 77301
E Essex Dr 77302
Estates Dr 77304
Estes Hill Ln 77302
Esther Dr 77384
Eva Ln 77306
Evangeline Blvd 77304
E, N, S & W Evangeline
Oaks Cir 77384
Evanhill Ct 77304
Everett St 77301
Evergreen Ln 77302
Evergreen Rd 77303
Evergreen Oak Dr 77384
Evergreen Park Ln 77385
Expedition Trl 77385
Explorer Way 77301
Exxon Rd 77302
Fairmont Ct 77304
Fairview Dr 77385
Fairway Ct 77302
Fairway Dr 77304
Fairway Oaks 77302
Fairwind Trail Ct & Dr .. 77385
Falcon Way 77304
Fall Forest Ct 77301
Fallen Timbers Dr 77385
Falling Pine Dr 77304
Fallow Ln 77303
Fallow Buck Ct & Dr ... 77384
Fallsbrook Ct 77302
Farmers Trl 77306
Fawn Trl
1-99 77302
8600-8899 77385
13400-13899 77302
Fawn Mist Ct & Dr 77303
Fawn Ridge Dr 77304
Fay Dr 77301
Felder Ln 77304
Fellowship Dr 77384
Fenley Rd 77302
Fenwick Ln 77384
Ferguson St 77301
Fern Ln 77306
Fields View Ct 77384
Fieldwood Ln 77304
Fife Dr 77301
Finch Ct 77385
Fir Ct 77302
Firehouse Rd 77385
Firetower Rd 77306
Firewood Dr 77303
Firthwood Dr 77301
Fitzroy Pl 77384
Five Guinea Ln 77302
Flamingo Ln & St 77385
Flint St 77301
Floating Heart Ct 77385
Florian Ct 77385
Florida Park 77302
Fm 1314 Rd
12200-12399 77301
12401-12497 77302
12499-19299 77302
Fm 1484 Rd 77303
Fm 1485 Rd
1000-1599 77301
2800-16999 77306
Fm 1488 Rd 77384
Fm 2090 Rd 77306
Fm 2432 Rd 77303
Fm 2854 Rd
600-699 77301
701-999 77301
1300-3498 77304
3500-14199 77304
Fm 3083 Rd
100-12499 77301
12500-17699 77302
15901-15999 77302
N Fm 3083 Rd 77301
N Fm 3083 Rd E 77303
N Fm 3083 Rd W
1-999 77303
1100-1700 77304
1702-2298 77304
Food For Life Way 77385
Forest Ct 77303
E Forest Ct 77384
W Forest Ct 77384
Forest Ln
9300-9999 77385
15100-15399 77306
E Forest Rd 77306
W Forest Rd 77306
Forest Trl 77306
Forest Way 77304
Forest Cliff Ct 77302
Forest Creek Dr 77304
Forest Glade Ct 77385
Forest Glen Dr 77303
Forest Haven Ct & Dr .. 77384
Forest Lane Ct & Dr ... 77302
Forest Oak Ln 77385
Forest Oak Park Ct 77385
Forest Park Ct & Trl ... 77385
Forest Pine Ct 77385
Forest Valley Bnd 77384
Forest View Dr 77384
Forest View Trl 77385
Forest West Dr 77304
W Fork Blvd 77304
S Fork Dr 77303
Fort Sumpter St 77302
Foster Dr 77301
Foster Oaks Dr 77301
Fountains Ln 77304
Foursquare Dr 77385
Fowler Park 77385
Foxcroft Park 77302
Foy Martin Dr 77304
Frank Beeson Dr 77306
Frank Plunk Dr 77306
Frankfort Dr 77385
Franklin Dr 77303
Franklin Woods Dr 77304
N Frazier St
100-2199 77301
2200-9799 77303
S Frazier St 77301
Friendship Ln 77385
Frontier Path Ct 77385
Fryer St 77301
Full Moon Ct 77302
Fullen St 77301
Fultz Ct & Rd 77304
Fussel Rd 77385
Gabriel Pl 77384
Galveston St 77301
Gandy Rd 77303
Gannet Ct 77385
Garden Ct W 77304
Garden Falls Dr 77384
Garden Shadow Dr 77384
Garrett Rd 77306
Garrett St 77301
Garrison Ct 77304
Gay Dr 77301
Gemini Ct 77306
General Thomas Kelly
Blvd 77303
Genesee Ridge Ct &
Dr 77385
Gentilly Ter 77304
Gentry Rd 77306
Gentry St 77301
George Strake Blvd 77304
Georgia Park 77302
Gerard Ct 77306
Geronimo Pl 77304
Gerry Dr 77303
Gettysburg Ct 77302
Gideon Rd 77306
Gilmore St 77301
Ginger Springs Pl 77385
Glade Meadow Ln 77302
Gladiola Ave 77301
Gladstell Rd 77304
Gladstell Rd E 77301
Gladstell St 77301
Glen Eagle Dr 77385
Glen Forest Dr 77385
Glen Haven Dr 77385
Glen Hollow Ct & Dr ... 77385
Glen Jay Ct 77385
Glen Oaks Dr 77385
Glen Rock Ln 77385
Gleneagle Dr N & S 77385
Gleneden Ct 77384
Glenmora Ct 77385
Gold Leaf Pl 77384
Golden Autumn Pl 77384
Golden Berry Dr 77384
Golden Eagle St 77385
Golden Oak Park Ln ... 77385
Golden Oaks Dr 77385
Golf Rdg 77304
Goodman Rd 77306
Goodwin Rd 77385
Gowan Dr 77301
Grace St 77303
Grahmann Ln 77301
Granby Ter 77304
Grand Isle 77304
Grand Lake Dr 77304
Grangerland Rd 77306
Granite Pass 77304
Grassy Ln 77306
Graystone Hills Ct &
Dr 77304
Graystone Ridge Dr 77304
Grazing Field Dr 77384
Great Oak Blvd & Ct ... 77385
Great Oaks Dr 77385
Grebe Dr 77385
N Green Cir 77303
Green Forest Rd 77303
Green Mesa Dr 77385
Greenbough St 77302
Greenbriar Dr 77304
Greenfield Dr 77303
Greenhouse St 77385
Greenleaf Cir 77302
Greenleaf Dr 77302
Greenleaf Ln 77304
E Greenleaf Ln 77306
W Greenleaf Ln 77306
Greenleaf Ridge Way ... 77385
Greenridge Rd 77303
Greentree Ln 77304
Greenway Dr 77304
Greenwich Pl 77384
Gregory Rd 77304
Grey Oaks Dr 77385
Griffith St 77301
Grove Park Ct 77385
Grove Ridge Trl 77301
Grovewood Park 77385
Guilford Park 77302
Guinevere Pl 77384
Gulf Coast Rd 77302
Gulfstream Dr 77303
N Gull Dr 77385
Gunder Moller Rd 77306
Gunston Ct 77302
Gwen Ct 77303
Hackberry Ln 77306
Hadden Park Ct 77385
Hailey St 77301
Haleanin Rd 77302
Half Hollow Ct 77304
Half Moon Ln 77301
Hall St 77301
Hallmark Dr 77304
Halo Dr 77301
Hamilton Cir 77304
Hampton Rd 77302
Hampton Hall Ln 77302
Hancock St 77301
Hanna Rd 77385
Hannah Way 77302
Hanover Ln 77304
Happy Trl 77384
N & S Harlan Ln 77385
Harmony Hollow Ct 77385
Harpers Way 77385
S Harpers Landing Dr .. 77385
Harris Blvd 77301
Hart Rd
1800-1899 77304
10200-10699 77306
Hartford Dr 77303
Hartwick Ct 77304
Harvill Dr 77303
Havenwood Dr 77303
Haversham Ct 77384
Hawknest Ct 77384
Hawthorne Dr 77301
N & S Hawthorne Hollow
Cir 77384
Hayden Rd 77306
Hayes Ranch Rd 77385
Hazelwood St 77301
Headland Ct 77302
Heathcliffe Ct 77384
Heather Ct & Ln 77385
Heidelberg St 77301
Hendricks Forest Ln 77384
Henry Ln
10200-10999 77306
11400-11599 77302
Henry Harris Rd 77306
Hereford Dr 77304
Heritage Ln 77304
Heritage Ranch Rd 77303
Hermitage Ct 77302
Heron Ln 77385
Hi Lo Ln 77303
Hickerson St 77301
Hickory Cir 77304
Hickory Rd 77302
Hickory Burl Ln 77301
Hickory Hollow Ln 77304
Hickory Ridge Dr 77303
Hicks St 77301
Hidden Deer Ln 77302
N & S Hidden Oaks 77384
Hidden Paradise Dr 77304
Hidden Park Ln 77385
Hidden River Ct 77302
Hideaway Ln 77304
High Lane Ct 77301
Highclere Holly Ct 77384
Highcrest Dr 77303
Highgrove Ct 77384
Highland Crossing Dr .. 77304
Highland Estates Ct 77385
Highland Hills Dr 77304
Highland Hollow Dr 77304
Highline Blvd 77306
Highline Oaks E & W ... 77306
Highpoint Mdw 77304
Highway 105 E
11000-11589 77301
Highway 105 E
11590-17899 77306
13901-13999 77306
Highway 105 W 77304
Highway 242
7900-11899 77385
11900-18599 77302
18801-19497 77306
19499-20499 77306
3100-3399 77384
Highway 75 N 77303
Hilbig Rd 77301
Hildred Ave 77303
Hill Dr 77304
Hill Rd 77306
Hill Brook Ln 77385
Hill Country Ct & Dr ... 77302
Hill Manor Dr 77304
Hill Top 77306
Hill Top Ct 77303
Hillcrest Dr
1-299 77303
800-1299 77301
10800-11499 77303
Hillgreen Dr 77303
Hilliard St 77301
Hillridge Dr 77385
Hilltop Dr 77303
Hillview Dr 77385
Hindo Dr 77303
Hiwon Dr 77304
Hobbit Glen Dr 77384
Hobbs 77306
Hockenberry Ct & Pl ... 77385
Hoda Ct & Dr 77303
Hogan Dr 77302
Hoke St 77301
Holder St 77301
Hollins Rd 77385
Holloman St 77301
Hollow Trl 77304
Hollow Glen Pl 77385
Hollow Oaks Dr 77385
Hollowbrook Ln 77384
Holly Cir 77302
Holly Ct 77304
Holly Dr
800-1199 77301
11700-11799 77303
Holly Gln 77306
Holly Grv 77304
Holly Ln
400-499 77304
15100-15599 77303
16300-18599 77302
Holly St 77301
Holly Chapple Dr 77384
Holly Crossing Dr 77384
Holly Forest Dr 77384
Holly Grove Ln 77384
Holly Springs Ct, Dr &
Ln 77302
Hollywood Dr 77303
Honey Laurel Dr 77304
Honey Tree St 77385
Hope Rd 77384
Hopkins St 77301
Hornsby Rd 77306
Horsepen Bend Dr 77385
Horseshoe Bnd 77384
Horsetail Ct 77385
House Rd 77304
Houston Ln 77306
Houston St 77301
Howards Way 77306
Hudson Rd 77304
Hues Ridge Dr 77302
Hulon Rd 77306
Humble Tank Rd 77304
Hummingbird 77385
Hummingbird Ln 77302
Hummingbird Pl 77385
Hunnington Dr 77303
Hunt St 77301
Hunter Park 77385
Hunter St 77301
Hunter Creek Ln 77304
Hunter Forest Dr 77384
Hunter Park Ct 77385
Hunter Ridge Ct 77384
Hunters Trl
100-298 77304
17200-17699 77306
Hunters Greens Rd 77306
Hurley Ln 77384
Hyacinth Way 77385
Ibis Ln 77385
Ike White Rd 77303
Imperial Crossing Dr 77385
Imperial Grove Ln 77385

Indian Pt 77306
Indian Corn Pl 77384
Indian Creek Dr 77304
Indian Hills Ln 77304
Indian Wells Ln 77304
Indigo Dr 77385
Industrial Ct 77301
Industrial Ln 77301
Industrial Way 77385
Infield Ct 77385
Interstate 45 N
2200B1-2200B9 77301
Interstate 45 N
100-2298 77301
101-10299 77304
2800-3498 77303
27000-27998 77385
Interstate 45 S
100-12298 77304
101-1799 77301
11101-11199 77302
12201-12299 77304
14500-18198 77384
14801-16999 77385
Iris Arbor Ct 77301
Irish Dr 77301
Iron Ore Rd 77303
Irwin Keel Ln 77306
Ivey St 77301
Ivy Ct 77304
Ivy Dr 77303
Ivy Wall Dr 77301
Jackrabbit Ln 77304
Jackson Sq 77304
Jackson Square Dr 77304
Jacobs Ct & Way 77384
Jacobs Forest Ct 77384
Jacobs Lake Blvd 77384
Jacobs Meadow Dr 77384
Jadecrest Ct 77304
Jake Goodrum Rd 77306
Jake Pearson Rd 77304
Janice St 77301
Jardine Ct 77385
Jarrell Dr 77304
Jeanette Ln 77303
Jeb Stuart Ln 77302
Jeff Davis Ct 77302
Jeffcote Rd 77303
Jefferson Chemical Rd
300-2299 77306
3700-10999 77301
Jefferson Crossing Dr 77304
Jernigan Rd 77306
Jessie Ann Ct 77304
Jetoma 77385
Jewel Ct 77385
Jewel St 77301
Jill St 77303
W Jimmy Ln 77385
Jireh Rd 77306
Joan Ln 77306
Jody Ln 77303
Johnson Rd
1600-1699 77304
12100-13399 77302
18700-19999 77385
Johnson Mallard Dr 77302
Johnson Martin Rd 77384
Jolin Ln 77306
Jones Rd 77384
Jonquil Path Way 77385
Joy Ln
100-199 77304
9400-9799 77303
Jubal Early Ln 77302
Judson Oak Dr 77384
Jules Anna Ln 77304
Juniper Knoll Way 77301
Kaleo Way 77304
Kalka Rd 77302
Kanani Ct 77302
Kane Ln 77385
Kathy St 77301
Katie Ln 77304
N Katydid Ct 77301

Kelley Rd 77303
Kellow St 77304
Kelly Rd 77303
Kellyn Ct 77306
Kellyn Oaks Dr 77306
Kensington Ct 77304
Kentucky Oaks Dr 77304
E & W Kentwick Pl 77384
Kenwood Dr 77301
Kerr Ln 77385
Keystone Mills Dr 77303
Keystone Timber Dr 77303
Kidd Rd 77302
Kids R Kids Dr 77304
Kimberly Ln 77301
Kimberly Trce 77304
Kimberly Dawn Dr 77304
King Ln 77306
Kingfisher Dr 77385
Kings Ct 77304
Kingsberry Ct 77304
Kingsley Ct 77304
Kingsway Dr 77304
Kirbee Rd 77302
Kirk Rd 77304
Kirkwood Ln 77304
Kirtland Ct 77384
Kittys Ln 77303
Kiwi Ln 77385
Kline Dr 77303
E & W Knightsbridge
Dr 77385
Knob Hollow Way 77385
Knoll Dale Trl 77385
Knotty Wood Ct 77301
Koalstad Rd 77302
Koenig Ln 77384
Kropik Rd 77306
Kuykendahl Ct 77384
Kyle Ln 77306
Kyle Reid Ct 77302
La Quinta Dr 77304
La Salle Ave, Br &
Xing 77304
La Salle Heights Ct 77304
La Salle Lake Rd 77304
La Salle Oaks 77304
La Salle Park Dr 77304
La Salle River Rd 77304
La Salle Springs Ct 77304
La Salle Woods 77304
Lace Flower Way 77385
Lake Cir 77302
Lake Dr 77384
Lake Rd 77303
Lake Business Dr 77304
Lake Conroe Dr W 77304
Lake Drive Ct 77384
E & W Lake Forest Cir,
Ct & Dr 77384
Lake Lamond Rd 77384
Lake Manor Dr 77304
Lake Ridge Dr 77304
S Lake Shore Dr 77303
Lake Windsor Cir 77384
Lakemere Park Ct 77385
Lakeshore Dr 77304
E Lakeshore Dr 77303
W Lakeshore Dr 77303
Lakeside Dr
9400-10199 77306
12000-12099 77303
Lakeview Ct 77302
Lakeview Dr
200-299 77301
3500-4399 77303
15200-15499 77302
Lakeway St 77304
Lakewood Dr
7400-10199 77306
10200-10499 77385
Lamesa Dr 77384
E Lana Ln 77385
Lancelot Ln 77304
Lancer Park 77385
Landfall Ln 77302

Landry Ln 77303
Landscape Ct 77301
Langtree Ln 77306
Lantern Ln 77303
Lantern Creek Ct 77303
Lapis Park Ln 77385
Lark Ln 77384
Larkspur Ln 77385
Laughing Falcon Trl 77385
Laura Ct & Ln 77385
Laureate Ct 77384
Laurelee Ln 77302
Lazy Ln 77301
Lazy Oaks Dr 77306
Lazy Pine Ct 77304
Lazy River Rd 77385
Leaf Cluster Ct E 77301
Leafhopper Ln 77301
Leafy Ln 77306
Leafy Meadow Dr 77302
League Line Rd
1000-1299 77303
1300-12299 77304
N Lee 77303
S Lee 77303
Lee Dr 77306
Leela Springs Dr 77304
Legacy Meadows Ln 77304
Leonidas Horton Rd 77304
Leslie Ct 77384
E & W Lewis St 77301
Lexington Ct
1-99 77302
200-299 77385
400-499 77302
Lexington Dr 77385
Lightningbug Ln 77301
W Lilac Ridge Ct & Pl 77384
Lillian St 77301
Lilly Blvd 77301
Lilly Dr 77384
Lily Landry Ct 77384
Lily Meadows Dr 77304
Lily Ranch Ln 77304
Limerick Ln 77384
Linda Ln 77306
Linda St 77301
Lindy Ln 77301
Linger Ln 77303
Linwood 77304
Liriope Ct 77384
Lisbon Meadows Dr 77304
Lismore Estates Ln 77385
Little Blue Heron Ln 77304
Little Egypt Rd 77304
Little John Ln
1-99 77301
100-299 77304
Little Scarlet St 77385
Little T 77302
Live Oak Dr
1800-1899 77301
18600-18899 77306
Llano Ct 77384
Logan Creek Ln 77304
Logan Grove Ct 77302
Lombard Rd 77306
S London Grn 77384
Lone Corral Ct 77302
Lone Oak Dr 77303
Lone Star Ranch Dr 77302
Long Dr 77302
Long St 77301
Long Branch Dr 77303
Long Haven Ln 77304
Long Leaf Dr 77303
Long Tree Ln 77303
Long Valley Ct 77302
Longacre Dr 77304
Longleaf Ct 77302
Longleaf Dr 77385
Longleaf Ln 77302
Longmire Cir, Ct, Cv,
Rd, Trce, Trl & Way 77304
Longmire Creek Ct &
Way 77304

Longmire Creek Estates
Dr 77304
Longmire Lakeview 77304
Longmire Pointe 77304
Longmire Way Ct 77304
Longview St 77301
Longwood Dr 77304
Longwood Ln 77302
E & W Loop Rd 77384
N Loop 336 E 77301
N Loop 336 W
100-1299 77301
N Loop 336 W
1300-3699 77304
S Loop 336 E 77301
S Loop 336 W 77304
Lorandis St 77301
Lori St 77301
Los Cabos Dr 77306
Lost Creek Ranch Dr 77303
Lost Pine Ct 77304
Louisiana Park 77302
Lovebug Ln 77301
Lovelady Dr 77302
Lovie Ln 77302
Lucas Ln 77306
Lucille Ln 77384
Lulach Cir & Ln 77301
Lynchester Ln 77306
Lyric Rd 77302
Mable St 77301
Macdonnel 77302
Mace St 77303
Macon Park 77302
Madeley St 77301
Magenta Mdw 77304
Magnolia Ct 77302
Magnolia Dr
3600-4999 77302
8200-9999 77306
10600-11399 77303
15200-15499 77384
N Magnolia Dr 77301
S Magnolia Dr 77301
Magnolia Ln 77304
Magnolia Park 77306
Magnolia Trl 77306
Magnolia Bend Dr 77302
Magnolia Grove Ln 77384
Magnolia Ridge Dr 77302
Mail Route Rd 77384
Main St 77385
N Main St 77301
S Main St 77301
Malaga Forest Dr 77384
Malagueta Ct 77384
Mallard Dr 77302
Mallie St 77301
Manassas Park 77302
Manchester Dr 77304
Mann Rd 77303
Mansion Woodland Dr 77384
Mansions View Dr 77384
Many Trees Ln 77302
Maple 77302
Maple Dr 77302
Maple Ln
200-499 77304
12000-12999 77303
Maple St 77301
Maple Ash St 77385
Maple Grove Dr 77384
Maple Mill Ct 77301
Maple Point Dr E & N 77301
Marie St 77301
Marilyn St 77301
Marissa Ln 77301
Mark Dr 77302
Mark Ln 77303
Marlberry Branch Ct &
Dr 77384
Marlowe Way 77384
Marshall Rd 77303
Martin Dr 77302
Mary Katheryns Xing 77304
Maryann Ln 77301

Marymont Park 77302
Marywood Dr 77384
Massey Rd 77306
Masters Dr & Vlg 77304
Masterson Ln 77301
Maurel 77304
Mcalister Rd 77302
Mcallister Rd 77306
Mccall Ave 77301
Mcclain Rd 77306
Mccloud St 77301
Mccomb Rd 77302
Mccowan St 77385
Mccrorey Rd 77303
Mcdade St 77301
Mcdonald Ct 77302
Mcdowell Rd 77306
Mcgoey Cir 77384
Mcgregor Rd 77302
Mckay Park 77304
Mcknight Rd 77303
Mcmillan St 77301
Mcqueen Rd 77302
Mcrae Cir & Lk 77303
Meachen Rd & Trl 77302
Meachen Meadow Trl 77302
Meachen Meadows Trl 77302
Meacom Dr 77384
Meador Ln & Rd 77303
Meadow Rd 77384
Meadow Creek Ln 77302
Meadow Grove Dr 77384
Meadow Landing Dr 77384
Meadow Run Dr 77384
Meadowhawk Pl 77384
Meadowlark St 77385
Medical Center Blvd 77304
Megan Rd 77303
Melanie Park 77304
Melmont St 77302
Melville Glen Pl 77384
Memorial Dr 77304
Memory Ln 77301
W Memory Ln 77303
Mercer Estates Ct 77385
Meridian Ct 77301
Merrimac Park 77302
N & S Merryweather Cir
& Pl 77384
Mesa Ct 77304
Mesa Ridge Dr 77303
Metcalf St 77301
Metts Rd 77306
Mid Pines Dr 77304
Middle Parkway Dr 77302
Midlake Park 77385
Midlane Cir & Dr 77301
Midwood Cir 77301
Military Dr 77303
Mill Ave 77301
Miller Cir 77302
Miller Rd 77303
Millmac Rd 77303
Mills Creek Rd 77304
Milroy Ln 77304
Mimosa 77302
Mindybrook Ct 77303
Minnow Lake Dr & Ln 77384
Miracle Dr 77301
Mirmar Estates Ct &
Ln 77385
Mississippi Park 77302
N & S Misty Canyon
Pl 77385
E, N & W Misty Dawn Ct
& Dr 77385
Misty Haven Dr 77304
Misty Oak Ct 77302
Misty Sage Dr 77302
Mizell Rd 77303
Moa Ct 77385
Mobile Ct 77302
Mockingbird Ct 77385
Mockingbird Hl 77303
Mockingbird Pl 77385
Mockingbird Rd 77303

Mohawk Dr 77304
Moller Rd 77306
Monitor Park 77302
Monroe Ct 77302
Montgomery Park Blvd 77304
Monticello Park 77302
Montrose Cir 77301
Moon Valley Ct 77304
Moonlight Trl 77384
Moorehead Rd 77302
Moorhead Rd 77302
Morgan St 77301
Moss Hill Ln 77303
Moss Oaks Dr 77385
Mosswood Dr 77302
Mossy Ln 77306
Mossy Cup St 77304
Muleshoe Dr 77384
Mulled Wine Ct 77384
Munger St 77301
Murmuring Creek Pl 77385
Murray St 77301
Mustang Dr 77384
Mystic Hill Dr 77302
Mystic Ridge Ct & Ln 77302
Nancy Ct & Ln 77385
Narcille St 77384
Natchez Park 77302
Natural Pine Trl 77301
Navajo Trl 77304
Needham Rd 77385
Nevin Ct 77301
New Dawn Pl 77385
New Harmony Dr 77304
Newton 77301
Newton Cir 77303
Newton Acres 77303
Nicholas Xing 77304
Nicholson Rd 77303
Nicklaus Ln 77302
Nightingale Dr 77302
Nikis Xing 77304
Nikita Ct 77302
Nila Grove Ct 77385
Noble Ct 77304
Nonesuch Rd 77306
Nora 77303
Noralean Rd 77306
Norene St 77301
Northampton Dr 77303
E & W Northcastle Cir &
Ct 77384
Northchase Ct 77301
Northern Flicker Trl 77385
Northline Rd 77384
Northline Oaks 77384
Northpine Dr 77301
Northridge Dr 77303
Northshore Dr & Loop 77304
Northwood Dr 77303
Nottingham Ln 77301
Nottinghill Ct 77304
Nugent St 77301
O Dr 77304
Oak Dr 77302
Oak Gln 77304
Oak Ln 77304
Oak Lndg 77304
Oak St 77301
Oak Arbor Dr 77384
Oak Bend Cir 77304
Oak Briar Ln 77384
Oak Canyon Dr 77385
Oak Chase Dr 77304
Oak Circle Ct & Dr 77301
Oak Cliff Ct 77304
Oak Cluster Ct 77301
Oak Cove Pt 77304
Oak Crest Ct 77385
Oak Estates Dr 77384
Oak Forest Dr
100-499 77303
1000-2599 77306
N Oak Forest Dr 77303
Oak Forest Ln 77385
Oak Gate Dr 77304

Oak Grove Ln 77304
Oak Haven Ln 77303
Oak Hollow St 77301
Oak Leaf Ct 77304
Oak Leaf Rd 77303
Oak Park Dr 77302
Oak Pass Ct 77385
Oak Ridge School Rd 77385
Oak Rise Dr 77304
Oak Shadow Cir 77302
Oak Stone Ln 77384
Oak Stream Dr 77304
Oak Summit Ln 77384
Oak Thicket Ct 77385
Oak Tree Dr 77303
Oakdale Dr 77304
Oakglen Dr 77303
Oakhill Dr 77304
Oakland Ct & Ln 77302
Oaklawn Dr 77304
Oakleaf Dr 77302
Oakleaf Hills Cir 77304
Oakmont Dr 77301
Oakridge Park Dr 77385
Oakshire Ln 77384
Oakville Dr 77304
Oconnor Dr 77304
Odaniel Ln 77301
Odd Fellow St 77301
Odd Fellows Ct 77304
Ogrady Dr 77304
Old Anderson Rd 77304
Old Castle Way 77304
Old Coffin Rd 77302
Old Conroe Rd 77384
Old Country Club Rd 77304
Old Hickory Dr 77302
Old Highway 105 E
2900-3399 77301
Old Highway 105 E
11300-11499 77303
16800-19799 77306
Old Highway 105 W 77304
Old Houston Rd 77302
Old Humble Pipeline
Rd 77302
Old Little Rd 77303
Old Magnolia Rd 77304
Old Montgomery Rd 77301
Old Oak Hill St 77301
Old Oaks Ln & St 77385
Old Sam Rd 77302
Old Smith Rd 77384
Old Texaco Rd 77302
Old Texaco Camp Rd 77302
Ollerton Dr 77303
Orangewood Dr 77302
Orchard Ln 77301
Orchid Grove Pl 77385
Orchid Hill Dr E & N 77301
Orinda Dr 77304
Oriole 77385
Oriole Ln 77306
Oriole Pl 77385
Orion Ln 77306
Orkney Ln 77301
Orleans Ct 77302
Orth Ln 77385
Orval Rd 77301
Our Ln 77304
Overbrook Dr 77304
Overlook Ct 77302
Owen Dr 77304
Owen Ridge Dr 77384
Owens 77301
Oxford Dr 77303
N & S Pacific St 77301
Paddington Ct & Way 77384
Paddocks Rd 77306
Pagemill Ln 77304
Palace 77306
Palestine St 77301
Pali Ct 77304
Palmer Dr 77302
Palmetto Dr 77302
Palmetto Pl 77304

Palomino Ct & Dr 77384
Palos Verde 77304
Pamela Ln 77306
Panorama Dr 77304
Paradise Ln 77302
Paradise Vly 77304
Paradise Valley Dr 77304
Park Ave 77384
N Park Ct 77306
N Park Dr 77306
Park Ln 77302
Park Mnr 77301
Park Pl 77301
Park Oak Dr 77304
Parkgate St 77304
Parkway Dr 77303
E Parkway Dr 77302
W Parkway Dr 77302
S Parkway St 77303
Parkwood 77303
Parkwood St E 77301
Parkwood St W 77301
Parsley Rd 77303
Parsons Ct & Vly 77303
Passage Ln 77301
Pat George Blvd 77303
Patricia Ln 77301
Patsy Ln 77385
Paula Ln 77385
E & W Pauline St 77301
Payne Ct 77385
Payne Rd 77302
Peach St
900-1109 77301
1110-1499 77304
Peach Creek Dr 77303
Peach Dale Ct 77301
Peachtree Park 77302
Peacock Ln 77302
Pearl Garden Ct 77384
Pearson Rd 77306
Pebble Ct 77304
Pebble Creek Dr 77304
Pebble Glen Dr 77304
Pebble View Ct & Dr 77304
Pebblebrook Cir 77384
Pebblestone 77304
Pecan Bnd 77304
Pecan Ln 77304
Pecan St 77301
Pegasus Ct 77306
Peggy St 77301
Pembrook Cir 77301
Penrod 77303
Peoples Rd 77384
Peppervine Ct 77385
Perkins Crossing Dr 77304
Perry Rd
14200-14899 77302
18600-18799 77306
Petty Dr 77306
Petty Walker Ln & Rd 77306
Pheasant Run Dr 77384
E & W Phillips St 77301
Philmore Ln 77306
Phyllis Ct 77303
Pickering Rd 77302
Pierson St 77385
Piglette Ln 77302
Pilot Pt 77304
Pin Oak Dr
1800-3799 77301
10600-10799 77302
11000-11299 77306
15400-15499 77384
Pin Oak Rd 77385
Pine Cir N 77304
Pine Cir S 77304
Pine Ct 77304
Pine Dr
100-3199 77304
14700-14798 77302
14800-14899 77302
Pine Hvn 77385
Pine St 77301
Pine Way 77304

Pine Acres Dr 77384
Pine Cluster Ct 77301
Pine Creek Ct & Dr 77301
Pine Crest Dr 77301
Pine Forest Dr 77384
Pine Grove Ln 77384
Pine Hill Dr 77301
Pine Knoll Ct 77384
Pine Manor Ct & Dr 77385
Pine Mist Ln 77304
Pine Oak Dr 77304
Pine Shadow Dr 77301
Pine Shadows Cir 77302
Pine Springs Ct & Dr 77304
Pine View Dr 77302
N & S Pinebark 77303
Pinecrest Ln 77304
Pinehurst Cir 77384
Pineridge Dr 77303
Pineview 77304
Pineview Dr 77303
Pinewood 77385
Pinewood Dr
100-306 77304
307-405 77385
308-406 77304
407-799 77385
16500-16599 77302
N Pinewood Ln 77306
Pinewood Plaza Dr 77303
Pinewood Village Dr 77302
Piney Meadow Dr 77301
Piney Point Ln 77303
Piney Point Rd 77301
Piney Shores Dr 77304
Pinkys End 77304
Pioneer Trce 77303
Pioneer Trl 77302
Pipeline Rd 77303
Piper Dr 77301
Pisces Rd 77306
Plantation Dr 77301
Plaster Cir 77303
Player Ct 77302
Pleasant Bnd & Dr 77301
Plum St
1000-1099 77301
11300-11399 77302
Point Clear Dr 77304
Pollok Dr 77303
Ponderosa Cir 77302
Ponderosa Trl 77301
Ponderosa Timbers Dr 77385
Poplar Cir 77304
Poplar Pine Ct 77385
Porter Rd 77301
Portman Rd 77306
Portman Terry Rd 77306
Possum Trot 77302
Post Oak Ct 77301
Post Oak Dr
100-399 77301
10100-12099 77385
Post Ridge Dr 77304
Pozos Ln 77303
W Prairie Dawn Cir 77385
Prairie Oak Dr 77385
Prentice Rd 77384
Prescott Dr 77301
Presswood Dr 77301
Primrose St 77385
Prince Ln 77306
Prince Of Wales St 77304
Privet Pl 77385
Pugh Ln 77306
S Pyeatt Ln 77385
Quail Run Cir 77302
Queens Ct 77304
Quiet Lake Dr 77304
Quince Tree Pl 77385
Quinette Rd 77302
Quinlan North Lake Dr 77303
Quinns Cabin Ct 77304
R D Andrus Rd 77302
N Rail Dr 77385
Raindance Ct 77385

Raleigh Dr 77302
N & S Rambling Ridge
Ct & Pl 77385
Rampart Ln 77302
Ramwind Ct 77385
Ramzi Dr 77303
Rapidan Park 77302
Ravensworth Dr 77302
E, N, S & W Rayburn
Dr 77302
Reaves St 77301
Rebecca Ln 77301
Red Bird Ln 77384
Red Fern Ct 77385
Red Leaf Ln 77306
Red Oak Ct 77301
Red Oak Dr 77301
Red Oak Ln
100-199 77304
800-2299 77306
Red Stag Ct & Ln 77303
Red Tail Hawk Ct 77302
Redbird 77385
Redbud Dr 77302
Redbud Grove Ct 77301
Reed Rd 77306
Reeves St 77301
Regal Park Ct 77385
Regency Ct & Way 77304
Reid Ridge Dr 77384
Reinhardt Rd 77306
Relissare Dr 77304
Reverse St 77301
Rhea Ct 77385
Rhodes Ln 77385
Rhodes St 77301
Rhoten Ct 77302
Richardson Rd 77304
Richmond Park 77302
Ridgemoor Estates Ct &
Ln 77385
Ridgewater Way 77302
Ridgeway Dr 77303
S Ridgeway Dr 77301
Ridgewood Rd 77304
Rifle Rd 77303
Rigby Owen Rd 77304
Riggs St 77301
Ripplewood Ct & Dr 77384
River Dr 77385
E River Rd 77302
River Rdg 77385
River Bend Dr 77302
River Crossing Dr 77384
River Fall Ct 77302
River Oaks Dr 77385
River Plantation Dr 77302
River Pointe Dr 77304
River Ranch Dr 77302
River Ridge Ln 77304
River Rouge 77304
Riverbrook Dr 77385
Riverhill Dr 77304
N & S Rivershire Dr 77304
Riverside Ln 77304
Riverway Dr 77304
Riverwood Ct 77304
Roanoke Dr 77302
Robbie Ln 77306
N Roberson St 77301
Robert E Lee Dr 77302
Robin Ct
9900-9999 77385
11500-11699 77303
Robin Ln 77303
Robin Trl
1-99 77304
15100-15399 77302
Robindale Cir 77384
Robinhood Dr 77301
Robinson Rd 77385
Rock Pt 77304
Rock Bass Rd 77384
Rockingham Pl 77304
Rocky Rd 77306
Rocky Ridge Dr 77302

Roda Dr 77303
Rogillio Rd 77306
Rolling Pnes 77301
E Rolling Hills Dr 77304
Rolling Ridge Ct 77385
Rollinghills Rd 77303
Rollingwood Loop 77303
Rookery Ct 77385
Rose Rd 77303
Rose Canyon Dr 77302
Rose Royal Dr 77303
Rosebud Ln 77303
Rosemere Dr 77304
Roughneck Rd 77306
Round Oak Ln 77304
Rowan Tree Pl 77384
Roxbury Dr 77304
Roy Harris Loop 77306
Royal Est 77303
E Royal Mews 77384
Royal Rdg 77302
Royal Adrian Dr 77303
Royal Andrews Dr 77303
Royal Campbell Dr 77303
Royal Cavins Dr 77303
Royal Coach 77306
Royal College Hill Rd 77304
Royal Creek Rd 77303
Royal Cullum Dr 77303
Royal Dalton Cir 77304
Royal Damon Dr 77303
Royal Duaine Dr 77303
Royal Estates Dr 77303
Royal Forest Dr 77303
Royal Green Dr 77303
Royal Highlands Ln 77304
Royal Karin Dr 77303
Royal Lake Dr 77303
Royal Magnolia Dr 77303
Royal Pines Dr 77303
Royal Ramsey Dr 77303
Royal Shores Dr 77303
Royal Springs Rd 77303
Royal Sterling Dr 77303
Royal Terrell Dr 77303
Royal Tricia Dr 77303
Royal West Dr 77303
Royal Woods Ct 77385
Royal York Dr 77303
Ruby Cir 77302
Runnels Rd 77303
Running Deer St 77385
Runnymede St 77384
Russell 77304
E & W Russet Grove
Cir 77384
Rustic Ln 77306
Rustling Dr 77303
Rustling Oaks 77303
Rustling Oaks Dr 77301
Rusty Oak Trl 77302
Rutledge Ct 77302
Ryan Ct 77304
Ryan Guinn Way 77303
Ryanwyck Pl 77384
Saddle And Surrey Ln 77385
Saddlewood Dr 77384
Sadie Ln 77303
Sage Brush Ct 77302
Sagestone 77304
Sagitarius Ct 77306
Saint Charles 77304
San Jacinto Dr 77302
N San Jacinto St 77301
S San Jacinto St 77301
Sand Shore Dr 77304
Sandalwood St 77303
Sandchester Trl 77306
Sandingham Way 77384
Sandpiper Ln 77306
Sandra Ct 77302
N Sandra St 77301
S Sandra St 77301
Sandy Beach Dr 77304
Sandy Oaks Dr 77385
Sandy Spring Rd 77302

E & W Santa Fe St 77301
Sapp Rd 77304
Sarah Lynn Ln 77303
Savanah Park 77302
Savannah Park 77302
Scarborough Dr 77304
Scarlet Mead Ct 77384
Scarlet Oak Trl 77385
Scenic Knl 77385
Scenic Forest Dr 77384
Scenic Woodland Dr 77384
Schank Rd 77306
Schnebelen Rd 77302
Scoldern Rd 77384
Scott St 77301
Searrid Dr 77385
Seay Ct 77306
E Semands St 77301
W Semands St
300-1399 77301
2000-2099 77304
Serenity Ln 77304
Serenity Rose Dr 77304
Setting Sun Ct 77302
Settlers Xing 77303
Seven Coves Dr 77304
Sewanee Park 77302
Sgt Ed Holcomb Blvd N
& S 77304
Shadow Ln
600-7899 77304
17100-17699 77306
Shadow Glenn Dr 77301
Shadow Oaks Dr 77303
Shadow Park Dr 77304
Shadow View Dr 77304
Shadowood St 77304
Shady Grv & Ln 77301
Shady Birch Dr 77301
Shady Glen Ln 77385
Shady Hollow Dr 77304
Shady Magnolia Ct &
Dr 77301
Shady Oak Ln 77304
Shady Oaks Dr
1600-1799 77301
6300-6400 77385
6402-7898 77385
Shady Pine Dr 77301
Shady Tree Ln 77301
Shadylyn Dr 77304
Shadywood Cir 77304
Shafer Loop 77306
Shakey Holw 77306
Shalimar Ln 77304
Shandy Way 77301
Shannon Green Ct 77384
Sharon Ln 77302
Sharon St 77301
Sharyn Dr 77384
Shasta Ridge Dr 77304
Shaw Cir 77302
Sheats Rd 77302
Sheffield Rd 77306
Shellee Dr 77303
Shenandoah Park 77302
Shepards Lndg 77304
Sherbrook Cir 77385
Sherman St 77301
Shetland Ln 77302
Shetland Way 77301
Shiloh Park 77302
Shimmer Pond Pl 77385
N & S Shore Dr &
Loop 77304
Short St 77306
Si Terry Rd 77306
Siegen Dr 77304
Sika Deer Ln 77384
Silk Tree Pl 77384
Silver Bayou Ct 77384
Silver City Loop 77304
Silver Creek Dr 77301
Silver Leaf Ct & Ln 77385
Silver Penny Dr 77384
Silver Shadow 77304

Silver Springs Rd 77303
Silverdale Dr 77301
Silveridge 77304
Silverstone Ln 77384
Silverstone Way 77304
E & W Silverwood Ranch
Dr & Est 77384
Simmons Dr 77385
Simms Rd 77385
Simon Ct 77302
Simons Ln 77385
Simonton St 77301
Skycrest Ct 77302
Skyline Dr & Ln 77302
Skyridge Dr 77385
Sleeping Creek Pl 77384
Sleepy Ln 77303
Sleepy Hollow Rd 77385
Slick Rock Dr 77304
Sloan Rd 77306
Snead Ct 77302
Snow Woods Ct 77385
Somerset St 77302
Sonali Springs Dr 77302
Songwood Dr 77385
Songwood Trl 77385
Sonoma Ct 77384
Southern Oaks Dr 77301
Southern Pines Dr 77302
Southline Rd 77384
Southmore Dr 77301
Southshore Dr 77304
Southwest Dr 77304
Sovereign Way 77384
Spanish Oak 77306
Spindle Oaks Dr 77385
Spoonbill Trl 77385
Sprawling Oaks Dr 77385
Sprayberry Ln 77303
Spreadwing St 77385
Spring Flower Ct 77302
Spring Forest Ct & Dr 77302
Spring Rain Ct 77302
Springfield Dr 77302
Springwood Dr 77385
Springwood Glen Ln 77304
Spruce Dr 77302
St Lukes Way 77384
Stableridge Dr 77384
Standing Oaks Dr 77385
Stark Ct & Ln 77385
Staton Rd 77303
E & W Stedhill Loop 77384
Steed Pl 77301
Steep Trail Pl 77385
Steitz Rd 77303
Stephen F Austin Ct &
Dr 77302
Sterling Place Dr 77303
Sterres Dr 77304
Steve Owens Rd 77304
Stevens Ave 77301
Stevenson Dr 77302
Stidham Rd 77302
Stinson St 77301
Stoltje Dr 77306
Stone Ct 77304
Stone Gate Dr 77385
Stone Mountain Dr 77302
Stonecrest Dr & Ln 77302
Stoneglade Dr 77301
Stonehedge Dr 77303
Stoneside Rd 77303
Stonewall Jackson Bnd,
Ct & Dr 77302
Stoney Brook Ct 77304
Stoneycreek Park 77385
Stoneycreek Park Ct 77385
Stony Creek Ct & Dr 77384
Stowe Rd
13100-13699 77306
13700-15099 77302
Strausie Ln 77302
Stubby Ln 77306
Sugarfoot Ln 77301
Summer Breeze Ct 77302

Summer Holly Ct & Dr 77384
Summer Oaks Dr 77303
Summer Park Blvd 77303
Summer Park Ln 77385
Summer Pine Ct 77304
Summer Rain Ct & Dr 77303
Summer Ridge Dr 77303
Summer Ridge Ln 77302
Summer Rose Ln 77302
Summer View Ct 77303
Summer Wood Blvd 77303
Summerdale Ln 77302
Summergate Dr 77304
E, N, S & W
Summerlin 77302
Summerset Estates
Blvd 77302
Summit Dr 77303
Summit Mist Ct & Dr 77304
Summitt Dr 77303
Sun City Ln 77304
Sun Perch Rd 77384
Sun View Ln 77302
Suncrest Estates Ct 77385
Sunny Morning Ct 77302
Sunny Oaks Pl 77385
Sunny Pines Ct 77302
Sunpark Dr 77303
Sunset Blvd 77303
Sunset Dr 77306
Sunset Ln 77385
Sunset Trl 77384
Sunset Heights Ln 77302
Sunset Mist Ln 77304
Sunset Park Ln 77302
Supreme Ct 77304
Surrey Run Pl 77384
Susan Ct & Ln 77385
Suzanne Dr 77303
Swallow Dr 77385
Swamp Bluet Ct 77385
Swan Ct 77385
Sweet Bay 77304
Sweet Garden Dr 77384
Sweet Gum Dr 77306
Sweet Leaf Grove Ln 77384
Sweetgum Dr 77304
Sweetgum St 77385
Sycamore Dr, St & Trl 77302
Sycamore Leaf Way 77301
Tableland Trl 77385
Tacoma Springs Dr 77304
Tallahassee Park 77302
Tallow Dr 77385
Talmalge Hall Ct & Dr 77302
Tambarisk Ln 77304
Tamina Mnr 77384
Tamina Rd 77385
Tamina Trl 77384
Tamra Ct 77306
Tanager Ln
9800-9899 77385
14300-14599 77306
Tanglewood Dr 77301
Tara Park 77302
Tarrytown Way 77384
N Tarrytown Crossing
Dr 77304
Tartan Ct & Ln 77301
Tate Ct 77385
Taupewood Pl 77384
Taurus Ct 77306
Tavish Ln 77301
Teakwood Pl 77384
Teas Ct 77304
Teas Rd 77303
Teas Cottage Dr 77304
Teas Crossing Ct &
Dr 77304
Teas Lakes Dr 77304
Teas Nursery Rd 77304
Teasdale 77301
Teaswood Dr 77304
Tennessee Park 77302
Tern Ct 77385
Terrell Trail Ct 77385

Terri Ln 77385
Terry Ave 77385
Texaco Rd 77302
Texas Park 77302
Texas Star Ct 77302
Thicket Grove Pl 77385
Thomas Ave 77301
Thomas Ln
4400-4899 77303
13100-13199 77302
N Thompson St
100-2199 77301
2200-2499 77303
1527-1-1527-2 77301
Thoroughbred Dr 77304
N Thrasher Dr 77385
Threadtail St 77385
Thrush Ln 77385
Thunderbird Ct & Dr 77304
Tickner St 77301
Timber Ln 77384
Timber Creek Dr 77301
Timber Hill Dr 77301
Timber West Ln 77304
Timber Wood Ln 77384
Timberfalls Dr 77384
Timberlane St 77301
Timberside Ct & Dr 77304
Timothy Ln 77303
Tims Ln 77301
Tink Calfee Rd 77304
Toby Ln 77301
Todd St
500-699 77385
17600-17799 77302
Toledo St 77301
Tolliver Rd 77306
Tom Stinson Dr 77303
Tommy Smith Rd 77306
Torrijos Ct 77384
Toucan Ln 77385
Tower Ln 77306
Tower Brook Dr 77306
Tower Glen Dr & Ln 77306
Towerwood Dr 77306
Traci Jo Ln 77302
Tracy Ct 77306
S Trade Center Pkwy 77385
Trafalgar Pl 77384
Trail Oak Dr 77302
Trails End Rd 77385
Trails Park Ln 77385
Tramonto Dr 77304
Tranquil Lake Way 77385
Traylor Ln 77303
Traylor Rd 77304
Tree Monkey Rd 77303
Trellis Ct 77304
Trenda Ct 77306
Trenton Ln 77303
Trevino Ln 77302
Trey Rogillios Way 77304
Trilling Bird Pl 77384
Triple Crown Way 77304
Tristan Way 77384
Troll Woods Ct 77384
Trophy Rack Dr 77303
E & W Trousdale Hills Dr 77304
Tubac St 77304
Tucker 77306
Tuffy Rd 77302
Tulip St 77385
Tupelo Ln 77304
Turner St
100-199 77304
500-799 77301
801-1099 77301
Tuscany Dr 77304
Twelve Oaks 77304
Twila Ln 77301
Twilight Star Ct 77302
Twin Deer Rd 77385
Twin Lake Dr 77306
Twin Lakes Cir 77306
Twin Oak Dr 77385

Twin Pines Rd 77303
E & W Twinvale Loop 77384
Tx Dot Rd 77303
Tyler Rd 77302
Tyler St 77301
Up Country Ln 77385
Upland Circle Dr 77303
Urquhart St 77301
Valance Way 77385
Vale Ln 77301
Valewood Pl 77384
Valiant Oak St 77385
Valley Dr 77303
Valley Ln 77306
Valley Mead Pl 77384
Valley View Xing 77304
Valwood Dr 77301
Vanamen Ct 77304
Vans Ln 77302
Vassal Xing 77304
Velda Rose Ln 77304
Velma St 77301
Velvet Rose Ct 77384
Veranda View Pl 77384
Vick Cemetery Rd 77306
Vicksburg Ct 77302
Victoria Glen Dr 77384
E & W Victory Lake Dr 77384
N View Ct 77302
Village Way 77302
E & W Village Green Cir 77304
Village Hill Dr & Ln 77304
Village Woods Dr 77302
Vine Rd 77301
Violet St 77301
Virginia Ln 77304
Voyager Ln 77301
Waak Rd 77306
Waco St 77301
Wade Cir N 77304
Wagers St 77301
Wagon Trl 77302
Wagon Wheel Ct 77302
Wahrenberger Rd 77304
Wakefield Way 77306
Walding Rd 77303
Walker Dr 77306
Walker Rd
3100-3799 77303
12900-15099 77302
Walnut Dr 77302
Walnut Hills Dr 77302
Walters Way 77385
Waltons Pt 77304
Wanda Ln 77303
Wannan Ln 77301
Warbler Dr 77385
Warbonnet Dr 77304
Ward Rd 77306
Water Buck Ct & Ln 77303
Waterford Ct 77304
Watergate Cir 77304
Watermint Pl 77384
Waukegan Rd 77306
Waxahachie St 77301
Waxwing Ln 77306
Wayne Bennette Ct 77304
Weaver Ln 77303
Webb St 77301
Wedgewood Blvd 77304
Weeping Spruce Ct & Pl 77384
Weisinger Ln 77304
Wellesley Dr 77304
Wellington Ln 77304
Wellman Rd 77384
Wells Ln 77385
Wells Rd 77306
Wells St 77301
Wellwood Ln 77304
West Ln 77303
E West Ln 77306
Westbrook Dr 77304
Westchester Dr 77304

Western Echo Rd 77302
Western Hill Dr 77302
Western Ridge Way 77385
Westgate Dr 77385
Westhoff Ct 77384
Westland Gate Dr 77384
Westleton Ln 77304
Westmont Park 77304
Westpark Dr 77304
Westview Blvd 77304
Westview Dr 77301
Westview Ln 77304
Westward Ridge Pl 77384
Westwood Cir 77301
Westwood Dr 77302
N Westwood Dr 77302
Wheatridge Ln 77302
Whiddon Ln 77306
Whipporwill Rd 77303
Whispering Pnes 77302
Whispering Oaks Dr 77385
Whispering Pines Dr 77302
Whispering Pines Cmtry Rd 77303
E Whistlers Bend Cir 77384
White Rd
1500-1999 77304
11300-11599 77303
White Bass 77384
White Birch Ln 77385
White Oak Blvd 77304
White Oak Ct 77301
White Oak Dr
2000-2099 77304
3600-3799 77301
9000-9199 77384
10900-10999 77303
17500-22699 77306
White Oak Ln 77303
White Oak Lndg 77385
White Oak Mnr 77304
White Oak Orch 77306
White Oak Pass 77385
White Oak Path 77385
White Oak Pl 77385
White Oak Pt 77304
White Oak Run 77385
E White Oak Ter 77304
W White Oak Ter 77304
White Oak Trce 77304
White Oak Trl 77385
White Oak Way 77304
White Oak Xing 77385
White Oak Creek Dr 77304
White Oak Point Dr 77304
White Oak Ranch Dr 77304
White Perch Lake Dr 77384
White Rock Rd 77306
Wiggins Rd 77302
Wigginsville Rd 77302
Wild Oak Ln 77302
Wild Oak Park Dr 77385
Wild Orchid Ct 77385
Wild Turkey Dr 77385
Wildwood Ln 77301
Wildwood Rd 77306
Wildwood Park Ln 77385
Wilkins Dr 77301
Will Anderson Rd 77303
William Ln 77302
E Williams Rd 77303
S Williams Rd 77303
Williams St 77304
Williamsburg Park 77302
Willingham Ln 77306
Willis Way 77384
Willis Waukegan Rd 77303
Willow Dr 77304
Willow Rd 77303
Willow Creek Park 77304
Willow Oaks 77385
Willow Point Dr 77303
Willow Springs Ln 77302
Willow Wind Ln 77302
Willow Wisp Pl 77385
Willowbend Ln 77303

Willowbend St 77301
Willowick Dr 77304
Willowisp Trl 77302
Willowridge Cir 77304
Wilmington Way 77384
Wilson Rd
300-1299 77301
1300-3199 77304
N Wimberly Way 77385
Winchester Dr 77385
Wind River Ct & Dr 77384
Winding Creek Way 77385
Winding Hollow Ct 77385
Windsor Dr 77304
Windsor Rd 77306
Windsor Bridge Dr 77384
E & W Windsor Hills Cir 77384
Windsor Lakes Blvd 77384
Windswept Dr 77301
Windswept Oaks Pl 77385
N Windvale Cir 77384
Windy Grove Ln 77301
Wing St 77385
Winged Foot Dr 77304
Winter Trail Dr 77304
Wolf Den St 77385
Wood Loop 77306
Wood Fern Ct 77385
Wood Hollow Dr 77304
Wood Loop Ct 77306
Wood Warbler Ln 77306
Woodcliffe Dr 77304
Woodcrest Ln 77306
Woodcroft Dr 77385
Wooded Ln 77301
Wooded Trl 77302
Woodgate Pl 77303
Woodgreen Ln 77306
Woodhaven Dr 77303
Woodhaven Est 77304
Woodhaven Ln 77304
Woodhaven Forest Dr 77304
Woodhollow Dr 77385
Woodland Ct 77302
Woodland Dr 77301
Woodland Ln 77302
Woodland Forest Dr 77306
Woodland Glen Ln 77385
Woodland Hills Dr 77303
N & S Woodloch St 77385
Woodman Rd 77306
E & W Woodmark 77304
Woodpecker Forest Ln 77384
Woodridge Dr
500-4699 77306
18000-19199 77302
Woods Estates Dr 77304
Woodside Estates Ln 77385
Woodson Rd 77385
Woodstock Ln 77302
Woodstone Ct 77384
N & S Woodsway St E & W 77301
Woodview Dr 77303
Woody Creek Dr 77301
Woolridge Dr 77301
Wrangler Ave 77302
Wren Ct 77385
Wren Rd 77303
Wren Hill St 77385
Wrenfield Pl 77384
Wroxton Dr 77304
Wynden Meadow Ln 77304
Yates St 77304
Yaupon Ct 77304
Yearling Pl 77385
York Ave 77301
N & W Yorkchase Ln 77304
Young Ln 77302
Young Sam Rd 77302
Youpon 77385
Youpon Ridge Way 77385
Yupon Dr
100-199 77304
11500-11699 77303

13800-13999 77304

NUMBERED STREETS

N & S 1st 77301
N & S 2nd 77301
N & S 3rd 77301
N 4th St 77301
N & S 5th 77301
N & S 6th 77301
N & S 7th 77301
N 8th St 77301
N & S 9th 77301
9th Tee St 77302
N & S 10th 77301
S 11th St 77301
S 12th St 77301
S 13th St 77301

CORPUS CHRISTI TX

General Delivery 78469

POST OFFICE BOXES MAIN OFFICE STATIONS AND BRANCHES

Box No.s
A - H 78469
1 - 2997 78403
3001 - 3974 78463
4000 - 4997 78469
5001 - 5999 78465
6001 - 6998 78466
7001 - 7998 78467
8000 - 8993 78468
9001 - 9940 78469
9998 - 9998 78426
10001 - 10940 78460
18001 - 18998 78480
23001 - 23120 78403
30014 - 31764 78463
50000 - 52800 78465
60001 - 61280 78466
71021 - 71920 78467
72001 - 72956 78472
81000 - 81549 78468
150000 - 152900 78403
181001 - 181598 78480
260001 - 261318 78426
270001 - 272000 78427
281000 - 281000 78403
331181 - 331720 78463
721001 - 721473 78472

RURAL ROUTES

02, 06 78410
07 78413
09 78414
03, 05 78415
03 78417

NAMED STREETS

A La Entrada St 78418
Aaron Cv & Dr 78413
Aava 78414
Abby Dr 78413
Aberdeen Ave
100-198 78411
200-299 78411
300-399 78412
Abeto Dr 78414
Abner Dr 78411
Aborigine St 78414
Acacia Dr 78408
Academy Dr 78407
Acapulco St 78417
Accrington Ct 78414
Action Ln 78412

Acushnet Dr 78413
Ada St 78405
Adair Dr 78413
Adams Dr 78415
Adbury Dr 78413
Adcote Dr 78413
Adel Dr 78412
Adina Way 78413
Adkins Dr 78411
Admiral Dr 78418
Adrian Dr 78414
Adrianna Dr 78413
Agen Dr 78413
Agnes St
1000-1699 78401
1701-1799 78401
1900-5699 78405
5701-5797 78406
5799-9399 78406
9401-10399 78406
Agrito St 78405
Agua Dulce Creek Dr 78410
Airdome Dr 78418
Airline Rd
500-2099 78412
2100-3799 78414
3801-4099 78414
Airport Rd 78405
Airstream Dr 78408
N Alameda St 78401
S Alameda St
200-799 78401
800-3299 78404
3300-4199 78411
4200-6199 78412
Alamo St 78405
Alaniz Dr 78415
Alazan Dr 78418
Albacore St 78418
Alberta Cir 78414
Alden Dr 78412
Alejandro St 78415
Alexandria Dr 78412
Alexis Dr 78414
Alhambra Dr 78418
Alice St 78411
Alisa Ann Dr 78418
Allamanda Dr 78418
Allen Pl 78411
Allencrest Cir & Dr 78415
Allier Dr 78414
Alma St 78411
Almeria Ave 78418
Aloha St 78418
Alta Plz 78411
Alta Gigonella 78415
Alta Vista Dr 78410
Althea Ct 78414
Alvin Dr 78415
Amadas Dr 78414
Amanda St 78414
Amazon Dr 78412
Ambassador Row 78416
Amber Dr 78418
Ambrosia St 78418
Amethyst Ct 78414
Amherst Dr 78412
Amistad St 78404
Ammer Lake Dr 78413
Amos Ct 78418
Ample Arbor Ct 78412
Anacua St 78414
Anastasia 78413
Anchor St 78418
Anderson St 78411
Andover Dr 78411
Andrea Ln 78414
Andrews Dr
1801-1897 78416
1899-1999 78416
2001-2299 78416
2200-2206 78415
2208-2298 78416
Angel Ave 78404
Angela Dr 78416
Angelique Ct 78415

Angelo Dr 78411
Angelwing Dr 78414
Angus Dr 78415
Anita Dr 78416
Annapolis Dr
1000-1299 78404
1300-1499 78415
Annaville Rd 78410
Annemasse Dr & St 78414
Annette Dr 78418
Annie Rae Way 78418
Antares Dr 78418
Antelope St
900-1300 78401
1302-1398 78401
2501-2697 78408
2699-3099 78408
3101-3399 78408
Anthony St 78415
Antigua Dr 78411
Antioch Cir 78413
Antoinette St 78418
Anvil Dr 78414
Apollo Rd 78413
Aquamarine Dr 78414
Aquaris 78418
Aquarius St 78418
Aquila St 78414
Aransas St 78411
Arapahoe St 78413
Arboleda 78417
Arbolito St 78414
Archdale Dr 78416
Archer Dr 78415
Archmont Dr 78414
Arctic Cir 78414
Argonne Dr 78412
Argus Cts 78415
Aristocrat Dr 78418
Arizona Trl 78410
Arlene Dr 78411
Arlington Dr 78415
Armada Park 78415
Arman St 78418
Armitage Dr 78418
Armstrong Dr 78413
Arnold Dr 78412
Arron Dr 78413
Arshia St 78414
Artesian St 78401
Aruba Dr 78418
Aryan Ct 78414
Ashdown Dr 78413
Ashland Dr 78412
Ashley 78414
Ashley Dr 78410
Ashlock Dr 78418
Aspen St 78411
Aspen Grove Dr 78413
Aspenwood Dr 78412
Aswan Dr 78412
Atascadera Ave 78418
Atlanta St 78410
Atlantic St 78404
Attoyac Dr 78410
Aubie Ct 78414
Audn Dr 78414
Augusta Cir & Dr 78413
Austin St
2800-3299 78404
3300-3699 78411
Auther St 78410
Autotown Dr 78411
Autumn Leaf 78410
Avalon St 78412
Avenida De San Nico 78418
Avenue A 78410
Avenue B 78410
Avenue C 78410
Avenue D 78410
Aviation Dr 78418
Avignon St 78414
Avondale Dr 78408
Axis Ln 78418
Ayers St
501-697 78404

699-999 ... 78404
902-902 ... 78463
1000-3098 ... 78404
1001-3099 ... 78404
3100-3198 ... 78415
3200-7499 ... 78415
Azalea Dr ... 78408
Azimuth Ct ... 78414
Azores Dr ... 78418
Aztec St ... 78405
Backside ... 78418
Baffin Bay Dr ... 78418
Bahama Dr ... 78411
Baker Dr ... 78408
Balboa St ... 78405
Balchuck Ln ... 78415
Baldpate Ct & Dr ... 78413
Baldwin Blvd
101-1397 ... 78404
1399-1999 ... 78404
2100-4299 ... 78405
4300-4899 ... 78408
Baldwin Cts ... 78405
Bali Dr ... 78418
Ballad Tree Dr ... 78410
Baltic Ct ... 78414
Bandera Dr ... 78410
Bar Le Doc Dr ... 78414
Bar T Dr ... 78414
Barataria Dr ... 78418
Barcelona Dr ... 78416
Barclay St ... 78414
Barlovento St ... 78414
Barlow Trl ... 78410
Barnard Dr ... 78413
Barnes St
3900-3999 ... 78415
4000-4199 ... 78411
Barness Dr ... 78415
Barons Dr ... 78415
Barracuda Pl ... 78411
Barrera Dr ... 78416
Barrogate Dr ... 78409
Barry St ... 78411
Barthelome St ... 78408
Bartlett Dr ... 78408
Barton St ... 78418
Bascule Dr ... 78416
Basin St ... 78414
Basswood Dr ... 78410
Bataan St ... 78419
Battlin Buc Blvd ... 78408
Bauer Dr ... 78414
Bay Dr ... 78414
Bay Area Dr ... 78415
Bay Bean Dr ... 78418
Bay Front Park ... 78401
Bay Moon Ct ... 78417
Bay Wind Dr ... 78414
E Bayberry Pl ... 78418
Baybrook Dr ... 78418
Baycliff Dr ... 78412
Baylark Dr ... 78412
Bayonne Dr ... 78414
Bayou St ... 78416
Bayridge Dr ... 78411
Bayshore Dr ... 78412
Bayside Dr ... 78411
Baywood Ln ... 78418
Beach Ave ... 78402
Beach Break ... 78418
Beach Way Dr ... 78418
Beacon St ... 78405
Beadwass Dr ... 78411
Beal Dr ... 78410
Bear Ln
4900-5098 ... 78405
5100-5700 ... 78405
5702-6098 ... 78405
6601-6699 ... 78406
Beard Dr ... 78413
Bearden Dr ... 78409
Beardmore Dr ... 78415
Beasley ... 78418
Beau Terre ... 78414
Beaufort Ct ... 78418
Beauregard Dr ... 78415
Beauvais Dr ... 78414
Beaver Creek Dr ... 78413
Beckford Cir ... 78414
Beckworth Trl ... 78410
Bedrock Dr ... 78410
Bee Mountain Dr ... 78410
Beechcraft Ave ... 78405
Beechwood Dr ... 78412
Behmann St ... 78418
Bel Air Dr ... 78418
Belden ... 78401
Belfast Dr ... 78413
Bell Isle ... 78414
Bell St ... 78417
Bellac St ... 78414
Belleview Dr ... 78412
Bello ... 78418
Belma St ... 78418
Belmeade Dr ... 78412
Belmont Dr ... 78418
Belton St ... 78416
Belvoir Ave ... 78414
Benchfield Dr ... 78413
Benice Dr ... 78415
Bennyville Dr ... 78410
Bent Trail Dr ... 78413
Bentridge ... 78413
Bentwood Ln ... 78415
Benys Rd ... 78408
Berens Ct ... 78418
Berkeley Dr ... 78414
Berlet Ln ... 78418
Bermuda Pl ... 78411
Bernandino St ... 78416
Bernice Dr ... 78412
Berrydale Cir ... 78413
Bertram St ... 78416
Besterio Dr ... 78415
Beta Ln ... 78418
Betel St ... 78416
Beth Creek Cir ... 78410
Bethlehem Dr ... 78413
Betty Jean Dr ... 78411
Bevecrest Dr ... 78415
Beverly Dr ... 78411
Bevington Dr ... 78413
Bevly Dr ... 78411
Bevo ... 78414
Bexar Dr ... 78415
Bickham Rd ... 78410
Big Cyprus Byu ... 78410
Big Dipper Dr ... 78412
Biltmore Dr ... 78413
Bimini Dr ... 78418
Binnacle St ... 78418
Birch Pl ... 78416
Birchwood Dr ... 78412
Bird Island Dr ... 78418
Birdwood Cir & Ln ... 78410
Birmingham St ... 78414
Bishops Mill Dr ... 78414
Bison Dr ... 78414
Bistineau Dr ... 78413
Black Bayou St ... 78410
Black Hawk Ct ... 78418
Black Oak Dr ... 78418
Black Peak Dr ... 78410
Blackbeard Dr ... 78418
Blackbuck Ln ... 78418
Blackjack Pl ... 78416
Blackstone Cir ... 78414
Blades St ... 78410
Blake St ... 78405
Blanch Moore ... 78411
Blanco Cts ... 78415
Blanco Rd ... 78409
Blankenberge Dr ... 78414
Blevins St ... 78415
Bloomington St ... 78416
Blossom St ... 78418
Blucher St ... 78401
Blue Angel St ... 78412
Blue Creek Cir ... 78410
Blue Grass Dr ... 78410
Blue Jay St ... 78418
Blue Lake Dr ... 78413
Blue Oak Dr ... 78418
Blue Sage Cir ... 78413
Blue Skyway Dr ... 78414
Blue Star ... 78414
Blue Water Dr ... 78415
Bluebelle Ln ... 78416
Bluebonnet Dr ... 78408
Bluefield Dr ... 78413
Bluefish St ... 78418
Blueridge Mnt Dr ... 78410
Bluff Trl ... 78410
Blundell Dr ... 78415
N Bluntzer St ... 78408
S Bluntzer St ... 78405
Boar Thicket Dr ... 78414
Boardwalk Ave ... 78414
Boat Hole Dr ... 78418
Bobalo Dr ... 78412
Bobcat Dr ... 78414
Bobolink Ln ... 78415
Bobtail Dr ... 78414
Boca Raton Cir & Dr ... 78413
Bockholt Rd ... 78406
Bodega Bay Dr ... 78414
Bois D Arc Pl ... 78416
Bolivar St ... 78416
Bollinger St ... 78414
Bon Soir ... 78414
Bonasse Ct ... 78418
Bondondi Dr ... 78414
Bonham St ... 78415
Bonita St ... 78404
Bonner Dr
4400-5599 ... 78411
5600-5899 ... 78412
Boomer St ... 78418
Boomerang Dr ... 78414
Booty St ... 78404
Bordeaux Dr ... 78414
Borden Cir ... 78413
Boros Dr ... 78413
Boston Dr ... 78413
Botsford St ... 78404
Boulder Cir ... 78409
Bounty Ave ... 78418
Bourbonais Dr ... 78414
Bourget Dr ... 78413
Bourgogre Dr ... 78414
Bowie St ... 78415
Bowsprit Ct ... 78418
Bradford Dr
3900-3999 ... 78415
4000-4199 ... 78411
Bradley Dr ... 78414
Bradshaw Dr ... 78412
Braeburn Dr ... 78415
Braesvalley Dr ... 78413
Braeswood Dr ... 78412
Braggs Dr ... 78413
Bramblebush Dr ... 78410
Bramling Cir ... 78418
Brandesky Dr ... 78415
Brandon Dr ... 78413
Brandywine Cts ... 78415
Braniff St ... 78405
Brannan St ... 78405
Branscomb Dr ... 78411
Bratton Rd ... 78413
Brawner Pkwy
2614A-2614Z ... 78415
400-1099 ... 78411
2600-2698 ... 78415
2901-3199 ... 78415
3200-4199 ... 78411
Bray Dr ... 78413
Brazos Dr ... 78412
Breckenridge Dr ... 78408
Breezeway Ave ... 78404
Brendel Ln ... 78410
Brennan St ... 78408
Brentwood Dr
1200-1299 ... 78404
1300-4399 ... 78415
Bretshire Dr ... 78414
Brett St ... 78411
Brewster St ... 78401
Brewton Dr ... 78415
Brezina Rd ... 78413
Brianna Cir ... 78414
Briarhurst St ... 78414
Briarwood St ... 78412
Bridgeport Ave ... 78402
Bridgett Dr ... 78414
Bridle Ln ... 78410
Briecesco ... 78414
Brigantine Dr ... 78418
Bright St ... 78405
Brighton Dr ... 78418
Brightwood Dr ... 78414
Brinkwood Dr ... 78413
Brisbane Dr ... 78413
Brisk Wind Dr ... 78414
Briston Dr ... 78418
Brittany Dr ... 78412
Broadmoor Dr ... 78413
N Broadway St ... 78401
W Broadway St
1101-1197 ... 78401
1199-1499 ... 78401
1501-1999 ... 78401
2301-2497 ... 78407
2499-2699 ... 78407
2701-3099 ... 78407
Brock Dr ... 78412
Brockhampton Ct & St ... 78414
Brockton Ln ... 78411
Broken Bough Cir ... 78413
Bromley Ct & Dr ... 78413
Brompton Dr ... 78418
Bronco Rd ... 78409
Brookdale Dr ... 78415
Brooke Rd ... 78414
Brookedge Ln ... 78414
Brookhaven Dr ... 78410
Brookhill Dr ... 78410
Brookhollow Dr ... 78410
Brooklane Dr ... 78410
Brooks Dr ... 78408
Brookside Dr ... 78410
Broomsedge St ... 78418
Broughton Dr ... 78415
Brown Dr ... 78414
N Brownlee Blvd ... 78401
S Brownlee Blvd
300-799 ... 78401
800-1899 ... 78404
Brownwood Cir ... 78410
Bruin ... 78414
Bruiser ... 78414
Brush Creek Dr ... 78414
Brushwood Ln ... 78415
Buccaneer Dr ... 78411
Buckaroo Trl ... 78404
Buckeye Loop ... 78418
W Buckhorn Dr ... 78410
Buckingham St ... 78410
Buddy Lawrence Dr
2901-2997 ... 78408
2999-3100 ... 78408
3102-3298 ... 78408
3800-3900 ... 78407
3902-3998 ... 78407
Buena Vista Dr ... 78418
Buenos Aires St ... 78417
Buffalo St
700-998 ... 78401
2701-2797 ... 78408
2799-3099 ... 78408
Buford St
400-1800 ... 78404
1802-1898 ... 78404
2000-3099 ... 78405
Buggywhip Dr ... 78415
Bullion Ct ... 78418
Burgandy Dr ... 78418
Burgentine Dr ... 78418
Burkshire Dr ... 78412
Burleson St ... 78402
Burnet St ... 78416
Burney Dr ... 78411
Burnham Dr ... 78413
Burning Tree Ln ... 78410
Burns St ... 78401
Burr Dr ... 78412
Burton Ln ... 78411
Bush Ave ... 78417
Bushick Pl ... 78402
Buttermilk Dr ... 78413
Buttes Dr ... 78410
E & N Cabana St ... 78418
Cabaniss Rd ... 78415
Cabo Blanco Dr ... 78418
Cactus Cir ... 78410
Cactus Dr ... 78415
Caddo St ... 78412
Cain Dr
4800-5599 ... 78411
5600-5899 ... 78412
Cairo Dr ... 78412
Calais St ... 78414
Calallen Dr ... 78410
Calamity Ct ... 78410
Calaveras Dr ... 78410
Caldwell St
1201-1497 ... 78401
1499-1699 ... 78401
2000-2198 ... 78408
Calgary Dr ... 78414
Caliche Creek Dr ... 78410
California St ... 78411
Callaway Dr ... 78415
Calle Cuernavaca ... 78417
Calle San Carlos ... 78417
Calle San Lucas ... 78417
Calle San Marcos ... 78417
Calle San Miguel ... 78417
Calle Vaca ... 78417
Callicoatte Rd ... 78410
Calvin Dr ... 78411
Camargo Dr ... 78415
Cambridge Dr
1200-1299 ... 78404
1300-4399 ... 78415
Camden Pl ... 78412
Camellia Dr ... 78404
Camino De Oro Ct ... 78418
Camino De Plata Ct ... 78418
Campbell St ... 78411
Campodolcino Dr ... 78414
Camway Dr ... 78415
Camwood Dr ... 78415
Canaan Pl ... 78413
Canadian Dr ... 78414
Canadian Mist Dr ... 78418
Candace St ... 78415
Candlewood Dr ... 78412
Candy Ridge Rd ... 78413
Cane Harbor Blvd ... 78418
Canis Dr ... 78412
Cannes Dr ... 78414
Cano Ln ... 78414
Cantera Trl ... 78418
Cantera Bay ... 78418
Canterbury Dr ... 78412
Cantwell Ln
300-598 ... 78408
600-910 ... 78408
911-1300 ... 78407
1302-1898 ... 78407
Canyon St ... 78410
Canyon Creek Dr ... 78413
Canyon Lake Cir ... 78413
Cape Ann Dr ... 78412
Cape Aron Dr ... 78412
Cape Cod Dr ... 78412
Cape Fear Dr ... 78412
Cape Hatteras Dr ... 78412
Cape Henry Dr ... 78412
Cape Lookout Dr ... 78412
Cape May Dr ... 78412
Cape Romain Dr ... 78412
Cape Vista Ct ... 78414
Capernaum Ct ... 78413
Capitan Dr ... 78414
Capitol Dr ... 78413
Caplin Dr ... 78410
Capri Dr
3600-3999 ... 78415
4000-4199 ... 78411
Caprice Dr ... 78418
Capstan St ... 78418
Captain Kidd Dr ... 78418
Captains Row ... 78418
N Carancahua St ... 78401
S Carancahua St
200-899 ... 78401
900-998 ... 78404
Caravel Dr ... 78418
Caravelle Pkwy ... 78415
Carbon Plant Rd ... 78410
Carbondale Dr ... 78413
Cardinal Ln ... 78410
Cardinales Ln ... 78414
Carencia Dr ... 78410
Caribbean Dr ... 78418
Caribe St ... 78418
Caribou Dr ... 78414
Carleta St ... 78418
Carline Aly ... 78401
Carlisle St ... 78401
Carlos Fifth Ct ... 78418
Carlow Cir & Dr ... 78413
Carlton St ... 78415
Carmel Pkwy ... 78411
Carmen St ... 78405
Carmer Cir ... 78413
Caroline Rd ... 78409
Carolyn Dr ... 78417
Carriage Ln ... 78415
N & S Carrizo St ... 78401
Carroll Ln
3800-4299 ... 78411
4301-4499 ... 78411
4500-5199 ... 78415
5201-5699 ... 78415
Carrolleton St ... 78411
Carson St ... 78412
E & W Cartagena Cir, Ct
& Dr ... 78418
Carver Dr ... 78405
Casa Blanca Ct ... 78418
Casa Blanca Dr ... 78411
Casa Bonita Dr ... 78411
Casa De Amigos Dr ... 78411
Casa De Oro Dr ... 78411
Casa De Palmas Dr ... 78411
Casa Grande Dr ... 78411
Casa Linda Dr ... 78411
Casa Rosa Dr ... 78411
Casa Verde Dr ... 78411
Cascade Dr ... 78413
Cassowary Ct ... 78414
Castenon St ... 78416
Castilla Cts ... 78415
Castle Forest Cir ... 78410
Castle Knoll Dr ... 78410
Castle Park Dr ... 78418
Castle Ridge Dr ... 78410
Castle River Dr ... 78410
Castle Rock Cir ... 78410
Castle Top Cir ... 78410
Castle Valley Dr ... 78410
Castle View Cir ... 78410
Castle Way Cir ... 78410
Castlewood St ... 78410
Catalina Pl ... 78411
Catamaran Dr ... 78418
Catcay Dr ... 78418
Cateau St ... 78414
Catfish Dr ... 78410
Catherwood Dr ... 78414
Cattail Ct ... 78414
Cattlemen Dr ... 78414
E & W Causeway
Blvd ... 78402
Cavendish Dr ... 78413
Cayo Cantiles St ... 78418
Cayo Gorda Ct ... 78418
Cedar St ... 78411
Cedar Brook Dr ... 78413
Cedar Brush Dr ... 78414
Cedar Creek Cir ... 78413
Cedar Hollow Ct ... 78414
Cedar Pass Dr ... 78413
Cedar Springs Rd ... 78414
Cedro Dr ... 78414
Celia St ... 78409
Celon Dr ... 78418
Cenizo Ave ... 78408
Centaurus St ... 78405
Center Dr
401-499 ... 78411
4201-4299 ... 78412
Central St ... 78418
Central Park Dr ... 78414
Cessna Dr ... 78412
Chachalaca St ... 78414
Chamberlain St ... 78404
Chamizal St ... 78410
Chamomile Ct ... 78414
Champions Dr ... 78413
Chancellor Row ... 78416
Chandler Ln ... 78404
Chanti Ln ... 78410
Chantilly Dr ... 78410
N & S Chaparral St ... 78401
Chapel Creek Dr ... 78414
Chapel View Dr ... 78414
Charlero Dr ... 78414
Charles Dr ... 78410
Charlotte Dr ... 78418
Charter Ln ... 78414
Chase Dr ... 78412
Chatfield Dr ... 78413
Chenoweth Dr ... 78404
Cherokee St ... 78409
Cherry St ... 78411
Cherry Hills Dr ... 78413
E & W Cherrystone Dr ... 78412
Cheryl Dr ... 78415
E & W Chesapeake ... 78418
Cheshire Dr ... 78414
Chester St ... 78411
Chestnut St ... 78411
Chevy Chase Dr ... 78412
Cheyenne St ... 78405
Chickery St ... 78409
Chimney Rock Dr ... 78410
China Berry Ln ... 78415
Chipito St ... 78401
Chippewa St ... 78405
Chisolm Trl ... 78410
Chispa Creek Dr ... 78410
Chiswick Dr ... 78413
Choctaw Dr ... 78415
Christie St ... 78415
Christine St ... 78415
Chuckster Dr ... 78414
Chula Vista St ... 78416
Church St ... 78410
Churchill Dr
2900-3099 ... 78404
3101-3197 ... 78415
3199-3200 ... 78415
3202-3398 ... 78415
Cibolo Crk ... 78410
Cimarron Blvd ... 78414
Cimarron Lake Dr ... 78414
Cindia St ... 78415
Cinnamon Oaks Dr ... 78414
Circle Dr
200-299 ... 78411
300-399 ... 78412
Cisco Cir ... 78413
Citation Dr ... 78417
Citrus Valley Dr ... 78414
Civitan St ... 78417
Clairfield St ... 78414
Clancey ... 78414
Clare Dr ... 78412
Claremore St ... 78412
Clarice Dr ... 78418
Claride St ... 78418
Clarion Dr ... 78412
W Clark Dr ... 78415
N Clarkwood Rd ... 78409
S Clarkwood Rd ... 78406
Claudia Dr ... 78418

Clear Creek Dr 78410
Clear Fork Ct & Dr 78410
Clearbrook Dr 78413
Clearlake Cir 78413
Clearview Dr 78418
Clearwater Dr 78413
Clement Dr 78414
Clemmer St 78415
Cleo St 78405
Cleopatra Dr 78412
Cleveland St
 701-799 78408
 900-999 78401
Cliff Crenshaw St 78410
Cliff Maus Dr
 1400-1498 78405
 1500-1598 78416
 1600-1999 78416
Clifford St 78404
Cliffwood St 78410
Clifton 78408
Cline St 78418
Clinton Dr 78412
Clodah Dr 78404
Clover Cir 78416
Cloyde St 78404
Clubgate Dr 78413
Coahuila St 78417
Coastal Wind Dr 78414
Cobblestone Ln 78411
Cobo De Bara Cir 78418
Coke St
 300-599 78408
 901-1199 78401
Cold Springs Dr 78413
Cole St 78404
Coleman Ave
 701-797 78401
 799-1899 78401
 2000-2999 78405
Coleta Creek Dr 78410
Collingswood Dr 78412
Collins St 78411
Colonial Cts 78408
Colony Dr 78412
Colorado Dr 78417
Columbia St 78416
Columbia River Dr 78410
Columbine Ln 78415
Comal St 78407
Comanche St
 701-1197 78401
 1199-1699 78401
 1800-1999 78408
 2001-2799 78408
Commerce St 78406
Commodores Dr 78418
Commodores Pointe 78418
Commonwealth Dr 78414
Community Dr 78412
Compass St 78418
Complex Rd 78409
Compton Rd 78418
Concho St 78407
Concord St 78415
Concrete St 78401
Condee Dr 78415
Congressional Dr 78413
Constance St 78413
Convair Dr 78412
Coody Ln 78413
Cool Breeze 78413
Cool Wind Ct 78414
Coopers Aly 78401
Coppedge Dr 78414
Copper Mountain Dr 78413
Copus St 78411
Coquina Bay Ave 78418
Cora Lee Dr 78418
Coral Pl 78411
Coral Gables Dr 78413
Coral Reef Dr 78418
Coralridge Dr 78413
Coralvine St 78418
Corban Dr 78415
Cordelia St 78412
Cordula St 78411
Corinth Dr 78413
Cork Dr 78413
Corn Product Rd 78409
E, N, S & W Cornelia Cir 78408
Cornell Dr 78414
Cornerstone Dr 78418
Cornett Dr 78410
Cornwall Dr 78404
Corona Dr 78411
Coronado Trl 78410
Coronation Dr 78414
Corporate Dr 78405
Corsica Rd 78414
Cortez St 78405
Cory St 78414
Cosner Dr 78415
Costa Bona St 78415
Cott St 78411
Cottage St 78415
Cotton Club Dr 78414
Cottonwood St
 3500-3699 78411
 6700-6798 78413
Cougar Dr 78414
Countiss Dr 78410
Country Club Dr 78412
N Country Club Pl 78407
S Country Club Pl 78408
Country Dawn Dr 78410
Country Estates Dr 78410
Country Side Cir 78410
County Rd 26a 78414
County Rd 55a 78406
County Rd 69 78410
County Rd 7b 78414
County Road 14a 78415
County Road 18 78415
County Road 20a 78415
County Road 20b 78415
County Road 22 78415
County Road 26 78415
County Road 26a 78415
County Road 30 78415
County Road 32 78415
County Road 33 78415
County Road 37 78417
County Road 41 78413
County Road 47 78415
County Road 49 78415
County Road 49a 78415
County Road 51 78415
County Road 53 78415
County Road 55 78415
County Road 55a 78415
County Road 57 78415
Courtland Dr 78418
Cousteau Ln 78414
Cove Way Dr 78418
Coventry Ln 78411
Covington Xing 78414
Cowhouse Creek Ct 78410
Cox Cir 78410
Coyote Trl 78415
Cozumel Dr 78418
Craig St
 500-1800 78404
 1802-1898 78404
 2000-2099 78405
Crane St 78411
Crapemyrtle Dr 78414
Crayton St 78418
Crecy St 78419
N & S Creek Cir & Dr 78410
Creekbend Rd 78413
Creekmont Dr 78413
Creekside Dr 78410
Crenshaw Dr 78413
Crescent Cir 78412
Crescent Dr
 1100-1400 78412
 1345-1345 78468
 1401-1499 78412
 1402-1498 78412
Crest Cir 78415
Crest Cliff Dr 78415
Crest Colony Ln 78415
Crest Elm Dr 78415
Crest Forest Dr 78415
Crest Lake Dr 78415
Crest Park Dr 78415
Crest Pebble Dr 78415
Crest Valley Cir 78415
Crest Veil Dr 78415
Crest Willow Dr 78415
Crestbrook Ct 78415
Crestdale Dr 78415
Crested Butte Dr 78413
Cresterrace Dr 78415
Crestford Dr 78415
Crestgrove Dr 78415
Cresthaven Dr 78415
Cresthill Dr 78415
Crestland Dr 78415
Crestlea Dr 78415
Crestline St 78418
Crestmeadow Dr 78415
Crestmont St 78418
Crestmore Dr 78415
Crestoak Dr 78415
Crestside Dr 78415
Crestview Dr 78412
Crestvilla Dr 78415
Crestwater Dr 78415
Crestwick Dr 78413
Crestwood Dr 78415
Crews St 78405
Cricket Hollow St 78414
Cripple Creek Dr 78410
Crockett St 78415
Cromwell Dr 78413
Crooked Creek Dr 78414
Cross River Dr 78410
Crossbill St 78418
Crossgate Dr N & S 78413
Crossjack St 78418
Crossridge Dr 78413
Crossstown Expy 78417
Crosstimbers Dr 78413
Crosstown Expy
 3801-3899 78416
 4000-5098 78415
 5200-6398 78417
 6400-6499 78417
E Crosstown Expy 78401
Crosstown Access 78416
Crossvalley Dr 78413
Crown Hbr 78402
Cruiser St 78418
Crystal Ln 78410
Cub St 78405
Cuiper St 78415
Culberson St 78408
Cullen St 78411
Cumana Dr 78418
Cumberland Cir 78414
Cunningham St 78411
Curtis Clark Dr
 4700-5599 78411
 5701-5737 78412
 5739-5740 78412
 5742-5758 78412
Curtiss St 78405
Cutlass Ave 78418
Cuttysark St 78418
Cynthia St 78410
Cypress St 78411
D St
 12-10598 78418
 9601-11099 78419
Dabney St 78411
Dagger Island Dr 78418
Dahlia Dr 78404
Daisy Dr 78410
Dakin Pl 78411
Dallas St 78413
Dalmation Dr 78414
Dalraida Dr 78411
Daly Dr 78412
Damascus 78413
Damsel St 78413
Dandridge Dr 78413
Dante Dr 78415
Darcey Dr 78416
Dasmarinas Dr 78418
Date St 78404
Date Palm Dr 78418
David St 78405
Dawn Breeze Dr 78412
Dawson Ct 78414
Days End Dr 78417
Daytona Dr
 1300-1599 78415
 3000-3099 78404
Debra Ln 78418
Deck St 78412
Deepdale Dr 78413
Deepwater Cir 78410
Deepwood Cir 78415
Deer Run & St 78410
Deer Creek Dr 78415
Deer Park Cir & Rd 78413
Deerwood Dr 78413
Deforrest St 78404
Del Mar Blvd 78404
Del Oso Rd 78412
Del Rio Dr 78413
Del Starr Dr 78413
Delaine Dr 78411
Delano Dr 78412
Delgado St 78416
Delphine St
 3801-3999 78415
 4001-4199 78411
Delta Dr 78412
Delwood St 78413
Dema St 78418
Dempsey St 78407
Denain Dr 78414
Denver Ave
 2700-2898 78404
 2900-2999 78404
 3300-3899 78411
Derby Dr 78414
Derry 78408
Devils Creek Dr 78410
Devon Dr
 1200-1299 78404
 1300-1699 78415
 2800-2899 78404
 4000-4400 78415
 4402-4498 78415
Devonshire Dr 78415
Dew Creek Cir 78410
Dewberry Dr 78414
Dewitt St 78418
Diamond Cut Dr 78409
Diamond Ridge Dr 78413
Diana Cir 78410
Dickens Dr 78412
Digger Ln 78415
Dijon Lake Dr 78413
Dillon Ln 78415
Dimmit Dr 78419
Dinn St 78415
Diver Duck Ct & Dr 78413
Division Rd 78418
Dixie St 78405
Dixon Dr 78408
Doberman St 78414
Dodd Dr 78415
Doddridge Cir & St 78411
Dody St 78411
Dogtooth Ct 78414
Dogwood St 78410
Dolores St 78405
Dolphin Pl 78411
Dolphin St 78418
Dolphin Ter 78418
Domingo Dr 78416
Domingo Pena 78417
Dominica Dr 78411
Don Patricio Rd 78418
Dona Dr 78407
Donaho Dr 78413
Donegal Dr 78413
Donington Dr 78414
Dorado St 78417
Dorchester Dr 78418
Doris Creek Cir 78410
Dorsal St 78418
Dorsey St 78414
Dorthy Dr 78412
Doss St 78408
Doubloon St 78418
Douglas Dr 78409
Dove Ln 78418
Dove Springs Dr 78414
Dover Ave 78408
Downing St 78414
Dragonet St 78418
Drake Dr 78413
Drexel Dr 78412
Driftwood Pl 78411
Driscoll Dr 78408
Dry Creek Dr 78410
Dryer Cir 78416
Dublin Dr 78413
Dubose St 78416
Ducat Ct 78418
Duchess St 78413
Duke Dr 78414
Dunbar St 78405
Dunbarton Oak St 78414
Dunbrook Dr 78415
Duncan St 78405
Dundee Dr 78413
Dune Dr 78418
Dungeoness Dr 78414
Dunns Point Dr 78414
Dunsford Dr 78413
Dunstain St 78410
Dunwick Pl 78411
Durant Cir & Dr 78414
Durham Dr 78414
Duseoboc 78414
Dusty Dawn Rd 78413
Dwyer Dr 78410
Dyna St 78418
E St 78419
Eagle Dr 78413
Eaglesnest Bay Dr 78418
Earnhart 78414
Easley St 78405
Easter Dr 78415
Eastern St 78405
Eastgate Dr 78408
Easthaven Dr 78412
Eastphal Ct 78413
Eastwind Dr 78413
Eastwood Dr 78410
Easy Cir & St 78418
Ebonwood Dr 78412
Eckner Dr 78414
Eden Ln 78407
Edgebrook Dr 78413
Edgewater Dr 78412
Edinburg Cir 78413
Edith St 78411
Edmonton Dr 78414
Edwards St 78404
Egyptian Cir & Dr 78412
Eider Dr 78413
Eikel Pl 78418
Eisenhower St
 2901-3099 78405
 3101-3299 78416
Eklund Ave 78406
El Chiflon 78414
El Gato Creek Cir 78410
El Monte St 78417
El Paso St 78417
El Soccorro Loop 78418
Elba Ct 78418
Elderberry Ln 78415
Eldon Cir & Dr 78412
Eldora Dr 78413
Eleanor St 78405
Elesa St 78405
Elgin St 78405
E Eliff St 78410
Elizabeth St 78404
Elizondo Dr 78414
Elk Dr 78414
Elk St 78410
Ellis Dr 78415
Elm Hollow Dr 78413
Elmdale St 78415
Elmhurst Ln 78413
Elmont Ave 78410
Elmore Dr 78408
Elvira Dr 78416
Elvis Dr 78414
Elwood Ct 78413
Embassy Dr 78411
Emelie Cir 78413
Emerald St 78418
Emerson Cir 78415
Emmaus Dr 78418
Emmord Loop 78410
Emory Dr 78410
Empire State Dr 78414
Emu Dr 78414
Encantada Ave 78418
Enchanted Hbr 78402
Encino Dr 78414
English Ln 78414
Ennis Joslin Rd 78412
Enterprise Ct 78404
S Enterprize Pkwy 78405
Ephesus Cir 78413
Erie Dr 78414
Erin Dr 78408
Erne St 78409
Erskine Dr 78412
Erwin Ave 78408
Escalante Trl 78410
Escapade St 78418
Escondido St 78417
Espinoza St 78405
Esplanade Dr 78414
Esquire Dr 78414
Essex Dr
 4500-4599 78413
 12421-12421 78419
Estate Dr 78412
Ester Dr 78418
Ethel St 78408
Etienne Dr 78414
Etring Ave 78415
Eucalyptus St 78414
Eunice Dr 78404
Evelyn St 78415
Evening Star Ln 78409
Evergreen Dr 78412
Everhart Rd
 401-497 78411
 499-4900 78411
 4801-4899 78466
 4901-5699 78411
 4902-5698 78411
 5700-7300 78413
 7302-7698 78413
Excalibur Rd 78414
Exchequer Dr 78410
Exeter 78414
Ezekiel Ct 78418
Fair Oaks Dr 78410
Fairchild St 78405
Fairfax Dr 78408
Fairfield Dr 78412
Fairmont Dr 78408
Fairview Dr 78408
Fairway Dr 78410
Falcon Cts 78415
Falcon Dr 78414
Falkinson St 78416
Falling Leaf Cir 78413
Fallow Ln 78418
Fannin St 78415
Fawn Ridge Dr 78413
Fenway Dr 78413
Fenwick Dr 78414
Fern St 78404
Fern Forest Cir 78413
Ficus Ct 78414
Fig St 78404
Figueroa St 78410
Fiji Cir 78418
Finistere St 78418
Fir St 78411
Fire Creek Dr 78413
First National Blvd 78418
Fisher Cir 78413
Fisk Ct 78401
Fitzgerald St 78401
Fitzhugh Dr 78414
Five Points Rd 78410
Flagstaff Dr 78414
Flagstone Creek Cir & Dr 78410
Flato Rd 78405
Flatrock Crossing Cir 78410
Fleece Dr 78414
Fleet Ave 78405
Fleetwood Ln 78410
Flintlock Dr 78418
Flood St 78408
Floral St 78407
Florida Ave
 1000-1299 78404
 1300-1399 78415
Flour Bluff Dr 78418
Floyd St 78411
Flyingfish St 78418
Flynn Pkwy
 5101-5397 78411
 5399-5499 78411
 5700-5899 78413
Fm 2292 78415
Fm 2444 78415
Fm 286 78415
Fm 43 78415
Fm 665 Rd 78415
Fm 763 78415
Foley Dr 78415
Fontana Ave 78410
Fonvilla Cir 78410
Forest Cir 78410
Forest Hill Ln 78410
Forestay St 78418
Foriven St 78419
S Fork Dr 78414
Fort Collins Dr 78413
Fort Griffin Dr 78414
Fort Stockton Dr 78413
Fort Worth St 78411
Fortuna Bay Dr 78418
Fortune Dr 78405
Foster Dr 78404
Fountain St 78416
Fox Dr 78414
Fox Glove Ln 78413
Fox Hill Dr 78413
Fox Hollow Cir 78413
Fox Run Cir & Dr 78413
Fox Tail Dr 78413
Fox Trot Dr 78413
Francesca St 78405
Francis St 78405
Franklin Dr 78415
Frederick Dr 78417
Freds Folly Dr 78414
French Dr 78411
Fresno Dr 78411
Friar Tuck Dr 78411
Friendship Dr 78416
Frio St 78417
Frontier Dr 78410
Frontside Dr 78418
Fruitwood Dr 78413
Fulton Dr 78414
Fulwell Dr 78413
Fumay St 78414
Furman Ave 78404
Gabriel Ct & Dr 78415
Gaines St 78412
Galatia Dr 78413
Galic Cir 78413
Galilee Cir 78413
Gallop Trl 78410
Galvan St 78405
Galway Dr 78413
Garallis St 78407
Garden Ct 78414

Garden Yard 78408
Gardenia Cts & Dr 78408
Garfield Dr 78408
Garnet Ct 78414
Gaslight St 78412
Gateridge Dr 78413
Gates Ln 78410
Gavilan St 78417
Gaviota St 78406
Gayle Cir & Dr 78413
Geiger Dr 78414
Gemini St 78405
Generiv Blvd 78402
Gentle Wind Ave 78414
Georgia Dr 78414
Geronimo Dr 78410
Gershwin Ln 78414
Gertie St 78412
Gertrude St 78418
Gethsemane Ct 78413
Gettysburg St 78410
Giants Dr 78414
Gibbs 78415
Gibraltar Dr 78414
Gibson Ln 78406
Gilliam St 78409
Gingerberry Dr 78414
Ginguite Dr 78414
Gladstone Dr 78414
Glasgow Dr 78413
Glasson 78406
Glazebrook St 78404
Glen Arbor Dr 78412
Glendale Dr 78404
Glenfield Dr 78416
Glenmont Dr 78415
Glenmore St 78412
Glenoak Dr 78418
Glenway St 78415
Glenwood St 78410
Gloria St 78405
Gold Nugget Cir 78417
Gold Ridge Rd 78413
Gold Rush Ln 78410
Goldcrest Cir 78418
Golden Canyon Dr 78414
Golden Gate Cir 78416
Golden Oak Dr 78418
Goldeneye Dr 78413
Goldfinch Cir 78418
Goldfish St 78418
Goldstar 78414
Goldston Rd 78409
Goliad St 78405
Golla Dr 78407
Gollihar Rd
1751-1997 78416
1999-2000 78416
2002-2198 78416
2200-3899 78415
3901-3999 78415
4001-4297 78411
4299-4799 78411
4900-5799 78412
Gordon St 78404
Goshen Ct 78413
Graciela Dr 78415
Graford Pl 78413
Graham Rd 78418
Granada Dr 78418
Granada St 78408
Grand Isle Cir 78414
Grand Junction Dr 78413
Grand Lake Dr 78413
Grand Park Ave 78418
Grand Teton Dr 78410
Grand View St 78418
Grandvilliers Dr 78414
Granite Peak Dr 78410
Grant Pl 78411
Grape Arbor Dr 78414
Grass Cay Ct 78418
Grassmere Dr 78415
Great Lakes Dr 78413
Greely Dr 78412
Green St 78415
Green Acre Dr 78405
Green Branch Dr 78405
Green Earth Dr 78405
Green Field Dr 78405
Green Gate Dr 78405
Green Grove Dr 78415
Green Jays Ct 78418
Green Lane Dr 78405
Green Leaf Dr 78405
Green Meadow Dr 78405
Green Oaks Dr 78405
Green Park Dr 78405
Green Pass Dr 78405
Green Path Dr 78405
Green Point Dr 78405
Green Trail Dr 78405
N & S Green Tree Dr 78405
Green Valley Dr 78405
Green View Dr 78405
Green Willow Dr 78405
Greenbay Dr 78418
Greenbriar Dr 78413
Greenough 78414
Greensboro Dr 78413
Greenway Dr 78412
Greenwich Dr 78414
Greenwood Dr
2501-2597 78405
2599-3299 78405
3301-3497 78416
3499-5099 78416
5100-5198 78417
5200-6499 78417
6800-7398 78415
Greer Dr 78418
Gregory Dr 78412
Grenade Ct & Dr 78414
Grenadine Dr 78418
Grenoble Dr 78414
Greystone Dr 78414
Griffith St 78410
Grisham Cts 78405
Grizzley Dr 78414
Grossman Dr 78411
Guadalupe St
2200-2699 78416
2700-2899 78405
Guadalupe River Dr 78410
Guatemozin St 78405
Guess Dr 78410
Guinevere St 78414
Gulf Shore Pl 78411
Gulf Stream Dr 78418
Gulfbreeze Blvd 78402
Gulfspray Ave 78402
Gulfton Dr 78418
Gun Cay Ct 78418
Gunwale Dr 78418
Guth Ln 78410
Gypsy St 78418
Hacala St 78417
Hackberry St 78410
Hailey Ct 78414
Hakel Dr 78415
Halcon St 78414
Halfpenny St 78414
Halifax Dr 78414
Hall Ave 78408
Hallmark Pl 78408
Halsey St 78405
Halyard Dr 78418
Hambendi St 78405
Hamlett Dr 78415
Hamlin Dr 78411
Hampshire Rd 78408
Hampton St 78414
Hancock Ave 78404
Handlin Dr 78418
Handover Dr 78412
Hangar Ln 78406
Hanley Dr 78412
Hannah Cir 78413
Hannigan Dr 78413
Hanzi Dr 78415
Harbor Dr 78401
Harbor Lights Dr 78412
Harbor Village Dr 78412
Hardwick St 78412
Hardwood St 78410
Harmon St 78405
Harney Rd 78410
Harold Dr 78415
Haroldson Dr 78412
Harpers Ferry St 78410
Harriett Dr 78416
E & N Harrington Dr 78410
Harris Dr 78411
Harrison St 78404
Harry St
4100-4199 78411
4200-4399 78412
Hart Rd 78410
Hartack Cir 78417
Hartford Dr 78411
Hartley Cir 78413
Harvard St 78416
Harvest Hill Rd 78414
Harwick Dr 78417
Hastings Dr 78414
Hatch St 78407
Hathor Dr 78412
Haubourdin 78414
Havana St 78405
Haven Dr 78410
Haverhill Ln 78411
Havre St 78414
Hawksnest Bay Dr 78418
Hawthorne Dr 78404
Hayes St 78402
Hayward Dr 78411
Hazel Dr 78412
Hazel Park 78410
Headley St 78405
Hearn Rd 78410
Heavens Gate Dr 78413
Hebert Ln 78413
Heinsohn Rd 78406
Heizer Dr 78410
Held Dr 78418
Helen St 78415
Hellcat Ln 78418
Hemlock Pl 78416
Hemlock Rd 78410
Hendricks St 78417
Hereford Rd 78408
Heritage Ln 78415
Hermine Dr 78418
Hermosa Dr 78411
Herndon Cir & St 78411
Herring Dr 78418
Hewit Dr & Pl 78404
Hialeah Dr 78418
Hiawatha St 78405
Hibiscus St 78405
Hickey Dr 78413
Hickory Pl 78416
Hidalgo St 78405
Hidden Cv, Lk & Way 78412
Hidden Oaks 78412
Hidden Wood 78412
Higgins Dr 78413
High Arch Ct 78412
High Bank Dr 78413
High Gun 78414
High Meadow Dr 78413
High Ridge Dr 78410
High Starr Dr 78408
Highland Ave 78405
Highland Mist Dr 78418
Highway 361 78418
Highway 44 78406
Highwood St 78410
Hill St 78417
Hill Country Ln 78410
Hill Crest Dr 78415
Hilldale Dr 78415
Hillwood Trl 78410
Hinman Dr 78412
Hitching Post Ln 78415
Hoffman St 78404
Hogan Dr 78413
Holiday Ln 78414
Holland Dr 78418
Hollister Dr 78414
Holly 78414
Holly Rd
1400-1999 78417
2001-2099 78417
2400-2598 78415
2600-3500 78415
3502-3998 78415
4000-5000 78411
5002-5598 78411
5601-5997 78412
5999-7500 78412
7502-8198 78412
Holly Ridge Dr 78413
Hollywood Ter 78415
Holmes Dr 78411
Homecrest St 78412
Hondo Creek Dr 78410
Honduras Dr 78411
Honey Creek Dr 78410
Honey Trail St 78410
Honeysuckle Ln 78415
Honeywood St 78410
Hopkins Rd 78409
Hopper Dr 78411
Horizon Dr 78408
Horne Rd
600-698 78416
700-2199 78416
2300-3199 78415
Horseshoe Dr 78410
Hosea Ct 78418
Hospital Blvd 78405
S Hotel 78402
Houston St
2600-2699 78415
2701-3199 78415
3200-3599 78411
Howard St
1400-1699 78401
1801-1997 78408
1999-2399 78408
Hudson St 78416
Huey 78418
Hugo Dr 78412
Huisache St 78408
Hulbirt St 78407
Hulen Dr 78413
Hull Dr 78414
Humble Rd 78418
Hunt Cir & Dr 78413
Hunter Cir & Rd 78409
Huntington Dr 78410
Hurlwood Cir 78410
Huron Dr 78405
Hurst Dr 78410
Hygeia 78415
Idle Hour Dr 78414
Idlewilde Pl 78408
Idylwood Dr 78412
Ih 37
301-399 78401
Ih 37
4301-5599 78408
4900-5698 78407
5900-9099 78409
9101-9399 78409
10400-10498 78410
10500-13499 78410
13501-14399 78410
Ih 37 Access Rd 78410
Impala Dr 78414
Imperial Cir 78416
Imperial Hbr 78402
Indarins St 78416
Indian Wells Ct 78414
Indiana Ave 78404
Indigo St 78418
Indio Creek Cir 78410
Industrial Rd 78408
Inglewood Dr 78415
Ingram Dr 78415
International Blvd 78406
Interstate Highway 69
Access Rd 78410
Inverness Dr 78413
Iris Ave 78406
Irma Dr 78410
Iron River Dr 78410
Iroquois Cir & Dr 78413
Isabel St 78404
Isabella Ct 78418
Isaiah Ct 78418
Isla Colon 78418
Isla Pinta Ct 78418
Island Park Ct 78414
Islander Dr 78418
Islla Dr 78416
Itaska Cts 78415
Iturbide St 78405
Ivy Dr 78418
Ivy Ln 78415
Ivy Ridge St 78413
Jacinto Cir 78413
Jackfish Ave 78418
Jackson Pl 78411
Jackson Ter 78410
Jacktar St 78418
Jacob St 78410
Jacquelyn Dr 78412
Jade Dr 78409
Jakes Wake Run 78414
Jamaica Dr 78418
James St 78408
Jane St 78418
Janssen Dr 78411
Japonica Dr 78410
Jarvis St 78412
Jasmine Cts 78408
Jasper Dr 78409
Javelina Dr 78413
Jay Hawk Loop 78418
Jean St 78411
Jefferson Rd 78413
Jeremiah Ct 78418
Jericho Rd 78413
Jerusalem Dr 78413
Jessamine St 78418
Jesse Jaye Dr 78410
Jessica Dr 78414
Jester St 78418
Jets Ct 78414
Jibstay St 78418
Jim Wells Dr 78413
Jo Ann St 78415
Joe Fulton Intl Tc 78402
Joe Fulton Intl Trade 78409
Joe Mireurn 78406
Joel Ct 78418
Johanna St 78415
John St 78407
John Lee St 78412
John Sartain St 78401
Johnston Dr 78415
Jolly Roger St 78418
Jonnell St 78418
Joplin Ln 78414
Jordan Dr 78412
Jose Dr 78416
Josephine St 78401
Joyce Dr 78417
Juanita St 78404
Juarez St 78416
Judie Cts 78418
Julia Cir & Ln 78414
Julianna Dr 78410
June Dr 78418
Junior Ter 78412
Junior Beck Dr 78405
Juniper Dr 78418
Kaipo Dr 78418
Kaler Dr 78407
Kangaroo Ct 78414
Karchmer Dr 78415
Karen Dr 78416
Karnak Dr 78412
Kasper St 78415
Katherine Dr 78404
Kathy Dr 78411
Kay St 78411
Kaycrest St 78415
Kazmir Dr 78418
Keegan 78410
Keel Ave 78418
Keelung Dr 78413
Keenland Rd 78418
Keighley Xing 78414
Kelly Dr 78409
Keltic Dr 78414
Kendall Dr 78415
Kenith Cir 78413
Kennedy Ave 78407
Kennsington Ct 78414
Kent Cir 78411
Kentner St 78412
Kentucky Derby Dr 78417
Kenwood Dr 78408
Kern Dr 78412
Kerrville Dr 78413
Kerry Dr 78413
Ketch St 78418
Kettlesing Ct 78414
Kevin Dr 78413
Key Largo Ct 78418
Key West Dr 78411
Keys St 78404
Keystone Dr 78413
Kickapoo Dr 78410
Kilgore St 78415
Killarmet Cir & Dr 78413
Killarney Dr 78413
Kimbrough Dr 78412
King Dr 78418
King Ln 78414
King St 78401
King Trl 78414
King Acres Dr 78414
King Arthur 78413
King David 78414
King George Pl 78414
King Henry Dr 78414
King Phillip Ct 78418
King Ranch Dr 78414
King Richard Dr 78411
Kings Cir, Ct & Lk 78413
Kings Point Hbr 78402
Kingsbury Dr 78410
Kingshire Dr 78413
Kingsland Dr 78414
Kingston Dr
3700-3999 78415
4000-4199 78411
Kingwood Dr 78410
Kinney St 78401
Kinsolving Ct 78405
Kirkwood Dr
4300-4499 78411
4500-4699 78415
Kitchener 78414
Kitchens St 78405
Kitty Ln 78414
Kitty Hawk Dr 78414
Kleberg Pl 78402
Knickerbocker St 78418
Knights Cir 78413
Knot Cir 78418
Knotty Oaks Trl 78414
Kodiak Dr 78414
Koepke St 78407
Kolda Dr 78414
Kosarek Dr 78415
Kostoryz Rd
1300-1398 78411
4100-4198 78415
4200-6299 78415
Kram St 78413
Kress Cir 78413
Krill St 78408
Kristin Dr 78414
Kush Ln 78404
La Bianca Dr 78414
La Blanquilla Dr 78418
La Branch Dr 78410
La Costa Dr 78414
La Crosse Dr 78415
La Joya St 78417
La Paz Dr 78415
La Playa Dr 78414
La Rochelle Way 78414
La Rue Ln 78411
La Salle Dr 78414
Labonte 78414
Labrador Dr 78414
Lady Diana Ct 78413
Laffite Cir, Ct & Dr 78418
Lago Vista Dr 78414
Laguna Shores Rd 78418
E Lake Dr 78414
S Lake Dr 78414
Lake St 78401
Lake Apache Dr 78413
Lake Baykal Dr 78413
Lake Bistineau Dr 78413
Lake Bolsena Dr 78413
Lake Buchanan Ct 78413
Lake Charles Dr 78413
Lake Como Dr 78413
Lake Conroe Ct 78413
Lake Geneva Dr 78413
Lake George Dr 78413
Lake Granbury Dr 78413
Lake Huron Dr 78413
Lake Livingston Dr 78413
Lake Maggorie Dr 78413
Lake Medina Dr 78413
Lake Micala Dr 78413
Lake Michigan Dr 78413
Lake Monticello Ct 78413
Lake Neuchatel Dr 78413
Lake Nocona Dr 78413
Lake Ontario Dr 78413
Lake Shore Dr 78413
Lake Superior Dr 78413
Lake Tahoe Dr 78413
Lake Travis Dr 78413
Lake View Dr 78412
Lake Whitney Dr 78413
Lake Windemere Dr 78413
Lakeside Dr 78418
Lakewood Cir 78413
Lamar St 78405
Lamont St
3400-3999 78415
4000-4699 78411
Lamp Post Ln 78415
Lando Ct 78414
Lands End 78414
Langton Ave 78416
Lanier Dr 78415
Lansdown Dr
600-1000 78412
1002-1098 78412
4501-4697 78411
4699-4999 78411
Lantana St
300-899 78408
1001-1197 78407
1199-1300 78407
1302-1398 78407
Lanyard Dr 78418
Laramie Ln 78414
Larcade Dr 78415
Laredo St
900-1699 78401
1800-1898 78405
1900-2399 78405
Lariat Ln 78415
Larkspur Ln 78416
Larkwood St 78410
Las Bahias Dr 78414
Las Brisas St 78414
Las Miras Ct 78414
Las Palmas Dr 78418
Latour Pl 78418
Laura Pl 78411
Laurel Dr 78404
Lauren Dr 78416
Lavaca Dr 78411
Lavaca River Ct 78410
Lavender Dr 78414
Lawnview St
1600-2298 78404
2300-3099 78404
3101-3299 78404

Street	ZIP
3300-3699	78411
Lawrence St	78401
Lawton St	78405
Lazio Ct	78410
Lazy Ln	78415
Lazy Willow Ct	78412
Le Pierre Dr	78414
Lea Ln	78415
Lear St	78417
Lee St	78411
Leeward Dr	78418
Legacy Pt	78414
Leicester	78414
Leigh Dr	78408
Lemans Dr	78414
Leming Ave	78404
Lens Dr	78414
Leon St	78416
Leonard Dr	78410
Leopard St	
600-612	78401
614-1699	78401
1800-1898	78408
1900-5899	78408
5900-9399	78409
9400-13499	78410
Leprechaun Dr	78413
Les Parre	78414
Lesle Ln	78412
Lester St	78408
Lethaby Dr	78413
Lewis St	
2900-3001	78404
3002-3198	78415
3003-3099	78404
3200-3500	78415
3502-3698	78415
Lexington Ave	78407
Lexington Blvd	78419
N Lexington Blvd	78409
Lexington Rd	78412
Liana Ln	78413
Liberty Dr	78408
Light Wind Dr	78414
Lighthouse Dr	78418
Ligustrum Dr	78408
Lily St	78408
Limerick Dr	78413
Limestone Dr	78412
Lincoln Cir	78411
Lincoln St	78415
Linda St	78407
Linda Vista Dr	78416
Linden St	78411
Lindenwood Dr	78414
Lindgreen St	78410
Lindgreen River St	78410
Lindo	78418
Linn St	78410
Linnet Cts	78418
Lipan St	
600-798	78401
800-1699	78401
1800-2799	78408
Lipes Blvd	
5500-5599	78413
5600-6098	78414
5601-7599	78413
7200-7598	78413
Liptonshire Dr	78415
Litewood St	78410
Little John Dr	78411
Live Oak St	78408
Liverpool Ln	78414
Llano Dr	78407
Lobo St	78401
Locke Ln	78415
Lockheed St	78405
Lodge Ln	78409
Logan Ave	
1000-1299	78404
1300-1399	78415
Loire Blvd	78414
Lois Dr	78410
Lola Johnson Rd	78418
Lolita St	78416
Loma Alta Rd	78410
Lombardy Dr	78418
Lomond Dr	78413
Londonderry Dr	78415
Long Cir	78413
Long Creek Dr	78414
Long Meadow Dr	78413
Long S Dr	78414
Longboat Dr	78418
E & W Longview St	78408
Loomis Dr	78414
Lori Dr	78410
Lorine Dr	78418
Loritte Dr	
1800-2000	78416
2002-2298	78416
2201-2205	78415
2207-2299	78416
Lorraine Dr	78411
Los Arroyos Dr	78414
Lost Creek Cir & Dr	78413
Lostgate Dr	78413
Lott Ave	78410
Lotus St	78408
Lou St	78405
Louis Lynch Dr	
800-952	78408
953-999	78407
Louise Dr	78404
Louisiana Ave	78404
Louisville Dr	78418
Lourdes St	78414
Lovain Dr	78414
Lovebird St	78418
Loveland Pass Ct	78413
Lovers Ln	78412
Lowell St	78401
N Lower Broadway St	78401
Lowman St	78411
Lucille Dr	78412
Lucinda Ln	78412
Lugano Dr	78413
Lula St	78412
Lum Ave	78412
Lumberdale Cir	78413
Luna St	78408
Luxor Dr	78412
Luzius Dr	78418
Luzon Dr	78418
Lynch St	78404
Lynda Lee Dr	78418
Lynhurst St	78418
Lynn St	78418
Lynncrest Dr	78415
Lynnwood Ln	78415
Lyons St	78414
Mable St	78411
Macarena Dr	78414
Macarthur St	
2900-3099	78405
3100-4099	78416
Macbeth Ln	78414
Macleod Dr	78408
Madiera Dr	78414
Madrid Cir & Dr	78416
Magee Ln	78410
Magnolia St	78408
Mahan Dr	78415
Mahony Cir	78413
Main Dr	78409
Main Royal Dr	78418
Mainsail St	78418
Makepeace Ln	78414
Malachite Dr	78414
Malden Dr	78413
Mallard Dr	78410
Man O War Ct	78418
Manassas Ln	78410
Manchester Ave	78407
Mandy Ln	78412
Mango Cts	78415
Manhattan Dr	78411
Manitoba Dr	78418
Manitou St	78411
Manitoulin Island Dr	78414
Mann St	78401
Manning Rd	78409
E & W Manor Dr	78412
Manresa St	78415
Mansfield Dr	78414
Manshein Blvd	78415
Mansions Dr	78414
Maple St	78411
Maple Leaf	78410
Maramet Dr	78414
Marans St	78414
Marauder Dr	78414
Marble Falls Dr	78414
Marblewing Dr	78414
Margaret Ave	78407
Margie Dr	78410
Margo Dr	78411
Marguerite St	
1000-1699	78401
1701-1799	78401
1901-1997	78405
1999-2999	78405
Mariana Dr	78418
Marie St	78411
Marine Dr	78418
Marion Cir	78411
Marion St	78415
Marissa Dr	78414
Markins Dr	78411
Marks Dr	78411
Marlin Dr	78418
Mars Ave	78409
Mars Hill Dr	78413
Marseille Dr	78414
Marshall St	78409
Martha Dr	78418
Martin	78417
Martin Luther King Dr	
900-2298	78401
2400-3098	78407
Martine St	78410
Martinique Dr	78411
Marvin L Berry Rd	78409
Mary St	
1001-1197	78401
1199-1799	78401
1801-1899	78401
2000-3099	78405
Maryland Dr	
1100-1299	78404
1300-1499	78415
Masada Ct	78413
Mason Dr	78407
Masterson Dr	78415
Matlock St	78418
Matteson St	78418
Matthew Dr	78418
Maui Dr	78418
Mavis Dr	78411
Maximus Dr	78414
Mayfield Dr	78410
Maylands Dr	78413
Mayo Dr	78413
Mcalpin Dr	78413
Mcardle Rd	
2801-3197	78415
3199-3200	78415
3202-3698	78415
4000-4198	78411
4200-5499	78411
5501-5597	78412
5599-7400	78412
7402-7598	78412
Mcbride Ln	
100-800	78408
802-898	78408
1100-1298	78407
Mcburnett Dr	78410
Mccain Dr	78410
Mccall St	78404
Mccampbell Rd	78408
Mcclendon St	78404
Mcdonald St	78418
Mcgloin Rd	
6900-7999	78415
8400-8499	78406
8900-8999	78415
Mcgregor Dr	78411
Mciver St	78418
Mckenzie St	78404
Mckinzie Rd	78410
Mcnorton Rd	78409
Meadow Cir	78413
Meadow Ridge Dr	78418
Meadow Vale Cir	78413
Meadow Wood St	78418
Meadowbreeze Pkwy	78414
Meadowbrook Dr	78412
Meadowcreek Dr	78414
Meadowgate Dr	78413
Meadowglen Dr	78414
Meadowgrove Dr	78414
Meadowheights Dr	78414
Meadowlane Dr	78412
Meadowlight Pkwy	78414
Meadowpass Dr	78414
Meadowview Dr	78414
Meadowvista Dr	78414
Meadowwalk Dr	78414
Meandering Ln	78413
Medina Spgs	78410
Mediterranean Dr	78418
Meeks Rd	78418
Megal Dr	78413
Megan Cir	78414
Melbourne Dr	
1200-1299	78404
1300-1599	78415
Meldo Park Dr	78411
Melex Dr	78410
Melisa Ln	78412
Melody Ln	78418
Melrose St	78404
Memphis Dr	78412
Mendenhall Dr	78415
Mendocino Cir & Dr	78414
Mendoza St	78416
Mercer Cir	78413
Mercury Ave	78409
Merganser Dr	78413
Meridian Pl	78411
Merlin Pl	78414
Mermaid Dr	78412
Merrill Dr	78408
Merrimac St	78415
Merriman Ave	78412
Mesa Ave & Cir	78410
N Mesquite St	78401
Mesquite Ridge Dr	78410
Mestina St	
1001-1497	78401
1499-1699	78401
1801-1897	78408
1899-2000	78408
2002-2198	78408
Meuly St	78405
Mexico St	78401
Miami Dr	
1200-1299	78404
1300-1499	78415
Michael Ct	78415
Michaux Dr	78414
Micheline Dr	78412
Middle Ln	78410
Middlecoff Cir & Rd	78413
Midwest Cir	78414
Milam Dr	78415
Milan St	78414
Mildred Dr	78411
Military Dr	78418
Milky Way Dr	78412
Mill Brook Dr	78418
Mill Wood Dr	78413
Miller Cir	78411
Milo St	78415
Mima Cir	78414
Mimosa Dr	78408
Mingo Cay Ct	78418
Minton St	78407
Miramar Pl	78411
Miranda Dr	78414
Miriam Vale Ct	78414
Mirror Cts	78418
Mission Dr	78417
Mistletoe Dr	78411
Misty Dr	78416
Misty Meadow Rd	78414
Mitchell St	78411
Mitra Pkwy	78414
Mizzen St	78418
Mobile Dr	78410
Modesto St	78417
Moffet Cir & Dr	78412
Mohawk St	78405
Mohican Cir	78414
Mokry Dr	78415
Molina Dr	78416
Mona Lisa Cir	78413
Monaco St	78411
Monarch St	78413
Monette Dr	78412
Monitor St	78415
Monmouth St	78418
Montclair Dr	78412
Montdidier St	78414
Montebello	78414
Montecita Dr	78413
Montego Dr	
3800-3999	78415
4000-4199	78411
4201-4399	78411
Montereau St	78414
Monterrey St	78411
Montgomery St	78405
Montreal Cir	78414
Montreal Dr	78418
Montserrat	78414
Moody Dr	78416
Moon Beam Trl	78409
Moon Light Dr	78409
Moon River Trl	78410
Moonglow Ln	78409
Moonlake Ridge Dr	78413
Moore St	78407
Moorhead Dr	78410
Mora Rd	78418
Morales St	78416
Moravian Dr	
4300-4499	78411
4500-5099	78415
Moray Pl	78411
Morgan Ave	
500-1999	78404
2000-4000	78405
4002-4098	78405
Moritz Cir	78416
Moritz Lake Dr	78413
Morning Star Ln	78409
N & S Morningside St	78404
Moro Ln	78418
Morris St	
1200-1899	78401
2000-2999	78405
Morrow Dr	78410
Motts Dr	78410
Moultrie Dr	78413
W Mount Dr	78414
Mount Rainer Dr	78410
Mount Vernon Dr	78411
Mountain Trl	78410
Mountain View Dr	78410
Mountain Wood Dr	78413
Mounts Dr	78418
Mt Zion	78413
Mueller St	78408
Mulberry St	78411
Mulholland Dr	78410
Mullet St	78418
Mulligan Dr	78413
Muntanya St	78415
Murphey Dr	78413
Musket Ln	78410
Mussett St	
1400-1699	78401
1901-1997	78408
1999-2100	78408
2102-2198	78408
Mutiny Ct	78418
Mystic Star Dr	78414
Nacogdoches Dr	78414
Nagle St	78418
Nancy St	78412
Nandina Dr	78408
Napa Dr	78414
Naples St	
100-3099	78404
3100-3398	78415
3400-4499	78415
Narsonne St	78414
Nas Dr	78418
Nassau Dr	78418
Natal Plum Dr	78418
Natchez Dr	78414
National Dr	78416
Nautical Wind Dr	78414
Navajo St	78405
Navarro St	78415
Navigation Blvd	
100-921	78408
922-1098	78407
923-999	78408
1100-1399	78407
1401-1599	78407
E Navigation Blvd	78402
N Navigation Blvd	78408
S Navigation Blvd	78405
Navy Dr	78418
N & S Naylor Cir	78408
Nazareth Dr	78413
Nela Rd	78414
Nell St	78411
Nelon St	78410
Nelson Ln	78411
Nemec St	78415
Nemesis Dr	78414
Nemo Ct	78418
Neptune St	78405
Nesbitt Dr	78415
Neustadt Dr	78414
New Bedford Dr	78414
New Brunswick Dr	78414
New House St	78405
New York Ave	78414
Newbury Ln	78411
Newcastle Dr	78418
Newman	78414
Newmarket Dr	78414
Newport Dr	78418
Niagara St	
2100-3000	78405
3002-3098	78405
3700-3900	78416
3902-4098	78416
Nichols Dr	78410
Nicholson St	78415
Nicklaus Ln	78413
Nicole Ct	78415
Night Hawk Ln	78410
Nile Dr	78412
Nimitz St	78405
Noakes St	78407
Nocona Cir	78413
Nodding Pines Dr	78414
Nogales St	
2200-2699	78416
2701-2719	78405
2721-2899	78405
Nolford Pl	78410
Nomad Ct	78414
Norchester Dr	78415
Norfolk Dr	78418
Normandy Dr	78415
Northfield Dr	78413
Northgate Cir & Dr	78413
Northwest Blvd & Trl	78410
Northwind Dr	78414
Northwood Dr	78410
Norton St	
100-399	78415
401-3099	78415
3300-3399	78411
Norvel Dr	78412
Norwich Ct	78413
Nottingham Dr	78411
Nueces St	
1400-1999	78401
2300-2308	78407
2310-2999	78407
Nueces Bay Blvd	
501-699	78408
800-1098	78408
809-809	78469
1700-1798	78407
1800-1899	78407
Nuecestown Rd	78410
Nuss Dr	78414
Oak Hl & Vw	78418
Oak Bay Dr	78413
Oak Crest St	78418
Oak Forest Dr	78413
Oak Harbor Dr	78418
Oak Hollow Dr	78414
Oak Knoll Cir	78413
Oak Park Ave	
701-797	78408
799-999	78408
1201-1297	78407
1299-1300	78407
1302-1398	78407
Oak Ridge Dr	78418
Oakbrook Dr	78413
Oakdale Dr	78418
Oakgate Dr	78413
Oakhurst Dr	78411
Oakmont Dr	78413
Oberste St	78418
Obrian Dr	78413
Ocasey Dr	78413
Ocean Dr	
11-11	78418
1100-3299	78404
3300-4299	78411
4300-6518	78412
6520-7098	78412
8801-8897	78419
8899-9099	78419
9600-9698	78418
11801-11899	78418
Ocean Park Dr	78404
Ocean View Pl	78411
Ocean Way St	78411
Oconnell St	78418
Oday Pkwy	
3701-3799	78415
4000-4299	78413
Odell Dr	78413
Odem Dr	78415
Odessa Dr	78413
Oglethorpe Dr	78410
Ogrady Dr	78413
Ohara Dr	78413
Ohio Ave	78404
Old Brownsville Rd	
1000-1099	78415
1101-1199	78415
3600-5399	78405
5400-5500	78417
5501-5599	78405
5501-6799	78417
5502-6598	78417
6600-6898	78415
6900-8299	78415
8301-8699	78415
Old Perimeter Rd	78406
Old Robstown Rd	78408
Old Square Dr	78414
Oleander Ave	78404
Olive Grove Dr	78414
Oliver Ct	78408
Ollie St	78418
Olmos Creek Cir	78410
Olmos River Ct	78410
Olsen Dr	78411
Olympia Dr	78413
Omaha Dr	78408
Omalley Dr	78413
Oneill St	78418
Ontario Dr	78418
Opal Dr	78409
Opengate Dr	78413
Opossum Creek Dr	78410
Opportunity Dr	78405
Orange St	78418

Orangetip Dr 78414
Orangewood Dr 78412
Orbit Ave 78409
Orchid Ln 78416
Oriental Ave 78414
Oriole St 78418
Orion Dr 78418
Orlando Dr 78411
Orleans Dr 78418
Ormond Dr 78415
Orms Dr 78412
Orrel Cir 78410
Ortiz 78414
Osage St 78405
Oso Dr 78415
Oso Pkwy
2801-2899 78414
4500-5599 78413
5600-6199 78414
6201-6399 78414
N Oso Pkwy 78414
S Oso Pkwy
4800-5399 78413
5600-5899 78414
Oso Bay Ranch Rd 78418
Oso Hills Dr 78413
Otoole Dr 78413
Otranto Dr 78418
Ottawa Cir 78414
Outpost Dr 78410
Outreau Dr 78414
Ovendara St 78404
Overbrook Cir 78413
Overland Trl 78410
Owen Ct 78413
Oxford Dr 78411
Paddlewheel Dr 78410
N Padre Island Dr
100-899 78406
901-999 78406
1500-1598 78408
1600-2299 78408
S Padre Island Dr
100-599 78405
600-1098 78416
1100-2100 78416
2102-2198 78416
2400-3999 78415
4000-5599 78411
5600-8300 78412
8302-8398 78412
9101-9297 78418
9299-15399 78418
15401-15999 78418
S Padre Staples Mall 78411
Paige Pl 78415
Paint Rock St 78410
Painter Dr 78415
Pajaro Ln 78414
Palm Dr
300-398 78408
400-699 78408
1200-2099 78407
Palmero St 78404
Palmetto St 78412
Palmira Ave 78418
Palo Alto St 78401
Palo Blanco St 78417
Palo Seco Dr 78418
Palo Verde St 78417
Paloma St 78412
Pamona St 78417
Panama Dr
3600-3931 78415
3933-3999 78415
4000-4099 78411
Panay Dr 78418
Pangani Dr 78415
Papaya Cts 78415
Parade Dr 78412
Paradise Dr 78418
Paris Dr 78414
Park Ave 78401
Park St 78412
Park Road 22 78418
Park Wind Dr 78414
Parkdale Plz 78411
Parkers Aly 78401
Parkgreen Dr 78414
Parkland Dr 78413
Parkview Dr 78415
Parkway 78414
Parkwood Pl 78408
Parliament Dr 78411
Parr St 78408
Parsley Ct 78414
Pasadena Pl 78411
Pato St 78414
Patrick Dr 78413
Patriot Dr 78413
Patti 78414
Patton St 78414
Paul Jones Ave 78412
Paula Dr 78410
Pavo Real St 78414
Peabody Ave
700-799 78408
1300-2199 78407
Peach Creek Ct 78410
Peachtree St 78410
Peacock Dr 78414
Pearse Dr 78415
Pearson St 78418
Pebble Beach Dr 78413
Pebble Springs Ct 78414
Pecan St 78411
Pecan Bayou Ct 78410
Pecan Valley Dr 78413
Pecos River Dr 78410
Peerman Pl 78411
Pegasus Loop 78418
Pels Ave 78416
Pembrock 78414
Pendleton Dr 78415
Pennington Dr 78412
Penny Ln 78414
Pensacola Cts 78415
Pentridge Dr 78410
Peoples St 78401
Peoples Street T Head
Blvd 78401
Pepper Mill Dr 78413
Pepper Ridge Rd 78413
Pernitas Creek Dr 78410
Perry Ln 78410
Persimmon St 78415
Perthshire Dr 78418
Pescadores Dr 78418
Peseta Ct 78418
Peterson Dr 78412
Petit Pointe 78414
Petronila Creek Ct 78410
Petty Dr 78408
Pharaoh Dr 78412
Pheasant Cir 78413
Philippine Dr 78411
Phillip Dr 78415
Philmont Lake Dr 78414
Philomena Dr 78412
Picadilly Ln 78414
Picante Dr 78414
Piedra Creek Dr 78410
Piedrabuena Dr 78414
Pieriden Dr 78410
Pimlico Ln 78418
Pine St 78405
Pinehollow Ln 78418
Pinehurst Dr 78413
Pinewood Dr 78412
Pink Cadillac Dr 78414
Pinson Dr 78406
Pinta Creek Cir 78410
Pintail Dr 78413
Pionciana St 78418
Pioneer Dr 78410
Piper Dr 78412
Platte River Dr 78410
Playa Del Rey 78418
Player St 78413
Pleiades Pl 78418
Plerrent St 78417
Pocono Cir 78414
Poenisch Dr 78412
W Point Rd 78416
Polaris Pl 78418
Pollex Ave 78415
Pompano Pl 78411
Ponder St 78404
Ponderosa Ln 78415
Ponil Creek Dr 78414
Pontchartrain Dr 78413
Poolside Dr 78409
Pope Dr 78411
Poplar St 78411
Porpoise St 78418
E Port Ave 78401
N Port Ave
101-197 78408
199-500 78408
502-798 78408
900-2599 78401
S Port Ave
400-1399 78405
1300-1398 78465
1400-3098 78405
1401-3099 78405
3101-3199 78416
3200-3298 78415
3300-4199 78415
4201-4299 78467
4201-4299 78415
4301-4499 78415
Port Royal Ct 78418
Portillo Dr 78418
Ports O Call Dr 78418
Portsmouth Dr 78418
Post Ave 78405
Post Oak Cir 78410
Poth Ln
900-961 78408
1800-1899 78407
Potomac Pl 78410
Powderhorn Ct 78413
Powell Dr 78410
Power St 78401
Prairie Dr 78413
S Prairie Rd 78415
Prairie Creek Dr 78410
Prairie Dog Fork Dr 78410
Prallak Dr 78418
Prax Morgan Pl 78414
Preakness Cir 78417
Premont Dr 78414
Presa St 78416
Prescott St
1600-2200 78404
2202-3098 78404
3100-3298 78415
3801-4397 78416
4399-4899 78416
Presidio Dr 78414
Pressler Dr 78413
Preston St 78418
Primavera Dr 78418
Primrose Dr 78404
Prince Dr 78412
Prince Charles 78414
Princess Dr 78410
Princess Jean 78414
Prinston Dr 78411
Priscilla Dr 78414
Private Rd 26b 78415
Promise Ln 78412
Prosper Dr 78415
Pueblo St 78405
Puget Sound Dr 78410
Punta Bonaire Dr 78418
Punta Espada Loop 78418
Purdue Rd 78413
Purl Pl 78412
Purplewing Dr 78414
Pyle Dr 78415
Pyramid Dr 78412
Pyrenees St 78414
Quail Creek Dr 78414
Quail Hollow Dr 78414
Quail Run Dr 78414
Quail Springs Rd 78414
Quaile Dr 78408
Quarterdeck Dr 78418
Quebec Dr 78414
Queen Dr 78415
Queen Bess Dr 78414
Queen Jane St 78414
Queen Johanna Ct 78418
Queens Ct 78413
Queensborough Cir 78413
Quetzal St 78418
Quig Cir 78410
Quincy Dr 78411
Rabbit Run 78418
Rackley Dr 78407
Radial Ct 78414
Railroad Ave 78410
Rain Mist Ln 78409
Rainbow Ln 78411
Raintree Dr 78410
Raintree Ln 78409
Rainy River Ct 78414
Ralston Ave 78404
Rambler Pl 78408
Ramfield Rd 78418
Ramirez St 78401
Ramona Dr 78416
Ramos St 78410
Ramsey St 78415
Ramsgate Cir 78414
Rancho Vista Blvd 78414
Rand Morgan Rd 78410
Randall Dr 78411
Randolph Cir 78410
Ranger Ave 78415
Ranger Cts 78404
Ranger Rd 78418
Ransom Island Dr 78418
Rapids Dr 78410
Rasputin Ct 78413
Raven St 78418
Raven Hill Rd 78414
Ravine Dr 78410
Rawleigh Dr 78412
Ray Dr 78411
Ray Ellison Dr 78415
Rayado Creek Dr 78414
Rayfish St 78418
Reagan Dr 78410
Reales Dr 78418
Rebecca Dr 78410
Recreation Dr 78418
Recycle 78409
Red Bishop Cir 78418
Red Bluff Rd 78410
Red Creek Cir 78410
Red Mile Rd 78418
Red Oak Dr 78418
Red Poll Cir 78418
Red River Dr 78410
Red Start Cir 78418
E & W Redbird Ln 78410
Redbud Dr 78410
Redfish St 78418
Redfish Bay Dr 78418
Redmond St 78418
Redwood St 78411
Reef Ave 78402
Reeves Dr 78408
Regal St 78413
Regency Dr 78414
Rehfeld Rd 78410
Reid Dr
3100-3299 78404
3700-3799 78411
Rene Dr 78416
Republic Dr 78413
Resaca St 78401
Retama Ave
800-900 78408
902-998 78408
1101-1199 78407
Retta Dr 78418
Reveille 78414
Revolution Dr 78413
Rex Ln 78418
Reyna St 78405
Reynosa St 78416
Rhew Rd 78409
Rhine Dr 78412
Rhodes Ct 78410
Rhonda Dr 78412
Rhumba Trl 78410
Riata Cir & Dr 78418
Ribbon Tail St 78418
Richard St 78415
Richland St 78418
Richmond St 78410
Richter St 78415
Richwood Cir 78410
Rick Ln 78418
Rickey Dr 78412
S Ridge Ct 78413
Ridge Creek Dr 78413
Ridge Stone Dr 78413
Ridge View Dr 78413
Ridgeline Ct 78413
Ridgewood Cts 78413
Riding Wind Dr 78414
Riggan St 78404
Riley Dr 78412
Rincon Rd 78402
Rio Grande Dr 78417
Rio Vista Ave 78412
Rippling Creek Cir &
Dr 78410
Rita Dr 78412
River Dr & Ln 78410
River Bend Ct 78415
River Canyon Dr 78410
River Crest Rd 78415
River East Dr 78410
River Forest Dr 78410
River Hill Dr 78410
River Home Dr 78410
River Oaks Dr 78413
River Park Dr 78410
River Ridge Cir & Dr 78410
River Rock Dr 78410
River Run Blvd 78410
River Valley Dr 78410
River View Trl 78410
River Walk Dr 78410
Riverdale Dr 78418
Rivergate Dr 78413
Riverside Blvd 78410
Riverton Dr 78416
Riverway Dr 78410
Riverwood Dr 78410
Riviera Dr 78418
Roanoke Dr 78414
Robb Pl 78415
Robby St 78410
Robert Dr 78412
Robertson Dr 78415
Robin Dr 78415
Robinhood Dr 78411
Robinson St 78404
Rock Creek Dr 78412
Rock Crest Dr 78414
Rockford Dr 78416
Rocklawn Dr 78416
Rocksprings Dr 78413
Rockwood St 78410
Rodd Field Rd
1300-1823 78412
1825-1999 78412
2101-2297 78414
2299-3600 78414
3602-3798 78414
Rogerio St 78415
Rogers St 78405
Rogerson Dr 78415
Rojo Cts & St 78415
Rolling Acres Dr 78410
Rolling Ridge Dr 78410
Romford Dr 78413
Ronald Dr 78412
Ronson Dr 78412
Rooney Dr 78413
Roosevelt Dr 78415
Root St 78409
Ropes St 78411
Rorer Cir 78410
Rosalie St 78416
Roscher Rd 78418
Rose St 78418
Rose Petal Dr 78415
Roseanne St 78418
Rosebud Ave 78404
Rosedale Dr 78411
Rosedown Dr 78418
Roseland Dr 78414
Rosemary St 78418
Rosewood St 78405
Roslyn St 78416
Ross St 78415
Rossi Dr 78411
Rossiter St 78411
Round Rock St 78410
Round Table St 78414
Roundtree Cir 78410
Royal Ct 78414
Royal Fifth Ct 78418
Royalton Dr 78413
Rudder Ct 78418
Rugged Ridge Dr 78413
Rushing Blvd 78410
Rusk St 78406
Russ Ln 78414
Russell Dr 78408
Rustic Oak St 78410
Rustling Cove Dr 78410
Ruth St 78405
Ryan St 78405
Saar Ct 78414
Sabal Dr 78414
Sabinal Dr 78417
Sabinas St 78405
Sabo Dr 78414
Sabre Dr 78418
Sacky Dr 78415
Saddle Ln 78410
Saddlewood 78413
Safari Dr 78411
Safety Steel Dr 78414
Sage Brush Dr 78410
Sahara Dr 78412
Sailfish St 78418
Sainchen Rd 78409
Saint Agatha Dr 78418
Saint Andrews Dr 78413
Saint Anthony Pl 78418
Saint Bartholomew St 78418
Saint Benedict Ct 78418
Saint Bernadine Dr 78418
Saint Bernard St 78418
Saint Charles St 78402
Saint Christopher St 78418
Saint Columban Pl 78418
Saint Denis St 78414
Saint Dominic Ct 78418
Saint Felicity 78418
Saint George Dr 78413
Saint Gregory St 78418
Saint James Ct 78413
Saint Joseph St 78418
Saint Laurent Dr 78414
Saint Lucy Dr 78418
Saint Luke St 78418
Saint Maria Dr 78418
Saint Martin St 78418
Saint Michael Ct 78418
Saint Paul Cir 78418
Saint Perpetua Dr 78418
Saint Peter St 78418
Saint Phillip Ct 78418
Saint Pius Dr 78412
Saint Timothy St 78418
Saint Tropez St 78414
Salazar St 78416
Salem Dr 78412
Salisong Dr 78413
Sally Ln 78414
Salsa Dr 78414
Salt Cay Ct 78418
Saluki St 78414
Sam St 78412
Sam Rankin St 78401
Samba Dr 78414
Sammons Dr 78410
Samoa Dr 78418
San Angelo Dr 78413
San Antonio St 78411
San Benito Dr 78414
San Blas Dr 78415
San Felipe Dr 78418
San Fernando Pl 78411
San Jacinto Dr 78405
San Juan St 78401
San Luis St 78401
San Pedro St 78401
San Rafael St 78416
San Ramon Dr 78413
San Roque Creek Dr 78410
San Saba Dr 78407
Sanbar Ln 78418
Sand Dollar Ave 78418
Sandalwood Dr 78412
Sanders Dr 78413
Sanderson Dr 78417
Sandpiper Cir & Dr 78412
Sandra Ln 78414
Sands Dr 78418
Sandstone Dr 78412
Sandy Way 78418
Sandy Creek Ct 78410
Sandy Hollow Dr 78410
Sandy Oaks Dr 78418
Sandy Ridge St 78410
Santa Ana St 78415
Santa Barbara St 78411
Santa Cruz Dr 78414
Santa Elena St 78405
Santa Fe St
1000-3000 78404
3002-3298 78404
3300-4299 78411
Santa Gertrudis Dr 78410
Santa Lucia St 78415
Santa Maria Ln 78415
Santa Monica Pl 78411
Santa Sofia St 78415
Santana Dr 78418
Sapphire Ct 78414
Sara Lynn Pkwy 78414
Sarah 78417
Saratoga Blvd
100-2399 78417
3000-3198 78415
3200-3999 78415
4000-5599 78413
5600-7100 78414
7102-7198 78414
Saratoga Cts 78404
Sarazen Dr
5500-5599 78413
6002-6098 78414
Sarita St
2100-2198 78405
2200-2999 78405
3101-3697 78416
3699-3999 78416
4001-4099 78416
Saskatchewan Dr 78414
Saskatoon Dr 78414
Saspamco Creek Dr 78410
Saturn Rd 78413
Sault Dr 78414
Sauve Terre 78414
Savage Ln
600-698 78408
700-899 78408
942-1099 78407
Savoy St 78414
N Saxet Dr 78408
Saxony Dr 78418
Scabbard Dr 78414
Scallop St 78418
Scapular St 78406
Scarlet Oak Dr 78418
Scenic Cir 78410
Schanen Blvd & Cir 78413
Schatzel St 78401
Schnauzer St 78414
Schooner Dr 78418

Schooner Hbr 78402
Schwerin Lake Dr 78413
Scotch Moss Dr 78414
Scotland Dr 78418
Scott Dr 78408
Sea Dr & Pnes 78418
Sea Anchor St 78418
Sea Horse Ave 78418
Sea Island Dr 78413
Sea Oak Dr 78418
Sea Side Dr 78418
Seadog Cir 78410
Seafarer Dr 78418
Seafoam Dr 78418
Seagrape St 78418
Seagull Blvd 78402
Seahawk Dr 78415
Sealane Dr 78412
Seamist Dr 78414
Seamount Cay Ct 78418
Sean Dr 78412
Seashore Dr 78412
Seaview Ln 78411
Sebastian Ct 78414
Security Dr
10139-10139 78418
10139-10139 78480
Sedwick Rd 78409
Segrest St 78405
Seguin Dr 78415
Seigler St 78402
Seine Dr 78412
Selkirk Dr 78418
Seminole St 78405
Senators Ct & Dr 78413
Sentinel Dr 78418
Sequoia St 78411
Serenity Ct 78414
Sessions Rd 78410
Sete Dr 78414
Seth St 78418
Seven Trees Dr 78410
Seville Dr 78416
Shadi St 78418
Shadow Wood Dr 78415
Shadowbend Dr 78413
Shady Ln 78410
Shady Creek Ln 78414
Shallow Creek Dr 78410
Shamrock Dr 78412
Shane Dr 78410
Shangrala St 78412
Sharolyn St 78415
Sharon Dr 78412
Sharpsburg Rd 78410
Shasta Ln 78415
Shaw St 78416
Shawnee St 78405
Shayan Ct 78414
N & S Shea Cir &
Pkwy 78413
Sheffield Ln 78411
Shelburne Dr 78414
Shelton Blvd 78410
Shely St
100-1899 78404
1901-1999 78404
2101-2199 78405
Shephard Dr 78412
Sheridan Dr 78412
Sherman St 78416
Sherwood Dr 78411
Shiels Dr 78412
Shilling Way Ln 78414
Shiloh Ln 78410
Shirley Dr 78416
Shoal Creek Cir 78410
Shopping Way 78411
Shore Dr 78418
N Shoreline Blvd
100-1999 78401
2700-2798 78402
2800-2999 78402
3001-3899 78402
S Shoreline Blvd 78401
Shoshone Dr 78410

Shower Dr 78416
Sierra Cir & St 78410
Sierra Blanca Blvd 78413
Silver Creek Dr 78410
Silver Hollow Dr 78413
Silver Sands Dr 78412
Silverberry Dr 78417
Silverspur Dr 78410
Silverton Dr 78410
Simon St 78406
Sinclair St 78411
Sir Galahad 78413
Sir Gawain 78413
Sir Geraint 78413
Sir Jack St 78414
Sir Lancelot 78413
Sir Moses 78414
Sir Palleas 78413
Siskin Cir 78418
Skipper Ln 78418
Sky Crest St 78418
Skyking Dr 78412
Skylark 78408
Skyline Dr 78408
Skysail St 78418
Slough Rd 78414
Smith Dr 78410
Smokewood Dr 78413
Snake River Dr 78414
Snead Dr 78413
Snow Peak Dr 78409
Snowbird Dr 78413
Snowfinch Cir 78418
Snowgoose Dr 78413
Snowmass St 78413
Snowridge Cir 78409
Snug Hbr 78402
Sobey Dr 78408
Softwood St 78410
Sokol Dr 78415
Soledad St
2200-2699 78416
2700-2999 78405
Solomon Ln 78415
Songbird Ln 78414
Sonoma Dr 78414
Sonora St 78405
Sorrell St 78404
Southbay Dr 78412
Southern St 78404
Southern Minerals Rd 78409
Southern Sun Dr 78415
Southgate Dr 78415
Southhaven Dr 78412
Southland Dr 78408
Southview Dr 78408
Southwind 78413
Southwood St 78415
Spanish Trl 78410
Spanish Wood Dr 78414
Sparkle Sea Dr 78412
Sparkleberry 78410
Spaulding Dr 78410
Spencer Dr 78412
Spicewood Dr 78412
Spitfire Dr 78412
Spohn Dr S 78414
Spring Ln 78418
Spring St 78415
Spring Brook Dr 78413
Spring Creek Dr 78410
Spring Fork Cir & Dr 78413
Spring Hill Ln 78410
Spring Wind 78413
Spruce St 78408
Sprucewood Dr 78412
Spurwood St 78410
Squaw Pass Ct 78413
Stacy Ln 78410
Stafford St 78416
Stag Hill Dr 78414
Stages Dr 78412
Stampede Dr 78414
Stanley St 78405
Stanton Dr 78418
N Staples St 78401

S Staples St
200-699 78401
800-3199 78404
3201-3297 78411
3299-5699 78411
5700-8599 78413
8800-8898 78414
7110-1-7110-2 78413
N Star Ln 78409
Star Cove Dr 78412
Star Glow Dr 78414
Star Harbor Dr 78414
Stardust Ln 78418
Starfish Cts 78418
Starlite Ln 78410
Starnberg Lake Dr 78413
Starr St 78401
Starry Cir & Rd 78414
Starshine Dr 78414
State Highway 286 78415
State Highway 44 Byp 78406
Steamboat Ln 78410
Sterling Dr 78414
Stetson Cir 78414
Stewart Pl 78402
Stewart St 78418
Still Brook Dr 78414
Stillman Ave 78407
Stillwell Ln 78409
Stingray St 78418
Stinson St 78405
Stirman St 78411
Stock Dr 78406
Stone St 78418
Stonegate Way 78411
Stonemill Cir 78413
Stonewall Blvd 78410
Stony Brook Dr 78413
Stony Creek Dr 78413
Strasbourg Dr 78414
Strateford Dr 78414
Stratton Dr 78412
Strom Rd 78418
Sudan Dr 78412
Sudbury 78414
Sue Cir 78410
Suffolk Dr 78414
Sugar Creek Dr 78413
Sugar Magnolia Dr 78410
Sugar Ridge Rd 78413
Sulaine Pl 78415
Sullivan St 78406
Sulu Dr 78418
Summer Breeze Ct 78418
Summer Ridge Dr 78414
Summer Time 78413
Summer Wind Dr 78413
Summers St 78407
Summit St 78418
Sumpter Ln 78410
Sumster Cts 78415
Sun Beam Dr 78412
Sun Belt Dr 78408
Sun Valley Dr 78413
Sun Wood Dr 78413
Sundown Dr 78410
Sunfish St 78418
Sunglo 78418
Sunlight Dr 78413
Sunny Dr 78410
Sunnybrook Rd 78415
Sunnycrest St 78418
Sunnyville Cir & Dr 78410
Sunray Cir 78409
Sunrise Ave 78405
Sunset Ave 78404
Sunshine Ave 78409
Suntan Ave 78418
Suntide Rd 78409
Surfside Blvd 78402
Surrey Ct & Ln 78415
Susan Dr 78412
Sussex Dr 78418
Sutherland Dr 78414
Sutton Ln 78411
Suwanee Cir 78413

Swansea Dr 78413
Swantner St 78404
Sweeney Dr 78413
Sweet Bay Dr 78418
Sweet Briar Cir 78413
Sweet Gum St 78415
Sweet Water Creek Dr 78410
Swift Cir 78418
Swiss Dr 78415
Sycamore Pl 78416
Sydney St 78414
Sylling Dr 78414
Sylvan Crest Dr 78415
Tahiti Dr 78418
Tahoe Cir 78413
Tajamar St 78418
Talbert Rd 78406
Taldora St 78414
Talisman St 78416
Talmadge St 78418
Tamarisk Dr 78418
Tamarron Ct 78413
Tampa Cts 78415
Tampico St 78405
N Tancahua St
400-499 78401
501-1799 78401
800-898 78403
802-1798 78401
S Tancahua St
200-799 78401
801-899 78401
900-999 78404
Tangled Ridge Ct 78413
Tanglewood Dr 78412
Tango Cir 78414
Tanzanite Dr 78414
Taos Dr 78413
Tapestry Dr 78414
Tara St 78412
Tarafaya Dr 78414
Tarlton St
100-1999 78415
2201-2497 78416
2499-2699 78416
2700-2799 78405
2801-2899 78405
Tarpon Pl 78411
Tartan Cir & Dr 78413
Tates Creek Rd 78418
Tawakoni St 78409
Taxiway Echo 78406
Taylor St 78401
Taylors Way Ct 78414
Teague Ln 78410
Teak St 78411
Teal Dr 78410
Teamwork Trl 78417
Terrace Cir 78411
Terrace St 78404
Terrace Bay Dr 78418
Terrell Cir 78413
Terrier St 78414
Tesoro Dr 78418
Texaco Rd 78402
Texan Trl 78411
Texas Ave 78404
Thames Dr 78412
The 600 Bldg 78401
Theda Dr 78412
Thelma Dr 78418
Theresa St 78416
Thirty Seven Ct 78409
Thomas Dr 78407
Thoreau Cir 78410
Thornberry Ct 78415
Three Fathoms Bank
Dr 78418
Thunder Bay Cts 78414
Thundersee Dr 78413
Tide St 78416
Tierra Grande 78415
Tierra Oriente 78415
Tierra Poniente 78415
Tiger Ln 78415
Tillet Ct 78414

Tim Ln 78412
Timber Crest Dr 78413
Timbergate Dr
5300-5599 78413
5700-5798 78414
5800-6099 78414
Timbergrove Ln 78410
Timberline Cir & Dr 78409
Timon Blvd 78402
Timrod St 78404
Tinian Dr 78418
Toben Dr 78412
Tocken Ct 78414
Toledo Dr 78413
Tolman St 78415
Tompkins St 78404
Tonga Dr 78418
Topaz Ct 78414
Topeka St
2800-3299 78404
3400-3799 78411
Topgallant St 78418
Topsail St 78418
Toronto Dr 78414
Torreon St 78405
Tortuga Ct 78418
Totton Dr 78411
Toulon Dr 78414
Tourmaline Dr 78414
Townhouse Ln 78412
Townsend St 78415
Tracy St 78404
Trail Creek Dr 78414
Trail Ridge Dr 78413
Trantella Ct 78414
Trappers Lake Dr 78413
Tree Top Pl 78413
Treebine Dr 78418
Trenton Dr 78404
Trestle Cir 78416
Treyway Cir & Ln 78412
Tribble Ln 78407
Trieste Dr 78413
Trinidad Dr 78418
Trinity Dr 78411
Trinity River Dr 78410
Triple Crown Dr 78417
Tripoli Dr
3600-3999 78415
4000-4400 78411
4402-5498 78411
Trixie Dr 78412
Trojan Dr 78416
Tropical Ln 78408
Tropical Wind Dr 78414
Troy Dr 78412
Truk Dr 78418
Truxton Dr 78414
Tudor Dr 78414
Tulane St 78418
Tulia St 78418
Tulip St 78408
Tuloso Cir & Rd 78409
Tumbleweed Dr 78410
Tuna St 78418
Tupper Ln 78417
Turkey Creek Dr 78410
Turkey Hollow Ct 78414
Turkey Springs Dr 78414
Turning Leaf Dr 78410
Tuscan Way 78410
Tuscarora Dr 78410
Tuskegee Ct 78401
Twilight Ridge Dr 78413
Twin Creek Dr 78414
Twin River Blvd 78410
Twine Dr 78414
Twite Cir 78418
Tyler Ave
1100-1299 78404
1300-1399 78415
Uninsou Dr 78415
Union St 78407
University Dr 78412
Up River Rd
3101-3197 78408
3199-4599 78408
4601-4699 78408
4800-4998 78407
5000-5900 78407
5902-5998 78407
6600-9200 78409
9202-9398 78409
9400-12699 78410
N & S Upper Broadway
St 78401
Urban St 78415
Ursa Dr 78412
Utica St 78418
Vail St 78413
Vaky St 78404
Valdemorillo Dr 78414
Valdez Dr 78416
Valencia Dr 78416
Valerie St 78418
Valhalla Dr 78415
Valley Cir & Cv 78413
Valley Mill Dr 78413
Valley Stream Dr 78413
Valley View Dr 78413
Valor Dr 78413
Valtourmanche Dr 78414
Van Cleve Dr 78408
Van Cura Dr 78408
Van Hyftte Cir 78414
Van Loan Ave 78407
Van Zandt Dr 78413
Vance Dr 78412
Vancouver Dr 78414
Vancrest Dr 78415
Vandemere Dr 78414
E & W Vanderbilt Dr 78415
Vanern Dr 78413
Vaquero Dr 78414
Vatter Dr 78413
Veda Dr 78410
Vega Dr 78418
Velda 78410
Venice Dr 78413
Ventoso St 78414
Ventura 78417
Venture St 78415
Venus Dr 78409
Vera Cruz St 78405
Verbena St 78405
Verde Cts 78415
Verdemar Dr 78418
Vermont St 78409
Verner Cir & Dr 78415
Vernon Dr 78407
Versailles Dr 78418
Vestal St 78416
Vetters Dr 78412
Vialoux Dr 78418
Vicksburg St 78410
Victor Lara Ortegon St 78417
Victoria Park Dr 78414
Victory Dr 78408
Vienna Dr 78414
Villa Dr 78408
Villa Maria Isabel 78418
Villarreal Dr 78416
Villefranche Dr 78414
Villonto St 78401
Vincent Dr
6100-6499 78412
14100-15798 78418
15800-15899 78418
Vineyard Dr 78414
Viola Ave 78415
Violet Rd 78410
Violeta Ct 78408
Virden Ct 78418
Virgil Dr 78412
Virginia Ave 78405
Virginia Hls 78414
Vista Cir 78410
Vista Ridge St 78410
Vitemb St 78416
Vivian Dr 78412
Volga Dr 78412
W.L. Breeding Dr 78414

Waco St 78401
Wagner Lee Dr 78418
Wagon Wheel Dr 78410
Wainwright St 78405
Wakeforest Dr 78413
Waldron Rd 78418
Wales Dr 78413
Walker Dr 78418
Walking Oaks 78418
Wall Dr & St 78414
Wallace Ave 78412
Walnut Hills Dr 78413
Waltham Dr 78411
Walton Pl 78412
Wandering Creek Dr 78410
Wapentate Dr 78413
Warlow Dr 78413
Warpath St 78410
Warwick Dr 78411
N & S Washam Dr 78414
Washington St 78405
Wasp St 78412
N Water St 78401
S Water St
301-899 78401
901-997 78404
999-1099 78404
Water Lily Dr 78415
Waterfall St 78416
Waterford 78414
Waterloo Dr 78415
Watson St 78415
Waverly Dr 78412
Waxwing St 78418
Wayside Dr 78415
Weaver St 78418
Webb St 78418
Weber Pkwy 78411
Weber Rd
5634A-5634C 78411
4000-4398 78411
4400-5400 78411
5402-5698 78411
5700-6799 78413
6700-6798 78427
6800-6898 78413
6801-6999 78413
7601-8399 78415
Wedgewood Ln 78411
Weir Dr 78415
Weiskopf Cir & Ln 78413
Welakens St 78408
Welianta St 78406
Wellington Cts 78408
Wellwood St 78410
Wentworth Dr 78413
Werner Ln 78408
Wesley Dr 78412
Westchester Dr 78408
Western Cir & Dr 78410
Westgard St 78415
Westgate Dr 78408
Westland Dr 78408
Westminster Dr 78415
Westphal Ct 78413
Westridge Blvd 78418
Westview Cir & Dr 78410
Westway Dr 78408
Westwood Dr 78410
Wexford Dr 78411
Whalen Dr 78413
Wharton St 78415
Whataburger Way 78411
Whirlwind St 78414
Whisper Wind St 78412
Whispering Oak Dr 78418
Whistler Dr 78414
Whitaker Dr 78412
White Bird Dr 78415
White Dove Dr 78414
White Oak Dr 78410
White Star 78414
White Tail Dr 78414
Whitecap Blvd 78418
Whitehall Dr 78412
Whiteley Dr 78418

Whitemarsh Dr 78413
Whitewing Dr 78413
Whiting Dr 78415
Whitman 78410
Whitman Pond 78418
Whitney Dr 78410
Whittier Dr 78415
Wickersham St 78415
Wicklow Dr 78413
Widgeon Dr 78410
Wild Horse Valley Dr ... 78410
Wild Olive Trl 78413
Wildcat Dr 78410
Wilderock Dr 78414
Wildfire Dr 78414
E & W Wildwood Dr 78410
Wilkins Dr 78410
Wilkinson Dr 78415
Willard St 78404
Williams Dr
4800-5599 78411
5600-5698 78412
5700-7099 78412
7101-7199 78412
Williams St 78401
Williamson Pl 78411
Williamsport 78418
Williston Dr 78415
Willow St 78411
Willow Oak Dr 78413
Willowbrook Dr 78411
Willowick Dr 78413
Willowood Creek Dr 78410
Wilma Dr 78412
Wilmont Dr 78410
Wilshire Pl 78411
Wilson Dr 78408
Wilson St 78418
Wimbledon St 78415
W Wind 78413
Wind Chime Dr 78413
Wind Rock Dr 78410
Windblown Dr 78414
Windbrook Ln 78414
Windfilled Cir 78414
Windhollow Dr 78414
Winding Star Dr 78413
Windjammer Dr 78418
Windows Dr 78413
Windrose Dr 78414
Windsong Dr 78414
Windsor Dr 78410
Windswept St 78415
Windvane Dr 78414
Windward Dr 78418
Windwillow Ct & Dr 78414
Windy Way 78413
Windy Bay Cir 78414
Windy Cove Cir 78414
Windy Creek Dr 78414
Windy House Cir 78414
Windy Ridge Dr 78413
Wingfoot Ln 78413
Winnebago St
600-998 78401
1000-2000 78401
2002-2298 78401
2300-2398 78407
2400-2499 78407
Winnie Dr 78404
Winnipeg Dr 78418
Winrock Ln 78413
Winston Dr 78412
Winter Park Pl 78413
Winters Dr 78415
Wirt Ave 78410
Wise Owl Ln 78418
Wishbone Ct 78414
Wittner Pl 78418
Wolf Dr 78414
Wolf Creek Ct 78410
Wolf Creek Dr 78413
Wolverine Dr 78414
Wood St 78417
Wood Creek Dr 78410
Wood Duck Dr 78413
Wood Iron Dr 78413
Wood River Dr 78410
Woodbend Dr 78412
Woodcrest Dr 78418
Woodgate Dr 78413
Woodhaven Dr 78412
Woodland St 78415
Woodland Creek Dr 78410
Woodlawn Dr 78412
Woodmere Dr 78414
Woodson Cir 78411
Woodstone Dr 78415
Woodway Dr 78414
Woodway Creek Dr 78410
Wool Dr 78414
Wooldridge Rd
4600-5599 78413
5600-8000 78414
8002-8298 78414
Wordsworth Crk 78410
Wow Rd 78413
Wray Ln 78412
Wright St 78405
Wyatt Dr 78410
Wyndale St 78418
Wynona Dr 78411
Wynwood St 78415
Xanadu St 78415
Xavier Ct 78401
Yale St 78416
Yardarm Ct 78418
Yaupon Dr 78414
Yeager Dr 78410
Yellow Oak Ave 78410
Yellowstone Dr 78410
Yerby Cir 78408
Yoakum Cir 78413
Yokosuka Dr 78413
Yolanda Dr 78416
York Ave
1000-1299 78404
1300-1399 78415
Yorkshire Dr 78413
Yorktown Blvd
101-497 78418
499-2199 78418
2201-2399 78418
4400-5099 78413
5101-5399 78413
5901-5997 78414
5999-8000 78414
8002-8598 78414
Yorktown Cir 78413
Yorktown Cts 78404
Yorktown Dr 78419
Yucatan St 78411
Yucca Cts 78415
Yucca St 78411
Yukon Dr 78412
Zamora St 78410
Zapata St 78405
Zaragosa St 78405
Zarsky Dr 78412
Zuza Dr 78418

NUMBERED STREETS

1st St SE 78419
2nd St 78404
3rd St 78404
5th St
600-799 78401
1201-1699 78404
5th St SE 78419
6th St
600-799 78401
1100-1599 78404
7th St 78404
10th St
500-598 78401
600-799 78401
800-1699 78404
1701-1799 78404
11th St
700-799 78401
800-1300 78404
12th St
300-799 78401
800-1299 78404
14th St
400-498 78401
800-1699 78404
15th St
700-799 78401
800-1799 78404
16th St
200-399 78405
600-798 78401
800-1198 78404
1200-2199 78404
2201-2299 78404
17th St
200-599 78405
601-1299 78405
1300-2099 78404
2101-2199 78404
18th St
400-1299 78405
1300-2100 78404
N 19th St 78408
S 19th St
201-397 78405
1400-1699 78404
20th St 78405
21st St 78405
22nd St 78405
23rd St 78405
S 24th St 78405
25th St 78405
44th St 78405
45th St 78405
600 Bldg 78401

CORSICANA TX

General Delivery 75110

POST OFFICE BOXES MAIN OFFICE STATIONS AND BRANCHES

Box No.s
All PO Boxes 75151

NAMED STREETS

A Ave 75110
Alan Brown Dr 75109
Albritton Rd 75110
N & S Allison Dr 75110
E & W Allyn Ave 75110
Ambassador Ln 75110
W Andy Rd 75109
Ann Arbor Dr 75110
Arcady Ln 75110
Arlington Cir & Dr 75110
W Asby Ln 75109
Ash St 75110
Austin Ave 75110
E Autrey St 75109
B Ave 75110
Balcom Ln 75110
Bayview Cir 75109
N & S Beaton St 75110
E & W Belclaire Cir 75110
Belmont Cir 75110
Ben Blackman Rd 75110
N & S Benton St 75110
Bentwood Cir 75109
E & W Beverly Dr 75110
Birdwell Rd 75110
Black Hills Rd 75110
Black Oak Dr 75110
Blackhills Sq 75110
Bluebonnet Rdg 75110
Blueridge Ct & Dr 75109
Bluffview Ln 75109
S Bonanza Dr 75110
Bonner Ave & Rd 75110
Borsellino Ln 75110
Bowie Cir & Dr 75110
Boyd Ave 75110
Bragg Ave 75110
Briarcrest Rd 75110
Briarwood Cir & St 75110
Bridle Path 75110
Brillhart St 75110
Brookhaven Dr 75110
Brooks Ave & Rd 75110
Brookshire 75109
Bryant S Way 75109
Bryn Mawr St 75110
Buchanan Blvd 75110
N & S Bunert St 75110
Bunert Park Rd 75110
Burr Oak Ln 75110
N Business 45 75110
S Business 45
1600-3099 75110
3100-3799 75109
Butler St 75110
C Regal Rd 75110
Caddo Trl 75109
Cajun Byu 75109
W Call Ave 75110
Cambridge St 75110
Canal St 75109
S Capehart 75109
Carol Ave 75110
Carter Dr 75109
Cedar Crest Ln 75110
Central St 75109
N & S Chambers Ave .. 75110
Chapel Rd 75110
Chaperial Rd 75110
E Chatfield Rd 75110
Cherry Ave 75110
Chewing St 75110
Christie Ln 75110
Christopher Dr 75110
Churchill Ave 75110
Circle Dr 75109
City Rd 75110
Clay St 75110
Clear Water Ct 75109
Clearbrook Ln 75110
Clubhouse Dr 75109
Cobalt Cv 75109
N & S Coker Ave 75109
E & W College Ave & Cir 75110
E & W Collin St 75110
Collins Ln 75109
Columbia Ave & Cir 75110
N Commerce St 75110
Confederate St 75110
Corinth Rd 75110
Corsicana St 75110
Corsicana Crossings Blvd 75109
Cotton Belt Dr 75110
Cottonwood Cir 75110
Country Club Rd 75110
Country Road Ranchette 75109
NW County Road 0001 75110
NW County Road 0002 75110
NW County Road 0003 75110
NW County Road 0004 75110
SW County Road 0005 75110
NW County Road 0006 75110
NW County Road 0007 75110
NW County Road 0008 75110
NW County Road 0009 75110
NW County Road 0010 75110
SE County Road 0010 . 75109
SW County Road 0010 75110
NW County Road 0011 75110
NW County Road 0012 75110
NW County Road 0013 75110
NW & SW County Road 0014 75110
NW County Road 0015 75110
NW County Road 0016 75110
NW County Road 0017 75110
NW & SW County Road 0018 75110
NW County Road 0020 75110
SE County Road 0020 . 75109
SW County Road 0020 75110
SW County Road 0021 75110
NW & SW County Road 0022 75110
NW County Road 0023 75110
NW County Road 0024 75110
NW County Road 0025 75110
SE County Road 0025 . 75109
SW County Road 0025 75110
NW County Road 0026 75110
NW County Road 0027 75110
NW County Road 0028 75110
NW & SW County Road 0030 75110
NW County Road 0040 75110
SE County Road 0040 . 75109
NE County Road 0050 . 75109
NW County Road 0050 75110
SE County Road 0050 . 75109
SW County Road 0050 75110
NW County Road 0060 75110
SE County Road 0060 . 75109
SW County Road 0060 75110
NE County Road 0070 . 75109
NW County Road 0070 75110
SE County Road 0070 . 75109
SW County Road 0070 75110
NE County Road 0080 . 75109
NW County Road 0080 75110
SE County Road 0080 . 75109
NW County Road 0090 75110
SE County Road 0090 . 75109
NE County Road 0091 . 75109
NE County Road 0092 . 75109
NE County Road 0093 . 75109
NE County Road 0094 . 75109
NE County Road 0095 . 75109
NE County Road 0100 . 75109
NW County Road 0100 75110
NE County Road 0110 . 75109
NW County Road 0110 75110
NE County Road 0120 . 75109
NW County Road 0120 75110
NE County Road 0130 . 75109
NW County Road 0130 75110
SE County Road 0130 . 75110
NE County Road 0170 . 75109
NE County Road 0220 . 75109
SW County Road 1000 75110
SW County Road 1005 75110
SW County Road 1006 75110
SW County Road 1007 75110
NW County Road 1010 75110
SE County Road 1010 . 75109
SW County Road 1010 75110
NW County Road 1020 75110
SE County Road 1020 . 75109
NW County Road 1021 75110
SW County Road 1025 75110
NW County Road 1030 75110
SE County Road 1030 . 75109
SW County Road 1030 75110
NE County Road 1040 . 75109
NW County Road 1040 75110
NW County Road 1041 75110
NW County Road 1050 75110
SE County Road 1050 . 75109
NW County Road 1052 75110
NW County Road 1053 75110
SE County Road 1060 . 75109
SE County Road 1070 . 75109
NW County Road 1080 75110
SE County Road 1080 . 75109
NW County Road 1081 75110
SE County Road 1081 . 75109
SW County Road 1081 75110
SE County Road 1086 . 75109
NW County Road 1090 75110
SE County Road 1090 . 75109
SW County Road 1090 75110
SE County Road 1095 . 75109
County Road 1098 ... 75109
NW & SW County Road 1100 75110
NW County Road 1110 75110
NW & SW County Road 1120 75110
NW & SW County Road 1130 75110
NW & SW County Road 1140 75110
NW & SW County Road 1150 75110
SW County Road 1160 75110
SW County Road 1161 75110
SW County Road 1162 75110
NW County Road 1170 75110
NW County Road 1180 75110
NW County Road 1250 75110
NW County Road 1260 75110
NW County Road 2000 75110
NW County Road 2002 75110
NW County Road 2004 75110
NW County Road 2005 75110
NW County Road 2006 75110
NW County Road 2007 75110
NW County Road 2010 75110
SE County Road 2010 . 75109
SW County Road 2010 75110
NW County Road 2020 75110
SE County Road 2020 . 75109
SW County Road 2020 75110
NW County Road 2030 75110
NW County Road 2040 75110
SE County Road 2040 . 75109
SE County Road 2050 . 75109
NW County Road 2060 75110
SE County Road 2070 . 75109
SE County Road 2080 . 75109
NW County Road 2090 75110
SE County Road 2090 . 75109
NW County Road 2091 75110
NW County Road 2100 75110
SE County Road 2100 . 75109
NW County Road 2107 75110
NW County Road 2109 75110
NW County Road 2110 75110
NW County Road 2120 75110
SE County Road 2120 . 75109
SE County Road 2130 . 75109
SE County Road 2135 . 75109
SE County Road 2140 . 75109
SE County Road 2145 . 75109
SE County Road 2150 . 75109
SE County Road 2160 . 75109
County Road 2163 75109
SE County Road 2170 . 75109
SE County Road 2171 . 75109
SE County Road 2175 . 75109
SE County Road 2190 . 75109
SE County Road 2200 . 75109
SE County Road 2210 . 75109
SE County Road 2215 . 75109
SE County Road 2218 . 75109
SE County Road 2220 . 75109
SE County Road 2230 . 75109
SE County Road 2230f 75109
SE County Road 2230k 75109
SE County Road 2231 . 75109
SE County Road 2240 . 75109
SE County Road 2247 . 75109
SE County Road 2250 . 75109
SE County Road 2260 . 75109
SE County Road 2270 . 75109
SE County Road 3010 . 75109
SE County Road 3015 . 75109
SE County Road 3020 . 75109
SE County Road 3030 . 75109
SW County Road 3030 75110
SE County Road 3032 . 75109
SE County Road 3040 . 75109
SW County Road 3040 75110

SE County Road 3040a 75109
SE County Road 3045 75109
SE County Road 3046 75109
SE County Road 3048 75109
SE County Road 3048a 75109
SE County Road 3048c 75109
SE County Road 3048d 75109
SE County Road 3048e 75109
SE County Road 3048f 75109
SE County Road 3050 75109
SE County Road 3060 75109
SE County Road 3070 75109
SE County Road 3071 75109
SE County Road 3072 75109
SE County Road 3080 75109
SE County Road 3085 75109
SE County Road 3090 75109
SE County Road 3100 75109
SE County Road 3101 75109
SE County Road 3104 75109
SE County Road 3105 75109
SE County Road 3110 75109
SW County Road 3110 75110
SE County Road 3115 75109
SE County Road 3120 75109
SW County Road 3120 75110
SE County Road 3121 75109
SE County Road 3122 75109
SE County Road 3123 75109
SE County Road 3123a 75109
SE County Road 3124 B 75109
SE County Road 3124a 75109
SE County Road 3124c 75109
SE County Road 3129 75109
SE County Road 3129a 75109
SE County Road 3130 75109
SE County Road 3132a 75109
SE County Road 3135 75109
SE County Road 3136 75109
SE County Road 3137 75109
SE County Road 3140 75109
SE County Road 3144 75109
SE County Road 3147 75109
SE County Road 3148 75109
SE County Road 3149 75109
SE County Road 3150 75109
SE County Road 3160 75109
SE County Road 3170 75109
SE County Road 3186 75109
SE County Road 3187 75109
SE County Road 3190 75109
SE County Road 4043 75109
SE County Road 4044 75109
SE County Road 4044b 75109
SE County Road 4045 75109
SE County Road 4045a 75109
SE County Road 4046 75109
Crestmont Ave 75110
Crestview Dr 75110
E Crocker St 75109
Crooked Ln 75109
Crown Central Rd 75109
Cumberland Cir & Dr 75110
Cypress Ave 75110
Dallas St 75110
Daniel Dr 75109
Dartmouth Ln 75110
Davis Ave 75110
Deep Water Cv 75109
Dobbins Cir & Rd 75110
Dogwood Trl 75110
Donaho Rd 75110
Donzi Ct 75109
E & W Drane Ave, Pl & Rd 75110
Dresden Rd 75110
Dyer Dr 75109
East Ln 75110
Edgewood Ave 75110
El Barco 75109
El Sueno 75109
Elm St 75110
Elmwood Ave & Cir 75110
Emhouse Rd 75110
Enfield Dr 75110
F Ave 75110
Factory Outlet Dr 75109
Fairfax Dr 75110
Fairmont Ave & Cir 75110
Fairoaks Dr 75110
Fairway Parks Dr 75110
Farmer Dr 75109
Ferguson Dr 75110
Fesmire Ave 75110
Ficklin Ave & Cir 75110
Fiddler Ln 75109
Fish Tank Rd 75110
Flint Cir 75109
Fm 1126 75110
Fm 1129 75109
Fm 1839 75110
Fm 2452 75110
Fm 2555 75110
Fm 2859 75109
Fm 3041 75109
Fm 3194 75110
Fm 3243 75109
Fm 3383 75110
Fm 637 75109
Fm 709 S 75110
Fm 739 75109
Fm 744 75109
Forest Lane Cir 75110
Forrest Ln 75110
S Fradonso St 75110
N & S Frey St 75110
Furrh 75109
G Ave 75110
G W Jackson Ave 75110
Gamble St 75110
E & W Garrity St 75110
Gioia Cir 75110
Gladstone St 75110
Glenbrook St 75110
Glenwood Cir 75110
S Goodin Ave 75109
S Goodwin 75109
Goodwin Ln 75110
Gorman St 75110
Governors Dr 75110
Grandview Cir & Dr 75109
Grandview Estate Dr 75109
Gray Thompson Rd 75110
Hackberry Ave 75110
Haeley Lou Ln 75110
Haggar St 75110
N & S Hall St 75110
Hamilton Ln 75109
Hamilton Rd
100-199 75110
201-299 75109
Hampton Ave 75110
Hardy Ave 75110
S & W Harris Rd 75110
N & S Harvard Ave 75109
Hatteras Dr 75110
Havner St 75110
Helm Pl 75110
Heritage Ln 75110
Hickory Hollow Ln 75110
Hidden Hills Dr 75110
Hidden Oaks 75110
Hidden Oaks Ln 75109
Hideaway Hbr 75109
Highland Cir 75110
Hillcrest Dr 75110
Hillsdale St 75110
Hillside Dr 75110
Hilltop Dr 75109
Hillview 75109
W Holsey Ave 75110
Home Ave 75110
N & S Hopkins Ave 75110
Hopwood St 75110
Horizon Rdg 75109
Horn St 75109
Hospital Dr 75110
Houston St 75110
Hutson Dr 75110
Imperial Ln 75110
SE Indondo 75109
Ingham Rd 75110
S Interstate Highway 45
1901-2197 75109
S Interstate Highway 45
2199-2299 75109
3400-3498 75110
S Interstate Highway 45 E 75109
S Interstate Highway 45 W 75109
Interurban Blvd 75110
Irene Ave 75110
James Ln 75109
Jennifer Cir 75110
Jester Dr 75109
Joe Johnson Dr 75110
John Rd 75110
E Jones St
100-599 75109
2100-2199 75110
Kelly St 75110
Kenwood St 75110
Kerr Ave 75110
Kings Cir 75110
Kingston Dr 75110
Kirk Dr 75109
Knight St 75110
La Bota 75109
Lafayette St 75110
Lake Halbert Rd 75109
Lakeshore Dr 75109
Lakeview Cir, Dr & Lndg 75109
Lakewood Ave 75110
Latta St 75110
Laura Ave 75110
Laura Ln
100-199 75109
1800-1899 75110
W Ledwell Rd 75109
Leesa Ln 75110
Lexington Cir, Dr & Sq 75110
Liberty Dr 75110
Linda Cir 75110
Liveoak Ave 75110
Lou Ann Ave 75110
Louis Ave 75110
Love Cir & St 75110
Lynne Ave 75110
Madison Cir, Dr & Sq 75110
Magnolia Ave 75110
E Main St 75109
N Main St 75110
S Main St 75110
W Mall Dr 75110
Mamie Ave 75110
W Maplewood Ave 75110
Martin Rd 75110
Martin Luther King Jr Blvd 75110
Max Ave 75110
Mckinney Ave 75110
Mcknight Ln 75110
Meadow Dr 75110
Meandering Way 75109
Medinah 75110
Mills Dr & Pl 75110
Mimosa Dr 75110
N Miracle Dr 75110
Mockingbird Ln & Pl 75110
Monte Carlo St 75110
Moonlight Dr 75109
Morgan Cir 75109
Morris Dr 75110
Mountain Dr 75109
Muirfield Way 75110
Mulberry Dr 75109
Navarro Cir 75110
Navarro Dr 75110
Navarro Rd 75109
N Navarro Rd 75109
S Navarro Rd 75109
Northpark Dr 75110
Northshore Blvd 75109
Northwood Blvd 75110
Oak St 75110
E Oak Grove Rd 75110
Oak Valley Ln & Rd 75110
Oaklawn Ave & Cir 75110
Oakridge Cir & Dr 75110
Old Waterworks Rd 75110
Olive St 75110
Orchard Dr 75109
Overlook Cir 75110
Oxford St 75110
Paradise Dr 75109
Paradise Bay Cir 75109
S Parham St 75110
E & W Park Ave & Pl 75110
W Park Row Blvd 75110
Parker 75110
Payne St 75110
Pecan Delight Ave 75109
Peggy Ln 75109
Phife Rd 75110
Pierce Dr 75110
Pin Oak Ln 75110
Pine St 75110
Pioneer Cir 75110
Post Oak Dr 75110
Powell Pike 75109
E Powell Pike 75110
N Powell St 75110
S Powell St 75110
Princeton Dr 75110
NW Private Road 100 75110
NW Private Road 105 75110
NW Private Road 1290 75110
NW Private Road 1295 75110
NW Private Road 2085 75110
SE Private Road 2163 75109
Private Road 3048f 75109
Private Road 3087 75109
SE Private Road 3178 75109
NW Private Road 90 75110
Professional Dr 75110
Pugh Ln 75109
Purdue Dr 75110
Rainbow Ln 75109
Ranch Rd 75109
Ranchland Rd 75110
Reagan St 75109
Red Oak Ln 75110
Regal Dr 75109
Renee St 75110
Ridgeway Dr 75109
Ritter St 75110
W Roane Rd 75110
E Rob Ave 75110
Rock Rd 75109
Royal Ln 75110
Sailboat 75109
Sandy Cir & Ln 75110
Scott Pl 75110
N & S Scruggs 75109
N & S Seely Ave 75110
Shady Ln 75109
Shady Creek Ln 75109
Shumard Oak Ln 75110
Southeast Dr 75109
N & S Spikes Rd 75110
Spur 294 75109
Stanford St 75110
Starcrest 75109
W State Highway 22 75110
E State Highway 31 75109
W State Highway 31 75110
Story Ln 75109
W Summitt Ave 75110
Sundance 75109
Sunny Ln 75110
Sunrise Dr 75109
Sunset Cir 75110
Sunset Dr 75110
Sunset Ln 75109
W Sycamore Ave 75110
T A Carroll Ave 75110
Tammy Ave 75110
S Tatum 75109
Tennyson St 75110
Territo Rd 75110
The Shores Dr 75109
E Thomas St 75110
E Thompson St 75110
Tilton Rd 75109
Tonkawa Trl 75109
Trailridge Cir, Dr & Pl 75110
N & S Trinity Ave 75110
Turnberry Ln 75109
Tyler Ave 75110
S Us Highway 287
1600-2800 75110
S Us Highway 287
2801-2897 75109
2802-2898 75110
2899-10499 75109
Valley Dr 75109
Varsity Dr 75110
View Ln 75110
Wade St 75110
Waller Dr 75110
Walnut St 75110
Walton St 75110
N & S Washington St 75110
Water Oak Ln 75110
Waters Edge Dr 75109
Waterside Dr 75109
Weaver Rd 75109
Wesley Dr 75110
White Oak Ln 75110
White Rock Rd 75109
Wichita Trl 75109
Williams Dr 75110
Willowcreek Cir 75110
Willowridge Cir & Trl 75110
Wilson Rd 75110
Winding Ridge Rd 75109
Windsor Dr 75110
Winfield Dr 75110
Winged Foot 75110
Woodcastle Dr 75110
Woodcrest Ave 75110
Woodland Ave & Pl 75110
Woodlawn Ave 75110
Woodside Ct 75109
Wright Way 75109
Wyona Dr 75109

NUMBERED STREETS

All Street Addresses 75110

CYPRESS TX

General Delivery 77429

POST OFFICE BOXES MAIN OFFICE STATIONS AND BRANCHES

Box No.s
All PO Boxes 77410

NAMED STREETS

Acorn Ridge Way 77429
Adams Run Dr 77429
Aldridge Creek Ct 77429
Alemarble Oak St 77429
Aliso Glenn Ln 77433
Allemand Ln 77429
Allen Pines Ln 77433
E & W Allen Shore Dr 77433
Allenwick Hills Ct 77429
Allysum Ct & Ln 77429
Almahurst Cir & Ln 77429
Almera Falls Dr 77433
Alpine Park Ln 77433
Alston Hills Dr 77433
Alto Peak Ln 77433
Alton Springs Dr 77433
Amalfi Coast Dr 77433
Amanda Grace Ln 77429
Amber Elm Trl 77433
Amber Grain Ln 77433
Amber Hollow Ct & Ln 77429
E & S Amber Willow Trl 77433
Amelia Island Dr 77433
American Holly Ct 77433
Amistad Lake Cir 77433
Amsbury Ln 77429
Amyford Bnd & Ct 77429
Anada Bay Ct 77429
Andalusian Dr 77433
Andover Harvest Ln 77429
Andover Manor Dr 77429
Andrew Arbor Ct 77433
Angler Cove Dr 77433
Annandale Terrace Dr 77429
Annfran Cir 77429
Anton Dr 77429
Antrim Pl 77429
Appian Oak St 77433
Apple River Dr 77433
Appleberry Dr 77433
Applemint Cir 77433
Applerock Trl 77433
E & W Apricot Blush Ct 77433
April Glen Ct 77429
April Mist Ct 77429
Aqua Bay Ct 77433
Aquilla Lake Cir 77433
Aragon Green Dr 77433
Arapaho Bend Ln 77429
Arapaho Shadow Ct 77429
Arapahoe Ridge Ln 77433
Arbor Blue Ln 77433
Arbor Lodge Dr 77433
Arbor Trace Ct 77429
Arbor Wind Ln 77433
Arbormont Dr 77429
Archcrest Ct 77433
Archwood Ln 77429
Arlington Pl 77429
Armadillo 77429
Armant Place Dr 77429
Arroyo Colorado Ct 77433
Ash Green Dr 77433
Ashland Landing Dr 77429
Ashland Springs Ln 77433
Ashley Terrace Ln 77433
Ashton Hills Ct & Dr 77429
Aspen Dr 77429
Aspen Terrace Ct 77433
Aspenwilde Dr 77433
Aster Estates Ln 77429
Aster Manor Ct 77429
Aster Petal Ct 77433
Astley Acres Ln 77429
Atherton Bend Ln 77433
Auburn Springs Ln 77433
Auburn Tree Dr 77429
Auburn Woods Dr 77429
Auckland Pt 77429
Audrie Rae Ln 77433
August Rd 77429
Augustin Landing Dr 77429
Augustus Venture Ct 77433
N & S Austin Shore Ct & Dr 77433
Austin Thomas Dr 77433
Autumn Glen Ct 77429
Autumn Gold Ct 77433
Autumn Haze Ln 77429
Autumn Mist 77429
Autumn Redwood Way 77433
Autumn Timbers Ln 77433
Autumn Valley Dr 77429
Autumnvale Ln 77429
Avalange Ct 77429
Avalon Point Ct 77429
Avanta Cove Dr 77433
Avery Brooke Ln 77429
Avery Grove Ct 77433
N & S Azure Mist Ct 77433
Bach Springs Ct 77429
Baden Hollow Ln 77433
Balcones Hills Ct 77433
Balcones Pine St 77429
Balsam Crossing Ln 77433
Bandera Falls Bnd 77429
Banner Meadow Ln 77433
Banyan Cove Ct & Ln 77433
Bare Branch Ln 77433
Barely Rose Ct 77433
Barker Bayou Ct 77429
Barker Bluff Ln 77433
Barker Cypress Rd
7000-12099 77433
12200-14499 77429
Barker Gate Ct 77433
Barker Grove Ct & Ln 77433
Barker Lake Ct 77433
Barker Marsh Dr 77429
Barker Park Ct 77433
Barker Pelican Ct 77429
Barker Ranch Ct 77429
Barker View Dr 77433
Barker West Dr 77433
Barklea Rd 77429
Barn Red Ct 77433
Barngate Ct 77429
Barngate Meadow Ln 77433
Baron Brook Dr 77433
Barons Lake Ln 77429
Barrone Dr 77429
Barrow Cove Dr 77429
Barrow Edge Ln 77433
Bartlett Landing Dr 77429
Bastrop Bayou Ct 77433
Bateau Ct & Dr 77429
Bauer Rd 77433
Bauer Ridge Dr 77429
Bay Blue Way 77433
Bay Tree Lndg 77429
Bayou Junction Ct & Rd 77433
Beacon Crossing Ln 77433
Beacon Hollow Ct 77429
Bear Song Ln 77429
Becker Cemetery Rd 77429
Becurtesy Ct 77433
Bedford Chase 77429
Bedford Falls Dr 77429
E, N, S & W Bee Cave Springs Cir 77433
Beech Creek Ct 77433
Begonia Creek Ct 77433
Begonia Estates Ct 77429
Belgrave Dr 77429
Bella Dr 77429
Bella Arbor Ln 77433
Bellavista Pt 77429
Belle Helene Cir 77433
Bellows Gate Ct 77429
Belton Bend Ct 77429
Belton Shore Dr 77433
Belvan Ct 77429
Belwood Park Ln 77433
Benbrook Manor Ln 77433
N Bend Ldg 77429
Bending Birch Ct & Dr 77433
Bending Branch Ln 77433
Bending Cypress Rd 77429
Bending Oak Ct 77429
Benford Ridge Ln 77433

Bennet Chase Dr 77429
Benson Landing Dr 77429
Bent Aspen Ct 77433
Bent Gulch Ln 77429
Bent Lake Ln 77429
Bent Pine Dr 77429
Bent Twig Way 77433
Bent Way St 77429
Bentgrove Ln 77433
Bergenia Dr 77429
Bering Landing Dr 77433
Berkshire Oak St 77429
Bernley St 77429
Berry Point Dr 77429
Bertani Ln 77429
Bertell Ln 77429
Bevken Ct 77429
Big Leaf Pasture Ln 77433
Billabong Crescent Ct 77429
N Birch Ln 77433
Birch Glen Dr 77429
Birdcall Ln 77429
Black Cherry Bend Ct 77433
Black Cove Dr 77433
Black Gap Dr 77433
Black Rose Trl 77429
Blackbird Dr 77429
Blackburn Cove Ct 77433
Blackfoot Trail Run 77429
Blackstream Ct 77433
Bladenboro Dr 77429
Blair Ridge Dr 77429
Blake Valley Ln 77429
Blanchard Park Ln 77433
N & W Blanco Bend Dr 77433
Blanco Falls Ln 77429
Blanco Trails Ln 77429
Blanton Brook Dr 77433
Blissfull Haven Ct 77433
Bloom Meadow Trl 77433
Blooming Pear Ct 77433
E & W Blooming Rose Ct 77429
Bloomingdale Manor Dr 77429
Blossom Field Ct 77433
Blossom Lake Ct 77433
Blossomheath Rd 77429
Blue Aaron Ct 77433
Blue Cove Ct 77433
Blue Egret Dr 77433
N Blue Hyacinth Dr 77433
Blue Shimmering Trl 77433
Blue Shine Trl 77433
Blue Thistle Dr 77433
Blue Wahoo Ln 77433
Bluebonnet Bnd 77429
Bluebonnet Dale Dr 77433
Blues Point Dr 77429
Bluff Haven Ln 77433
Bluff Park Ct 77429
Blushing Meadow Dr 77433
Bobcat Trl 77429
Boerne Canyon Ln 77433
Boerne Country Dr 77433
Bonaparte Dr 77429
Bonnywood Ln 77429
Bontura St 77429
Boston Post Rd 77429
Boudreaux Rd 77429
Bouganvilla Blossom Ln 77433
Boulder Hollow Ln 77429
Bowden Creek Dr 77433
Bowdin Crest Dr 77433
Bowing Oaks Dr 77433
Braddocks Rd 77429
Bradford Creek Ct 77433
Bradford Forest Dr 77433
Bradford Shores Dr 77433
Brady Branch Ln 77433
Braley Ct 77433
Branch Creek Dr 77433
Branson Ln 77429
Breckan Ct 77429
Breet Creek Ct 77429
Breezeloch Dr 77433
Breezeway Cove Dr 77433
Breezy Cypress Creek Trl 77429
Breezy Glen Ln 77433
Breezy Oak Ct 77433
E & W Bremonds Bend Ct 77433
Brenly Dr 77429
Bresslyn Ln 77429
Breton Bridge Ct 77433
Brett Creek Ct 77429
Briarwood Cove Cir 77433
Bridgeland Ldg 77433
N Bridgeland Lake Pkwy 77433
E, N, S & W Bridgeport Pass Cir 77433
Bridle Oak Dr 77433
Bridoon Dr 77433
Bright Angel Ln 77433
Bright Canyon Ln 77433
Brigid Place Dr 77429
Brinklow Point Dr 77433
Bristol Berry Dr 77429
Bristol Meadow Ln 77433
Broad Bend Dr 77433
Broadbluff Ln 77433
Brock Creek Way 77429
Brockland Ln 77433
Broken Brook Ct 77429
Broken Lance Ln 77433
Broken Limb Trl 77433
Broken Pine Ln 77433
Bronze Finch Dr 77433
Bronze Leaf Ct & Dr 77433
Brook Cove Dr 77433
Brook Rise Ln 77433
Brookchase Loop & Way 77433
Broomingdale Manor Dr 77429
Brothers Purchase Cir 77433
Broway Ln 77429
Brown Eyed Susan Ct 77433
Brown Redbud Ct 77433
Brownstone Mills Dr 77433
Brownwood Bend Ct 77433
Brydan Dr 77429
Buchanan Bend Ct 77433
Buffalo View Ln 77433
Buhler Ct 77429
Bunker Cove Dr 77433
Burgundy Sky Way 77433
Burham Park Dr 77433
Bush Sage Dr 77429
Buttercup Hill Ct 77433
By The Lake Ct & Way 77429
Cabot Lodge Ln 77429
Cabot Ridge Ln 77433
Cactus Blossom Trl 77433
Cactus Thorn Dr 77433
Caddo Springs Ct 77433
Cahill Ct & Ln 77429
Calcaterra Ct 77429
Caldera Ln 77433
Calico Field Dr 77429
Calico Heights Ln 77429
Calico Peak Way 77433
Calico Place Ln 77429
Calla Spring Dr 77429
Calvano Dr 77429
Cambridge Vale Ct 77429
Camden Bay Ct 77433
Camden Glen Ct & Ln 77433
Camellia St 77429
Camellia Estates Ln 77429
Cameo Rose Dr 77433
E & W Cameron Ridge Dr 77433
Camp Cove Dr 77429
Campsite Trl 77429
Campwood Ln 77429
E Canary Yellow Cir 77433
Canby Point Ln 77433
Canton Common Ln 77433
Canton Pass Ln 77433
Cantrell Mnr 77429
Cantwell Bnd 77429
E Canyon Lake Springs Dr 77433
Canyon Maples Ln 77429
Canyon Walk Ln 77433
Canyon Whisper Dr 77429
Cape Royal Dr 77433
E Caramel Apple Trl 77433
Caraway Ridge Dr 77433
Cardinal Cove Ct 77429
Cardinal Flowers Dr 77429
Cardinal Grove Ct 77429
Cardinal Landing Ln 77433
Carla Way 77429
Carolina Falls Ln 77433
E & N Carolina Green Dr 77433
Carolina Hills Dr 77433
Carolina Oaks Ct & Dr 77433
Carousel Creek Ct 77429
Carraway Ct 77429
Carriage Crossing Ln 77429
Carrington Ln 77429
Carsen Bnd 77433
Carsenwood Ln 77433
Carson Field Ln 77433
Cartage Knolls Dr 77433
Casa Blanca Cir 77433
Casaba Ct 77429
Cascade Bend Ln 77429
Cascade Caverns Ct 77429
Cascade Woods Ln 77433
Cascading Brook Ct & Way 77433
Castlemoor Ct 77433
Cat Hollows Ct 77433
Catalano Ct 77429
Cathedral Falls Dr 77429
Catherine Anne Ct 77433
Catrose Ln 77433
Cavesson Dr 77433
Cedar Canyon Dr 77433
Cedar Cliff Ln 77429
Cedar Manor Ct 77429
Cedar Point Dr 77429
Cellini Dr 77433
Central Dr 77433
Central Creek Dr 77433
Chaco Canyon Ct & Dr 77429
Chad Arbor Trl 77433
Chalmette Park St 77429
Chandler Ridge Ln 77429
Channel Bend Dr 77433
Channel Hill Dr 77433
Channing Way 77429
Chaparralberry Dr 77433
Chapel Cove Ct 77429
Chapel Hollow Ln 77429
Chapel Lake Dr 77429
Chapmans Count Rd 77433
Chappell Knoll Dr 77433
Charlottes Bequest Cir 77433
Charolais Dr 77429
Charter Mill Ln 77433
Chatfield Run Ct 77433
Chatham Springs Ln 77433
Chavile 77429
Chelsea Dell Dr 77429
Cherry Cove Ln 77433
Chestnut Falls Dr 77433
Chestnut Glen Ln 77429
Cheval Dr 77433
Chianti Ridge Dr 77433
Chiefs Honor Ct 77433
China Blue Ln 77433
China Green Dr 77433
Chipstone Ct 77433
Cholla Canyon Ln 77433
Cholla View Ln 77433
Chopin Ct 77429
Christopher Lake Ct 77433
Chriswood Dr 77429
E & W Cibolo Creek Ct 77433
Cinderwood Dr 77429
Cinnamon Ash Ct 77433
Circular Quay Ln 77429
Cisco Ct 77433
E & W Citrus Rose Ct 77433
Clairson Ln 77433
Clareton Ct & Ln 77429
Clarkman Ridge Ln 77433
Claycreste Ct 77429
Claycroft Ct 77429
Claymont Hill Dr 77433
Clayton Bluff Ln 77433
Clear Pointe Dr 77433
Clearhaven Ct 77429
Clemens Dr 77433
Cliff Sage Ct 77433
Clipper Pointe Dr 77433
Cloaksdale Ln 77433
Clois Vista Dr 77433
Closewood Terrace Dr 77429
Clover Nut Ct 77433
Cloverland Park Ln 77433
Cloverwood Dr 77429
Cluster Pine Dr 77429
Coalfield Ln 77433
Cobble Cove Cir 77433
Cobble Meadow Ct 77433
Cobblestone Dr 77429
Coco St 77433
Cocobola Ln 77433
Codys Run 77429
Coffee Mill Lake Ct 77433
Coldwater Cove Ln 77433
Cole Bridge Ct & Ln 77429
Colecrest Ct 77429
N Coles Crossing Dr 77429
E, N, S & W Colony Shore Dr 77433
Colt Springs Ct & Ln 77429
Columbia Pines Ln 77433
Columbia Springs Ct 77433
Comal Bend Ln 77429
E Comal River Dr 77433
Comfort Ct 77429
Concho Creek Ln 77433
Concord Hill Dr 77433
Connemara Dr 77433
Conner Landing Ln 77433
Conner Park Dr 77429
Contado Ct 77429
Conway Lndg & Pl 77429
Copeland Oaks Blvd 77429
Copper Gables Ln 77429
Copper Trace Ln 77429
E, N, S & W Coral Honeysuckle Loop 77433
Coral Leaf Trl 77433
Coreland Ln 77429
Corktree Knls 77429
Cornelia Dr 77429
Coronado Ridge Ct 77433
Corral Dr 77433
Corrigan Springs Dr 77429
Cortina Valley Dr 77429
Cortland Ridge Ln 77433
Costa Brava Dr 77433
Cottage Cypress Ln 77433
Cottage Rose Trl 77429
Cottonwood Ln 77429
N & S Cottonwood Green Ln 77433
Country Cv 77433
Country Cove Ct 77433
Country Fair Ln 77433
Country Park Way 77433
Country Rose Ln 77429
Court Amber Trl 77433
Court Green Trl 77433
Courtly Estates Ln 77429
Coushatta Ct 77429
Cove Bend Ln 77433
Cove Bluff Ct 77433
Cove Edge Ln 77433
Cove Forest Ln 77433
Cove Harbor Ln 77433
Cove Hill Ln 77433
Cove Landing Dr 77433
Cove Manor Dr 77433
Cove Mill Ln 77433
Cove Pointe Dr 77433
Cove Ridge Ln 77433
Cove Springs Ct & Dr 77433
Cove Vista Ln 77433
Crab Apple Ct 77429
Cragmont Bridge Dr 77433
Craigwood Ln 77429
Creek Bluff Ln 77433
Creek Hill Ln 77429
Creek Mill Ct 77429
Creek Mist Ct & Dr 77433
Creekline Glen Ct 77429
Creekline Green Ct 77429
Creekline Meadow Ct 77429
Creekview Ln 77429
Creekway Dr 77429
Crescent Haven Dr 77433
Crescent Lilly Dr 77433
Crescent Meadow Dr 77433
Crest Cove Dr 77433
Crest Haven Ln 77433
Crestbrook Manor Ln 77433
Crestbury Ct & Ln 77433
Crested Hill Ln 77433
Crested Iris Dr 77429
Crested Peak Ln 77433
Creston Acres Ln 77433
Creston Cove Ct 77433
Crestwood Creek Ln 77433
Cretian Point Ct 77429
Cricket Hollow Ln 77429
Crim Lilly Ct 77433
Crimson Flower Ln 77433
Crimson Leaf Ct 77433
Crooked Lake Way N & S 77433
Crooked Oak Dr 77429
Crooked Pine Dr 77429
Cross Canyon Ln 77433
Cross Hollow Ln 77433
Cross Stone Ct 77433
Crossfalls Ln 77433
Crossland Ct 77433
Crossland Park Ln 77433
Crosslyn Ln 77429
Crossview Lake Dr 77433
Crossvine Trail Ct & Ln 77433
Crosswood Trails Ln 77433
Crow Court Dr 77429
Crow Ridge Ct 77433
Crystalynn Ln 77429
Cumberland Trl & Way 77429
Cumberland Oak Ct & Way 77433
Cupshire Dr 77433
Curio Gray Trl 77433
Curlew Dr 77433
Cy Fair Fire Rd 77433
Cypress Cir 77429
Cypress Dr 77433
Cypress Ln 77429
Cypress Vlg 77429
Cypress Bend Dr 77429
Cypress Bluff Dr 77433
Cypress Branch Dr 77429
Cypress Breeze Ct
7300-7399 77433
14000-14099 77429
Cypress Breeze Dr 77433
Cypress Bridge Dr 77429
Cypress Brook Ct 77429
Cypress Brook Willow Dr 77429
Cypress Church Rd 77433
Cypress Cottage Ct 77429
Cypress Creek Blvd 77429
Cypress Creek Bank Dr 77429
Cypress Creek Bend Dr 77433
Cypress Creek Forest Dr 77429
Cypress Creek Lakes Dr 77433
Cypress Creek Willow Dr 77429
Cypress Crescent Ln 77433
Cypress Crest Dr 77429
Cypress Crossing Dr 77429
Cypress Downs Dr 77429
Cypress Echo Dr 77433
Cypress Edge Dr 77433
Cypress Falls Dr 77429
Cypress Farms Ranch Rd 77429
Cypress Fields Ave 77429
Cypress Glade Dr 77429
Cypress Glen St 77429
Cypress Green Dr 77429
Cypress Green Ln 77433
Cypress Gully Dr 77433
Cypress Hall Dr 77429
Cypress Heath Ct 77429
E & W Cypress Hill Cir 77433
Cypress Hollow St 77429
Cypress Knee Dr 77429
Cypress Lake Village Dr 77429
Cypress Leaf Dr 77429
Cypress Lilly Dr 77433
Cypress Links Trl 77429
Cypress Marsh Ct 77429
Cypress Meade Ct & Ln 77429
Cypress Meadow Dr 77433
Cypress Meadows Dr 77429
Cypress Mill Place Blvd 77429
Cypress Mist Ct 77433
Cypress North Houston Rd
12925A-12925B 77429
11300-15999 77429
19300-19599 77433
Cypress Oaks Dr 77429
Cypress Orchard Ln 77429
Cypress Palms Ct 77429
Cypress Park Dr 77429
Cypress Pass Loop E & W 77429
Cypress Path Ct 77429
Cypress Pelican Dr 77429
Cypress Point Dr 77429
Cypress Poll Dr 77433
Cypress Pond Cir, Dr & Rd 77429
Cypress Post Dr 77433
Cypress Post Ln 77429
Cypress Prairie Dr 77433
Cypress Ridge Dr 77429
Cypress Ridge Grove Ln 77433
Cypress Rosehill Rd 77429
Cypress Sage Dr 77429
Cypress Side Dr 77433
Cypress Springs Ln 77433
Cypress Star Ln 77429
Cypress Steepe Ln 77433
Cypress Stone Ln 77433
Cypress Thicket Dr 77429
Cypress Timber Dr 77429
Cypress Trace Dr 77429
Cypress Vale Dr 77433
Cypress Valley Dr, Ln & Rd 77429
Cypress View Dr 77429
Cypress Waters Ct & Dr 77429
Cypressedge Ct 77429
Cypresswood Dr
18700-18799 77429
20000-21599 77433
Cypriate Trl 77429
Da Vina Ln 77429
Dahlia Glen Ln 77429
Daisy Bloom Ct 77433
Daisy Creek Trl 77433
Dakota Bend Dr 77429
Dakota Hill Ct 77433
Dale Dr 77429
Dale Hollow Ln 77429
Dalton Crest Dr 77433
Dancing Green Dr 77433
Dappled Walk Way 77433
Darby House Ct & St 77429
Darby Retreat Ln 77429
Darby Springs Way 77429
Darling Point Ct 77429
Darmera Ct 77429
Daubern Ct 77429
Dawnheath Dr 77433
Dawntreader Dr 77429
Day Trip Trl 77429
Daybreak Ln 77429
Dayton Ridge Ln 77433
Dayton Springs Dr 77429
Debbie Terrace Dr 77433
Deep Woods Dr 77429
Delacey Ln 77429
Delta Estates Ct 77429
Desert Moon Dr 77433
Desert Shadows Ln 77433
Desert Star Ct 77429
Destrehan Dr 77429
Deval Dr 77429
Dexter Point Dr 77429
Diamond Rock Dr 77429
Dickinson Manor Ln 77433
Diven Cir 77429
Dockside Arbor Dr 77433
Dogwood Ln 77429
Dogwood Glen Ct 77429
Dolan Heights Ct 77433
Dolben Meadows Ln 77433
Dolgo Dr 77429
Dominique Dr 77429
Doral Chase Ln 77433
Doral Rock Ct 77433
Doric Ct 77429
Double Bay Rd 77429
Double Bayou Ct 77433
Double Meadows Ct & Dr 77433
Dove Creek Springs Trl 77433
Dove Run Ct 77433
Dove Trail Ct 77433
Dovefield Ln 77433
Drake Prairie Ln 77429
Drifting Rose Cir & Dr 77429
Drifting Willow Ct 77429
Driftwood Shores Ct 77433
Drumwood Ln 77429
Dry Creek Dr 77429
Dry Creek Ranch Rd 77429
Dual Circle Ct 77429
Duffton St 77433
Dula Ln 77429
Duncan Grove Dr 77429
Dundee Ct & Rd 77429
Dunlay Springs Dr 77433
Dunleith Cir 77429
Dunnel Rdg 77429
Dunoon Bay Point Ct 77429
Dunsmore Pl 77429
Dunwoody Bnd 77429
Durand Oak Ct & Dr 77433
Durango Path Ln 77433
Durango Valley Ln 77433
Durham Canyon Ln 77433
Durham Cove Ln 77429
Dusty Path Ln 77429
Dusty Yaupon Ln 77433
Eagle Fields Dr 77429
Eagle Valley Dr 77429
Early Hollow Ln 77429
Earlywood Ln 77429
Eastcrest Park Dr 77429
Eastern Fork Ct 77433

Easton Bend Ln 77429
Easton Sky Ln 77433
Echo Stable Ln 77429
Edenstone Dr 77429
Edgewood Haven Dr ... 77433
Edison Light Trl 77429
Edworthy Rd 77433
Egret Glen Ct 77429
Egret Haven Ln 77433
Egret Wood Way 77429
Eldon Park Ct 77429
N Eldridge Pkwy 77429
Elinor Ct 77429
Elizabeth Bay Rd 77429
E, N, S & W Elizabeth Shore Loop 77433
Ellendale Ct 77429
Ellerslie Ln 77429
Elm Dr 77429
Elm Leaf Pl 77429
Elm Square Ct & St 77429
Elmington Ct & Dr 77429
Elmwood Brook Ct 77433
Elmwood Manor Dr 77429
Emerald Cypress Ln 77429
Emerald Moss Ct 77429
Emery Spur Ln 77433
Emily Anne Ct 77433
Emory Hill St 77429
Empire Gold Dr 77433
Empire Heights Ct 77429
Emptyness Dr 77429
Emrose Ln 77429
Enchanted Dr 77429
Enchanted Creek Dr 77433
Enchanted Rose Ln 77433
Enchanted Valley Dr 77433
Englewood Park Ln 77429
Enola Dr 77429
Epsom Downs Dr 77433
Escalante Dr 77433
Escher Rd 77433
Evanfield Ct 77433
Evensong Ln 77429
Eventide Dr 77429
Evergreen Knoll Ln 77433
Evergreen Lake Ln 77429
Everhart Springs Ln 77433
Fable Ct 77429
Fair Castle Dr 77433
Fair Falls Way 77433
Fair Glade Ct & Ln 77429
Fair Grange Ln 77433
Fairbridge Ln 77429
Fairfield Falls Way 77433
Fairfield Green Blvd 77433
Fairfield Lakes Ct 77433
Fairfield Park Way 77433
Fairfield Place Dr 77433
Fairfield Trace Dr 77433
Fairfield Village Square Dr 77433
Fairhaven Creek Dr 77433
Fairhaven Crossing Dr .. 77433
Fairhaven Falls Dr 77433
Fairhaven Forest Dr 77433
Fairhaven Gateway Dr .. 77433
Fairhaven Hills Dr 77433
Fairhaven Island Ct 77433
Fairhaven Lake Dr 77433
Fairhaven Manor Cir 77433
Fairhaven Meadow Dr .. 77433
Fairhaven Park Ct 77433
Fairhaven Sunrise Ct ... 77433
Fairhaven Sunset Ct 77433
Fairwood Breeze 77429
Fairwood Springs Ct & Dr 77429
Fairworth Place Ln 77433
Faith Valley Dr 77429
Falcon Heights Dr 77429
Falcon Hill Ct 77433
Fall Fair Ct & Ln 77429
Falling Cedar Ct 77429
Falling Rain Ct 77429
Far Point Manor Ct 77429

Farentre Dr 77429
Farrawood Dr 77429
Farriswood Ct 77433
E & W Farwood Ter 77433
Fawn Canyon Ct 77433
Fawn Lily Dr 77429
Fawn Springs Ct 77433
Feather Lance Dr 77433
Felicity Aime Ln 77429
Fenske Rd 77433
Fern St 77429
Fernwick Village Dr 77433
Feron Ln 77433
Field Cypress Ln 77433
Field Green Dr 77433
Field Haze Trl 77433
Field Yucca Ln 77433
Fieldhaven Ct 77433
Fiery Brown Ln 77433
Fiesta Rose Ct 77433
Filly Pass Ct 77433
Filmont Ct 77433
Finch Brook Dr 77433
Fir Canyon Trl 77433
Fir Glen Ln 77433
Fir Knoll Way 77429
Fir Woods Ln 77429
Fire Thorn Ln 77433
E & W Firemist Ct & Way 77433
First Bend Ct & Dr 77433
First Voyage Ct 77433
Flagstone Trail Ct 77433
Flameleaf Gardens Ct .. 77433
Flaming Amber Way 77433
Fleur De Lis Blvd 77429
Flintridge Lake Ln 77433
Florafield Ln 77429
Floret Estates Ct & Ln .. 77429
Flowercroft Ct 77429
Flowing Oak Ln 77433
Fm 529 Rd 77433
Foley Park Ct 77433
Folly Fields Dr 77433
Folly Point Dr 77433
Forest Cove Dr 77429
Forest Creek Farms Dr 77429
Forest Forge Dr 77433
Forest Meadow Dr 77429
Forest Moon Dr 77433
Forest Run Dr 77433
Fosters Creek Dr 77429
N & S Founders Shore Dr 77433
Fragrant Rose Ct 77429
Francel Ln 77433
Freer Ct 77429
Freestone Peach Ln 77433
N Frio River Cir 77433
Frio Springs Ct & Ln ... 77429
Fritsche Cemetery Rd .. 77429
Fry Rd 77429
Fullers Grant Ct 77433
Gable Cove Ln 77433
Gable Mills Dr 77433
Gable Oak Ln 77433
Gail Shore Dr 77433
Gainesway Dr 77429
Galentine Pt 77433
Galleon Field Ln 77433
Galvani Dr 77429
Galveston Dr 77433
Garden Bend Cir 77433
Garden Bloom Ln 77433
Garden Falls Ct 77433
Garden Landing Dr 77433
Garden Shadows Ln 77433
Garden Vista Dr 77433
Garner Walk 77433
Garnet Red Rd 77433
Gary Ct 77429
Gaslamp Point Ct 77433
Gearen Ct 77429
General Gresham Ln 77429
Geneva Fields Dr 77429

Gentle Breeze Ct 77429
Gentle Creek Way 77429
Gentle Mist Ct & Ln 77433
Gentle Ridge Ct 77433
Gentry Rd 77429
Georgetown Glen Cir ... 77433
Gervaise Dr 77429
Gibbons Creek Way 77433
E & W Ginger Pear Ct . 77433
E Ginger Spice Ct 77433
Ginnydale Dr 77433
Glade Bridge Ct 77429
Glade Point Dr 77429
Glademill Ct 77433
Gladewater Ct 77433
Gleaming Rose Dr 77429
Glenbriar Spring Ln 77433
Glenfield Hollow Ln 77433
Glenwick Ct 77433
Glenwood Canyon Ln .. 77433
Glenyork Ct 77429
Glory Rose Ct 77429
E & W Gold Buttercup Ct 77433
Gold Leaf Trl 77433
Golden Cactus Ln 77433
Golden Cedar Dr 77433
Golden Cypress Ln 77429
Golden Gate Ct 77433
Golden Hawk Trl 77433
Golden Hearth Ln 77433
Golden Legion Ln 77433
Golden Manor Ln 77429
Golden Rainbow Dr 77433
Golden Ray Dr 77429
Golden Sage Ln 77429
Golden Sycamore Trl ... 77433
Golden Thistle Ct & Ln 77433
Golden Valley Dr 77429
Goldendale Ct 77433
Goodley Ct 77429
Grackle Dr 77433
Gran Villa Dr 77433
Granbury Ct 77433
Grand Corral Ct & Ln .. 77429
Grandbluff Ct 77433
Granger Blf 77433
Granite Birch Ct 77433
Granite Knoll Ln 77433
Granite Park Ct 77433
Granite Shoals Ct 77433
Granite Valley Ln 77433
Grant Rd 77429
Grants Manor Ct 77429
Grape Creek Grove Ln 77433
Grape Orchard Ct 77433
Grapevine Glen Dr 77433
Grasmere Dr 77429
Gray Bear Cir 77429
N & S Gray Heron Ct .. 77433
Gray Oak Ct 77433
Gray Pearl Ct 77433
Grayden Dr 77433
Great Elms Ct & Dr 77433
Great Pines Dr 77433
Green Canary Cir 77433
Green Cypress Ct 77433
Green Fir Trl 77433
Green Jewel Dr 77433
E Green Ripple Cir 77433
Green Star Ln 77429
Green Tavern Ct 77429
Green Valley Way 77433
Green Whisper Dr 77433
Greenhaven Lake Ln 77429
Greenleaf Ridge Ct 77433
Greenwood Manor Dr .. 77429
Greenwood Point Dr 77433
Grey Hollow Ln 77429
Grey Springs Ct 77429
Grotto Point Dr 77429
Grove Brook Ln 77429
Grove Estates Ln 77429
Groveland Hills Dr 77433

Groveleigh Ln 77429
Guadalupe Springs Ln .. 77429
Gypsy Red Dr 77433
Haden Crest Ct 77429
Hailey Paige Dr 77433
Halamar Ln 77433
Hallowed Stream Ln 77433
Hallwell Ct 77429
Halpren Falls Cir & Ln .. 77429
Halprin Creek Dr 77429
Hamblin Rd 77429
Hamilton Hills Dr 77433
Hamilton Park Dr 77429
Hamlet Shadow Ln 77433
Hammondsport Ln 77429
Hanberry Ln 77433
Hancock Elm St 77429
Hancock Oak St 77429
Hannah Glen Ln 77429
Happy Ln 77429
Harbor Water Dr 77433
Harbour Bridge Point Dr 77429
Hardwood Ridge Trl 77429
Harmony Estates Ln 77429
Harnett Dr 77429
Harris Canyon Ln 77429
Harris Settlement Ct 77433
Hartaway Ln 77429
Hartcrest Dr 77429
Hartfield Bluff Ln 77433
Harvest Chase Ct 77429
Harvest Landing Ln 77433
Harvrenee Dr 77429
Hasina Knoll Dr 77429
Haughland Dr 77433
Haven Arbor Dr 77433
Haven Creek Dr 77433
Haven Forest Ct 77433
Haven Hollow Ct 77429
Haverfield Ct 77429
Hawksmoor Ct 77429
Hayden Grove Dr 77433
Hayesford Ln 77429
Hazel Thicket Trl 77429
Hazeldale Dr 77433
Hazelway Ln 77429
Hazen Point Dr 77433
Hazy Ridge Ln 77429
Headland Dr 77433
Heartwood Way 77433
Heartwood Oak Trl 77429
Hearty Orange Ct & Dr 77433
Heath Falls Ln 77429
Heathcrest Ct 77429
Heather Mist Ct 77429
Heatherwick Dr 77429
Heathridge Ln 77433
Heights Harvest Ln 77429
Hempstead Rd 77429
Hemwick Dr 77429
Henderson Point Dr 77429
Hentinco Dr 77433
Heron Marsh Dr 77429
Heron Meadow Ln 77433
Heron Point Dr 77429
Hickory Dale St 77429
Hickory Field Ct 77433
Hickory Hill Ln 77429
Hidden Clover Cir 77433
Hidden Dale Pt 77429
Hidden Falls Dr 77429
Hidden Shadow Ln 77433
Hidden Valley Waters Dr 77429
Hideaway Park Dr 77429
High Ferry Ln 77429
High Noon Ct 77433
High Valley Way 77433
Highland Elm St 77433
Highland Hills Dr 77429
N Highlands Bayou Dr .. 77433
Highway 290 14200-26299 77429

Highway 290 27000-30099 77433
Hill Lakes Ct 77429
Hillock Glen Ln 77429
Hillsdale Park Ct & Dr .. 77433
Hillside Park Way 77433
Hillside Terrace Ln 77433
Hilltop Park Ln 77433
Hilltop View Dr 77429
Hilton Head Ln 77429
Hitching Post Ct 77429
Hollow Branch Ct 77429
Hollow Cove Ct 77433
Hollow Field Ct & Ln ... 77433
Hollow Stone Ln 77433
Holly Ln 77429
Holly Barr Ln 77433
Holly Berry Ct 77433
Holly Branch Ct 77433
Hollygate Ln 77429
Holts Landing Dr 77433
Honey Daisy Ct 77433
Honey Pine Ln 77433
Honeycomb Ln 77429
Hope Farm Ln 77429
Hope Shadow Ct 77429
Horseshoe Canyon Dr .. 77433
Horseshoe Falls Ln 77433
Horseshoe Hill Ct 77429
House Hahl Rd 77433
Houston Dr 77433
Hubbard Creek Ct 77433
Huddlestone Dr 77429
Huffmeister Rd 77429
Hughlett Dr 77433
Hunterfield Dr 77429
Hunters Cyn 77429
Huntmont Dr 77429
Hurst Ct 77429
Hurstfield Pointe Ct & Dr 77429
Hyde Park 77429
Idylwild Wood Way 77429
Imperial Springs Ct 77429
Imperial Woods Ln 77429
Indian Cherry Forest Ln 77433
Indian Cypress Dr 77429
Indian Desert Dr 77433
Indigo Key Ct 77433
Indigo Spires Ct & Dr .. 77429
Ingleside Park 77429
Inland Grove Ct 77429
Invergarry Way 77429
Iris Edge Way 77429
Irish Elm Ct 77429
Ivory Crossing Ln 77433
Ivy Hollow Ln 77433
Ivy Manor Ct 77433
Ivyford Ct 77429
Ivyforest Dr 77429
Jacaranda Pl 77429
Jackson Brook Way 77429
Jadestone Creek Ln 77433
Jaquine Dr 77433
Jarvis Rd 77429
Jasmine Bloom Ln 77433
Jasper Ln 77433
Jasper Oaks Dr 77433
Jast Dr 77429
Jefferson Oaks 77433
Jelly Park Stone Dr 77433
Jenista Ln 77433
Jenny Wood Ct 77433
Jills Way Ln 77433
Jodie Lynn Cir 77433
Johns Enterprise Ct 77433
Johns Purchase Ct 77433
Johns Stake Ct 77433
Jordan Canyon Ln 77429
Josey Creek Ct 77433
Joshnomi Ln 77433
Judge Bry Rd 77429
Juergen Rd 77433
Julington Ln 77429
Junction Creek Ln 77429

June Oak St 77429
Juniors Map Ct 77433
Juniper Bend Ct & Ln .. 77429
Juniper Cove Ct & Dr .. 77433
Juniper Creek Ln 77429
Juniper Hollow Way 77433
Juniper Woods Ct 77429
Kanai Ct 77429
Kaston Dr 77433
Kathy Ln 77429
Katie Marie Ct 77433
Katy Hockley Rd 77433
Kavanaugh Ln 77429
Keegans Ledge Ln 77433
Keepers Trl 77429
Keesey Creek Cir 77433
Kellan Ct 77429
Kellerton Ct & Ln 77429
Kelley Green Ct 77429
E & W Kelsey Creek Trl 77433
Kelsey Gap Ct 77433
Kelsey Woods Ct 77433
Kendal Ridge Ln 77433
Kendons Way Ln 77433
Keneva Dr 77429
Kenmark Ct & Ln 77433
Kenson Ln 77429
Kentley Orchard Ln 77433
Kenwood Haven Dr 77433
Kerby Pl 77433
Kerman Dr 77429
Kerrington Glen Dr 77433
Kerrville Ct 77429
Key Crest Ln 77429
Key Oak Ln 77429
Key Ridge Ln 77433
Keystone Bend Ln 77433
Keystone Green Dr 77429
Kiawah Dr 77429
Kicking Horse Pass 77433
King Cir 77429
Kings Ct 77429
Kings Cypress Ln 77429
Kingston Creek Ln 77433
Kirby Hill Ct 77433
Kitzman Rd 77433
Kluge Rd 77429
Kluge Bend Cir 77429
Kluge Corner Ln 77429
Knauff Ranch Ct 77429
Knigge Cemetery Rd ... 77429
Knoll Dale Ct 77433
Knotty Chestnut St 77429
N & S Kolbe Cir & Dr .. 77429
S Kolbe Spur Dr 77429
Kransburg Ranch Ct & Dr 77433
Kurtell Ln 77429
Kwik Kopy Ln 77429
Kyle Crest Trl 77433
Kz Rd 77433
La Paloma Estates Dr .. 77433
Labarre Dr 77429
Ladino Rd 77429
Ladino Run St 77429
Lady Shery Ln 77429
Laffite Dr 77429
Lake Prt 77429
Lake Cypress Hill Dr ... 77429
Lake Forest Dr 77429
Lake Fork Ct 77433
Lake Haven Dr 77433
Lake Leon Ct 77433
Lake Lewisville Ct 77433
Lake Loop Dr 77433
Lake Louise Ct 77433
Lake Mist Ct & Dr 77429
Lake Nocona Ct 77433
Lake Parc Bend Dr 77429
Lake Raven Ct 77433
Lake Riata Ln 77433
E & W Lake Rose Ct ... 77429
Lake Spring Ct 77433
Lake Texoma Cir 77433
Lake Timber Ct 77429

Lakecrest Cir & Dr 77429
Lakecrest View Dr 77433
Lakehills View Cir 77429
Lakeland Falls Dr 77433
Lakepointe Bend Ln 77429
Lakeport Crossing Dr ... 77429
Lakeridge Park Ln 77433
Lakeside Haven Dr 77433
Lakeside View Way 77429
Lakeview Dr 77429
Lakewood Bnd 77429
Lakewood Glade Ct 77429
Lakewood Glen Ct 77429
Lakewood Meadow Dr .. 77429
Lakewood Valley Ct 77429
Lakewood West Dr 77429
Lantana Ridge Ct 77433
Lantern Springs Ln 77433
Lapis Meadow Dr 77433
Larch Grove Ct 77429
Larkspur Hills Dr 77433
Laskey Manor Ct 77429
Lasting Rose Dr 77429
Latticevine 77429
Laumar Ct 77429
Laura Cir 77429
E & W Laura Shore Ct & Dr 77433
Laurel Knoll Cir 77433
Laurel Trail Dr 77433
Laurus Estates Ln 77429
Lavender Bay Ln 77429
Lavender Creek Ct 77433
Lavender Landing Ln ... 77433
Lavender Run Dr 77433
Lawrence Trace Ct 77429
Lawton Ridge Dr 77433
Layton Castle Ln 77429
Layton Hills Dr 77433
Lazdins Cir 77429
E & S Lazy Daisy Cir .. 77433
Leaf Chase Ct 77429
Leafwind Dr 77433
Leaning Aspen Ct 77429
Ledgefield 77433
Ledgewood Park Dr 77429
Lee Way Dr 77429
Legacy Pines Dr 77433
Leigh Woods Dr 77433
Leightonfield Ct 77433
Lemur Ln 77429
Lentando Ln 77429
Leon Springs Ln 77429
Lesota Ct 77429
Lewis Dr 77433
Lexxe Creek Ct 77433
Liberty Stone Ln 77429
Light Falls Ct 77429
Lighthouse Scene Ln ... 77433
Lilac Breeze Ct 77429
Lilly Hollow Dr 77429
Limber Pine Pl 77429
E & W Lime Blossom Ct 77433
Lime Green Trl 77433
Limestone Ridge Trl 77433
Lindall Ct 77429
Lindenwick Ct 77433
Lindsey Rd 77429
Lindsey Hill Ln 77429
Linwood Manor Ct 77429
Lippizaner Dr 77433
Lismore Pt 77429
Lismore Lake Dr 77429
Little Creek Ct 77433
Little Cypress Dr & Ln .. 77433
Little Miss Creek Dr 77429
Little Ranch Rd 77429
Little Rock Ct 77429
Little Thicket Ct 77433
Live Oak Trl 77429
Live Oak Bend Way 77429
Live Oak Glen Ln 77429
Livery Ln 77433
Llano Pass Ct 77429
Llano River Ln 77433

Lockdale Ln 77429
Lodgepole Pine St 77429
Lone Star Oak Ct & St 77433
Long Haven Dr 77433
Long Key Dr 77433
Longdale Ct 77433
Longhurst Hills Ln 77429
E & W Longwood Mdws & Spur 77429
Longwood Spur Rd 77429
Longwood Trace Dr 77429
Lost Cypress Dr 77429
Lothbury Dr 77429
Louetta Rd 77429
Lower Lake Dr 77433
Loyola Dr 77429
Lusterleaf Dr 77429
Lutheran Cemetary Rd 77433
Lyndbrook Ln 77433
Lynn Haven St 77429
Mablehurst Dr 77429
Mackinaw Isle Ct 77429
Macy Dr 77429
Madewood St 77429
Madison Claire Ct 77433
Magic River Dr 77429
Magnolia Brook Ln 77433
Magnolia Dell Dr 77433
Magnolia Manor Dr 77429
Magnoliabough Pl 77429
Mahogany Crest Dr 77429
Majestic Landing Ln 77433
Major Elm St 77433
Malango Point Dr 77433
Mallard Estates Ct 77429
Mallard Point Ct 77433
Manning Dr 77429
Manor Bend St 77433
Manorwood Ln 77429
Mansion Ct 77429
Maple Arbor Ct 77429
Maple Cliff Ln 77429
Maple Meadows Ct & Dr 77433
Maple Mill Dr 77429
Maple Point Ct & Dr 77433
Maple Village Ct & Dr 77433
Maranta Estates Ct 77433
Marble Ridge Ct 77433
Marblepointe Ln 77429
Mariah Rose Ct 77433
Marigold Creek Ct 77433
Marin Dr 77429
Marin Hill Ct 77429
Mariposa Blue Ln 77433
Markhurst Dr 77429
Marklena Dr 77429
Marks Way 77429
Marlan Forest Ln 77433
Marron Ct & Dr 77429
Marwell Ln 77429
Mary Ann St 77429
Mason Rd 77433
Mason Terrace Ln 77429
Mathis Landing Dr 77433
Matlock Ct 77433
Mauve Orchid Way 77433
Maverick Creek Ln 77433
Maverick Trace Ln 77433
Maverick Valley Ln 77429
Maxted Ct 77429
Maxwell Rd 77429
May Apple Ct 77433
Mayberry Heights Dr 77433
Mcalexander Dr 77429
Mccamey Dr 77429
Mccearley Dr 77429
Mcclurd Ct 77429
Mccracken Cir 77429
Mcswain Rd 77429
Meadow Blossom Ln 77433
Meadow Breeze Dr 77433
Meadow Estates Ln 77429
Meadow Palm Dr 77433
Meadow Sage Ct 77433
Meadow Sweet Dr 77429
Meadowview Dr 77429
Meandering Oak Ln 77433
Medina Lake Ct & Ln 77429
Medio Vista Ln 77433
Medlowe Ct 77429
Melba Rose Cir 77433
Mellenbrook Ln 77433
Melody Gdn 77429
Melody View Ct 77429
Merilee Ct 77429
Merle Rd 77433
Mesa Creek Ln 77433
Mesa Falls Ln 77433
Mesa Red Ct 77433
Mesquite Bend Ln 77433
Mesquite Estates Ln 77429
Micmac Ct 77429
Middle Bluff Trl 77429
Midnight Glen Dr 77429
Mierwood Manor Dr 77429
Milestone Ln 77429
Mill Canyon Ct 77429
Mill Haven Cir 77433
Mill Ridge Dr 77429
Miller Meadows Ln 77433
Millies Creek Ln 77433
Mills Rd 77429
Mills Fork Dr 77433
Mills Glen Dr 77429
Mills Park Ln 77429
Mills Station Ct 77429
Millstone Estates Ln 77429
Mimosa Ln 77429
Miscindy Pl 77429
Missarah Ln 77429
Misty Arch Ln 77433
Misty Cypress Ct 77429
Misty Dawn Trl 77433
Misty Hills Dr 77429
Misty Jade Ln 77429
Misty Pond Ct 77429
Misty River Way 77433
Mitchell St 77429
Mohave Way Ct & Dr 77429
Mohican Dr 77429
Molly Winters Ln 77433
Monarch Creek Ln 77433
Montaigne Dr 77429
Montana Bend Ln 77433
Monteigne Ln 77429
Montes Landing Dr 77429
Moon Harvest Ln 77433
Moon Vista Ln 77433
Moonlit Falls Dr 77433
Moonlit Haven Cir 77433
Moonrise River Ln 77433
Morgan Jane Way 77433
Morgan Willow Ln 77429
E & W Morgans Bend Dr 77433
Morgans Gold Dr 77433
Morgans Lake Dr 77433
Morgans Mill Ct 77433
Morgans Secret Dr 77433
Morley Dr 77429
Morning Cypress Ln 77433
Morning Glory Terrace Ct 77433
Morning Oak Ln 77433
Morning Pine Trl 77433
Moss Bay Ct & Ln 77429
N & S Moss Creek Dr & Ln 77429
Moss Green Ct 77429
Moss Springs Ct 77433
Moss Valley Dr 77429
Mosshill Estates Ln 77429
Mossy Park 77429
Mossy Brook Ct & Ln 77433
Mossy Leaf Ln 77433
Mount Airy Ct & Dr 77429
Mountain Dale Ct & Dr 77433
Mountaindale Dr 77433
Muddobber Ln 77433
Mueller Cemetary Rd 77429
Mueschke Rd 77433
E, N, S & W Mulberry Field Cir 77433
Muley Ct & Ln 77433
Musetta Ct 77429
Musket Trail Dr 77429
Mustang Bend Cir 77429
Mustang Creek Cir 77429
Mustang Crossing Cir 77429
Mustang Glen Ln 77429
Mustang Valley Cir 77429
Mystic Bend Dr 77429
Mystic Blue Trl 77433
Mystic Bluff Ln 77433
Naples Cliff Ct 77433
Narcissus Brook Ln 77433
Narnia Vale Ct 77429
Natchez Creek Ln 77429
Nathan Ridge Ln 77429
Navidad Bend Ct 77433
Nevermore Dr 77429
New Ann St 77429
New Cypress Dr 77429
New Kentucky Rd 77429
Nicholas Pass Ln 77433
Nightingale Falls Ct 77429
Norstrom Falls Ct 77429
Norstrum Falls Ct 77429
Northface Manor Ct 77429
Northlake Forest Dr 77429
Northpointe Ridge Ln 77429
Northspring Bend Ct & Ln 77429
Northsun Ln 77429
Northwest Fwy 77429
Norwood Peak Ln 77433
Nottoway Cir 77429
Nueces Springs Ln 77429
Oak Alley Ln 77429
Oak Arbor Way 77433
Oak Cluster Ct 77429
Oak Fair Bnd 77429
Oak Harbor Bnd & Mnr 77429
Oak Hollow Cir & Dr 77429
Oak Lake Bnd 77429
Oak Orchard Ct & Ln 77433
Oak Park Bend Ln 77433
Oak Plaza Dr 77429
Oak Sage Dr 77433
Oak Spring Rd 77433
Oakfield Dr 77429
Oakfield Glen Ln 77433
Oakleigh Dr 77433
Oakshield Ln 77433
Oakwood Canyon Dr 77433
Oakwood Manor Dr 77429
Obelisk Bay Dr 77429
N Oblong Cir 77429
Ochre Leaf Trl 77433
Ochre Willow Trl 77433
Oddom Ct 77429
Old Gruene Ct 77429
Old Hickory Dr 77429
Old Huffmeister Rd 77429
Old Kluge Rd 77429
Old Spring Cypress Rd 77429
Olden Ct 77429
Oldgate Pass Ln 77433
Oleander Ridge Way 77433
Olive Tree Ct 77429
Olmstead Park Dr 77429
Oneida Ct 77429
Opal Hollow Ln 77429
Opera House Row Dr 77429
Orange Bloom Ct 77433
Orange Maple Ct 77433
Orange Poppy Dr 77433
Orchid Blossom Way 77433
Orchid Cove Ct 77433
Orchid Mist Dr 77433
Orchid Trail Ln 77429
Oriole Point Ct 77429
Ormonde Crossing Dr 77429
Owens Canyon Ln 77433
Oxford Haven Dr 77433
Oxton Ct 77429
Packard Falls Ct 77429
Paddock Bend Dr 77433
Page Rock Dr 77433
Paige Terrace Ct 77433
Paint Bluff Ln 77433
Painted Desert Dr 77433
Painted Stone Ct 77433
Palladio Dr 77429
Pallwood Ln 77429
Palmer Manor Dr 77429
N Palo Duro Lake Trl 77433
E & W Paloma Dr 77433
Paloma Bay Ct 77433
Paloma Crossing Ct 77429
W & E Paloma Lago Cir & Ct 77433
Paloma Ranch Ct 77433
Palos Park Dr 77429
Panola Pointe 77429
Parable Ln 77429
Paradise Meadow Ct 77433
Parc Cove Ct 77429
Parc Lake Edge Dr 77433
Parish Timbers Ct 77433
Park Antique Ln 77429
Park Arbor Ct 77429
Park Forest Dr & Trl 77429
Park Oak Ct 77433
Park Overlook Ct 77433
Park Sage Ct & Ln 77433
Parkcross Pl 77433
Parkford Meadow Dr 77433
Parkland Manor Dr 77433
Parkwille Ln 77433
Parmley Creek Ct 77429
Parsons Knoll Dr 77433
Partners Voice Dr 77433
Pasture Bend Ct & Ln 77433
Pasture Spring Ln 77433
Pawnee Bend Dr 77429
Pawnee Trails Dr 77429
Paxton Landing Ln 77433
Paynes Creek Dr 77433
Payton Haven Dr 77433
Peach Bluff Ln 77429
Peach Meadow Dr 77433
Peach Mill Ct 77433
Peach Mountain Ln 77433
Pebble Creek Ln 77429
Pebble Creek Trl 77433
Pebble Meadow Ct 77429
Pebble Pine Ct & Trl 77433
Pecos Bend Ct 77433
Pecos Pass Ct 77433
Pecos River Bend Cir & Dr 77433
E & W Pedernales River Dr 77433
Pegasus Cir & Rd 77429
Pelican Marsh Dr 77429
Pence Hills Ct 77433
Pennland Ln 77429
Pepper Creek Ln 77433
Petal Rose Ct 77433
Petina Cypress Ct 77433
Petties Way 77429
Pheasant Grove Dr 77433
Pin Oak Bend Dr 77433
Pin Oak Glen Ln 77433
Pine Dr 77429
Pine Arbor Way 77433
Pine Belt Dr 77429
Pine Bough Ln 77429
Pine Brook Trl 77429
E & W Pine Creek Bnd 77433
Pine Glen Ln 77433
Pine Spring Ln 77429
Pine Valley Trl 77433
Pine View Dr 77429
Pinedell Dr 77429
Pinefrost Ln 77429
Pinos Verde Dr 77433
Pinson Dr 77429
Pioneer Ridge Dr 77433
Piper Hill Ln 77429
Placid Oak Ct 77433
Plains River Dr 77429
Plattsmouth Ln 77429
Pleasant Grove Rd 77429
Pleasant Knoll Ln 77433
Plum Green Ct 77429
Plum Springs Dr 77429
Plumwood Dr 77429
Point Village Ln 77429
Pointer Ridge Ln 77433
Polaris Point Ln 77433
Pondwood Dr 77429
Poppy Grove Ln 77433
Poppys Point Ct 77433
Port Barrow Dr 77429
Post Oak Glen Ln 77429
Postano Bluff Dr 77433
Powell Ridge Dr 77433
Poydras Ct 77429
Prade Ranch Ln 77429
Prado Woods St 77429
Prairie Bend Ct 77433
Prairie Bluff Dr 77433
Prairie Fire Ln 77433
Prairie Flax Ct 77433
Prairie Haven Ct 77429
Prairie Lea St 77429
Prairie Mill Ln 77433
Prairie Village Dr 77433
Preece Ct 77429
Prescott Mnr 77433
Preston Bloom Cir & Ct 77429
Pricewood Manor Ct 77433
Prim Pine Ct 77433
Prima Vista Dr 77433
Primrose Edge Ct 77429
Primrose Glen Ln 77433
Primrose Park Ln 77433
Primrose Prairie Ct 77433
Primula Ct 77429
Pristine Lake Ln 77429
Privet Ln 77429
Progress Ridge Way 77429
Promenade Park 77429
Prospect Canyon Ln 77433
Prospect Point Dr 77429
Prosper Ridge Dr 77433
Providence Shore Way 77433
Pueblo Run 77429
Pueblo Run Dr 77429
Purple Finch Ct 77433
Quail Farms Rd 77429
Quail Forest Dr 77429
Quail Park Dr 77429
Quarry Vale Dr 77429
Queen Of Scots Dr 77429
Queenslake Dr 77429
Quiet Ridge Ln 77429
Radiant Lilac Trl 77433
Rain Meadow Ln 77433
Raleigh Green Trl 77433
Raleigh Oak Ln 77433
Rambling River Way 77433
Ramona 77429
Ranch Mill Ln 77433
Ranchland Ln 77429
Randall Ridge Ln 77429
Range Valley Ln 77429
Ranger Rdg 77429
Rankin Meadows Ct 77433
Raven Creek Ln 77433
Raven Flight Dr 77429
Raven Hill Dr 77429
Raven Lake Ct 77433
Raven Rook Dr 77429
Raven Roost Ct & Dr 77429
N & S Raven Shore Ct & Dr 77433
Raven South Dr 77429
Raven Tree Dr 77429
Ravens Caw Dr 77429
Ravens Chase Ln 77429
Ravens Glen Ct 77429
Ravens Mate Dr 77429
Ravensbrook Ln 77429
Ravensong Dr 77429
Ravensway Dr 77429
Ravensway Center Dr 77429
Ravenwing Dr 77429
Rawhide Trl 77429
Red Ashberry Trl 77433
E & W Red Bayberry Ct 77433
Red Bud Ln 77429
Red Canary Ct 77433
Red Cedar Bluff Ln 77433
Red Cedar Canyon Ln 77433
Red Cedar Cove Ln 77433
Red Laurel Ct 77429
Red Oak Bend Dr 77433
Red Oak Glen Dr 77429
Redbud Berry Ln & Way 77433
Redbud Dale Ct 77429
Redbud Leaf Ln 77433
Redbud Terrace Ln 77433
Redding Crest Ln 77429
Redgrove Falls Ct 77433
Redoak Manor Ln 77433
Redondo Valley Ct & Dr 77433
Redstone Hills Dr 77433
Redwood Manor Ln 77433
Reflection Point Dr 77433
Refuge Creek Dr 77433
Refuge Lake Dr 77433
Regatta Cove Ct 77433
Regency Ash Ct 77429
Regency Forest Dr 77429
Regency Green Dr 77429
Regency Oak Ln 77429
Regency Pine Dr 77429
Remington Grove Ct 77433
Remington Manor Dr 77433
Reston Bridge Dr 77429
Reston Run Ct & Ln 77433
Retreat Trl 77429
Rexine Ln 77433
Riata Canyon Ct & Dr 77433
Riata Crossing Dr 77433
N Riata Lake Dr 77433
Riata Manor Ln 77433
Riata Prairie Ln 77433
Riata Springs Ln 77433
E & W Rice Meadow Cir 77433
Ridge Cove Ln 77433
Ridge Falls Ct 77433
Ridge Stream Ln 77433
Ridgefield Park Ln 77433
Ridgegrove Ln 77433
Ridgestone Park Ln 77433
Rifleman Cir & Trl 77429
Riford Dr 77429
Rigby Point Ln 77433
Riley Ridge Ln 77429
Rion Hill Ct 77429
Ripping Lake Ct 77429
Rippling Springs Dr 77429
Rising Bluff Ln 77429
Rising Brook Dr 77429
Riven Oaks Ct 77433
Rivenwood 77433
River Pines Dr 77433
River Raven Ct 77429
Riverbend Point Ln 77433
Riverlet Ct 77429
Riverton Ash Ct 77433
Riverton Crest Ct 77433
Riverton Manor Ct 77429
Riverton Ranch Dr 77433
Roanoke Falls Dr 77433
Robbins Rd 77429
Robin Grove Ct 77433
Robison Woods Rd 77429
Rochelle Ct 77429
Rock Creek Villa Dr 77429
Rock River Ln 77433
Rockhill Point Dr 77429
Rockledge Dr 77429
Rocksprings Rdg 77429
Rockwood Park Ln 77433
Rocky Bridge Ln 77433
Rocky Mill Dr 77429
Rocky Trace Ln 77433
Roland Canyon Dr 77433
Rolling Valley Dr 77429
Rolling View Trl 77433
Rose Trl 77429
Rose Bay Trl 77429
Rose Down Cir 77429
Rose Garden Trl 77429
Rose Hill Park Ln 77429
Rose Pine Ct 77429
Rose View Ct 77429
Rosebud Knoll Ct 77429
Roseglade Dr 77429
Rosehill Estates Ln 77429
Rosemont Estates Ln 77429
Rosethorn Ct 77429
Rosetta Dr 77429
Rosevale Ct 77429
Roseview Ln 77429
Rosewood Glen Dr 77429
Rosy Hill Ct 77429
Royal Cove Cir 77433
Royal Haven Ln 77433
Ruby Valley Ct 77433
Running Cypress Dr 77429
Russet Bend Ln 77429
Rustic Brook Ct 77429
Rustic Cape Dr 77433
Rustic Fields Ln 77429
Rustic Gate Dr 77433
Rustic Hills Ln 77429
Rustic Lake Ln 77433
Rustic Rail Ct 77433
Rustic Stable Ln 77429
Rustler Gate Ln 77433
Rustlers Trail Ln 77429
Rustling Glen Ln 77429
Rusty Rock Ln 77433
Saathoff Dr 77429
Sabinal River Ct 77433
Sabine River Ct 77433
Sable Acre Ct 77433
Sable Key Ct 77429
Sable Oaks Ln 77433
Sableleaf Dr 77429
Sableton Crest Ln 77429
Sac Ct 77429
Saddle Briar Ln 77429
Saddle Ridge Pass 77433
Saddleback Chase Ln 77433
Saddleville Mills Ln 77433
Safe Haven Dr 77433
Sage Cypress Ct 77433
Sagebrush Valley Ln 77433
Sagemark Ridge Dr 77433
Saint Pierre Ct & Ln 77429
Salado Creek Ct 77433
Salamanca Ct 77429
Salem Blue Ct 77433
Salida Creek Cir 77433
Salt Grass Trl 77429
Salt Grass Meadow Dr 77433
Sam Rayburn Ct 77433
N San Gabriel River Cir 77433
San Saba Canyon Cir & Ln 77429
San Saba Creek Cir 77433
San Saba River Ct 77433
San Solomon Springs Ct 77433
Sandalin Ct & Dr 77433
Sanderling Dr 77433
Sandia Springs Cir 77433
Sandler Bnd & Ct 77433
Sandlight Ln 77433
Sandy Ct 77433
Sandy Brook Ln 77429
Sandy Cypress Ct 77433
Sandy Hill Cir 77433

Sandy Ring Ct 77429
Santee Pass Dr 77429
Santos St 77433
Sapulpa Ln 77429
Saracen Dr 77429
Saras Walk 77429
Sarasam Creek Ct 77429
Sardina Shore Dr 77433
Sasher Ln 77429
Satinwood Hills Ln 77433
Satsuma Vale St 77433
Savannah Bay Rd 77433
Savannah Park Dr 77429
Sawmill Creek Dr 77433
Sawyer Run Ln 77429
Saxon Meadow Ln 77433
Saxon Place Ct 77433
Scamp Dr 77429
Scenic Brook Dr 77433
Scenic Lake Ct 77429
Scenic Path Ct 77429
Scenic Point Ct 77433
Scenic Woods Cir & Dr 77433
Schiel Rd 77433
Schmidt Rd 77429
Scott Cir 77429
Scouts Ln 77429
Seabluff Ct 77433
Secret Branch Ct & Ln 77433
Secret Forest Ct 77429
Sedona Oaks Dr 77433
Sedona Ridge Dr 77433
Sedona Run Dr 77433
Seminole Ridge Dr 77433
Sendera Oaks Ct & Ln 77433
Serendipity Ln 77429
Serene Shore Dr 77429
Serene Wood Ln 77433
Serrano Gap Ct 77429
W, N & S Settlers Shore Cir & Dr 77433
Shadow Ln 77429
Shadow Cypress Ct 77433
Shadow Grange Ct 77433
E Shadow Lake Ln 77429
Shady Bliss Cir 77433
Shady Blossom Dr 77433
Shady Cypress Ln 77429
Shady Edge Dr 77433
Shady Gate Ct 77429
Shady Haven Cir 77433
Shady Knoll Ln 77429
Shady Loch Ln 77433
Shady Pecan Ct 77429
Shadydale Rd 77429
Shaft Dr 77429
Shallow Cove Ct 77429
Shallow Leaf Ln 77433
Shavano Ct & Ln 77433
Shaw Rd 77429
Shawnee Forest Dr 77433
Sheffield Gray Trl 77433
Sheffield Park Dr 77433
Shellmont Ct 77433
Sherburn Manor Dr 77429
Shetstone Cir 77433
Shiloh Springs Dr 77433
Shimmering Green Trl 77433
Shimmering Lake Dr 77433
Shoal Hollow Ct 77433
Shoal Park Dr 77433
Shoal Springs Ln 77433
Shore Lands Rd 77433
Shore Park Rd 77433
Shorebridge Rd 77433
Short Ct 77429
Shurlin Pl 77429
Sienna Glen Ct 77429
Sienna Oak Dr 77433
Sienna Peak Ln 77429
Sienna Shadow Ln 77433
Signal Ridge Way 77429
Silent Jasmin Ct 77433
Silver Blueberry Trl 77433
Silver Sagebrush Ct 77433
Silverbluff Ct 77433
Silverheels Dr 77433
Silverton Stone Ln 77429
Silverwood Trl 77433
Silverwood Bend Ln 77433
Single Ridge Way 77429
E & W Single Rose Ct 77429
Sioux Run 77429
Sisterdale Dr 77433
Skinner Ct & Rd 77429
Sky Ridge Dr 77433
Sky Way St 77433
Skyhill Dr 77433
Sloan Ridge Ln 77429
Smoke Creek Ct 77429
Smokey Saddle Ln 77429
Snowberry Dr 77433
Snowny Hills Dr 77433
Solace Vista Dr 77433
Solvista Creek Ln 77429
Sonata Creek Ln 77429
South Dr 77433
Southern Cypress Ct & Ln 77429
Spanish River Ln 77429
Spiced Cider Ln 77433
Spindle Arbor Rd 77429
Spinney Lane Dr 77429
Spreading Oak Dr 77429
Sprila Park Dr 77429
Spring Barker Dr 77429
Spring Cypress Rd
  13000-16700 77429
  16635-16635 77410
  16701-17999 77429
  16702-17998 77429
Spring Glade Dr 77429
Spring Marsh Ct 77429
Spring Walk Ln 77429
Spring Wreath Ln 77433
Springhill Bend Ln 77433
Springmint Ct & Dr 77433
Spur Canyon Ct 77429
Spyglen Ct & Ln 77429
Stable Bend Cir 77429
Stable Brook Cir 77429
Stable Creek Cir 77429
Stable Lake Dr 77429
Stable Manor Ln 77429
Stable Oak Dr 77429
Stable Park Ct & Dr 77429
Stable Run Dr 77429
Stable Springs Cir 77429
Stable Star Cir 77429
Stable Trail Dr 77429
Stable View Ct 77429
Stablepoint Ln 77429
Stablewood Downs Ln 77429
Stablewood Farm Dr 77429
Staffordale Ct 77433
Stallings Gate Ln 77433
Stallion Peak Cir 77433
Stallion Point Cir 77429
Standing Field Ct 77433
Stanfield Ct 77433
Stanton Lake Dr 77433
Star Canyon Ct 77429
Star Haven Dr 77433
Star Thistle Ct 77433
Steelwood Dr 77429
Steinhagen Rd 77429
Stem Green Ct 77433
Stenbury Ct 77429
Stephens Charge Ct 77433
Sterling Moon Ln 77433
Sterling Park Ln 77429
Stewart Crest Ln 77433
Still Oak Ln 77433
Stillbrook Cir 77429
Stiller Park Ct & Dr 77429
Stillwood Park Ct 77433
Stone Bank Ct 77429
Stone Falls Ct 77433
Stone Field Canyon Ln 77433
Stone Oak Estates Ct 77429
Stone Ridge Crossing Ln 77433
Stone Stable Ln 77429
Stonecreek Bend Ln 77433
Stonecross Glen Ln 77433
Stonemeade Pl 77429
Stoneridge Park Ct & Ln 77429
Stoney Haven Dr 77433
Stoney Mill St 77429
Story Glen Dr 77429
Strat Wood Ct 77433
Stratford Canyon Dr 77433
Streetcar Ct 77429
Stroman Dr 77429
Sublime Point Dr 77433
Sugarloaf Bay Dr 77429
Summer Cypress Ct & Dr 77429
Summer Retreat Ln 77433
E & W Summer Rose Ct 77429
Summer Shower Ct & Dr 77433
Summerfern Ct 77429
Summerland Cir 77429
Summit Crest Ct 77429
Sunbluff Ct 77429
Sunburst Trail Dr 77433
Sunburst View Dr 77433
Sundance View Ln 77433
Sundial Stone Ln 77433
Sunlight Bay Ct 77429
Sunmill Ct 77429
Sunny Springs Ln 77433
Sunset Green Ct 77433
Sunset Haven Dr 77433
Sunset Valley Dr 77433
Sunshine Park Dr 77429
Sunshine Ridge Ln
  20000-20098 77429
  20000-20198 77433
  20001-20099 77429
  20001-20199 77433
Sutton Falls Dr 77433
Swan Valley Dr 77433
Swansbury Dr 77429
Sweet Gardens Ct 77433
Sweet Springs Ln 77429
Sweetgum Way 77433
Sweetstone Bluff Ln 77433
Sweetstone Estates Ct 77429
Sweetstone Field Ct 77433
Sweetstone Grove Ct & Ln 77433
Sweetstone Springs Ct 77433
Sweetwater Lake Ct 77433
N & S Swirling Cloud Ct 77433
Sycamore Leaf Ln 77429
Sycamore Valley Dr 77433
Sylvia Dr 77429
Tall Forest Dr 77429
Tall Haven Ln 77433
Tall Spruce Dr 77433
Tallow Glen Ln 77433
Tallow View Ln 77433
Tangler Ln 77429
Tanglewood Trails Dr 77433
Taos Creek Ct 77433
Tara Ashley St 77433
Tarbet Place Ct 77433
Taren Ct 77429
Tawnas Way Ln 77429
Tawny Bluff Ct 77433
Taylor Cove Ct 77433
Tayman Oaks Dr 77433
Teal Haven Ln 77429
Teal Hollow Dr 77433
Teal Shadow Ct 77433
Teal Wind Dr 77433
Tealbrook Dr 77433
Tejas Trl 77429
Telge Rd 77429
Telge Lake Trl 77429
N & S Telge Manor Dr 77429
Temple Hill Ln 77433
Temple Park Ln 77433
Tenaya Falls Dr 77433
Terra Canyon Ln 77433
Terra Point Dr 77429
Terra Stone Ct 77433
Terrace Bnd 77429
Terrace Cove Ln 77433
Terrebone Dr 77429
Texas Army Trl 77429
Texas Redbud Ct 77433
Texas Sage Way 77433
Thatcher Hills Ct 77429
Thicket Hollow Ln 77433
Thicket Trace Ct 77433
Thistle Down 77433
Thistle Meadow Ln 77433
Thistle Rock Ln 77429
Thistlebridge Ct 77429
Thomas Ridge Ln 77433
Thomas Shore Ct & Dr 77433
Thomas Survey Dr 77429
Thorn Cypress Dr 77429
Thornbluff Ct 77429
Thornmeadow Ln 77433
Three Rivers Way 77429
Thyme Green Ln 77433
Tilbury Woods Ln 77433
Tiltwood Ln 77429
Timber Cliff Ct & Ln 77433
Timber Crossing Ln 77433
Timber Manor Dr 77433
Timber Mist Ct 77433
Timber Trail Way 77433
Timberchase Pl 77429
Timberidge Ct 77429
Timberlake Dr 77429
Timberline Trl 77433
Timberly Park Ln 77433
Timbermoss Ct 77433
Timberstone Ct 77433
Tipshire Ln 77433
Toas Creek Ct 77429
Tobinn Manor Dr 77429
Tonsley Springs Dr 77433
Toprock Ln 77433
Tower Bluff Ln 77433
Towering Cypress Dr 77433
Town Glade Dr 77429
Townsend Ct 77429
Township Glen Ct & Ln 77433
Traceton Cir 77429
Trail Meadow Ln 77429
Trailmeadow Ct 77429
Tranquility Park Dr 77429
Tree Arbor Ln 77429
Tree Star Ln 77433
Treeline Ln 77429
Trellis Estates Ct 77429
Tribe Dr 77429
Trinity Trl 77429
Trinity Trail Ct 77429
Triston Hill Ct 77433
Troon Oak St 77433
Trumbull Ridge Dr 77433
Trumpet Vine Ln 77433
Tuckerton Rd 77429
Tuhati Forest Ln 77433
Tulip Blossom Ct 77433
Tupelo Dr 77429
Tupper Bend Ct & Ln 77433
Turning Leaf Lake Ct 77433
Turning Limb Ct 77433
Turning Tree Way 77433
Turquoise Mist Dr 77433
Tuscana Shores Dr 77433
Tuskin Oaks Dr 77433
Twilight Creek Ln 77433
Twilight Grove Ln 77433
Twilight Knoll Trl 77429
Twin Sisters Dr 77429
S Twinberry Field Dr 77433
Twinkle Sky Ct 77433
Twisted Canyon Dr 77429
Twisted Leaf Dr 77433
Twisting Ivy Ln 77429
Twisting Springs Dr 77433
Twlight Knoll Trl 77429
Tyler Trails Ct 77433
Tylermont Dr 77429
Union Pointe Ct 77429
Urban Elm St 77429
Urbanna Ct 77429
Utah Oaks Ct 77433
Uvalde Springs Ln 77429
Val Verde Springs Ct 77433
Valebluff Ln 77429
Valley Cove Dr 77433
Valley Moon Ln 77433
Valley Plum Ct 77433
Valley Stone Ct 77429
Vanover Ln 77429
Vaulted Chestnut Ln 77433
Venezia Terrace Ct 77433
W Verde Creek Cir 77433
Vernon Rd 77429
Via Barolo 77429
Via Chianti Ct & Ln 77429
Via Davina Ln 77429
Via Davinci Ln 77429
Via Firenze Ln 77429
Via Michaelangelo Ct 77429
Via Palazzo Ln 77429
Via Pinetta 77429
Via Ponte Vecchio Ln 77429
Via Porta Rosa 77429
Via San Rocco Ct 77429
Via Siena Ct & Ln 77429
Via Torre De Pisa Ln 77429
Via Toscano Ct & Ln 77429
Vickers Rd 77433
Vicki Ln 77429
Victory Trace Ct 77429
Vidailia Pointe Dr 77429
Vienna Ct 77429
Village Cir 77429
Village Lake Dr 77429
Village Square Dr 77433
Vinca Ct 77429
Vincennes Oak St 77429
Vine Grove Ct 77433
Vinegrove Falls Ct 77433
Vinemoss Ln 77433
Vinery Ct & Ln 77429
Vintage Falls Dr 77433
Violet Haze Trl 77433
Violet Trace Ct 77433
Vista Heights Dr 77433
Vista Lake Ct 77433
Viviene Westmoreland Dr 77429
Waco Trails Cir 77429
Wade Haven Dr 77433
Wagon Bridge Ln 77433
Walbrook Meadows Ln 77433
Walden Gate Ln 77433
Wallach Dr 77429
Walnut Leaf Ln 77433
Warner Smith Blvd 77433
Water Bridge Dr 77433
Water Dance Ct 77433
Water Mill Dr 77429
Water Oak Ln 77429
Water Oak Bend Ct 77429
Water Oak Park Cir 77429
Water Scene Trl 77429
Watercypress Ct 77433
Watsons Bay Dr 77429
Waverly Bend Ln 77433
Waverly Canyon Ct 77429
Waverly Crest Ct 77429
Waverly Hill Ln 77429
Waverly Hollow Ln 77429
Waverly Springs Ln 77429
Wayfare Ct 77429
Wayne River Ct 77433
Waynewood Dr 77429
Wedgewood Park
  15400-15599 77429
  26300-26799 77433
Wedgewood Park Ct 77433
Welham Hester Cir 77429
Wenbury Dr 77429
Wendover Creek Ct 77429
Wessex Park Dr 77429
West Dr & Rd 77433
Westcliffe Ct 77433
Westgate Dr 77429
Westgate Park Dr 77433
Westgate Pasture Ln 77433
Westgate Springs Ln 77433
Westmore Dr 77429
Weston Oaks Dr 77429
Weston Park Dr 77433
Westover Dr 77429
Westridge Bend Ln 77433
Westwego Trl 77433
Wetherfield Ln 77429
S Whimsey Dr 77433
Whispering Cypress Dr 77429
Whispering Daisy Ct 77429
Whispering Green Dr 77429
Whispering Lake Ct 77429
Whispering Oak Dr 77429
Whispering Valley Dr 77429
Whispering Water Way 77433
Whispy Green Ct 77433
Whistling Wind Ln 77429
White Ash Ln 77433
White Barnwood Ct 77433
White Heron Dr 77433
White Hyacinth Ct & Dr 77433
White Oak Hl 77429
White Oak Creek Ct 77429
White Oak Falls Ct 77429
White Oak Gardens Dr 77429
White Oak Glen Ct 77429
White Oak Park Ct 77429
White Oak Point Ct 77429
White Oak Springs Dr 77429
White Oak Trace Ct & Dr 77429
White Rock Lake Trl 77433
White Sage Ct 77433
White Truffle Trl 77433
Wickhurst Pl 77429
Wilcant Ln 77429
Wild Current Way 77433
Wild Dove Ct 77429
Wild Ivy Ct 77429
Wild Rose Trl 77429
Wild Timber Trl 77433
Wild Turkey Dr 77429
Wild Yaupon Dr 77433
Wildberry Creek Ct 77433
Wilderness Rd 77429
Wildhurst Ln 77429
Wildwood Run 77429
Wildwood Bend Ln 77433
Wiley Martin Dr 77429
Wilks Dr 77433
William Dowdell Dr 77429
E & W Williams Bend Cir & Dr 77433
Williams Elm Dr 77433
Williams Oak Dr 77433
Williams Pine Dr 77433
Williams Ridge Ct 77433
Williams Willow Ln 77433
Willow Ln 77429
Willow Cliff Ln 77429
Willow Field Dr 77429
E & W Willow Oak Bend Dr 77433
Willow Trace Dr 77433
Willowbrook Dr 77429
Willowhurst Dr 77429
Wimberly Way 77429
Winbush Ct 77429
Wincrest Ct 77429
Wincrest Falls Dr 77429
Wind Mist Ln 77433
Windgate Ct 77433
E & W Windhaven Terrace Ct & Trl 77433
Winding Ln 77429
Winding Black Cherry Ln 77433
Winding Cypress Brook Dr 77429
Winding Oak Ct 77429
Winding Springs Dr 77429
Winding Waco Ct 77433
Winding Waters Dr 77433
Windmill Cove Ln 77429
Windsdowne Ln 77429
Windwood Park Ln 77429
Windy Grove Ln 77433
Windy Path Ln 77433
Windy Peak Ln 77433
Windy Thicket Ln 77433
Wine Meadow Ct 77429
Winebrook Ct 77429
Winesap Ln 77429
Wingborne Ln 77429
Winsome Rose Ct 77433
Winston Hill Dr 77433
Winter Rose Ct 77429
E & W Winter Violet Ct 77433
Wisteria Estates Ln 77429
Wisteria Springs Ct & Dr 77433
Wolf Branch Ct 77429
Woodcypress Ln 77429
Wooded Creek Ln 77433
Wooded Field Trl 77429
Wooded Glen Ct 77429
Wooded Tree Ln 77429
Woodford Hollow Ct & Ln 77429
Woodland Knoll Ln 77433
Woodland Orchard Ln 77433
Woodlawn Manor Ct 77429
Woods Spillane Blvd 77429
Woodsburgh Ln 77433
Woodside Dr & Ln 77429
Woodwind Shadows Dr 77433
Woodworth Dr 77429
Wrangler Run Ct 77429
Wynfield Dr 77429
Wynmar Ln 77429
Wytchwood Cir 77429
Yarrow Dr 77433
Yaupon Creek Dr 77433
Yaupon Mist Dr 77433
Yaupon Pass Dr 77433
Yaupon Point Ct 77433
Yaupon Ranch Ct & Dr 77433
Yaupon Ridge Ct 77433
Yaupon View Dr 77433
Yellow Begonia Dr 77433
N & W Yellow Bud Ct 77433
Yellow Daisy Ct 77433
Yellow Oak Trl 77433
Yellow Thrush Dr 77433
Yorkmont Dr 77429
Youngfield Dr 77429
Yucca Field Dr 77433
Yucca Valley Ln 77433
Yuma Ridge Ln 77433
Zenith Glen Ln 77429

NUMBERED STREETS

All Street Addresses 77429

DALLAS TX

General Delivery 75221

POST OFFICE BOXES MAIN OFFICE STATIONS AND BRANCHES

Box No.s
A - G 75208

3 - 2553 75221
2525 - 2525 75357
2634 - 3188 75221
3701 - 6401 75208
7000 - 7999 75209
7474 - 7474 75357
9001 - 9299 75209
9930 - 9930 75208
12000 - 25663 75225
29001 - 29972 75229
35001 - 36670 75235
38001 - 38902 75238
41001 - 41900 75241
50014 - 50965 75250
59001 - 59997 75229
75265 - 75265 75265
130001 - 139100 75313
140001 - 141380 75214
150001 - 159090 75315
170001 - 179130 75217
180001 - 189000 75218
190101 - 199810 75219
210001 - 212100 75211
214062 - 219099 75221
222000 - 229992 75222
259000 - 259005 75225
270001 - 279080 75227
299000 - 299625 75229
360001 - 362098 75336
397501 - 399100 75339
411001 - 411600 75241
420001 - 421502 75342
501013 - 509012 75250
515001 - 517036 75251
540001 - 549045 75354
550121 - 559500 75355
560001 - 569810 75356
570001 - 572136 75357
595004 - 596671 75359
600001 - 609008 75360
610001 - 619999 75261
620002 - 620068 75262
630005 - 630061 75263
640025 - 640025 75264
650001 - 659000 75265
660002 - 669100 75266
670000 - 670005 75267
670001 - 671392 75367
670200 - 679002 75267
679001 - 679012 75367
679738 - 679762 75267
700001 - 709020 75370
710001 - 711076 75371
720001 - 729083 75372
740001 - 749097 75374
761101 - 769100 75376
780001 - 781932 75378
793251 - 799900 75379
800001 - 809118 75380
810001 - 819120 75381
820001 - 829018 75382
902068 - 80902068 75380

RURAL ROUTES

78 75211
02 75241
08, 10, 12, 17, 19, 25, 26, 29, 39, 47, 48 75252
05, 06, 14 75253
07, 09, 11, 15, 16, 18, 22, 23, 28, 31, 33, 36, 37, 38, 40, 44 75287

NAMED STREETS

Aaron Cir 75233
Abbey Ct 75214
Abbey Ln 75234
Abbey Woods Ln 75248
Abbotsford Ct 75225
Abbott Ave 75205
Aberdeen Ave 75230
Aberdon Rd 75252
Abernathy Ave 75220
Abigale Ln 75253
Abilene St 75212
Ables Ln 75229
Ablon Dr 75234
Abraham Dr 75227
Abrams Ct 75231
Abrams Pkwy 75214
Abrams Rd
1200-5899 75214
5900-5998 75231
6000-6599 75231
6601-7399 75231
6640-8298 75231
6640-6640 75382
8300-9598 75243
9600-13000 75243
13002-13098 75243
Abrams Place Ct 75231
Abramshire Ave 75231
Abshire Ln 75228
Abston Ln 75218
Abuelo Ct 75211
Acacia St 75203
Academy Dr 75227
Academy Ln 75234
Acapulco Dr 75232
Accent Dr 75287
Acklin Dr 75243
Acme St 75241
Acoca St 75228
N & S Acres Dr 75217
Acuna Cir & St 75217
Adair St 75204
N & S Adams Ave 75208
Adbritain Dr 75211
Addeline St 75235
Addie Rd 75217
Addison Rd 75287
Addison St 75203
Adelaide Dr 75216
Adell Dr 75217
Adler Dr 75211
Adleta Blvd & Ct 75243
Adlora Ln 75238
Adolph St 75204
Adrian Dr 75209
Aero Dr 75209
Afton St 75219
Agnes St 75210
Ainsdale Ct 75252
Ainsworth Dr 75229
Aintree Cir 75214
Ainwick Ct 75227
Airelara Rd 75253
Airellia Ave 75209
E, N, S & W Airfield Dr 75261
Airhaven St 75229
Airline Ext 75205
Airline Rd
4901-4997 75205
4999-6700 75205
6702-7098 75205
9600-9699 75225
9701-9899 75230
N Akard St 75201
S Akard St
101-197 75202
199-812 75202
814-816 75202
1011-1097 75215
1099-1722 75215
1724-1928 75215
Akron St 75212
Al Patterson Dr 75241
Alabama Ave 75216
Aladdin Dr 75229
Alamain Dr 75241
Alamo St 75202
Alamosa Dr 75232
Alan Dale Ln 75209
Alaska Ave 75216
Albany St 75201
Albemarle Dr 75234
Albert Williams Dr 75241
Alberta Dr 75229
Albright St 75203
N Albrook Dr 75211
Alcalde St 75246
Alcazar Plz 75211
Alco Ave 75211
Alcorn Ave 75217
Alcott St
4700-4898 75204
4900-5299 75206
Alcova Ln 75249
Alden Ave 75211
Aldenwood Dr 75232
Alder Cir 75238
Alderson St 75214
Aldwick Cir & Dr 75238
Aledo Dr 75228
Alex St 75203
Alex David Cir 75232
Alexander Dr 75214
Alexander Ln 75247
Alexis Dr 75254
Alfalfa Dr 75248
Algebra Dr 75232
Algiers St 75207
Algonquin Dr 75217
Alhambra St 75217
Alicante Ave 75248
Alice Cir 75205
Alicia Cir 75287
Allegheny Ct & Dr 75229
Allegiance Dr 75237
Allegro Dr 75241
Allen St 75204
Allenbrook Ct 75243
Allencrest Ln 75244
Allentown Dr 75217
Allie Ln 75253
Allison Dr 75208
Allister St 75229
Allview Ln 75227
Allwood Ln 75229
Alma St 75215
Almazan Dr 75220
Almeda Dr 75216
Almond Ave 75247
Almorgodo Ave 75233
Alonzo Pl 75204
Alpaca Pass 75211
Alpha Rd
4000-4912 75244
4914-5098 75244
5200-7899 75240
7901-7999 75240
Alpine St 75223
Alsatian Ct 75253
Alsbury St 75216
Alta Ave 75206
Alta Mesa Dr 75241
Alta Mira Dr 75218
Alta Oaks Dr 75243
Alta Vista Cir & Ln 75229
Altacrest Dr 75227
Altadena Ln 75232
Altaire Ave 75241
Altamore Dr 75241
Altman Dr 75229
Alto Caro Dr 75248
Alto Garden Dr 75217
Alton Ave 75214
Altoona Dr 75233
Altura Ave 75228
Alva Ct 75220
Alvarado St 75233
Alvin St 75218
Amador Ave 75252
Amanda Ln 75238
Amapola Ave 75248
Amarosa Rd 75217
Ambassador Row 75247
Amber Dr 75241
Amber Ln 75234
Amber Hills Dr 75287
Ambergate Ln 75287
Amberley Dr 75243
Amberton Pkwy 75243
Amberwood Rd 75248
Ambrose Cir, Ct & Dr 75241
Amelia Ct & St 75235
Amerada Plz 75243
American Way 75237
Ames St 75225
Amesbury Dr 75206
Amherst Ave 75225
W Amherst Ave
2100-2699 75235
4500-5799 75209
Amherst Cir 75209
Amity Ln 75217
Amos St 75212
Amsterdam Rd 75234
Amy St 75217
Anaconda Dr 75217
Anaheim Dr 75229
Ancestry Ct & Ln 75217
Anchor Ridge Dr 75249
Anchorage Cir 75217
Andalusia Ave 75248
Anderson Ave 75211
Anderson St 75215
Andjon Dr 75220
Andora Ct 75287
Andover Dr 75228
Andrea Ln 75228
Andrews Ave 75211
Andy St 75212
Angel Fire Dr 75253
Angelica Way 75217
Angelina Dr 75212
Angelo St 75217
Angelus Rd 75217
Angier Way 75228
Angle View Dr 75248
Anglebluff Cir 75248
Anglecrest Dr 75227
Angleridge Rd 75238
Angleton Pl 75243
Angora St 75218
Angus Dr 75217
Anise Ln 75217
Anita St
5300-6099 75206
6100-6799 75214
Ann Ave 75223
E Ann Arbor Ave 75216
W Ann Arbor Ave 75224
Ann Kathryn Way 75236
Annabelle Ln 75217
Annapolis Ln 75214
Annarose Dr 75232
Annex Ave 75204
Anode Ln 75220
Ansley Ave 75235
Anson Cir & Rd 75235
Antares Ct 75252
Anthony St 75203
Antigua Cir & Dr 75244
Antler Ave 75217
Antoinette St 75217
Antrim Dr 75218
Anzio Dr 75224
Apache Dr 75217
Apollo Dr 75237
Appaloosa Dr 75237
Appian Way 75216
Apple Rdg 75287
Apple St 75204
Apple Creek Dr 75243
Apple Valley Dr 75234
Apple Valley Way 75227
Appleberry Dr 75253
Applecross Ln 75248
Appledale Ln 75287
Applegate Dr 75253
Appleton Dr 75216
Appollonia St 75204
Apricot St 75247
April Hill Ln 75287
Aqua Dr 75218
Araglin Ct 75230
Aramis Ln 75252
Aransas St 75212
Arapaho Rd 75248
Arawak Pl 75234
Arbargee Cir 75230
Arbol Verde Ct 75217
Arboleda Way 75248
Arbor Branch Dr 75243
Arbor Downs Dr 75248
Arbor Oaks Dr 75248
Arbor Park Ct & Dr 75243
Arbor Trail Dr 75243
Arborcrest Dr 75232
Arboreal Dr 75231
Arborgate St 75231
Arborhill Dr 75243
Arborside Dr
7700-7798 75231
8501-8997 75243
8999-9100 75243
9102-9198 75243
Arborvitae Ave 75224
Arbuckle Ct 75229
N & S Arcadia Dr 75211
Arcady Ave
4200-4599 75205
4600-4699 75209
Archbrook Dr 75232
Archdale Dr 75230
Archer Ave 75211
Archer Ct 75252
Archwood Ln 75248
Arden Rd 75241
Areba St 75203
Argentia Dr 75224
Argo St 75214
Argonne Dr 75208
Argyle Ave 75203
Ariel Dr 75232
Arizona Ave 75216
Arkan Pkwy 75241
Arlene Ln 75217
Arlington Park Dr 75235
Armstrong Ave & Pkwy 75205
S Army Ave 75211
Arnoldell St 75211
Arpege Cir 75224
Arrowdell Rd 75253
Arrowhead Dr 75204
Arroyo Ave 75219
Arroyo Verda Dr 75249
Artful Dr 75235
Arts Plz 75201
Arturo Dr 75228
Asbury St 75205
Ascot Ln 75214
Ash Ln
3201-3599 75226
4000-6200 75223
6202-6298 75223
Ash Bluff Ln 75248
Ash Creek Dr 75228
Ash Grove Way 75228
Ash Leaf Ct 75212
Ashbourne Dr 75248
Ashbrook Rd 75227
Ashby St 75204
Ashcrest Ln 75249
Ashcroft Ave 75243
Ashford Dr 75214
Ashglen Cir 75238
Ashington Dr 75225
Ashley Trl 75211
Ashmere Ct 75225
Ashmont Ct 75287
Ashridge Dr 75240
Ashton Ct 75230
Ashview Cir 75217
Ashwood Dr 75253
Asled Ct 75241
Aspen Dr 75227
Aspen Creek Ln 75252
Aspendale Dr 75253
Aspermont Ave 75216
Aster St 75211
Astoria Dr 75227
Atha Dr 75217
Athens Ave 75205
Atherton Dr 75243
Athlone Dr 75218
Atlanta St 75215
Atlantic St 75208
Atlas Dr 75216
Atoka St 75204
E & N Atoll Dr 75216
Aton St 75208
Atwell St
3300-3699 75235
3701-3799 75209
Atwood St 75203
Aubrey Ave 75235
Auburn Ave 75214
Auburndale Ave 75205
Audelia Rd
8501-9397 75238
9399-10899 75238
10900-11298 75243
11300-13100 75243
13102-13398 75243
Audrey St 75210
Audubon Pl 75220
N & S Augusta St 75214
Aurora Ave 75217
Authon Dr 75248
Autobahn Dr 75237
Autumn Way 75252
Autumn Leaves Trl 75241
Autumn Meadow Trl 75232
Autumn Oaks Dr 75243
Autumn View Cir 75249
Autumn Woods Trl 75232
Autumncrest Ct 75249
Ava Ln 75227
Avalon Ave 75214
Avalon Creek Ct 75230
Avant St 75215
Avenel Dr 75234
Avenue E 75203
Avenue A 75203
Avenue B 75203
Avenue D 75203
Avenue F 75203
Avenue G 75203
Avenue H 75203
Avenue I 75203
Avenue J 75203
Avenue L 75203
Avenue Q 75228
Averill Way 75225
Avery St 75208
Aviation Pl 75235
Avila Plz 75201
Avocado Dr 75241
Avon St 75211
Avondale Ave 75219
Axminster Ct 75214
Axton Cir & Ln 75214
Aylesport Dr 75201
Azalea Ln 75230
Aztec Dr 75216
Babalos Ln 75228
Babcock Dr 75212
Bacardi Dr 75238
Bachman Dr 75220
Baden St 75203
N & S Bagley St 75211
Bahama Dr 75211
Bainbridge Ave & Dr 75237
Baker Ave 75212
Bakersfield St 75233
Balalaika Rd 75241
Balboa Dr & Pl 75224
Balch Dr 75216
Balcony Ln 75241
Baldcypress Dr 75253
Baldwin St 75210
Balfour Pl 75219
Ball St 75216
Ballard Ave 75208
Bally Mote Dr 75218
Ballycastle Dr 75228
Baltimore Dr
6801-6897 75205
6899-7099 75205
7100-8698 75225
Balvanera Plz 75211
Bambi St 75217
Band Box Pl 75244
Bandera Ave 75225
Bandit Dr 75249
Banff Dr 75243
Bank St 75223
Banner Dr 75251
Banning St 75233
Bannister St 75252
Bannock Ave 75215
Banquo Dr 75228
Banting Way 75227
Bantry Cir & Ln 75248
Banyan Ln 75287
Bar Harbor Cir & Dr 75232
Bar X St 75228
Baraboo Dr 75241
Baralinc St 75212
Barbados Ct 75217
Barbaree Blvd 75228
Barbarosa Dr 75228
Barber Ave 75210
Barberry Dr 75211
Barcelona Dr 75254
Barclay St 75227
Bardwell Ave 75216
Barfield Dr 75252
Barge Ln 75212
Bargiames Ln 75238
Barksdale Ct 75211
Barkwood Ln 75248
Barkworth Dr 75248
Barlow Ave
1200-2399 75224
2400-2599 75233
Barnabus Dr 75241
Barnaby St 75243
Barnacle Dr 75249
Barnard Blvd 75211
Barnes Ave 75218
Barnes Bridge Rd
1600-1699 75218
1700-3300 75228
3302-4014 75228
N & S Barnett Ave 75211
Barney St 75217
Barnsbury Ct 75248
Baroness Dr 75229
Baronne Cir 75218
Barredo St 75217
Barree Dr 75241
Barrett Dr 75217
Barrington Ct 75252
Barry Ave 75223
N Barry Ave 75214
S Barry Ave 75223
Barrywood Dr 75230
Barstow Blvd 75236
Bartlett Ave 75216
Baseline Dr 75243
Basil Ct 75204
Bass Dr 75235
Basswood Dr 75241
Bastille Rd 75212
Bataan St 75212
Bateman Ave 75216
Bates St 75227
Baumgarten Dr 75228
Baxtershire Dr 75230
W Bay Cir 75214
Bay Meadows Cir & Ct 75234
Bay Oaks Dr 75229
Bay Pines Ln 75287
Bay Point Dr 75248
Bayard Cir 75243
Bayberry Ln 75249
Baylor St 75226
Baymar Ln 75252
Bayonne St 75212
Bayshore Pl 75217
Bayside St 75212
Baystone Dr 75211
Baythorne Dr 75243

Bayview Dr 75211
Baywood Dr 75217
Beachview St 75218
N Beacon St
100-398 75214
400-799 75214
801-999 75214
1200-1299 75206
S Beacon St
100-398 75214
400-1199 75223
Beacon Hill Cir 75217
Beaker Dr 75241
Beall St 75223
Beansout Dr 75248
Bearden Ln 75227
Beatrice St 75208
Beau Purple Dr 75211
Beauchamp Ave 75216
Beauford Rd 75253
Beaumont St 75215
Beauregard Dr 75225
Beauty Ln 75229
Beautycrest Cir, Ct & Dr 75217
Beaver St 75208
Beaver Brook Ln & Pl 75229
Beck Ave 75228
Becket Ridge Ct 75234
Beckington Ln 75287
N Beckley Ave
100-1899 75203
1900-2800 75208
2802-2998 75208
S Beckley Ave
100-1199 75203
1301-1397 75224
1399-3400 75224
3402-3898 75224
Beckley Hills Dr 75241
Beckley View Ave 75232
Beckleycrest Ave 75232
Beckleymeade Ave
200-798 75232
800-900 75232
902-2398 75232
2500-2598 75237
Beckleyside Dr 75241
Beckleywood Blvd 75224
Beckwith Ct 75248
Bedford St 75212
Bedivere Ct 75254
Bee St 75234
Beechmont Dr & Pl 75228
Beechnut St 75237
Beechwood Ln 75220
Beeman Ave 75223
Beeville St 75212
Begonia Ln 75233
Bekay St 75238
Bel Aire Dr 75218
Belclaire Ave
4200-4599 75205
4600-4699 75209
Belfield Dr 75234
Belford Dr 75214
Belfort Ave 75205
Belgrade Ave 75227
Belinda Ln 75227
Belknap Ave 75216
Bell Ave 75206
Bella Vista Dr 75218
Bellafonte Dr 75243
Bellbrook Dr
6300-6399 75217
14800-15099 75254
Bellcrest Dr 75241
Belle Starr Dr 75227
Belleau Dr 75208
Bellerive Dr 75287
Bellewood Dr 75238
Bellingham Ct & Dr 75228
Bellknoll Ln 75229
Bellview St 75215
Bellville Dr 75228
Belmar Ct 75287
Belmark Cir 75243
Belmead Dr 75230
Belmont Ave
4301-4497 75204
4499-4899 75204
4901-4997 75206
4999-5699 75206
5650-5650 75372
5700-6098 75206
5701-6099 75206
6100-6399 75214
Belrose Pl 75228
Belt Line Rd
3200-3498 75234
3500-3600 75234
3602-3698 75234
4800-7980 75254
7982-7998 75254
7989-7999 75248
S Belt Line Rd 75253
Belteau Ln 75227
Belton Dr 75287
E, N, S & W Beltwood Pkwy 75244
Belvoir Cir 75233
Ben Hur St 75253
Benares Dr 75243
Benavides Dr 75217
Benbow Dr 75232
Benbrook Dr 75228
Benchmark Dr
13700-13799 75234
17700-18099 75252
Bencrest Pl 75244
N & S Bend Dr 75229
Bending Oaks Trl 75217
Bendwood Ln 75287
Benedict Dr 75214
Bengal St 75235
Bennett Ave 75206
Benning Ave 75227
Bennington Dr 75214
Benrock St 75241
Benson St 75226
Bent Trl 75248
Bent Branch Ln 75243
Bent Brook Ct 75252
Bent Creek Trl 75252
Bent Oak Ct 75248
Bent Oak Ln 75287
Bent Oak Pl 75248
Bent Tree Dr 75248
Bent Tree Forest Cir & Dr 75248
Bentgreen Dr 75248
Bentham Ct 75227
Bentley Ave 75211
Bentwood Ct & Trl 75252
Bergen Ln 75234
Bergstrom Dr 75227
Berierin Dr 75241
Berkinshire Dr 75218
Berkley Ave 75224
Berkshire Ln
5700-5899 75209
5901-5947 75225
5949-6199 75225
Bermuda Rd 75241
Bermuda St 75214
Bernal Dr 75212
Bernardin Cir 75243
Bernice St 75211
Berridge Ln 75227
Berry Trl 75248
Berry Knoll Dr 75230
Berry Trail Ct 75248
Berryhill St 75231
Berrymeade Ln 75234
Bersount St 75208
Bert Ln 75240
Berthoud Pass 75252
Bertrand Ave
3101-3399 75215
3500-3598 75210
3600-4200 75210
4202-4398 75210
Berwick Ave 75203
Berwyn Ln 75214
Bessie Dr 75211
Best Dr 75229
Beta Rd 75244
Bethany Dr 75228
Bethpage Ave 75217
Bethurum Ave 75215
S Better Dr 75229
Betterton Cir 75203
Betty Jane Ln & Pl 75229
Bettyrae Way 75232
Bettywood Ln 75243
Beutel Ct 75229
Bevann Dr 75234
Beverly Dr
3100-4599 75205
4600-4699 75209
W Beverly Dr 75209
Bevington Rd 75248
Bexar St 75215
Bicentennial Ln 75253
Bickers St 75212
Bickham Rd 75220
Big Bend Dr 75287
Big Oaks St 75217
Big Sky Dr 75249
Big Thicket Dr 75217
Big Town Blvd 75227
Biggs St 75253
Biglow Dr 75216
Bigwood St 75211
Bilbrook Ln 75287
Bilco St 75232
Bill Browne Ln 75243
Bill Harrod St 75212
Bill Moses Pkwy 75234
Billie Dr 75232
Bimebella Ln 75211
Binkley Ave 75205
Birch Ave 75217
Birch St 75223
Birchbrook Dr 75206
Birchcroft Dr 75243
Birchlawn Dr 75234
Birchleaf Ct 75249
Birchmont Ln 75230
Birchridge Dr 75254
Birchwood Dr 75240
Bird Ln 75241
Birdsong Dr 75203
Birkenhead Ct 75204
Birmingham Ave 75215
Bisbee Dr 75227
Biscayne Blvd 75218
N Bishop Ave 75208
S Bishop Ave 75208
Bishop Ln 75244
Bishop Allen Ln 75237
Bishop College Dr 75241
Bismark Dr 75216
Bison Trl 75208
Bissonet Ave 75217
Bitter Creek Dr 75217
Bizerte Ave 75224
Black Berry Ln 75248
Black Gold Dr 75247
Black Hawk St 75212
Black Hickory Rd 75243
Black Oak Dr 75241
Black Otter Trl 75287
Black Rock Dr 75211
Black Walnut Ct & Dr 75243
Blackbird Ln 75238
Blackburn St
2900-3298 75204
3300-3399 75204
3400-3520 75219
3601-3799 75219
Blackheath Rd 75227
Blackjack Oaks Dr 75227
Blacksmith Dr 75253
Blackstone Dr 75237
Blackwell St 75231
Blackwillow Ct & Ln 75249
Blackwood Dr 75231
Blair Blvd 75223
Blair Rd 75231
Blairview Dr 75230
Blake Ave 75228
Blakeney St 75215
Blanch Cir 75214
Blanchard Dr 75227
Blaney Way 75227
Blanning Dr 75218
Blanton St 75227
Blaydon Dr 75228
Blaylock Dr 75203
Blessing Cir & Dr 75214
Bliss St 75203
Bloomfield Dr 75217
Blossom Ln 75227
Blossomheath Ln 75240
Blue Bay Dr 75248
Blue Bayou Dr 75253
Blue Bird Ave 75237
Blue Bonnet Rd 75209
Blue Creek Dr 75216
Blue Fire Ct 75248
Blue Grass Dr 75211
Blue Lake Cir 75244
Blue Meadow St 75217
Blue Mesa Dr 75252
Blue Mist Ln 75248
Blue Myrtle Way 75212
Blue Quail Ct 75241
Blue Ridge Blvd 75233
Blue Sage Dr 75249
Blue Scope Ln 75211
Blue Trace Ln 75244
Blue Valley Ln 75214
Bluebank Rd 75229
Blueberry Blvd 75217
Bluecrest Dr 75232
Bluefield Dr 75248
Bluestar Ln 75235
Bluestem Cir & Rd 75249
Bluewood Dr 75232
Bluff Park 75220
Bluff Dale Dr 75218
Bluff Point Dr 75248
Bluff Ridge Way 75206
Bluffcreek Dr 75227
Bluffman Dr 75241
Bluffton Dr 75228
Bluffview Blvd 75209
Bluitt Ave 75215
Blunter St 75241
Blystone Ln 75220
Blyth Dr 75228
Blythdale Dr 75248
Boaz St 75209
Bob O Link Dr 75214
Bobbie St 75203
Bobbitt Dr 75229
Boca Bay Dr 75244
Boca Chica Cir & Dr 75232
Boca Raton Dr
5100-5499 75229
5500-6199 75230
6201-6299 75230
Bocowood Dr 75228
Bodine Ln 75217
Boedeker Cir 75225
Boedeker Dr
6100-6198 75205
7700-8898 75225
9001-9599 75225
Boedeker St 75230
Boeing Ct 75228
Bogata Blvd & Pl 75220
Bohannon Dr 75217
Boisenberry Ln 75249
Bolero Ave 75217
Bolivar Dr 75220
Boll St 75204
Bolton Boone Dr 75237
Bomar Ave 75235
Bombay Ave 75235
Bon Aire Dr
100-299 75218
301-499 75218
5600-5799 75241
Bon Park Ct 75228
Bonanza Ct & Ln 75211
N & S Bond Ave 75211
Bondstone Dr 75218
Bonham St 75229
Bonita Ave 75206
Bonkirk Ln 75232
Bonnard Dr 75230
Bonnie View Rd
300-1799 75203
1800-2798 75216
2800-4899 75216
4900-8699 75241
8701-8899 75241
Bonnywood Ln 75233
Booker St 75215
Bookhout St 75201
Boomer Cir 75238
Boquillas Ct 75217
Bordeaux Ave
4200-4599 75205
4600-5698 75209
5700-6499 75209
Borger St 75212
Borich St 75210
Boston Pl 75217
Boswell St 75203
Botany Bay Dr 75211
Boulder Dr 75233
N Boulevard Ter 75211
Boundbrook Ave & Cir 75243
Bourbon St 75226
Bourquin St 75210
Bow Arrow Dr 75224
Bowen St 75204
Bowles Ln 75253
Bowling Ave 75210
Bowling Brook Dr 75241
Bowling Green Ave 75216
Bowman Blvd
9800-9999 75220
10000-10098 75229
Bowser Ave
3700-3798 75219
3800-4731 75219
5000-5200 75209
5202-5498 75209
Bowser Ct 75219
Boyd St 75224
Boynton St 75212
Bradbury Ln 75230
Braddock Pl 75232
Bradfield Rd 75217
Bradford Dr
4700-4899 75219
5000-5499 75235
Bradgate Ct 75248
Bradley St
400-499 75224
1600-1699 75208
Bradshaw St 75215
Brady Dr 75243
Brae Loch Dr 75217
Braeburn Dr 75214
Braemar Cir & Dr 75234
Braemore Pl 75230
Braewick Ct 75225
Braewood Pl 75248
Brahma Dr 75241
Braliso Row 75247
Bramlett Dr 75217
Branch Hollow Dr 75243
Branch Oaks Cir 75230
Branch View Ln 75234
Branchcrest Cir 75248
Branchfield Dr 75214
Brandeis Ln 75214
Brandenburg Ct 75287
Brandon St
1600-1799 75208
1801-2099 75208
2400-4599 75211
Brandywine Dr 75234
Brantley St 75212
Branwood Ln 75243
Brashear St 75210
Brass Way 75236
Bravura Ln 75217
Breakers Pt 75243
Breakpoint Trl 75252
Breakwood Dr 75227
Breckenridge Dr 75230
Bremen St 75206
Bremerton Ct & Dr 75252
Brendenwood Dr 75214
Brennans Dr & Pl 75214
Brenner Dr 75220
Brent Dr 75287
Brentcove Cir 75214
Brentfield Ct & Dr 75248
Brentgate Dr 75238
Brentridge Ct & Dr 75243
Brentwood Ave 75248
Bretshire Dr 75228
Bretton Bay Cir & Ln 75287
Bretton Creek Ct 75220
Bretton Woods Way 75220
Brewster St 75227
Briar Dr 75243
Briar Brook Ct 75218
Briar Cove Dr 75254
Briar Creek Ln 75214
Briar Oaks Cir 75287
Briar Ridge Rd 75287
Briar Tree Dr 75248
Briarbank Cir 75227
Briarbend Rd 75287
Briarbrook Dr 75234
Briarcliff Rd 75235
Briarcrest Cir & Dr 75224
Briarglen Cir & Dr 75211
Briargrove Ln 75287
Briarhaven Dr 75240
Briarhurst Dr 75243
Briaridge Rd 75248
Briarmeade Dr 75254
Briarmeadow Dr 75230
Briarnoll Dr 75252
Briarwood Ln & Pl 75209
Brichelm Dr 75287
Bridal Wreath Ln 75233
Bridge Hollow Ct 75229
Bridgegate Cir, Ct, Ln & Way 75243
Bridges St 75217
Bridget Ln 75218
Bridgeview Ln 75253
Bridgewater Ln 75211
Bridle Wood Dr 75211
Briercrest Dr 75217
Brierfield Cir & Dr 75232
Brierhill Dr 75217
Brierwood Ln 75217
Brierwyck Dr 75217
Brigade Ct 75225
Brigadoon Ln 75216
Briggs St 75227
Brigham Ln 75215
N Brighton Ave 75208
S Brighton Ave 75208
Brighton Grn 75252
Brightwood Dr 75217
Briley Rd 75217
Brincrest Cir & Dr 75234
Brisbane Ave 75234
N & S Briscoe Blvd 75211
Bristol Dr 75224
Britainway Ln 75228
Britt St 75236
Brittania Ct & Way 75243
Brittany Cir 75230
Britton Dr 75216
Brixey Dr 75216
Broadmoor Dr 75218
Brock St 75203
Brockbank Ct
3000-3099 75220
10737-10771 75229
Brockbank Dr
9500-9999 75220
10000-11099 75229
Brockham Cir 75217
Brockton Dr 75217
Brockway Dr 75234
Brockwood Rd 75238
Brodie St 75224
Broken Arrow Ln 75209
Broken Bow Rd 75238
Broken Tree Trl 75232
Bromfield St 75216
Bromwich Ct 75252
Bronco Dr 75237
Bronx Ave 75241
Bronze Way
4000-4399 75237
4400-4799 75236
Brook Lake Dr 75248
Brook Spring Dr 75224
Brook Terrace Trl 75232
Brook Valley Cir, Ct, Ln & Pl 75232
Brookcove Ln 75214
Brookcrest Dr 75240
Brookdale Dr 75235
Brooke Forrest Dr 75253
Brookfield Ave 75235
Brookgreen Cir & Dr 75240
Brookhaven Dr 75224
Brookhaven Club Dr 75234
Brookhill Ln 75230
Brookhollow Dr 75234
Brookhollow Rd 75235
Brookhurst Dr 75218
Brooklawn Dr 75237
Brookline Ln 75234
E Brooklyn Ave 75203
W Brooklyn Ave
200-2399 75208
2400-2899 75211
Brooklyndell Ave 75211
Brookmeadow Ln 75218
Brookmere Dr 75216
Brookport Dr & Pl 75229
Brookridge Cir 75254
Brookridge Dr 75240
Brookriver Dr 75247
Brooks Ave 75208
Brookshire Cir & Dr 75230
N & S Brookside Dr 75214
Brookstown Dr 75230
Brooktree Ln 75287
Brookview Dr 75220
Brookwood Dr 75224
Broom St 75202
Browder St
200-598 75201
600-999 75201
1101-1397 75215
1399-2000 75215
2002-2198 75215
Brown Pl & St 75219
Browning Ln 75230
E Brownlee Ave 75216
W Brownlee Ave 75224
Brownstone Ct 75204
Brownsville Ave 75216
Brownwood St 75217
Brundrette St
2001-2099 75208
4000-4099 75212
Brunner Ave 75224
Brunswick Dr 75220
Brushcreek Ln 75240
Brushfield Dr 75248
Brushy Creek Trl 75252
Bruton Rd 75217
Bruton Springs Dr 75227
Bryan Pkwy
5500-5506 75206
5508-6199 75206
6200-6499 75214
Bryan St
1503-1697 75201
1699-2299 75201
2301-2399 75201
2700-2998 75204
3000-4899 75204

4900-5499 ... 75206
5501-5513 ... 75206
Bryce Canyon Rd ... 75211
Bryn Mawr Dr
2900-4499 ... 75225
5400-5799 ... 75209
7600-7999 ... 75225
Bryson Dr ... 75238
Buchanan Dr ... 75228
Buckalew St ... 75208
Buckeye Cmns ... 75215
Buckeye Dr ... 75217
Buckingham Ct ... 75254
Buckingham Rd ... 75243
Bucknell Dr ... 75214
N Buckner Blvd
100-198 ... 75218
200-1599 ... 75218
1601-1699 ... 75218
1800-1998 ... 75228
2000-3799 ... 75228
S Buckner Blvd
100-2099 ... 75217
2100-5000 ... 75227
5002-5398 ... 75227
5501-5699 ... 75228
Buckskin Dr ... 75241
Buckthorne Cir ... 75243
Budd St ... 75215
Budeudy Dr ... 75253
Budtime Ln ... 75217
Buena Vista St
3900-4199 ... 75204
4200-4500 ... 75205
4502-4598 ... 75205
Buffalo Creek Pl ... 75230
Buffridge Trl ... 75252
Buford Dr ... 75241
Buick Ave ... 75203
Bulova St ... 75216
Bumelia Ct ... 75253
Buna Dr ... 75211
Bunchberry Dr ... 75243
Bunche Dr ... 75243
Burbank St ... 75235
Burger Ave ... 75215
Burgoyne St ... 75233
Burgundy Rd ... 75230
Burleson Dr ... 75243
Burlew St ... 75204
Burlingdell Ave ... 75211
Burlington Blvd
900-2299 ... 75208
2301-2399 ... 75208
2401-2497 ... 75211
2499-2899 ... 75211
Burlywood Dr ... 75217
Burma Rd ... 75216
Burnet Ct ... 75217
Burney Dr ... 75243
Burnham Dr ... 75243
Burning Light Dr ... 75228
Burninglog Ln ... 75243
Burns Ave ... 75211
Burns Ct ... 75235
Burns Run ... 75248
Burnside Ave
4800-5099 ... 75216
5100-5199 ... 75241
Burrell Dr ... 75232
Burroaks Cir & Dr ... 75217
Burwood Ln ... 75214
Bushel Ln ... 75241
Bushire Dr ... 75229
Bushmills Rd ... 75243
Butler St ... 75235
Buttercup Ln ... 75217
Butternut St ... 75212
Buttonwood Ct ... 75287
Buxhill Dr ... 75238
Byron Ave ... 75205
Byway St ... 75211
C F Hawn Fwy
6200-11299 ... 75217
11300-14099 ... 75253
Caballero Cir ... 75236

Cabana Ln ... 75229
Cabell Dr ... 75204
Cablewood Cir ... 75227
Cabo San Lucas Dr ... 75217
Cabot Dr ... 75217
Cabrera Dr ... 75228
Cabrillo Ln ... 75253
Cactus Ln ... 75238
Caddo St ... 75204
Caddo Leaf Ct ... 75212
Cade Pkwy & Rd ... 75217
Cadenza Ln ... 75228
Cadillac Dr ... 75203
Cadiz St
100-298 ... 75207
300-399 ... 75207
800-1098 ... 75215
1100-1199 ... 75215
1400-2299 ... 75201
Cahuenga Ave ... 75248
Caillet St ... 75209
Cain Blvd ... 75211
Caladium Dr
5200-5499 ... 75229
5500-5899 ... 75230
Calais Dr ... 75254
Calculus Dr ... 75244
Calcutta Dr ... 75241
Calder St ... 75216
Caldwell St ... 75223
California Dr ... 75204
California Crossing Rd ... 75220
Calla Dr ... 75252
Calle Bella Dr ... 75211
Calle Del Oro Ln ... 75217
Calm Meadow Rd ... 75248
Calmar St ... 75217
Caltha Dr ... 75253
Calumet Ave ... 75211
Calvary Ave ... 75204
Calvert St ... 75247
Calvin St ... 75204
Calypso St ... 75212
Calyx Cir ... 75216
Camacho Plz ... 75201
Cambria Blvd ... 75214
Cambrick St ... 75204
Cambridge Ave ... 75205
Cambridge Gate Dr ... 75252
Cambridge Square Dr ... 75228
Camden Ave ... 75206
Cameanc Dr ... 75249
Camel Ct ... 75241
Camellia Dr ... 75230
Camelot Dr ... 75229
Cameo Ln ... 75234
Cameron Ave ... 75223
Camille Ave ... 75252
E Camp Wisdom Rd ... 75241
W Camp Wisdom Rd
101-197 ... 75232
199-1899 ... 75232
1901-1999 ... 75232
2601-2797 ... 75237
2799-4356 ... 75237
4358-4398 ... 75237
6363-6997 ... 75236
6999-7404 ... 75236
7406-7502 ... 75236
8100-8498 ... 75249
8500-8999 ... 75249
Campanella Dr ... 75243
Campbell Rd
5900-7699 ... 75248
17200-19799 ... 75252
Campbell St ... 75204
Campfire Cir ... 75232
Campus Dr ... 75217
Canaan St ... 75215
Canada Dr ... 75212
Canal St ... 75210
Canary Dr ... 75216
Canary Island Ct ... 75217
Canberra St ... 75224
Canby St ... 75235
Cancun Ln ... 75287

Candlebrook Dr ... 75243
Candlefire Ct ... 75248
Candlelight Ln ... 75229
Candlenut Ln ... 75244
Candlewick Ln ... 75234
Candlewood Pl ... 75217
Canelo Dr ... 75232
Cannan St ... 75215
Cannen John Ln ... 75204
Canongate Dr ... 75248
Cansler Dr ... 75252
Canson St ... 75233
Cantabria Dr ... 75248
Cantata Ct ... 75241
Cantegral St ... 75204
Canter Dr ... 75231
E, N, S & W Canterbury Ct ... 75208
Canterview Cir & Dr ... 75228
Canton St
1701-1797 ... 75201
1799-2300 ... 75201
2302-2498 ... 75201
2425-2697 ... 75226
2699-3799 ... 75226
Cantura Dr ... 75217
E Canty St ... 75203
W Canty St ... 75208
Canvasback Ln ... 75249
Canyon Crst ... 75248
Canyon Dr ... 75209
Canyon St ... 75203
Canyon Lake Dr ... 75249
Canyon Ridge Dr ... 75227
Canyon Springs Rd ... 75248
Cape Ct ... 75230
Cape Cod Dr ... 75216
Cape Coral Dr ... 75287
Capella Park Ave ... 75236
Capestone Dr ... 75217
N & S Capistrano Dr ... 75287
Capitol Ave
3922-3998 ... 75204
4000-4810 ... 75204
4900-5199 ... 75206
5201-5299 ... 75206
Capps Dr ... 75209
Capri Ct & Dr ... 75238
Capridge Dr ... 75238
Capriola Ln ... 75228
Caprock Cir ... 75218
Captains Cv ... 75249
Capulet Pl ... 75252
Caracas Dr ... 75232
Caravan Trl ... 75241
Caravelle Ct ... 75217
Carbona Dr ... 75217
Carbondale St ... 75216
Cardella Ave ... 75217
Cardiff St ... 75241
Cardinal Dr ... 75216
Carey Ln ... 75253
Caribou Trl ... 75238
Carillon Dr ... 75240
Carioca Cir, Dr & Pl ... 75241
Carissa Cir & Dr ... 75218
Carl St ... 75210
Carlin Dr ... 75209
Carlisle St
2501-2599 ... 75201
2801-2897 ... 75204
2899-3300 ... 75204
3302-3498 ... 75204
Carlson Dr ... 75235
Carlton Garret St ... 75215
Carmarthen Ct ... 75225
Carmel St ... 75204
Carnegie Dr & Pl ... 75228
Carnes St ... 75208
Carol Ln ... 75247
Carolina Oaks Dr ... 75227
Carolyncrest Dr ... 75214
Carom Way ... 75217
Caroridge Dr ... 75248
Carpenter Ave
2500-3399 ... 75215

3501-3597 ... 75210
3599-4399 ... 75210
Carr St ... 75227
Carriage Ln ... 75248
Carrick St ... 75234
Carrington Dr ... 75254
Carrizo St ... 75229
N Carroll Ave
111-115 ... 75226
205-313 ... 75246
315-319 ... 75246
321-899 ... 75246
1000-1012 ... 75204
1014-2700 ... 75204
2702-2898 ... 75204
S Carroll Ave
104-112 ... 75226
114-133 ... 75226
135-305 ... 75226
402-412 ... 75223
414-1016 ... 75223
1018-1114 ... 75223
Carrollwood Dr ... 75252
Carrousel Cir ... 75214
Carry Back Cir & Pl ... 75229
Carson Dr ... 75287
Carson St ... 75216
Carta Valley Ct & Dr ... 75248
Cartagena Pl ... 75228
Carter Rd ... 75217
Carter St ... 75210
Carterette Ln & Pl ... 75229
Carthage Ln ... 75243
Carthay Ave ... 75248
Cartwright St ... 75212
Caruth Blvd
3100-4499 ... 75225
5415-5423 ... 75209
5425-5764 ... 75209
7400-7799 ... 75225
Caruth Ct ... 75225
Caruth Haven Ln
5445-5497 ... 75225
5499-5599 ... 75225
5700-5799 ... 75206
Cary St ... 75227
Casa Del Sol Ln ... 75228
Casa Grande Dr ... 75253
Casa Loma Ave ... 75214
Casa Oaks Dr ... 75228
Casa Vale Dr ... 75218
Casa View Dr ... 75228
Casablanca Ct ... 75248
Casaverde Ave ... 75234
Cascade Ave ... 75224
Casey St ... 75215
Cash Rd ... 75247
Casino Dr ... 75224
Casnett Dr ... 75217
Cass St ... 75235
Cassandra Way ... 75228
Cassia Dr ... 75232
Cassidy Ln ... 75217
Cassie Ct ... 75232
Castillo Dr ... 75236
Castle St ... 75208
Castle Bay Dr ... 75227
Castle Bend Dr ... 75287
Castle Hills Dr ... 75241
Castle Pines Dr ... 75252
Castlecreek Ct ... 75225
Castlefield Dr ... 75227
Castlegate Dr ... 75229
Castlerock Dr ... 75217
Castleton Cir, Dr & Pl ... 75234
Castlewood Rd ... 75229
Castolon Dr ... 75228
Catalonia Dr ... 75217
Catalpa Rd ... 75243
Catamore Ln ... 75229
Catawba Rd ... 75209
Cathedral Dr ... 75214
Catherine St ... 75211
Cathys Pl ... 75252
Catina Ln ... 75229
Catron Dr ... 75227

Catskill St ... 75217
Cattle Dr ... 75241
Caulfield Dr ... 75248
Cauthorn Dr ... 75210
Cavalier Cir ... 75227
Cave Dr ... 75249
N & S Cavender St ... 75211
Cavendish Ct ... 75225
Cayo Blanco Ct ... 75217
Cayuga Dr ... 75228
Cecille Ave ... 75214
Cedar Ln ... 75234
Cedar Bayou Dr ... 75244
Cedar Bend Dr ... 75244
Cedar Bluff Ln ... 75253
N & S Cedar Circle Dr ... 75237
Cedar Creek Ln ... 75252
Cedar Creek Canyon Dr ... 75252
Cedar Crest Blvd ... 75203
Cedar Elm Cir ... 75211
Cedar Elm Ln ... 75212
Cedar Falls Dr ... 75232
Cedar Forest Trl ... 75236
Cedar Glen Dr ... 75232
Cedar Grove Dr ... 75241
Cedar Haven Ave ... 75216
Cedar Hill Ave ... 75208
Cedar Hollow Dr ... 75248
Cedar Knoll Dr ... 75236
Cedar Lake Dr ... 75227
Cedar Mound Dr ... 75241
Cedar Mountain Cir ... 75217
Cedar Oaks Blvd ... 75216
Cedar Path Dr ... 75211
Cedar Point Dr ... 75241
Cedar Post Ct ... 75227
Cedar Ridge Dr ... 75236
Cedar Rock Dr ... 75241
Cedar Run Dr ... 75227
Cedar Shadow Dr ... 75236
Cedar Springs Rd
1600-1698 ... 75202
1700-1799 ... 75202
1900-2699 ... 75201
2701-2799 ... 75201
3401-3497 ... 75219
3499-4899 ... 75219
4900-8099 ... 75235
Cedar Thicket Dr ... 75249
Cedar Tone Dr ... 75211
Cedar Tree Ln ... 75236
Cedar Valley Ln ... 75232
Cedar Waxwing Ln ... 75236
Cedar Way Dr ... 75241
Cedar Wood Dr ... 75241
Cedarbrier Dr ... 75236
Cedarbrook Dr ... 75248
Cedarbrush Dr ... 75229
Cedarcliff Dr ... 75217
Cedarcroft Ln ... 75233
Cedardale Dr & Rd ... 75241
Cedarhurst Dr ... 75233
Cedarplaza Ln
3100-3499 ... 75235
3500-3799 ... 75209
Cedarvale Ct ... 75217
Cedarview Rd ... 75287
Cedro Pl ... 75230
Celeste Dr ... 75217
Celestial Pl & Rd ... 75254
Centenary Ave ... 75225
Centennial Dr ... 75217
SW Center Mall ... 75237
Center Court Dr ... 75243
Centeridge Dr ... 75249
Centerville Rd
1201-1297 ... 75218
1299-1300 ... 75218
1302-1398 ... 75218
1500-2800 ... 75228
2802-2998 ... 75228
Central Ct ... 75204
N Central Expy
100-104 ... 75201
802-2298 ... 75204

2300-4199 ... 75204
4200-8398 ... 75206
4201-6499 ... 75205
8201-8699 ... 75225
8500-8798 ... 75231
8800-10900 ... 75231
10902-10998 ... 75231
11100-13999 ... 75243
S Central Expy
3000-3598 ... 75215
3600-5099 ... 75215
5101-5599 ... 75215
6901-6997 ... 75216
6999-7900 ... 75216
7902-7998 ... 75216
8100-9599 ... 75241
9601-10399 ... 75241
Central Market Ln ... 75201
Centre St ... 75208
S Cesar Chavez Blvd
101-397 ... 75201
399-800 ... 75201
802-1230 ... 75201
1700-1898 ... 75215
1900-2699 ... 75215
Cessna Ct ... 75228
Chackbay Ln ... 75227
Chadbourne Rd ... 75209
Chadwell Dr ... 75234
Chadwick Ct ... 75248
Chairman Dr ... 75243
Chalet Ln ... 75232
Chalfont Cir, Ct & Pl ... 75248
Chalk Canyon Dr ... 75249
Chalk Hill Rd ... 75212
Chalkstone Dr ... 75248
Challaburton Dr ... 75234
Challedon Ln ... 75211
Challenger Dr ... 75237
Chalmers St
900-1000 ... 75211
1002-1098 ... 75211
2600-2899 ... 75233
Chambers St ... 75206
Champa Dr ... 75218
Champagne Dr ... 75224
Chancellor Row ... 75247
Chandler Ct & Dr ... 75243
Channel Dr ... 75229
Channelbrook Ct ... 75287
Channing Cir ... 75224
Chantilly Ct & Ln ... 75214
Chanute Ct ... 75211
Chaparral Dr ... 75234
Chapel Creek Cir & Dr ... 75220
Chapel Downs Dr ... 75229
Chapel Hill Rd ... 75214
Chapel Mesa Ct ... 75249
Chapel Valley Rd ... 75220
Chapel View Dr ... 75234
Chapelridge Ct & Dr ... 75249
Chapelwood Way ... 75228
Chaporal Pl ... 75253
Chappell St ... 75208
Chapultepec Plz ... 75201
Charade Dr ... 75214
Charba St ... 75210
Charcoal Ln ... 75234
Charing Cross Ln ... 75238
Chariot Dr ... 75227
Charlemagne Dr ... 75216
Charles Ct ... 75217
Charles St ... 75228
Charlestown Dr ... 75230
Charlie Bird Pkwy ... 75234
Charlmont Cir ... 75248
Charmwood St ... 75211
Charolais Dr ... 75241
Chart Dr ... 75228
Chartwell Dr ... 75243
Chateau Dr ... 75217
Chatham Hill Rd
5401-5497 ... 75220
5499-5599 ... 75220
5700-5799 ... 75225
Chatham Square Ct ... 75227
Chatsworth Dr ... 75234

Chattanooga Pl ... 75235
Chattington Dr ... 75248
Chaucer Ln ... 75244
Chaucer Pl ... 75237
Checota Dr ... 75217
Chellen Dr ... 75234
Chelmsford Dr ... 75217
Cheltenham Way ... 75230
Chemical St ... 75207
Chenault St ... 75228
Chepstow Ct ... 75248
Cherbourg St ... 75216
Cherokee Trl ... 75209
Cherry Glen Ln ... 75232
Cherry Hill Dr ... 75243
Cherry Hills Dr ... 75234
Cherry Laurel Ln ... 75211
W Cherry Point Dr ... 75232
Cherry Ridge Ct ... 75229
Cherry Tree Dr ... 75243
Cherry Valley Blvd ... 75241
Cherrybrook Dr ... 75217
Cherrycrest St ... 75228
Cherrystone Rd ... 75253
Cherrywood Ave ... 75235
Cheryl Ln ... 75224
Chesapeake Dr ... 75217
Chesley Ln ... 75214
Chesterfield Dr ... 75237
Chesterton Dr ... 75238
Chestnut St ... 75226
Cheswick St ... 75218
Chevella Dr ... 75232
Chevez Dr ... 75211
Chevy Chase Ave ... 75225
Cheyenne Rd ... 75217
Chicago St ... 75212
Chicory Ct ... 75214
Chicot Dr ... 75230
Chihuahua Ave ... 75212
Childers St ... 75203
Childs St ... 75203
Chilmark Ct & Way ... 75227
Chilton Dr ... 75227
Chimney Corner Ln ... 75243
Chimney Hill Ln ... 75243
Chimney Sweep Ln ... 75243
China Elm Dr ... 75212
China Lake Dr ... 75253
China Tree Dr ... 75249
Chinaberry Rd ... 75249
Chinkapin Way ... 75212
Chippendale Dr ... 75238
Chipperton Dr ... 75225
Chippewa Dr ... 75212
Chipping Way ... 75252
Chireno St ... 75220
Chisholm Trl ... 75243
Chiswell Rd ... 75238
Chloe Way ... 75236
Choate Rd ... 75241
Choice St ... 75215
Choir St ... 75237
Chorus Way ... 75237
Christensen Dr ... 75227
Christian Ct ... 75237
Christian Pkwy ... 75234
Christie Ln ... 75249
Christopher Pl ... 75204
Chrysalis Dr ... 75237
Chrysler Dr ... 75203
Chuck Taylor Dr ... 75232
Chula Vista Dr ... 75227
Church Cir ... 75238
Church Rd
9000-9299 ... 75231
9401-9597 ... 75238
9599-10699 ... 75238
Church St ... 75203
Churchill Ave ... 75227
Churchill Ct ... 75230
Churchill Way
6000-6999 ... 75230
7001-7199 ... 75230
7601-7897 ... 75251
7899-7900 ... 75251

7902-7978 75251
Churchill Green Dr 75228
Cibola Dr 75211
Cicero St 75216
Cimarec St 75218
Cimmaron Trl 75243
Cinco St 75234
Cinda Ree Ln 75216
Cinderella Ln 75229
Cindy Ln 75229
Cinnabar Dr 75227
Cinnamon Oaks Ct &
Dr 75241
Circle Dr 75224
W Circle Dr 75214
Circle Bluff Ct 75244
Circlewood Dr 75217
N Cisco St 75246
Citadel Dr 75217
Citation Dr 75229
City Market Ln 75201
City Side Ln 75201
Cityplace West Blvd 75204
Claibourne Blvd 75212
Clamath Dr 75204
Claremont Dr 75228
Claren Ct 75252
Clarence St 75215
E Clarendon Dr 75203
W Clarendon Dr
100-2399 75208
2400-2598 75211
2600-4400 75211
4402-4598 75211
Clark Rd
8100-8200 75236
8202-8398 75236
8401-10399 75249
Clark St 75204
Clark College Dr 75241
Clark Vista Dr 75236
Clarkridge Dr 75236
Clarksdale Dr & Pl 75228
Clarksprings Dr 75236
Clarktown Ct 75236
Clarkview Dr 75236
Clarkwood Dr 75236
Clary Dr 75218
Classen Dr 75218
Claude St 75203
Claudette Ave 75211
Claudia Ln 75217
Clay St 75204
Clay Academy Blvd S .. 75236
Claybrook Dr 75231
Clayco Dr 75243
Claymont Dr 75227
Claymore Dr 75243
Clayshire Cir 75231
Clayton Ave 75214
Clayton Oaks Dr 75227
Clear Bay Dr 75248
Clear Cove Ln 75244
Clear Creek Rd 75232
Clear Fork Dr 75232
Clear Ridge Dr 75248
Clear Springs Rd 75240
Clearbrook Ln 75218
Clearcrest Dr 75217
Cleardale Dr 75232
Clearfield Rd 75217
Clearglen Dr 75232
Clearhaven Cir & Dr 75248
Clearhurst Dr 75238
Clearlake Dr 75225
Clearmeadow Dr 75238
Clearpoint Dr 75217
Clearview Cir
2000-2399 75224
2400-2799 75233
Clearwater Dr 75243
Clearwood Dr 75232
Cleary Cir 75248
Cleaves St 75203
Clements St 75214
Clemson Dr 75214

Clendenin Ave 75228
Clermont St 75223
Cleveland Rd 75241
Cleveland St 75215
N & S Cliff St 75203
Cliff Creek Dr 75233
Cliff Creek Crossing
Dr 75237
Cliff Gables Dr 75211
Cliff Haven Ct & Dr 75236
Cliff Heights Cir 75241
Cliff Ridge Dr 75249
Cliff Teen Ct 75233
Cliffbrook Dr 75254
Cliffdale Ave 75211
Cliffmere Dr 75238
Cliffoak Dr 75233
Clifford Dr 75220
Clifford Jackson St 75210
Cliffside Dr 75227
Cliffview Dr 75217
Cliffwood Dr 75237
N Clinton Ave 75208
S Clinton Ave
100-1099 75208
1400-1498 75224
1601-1799 75224
Clodus Fields Dr 75251
Cloister Dr 75228
Cloudcroft Cir 75224
Clover Ln 75220
Clover St 75226
Clover Haven Cir, Ct &
St 75227
Clover Meadow Dr
8400-8499 75231
8500-8799 75243
Clover Ridge Dr 75216
Clover Valley Dr 75243
Cloverbrook Ln 75253
Cloverdale Ln 75234
Cloverglen Dr 75249
Cloverhill Rd 75253
Clovis Ave 75233
Club Cir 75208
Club Creek Cir 75238
Club Crest Dr 75248
Club Glen Dr 75243
Club Hill Cir, Ct, Dr, Ln
& Pl 75248
Club Lake Ct 75214
Club Manor Dr 75237
Club Meadows Dr 75243
Club Oaks Cir, Ct, Dr, Pl
& Plz 75248
Club Terrace Dr 75237
Club Wood Dr 75237
Clubhouse Cir 75240
Clubview Dr 75232
Clubway Ln 75244
Clydedale Dr 75220
Clymer St 75212
Coach Light Rd 75237
Coahuila Dr 75217
Coalson Ave 75216
Cobblers Cir & Ln 75287
Cobblestone Cir 75229
Cobblestone Dr
3900-3999 75229
13600-13699 75244
Cochran Bluff Ln 75220
Cochran Chapel Cir &
Rd 75209
Cochran Creek Ct 75220
Cochran Heights Ct &
Dr 75220
Cochran Oaks Ln 75220
Cockatiel Ln 75236
Cockrell Ave 75215
S Cockrell Hill Cir 75211
N Cockrell Hill Rd
100-118 75211
120-1719 75211
1721-1799 75211
2201-2299 75212
S Cockrell Hill Rd
101-147 75211

149-2500 75211
2502-2898 75211
2900-6200 75236
6202-8198 75236
Cody Dr 75228
Coelum Ct 75253
Coit Rd
11901-12097 75251
12099-12300 75251
12302-12998 75251
13000-14099 75240
14101-14799 75254
14801-17299 75248
17300-18199 75252
Colada Ct 75248
Colbert Way 75218
Colby St
2501-2599 75201
2600-2699 75204
Colchester Dr 75234
Cold Harbor Ln 75244
Cold Springs St 75217
Cold Town Ln 75211
Coldbrook Ln 75253
Coldwater Cir 75228
Cole Ave
2600-2700 75204
2702-4199 75204
4200-4999 75205
Cole St 75207
Colebrook Dr 75217
Colegrove Dr 75248
Coleman Ave 75215
Coleridge St 75218
Coles Manor Pl 75204
Coleshire Dr 75232
Colewood Ln 75243
Colfax Dr 75231
Colgate Ave 75225
Colhurst St 75230
College Way 75241
College Park Dr 75229
N Collett Ave 75214
Collier St 75223
Collingwood Dr 75234
Collins Aly & Ave 75210
Collinway Pl 75230
Collville Ave 75235
Colmar St 75218
Colonial Ave 75215
Colony Ct 75235
E Colorado Blvd 75203
W Colorado Blvd
100-198 75208
200-2099 75208
2100-3199 75211
3201-3299 75211
N Colson St 75246
Colt Ln 75237
Colten James Ln 75204
Colter Way 75227
Columbia Ave
4500-4899 75226
4900-5899 75214
5901-5999 75214
Columbia Center Dr 75229
Columbine Ave 75241
Columbus St 75204
Colwick Dr 75216
Comal St 75203
Comer Dr 75217
Comerica Ctr 75201
Commerce St
100-399 75207
500-598 75202
600-1099 75202
1100-1114 75242
1101-1399 75202
1200-1230 75202
1401-1497 75201
1499-2299 75201
2600-4199 75226
W Commerce St
100-2099 75208
2101-2297 75212
2299-3099 75212
3101-3299 75212

Commodore Dr 75215
Commonwealth Dr 75247
Communications Dr 75211
Community Dr 75220
Compass Ridge Dr 75249
Composite Dr
10700-10999 75220
11001-11099 75229
Compton St 75203
Comstock St 75208
Conant St 75207
Concerto Ln 75241
Concho St 75206
Concord Ave 75235
Concordant Trl 75237
Concordia Ln 75241
Congo St 75223
Congress Ave & Pl 75219
Congressman Ln 75220
Conklin St 75212
Connaught Ct 75225
Connecticut Ln 75214
Connector Dr 75220
Conner Dr 75217
Conner St 75204
Connerly Dr 75205
Conrad St 75224
Conroe St 75212
Constance St 75220
Constitution Dr 75229
Continental Ave 75207
Contour Dr 75248
Control Pl 75238
Convent St 75204
Converse St 75207
Conveyor Ln 75247
Conway St 75224
Coogan Dr 75229
Cookscreek Pl 75234
Cool Mist Ln 75253
Cool Morn Dr 75241
Coolair Dr 75218
Coolglen Dr 75248
Coolgreene Dr 75228
Coolidge St 75215
Coolmeadow Ln 75218
Coolwater Cv 75252
Coolwood Dr 75248
Coombs St 75215
Coombs Creek Dr
400-598 75211
600-2599 75211
2601-2799 75211
2900-3199 75233
Coombsville Ave 75212
Cooper St 75215
Copeland St 75210
Copenhill Rd 75240
Coppedge Ln
9900-9999 75220
10000-10499 75229
Copper Creek Dr 75248
Copper Stone Dr 75287
Copperhill Dr 75248
Coppertowne Ct & Ln .. 75243
Copperwood Ln 75248
Coral Dr 75243
Coral Cove Dr 75243
Coral Gables Dr 75229
Coral Harbour Cir &
Ct 75234
Coral Hills Ct, Dr & Pl .. 75229
Coral Ridge Dr 75287
Coral Rock Ln 75229
Corday St 75218
Cordova St 75223
Core St 75207
Coriander Pl 75217
Corinth St
100-198 75207
200-599 75207
1001-1297 75215
1299-2199 75215
Corinth Street Rd 75216
N Corinth Street Rd 75203
S Corinth Street Rd 75203

Cork Ln 75231
Cork Oak Cir 75227
Corkwood Rd 75238
Cornelia Ln 75214
Cornell Ave 75205
Cornerstone Pkwy 75225
E Corning Ave 75216
W Corning Ave 75224
Corona St 75214
Coronado Ave & Way .. 75214
Coronet Blvd 75212
Corporate Dr 75228
Corral Dr 75237
Corregidor St 75216
Corrigan Ave
4500-4899 75216
4900-5199 75241
Corrigan Ct 75241
Corsicana St 75201
Cortez Dr 75220
Cortland Ave 75235
Cortleigh Pl 75209
Corto Dr 75218
Corvallis Dr 75229
Corvette Dr 75217
Cory St 75217
Cosgrove Dr 75231
Cosmo Ave 75248
Costa Mesa Dr 75228
Costera Ln 75248
Coston Dr 75217
Coteau Way 75227
Cotillion Ct & Dr 75228
Cotswold Ct 75220
Cottage Ln 75204
Cotton Ln 75216
Cottonseed Ter 75253
Cottonvalley Rd 75232
Council St 75215
Countess Dr 75229
Country Ln 75253
Country Brook Dr 75287
Country Club Cir 75214
Country Club Dr 75218
Country Creek Ct &
Dr 75236
Country Market Ln 75201
N & S Counts Blvd 75211
County Cork Dr 75218
County View Rd 75249
Courtdale Dr 75234
Courtland Dr 75287
Courtney St 75217
Courtshire Dr 75229
Courtyard Cir & Pl 75234
Cove Dr 75216
Cove Hollow Dr 75224
Covecreek Pl 75240
Covehaven Dr 75252
Covemeadow Dr 75238
Coventry Ct 75230
Cover Dr 75241
Coveridge Dr 75238
Covewood Cir 75248
Covey Ct 75238
Covington Ln 75214
Cowan Ave 75209
Cowart St 75211
Cowboy Dr 75237
Cox Ln
10500-10800 75229
10802-11398 75229
11901-12197 75244
12199-12300 75244
12302-12398 75244
Coxville Ln 75253
Coyote Trl 75227
Cozumel Plz 75211
Craddock St 75216
Cradlerock Dr 75217
Cragmont Ave 75205
Craige Dr 75217
Craighill Ave 75209
Craigshire Ave 75231
Crampton St 75207
Cranberry Ln 75244

Crane St 75212
Cranfill Dr
4201-4497 75216
4499-4900 75216
4902-4998 75216
5000-5099 75241
Cransbrook Ct 75225
N & S Crawford St 75203
Creative Pl 75211
W Creek Ct 75287
Creek Dr 75252
W Creek Dr 75287
Creek Arbor Ct 75287
Creek Bend Rd 75252
Creek Cove Dr 75217
Creek Crossing Dr 75253
Creek Forest Dr 75230
Creek Hollow Dr 75252
Creek View Cir & Dr ... 75233
Creek Vista Ct 75252
Creekbluff Dr 75249
Creekdale Dr 75229
Creekglen Dr 75227
Creekhaven Pl 75240
Creekmeadow Dr 75287
Creekmere Cir & Dr 75218
Creekridge Dr 75218
Creekside Dr 75217
Creekside Pl 75240
Creekspan Dr 75243
Creekwood Dr 75228
Creel Creek Cir & Dr ... 75228
Creighton Dr 75214
Crenshaw Dr 75217
Crepe Myrtle Cir & Ln .. 75233
Crescendo Dr 75238
Crescent Ave 75205
Crescent Ct 75201
Crest Ave 75216
Crest Brook Dr 75230
Crest Cove Cir 75244
Crest Meadow Dr 75230
Crest Ridge Dr 75228
Crested Butte Dr 75252
Crestedge Cir & Dr 75238
N & S Cresthaven Rd .. 75209
Cresthill Rd 75227
Crestlake Dr 75238
Crestland Ave 75252
Crestline Ave
9901-9999 75220
11300-11398 75229
12101-12499 75244
Crestmere Dr 75254
Crestmont Dr 75214
Crestmoor Dr 75234
Crestover Cir & Dr 75229
Crestpark Dr 75244
Crestpoint Dr 75254
Crestshire Dr 75227
Creststone Dr 75287
Crestview Dr 75235
Crestway Ct & Dr 75230
Crestwick Dr 75238
Crestwood Dr 75216
Crete St 75203
Cricket Dr 75217
Crimnson Ct 75217
Cripple Creek Dr 75224
Cristler Ave 75223
Crittendon Dr 75229
Crocker Dr 75217
Crofton Dr 75231
Cromwell Cir 75229
Cromwell Ct 75229
Cromwell Dr
10000-10098 75229
10100-11400 75229
11402-11798 75229
11800-12199 75234
Cronk Ln 75227
Crooked Ln 75229
Crooked Creek Cir, Ct &
Dr 75229
Crooked Oak Dr 75248
Cross St 75210

Cross Creek Ct & Dr ... 75243
Cross Timbers Ln 75252
Crossing Ln 75220
Crossman Ave 75212
Crosstown Expy 75223
Crosswood Ln 75241
Crouch Rd 75241
Crow Creek Cir 75224
Crow Creek Dr 75233
Crowberry Dr 75228
N & S Crowdus St 75226
Crowley Dr 75229
Crown Dr 75234
Crown Rd 75229
Crown Knoll Cir 75232
Crown Shore Dr 75244
Crownfield Ln 75217
Crownover Ct 75252
Crownpoint Cir 75232
Crownrich Ln 75214
Crownwood Ct 75225
Crozier St 75215
Crusader Dr 75217
Crutcher St 75246
Crystal Lake Blvd 75236
Crystal Valley Way 75227
Crystalwood Ct & Dr ... 75249
Cuba St 75217
Culberson St 75227
Culcourt St 75209
Cullen Dr 75206
Culpepper Ave 75235
Culver St 75223
Cumberland St 75203
Cummings St 75216
Cup Cir 75217
Cupertino Trl 75252
Currin Dr 75230
Curvilinear Ct 75227
Cushing Dr 75217
Custer Dr 75216
Cutleaf Ct 75249
Cutter Mill Dr 75248
Cy Blackburn Cir 75217
Cymbal Dr 75217
Cypress Ave 75227
Cypress Falls Dr 75287
Cypress Hills Dr 75248
Cypress Point Dr 75253
Cyprus Point Dr 75234
Da Vinci Dr 75287
Dacki Ave 75211
Dahlia Ct & Dr 75216
Dahman Cir 75238
Daingerfield Dr 75227
Dairy Milk Ln 75229
Dale St 75203
Dale Crest Dr
9700-9899 75220
9901-9999 75220
10001-10299 75229
Dale Glade Dr 75217
Dalehurst Dr 75228
Daleport Cir 75248
Dalewood Ln 75214
Dalgreen Cir & Dr 75214
Dalhart Ln 75214
Dali Dr 75287
Dallas Pkwy
13200-13698 75240
13700-14099 75240
14100-14799 75254
14801-14999 75254
15100-17298 75248
17300-17399 75248
17400-19003 75287
19005-19199 75287
Dallas St 75210
Dallas Fort Worth
Tpke 75208
Dalmalley Ln 75248
Dalny St 75214
Dalron Dr 75218
Dalton Dr 75216
Dalview Ave 75203
Damascus Way 75234

Street	ZIP
Damon Ln	75229
Dan Morton Dr	75236
Danashire Ave	75231
Danbury Ln	
6001-6099	75206
6100-6599	75214
Dancliff Dr	75224
Dandelion Dr	75217
Dandridge Dr	75243
Dandy Ln	75227
Danfield Ct	75252
Daniel Ave & Ct	75205
W Danieldale Rd	
201-497	75232
499-799	75232
801-1299	75232
2301-2399	75237
Danny Ln	75234
Danson Dr	75253
Dante Dr	75235
Danube Dr	
1500-1598	75216
1600-1699	75216
1701-1799	75216
1800-1999	75203
Danvers Dr & Pl	75240
Danville Dr	75217
Darby Dr	75227
Darbyshire Dr	75229
Daria Dr & Pl	75229
Darien St	75212
Dark Star Ln	75211
Darko Dr	75232
Darlene St	75232
Darrington Dr	75249
Dart Ave	75217
Dartbrook Dr	75254
Dartcrest Dr	75238
Dartmoor Ct & Dr	75229
Dartmouth Ave	75205
Dartridge Cir & Dr	75238
Dartstone Dr	75244
Dartway Dr	75227
Dartwood Ln	75225
Darvany Dr	75220
Darwin St	75211
Dasch St	75217
Data Dr	75218
Dathe St	75215
Daven Oaks Dr	75248
Davenport Ct	75248
Davenport Rd	
6000-17399	75248
17400-18099	75252
18101-18399	75252
David Phillips St	75227
Davila Dr	75220
Davilla Ave	75228
E Davis St	75203
W Davis St	
100-198	75208
200-2300	75208
2302-2398	75208
2401-2497	75211
2499-6099	75211
Dawes Dr	75211
Dawn Dr	75228
Dawnridge Dr	75249
Dawnview Ct	75249
Dawson St	75226
Day Blvd	75203
Day St	75227
Day Star Dr	75224
Daybreak Dr	75287
Daystrom Ct	75243
Daytonia Ave	75218
Dazzle Dr	75232
De Bercy Ct	75229
De Haes Ave	75224
De Kalb Ave	75216
De Lee St	75227
De Maggio St	75210
De Or Dr	75230
De Ville Cir	75224
De Witt Cir	75224
Debbe Dr	75252
Debshire Cir	75231
Deep Green Dr	75249
Deep Haven Dr	75249
Deep Hill Cir	75233
Deep Valley Dr	75244
Deepwood St	75217
Deer Creek Dr	75228
Deer Hollow Dr	75249
Deer Meadow Ln	75287
Deer Park Dr	75248
Deer Path Dr	75216
Deer Run Trl	75243
Deer Trail Dr & Pl	75238
Deere St	75204
Deermont Trl	75243
Deerwood Dr	75232
Degas Ln	75230
Del Monte Dr	75217
Del Norte Ln	75225
Del Prado Dr	75254
Del Roy Dr	
5100-5499	75229
5500-6199	75230
Delafield Ln	75227
Delano Pl	75204
Delaware St	75208
Delford Cir	75228
Delhi St	75212
Delicias Plz	75211
Dell Garden Ave	75217
Dell Oak Dr	75217
Dell View Dr	75253
Delmac Dr	75233
Delmar Ave	75206
Delmeta Dr	75248
Deloache Ave	
4900-5600	75220
5602-5698	75220
5700-7099	75225
Delphinium Dr	75217
Delrose Dr	75214
Demetra Dr	75234
Dempster Ave	75211
Denham Cir, Ct, Dr & Pl	75217
N Denley Dr	75203
S Denley Dr	
613-629	75203
631-899	75203
900-1198	75216
1200-5099	75216
5101-5199	75241
Denmark St	75253
Dennis Ln	75234
Dennis Rd	75229
Dennison St	75212
Dentcrest Dr	75254
Denton Dr	
4701-4799	75219
4900-9399	75235
9601-10097	75220
10099-10799	75220
10801-10999	75220
11000-11499	75229
11501-11699	75229
11901-12197	75234
12199-13999	75234
14001-14099	75234
Denton Drive Cut Off	75235
Dentport Dr	75238
N & S Dentwood Dr	75220
N & S Denver St	75203
Depaul Ave	75241
Derby Ln	75227
Derek Trl	75252
Desco Cir, Dr, Pl & Sq	75225
Desdemona Dr	75228
Deseret Trl	75252
Desert Willow Dr	75243
Destiny Way	75237
Detonte St	75223
Detroit St	75217
Deveron St	75232
Devilwood Ct	75253
Devon Cir	75217
Devonshire Dr	75209
Dex Dr	75244
Dexter Dr	75230
Dfw Tpke	
401-403	75260
401-401	75222
2400-2400	75398
4201-4297	75211
4299-4499	75211
Diamond Ave	75215
Diamond Head Cir	75225
Dibsworth Ln	75238
Diceman Ave	75203
Diceman Dr	75218
Dickason Ave	75219
Dickens Ave	75205
Dickerson St	75252
Didsbury Cir	75224
Dilbeck Ln	75240
Dildock St	75215
Dilido Rd	75228
Dillard Ct & Ln	75209
Dillon Dr	75227
Dilworth Rd	75243
Dinsdale Dr	75218
Diplomacy Row	75247
Diplomat Dr	75234
Directors Row	75247
Dismount St	75211
Distribution Way	75234
Dittmar Pl	75229
Diversey St	75201
Division St	75211
Divot Cir	75232
Dixfield Dr	75218
Dixiana Dr	75234
Dixie Ln	75228
Dixie Garden Ct & Ln	75236
Dixon Ave & Cir	75210
Dixon Branch Dr	75218
Doak St	75217
Dodd St	75203
Doe Ct	75249
Dogwood Trl	75224
Dogwood Creek Ln	75252
Dolores Way	75232
Dolphin Rd	75223
Dolton Dr	75207
Dominion St	75208
Dominique Dr	75214
Don Dr	75247
Don St	75227
Donald St	75215
Donegal Dr	75218
Donna Dr	75227
Donnybrook Cir, Ln & Pl	75217
Donore Ln	75218
Donosky Dr	75203
Doolin Ct	75230
Dorado Beach Dr	75234
Doral Dr	75287
Doran Cir	75238
Dorchester Dr	75218
Dorfspring St	75217
Doric St	75220
Dorinda Cir	75217
Dornoch Ln	75248
Dorothy Ave	75209
Dorothy Nell Dr	75253
Dorrington Cir & Dr	75228
Dorris St	75215
Dorset Pl & Rd	75229
Dothan Ln	75229
Doug Dr	75247
Douglas Ave	
2201-2297	75219
2299-4416	75219
4418-4498	75219
6201-6297	75205
6299-6399	75205
7301-8097	75225
8099-9600	75225
9602-9698	75225
4415 1/2-4415 1/2	75219
Dove Dr	75236
Dove Brook Cir	75230
Dove Creek Way	75232
Dove Meadow Dr	75243
Dove Trail Cir	75238
Dover St	75216
Dow Ct	75212
Dowdy Ferry Rd	75217
Dowell Cir	75252
Downhill Dr	75217
Downing Ave	75216
Downs Lake Cir	75230
Doyle Ave	75203
Dragon St	75207
Drake St	75228
Drane Dr	75209
Dresden Dr	75220
Drew St	75212
Drexel Dr	75205
Driftway Dr	75228
Driftwood Dr	
1500-1699	75224
3200-3299	75227
Driskell St	75215
Drowsy Ln	75233
Druid Ln	
4000-4599	75205
5400-5599	75209
Druid Hills Dr	75224
Drujon Ln	75244
Drumcliffe Ln	75231
Drummond Cir, Ct, Dr & Pl	75228
Drury Dr & Pl	75232
Drycreek Ln	75237
Dryden Ave	75216
Dryden Dr	75211
Dublin St	75205
Dubois Ave	75203
Duchess Cir & Trl	75229
Dudley Ave	75203
Duet Dr	75241
Duff St	75204
Duffield Ct	75248
Duffield Dr	
6300-7399	75248
7400-7499	75252
Dugald Pl	75216
Dugan St	75217
Dujon Ln	75218
Dulaney Dr	75228
Duluth St	75212
Dumane St	75211
Dumas St	75214
Dumbarton Dr	75228
Dumfries Dr	75227
Dumont St	75214
Dunaway Dr	75228
Dunbar St	75215
Duncannon Ct	75225
Duncanville Rd	
1525-2399	75211
2600-3198	75211
3200-5799	75236
Dundrennan Ln	75248
Dunhaven Rd	75220
Dunhill Dr	75228
Dunintra Ave	75214
Dunlap St	75217
Dunleer Way	75248
Dunloe Ave	75228
Dunminster Ct	75219
Dunmore Dr & Pl	75231
Dunoon Ave	75248
Dunreath Dr	75227
Dunrobin Ln	75232
Dunstan Ln	75214
Duntredg St	75270
Dupont Cir & Dr	75216
Dupper Ct & Dr	75252
Durango Dr	75220
Durant St	75215
Durham St	
2600-2699	75241
7000-7098	75205
Durrett St	75223
Dusk Ln	75237
Dusti Dr	75243
Dusty Oak Dr	75227
Dutton Dr	75211
Duval Dr	75211
Duxbury Dr	75218
Dwarfs Cir	75229
N & S Dwight Ave	75211
Dye Dr	75248
Dyer Ct	75205
Dyer St	
2800-3000	75205
3002-3198	75205
5500-5699	75206
Dykes Way	75230
Dysart Cir	75214
Dyson St	75215
Eads Ave	75203
Eagle Dr	75216
Eagle Trl	75238
Eagle Bend Ct	75249
Eagle Ford Dr	75249
Eagle Heights Dr	75212
Eagle Place Dr	75236
Eagle Rock Dr	75253
Earlcove Dr	75227
Earlport Cir & Dr	75248
Earlshire Dr	75229
Early Dawn Trl	75224
Earlywood Dr	75218
Earnhardt Way	75217
Earthwind Dr	75248
Easley St	75215
East Pl	75210
Eastcliff Dr	75217
Eastcrest Ln	75217
Easter Ave	75216
Eastern Ave	75209
Eastern Oaks Dr	75227
Eastgate Cir	75216
Eastgrove St	75211
Eastham Dr	75217
Eastlawn Dr	75229
Easton Pl & Rd	75218
Eastpoint Dr	75227
Eastridge Dr	75231
Eastus Dr	75208
Eastview Cir	75230
Eastwood Dr	75228
Easy St	75247
Eaton Dr	75220
Ebbtide Ln	75224
Ebenezer Mews	75236
Ebony Dr	75243
Eccles Dr	75227
Echo Ave	75215
Echo Bluff Dr	75248
Echo Brook Ln	75229
Echo Glen Dr	75244
Echo Lake Dr	75253
Echo Ridge Ct	75243
Echo Valley Dr	75243
Ector Ct	75227
Edd Rd	75253
Eddy Sass Ct	75227
Edelweiss Cir	75240
Eden Dr	75287
Eden Roc Dr	75238
Eden Valley Ln	75217
Edgar Pl	75204
Edgecliff Cir & Dr	75238
Edgecove Dr	75238
Edgecreek Dr	75227
Edgecrest Dr	75254
Edgedale Dr	75232
N Edgefield Ave	75208
S Edgefield Ave	
100-1399	75208
1700-3399	75224
Edgeglen Dr	75217
Edgehollow Pl	75287
Edgelake Dr	75218
Edgemere Rd	
8500-8699	75225
9901-10997	75230
10999-11199	75230
Edgemont Ave	75216
Edgepine Dr	75238
Edgerton Dr	75231
Edgestone Rd	75230
Edgewater St	75205
Edgewood St	75215
Edgeworth Dr	75217
Edinburgh Ct & St	75252
Edison St	75207
Edith Ct & Ln	75220
Edlen Dr	75220
Edmondson Ave	
4200-4599	75205
4600-5399	75209
Edwards Ave	75235
Edwards Cir	75224
Egan Ave	75235
Egret Ln	75230
Egyptian Dr	75232
Eisenhower Dr	75224
Ekukpe Dr	75217
El Benito Dr	75212
El Campo Dr	75218
El Capitan Dr	75228
El Centro Dr	75220
N El Centro Way	75241
S El Centro Way	75241
El Cerrito Dr	75228
El Estado Dr	75248
El Greco Ln	75287
El Hara Cir	75230
El Padre Ln	75248
El Pastel Dr	75248
El Patio Dr	75218
El Pensador Dr	75248
El Rito St	75220
El Santo Ln	75248
El Sol St	75236
El Tivoli Dr	75211
El Torro St	75236
El Tovar Ave & Cir	75233
El Triumfo St	75212
Elaine Dr	75227
Elam Rd	75217
Elam Heights Dr	75217
Elbow St	75232
Elder St	75234
Elder Grove Dr	75232
Elderberry Cir, Ct & Ln	75249
Elderleaf Dr	75232
Elderoaks Ln & Pl	75232
Elderwood Dr	75230
Eldon Dr	75217
Eldorado Ave	75208
Electra St	75215
Electronic Ln	75220
Elena St	75216
Elf St	75217
Elfland Cir	75229
Eli Ave	75211
Elice Ct	75233
Elihu St	75210
Elise Way	75236
Elizabeth St	75204
Elk Creek Rd	75253
Elk Horn Trl	75216
Elkhart Ave	75217
Elkridge Dr	75227
Elkton Cir	75217
Elkwood Dr	75217
Ella Ave	75217
Ellensburg Dr	75244
Ellenwood St	75217
Ellery Dr	75243
Elliott Dr	75227
Ellis St	75204
Ellsworth Ave	
5301-5397	75206
5399-6099	75206
6100-6999	75214
Elm St	
403-497	75202
499-1100	75202
1102-1414	75202
1201-1201	75270
1401-1405	75202
1500-1500	75201
1502-1938	75201
1940-2298	75201
2500-2598	75226
2600-4499	75226
Elm Creek Ln	75252
Elm Hollow Dr	75229
Elm Lawn St	75228
Elm Leaf Ct & Dr	75236
Elm Shadows Dr	75232
Elm Valley Ln	75232
Elmada Ln	75220
Elmbrook Dr	75247
Elmcrest Dr	75238
Elmdale Pl	75224
Elmhurst Pl	75224
Elmira St	75227
E Elmore Ave	75216
W Elmore Ave	75224
Elmridge Dr	75240
Elmspring Rd	75253
Elmwood Blvd	75224
Eloise St	75217
Elsa Ln	75217
Elsberry Ave	75217
Elsbeth St	75208
Elsby Ave	75209
Elston Dr	75232
Elva Ave	75227
Elvedon Dr	75248
Elwayne Ave	75217
Elysian Ct	75230
Embassy St	75217
Ember Crest Rd	75241
Emberglow Ln	75243
Embers Rd	75248
Emberwood Dr	75232
Embrey Dr	75232
Emeasho Dr	75243
Emeline St	75234
Emerald St	75229
Emerald Isle Dr	75218
Emeraldwood Dr	
6000-6099	75248
6400-6498	75254
Emeraldwood Pl	75254
Emerson Ave	
4100-4599	75205
5300-5599	75209
Emery St	75215
Emhouse St	75232
Emily Rd	75240
Emily St	75203
Emma Dr	75241
Emmett St	
1801-1997	75208
1999-2399	75208
2400-3399	75211
Emory Oak Cir & Ln	75249
Empire Dr	75214
Empire Central	75235
Empire Central Dr	75247
Empire Central Pl	75247
Empress Row	75247
Emrose Cir & Ter	75227
Enchanted Ln	75227
Encino Dr	75228
Enclave Way	75218
Encore Dr	75240
Enderly Pl	75227
Endicott Ln	75227
Energy Ln	75252
Energy Pl	75211
Enfield Dr	75220
Engle Ave	
1101-1297	75224
1299-2399	75224
2400-2799	75233
Englewood Rd	75203
Enola Gay Ave	75227
Ensenada Plz	75211
Enterprise Dr	75234
Envoy Ct & St	75247
Epenard St	75211
Epping Ln	75229
Epps Field Rd	75234

Erhard Dr 75228
Eric Ln 75234
Erie Ct 75218
Erikaglen Dr 75241
Eriksson Ln 75204
Erin Dr 75218
Ermine Way 75234
N Ervay St
201-297 75201
299-399 75201
400-498 75201
400-400 75221
400-400 75250
400-400 75313
401-599 75201
S Ervay St
200-798 75201
800-1099 75201
1201-1297 75215
1299-2999 75215
Escada Dr 75234
Esmalda St 75212
Espanola Dr 75220
Esplanade Dr 75220
Essex Ave 75203
Esta Buena Dr 75218
Estacado Dr 75228
Estancia Cir 75248
Estate Ln 75238
Esterbrook Dr 75234
Esterine Rd 75217
Ethel Dr 75227
Etta Dr 75227
Euclid Ave
1800-2099 75206
3500-4099 75205
Eudora Dr 75230
Eugene St 75215
Eunice St 75234
Eustis Ave 75218
Evangeline Way 75218
Evanston Ave 75208
Evelyn St 75216
Everglade Cir & Rd 75227
Evergreen Hills Rd 75208
Everton Pl 75217
Everwood Ct 75252
N Ewing Ave 75203
S Ewing Ave
201-397 75203
399-800 75203
802-998 75203
1000-4699 75216
Excelsior Way 75230
N Exchange Park 75235
Exchange Park Mall 75235
Exchange Service Dr 75236
Executive Cir 75234
Executive Dr 75238
Exeter Ave 75216
Exline St 75215
Exposition Ave 75226
Express St 75207
Ezekial Ave 75217
Fabens Rd 75229
Fabric Xpress Way 75234
Fabrication St 75212
Fadeway St 75211
Fair Oaks Ave 75231
Fair Oaks Xing
8201-8201 75231
8500-8899 75243
Fair Vista Dr 75227
Faircloud Dr 75217
Faircrest Dr 75238
Fairdale Ave 75227
Fairfax Ave
3600-3999 75209
4200-4599 75205
4600-4699 75209
Fairfield Ave 75205
Fairfield St 75212
Fairglen Dr 75231
Fairhaven Ln 75227
Fairhope Ave 75217
Fairlakes Cir, Ct & Dr 75228

Fairley Ln 75209
Fairmount St
2400-2498 75201
2500-3100 75201
3102-3398 75201
3400-3498 75219
3500-4899 75219
Fairport Rd 75217
Fairview Ave 75223
Fairway Ave 75227
Fairway St 75219
Fairwood Dr 75232
Faithful Trl 75237
Fakes Dr 75224
Fall Manor Dr 75243
Fall River Dr 75228
Fallbrook Dr 75243
Fallen Leaf Dr 75253
Falling Springs Rd 75253
Fallkirk Dr 75248
Fallmeadow Ln 75248
Fallon Pl 75227
Falls Dr 75211
Falls Rd
5300-5599 75220
5800-5998 75225
Falls Bluff Dr 75211
Falls Creek Ct 75254
Fallsview Ln 75252
Famous Dr 75208
Fannie St 75212
Fantasia Ln 75229
Far Hills Ln 75240
Farancou Dr 75231
Fargo St 75223
Farley Trl 75287
Farmers Branch Ln 75234
Farmers Market Way 75201
Farnsworth Dr 75236
N & S Farola Dr 75228
Farquhar Cir & Ln 75209
Farragut St 75215
Farrar St 75218
Farrington St 75207
Fatima Ave 75241
Faulk St 75203
Faultless Dr 75211
Fawn Dr 75238
Fawn Ridge Dr 75224
Fawn Valley Dr 75224
Fawnhollow Dr 75244
Faye St 75215
Fayette St 75203
Featherbrook Dr 75228
Featherstone Dr 75216
Featherwood Dr 75252
Federal St 75201
Felicia Ct 75228
Fellows Ln 75216
Felton Ct 75215
Fenchurch Rd 75238
Fenestra Dr 75228
Fenton Dr 75231
Fenway St 75217
Fenwick Dr 75228
Ferantra Dr 75218
Ferdinand Dr 75248
Ferguson Rd 75228
Fermapl Dr 75254
Fern Ave 75217
Fern Dr 75228
Fern Creek Dr 75253
Fern Glen Trl 75241
Fern Hollow Dr 75238
Fern Valley Ct 75287
Fernald Ave 75218
Ferncliff Trl 75232
Ferncroft Dr 75233
Ferndale Ave 75224
Ferndale Rd 75238
Fernheath Ln 75253
Fernmeadow Cir & Dr 75248
Fernshaw Dr 75248
Fernwood Ave
700-899 75203
901-1197 75216
1199-4300 75216
4302-4498 75216
Ferrell Dr
11300-11399 75229
11400-11499 75234
Ferris St 75226
W Ferris Branch Blvd 75243
Ferris Creek Ln & Pl 75243
Fess St 75212
Few St 75212
Fidelis Ave 75241
N Field St
300-399 75202
2201-2599 75201
S Field St 75202
Field View Ln 75249
Fieldale Dr 75234
Fieldcrest Ct & Dr 75238
Fielder Ct 75235
Fieldfare Cir & Ct 75229
Fieldgate Dr 75230
Fieldstone Dr 75252
Fieldwood Ln 75244
Files St 75217
Fillmore Dr 75235
Fin Castle Dr 75287
Finis Ln 75212
Finklea St 75212
Finnell St 75220
Firebird Dr 75241
Firebrick Ln 75287
Firecrest Ct 75252
Fireflame Dr 75248
Fireglow Walk 75243
Firelight Ln 75248
Firelog Ln 75243
Fireside Dr 75217
Firestone Dr 75252
Firethorn Dr 75249
Firewood Dr 75241
Fish Rd 75253
Fish Trap Rd 75212
Fisher Rd 75214
Fitchburg St 75212
Fite Cir & Ln 75236
N Fitzhugh Ave
100-200 75246
202-500 75246
502-898 75246
909-1405 75204
1407-3404 75204
3406-3626 75204
S Fitzhugh Ave
106-298 75226
301-315 75226
402-412 75223
414-1641 75223
1643-1661 75223
3400-4250 75210
4301-4301 75210
4500-4598 75223
Fitzroy Cir & Dr 75238
Fitzsimmons St 75216
Five Mile Cir 75233
Five Mile Ct 75224
Five Mile Dr 75216
E Five Mile Pkwy 75216
W Five Mile Pkwy
400-2398 75224
2400-2699 75233
Flagstaff Dr 75241
Flagstone Ln 75240
Flair Dr 75229
Flameleaf Pl 75249
Flamingo Ln 75218
Flanary Ln 75252
Flanders St 75208
Flask Dr 75241
Flatstone Cir & Ct 75252
Flaxley Dr 75229
Fleetwood St 75223
Fleetwood Oaks Ave 75235
S Fleming Ave 75203
Fletcher St 75223
Flicker Ln 75238
Flickering Shadow Dr 75243

Flint Falls Dr 75243
Flintcove Dr 75248
Flintridge Dr 75244
Flintshire Ln 75252
Flo Ave 75211
Flora St
2000-2700 75201
2702-2798 75201
3100-3198 75204
3201-3299 75204
Florence St 75204
Florencia Plz 75211
Florina Pkwy 75249
Flower Meadow Dr 75243
Flowerdale Ln 75229
Flowers Ave 75211
Floyd Cir 75243
Floyd St 75204
Floyd Lake Dr 75243
Flynn St 75201
Fm 1382 75249
Foley St 75223
Folklore Trl 75224
Folkstone Rd 75220
Folsom St 75208
Fondren Dr
2601-2799 75206
2800-3199 75205
5600-5698 75206
Fontana Dr 75220
Fonville Dr 75227
Foothill Dr 75253
Ford Rd 75234
Fordham Rd 75216
Fore Cir 75234
Foreman St 75210
Forest Ave 75215
Forest Ct 75230
Forest Ln
2300-2698 75234
2700-3699 75234
3700-5499 75244
5500-5598 75230
5600-7999 75230
8000-8132 75243
8134-10898 75243
8135-8135 75230
8201-10899 75243
Forest Pkwy 75241
Forest Trl 75238
Forest Bend Rd 75244
Forest Central Dr 75243
Forest Cliff Dr 75228
Forest Cove Cir 75230
Forest Creek Dr & Pl 75230
Forest Glade Cir 75230
Forest Glen Dr 75230
Forest Green Dr 75243
Forest Grove Dr 75218
Forest Haven Trl 75232
Forest Heights Dr 75229
Forest Hills Blvd & Pl 75218
Forest Hollow Park 75228
Forest Knoll Trl 75232
Forest Lakes Ln 75230
Forest Lane Cir & Pl 75244
Forest Meadow Trl 75232
Forest Oaks Dr 75228
Forest Park Rd 75235
Forest Springs Dr 75243
Forest View St 75243
Forest Vista Ct 75249
Forestdale Ln 75234
Forester Dr 75216
Forestgate Dr 75243
Forestridge Cir & Dr 75238
Forestshire Dr 75230
Forestway Dr 75240
Forestwood Cir & Dr 75244
Formosa Ave 75248
Forney Br 75227
Forney Rd
3401-3599 75223
5300-9299 75227
Forsythe Dr 75217
Fort Bend Dr 75227

Fort Worth Ave
600-2099 75208
2100-3399 75211
Fortson Ave 75252
Fortune Ln 75216
Foster Ave 75203
Fostoria Dr 75217
Fountain Dr 75224
Fountaindale Dr 75217
Fountainhead Ln 75233
Fouraker St 75208
Fouts Ln 75208
Fowler St 75216
Fox Trl 75248
Fox Creek Trl 75249
Fox Crossing Ct 75232
Fox Fire Dr 75287
Fox Hill Ln 75232
Fox Point Trl 75249
Fox Ridge Cir 75249
Fox Run Dr 75217
Foxboro Ln 75241
Foxglove Ln 75249
Foxgrove Cir 75228
Foxhaven Dr 75249
Foxwood Ln 75217
Foxworth Dr 75248
Fran Way 75203
N & S Frances St 75211
Frank St 75210
Frank Jackson Dr 75252
Frankford Ct 75252
Frankford Rd
2501-2597 75287
2599-5099 75287
5101-5299 75287
5500-8100 75252
8102-8498 75252
Frankford Lakes Cir 75252
N Franklin St 75211
S Franklin St
900-2000 75211
2002-2098 75211
2300-3999 75233
Franwood Dr 75217
Frazier St 75210
Freddie St 75217
Free Range Dr 75241
Freedom Cir 75287
Freeland Way 75228
Freemont St 75231
Freeport Dr 75228
Freestone Cir 75227
Freewood Dr 75220
French Settlement Rd 75212
Frenchmans Way 75220
Fresno St 75217
Friendship Dr 75217
Friendway Ln 75237
Fringewood Dr 75228
Frio Dr 75216
E Frio Dr
4500-5098 75216
5100-5198 75241
5201-5299 75241
W Frio Dr 75216
Frito Lay Towers 75235
Fritz St 75241
Front St 75203
Frontier Ln 75214
Frost Ave 75215
Frostwood St 75217
Frosty Trl 75241
Fruitland Ave 75234
Fuller Dr
1100-1198 75218
1200-1499 75218
1501-1599 75218
1600-1899 75228
Fullerton Dr 75211
N & S Fulton St 75214
Fuqua St
4801-4899 75204
5001-5197 75206
5199-5200 75206
5202-5298 75206

Furey St 75212
Furlong Dr 75211
Fyke Rd 75234
Gable Cir & Dr 75229
Gabriel Ct 75233
Gadberry Dr 75241
N & S Gail St 75211
Gailbrook Ln 75228
Gainesborough Dr 75287
Galahad Dr 75229
Galemeadow Cir 75214
Galen Ln 75217
Galena St 75228
Galicia Ln 75217
Gallagher St 75212
Gallant Fox Dr 75211
Gallatin St 75203
Galleria Pl 75244
Gallery Dr 75252
Galloway Ave 75216
Galva Dr 75243
Galway Dr 75218
Game St 75203
Gamma Rd 75244
Gannon Ln 75237
Gano St 75215
Garapan Dr 75224
Garden Dr 75215
Garden Ln
3200-3499 75215
3700-3898 75210
Garden Brook Dr 75234
Garden Crest Ln 75232
Garden Grove Dr 75253
Garden Springs Dr 75253
Garden Terrace Dr 75243
Gardendale Dr 75228
Gardenia Dr & Pl 75218
Gardenside Dr 75217
Gardenview Dr 75217
Gardner Rd 75220
Garfield Ave 75211
Garland Ave 75223
Garland Rd 75218
Garlinghouse Ln 75252
N Garrett Ave
100-198 75214
1401-1497 75206
1499-2699 75206
S Garrett Ave
100-300 75214
302-398 75214
400-499 75223
Garrison Ave 75216
Garwood Dr 75238
Garza Ave 75216
Gaslite Cir 75234
Gaspar Dr 75220
Gaston Ave
2500-2598 75226
2600-3299 75226
3300-4899 75246
4900-7399 75214
Gaston Pkwy
7001-7099 75214
8701-11999 75218
Gatecove Dr 75227
Gatecrest Dr 75238
Gateridge Dr 75254
Gatesworth Ln 75287
Gatetrail Dr 75238
Gateway Ln 75218
Gatewood Dr & Pl 75218
Gatsby Ln 75253
Gatwick Pl 75234
Gaucho St 75211
Gause Ln 75217
Gay St 75210
Gayglen Dr 75217
Gaylord Dr
1300-2099 75217
2100-2299 75227
2301-2399 75227
Gaywood Rd 75229
Gemini Ln 75229
Genesis Dr 75232

Genetta Dr 75228
Gennaro St 75204
Genoa Ave 75216
Genstar Ln 75252
Gentle Knoll Ln 75248
Gentle River Dr 75241
Gentle Wind Ln 75248
Gentry Dr 75212
George Ct & St 75234
Georgia Ave
600-998 75216
1000-1599 75216
1600-1699 75203
Georgian Ct 75254
Gertrude Ave 75210
Ghent St 75215
Gibbons Dr 75287
Gibbs Williams Cir 75224
Gibbs Williams Rd 75233
Gibsondell Ave 75211
Giddings Cir 75238
Gideons Way 75236
Gifford St 75223
Gilbert Ave
3701-3797 75219
3799-4600 75219
4602-4698 75219
5100-5199 75209
Gilford St 75235
Gill St 75227
Gillarel Springs Ln 75241
Gillespie St 75219
Gillette Cir & St 75217
Gillis Rd 75244
Gillon Ave 75205
Gilmer St 75212
N & S Gilpin Ave 75211
Ginger Ave 75211
Ginseng Dr 75217
Givendale Rd 75241
Glacier Dr 75227
Glad Acres Dr 75234
Glade St 75232
Glade Creek Ct 75218
Glade Forest Dr 75218
Glade Hill Ct 75218
Gladeside Ct 75248
Gladewater Rd 75216
Gladiolus Ln 75233
Gladstone Dr
2300-2399 75208
2400-2899 75211
Gladwood Ln 75243
N Glasgow Dr 75214
S Glasgow Dr
100-398 75214
400-1099 75223
1101-1199 75223
Glass St 75207
Glen Ave 75216
Glen Abbey Dr 75248
Glen Albens Cir 75225
Glen America Dr 75225
Glen Arbor Ct & Dr 75241
Glen Canyon Dr 75243
Glen Creek Ct 75243
Glen Cross Dr 75228
Glen Echo Ct 75238
Glen Falls Ln 75209
Glen Forest Ln 75241
Glen Heather Dr 75252
Glen Heights Dr 75287
Glen Hill Dr 75287
Glen Lakes Dr 75231
Glen Oaks Blvd & Cir 75232
Glen Park Dr 75241
Glen Regal Dr 75243
Glen Springs Cir & Dr 75243
Glen Stone Ln 75232
Glen Vista Dr 75217
Glenacre 75243
Glenaire Dr 75229
Glenbrook Ln 75252
Glencairn Dr 75232
Glenchester Ct 75225
Glencliff Cir, Ct & Dr 75217

Glencoe St 75206
Glencrest Ln 75209
Glenda Ln 75229
Glendale St 75214
Glendora Ave 75230
Glenfield Ave
1300-2399 75224
2400-2999 75233
3001-3299 75233
Glenfinnin Ln 75232
Glengariff Dr 75228
Glengold Dr 75234
Glengreen Dr 75217
Glenhaven Blvd 75211
Glenheather Ct 75225
Glenhollow Ct 75248
Glenhurst Dr 75254
Glenkirk Ct 75225
Glenleigh Dr 75220
Glenlivet Dr 75218
Glenmeadow Ct & Pl 75225
Glenmont Ln 75228
Glenncreek Xing 75230
Glenneagle Dr 75248
Glennox Ln 75214
Glenridge Rd 75220
Glenrio Ln
9900-9999 75220
10000-10098 75229
Glenrose Ct 75214
Glenshannon Cir 75225
Glenshire Ct 75225
Glenside Cir & Dr 75234
Glenview Ln 75234
Glenview St 75217
Glenway Dr 75249
Glenwick Ln
3900-4599 75205
5300-5599 75209
Glenwood Ave 75205
Glesman St 75232
Glidden St 75203
Globe Ave 75228
Glorietta Ln 75241
Gloster Rd 75220
Glover Pass 75227
Gloyd St 75203
Goddard Ct 75218
Godfrey Ave 75217
Goforth Cir & Rd 75238
Gold Rd 75237
Gold Dust Trl 75252
Golden Creek Rd 75248
Golden Gate Cir & Dr 75241
Golden Hills Dr 75241
Golden Oak 75234
Golden Trophy Dr 75232
Goldendale Dr 75234
Goldeneye Ln 75249
Goldfield Dr 75217
Goldfinch Way 75249
Goldie Ave 75211
Goldman St 75212
Goldmark Dr 75240
Goldspier Dr 75215
Goldwood Dr 75232
Golf Dr 75205
Golf Hill Dr 75232
Golf Lakes Trl 75231
Golfing Green Cir, Ct, Dr & Pl 75234
Goliad Ave
5700-6099 75206
6100-6499 75214
Gonzales Dr 75227
Gooch St 75241
N Good Latimer Expy 75204
S Good Latimer Expy
500-2198 75226
521-525 75201
717-2299 75226
2400-2498 75215
2500-2699 75215
Goodfellow Dr 75229
Gooding Dr
9800-9999 75220
10000-10198 75229
10200-10599 75229
Goodland Pl & St 75234
Goodman St 75211
Goodnight Ln
10500-10799 75220
10801-10899 75220
11100-11600 75229
11602-11698 75229
Goodshire Ave 75231
Goodwater St 75234
Goodwill Ave 75210
Goodwin Ave 75206
Goodyear Dr 75229
Gorman St 75223
Gospel Dr 75237
Gossage Ln 75227
Gould St 75215
Governors Row 75247
Gracefield Ln 75248
Gracey St 75216
Grader St 75238
Grady Ln 75217
Grady Niblo Rd 75236
Grafton Ave 75211
Graham Ave 75223
Grambling Dr 75241
Gramercy Pl 75230
Gramercy Oaks Dr 75287
Granada Ave 75205
Granbury Dr 75287
Grand Ave
1200-1498 75215
1500-3100 75215
3055-3055 75315
3101-3199 75215
3102-3198 75215
3200-3599 75210
3601-3899 75210
E Grand Ave
4200-4298 75223
4300-7199 75223
7201-7397 75214
7399-7599 75214
Grand Oaks Rd 75230
Grandview Ave 75223
Grandvista Ln 75249
Granger St 75224
Granis St 75243
Granite Hill Dr 75241
Grant St 75203
Grantbrook Ln 75228
Grantley Ct 75230
Grantwood Dr 75229
Granville Ct & Dr 75249
Grassmere Ln 75205
Grassy Ridge Trl 75241
Gray Oak Pl 75212
Gray Rock 75243
Gray Wolf Trl 75252
Graycliff Dr 75228
Grayport Dr 75248
Grayson Dr 75224
Graystone Dr 75248
Graywood Dr 75243
Great Light Dr 75228
Great Oak Dr 75253
Great Plains Ave 75241
Great Trinity Forest Way
3100-3300 75216
3302-4598 75216
4201-4299 75241
4701-4799 75216
5400-6298 75217
6300-8099 75217
Green St 75208
Green Acres Ter 75234
Green Ash Rd 75243
Green Castle Dr 75232
Green Cove Ln 75232
Green Hill Rd 75232
Green Meadow Dr 75228
Green Oaks Cir 75243
Green Park Dr 75248
Green Terrace Dr 75220
E Greenbriar Ln 75203
W Greenbriar Ln 75208
Greenbrier Dr
3100-4499 75225
5400-5799 75209
7400-7599 75225
Greenbrook Ln 75214
Greencrest Dr 75241
Greendale Dr 75217
Greenfield Dr 75238
Greengate Dr 75249
Greengrove Ln 75253
Greenhaven Dr 75217
Greenhaw Ln 75253
Greenhollow Ln 75240
Greenhurst Dr 75234
Greenland Dr 75228
Greenlawn Dr 75253
Greenleaf St 75212
Greenmere Pl 75227
Greenmound Ave & Cir 75227
Greenpoint St 75228
Greenport Dr 75228
Greenside Dr 75252
Greenspan Ave 75232
Greensprint Dr 75238
Greenstone Dr 75243
Greentree Ln 75214
Greenville Ave
1300-1598 75206
1600-5200 75206
5111-5111 75360
5111-5111 75372
5201-6499 75206
5202-6598 75206
6700-6798 75231
6800-8299 75231
8301-8499 75231
8501-8597 75243
8599-12699 75243
12701-13099 75243
Greenway Blvd 75209
Greenwich Ln 75230
Greenwood St 75204
Greer St 75215
Gregg St 75235
Gregory Dr 75232
Grenadier Ct & Dr 75238
Grenore Dr 75218
Gretchen Ln 75252
Gretna St 75207
Grey Dawn Ln 75227
Greyfriars Ln 75238
Greystone Dr 75244
Griffin St E 75215
Griffin St W 75215
N Griffin St 75202
S Griffin St 75202
Griffith Ave 75208
Grigsby Ave 75204
Grinnell St 75216
Grissom Ln 75229
Grogan St 75253
Groom Ln 75227
Gross Rd 75228
Groton Ln 75217
Grove Hill Rd 75227
Grove Oaks Blvd 75217
Grovecrest Dr 75217
Groveland Dr 75218
Grovenor Ct 75225
E Grover C Washington Ave 75216
Groveridge Dr 75227
Grovetree Ln 75253
Groveview Dr 75233
Groveway Dr 75232
Grovewood St 75210
Grumman Dr 75228
Guadalupe Ave 75233
Guam St 75212
Guaranty St 75215
Guard Dr 75217
Guaymas Plz 75211
Guernsey Ln 75220
Guest St 75208
Guiding Light Dr 75228
Guildhall Dr 75238
Guillot St 75204
Gulden Ln 75212
Gulf Palms Dr 75227
Gulfstream Dr 75244
Gulledge Ln 75217
Gunnison Dr 75231
Gunter Ave 75210
Gurley Ave 75223
Gus Thomasson Rd 75228
Guthrie St 75224
Guymon St 75212
Haas Dr
4600-4899 75216
5000-5098 75241
Habersham Ln 75248
Hacienda Dr 75233
Hackney Ln 75238
Haddington Ln 75287
Hadley Dr 75217
Hagen Ct 75252
Haggar Way
3300-3599 75235
3700-3798 75209
Hague Dr 75234
Haines Ave 75208
Halcyon Pl 75206
Hale St 75211
Haley Dr 75253
Half Crown Dr 75237
Halifax St 75247
Hall Ct 75219
N Hall St
210-298 75226
300-335 75226
337-621 75226
900-3299 75204
3401-3623 75219
3625-4499 75219
4501-4525 75219
4800-5199 75235
4525 1/2-4525 1/2 75219
S Hall St 75226
Hallmark Dr 75229
Hallshire Ct 75225
Hallsville St 75204
Hallum St 75243
Halprin Ct & St 75252
Halsey St 75224
Halsley Rd 75217
Halstead Ct 75243
Halwin Cir 75243
Hamblen Dr 75232
Hambrick Rd 75218
Hamburg Ct & St 75215
Hamilton Ave
3200-4599 75210
4600-4898 75223
Hamilton Dr 75203
Hamlet Ave 75203
Hamlin Dr 75217
Hammerking Rd 75232
Hammerly Dr 75212
Hammond Ave 75223
Hampstead Ln 75230
Hampton Ct 75254
N Hampton Rd
100-1900 75208
1902-2398 75208
2600-4199 75212
S Hampton Rd
200-1899 75208
2101-2197 75224
2199-4100 75224
4102-4198 75224
4300-9000 75232
9002-9298 75232
Hancock St 75210
Handicap Cir 75211
Handley Dr 75208
Handlin Rd 75253
Hanford Dr 75243
Hanging Cliff Cir & Dr 75224
Hannah Way 75253
W Hanover Ave 75209
Hanover St 75225
Hansboro Ave
1100-1899 75224
2800-3399 75233
Happy Ln 75230
Happy Canyon Cir, Ct & Dr 75241
Happy Hollow Ln 75217
Happy Trails Dr 75241
Haraby Ct 75248
Harbin St 75208
Harbinger Ln 75287
Harbor Rd 75216
Harbor Glen Dr 75249
Harbor Town Dr 75287
Harbord Oaks Cir 75252
Harding St 75215
Hardned Ln 75217
Hardwick St 75208
Hardwood Trl 75249
Hargrove Dr 75220
Harkness Dr 75243
Harlandale Ave 75216
Harlee Dr 75234
Harlingen St 75212
Harmon St 75215
Harmony Ln 75241
Harmony Creek Rd 75237
Harold Walker Dr 75241
Harrell Ave 75203
Harriet Cir 75244
Harris Ct 75223
Harrisburg Cir 75234
Harrison Ave 75215
Harry Hines Blvd
2500-2598 75201
2600-3099 75201
3101-3399 75201
3600-4498 75219
4500-4599 75219
4600-9399 75235
9500-9698 75220
9700-10999 75220
11000-11699 75229
11800-13098 75234
13100-14099 75234
Harrys Ln 75229
Harston St 75212
Hart St 75203
Harter Rd 75218
Hartford St 75219
Hartline Dr 75228
Hartman St 75204
Hartsdale Dr 75211
Harvard Ave 75205
Harvest Rd 75217
Harvest Glen Dr 75248
Harvest Hill Rd
3900-5099 75244
5101-5199 75244
5300-5498 75230
5500-5999 75230
Harwell Dr 75220
Harwich Dr
9900-9998 75220
10000-10099 75229
N Harwood St 75201
S Harwood St
100-298 75201
300-1299 75201
1500-1798 75215
1800-3600 75215
3602-4998 75215
Haselwood Ln 75238
N Haskell Ave
113-123 75226
408-503 75246
502-502 75371
505-711 75246
608-898 75246
911-919 75204
921-3263 75204
3265-3329 75204
S Haskell Ave
100-110 75226
112-420 75226
422-498 75226
500-3301 75223
3303-3333 75223
Haskell Ct 75204
Haskell Dr 75204
Haslett St 75208
Hasty St 75228
Hatcher St
1600-3300 75215
3302-3398 75215
3500-4899 75210
Hathaway St 75220
Hatton St 75203
Havana St 75215
Haven St 75215
Haven Creek Ct 75238
Havencove Dr 75227
Havendon Cir 75203
Havenglen Dr 75248
Havenhurst St 75234
Havenport Ln 75287
Havenrock Cir 75248
Havenshire Pl 75254
Havenwood Dr 75232
Haverford Rd 75214
Haverhill Ln 75217
Haverwood Ln 75287
Hawes Ave 75235
Hawick Ln 75220
N Hawkins St
400-498 75204
1001-1099 75201
Hawks Nest Ct 75227
Hawley Ln 75217
Hawthorne Ave 75219
Hay St 75223
Hayfield Dr 75238
Haymarket Rd
500-1299 75217
1300-2799 75253
Haymeadow Cir & Dr 75254
Haynie Ave 75205
Haywood Pkwy 75232
Hazel Rd 75217
Hazelcrest Dr 75253
Hazelhurst Ln 75227
Healey Dr 75228
Hearne Ave 75208
Hearthstone Dr 75234
Heartside Pl 75234
Heartsill Dr 75235
Heashene Rd 75244
Heather Ln 75229
Heather Glen Dr 75232
Heatherbrook Dr 75244
Heatherdale Dr 75243
Heatherfield Ln 75287
Heatherknoll Dr 75248
Heathermore Dr 75248
Heatherwood Dr 75228
Heavenly Way 75237
Hector St 75210
Hedgdon Dr 75216
Hedge Dr 75249
Hedgeapple Dr 75243
Hedgebrook Dr 75249
Hedgerow Dr 75235
Hedgeway Dr 75229
Heinen Dr 75227
Helen St 75223
Helena St 75217
Helsem Bnd & Way 75230
Helsminster Dr 75201
Hemington Ct 75252
Hemlock Ave 75231
Hemphill Dr 75216
N Henderson Ave
100-198 75214
200-400 75214
402-698 75214
1601-1697 75206
1699-3099 75206
S Henderson Ave
100-199 75214
201-399 75214
400-1799 75223
Hendricks Ave 75216
Henry St 75226
Hensley Ct 75211
Hensley Field Cir & Dr 75211
Herald St 75215
Herbert St 75212
Heritage Cir 75234
Heritage Pl 75217
Hermitage St 75234
Hermosa Dr 75218
Hermosillo Plz 75211
Heron Trl 75236
Herrling St 75210
Herschel Ave 75219
Hester Ave 75205
Heyser Dr 75224
Heyworth Ave 75211
Hi Line Dr 75207
Hialeah Dr 75214
Hiawatha St 75212
Hibernia St 75204
Hibiscus Dr 75228
Hichert Dr 75251
Hickman St 75215
Hickory St
1400-1498 75215
1500-2499 75215
2500-2799 75226
2801-3299 75226
Hickory Xing 75243
Hickory Creek Ln 75252
Hickory Hill Dr 75248
Hidalgo Dr 75220
Hidden Cove Dr 75248
Hidden Glen Dr 75248
Hidden Trail Dr 75241
Hidden Valley Dr 75241
Hiddencreek Dr 75252
Hideaway Dr 75214
Higgins Ave 75211
High St 75203
High Bluff Dr 75234
High Brook Dr 75234
High Brush Cir & Dr 75249
High Court Pl 75254
High Creek Dr 75249
High Dale Dr 75234
High Forest Dr 75230
High Harvest Rd 75241
N & S High Hill Blvd & Pl 75203
High Hollows Dr 75230
High Lark Dr 75234
High Market St 75219
High Meadow Cir 75234
High Meadow Ct 75234
High Meadow Dr
11800-12376 75234
12378-12398 75234
12400-12799 75244
High Meadow Mews 75244
High Meadow Pl 75234
High Mesa Dr 75234
High Oaks Cir 75231
High Plain Ln 75249
High Point Cir 75243
High School Ave 75205
High Star Ln 75287
High Summit Dr 75244
High Tech Dr 75220
High Timber Dr 75236
High Valley Dr 75234
High Vista Dr
3200-3699 75234
3700-3799 75244
Highcrest Dr 75232
Highedge Cir & Dr 75238
Highfall Dr 75232
Highfield Dr 75227
Highgate Ln 75214
Highgrove Dr 75220
Highland Dr 75205
Highland Rd
1300-1698 75218
1800-1998 75228
2000-2699 75228
2701-3499 75228

Street	ZIP
Highland Creek Ln	75252
Highland Glen Trl	75248
Highland Heather Ln	75248
Highland Hills Dr	75241
Highland Hills Shp Ctr	75241
Highland Meadow Dr	75234
Highland Oaks Dr	75232
Highland Park Vlg	75205
Highland Place Dr	75236
Highland View Dr	75238
Highland Village Dr	75241
Highland Woods Cir & Dr	75241
Highlander Dr	75287
Highmark Sq	75254
Highmont St	75230
Highplace Cir	75254
Highridge Dr	75238
Highspire Dr	75217
Hightower Pl	75244
Highview St	75211
Highwood Dr	75228
Hilandale St	75216
Hilda Cir	75241
Hildebrand St	75211
N Hill Ave	75246
S Hill Ave	
100-198	75226
601-699	75223
Hill Country Ln	75249
Hill Forest Dr	75230
Hill Haven Dr	75230
Hill View Dr	75231
Hillard Dr	75217
Hillbriar Dr	75248
Hillbrook St	75214
Hillburn Dr	
100-198	75217
200-2099	75217
2100-2599	75227
2601-2699	75227
Hillcrest Ave	
5501-5897	75205
5899-7099	75205
8500-8599	75225
8601-9599	75225
Hillcrest Rd	
9900-10898	75230
10900-12800	75230
12802-12898	75230
13001-13097	75240
13099-14000	75240
14002-14098	75240
14100-14200	75254
14202-14798	75254
14800-17299	75248
17300-18799	75252
Hillcrest Plaza Dr	75230
Hillcroft St	75227
Hilldale Dr	75231
Hillfawn Cir	75248
Hillglenn Rd	75228
Hillgreen Cir & Dr	75214
Hillguard Rd	75243
Hillhouse Ln	75227
Hillmont Dr	75217
Hillpark Dr	75230
Hillpoint Dr	75238
Hillsboro Ave	75228
Hillside Dr & Vlg	75214
Hillstar Cir	75217
Hilltop Ln	75205
Hilltop St	75227
Hillvale Dr	75241
Hillwood Cir & Ln	75248
Hilton Head Dr	75287
Hines Pl	75235
Hinton St	75235
Hobart St	75218
Hoblitzelle Dr	75243
E Hobson Ave	75216
W Hobson Ave	75224
Hockaday Dr	75229
Hodde St	75217
Hodge St	75215
Hoel Dr	75224
Hohen Ave	75215
Hoke Smith Dr	75224
Holbrook Dr	75234
Holcomb Rd	75217
Holland Ave	
3700-4599	75219
5000-5099	75209
5101-5599	75209
Hollandale Ln	75234
Holliday Cir, Ct & Rd	75224
Hollis Ave	75227
Hollow Bend Ln	75227
Hollow Creek Dr	75253
Hollow Crest Ct	75287
Hollow Oak Ct & Dr	75287
Hollow Ridge Rd	75227
Hollow Way Rd	
9200-9999	75220
10000-10250	75229
10252-10298	75229
Holly Ave	75204
Holly Glen Cir, Dr & Pl	75232
Holly Hill Cir & Dr	75231
Holly Leaf Ct	75212
Holly Tree Dr	75287
Hollybush Dr	75228
Hollywood Ave	
100-1699	75208
2300-2399	75224
2401-2499	75224
Holmes St	75215
Holt Dr	75218
Holyoke Dr	75248
Holystone St	75212
Homeland St	75212
Homeplace Dr	75217
Homer St	
2400-2798	75206
3201-3499	75206
4700-4799	75204
4801-4899	75204
4900-5299	75206
Homestead Ct	75252
Homeview St	75217
Homeway Cir	75228
Homewood Pl	75224
Hondo Ave	75219
Honey Creek Ln	75287
Honey Locust Dr	75217
Honey Tree Ln	75211
Honeysuckle Ln	75241
Hood St	75219
Hooper St	75215
Hope St & Way	75206
Hopeful Vista Ln	75253
Hopetown Dr	75229
Hopewell St	75215
Hopkins Ave	75209
Horizon Dr	75216
Horizon Hills Dr	75253
Horizon North Pkwy	75287
Hornbeam Dr	75243
Horseshoe Trl	75209
Hortense Ave	75216
Hot Springs Ct	75241
Houghton Rd	75217
Hour Glass Cir	75252
Housley Dr	75228
N Houston St	
401-499	75202
2201-2297	75219
2299-2599	75219
S Houston St	75202
Hovenkamp Dr	75227
Howard Ave	75227
Howell St	
100-399	75207
2600-2698	75204
2700-3499	75204
Hoyle Ave	75227
Hubert St	75206
Huckleberry Cir	75216
Hudnall St	75235
Hudson St	75206
Hudspeth Ave	75216
Huey St	75210
Huff Trl	75214
Hughes Cir	75240
Hughes Ln	
13000-13999	75240
14000-14399	75254
Hughes Pl	75240
Hugo Pl & St	75204
Hull Ave	75216
Hulse Blvd	75203
Hume Dr	75227
Humoresque Dr	75241
Humphrey Dr	75216
Hundley Blvd & Ct	75231
Hunnicut Cir	75227
Hunnicut Ct	75227
Hunnicut Pl	75227
Hunnicut Rd	
6500-7400	75227
7402-7598	75227
7601-7997	75228
7999-8599	75228
Hunt St	75201
Hunters Bend Ln	75249
Hunters Creek Dr	75243
Hunters Glen Rd	75205
Hunters Point Dr	75248
Hunters Ridge Dr	75248
Hunters Run Cir, Ct & Dr	75232
Hunters View Ln	75232
Hunterwood Dr	75253
Huntingdon Ave	75203
Huntley St	75214
Hurley Way	75220
Huron Dr	75235
Hursey St	75205
Hustead St	75217
Hutchins Ave & Rd	75203
Huttig Ave	75217
Hutton Ct & Dr	75234
Hyacinth Ln	75252
Hyatt Ct	75253
Hyde Park Dr	75231
Hyer St	75205
Hymie Cir	75217
Iberia Ave	75207
Idaho Ave	75216
Idlewheat Ln	75241
Idlewood Ln	75230
Ike Ave	75241
Ikel Dr	75248
Ila Dr	75220
Ilahe Dr	75233
E Illinois Ave	75216
W Illinois Ave	
100-2399	75224
2400-2899	75233
3100-3298	75211
3300-5600	75211
5602-5698	75211
Image Cir, Ct, Ln & Pl	75211
Imperial St	75210
Inadale Ave	75228
Inca Dr	75216
Independence Dr	75237
Indian Trl	75229
Indian Creek Trl	75241
Indian Ridge Trl	75232
Indian Springs Rd	75248
Indian Summer Trl	75241
Indian Wells Rd	75253
Indiana Blvd	75226
Indianola St	75227
Inge St	75235
Ingersoll St	75212
Inglecliff Dr	75230
Ingleside Dr	75229
Inspiration Dr	75207
Insurance Ln	75205
Interlachen Cir	75287
Interlude Dr	75241
International Pkwy	75228
Interstate Highway 30	75211
Inverness Ln	75214
Inverrary Ct	75287
Investment Dr	75236
Investor Dr	75237
Inwood Cir	75244
Inwood Rd	
1100-1298	75247
1300-1399	75247
1401-1699	75247
1701-1797	75235
1799-3399	75235
3401-3499	75235
3500-9199	75209
9200-9398	75220
9400-9999	75220
10000-10198	75229
10200-11399	75229
11401-11699	75229
11800-14199	75244
14201-14399	75244
Iowa Ave	75216
N & S Ira Ave	75211
Ireland Ave	75227
Iron Ridge St	75247
Irongate Ln	75214
Ironhorse Dr	75227
Irons St	75217
Ironwood Ln	75249
Ironworks Dr	75253
Iroquois Dr & St	75212
Irvin Simmons Dr	75229
Irving Ave	75219
Irving Blvd	
1600-1698	75207
1700-2799	75207
2801-2899	75207
2900-4799	75247
Irwindell Blvd	75211
Isabella Ln	75229
Isla Verde Plz	75211
Itasca Dr & Pl	75228
Ivan St	75201
Ivandell Ave	75211
Ivanhoe Ln	
1900-2199	75208
2201-2299	75208
4000-4099	75212
Ivory Ln	75216
Ivy Ln	75241
Ivy Hill Dr	75287
Ivy Ridge St	75241
Ivygate Cir	75238
Ivyglen Dr	75254
Ivywood Dr	75232
J J Lemmon Rd	75241
Jack Casey Ct	75217
Jackson St	
500-1198	75202
1200-1300	75202
1302-1398	75202
1400-1598	75201
1600-2199	75201
Jackson Creek Dr	75243
Jacob Way	75211
Jacobie Blvd	75217
Jacobson Dr	75253
Jacotte Cir	75214
Jadaglen Dr	75241
Jade Dr	75232
Jadewood Dr	75232
Jaffee St	75216
Jaguar Ln	75226
Jalisco Plz	75211
Jamaica St	75210
James Dr	75227
Jameson Dr	75220
Jamestown Rd	75230
Jamie Way	75236
Jane Ln	75247
Janlyn Ln	75234
N & S Janmar Ct & Dr	75230
Jantez St	75212
Janwood Ln	75234
Jared Dr	75217
Jarvis Cir	75215
Jason Dr	75206
Jasoncrest Trl	75243
Jb Jackson Jr Blvd	75210
Jeane St	75217
Jeff St	75212
E & W Jeffaline Ln	75233
E Jefferson Blvd	75203
W Jefferson Blvd	
100-2199	75208
2201-2299	75208
2400-6000	75211
6002-9314	75211
Jeffries St	
1400-1698	75226
1701-1799	75226
2400-2598	75215
2600-3600	75215
3602-3698	75215
Jennie Lee Cir & Ln	75227
Jennifer Pl	75243
Jennings Ave	75216
Jenny Ln	75227
Jenny Dale Dr	75212
Jensen Ct	75204
Jeran Dr	75217
E Jerden Ln	75203
W Jerden Ln	75208
Jereme Trl	75252
Jericho Ct	75248
Jerome St	75223
Jerridee Cir	75229
Jessica Ln	75217
N & S Jester Ave	75211
Jesus Maria Ct	75236
Jett St	75234
Jewell Pl	75215
Jill Ln	75227
Jim St	75212
Jim Loftin Rd	75224
N Jim Miller Rd	
101-197	75217
199-2099	75217
2301-2497	75227
2499-5499	75227
5500-6399	75228
S Jim Miller Rd	75217
Jim Reinthal Ct	75217
Jo Pierce St	75217
Joan Dr	75217
Joanna Dr	75234
Joaquin Dr	75228
Joe Field Rd	75229
John Mccoy Dr	75227
John W Carpenter Fwy	75247
John West Rd	75228
Johnson Ln	75241
Jollyn Ct	75241
Jonelle St	75217
Jones St	75210
Jonesboro Ave	75228
Jordan St	75215
Jordan Ridge Dr	75236
Jordan Valley Rd	75253
Joseph Hardin Dr	75236
Joseph Wiley St	75210
Josephine St	75246
Josey Ln	
11800-11898	75234
11900-13999	75234
13904-13904	75381
14000-14598	75234
14001-14199	75234
Joshua Ln	75287
Jourdan Way	
8500-8699	75225
8701-8899	75225
9600-9999	75230
Joy St	75203
Joyce Way	75225
Joymeadow Dr	75218
Jubilant Dr	75237
Jubilee Trl	75229
Judd Ct	75243
Judge Dupree Dr	75241
Judi Ct & St	75252
Julian St	75203
Julianna Cir	75229
Juliet Pl	75252
Juliette Fowler St	75214
Julius Schepps Fwy	
3201-3799	75215
7301-7399	75216
Junction St	75210
June Dr	75211
Junior Dr	75208
Juniper Cv	75234
Juniper Dr	75220
Junius St	
3500-3698	75246
3700-4899	75246
4900-5800	75214
5802-6298	75214
Junkin Ct	75249
Jupiter Rd	
10801-11297	75218
11299-12499	75218
12600-12899	75238
12901-13799	75238
Justice Ln	75287
Justice Way	75220
N & S Justin Ave	75211
K St	75215
Kahala Dr	75218
Kahn St	75241
Kalani Pl	75240
Kansas Ave	75241
Karen Ln	75217
Karlie Way	75236
Kate St	75225
Kathleen Ave	75216
Kavasar Dr	75241
Kaw St	75241
Kaywood Dr	75209
Keats Dr	75211
Keeler St	75215
Keenan Bridge Rd	75234
Keeneland Ct & Pkwy	75211
Keepers Green St	75240
Kelann Ct	75253
Keller Springs Rd	75248
Kellogg Ave	75216
Kelly Ave	75215
Kelly Blvd	75287
Kelly Cir	75287
Kelly Cave Trl	75252
Kelman St	75214
Kelsey Rd	75229
Kelso Dr	75211
Kelton Dr	75209
Kelvingate Ct	75225
Kemp St	75241
Kemper Ct	75220
Kempwood Ln	75253
Kemrock Dr	75241
Kendale Dr	75220
Kendall Square Dr	75217
Kendallwood Dr	75240
Kenesaw Dr	75212
Kenilworth St	75210
Kennington Ct	75248
Kennison Dr	75227
Kenny Ln	75230
Kenshire Ln	75230
Kensington Ln	75208
Kenswick Ct	75252
Kent St	75203
Kenton Dr	75231
Kentshire Ln	75287
Kenwell St	75209
Kenwhite Dr	75231
Kenwood Ave	
5700-6099	75206
6100-6999	75214
Kernack St	75211
Kerr Cir, Ct, Pl & Trl	75244
Kerrville St	75227
Kessler Ct & Pkwy	75208
Kessler Canyon Dr	75208
Kessler Lake Dr	75208
Kessler Springs Ave	75208
Kessler Woods Ct & Trl	75208
Keswick Dr	75232
Kettering Ct	75248
Kevin Dr	75248
Key St	75205
Key Biscayne Dr	75217
Key Haven Dr	75236
Keyhole Ln	75229
Keyport Dr	75234
Keyridge Dr	75241
Kidd Springs Dr	75208
Kidwell St	75214
E Kiest Blvd	
1101-1197	75216
1199-3100	75216
3102-3198	75216
3200-3899	75203
W Kiest Blvd	
101-297	75224
299-1200	75224
1202-2398	75224
2400-3900	75233
3902-4298	75233
4400-6099	75236
6101-6799	75236
7777-7799	75211
Kiest Forest Ct & Dr	75233
Kiest Knoll Dr	75233
Kiest Polk Vlg	75224
Kiest Valley Ct & Pkwy	75233
Kiestcrest Dr	75233
Kiesthill Dr	75233
Kiestmeadow Dr	75233
Kiestridge Dr	75233
Kiestwood Dr	75233
Kilarney Dr	75218
Kilbride Cir & Ln	75248
Kilburn Ave	75216
Kildare Ave	75216
Kilgore St	75212
Kilkenny Pl	75228
Kilkirk Ln	75228
Killion Dr	75229
Kilmichael Ln	75248
Kiltartan Dr	75228
Kimball Ridge Cir, Ct, Dr & Pl	75233
Kimballdale Dr	75233
Kimberly Ln	75214
Kimble St	75215
Kimsey Dr	75235
King Arthur Dr	75247
King Cole Cir, Ct & Dr	75216
King Edward Dr & Pl	75228
King George Dr	75235
King James Dr	75247
King Of Spain Ct	75248
King William Dr	75220
Kingbridge St	75212
Kingdom Estates Dr	75236
Kingfisher Dr	75236
Kings Hwy	75208
Kings Rd	75219
Kings Hollow Ct	75248
Kingsbury Dr	75231
Kingscrest Cir	75248
Kingsfield Rd	75217
Kingsford Ave	75227
Kingsgate Ct	75225
Kingshollow Dr	75248
Kingsley Dr	75216
Kingsley Rd	
8801-8899	75231
11333-11333	75238
Kingsley Creek Cir	75231
Kingsman Dr	75228
Kingspoint Dr	75238
Kingsridge Dr	75287
Kingston St	75211
Kingstree Dr	75248
Kingswood Dr	75228
Kinkaid Cir & Dr	75220
Kinmore St	75223
Kinross Dr	75232
Kinslow Dr	75217
Kipling Dr	75217
Kirby St	75204
Kirkham Dr	75252

Street	ZIP
Kirkhaven Dr	75238
Kirkland Ct	75237
Kirkley St	75241
Kirkmeadow Ln	75287
Kirkwood Dr	75218
Kirnwood Ct	75232
Kirnwood Dr	
300-398	75232
400-1500	75232
1502-2498	75232
3201-3299	75237
E Kirnwood Dr	75241
Kirnwood Pl	75232
Kirven St	75227
Kiska St	75216
Kissell Ln	75217
Kit Ln	75240
Kittiwake Cir	75211
Kitty St	75241
Kittyhawk Ln	75217
Kiva Ln	75227
Kiwanis Rd	75236
Kleberg Rd	75253
Kline Dr	75229
Klondike Dr	75228
Knight St	75219
Knightsbridge Dr	75252
Knightwood Ct	75225
Knobby Tree	75243
Knoll Krest Dr	75238
Knoll Manor Ln	75206
Knoll Ridge Dr	75249
Knoll Trail Dr	75248
Knollmeadow Ln	75287
Knollview Dr	75248
Knollwood Dr	75240
Knott Pl	75208
Knox St	75205
Knoxville Rd & St	75211
Kodiak Dr	75217
Koi Pond Ct	75248
Koko Head Cir	75218
Kolloch Dr	75216
Komalty Dr	75217
Konawa Dr	75217
Kool Ave	75241
Korgan St	75216
Kostner Ave	75216
Kraft St	75212
N Kramer Dr	75211
Kristen Dr	75216
Krueger St	75224
Kushla Ave	75216
Kyle Ave	75208
Kynard St	75215
Kyser St	75216
La Avenida Dr	75248
La Barba Cir	75227
La Bolsa Dr	75248
La Cabeza Dr	75248
La Cosa Dr	75248
La Estrella Plz	75203
La Flor Ln	75241
La Fonda Blvd	75228
La Foy Blvd	75209
La Grange Cir & Dr	75241
La Jolla Ln	75236
La Joya Dr	75220
La Kenta Cir	75234
La Mancha Dr	75248
La Manga Dr	75248
La Palma Dr	75253
La Paloma Dr	75236
La Paz St	75217
La Place Dr	75220
La Playa Dr	75233
E La Prada Dr	75228
La Reunion Pkwy	75212
La Rioja Dr	75217
La Risa Dr	75248
La Rue St	75211
La Senda Pl	75208
La Sierra Dr	75231
La Sobrina Dr	75248
La Strada Ct	75220
La Verdura Dr	75248
La Verne Ave	75227
La Vista Ct	75206
La Vista Dr	
5700-6028	75206
6030-6038	75206
6101-6197	75214
6199-7499	75214
Labett St	75217
Labron Ave	75209
Lacamp St	75232
Lacehaven Cir & Dr	75248
Lacewood Dr	75224
Laclede Ave	75204
Lacompte Dr	75227
Lacrosse Dr	75231
Lacy Blvd	75227
Lacywood Ln	75227
Ladale Dr	75212
Ladd St	75212
Ladera Dr	75248
Ladonia Dr	75217
Ladybird Ln	75220
Lafayette St	75204
Lafayette Way	75230
Lago Vis W	75234
Lago Vista Ct	75236
Lagoon Dr	75207
Lagow St	75210
Laguna Dr	75287
Lahoma St	75235
Laingtree Dr	75243
Lairds Ln	75248
Lakawana St	75247
Lake Ave	75219
Lake Anna Dr	75217
Lake Bend Dr	75212
Lake Bluff Dr	75249
Lake Circle Dr	75214
Lake Cliff Dr	75203
Lake Country Ct	75234
Lake Edge Dr	75230
Lake Forest Dr	75254
Lake Gardens Dr	75218
Lake Grove Ln	75211
Lake Haven Dr	75238
E & W Lake Highlands Dr & Pl	75218
Lake Hollow Dr	75212
Lake June Pl & Rd	75217
Lake North Cir	75220
Lake Placid Dr	75232
Lake Pointe Dr	75212
Lake Terrace Cir & Dr	75218
Lake Vista Dr	75249
Lakedale Dr	75218
Lakefair Cir	75214
Lakefield Blvd	75220
Lakeforest Ct	75214
Lakehill Ct	75220
Lakehurst Ave	75230
Lakehurst Ct	75211
Lakeland Dr	
1600-2098	75218
2100-2699	75228
Lakemere Dr	75238
Lakemont Dr	
8400-8899	75209
9500-9999	75220
Lakenheath Pl	75204
Lakeridge Dr	75218
Lakeshore Dr	75214
Lakeside Dr	
2400-2699	75253
4201-4399	75219
4400-4998	75205
Lakeside Park	75225
E & W Lakeview Dr	75216
Lakeway Ct	75230
Lakewood Blvd	75214
N Lamar St	75202
S Lamar St	
205-897	75202
899-999	75202
1000-6099	75215
Lambert St	75203
Lamesa St	75215
Lamont Ave	75216
Lampasas Ave	75233
Lamplighter Ln	75229
Lanark Ave	75203
Lanarkshire Dr	75238
N Lancaster Ave	75203
S Lancaster Ave	75203
S Lancaster Rd	
2300-5099	75216
5100-8899	75241
Lancelot Dr	75229
Land Dr	75253
Landis St	75203
Landlewood Ct	75287
Landlock Dr	75218
Landmark Blvd & Pl	75254
Landpiper Ct	75287
Landrum Ave	75216
Landrum Lakes Ct	75212
Lane Park Ct & Dr	75225
Lanecrest Dr	75228
Laneri Ave	75206
Lanett Cir	75238
Lanewood Cir	75218
Laneyvale Ave	75217
Langdale Cir	75238
Langdon Ave	75235
Langdon Rd	75241
E Langdon Rd	75241
Lange Cir	75214
Langford St	75208
Langland Rd	75244
Langston Ct	75235
Lanoue Dr	75220
Lansdowne Dr	75217
Lansford Ave	75224
Lanshire Dr	75238
Lansing St	75203
Lantana Ln	75241
Lantern Ln	75236
Lanward Cir & Dr	75238
Lanyon Dr	75227
Lapanto Ln	75227
Lapsley St	75212
Larailla St	75203
E & W Laramie Ln	75217
Larchbrook Cir & Dr	75238
Larchcrest Dr	75238
Larchfield Ln	75238
Larchgate Dr	75243
Larchmont Dr	75252
Larchmont St	75205
Larchridge Dr	75232
Larchview Dr	75254
Larchway Dr	75232
Larchwood Dr	75238
Laredo Plz	75211
Laren Ln	75244
Larga Dr	75220
Largent Ave	75214
Larimore Ln	75236
Lark Ln	75209
Lark Meadow Way	75287
Larkglen Cir	75230
Larkhill Dr	75211
Larkin Dr	75227
Larkspur Ln	75233
Larmanda St	75231
Larry Dr	75228
Larson Ln	75229
Las Brisas Dr	75243
Las Campanas Dr	75234
Las Cruces Ln	
1700-2099	75217
2300-2399	75227
Las Flores Dr	75254
Las Haciendas Dr	75211
Las Pinas Ct	75211
Las Villas Ave	75211
Lasalle Dr	75203
Lasater Rd	75253
Lasca St	75227
Lashley Dr & Pl	75232
Latham Dr	75229
Lathrop Dr	75229
Latimer St	75215
Latta Cir, Pkwy & St	75227
Lattimore Dr	75252
Lauder Ln	75248
Lauderdale St	75241
Laughlin Dr	75228
Laura Ln	75241
Lauraette Dr	75208
Laurel Canyon Dr	75233
Laurel Hill Dr	75253
Laurel Leaf Ct	75212
Laurel Oaks Dr	75248
Laurel Valley Rd	75248
Laurel Wood Ln	75240
E Laureland Rd	75241
W Laureland Rd	75232
Lauren Ln	75227
Laurenwood Dr	75217
Laureston Pl	75225
Lausanne Ave	75208
Lavalle Ln	75243
Lavano Ln	75228
Lavendale Ave & Cir	75230
Lavita Ln	75234
Lawler Rd	75243
Lawndale Dr	75211
Lawngate Dr	75287
Lawnhaven Rd	75230
Lawnview Ave	75227
Lawrence St	75215
Laws St	75202
E & W Lawson Rd	75253
E Lawther Dr	75218
W Lawther Dr	
3401-4797	75214
4799-4899	75214
4901-4999	75238
Lawtherwood Ct & Pl	75214
Lawton Dr	75217
Laysan Ct	75249
Lazy Acres Cir	75240
Lazy River Cir & Dr	75241
Lazydale Dr	75228
Le Clerc Ave	75210
Le Forge Ave	75216
Le Harve Dr	75211
Le Mans Dr	75238
Le May Ave	75216
Lea Crest Dr	75216
Leachman Cir	75229
Leads St	75203
Leafwood Dr	75253
Leafy Ln	75248
Leahy Dr	75229
Leameadow Dr	75248
Leana Ave	75241
Leander Dr	75211
Leaning Oaks St	75241
Lear St	75215
Leaside Dr	75238
Leath Ct & St	75212
Leatherneck Pl	75211
Leatrice Dr	75208
Leavalley Cir & Dr	75248
Lebanon Ave	75208
Lebrock St	75241
Lechlade Ln	75252
Leda Dr	75218
E Ledbetter Dr	
201-297	75216
299-3299	75216
3301-3499	75216
4000-4100	75241
4102-4298	75241
S Ledbetter Dr	
2501-2799	75211
3400-4299	75236
W Ledbetter Dr	
101-397	75224
399-2399	75224
2400-4399	75233
4400-5799	75236
Ledgestone Dr	75214
Ledyard Dr	75248
Lee Pkwy	75219
Lee St	
2700-2899	75206
3201-3297	75205
3299-3300	75205
3302-3398	75205
Lee Hall Dr	75235
Leesburg St	75212
Leeshire Dr	75228
Leeway Dr	75236
Leewood St	75212
Legacy Dr	75217
Legendary Ln	75224
Legters Dr	75236
Lehigh Dr	75214
Leigh Ann Dr	75232
Leinsper Green St	75240
Leisure Dr & Way	75243
Leland Ave	75215
Leland College Dr	75241
Lemmon Ave	
2501-2797	75204
2799-3199	75204
3201-3299	75204
3701-3797	75219
3799-4804	75219
4806-4850	75219
4901-4997	75209
4999-8199	75209
8201-8699	75209
E Lemmon Ave	75204
Lemmonwood Dr	75231
Lenel Dr & Pl	75220
Lennox Dr	75244
Lennox Ln	75229
Lenosa Ln	75253
Lenway St	75215
Leo Ln	75229
Leon Dr	75217
Leona Ave	75231
Leonard St	75201
Leonila Plz	75211
Leota Dr	75217
Leroy Ct & Rd	75217
Les Chateaux Dr	75235
Les Jardins Dr	75229
Leslie St	75207
Lester Dr	75219
Leston St	75247
Leta Mae Cir & Ln	75234
Levant Ave	75217
E Levee St	75207
Levelland Rd	75252
Lewis Ct & St	75206
Lewisburg Ln	75237
Lewiston Ave	
2000-2099	75217
2100-2999	75227
Lexington Ave	75205
Libby Ln	75228
Liberation Ct	75287
Liberty Ct	75204
Liberty Hl	75248
Liberty St	75204
Library Ln	75232
Licorice Pl	75217
Life Ave	75212
Light Point Dr	75228
Light Shore Dr	75228
Lighthouse Way	75249
Lilac Ln	75209
Lilgreen St	75223
Lillard Ln	75234
Lillian St	75211
Lima St	75232
Limerick Dr	75218
Limestone Dr	75217
Lina St	75287
Linchins Dr	75235
Lincoln Plz	75201
Lincolnshire Ct	75287
Linda Dr	75220
Linda Ln	75241
Lindaloe St	75236
Lindaro Ln	75228
Lindbergh Dr	75228
Lindell Ave	75206
Linden Ln	75230
Lindenshire Ln	75230
Lindenwood Ave	75205
Linder Ave	75215
N & S Lindhurst Ave	75229
Lindsley Ave	75223
Lineville Dr	75234
Linfield Rd	75216
Lingo Ln	75228
Linkwood Dr	75238
Linnet Ln	75209
Linwood Ave	75209
Lippitt Ave	75218
Lipscomb Ave	75214
Lipton Ln	75217
Liptonshire Dr	75238
Listi Dr	75238
Little Canyon Rd	75249
Little Fawn Ln	75249
Little Fox Dr	75253
Little Pocket Rd	75228
Little River Dr	75241
Littlecrest Dr	75234
Live Oak St	
2000-2098	75201
2500-2598	75204
2600-4899	75204
4900-5799	75206
5800-5899	75214
Lively Cir & Ln	75220
Livenshire Dr	75238
Livingston Ave	
4201-4297	75205
4299-4599	75205
4600-5399	75209
Livvie Meador Ln	75227
Lizshire Ave	75231
Lizzy Dr	75211
Llano Ave	
5700-6099	75206
6100-6399	75214
N Llewellyn Ave	75208
S Llewellyn Ave	
200-298	75208
300-1099	75208
1300-1898	75224
1900-3299	75224
Lloyd Cir, Ct & Dr	75252
Lloyd Valley Ln	75230
Lobdell St	75215
Lobello Dr	75229
Local Vista Dr	75217
Locarno Dr	75243
Loch Maree Ln	75248
Loch Ness Dr	75218
Lochinvar Ct & Dr	75254
Lochlynn Cir	75228
Lochmeadows Dr	75244
Lochmond Cir	75218
Lochspring Dr	75218
Lochwood Blvd	75218
Lockhart Ave	75228
Lockhaven Dr	75238
Lockheed Ave	75209
Lockmoor Ln	75220
Lockridge Cir	75233
Locksley Ave	75209
Locust Ave	75216
Lodge St	75204
Lofland St	75235
Log Cabin Rd	75253
Logan St	75215
Logancraft Dr	75227
Loganwood Dr	75227
Lolita Dr	75227
Loma Garden St	75217
Loma Vista Dr	75243
Lomax Dr	75227
Lombardy Ln	75220
Lomita Ln	75220
Lomo Alto Ct	75219
Lomo Alto Dr	
4100-4399	75219
4401-5897	75205
5899-6699	75205
6701-6999	75205
8100-8198	75225
Londenberry Dr	75217
London Ct & Ln	75252
London Fog Dr	75227
Londonderry Ln	75228
Lone Moor Cir	75248
Lone Oak Dr	75232
Lone Star Dr	75212
Lone Tree Ln	75218
Lonesome Dove Ln	75237
Long Canyon Trl	75249
Long Grove St	75253
N & S Longacre Ln	75217
Longbow Ct	75229
Longbranch Ln	75217
Longfellow Dr	75230
Longhorn St	75228
Longleaf Ln	75232
Longley Ct	75252
Longmeade Dr	75234
Longmeadow Ct & Dr	75238
Longmont Dr	75238
Longpoint Ave	75247
Longridge Dr	75232
Longview St	75206
Longvista Dr	75248
Longwood Ln	75228
Lonsdale Ave	75217
Lontos Dr	75214
Loomis Ave	75215
Loree Dr	75228
Lorelle Pl	75204
Loring Dr	75209
Lorinser Ln	75220
Loris Ln	75216
Lorna Ln	75214
Lorraine Ave	
4200-4599	75205
4600-4699	75209
Lorwood Dr	75238
Los Alamitos Dr	75232
Los Altos Dr	75248
Los Angeles Blvd	75233
Los Arboles Ct	75230
Los Cabos Dr	75232
Los Gatos Dr	75232
Losa Dr	75218
Lost Canyon Dr	75249
Lost Creek Dr	75224
Lost Mirage Dr	75232
Lost Valley Dr	75234
Lost View Rd	75252
Lottie Ln	75253
Lotus St	75203
Louise Ave	75226
E Louisiana Ave	
100-398	75216
400-1499	75216
1500-1699	75203
W Louisiana Ave	75224
Louniani Dr	75252
Lourdes St	75211
Love Pl	75237
Love Field Dr	75235
Lovedale Ave	75235
Lovejoy Dr	75217
Loveland Dr	75252
Lovers Ln	75225
E Lovers Ln	
5700-5798	75206
5800-5900	75206
5902-6072	75206
6100-6699	75214
W Lovers Ln	
2100-2699	75235
4001-4197	75209
4199-5799	75209
5800-5898	75225
Lovers Lane Cir	75225
Lovett Ave	75227
Loving Ave	75214
Lovingood Dr	75241
Lovington Dr	75252
Lowell St	75214
Lowery St	75215
Lubbock Dr	75238
Lucas Dr	75219
Lucchese Ln	75253

Lucerne St 75214
Lucile Herrin Ln 75227
Lucille St 75204
Lucky Ln
2700-2798 75241
4701-4899 75247
Lucy St 75217
Lueders Ln 75230
Lufield Dr 75229
Lufkin St 75217
Lullwater Dr
8200-8499 75218
8500-8799 75238
Luna Rd
10500-10698 75220
10700-10800 75220
10802-10898 75220
11201-11247 75229
11249-11300 75229
11302-11398 75229
11400-11498 75234
11500-11799 75234
Lunar Ln 75218
Lupo Dr 75207
Lupton Cir & Dr 75225
Luther Ln 75225
Luxar Way 75233
Luzon St 75216
Lyddon Ln 75232
Lydgate Dr 75238
Lydia Dr 75217
Lyman Cir 75211
Lynbrook Dr 75238
Lyndon B Johnson Fwy
1500-3100 75234
3102-3498 75234
3800-3998 75244
4000-4299 75244
4301-5099 75244
5301-5397 75240
5399-6700 75240
6702-6898 75240
7500-7598 75251
7600-8140 75251
8142-8198 75251
8330-9098 75243
9100-9500 75243
9502-9798 75243
11300-11598 75238
12600-12698 75228
34100-34198 75241
34200-34900 75241
34902-35698 75241
39000-39598 75232
39600-39698 75237
39700-39799 75237
Lynford Dr 75238
Lynn Haven Ave 75216
Lynnacre Cir & Dr 75211
Lynngrove Dr 75238
Lynworth Dr 75248
Lyola St 75241
Lyoncrest Ct 75287
Lyons St 75210
Lyre Ln 75214
Lyte St 75201
Lytham Dr 75252
Mabel Ave 75209
Macarthur Ave 75209
Macbeth Pl 75252
Maceo Cir 75216
Mack Cir & Ln 75227
Macmanus Dr 75228
Macomba Ct 75217
Macon St 75215
Macy Ln 75253
Maddox St 75217
Madeleine Cir 75230
Madera St 75206
N Madison Ave
203-397 75208
399-1299 75208
1300-1399 75203
S Madison Ave 75208
Madras Dr 75217
Madrid St 75216
Magdeline St 75212

Magna Vista Dr 75216
Magnolia Hill Ct 75201
Maguires Bridge Dr 75231
Maham Rd 75240
Mahanna St
3100-3399 75235
3401-3499 75209
Mahanna Springs Dr 75235
Mahogany Trl 75252
Mahon St 75201
Maiden Ct 75254
Mail Ave 75235
Main Pl 75226
Main St
500-1419 75202
1500-2206 75201
2208-2298 75201
2501-2597 75226
2599-4499 75226
S Main St 75261
W Main St 75208
Majesty Dr 75247
Major Dr 75227
Majorca St 75248
Malabar Ln 75230
Malcolm Cir, Ct & Dr 75214
Malcolm X Blvd 75215
N Malcolm X Blvd 75226
S Malcolm X Blvd 75226
Malden Ln 75216
Malibu Dr 75229
Mallard Dr 75236
Mallory Dr 75216
Malmesbury Rd 75252
Malone Cliff Vw 75208
Manana Dr 75220
Manchester Dr 75220
Mandalay Dr 75228
Mandarin Way 75249
Manderville Ln 75231
Manett St
4600-4899 75204
4900-5399 75206
Mangold Cir 75229
Manhattan Dr 75217
Manila Rd 75212
Manitoba Ave 75241
Manning Ln 75220
Mannington Dr 75232
Manor Way 75235
Manor Oaks Dr 75248
Manorview Cir & Ln 75228
Manson Ct 75229
Manuel Plz 75201
Manufacturing St 75207
N & S Manus Dr 75224
Manzano Cir 75230
Maple Ave
2500-2798 75201
2800-3144 75201
3146-3298 75201
3500-4899 75219
4900-6999 75235
Maple Creek Ln 75252
Maple Glen Dr 75231
Maple Routh
Connection 75201
Maple Springs Blvd 75235
Maplecrest Dr 75254
Mapledale Cir & Dr 75234
Maplegrove Ln 75218
Maplehill Dr 75238
Mapleleaf Cir & Ln 75233
Mapleridge Dr 75238
Mapleshade Ln 75252
Mapleton Dr 75228
Mapletree Ln 75252
Mapleview Cir 75248
Maplewood Ave 75205
Mar Vista Trl 75236
Marbella Ln 75228
Marble Falls Dr 75287
Marblehead Dr 75232
Marbrook Dr 75230
Marburg St 75215
Marcell Ave 75211

March Ave 75209
Marchant Cir 75218
Marco Island Ct 75217
Marcole St 75212
Marder St 75215
Marena Moore Ct 75232
Marfa Ave 75216
Margarita Dr 75232
Margate Dr 75220
Margewood Dr 75236
Marianne Cir 75252
Mariano Plz 75211
Maribeth Dr 75252
Marideen Ave 75233
Marie St 75204
Marielle Cir 75232
Marietta Dr 75234
Marietta Ln 75241
Marigold Dr 75241
Marilla Ct & St 75201
Marimont Ln 75228
Marine Way 75211
Mariner Dr 75237
Maringo Dr 75227
Marion Dr 75211
Mariposa Dr 75228
Marjorie Ave 75216
Mark Trail Way 75232
Mark Twain Cir & Dr 75234
Markanne Dr 75243
N & S Market St 75202
Market Center Blvd 75207
Markison Rd
10300-10398 75238
10400-10599 75238
10502-10502 75355
10600-10698 75238
Marks Dr 75217
Markville Dr
9000-9199 75243
9130-9130 75374
9200-9298 75243
Marla Dr 75217
N & S Marlborough
Ave 75208
Marlette Ln 75235
Marlin Dr 75228
Marlow Ave 75252
Marne St 75215
Marquette St 75225
Marquis Ln 75229
Marquita Ave
5700-6099 75206
6100-6499 75214
N Marsalis Ave 75203
S Marsalis Ave
100-1199 75203
1200-4899 75216
5100-5899 75241
5901-5999 75241
Marsalis Pkwy 75203
Marsann Ln 75234
Marseille Pl 75204
Marsh Ln
9400-9999 75220
10000-11500 75229
11502-11798 75229
11800-11898 75234
11900-13099 75234
13101-14999 75234
17400-17598 75287
17600-19099 75287
Marsh Lane Pl 75220
Marshall Dr 75210
Marshalldell Ave 75211
Mart St 75212
Martel Ave
5200-5398 75206
5400-6099 75206
6100-6399 75214
Martha Ln 75229
Martin Luther King Jr
Blvd
1000-1398 75215
1400-3199 75215
3200-3399 75210
3401-3999 75210

Martindell Ave 75211
Martinez Trl 75212
Martinique Ave 75223
Marvel Dr 75217
Marview Ln 75227
Marvin Ave 75211
Marvin D Love Fwy
3300-3799 75224
3801-4199 75224
5300-5399 75232
5401-5799 75232
5801-6197 75237
6199-8099 75237
Mary St 75206
Mary Cliff Rd 75208
Mary Dan Dr 75217
Mary Margaret St 75287
Marydale Dr 75208
Maryibel Cir 75237
Maryland Ave
1700-4300 75216
4302-4698 75216
5100-5299 75241
Mask Dr 75241
Masland Cir 75230
Mason Pl 75204
Mason Dells Dr 75230
N Masters Dr
106-114 75217
116-2099 75217
2100-2999 75227
S Masters Dr 75217
Masters Rd 75217
Matador Dr 75220
Matagorda Dr 75232
Matalee Ave 75206
Matamoros Plz 75211
Matchpoint Pl 75243
Materhorn Dr 75228
Mateur St 75211
Mather Ct 75211
Mathis Ave
11300-11399 75229
11400-11499 75234
Matilda St 75206
Matisse Ln 75230
Matland Dr 75237
Mattison St 75217
Mattney Cir & Dr 75237
Maureen Dr 75232
Maurine F Bailey Way 75215
Maverick Ave 75228
Max Dr 75249
Max Goldblatt Dr 75227
Maxim Dr 75244
Maxine Dr 75241
Maxwell Ave 75217
May St 75208
Maybank Dr 75220
Maybeth St 75212
Mayblossom Way 75217
Maydelle Ln 75234
Mayfair Blvd 75218
Mayflower Dr 75208
Mayhall St 75203
Mayhew Dr 75228
Maylee Blvd 75228
Mayo St 75204
Mayrant Dr 75224
Maywood Ave 75216
Mazatlan Ave 75232
Mcadams Ave 75224
Mcbroom St 75212
Mccain Ct & Dr 75249
Mccallum Blvd 75252
Mcclintock St 75234
Mcclung Ln 75217
Mccommas Blvd
5200-6099 75206
6100-6599 75214
Mccommas Bluff Rd 75241
Mccosh Dr 75228
Mccoy Pl & St 75204
Mccraw Dr 75209
Mccree Rd 75238
Mccutcheon Ln 75227

Mcdaniel Dr 75212
Mcdermott Ave 75215
Mcdonald Ave 75215
Mcdowell Ave 75216
Mcelree St 75217
Mcewen Rd 75244
Mcfarlin Blvd 75205
Mcgowan St 75203
Mcgregor St 75217
Mcintosh Ct 75238
Mckamy Blvd 75248
Mckee St 75215
Mckell St 75204
Mckenzie St 75223
Mckim Cir & Dr 75227
Mckinney Ave
701-997 75202
999-1099 75202
1101-1799 75202
1801-2599 75201
2600-4199 75204
4200-5300 75205
5302-5398 75205
Mckinnon St 75201
Mclarty Dr 75241
Mclean Ave 75211
Mcmillan Ave 75206
Mcnabb Dr 75217
Mcneil St 75227
Mcpherson St 75212
Mcrae Rd 75228
Mcshann Rd 75230
W Mcvey Ave 75224
E Mcvey St 75216
Meade St 75232
Meaders Cir 75229
Meaders Ln
5100-5699 75229
5701-5799 75229
5800-5999 75230
Meadow Rd
6000-7799 75230
8000-8399 75231
Meadow St 75215
Meadow Bluff Ln 75237
Meadow Crest Dr 75229
Meadow Dawn Ln 75237
Meadow Gate Ln 75237
Meadow Green Dr 75234
Meadow Grove Ln 75287
Meadow Harvest Ln 75237
Meadow Heath Cir &
Ln 75232
Meadow Isle Ln 75237
Meadow Lake Ave &
Cir 75214
Meadow Nest Dr 75236
Meadow Oaks Dr 75230
Meadow Park Dr 75230
Meadow Port Dr 75234
Meadow Ridge Dr 75236
Meadow Stone Ln 75237
Meadow Trail Dr 75236
Meadow Tree Cir 75248
Meadow Valley Ln 75232
Meadow Vista Dr & Pl 75248
Meadow Way Ct & Ln 75228
Meadowbriar Ln 75230
Meadowbrook Dr
9200-9999 75220
10000-10099 75229
Meadowchase Way 75287
Meadowcliff Ln 75238
Meadowcreek Dr
4500-4798 75248
4800-6099 75248
6100-6498 75254
6500-7199 75254
Meadowcrest Dr 75230
Meadowdale Ln 75229
Meadowglen Dr 75238
Meadowhaven Dr 75254
Meadowhill Dr 75238
Meadowick Ln 75227
Meadowknoll Cir & Dr 75243
Meadowlark Ln 75214

Meadowood Rd 75220
Meadowshire Dr 75232
Meadowside Dr 75240
Meadowspring Ln 75218
Meadowview St 75210
Meandering Pl 75248
Meandering Way
13000-13400 75240
13402-13898 75240
14101-14297 75254
14299-14600 75254
14602-14798 75254
15201-16299 75248
17400-18299 75252
Mecca St 75206
Medalist Dr 75232
Medallion Ln 75229
Medallion Shp Ctr 75214
Medical Pkwy 75234
Medical District Dr
1200-1299 75207
1301-1499 75207
1900-2299 75235
2301-2399 75235
Medici Pl 75252
Medill St 75215
Medina Dr 75287
N & S Mediterranean Cir
& Dr 75238
Medlock Dr 75218
Meek St 75216
Megan Way 75232
Mehalia Dr 75241
Melba St
100-899 75208
2800-2899 75211
Melbourne Ave
1100-2299 75224
2500-2599 75233
Meletio Ln 75230
Melinda Ln 75217
Melinda Hills Dr 75212
Melissa Ln 75229
Melissa River Way 75212
Melody Ln 75231
Melrose Ave 75206
Melshire Dr 75230
Memory Ln 75217
Memory Lane Blvd 75241
Memphis St 75207
Mendenhall Dr 75244
Mendocino Dr 75248
Mendosa Ln 75227
Menefee Dr 75227
Menger Ave 75227
Menier St 75209
Mentor Ave 75216
Merallak St 75215
Mercantile Row 75247
Mercedes Ave
5200-6099 75206
6101-6197 75214
6199-6699 75214
Mercer Cir, Dr & Pl 75228
Meredith Ave 75211
Merit Dr 75251
Merlin St 75215
Merrell Cir & Rd 75229
Merrifield Ave 75223
N Merrifield Rd 75211
S Merrifield Rd
100-399 75211
401-1499 75211
3300-3698 75236
3700-3999 75236
4001-4099 75236
Merrilee Ln 75214
Merrimac Ave 75206
Merriman Pkwy 75231
Merriweather Dr 75236
Merrydale Dr 75253
Mesa Cir 75235
Mesa Glen Ln 75233
Mesa Verde Trl 75232
Mesa View Dr 75241
Mesita Dr 75217

Method St 75243
Methuen Green St 75240
Metric Dr 75243
Metro Media Pl 75247
Metropolitan Ave
1400-3199 75215
3200-4600 75210
4602-4698 75210
Metz Ave 75232
Mevis Ln 75232
Mexicana Rd 75212
Mexico Ct 75236
Meyers St 75215
Meyersville Ave 75212
Miami Dr 75217
Mican Dr 75212
Michael Ln 75228
Michaelangelo Dr 75287
Michelle Dr 75217
Michigan Ave 75216
Mickey Dr 75217
Mid Surrey Ct 75229
Midbury Dr 75230
Midcrest Dr 75254
Middle Cove Dr 75248
Middle Downs Dr 75243
Middle Glen Dr 75243
Middle Knoll Dr 75238
Middlebrook Pl 75208
Middlefield St 75253
Middleton Rd 75229
Midlake Dr 75218
Midland Ln 75217
Midpark Rd 75240
Midpines Dr 75229
Midrose Trl 75287
Midvale Dr 75232
Midway Rd
8200-8799 75209
8801-9099 75209
9201-9999 75220
10001-10197 75229
10199-11500 75229
11502-11598 75229
12700-14000 75244
14002-14998 75244
17600-19100 75287
19102-19398 75287
Midway Plaza Blvd 75241
Mike St 75212
Milam St 75206
Miles St 75209
Milford Pl 75230
Milhof Dr 75228
Military Cir 75227
Military Pkwy
4700-4899 75223
4900-4998 75227
5000-9800 75227
9802-9898 75227
Mill Creek Cir, Pl &
Rd 75244
Mill Falls Dr 75248
Mill Grove Ln 75240
Mill Hollow Dr 75243
Mill Point Cir 75248
Mill Run Rd 75244
Mill Stream Dr 75232
Mill Valley Ln 75217
Millar Dr 75236
Millard St 75203
Millbrook Dr 75237
Miller Ave 75206
Miller Rd 75238
Millerdale Ln 75227
Millermore St 75216
Millers Ferry Row 75215
E Millett Dr 75241
W Millett Dr 75232
Millmar Cir & Dr 75228
Millridge Cir & Dr 75243
Millstone Dr 75228
Milltrail Dr 75238
Millview Ln 75287
Millwheat Trl 75252
Millwood Cir 75234

Millwood Dr 75234
Millwood Pl 75287
Milton Ave 75205
Milton St 75206
Milverton Dr 75217
Mimi Ct 75211
Mimms Dr 75252
Mimosa Ln 75230
Minehampton Ln 75201
Minert St 75219
Mingo St 75223
Minoco Dr 75227
Mint Way
4000-4300 75237
4302-4398 75237
4400-4699 75236
Minuet Ln 75241
Mira Lago Blvd 75234
Mira Vista Ct 75236
Miradero St 75211
Mirage Canyon Dr 75232
Mirage Valley Dr 75232
Miramar Ave 75205
Miramax Trl 75249
Miranda St 75204
Miro Pl 75204
Miron Dr 75220
Mirror Lake Dr 75217
Mission St 75206
Mission Hills Ln 75217
Mississippi Ave 75207
E Missouri Ave 75216
W Missouri Ave 75224
Missy Dr 75252
Misthaven Pl 75287
Mistletoe Dr 75223
Misty Trl 75248
Misty Bluff Ct 75249
Misty Glen Ln 75232
Misty Grove Dr 75287
Misty Lake Xing 75287
Misty Meadow Dr 75287
Misty Wood Dr 75217
Mitchell St 75210
Mitchwin Rd 75234
Mitscher Dr 75224
Mixon Dr 75220
Moberly Ln 75227
Mobile St 75208
Mockingbird Ln
2900-2998 75205
3000-4599 75205
4601-4699 75209
E Mockingbird Ln
5200-5298 75205
5300-6099 75206
6100-7299 75214
W Mockingbird Ln
200-298 75247
300-1499 75247
1501-4299 75235
4401-4497 75209
4499-5351 75209
5353-5519 75209
Mockingbird Pkwy 75205
Modella Ave 75229
Modern Pl 75214
Modesto Dr 75227
Modlin St 75228
Modree Ave 75216
Moffatt Ave 75216
Mohawk Dr 75235
Mojave Ct & Dr 75241
Moler St 75211
Mona Ln 75236
Monaco Ln 75233
Monaghan Ct 75203
Monarch St
4500-4799 75204
4801-4899 75204
4901-5197 75206
5199-5299 75206
Monet Pl 75287
Moneta Ln 75236
Monitor St 75207
Monmouth Ln 75211

Monroe Dr
9800-9999 75220
10000-10200 75229
10202-10298 75229
Monssen Dr & Pkwy 75224
Montague Ave 75216
Montalba Ave 75228
E Montana Ave 75216
W Montana Ave 75224
N & S Montclair Ave 75208
Montclova Ct 75217
Monte Carlo St 75224
Monte Vista Dr 75223
Montecito Ave 75248
Montego Plz 75230
Monteleon Ct 75220
Monterrey Ave 75228
Monterrey Plz 75201
Montezuma St 75204
Montfort Dr
12601-12697 75230
12699-12899 75230
13100-14099 75240
14100-14899 75254
14901-14999 75254
Montfort Pl 75240
Montfort Rd 75248
Montgomery St 75215
Monticello Ave
3000-3199 75205
5100-6099 75206
6100-6399 75214
Montie St 75210
N Montreal Ave 75208
S Montreal Ave
100-1699 75208
2201-2597 75224
2599-2999 75224
Montrose Dr 75209
Montvale Dr 75234
Montwood Ln 75229
Moondale Ln 75217
Moondust Dr 75248
Moonglow Dr 75241
Moonhill Dr 75241
Moonlight Ave 75217
Moonmist St 75217
Moonriver Ln 75234
Moonstone Dr 75241
Moorcroft Dr 75228
N & S Moore St 75203
Moran Dr 75218
Moreland Ave 75204
Morgan Ave 75203
Morgan Dr 75241
Morgan Meadow Ln 75243
Morning Ave 75210
Morning Dew Cir & Trl 75224
Morning Frost Trl 75224
Morning Glory Dr 75229
Morning Light Dr 75228
Morning Springs Trl 75224
Morningmist Dr 75217
Morningside Ave
5200-6099 75206
6100-6199 75214
Morningstar Cir & Ln 75234
Morningview Dr 75241
N & S Morocco Ave 75211
Morrell Ave 75203
Morris St 75212
Morrison Ln 75229
Morrow St 75217
Morse Dr 75236
Morton St 75209
Moser Ave 75206
Moss Trl 75231
Moss Circle Dr 75243
Moss Creek Ct & Trl 75252
Moss Farm Ln 75243
Moss Haven Dr 75231
Moss Meadows Dr 75231
Moss Point Rd 75232
Moss Rose Ct 75217
Mossbrook Trl 75252
Mosscove Cir 75248

Mosscrest Dr 75238
Mossglen Dr 75227
Mossridge Cir & Dr 75238
Mossvine Cir, Dr & Pl 75254
Mosswood Dr 75227
Mossy Oak Dr 75248
Motor Cir 75207
Moulin Rouge Dr 75211
Mount Ararat St 75211
Mount Auburn Ave 75223
Mount Castle Dr 75234
Mount Everest St 75211
Mount Hood St 75211
Mount Lookout St 75211
Mount Nebo St 75211
Mount Pleasant St 75211
Mount Ranier St 75211
Mount Royal St 75211
Mount Shasta St 75211
Mount Vernon St 75205
Mount View Dr 75234
Mount Washington St 75211
Mountain Blf 75227
Mountain Trl 75236
Mountain Bend Cir 75217
Mountain Cabin Rd 75217
Mountain Cedar Ln 75236
Mountain Creek Pkwy
1800-2198 75211
2200-2300 75211
2302-3098 75211
3200-3698 75236
3700-4899 75236
5500-7799 75249
Mountain Hollow Dr 75249
Mountain Knoll Ct 75249
Mountain Lake Rd
1100-2399 75224
2500-2699 75233
Mountain Valley Ln 75211
Mountainview Dr 75249
Mounts Run Dr 75218
Mouser Ln 75203
Muir Cir 75287
Muirfield Dr 75287
Mulberry St 75217
Muleshoe Rd 75217
Mullins Ln 75227
Mullrany Dr 75248
Mumford Ct & St 75252
Muncie Ave 75212
Mundy Cir & Dr 75216
Munger Ave
601-699 75202
800-1098 75202
3301-3397 75204
3399-4799 75204
S Munger Blvd
101-197 75214
199-299 75214
301-399 75214
400-499 75223
501-799 75223
Municipal St 75215
Mural Ln 75210
N & S Murdeaux Ln 75217
Murdock Rd 75217
Murray St 75226
Musgrave Dr 75217
Muskogee Cir & Dr 75217
Myers Cir 75217
Myerwood Ln 75244
Myra Ln 75234
Myrtice Dr 75228
Myrtle St 75215
Myrtle Springs Ave 75220
Myrtlewood Dr 75232
Mystic Trl 75241
Nabers Ct 75249
N & S Nachita Dr 75217
Nagle St 75220
Nailsworth Way 75252
Naira Dr 75217
Nakoma Dr 75209
Nall Rd 75244
Namur St 75227

Nan Way Cir 75225
Nandina Dr 75241
Nantucket Village Cir 75227
Nantucket Village Ct 75227
Nantucket Village Dr
2000-2099 75217
2101-2213 75227
2215-2269 75227
2271-2271 75227
Nantuckett Dr 75224
Nanwood Ln 75244
Naoma St 75241
Naples Dr 75232
Naravista Dr 75249
Narboe St 75216
Nash St 75235
Nashwood Ln 75244
N & S Nassau Cir 75217
National St 75215
Natures Way 75236
Navajo Cir, Ct, Dr &
Pl 75224
Navaro St
1600-1799 75208
3000-3699 75212
S Navy Ave 75211
Nayarit Dr 75217
Naylor St
1400-1598 75218
1800-1899 75228
Neal St 75208
Nebraska Ave 75216
Neches St 75208
Nedra Way 75248
Needle Leaf Ln 75236
E Neely St 75203
W Neely St 75208
Neering Dr 75218
Nelson Dr 75227
Nemechek Dr 75217
Neola Dr 75209
Neomi Ave 75217
Neosho Dr 75217
Neptune Rd 75216
Nesbitt Dr 75214
Nestle Dr 75234
Netherland Ct & Dr 75229
Nettleton Dr 75211
Neuhoff Dr 75217
Neutron Rd 75244
Nevis Ln 75218
New Bark Cir 75244
New Bedford Dr 75217
New Castle Dr 75244
New Haven Dr 75217
New Moon Ln 75235
New Orleans Pl 75235
Newberry St 75229
Newcastle Dr 75220
Newcombe Dr 75228
Newell Ave 75223
Newhall St 75232
Newheart St 75232
Newkirk St
10500-10699 75220
10701-10799 75220
11201-11297 75229
11299-11499 75229
Newmore Ave 75209
Newport Ave 75224
Newt Dr 75252
Newton Ave & Ct 75219
Niblick Cir 75232
Nicholson Dr 75224
Nicholson Rd 75234
Nicki Ct & St 75252
Nicole Pl 75252
Nile Dr 75253
Nimitz Dr 75224
Nimrod Trl 75238
Nisqually St 75217
Noah St 75203
Nob Hill Pl & Rd 75208
Noel Rd
12800-12898 75230
13101-13327 75240
13329-13799 75240
13770-13770 75380
13801-14099 75240
13900-14098 75240
14100-14199 75254
Nogales Dr 75220
Nokomis Ave 75224
Nolte Dr 75208
Nomas St 75212
Nome St 75216
Nonesuch Ct & Rd 75214
Norbury Dr 75248
Norco St 75212
Norcross Ln 75229
Norfolk Ave 75203
Norlock Ln 75201
Norma St 75247
Normah St 75206
Norman Dr 75211
Normandy Ave 75205
Norris St 75214
Norsworthy Dr 75228
North Dr 75207
North St 75203
Northaven Ct 75229
Northaven Rd
2600-5499 75229
5501-5599 75229
5600-7999 75230
Northboro St 75230
Northbrook Dr 75220
Northcliff Dr 75218
Northcreek Ln 75240
Northcrest Rd 75229
Northernmost Dr 75252
Northgate Cir 75230
Northlake Dr 75218
Northland Cir 75230
Northlawn Dr 75229
Northmeadow Cir 75231
Northmoor Dr
5200-5499 75229
5500-5899 75230
Northpark Ctr 75225
Northpoint Dr 75238
Northport Dr 75230
Northridge Dr 75214
Northview Ln 75229
Northway Dr 75206
E Northwest Hwy
5701-6699 75231
6400-6498 75214
6500-7498 75231
7500-11399 75238
11400-12000 75218
12002-12198 75218
12201-12297 75228
12299-12600 75228
12602-12698 75228
W Northwest Hwy
1600-2356 75220
2341-2341 75378
2341-2341 75354
2341-2341 75209
2357-5699 75220
2358-5598 75220
5800-5898 75225
5900-7500 75225
7502-7700 75225
Northwest Pkwy 75225
Northwood Rd 75225
N & S Norvell Dr 75227
Norwalk Ave 75220
Norway Pl & Rd 75230
Norwich Ln 75212
Norwood Dr 75228
Norwood Rd
5001-5099 75247
5055-5055 75235
5055-5055 75342
5055-5055 75356
5101-5197 75247
5199-5299 75247
Nottingham Ln 75217
Nova Dr 75229
Nuestra Dr 75230
Nueva Leon Plz 75211

Nuevo Laredo Ct 75236
Nussbaumer St 75226
Nuthatch St 75236
Nutmeg Ln 75249
Nutting Dr 75227
Nutwood Cir 75252
Nyman Dr 75236
O B Crowe Dr 75227
O Bannon Dr 75224
O Hare Ct 75228
Oak Ln
2800-2998 75215
3001-3097 75226
3099-3100 75226
3102-3198 75226
Oak Plz 75253
Oak St 75204
Oak Strm 75243
Oak Trl 75232
Oak Arbor Dr 75233
Oak Bend Ln 75227
Oak Branch Ln 75227
N & S Oak Cliff Blvd 75208
Oak Creek Cir 75227
Oak Dale Rd 75241
Oak Falls Cir 75287
Oak Farms Blvd 75241
Oak Forest Dr 75232
Oak Garden Ct & Trl 75232
Oak Gate Ln 75217
Oak Glen Trl 75232
Oak Grove Ave 75204
Oak Haven Ln 75217
Oak Highland Dr 75243
Oak Hill Cir & Pl 75217
Oak Hollow Dr 75217
Oak Knoll St 75208
Oak Lake Dr 75287
Oak Lawn Ave
100-1799 75207
2101-2497 75219
2499-4299 75219
4301-4499 75219
Oak Manor Dr 75230
Oak Meadows Dr 75232
Oak Mount Pl 75287
Oak Park Dr 75232
Oak Point Dr 75254
Oak Shadow Ct 75287
Oak Terrace Cir 75227
Oak Tree Cir 75287
Oak Valley Ln 75232
Oak Vista Dr 75232
Oakbluff Dr 75254
Oakbrook Blvd 75235
Oakcrest Rd 75248
Oakdale St 75215
E Oakenwald St 75203
Oakhurst St 75214
Oakington Ct 75252
Oakland Cir 75215
Oakleaf Rd 75248
Oakley Ave 75216
Oakmont Dr 75234
Oakmore Dr 75249
Oakpath Ln 75243
Oaks North Dr & Pl 75254
Oakshire Pl 75243
Oakstone Dr 75249
Oakvale Ct 75217
Oakwind Ct 75243
Oakwood Dr 75217
Oakwood Ln 75214
Oates Cir & Dr 75228
Obenchain St
2101-2299 75208
2400-3599 75212
Oberlin Dr 75243
Ocalla Ave 75218
Oceanview Dr 75232
Octavia St 75215
Odair Ct 75218
Odeneal St 75217
Odessa St 75212
Odette Ave 75228
Odom Dr 75217

Office Pkwy 75204
Ogden Ave 75211
Ohana Pl 75237
E Ohio Ave 75216
W Ohio Ave 75224
Oklaunion Dr 75217
Old Bent Tree Ln 75287
Old Colony Rd 75233
Old Gate Ln 75218
Old Glory Dr 75237
Old Hickory Trl 75237
Old Homestead Dr 75217
Old Jamestown Ave &
Ct 75217
Old Mill Ct 75217
Old Mill Ln 75217
Old Mill Rd 75287
Old Moss Rd 75231
Old North Rd 75234
Old Oaks Dr 75211
Old Orchard Dr 75208
Old Ox Dr & Rd 75241
Old Pond Dr 75248
Old Preston Ct & Pl 75252
Old Seagoville Rd 75217
Old Settlers Way 75236
Old South Pkwy 75217
Old Spanish Trl 75211
Old Town Dr 75206
Oldbridge Dr 75228
Olde Forge Rd 75211
Olde Towne Row 75227
Olde Village Ct 75227
Olden St 75211
Oldfield Dr 75217
Oleta Dr 75217
Olin Rd 75244
Olin Welborn St 75201
Olive St
400-698 75201
700-2199 75201
2201-2399 75201
2990-3992 75219
Olive Tree Rd 75252
Oliver Ave 75205
Olmos Dr 75218
Olney Ct 75241
Olson Dr 75227
Olusta Dr 75217
Olympia Dr 75208
Olympic Ct 75234
Olympic Dr
10300-10599 75220
14300-14348 75234
14350-14399 75234
Omar St 75232
Omega Rd 75244
Ontario Ln
9801-9897 75220
9899-9999 75220
10000-10098 75229
Onyx Ln 75234
Opal Ave 75216
Opera St 75203
Oradell Ln 75220
Oram St
5720-5798 75206
5800-6099 75206
6100-6299 75214
6301-6399 75214
Orangeville Dr 75237
Orangewood Dr 75248
Orbiter Cir & Dr 75243
Orchard Hl 75243
Orchard Ln 75253
Orchard Ridge Ct 75229
Orchid Ln 75230
Oregon Ave 75203
N & S Orient St 75203
Orinda Dr 75248
Orinoco Dr 75217
Oriole Dr 75209
Orlando Ct 75211
Orleans St 75226
Ormond St 75217
Oro Way 75211

Ortega St 75253
Osage Cir 75223
Osage Plaza Pkwy 75252
Osborn Rd 75227
Oslo Ln 75217
Othello Pl 75252
Otomi St 75236
Ott Cir 75211
Ottawa Rd 75212
Ouida Ave 75211
Outrider Ln 75211
Ovella Ave 75220
Over Downs Cir & Dr 75230
Overbrook Dr 75205
Overcrest St 75211
Overdale Dr 75254
Overglen Dr 75218
Overhill Dr 75205
Overhill Ln 75216
Overlake Dr 75220
Overland Dr 75234
Overlook Dr 75227
Overmead Cir 75248
Overpark Ct & Dr 75217
Overridge Dr 75232
Overton Ct 75216
E Overton Rd 75216
W Overton Rd 75224
Overview Dr 75254
Overwood Rd 75238
Ovid Ave 75224
Owega Ave 75216
Owens St 75235
Owensons Dr 75224
Owenwood Ave 75223
Oxbow Ln 75241
Oxford Ave 75205
Oxford Dr 75252
Oxfordshire Ln 75234
Ozona St 75216
Pace St 75207
Pacesetter Dr 75241
Pachuca Ct 75236
Pacific Ave
900-1098 75202
1301-1499 75202
1510-1624 75201
1626-1800 75201
1802-1998 75201
2401-2497 75226
2499-2599 75226
4901-4999 75210
S Pacific Ave 75223
Packard St
700-1099 75203
3500-3599 75215
Paddock Cir 75238
Padgitt Ave 75203
Paducah Ave 75216
E Page Ave 75203
W Page Ave 75208
Pageant Pl 75244
Pagemill Rd 75243
Pagewood Dr & Pl 75230
Painted Trl 75237
Palace Way 75218
Palacios Ave 75212
Paladium Dr
5300-5399 75254
5500-5699 75249
Paldao Dr 75240
Palisade Dr 75217
Pall Mall Ave 75241
Pallos Verdas Dr 75229
Palm Ln 75206
Palm Beach Ave 75217
Palm Desert Dr 75287
Palm Island St 75241
Palm Oak Dr 75217
Palmdale Cir 75234
Palmer Dr 75211
Palmetto Dr 75217
Palo Alto Dr 75241
Palo Duro Ln 75216
Palo Pinto Ave
5700-6099 75206
6100-6399 75214
Palomar Ln 75229
Palomino Rd 75253
Pampas St 75211
Pampas Creek Dr 75227
Panama Pl 75215
Panavision Trl 75249
Pandora Cir & Dr 75238
Panola Dr 75241
Panoramic Cir 75212
Panther Ridge Trl 75243
Papa Ct 75211
Parader Ct 75228
Paramount Ave 75217
Park Ave
400-1199 75201
1400-1798 75215
1800-1999 75215
2001-2299 75215
Park Ln
3000-3042 75220
3044-5699 75220
5700-7899 75225
7901-7999 75225
8000-8999 75231
Park Bend Dr 75230
Park Bridge Ct 75219
Park Brook Dr 75218
Park Central Dr 75251
Park Central Pl 75230
Park Forest Ctr 75234
Park Forest Dr 75230
Park Forest Shopping Ctr 75229
Park Grove Ln 75287
Park Highland Pl 75248
Park Highlands Dr 75238
Park Hill Dr 75248
Park Lake Ct 75234
Park Lake Dr 75230
Park Lane Ct & Pl 75220
Park Manor Dr 75241
Park Oak Cir 75228
Park Preston Dr 75230
Park Row Ave
1800-3099 75215
3200-3298 75210
Park Village Pl 75230
Park Vista Dr 75228
Parkchester Dr 75230
Parkcliff Dr 75253
Parkdale Dr 75227
Parker St 75215
Parkford Dr 75238
Parkhaven Ct 75252
Parkhouse St 75207
Parkhurst Dr 75218
Parkland Ave 75235
Parkmont St 75214
Parkridge Dr 75234
Parksedge Ln 75252
Parkshire Ave 75231
Parkside Dr 75209
Parkside Center Blvd 75244
Parkstone Way 75249
Parkview Ave 75223
Parkway Ave 75203
Parkwood Dr 75224
Parlay Cir 75211
Parliament Pl 75225
Parnell St 75215
Parral Plz 75211
Parrott St 75216
Parry Ave
3601-3797 75226
3799-3899 75226
4101-4197 75223
4199-5499 75223
Parsons Ave 75215
Parvia Ave 75212
Parwelk St 75235
Parwen Dr 75230
Pasadena Ave & Pl 75214
Paschall Rd 75217
Paseo Bonita Dr 75227
Paseo Paraiso Dr 75227
Passage Dr 75236
Pasteur Ave 75228
Pastor St 75212
Pastor Bailey Dr 75237
Pat Dr 75228
Patience Blvd E 75236
Patito Pl 75240
Patonia Ave 75241
Patricia Ave 75223
Patrick Cir & Dr 75214
Patrol Way 75241
Patterson St
1300-1398 75202
1602-1698 75201
N & S Patton Ave 75203
Paulus Ave 75214
Pauma Valley Cir & Dr 75287
Pavillion St 75204
Pavonia Dr 75204
Paxson Trl 75249
Payne St
100-199 75207
201-299 75207
1600-1698 75201
1801-1999 75201
Peabody Ave 75215
Peaceful Bend Dr 75237
Peachtree Rd 75227
N Peak St
100-200 75226
202-208 75226
402-402 75246
404-803 75246
805-899 75246
910-2299 75204
2301-2599 75204
S Peak St
209-297 75226
299-398 75226
500-916 75223
918-928 75223
Peangert Dr 75233
Pear St 75215
Pear Ridge Dr 75287
N & S Pearl Expy & St 75201
Pearlstone St 75226
Pearson Dr 75214
Peary Ave 75215
Peavy Cir 75228
Peavy Pl 75228
Peavy Rd
400-498 75218
500-1300 75218
1302-1598 75218
1600-2999 75228
3001-3199 75228
Pebble Ave 75217
Pebble Beach Dr
3100-3699 75234
6900-6999 75252
Pebble Valley Ln 75217
Pebblebrook Dr 75229
Pebbleshores Dr 75241
Pebblestone Dr 75230
Pebblewood Dr 75217
Pecan Dr 75203
Pecan Creek Ln 75252
Pecan Forest Dr 75230
Pecan Grove Ct 75228
Pecan Meadow Dr 75236
Pecan Ridge Dr 75237
Pecan Springs Ct 75252
Pecos St 75204
Peeler St 75235
Peerless Ln 75235
Pegasus St 75238
Pegasus Park Dr 75247
Pegshire Ave 75231
Pekoe Park 75217
Pelican Dr 75238
Pelman St 75224
Pemberton Dr 75230
Pemberton Hill Rd 75217
E Pembroke Ave 75203
W Pembroke Ave 75208
Pencross Ln 75248
Pendleton St 75252
Penelope St 75210
Penguin Dr 75241
Peninsula Dr 75218
Penland St 75224
Pennridge Ln 75241
Pennsylvania Ave
1200-3199 75215
3201-4297 75210
4299-4399 75210
Pennyburn Dr 75248
Pennystone Dr 75244
Penrod Ave 75211
Penrose Ave
5700-6099 75206
6100-6299 75214
Pensacola Ct 75211
Penshire Ln 75227
Pensive Dr 75229
E Pentagon Pkwy
701-1297 75216
1299-1399 75216
2201-2599 75241
W Pentagon Pkwy
601-1699 75224
2400-3699 75233
W Pentagon Parkway Cir 75224
Peoria St 75212
Pepperidge Cir 75228
Peppermill Ln 75287
Peppertree Ln 75211
Pepperwood St 75234
Peppy Pl 75252
Perelari Dr 75229
Perimeter Rd 75228
Periwinkle Dr 75233
Perryton Dr
1500-2400 75224
2402-2598 75224
2515-2523 75233
E Perryton Dr 75224
Pershing St 75206
Persimmon Rd 75241
Perth St 75220
Peru St 75203
Petain Ave 75227
Petal St 75238
Peter Pan Dr 75229
Peterbilt Blvd 75241
Peterborough Mews 75236
Peters St 75215
Peterson Ln 75240
Petty Ln 75217
Petunia St 75228
Peyton Dr 75240
Phantom Hill Rd 75217
Pheasant Park 75236
Phelps Dr 75253
Philip Ave 75223
Phinney Ave 75211
Phoenix Dr 75231
Phyllis Ln 75234
Picasso Pl 75287
Pickens St 75214
Pickfair Cir 75235
Pickrell Dr 75227
Pickwick Ln 75225
Pictureline Cir & Dr 75233
Piedmont Dr 75227
Piedmont Park Shopping Vlg 75217
Pierce St
500-598 75211
600-799 75211
801-999 75211
2600-2698 75233
2700-2799 75233
2801-2899 75233
Pike St 75234
Pilgrim Dr 75215
Pilgrim Rest Dr 75237
Pilot Dr 75217
Pimlico Dr 75214
Pin Oak Ct 75234
Pin Oak Ln 75253
Pin Tail Ct 75232
Pinchalt Dr 75236
Pindar Ave 75217
Pine St
1600-3499 75215
3600-3622 75210
3624-3900 75210
3902-3998 75210
Pine Forest Dr 75230
Pine Trail Ct & Rd 75241
Pine Tree Cir & Ct 75234
Pine Valley Dr
3600-3699 75234
13200-13298 75253
13300-13399 75253
Pineberry Rd 75249
Pinebluff Dr 75228
Pinebrook Dr 75241
Pinecliff St 75235
Pinecrest Dr 75228
Pinedale Ln 75241
Pinehaven Dr 75227
Pinehurst Cir 75234
Pinehurst Ln 75227
Pineland Dr 75231
Pineview Rd 75248
Pinewood Dr 75243
Pink Star Dr 75211
Pinnacle Park Blvd 75211
Pinnacle Point Dr 75211
Pinocchio Dr 75229
Pinto St 75211
Pinwherry Ln 75232
Pinyon Tree Ln 75243
Pioneer Dr 75224
Piper Ln 75228
Pipestone Rd 75212
Pisa Mews 75236
Pittman St 75208
Pittsburg St 75207
Placid Way 75244
Placid Way Pl 75244
Plainview Dr 75217
Plano Pkwy 75238
Plano Rd
8500-8898 75238
8900-11199 75238
11200-11799 75243
11801-12499 75243
Plantation Rd 75235
Planters Glen Dr 75244
Plata Way 75211
Platas St 75227
Plate Dr 75217
Platinum Way 75237
Platte River Way 75287
Plaudit Pl 75229
Playa Vista Dr 75236
Players Ct 75287
Plaza Blvd 75241
NW Plaza Dr 75225
Pleasant Dr
100-118 75217
120-2099 75217
2101-2197 75227
2199-3600 75227
3602-3698 75227
Pleasant Grove Ctr & Mall 75217
Pleasant Hills Dr 75217
Pleasant Meadows Ln 75217
Pleasant Mound 75227
Pleasant Oaks Dr 75217
Pleasant Ridge Rd 75236
Pleasant Valley Dr 75243
Pleasant View Dr 75231
Pleasant Vista Ct & Dr 75217
N & S Pleasant Woods Dr 75217
Plowman Ave 75203
Plum St 75203
Plum Dale Rd 75241
Plum Grove Ln 75211
Plum Leaf Ct 75212
Plummer Dr 75228
Plumstead Dr 75228
Plumtree Dr 75252
Pluto St 75212
N Plymouth Rd
401-597 75211
599-799 75211
801-899 75211
1001-1399 75208
S Plymouth Rd 75211
Pocono Trl 75217
Poe St 75212
Poinciana Pl 75212
Poinsettia Dr 75211
Pointer St 75212
N Polk St 75208
S Polk St
100-198 75208
200-1199 75208
1300-2198 75224
2200-4099 75224
4101-4299 75224
4600-5398 75232
5400-9700 75232
9702-9998 75232
Polk Vlg 75232
Polk Plaza Ln 75232
Pollard St 75208
Polly St 75210
Pomeroy Dr 75233
Pomona Rd 75209
Pompton Ct 75248
Pond St 75217
Ponder Dr & Pl 75229
Ponderosa Cir & Way 75227
Pondrom St 75215
Pondview Dr 75217
Pondwood Dr 75217
Pontiac Ave 75203
Pontinti St 75207
Pool View Ct & Dr 75249
Poplar St 75215
Poplar Springs Ln 75227
Poppy Dr 75218
Poquita Dr 75220
Poradinc Rd 75240
Port Blvd 75241
Port Royal Dr 75244
Porter Ave 75220
Portico Ln 75241
Portlock Dr 75234
Portnoma Ln 75217
Portobello Trl 75252
Portrush Dr 75243
Portside Ridge Ln 75249
Portsmouth Ln 75252
Posada Dr 75211
Post Dr 75220
Post Oak Cir 75217
Postage Due St 75204
Postal Way 75212
Potomac Ave 75205
Potters House Way 75236
Power Dr 75227
Powhattan St 75215
Prague Mews 75236
N Prairie Ave
101-197 75246
199-600 75246
602-698 75246
1200-2499 75204
Prairie Bluff Dr 75227
Prairie Creek Rd 75227
N Prairie Creek Rd
200-498 75217
500-1700 75217
1702-1998 75217
2100-2198 75227
2200-3000 75227
3002-3798 75227
Prairie Flower Trl 75227
Prairie Grove Dr 75217
Prairie Hill Ln 75217
Prairie Oak Dr 75217
Prairie View Dr 75235
Prairie Vista Dr 75217
Prairie Wood Pl 75217
Prater St 75217
Pratt St 75224
Preakness Ln 75211
Preferred Pl 75237
Prelude Dr 75238
Premier Row 75247
Prentice St 75206
Prescott Ave 75219
Preservation Ln 75236
President George Bush Tpke
3300-3398 75287
7900-8098 75252
Presidential Dr 75243
Presidio Ave 75216
Preston Cir 75211
Preston Pkwy 75205
Preston Rd
4400-4698 75205
4700-6999 75205
7001-7099 75205
7100-7298 75225
7300-8599 75225
8601-9699 75225
9701-9797 75230
9799-12999 75230
13000-13699 75240
13701-13799 75240
14000-15000 75254
15002-15098 75254
15101-15111 75248
15113-17195 75248
17197-17199 75248
17201-17215 75252
17217-19599 75252
Preston Bend Dr 75248
Preston Brook Pl 75230
Preston Center Plz 75225
Preston Creek Ct, Dr & Pl 75240
Preston Crest Ln 75230
Preston Fairways Cir & Dr 75252
Preston Gate Ct 75230
Preston Glen Dr 75230
Preston Grove Ln 75230
Preston Haven Dr
5200-5499 75229
5500-6199 75230
Preston Hollow Ln 75225
Preston Oaks Rd 75254
Preston Trail Dr 75248
Preston Valley Dr & Pl 75240
Preston View Blvd 75240
Prestondell Ct 75240
Prestondell Dr
6109-6178 75240
6180-6194 75240
6200-6299 75254
Prestondell Pl 75240
Prestonridge Rd 75230
Prestonshire Ln 75225
Prestonwood Blvd 75248
Prestwick Dr 75234
Prestwick Ln 75252
Prichard Ln
1300-2099 75217
2100-2700 75227
2702-2998 75227
Prime Ln 75236
Primrose Ln 75234
Prince St 75214
Prince Hall Ct, Ln, Sq & St 75216
Princess Cir & Ln 75229
Princeton Ave 75205
Pringle Dr 75212
Production Dr 75235
Profit Dr 75247
Program Dr 75220
Progressive Dr 75212
Promenade Ln 75238
Prominence Dr 75238
Prospect Ave
5700-6099 75206
6100-6399 75214

Prosper St 75209
Prosperity Ave 75216
Proton Rd 75244
Province Ln 75228
Prudential Dr 75235
Pruitt Ave 75227
Pryor St 75226
Pueblo St 75212
Puerto Rico Dr 75228
Puget St 75212
Pulaski St 75247
Purcell Ct 75209
Purdue Ave
2700-4499 75225
4600-5699 75209
7800-7999 75225
Purple Sage Rd 75240
Putting Green Dr 75232
Pyka Dr 75233
Pyramid Dr 75234
Quadrangle Dr 75228
Quail Ct 75249
Quail Trl 75253
Quail Hollow Rd 75287
Quail Lake Dr 75287
Quail Run St 75238
Quaker St 75207
Quality Ln 75231
Quanah St 75228
Quarry St 75212
Quartermile Ln 75248
Quarterway Dr 75248
Quartet Dr 75241
Quebec St 75247
Queens Chapel Rd 75234
Queens Ferry Ln 75248
Queens Garden Dr 75248
Queensview Ct 75225
Queensway St 75217
Queenswood Ln 75238
Queretaro Plz 75211
Querida Ln 75248
Quicksilver Dr 75249
Quiet Ln 75211
Quietwood Dr 75253
Quincy Ln 75230
Quincy St 75212
Quinella Dr 75211
Quinn St 75217
Quinto Dr 75227
Quorum Dr 75254
E R L Thornton Fwy
2400-2498 75226
4501-5097 75223
5099-5700 75223
5702-5798 75223
7701-7797 75228
7799-9399 75228
9401-9699 75228
S R L Thornton Fwy
100-298 75203
300-899 75203
2200-2298 75224
2300-4600 75224
4602-4698 75224
5000-5398 75232
5400-9500 75232
9502-9798 75232
Race St 75246
Racell St 75210
Racine Dr 75232
Radar Way 75211
Radbrook Pl 75220
Radcliff Dr 75227
Raeford Dr 75243
Railway St 75215
Rain Dance Trl 75252
Rain Forest Ct & Dr 75217
Rainbow Dr 75208
Rains Run 75252
Rainsong Dr 75287
Raintree Ct 75254
Raleigh Pl & St 75219
Ralph Ln 75227
Ralston Ave 75235
Rambler Rd 75231
Ramblewood Trl 75240
Rambling Dr 75228
Ramona Ave 75216
Rampart St 75235
Ramsey Ave 75216
Ranchero Ln 75236
Ranchita Dr 75248
Rand Ave 75216
Randall St 75201
N Randolph Dr 75211
S Randolph Dr 75211
Randolph St 75241
Randy Ln 75234
Ranger Dr 75212
Ranier St 75208
Rankin St 75205
Raphael Ln 75287
Ravehill Ln 75227
Raven Row 75236
Ravendale Ln
5800-5899 75206
6100-6899 75214
Ravenglen Ct 75287
Ravenscroft Dr 75230
Ravensway Dr 75238
Ravenview Rd 75253
Ravenwood Dr 75217
Ravine Dr 75220
N Ravinia Dr 75211
S Ravinia Dr
101-113 75211
115-2300 75211
2302-2398 75211
3200-3599 75233
3601-3699 75233
Rawhide Pkwy 75234
Rawlins St
3700-4599 75219
5100-5699 75235
Ray Rd 75241
Raydell Pl 75211
Rayenell Ave 75217
Rayville Dr 75217
Reading St 75247
Reagan St 75219
Real Oaks Dr 75217
Reaumur Dr 75229
N & S Record St 75202
Record Crossing Rd 75235
Rector St 75203
Red Bird Ct 75232
E Red Bird Ln 75241
W Red Bird Ln
600-2299 75232
2301-2399 75232
2400-4298 75237
4401-5997 75236
5999-6599 75236
Red Bird Center Dr 75237
Red Bud Dr 75227
Red Bud Ln 75211
Red Cedar Trl 75248
Red Chute Dr 75253
Red Cloud Dr 75217
Red Elm Rd 75243
Red Fern Ln 75240
Red Hickory Ln 75206
Red Maple Dr 75249
Red Mesa Dr 75249
Red Oak St 75203
Red Osier Rd 75249
Red Raider Ln 75237
Red Spring Rd 75241
Red Willow Ln 75249
Red Wing Dr 75241
Redcrest Ct 75249
Redfield St 75235
Redkey St 75217
Redman Cir 75223
Redondo Dr 75218
Redpine Rd 75248
Redstart Ln 75214
Redstone Cir 75252
Redwood Cir 75218
Redwood Ct 75209
Redwood Ln 75209
Reed Ln
2800-3399 75215
3401-3499 75215
3500-3699 75210
Reedcroft Dr 75234
Reeder Rd 75229
Reese Dr 75210
Reeves St 75235
Reforma Dr 75254
Regal Row
100-1699 75247
1700-1798 75235
1800-1999 75235
Regal Hill Cir 75248
Regal Oaks Dr 75230
Regal Park Ln 75230
Regalbluff Dr 75248
Regalview Cir 75248
Regatta Cir, Dr & Pl 75232
Regency Pl 75254
Regency Crest Dr 75238
Regent Blvd 75261
Regent Cir 75229
Regent Dr 75229
Reiger Ave
4500-4899 75246
4900-6399 75214
Rembrandt Ter 75287
Remington Ln 75229
Remington Park Cir, Dr,
Pl & Sq 75252
Remond Dr 75211
Rena Rd 75228
Renaissance Cir, Ct &
Dr 75287
Renner Dr 75216
N & S Reno Ct 75217
Renoir Ln 75230
Renova Dr 75227
Rentzel St 75220
Republic St 75208
Research Row 75235
Reservoir St 75211
Restland Rd 75243
Retail Rd 75231
Reunion Blvd E 75207
Reva St 75227
Reverchon Dr 75211
Revere Pl
5900-6099 75206
6100-6399 75214
Reverend Cbt Smith
St 75203
Reward Ln 75220
Rex Dr 75230
Rexford Dr 75209
Rexlawn Dr 75227
Rexton Ln 75214
Reyna Ave 75236
Reynolds Ave 75223
Reynoldston Ln 75232
Rhapsody Ln 75241
Rheims Pl 75205
Rhoda Ln 75217
Rhodes Ln 75241
Rhome St 75229
Rialto Dr 75243
Ricardo Dr 75227
Rice Ln 75241
Rich St 75227
Rich Acres Dr 75253
Richard Ave 75206
Richardson Ave 75215
Richardson Branch Trl 75243
Richey St 75212
Richinte Dr 75237
Richland Ave 75234
Richmond Ave
5400-6099 75206
6100-6399 75214
6401-6499 75214
Richmondell Ave 75211
Richwater Dr 75252
Richwood Dr 75237
Rickenbacker Dr 75228
Rickover Cir, Ct & Dr 75244
E & W Ricks Cir 75230
Rickshaw Dr 75229
Ridan Ln 75211
Riddick Ct 75218
Ridge Rd 75229
Ridge Creek Dr 75249
Ridge Crossing Dr 75227
Ridge Elm Dr 75227
Ridge Oak St 75227
Ridge Park Ln 75232
Ridge Spring Dr 75218
Ridgebriar Dr 75234
Ridgecove Dr 75234
Ridgecrest Dr 75253
Ridgecrest Rd 75231
Ridgedale Ave 75206
Ridgedorf Dr 75217
Ridgefair Pl 75234
Ridgefrost Cir 75228
Ridgegate Dr 75232
Ridgehaven Dr 75238
Ridgelake Dr 75218
Ridgelawn Dr 75214
Ridgelea St 75209
Ridgell Row 75253
Ridgemar Dr 75231
Ridgemeadow Dr 75218
Ridgemont Dr 75214
Ridgemoor Cir 75241
Ridgeoak Way
3301-3397 75234
3399-3600 75234
3602-3698 75234
3700-3999 75244
Ridgepoint Dr 75211
Ridgeside Dr 75244
Ridgestone Dr 75287
Ridgetown Cir 75230
Ridgeview Cir 75240
Ridgeway St 75214
Ridgewick Dr 75217
Ridgewood Dr 75217
Riek Rd 75228
Rilla Ave 75217
E & W Rim Rd 75211
Rim Rock Rd 75253
Rimdale Dr 75228
Rimwood Ln 75235
Rincon Way 75214
Ring St 75223
Rio Blanco Dr 75227
Rio Branco St 75234
Rio Doso Dr 75227
Rio Grande Ave & Cir 75233
Rio Hondo Dr 75218
Rio Verde Way 75228
Rio Vista Dr 75208
Ripley St 75204
Ripple Rd 75241
Ripplewood Dr 75228
Riseden Dr 75252
Riser St 75212
Rising Sun Ln 75227
Risinghill Dr 75248
Rita Rd 75243
River Bend Dr 75247
River Chase Dr 75287
River Hill Cir & Dr 75287
River Oaks Rd 75241
River Rock Dr 75217
River Wharf Dr 75212
Riverbrook Dr 75230
Rivercrest Dr 75228
Riverdale Dr 75208
Riveredge Dr 75207
Riverfall Dr 75230
N & S Riverfront Blvd 75207
Riverside Dr 75235
Riverside Rd 75241
Riverstone Ct 75252
Riverton Ave 75218
Riverview Ln 75248
Riverway Cir 75217
Riverway Dr
1600-2099 75217
2100-2399 75227
Riverway Pl 75217
Riverway Bend Cir 75217
Riverwood Rd 75217
Riviera Dr 75211
Road Runner Ln 75217
Roanoke Ave 75235
Roaring Springs Ln 75240
Robert B Cullum Blvd 75210
Roberta St 75203
Roberts Ave 75215
Robertson Dr 75241
Robin Rd 75209
Robin Glen Dr 75232
Robin Hill Cir & Ln 75238
Robin Meadow Dr 75243
Robin Oaks Dr 75216
Robin Song 75243
Robin Willow Ct & Dr 75248
Robincreek Dr & Pl 75232
Robindale Dr 75238
Robingreen Ln 75232
Robledo Dr 75230
Roby St 75215
Rochelle Dr 75220
Rochester St 75215
Rock Bluff Dr 75227
Rock Branch Dr 75287
Rock Canyon Cir & Trl 75232
Rock Cliff Pl 75209
Rock Creek Dr 75204
Rock Garden Trl 75232
Rock Hill Ln 75229
Rock Island St 75207
Rock Quarry Rd 75211
Rockaway Dr 75214
Rockbend Pl 75240
Rockbrook Dr 75220
Rockcraft St 75218
Rockdale Dr 75220
Rockefeller Blvd 75203
Rockford Dr 75211
Rockhaven Pl 75243
Rockhurst Dr 75214
Rockingham St 75217
Rockland Dr 75243
Rockledge Dr 75217
Rockmartin Dr 75234
Rockmoor Ct & Dr 75229
Rockpoint Ct 75238
Rockport Dr 75232
Rocksprings Ct 75254
Rockview Ln 75214
Rockwall Rd 75238
Rockwood St 75203
Rocky Rd 75244
Rocky Branch Dr 75243
Rocky Cove Cir 75243
Rocky Place Ct 75217
Rocky Ridge Rd 75241
Rocky Top Cir 75252
Rockyglen Dr 75228
Rodale Way 75287
Rodney Ln 75229
Roe St 75215
Roehampton Dr 75252
Roger Hollow Cir 75232
Rogers St 75215
Rogue Way 75218
Roland Ave 75219
Rolinda Dr 75211
Rolling Acres Dr 75248
Rolling Creek Ln 75236
Rolling Fork Dr 75227
Rolling Hills Ln 75240
Rolling Knoll Ct, Dr &
Pl 75234
Rolling Meadows Dr 75211
Rolling Rock Ln 75238
Rolling Vista Dr 75248
Rollingdale Ln 75234
Romanway Dr 75249
Romine Ave 75215
Romo Plz 75211
Ron Baker Dr 75227
Rondo Dr 75241
Ronnie Dr 75252
Ronryan Rd 75236
Rooster Ln 75287
Roper St 75209
Rosa Ct & Rd 75220
Rosalie Dr 75236
Rosalinda Ln 75217
Rose Ln 75215
Rose Creek Ct 75238
Rose Garden Ave 75217
Rose Grove Ct 75248
Rosebank Dr 75228
Rosebud Dr 75252
Rosecliff Dr 75217
Rosedale Ave 75205
Roseland Ave 75204
Rosemary Dr 75206
Rosemary Ln 75211
Rosemead Dr 75217
Rosemeade Pkwy 75287
N Rosemont Ave 75208
S Rosemont Ave 75208
Rosemont Rd 75217
Roseville Dr 75241
Rosewood Ave 75219
Rosine Ave 75215
Ross Ave
501-697 75202
699-1201 75202
1203-1499 75202
1801-1897 75201
1899-2699 75201
2701-2899 75201
3000-3098 75204
3100-4899 75204
4900-6099 75206
Rosser Cir 75229
Rosser Ct 75229
Rosser Rd
10101-10197 75229
10199-11099 75229
11101-11599 75229
11800-13199 75244
Rosser Sq 75244
Rossford St 75234
Roswell St 75219
Rotan Ln 75229
Rothington Rd 75227
Rothland St 75227
Rough Bark Dr 75217
Round Table Dr 75247
Roundrock Rd 75248
Routh St
1700-3199 75201
3500-3699 75219
3701-3799 75219
Rowan Ave 75223
Rowden Trl 75252
Rowena St 75206
Rowland Ave 75217
Roxana Ave 75217
Roxbury Ln 75229
Royal Cir 75230
Royal Ln
1701-1803 75229
1805-5699 75229
5701-5799 75229
5800-5958 75230
5959-7999 75230
5959-5959 75367
5960-7998 75230
8800-9699 75243
9700-9798 75231
9800-9999 75231
10000-10199 75238
Royal Pl 75230
Royal Way 75229
Royal Cedar Dr 75236
Royal Chapel Dr 75229
Royal Club Ln 75229
Royal Cove Dr 75229
Royal Crest Dr
5100-5599 75229
5800-6399 75230
6401-6899 75230
Royal Crown Dr 75243
Royal Gable Dr 75229
Royal Haven Ln 75229
Royal Highlands Dr 75238
Royal Oaks Dr 75253
Royal Palms Ct 75244
Royal Park Dr 75230
Royal Ridge Dr 75229
Royal Springs Dr 75229
Royal Terrace Ct 75225
Royalbrook Ct 75243
Royalpine Dr 75238
Royalshire Dr 75230
Royalton Dr 75230
Royalwood Dr 75238
Royce Dr 75217
Rubens Dr 75224
Ruby Dr 75237
Ruder St 75212
Rue Du Lac St 75230
Rugby Ln 75234
Rugged Cir & Dr 75224
Ruidosa Ave 75228
Runnemede Dr 75214
Running Brook Ln 75228
Rupert St 75212
Rupley Ln 75218
Rushing Rd 75287
Rusk Ave, Ct & Pl 75204
Ruskin St 75215
Russcrest Dr 75227
Russell St 75204
Russell Glen Ln 75232
Russwood Cir 75229
Rust College Dr 75241
N & S Rustic Cir 75218
Rustic Meadows Dr 75248
Rustic Valley Dr 75248
Rustleleaf Dr 75238
Rustown Dr 75228
Rustrelm St 75246
Rutgers Dr 75214
Ruth Ann Dr 75228
Ruthdale Dr 75244
Rutherglen Dr 75227
Rutledge St 75215
Rutz St 75212
Ryan Cir 75224
Ryan Rd
500-999 75224
1800-1899 75220
Ryanridge Dr 75232
Ryddington Pl 75230
Rylie Rd
8100-10499 75217
10500-10699 75253
Rylie Crest Dr
9500-11099 75217
12000-12399 75253
Ryliewood Dr 75217
Ryoaks Dr 75217
Sabine St 75203
Sable Ridge Dr 75287
Sacro Monte Dr 75248
Saddleback Dr 75227
Saddlegate Ln 75287
Saddleridge Dr 75249
Sadler Cir 75235
Sage Valley Ln 75211
Sagecliff Ct 75248
Sagewood Dr 75252
Sahara Way 75218
Saint Albans Dr 75214
Saint Albert Dr 75233
Saint Andrews Dr 75205
Saint Anne Ct & St 75248
N Saint Augustine Dr
128-130 75217
132-2019 75217
2021-2099 75217
2100-3099 75227
3101-4199 75227
S Saint Augustine Dr 75217
S Saint Augustine Rd 75253
Saint Bernard Dr 75233
Saint Brigid Dr 75233
Saint Charles Ave 75223
Saint Christopher Ln 75287
Saint Clair Dr 75215

Saint Cloud Cir 75229
Saint Croix Dr 75229
Saint David Dr & St 75233
Saint Dominic Cir 75233
Saint Faustina Cir 75233
Saint Francis Ave
1600-1699 75218
1800-1998 75228
2000-3999 75228
4001-4099 75228
4200-4498 75227
4500-4799 75227
Saint Gabriel Dr 75233
Saint George Dr 75237
Saint Germain Rd 75212
Saint James Ln 75238
Saint Johns Dr 75205
Saint Joseph St
901-999 75246
1101-1297 75204
1299-1399 75204
Saint Judes Dr 75230
Saint Landry Dr 75214
Saint Laurent Pl 75225
Saint Lawrence Cir 75244
Saint Lazare Dr 75229
Saint Louis St 75226
Saint Luke Ln 75237
Saint Malo Cir 75224
Saint Marks Cir 75230
N Saint Mary Ave 75214
S Saint Mary Ave
100-399 75214
401-897 75223
899-999 75223
1001-1199 75223
Saint Michaels Dr 75230
Saint Monica Dr 75233
Saint Moritz Ave 75214
Saint Nicholas Dr 75233
N & S Saint Paul St 75201
Saint Regis Dr 75217
Saint Rita Dr 75233
Saint Rosalie Dr 75217
Saint Sophia Dr 75233
Saint Thomas Cir 75228
Saint Ursula Dr 75233
Saint Zachary Dr 75233
Saipan St 75216
Salado Dr 75248
Salamanca Ave 75248
Sale St 75219
Salerno Dr 75224
Salisbury Dr 75229
Salmon Dr 75208
Saltillo Plz 75211
Sam Dealey Dr 75208
Sam Houston Rd 75227
Sam Rayburn Trl 75287
Samaritan Rd 75236
Samcar Trl 75241
Sammy Cir 75237
Samuell Blvd
2700-3498 75223
3500-3600 75223
3602-3698 75223
3700-3898 75228
3900-7500 75228
7502-7898 75228
San Benito Way 75218
San Carlos St 75205
San Cristobal Dr 75218
San Diego Dr 75228
San Felipe Dr 75218
San Fernando Way 75218
San Francisco Dr 75228
San Gabriel Dr 75229
San Jacinto St
901-1099 75202
1701-1997 75201
1999-2099 75201
2101-2699 75201
2901-2997 75204
2999-4899 75204
4900-5099 75206
San Jose Ave 75241
San Jose Dr 75211
San Juan Ave 75228
San Lea Dr 75228
San Leandro Dr 75218
San Leon Ave 75217
San Lorenzo Dr 75228
San Lucas Ave 75228
San Marcus Ave 75228
San Marino Ave 75217
San Mateo Blvd 75223
San Medina Ave 75228
San Pablo Dr 75227
San Patricio Dr 75218
San Paula Ave 75228
San Pedro Pkwy 75218
San Rafael Dr 75218
San Saba Dr 75218
San Simeon Cir 75248
San Souci Dr 75238
San Vicente Ave 75228
Sanabel Dr 75218
Sancolis Dr 75227
Sand Shell Ct 75252
Sand Springs Ave 75227
Sandal St 75217
Sandalwood Dr 75228
Sanden Dr 75238
Sanderson Pl 75210
Sandestin Dr 75287
Sandhill Rd 75238
Sandhurst Ln 75206
Sandos Dr 75253
Sandpebble Ct 75254
Sandpiper Ln 75230
Sandra Lynn Dr 75228
Sandstone Dr 75227
Sandy Ln 75220
Sandydale Dr 75248
Sandyhook Cir 75227
Sandyland Blvd 75217
Sane Dr 75203
E Saner Ave 75216
W Saner Ave
100-298 75224
300-1699 75224
2801-3299 75233
Sanger Ave 75215
Sanshire Ave 75231
Santa Anita Dr 75214
Santa Anna Ave 75228
Santa Barbara Dr 75214
Santa Clara Dr 75218
Santa Cruz Dr 75227
Santa Elena Plz 75211
Santa Fe Ave
200-298 75203
1600-1698 75215
2601-2699 75226
4600-7198 75223
5101-5899 75214
6501-7199 75223
Santa Garza Dr 75228
Santa Gertrudis Dr 75241
Santa Maria Ln 75214
Santa Monica Dr 75223
Santa Rosa Way 75241
Santa Teresa Ave 75228
Santerre Ave 75211
Santiago Plz 75201
Sapphire St 75223
Sarah Dr 75236
Sarah Ln 75253
Sarah Lee Ln 75217
Sarah Nash Ct 75225
Saranac Dr 75220
Sarasota Cir 75223
Saratoga Cir 75214
Sargent Rd 75203
Sarita Ct 75211
Sasanqua Ln 75218
Sassafras Dr 75217
Satinwood Dr 75217
Satsuma Dr 75229
Saturn Dr 75237
Sausalito Dr 75287
Savoy St 75224
Sawgrass Dr 75252
Sawmill Rd 75252
Sax Leigh Dr 75241
Saxon St 75218
Scammel Dr 75227
Scarborough Ln 75287
Scarlet Dr 75253
Scarlet Oak Ct 75234
Scarsdale Ln 75227
Scenic Cir 75216
Scenic Bluff Cir 75227
Schafer St 75252
Schepps Pkwy 75217
Schofield Dr 75212
Schooldell Dr 75211
Schooner Ct 75217
Schroeder Rd 75243
Schuster Dr 75212
Scotia Dr 75248
Scotland Dr 75216
Scotsmeadow Dr 75218
Scotspring Ln 75218
Scott St 75215
Scottsbluff Dr 75228
Scottsboro Ln 75241
Scottsdale Dr 75227
Scurry St 75204
Scyene Cir 75227
Scyene Ct 75227
Scyene Rd
4000-4498 75210
4500-4799 75210
4801-4899 75210
5800-5998 75227
6000-10399 75227
Sea Harbor Rd 75212
Sea Island Dr 75232
Sea Pines Dr 75287
Seabeach Rd 75232
Seabury Dr 75287
Seacrest Ln 75253
Seaford Dr 75217
Seagoville Rd 75253
N Seagoville Rd 75217
S Seagoville Rd 75217
Seagrove Dr 75243
Seale St 75208
Searcy Dr 75211
Sears St 75206
Seaside Dr 75232
Seaton Dr 75216
Seaway Dr 75217
Seay Dr 75216
Sebring Dr 75241
Seco Blvd 75217
Secret Forest Dr 75249
Security Dr 75247
Sedalia St 75216
Sedgemoor Ave 75232
Sedgwick Dr 75231
Sedona Ln 75232
Seedling Ct & Ln 75287
Seegar St 75215
Seelcco St 75235
Seevers Ave 75216
Segovia Dr 75248
Seguin Dr 75220
Seldon Way 75227
Selecman Dr 75248
Self Plaza Dr 75218
Selkirk Dr 75216
Selma Ln 75234
N & S Selva Dr 75218
Seminole Dr 75217
Senate St 75228
Seneca Dr 75209
Senlac Dr 75234
Sentinel Ln 75287
Serenade Ln 75241
Sereno Dr 75218
Serrano Ave 75248
Sesame St 75238
Sewell Cir & Dr 75253
Sexton Ln 75229
Seydel St 75217
Seymour Dr 75229
Shadow Ln 75236
Shadow Way 75243
Shadow Bend Dr 75230
Shadow Creek Dr 75241
Shadow Gables Dr 75287
Shadow Glen Dr 75287
Shadow Ridge Dr 75287
Shadow Wood Dr 75224
Shadrack Dr 75212
Shady Ln 75208
Shady Trl
10200-10298 75220
10300-10999 75220
11000-11199 75229
11201-11299 75229
Shady Bend Dr 75244
Shady Brook Ln 75206
Shady Crest Trl 75241
Shady Downs Ct 75238
Shady Glen Ln 75232
Shady Hill Dr 75229
Shady Hollow Cir, Ct &
Ln 75233
Shady Valley Dr 75238
Shadybank Dr 75248
Shadybay Cir 75229
Shadybrook Ln 75231
Shadycliff Dr 75240
Shadycreek Ln 75229
Shadydale Ln 75238
Shadymeadow Dr 75232
Shadyoak Ln 75229
Shadyridge Ln 75234
Shadyview Dr 75238
Shadyway Dr 75232
Shadywood Ln 75209
Shafter Dr 75227
Shagrock Ln 75238
Shahan Dr 75234
Shakespeare Pl 75252
Shallewo St 75210
Shanna Ct 75227
Shannon Ln 75205
Sharon St 75211
Sharondale Dr 75228
Sharp St 75247
Sharpview Cir & Ln 75228
Shasta Ave 75211
Shaw St 75212
Shayna Ct & Dr 75217
Shea Rd 75235
Shelburne Ct & Dr 75227
Shelby Ave 75219
Sheldon Ave 75211
Shelia Ln 75220
Shell Flower Ln 75252
Shelley Blvd 75211
Shellhorse Rd 75241
Shelmire Dr 75224
Shelter Pl 75203
Shelterwood Cir & Ln 75229
Shelton Way 75252
Shenandoah St 75205
Shenstone Dr 75228
Shepherd Ln 75253
Shepherd Rd 75243
Sheraton Dr 75227
Sherbrook Ln 75229
Sherburne Dr 75231
Sheridan St 75235
Sherman Ave 75229
Sherry Ln 75225
Sherwood Gln 75228
Sherwood Forest Dr 75220
Shetland Dr 75230
Shilling Way 75243
Shiloh Rd 75228
Shindoll St 75216
Shining Light Dr 75228
Shining Willow Ln 75230
Shiremont Dr 75230
Shirestone Ln 75244
Shirley Dr 75229
Shook Ave 75214
E Shore Cir 75217
E Shore Dr 75217
N Shore Dr 75216
S Shore Dr 75216
W Shore Dr 75214
Shorecrest Dr
2100-3699 75235
3700-4299 75209
Shoredale Ln 75234
Shorelark Dr 75217
Shoreline Dr 75233
Shoreview Rd 75238
Shorewood Dr 75228
Short Blvd 75232
Shortal St 75217
Shortland Dr 75248
Shortleaf Dr 75253
Shortmeadow Dr 75218
Shubert Ct 75252
Sibley Ave 75223
Sicily St 75203
Sickle Cir 75241
E Side Ave
3800-4800 75226
4802-4898 75226
4900-5700 75214
5702-5798 75214
Sidney St 75210
Sidwin St 75228
Sienna Ct 75204
Sierra Way 75241
Siesta Dr 75224
Sigma Rd 75244
Signet St 75203
Sikorski Ln 75228
Silent Oak 75234
Silkwood St 75215
Silver Ave 75223
Silver Brook Rd 75253
Silver Creek Rd 75243
Silver Falls St 75217
Silver Lake Dr 75211
Silver Meadow Dr 75217
Silver Spruce Dr 75252
Silverado Dr 75253
Silverdale Dr 75232
Silverhill Dr 75241
Silverock Dr 75218
Silversprings Cir & Dr 75211
Silverthorne Dr 75287
Silverton Dr 75229
Silvertree Dr 75243
Silverwood Ln & Pl 75233
Silvery Moon Cir & Dr 75241
Simonton Rd 75244
Simpson St 75246
Simpson Stuart Rd 75241
Sinbad Cir & Trl 75234
Sinclair Ave 75218
Singing Hills Dr 75241
Singleton Blvd 75212
Sistine Mews 75236
Skelton Pl 75248
Skiles St 75204
Skillman St
701-729 75214
731-899 75214
1200-1698 75206
1700-5799 75206
5900-5998 75231
6000-8307 75231
8309-8499 75231
8600-8898 75243
8900-9799 75243
Sky High Cir 75253
Skyfrost Dr 75253
Skylark Dr 75216
Skyline Dr 75243
Skyview Dr 75228
Slade St 75203
Slagle St 75216
Slaughter Ave 75214
Slay St 75217
Sleepy Ln 75229
Sleepy Hollow Dr 75235
Sleeth St 75216
Slocum St 75207
Slopes Dr 75231
N & S Smith St 75211
Smoke Glass Trl 75252
Smoke Tree Ln 75253
Smokefeather Ln 75243
Smu Blvd
2800-2898 75205
2900-3000 75205
3002-3098 75205
5501-5597 75206
5599-5699 75206
Sneed St 75204
Snider Plz 75205
Snow White Dr
10800-11299 75229
11301-11499 75229
12001-12197 75244
12199-12299 75244
Snowbird Ln 75252
Soft Wind Dr 75241
Softcloud Dr 75241
Soho Ln 75204
Solana Dr 75253
Solar Ln 75216
Solitude Dr 75241
Soloman Dr 75212
Solta Dr 75218
Sombrero Dr 75229
Somerset Ave 75203
Somerton Dr 75229
Somerville Ave 75206
Sonata Ln 75241
Sondra Dr 75214
Songwood Dr 75241
Sonnet Dr 75229
Sonny Cir 75210
Sonora Ave 75216
Sophora Cir & Dr 75249
Sorcey Rd 75249
Sorenson Cir 75227
Sorrento St 75228
South Blvd 75215
Southbrook Dr 75209
Southcrest Rd 75229
Southeast Dr 75217
Southerland Ave 75203
Southern Ave
4300-4599 75205
4600-5373 75209
Southern Blvd 75240
Southern Hills Dr 75216
Southern Knoll Dr 75248
Southern Oaks Blvd 75216
Southern Pines Ct, Cv &
Dr 75234
Southgate Ln 75217
Southland St 75215
Southmeadow Cir 75231
Southpoint Dr 75248
Southport Dr 75232
Southridge Dr 75214
Southside Terrace Dr 75232
Southview Ln 75240
Southwell Rd 75229
Southwestern Blvd
2900-4499 75225
5400-5799 75209
7600-7800 75225
7802-7998 75225
8100-8899 75206
8900-9198 75214
Southwestern Medical
Ave 75235
Southwick Dr 75241
Southwood Dr
2300-2399 75224
2400-2999 75233
Sovereign Row 75247
Spa Ct 75241
Spangler Rd 75220
Spanish Vlg 75248
Spanish Bay Dr 75253
Spanky Pl 75248
Spanky Branch Ct &
Dr 75248
Spann St 75203
Sparkman Rd 75220
Sparks St 75203
Sparrow Ln 75217
Speight St 75232
Spelt Ln 75241
Spence St 75215
Spenwick Ter 75204
Sperry St 75214
Spiceberry Ct 75217
Spicewood Dr 75253
Spikerush Ct 75241
Spirehaven Ln 75238
Spivey St 75203
Spokane Cir 75229
Sports St 75207
Sprague Dr 75233
Spring Ave
3200-3499 75215
3500-4999 75210
Spring Branch Dr 75238
Spring Creek Pl, Rd &
Vlg 75248
Spring Flower Trl 75248
Spring Garden St 75215
Spring Glen Dr 75232
Spring Grove Ave 75240
Spring Hollow Cir &
Dr 75243
Spring Valley Rd
3940-4198 75244
4200-5099 75244
5200-7999 75254
8000-8898 75240
Springbrook St 75205
Springdale St 75210
Springer St 75216
W Springfield Ave 75232
Springford Dr 75238
Springhaven Dr 75217
Springhill Dr 75228
Springlake Dr 75217
Springlake Rd 75234
Springmeadow Dr 75229
Springside Ln 75214
Springtree Ln 75243
Springvale Dr 75234
Springview Ave 75216
Springwater Dr 75228
Springwood Ln & Pl 75233
Sprowles St 75229
Spruce St 75211
Spruce Creek Ln 75252
Spruce Valley Ln 75233
Spruce View Dr 75232
Sprucewood Cir & Dr 75240
Spur Trl 75234
Spur 408 75236
Spurling Dr 75230
Spurlock St 75223
Spyglass Cir & Dr 75287
Square Dr 75238
Squaw Valley Dr 75252
Squire Pl 75234
Stable Glen Dr 75243
Stables Ln 75229
Stacy St 75204
Stafford St 75208
Staffordshire Dr 75238
Stag Rd 75241
Stagecoach Cir & Trl 75241
Stallcup Dr 75228
Stampley St 75203
Stanford Ave
2700-4499 75225
4600-5799 75209
7800-7999 75225
Stanford Ct 75254
Stanhope St 75205
Stanley Smith Dr 75216
Stanwood Dr 75228
Stanworth Dr
6700-6899 75252
17300-17399 75248
17500-17599 75252
Stapleford Cir & Way 75252
Star Crossed Pl 75252
Starbuck Dr 75252

Street	ZIP
Starcrest Ln	75234
Stardale Ln	75217
Stardust Ln	75234
Staretta Ln	75211
E Stark Rd	75253
Starkey St	75232
Starks Ave	75215
Starlight Rd	75220
Starling Cir	75209
Starr St	75203
Starwood Cir	75253
State St	
2500-2599	75201
2600-3199	75204
3201-3299	75204
Stately Ct	75252
Stateoak Dr	75241
Steamboat Dr	75230
Stebbins St	75217
Stedman Cir & Dr	75252
Stefani Dr	75225
Steinhagen Ln	75287
Steinman Ave	75203
Stella Ave	
800-998	75216
1000-1599	75216
1601-1699	75216
1700-1899	75203
Stellariga Pl	75203
Stemmons Ave	75208
N Stemmons Fwy	
201-797	75207
799-2799	75207
2900-8900	75247
8902-9098	75247
10200-10598	75220
10600-10899	75220
10901-10999	75220
11000-11098	75229
11100-11500	75229
11502-11698	75229
12101-12197	75234
12199-14099	75234
Stemmons Trl	75220
Stephenson Dr	75215
Steppington Dr	75230
Steuben Ct	75248
Stevens St	
1500-1599	75218
1600-1699	75228
Stevens Crest Dr	75211
Stevens Forest Dr	75208
Stevens Point Ln	75287
Stevens Ridge Dr	75211
Stevens Village Dr	75208
Stevens Woods Ct & Ln	75208
Stewart Dr	75208
Stichter Ave	75230
Stigall Dr	75209
Still Forest Dr	75252
Stillmeadow Rd	75232
Stillwater Cir & Dr	75243
S Stillwell Blvd	75211
Stillwood St	75248
Stinson Dr	75217
Stirling Ave	75216
Stockton Ln	75287
Stokes St	75216
Stone Pl	75201
Stone Arbor Ct	75287
Stone Canyon Pl & Rd	75230
Stone Cliff Ct	75287
Stone Creek Pl	75243
Stone Falls Ln	75287
Stone Meadow Dr	75230
Stone River Cir	75231
Stoneboro Trl	75241
Stonebriar Ct	75206
Stonebridge Dr	75204
Stonebrook Cir	75240
Stonecourt Cir & Dr	75225
Stonecrest Dr	75254
Stonegate Rd	75209
Stonehaven Dr	75254
Stonehearth Pl	75287
Stonehill Dr	75254
Stonehollow Way	75287
Stonehurst St	75217
Stoneleigh Ave	75235
Stoneman St	75215
Stonemoss Dr	75240
Stoneport Dr	75217
Stoneridge Dr	75252
Stoneshire Ct	75252
Stonetrail Dr	75230
Stoneview Dr	75237
Stonewall St	75223
Stonewood Dr	75227
Stony Creek Dr	75228
Stony Ford Dr	75287
Storey Ln	75220
N Storey St	75203
S Storey St	75203
Stovall Cir & Dr	75216
Strait Ln	
9900-9999	75220
10000-11500	75229
11502-11598	75229
Strait Lane Cir	75229
Strand St	75218
Strasbourg Mews	75236
Stratford Ave	75205
Stratford Way	75220
Strathmore Dr	75238
Stratton Dr	75241
Strawberry Trl	75241
Strayhorn Dr	75228
Stretch Dr	75211
Strickland St	75216
Strobel Ave	75216
Strong St	75208
Stubbs Dr	75253
Stults Rd	75243
Stutz Dr	75235
Sudbury Dr	75214
Sue St	75203
Suetelle Dr	75217
Suewood Ln	75217
E Suffolk Ave	75203
W Suffolk Ave	75208
Sugar Mill Rd	75244
Sugarberry Pl & Rd	75249
Sugarleaf Ln	75249
Sul Ross Ln	75214
Sullivan Dr	75215
Sullivan Rd	75253
Sulphur St	75208
Sultana St	75253
Sumac Ct & Dr	75217
Sumac Leaf Ct	75212
Sumatra Dr	75241
Summer Creek Cir	75231
Summer Glen Ln	75243
Summer Meadow Ln	75252
Summer Oaks Dr	75227
Summer Place Ct	75234
Summerfield Dr	75287
Summerhill Ln	75238
Summerset Dr	75249
Summerside Dr	
5995-5995	75248
5995-5995	75379
5999-6099	75252
Summertime Ln	75241
Summertree Ln	75243
Summerwood Cir	75243
Summit Ln	75227
Summit Hill Dr	75287
Summit Oak Cir	75227
Summit Parc Dr	75249
Summitt Ave	75206
Summitt Ridge Dr	75216
Sumter Dr	75220
Sun Valley Dr	75216
Sunbeam Ave	75217
N & S Sunbeck Cir	75234
Sunberry St	75227
Sunbriar Ave	75217
Sunburst Dr	75217
Sunburst Ln	75234
Suncrest Dr	75228
Sundance Ln	75287
Sundial Dr	75229
Sundown Trl	75234
Sunglow Ln	75234
Sunhaven Ln	75252
Sunland St	75218
Sunlight Dr	75230
Sunmeadow Dr	75252
Sunny Brae Dr	75204
Sunny Crest Ln	75241
Sunny Glen Dr & Pl	75232
Sunny Hill Ln	75234
Sunnybrook Ln	75220
Sunnydale Dr	75217
Sunnyland Ln	75214
Sunnyside Ave	75211
Sunnyvale St	75216
Sunnywood Dr	75228
Sunridge Trl	75243
Sunrise Hill Ln	75241
Sunrose Ln	75234
Sunscape Ln	75287
Sunset Ave	
101-197	75208
199-999	75208
1001-1099	75208
2400-2799	75211
Sunset Pt	75249
Sunset Inn Cir	75218
Sunset Valley Dr	75248
Sunshine Cir	75238
Sunview Dr	75253
Superior St	75211
N Support Rd	75261
Surf Dr	75214
Surrey Ave	75203
Surrey Cir	75209
Surrey Oaks Dr	75229
Surrey Square Ln	75209
Susan St	75211
Sussex Ave	75203
Sutter St	75216
Sutton St	75210
Swaffar Dr	75228
Swaindell St	75211
Swallow Ln	75218
Swan Dr	75228
Swananoah Rd	75209
Swansee Dr	75232
Swanson Ct & St	75210
Sweet Gum St	75249
Sweet Sue Ln	75241
Sweetbay Ct	75253
Sweetbriar Dr	75228
Sweetwater Dr	75228
Sweetwood Dr	75228
Swift Ave	75228
Swiss Ave	
2400-4899	75204
4900-6100	75214
6102-6298	75214
Swiss Cir	75204
Switzer Ave	75238
Swor St	75235
Sycamore St	75204
Sylvan Ave	
1201-1397	75208
1399-2200	75208
2202-2398	75208
2400-3499	75212
Sylvania Dr	75218
Sylvester St	75219
Sylvia Dr	75228
Sylvia St	75241
Symphony Ln	75227
Syracuse Dr	75214
T I Blvd	75243
Tabasco Plz	75211
Tabor Dr	75231
Tackett St	75217
Tacoma St	75216
Taft St	75208
Tahoe Dr	75240
Talbot Pkwy	75232
Talco Dr	75241
Talina Dr	75228
Talisman Dr	75229
Tall Oak Dr	75287
Tallow Berry Dr	75249
Tally Ho Ln	75212
Talmadge Ln	75230
Talmay Dr	75230
Tamalpais Dr	75217
Tamarack Dr	75228
Tamaron Ct & Dr	75287
Tamerisk Ln	75234
Tamintri Dr	75230
Tampa Bay Dr	75217
Tampas Ln	75227
Tamworth Dr	75217
Tan Oak Dr	75212
Tanbark Rd	75229
Tandem Trl	75217
Tangiers Dr	75211
Tangle Ter	75233
Tanglecrest Dr	75254
Tangleglen Cir, Dr & Pl	75248
Tangleridge Ln	75240
Tanglevine Dr	75238
Tanglewood Cir, Ct, Dr & Pl	75234
Tanner St	75215
Tantor Rd	75229
Tanzy Ln & Rd	75236
Taos Rd	75209
Taperwicke Dr	75232
Tara Ln	75217
Tarleton St	75218
Tarna Dr	75229
Tarpley Ave	75211
Tarrant Pl	75208
Tarryall Dr	75224
Tascosa St	75228
Tato Dr	75211
N & S Tatum Ave	75211
Tavaros Ave	75218
Tavel Cir	75230
Tayloe St	75227
Taylor St	
2001-2297	75201
2299-2499	75201
2700-3099	75226
Taylorcrest Dr	75253
Teagarden Ct & Rd	75217
Teague Dr	75241
Teakwood Dr	75240
Tealford Dr	75228
Tealglen Dr	75241
Tealmont Trl	75211
Tecate Ct	75236
Technology Blvd E & W	75220
Telegraph Ave	75228
Telephone Rd	75241
Tellerson Ave	75228
Telluride Ln	75252
Telstar Dr	75233
Temper Ln	75253
Tempest Dr	75217
Templecliff Dr	75217
Templeton Trl	75234
Tenino St	75217
Tenison Memorial Dr	75223
Tenna Loma Ct	75208
N Tennant St	75208
Tennessee Ave	75224
Tennington Park	75287
Teresa Dr	75217
Teresita Trl	75227
Terminal St	75202
Terra Alta Cir	75227
Terra Forest Dr	75217
Terrace Dr	75224
Terrace Lawn Cir	75248
Terre Colony Ct	75212
Terrell St	75223
Terry St	75223
Tessla Dr	75241
Tetley Dr	75201
Tettenhall Dr	75252
Tewkesbury Way	75252
Tex Oak Ave	75235
Texas Dr	75211
Texas St	75204
Texas College Dr	75241
Texoma Way	75241
Texridge Dr	75232
Thackery St	
6600-6698	75205
8301-8497	75225
8499-8699	75225
8701-9599	75225
9701-9799	75230
Thale Dr	75228
Thames Ct	75252
The Mall	75219
Thedford Ave	75209
Thedford Dr	75217
Thelma St	75217
Thibet St	75211
Thistle Ln	75240
Thomas Ave	
2400-2599	75201
2600-3299	75204
3301-3399	75204
Thomas Chapel Dr	75248
Thomas Tolbert Blvd	75215
Thomasson Dr	75208
Thomaswood Ln	75253
Thoriv Ave	75223
Thornberry Ln	75220
Thorne St	75217
Thornhill Dr	75217
Thorntree Ln	75252
Thornwood Dr	75227
Throckmorton St	75219
Thrush St	75209
Thunder Rd	75244
Thunderbird Ln	75238
Thurgood Ln	75238
Thursby Ave	75252
Thurston St	75235
Tiawah Dr	75217
Tibbs St	75230
Tierra Dr	75211
Tiffany St	75211
Tiffany Way	75218
E Tilden St	75203
N & S Tillery Ave	75211
Tillman St	75217
Tim Tam Cir	75229
Timber Creek Ln	75248
Timber Dell Ln	75232
Timber Falls Dr	75249
Timber Oaks Dr	75287
Timber Trail Dr	75229
Timber Wood Dr	75211
Timberbent Dr	75252
Timberbluff Cir, Ct & Rd	75249
Timberbrook Ln	75249
Timbercrest Ln	75233
Timberglen Rd	75287
Timbergrove Cir	75208
Timberhollow Cir	75231
Timberidge St	75227
Timberlake Ct	75230
Timberleaf Dr	75243
Timberline Dr	75220
Timberloam Dr	75217
Timberview Cir & Rd	75229
Timothy Dr	75227
Timplemore Dr	75218
Tioga Cir, Ct, Pl & St	75241
Tippecanoe Cir	75215
Tipperary Dr	75218
Tips Blvd	75216
Tisinger Ave	75228
Titan Dr	75247
Todd St	75210
Todville Pl	75228
Tokalon Dr	75214
Tokay St	75212
Tokowa Dr	75217
Toland St	75227
Tolbert St	75227
Toler Trl	75249
Tolosa Dr	75228
Toltec Dr	75232
Toluca Ave	75224
Tom Braniff Ln	75235
Tom Field Rd	75234
Tomahawk Dr	75253
Tomberra Way	75220
Tomkins Ln	75217
Tomlinson St	75248
Tonawanda Dr	75217
Tooms St	75227
Top Flight Dr	75211
Top Line Dr	75247
Topaz Ln	75234
Topeka Ave	
2300-2399	75208
2600-3499	75212
Tophill Cir & Ln	75248
Topsfield Dr	75231
Toro	75217
Toro Bravo Dr	75236
Toronto St	75212
Torreon Ct	75217
Torrey Pine Dr	75287
Tory Sound Dr	75231
Tosca Ln	75224
Toston St	75203
Toulon Ln	75227
Touraine Dr	75211
Tower Trl	75229
Towerwood Dr	75234
N Town Mall	75234
Town Bluff Dr	75248
Town Creek Dr	75232
Town Hill Ln	75214
Town House Row	75225
Town North Dr	75231
Towneship Ln	75243
Towns St	75243
Townsend Dr	75229
Townsley Ct	75248
Tractor Dr	75241
Tracy Rd	75241
Tracy St	75205
Trade Village Pl	75217
Trade Winds Dr	75241
Trafalgar Ct	75254
Trail Ave	75217
Trail Glen Dr	75217
Trail Hill Dr	75238
Trail Meadow Dr	75230
Trailblazer Way	75236
Trailcliff Dr	75238
Trailcrest Dr & Pl	75232
Traildust Dr	75237
Trailhouse Dr	75237
Trailpine Dr	75238
Trailridge Dr	75224
Trails End Dr	75248
Trailview Dr	75238
Trailwood Dr	75241
Tralee Dr	75218
Trallam Dr	75217
Trallorn Dr	75211
Tram Dr	75212
Trammel Dr	75214
Trammel Crow Ctr	75201
Tranquil Way	75237
Tranquilla Dr	75218
Transit St	75217
Transport Dr	75247
Traviate Ave	75248
Travis St	
3500-4199	75204
4200-4799	75205
Travis Trl	75241
Traymore Ave	75217
Treadway Plz & St	75235
Tree Shadow Ct, Pl & Trl	75252
Treehaven St	75215
Treehouse Ln	75231
Treeline Cir & Dr	75224
Treetop Ln	75241
Treeview Ln	75234
N & S Trego Ct	75217
Trellis Ct	75246
Tremont St	
4700-4899	75246
4900-6399	75214
Trend Dr	75234
Trent Pl	75252
Trenton Dr	75243
Tres Logos Ln	75228
Trevolle Pl	75204
Trevor Dr	75243
Trew Dr	75228
Trewitt Rd	75217
Trezevant St	75210
Tribeca Way	75204
Tribune Dr	75224
Trinidad Dr	75232
Trinity Ln	75241
Trinity Creek Dr	75217
Trinity Cross Ct	75236
Trinity Gate Dr	75237
Trinity Mills Rd	
3301-4219	75287
4221-4500	75287
4475-4475	75370
4502-4598	75287
Trinity River Cir	75203
Trio Ln	75241
Tristian Ct	75211
Triton Ln	75227
Triumph Rd	75241
Trojan St	75216
Troon Cir	75287
Troy St	75210
Troy Glen Dr	75241
Truelite Ln	75211
Truesdell Pl	75244
N Trunk Ave	75226
S Trunk Ave	
701-899	75210
3501-3599	75215
Truth Dr	75236
Truxillo St	75228
Truxton Dr	75231
Tucker St	75214
Tudor Pl	75228
Tufts Rd	75217
Tulane St	
7101-8099	75225
8400-8498	75225
9701-9799	75230
10000-10098	75230
Tulip Ln	75230
Tumalo Trl	75212
Tumble Ridge Ct	75227
Tumbleweed Dr	75217
Tumbling Creek Trl	75241
Tune Ave	75217
Tupelo Ln	75287
Turbeville Dr	75243
Turf Dr	75217
Turfway Cir & Dr	75227
Turin Dr	75217
Turnberry Ln	75248
Turnbow Dr	75217
Turnbridge Dr	75252
Turner Ave	75208
Turner Way	75230
Turnout Ln	75236
Turtle Creek Blvd	
100-1499	75207
1501-1599	75207
2401-3497	75219
3499-3699	75219
3701-4125	75219
6500-7047	75205
7049-7099	75205
7100-8500	75225
8502-8616	75225
Turtle Creek Bnd	75204
Turtle Creek Cir	75219
Turtle Creek Dr	75219
Turtle Creek Ln	75205
Tuscany Way	75218
Tuskegee St	75215
Tuxedo Cir & Ct	75215

Street	ZIP
Tweed Dr	75227
Twin Branch Dr	75287
Twin Bridge Ct	75243
Twin Brooks Dr	75252
Twin Coves St	75248
Twin Creek Cir & Dr	75228
Twin Hills Ave	75231
Twin Oaks Cir	75240
Twin Post Rd	75244
Twin Tree Ln	75214
Twineing St	75227
Twinlawn Dr	75228
Twisted Oaks Cir	75231
Twyman Ave	75215
N Tyler St	75208
S Tyler St	
100-1299	75208
1301-1497	75224
1499-3600	75224
3602-3898	75224
Tyree St	75209
Tyrone Dr	75236
Uarda Dr	75217
Udal Ave	75217
Ukiah Dr	75227
Ulloa Ln	75228
Umphress Ct & Rd	75217
Undercliff Dr	75217
Underwood St	75216
Uninchit St	75204
Union Aly	75204
University Blvd	
2501-2599	75206
2800-4500	75205
4502-4538	75205
E University Blvd	
5501-5597	75206
5599-6099	75206
6100-6399	75214
W University Blvd	75209
University Hills Blvd	75241
Upcreek Ct	75253
Upshur St	75223
Upton St	75203
Urban Ave	75227
Urban Crest Rd	75227
Urban Lofts Dr	75215
Ursula Ln	75229
Uruapan Plz	75211
Us Highway 75	75241
Utah Ave	75216
Utica Dr	
1900-2099	75217
2100-2599	75227
Vacek Rd	75212
Vacherie Ln	75227
Vada Dr	75214
Vagas St	75219
Vail St	75287
Vail Meadow Ln	75253
Valdez Dr	75253
Valdina St	75207
Vale St	75211
Valencia St	75223
Valentine Ct	75217
Valentine St	75215
Valiant Dr	75229
Vallejo Dr	75227
Valleria Dr	75211
Valley St	75203
Valley Branch Cir & Ln	75234
Valley Chapel Ln	75220
Valley Creek Dr	75254
Valley Glen Dr	75228
Valley Hi Cir	75234
Valley Lawn Pl	75229
Valley Meadow Ct, Dr & Pl	75220
Valley Mills Ln	75227
Valley Ridge Rd	75220
Valley Spring Dr	75218
Valley View Ln	
1601-1697	75234
1699-3400	75234
3402-3698	75234
3700-4099	75244
6901-7297	75240
7299-7399	75240
Valley View Mall	75240
Valley View Pl	75240
Valleybrook Dr	75254
Valleydale Dr	75230
Valwood Cir, Ctr & Pkwy	75234
N & S Van Buren Ave	75208
Van Cleave Dr	75216
Van Dyke Rd	75218
Van Gogh Pl	75287
Van Hise Dr	75212
Van Hook Dr	75248
Van Ness Ln & Pl	75220
Van Pelt Dr	75228
Van Winkle Blvd	75235
Vance Dr	75203
Vancouver Cir & Dr	75229
Vandelia St	
4300-4599	75219
4900-5699	75235
Vanderbilt Ave	
5100-6099	75206
6100-6799	75214
Vandervort Dr	75216
Vanette Ln	75216
Vanguard Way	75243
Vannerson Dr	75215
Vantage St	75207
Vantage Point Dr	75243
Vaquero Dr	75217
Vargon St	75243
Vassar Ave	75205
Vatican Cir & Ln	75224
Vecino Dr	75241
Vecinos Blvd	75212
Velasco Ave	
5700-6099	75206
6100-6899	75214
Vendome Pl	75230
Venetian Way	75229
Ventana Trl	75252
Venture Dr	75234
Vera Cruz Plz	75201
W Verallar Dr	75261
Veranda Way	75241
Verano Dr	75218
Verde Way	75211
Verde Valley Ln	75254
Verde Vista Trl	75236
Verdun Ave	75215
Vereldel Dr	75232
Verierne Dr	75228
Vermont Ave	75216
N Vernon Ave	75208
S Vernon Ave	
400-498	75208
500-1099	75208
1401-2097	75224
2099-3399	75224
3401-3499	75224
Veronica Cir & Rd	75234
Versailles Ave	75205
N Versailles Ave	
3508-3514	75209
3516-3851	75209
4400-4498	75205
4500-4547	75205
4600-4698	75209
S Versailles Ave	
3515-3515	75209
3517-3857	75209
3859-3877	75209
4401-4497	75205
4499-4599	75205
4600-4696	75209
4698-4698	75209
Vesper St	75215
Veterans Dr	
4601-4697	75216
4699-4800	75216
4802-4898	75216
4900-5199	75241
Via Estrella	75211
Via Helena Dr	75211
Via James Jacob	75211
Via Jesse Elias	75211
Via San Antonio	75211
Via San Eduardo	75211
Via St Catherine	75211
Viaduct St	75203
Vicarage Ct	75248
Viceroy Dr	
1200-1300	75247
1302-1398	75247
1400-1498	75235
1500-1799	75235
Vickery Blvd	
5000-6099	75206
6100-6499	75214
Vicksburg St	75207
Victor St	
4301-4497	75246
4499-4899	75246
4900-6299	75214
Victoria Ave	75209
Victorian Ct	75243
Victorian Forest Dr	75227
Victory Ave	75219
Victory Park Ln	75219
Vida Ct & Ln	75253
Vienna Cir	75228
Viera Plz	75211
Viewcrest Dr	75228
Viewside Dr	75231
Vilbig Rd	
1600-1899	75208
1901-1999	75208
2400-4099	75212
Villa Rd	75252
Villa Cliff Dr	75228
Villa Creek Dr	75234
Villa Grove Dr	75287
Villa Haven Dr	75238
Villa Park Cir	75225
Villa Sur Trl	75228
Village Cir	75248
Village Ct	75248
Village Ln	75248
Village Pl	75248
Village Way	75216
Village Bend Dr	75206
Village Fair Dr	75224
Village Green St	75227
Village Star Ln	75217
Village Trail Dr	75254
Villager Rd	75230
Villanova St	75225
Villars St	75204
Villaverde Ave	75234
Vincent Ave	75211
Vine Ln	75217
Vine St	75204
Vine Maple Pl	75212
Vinecrest Dr	75229
Vinemont St	75218
Vineridge Dr	75248
Vinewood Dr	75228
Vineyard Dr	75212
Vineyard Way	75234
Vinland St	75227
Vinson St	75212
Vintage Pl	75214
Vintage St	75234
Viola St	75203
Virgil St	75226
Virginia Ave	75204
Virginia Blvd	75211
W Virginia Dr	75237
Virgo Ln	75229
Visalia Dr	75228
Viscount Row	75247
Vista Ct	75217
Vista Creek Dr	75243
Vista Del Sol	75287
Vista Gate Dr	75243
Vista Grande Dr	75249
Vista Hill Ln	75249
Vista Meadow Cir & Dr	75248
Vista Oaks Cir, Dr & Pl	75243
Vista Park Rd	75238
Vista Real Dr	75211
Vista Tree Cir	75248
Vista View Dr	75243
Vista Willow Dr	75248
Vistadale Cir & Dr	75238
Vistaridge Dr	75248
Vivian Ave	75223
Vizcaya Dr	75248
Volga Ave	75216
Voss Rd	75287
Voss Hills Pl	75287
Voyage Trl	75215
Voyager Dr	75237
Wabash Cir	75214
E Waco Ave	75216
Waddell Ave	75235
Waddy Ave	75208
Wadlington Ave	75217
Wadsworth Dr	
4600-4999	75216
5000-5099	75241
Waggoner Dr	75230
Wagon Wheels Trl	75241
Wahoo St	75210
Wainsborough Ln	75287
Wake St	75212
Wake Forrest Dr	75214
Wakefield Cir & St	75231
Walden Way	75287
Waldorf Cir & Dr	75229
Waldron Ave	75215
Waldrop Dr	75229
Wales Ln	75244
Waleska Plz	75211
Walker St	75211
Walkway St	75212
Wall St	75215
Wallace St	75217
Wallbrook Dr	75238
Waller Dr	75229
Walling Cir & Ln	75231
Walmsley Ave	75208
Walnut St	75243
Walnut Glen Pl	75229
Walnut Hill Cir	75230
Walnut Hill Ln	
2000-2098	75229
2100-5599	75229
5601-5699	75229
5701-5797	75230
5799-7799	75230
7801-7899	75230
8000-8400	75231
8402-8898	75231
9700-11199	75238
Walnut Meadow Ln	75229
Walnut Ridge St	75229
Walnut Springs Ct	75252
Walraven Ln	75235
Walter Dr	75211
N & S Walton St	75226
N Walton Walker Blvd	
1200-1298	75211
1300-1399	75211
1401-1699	75211
2200-3099	75212
10101-10197	75220
10199-10299	75220
S Walton Walker Blvd	
400-798	75211
800-2999	75211
3001-3099	75211
3200-4299	75236
Wanda St	75215
Wander Ln & Pl	75230
Wandt Dr	75236
Wanebe Dr	75235
Waneta Dr	75209
Wanklyn Ct & St	75237
Warancou Dr	75225
Warbler St	75227
Ware St	75223
Warick Dr	75229
Warm Breeze Ln	75248
Warm Mist Ln	75248
Warm Moon Ln	75241
Warren Ave	75215
Warrington Dr	75227
Warrior Dr	75253
Wasco Ln	75241
N Washington Ave	
100-199	75226
301-397	75246
399-999	75246
1000-1198	75204
1200-2499	75204
Washington Ct	75204
Washington Row	75204
Wasina Dr	75234
Waskom St	75228
Watauga Rd	75209
Wateka Dr	75209
Water Oak Ct	75234
Water Oaks Dr	75227
Waterbridge Cir	75218
Waterbury Dr	75217
Watercrest Ct	75234
Watercrest Pkwy	75231
Waterfall Pl & Way	75240
Waterford Dr	75218
Waterhouse Dr	75241
Watership Ln	75237
Waterside Cir, Ct & Dr	75218
Watervaliet Dr	75224
Waterview Pkwy	75252
Waterview Rd	75218
Waterway Rd	75287
Waterwood Ln	75217
Watkins Ave & Ct	75204
Watson Ave	75225
Watson Cir	75225
Watson Dr	75241
Watsonwood St	75253
Watt St	75204
Watterson Dr	75228
N Waverly Dr	75208
S Waverly Dr	
100-198	75208
200-1499	75208
1600-2598	75224
2600-2699	75224
Waweenoc Ave	75216
Wax Berry Dr	75249
Waycrest Dr	75232
Waycross Dr	75227
Wayne St	75223
Wayside Dr	75235
Weald Green St	75240
Weather Vane Ln	75228
Weaver St	75253
Webb Ave	75205
Webb Chapel Ct	75229
Webb Chapel Ext	75220
Webb Chapel Rd	
9400-9999	75220
10200-10298	75229
10301-11799	75229
11800-14500	75234
14502-14998	75234
Webb Garden Dr	75229
Webb Kay Dr	75243
Webb Royal Plz	75229
Webster St	75209
Webster Ter	75229
Wedgecrest Dr	75232
Wedgemere Dr	75232
Wedgewood Ln	75220
Wedglea Dr	75211
Weeburn Dr	75229
Weehaven Dr	75232
Weir St	75212
Weisenberger Dr	75212
Weiss St	75235
Welborn St	75219
Welch Rd	
10500-11698	75229
11701-11799	75229
11801-12597	75244
12599-14099	75244
14101-14399	75244
Weldon St	75204
Weldon Howell Pkwy	75225
Wellcrest Dr	75230
Welleart Ave	75216
Wellingshire Ln	75220
Wellington St	75210
Wells St	75215
Wembley Ter	75220
Wemdon Dr	75220
Wenatche Dr	75233
Wendelkin St	75215
Wendell Rd	75243
Wendover Rd	75214
Wendy Ln	75214
Wenonah Dr	75209
Wentwood Dr	75225
Wentworth St	
1301-1697	75208
1699-2299	75208
2401-2497	75211
2499-2599	75211
Wes Hodges Rd	75217
Wescott Ln	75287
Wesley Chapel Ln	75236
Wesleyan Dr	75241
Wessex Dr	75217
West Aly	75223
Westbend Dr	75231
Westbriar Dr	75228
Westbrook Ln	75214
Westburg Aly	75204
Westchester Dr	
6300-7099	75205
7500-7998	75225
8000-8499	75225
Wester Way	75248
Wester Way Ct & Pl	75248
Westerham Dr	75232
Western St	75211
Western Hills Dr	75217
Western Oaks Dr	75211
Western Park Ct, Dr & Plz	75211
Western Park Shopping Vlg	75211
Westfield Dr	75243
Westforest Dr	75229
Westgate Dr	75254
Westglen Dr	75228
Westgrove Cir, Dr & Pl	75248
Westlake Ave	75214
Westlawn Dr	75229
Westmere Cir	75230
Westminster Ave	75205
Westminster Dr	75234
Westminster Ter	75243
N Westmoreland Rd	
106-1499	75211
1700-4299	75212
S Westmoreland Rd	
100-2699	75211
2700-4299	75233
4401-4597	75237
4599-7800	75237
7802-8498	75237
Westmount Ave	75211
Westover Dr	75231
Westpark Dr	75231
Westport Ave	75203
Westrock Dr	75243
Westshire Ln	75287
Westside Dr	75209
Westview Cir	75231
Westway Ave	75205
Westwick Rd	75205
Westwind Ct	75231
Westwood Pl	75287
Weymouth Dr	75252
Wharton Dr	75243
E Wheatland Rd	75241
W Wheatland Rd	
300-398	75232
400-2399	75232
2400-4099	75237
4101-4399	75237
7000-7599	75249
Wheatley Pl	75204
Wheeler St	75209
Wheelock St	75220
Whintatt St	75226
Whippoorwill Dr	75224
Whirlaway Rd	75229
Whispering Cir, Ct & Trl	75241
Whispering Cedar Dr	75236
Whispering Gables Ln	75287
Whispering Hills Dr	75243
Whispering Oak	75234
Whispering Oaks Dr	75236
Whispering Pines Dr	75248
Whistler Dr	75217
Whitaker Ave	75216
Whitby Ave	75237
White Ash Rd	75249
White Elm Rd	75243
White Oak Dr	75227
White Pine Ln	75238
White River Dr	75287
White Rock Cir	75238
White Rock Pl	75238
White Rock Rd	75214
White Rock Trl	75238
White Rose Trl	75248
White Star Ln	75217
White Valley Dr	75249
Whitedove Dr	75224
Whitehall Dr	75229
Whitehall Ln	75232
Whitehaven Dr	75218
Whitehill St	75231
Whitehurst Dr	75243
Whitemarsh Cir	75234
Whiteridge Dr	75217
Whitestone Ln	75232
Whitewater Ln	75287
Whitewing Ln	75238
Whitewood Dr	75233
Whitingham Dr	75227
Whitley Dr	75217
Whitman Ln	75230
Whitneyglen Dr	75241
Whittenburg Gate	75243
Whittier Ave	75218
Whitworth St	75227
Wicker Ave	75234
Wickersham Rd	75238
Wickerwood Dr	75248
Wickford St	75208
Wicklow Dr	75218
Wickmere Mews	75208
Wideman Dr	75217
Widgeon Way	75249
Wightman Pl	75243
Wilada Dr	75220
Wilbarger Dr	75227
Wilbur St	
1100-2399	75224
2500-2799	75233
Wilburton Dr	75227
Wilcox Dr	75232
Wild Brick Dr	75249
Wild Cherry Way	75206
Wild Creek Ct	75253
Wild Honey Dr	75241
Wild Valley Dr	75231
Wildbriar Dr	75214
Wildcat Rd	75217
Wilder St	75215
Wilderness Ct	75254
Wildflower Dr	75229
Wildglen Dr	75230
Wildgrove Ave	75214
Wildhaven Dr	75238
Wildoak Cir & Dr	75228
Wildrose Dr	75224
Wildvine Dr	75248
Wildwood Rd	75209
Wiley College Dr	75241
Wilhelmina Dr	75237
Wilhurt Ave	75216

William Dodson Pkwy 75234
Williams Pkwy 75205
Williams Way Ct & Ln 75228
Williamsburg Rd 75220
Williamson Cir & Rd 75214
Williamstown Rd 75230
Williamswood Dr 75252
Willis Ave 75206
N & S Willomet Ave 75208
Willoughby Blvd 75232
Willow Ln
4300-5100 75244
5102-5198 75244
5500-6800 75230
6802-6898 75230
Willow St 75226
Willow Bend Rd 75240
Willow Crest Ln 75233
Willow Glen Dr 75232
Willow Grove Rd 75220
Willow Leaf Ct 75212
Willow Ridge Dr 75244
Willow Springs Ln 75210
Willow Wood Ln 75252
Willowbrook Rd 75220
Willowdell Dr 75243
Willowgate 75230
Willowood St 75205
Wilma St 75241
Wilmington Dr 75234
Wilshire Blvd 75241
Wilson St 75212
Wilton Ave 75211
Wimberley Ct 75229
Wimbleton Way 75227
Winchester St 75231
Wind River Dr 75216
Windbreak Trl 75252
Windchime Dr 75224
Windcrest Dr 75243
Windfall Cir 75253
Windflower Way 75252
Windham Dr 75243
Windhaven Ln 75287
Winding Brook Cir & Ln 75208
Winding Creek Ct & Rd 75252
Winding Lake Dr 75230
Winding Ridge Dr 75238
Winding Rose Trl 75252
Winding Way Ct 75287
Winding Woods Trl 75227
Windlake Cir 75238
Windledge Dr 75238
Windmier Cir, Ct & Ln 75252
Windmill Cir 75252
Windmill Ln
2900-3099 75234
19100-19299 75252
N & S Windomere Ave 75208
Windpiper Dr 75252
Windridge Way 75217
Windrock Rd 75252
Windsong Dr 75252
Windsor Ave, Ln & Pkwy 75205
Windtop Ln 75287
Windward Cir 75287
Windwood Dr 75249
Windy Crest Ct & Dr 75243
Windy Hill Rd 75238
Windy Knoll Dr 75243
Windy Meadow Dr 75248
Windy Ridge Dr 75248
Windy Terrace Cir & Dr 75231
Winecup Rdg 75249
Winedale Dr 75231
Wing Point Dr 75248
Wing Tip St 75227
Wingate Dr 75209
Winged Foot Ct 75229
Winn Pl 75204
Winnequah St 75212
N Winnetka Ave
100-1900 75208
1902-1998 75208
2400-3699 75212
S Winnetka Ave 75208
Winnwood Rd 75254
Winonly Cir 75211
Winslow Ave 75223
Winsor Dr 75244
Winsted Dr 75214
Winston Ct 75220
Winston St 75208
Winter Oak St 75227
Winterberry Dr 75249
Wintercreek Way 75287
Winterhaven Dr 75234
Winters St 75216
Winterset Ave 75232
Winterwood Ln 75248
Winthrop Dr 75228
Winton St
5300-5498 75206
5500-6099 75206
6100-6498 75214
6500-6799 75214
Wireway Dr 75220
Wisconsin St 75229
Wisdom Creek Dr 75249
Wisteria St 75211
Wisterwood Dr 75238
Witham St 75220
Witherspoon Dr 75217
Wittington Pl 75234
Wittmore Cir 75240
Wixom Ln 75217
Wofford Ave 75227
Wolcott Dr 75241
Wolf St 75201
Wolf Creek Cir & Trl 75232
Wolf Run Dr 75227
Wolfwood Ln 75217
Wonderland Trl 75229
Wonderlight Ln 75228
Wood St 75201
Wood Dale Dr 75228
Wood Forest Dr 75243
Wood Heights Dr 75227
Wood Homestead Dr 75249
Wood Manor Cir 75234
Wood River Rd 75232
Wood Slope Dr 75249
Wood Valley Dr & Pl 75211
Woodacre Cir & Dr 75241
Woodall St 75247
Woodall Rodgers Fwy
1600-1698 75202
1801-1997 75201
1999-2099 75201
2901-2999 75204
Woodard Ave 75227
Woodbend Ct & Ln 75243
Woodbine Ave 75203
Woodbluff Ct 75243
Woodbriar Dr 75248
Woodbridge Dr 75243
Woodbrook Dr 75243
Woodburn Trl 75241
Woodcastle Dr 75217
Woodcliff Dr 75224
Woodcreek Dr 75220
Woodcrest Ln
4300-4399 75206
6100-6499 75214
Wooded Trl 75249
Wooded Beck Ct 75249
Wooded Creek Ct & Dr 75244
Wooded Gap Dr 75249
Wooded Gate Dr 75230
Woodfell Ct 75249
Woodfin Dr 75220
Woodford Dr 75229
Woodgreen Dr 75217
Woodgrove Dr 75218
Woodhaven Ct & Dr 75234
Woodhill Rd 75217
Woodhollow Dr 75237
Woodhome Dr 75249
Woodhue Cir & Rd 75228
Woodhurst Dr 75243
E Woodin Blvd
100-1299 75216
1500-1699 75203
W Woodin Blvd 75224
Woodlake Cir & Dr 75243
Woodland Dr 75225
Woodland Terrace Dr 75232
Woodlark St 75227
Woodlark Trl 75241
Woodlawn Ave 75208
Woodleaf Dr 75227
Woodleigh Ct & Dr 75229
Woodlot Dr 75217
Woodmark Ct 75230
Woodmeadow Cir & Pkwy 75228
Woodmen Cir 75238
Woodmere Dr 75233
Woodmont Dr 75217
Woodoak Dr 75249
Woodpond Pl 75252
Woodridge Dr 75218
Woodrigg Dr 75249
Woodrock Dr 75217
Woods Edge Dr 75287
Woodsboro Ln 75241
Woodshadow Dr 75249
Woodshire Dr 75232
Woodshore Cir & Dr 75243
Woodside St 75204
Woodspan Dr 75232
Woodstock Dr 75232
Woodstone Ln 75248
Woodstream Ct 75240
Woodthrush Dr 75230
Woodvale St 75217
Woodview Ln 75216
Woodvista Ct 75217
Woodway Dr 75217
Woodwick Dr 75232
Woodwind Ln 75229
N & S Woody Rd 75253
Woolsey Dr 75224
Worcola St 75206
Word St 75204
Works Ave 75216
World Store Ct 75217
Worth St
3201-3299 75226
3400-3400 75246
3402-4899 75246
4900-6299 75214
Wortham Ln 75252
Worthing St 75252
Worthington St 75204
Wren Way 75209
Wrenwood Dr 75252
Wright St 75208
Wullschleger Ln 75210
Wyatt Cir & St 75218
Wyche Blvd 75235
Wycliff Ave
1201-1297 75207
1299-1399 75207
1401-1599 75207
2101-2197 75219
2199-4299 75219
Wylie Dr 75235
Wyman St 75235
Wynell St 75241
Wynnewood Dr 75224
Wynnewood Village Shp Ctr 75224
Wyoming St 75211
X St 75229
X Ray Ln 75236
Xavier Ct 75218
Y St 75229
Yadak Rd 75249
Yakimo Dr 75208
Yamini Dr 75230
Yancy St 75216
Yardley Ct 75248
E Yarmouth St 75203
W Yarmouth St 75208
Yarrow Cir 75217
Yeager Dr 75218
Yellow Rock Trl 75248
Yellowstone Rd 75235
Yewpon Ave 75216
Yolanda Cir & Ln 75229
York St 75210
Yorkford Dr 75238
Yorkmont Cir 75218
Yorkshire Dr 75230
Yorkspring Dr & Pl 75218
Yorktown St 75208
Yorkville Ct 75248
Yosemite Ln 75214
Young St
500-898 75202
1001-1399 75202
1400-2299 75201
Youngblood Rd 75241
Youngstown St 75253
Yucatan Plz 75211
Yucca Dr 75217
Yukon Cir 75216
Yuma Ct 75208
Yuma St
2300-2398 75208
2600-2699 75212
Z St 75229
E Zacha St 75228
N Zang Blvd
101-197 75208
199-1099 75208
1100-1199 75203
1201-1499 75203
S Zang Blvd
100-699 75208
701-1099 75208
1400-1598 75224
1600-1700 75224
1702-2798 75224
Zaragoza Plz 75211
Zealand St 75216
Zeb St 75211
Zelkova Cir 75249
Zelrich Ln 75229
Zenia Dr 75204
Zenith St 75212
Zodiac Ln 75229
Zola Ln 75217
Zonie Rd 75241
Zorro Ave 75248
Zuni St 75236

NUMBERED STREETS

1st Ave 75226
1st Ave 75226
1st Ave 75226
901-1097 75210
1099-4299 75210
1st St 75203
S 2nd Ave 75226
S 2nd Ave 75226
S 2nd Ave 75226
1300-2102 75210
2104-5399 75210
5700-5798 75217
3rd Ave 75226
4th Ave 75226
E 5th St 75203
W 5th St 75208
E 6th St 75203
W 6th St 75208
E 7th St 75203
W 7th St 75208
E 8th St 75203
W 8th St
100-1199 75208
1201-1799 75208
2800-3200 75211
3202-3798 75211
E 9th St 75203
W 9th St
101-197 75208
199-1000 75208
1002-1598 75208
2701-2797 75211
2799-3300 75211
3302-3398 75211
E 10th St 75203
W 10th St
101-197 75208
199-2100 75208
2102-2398 75208
2400-2799 75211
E 11th St 75203
E 12th St 75203
W 12th St
200-1900 75208
1902-2398 75208
2401-2497 75211
2499-2899 75211
2901-2999 75211
18th St 75216
W 23rd St 75261
N 28th St 75261
W 32nd St 75261
50th St 75216
51st St 75216
52nd St 75216
54th St 75216
56th St 75241
N 40 Pl 75252

DEL RIO TX

General Delivery 78840

POST OFFICE BOXES MAIN OFFICE STATIONS AND BRANCHES

Box No.s
1 - 4379 78841
420001 - 428005 78842

HIGHWAY CONTRACTS

01, 02, 03, 04 78840

NAMED STREETS

E & W Academy St 78840
Adobe St 78840
Adriana Loop 78840
Aduna St 78840
Agarita Dr 78840
Agave St 78840
Agua Azul 78840
Agua Dulce Trl 78840
Agua Linda 78840
Agua Serena 78840
Agua Verde Rd 78840
Aguinaldo St 78840
Aguirre St 78840
Airport Blvd 78840
Ajo Ln 78840
Alabama Ave
100-198 78840
100-199 78843
Alambre Dr 78840
Alamo Dr 78840
Albert St 78840
Alderete Ln 78840
Algerita Dr 78840
Alice Dr 78840
Allen Ranch Rd 78840
Alma 78840
Alta Vista Dr 78840
Alyssa Dr 78840
Ama Caro Dr 78840
Amistad Ave & Blvd 78840
N & S Amistad Village Rd 78840
Anchor St 78840
Anderson Cir 78840
Andrade St 78840
Angela Dr 78840
Apache Trl 78840
Arantz St 78840
Arapahoe Trl 78840
Arbor Ave 78840
Arbor Hills Ave 78840
Arkansas Ave 78843
Arnold Blvd 78840
Arranaga Ave 78840
Arrowhead St 78840
Arroyo Dr 78840
Arteaga St 78840
Ash St 78840
Ashenwoo St 78840
Austin Cts 78840
Avant St 78840
Avenue E 78840
Avenue 4 78840
Avenue A 78840
Avenue B 78840
Avenue C 78840
Avenue D 78840
Avenue G 78840
Avenue H 78840
Avenue I 78840
Avenue J 78840
Avenue K 78840
Avenue L 78840
Avenue M 78840
Avenue O 78840
Avenue P 78840
Avenue Q 78840
Avenue R 78840
Avenue T 78840
Avenue U 78840
Avenue V 78840
Avila Ln 78840
Avondale St 78840
Baja St 78840
Barbara Way 78840
Barrera Ave 78840
Barron St 78840
Barton Ave 78840
Bauer Ave 78840
S Bayview Dr 78840
E & W Bean St 78840
Beard St 78840
N Bedell Ave
200-2000 78840
2001-2499 78840
2001-2001 78842
2002-2498 78840
S Bedell Ave 78840
Benita Ln 78840
Betty Lou Dr 78840
Birch St 78840
Blackbuck Trl 78840
Blaine Rd 78840
Blossom Rd 78840
Blue Rdg 78840
Blue Sage Rd W 78840
Bluebonnet Rd 78840
Bluebonnett Dr 78840
Bolner Ln 78840
Boot Hill Trl 78840
Borroum St 78840
Bouganvilla St 78840
Boulder Ridge Dr 78840
E & W Bowie St 78840
Bowling St 78840
Braddie Dr 78840
Braun St 78840
Brewer 78840
Brian Ave 78840
Bridge St 78840
Brinkley Cir 78840
Brite Rd 78840
N & S Broadview St 78840
E Broadway St
100-199 78840
114-114 78841
200-398 78840
201-499 78840
W Broadway St 78840
Brodbent Ave 78840
Brown St 78840
Bryce Canyon Dr 78840
Buck Trl 78840
Buck Horn St & Trl 78840
Buena Vista Cir 78840
Bullis Well Rd 78840
Bundy Trl 78840
Bunting Dr 78840
Burge Dr 78840
Burk Rd 78840
Burnett St 78840
Burwood Ln 78840
Butch Cassidy Trl 78840
Butte Cir 78840
Caballo Dr 78840
Cabarnet Ln 78840
Cactus Ln & St 78840
Calderon Ln 78840
California Ave 78843
Calle Cocobolo 78840
Calle Del Verdelgal 78840
Camino Real St 78840
Cana Cir 78840
E Canal St 78840
Cano St 78840
Canon St 78840
E & W Cantu Rd & St 78840
Canyon Dr 78840
Canyon Creek Dr 78840
Capri Cv & Rd 78840
Cardenas St 78840
Carla Dr 78840
Carlson St 78840
Casa Blanca St 78840
Casa Grande 78840
Cassenelli St 78840
Catherine St 78840
Cedar St 78840
Cedro St 78840
Ceniza St 78840
Ceniza Hills Cir 78840
Ceniza Ridge Dr 78840
Center Ave & Dr 78840
Central St 78840
Centro Ave 78840
Centurion St 78840
Cerezo Ave 78840
Chalupa Cir 78840
Chapman Rd 78840
E & W Chapoy St 78840
Chardonnay Way 78840
Charles Dr 78840
Cherokee Trl 78840
Cherry Dr 78840
Chestnut St 78840
Chevrolet Dr 78840
Chihuahua St 78840
Chisolm Trl 78840
Christie Ln 78840
Ciarfeo St 78840
Cienegas Rd 78840
Cipri Rd 78840
Circle Dr 78840
Circle East Dr 78840
Cisneros St 78840
Clayton St 78840
Clouse Dr 78840
Cochran St 78840
Colorado Ave 78843
Comanche Trl 78840
Concepcion Cir 78840
Condry Rd 78840
Contreras St 78840
Converse St 78840
Coon Canyon Rd 78840
Cora Ave 78840
Cordelia St 78840
Cordona St 78840
Cordova Ln 78840
E & W Cortinas St 78840
Cottontail Ln 78840
County Road 630 78840
County Road 635 78840
County Road 650 78840

Covey Ridge Dr 78840
Coyote 78840
Crest Ave 78840
Crestline Dr 78840
Cribb St 78840
Crosswinds Way 78840
Cuellar St 78840
Culp Rd 78840
Currency Dr 78840
Cypress St 78840
Dallas Dr 78840
Danda Ln 78840
Danielle Dr 78840
Darrell Dr 78840
Dawson Dr 78840
E & W De La Rosa St 78840
De Leon St 78840
Deborah Kay St 78840
Deer Trl 78840
Deer Draw 78840
Delmar Ln 78840
Dennis Dr 78840
Devils Clf 78840
Diablo Rd 78840
Diablo East Rd 78840
Diaz St 78840
Diego Loop Rd 78840
E & W Dignowity St 78840
Dobkins St 78840
Dodson Ave 78840
Dogwood St 78840
Dolan Creek Rd 78840
Don Martin 78840
Don Pedro Dr 78840
Dona Ruth Rd 78840
Doodles St 78840
Dos Caballos 78840
Dos Pistolas 78840
Dove Ave 78840
Dr Fermin Calderon Blvd 78840
Duck St 78840
Duck Pond Rd 78840
E & W Duke St 78840
Echo Valley Dr 78840
Edna St 78840
Eduardo St 78840
Edward Dr & St 78840
Edwards St 78840
El Dorado St 78840
El Lago Camino 78840
Ela St 78840
Elder St 78840
Elises Cir 78840
Elizabeth Dr 78840
Ellis St 78840
Enchanted Way 78840
Encinal Dr 78840
Encino Dr 78840
Espuela Dr 78840
Esquivel St 78840
Evans St 78840
Fairway Dr 78840
Far Hills Dr 78840
Farley Ln 78840
Farrow St 78840
Fast Draw 78840
Fawcett Dr 78840
Fawn Dr 78840
Federico St 78840
Fiesta Dr 78840
Figueroa Dr 78840
Finegan Rd 78840
Fir St 78840
Fletcher Dr 78840
Flint Rock Trl 78840
Flores St 78840
Floyd Ave 78840
Fm 2523 78840
Fokes St 78840
Foster Cir, Dr & St 78840
Fox Dr & Trl 78840
N & S Frank St 78840
Frausto St 78840
Frazier St 78840
Freedom Way 78843

Frontera Rd 78840
Fury Creek Trl 78840
Gabriellas Way 78840
Gaila Ln 78840
Gaitan St 78840
Galveston 78840
Gancho 78840
Garden Cts 78840
Garden Crest Cir 78840
E & W Garfield St 78840
Garner Dr 78840
E & W Garza St 78840
Georgia Ave 78843
E & W Gibbs St 78840
Gilberto St 78840
Gilchrist Ln 78840
Gillis Ave 78840
Givens Ave 78840
Glen Canyon Dr 78840
Glendale Dr 78840
Gonzalez 78840
Graham St 78840
Grand Teton Dr 78840
Grandview Dr 78840
Greenway Ln 78840
Greenwillow St 78840
E & W Greenwood St 78840
Gregory Dr 78840
Griner St 78840
Grissom Dr 78840
Guajalote St 78840
Guayacan St 78840
Guillen St 78840
E & W Gutierrez St 78840
Guyler Ln 78840
Gyna Dr 78840
Hackberry Ln 78840
Hall St 78840
Hamilton Ln 78840
Happy Ln 78840
Harbor St 78840
Harness Rd 78840
Harris Dr 78840
Hartgrove St 78840
Harvey Dr 78840
Hermosa Dr 78840
Hernandez St 78840
Herrmann Dr 78840
Hetrick St 78840
Hidden Meadows Ln 78840
Highland St 78840
E Highway 90 78840
Hill St 78840
Hillcrest Rd 78840
Hillside Ave 78840
Hitching Post Rd 78840
Hodge St 78840
Hogan Dr 78840
Hold Up Pass Rd 78840
Holly Ave 78840
Holman Dr 78840
Holmig St 78840
Holt St 78840
Horseshoe Bnd 78840
Hortencia St 78840
Houston Ave 78840
Howell St 78840
Hudson Dr 78840
Hutchinson St 78840
Illinois 78840
Indian Pt 78840
Indian Head Ranch Rd 78840
Indian Springs Ave 78840
Industrial Blvd 78840
Inspiration Cir & Way 78840
W Inverness Ave 78840
Irene Ave 78840
Ivy Dr 78840
J S Murray Rd 78840
Jaimie Way St 78840
James Dr 78840
Jap Lowe Dr 78840
Jara Dr 78840
Jason Cir 78840
Jasper St 78840

Javalina Trl 78840
Javier Dr 78840
Jeffery Dr 78840
Jessica Ln 78840
Jodobo Dr 78840
Joe Rice Dr 78840
John Glenn Dr 78840
Johnson St 78840
Jones Cir & St 78840
Juanita St 78840
June Ave 78840
Kansas Ave 78843
Karen St 78840
Katrina St 78840
Kelly Rd 78840
Kennedy Dr 78840
Kentucky Ave 78843
Kenwood Ave 78840
Kenyon St 78840
Khoury Dr 78840
Kim Dr 78840
King Dr 78840
King Charles Pl 78840
King Georges Pl 78840
King Henrys Pl 78840
King Johns Pl 78840
King Richards Pl 78840
Kings Way 78840
Knight St 78840
Knowlton Rd 78840
La Carnada Dr 78840
La Grande St 78840
La Paloma Dr 78840
La Peggy 78840
Lago Azul Cir 78840
Lago Camino Dr 78840
Lago Vista Dr 78840
Lake Dr 78840
Lakeshore Dr 78840
Lakeview Loop 78840
Lantana Ln 78840
Laredo St 78840
Larkwood Ln 78840
Larson Dr 78840
Las Brisas Blvd 78840
Las Chispas St 78840
Las Palmas 78840
Las Vacas St 78840
Laughlin Afb 78843
Laurel Ln 78840
Lawhon St 78840
Lawmen Trl 78840
Lee St 78840
Lena Dr 78840
Lenawee Ave 78840
Lenise Ter 78840
Lenora Ave 78840
Leon St 78840
Lerdo 78840
Leticia St 78840
Lewis Dr 78840
Liberty Dr 78843
Lilac Ln 78840
Lima St 78840
Linda Vista Dr 78840
Linea Cir 78840
Lisa Dr 78840
Live Oak Dr & St 78840
Lodgepole Trl 78840
Loma Linda 78840
Lomita St 78840
Long Dr 78840
Longhorn St 78840
Lookout Dr 78840
Lorean Dr 78840
E & W Losoya St 78840
Lowe Dr 78840
Lubbock 78840
Lupita Cir 78840
Magnolia St 78840
N & S Main St 78840
Mangum 78840
Maple St 78840
Margaret Ln 78840
Margo Dr 78840
Marina Access Rd 78840

Mario Salas Ave 78840
Mariposa Dr 78840
Marshall Smith Dr 78840
E & W Martin St 78840
W Martinez St 78840
Mary Lou Dr 78840
Massie St 78840
Mata Ln 78840
Mathews Cir 78840
Maude Ln 78840
Maverick Trl 78840
Maximo St 78840
Mayfield Dr 78840
Mcconnell St 78840
Mcgregor Ct 78840
Mckee St 78840
Mclymont St 78840
Meadow Ln 78840
Meandering Way 78840
Medicine Bow Trl 78840
Melody Rd 78840
Memorial Dr 78840
Mendez St 78840
Mercedez Dr 78840
Mereenti St 78843
Mesa Dr 78840
Mesa Venado 78840
Mesquite St & Trl 78840
Michelle Dr 78840
Miers St 78840
Miers Ranch Rd 78840
Miguel Angels Ct 78840
Milagro Rd 78840
Mill St 78840
Miller Dr & St 78840
Mimosa Ln 78840
Minjares St 78840
W Mitchell Blvd 78843
Moore St 78840
Morales St 78840
E & W Morin St 78840
Mountain Laurel Rd 78840
Mountain View Dr & Rd 78840
Mumbrue St 78840
Nancy St 78840
Nannette Dr 78840
E & W Ney St 78840
Nicholas St 78840
E & W Nicholson St 78840
Nighthawk Trl 78840
Noriega St 78840
Northill Dr 78840
Northline Rd 78840
Nueces St 78840
Oakwalk St 78840
Obrien St 78840
E & W Ogden St 78840
Ohio St 78840
Old Foster Rd 78840
Old Hamilton Rd 78840
Oneal Cir 78840
N & S Orbit Cir & St 78840
Outlaw Xing 78840
Owens 78840
Pace Miller Dr 78840
Packsaddle Cir 78840
E & W Pafford St 78840
Page Ave 78840
Painted Rock 78840
Paisano Dr 78840
Palm Dr 78840
Palma St 78840
Palo Alto Dr 78840
Paloma Dr 78840
Palomino Rd 78840
Papalote Dr & Rd 78840
Paredes St 78840
Park Ave 78840
Parkway Ave 78840
Patos 78840
Pauline Ave & Cir 78840
Paulito Dr 78840
Peacepipe Trl 78840
Pecan St 78840
Pecos Cir & St 78840

Peggy St 78840
Pepper Ln 78840
Perry St 78840
Persimon Dr 78840
Pete Dr 78840
Phil St 78840
Philemon St 78840
Pierce St 78840
Pike Rd 78840
Pilot Point Rd 78840
Pine St 78840
Playground Walk 78840
Plaza Ave 78840
W Plomada Dr 78840
Poindexter Dr 78840
N Pond St 78840
Prairie Flower Path 78840
Private Road 1500 78840
Private Road 1800 78840
Private Road 1950 78840
Private Road 2000 78840
Private Road 2523 78840
Private Road 4900 78840
Private Road 4910 78840
Profit Dr 78840
Pulliam St 78840
Puma St 78840
Purple Sage St 78840
Pushkar St 78840
Quail Rd & Trl 78840
Quail Creek Dr 78840
Qualia Dr 78840
Quanah Pass 78840
Quick Draw Dr 78840
Railroad Ave 78840
Railway Ave 78840
Rainbow Ave 78840
Ramirez St 78840
Ramon St 78840
Ramon Cardenas Dr 78840
N Ranch Road 2523 78840
Rancho Del Rio Rd 78840
Rapala Dr 78840
Rawhide Trl 78840
Ray Dr 78840
Rays Ct 78840
Regin St 78840
Rehm Rd 78840
Rhonda St 78840
Riata Dr 78840
Ricco Dr 78840
Richards Ct 78840
Rickenbacker Cir 78840
Ricks Dr 78840
Ridgeline Dr 78840
Ridgemont St 78840
Ridgewood Dr 78840
E & W Rimfire Rd 78840
Rincon Dr 78840
Rio Loop 78840
Rio Diablo Pkwy 78840
Rio Grande St 78840
Rio Vista Dr 78840
Riojas St 78840
River Rd & St 78840
Riverview Ln 78840
Roadrunner St 78840
Rockwell Way 78840
Rodeo Trl 78840
Rodriguez St 78840
Rolling Ridge Dr 78840
Rosalinda Dr 78840
Rose Ave 78840
Rosita St 78840
Round Mountain Rd 78840
Rowland Dr 78840
Royal Falcon Dr 78840
Royal Way Dr 78840
Rubio St 78840
Running Bear Trl 78840
Running Deer Mdws 78840
Rusty Dr 78840
Sabrina Dr 78840
Saddle Blanket 78840
Saddletree Trl 78840
Sage Dr 78840

Sage Brush Trl 78840
Sage Hill Dr 78840
Sailboat Ln 78840
Saint Joseph St 78840
Saint Peter St 78840
San Felipe Ave & Spgs 78840
San Jose Cts 78840
San Juan St 78840
San Marcos Dr 78840
San Pedro Dr 78840
Sanchez St 78840
Sanders Point Rd 78840
Santa Maria Dr 78840
Santiago St 78840
Sartwelle St 78840
Sawtooth Rd 78840
Schwalbe Rd 78840
Scott Dr & Ln 78840
Sd 49000 78840
Sd 63025 78840
Sd 65010 78840
Sequoia Dr 78840
Serafini Dr 78840
Shadow Mountain Dr 78840
Shannon Cir 78840
Shawnee Trl 78840
Shirley Raye Dr 78840
Shoreline Dr 78840
Shorty Dr 78840
Sierra Dr & Rd 78840
Siesta Cir 78840
Silver Sage Dr 78840
Silverado Rd 78840
Skyline Rd & St 78840
E & W Skyview Dr 78840
Sleeping Lady Mountain Dr 78840
Smith Rd 78840
Sombrero Dr 78840
Sotol St 78840
Spaatz Cir 78840
Space Blvd & Cir 78840
Speer St 78840
Spike Run 78840
Spring St 78840
Spur 239 78840
St Andrews Ave 78840
Stampede Creek Rd 78840
Stanley St 78840
State Loop 79 78840
E & W Strickland St 78840
Stricklen Ave 78840
Striper Rd 78840
Sultenfuss St 78840
Suma St 78840
Summit Dr 78840
Summitt Ave 78840
Sundance Kid Trl 78840
Sunny Ln 78840
Sunrise Ave & Trl 78840
Sunset Ave 78840
Susie St 78840
Taini Ave 78840
Talley Trl 78840
Tamara Ln 78840
Tardy St 78840
Taylor Rd 78840
Tenderfoot Trl 78840
Tepee Trl 78840
Teresa Dr 78840
Terrace Cir 78840
N & S Terry St 78840
Tesoro Hls, Park, Pass, Pl & Run 78840
Tesoro Stone 78840
Texas Dr & St 78840
Texas R 2 78840
Texas Spur 239 78840
Texas Spur 349 78840
Texas Spur 454 78840
The Oak 78840
Thunderbird Ave 78840
Tierra Blanca St 78840
Timber Rock Dr 78840
Tomahawk Trl 78840

Top Dr 78840
Tower Trl 78840
Trey Dr 78840
Tule St 78840
Uco Dr 78840
Un Amor Ct 78840
Urista St 78840
N & S Us Highway 277 78840
S Us Highway 377 78840
E & W Us Highway 90 78840
Val Verde St 78840
Valenti Ln 78840
Vega Verde Rd 78840
Venice Dr 78840
Veterans Blvd 78840
Vic Bolner Ln 78840
Vicky Dr 78840
Victor Dr 78840
E & W Viesca St 78840
Virgie St 78840
Virginia St 78840
Vista Park 78840
Vista Hermosa 78840
Vista Loma 78840
Vista Oriente 78840
Vitela St 78840
Wade Cir 78840
Wagon Wheel Rd 78840
Wall St 78840
Wallen St 78840
Walnut St 78840
Warbonnet Trl 78840
Ware St 78840
Warner St 78840
Washington St 78840
Water Dr 78840
Waters Ave 78840
Weather Station Rd 78840
Wells Ave 78840
Wendy Dr 78840
Wernett St 78840
West Dr 78840
Western Dr & Trl 78840
Westward Way 78840
Westwind Ln 78840
Whispering Ln 78840
White St 78840
White Dove 78840
White Feather Trl 78840
Whitetail Rd 78840
Whitewing Ln 78840
Wild West Dr 78840
Wildcat Dr 78840
Willow Cir 78840
Windcrest Cir 78840
Winding Way St 78840
Windlake Loop 78840
Windmill Trl 78840
Y Dr N & S 78840
Yarbrough St 78840
Yellowstone Dr 78840
Yosemite Dr 78840
Yucca Dr & St 78840
Yucca Trailer Park Rd 78840
Yvonne Dr 78840
Zacatecas 78840
Zertuche St 78840

NUMBERED STREETS

E & W 1st 78843
E & W 1st 78840
E & W 2nd 78843
E & W 2nd 78840
E & W 3rd 78840
E & W 4th 78843
E & W 4th 78840
E & W 5th 78843
E & W 5th 78840
E & W 6th 78840
7th St 78840
E & W 8th 78840
E & W 9th 78840
E & W 10th 78840
E & W 11th 78840

E & W 12th 78840
E & W 13th 78840
E & W 14th 78840
E & W 15th 78840
E 16th St 78840
E & W 17th 78840

DENISON TX

General Delivery 75020

POST OFFICE BOXES MAIN OFFICE STATIONS AND BRANCHES

Box No.s
All PO Boxes 75021

RURAL ROUTES

02, 03, 06 75020
01, 04, 05 75021

NAMED STREETS

E Acheson Rd 75021
E Acheson St 75021
W Acheson St
100-199 75021
200-1699 75020
Adobe Ln 75020
Agape Ct 75021
Airport Dr 75020
Alexander Dr 75020
Allred Cir 75020
Alpine Dr 75020
Alta Vista Dr & St 75020
Ambassador Ct & St ... 75020
Amsden Cir 75020
Amsden St
500-599 75021
800-999 75020
Anderson St 75020
Angus Ln 75020
Ann St 75020
W Anne St 75020
Ansley Blvd 75020
Arapaho Cir, Cv, Dr & Pl 75020
Arboretum 75020
Armadillo Hill Dr 75020
N & S Armstrong Ave ... 75020
Arthur Rd 75021
Ash Dr 75020
Aspen St 75020
N & S Austin Ave 75020
Ave A 75021
Avon Dr 75020
B Ave 75021
Baby Bird Ln 75021
Bailey Dr 75021
Baker Ln 75021
Baker St 75020
Balboa St 75020
Ball Park Loop 75020
N & S Barrett Ave 75020
Belle Ave & Cir 75020
Bells Dr 75021
Berry Ridge Dr 75021
Big Cedar Ln 75020
Birchwood Dr 75020
Bledsoe 75021
Bluebonnet Ave & Cir .. 75020
Bob White Rd 75020
Bois D Arc Rd 75020
E Bond St 75021
W Bond St
100-199 75021
200-2499 75020
Brannum Ln 75021
Brenda Ave 75020
Brewster St 75020
Briarwood Dr 75020
Brink Dr 75021
W Brock St 75020
Brookhaven Cir & Dr ... 75020
Brookhollow St 75020
Brookside Dr 75020
N & S Brown Ave 75020
Bruce Dr 75020
Bryan Dr 75020
E Bullock St 75021
W Bullock St
100-199 75021
200-1799 75020
N & S Burnett Ave 75020
E Burrell St 75021
W Burrell St
100-199 75021
200-599 75020
N Bush Ave 75020
Butterfield Rd 75021
Candy Deann 75020
Caprice Ave 75020
Carla St 75020
Carpenters Bluff Rd 75021
Cathey Dr 75020
Cedar Dr 75020
Cedar Hills Dr 75021
S Center St 75021
N & S Chandler Ave ... 75020
Chaparral Estates Dr ... 75021
Charlsie Dr 75020
Chase St 75020
Cherry Mound Ln 75021
E Chestnut St 75021
W Chestnut St
100-199 75021
200-1699 75020
1701-2599 75020
Chickadee Ln 75020
Chiles Ln 75020
Choctaw Cir 75020
Choctaw Bottom Rd 75021
Ciaccio Rd 75021
Cindy Ln 75020
Circle Dr 75021
Clark Dr 75020
Cleve Cole Rd 75021
Coe Rd 75021
E Coffin St 75021
W Coffin St
100-199 75021
200-2699 75020
Cold Creek Ct & Dr 75020
Cole Dr 75020
S College Blvd 75020
College Creek Dr 75020
Collier Dr 75020
W Collins St 75020
Colonna Dr 75021
Commerce Blvd 75020
Cook Ln 75021
Coronado St 75020
Corp Rd 75020
Cortez St 75020
Country Ln 75020
Coushatta Dr 75020
Cowbird Ln 75021
Crabtree Rd 75021
Crawford Ln 75020
E Crawford St 75021
W Crawford St
100-199 75021
200-6399 75020
Creekside Dr 75020
Crescent Valley Cir 75020
Crestview Dr 75020
N & S Crockett Ave 75021
Crone Rd 75021
Cross Creek Ln 75021
Cross Timber Estates Dr 75020
Crosstimbers Ln & Rd .. 75020
Cumberland Cir 75021
Cumberland Dr 75020
Cynthia Dr 75020
Daisy Hill Ln 75021
Dana Ln 75021
Darryl Dr 75021
Davis Ave 75020
Davy Ln 75020
E Day St 75021
W Day St
100-199 75021
200-2999 75020
Dean Dr 75020
Debaca St 75020
Debra Ave 75020
Deer Mdw & Run 75020
Deer Creek Cir & Dr ... 75020
Deer Lake Dr 75020
Deleon St 75020
Delphia Dr 75021
Delton St 75020
Demarco St 75021
N & S Derby St 75020
Desvoignes Rd 75021
Diamond Pointe Loop .. 75020
Diana Dr 75021
Diane Dr 75020
Dillard Dr 75020
Dinn St 75020
Dogwood Dr 75020
Doolittle St 75020
Doris Dr 75021
Doty Dr 75021
Doubletree Dr 75020
Dove Ln 75020
Driggs Dr 75020
Dripping Springs Rd 75021
Dubois St 75020
Dugan Chapel Rd 75021
Duncan Dr 75021
Dyess St 75020
Eagle Crest Ln 75020
Eastwood Ter 75020
Eastwood Terrace Dr ... 75020
Easy St 75020
Echo Ridge Ct 75020
N & S Eddy Ave 75020
Edgewood Ter 75020
Edgewood Terrace Dr .. 75020
Edmonds Rd 75020
Edwards Dr 75020
S Eisenhower Blvd, Pkwy & Rd 75020
E Elm St 75021
W Elm St 75020
Elmore Rd 75021
Elmridge Rd 75020
Emerald Dr 75021
E End Rd 75021
England Dr 75021
Esquire Dr 75021
Ester Ln 75021
Esther Dr 75020
Executive Hanger Dr ... 75020
N & S Fairbanks Ave ... 75020
Falling Star Dr 75020
Family Pl 75020
N Fannin Ave 75020
S Fannin Ave
100-2899 75020
2900-5799 75021
Fantasy Ln 75021
Fawn Hollow Cir & Trl .. 75020
Fern Trl 75021
Fielder Dr 75020
Flora Ln 75020
E Florence St 75021
W Florence St 75020
Flowers Dr 75020
Flying M Dr 75020
E Fm 120 75021
W Fm 120 75020
S Fm 131 75020
Fm 1310 75020
N Fm 1417 75020
Fm 1753 75020
Fm 1897 75021
Fm 406 75020
Fm 691 75020
W Fm 84 75020
Fm 996 75020
E Ford St 75021
W Ford St 75020
Forest Ln 75021
Fossil Ridge Dr 75020
Fox Cir & Trl 75020
Frances Dr 75020
Frank Cir 75020
Freeman Rd 75021
S French Ave 75020
Friends Rd 75021
Frosty Hollow Rd 75021
Fuller St 75020
N Gail Dr 75020
Galley Dr 75021
Game Farm Rd 75021
E Gandy St 75021
W Gandy St
100-199 75021
200-1699 75020
Georgetown Rd 75020
Geraldine Ln 75020
S Gerrard St 75020
Glen Key St 75020
Glenda Ln 75021
Glenwood Dr 75020
Golf Dr 75020
Golf Walk Cir 75020
Grandpappy Dr 75020
Grayson Dr 75020
Green Oaks Dr 75021
Greenbrier St 75020
Greenwood Cir 75020
Gun Club Rd 75021
Hackberry St 75020
Hallie Rd 75020
Handark Rd 75021
Hanna Dr 75020
E Hanna St 75021
W Hanna St 75020
Hanna Cove Dr 75020
Harbor Rd & Vw 75020
Harborview Cir & Dr 75020
Hardy Ln 75020
Hargos Rd 75021
Harrison Rd & St 75021
Harvey Ln 75020
Hathaway 75020
Haven Cir 75020
Hayden Ln 75020
Heironimus Ln 75020
Helen Dr 75020
E Heron St 75021
W Heron St
100-199 75021
200-1699 75020
N & S Hickory Ave 75020
Hidden Trl 75020
Hidden Hills Ln 75020
Hidden Meadows Ln 75021
Hidden Valley Dr 75020
Hide A Way Cir 75020
Higgins Trl 75021
High Point Cir 75020
High View Dr 75020
Highland Dr & Ter 75020
Highland Park Dr & Plz 75020
Highland Terrace Cir ... 75020
Hill Dr 75020
Hill Clark Rd 75020
Hilltop Dr 75020
Hitchcock Dr 75020
Hodges Rd 75021
Hoffman Ln 75020
Holder Ln 75020
Holiday St 75020
Holland Dr 75020
Holly St 75020
Horse Apple Ln 75020
N & S Houston Ave 75021
Huggins Ln 75020
E Hull St 75021
W Hull St
100-199 75021
200-2299 75020
Hyde Park Ave & Cir ... 75020
Idlewood Dr 75020
Immigrant Trail Rd 75021
N & S Imperial Dr 75020
Ina Ln 75021
Interurban Rd 75021
Inwood Rd 75020
Isaacs Cir 75020
Ivey Dr 75020
Ivy Dr 75021
Jack Barnett Dr 75020
Jack Cole Rd 75021
Jacqueline Ln 75020
Jade Ln 75021
Janice Dr 75020
Jefferson Dr 75020
Jennettes Rd 75020
Jennie Ln 75020
Jennifer Ave 75020
Jerry St 75020
Jerry Pedigo Rd 75021
Joe Washburn Rd 75021
Johnson Rd 75021
E Johnson St 75021
W Johnson St
100-199 75021
200-2699 75020
Joy Ln 75021
Juanita Dr 75020
Julian C Fields Rd 75020
Karen Dr 75021
Kawahee Ln 75020
Kegelman St 75020
W Kelantow St 75020
S Kelly Ave 75020
Kelsey Rd 75021
Kelsoe Rd 75020
Kerby Dr 75020
Kiefer Ct 75021
King Ave & St 75020
Knight Rd 75020
Knob Cir 75021
Knob Hill Loop 75020
Kool Ln 75021
Lafayette Dr 75020
Lake Dr 75020
Lakeridge Dr 75020
Lakeview Dr 75020
Lakewood Rd 75020
N & S Lamar Ave 75021
S Lang Ave 75020
Lariat Dr 75021
Layne Dr 75020
Lazy River Trl 75021
Leafy Ln 75020
Ledbetter Ln 75021
Leeper Dr 75020
Lifesearch Way 75020
Lil Old Rd 75020
N & S Lillis Ln 75020
Lillis Park Cir 75020
Links Est 75020
Little Creek Dr 75020
Lockloma Ct & St 75020
Lockwood Dr 75020
Lonesome Dove Trl 75021
Longhorn Blvd 75020
Loy Dr 75020
W Loy Lake Rd 75020
Lucas Ct 75020
Luke Dr 75021
Lum Ln 75020
Lyndana Ave 75021
Lynlee Ln 75020
N & S Lynn Ave 75020
Macarthur Dr 75020
Maccallum Ave 75020
Macgregor Dr 75020
Mack Nelsen Ln 75021
Magnus Rd 75021
E Main St 75021
W Main St
100-199 75021
200-1599 75020
Maine Ln 75020
E Maple Row 75021
Marcel Dr 75020
Marcus Cir 75020
Mark Dr 75021
Marlin Dr 75020
Marrett Ave 75020
Martin Dr 75021
Martin Luther King St ... 75020
Mauk Cir 75020
N & S Maurice Ave & Cir 75020
Maxwell Ln 75020
Mayes Dr 75021
Mccraw Ln 75021
Mccullum Ave 75020
Meadow Lake Estates Rd 75021
Meadowlark Ln 75020
Meadows Dr 75020
Melrose Cir 75020
Memorial Dr 75020
Memory Ln 75021
Micajah Davis Ln 75020
Middle Rd 75021
Miller St 75020
N & S Mirick Ave 75020
Mitchell Snider St 75020
Mockingbird Ln 75020
Mollenhour Dr 75020
W Molly Cherry Ln 75020
Monarch Dr 75020
Monarch Ridge Rd 75020
E Monterey St 75021
W Monterey St
100-199 75021
200-1999 75020
Montes Ln 75021
E Morgan St 75021
W Morgan St 75020
Morningside Cir 75020
Morrison Dr 75020
E Morton St 75021
W Morton St
100-199 75021
200-3259 75020
3261-3299 75020
Mountain Creek Dr 75021
Mourning Dove Ln 75020
Mundt St 75020
E Munson St 75021
W Munson St
100-199 75021
200-2199 75020
Murphy Ln 75021
E Murray St 75021
W Murray St
100-199 75021
200-1899 75020
Nancy Ln 75020
Nash Dr 75021
E Nelson St 75021
W Nelson St 75020
Neva Ln 75020
Nita Rd 75021
Ntech Dr 75020
Oak Dr 75020
Oak Ridge Dr 75020
Oak Ridge Rd 75021
Oakwood Dr & St 75020
Oasis Dr 75020
Odell Ave 75020
Old Airport Rd 75021
Old State Ln 75020
Old Turkey Farm Rd ... 75021
E Owing St 75021
W Owing St 75020
Pappys Rd 75020
S Park Ave, Cir, Dr, Rdg & Vlg 75020
Park Road 20 75020
N Parkdale Dr & Ln 75020
Parkway Dr 75021
E Parnell St 75021
W Parnell St 75020
Pat Ct 75021
Paula Dr 75020
Pavillion Cir 75020
Peachtree Ct & Ln 75020
Pecan St 75020
Pecan Gap St 75020
Pecan Orchard Rd 75020
Pelican Trl 75021
Pelts Dr 75021
N & S Perry Ave 75020
Pershing Cir & Dr 75020
Persimmon St 75020
Peterson Rd 75020
Pheasant Trl 75021
Pineway Dr 75020
Plum Tree Ln 75021
N Point Lookout Dr 75020
S Polaris St 75020
Pool Rd 75020
Post Oak St 75020
Pottsboro Rd 75020
Power Plant Rd 75020
Preston Rd 75020
Private Road 1 75021
Private Road 192 75021
E & W Prospect St 75021
Putnam Ln 75021
Pyramid Cir 75020
Quarter Mile Rd 75020
Queens Rd 75020
R L Franks Rd 75021
Railroad Blvd 75020
Ramblin Oaks Dr 75021
Randell Dr & Ter 75020
Randell Lake Rd 75020
Randell Terrace Dr 75020
Ransom Cir 75020
Rawhide Trl 75021
Ray Dr 75020
Rc Vaughan Rd 75020
Reality Rd 75021
Reba Dr 75020
Reba Macentire Ln 75020
Red Oak Dr 75020
Redbud St 75020
Refuge Rd 75020
Regal Dr 75020
Regency Ln 75020
Regina Ln 75020
Renaissance Cir & Dr .. 75020
Rent A Shop Ct 75021
Reservoir Dr 75020
Rice St 75020
Richerson Rd 75021
Ridgeway Cir 75020
Ridgewood Rd 75020
River Rd 75021
River Hills Dr 75020
River Oaks Ln 75021
Riverbend Dr 75021
Riverboat Dr 75021
Rivercrest Cir 75020
Roberts Ave 75020
Rockey Ln 75020
Rolen Dr 75021
Rolling Acres Rd 75021
Ross Ave 75020
Royal Ridge Dr 75020
N & S Rusk Ave 75020
Russell Ln 75021
Saddle Tree Ln 75021
Sage Brush Ln 75021
Sanford Rd 75021
Scott Ave 75020
N & S Scullin Ave 75020
E Sears St 75021
W Sears St
100-199 75021
200-1599 75020
Sequoia Dr 75020
Seven Hills Rd 75021
Seymore Cir & St 75020
Seymore Bradley Rd ... 75020
Shadow Cir 75020
Shady Ln 75020
Shady Woods Ln 75021
Shaffer Rd 75021
Shane Ct 75020

Shannon Rd
1900-2000 75020
2001-2037 75021
2002-2020 75020
2039-2599 75021
Sharon Cir 75020
Sharpes Pecan Rd 75021
Shawn Dr 75020
Shawnee Cir 75020
E Shepherd St 75021
W Shepherd St 75020
Sheryl Ln 75021
Shiloh St 75020
Sidney Dr 75020
Sierra Dr 75020
Silver Spur Dr 75021
Singletree Rd 75021
Smith Dr 75020
Smith Creek Rd 75021
Snow Rd 75021
Southgale Rd 75021
Southwestern Dr 75020
Spring Creek Dr 75020
Spring Valley Dr 75020
Spur 503 75020
Square Dance Rd 75021
W Stafford Dr 75020
Stagecoach Trl 75021
Star St 75020
Starling Dr 75021
Starr Rd 75021
N & S State Highway
91 75020
Steven Dr 75020
Stinson Rd 75020
Stowers Dr 75021
Summit Oaks Cir 75020
Sunrise Rd 75021
Sunset St 75020
Sweet Gum St 75020
Sycamore St 75020
Tananger Springs Dr 75021
Tejas Dr 75020
E Texas St 75021
W Texas St
100-199 75021
200-1599 75020
Texoma Dr & Ter 75020
Texoma Terrace Rd 75020
Thatcher St 75020
S Theresa Dr 75020
Thomas St 75020
Thompson Rd 75020
Thompson Heights Dr 75020
Thornbird Dr 75021
Thorsen St 75020
Thousand Oaks Dr 75021
Timber Brook Cir 75021
Timber Ridge Dr 75021
Timbercreek Dr 75021
Timberview 75020
Timberwood Dr 75021
Tom Tynes Rd 75020
N & S Tone Ave 75020
Tower Ln 75020
Tracey St 75020
Tracy Ln 75021
Trail Dr 75020
Trail Rd 75021
N & S Travis Ave 75021
Treece Ave 75020
Trout Ln 75020
Tuckaway St 75020
Tumbleweed Trl 75021
Turney Ln 75020
Turtlecreek 75020
Twining Dr 75020
Us Highway 69 75021
E Us Highway 69 75021
N Us Highway 69 75020
W Us Highway 69 75021
N & S Us Highway 75 75020
Valentine Dr 75020
Valley View Cir
1-299 75021
3900-4099 75020
Vandenburg Dr 75020
Vaughn Dr 75020
Venture Cir 75020
Verna Ln 75020
Via Esplanade Dr 75021
Vickery St 75020
Victoria Ln 75021
Village Cir 75020
Village Green Ct 75020
Vine Ln 75020
Wagner Rd 75021
E Walker St 75021
W Walker St
100-199 75021
200-2899 75020
Warehouse Rd 75020
E Washington St 75021
W Washington St 75020
Waterloo Ave 75020
Waterloo Lake Dr 75020
Wayne Cabaniss Dr 75020
Webster Ln 75020
Well Rd 75020
Wells Dr 75020
Westridge Dr 75020
Whispering Oaks Dr 75020
White Dove Trl 75020
Whitney Rd 75021
Wild Kingdom Rd 75021
Wilde St 75020
Willow Grove Rd 75020
Willow Tree Rd 75020
N & S Wood Ave 75020
E Woodard St 75021
W Woodard St
100-199 75021
200-232 75020
231-239 75021
234-1698 75020
301-1699 75020
Woodcroft Ln 75021
Woodlake Rd 75021
Woodland Park Dr 75020
Woodlawn Blvd 75020
Woodlawn Cir 75020
Woodlawn Rd 75021
Woodruff Rd 75020
Woodview Ter 75020
Yellow Jacket Rd 75020
N York Ave 75020
Young Rd 75021

NUMBERED STREETS

All Street Addresses 75021

DENTON TX

General Delivery 76201

POST OFFICE BOXES MAIN OFFICE STATIONS AND BRANCHES

Box No.s
A - U 76202
AC - AC 76202
1 - 9976 76202
9998 - 52418 76206
90204 - 90224 76202
424001 - 425979 76204

RURAL ROUTES

01, 08, 10, 16, 29, 37, 39, 41 76207
02, 04, 05, 07, 11, 20, 21, 27, 32, 36, 40, 42 76208
03, 06, 09, 12, 13, 15, 17, 19, 22, 23, 24, 25, 26, 28, 30, 31, 33, 34, 35, 38, 43 76210

NAMED STREETS

Abbots Ln 76205
Abby Way 76208
Acme St 76205
Acorn Bnd 76210
Acorn Ranch Mhp 76208
Acropolis Dr 76210
Aeronca Dr 76207
Aileen St 76201
Ainsley Ct 76210
Airport Rd 76207
Alamo Pl 76201
Alan A Dale Cir 76209
Alcove Ln 76210
Alderbrook Dr 76210
Alegre Vista Dr 76205
Alexander St 76205
Algarve Dr 76210
Alice St 76201
Allen Ct 76209
Allen St 76205
Allise Cir 76209
Allison Dr 76207
Alta Vista Dr 76210
Altius Ln 76210
Amarillo St 76201
Amber Ct 76207
Ame Dr 76207
Amherst Dr 76201
Andalusian Dr 76210
Anderson St 76201
Andover Ln 76210
Andrew Ave & Ct 76210
Angel Bnd 76208
Angelina Bend Dr 76205
Angus Ln 76208
Anna St 76201
Antler Cir 76208
Anysa Ln 76209
Apache Trl 76210
Apollo Dr 76209
Appaloosa Ct & Dr 76208
Apple Valley Ct & Ln 76208
Applewood Trl 76207
Aqueduct Dr 76210
Arabian Ave 76210
Archer Rd 76208
Archer Trl 76209
Ardglass Trl 76210
Arrowhead Dr 76207
Ascot Ln 76209
Ash Ln
1500-1799 76210
4000-4099 76208
Ashcroft Ln 76207
Asheann Dr 76209
Ashley Cir 76207
Ashton Gardens Ln 76210
Ashwood Ln & Pl 76210
Aspen Dr 76209
Aspen St 76210
Aspenhill Dr 76209
Aster Ct 76208
Athens Dr 76209
Atlanta Dr 76208
Atlantic Dr 76210
Atlas Dr 76209
Attaway Cir & Cv 76208
Atwell Ln 76208
Auburn Dr 76201
Audra Ln
300-498 76209
500-2099 76209
3100-4099 76208
Augusta Dr 76207
N Austin St 76201
Autumn Oak Dr 76209
Autumn Path Rd 76208
Avalon Dr 76207
Avenue S 76205
Avenue A
101-397 76201
Avenue A
399-401 76201
403-1299 76201
410-410 76203
900-1298 76201
N & S Avenue B 76201
Avenue C
600-898 76201
900-1199 76201
1200-1599 76205
Avenue D 76201
Avenue F 76201
Avenue G 76201
Avenue H 76201
Avon Dr 76210
Avon St 76209
Azalea St 76205
Bailey St 76205
Baker Dr 76210
Balboa Ct 76207
Baldwin St 76205
Balentine St 76207
Balladeer 76210
Ballycastle Ln 76210
Bandera St 76207
Barbara St 76209
Barber St 76209
Barberry Ave 76208
Barcelona St 76207
Bareback Ln 76210
Barnes Dr 76209
Barnhill Ct 76208
Barrow Dr 76207
Barrydale Dr 76208
Barrymore Rd 76208
Barthold Rd 76207
Barton Springs Dr 76210
Batey Bnd 76208
Bauer Dr 76207
Bay Meadow Dr 76210
Bayberry St 76205
Baybrooke Dr 76210
Bayfield Dr 76209
Baytree Ave 76208
Beatriz Dr 76207
Beckley Ct 76210
Beechwood Dr 76210
Belhaven St 76201
N Bell Ave
201-299 76201
300-3000 76209
3002-3098 76209
3100-3399 76207
S Bell Ave 76201
Bell Pl 76209
Bella Lago Dr 76210
Bellaire Dr 76209
Bellemead Dr 76201
Bellview Dr 76210
Belmont St 76210
Belmont Park Dr 76210
Belvedere Dr 76207
Benbrook Cv 76208
Benjamin St 76207
Bent Creek Dr 76210
Bent Oaks Ct & Dr 76210
Bentgate Ct 76208
Bentley Ct 76210
Bentwood Ct 76210
Benwick Dr 76210
Berkshire Ln 76210
Bernard St
100-102 76201
104-1500 76201
1502-1698 76201
1700-2499 76205
2501-2699 76205
Berry Ln 76208
Berry Down Ln 76208
Beverly Dr 76209
Biddy Bye Ln 76210
Big Horn Trl 76210
Birch Ln 76210
Birchbrook Ct 76205
Birdwood Cir 76210
Bishop Pine Rd 76208
Bishops Park St 76205
Bissonet Dr 76210
Black Butte Dr 76210
Black Jack Dr 76208
Black Oak St 76209
Black Walnut 76208
Blackberry Way 76210
Blackford Oakes 76209
Blagg Rd 76208
Blake St 76210
Blue Holly Dr 76210
Blue Jay Dr 76210
Blue Ridge Ct 76210
Blue Sky Ln 76210
Bluebird Cir 76209
Bluebonnet Pl 76209
Boardwalk Ln 76205
Bob O Link Ln 76209
Bolivar St 76201
Bonita Ave 76210
N Bonnie Brae St
100-1200 76201
1202-1298 76201
1400-4899 76207
S Bonnie Brae St
101-197 76201
199-203 76201
205-217 76201
1301-1697 76207
1699-3200 76207
3202-3398 76207
Boulder Dr
2500-2699 76210
11900-11999 76207
Bowie Ln 76210
Bowling Green St 76201
Boxwood Ct & Dr 76208
Boyd St 76209
Bradford Ct 76210
Bradford St 76207
Bradley St 76201
N Bradshaw St
100-198 76205
300-799 76209
S Bradshaw St 76205
Brampton Dr 76210
Brandi Ln 76210
Brandon Dr 76207
Brandywine Cir & St 76209
Bray Village Dr 76207
Brazos Dr 76210
Breezehollow Way 76210
Breton Dr 76210
Brett Rd 76210
Briar Forest Dr 76210
Briarwood St 76209
Briarwyck Ct 76205
Briary Trace Ct 76210
Bridges St 76208
Bridgestone Ct & Dr 76210
Briercliff Dr 76210
Brighton Cir & Dr 76210
Brightwood Ter 76209
Brinker Rd 76208
Brisas Ct 76210
Bristol St 76209
Brittany Dr 76209
Broadway St 76201
Brock Cir 76209
Broken Arrow Rd 76209
Broken Bow St 76209
Bronco Cir 76208
Brooke St 76207
Brookfield Ln 76209
Brookhollow Dr 76207
Brooklake St W 76207
Brookshire Run 76210
Brookside Dr 76208
Brookview Dr 76210
Brown Dr 76209
Brown Ter 76208
S Brown Brothers Trl 76207
Browntrail Ct 76208
Bryan St 76201
Bryn Mawr Pl 76201
Buckboard Cir 76208
Buckingham Dr
200-2699 76209
3500-3599 76210
Buena Vista Cir & Dr 76210
Bull Run 76209
Burl St 76208
Burning Tree Ln &
Pkwy 76209
Burrwood Cir 76208
Bushey St 76205
Butler Dr 76210
Byram Ln 76208
Cactus Cir 76209
Caddo Cir 76210
Cadena Rd 76210
Cahill Way 76208
Caladium Dr 76210
Callaway Ct 76207
Calvert Ln 76208
Cambridge Ln 76209
Camden Ct 76205
Camellia St 76205
Camelot St 76209
Camino Real Trl 76208
Campbell Ln 76209
Cannes Dr 76210
Canoe Ridge Ln 76210
Canterbury Ct 76205
Canton Ct 76208
Canyon Ct 76205
Cape Hatteras Ct 76210
Capetown Dr 76208
Cardinal Cir 76208
Cardinal Dr 76209
Caribou Ct 76208
Carlton Ln 76208
Carlton St 76201
Carmel St 76205
Carolyn Ln 76208
Carpenter Rd & St 76208
Carriage Hl 76207
Carriage Lane Cir 76208
Carriage Wheel 76210
Carrigan Ln 76207
N & S Carroll Blvd 76201
Carson Dr 76209
Casa Grande Dr 76210
Cascade Dr 76207
Casie Ct 76207
Cassidy Ln 76210
Castle Ln 76209
Castlegate Dr 76210
Cattail Ln 76208
Cavender Cir 76205
Cedar Cir 76208
Cedar St 76201
Cedar Creek Ln 76210
Cedar Elm Dr 76210
Cedar Hill St 76209
Centenary Dr 76210
Central Ave 76201
Central Village Dr 76210
Centre Place Dr 76205
Chalkstone Cir & Cv 76208
Chambers St 76205
Chambray Dr 76210
Champlain Ln 76210
Chaparral Ct 76209
Chaparral Est 76208
Chapel Dr 76205
Chapel Pl 76210
Chapel Hill Ln 76207
Charles St 76209
Charleston Ct 76210
Charlotte St 76201
Charter Bnd 76210
Chase Ln 76209
Chasewood Ln 76205
Chateau Ct 76209
Chaucer Dr 76210
Chebi Ln 76209
Chelsea Ct 76210
Cherokee Trl 76210
Cherry Ln 76210
Cherry Tree Ln 76210
Cherrywood Ln 76209
W Chestnut St 76201
Chevelly Ct 76209
Cheyenne Ct 76208
Cheyenne Trl 76210
Chimney Rock Dr 76210
Chinn Rd 76207
Chippewa Ct 76210
Chiquita St 76205
Chisholm Trl
500-799 76209
2800-2999 76210
Chittamwood Ct & Dr 76208
Choctaw Ave 76209
Chon Dr 76207
Christopher Dr 76209
Church Dr 76210
Churchill Cir & Dr 76209
Cielo Ln 76208
Cindy Ln 76207
Circle View Ln 76210
Citadel 76207
Clarendon Dr 76207
Claridge Ct 76207
Clark Dr 76210
Clay Trl 76210
Claydon Dr 76207
Clear River Ln 76210
Clear Star 76207
Clearview Dr 76210
Clemson Dr 76207
Clermont Ln 76205
Cleveland St 76201
Cliff Oaks Dr 76210
Cliffside Dr 76208
Cliffview Dr 76210
Clover Ln 76209
Club View Cir 76210
Clubhouse Dr 76210
Clubside Dr 76210
Clydesdale Dr 76210
Cobb Dr 76210
Cobblestone Row 76207
Cochise Ct 76210
Coe Rd 76208
Coffey Dr 76207
Cogburn Ct 76208
Coit St 76201
Colbert Cv 76207
Cole Ave 76208
Colina Ave 76210
E College St 76209
W College St 76201
College Park Dr 76209
Collier St 76201
Collins Rd 76208
E Collins St 76205
W Collins St 76201
Colonial St 76207
Colorado Blvd
1900-2100 76205
2101-2399 76205
2101-2101 76206
2102-2398 76205
2700-3699 76210
Comanche Cir & Dr 76208
Comer St 76207
Como Lake Rd 76210
Compton St 76207
Concord Ln 76205
Conditt Cir 76209
E & W Congress St 76201
Constantina Dr 76207
Cook St 76205
Cooper Br E & W 76209
Cooper Creek Rd 76208
Copper Leaf Dr 76210
Copper Ridge St 76209
Coral Cv 76210
Corbin Rd 76207
Cordell St 76201
Cordero Ct 76210
Cordova Cir 76209
Corinth Bnd 76208
Corinth Pkwy 76208
N Corinth St 76208
S Corinth St 76210
Cornell Ln 76201
Coronado Dr 76209
Corral Ln 76210

Cotten Dr 76207
Cottonwood Ln 76207
Cottonwood Trl 76208
Countess Ln 76210
Country Club Rd 76210
Country Home Dr 76210
Countryside Dr
100-3199 76208
9900-10799 76207
Cove Dr 76208
Coventry Ct 76207
Covington Ln 76210
Coyote Pt 76208
Craig Ln 76209
Crapemyrtle 76208
Crater Lake Ln 76210
Crawford Dr 76210
N Crawford St 76209
S Crawford St 76205
Creek Ave 76209
Creek Bend Ct & Dr 76208
Creek Crossing Dr 76210
Creek Falls Dr 76208
Creek Hill Ln 76208
Creekdale Dr 76210
Creekedge Ct 76210
Creekside Dr 76210
Creekwood St 76210
Crenshaw Ln 76210
Crescent St 76201
Crestmeadow St 76207
Crestoak Pl 76209
Crestridge Ct & Dr 76207
Crestview Dr 76207
Crestwood Pl 76209
Crisoforo Dr 76207
Crockett Dr 76210
Cromwell Dr 76209
Cross Timber St 76205
Crossvine 76208
Crow St 76201
Croydon St 76209
Cruden Bay Ct 76210
Cruise St 76207
Crystal Springs Dr 76210
Cumberland Ct 76210
Cunningham Rd 76208
Custer Dr 76208
Cypress St 76207
Cyrus Way 76208
Daisy Dr 76208
Dakota Ln 76207
Dallas Dr 76205
Dalton Dr 76208
Dana Ln 76209
Danbury Cir & Cv 76208
Daniels St 76205
Darby Ln 76207
Darien Pl 76210
Dartmouth Pl 76201
Daugherty St 76205
Davis St 76209
Dawnlight Dr 76210
Dayspring Dr 76210
Deer Trl 76205
Deer Forest Dr 76208
Deerfield Dr 76208
Deerwood Pkwy 76208
Del Dr 76207
Del Mar Ct 76210
Del Rey Cir & Dr 76208
Denison St 76201
Denton St 76201
Denton Estates Mhp 76207
Depaul Dr 76210
Derby Run 76210
Desert Dr 76210
Desert Holly Way 76208
Desert Willow Dr 76208
Destin Dr 76205
Devonshire Dr 76209
Di Lago Park Place Dr 76208
Diamond Dr 76208
Diamond Leaf Dr 76208
Diane Cir 76209
Dixon Ln 76207

Dobbs Rd 76208
Doecrest Dr 76210
Dogwood Dr & Trl 76208
Dolores Pl 76208
Donaldson Ct 76210
Donna Rd 76207
Donner Lake Cir 76210
Doris Dr 76207
Dotson St 76205
Double Oak Ct & St 76209
Dover St 76209
Downing Dr 76207
Drexel Dr 76210
Driftwood Dr 76208
Driftwood Trl 76209
Driskell Dr 76210
Duchess Dr 76208
Dudley St 76205
Duncan St 76205
Dundee Dr 76210
Dunes Pl & St 76209
Dunlavy Rd 76210
Durance Ct 76210
Durango Cir 76208
Eagle Dr 76201
Eagle Nest Ct 76209
Eagle Ridge Dr 76210
Eagle Wing Ln 76210
Early Dawn Trl 76210
Eason Rd 76208
Ector St 76201
Ed Robson Cir 76207
Edgefield Dr 76210
Edgewood Pl 76209
Edinburg Ln 76209
Edmondson Dr 76207
Edwards Rd 76208
Egan St 76201
El Cielito St 76205
W El Paseo St 76205
Eldorado Dr 76210
Ellison Park Cir 76205
N Elm St
101-197 76201
199-2999 76201
3000-6499 76207
S Elm St 76201
Elysian St 76210
Emerald Park Ct & Dr 76208
Emerson Cir & Ln 76209
Emery St 76201
Enchanted Oaks Cir 76210
Energy Pl 76207
Englefield Grn 76207
English Manor Rd 76210
English Saddle Ln 76210
Estacado Dr 76210
Eton Pl 76207
Eufemia Dr 76207
Evan Dr 76207
Evening Wind Rd 76208
Everett Ct 76208
Evergreen Cv 76208
Evers Pkwy 76207
Exposition St 76205
Fain St 76201
Fair Oaks Cir 76210
Fairfax Rd & Trl 76205
Fairmount Park Dr 76210
Fairview Dr 76210
Fairway Dr 76210
Fairway Vista Dr 76210
Falcon Ct & Dr 76210
Fallmeadow Ct & St 76207
Fannin St 76201
Farris Rd 76208
Fawn Dr 76208
Fereenso St 76205
Ferguson St 76201
Fieldstone St 76207
Fieldwood Dr 76208
First St 76201
Fishtrap Rd 76208
Fiste 76207
Fladger St 76207
Flagstone Ct 76207

Flariank Rd 76207
Fm 2181 76210
Fm 428 76208
Fondren Rd 76210
Fordham Ln 76201
S Forest Hls 76210
Forest St 76209
Forest Glen Dr 76210
Forestview Dr 76210
Forestwood Dr 76210
Forrestridge Dr
2800-3499 76205
3500-3699 76210
Fort Worth Dr
200-737 76201
739-799 76201
900-3400 76205
3402-3598 76205
Foster Rd 76208
Fountainview Dr 76210
Fowler Dr 76209
Fox Holw 76205
Fox Creek Ct 76209
Fox Hollow Run 76208
Fox Sedge Ln 76208
Foxcroft Cir 76209
Foxwood Cir 76207
Frame St 76209
Francks Cir 76208
Franklin Dr 76207
Freedom Ln 76209
Freeport Dr 76207
Friar Tuck Cir 76209
Friesian Ct 76210
Fritz Ln 76208
Frontier Dr 76210
Frost Ln 76210
Fry St 76201
Fulton St 76201
Gabe Ct 76207
Gable Ct 76209
Gaelic Ct 76208
Galante Ln 76208
Gallery St 76207
Ganzer Rd 76207
Gardenia Dr 76207
Gardenview Cir & St 76207
Gardner Trl 76207
Garrison Rd 76210
N Garza Rd 76208
Gatewood Dr 76205
Gayla Ln 76208
Geesling Rd 76208
Geneva Cir 76210
Georgetown Dr 76201
Georgia Ave 76207
Geronimo Dr 76210
Gessner Dr 76210
Glen Aerie Ln 76210
Glen Crest Ln 76208
Glen Falls Ln 76210
Glen Garden St 76207
Glen Manor Rd 76208
Glenbrook St 76207
Glencoe Rd 76208
Glendale Dr 76207
Glendora Ct 76210
Glenhaven Dr 76210
Glenngary Way 76208
Glenview Dr 76210
Glenwood Dr 76208
Glenwood Ln 76209
Gober St 76201
Gold Rush Ct & St 76210
Golden Cir 76208
Golden Meadow Dr 76208
Golden Sand Dr 76210
Goldenrod Dr 76208
Golf Ct 76205
Goliad Ct 76210
Goodland Dr 76207
Goodnight Trl 76210
Goodson Way 76207
Goshawk Ln 76210
Granada Trl 76205
Grancens Dr 76210

Grandview Dr 76207
Grant Pkwy 76208
Grassy Glen Dr 76208
Graystone Ln 76210
Great Bear Ln 76210
Gree River Dr 76208
Green Ivy Rd 76210
Green Oaks St 76209
Greenbend Dr 76210
Greenbriar St 76201
Greenleaf Cir 76208
Greenlee St
900-1200 76201
1202-1298 76201
1500-1699 76205
Greenspoint Cir 76205
Greenway St 76207
Greenwood Dr 76209
Gregg St 76201
Grissom Rd 76208
Grove St 76209
Groveland Ct & Ter 76210
Guadalupe Pl 76205
Gunnison Dr 76208
Haggard Ln 76201
Hallmark Dr 76207
Hallum Dr 76209
Hampton Rd 76207
Hanford Dr 76207
Hann St 76201
Hanover Dr 76209
Hardaway Rd 76207
Harrison Ct 76208
Hartee Ct 76208
Hartlee Ct & Trce 76208
Hartlee Field Rd 76208
Harvard Dr 76210
Harvest Glen Dr 76208
Harvest Hill Dr 76208
Harvest Moon Trl 76210
N Haven Dr 76210
Hawks View Ln 76208
Hawthorn Dr 76208
Hayden Ln 76210
Hayes 76207
Hayling Way 76210
Haynes St 76201
Hazel Wood Dr 76210
Headlee St 76201
Heather Ln 76209
Helm Ln 76210
Hemingway Dr 76210
Henderson Dr 76209
Hercules Ln
100-399 76207
500-698 76209
700-800 76209
802-898 76209
W Hercules Ln 76207
Hereford Rd 76210
Heritage Ln 76209
Hermalinda Dr 76207
Heron Pond Ln 76208
Herring Ct 76210
Hettie St 76209
Hickory Ln 76208
E Hickory St
101-197 76201
199-499 76201
500-598 76205
600-1299 76205
W Hickory St 76201
Hickory Creek Rd 76210
Hidden Oaks Cir 76210
Hidden Path Ln 76210
Hidden Springs Dr 76210
Hidden Valley Airpark 76208
High Meadow Dr 76208
High Pointe Dr 76210
Highfield Park 76210
W Highland St
200-298 76201
300-499 76201
501-1099 76201
1506-1506 76203

Highland Park Cir & Rd 76205
Highlands Dr 76210
Highpoint Dr 76210
Highview Cir & Ct 76205
Hilcroft Ave 76210
Hill St 76205
Hill Alley St 76205
Hillcrest St 76201
Hillside Dr 76210
Hilltop Ln 76208
Hillview Ct & St 76209
Hilton Pl 76209
Hinkle Dr 76201
Hinkley Oak Ct & Dr 76208
History Cres 76210
Hobson Ln 76205
Hofstra Dr 76210
Holland Ln 76208
Hollis Dr 76210
Hollow Ridge Dr 76210
Hollycreek 76207
Hollyhill Ln 76205
Homer Rd 76208
Hope St 76205
Hopkins Dr 76205
Houston Pl 76201
Howard Ct 76209
Hudson St 76210
Hudsonwood Dr 76208
Huisache St 76209
Hummingbird Ln 76209
Hunters Ridge Cir 76205
Huntington Dr 76209
Huron Cir 76210
Hutchinson Ln 76210
I O O F St 76201
Imperial Dr 76209
Inca Rd 76209
Indian Lake Trl 76210
Indian Paint Way 76208
Indian Ridge Dr 76205
Indigo Ter 76209
Industrial St
100-300 76201
302-398 76201
900-999 76205
Inglewood St 76209
Inman St 76205
Interstate 35 76207
Interstate 35 W 76207
N Interstate 35
2419-9999 76207
N Interstate 35
2500-3198 76201
3200-8998 76207
N Interstate 35 E 76205
S Interstate 35 E
201-219 76205
221-2400 76205
2401-2597 76210
2402-2598 76205
2599-8200 76210
7701-7899 76210
8202-8298 76210
Inwood Ct 76208
Island Cir 76208
Jackpine Dr 76208
Jackson St 76205
Jacqueline Dr 76205
Jagoe St 76201
James St 76205
Jamestown Ln 76209
Jannie St 76209
Jasmine St 76205
Jason Dr 76205
Jay St 76208
Jefferson Trl 76205
Jeffrey Dr 76208
Jesse Way 76210
Jim Christal Rd 76207
John Dr 76207
John Carrell Rd 76207
Johnson St 76205
Jones St 76208
Joshua St 76209

Joyce Ln 76207
June Rd 76208
Juneau Ct & Dr 76210
Juno Ln 76209
Jupiter Dr 76209
Kappwood Ct 76210
Kariba Ln 76210
Karina Ln 76208
Kayanne Ln 76208
Kayewood Dr 76209
Keating Kove 76208
Kelistow 76203
Kendolph Dr 76205
Kenilworth Dr 76208
Kent St 76209
Kentucky Derby Dr 76210
Kenwood St 76205
Kerley St 76205
Key Largo Ct 76208
Kilkenny Ct 76210
Kiln Dr 76210
Kimberly Dr 76208
Kingfisher Ct & Ln 76209
Kings Ct 76209
Kings Row
600-798 76209
800-3099 76209
3100-3200 76208
3202-3698 76208
Kingsley Dr 76207
Kingston Dr 76207
Kingston Trce 76209
Kingswood Ct 76205
Kirby Dr 76210
Knight St 76205
Knob Hill Dr 76210
Knoll Pines Rd 76208
Knoll Ridge Cir, Ct & Dr 76210
Kootenay Cir 76210
Kossman Dr 76208
La Croix Rd 76208
La Fonta 76208
La Jolla Way 76207
La Mancha Ln 76205
La Mirada 76208
La Paloma Dr 76209
La Vista Ct 76208
Lafayette Dr 76205
Laguna Dr 76209
N Lake Trl 76201
Lake Bluff Cir & Ct 76210
Lake Country Dr 76210
Lake Cove Ct 76210
Lake Crest Ln 76208
Lake Fork Cir 76210
Lake Grove Ct 76210
Lake Haven Ln 76208
Lake Sharon Dr 76210
Lake Shore Est & Ln 76208
Lake Vista Ln 76208
Lakeshore Rd 76208
Lakeside Ct 76210
Lakeside Dr 76208
Lakeview Blvd & Ln 76208
Lakewood Dr 76207
Lakey St 76205
Lamplighter Dr 76210
Lamprey Cir 76210
Lance Ln 76209
Landmark Ct & Ln 76207
Landwick Ct 76210
Lane St 76209
Laney Cir & Rd 76208
Lantana Dr 76208
Laredo Ct 76205
N Lariat Rd 76207
Las Brisas Ct 76210
Lattimore St 76209
Laura St 76208
Laurel St 76205
Laurelwood Dr 76209
Laurens Place Rd 76210
Le Sage Ct 76208
Lea Meadow Cir 76208
Leatherwood Ln 76210

Ledgestone Dr 76210
Lee Dr 76209
Leeds Ct 76210
Legacy Ct 76207
Lehrman St 76209
Leisure Ln 76210
Leslie St 76205
Lexington Ln 76205
Liberty Ln 76209
Lido Way 76207
Lighthouse Dr 76210
Lillian Miller Pkwy
2400-2499 76205
2500-3199 76210
Lincoln Pl 76205
Linda Ln 76207
Linden Dr 76201
Lindenwood Trl 76207
Lindsey St
900-1099 76201
1100-1699 76205
Linwood Dr 76209
Lipizzan Ct & Dr 76210
Liveoak St 76209
Livingston Dr 76210
Lochwood Cir 76208
Lockhart Ct 76207
Lockheed Ln 76207
Lockhurst Ln 76208
Locksley Ln 76209
N Locust St
100-198 76201
200-1499 76201
1501-1899 76201
1900-3021 76209
3023-3099 76209
3200-8399 76207
S Locust St
100-1100 76201
1102-1498 76201
1900-2098 76205
Logan Dr 76207
Loma Linda Ter 76210
Londonderry Ln 76205
Lone Star Ln 76210
Lonesome Trl 76210
Lonesome Oak Dr 76208
Long Rd 76207
Longfellow Ln 76209
Longhorn Dr 76210
Longleaf Ln 76210
Longmeadow Ct & St 76209
Longmont Dr 76208
Longridge Dr 76205
Longview Dr 76210
Lookout Ln 76207
Loon Lake Rd 76210
N Loop 288
100-1199 76209
N Loop 288
1201-1499 76209
3400-4899 76208
S Loop 288
100-199 76209
500-2300 76205
2302-2398 76205
Los Colinas 76207
Lost Pony Dr 76210
Louise St 76201
Loveland Dr 76208
Lovell St 76201
Lovers Ln 76207
Lubbers Ln 76208
Luck Hole Dr 76210
Lula Ct 76210
Lutha Ln 76208
Lynchburg Dr 76208
Lynda Ln 76208
Lynhurst Ln 76205
Lynnbrook Dr 76207
Macbey Dr 76208
Mack Dr & Pl 76209
Maddox St 76205
Madison Ln 76208
Maggies Mdw 76210
Magnolia St 76201

Maid Marion Pl 76209
Maiden Ct 76210
Makena Ct 76210
Malibu Ct 76207
Mallard Dr 76210
Malli Ct 76209
Mallory Dr 76210
Malone St 76201
Manchester Ct & Way 76210
Manhattan Dr 76209
Manor Ct N 76210
Manor Ct S 76210
Manor Ln 76208
Manten Blvd 76208
Maple St 76201
Marbellas Ct 76210
Marble Cove Ln 76210
Margie St 76201
Marianne Cir 76209
Marietta St 76201
Marina Dr 76208
Mark Ln 76210
Mark Twain Ln 76210
Market St 76209
Marquette Dr 76210
Marseilles Ln 76210
Marsh Rail Dr 76208
Marshall Rd 76207
Marshall St 76201
Martin St 76205
Mary Ln 76208
Maryland Ct 76207
Marymount Dr 76210
N & S Masch Branch Rd 76207
Mason Ave 76210
Massey St 76205
Matt Wright Ln 76207
Matthew Ave 76210
May St 76209
Mayfield Cir 76208
Mayfield Dr 76207
N & S Mayhill Rd 76208
Mcclintock Dr 76208
Mccormick St
900-1299 76201
1500-2499 76205
Mcdonald Dr 76205
Mckamy Blvd 76207
E Mckinney St
100-102 76201
101-103 76202
104-398 76201
105-399 76201
400-3699 76209
3700-8599 76208
W Mckinney St 76201
Meadow Ln
100-499 76207
4000-4099 76208
Meadow St 76205
Meadow Oak St 76209
Meadow Oaks Dr 76210
Meadow Ridge Dr 76201
Meadow View Ct 76207
Meadowbrook Cir 76209
Meadowedge Ln 76207
Meadowlands Dr 76210
Meadowlark Ln
100-499 76208
3300-3599 76209
Meadows Dr 76208
Meadowview Dr 76210
Medpark Dr
3100-3198 76208
3200-3299 76208
3301-3399 76210
Melrose Dr 76207
Memorial Dr 76210
Memory Ln 76207
Meng Cir 76209
Mercedes Rd 76205
Mercer Way 76209
Meredith Ln 76210
Merrimack Dr 76210
Mesa Ct 76208

Mesa Dr 76207
Mesquite St 76201
Metro St 76207
Michael John Rd 76210
Michelle Way 76207
Michial St 76205
Milam Rd 76207
Mild Creek Ln 76210
Mill St 76205
Mill Pond Rd 76209
Mills Rd 76208
Millwood Dr 76210
Mimosa Dr 76201
Mingo Rd
1401-1597 76209
1599-2599 76209
2601-2699 76209
3100-6199 76208
Minor Cir 76205
Mira Vista Dr 76210
Miramar Dr 76210
Miranda Pl 76210
Mirror Rock Ln 76210
Mission St 76205
Mission Hills Ln 76210
Misty Gln 76210
Misty Hollow St 76209
Mistywood Ln 76209
Mockingbird Ct & Ln 76209
Mohican St 76209
Monaco Dr 76210
Moncayo Dr 76209
Montclair Pl 76209
Monte Carlo Ln 76210
Monte Verde Way 76208
Montebello Dr 76210
Montecito Dr
2800-3899 76205
3900-8399 76210
Montecristo Ct 76210
Monterey Dr 76209
Montevideo Ct 76210
Moonlight Dr 76208
Moonlit Path Dr 76208
Moor Hen Dr 76208
Morgan Dr 76210
Morin Dr 76207
Morning Glory Dr 76210
Morningside Dr 76208
Morse St
600-698 76205
700-1899 76205
3800-3999 76208
Mosscreek Dr 76210
Mosspoint Ct 76210
Mountainview Dr 76210
Mounts Ave 76201
Mozingo St 76209
Muirfield St 76210
E Mulberry St
201-297 76201
299-300 76201
302-398 76201
1100-1198 76205
W Mulberry St 76201
Mulholland Rd 76210
Mulkey Ln 76209
Munden Dr 76207
Munro Park Ave 76208
Murray S Johnson St 76207
Mustang Dr
3300-3599 76210
4700-5099 76207
Mustang Trl 76208
Myrtle St 76201
Nash Dr 76210
Natchez Trce 76210
Nautical Ln 76210
Navajo Rd 76210
Navajo St 76209
Neff St 76201
Neptune Dr 76209
Nevada St 76209
Newport Ave 76209
Newton St 76205
Nightfall Dr 76210

Nightingale Ln 76210
Noble St 76209
Nome Ct 76210
Nora Ln 76210
Norfolk Ct 76210
Normal St 76201
Norman St 76201
Northcrest Rd 76209
Northpointe Dr 76207
Northridge St 76201
Northway 76207
Northwood Ter 76209
Norwich Ln 76210
Norwood Ct 76210
Nottingham Dr 76209
Nowlin Rd 76210
Oak Ln 76208
E Oak St
100-499 76201
701-997 76205
999-1171 76205
1173-1199 76205
W Oak St 76201
Oak Vly 76209
Oak Bend Cir 76208
Oak Bluff Dr 76210
Oak Brook Ct 76207
Oak Creek Dr 76210
Oak Creek Ln 76208
Oak Forrest Cir 76210
Oak Hill Dr 76210
Oak Lawn St 76209
Oak Park Dr 76209
Oak Ridge Dr 76210
Oak Tree Dr 76209
Oakcrest Ct 76210
Oakhill Dr 76201
Oakhollow Ct & Dr 76210
Oakhurst St 76210
S Oakland St 76201
Oakmont Dr 76210
Oakridge St 76209
Oakshire St 76209
Oakview Pl 76210
Oakwood Cir 76208
Oakwood Dr 76205
Oberman Ln 76208
Ocean Dr 76210
Oceano Dr 76210
Oceanview Dr 76208
Old Alton Dr & Rd 76210
Old Lee Ct 76209
Old North Rd 76209
Old Orchard Ln 76209
Olives Br 76208
Olmos Creek Pl 76205
Olympia Dr 76209
Olympus Ct 76210
Orangewood Trl 76207
Oriole Ln 76209
Orr Rd 76208
Osage Ln 76210
Osprey Ct 76210
Ottowa Ln 76210
Overlake Dr 76210
Overlook Ln 76207
Owens Ln 76209
Oxford Ct & Ln 76209
Oxford Oaks Ln 76210
Pace Dr 76209
Pacific St 76201
Paco Trl 76209
Paddock Way 76210
Paige Rd 76208
Paint Dr 76210
Painted Ridge Rd 76207
Paisley St 76209
Palace Ct 76210
Palamino Ct 76210
Palmares Ct 76210
Palmer Dr 76209
Palmetto Ct 76210
Palmwood Pl 76209
Palo Verde Dr 76210
Palomino Ct 76208
Palos Verdes Dr 76210

Panhandle St 76201
Par Dr 76208
Paradise Cv 76208
Paradise Ln 76210
Park Ln 76205
E Park Ln 76208
Park Pl 76208
Park Palisades Dr 76210
Park Wood Ct & Dr 76208
Parkcrest Ct & Dr 76207
Parkhaven Dr 76210
Parkridge Dr 76210
Parkside Dr 76201
Parkview Cir 76210
Parkview Ct 76207
Parkview Dr 76210
Parkview St 76207
W Parkway St 76201
Parvin St 76205
Paulie Dr 76208
Pauline St 76201
Peach St 76209
Peacock Ln 76210
Peak St 76201
Peakview Dr 76210
Pear Tree Pl 76207
Pearl St 76201
Pebble Beach Trl 76208
Pecan Ct 76208
Pecan St 76209
W Pecan St 76201
E Pecan Creek Cir 76210
Pecan Creek Rd 76207
Pecan Grove Dr 76209
Pecan Tree Dr 76210
Pecan Valley Ct 76210
Pelican Ct 76208
Pembrooke Pl 76205
Penina Trl 76210
Peninsula Bnd & Trl 76208
Penniman Rd 76209
Pennsylvania Ct & Dr 76205
Pepperidge Ave 76207
Pepperwood Trl 76207
Peregrine Dr 76210
Perimeter St 76207
Pershing Dr 76209
Pertain St 76209
Pheasant Holw 76207
Phoenix Ct 76205
Photinia Ave 76208
Picadilly Ln 76209
Pickwick Ln 76209
Pierce St 76201
Pimlico Ct 76210
Pin Oak Dr 76209
Pinckney Dr 76209
Pine Trl 76208
Pine Glen Rd 76208
Pine Hills Ln 76210
Pinehurst Ct 76210
Pineoak Ln 76210
Piner St 76201
Pinewood Dr 76207
Piney Creek Blvd 76205
Pinnell Ct 76210
Pinto Dr 76210
Pioneer Dr 76210
Piper Dr 76210
Piping Rock St 76205
Pirtle St 76209
Plum Holw 76207
Plumbago Dr 76208
E Pockrus Paige Rd 76208
Poinsettia Blvd 76208
Ponder St 76201
Poseidon Dr 76207
Post Oak Cir 76210
Post Oak Ct
1700-1799 76209
2100-2299 76210
Post Oak Dr 76210
Post Oak Trl 76210
Post Ridge Cir 76210
Postwood Ct & Dr 76210
Potomac Pkwy 76210

Potterstone St 76208
Pottery Trl 76210
E Prairie St
100-299 76201
301-399 76201
400-1100 76205
1102-1198 76205
W Prairie St
300-2600 76201
2602-2698 76201
3100-3199 76207
Preakness St 76210
Precision Dr 76207
Pres Ct 76209
Prescott Downs Dr 76210
Preston Pl 76209
Primrose Ln 76201
Princeton Ct 76201
Private Road 1001 76210
Private Road 502 76210
Private Road 505 76210
Private Road 508 76210
Private Road 803 76208
Private Road 806 76208
Private Road 816 76208
Providence St 76205
Purbeck Trl 76210
Purdue Dr 76210
Quail Cir 76208
Quail Creek Dr 76208
Quail Ridge Dr 76209
Quail Run Dr 76208
Quailcreek Rd 76208
Railroad Ave 76209
Raintree Way 76210
Raleigh Path Rd 76208
Rambling Brook Trl 76210
Ramey Cir 76205
Ramsey Ct 76209
Ranch House Dr 76210
Ranchman Blvd 76210
Rancho Domingues Rd 76210
Rankin Dr 76210
Ravenwood Dr 76207
Ravinia Dr 76208
Reata Ct 76210
Rector Rd 76207
Red Cedar Ct 76208
Red Oak Ct 76209
Red Oak Dr 76208
Red Wolfe Rd 76208
Redbud Dr & Trl 76208
Redondo Rd 76210
Redrock Dr 76210
Redstone Rd 76209
Redwood Dr 76210
Redwood Pl 76209
Reed St 76205
Regal Rd 76210
Regency Ct 76210
Regent Ct 76210
Regina Dr 76210
Remington St 76210
Retama St 76209
Rich St 76205
Richmond Ct 76210
Ricks Rd 76210
Ridge Ln 76208
Ridgecrest Cir 76205
Ridgedale Ct 76207
Ridgemont Ln 76208
Riley Rd 76210
Riney Rd 76207
Rio Bravo Way 76208
Rio Grande Blvd 76205
Riverchase Trl 76210
Rivercrest Dr 76207
Riverside Dr 76208
Riverview Dr 76210
Robbie O St 76207
Roberts St 76209
Robertson St 76205
Robin Cir 76209
Robinson Rd 76210
Robinwood Ln 76209

Rockwood Ln 76209
Rocky Ct 76208
Rocky Bend Ct 76208
Rodeo Dr 76208
Roland Rd 76207
Rolling Hills Cir 76205
Ropers Rd 76207
Rose St 76209
Roselawn Dr
2300-3198 76205
3200-3399 76205
3401-3599 76205
3800-3999 76207
Rosemont Ct 76207
Rosewood Dr 76207
Ross St 76201
Royal Ln 76209
Royal Acres Dr 76209
Royal Belfast Ct 76210
Royal Meadow St 76209
Royal Oaks Cir, Ct & Pl 76210
N Ruddell St
100-299 76205
300-1600 76209
1602-1998 76209
S Ruddell St 76205
Rugby Ln 76209
Ruidosa Ct 76205
Russell Newman Blvd 76208
Ruth St 76205
Ryan Rd 76210
Sabre Ln 76207
Sadau Ct 76210
Saddle Ct & Dr 76210
Saddleback Dr 76210
Sagebrush Dr 76209
Sagewood St 76207
Saint Claire Dr 76210
Saint James Ct 76210
Saint Johns Dr 76210
Saints Cir 76209
Salado St 76209
Salon Ct 76210
Sam Bass Blvd 76205
San Felipe Dr 76210
San Gabriel Dr 76205
San Jacinto Blvd 76205
San Lorenzo Dr 76210
San Lucas Ln 76208
San Marino Ln 76210
San Sebastian Pl 76205
Sand Jack Dr 76208
Sanders Rd 76210
Sandestin Dr 76205
Sandhurst Dr 76207
Sandlewood Dr 76207
Sandpiper Dr 76205
Sandstone Dr 76207
Sandy Creek Dr 76205
Santa Fe St 76205
Santa Monica Dr 76205
Santiago Pl 76205
Santos Dr 76207
Saranac Cir 76210
Sarasota 76207
Sauls Ln 76209
Savage Dr 76207
Savannah Trl 76205
Savill Gdn 76207
Sawyer Ave 76201
Schmitz Ave 76209
Schuyler St 76207
Scott Dr 76205
Scripture St 76201
Sea Cove Ln 76208
Seaside Dr 76208
Second St 76201
Selene Dr 76209
Seminole Ave 76209
Sena St 76201
Serendipity Hills Ct & Trl 76210
Serene Ct 76207
Serenity Way 76210
Settlement Dr 76210

Settlers Creek Rd 76210
Seven Oaks Ln 76210
Seville Rd 76205
Shadow Ln 76208
Shadow Trl 76207
Shadow Brook Ct 76210
Shadow Crest Dr 76210
Shadow Oak Dr 76208
Shady Ln 76208
Shady Oaks Cir 76208
Shady Oaks Dr 76205
Shady Oaks Pl 76210
Shady Rest Ln 76208
S & W Shady Shores Rd 76208
Shahan Dr & Ln 76208
Shalimar Dr & Way 76207
Shards Ct 76210
Sharon Dr 76210
Sharon Rose Ct 76210
Shaw Ln 76208
Shawnee St 76209
Shelby Ln 76207
Shell Dr 76208
Shenandoah Trl 76210
Shepard Ln 76210
Sheraton Pl & Rd 76209
E Sherman Dr
100-2299 76209
2301-3899 76209
4100-7999 76208
W Sherman Dr 76201
Sherwood St 76209
Sherwood Mhp 76208
Shiloh Ln 76208
Shiloh Rd 76210
Shoal Bnd 76210
Shoreline Dr 76210
Siena Dr 76210
Sierra Dr 76209
Silent Star Ln 76210
Silktree Ct 76208
Silver Dome Rd 76208
Silver Sage Dr 76209
Silverdome Mhp 76208
Silvermeadow Ln 76210
Simmons St 76205
Sioux Ct 76210
Sirius Rd 76208
Skelton St 76207
Skinner St 76205
Skylane 76207
Skylark Dr 76205
Skyview Dr 76210
Smith St 76205
Smokerise Cir 76205
Smoketree Trl 76208
Smokey Ln 76208
Snyder St 76209
Solar Way 76207
Soledad Dr 76208
Sombre Vista Dr 76205
Sombrero Dr 76210
Soriano St 76207
Southerland Dr 76207
Southmont Dr 76205
Southpoint Ct 76207
Southridge Dr
1700-2599 76205
2800-2899 76210
Southway 76207
Spanish Ln 76210
Spanish Oak Cir 76208
Sparta Dr 76210
Spartan Dr 76207
Spencer Rd
1500-2599 76205
2800-2999 76208
Spenrock Ct 76210
Spring Dr 76208
Spring Park Rd 76208
Spring Side Rd 76207
Spring Valley Dr 76208
Springbrook St 76210
Springcreek Dr 76210
Springfield St 76208

Springhill Dr 76209
Springside Dr 76207
Springtree Rd 76208
Springtree St 76209
Spur Ct 76210
Spyglass Hill Ln 76208
St James Pl 76210
Stacy Ct 76209
Staghorn Cir 76208
Stallion Ct & St 76208
Stanefer Cir 76205
Stanford Ct, Dr & Ln 76210
Stanley St 76201
Stapler Dr 76208
Starwood Ln 76207
State School Rd 76210
Steedman Ln 76208
Stella St 76201
Stephen Dr 76207
Stockade Ln 76205
Stockbridge Rd 76208
Stockton St 76209
Stone Creek Ln 76210
Stone Mountain Dr 76210
Stone Oak Blvd 76210
Stone Wood Dr 76207
Stonegate Cir & Dr 76205
Stoneway Dr 76210
Stonewick Dr 76210
Straightway Ln 76208
Strata Dr 76201
Stratford Ln 76209
Stroud St 76201
Stuart Rd
900-4499 76209
4500-4999 76207
Summerwind Ct 76209
Summerwood Ct 76210
Summit Ct 76210
Summit Ridge Dr 76210
Sun Ray Dr 76208
Sun Valley Dr 76209
Sunburst Trl 76210
Sundown Blvd 76210
Sunflower Dr 76210
Sunny Oak Dr & Ln 76208
Sunnydale Ln 76209
Sunrise Cv 76209
Sunset Cir 76208
Sunset St 76201
Surf St 76208
Surrey Oaks Ct 76210
Susie Ln 76208
Sussex Ct & Way 76210
Swan Park Dr 76210
Sweet Cloud Way 76210
Sweet Gate Ln 76208
Sweetgate Ln 76208
Sweetgum Dr 76208
Swisher Rd 76208
Swiss Pine Rd 76210
E Sycamore St
100-298 76201
300-399 76201
400-1165 76205
1167-1199 76205
W Sycamore St 76201
Syracuse Dr 76210
Tahoe Ln 76210
Taliaferro St 76201
Tallahassee Dr 76208
Tanglewood St 76207
Tartan Cir 76208
Taylor Cir 76210
Teakwood Ave 76207
Teal Dr 76208
Tealwood Ln 76210
Teasbend Ct 76210
Teasley Ln
1100-3100 76205
3102-3198 76205
3200-9199 76210
Telese Ct 76209
Tennessee Dr 76210
Tennyson Trl 76205
Terra Evergreen Dr 76208

Terry Ct 76209
N Texas Blvd
100-198 76201
200-599 76201
601-1099 76201
700-700 76203
1000-1098 76201
1101-1199 76205
Texas St
300-498 76201
500-999 76209
1001-1199 76209
Thackery Dr 76210
The Grv & Rdg 76210
The Briars 76210
The Downs 76210
The Retreat 76210
The Woods 76210
E Third St 76201
Thistle Hl, Rdg & Way 76210
Thomas St 76201
Thomas J Egan Rd 76207
Thorndale Ct 76210
Thoroughbred Trl 76210
Thunderbird Dr 76207
Ticonderoga Dr 76205
Tieszen St 76207
Timber Trl 76209
Timber Ridge Cir 76210
Timbergreen Cir 76205
Timberidge St 76205
Timberview Cir, Ct & Dr 76210
Titan Trl 76209
Tomlee St 76210
Topanga Canyon Dr 76210
Tori Oak Trl 76210
Tower Ridge Dr 76210
Trailhead Ln 76205
Trailwood Dr 76207
Travis St 76205
Tree House Ln 76208
Tremont Cir 76205
Trencon Rd 76208
Trenton Pl 76208
Trinity Rd 76208
N Trinity Rd 76208
S Trinity Rd 76208
Trinity Ter 76210
Trinity Oaks Mhp 76208
Triple Crown Ct 76210
Tripp Trl 76207
Tristan Ct 76208
Troy H Lagrone Dr 76205
Trumpet Vw 76208
Trumpet Vine 76208
Tulane Dr 76201
Tuscan Hills Cir 76210
Tuscany Dr 76210
Twilight Dr 76208
Twin Brook Turn 76210
Twu Student Building 76204
Tyler St 76209
Uland St 76209
Underwood Rd 76207
Underwood St 76201
Unicorn Lake Blvd 76210
Union Cir
1100-1199 76201
1155-1155 76203
Union Lake Rd 76210
E University Dr
101-597 76209
599-3099 76209
3100-5399 76208
W University Dr
100-2400 76201
2402-3098 76201
3100-9099 76207
Val Verde Ct 76210
Valderamma Ln 76210
Valencia Ln 76210
Valley Creek Rd 76205
Valley Stream Rd 76208
Valley View Dr 76210
Valley View Rd 76209

Vanderbilt Ct & St 76201
Vickery Way 76210
Victoria Dr 76209
Villa Ct 76210
E Village St 76209
Villanova Dr 76210
Vine St 76209
Vinsonville Ln 76208
Vintage Cir, Ct & Dr 76210
Virginia Cir 76209
Visalia Ln 76210
Vista Ct 76210
Vista Verde St 76210
Vistaview Dr 76210
Wagon Trail Dr 76205
Wagon Wheel Trl 76208
Wainwright St 76201
W Walnut St 76201
Walton Dr 76208
Wandering Oak Dr 76208
Warbird Dr 76207
Warren Ct 76201
Warwick Dr 76210
Wasatch Dr 76208
Water Front Ct 76210
Water Oak 76209
Waterford Way 76210
Waterside Pl 76210
Waterton Cir 76210
Waterwood Cir 76208
Wavecrest Ln 76208
Waverly Rd 76208
Wayne St 76209
Webb Rd 76208
N & S Welch St 76201
Wellington Dr 76209
Wellington Oaks Cir, Ct & Pl 76210
Wellston Ln 76210
Wendell Dr 76207
Wentwood Dr 76210
Weslayan Dr 76210
Wessex Ct 76210
Westchester St 76201
Westcourt Rd 76207
Westgate Dr 76207
Westglen Dr 76207
Westheimer Rd 76210
Westminster St 76205
Weston Dr 76209
Westridge St 76205
Westview Trl 76207
Westway St 76201
Westwind Dr 76210
Westwood Dr 76205
Whetstone Dr 76210
Whippoorwill Cir 76208
Whippoorwill Ln 76205
Whispering Oaks 76209
White Dove Ln 76210
White Oak Ct 76209
Whitefish Ct 76210
Whitehall Dr 76210
Whiterock Rd 76208
Whitetail Dr 76208
Whiting Way 76208
Whitney Ct 76205
Wicker Way 76209
Wickersham Ln 76210
Widgeon Ln 76210
Wilderness St 76205
Wildwood Ln
1101-1199 76208
2200-2499 76210
Wildwood St 76210
Williams Ln 76209
Williams St 76201
Williamsburg Row 76209
Willow Ln
1100-1299 76207
6500-6599 76208
Willow Stone St 76207
Willowcrest Loop 76205
Willowick Cir 76210
Willowwood St 76205
Wilmette Dr 76208

Wilshire St 76201
Wilson St 76205
Wilsonwood Dr 76209
Winchester Ct
2700-2799 76209
3600-3699 76210
Wind River Ln 76210
Windbrook Ct & St 76207
Windfields St 76209
Winding Stream Ln 76210
Windmere Cir 76210
Windmill Hill Cir 76208
Windridge Ln 76208
E Windsor Dr 76209
W Windsor Dr 76207
Windsor Pkwy 76210
Windsor Farms Dr 76207
Windstone Way 76210
Windstream St 76209
Windswept Ct 76209
Windy Hl 76209
Windy Meadow Dr 76208
Windy Point Dr 76208
Wing Way 76208
Winnetka Rd 76208
Winslow Dr 76207
Winston Dr 76210
Wintercreek Dr 76210
Wisteria St 76205
Withers St
301-499 76201
501-597 76209
599-699 76209
Wolftrap Dr 76209
N Wood St
100-298 76205
300-999 76209
S Wood St 76205
Wood Hollow Rd 76208
Wood Ridge Ct 76210
Wood Stone Cir 76208
Woodbrook St 76205
Woodcrest Cir 76210
Woodford Ct & Ln 76209
Woodhaven St 76209
Woodlake Ct & Dr 76210
Woodland St 76209
Woodland Hills Dr 76208
Woodlands Hills Dr 76208
Woodmount Ct 76209
N & S Woodrow Ln 76205
Woods Edge Ct 76210
Woodson Cir 76209
Woodthrush Ln 76209
Worthington Dr 76207
Wrangler Ln 76205
Wright Ct 76210
Wye St 76205
Yale Dr 76210
Yellowstone Ln 76210
Yellowstone Pl 76209
Yellowstone Park Ln 76210
Yorkshire St 76209
Yucca Dr 76208
Yukon Dr 76210
Zachary Dr 76210
Zilda Way 76208

NUMBERED STREETS

All Street Addresses 76208

DESOTO TX

General Delivery 75115

POST OFFICE BOXES MAIN OFFICE STATIONS AND BRANCHES

Box No.s
All PO Boxes 75123

RURAL ROUTES

01, 03, 04 75115

NAMED STREETS

Abbey Ln 75115
Abbott Ave 75115
Ace Dr 75115
Adam Pl 75115
Aerie Pl 75115
Almond Ln 75115
Alpine Dr 75115
Alverstone St 75115
Amanda Ave 75115
Amber Cir & Ln 75115
Amherst Dr 75115
Amsbury Dr 75115
Andalusia Trl 75115
Angie Ln 75115
Anglebluff Dr 75115
Apache Ct 75115
Arbor Creek Dr 75115
Armstrong Dr 75115
Arthurs Dr 75115
Ash Grove Ln 75115
Ashbrook Dr 75115
Ashford Dr 75115
Ashington Pl 75115
Aspen Ct, Dr & Ln 75115
Augusta Ct 75115
Austin Dr 75115
Avalon Dr 75115
Aviary Ct & Dr 75115
Azalea Dr 75115
Bailey Dr 75115
Balsam Grove Cir, Ct & Ln 75115
Barrington Dr 75115
Barrows Pl 75115
Bayberry Ln 75115
Beaver Brook Ln 75115
Beeblossom Dr 75115
Beechwood Dr 75115
Belclaire Ter 75115
E & W Belt Line Rd 75115
Beltwood Ct & Pl 75115
N & S Beltwoods Dr 75115
Bennett Cir 75115
Bent Creek Cir & Dr 75115
Berry Ln 75115
Beverly Dr 75115
Big Bend Dr 75115
Birchwood Ln 75115
Bittersweet Cv 75115
Blue Sky Dr 75115
Blue Stream Dr 75115
Bluebird Ln 75115
Bluebonnet Ct & Dr 75115
Bluffview Dr 75115
Bob White St 75115
Bolton Boone Dr 75115
Bordeaux Ave 75115
Boulder Creek Dr 75115
Boysenberry Dr 75115
Bramble Creek Cir & Dr 75115
Breckenridge Dr 75115
Brees Dr 75115
Brentwood Dr 75115
Briarbrook Dr 75115
Briarwood Ln 75115
Bridgeport Dr 75115
Bridle Dr 75115
Bright Angel Trl 75115
Brighton Dr 75115
Bristol Cir & Trl 75115
Broken Crest Dr 75115
Brook Hollow Cir & Dr 75115
Brooks St 75115
Brookview Dr 75115
Brookwood Dr 75115
Brownstone 75115
Buckingham Pl 75115
Buelwood Ct 75115
Buffalo Creek Dr 75115

Buxton Dr 75115
Calgary Dr 75115
Callalily Dr 75115
Cambridge Dr 75115
Camden Ct 75115
Camelia Ct 75115
Campbell St 75115
Camrose Ln 75115
Canary Ct & Ln 75115
Candelila Dr 75115
Candellia Dr 75115
Candle Meadow Blvd 75115
Candlenut Ct 75115
Canterbury Trl 75115
Canyon Pl 75115
Canyon Ridge Dr 75115
Caraway Ln 75115
Cardigan Ln 75115
Cardinal Dr 75115
Carey Dr 75115
Carmela Dr 75115
Carriage Creek Ct & Dr 75115
Cassandra Cir 75115
Castle St 75115
Castlewood Ct 75115
Cattail Creek Dr 75115
Cedar Brook Dr 75115
Cedar Rapids Ln 75115
Cedar Ridge Cir & Dr 75115
E Centre Park Blvd 75115
Chacon Canyon Dr 75115
Chalet Dr 75115
Chalk Hill Ln 75115
Channel View Ct & Ter 75115
Chaparral Dr 75115
Chapel Hill Dr 75115
Charles St 75115
N Chattey Rd 75115
Cherokee Ln 75115
Cherry Hill Ln 75115
Chestnut Ln 75115
Cheyenne Dr 75115
Chowning Dr 75115
Church St 75115
Cimmarron Dr 75115
Cindy Way 75115
Circle Creek Dr 75115
City Park Dr 75115
Claire View Dr 75115
Clear Creek Dr 75115
Clear Springs Dr 75115
Cliff Trl 75115
Clifton Ln 75115
Cloudcrest Dr 75115
Clover Hill Ln 75115
Cloverdale Ln 75115
Clubbrook Cir 75115
Clubwood Ct 75115
Cobblestone Dr 75115
N & S Cockrell Hill Rd 75115
Cold Water Dr 75115
Connie Dr 75115
Conures Dr 75115
Cool Meadow Ct 75115
Copper Dr 75115
Coral Ridge Ln 75115
Cordell Dr 75115
Cornerstone Ln 75115
Cottonwood Cir & Dr 75115
Country Ridge Dr 75115
Courson Dr 75115
Cove Mdw 75115
Covington Dr 75115
Crane Cir 75115
Creek Tree Dr 75115
Creekbend Cir 75115
Creekview Ct 75115
Cresent Cir & Dr 75115
Crestone St 75115
N & S Crestwood Blvd & Ct 75115
Cripple Creek Ct 75115
Crooked Creek Ln 75115
Crossbow Trl 75115

Crystal Lake Dr 75115
Cypress Ln 75115
Daisy Dr 75115
Dalton Dr 75115
E Danbury Dr 75115
E & W Danieldale Rd 75115
Danny Dr 75115
Dartbrook Dr 75115
Dashing Creek Dr 75115
Daventry Dr 75115
David Ave 75115
Davis Dr 75115
Deborah Ave 75115
Deer Creek Cir & Dr 75115
Dennis Dr 75115
Derby Ln 75115
Desoto Dr 75115
Devonshire Dr 75115
Diamond Dr 75115
Dogwood Trl 75115
Dorchester Dr 75115
Dove Ln 75115
Dreama Dr 75115
Dreda Cir 75115
Drexel Dr 75115
Driftwood Ln 75115
Dry Creek Cir 75115
Duke Dr 75115
Duke Of Gloucester St 75115
Dusky Thrush St 75115
Dutchman Creek Dr 75115
Dynamic Dr 75115
Eagle Ct & Dr 75115
Eagle Point Dr 75115
Echobrook Pl 75115
Eddie Ct 75115
Edgebrook Dr 75115
Edgewood Dr 75115
Edmonds Way 75115
Elder Oak Dr 75115
Eldorado Dr 75115
N & S Elerson Rd 75115
Emerald Dr 75115
Emery Oak Ct 75115
Essex Ct & Dr 75115
Estate Ln 75115
Evelyn St 75115
Evergreen Cir 75115
Executive Way 75115
Ezell Dr 75115
Faircrest Dr 75115
Fairweather St 75115
Falcon Dr 75115
Fall Wheat Ct & Dr 75115
Faye St 75115
Fern Dr 75115
Fieldstone Dr 75115
Finch Dr 75115
Flagstaff Dr 75115
Flagstone Ln 75115
Foraker St 75115
Forest Crk 75115
Forest Glen Dr 75115
Forestbrook Dr 75115
Foxwood Dr 75115
Fraderl Dr 75115
Franklin St 75115
Frenchmans Dr 75115
Frost Hollow Dr 75115
Galleria Dr 75115
Gannon Ln 75115
Garden Brook Ln 75115
Garden Grove Ln 75115
Gardenia St 75115
Garner Ct 75115
Gatewood Dr 75115
Gatlinburg Cir 75115
Gilbert Ave 75115
Ginger Trl 75115
Glacier St 75115
Glen Ave & Ct 75115
Glenwick Dr 75115
Goffin Dr 75115
Gold Finch Dr 75115
Golden Meadow Dr 75115
Goldeneye Dr 75115

Goldenrod Ct ... 75115
Gracelane Dr ... 75115
Granada Dr ... 75115
Grand Teton Ct & Dr ... 75115
Granite Ct & Ln ... 75115
Greenbriar Cir & Dr ... 75115
Greenbrook Cir & Dr ... 75115
Gregory Dr ... 75115
Greyhawk Dr ... 75115
N Hampton Rd ... 75115
S Hampton Rd
100-300 ... 75115
229-229 ... 75123
301-1599 ... 75115
302-1598 ... 75115
Hanna Ave & Cir ... 75115
Harvest Hill Cir ... 75115
Havencrest Dr ... 75115
Haverford Ln ... 75115
Heather Knoll Dr ... 75115
Hemlock Ct & Dr ... 75115
Heritage Hill Dr ... 75115
Heron Ct ... 75115
Hickory Bend Dr ... 75115
Hidden Brooke Dr ... 75115
Hidden Meadow Ct ... 75115
Hideaway Pl ... 75115
High Bluff Dr ... 75115
Highlands Dr ... 75115
Highridge Dr ... 75115
Hillcrest Dr ... 75115
Hillside Ln ... 75115
Hilltop Cir ... 75115
Hollaway Cir ... 75115
Hollow Crest Dr ... 75115
Hollow Oak Dr ... 75115
Holt Ave ... 75115
Honey Tree Cir, Ct &
Ln ... 75115
Honeysuckle Way ... 75115
Honor Cir & Dr ... 75115
Hoover St ... 75115
Horseshoe Ct ... 75115
Hubert Dr ... 75115
N Hulgan Cir ... 75115
Hummingbird Dr ... 75115
Hunters Creek Dr ... 75115
Ida Bess Ave ... 75115
Idle Creek Ct & Ln ... 75115
Indian Creek Dr ... 75115
Inglewood Ct & Trl ... 75115
N & S Interstate 35 ... 75115
Ironwood Ct & Dr ... 75115
Jamille Dr ... 75115
Janeil Ln ... 75115
Jasper Dr ... 75115
E & W Jay Ct ... 75115
Jeff Grimes Blvd ... 75115
Jefferson Ave ... 75115
Jewelflower Dr ... 75115
Jewett Ln ... 75115
Jo Dr ... 75115
Joanna Ave & Cir ... 75115
Joe Boy Ct ... 75115
Johns Dr ... 75115
Jordan Dr ... 75115
Juniper Ridge Cir & Ct ... 75115
Kari Ann Ln ... 75115
Kathy Dr ... 75115
Kaylor Dr ... 75115
Kearsarge St ... 75115
Keats Dr ... 75115
Kelly Ln ... 75115
Kelsie Cir, Ct & Ln ... 75115
Kensington Dr ... 75115
Kentsdale Pl ... 75115
Kestrel Ave ... 75115
Keswick Dr ... 75115
Keysville Ave ... 75115
Killdee Ct ... 75115
Kimberly Dr ... 75115
Kinglet St ... 75115
Kings Ln ... 75115
Kirnwood Dr ... 75115
Kite St ... 75115
Kittery Dr ... 75115

Knob Hill Dr ... 75115
Knollwood Dr ... 75115
Ladner Ln ... 75115
Lake Grove Ln ... 75115
Lakeside Dr ... 75115
Lakeview Dr ... 75115
Lakewood Dr ... 75115
E & W Lanett Cir &
Dr ... 75115
Laon Ln ... 75115
Laramie Ln ... 75115
Larchbrook Dr ... 75115
E & W Lark Ct ... 75115
Larry Dr ... 75115
N & S Laurel Springs
Cir, Ct & Dr ... 75115
Laurie Ave ... 75115
Leisure Ln ... 75115
Lemontree Ln ... 75115
Lexington Cir & Ln ... 75115
Lilac Ln ... 75115
Lion St ... 75115
Lisa Ln ... 75115
Little John Dr ... 75115
Little River Ct ... 75115
Live Oak Ct & Dr ... 75115
Longleaf Cir & Dr ... 75115
Longmeadow Ct & Ln ... 75115
Lost Creek Dr ... 75115
Lucile Cir ... 75115
N & S Lyndalyn Ave ... 75115
Lyndon Ave ... 75115
Macaw Way ... 75115
Madera Dr ... 75115
Magnolia Trl ... 75115
Mai Ave ... 75115
Mallard Dr ... 75115
Manor Dr ... 75115
Mantlebrook Dr ... 75115
Maple Ln ... 75115
Maplecrest Dr ... 75115
Marantha St ... 75115
Marble Canyon Dr ... 75115
Marilyn Ave ... 75115
Marisa Ct & Ln ... 75115
Marlene Pl ... 75115
Marsha Ln ... 75115
Martin Dr ... 75115
Masters Cir & Dr ... 75115
Matagorda Ln ... 75115
Maywood Ln ... 75115
Meadow St ... 75115
Meadow Hill Dr ... 75115
Meadow Wood Ct ... 75115
Meadowbrook Dr ... 75115
Meadowcreek Dr ... 75115
Meadowcrest Dr ... 75115
Meadowlark Ln ... 75115
Melody Ln ... 75115
Meriweather Pl ... 75115
Michael Dr ... 75115
Mill Creek Dr ... 75115
Millington Cir, Ct & Dr ... 75115
Minah Dr ... 75115
Minden Ln ... 75115
Miramar Ave ... 75115
Mirkes Pkwy ... 75115
Missionary Rdg ... 75115
Misty Glen Dr ... 75115
Mockingbird Ln ... 75115
Monahan Dr ... 75115
Montauk Way ... 75115
Montridge Ln ... 75115
Montrose Ln & Trl ... 75115
Morningside Dr ... 75115
Morris St ... 75115
Mosslake Dr ... 75115
Mossy Rdg ... 75115
Mountain Cir & Pl ... 75115
Mountain Laurel Ct &
Ln ... 75115
Mulberry Ln ... 75115
Nancywood Ave ... 75115
Neal Rd ... 75115
Neff Ct ... 75115
Nelson Ct ... 75115

Nettleton Dr ... 75115
Newberry Ct ... 75115
Newcastle Dr ... 75115
Newport Way ... 75115
Nightingale Ct ... 75115
Nobleman Ln ... 75115
Nora Ln ... 75115
Normandy ... 75115
Northgate Dr ... 75115
Northlake Dr ... 75115
Norwood Ct ... 75115
Oak Trl ... 75115
Oak Meadow Ln ... 75115
Oakmont Ct ... 75115
Old Hickory Trl ... 75115
Oleander Dr ... 75115
Olympia St ... 75115
Opal Dr ... 75115
Open Ct ... 75115
Oriole St ... 75115
Osprey Dr ... 75115
Oteca Dr ... 75115
Oxford Dr ... 75115
Painted Redstart St ... 75115
Pajarito Ct ... 75115
Palisades Dr ... 75115
Palo Duro Cir ... 75115
Parakeet Dr ... 75115
Park Row Ln ... 75115
Parkdale Ln ... 75115
Parker Rd ... 75115
E & W Parkerville Rd ... 75115
N & S Parks Ct & Dr ... 75115
Parrot Ct ... 75115
Partridge Cir ... 75115
Peach Ln ... 75115
Peacock Dr ... 75115
Pebblebrook Dr ... 75115
Pecan Dr ... 75115
Pecan Crossing Dr ... 75115
Peggs St ... 75115
Pelican Ct ... 75115
Pheasant Ln ... 75115
Pidgeon Ct ... 75115
Pin Oak Dr ... 75115
Pine Hollow Dr ... 75115
Pine Tree Ln ... 75115
Pinnacle Peak Dr ... 75115
Pintail Ct & Dr ... 75115
Place Louie ... 75115
Plantation Dr ... 75115
Plaza Rd ... 75115
E & W Pleasant Run
Rd ... 75115
Plum Creek Dr ... 75115
N & S Polk St ... 75115
Post Oak Ln ... 75115
Prairie Creek Dr ... 75115
Prestonwood Trl ... 75115
Primrose Ct & Ln ... 75115
Prince George Ave ... 75115
Princeton Dr ... 75115
Priscilla Ln ... 75115
Private Dr ... 75115
Quail Ln ... 75115
Quick Silver Dr ... 75115
Rain Lily Dr ... 75115
Rainier St ... 75115
Raintree Cir, Ct & Ln ... 75115
Ramblewood Cir ... 75115
Ranch Valley Dr ... 75115
Randa Ln ... 75115
Rapid Falls Dr ... 75115
Raspberry Ln ... 75115
Ray Ave ... 75115
Ray Andra Dr ... 75115
Rayburn Dr ... 75115
Reagan Ct ... 75115
Red Bud Dr ... 75115
Redman Dr ... 75115
Reedsport Pl ... 75115
Regal Bluff Ln ... 75115
Regalwood Dr ... 75115
Regents Park Ct ... 75115
Registry Dr ... 75115
Renee Ln ... 75115

Reunion Rd ... 75115
Richards Cir ... 75115
Richlen Way ... 75115
Rickey Canyon Ave ... 75115
Ridgewood Dr ... 75115
Rio Bravo Dr ... 75115
Rio Grande Dr ... 75115
Rio Rojo Dr ... 75115
Rio Verde Dr ... 75115
Rio Vista Dr ... 75115
Ripplewood Dr ... 75115
Rising Ridge Cir & Dr ... 75115
Riverwood Dr ... 75115
Roaring Springs Dr ... 75115
Rob Ln ... 75115
Robbie Mince Way ... 75115
E & W Robin Ct ... 75115
Robin Meadow Ct &
Dr ... 75115
Rock Glen St ... 75115
Rockcreek Dr ... 75115
Rolling Hills Ln ... 75115
Rose Cir ... 75115
Rosemont Dr ... 75115
Rosewood Dr ... 75115
Round Rock Dr ... 75115
Royal Crest Dr ... 75115
Royal Oak Dr ... 75115
Ruffian Rd ... 75115
Running River Dr ... 75115
Rusticwood Dr ... 75115
Sabona Dr ... 75115
Saddle Head Dr ... 75115
Saddlebrook ... 75115
Sagewood Dr ... 75115
Saint Andrews Pl ... 75115
Saint George Pl ... 75115
San Moritz Ct ... 75115
Sandalwood Ln ... 75115
Sandstone Ct ... 75115
Sandy Creek Ct, Dr &
Pl ... 75115
Sapling Way ... 75115
Sawsawi Trl ... 75115
Scenic Way ... 75115
Scotland Dr ... 75115
Seahawk Dr ... 75115
Senegal Dr ... 75115
Sequoia Ct & Dr ... 75115
Settlers Creek Dr ... 75115
Shadow Wood Trl ... 75115
Shady Cove Pl ... 75115
Shadybrook Cir & Dr ... 75115
Shadywood Ln ... 75115
Shallow Bend Dr ... 75115
Shannon Cir ... 75115
Sharp Dr ... 75115
Shasta St ... 75115
Shavano St ... 75115
Shennandoah Dr ... 75115
Sherod Dr ... 75115
S Sherrie Ln ... 75115
Sherry Ln ... 75115
Sherwood Ln ... 75115
Shiloh Dr ... 75115
Shockley Ave ... 75115
Shoreline Dr ... 75115
Sierra Dr ... 75115
N & S Silver Creek Cir,
Ct & Dr ... 75115
Skyflower Ct ... 75115
Snapdragon Ln ... 75115
Snowy Orchid Ln ... 75115
Southlake Dr ... 75115
Southpointe Dr ... 75115
Southwood Dr ... 75115
Sparrow Ct & Ln ... 75115
Spice St ... 75115
Spicewood Dr ... 75115
Spindle Top Dr ... 75115
Spinner Cir & Rd ... 75115
Springbrook Cir & Dr ... 75115
Spruce Wood Cir ... 75115
Squirebrook Dr ... 75115
Stain Glass Dr ... 75115
Stardust Ln ... 75115

Starling Dr ... 75115
Stellaway Dr ... 75115
Stinnett Pl ... 75115
Stone Ridge Ln ... 75115
Stonebridge Dr ... 75115
Stony Creek Dr ... 75115
Stray Horn Dr ... 75115
Streamside Dr ... 75115
Sumac Pl ... 75115
Summerside Dr ... 75115
Summertree Ln ... 75115
Summerwood Ct ... 75115
Summit Dr ... 75115
Sundown Ln ... 75115
Sunrise Dr ... 75115
Sunset Dr ... 75115
Surrey Dr ... 75115
Swan Dr ... 75115
Sweet Gum Dr ... 75115
Sycamore Dr ... 75115
Tanglerose Ct & Dr ... 75115
Tanglewood Dr ... 75115
Tara Dr & Pl ... 75115
Tate Dr ... 75115
Teakwood Ln ... 75115
Tealridge Ct & Ln ... 75115
Ten Mile Dr ... 75115
Tenderfoot Ln ... 75115
Teresa Ct & Dr ... 75115
Terrace Dr ... 75115
Tewa Trl ... 75115
The Meadows Pkwy ... 75115
Thistlewood Dr ... 75115
Thomasson Cir ... 75115
Thorntree Dr ... 75115
Thunderbrook Cir & Dr ... 75115
Timber Trl ... 75115
Timberlake Dr ... 75115
Timberline Ave & Ct ... 75115
Toucan Ct ... 75115
Townsend Ln ... 75115
Trail Ridge Dr ... 75115
Trailwood Dr ... 75115
Travis Dr ... 75115
Treeline Dr ... 75115
Trillium Ct & Ln ... 75115
Tumble Creek Dr ... 75115
Turnstone Ct ... 75115
Turtle Point Ct & Dr ... 75115
Twilight Cir ... 75115
Twin Creek Dr ... 75115
Twin Falls Dr ... 75115
Twin Hills Ln ... 75115
Twin Pines Dr ... 75115
S Uhl Rd ... 75115
Urban Dr ... 75115
Valley Ridge Dr ... 75115
Valleyglen Dr ... 75115
Vanilla Ct ... 75115
Venture Ln ... 75115
Versailles Ave ... 75115
Vickery Dr ... 75115
Village Green Dr ... 75115
Vince Ln ... 75115
Vincent Cemetery Rd ... 75115
Walker Way ... 75115
Walnut Hill Ln ... 75115
Wandering Way Trl ... 75115
Warbler Dr ... 75115
Warren Dr ... 75115
Water Crest Dr ... 75115
Waterford Ct ... 75115
Waterthrush Ct ... 75115
Waterview Ln ... 75115
Weatherstone Dr ... 75115
Wedgewood Dr ... 75115
Wellington Dr ... 75115
Wendy Ln ... 75115
Wentwood Ct & Dr ... 75115
Wesley Dr ... 75115
Westlake Dr ... 75115
N & S Westmoreland
Rd ... 75115
Wexford Ln ... 75115
Whetstone St ... 75115
Whispering Oaks Dr ... 75115

White Ash Rd ... 75115
White Cap Ct ... 75115
White Falls Dr ... 75115
White Stone Hill Dr ... 75115
Whitewater Trl ... 75115
Wildvine Dr ... 75115
Wildwood Ct & Dr ... 75115
Williams Ave & Cir ... 75115
Willow Cv ... 75115
Willow Wood Ln ... 75115
Willowsprings Ct ... 75115
Winding Brook Dr ... 75115
Windmill Cir & Trl ... 75115
Windmill Hill Ln ... 75115
Windwood Dr ... 75115
Windy Meadow Cir &
Dr ... 75115
Winning Colors Ct ... 75115
Winston Dr ... 75115
Winterbury Ct ... 75115
E & W Wintergreen Ct &
Rd ... 75115
Wisterglen Dr ... 75115
Wolf Dr & Trl ... 75115
Wolf Creek Dr ... 75115
Wood Gln ... 75115
Wood Hollow Way ... 75115
Woodbrook Dr ... 75115
Woodhaven Dr ... 75115
Woodland Hills Ave ... 75115
Woodlawn Dr ... 75115
Woodridge Cir, Ct &
Dr ... 75115
Worley Glen Ave ... 75115
Worthington Dr ... 75115
Wren St ... 75115
Wylie Creek Dr & Pl ... 75115
Wyndmere Ct & Dr ... 75115
Yardley Pl ... 75115
Yellowbird Ct ... 75115
York Dr ... 75115
N & S Young Blvd ... 75115

NUMBERED STREETS

All Street Addresses ... 75115

DUNCANVILLE TX

General Delivery ... 75138

POST OFFICE BOXES MAIN OFFICE STATIONS AND BRANCHES

Box No.s
All PO Boxes ... 75138

NAMED STREETS

Aaron Pl ... 75137
Acton Ave & Ct ... 75137
Adams Dr ... 75137
Alameda Ave ... 75137
N Alexander Ave ... 75116
S Alexander Ave
100-500 ... 75116
502-598 ... 75116
600-1499 ... 75137
S Alexander Ct ... 75116
Allen Ave ... 75137
Amelia St ... 75137
Anzio Dr ... 75116
Apollo Ave
300-399 ... 75116
700-999 ... 75137
Ascot Dr ... 75116
Aspen Dr ... 75116
Astaire Ave ... 75137
Athenia Way ... 75137
Austin Stone Dr ... 75137

Avenue C
200-699 ... 75116
Avenue C
800-1099 ... 75137
Avenue Of The Stars ... 75137
Azalea Ln ... 75137
Barrymore Ln ... 75137
Bayless Ln ... 75116
Beaver Creek Cir, Ct, Dr
& Pl ... 75137
Bella St ... 75137
Belmont Pl ... 75116
Big Stone Gap Rd ... 75137
Birdwood Cir & Dr ... 75137
Blanco St ... 75137
Blossom Dr ... 75137
Blueberry Dr ... 75116
Blueridge Dr ... 75137
Bogart Cir ... 75137
Bow Creek Ct & Dr ... 75116
Bradley Dr ... 75137
Braewood Pl ... 75137
Briar Hill Cir ... 75137
Briarmeade Dr ... 75137
Brooke Ct ... 75137
Brooks Dr ... 75116
Brookside Dr ... 75137
Brookstone Ln ... 75137
Brookwood Dr ... 75116
Cactus Dr ... 75137
Calder Ave ... 75116
Cambridge Dr ... 75137
Camellia Cir & Dr ... 75137
E & W Camp Wisdom
Rd ... 75116
Candlelight Ave ... 75137
N & S Capri Dr ... 75116
Caravan Trl ... 75116
Carder St ... 75116
Cardinal Creek Dr ... 75137
Carr Ln ... 75116
Carriage Way ... 75137
Carroll Ave ... 75137
N & S Casa Grande Cir
& Pl ... 75116
Cavan Rd ... 75116
Cedar St ... 75137
Cedar Creek Dr ... 75137
Cedar Hill Pl & Rd ... 75137
N Cedar Ridge Dr ... 75116
S Cedar Ridge Dr
100-399 ... 75116
600-800 ... 75137
711-711 ... 75138
801-1299 ... 75137
802-1298 ... 75137
Cedar Run Dr ... 75137
E & W Center Cir &
St ... 75116
Center Ridge Dr ... 75116
Charlotte St ... 75137
Chatfield Dr ... 75116
E & W Cherry Cir, Ct &
St ... 75116
Churchill Downs ... 75116
Circle Dr ... 75137
N Clark Rd ... 75116
S Clark Rd
100-598 ... 75116
600-1798 ... 75137
Cliffcrest Dr ... 75137
Cliffwood Cir, Ct & Dr ... 75116
Clint Smith Dr ... 75137
N Cockrell Hill Rd ... 75116
S Cockrell Hill Rd
101-599 ... 75116
600-2199 ... 75137
Colbert Ln ... 75137
Commons Gate St ... 75137
Corinthian Pl ... 75137
Coronado Ln ... 75137
Country Bnd ... 75137
Countryside Ct ... 75137
Coventry Ln ... 75137
Crankshaft Dr ... 75116
Creekhaven Dr ... 75137

Creekwood Ct 75116
Crescent Ln 75137
Crest Lane Dr 75137
Crestdell Dr 75137
Crestside Dr 75137
Cripple Creek Dr 75116
Crosspointe St 75137
Crystal Springs Dr 75137
Cypress St 75137
Dalleri Dr 75137
E & W Danieldale Rd 75137
W Daniels St 75116
E & W Davis Cir & St 75116
Dawn Dr 75137
Dawson Dr 75116
De Haviland Ave 75137
Dean Ct 75137
Deer Ridge Dr 75137
Del Lenora Dr 75116
Delphi Dr 75137
Dove Creek Dr 75116
Dow Ross Blvd 75116
Driftwood Dr 75116
Dula Cir 75116
N Duncanville Rd 75116
Eaton Cir 75137
Echo Dr 75116
Eisenhower Dr 75137
Elm Ln 75137
Elsmere Dr 75116
Emporia Ln 75116
Equestrian Trl 75116
Escuela Dr 75116
Explorer St 75137
E & W Fain St 75116
Fairbanks Cir 75137
Fairlawn Dr 75116
E & W Fairmeadows Cir & Dr 75116
Fairway Cir & Dr 75137
Fairwood Pl 75116
Falling Leaves Dr 75116
Fawn Ridge Dr 75137
Ferguson Ln 75137
Flamingo Way 75116
Florence Dr 75116
N & S Forest Cir, Ct & Ln 75116
Fouts Ave 75116
Frank Keasler Blvd 75116
E & W Freeman St 75116
Gable Ave 75137
Gardenia Cir 75137
Gaynor Ave 75137
Gemini Ave 75137
Genoa Dr 75116
Gentle Meadow Ln 75137
Georgeland Dr 75116
Godwin Ln 75116
Golden Meadows Ln 75116
Goldman St 75116
Granada Dr 75116
Grant Ct 75137
Grape St 75137
Graystone Pl 75137
Green Hills Ct & Rd 75137
Green Leaf Ln 75137
Green Ridge Dr 75137
Green Rock Dr 75137
Green Terrace Ln 75137
Green Tree Ct, Ln & Pl 75137
Green Valley Ln & Pl 75137
Greenbriar Ln 75137
Greenstone Cir 75116
Greenstone Ct 75116
N Greenstone Ln 75116
S Greenstone Ln
100-399 75116
600-1699 75137
Greenway Cir, Ct & Dr 75137
Greenwood Pl 75137
Halo St 75137
Halsey Dr 75137
Hamilton St 75116
Harlow Ln 75137

Harman St 75116
Harrington Cir & Dr 75116
N & S Hastings St 75116
Hayworth Ave 75137
Heather Glen St 75137
Heather Run Dr 75137
Heather Wood Dr 75137
Hepburn Ln 75137
Hickory Dr 75137
High Ridge Dr 75137
Highgate Dr 75137
Highland Dr 75137
Highmore Dr 75116
E & W Highway 67 75137
Hill City Dr 75116
Hill Terrace Dr 75116
Hillcroft Cir & Dr 75137
Hitchcock Cir 75137
Holliday Ln 75116
Holly Ln 75116
Hopkins Ave 75116
Horizon St 75137
N & S Horne St 75116
Hummingbird Ln 75137
Huntington Dr 75137
Hustead St 75116
Hyde Park Pl 75137
Ida Vista Ct 75116
E Interstate 20 75116
James Collins Blvd 75116
Jellison Blvd 75116
Jewell Dr 75137
Joe Wilson Rd 75137
Joes Dr 75116
Johnson Dr 75116
Jungle Dr 75116
Katherine Ct 75137
Kelly Ct 75137
Kennedy Ave 75116
Kensington Dr 75137
Keywe Pl 75116
Kinestow Dr 75116
Kings Ct 75137
La Plata Dr 75116
Lady Ln 75116
Lakeside Dr 75116
Lakeview Cir 75137
Lamar Ave 75137
Lansdale Dr 75116
Larry Dr 75137
Lazy River Cir & Dr 75116
Leigh Ln 75137
Lime Leaf Ct & Ln 75137
Limetree Ln 75137
S Lincoln Dr 75137
Linda Ln 75137
Link Dr 75116
Linkcrest Cir, Ct & Dr 75137
Linkhaven Dr 75137
Linklea Dr 75137
Linkmeadow Dr 75137
Linkview Dr 75137
Linkwood Dr 75137
E Little St 75137
Little Creek Dr 75116
Lloyd Dr 75137
Lodema Ln 75116
Lombard Ln 75137
London Ln 75116
Longworth Blvd 75137
Los Altos Ln 75116
Lou Ave 75137
Louise Ave 75137
Madison Ct 75137
Madrid Dr 75116
E & W Magnolia Ln 75137
N Main St 75116
S Main St
100-699 75116
700-2199 75137
2201-2599 75137
Main Park Ln 75137
Mansfield Ln 75137
Maple Leaf Dr 75137
Markwood Dr 75116
Marshall Dr 75137

Martin Luther Cir 75116
Mcarthur Dr 75137
Mccall Dr 75137
Mcmurry Ave 75116
Meadow Grn 75137
Meadow Crest Ln 75137
Meadow Ridge Dr 75137
Meadow Run Cir & Dr 75137
Meadowbrooke Cir, Ct, Dr & Pl 75137
Meadowcreek Dr 75137
Meadowglen Dr 75137
Meadowlark Ln 75137
Meadowwood Dr 75137
Melody Ln 75116
Memory Ln 75116
Mercury Ave 75137
Merribrook Trl 75116
N & S Merrill Ave 75116
Michaels Dr 75116
Middale Rd 75116
Middle Run 75137
Middle Run Ct & Pl 75137
Minuet Ln 75116
Mission St 75137
Misty Ln 75116
Mizell St 75116
Mockingbird Ct 75137
E & W Mona Ave 75137
Monroe Dr 75137
Moore St 75116
Morning Dove Dr 75137
Moss Hill Ln 75137
E & W Nance St 75116
Naples Dr 75116
Natalie Ln 75137
Nature Dr 75116
Nimitz Dr 75116
Nob Hill Cir & Dr 75137
Oak Leaf Dr 75137
Oak Ridge Dr 75137
Oak Run Dr 75137
Oak Village Cir 75137
Oakwood Dr 75137
Old Country Rd 75137
Oleander St 75137
Olson Pl 75137
Olympia Dr 75137
Omaha Ln 75116
E & W Orange St 75116
Orchard Ct 75137
Oriole Blvd & Cir 75116
Oxford Dr 75137
Palm Ave 75137
Panther Dr 75116
Park Ln 75116
Parkview Ct & Dr 75137
Parkwood Cir 75137
Partridge Run Dr 75137
Patton St 75116
N Peach St 75116
S Peach St
100-699 75116
700-1099 75137
Peacock Cir 75137
Pebble Rd 75116
Pebble Springs Pl 75137
Pecan Ln 75137
Pelt Pl 75116
Penn Springs Dr 75137
Pepperidge Dr 75137
Plateau Dr 75116
Plaza Ln 75116
Polo Ct 75116
Power Dr 75116
Prairie Smoke Ln 75137
Quail Run 75116
E & W Red Bird Ln 75116
Red Bud Dr 75137
Red Clover Ln 75137
Red Sage Ln 75137
Redman Ln 75137
Rew Ave 75137
W Ridge Dr 75116
Ridge Crest Dr 75116
Ridge Rock Ln 75116

Rita Ln 75116
Robin Hill Ln 75137
Rock Canyon Dr 75137
Rock Rose Dr 75137
Rock Springs Rd 75137
Rockaway Dr 75116
Rockcrest Dr 75137
Rocky Creek Dr 75137
Rogers Ln 75137
Rolling Ridge Ln 75116
Roma Dr 75116
Roundtop Blvd 75116
Royal Ave 75116
N & S Royal Oak Dr 75116
Sagebrush Trl 75137
San Juan Dr 75116
San Miguel Dr 75137
San Pedro Ave 75137
Sanders Dr 75137
Santa Fe Trl
100-699 75116
700-1699 75137
Scio Dr 75116
Seabrook Dr 75137
Shady Trail Dr 75137
Shady Tree Pl 75137
Shamrock Dr 75137
Shannon Dr 75137
Sharon Dr 75137
W Shaw St 75137
Shelly Ct 75116
Shenandoah Ct 75137
Sheree Ln 75116
Sherrill Blvd 75116
Shorewood Dr 75116
Sierra Blanca Dr 75116
Silver Creek Dr & Pl 75137
Sims St 75137
Ski Dr 75116
Skyline Dr 75116
W Sliger Dr 75137
Smith St 75116
Softwood Cir & Dr 75137
Sorrel St 75137
Southloop Dr 75137
Southwood Cir, Ct & Dr 75137
Space Way Dr 75137
Sparta Dr 75137
Spindletop Dr 75137
Spring Lake Dr 75137
Springwood Ln 75137
Stanwyck Ave 75137
Starnes Dr 75116
Statler Dr 75116
Steeplechase Trl 75116
Steger Dr 75116
Stewart Ave 75137
Stratford Ln 75137
Summit Ridge Dr 75116
Sun Valley Dr 75116
Sunrise Ln 75137
Sunset Ln 75137
Sunset Village Dr 75137
Swan Ridge Dr & Pl 75137
Tampico Cir 75116
Tanco Ln 75116
Tanglewood Dr 75116
Taylor Ct 75137
Teakwood Dr 75137
Ten Mile Ln 75137
Tenery Ln 75116
Thistle Green Ln 75137
Thoroughbred Hls 75116
Thrush Ave 75116
Timber Trl 75137
Timberline Cir, Ct & Dr 75137
Timothy Trl 75137
Tower Crest Dr 75116
Towne Pl 75116
Tracy Ave & Ct 75137
Trail Ridge Dr 75116
Truman Ct 75137
Tucson Dr 75116
Tyler Ct 75137

Upland Ln 75116
Vail Dr 75116
Valley Ln 75137
Valley Hill Rd 75137
Valleyview Ln 75137
Van Rowe Ave 75116
N & S Venice Cir & Dr 75116
Villa Creek Dr 75137
E & W Vinyard Rd 75137
Walnut Cir & St 75116
Watwick Ln 75137
Wayne Ave 75137
Wellington Dr 75137
Wembley Cir 75137
Wesley Ln 75137
West Ln 75116
Westminister Ln 75137
Westwood Ct & Sq 75116
E & W Wheatland Rd 75116
Whippoorwill Plz 75137
Whispering Hills Dr 75137
Whitecliff Dr 75137
Wicken Ln 75137
Wildwood Dr 75137
Willow Cir 75116
Willow Run Cir & Dr 75137
Willowbrook Cir & Dr 75116
Willowwood Pl 75116
Wilson Ct 75137
Wind Ridge Cir & Dr 75137
Wind River Dr 75116
Winding Trl 75116
Windsor Dr 75137
E & W Wintergreen Rd 75137
Wishing Star Dr 75116
Woburn Ln 75137
Wood Crk 75137
Wood Ln 75116
Woodacre Cir 75116
Woodhaven Blvd 75116
Woodridge Pl 75116
Wren Ave & Cir 75116
Wyndham Dr 75137

EAGLE PASS TX

General Delivery 78852

POST OFFICE BOXES MAIN OFFICE STATIONS AND BRANCHES

Box No.s
All PO Boxes 78853

HIGHWAY CONTRACTS

01, 02, 03, 04, 05, 06, 08 78852

NAMED STREETS

A E Stock Dr 78852
Abeto Cv 78852
Academy Rd 78852
Acapulco Dr 78852
N & S Adams Cir & St 78852
Adolphus St 78852
Agarita Dr 78852
Agua Dulce Rd 78852
Aim St 78852
Aj Dr 78852
Alamo St 78852
Alamosa St 78852
Alazan Dr 78852
Albores 78852
Alegre 78852
Alexander Dr 78852
Alice Dr 78852

Alvin 78852
Amanda 78852
Amy Dr & St 78852
Ana Karen Ln 78852
Anacua St 78852
Anezo Dr 78852
Angie Dr 78852
Antelope Dr 78852
Antonio M Garcia St 78852
Apple Wood St 78852
Arce Ln 78852
Argelia St 78852
Argos Cir 78852
Arlington St 78852
Armando Cir 78852
Arnulfo Diaz St 78852
Arrow Point Blvd 78852
Arturo Dr 78852
Austin St 78852
Avenida Linares 78852
Avenue A 78852
Avenue B 78852
Avenue C 78852
Avenue D 78852
Aztec Mall Dr 78852
B Alonzo Cir 78852
Balcones Blvd 78852
Baltica 78852
Barbara 78852
Barranca 78852
Barrera St 78852
Basswood St 78852
Bayo Dr 78852
Becker St 78852
Becos St 78852
Bella Vista Cir 78852
Benavides Rd 78852
Beverly Hills Blvd 78852
Bianca 78852
N Bibb Ave 78852
S Bibb Ave
200-455 78852
410-410 78853
456-798 78852
457-799 78852
Big Lake Blvd 78852
Bishop Gracida Dr 78852
Bison Dr 78852
Black Tail Dr 78852
Blanca Cir 78852
N Blanco St 78852
Blesse St 78852
Bliss St 78852
Blue Cloud 78852
Bob Rogers Dr 78852
Boehmer Ave 78852
Bonaza Hts 78852
Bonita Cir 78852
Bonnet Ave 78852
Borjon Dr 78852
Boulder Ridge Dr 78852
Bowles St 78852
Branch Cir 78852
N & S Brazos St 78852
Brown St 78852
Bryan St 78852
Buck Dr 78852
Buckley Ave 78852
Buena Vista Dr 78852
Bullis 78852
Butler Rd 78852
Caida Del Sol Ave 78852
Caleta Cir 78852
Calle Alegre 78852
Calle Carr 78852
Calle Coahuila 78852
Calle De Los Santos 78852
Calle Jalisco 78852
Calle Linda Vis 78852
Calle Loma 78852
Calle Oaxaca 78852
Calle Potro 78852
Calle Santos 78852
Calle Teresa 78852
Callejon Teran 78852
Camarinos Dr 78852

Camino Del Sol 78852
Canal Dr 78852
Candelario Montalvo 78852
Cantera Cir 78852
Caoba St 78852
Caribou Trl 78852
Carla Cir & Dr 78852
Carleton Dr 78852
Carlotta 78852
Carolina St 78852
Carthage Ave 78852
Cary Rd 78852
Casales Rd 78852
Cathleen 78852
Catrina 78852
Cecilio St 78852
Cedar Dr 78852
Cedro 78852
Cendero St 78852
Ceniza Dr 78852
Cenizo Hts & Trl 78852
Center St 78852
Cerna Cir 78852
Cesar Chavez Cir 78852
N & S Ceylon St 78852
Champion Cir 78852
Chapala Dr 78852
Chaparral Cres & Run 78852
Chapote Loop 78852
Chapultepec Dr 78852
Charlie Cir 78852
Chavarria Rd 78852
Chelo St 78852
Chick Kazen 78852
Chico St 78852
Chilo St 78852
Chittim Trl 78852
Christian 78852
Christina Pkwy 78852
Chucho Dr 78852
Chuck Wagon Rd 78852
Chula St 78852
Chula Vista Rd 78852
Church St 78852
Cindy Marie 78852
Cipres Dr 78852
Clarkson Dr 78852
Clavel St 78852
Cody Dr 78852
Cole St 78852
Colorado St 78852
Columbine Curv 78852
Columbino Dr 78852
N & S Comal St 78852
Commercial St 78852
Commissary Ave 78852
Concho St 78852
N & S Converse St 78852
Coolidge St 78852
Cortinas Cir 78852
Cory Cir 78852
Costa Rica Dr 78852
Cotorra 78852
County Road 207 78852
County Road 209 78852
County Road 215 78852
County Road 223 78852
County Road 226 78852
County Road 227 78852
County Road 229 78852
County Road 237 78852
County Road 243 78852
County Road 251 78852
N County Road 253 78852
County Road 298 78852
County Road 301 78852
County Road 305 78852
County Road 307 78852
County Road 501 78852
County Road 503 78852
County Road 505 78852
County Road 509 78852
County Road 515 78852
County Road 519 78852
County Road 521 78852
County Road 529 78852

County Road 531 78852
Cox St 78852
Coyunda 78852
Crane St 78852
Crescent Blvd 78852
Crestwind Cir 78852
Cristin Dr 78852
Crockett St 78852
Cross Creek Dr 78852
Crown Hl, Pt & Way 78852
Crown Ridge Blvd 78852
Crown View Dr 78852
Cypress 78852
Daisy Diaz Dr 78852
Dalia St 78852
Dance Cir 78852
Darrel Dr 78852
De Bona Dr 78852
De Los Santos 78852
Deer Run Blvd 78852
Del Rio Blvd 78852
Democracy 78852
Desirable St 78852
Desolation Dr & Row 78852
Diaz St 78852
Distribution Dr 78852
Doe Ln 78852
Dolch Dr 78852
Don Martin Dr 78852
Dr Gates Rd 78852
Dr Mittal Dr 78852
Dub Dr 78852
Duffy St 78852
Dupui Cir 78852
Eagle 78852
Eagle Nest Rd 78852
Eagle Point Rd 78852
Eagle View Rd 78852
Ebano St 78852
Edna Dr 78852
Eidson Rd 78852
El Indio Hwy 78852
El Venado Dr 78852
Elaine Cir 78852
Elia Santos 78852
Elizabeth Cir 78852
Elizondo Rd 78852
Elk Ln 78852
Ella 78852
Elm Crk 78852
Emilio Cir 78852
Encinal Dr 78852
Encino Park & St 78852
Encuentro 78852
End St 78852
Epting Cir 78852
Erika St 78852
Erline Dr 78852
Escondido 78852
Esquenazi Dr 78852
Evans Ave 78852
Fairhaven Dr 78852
Falcon Blvd 78852
Fallow Ln 78852
Fawn Dr 78852
Ferrer Rd 78852
Ferry St 78852
Fig 78852
Fletcher Rd 78852
Florence St 78852
Flores Dr 78852
Flowers St 78852
Fm 1021 78852
Fm 1588 78852
Fm 1589 78852
Fm 1907 78852
Fm 2030 78852
Foothills St 78852
Ford St 78852
N Foster Maldonado Blvd 78852
Fox Pl, Run & St 78852
Fox Cove Dr 78852
Foxborough 78852
Foxfire 78852
Frances Gates Loop 78852

Francis St 78852
Frente 78852
Fresno Dr, Loop & St 78852
Frick St 78852
Friendly Rd 78852
Frontier Rd 78852
Garcia St 78852
E Garrison St 78852
Garza St 78852
Gazelle Dr 78852
Gennter Dr 78852
George St 78852
Ghost Rider Dr 78852
Ginebra 78852
Glen Haven Dr 78852
Golfcrest Dr 78852
Gomez St 78852
Grand Haven Dr 78852
Grand Park Ln 78852
Grangeno Dr 78852
Grass Valley Rd 78852
Graytex 78852
Greasewood Dr 78852
Guadalajara Dr 78852
Guisseppi 78852
Hacienditas Rd 78852
Harding St 78852
Harold Ave 78852
Hawk St 78852
Hc 9 Box 78852
Henry Bonilla 78852
Heritage Farms Dr 78852
Herring St 78852
Hewatt Cir 78852
Hicks Cv 78852
Hidalgo St 78852
High St 78852
High Noon 78852
Hillcrest Blvd 78852
Hillside Cir 78852
Hilltop Cir 78852
Hoover St 78852
Hopedale Rd 78852
Horse Shoe Cir 78852
Ibarra Rd 78852
Imelda Dr 78852
Industrial Blvd 78852
Iris St 78852
Irma Morales 78852
J M Wheeler St 78852
J R Rodriguez Cir 78852
Jacaranda Dr 78852
Jalisco Cir 78852
Jane St 78852
Jardines Verdes Dr 78852
Jasmine Dr 78852
Jefferson St 78852
Jodobo Dr 78852
Jose Dr 78852
Juan Cir 78852
Juanita Dr 78852
Juarez St 78852
Karen Dr 78852
Katy Dr 78852
Kayleigh St 78852
Keli Cir 78852
Kelso Dr 78852
Kennor Dr 78852
Kickapoo St 78852
Kid Cir 78852
Kifuri St 78852
Kilowatt Dr 78852
King Arthur St 78852
King David St 78852
Kioske Ave 78852
Kiriaka Dr 78852
Kurt Bluedog 78852
Kypuros Rd 78852
La Grande 78852
La Herradura Rd 78852
La Jolla St 78852
La Loma St 78852
La Paloma Dr 78852
Lago Vis 78852
Lago Vista Dr 78852
Lagos Dr 78852

Laguna Cir 78852
Lakonia Dr 78852
Lance Dr 78852
Lancon Cir 78852
Landin Cir 78852
Laredo St 78852
Lariat 78852
Larisa Cir 78852
Las Brisas Dr 78852
Las Cimas Dr 78852
Las Haciendas St 78852
Las Moras 78852
Las Quintas Blvd 78852
Latigo 78852
Laura St 78852
Lazar Dr 78852
Lehmann St 78852
Lehmann Ranch Rd 78852
Leona St 78852
Leonel St 78852
Lety St 78852
Lewis St 78852
Lila Dr 78852
Linda Cir 78852
Linda Vista Rd 78852
Lindburgh Cir & St 78852
Lisa Blvd 78852
Lizette Cir 78852
Loma Linda 78852
Long Horn Rd 78852
Lorilee Dr 78852
Los Angeles Dr 78852
Los Guajillos Rd 78852
Los Sauces Rd 78852
Lucino Loop 78852
Lucky Eagle Dr & Trl 78852
Luis St 78852
Macarena 78852
Mack Cir 78852
Madison St 78852
Madrono Dr 78852
Magnum Dr 78852
E & W Main St 78852
Malibu Blvd 78852
Maple St 78852
Marble St 78852
Marco Dr 78852
Margarita Dr 78852
Mari Dr 78852
Maria Del Refugio Dr 78852
Maria Esther Dr 78852
Mariana St 78852
Marion Dr 78852
Mariza St 78852
Mark Anthony 78852
Marquez Dr 78852
Marselles Dr 78852
Mary Dr 78852
Mathiwos Dr 78852
Maverick Dr 78852
Maverick Industrial Park Rd 78852
Mayan Cir 78852
Mazatlan Cir 78852
Mazza Dr 78852
Meadow Briar Ln 78852
Meadow Point Dr 78852
Meadow Wood Dr 78852
Medina St 78852
Megan St 78852
Mela Garcia Rd 78852
Mello Dr 78852
Memo Robinson Rd 78852
Memorial Dr 78852
Memorial Jr High Dr 78852
Merida 78852
Mesa Dr 78852
Mesquite St 78852
Meyers St 78852
Michael Dr 78852
Michelle Dr 78852
Michigan Dr 78852
Mikulinski 78852
Minerva Dr 78852
Mirasol Dr 78852
Misty Hollow Dr 78852

Misty Willow Dr 78852
Mochelle Dr 78852
Molina Loop 78852
Monarch Path 78852
Mondragon Blvd 78852
Monica Rhia Dr 78852
N & S Monroe St 78852
Montana St 78852
Montemayor St 78852
Monterrey Cir 78852
Moonlight Trl 78852
Mora 78852
Morales Cir & St 78852
Morning Star Dr 78852
Nacimiento Ln 78852
Nancy Dr 78852
Nava 78852
Nelly Mae Glass Dr 78852
Neviesca 78852
Nicolas 78852
Nogal St 78852
Nopal St 78852
North St 78852
Nueces St 78852
Oak Cir 78852
Oak Breeze 78852
Oak Manor Dr 78852
Ocampo 78852
October 28th 78852
Old Pioneer Rd 78852
Olive St 78852
Olmos Cir 78852
Olmos Park Cir 78852
Ontario Dr 78852
Paco St 78852
Paisano Dr 78852
Palma St 78852
Palo Blanco Rd 78852
Paloma Pl 78852
Parks St 78852
Paseo Dr 78852
Paseo De Encinal Dr 78852
Paso Caballero 78852
Paso Del Rio Blvd 78852
Patricio Cir 78852
Patzcuaro Dr 78852
Peach St 78852
Pecan Dr 78852
Pecos St 78852
Pershing Cir 78852
N & S Pierce St 78852
Pino St 78852
Pirul 78852
Pleasant 78852
N Point 78852
Point Loma Dr 78852
E Potro 78852
Power Plant Rd 78852
Prairie View Dr 78852
Private Road 215 78852
Private Road 221 78852
Private Road 260 78852
Private Road 261 78852
Private Road 302 78852
Progreso 78852
Pueblo N 78852
Pueblo Nuevo Dr 78852
Quail Valley Rd 78852
Quarry St 78852
Rafael St 78852
Rainbow Cir 78852
Raintree Dr 78852
Ralph Dr 78852
Ramirez Rd 78852
Ramos Loop 78852
Ranchitos Rd 78852
Randall Cir 78852
Rebecca Ln 78852
Reindeer Dr 78852
Remington Dr 78852
Renee Dr 78852
Resolution Run 78852
Richard Ln 78852
Richland Hills Blvd 78852
Ricks Dr 78852
Ricky Dr 78852

Riddle St 78852
Rio Cir, Dr, Rd & Vis 78852
E Rio Grande St 78852
Riojas Rd 78852
Rios Ave 78852
Riskind Cir 78852
Ritchie Rd 78852
Rivera Dr 78852
Riverpark Rd 78852
Riverside Dr 78852
Robert Cir 78852
Roberto Manuel Cir 78852
Robins Row 78852
Robles 78852
Rock Hill Dr 78852
Rodriguez St 78852
Roman Cir 78852
Romel St 78852
Romemarie Dr 78852
Roosevelt St 78852
Rosa 78852
Rose Mary 78852
Rosewood 78852
Rosita Gdns 78852
Rosita Valley Rd 78852
Roswell St 78852
Round Rock Dr 78852
Royal Bend Dr 78852
Royal Club Dr 78852
Royal Crown Dr 78852
Royal Haven Dr 78852
Royal Park Dr 78852
Royal Point Dr 78852
Royal Ridge Dr 78852
Ruela Dr 78852
Ryan St 78852
Sahara Dr 78852
Saint Anne 78852
Salinas St 78852
Salonika Dr 78852
Saltillo Cir 78852
San Felipe 78852
San Juan Dr 78852
N & S San Marcos St 78852
San Miguel 78852
Sanchez Ave 78852
Sandalo St 78852
Santa Ana Cir 78852
Santa Fe Trl 78852
Santos Cir 78852
Sauz Dr & St 78852
School Cir 78852
Seadind St 78852
Seco Rd 78852
Seymour St 78852
Siesta Dr 78852
Siete Lomas St 78852
Silver Oak Cir 78852
Silver Spur Cir 78852
Simpson Dr 78852
Sioux Cir 78852
Siwel St 78852
Six Shooter Rd 78852
Sosa Rd 78852
Southwood Dr 78852
Spicewood Dr 78852
Spies Dr 78852
Spike Hill Dr 78852
Spirit Ln 78852
Spring View Dr 78852
Springwood Dr 78852
Stafford Dr 78852
Stag Ln 78852
Stanley Dr 78852
Stephanie Dr 78852
Steven Dr 78852
Stone Ln, St, Trl & Way 78852
Stone Hedge 78852
Stroman Dr 78852
Sueno Cir 78852
Sun Valley Trl 78852
Suncrest Dr 78852
Sunrise Loop & Run 78852
Sunset Loop & Rd 78852
Superior Dr 78852

Surita Cir 78852
Susan Cir 78852
T Curi 78852
Tabachin Dr 78852
Taft St 78852
Tahoe Dr 78852
Tampico Cir 78852
Tanglewood Dr 78852
Tehuacan Dr 78852
Tesoro Loop 78852
S Texas Dr 78852
Texas Highway 131 78852
Texcoco Dr 78852
Thompson Dr & Rd 78852
Timber Valley Dr 78852
Timberwood Dr 78852
Tina Dr 78852
Tita St 78852
Toni 78852
Town Square Blvd 78852
E Travis St 78852
Trey 78852
N Trinity St 78852
Tron Ln 78852
Turkey Trl 78852
Turnpike 78852
N Us Highway 277 78852
Us Highway 57 78852
Valencia Dr 78852
Valerie Dr 78852
Valley View Rd 78852
Van Green St 78852
Venado Dr 78852
Venado Grande Rd 78852
Venesa Dr 78852
Vera Cruz Cir 78852
N & S Veterans Blvd 78852
Victoriano Ave 78852
Vid Cir 78852
Vienna 78852
View Dr 78852
Villa Cir 78852
Villareal 78852
Vista Dr 78852
Vista Bonita Dr 78852
Vista Hermosa Dr 78852
Wagon Wheel Cir & Rd 78852
Walkabout Cir 78852
Washington St 78852
Webster St 78852
Wedgefield Dr 78852
Westlake Blvd 78852
Weyrich Rd 78852
Whitetail 78852
Wichita Cir 78852
Wild Oak Dr 78852
Wild Turkey Dr 78852
Wildwood Dr 78852
Williams St 78852
Willie St 78852
Willobrae Dr 78852
Willow Rdg & Trl 78852
Willow Creek Dr 78852
Willow Garden Dr 78852
Willow Wood Dr 78852
Wilson St 78852
Winchester Rd 78852
Winding Ridge Cir & Dr 78852
Windmill 78852
Wipff Rd 78852
Woodway 78852
Yoblanda Dr 78852
Yolanda Blvd 78852
Yolis 78852
Yota Dr 78852
Ysaiz Dr 78852
Yucca Cir & Loop 78852
Yvonne Cir 78852
Zacatecas Dr 78852
Zamora Medical Cir 78852
Zaragoza St 78852
Zarate Cir 78852

NUMBERED STREETS

All Street Addresses 78852

EARLY TX

POST OFFICE BOXES MAIN OFFICE STATIONS AND BRANCHES

Box No.s
All PO Boxes 76803

RURAL ROUTES

02, 04, 06 76802

HIGHWAY CONTRACTS

31 76802

NAMED STREETS

Abby Rd 76802
Airport Rd 76802
Allen Dr 76802
Autumn Dr 76802
Bevrodon St 76802
Bluebonnet Dr 76802
Bluebonnet Hills Dr 76802
Bonnie Ave 76802
Briarcrest 76802
S Broadway St 76802
Broken Arrow St 76802
Buffalo Trl 76802
C C Woodson Rd 76802
Cactus Ln 76802
Campbell Trl 76802
Canal St 76802
Chaparral Dr 76802
Cooks Ln 76802
County Road 257 76802
County Road 258 76802
County Road 264 76802
County Road 267 76802
County Road 269 76802
County Road 270 76802
County Road 291 76802
County Road 292 76802
County Road 294 N 76802
County Road 308 76802
County Road 309 76802
N County Road 310 76802
County Road 312 76802
County Road 315 76802
County Road 317 76802
County Road 318 76802
County Road 319 76802
County Road 334 76802
County Road 336 76802
County Road 337 76802
County Road 338 76802
County Road 339 76802
County Road 340 76802
County Road 342 76802
County Road 344 76802
County Road 345 76802
County Road 346 76802
County Road 347 76802
County Road 348 76802
County Road 367 76802
County Road 369 76802
County Road 371 76802
County Road 372 76802
County Road 381 76802
County Road 382 76802
County Road 404 76802
County Road 405 E 76802
County Road 592 76802
County Road 613 76802
County Road 614 76802
County Road 615 76802
County Road 616 76802
County Road 618 76802
Crescent Dr
101-101 76802
101-101 76803

103-299 76802
Cudaville Ln 76802
Early Blvd 76802
Eastover Dr 76802
Eastwind Dr 76802
Fm 2126 76802
Fm 2525 76802
Fm 3100 76802
Fox Hollow Ln 76802
Gahanna Dr 76802
Garmon Dr 76802
Gobbler Ln 76802
Grandview Dr 76802
Green Oak Dr 76802
Greentree Cir 76802
Half Moon Cir 76802
E Hall Ct 76802
Hanson Ln 76802
Highway 183 N 76802
Highway 377 N 76802
Highway 84 E 76802
Hillcrest Rd 76802
Homewood Cir 76802
Horse Hollow Ln 76802
Hudson Ln 76802
E Industrial Blvd 76802
Inez St 76802
Jakewood Ln 76802
James Blvd 76802
Jenkins Spring Rd 76802
Johnathan Ln 76802
Keldenso 76802
Kim Ave 76802
Kings Court Dr 76802
Linda Ln 76802
Lisa Ln 76802
Lisa May Ln 76802
Live Oak Rd 76802
Longhorn Dr 76802
Lucas Dr 76802
Mark Allen Dr 76802
Mcdonald Dr 76802
Meadow Ln 76802
Meadow Glen Dr 76802
Mesquite Dr 76802
Mistletoe Ln 76802
Mitsy Ln 76802
Mockingbird Cir 76802
Monte Vista St 76802
Morning Dove Ln 76802
Morton Ln 76802
Northline Dr 76802
Nottingham Oaks Ln 76802
Oak Cir & St 76802
Oak View Cir 76802
Old Comanche Rd 76802
Old May Rd 76802
E Orchard Dr 76802
Park Dr 76802
Pine Dr 76802
Post 138 76802
Post 44 76802
Post 45 76802
Post 73 76802
Price Ln 76802
Rainbo Valley Dr 76802
Rainbow Dr 76802
Reagor Ln 76802
Richland Dr 76802
E River Oaks Rd 76802
Roberts Ln 76802
Rosedale Dr 76802
Ross Dr 76802
Salt Creek Dr 76802
Scarlet Dr 76802
Sendera Dr 76802
Sherry Ln 76802
Silent Timbers Ln 76802
Skyview Dr 76802
Sleepy Oaks 76802
Sonjia Dr 76802
Stage Coach Dr 76802
Sudderth Dr 76802
Sundown St 76802
Sunny Vale Dr 76802
Sunnydale Dr 76802
Sunrise St 76802
Sunset Cir & Dr 76802
Suttee Rd 76802
Terraha Dr 76802
Todd Ln 76802
Trailer Dr 76802
Turtle Creek Dr 76802
Valley Vista St 76802
Virginia Ave 76802
Wallace Trl 76802
West St 76802
Wheat 76802
Whispering Oaks Ln 76802
Wild Tree Ln 76802
Wildwood Dr 76802
Williams Dr 76802
Wills Way 76802
Windcrest Dr 76802
Woodway Ln 76802
Yucca Tree Cir 76802

EDINBURG TX

General Delivery 78539

POST OFFICE BOXES MAIN OFFICE STATIONS AND BRANCHES

Box No.s
All PO Boxes 78540

RURAL ROUTES

02, 19, 23, 30 78539
03, 04, 05, 07, 09, 13, 22, 25, 26, 29, 33, 38 78541
01, 06, 10, 11, 12, 14, 15, 16, 20, 24, 27, 31, 32, 34 78542

NAMED STREETS

Abbott Ave 78541
Abby St 78542
Abdon Cir 78541
Abel Dr 78542
N Abram Rd 78541
Acacia Ln 78541
Academy Ave 78541
Aceves St 78541
Acme Ln 78541
Aconcagua St 78541
Adam Lee Dr 78541
E Adams Ave & Ln 78542
Adriana 78542
Adriel Dr 78542
Adventure Ave 78542
Affirmed Ave 78539
Agate St 78541
Agave Ave & Cir 78542
Aggie Dr 78542
Agua Fina 78541
Aguajito St 78542
W Aguilar St 78541
Ake Ave 78539
N Alamo Est 78542
N Alamo Rd 78542
S Alamo Rd 78542
Alamo St 78541
Alanzo Ave 78542
Alazan St 78542
Albanian St 78542
E Alberta Rd
201-299 78539
501-797 78541
799-8299 78542
W Alberta Rd 78539
Alberto Rd 78542
Alcaniz Dr 78539
Alcatraz St 78542
Alexander Dumas Dr S & W 78542
Alice Ln 78541
Aliyah St 78542
Allen Dr 78539
Allison St 78539
Aloe Vera St 78541
Alquds Ave 78539
N & W Alteza Dr 78541
Alvacan St 78541
Alvarado St 78539
Alyanna St 78542
Amanda Dr 78542
Amando St 78539
Amapola St 78542
Ambassador St 78541
Amber Dr 78541
America St 78542
Amistad Cir 78539
Amos St 78542
Anacua Cir 78539
Anacua Dr 78541
Anaya St 78539
Ancira Ln 78539
Anderson Rd 78542
Andrea Ave 78539
Angela Ave 78542
Angie Ln 78541
Ann St 78539
E Ann St 78542
Annette Ave 78542
Ansley Dr 78542
Apache Dr 78542
Appaloosa St 78542
Apple St 78539
April Ave 78541
Aquamarine Ln 78541
Arain Ct 78541
Arcola Ln 78542
Argentine Ct & Rd 78542
Ariel Ln 78539
Arlina Dr 78542
Arlington 78541
N Armagoza Dr 78541
Art Y Jo Dr 78541
Arthur Ave 78542
Aruba Dr 78541
Ascot Dr 78542
Ash Ave 78542
Ash Cir 78539
Ashley Ave 78542
Asilmar St 78542
Aspen Dr 78542
Astaire Ave 78542
Atlanta 78541
Atlas Peak Ct 78541
Audrey Ln 78541
Aurora Rd 78541
Austin Blvd 78539
Autumn Chase Ave 78541
Avenida De Palmas Ave 78542
Avenida Dulce 78541
Axis Ln 78542
Ayssa Ct 78541
Azalea Ave 78542
Azul St 78542
Baccaret St 78542
Bahamas Dr 78541
Bail Bond Dr 78542
E & W Baker Dr 78539
Baltic Ave 78539
Bandera Ln 78542
Barb Mar Ln 78541
Barbara Ln 78542
Barcelona St 78542
Barreda Cir 78542
Barry Dr 78542
Barton Dr 78541
Bass Blvd 78542
Battey Rd 78539
Battista St 78542
Baylor Ave 78542
Baywood St 78541
Beatrice Ave 78539
Beaulieu Dr 78541
Beaumont Ave 78542
Becky Ln 78541
Beduino Ave 78542
Beech Ave 78542
Belinda St 78541
Bell 78541
Benchmark Dr 78542
Benites St 78539
Benito A Ramirez Rd 78542
Benji Cir 78541
N Bentsen Rd 78541
Berkely Dr 78539
Bermea Rd 78542
Bernal St 78539
Beth Dr 78542
Betty Blvd 78542
Beverly Hills Ln 78542
Bianca 78539
N Big 5 Rd 78541
Big Valley Cir 78541
Billy Hart Dr 78542
Biltmore Ave 78539
Birch St 78541
Bishop St 78539
Black Buck Dr 78542
Black Jack St 78542
Black Stone St 78542
Blackhawk St 78539
Blanco St 78542
Blaze Blvd 78539
Blood Stone St 78542
Blue Jay Ln 78542
Blue Ridge Dr 78539
Blue Stone St 78542
Bluebonnet Ave 78539
Boardwalk St 78539
Bogart Dr 78542
Bold Ruler Ave 78539
Bonanza Rd 78542
Bonnie Dr 78539
Borders Dr 78542
Borolo Dr 78541
Boston 78541
N Boston College Dr 78541
Bougainvillea Ave 78542
Bract St 78542
Brandi Ln 78539
Brandon St 78542
Brazil Ave 78542
Brenda 78541
Bridget St 78539
Brightwood Ave 78539
Bristol 78539
Bronze Ave 78542
Brooklyn St 78542
Brushline Rd 78542
Buck Dr 78542
Buck Fawn Dr 78542
Buckles Blvd 78542
Buenos Aires St 78539
Buffalo St 78542
Bunker Ave 78542
E Burns Rd 78542
Burr Dr 78542
S Business Highway 281 78539
Butkus Dr 78542
Butterfly 78539
Caballete St 78542
Caballo Ln 78542
Cabana St 78542
Cactus Ln 78541
Cain St 78542
Calahan Ave 78541
Caleb Ct 78541
Caledonia St 78542
Calichera Rd 78541
W Calle Cedro 78541
Calle Cuates 78542
Calle De Amanda 78542
Calle De America 78542
Calle De Los Aguacates 78542
Calle De Los Arboles 78542
Calle De Rebecca 78542
Calle Divina 78539
Calle Encantada 78539
Calle Nicky 78542
Calle Paris 78542
Calle Tranquilo 78539
Calma Est & St 78541
Cambridge Ln 78542
E Cameron Rd 78542
Campanario Cir 78539
Candlelight Ln 78541
Candy Ln 78539
E Cano St
100-198 78539
200-1499 78539
1600-1999 78542
W Cano St 78539
E Canton Rd
101-197 78539
199-1299 78539
1601-1997 78542
1999-8999 78542
W Canton Rd 78539
Cantu Dr 78542
Cantu Rd 78541
Cardinal Ave, Ct & Ln 78542
Carl St 78542
Carla Marie Way 78542
Carlos St 78541
W Carmen Ave 78541
Carmen Avila Rd 78542
Carnation St 78542
Carolina Ave 78541
Carpintero St 78542
Carranza Ave 78542
Carricero St 78542
Carson St 78539
Casa Vieja St 78539
Cascada Dr 78541
Cascade Ave 78539
Cassie 78541
Castille Ct 78539
Cavasos Rd 78541
Cavazos St 78539
Cedar Ave 78542
Cedar St 78539
Celebrity St 78542
Celeste Dr 78539
Cenizo St 78542
Center Point Dr 78539
Centurion Ave 78542
Cereza Ln 78542
Cerrito Linda Dr 78541
Cervantes Ave 78541
N & S Cesar Chavez Rd 78542
Cessna Ave 78542
Chachalaca St 78539
Champagne Dr 78542
E & W Champion St 78539
Chance Dr 78539
Chance Ln 78542
Chandler Cir 78542
Chapa Rd 78542
E Chapin St
100-700 78541
702-1098 78541
1300-6700 78542
6702-6798 78542
W Chapin St 78541
N Chapoto Cir 78541
Charlene St 78539
Charles Cir 78541
Charlie Pl 78542
Chateau St 78539
E & W Chavez St 78541
Chavez Private Dr 78542
Chayna Ave 78539
Chelsea Ln 78542
Cherokee Ave 78542
Cherry Ln 78542
Cherry St 78541
Chestnut Dr 78541
Chetumal Ave 78542
Cheyenne Ave 78542
Chicago 78541
Chinese St 78541
Chinook Dr 78542
Chippewa Ave 78541
Chola St 78541
Chris Cir 78539
N Christopher Ln 78542
Chukar Ln & St 78542
Churchill Ave 78539
Cibolo Dr 78542
Ciguena Dr 78541
Citation Ave 78539
Citation Dr 78542
Citation St 78542
Citrus Dr 78541
Citrus Ln 78542
Citrus Rd 78541
Clarissa Ct 78542
Claudia Ct 78541
Clay St 78542
Cleveland Ave 78542
Closner Blvd 78541
N Closner Blvd
100-198 78539
200-3699 78541
3701-4499 78541
S Closner Blvd 78539
S Closner Ln 78539
Clubhouse Dr 78542
Cochise Dr 78542
Coffee Mill Dr 78541
Colibri St 78542
Collin Dr 78542
E Colorado 78542
Colton St 78542
N Columbia Dr 78541
Comanche Dr 78542
Comedy Ln 78542
Comino St 78541
Concepcion St 78541
Conquest 78539
Continental St 78541
W Cooper St 78541
Copa De Oro St 78542
Coral Ct 78541
Cordoba Dr 78541
Corina Dr 78542
W Corina Ln 78541
Cornerstone Blvd 78539
Corrion Dr 78541
Cortez Dr 78542
Cory Acres 78541
Cosentin0 Dr 78541
Cosentino Dr 78541
Cottonwood Dr 78541
Country St 78541
Country Vw 78542
Country Club Dr N & S 78542
Country Colony St 78541
Country Meadows Dr 78541
County Road 4510 78541
County Road 4521 78541
County Road 4611 78541
County Road 4640 78541
Cove Ln 78542
Cowboy Dr 78542
Crawfish Dr 78542
Crestview Dr 78539
Crimson St 78541
Cristen Ave 78542
Cristobal Dr 78542
N Cross Ln 78541
Crown Cir 78539
Crown Point St 78541
Cruz Cir 78541
Crystal Falls Ave 78539
Cuco Ln 78539
Cuesta Del Sol 78542
Cuevas Rd 78542
Cullen St 78541
Cumbia St 78542
E Curry Rd 78541
E Curve Rd 78542
Cynthia St 78539
Cypress St 78542
Daisy Ave 78542
Dallas Ave 78542
Dalobo Blvd 78541
Damasco Ave 78541
Dan Dr 78539
Dana Dr 78542
Dantes Dr 78542
Danubio Dr 78539
Dartmouth Ave 78539
Date Palm St 78541
E David Dr 78539
E Davis Rd 78542
W Davis Rd 78541
Dawson St 78539
E De La Rosa St 78542
Debbie Dr 78542
Debby Ave 78542
Deborah St 78539
W Del Mar St 78541
Del Rio St 78542
Delia Dr 78542
Denise Cir 78541
N Denkhaus Blvd 78541
Denver 78541
N Depot Rd 78541
Desert Diamond St 78542
S Dfw Dr 78539
Diamond Ave 78542
Diana Dr 78542
Diedorf Dr 78542
Dillon Rd 78542
Dinastia Dorada 78542
Dios St 78542
Diplomat Dr 78542
Dishman St 78542
Doctors Dr 78539
Dolly St 78539
Don Hugo Dr 78542
N & S Doolittle Rd 78542
Dorris 78539
Dorthy St 78542
Dove Ave 78542
Dowitcher 78542
Dreamer Rd 78541
Drennan St 78541
Drury Dr 78542
Duberney Blvd 78541
Dude Ln 78542
Dulcenea St 78539
Dunes Rd 78542
Durango St 78542
Durmiendo St 78539
Dutchess St 78539
Eagle Landing Dr 78542
Earth Dr 78542
Easy St 78539
Eben Ezer Dr 78542
Ebony Ave 78542
W Ebony Dr 78539
E Ebony Ln 78539
Ebony St 78541
Ebro Dr 78539
Eclipse St 78542
Ector Dr 78542
Edgewood Ave 78541
N Edison Rd 78541
Edna Cir 78539
Edward Dr 78539
E Efrain St 78542
W Efrain St 78541
Eisenhower St 78541
El Bienestar Rd 78541
El Bosque Dr 78542
El Centro St 78542
E El Cibolo Rd
700-799 78542
800-899 78541
1200-1204 78542
1205-1299 78541
1206-1298 78542
W El Cibolo Rd 78541
El Dorado 78542
El Jardin Cir 78541
N El Mundo Dr 78541
El Paso St 78542
El Recreo Cir 78539
El Rucio Rd 78542
El Sauz St 78542
Eleanor St 78542

W Elisa Ln 78541
Elizabeth Ave 78541
E Elizabeth St 78542
Elizabeth Moya St 78542
Elizondo Dr 78542
Elk Ln 78539
Elk Run Ct & Dr 78541
Elma Cir 78542
Elsham Rd 78539
Empress St 78539
En Sueno 78539
Encanto Ave 78541
Encinitos Rd 78542
Encino Ct 78539
Encore Ave 78542
Enfield Rd 78539
English Ave 78541
Enron St 78542
Enterprise St 78541
Ernesto Dr 78539
Escondido Ln 78542
Esperanza Dr & St 78542
Esther Ave 78539
Eubanks Rd 78541
Eucalipto 78541
Eunice Garcia Dr 78541
Eva 78539
Eva Ave 78542
S Evangelina St 78539
Evaristo Ln 78541
Everest St 78541
Everhard St 78542
S Excalibur St 78539
N & S Expressway
281 78542
Ezekiel St 78542
Fabulous Dr 78542
Faccio St 78542
Fairway Dr 78539
W Faith Hill St 78541
Falcon Crest Ln 78542
Fallow Ln 78542
Fatima Ave 78541
Fawn Cir 78539
E Fay St
200-1499 78539
1601-1899 78542
W Fay St 78539
Fe Dr 78542
Featherie St 78542
Figueroa 78539
Flag Dr 78542
Flamingo Ave 78542
Fleur Ln 78542
Flipper Dr 78541
Floral Rd 78541
N Flores St 78541
Floresta St 78541
Fm 1017 78541
W Fm 1925 78541
Fm 2058 78541
E Fm 2812 78542
W Fm 2812 78541
Fm 3250 78541
Fm 490 78541
E Fm 490 78542
W Fm 490 78541
N & S Fm 493 78542
Fm 681 78541
Fontana St 78541
Forego Ave 78539
Forrest Dr 78539
Fort Brown Ave 78539
Fort Hood Ave 78539
Fortress St 78539
Fortune Ave 78542
N Foster Dr 78542
Fountain Plaza Blvd 78539
Fox Ln 78542
Fran Boyllan St 78541
Franchesca Ave 78542
Francis Dr & Ln 78542
N Franklin Rd 78541
E Freddy Gonzalez Dr
100-198 78539
201-999 78539
1401-1999 78542
2300-2398 78542
W Freddy Gonzalez
Dr 78539
Freedom Dr 78542
French Ave 78541
Fresno Dr
1-799 78542
1100-1399 78541
Friday St 78542
Friendly Dr 78542
Frio Dr 78539
Frontera Rd 78541
Frontier Dr 78539
Fudge St 78542
Fuente De Gozo 78539
Fuente De Paz 78539
Gabbie Ln 78542
Gala Ave 78542
Garcia Ave 78541
Gardenia Dr 78541
Gardenia St
5100-5498 78541
5500-5899 78541
8000-8299 78542
W Garner St 78541
Gary Ln 78542
Garza St 78539
Gastel Cir 78539
N Gaston Cir 78542
Gateway Dr 78539
Gayle 78541
Geena St 78539
Gemini Ave 78542
Geoffrey Ln 78539
George St 78539
Geranio Dr 78541
German Ave 78541
Geronimo Dr 78542
Geronimo Molina St 78542
Gibson Dr 78542
Ginger Ave 78539
Ginko Dr 78542
Gisselle St 78541
Gladiola Dr 78541
Glamour Dr 78542
Glasscock 78541
Glen St 78542
Glendale Dr 78541
Gloria Ann Dr 78539
Gold Ave 78542
Gondola Ave 78542
Gonzalez St 78542
Goodrich Dr 78539
Grace Ln 78542
Granada Cir & St 78542
E Granjeno Ave 78542
Granrey Dr 78541
Grapefruit Dr 78541
Grapefruit St 78539
Greenbriar Dr 78539
Gregg Dr 78542
Grizzly Ln 78542
Guadalupe Dr 78539
Guajillo St 78541
Guava 78541
Gulf Cir 78542
N Gwin Rd 78542
Gyr St 78539
Habanero Ln 78539
Hackberry Ln 78539
Haddonfield St 78542
Haidee Dr 78542
Hallam Ave 78542
W Hampton 78539
Hannah Dr 78542
Happy Valley Dr 78539
Harmony Dr & Ln 78542
Harrah Dr 78542
Harrods St 78542
Harvest St 78539
Haven Ln 78542
Hawthorne Ave 78539
Hayden St 78542
Heartbreak Dr 78542
Heather Ave 78542
Hedfelt Dr 78539
Helen St 78542
Hendrix Dr & St 78542
Herb St 78542
Herieree St 78541
Heritage Oaks Rd 78539
Hernandez Dr & Rd 78542
Hickory St 78541
Hidden Forest Dr 78539
High Ridge Ln 78539
Highland Ave 78542
Highland St 78541
W Hill Dr 78539
Hill Country Rd 78539
Hillcrest Ln 78542
Hinojosa Rd 78541
Hobbs Dr 78539
N Hoehn Rd 78541
Hollis Dr 78542
Hollywood Dr 78539
Holmes Rd & St 78542
Horizon Trl 78541
Horizon Peak 78539
Horsetail Fls 78539
Hudson St 78542
Huisache 78539
S Hummer Ln 78539
Hummingbird Ln 78542
Humphrey St 78542
Hunters Chase Dr 78539
Hylton Ave 78539
S I Rd 78542
Ichabod Ln 78539
Ida St 78539
Illeana St 78539
Illusivo Ave 78542
Ima St 78539
Imelda 78541
Imperial Ln & St 78542
Independence Dr 78541
Indigo St 78541
Industrial Dr 78542
Inez Ave & St 78539
E Ingle Rd 78542
W Ingle Rd 78541
N Inspiration Rd 78541
International St 78539
E Iowa Rd 78542
N Iowa Rd 78541
Iris Ave 78539
Irongate Dr 78539
Isabella St 78541
Isiah St 78542
Ivory St 78541
Ivy Ln 78539
Jacaranda St 78541
Jackie St 78539
Jackpot Blvd 78542
Jacks St 78542
Jackson Crk 78539
Jackson Rd 78540
N Jackson Rd 78541
S Jackson Rd 78539
Jacob St 78542
Jade St 78542
Jake 78541
Jalapeno Ln 78539
Jam Sq E 78542
James Ave 78539
Janet Dr 78541
Janie St 78542
Jared St 78542
N Jasman Rd 78542
Jasmine Rd 78542
Jason Ave 78539
Jasper St 78541
Jeanine St 78542
Jefferson Ave 78542
Jeffrey Dr 78542
Jeni Rey Ln 78542
Jennifer Rd 78541
Jennifers Dr 78541
Jeremiah St 78542
Jerry Ann Dr 78542
Jessica 78541
Jessica Ln 78542
Jewel Cir 78539
Jo Din St 78542
Joan Dr 78541
Joann St 78539
Joby St 78541
John Ave 78539
W Jordan Dr 78539
Joscelyn Dr 78541
Josephine Rd 78542
Joy St 78539
N Juan St 78541
Jubilee Blvd 78542
Julie Ln 78542
Juniper Dr 78542
Jutland 78542
Kaat St 78539
Kamien Rd 78541
Kansas Dr 78542
Karen Ln 78539
Katherine Ave 78539
Kathleen Ave 78541
Kayla Ave 78539
Kellie Dr 78542
Kelsey Dr 78542
Kendlewood St 78541
Kenyon Dr & Rd 78542
Keralum Dr 78542
Keri Dr 78542
Kestrel Dr 78542
Keystone 78541
Kiana Ln 78542
Kika De La Garza St 78539
Killebrew St 78539
Kimberly Ln 78541
Kings Dr 78539
Kiskadee Trl 78539
Kiwi Ln 78541
Knight Ave 78539
Kokopelli Dr 78541
Kotzur Rd 78541
Kristie Dr 78541
E Kuhn St
201-297 78541
299-1499 78542
1600-1799 78542
1801-1899 78542
W Kuhn St 78541
Kyle Ave 78542
La Blanca Cir & Dr 78542
La Cantera St 78541
La Condesa 78539
La Cuchilla Rd 78542
La Flor St 78542
W La Guardia Ln 78539
N La Homa Rd 78541
La Jarita Rd 78541
La Luna Dr 78541
La Mancha Dr 78541
La Mora Ln 78541
La Paloma St 78542
La Paz St 78542
La Puerta Ave 78541
La Quinta Ln 78542
Labrador Dr 78542
Lacywood 78539
Laguna Seca Rd N, S &
W 78541
Lake Citrus Dr 78541
Lake Point Dr 78541
Lake Shore Dr 78539
Lakeshore Dr 78541
Lakeside Dr 78541
Lakeview Dr 78541
Lakeway Dr 78541
Lakota Dr 78542
Lamar Ave 78541
Lancelot Ln 78539
Lane Rd 78541
Langer Dr 78542
Lantana Dr 78542
Laredo St 78542
Largo Dr 78542
Larry Twayne Way 78541
Las Alamedas 78541
Las Brisas Cir 78542
Las Canas Rd 78541
Las Cruces Dr 78539
Las Palmas Dr 78539
Las Vegas Dr 78539
Lasso Trl 78541
Laurel Oak Way 78539
Laurie Ln 78539
Lavender St 78541
Lazaro St 78542
Lazy Palm Dr 78541
Leann Rimes Rd 78542
Lebanon 78539
Lee Cir 78539
Legna St 78542
Leigh Ann Dr 78542
Lemon Dr 78541
Lemon St 78539
Lemon Tree Ct 78539
Lerma Dr 78539
Leslie St 78539
Leticia St 78542
Lexington Cir 78539
N Liberty 78541
Lilac St 78541
Lily Ln 78541
Lime St 78539
Linan 78542
Lincoln Ave 78542
W Lindsay Blvd 78539
Links Dr 78542
Linva Ave 78541
Lipsey Dr 78542
Lisa St 78541
Live Oak Rd 78539
Liz Rios Dr 78542
Lizette Dr 78542
Llano Grande Ln 78542
Llano Mediano Ln 78542
Llano Molano Ln 78542
Locker Ave 78542
Loda Ln 78542
E Loeb St
100-1499 78541
1600-1799 78542
W Loeb St 78541
S Logan Dr 78539
Loma Dr 78542
Lomita St 78541
Longoria Ln 78541
Lonny Ln 78542
Lookout 78541
E Lopez Dr 78542
Loretta Lynn Dr 78541
Lori Ln 78542
Lori Morgan Dr 78541
Los Azares 78542
Los Cerritos Cir N 78541
Los Ebanos Ct 78541
Los Lagos Dr 78542
Los Pinos Ln 78541
Los Terrazos Blvd 78541
Los Venados Dr 78542
N Los Veteranos Dr 78541
Lotto Ln 78541
Louisiana Dr 78542
E & W Lovett St 78541
Lowry Ln 78539
Loyola Dr 78541
Lucca St 78542
Lucy Ct 78541
Ludden 78542
Lula St 78539
Lupita St 78542
Luxury Ln 78542
Luz Escobedo St 78542
Lydia Dr 78542
Lynn Dr 78539
N M Rd 78542
Mabel St 78542
Macquarie Dr 78542
Madero Dr 78542
Mae St 78542
Magella St 78542
Magic Ave 78542
Magnolia Cir 78542
Magnolia Village Dr 78542
E & W Mahl St 78539
Majella St 78542
Majestic Ave 78542
Malachi St 78542
Malibu Dr 78542
Mallory Dr 78541
Maltese St 78539
Manana St 78539
Mandela Cir 78541
Manzano St 78539
Maple St 78539
Marc Ave 78539
Marcy St 78541
Margarita St 78542
Maria Luiza Dr 78539
Marigold St 78542
Marion Ln 78539
Mariposa St 78542
Marisol Dr 78542
Marissa Ct 78542
Marlin Ct 78542
Martha Louise Ave 78539
Martin St 78539
Mary Ave 78539
Mathews Ave 78539
Mauritius Ln 78542
Maxium 78541
Mayberry 78541
N Mccoll Rd 78541
S Mccoll Rd 78539
Mccook Acres 78541
Mccormack Dr 78542
E Mcintyre St
101-597 78541
599-1499 78541
1600-1799 78542
W Mcintyre St 78541
Mckee Dr 78539
Meadow Ln 78542
Megan Dr 78539
Melinda Dr 78539
Melissa Loop 78542
Melody Ln 78542
Melroy Dr 78539
Merak St 78542
Mercado Dr 78539
Mercedes Dr 78542
Mesa Dr 78539
Mesquite Ave 78542
Mesquite St 78539
E Mesquite St 78542
Michael Blvd 78539
Michael Angelo 78539
Michelle Dr 78541
Midlands Cir 78539
Midtown Cir 78539
W Mile 10 Rd 78541
N Mile 10 1/2 Rd 78541
Mile 10 1/3 78541
W Mile 11 78541
Mile 12 Rd 78541
Mile 14 Rd 78541
E Mile 15 1/2 N 78542
Mile 16 N 78542
Mile 16 Rd 78541
W Mile 16 1/2 Rd 78541
E Mile 17 N 78542
Mile 17 Rd N 78541
E Mile 17 Rd 78542
E Mile 17 1/2 N 78542
E Mile 17 1/2 Rd 78542
W Mile 17 1/2 Rd 78541
E Mile 18 Rd 78542
Mile 19 Rd N 78542
E Mile 20 Rd 78542
W Mile 21 Rd 78541
Mile 22 1/2 N 78542
Mile 8 Rd 78542
Mile 8 1/2 Rd 78541
Mile 9 Rd 78541
Milestone 78541
Miller Rd 78542
Millwood St 78541
Milwaukee Ave 78539
Mina De Oro 78542
Mineral Rights 78541
Minnie Ln 78542
Mirage Dr 78542
Mirasoles Ln 78542
Mission St 78542
Mockingbird Ln & St 78542
Mohawk Ave 78542
N Mojave 78541
Molly St 78542
Monday St 78542
Mondego Dr 78542
Monette St 78539
N Monmack Rd 78541
S Monmack Rd 78539
Monreal Rd 78541
Monroe Ave 78539
Monserat Dr 78539
Monte Alto Dr 78541
Monte Bello Ln 78541
Monte Bonito Ln 78541
Monte Calvario Dr 78541
Monte Carlo Ln 78541
E Monte Cristo Rd
100-900 78541
902-998 78541
1300-14199 78542
W Monte Cristo Rd 78541
W Monte Cristo Heights
Rd 78541
N Monte Cristo Ranch
Rd 78541
Monte Morelos Ln 78541
Monte Rey Ln 78541
Monte Sinai Dr 78541
Monte Suma Dr 78541
Monte Video Ln 78541
Montegue St 78542
Montelongo Rd 78541
Montemayor Ln 78541
Monterrey St 78539
N Montevideo Ave 78541
S Montevideo Ave 78539
Montreal St 78539
Moonlight Ln 78541
N Moorefield Rd 78541
Mora St 78542
Morris St 78542
Morroco Dr 78542
Mossy Oak Dr 78542
Mountain View Ln E 78542
Munoz St 78541
Murillo St 78541
Muse Dr 78542
Mustang St 78542
Myra Ct 78541
Nacona Dr 78542
Nadia Ln 78542
Nancy St 78542
Nardo St 78541
Nassau St 78541
Nature Trl 78542
Nautical Ln 78539
E Nava Rd 78542
Navarro Ln 78542
Navigator Dr 78541
Neighborhood St 78542
Nelda St 78542
Nellie Ave 78541
Neptune St 78542
Nessuh Ave 78541
New York Dr 78542
Nicole Dr 78542
Nikkie Ln 78542
Nitsche Dr 78542
Nobis Ave 78542
Nogales St 78541
Nohemi Ct 78541
Nominee St 78542
E Nopal Dr 78542
Nora Dr 78539
Norma Ln 78539
Northern Dancer Ave 78539
Northern Lights Ave 78541
Northridge Dr 78539
W Notre Dame Dr 78541
N Nowell Dr 78542
Nuilguy Dr 78542
Oaks Pl & Rd 78539

Ocean View Dr 78539
Ocotillo Ave 78542
S Ohare Dr 78539
Okeechobee Ln 78542
S Old Alamo Rd 78542
Oliva St 78539
Olmo Ln 78541
Omega St 78539
N Opal St 78541
Opuntia Ln 78541
Ora St 78539
W Orange Ave 78541
Orange Dr 78541
Orange St 78539
Orchard Ave 78542
Orchid St 78542
Oregano St 78541
Oregon Dr 78542
Oriente St 78541
Orlando St 78541
Orquidea St 78541
Oscar 78541
Oscar Loop 78542
E Owassa Rd 78542
W Owassa Rd 78539
Owen Cir & Dr 78542
Oxford St 78539
N Pablo St 78541
Pacific Ave 78539
Padre Ln 78539
Page Ave 78539
Pajarillos St 78542
Palace St 78539
Palacios Dr 78539
Palm Cir 78542
E Palm Dr 78539
W Palm Dr
100-199 78541
201-299 78541
300-399 78539
301-397 78541
399-1200 78541
1202-2198 78541
Palm Circle Dr 78542
Palm Lake Dr 78541
Palmera Cir 78542
Palmeras Cir N & S 78542
Palomino St 78542
Pancho Villa Dr 78542
Park Cir & St 78539
Park Place Dr 78539
Paseo Ave 78542
Paseo Del Prado Ave 78539
Paseo Del Rey 78542
Paseo Encantado 78542
Pat St 78542
Patsy Cline Dr 78541
Patterson St 78542
E Pauline Ln 78542
Pavo Real Ln 78542
Payton Dr 78542
Peach St 78539
E Peadwalt Sq E 78542
Pebble Crk 78539
W Pecador Dr 78541
Pecan Ridge Ln 78539
Pelican Dr 78541
Pelican Lake Ave 78539
Penelope Dr 78542
Penpal St 78542
Pequena Dr 78541
Perch Ave 78542
Peregrin Dr 78542
Peridot St 78541
Persimmon Ave 78539
Petal St 78542
E & W Peter St 78541
Petirrojo St 78542
Petra St 78542
Petunia St 78542
Pfeiffer St 78542
Pheasant Dr 78539
Phoenix St 78541
Phyllis Ln 78542
Pigeon Dr 78542
Pike Ave 78542

S Pin Oak Rd 78539
Pine Ridge Dr 78539
Pioneer St 78542
Piquin St 78539
Pirul St 78541
Pistil St 78542
Pizzaro Dr 78542
Plantation Oaks Dr 78541
Plaza Cir 78539
Plazas Del Lago Dr 78539
Plum St 78539
Pluto St 78542
Poblano Ln 78539
Poinsetta St 78542
Point West Dr 78539
Pollen St 78542
Ponciana Dr 78542
N Popotillo Ave 78541
W Portales Dr 78541
Portillo St 78542
Post Oak Pl 78539
Post Oaks Rd 78539
Postage Due St 78539
Prairie Ln 78542
E Prandard Sq 78539
Premiere Ln 78542
Presidente Dr 78539
Presidio Dr 78539
Presley Dr 78542
Prestwick St 78542
Prickly Pear St 78541
Primavera St 78542
Primos Cir 78542
Princess St 78539
Priscilla Ln 78539
S Professional Dr 78539
Promenade Ave 78542
Prosperity Dr 78541
Providence Dr 78542
W Puente St 78541
Puffin St 78542
Quail Ave 78542
Quartz St 78539
Queens Dr 78542
Quietud St 78542
Quilicy 78539
Rachel Dr 78539
Rafael Dr 78539
Railroad Dr 78541
Ram Cir 78542
Rambo Dr 78542
E Ramseyer Rd 78542
Rancho Alto Dr 78542
Rancho Del Rey 78542
Rangel Dr 78541
Rankin Dr 78542
Rattlesnake Dr 78542
S Raul Longoria Rd 78542
Raven Cir E 78542
Rawlings St 78542
Rebecca Dr 78542
Red Gate Rd 78541
Redbird St 78542
Redwood St 78541
Reef Ln 78542
Regal Dr 78539
Regency Dr 78539
Regency Acres Dr 78541
Relaxation St 78539
Remington Ave 78539
Renarea St 78542
Renee Ln 78539
N Republic Dr 78541
Retama St 78541
Revilla St 78542
Reymundo St 78542
W Rhin Dr 78539
S Rhonda St 78539
Rhythm Dr 78542
Ric Mar St 78541
Ricco St 78539
Rice Ln 78542
E Richardson Rd 78542
Ringold Cir 78539
Rio Bravo Dr 78542
Rio De Janeiro St 78539

Rio Grande Care Rd 78541
Rio Rebuelto Ln 78542
Rio Red Cir & Ln N, S & W 78541
Rios Private Rd 78542
Ripple Dr 78541
Ritz Ave 78542
River Dr 78539
River Oaks Dr & Ln 78539
River Rock Dr 78539
Riverbend Dr 78541
W Roadrunner Dr 78541
Robbie Ln 78542
N Roberts St 78541
Robin Ln & St 78542
Rochester St 78539
Rock Ct 78542
Rockwood Dr 78541
Rocotillo Ln 78539
Rodeo Dr 78539
Rodrigo Ave 78541
Rodriguez Blvd 78541
N Roegiers Rd 78541
N Roel Bazan 78541
E Rogers Rd
400-498 78541
500-924 78541
940-1298 78542
1300-12700 78542
12702-14098 78542
W Rogers Rd 78541
E Rojas St 78542
Roman Cir 78542
W Ron Case 78541
Roosevelt Ave 78542
N Rooth Rd 78541
Rosalia Cir 78541
Rose Gdn 78542
Rosewood St 78541
Roulette St 78542
Round Up Cir 78539
N Roy Dr 78541
Royal St 78539
N Ruby St 78541
Ruidoso 78541
E Russel Rd 78542
E & W Russell Rd 78541
Russet St 78541
Russian Ave 78541
Sabal Ave 78539
Sabinito Dr 78542
Sage Ln 78539
Saginaw Ave 78541
Saker St 78539
N Sal St 78541
Saldana Dr 78539
N Salinas St 78541
Saltillo St 78539
Saltwater Ave 78542
Salvador Ave 78539
Salvatierra Ave 78541
E & W Samano St 78539
Samgar St 78539
San Alejandro St 78539
San Antonio St 78542
San Carlos Cir 78542
San Clemente Ave 78542
San Felipe St 78541
San Francisco Ave & Dr 78542
San Gabriel St 78539
San Guillermo St 78542
San Jacinto Ave 78542
San Jose Ave 78542
San Jose Dr 78541
San Jose St 78542
San Luis St 78542
San Manuel St 78539
San Marcos St 78542
San Pedro St 78542
San Santiago St 78542
Sanchez St 78542
Sand Ct 78542
Sandia Ln 78541
Sandie Ln 78542
Sandstone 78541

Santa Ana Ave
600-699 78541
1100-1400 78542
1402-1498 78542
Santa Elena Ave 78542
Santa Fe St 78541
Santa Maria 78541
Santa Maria St 78542
Santiago St 78542
Sapphire St 78539
W Sarah Evans 78541
Saturday St 78542
Saturn St 78542
Sauceda Dr 78542
E & W Schunior St 78541
Scotland Dr 78539
Seattle Slew St 78539
Secretariat 78539
Seguin Ave 78542
Segura Mendoza Dr 78541
Selena Dr 78542
N Seminary Est, Rd & Vlg 78541
Seminary Acres 78541
Sendero Ave 78542
Sepal St 78542
Serenity Dr 78539
Sernas Private Dr 78542
Serrano St 78539
Seton St 78542
Sevilla Blvd 78542
Shadow Wood St 78541
Shalom Dr 78539
Shania Twain Dr 78541
Sharon St 78541
N & S Sharp Rd 78542
Shavano St 78541
Shay Ln 78539
Sheffield St 78539
N Shelly Ave 78542
Shelly Lori Rd 78541
Sherman St 78542
Short Line St 78539
Sierra Cir 78539
Siesta Dr 78539
Silver St 78542
Silver Shadow Dr 78541
Simpson Rd 78542
Sin Tacha St 78542
Sinatra Dr 78542
Singletary Dr 78542
N & S Skinner Rd 78542
Skyhawk Dr 78542
Skylark Ave 78542
Slaughter Dr 78542
Slots Dr 78542
W Smith St 78541
Snapper St 78541
Snook Ct 78542
Snowdrop Dr 78542
Socata Dr 78542
Sol Dorado 78542
Soledad Dr 78541
Solera St 78541
Solis Ln 78542
Sophia Ave 78542
Sorrento St 78542
Soto Dr 78542
Southern Breeze Ave 78541
Southfork 78542
Southland Ave 78539
Southport Dr 78542
Southridge Dr 78539
Spades Ave 78542
Spicewood Dr 78542
E Sprague St
200-1199 78539
1201-1499 78539
1600-1698 78542
1801-2399 78542
W Sprague St 78539
Spring St 78542
Stacey St 78539
Stags Leap 78541
Stallion St 78542
Stanford Ct 78541

Star Ln 78542
Starshine Dr 78542
E State Highway 107 78542
W State Highway 107 78539
S State Highway 336 78539
Steamboat Dr 78541
E Steel Ave 78542
Stephen 78539
Stillwater Cv 78542
Stirling Ave 78539
Stonecrest 78541
Stonehaven Blvd 78539
Stonehill 78541
Stoneview 78541
Stratosphere Dr 78539
Strupie St 78542
Stuart Dr 78539
E & W Stubbs St 78539
Studio Ln 78542
Stumpy Ln 78542
Suaze 78541
N Sugar Rd 78541
S Sugar Rd 78539
Sugarbird Ln 78542
Sugarland Dr 78542
E Sullivan Ave 78542
Summerfield Dr 78539
Summit Cir 78539
Sundance Dr 78542
Sunday St 78542
N & S Sunflower Rd 78542
Sunny Ln 78541
Sunnyside Dr & Ln 78542
Sunrise Cir & Ln 78542
Sunset Dr 78539
Susan Dr 78539
Suzette Ln 78541
Sweet Ln 78539
Sycamore Dr 78542
Sydney St 78539
Sylvia St 78541
Tagle St 78541
Tahiti Dr 78541
Tallow Cts 78539
Tamesis Dr 78539
Tampa St 78541
Tangelo 78539
Tangerine 78539
Tanglewood Dr 78539
Tanguma Ave 78541
Tanya Tucker Dr 78541
Tapadillo Dr 78541
Tarpon Ct 78542
Tassajara St 78542
N Taylor Rd 78541
Tecate St 78542
Tejano Dr 78542
W Temple Dr 78541
Tepoztlan St 78542
Terne Ave 78541
Terranova Cir 78541
N Terry Rd 78542
Tex Mex Rd 78542
N Texan Rd 78541
E Texas Rd 78542
The Hills Dr 78542
Thelma Dr 78539
E Thompson Rd 78542
Thora Dr 78539
Thursday St 78542
Tierra Buena 78541
Tierra Dulce Dr 78539
Tiffany St 78542
Tigris 78539
Tillmin Dr 78542
Timberwood Dr 78542
E Tin Ave 78542
Tiquisate Ave 78541
Toffee Ln 78539
Toledo Ave 78541
Tori Ln 78539
Tortolita St 78542
Toucan Dr 78542
Tourist Dr 78539
N & S Tower Rd 78542
S Trail Dr 78542

Trailblazer Ave 78541
E Trenton Rd
101-699 78539
800-1498 78542
1500-8299 78542
W Trenton Rd 78539
S Tres Hermanos 78542
Trey Dr
2800-3199 78541
3900-4199 78542
Trinity Ln 78542
Trisha St 78539
Trophy Dr 78542
Tropicana St 78542
Trout Ct 78542
Tuesday St 78542
Tulipan Ave 78542
Turquoise Rd 78542
N Turquoise Rd 78541
Turtle Lake Ave 78539
Twin Cir 78542
S Union St 78539
E University Dr
200-1499 78539
1600-5299 78542
W University Dr 78539
Upland Dr 78539
Uranus St 78542
Urbina St 78542
Uresti St 78542
N Us Highway 281
200-3298 78542
N Us Highway 281
8501-8599 78541
N & S Val Verde Rd 78542
Val Verde Vsta St 78542
Valencia Dr 78541
Valentine Dr 78542
Valero Ln 78542
Valle Cir 78539
Valparaiso St 78539
Valverde Vista Rd 78542
Van Tassel Cir 78539
E & W Van Week St 78541
Vance St 78539
Vegas Private Rd 78542
Venus Dr 78542
Vera Ave 78539
Verbena Ave & St 78542
Verde Ave 78542
N Veronica Ln 78542
N Veterans Blvd 78541
S Veterans Blvd
201-297 78539
299-2500 78539
2502-2598 78539
3200-5699 78542
Via Blanca 78542
Via Del Oro 78541
Via Fernandez 78541
Via Paseo 78541
Via Plata 78541
Via Rojo 78542
Via Sol Dr 78541
Via Verde 78542
Vicksburg Dr
1200-1299 78541
12301-12399 78542
12401-12499 78542
Victoria Ave 78539
Victory Ave 78542
Viento St 78542
View Point Dr 78542
Villa Allegre 78539
Villa Linda Ave 78541
Village Dr 78541
Villarreal St 78542
Vina Ave 78539
Violeta Dr 78542
Virginia Dr & St 78542
Vista Bonita Dr 78542
Vista Chula St 78539
Vista Del Cielo 78542
Vista Florida St 78539
Vista Hermosa St 78539
Vista Linda St 78539

Vista Tropical St 78539
Vivian Ln 78542
Vivian St 78541
Wagon Trl 78541
Wakita Dr 78542
Wallace Rd 78541
Walnut St 78541
Wane Cir & St 78542
N Ware Rd 78541
Washington Ave 78542
Wassell Cir, Dr & St 78542
Water Oak Dr 78542
Wayne Dr 78542
Webster Dr 78542
Wedda Ln 78539
Wednesday St 78542
Wellington Ave 78539
E Wells St 78541
Wendy Dr 78539
W Western Dr 78539
Western Rd 78541
N Western Rd 78541
Whitewing Ave 78539
Wilcox Dr 78542
Wilderness Dr 78542
Wildflower Dr 78539
Wilson Ave 78542
E, N, S & W Wind Dr 78542
Windjammer Dr 78542
Windsor Ave 78542
E Wisconsin Rd 78542
Wither Rd 78541
Wolf Dr 78541
Woods Dr E 78542
Woodstone St 78542
W Worthington 78539
Wyoming St 78542
Xander St 78542
N Yale Dr 78541
Yandel St 78542
Yary Dr 78542
Yellow Rose Dr 78539
Yellow Stone St 78542
Yosemite St 78542
Yucca Ave 78542
N Yvette St 78542
E Yvonne St 78542
Zeke Ave 78542
W Zelma St 78541
Zenon Moya St 78542
Zimmerman St 78539
Zircon Dr 78541
Zoe Ave 78539

NUMBERED STREETS

N 1st Ave 78541
S 1st Ave 78539
N 1st St 78542
S 2nd Ave 78539
2nd St 78541
N 2nd St 78542
S 2nd St 78539
N 3rd Ave 78541
S 3rd Ave 78539
N 4th Ave 78541
S 4th Ave 78539
N 5th Ave 78541
S 5th Ave 78539
N 6th Ave 78541
S 6th Ave 78539
N 7th Ave 78541
S 7th Ave 78539
N 8th Ave 78541
S 8th Ave 78539
9 Mile Line Rd 78541
N 9th Ave 78541
S 9th Ave 78539
N 10th Ave 78541
S 10th Ave 78539
N 10th St 78541
N 12th Ave 78541
S 12th Ave 78539
N 13th Ave 78541
S 13th Ave 78539
N 14th Ave 78541

S 14th Ave 78539
N 14th Pl 78541
N 15th Ave 78541
S 15th Ave 78539
N 16th Ave 78541
S 16th Ave 78539
N 17th Ave 78541
S 17th Ave 78539
N 19th Ave 78541
S 19th Ave 78539
N 20th Ave 78541
S 20th Ave 78539
N 21st Ave 78541
S 21st Ave 78539
N 22nd Ave 78541
S 22nd Ave 78539
S 23rd Ave 78539
N 23rd St 78541
S 24th Ave
100-198 78539
201-799 78539
1001-1099 78542
1901-1999 78539
S 25th Ave 78542
S 26th Ave 78542
N 26th St 78539
N & S 27th 78542
N & S 28th 78542
N 29th Ave 78542
S 29th Ave 78542
N 29th Ln 78541
N 29th St 78541
33rd Ln & St 78541
34th St 78542
N 34th St 78541
N 35th St 78541
N 36th Ln 78541
N 37th Ln 78541
38th Ln & St 78541
N 39th St 78541
N 40th St 78541
41st Ln & St 78541
S 82nd 1/2 St 78542
N & S 83rd 78542
S 83rd 1/2 St 78542
N & S 84th 78542
N & S 85th 78542
N & S 86th 78542
N 87th St 78542
N 111th St 78541
N 113th St 78541

EL PASO TX

General Delivery 79910

POST OFFICE BOXES MAIN OFFICE STATIONS AND BRANCHES

Box No.s
1 - 60 79940
11 - 20 79999
61 - 139 79941
125 - 125 79999
141 - 240 79942
241 - 513 79943
313 - 455 79999
521 - 740 79944
741 - 920 79945
927 - 1110 79946
1111 - 1111 79999
1121 - 1340 79947
1341 - 1612 79948
1621 - 1830 79949
1799 - 1799 79999
1831 - 2040 79950
1919 - 1977 79999
2041 - 2250 79951
2251 - 2460 79952
2700 - 2992 79999
3000 - 3997 79923
4001 - 4999 79914
5001 - 5311 79953
5050 - 5050 79999
5321 - 5471 79954
5481 - 5791 79955
6000 - 6990 79906
9000 - 11600 79995
12001 - 13790 79913
16000 - 16400 79906
17000 - 17996 79917
20022 - 20998 79998
23000 - 23269 79923
24000 - 24902 79914
26001 - 27275 79926
31001 - 31850 79931
71001 - 71740 79917
95002 - 95025 79995
98129 - 98129 79998
99001 - 99124 79999
130002 - 130023 88513
170761 - 170999 88517
200025 - 200025 88520
220001 - 222238 79913
290001 - 292825 79929
293000 - 293000 88529
310032 - 317202 88531
370001 - 372396 79937
390261 - 390261 88539
400033 - 400139 88540
410298 - 410391 88541
420516 - 420687 88542
430796 - 430846 88543
440002 - 440155 88544
450344 - 450469 88545
460729 - 460729 88546
470823 - 470828 88547
500001 - 500001 88550
512301 - 512362 79951
522501 - 522562 79952
540001 - 540156 88554
640001 - 641558 79904
650001 - 652577 88565
660800 - 660810 88566
670800 - 670810 88567
680800 - 680810 88568
690800 - 690810 88569
700800 - 700810 88570
710800 - 710810 88571
720800 - 720810 88572
730800 - 730810 88573
740001 - 740925 88574
750001 - 758999 88575
760001 - 760037 88576
870016 - 870149 88587
880001 - 880997 88588
890537 - 890537 88589
900002 - 900244 88590
902900 - 902999 79990
920001 - 920838 79902
937003 - 937003 79937
960001 - 964028 79996
971001 - 975074 79997
981003 - 982402 79998

NAMED STREETS

A L Gill Dr 79936
Aaker St 79927
Aaron St 79924
Abbey Woods Pl 79936
Abdou Pl 79905
Abedul Pl 79932
Abejeno Rd 79927
Aberdeen St 79925
Abigail St 79936
Abilene Ave 79924
Ability Dr 79936
Abington Dr 79912
Abraham Ct 79915
Abril Dr 79935
Abston St 79906
Acacia Cir 79912
Academy Cir 79924
Acapulco Ave 79915
Acatlan Ln 79907
Accrington Ct 79928
Acer Ave 79925
Achilles Dr 79924
Achim Dr 79928
Ackerman Dr 79928
Acoma St 79934
Acorn Pl 79925
Acra Ct 79928
Ada Ln 79932
Adabel Dr 79936
Adan Fuentes St 79938
Adauto Ct 79935
Addison St 79928
Addy Ct 79928
Adeline Ave 79938
Adin St 79924
Admiral St 79925
Adobe Dr 79915
Adolph Carson Pl 79936
Adolphus Ave 79904
Adonis Dr 79924
Adrian Ct 79928
Adrian Campos St 79938
Adrian George Ct 79907
Adriana Ct 79907
Aero Vista Dr 79908
Affection Ct 79924
Agave Cir 79907
Agave Park Ct 79932
Agena Ln 79924
Aggie Ct 79924
Agua Azul Pl 79928
Agua Brava Pl 79928
Agua Caliente Dr 79912
Agua Clara St 79928
Agua De Brisa 79928
Agua De Flor 79928
Agua De Lluvia 79928
Agua De Mar 79928
Agua Del Rio 79928
Agua Dulce St 79936
Agua Fria Pl 79928
Agua Limpia Pl 79928
Agua Marina Pl 79928
Agua Mineral Pl 79928
Agua Nieve Pl 79928
Agua Pesada Pl 79928
Agua Prieta Dr 79907
Agua Pura Pl 79928
Agua Rica 79928
Agua Tibia Pl 79928
Ahumada Dr 79927
Aiken Ln 79924
Air Coupe 79928
Air Force 79924
Aire Rock Ct 79935
Airport Rd
6200-6699 79925
7000-7199 79906
Airway Blvd 79925
Aja Koren Pl 79938
Ajax Ct 79924
Akron St 79907
Al Hernandez St 79938
Al Roberts Dr 79936
Al Smith 79932
Alabama St
1201-5099 79930
5501-6297 79904
6299-7899 79904
Aladdin Ave 79924
Alameda Ave
2300-2413 79901
2415-2499 79901
2900-6899 79905
6900-8129 79915
8130-9399 79907
9401-9499 79907
9500-11999 79927
Alamo Ave 79907
Alamosa Way 79912
Alan A Dl 79924
Alan Duncan Ln 79936
Alan Shepard Ln 79936
Alandalus Dr 79932
Alaska St 79915
Alba Ln 79936
Alba Del Sol 79911
Albacore Ln 79924
Albany Dr 79924
Albert Saab Dr 79907
Alberta Ave 79905
Alberton Ave 79928
Album Ave
9400-10299 79925
10301-10399 79925
10400-10500 79935
10502-10698 79935
Alcala Ct 79932
Alcalde St 79912
Alcan St 79924
Alcazar Ct 79935
Alcon Dr 79928
Alcott Rd 79928
Aldama Ct 79935
Alderette Ave 79907
Alderwood Manor Dr 79928
Aldo Pl 79928
Aldrin Cir 79927
Aleppo St 79936
Alethea Park Dr 79902
Alex Guerrero Cir 79936
Alex Nicholas Ct 79932
Alexander Pl 79915
Alfonsito Ct 79938
Alfred Subia Pl 79901
Alfredo Apodaca 79938
Alfredo Vasquez Dr 79934
Algerita Ct 79915
Algiers Ct 79925
Algonquin Rd 79905
Alhambra Ln 79936
Alicante Way 79912
Alice Walther 79932
Alicia Dr 79905
Alicia Arzola Dr 79928
Alicia Chacon Ln 79936
Alina Baltazar 79932
Alison Dr 79927
Alkali 79938
Allegheny Dr 79925
Allemande Rd 79938
Allemands 79928
Alley E 79901
Alley J 79901
Alliance Ct 79904
Alline Pl 79936
Allway Dr
10200-10399 79925
10400-10499 79935
Alma Way 79927
Alma Point Dr 79938
Almedia Pl 79936
Almond Ct 79915
Almond Beach Dr 79936
Alondra Way 79907
Alop St 79906
Alovera Ln 79912
Alpha 79938
Alpha Ave 79915
Alpine Dr 79915
Alps Dr
4800-5399 79904
9100-9199 79924
Alta St 79903
Alta Cumbre Pl 79912
Alta Loma Dr 79935
Altadena Pl 79912
Altar Del Sol 79911
N & S Alto Mesa Dr 79912
Alto Penasco Pl 79912
Alto Rey Ave 79912
Alton Griffin St 79907
Alton Oaks Ave 79938
Altura Ave
2400-3700 79930
3702-3798 79930
3800-4399 79903
Alvarez Dr 79932
Am Cir 79927
Amado Pl 79927
Amalia Dr 79928
Amarillo St 79936
Amazon Ct 79904
Ambassador Dr 79924
Amber Dr 79904
Amber Morgan Dr 79936
Amber Point Pl 79938
Amberwood Pl 79932
Ambrose 79938
Ameca St 79915
Amelia Dr 79912
Amen Cor 79922
American Dr 79925
N & S Americas Ave 79907
Ames Ct 79907
Amethyst Rd 79915
Amherst Dr 79928
Amiens Ln 79907
Amigo Dr 79907
Amistoso St 79938
Amposta Dr 79912
Amstater Cir 79936
Amsterdam Way 79912
Amur Way 79907
Amy Sue Dr 79936
Ana Way 79912
Anaheim Ln 79927
Anahi Ct 79927
Anahuac Ave 79932
Anapaula Dr 79932
Anasazi Ct 79912
Anchorage Ave 79924
Andalucia Dr 79935
Andalusian Pl 79938
Anderson Ave 79904
Anderson Rd 79927
Andes Dr 79904
Andre Agassi Dr 79938
Andrea Pl 79915
Andrea Kufner 79928
Andrea Micaela Pl 79928
Andreport St 79928
Andrew Wiseman St 79938
Andrews Pl 79928
Andrienne Dr 79936
Andy Ct 79927
Andy Williams Pl 79936
Ange St
101-299 79901
600-2399 79902
Angel St 79932
Angel Face Dr 79936
Angel Falls Pl 79924
Angel Wings Ct 79936
Angelica Ct 79936
Angie Bombach Ave 79928
Angora Loop St N & S 79934
Angus Dr 79927
Aniceto Granillo Ln 79927
Anise Dr
1900-1999 79935
2001-2299 79935
2300-2899 79936
Anita Cir 79905
Anita Way 79938
Ankerson St 79904
Anna Marie Ct 79928
Anna Martha Way 79907
Annagill St 79936
Annegret Dr 79928
Annette Ave 79924
Annie Rd 79932
Ansback St 79916
Ansley 79928
Antelope Ct 79924
Antero Pl 79904
Anthony St 79901
Antigua Dr 79927
Antilles Pl 79927
Antler Dr 79924
Antoinette 79938
Anton Ave 79938
Antonia Arco Ct 79924
Antonio Ave 79924
Antonio Santos Way 79934
Antwerp Dr & St 79928
Anvil Pl 79924
Apache St 79925
Apache Canyon Rd 79906
Apache Plume Ct 79928
Apache Point Dr 79938
Aparicio Dr 79907
Aphonia Dr 79924
Aphrodite Dr 79924
Apis Ct 79924
Apodaca Pl 79907
Apodaca Rd 79927
Apollo Ave 79904
Apostle 79928
Appaloosa Pl 79924
Appeling Dr 79907
Apple Ln 79925
Apple Gate Way 79936
Apple Point Ct 79938
April Ruth Way 79936
Aqua Ct 79936
Aquamarine St 79924
Aquarius Ln 79925
Aquatic Ln 79936
Aquifer Ct 79936
Aquilla Jane Ct 79928
Arabian Nights St 79924
Arabian Point Ave 79938
Araceli Ave 79938
Aranda Ln 79907
Arango Dr 79928
Arapaho Rd 79905
Araquaia Way 79907
Arbol Pl 79932
Arboleda Dr 79907
Arboles Dr 79932
Arbor Pl 79915
Arcadia Pl 79902
Arce Dr 79932
Arch Bridge Dr 79934
Archer Tower Ct 79936
Archie Dr 79935
Archuleta Dr 79938
Ardelle Ave 79936
Ardennes Ct 79924
Argal Ct 79935
Argentina St 79903
Argonaut Dr 79912
Arian Pl 79911
Ariel Rico Ct 79907
Aries Dr 79924
Arisano Dr 79932
Arizona Ave
101-397 79902
399-1999 79902
2000-2798 79930
Arkville 79928
Arlen Ave 79904
Arlene Cir 79927
Arlington St 79915
Armadillo Ln 79934
Armando Rd 79938
Armington Dr 79928
Armistad Ave 79912
Armour Dr 79935
Armstrong Dr 79927
Arnaz Ct 79936
Arnold Dr 79908
Arnold Pl 79907
Arnold Palmer Dr 79935
Arnulfo Pl 79905
Arrambide St 79936
Arratia Ave 79938
Arredondo Dr 79912
Arrollo Rd 79922
Arrow Knoll Cir 79936
Arrow Ridge Way 79912
Arrow Rock Dr 79936
Arrow Weed Dr 79928
Arrowhead Dr 79924
Arroyo Grande Dr 79932
Arroyo Sereno Ct 79932
Arroyos Pl 79936
Art Cir 79905
Art Wall Dr 79936
Artcraft Rd 79932
Artemediano St 79927
Artesano Rd 79927
Arthur Ashe Ct 79938
Artillery Rd 79906
Arts Festival Plz 79901
Arvana Ct 79927
Arvin Cir & Rd 79907
Arzate Pl 79927
N & S Ascarate St 79905
Ascarate Park Rd 79905
Ascencion St
100-2399 79928
3301-3397 79938
3399-3499 79938
Ash Ln 79925
Ashburn St 79906
Ashearl Dr 79934
Asherton Pl 79928
Ashford St 79928
Ashley Rd 79934
Ashridge Dr 79925
Ashwood Dr
10200-10399 79925
10400-10599 79935
Aspen Rd 79915
Assyria Dr 79907
Aster Ct 79924
Astoria Dr 79928
Astronaut Pl 79936
Athens Ave 79938
Athens Ct 79905
Atkinson Way 79915
Atlanta Ave
2000-2099 79902
2100-2199 79930
Atlantic Rd 79922
Atlantus Dr 79928
Atlas Ave 79904
Atoka St 79905
Attrill St 79928
Atun Way 79907
Atwood Dr 79907
Auburn Ave 79905
Auburn Sands Dr 79934
Audobon St 79924
Augusta Rd 79938
Aurea St 79928
Aurora Ave 79930
Austin Rd 79906
Autumn Gate Dr 79936
Autumn Sage Dr 79911
Autumn Wheat Dr 79934
Autumn Willow Way 79922
Ava Leigh Ave 79938
Avalon Dr 79925
Aviation Way 79928
Avila Ln 79922
Avondale St 79927
N & S Awbrey St 79905
Ayeta Ln 79907
Ayla Rd 79938
Azalea Pl 79922
Azogue Ave 79938
Aztec Rd 79925
Azteca Trl 79938
Azulejos St 79928
Azulito St 79928
Azure Point Ave 79938
Azure Sky Pl 79938
E B Taulbee Dr 79924
Babe Hiskey Ln 79936
Babe Ruth St 79934
Babylonia Dr 79907
Bacalao Ln 79907
Bacerac Ct 79902
Bach Way 79936
Bachimba Dr 79928
Backus St 79925
Baeza Way 79907
Bagdad Way 79924
Bagwell Ct 79932
Bahamas St 79927
Bahia Kino Way 79915
Bailee Point Ln 79938
Bailey Rd 79932
Bain Ct 79928
Bain Pl 79927
Bainbridge Ave 79924
Bakersfield Rd 79927
N & S Balboa Rd 79912

Balcones Ct 79912
Bales Dr 79928
Balko Way 79911
Ball Park Plz 79901
Balladeer Ave 79936
Ballard 79938
Ballerina Dr 79922
Ballinger Dr 79924
Ballistic St 79924
Ballymote Dr 79925
Balmorhea St 79936
Balsam Dr 79915
E Baltimore Dr 79902
Banana Tree Ln 79915
Bancroft Dr 79902
Bandolero Dr 79912
Bandolina Dr 79927
Bandy Ct 79903
Banner Ct 79903
Banner Crest Dr 79936
Banner Hill Ave 79936
Banner Run Dr 79936
Bara Dr 79935
Barandal Dr 79907
Barbaree Dr 79912
Barcelona Dr 79905
Bari Ave 79938
Barkarian Pl 79936
Barker Rd 79915
Barnard Dr 79928
Barney St 79905
Barnhart Dr 79927
Barnsworth 79932
Baron Pl 79936
Barranca Dr 79935
Barrel Cactus Dr 79928
Barrett Allen Ln 79932
Barstow Ave 79928
Bartlett Dr 79912
Bartlett Landing Ct 79912
Barton St 79915
Barzon St 79927
Bashkir Trl 79938
Basil Ct 79925
Bassett Ave 79901
Basswood Ave 79925
Bastille Ave 79924
Bat Masterson Dr 79936
Bataan Cir 79903
Bates Way 79915
Batiste Ln 79932
Battalion Way 79938
Bauman Rd 79927
Bauxite Ave 79932
Bay Ct 79902
Bay Bridge St 79934
Bay City Pl 79936
Bay Willow Way 79922
Baylor Pl 79907
Baynard Ct 79928
Bayo Ave 79925
Bayonet Ave 79916
Bayonne Ln 79907
Bayview Ln 79936
Baywood Rd 79915
Bea Martinez 79932
Beach Ave 79904
Beach Front Dr 79936
Beacham St 79938
Beachcomber Dr 79936
Beacon Ave 79905
Beall Ave 79904
Beals Dr 79924
Bean Ct 79927
Bear Cat Ridge Dr 79912
Bear Lake Pl 79936
Bear Ridge Dr 79912
Bear Rock Pl 79938
Beatrix Ave 79907
Beaumont Pl 79912
Beautonne Ave 79924
Beaver Ln 79927
Becknell Ln 79924
Becky Ln 79915
Bedford Rd 79922
Bedouin Ct 79934
Beech St 79925
Beechnut Rd 79912
Beechwood Pl 79932
Beethoven Pl 79936
Begonia Pl 79907
Behr Pl 79906
Bejar Dr 79927
Bel Mar Ave 79912
Belding Dr 79925
Belen Rd 79915
Belen St 79927
Belfast Ave 79925
Belfry Park Dr 79936
Belgian Trl 79938
Belinda Ann Ln 79924
Belk St 79904
Bell Point Dr 79938
Bell Tower Dr 79936
Bella Cumbre Dr 79912
Bella Vista Dr 79935
Belladonna Cir 79924
Bellagio Ln 79907
Bellaire Ln 79924
Bellas Artes Dr 79912
Bellis Ave 79925
Bellows Ct 79936
Bellrose Dr 79925
Bells Corner Ave 79932
Bellview Ct 79912
Bellwether Dr 79936
Bellwoode Ave 79932
Belmont St 79903
Belton Rd 79912
Belva Way 79922
S Belvidere St 79912
Ben Brook Dr 79936
Ben Crenshaw Dr 79935
Ben Garza Dr 79905
Ben Gurion St 79928
Ben Hogan Dr 79935
Ben Proctor Dr 79936
Ben Swain Dr 79915
W Bend Ln 79912
Benedict Rd 79922
Benfield Ct 79928
Bengal Dr 79935
Benito Way 79907
Bennett Pl 79907
Benning Ave 79904
Benny Emler Dr 79934
Benson Dr 79915
Benteoni Ave 79904
Benton St 79928
Bentridge 79932
Berger Ct 79928
Bergerac Ln 79907
Bergstrom St 79908
Berkshire Pl 79902
Bermuda Ave 79925
Bernadine Ave 79915
Bernard Dr 79938
Bernard Kern Dr 79936
Bernice Ct 79927
Berrel Ct & Pl 79928
Berringer St 79932
Berry Cir 79906
Berryville St 79928
Bert Green Dr 79936
Bert Yancey Dr 79936
Berwick Rd 79925
Beryl Ln 79904
Bessemer Dr 79936
Betel Dr 79907
Beth View Dr 79932
W Beth Wald St 79938
Bethany Dr 79925
Beto Portugal Ln 79938
Bettina Ave 79938
Betts Dr 79938
Beverly Pl 79907
Bhopinder Cir 79927
Big Acacia Dr 79938
Big Bear Ct 79936
Big Bend Dr 79904
Big Horn Ln 79924
Big John Dr 79938
Big Low Pl 79928
Bill Bart 79938
Bill Burnett Dr 79928
Bill Collins Ct 79935
Bill Hill Dr 79936
Bill Horn Way 79936
Bill Howard Pl 79936
Bill Mitchell Dr 79938
Bill Mueller Pl 79912
Bill Ogden Dr 79936
Billet Hill St 79936
Billie Marie Dr 79936
Billston Rd 79928
Billy Casper Dr 79936
Billy The Kid St 79907
Bing Crosby Dr 79936
Bingham Ct 79936
Birch St
700-998 79903
1000-1099 79903
1100-1199 79930
Bird Ave 79922
Bird Song St 79938
Birdsview Cir 79938
Birthstone Dr
10401-10407 79925
10409-10639 79925
10640-10699 79935
Bisbee Ave 79903
Biscaine St 79924
Bishop Ave 79904
Bishop Way 79903
Bishop Flores Dr 79912
Bissonet Ave 79915
Bittersweet Pl 79922
Black Dr 79907
Black Bear Ln 79938
Black Elk Pl 79936
Black Mallard Pl 79932
Black Mesa Dr 79911
Black Ridge Dr 79912
Black Sage Dr 79911
Black Sands Ln 79924
Blackberry Ct 79936
Blacker Ave 79902
Blackfoot 79928
Blackhawk Dr 79924
Blackmon Pl & St 79928
Blackstone Ct 79922
Blacktail Deer Ln 79938
Blackwood Ave 79925
Blaeu Dr 79938
Blair Dr 79928
Blake Pl 79928
Blakey Way 79907
Blanchard Ave 79902
Blanco Ave 79905
Blanda Ct 79936
Blazing Star Dr 79928
Blazon Gold Way 79936
Bliss Ave 79903
Blooming Desert Dr 79928
Blossom Ave 79924
Blue Barrel Dr & St 79934
Blue Bell Dr 79938
Blue Bonnet Ct 79936
Blue Dirt Cir 79938
Blue Earth Ln 79936
Blue Feather Ct 79936
Blue Grove Ln 79936
Blue Heron Dr 79928
Blue Moon Dr 79936
Blue Moon Way 79927
Blue Palm Pl 79936
Blue Quail Ave 79936
Blue Ridge Cir & Dr 79904
Blue River Way 79907
Blue Sage Cir 79924
Blue Wing Dr 79924
Blueberry Ct 79936
Bluesky Point Ct 79938
Bluff Canyon Cir 79912
Bluff Creek St 79911
Bluff Ridge Dr 79912
Bluff Trail Ln 79912
Bluff View Pl 79912
Blythe Dr 79924
Bo Ln 79938
Bob Gilder Pl 79936
Bob Goalby Ln 79935
Bob Heasley Dr 79938
Bob Hope Dr 79936
Bob Kennedy Way 79907
Bob Lunn Pl 79935
Bob Mitchell Dr 79936
Bob Murphy Dr 79936
Bob Smith Dr 79936
Bob Stone Dr 79936
Bobby Fuller Dr 79936
Bobby Jones Dr 79936
Bobcat Ct 79924
Bobolink Way 79922
Bobwhite Ave 79924
Bocalusa Ave 79928
Bodega Pl 79935
Boeing Dr
6400-8400 79925
8401-8401 79910
8401-8401 79997
8402-8798 79925
8403-8799 79925
Boer Trail Ave 79938
Bogart Pl 79936
Boggiano Dr 79912
Bogota Pl 79928
Bois D Arc Dr 79925
Bold Ruler Ct 79936
Bolin Pl 79928
Bolivia St 79903
Bolling St 79918
Bolton Pl 79903
Bomarc St 79924
Bombay Ct 79928
Bon Aire Dr 79924
Bonds Ct 79903
Bonfire Hill Way 79936
Bonneville Ln 79912
Boody Ct 79928
N Boone St
1-199 79905
801-1197 79903
1199-2199 79903
Boots Green Rd 79938
Borcana Ct 79928
Bordeaux Dr 79907
Bordelon Pl 79928
Border Rd 79906
E & W Borderland Rd 79932
Borealis Ln 79912
Boris Becker Pl 79938
Borrett St 79907
Borunda Ln 79907
Bosham Dr 79925
Bosserman Ave 79906
Boston Ave 79902
Bothwell St 79927
Boulder Rdg 79912
Bourbon St 79924
Bouvier Way 79907
Bovee Rd 79927
Bowdoin St 79928
Bowen Rd 79915
Bowers Ave 79907
Bowman Cir 79904
Box Elder Rd 79932
Boxwood Cir 79925
Boy Scout Ln 79922
Boyne Ave 79904
Bradbury Dr 79928
Bradford St 79928
Bradley Rd 79938
Bradshaw Ave 79906
Brady Ln 79904
Brady Pl 79935
Bragg Ave 79904
Brahman Way 79925
Bram Pl 79928
Brand Ct 79905
Brandeis Dr 79928
Brandwood Ct 79925
Brandywine Rd 79907
Branell Ln 79928
Brangus Dr 79927
Branon St 79924
Brasher St 79938
Braveheart Ave 79936
Brayman Pl 79938
Brays Landing Dr 79911
Brazil Pl 79903
Brazos Ave 79905
Breaux St 79928
Breckenridge Dr 79936
Breean Isabell Pl 79938
Breeze Ct 79936
Breezeway Ave 79925
Breish Ct 79925
Bremerton Dr 79928
Brentwood Ave 79902
Bressler 79938
Bret Harte Dr 79928
Brewster Pl 79928
Brezo St 79928
Brian Allin Dr 79936
Brian Mooney Ave 79935
Brian Ray Cir 79936
Brianna Ct 79932
Briarcliff Ct 79932
Briarside Ln 79932
Brice Ct 79928
Brick Dust St 79934
Bridal Way 79932
Bridalveil Dr 79924
Bridget St 79924
Bright Water Ln 79912
Brighton Ln 79902
Brill Cir 79928
Brillo Del Sol 79911
Brillo Luna 79932
Brisa Del Mar Dr 79912
Brisa Del Valle Dr 79927
Brisbane Way 79924
Bristol Dr 79912
Britton Ave 79904
Broad Autumn Ct 79928
Broaddus Ave 79904
Broadmoor Dr 79912
Broadway Dr 79915
Brogan Dr 79915
Broken Arrow Dr 79936
Broken Bow St 79936
Bronce St 79928
Bronco Buster Ln 79936
Bronze Way 79930
Bronze Crest Ln 79902
Brook Hollow Dr 79925
Brook Ridge Cir 79912
Brooke Lauren Pl 79927
Brookhaven Dr 79925
Brookrock St 79935
Brooks Earl Dr 79938
Brookside Pl 79938
Brosius Cir 79904
Brown Rd 79927
Brown St
140-199 79901
600-1699 79902
1701-1999 79902
Brown Ridge Pl 79912
Brownfield Dr
10800-10899 79935
10900-10941 79936
10943-10999 79936
Brownlee Cir 79906
Bruce Pl 79928
Bruce Bissonette Dr 79912
Bruce Devlin Dr 79935
Bruce Jenner 79938
Bruce Jenner Ln 79936
Brunner Pl 79903
Brussels Way 79912
Bryce Dr 79928
Bryn Mawr Ct 79928
Bucher Rd 79915
Buck St 79938
Buckingham Dr 79902
Buckley Dr 79912
Bucknell Dr 79928
Buckner St 79925
Buckwheat St 79938
Buckwood Ave 79925
Bud Allin Pl 79935
Buena Park Dr 79907
Buena Suerte Dr 79912
Buena Vista St 79905
Buffalo 79938
Buffalo Bill Dr 79938
Buffalo Creek Dr 79938
Buffalo Gap Pl 79936
Buffalo Soldier Cir 79936
Buford Rd 79927
Bugler Hoover Ave 79906
Bull Elk Dr 79938
Bull Moose Ct 79938
Bullseye St 79934
Bundala Dr 79927
Bunker St 79906
Bunker Forge Pl 79936
Bunky Henry Ln 79936
Buntline Dr 79938
Bunyan Way 79928
Bur Oak Cir 79907
Burciaga Dr 79912
Burgess Dr 79907
Burgundy Dr 79907
Burma Pl 79927
Burnham Rd 79907
Burning Tree Dr 79912
Burnside Ln 79934
E & W Burt Rd 79927
Bush Ln 79925
Butchofsky Pl 79907
Butte Cir 79902
Butterfield Cir 79906
Butterfield Dr 79932
Butterfield Trail Blvd 79906
Butterfly Pl 79907
Butternut St 79907
Buxton Dr 79928
Byron St
1800-4899 79930
4901-4999 79930
5501-5997 79904
5999-6800 79904
6802-6898 79904
Byway Dr
10200-10399 79925
10400-10499 79935
Bywell 79928
Bywood Dr
10400-10899 79935
10900-10999 79936
Byzantium Ln 79924
C J Levan Ct 79924
Caballo Lake Dr 79936
Cabana Dr 79928
Cabana Del Sol 79911
Cabaret Dr 79912
Cabeza De Vaca Rd 79927
Cabot Pl 79935
Cabrillo Dr 79912
Cachet Pl 79936
Cactus Bloom Ct 79928
Cactus Blossom Dr 79938
Cactus Creek Pl 79928
Cactus Crossing Dr 79928
Cactus Flower 79938
Cactus Hill Dr 79912
Cactus Pointe Ct 79912
Cactus Ridge Ln 79928
Cactus Rose Pl 79934
Cactus Spine Ln 79912
Cactus Thrush 79911
Cactus View Ct 79928
Cactus Wren 79928
Cadiz St 79912
Cadwallader Dr 79915
Cairo Ave 79938
Calais Ln 79907
Calcote Pl 79906
Calcutta Dr 79927
Calgary Ave 79924
Calhoun Dr 79928
Caliche Dr 79915
E & W California Ave 79902
Calla Lily Pl 79928
Calle Alta 79912
Calle Asti St 79932
Calle Azul Way 79912
Calle Bonita Ln 79912
Calle Colina 79912
Calle Corrales 79912
Calle Cuesta 79912
Calle Cumbre 79912
Calle Del Oro 79912
Calle Del Rio 79912
Calle Del Sol Dr 79912
Calle Del Sur 79912
Calle Flor Pl 79912
Calle Lago 79912
Calle Lisa Way 79912
Calle Lomas Dr 79912
Calle Milagro Dr 79912
Calle Olaso Dr 79932
Calle Parque Dr 79912
Calle Paz Pl 79935
Calle Pino 79912
Calle Placido Dr 79912
Calle Roja 79912
Calle Vista Dr 79912
Calleros Ct 79901
Callison Rd 79907
Callisto Ct 79927
Calvary Rd 79928
Camarena Pl 79936
Camargo Ct 79907
Camaro Ct 79935
Cambria Cove Pl 79912
Cambridge Ave 79903
Camden Cir 79924
Camden Lake St 79932
Cameldale Dr 79928
Camelot Hts 79912
Camichin Pl 79927
Camille Dr 79912
Camino Alegre Dr 79912
Camino Alto Rd 79902
Camino Azteca St 79938
Camino Barranca 79912
Camino Bello Ln 79902
Camino Buena Vis 79938
Camino Buena Suerte 79938
Camino Buena Vida 79938
Camino De La Vista Dr 79932
Camino De Paz Ct 79922
Camino De Tierra Rd 79938
Camino Del Sol 79911
Camino Estancias 79912
Camino Fuente Dr 79912
Camino Monte Vis 79938
Camino Norte Ct 79932
Camino Penasco 79912
Camino Real Ave 79922
Camino Vista Linda 79938
Campana Ct 79907
N Campbell St
100-118 79901
120-200 79901
202-498 79901
700-2899 79902
2901-3099 79902
S Campbell St 79901
Campeche Rd 79927
Campestre Ln 79936
Campfire 79936
Campo Verde Ln 79915
Campus Park Dr 79932
Camwood Dr 79925
Can Cun Ln 79912
Cana Ave 79907
Canal Rd 79901
Cananea Ln 79907
Canario Dr 79928
Canary Ct 79915
Canary Palm Ct 79936
Cancellare Ave 79932
Candace Ln 79928
Candado Pl 79912
Candelaria St 79907

Candlewood Ave
7800-10599 ... 79925
10600-10699 ... 79935
Cannes Cir ... 79907
Cannon Forge Pl ... 79936
Cannon Hill Dr ... 79936
Canopy Pl ... 79936
Canterbury Dr ... 79902
Canton Ct ... 79905
Cantona Silvas Ln ... 79927
Canyon Breeze Ln ... 79928
Canyon Point Ln ... 79904
Canyon Ridge Way ... 79912
Canyon Run Dr ... 79912
Canyon Sage Dr ... 79924
Canyon Springs Dr ... 79912
Canyon Terrace Dr ... 79902
Canyon View Ln ... 79912
Canyon Wren Ave ... 79911
Cape Cod Way ... 79907
Capella Ave ... 79904
Capello Way ... 79907
Caper Rd ... 79925
Capistrano Dr ... 79924
Capitan Cir ... 79904
Capitan Rdg ... 79912
Caples Cir ... 79903
Caporal Ct ... 79932
Capricho Ln ... 79907
Capricorn Dr ... 79924
Caprock Ct ... 79912
Captain Valtr St ... 79924
Cara Mia Way ... 79936
Carabinas Way ... 79922
Carablanca Dr ... 79927
Carat Ct ... 79924
Carbajal Rd ... 79927
Cardigan Dr
10200-10639 ... 79925
10640-10899 ... 79935
10900-10999 ... 79936
Cardis Ct ... 79905
Cardon St ... 79903
Carey Way ... 79915
Cargill St ... 79905
Caribe Cir ... 79927
Caribou Dr ... 79924
Carinha Ave ... 79938
Carl Longuemare Rd ... 79907
Carlin Dr & Rd ... 79927
Carlos Bombach Ave ... 79928
Carlos Moran Ct ... 79936
Carlotta Dr ... 79907
Carls Ave ... 79938
Carlsbad Rd ... 79916
Carlson Way ... 79915
Carlyle Pl ... 79903
Carmelita Cir ... 79907
Carmen Rd ... 79928
Carnegie Ave ... 79925
Carnes Rd ... 79907
Carnival Dr ... 79912
Carol St ... 79907
Carole Jeschke Ct ... 79924
N & S Carolina Dr ... 79915
Carousel Dr ... 79912
Carpenter Dr
8000-8099 ... 79915
8101-8197 ... 79907
8199-8348 ... 79907
8350-8398 ... 79907
Carr ... 79927
Carranza Dr ... 79907
Carreta Ln ... 79927
Carrillo Ln ... 79927
Carrington Rd ... 79916
Carrol St ... 79930
Carryback Ct ... 79938
Carson Dr ... 79928
Carswell Ct ... 79908
Cartagena Cir ... 79932
Carter Rd
300-6599 ... 79906
1000-1099 ... 79916
Carter Scott Pl ... 79927
Cartway Ln ... 79925

Casa St ... 79925
Casa Blanca Ave ... 79938
Casa Grande Pl ... 79907
Casa Loma Cir ... 79912
Casa View Dr ... 79936
Cascada St ... 79928
Cascade Dr ... 79928
Cascade Ln ... 79912
Cascade Pt ... 79938
Caseta Rd ... 79922
Casey Stengel Pl ... 79934
Cashew Dr ... 79907
Casino Dr ... 79938
Casitas Del Este Ln ... 79935
Casper Rdg ... 79912
Cassatt Pl ... 79936
Cassidy Dr ... 79938
Cassidy Rd
1400-1499 ... 79906
2400-2999 ... 79916
Cassiopeia Ct ... 79907
E & W Castellano Dr ... 79912
Castile Ave ... 79912
Castillo Ct ... 79932
Castle Ct ... 79908
Castle Dr ... 79908
Castle Way ... 79932
Castle Gate Way ... 79936
Castle Hill Cir ... 79936
Castle Keep Cir ... 79936
Castle View Way ... 79936
Castle Woods Dr ... 79936
Castlefin Dr ... 79927
Castleman Ave ... 79904
Castlerock Ln ... 79912
Castletown Dr ... 79925
Castner Dr ... 79907
Catalina Way ... 79925
Catalpa Ln ... 79925
Catesby Way ... 79911
Catham Cir ... 79928
Cathedral Cir ... 79907
Catherine Ann Dr ... 79936
Catherine Jane Dr ... 79938
Catnip St ... 79925
Catskill Ave ... 79904
Cattle Ln ... 79934
Cattle Ranch St ... 79934
Causeway Dr
10500-10599 ... 79925
10600-10699 ... 79935
Cavalier St ... 79924
E, S & N Cave Ave &
Dr ... 79938
Cave Palm Pl ... 79936
Cayman Ln ... 79927
Cayuga Cir ... 79936
N Cebada St
100-154 ... 79905
156-399 ... 79905
500-598 ... 79903
600-1300 ... 79903
1302-1498 ... 79903
S Cebada St ... 79905
Cecilia Ct ... 79915
Cedar Crk ... 79938
Cedar St
1000-1099 ... 79903
1100-1199 ... 79930
Cedar Breaks Ln ... 79904
Cedar Crest Dr ... 79936
Cedar Oak Dr ... 79936
Cedar Sands Ln ... 79924
Cedardale Pl ... 79925
Cedarwood Ave ... 79928
Celaya Way ... 79927
Celedon Cir ... 79927
Celerity Wagon St ... 79906
Celestial Pl ... 79904
Celia Way ... 79922
Celina Ct ... 79915
Celso Pl ... 79928
Celtic ... 79928
Cemetery Rd ... 79907
Centaur Dr ... 79924
Centennial Dr ... 79912

Center Way ... 79915
Central Ave ... 79905
Century Dr ... 79938
Century Way ... 79924
Century Plant Dr ... 79912
Ceres Pl ... 79907
Cermac St ... 79924
Cerrito Ct ... 79927
Cerrito Alegre Ln ... 79912
Cerrito Alto Ln ... 79912
Cerrito Bajo Ln ... 79912
Cerrito Bello Ln ... 79912
Cerrito Bonito Ln ... 79912
Cerrito Feliz Ln ... 79912
Cerrito Grande Ln ... 79912
Cerrito Perdido Ln ... 79912
Cerro Azul Dr ... 79902
Cerro De Paz St ... 79902
Cerro Negro Dr ... 79912
Cervantes Ct ... 79922
Cessna Dr ... 79925
Ceylon Dr ... 79925
Cezanne Cir ... 79936
Cf Jordan Dr ... 79912
Ch Hunton St ... 79938
Chadbourne St ... 79903
Chaffee Rd ... 79916
Challenger Ln ... 79936
Chama St ... 79905
Chamois Ln ... 79938
Champie Ln ... 79915
Champions Pl ... 79912
Champlain St ... 79924
Chandelier Rd ... 79928
Chandler St ... 79904
Chanticleer Pl ... 79915
Chantilly Dr ... 79907
Chapala Ct ... 79907
Chaparral Pl ... 79902
Chaparral Rd ... 79916
Chapel Pl ... 79907
Chapel Hill Rd ... 79928
Chapel Run Pl ... 79936
Chaplin Ct ... 79936
Chardon Rd ... 79938
Chariot Way ... 79902
Charl Ann St ... 79932
Charles Rd ... 79901
Charles Boyle Pl ... 79934
Charles Coody Ln ... 79935
Charles Maiz Ln ... 79934
Charles Owens Dr ... 79936
Charles Reynolds Ln ... 79934
Charles Young Ave ... 79904
Charleston St ... 79924
Charlie Smith Dr ... 79936
Charlotte Ct ... 79924
Charolais Dr ... 79938
Charro Pt ... 79938
Charter Park Ave ... 79936
Chaswood St ... 79935
Chateau Ave ... 79924
Chato Villa Dr ... 79936
Chaucer Dr ... 79928
Chauvin ... 79928
Chazy Ct ... 79928
Chelita Dr ... 79936
Chelsea St
100-499 ... 79905
501-597 ... 79903
599-1799 ... 79903
1801-1899 ... 79903
Cheltenham Dr ... 79912
Cherbourg Ave ... 79925
Chermont Dr ... 79912
Cherokee Ct ... 79924
Cherokee Ridge Dr ... 79912
Cherrington St ... 79928
Cherry St ... 79915
Cherry Hill Ln ... 79912
Chert St ... 79924
Chesak Cir ... 79905
Chesapeake Ln ... 79912
Cheshire Way ... 79912
Chester Ave ... 79903
Chesterfield Ave ... 79903

Chestnut Ct ... 79915
Chetumal Ln ... 79925
Cheyenne Trl ... 79925
Cheyenne Ridge Dr ... 79912
Chezelle Dr ... 79925
Chianti Dr ... 79928
Chick A Dee St ... 79924
Chickasaw Dr ... 79936
Chico Ct ... 79903
Chihuahua St ... 79901
Childress Ave ... 79936
Chile Pl ... 79903
Chime Tower Pl ... 79936
Chinaberry Dr ... 79925
Chinchilla Ln ... 79907
Chino Dr ... 79915
Chinook Ln ... 79912
Chip Chip Way ... 79915
Chippendale Ave ... 79934
Chiquis Ln ... 79936
Chiricahua Dr ... 79912
Chisholm Pass Dr ... 79936
Chisolm Trail Dr ... 79927
Chisos Ln ... 79904
Chito Samaniego Dr ... 79936
Cholla Dr ... 79928
Chris Evert Pl ... 79938
Chris Forbes ... 79927
Chris Roark Pl ... 79936
Chris Scott Dr ... 79936
Christenson Cir ... 79904
Christian Castle ... 79938
Christian Cunningham ... 79938
Christian Isaiah Ct ... 79928
Christopher Ave ... 79912
Christy Ave ... 79907
Chromite St ... 79932
Chula Vista St ... 79915
Church Ave ... 79930
Cibolo Ct ... 79905
Cibolo Creek Dr ... 79911
Cidra Del Sol ... 79911
Cielito Lindo Dr ... 79938
Cielo Azul Dr ... 79927
Cielo De Oro Pl ... 79924
Cielo Del Rey Pl ... 79924
Cielo Del Rio Pl ... 79932
Cielo Lindo Dr ... 79927
Cielo Mistico Dr ... 79927
Cielo Vista Dr ... 79925
Cimarron Rdg ... 79912
Cimarron St ... 79915
Cincinnati Ave ... 79902
Cindy Ln ... 79927
Cinecue Way ... 79907
Cinnamon Teal Cir ... 79932
Circle Dr ... 79902
Circus Ln ... 79912
Cirwood Dr ... 79935
Cisco Ln ... 79924
Cisneros Pl ... 79904
Citadel Dr ... 79928
Citation Dr ... 79936
Citrus Pl ... 79901
Civic Center Plz ... 79901
Claiborne St ... 79928
Claire Pl ... 79904
Clairemont Dr ... 79912
Clancy Ln ... 79928
Clara Barton Dr ... 79936
Claralli Ave ... 79903
Claravista Ln ... 79912
Clarisa Ln ... 79907
N & S Clark Dr & Pl ... 79905
Clarkstone Ct ... 79932
Claudia Dr ... 79927
Clausen Dr ... 79925
Clavel Dr ... 79907
Clay Ct ... 79932
Clay Basket Cir ... 79936
Clay Springs Rd ... 79938
Clayton Rd ... 79932
Clayton St ... 79902
Clear Lake Way ... 79936
Clearbrook Pl ... 79938
Clearview Ln ... 79904

Clearwater St ... 79924
Clemente Ave ... 79912
Clems Rd ... 79927
Clemson Ln ... 79928
Cleo Amelia Ln ... 79938
Cleralea Ave ... 79905
Cleto Rodriguez ... 79938
Cleveland Ave
5700-5799 ... 79925
5800-6299 ... 79905
E & W Cliff Dr ... 79902
Cliff Rock Ln ... 79935
Cliff Rose Ct ... 79928
Clifford Ct ... 79907
Clifton Ave ... 79903
Clio St ... 79904
Clistric Dr ... 79922
Cloud Ridge Dr ... 79912
Cloudburst Dr ... 79912
Cloudview Dr ... 79912
Cloudy Sky Dr ... 79932
Clover Way ... 79915
Cloverdale Dr ... 79928
Clyde Rd ... 79925
Clydesdale Dr ... 79924
Coachwhip Dr ... 79938
Coat Of Arms Pl ... 79936
Coates Dr ... 79932
Cobre St ... 79928
Cochise Ln ... 79912
Cockrell Ln ... 79924
Coco Palm ... 79936
Coconut Tree Ln ... 79915
Cocotitlan ... 79928
Cocoyoc Ct ... 79932
Cocula Ave ... 79932
Coe ... 79904
Coeur Dalene Cir ... 79922
Coffin Ave ... 79902
Cohen Ave ... 79924
Coker Rd ... 79927
Colby Dr ... 79928
Colchester Dr ... 79912
Cold War St ... 79916
Coldridge Valley Pl ... 79928
N Coldwell St ... 79901
Cole Rd ... 79906
Coleen Way ... 79936
Coleridge Rd ... 79928
Coles St ... 79901
Colette St ... 79924
Colfax St ... 79905
Colin Powell Ave ... 79934
Colina Pl ... 79907
Colina Alta Dr ... 79912
Colina Baja Way ... 79928
Colina Bella Dr ... 79928
Colina Blanca Pl ... 79928
Colina Corona Dr ... 79928
Colina De Luz ... 79928
Colina De Oro St ... 79928
Colina De Paz ... 79928
Colina De Rio St ... 79928
N & S Collingsworth
St ... 79905
Collins Dr ... 79906
Colmenero Ct ... 79907
Colmillo Dr ... 79907
Coloma Cir ... 79907
Colonia Campo Dr ... 79928
Colonia Granja Dr ... 79928
Colonia Morales ... 79928
Colonia Tierra Dr ... 79928
Colonial Blf ... 79928
Colt Ln ... 79907
Colter Ct ... 79904
Columbia Ave ... 79907
Columbine St ... 79922
Columbus Way ... 79903
Colville Dr ... 79928
Comanche Ave ... 79905
Comet St ... 79904
Comice Ln ... 79912
Comington St ... 79930
Commerce Ave ... 79915
Commerce Park Dr ... 79912

Commercial Dr ... 79938
Commodore St ... 79924
Common Dr ... 79936
Comstock Ct ... 79904
N & S Concepcion St ... 79905
Concha St ... 79907
Concord St ... 79906
Conejo Ln ... 79907
Conere Dr ... 79938
Confederate Rd ... 79936
Confetti Dr ... 79912
Congo Way ... 79907
Conifero Ct ... 79932
Conley Rd ... 79932
Connolly Dr ... 79938
Connors Ln ... 79932
Conover Ln ... 79924
Conquistador Dr ... 79927
Conrad Ct ... 79927
Conrad Nathan Pl ... 79936
Constellation Dr ... 79912
Constitution Ave ... 79918
Constitution Blvd ... 79938
Constitution Dr ... 79922
Contessa Rdg ... 79912
Continental Dr ... 79925
Convair Rd ... 79925
Cook Dr ... 79907
Cool Brook Dr ... 79936
Cooley Ave ... 79907
Copa De Oro Ct ... 79936
N Copia St
100-399 ... 79905
500-1600 ... 79903
1602-1698 ... 79903
1900-2098 ... 79930
2100-3599 ... 79930
3601-5099 ... 79930
S Copia St ... 79905
Copper Ave ... 79930
Copper Canyon Dr ... 79934
Copper Cloud Cir ... 79912
Copper Crest Ln ... 79902
Copper Gate Pl ... 79936
Copper Head Ln ... 79934
Copper Hill Pl ... 79934
Copper Mine Ln ... 79934
Copper Nail Ln ... 79934
Copper Point Pl ... 79934
Copper Ranch Ave ... 79934
Copper Ridge Dr ... 79912
Copper Sky Ct ... 79934
Copper Town Dr ... 79934
Copper Trail Ave ... 79934
Copper Valley Ln ... 79934
Copperfield Ln ... 79912
Copperqueen Dr ... 79915
Cora Pl ... 79915
Cora Bell Pl ... 79936
Cora Ruecker ... 79928
Cora Viescas Ln ... 79936
Coral Gate Dr ... 79936
Coral Hills Rd ... 79912
Coral Palm Ct ... 79936
Coral Sands Dr ... 79924
Coral Sky Ln ... 79912
Coral Willow Dr ... 79922
Coralstone Dr
10500-10639 ... 79925
10640-10699 ... 79935
Corby Pl ... 79928
Cordero Way ... 79922
Corey Creek Dr ... 79912
Corinth Ct ... 79927
Cork Dr ... 79925
Cornelius Dr ... 79907
Cornell Ave ... 79924
Cornhusk Ln ... 79932
Cornus Ln ... 79925
Cornwall Rd ... 79925
Corona Ave ... 79905
Corona Crest Ave ... 79936
Corona Del Sol ... 79911
Coronado Rd ... 79915
Coronado Ridge Dr ... 79912
Coronel Dr ... 79928

Corozal Dr ... 79915
Corral Dr ... 79915
Corralitos Ave ... 79907
Corsicana Ave ... 79924
Corte Del Rey ... 79932
Corte Del Sol St ... 79930
Corte Rimini Way ... 79932
Cortesano Ct ... 79912
Cortez Dr ... 79905
Cortijo Dr ... 79912
Cortina Dr ... 79912
Corto Way ... 79902
Cortona Pl ... 79928
Corvena Way ... 79922
Cory Dr ... 79932
Corzo Pl ... 79928
Cosecha Luna ... 79932
Cosmos Ave ... 79925
Costa Blanca Pl ... 79932
Costa Brava ... 79938
Costa De Oro Rd ... 79922
N Cotton St
100-299 ... 79901
600-1299 ... 79902
1301-1399 ... 79902
S Cotton St ... 79901
Cottontail Dr ... 79938
Cottonwoods ... 79925
Cougar Rdg ... 79912
Cougar St ... 79934
Country Abby Dr ... 79932
Country Club Pl ... 79922
Country Club Rd ... 79932
Country Oaks Dr ... 79932
Coupland Ct ... 79922
Courchesne Rd ... 79922
Courtland Dr ... 79907
Coventry Cir ... 79907
Covey Way ... 79936
Covington Ridge Way ... 79928
Cow Tongue Dr ... 79928
Cowan Cir ... 79904
Cowlitz Ln ... 79938
Cox Rd ... 79932
Coxe Ave ... 79904
Coyote Ln ... 79912
Coyote Bluff Ct ... 79938
Coyote Draw Pl ... 79938
Coyote Drift Ct ... 79938
Coyote Hill Ln ... 79938
Coyote Park Dr ... 79938
Coyote Pass Ln ... 79938
Coyote Point Pl ... 79938
Coyote Ranch Ln ... 79934
Coyote Trail Dr ... 79938
Coyote View Pl ... 79938
Cozumel Ln ... 79925
Cozy Cv ... 79938
Cozy Creek Dr ... 79938
Cozy Edge Way ... 79928
Cozy Prairie Dr ... 79938
Cpl Anthony J Carson
St ... 79908
Cpl Rigo Gutierrez Rd ... 79927
Craddock Ave ... 79915
Craggy Rock Ave ... 79938
Craig Way ... 79907
Craigo Ave ... 79904
Cramer Ln ... 79915
Cramer Rd ... 79916
Crane Ave ... 79922
Crater Lake Ave ... 79936
Crawford Ct ... 79907
Crazy Horse Dr ... 79936
Cree Ct ... 79936
Crenshaw Dr ... 79924
Creosote ... 79928
Crescent Cir ... 79903
Crescent Moon Pl ... 79932
Crest Creek Ln ... 79911
Crest Gate Way ... 79936
Cresta Alta Dr ... 79912
Cresta Bonita Dr ... 79912
Cresta Mira Dr ... 79912
Crested Quail Dr ... 79936
Crestmont Dr ... 79912

Creston Ave 79924
Crestwood Pl 79907
Crete Dr 79924
Cribbs Pl 79904
Crimson Cloud Ln 79912
Crimson Crest Ln 79936
Crimson Sky Dr 79936
Cristal Point Way 79938
Cristian Ct 79928
Cristo Viene Dr 79907
Criswell Ln 79932
Crocker Dr 79928
Crockett St 79922
Cromo Dr 79912
Cronus Dr 79924
Croom Rd 79915
E & W Crosby Ave 79902
Cross St 79924
Cross Canyon Pl 79912
Cross Ridge Dr 79912
Cross River Rd 79928
Cross Timbers Ct 79932
Crossbend Ct 79932
Crossland Ct 79938
Crosson Cir 79904
Crossroads Dr
  4901-4999 79922
  5000-5099 79932
Croton Cir 79924
Crow Dr 79935
Crowell Dr 79927
Crown Hill Pl 79936
Crown Oaks Ct 79936
Crown Point Dr 79912
Crown Ridge Dr 79912
Crown Rock Dr 79938
Crown Royal Dr 79936
Crown Woods Ct 79936
Crucebello Way 79912
Crucero Del Sol 79911
Crusade Dr 79912
Cruz Tierra St 79938
Crystal Dr 79912
Crystal Cove Pl 79912
Crystal Gate Dr 79936
Crystal Ridge St 79938
Crystal Sands Ct 79924
Cuartel Ln 79912
Cuatro Vistas Dr 79935
Cuba Dr 79915
Cuernavaca Dr 79907
Cuesta Brava Ln 79935
Cueva De Oro Ct 79902
Cullen Ave 79915
Cullins Ave 79938
Cumberland Ave & Cir 79903
Cumbre Negra St 79935
Cumbrian Ln 79912
Cuna Pl 79928
Cupid Dr 79924
Cuprite Dr 79932
Curie Dr 79902
Curlew Ln 79924
Curley Ave 79938
Curt Byrum Pl 79928
Cutlass Dr 79932
Cutler Pl 79928
Cutty Sark Dr 79936
Cynthia Farah Pl 79936
Cypress Ave 79905
Cypress Point Ct 79928
Cypress Ridge Dr 79912
Da Vinci St 79936
Dade Rd 79938
Daffodil Pl 79928
Dahl Cir 79906
Dahlia Ct 79922
Dailey Ave 79905
Dairyland Ave 79928
Daisy St 79925
Dakota St 79930
Dakota Ridge Dr 79912
Dakota River Ave 79932
Dale Rd 79915
Dale Douglas Dr 79936
Dalhart Dr 79924
Dali Way 79936
Daljit Ct 79927
Dallas St
  1-297 79901
  299-399 79901
  600-999 79902
  1001-1099 79902
Dalton Ave 79924
Damacio Colmenero Ct 79927
Damasco Dr 79936
Damian Dr 79938
Damsel Point Pl 79938
Dan Sikes Dr 79936
Dana Bree Dr 79936
Dana Michelle Dr 79928
Danbury Rd 79907
Dandelion Way 79936
Daniels Ln 79936
Danny Dr 79924
Dantin Ct 79907
Danube Cir 79907
Danube Dr 79928
Danube Way 79928
Daphne Ct 79925
Daplin Way 79934
Darby Way 79912
Darin Rd 79925
Darius Ct 79927
Darkshire Ct 79928
Darley Dr 79928
Darlina Dr 79925
Darnall St 79930
S Darrington Rd 79928
Dartmouth Dr 79928
Darway Dr 79925
Darwin Rd 79928
Darwood Dr 79902
Date Tree Ln 79915
Datil Dr 79924
Datsun Dr 79927
Daugherty Dr 79925
Dave Elliott Dr 79936
Dave Head Loop 79938
Dave Marr Ct 79935
Davenport Rd 79907
Daventry Ct 79928
David Barkey 79938
David Bret 79936
David Carrasco Dr 79936
David Forti Dr 79936
David Garcia Rd 79907
David Lee Ct 79936
David M Brown Ct 79934
David Ray Way 79936
Davidson Blvd 79938
N & S Davis Dr 79907
Davis Cup Ct 79932
Davis Seamon Rd 79930
Davwood Ln 79925
Dawkins Ct 79904
Dawn Dr 79912
Dawnlight Ln 79911
Daybreak 79932
Dayna Ct 79928
De Anza Cir 79925
De Bartolo Ln 79928
De Gaulle Pl 79928
De Havilland Dr 79925
De Leon Ct & Dr 79912
De Lucio Rd 79927
De Palma Pl 79928
De Quincy 79928
De Soto Ave 79912
De Stefano Ln 79928
De Vaca Ct 79927
De Vargas Dr 79905
Dean Rd 79938
Dean Jones St 79936
Dean Martin Dr 79936
Dean Refram Dr 79936
Dearborne Dr 79924
Death Valley Ln 79938
Debbie Dr 79925
Debbie Rd 79938
Debbie Good 79932
Debeers Dr 79924
Deborah Dr 79927
Debra Kaye Ave 79938
Decamp Point Pl 79938
Decatur Way 79924
Dede Ln 79902
Deepwood Ct 79925
Deer Ave 79924
Deer Rdg 79912
Deer Grass Cir 79936
Deer Track Ct 79938
Deerfield Park Dr 79938
Defoe Rd 79928
Deke Slayton Ln 79936
Del Mar Dr 79932
Del Monte St 79915
Del Norte St 79915
Del Rio St 79915
Del Rivers 79907
Del Valle Pl 79932
Delacroix Dr 79936
Delafield Dr 79936
Delano Dr 79927
Delaware St 79905
Delfina Dr 79907
Delhi Dr 79927
Delhi Pl 79928
Delia Ave 79938
Delicias Ct 79907
Delilah Ave 79927
Dell Haven Ave 79907
Dellwood Dr 79924
Delta Dr
  901-1197 79901
  1199-1500 79901
  1502-1798 79901
  3900-4298 79905
  4300-6999 79905
Delta Point Dr 79938
Demerritt Ave 79916
Dempsey Ave 79925
Dennis Cir 79925
Dennis Babjack Dr 79936
Dennis Cavin Ln 79934
Denver Ave 79902
Depalm Island Pl 79936
Derby Point Dr 79938
Derick Rd 79925
Derrickson Dr 79912
Derringer Rd 79938
N Desert Blvd 79912
S Desert Blvd 79932
Desert Loop 79938
Desert Pass 79912
Desert Ash Dr 79928
Desert Bloom Dr 79938
Desert Blossom Dr 79938
Desert Breeze Dr 79928
Desert Bush Dr 79928
Desert Cactus Dr 79928
Desert Canyon Dr 79912
Desert Chicory St 79928
Desert Cloud Dr 79928
Desert Cove Ln 79912
Desert Crest Way 79928
Desert Dandelion St 79928
Desert Eagle Dr 79912
Desert Fire Ct 79928
Desert Gold Dr 79938
Desert Highlands Ln 79928
Desert Hills Ln 79925
Desert Jewel Dr 79912
Desert Keep Dr 79936
Desert Lily Pl 79928
Desert Marigold St 79928
Desert Meadows Rd 79938
Desert Mesa Dr 79928
Desert Mesquite Dr 79928
Desert Moon Dr 79928
Desert Ocotillo Dr 79928
Desert Orchid Dr 79928
Desert Point Dr 79928
Desert Quail Ave 79936
Desert Rain Dr 79936
Desert Ridge Dr 79925
Desert Rose Ct 79928
Desert Sage Dr 79928
Desert Sands Pl 79924
Desert Shadow Dr 79928
Desert Silver Dr 79928
Desert Skies Pl 79912
Desert Sky Dr 79928
Desert Song Dr 79928
Desert Spring Dr 79928
Desert Star Dr 79928
Desert Stone Dr 79928
Desert Storm 79938
Desert Sun Dr
  1700-1799 79928
  1900-2099 79938
Desert Sunset Dr 79928
Desert View Ln 79934
Desert Wildflower Pl 79928
Desert Willow Dr 79938
Desert Willow Way 79924
Desert Wind Dr 79928
Desert Yucca Pl 79928
Desierto Azul Dr 79912
Desierto Bello Ave 79928
Desierto Bonito Ave 79928
Desierto Bueno Ave 79928
Desierto Lindo Ave 79928
Desierto Luna St 79912
Desierto Maiz Ct 79912
Desierto Oro Ct 79912
Desierto Pais Dr 79912
Desierto Rico Ave 79912
Desierto Rojo Ct 79912
Desierto Rosa Pl 79912
Desierto Seco Dr 79912
Desierto Sol Ct 79912
Desierto Verde Ct 79928
Desierto Vista Ct 79928
Destello Rd 79907
Destiny Ave 79938
Destiny Point Dr 79938
Detroit Ave
  1901-1997 79902
  1999-2099 79902
  2401-2499 79930
Devils Tower Cir 79904
Devon Ave 79924
Devonshire Dr 79925
Devontry Dr 79934
Devore Ct 79904
Dew Dr 79912
Dewberry Dr 79911
Dial Rock Ln 79935
Diamond Dr 79904
Diamond Cove Pl 79912
Diamond Crest Ln 79902
Diamond Gate Pl 79936
Diamond Head Dr 79936
Diamond Point Cir 79912
Diamond Ridge Dr 79912
Diamond Springs Dr 79928
Diana Dr
  7400-8098 79904
  8100-9099 79904
  9100-9298 79924
  9300-9499 79924
  9501-9599 79924
Diana Candia 79936
Diana Natalicio Dr 79936
Diane Lynn Ct 79936
Diane Troyer Way 79936
Dianjou Dr 79912
Diciembre Dr 79935
Dick Lotz Ln 79936
Dick Mayers Dr 79936
Dick Ritter Dr 79936
Dickens Rd 79928
Dickman Rd 79906
Diego Ave 79938
Diego Aidan Dr 79938
Diego Rivera Dr 79936
Diesel Dr 79907
Dijon Pl 79927
Dilly Ct 79928
Dina Ct 79907
Dindinger Rd 79927
Dini Rozi Dr 79927
Dipp Ave 79938
Dirk Ct 79925
Disney Dr 79907
Disraeli Way 79928
Dixon Pl 79907
Dizzy Dean Pl 79934
Dobbs Ave 79904
Doc Holiday Pl 79936
Dodge Rd 79915
Doe Ct 79924
Doe Ln 79938
Dogwood St 79925
Dolan Ct & St 79905
Dolomite Dr 79904
Dolores Ct 79915
Dolph Quijano Pl 79936
Dolphin Dr 79924
Dome Ct 79928
Domingo St 79932
Dominic Anakin Dr 79928
Dominican St 79936
Don Budge Way 79936
Don Haskins Dr 79936
Don January Dr 79935
Don Meredith Ln 79936
Don Morril St 79938
Don Quixote Ct 79922
Dona Beatriz Cir & Ln 79932
Donahue Ave 79904
Doncaster St 79928
Donegal Rd 79925
Doniphan Dr
  1081-3297 79922
  3299-4999 79922
  5000-6499 79932
Doniphan Rd 79906
Doniphan Park Cir 79922
Donna Caponi Ln 79936
Donna Kvapil Pl 79932
Donna Marie Dr 79927
Donny Murray Ln 79928
Donnybrook Pl 79902
Donway Pl 79925
Dorbandt Cir 79907
Doris Rd 79927
Doris St 79938
Dornoch St 79925
Dorothy Way 79936
Dorsey Dr 79912
Dos Deannas Dr 79936
Dos Palmas Dr 79936
Dos Reyes Pl 79936
Dos Rios Dr 79936
Double Jay Dr 79936
Doug Allan 79932
Doug Ford Dr 79935
Doug Olson Dr 79936
Douglas Ave 79903
Dover Ct 79922
Dow Ln 79938
Downs Ct 79924
Doy Dr 79928
Doyle Pl 79907
Draco Pl 79907
Dragon Crest Dr 79936
Dragonfly Way 79936
Drake Pl 79907
Drammen Way 79927
Dreamlight Pl 79911
Drillstone Dr 79925
Driver Cir & Ln 79903
Drugan Ave 79907
Drummer Boy 79932
Drumond Rd 79925
Drury Ln 79915
Dryden Pl 79928
Dryden Rd 79907
Duanesburg St 79928
Dublin Rd 79925
Duchess St 79904
Dudley Rd 79906
Duke Ct 79903
Duke Snider Cir 79934
Dulce Cir 79907
Dulce Tierra Dr 79912
Dulcinea Ct 79922
Dumas Dr 79927
Dumont Ln 79912
Dunbarton Dr 79925
Dundee St 79925
Dungarvan Dr 79925
Dunlap Dr 79924
Dunlin Pl 79928
Dunne Ave 79905
Dunoon Dr 79925
Dunterad Dr 79908
Duplex Blvd 79938
Duran Pl 79915
S Durango St 79901
Durazno Ave 79905
Durrill Rd 79915
Dusk Creek Pl 79911
Duskin Dr 79907
Duskwood St 79928
Duson 79928
Dust Devil Ct 79928
Duster Dr 79934
Duval Pl 79924
Duwamish Dr 79938
Duxbury Dr 79912
Dyer St
  2400-2498 79903
  2800-2998 79930
  3000-4199 79930
  4116-4116 79931
  4200-5098 79930
  4201-5099 79930
  5300-9099 79904
  9100-10600 79924
  10602-10798 79924
  10800-12499 79934
  12501-13799 79934
Eads Pl 79935
Eagle Dr 79912
Eagle St 79918
Eagle Crest Pl 79936
Eagle Heart Dr 79936
Eagle Pass Ln 79924
Eagle Point St 79912
Eagle Ridge Dr 79912
Eagles Den Ln 79927
Eaglestone Way 79925
Early Morn Ave 79938
East Rd 79915
Eastbrook Dr 79938
Easter Way 79915
Eastern Sky 79938
Eastlake Dr 79928
Eastland St 79907
Eastman Ct & St 79930
Eastridge Dr 79925
Eastside Rd 79915
Easy Way 79932
Eaton Ct 79915
Ebb Tide Dr 79936
Echo St 79904
Echo Cliffs Dr 79912
Eclipse St 79904
Ed Furgol Ct 79936
Ed Merrins Dr 79936
Ed White Way 79936
Edgar Rd 79932
Edgar Degas St 79936
Edgar Park Ave 79904
Edge Of Texas 79934
Edgemere Blvd
  6200-10699 79925
  10800-10899 79935
  11101-11497 79936
  11499-11599 79936
  11601-11799 79936
  12300-12999 79938
  13001-14399 79938
Edgerock Dr 79935
Edinburg Dr 79924
Edison Way 79925
Edith Dr 79915
Edmonton Ave 79924
Edna Ave 79905
Edsel Ct 79903
Edward James Ave 79936
Edward Williams Dr 79938
Edwards St
  1500-1598 79903
  1600-1699 79903
  11100-11198 79908
  11156-11158 79918
Egret Way 79922
Eichelberger Ave 79938
Eileen Dr 79904
Eisenberg Ave 79938
Eisenhower Ave 79924
Ekery Ave 79938
El Arco Dr 79907
El Cajon Dr 79912
El Camino Dr 79912
El Campo Dr 79924
El Castillo Pl 79912
El Centauro Dr 79922
El Cid Dr 79927
El Dorado Dr 79925
El Encanto Pl 79902
El Greco Cir 79936
El Gusto Dr 79912
El Morro Rd 79904
El Nido Ct 79905
El Parque Dr 79912
El Paso Dr 79905
N El Paso St
  600-699 79901
  701-897 79902
  899-1599 79902
  1601-1699 79902
S El Paso St 79901
El Pedregal Way 79912
El Pinal Pl 79912
El Portal Dr 79903
El Poste Ct 79912
El Puente Dr 79912
El Quelite Pl 79932
El Risco St 79912
El Rosio Ave 79928
El Salto Dr 79927
El Tepeyac Ave 79927
El Vergel Dr 79907
Elaine Pl 79915
Elba Margarita Cir 79927
Elberton Way 79907
Elder Rd 79915
Eleanor Way 79922
Elena Ave 79905
Elgin Dr 79907
Elgin Ln 79928
Elias Pl 79936
Eligio Dr 79927
Elise St 79924
Elizabeth Dr 79927
Elk Pt 79938
Elk Rock Way 79938
Elkhart Dr
  10800-10899 79935
  10900-10999 79936
Elkhorn Ct 79936
Elkton Way 79924
Ellen Dr 79927
Ellen Sue St 79927
Ellendale 79928
Ellerthorpe Ave 79904
Ellington Ct 79908
Elliott Dr 79915
Ellis St 79903
Elm St
  1001-1099 79903
  1101-1197 79930
  1199-3700 79930
  3702-4498 79930
Elmhurst Dr 79925
Elmo Ln 79928
Elmridge Ct 79925
Elmwood Ct 79932
Eloice Rd 79924
Elon Ln 79912
Eloy Tellez Ln 79934
Elsa Pl 79924
Elsworth Dr 79928
Elvin Way 79907
Elvira Way 79922
Emerald Dr 79904

Emerald Acres 79928
Emerald Bay Way 79928
Emerald Bluff Dr 79928
Emerald Brook Dr 79928
Emerald Butte Pl 79928
Emerald Cloud Ln 79928
Emerald Coast Ln 79928
Emerald Cove Way 79928
Emerald Creek Dr 79928
Emerald Crest Way 79902
Emerald Draw Dr 79928
Emerald Dunes Pl 79928
Emerald Falls Dr 79928
Emerald Forest Pl 79928
Emerald Gate Ln 79936
Emerald Gem Ln 79928
Emerald Glen St 79928
Emerald Glow Ln 79928
Emerald Green Dr 79928
Emerald Hills St 79928
Emerald Isle St 79928
Emerald Lake Pl 79928
Emerald Manor Dr 79928
Emerald Mist Dr 79928
Emerald Nook Ct 79928
Emerald Park Dr 79928
Emerald Pass Ave 79928
Emerald Point Dr 79938
Emerald Pond Dr 79928
Emerald Reef Dr 79928
Emerald Rise Dr 79928
Emerald River St 79928
Emerald Run St 79928
Emerald Seas Way 79928
Emerald Shore Ln 79928
Emerald Skies Way 79928
Emerald Sky Pl 79928
Emerald Springs Ln 79928
Emerald Terrace Dr 79928
Emerald Tide Way 79928
Emerald Trail Way 79928
Emerald View Dr 79932
Emerald Vista Pl 79928
Emerald Way St 79928
Emerald Woods St 79928
Emerson St 79915
Emily Ct 79936
Emma Ln 79938
Emma Way 79907
Emmett Larkin Pl 79904
Emory Rd 79922
Empire Ave 79925
Encantado Dr 79928
Encanto Way 79912
Encino Dr 79905
Endeavor Pl 79934
Endwall St 79928
Enero Dr 79935
Enfield Way 79907
England Pl 79934
English Ave 79938
English Point Ave 79938
Enid Ct 79912
Enid Wilson Ln 79936
Ennis St 79928
Enrique Ln 79907
Enrique Gomez Ln 79938
Ensenada Way 79927
Enterprise Ct 79912
Envoy Way 79907
Ephesus Ct 79927
Episo Rd 79927
Equestrian Rd 79928
Equinox Ct 79924
Eric Payne Ct 79936
Erica St 79925
Ernest Rd 79927
Ernesto Serna Pl 79936
Ernie Banks Dr 79934
Eron Way 79915
Escalante Dr 79927
Escalera Dr 79928
Escalon Way 79912
Escape Point St 79938
Escarpa Dr 79935
Escobar Dr 79907
Escondida Pl 79927
Escondido Dr 79912
Escudo Rd 79927
Esmara Ct 79936
Esmeralda Armendariz 79932
Espada Dr 79912
Espana Ln 79912
Espanola Ln 79912
Esparza Ln 79934
Esper Dr 79936
Esperanza Cir 79922
Espina Dulce Pl 79912
Esplanada Cir 79932
Espolon Dr 79912
Essex Falls Ln 79934
Estancia Way 79927
Estancia Clara Ln 79927
Esteban Ln 79905
Esther Rd 79907
Esther Lama Dr 79936
Eston Pl 79928
Estrada Dr 79936
N Estrella St
 100-148 79905
 150-200 79905
 202-398 79905
 500-1299 79903
 1301-1399 79903
S Estrella St 79905
Ethel Rd 79932
Ethyl Hart St 79927
Etling Way 79911
Eubanks Ct 79902
N Eucalyptus St
 1-5 79901
 7-99 79901
 101-199 79901
 800-899 79903
S Eucalyptus St 79905
Euclid St 79905
Eugene Cir 79907
Eugenia Ct 79925
Euphrates Dr 79907
Evalyn Ave 79904
Everest Dr 79912
Evergreen St 79905
Everlook Ln 79928
Evert Dr 79932
Everwood St 79925
Excalibur Dr 79902
Executive Center Blvd
 100-599 79902
 701-799 79922
Exeter Dr 79928
Exodus St 79936
Ezekiel Ln 79938
Ezequiel Coca Way 79927
Fabian 79932
Fabled Point Ave 79938
Faena 79927
Fair Lawn Ln 79922
Fairbanks Dr 79924
Fairchild St 79908
Fairfax St 79924
Fairfield Dr 79925
Fairview Ct 79932
Fairway Cir 79922
Fairwood Ct 79928
Faith Rd 79938
Falby Ct 79915
Falcon Ave 79924
Falcon Head Ln 79912
Falcon Point Ln 79938
Falk St 79927
Falkirk Ave 79925
Fall River Rd 79907
Fallen Hero Ln 79938
Falling Leaf Cir 79934
Falling Rock Pl 79938
Falling Star Way 79912
Fandango Pl 79912
Far View Ct 79928
Faraings Ave 79904
Farrell Rd 79927
E & W Father Rahm Ave 79901
Fatima Ave 79915
Faust Wardy Ct 79924
Favila Rd 79927
Fawn Dr 79938
Fawn Passage Pl 79936
Faxon Dr 79924
Fay Rd 79907
Fe Jackson Rd 79927
Feather Hawk Dr 79912
Febrero Dr 79935
Federal Ave 79930
Felix Rd 79938
Feliz Pl 79905
Fenway Dr 79925
Ferguson Dr 79938
Ferinand Ct 79932
Fern Way 79902
Fernando Zubia Ave 79938
Fernridge Ct 79925
Fernwood Cir 79932
Ferrari Ct 79912
Fertell Dr 79924
N & S Festival Dr 79912
Fewel St 79902
Fiddlewood Cir & Ln 79936
Fieldrock Ct 79935
Fierro Dr 79935
Fiesta Dr 79912
Figueroa Rd 79927
Fiji Palm Pl 79936
Fillmore Ave 79930
Finch Way 79922
Findley Ave 79905
Fineman Cir 79904
Finita Ln 79907
Finsterwald Pl 79936
Fir St 79925
Fire Barrel Way 79934
Fire Fighter 79938
Fire Ridge Cir 79932
Firedale Ln 79912
Firefly Way 79936
Firehouse Dr 79936
Fireside Ln 79912
Firestar Ln 79912
Firestone Dr 79925
Firewood Dr 79938
Firstwood 79905
Fishkill Dr 79928
Fito Hernandez St 79928
Fito Molina Ln 79934
Fitzpatrick Way 79928
Flaca Ln 79927
Flager St 79938
Flagon Pl 79936
Flagstaff Ct 79915
Flamingo Dr 79902
Flanagan Pl 79928
Flariewo Dr 79927
N Flarkern St 79902
Flax St 79925
Fleetwood Rd 79932
Flemish Cir 79912
Fletcher Pl 79936
Flicker Way 79915
Flint Cir 79915
Flor Acacia Ct 79927
Flor Amarilla Ave 79927
Flor Azucena Ln 79927
Flor Blanca Ave 79927
Flor Bonita Ave 79927
Flor Del Rio St 79927
Flor Del Sol St 79927
Flor Del Sur Ave 79927
Flor Eucharis Dr 79927
Flor Gentiana Dr 79927
Flor Liatris Dr 79927
Flor Marsha St 79927
Flor Morada Rd 79927
Flor Preciosa Ln 79927
Flor Prunus Ln 79927
Flor Rubus Ct 79927
Flor Scabiosa Dr 79927
Flor Tulipan St 79927
Flor Veronica Dr 79927
Flora Ct 79928
Flora Ln 79938
Flora Alba Dr 79928
Floralia St 79927
N Florence St
 100-198 79901
 200-299 79901
 900-3099 79902
S Florence St 79901
Flory Ave 79904
Flounder Dr 79924
Flower Dr 79905
Flowering Cactus Pl 79928
Flowers Dr 79938
Floyd Way 79915
Floyd Childs Ct 79936
Fluff Grass Ln 79928
Fluorite Dr 79932
Flynn Dr 79932
Fody Ave 79904
Foggy Pt 79938
Folklore Ct 79936
Fonseca Dr 79905
Foothills Dr 79924
Forbes Dr 79908
Fordham Dr 79928
Forest Ridge Ln 79935
Forest Willow Cir 79922
Forgan Way 79911
Forney Ln 79935
Forrest Rd 79916
Forrest Way 79903
Forrest Haven Ct 79907
Forrest Hills Dr 79932
Forsan Dr 79927
Fort Blvd 79930
Fort Apache Ln 79938
Fort Davis 79938
Fort Defiance Dr 79938
Fort Worth St 79924
Fortenberry Pl 79928
Fortuna St 79928
Fortune Ct 79907
Foster Dr 79907
Founders Blvd 79906
Fountain Rd 79912
Fountain Hills Pl 79932
Fourth Of July 79938
Fox Pl 79905
Fragrant Ash Pl 79907
Frances Silva 79938
Francesca Dr 79936
Francine St 79907
Francis St 79905
Francis Scobee Dr 79936
Francisco Ave 79912
Francisco Paz Dr 79938
Francisco Roque Dr 79934
Frank Beard Dr 79935
Frank Cordova Cir 79936
Frank Shorter Ln 79936
Frank Sinatra Pl 79936
Frank Valdez Dr 79905
Frank West Ave 79904
Frankfort Ave
 2400-3999 79930
 4100-4799 79903
Frankie Ln 79938
E Franklin Ave 79901
W Franklin Ave 79901
Franklin Dr 79915
Franklin Loop 79915
Franklin Bloom Ct 79912
Franklin Bluff Dr 79912
Franklin Cove Pl 79912
Franklin Crest Dr 79912
Franklin Dell 79912
Franklin Desert Dr 79912
Franklin Dove Ave 79912
Franklin Eagle Ct 79912
Franklin Gate Dr 79912
Franklin Hawk Ave 79912
Franklin Jay Ln 79912
Franklin Lair 79912
Franklin Moor 79912
Franklin Nook Way 79912
Franklin Perch Pl 79912
Franklin Point Dr 79912
Franklin Quail Pl 79912
Franklin Raven Pl 79912
Franklin Red Dr 79912
Franklin Ridge Dr 79912
Franklin Summit Dr 79912
Franklin Trail Dr 79912
Franklin View Dr 79912
Franklin Vista Dr 79912
Franklin Wind Pl 79912
Franklin Wren Way 79912
Fray Pl 79907
Fray Olguin Ct 79927
Fray Vargas Ct 79927
Frazier Ct 79935
Fred Adkins Ln 79936
Fred Carter Dr 79936
Fred Griffin Ave 79904
Fred Marti Ln 79936
Fred Perry Dr 79936
Fred Wilson Ave
 3401-4399 79904
 4400-5099 79906
Freddy Way 79907
Frederick Rd 79905
Fredonia St 79927
Freedom Dr 79925
Freeport Dr 79935
Freight Ln 79936
Fremont Ln 79912
French Pl 79905
French Rd 79906
Fresno Dr
 191-197 79915
 199-299 79915
 301-399 79915
 400-426 79907
 428-599 79907
Fresquez Dr 79927
Fressia Pl 79928
Friar Tuck Ct 79924
Friendship Seven St 79924
Friesian Trl 79938
Friona Dr 79927
Frisco Dr 79938
Frontera Rd 79922
Frutas Ave 79905
Fuchsia Ct 79925
Fuente St 79927
Fuji Ct & Ln 79928
Fullerston 79928
Funston Pl 79936
Furman Pl 79907
Fury Ln 79935
Fury Point Pl 79938
G J Forster Pl 79924
G T Powers Dr 79924
G V Underwood Dr 79924
Gabel Ave 79904
Gabriel Dr 79924
Gabriela Ln 79938
Gail Pl 79927
Gail Borden Pl 79935
Gairloch Dr 79925
Gaius Dr 79924
Gajeske Ave 79938
Gala Pl 79924
Galahad Way 79924
Galatea Pl 79924
Galaxie Dr 79924
Galena Dr 79904
Galestro Pl 79928
Galilee Dr 79927
Galindo Ave 79932
Gallagher St 79915
Galleon Ln 79927
Gallic Ct 79925
Galloway Dr 79902
Galsworthy Way 79928
Galvan Pl 79907
Galveston Dr 79924
Gambel Quail Dr 79936
Gambusino Ave 79938
Ganado Dr 79927
Garcia Cir 79904
Gardella Cir 79904
Garden Pl 79915
Garden Gate Way 79936
Garden Grove Ln 79912
Garden Point Dr 79938
Garden Rock Dr 79938
Gardenia Ct 79925
Gardner Rd 79932
Garfield Rd 79938
Garibay Ct 79936
Garland Ln 79924
Garment St 79938
Garnet Dr 79904
Garnet Crest Way 79902
Garry Owen Rd 79903
Garwood Ct 79925
Gary Ln 79922
Gary Lee 79938
Gary Player Dr 79935
Gaspar St 79907
Gaston Dr 79935
Gate Pl 79936
Gate Ridge Cir 79932
Gateway Blvd E
 2600-6598 79905
 6600-7398 79915
 7314-7314 79926
 7400-7958 79915
 7960-9598 79907
 10500-12498 79927
 13000-13098 79936
Gateway Blvd N
 600-698 79905
 1000-2098 79903
 7500-8298 79904
 8300-9000 79904
 9002-9098 79904
 9100-10598 79924
 10600-10700 79924
 10702-10798 79924
 11300-11398 79934
Gateway Blvd S
 901-2399 79903
 3801-3899 79930
 5400-5499 79904
 5501-9039 79904
 9201-9299 79924
 10701-10899 79934
Gateway Blvd W
 2801-3799 79903
 5601-6097 79925
 6099-10599 79925
 10601-11299 79935
 11301-12299 79936
 12301-13597 79928
 13599-14799 79928
 14801-15499 79928
Gatewood St 79904
Gatlin Ct 79938
Gato Rd 79932
Gaudi Way 79938
Gay Brewer Dr 79935
Gay Lynn Rd 79938
Gaynor 79938
Gaza Dr 79927
Gazelle Dr 79925
Geiger Ave 79905
Geisler Ct 79907
Gema Marie Pl 79928
Gemini St 79904
Gemotes Pl 79907
Gemstone St 79924
Gen Maloney Cir 79924
Gene Littler Dr 79936
Gene Sarazen Dr 79936
Gene Torres Dr 79936
Genevieve Cir 79927
Genie Dr 79924
Gensour Rd 79916
Gentry Way 79928
George Archer Dr
 10700-10899 79935
 10900-10999 79936
George Dickens Pl 79938
George Dieter Dr
 1300-1999 79936
 2001-3399 79936
 2100-3698 79936
 2100-2100 79996
George Fernandez Dr 79938
George Jean Ln 79927
George Jordan Ave 79904
George Orr Rd 79915
George Patton Ln 79924
George Perry Blvd 79925
Georgetown St 79924
Georgia Pl 79902
Gerald Dr 79925
Geranium Dr 79907
Gerard 79938
Geronimo Dr
 700-898 79905
 900-1099 79905
 1100-1499 79925
Geronne Dr 79907
Geyser 79932
Ghost Dance Cir 79936
Ghost Flower St 79928
Gibb Mls 79938
Gibbs St 79907
N & S Gibraltar Dr 79905
Gideon Cir 79927
Gifford Dr 79927
Gil Reyes Dr 79938
Gila Rd 79905
Gila River Ln 79938
Gilbert Dr 79907
Gilberto Avila St 79936
Gilded Sun Dr 79938
Giles Rd 79915
Gilmore Way 79907
Gils Magic Dr 79932
Ginger Kerrick 79938
Girl Scout Ln 79922
Girl Scout Way 79924
Glacier Peak Dr 79904
Gladys Ave 79915
Glardon Cir 79915
Glasgow Rd 79925
Glassburn Rd 79906
Glaze Dr 79928
Glemmway Pl 79925
Glen Cv 79938
E Glen Dr 79936
Glen Arbor St 79924
Glen Campbell Dr 79936
Glen Haven Pl 79907
Glendale Ave 79907
Glendive Dr 79928
Glendora Ln 79912
Glenn James Pl 79936
Glenosa Dr 79928
Glenwood Pl 79903
N Glenwood St 79905
S Glenwood St 79905
Glitter Pt 79938
Globe Cir 79915
Globe Mallow Dr 79928
Globe Willow Dr 79922
Gloria St 79907
Glorieta 79927
Glorieta Pass Rd 79906
W Glory Rd 79902
Gloster Ct 79935
Goby St 79924
Gohman St 79927
Gold Ave 79930
Gold Crown Rd 79928
Gold Point Dr 79938
Gold Ranch Ave 79934
Golden Arrow Pl 79924
Golden Barrel Pl 79928
Golden Eagle Dr 79928
Golden Edge 79928
Golden Gate Rd 79936
Golden Hawk Dr 79912
Golden Hill Ter 79902
Golden Key Cir 79925
Golden Knight 79904
Golden Mesa Ct 79928
Golden Pond Dr 79934
Golden Sage Dr 79911
Golden Sands Dr 79924
Golden Springs Dr 79912

Golden Sun Dr 79938
Golden Trail Ln 79936
Golden Willow Way 79922
Goldfield St 79938
Goldshire Pl 79928
Golf View Ln 79928
Goliad Dr 79924
Golondrina Cir 79907
Gomez Rd 79932
Gondola Ln 79912
Gonzales St 79907
Good Samaritan Ct 79912
Goodman St 79924
Goodwin Dr 79902
Goodyear Dr 79936
Gordon Bays Way 79936
Gordon Cooper Ln 79936
Gorman Pl 79936
Goucher Dr 79928
Gourd St 79925
Goya Ct 79936
Grace Pl 79915
Grace Madriles 79932
Gracecus Way 79924
Graham Ct 79903
N Grama St
  100-299 79905
  301-399 79905
  500-1599 79903
S Grama St 79905
Grambling Ct 79907
Gran Cima Ln 79935
Gran Quivira Dr 79904
Gran Vida Dr 79912
Gran Vista Dr 79907
Granada Ave 79912
Granby St 79932
Grand Bahamas Dr 79936
Grand Canyon Pl 79904
Grand Cayman Ln 79936
Grand Ridge Dr 79912
Grand River Dr 79928
Grand Teton Dr 79912
Grandview Ave 79902
Granero Dr 79912
Granillo St 79907
Granite Rd 79915
Granite Rock Dr 79938
Granite Trail Ct 79912
Grant Ave 79930
Grapeland Dr 79924
Graphite Dr 79932
Greasewood Rd 79928
Great Abaco Ct 79936
Great Bear Ct 79905
Great Spirit Cir 79936
Greco Ct 79924
Green Castle Rd 79932
Green Cove Dr 79932
Green Desert Cir 79928
Green Gate Way 79936
Green Harvest Dr 79938
Green Haven Pl 79907
Green Lilac Cir 79915
Green Pear Dr 79928
Green Valley Pl 79915
Green Village Ct 79912
Green Vine Ct 79936
Greenbrier Rd 79912
Greendale Dr 79928
Greenhill Ln 79912
Greenlee Dr 79936
Greenock St 79925
Greenveil Dr 79936
Greenway Ave 79925
Greenwich Dr 79902
Greenwood Cir 79925
Greg Dr 79938
Greg Martinez 79928
Greg Powers Dr 79936
Greggerson Dr 79907
Gregory Ave 79902
Gregory Jarvis Dr 79936
Grenada Way 79927
Grenoble Dr 79907
Greta Ln 79938
Gretna 79928
Griems Ct 79905
Griffin Way 79907
Grijalva Dr 79927
Grissom Ln 79903
Grizzly Bear Ln 79938
Grotto Bay Ct 79936
Grouse Rd 79924
Grover Dr 79925
Groverock Ct 79935
Gruenther Rd 79938
Gschwind St 79924
Guadalajara Dr 79907
Guadalupe Dr 79904
Guerra Ct 79927
Guerrero Dr 79928
Guido Ln 79903
Guilford Pl 79928
Guillermo Espinoza 79938
Guillermo Frias Ln 79934
Gulf Pl 79915
Gulf Creek Dr 79911
Gulf Star Ct 79936
Gulfport Dr 79924
Gull Lake Pl 79936
Gum Ln 79925
Gunnison Dr 79904
Gunter Ave 79904
Gurdev Cir 79927
Gurss Pl 79902
Gus Grissom Way 79936
Gus Moran St 79936
Gus Rallis Dr 79932
Gus Salcido Ln 79928
Gustavo 79936
Gustavo Madrid Ln 79934
Guthrie St 79935
Guy Way 79935
Gwen Evans Ln 79936
Gwendolyn Dr 79938
Gypsum Hills Cir 79936
H P Martinez Way 79934
H S Sibley Ct 79924
Haan Rd 79916
Hacienda Ave 79915
Hacienda Rock Dr 79938
Hacienda Roja 79922
Haddad Ct 79936
Hadley Pl 79928
Hadlock St 79905
Hagood Ave 79906
E & W Hague Rd 79902
Hal Marcus Pl 79936
Half Moon Dr 79915
Half Moon Pass 79927
Halifax St 79928
Hallmark Ct 79904
Hamilton Ave 79930
Hamline Rd 79928
Hammer Way 79907
N Hammett St 79905
Hampshire Ln 79902
Hampton Rd
  500-613 79915
  614-799 79907
Hanawalt Dr 79903
Hancock Rd 79907
Handy Cir 79906
Haney Rd 79927
Hank Aaron Dr 79934
Hanley Way 79905
Hannah Leigh St 79938
Hanoverian Pl 79938
Hansen Ln 79938
Happer St 79903
Harcourt Dr 79924
Hardaway St 79903
Hardesty Pl 79905
Harding Way 79907
Hardwick Pl 79928
Hardy Cir 79905
Harkis Rd 79936
Harlan Dr 79924
Harmony Dr 79924
Harnose Dr 79928
Harold Pl 79907
Harrier Dr 79907
N & S Harris St 79907
Harrison Ave 79930
Harrison Rd 79928
Hartford Dr 79907
Hartlepool Dr 79928
Hartsdale Dr 79928
Harvard Ave 79907
Harvest Dr 79927
Harvest Ln 79924
Harvey St 79922
Harwood Dr 79925
Hasan Ave 79924
Hase St 79906
Haselden Rd 79928
Haskell Pl 79927
Hastings Dr 79903
Hatch Ave 79904
Hatchett Rd 79927
Hathaway Ct 79904
Hauck St 79906
Havenrock Dr 79935
Haverhill Rd 79907
Hawaii St 79915
Hawick Rd 79925
Hawk Rd & St 79916
Hawk Point Dr 79938
Hawkins Blvd
  501-797 79915
  799-1099 79915
  1100-2099 79925
Hawley Cir 79903
Hawthorne St 79902
Hayes Ave
  2100-2199 79906
  3300-4098 79930
  4100-4199 79930
Haynes Rd 79927
Haynesworth Ave 79903
Haystack Ln 79932
Hazel Ct 79922
Hazelnut Ct 79907
Hazeltime St 79936
Hazelwood St 79928
Healy Dr 79936
Heantriv Dr 79935
Heard Ln 79904
Heartstone Ct 79924
Heatfield St 79901
Heath Way 79912
Heather Ave 79925
Heathrow Ct 79928
Hector Dr 79935
Hedgerow Ct 79925
Heid Ave 79915
Heisig Ave 79902
Helen Of Troy
  6900-6999 79911
Helen Of Troy
  7300-7369 79912
Helen Of Troy Dr 79912
Helen Of Troy Plz 79912
Helen Wynn Ct 79936
Helena Ct 79905
Helena St 79928
Helican Pl 79924
Hellas Dr 79924
Helms Rd 79907
Hemlock St 79925
Hemmingway Dr 79924
Hemphill Ct 79907
Hempstead Dr 79912
Hencenco Dr 79912
Henderi Ave 79910
Henderson Pl 79907
Hendrik Dr 79928
Henri Dunant Way 79936
Henri Matisse Ave 79936
Henry Way 79907
Henry Brennan Dr 79936
Henry Phipps Dr 79936
Herbert St 79904
Hercules Ave 79904
Hercules St 79916
Hereford Dr 79928
Heritage Ridge Way 79912
Herlinda Chew Way 79936
Hermes Dr 79924
Hermit Thrush 79911
Hermosa Ln 79922
Hermosillo Dr 79915
Hermoso Del Sol 79911
Hernandez St 79905
Hero Ave 79904
Hero Point Dr 79938
Hesse Dr 79927
Hester St 79907
Hiawatha Dr 79936
Hibbert Pl 79903
Hibiscus Ct 79928
Hickman St 79936
Hickory Ln 79915
Hiday Cir 79904
Hidden Crk 79938
Hidden Way 79922
Hidden Bend Pl 79928
Hidden Crest Cir 79912
Hidden Grove Dr 79938
Hidden Hills Dr 79902
Hidden Sun Ct 79938
Hidden Valley Dr 79938
Higgins Pl 79907
High Campus Rd 79928
High Plains Dr 79911
High Point Dr 79904
High Ridge Dr 79912
High Rock Dr 79938
Highland Ave 79907
Highweed Dr 79928
Highwood Way 79936
Higley Cir 79928
Hilario Hernandez 79938
Hillcrest Dr 79902
Hiller St 79925
S Hills St 79901
Hillside Dr 79922
Hillview Ave 79932
Hilton Ave 79907
Hinman Rd 79916
Hipolito Ln 79907
Hitchcock Ave
  10700-10899 79935
  11001-11017 79936
Hixson St 79902
Hockney St 79915
Hodaka Way 79927
Hodges Cir 79924
Holden Cir 79928
Holguin Rd 79927
Holiday St 79905
Hollings St 79924
Holloway Pl 79907
Holly Pl 79915
Holly Springs Ave 79938
Hollydale Dr 79912
Hollyglen St 79936
Hollyhock Dr 79924
Hollywood Dr 79928
Holmes Dr 79924
Holmsley Trl 79907
Holstein Dr 79936
Holstein Rd 79927
Holsteiner Ct 79938
Holy Cross St 79928
Holy Springs Ct 79928
Homan Dr 79927
Home Show Ln 79936
Homedale Dr 79928
Homer Cir 79904
Homestead Dr 79928
Hondo Pass Dr
  3400-4899 79904
  4900-5799 79924
Honey Comb Pl 79938
Honey Dew 79938
Honey Locust Ln 79924
Honey Mesquite 79928
Honey Point Dr 79938
Honey Willow Way 79922
Honeybee Ct 79924
Honeysuckle Dr 79925
Honolulu Dr 79925
Honour Point Pl 79938
Hookheath Dr 79922
Hookridge Dr 79925
Hoover Ave 79912
Hope Ave 79938
Hopewell Dr 79925
Horizon Blvd
  100-1099 79927
  1100-1299 79927
  1300-16200 79928
  1500-12998 79928
  13000-15370 79928
  15372-15398 79928
  16202-16398 79928
Horizon Heights Cir 79928
Horizon Point Cir 79928
Horizon View Dr 79928
Horizon Vista Ave 79928
Horn Cir 79927
Horncastle Rd 79907
Horse Creek Ln 79938
Horse Ranch St 79934
Hosea St 79936
Hosston 79928
Hough Way 79911
Houghton Spgs 79928
Houma Ave 79928
Hourglass Dr 79915
Houston St 79903
Hovey Dr 79927
Hovland Ln 79938
Howard St 79904
Howze St
  400-599 79906
  1001-1097 79903
  1099-2199 79903
  2201-2499 79903
Hubbard Ct 79935
Hubble Dr 79904
Huckleberry St 79903
Huddersfield St 79928
Hudson Way 79907
Hudspeth Pl 79901
Hueco Ave 79903
Hueco Cave Dr 79938
Hueco Club Rd 79938
Hueco End Dr 79938
Hueco Hill Dr 79938
Hueco Land Ln 79938
Hueco Mine Dr 79938
Hueco Mountain Rd 79938
Hueco Pit Dr 79938
Hueco Ranch Rd 79938
Hueco Sands Dr 79938
Hueco Tanks Rd 79938
Hueco Valley Dr 79938
Hueco View Dr 79938
Huereque Dr 79927
Huerta St 79905
Hugg St 79924
Hugh Herr Ct 79938
Hugh Royer Pl 79936
Hughes Cir 79907
Hughey Cir 79925
Hugo Reyes Dr 79938
Humberto Ln 79907
Humble Pl 79915
Hume St 79930
Humphrey Rd 79906
Hunnicutt Rd 79938
Hunt Ct 79903
Hunter Crk 79938
Hunter Dr 79915
Hunter Hill Way 79936
Hunters Glenn Ct 79932
Hunters Grove Ave 79938
Hunters Ridge Pl 79912
Hurd Pl 79912
Husky Ct 79924
Hutsell Pl 79932
Hyde Park Pl 79904
Ibex Ave 79924
Idaho St 79902
Idalia Ave 79930
Idlewilde Dr 79925
Iglesia Cir 79907
Ignacio St 79932
Ignacio Almanzar Ln 79934
Ignacio Frias Dr 79934
Igoe Pl 79924
Igor Kaleri Ave 79938
Iguana Pl 79928
Ike St 79938
Ilan Ramon Pl 79934
Immanuel Vista Dr 79938
Imogene Ct 79928
Impala Ave 79924
Imperial St 79924
Imperial Gem Ave 79936
Imperial Ridge Dr 79912
Imus Dr 79912
Inca Ave 79912
Inca Dove 79911
Independence Dr 79907
Independent Dr 79938
India Ct 79927
Indian Pl 79907
Indian Bluff Rd 79912
Indian Hills Dr 79938
Indian Trail Rd 79938
Indian Wells Dr 79938
Indiana St 79930
Indio Ct 79927
Industrial Ave 79915
Ingersoll Way 79930
Ingham St 79928
Inglewood Dr 79927
Ingram Ave 79938
Ingram Ct 79928
Innsbruck Ave 79927
Inspiration Ct 79928
Interlachen Ct 79928
International Rd 79925
Intrigue Ct 79928
Inverness Dr 79928
Ipswich Pl 79928
Ira Way 79935
Ireland Cir & Ct 79930
Irene Dr 79927
Irene Agnes Rd 79938
Iris Dr 79924
Irma Rd 79907
Iron Gate Way 79936
Iron Ridge Pl 79912
Irondale Dr 79912
Ironwood Cir 79915
Iroquois Dr 79912
Irwin Ave 79907
Isaac Dr 79927
Isabel Way 79927
Isabella Dr 79912
Isaiah Dr 79927
Isaias Avalos Ln 79934
Isha Way 79925
Isla Azul Pl 79912
Isla Bahia Way 79925
Isla Banderas Way 79925
Isla Cocoa Ln 79925
Isla Del Rey Dr 79912
Isla Marino St 79925
Isla Morada Dr 79925
Isla Mujeres Ln 79925
Isla Verde Cir 79925
Island Point Dr 79938
Islerock Dr 79935
Isola 79928
Isomedix Pl 79936
Istanbul Cir 79907
Itasca St 79936
Ivan Smith Way 79936
Ivanhoe Dr
  10700-10899 79935
  11193-11197 79936
  11199-11399 79936
Iverson Ct 79928
Ivey Rd 79927
Ivory Gate Way 79936
Ivory Point Pl 79938
Ivy Point Way 79938
Jacaranda Ln 79922
Jacey Ct 79925
Jacinto Ramos Ave 79938
Jack Way 79927
Jack Cupit Ln 79936
Jack Fleck Dr 79935
Jack Marcus Dr 79934
Jack Nicklaus Dr 79935
Jackie Pl 79936
Jackrabbit Rd 79928
Jackson Ave 79930
Jacob Kuechler Dr 79938
Jacquelin Ann Ct 79936
Jade Ln 79904
Jadestone St 79924
Jaffee Pl 79905
Jaime Rd 79927
Jalapa Dr 79907
Jalisco Ln 79912
Jamaica St 79924
Jamaican Palm Dr 79936
James St 79915
James Chisum Dr 79936
James Cravens Ct 79936
James Dudley Dr 79936
James Grant Dr 79936
James Guines Dr 79936
James Kelley Dr 79936
James Rey Cir 79938
James Watt Dr 79936
Jamestown Rd 79907
Jamin Pl 79928
Jamocha Way 79934
Jan Pl 79938
Jan De Roos Pl 79936
Jan Ellyn Ln 79912
Jan Herring Way 79936
Janet Coles Ln 79936
Janis Ave 79927
Janway Dr
  10400-10599 79925
  10600-10799 79935
Japonica St 79924
Jaquez Rd 79907
Jardin Bello 79932
Jardines Pl 79932
Jarman Rd 79906
Jarvis Dr 79935
Jasmine Ali 79938
Jason Way 79935
Jason Crandall Dr 79938
Jasper Ct 79927
Jasper Dr 79928
Java Sun Pl 79934
Javier St 79932
Jay R Vargas 79938
Jean Kennedy Ln 79907
Jean Louise St 79928
Jeanny Marie Ct 79932
Jeb Stuart Rd 79916
Jebel Way 79912
Jeff Winton Dr 79928
Jefferson Ave 79930
Jemez Dr 79905
Jen Renee Ln 79932
Jennifer Dr 79936
Jenny Rd 79927
Jenny Laurie Ct 79928
Jennys Pl 79938
Jensen Ave 79915
Jeremiah Dr 79928
Jericho Dr 79927
Jericho Tree Dr 79934
Jerry Dr 79924
Jerry Abbott St 79936
Jerry Lewis Way 79936
Jerry Pate Pl 79935
Jerry Turner 79932
Jersey St 79915
Jervis Dr 79927
Jessica St 79932
Jesuit Dr 79907
Jesus Almeida 79938
Jesus Chavez Pl 79928
Jetrock Dr 79935
Jettie Ray Way 79936
Jewel Dr 79927
Jewel Ridge Way 79912
Jeweled Desert Dr 79928

Jeweled Mesa Ct 79928
Jewell Dr 79928
Jim Bean Dr 79927
Jim Bridger Rd 79938
Jim Castaneda Dr 79934
Jim Colbert Ln 79936
Jim De Groat Dr 79912
Jim Dent Ct 79936
Jim Ferriell Dr 79936
Jim Hofher Pl 79928
Jim Knowles Pl 79928
Jim Larabel Dr 79936
Jim Paul Dr 79936
Jim Ryan Ln 79936
Jim Thorpe Dr 79936
Jim Webb Dr 79934
Jimenez Ln 79927
Jimmy Connors Ct 79938
Jimmy Don Ct 79927
Jivaro Pl 79912
Jm Browning St 79938
Jo Way 79927
Jo Ann Dr 79938
Joan Francis Dr 79928
Joaquin Ct 79907
Joe Battle Blvd
1100-1899 79936
1900-2300 79938
2302-3698 79938
Joe Dimaggio Cir 79934
Joe Herrera Dr 79924
Joe Kennedy Way 79907
Joe Manago St 79924
Joe Perez Ct 79905
Joe Plise Way 79927
Joe Porter Dr 79936
Joe Ray Way 79936
Joe Rodriguez 79927
Joe Turner Ct 79915
Joe Watson Ct 79936
Joel Dr 79924
Joel King Pl 79932
Johannsen Rd 79932
John Andreas Dr 79907
John B Oblinger Dr 79934
John Christopher Dr 79938
John Cox Pl 79936
John Glenn Dr 79936
John Henry St 79938
John Kennedy Way 79907
John Macguire Pl 79912
John Martin Ct 79932
John Mcenroe Pl 79938
John Paul St 79938
John Phelan Dr 79936
John Polley Cir 79936
John Ring Ln 79936
John Schlee Ct 79935
John Weir Dr 79936
Johnny Mata Dr 79938
Johnny Miller Dr 79936
Johnson Ave 79930
Jolla Del Sol 79911
Jon Cunningham Blvd 79934
Jon Evans Dr 79938
Jon Meier Ct 79912
Jonah Ct 79938
Jonathan Elias Ct 79938
Jones Ln 79936
Jones Point Pl 79928
Jonkoping Rd 79927
Jonwood St 79925
Joon Rd 79938
Jorado Ln 79938
Jordan Ln 79922
Jordan Emily Ln 79932
Jorge Rd 79927
Jorge Grajeda 79938
Jose Bombach Dr 79936
Jose Cardenas Ln 79912
Jose Cisneros Dr 79936
Jose Cueto Ct 79912
Jose Duran Ln 79934
Jose Granillo St 79927
Jose Ortiz Ln 79936
Joseph St 79927
Joseph Dewayne 79932
Joseph Rodriguez Dr 79932
Josephine Cir 79907
Joshua Ct 79915
Joshua Louis Dr 79938
Josie Pl 79924
Journey Ct 79912
Joya Del Valle 79927
Joyce Cir 79904
Jt Hourigan Pl 79936
Juan De Herrera
Lateral 79927
Juan Munoz 79932
Juanchido Ln 79907
Juanita Way 79907
Juanita Duran Way 79927
Judith Resnik Dr 79936
Judy Ln 79927
Judy Marie Ln 79938
Julia May Pl 79935
Juliandra Ave 79924
Julie Ln 79938
Julie Marie Pl 79938
Juliet Way 79915
Juliette Low Dr 79936
Julius Boros Dr 79936
Junction Ave 79924
Juno Pl 79907
Justice Rd 79938
Justin Ct 79927
Justus St 79930
Kachina Dr 79936
Kaitlyn Reece 79938
Kalpana Chawla Ct 79934
Kane Way 79928
N Kansas St
200-210 79901
212-299 79901
301-599 79901
800-1198 79902
1200-2799 79902
2801-2899 79902
S Kansas St 79901
Kapilowitz Ct 79905
Kapriz Ave 79932
Karachi Way 79927
Karen Pt 79938
Karen St 79925
Karen Kay Dr 79938
Karen Sue Pl 79936
Kari Anne Dr 79928
Karl Ct 79938
Karl Wyler Dr 79936
Karon St 79927
Kasey Way 79927
Kaspar Way 79904
Kastrin St 79907
Katelyn Gray Cir 79924
Katherine Ct 79932
Katherine Dr 79928
Katherine Mengas St 79908
Kathy Ave 79927
Katie Ln 79932
Kaufman 79932
Kaws Pl 79934
Kayser Cir 79904
Kaywood Dr 79925
Keagle Rd 79927
Kearney Way 79928
Kearny Loop 79906
Keats Rd 79928
Keeny Ct 79907
Keith Rd 79938
Kellogg St 79924
Kelly Ave 79938
Kelly Way 79902
Kelso St 79932
Keltner Ave 79904
Kelton Ct 79938
Kelvin Ave 79915
Kemp Ave 79904
Ken Still Ln 79935
Ken Venturi Ln 79936
N & S Kenazo Ave 79928
Kendall St 79924
Kendrick Cir 79927
Kenmore 79932
Kenna Ln 79938
Kennarmont Dr 79928
Kennestrom Ct 79927
Kenneth St 79904
Kenneth Capshaw 79932
Keno Dr 79928
Kensington Cir 79924
Kent Ave 79922
Kenton Rd 79928
Kentucky St 79930
Kentwood Ave 79928
Kenworthy St 79924
Kenyon Joyce Ln 79902
Kerbey Ave 79902
Kerfoot St 79904
Kermit Ln 79935
Kern Dr 79902
Kerriel Cir 79907
Kerrville Pl 79924
Kessler Dr 79907
Kestrel Ave 79928
Ketchikan St 79924
Kevin Rd 79928
Keystone Dr 79924
Khalsa Way 79927
Khouri Cir 79915
Khyber Rd 79927
Kieffer Ln 79912
Kiko A Fierro Pl 79938
Kiko Duran 79934
Kila St 79928
Kilburn Way 79907
Kilgore Pl 79936
Kilkenny Rd 79925
Killarney St 79925
Killeen Pl 79936
Kilmaltie Dr 79925
Kilmarnock Dr 79925
Kimberley St 79932
Kimberly 79938
Kimi Ct 79938
Kincade Ct 79938
Kindling Ct 79936
King Pl 79932
King Arthur Ct 79903
King James Pl 79903
King Palm Dr 79936
King Richard Ct 79924
Kingdom Ave 79936
Kingery Dr 79902
Kingfish Ct 79936
Kingman Dr 79915
Kings Arms Ct 79936
Kings Bridge Dr 79934
Kings Crest Dr 79936
Kings Crown Pl 79936
Kings Guard Dr 79936
Kingsfield Ave 79912
Kingsgate Ct 79928
Kingsley Dr 79928
Kingspoint Dr 79912
Kingston Dr 79928
Kingswood Ct 79938
Kingswood Dr 79932
Kingswreath Pl 79907
Kinross Ave
10300-10599 79925
10600-10621 79935
10623-10799 79935
Kioka Ln 79928
Kiowa Ct 79925
Kiowa Creek Dr 79911
Kiowa Point Ave 79938
Kipling Way 79928
Kira Christel Ln 79936
Kirby St 79938
Kirkcaldy Rd 79925
Kirkland St 79927
Kirkpatrick St 79906
Kirkwall St 79925
Kirwood St 79924
Kit Carson Dr 79936
Kitt Rd 79915
Kleppin Ct 79927
Klondike Ct 79904
Knights Dr 79915
Knollwood 79932
Knorr Pl 79912
Knowles Way 79907
Knox Dr 79904
Kodiak Ave 79924
Kokopelli Way 79912
Kolliker Dr 79936
Konya Pl 79927
Koshare Ct 79938
Krag St 79938
Kramer 79938
Kreuger St 79938
Krista Ilee Pl 79938
Kristy Weaver Dr 79936
Krupp Dr 79902
Kuna Loop 79936
Kurita Ave 79905
Kurler Ave 79938
Kurthwoods 79928
Kyle Rd 79938
Kyle St 79905
Kyle Wendelin Ln 79936
La Adelita Dr 79922
La Barca Dr 79907
La Batalla Ct 79928
La Brigada Ln 79922
La Cabana Pl 79912
La Cadena Dr 79912
La Cantera Dr 79912
La Chapa Ave 79912
La Cienega Dr 79927
La Cruz Dr 79902
La Cuesta Dr 79936
La Cumbre Ln 79912
La Estancia Cir 79932
La Fogata Rd 79927
La Gente Way 79907
La Gotera Pl 79912
La Grange Ct 79915
La Grange St 79938
La Huasteca Way 79907
La Jolla Dr 79915
La Luz Ave 79903
La Mancha Ct 79922
La Mirada Cir 79932
La Morenita Cir 79927
La Paloma Cir 79907
La Paz Dr 79915
La Poblana Dr 79927
La Posta Dr 79912
La Puente 79927
La Puesta Dr 79932
La Quebrada Pl 79912
La Quinta Pl 79936
La Senda Dr 79915
La Sombra Way 79912
La Subida Dr 79935
La Taste Ave 79924
La Vista Pl 79924
La Von Ave 79938
Labreck Ave 79938
Lacebark Elm Dr 79907
Lackland St
2901-4097 79930
4099-4499 79930
4501-4899 79930
5401-6097 79904
6099-6200 79904
6202-6298 79904
Lacota Point Dr 79938
Ladera Rd 79915
Ladrillo Pl 79901
Lady Hawk Ct 79912
Ladybird Cir 79904
Lafayette Dr
101-197 79915
199-699 79915
700-1299 79907
Lafitte 79928
Lago Pt 79938
Lago Azul St 79928
Lago Chico Pl 79928
Lago Claro Dr 79928
Lago De Oro Dr 79928
Lago Di Como Ct 79928
Lago Di Garda Ct 79928
Lago Di Iseo Ct 79928
Lago Grande Dr 79928
Lago Lindo Dr 79928
Lago Maggiore St 79928
Lago Seco Dr 79928
Lagrimas Rd 79927
Laguna Pl 79902
Laguna Azul Ave 79928
Laguna Vista Dr 79932
Lagunillas Pl 79907
Lainy Rd 79927
Lait Dr 79925
Lajitas Pl 79928
Lake St 79905
Lake Alice Dr 79936
Lake Arrowhead 79928
Lake Austin Pl 79936
Lake Bonito 79928
Lake Candlewood 79928
Lake Champlain St 79936
Lake Champlin 79928
Lake Charles Pl 79936
Lake Cumberland 79928
Lake Erie Dr 79936
Lake Geneva Dr 79936
Lake George Pl 79936
Lake Granada 79928
Lake Hickory 79928
Lake Huron Dr 79936
Lake Kentucky 79928
Lake Loy Dr 79936
Lake Mead Ct 79928
Lake Mead Pl 79936
Lake Michigan Dr 79936
Lake Moss Pl 79936
Lake Nasser Dr 79936
Lake Nemi Dr 79936
Lake Omega St 79936
Lake Oneida Ct 79936
Lake Ontario 79928
Lake Ontario Dr 79936
Lake Ozarks Dr 79936
Lake Powell Pl 79936
Lake Saint Pierre 79928
Lake Seminole Dr 79928
Lake Spier Dr 79936
Lake Summer 79928
Lake Superior Ln 79936
Lake Tahoe Pl 79936
Lake Tana Dr 79936
Lake Tillery 79928
Lake Travis Pl 79936
Lake Victoria Dr 79936
Lake Volta Pl 79936
Lake West Pt 79928
Lakehurst Rd 79912
Lakeshore Ct & Dr 79932
Lakeview Dr 79924
Lakeway Dr 79932
Lakewood Ave
10500-10599 79925
10600-11099 79935
Lamar St 79903
Lambda Dr 79924
Lampliter Pl 79925
Lana Pl 79924
Lancaster Ave 79938
Lancaster Dr 79907
Lancer Way 79912
Land Rush St 79911
Landgren Dr 79927
Landon Way 79907
Landry Mckee Ln 79907
Langhorn Ave 79904
Langtry St
100-198 79901
201-299 79901
600-899 79902
Lanka St 79936
Lankmoore Ave 79904
Lanner St 79928
Lantana Ln 79936
Lanward Ct 79932
Lanza Ln 79927
Lanza Del Sol 79911
Lapstone Way 79934
Laralint Dr 79925
Laramie Cir 79924
Laramie Ridge Ln 79912
Laramie River Ave 79932
Larchmont Dr 79902
Laredo Ave 79905
Lariat St 79915
Lark Ln 79927
Lark Bunting Ln 79911
Larkspur Ct 79924
Larrinso Dr 79907
Larry Hinson Dr 79936
Larry Mahan Dr 79925
Larry Mize Way 79936
Larry Wadkins Dr 79936
Larry Wood Pl 79936
Las Aguilas Dr 79928
Las Aves Pl 79912
Las Brisas Cir 79905
Las Casitas Dr 79938
Las Colinas Dr 79928
Las Colonias Rd 79928
Las Flores Dr 79938
Las Granjas Dr 79932
Las Hadas Ln 79907
Las Olas Ct 79932
Las Palmas Way 79912
Las Palomas Dr 79928
Las Pistas Pl 79912
Las Playas Ct 79932
Las Quintas Dr 79938
Las Varas Rd 79928
Las Vegas Dr 79902
Lasso Cir 79907
Lasso Rock Dr 79938
Last Waltz Dr 79932
Lata Pl 79928
Latimer Pl 79932
N & S Latta St 79905
Laura Ln 79938
Laura Way 79915
Laura Marie Dr 79936
Lauree Zelt St 79928
Laurel Cyn 79912
N Laurel St
600-699 79903
801-897 79902
899-1399 79902
S Laurel St 79901
Laurel Clark Ln 79934
Laurel Springs Ct 79932
Lauren St 79928
Laurie Jo Ln 79927
Laverne Ave 79915
Lavina St 79928
Lawkland St 79928
Lawndale Dr 79912
Lawrence Ave 79904
Lawson St 79904
Lawton Dr 79902
Lawton St 79928
Lazarus Ct 79927
Lazear St 79930
Lazy Ln 79902
Lazy Willow Dr 79922
Le Barron Rd 79907
Le Compte St 79928
Le Conte Dr 79912
Le Lois St 79927
Le Marche Ln 79907
Le Sabre Ln 79907
Lead Tree Pl 79907
Leafy Point Pl 79938
League Rd 79938
Leah Point Ln 79938
Leavell Ave 79904
Leavell Dr 79906
Lebanon Ave 79930
Lechugilla Ct 79912
Lee Blvd 79936
N Lee St
200-299 79901
601-697 79902
699-999 79902
S Lee St 79901
Lee Elder Dr 79936
Lee Shannon Rd 79932
Lee Starling Dr 79907
N Lee Trevino Dr
600-698 79907
1201-1299 79907
1300-3199 79936
3201-3599 79936
S Lee Trevino Dr 79907
Leeann Pl 79911
Leeds Ave 79903
Leewood Dr
10300-10326 79925
10328-10399 79925
10400-10498 79935
Legacy Ct 79912
Legacy Ridge Way 79912
Lehigh Ln 79928
Lehr St 79906
Leigh Fisher Blvd 79906
Lemo St 79904
Lemon Tree Ln 79915
Lemonade St 79924
Lemuel Cir 79938
Lenox Ct 79912
Leo St 79904
Leo Collins Dr 79936
Leon St 79901
Leonardo Ave 79907
Leonor Ct 79907
Leopoldo St 79907
Leroy Bonse Dr 79936
Les Halles Pl 79907
Les Peterson Ln 79936
Lesa Ln 79915
Leslie Ct 79932
Leslie Ann Ln 79936
Leslie Harmon St 79938
Leslie Ross Rd 79906
Leslie Ward Ct 79922
Leticia St 79936
Letona St 79927
Letterman Ct 79930
Lettie Ct 79915
Levelland Pl 79924
Lewis Pl 79938
Lewis Lee Ct 79936
Lexa Dean 79938
Lexington Dr 79924
Liahona Dr 79927
Liana Ct 79932
Liberator Dr 79938
Liberty St 79907
Libra Ln 79904
Lico Ln 79927
Lienege Rene Ct 79932
Likins Dr 79925
Lilac Way 79915
Lilly Dr 79927
Limas Dr 79935
Limerick Rd 79925
Limonite Cir 79932
Linares Ln 79907
Lincoln Ave 79930
Linda Ave 79922
Linda Johnson 79932
Linda Rene Ln 79938
Linda Roberts 79938
Linda Ruby Dr 79936
Linda West Dr 79938
Lindbergh Ave 79932
Linden St 79905
Lindenwood Ave 79936
Lindsey Dr 79924
Linger Ln 79928
Link Dr 79907
Linwood Dr 79928
Lionel Dr 79936
Lions Gate Ln 79936
Lipizzan Ct 79938
Lippert Rd 79927
Lirio Rd 79915
Lisa Denise Ct 79938
Lisa Diane Rd 79927
Lisa Sherr St 79938
Lisbon St 79905

Liston Pl 79928
Litchfield St 79928
Little Ln 79922
Little Corrina Ave 79927
N & S Little Flower Rd 79915
Little John Ct 79924
Little Missy Ln 79938
Live Oak Dr 79932
Llano Way 79904
Llano Libre Way 79912
Loana Dr 79928
Loanda Ln 79928
Lobo Ln 79935
Lockerbie Ave 79925
Lockheed Dr 79925
Locust St 79905
Lodge Ct 79936
Loera St 79928
Lois Brooks St 79908
Lois Hollingsworth St 79908
Lolita Pl 79907
Lolo Caldera Way 79938
Loma Ln 79938
Loma Alegre Dr 79934
Loma Alta Ln 79934
Loma Azteca Ct 79934
Loma Azul Ct 79934
Loma Baja Pl 79934
Loma Blanca Dr 79934
Loma Bonita Dr 79934
Loma Canada Ct 79934
Loma Casitas Rd 79934
Loma Clara Ct 79934
Loma Colorada Ct 79934
Loma Corta Pl 79934
Loma Crystal Pl 79934
Loma De Alma Dr 79934
Loma De Amor Ln 79934
Loma De Arena Ct 79934
Loma De Brisas Dr 79934
Loma De Cobre Dr 79934
Loma De Color Dr 79934
Loma De Cristo Dr 79912
Loma De Indios Ln 79934
Loma De Luna Dr 79934
Loma De Luz Pl 79934
Loma De Oro Dr 79934
Loma De Paz Dr 79934
Loma De Plata Dr 79934
Loma De Rio Pl 79934
Loma De Vida Ln 79934
Loma Del Norte Dr 79934
Loma Del Rey Cir 79934
Loma Del Sol Dr 79934
Loma Del Sur Dr 79934
Loma Diamante Dr 79934
Loma Dorada Ln 79934
Loma Escondida Dr 79934
Loma Feliz Ct 79934
Loma Franklin Dr 79934
Loma Fria Pl 79934
Loma Grande Dr 79934
Loma Hermosa Dr 79934
Loma Isla 79934
Loma Linda Blvd 79938
Loma Linda Cir 79934
Loma Portal Pl 79934
Loma Rica Way 79934
Loma Roja Dr 79934
Loma Rosada Dr 79934
Loma Royal Pl 79934
Loma Seca Pl 79934
Loma Serena Pl 79934
Loma Suave Ln 79934
Loma Taurina Dr 79934
Loma Terrace Rd 79907
Loma Triste Pl 79934
Loma Verde Dr 79936
Loma Vista Pl 79907
Lomaland Dr
300-1299 79907
1300-1332 79935
1334-1699 79935
1701-1899 79935
Lombardy Ave 79922
Lomita Dr 79907

Lomont Dr 79912
London Bridge Dr 79934
Londonderry Rd 79907
Lone Cactus Ct 79934
Lone Crest Dr 79902
Lone Star Pl 79907
Lone Wolf Cir 79936
Lonesome Dove Cir 79936
Lonewood Dr 79925
Long John Dr 79936
Long Shadow Ave 79938
Longhorn Dr 79907
Longleaf Pl 79928
Longspur 79911
Longstreet 79904
Longview Cir 79924
Lookout Point Pl 79938
N Loop Dr
6901-7097 79915
7099-8099 79915
8100-9599 79907
9600-12099 79927
10550-10550 79929
Lopez Rd 79938
Lorenzo Frias Dr 79938
Lorenzo Ponce Dr 79938
Lorenzo Ruiz Ave 79936
Loretta Ken St 79927
Loretto Rd 79903
Loring Pl 79928
Lorne Rd 79925
Lorri Dr 79936
Los Adobes Dr 79927
Los Altos Dr 79912
Los Angeles Dr 79902
Los Bancos Dr 79912
Los Cerritos Dr 79912
Los Felinos Cir 79912
Los Frias 79927
Los Fuentes Dr 79912
Los Jardines Cir 79912
Los Lagos Way 79907
Los Magos Cir 79927
Los Miradores Dr 79912
Los Moros Dr 79932
Los Nietos Ct 79932
Los Olivos Ct 79912
Los Pinos Way 79912
Los Pueblos Dr 79912
Los Reales Dr 79912
Los Robles Dr 79912
Los Seris Pl 79912
Los Siglos Dr 79912
Los Surcos Rd 79907
Los Vientos Way 79927
Lost Padre Mine Dr 79902
Lost Pines Ln 79936
Lottie Ln 79932
Lou Brock Pl 79934
Lou Graham St 79936
Louis Dr 79904
Louisiana St 79930
Louisville Ave 79930
Lounint Dr 79924
Louvre Dr 79907
Love Rd 79922
Lovebird Ln 79924
Loving Ln 79938
Lowd Ave
8000-8014 79915
8016-8199 79907
Lowell Rd 79928
Lowenstein Ave 79907
Loweree Ave 79938
Loya Rd 79927
Loyola Ln 79928
Lozano Ln 79927
Lt Luis Peralta Rd 79927
Ltv Dr 79928
Lubbock Dr 79924
Lucas Ave 79904
Lucas Rd 79938
Lucas Marcelo Dr 79912
Lucero Ln 79907
Lucio Moreno Dr 79934
Luckett Ct 79932

Lucknow Rd 79927
Lucky Dr 79907
Lucy Dr 79924
Lucy Acosta Way 79936
Luella Ave 79925
Lufkin Way 79924
Luis Ln 79907
Luis Cortinas 79938
Luis Gomez Pl 79936
Luis Lares Pl 79938
Luis Mendivil Ct 79927
Luke St
5000-10098 79908
10100-10499 79908
11100-11299 79918
Lulac Dr 79905
N Luna St
100-300 79905
302-398 79905
601-697 79903
699-1399 79903
1401-1499 79903
S Luna St 79905
Lupe Anna Ln 79927
Lupe Rivera Dr 79936
Lupelenes Way 79907
Lutes Cir 79906
Luz Carpio Way 79936
Luz De Agua Pl 79912
Luz De Camino Way 79912
Luz De Casita Ct 79912
Luz De Ciudad Ct 79912
Luz De Color Ct 79912
Luz De Cueva Ln 79912
Luz De Dia Ct 79912
Luz De Espejo Dr 79912
Luz De Estela Ct 79912
Luz De Lumbre Ave 79912
Luz De Luna Pl 79912
Luz De Ojos Ct 79912
Luz De Paseo Rd 79912
Luz De Pueblo Ct 79912
Luz De Sol Dr 79912
Luz De Villa Ct 79912
Lydia Rd 79927
Lyle Ln 79936
Lyman Ln 79938
Lyman Dutton Cir 79936
Lynch Ln 79932
Lynn Haven Ave 79907
Lynn Hill St 79938
Lynne Way 79915
Lynwood St 79936
S M Mellnik Dr 79924
Mabel Pl 79928
Mac Kenze Ann Pl 79927
Macadamia Cir 79907
Macaw Ave 79924
Macaw Palm Dr 79936
Macdill Ct 79908
Mace St 79932
Macias St 79905
Mackenzie Dr 79907
Mackerel Ln 79924
Mackinaw St 79924
Macon Ln 79924
Madeline Dr 79902
Madera Ave 79903
Madero Dr 79928
Madison Lee Dr 79927
Madrid Way 79915
Madrigal Rd 79927
Madrone Way 79907
Madtone Dr 79907
Magdalena Ave 79922
Mager 79938
Magic Rock Dr 79938
Magnetic St 79904
Magnolia St 79903
Mago Pl 79936
Magoffin Ave
501-597 79901
599-2399 79901
2900-3000 79905
3002-3098 79905
Magruder St 79925

Maguire St 79928
Mahogany Ln 79922
E Main Dr 79901
W Main Dr
201-299 79901
701-1399 79902
Mainzer Ave 79905
Maj Sprague Ave 79924
Majestic Crown Rd 79928
Majestic Mountain Dr 79912
Majestic Ridge Dr 79912
Majorca Ct 79912
Malachite Ct 79924
Malaga Pl 79905
Malapai Ln 79904
Mallett St 79907
Mallory Ct 79912
Mamba Ct 79924
Mamie Rd 79932
Mammoth Ln 79911
Man O War St 79932
Manatee St 79938
Manchester Ave 79903
Mandeville Ave 79928
Mandy Way 79927
Mango Rd 79915
Mangrum Cir 79912
Manila Dr 79924
Manitoba St 79924
Manning Way 79915
Manny Aguilera Dr 79936
Manor Pl 79915
Mansfield Ave 79915
Manso Ct 79927
Manuel Dr 79907
Manuel Acosta Dr 79936
Manuel Gameros Dr 79934
Manuel Moreno Dr 79934
Manuel Ortega Ave 79927
Manuel Puentes Ct 79934
Manzana Ave 79905
Manzana Rd 79927
Manzanilla Pl 79928
Maple St 79903
Maple Landing Ct 79912
Maple Leaves Ct 79938
Maple Point Dr 79938
Maple Ridge Way 79912
Mapula Loop & Pl 79938
Maquitico Ct 79936
Mara Pl 79932
Marathon Pl 79928
Maravilla Dr 79907
Maravillas St 79938
Marbella Dr 79932
Marble Dr 79904
Marble Canyon Dr 79912
Marble Gate Way 79936
Marburn Ct 79928
Marcena St 79912
March Ct 79908
Marciano St 79932
Marcillus Ave 79924
Marconi Ln 79935
Marcos Lucero Pl 79934
Marcus Uribe Dr 79934
Mardi Gras Dr 79912
Marfa Pl 79928
Marfil Dr 79907
Margaret Ln 79907
Margaret Jean Dr 79938
Maria Ct 79907
Maria Seanes Dr 79936
Mariana Cir 79915
Maribeth Pl 79924
Maricela Dr 79915
Maricopa Dr 79912
Marie Tobin Dr 79924
Marietta St 79932
Marigold Way 79907
Marimba Dr 79912
Marina Ave 79938
Marine 79924
Mariposa Dr 79912
Marisa Atilano Way 79938
Marisma Ct 79936

Marissa Dr 79924
Mark Jason Dr 79938
Mark Mabon Ct 79927
Mark Twain Ave 79928
Mark Wallace Ln 79912
Market Ave 79915
Market Center Ave 79912
Markham Ct 79904
Marks St 79904
Marlicia Dr 79907
Marlin Dr 79924
Marlow Rd 79905
Marlys Larson St 79936
Marne Dr 79907
Marquez Rd 79927
Marquis St 79936
Marquita Ln 79915
Marr St
400-499 79905
601-797 79903
799-2300 79903
2302-2798 79903
Marsh Mccall Way 79936
Marsha Rd 79938
Marshall 79908
Marshall Rd 79906
Marta Duron Ln 79936
Martha Ln 79938
Martha Way 79907
Martha Gale Dr 79912
Marthmont Way 79912
Martin Ln 79903
Martin Bauman Dr 79928
Martin Forman 79938
Martina Pl 79936
S Martinez St 79905
Martinique Dr 79927
Marvin Ln 79938
Mary Alice Pl 79936
Mary Jeanne Ln 79915
Mary Megan Ct 79935
Mary Stuart Dr 79912
Mary Tarango Pl 79932
N & S Maryland St 79905
Masada Dr 79938
Mascotte St 79938
Masquerade Ln 79912
Matador St 79924
Matagorda St 79936
Matamoros Dr 79915
Mathias Dr 79903
Matkin St 79906
Matterhorn Dr
8900-9099 79904
9100-9199 79924
Matthew Lutz Pl 79938
Mattox St 79925
Mauer Rd 79915
Maureen Cir 79924
Maurice Rd 79927
Maurice Bell Dr 79932
Maverick Ave 79915
Maxie Marie 79932
Maximo St 79932
Maximo Yabes St 79938
Maxine Dr 79927
Maxwell Ave 79904
Maxwood Dr
10200-10399 79925
10400-10499 79935
May Cir 79938
Maya Ave 79912
Maya Lizabeth Pl 79938
Maya Point Dr 79938
Maya Rock Way 79938
Mayfield Terrace St 79930
Mayflower Ave 79925
Mazatlan Dr 79915
Mcadoo Dr 79927
Mcaffee Pl 79903
Mcallen Pl 79924
Mcauliffe Dr 79936
Mcbryar Ave 79904
Mccabe Dr 79925
Mccamey Rd 79907
Mccarthy Ave 79915

Mcclintock Dr 79932
Mccombs St
9200-9544 79924
9546-10610 79924
10612-10898 79924
10900-11298 79934
11300-11400 79934
11402-13698 79934
Mcconnell Ave 79904
Mccormick Ln 79924
Mccracken Dr 79938
Mccune Rd 79915
Mccutcheon Ln 79932
Mcdougal Ln 79912
Mceachern Pl 79938
Mcelroy Ave 79907
Mcfall Dr 79925
Mcgregor Dr 79904
Mcintosh Dr 79925
Mckelligon Dr 79902
Mckelligon Canyon Rd 79930
Mckesson St 79927
Mckinley Ave 79930
Mclean St 79936
Mcmahon Ave 79928
Mcmahon Cir 79904
Mcnair Rd 79906
N & S Mcneil Dr 79906
Mcpharlin St 79930
Mcrae Blvd 79925
Mcreynolds Pl 79906
Mcveigh Dr 79912
Meade Ct 79904
Meadow Lk 79938
Meadow Gate Dr 79936
Meadow Lawn 79938
Meadow Oaks Ct 79932
Meadow Sage Dr 79911
Meadow West Dr 79932
Meadow Willow Dr 79922
Meadowbrook Dr 79936
Meadowdale Dr 79928
Meadowlark Dr 79922
Meadowview Dr 79925
Mecca Dr 79907
Mechem St 79928
Medalla St 79927
Medano Dr 79912
Medical Center Dr 79902
Medill Pl 79928
Medina St 79905
Medwood Dr
10301-10399 79925
10400-10425 79935
10427-10499 79935
Mel Cole Dr 79928
Melendez St 79927
Melicent St 79912
Melinda St 79927
Melissa Cir 79927
Mellon Dr 79907
Mellward Rd 79927
Melody Ln 79932
Melrose Ct 79932
Melton Rd 79927
Melville Ln 79912
Memory Dr 79932
Memphis Ave
2400-3934 79930
3936-3998 79930
4001-4097 79903
4099-4699 79903
Menard Ln 79936
Menlo Ave 79936
Mentone Dr 79927
Menzies St 79924
Meraz Ave 79907
Mercantile Ave 79928
Mercedes St 79924
Mercer Ln 79928
Merchant Ave 79915
Mercury St 79904
Mercy Rock Pl 79938
Merejildo Madrid St 79934
Meribeth Ln 79938
Merida Ln 79905

Meriden Ln 79912
Meril Rd 79925
Mermaid Dr 79936
Merriam Ave 79904
Merriman Dr 79912
Merritt Rd 79906
N Mesa St
101-197 79901
199-699 79901
701-797 79902
799-4499 79902
4500-5980 79912
5981-5981 79902
5982-7698 79912
5985-7699 79912
7700-8099 79932
S Mesa St 79901
Mesa Drain Rd 79927
Mesa Grande Ave 79912
N & S Mesa Hills Dr 79912
Mesa Park Dr 79912
Mesa Rock Pl 79938
Mesa Verde Ln 79904
Mescal Ln 79912
Mescalero Dr 79925
Mesilla Ct 79932
Mesilla Vista Ln 79912
Mesita Dr 79902
Mesquite Ct 79922
Mesquite Bush Dr 79934
Mesquite Flor Dr 79934
Mesquite Gum Ln 79934
Mesquite Lake Ln 79934
Mesquite Miel Dr 79934
Mesquite Rock Dr 79934
Mesquite Sun Ln 79934
Mesquite Tree Ln 79934
Metate Pl 79912
Meteor Way 79912
Meteor Rock Pl 79938
Metetuye Ln 79902
Mettler Dr 79925
Mew Gull Ln 79928
Miami Ct 79924
Mica Dr 79928
Michael Ave 79938
Michael Dr 79927
Michael Chang Pl 79938
Michael P Anderson Ln 79934
Michael Smith Dr 79936
Michael Torres Dr 79938
Michel 79932
Michelangelo Dr 79936
Michele Ann Dr 79938
Michelle Ln 79924
Mickey Mantle Ave 79934
Midas Dr 79924
Middle Drain Rd 79927
Middledale St 79934
Middlesboro Ave 79924
Midianite Dr 79927
Midland Ct 79928
Midnight Sun Dr 79927
Midway Dr 79915
Miguel St 79928
Miguel Pedraza Sr Ct 79927
Miguel Terrazas 79938
Miguel Varela Ln 79936
Mike Ln 79932
Mike Andrade Pl 79936
Mike Carbajal Rd 79927
Mike Godwin Dr 79936
Mike Hill Dr 79936
Mike Vane Dr 79934
Milan St 79924
Milan Ridge Dr 79912
Milky Way Ct 79904
Mill Gate Way 79936
Mill Valley Rd 79927
Miller Cir 79915
Miller Barber Dr
10700-10899 79935
10900-10920 79936
10922-10998 79936
Millicent Dr 79938

E Mills Ave
100-198 ... 79901
200-300 ... 79901
219-219 ... 79940
219-219 ... 79941
219-219 ... 79942
219-219 ... 79943
219-219 ... 79944
219-219 ... 79945
219-219 ... 79946
219-219 ... 79947
219-219 ... 79948
219-219 ... 79949
219-219 ... 79950
219-219 ... 79951
219-219 ... 79952
219-219 ... 79953
219-219 ... 79954
219-219 ... 79955
301-2399 ... 79901
302-2398 ... 79901
W Mills Ave ... 79901
Millstone Ct ... 79932
Milo Dr ... 79927
Milpas Ln ... 79907
Milray Dr ... 79932
Milton Rd ... 79915
Milton Henry ... 79932
Mimosa Ave ... 79915
Mina Perdida St ... 79902
Minas Ct ... 79928
Mineola Dr ... 79925
Miner St ... 79938
Mineral Ct ... 79928
Mineral Ridge Dr ... 79912
Mink Pl ... 79928
Minnesota Ct ... 79927
Minue Dr ... 79916
Minuteman St ... 79924
Mira Grande Dr ... 79912
Mira Hermosa Dr ... 79912
Mira Serena Dr ... 79912
Mira Sierra Ln ... 79912
Miracle Ln ... 79938
Miracle Way ... 79925
Mirage Ct ... 79936
Miranda Ct ... 79932
Mirasol Dr ... 79907
Mireles Ct ... 79927
Miriam Dr ... 79936
Mirisa St ... 79927
Missbev Ave ... 79932
Mission Rd ... 79903
Mission Viejo Dr ... 79912
Mississippi Ave ... 79902
E Missouri Ave
300-398 ... 79901
401-499 ... 79901
801-1799 ... 79902
1901-2997 ... 79903
2999-4499 ... 79903
4501-4599 ... 79903
W Missouri Ave
101-497 ... 79901
499-600 ... 79901
602-606 ... 79901
700-1399 ... 79902
Missy Yvette Dr ... 79936
Misty Ct ... 79928
Misty Point Dr ... 79938
Mitchell Dr ... 79928
Mitchell Jones Dr ... 79936
Mitzi Bond ... 79932
Mitzie Ram Pl ... 79904
Mobile Ave
2500-2598 ... 79930
2600-4099 ... 79930
4300-4499 ... 79903
Mocha Dune Dr ... 79934
Mockingbird Rd ... 79907
Moctezuma Pl ... 79928
Modesta Rd ... 79932
Moffat Ln ... 79912
Mogollon Cir ... 79912
Mohair Dr ... 79934
Mohawk Ave ... 79925
Mohegan Ln ... 79912
Mojave Dr ... 79915
Molly Marie Ct ... 79936
Monaco Dr ... 79925
Monahans Dr ... 79924
Monarch Dr ... 79912
Monclova Ln ... 79907
Mondel Pine Pl ... 79907
Monica Ct ... 79932
Monica Seles Pl ... 79938
Monroe Ave ... 79930
Mont Blanc Dr ... 79907
Montague Loop ... 79906
Montana Ave
101-197 ... 79902
199-1915 ... 79902
1916-5499 ... 79903
5501-5599 ... 79903
5600-10500 ... 79925
10502-10598 ... 79925
10600-10698 ... 79935
10700-10800 ... 79935
10802-10898 ... 79935
10900-11298 ... 79936
11300-11800 ... 79936
11802-12098 ... 79936
12100-12298 ... 79938
12300-18000 ... 79938
18002-19898 ... 79938
Montclair Dr ... 79932
Monte Alto Rd ... 79927
Monte Carlo Pl ... 79927
Monte Del Sol ... 79911
Monte Mayor Dr ... 79927
Monte Negro Dr ... 79935
Monte Rubio Ct ... 79927
Monte Sanders Ln ... 79935
Monte Sur Dr ... 79935
Montebello Dr ... 79912
Montecito Rd ... 79915
Montego Bay Dr ... 79912
Montell Dr ... 79927
Montera Rd ... 79907
Monterrey Dr ... 79915
Montestruc Ct ... 79901
Montevideo St ... 79927
Montgomery Dr ... 79924
Montmartre Dr ... 79907
Montoya Dr
4901-4929 ... 79922
4931-5099 ... 79922
5150-6099 ... 79932
Montoya Ln ... 79932
Montoya Rd ... 79932
Montoya Oak Ln ... 79932
Montreal Cir ... 79927
Montridge Ct ... 79904
Montrose Ct ... 79925
Montsarrat ... 79938
Montview Ct ... 79905
Montwood Dr
9200-10399 ... 79925
10400-10498 ... 79935
10500-10600 ... 79935
10602-10998 ... 79935
11000-11098 ... 79936
11100-12199 ... 79936
12200-12498 ... 79928
12201-12299 ... 79938
Monument Ave ... 79938
Monville Cir ... 79904
N & S Moon Rd ... 79927
Moon Point Pl ... 79938
Moon Ranch Ln ... 79934
Moon River Ln ... 79912
Moon Rock Pl ... 79938
Moondale Dr ... 79912
Moonglow Dr ... 79912
Moonlight Ave ... 79904
Moore Rd ... 79932
Moore St ... 79902
Mooreland St ... 79907
Moose Ct ... 79924
Mora Cir & Dr ... 79932
Morales St ... 79907
Morehead Ave ... 79930
Morelia Rd ... 79907
Morenci Rd ... 79903
Moreras Ct ... 79907
Morgan Ave ... 79906
Morgan Bay St ... 79936
Morgan Marie St ... 79936
Morissey Way ... 79928
Morley Dr ... 79925
Morning Dawn Ave ... 79932
Morning Dew Ct ... 79936
Morning Glory Cir ... 79924
Morning Mist Pl ... 79938
Morning Star Dr ... 79912
Morningside Cir ... 79904
Morocco Cir ... 79927
Morrill Rd ... 79932
Morrow Ct ... 79902
Moser Pl ... 79904
Moses Dr ... 79927
Mosher Way ... 79927
Moss Point Pl ... 79938
Mosswood St ... 79935
Mount Abbott Dr ... 79904
Mount Baldy Dr ... 79904
Mount Bona Pl ... 79904
Mount Boucherie Ln ... 79924
Mount Capote Dr ... 79904
Mount Carmel Ave ... 79907
Mount Chinati Dr ... 79904
Mount Cristo Rey Ln ... 79922
Mount Delano Dr ... 79904
Mount Elbert Dr ... 79904
Mount Etna Dr
8900-9099 ... 79904
9100-9199 ... 79924
Mount Everest Dr ... 79904
Mount Hagan Dr ... 79904
Mount Hood Dr ... 79904
Mount Latona Dr ... 79904
Mount Olympus Dr
8900-9099 ... 79904
9100-9299 ... 79924
Mount Ranier Dr ... 79904
Mount Rushmore Ln
5201-8933 ... 79904
8935-9099 ... 79904
9100-9199 ... 79924
Mount San Berdu Dr
8900-9099 ... 79904
9100-9299 ... 79924
Mount Scott Dr ... 79904
Mount Shasta Dr
8600-9099 ... 79904
9100-9299 ... 79924
Mount Tibet Dr ... 79904
Mount Vernon Ct ... 79904
Mount Whitney Dr ... 79904
Mountain Ave ... 79930
Mountain Ash Dr ... 79904
Mountain Breeze Ave ... 79928
Mountain Ridge Dr ... 79904
Mountain Sun Dr ... 79938
Mountain View Dr ... 79904
Mountain Walk Dr ... 79904
Mountain Willow Dr ... 79904
Mountain Wind Dr ... 79904
Moye Dr ... 79925
Msg R Miller St ... 79918
Msg Thomas J Sanchez
St ... 79908
Muddy Point Ln ... 79938
Mulberry Ave ... 79932
Mule Deer Dr ... 79938
Mumm Ln ... 79924
Mundy Dr ... 79902
Mundy Creek Dr ... 79911
Mura Pl ... 79928
Muralla Way ... 79907
Murchison Dr
1300-2000 ... 79902
2002-2098 ... 79902
2100-2499 ... 79930
Muro Way ... 79927
Murphy St ... 79924
Murray Pl ... 79902
Muscat Rd ... 79927
Mustang Ave ... 79915
Myles St ... 79930
Myra St ... 79915
Myrna Deckert Dr ... 79936
Myrtle Ave ... 79901
Mystic Desert Dr ... 79928
Mystic Valley Ct ... 79938
Nabhan Dr ... 79915
Nachito Way ... 79938
Nairn St ... 79925
Nakitu Dr ... 79907
Nancy Dr ... 79927
Nancy Lee Ave ... 79928
Nancy Lopez Ln ... 79936
Nancy Mcdonald Dr ... 79936
Naomi Dr ... 79927
Naples St ... 79924
Napolske Ct ... 79936
Naranjos Dr ... 79907
Narciso ... 79928
Nardo Goodman Dr ... 79912
Nasa Way ... 79936
Nashville Ave
2400-3999 ... 79930
4000-4599 ... 79903
Nassau Way ... 79927
Nastase Pl ... 79932
Natalicio Ln ... 79912
Natchez Ave ... 79928
Natchez Ln ... 79924
Natchitoches ... 79928
Nathan Bay Dr ... 79934
Nations Ave ... 79930
Native Dancer St ... 79938
Nato Ct ... 79924
Nautical Dr ... 79936
Navajo Ave ... 79925
Navajo Point Dr ... 79938
Navarie Pl ... 79932
Navarrette Cir ... 79907
Navasota Pl ... 79905
Navy ... 79924
Nayarit Dr ... 79928
Nazareno St ... 79928
Nearpoint Dr ... 79911
Neches Ave ... 79905
Nederland Ln ... 79936
Nehemiah Pl ... 79936
Neil Armstrong Ln ... 79936
Nelda Candelaria Ln ... 79927
Nell Pl ... 79924
Nenna Ct ... 79932
Neptune St ... 79904
Nesbit Ave ... 79924
Nesting Pl ... 79936
Nettie Rose Cir ... 79936
E & W Nevada Ave ... 79902
N & S Nevarez Rd ... 79927
New Britton Dr ... 79928
New Harvest Pl ... 79912
New Haven Dr ... 79907
New Orleans Dr ... 79912
New World Dr ... 79936
New York Ave ... 79902
Newcastle Dr ... 79924
Newell Hays St ... 79927
Newell Heights Ln ... 79938
Newkirk Rd ... 79928
Newland Ct ... 79907
Newman St
100-166 ... 79901
168-198 ... 79901
600-1099 ... 79902
Newport Dr ... 79924
Neyla Dr ... 79932
Niagara Falls Pl ... 79924
Nicholas Rd ... 79927
Nichols Rd
301-397 ... 79915
399-499 ... 79915
500-599 ... 79927
Nick Faldo Pl ... 79936
Night Fall Pl ... 79932
Night Hawk Dr ... 79912
Night School ... 79928
Nighthaven St ... 79928
Nike Ln ... 79924
Niles St ... 79907
Nimbus Rd ... 79912
Nimitz Pl ... 79915
Nina Dr ... 79907
Nina Pearl Dr ... 79938
Nino Aguilera St ... 79901
Nirmal Dr ... 79927
Nita Pl ... 79928
Nita Fay Dr ... 79912
Nitron Ave ... 79938
Nixon Way ... 79905
Nobel Rock Ct ... 79938
Noble St
100-200 ... 79901
202-298 ... 79901
600-1200 ... 79902
1202-1398 ... 79902
Noble Path Pl ... 79928
Noble Ridge Way ... 79912
Noel Espinoza Cir ... 79936
Nogal Pl ... 79915
Nolan Dr ... 79924
Nolan Richardson Dr ... 79936
Nolton Ave ... 79938
Nome Ave ... 79924
Nonap Rd ... 79928
Nooch Rd ... 79927
Nopal Ave ... 79922
Nopales Ln ... 79912
Norcross Pl ... 79928
Nordstrom Ave ... 79932
Norfolk Ln ... 79902
Norma St ... 79938
Norma Rae Ct ... 79932
Norman Montion Dr ... 79936
Normandy Dr ... 79925
Normont Way ... 79912
Norte Pl ... 79904
Northampton St ... 79934
Northbrook Ct ... 79932
Northfield Ave ... 79936
Northport Ct ... 79928
Northridge Dr ... 79912
Northrop Rd ... 79925
Northview Dr ... 79934
Northwestern Dr ... 79912
Northwind Dr ... 79912
Northwyck Way ... 79928
Norton St ... 79904
Norwich Way ... 79907
Norwood Ct ... 79924
Nostalgia Ct ... 79912
Notre Dame Rd ... 79928
Nottingham Dr
100-198 ... 79924
9100-9168 ... 79907
9170-9466 ... 79907
9468-9498 ... 79907
Notus Ln ... 79935
Nova Way ... 79924
Noviembre Dr ... 79935
Novilla Pl ... 79932
Nueces Way ... 79925
Nueva Mission Rd ... 79927
Nunda Ave ... 79928
Nutmeg Dr ... 79907
Oak Ct ... 79905
Oak Rdg ... 79912
Oak Abbey Ct ... 79936
Oak Arrow Way ... 79936
Oak Cliff Dr ... 79912
Oak Crest Cir ... 79936
Oak Crossing Dr ... 79936
Oak Landing Dr ... 79912
Oak Point Pl ... 79938
Oak Tower Pl ... 79936
Oak Tree Ct ... 79932
Oakbriar Cir ... 79932
Oakdale St ... 79925
Oakhill Ct ... 79928
Oakhurst Ln ... 79928
Oakwood Dr ... 79924
Oasis Dr ... 79936
Oaxaca Ct ... 79907
Obadiah Ln ... 79938
Obrady Pl ... 79934
Obrian St ... 79934
Obsidian St ... 79924
Ocala Ave ... 79938
Occidental Ave ... 79928
Ocean Ct ... 79928
Ocean Park St ... 79936
Ocean Point Dr ... 79938
Ocean Side Dr ... 79936
N Ochoa St
100-200 ... 79901
202-298 ... 79901
700-798 ... 79902
800-1799 ... 79902
1801-2399 ... 79902
S Ochoa St ... 79901
Ochre Bluff Ln ... 79934
Oconnor Dr ... 79934
Ocotal Rd ... 79928
Ocotillo St ... 79932
Octavia St ... 79902
N Octavia St ... 79901
Octubre Dr ... 79935
Odell Ln ... 79934
Oden Dr ... 79927
Odessa Ln ... 79924
Odonnell St ... 79934
Offutt Cir ... 79908
Ohara Dr ... 79934
Ohio St ... 79930
Ojinaga Rd ... 79928
Ojo De Agua Dr ... 79912
Okeefe Dr ... 79902
Oklahoma St ... 79930
Olan Ct ... 79924
Olano Ct ... 79927
Old Butterfield Trl ... 79938
Old Castle St ... 79936
Old County Dr ... 79907
Old Hatchita Rd ... 79938
Old Hueco Tanks Rd ... 79927
Old Paint Dr ... 79911
N & S Old Pueblo Dr ... 79907
Old Rim Ct ... 79938
Old Spanish Trl ... 79904
Oldenberg Ct ... 79938
Oleander Way ... 79922
Oleary Dr ... 79938
Oleaster Dr ... 79932
Olga St ... 79924
Olga Mapula Dr ... 79936
Olive Ave ... 79901
Olive Point Dr ... 79938
Olivia Cir ... 79912
Olmeca Dr ... 79912
Olmos St ... 79922
Olson St ... 79903
Olympic Ave ... 79904
Omalley Dr ... 79934
Omar Bradley Dr ... 79924
Omega Cir ... 79924
Omicron Pl ... 79924
Onate Way ... 79907
Oneida Dr ... 79912
Onix Dr ... 79912
Onizuka Dr ... 79936
Onnie Kirk Ave ... 79938
Ontario St ... 79924
Ontiveros St ... 79932
Onyxstone St ... 79924
Opal Gate Way ... 79936
Opalstone St ... 79924
Ophelia Way ... 79915
Opossum Cir ... 79928
Optima Way ... 79911
Oran Ct ... 79924
Orange Tree Ln ... 79915
Orantes Pl ... 79932
Orbit Way ... 79936
Orchard Ave ... 79905
Orchid Dr ... 79928
N Oregon St
100-521 ... 79901
523-699 ... 79901
700-2500 ... 79902
2502-2698 ... 79902
S Oregon St ... 79901
Oreilly St ... 79930
Orgain Way ... 79915
Oriley Ln ... 79934
Orinoco Way ... 79907
Orio Palmer Dr ... 79938
Oriole Way ... 79915
Orion Pl ... 79904
Orizaba Ave ... 79912
Orkney Rd ... 79925
Orlando Ln ... 79924
Orleans Ave ... 79924
Ormsby Ct ... 79927
Orndorff Dr ... 79915
Oro Pl ... 79928
Orourke Ln ... 79934
Orozco Pl ... 79907
Orpheus Dr ... 79924
Orr Cir ... 79904
Ortega Ct ... 79907
Ortiz Ln ... 79927
Orville Moody Ln ... 79935
Orwell Way ... 79912
Oryx Cir ... 79924
Osage Ln ... 79925
Osaple Cir ... 79932
Osborne Dr ... 79922
W Osborne Rd ... 79924
Oscar Alvarez Ct ... 79927
Oscar Perez ... 79932
Osceola St ... 79938
Oshea St ... 79938
Oslo Dr ... 79927
Oso Rock Way ... 79938
Osullivan Dr ... 79928
Otero Ct ... 79915
Otoole Dr ... 79934
Otter Ct ... 79924
Otter Point Dr ... 79938
Otto Way ... 79915
Otyokwa Way ... 79907
Oval Rock Dr ... 79912
Ovalo Way ... 79927
Oveja Ave ... 79912
Overbrook Pl ... 79938
E & W Overland Ave ... 79901
Overland Stage Rd ... 79938
Overlook Ridge Ln ... 79912
Owl Ct ... 79924
Owl Point Ave ... 79938
Owl Rock Pl ... 79938
Oxbow Dr ... 79928
Oxcart Run St ... 79936
Oxford Ave ... 79903
Pablino Pl ... 79927
Pablo Sanchez Pl ... 79938
Pablo Silvas Sr St ... 79927
Pacheco Dr ... 79935
Pacific Dr ... 79922
Pacific Point Dr ... 79938
Paddlefoot Ln ... 79907
Paden St ... 79905
Padilla Dr ... 79907
Padres Dr ... 79907
Paducah Ave ... 79936
Page Ct ... 79928
Page St ... 79927
Pageant Ct ... 79912
Pagosa Ct ... 79904
Painted Quail Pl ... 79936
Painted Sky Ln ... 79912
E Paisano Dr
100-1700 ... 79901
1702-1798 ... 79901
2000-4399 ... 79905
4400-5598 ... 79905
4400-4400 ... 79995
4401-5599 ... 79905
5600-5999 ... 79925
W Paisano Dr
100-799 ... 79901
1700-1798 ... 79922
1800-2799 ... 79922
2801-2899 ... 79922
Paisley Ln ... 79928
Paiute Way ... 79912
Pali Dr ... 79936

Palla Pl 79907
Palm St
1-200 79901
202-298 79901
800-898 79903
Palm Grove Cir 79936
Palma Sola Dr 79907
Palmary Dr 79912
Palmdale St 79932
Palmer Pl 79928
Palmetto Dr 79925
Palo Alto Ave 79912
Palo Verde Pl 79912
Paloma Dr 79924
Palomino St 79924
Pam Mccall Dr & Ln 79924
Pamela Anne Ln 79936
Pamela Raye Rd 79927
Pamlico Dr 79912
Pamplona Ct 79932
Pan American Dr
400-499 79907
9500-9799 79927
Panahi Rd 79927
Panama Way 79922
Panama Palm Ct 79936
Pancho Gonzalez Ct 79938
Pandora St 79904
Pansy Ct 79932
Panther Dr 79924
Papago Rd 79905
Papaya St 79915
Parade Ln 79925
Parade Willow Dr 79922
Paradise Ln 79924
Paradise Cove Ln 79938
Paragon Ln 79912
Paraguay Ct 79903
Parakeet Ct 79924
Parchment Pl 79936
Paredon Dr 79928
Paridise Breeze Ave 79928
Paris Ave 79924
Park Crk 79938
Park Dr 79902
Park St 79901
Park Haven Ave 79907
Park Hill Dr 79902
Park North Dr 79904
Park View Cir 79935
Parker Rd 79927
Parkland Dr 79925
Parkmont Pl 79912
Parkwood St 79925
Parque Del Sol 79911
Parral Dr 79915
Parrot Way 79922
Partello St
2500-4798 79930
4801-4899 79930
5800-6098 79904
6100-6200 79904
6202-6298 79904
Partisan Rock Ln 79938
Pasadena Cir 79924
Pasaje Pl 79928
Pasatiempo Cir 79912
Pascal St 79932
Pasco Ct 79905
Paseo Alegre Ave & Dr 79928
Paseo Alto Pl 79928
Paseo Amado Pl 79928
Paseo Antiguo Dr 79936
Paseo Arena Pl 79936
Paseo Azul Dr 79928
Paseo Blanco Dr 79928
Paseo Bonito Way 79936
Paseo Central Ave 79928
Paseo Chico Dr 79928
Paseo Clara Pl 79928
Paseo Colina Pl 79936
Paseo Corona 79936
Paseo Corto Cir 79928
Paseo De Amor Ln 79936
Paseo De Arco Ct 79928
Paseo De Cruz Ct 79928
Paseo De Fe Cir 79928
Paseo De Flor Cir & St 79928
Paseo De Luna Ln 79912
Paseo De Luz 79936
Paseo De Oro Ln 79936
Paseo De Suerte Dr 79928
Paseo De Vida Ct & Dr 79928
Paseo Del Este Dr 79928
Paseo Del Mar Dr 79928
Paseo Del Monte Pl 79928
Paseo Del Norte 79912
Paseo Del Prado Dr 79936
Paseo Del Rey Dr 79936
Paseo Del Rio Ct 79936
Paseo Del Sol Pl 79936
Paseo Del Sur Ct 79928
Paseo Dorado Cir 79936
Paseo Feliz Dr 79928
Paseo Festivo Ct 79936
Paseo Florido Way 79936
Paseo Fresco Way 79936
Paseo Granada Ln 79936
Paseo Grande St 79928
Paseo Hermoso Dr 79928
Paseo Lago Dr 79928
Paseo Largo Cir 79928
Paseo Las Nubes Dr 79928
Paseo Lindo Dr 79928
Paseo Milagro Ave 79928
Paseo Mision St 79928
Paseo Nuevo Dr 79928
Paseo Rae Ave 79928
Paseo Randy Ln 79928
Paseo Real Cir 79936
Paseo Redondo Ave 79912
Paseo Rico Cir 79928
Paseo Rojo Dr 79928
Paseo Rosannie Ave 79928
Paseo Royal Way 79936
Paseo Segovia Pl 79936
Paseo Sereno Dr 79928
Paseo Solo Ln 79936
Paseo Unido St 79928
Paseo Valle Ln 79928
Paseo Verde Dr 79928
Pasillo Rock Pl 79938
Paso Noble Dr 79912
Paso View Dr 79938
Pasodale Rd 79907
Passage Pl 79936
Passero Dr 79903
Passmore Rd 79927
Pat Rd 79928
Pat Cruz 79932
Patio Feliz Ln 79912
Patria 79932
Patrice Promak St 79938
Patricia Ave 79936
Patrick James Ct 79936
Patriot St 79916
Patriot Point Dr 79938
Patrol Ave 79907
Patsy Pl 79938
Patterson Pl 79903
Patti Jo Dr 79927
Patton St 79924
Patty Berg Way 79912
Paul Harney Dr 79936
Paul Jason Dr 79927
Paul Klee Dr 79936
Paul Moran Pl 79936
Paul Todd Dr 79936
Paula Ct 79915
Pavo Ln 79907
Pawling Dr 79928
Pawnee Ct 79912
Payne Cir 79930
Peacepipe Ln 79936
Peach Tree Ln 79915
Peacock Ln 79924
Peadond St 79918
Pear Tree Ln 79915
Pearl Ln 79915
Pearl Gate Pl 79936
Pearl Ridge Dr 79912
Pearl Sands Dr 79924
Pebble Beach Dr 79912
Pebble Hills Blvd
10700-10748 79935
10750-10799 79935
10801-10899 79935
10900-10998 79936
11000-11900 79936
11902-12198 79936
12400-14100 79938
14102-14498 79938
Pebble Rock 79938
Pecan Ct 79915
Pecan Park Pl 79932
Pecos St 79905
Pedernales Dr 79907
Pedro Figari Ave 79936
Pedro Lucero Dr 79934
Peerless Pl 79925
Pegasus Ct 79904
Peggy Hopkins 79938
Peggy Rosson Way 79936
Peinado Ln 79903
Pelhem Rd 79936
Pell Way 79907
Pellicano Dr
10800-11299 79935
11300-11320 79936
11322-12300 79936
12302-12398 79936
12400-13599 79928
Pembroke Ln 79924
Pence Way 79907
Pendale Rd
100-1199 79907
1201-1299 79907
1301-1447 79936
1449-1450 79936
1452-1598 79936
N & S Pendell Rd 79905
Pendleton St 79936
Penjamo Dr 79927
Pennsylvania Cir & Pl 79903
Penroy Ln 79928
Pentantr Dr 79936
Penwood Dr 79935
Pera Ave 79905
Percheron 79938
Perla Point Dr 79938
Perlette St 79927
Perlite Dr 79928
Perry Ave 79938
Persephone Dr 79924
Pershing Dr 79903
Pershing Rd
1-99 79916
1400-1599 79906
Persimmon St 79924
Perth Ct & Dr 79922
Peru Pl 79903
Peruvian Paso 79938
Pescador Dr 79935
Petaya Ln 79912
Pete Brown Dr 79936
Pete Faulkner Pl 79936
Pete La Rue Cir 79928
Pete Payan Dr 79912
Pete Rose Dr 79936
Pete Sampras Pl 79938
Peter Cooper Dr 79936
Peter Hurd Dr 79936
Peter Noyes Dr 79928
Peters Rd 79927
Petty Ln 79907
Petty Fields Dr 79938
Petty Prue St 79938
Peyton Rd 79928
Pheasant Rd 79924
Phil Gibbs Dr 79936
Philip Dr 79927
Phillip Bazaar 79938
Phillips Pl 79938
Phillips St 79906
Phillipy Ct 79907
Phillis Wheatly Way 79938
Phoenix Ave 79915
Physicians Dr 79936
Picacho Hls 79912
Picasso Dr 79936
Pickerel Dr 79924
Pico Alto Dr 79935
Pico Norte Rd 79935
Piedmont Dr 79902
Piedra Roja St 79936
N Piedras St
100-300 79905
302-398 79905
500-598 79903
600-900 79903
902-1198 79903
1201-1397 79930
1399-5001 79930
5002-5099 79920
S Piedras St 79905
Pier Ln 79936
Pierce Ave 79930
Pifas Nevarez Pl 79934
Pike Rd 79906
Pikes Peak Dr 79904
Pilar Cir 79907
Pilgrimage Cir 79912
Pima Ln 79915
Pin Cushion Rd 79928
Pinal Ct 79928
Pinar Del Rio Dr 79932
Pine Pl 79905
Pine Creek Ln 79922
Pine Point Ct 79938
Pine Ridge Way 79912
Pine Springs Dr
12200-12299 79936
12300-12380 79928
12382-12498 79928
Pine Valley Ave 79928
Pinehurst Dr 79912
Pinewood St 79907
Pink Coral Dr 79936
Pinnacle St 79902
Pino Ct 79928
Pino Alto 79912
Pino Blanco Pl 79938
Pino Real Dr 79912
Pino Seco Pl 79938
Pino Triste Dr 79938
Pinon St 79907
Pinta Way 79912
Pintada Pl 79912
Pinto Pony Ln 79938
Pintoresco Dr 79935
Pioneer Ln 79927
Pioneer Rdg 79912
Pipecreek Ct 79936
Piro Ct 79927
Pisces Pl 79924
Pistachio St 79924
Pistolero 79912
Pitts St 79912
Pittsburg Ave 79930
Pizarro Dr 79912
Place Rd 79927
Placida Rd 79932
Plains Dr 79907
Plainview Dr 79924
Plant Rd 79907
Plaquemine Dr 79928
Plata Pl 79928
Platino Pl 79928
Plautus Ct 79936
Playa Pt 79938
Playa Del Sol 79911
Plaza Cir 79927
Plaza Azul Rd 79912
Plaza Blanca St 79912
Plaza Canada Ct 79912
Plaza Central Ln 79912
Plaza Chica Way 79912
Plaza Del Sol Ct 79912
Plaza Del Sur Ct 79912
Plaza Fatima Ct 79912
Plaza Redonda Dr 79912
Plaza Rica Ct 79912
Plaza Roja Ct 79912
Plaza Serena Rd 79912
Plaza Taurina Dr 79912
Plaza Verde Dr 79912
Plazer Pl 79928
Pleasant Crst 79928
Pleasant Gdn 79938
Pleasant Hill Dr 79924
Pleasant Manor Ct 79938
Pleasant Sand Dr 79924
Pleasant View Ct 79912
Pleasonton Rd
500-4899 79906
1000-1799 79916
Plereenw Dr 79915
Plum Ave 79915
Plumed Quail Ln 79936
Plymouth Dr 79907
Pocahantas Pl 79936
Pocano Ln 79912
Poet Point Pl 79938
Poets Rock Ln 79938
Poinciana St 79924
N Point Ave 79938
Point Ct 79904
W Point Dr 79907
Pointe Ln E 79936
Polaris St 79904
Polep Way 79927
Polk Ave 79930
Pollard St
3600-5099 79930
5400-5799 79904
Polly Harris Dr 79936
Polo Inn Rd 79915
Polvadera Dr 79912
Polvo Way 79907
Polycrates Pl 79924
Pomeroy Pl 79928
Pomona Ct 79912
Pompano Ave 79924
Pompeii St 79924
Ponca Way 79907
Ponce Dr 79915
Ponder Dr 79906
Ponderosa St 79924
Pony Express Rd 79938
Pony Soldier Ave 79936
Pony Trail Pl 79936
Poona Rd 79927
Poplar St
100-198 79901
200-299 79901
801-899 79903
Poquita Ct 79904
Por Fin Ln 79907
Porche St 79915
Porfirio Diaz St 79902
Porfirio Payan Dr 79934
Porpoise Dr 79924
Porras Dr 79912
Porsel Dr 79927
Port Arthur Ln 79924
Port Lavaca Dr 79924
Port Royal Pl 79928
Portage Pl 79928
Portales Ave 79938
Porter Ave 79930
Portillo Dr 79932
Portland Ave 79930
Portofino Ave 79938
Portsmouth Blvd 79922
Portugal Dr 79912
Porvenir Ct 79927
Post Rd 79903
Post Oak Ct 79932
Potencia Dr 79927
Potomac St 79924
Pow Wow Canyon Rd 79938
Powder River Ln 79938
Poza Rica Ct 79935
S Prado Rd 79907
Prado Del Sol Dr 79936
Prairie Dr 79925
Prairie Rose St 79936
Pranchen St 79901
Pratt Ave 79936
Pratt Way 79915
Presa Pl 79907
Prescott Dr 79915
Preston Dr 79924
Prestwick Rd 79925
Pretty Acres 79927
Preview Pl 79936
Prickley Pear Dr 79912
Primrose Ln 79928
Prince Edward Ave 79924
Prince George Ln 79924
Princeton Way 79907
Priscilla Cir 79936
Pritam Dr 79927
Privada Ct 79936
Private Factor Ave 79906
Private Walley Ave 79906
Prospect St
300-398 79901
500-1299 79902
Proud Eagle Dr 79936
Provincial Dr 79932
Pueblo St 79903
Pueblo Alegre Dr 79936
Pueblo Amable Way 79936
Pueblo Azul Ln 79936
Pueblo Bonito Ct 79936
Pueblo Carmel Way 79936
Pueblo Chico Ct 79936
Pueblo Corona Ln 79936
Pueblo Del Rio Way 79936
Pueblo Dormido Way 79936
Pueblo Fuerte Ct 79936
Pueblo Laguna Dr 79936
Pueblo Lindo Ct 79936
Pueblo Nubes Ln 79936
Pueblo Nuevo Cir 79936
Pueblo Seguro Way 79936
Pueblo Sereno Way 79936
Puentecillas 79928
Puerto Del Carmen Dr 79928
Puerto Rico St 79915
Puesta Del Sol Ln 79912
Pullman Dr 79936
Puma Cir 79912
Pumice Dr 79928
Pumpkin Patch Ln 79932
Punjab Dr 79927
Punto Reyes Ln 79912
Purple Hills Way 79912
Purple Sage Ct 79938
Putter Ln 79934
Pvt Juan Garcia Rd 79927
Pygmalion Ct 79924
Pyrite Dr 79932
Quadri Ct 79907
Quail Ave 79924
Quail Bush Cir 79936
Quail Cove Ct 79912
Quail Harvest Ln 79936
Quail Mesa Dr 79927
Quail Spring Dr 79928
Quaker Ridge Dr 79928
Quanah Pl 79936
Quartz St 79924
Quasar Ct 79904
Quebec St 79924
Queens Garden Cir 79936
Queretaro Dr 79912
Quezada Ave 79935
Quill Ct 79904
Quillayute Dr 79938
Quillen Cir 79904
Quinault Dr 79912
Quincy Ave 79922
Quinn Ave 79938
Quinta Antigua Ln 79912
Quinta Del Sol 79938
Quinta Luz Cir 79922
Quinta Real Ct 79912
Quintana Dr 79936
Quitman Ave 79903
R J Lunn Ct 79924
R J Wood Rd 79924
R L Shoemaker Dr 79924
R T Cassidy Dr 79924
R W Hoyt Way 79924
Rabe Ct 79907
Rachel Dr 79927
Rachel Crystel Pl 79938
Racoon Dr 79924
Radford St
401-499 79905
500-598 79903
600-2299 79903
2301-2799 79903
Radlite Dr 79928
Rafael Septien Ln 79927
Rafael Serna Ln 79934
Railroad Dr
8601-8899 79904
9101-9497 79924
9499-10599 79924
10901-11697 79934
11699-11799 79934
11801-12099 79934
Rain Cloud Dr 79927
Rain Dance Dr 79936
Rainbow Cir 79912
Rainbow Point Dr 79938
Rainbow Ridge Dr 79912
Raindrop Way 79924
Raintree Ave 79924
Rainwater Ct 79912
Rakocy Ct 79936
Raleigh Dr 79924
Ralph Janes Pl 79936
Ralph Seitsinger 79938
Ralpheene St 79907
Ramada Dr 79912
Ramey Cir 79908
Ramirez Ct 79907
Ramon Prieto 79938
Ramon Vega 79938
Ramona Ave 79915
Ramos Ct 79915
Rampart Pl 79902
Ramsgate Rd 79907
Ranchito Ave 79924
Ranchitos Del Este Rd 79938
Ranchland Dr 79915
Rancho Alegre Way 79915
Rancho Del Sur Dr 79938
Rancho Grande Dr 79936
Rancho Miraval Way 79927
Rancho Sereno Pl 79932
Rancho Trail Dr 79936
Rancho Verde Way 79907
Rancho Viejo Dr 79927
Rancho Vista Ln 79938
Rancich St 79904
Randall Cunningham 79938
Randolph Dr 79902
Randy Petri Ln 79936
Randy Wolff Pl 79935
Range War Ct 79927
Ranger St 79907
Ranier Point Dr 79938
Rankin Dr 79927
Raphael Cir 79936
Raquel St 79928
Rasnick Ln 79928
Rathmore Dr 79928
Ratner Cir 79936
Raton Dr 79915
Rattler Point Dr 79938
Rattlesnake Springs Rd 79906
Raul Mendiola Ln 79938
Raven Ct 79924
Rawhide Way 79938
Ray Way 79907
Ray Juarez Pl 79938
Ray Mena Ln 79934
Raya Del Sol 79911
Rayado Creek Ln 79911
Rayito Pl 79924
Raymond 79938
Raymond Jays Rd 79903
Raymond Telles Dr 79924

Raymundo St 79927
Raynolds St
100-298 79905
300-499 79905
500-1899 79903
N Raynor St
115-199 79905
300-398 79905
500-1099 79903
1101-1199 79903
1700-3700 79930
3702-3898 79930
S Raynor St 79905
Rc Poe Rd 79938
Rebecca Ct & Ln 79938
Rebecca Ann Dr 79936
Rebel Ct 79936
Rebonito Dr 79938
Red Barrel Pl 79934
Red Bluff Rd 79930
Red Bud Way 79915
Red Canyon Ct 79934
Red Cedar Dr 79911
Red Cloud Dr 79928
Red Cloud Pl 79936
Red Coral Way 79936
Red Deer Rock Dr 79938
Red Fox Way 79936
Red Hawk Ln 79936
Red Maple 79938
Red Oak Ct 79924
Red Orchard Dr 79938
Red Palm Pl 79936
Red Robin Dr 79915
Red Rock Cyn 79930
Red Sails Dr 79936
Red Sands Ct 79924
Red Sky Ln 79930
Red Sun Dr 79938
Redd Rd 79911
E Redd Rd
100-199 79932
201-299 79932
400-900 79912
902-998 79912
W Redd Rd 79932
Redstone Ln 79924
Redstone Cove Dr 79934
Redstone Mesa Ct 79934
Redstone Pass Ct 79934
Redstone Peak Pl 79934
Redstone Rim Dr 79934
Redstone Wash Pl 79934
Redwing Way 79922
Redwood St 79924
Reed Loop 79906
Reeder Rd 79906
Reef Sands Dr 79924
Reese Ct 79927
Regal Ln 79904
Regal Banner Ln 79936
Regal Palm Ct 79936
Regal Ridge Dr 79912
Regan Dr 79903
Regency Dr 79912
Regina Dr 79927
Regulus Dr 79924
Reid Rd 79927
Reilly Ln 79928
Reindeer Ave 79907
Rembrandt Ln 79936
Remcon Cir
7300-7382 79912
7383-7599 79912
7383-7383 79913
7384-7598 79912
Remine Ave 79938
Remington Rd 79938
Rene 79938
Renee Weeks Ct 79924
Renfrew Dr 79925
Reno Ct 79907
Renoir Pl 79936
Republic Blvd 79938
Resler Dr 79911
N Resler Dr 79912
S Resler Dr 79912
Resler Ridge Dr 79912-
Resoland Blvd 79938
Retta Ct 79907
Reveles Way 79927
Revere St 79905
Rex Ct 79925
Rex Baxter Dr 79936
Rey Del Sol 79911
Rhaelynne Dr 79932
Rhea Ln 79924
Rheims Ct 79924
Rhine Bridge Dr 79934
Rhutan Rd 79927
Rhyolite Dr 79924
Riane Chantee Dr 79936
Rich Beem 79938
Richard Dr 79907
Richardson Dr 79907
Richardson Rd 79927
Richmond Ave 79930
Rick Husband Dr 79934
Rick Rhodes Dr 79936
Rickbeem 79938
Ricker Rd 79916
Ricky Zelt Dr 79928
Rico Valles 79932
Ridge St 79932
Ridge Top Dr 79904
Ridge View Ln 79904
Ridgecrest Ct & Dr 79902
Ridgemont Dr 79912
Ridgewood Dr 79925
Ridgley Way 79904
Rifton St 79928
Riley Ct 79904
Rim Rd 79902
Rinconada Ln 79922
Rinconcito Way 79912
Ringold Rd 79912
Rio Rd 79922
Rio Arriba Dr 79907
Rio Bravo St 79902
Rio Del Norte 79927
Rio Dulce 79932
Rio Estancia Dr 79932
Rio Fango 79932
Rio Flor Pl 79912
E & W Rio Grande
Ave 79902
Rio Mira Rd 79932
Rio Monte St 79915
Rio Penasco Ave 79928
Rio Tinto Dr 79912
Rio Valle Ct 79932
Rio Verde Dr 79912
N & S Rio Vista Rd 79927
Rio West Dr 79932
Ripley Dr 79922
Rising Star Ct 79936
Rising Sun St 79936
Risner Pl 79936
Rita Pl 79907
Ritz Pl 79936
E River Ave 79902
W River Ave 79902
E River Ln 79932
River Run 79932
River Bend Dr 79922
River Creek Pl 79922
River Elms Ct 79922
River Hollow Ct 79905
River Oaks Dr 79912
River Park Pl 79932
River Valley St 79915
Rivera Ave 79905
Riverdale St 79907
Riverside Dr 79915
Riverside Rd 79927
Riverstone Dr 79936
Riverview Cir 79915
Riverwood Dr 79935
Rives Mcbee Ln 79936
Road House Dr 79936
Road Runner St 79934
Roadside Ct 79922
Roanoke Dr
9000-9099 79904
9100-9621 79924
9623-9699 79924
Roaring Springs Dr 79928
Robert Dr 79904
Robert Acosta Dr 79934
Robert Alva Ave 79905
Robert Dahl Dr 79938
Robert David Dr 79928
Robert E Lee Rd 79925
Robert Holt Dr 79924
Robert Ituarte Dr 79938
Robert Kirtley Dr 79936
Robert Lennox Dr 79934
Robert Rivera Ln 79936
Robert Wynn St 79936
Roberta Lynne Dr 79936
Roberto Avalos Ct 79934
Roberto Nunez Ln 79938
Roberts Ranch Rd 79928
Robin Rd 79927
Robin Hood Pl 79924
E & W Robinson Ave 79902
Rocca Ln 79915
Rochester Dr 79912
Rocio St 79936
Rock Canyon Dr 79912
Rock Dove 79911
Rock Wall Ln 79936
Rockbridge Ave 79938
Rockdale St 79934
Rocking M Ranch Rd 79938
Rockwood Rd 79932
Rocky Bluff Dr 79902
Rocky Ridge Dr 79904
Rocoso Pl 79912
Rod Curl Ln 79935
Roden Rd 79927
Rodeo Ave 79915
Rodman St 79928
Rodolfo Anchondo Ct 79938
Rodriguez Rd 79927
Rodriguez St 79930
Rodulfo Ln 79907
Rogelio Ave 79902
Roger Bombach Dr 79936
Roger Chaffee Ln 79936
Roger Joseph Dr 79938
Roger Maris Dr
5100-5138 79924
5140-5198 79924
5200-5499 79934
Roger Torres Pl 79938
Rogers Rd
1562A-1562B 79906
1500-1599 79906
8100-8199 79907
Rogers Hornsby St 79934
Rojas Dr
11100-11299 79935
11300-12294 79936
12295-12297 79928
12299-12499 79928
Rolland Ct 79907
Rolling Stone Ave 79924
Rollins Ct 79932
Roma Ave 79938
Roman Gabriel Ln 79927
Roman Ruler Ct 79938
Romer Ray Dr 79932
Romeria Dr 79907
Romero Dr 79935
Romulus Pl 79915
Romy Ledesma 79936
Ron St 79927
Ron Cerrudo St 79936
Ronald Mcnair Dr 79936
Ronnie Reif Dr 79936
Ronquillo Ln 79907
Roosevelt St 79905
Rorenstock St 79906
Rosa Ave 79905
Rosa Azul Dr 79927
Rosa Blanca Dr 79927
Rosa Gandara Pl 79932
Rosa Guerrero 79936
Rosa M Richardson
Ave 79927
Rose Ln 79915
Rose Bud Ln 79936
Rose Colleng Pl 79932
Rose Gate Way 79936
Rose Haven Ave 79907
Rose Kennedy Dr 79907
Rose Lane Cir 79915
Roseann Ct 79936
Rosedale St 79915
Rosemary St 79915
Rosemont Dr 79922
Rosenbaum Ln 79912
Roseville Dr 79927
Roseway Dr 79907
Rosewood St
600-799 79903
801-999 79903
1100-1198 79930
Rosinante Rd 79922
Rosinie Rose Pl 79936
Roslyn Dr 79928
Rosston Way 79911
Roswell Rd 79915
Roth Pl 79906
Rotterdam Way 79912
Round Dance Rd 79938
Round Oak 79928
Round Rock Dr 79924
Roxanna Ave 79932
Roxbury Dr 79922
Roy Pace Dr 79936
Royal Dr 79924
Royal Arms Dr 79912
Royal Banner Ln 79936
Royal Crest St 79936
Royal Crown Rd 79928
Royal Gorge Dr 79934
Royal Jewel St 79936
Royal Knoll Dr 79936
Royal Oak Ct 79932
Royal Palm St 79912
Royal Ridge Dr 79912
Royal Run St 79936
Royal Terrace Ln 79936
Royal Willow Way 79922
Royal Woods Dr 79936
Ruben Soto Dr 79938
Rubicon Way 79907
Rubin Dr 79912
Ruby Dr 79932
Ruby Gate Way 79936
Rubye Mae Pl 79912
Ruckman St 79904
Rudder Pl 79936
Ruddy Quail Ln 79936
Rudi Kuefner Dr 79928
Rudy Montoya Dr 79936
Rudy Valdez Dr 79938
Rudy Vidovic 79932
Ruewood Pl 79935
Rufus Brijalba Dr 79936
Ruhlen Ct 79922
Ruiz Ct 79907
Rule Dr 79924
Running Deer Dr 79936
Rushing Rd 79924
Rusk Ave 79905
Russ Rd 79927
Russ Randall St 79936
Russell St
1900-2698 79930
2700-3600 79930
3602-4298 79930
5500-5598 79904
6201-6299 79904
Russell Borea Ave 79938
Russett Ln 79912
Russolo Dr 79936
Rustic Mnr, Riv & Vly 79938
Rustic Bend Pl 79928
Rustic Hidden Dr 79938
Rusty Bucket Ct 79932
Ruth Deerman Pl 79912
Rutherford Dr 79924
Rutherglen St 79925
Rutledge Pl 79924
Rv Dr 79928
Ryan Cir 79915
Ryan Steven Pl 79936
Ryan Wesley St 79938
Ryderwood Dr 79928
Rye Ln 79927
Ryland Ct 79907
Sabine Ct 79905
Sabio Dr 79928
Sabrina Lyn Dr 79936
Sachet Cliff Dr 79934
Saco Way 79928
Sacramento Ave 79930
Saddle Bronc Dr 79925
Safari Ln 79907
Safford Ct 79915
Sage Ct 79924
Sagebrush Cir 79938
Sagebrush Way 79936
Sageland Way 79907
Sagitta Ct 79907
Sagittarius Ave 79924
Sagrado Ln 79905
Saguaro Park 79932
Saguaro Way 79907
Sahuaro Dr 79928
Saigon Dr 79925
Saint Abraham 79936
Saint Andrew Ln 79907
Saint Anthony St 79907
Saint Armand Ct 79936
Saint Cassian Dr 79936
Saint Catherine Dr 79907
Saint Charles St 79904
Saint Clare Pl 79936
Saint Crispin 79936
Saint Francis 79936
Saint James 79936
Saint Jerome Pl 79936
Saint Johns Dr 79903
Saint Jude Ave 79936
Saint Laurence 79936
Saint Laurent Dr 79907
Saint Lo Dr 79925
Saint Lucia 79936
Saint Luke 79936
Saint Mark Ave 79936
Saint Martin Way 79936
Saint Marys Dr 79907
Saint Matthews St 79907
Saint Moritz Way 79907
Saint Paul 79936
Saint Pius 79936
Saint Romeo 79936
Saint Stephen Pl 79936
Saint Thomas Way 79936
Saint Vitus 79936
N Saint Vrain St
101-107 79901
109-200 79901
202-298 79901
601-697 79902
699-2400 79902
2402-2598 79902
S Saint Vrain St 79901
Saker Dr 79928
Sal Berroteran Dr 79936
Sal Rasura 79936
Salamanca Ln 79927
Salas Ln 79932
Salem Dr 79924
Salerell Ave 79930
Salette Way 79936
Salgado Cir 79904
Salisbury Dr 79924
Sally Ray Way 79936
Sallybrook St 79925
Salt Bush Dr 79938
Saluki Dr 79924
Sam Hawken Rd 79938
Sam Horrell Way 79912
Sam Snead Dr
10700-10719 79935
10721-10899 79935
10900-11199 79936
Sam Ward Pl 79936
Samalayucca Rd 79927
Samantha Ln 79907
Samantha Rae Pl 79938
Sambrano Ave 79905
Sami Ct 79936
Sammy Davis Pl 79936
Sammy Reece Pl 79938
Samoa Dr 79925
Sampson Ct 79925
Samuel 79927
San Angelo Pl 79912
E San Antonio Ave
100-1699 79901
1701-2299 79901
2900-3700 79905
3702-3898 79905
W San Antonio Ave 79901
San Blas Dr 79912
San Clemente 79912
San Diego Ave 79930
San Fernando Ct 79907
San Francisco Ave 79901
San Gabriel St 79905
San Jose Ave
2000-2099 79902
2100-2899 79930
San Jose Rd
7800-8099 79915
8100-8287 79907
8289-8299 79907
San Juan Ln 79907
San Lorenzo Ave 79907
N San Marcial St
100-399 79905
500-598 79903
600-1299 79903
2001-2097 79930
2099-2800 79930
2802-2998 79930
S San Marcial St 79905
San Marcos Dr 79922
San Marino Dr 79912
San Martin Ct 79905
San Mateo Ln 79902
San Miguel Dr 79907
San Miguel St 79927
San Pablo Pl 79915
San Paulo Dr
7900-7957 79915
7958-7999 79907
San Pedro Dr 79907
San Saba Rd 79912
San Simon Ln 79907
San Ysidro Rd 79927
Sand Dune St 79934
Sand Gate Dr 79928
Sand River Pl 79932
Sand Verbena St 79928
Sandbar Ct 79922
Sandcastle Ct 79936
Sanddrift Rd 79928
Sanders Ave
5100-5198 79924
5200-5248 79924
5249-5249 79914
5249-5799 79924
5250-5798 79924
Sanderson Way 79915
Sandhill Ct 79907
Sandia Way 79927
Sandland Dr 79907
Sandoval Ct 79907
Sandra Way 79907
Sands Ave 79904
Sandy Ln 79907
Sandy Hills Ln 79928
Sandy Koufax Dr
10800-10899 79924
10900-10999 79934
Sandy Plateau Cir 79936
Sandy Point Ln 79938
Sandy Rock Dr 79938
Santa Ana Dr 79902
Santa Anita Dr 79902
Santa Barbara Dr 79915
Santa Clara Ct 79915
Santa Cruz Ct 79915
Santa Elena Cir 79932
N Santa Fe St 79901
S Santa Fe St 79901
Santa Fe Trl 79938
Santa Gertrudes Dr 79927
Santa Maria 79907
Santa Maria Ct 79915
Santa Martina Dr 79927
Santa Monica Ct 79915
Santa Paula Dr 79927
Santa Rita St 79902
Santa Rosa St 79922
Santa Rosalia Ct 79907
Santa Teresa Dr 79932
Santiago St 79932
Santiago Bustamante
Ave 79927
Santiago Roque Dr 79934
Santiesteban Ln 79938
Santini Pl 79915
Santis Ct 79932
Santorini Ct 79927
Santos Sanchez St 79927
Saplinas Rd 79932
Sapphire St 79924
Sara Danielle Pl 79936
Sara Lynn Ct 79932
Sara Suzann Ln 79932
Sarah Anne Ave 79924
Sarah Lisa Ln 79936
Sarah Rachel Ct 79928
Saratoga Dr 79912
Sargeant Ln 79907
Sargent Denny Ave 79906
Sargent Lytle Ave 79906
Sargent Shaw Ave 79906
Sarina Cir 79938
Sarum 79928
Satelite Dr 79912
Satiacum Ln 79938
Satterlee Pl 79906
Saturn Pl 79904
Saucillo Rd 79928
Saul Ct 79927
Saul Kleinfeld Dr 79936
Savannah Ave 79930
Saxon Dr 79924
Sayers Dr 79927
Scarlet Ct 79927
Scarlet Point Dr 79938
Scenic Dr 79930
Scenic Crest Cir 79930
Schenck St 79906
Schoellkope Pl 79936
Schoenfelder Ln 79928
School Ln 79936
Schooner Dr 79936
E & W Schuster Ave 79902
N & S Schutz Dr 79907
Schwabe St 79907
Schwarzkopf Dr 79934
Schwood Dr 79925
Scobey Dr 79928
Scooter Ln 79907
Scorpio Pl 79928
Scorpius Ln 79907
Scott 79932
Scott Ave 79906
Scott Ray Way 79936
Scott Simpson Dr 79936
Sea Biscuit Ct 79938
Sea Breeze Dr 79936
Sea Cove Dr 79936
Sea Foam Way 79936
Sea Gull Dr 79936
Sea Horse Dr 79936
Sea Palm Dr 79936
Sea Side Dr 79936
Sea View Dr 79936
Seabrook St 79936
Seale Ct 79907

Sean Haggerty Dr
4900-4999 79934
5000-5900 79924
5902-5998 79924
11100-11499 79934
Sean Sims St 79938
Sears Way 79927
Seattle Slew Ave 79938
Seawood Dr 79925
Sebastian Ave 79938
Sebastian Ln 79928
Seco Palm St 79912
Secretariat Dr 79932
Seguin Ct 79924
Seitler Pl 79906
Selden Dr 79903
Selfridge Pl 79908
Selkirk Dr 79925
Selma Ct 79936
Seminole Dr 79928
Senda Del Sol 79911
Seneca Dr 79915
Senor Tedd Way 79907
Septiembre Dr 79935
Sequeiros 79932
Sequoia Way 79915
Serena Ct 79928
Serendipity St 79936
Sereno Dr 79907
Serrania Dr 79932
Seth Cir 79927
Setting Sun Dr 79938
Settler Rd 79927
N & S Seville Dr 79905
Sgm Christian Fleetwood St 79908
Sgt Alchesay Ct 79908
Sgt Alexander Kenaday St 79908
Sgt E Churchill St 79918
Sgt F Markle St 79918
Sgt Koehler Ct 79908
Sgt Major Blvd 79916
Sgt Mckibben Ct 79908
Sgt Patrick Gass St 79908
Sgt Quinn Ct 79908
Shadow Canyon Pl 79912
Shadow Glen Ct 79928
Shadow Mountain Dr 79912
Shadow Ridge Dr 79938
Shadow Willow Dr 79922
Shady Ln 79922
Shady River Ave 79938
Shady Valley Cir 79927
Shady Willow Dr 79922
Shaef Pl 79924
Shakespeare Dr 79928
Shamrock Ct 79925
Shanda Cir 79927
Shannon Pl 79925
Shape Dr 79928
Shapleigh Ct 79936
Sharondale Dr 79912
Sharp Dr 79924
Sharp Rd 79907
Shaver Dr 79925
Shawna Laurie Ct 79928
Shawnee Dr 79912
Shawnee Ln 79938
Shedd Rd 79906
Shedfield Dr 79925
Sheffield Dr 79927
Sheila Dr 79936
Shelby Ridge Dr 79912
Shell St 79925
Shelly Ln 79938
Shelter Pl 79905
Shenandoah St 79924
Sheppard Ave 79904
Sherbrooke Ave 79924
Sheridan Rd
1-99 79916
200-4499 79906
Sherwin Way 79924
Sherwood Dr 79924
Sherwood Forest Ct 79924

Sheryl Cir 79927
Shetland Rd 79925
Shifrin Ave 79938
Shifting Sand Dr 79938
Shiley St 79906
Shiner Ave 79936
Shipley Ave 79925
Shire Way 79912
Shirley Ave 79905
Shockley Ct 79930
Shogun Ct 79938
Shoreline Dr 79936
Shorty Ln 79922
Shoshone St 79924
Shreya St
1700-1899 79928
1900-2199 79938
Shriver Ln 79907
Shrub Oak Dr 79924
Shuttle Columbia Dr 79925
Sidewinder St 79924
Sidney St 79924
Siegel Ln 79938
Sierra St 79903
Sierra Azul Dr 79936
Sierra Bonita Dr 79936
Sierra Crest Dr 79902
Sierra De Oro Dr 79936
Sierra Fria Ct 79912
Sierra Madre Dr 79904
Sierra Morena Dr 79936
Sierra Valle Ln 79912
Sierra Vista Dr 79904
Siesta Way 79922
Siete Leguas Rd 79922
Sigala Ct 79924
Sigma St 79924
Signal Peak Pl 79904
Signal Ridge Dr 79936
Sikorsky St 79925
Silao Ct 79927
Silent Crest Dr 79902
Silent Sun Ln 79912
Silent View Pl 79928
Silvas Way 79907
Silver Ave 79930
Silver Cholla Dr 79934
Silver Crest Dr 79902
Silver Crown Rd 79928
Silver Gate Pl 79936
Silver Lake Pl 79936
Silver Palm Dr 79936
Silver Point Ave 79938
Silver Ranch Ave 79934
Silver Sands Ave 79924
Silver Shadow Dr 79912
Silver Springs Dr 79912
Silver Spur St 79938
Silver Star 79912
Silver Strand Pl 79924
Silverbell Ln 79932
Silverberry Ln 79936
Silvercloud Dr 79924
Silverwood Way 79922
Silvestre Rd 79907
Simon Ct 79932
Simpia Dr 79905
Simpson Rd 79938
Sims Dr 79925
Sinaloa Ln 79907
Sinclair St 79924
Singapore Ave 79925
Singh St 79907
Singing Hills Dr 79912
Singing Oaks Ct 79932
Singing Quail Dr 79936
Sinking Rock Pl 79938
Sioux Dr 79925
Sir Gareth Dr 79902
Sirius Ave 79904
Sisal Dr 79925
Sitting Bull Dr 79936
Sixta Dr 79932
Skipper Dr 79936
Sky Hawk Ave 79924
Skydale Dr 79912

Skylark Way 79922
Skylight Cir 79927
Skyline Ave 79904
Skymont Way 79912
Skyrocket Dr 79911
Skyview St 79912
Skyway Ln 79912
Slamen Cir 79904
Slater Rd 79906
Sleepy Hollow St 79932
Sleepy Willow Dr 79922
Slippery Rock Rd 79928
Slocum Ave 79904
Slocum St 79936
Smith Rd 79907
Smoketree Ct 79938
Smokey Point Dr 79938
Smokey Ridge Ct 79932
Snark Ln 79924
Snelson Dr 79907
Snohomish Loop 79938
Snoqualime Dr 79938
Snow St 79906
Snow Cloud Ct 79936
Snow Fall Pl 79936
Snow Hawk Dr 79936
Snowflake Ct 79904
Snowheights Ct 79912
Snowy Plover 79928
Snowy Point Dr 79938
Snowy River Pl 79932
Snowy Rock Pl 79938
Soapberry Way 79907
Soaring Eagle Pl 79936
Soberana Ln 79936
Socorro Rd
9000-9399 79907
9401-9499 79907
9500-11799 79927
Sofia Pl 79907
Sol De Alma 79922
Solano Dr 79935
Solar Pl 79904
Solar Point Ln 79938
Soledad Ln 79932
Soleen Rd 79938
Sombra Alegre Dr 79938
Sombra Fuerte Dr 79938
Sombra Grande Dr 79938
Sombra Verde Dr 79935
Somerset Dr 79912
Somerville Ave 79906
Sonaran Ct 79932
Song Point Ct 79938
Songland Rd 79932
Sonia Rose Pl 79936
Sonny Madrid Ln 79934
Sonoma Pl 79936
Sonoma Breeze Ct 79928
Sora Way 79911
Sorbonne Dr 79907
Sorrel Dr 79932
Sorrento St 79924
Soto Ln 79927
Sotol Ct 79912
Souda Dr 79924
Southshore Pl 79928
Southside Rd
201-399 79907
500-698 79907
800-10099 79927
Southview Dr 79928
Southwestern Dr 79912
Southwick Dr 79928
Southwind Dr 79912
Soya Dr 79927
Space Shuttle Ln 79936
Spalding Way 79907
Spanish Pl 79932
Spanish Point Dr 79938
Sparkman St
2301-2397 79903
2399-2400 79903
2402-2498 79903
2501-2799 79930
Sparks Cir 79927

Sparks Dr 79928
Sparrow Dr 79915
Sparrow Point St 79938
Spencer Dr 79936
Spinnaker Ln 79936
Spire Hill Dr 79936
Spire Terrace Dr 79936
Spiritus Pl 79932
Splendid Sun 79912
Splendor Ct 79936
Spofford Pl 79928
Sports Ct 79935
Spotted Eagle Dr 79924
Spotted Horse Dr 79936
Spring Crest Dr 79912
Spring Valley Cir 79927
Springdale St 79928
Springfire Dr 79912
Springhill Cir 79912
Springwood Dr
7600-10599 79925
10600-10699 79935
Spruce Creek Ln 79932
Spur Dr 79906
Spur Pl 79927
Spyglass Hill Ct 79928
Square Dance Rd 79938
Squires Ct 79924
Ssg Rivers Ct 79908
Ssg Robert T Kuroda St 79908
Ssg Sims St
11100-11299 79918
11301-11399 79918
11600-11698 79908
Stable Rd 79938
Staci Ln 79927
Stack Pole Rd 79938
Stacy Ln 79938
Stacy Ann Dr 79938
Stagecoach Ct 79932
Stagecoach Dr 79938
Staghorn Dr 79907
Stahala Dr 79924
Stallion Way 79922
Stampede Dr 79934
Stan Musial Ct 79934
Stan Roberts Sr Ave 79934
Stanford Ct 79907
Stanley St 79907
Stanley Green Way 79934
Stansbury Dr 79928
N Stanton St
100-599 79901
601-699 79901
700-4500 79902
4502-4898 79902
5501-5597 79912
5599-5699 79912
5701-5799 79912
S Stanton St 79901
Star Beach Ln 79936
Star Flower Ln 79934
Star Lake Pl 79936
Star Of India Ln 79924
Star Ridge Pl 79912
Star View Dr 79912
Starboard Ln 79936
Stardust Dr 79912
Starduster 79928
Starfish Ct 79936
Stargazer Ct 79904
Starlight Ct 79904
Starlit Pl 79912
Starr Ave 79907
Starry Night Dr 79932
State Jail Rd 79938
Stateline Rd 79934
Statler St 79904
Staubach Dr 79927
Stedham Cir 79927
Steele Rd 79904
Steeplerock Ridge Rd 79938
Steffers Ln 79932
Steffi Graf Dr 79938
Stennis Rd 79916

Stephanie Dr 79936
Stephanie Frances St 79924
Stephanotis Ct 79928
Stephenson Ave 79905
Sterling Pl 79932
Sterling Mary Way 79936
Stern Dr 79932
Sternberg St 79930
Steve Degroat Ln 79911
Steve Spray St 79936
N Stevens St
100-199 79905
201-299 79905
501-997 79903
999-1399 79903
1401-1899 79903
2100-5099 79930
6200-6299 79904
S Stevens St 79905
Stevie Ln 79927
Stewart Ct 79902
Stewart Dr 79915
Stiles Dr 79915
Still Water Ct 79936
Stinson Ave 79910
Stockmeyer Dr 79936
Stockton St 79906
Stockwell Ln 79902
Stockyard Dr 79927
Stone Ct 79924
Stone Canyon Way 79936
Stone Castle Dr 79936
Stone Edge Rd 79904
Stone Gate Ln 79936
Stone Lake Pl 79936
Stone Pine Ln 79907
Stone Pointe Way 79936
Stone Ridge Pl 79912
Stone Rock St 79938
Stone View Way 79936
Stonebluff Rd 79912
Stonebridge Dr 79934
Stonehaven Dr 79925
Stoneheath Ct 79932
Stoneman Rd 79906
Stonewall Rd 79924
Stoneway Dr 79925
Stonington Ln 79938
Stormy Point Dr 79938
Story St 79904
Stotts Ave 79932
Stoutland Ln 79928
Strahan Rd 79932
Strain Ct 79924
Strand Ln 79904
Strata Rock Dr 79938
Stratford Rd 79928
Stratford Hall Cir 79912
Stratus Rd 79912
Strawberry Cir 79932
Strickland Dr 79907
Stubing Pl 79925
Stumm Pl 79928
Sturgeon Dr 79924
Sudan Dr 79927
Sudderth St 79928
Sue Hall Dr 79905
Suewood Ct 79925
Suez Dr 79925
Suffolk Rd 79925
Sugar Bay Way 79936
Sugar Goodman 79911
Sugar Hills Dr 79928
Sugarberry Dr 79925
Sugarland Dr 79924
Sullivan Dr 79938
Sumac Dr 79925
Sumatra St 79925
Summer Sun 79932
Summerbrooke Ct 79932
Summerford Ln 79907
Summit Breeze Ave 79928
Sun Arbor Pl 79928
Sun Beam Dr 79938
Sun Bolt Way 79938
Sun Bowl Dr 79902

Sun Bridge Pl 79928
Sun Canyon Ln 79912
Sun Chariot Dr 79938
Sun City Pl 79928
Sun City Park Ct 79932
Sun Country Dr 79938
Sun Court Cir 79924
Sun Cove Ave 79938
Sun Dial Ct 79915
Sun Empress Dr 79938
Sun Fire Blvd 79938
Sun Fire St 79928
Sun Flare Dr 79938
Sun Gate 79938
Sun Haven Dr 79938
Sun King Ct & St 79928
Sun Kings St 79928
Sun Manor Dr 79938
Sun Meadow Ln 79936
Sun Mist Ct 79938
Sun Mountain Dr 79938
Sun Park Rd 79927
Sun Point Ln 79912
Sun Port Way 79938
Sun Quest St 79938
Sun Ray Way
500-699 79928
11000-11099 79927
12100-12199 79928
Sun Ridge Dr 79912
Sun Rock Way 79938
Sun Seeker 79938
Sun Shadow Dr 79912
Sun Spirit Dr 79938
Sun Spot St 79938
Sun Spring Way 79938
Sun Spur Way 79938
Sun Sweet Way 79938
Sun Terrace Ave 79938
Sun Tide Dr 79938
Sun Trail Dr 79938
Sun Valley Dr 79924
Sun View Ln 79928
Sun Willow Ave 79938
Sunburst Dr 79925
Suncrest Dr 79912
Sundale Rd 79912
Sundance Ave 79936
Sundown Pl 79912
Sundrop Ct 79936
Sundrop Dr 79938
Sunflower Ln 79907
Sunhaven Dr 79927
Sunland Rd 79907
Sunland Park Dr
100-899 79912
900-1299 79922
Sunmount Dr 79925
Sunny Land Ave 79938
Sunny Prairie Dr 79938
Sunny Sky Pl 79928
Sunny Vale Cir 79924
Sunnybrook Ln 79927
Sunnyfields Ave 79915
Sunnymead Pl 79924
Sunnyside Ave 79904
Sunnyview Pl 79915
Sunrise Ave 79904
Sunrise Hills Dr 79928
E & W Sunset Rd 79922
Sunset Hills Dr 79928
Sunset Park Dr 79932
Sunset Point Dr 79938
Sunset Rose Dr 79936
Sunshine Ct 79936
Sunstone St 79924
Supima Dr 79927
Surety Dr 79905
Surf Scoter Pl 79928
Susan Way 79915
Susan Edge Pl 79936
Susan Jean 79932
Susser Dr 79928
Suwanee St 79938
Suzi Way 79927
Swain St 79906

Swallow Ln 79924
Swan Dr 79922
Swaps Dr 79936
Swede Johnsen Dr 79912
Sweet Acacia Ln 79907
Sweetbriar Ct 79907
Sweetwater Dr 79924
Sword Dancer Ct 79938
Swordsmen Pl 79936
Sycamore Way 79915
Sycene Ct 79924
Sylvan Lake Pl 79936
Sylvania Way 79912
Sylvia Ct & Dr 79927
Tabasco Pl 79928
Tablerock Dr 79912
Taffy Bagley Dr 79936
Tag Rock Pl 79938
Tahiti Dr 79925
Tahoka Ave 79936
Tailwind 79928
Tait Ct 79936
Taj Mahal St 79924
Talent Way 79928
Talking Rock Pl 79938
Talon Pl 79912
Tamara Dr 79938
Tamburo Ct 79905
Tammy Ct 79904
Tampa Ave 79905
Tampico Dr 79915
Tangerine Ave 79938
Tangerine Ln 79915
Tangier Pl 79905
Tania Dr 79927
Tannery Way 79934
Tanning Rock Way 79938
Tanton Rd 79927
Taos Dr 79905
Tapir Ct 79924
Tara Point Pl 79938
Tarango 79932
Tarascas Dr 79912
Tarek Ln 79912
Tareyton St 79924
Tarpon Dr 79924
Tarrant Rd 79907
Tascosa St 79936
Tassie Way 79927
Taurus Ct 79904
Tautoga Dr 79924
Tawny Oaks Pl 79912
Taxco Dr 79915
Taxiway 79928
Taylor Ave 79930
Tayopa Ct 79932
S Tays St 79901
Tea Rose Pl 79936
Teachers Dr 79936
Teakwood Rd 79915
Teal Ln 79924
Tecate Pl 79912
Ted Houghton 79936
Ted Kennedy Way 79907
Ted Williams Pl 79934
Tedd Floyd Ln 79907
Tee Ct 79934
Teichelkamp Dr 79928
Teja Rock Pl 79938
Tejas Dr 79905
Tekoa Ct 79936
Telescope Ct 79904
Telles Rd 79938
Telop Rd 79927
Temperence St 79928
Temple Ct 79924
Tenaha Ave 79936
Tenango Dr 79907
Tender Foot Ct 79936
Tennis West Ln 79932
Tennyson Dr 79928
Teodoso Dr 79907
Tepic Dr 79912
Teramar Way 79922
Teresa Pl 79924
Teresa Del Mar 79912

Terrace Ct 79902
Terrell Ave 79936
Territory Dr 79932
Terry Ct
300-399 79915
400-599 79927
Tesuque Dr 79905
Tetons Dr 79904
Texaco Rd 79905
Texarkana Pl 79924
Texas Ave 79901
Texas Oak Dr 79924
Texas Rainbow Dr 79928
Texas Red Dr 79907
Texas Star St 79936
Texwood Ave 79925
Thackery Dr 79928
Thames Dr 79907
Thatcher Pond Ln 79934
Thayer Pease Ave 79928
Thea Smith Dr 79928
Thelma Ln 79938
Tholos Ct 79924
Thomas Pl 79915
Thomas Granillo Ln 79927
Thomason Ave 79904
Thompson Loop 79906
Thor St 79924
Thorn Ave
100-399 79932
400-598 79912
600-799 79912
801-899 79912
Thorn Ridge Cir 79932
Thornton St 79932
Threadgill Ave 79924
Three Missions Dr 79927
Three Rivers Dr 79912
Throne Pl 79936
Thrush Way 79922
Thunder Rd 79927
Thunder Bluff Pl 79928
Thunder Bolt Ct
1300-1399 79936
14100-14199 79938
Thunder Crest Ln 79912
Thunder Ridge Dr 79938
Thunder River Pl 79932
Thunder Storm Dr 79932
Thunder Trail Way 79936
Thunderbird Dr 79912
Thundercloud Dr 79936
Thygerson Ln 79927
Tiber Pl 79924
Tibuni Pl 79904
Tiercel Pl 79928
Tierra Agave Dr 79938
Tierra Agua Pl 79938
Tierra Aida Ln 79938
Tierra Aire Pl 79938
Tierra Alamo Dr 79938
Tierra Alaska Ave 79938
Tierra Alba Dr 79938
Tierra Alegre Way 79938
Tierra Alexis Dr 79938
Tierra Allen Pl 79938
Tierra Alma Ln 79938
Tierra Alta Ave 79912
Tierra Alyssa Dr 79938
Tierra Alzada Dr 79938
Tierra Amanda Ln 79938
Tierra Ana Ct 79938
Tierra Angel Dr 79938
Tierra Apache Dr 79938
Tierra Arena Dr 79938
Tierra Aries Pl 79938
Tierra Arleth Dr 79938
Tierra Arroyo Dr 79938
Tierra Asia 79938
Tierra Aspid Way 79938
Tierra Aurora Dr 79938
Tierra Ave Pl 79938
Tierra Ayala 79938
Tierra Azteca Dr 79938
Tierra Azul Way 79938
Tierra Bahia Dr 79938
Tierra Baja Dr & Way 79938
Tierra Balsa Ct 79938
Tierra Bella Dr 79938
Tierra Berlin Ln 79938
Tierra Blanca Way 79938
Tierra Blanda Dr 79938
Tierra Bonita Way 79938
Tierra Bowles 79938
Tierra Brisa Dr 79938
Tierra Bronce Dr 79938
Tierra Buena Dr 79938
Tierra Cabo 79938
Tierra Cadena Dr 79938
Tierra Cafe Dr 79938
Tierra Calida Dr 79938
Tierra Campa Dr 79938
Tierra Canada Dr 79938
Tierra Cara Dr 79938
Tierra Casa 79938
Tierra Cebada Dr 79938
Tierra Cecil Pl 79938
Tierra Chica Way 79938
Tierra China Ct 79938
Tierra Chisum Dr 79938
Tierra Cipres Dr 79938
Tierra Clara Rd 79938
Tierra Cobre Dr 79938
Tierra Coral Ct 79938
Tierra Corta Ln 79938
Tierra Cortez Ave 79938
Tierra Creel Ln 79938
Tierra Cromo Dr 79938
Tierra Cuervo Dr 79938
Tierra David Ct 79938
Tierra De Oro Way 79938
Tierra De Paz Way 79938
Tierra Del Mar 79912
Tierra Delfin Dr 79938
Tierra Dulce Dr 79938
Tierra Dura Dr 79938
Tierra Encino Dr 79938
Tierra Espada Dr 79938
Tierra Este Rd 79938
Tierra Eva Pl 79938
Tierra Feliz Dr 79938
Tierra Fertil Dr 79938
Tierra Fiji Ln 79938
Tierra Fina Dr 79938
Tierra Flor Pl 79938
Tierra Flores Dr 79938
Tierra Fresa Way 79938
Tierra Fresca Ct 79938
Tierra Fresno Dr 79938
Tierra Fuego Ct 79938
Tierra Galvez 79938
Tierra Gema Ct 79938
Tierra Grande Way 79938
Tierra Gris Way 79938
Tierra Halcon Dr 79938
Tierra Humeda Dr 79938
Tierra Inca Dr 79938
Tierra India Way 79938
Tierra Inez Pl 79938
Tierra Iris Pl 79938
Tierra Isela 79938
Tierra Isla Way 79938
Tierra Jazmin Ln 79938
Tierra Jezrel 79938
Tierra Joya Pl 79938
Tierra Karla Dr 79938
Tierra Keto Pl 79938
Tierra Kino Way 79938
Tierra Lago Way 79938
Tierra Laguna Dr 79938
Tierra Lana Way 79938
Tierra Laurel Dr 79938
Tierra Lazo Ct 79938
Tierra Leon Way 79938
Tierra Leona Dr 79938
Tierra Libre Way 79938
Tierra Lily Ct 79938
Tierra Lima Dr 79938
Tierra Limon Dr 79938
Tierra Limpia Dr 79938
Tierra Lince Dr 79938
Tierra Linda Dr 79928
Tierra Lirio Pl 79938
Tierra Lisa Dr 79938
Tierra Lisboa Ln 79938
Tierra Lobo Way 79938
Tierra Loma Rd 79938
Tierra Lorena Dr 79938
Tierra Lucero Ln 79938
Tierra Lucia Ct 79938
Tierra Luz Way 79938
Tierra Madre Rd 79938
Tierra Madrid 79938
Tierra Mar Way 79938
Tierra Marfil Rd 79938
Tierra Maria Ct 79938
Tierra Marta Ct 79938
Tierra Maya Dr 79938
Tierra Meca Dr 79938
Tierra Mesa Ct 79938
Tierra Mia Way 79938
Tierra Mina Dr 79938
Tierra Mision Dr 79938
Tierra Mona 79938
Tierra Monje 79938
Tierra Morena Dr 79938
Tierra Negra Dr 79938
Tierra Nevada Dr 79938
Tierra Nido Pl 79938
Tierra Nogal Dr 79938
Tierra Nora 79938
Tierra Norte Rd 79938
Tierra Nube 79938
Tierra Nueva Dr 79938
Tierra Nuez Pl 79938
Tierra Nunez Dr 79938
Tierra Oso Pl 79938
Tierra Padre Ln 79938
Tierra Palma Dr 79938
Tierra Paola 79938
Tierra Paris 79938
Tierra Patino Ln 79938
Tierra Pera Ct 79938
Tierra Perla Ct 79938
Tierra Pez Way 79938
Tierra Pino Dr 79938
Tierra Plata Dr 79938
Tierra Point Ct 79938
Tierra Polar Dr 79938
Tierra Pueblo 79938
Tierra Pura Dr 79938
Tierra Rancho St 79938
Tierra Real Dr 79938
Tierra Rey Ct 79938
Tierra Rica Way 79938
Tierra Rio Rd 79938
Tierra Robles Dr 79938
Tierra Roca Pl 79938
Tierra Roja St 79912
Tierra Roma 79938
Tierra Roman Dr 79938
Tierra Rosa Dr 79938
Tierra Ruby Dr 79938
Tierra Salada Dr 79938
Tierra Salas 79938
Tierra Santa Pl 79922
Tierra Sara Ln 79938
Tierra Sauz Dr 79938
Tierra Seca Way 79938
Tierra Serena Dr & Rd 79938
Tierra Sol Rd 79938
Tierra Sonora 79938
Tierra Sophia Dr 79938
Tierra Sur Pl 79938
Tierra Tania Pl 79938
Tierra Taos Dr 79912
Tierra Tigre Ave 79938
Tierra Tina Pl 79938
Tierra Toro 79938
Tierra Tuna Dr 79938
Tierra Valle Dr 79938
Tierra Vela 79938
Tierra Venado Dr 79938
Tierra Verde Dr 79907
Tierra Vergel 79938
Tierra Vianey Dr 79938
Tierra Vida Way 79938
Tierra Vista Ln 79932
Tierra Volcan Ave 79938
Tierra Westex Ln 79938
Tierra Yamila Ln 79938
Tierra Yukon Ln 79938
Tierra Yvette Ln 79938
Tierra Zafiro Dr 79938
Tierra Zulema Ct 79938
Tiffany Ct 79938
Tiger Eye Dr 79924
Tigris Dr 79907
Tigua Cir 79907
Tim Foster 79938
Timber Pl 79938
Timber Oaks Dr 79932
Timberwolf Dr 79903
Time Rock Pl 79938
Timothy Dr 79928
Timothy Drew Way 79936
Tin Star St 79911
Tio Dink Cir 79907
Tirres Pl 79936
Titan St 79924
Titanic Ave 79904
Tivoli St 79924
Tiwa Blvd 79927
Tobacco Rd 79938
Tobar Way 79912
Tobin Pl 79905
Todd Skinner Dr 79938
Tokay Ave 79927
Toledo Pl 79905
Toltec Dr 79912
Toluca Dr 79912
Tom Bolt Dr 79936
Tom Fiore Ct 79936
Tom Kite Ct 79935
Tom Shaw Dr 79936
Tom Ulozas Dr 79936
Tom Watson Ct 79936
Tom Weiskopf Dr 79936
Tomahawk St 79936
Tomahawk Trail Dr 79938
Tomas Granillo St 79927
Tommy Aaron Dr 79936
Tompkins Ave 79904
Tompkins Rd 79930
Tomwood Ave 79925
Tonantzin Pl 79911
Tonto Pl 79904
Tony Acosta Ct 79936
Tony Jacklin Dr 79935
Tony Lama St 79915
Tony Ponce Dr 79936
Tony Tejeda Dr 79936
Toreador Pl 79927
Tornillo St 79901
Torres St 79922
Torrey Dr 79924
Torrey Pines Dr 79912
Totonaca Ln 79912
Toucan Ct 79924
Touchstone Pl 79936
Tourmaline St 79924
Tower Arms Dr 79936
Tower Hill Dr 79936
Tower Knoll Ln 79936
Tower Point Way 79938
Tower Trail Ln 79907
Tower View Dr 79936
Tower Wall Ln 79936
Town Lake Ln 79936
Townsley St 79904
Toyota Rd 79927
Tracy Pl 79902
Tracy Austin Ln 79936
Trade Center Ave 79912
Tradewind Ct 79904
Trail Blazer Dr 79936
Trail Land Ave 79938
Trail Ridge Dr 79912
Trails End Ct 79932
Tranquilo Dr 79907
Transpark Dr 79927
Travelo Rd 79928
Travis St 79903
Trawood Dr
1201-1219 79925
1221-1799 79925
1800-2299 79935
2400-2498 79936
2500-3199 79936
3201-3399 79936
Traymore Rd 79928
Treasure Hill Pl 79936
Tredlow Ct 79905
Tree Quail Ct 79936
Trejo Rd 79927
Tremont Ave 79930
Tres Caballos Dr 79927
Trew Ct 79924
Trey Burton Dr 79936
Trice Cir 79907
Tricia Rd 79938
Trident Pl 79924
Trigger Rock Ln 79938
Trimona Way 79915
Trina Pl 79936
Trinidad Dr 79925
Trinidad Granillo St 79927
Trinity Pl 79905
Triplex Blvd 79938
Triumph Dr 79924
Trojan Dr 79924
Trollope Dr 79928
Tropicana Ave 79924
Trout Ct 79924
Trowbridge Dr
3701-3797 79903
3799-5399 79903
5401-5499 79903
5600-5899 79925
5900-6599 79905
Troy Ave 79907
Trudy Elaine Dr 79936
True Blue Rd 79928
Truman Ave 79930
Truscott Ave 79938
Tuckey Ln 79928
Tudor Way 79912
Tulane Dr 79907
Tularosa Ave 79903
Tulip Ct 79915
Tumbleweed Ave 79924
Tungsten Rd 79938
Tunisia 79938
Tunnel Point Way 79938
Turf Rd 79938
Turk Ct 79907
Turn To Dr 79936
Turnberry Rd 79912
Turner Rd 79936
Turney Dr 79902
Turnstone Dr 79922
Turquoise St 79904
Turrentine Dr 79925
Turtle Dove Ct 79922
Tuscan Hills Pl 79938
Tuscan Rose Ln 79938
Tuscan Sun Ct 79938
Tuscany St 79924
Tuscany Hills Pl 79938
Tuscany Ridge Dr 79912
Tuscarora Ave 79912
Twilight Ln 79912
Twilight View Way 79932
Twin Hills Dr 79912
Twin Leaf Dr 79928
Twin Oaks Pl 79912
Two Towers Dr 79936
Ty Cobb Pl 79934
Tyler Ave 79930
Tyler Seth Ave 79932
Tyra Rd 79927
Tyrone Rd 79925
Ubeda Ct 79932
Uli Ruecker Dr 79928
Ululani Dr 79927
Ulysses Pl 79904
Umbria Dr 79904
Union Fashion Ctr 79901
E & W University Ave 79902
Untermyer St 79928
Upland St 79907
Upper Canyon Pl 79912
Upper Valley Rd 79932
Upsala Dr 79928
Upson Dr 79902
Ural Way 79907
Urania St 79928
Uranio Pl 79928
Urbici Soler Dr 79936
Urrunaga St 79927
Ury St 79928
Us Highway 62/180 79938
Ute Ln 79905
Uva Pl 79905
Uvalde Pl 79924
Val Verde St 79905
Valdespino St 79907
Valdiviez St 79907
N & S Valencia Pl 79905
Valentin Ave & Dr 79928
Valentino Perez 79938
Valeria Ln 79912
Vallarta Dr 79927
Valle Alegre Dr 79907
Valle Azul Dr 79927
Valle Bajo Rd 79927
Valle Bello Ave 79932
Valle Blanco Dr 79927
Valle Bonito Rd 79927
Valle Buenavida 79927
Valle Calido Dr 79927
Valle Cromo Way 79927
Valle De Bravo Pl 79928
Valle De Oro Dr 79927
Valle Del Carmen Dr 79927
Valle Del Centro Dr 79927
Valle Del Este Dr 79927
Valle Del Mar Dr 79927
Valle Del Paseo Dr 79927
Valle Del Rio Dr 79927
Valle Del Sol Dr 79924
Valle Dorado Rd 79927
Valle Espanola 79932
Valle Fertil Dr 79927
Valle Florido Dr 79927
Valle Frondoso Rd 79927
Valle Grande Ct 79935
Valle Grande Rd 79927
Valle Hermoso Dr 79927
Valle Koki Dr 79927
Valle Lindo Dr 79927
Valle Liso Ln 79927
Valle Los Coronados 79927
Valle Los Nogales Dr 79927
Valle Negro Dr 79927
Valle Olivia Rd 79927
Valle Palomar Rd 79927
Valle Palos Verdes Dr 79927
Valle Pintoresco Dr 79927
Valle Placido Dr 79907
Valle Rico Dr 79927
Valle Rojo Dr 79927
Valle Romero Dr 79927
Valle Rubio Dr 79927
Valle Sereno Dr 79907
Valle Sonata Way 79907
Valle Suave Dr 79927
Valle Tila Dr 79927
Valle Verde Rd 79927
Valle Viejo Dr 79927
Valley Cir, Dr & Rd 79932
Valley Cedar Dr 79932
Valley Crest Dr 79907
Valley Dale Rd 79927
Valley Elder Ln 79932
Valley Elm Dr 79932
Valley Fair Way 79907
Valley Laurel St 79932
Valley Light Ct 79938
Valley Lilac Ln 79932
Valley Maple Dr 79932
Valley Oak Dr 79932
Valley Plum Ave 79932
Valley Quail Dr 79936
Valley Ridge Dr 79927
Valley Spring Way 79932
Valley View Dr 79907
Valley West St 79932
Valley Willow Way 79922
Valor Ct 79936
Valour Point Ave 79938
Valplano Dr 79912
Van Ln 79938
Van Buren Ave 79930
Van Dyke Ct 79936
Van Fleet Rd 79938
Van Gogh Dr 79936
Van Haselen Ct 79907
Van Horn Dr 79924
Van Nuys Dr 79927
Vance Pl 79907
Vancouver St 79924
Vandenburg St 79924
Vanderbilt Dr 79935
Vanderveer Dr 79938
Vanessa Leigh Dr 79936
Vanguard Ct 79924
Vaquero Ln
100-199 79912
200-299 79902
Vaquero Rock Dr 79938
Vasco Way 79912
Vashon Ln 79938
Vassar Dr 79928
Vaudeville Dr 79912
Vaughn Ct 79905
Vechot Dr 79938
Vega Ct 79904
Velia Ct 79928
Velma Miles Pl 79912
Velvet Willow Dr 79938
Venado Dr 79915
Venecia Dr 79928
Venezuela Rd 79903
Venice Ct 79924
Ventana Ave 79938
Ventana Del Sol Dr 79912
Ventura Dr 79907
Venture 79927
Venusiano St 79932
Veny Webb St 79928
Vera Ct 79932
Vera Ln 79927
Veracruz Ave 79915
Veranda 79927
Verbena Dr 79924
Verde Cir 79907
Verde Lagos Pl 79932
Verde Mar Pl 79912
Verdeland Dr 79907
Verdi Pl 79936
Verdun Way 79907
Vere Leasure Dr 79936
Vereda Del Valle Ave 79932
Vern Butler Dr 79932
Vernoy Way 79907
Verona Cir 79915
Veronica St 79938
Versailles Dr 79907
Vesta Loop Ct 79904
Veta Rica Ave 79938
Via Alegre Ln 79912
Via Alta Ln 79912
Via Appia St 79912
Via Aventura Dr 79912
Via Azteca 79936
Via Bella 79928
Via Bonita Ln 79912
Via Campo Dr 79936
Via Canutillo 79911
Via Cipro St 79912
Via Corta Ct 79912
Via Cremonia Way 79932
Via Cuesta Dr 79912
Via Cumbre Linda 79928
Via De Albur Ct 79912
Via De La Paz Dr 79912
Via De Los Arboles 79932
Via Del Rio 79936
Via Descanso Dr 79912
Via Fortuna Ln 79912

Via Granada Dr 79936
Via Hermosa Ct 79912
Via Inca Dr 79936
Via Lanza St 79912
Via Linda Ct 79912
Via Loma Dr 79912
Via Mirada Ln 79922
Via Monte St 79912
Via Norte Ln 79912
Via Penasco 79912
Via Placita 79927
Via Quijano 79912
Via Redonda Ct 79912
Via Riqueza St 79912
Via Robles Ln 79912
Via Seca Dr 79936
Via Serena Dr 79912
Via Suceso Dr 79912
Via Suerte Ave 79912
Via Verde St 79912
Viale Del Sol Ave 79932
Viale Lungo Ave 79932
Vianney Way 79912
Vic Clark Ct 79912
Vicente Gomez 79932
Viceroy Dr 79924
Vicksburg Dr 79924
Vicolo Pavia Ln 79932
Victor Ln 79907
Victor Flores Pl 79934
Victor Lopez Dr 79936
Victoria Ln 79905
Victoria Ruiz Ct 79904
Victory Ave 79906
S Vienna St 79938
Viewmont Ln 79912
Viking Dr 79912
Vikki Carr Ln 79936
Villa Pl 79907
Villa Antigua Ct 79932
Villa Canto St 79912
Villa Del Mar Rd 79927
Villa Del Sol 79911
Villa Encanto 79922
Villa Flores Dr 79912
Villa Hermosa Dr 79912
Villa Linda Way 79932
Villa Madero Dr 79907
Villa Milagro St 79924
Villa Nueva Pl 79907
Villa Plata Dr 79935
Villa Romero Dr 79928
Villa Santos Cir 79935
Villa Serena Ct 79922
Villa Vanessa Dr 79912
Villa Victoria Dr 79928
Village Ct 79922
Village Gate Dr 79936
Villanova Dr 79907
Villas Del Sur Rd 79927
Villas Del Valle Rd
500-799 79927
600-799 79928
Vineyard Rd 79927
Vinson Way 79915
Violet Way 79925
Viramontes St 79932
N Virginia St
101-197 79901
199-200 79901
202-298 79901
600-2399 79902
S Virginia St 79901
Virgo Ln 79904
Visa Rd 79927
Viscount Blvd 79925
Vista Alegre Dr 79935
Vista Allura Pl 79935
Vista Bonita St 79912
Vista Clara Dr 79912
Vista Corona Ct 79912
Vista De Oro Dr 79935
Vista Del Este St 79938
Vista Del Monte St 79922
Vista Del Rey Dr 79912
Vista Del Sol Dr
10400-10599 79925
10600-11199 79935
11200-11498 79936
11500-12299 79936
Vista Granada Dr 79936
Vista Grande Cir 79922
Vista Hill Dr 79922
Vista Lago Pl 79936
Vista Laguna Dr 79935
Vista Linda St 79932
Vista Lomas Dr 79935
Vista Mia Ct 79922
Vista Real Dr 79935
Vista Rio Cir 79912
Vista Sierra Ln 79938
E & W Vitex Cir 79936
Vivian Dr 79915
Vocational Dr 79915
Vogue Dr 79935
Volans Pl 79907
Volare Dr 79936
Volcanic Ave 79904
Volcanic Rock Dr 79938
Von Bargen Dr 79928
Voss Dr 79936
Voyager Cove Dr 79936
Vulcan Ave 79904
Vulcan Rd 79916
Wadsworth Ave 79924
Wagner Ln 79903
Wagon Pl 79934
Wagon Trail Dr 79938
Wagon Wheel 79916
Wagon Wheel Dr 79938
Wagon Wheel Pl 79938
Wahoo Ln 79924
Wainwright Dr 79903
Wake Forest Ln 79928
Wakefield Ct 79922
Walcott Rd 79927
Walden Pond Ln 79934
Walden Pond St 79924
Waldorf Dr 79924
Walearle Dr 79932
Walker St 79905
Walker Post Ave 79928
Wall St 79915
Wallenberg Dr 79912
Wallington Dr 79902
Wally Dr 79924
N Walnut St
78A-78B 79901
1-100 79901
102-298 79901
701-797 79903
799-899 79903
1100-1122 79930
1124-1199 79930
S Walnut St 79905
Walsh Ln 79915
Walter Ln 79903
Walter Jones Blvd 79906
Waltham Ct 79922
Wanda Ct 79928
Wapiti St 79924
War Arrow Pl 79936
War Feather Dr 79936
Waraingt Rd 79906
Warbler Ave 79922
Warbonnet Dr 79936
Warcloud Ave 79936
Ward St 79901
Ward Robert Pl 79936
Warhol Dr 79936
Warner Pl 79907
Warnock Way 79915
Warren Dr 79928
Warren St 79924
Warren Belin Dr 79928
Warriors Dr 79932
Warwick Rd 79907
Washington St 79905
Waterfall Dr 79907
Waterhouse Dr 79912
Waters St 79906
Waterside Dr 79936
Waterspring Ln 79936
Waterstone Ln 79934
Waterview Ave 79915
Waterville St 79928
Waverly Dr 79924
Wax Palm Pl 79936
Waycross Ave 79924
Waymore Dr 79902
Wayne Way 79915
Wayside St 79936
Weatherford Ln 79924
Weaver Rd 79928
Webster Ave 79905
Wedge Ln 79934
Wedgewood Dr 79925
Weems Ct 79905
Weeping Willow Dr 79922
Weiermann 79928
Weightman Cir 79903
Welch Ave 79905
Wellesley Rd 79902
Wellettka Dr 79927
Wellington 79928
Wellman Dr 79927
Wells Rd 79907
Wells Branch Pkwy 79928
Wenda Dr 79915
Wendover 79908
Wendy Reed Dr 79928
Werling Ct 79928
Wes Ellis Ln 79936
Wesley St 79927
Wesleyan 79928
West Dr 79915
Westcity Ct 79902
Westeria Ln 79924
Western Ct 79901
Western Gull Dr 79928
Western Sage Pl 79912
Western Skies Dr 79912
Western Spur Ln 79936
Westfield Dr 79932
Westlake Ct 79912
Westline Dr 79904
Westmoreland Dr 79925
Weston St 79928
Weston Brent Ln 79935
Westover Dr 79912
Westside Dr 79932
Westvale Ct 79932
Westview Ave 79912
Westwind Dr 79912
Wetumka Ln 79927
Wewoka Dr 79927
Wexford Dr 79925
Wh Burges Dr 79925
Wharf Cove Dr 79936
Wheeling Ave 79930
Whirl Away Dr 79936
Whisper Canyon Dr 79912
Whisper Mare Ct 79938
Whispering Wind Dr 79938
Whistler Ln 79936
Whistling Swan Pl 79932
Whitaker Ln 79902
Whitcomb St 79925
White Rd 79907
White Bird Dr 79936
White Cliffs Dr 79912
White Cloud Rd 79928
White Oak Dr 79932
White Sands Dr 79924
White Spring Dr 79928
Whitehall Dr 79934
Whitetail Dr 79924
Whitetail Deer Dr 79938
Whitewater Ln 79907
Whitey Ford St 79934
Whitney Way 79907
Whitney Ann 79932
Whittier Dr 79907
Whitus Dr 79925
Whyburn St 79924
Wichita Cir 79904
Wick Way 79925
Wickham Ave 79904
Wieland Way 79925
Wier Ln 79907
Wilcox Dr 79915
Wild Flower Dr 79938
Wild Point Pl 79938
Wild Ridge Way 79936
Wild Sage Ct 79932
Wild Sands Ct 79924
Wild Willow Dr 79922
Wildwood Ct 79912
Wilkinson Dr 79936
Will Rand Dr 79912
Will Ruth Ave 79924
Will Scarlet Ct 79924
Willa Pl 79928
William Mccool St 79934
William Payne Ct 79936
Williamette Ave 79907
Williams St
301-399 79901
601-797 79902
799-999 79902
Williamsburg Dr 79912
Willie Mays Dr 79934
Willie Sanchez Ln 79925
Willow St
1-199 79901
201-299 79901
800-898 79903
Willow Bark Way 79922
Willow Brook Way 79922
Willow Creek Cir 79932
Willow Glen Dr 79922
Willow West Dr 79922
Willowmist Ave 79936
Wilmoth Ct 79904
Wilshire Dr 79924
Wilson Way 79903
Wilson Park Rd 79908
Wilton Pl 79927
Wimbledon Way 79932
Winchester Rd 79907
Wind Ct 79936
Wind Ridge Dr 79912
Wind River Ave 79932
Wind Song Dr 79912
Windcrest Dr 79912
Windermere Dr 79928
Windfall Way 79938
Windmill Palm Ct 79936
Windrift Ct 79934
Windrock St 79925
Windrose Pl 79912
Windsor Dr 79924
Wingard Dr 79938
Wingfoote Rd 79912
Wingo Way 79907
Winn Rd 79927
Winner Pl 79907
Winslow Rd 79915
Winston Pl 79907
Winter Dr 79902
Winter St 79930
Winter Spring Pl 79928
Winterspring Pl 79928
Winthrop Dr 79924
Wisconsin Ct 79927
Wiseman Cir 79927
Wisteria Ave 79915
Wolf Berry Dr 79928
Wolf Creek Dr 79911
Wolff Ave 79906
Wolverine Dr 79924
Wonder Rock Pl 79938
Wonderland Ln 79907
Wong Pl 79936
Wood Quail Way 79936
Wood Sugar Ct 79938
Woodale Dr 79928
Woodall St 79925
Woodard Ct 79925
Woodberry Ct 79924
Woodbine Ln 79912
Woodchuck Ct 79924
Woodcrest Ln 79912
Woodfield Dr 79932
Woodfin Dr 79925
Woodgreen Dr 79932
Woodhead Pl 79938
Woodhill Ct 79928
Woodland Ave 79922
Woodlark Pl 79912
Woodrow Rd 79938
Woodrow Bean 79924
Woodruff Ct 79925
Woods Point Ave 79938
Woodside Dr 79925
Woodway Dr 79925
Woody Dr 79925
Wooldridge Dr 79915
Wooster Ln 79936
Worsham Rd 79927
Worth Ct 79925
Wrangler Dr 79924
Wren Ave 79924
Wright St
1200-1300 79902
1302-1398 79902
11274-11274 79908
Wyatt Dr 79907
Wyatt Earp St 79936
Wycliffe St 79928
Wymond Ct 79905
Wyoming Ave
600-1809 79902
1810-4499 79903
Yale Ave 79907
Yamaha Dr 79927
Yanagisako Ave 79938
E Yandell Dr
100-198 79902
200-1820 79902
1822-1828 79902
1900-3000 79903
3002-5698 79903
3011-3011 79923
3013-5299 79903
5700-5799 79925
5800-6299 79905
W Yandell Dr 79902
Yaqui Way 79925
N Yarbrough Dr
300-398 79915
400-922 79915
924-998 79915
1100-2599 79925
2601-3599 79925
3100-3598 79925
3100-3100 79937
S Yarbrough Dr 79915
Yarmouth Ln 79924
Yarwood Dr 79935
Yasmin Dr 79932
Yates Pl 79928
Yaya Ln 79907
Ybarra Ct 79905
Yellow Rose St 79936
Yellowstone St 79924
Yerba Verde St 79932
Yermoland Dr 79907
Yeshiva Ln 79928
Yogi Berra Dr 79934
Yolanda Dr 79915
Yorkshire Ct 79922
Yorktown Way 79907
Yosemite Pl 79904
Young St 79906
Ysleta Ln 79907
Yucatan Ln 79907
Yucca Pl 79932
Yucca Trl 79938
Yukon St 79924
Yuma Dr 79915
Yvette Ave 79924
Yvonne Ct 79915
Yvonne Diane Dr 79936
Yvonne Richardson Ave 79936
Zabel Ln 79928
Zacatecas Ct 79907
Zach Rd 79927
Zachariah Rd 79938
Zacharias Ct 79927
Zambia Ct 79928
Zane Grey St 79906
Zane Richards 79938
Zanzibar Rd 79925
Zapal Ave 79922
Zapata St 79928
N Zaragoza Rd
100-168 79907
170-899 79907
880-880 79917
901-1299 79907
1000-1098 79907
1300-1899 79936
1900-3800 79938
3802-3998 79938
S Zaragoza Rd 79907
Zebra Ct 79924
Zebu Rd 79927
Zellige St 79928
Zelt St 79928
Zena Bliss Ave 79904
Zenaida Ln 79907
Zenith Dr 79912
Zinc Pl 79928
Ziner Pl 79928
Zinnia Pl 79907
Zion Ln 79904
Zircon Dr 79904
Zonobia Ave 79938
Zorrillo Ln 79907
Zulema St 79928
Zuni Pl 79925

NUMBERED STREETS

1st Ave 79901
1st Dragoons Ave 79904
2nd Cavalry Cir 79904
E 3rd Ave 79901
3rd Infantry Rd 79904
E 4th Ave 79901
E 6th Ave 79901
E 7th Ave 79901
E 8th Ave 79901
8th Cavalry Cir 79904
E 9th Ave 79901
9th Cavalry Cir 79904
10th Cavalry Cir 79904
13th Cavalry Cir 79904
25th Infantry Rd 79904

ENNIS TX

General Delivery 75119

POST OFFICE BOXES MAIN OFFICE STATIONS AND BRANCHES

Box No.s
All PO Boxes 75120

RURAL ROUTES

01, 02, 03, 04, 05, 06, 07, 08, 09 75119

NAMED STREETS

All Street Addresses 75119

NUMBERED STREETS

All Street Addresses 75119

EULESS TX

General Delivery 76039

POST OFFICE BOXES MAIN OFFICE STATIONS AND BRANCHES

Box No.s
All PO Boxes 76039

RURAL ROUTES

02, 04, 06, 08, 10 76039
01, 03, 05, 07 76040

NAMED STREETS

Abbey Rd 76039
Acorn Dr 76039
S Airport Cir 76040
Airport Fwy
100-1098 76039
101-2399 76040
E Airport Fwy
600-698 76040
601-699 76039
Alberi Dr 76039
Alder Trl 76040
E & W Alexander Ln 76040
Allante Ct 76040
Allen Dr 76039
Almond Ln 76039
Amber Hill Ln 76039
Amberton Pl 76040
American Blvd 76040
Amy Way 76039
Ancient Oak Dr 76040
Angela Ln 76039
Angelman Dr 76039
Anice Ln 76039
Ansley Ct 76039
Anthem Ave 76040
Anthony Dr 76039
Apple St 76040
Aransas Dr 76039
Arbor Ct, Ln & Trl 76039
Arbor Club Ln 76039
Arbor Creek Dr 76039
Arbor Crest Ln 76039
Arbor Glen Dr 76039
Arbor Park Dr 76039
Argone Ct 76039
Aries Dr 76040
Arnett Dr 76040
Arwine Ct 76040
Asbury Cir 76039
Ascot Dr 76040
E & W Ash Ln 76039
Ashbrook Ct 76039
Ashleaf Ln 76040
Aspenway Cir 76039
Atkerson Ln 76040
Attaway Dr 76039
Auburndale Dr 76040
Augustine Dr 76039
Aurora Ct & Dr 76039
Baccarac Ct 76040
Balsam Dr 76039
Basswood Dr 76039
Bay Ave 76040
Bayberry Ln 76039
Bayless Dr 76040
Baze Rd 76039
Bear Creek Dr & Pkwy 76039
Bear Lake Dr 76039
Becker Dr 76039
Beech Dr 76039
Beech Tree Ln 76040
Bell Dr 76039
Bell Ranch Cir 76040
Bent Tree Ct & Dr 76039
Black Bear Dr 76039

Black Cherry Ln 76040
Black Gum Trl 76040
Blanco Dr 76039
Blessing Creek Dr 76039
Blue Ash Ln 76040
Blue Spruce Dr 76040
Bluegrass Ln 76039
Bocowood Cir & Dr 76039
Bordeaux Dr 76039
Boulder Park Dr 76040
Boxwood Ct 76039
Bradbury Dr 76040
Branch Bnd 76039
Brasher Ln 76040
Brazos Blvd 76039
Brenda Ln 76039
Briarwood Ct 76040
Bridgegate St 76040
Bridle Dr 76039
Bristol Ave 76040
Brittany Ct & Dr 76039
Broadway Ave 76040
Brook Forest Ln 76039
Brook Glen Dr 76039
Brook Grove Dr 76039
Brook Hollow Dr 76039
Brown Bear Ct & Way 76039
Brownstone St 76039
Buck Trl 76039
Buckingham Ave 76040
Byers St 76039
Cadbury Dr 76040
Calais Ct 76039
Calloway Cemetery Rd 76040
Calvary Dr 76040
Candace Ct 76039
Cannon Dr 76040
Canterbury St 76039
Canvasback Ct 76039
N Canyon Trl N & S 76040
Canyon Ridge Dr 76040
Caraway Ln 76039
Caribou Way 76039
Carol Way 76039
Carter Dr 76039
Catalpa Ln 76039
Cecil Ln 76039
Cedar Ct 76040
Cedar Elm Dr 76039
Cedar Ridge Ter 76039
Channing Ln 76039
Cherry Ann Ct & Dr 76039
Chesapeake Ct & St 76040
Chestnut Oak Ct 76039
Chinaberry Ct 76040
Chipwood Ct 76039
Chittam Dr 76039
Chittamwood Trl 76040
Chrissy Creek Ln 76040
Christine Ct 76039
Christopher Ln 76040
Churchill Ln 76039
Cinnamon Ct & Ln 76039
Clairemont Ln 76039
Claymore Dr 76040
Clebud Dr 76040
Cliffdale Dr 76040
Cliffwood Rd 76040
Clinic Dr 76039
Clisterl Dr 76039
Clove Ln 76039
Clover Ln 76039
Cold Bay Ln 76039
Collin Dr 76039
Colonial Ln 76040
Colton Ct 76040
Commerce St 76040
Conifer Dr 76039
Conifer Ln 76040
Constitution Dr 76040
Copher Ct 76039
Country Ln 76039
Coyote Dr 76040
Cranberry Ln 76039
Crane Dr 76039
Creekside Dr 76040
Crepe Myrtle Dr 76039
Cresthaven Dr 76040
Crestridge Cir 76040
Cripple Creek Dr 76039
Crowberry Way 76040
Crowe Dr 76040
Cullum Dr 76040
Cypress Cir 76039
Dallas Dr 76039
Danny Creek Dr 76040
Darlene Trl 76039
David Dr 76040
Deacon Dr 76039
Debra Dr 76040
Deedee Creek Dr 76040
Del Paso St 76040
Del Prado Dr 76040
Delta Dr 76039
Denali Dr 76039
E Denton Cir & Dr 76039
Desert Ct 76040
Devon Dr 76039
Dickey Dr 76040
Dogwood Cir 76039
Donley Ct & Dr 76039
Double Barrel Dr 76040
Douglas St 76039
Drake Dr 76039
Driftwood Dr 76040
Driskill Dr 76039
Dunaway Ct & Dr 76040
Eagles Nest Dr 76039
Eastcliff Dr 76039
N Ector Dr 76039
S Ector Dr 76039
Eden Trl 76039
Edinborough Ct & Dr 76039
Edury Ct 76039
El Camino Real 76040
Elm St 76039
Elmwood Ct 76039
Emerson Dr 76039
Erica Ln 76039
Erwin Dr 76039
Essex Pl 76039
Eugene Cir 76040
E & W Euless Blvd & St 76040
Eva Ln 76040
Evans Dr 76040
Evergreen Dr 76040
Evita Ln 76039
F A A Blvd 76039
Fair Oaks Blvd 76039
Fairlawn Ct 76039
Falling Leaf Ln 76040
Falls Dr 76039
Fannin Dr 76039
Faun Dr 76040
Fayette Ct & Dr 76039
Fernando Dr 76039
Ferris St 76040
Fiori Way 76039
Fite St 76040
Flint Ct 76040
Foreman Dr 76039
Forest Trail Ct 76039
Forestcrest Ct 76039
Fountain Gate Dr 76039
Fountain Meadows Dr 76039
Fountain Park Dr 76039
Fountain Wood Dr 76039
Fountainside Dr 76039
Fountainview Dr 76039
Foxbury Dr 76040
Franklin Dr 76040
Frazier Ct 76040
Freestone Dr 76039
E & W Fuller Dr 76039
Fuller Wiser Rd 76039
Garrett Rd 76040
Gaye Ct 76040
Gazebo Ct & Ln 76040
Ginger Ln 76039
E & W Glade Rd 76039
Glade Shadow Dr 76039
Glenn Dr 76039
Goldenrain Tree Dr 76039
Granite Ct 76039
Gray Oak Ct & Dr 76039
Great Oak Dr 76040
Greenbriar Dr 76040
Greenhill St 76039
Greenridge Ct 76039
Grizzly Run Ln 76039
Hammerhead Turnaround St 76040
Hanover Dr 76040
Harbor Ct 76040
Harrington Ct & Ln 76039
Harris Dr 76039
Harston Woods Dr 76040
E & W Harwood Cir, Ct & Rd 76039
Hawthorn Dr 76039
Heather Dr 76040
Henslee Dr 76040
Heritage Ave 76039
Hickory Springs Dr 76039
Hideaway Ct 76039
Hideout Trl 76040
High Creek Dr 76040
High Hawk Trl 76039
Highland Dr 76040
Highview Dr 76039
S Highway 157 76040
Highway 360 76039
Hill Trail Dr 76039
Hillcrest Dr 76039
Hilltop Dr 76039
Hilton Dr 76040
Himes Dr 76039
Hodges Dr 76040
Holder Dr 76039
Holliday Ln 76039
Hollow Oak Dr 76040
Holly Ct & Dr 76039
Hollywood Blvd 76040
Holton Cir 76040
Honey Locust Cir 76040
Honey Locust Dr 76039
Horse Shoe Dr 76039
House Anderson Rd 76040
Huffman Rd 76039
E & W Huitt Ln 76040
Huntington Dr 76040
N Industrial Blvd 76039
S Industrial Blvd 76040
International Dr 76039
Irion Dr 76039
Ironbridge Pl 76040
Ivory Ct 76040
Jamboree Way 76039
Jamestown Ct 76040
Janann St 76039
Jean Ln 76040
Jefflyn Ct 76040
Jenny Ln 76039
Jimison Ln 76040
John Vernon Ln 76040
Johns Dr 76039
Jonathan Ct & Dr 76040
Jones St 76039
Joyce Ct 76039
Juniper Ct 76040
Juniper Dr 76039
Justice Ct 76040
Karen Ln 76040
Kathleen Ln 76040
Kayli Ln 76039
Kelly Cir 76040
Kenneth Dr 76040
Kensinger Ct 76039
Kessler Dr 76039
Kevin Dr 76040
Kimble Dr 76039
Knapford Sta 76040
Knapp Ln 76040
Knoll Trl 76039
Knoll Wood Ct 76039
Knott Ct 76039
Kodiak Cir 76039
Koen Ln 76040
Kynette Dr 76039
Lake Eden Dr 76039
Lakeshore Dr 76039
Lakewood Blvd 76039
Lamar Dr 76039
Landover Dr 76040
Lantana Dr 76039
Lark Ln 76039
Laurel Ln 76039
Lawndale Ln 76039
Lee Dr 76039
Lemon Ln 76039
Lexington Ln 76039
Libra Ln 76040
Limestone Ct & Dr 76039
Linda Ln 76040
Linkwood Dr 76040
Liston Ln 76040
Little Bear Ct & Trl 76039
Little Creek Dr 76039
Little Cub Way 76039
Live Oak Ct & Dr 76040
Loblolly Ln 76040
Lois Ln 76040
London Ct 76039
Lone Oak Cir 76039
Long Bow Ct & Trl 76040
Lost Valley Dr 76039
Mack Dr 76039
Madisson Dr 76039
Magnolia Ln 76039
Main Pl 76040
N Main St
100-199 76040
200-3099 76039
S Main St 76040
Maloney Ct 76040
Manchester Dr 76039
Manor Green Blvd 76039
Maplewood Ct 76039
Marlene Ct & Dr 76040
Marshall Dr 76039
Martha St 76040
Martin Ln 76040
Mary Dr 76040
Maxwell Ct 76039
Mccormick Ct 76039
Mcdowell Dr 76039
Meadowview Dr 76039
Mel Ct 76039
Merlin Way 76039
Mesa Dr 76040
E Mid Cities Blvd 76039
Midcreek Dr 76039
Middlebury Ln 76040
Midland St 76039
Midpark Dr 76039
Midway Dr E & W 76039
Milam Dr 76039
Milla Ct & Ln 76039
S & W Mills Dr 76040
Mimosa Ln 76039
Mint Ln 76039
Minters Chapel Rd 76039
Mirage Ct 76040
Monterrey Blvd 76040
Monument Way 76040
Moonlight Dr 76039
Moose Hollow Ln 76039
Morningside Dr 76040
Morrison Ct & Dr 76039
Mosier Valley Rd 76040
Moss Hill Ln 76039
Mossy Grove Ln 76040
Mountain Ash Ln 76040
Muskeg Ln 76039
Nautical Dr 76040
Needles St 76040
Nettle Ln 76039
Newkirk Ct 76039
Newport Cir & Way 76039
Nita Ln 76040
Norman Dr 76040
Normandy Ct & Dr 76039
Northcliff Dr 76040
Northrope St 76039
Nutmeg Ln 76039
Oak Ln 76039
Oak St 76040
Oak Forest Trl 76039
Oak Timber Dr 76039
Oakridge Dr 76040
Oakwood Cir & Dr 76040
Oasis Ct 76040
Oceanside Dr 76040
Old English Ct 76039
Overlake Ct 76039
Paint Rock Ct 76040
Palomino Dr 76039
Pamela Dr 76040
Paradise Hills Dr 76040
Paradise Oaks Dr 76040
Park Dr 76040
Park Crest Ave 76039
Park Grove Dr 76039
Park Haven Blvd 76039
Park Hill Dr 76040
Park Manor Ct 76039
Park Meadows Dr 76039
Park Vista Ln 76039
Parker Dr 76039
Parsley Ln 76039
Patriot Ln 76040
Paula Ln 76040
Pauline St 76040
Peach St 76040
Peach Tree Way 76040
Pebble Creek Dr 76040
Pecos Dr 76039
Penny Ln 76039
Penoak Ct 76039
Peppercorn Dr 76039
Peterstow Dr 76039
Pin Oak Ter 76040
Pinion Dr 76039
Pinnacle Cir E & W 76040
Pintail Pkwy 76039
S & W Pipeline Rd E & W 76040
Plank St 76040
Pleasant Trl 76039
Plum St 76040
Ponciana Dr 76039
Poppy Ln 76039
Port Royale Way 76039
Post Oak Blvd 76040
Post Oak Dr 76039
Potomac Dr 76039
Presidio Cir 76040
Priest Ln 76039
Primrose Ct & Hl 76039
Princeton Pl 76040
Quarry Trce 76040
Raider Ct & Dr 76040
Raines Ct 76039
Rambling Ct & Ln 76039
Ranger St 76040
Reaves Ct 76040
Red Bud Ln 76039
Red Cedar Dr 76039
Red Hawk Ln 76039
Regal Pkwy 76040
Regina Ct 76039
Renee Dr 76040
Republic Ln 76040
Reveille Cir 76040
Revolution Ln 76040
Rexana St 76039
Ridgecrest Dr 76040
Ridgewood Dr 76039
W Rim Dr 76039
Rippling Brook Way 76040
Roaring Canyon Rd 76039
Rock Creek Dr 76039
Rockwall Dr 76039
Rodolphus St 76040
Rollingwood Dr 76040
Rosemary Ln 76039
Rosemead Dr 76039
Rosewood Ct 76039
Ross Ave 76040
Roundtree Dr 76039
Roxboro Rd 76039
Royal Pkwy 76040
Royce Dr 76040
Running Bear Ct 76039
Rusk Dr 76039
Saddle Dr 76039
Saffron Ln 76039
Sage Ln 76039
Sagebrush Trl 76040
Salem Dr 76039
Salient Pt 76040
Salmon Run Ct & Ln 76039
Salsbury Dr 76040
Sandlewood Ln 76039
Saratoga Dr 76040
Scarlet Oak Ln 76040
Scotch Elm St 76039
Scrimshire Ct 76039
Seaside Ct & Dr 76040
Serenade Ln 76039
Serenity Hill Dr 76040
Shadow Ln 76039
Shady Holw 76039
Shady Creek Dr 76040
Sharpsbury Dr 76040
Sheenjack Holw 76039
Shelmar Dr 76039
Shenandoah Dr 76039
N Sheppard Dr 76039
S Sheppard Dr 76040
Sierra Dr 76040
Signet Dr 76040
Silent Oak Dr 76040
Silk Tree Ln 76040
Silver Creek Dr 76040
Simmons Dr 76040
Sixpence Ln 76039
Skyway Dr 76040
Slaughter Ln 76040
Slick Rock Chase 76040
Smoke Tree Trl 76040
Sotogrande Blvd 76040
Spicebush Ln 76039
Spinning Glen St 76040
Spring Oak Ct 76039
Springridge Ln 76039
Springwood Ct 76039
Sprucewood Ln 76039
Stage Line Dr 76039
Stanley Dr 76039
Stardust Ct 76040
Starlight Ct 76039
State Highway 121 76039
Steeps Ct 76039
Stewart Ln 76039
Stone Hollow Way 76040
Stonewall Dr 76039
Stony Creek Dr 76039
Stratford Ct 76039
Summerbrook Dr 76040
Summit Ridge Dr 76039
Sunny Creek Ln 76040
Sunset Dr 76040
Surrey Ln 76039
Susan St 76040
Sweet Bay Dr 76040
Sweet Gum Dr 76039
Swor St 76040
W Sycamore Cir 76040
Sycamore Ln 76039
Tall Timbers Dr 76039
Tallow Dr 76039
Tallwood Dr 76040
Tanbark Dr 76040
Tanglecrest Ct 76039
Tangleridge Ct 76039
Tanglewood Trl 76040
Tarragon Ln 76039
Tarrant Dr 76039
Tarrant Main St 76040
Teal Wood Ln 76039
Tennison Dr 76039
Texas Star Ct, Dr & Pkwy 76040
Thistle Ct 76039
Thoreau Ln 76039
Thorn Wood Dr 76039
Timber Ridge Dr 76039
Timberland Trl 76040
Timberlane Ter 76039
Timothy Ln 76039
Toplea Dr 76040
Town Creek Dr 76039
Trail Lake Dr 76039
Trailwood Dr 76039
Tranquil Cv 76040
Travis Dr 76039
Treetop Dr 76040
Trenton Ln 76040
Trinity Blvd 76040
Trinity Hills Ln 76040
Trinity Terrace Ln 76040
Tristan Ln 76040
Trojan Trl 76039
Twin Oaks Ct 76039
Tyler Ave 76040
Underwood Ln 76039
Valley Ct 76039
Vaucluse Dr 76040
Victoria Dr 76039
Villa Dr 76040
Village Dr 76039
N Vine St 76040
Violet St 76040
Vista Glen Ln 76040
Vista Mar Dr 76040
Wade Ct 76039
Walden Trl 76039
Walnut Way 76039
Waterford Way 76039
Waterside Dr 76039
Wellington Dr 76040
Westcliff Dr 76040
Westover Dr 76039
Westpark Ct & Way 76040
Westpark Way Cir 76040
Westport Cir 76039
Westwood Dr 76039
Whetstone Ln 76039
White Birch Way 76040
E Whitener Rd 76040
Wigeon Way 76039
Wild Ivy Way 76040
Wild Oak Ln 76039
Wildbriar St 76039
Wildwood St 76040
Willow Ln 76039
Wilshire Dr 76040
Winchester Dr 76039
Windlea Dr 76040
Windward Way 76040
Windy Hollow Way 76040
Winston Ct & Dr 76039
Witten Ct 76039
Woodberry Ct 76039
Woodcreek Ct 76039
Wooddale 76039
Wooded Glen Way 76040
Woodhaven Ct 76039
Woodhollow Dr
1700-1799 76039
3600-3899 76040
Woodpark Ln 76039
Woodpath Dr 76039
Woodridge Cir 76040
Woodvine Dr 76040
Yoristow Dr 76040
Yorkshire Ct & Dr 76040

FLOWER MOUND TX

POST OFFICE BOXES MAIN OFFICE STATIONS AND BRANCHES

Box No.s
All PO Boxes 75027

NAMED STREETS

Abbey Ln 75028
Abbey Glen Dr 75028
Aberdeen Dr
2000-2098 75028
2701-2709 75022
2711-2900 75022
2902-2998 75028
Abron Ln 75022
Acacia St 75028
Acorn Trl 75028
Acropolis Dr 75028
Acton Dr 75022
Ada Dr 75022
Addington Pl 75028
Ainsley Dr 75028
Albero Ln 75028
Alberta Ln 75022
Alexander Dr 75028
Almond Dr 75028
Alpine Cv 75028
Altoga Ct 75028
Amador Ct 75022
Amber Ct & Ln 75028
Amberwood Gln 75028
Amen Cor 75022
Amhearst Ct & Ln 75028
Amy Ln 75028
Anchor Ct 75022
Andean Teal Ln 75028
Andover Ln 75028
Andrea Dr 75022
Annabel Ave 75028
Anne Cir 75022
Apache Trl 75022
Appalachian Way 75022
Appleton Ln 75022
Arabian Cir 75022
Arbor Creek Ln 75022
Arbor Oaks Ct 75022
Archer Ct 75028
Argos Way 75028
Armstrong Dr 75028
Arrow Wood Dr 75028
Arrowhead Dr 75028
Ash St 75028
Ash Grove Ct 75028
Ash Leaf Ln 75022
Ashburton Way 75022
Ashby Dr 75022
Aspen Way 75028
Atwood Dr 75028
Auburn Dr
3700-3799 75022
4201-4297 75028
4299-4499 75028
Augusta Ct, Dr & Pl 75022
Aurora Ct 75028
Austin Ct 75028
Autumn Ln 75028
Autumn Sage Trl 75022
Avon Ct 75028
Azalea Ct 75028
Bachman Dr 75028
Bainbridge Ln 75022
Baker Ct 75028
Baldcypress Ln 75028
Balmoral Ln 75028
Balmoral Castle Ct 75022
Baltusrol Dr 75022
Bancroft Way 75022
Banner Ct 75028
Bar Harbor Dr 75028
Barkridge Trl 75028
Barrens Cir 75028
Barton Creek Ln 75028
Basil Dr 75028
Bay Park Ct 75022
Bay Valley Ct 75022
Bayberry St 75028
Baybreeze Dr 75028
Bayshore Dr 75022
Beach Pl 75022
Beachview Dr 75022
Beacon Ct & St 75028

Beau Ridge Ct 75028
Beaver Creek Dr 75022
Becket Dr 75028
Beckingham Ct 75022
Beckworth Dr 75022
Beechwood Ln 75028
Belair Ln 75022
Bella Lago Dr 75022
Bellanca Ct 75028
Belmeade Ln 75028
Belmont Ct 75028
Belstrum Ct & Dr 75028
Bennington Ave 75028
Bent Grass Way 75028
Bent Oak Cir 75022
Bentley Dr 75028
Beretta Dr 75028
Beringer Ct 75022
Berry Hill Ct 75028
Bershire Ct & Dr 75028
Beth Dr 75022
Beverly Dr 75022
Big Canyon Dr 75022
Big Falls Dr 75028
Birch St 75028
Birch Leaf Pl 75022
Birchbrook Dr 75028
Birchmont Dr 75022
Birchwood Dr 75028
Biscayne Dr 75028
Bishop Dr 75028
Black Walnut Dr 75022
Blairwood Dr 75028
Blossom Trl 75028
Blue Bird Dr 75022
Blue Bonnet Ct 75028
Blue Grass Ct & Dr 75028
Blue Leaf Dr 75028
Blue Moon St 75028
Blue Ridge Dr & Trl 75028
Blue Sage Ct & Dr 75022
Blue Sky Ln 75028
Blue Wood Trl 75022
Bluebonnet Grn 75028
Bluestem St 75028
Bluffview Ct & Ln 75022
Blum Ct 75028
Blustery Ct 75028
Bob White Ln 75022
Bois D Arc Ct 75028
Bolo Ln 75022
Bonanza Ln 75022
Bonita Dr 75022
Bordeaux Cir, Ct &
Way 75022
Bosbury Dr 75028
Bosque Ct 75028
Boulder Way 75022
Bourne Ln 75022
Bradford Dr 75028
Bramwell Dr 75028
Branch Hollow Cir 75028
Branch Oaks Ln 75028
Branchwood Trl 75028
Brandywine Dr 75028
Braxton Ln 75028
Breaker Ln 75022
Breckenridge Dr 75022
Breezywood Dr 75022
Brenda Dr 75022
Briar Ln 75028
Briar Patch Ln 75022
Briarcreek Dr 75028
Briaridge Ln 75028
Briaroaks Dr 75028
Bridgewater Pl 75028
Bridle Bit Rd 75022
Bridlewood Blvd 75028
Brighton Dr 75028
Brightstone Ct 75022
Bristol Dr 75028
Britford Dr 75028
Brittany Dr 75022
Broadmoor Ln 75022
Broadway Ave 75028
Brook Ln 75028

Brookhollow Ln 75028
Brookville Ln 75028
Brookwood Dr 75028
Broughton Dr 75028
Brown Dr 75022
Brownstone Dr 75028
Brush Creek Ln 75028
Bruton Orand Blvd 75022
Buckeye Ct & Dr 75028
Buckner Ct & Dr 75028
Buckthorn Ct & St 75028
Bur Oak Dr 75028
Burlington Dr 75022
Burning Tree Dr 75022
Buttonwood Dr 75028
Caddo Trl 75022
Caladium Cir & Dr 75022
Calisto Way 75028
Calloway Ct 75028
Camara Ct 75022
Cambridge Dr 75028
Camden Dr 75028
Candlebrook Dr 75028
Candlelight Cv 75028
Canongate Dr 75022
Canter Way 75028
Canterbury Ln 75028
Canvasback Ln 75028
Cape Brett Dr 75022
Capri Ln 75028
Caprock Cv 75028
Cardinal Dr 75022
Carlisle Ct 75022
Carnaby Ln 75028
Carriage Ct 75028
Carrington Ave 75028
Carroll Ct 75022
Carterton Ct & Way 75022
Cartwright Ct 75028
Caruth Ct 75022
Cassandra Dr 75022
Castle Ct 75028
Castlewood Ct 75022
Catalpa Rd 75028
Cavalier Way 75022
Cayenne Dr 75028
Cedar St 75028
Cedar Bluff Ln 75028
Cedar Pass Ct 75028
Cedar Ridge Dr 75022
Cedarcrest Ct 75022
Cedarwood Dr 75028
Cenerlia Dr 75022
Centenary Dr 75028
Central Park Ave 75028
Chadwick Dr 75022
Champions Ct 75028
Chancellor Dr 75022
Channing Ct 75028
Chaparral 75022
Chapel Ct 75028
Chatham Dr 75028
Chaucer Ln 75022
Chelsea Ln 75022
Cherokee Path 75022
Cherokee Trl 75022
Cherry Brook Way 75028
Cherry Sage Dr 75022
Cheshire Dr 75028
Chestnut Ct 75028
Cheyenne Cir 75022
Chilton Ln 75028
Chimney Rock Dr 75022
Chinaberry Dr 75028
Chinkapin Ln & Pl 75028
Chinn Chapel Rd 75022
Choctaw Trl 75022
Christie Ct 75028
Christopher Ct 75022
Churchill Dr
2601-2699 75028
3001-3097 75028
3099-3199 75022
3900-4199 75028
Cilantro Dr 75028
Claremont Ct 75028

Clayton Dr 75028
Clear Creek Dr 75022
Clear Ridge Ln 75028
Clearpoint Dr 75022
Clearwood Ln 75028
Cobble Trl 75028
Coker Dr 75028
Coldwater Ln 75028
W College Pkwy 75028
Colli Ctr 75022
Colonial Ct, Dr & Pl 75028
Colony Ct & St 75028
Columbia Dr 75022
Commonwealth Dr 75028
Compton Ct 75028
Concord Dr 75022
Condor St 75028
Connors Dr 75028
Conroe Ct 75028
Consolvo Dr 75022
Copperhill Ct 75022
Coral Springs Dr 75022
Corkwood Cir 75028
Cornell Dr 75022
Corporate Cir & Ct 75028
Cortadera Ct 75028
Cottage Ln 75028
Cottonwood Dr 75028
Cottrell Dr 75022
Country Club Dr 75028
Country Oaks Dr 75022
Courtney Dr 75022
Covington Dr 75028
Crabapple Ln 75028
Crandon Dr 75022
Crawford Ct 75028
N Creek Xing 75022
Creek View Dr 75022
Creekhaven Dr 75022
Creekside Pl 75022
Creekwood Ct & Dr 75022
Crepe Myrtle Dr 75022
Crescent Ct & Dr 75028
Crescent Oaks Rd 75022
Crestbrook Dr 75028
Crested Butte Trl 75022
Crestfield Dr 75022
Crestside Dr 75028
Crestwood Cir 75022
Cripple Creek Dr 75028
Cromwell Way 75022
Crooked Ln 75028
Crooked Creek Ct 75028
Cross Haven Dr 75028
Cross Timbers Rd
601-2097 75028
2099-4600 75028
4602-5198 75028
5501-5597 75022
5599-8099 75022
8101-9299 75022
Crossbow Ln 75028
Crown Knoll Cir 75028
Crownwood Ct 75022
Culwell St 75028
Currant Way 75028
Cypress Ct 75028
Cypress Leaf Ln 75022
Dade Dr 75028
Daisy Ln 75028
Dalton Dr 75022
Dana Ct & Dr 75028
Danley Ct 75028
Darcey Ct 75028
Dartmouth Dr 75022
Dawn Dr 75022
Dayflower Dr 75028
Deer Path 75022
Del Pino Ct 75022
Delaina Dr 75028
Delaney Ter 75028
Dendron Dr 75028
Derbyshire Ct 75022
Devereux Ct 75028
Devonshire Ct 75022
Dexter Ct 75028

Diamond Point Dr 75022
Diana Ln 75028
Dickens Ln 75028
Dillon Ct 75028
Dixon Ln 75028
Dogwood St 75028
Dominion Ct 75022
Donnoli Dr 75022
Doral Ct E & W 75022
Dorchester Ct 75022
Doubletree Trl 75028
Dove Meadow Dr 75028
Dover Dr 75028
Dowland Dr 75022
Downing St 75028
Drake Trl 75028
Dresage Ct & Ln 75022
Driftwood 75022
Druid Way 75028
Dumas Ct 75022
Duncan Ln 75028
Durango Pl 75028
Durham Ln 75022
Dwyer Ln 75022
Eads St 75028
Eagle Creek Dr 75028
Eastbourne Ln 75022
Eastglen Dr 75028
Echo Blf 75028
Edgefield Trl 75028
Edinburg Ln 75028
Edna Valley Ct 75022
Ellis Dr 75028
Elm St 75028
Elm Creek Ln 75028
Elm Crest Ct 75022
Elmhurst Ln 75028
Elmridge Dr 75022
Elmwood 75022
Emerald Cove Dr 75022
Emerson Ln 75022
Emory Dr 75022
Enchantress Ln 75028
Enterprise Dr 75028
Equestrian Ct & Way 75028
Essex Ct 75028
Everton Dr 75022
Fair Lake Rd 75022
Fairbank Ln 75028
Fairfax Ct & Way 75022
Fairfield Ln 75028
Fairhaven Ct 75028
Fairmont Dr 75028
Fairway Dr 75028
Falcon Dr 75022
Fallbrook Dr 75028
Fallow Cir 75028
Fawn Run Dr 75028
Ferndale Dr 75028
Fieldcrest Rd 75022
Fireside Dr 75028
Firestone Dr 75022
Firewheel Dr 75028
Flamingo Dr 75028
Flatwood Dr 75022
Flint Ridge Dr 75028
Flower Mound Rd
100-998 75028
1000-2699 75028
2700-2900 75022
2902-3798 75022
Fordham Ct 75022
Forest Glen Dr 75028
Forest Hill Cir & Dr 75028
Forest Meadow Dr 75028
Forest Oak Ct 75022
Forest Vista Dr 75028
Forestwood Dr 75022
Forums Dr 75028
Fox Glen Ln 75028
Fox Hollow Ct 75028
Foxborough Trl 75028
Foxglove Ct 75022
Fradench Dr 75022
Francis Ct 75028
Friar Ct 75028

Frontier Dr 75022
Frost Ln 75028
Fuqua Dr 75028
Furlong Ct & Dr 75022
Gaitland Cir 75022
Gallant Ct 75028
Gallop Ct 75028
Gamma Rd 75028
Garden Ridge Blvd &
Pkwy 75028
Garwood Cir 75022
Gateridge Dr 75028
Gatwick Ct 75028
Gayle Ct 75028
Genevieve Ct 75022
Gentle Dr 75022
Gentry Ln 75028
Georgetown Dr 75028
Geranium St 75028
Gerault Rd 75028
Gilbert Ct 75022
Ginger Dr 75028
Gisbourne Dr 75028
Giverny 75022
Glasgow Ct 75028
Glen Chester Dr 75022
Glen Ellen Dr 75022
Glen Garry Dr 75022
Glen Heather Dr 75028
Glen Hollow Ln 75028
Glen Oaks Dr 75022
Glenbrook St 75022
Glenmoor Dr 75022
Glenridge Dr 75028
Glenshannon Ln 75022
Glenshire Dr 75028
Glory Creek Cir 75022
Golden Arrow Dr 75028
Golden Aspen Dr 75022
Good Morning Ct 75028
Grady Ct 75028
Granby Ln 75022
Grand Meadow Ln 75028
Grand Park Place Ln 75028
Grandview Ct & Dr 75028
Grapevine Rd 75022
Graystone Dr 75028
Green Briar Ln 75022
Green Meadow Ct &
Ln 75022
Green Tree Ln 75022
Greenleaf 75022
Greenwood Ct & Dr 75022
Gregory Dr 75028
Gremar St 75022
Griffis Rd 75022
Guardian Ct 75022
Gunnison Trl 75028
Hackberry St 75022
Haley Dr 75028
Hallford Ct 75028
Halsey Dr 75028
Halter Way 75028
Hamilton Dr 75022
Hamlett Ct & Ln 75028
Hampshire Dr 75028
Hanover Ct & Dr 75028
Harbor Ct & Dr 75022
Harbor View Dr 75022
Hardy Ln 75028
Harris Rd 75022
Hartford Dr 75028
Harvard Dr 75022
Harvest Glen Dr 75028
Hasland Dr 75028
Hastings Way 75022
Havenlake Dr 75022
Haversham Dr 75022
Hawk Rd 75022
Hawthorne Ct 75022
Hazel St 75028
Hazy Meadows Ln 75022
Hearthstone Dr 75022
Heatfield Dr 75022
Heather Ct 75022
Heather Glen Dr 75028

Heather Ridge Ct &
Dr 75028
Heather Wood Dr 75022
Heiden Ct 75028
Helmsford Dr 75028
Hemlock Ln 75022
Henley Ct 75028
Heritage Ln 75022
Heron Ct 75022
Hickory Dr 75028
Hickory Leaf Ln 75022
Hickory Springs Rd 75022
Hidden Trl 75022
Hidden Brook Trl 75028
Hidden Forest Dr 75028
Hidden Trail Ct 75022
Hidden Valley Rd 75022
Hide A Way Ln 75022
High Rd 75022
High Chaparral Dr 75022
High Meadow Rd 75022
High Point Dr 75022
High View Rd 75022
Highdale Ct 75028
Hill Ridge Dr 75028
Hillcrest Rd 75022
Hillsdale Dr 75022
Hillshire Ct 75028
Hillside Ln 75028
Hilltop Ct 75028
Holly Ln & Pl 75022
Holly Leaf Ln 75022
Holly Oak Ct 75028
Homestead St 75028
Honey Mesquite Ln 75028
Honeysuckle Way 75028
Horizon St 75028
Hornby Ln 75022
Hugo Ct 75022
Hunters Run 75028
Huntly Ln 75022
Huntwick Ln 75028
Hyde Park Ct 75028
Immel Dr 75022
Imperial Dr 75028
Indale Way 75028
Indian Trl 75022
Indian Blanket Trl 75028
Indian Cherry Ln 75028
Ingleside Dr 75022
Inglewood Dr 75028
Inverness Ct 75022
Ironwood Ct & Dr 75028
Ivywood Dr 75028
Jackson Way 75022
Jaclamo St 75022
Jameston Dr 75028
Jenbri St 75022
Jennifer Dr 75022
Jenny Ln 75028
Jester Ln 75028
John Ct 75028
Johnson Pl 75028
Joshua Dr 75028
Jubilee Dr 75028
Juniper St 75028
Justin Rd 75028
Kales Ln 75022
Karla Dr 75022
Karnes Rd 75022
Katherine Ct & St 75022
Katina Dr 75028
Kelcourt Dr 75022
Kelsey Ct 75028
Kensington Ct 75022
Kent Dr 75022
Kentmere Ct 75022
Kenwood Dr 75022
Kiley Ln 75022
Kimberly Dr 75022
Kingfisher Ct 75022
Kings Ct & Dr 75028
Kings Forest Ln 75028
Kingston Ln 75028
Kingswood Dr 75028
Kinross Ct 75028

Kipling Dr 75022
Kirkpatrick Ln 75028
Knights Ct 75022
Kyle Ln 75028
La Cima Rd 75028
La Maison Pl 75022
La Rochelle 75022
La Salle 75022
Lake Bluff Ct & Dr 75028
Lake Breeze Ln 75022
Lake Coves Dr 75022
Lake Crest Ct & Dr 75022
Lake Flower Dr 75022
Lake Forest Blvd 75028
Lake Geneva Ct 75022
Lake Lucern Ct 75022
Lake Lugano Dr 75022
Lake Ridge Rd 75022
Lake Victoria Ct 75022
Lake Ville Dr 75022
Lake Vista Dr 75022
Lake Windermere Dr 75022
Lakehollow Ln 75028
Lakehurst Dr 75022
Lakemont Dr 75022
Lakeshore Dr 75028
Lakeside 75022
Lakeside Pkwy 75028
Lakeview Ln 75022
Lakeway Ter 75028
Lakewood Ln 75022
Lambda Ln 75028
Lamplighter Dr 75028
Lancashire Dr 75028
Lance Dr 75022
Landwyck Ln 75028
Langley Ct 75022
Lansdale Dr 75028
Largo Ct & Dr 75028
Larkspur St 75028
Latigo Ln 75022
Latigo Hills Rd 75022
Laurel Hill Dr 75028
Laurel Oak Dr 75028
Lauren Way 75028
Lavender Ln 75028
Lavon Dr 75028
Lavorton Pl 75022
Lazy Riv 75022
Leafspray Ln 75022
Leanne Dr 75022
Leese Dr 75028
Lexington Ave 75028
Liberty Ct 75028
Lighthouse Dr 75022
Lincoln Ct 75028
Lindby Dr 75028
Lionheart Ct 75028
Lippizaner Ct & Dr 75028
Lismore Dr 75022
Litchfield Ct 75022
Littlejohn Ct 75028
Live Oak Ln 75022
Liverpool Dr 75028
Livingston Ln 75028
Lloyd Ct 75028
Loblolly Ct 75028
Locke Dr 75028
Lockesley Dr 75028
Lockspur Ct 75022
Lofty Pines Ln 75028
Loma Alta Dr 75022
London Ln 75028
Lone Oak Way 75028
Lonebuck Dr 75028
Long Ln 75022
Long Meadow Dr 75022
Long Prairie Rd
1-97 75022
99-3600 75022
3602-3698 75022
3700-3798 75028
3800-6299 75028
Longbow Trl 75028
Longfellow Ln 75028
Lopo Cir & Rd 75028

Lori Ct 75028
Lost Crk 75022
Loyola Dr 75022
Lusk Ln 75028
Luther Ln 75028
Luttrell Ct 75028
Maddy Ln 75028
Madeline Ln 75028
N & S Magnolia Ct 75028
Magnolia Leaf Ln 75022
Mahogany St 75022
Mallard Way 75028
Mandalay Dr 75022
Manor Way 75028
Maple Ct 75028
Maple Grove Dr 75028
Mapleleaf Ln 75028
Maplewood Ln 75028
Marbella Dr 75022
Marble Pass Dr 75028
Marcus Ct & Dr 75028
Margie Ct 75028
Marian Ln 75028
Mariner Ct 75022
Marlow Ct & Dr 75028
Marquette Dr 75022
Marshall Crk 75028
Mary Ct 75022
Masters Ct 75022
Matterhorn Ln 75022
Mattise Dr 75022
Mayhaw Dr 75028
Maywood Ct 75028
Mazzini Ct 75028
Mcpherson Ln 75022
Meadow Dr 75022
Meadow Chase Ln 75028
Meadow Glen Dr 75022
Meadow Green Dr 75022
Meadow Ridge Dr 75022
Meadow Vista Dr 75022
Meadow Wood Dr 75022
Meadowbrook Ln 75022
Meadowcrest Ln 75022
Meadowlark 75022
Meandering Creek
Path 75028
Medical Arts Dr 75028
Medlin Ct 75028
Melinda Ct 75028
Melody Ct 75028
Merrimack Ln 75022
Merritt Dr 75028
Merryglen Ln 75022
Mesa Dr 75022
Mesquite St 75028
Meyerwood Ln N & S 75028
Midnight Ct 75028
Midway Rd 75022
Milford Dr 75028
Mimosa Ct 75028
Miracle Ln 75022
Mission Ridge Dr 75022
Mistletoe Dr 75022
Misty Glen Dr 75028
Misty Trail Ln 75028
Mockingbird Ln 75022
Mohawk 75022
Monet Ct 75022
Mont Clair Dr 75028
Montalcino Blvd 75022
Monticello Ct 75028
Montrose Ct 75022
Moonlight Bay 75022
Morgan Dr 75028
Morning Mist Trl 75028
Morningstar Cir & Dr 75028
Morriss Ct & Rd 75028
Moss Haven Cir 75022
Mossey Oak Ct 75022
Mount Vernon Ct 75028
Muirfield Ct 75022
Mulberry St 75028
Murrell Park Rd 75022
Mustang Trl 75028
Myrtice Dr 75022

Mystic Hollow Ct 75028
Nan Ln 75022
Nandina Dr 75022
Nantucket Ct 75022
Napa Ct 75022
Napier Ln 75022
Naples Dr 75028
Narrowbrook Dr 75028
Native Oak Ct & Dr 75022
Nautilus Ct 75022
Neptune Ct 75022
Newcastle Ct 75028
Newcomer Ln 75022
Newport Dr 75028
Newton Dr 75028
Noble Way 75022
Normandy Dr 75028
North Dr 75028
Northcrest Dr 75028
Northfalls Ct 75022
Northridge Ct 75022
Northshore Blvd
1601-1699 75022
2300-2398 75028
2400-2599 75028
2700-2999 75022
Northview Ct 75022
Northwood Dr 75022
Norwich St 75028
Nottingham St 75028
Oak Dr 75028
Oak Rdg 75022
Oak Bend Ct 75028
Oak Bluff Dr 75028
Oak Brook Pl 75022
Oak Creek Cir 75028
Oak Crest Dr 75028
Oak Dell Way 75022
Oak Grove Ct 75028
Oak Hollow Ln 75028
Oak Leaf Cir 75022
Oak Meadow Dr 75028
Oak Park Dr 75028
Oak Springs Dr 75022
Oak Tree Ln 75028
Oakdale Ln 75022
Oakmont Ct 75022
Oakview Dr 75022
Oakwood Ct 75028
Old Cross Timbers Rd 75022
Old Hickory Ln 75028
Old Mill Dr 75028
Old Oak Trl 75028
Old Settlers Rd 75022
Olympia Dr
2201-2399 75028
2300-2300 75027
2300-2398 75028
Opus Ct 75022
Orchard Dr 75028
Orchid Ct 75028
Oriole Dr 75022
Orion Ct 75028
Orly Dr 75022
Outlook Cv 75022
Oxford Ct & Ln 75022
Pacer Way 75028
Pack Saddle Way 75028
Paddock Cir 75022
Paisley Dr 75028
Palomino Cir 75022
Paluxy Ct 75028
Paprika Dr 75028
Par Dr 75028
Paradise Ln 75022
N Park Dr 75022
Park Ln 75028
Park Pl 75028
Park Bend Dr 75022
Park Ridge Rd 75022
Park View Dr 75028
Parker Dr & Sq 75028
Parkhaven Dr 75022
Parkside Pl 75022
Parkwood Dr 75022
Pasadena Pl 75022

Peaceful Cv 75022
Peachleaf Ln 75022
Pearl Ln 75022
Pearl River Dr 75028
Pecan Dr 75022
Pecan Hollow Ct 75028
Pecan Leaf Ln 75022
Pecan Meadows Dr 75028
Pecan Park Dr 75022
Pelican Ct 75022
Pendleton Ln 75028
Peninsula Dr 75022
Pepperport Ln 75022
Pepperwood Dr 75028
Peters Colony Rd 75022
Peterson Ct 75028
Petunia Dr 75028
Pheasant Ct 75022
Piedmont Ct 75022
Pierre Ln 75022
Pin Oak Ct & Dr 75028
Pine Ct 75028
Pine Valley Dr 75022
Pinehurst Dr 75028
Piney Point Dr 75022
Ping Dr 75028
Pinon St 75028
Pintail Pl 75028
Pioneer Park Dr 75022
Plantation Ln 75022
Plum St 75028
Plum Tree Ln 75022
Pocahontas 75022
Point De Vue Dr 75022
Polo Run Dr 75022
Pond Wood Dr 75022
Ponder Pl & Way 75028
Ponderosa Pine Dr 75022
Poplar Dr 75028
Porter Rd 75022
Portsmouth Ct 75022
Post Oak Rd 75028
Potomac Dr 75022
Prairie Ct 75028
Prairie Creek Ct, Dr &
Pl 75028
Prairie Hill Ln 75028
Preakness Dr 75022
Prescott Cir, Ct & Dr 75028
Prestwick Ln 75022
Prince Ln 75022
Prince Edward Ct 75022
Princeton Dr 75028
Princewood Dr 75028
Prospect Dr 75028
Providence Ln 75022
Purple Sage Dr 75028
Quail Run 75022
Queen Mary Dr 75022
Rainbow Ct 75028
Rainier Way 75028
Raintree Dr & Pl 75022
Ranch Rd 75022
Ranchero Way 75028
Rangewood Dr 75028
Raven Cir 75022
Rawlings Ct & St 75022
Red Bud Cv 75028
Red Bud Dr 75022
Red Cedar Ln 75022
Red Maple Rd 75022
Red Oak Ln 75028
Red Rock Cir & Ln 75022
Redcliff Ln 75028
Redwood Crest Ln 75022
Reflection Ct 75022
Regency Dr 75028
Regency Park Ct 75022
Reid Dr 75022
Remington Dr 75028
Remington Park Ct &
Dr 75028
Reserve Ct 75028
Richland Rd 75022
Ridge View Ct 75022
Ridgecrest Dr 75022

Ridgemere Dr 75028
Ridgemont Dr 75028
Ring Teal Ln 75028
Rippy Rd 75028
River Bend Ct & Trl 75022
River Birch Dr 75028
River Hill Ct & Dr 75022
River Oaks Dr 75028
Riverplace Dr 75028
Riviera Ct 75022
Roadrunner Dr 75022
Robin Ln 75028
Rochdale Dr 75028
Rock Cv 75028
Rock Cliff Ln 75028
Rock Haven Ct & Dr 75022
Rock Ridge Dr 75028
Rockcreek Ct 75028
Rocky Point Rd 75022
Rodney Cir 75022
Rolling Hls 75022
Rolling Oaks Dr 75022
Rollo Ct 75028
Romana Ct 75022
Rose Bluff Ter 75028
Rosebud Ct 75028
Rosemary Dr 75028
Rosena Trl 75028
Rosewood Trl 75028
Rothschild Dr 75022
Roundrock Way 75022
Royal Ct 75028
Royal Oaks Dr 75022
Ruby Crest Ct 75022
Rue De Isabelle 75022
Rue Jordan 75022
Russwood Dr 75028
Rustic Timbers Ln 75028
Ryans Pl 75022
Saddle Dr 75022
Saddle Ridge Trl 75028
Saddleback Ln 75028
Sagebrush Dr
2100-2699 75028
2800-3299 75022
Saint Andrews Dr 75022
Saint Charles Ct 75022
Saint Clair Ct 75022
Saint Francis Ln 75028
Saint James Ct 75028
Saint Mark Dr 75022
Salisbury Ln 75022
Samuel Ct 75028
San Bernard Ct 75028
San Jacinto Dr 75028
San Paula Dr 75022
Sandera Ct & Ln 75028
Sandhurst Dr 75022
Sandra Lynn Dr 75022
Sandstone Ct 75022
Sandy Ln 75022
Sanmar Dr 75028
Santa Monica St 75022
Sarah Springs Trl 75022
Saturn St 75028
Savannah Ct 75028
Sawgrass Ct 75022
Scenic Dr 75022
Scenic Fir Pl 75028
Schooner Ct 75022
Scott Dr 75022
Seafarer Ct 75022
Seascape Ct 75022
Seaton Ct 75028
Seaview Dr 75022
Sedalia Ct & Dr 75028
Sedona St 75022
Seminole Cir 75022
Sentinel Oaks Dr 75022
Seville Ln 75022
Shadow Oak Ct 75028
Shady Trl 75022
Shady Creek Dr 75022
Shady Oaks Dr 75022
Shadywood Ct & Ln 75022
Shamrock Dr 75028

Sharondale Dr 75022
Shasta Ln 75028
Shawnee Trl 75022
Sheffield Ct & Ln 75028
Shelby Ct 75022
Shelley Dr 75022
Shelmar Dr 75028
Shenandoah Ln 75028
Shepherd Pl 75028
Sherri Ln 75028
Sherwood Dr 75028
Sheryl Dr 75022
Shiloh Rd 75028
Shorecrest 75022
Shorefront Ln 75022
Shoreline Dr 75022
Shoshone Trl 75022
Shumard Ln 75028
Sicily Way 75028
Sidney Ln 75022
Sierra Ln 75028
Silver Maple Ct 75028
Silverleaf Ct 75028
Silveron 75028
Silverthorn Ln 75028
Silverwood Dr 75028
Simmons Rd 75022
Simmons Creek Ct &
Ln 75022
Singing Brook Rd 75028
Skelton St 75022
Skillern Blvd 75022
Skinner Dr 75022
Skyline Dr 75028
Slash Pine Dr 75028
Sleepy Lagoon 75022
Solano Dr 75022
Somerset Dr 75022
Sonoma Bnd 75022
Sorrel Ct 75028
South Dr 75022
Southern Hills Ct & Dr 75022
Southernwood Ct 75022
Southfalls Ct 75022
Southampton Ct 75028
Southmoor Trl 75022
Southwestern Dr 75028
Southwicke Dr 75022
Spanish Oak Dr 75028
Spinks Rd
1000-1398 75028
1400-1500 75028
1502-2098 75028
2601-2697 75022
2699-2700 75022
2702-2798 75022
Spinniker Ct 75028
Spring Meadow Ln 75028
Spring Ridge Ln 75028
Springwater Dr 75028
Springwood Cir & Rd 75028
Spruce St 75028
Squires Dr 75028
Stallion Cir 75022
Stanford Ct & Dr 75022
Stanton Ct 75028
Stapleton Ln 75028
Starleaf Pl 75022
Starlight Trl 75022
Staton Oak Dr 75022
Steamboat Dr 75022
Steeple Point Pl 75022
Steppington Ave 75022
Stevenson Ln 75028
Stewart Way 75022
Stillwater Ct 75022
Stone Ct 75028
Stone Bend Ln 75028
Stone Bridge Dr 75028
Stone Creek Dr 75028
Stone Crest Dr 75028
Stone Hill Farms Pkwy 75022
Stone Trace Ln 75028
Stone Trail Dr 75028
Stonehedge Pl 75028
Stonehenge Ln 75028

Stonehill Ct 75022
Stonewood Ct 75028
Stoney Brook Ln 75028
Strait Ln 75028
Stratford Ln 75028
Strawn Ct 75028
Sugarberry Ln 75028
Sumac Dr 75028
Summer Trl 75028
Summerfields Dr 75028
Summit Cir 75028
Sun Meadow Dr 75022
Sun Ridge Dr 75028
Sunbrook Cir 75028
Suncreek Path 75028
Suncrest Dr 75028
Sundale Dr 75028
Sundown Dr 75028
Sunflower Ln 75028
Sunlight Dr 75028
Sunnyside Dr 75028
Sunnyview Ln 75022
Sunset Trl 75022
Sunstar Ln 75028
Suntree Ln 75022
Superior Ct, Dr & Pl 75028
Surrey Ct, Dr & Ln 75022
Surrey Woods Ct &
Rd 75028
Surveyors Ln 75022
Sutters Way 75022
Sweet Grass Trl 75028
Sweetgum Ct 75028
Sweetwater Ln 75028
Sycamore Dr 75028
Sycamore Leaf Ln 75022
Tanglewood Ln 75028
Tanyard Ct 75022
Tara Ct 75028
Tarragon Dr 75028
Taylor Ct 75028
Teaberry Ct 75028
Teakwood Ct & Dr 75028
Tealwood Blvd, Cir &
Ln 75028
Telluride Dr 75028
Temple Dr 75028
Tennyson Dr 75028
Teresa Dr 75022
Termaine Dr 75022
Thames Ct 75028
Thistle Hill Cir 75022
Thistlewood Ct 75022
Thomas Rd 75022
Thompson Ct 75028
Thoreau Cir 75022
Thorn Trl 75028
Thrush Rd 75028
Tiffany Dr 75022
Timber Ct 75022
Timber Creek Rd &
Trl 75028
Timber Meadow Dr 75028
Timber Park Dr 75028
Timber Ridge Ln 75028
Timber Trail Dr 75028
Timber Valley Cir & Dr 75028
Timberglen Dr 75028
Timberhaven Ct & Dr 75028
Timberhill Dr 75028
Timberlake Ct 75022
Timberland Pkwy 75028
Timberline Dr 75028
Timberview Ct & Dr 75028
Timberwood Dr 75028
Timothy Dr 75022
Tinsdale Dr 75022
Tony Dr 75022
Topaz Ct 75022
Tophill Dr & Ln 75022
Torrey Pine Dr 75028
Torreya Ct 75022
Tour 18 Dr 75022
Tournament Ln 75028
Towne View Blvd & Ct 75028
Townsend Dr 75028

Trail Ridge Ln 75028
Trails End Dr 75028
Trailwood Ln 75028
Travis Ct 75028
Tree Line Rd 75028
Trellis Trl 75022
Trevor Ct 75028
Trinity Ct 75028
Trogdon Ct 75022
Trotter Ln 75028
Tulane St 75022
Turtle Cv 75028
Twain Dr 75028
Twilight Dr 75028
Twin Oaks Ct 75028
Upton Ln 75028
Vail Ln 75028
Valencia Ct 75022
Valencia Dr 75028
Valley View Ln 75022
Valleydale Dr 75028
Valleywood Dr 75028
Vanderbilt Dr 75022
Veronica Dr 75022
Versailles Pl 75022
Vicksberry Trl 75022
Victory Ct & Dr 75028
Village Crest Ct & Dr 75022
Village Oaks Trl 75022
Vintage Pl 75028
Virginia Pkwy 75022
Wager Rd 75028
Waketon Rd 75028
Walden Blvd & Ct 75022
Walnut St 75028
Walnut Grove Pl 75022
Wanda Ln 75022
Wareham Ln 75022
Warrington Ave 75028
Warwick Ave 75028
Water Oak Ct & Dr 75028
Waterbend Dr 75028
Waterford Dr 75028
Waterstone Trl 75028
Waterview 75022
Waverly Rd 75028
Wayne Ct 75028
Wayside Ln 75022
Weathervane Ln 75028
Weatherwood Dr 75028
Welborne Ln 75022
Welch Ct 75028
Wembley Cir 75022
Wennington Dr 75022
Wentworth Dr 75028
Westerville Ct 75028
Westin Ln 75028
Westminister Trl 75022
Westwood Dr 75028
Whispering Oaks 75022
White Bud Ct 75028
White Oak Ct 75028
White Pine Dr 75028
Whitman Ln 75028
Whitney Ln 75028
Whittier St 75028
Wichita Trl 75022
Wickersham Dr 75022
Wicklow Ct 75022
Widgon Way 75028
Wild Honey Ct 75022
Wildflower Ln 75028
Wildgrove Ct & Dr 75022
Wildwood Dr 75028
Willow Ct, Run & St 75028
Willowood Ln 75028
Willowross Way 75028
Wilshire Ln 75028
Wimbledon Dr 75028
Wind Swept Ct 75022
Windchase Dr 75028
Winding Creek Blvd 75022
Winding Oaks Dr 75022
Winding Path Way 75022
Windmill Ct & Ln 75028
Windridge Ln 75028
Windsor Dr 75028
Windsor Centre Trl 75028
Winnpage Rd 75022
Winslow Ave & Ct 75028
Wisdom Creek Ct & Dr 75022
Wise Ln 75022
Wisteria Ct 75028
Withers Ave 75028
Withers Rd 75022
Witherspoon Way 75022
Wolcott Dr 75028
Wolf Creek Trl 75028
Wood Trl 75022
Wood Creek Cir & Dr 75028
Wood Duck Way 75028
Woodberry Dr 75022
Woodbine St 75028
Woodbury Dr 75028
Woodhaven Dr 75028
Woodhill Dr 75022
Woodhollow Dr 75022
Woodland Blvd 75022
Woodland Hills Ct 75022
Woodmont Dr 75022
Woodpark Dr 75022
Woodridge Dr 75022
Woodstone Ct 75022
Woodview Dr 75028
Woodway Dr 75028
Yaggi Dr 75028
Yale Dr 75022
Yeddo Path 75028
Yorkshire Ct 75028
Youngworth Dr 75028
Youpon St 75028
Yucca Dr 75028
Zachary Way 75028
Zane Dr 75028

NUMBERED STREETS

1 Place Ln 75028
3 Bridges Dr 75022

FORT WORTH TX

General Delivery 76102
General Delivery 76161

POST OFFICE BOXES MAIN OFFICE STATIONS AND BRANCHES

Box No.s
1 - 1996 76101
2001 - 3572 76113
4000 - 4938 76164
6000 - 6995 76115
7000 - 7959 76111
8001 - 8996 76124
9000 - 9880 76147
9997 - 9997 76110
10001 - 10998 76114
11001 - 12920 76110
15000 - 15976 76119
16001 - 16994 76162
17001 - 17919 76102
19001 - 19436 76119
24001 - 25636 76124
26500 - 26996 76126
33001 - 35436 76162
40001 - 41320 76140
48001 - 48960 76148
50001 - 51618 76105
60000 - 60835 76115
64001 - 64956 76164
76191 - 76199 76161
77001 - 77980 76177
79001 - 79779 76179
99001 - 99429 76161
100001 - 102034 76185
107001 - 107120 76111
121001 - 124056 76121
126001 - 127354 76126
136001 - 137560 76136
150001 - 152296 76108
155001 - 156560 76155
161001 - 165194 76161
185001 - 185896 76181
330001 - 331976 76163
470001 - 472600 76147
900000 - 900000 76161
901001 - 901105 76101
902001 - 902010 76102
908001 - 908001 76108
911004 - 911004 76111
915001 - 915426 76115
916046 - 916820 76161
919002 - 919002 76119
921001 - 921554 76121
924003 - 924998 76124
926001 - 926002 76126
947001 - 947998 76147
950002 - 955986 76155
961001 - 961998 76161
962001 - 962020 76162
964998 - 964998 76164
970525 - 970765 76161
977001 - 977002 76177
980004 - 980004 76161
985001 - 985015 76185
994111 - 994113 76161

RURAL ROUTES

08, 106, 108, 11, 15, 18, 20, 30, 44, 58, 63, 86, 91 76108
36, 52, 64 76118
42 76119
04, 136, 16, 24, 29, 37, 69 76120
101, 115, 26, 33, 45, 48, 50, 54, 65, 72, 76, 81, 92 76123
05, 110, 135, 17, 53, 90 76126
102, 113, 117, 127, 133, 51, 60, 62, 75, 85, 88, 94 76131
93 76132
79 76133
126, 31, 32, 89 76134
02, 10, 25, 97 76135
100, 129, 74 76137
03, 07, 112, 40, 83 76140
131, 38, 39, 55 76155
01 76177

HIGHWAY CONTRACTS

01 76177
01, 06, 09, 104, 105, 107, 114, 118, 134, 137, 14, 28, 43, 47, 56, 66, 68, 87, 95, 96 76179

NAMED STREETS

Abaco Way 76123
Abbey Ct 76119
Abbott Dr 76108
Abelia Ct 76108
Aberdeen Dr 76116
Abney Ave 76110
Acacia St 76109
Academy Blvd 76108
Acapulco Rd 76112
Acme Brick Plz 76109
Acoma Trl 76177
Acorn Ct 76179
Acorn Run 76109
Ada Ave 76105
Adallont Dr 76109
Adam Ave 76164
Adam Grubb 76135
Adams Dr 76117
S Adams St
100-1699 76104
1700-4099 76110
4100-5699 76115
Adams Fall Ln 76123
Adcock Ct 76137
Addington Dr 76135
Addison Dr 76244
Adelbert Dr 76135
Adell St 76108
Aden Rd 76116
Adler Trl 76179
Admiralty Way 76108
Adobe Dr 76123
Adolph St 76107
Adolphus Cir 76120
Adonia Dr 76131
Adrian Dr 76107
Adriana Ave 76120
Aeronca Dr 76179
Afton Rd 76134
Agate Pl 76135
Agave Way 76126
Aidan Ct 76244
Aiken Ln 76123
Aimsley Ct 76137
Ainsdale Dr 76135
Ainsly Ln 76244
Airline Dr 76118
Airport Fwy
2200-2299 76102
2400-4099 76111
4100-6899 76117
6900-7000 76118
7001-7699 76118
7002-7698 76118
15000-15098 76155
Airway Dr 76106
Akers Ave 76111
Ala Dr 76108
Alabama Ave 76104
Alaire Dr 76132
Alamo Ave 76107
Alamosa St 76119
Alan Ct 76148
Alanbrooke Ct & Dr 76140
Alandale Dr 76119
Alava Dr 76133
Albany Dr 76131
Albatross Ct 76126
Albatross Ln 76177
Albermarle Ct & Dr 76132
Albert Ave 76116
Albert St 76108
Alcannon St 76119
Alcatel Ln 76102
Alden Dr 76134
Aldersyde Dr 76244
Aldra Dr 76120
Aledo Rd 76126
Aledo Creeks Rd E 76126
Aledo Grove Ct 76126
Aledo Iona Rd 76126
Aledo Oaks Ct 76126
Aledo Ridge Rd 76126
Aledo Springs Ct 76126
Alemeda Ct 76108
Alemeda St
2900-2998 76108
3000-3098 76116
3301-3399 76116
3400-3698 76126
Alex St 76179
Alexander Dr 76112
Alexandra Ct 76244
Alexandra Meadows Dr 76131
Alexandria Ct 76133
Alexandria Sky Ln 76119
Alexis Ave 76120
Algerita St 76119
Alhambra Ct & Dr 76119
Alicante Ave 76133
Alice Rd 76135
Alice St 76110
Alicia Dr 76133
All Saints Ave 76104
E Allen Ave
100-299 76110
600-1599 76104
W Allen Ave 76110
Allen Mill Ct 76135
Allen Place Dr 76116
Allena Ln 76118
Allencrest Dr 76108
Allenwood Dr 76134
Alliance Blvd 76177
Alliance Gateway Fwy 76177
Allison Ln 76140
Alloway Dr 76119
Alma St 76140
Almena Rd 76114
Almond Ln 76244
Almondale Dr 76131
Almondtree Dr 76140
Alpena Dr 76131
Alpine St 76126
Alread Ct 76102
Alsace Ct 76134
Alston Ave
300-1699 76104
1700-2399 76110
Alsue St 76140
Alta Dr 76107
Alta Canada Ln 76177
Alta Loma Dr 76244
Alta Mere Dr
401-497 76114
499-599 76114
600-698 76116
601-699 76114
700-3599 76116
E Alta Mesa Blvd 76140
N Alta Mesa Ct 76108
S Alta Mesa Ct 76108
Alta Mesa Dr 76108
Alta Mira Cir 76132
Alta Sierra Dr 76126
Alta View St 76111
Alta Vista Dr 76148
Alta Vista Rd 76244
Altamesa Blvd
101-1003 76134
1001-1005 76115
1900-1998 76134
2000-2299 76134
2300-3702 76133
3701-3701 76163
3703-5251 76133
3704-5098 76133
5200-5250 76123
5252-5299 76123
5300-5498 76133
5301-5499 76123
5900-6899 76132
6901-6999 76123
Altamesa Blvd E 76134
Altamont Dr 76106
Alter Dr 76119
Altomonte Dr 76132
Alton Rd 76109
Altura Ct & Rd 76109
Alverstone Dr 76120
Alvord Ave 76111
Alwood Ct 76135
Alyse Dr 76137
Alyssa Ct & Dr 76108
Alysse Way 76179
Alyssum Dr 76244
Amador Dr 76244
Amanda Ave 76105
Amaryllis Ln 76108
Amber Ct 76133
Amber Dr
700-899 76179
6800-6999 76133
7300-7499 76148
Amber Dr S 76133
Amberdale Dr 76137
Amberjack Trl 76179
Ambling Trl 76108
Ambrosia Dr 76244
American Blvd 76155
American Flyer Blvd 76108
Americana Blvd 76131
Amethyst Dr 76131
Amherst Ave 76114
Amhurst Cir 76132
Amistad Ct & St 76137
Ammons St 76117
Amon Carter Blvd 76155
Amon Carter Sq 76107
Amory Dr 76126
Amspoker Ave 76115
Anahuac Ave 76114
Anchor Ct 76135
Anchorage Ct 76179
Anchorage Pl 76135
Anchura Ct 76137
Andante Dr 76134
Andenwood Ct & Dr 76140
Anderson Blvd
4400-4599 76117
6800-8699 76120
Anderson Rd 76117
Anderson St
100-299 76179
5100-5499 76105
5500-5799 76119
Andora Ave 76133
Andover St 76114
Andrea Ct 76114
Andrea Ln 76119
Andress Dr 76132
Andrew Ave 76105
Anewby Ct & Way 76133
Angel Fire Rd 76244
Angel Food Ln 76244
Angela Ct 76140
Angelica St 76244
Angelina Way 76137
Angle Ave
2600-2799 76164
2800-4499 76106
Angle Dr 76117
Anglin Cir 76140
Anglin Dr
3500-3800 76119
3802-3898 76119
6100-6619 76119
6620-7499 76140
7500-8499 76140
Angoni Way 76131
Angus Dr
3900-4699 76116
5900-6199 76179
Animas Ct 76140
Anita Ave 76109
Anmar Ct 76140
Ann Ct 76108
Ann Ln 76140
Ann Ln N 76140
Ann St 76104
Ann Arbor Ct 76109
Anna St 76103
Annabelle Ln 76119
Annalea Dr 76123
Annandale Dr 76132
Annapolis Dr 76108
Anne Ct 76148
Annels Ct 76109
Annette Dr 76108
Annglen Dr 76119
E & W Annie St 76104
Ansley Dr 76114
Ansley Rd 76179
Anthony Dr 76108
E Anthony St 76115
W Anthony St 76115
Anvil Ct 76179
Apache Ct 76119
Apache Trl 76135
Apalachee Trl 76179
Apollo Dr 76108
Appalachian Way 76123
Appaloosa Cir & Dr 76179
Appian Way 76135
Apple Tree Ct 76179
Applesprings Dr 76244
Appletree Ct 76140
Appletree Way 76244
Applewood Rd 76133
Appleyard Dr 76137
Appomattox Dr 76140
April Ln 76148
April Breeze Ct 76120
April Sound Ct 76120
April Springs Dr 76134
Aquilla Dr 76108
Arabella Ct 76120
Arabian Ave 76179
Arado Dr 76131
Aragon Dr 76133
Aransas Dr 76131
Arbol Ct
100-199 76108
4900-4999 76126
Arbor Ave
3500-4399 76119
7100-8299 76116
Arbor Bnd 76132
Arbor Dr 76123
Arbor Ln 76132
Arbor Pl 76132
Arbor Rdg 76132
Arbor Crest Ct 76179
Arbor Gate St 76133
Arbor Glen Ct & Dr 76140
Arbor Hill Ct & Dr 76120
Arbor Mill Dr 76135
Arbor Park Dr 76120
Arbor Ridge Ct & Dr 76112
Arborlawn Dr 76109
Arborwood Trl 76123
Arc Dr 76114
Arcadia Ct 76137
Arcadia St 76179
Arcadia Trl 76137
Arcadia Park Dr 76244
Arch St 76105
Arch Adams Ln & St 76107
Archer Dr 76244
Archer Ln 76119
Arden Pl 76103
Ardenwood Dr 76123
Arena Cir 76179
Ariel Ln 76119
Arizona Ave 76104
Arlan Ln 76109
Arlene Dr 76108
Arles Ct 76107
Arlie Ave 76116
E Arlington Ave 76104
W Arlington Ave 76110
Arlington Lakeshore Dr 76119
Armando Ave 76133
Armour Dr 76244
Armstrong Ct
6700-6799 76137
8900-8999 76126
Arnold Ct 76111
Arnold Dr 76140
Arrendondo Way 76126
Arrow Ln 76114
Arrow Wood St 76126
Arrowhead Ct 76103
Arrowhead Rd 76132
Arrowhead St 76108
Arrowwood Dr 76115
Arroyo Ct 76108
Arroyo Dr 76108
Arroyo Ln 76126
Arroyo Rd 76109
Arroyo Trl 76135
Arthur Dr 76134
Arthur St 76107
Aruba Ln 76123
Arundel Ave 76109
Asbury Ave 76119
Asbury Dr
200-599 76179
5500-5502 76114
5501-5503 76114

5504-5599 76114
Ash Ct
1100-1199 76126
6500-6599 76148
Ash Creek Ln 76177
Ash Crescent St 76104
Ash Flat Dr 76131
Ash Grove Trl 76112
Ash Meadow Cir & Dr 76131
Ash Park Dr 76118
Ash River Ct & Rd 76137
Ashancol Rd 76131
Asharint Dr 76179
Ashberry St 76106
Ashbourne Way 76133
Ashbriar Ln 76126
Ashbrook Dr 76132
Ashbury Dr 76133
Ashcroft Cir 76120
Ashdale Dr 76140
Ashe Ct 76112
Asher Ct 76131
Asheville Ln 76123
Ashford Ave & Ct 76133
Ashland Ave 76107
Ashley Ct 76123
Ashley Dr
1900-1999 76134
5300-5399 76137
Ashley Ln
100-199 76108
3700-3899 76123
Ashmont Ct & Ln 76244
Ashmore Dr 76131
Ashridge Rd 76134
Ashton Ave 76137
Ashville Ave 76116
Ashwood Cir 76123
Askew St 76244
Aspen Ct 76126
Aspen Ct N 76137
Aspen Ln 76112
Aspen Way 76137
Aspen Creek Dr 76244
Aspen Ridge Dr 76108
Aspen Wood Cir 76132
Aspen Wood Ct 76179
Aspen Wood Trl 76132
Assembly Ct & Rd 76179
Asta Ct 76126
Aster Ave & Ct 76111
Aster Ridge Dr 76244
Astor Dr 76244
Astoria Ct 76148
Atascosa Ave 76120
Atchison Dr 76131
Atco Dr 76118
Athenia Dr 76114
Athens Way 76123
Atkins St 76115
Atlanta St 76104
Aton Ave 76114
Aubrac Way 76131
Aubrey Ct 76140
Auburn Dr 76123
Auburn St 76114
Auburn Ridge Dr 76123
Audras Way E 76116
Audubon Trl 76132
Augusta Ct 76132
Augusta Dr 76106
Augusta Ln 76137
Augusta Rd
1100-1599 76126
6600-6699 76132
6701-6799 76132
Aurora Ct 76117
Aurora Dr 76108
Aurora St 76117
Austin Ln 76111
Austin Pl 76135
Austin Rd 76118
Austin St 76107
Austin Creek Ct 76140
Austin Ridge Dr 76179
Auto Ct 76179

Autumn Ct 76109
Autumn Dr 76109
Autumn Ln 76148
Autumn Park 76140
Autumn Breeze Cir 76140
Autumn Creek Trl 76134
Autumn Falls Dr 76118
Autumn Glen Dr 76140
Autumn Hills Dr 76140
Autumn Lea Dr 76140
Autumn Leaves Trl 76244
Autumn Meadow St 76155
Autumn Moon Dr 76140
Autumn Park Ct & Dr 76140
Autumn Run Dr 76140
Autumn Sage Dr 76108
Ava Court Dr 76112
Avalon Ct 76103
Avalon Dr 76148
Avenel Ct & Way 76177
Aventine Ln 76244
Avenue E
1400-2099 76104
Avenue E
2700-3699 76105
Avenue N 76105
Avenue A 76105
Avenue B
1700-2299 76104
2500-3399 76105
Avenue C
1900-2199 76104
2700-3499 76105
Avenue D
1400-2199 76104
2700-3599 76105
Avenue F 76105
Avenue G 76105
N Avenue H 76105
Avenue I 76105
Avenue J 76105
Avenue K 76105
Avenue L 76105
Avenue M 76105
Avery Dr 76132
Aviation Way 76106
Aviator Dr 76179
Aviator Way 76177
Aviemore Dr 76109
Avington Way 76133
Avoca St 76132
Avon St 76134
Avondale St 76109
Avondale Ridge Dr 76179
Avonshire Ln 76137
Avril Ct N & S 76116
Axis Ct 76132
Axis Deer Run 76179
N Ayers Ave 76103
S Ayers Ave
300-999 76103
1000-2799 76105
Azalea Ave 76107
Azalea Dr 76137
Azle Ave
2000-2399 76164
2400-3600 76106
3602-5898 76106
5001-5999 76114
6000-6899 76135
Azle Way 76135
Aztec Ct & Dr 76135
Azteca Dr 76112
Babbling Brook Dr
600-699 76179
11700-11799 76244
Baby Doe Ct 76137
Bachman Dr 76108
Backstretch Ct 76126
Bacon Dr 76244
Badger Creek Ln 76177
Badlands Dr 76179
Bailey Ave 76107
N Bailey Ave 76107
Bailey St 76179

E Bailey Boswell Rd
100-199 76179
200-1199 76131
W Bailey Boswell Rd 76179
Baird Dr 76134
Baker Blvd 76118
Baker St 76104
Bakers Ln 76117
Bal Harbour Ct 76179
Bal Lake Dr 76116
Balanced Rock Dr 76131
Balboa Dr 76133
Balcones Ct & Dr 76108
Balcony Dr 76132
Bald Eagle Ct 76135
Baldemar Ln 76102
Baldwin Ave
3500-3799 76110
4100-4399 76115
Baldwin Ln E 76140
Baldwin Ln W 76140
Balfour Dr 76140
Ball Rd 76140
Ballinger St 76102
S Ballinger St 76104
Ballington Dr 76116
Balsam St 76111
Balsam Wood Ct 76179
Balta Dr 76244
E Baltimore Ave 76104
W Baltimore Ave 76110
Baltusrol Rd 76132
Balwood Dr 76134
Bamberg Ln 76244
Bamberry Dr 76133
Banbury Ct & Dr 76119
Bancroft Cir 76120
Bancroft Dr 76126
Bandelier Trl 76137
Bandera Rd 76116
Bandera St 76126
Bandy Ave 76134
Bangor Dr 76116
Baninced Rd 76140
W Bank Landing St 76107
Banks Rd 76140
Banks St 76114
Banner Dr 76137
Bannock Dr 76179
Bar Wood Dr 76179
Barada Ct 76133
Barbara Ct 76148
Barbara Dr
1101-1199 76126
9100-9299 76108
Barbara Rd 76114
Barbell Ln 76111
Barber Ln 76126
Barberry Dr 76133
Barcelona Dr 76133
Barclay Ave 76111
Barcus Cir 76134
Barden St 76107
Bareback Ln 76131
Barenney Ave 76106
Bark Wood Ct 76135
Barkridge Trl 76109
Barksdale Dr 76244
Barley Dr 76179
Barnett St
3800-5099 76103
5100-5199 76112
Barneys Pl 76126
Barnhill Ln 76135
Baroque Dr 76119
Barr St 76110
Barracks Dr 76177
Barrier Reef Dr 76179
E Barron Ave 76140
W Barron Ave 76140
Barron Ln 76112
Barron St 76103
Barron Way 76140
Barry Dr 76148
Barrywood Ct & St 76112
Bartlett Cir 76108

Barton Hills Dr 76112
Barwick Dr 76132
Basalt Way 76131
Base St 76135
Baseline Ln 76133
Basil Ave 76134
Basil Leaf St 76244
Basilwood Dr 76244
Basset Locke Dr 76108
Basswood Blvd
801-899 76131
3000-3098 76137
3100-5699 76137
Basswood Ct
1100-1199 76131
5000-5099 76135
Basswood Dr 76135
Battle Creek Ct & Rd 76116
Baugh Ln 76244
Baurline St 76111
Baxter Ln 76119
Bay Ct 76179
N & S Bay Breeze Ct & Ln 76179
Bay Hill Ct 76132
Bay Lake Dr 76179
Bay Laurel Ln 76108
Bay Oaks Ct 76112
Bay View Dr 76244
Bayard St 76244
Bayberry Dr 76137
Bayline Dr 76133
Baylor Ave 76114
Baylor St 76119
Baymort Ct 76112
Bayridge Ct 76179
Bayshore Ct 76179
Bayside Dr 76132
Baytree Dr 76137
Baywater Ct 76179
Bea Ct 76135
Beach Dr 76179
Beach Rd 76126
Beach St
100-299 76111
301-899 76111
1700-2499 76103
N Beach St
100-1299 76111
1300-1898 76111
1301-3599 76111
1900-2300 76111
2302-3598 76111
3600-6598 76137
3601-6597 76137
6599-7999 76137
8200-12699 76244
S Beach St 76105
W Beach St 76111
Beachview Ln 76179
Beacon Ct & Way 76140
Beal St 76103
Bear Trl 76126
Bear Creek Dr E 76126
Bear Creek Trl 76244
Bear Hollow Ct 76137
Bear Hollow Dr 76244
Bear Hollow Ln 76137
Bear Lake Dr 76137
Bear Path Trl 76126
Beasley Ct 76126
Beaty Ct & St 76112
Beaufort Ct 76123
Beaumont St 76106
Beauvior Dr 76120
Beaver Trl 76134
Beaver Creek Dr 76177
Beaver Head Rd 76137
Beaver Ridge Dr 76137
Beckham Pl 76104
Beckwood Dr 76112
E Beddell St 76115
W Beddell St
400-1699 76115
3600-3699 76133
Bedford St 76107

Bedfordshire Dr 76135
Bedington Ln 76244
Bedrock Dr 76123
Bee Balm Dr 76123
Bee Creek Ln 76120
Bee Tree Ln 76133
Beechcreek Dr 76134
Beechgrove Ct & Ter 76140
Beechwood Dr 76116
Beekman Dr 76244
Beetle Dr 76148
Begonia Ct 76244
Belcross Ln 76133
Belden Ave 76132
Belford Ave 76103
Belfry Ct 76179
E Belknap St
100-1699 76102
2400-3900 76111
3901-3997 76111
3902-3998 76111
3999-4199 76111
4200-6299 76117
W Belknap St 76102
Bell Ave 76131
W Bell St 76140
Bell Helicopter Blvd 76118
Bella Cir 76120
Bella Amore Dr 76126
Bella Angelo Ct 76126
Bella Colina Dr 76126
Bella Flora Ct & Dr 76126
Bella Italia Ct & Dr 76126
Bella Milano Dr 76126
Bella Palazzo Dr 76126
Bella Roma Dr 76126
Bella Rosa Ct 76126
Bella Sereno Ct 76126
Bella Terra Dr 76126
Bella Villa Dr 76126
Bella Vino Dr 76126
Bella Vista Dr 76112
Bella Vita Dr 76126
Belladonna Dr 76123
Bellaire Cir 76109
Bellaire Ct S 76132
Bellaire Dr 76132
Bellaire Dr N 76109
Bellaire Dr S
3400-5522 76109
5524-5608 76109
5601-5609 76109
5611-5699 76109
5701-5799 76109
6200-7699 76132
7701-7799 76132
Bellaire Dr W 76109
Bellaire Country Pl 76132
Bellaire Park Ct 76109
Bellaire Ranch Dr 76109
Bellchase Dr 76120
Bellcrest Ct 76135
Belle Ave 76164
Belle Pl 76107
Bellflower Way 76123
Bellis Dr 76244
Bellvue Ct & Dr 76134
Bellwood Ct 76109
Belmeade Dr 76115
Belmont Ave 76164
Belmont St 76179
Belmont Stakes Dr 76179
Belshire Ct 76140
Belstrum Pl 76137
Belton St 76118
Belvedere Dr 76244
Belzise Ter 76104
S Ben Ave & St 76103
Ben Day Murrin Rd N 76126
Ben Hall Ct 76110
Ben Hogan Ln 76244
Benares Ct 76133
Benavente Ct 76126
Benbridge Dr 76107
Benbrook Blvd
2300-2499 76110

2500-3399 76109
4734-5098 76116
Benbrook Dr 76110
Benbrook Hwy 76116
Benbrook Pkwy 76126
Benbrook Ter 76126
Benbrook Lake Dr 76123
Bend Ct 76177
Bendale Rd 76116
Bending Oak Dr 76108
Bendry St 76119
Benito Ct 76126
Benjamin St 76164
Benmar St 76103
Bennett St
800-999 76102
8301-8399 76108
Benning Way 76177
Bennington Dr 76148
Bens Trl 76120
Bent Creek Ct & Dr 76137
Bent Creek Ranch Ct 76126
Bent Green Way 76179
Bent Oak Dr 76131
Bent Rose Way 76177
Bent Spur Dr 76179
Bentley Ave 76137
Bentley Gate St 76120
Benton Ave 76112
Bentree Dr 76120
Bentwood Ct 76132
Benview Ct 76126
Berend Ct 76116
Bergstrom Ln 76155
Berke Pl 76116
Berke Rd 76115
Berkeley Pl 76110
Berkshire Dr 76137
Berkshire Dr E 76137
Berkshire Ln 76134
Bermejo Rd 76112
Bernadine Dr 76148
Berner St 76111
Bernese Ln 76131
Bernice St 76117
Bernie Anderson Ave 76116
Berrenda Dr 76131
E Berry St
100-1299 76110
1300-2399 76119
2400-4999 76105
5000-6099 76119
E Berry St S 76119
W Berry St
100-2499 76110
2500-3399 76109
Berrybrook Dr
1900-1999 76134
7900-8099 76148
Berrybush Ln 76137
Berryhill Dr 76105
Berrywood Trl 76244
Bert St 76117
Bertha Ave 76105
Bertha Ln 76117
Bertrose St 76107
Beryl St 76111
Bessie St 76104
Bethlehem St 76111
Bethune St 76105
Betsy Ross Ct 76148
Bettibart St 76134
Bettis Dr 76133
Betty Dr 76148
Betty Ln 76117
Bevans St 76111
Beverly Ave 76104
Beverly Dr 76117
Beverly Dr E 76132
Beverly Dr W 76132
Beverly Glen Dr 76132
Beverly Hills Dr 76114
E Bewick St 76110
W Bewick St
100-1799 76110
2600-2899 76109

Bewley Ct 76244
Bewley Dr 76244
Bewley St 76117
Bianca Cir 76132
Bickmore Ln 76244
E Biddison St 76110
W Biddison St
100-2499 76110
2700-3999 76109
Bideker Ave 76105
Big Bear Ln 76126
Big Bend Ct 76137
Big Bend Dr 76137
Big Bend St 76114
Big Bend Trl 76135
Big Creek Ct 76132
Big Cypress Ct 76137
Big Flat Dr 76131
Big Fork Rd 76119
Big Horn Ct 76108
Big Horn Way 76137
Big Oak Dr 76131
Big Sky Ln 76131
Big Spring Ct & Dr 76120
Big Spruce Ln 76123
Big Stone Ct 76123
Big Thicket Dr 76244
Big Wichita Dr 76179
Big Willow Ct & Dr 76179
Big Wood Ct 76135
Biggs St 76177
Bigham Blvd 76116
Bigleaf Ln 76137
Bilglade Rd
2400-2599 76115
2700-3899 76133
3900-4399 76109
Billings Rd
4301-4397 76108
4399-4499 76108
5700-6199 76135
Billy Mitchell Ave 76114
Biloxi Dr 76133
Bilsky Bay Dr 76140
Bindweed St 76123
Bing Dr 76108
Bingham Dr 76117
Binkley St 76105
Binyon Ave 76133
Birch Creek Rd 76244
Birch Grove Ln 76137
Birch Hollow Ln 76132
Birch Park Dr 76118
Birchbend Ln 76137
Birchill Rd 76148
Birchman Ave 76107
Birchwood Ln 76108
Bird Ct, Pl & St 76111
Birdell St 76105
Birds Eye Rd 76177
Birdsong Dr 76140
Birdville Way 76244
Birkdale Dr 76116
Bisbee St 76119
Biscayne Ct 76117
Biscayne Dr 76117
Biscayne Ln 76133
Bishop Ave 76105
Bishop Ct 76179
Bishop St
1000-3299 76105
3400-3599 76119
Bishops Flower 76109
Bison Ct
5300-5399 76137
9700-9999 76244
Bison Trl
6700-6799 76137
11200-11298 76108
Bittersweet Dr 76120
Biway St 76114
Black Dr 76137
Black Ash Dr 76131
Black Bass Dr 76179
Black Bear Ct 76137
Black Canyon Rd 76109

Black Forest Ct & Ln ... 76140
Black Hills Ct & Ln ... 76137
Black Leaf Ct ... 76135
Black Maple Dr ... 76244
Black Mesa Ct ... 76179
Black Oak Ln ... 76114
Black Sumac Dr ... 76131
Black Wing Dr ... 76137
Blackberry Trl ... 76120
Blackburn Dr ... 76120
Blackerby Cv ... 76140
Blackhaw Ave ... 76109
Blackmon Ct ... 76137
Blackmore Ave ... 76107
Blackstone Dr ... 76114
Blackthorn Dr ... 76137
Blair Ct ... 76132
Blair St ... 76108
Blairwood Dr ... 76134
Blake Ct ... 76137
Blaketree Dr ... 76177
Blalock Ave ... 76115
Blanca Ct ... 76179
Blanch Cir ... 76107
Blanchard Dr ... 76131
Blanchard Way ... 76126
Blanco Ct ... 76126
Blanco Dr ... 76137
Blanco Creek Trl ... 76244
Blandin St ... 76111
Blazing Star Dr ... 76179
Bledsoe St ... 76107
Blenheim Pl ... 76120
Blessing Ln ... 76140
Blevins St ... 76111
Bliss Rd ... 76177
Blodgett Ave ... 76115
Bloomfield Ct & Ter ... 76123
Blooming Ct ... 76244
Blossom Dr
6200-6299 ... 76148
7600-7899 ... 76133
Blue Cir ... 76137
Blue Bell Dr ... 76108
Blue Bird Dr ... 76135
Blue Bonnet Cir ... 76109
Blue Bonnet St ... 76179
Blue Carriage Ct & Ln ... 76120
Blue Crescent St ... 76116
Blue Flag Ln ... 76137
Blue Grass Dr ... 76148
Blue Grass Ln ... 76133
Blue Grove Ave ... 76111
Blue Haze Dr ... 76108
Blue Heron Ct ... 76108
Blue Jack Trl ... 76244
Blue Lake Ct & Dr ... 76103
Blue Leaf Ct ... 76135
Blue Meadow Dr ... 76132
Blue Mound Rd
4100-5499 ... 76106
5500-9999 ... 76131
Blue Mound Rd W ... 76179
N Blue Mound Rd ... 76131
S Blue Mound Rd ... 76131
Blue Periwinkle Ln ... 76123
Blue Pine Dr ... 76134
Blue Pond Cir ... 76123
Blue Prairie Trl ... 76179
Blue Quartz Rd ... 76179
Blue Ribbon Rd ... 76179
Blue Rider Ct ... 76126
Blue Ridge Trl
200-899 ... 76179
9000-9199 ... 76118
Blue Sage Cir ... 76123
Blue Sage Ct ... 76132
Blue Sage Rd ... 76132
Blue Smoke Ct N ... 76105
Blue Springs Dr ... 76123
Blue Spruce Cir ... 76137
Blue Stem Ct ... 76108
Blue Top Dr ... 76179
Blue Valley Ct ... 76112
Blue Water Lake Dr ... 76137
Blue Wood Dr ... 76179

Bluebell Dr ... 76140
Bluebird Ave ... 76111
Bluebird St ... 76140
Bluebonnet Cir ... 76126
Bluebonnet Dr ... 76111
Bluebonnet Hilltop Dr ... 76126
Bluecrest Dr ... 76126
Bluejay Dr ... 76131
Blueridge Ct ... 76112
Blueridge Dr
5600-5899 ... 76112
6000-6099 ... 76148
Bluestone Rd ... 76108
Bluewood Dr ... 76244
E & W Bluff St ... 76102
Bluff Oak Way ... 76131
E Bluff Springs Rd ... 76108
Bluff View Dr ... 76137
Bluffview Dr ... 76132
Boat Club Rd
3700-5699 ... 76135
5700-10000 ... 76179
10002-10098 ... 76179
Bob Hanger St ... 76179
Bob Wills Dr ... 76244
Bobcat Dr ... 76244
Bobs Pl ... 76126
Bobwhite Dr ... 76112
Boca Ln ... 76112
Boca Agua Dr ... 76112
Boca Bay Dr ... 76112
Boca Canyon Dr ... 76112
Boca Circa ... 76112
Boca Hill Cir ... 76112
Boca Raton Blvd ... 76112
Bodart Ln ... 76108
Boicourt St ... 76114
Bois D Arc Ct ... 76126
Boland St ... 76107
Bolen St ... 76244
Bolero Ct ... 76135
Bolingbroke Ct & Pl ... 76140
Bolliger Blvd ... 76108
E & W Bolt St ... 76110
Bolton St ... 76111
Bomar Ave ... 76103
Bombay Ct ... 76116
Bomber Rd ... 76108
Bomford Dr ... 76244
Bonaire Cir ... 76140
Bonanza Dr ... 76137
Bonanza Trl ... 76135
Bonaventure Blvd N & S ... 76140
Bond St ... 76114
E Bonds Ranch Rd ... 76131
W Bonds Ranch Rd
100-799 ... 76131
2200-4299 ... 76179
Bong Dr ... 76112
Bonita Dr ... 76114
Bonita Springs Dr ... 76123
Bonnell Ave ... 76107
Bonner Dr ... 76148
Bonnet Ct & Dr ... 76131
Bonnie Dr
2900-4599 ... 76116
5600-5899 ... 76148
Bonnie Brae Ave ... 76111
Bonnie Wayne St ... 76117
Booker St ... 76111
Booker T St ... 76105
Boot Hill Ln ... 76177
Booth Pl ... 76118
Booth Calloway Rd ... 76118
Boothbay Way ... 76179
Borden Dr ... 76116
Bosque Ct ... 76108
Bostick St ... 76105
Boston Ave
300-2699 ... 76103
3400-3699 ... 76116
Boswell Meadows Dr ... 76179
Botanic Garden Blvd ... 76107
Boulder Cir ... 76123
Boulder Run ... 76109

Boulder Canyon Trl ... 76123
Boulder Lake Ct & Rd ... 76103
Boulder Ridge Dr ... 76140
Boulevard 26 ... 76180
Bounty Rd E & W ... 76132
Bourbon St ... 76123
Bourine St ... 76107
Bourland Dr ... 76108
Bowfin Dr ... 76179
Bowie St ... 76148
E Bowie St
100-199 ... 76110
300-1199 ... 76104
W Bowie St
100-2499 ... 76110
2500-2821 ... 76109
2823-2999 ... 76109
Bowin Dr ... 76132
Bowline Ct ... 76135
Bowling Dr ... 76148
Bowling Green St ... 76119
Bowman Dr ... 76244
Bowman Roberts Rd ... 76179
Bowman Springs Rd ... 76119
Bowood Ct ... 76112
Boxcar Blvd ... 76107
Boxthorn Ct ... 76177
Boxwood Ct ... 76133
Boxwood Dr ... 76120
E Boyce Ave ... 76115
W Boyce Ave
300-2699 ... 76115
2700-3699 ... 76133
N Boyce Ln ... 76108
S Boyce Ln ... 76108
Boyd Ave ... 76109
Boylan Dr ... 76126
Boylston Dr ... 76137
E & W Bozeman Ln ... 76108
Bracken Dr ... 76137
Brad Dr ... 76134
Bradbury Ct ... 76132
Bradford Ct ... 76132
Bradford Pl ... 76112
Bradford Creek Dr ... 76116
Bradford Park Ct ... 76107
Bradford Pear Ct ... 76244
Bradley Ave ... 76117
Bradley St
600-899 ... 76103
900-1299 ... 76105
Bradshaw Dr ... 76108
Brady Ave ... 76109
Brady Dr ... 76119
Brady Creek Rd ... 76131
Brady Oaks Ct & Dr ... 76135
Brae Ct ... 76111
Braeview Dr ... 76137
Braewick Dr ... 76131
Braewood Dr ... 76131
Braewood Ln ... 76244
Bragg Rd ... 76177
Brahma Trl ... 76179
Bramble Dr ... 76133
Brambleton Pl ... 76119
Bramblewood Rd ... 76133
Brampton Ct ... 76116
Branch Cir E ... 76108
Branch Cir W ... 76108
N Branch Dr ... 76132
Branch Rd ... 76109
Branch Way ... 76116
Branch Creek Dr ... 76132
Branch Hollow Trl ... 76123
Branchwater Trl ... 76116
Branchwood Trl ... 76116
Brandies St ... 76111
Branding Iron Trl ... 76131
Brandingshire Pl ... 76133
Brandon Ln ... 76116
Brandy Ct ... 76179
Brandywine Ln ... 76244
Brandywine St ... 76148
Bransford St ... 76104
Brants Ln ... 76116

Braswell Dr
2800-3099 ... 76111
3200-3299 ... 76106
Bratcher St ... 76119
Bray Birch Dr & Ln ... 76244
Brazendine Dr ... 76244
Brazoria Trl ... 76126
Brazos Ave ... 76116
Brazos Dr
1200-1399 ... 76126
5700-5799 ... 76137
Brazos Trl ... 76116
Brea Canyon Rd ... 76108
Breckenridge Ct ... 76177
Bree Ct ... 76131
Breeders Cup Dr ... 76179
Breeze Bay Pt ... 76131
Breeze Hollow Ct ... 76179
Breeze Water Way ... 76244
Breezewind Ln ... 76123
Breezewood Dr ... 76155
Breezy Bluff Ct ... 76126
Brekenridge Dr ... 76179
Brenden Dr ... 76108
Brennan Ave ... 76106
Brent Dr
5600-5799 ... 76148
8300-8399 ... 76120
Brenton Rd ... 76134
Brents St ... 76102
Brentwood Dr ... 76112
Brentwood Stair Rd
4200-4999 ... 76103
5000-7899 ... 76112
8200-8499 ... 76120
Brett Dr ... 76123
Brett Jackson Rd ... 76179
Bretton Wood Dr ... 76244
Brevet Ln ... 76244
Brewster Ln ... 76244
Brian Way Cir ... 76116
Brianhill Dr ... 76135
Briar Ct & Run ... 76126
Briar Cove Ct ... 76112
Briar Creek Dr ... 76126
Briar Forest Rd ... 76244
Briar Rose Ln ... 76140
Briarcliff Rd ... 76117
Briarcreek Dr ... 76244
Briarcrest Ct ... 76132
Briardale Rd ... 76119
Briarhaven Ct & Rd ... 76109
Briaroaks Dr ... 76140
Briarstone Ct ... 76112
Briarwild Ct ... 76133
Briarwood Dr ... 76132
Briarwood Ln
4800-4899 ... 76103
5100-5299 ... 76112
Briarwyck Ct ... 76137
Brice Ct ... 76140
Bridal Trl ... 76179
Bridalwreath Dr ... 76133
Bridge St
4200-5299 ... 76103
5500-6799 ... 76112
Bridge Creek Cir ... 76112
Bridge Hill Dr ... 76116
Bridgeman St ... 76114
Bridgeport Ct ... 76137
Bridges Ave ... 76118
Bridgestone Dr ... 76123
Bridgeview Dr ... 76109
Bridgewood Cir & Dr ... 76112
Bridle Ave ... 76108
Bridle Trl ... 76179
Bridle Bit Trl ... 76135
Bridle Path Way ... 76244
Briercliff Ct ... 76132
Brierhill Ct ... 76132
Brierhollow Ct ... 76132
Briery Dr & St ... 76119
Bright St
2800-3299 ... 76105
3300-3999 ... 76119
Brighton Ct ... 76137

Brighton Rd ... 76109
Brightwater Rd ... 76132
Brimstone Dr ... 76244
Brinson Dr ... 76244
Briscoe Dr ... 76108
Bristlecone Ct & Ln ... 76137
Bristol Ave ... 76179
Bristol Pt ... 76148
Bristol Rd ... 76107
Bristol Trace Ct & Trl ... 76244
Brittain St ... 76111
Brittany Pl ... 76137
Brittlebrush Trl ... 76177
Britton Ave ... 76115
Britton Ridge Ln ... 76179
Brixton Dr ... 76137
Broad Ave ... 76107
Broadcast Hill St ... 76103
Broadleaf Dr ... 76108
Broadmoor Dr ... 76116
E & W Broadus Ave ... 76115
Broadview Dr
2900-3799 ... 76114
4500-4599 ... 76135
Broadway Ave ... 76117
E Broadway Ave ... 76104
W Broadway Ave ... 76104
W Broadway St ... 76102
Brocks Ln ... 76114
Brockton Ct ... 76132
Broken Arrow Rd ... 76137
Broken Arrow Trl ... 76108
Broken Bend Blvd ... 76244
Broken Bow Dr ... 76137
Broken Gap Dr ... 76179
Broken Horn Trl ... 76126
Broken Pine Trl ... 76137
Broken Spoke Ct ... 76131
Brom Bones Aly ... 76114
Bronco Crossing Ct & Trl ... 76123
Bronze River Rd ... 76179
Brook Ann Ct ... 76137
Brook Hill Ln ... 76244
Brook Hollow Dr ... 76114
Brook Meadow Ln ... 76133
Brook Ridge Dr ... 76120
Brook Tree Dr ... 76109
Brook Water Dr ... 76120
Brookdale Ct ... 76148
Brookdale Dr ... 76148
Brookdale Rd ... 76116
Brookglen Ln ... 76179
Brookhaven Cir ... 76109
Brookhaven Ct ... 76133
Brookhaven Trl ... 76133
Brookhollow Ln ... 76131
Brookland Ave ... 76116
Brookline Ave ... 76119
Brooklynn Ct ... 76137
Brooklynn Dr ... 76179
Brooks Ave ... 76118
Brooks St ... 76105
Brooks Baker Ave ... 76135
Brookside Ct ... 76148
Brookside Dr
5600-5699 ... 76109
6200-6599 ... 76148
Brookstone Ln ... 76179
Brookvale Rd ... 76132
Brookway Dr ... 76123
Brothers St ... 76106
Brown Ave ... 76111
Brown Dr ... 76115
Brown Ln ... 76140
Brown Fox Dr ... 76244
Browning Ct E & W ... 76111
Brubeck Ln ... 76132
Bruce St ... 76111
Brunston Rd ... 76244
Brunswick St ... 76107
Brush Creek Rd ... 76119
Brushy Trl E & W ... 76108
Brushy Creek Trl ... 76118
Bryan Ave
100-1399 ... 76104

1600-1799 ... 76110
2700-2999 ... 76104
3000-4099 ... 76110
Bryant St ... 76126
Bryant Irvin Ct ... 76107
Bryant Irvin Rd
3100-4199 ... 76109
4200-4298 ... 76109
4201-4299 ... 76109
4301-4397 ... 76132
4399-7099 ... 76132
7101-7101 ... 76132
7101-7101 ... 76162
Bryant Irvin Rd N ... 76107
Bryce Ave ... 76107
Bryce Canyon Ct & Dr ... 76137
Bryson Ln ... 76179
Buccaneer Ct ... 76179
Buchanan St ... 76114
Buck Ave ... 76110
Buckboard Ln ... 76123
Buckeye St ... 76137
Buckhorn Ct & Pl ... 76137
Bucking Bronc Dr ... 76126
Buckingham Rd ... 76155
Buckskin Ct ... 76137
Buckskin Dr ... 76137
Buckskin Run ... 76116
Buckstone Dr ... 76179
Buckwheat Ct & St ... 76137
Bud Cross Rd ... 76179
Buddy L Dr ... 76108
Buelter Ct ... 76126
Buena Vis ... 76126
Buena Vista Ave ... 76107
Buena Vista Dr ... 76137
Buffalo Ct N ... 76119
Buffalo Ct S ... 76119
Buffalo Rd ... 76135
Buffalo Bend Ct & Pl ... 76137
Buffalo Creek Dr ... 76131
Buffalo Gap Trl ... 76126
N Buffalo Grove Rd ... 76108
Buffalo Springs Ct & Dr ... 76140
Bugbee St ... 76116
Buggs Pl ... 76126
N Bugle Ct & Dr ... 76108
Buie Dr ... 76140
Bull Run ... 76177
Bull Shoals Dr ... 76131
Bullfinch Ct ... 76133
Bullhead Dr ... 76179
Bunch Dr ... 76112
Bundy St ... 76119
Bunk House Dr ... 76179
Bunker Blvd ... 76148
Bunker Ct ... 76126
Bunker Hill Dr ... 76140
Bunting Ave ... 76107
Burchill Rd ... 76105
Burge St ... 76118
Burgee Ct ... 76244
Burgess Dr ... 76132
Burgundy Dr ... 76133
Burgundy Rose Dr ... 76123
Burke Rd ... 76119
Burkett Dr ... 76116
Burleson St ... 76119
Burleson Cardinal Rd ... 76140
Burlington Ave ... 76108
Burlington Blvd ... 76131
Burlington Rd ... 76179
Burly St ... 76119
Burmeister Rd ... 76134
Burnett St ... 76102
Burnett Tandy Dr ... 76107
Burnice Dr ... 76119
Burns St ... 76118
Burnside Dr ... 76177
Bursey Rd ... 76148
Burson Ave ... 76110
Burton Ave
2500-4799 ... 76105
5500-5799 ... 76119

Burton Hill Rd
100-599 ... 76114
600-1299 ... 76114
1400-2199 ... 76107
Burts Dr ... 76244
Burwell Dr ... 76244
Busch Gardens Dr ... 76123
Bush Buck Run ... 76179
Bushnell Dr ... 76116
Business Highway 287 N ... 76179
Busseron Dr ... 76116
Buster Ct ... 76111
Buster Dr ... 76117
Butler Ct ... 76116
E Butler St
100-1099 ... 76110
1100-1499 ... 76115
1500-1599 ... 76119
W Butler St
100-2399 ... 76110
2900-3199 ... 76109
Butte Meadows Dr ... 76177
Buttercup Cir N & S ... 76123
Butterfield Cir ... 76112
Butterfield Dr ... 76133
Butterfly Way ... 76244
Butternut Ct ... 76137
Butterwick St ... 76134
Button Bush Dr ... 76244
Button Willow Dr ... 76123
Buttonwood Dr ... 76137
Buttonwood Rd ... 76133
Byers Ave ... 76107
Byrd Dr ... 76114
Byron St ... 76114
Caballo St ... 76179
Cabela Dr ... 76177
Cable Dr ... 76137
Cabot Dr ... 76114
Cabral Cir ... 76102
Cacti Dr ... 76108
Cactus Ct ... 76112
Cactus Dr ... 76135
Cactus Ln ... 76108
Cactus Trl ... 76108
Cactus Flower Dr ... 76131
Cactus Patch Way ... 76131
Cactus Springs Dr ... 76244
Caddo Ct ... 76132
Caddo Dr ... 76244
Caddo Trl ... 76135
Caddy Cir ... 76140
Cade Trl ... 76244
Caden Ct ... 76148
Cadiz Dr ... 76133
Cagle Dr ... 76118
Cahill Oval St ... 76114
Cahoba Ct, Dr & Ter E & W ... 76135
Cain Ct ... 76103
Cairn Cir ... 76134
Caladium Ln ... 76140
Calais Rd ... 76116
Calamar St ... 76106
Calder Ct ... 76107
Caldwell Ln ... 76179
Calender Ct ... 76131
Calera Pl ... 76114
Calf Creek Dr ... 76179
Calf Meadows Ln ... 76126
Calhoun St ... 76102
N Calhoun St
600-2299 ... 76164
3000-3499 ... 76106
S Calhoun St ... 76104
Caliche Rd ... 76108
Calico Rock Dr ... 76131
California Pkwy N ... 76115
California Pkwy S ... 76134
E California Pkwy ... 76119
Caliope Ct ... 76120
Calla Ct ... 76123
Callahan Ct ... 76112
Callahan St ... 76105
Callaston Ln ... 76112

Callaway Dr 76111
Calle De Establo 76108
Callender Dr 76108
Calloway Ct, Dr & St N & S 76114
Calmar Ct & Rd 76112
Calmont Ave
3600-4198 76107
4200-5199 76107
5201-5999 76107
6000-8799 76116
8801-8899 76116
Calumet St 76105
Calvert St 76107
Camarillo Dr 76244
Cambrian Way 76137
Cambridge Cir 76108
Cambridge Dr 76179
Cambridge Rd 76155
Cambridge St 76114
Camden St 76133
Camden Bluff St 76244
Camellia Rose Ct & Dr 76116
Camelot Rd 76134
Cameo Dr 76134
Cameron St
900-1599 76115
5400-5499 76119
Cameron Creek Cir, Ct, Cv, Ln & Pl 76132
Cameron Hill Pt 76134
Camilla St 76105
Camille Ct 76135
Camino Ct 76126
S Camp Ct 76179
Camp Bowie Blvd
3100-3298 76107
3300-5999 76107
6000-7299 76116
Camp Bowie West Blvd 76116
Camp Worth Trl 76244
Campana St 76133
Campbell Cir 76119
Campbell St 76105
Campfire Ct 76244
Campion Ln 76137
Campolina Way 76244
Campus Dr
4000-5399 76119
5500-5599 76140
5601-5799 76140
Camrose Ct & St 76244
Canary Dr 76131
Canary Ln 76244
Canberra Ct 76105
Canchim St 76131
Candace Dr 76119
Candleberry Ct 76133
Candlelite Ct & Ln 76109
Candler Dr 76131
Candleridge Cir 76133
Candlestick Ct 76133
Candlestick Trl 76179
Candlewick Ct 76140
Candlewind Ln 76133
Candlewood Rd 76103
Candlewyck St 76244
Cando Dr 76134
Cane River Rd 76244
Canfield Dr 76120
Canisius Ct 76120
Canja Dr 76126
Cannas Ct 76123
E & W Cannon St 76104
Cannonwood Dr 76137
Canoga Cir 76137
Cantabria Ct 76114
Cantana Ct 76244
Cantera Way 76126
Canterbury Cir 76112
Canterbury Ct 76132
Canterbury Dr
100-999 76179
1900-2299 76107

E Cantey St 76104
W Cantey St
300-2499 76110
2500-3399 76109
S Canton Dr 76112
Cantrell St 76116
Cantrell Sansom Rd 76131
Canyon Cir 76133
Canyon Ct 76137
Canyon Dr
600-699 76179
5600-5699 76137
Canyon Rd 76126
Canyon Trl 76135
Canyon Creek Trl 76112
Canyon Crest Ct 76179
Canyon Crest Dr 76132
Canyon Crest Rd 76179
Canyon Lands Dr 76137
Canyon Oak Ct & Dr 76112
Canyon Ridge Ave 76103
Canyon Ridge St 76131
Canyon Rim Dr 76179
Canyon Springs Rd 76132
Cap Rock Ln 76133
Cape St 76179
Cape Cod Dr 76133
Cape Royale Ct & Dr 76179
Capers Ave 76112
Capilla Ct & St 76133
Capital St 76119
Capital Reef Ct 76137
W Capps St 76110
Capra Way 76126
Capri Dr 76114
Capstone Dr 76244
Capulin Rd 76131
Caravan Dr 76131
Caravelle Ct 76108
Caraway Dr 76179
Carb Dr 76114
Cardiff Ave 76133
Cardinal Dr 76131
Cardinal Ln 76111
Cardinal Rdg 76119
Cardinal Ridge Ave 76115
Cardinal Wood Ct 76112
Cardona Ct 76126
Carette Dr 76108
Carey Rd 76140
Carey St 76119
Cargill Cir 76244
Caribia Ct 76123
Caribou Ct 76137
Caribou Trl 76135
Caribou Ridge Dr 76137
Carl St 76103
Carleton Ave 76107
Carlin Dr 76108
Carlock St 76110
Carlos St 76108
Carlotta Dr 76177
Carlsbad Way 76244
Carlson Ct 76119
Carlton St 76133
Carlton Oaks Dr 76177
Carlyle Dr 76132
Carman Dr 76116
Carmel Ave 76119
Carnation Ave 76111
Carnett Ct 76133
Carol Ave 76105
Carol Dr 76108
Carol Oaks Ln & Trl 76112
Caroldean Ct & St 76117
Carolea Dr 76111
Carolina Dr 76123
Carolina Trace Trl 76244
Caroline Ct 76137
Carolyn Rd 76109
Carondolet Ct 76114
Carousel Dr 76148
Carriage Ln
300-699 76179
7500-7699 76112
Carriage Hill Dr 76140

Carrick St 76116
Carrington Ln 76137
Carroll St 76107
Carrotwood Dr 76244
Carruthers Dr 76112
Carson St 76117
N Carson St 76140
Cartagena Ct & Dr 76133
Carten St 76112
Carter Ave 76103
Cartist Dr 76116
Cartwright Ave 76111
Cartwright Dr
300-398 76126
400-499 76126
2900-2999 76117
Carver Ave 76102
Carver Dr 76107
Carverly Ave 76119
Carverly Dr 76112
Casa Blanca Ave & Cir 76107
Casa Loma Ter 76119
Casburn Ct 76120
Cascade Cir 76148
Cascade Ct
6200-6299 76148
7200-7499 76137
8500-8599 76179
Cascade Canyon Trl 76179
N Cascades St 76137
Casey Ct 76140
Casino Cir 76119
Casita Ct 76116
Cason Ct 76135
Caspian Cv 76244
Cass Dr 76119
Cass St 76112
Cassandra Ct 76131
Cassidy Ln 76244
Cassie Ln 76134
Casstevens St 76114
Castanada Cir 76112
Castile St 76133
Castillo Rd 76112
Casting Ct 76126
Castle Cir 76108
Castle Creek Ct & Dr 76132
Castle Oak Ln 76108
Castle Pines Rd 76132
Castle Ridge Rd 76140
Castle Springs Rd 76134
Castleberry Cut Off Rd 76114
Castlebrook Ct 76179
Castleman St 76119
Castleroy Ln 76135
Castleview Dr 76120
Castlewood Dr 76131
Castro Ln 76108
Catalina Ct & Dr 76107
Catalpa Rd 76131
Catalpa St 76117
Catamaran Dr 76135
Catbrier Ct 76137
Cathedral Dr 76119
Catherine St 76103
Cathy Ct & Dr 76148
Catlow Ct 76137
Catlow Valley Rd 76137
Cats Eye Dr 76179
Cattail Ct 76108
Cattle Dr 76179
Cattle Creek Rd 76134
Cattle Crossing Dr 76131
Cattlebaron Dr 76108
Cattlebaron Parc Dr 76108
Cattlemans Way 76131
Cavalry Dr 76177
Cave Cove Ct 76244
Cave Creek Ct 76137
N & W Caylor Rd 76244
Cayman Dr 76123
Cecelia Ln 76140
Cecil Dr 76118
Cedar St 76102

Cedar Breaks Dr 76137
Cedar Brush Ct & Dr 76123
Cedar Creek Ct 76103
Cedar Creek Dr 76109
Cedar Falls Dr 76244
Cedar Glen St 76244
Cedar Hill Rd 76116
Cedar Hollow Dr 76244
Cedar Lake Ln 76123
Cedar Park Blvd 76118
Cedar Ridge Ln 76177
Cedar River Trl 76137
Cedar Springs Dr 76179
Cedar Tree Dr 76131
Cedar View Ct & Trl 76137
Cedarcrest Dr 76117
Cedarcrest Ln 76123
Cedardale Ct 76148
Cedarhill Rd 76148
Cedarview Ct & Dr 76123
Celeste St 76140
Centaur Ct 76120
Centennial Ct 76244
Centennial Dr 76244
Centennial Rd 76119
Center Ln 76140
Center Ridge Dr 76131
Centerboard Ln 76179
E & W Central Ave 76164
Centre Ct 76116
NW Centre Dr 76135
Centre Station Dr 76155
Centreport Dr 76155
Centreport Landing Cir 76155
Century Dr 76140
Century Pl 76133
Cervantes Ave 76133
Cessna Ct 76179
Chaco Trl 76137
Chadbourne Dr 76140
Chadbourne Rd 76244
Chaddybrook Ln 76137
Chadsford Ct 76148
Chadwick Dr 76131
Chaffin Dr 76118
Chalk Hills Ct 76126
Chalk Hollow Dr 76179
Chalk Knoll Rd 76108
Chalk Mountain Dr 76140
Chalk River Dr 76179
Chalkstone Dr 76131
Chalmette Ct 76140
Chama Dr 76119
Chama Valley Rd 76244
Chambers Ave 76107
Chambers Ln 76179
Chambers St 76102
Chambers Creek Dr S 76140
Chamita Ln 76116
Chamizal Dr 76137
Chamness Ct 76117
Champions Ave 76119
Champions View Pkwy 76244
Championship Pkwy 76177
Champlain Dr 76137
Chance Blvd 76134
Chancellorsville Dr 76140
N & S Chandler Dr E & W 76111
Chandler Lake Ct & Rd 76103
Chandra Ln 76134
Chaney St 76117
Channel View Dr 76133
Channing Rd 76244
Chantilly Ln 76134
Chaparral Dr 76108
Chaparral Ln 76109
Chaparral Creek Dr 76123
Chapel Ave 76116
Chapel Ln 76135
Chapel Creek Blvd
2001-2099 76108
3200-3299 76116
N Chapel Creek Blvd 76108
Chapel Glen Ter 76116

Chapel Hill Ct 76116
Chapel Oak Trl 76116
Chapel Pointe Trl 76116
Chapel Ridge Dr & Way 76116
Chapel Rock Dr 76116
Chapel Springs Trl 76116
Chapel Wood Ct 76116
Chapin Ct 76116
Chapin Rd
7500-9499 76116
7701-7997 76116
7999-8199 76116
8201-9299 76116
9500-9598 76126
9600-9700 76126
9702-9798 76126
Chapman Rd 76148
Chapman St 76105
Chapperal Dr 76117
Chaps Ave 76244
Charbonneau Rd 76135
Charbray Ct & Rd 76131
Chardin Park Dr 76244
Chariot Dr 76107
Charisma Ct & Dr 76131
Charlene St 76105
Charles Ct 76116
Charleston Ave 76123
Charlestown Ln 76140
Charlie Ln 76104
Charlott St 76112
Charlotte Dr 76119
Charmaine Dr 76148
Charmion Ln 76131
Charron Ln 76116
Charter Oak Ct 76179
Chartwell Ln 76120
Chase Ct 76110
Chase Ridge Trl 76137
Chasmier Way 76134
Chastien Ct 76131
Chatburn Ct 76110
Chateau Dr 76134
Chatham Ct 76140
Chatsworth Ln 76244
Chattaroy Ln 76244
Chaucer St 76112
Chauncery Pl 76116
Cheatham Ct 76244
Cheatham Dr 76148
Chedlea Ave 76133
Chelan Ct & Way 76244
Chelsea Ct 76132
Chelsea Dr
1-2199 76134
2300-2399 76119
Chelsea Rd 76103
Cheltenham Dr 76140
Chenault St 76111
Cherbourg Dr 76120
Cherilee Ln 76148
Cherokee Trl 76133
Cherry Ln
2600-3021 76116
3020-3020 76121
3022-3398 76116
3023-3399 76116
N Cherry Ln 76108
S Cherry Ln 76108
Cherry St 76102
N Cherry St 76102
Cherry Bark Ln 76140
Cherry Hills Dr 76132
Cherry Tree Ct 76179
Cherrycrest 76126
Cherrylawn Ct 76131
Cherryridge Dr 76134
Cherrytree Ln 76140
Cheryl Ct 76148
Cheryl Ln 76117
Cheryl St 76117
Chesapeake Pl 76132
Chesapeake St 76148
Chesapeake Bay Dr 76123
Cheshire St 76134

Chesington Dr 76137
Chesser Boyer Rd 76111
Chessie Cir 76137
Chestalynn Ct 76117
Chester Ave 76106
Chester St 76103
N & S Chesterfield Dr 76179
Chestnut Ave
2000-2799 76164
2800-3599 76106
Chestnut Ct 76137
Chestnut Ln 76179
Chestnut St 76137
Cheswick Dr 76123
Chevy Chase Dr 76134
Cheyenne Ct 76131
Cheyenne St 76114
Chicago Ave 76103
S Chicago Ave 76105
Chickadee Dr 76108
Chickasaw Ave 76119
Chickering Rd 76116
Chico St 76132
Chicora Ct 76116
Chiefton Way 76244
Childers Ave 76126
Childress St 76119
Chiltern Hills Dr 76112
Chilton St 76112
Chimney Meadow St 76155
Chimney Rock Ct 76112
Chimney Rock Dr 76140
Chimney Rock Rd
300-599 76140
5400-5599 76112
Chimney Wood Cir 76112
China Rose Dr 76137
Chinkapin Ln 76244
Chippendale Dr 76134
Chippewa Trl 76135
Chisholm Trl
3100-3199 76116
5900-5999 76148
Chisos Rim Ct & Trl 76244
Chivalry Ln 76140
Chloe Ln 76244
Choate Ln 76108
Choctaw Trl 76116
Cholla Ct & Dr 76112
Cholla Cactus Trl 76177
Chris Dr 76244
Chris Grubbs Rd 76179
Christie Ave & Ct 76140
Christina Ct 76179
Christine Ave 76105
Christine Ct 76105
Christine St 76114
Christopher Cir & Dr 76140
Christy Ct 76112
Christy Ln 76137
Chrysalis Dr 76131
Chuck Wagon Trl 76108
Chuparosa Dr 76177
Church Dr 76135
Church St 76112
Church Park Ct & Dr 76133
Churchhill Dr 76131
Churchill Rd 76114
Cibolo Dr 76133
Ciello Ct 76108
Cienegas Cir 76112
Cimarron Trl 76148
Cimmaron Trl 76116
Cindy Ct 76111
Cindy Dr 76111
Cindy Ln
300-399 76179
5400-5699 76135
Cinnabar Ct 76114
Cinnamon Hill Dr 76133
Circle Dr 76119
Circle Trl 76135
Circle Park Blvd 76164
Circle Park St 76106
Circle R Rd E 76140
Circle Ridge Dr W 76114

Circle S Rd 76116
Cisco Ct 76108
Citation Ct 76112
Citation Dr 76106
Citrine Pass 76137
Citrus Dr 76244
Citylake Blvd E & W 76132
Cityview Blvd 76132
Claer Dr 76115
Claiborn St 76135
Clairborne Dr 76177
Claire Dr 76131
Clairemont Ave 76103
Clara St 76110
Clarence St
300-399 76111
1200-1299 76117
1300-1399 76117
1000-1099 76117
1000-1099 76117
Clarendon St 76134
Claridge Ct 76109
Clarity Dr 76123
Clarke Ave 76107
Clarke Dr 76135
Clarks Mill Ln 76123
Clarksburg Trl 76244
Clary Ave 76111
Claude Ct 76135
Claudia Dr 76134
Clay Ave
4000-4399 76117
4300-4399 76109
Clay Mountain Trl 76137
Claycourt Cir 76120
Claymore Ln 76244
Clayton Rd E & W 76116
Clear Brook Cir 76123
Clear Creek Dr 76137
Clear Creek Ln 76131
Clear Fork Trl 76109
Clear Lake Cir 76109
Clear Lake St 76102
Clear Spring Dr 76132
Clearbrook Ct 76148
Clearbrook Dr 76123
Clearview Ct 76126
Clearview Dr 76119
Clearview Ln 76126
Clearwood Dr 76108
Cleburne Ct 76133
Cleburne Rd 76110
W Cleburne Rd
6800-7599 76133
7900-8499 76123
Cleckler Ave 76111
Cleveland Ave 76104
Cliburn Dr 76244
Cliff Ct 76134
Cliff Park 76134
Cliff St 76164
Cliff Oaks Dr 76179
Cliffbrook Ct 76112
Clifford St 76108
Clifford Center Dr 76108
Cliffridge Ln 76116
Cliffrose Ln 76109
Cliffside Ct & Dr 76134
Cliffview Dr 76112
Clifton St 76107
Clinton Ave
1200-2799 76164
2800-3799 76106
Clipper Ln 76179
Cloer Dr 76109
Cloisters Dr 76131
Clotell Ct & Dr 76119
Cloudcroft Ln 76131
Cloudview Rd 76109
Clover Ct 76132
Clover Dr 76179
Clover Ln
1200-3499 76107
7500-7699 76148
Clover St 76102
E & W Clover Park Dr 76140

Cloverdale Dr 76134
Cloverglen Ln 76123
Cloveridge 76126
Cloveridge Dr 76244
Clovermeadow Dr 76123
Clovis Ct 76148
Club Ct 76179
Club Creek Dr 76137
Club Oak Dr 76114
Clubgate Dr 76137
Clyde St 76108
Clymer St 76107
Coach House Cir 76108
Coachwood Cir 76133
Coad St 76140
Coastal Pt 76131
Coates Cir 76116
Coates Dr 76114
Cobb Dr 76103
S Cobb Dr 76105
Cobb Park Dr 76105
Cobblestone Ct
1900-1999 76112
6900-6999 76140
Cobblestone Dr
3400-3799 76140
10600-10899 76126
Cobham Way 76132
Cochran Way 76108
Cockrell Ave
2500-3499 76109
3700-3899 76110
4100-5299 76133
Coconino Ct 76137
Cody Ct 76114
Coffee Rd 76117
Cog Hill Dr 76120
Cogley Dr 76244
Coin St 76140
Colbert Dr 76131
Colbi Ct & Ln 76120
Cold Harbor St 76123
Cold Mountain Trl 76131
Cold Springs Rd
1000-1999 76102
2300-2799 76106
Coldstream Dr 76123
Coldwater Canyon Rd 76132
Cole Ave 76179
Cole Ct 76115
Cole St 76115
Coleman Ave 76105
Coleman St 76114
Coleto Creek Cir 76179
Colfax Ln 76134
Colgate Ct 76112
Colina Cir & Dr 76108
Colinas Trl 76177
Collado Ct 76108
Collard St 76103
S Collard St
300-799 76103
901-997 76105
999-3299 76105
College Ave
100-1699 76104
1700-4099 76110
4100-4899 76115
NW College Dr 76179
Collett Dr 76108
Collett Little Rd 76119
Collier St 76102
Collin St 76119
Collins Ct 76131
N Collins St 76155
Collinsworth St 76107
Collinwood Ave 76107
Colonial Dr 76140
Colonial Pkwy
1900-1999 76110
2100-2899 76109
Colonial Pl 76140
Colonial St 76111
Colonial Heights Ln 76179
Colonial Park Dr 76117
Colony Ct
800-899 76131
1300-1399 76117
Colony Hill Rd 76112
Colorado Ct 76137
Colorado Dr 76126
Colorado Creek Ct 76133
Colorado Springs Dr 76123
Colt Ct 76179
Colt St 76116
Colter Ct 76108
Colton Dr 76108
Coltrane St 76132
Colts Foot St 76244
Columbia Ave 76114
Columbia Ct 76131
Columbine Dr 76140
Columbus Ave
1900-2799 76164
2800-3599 76106
Columbus Trl
3500-4798 76133
3501-5099 76123
5300-5398 76123
Colusa Dr 76133
Colvin St 76104
Colwick Ct 76133
Comal Ave 76108
Comanche Ave 76114
Comanche St 76119
Comanche Trl 76135
Comanche Moon Dr 76179
Comanche Peak Dr 76179
Comanche Ridge Dr 76131
Comanche Springs Dr 76131
Comer Dr 76134
Comfort Dr 76132
Comfrey St 76244
Comiskey Ct 76179
Comita Ave 76132
Commander Rd 76106
Commerce St 76102
N Commerce St
100-299 76102
500-2299 76164
2800-2899 76106
2900-2999 76164
3300-3899 76106
N & S Commercial St 76107
Commonwealth Ct &
Dr 76179
Community Ln 76133
Como Dr 76107
Compass Ct 76135
Competition Cir 76179
Compton Trl 76244
Comstock Cir 76244
Concho Dr 76126
Concho Trl
100-399 76108
2800-2899 76118
Concho Valley Trl 76126
Concina Way 76108
Concord Ct 76140
Concord St 76148
Concrete St 76107
Condor Trl 76131
Coneflower Rd 76123
Coneflower Trl 76131
Conejos Dr 76116
Conestoga Dr 76131
Confederate Park Rd
6900-9898 76108
6901-8199 76108
9100-9599 76135
Confidence Dr 76244
Congress St 76107
Conklin Ave 76117
Conlin Dr 76134
Connemara Ln 76244
Conner Ave 76105
Conroy St 76134
Constance Dr 76131
Constellation Blvd &
Ct 76108
Constitution Ct & Dr 76148
Contender Ln 76132
Contento St 76133
Continental Dr 76131
Conway St 76111
Cook Ct 76244
Cook Ranch Rd 76126
Cooks Ln 76120
Cool Brook Ct 76244
Cool Meadow Dr 76132
Cool Ridge Ct 76133
Cool Spring Dr 76108
Coolwater Trl 76179
Cooper St 76104
Copper Creek Dr 76244
Copperfield Dr 76132
Copperstone Dr 76112
Copperwood Dr 76108
Copperwood Ln 76140
Coppin Dr 76120
Coral Cir 76126
Coral Ln 76140
Coral Creek Dr 76135
N, S & W Coral Springs
Ct & Dr 76123
Cordes Ct 76112
Cordone Ct & St 76133
Cordova Ave 76132
Coriander Ct 76244
Corina Dr 76108
Cork Pl 76116
Corky Ct 76179
Corn Field Dr 76179
Cornell Ave 76114
Corner Brook Ln 76123
Cornerstone Dr 76123
Cornerwood Dr 76244
Corning Ave 76106
Cornish Ave 76133
Cornwallis Ct 76148
Corona Ct 76108
Coronada Dr 76116
Coronado Bnd 76108
Coronado Ct 76116
Coronado Bend Ct 76108
Corporation Pkwy 76126
Corral Cir 76244
Corral Ct 76148
Corral Dr
100-199 76244
2300-2399 76133
9700-9799 76244
Corral Dr N 76244
Corriente Ln 76126
Corrin Ave 76131
Cortez Ct 76119
Cortez Dr 76116
Corto Ave 76109
Costa Mesa Dr 76244
Costen Ln 76114
Cotillion Rd 76134
Cotswold Hills Dr 76112
Cottage Dr 76135
Cottageview Ln 76155
Cottageville Ln 76244
Cottey St
5000-5499 76105
5500-5599 76119
Cotton Creek Ln 76123
Cotton Depot Ln 76102
Cottonbelt Dr 76131
Cottontail Dr 76244
Cottonwood Ct 76135
Cottonwood St 76111
Cottonwood Trl 76126
Cottonwood Creek Rd 76135
Cottonwood Village Dr 76120
Cougar Trl 76108
Cougar Ridge Rd 76126
Council Dr 76126
Count Dr 76244
Country Ln
3800-4099 76123
5600-5699 76109
Country Pl 76109
Country Club Cir 76109
Country Club Ln 76112
Country Creek Ln 76123
Country Day Ln 76109
Country Day Trl 76132
Country Hill Ct & Rd 76140
Country Manor Rd 76134
Country Valley Ln 76179
Countryside Ct E 76132
Countryside Ct W 76132
Countryside Ln 76133
N County Rd 76179
County Loop Rd 76179
Court St 76105
Courtney Cir 76137
Courtney Way 76148
Courtney Oaks Dr 76112
Courtright Dr 76244
Courtside Dr
4800-7099 76133
6100-6399 76148
Coury Rd 76140
Cousins Dr 76134
Cove Meadow Ln 76123
Covelo Ave 76111
Coventry Park Dr 76117
Covered Bridge Ct &
Dr 76108
Covert Ave
2400-2699 76115
2700-3599 76133
Covington Ct 76108
Covington Dr 76126
Cowan St 76105
Cowden St
5000-5999 76114
6000-6099 76135
Cowhand Ct 76131
Cowley Rd 76119
Cox St 76105
Coyote Hill Dr 76177
Coyote Ridge Dr 76244
Cozby Ct & St W, E, N
& S 76126
Cozy Cir 76120
Crabapple Ct & St 76137
Crabtree St 76111
Cracked Wheat Trl 76179
Cradle Rock Ct 76108
Craig Ct & St 76112
Cranberry Dr 76137
Cranbrook Dr 76131
Crandall Dr 76244
Crandle Dr 76108
Crane Cir 76131
Cranwell Ct 76134
Crater Lake Dr 76137
Cravens Rd 76112
S Cravens Rd
1700-2599 76112
2700-4399 76119
Crawford Ct 76119
Crawford Ln 76119
Crawford Ln E 76119
Crawford Ln W 76119
Crawford Rd 76244
Crawford St 76104
Crawford Farms Ct &
Dr 76244
Crazy Horse Ln 76137
Creamello Ave 76244
Creech St
3900-4199 76111
4200-4299 76117
Creede Trl 76118
N Creek Dr 76179
S Creek Dr 76133
Creek Bank Ct 76126
Creek Bed Dr 76244
Creek Bend Dr
400-499 76131
5100-7099 76137
Creek Hill Ln 76179
Creek Hollow Ln 76131
Creek Meadow Dr 76123
Creek Meadows Dr 76133
Creek Point Dr 76179
Creek Ridge Trl 76179
Creek Run Rd 76120
Creek Terrace Dr 76131
Creekfall Dr 76137
E & W Creekhaven Dr 76137
Creekhollow Dr 76137
Creekland View Dr 76244
Creekmoor Dr 76133
Creekside Cir 76106
Creekside Dr
200-299 76131
3000-3199 76106
4500-4699 76137
9800-9899 76126
Creekstone Ct 76112
Creekview Ct 76112
Creekview Ln 76123
Creekwood Ct 76108
Creekwood Dr 76109
Creekwood Ln
200-399 76134
2500-3499 76123
Creighton Ct 76120
Crenshaw Ave 76105
Crenshaw Dr 76126
Creosote Dr 76177
Crepe Myrtle Ct 76126
Crescent Creek Ln 76140
Crescent Lake Ct &
Dr 76137
Crescent Ridge Dr 76140
Crest Dr 76179
Crest Canyon Dr 76108
Crest Point Dr 76179
Crest Ridge Cir 76108
Crest Ridge Ct 76179
Crest Ridge Dr
201-497 76108
499-599 76108
8900-8999 76179
Crest Wood Dr 76179
Crestbrook Dr 76179
Crested Butte Dr 76131
Crested Elm Ct 76108
Crested Oak Ct 76108
Crested Ridge Ln 76108
Cresthaven Ter 76107
Cresthill Rd 76116
Cresting Creek Dr 76108
Crestline Rd 76107
Crestmont Ct 76133
Crestmore Rd 76116
Creston Ave & Ct 76133
Crestover Ct 76117
Crestview Ct
600-699 76179
7700-7799 76148
Crestview Dr
2100-4199 76103
9200-9299 76126
Crestway Dr 76244
Crestwick Ct 76112
Crestwood Dr 76107
Crestwood Ln 76132
Crestwood Ter 76107
Cricket Ct 76135
Cripple Creek Dr 76179
Cripple Creek Rd 76137
Crites St 76118
Crix Ln 76140
Crockett St 76107
Crofton Ct 76126
Crofton Dr 76137
Croftway Ct 76131
Cromart Ave & Ct 76133
Cromwell St 76104
Cromwell Marine Creek
Rd 76179
Crooked Ln 76112
Crooked Stick Ct & Dr 76132
Crosby Ave 76108
Cross Plains Ct 76126
Cross Ridge Cir & Ct 76120
Cross Timbers Dr 76108
Crossbow Ct
7200-7299 76133
7700-7799 76148
Crosscreek Ln 76109
Crosslands Ct 76132
Crosslands Rd
1-99 76132
3800-3999 76109
4100-4199 76132
Crosstie Cir 76116
Crosswicks Cir & Ct 76137
Crosswind Dr 76179
Crouch St 76105
Crouse Dr 76137
Crowder Dr 76179
Crowley Rd 76134
Crowley St 76114
Crown Rd 76114
Crown Oaks Dr 76131
Crown Ridge Ct 76108
Crowne Pointe Ln 76244
Crownwood Dr 76137
Croydon Dr 76140
Crumbcake Dr 76244
Crump St 76102
N Crump St 76106
Crystal Brook Dr 76179
Crystal Creek Cir 76137
Crystal Falls Dr 76244
Crystal Lake Dr 76179
Crystal Springs Dr 76108
Crystal View Dr 76244
Cuculu Dr 76133
Culberson Ct 76244
Cullen St 76107
Culver Ave 76116
Cumberland Pass &
Rd 76116
Cumberland Gap Dr 76244
N Cummings St 76102
Cunningham St 76134
N Cunningham St 76140
Cupp Ct 76126
Curacao Dr 76123
Currie St
100-1199 76107
3200-3299 76133
Curtis Ct 76110
Curtis Dr 76116
Curzon Ave
4000-5999 76107
6000-6799 76116
Custer Dr 76114
Cut Bank Trl 76134
Cutler Ln 76179
Cutter St 76119
Cutter Hill Ave 76134
Cynthia Ct 76140
Cypress Dr 76148
Cypress St
1300-2499 76102
1600-1899 76117
Cypress Club Dr 76137
Cypress Gardens Ct &
Dr 76123
Cypress Hills Dr 76108
Cypress Point Dr 76132
Cypress Point Ln 76137
Cypress Wood Ct 76133
Dacy Ln 76116
Daffodil Ct 76137
E Daggett Ave 76104
W Daggett Ave
100-1299 76104
1500-2399 76102
Dahlen St 76116
Dahlia Dr 76123
Daily Double Dr 76126
Daisy Ln 76111
Daisy Leaf Dr 76244
Dakar Rd E & W 76116
Dakota St 76107
Dakota Trl 76135
Dakota Ridge Dr 76134
Dale Ln 76108
Dale Hollow Rd 76103
Dale Lane Ct 76108
Dalerosa Ct 76126
Dalevale Ct 76135
Dalewood Ct 76112
Dalford St 76111
Dalhart Dr 76179
Dallam Ln 76108
Dallas Ave 76112
Dalrock Rd 76131
Dalton St 76244
Damascus Ct & Dr 76112
Damon Ave 76111
Dan Danciger Rd 76133
Dana Dr
3700-3899 76111
3900-5899 76117
Dana Lynn Dr 76137
Danciger Dr 76112
Dancy Dr N & S 76131
Dandelion Dr 76137
Danele Ct 76118
Daniel St 76104
Danieldale Dr 76137
Danner St 76105
Danube Ct 76118
Danville Dr 76244
Dapple Dr 76244
Darcy St 76107
Daren Dr 76137
Darien St 76140
Dark Leaf Ct E & W 76135
Darkento St 76111
Darla Dr 76132
Darlington Trl 76131
Darlisti Trl 76118
Darnell Ave 76126
Darnell St 76107
Dartmoor Ct 76110
Dartmouth Ave 76114
Darwood Ave 76116
E & W Dashwood St 76104
Davenport Ave 76116
David Dr 76111
David Ln 76119
David Strickland Rd 76119
Davidson St
300-498 76126
6500-6899 76118
E Davis Ave 76104
Davis Rd 76140
Davy Crockett Trl 76137
Dawn W 76116
Dawn Ct 76133
Dawn Dr 76116
E Dawn Dr 76244
Dawn Hills Dr 76132
Dawson Trl 76108
Dax Dr 76135
Day Dr 76132
Daylily Ct 76123
Daymist Dr 76140
Dayspring Dr 76140
Daystar Dr 76123
Dayton Rd 76140
Dayton St
1000-1099 76111
2000-2199 76117
De Cory Rd 76134
N De Costa St 76111
De Ridder Ave 76106
Deal Ct & Dr 76135
Dean Ln 76107
Deanne Ct 76123
Deauville Cir E 76108
Deauville Cir N 76108
Deauville Cir S 76108
Deauville Cir W 76108
Deauville Ct 76112
Deauville Dr 76108
Deauville Dr E 76108
Deavers Ln 76114
Debbie Ct & St 76115
Deborah Ln
6000-6099 76148
7600-7699 76118
Debra Ct 76112
Debra Court Dr 76112
Decatur Ave 76106
Deck House Rd 76179

Declaration St 76148
Decoy Ln 76120
Dee Ct 76135
Dee Ln 76117
Deen Rd 76106
Deep Valley Ln 76132
Deepdale Dr 76107
Deepwood Ln 76123
Deer Trl 76140
Deer Bluff Ln 76179
Deer Creek Rd 76140
Deer Glen Trl 76140
Deer Hollow Dr 76132
Deer Horn Dr 76179
Deer Lake Dr 76140
Deer Park Dr 76137
Deer Ridge Ct & Dr 76137
Deer Run Dr 76137
Deerbrook Dr 76108
Deerfoot Trl 76131
Deering Dr 76114
Deerlodge Trl 76137
Deerwood Forest Dr 76126
Deewood Ct 76112
Defiel Rd 76179
Degaulle St 76155
Del Mar Ct 76126
Del Prado Ave 76133
Del Ridge Rd 76126
Del Rio Ave 76126
Del Rio Ct 76133
Del Rio Dr 76133
Delafield Dr 76131
Delamere Dr 76244
Delaney Dr 76244
Delano Ct 76244
Delante St 76117
Delaware Trl 76135
Delga St 76102
Dell St
  1100-1199 76108
  2300-2999 76111
Delmar Ct
  300-399 76108
  300-399 76179
Delmar St 76108
Delmas Dr 76116
Delmonico Dr 76244
Deloache Cres & St 76114
Delta Ct 76126
Delta Way 76123
Delta Way Ct 76123
Denair St 76111
Denali Dr 76137
Denbury Dr 76133
Dencherl St 76105
Deniro Dr 76134
Denise Dr 76148
Denise St 76179
Denman St 76119
Dennis Ave 76114
Dennis Dr 76179
Denton Hwy
  2701-2797 76117
  2799-5003 76117
  5005-5099 76117
  5200-5899 76148
  5900-6298 76148
  5901-6299 76148
  6300-8499 76148
  8801-9899 76244
Denver Ave 76164
Denver City Dr 76179
Depot Rd 76131
Derby Ct & Ln 76123
Derbyshire Dr 76137
Derek Dr
  2900-2999 76116
  5900-5999 76148
Descanso Gardens Dr 76132
Desert Falls Dr 76137
Desert Highlands Dr 76132
Desert Prairie Dr 76112
Desert Ridge Dr 76116
Desert Willow Ct 76137
Desmond Ln 76120

Desoto Ct N & S 76119
Desperado Rd 76131
Destin Dr 76131
Devalcourt Ave 76119
Devinstone Ct & Dr 76177
E Devitt St
  100-1299 76110
  1400-1499 76119
W Devitt St
  100-2499 76110
  2700-3199 76109
Devon Ct 76109
Devonshire Dr 76131
Dew Plant Way 76123
Dewdrop Ln 76123
Dewey St 76106
Dewey Scott St 76126
Dewolfe Ln 76135
Dexter Ave 76107
Diamond Ave 76102
Diamond Rd 76106
Diamond Oaks Ct & Dr 76117
Diamond Peak Dr 76177
Diamond Ridge Dr 76244
Diamond Springs Ct & Trl 76123
Diamond Trace Trl 76244
Diamond Valley Dr 76179
Diana Dr 76118
Diane Dr
  5500-5599 76133
  9200-9299 76108
Diaz Ave 76107
Dick Price Rd 76140
Dickens Dr 76126
Dickinson Ave 76120
Dickson Rd 76179
E Dickson St 76110
W Dickson St 76110
Dido Hicks Rd 76179
Dido Vista Ct 76179
Dillard St 76105
Dillon Cir 76137
Dillon St 76179
Dillow St 76105
Dilworth Ct & St 76116
Dinette St 76244
Diplomacy Rd 76155
Disraeli Dr 76119
Diver Ct 76119
Dixie St 76106
Dodge St
  2200-2499 76164
  2500-2599 76106
N Dodson Dr 76108
S Dodson Dr 76108
Dodson Ter 76135
Doe Creek Trl 76244
Doeline St 76117
Dogleg Dr 76117
Dogwood Ct 76137
Dogwood Dr 76126
Dogwood Ln 76137
Dogwood Park Dr 76118
Dogwood Springs Dr 76244
Dollar Ln 76126
Dolores St 76102
Dolphin Way 76132
Dominion Ct 76179
Dominion Dr 76131
Dominy Ln 76116
Donald St 76108
Donalee St
  2300-3199 76105
  3200-4199 76119
Dondo Ct 76106
Donna Ln 76119
Donna St 76110
Donnelly Ave & Cir 76107
Donnis Dr 76244
Donnyville Ct 76119
Dooling St 76111
Doral Ct & Dr 76112
Dorchester St 76134
Doreen Ave 76116

Doreen St 76108
Dorfan St 76108
Dorman St 76119
Dorothy Ln 76107
Dorothy Ln N 76107
Dorothy Ln S 76107
Dorothy Rd 76119
Dorset Dr 76244
Dorsey St 76119
Dosier Cv E & W 76179
Dottie Lynn Pkwy 76120
Double Oak Ln 76123
Dougal Ave 76137
Douglas Dr 76148
Douglas St 76114
Dove Cir 76131
Dove Ct
  7700-7799 76148
  9100-9199 76126
Dove Dr 76120
Dove Ln 76108
Dove Creek Dr 76244
Dove Meadow Ct 76133
Dove Tree Ct 76137
Dovenshire Ter 76112
Dover Ln 76118
S Dover Ter 76132
W Dover Ter 76132
Dovercliff Ct 76112
Dowdell Rd & St 76119
Down Hill Dr 76120
Downe Dr 76108
Downeast Dr 76179
Downey Ct & Dr 76112
Downing Dr 76106
Downs Dr 76179
Downshill Ct 76112
Downwood Ct 76108
Doyle St 76117
Dragon Dr 76132
Dragonfly Way 76244
Drake Ln 76137
Draper St 76105
Dream Ln 76148
Dreeben Dr 76118
E & W Drew St 76110
Drews Ln 76120
Drexel Dr 76137
Drexler Pl 76126
Drexmore Rd 76244
Driess St 76104
Driftway Dr 76135
Driftwood Ct 76179
Driftwood Ln 76140
Dripping Springs Dr 76134
Driskell Blvd 76107
Driver Ave 76107
Drop Tine Ct & Dr 76126
Drover Dr 76244
Drovers View Trl 76131
Druid Ct & Ln 76112
Drummond Ln 76108
Drury Ln 76116
Dry Creek Dr 76244
Dry Valley Ct 76108
Dryden Rd 76109
Duane St 76126
Dublin Dr 76134
Duboise St 76107
Duer Dr 76119
Duff Ct 76112
Dulles Dr 76155
Dunbar St 76105
Duncan Dr 76119
Duncan St 76114
Duncan Way 76244
Dundee Ave 76106
Dunford St 76105
Dunham Close 76114
Dunigan Ct 76126
Dunlap Dr 76119
Dunn St 76244
Dunn Hill Dr 76137
Dunraven Trl 76244
Dunson Ct & Dr 76148
Dunwick Ln 76109

Dunwoody Ct 76244
Dupont Cir 76134
Durado Dr 76179
Durango Rd 76116
Durango Root Ct & Dr 76244
Durgans Hill Ct 76137
Durham Ave 76114
Duringer Rd 76133
Durness Dr 76179
Durrett St 76244
Dustin Ct 76148
Dustin Dr 76148
Dustin St 76179
Dusty Rd 76148
Dusty Way 76123
Dusty Palomino Dr 76179
Dutch Branch Rd 76132
Dutch Iris Ln 76140
Duval St 76104
Dwarf Nettle Dr 76244
Dwight St 76116
Dynasty Dr 76123
Eagle Ct 76126
Eagle Dr
  700-899 76131
  900-1899 76111
Eagle Pkwy 76177
Eagle Heights Dr 76135
Eagle Lake Dr 76135
Eagle Mountain Cir & Dr 76135
Eagle Mountain Dam Rd 76135
Eagle Narrows Ct & Dr 76179
Eagle Pass Dr 76179
Eagle Ranch Blvd 76179
Eagle Ridge Cir 76179
Eagle Ridge Dr 76112
Eagle Rock Dr 76133
Eagle Trace Dr 76244
Eagle Vista Dr 76179
Eagles Rest Dr 76179
Eaglestone Way 76244
Eagleview Ct 76179
Earl Ln 76107
Earl St 76111
Earle Dr 76117
Early Fawn Ct 76108
Easley St 76108
East Ave 76103
East Fwy 76120
East Ln 76116
East Pl 76108
Eastchase Pkwy 76120
Eastcrest Ct 76105
Eastern Dr 76120
Eastland Ave 76135
Eastland St 76119
Eastline Dr 76119
Easton Ln 76120
Eastover Ave
  2200-2399 76105
  3400-5099 76119
Eastridge Dr
  1800-3799 76117
  10500-10599 76126
Eastview St 76134
Eastwedge Dr 76137
Eastwind Dr 76137
Eastwood Ave 76107
Easy St 76117
Ebbtide Ct 76135
Echo Trl 76109
Echo Bluff Dr 76137
Echo Hill Dr 76148
Echo Hills Ct N & S 76126
Echo Point Dr 76123
Ector Dr 76108
Ed Coady Rd 76134
Eddie Pl 76140
Eddleman Ct & Dr 76244
Eden Ave & Dr 76117
Edenwood Dr 76123
Eder St 76112
Ederville Cir 76120

Ederville Rd
  6600-7700 76112
  7702-7898 76112
  8200-8599 76120
Ederville Rd S 76103
Edge Hill Rd 76126
Edgebrook Ter 76116
Edgecliff Rd
  1300-2299 76134
  2500-2599 76133
Edgefield Rd 76107
Edgehill Rd 76116
Edgemere Pl 76135
Edgewater Dr 76126
Edgewater Trl 76135
Edgewest Ter 76108
Edgewood Dr 76137
N Edgewood Ter 76103
S Edgewood Ter
  400-899 76103
  1000-3199 76105
  3200-4799 76119
Edgewood Trl 76126
Edith Ln 76117
Edmonds Dr 76244
Edmonia Ct 76105
Edmund Dr 76126
Edna Ct 76140
Edna Dr 76140
Edna St 76117
Edney St 76115
Educators Way 76179
Edwards Dr 76179
Edwards St 76117
Edwards Ranch Rd 76109
Edwards View Ct 76132
Edwin St 76110
Effie St 76105
Effie Morris Ln 76135
Egan Way 76137
Egg Farm Rd 76244
Egg Store Rd 76244
Egret Dr 76120
Eight Twenty Blvd 76106
Eileen St 76117
Eisenhower Dr 76112
El Camino Dr 76177
El Campo Ave 76107
El Capitan St 76179
El Cid Pl 76133
El Dorado Dr 76107
El Greco Ave 76133
El Lago Bnd 76119
E & W El Paso St 76102
El Rancho Rd 76119
El Retiro Rd 76116
El Toro Ct 76133
Elaine Ct & Pl 76106
Eland Run 76179
Elbe Trl 76118
Elderberry Ct 76126
Elderwood Trl 76120
Eldon Martin St 76179
Eldridge St 76107
Eleanor Dr 76108
Elektoy Way 76108
Elgin St 76105
Elinor St 76111
Elizabeth Blvd 76110
Elizabeth Ct 76104
W Elizabeth Ln 76116
Elizabeth Rd 76119
Elizabeth Nicole Ln 76119
Elk Creek Ln 76123
Elk Hollow Dr 76140
Elk Ridge Dr 76137
Elk Run Dr 76140
Elkins Dr 76179
Elkins School Rd 76179
Elko Ln 76108
Ella Young Dr 76135
Elle Cir 76120
Ellenboro Ln 76244
Ellington Dr 76112
Elliot Ave 76111
Elliott Reeder Rd 76117

Ellis Ave
  1400-2799 76164
  2800-3799 76106
Ellis Rd 76112
Ellis Ranch Trl 76119
Ellison Ave 76117
Ellison Ct 76244
Ellison St 76244
Ellsmere Ct 76103
Elm Park 76118
Elm St 76102
N Elm St
  200-399 76102
  3000-3899 76106
Elm Creek Ct 76109
Elm Creek Way 76140
Elm Crest Ct 76132
Elm Grove Dr 76244
Elm River Ct & Dr 76116
Elmdale Dr 76137
Elmhurst Dr & Ln 76244
Elmwood Ave 76104
Elmwood Dr 76116
Elsie St 76105
Elsinor Dr 76116
Elton Rd 76117
Elva Warren St
  1100-1399 76115
  1400-1499 76119
Elvis Ct 76134
Embassy Dr 76119
Ember Ln 76131
Ember Glen Dr 76137
Embercrest Ln 76123
Embry Pl 76111
Emerald Dr 76133
Emerald Creek Dr 76131
Emerald Crest Dr 76108
Emerald Glen Way 76115
Emerald Lake Ct & Dr 76103
Emerald Oaks Dr 76117
Emerald Trace Way 76244
Emerson Dr 76148
Emerson St 76119
Emery Ave 76244
Emerywood Ln 76137
Emily Dr
  301-397 76108
  399-599 76108
  2300-2899 76112
  6600-6699 76148
Emma St 76111
Emma Way 76148
Emmeryville Ln 76244
Emory Trl 76244
Emperor Dr 76119
Empire Rd 76155
Ems Ct & Rd 76116
Encanto Dr 76109
Enchanted Rock Ln 76244
Encino Dr 76116
Enclave Cir & Dr 76132
End O Trl 76112
S Enderly Pl 76104
Endicott Ave 76137
Energy Way 76102
Engblad Dr 76134
Engleman Ct & St 76137
Englewood Ln 76107
English Oak Dr 76244
Ennis Ave 76111
Enoch Dr 76112
E & W Enon Ave & Rd 76140
Ensenada Ln 76108
Ensign Dr E & W 76119
Enterprise Ave 76118
Ephriham Ave & Ct 76164
Epoch Cir 76116
Epps Ave 76104
Equestrian Trl 76244
Erath St 76119
Eric Ln 76126
S Erie St 76112
Erikson Dr 76114
Erin Ln 76179

Ermis St 76111
Ernest Ct 76116
Ernest St 76105
Errandale Dr 76179
Escalante Ave & Ct 76112
Escambia Ter 76244
Esco Dr 76140
Espana Dr 76133
Essex St 76105
Estancia Ct & Way 76108
Estandarte Ct 76126
Estate Pl 76140
Estates Ln 76137
Ester Dr 76114
Estes Ave 76119
Estes St 76126
Estes Park Cir, Ct & Rd 76137
Estill Dr 76148
Estrella Ct 76106
Estrella Ln 76126
Estrella St 76106
Estribo Cir 76126
Eton Ct 76132
Etsie St 76117
Etta Dr 76108
Etta St 76105
Eugene Ave 76115
Eura St 76116
Eureka Springs Ct 76108
Evangeline Rd 76140
Evans Ave
  900-3099 76104
  3100-3899 76110
  4100-4899 76115
Evans Rd 76135
Evelyn Dr 76118
Evening Shade Dr 76131
Evening Star Dr 76133
Evening View Dr 76131
Everest Dr 76132
Everglades Cir 76137
Evergreen Dr
  7500-7613 76148
  7615-7621 76148
  13000-13399 76244
Evergreen Rd 76118
Everman Pkwy 76140
W Everman Pkwy 76134
Everman Kennedale Rd 76140
Evonshire Dr 76119
Ewing Ave 76116
Excelsior Ln 76244
E & W Exchange Ave 76164
Exeter St 76104
Exmore Pony Way 76244
Expedition Ave & Dr 76108
Exposition Way 76244
Ezell St 76117
Faa Blvd 76155
Fabons St 76104
Faett Ct 76119
Fagan Dr 76131
Fain St 76117
Fair Dr 76131
Fair Haven Ct & St 76179
Fair Meadows Dr
  700-799 76179
  6600-6699 76148
Fair Oaks Dr 76148
Fair Park Blvd 76115
Fair Wind St 76135
Fairbrook Ln 76140
Faircrest Ct & Cv 76137
Fairfax Ave 76119
Fairfax St 76116
Fairfield Ave 76116
Fairfield Ct 76126
Fairglen Ave 76137
Fairgrounds Ln 76140
Fairhaven Dr 76123
Fairland St 76116
Fairlane Ave 76119
Fairmeadows Ln 76123

Fairmount Ave
1100-1699 76104
1700-2299 76110
Fairmount St 76179
Fairview Dr 76148
Fairview St 76111
Fairway Cir 76117
Fairway Dr
2100-4699 76119
6600-6699 76114
8500-8599 76179
Fairway Crossing Dr 76137
Fairway Gate Ln 76137
Fairway Meadows Dr 76179
Fairweather Dr 76120
Fairwood Ct 76179
Faith Dr 76120
Faith Creek Ln 76118
Falabella Way 76244
Falcon Dr 76119
Falcon Rd 76131
Falcon Way W 76106
Falcon Ridge Ct 76137
Falcon Ridge Dr
4000-4099 76137
5400-5499 76112
Falconer Way 76179
Fall Ct 76133
Fall Cedar Dr 76108
Fall Creek Ct
5746-5750 76137
5759-5763 76137
7000-7099 76148
Fall Creek Dr 76137
Fall Meadow Dr 76132
Fall River Dr 76103
Fallbrook Ct 76120
Fallen Trl 76123
Falling Springs Rd 76116
Fallow Ct 76132
Fallworth Ct 76133
Falmouth Dr 76140
Family Dr 76179
Family Pl 76134
Fandor St 76108
Fannin St 76148
Fantail Dr 76179
Fargo Ct 76133
Farleigh Ct 76140
Farm Field Ct & Ln 76137
Farmer Dr 76244
Farmers Rd 76108
Farmers Branch St 76108
Farmington Dr
9900-9999 76126
12800-12999 76244
Farnswood Ln 76112
Farnsworth Ave 76107
Faron St 76107
Farradow Dr 76148
Farrah Dr 76131
Farrell Ln
2000-2599 76112
2800-3699 76119
Farris Ct 76133
Farris Way 76126
Fathom Dr 76135
Fawn Ct 76137
Fawn Dr 76132
Fawn Hill Ct & Dr 76134
Fawn Meadow Ct & Dr 76140
Fawn Valley Dr 76140
Fay Blvd 76120
Faye Dr 76118
Fayetteville Dr 76244
Feather Grass Ln 76177
Feather Wind Ct, Dr & Way 76135
Feathercrest Dr 76137
Featherstone Dr 76140
Feed Mill Dr 76244
Felder Ln 76112
Feldspar Dr 76131
Feliks Gwozdz Pl 76104
Felisa Pl 76133

E Felix St 76115
Fencerow Rd 76244
Fender Ct 76148
Fennel St 76244
Fenton Ave 76133
Fenway Ct 76137
Fenway Ln 76179
Ferguson Ct & Dr 76115
Feriewoo St 76103
Ferlinco Blvd 76155
Fern Lake Ct & Dr 76137
Fern Meadow Dr 76179
Fern Valley Dr 76244
Fernander Dr 76107
Fernbury Ct & Dr 76179
Ferncreek Ln 76179
Ferndale Dr 76116
Fernhill Dr 76123
Fernleaf Dr 76137
Fernwood St 76114
Fershaw Pl 76116
Fescue Dr 76179
Fewell Dr 76135
Fianna Hills Dr 76132
Ficus Dr 76244
Fiddlers Trl 76244
Field St 76117
Field Creek Ct 76134
Fieldcrest Dr
4600-4799 76109
10100-10299 76126
Fielder St 76164
Fieldstone Rd 76244
Fiesta Cir & St 76133
Filbert Cir 76123
Fillmore St 76105
Finbro Ct & Dr 76133
Finch Cir 76131
Finch Dr 76244
Fincher Rd 76117
Finley St 76111
Fir Dr 76244
Fir Park 76118
Fir Tree Ln 76123
Fire Creek Ln 76177
Fire Hill Dr 76137
Firebird Dr 76148
Firefly Dr 76137
Firehall Dr 76135
Firenze Dr 76140
Firestone Rd 76132
Firewheel Trl 76112
First Chapel Dr 76108
Firstcomm Plz 76109
Firth Rd 76116
Fiscal Ct 76244
Fisher Ave 76111
Fishhook Ct 76179
Fitzgerald St 76179
Fitzhugh Ave
2700-5199 76105
5500-5999 76119
Flagstaff Run 76140
Flagstone Dr 76114
Flagstone St 76118
Flamewood Dr 76140
Flamingo Dr 76131
Flamingo Rd 76119
Flanders Ln 76134
Flat Creek Dr 76179
Flat Rock Ct & Rd 76132
Flatiron St 76244
N Flaxseed Ln 76108
Fleetwing Trl 76131
Fleetwood Dr 76123
Fleetwood Rd 76155
Fleishman Way 76108
Fleming Ct & Dr 76148
Flemming Dr 76112
Fletcher Ave 76107
Flicka Ct 76126
Flight Line Rd 76177
Flint St 76115
Flint Rock Dr 76131
Flintwood Trl 76137
Flippo St 76137

Flo Ct 76118
Flora Dr 76126
Florence St 76102
Florentine Dr 76134
Florian Ln 76108
Flowering Plum Ln 76140
Flowertree Ct & Dr 76137
Flowing Springs Dr 76177
Floyd Dr 76116
Flyaway Ln 76120
Flying Ranch Rd 76134
Flynn Ct 76137
Fm 1187 E 76126
Fm 156
10000-10399 76131
Fm 156
11700-11799 76179
Fm 2871 76126
Fm 718 76179
Foard St 76119
N Foch St 76107
E Fogg St
100-699 76110
1100-1399 76115
W Fogg St 76110
Folkstone Dr 76140
Folwell Blvd 76119
Fondren Pl 76126
Fontaine St 76106
Fools Gold Dr 76179
Foothill Dr 76131
Forbes Ct & St 76105
Forby Ave 76103
Forest Ave 76112
S Forest Ave 76112
Forest Dr S
2400-2498 76110
2601-2699 76109
Forest Ln 76112
Forest Acre Cir N & S 76140
Forest Bend Pl 76112
Forest Creek Dr 76123
Forest Creek St 76126
Forest Edge Dr 76119
Forest Glen Dr 76119
Forest Haven Dr 76119
Forest Highlands Dr 76132
Forest Hill Cir 76140
Forest Hill Ct 76119
Forest Hill Dr
5300-6549 76119
6550-7499 76140
7500-8999 76140
N Forest Hill Dr 76140
S Forest Hill Dr 76140
Forest Hill Everman Rd 76140
Forest Knoll Dr 76119
Forest Oaks Dr 76119
Forest Park Blvd
800-899 76102
900-3499 76110
N Forest Park Blvd 76102
Forest Ridge Ct 76137
Forest River Cir, Ct & Dr 76112
Forest Wood Dr 76119
N Fork Rd 76179
Forney Trl 76244
Fort Concho Dr 76137
Fort Union Ct 76137
Fort Worth Ave 76112
Fortner Way 76116
Fortuna St 76119
Fortune Rd 76116
Forum Way S 76140
Fossil Dr
3400-3899 76111
3900-5499 76117
Fossil Bluff Dr 76137
Fossil Bridge Dr 76131
Fossil Creek Blvd 76137
Fossil Hill Dr 76131
Fossil Park Ct & Dr 76137
Fossil Ridge Dr 76137
Fossil Ridge Rd 76135

Fossil Run Blvd 76131
Fossil Valley Dr 76131
Fossil Vista Dr 76137
Fossil Wood Dr 76179
Fossile Butte Dr 76244
Foster Ct 76126
Foster Dr 76135
Fountain Flat Dr 76244
Fountain Ridge Dr 76123
Fountain Square Dr 76107
Four Oaks Ln 76107
Four Seasons Ln 76140
Four Sixes Dr 76108
Four Winds Dr 76133
Fournier St 76102
Fox Dr
400-599 76179
4100-4299 76117
Fox Trl 76109
Fox Chase Dr 76137
Fox Hill Dr 76131
Fox Hollow St 76109
Fox Hunt Trl 76179
Fox Meadow Way 76123
Fox River Ct & Ln 76120
Fox Run Ct 76137
Fox Run Dr
3800-3999 76123
5300-5599 76137
Fox Run Trl 76179
Fox Trot Dr 76123
Foxboro Ct 76133
Foxcraft Dr 76131
Foxfire Ln 76108
Foxfire Way 76133
Foxglen Ct 76131
Foxglove Ct 76112
Foxhound Ln 76123
Foxpaw Trl 76244
Foxpointe Rd 76132
Foxridge Ct 76133
Foxwood Dr 76244
Frances Dr 76104
Francesca Dr 76108
Francis Dr 76116
Francis St 76164
Franciscan Dr 76134
Francisco Ct & Dr 76133
W Franklin Ave 76179
Franklin Dr 76106
Franks St 76177
Franseri Dr 76108
Franwood Ter 76112
Frazier Ave
2500-4099 76110
4100-5299 76115
Frazier Dr E 76115
Freddie St
2900-2999 76105
3200-4199 76119
Frederick St 76107
Fredricksburg Dr 76140
Freedom Way 76244
Freeland Ridge Dr 76177
Freeman Dr 76140
Freeman St 76104
Fremont Trl 76244
French Ave 76106
French Lake Dr 76133
French Quarter Ln 76123
Fresh Springs Rd 76120
Freshfield Rd 76119
Freshwater Ln 76179
Fresno Ct 76244
Fressia Ln 76108
Friar Ct 76119
Friar Dr 76179
Friarford Rd 76112
Friedman Ln 76244
Friend Dr 76120
Friendly Ln 76117
Friendship Oak St 76116
Friendsway Ct & Dr 76137
Friendswood Dr 76123
Fringewood Dr 76120
Frio Dr 76137

Frisco Ave 76119
Frisco Dr 76131
Frisco Wood Dr 76244
Fritz Allen St 76114
Frontier St 76114
Frosted Willow Ln 76177
Fry St 76115
Frye Rd 76155
Full Moon Ct & Dr 76132
E Fuller Ave 76115
W Fuller Ave
800-1798 76115
1800-2699 76115
2700-3699 76133
Fuller Cir 76133
Fulton St 76104
Fumar Ln 76244
Funtier Ct 76179
Furlong Way 76244
Furman Ct & Dr 76244
Fursman Ave 76114
Gable Ln 76155
Gabriel Ln 76116
Gabriella Dr 76108
Gadsden Ave 76244
Gage St 76117
Gaines Ct 76117
Gaines Dr 76244
Gainsborough Ct & Way 76134
Gairlock Dr 76179
Gale Ln 76119
Gale St 76114
Galemeadow Ct & Dr 76123
Gallahad Dr 76179
Gallant Ct & Trl 76244
Gallatin Ln 76177
Galleria Dr 76119
Galley Cir 76135
Gallina Trl 76119
Galt Ave 76109
Galveston Ave
100-1299 76104
1700-1999 76110
Galvez Ave 76111
Galway Ave 76109
E Gambrell St 76115
W Gambrell St
301-397 76115
399-2699 76115
2700-3699 76133
Gammer Dr 76116
Garber Ln 76244
Garcia Ln 76140
Garden Ln 76119
Garden St 76117
Garden Acre Dr 76140
Garden Acres Dr 76140
Garden Bell Way 76118
Garden Bluff Trl 76118
Garden Gable Rd & Way 76118
Garden Springs Dr 76123
Garden Wood Dr 76118
Gardendale Dr 76120
Gardengate Ct & Ln 76137
Gardenia St 76119
Garfield Dr 76105
Garland Ave 76116
Garland Dr 76117
Garmon Dr 76105
Garnet Ln 76112
Garrick Ave 76133
Garrison Ave
2200-2399 76105
3900-4199 76119
Garvey St 76102
Garwin Dr 76132
Gary Dr 76117
Gary Ln 76112
Garza Ave 76116
Gascony Pl 76132
Gaston Ave 76116
Gateway Dr 76119
Gateway Alliance Dr 76244
Gateway Park Dr 76111

Gatineau Ct 76118
Gatlinburg Dr 76123
Gatwick Cir & Ct 76155
Gavin Ct 76179
Gay St 76111
Gayle Dr 76148
Gebron Ct & Dr 76126
Geddes Ave 76107
Gelbray Pl 76131
Gemini Pl 76106
Gendy St 76107
Gene Ln 76117
General Arnold Blvd 76114
General Ramey Dr 76114
General Worth Dr 76244
Genessee Ct 76118
Geneva Ln 76131
Genevieve Dr 76137
Genoa Rd 76116
Gentian Dr 76123
Gentilly Ln 76123
Gentle St 76140
George Ave 76119
George St 76108
Georgetown Dr 76140
Georgetown Pl 76244
Georgian Ct 76117
Georgian Dr 76117
Georgian Rd 76134
E Georgian Rd 76179
Gerald Ct 76244
Geranium Ln 76123
German Pointer Way 76123
Gerome St 76118
Geronimo Trl 76116
Gertie Barrett Rd 76119
Gessner Dr 76244
Gettysburg Dr 76140
Gettysburg Ln 76123
Geyser Trl 76137
Ghost Flower Dr 76177
Gibbs Dr 76108
Gibson Ln 76117
Giddyup Ln 76179
Gidran Dr 76244
Gila Bend Ln 76137
Gilbert Dr 76116
Gilbow Ave 76114
Gilcrest Dr 76111
Gill St 76131
Gillham Rd 76114
Gillis St 76111
Gillis Johnson St 76179
Gillispie Dr 76132
Gilman Rd 76140
Gilmore St 76111
Gilmore Creek Rd 76179
Gilvin St 76102
Gimper Dr 76119
Ginger Ct 76119
Gingerwood Ct 76123
Giordano Way 76244
Gipson St 76111
Giverny Ln 76116
Glacier Ct 76137
Glacier St 76115
Glade St 76114
Glade Oaks Dr 76120
Gladewater Dr 76134
Gladiola Ln 76123
Gladney Ln 76244
Gladys Ct 76116
Glasgow Rd 76134
Glassenberry St 76244
Glazier Bay Ln 76133
Gleashes St 76102
Glen Dr 76148
Glen Canyon Rd 76137
Glen Eden Dr 76119
Glen Garden Ave 76119
Glen Garden Dr
700-1799 76104
2500-2698 76119
2700-2999 76119
N Glen Garden Dr 76119
S Glen Garden Dr 76119

Glen Haven Dr 76133
Glen Hills Rd 76118
Glen Hollow Dr 76179
Glen Knoll Dr 76179
Glen Meadow Dr 76132
Glen Mills Trl 76179
Glen Park Dr 76119
Glen Springs Trl 76137
Glen Vista Dr 76244
Glenavon Ct 76109
Glenbrook Ln 76133
Glenbrook St 76126
Glenburne Dr 76131
Glenco Ter 76110
Glencrest Dr 76119
Glenda Ave 76111
Glenda St 76117
Glendale Ave 76106
Glendora St 76106
Gleneagles Cir 76137
Gleneagles Way 76179
Glenhaven Dr 76117
Glenmont Ct & Dr 76133
Glenmore Ave 76102
Glenn Ct 76140
Glenn Dr
1600-1799 76131
9000-9099 76108
Glenndon Dr 76120
Glenscape Ct & Trl 76137
Glenshee Dr 76135
Glenvar Rd 76135
Glenview Dr
5100-5598 76117
5600-5699 76117
5701-5999 76117
7200-7999 76180
Glenville Ct 76244
Glenwick Dr 76114
Glenwillow Ct 76132
Glenwood Ct & Dr 76109
Gleralto Dr 76135
Globe Ave 76131
Gloriosa Dr 76244
Gobi Dr 76131
Goddard Rd 76111
Goforth Rd 76126
Gold Basin Rd 76179
Gold Creek Dr E 76244
Gold Dust Ln 76131
Gold Spike Dr 76106
Golden Ln 76123
Golden Gate Dr E 76132
Golden Heights Rd 76177
Golden Horn Ln 76123
Golden Meadow Trl 76134
Golden Oak Ct 76108
Golden Oaks Dr 76117
Golden Sunset Ct & Trl 76244
Golden Triangle Blvd
2700-2898 76177
3500-5999 76244
Golden Triangle Cir 76244
Golden Triangle Dr 76177
Golden Yarrow Dr 76244
Goldeneye Ln 76120
Goldenrod Ave 76111
Goldenview Dr 76244
Goldenwood Dr 76112
Goldfield Ln 76108
Goldfinch Dr 76108
Goldie St 76111
Goldleaf Ct 76131
Goldrock Dr 76137
Goldrush Dr 76244
Goldstein Gate Dr 76140
Goldstone Ln 76131
Golf Club Cir & Dr 76179
Golfview Way 76126
Goliad St 76126
Gonzalez Dr 76105
Good Shepherd Way 76119
Goodfellow Ave 76112
Goodland Ter 76179
Goodman Ave 76107

Goodnight Cir
4100-4299 76137
9800-9898 76108
Goodnight Dr 76137
Gordon Ave
2700-3999 76110
4600-5399 76115
Gorman Dr 76132
Gothic Dr 76119
Gould Ave
1200-2699 76164
2800-3199 76106
Gounah St 76102
Goya St 76133
Grace Ave 76111
Grace Ln 76179
Grace Cozby Dr 76126
Grady St 76119
Grady Lee St 76134
Grafton St 76103
Graham St
5200-5899 76114
6000-6199 76135
Graham Ranch Rd 76134
Grainger St
400-1299 76104
1900-2299 76110
Grainger Trl 76137
Grainland Ct 76179
Granada Dr 76118
Granada Rd 76116
Granbury Rd
3300-4400 76109
4402-4498 76109
4600-7099 76133
7100-7899 76123
Granbury Cut Off 76132
N Grand Ave 76164
Grand Central Ct & Pkwy 76131
Grand Champion Blvd 76179
Grand Gulf Rd 76123
Grand Junction Dr 76179
Grand Lake Dr 76135
Grand Meadow Ct & Dr 76108
Grand Mesa Dr 76137
Grand National Blvd 76179
Grand Rapids Dr 76177
Grand River Rd 76155
Grand Teton Trl 76137
Grande Ct 76112
Grandstand Way 76244
Grandview Dr 76112
Granger Ln 76244
Granite Ct 76179
Granite Path 76244
Granite Creek Dr 76179
Granite Ridge Dr 76179
Granite Shoals Ave 76103
Grant Ave 76102
Grant Cir 76108
Grant Park Ave 76137
Grantland Cir 76112
Grants Ln 76179
N Grants Ln 76108
S Grants Ln 76108
Grants Lndg 76179
Grantsville Dr 76244
Grapeleaf Dr 76244
Grapevine Ter 76123
Grapewood St 76111
Grass Valley Trl 76123
Grasshopper Dr 76148
Grassland Ct 76179
Grassland Dr 76133
Grassmere Rd 76244
Grassy Glen Dr 76244
Grassy Hill Ln 76123
Grassy View Dr 76177
Grattan Dr 76112
Gravel Dr 76118
Gray Fox Ct & Dr 76123
Gray Oak Ln 76108
Gray Rock Dr 76131
Gray Shale Dr 76179

Grayhawk Ct & Ln 76244
Grayson Ave 76106
Grayson Ct 76148
Grayson St 76119
Grayson Way 76148
Grayson Ridge Dr 76179
Graywolf Ridge Trl 76244
Grazing Ln 76123
Great Basin Ln 76133
Great Divide Dr 76137
Great Southwest Pkwy 76106
Greble Ct 76244
Green Dr 76117
W Green St 76179
Green Apple Ct 76148
Green Apple Dr 76140
Green Arbor Ct 76109
Green Ash Dr 76244
Green Heath Ave 76120
Green Hill Cir 76112
Green Jacket Dr 76137
Green Links Dr 76126
Green Meadow Ct & Dr 76112
Green Oaks Dr 76114
Green Oaks Rd 76116
Green Ridge Dr 76148
Green Ridge St 76133
Green Ridge Ter 76179
Green River Ct & Trl 76103
Green Willow Dr 76134
Greenacres Dr
6600-6699 76148
7300-7399 76112
Greenbelt Rd 76118
Greenbriar Ct 76179
Greenbriar Ln 76132
Greenbriar Crescent St 76135
Greenbrier Dr 76114
Greenbrook Pl 76116
Greendale Ct 76112
Greendale Dr 76148
Greene Ave
2500-3299 76109
4300-5299 76133
Greenfern Ln 76137
Greenfield Ave 76102
Greenfield Ct 76148
Greenfield Dr 76148
Greenfield Rd 76135
Greengage Dr 76133
Greenhaven Dr 76179
Greenleaf St 76107
Greenlee St 76112
Greenshaven Dr 76112
Greenshire Pl 76133
Greenspoint Cir, Ct, Dr & Ter 76112
Greenstone Dr 76137
Greentree Ct 76179
Greenvale Ct 76179
Greenview Cir N 76120
Greenview Cir S 76120
Greenview Ct 76126
Greenway Dr 76179
Greenway Rd 76116
Greenwood Way 76244
Greenwood Creek Dr 76109
Greer St 76102
Grenada Ct & Dr 76119
Greta Ln 76120
Grey Crow Dr 76177
Grey Twig Dr 76244
Greybull Trl 76134
Greylock Ct & Dr 76137
Griffin St 76133
Griffith Dr 76179
Griggs Ave
600-899 76103
900-3099 76105
3300-3799 76119
Griggs Ct
3900-3999 76119
4500-4599 76140

Griggs St
6100-6399 76119
6800-6999 76140
Grigsby Dr 76140
Grinstein Dr 76244
Grisham Way 76109
Gristmill Ct 76179
Gristmill Ln 76140
Grizzly Bear Dr 76244
Grizzly Hills Cir 76244
Gross St 76111
Grossman Groove Ln 76140
Grove St 76102
N Grove St
100-299 76102
1300-2099 76164
3200-3899 76106
S Grove St
2700-3099 76104
3100-3899 76110
Grover Ave 76106
Guadalupe Ct 76137
Guadalupe Dr 76179
Guadalupe Rd 76116
Guard Hill Dr 76123
Guenther Ave 76106
Guilford Rd 76107
Guilford St 76119
Gulfstream Rd 76106
Gulfwind Ct & Ln 76123
Gull Cir 76131
Gum Dr 76119
Gumm Rd 76134
Gumper Ct 76126
Gumwood Park 76118
Gunnison Trl 76116
Gustave St 76114
Gutierrez Dr 76177
Guyana Rd 76123
Gwynne St 76111
Gypsy Gulch St 76119
H C Meacham Blvd 76135
SE Ha Payak Rd 76244
Haas Dr 76244
Hackamore St 76108
Hadley St 76117
Hagan St 76106
Hagg Dr 76114
Hahn Blvd 76117
Haig Point Ct 76132
Halbert St 76112
Hale Ave 76106
Hale Ct 76116
Haley Ave 76117
Haley Ln 76132
Half Moon Dr 76111
Half Moon Bay Ln 76177
Halifax Rd 76116
Hall St 76105
Halladay Trl 76108
Hallbrook Dr 76134
Hallmark Dr S & W 76134
Halloran St 76107
Hallum St 76114
Hallvale Dr 76108
Halter Dr 76126
Haltom Rd
100-1299 76117
1300-5099 76117
5500-6199 76137
6700-6899 76137
Halyard Ct 76135
Hamilton Ave 76107
E & W Hammond St 76115
Hampshire Blvd 76103
N Hampshire Blvd
5000-5099 76103
5100-5114 76112
5116-5499 76112
S Hampshire Blvd
5000-5099 76103
5100-5102 76112
5104-6099 76112
N Hampshire St 76179
S Hampshire St 76179
Hampton St 76102

N Hampton St
100-799 76102
3000-3599 76106
Hamsted St 76115
Hancock Ct 76108
Handley Dr
1400-1476 76112
1475-1475 76124
1477-3199 76112
1478-3198 76112
S Handley Dr 76112
Handley Ederville Rd
100-199 76112
1700-2499 76118
2500-3299 76118
Haney Ct & Dr 76148
Hangar Rd 76179
Hanger Ave 76105
Hanger Cutoff Rd 76135
Hanger Park Dr 76119
Hanna Ave
2300-2799 76164
2800-3199 76106
Hanna Ct 76126
Hanna Ranch Blvd 76140
Hanna Rose Ln 76244
Hannahsville Ln 76244
Hanon Ct & Dr 76108
Hanover Rd 76116
N & S Hansbarger St 76140
Hanson Dr 76148
Happy Trl 76244
Harbor East Dr 76179
Harbour Breeze Ln 76179
Harbour Creek Ct 76179
Harbour Point Cir 76179
Harbour Town Ln 76132
Harbour View Ct & Ln 76179
Hardback Ct 76135
Hardeman St 76119
Harding St 76102
N Harding St
200-599 76102
3000-3899 76106
Hardisty St 76118
Hardnose Ln 76135
Hardwood Ct 76135
Hardy St 76106
Harlan Ave 76132
Harlanwood Dr 76109
Harlem St 76105
Harley Ave 76107
Harmon Rd
100-1800 76177
1802-3098 76177
8600-8699 76131
8700-13299 76177
E Harmon Rd 76131
Harmony Dr 76133
Harness Cir 76179
Harney Dr 76244
Harold Creek Dr 76179
S Harper St 76111
Harriman Dr 76131
Harrington Ave 76164
Harris Ln 76117
Harris Pkwy 76132
Harrisdale Ave 76114
Harrison Ave 76110
Harrison Way 76148
Harrold St 76107
Harrow Ln 76117
Hart St 76112
Hartford Dr 76114
Hartman Rd
5400-5899 76119
5900-6499 76119
6500-6599 76140
Hartsfield Pl 76155
Hartwood Cir, Ct & Dr 76109
Harvard Ave 76118
Harvard Ct 76123
Harvard St 76114
Harvest Ln 76133
Harvest Glen Ct 76108
Harvest Grove Dr 76244

Harvest Moon Dr 76123
Harvest Ridge Rd 76244
Harvestmeade St 76155
Harvestwood Cir 76112
E Harvey Ave 76104
Harwell St 76108
Harwen Ter
3400-3699 76109
4300-4699 76133
Harwood St 76103
Haskell St 76107
Hassett Ave 76114
Hasten Ct 76120
Hastings Dr 76133
Hatch Rd 76135
Hatcher St
2900-3099 76105
3200-4199 76119
Hatchery Rd 76114
Hathaway Dr 76108
Hathcox Ave 76115
Hathman Ln 76244
E Hattie St 76104
Haun Dr 76137
N Haven Dr 76126
Haven Ln 76112
Haven Lake Way 76244
Havenview Ct 76132
Havenwood Ct & Ln 76112
Hawkeye Ct 76119
Hawkins St 76105
Hawkins Home Blvd 76126
Hawkins View Dr 76132
Hawks Nest Dr 76131
Hawkshaw Ct 76137
Hawkview Dr 76179
Hawkwood Ct & Trl 76123
Hawlet St 76103
Hawley Dr 76244
Hawrylak St 76135
Hawthorn Ln 76137
Hawthorne Ave 76110
Hawthorne Park Dr 76132
Hayden Pl 76155
Hayes Ct 76108
Hayfield Ct 76137
Haylee Dr 76131
Hayloft Ct 76123
Haynes Ave 76103
S Haynes Ave
300-999 76103
1000-1299 76105
Haynie St 76112
Hays St 76102
N Hays St
100-699 76102
3000-3199 76106
Haystack Blvd 76116
Haywire Ranch Rd 76108
Haywood Ct & Dr 76126
Hazel Dr 76244
Hazel Leigh Ln 76134
Hazeline Rd 76103
Hazelnook Rd 76134
Hazelnut Ct 76179
Hazelnut Dr 76140
Hazeltine Dr 76132
Hazelwood Dr W 76107
Headless Horseman Rd 76114
Hearthstone Ct 76123
Hearthstone Ln 76135
Heartwood Dr 76244
Heath St 76137
Heathcliff Dr 76140
Heathcote St 76102
Heather Ct 76126
Heather Dr 76148
Heather Ln 76140
Heather Trl 76119
Heatherbend St 76123
Heatherglen Ter 76179
Heatherwood Ct 76179
Heathrow Ct 76123
Heavenway Dr 76148
Heber Springs Trl 76244

Hedge Apple Ct 76244
Hedgeoak Ct 76112
Hedgewood Ct & Trl 76112
Hedrick St 76111
Heidelberg Dr 76134
Heidi Ct 76108
Heidi Ln 76116
Heights Dr & Ln 76112
Heights View Dr 76126
Heightsview Ln E 76132
Heirloom Dr 76134
Heirship Ct 76244
Helmick Ave 76107
Helms St 76114
Helmsford Trl 76179
Hemlock Dr 76117
Hemlock St 76137
Hemlock Trl 76131
Hemphill St
100-1699 76104
1700-4099 76110
4100-5500 76115
5502-5598 76115
9901-9999 76134
Hemsell Pl 76116
Hen House Rd 76244
Hencken Ct 76126
Henco Dr 76119
Henderson St 76102
N Henderson St
100-112 76102
114-599 76102
600-1099 76107
S Henderson St
200-1699 76104
1700-4099 76110
4100-4399 76115
Hendricks St 76105
Henna Ln 76108
Hennessey Ct & Trl 76131
Henry Ave 76106
Henry Dr 76118
Hensley Dr 76134
Hereford Dr 76179
Heritage Ave 76131
Heritage Ln
3000-3499 76140
6900-6999 76134
Heritage Pkwy 76177
Heritage Glen Dr 76244
Heritage Hills Ct & Dr 76109
Heritage Place Dr 76137
Heritage Trace Pkwy
2400-3499 76177
3500-5299 76244
Heritage Way Dr 76137
Herkes Ct & Pl 76126
Herman St 76108
Hermosa St 76107
Herndon Dr 76116
Heron Dr 76108
Herrick Ct 76117
Herring Dr 76179
Herschel Dr 76148
Hervie St 76107
Heywood Ave 76109
Hialeah Ct 76179
Hialeah Park St 76179
Hiawatha Ct 76131
Hiawatha Ln 76131
Hiawatha Trl 76135
Hibbs Dr 76137
Hibiscus St 76137
Hickende Dr 76137
Hickock Dr 76116
Hickory Cir 76244
Hickory Cir S 76244
Hickory Dr 76117
Hickory Pl 76137
Hickory Bend Ln 76108
Hickory Meadows Ln 76244
Hickory Springs Rd 76116
Hickory Upland Dr 76131
Hickoryhill Rd 76148
E Hicks Field Rd 76179
Hidden Ln 76107

Hidden Pl 76135
Hidden Rd 76107
Hidden Brook Dr 76120
Hidden Cove Ct 76179
Hidden Creek Cir 76109
Hidden Creek Ct 76107
Hidden Creek Rd 76107
Hidden Dale Dr 76140
Hidden Ford Dr 76131
Hidden Gate Ct 76120
Hidden Hill Dr 76179
Hidden Hills Ct & Ln 76108
Hidden Meadow Dr 76179
Hidden Oaks Dr 76120
Hidden Point Dr 76120
Hidden Springs Dr 76109
Hidden Valley Ct & Dr 76177
Hidden View Cir 76109
Hideaway Trl 76131
Hiett Ct 76112
Higgins Ln 76111
High St 76110
High Bluff Dr 76108
High Brook Dr 76132
High Cotton Trl 76179
High Country Dr 76132
High Country Trl 76131
High Creek Dr 76119
High Crest Ave 76111
High Desert Dr 76131
High Eagle Trl 76108
High Lawn Ter 76148
High Meadow Ct
6500-6599 76148
7600-7699 76112
High Meadow Trl 76135
High Plains Ct 76179
High Point Hl 76126
High Point Rd 76119
High Ridge Rd
1400-1899 76126
5200-5299 76119
5300-5399 76119
5400-5499 76140
High River Rd 76155
High Vista Ct 76112
Highbush Dr 76126
Highcrest Dr 76148
Highgate Rd 76244
Highgrove Dr 76132
Highland Ave
1800-1999 76164
5600-6222 76117
6224-6228 76117
N Highland Cir 76117
S Highland Cir 76117
Highland Ter S 76134
Highland Trl 76155
Highland Lake Dr 76135
Highland Meadow Ct & Dr 76132
Highland Oaks St 76107
Highland Orchard Dr 76179
Highland Park Cir 76107
Highland Park Cir W 76107
Highland Park Dr 76132
Highland Ridge Rd 76108
Highland Station Dr 76131
Highlawn Ter 76133
Hightower Dr 76148
Hightower St 76112
Highview Rd 76140
Highview Ter
2500-2799 76109
6400-6599 76148
Highway Dr 76116
Highway 114 76177
Highway 360 76155
Highway 377 S 76126
Highwoods Ct & Trl 76112
Hilcroft Rd 76244
Hildring Ct 76109
Hildring Dr E
4000-4999 76109
5000-5299 76132
Hildring Dr W 76109

Street	ZIP
Hill Ave	76116
Hill Ct	76148
N Hill Ln	76135
Hill Pl	76164
Hill Ridge Dr	76135
Hill Top Pass	76126
Hillard Heights Ct	76132
Hillbrook Ct	76126
Hillcrest Blvd	76244
Hillcrest Cir	76116
Hillcrest Ct E	76244
Hillcrest Dr	76148
Hillcrest St	76107
Hillcroft Rd	76108
Hilldale Ct	76116
Hilldale Rd	
3100-3499	76116
3900-4699	76119
6400-6499	76116
Hillgard Dr	76108
Hillglen Dr	76148
S Hills Ave	76109
S Hills Cir	76109
N Hills Dr	76117
W Hills Ter	76179
Hillside Ave	76119
Hillside Ct	76132
Hillside Dr	
1500-1799	76114
4800-4858	76114
4860-4999	76114
6600-6799	76132
Hillstone Dr	76126
Hilltop Cir	76114
Hilltop Ct	76134
Hilltop Dr	
5900-6099	76148
7400-7499	76108
Hilltop Rd	76109
Hillview Dr	
2400-2499	76119
5900-6099	76148
Hillwood Dr	76179
Hires Ln	76117
Hitson Ln	76112
Hobart St	76134
Hobby Ln	76155
Hodgkins Rd	76135
Hodgson St	76115
Hogan Dr	76126
Holden St	76111
Holder St	76118
Holland St	76164
Holley St	76140
Holliday Dr	76244
Hollis St	
2600-3699	76111
3700-3706	76111
3701-3707	76111
3708-4299	76111
4300-4599	76117
Hollister Dr	76244
Holliwell Ln	76179
Hollow Creek Rd	76116
Hollow Forest Dr	76123
Hollow Hills St	76120
Hollow Point Dr	76123
Hollow Valley Dr	76244
Holloway St	76114
Hollowbrook Ct & Rd	76103
Holly Ct	76126
Holly Bend Dr	76116
Holly Grove Ct & Dr	76108
Holly Hock Ln	76244
Holly Springs Dr	76133
Hollyberry Ct	76133
Hollyridge Ln	76108
Holmes St	76105
Holt St	
1500-1799	76103
8800-8999	76135
Homan Ave	76164
Home Port Dr	76131
Homedale Dr	76112
Homelands Way	76135
Homestead Cir	76133
Homestretch Ct & Dr	76244
Honey Dew Ln	76120
Honeybee Ct & Ln	76137
Honeycomb Ct	76131
Honeysuckle Ave	76111
Hood St	76135
Hooks Ln	76112
Hooper St	76107
Hope St	76114
Hopewell Cv & Ln	76179
Hopi Trl S	76108
Hopke Ct	76126
Hopkins Ct & St	76107
Horace Ave	76244
Horizon Dr	76177
Horizon Pl	76133
Horn Cap Dr	76179
Horn Frog St	76108
Hornaday Cir N & S	76120
Hornbeam Dr	76123
Hornby St	76108
Horncastle Ct & St	76134
Horne St	76107
Horse Trap Dr	76179
Horse Whisper Ln	76131
Horseback Trl	76177
Horseshoe Bend Ct & Dr	76131
Horseshoe Ridge Dr	76244
Horton Cir	76133
Horton Rd	76119
Hosta Way	76123
Hot Springs Ct	76123
Hot Springs Trl	76137
Houghton Ave	76107
Hounds Tail Ln	76244
House St	76103
Houston St	76102
N Houston St	
100-399	76102
500-2799	76164
2800-3799	76106
Houston Hill Rd	76179
Houston Wood Dr	76244
Hovenkamp Ave	76118
Howard St	76119
Howling Coyote Ln	76131
Huckleberry Dr	76137
Huddleston St	76137
Hudgins Ave	76111
Hudson St	76103
Huffines Blvd	76135
Huffman St	76111
N Hughes Ave	76103
S Hughes Ave	
600-899	76103
900-3099	76105
3300-4999	76119
Hughes Ct	76148
Hughes Dr	76148
Hulen Cir E	76133
Hulen Cir W	76133
Hulen Ct	76109
Hulen Pl	76107
Hulen St	76107
S Hulen St	
2600-4599	76109
4600-6099	76132
6100-7899	76133
8100-8498	76123
8500-8800	76123
8802-9198	76123
Hulen Bend Blvd, Cir, Ct, Ln & Ter	76132
Hulen Park Cir	76123
Hulen Park Dr	
3700-3799	76109
4400-4798	76132
Humbert Ave	76107
Humble Ct	76107
Humboldt Bay Trl	76177
E & W Humbolt St	76104
Hummingbird Ct	76137
Hummingbird Trl	76131
Hunt Club Pl	76244
Huntdale Ct	76135
Hunter St	
2700-3199	76112
4400-4599	76117
Hunter Park Cir	76116
Hunters Trl	76123
Hunters Creek Ct & Dr	76123
Hunters Glen Ct	76120
Hunters Glen Dr	76148
Hunters Glen Trl	76120
Hunters Hill Dr	76123
Hunters Point Way	76123
Hunters Ridge Rd	76132
Hunting Dr	76119
Hunting Green Ct & Dr	76134
Huntington Dr	76137
Huntington Ln	76110
Huntwick Dr	76123
Hurley Ave	
1100-1699	76104
1700-2299	76110
Huron Trl	76135
Hurricane Ln	76244
Hutchinson St	76106
Hyacinth Dr	76244
Hyatt Ct	76116
Hyde Ct	76112
Hyde Rd	76179
I M Terrell Cir & Way	76102
Ibis Ct	76131
Ichabod Crane Rd	76114
Ida Way	76119
Idledell Dr	76116
Idlewild Dr	76107
Illinois Ave	
100-1599	76104
3100-3299	76110
Image Cir	76116
Imes Ln	76179
Imperial Dr	76119
Inca Rd	76116
Incline Ter	76179
Indale Rd	76116
Independence Ln	76140
Independence Pkwy	76177
Independence Rd	76131
Indian Ct	76244
Indian Bluff Trl	76131
Indian Cove St	76108
Indian Creek Ct	76107
Indian Creek Dr	
1400-6299	76107
6300-6399	76116
12100-12699	76179
E Indian Creek Dr	76179
W Indian Creek Dr	76179
Indian Creek Rd	76179
Indian Crest Dr	76179
Indian Hills Ct	76126
Indian Mound Ct	
200-299	76108
4700-4799	76132
Indian Mound Rd	76108
Indian Pony Way	76244
Indian Rock Dr	76244
Indian Springs Rd	76148
Indian Tree Ct	76126
Indian Valley Dr	76123
Indiana Ave	76137
Indianwood Ln	76132
Indigo Ct	76112
Indigo Ridge Dr	76131
Indio St	76133
Industrial Ave	76104
E Industrial Ave	76131
Industrial Dr	76111
Inez Dr	76114
Ingle Ct	76117
Ingram St	
500-598	76108
800-899	76104
Ingrid Ln	76131
Inman Ct	76109
Innisbrook Ln	76179
Innovation Way	76244
Inspiration Dr	76126
Inspiration Ln	76114
Insurance Ln	76109
Intermodal Pkwy	76177
International Plz	76109
Interstate 20	
5600-5698	76140
Interstate 20	
5901-5997	76132
5999-6199	76132
E Interstate 20	76119
Inverness Ave	
4600-4799	76109
4800-5199	76132
Inwood Dr	76148
Inwood Rd	76109
Inwood St	76126
Iola St	76119
Iona Dr	76120
Ira St N	76117
Irene St	76116
Irion Ave	76106
Iris Ave, Cir, Ct & Dr	76137
Irish Bend Dr	76123
Irish Mountain Dr	76123
Irish Setter Dr	76123
Irish Valley Trl	76123
Irma St	76104
Iron Dr	76137
Iron Gate Ct	76179
Iron Horse Dr	76131
Iron Horse Ln	76107
Iron Ore Trl	76131
Iron Ridge Dr	76140
Ironsides Ln	76131
Ironstone Trl	76179
Ironwood Ct	76140
Irwin St	76110
Isadora Ln	76131
Isbell Ct, Rd & St	76114
Isham St	76112
Island Cir & Ct	76137
Island Park Ct & Dr	76137
Island View Dr	76135
Isle Royale Dr	76137
Islip Cir	76155
Ivanhoe Dr	76132
Ives St	76108
Ivey St	76111
Ivy Ct	76244
Ivy Creek Ln	76140
Ivy Glen Ln	76140
Ivy Hill Ct & Rd	76135
Ivy Leaf Ln	76108
S Ivy Way Ct & Pl	76118
Ivy Wood Ln	76115
J T Luther Dr	76115
J W Delaney Rd	76112
Jack Atkins Ct	76117
Jack Newell Blvd N & S	76118
Jackie Ct & Ter	76148
Jacksboro Hwy	
1100-5998	76114
1101-1111	76107
1113-5999	76114
2601-2699	76114
7300-12199	76135
8201-9099	76135
Jackson Ct	76118
Jackson St	76119
Jackson Way	76244
Jacob Ct	76116
Jacocks Ln	76115
Jacqueline Ct & Rd	76112
Jade St	76244
Jaden Ln	76116
Jakmar Rd	76126
Jalah Ct	76114
Jamaica Ln	76103
Jambeass Dr	76132
Jameanti Rd	76177
James Ave	
2900-4099	76110
4100-5599	76115
5600-5799	76134
James Ct	76108
James Dr	76114
Jameson St	76118
Jamestown Dr	76140
Jamesway Ct & Rd	76135
Jamies Rdg	76126
Jan Ct	76179
Jana Dr	76119
Janada St	76117
Jane Ln	76117
Jane Anne St	76117
Janice Ln	76112
Janrue Ct	76117
January Cir	76126
Japanese Garden Ln	76107
Japonica St	76123
Jarvis Rd	76179
Jarvis St	76104
Jarvis Way	76135
Jasmine Dr	76137
Jason Ct	
2900-2999	76112
9300-9399	76108
Jason Dr	76108
Jasper St	76106
Jay St	
3500-3599	76140
8400-8699	76108
Jaybird Dr	76244
Jaycrest Ct	76135
Jaylin St	76244
Jazmine Dr	76140
Jean Ave	76119
Jean Hills Ln	76119
Jeaneta Ave	76126
Jeanette Dr	76109
Jeff St	76111
E Jefferson Ave	76104
W Jefferson Ave	76110
Jefferson Pkwy	76107
Jeffries Ln	76117
Jennie Dr	76133
Jennifer Ct	76119
Jennifer Dr	76118
Jennifer Leigh Ct	76118
Jennings Ave	76102
S Jennings Ave	
100-1699	76104
1700-3799	76110
Jenny Lake Trl	76244
Jenson Cir, Ct & Rd	76112
Jeremiah Dr	76108
Jericho Ln	76108
Jerome St	
900-998	76104
1000-1799	76110
Jerri Ln	76117
Jerri Lynn Ct & Dr	76148
Jerry Ln	76117
Jerry Dunn Pkwy	76126
Jersey Ln	76102
E Jessamine St	76104
W Jessamine St	76110
Jessica St	76244
Jessica Kay Ln	76119
Jessica Marie Ln	76119
Jessie Pl	76134
Jewell Ave	76112
Jill Ln	76112
Jill St	76108
N Jim Wright Fwy	76108
NW Jim Wright Fwy	76135
S Jim Wright Fwy	76108
Joanne Ct	76118
Jockey Dr	76244
Jockey Club Ln	76179
Jodi Dr	76244
Joe B Rushing	76119
Joe Elle Ln	76135
Joel East Rd	76140
John Dr	76118
John B Sias Memorial Pkwy	76134
John Burgess Dr	76140
John Kennedy Dr	76179
John Reagan St	76126
John Ryan Dr	76132
John T White Rd	
6700-6799	76112
6801-9099	76120
John T White Rd N	76120
Johnnie Ct & St	76148
Johns Ter	76115
Johns Way	76135
Johnson Ave	76140
Johnson St	
1000-1299	76126
1300-1399	76102
2400-2499	76105
Johnstone Ln	76133
Jolie Dr	76137
Jolley Ct	76135
Jonah Dr	76108
N Jones Cir	76104
S Jones Cir	76104
W Jones Cir	76104
Jones St	76102
N Jones St	
600-1499	76164
3300-3499	76106
S Jones St	
2400-3099	76104
3200-4099	76110
Jonette Dr	76118
Jonquil St	76133
Joplin Ln	76108
Joplin St	76117
Jordan Trl	76126
Jordan Park Dr	76117
Joseph Ln	76112
Josh Rd	76177
Joshua Ct	76114
Joshua Dr	76134
Joy Dr	76108
Joy Grace Dr	76137
Joy Lee St	76117
Joyce Dr	76116
Joymeadow Dr	76123
Joyner Ranch Rd	76134
Juanita St	76111
Judd St	76104
N Judd St	76108
S Judd St	76108
Judie Ct	76148
Judith Way	76137
N & S Judkins St	76111
Judy Ave	76126
Judy Ct	76148
Judy Dr	76148
Judy Ln	76103
Judy St	76108
Julian St	76244
Julie Ave	76116
N Juliet Ln	76137
June Dr	76108
Juneau Ct & Rd	76116
Juneberry St	76137
Juniper Ln	76126
Juniper St	76117
Junius St	76103
Juran Ct	76135
Just Dr	76140
Justin Ct	76148
Justin Dr	76244
Justine Pl	76126
Kachina Lodge Rd	76131
Kalgary Ct	76179
Kaltenbrun Rd	76119
Kane St N	76126
Kansas St	76107
Kaplan Ct	76155
Karen Cir	76116
Karen Ct	76126
Karen Ln	
4200-4299	76135
6000-6099	76148
Karen St	76116
Karnes St	76111
Kary Lynn Dr E	76148
S Kate St	76108
Katherine Ct	76118
Kathleen Ct & Dr	76137
Kathy Ln	
3100-3299	76123
7500-7599	76126
Kathy Ann Ct	76126
Katie Ln	76148
Katie Corral Dr	76126
Katie Joyce Ct	76135
Katrina Ct	76114
Katrine Ct & St	76117
Katy Dr	76131
Katy Rd	76244
Katy St	
300-499	76119
4900-5199	76105
Katy Rose Ct	76126
Kay Dr	76119
Kay Ln	
100-106	76179
100-116	76114
108-399	76179
118-198	76114
Kay Lea Dawn Ct	76135
Kearby St	76111
Kearney Ave	76106
Keating Rd	76137
Keating St	76244
Keechi Creek Ct	76137
Keith Dr	76244
Keith Pumphrey Dr	76114
Kell Dr	76112
Kell St	76109
Keller Ave	76126
Keller Haslet Rd	76244
Keller Hicks Rd	
1700-2599	76177
2600-2898	76244
2900-4200	76244
4202-4998	76244
Kelley Ct	76120
Kelley Dr	76140
Kelli Ct	76106
Kellis St	76119
E Kellis St	76119
W Kellis St	76115
Kelly Ct	76137
Kelly Rd	76126
Kelly Lynn Ln	76148
Kelpie Ct	76111
Kelroy St	76119
Kelton St	76133
Kelvin Ave	76133
Kemble Ct & St	76103
Kemp Rd	76118
Kempson Ct	76179
Kender Ln	76108
Kenilworth Dr	76244
Kenley St	76107
Kennedale Pkwy	76140
W Kennedale Pkwy	76140
Kennedale Rd	76119
Kennedale St	76140
Kennedale New Hope Rd	76140
Kennedy Ct	76148
Kennedy Ln	76131
Kennedy St	
1300-1699	76102
5700-5899	76148
Kenny Ct & Dr	76244
Kenshire Dr	76126
Kensington Dr	76110
Kent St	76109
Kentish Dr	76137
S Kentucky Ave	76104
Kentucky Derby Ln	76179
Kentwood Pl	76112
Kenway Ct	76132
Kenwick Ave	76116
Kenwood Ave	76116
Kenwood Ct	76103
Kenya Ct	76106
Kermit Ave	76116
Kern Ct & Ln	76137
Kerr St	76112
Kerry Ln	76117
Kerry St	76126

Kessler Rd 76114
Keswick Ave 76133
Kevin Dr 76118
Key West Ct 76133
Keyhole Cir 76135
Kickapoo Dr 76179
Kielder Cir & Ct 76134
Kildee Ln 76133
Killdeer Cir 76108
Killian St 76119
Kilpatrick Ave 76107
Kimbell Dr 76244
Kimberly Ct 76137
Kimberly Ln 76133
Kimberly Kay Dr 76133
Kimbo Ct 76111
Kimbo Rd
  2600-3899 76111
  3900-4099 76117
Kimbrough St 76108
Kimzey St 76107
Kincaid Ct & Dr 76116
Kinchani Dr 76116
Kind St 76140
King Ct 76112
King St 76140
King Arthurs Ct 76140
King George Dr 76112
King Ranch Ct 76108
King Ranch Rd 76132
King Richards Ln 76133
Kingfisher Dr 76131
Kings Ave 76117
Kings Cir N 76111
Kings Cir S 76111
Kings Ct 76118
Kings Hwy 76117
Kings Trl 76133
Kings Canyon Cir 76134
Kings Cross Dr 76131
Kings Glen Ln 76140
Kings Oaks Ln 76111
Kingsbrook Ln 76179
Kingsbrook Trl 76120
Kingsbury Ave 76118
Kingsdale Dr 76119
Kingsknowe Pkwy 76135
Kingsley Dr
  900-1099 76179
  6900-6999 76134
Kingslink Cir 76135
Kingsmill Ter 76112
Kingspoint Blvd 76140
Kingsport Rd 76155
Kingsridge Rd 76109
Kingston Ct 76109
Kingswood Cir & Dr 76133
Kinman St 76117
Kinsale Ct 76116
Kinsey Dr 76126
Kinston Cv & St 76179
Kiowa Ave 76114
Kiowa Trl W 76108
Kipling St 76112
Kirby Dr 76155
Kirk Dr 76116
Kirkland Ct & Dr 76109
Kirkwall Dr 76134
Kirkwood Rd 76116
Kittansett Ct 76132
Kitty Dr 76148
Kitty Hawk Ln 76123
Kittyhawk Ct & Ln 76108
Klamath Rd 76116
Klamath Mountain Rd 76137
Kleinert St 76134
Knight Dr 76140
Knight Way 76126
Knight Island Ln 76120
Knights Ct 76244
Knob Hill Rd 76140
Knowledge Dr 76117
N & S Knowles Dr 76179
Knox St 76119
Koch St 76105
Kodiak Ct 76137
Koen Ln 76155
Koldin Ln 76114
Koldin Trl 76140
Kollmeyer Way 76126
Korth St 76114
Kramer Ct 76112
Krista Ln 76120
Kristen Ct & Dr 76131
Kroger Dr 76244
Kuban Blvd 76120
Kuroki St 76104
Kurtz Ct 76120
Kutman Ct 76105
Kyle Ave 76133
Kyledale Ct 76135
Kyleigh Dr 76123
La Bandera Trl 76126
La Barranca St 76114
La Cantera Ct & Dr 76108
La Jitas Ct 76108
La Jolla Ct 76116
La Jolla Cv 76114
La Junta St 76114
La Monde Ter 76114
La Palma Dr 76116
La Plaza Dr 76108
La Sierra Rd 76134
Labadie Dr 76118
Lacebark Ln 76244
Lacebark Elm Dr 76123
Lacey Ln 76244
Lackland Rd 76116
Lacy Dr 76177
Ladera Ct
  4100-4199 76133
  8900-8999 76126
Ladera Dr 76108
Ladera Pl 76133
Ladigo Ln 76126
Ladina Pl 76131
Ladona Dr 76133
Lady Rachael Ct 76134
Lafayette Ave 76107
Lago Vista Dr 76132
Lagonda Ave 76164
Lagoona Ln 76134
Laguardia Ln 76155
Laguna Ct & Dr 76119
Lahontan Dr 76132
Lake Dr 76117
N Lake Dr 76135
Lake St 76102
S Lake St 76104
Lake Arlington Rd 76119
Lake Arrowhead Dr 76137
Lake Bluff Dr 76137
Lake Breeze Ct & Dr 76132
Lake Charles Ave N 76103
Lake Chelen Dr 76137
Lake Como Dr 76107
Lake Country Ct & Dr 76179
Lake Falls Dr 76118
Lake Harbor Ct 76179
Lake Havasu Trl 76103
Lake Haven Cir 76108
Lake Highlands Dr 76179
Lake Louise Ct & Rd 76103
Lake Mead Trl 76137
Lake Meredith Way 76137
Lake Oaks Cir 76108
Lake Powell Dr 76137
Lake Rock Ct & Dr 76179
Lake Shore Ct 76103
Lake Shore Ct N 76179
Lake Shore Dr
  1400-1799 76103
  6100-6199 76179
Lake Side Dr 76132
Lake Stone Trl 76123
Lake Tahoe Trl 76137
Lake Valley Ct 76123
Lake View Dr 76179
Lake View Rdg 76108
Lake Villas Dr 76137
Lake Vista Dr 76132
Lake Vista St 76135
Lake Worth Blvd 76135
Lakecliff Dr 76179
Lakeland St 76111
Lakepoint Dr 76119
Lakeridge Rd 76108
Lakeside Ct 76179
Lakeside Cv 76135
Lakeside Dr
  5600-11099 76179
  6100-6899 76135
N Lakeside Dr 76134
Lakeside Oaks Cir 76135
Lakeview Cir 76179
Lakeview Ct
  5900-5999 76137
  12600-12699 76179
Lakeview Dr
  300-400 76126
  402-498 76126
  4300-4599 76135
Lakeway Cir 76179
Lakeway Ct 76126
Lakeway Dr 76126
Lakewood Dr 76135
Lakewood Rd 76107
Lakewood Heights Ct 76179
Lalagray Ln 76148
Lamar St
  101-197 76102
  199-1299 76102
  5600-5699 76148
N Lamar St 76102
Lamb Creek Dr 76179
Lambert Ave 76109
Lamberton Ter 76244
Lambeth Ln
  4300-4399 76103
  5200-6499 76112
Lamesa Pl 76109
Lamington Dr 76244
Lamond Ct 76117
Lamont St 76110
Lampasas Dr 76126
Lampe Ct & Dr 76148
Lamplighter Ln 76134
Lamplighter Trl 76244
Lana Cir 76140
Lanae Ln 76134
Lanark Ave 76109
E Lancaster Ave
  100-1749 76102
  1750-5099 76103
  5100-7999 76112
  8000-8099 76120
W Lancaster Ave
  200-250 76102
  251-299 76101
  251-299 76102
  251-299 76113
  252-1698 76102
  301-1699 76102
  2700-3599 76107
E Lancaster St 76102
Lance Ct 76148
Lance Leaf Dr 76244
Lancelot Cir 76140
Lancelot Ct 76133
Lanchant St 76107
Landers Ln 76135
Landers St 76107
Landing Way 76179
Landing Way Ct 76179
Landino St 76114
Landisburg Trl 76244
Landmark Dr 76244
Landmark Ln 76119
Landmark Ridge St 76133
Lands End Blvd 76116
Lands End Ct 76116
Lands End St 76109
Landsdale Ln 76179
Landview Dr 76133
Landwood Ct 76120
Landy Ln 76118
Lanewood Dr 76112
Langley Ave 76140
Langley Rd 76114
Langley Hill Dr 76244
Langston St 76105
Lanham Ct & St 76108
Lankford Trl 76244
Lanola Ct 76103
Lansdale Rd 76116
Lansdowne Ave 76135
Lansford Ct & Dr 76126
Lantana Ct & Ln 76112
Lantern Hollow St 76109
Lara Ct 76133
Lara Ln 76148
Laramie Trl 76116
Larch St 76135
Laredo Dr 76116
Lariat Cir 76244
Lariat Dr 76131
Lariat Ln 76108
Lark St 76117
Larkin Ave 76133
Larks View Pt 76244
Larkspur Dr 76137
Larkspur Ln 76112
Larry St 76117
Larson Ct & Ln 76115
Las Brisas St 76119
Las Cimas Ct 76132
Las Cruces Dr 76119
Las Vegas Ct
  8600-8710 76116
  8712-8756 76116
  8800-8899 76108
Las Vegas Trl 76116
N Las Vegas Trl 76108
S Las Vegas Trl 76108
Las Ventanas Trl 76131
Lasalle St 76111
Lashburn Ct 76109
Lassen Ct 76132
Laster Rd 76119
Latania Ln 76244
Latham Dr 76118
Latigo Cir 76244
Latrobe Trace Way 76244
Laughlin Rd 76177
Laughton St 76110
Laura Rd 76114
Laura Ann Ct 76118
Laurel Canyon Ter 76132
Laurel Forest Dr 76177
Laurel Glen Dr 76244
Laurel Oak Dr 76131
Laurel Valley Ct 76132
Laurel Valley Dr 76132
Laurel Valley Ln 76137
Laurelhill Ct & Ln 76133
Laurelwood Ct 76131
Lauren Way
  8200-8299 76148
  11400-11699 76244
Lauretta Dr 76119
Laurie Dr 76112
Lava Rock Dr 76179
Lavano Dr 76134
Lavender Dr 76244
Laver Ct 76112
Laverda Dr 76117
Lavon Dr 76118
Lawndale Ave 76133
Lawndale Dr 76134
Lawnsberry Dr 76137
Lawnwood St 76111
Lawrence Rd 76114
Lawrence Lake Rd 76135
Lawson Rd 76131
Lawther Dr 76114
Lax Dr 76126
Laysan Teal Way 76118
Layton Ave 76117
Lazy Brook Dr 76148
Lazy Crest Dr 76140
Lazy Spur Blvd 76131
Lea Pl 76140
Lea Crest Ln 76135
Lea Shore Ct & St 76179
Lead Cir 76137
Lead Creek Dr 76131
Leaf Hollow Dr 76244
Leaflet Dr 76244
Leafy Trl 76123
Leah Ln 76140
Leandra Ln 76131
Leaping Buck Pt 76126
Lear Rd 76106
Leatherman Dr 76179
Leatherwood Dr 76108
Lebow St 76106
Lechner Rd 76179
Ledgestone Ct & Dr 76132
Ledgeview Ct & Rd 76109
Ledoux Dr 76134
Lee Ave
  1200-2799 76164
  2800-3299 76106
Lee Dr 76140
Lee St 76140
Leeray Rd 76244
Leeward Ln 76135
Legacy Dr 76108
Legacy Downs Dr 76126
Legato Ln 76134
Legend Rd 76132
Lehman St 76108
Leigh Dr 76118
Leisure Dr 76120
Leith Ave 76133
Leland Ln 76126
Leming St 76106
W Lemon St 76179
Lemon Grove Dr 76135
Lemons Rd 76140
Lemonwood Ln 76133
Lena St 76105
Lena Pope Ln 76107
Lenore St 76134
Lenox Dr 76107
Lenway Ave 76116
Leo Ct 76116
Leona Ln 76117
Leonard St 76119
Leonard Trl 76114
Leppee Way 76126
Lesley Ln 76148
Leslie Ct 76126
Leslie Dr 76118
Leslie St 76104
Lester Granger Dr 76112
E & W Leuda St 76104
Levee Cir E & W 76109
Levelland Dr 76107
Levitt Ct & Dr 76148
Lewis Ave 76103
Lewis Deas Rd 76108
Lexington Ct 76140
Lexington St 76102
N Lexington St 76102
Lexus Dr 76137
Leyland Pl 76137
Libbey Ave 76107
Liberty Ln 76131
Liberty St 76105
Liberty Way 76177
Liberty Crossing Dr 76131
Library Ln 76109
Lifford Pl & St 76116
Lighthouse Ct & Dr 76135
N & S Lighthouse Hill Ln 76179
Lightland Rd 76137
Lilac Ln 76135
Lilac St 76110
Lillian St 76111
Lillybrook Ln 76244
Lily Dr 76244
Limerick Dr 76134
Limestone Dr 76244
Limestone Trl 76134
Lincoln Ave
  1200-2799 76164
  2800-4199 76106
Lincoln Meadows Cir, Ct, Ln & Pl 76112
Lincoln Oaks Dr N & S 76132
Lincoln Terrace Dr 76107
Lincolnshire Way 76134
Linda Ct 76116
Linda Dr 76148
Linda Ln 76119
Lindale Rd 76140
Lindell Ave 76116
Linden Ave & Ln 76107
Lindentree Ln 76137
Lindenwood Dr 76107
Lindsay Ln 76117
Lindsey St 76105
Lindstrom Dr 76131
Lindy Ln 76148
Link St 76140
Linley Ln 76244
Linna Dr 76134
Linton Dr 76108
Linton St 76117
Linville Ln 76140
Linwood Ln 76134
Lionel Way 76108
Lionfish Way 76131
Lipan Trl 76108
Lipps Dr 76134
Lipscomb St
  100-1699 76104
  1700-4099 76110
Lisa Ct
  7500-7699 76112
  9300-9399 76108
Lisbon St 76107
Little Rd 76140
Little St 76105
Little Bend Ct 76244
Little Deer Ln 76131
Little Fossil Rd 76117
Little Fox Ct & Ln 76108
Little Horse Trl 76108
Little James Ln 76119
Little John Ct & Dr 76179
Little Leaf Ct E & W 76135
Little Mohican Dr 76179
Little Natalie Ln 76119
Little Reata Trl 76126
Little Road Cir 76140
Little Rock Ln 76120
Little Short Rd 76119
Little Valley Ct & Rd 76108
Little Wood Ct 76135
Littlejohn Ave 76105
Littlepage St 76107
Live Oak Ct 76108
Live Oak Ln 76179
Live Oak Rd 76108
Live Oak St 76102
N Live Oak St 76102
Live Oak Trl 76135
Live Oak Creek Dr 76108
Livingston Ave 76110
Liz Ln 76148
Lizzie Pl 76244
Lizzie Davis St 76105
Llano Ave 76116
Llano Dr 76134
Lloyd Ave
  600-799 76103
  1100-1999 76105
Lloyd Ct 76134
Loadstar Ln 76108
Lobos Ct 76137
Loch Lomond Ln 76148
Lochmoor Dr 76179
Lochness Ct & Ln 76126
Lochshire Dr 76179
Lochwood Ct 76179
Locke Ave
  3300-5999 76107
  6000-6799 76116
Lockheed Blvd 76108
Locksley Ct 76179
Locksley Dr
  900-999 76179
  10100-10199 76126
Lockwood St 76108
Locust St
  900-1199 76102
  1000-1099 76126
Lodestone Ln 76123
Lodgepole Ln 76137
Lofton Ter 76109
Loftsmoor Ct 76244
Log Cabin Village Ln 76109
Logan St 76104
Logans Ln 76135
Lohani Ln 76131
Lois St 76119
Lollita Ct 76119
Loma Linda Ct 76112
Loma Vista Dr
  6400-6499 76148
  6700-6999 76133
Lombardy Ct
  1-99 76132
  800-899 76112
Lombardy Ter 76132
Lomita St 76119
Lomo St 76110
Lomo Alto Dr 76132
Lon Morris Ct 76135
Lon Stevenson Rd 76140
London Ln 76118
Lone Brave Dr 76244
Lone Eagle Ct & Dr 76108
Lone Oak Dr 76107
Lone Pine Ct & Ln 76108
Lone Star Blvd 76106
Lone Star Cir 76177
Lone Tree Ln 76244
Lonely Oak Ln 76135
Lonesome Pine Pl 76244
Loney St 76104
Lonez Ct 76140
Long Ave 76114
E Long Ave
  100-2549 76106
  2550-3899 76137
W Long Ave 76106
Long Cove Ct 76132
Long Pointe Ave 76108
N Long Rifle Dr 76108
Long Stem Trl 76244
Longbranch Trl 76116
Longfellow Ln 76120
Longfield Dr 76108
Longford Dr & St 76116
Longhorn Ln 76179
Longhorn Rd 76179
Longhorn Trl 76135
Longleaf Ln 76137
Longmeadow Way 76133
Longmont Trl 76179
Longstraw Dr 76137
Longvue Ave
  2800-2898 76108
  3400-3699 76116
  3900-5298 76126
Lookout Dr 76140
Lookout Way 76126
E Loop 820
  100-3098 76112
E Loop 820
  101-1399 76120
  1401-3099 76112
E Loop 820 N 76118
E Loop 820 S
  1000-2399 76112
  2600-6499 76119
NE Loop 820
  643-653 76118
  1000-2598 76106
  1001-1399 76131
  3101-3397 76137
  3399-3899 76137
  3901-5099 76137
  4800-5698 76117
NW Loop 820
  100-598 76179

3400-6698 76135
3501-3699 76106
3901-6499 76135
SE Loop 820
1200-1399 76134
1900-5298 76140
1901-5299 76119
6601-6699 76140
SW Loop 820
500-2698 76115
701-2299 76134
2401-2697 76133
2699-3999 76133
4001-5999 76132
4100-5398 76109
5500-5998 76132
7801-7997 76126
7999-8099 76126
8101-8199 76126
W Loop 820 N 76108
W Loop 820 S
100-800 76108
2800-3599 76116
4801-4899 76126
E Loraine St 76106
NE Loraine St 76117
NW Loraine St 76106
W Loraine St 76164
Loreto Dr 76177
Lori Ln 76126
Lori Valley Ln 76244
Lorin Ave 76105
Los Alamitos Ln 76140
Los Alamos Trl 76131
Los Altos Rd 76244
Los Barros Trl 76177
Los Cabos Trl 76177
Los Gatos Ln 76131
Los Olivos Ln & Trl 76131
Los Osos Dr 76131
Los Padres Ct & Trl 76137
Los Rios Dr 76179
Lost Horizon Dr 76126
Lost Prairie Dr 76244
Lost Star Ct & Ln 76132
Lottie Ln 76179
Lotus Ave 76111
W Lotus Ave 76111
Lotus Trl 76135
Lou Menk Dr 76131
Louis St 76112
S Louise St 76112
Louisiana Ave 76104
Loutheld St 76119
Love Cir & Ct 76135
Love Chapel Ct 76119
Lovell Ave
3200-3498 76107
3500-5999 76107
6000-6099 76116
Lovelock Dr 76108
Lovely Dr 76140
Loving Ave
2000-2799 76164
2800-3299 76106
Low Iron Crossing Dr 76131
Lowden Cir 76104
E Lowden St 76104
W Lowden St
100-2499 76110
2500-2800 76109
2802-2998 76109
Lowe St 76110
Lowell Ln 76133
Lower Birdville Rd 76117
Lowery Rd 76120
Lowery Oaks Trl 76120
Lowline Dr 76131
Lowriemore Ln 76105
Loyal Dr 76140
Loydhill Ln 76135
Lozier Heights Ct 76132
Lt Jg Barnett Rd 76114
Lubbock Ave
2500-3299 76109
3900-4099 76110
4100-4198 76115

4200-5299 76115
5300-6099 76133
Lucas Ct 76119
Lucas Dr
1800-2599 76112
2600-2699 76119
Lucas Ln 76134
Lucca Dr 76140
Lucerne Dr 76135
Lucilla Ct 76134
Lucille St 76117
Lucinda Ln 76119
Lucy Ln 76133
Ludelle St 76105
Luella St 76102
Luke Dr 76108
Lulu St 76106
Lumber St 76112
Luna Ln 76244
Luna Vista Dr 76108
Lunar Dr 76134
Lupine Cir & St 76135
Luther Ct 76119
Luxton St 76104
Lyday Dr 76140
Lydick Ln 76114
Lydon Ave 76106
Lyle St 76114
Lynda Dr 76114
Lyndale Ct & Dr 76148
Lyndon Dr 76116
Lynncrest Dr 76109
Lynndale Pl 76133
Lynnfield Dr 76103
Lynnhaven Rd 76103
Lynnwood Hls 76112
Lynwood St 76134
Lynx Ln 76244
Lyric Dr 76134
Mable Ct 76104
Macaroon Ln 76244
Macarthur Dr
5500-5699 76112
6300-6499 76148
Macaskill Dr 76148
Macaw Dr 76120
Macdougall Dr 76148
Maceo Ln 76112
Macgregor Dr 76148
Macie Ave 76106
Macie St 76114
Mack Rd 76117
Mackerel Dr 76179
Mackey Ct 76117
Mackneal Trl 76148
Macneill Dr 76148
Macon St 76102
Macrae St 76148
Macy Ln 76244
Maddie Ave 76244
E Maddox Ave
500-2399 76104
2400-2599 76105
W Maddox Ave 76104
Madeira Dr 76112
Madeline Pl 76107
Madella St 76117
Madge Pl 76117
Madison Ave 76134
Madoc Fork Dr 76116
Madrid Dr 76133
Madyson Ridge Dr 76133
Maegen Cir 76112
Magellan Dr 76114
Magma Dr 76131
E Magnolia Ave 76104
W Magnolia Ave
100-1699 76104
2100-2399 76110
Magnolia Grn 76104
Magnolia Park 76118
Magnolia Pkwy 76126
Magnolia Blossom Trl 76131
Mahafy St 76135
Mahan Dr 76116
Mahaney Pl 76119

Mahonia Dr 76133
Maiden Ln
5700-5999 76131
6000-6099 76119
Main St
100-198 76102
200-1699 76102
5600-5799 76148
N Main St
400-2799 76164
2800-4799 76106
4901-5097 76179
5099-6099 76179
S Main St
100-1699 76104
1700-3899 76110
Maize Rd 76133
Majestic Ct 76244
Major St 76112
Major Oak St 76116
Makarwich Ct 76114
Makiposa Ln 76177
Malabar Trl 76123
Malaga Dr 76135
Malcolm St 76112
Maley St 76114
Malibar Rd 76116
Malibu St 76244
Malibu Sun Dr 76137
Malinda Ln N & S 76112
Mall Cir 76116
Mallard Ct 76108
Mallard Dr 76131
Mallard Ln 76148
Mallory Dr 76117
Mallow Oak Dr 76123
Malone Dr 76140
Malone St 76106
W Malta Ave 76115
Malta St 76135
Malvern Trl 76105
Malvey Ave
5401-5597 76107
5599-5999 76107
6000-6699 76116
Malvey Ct 76116
Manana St 76244
Manassas Rd 76177
Manchester St 76109
Manderly Pl 76109
Mandy Ln 76112
Manell Ln 76126
Manhassett Ct & Dr 76140
Manhattan Blvd 76120
Manhattan Dr 76107
Manitoba St 76179
Manning St 76126
Manor Ct 76134
Manor Ridge Way 76120
Manordale Ct 76140
Manorwood Trl 76109
Mansel Ln 76134
Mansfield Ave 76104
Mansfield Hwy 76119
Manta St 76108
Mantis St 76106
Many Oaks Dr 76140
Manzinita St 76137
Maple Creek Dr 76177
Maple Hill Dr 76123
Maple Park Dr 76118
Maple Stream Dr 76177
Maplehill Rd 76148
Mapleleaf St 76111
Maplewood Dr 76244
Marbella Cir & Dr 76126
Marble Canyon Ct & Dr 76137
Marble Creek Dr 76131
Marble Falls Ct & Rd 76103
Marblehead Ct 76108
Marbury Dr 76133
Marci Ln 76140
Marcille Ct 76118
Marfa Ave 76116
Margaret Dr 76140

Margaret St 76107
Margarita Dr 76137
Marguerite Ln 76123
Maria Dr 76108
Marie Ct 76108
Marie Ln
1300-1399 76108
3200-8299 76123
Marie Jones Rd 76119
Marietta Ct 76123
Marigold Ave 76111
Marigold Dr
4000-4099 76137
6000-6099 76148
Marilyn Ct & Dr 76108
Marina Dr 76135
Marina Club Blvd 76132
Marina Del Rd 76179
Marine Cir 76106
Marine Ct E 76106
Marine Ct W 76106
Marine Ln 76179
Marine Creek Pkwy
4400-4699 76106
4700-4899 76179
4901-5599 76179
Mariner Cir 76179
Marineway Dr 76135
Marion Ave 76104
Marist Dr 76120
Maritime St 76179
Mark Ct 76108
Mark Ln 76148
Mark Iv Pkwy
4000-4099 76106
4101-5299 76106
4600-4602 76161
4604-5298 76106
5300-6099 76131
Market Ave
2000-2799 76164
2800-2999 76106
Marklin Dr 76108
Marko Ct 76133
Marks Ln 76135
Marks Pl 76116
Markum Dr 76117
Markum Ranch Rd 76126
Marlborough Dr W 76134
Marlene Dr
800-1199 76140
5600-5799 76148
Marlin St 76105
Marlinda Cir 76140
Marlow Ln 76131
Maroon Dr 76120
Marquette Ct 76109
Marquita Dr 76116
Marrett Dr 76108
Marrs Dr 76140
Marsalis St 76117
Marsarie Ct & St 76137
Marsh Ct & Ln 76123
Marsha St 76179
Marshall St
2400-2799 76111
4300-4899 76119
Martel Ave 76103
Martha Ct 76148
Martha Dr 76148
Martha Ln
100-399 76126
4300-4899 76103
6400-7399 76112
Martha Jean St 76108
Martin St 76119
Martin Luther King Fwy
300-2099 76104
2500-2699 76105
3301-3497 76119
3499-5152 76119
5154-5198 76119
1501-1599 76102
Martin Lydon Ave
1801-2397 76115
2399-2699 76115
2700-3599 76133

Martindale Cir 76112
Martingale View Ln 76244
Martinique Ln 76123
Martinsburg Dr 76244
Marvin Brown St 76179
Mary St 76106
Mary Boaz St 76118
Mary K Ln 76108
Maryann Dr 76119
Maryanne Pl 76137
Maryannes Ct 76135
Maryannes Meadow Dr 76135
Marydean Ave 76116
Maryel Dr 76112
Maryhill Rd 76140
Maryland Ave 76104
Marys Ln 76116
Marys Creek Dr 76116
Maryview Ct & Ter 76117
Maryville Ln 76108
E & W Mason St 76110
E, N, S & W Masters Dr 76137
Matador Ct 76108
Matador Ranch Rd 76134
Matar St 76117
Matisse Dr 76107
Matt St 76179
Matthew Dr 76244
Matthews Ct 76119
Matthews Dr 76118
Mattison Ave 76107
Maui Dr 76119
Maurice Ave 76111
Maurice Ct 76140
Maurie Cir, Ct & Dr 76148
Maverick Dr 76108
Maverick St 76116
Max St 76108
Maxey Rd 76119
Maxine St 76117
Maxwell Blvd & Ct 76179
May St
400-1699 76104
1700-4099 76110
4551-4697 76115
4699-4700 76115
4702-4798 76115
Mayan Ct 76135
Mayan Ranch Rd 76132
Mayberry Ln 76123
Maydell St 76106
Mayfair Cir 76123
Mayfair St 76116
Mayfield St 76102
Maywood St 76116
Mc Clure St 76115
Mcadoo Ln 76131
Mcbreyer Pl 76244
Mccandless St 76106
Mccarran Ave 76155
Mccart Ave
2500-2900 76110
2901-2999 76109
2902-4098 76110
3001-4099 76110
4100-5299 76115
5300-7500 76133
7501-7897 76123
7502-7798 76133
7899-8799 76123
Mccauley Dr 76244
Mcclellan Ct 76112
Mccleskey Ct 76112
Mccomas Rd
3801-3899 76111
3900-4299 76117
Mcconnell Dr
5200-5399 76115
5400-5499 76134
Mccormick Ct 76179
Mccoy Ct & Dr 76148
Mccracken Ct 76132
Mccullar St 76117
Mccully St 76108

Mccurdy St 76104
Mcdaniel Rd 76126
N & S Mcentire Ct 76108
Mcewen Ct 76112
Mcfadden Ln 76108
Mcfarland Way 76244
Mcfarring Dr 76244
Mcgee Dr 76114
Mcgee St 76112
Mcgown Ave 76106
Mcguire St 76117
Mcivey St 76111
Mckaskle Dr 76119
Mckavett Dr 76140
Mckenzie St 76105
Mckibben St 76117
Mckinley Ave
2100-2799 76164
2800-3299 76106
Mckinley St 76126
Mclean Rd 76117
Mclean St 76103
Mclemore Ave 76111
Mclennan St 76106
E & W Mcleroy Blvd 76179
Mcmillian Pkwy 76137
Mcnaughton Ln 76114
Mcnay Rd 76135
Mcneill Ln 76179
Mcnutt St 76117
Mcpherson Ave
1800-1898 76110
2401-2499 76110
2500-3499 76109
Mcpherson Blvd 76123
Mcpherson Rd 76140
Mcquade St 76117
Mcree Rd 76179
Meacham Blvd
300-2549 76106
2550-3899 76137
3900-4299 76117
Meacham Airport Cir 76106
Meaders Ave 76112
Meadow Ct 76112
Meadow Dr 76119
S Meadow Dr 76133
S Meadow Dr E 76133
Meadow Rd 76109
Meadow St 76179
Meadow Breeze Ct 76140
Meadow Creek Dr
7300-7499 76133
7500-7999 76123
Meadow Crest Rd 76108
Meadow Haven Dr 76132
Meadow Hill Ct & Rd 76108
Meadow Lane Ct & Ter 76112
Meadow Oak Ct 76137
Meadow Oaks Dr 76117
Meadow Park Dr 76108
Meadow Ridge Dr 76133
Meadow Spring Ln 76120
Meadow Sweet Ln 76123
Meadow Trails Dr 76244
Meadow Valley Dr 76123
Meadow View Trl 76120
Meadow Way Ln 76179
Meadow Wood Ln 76112
Meadowbrook Blvd 76120
Meadowbrook Dr
2600-5099 76103
5100-7999 76112
7100-8299 76148
8000-8708 76120
8710-8798 76120
Meadowbrook Gardens Dr 76112
Meadowcrest Dr
7400-7499 76112
10100-10199 76126
Meadowdale Dr
700-799 76179
7400-7499 76148
Meadowglen Cir 76116

Meadowhill Dr 76126
Meadowknoll Dr 76123
Meadowland Dr 76123
Meadowlark Dr
800-1099 76131
7600-7899 76133
Meadowlark Ln E 76148
Meadowlark Ln N 76148
Meadowmoor St 76133
Meadowood Village Dr 76120
Meadowpark Ct 76132
Meadows Dr N & S 76140
Meadows West Dr S 76132
Meadowside Dr 76116
Meadowside Rd 76132
Meadowside Rd S 76132
Meadowview Dr 76179
Meadowview Ln 76148
Meandering Ct 76135
Meandering Rd 76114
Meandering Creek Ct & Ln 76179
Meares Dr 76137
Mecca St 76119
Mechanic St 76111
Medford Ct E 76109
Medford Ct W 76109
Medford Rd 76103
Medical Dr 76120
Medina Ave 76133
Medinah Dr 76132
Medlock Dr 76120
Meeker Blvd 76114
Mel St 76112
Melanie Ct & Dr 76131
Melba Ct 76114
Melbourn St 76117
Melbourne Dr 76114
Melinda Ct 76148
Melinda Dr
4700-6599 76119
6100-6399 76148
Melinda St 76117
Melissa Ct 76108
Melissa Dr 76108
Melissa St 76117
Melita Ave 76133
Mellie Ct 76123
Melody Ln 76148
Melody St 76134
Melody Hills Dr 76137
Melodylane St 76137
Melrose Ct 76108
Melrose Ln 76244
Melrose St E 76108
Melrose St W 76108
Melville Ln 76120
Melvin Dr 76126
Melwood St 76112
Memorial Dr 76244
Memory Dr 76108
Memory Ln 76148
Memphis Ln 76132
Mendosa Ct 76126
Menefee Ave 76106
Menn St 76117
Menzer Ct & Rd 76103
Mercado Dr 76106
Mercantile Dr 76137
Mercantile Plaza Dr 76137
Merced Dr 76137
Merced Lake Rd 76177
Mercedes Ave 76107
Mercedes St 76126
Mercury St 76111
Meredith Ln
5900-6199 76134
8600-8699 76244
Meredith Creek Ln 76179
Merganser Dr 76118
Meribee Dr 76244
Merida Ave
2700-3299 76109
3700-4099 76110
4100-5099 76115
Meridian Ln 76244

Meriweather Ave ... 76115
Merlotte Ln ... 76244
Mermaid Ln ... 76106
Merrett Dr ... 76135
Merrick Ct & St ... 76107
Merrill Ln ... 76177
Merrimac Cir ... 76107
Merrimac Dr ... 76140
Merrimac St ... 76107
Merritt St ... 76114
Merry Ln ... 76112
Merry Lane Ct ... 76112
Merry View Ln ... 76120
Merrymount Rd ... 76107
Mesa Ct ... 76179
Mesa Dr ... 76132
Mesa Grande Dr ... 76108
Mesa Ridge Ct & Dr ... 76137
Mesa Springs Dr ... 76123
Mesa Verde Ct ... 76137
Mesa Verde St ... 76108
Mesa Verde Trl ... 76137
Mesa View Trl ... 76131
Mesilla Ln ... 76131
Mesquite Rd ... 76111
Mesquite Trl ... 76126
Mesquite Meadow Ln ... 76126
Messer Ct & Pl ... 76126
Meyers Ln ... 76244
Miami Springs Dr ... 76123
Michael Dr ... 76140
Michael Ln ... 76126
Michael St
1300-1699 ... 76106
2400-2499 ... 76112
8500-8699 ... 76108
Michelle Dr ... 76140
Michelle Ridge Dr ... 76123
Michigan Ave ... 76114
Mickey Dr ... 76148
Micki Lynn Ave ... 76107
Mid Ct ... 76109
Midcentral Dr ... 76244
Middle Rd ... 76116
Middlebrook Rd ... 76116
Middleview Rd ... 76108
Middlewood Dr ... 76109
Midland Dr ... 76135
Midland St ... 76105
Midtown Ln ... 76104
Midway Rd
5200-5498 ... 76117
5500-6899 ... 76117
6900-7199 ... 76118
7200-7299 ... 76118
Mighty Mite Dr ... 76105
Mike Ln ... 76116
Mike Lane Ct ... 76116
Mil Oaks Ln ... 76135
Milam St ... 76112
Milan Ln ... 76244
Milano Ct ... 76126
Milburn St ... 76116
Milby Oaks Dr ... 76244
Mildred Ln
100-100 ... 76126
102-1399 ... 76126
3700-3799 ... 76117
E Mildred Ln ... 76126
Miles Dr
5500-5698 ... 76132
7900-8099 ... 76148
Milestone Ct ... 76244
Milford Dr ... 76137
Mill Creek Trl ... 76179
Mill Pond Ct ... 76133
Mill Springs Pass ... 76123
Mill Valley Cir, Ct & Sq ... 76120
Mill Water Dr ... 76120
Miller Ave
1000-3199 ... 76105
3200-5499 ... 76119
Miller Ct ... 76108
Millet Ave ... 76105
Mills St ... 76102
Millwood St ... 76131
Milmo Dr ... 76134
Milton St ... 76105
Mimosa Ct ... 76137
Mimosa Park Dr ... 76118
Mims St ... 76112
Minden St
700-1099 ... 76110
1100-1499 ... 76115
1500-1599 ... 76119
Mindys Rdg ... 76126
Mineola St ... 76106
Mineral Creek Dr ... 76179
Minette Rd ... 76135
Ming Dr ... 76134
Minister Dr ... 76119
Mink Dr ... 76117
Minnie St ... 76117
Minnis Dr ... 76117
Minnow Dr ... 76179
Minot Ave ... 76133
Mint Springs St ... 76179
Minten Dr ... 76108
Minton Rd ... 76179
Mintrelm Ave ... 76110
Minturn Dr ... 76131
Minuteman Dr ... 76131
Mira Lago Ln ... 76179
Mira Monte Ln ... 76179
Mira Vista Blvd ... 76132
Mirage Dr ... 76244
Miraloma Dr ... 76126
Miramar Cir ... 76126
Miranda Dr ... 76131
Mirasol Dr ... 76177
Mirike Dr ... 76108
Miro Ct ... 76107
Mirror Lake Dr ... 76117
Mirror Ridge Dr ... 76179
Missent ... 76161
Missequenced ... 76161
Mission St ... 76109
Missionary Ridge Trl ... 76131
Mississippi Ave
1600-3099 ... 76104
3100-3299 ... 76110
Missorted ... 76161
Missouri Ave ... 76104
Missouri Ln ... 76131
Missy Ln ... 76131
Mist Hollow Ct ... 76109
Mister G Dr ... 76126
Mistletoe Ave ... 76110
Mistletoe Blvd
1600-2099 ... 76104
2100-2599 ... 76110
Mistletoe Dr ... 76110
Mistletoe Rd ... 76126
Misty Ct ... 76133
Misty Trl ... 76123
Misty Breeze Dr ... 76179
Misty Dawn Dr ... 76140
Misty Glen Ct ... 76120
Misty Meadow Ct & Dr ... 76133
Misty Mountain Dr ... 76140
Misty Oaks Dr & Pl ... 76112
Misty Redwood Trl ... 76177
Misty Ridge Dr N ... 76137
Misty Valley Dr ... 76123
Misty Water Dr ... 76131
Mistys Run ... 76244
Mitch St ... 76179
Mitchell Ave ... 76110
Mitchell Blvd
1400-3999 ... 76105
4201-4299 ... 76119
4500-4598 ... 76119
Mitchell Saxon Ct & Rd ... 76140
Mizzenmast Ct ... 76135
Moberly St ... 76119
Mobile Dr ... 76137
Moccassin Ln ... 76177
Mockingbird Ct ... 76109
Mockingbird Dr ... 76131
Mockingbird Ln ... 76109
Modena Ct & Dr ... 76126
Modlin Ave ... 76107
Mohawk Ave ... 76116
Mohawk Trl ... 76135
Mojave Trl ... 76116
Molasses Dr ... 76179
Molina Ln ... 76179
Moline Dr ... 76117
Mona Lisa Ave ... 76148
Mona Lisa St ... 76137
Monarch Dr ... 76119
Monarch Hills Dr ... 76132
Monarda Way ... 76123
Monastery Dr ... 76119
Moncrief St ... 76244
Monda St ... 76110
Moneda Ave, Cir & St ... 76117
Monette St ... 76117
Money Ln ... 76126
Monica Ct & Ln ... 76244
Monmouth Dr ... 76116
Monna Ct & St ... 76117
Monnig Ln ... 76244
Mono Lake Rd ... 76177
Monroe St ... 76102
Mont Dr ... 76132
Mont Del Dr ... 76132
Montague Ct & St ... 76119
Montane Ct ... 76137
Montclair Dr ... 76103
Monte Vista Ln ... 76132
Montecito Way ... 76106
Montego Ct & Rd ... 76116
Montego Bay Ln ... 76123
Monterra Blvd ... 76177
Monterra Cir ... 76114
Monterra Bluff Ln ... 76177
Monterra Creek Dr & Ln ... 76177
Monterra Crest Dr ... 76177
Monterra Oaks Pl ... 76177
Monterra Ranch Cir & Dr ... 76177
Monterra Villa Trl ... 76177
Monterrey Dr ... 76112
Monterrey Manor Dr ... 76116
Montford Ct ... 76126
Montgomery St ... 76107
Monthaven Dr ... 76137
Monticello Dr ... 76107
Monticello Park Pl ... 76107
Montoya Ln ... 76119
Montreal Cir ... 76117
Montrose Dr ... 76114
Montserrat Rd ... 76126
Monument Ct ... 76244
W Mony St ... 76102
Moon Dr ... 76244
Moon Flower Ct ... 76244
Moon Ridge Ct ... 76133
Moon Rise Ct ... 76244
Mooney Dr ... 76179
Moonglow Ln ... 76148
Moonmist Cir ... 76140
Moor Ct ... 76140
Moore Ave ... 76106
Moorhen Cir ... 76244
Moorview Ave ... 76119
Mopac Rd ... 76107
Morab St ... 76244
Morales Dr ... 76126
Moran St ... 76108
Moreau Ct ... 76118
Morein St ... 76140
Moresby St ... 76105
Morgan St ... 76102
Morley Ave ... 76133
Mormon Trl ... 76137
Morning Ln ... 76123
Morning Dew Dr ... 76132
Morning Dew St ... 76108
Morning Glory Ave ... 76111
Morning Meadow Dr ... 76244
Morning Song Dr ... 76244
Morning Star Dr ... 76131
E Morningside Dr ... 76104
W Morningside Dr ... 76110
E Morphy St ... 76104
W Morphy St
300-1999 ... 76104
2100-2199 ... 76110
Morrell St ... 76133
Morris Ave
4700-5099 ... 76103
5200-5399 ... 76112
Morris Blvd ... 76148
Morris Ct ... 76103
Morris Dido Newark Rd ... 76179
Morrison Ct ... 76112
Morrison Dr
900-1299 ... 76120
1300-2199 ... 76112
Morrison St ... 76102
Morton St ... 76107
Mosaic Dr ... 76179
Mosier View Ct ... 76118
Moss Holw ... 76109
Moss Ln ... 76148
Moss Hollow Ct ... 76109
Moss Rock Dr ... 76123
Moss Rose Ct & Dr ... 76137
Mossbrook Dr ... 76244
Mosson Rd ... 76119
Mosstree Dr ... 76120
Mosswood Ct ... 76131
Mossy Oak Trl ... 76131
Moulton Rd ... 76111
Mount Bonnel Ct ... 76108
Mount Hood Rd ... 76137
Mount Horum Way ... 76105
Mount Pheasant Ct & Rd ... 76108
Mount Plymouth Pt ... 76179
Mount Royal Ter ... 76107
Mount Shasta Cir ... 76137
Mount Storm Way ... 76179
Mountain Lk ... 76179
Mountain Air Trl ... 76131
Mountain Bluff Dr ... 76179
Mountain Cedar Dr ... 76131
Mountain Crest Dr ... 76123
Mountain Hawk Dr ... 76177
Mountain Home Ln ... 76131
Mountain Lake Cir & Ct ... 76179
Mountain Lion Dr ... 76244
Mountain Oak St ... 76244
Mountain Ridge Ct E & W ... 76135
Mountain Robin Ct ... 76244
Mountain Spring Trl ... 76123
Mountain Stream Trl ... 76244
Mountain Valley Ct ... 76123
Mountain Vista Dr ... 76126
Mountcastle Dr ... 76119
Mourning Dove Ln ... 76244
Mt Mckinley Rd ... 76137
Mt Vernon Ave ... 76103
Mt View Ave ... 76103
Muir Dr ... 76244
Muirfield Rd ... 76132
Muirwood Trl ... 76137
Mulberry Ct ... 76137
Mulberry Dr ... 76126
Mule Deer Run ... 76179
Muleshoe Ln ... 76179
E Mulkey St ... 76104
W Mulkey St ... 76110
Mulligan Pass ... 76179
Mullins Crossing Dr ... 76126
Munson Way ... 76126
Murel Dr ... 76148
Murphy St ... 76111
Murray Ave ... 76117
Murray Ct ... 76107
Murrieta Way ... 76244
Murton Pl ... 76137
Muse Ct & St ... 76112
Museum Way ... 76107
Muskrat Dr ... 76244
Mustang Ct ... 76137
Mustang Dr
300-899 ... 76179
4500-4699 ... 76137
Mustang St ... 76114
Mustang Creek Ct & Dr ... 76126
Mustang Downs Dr ... 76126
Mustang Wells Dr ... 76126
Myers Dr ... 76108
Myra St ... 76108
E & W Myrtle St ... 76104
Myrtle Springs Rd ... 76116
Mystic Trl ... 76118
Mystic Falls Dr ... 76179
Mystic River Trl ... 76131
Nacona Dr ... 76135
Nadine Dr ... 76117
Nafex Way ... 76131
Nail Ln ... 76126
Nanci Dr ... 76148
Nancy Ln ... 76114
Nandina Ct ... 76137
Nannette St ... 76114
Nantucket Dr ... 76140
Napa Valley Trl ... 76244
Nara Vista Trl ... 76119
Nash Ln ... 76244
Nashville Ave ... 76105
Natalie Dr ... 76134
Natchez Ct ... 76133
Natchez Trce ... 76134
Natchez Trl ... 76137
Nathan Ct ... 76108
Nathan Dr ... 76108
Nathan St ... 76179
Nathaniel Dr ... 76179
Native Dr ... 76179
Nature Dr ... 76244
Nauert Rd ... 76140
Nautilus Cir ... 76106
Navajo Ct ... 76137
Navajo Trl ... 76135
Navajo Way ... 76137
Navajo Bridge Trl ... 76137
Navasota Cir ... 76131
Navigation Ct & Dr ... 76179
Neal St ... 76106
Nebraska Ave ... 76107
Neches St ... 76106
Neeley Dr ... 76244
Negril Ct ... 76137
Nehemiah Dr ... 76108
Neill Ave ... 76140
Nell St ... 76119
Nelms Dr ... 76119
Nelson Ave ... 76111
Nelson Dr ... 76126
Nelson Ter ... 76148
Neptune St ... 76179
Netleaf Ln ... 76244
Nettie St ... 76244
Neville St ... 76107
Nevis Dr ... 76123
New Castleton Ct & Ln ... 76135
New Day Dr ... 76179
New Harbor Ln ... 76179
New Hope Rd ... 76140
New York Ave
100-3099 ... 76104
3100-3799 ... 76110
Newark Ave ... 76103
S Newark Ave ... 76105
Newberry Ct & Trl ... 76120
Newburg Way ... 76244
Newcastle Ln ... 76135
Newman Dr ... 76117
Newport Ct ... 76116
Newport Rd ... 76120
Newton Dr ... 76132
Newton St
700-799 ... 76131
5300-5399 ... 76117
Neystel Rd ... 76134
Nichols St ... 76102
N Nichols St
100-599 ... 76102
2600-3899 ... 76106
Nicole St ... 76120
Nies St ... 76111
Night Wind Ln ... 76244
Nighthawk Rd ... 76108
Nightheart Dr ... 76112
Nightingale Dr ... 76123
Nikos Pl ... 76120
Niles Ct ... 76244
Nimitz Dr ... 76114
Nina Ln ... 76117
Nina Maria St ... 76114
Nine Mile Azle Rd ... 76135
Nine Mile Bridge Rd ... 76135
Nixon St ... 76102
Noble Ave
100-499 ... 76140
2600-3799 ... 76111
Noble Grove Ln ... 76140
Noe St ... 76105
Noelle Way ... 76179
Nogales Dr ... 76108
Nohl Ranch Rd ... 76133
Nola Ct & Dr ... 76148
Nolan St ... 76119
Noontide Ct & Dr ... 76179
Nordland Ln ... 76244
Norfleet St ... 76114
Norfolk Dr ... 76131
Norfolk Rd ... 76109
Noric Way ... 76244
Norma Ct ... 76103
Norma Dr ... 76114
Norma Ln ... 76118
Norma St
4500-5099 ... 76103
5100-7399 ... 76112
Norman Ave ... 76116
Norman St ... 76106
N Normandale St
100-299 ... 76108
8600-9299 ... 76116
S Normandale St ... 76116
W Normandale St ... 76116
Normandy Ct ... 76133
Normandy Ln ... 76179
Normandy Rd
4100-4899 ... 76103
6400-7399 ... 76112
Normont Cir ... 76103
Norris St
4600-4799 ... 76105
5500-5799 ... 76119
Norris Valley Dr ... 76135
North Fwy
500-999 ... 76102
2800-3398 ... 76111
2901-5199 ... 76106
3700-7298 ... 76137
5501-8299 ... 76131
8300-13699 ... 76177
13701-14599 ... 76177
Northbrook Dr ... 76116
Northcrest Ct & Rd ... 76107
Northeast Pkwy ... 76106
W Northern Ave ... 76179
Northern Cross Blvd
2900-3499 ... 76137
4200-4299 ... 76137
4400-4599 ... 76117
Northern Pine Dr ... 76244
Northfield Dr ... 76179
Northfork Rd ... 76119
Northglen Dr ... 76119
Northland Dr ... 76137
Northpark Dr ... 76102
E Northside Dr
100-699 ... 76164
800-1399 ... 76102
1500-1699 ... 76106
1900-1999 ... 76111
W Northside Dr ... 76164
Northton St ... 76104
Northway Dr ... 76131
Northwood Rd ... 76107
Norton Dr
800-899 ... 76179
3200-3999 ... 76118
Norvell Dr ... 76117
Norwich Dr ... 76109
Norwood St ... 76107
Nosilla St ... 76112
Notre Dame Ave ... 76114
Notting Hill St ... 76244
Nottingham Blvd ... 76112
Nottingham Ct ... 76179
Nottingham Trl ... 76179
Novato Pl ... 76244
Novella Ct & Dr ... 76134
Nowlin St ... 76102
Nueces Ct ... 76126
Nuggett Ln ... 76126
Nursery Ln ... 76114
Nutwood Pl ... 76133
Oak Ct
800-899 ... 76179
1100-1199 ... 76126
5300-5399 ... 76140
Oak St ... 76140
Oak Trl ... 76109
Oak Bluff Ct ... 76108
Oak Branch Ln ... 76140
Oak Cliff Rd ... 76103
Oak Creeks Ct ... 76135
Oak Crest Dr ... 76120
Oak Crest Dr E ... 76140
Oak Crest Dr W ... 76140
Oak Forest Ct ... 76112
Oak Forest Dr
600-1199 ... 76114
1500-1699 ... 76107
Oak Glen Cir ... 76114
Oak Grove Ct N ... 76115
Oak Grove Ct S ... 76115
Oak Grove Rd
800-1025 ... 76115
1027-1099 ... 76115
1100-5899 ... 76134
5901-6699 ... 76134
7000-10799 ... 76140
Oak Grove Rd W ... 76134
Oak Grove St ... 76104
Oak Grove Shelby Rd ... 76140
Oak Haven Dr
200-5699 ... 76244
3300-3899 ... 76119
Oak Hill Cir ... 76109
Oak Hill Ct ... 76132
Oak Hill Dr ... 76132
Oak Hill Rd
1400-2299 ... 76112
5700-6099 ... 76148
Oak Hill St ... 76119
Oak Hollow Ct ... 76112
Oak Hollow Ln ... 76112
Oak Hollow Trl ... 76179
Oak Knoll Dr ... 76117
Oak Manor Dr ... 76116
Oak Mill Ct & Dr ... 76135
Oak Park Cir ... 76109
Oak Park Ct ... 76109
Oak Park Dr ... 76118
Oak Park Ln
4300-4398 ... 76109
4400-4451 ... 76109
4450-4450 ... 76185
4453-4499 ... 76109
Oak Ridge Dr ... 76117
Oak Springs Ln ... 76123
Oak Timber Dr E ... 76119
Oak Tree Cir ... 76133
Oak Tree Ct ... 76140
Oak Tree Dr ... 76140
Oak View Dr ... 76112
Oakbend Trl ... 76132
Oakbriar Trl ... 76109
Oakcrest Ln ... 76126
Oakdale Ct ... 76148
Oakdale Dr
101-197 ... 76108

199-399 76108
401-599 76108
5800-5999 76119
Oakhurst Scenic Dr 76111
S Oakland Blvd & Pl 76103
Oakland Bend Dr 76112
Oakland Hills Dr & Ln 76112
Oakland Knoll Dr 76112
Oaklawn Dr
600-699 76114
3700-3899 76107
6600-6699 76148
Oakleaf Dr 76132
Oakline Trl 76112
Oakmeadow Dr 76132
Oakmont Blvd 76132
Oakmont Ct 76112
Oakmont Ln
5500-5899 76112
5700-5799 76137
Oakmont Ln N 76112
Oakmont Ter 76132
Oakmont Trl 76132
Oakmount Dr 76137
Oakridge Cir 76155
Oakridge Ct 76155
Oakridge Rd 76135
Oakton Rd 76116
Oakview Ct 76148
Oakview St
1100-1299 76117
1300-1399 76117
4300-4399 76119
Oakville St 76244
Oakway Ln 76112
Oakwood Ct
100-199 76135
7800-7899 76126
Oakwood Ln 76179
Oakwood St 76117
Oakwood Ter 76117
Oakwood Trl 76112
Oarlock Dr 76135
Oates Dr 76114
Obrien Ct & Way 76244
Observation Dr 76135
Ocean Ct 76133
Ocean Dr 76123
Oceano Ter 76132
Ocho Rios Dr 76137
Ocotillo Ln 76177
Odd St 76164
Odell Dr
5300-5399 76115
5400-5499 76134
Odessa Ave
3000-3299 76109
4300-5699 76133
Odeum Ct & Dr 76244
Odie Dr 76108
Odom Ave 76114
Oels St 76108
Ohara Ln 76123
Ohare Ct 76155
Ohio St 76106
Ohio Garden Rd 76114
Okelly Dr 76126
Ola Ln 76111
Ola St 76105
Old Benbrook Rd
3900-4999 76116
5001-5199 76116
5200-8198 76126
5201-5299 76126
8200-8299 76126
Old Blue Cir 76119
Old Blue Mound Rd 76177
Old Burleson Rd 76140
Old Clydesdale Dr 76123
Old Crowley Rd 76134
Old Decatur Rd
400-1398 76179
1400-1699 76179
4300-4599 76106
6000-6598 76179
6600-9899 76179
Old Denton 76137
Old Denton Rd
3900-5099 76117
6101-6197 76131
6199-6599 76131
8200-11400 76244
11402-11998 76244
12500-13399 76177
Old Garden Rd 76107
Old Gate Rd 76108
Old Glory Trl 76134
Old Handley Rd 76112
Old Hemphill Rd 76134
Old Hickory Trl 76140
Old Homestead Rd 76132
Old Kent Ct 76244
Old Leonard St 76119
Old Macgregor Ln 76244
Old Mansfield Rd 76119
Old Mill Cir 76148
Old Mill Ct
4100-4199 76133
6000-6099 76148
Old Mill Dr 76137
Old Mill Run 76133
Old Mill Creek Rd 76135
Old Orchard Dr 76123
Old Pecos Trl 76131
Old Randol Mill Rd 76120
Old Richwood Ln 76244
Old Santa Fe Trl 76131
Old Squall Dr 76118
Old Stone Dr 76137
Old Trinity Way 76116
Old University Dr 76107
Old Whitley Rd 76148
Oldfield Ct 76244
Oldham Ct 76140
Oldwest Trl 76131
E & W Oleander St 76104
Olinger Dr 76108
Olive Pl 76116
Oliver Dr 76244
Olivewood Ln 76140
Olivia Dr 76108
Ollie St 76119
Olympia Trl 76137
Olympia Hills Rd 76132
Olympia Trace Cir 76244
Omaha Dr 76108
One Main Pl 76126
One Tandy Ctr 76102
Ontario Dr 76108
Opal Ct & St 76179
Open Range Dr 76177
Orange St 76110
Orcas St 76106
Orchard Dr 76148
Orchard St 76119
Orchard Creek Rd 76123
Orchard Grove Dr 76244
Orchid Dr 76137
Oregon Trl Ct 76148
Orien St 76117
Orilla Ln 76108
Orinda Dr 76108
Oriole Ct 76137
Oriole Dr 76131
Orland Park Cir 76137
Orlando Dr 76126
Orlando Springs Dr 76123
Orleans Ln 76123
Orval Ct 76117
Osage St 76114
Osage Trl 76135
Osborne Ln 76112
Osbun St 76116
Oscar Ave 76106
Osprey Ct & Dr 76108
Otero Pass 76131
Otter Ct 76134
Otto St 76105
Ouray Pass 76244
Outlook Ave & Ct 76244
Over Lake Dr 76135
Overcrest Dr 76126
Overhill Rd 76116
Overland Dr 76179
Overland St 76131
Overlook Dr
4200-4299 76119
6700-6899 76126
Overlook Ter 76112
Overlook Trl 76108
Overton Ave 76133
Overton Plz 76109
Overton Ter 76109
Overton Commons Ct 76132
Overton Crest St 76109
Overton Hollow St 76109
Overton Park Dr E &
W 76109
Overton Ridge Blvd &
Cir 76132
Overton Terrace Ct 76109
Overton View Ct 76109
Overton Woods Ct &
Dr 76109
Overview Ct 76140
Ovid Dr 76114
Owasso St 76107
Owendale Dr 76116
Owens St 76117
Owenwood Dr 76109
Owl Creek Dr 76179
Oxford St
1100-1299 76114
2400-2599 76106
Oxley Dr 76118
Ozark Dr 76131
Pace Ct 76179
Pacers Ln 76179
Pacific Ct 76109
Pacific Pl 76112
Pacino Dr 76134
Pack Saddle Cir, Ct &
Trl 76108
Packard Ct 76119
Packers St 76106
Paddington Dr E 76131
Paddlefish Dr 76179
Paddock Dr 76244
Padre Ave & Ct 76244
E & W Pafford St 76110
Page Ave 76110
Pagosa Dr 76116
Paine Ave 76120
Paint Trl 76116
Paint Brush Rd 76108
Paint Horse Trl 76131
Paint Pony Trl N 76108
Paint Rock Ct 76132
Paint Trail Ct 76116
Paintbrush Dr 76244
Painted Canyon Dr 76131
Painted Tree Trl 76131
Paladin Pl 76137
Palasades Dr 76108
Palcheff Dr 76126
Palencia Ct & Dr 76126
Palisades Ct 76244
Pallas Ct 76123
Pallette St 76140
Palm Dr 76244
Palm Ridge Dr 76133
Palmer Dr
5200-5499 76117
12500-12599 76179
Palmetto Dr
200-699 76114
7500-7599 76133
Palmnold Cir E & W 76120
Palo Alto Dr 76116
Palo Duro Cir 76179
Palo Duro Ct 76116
Palo Pinto Rd 76116
Paloma Ct 76179
E Paloma Ct 76108
W Paloma Ct 76108
Paloma Blanca Dr 76179
Palomino Ct 76179
Palomino Dr
100-899 76179
3800-4099 76116
Paloverde Ct 76112
Paloverde Dr 76137
Paloverde Ln 76112
Paluxy Dr
1300-1399 76126
9200-9299 76244
Paluxy Sands Trl 76179
Pamela Dr 76116
Pamela Ln 76112
Pamlico Rd 76116
Pampas Dr 76133
Panama St 76119
Panay Way Ct & Dr 76108
Panda Ct 76119
Pangolin Ct & Dr 76244
Panola Ave
3100-5099 76103
5100-5199 76112
Pansy Rd 76123
Pantego Dr 76134
Panther Dr 76116
Paper Birch Ln 76123
Paper Shell Way 76179
Papurt Dr 76106
Parade Grounds Ln 76244
Paradise St 76111
Paradise Valley Rd 76112
Paralewo Ave 76104
Parham Ct 76112
Paris St 76119
Park Ave 76140
Park Brk 76140
Park Ct 76137
Park Dr
1000-1099 76126
5200-5299 76114
5501-5597 76179
5599-10099 76179
E Park Dr 76132
N Park Dr
500-599 76179
5700-6699 76148
Park Ln 76132
Park Rd 76135
Park St 76164
Park Trl 76132
Park Arbor Ct 76116
Park Bend Dr 76137
Park Brook Dr 76137
Park Canyon Dr 76108
Park Center Blvd 76179
Park Center Ct 76179
Park Center St 76126
Park City Trl 76140
Park Creek Cir, Ct & Dr
E, N & W 76137
Park Downs Ct & Dr 76137
Park Falls Ct 76137
Park Forest Dr 76137
Park Haven Pl 76137
Park Hill Dr
1800-2499 76110
2500-3699 76109
Park Hollow St 76109
Park Lake Dr 76133
Park Manor Ct 76119
Park Manor Dr 76104
Park Meadow Ct 76112
Park Oak Ct 76137
Park Oaks 76140
Park Place Ave 76110
Park Place Dr 76118
Park Ridge Blvd 76109
Park Ridge Dr 76137
Park Ridge Trl 76179
Park River Ct 76137
Park Run Rd 76137
Park Trails Dr 76137
Park Village Ct 76137
Park Vista Blvd
6700-6799 76137
7400-8499 76137
13000-13199 76244
13200-13298 76177
13200-13298 76244
13201-13299 76177
13201-13299 76244
13300-13600 76177
13602-14198 76177
Park Vista Cir 76244
Park West Cir 76134
Parkcrest Ct 76109
Parkdale Ave 76105
Parker Rd 76117
Parker Rd E 76117
Parker Rd W 76117
Parker St 76112
S Parker St 76140
Parker Henderson Rd 76119
Parkersburg Dr 76244
Parkgate Dr 76137
N Parkhaven Dr 76137
Parkhill Ave 76179
Parkland Ct 76137
Parkmere Dr 76108
Parkmount Ct & Dr 76137
Parkrise Dr 76179
Parks Ct 76244
Parkside Dr 76108
Parkside Trl 76137
Parkside Way 76137
Parkview Dr
100-399 76179
2500-2699 76102
5200-5499 76148
9200-9699 76134
Parkview Ln 76137
Parkview Hills Ln 76179
Parkway Dr 76134
Parkwest Blvd 76179
Parkwood Dr
4300-4799 76140
6600-6699 76148
Parkwood Ln 76133
Parkwood Trl 76137
Parkwood Hill Blvd 76137
Parkwood Plaza Dr 76137
Parmer Ave 76109
Parrish Rd 76117
Parsons Ln 76106
Partridge Dr
600-799 76131
7700-7799 76148
Partridge Rd 76132
Pascal Way 76137
Paseo Trl 76177
Passage Dr 76135
Pasteur Ct 76133
Pastime Ct 76244
Pate Dr
2400-3099 76105
3200-4499 76119
Pate Rd 76126
Pathway Dr 76119
Patino Ct 76148
Patino Rd 76112
Pato Ct 76126
Patreota Dr 76126
Patricia St 76117
Patricias Rdg 76126
Patrick Ln 76120
Patron Trl 76108
Patsy Cir 76134
Patsy Ct 76148
Patsy Ln 76148
Patterson Dr 76117
Patton Ct 76110
Patton Dr 76112
Paul Meador Dr 76135
Paula Ridge Ct 76137
Pauls Ct & Dr 76179
Pavillion Ct & St 76102
Pawnee Trl 76135
Pawpaw Ridge Dr 76179
Payton Dr 76131
Peace St 76244
Peaceful Ter 76123
E & W Peach St 76102
Peach Orchard St 76244
Peach Tree Ct 76179
Peach Willow Ln 76109
Peacock Dr 76131
Peak St 76106
Pear St 76244
Pear Tree Ct 76140
Pear Tree Ln
7500-7699 76133
7700-7799 76148
Pearl Ave
2000-2720 76164
2721-2721 76106
2722-2722 76164
2723-3499 76106
Pearl Oyster Ln 76179
Pearl Ranch Rd 76126
Pearson Ct 76126
Peat Ct 76244
Pebble Dr 76118
Pebble Beach Way 76137
Pebble Creek Rd 76107
Pebble Ridge Dr 76132
Pebble Stone Dr 76123
Pebblebrook Ct 76109
Pebblebrook Dr 76148
Pebblecreek Ct 76126
Pebbleford Rd 76134
Pebblestone Dr 76126
Pecan Ct 76117
Pecan Dr 76114
Pecan Ln 76116
Pecan St 76102
N Pecan St 76106
Pecan Chase 76132
Pecan Creek Cir 76244
Pecan Meadow Ct &
Dr 76140
Pecan Orchard Ct &
Way 76179
Pecan Park Dr 76118
Pecan Valley Dr 76132
Pecantree Ln 76140
Pecos St 76119
Pecos Trl 76116
Pecos River Trl 76132
Peden Rd 76179
Pedernales Trl 76118
Pedigree Trl 76244
Peggy Dr 76133
Pelham Rd 76116
Pelican Way 76131
Pemberton Ct & Dr 76108
Pembroke Dr 76110
Pendery Ln 76244
Pendleton Dr 76244
Penhurst Dr 76133
Peninsula Ln 76244
Peninsula Club Cir 76135
Penland St 76111
Penn St 76102
Pennerid Dr 76112
Pennington 76126
Pennsylvania Ave 76104
Pennsylvania Dr 76131
Penny Ln 76123
Penny Royal Dr & St 76244
Penrod Ct 76114
Penrose Ave 76116
Pensacola Ave 76116
Penta Rd 76108
Penticost St 76107
Penwell Dr
2300-2399 76120
5501-5697 76135
5699-5799 76135
Peony Ct 76123
Pepperbush Dr 76137
Pepperidge Ln 76131
Peppermill Ln 76140
Peppertree Ln 76108
Pepperwood Trl 76108
Perch Dr 76179
Perdido Dr 76148
Peregrine Trl 76108
Perisho Ct 76126
Periwinkle Dr 76137
S Perkins St 76103
Permian Ln 76137
Perry Dr 76108
Perry Ln 76133
Perry St 76106
Pershing Ave
3600-6199 76107
6200-6299 76116
Persimmon Ct 76244
Perth Ct 76179
E Peter Smith St 76104
W Peter Smith St
200-1599 76104
2000-2399 76102
Petersburg Dr 76244
Peterson Ct 76177
Peterson Dr E 76140
Peterson Dr W 76140
Petty Pl 76177
Petunia Dr 76244
Petworth Pl 76103
Peyton Ln 76134
Peyton Brook Dr 76137
Phantom Hill Rd 76140
Pharr St 76102
Pheasant Gln 76140
Pheasant Rd 76131
Pheasant Creek Dr 76244
Pheasant Run Trl 76131
Pheasant Walk St 76133
Philadelphia Ct 76148
Phillip Ct 76116
Phillips Cir 76114
Phoenix Dr 76116
Photo Ave 76107
Picasso Dr 76107
Pico Ln 76126
Piedmont Rd 76116
Piedra Dr 76179
Pier 1 Pl 76102
Pierce Ave 76119
Pilot Point St 76108
Pima Ln 76119
Pimlico Way 76179
Pin Tail Ct 76244
Pine Ln 76140
Pine St
2100-2699 76102
6100-6299 76148
Pine Bluff Ct 76123
Pine Flat Ct 76179
Pine Grove Ln 76123
Pine Hurst Trl 76137
Pine Park Dr 76118
Pine Ridge Ln 76123
Pine Tree Cir E, S &
W 76244
Pine Valley Pl 76132
Pinehill Ct 76148
Pinehurst Dr W 76134
Pinellas Ave 76244
Pineview Ln 76140
Pinewood Dr 76116
Piney Point St 76108
Pinionpark Way 76179
Pinkeys Ct 76126
Pinon St 76116
Pinson St
5000-5499 76105
5500-5799 76119
Pinto Ln 76179
Pinto Trl 76116
Pinyon Pine Dr 76244
Pioneer St 76119
Piper Ct 76126
Piper Dr 76179
Pipestone Dr 76137
Pitchfork Ranch Rd 76134
Pittman Ave 76140
Pitts St 76244
Pittsburg Pl 76111
Placid Dr 76117
Placitas Trl 76131
Plainfield Dr 76108
Plamera Ln 76131
Plantation Dr 76116
Plantation Ln 76123
Plantation Rd 76140

Plants Ave 76112
Plassmeyer Ct 76126
Plata Ln 76126
Plateau Dr 76120
Platt Ct & Trl 76137
Platte Pl 76137
Plaza Cir 76112
Plaza Dr 76140
Plaza Pkwy 76116
Plaza Ridge Ct 76179
Pleasant St 76115
Pleasant Mound Dr 76108
Pleasant Wood Ln 76140
Plover Cir 76135
Plover Rd 76126
Plum St 76148
Plum Valley Pl 76116
Plumtree Ln 76140
Plumwood St 76111
Plymouth Ave 76109
Plymouth Dr 76140
Poco Ct 76133
Poindexter St 76102
Poinsetta Dr 76114
Point Lobos Trl 76177
Point Reyes Dr 76137
Polar Brook Dr 76244
S Polaris Dr 76137
Polk Ave 76177
Pollard Dr 76114
Pollard St 76112
Pollys Way 76126
Polo Dr 76123
Polo Club Dr N & S 76133
Pomona Ave 76114
Ponce Ave 76133
Pond Dr 76109
Ponder St 76244
Ponderosa Ct 76244
Ponderosa Dr 76117
Ponderosa Pine Dr 76244
Pope Dr 76104
Popken Dr 76114
Poplar St
  1000-1099 76126
  2200-2499 76102
Poplar Ridge Dr 76123
Poplar Spring Rd 76123
Pople Dr 76126
Popplewell St 76118
Poppy Ct & Dr 76137
Poppy Hill Ln 76244
Porche Ct & Dr 76116
Porcupine Dr 76244
Poreeney Dr 76123
Porichal St 76117
Poriela Dr 76133
Pork Chop Hl 76126
Porta St 76120
Portales Ct & Dr 76116
S Porter St 76140
Portico Dr 76132
Portifino St 76126
Portland Ave 76102
Portman Ave 76112
Porto Vila Ct 76126
Portridge Dr 76135
Portrush Dr 76116
Portside Pl 76135
Portview Dr 76135
Portwood Ct 76117
Portwood Way 76179
Posey Ln 76117
Post Oak Ter 76112
Post Ridge Dr 76123
Postwood Dr 76244
Potomac Ave 76107
Potrillo Ln 76131
Powder Ct 76108
Powder Horn Ct & Rd 76108
E Powell Ave 76104
W Powell Ave 76110
Poynter St 76123
E & W Pradera Ct 76108
Prairie Ave
  1900-2799 76164
  2900-3399 76106
Prairie Ct
  500-599 76179
  6200-6299 76148
  9700-9799 76244
Prairie Dr 76148
Prairie St 76140
Prairie Clover Trl 76131
Prairie Creek Trl 76179
Prairie Crossing Dr 76244
Prairie Dawn Dr 76131
Prairie Fire Dr 76131
Prairie Gulch Dr 76140
Prairie Heights Ct & Dr 76108
Prairie Hen Dr 76177
Prairie Hill Rd N & S 76131
Prairie Lookout Dr 76119
Prairie Meadow Ct 76244
Prairie Ridge Ct & Trl 76179
Prairie Rose Ln 76123
Prairie Wind Trl 76134
Prairieview Dr 76134
Prandarn St 76114
Preakness Cir 76123
S Precinct Line Rd 76118
Preferred Dr 76179
Prelude Dr 76134
Premier Ct 76132
Premier St 76111
E & W Presidio St 76102
Presidio Vista Dr 76177
Prestige Rd 76244
Preston Dr 76119
Preston Hollow Rd 76109
Prestwick Dr 76135
Pretoria Pl 76123
Prevost St 76107
Prewett Rd 76137
Prickly Pear Dr 76244
Pricklybranch Dr 76244
Priddy Ln 76114
Priest Ct 76126
Primrose Ave 76111
Prince Ct 76126
Prince Dr 76126
E Prince St 76115
Prince John Dr 76179
Princess Victoria Ct 76137
Princeton St 76109
Priscella Dr 76131
Private Road 4716 76177
Proctor St 76112
Pronghorn Ln 76108
Prospect Ave
  2001-2097 76164
  2099-2699 76164
  2800-3299 76106
Prospect Heights Dr 76110
Prospect Hill Dr 76123
Prospector Ct 76108
Prothrow St 76112
Provinces St 76179
Provine St 76103
Pruitt St 76104
Pueblo Trl 76135
Puerto St 76133
Puerto Vista Dr 76179
E & W Pulaski St 76104
Pulido St 76107
Pullman Dr & Ln 76131
Pumice Dr 76131
Pumphrey Dr 76114
Pumpkin Dr 76114
Purcey St 76102
Purdue Ave 76114
Purington Ave
  2700-3699 76103
  5200-6399 76112
Purple Sage Ct & Trl 76179
Purselley Ave 76112
Putnam St 76112
Putter Dr 76112
Pylon St 76106
Pyramid Blvd 76126
Pyrite Dr 76131
Pyron Ave 76112
Quachita Crossover 76137
Quail Ct
  100-199 76135
  7400-7499 76148
Quail Dr 76131
Quail Rd 76119
Quail Run 76148
Quail Trl 76114
Quail Creek Ct 76244
Quail Creek St 76126
Quail Feather Dr 76123
Quail Glen Dr 76140
Quail Grove Dr 76177
Quail Hollow Ct & Rd 76133
Quail Meadow Dr 76148
Quail Ridge Ct 76132
Quail Ridge Rd 76132
Quail Ridge St 76179
Quail Run St 76107
Quail Springs Cir 76177
Quail Valley Dr 76244
Quail Wood Ct & Ln 76112
Quails Ln 76119
Quails Nest Dr 76177
Quanah Dr 76244
Quarry Cir 76244
Quarry Hill Ct 76179
Quarry Ridge Trl 76244
Quarter Horse Ln 76123
Quartz Ct 76244
Quebec Dr 76108
Quebec St 76135
Queen Ct & St 76103
Queen Ann Dr 76119
Queens Brook Ct & Ln 76140
Queensbury Cir 76133
Queenswood Ct 76244
Quentin Ct 76106
Quest Ct 76179
Queta St 76133
Quinn St 76105
Quorum Dr 76137
Race St 76111
N Race St 76140
S Race St 76140
Racebrook Ct 76137
Rachel Ct 76137
Rachel Lea Ln 76179
Racquet Club Dr 76120
Radford Rd 76119
Radioshack Cir 76102
Radstock Ave & Ct 76133
Railfence Ct & Rd 76119
Railhead Dr 76177
Railhead Rd 76106
Railridge Cir N & S 76133
Rain Dance Ct & Trl 76123
Rain Forest Ln 76123
Rain Lily Trl 76177
Rainbow Trl 76135
Rainbow Creek Dr 76123
Rainier Rd 76137
Raintree Ct & Rd 76103
Rainwater Way 76179
Rainy Lake Dr 76244
Raisintree Dr 76244
Raleigh Ct & Dr 76123
Rall Cir 76132
Ralph St 76108
Ram Ridge Ct & Rd 76137
Ramble Wood Trl 76132
Rambler Rose St 76137
Ramey Ave
  3800-5499 76105
  5500-6599 76112
Ramhead Dr 76112
Ramona Dr 76116
Rampston Pl 76137
Rams Lake Rd 76179
E Ramsey Ave 76104
W Ramsey Ave 76110
Ranch Ct 76126
Ranch Rd
  1-499 76126
  700-999 76131
  5900-6099 76148
Ranch Bluff Ct 76126
Ranch Hand Trl 76131
Ranch House Dr E & W 76116
Ranch View Ct, Rd & Ter 76109
Rancho Ct 76244
Rancho Dr
  1-20 76244
  100-499 76108
  200-299 76179
  9700-9799 76244
Rancho Dr N 76244
Rancho Pl 76244
Rancho Blanca Ct 76108
S Rand St 76103
Randell Ave 76134
Randell Way 76116
Randle Ln 76179
Randol Crossing Ln 76120
Randol Mill Rd
  5100-6799 76112
  6800-9199 76120
Randolph Ct 76114
Random Rd 76179
Ranger Dr 76120
Ranger Way 76133
Ranier Ct 76109
Rankin Rd 76135
Ransom Ter 76112
Ranya 76126
Raphael St 76119
Rashti Ct 76109
Raton Dr 76116
Raton Ln 76112
Rattikin Rd 76105
Rattler Way 76126
Raven Dr 76131
Ravens Nest Dr 76177
Ravensbrook Ct 76244
Ravensway Dr 76126
Ravenswood Dr 76112
Ravenya St 76179
Ravine Rd 76105
Rawleigh Dr 76126
Ray Ct & Dr 76117
Ray Alvin St 76119
Ray Simon Dr 76106
Ray White Rd 76244
Rayburn Ct & Dr 76133
Raymond Ave 76108
Raymond Dr 76244
N & S Rayner St 76111
Reaford Dr 76117
Reagan Dr 76116
Realoaks Dr 76131
Reata Place Trl 76126
Reata West Dr 76126
Reba Ct 76115
Rebecca Ln 76148
Rebel Rd 76140
Receda Ct 76131
Rector Ave 76133
Red Bark Ct 76135
Red Birch Ln 76244
Red Bird Ln 76114
Red Bluff Ln 76177
Red Brangus Trl 76131
Red Bud Ln
  5100-5399 76114
  6900-7599 76135
Red Bud Rd 76135
Red Cardinal Ln 76114
Red Drum Dr 76179
Red Elm Ln 76131
Red Fox Trl 76137
Red Hawk Ct 76132
Red Moon Trl 76131
Red Oak Ct 76135
Red Oak Ln 76114
Red Oak Ln W 76114
Red Robin Ct & Dr 76244
Red Rock Trl 76137
Red Sierra Dr 76112
Red Tail Ct 76244
Red Velvet Rd 76244
Red Willow Rd 76133
Red Wolf Dr 76244
Redbrook Ln 76140
Redbud Dr 76148
Redcloud Dr 76120
Reddenson Dr 76132
Redding Ct & Dr 76131
Redeagle Creek Dr 76179
Redear Dr 76179
Redfield Dr 76133
N & S Redford Ln 76108
Redgum Dr 76244
Redonda St 76108
Redstone Dr 76112
Redwine Ct 76140
Redwing Dr 76131
Redwing Ln 76123
Redwood Blvd 76119
Redwood Cir 76119
Redwood Dr 76116
Redwood Dr E 76119
Redwood Dr N 76119
Redwood Dr S 76119
Redwood Dr W 76119
Redwood Trl 76137
Redwood Creek Ln 76137
Reed Ave 76179
Reed St 76119
Reef Point Ln 76135
Reeves Pl 76118
Reeves St
  3100-3499 76117
  6500-6899 76118
Refinery St 76106
Refugio Ave
  2101-2197 76164
  2199-2799 76164
  2800-3299 76106
Regal Dr 76132
Regal Rd
  3500-3599 76111
  6300-6499 76119
Regal Ridge Dr 76119
Regal Royale Dr 76108
Regatta Ct 76179
Regency Cir 76137
Regency Ln 76134
Regent Row St 76126
Regents Ct 76179
Reggis Ct 76155
Regina Dr 76131
Reginald Rd 76112
Reid River Dr 76116
Reidy St 76116
Remington Cir 76132
Remington Dr 76131
Remington Lk 76132
Remington Rdg 76132
Remington St 76116
W, E, N & S Remuda Cir, Ct & Dr 76108
Rena Dr 76118
Renaissance Sq 76105
Rench Rd 76135
Rendon Rd 76140
Rendon Bloodworth Rd 76140
Rendon New Hope Rd 76140
Renee Cir 76116
Renfro Dr 76108
Renner Ave 76104
Reno Rd 76116
Renwick Cv 76244
Renwood Dr 76140
Renzel Blvd 76116
Repper St 76106
Republic Dr 76140
Resource Dr 76119
Retriever Ln 76120
N & S Retta St 76111
Reunion Ranch Rd 76134
Reveille Rd 76108
Revere Dr 76134
Revere St 76117
N Rhea Ct & Dr 76108
Rhea Ridge Dr 76135
Rhineland Rd 76126
Rhonda Ct 76148
Rhoni Ct 76140
Riata River Rd 76132
Ribinskas Ct 76126
Rice Ln 76103
Rich St 76112
Richard Dr 76148
Richard St
  4300-4799 76119
  8100-8299 76108
Richard Legacy Way 76105
Richardo Ln 76244
Richards Ter 76115
Richards Ranch Rd 76134
Richardson Ct 76119
Richardson Ct E 76119
Richardson Ct W 76119
Richardson Dr 76148
Richardson St 76119
Richardson Ranch Rd 76126
Richland Rd 76118
Richland St 76116
Richlynn Ter 76118
E Richmond Ave 76104
W Richmond Ave 76110
Richmond Park Ln 76140
Rickee Ct 76148
Rickee Dr
  4600-4999 76115
  5900-6099 76148
Rickenbacker Pl 76112
Ricky Ranch Rd 76126
Ricochet Dr 76131
Ridge Cir 76126
Ridge Dr 76140
N Ridge Dr 76108
Ridge Ln 76114
Ridge Rd N
  2600-2899 76133
Ridge Rd W 76133
N Ridge Rd
  6000-6399 76135
S Ridge Rd 76135
S Ridge Ter 76133
Ridge Lake Dr 76244
Ridge North Rd 76126
Ridge Oak St 76112
Ridge View Dr 76137
Ridgecrest Cir
  500-699 76179
  4100-6499 76135
Ridgecrest Ct 76133
Ridgecrest Dr
  200-899 76179
  2700-2899 76133
  5900-6099 76148
Ridgecrest Ln 76132
Ridgecrest Trl 76132
Ridgecrest Way 76132
Ridgehaven Ct & Rd 76116
Ridgeline Dr 76135
Ridgemont Rd 76117
Ridgepointe Rd 76244
Ridgerock Ct & Rd 76132
Ridgeton Rd 76116
Ridgetop Ct 76131
Ridgetop Dr 76148
Ridgevale Rd 76116
Ridgeview Cir 76244
Ridgeview Dr 76137
Ridgeview St 76119
Ridgewater Trl 76131
Ridgeway Rd 76126
Ridgeway St 76116
Ridgewood Dr 76132
Ridgewood Rd 76107
Ridgewood Trl 76148
Ridglea Ave 76116
Ridglea Dr 76148
Ridglea Ln 76116
Ridglea Pl 76116
Ridglea Country Club Ct 76116
Ridglea Country Club Dr
  3500-3799 76116
  3800-4099 76126
  4100-4399 76126
Ridglea Crest Dr 76116
Ridglea Hills Ct 76116
Ridgmar Blvd & Plz 76116
Ridgmar Meadow Rd 76116
Ridgmar West Ct 76116
Riding Stable Ln 76123
Rigewater Trl 76131
Riley St 76115
Riley Ridge Rd 76126
Rim Rock Dr 76108
Rimbey Rd 76119
Rimstone Dr 76108
Rincon Way 76137
Ringold Dr 76133
Ringtail Dr 76244
Rio Blanco Ct 76137
Rio Frio Trl 76126
W Rio Grande Ave 76102
Rio Grande Dr
  1000-1100 76126
  1100-1323 76126
  1102-1398 76126
  1325-1399 76126
  5700-5799 76137
Rio Salado Dr 76179
Rio Viento 76135
Rio Vista Rd 76116
Rip Johnson Dr 76107
Ripley St 76244
Ripple Creek Ct 76120
Ripple Springs Dr 76148
Riptide Ct 76135
Ripy Ct 76110
E Ripy St
  100-1099 76110
  1100-1399 76115
W Ripy St 76110
Riscky Trl 76244
Rising Knoll Ln 76131
E Risinger Rd 76140
W Risinger Rd
  100-1099 76140
  1100-2599 76134
  3000-3098 76123
  3100-5399 76123
Riss Ct 76126
Rita Ln 76117
Rita Kay Ln 76119
Ritter Ln 76137
River Rd 76114
River Run 76107
River Bend Blvd 76116
River Bend Dr 76132
River Bend Rd 76132
River Birch Rd 76137
River Bluff Dr 76132
River Brook Ct 76116
River Cross Dr 76114
River Falls Dr 76118
River Forest Dr 76116
River Garden Dr 76114
River Hill Ln 76114
River Lodge Trl N & S 76116
River Meadows Pl 76112
River Oaks Blvd 76114
River Park Cir, Dr, Ln & Plz N & S 76116
River Pass St 76109
River Pine Ln 76116
River Pointe Dr 76114
River Ranch Blvd 76132
River Ridge Ct & Dr 76137
River Rock Blvd 76179
River Trails Blvd 76118
River Valley Blvd 76132
River Valley Ct 76116
River View Ct & Dr 76132
Riverbend Ct 76109
Riverbend Dr 76109
Riverbend Pkwy 76112
Riverbend Pl 76112
Riverbend Estates Dr 76112

Riverbend West Dr 76118
Riverchase St 76126
Rivercove Ct 76116
Rivercreek Ranch Ln 76126
N Rivercrest Ct & Dr 76107
Riverdale Dr 76132
Riverflat Ct & Dr 76179
Riverfront Dr 76107
Riverglen Dr 76109
Rivergrove Ct 76116
Riverhills View Dr 76109
Riverhollow Ct & Dr 76116
Riveridge Ct & Dr 76109
Rivermoor Ct 76116
Riveroad Ct 76116
Riverpark Ct & Dr 76137
Riverport Rd 76116
Riverridge Rd 76116
Rivers Edge Dr 76118
Riverside Dr
100-1799 76111
2101-2197 76103
2199-2499 76103
N Riverside Dr
100-2399 76111
5001-5197 76137
5199-7999 76137
S Riverside Dr
100-2849 76104
3000-4899 76119
Riverstone Cir, Ct, Trl
& Way E & N 76116
Rivertree Blvd 76109
Riverview Cir 76112
Riverview Ct 76126
Riverwalk Dr 76109
Riverwater Trl 76179
Riverway Ct 76116
Riverwell Ct 76116
Riverwood Ct 76116
Riverwood Dr 76116
Riverwood Trl 76109
Road Runner Cir 76135
Roadrunner Rd 76135
Roanoke St 76116
Roaring Fork Dr 76133
Roaring Springs Rd
105-313 76114
315-599 76114
600-698 76114
601-699 76114
700-1399 76114
1400-2299 76107
N Roaring Springs Rd 76114
Robbins Dr 76108
Robbins Way 76179
E Robert St 76104
W Robert St
1000-2499 76110
2700-2799 76109
Robert Burns Dr 76119
Roberts Dr 76179
Roberts Ln 76140
S Roberts Cut Off Rd 76114
Robertson Rd 76135
Robin Ave 76164
Robin Ct 76148
Robin Dr
900-999 76179
5700-5899 76148
5900-6099 76148
Robindale Rd 76140
Robinhood Ln 76112
Robinson St
2300-3199 76106
4700-4999 76114
Robinwood Dr 76111
Robotics Pl 76118
Robs Ct 76126
Rochester Dr 76244
Rock Canyon Ct 76123
Rock Creek Dr 76123
Rock Creek St 76126
Rock Crest Dr 76114
Rock Dove Cir
900-999 76131
9700-9799 76244
Rock Elm Rd 76131
Rock Garden Trl 76123
Rock Island St 76106
Rock Prairie Ln 76140
Rock Quarry Rd 76132
Rock Ridge Blf 76112
Rock River Dr 76103
Rock Springs Rd 76107
Rock Valley Dr 76244
Rock View Ct 76112
Rockbrook Ct 76112
Rockdale Rd 76134
Rocket Ln 76131
Rockhaven Dr 76179
Rockhill Ct & Rd 76112
Rockledge Dr 76179
Rockledge Rd 76108
Rockmill Trl 76179
Rockmoor Dr 76134
Rockmoor Ln 76116
Rockport Ln 76137
Rockridge Ter 76110
Rockway St 76108
Rockwell Ln 76179
Rockwood Dr & Ln 76114
Rockwood Park Dr 76107
Rockwood Park Dr N 76114
Rocky Ct 76123
Rocky Chris Ct 76126
Rocky Ford Rd 76179
Rocky Mountain Rd 76137
Rocky Point Trl 76135
Rocky Ridge Ter 76108
Rocky Top Cir 76131
Roddy Dr 76123
Rodeo Plz 76164
Rodeo St 76119
N & S Roe St 76108
Rogers Ave
2300-3699 76109
4300-4499 76133
Rogers Rd
500-599 76126
1600-1800 76107
1802-1898 76107
Rogers St 76140
Rogue River Trl 76137
Roky Ct 76114
Roland Ct 76140
Rollie Michael Ln 76179
Rolling Creek Run 76108
Rolling Hills Ct 76126
Rolling Hills Dr
2100-4699 76119
7400-10000 76126
10002-10198 76126
10100-10299 76126
Rolling Meadow Trl 76135
Rolling Meadows Dr 76123
Rolling Rock Dr 76123
Rolling Springs Ct 76120
Rolling Wood Trl 76135
Roma Dr 76126
Roma Ln 76134
Romeo Ln 76126
Romney Rd 76134
Ronald Dr 76134
Ronald St 76108
Ronay Dr 76140
Rondo Dr 76106
Ronnie St 76108
Roosevelt Ave
2000-2799 76164
2800-3399 76106
Roosevelt Gap Ct 76140
Rooster St 76244
Rosa Ct 76134
Rosalyn Dr 76148
Rose Ct
6500-6599 76140
9100-9199 76244
Rose Crest Blvd 76140
Rose Crystal Way 76179
Rose Lea Ct 76137
Rose Of Sharon Ln 76137
Rose Quartz Ct 76132
Rose Tree Ct 76137
Rosebriar Way 76244
Rosebud Ln 76118
E Rosedale St
100-2199 76104
2200-5499 76105
5500-6999 76112
W Rosedale St
100-2199 76104
4501-5629 76107
W Rosedale St N 76110
W Rosedale St S 76110
Rosedale Springs Ln 76134
Rosehaven Dr 76116
Rosehill Dr 76112
Roseland St 76103
E & S Roselane St 76112
Roseman Ct 76179
Rosemary Ct 76244
Rosemary Dr 76126
Rosemeade Dr 76116
Rosemere Ave 76111
Rosemont Ave 76116
Rosen Ave
2300-2799 76164
2800-3299 76106
Rosewood St 76116
Rosita St 76119
Ross Ave
2000-2699 76164
2800-3799 76106
Ross Lake Dr 76137
Rosser St 76112
Rota Cir 76133
Rothington Rd 76116
Rough Creek Rd 76140
Round Hill Rd 76131
Round Leaf Dr 76244
Round Rock Rd 76137
Round Rock Trl 76135
Roundhouse Dr 76131
Roundrock Dr 76179
Roundrock Ln 76140
Roundrock Loop E 76179
Roundrock Loop N 76179
Roundtree Ct 76137
Roundup Rd 76179
Rouse St 76111
Route 66 76148
Routt St 76112
Rowan Dr 76116
Rowland Dr 76108
Roxanne Ct & Way 76135
Roxie St 76117
Roy C Brooks Blvd 76140
Royal Dr 76116
Royal Ln 76109
Royal Ascot Dr 76244
Royal Birkdale Dr 76135
Royal Burgess Dr 76135
Royal Crest Dr 76140
Royal Harbor Ct 76179
Royal Lytham Rd 76244
Royal Meadows Trl 76140
Royal Oak Ct 76155
Royal Oak Dr 76126
Royal Oaks Dr 76119
Royal Terrace Ln 76120
Royal Troon Dr 76179
Royalwood Dr 76131
Royster Rd 76134
Ruben Ln 76126
Ruby Pl 76116
Ruby Lea Ln 76179
Rudd St 76105
Rue Chateau St N 76132
Rufe Snow Dr
2800-3399 76118
3400-3599 76118
5900-8299 76148
Ruff Rd 76140
Rufus St
3100-3199 76105
3200-3999 76119
Rugged Ave 76179
Ruidosa Trl 76116
Ruidoso Ct & Dr 76179
Rum St 76244
Rumfield Rd 76108
Runnels St 76106
Running River Ct & Ln 76131
Running Water Trl 76131
Runnymeade Pl 76108
N Rupert St 76107
Ruse Springs Ln 76131
Rush St 76116
Rush Creek Ct 76244
Rush River Trl 76123
Rushing Creek Ct 76137
Rushing River Dr 76118
Rushing Springs Dr 76118
Rushmore Ct & Rd 76137
Rushwood Ct 76135
Rusk St 76137
Russell Rd 76140
Russell St 76108
Russet Trl 76140
Rustic Dr
900-999 76179
6700-6899 76140
Rustic Forest Rd 76140
Rustic View Rd 76140
Rusticwood Ct 76140
Ruston Ave 76133
Rustwood Ct 76109
Rusty Dell St 76111
Rutan St 76119
Rutgers Ct 76120
Ruth Rd 76118
Ruth St 76112
Ruthann Dr 76119
Ruthdale Dr 76134
Ruths Ct 76179
Rutland Ave 76133
Rutledge St 76107
Ryan Ave
2300-4099 76110
4400-4799 76115
Ryan St 76179
Ryan Creek Rd 76179
Ryan Place Dr 76110
Rye Dr 76179
Rye Glen Ct 76179
Saba Dr 76119
Sabbatical St 76131
Sabelle Ln 76117
Sabinas Trl 76118
Sabine St
3100-3199 76119
4700-4899 76137
Sabrosa Ct E & W 76133
Sackett Lndg 76116
Saddle Rd 76108
Saddle Trl
300-399 76179
8300-8399 76116
Saddle Bag Dr 76179
Saddle Blanket Ct 76131
Saddle Creek Dr 76177
Saddle Flap Dr 76179
Saddle Horse Ln 76119
Saddle Ridge Cir 76123
Saddle Ridge Ln 76179
Saddleback Cir 76148
Saddlebrook Dr 76116
Saddlehorn Dr 76116
Saddleway Dr 76179
Sadie Trl 76137
Sadler Ave 76133
Saffron Dr 76123
Sage Ct 76132
Sage Meadow Trl 76177
Sage Wind Cir 76177
Sagebrush Rd 76116
Sagecrest Ter 76109
Sagehill Ct & Dr 76123
E Sagelake Rd 76109
Sagestone Dr 76177
Sagewood Ln 76131
N & S Saginaw Blvd 76179
Sagrada Park 76126
Sahalee Dr 76132
Sahara Pl 76115
Saharra Slew Ct 76126
Sailwind Dr 76135
Saincona Dr 76126
Saint Andrews Ct 76132
Saint Andrews Ln 76137
Saint Andrews Rd 76132
Saint Annes Ct 76179
Saint Barts Rd 76123
Saint Benet Ct 76126
Saint Charles Pl 76107
Saint Christian St 76119
Saint Croix Ct 76118
Saint Croix Ln 76137
Saint Donovan St 76107
Saint Edwards St 76114
Saint James St 76244
Saint Johns Dr 76132
Saint Johns Ln 76114
Saint Joseph Ct 76110
Saint Juliet St 76107
Saint Kitts Rd 76123
Saint Laurent Ct 76126
Saint Lawrence Rd 76103
Saint Louis Ave
100-1699 76104
1700-4099 76110
Saint Lucia Rd 76123
Saint Martin Rd 76123
Saint Thomas Pl 76135
Saint Veran Park 76114
Saint Vincent Rd 76123
Saints Cir 76108
Salado Trl 76118
Saldana Dr 76133
Salem Cir 76132
Salem Ct
100-199 76134
3300-3399 76140
Salem Dr 76140
Salem Trl 76132
Salisbury Ave 76106
Salix Ct 76109
Sallee Way 76126
Sally St 76137
Salmon Run Way 76137
Salt Rd 76140
Salt Creek Trl 76131
Salt River Rd 76137
Saltbrush St 76177
Saludo St 76133
Salvia Dr 76177
Sam Bass Ct & Trl 76244
Sam Calloway Rd 76114
Sam Cantey Rd 76179
Sam Houston Ave 76119
Samantha Dr 76134
Samora Ct 76135
Samuels Ave 76102
San Angelo Ave 76126
San Antonio Dr 76131
San Benito St 76114
San Carlos Way 76244
San Diego Trl 76131
San Felipe Dr 76137
San Fernando Dr
3000-3199 76177
6800-7099 76131
San Francisco Trl 76131
San Gabriel Ct 76118
San Isabel Ct 76137
San Jacinto Dr
3100-3399 76116
5000-5099 76137
San Joaquin Trl 76118
San Jose Dr 76112
San Juan Ave 76133
San Luis Trl 76131
San Marcos Ct & Dr 76116
San Pedro Ct 76179
San Rafael St 76134
San Rocendo St 76116
San Rose Dr
2900-2999 76105
3600-3899 76119
San Saba Ave 76126
San Saba Dr 76114
San Simeon Ln 76179
San Tejas Dr 76177
San Villa Dr 76135
Sanborn St 76103
Sanctuary Ln 76132
Sanctuary Heights Ct &
Rd 76132
Sand St 76118
Sand Dune Rd 76135
Sand Springs Rd 76114
Sand Verbena Way 76177
Sandage Ave
2500-2698 76109
2700-3299 76109
4000-4099 76110
4100-5199 76115
Sandalwood Dr 76140
Sandalwood Ln 76116
Sandcastle Ct 76179
Sandcherry Dr 76244
Sandell Dr 76108
Sanderson Ave 76103
Sandgate St 76105
Sandhill Crane Dr 76118
Sandoval Dr 76131
Sandpiper Cir & Ct S 76108
Sandra Dr 76133
Sands Ct 76108
Sandshell Blvd, Cir, Ct
& Dr E & W 76137
Sandstone Ct & Dr 76120
Sandy Ct 76140
Sandy Ln
100-1299 76120
1400-3299 76112
5600-5699 76114
6100-6199 76148
6400-6599 76140
Sandy St 76140
Sandy Trl 76120
Sandy Creek Dr 76131
Sandy Lane Park Dr 76112
Sandy Ridge St 76133
Sandy Shores Ct 76179
Sandybrook Dr 76120
Sandywoods Ct 76112
Sanford St 76117
Sangers Ct 76244
Sanguinet Ct & St 76107
Sansom Blvd 76179
Sansom Cir 76114
Santa Ana Dr 76131
Santa Barbara Ave 76114
Santa Clara Dr 76116
Santa Cova Ct 76126
Santa Fe Dr 76131
Santa Fe Trl
2900-3199 76116
5600-5699 76148
Santa Gertrudis St 76179
Santa Marie Ave 76114
Santa Monica Dr 76116
Santa Paula Dr 76116
Santa Rita Ct & Dr 76133
Santa Rosa Dr 76117
Santiago Ave 76133
Santos Dr 76106
Sapphire St 76244
Sapphire Pool Trl 76244
Sappington Pl 76116
Sarah Ct 76148
Sarah Ln 76179
Sarah Jane Ln 76119
Saramac Dr 76148
Saranac Trl 76118
Sarasota Springs Ct &
Dr 76123
Saratoga Ct 76131
Saratoga Rd 76244
Saratoga Downs Ct &
Way 76244
Saratoga Springs Cir 76244
Sargent St 76103
S Sargent St
300-999 76103
1000-1299 76105
Sarita Ct, Dr & Park 76109
Sarita Park Ct 76109
Sarsard Ct 76126
Sartain Dr 76120
Saslow Skwy 76140
Satellite Dr 76244
Saturn Pl 76106
Saucer Dr 76117
Saucon Valley Dr 76132
Saunders Rd 76119
Savage Dr 76134
Savannah Ln 76132
Savanno Ln 76244
Savory Dr 76244
Savoy Ct & Dr 76133
Sawgrass Dr 76132
Sawtimber Trl 76244
Sawyer Dr 76179
Saxony Rd 76116
Saybrook Ct 76131
Scarlet Trl 76179
Scarlet Sage Ct 76112
Scarlet View Trl 76131
Scenery Hill Ct & Rd 76103
Scenic Green Cir 76244
Scenic Hill Dr 76111
Scenic Point Dr 76244
Scenic View Dr 76244
Scenic Vista Dr 76108
Schadt Ct & St 76106
Scharf Ct 76116
Scharmels Ln 76126
Schieffer Ave 76110
Schieme St 76114
Schilder Dr 76114
Schley Ct 76116
Schmidt St 76105
Schwartz Ave 76106
Scoggins St 76114
Scots Briar Ct & Ln 76137
Scotsdale Dr 76119
Scott Ave 76103
Scott Ct 76148
Scott Rd 76114
Scott St 76108
Scotts Way 76111
Scotts Bluff Ct 76244
Scotts Valley St 76244
Scranton Dr 76118
Scrub Oak Ct 76108
Scruggs Dr 76118
Scruggs Park Dr 76118
Scurry Ct 76108
Sea Bass Ct & Dr 76179
Sea Breeze Ln 76135
Sea Meadow Dr 76132
Sea Ridge Ct & Dr 76133
Sea Tac Dr 76155
Sea Turtle Way 76135
Seabrook Dr 76132
Seabury Dr 76137
Seafield Ln 76135
Seahorse Cv 76179
Seal Cv 76179
Sealands Ln 76116
Seaman St 76111
Searcy Dr 76131
Sears Dr 76105
Seascape Pt 76131
Seaton Ct 76132
Seattle Slew Ct & Dr 76112
Seawood Dr 76123
Secco Ct & Dr 76179
Secretariat Ct & Dr 76112
Sedalia Dr 76108
Sedalia Trl 76126
Sedgewick Rd 76244
Sedona Ranch Dr 76131
Seguin Trl 76118
Segura Ct N & S 76132
Selago Dr 76244
Selene St 76106
Selk Ave 76111

Selkirk Dr W 76109
Selma St 76111
E Seminary Dr
100-1499 76115
1800-3599 76119
3000-3099 76119
W Seminary Dr
100-2600 76115
2602-2698 76115
2700-3599 76133
3600-3626 76109
3628-3698 76109
Senator Dr 76244
Sendera Ln 76126
Sendero Trl 76177
Seneca Ct & Dr 76137
Senepol Way 76131
Senita Cactus St 76177
Sentinel Way 76244
Sequoia Ct 76135
Sequoia Dr 76140
Sequoia Way
800-999 76131
8300-8499 76137
Sera Roma Dr 76126
Sereno Ln 76244
Serrano Dr 76126
Sessums Pl 76126
Seth Barwise St 76179
Seton Hall Dr 76120
Settlement Plaza Dr 76108
Settlers Trl 76244
Seven Gables St 76133
Sevenoaks Dr 76244
Sevilla Rd 76116
Seville Dr 76179
Sewell Ave 76114
Sexton Ln 76126
Seymour Ave 76114
Shackleford St 76119
Shad Dr 76179
Shaddox Dr 76244
Shadow Dr 76116
Shadow Ln 76117
Shadow Bend Dr 76137
Shadow Creek Ct
5600-5699 76112
6800-7099 76132
Shadow Grass Ave 76120
Shadow Hill Dr 76112
Shadow Trace Dr 76244
Shady Ln 76126
Shady Cedar Dr 76244
Shady Cliff Ln 76179
Shady Creek Dr 76109
Shady Elm Ct 76108
Shady Glen Cir 76132
Shady Glen Ct 76120
Shady Glen Way 76132
Shady Grove Dr 76244
Shady Hill Dr E 76119
Shady Hollow Dr 76123
Shady Lane Dr 76112
Shady Oaks Ln 76107
Shady Oaks Manor Dr 76135
Shady Ridge Ct 76109
Shady River Ct N & S 76126
Shady Side Trl 76116
Shady Springs Trl 76179
Shady Valley Dr 76116
Shadybrook Dr 76244
Shadydale Ct 76148
Shadydell Dr 76135
Shadymeadow Dr 76123
Shadywood Dr 76140
Shafer Pl 76126
Shagbark Ct & St 76137
Shalako Dr 76116
Shale Dr 76244
Shalimar Dr 76131
Shallow Run 76109
Shallow Creek Dr 76179
Shallow Water Ct 76120
Shalon Ave 76112
Shamrock Ave 76107
Shamrock Ct 76119

Shamrock Ln 76119
Shane Ave 76134
Shane Dr 76117
Shannon Dr 76116
Sharon Rd 76116
Sharondale St 76115
Sharpview Ct & Dr 76116
Shasta Ct & Trl 76133
Shasta Ridge Ct 76123
Shavano Dr 76123
E & W Shaw St 76110
Shawnee Trl 76135
Shaye Ln 76112
Shea Ln 76179
Sheffield Dr 76134
Sheffield Pl 76112
Sheilagh Pl 76126
Shelburne Rd 76244
Shelby Dr 76109
Shelby Ln 76135
Shelby Rd 76140
Shelby Oaks Ct 76140
Sheldon Trl 76244
Shell Creek Dr 76137
Shell Ridge Dr 76133
Shellbrook Ave 76109
Shelly Ray Rd 76244
Shelman Trl 76112
Shelter Grove Rd 76131
Shelton Dr 76120
Shelton St 76112
Shenandoah Dr 76140
Shenandoah Rd 76116
Shenna Blvd 76114
Shepheard Dr 76114
Shepherd Oaks Cir 76112
Sheppard St 76119
Sheridan Cir & Rd 76134
Sherman Ave 76106
Sherry Ct 76108
Sherry Dr 76108
Sherry Ln
401-699 76114
900-999 76179
Sherwood Ave 76107
Sherwood Dr 76114
Sherwood Trl 76179
Shields St 76244
Shilling Dr 76103
Shiloh Ct 76140
Shiloh Dr 76107
Shiner Dr 76179
Shinnecock Hills Dr 76132
Shiny Oaks Trl 76112
Shipley Ct 76116
Shipp Dr 76148
Shipps Rd 76126
Shire Ct 76140
Shirley Ave 76109
Shiver Rd 76244
Shoal Creek Rd 76132
N Shore Dr 76135
Shore Front Ct & Dr 76135
Shorecrest Ct 76132
Shorehaven Pl 76116
Shoreline Cir N 76119
Shores Ct 76137
N Shores Dr 76179
Shoreview Dr 76108
Short St 76179
Shortcake Ct 76135
Shotts St 76107
Shoveler Trl 76118
Show Master Ln 76179
Shropshire St 76105
Shumer Shuffle Dr 76140
Side Saddle Trl 76131
Sidewinder Trl 76131
Sidonia Ct 76126
Sienna Dr 76133
Sienna Ridge Ln 76131
Sierra Ct 76109
Sierra Dr 76116
Sierra Blanca Dr 76179
Sierra Estate Trl 76119
Sierra Madre Dr 76179

Sierra Ridge Dr 76123
Sierra View Dr 76244
Signal Hill Ct N & S 76112
Sika Deer Run 76179
Sikes Ct 76126
Silent Brook Ct & Ln 76244
Silent Hollow Dr 76140
Silent Ridge Ct E & W 76132
Sills Way 76177
Silsby Dr 76244
Siltstone Ln 76137
Silver Canyon Ct & Dr 76108
Silver City Dr 76179
Silver Creek Rd 76108
Silver Fox Ct 76108
Silver Hill Ct 76108
Silver Hill Dr
100-199 76108
2500-2799 76131
Silver Horn Dr 76108
Silver Lake Ct 76117
Silver Lake Dr 76117
Silver Lake Trl 76140
Silver Maple Dr 76244
Silver Mesa Ln 76108
Silver Oak Ln 76135
Silver Ridge Blvd E 76108
Silver Rock Ln 76135
Silver Saddle Ct & Rd 76126
Silver Sage Dr 76137
Silver Spring Ln 76135
Silver Springs Dr 76123
Silver Spur Ln 76179
Silver Streak Dr 76131
Silver Valley Ct & Ln 76108
Silver View Ln 76135
Silverbell Ln 76140
Silverberry Ave 76137
Silverbrook Dr 76179
Silveridge Dr 76133
Silverleaf Ct & Dr 76112
Silverthorn Ct 76177
Silverton Cir 76133
Silverwood Trl 76244
Silvinia Ct 76126
Simiford St 76131
Simondale Dr 76109
Simpson Ct 76244
Sims Dr 76119
Sinclair St 76244
Singleleaf Ln 76133
Singleton Rd 76179
Singletree Ct 76132
Sioux Creek Ln 76244
Sir Guy Dr 76179
Sirocka Dr 76116
Sirron St 76105
Sitka St 76137
Sixpence Ln 76108
Skipador Dr 76179
Sky Acres Dr 76114
Sky Creek Ct 76179
Sky Harbor Way 76155
Sky Wood Ct 76179
Skylake Ct & Dr 76179
Skylark Ln 76148
Skyline Dr 76114
Skyline Bluff Ct & Dr 76102
Skyline Park Dr 76108
Skymeadow Dr 76135
Skyview Ter 76116
Skyway Ct 76179
Slade Blvd 76116
Slate St 76114
Slay St 76135
Sledge Loop 76126
Sleeping Doe Dr 76179
Sleepy Creek Ln 76179
Sleepy Hollow Dr 76114
Sleepy Meadows Dr 76244
Sleepy Ridge Cir 76133
Slide Rd 76244
Slide Rock Rd 76137
Slim Ridge Rd 76119
Slippery Rock Dr 76123
Slocum Ave 76116

Slover Dr 76137
Smallwood Dr 76114
Smilax Ave 76111
Smith Ave 76140
Smith St
1700-1799 76110
7700-7798 76108
7800-7899 76108
Smokethorn Dr 76244
Smokey Ridge Dr 76123
Snapdragon Dr 76244
Snapper Ct 76135
Snipe Ct 76126
Snow Egret Way 76118
Snow Goose Way 76118
Snow Ridge Ct & Dr 76133
Snowbird Ct 76126
Snowden Rd 76140
Snowdrop Ct 76123
Soapberry Dr 76244
Soaptree Ln 76177
Socorro Rd 76116
Soft Shell Dr 76135
Softwind Ct & Trl 76116
Softwood Cir 76244
Sohi Dr 76137
Solomon Dr 76108
Solona Cir & St 76117
Somerset Ln 76109
Somerset Hills Ct 76132
Somervell St 76120
Sommerville Place Rd 76135
Sondra Dr 76107
Songbird Ln
7700-7899 76133
7900-7999 76123
Sonoma Dr 76244
Sonora Trl 76116
Sopwith Ct 76126
Sorghum Dr 76179
Sorrel Ct 76126
Sorrell Ct 76137
Sourwood Dr 76244
South Ct 76133
South Dr
3500-4799 76109
4800-5399 76132
South Dr W 76132
South Fwy
100-3099 76104
3100-4099 76110
4200-5100 76115
5102-5598 76115
5800-6198 76134
6200-8699 76134
8700-10803 76140
N South Fwy 76102
Southbend Dr 76123
Southbrook Cir 76134
Southbrook Dr 76114
Southcrest Ct & Dr 76115
W Southern Ave 76179
Southern Ct 76179
Southern St 76106
Southern Cross 76111
Southern Hills Dr 76132
Southern Pine Way 76123
Southern Prairie Dr 76123
Southgate Dr 76133
Southland Ave 76104
Southpark Ln 76133
Southridge Trl 76133
Southview Dr 76134
Southview Rd 76108
Southway Cir 76115
Southway Dr 76140
Southwest Blvd
3700-5099 76116
5100-5398 76109
6000-6698 76109
6201-6799 76132
6801-6899 76132
Southwest Dr 76134
Southwind Ct 76137
Southworth Dr 76134
Sovereign Rd 76155

Soy Seed Trl 76179
Spanish Trl
1900-2499 76107
6500-6999 76135
Spanish Hills Dr 76126
Spanish Needle Trl 76177
Spanish Oak Dr 76109
Spanish River Trl 76137
Sparrow Ct
4300-4399 76133
5800-5899 76135
Sparrow Dr 76131
Sparrow Pt 76133
Sparrow Hawk Ln 76108
Sparrow Wood Ct &
Ln 76112
Spaugh Ct 76108
Spear St 76103
Speckle Dr 76131
Specklebelly Ln 76120
Spencer Ct 76120
Spencer St
3600-4099 76244
5700-6099 76119
Spicebush Rd 76133
Spicewood Trl 76134
Spiller St 76105
Spindletree Ln 76137
Spindrift Ct & St 76137
Spinnaker Ct 76135
Spinnaker Way 76132
Spirit Lake Dr 76179
Splitridge Ct 76108
Spoon Drift Dr 76135
Spoonbill Ct 76108
Spoonwood Ln 76137
Spotted Owl Dr 76244
Spring Dr 76131
Spring St 76179
Spring Buck Run 76179
Spring Creek Trl 76148
Spring Garden Dr
1-99 76134
8600-8699 76244
Spring Haven Dr 76244
Spring Hollow Dr 76131
Spring Meadow Ct 76132
Spring Mist Cv 76244
Spring Ranch Dr 76179
Spring Ridge Dr 76137
Spring Tree Ln 76244
Spring Valley Way 76132
Spring View Ln 76244
Springbranch Dr 76116
Springbrook Dr 76107
Springcreek Ct 76112
Springdale Ct 76148
Springdale Rd 76111
Springer Ave 76114
Springfield St 76112
Springford Cir 76244
Springhill Dr
1000-1054 76179
1055-1199 76179
6600-6699 76148
Springhill Rd 76116
Springlake Pkwy 76117
Springleaf Cir & Ct 76133
Springmont Ln 76244
Springrock Dr 76244
Springs Rd 76107
Springside Dr 76137
Springtide Dr 76135
Springview Ct 76117
Springway Ln 76123
Springwillow Rd 76109
Springwood Dr 76179
Sproles Dr 76126
Spruce Dr 76244
Spruce Ln 76126
Spruce Park Dr 76118
Spruce Pine Ct 76244
Spruce Springs Way 76177
Spruce Valley Dr 76137
Sprucebark Dr 76244
Spur Ridge Ct 76244

E Spurgeon St 76115
W Spurgeon St
300-2099 76115
3600-3999 76133
Spyglass Way 76137
Spyglass Hill Ct 76132
E Square St 76120
Squaw Creek Ct 76137
Stable Door Ln 76244
Stacey Ave 76132
Stackhouse St 76244
Stadium Dr
2300-3999 76109
4100-5199 76133
Stafford Dr 76134
Stafford Station Dr 76131
Stage Coach Rd 76244
Stagecoach St 76133
Staghorn Cir N & S 76137
Stalcup Rd
1500-2499 76112
2500-3899 76119
Stallion Ln 76179
Stampede Ct 76131
Stamps Ave 76114
Stancour Rd 76120
Standering Rd 76116
Standifer St 76164
Standish Rd 76133
Stanford Ave 76114
Stanley Ave
2100-4099 76110
4401-4497 76115
4499-5399 76115
Stanley Keller Rd 76117
Stanphill St 76119
Stansfield Dr 76137
Stanton Ct 76120
Staples Ave 76133
Stapleton Ln 76155
Star Dr
1000-4299 76244
5100-5299 76132
Star Fish St 76244
Star Gazer Ln 76140
Star Ridge Dr 76133
Star Thistle Dr 76179
Starboardway Dr 76135
Starburst Dr 76244
Starcrest Ct 76132
Stardust Dr 76148
Stardust Dr S 76148
Stardust Ln 76119
Staree Ln 76179
Stark St 76112
Starlight Ct 76117
Starlight Dr
1-99 76126
4400-5899 76117
Starlight Dr N 76126
Starlight Dr S 76126
Starling Cir 76117
Starling Dr 76112
Starnes Rd 76148
Starry Ct 76123
Starwood Ct & Dr 76137
Stately Ct 76244
Statesman Ln 76244
Station Way Dr 76131
Statler Blvd & Ct 76155
Stauss Ln 76155
Stayton St 76107
Steagall Ct 76244
Steamboat Ct & Dr 76123
Stearns St 76105
Stedman Trl 76244
Steel St 76137
Steel Dust Dr 76179
Steeple Ridge Ct &
Rd 76140
Steeplechase Dr 76123
Steerman Ct 76179
Steinburg Ln 76134
Steiner St 76244
Stella St 76104
Stephanie Dr 76117

Stephanie Ln 76134
Stephen Lee Dr 76119
Stephens Hill Rd 76140
Stephenson St 76102
Stephenson Levy Rd 76140
Stepping Stone Dr 76123
Sterling Dr 76126
Sterling Hill Dr 76108
Sterling Trace Cir 76244
Stetson Dr 76244
Stetson Dr N 76244
Stetson Dr S 76244
Stetson Trl 76131
Stevens Dr 76126
Stevens St 76114
Stevens Trl 76179
Stewart Ln 76126
Stewart St 76104
Still Meadow Dr 76132
Stillwater Ct 76137
Stillwater Dr 76137
Stillwater Trl 76118
Stirrup Way 76244
Stirrup Bar Dr 76179
Stirrup Iron Dr 76179
Stockton Dr 76132
Stockwood Dr 76135
Stockyards Blvd
100-199 76106
301-399 76164
Stone Ct & Dr 76108
Stone Canyon Cir 76108
Stone Chapel Way 76179
Stone Creek Ct, Ln,
Pkwy, Ter, Trl & Way N
& S 76137
Stone Creek Canyon
Ct 76137
Stone Creek Meadow
Ct 76137
Stone Crossing Ln 76140
Stone Garden Dr 76134
Stone Lake Ct & Dr 76179
Stone Meadow Ln 76179
Stone Mill Ln 76179
Stone Mountain Dr 76123
Stone Oak Ct, Dr &
Ln 76109
Stone Top Dr 76179
Stone Valley Dr 76244
Stone Water Dr 76120
Stonebank Ct 76112
Stonebriar Ln 76123
Stonebridge Pl 76110
Stonebrook Ct 76179
Stonecrest Ct 76244
Stonedale Rd 76116
Stonegate Blvd 76109
Stonegate Dr
1-99 76134
7100-7299 76126
Stonehaven Ct 76179
Stonehenge Rd 76109
Stonehill Dr 76126
Stoneleigh Dr 76126
Stoneshire Ct 76179
Stoneside Ct & Trl 76244
Stonewall Ct 76123
Stonewall Ln 76123
Stonewall Rd 76140
Stonewater Bend Trl 76179
Stoneway Dr N & S 76118
Stonewick Ct 76123
Stonewood Dr 76179
Stoney Bridge Ct &
Rd 76108
Stoney Creek Ct & Rd 76116
Stoney Gorge 76177
Stoneybrook Dr 76112
Storm Dr 76148
Storm Chaser Dr 76131
Stormydale Ln 76140
Story Ln 76108
Story St 76119
Stove Foundry Rd 76116
Straightaway Dr 76117

Straley Ave ... 76114
Stratford Ct ... 76103
Stratford Dr ... 76126
Stratford Park Dr ... 76103
Stratton Rd ... 76134
Stratum Dr ... 76137
Straw Rd ... 76179
Strawberry Ct & Way ... 76137
Strawberry Creek Ln ... 76135
Streamwood Rd ... 76116
Striper Dr ... 76179
Stripling Dr ... 76244
Strohl St ... 76106
Strong Ave ... 76105
Stroup Dr ... 76126
Stuart Dr
2400-3099 ... 76104
3100-3899 ... 76110
Stubbs Trl ... 76108
Sturges Dr ... 76112
Styles St ... 76114
Sue Cir ... 76119
Sue Ct ... 76135
Sue Dr ... 76118
Suellen Ln ... 76119
Suffolk Dr
2900-3399 ... 76133
3400-3699 ... 76109
Sugar Bush Ct ... 76137
Sugar Lake Rd ... 76103
Sugar Maple Dr ... 76244
Sugar Ridge Rd ... 76133
Sugarland Dr ... 76179
Sumac Rd ... 76116
Sumac Hill St ... 76120
Sumerlin ... 76126
Summer Ct ... 76123
Summer Creek Dr ... 76123
Summer Hill Ln ... 76148
Summer Lake Dr ... 76119
Summer Meadows Dr ... 76123
Summer Oaks Ln ... 76123
Summer Park Dr ... 76123
Summer Star Ln ... 76244
Summer Stream Dr ... 76134
Summer Sun Dr ... 76137
E & N Summer Trail Dr ... 76137
Summerbrook Cir ... 76137
Summercrest Ct & Dr ... 76109
Summerdale Ct ... 76148
Summerfields Blvd & Ct ... 76137
Summerglen Rd ... 76133
Summerhill Ln ... 76244
Summers Dr E ... 76137
Summerset Dr ... 76126
Summersville Ln ... 76244
Summertime Ln ... 76148
Summerview Ct ... 76123
Summerwind Dr ... 76244
Summit Ave ... 76102
S Summit Ave ... 76104
Summit Cv ... 76179
Summit Dr ... 76126
Summit Ln ... 76112
Summit Park Cir & Dr N, S & W ... 76135
Summit Point Ct ... 76179
Summit Ridge Dr ... 76148
Sumter Way ... 76244
Sun Dr ... 76244
Sun Haven Way ... 76244
Sun Meadow Ln ... 76140
Sun Meadows Ct ... 76123
Sun Valley Dr ... 76119
Sun View Dr ... 76108
Sunburst Dr ... 76140
Suncrest Dr ... 76180
Sundale Ct ... 76123
Sundance Cir ... 76148
Sundance Ln ... 76179
Sunday Pl ... 76133
Sunday St ... 76117
Sunderland Ct & Ln ... 76134
Sundial Dr ... 76244

Sundog Way ... 76244
Sundown Dr
3800-8699 ... 76116
4000-4099 ... 76116
5900-6099 ... 76148
6000-6299 ... 76114
Sundrop Ct ... 76108
Sunfish Dr ... 76132
Sunflower Cir N ... 76120
Sunflower Cir S ... 76120
Sunflower Ct ... 76133
Sunny Glen St ... 76134
Sunny Hill Dr ... 76148
Sunny Hollow Dr ... 76179
Sunnybank Ct & Dr ... 76137
Sunnybrook Dr ... 76148
Sunnydale Ct ... 76137
Sunnydale Dr ... 76116
Sunnyside Dr ... 76119
Sunnyview Ct ... 76137
Sunnyway Dr ... 76123
Sunnywind Ct ... 76137
Sunray Dr ... 76120
Sunridge Cir ... 76120
Sunridge Dr ... 76126
Sunrise Ct ... 76120
Sunrise Dr
7900-7999 ... 76148
9200-9499 ... 76134
Sunrise Lake Dr ... 76179
Sunrise Point Ct ... 76135
Sunscape Ct & Ln ... 76123
Sunset Blvd ... 76135
Sunset Cir N ... 76244
Sunset Cir S ... 76244
Sunset Dr ... 76116
E Sunset Dr ... 76244
Sunset Ln
1-99 ... 76108
200-5099 ... 76114
Sunset Rd ... 76114
Sunset St ... 76107
Sunset Ter ... 76102
Sunset Trl ... 76135
Sunset Cove Ct & Dr ... 76179
Sunset Hills Dr ... 76244
Sunset Oaks Dr ... 76112
Sunset Ridge Dr ... 76123
Sunset Trace Dr ... 76244
Sunset View Dr ... 76108
Sunshine Dr ... 76105
Sunswept Ct ... 76137
Sunwood Cir & Ct ... 76123
Superior Pkwy ... 76106
N Surfside Dr ... 76135
Surrey St ... 76133
Surry Ct ... 76179
Susan Ct ... 76148
Susan Ln ... 76120
Sussex Ct & St ... 76108
Sutter Ct ... 76137
Sutter St ... 76107
N Suttonwood Dr ... 76108
Suzie Rich Dr ... 76244
Swan Cir ... 76131
Swan Ct ... 76117
Swan St ... 76117
Swanee Ct ... 76148
Swayne Ave ... 76111
Sweet Birch Ct ... 76244
Sweet Cherry Ct ... 76244
Sweet Flag Ln ... 76123
Sweet Leaf Ct ... 76244
Sweet Meadows Dr ... 76123
Sweetbriar Ln ... 76109
Sweetgum Way ... 76133
Sweetwater Ln ... 76134
Sweetwood Ct ... 76137
Sweetwood Dr ... 76131
Swift St ... 76102
Swift Current Ct & Trl ... 76179
Swinson Dr ... 76126
Switchyard St ... 76107
Swords Dr ... 76137
Sycamore Dr ... 76120
Sycamore Ln ... 76179

Sycamore St ... 76104
Sycamore Ter ... 76104
Sycamore Creek Rd ... 76134
Sycamore Ridge Dr ... 76133
Sycamore School Rd
100-2399 ... 76134
2400-4698 ... 76133
2401-3499 ... 76123
3501-4699 ... 76133
5400-5499 ... 76123
Sycamore Trace Dr ... 76133
Sydney St
2800-3299 ... 76105
3300-3999 ... 76119
Sylvan Ct & Dr ... 76120
Sylvan Meadows Dr ... 76120
N Sylvania Ave
100-3699 ... 76111
3700-4999 ... 76137
S Sylvania Ave ... 76111
Sylvania Ct ... 76111
Sylvania Cross Dr ... 76137
Sylvania Park Dr ... 76111
T L Ferguson Dr ... 76115
T Square Dr ... 76120
Table Rock Dr ... 76131
Tackett Ct ... 76112
Tacoma Dr ... 76108
Tacoma Ter ... 76123
Tacoma Ridge Dr ... 76244
Tadpole Dr ... 76244
Taft St ... 76103
Tahoe Dr ... 76119
Tahoe Springs Dr ... 76179
Talgarth Ct ... 76133
Tall Meadow Ln ... 76133
Tall Oak Dr ... 76108
Tallahassee Ln ... 76123
Talleyrand Ct ... 76108
Tallgrass Trl ... 76244
Tallie Rd ... 76112
Tallman St ... 76119
Tallow Wind Trl ... 76133
Tallowood Ct ... 76131
Tallwood Ln ... 76134
Talons Crest Cir ... 76179
Talton Ave ... 76104
Talus Dr ... 76131
Tam O Shanter Dr ... 76111
Tamar Trl ... 76118
Tamarack Ct & Rd ... 76116
Tamarron Dr ... 76135
Tameron Trl ... 76132
Tamiami Trl ... 76137
Tammaron Trl ... 76140
Tammy Ct ... 76148
Tamworth Rd ... 76116
Tanacross Dr ... 76137
Tanbark Trl ... 76109
Tandy Ave ... 76103
Tangleridge Dr ... 76123
Tanglewood Park & Trl ... 76109
Tankersley Ave ... 76106
Tanna Ln ... 76134
Tanner Ave ... 76116
Tanneyhill Ln ... 76112
Tanny St ... 76114
Tanque Dr ... 76137
Tanqueray Pl ... 76116
Taos Ct ... 76179
Taos Dr ... 76180
Tapatio Springs Rd ... 76108
Tapestry Ct & St ... 76244
Tappanzee Ct ... 76114
Tar Heel Dr ... 76123
Tara Dr ... 76116
Tarpon Springs Dr ... 76123
N Tarrant Pkwy
1300-1399 ... 76131
2700-3499 ... 76177
4400-5199 ... 76244
5200-5298 ... 76137
5201-5999 ... 76244
5300-5998 ... 76244
Tarrant Rd ... 76105

Tasman St ... 76134
Tasselwood Dr ... 76244
Tate Ave ... 76244
Taxco Rd ... 76116
Taylor Rd ... 76114
Taylor St
100-1199 ... 76102
300-499 ... 76179
N Taylor St ... 76102
Tayside Ct ... 76179
Teaberry Ln ... 76133
Teague Rd ... 76140
Teakwood Ct & Trce ... 76112
Teal Dr ... 76137
Team Ranch Rd ... 76126
Tearose Trl ... 76123
Technology Blvd ... 76140
Tee Dr ... 76117
Tee Head Dr ... 76135
Tehama Ct ... 76177
Tehama Ridge Pkwy ... 76177
Teja Trl ... 76126
Tejas Ave ... 76116
Tejas Trl ... 76135
Telephone Rd
3900-3929 ... 76135
3930-3930 ... 76136
3931-7599 ... 76135
3932-7598 ... 76135
Temecula Rd ... 76244
Templeton Dr ... 76107
Ten Bears Ct ... 76179
Ten Mile Bridge Rd ... 76135
Tenderfoot Trl ... 76135
Tennessee Ave ... 76104
Tennis View Ct ... 76120
Tension Dr ... 76112
Tequilla Ct ... 76112
Terbet Ct & Ln ... 76112
Terlingua Ct ... 76108
Terminal Rd ... 76106
Terra Ct & Trl ... 76106
Terra Brook St ... 76106
Terra Chase Cv ... 76137
Terra Cota Ln ... 76123
Terra Meadows Ln ... 76137
Terrace Ave ... 76164
Terrace Trl ... 76114
Terrace Green St ... 76179
Terrace Landing Ct ... 76179
Terrace Oaks Ln ... 76112
Terrace View Dr ... 76108
Terrance St ... 76111
E Terrell Ave ... 76104
Terry St ... 76108
N Terry St ... 76106
Teton Trl ... 76137
Tex Blvd ... 76116
Texas St ... 76102
Texas Way ... 76106
Texas Health Trl ... 76244
Texas Longhorn Way ... 76177
Texas Sage Trl ... 76137
Texas Shiner Dr ... 76179
Thaddeus Dr ... 76137
Thames Trl ... 76118
Thannisch Ave ... 76105
Thaxton Trl ... 76137
The Resort Blvd ... 76179
Thelin St ... 76115
Thersa Dr ... 76114
Thicket Ct ... 76123
Thicket Bend Ct & Dr ... 76244
Thistle Ct ... 76126
Thistle Dr ... 76132
Thistle Ln ... 76109
Thistle Creek Ct ... 76179
Thistle Hill Dr ... 76110
Thistle Ridge Ter ... 76123
Thistledown Dr ... 76137
Thomas Ln ... 76114
Thomas Pl
200-599 ... 76140
1200-2400 ... 76107
2402-2698 ... 76107
7000-7099 ... 76148

Thomas Rd ... 76117
Thompson Ct ... 76179
Thompson Dr ... 76179
Thompson Rd ... 76244
Thompson St
101-197 ... 76140
199-299 ... 76140
300-399 ... 76134
600-799 ... 76140
Thoms Ct ... 76126
Thoreau Ln ... 76120
Thorn Hollow Dr ... 76244
Thornberry Dr ... 76137
Thornbush Dr ... 76179
Thorncreek Ln ... 76177
E Thornhill Dr ... 76115
W Thornhill Dr ... 76115
Thornhill Rd ... 76132
Thornton St ... 76106
Thoroughbred Ct ... 76179
Thoroughbred Trl ... 76123
Thorp Ln ... 76244
Thrall Ct & St ... 76105
Thrash Ct ... 76126
Thrasher Ct ... 76137
Three Bars Dr ... 76179
Three River Ct ... 76103
Three Wide Dr ... 76177
Threshing Dr ... 76179
Throckmorton St ... 76102
N Throckmorton St ... 76164
Thunder Bay Dr ... 76119
Thunderhead Trl ... 76135
Thurman Rd ... 76244
Thurmond Sail Ct ... 76179
Thurston Rd ... 76114
Tiara Trl ... 76108
Tiburon St ... 76106
Tidball Dr ... 76244
Tideway Dr ... 76135
Tidwell Dr ... 76114
Tierney Ct N ... 76112
Tierney Ct S ... 76112
Tierney Rd ... 76112
S Tierney Rd ... 76105
Tierra Verde Dr & Trl ... 76177
Tierra Vista Way ... 76131
Tiffany Meadows Ln ... 76140
Tiger Trl ... 76126
Tigris Trl ... 76118
Tiki Trl ... 76112
Tilapia Dr ... 76179
Tilden Ct ... 76132
Tillar St ... 76107
S Timber Ct ... 76126
Timber Trl ... 76134
Timber Creek Trl ... 76118
Timber Fall Ct & Trl ... 76131
Timber Oaks Dr ... 76179
Timber Ridge Ct
5500-5599 ... 76137
7500-7599 ... 76179
Timber Ridge Dr ... 76137
Timber Ridge Ter ... 76123
Timbercreek Rd ... 76126
Timbercrest Dr ... 76126
Timberland Blvd
11200-11298 ... 76177
11800-12499 ... 76244
Timberland Dr ... 76244
Timberline Ct ... 76126
Timberline Dr
1400-1899 ... 76126
2100-3199 ... 76119
S Timberline Dr
900-1299 ... 76126
1300-1499 ... 76126
3800-3900 ... 76119
3902-3998 ... 76119
Timberview Ct N ... 76112
Timberview Ct S ... 76112
Timberview Dr ... 76140
Timberwilde Cir ... 76112
Timberwolfe Ln ... 76135
Timberwood Ct ... 76179
Timken Trl ... 76137

Timothy Rd ... 76115
Tin Star Dr ... 76179
Tina Ct ... 76140
Tindall Dr ... 76244
Tinker Dr ... 76114
Tinkerbell Ln ... 76119
Tinsley Ct ... 76126
Tinsley Dr ... 76126
Tinsley Ln
2800-3499 ... 76179
3501-3599 ... 76179
8100-8199 ... 76108
Tioga Ct ... 76116
Tioga Downs Ct ... 76126
Tippy Ter ... 76134
Tipton Ct ... 76135
Tipton St ... 76114
Tiptop St ... 76117
Titan St ... 76108
Titus St ... 76106
Tobago Rd ... 76123
Tobey Ct ... 76126
Tobie Layne St ... 76126
Todd Ave ... 76110
Toffee St ... 76244
Toledo Ave & Ct ... 76133
Tom Ellen St ... 76111
Tom Stock St ... 76116
Tomahawk Trl ... 76244
Tommy St ... 76112
Tommy Hays Dr ... 76117
Tommy Watkins Dr ... 76117
Tompkins Cor ... 76135
Tony Ct ... 76135
Top Hill Ct ... 76126
Top Rail Run ... 76179
Topanga Ter ... 76132
Topaz Trl ... 76108
Topeka Dr ... 76131
Topper St ... 76134
Topperwind Ct ... 76134
Tori Trl ... 76244
Toronto St ... 76103
Torrey Pines Dr ... 76109
Tortoise Ln ... 76135
Tosca Dr ... 76180
Toscana Cir ... 76140
Tosoro Cir ... 76106
Toto Rd ... 76108
Toulouse Ln ... 76133
Tower St ... 76118
Towerwood Dr ... 76140
Town Center Dr ... 76115
Town Square Dr ... 76116
Towne Ct ... 76179
Townes Dr ... 76108
Townley Dr ... 76140
Townsend Dr
2600-4099 ... 76110
4100-5399 ... 76115
Township Ct ... 76179
Trabuco Canyon Rd ... 76108
Trace Ridge Pkwy
8300-8499 ... 76137
8500-8900 ... 76244
8902-9398 ... 76244
Tracy Dr ... 76117
Tracyne Dr ... 76114
Trade Wind Dr E ... 76177
Tradewind Dr ... 76131
Trading Post Dr ... 76131
Tradition Dr ... 76140
Trafalgar Rd ... 76116
Trail Dr ... 76119
Trail Bend Cir ... 76109
Trail Blazer Dr ... 76131
Trail Cliff Way ... 76132
Trail Creek Dr ... 76244
Trail Hollow Dr ... 76244
Trail Lake Dr
3601-3747 ... 76109
3749-4209 ... 76109
4211-4499 ... 76109
4500-6999 ... 76133
7000-7398 ... 76123
7001-7599 ... 76133

Trail Ridge Ct & Dr ... 76126
Trailhead Dr ... 76177
Trailridge Ct & Dr ... 76179
Trails Edge Rd ... 76109
Trails End Dr ... 76116
Trails End St ... 76114
Trailside Ct E & W ... 76135
Trailview Dr ... 76132
Trailwood Dr ... 76140
Trailwood Ln ... 76109
E Trammell Ave ... 76140
W Trammell Ave ... 76140
Trammell Dr ... 76126
Tranquil Acres Rd ... 76179
Tranquility Cir ... 76140
E Tranquility Cir ... 76140
W Tranquility Cir ... 76140
Tranquility Dr
4200-4399 ... 76244
5900-6114 ... 76140
Transport Dr ... 76177
Trappingham Ter ... 76116
Travers Trl ... 76244
Travertine Ln ... 76137
Travis Ave
400-1099 ... 76104
1900-4099 ... 76110
Travis Ct ... 76148
Travis St ... 76148
Traymore Dr ... 76244
Tree Ln ... 76114
Tree Leaf Ln ... 76123
Tree Ridge Ct ... 76133
Treehaven Rd ... 76116
Treeside Dr ... 76123
Treetop Ct ... 76179
Treetop Dr ... 76126
Treeview Ct ... 76126
Tremont Ave ... 76107
Trena St ... 76114
Trent Trl ... 76118
Trentman St ... 76119
Trenton Ct ... 76148
Trevino Ln ... 76126
Trevino Rd ... 76116
Trey Riata Dr ... 76123
Triad Blvd ... 76131
Triangle Leaf Dr ... 76244
Tribute Ln ... 76131
Trice Ct ... 76120
Trifecta Ln ... 76126
Trigg Dr ... 76114
Trilobite Trl ... 76137
Trimble Dr ... 76134
Trina Dr ... 76131
Trinidad Ct ... 76126
Trinidad Dr ... 76140
Trinity Blvd
7300-9100 ... 76118
9102-9598 ... 76118
13701-14097 ... 76155
14099-15699 ... 76155
15701-15899 ... 76155
Trinity Ct ... 76120
Trinity Dr ... 76126
Trinity Ln ... 76137
Trinity Trl ... 76131
Trinity Campus Cir ... 76102
Trinity Creek Dr ... 76179
Trinity Fork Dr ... 76116
Trinity Garden Dr ... 76118
Trinity Heights Blvd ... 76132
Trinity Landing Dr N ... 76132
Trinity Oaks Rd ... 76114
Trinity Ranch Rd ... 76126
Trinity Valley Ct ... 76133
Trinity View Dr ... 76116
Triple Crown Dr ... 76179
Triumph St ... 76119
Troon Rd ... 76132
Troost St ... 76104
Tropical Pt ... 76131
Trotter Ct ... 76123
Trout Dr ... 76179
Trout Creek Ct ... 76137
Troy Ct ... 76114

Troy Dr 76123
True Ave 76114
Trueland Dr 76119
Truelson Dr 76134
Truett St 76119
Truitt Dr 76126
Truman Ct & Dr 76112
Truxton Ct 76137
Trysail Dr 76135
E Tucker St 76104
W Tucker St
100-1499 76104
2200-2299 76102
Tucson Trl 76116
Tudanca Trl 76131
Tudor Dr 76119
Tulane Ave 76114
Tulare Ln 76177
Tularosa Ct & Dr 76137
Tule Ave 76116
Tuleys Creek Dr 76137
Tulip Ln 76137
Tulip Tree Ct & Dr 76137
Tulsa Way 76107
Tumbleweed Ct & Trl 76108
Tumbling Trl 76116
Tumbling Trail Ct 76116
Tupelo Trl 76244
Turkey Trl 76126
Turkey Creek Dr 76244
Turnberry Ct 76179
Turnberry Dr 76132
Turner St
4900-5499 76105
5500-5599 76119
Turner Ridge Dr 76110
Turning Leaf Trl
10400-10599 76131
11400-11499 76244
Turquoise Dr 76131
Turtle Pass 76177
Turtle Creek Ct 76116
Turtle Pass Trl 76135
Turtle River Ct 76137
Turtle Stream Dr 76179
Tuscan View Dr 76131
Tuscany Trl 76179
Tustin Ter 76108
Twain Ave 76120
Tweeter Dr 76108
Twilight Cir 76179
Twilight Dr S 76116
Twilight Dr W 76116
Twilight Trl 76126
Twin Ln 76114
Twin Creeks Dr 76244
Twin Mills Blvd 76179
Twin Oaks Dr
5500-5799 76148
6100-6399 76119
6800-6899 76140
Twin Oaks Trl 76134
Twin Pines Dr 76244
Twinflower Dr 76244
Twisting Way 76131
Two Hawks Dr 76131
Tyler Ct 76108
Tyler Pl 76135
Tyne Trl 76118
Tyra Ct 76148
Tyra Ln 76114
Tyson St 76131
Underwood St 76105
Union Dr 76131
Union Lake Ct & Dr 76137
Union Valley Ct 76179
Unity Dr 76108
University Dr 76107
N University Dr
100-108 76107
110-200 76107
202-398 76107
700-898 76114
900-1000 76114
1002-1098 76114
S University Dr
1300-1398 76107
1400-1799 76107
2400-3799 76109
3800-3899 76110
Upton Ave 76103
Urban Dr 76106
Urban Ridge Dr 76179
Urbanview St 76114
Us Highway 287
7400-9198 76177
Us Highway 287
9200-10498 76131
10500-10699 76131
10701-10899 76131
12801-14499 76179
12201-12299 76179
Usher St 76126
Utica St 76114
Uvalde St 76104
N Vacek St 76107
Vaden Ave 76140
Val Verde Dr
7600-7899 76133
7900-7999 76123
Valencia Ct 76116
Valencia Grove Ct &
Pass 76132
Valentine St 76107
N & S Valera Ct & St 76134
Valhalla Rd 76116
Valkus St 76105
Valle Ct & St 76108
Valley Dr 76140
Valley St 76102
Valley Creek Dr 76179
Valley Crest Dr 76120
Valley Dale Ct 76116
Valley Ford Ct 76148
Valley Forge Trl
2000-2199 76177
3000-3399 76140
Valley Haven Way 76244
Valley Hill Ln 76116
Valley Ridge Dr 76140
Valley Ridge Rd 76107
Valley River Dr 76244
Valley Springs Trl 76244
Valley Stream Way 76244
Valley View Dr
6000-6199 76116
6600-6699 76148
Valley View Trl 76137
Valley Village Dr 76123
Valleyside Dr 76123
Van Cliburn Way 76107
Van Deman Ct & Dr 76116
Van Horn Ave 76111
Van Natta Ln 76112
Van Zandt Dr 76244
Vance Rd 76118
Vancouver Dr 76119
Vanderbilt Ct, Dr, Ln &
St E & W 76120
Vandergriff Ct 76106
Vanessa Dr 76112
Vanshire Rd E & W 76108
Vaquero St 76108
Varden St 76244
Vaughn Ave 76140
Vaughn Blvd
1400-3299 76105
3401-3597 76119
3599-4399 76119
Vdali Ct 76135
Veal St 76104
Vega Ct & Dr 76133
Vega Place Cir 76133
Vel Dr 76112
Velma Dr 76105
Venado Ct 76108
Venera Ct & St 76106
Ventura St 76244
Vera Ave 76105
Vera Cruz St 76106
Verandas Cir 76132
Verano Ct 76108
Verbena Dr 76244
Verbena St 76104
Verde Dr 76244
Verde Oaks Ln 76135
Vermillion St 76119
Vermont Ave 76115
Verna Trl N 76108
Vernon Way 76244
Vernon Castle Ave 76126
Veronica Cir 76137
Versailles Rd 76116
Vesta Farley Rd 76119
Vestia Dr 76244
Via Azalee 76109
Via Bologna 76109
Via Firenze 76109
Via Medici 76109
Via Nice 76109
Via Nicola 76109
Via Palermo 76109
Via Trieste 76109
Via Venicia 76109
Via Villani 76109
Via Vista Ln 76135
Vichendi Dr 76164
E Vickery Blvd
100-2443 76104
2445-3699 76105
W Vickery Blvd
100-1199 76104
1400-2799 76102
3200-5999 76107
6000-7799 76116
7101-7499 76116
Vickery Loop E 76116
Vickery Loop W 76116
Vicki Ln 76104
Vicki St 76117
Vicksburg Ln 76123
Victor Ln 76140
Victoria Dr 76131
Victoria Pl 76112
Victoria Ash Dr 76244
Victorian Dr 76134
Viejo Ln 76244
Vienna Apple Rd 76244
Vienne Pl 76244
Viento Oaks Ln 76135
View St 76103
Villa Dr 76120
Villa Lago Dr 76179
Villa Milano Dr 76126
Villa Ridge Dr 76108
Village Ct 76117
Village Ln 76119
Village Pkwy 76134
Village Pl 76112
Village Course Cir 76119
Village Creek Rd
2400-3099 76105
3600-4499 76119
4501-5199 76119
Village Point Ln 76108
Village Stone Ct 76179
Vinca Cir 76135
Vincennes St 76105
Vincent St 76120
Vincent Ter 76137
Vinetta Dr 76119
Vinewood Ct & St 76112
Vineyard Ln 76123
Vino Dr 76126
Vinson St
4300-5099 76103
5100-5399 76112
Vintage Dr 76244
Viola St 76107
Virgie Ct 76148
Virgil St 76119
Virgil Anthony Blvd 76148
Virginia Ave 76102
S Virginia Ave 76104
Virginia Ct 76111
Virginia Ln
900-999 76179
4200-4799 76103
Virginia Pl 76107
Viridian Ln 76123
Vista St 76105
Vista Way 76126
Vista Cliff Dr 76179
Vista Del Sol Dr 76119
Vista Greens Dr 76244
Vista Heights Blvd 76108
Vista Meadows Dr 76244
Vista Mill Dr & Trl 76179
Vista Ranch Ct & Way 76179
Vista Ridge Cir 76179
Vista Ridge Ct
100-199 76126
6900-6999 76132
Vista Ridge Dr E 76132
Vista Ridge Dr N 76132
Vista Ridge Dr S 76132
Vista Ridge Dr W 76132
Vista Royale Ct & Dr 76108
Vista Verde Dr 76120
Vista Way Dr 76179
Vistas Dr 76135
Vistaview Dr 76112
Vivian Ln 76180
Vogt St 76105
Volare Dr 76126
Volder Dr 76114
Volga Ct 76118
Volk Ct 76244
Volley Ct 76133
Voltamp Dr 76108
Von St 76106
Voncille St 76117
Voss Ave 76244
Wabash Ave
1600-1699 76107
2400-3299 76109
4300-4599 76133
Wabash Ct 76131
Waco Way 76133
Waddell St 76114
Wade Ave 76111
Wade Hampton Ct 76132
Wade Hampton St 76126
Waggoman Rd 76131
E Waggoman St 76110
W Waggoman St 76110
Waggoner Ct 76108
Waggoner Ln 76114
Waggoner Ranch Rd 76134
Wagley Robertson Rd 76131
Wagner Ave 76106
Wagnon St 76108
Wagon Ct 76244
Wagon Trl 76140
Wagon Run Dr 76137
Wagon Rut Ct 76108
Wagon Track Ct 76132
Wagonet Rd 76140
Wagonwheel Rd 76133
Wainwright Dr 76112
Waits Ave
2500-3299 76109
4300-5999 76133
Wake Robin Dr 76123
Wakecrest Dr 76108
Wakeland Ct 76133
Walburn Ct 76133
Walcott Ln 76179
Waldemar St 76117
Walden Ave
4900-4999 76109
5000-5199 76132
Walden Wood Dr 76244
Waldorf St 76119
Waldron Ave 76133
Wales Ave & Ct 76133
Walker St
2400-3199 76105
5901-5997 76117
5999-6000 76117
6002-6098 76117
Wall Ave 76117
Wall Rd 76244
Wall St 76102
Wall Price Keller Rd 76244
Walla Ave 76133
Wallace Rd 76135
Wallace St 76105
Wallen Ave 76133
Walleye Dr 76179
Wallingford Dr 76133
Wallis Rd 76135
Walnut Dr 76114
Walnut Creek Ct & Dr 76137
Walnuthill Ct 76148
Walraven Cir 76133
Walsh Ct 76109
Walter Ct 76108
Walter Dr 76114
Walthall St 76117
Waltham Ave 76133
Walton Ave 76133
Wanda Ln
6100-6399 76119
6800-6999 76140
Wandering Way St 76126
Warbler Ln 76244
Ward Pkwy 76110
Ward St 76103
Warden St 76126
Warehouse Way 76179
Warfield St 76106
Warkendi Dr 76134
Warm Springs Trl 76137
Warmouth Dr 76179
Warner Rd 76110
Warnock Ct 76109
Warren Ave 76115
Warren Ln 76112
Warrington Ct & Pl 76112
Warrior Cir 76119
Warwick Ave 76106
Warwick Hills Dr 76132
Washburn Ave 76107
Washer Ave 76133
Washington Ave
200-399 76179
1000-1699 76104
1700-2299 76110
Washington Ter 76107
Washington Irving Dr 76114
Washita Ct & Way 76137
Watauga Ct E 76111
Watauga Ct W 76111
Watauga Rd
1600-1698 76131
1601-1699 76131
1700-1799 76106
1700-1999 76131
2000-2999 76111
5101-5599 76137
5200-5598 76137
5600-6699 76148
Water St 76102
Water Birch Dr 76244
Water Buck Run 76179
Water Meadows Dr 76123
Water Oak Dr 76244
Water Ridge Ct & Ln 76179
N & S Water Tower Ct
& Rd E, N & W 76179
Water Wood Dr 76179
Waterbird Ln 76137
Waterbrook St 76244
Waterchase Cir & Dr 76120
Watercress Dr
7400-9747 76135
8800-9298 76135
9748-9898 76108
Waterford Dr 76179
Waterfront Ct & Dr 76179
Waterhill Ct & Ln 76179
Waterloo Ln 76179
Waterman St 76102
Watermark Ct & Dr 76135
Watermill Dr 76132
Waters Edge Ln 76116
Waterside Ct & Trl 76137
Waterview Ct 76179
Waterway Dr N 76137
Waterwell Trl 76140
Waterwood Cir & Trl 76132
Watkins Ct 76116
Watonga St 76107
Watson Ct, Rd & St
W 76103
Watters Pl 76114
Watts Ct 76126
Waverly Ln 76244
Waverly Way 76116
Waxwing Cir S & W 76137
Waycrest Dr 76180
Wayfarer Trl 76137
Wayland Dr 76133
Wayne Ct 76116
Wayne Ct N 76117
Wayne Ct S 76117
Wayne St
200-399 76111
1000-1399 76117
1100-1299 76117
Waynell St 76108
Waynewood Ct 76135
Wayside Ave
2500-4099 76110
4100-5399 76115
5400-5499 76134
Wayside Cir 76115
Wayside Ct 76115
Wayside Ln 76115
Wayward Ct 76244
Weather Rock Ln 76179
Weatherbee St 76110
E & W Weatherford St 76102
Weatherstone Dr 76137
Weatherwood Ct & Rd 76133
Weaver St 76117
Weber St 76106
Weber River Trl 76140
Webster St 76117
Weddington Ct 76133
Wedghill Way 76133
Wedgmont Cir N & S 76133
Wedgway Dr 76133
Wedgwood Dr 76133
Wedgworth Ct & Rd 76133
Weepy Hollow Trl 76179
Wehring St 76118
Weiler Blvd 76112
Weir Way 76108
Weisenberger St 76107
Welarana Ave 76115
Welch Ave & Ct 76133
Welden Ct 76132
Weller Ln 76244
Wellesley Ave 76107
Wellington Rd 76116
N Wells Cir 76114
S Wells Cir 76114
Wells Dr 76135
Wells Burnett Rd 76135
Wells Ranch Rd 76140
Wellsburg Way 76244
Wellview Ave 76115
Welsh Ct & Walk 76244
Welshman Dr 76137
Wendel Dr 76133
Wendover Dr 76133
Wendy Ln
5300-5499 76140
8100-8199 76116
Wenneca Ave 76102
Wentworth Ct & St 76132
Wescott St 76109
Wesley St 76111
Wesley Way 76118
Wesleyan Dr & St 76105
Wessex Ave 76133
Wessex Ct 76134
West Fwy
1100-2799 76102
3301-3497 76107
3499-5299 76107
6300-7399 76116
7401-8999 76116
7600-9098 76108
9901-10199 76108
West Ln
1000-1199 76120
3500-3599 76119
West Pl 76108
Westbend Ln 76244
Westbriar Dr 76109
Westbrook Ave 76111
Westbury Ct 76132
Westchester Dr 76117
Westcliff Ave 76179
Westcliff Rd N 76109
Westcliff Rd S 76109
Westcliff Rd W 76109
Westcreek Cir 76126
N Westcreek Ct 76133
S Westcreek Ct 76133
Westcreek Dr 76133
Westcrest Dr
5200-5299 76115
5400-5799 76134
5900-5999 76134
5800-5999 76134
Westdale Ct & Dr 76109
Wester Ave 76133
Westerly Rd 76116
Western Ave
100-399 76179
1200-3599 76107
Western Cir 76148
Western Pass 76179
Western Pl 76107
Western Breeze Dr 76126
Western Center Blvd
1600-1602 76131
1604-3099 76131
3201-3297 76137
3299-4499 76137
4500-5298 76137
4501-5199 76137
Western Creek Ln 76137
Western Hills Blvd 76108
Western Meadows Ct &
Dr 76244
Western Oaks Rd 76108
Western Star Dr 76179
Western Trails Rd 76135
Westfield Ave 76133
Westfork Dr 76114
Westfork St 76114
Westfork Trl 76179
Westgate Dr 76179
Westglen Dr 76133
Westgrove Blvd 76117
Westgrove Dr 76179
Westhaven Ct & Dr 76132
Westheimer Rd 76244
Westhill Rd 76105
Westlake Dr
4300-4500 76109
4502-4598 76109
4600-4999 76132
8500-8599 76108
Westlake Ter 76108
Westland Ave
3200-3299 76108
3300-3699 76116
Westmere Ct & Ln 76108
Westminster Ct N & S 76133
Westmont Ct 76109
Westmoor Ln 76132
Westmoreland Rd 76126
Westover Ct, Dr, Ln, Rd,
Sq & Ter 76107
Westpark Dr 76126
Westpark View Dr 76108
Westpoint Blvd 76108
Westport Pkwy 76177
Westridge Ave 76116
Westridge Dr 76148
Westridge Ln 76116
Westridge Rd 76126
Westrock Dr 76133
Westvale Dr 76116
Westview Ave 76107

Westview Ave N 76107
Westview Rd 76179
Westvista Cir 76133
Westward Dr 76108
Westway Ter 76179
Westwick Dr 76114
Westwind Cir 76116
Westwind Ct 76179
Westwind Dr 76179
Westwood Ave 76107
Westwood Shores Ct & Dr 76179
Westworth Blvd 76114
Wexford Dr 76244
Weyburn Dr 76109
Whalin Ln 76126
Wharton Dr 76133
Wheat Ave 76133
Wheat Sheaf Trl 76179
Wheatfield Trl 76179
Wheatland Dr 76179
Wheaton Dr 76133
Wheel Stone Dr 76120
Wheeler St
3900-4099 76111
4100-5098 76117
4101-5099 76117
Wheeling Dr 76244
Wheelock Dr 76133
Whippoorwill Dr 76123
Whipporwill Ln 76140
Whirlwind Dr 76133
Whisper Ct & Dr 76123
Whisper Hollow Way 76137
Whisper Woods Cir 76120
Whispering Ct 76133
Whispering Ln 76148
Whispering Brook Ln 76140
Whispering Cove Trl 76134
Whispering Creek Trl 76134
Whispering Oaks Ln 76140
Whispering Pines Dr 76177
Whispering Stream Ct 76179
Whispering Willow Ln 76134
Whispering Wind St 76108
Whistle Stop Dr 76131
Whistler Ct & Dr 76133
Whistler Creek Dr 76177
Whistletop Dr 76131
Whistlewood Dr 76244
Whistling Duck Dr 76118
White St
700-1399 76104
4100-4299 76135
White Ash St 76131
White Creek Dr 76137
White Dove Dr 76112
White Falcon Way 76131
White Feather Ln 76131
White Hart Dr 76179
White Hills Dr 76137
White Lake Ct 76103
White Leaf Ct E & W 76135
White Oak Ln 76114
White River Dr 76179
White Rock Dr 76131
White Rock St 76179
White Sands Dr 76137
White Settlement Rd
1600-4099 76107
4400-5499 76114
5500-6699 76114
7600-16399 76108
White Swan Pl 76177
White Tail Ct & Trl 76132
White Willow Dr 76244
Whitefern Dr 76137
Whitehall St
4200-4299 76119
7300-7499 76118
Whitehurst Dr
2500-3299 76133
6400-6499 76148
Whitelake Rd E 76112
Whitestone Ranch Rd 76126
Whitethorn Ct 76137
Whitewater Ct 76123
Whitewood Dr 76137
Whitfield Ave 76109
Whitley Rd 76148
Whitman Ave 76133
Whitmore St 76107
Whitney Ct 76120
Whitney Dr
500-599 76179
7800-8599 76108
Whitney Ln
7800-7999 76112
8000-8199 76120
Whitten St 76134
Whittenburg Dr 76134
Whittier St 76133
Whittlesey Rd 76119
Wichita Ct 76140
Wichita St
100-799 76140
3500-5299 76119
5300-6549 76119
6550-7399 76140
7400-8069 76140
8071-8099 76140
Wicker Dr 76133
Wicklow Ct 76116
Wicks Trl 76133
Wickwood Ct 76131
Widgeon Ave 76116
Wiggins Dr 76244
Wilbarger St 76119
Wilbur St 76108
Wild Azalea Ave 76116
Wild Oak Dr 76140
Wild Oats Dr 76179
Wild Pear Ln 76244
Wild Plum Dr 76109
Wild Rose Ct 76137
Wild Rye Trl 76177
Wild Stallion Ct & Rd 76126
Wild Willow Trl 76134
Wild Wing Dr 76120
Wildbriar Ct E & W 76120
Wildcreek Way 76179
Wilderman St 76102
Wildflower Way 76123
Wildfowl Dr 76177
Wildhaven Dr 76137
Wildridge Ct 76108
Wildriver Trl 76131
Wildwest Dr 76131
Wildwood Cir E 76132
Wildwood Cir N 76132
Wildwood Cir S 76132
Wildwood Cir W 76132
Wildwood Rd 76107
Wilhelm St 76119
Wilkes Dr 76119
Wilkie Way 76133
Wilkinson Ave 76103
Will Rogers Blvd
6401-6497 76134
6499-6500 76134
6502-6598 76134
6600-8699 76140
Will Rogers Rd 76107
Willard Rd 76119
William Fleming Ct 76115
Williams Pl 76111
Williams Rd
100-1399 76120
3400-3798 76116
3401-3799 76116
3800-4999 76116
S Williams St 76104
E Williams Spring Ct & Rd 76135
Williamsburg Ln 76107
Willie St 76105
Willing Ave 76110
Willingham Ct 76244
Willis Ave 76116
Willis Ln 76148
Willman Ave 76180
Willmon St 76164
Willomet Ave 76133
Willoughby Ct 76134
Willow Cir 76112
Willow Ct 76179
Willow Dr 76120
Willow Way 76126
Willow Bend Rd 76116
Willow Creek Ct 76134
Willow Creek Ln 76134
Willow Creek Rd 76135
Willow Glen Cir & Ct 76134
Willow Lake Cir 76109
Willow Oak Ct & Dr 76112
Willow Park Dr 76134
Willow Park St 76118
Willow Ridge Ct & Rd 76103
Willow Rock Ln 76244
Willow Run Ct 76132
Willow Springs Rd 76119
Willow Vale Dr 76134
Willow View Dr 76148
Willow Vista Dr 76179
Willow Way Rd 76133
Willow Wood Dr 76179
Willowbrook Dr 76133
Willowick Ave 76108
Willowood Ct 76112
Willowstone Trl 76179
Willowview Dr 76179
Willowview St 76133
Wills Pl 76133
Wills Creek Ln 76179
Wills Point Ct 76105
Wilmington Ct & Dr 76107
Wilshire Blvd 76110
Wilson Ct 76135
Wilson Ln 76133
Wilson Rd
1400-2699 76112
5100-5799 76140
Wilton Dr 76133
Wiltshire Dr 76135
Wiman Dr 76119
N Wimberly St 76107
Wimbledon Cir 76137
Wimbleton Way 76133
Wimpy St 76164
Winbrook Dr 76126
Wincherr Ave E 76244
Winchester Ct & Pl 76133
Wind Cave Ct 76137
Wind Chime Ct & Dr 76133
Wind Dancer Trl 76131
Wind Hill Ct E & W 76179
Wind River Ct 76116
Wind River Dr 76179
Wind Star Way 76108
Windblow Ct 76123
Windchase Dr 76112
Windcrest Ln 76133
Winder St 76104
Windermere Pl 76112
Windflower Ln 76137
Windham St 76103
Windhaven Rd 76133
Winding Ln 76120
Winding Rd 76133
Winding Way 76126
Winding Brook Dr 76244
Winding Hollow Dr 76179
Winding Passage Way 76131
Winding River Dr 76118
Winding Valley Dr 76244
Windmere Ln 76137
Windmill Way W 76132
Windmill Run St 76112
Windowmere St
4300-4799 76105
5300-5399 76112
Windrock Dr 76148
Windrush Dr N & S 76116
Windsong Trl 76120
Windsor Cir 76140
Windsor Dr
600-799 76140
900-1099 76179
Windsor Pl 76110
Windswept Cir 76135
Windswept Dr 76116
Windward Rd 76132
Windward Way 76140
Windway Dr 76116
Windwillow Ct & Dr 76137
Windwood Ct & Trl 76132
Windy Ln 76140
Windy Canyon Way 76126
Windy Hill Ct 76116
Windy Hill Ln 76108
Windy Hill Rd 76140
Windy Ridge Dr 76123
Windy Ryon Way 76179
Wineberry Dr 76137
Winecup Trl 76131
Winesanker Way 76133
Winfield Ave 76109
Wing Rail Rd 76131
Wingate St 76107
Winged Foot Cir 76132
Winifred Dr 76133
Winkler Dr 76108
Winn Dr 76134
Winn Pl 76134
Winn Pl W 76134
Winn St 76133
Winnebago Ct 76179
Winnie St 76112
Winscott Rd 76126
Winscott Plover Rd 76126
Winslow Dr 76109
Winston Rd 76109
Winter Hawk Dr 76177
Winter Springs Dr 76123
Winterberry Ct & Ln 76244
Winterhazel Ct & Dr 76137
Winters St
300-799 76114
7200-7399 76120
Winthrop Ave
2400-2499 76107
3100-3299 76116
3301-3399 76116
4600-4999 76116
4700-4999 76116
Winton Ter E & W 76109
Wirfield St 76107
Wiseman Ave 76105
Wisen Ave 76133
Wiser Ave 76133
Wispwillow Dr 76244
Wispy Trl 76108
Wister Dr 76123
Wisteria Ct 76111
Wisteria Dr 76140
Wisteria Ln 76137
Withers St 76105
Wj Boaz Rd 76179
Wofford Way 76179
Wolens Way 76133
Wolf Mountain Ln 76140
Wolf Ridge Way 76244
Wolfcreek Ln 76244
Wonder Ct & Dr 76133
Wood Dr 76179
Wood Duck Dr 76118
Wood Hollow Ct 76135
Wood Leaf Ct 76244
Wood Rose Dr 76111
Woodacre Rd 76133
Woodbeach Dr 76133
Woodbend Ct 76132
Woodberry Ct & Dr 76112
Woodbine Dr 76112
Woodbine Cliff Dr 76179
Woodbridge Ct 76137
Woodbridge Dr
3400-7399 76140
6700-6799 76112
Woodchase Dr 76120
Woodchucker Dr 76112
Woodcreek Trl 76179
Woodcrest Ct 76137
Woodcrest Dr
300-399 76179
5600-5799 76140
Wooddale Dr 76148
Wooded Ct 76244
Woodfield Rd 76112
Woodforest Way 76155
Woodgarden Ln 76132
Woodgate Dr 76137
Woodglen Dr & Ln 76126
Woodhall Ct & Way 76134
Woodharbor Dr 76179
Woodhaven Blvd 76112
Woodhaven Ln 76137
Woodhinge Dr 76126
Woodie Way 76108
Woodlake Cir 76179
Woodlake Dr 76135
Woodland Ave 76110
Woodland Way 76137
Woodland Springs Dr 76244
Woodlands Cir 76120
Woodlane Ave 76117
Woodlark Dr 76123
Woodlawn St 76114
Woodmeadow Dr 76135
Woodmont Ct 76133
Woodmont Dr 76117
Woodmont Trl 76133
Woodmoor Rd 76133
Woodoak Ct 76112
Woodpecker Ln 76108
Woodridge Ct 76179
Woodridge Dr 76120
Woodrill Ct 76112
Woodrock Ct 76137
Woodrow Ave 76105
Woodruff Ct 76244
Woodrun Ct 76155
Woods Ave 76102
Woods Ln 76117
Woods Edge Trl 76244
Woodside Hl 76179
Woodside Hill Ct 76179
Woodslane Dr 76179
Woodsmoke Way 76137
Woodstock Dr 76137
Woodstock Rd 76116
Woodstream Trl 76133
Woodthrush Dr 76112
Woodvale Rd 76135
Woodview Dr 76112
Woodview Ln 76140
Woodvine Ct 76140
Woodward St 76107
Woodway Dr 76133
Woodwick Ct 76109
Woody Ln 76140
Woolery St 76107
Wooten Dr 76133
Works St 76112
World Champion Ct 76179
World Wide Dr 76177
Wormar Ave 76133
Worrell Dr 76133
Worth St 76104
Worth Hills Dr 76109
Worthview Dr 76114
Worthy St 76179
Wosley Dr 76133
Wreay Dr 76119
Wren Ave 76133
Wren Haven Dr 76135
Wrentham Dr 76179
Wrenwood Dr 76137
Wright Armstrong St 76179
Wrigley Way
900-999 76179
6000-6699 76133
Wurzburg Dr 76134
Wyatt Ct 76119
Wyatt Dr
1-95 76107
96-8599 76108
Wycliff St 76116
Wylie Thompson Cv 76179
Wyndale Ct 76109
Wyndham Crst 76114
Wyndham Dr 76244
Wyndrook St 76244
Wyoming Dr 76131
Xavier Dr 76133
Yale St 76114
Yale Trl 76179
Yampa Trl 76137
Yancey Ln 76244
Yarmouth Ln 76108
Yates St
1700-2699 76115
2700-2999 76133
Yeager St 76112
Yeary St
5000-5899 76114
6000-6199 76135
Yellow Birch Dr 76244
Yellow Buckeye Dr 76140
Yellow Cedar Trl 76244
Yellow Rose Cir 76115
Yellow Stone Rd 76126
Yellow Wood Dr 76244
Yellowleaf Ct & Dr 76133
Yellowstone Ct & Trl 76137
Yeoman Ln 76179
Yoakum St 76108
Yolanda Dr 76112
Yorba Linda Dr 76108
York Dr 76134
York St 76132
Yorkshire Dr 76119
Yorkshire St 76134
Yorkston St 76148
Yorktown Dr 76140
Yosemite Ct & Dr 76112
Young St 76103
Youngtree Ct 76123
Yucca Ave 76111
Yucca Flats Rd & Trl 76108
Yuchi Ct & Trl 76108
Yuma Ave 76104
Yuma Dr 76119
Z Boaz Pl 76116
S Z Boaz Park Dr 76126
Zachary Ct 76244
Zane Ct 76137
Zelma St 76117
Zeloski St 76107
Zephyr Way 76131
Zinna Ln 76140
Zion Trl 76137
Zoological Park Dr 76110
Zuni Trl N & S 76108
Zwolle St 76106

NUMBERED STREETS

1st Rd 76126
E 1st St
100-2299 76102
2400-2498 76111
2500-4099 76111
4100-4399 76117
4500-5699 76103
W 1st St 76102
E & W 2nd 76102
E & W 3rd 76102
E 4th St
100-2399 76102
2400-4099 76111
NE 4th St 76164
NW 4th St 76164
W 4th St
100-699 76102
3100-4099 76107
5th Ave
600-1699 76104
1700-4099 76110
4100-4899 76115
E 5th St 76102
NE 5th St 76164
NW 5th St 76164
W 5th St
100-1699 76102
2000-4099 76107
6th Ave
600-1699 76104
1700-4099 76110
4101-4497 76115
5700-5799 76134
E 6th St 76102
NE 6th St 76164
NW 6th St 76164
W 6th St
100-699 76102
2200-3102 76107
3101-3101 76147
3103-4099 76107
7th Ave 76104
E 7th St 76102
NE 7th St 76164
NW 7th St 76164
W 7th St
101-1799 76102
2100-4299 76107
8th Ave
500-1699 76104
1700-4099 76110
E 8th St 76102
W 8th St 76102
9th Ave 76104
E 9th St 76102
NE 9th St 76106
W 9th St 76102
9th Hole Dr 76179
10th Ave 76104
NE 10th St
100-299 76106
1016-1024 76102
1026-1199 76102
NW 10th St 76106
W 10th St 76102
11th Ave
700-798 76104
800-899 76104
1500-1899 76102
E 11th St 76102
NE 11th St
100-399 76164
1000-1099 76102
12th Ave 76104
E 12th St
200-1399 76102
2600-3299 76111
NE 12th St 76102
E 13th St 76102
14th Ave 76102
E 14th St 76102
NE 14th St
100-399 76164
1000-1099 76102
NW 14th St 76164
15th Ave 76102
15th Pl 76164
E 15th St 76102
NW 15th St 76164
W 15th St 76102
NE 16th St 76102
400-1399 76164
2600-2899 76106
NW 17th St 76106
E 18th St 76102
700-1499 76164
2400-2999 76106
E 19th St 76102
1200-1499 76164
2400-3099 76106
NE 20th St 76164
NW 20th St
100-2099 76164
2400-2498 76106
NE 21st St 76164
100-2199 76164
2400-3199 76106
NE 22nd St 76164
100-2299 76164
2400-2999 76106
NE 23rd St 76164
100-2299 76164
2600-3499 76106

NW 24th St
100-2399 ... 76164
2400-3599 ... 76106
NW 25th St
100-2399 ... 76164
2400-3599 ... 76106
NW 26th St
100-2399 ... 76164
2400-3599 ... 76106
NW 27th St
100-1999 ... 76164
2400-3599 ... 76106
NE 28th St
100-499 ... 76164
900-2545 ... 76106
2546-2548 ... 76111
2547-2549 ... 76106
2550-3700 ... 76111
3701-3719 ... 76111
3702-3720 ... 76111
3721-4199 ... 76111
4200-5099 ... 76117
5101-5199 ... 76117
NW 28th St
100-1999 ... 76164
2400-3599 ... 76106
NE 29th St
100-2499 ... 76106
3300-3499 ... 76111
NW 29th St ... 76106
NE & NW 30th ... 76106
NE & NW 31st ... 76106
NE & NW 32nd ... 76106
NE 33rd St
1400-2099 ... 76106
2500-2599 ... 76111
NW 33rd St ... 76106
NE & NW 34th ... 76106
NE 35th St
200-1699 ... 76106
2400-2599 ... 76111
NW 35th St ... 76106
NE 36th St
100-2399 ... 76106
2400-2599 ... 76111
NW 36th St ... 76106
NE & NW 37th ... 76106
NE & NW 38th ... 76106

FREEPORT TX

General Delivery ... 77541

POST OFFICE BOXES MAIN OFFICE STATIONS AND BRANCHES

Box No.s
All PO Boxes ... 77542

RURAL ROUTES

01 ... 77541

NAMED STREETS

All Street Addresses ... 77541

NUMBERED STREETS

All Street Addresses ... 77541

FRIENDSWOOD TX

General Delivery ... 77546

POST OFFICE BOXES MAIN OFFICE STATIONS AND BRANCHES

Box No.s
All PO Boxes ... 77549

NAMED STREETS

Abercreek Ave ... 77546
Abigail Ln ... 77546
Acorn Ct ... 77546
Affirmed Way ... 77546
Airline Dr ... 77546
Aladdin Ct ... 77546
Alder Cir ... 77546
Allan St ... 77546
Alysheba Ln ... 77546
Anchor Park ... 77546
Anderson Ranch Ln ... 77546
Anna Ln ... 77546
Annette Ln ... 77546
Antique Meadows Dr ... 77546
Apple Blossom Ln ... 77546
Applewood Dr ... 77546
Arbor Point Ln ... 77546
Arborlea Dr ... 77546
Arbre Ln ... 77546
Arezzo Cir ... 77546
Aspen Arbor Ct ... 77546
Autumn Bay Ct ... 77546
Autumn Cove Ct ... 77546
Autumn Creek Dr ... 77546
Autumn Crest Dr ... 77546
Autumn Harvest Dr ... 77546
Autumn Hills Ct ... 77546
Autumn Leaf Dr ... 77546
Autumn Park Ct ... 77546
Avondale Ln ... 77546
Azalea Trl ... 77546
Backenberry Ct & Dr ... 77546
Baker Rd ... 77546
Baker Springs Ct ... 77546
Balmoral Ct ... 77546
Bandera Creek Ln ... 77546
Barcelona Dr ... 77546
Barillos Creek Ln ... 77546
Barkentine Ln ... 77546
W Bay Area Blvd ... 77546
Bay Ledge Ct ... 77546
Bay Ridge Ct ... 77546
Bayboro Park Ct & Dr ... 77546
Baybrook Mall ... 77546
Bayou Oak Dr ... 77546
Beacon Bay Cir ... 77546
Beacons Vw ... 77546
Beamer Rd ... 77546
Beechwood Dr ... 77546
Bellmar Ln ... 77546
Belmont Dr ... 77546
Bending Creek Ln ... 77546
Bending Stream Dr ... 77546
Bentwood Ct & Ln ... 77546
Birch Ct ... 77546
Biscayne Shoals Dr ... 77546
Bisontine St ... 77546
Blackhawk Blvd ... 77546
Blue Heron Dr ... 77546
Blue Mesa Ridge Dr ... 77546
Blue Quail Dr ... 77546
Blueberry Ln ... 77546
Bob White Dr ... 77546
Bolivar Point Ln ... 77546
Bonnie Doon St ... 77546
Bougainvilla Ln ... 77546
Boundry Ct ... 77546
Boy Scout Dr ... 77546
Brandywyne Dr ... 77546
Breakers Point Dr ... 77546
Brendon Park Ln ... 77546
Briar Bend Dr ... 77546
Briar Creek Dr ... 77546
Briar Glen Ct ... 77546
Briarmeadow Ave ... 77546
Brideria Dr ... 77546
Bridle Path Ln ... 77546
Brigadoon Ln ... 77546
Brighton Park Ln ... 77546
Brill Dr ... 77546
British Woods Ln ... 77546
Broadmoor St ... 77546
Brookside Dr ... 77546
Brown St ... 77546
Bubbling Well Ct ... 77546
Buckingham Ct & Dr ... 77546
Bulen Ave ... 77546
Burr Oak Dr ... 77546
Butler Dr ... 77546
Buttonwood Dr ... 77546
Cactus Ridge Ct ... 77546
Cambridge Dr ... 77546
Cambridge View Dr ... 77546
Camellia Ct ... 77546
Camelot Ln ... 77546
Camp Fire Rd ... 77546
Camp Manison Rd ... 77546
Canal Dr ... 77546
Candlelight Ct ... 77546
Canyon Springs Ln ... 77546
Capistrano Falls Dr ... 77546
Cardinal Ridge Ct ... 77546
Carey Ln ... 77546
Carolina Ct ... 77546
Carrack Turn Dr ... 77546
Carriage Creek Ln ... 77546
Cascade Falls Dr ... 77546
E & W Castle Harbour Dr ... 77546
Castlelake Dr ... 77546
E & W Castlewood Ave ... 77546
Cavern Dr ... 77546
Cedar Gully Dr ... 77546
Cedar Oak St ... 77546
Cedar Ridge Ct & Trl ... 77546
Cedarwood Dr ... 77546
Centennial Ln ... 77546
Centerfield Dr ... 77546
N & S Century Cir, Ct & Dr ... 77546
Chappell Hill Dr ... 77546
Charleston St ... 77546
Charro St ... 77546
Chelsea Ln ... 77546
Cherry Tree Ln ... 77546
Chester Dr ... 77546
Chestnut Cir ... 77546
Chevy St ... 77546
Chiselstone Ct ... 77546
Christina Ln ... 77546
Chuck Dr ... 77546
N & S Clear Creek Dr ... 77546
Clearview Ave ... 77546
Clobourne Crossing Ln ... 77546
Cloud Croft Dr ... 77546
Clover Ridge Ave ... 77546
Clubhouse Dr ... 77546
Coachmaker Dr ... 77546
Cobblers Way ... 77546
Colonial Dr ... 77546
Colonial Ridge Dr ... 77546
Colony Bend Dr ... 77546
Condor Dr ... 77546
Constitution Ln ... 77546
Contender Ln ... 77546
Coopers Draw Ln ... 77546
Copper Canyon Dr ... 77546
Coronado St ... 77546
Corral Trl ... 77546
Cortona Ln ... 77546
Cottonwood Dr ... 77546
Country Club Dr ... 77546
Courtlandt Pl ... 77546
Coventry Ct ... 77546
Cowards Creek Ct & Dr ... 77546
Cozy Hollow Ct ... 77546
Crawford Dr ... 77546
Creek Bend Dr ... 77546
Creek Line Dr ... 77546
Creekside Dr ... 77546
Creekview Ct ... 77546
Creekwood Ln ... 77546
Crofter Glen Dr ... 77546
Cross Tide Ln ... 77546
Darden Springs Ln ... 77546
David St ... 77546
David Glen Dr ... 77546
Dawn Ave ... 77546
Dawn Hill Dr ... 77546
Daytona Ct ... 77546
Deepwood Dr ... 77546
Del Monte Dr ... 77546
Deseret Dr ... 77546
Desert Aire Dr ... 77546
Desota St ... 77546
Destin Ln ... 77546
Diamond Ln ... 77546
Dirt Rd ... 77546
Dock Bar Ct ... 77546
Dogwood Cir ... 77546
Dolan Springs Ln ... 77546
Dominion Ct ... 77546
Dorado Dr ... 77546
Doral Ct ... 77546
Dove Ct ... 77546
Dover Ln ... 77546
Duchess Park Ct & Ln ... 77546
Duke Ln ... 77546
Dunbar Estates Dr ... 77546
Durango Bend Ln ... 77546
Eagle Creek Dr ... 77546
Eagle Falls Dr ... 77546
Eagle Lakes Dr ... 77546
Eagles Cv ... 77546
Earlham Dr ... 77546
Easthaven Ct ... 77546
Echo Ave & Hbr ... 77546
Edenvale Ct & St ... 77546
Edgewater Dr ... 77546
E & W Edgewood Dr ... 77546
Edinburgh Dr ... 77546
W El Dorado Blvd & Dr ... 77546
Ella Ct ... 77546
Elmwood Cir ... 77546
Ember Hills Ln ... 77546
Emerald Cir ... 77546
Encino Dr ... 77546
Essex Dr ... 77546
Estate Dr ... 77546
Everett Dr ... 77546
Evergreen Dr ... 77546
Excalibur Ct ... 77546
Fairdale St ... 77546
Fairway Dr ... 77546
Falcon Lake Cir & Dr ... 77546
Falcon Ridge Blvd ... 77546
Falling Leaf Ct & Dr ... 77546
Fallow Ln ... 77546
Farriers Bend Dr ... 77546
Farris Valley Ln ... 77546
Fence Post Rd ... 77546
Ferndale Ct ... 77546
Fernwood Dr ... 77546
Fieldcreek Dr ... 77546
Fincher Dr ... 77546
Firenze Dr ... 77546
Five Knolls Dr ... 77546
Flamingo Ct ... 77546
Flat Rock St ... 77546
Fm 2351 Rd ... 77546
E Fm 528 Rd ... 77546
Forest Bend Ave & Ln ... 77546
Forest Pines Ct ... 77546
Forest View St ... 77546
Forge Stone Dr ... 77546
Friends Knoll Ln ... 77546
N & S Friendswood Dr ... 77546
Friendswood Lakes Blvd ... 77546
Friendswood Link Rd ... 77546
Frigate Dr ... 77546
Frontier Ln ... 77546
Frost Creek Ln ... 77546
Garden Dr ... 77546
Garden Lakes Dr ... 77546
Garnetfield Ln ... 77546
General Colony Dr ... 77546
Genessee Creek Ln ... 77546
Geneva Dr ... 77546
Girl Scout Ln ... 77546
Gleneagles Dr ... 77546
Glenlea Ct & Dr ... 77546
Glenshannon Ave ... 77546
Glenwest Dr ... 77546
Glenwood Dr ... 77546
Golden Leaf Dr ... 77546
Grand Hills Ln ... 77546
Grand Ranch Ln ... 77546
Greenbriar Ave ... 77546
Grey Mist Ct & Dr ... 77546
Gulf Fwy ... 77546
Hackberry Ln ... 77546
Hackberry Branch Ln ... 77546
Halls Creek Ct ... 77546
Hamilton Pool Ln ... 77546
Hampton Ct ... 77546
Hancock Springs Ln ... 77546
Harbor Pass Ln ... 77546
Harvest Cv ... 77546
Harvest Hill Ct & Dr ... 77546
Hatcher Ln ... 77546
Hatteras Point Dr ... 77546
Haverford Ln ... 77546
Hawke Bay Ln ... 77546
Hawkhill Dr ... 77546
Haye Rd ... 77546
Heather Ln ... 77546
E & W Heritage Dr ... 77546
Heritage Colony Dr ... 77546
Heritage Country Ct & Ln ... 77546
Heritage Falls Dr ... 77546
Heritage Plains Dr ... 77546
Hewing Dr ... 77546
Hibiscus Ln ... 77546
Hickory Ter ... 77546
Hickory View Ct ... 77546
Hidden Creek Ln ... 77546
Hidden Oak Ln ... 77546
Hidden Pine Ln ... 77546
Hidden Treasure Cir ... 77546
Hidden Woods Ln ... 77546
Hideaway Dr ... 77546
High Ridge Cir & Dr ... 77546
Hollier Rd ... 77546
Holly Springs Dr ... 77546
Hope Village Rd ... 77546
Hunt Dr ... 77546
Hunters Bnd, Cv, Frst, Ln & Trl ... 77546
Huntington Ln ... 77546
Idlewood Ct & Dr ... 77546
Imperial Dr ... 77546
Independence Dr ... 77546
Indian Summer Ct & Trl ... 77546
Indigo Pass Ct ... 77546
Inverness St ... 77546
Inwood Dr ... 77546
Ivy Stone Ln ... 77546
Janet Ln ... 77546
John Ave ... 77546
Jordan Bend Ln ... 77546
Judy Ave ... 77546
Juliabora Ct ... 77546
Kent Way ... 77546
Keowee Ct ... 77546
Keystone Dr ... 77546
Killarney Ave ... 77546
King George Ln ... 77546
Kings Chapel Ct & Rd ... 77546
Kingsbury Ln ... 77546
Kingsmill Rd ... 77546
Kingston Dr ... 77546
Knights Ct ... 77546
Knoll Bridge Ln ... 77546
La Salle St ... 77546
Lake Cir & Dr ... 77546
Lake Forest Dr ... 77546
Lake Mist Ln ... 77546
Lakeside Ln ... 77546
Lakeview Cir ... 77546
Lakeway Dr ... 77546
Lamar Canyon Ln ... 77546
Lancaster Dr ... 77546
Laura Leigh Dr ... 77546
Laurel Dr ... 77546
Laurelfield Dr ... 77546
Lavaca St ... 77546
Layfair Pl ... 77546
Leading Edge Dr ... 77546
Ledgebrook Ln ... 77546
Leigh Canyon Dr ... 77546
Leisure Ln ... 77546
Leslie Ln ... 77546
Leslies Ct ... 77546
Lexington St ... 77546
Liberty Cir ... 77546
Lighthouse View Dr ... 77546
Linda Ln ... 77546
Linkwood St ... 77546
Linson Ln ... 77546
Lisa Ct ... 77546
Live Oak Ln ... 77546
Livorno Ln ... 77546
Lochmoor Ln ... 77546
Londonderry Ave ... 77546
Longleaf Ct ... 77546
Los Frailes Dr ... 77546
Lost River Dr ... 77546
Lottie Ln ... 77546
Love Ct & Ln ... 77546
Lucian Ln ... 77546
Lundy Ln ... 77546
Lunsford Hollow Ln ... 77546
Lynn Cir ... 77546
Mae St ... 77546
E Magnolia St ... 77546
Mahrian Ct ... 77546
Majestic Ln ... 77546
Man O War Ln ... 77546
Mandale Rd ... 77546
Manison Pkwy ... 77546
W Maple Dr ... 77546
Maple Cliff Ln ... 77546
Maple Hill Dr ... 77546
Maplewood Dr ... 77546
Martina Dr ... 77546
Martinez Ct ... 77546
Mary Ann Dr ... 77546
Marys Ct ... 77546
Marys Creek Ln ... 77546
Matagorda Ln ... 77546
Match Point Ln ... 77546
Maxi Cir ... 77546
Mckissick Dr ... 77546
Meadow Ct ... 77546
Meadow Bend Dr ... 77546
Meadow Glen Rd ... 77546
Meadow Lark Ave ... 77546
Meadow Run Dr ... 77546
Meadow Trail Ct & Ln ... 77546
Meadow View Ct ... 77546
Meadow Wood Ln ... 77546
Meadowthorn Ct ... 77546
Melody Ln ... 77546
Melodywood Ct & Dr ... 77546
Merribrook Ln ... 77546
Merriewood Dr ... 77546
Merriman Ct ... 77546
Mesquite Falls Ln ... 77546
Miami Ct ... 77546
Middlecreek St ... 77546
Midnight Star Cir ... 77546
Mighty Buccaneer Dr ... 77546
Mills Ln ... 77546
Minglewood Ln ... 77546
Mirage Ct ... 77546
N & S Mission Cir ... 77546
Misty Ln ... 77546
Misty Falls Ln ... 77546
Misty View Ln ... 77546
Mockingbird Ln ... 77546
Monte Bello Dr ... 77546
Moore Rd ... 77546
Morning Dove Ln ... 77546
Morningside Ct ... 77546
Morningside Dr
200-399 ... 77546
310-310 ... 77549
400-498 ... 77546
401-499 ... 77546
Moss Point Dr ... 77546
Mossy Oak Ct ... 77546
Mossy Stone Dr ... 77546
Mountain Falls Ct ... 77546
Mountain Timber Ct & Dr ... 77546
Murphy Ln ... 77546
Mustang Dr ... 77546
Myra St ... 77546
Myrtlewood Dr ... 77546
Mystic Meadows Ln ... 77546
Narnia Way ... 77546
Nilelake Ct ... 77546
Nina Dr ... 77546
Northcliff Ridge Ln ... 77546
Northfield Dr ... 77546
Northstone Ln ... 77546
Northview Dr ... 77546
Norwood Glen Ln ... 77546
Nottingham Way ... 77546
Oak Dr ... 77546
Oak Hollow Dr ... 77546
Oak Park Ct & Ln ... 77546
Oak Vista Ct & Dr ... 77546
Oakland Dr ... 77546
Oaktree St ... 77546
Old Rd ... 77546
Old Course Dr ... 77546
Onion Gulch Cir ... 77546
Opal Springs Ln ... 77546
Orlando St ... 77546
Osborne Dr ... 77546
Osprey Ct ... 77546
Overlook Dr ... 77546
Oxnard Ln ... 77546
Paint Rock Rd ... 77546
Palm Aire Dr ... 77546
Palmer Dr ... 77546
Palo Duro St ... 77546
Pampas Trail Dr ... 77546
Park Ln ... 77546
Park Bend Dr ... 77546
Parkview Dr ... 77546
E & W Parkwood Ave ... 77546
Parkwood Village Dr ... 77546
Payson Pl ... 77546
Pebble Ln ... 77546
Pebble Lodge Ln ... 77546
Pecan Dr ... 77546
Pecan Valley Ct ... 77546
Penn Cir & Dr ... 77546
Penny Ln ... 77546
Pennystone Ct & Way ... 77546
Pennywayne St ... 77546
Pensacola Ln ... 77546
Peregrine Dr ... 77546
Peridot Ln ... 77546
Pilgrim Ln ... 77546
Pilgrim Hall Dr ... 77546
Pilgrim Harbor Dr ... 77546
Pilgrims Bend Dr ... 77546
Pilgrims Hall Dr ... 77546
Pilgrims Point Dr ... 77546
Pin Oak Dr ... 77546
Pine Dr ... 77546
Pine Bluff Dr ... 77546
Pine Breeze Dr ... 77546
Pine Cone Ln ... 77546
Pine Creek Dr ... 77546
Pine Hollow Dr ... 77546
Pine Hurst Ct ... 77546
Pine Needle Dr ... 77546
Pine Ridge Ct ... 77546
Pine Willow Ct ... 77546
Pinecrest Ct ... 77546
Piney Ridge Dr ... 77546
Piney Woods Dr ... 77546
Pirates Gold Cir ... 77546
Plantation Dr ... 77546
Planters Way ... 77546
Pleasant Plains Dr ... 77546
Point Clear Dr ... 77546
Point Isabel Ln ... 77546
Port Carissa Dr ... 77546
Portage Ln ... 77546
Post Oak Ct ... 77546
Prairie Wilde St ... 77546
Presidio St ... 77546

Prince George Dr 77546
Providence Dr 77546
Quaker Dr 77546
Quaker Bend Dr 77546
Queens Ln 77546
Queensburg Ln 77546
Quiet Canyon Ct & Dr 77546
Quillback Dr 77546
Rachael Ln 77546
W Ranch Dr 77546
Rancho Cir 77546
Ranchwood Ln 77546
Raven Falls Ln 77546
Raven Star Dr 77546
Ravine Cir & Dr 77546
Red Bud Ct 77546
Red Lantern Dr 77546
Red Maple Ct & Dr 77546
Red Oak Ln 77546
Red Wing Dr 77546
Regal Pine Way 77546
Regata Run Dr 77546
Regency Ct 77546
Remington Ct 77546
Rex Rd 77546
Richard Ln 77546
Richards Dr 77546
Richford Dr 77546
Richland Hollow Ln 77546
Richmond Ln 77546
Rigel St 77546
Ringwood Way Ln 77546
Riverrock Ct 77546
Riverside Ct 77546
Robin Ridge Cir 77546
Rockygate Ln 77546
Rolling Fog Dr 77546
Rolling Stone Dr 77546
Ron Cir 77546
Rosewood Ct 77546
Round Rock St 77546
Royal Ct & Pkwy 77546
Royal Oaks Dr 77546
Ruffian Ct & Dr 77546
Running Tide 77546
Rushwater Ln 77546
Rustic Ln 77546
Rymers Switch Cir & Ln 77546
Sable Dr 77546
Safe Harbour Cir 77546
Saffron Ln 77546
Sailors Moon Ct & Dr 77546
Saint Andrews Dr 77546
Saint Cloud Dr 77546
Saint Lawrence Cir, Ct, Cv & Dr 77546
Salisbury Ct 77546
Salmon Creek Ln 77546
Salton Point Dr 77546
San Augustine Ln 77546
San Joaquin Pkwy 77546
San Jose St 77546
San Miguel Dr 77546
Sand Sage Ln 77546
Sandringham Dr 77546
Sandy Lake Dr 77546
Sandy Reef Ct 77546
Sarasota Dr 77546
Saxon Hollow Ct 77546
Scarlet Oak Ct & Dr 77546
Scenic Vw 77546
Schooners Way 77546
Schulte Ln 77546
Sedora Dr 77546
Selder Dr 77546
Serenity Cove Cir 77546
Shadie Pine Ln 77546
E, N, S & W Shadowbend Ave 77546
Shadwell Way 77546
Shady Bend Ln 77546
Shady Nook Ln 77546
Shady Oaks Ln 77546
Shadywood Dr 77546
Sheet Bend Way 77546
Shiloh Park Ct 77546
Ship Anchor Dr 77546
Shooting Star St 77546
Sierra Madre St 77546
Signal Hill Dr 77546
Silouette Cv 77546
Silver Cliff Ln 77546
Silver Maple Ct 77546
Silver Spruce Ln 77546
Silverleaf Dr 77546
Silverstone Dr 77546
Skip Rock St 77546
Sky Harbor Ct 77546
Skyview Ter 77546
Somerset Ln 77546
Southfield Dr 77546
Sparrow Cir 77546
E & W Spreading Oaks Ave 77546
Square Rigger Ln 77546
St George St 77546
E & W Stadium Cir, Ct & Ln 77546
Staghorn Ln 77546
Stanley Ct 77546
Stapleton Dr 77546
Starboard View Cir & Dr 77546
Stardale Ln 77546
Steele Dr 77546
Steele Ranch Ct 77546
Stephen Ct 77546
Sterling Creek Dr 77546
Steven Luke Ln 77546
Stillhouse Hollow Ln 77546
Stillwater Dr 77546
Stone Creek Ct 77546
Stone Harbor Dr 77546
Stone Stile Dr 77546
Stonecreek Cir 77546
Stonehenge Ln 77546
Stoneledge Dr 77546
Stonemede Dr 77546
Stonesthrow Ave 77546
Stoney Lake Dr 77546
Stratmore Dr 77546
Streamside Dr 77546
Sugar Bars Dr 77546
Sugar Maple Ct 77546
Summer Cove Ct 77546
Sun Ct 77546
Sun Meadow Blvd 77546
Sun Park Dr 77546
Sunnyview Ave 77546
Sunset Dr 77546
Surrey Ln 77546
Surrey Woods Dr 77546
Sussex Way 77546
Sydney Ln 77546
Tall Pines Dr 77546
Tall Ships Dr 77546
Tall Timbers Ct, Ln & Way 77546
Talon Dr 77546
Tammony Park Ct & Ln 77546
Tampa St 77546
Tanglewood Dr 77546
Tashkent Dr 77546
Taylor Sky Ln 77546
Teal Manor Ct 77546
Ten Sleep Ln 77546
Tenison Way 77546
Terra Nova Ct 77546
Texoma Bend Ln 77546
Thomas Dr 77546
Thornwood Dr 77546
Thursa Ln 77546
Tibet Rd 77546
Timber Ln & Vw 77546
Timber Creek Ct & Dr 77546
Timber Grove Pl 77546
Timber Trail Ct 77546
Timberstone Ln 77546
Timpani Dr 77546
Tipperary Ave 77546
Torchwood Dr 77546
Tower Dr & Rdg 77546
Townes Rd 77546
Townes Forest Rd 77546
Trail Vw 77546
Trail Bend Ct & Ln 77546
Trail Head St 77546
Trail View Way 77546
Trevino Ct 77546
Tropicana Ct 77546
Tuscania Ln 77546
Twin Oaks St 77546
Twin Pines Dr 77546
Tyler Ct 77546
Valero St 77546
Vaquero St 77546
Verdun Ln 77546
Victoria Way 77546
Victory Terrace Ln 77546
E & W Viejo Dr 77546
Virginia Ln 77546
Volterra Cir 77546
Wagoner Branch Ct 77546
Wake Village Dr 77546
Walnut Cove Ct 77546
Wandering Trl 77546
Ware Dairy Rd 77546
Waterfall Dr 77546
Waters Edge Dr 77546
Waterwind Ct 77546
Watkins Way 77546
Webelos Ct & St 77546
Webster Ranch Rd 77546
Westfield Ln 77546
Westwood Dr 77546
Wheelwright Ln 77546
Whispering Pines Ave 77546
Whitaker 77546
White Pine Dr 77546
White Wing Cir 77546
Whitehall Ln 77546
Whitman Way Dr 77546
Whittier Dr 77546
Whittier Oaks Dr 77546
Widerop Ln 77546
Wilderness Trl 77546
Wilderness Pines Ct & Dr 77546
Wildwood Dr 77546
Williamsburg Cir 77546
E & W Willowick Ave 77546
Wimbledon Ln 77546
Winchester Ct 77546
Windcreek St 77546
Winding Rd 77546
Winding Way Dr 77546
Windsong Ln 77546
Windsor Dr 77546
Windwood St 77546
Winners Cir 77546
Woodcrest Dr 77546
Woodland Trail Dr 77546
Woodlawn Dr 77546
Woodstream Cir 77546
Woodview Dr 77546
Woodvine St 77546
Worden Ln 77546
Wynnview Dr 77546
Yorkshire Dr 77546
Zavalla Cir 77546

FRISCO TX

General Delivery 75034

POST OFFICE BOXES MAIN OFFICE STATIONS AND BRANCHES

Box No.s
1 - 5000 75034
5001 - 6200 75035
6000 - 9000 75034

NAMED STREETS

Abberley Ln 75033
Abbey Rd 75035
Abbott Dr 75035
Abercrombie Trl 75035
Aberdeen Pl 75034
Ablingdon Dr 75035
Academy Dr 75034
Acorn Ln 75034
Adams Ln 75034
Adare Manor Ln 75035
Addax Trl 75034
Adderberry Dr 75035
Adela Dr 75035
Adirondack Ln 75033
Adobe Trl 75033
Adolphus Dr 75035
Aerial Dr 75033
Agnes Creek Dr 75034
Alamo Ct 75033
Alamosa Dr 75033
Alberta Ct 75033
Albritton Dr 75034
Alcove Dr 75034
Alden Ln 75035
Alderon Ln 75034
Alderwood Dr 75035
Aldridge Dr 75035
Alexandria Dr 75035
Alfa Romeo Way 75033
Alis Ln 75035
All Stars Ave 75033
Allegheny Dr 75035
Allendale Dr 75034
Allorist Dr 75035
Alpha Ave 75034
Alpine Ct 75035
Alstone Dr 75035
Alta Vista Dr 75033
Altamont Dr 75033
Amalfi Dr 75033
Amber Valley Dr 75035
Amberdale Ln 75034
Ambergate Ln 75035
Amberly Pl 75034
Amberwood Ln 75034
Amberwoods Ln 75035
Ambrose Dr 75035
Amelina Ln 75035
Amesbury Dr 75034
Amherst Ln 75035
Amilfi Dr 75035
Anchor St 75035
Andover Dr 75035
Angel Falls Dr 75034
Angel Trace Dr 75034
Angelica Ln 75033
Angelo Dr 75035
Anita Ct 75035
Anne Dr 75035
Antelope Hills Dr 75034
Anthem Dr 75034
Apache Cir 75034
Apollo Ct 75033
Appalachian Ln 75033
Appaloosa Dr 75035
Appian Ln 75035
Apple Valley Dr 75033
Appleblossom Dr 75033
Apricot Ln 75035
April Sound Ln 75033
Arabian Way 75034
Arbor Cir 75034
Arboretum Dr 75034
Arborwood Ln 75033
Arbuckle Dr 75033
Arcadia Dr 75035
Arcadia Park Ln 75034
Arches Ln 75035
Aristocrat Ln 75033
Ark Rd 75035
Arlington Dr 75035
Arminta Ave 75034
Armistice Dr 75034
Armor Ln 75035
Armstrong Dr 75034
Arrowhead Dr 75034
Arrowwood Dr 75033
Arroyo Ln 75034
Ascot Dr 75033
Ash St 75034
Ashaway Ln 75035
Ashbury Ct 75033
Ashcroft Ln 75034
Ashdon Ln 75035
Asheboro St 75035
Ashland Belle Ln 75035
Ashley Ln 75035
Ashmont Dr 75035
Aspen Ln 75034
Aspermount Dr 75033
Astoria Dr 75035
Athenee Ln 75035
Athens Dr 75035
Atkins Ln 75035
Atlanta Dr 75035
Attleborough Dr 75035
Aubrey Ln 75033
Auburn Ln 75035
Augusta Dr 75034
Aurora Ln 75035
Autumn Ln 75034
Autumn Crest Dr 75035
Autumnwood Dr 75035
Avalon Dr 75035
Avanti Dr 75035
Avenue Of The Stars 75034
Avery Cir 75035
Avondale Dr 75033
Aylworth Dr 75035
Azalea Ln 75033
Azteca Ln 75033
Badger Creek Dr 75034
Badlands Dr 75035
Bainbridge Ln 75034
Baker Valley Rd 75034
Bakersfield Dr 75035
Bal Harbour Ln 75033
Balboa Ct 75034
Balch Springs Ct 75035
Balcones Dr 75033
Baldcypress Dr 75033
Balez Dr 75035
Balfour Ct 75034
Balint Ln 75035
Ball Dr 75034
Ballentrae Dr 75035
Ballymena Dr 75034
Balmoral Dr 75034
Balsam Ct & Dr 75033
Bamberg Ln 75035
Bancroft Ln 75035
Bandolier Ln 75033
Banner Dr 75034
Bannister Dr 75034
Bannock Rd 75034
Barbarosa Dr 75035
Bardwell Ln 75035
Bareback Ranch Rd 75034
Barkwood Ln 75033
Barlow Dr 75034
Barnhill Ln 75034
Baroque Way 75033
Barret Dr 75033
Barrymore Dr 75035
Bartlett Dr 75035
Barton Cir 75035
Basilwood Dr 75035
Bass Pond Dr 75034
Basswood Dr 75033
Bastille Way 75033
Baton Rouge Blvd 75035
Battle Creek Dr 75034
Bavarian Dr 75033
Bay St 75035
Bay Harbor Ln 75034
Bay Hill Dr 75034
Bay Meadows Dr 75034
Bayberry Ln 75034
Bayfield Dr 75033
Bayton Dr 75035
Beach St 75034
Beachwood Dr 75033
Beacon Hill Dr 75034
Bear Run 75033
Bear Creek Ln 75033
Bear Lake Rd 75034
Beartooth Dr 75034
Beckington Dr 75035
Beckley Ln 75035
Beech St 75033
Beeville Dr 75035
Begonia Dr 75035
Belclaire Dr 75034
Belcrest Dr 75034
Belfort Dr 75035
Belgrade Dr 75035
Bell Rock Rd 75035
Bellaire Ct 75034
Belle Chasse Ln 75035
Belle Isle Ln 75033
Bellevue Pl 75034
Bellingham Dr 75035
Bellingrath Dr 75035
Bells St 75035
Benalla Dr 75034
Benchmark Ln 75034
Bendbrook Dr 75035
Bent Creek Trl 75033
Bent Hook Dr 75034
Bent Tree Dr 75034
Bentgrass Dr 75033
Bentley Dr 75033
Benwick Dr 75035
Berkeley Hall Ln 75033
Berkley Ln 75034
Berkshire Dr 75035
Berkwood Pl 75034
Bermuda Way 75033
Bermuda Dunes Ct 75034
Berry Brook Ln 75034
Berry Ridge Ln 75033
Bethel Dr 75033
Beverly Dr 75034
Big Horn Trl 75035
Big Springs Dr 75035
Big Tree Ln 75034
Billy Dale Ct 75034
Biloxi Dr 75035
Biltmoore Dr 75034
Binkley Dr 75035
Birch Valley Ct 75034
Birchridge Dr 75033
Birkdale Ln 75035
Birmingham Dr 75035
Birmingham Forest Dr 75034
Biscayne St 75035
Bishop Dr & Hl 75035
Bison Trl 75033
Black Rock Cv 75034
Blackberry Ln 75034
Blackhawk Dr 75033
Blackstone Dr 75035
Blackthorn Trl 75033
Blackwolf Run Trl 75035
Blakehill Dr 75035
Blanchard Dr 75035
Blarney Stone Ct 75034
Blazing Star Rd 75034
Blitz Dr 75035
Bloomfield Ln 75033
Bloomsbury Pl 75033
Blossom Ln 75034
Blue Bay Dr 75035
Blue Grass Trl 75035
Blue Lake Dr 75033
Blue Oak Dr 75033
Blue Ridge Dr 75033
Bluewater Dr 75034
Bluff Top Rd 75035
Bluffview Dr 75034
Boardwalk Dr 75034
Boaz Dr 75035
Bobwhite Dr 75034
Bodega Trl 75035
Bois D Arc Ln 75035
Bolliger Ct 75035
Bonanza Creek Rd 75034
Bonham Ct 75035
Bonneville Rd 75034
Booker Trl 75035
Boone Cir 75033
Bordeaux Ave 75035
Boston Dr 75035
Botanical Ln 75035
Boulder Way 75034
Bouquet Dr 75035
Bow Ct 75035
Bowie Ln 75033
Bowling Green Dr 75035
Box Elder Ln 75035
Boxwood Ln 75034
Boyd Rd 75034
Boyle Ln 75034
Boyton Canyon Rd 75035
Bradford Grove Dr 75035
Bradley Ct 75035
Braemar Dr 75034
Bramblebush Dr 75035
Branch Trl 75035
Brandenberg Dr 75035
Brandywine Ln 75034
Brazos Dr 75033
Breakwater Dr 75034
Breckenridge Ct 75034
Breezewood Dr 75033
Breezy Point Ln 75034
Brentwood Dr 75034
Breton Dr 75035
Brett Dr 75035
Brianna Dr 75033
Briar Ct 75034
Briar Brook Ln 75033
Briar Hollow Ln 75033
Briar Tree Ln 75034
Briardale Dr 75035
Briarwood Ln 75034
Bridge St 75035
Bridge Water Cir 75034
Bridle Blvd 75033
Brighton Ln 75033
Brightside Ln 75033
Brijetta Dr 75034
Brin Dr 75035
Bristol Pl 75035
Brittany Ct 75034
Broadgreen Rd 75035
Broadhurst Dr 75033
Broadmoor Way 75033
Broken Bend Ln 75034
Brook Ridge Dr 75035
Brookhill Ln 75034
Brookhollow Blvd 75034
Brooks Ln 75034
Brookview Dr 75034
Brookwood Dr 75034
Brown Stone Ln 75033
Brownwood Dr 75035
Bruce Dr 75034
Bruschetta Dr 75034
Brushy Creek Dr 75035
Bryant Dr 75033
Bryce Canyon Dr 75035
Bryson Dr 75035
Buccaneer Pt 75034
Buchanan Ave 75033
Buckhorn Dr 75033
Buckingham Ln 75035
Buena Park Dr 75033
Buena Vista Dr 75034
Buffalo Creek Dr 75035
Bugatti Dr 75035
Bull Run Dr 75035
Bumelia Dr 75033
Bungala Ln 75034
Bunkhouse Rd 75034
Bunnels Fork Rd 75034
Bunny Run Ln 75034
Burbank 75034
Burgess Ln 75035
Burgundy Dr 75035
Burkett Dr 75034
Burleigh St 75035

Burnham St 75034
Burning Oak Dr 75034
Burnswick Isles Way 75034
Burnt Mill Ln 75035
Burr Oak Dr 75033
Bushwoods Dr 75034
Butterfly Trl 75035
Byron Dr 75035
Byron Nelson Ct 75034
Cactus Trl 75033
Caddo Ct 75033
Cain River Dr 75035
Cajun Dr 75035
Caladium Ln 75035
Calico Ct 75035
California Dr 75033
Calihan Ct 75035
Calimar Dr 75035
Calla Lilly Ln 75034
Calloway Ln 75034
Calm Meadow Dr 75035
Calvery Ct 75035
Cambridge Dr 75035
Camden Ln 75035
Camden Bluff Rd 75034
Camellia Ln 75033
Camelot Dr 75035
Cameron Rd 75033
Camfield Ave, Rd &
Way 75033
Camino Real 75035
Campbell Ct 75034
Campfire Ln 75033
Candle Island Dr 75034
Candlewood Dr 75033
Cane Hill Dr 75034
Canoe Rd 75035
Canondale Dr 75033
Canterbury Dr 75035
Canvas Back Dr 75034
Canyon Dr 75033
Canyon Crest Ct 75034
Canyon Lake Dr 75034
Canyon Oaks Dr 75033
Canyon Ranch Rd 75034
Cape Buffalo Trl 75034
Cape Cod Dr 75034
Cape Cod Springs Dr 75034
Cape Royal Ln 75033
Capitan Ln 75033
Capitol Ln 75034
Captains Cv 75034
Cardiff Ln 75035
Cardinal Creek Dr 75033
Carlisle Ct 75034
Carly Ln 75035
Carmack Dr 75033
Carmel Valley Dr 75035
Carnegie Dr 75034
Caroline Dr 75034
Carraway Dr 75034
Carrera Dr 75033
Carriage Hill Ln 75035
Carrington Greens Dr 75034
Carroll Cir 75034
Carson Ln 75033
Caruth Ln 75034
Casa Grande Trl 75034
Casabella Dr 75035
Cascade Creek Trl 75035
Cascata Dr 75034
Casetta Dr 75035
Castello Ct 75035
Castle Dr 75035
Castle Bank Ln 75033
Castle Brook Ln 75035
Castle Pines Dr 75034
Castlegate Dr 75035
Castlerock Trl 75033
Cathedral Lake Dr 75034
Cattail Ct 75034
Cattail Pond Dr 75034
Cava Rd 75035
Caveson Dr 75034
Cecile Dr 75035
Cecina Dr 75034
Cedar Ln 75033
Cedar Bluff Ln 75033
Cedar Cove Dr 75035
Cedar Creek Trl 75034
Cedar Ranch Rd 75034
Cedar Springs Dr 75035
Cedar Wood Dr 75033
Celebration Dr 75034
Centennial Mill Ln 75034
Chablis Ln 75035
Challaway Ln 75033
Chamber Hall Dr 75033
Chamberlyne Dr 75034
Chamomile Ln 75035
Champions Ct 75034
Chanay Dr 75035
Chandler Dr 75034
Chantilly Ln 75034
Chantrye Ln 75035
Chaparral Dr 75035
Chapel Trl 75035
Charanna Cir 75033
Chardonnay Dr 75035
Charleston Dr 75035
Charlotte Ln 75035
Charter Dr 75034
Chase Oaks Ct 75034
Chasemoor Pl 75035
Chateau Dr 75035
Chatham Dr 75035
Chattanooga Dr 75035
Chaucer Dr 75035
Chaves Ct 75033
Cheetah Trl 75034
Chelsea Dr 75033
Chenault Dr 75033
Cherry St 75033
Cherry Brook Ln 75033
Cherry Hills Dr 75034
Cherry Ridge Dr 75033
Cherry Springs Ct 75034
Cheryl Dr 75033
Chesapeake Dr 75034
Chester Dr 75035
Chestnut Dr 75034
Chevy Chase Ln 75033
Cheyenne Way 75033
Chico Basin Rd 75034
Childress Trl 75034
Chilmark Ct 75035
Chimney Peak Ln 75034
Chimney Rock Trl 75035
Chinaberry Ln 75033
Chinquapin Dr 75033
Chippewa Trl 75034
Chisholm Trl
1801-1897 75033
1899-2099 75033
9500-9599 75034
Chittamwood Ln 75035
Chivalry Ct 75033
Choctaw Pl 75034
Christie Dr 75033
Christopher Ln 75035
Church St 75034
Churchill Dr 75035
Cinch Dr 75035
Cinnabar Dr 75035
Cipriani Dr 75034
Citrus Ln 75035
Claiborne Ln 75033
Clairmont Ct 75035
Clancy Dr 75035
Claridge Ln 75035
Clarkson St 75034
Classic Ln 75033
Clayton Ct 75035
Clear Lake Dr 75035
Clear Pond Dr 75034
Clearcreek Cir 75034
Clearfield Ln 75033
Clearfork Trl 75034
Clearstream Ln 75033
Clearwater Dr 75034
Cleburne Dr 75035
Cliff Trl 75034
Clifton Dr 75035
Clipper Cir 75034
Clipper St 75035
Clover Knoll Dr 75035
Club Oak Ct 75034
Club Terrace Ln 75034
Clusterberry Dr 75035
Clydesdale Ct 75034
Coach House Ln 75035
Cobalt Dr 75034
Cobb Hill Dr 75033
Cobbie Creek Dr 75034
Cobblestone Dr 75035
Cody Ln 75033
Coit Rd 75035
Colborne Dr 75033
Colby Dr 75035
Coldstone Dr 75035
Coldwater Ln 75033
Coleman Blvd 75034
Coleto Creek Dr 75033
College Pkwy 75035
Colleton Ln 75033
Collinwick Dr 75035
Colonial Ct 75034
Colonnade Grove Dr 75033
Colorado Dr 75035
Colt Ct 75033
Columbia Dr 75035
Columbus Dr 75034
Commonwealth Dr
8900-8999 75034
9000-9298 75033
Compass Dr 75035
Compton Ct 75033
Concho Dr 75033
Concord Dr 75035
Coney Island Dr 75034
Connely Dr 75035
Connemara Dr 75034
Constitution Dr 75034
Continental Dr 75034
Coolwater Cv 75034
Copper Lake Trl 75035
Copper Point Ln 75034
Copperfield Ct 75034
Copperwood Dr 75035
Coral Dr 75034
Coral Ridge Ct 75034
Coralberry Dr 75035
Cordellera Ln 75035
Cordova Dr 75034
Cori Ln 75033
Corinthian Bay Dr 75034
Corkwood Dr 75033
Cornell Way 75034
Coronado Trl 75033
Corsicana Dr 75035
Cortez Ct 75033
Cortona Ln 75034
Cotley Dr 75034
Cotswold Dr 75035
Cottage Grove Dr 75033
Cotton Gin Rd 75033
Cotton Patch Ln 75035
Cottonwood St 75033
Coulter Lake Rd 75034
Country Club Dr 75034
Country Forest Ln 75034
Country Glen Trl 75034
Country View Ln 75034
Country Walk Ct 75034
Countrybrook Dr 75035
Countryside Dr 75034
N County Rd 75033
S County Rd 75034
County Down Ln 75033
County Road 112 75035
County Road 22 75035
County Road 23 75035
County Road 24 75033
County Road 26 75033
County Road 710 75033
County Road 72 75035
Courtland Dr 75034
Courtney Dr 75033
Cove Creek Ln 75034
Cove Meadow Ln 75033
Coventry Ln 75035
Covey Ln 75035
Covey Point Ln 75035
Covington Ln 75035
Cowper Dr 75035
Crab Apple Ln 75035
Crab Creek Dr 75034
Crampton Ln 75035
Crazy Horse Dr 75034
Cree Dr 75034
W Creek Dr 75033
Creek Point Dr 75035
Creekmere Dr 75035
Creekridge Dr 75034
Creekside Cir 75034
Creekview Dr 75034
Creekwood Dr 75035
Crenshaw Ln 75033
E & W Crescent Way 75034
Cresson Dr 75035
Crest Pointe Pl 75034
Crestridge Dr 75033
Crestview Dr 75033
Crianza Rd 75035
Crimson Oaks Dr 75035
Cripple Crk 75034
Crockett Dr 75033
Cromwell Ct 75033
Crooked Creek Dr 75034
Crooked Stick Dr 75035
Cross Bend Cir 75033
Crossbow Dr 75033
Crosshaven Ln 75033
Crossvine Ln 75033
Crowbridge Dr 75033
Crown Colony Dr 75033
Crown Cove Ln 75035
Crown Meadow Dr 75035
Crown Point Dr 75033
Crown Ridge Dr 75034
Crystal Ln 75034
Crystal Beach Ln 75035
Crystal Creek Dr 75034
Crystal Falls Dr 75034
Crystal Lake Dr 75034
Cumberland Ln 75033
Custer Rd & Trl 75035
Cypress Pt 75034
Cypress Point Ct 75034
Dabney Ct 75034
Daffodil Way 75033
Daimler Dr 75033
Daisy Ln 75035
Dallas Pkwy
1601-3497 75034
3499-6500 75034
6502-8198 75034
9200-9298 75033
9300-11699 75033
11701-12099 75033
Dalworth Dr 75035
Dampton Dr 75033
Danbridge Ln 75035
Danbury Dr 75035
Dancliff Dr 75035
Daneway Dr 75035
Daniel Way 75035
Danville 75033
Darkwood Dr 75035
Darnell Cir 75034
Dartmouth Dr 75035
Dashwood Dr 75035
David Dr 75034
Davis Dr 75034
Dawson Ct 75034
Daylily Way 75033
Deacon Dr 75034
Dearborn Ln 75035
Decatur Ct 75035
Declaration Dr 75035
Deep Canyon Trl 75033
Deep River Dr 75035
Deer Lake Dr 75034
Deerbrook Dr 75035
Deercreek Trl 75035
Deerfield Dr 75033
Deerwood Ln 75034
Del Largo Way 75033
Del Rio Dr 75035
Delaga Dr 75035
Delford Dr 75033
Deloach Ct 75034
Democracy Ln 75035
Denmere Ln 75035
Desert Fls 75034
Detweiller Dr 75033
Devenish Dr 75035
Dewberry Dr 75035
Dewees Ln 75034
Dexter Ln 75034
Diablo Grande Dr 75034
Diamond Spur 75034
Diamond Oaks Ct 75035
Dianna Dr 75033
Dickens Ln 75033
Dietz Dr 75033
Dillon Dr 75033
Discovery Bay Dr 75034
Divine Ct 75033
Dixon Ct 75033
Dock St 75035
Doctor Pink Rd 75033
Dodgeton Dr 75033
Doe Creek Trl 75034
Dogwood St 75033
Dominion Cir 75033
Donegal Dr 75034
Donley Dr 75034
Doonan Xing 75035
Doonbeg Dr 75035
Doral Ct 75034
Dorchester Ln 75033
Dotter Dr 75035
Dottier Dr 75035
Double Creek Rd 75035
Double Falls Dr 75034
Douglas Ave 75034
Dove Cv 75034
Dover Ct 75034
Dowelling Ct & Dr 75034
Downbrook Dr 75035
Dragonback Pass 75034
Dragonfly Dr 75035
Drawbridge Dr 75035
Dreammaker Way 75035
Drew Dr 75035
Drexel St 75035
Driftwood Dr 75034
Dripping Springs Dr 75034
Dromoland Dr 75035
Druid Hills Dr 75035
Drummond Dr 75035
Dry Canyon Dr 75034
Dry Creek Ln 75035
Dublin Ln 75035
Ducks Lndg 75033
Ducote Dr 75035
Duesenberg Dr 75033
Dumas Dr 75034
Dunafan Ct 75034
Dunhill Ln 75034
Dunsford Dr 75033
Durango Dr 75035
Durham Dr 75035
Dustin Trl 75034
Dutch Hollow Dr 75033
Duval Dr 75034
Duxbury Dr 75035
Eagle Point Ln 75035
Eaglebend Ln 75035
Early Wood Dr 75035
Eastpark Ln 75033
Eastwick Ct 75035
Echo Bend Ct 75034
Edelweiss Trl 75034
Eden Ln 75033
Eden Valley Dr 75034
Edgewater Dr 75034
Edgewood Cv 75033
Edinburgh Ln 75035
Edna Ln 75035
El Camino Dr 75034
El Cinco Dr 75033
El Dorado Pkwy 75035
El Paso Ln 75033
Eldorado Pkwy
2800-6600 75033
6602-8098 75033
12200-15998 75035
16101-16199 75035
Eleanor Ave 75035
Elite Dr 75033
Elizabeth Ave 75035
Elk Mound Dr 75033
Elm Ct 75033
Elm Ln 75034
Elm St 75034
Elm Spring Ln 75034
Elmhurst Ln 75034
Emerald Gate Dr 75035
Emerald Glen Ln 75033
Emerald Pond Dr 75034
Emerald View Dr 75034
Emilie Ln 75035
Enchanted Meadow Dr 75033
Enclave Dr 75034
Enfield Dr 75034
Englewood Ct 75034
Enmore Ln 75035
Erudia Rd 75033
Estacado Dr 75033
Estancia Dr 75034
Esther Way 75034
Eubanks St 75034
Euclid Dr 75035
Evening Sun Dr 75034
Evergreen Dr 75035
Everson Dr 75035
Evita Dr 75034
Excaliber Rd 75035
Excelsior Pl 75035
Exeter Dr 75033
Explorer Dr 75034
Fair Ln 75034
Fair Oaks 75033
Fairfax Dr 75034
Fairfield Pl 75035
Fairlawn Dr 75035
Fairmont Dr 75035
Fairway Dr 75035
Faith Dr 75034
Falcon Head Ct 75034
Falcon Point Dr 75033
Faldo Ct 75034
Fall Harvest Dr 75033
Fall River Dr 75033
Fallbrook Dr 75033
Falling Leaf Dr 75035
Fallmeadow Dr 75033
Fargo Dr 75033
Farmcote Dr 75035
Fawn Mist Dr 75034
Fayette Trl 75034
Feathering Dr 75034
Ferndale Ln 75034
Fernwood Pl 75034
Ferry Farm Ln 75035
Festival Ln 75034
Fiddlers Green Rd 75034
Fields Rd 75033
Fieldstone Dr 75034
Finch St 75034
Fiore Ln 75034
Fire Creek Trl 75034
Fire Ridge Dr 75033
Fireberry Ct 75033
Firefly Ln 75033
Firenze Ln 75034
Firestone Dr 75034
Firewheel Ln 75034
First St 75033
Fisher Dr 75033
Five Bar Dr 75035
Flagstone St 75034
Flamingo Ct 75033
Flanagan Cir 75034
Flanders Dr 75033
Flat Crk 75034
Flatiron Trl 75035
Fleetwood Dr 75035
Flemington Dr 75034
Flickers St 75034
Flintrock Dr 75034
Florence Dr 75034
Flores Dr 75035
Flowering Dr 75035
Flynt Dr 75035
Fm 423
1801-1899 75033
Fm 423
3000-3098 75033
5000-5498 75034
5500-8899 75034
8901-9001 75034
9000-9398 75033
9400-11700 75033
11702-18098 75033
Fm 720 75033
Foard Dr 75034
Folsom Dr 75033
Fondren Ln 75035
Foothill Ln 75035
Forest Breeze Dr 75034
Forest Creek Dr 75035
Forest Haven Ln 75035
Forest Manor Dr 75034
Forest Oaks Ct 75034
Forest Park Ln 75033
Forestbrook Dr 75035
Forge Dr 75035
Forrest Dr 75035
Fossil Lake Dr 75034
Fossil Ridge Dr 75034
Founders Ln 75034
Fountain Glen Ln 75034
Fountainbleau Ln 75033
Fountainbridge Dr 75035
Four Willows Dr 75035
Fowler Dr 75035
Fox Crossing Ln 75034
Fox Glen Run 75034
Fox Meadow Ln 75035
Fox Ridge Trl 75034
Foxbriar Ln 75035
Foxcreek Dr 75033
Foxwood Ln 75035
Fragrant Dr 75035
Francis Ln 75035
Franklin Ct 75033
Fredrick Dr 75033
Freedom Ln 75033
Freemont Trl 75033
Freestone Dr 75033
Frio Way 75034
Frisco St 75033
Frisco Lakes Dr 75034
Frisco Square Blvd 75034
Frontier Dr 75033
Fullerton Cir 75033
Gables Ct 75035
Gadwall Dr 75034
Gaited Trl 75034
Galaxy Dr 75035
Gallant Run 75033
Galleon Rd 75035
Galley St 75035
Gamay Cir 75035
Garden Cir 75034
Gardendale Dr 75035
Garrison Dr 75033
Gary Burns Dr 75034
Gaspard Ct 75033
Gatesville Dr 75035
Gatewick Dr 75035
Gaylord Pkwy
3000-3098 75034
3100-8699 75034
8701-8999 75034
9100-9198 75035
Geese Valley Dr 75033
Gem River Rd 75034
Genesis Ct 75034

Street	ZIP
Genova Ct	75035
Gentle Wind Ln	75034
Gentry Dr	75035
Georgian Trl	75033
Geranium	75035
Germantown Ln	75035
Gerrard St	75034
Giddings Dr	75035
Gillon Dr	75035
Glademeadow Dr	75035
Gladewater Dr	75033
Gladstone Ct	75035
Glasshouse Walk	75035
Glen Abbey Ct	75034
Glen Heather Dr	75034
Glen Meadow Ct	75033
Glen Rose Dr	75035
Glendale	75033
Gleneagle Ln	75034
Glenhurst Ln	75033
Glenmoor Ct	75034
Glenoaks Dr	75034
Glistening Pond Dr	75034
Gloryview Rd	75033
Godfrey Dr	75035
Gold Camp Rd	75033
Golden Spur	75034
Golden Bell Ln	75035
Golden Fountain Dr	75033
Golden Sunset Ct	75034
Goldenrod Dr	75035
Golfside Dr	75035
Goliad Cir	75033
Gonzales Dr	75035
Goodnight Trl	75034
Goose Creek Rd	75034
Gordon St	75034
Graceland Ln	75033
Gracie Ln	75035
Grand Arbor Ln	75035
Grand Canal Dr	75033
Grand Valley Dr	75033
Grandview Dr	75035
Granite Falls Trl	75035
Granite Rapids Dr	75034
Grant Ct	75035
Grapevine Ln	75035
Grassland Dr	75035
Grayhawk Blvd	75033
Great Basin Dr	75035
Greenbrier Dr	75033
Greenfield Dr	75035
Greenhaven Dr	75035
Greens Ct	75034
Greensboro Dr	75035
Greenvalley Ln	75033
Greenway Dr	75034
Greenwood Dr	75034
Gregory Ln	75035
Greymoore Dr	75034
Greystone Ln	75034
Griffin Rd	75034
Grosseto Dr	75034
Grosvenor Pl	75035
Grove Crest Dr	75035
Guadalupe Ln	75034
Guerin Dr	75035
Guinn Gate Dr	75034
Gulf St	75035
Gulf Shores Dr	75034
Gunnison Trl	75033
Hacienda Heights Ln	75034
Hackberry Ct & Rd	75034
Hackberry Creek Park Rd	75034
Hadlow Dr	75035
Hague Dr	75033
Haley Way	75034
Half Elm St	75034
Half Hitch Trl	75035
Half Main St	75034
Haltered Horse Ln	75034
Hamilton Ln	75034
Hampshire Ct	75034
Hampton Ct	75035
Hancock Dr	75033
Hannah Cir	75033
Harbor Rd	75035
Harbor Hideaway	75034
Harbor Springs Dr	75034
Harbour Town Ct	75034
Harliquin Ct	75035
Harmony Ln	75035
Harrisburg Dr	75035
Hartbeest Trl	75034
Hartford Ln	75033
Harvard Ln	75034
Harvest Glen Dr	75034
Hathaway Ln	75033
Havasu Dr	75034
Havenbrook Ln	75034
Haverford Dr	75034
Haverhill Ln	75033
Haversham Dr	75035
Hawk Creek Dr	75033
Hawks Landing Dr	75033
Hawktree Rd	75033
Hawthorne St	75034
Hay Meadow Dr	75033
Haywood Ct	75035
Hazel Green Dr	75033
Hearthstone Dr	75034
Heather Brook Ln	75033
Heather Ridge Trl	75033
Heathrow Dr	75034
Helen Dr	75035
Hemlock Trl	75033
Henderson Dr	75035
Heritage Oaks Dr	75034
Hermitage Ln	75035
Herrington Dr	75033
Hickory St	
7000-8499	75034
8501-8699	75034
9600-9698	75035
9700-9799	75035
Hickory Grove Ln	75034
Hicks Blvd	75034
Hidalgo Ln	75034
Hidden Cove Ln	75034
Hidden Creek Ln	75034
Hidden Knoll Trl	75035
Hidden Pond Dr	75034
Hidden River Dr	75034
Hidden Run Dr	75035
Hidden Spring Dr	75034
Hideaway Ln	75034
High Meadow Rd	75033
High Shoals Dr	75034
Highland Ct	75033
Highland Hills Dr	75034
Highpoint Rdg	75035
Hill Creek Trl	75035
Hill Haven Ct	75035
Hillcrest Rd	75035
Hillsdale Ln	75033
Hillside Dr	75033
Hilton Head Ln	75034
History Cir	75034
Hogan Ct	75034
Hollister Dr	75033
Hollow Falls Ct	75034
Hollowbrook Ln	75034
Holly St	75034
Holly Leaf Dr	75035
Holly Tree Ln	75035
Home Rd	75033
Homestead Ln	75033
Honeybee Ln	75035
Honeyflower Dr	75035
Honeygrove Dr	75035
Honeysuckle Dr	75035
Honor Dr	75034
Horizon Pt	75034
Horse Creek Dr	75034
Horseshoe Trl	75033
Hot Springs Ln	75035
Huffman Ln	75035
Humberside Dr	75035
Hummingbird Dr	75034
Hunt Club Trl	75035
Hunter Run	75035
Hunters Pkwy	75035
Hunters Creek Trl	75034
Hunting Dog Ln	75034
Huntington Rd	75035
Hursey Dr	75035
Hyde Park Dr	75035
Idlewild Dr	75034
Ikea Dr	75034
Impala Trl	75034
Imperial Meadow Dr	75035
Imperial Valley Ln	75034
Independence Pkwy	75035
Indian Wls	75034
Indian Blanket Dr	75034
Indian Creek Ln	75033
Indianola Dr	75033
Indigo Sky Dr	75034
Inglenook Dr	75035
Inlet St	75035
Innisbrook Ct	75034
Internet Blvd	75034
Ireland Ln	75035
Irongate Pl	75034
Ironhorse Dr	75035
Ironwood Dr	75033
Iroquois Dr	75035
Ivanhoe Dr	75033
Ivygreen Rd	75034
Izabella Ct	75033
Jack Pine Ct	75035
Jackson Ln	75035
Jadi Ln	75033
Jaguar Dr	75033
Jamestown Rd	75035
Janet Dr	75033
Jasmine Ln	75035
Jasper Dr	75035
Jefferson Dr	75034
Jeffreys Bay	75035
Jennifer Ln	75034
Jereme Trl	75035
Jernigan Dr	75035
Jerral Dr	75034
Jessica Ln	75034
Jester Ct	75034
Jewel Ln	75035
Jewelweed Dr	75033
John Hickman Pkwy	75034
John Q Hammons Dr	75034
John W Elliott Dr	
8700-8998	75034
9100-10598	75033
10600-10899	75033
John Wesley Dr	75034
Johnson St	75033
Joplin Dr	75035
Jordan Way	75034
Joy Dr	75035
Jules Dr	75033
Juneau Dr	75033
Junegrass Ln	75035
Juniper Dr	75033
Kara Creek Rd	75034
Karens Ct	75034
Kasba Dr	75035
Kathryn Dr	75035
Katiliz Pl	75035
Katy Ct	75035
Keathley Dr	75035
Kelmscot Dr	75035
Kelsey Ct	75035
Kelvington Dr	75035
Kemps Ldg	75035
Kendalwood Dr	75035
Kenmare Trl	75035
Kennedale Dr	75033
Kennedy Dr	75034
Kennsington St	75034
Kent Dr	75034
Kentshire Ln	75035
Kentwood Dr	75034
Kerry Dr	75035
Kerstyn Dr	75035
Kerway Dr	75034
Kessler Dr	75033
Keswick Dr	75034
Kettle Creek Dr	75034
Keystone Dr	75033
Kickapoo Dr	75034
Kiest Forest Dr	75035
Kilgore Dr	75035
Kilkenny Pl	75034
Killdeer Dr	75035
Kiltartan Dr	75035
Kimber Ln	75034
Kimberly Ln	75033
Kimblewick Dr	75034
King Rd	75034
King Arthur Rd	75035
King George Ln	75033
King Louis Dr	75033
Kingfisher Ln	75033
Kings Ridge Rd	75035
Kings View Dr	75034
Kingsford Ln	75035
Kingsley Ln	75034
Kingston Ln	75034
Kingsville Dr	75035
Kiowa Dr	75034
Kirby Ln	75035
Kirkhaven Dr	75034
Kite Ln	75034
Kittyhawk Dr	75033
Knight Ln	75035
Knight Trl	75034
Knightsbridge Dr	75034
Knoll Trace Way	75035
Knoll Wood Ct	75034
Knots Ln	75034
Knoxville Ln	75035
Kristina Dr	75034
Kruger Ln	75034
Kyser Way	75033
La Cantera Trl	75033
La Costa Ct	75034
La Grange Dr	75035
La Jolla Dr	75034
La Mesa Dr	75033
La Vista Ln	75033
Labrador Run Dr	75033
Lafayette Dr	75035
Lago Vista Ln	75034
Lagonda Ln	75033
Laguna Dr	75033
Lajoyce Ct	75034
Lake Creek Ct	75035
Lake Mead Ct	75034
Lake Placid Dr	75034
Lake Tahoe Dr	75034
Lake Trails Dr	75034
Lake Travis Dr	75034
Lakebluff Way	75035
Lakehill Blvd	75034
Lakeland Dr	75035
Lakeshore Dr	75034
Lakota Trl	75033
Lamar Ln	75033
Lampton Cir	75035
Lampwick Ln	75035
Lancaster Gate	75035
Lance Dr	75035
Lancelot Rd	75035
Landmark Pl	75035
Langdon Dr	75033
Lanier Dr	75035
Lantana Ln	75033
Lante Cir	75033
Lantern Trl	75033
Laramie Ln	75033
Lariat Trl	75034
Larkin Dr	75035
Larkspur Ln	75034
Larkwood Cir	75035
Las Polamas Dr	75033
Lasso Dr	75033
Last Stand Cir	75035
Lathem Dr	75034
Latigo Dr	75035
Latimer Dr	75033
Laurel Ln	75035
Laurel Valley Ln	75034
Laurelhurst Ln	75033
Lauren Way	75035
Laverton Dr	75034
Lawler Park Dr	75035
Lawton Ct	75033
Lazio Ln	75035
Lazy Meadow Ln	75033
Lazy Rock Ln	75034
Leann Dr	75033
Leatherwood Dr	75033
W Lebanon	75034
Lebanon Rd	
2301-6497	75034
6499-8899	75034
9101-9197	75035
9199-12599	75035
Lebaron Ln	75034
Lebeau Ln	75035
Ledge Dr	75034
Ledgestone Ct	75034
Lee Meadow Dr	75035
Legacy Dr	
1101-1497	75034
1499-8400	75034
8402-9998	75034
9001-10297	75033
10299-11699	75033
11701-13199	75033
Legend Trl	75035
Legendary Dr	75034
Legrand Dr	75033
Leland Dr	75035
Lenox Ln	75033
Lesli Ln	75034
Lewis Canyon Dr	75034
Lexington Pl	75035
Liam Dr	75034
Liberty Ct	75035
Library St	75034
Lido Ct	75035
Lilac Ln	75034
Limbercost Ln	75035
Lime Ridge Dr	75033
Limerick Ln	75034
Limestone Dr	75033
Lincoln Dr	75035
Lincoln Hills Ct	75034
Lincolnshire Ln	75035
Linda Ln	75033
Lindenwood Dr	75034
Lineberry Ln	75035
Lionheart Dr	75034
Lionshead Ln	75034
Liptonshire Dr	75034
Lismore Dr	75034
Little Horn Cir	75035
Little River Rd	75033
Littlefield Dr	75035
Live Springs Rd	75034
Liverpool Ln	75034
Livingston Dr	75033
Livorno Ln	75033
Loch Haven Ct	75034
Lockshire Dr	75035
Locust Dr	75033
Lofland Dr	75033
Logan Ct	75035
Loma Alta Dr	75034
London Dr	75035
Lone Falcon Ln	75034
Lone Grove Ct	75034
Lone Rock Rd	75034
Lone Star Ranch Pkwy	75034
Long Branch Dr	75034
Long Hollow Cir	75033
Long Valley Ct	75034
Longaberger Dr	75034
Longhorn Trl	75034
Longmont Ct	75035
Longvue Dr	75034
Lookout Point Cir	75035
Lorraine Dr	75034
Lorwood Dr	75035
Los Rios Ct	75033
Lost Creek Dr	75033
Lotus Cir	75035
Loudoun Springs Dr	75034
Louis Ln	75035
Louisiana Ln	75035
Louisville Dr	75035
Lourdes Ln	75035
Lovers Ln	75035
Loving Trl	75034
Loving Trail Dr	75035
Loxley Dr	75035
Lu Ln	75034
Lucca Ln	75033
Lucerne Dr	75035
Luckenbach Dr	75035
Ludlow Dr	75034
Ludwick Ln	75035
Luxembourg Ln	75033
Lynchburg Dr	75035
Lyndhurst Dr	75035
Mackinac Dr	75033
Madison Dr	75035
Madrone Dr	75033
Magnolia Rd	75033
Maiden Ln	75035
Main St	
201-8999	75034
1100-8998	75033
10501-13499	75035
Majestic Dr	75034
Malibu St	75033
Mallard Ct & Trce	75034
Mallory Dr	75035
Maltby Dr	75035
Maltese Ln	75034
Mammoth Cave Ln	75035
Mannheim Dr	75033
Manor Ln	75034
Mansfield Dr	75035
Maple St	75033
Mapleshade Dr	75035
Mapleton Dr	75033
Marble Falls Dr	75034
Marigold Dr	75035
Marilyn Dr	75033
Marine Blue Dr	75035
Mariner Dr	75034
Marion Dr	75034
Mariposa Ln	75034
Markham Dr	75035
Maroon Bells Ln	75035
Marquette Dr	75033
Marrietta Dr	75035
Marsalis Ln	75034
Marshall Dr	75033
Martel Pl	75035
Maserati Dr	75033
Mason Dr	75034
Massa Ln	75034
Masters Ln	75035
Matagorda Ln	75034
Matthew Ln	75035
Maumee Valley Ct	75034
Max Ln	75035
Maxwell Rd	75034
May Hall Dr	75034
Mayflower Dr	75034
Mccord Way	75035
Mcgregor Dr	75033
Mckamy Dr	75034
Mckenzie Ct	75034
Mckinney Rd	75033
Meadow Ln	75033
Meadow Glade	75035
Meadow Hill Dr	75033
Meadow Landing Dr	75034
Meadow Spring Dr	75035
Meadowbrook Ave	75033
Meadowcrest St	75033
Megan Ct	75035
Melrose Ln	75035
Melton Ln	75033
Memorial Dr	75034
Memphis Dr	75035
Menominee Dr	75033
Mensano Dr	75034
Mercedes Ln	75035
Mercy Rd	75035
Meridian Dr	75035
Merlot Ct	75035
Merrimac Dr	75033
Mesa Verde Dr	75033
Michelle Dr	75035
Middlegate Rd	75034
Middleton Dr	75033
Midnight Moon Dr	75034
Midway Dr	75035
Migratory Ln	75033
Milano Ln	75034
Milestone Ridge Dr	75035
Mill Pond Dr	75034
Mill Run Dr	75035
Mill Town Dr	75033
Miller Pl	75033
Millie Ln	75035
Millstream Dr	75033
Millvale Ct	75035
Milsap Ln	75035
Mimosa Ln	75034
Mimosa Rd	75033
Mineral Point Dr	75033
Minnow Way	75035
Mira Vista Dr	75034
Mirage Ln	75033
Miramar Dr	75034
Miranda Way	75035
Mirror Fountain Cir	75033
Mission Hills Dr	75034
Misty Oaks Ln	75034
Misty Pond Dr	75034
Misty Shores Ln	75034
Mobile Bay Ct	75034
Modena Dr	75033
Mohawk Dr	75034
Mohegan Ln	75034
Monarch Dr	75033
Mondovi Dr	75033
Monstrell Rd	75035
Montague Ln	75034
Montana Dr	75033
Monterey Dr	75034
Montezuma Way	75035
Montfair Blvd	75033
Montgomery Dr	75035
Monticello Dr	75035
Montreaux Dr	75034
Montura Ln	75033
Montwood Dr	75034
Monument Ln	75034
Moody Ave	75035
Moonlight Ln	75034
Moore St	75034
Moraine Dr	75034
Mordor Ln	75034
Morgan Hill Ln	75034
Morley Dr	75035
Morning Glory Ln	75035
Morningside Dr	75035
Morris Ln	75034
Morro Bay Ln	75035
Mosaic Dr	75035
Moss Glen Dr	75034
Mosscreek Ln	75035
Mossvine Dr	75035
Mount Hawley Rd	75035
Mount Vernon Dr	75035
Mountain Creek Trl	75035
Mountain Laurel Ln	75035
Mountain Sky Rd	75034
Mountain View Ln	75035
Muirfield Ct	75034
Mulberry Ln	75033
Mulch Ln	75035
Munira Dr	75035
Munstead Trl	75033
Murray Ln	75035
Musketeer Dr	75035
Musselburgh Dr	75034
Mustang Trl	75035
Myatt Ave	75035
Myers Ave	75034
Myrtle Ln	75034
Myrtle Beach Ln	75033
Nancy Jane Ln	75035

Nandina Ln 75035
Nantucket Ct 75035
Napa Valley Dr 75035
Naples Ln 75035
Nash Ln 75035
Nashville Dr 75035
Natalie Dr 75035
Nation Dr 75034
Native Ln 75035
Natural Bridge Dr 75034
Nautical Dr 75034
Navajo Dr 75034
Navarro Way 75034
Neches Pine Dr 75034
Neptune Cir 75033
Network Blvd 75034
New Kent Rd 75035
New Orleans Dr 75035
Newberry Dr 75035
Newcastle Dr 75034
Newgate Dr 75035
Newman Blvd 75033
Newman Rd 75034
Newport Dr 75035
Nichols Trl 75034
Nicholson Dr 75034
Nicklaus Ct 75034
Nightfall Dr 75035
Nighthawk Dr 75033
Nightwind Ct 75034
Noble Oak Ln 75033
Nobleman Dr 75033
Noel Dr 75035
Nogales Ln 75033
Norcross Dr 75034
Norfolk Ln 75035
Normandy Dr 75034
North St 75033
Northshore Dr 75034
Norwich Ln 75033
Norwood Dr 75034
Nottingham Ln 75035
Nottoway Ct 75035
Nutmeg Cir 75034
Nyala Trl 75034
Oak St 75033
Oak Knoll Ln 75034
Oak Point Dr 75034
Oakcrest Dr 75034
Oakhurst Ln 75034
Oakland 75033
Oakland Hills Ln 75034
Oakleaf Dr 75035
Oakleigh Ln 75033
Oakmont Dr 75034
Oakwood Ln 75035
Ocean Rd 75035
Ocean Spray Dr 75034
Oceana Dr 75034
Oconnor Ln 75035
Odessa Dr 75035
Ohio Dr 75035
Old Hawkins Ln 75033
Old Newman Rd 75034
Old Oak Ct 75034
Old Orchard Rd 75033
Old Province Way 75034
Old Saybrook Ln 75033
Old Works Dr 75035
Oleander 75035
Oliver Ln 75035
Olivia St 75035
Olton Dr 75035
Oneida Dr 75034
Ontario Dr 75034
Orange Ct 75035
Orchard Hill Ln 75035
Orchard Park Dr 75034
Orchid Dr 75035
Ormond Ln 75035
Oryx Trl 75034
Osage Pl 75034
Osr 75034
Otis Dr 75034
Outpost Trl 75033
Overhill Dr 75033
Overland Park Ln 75035
Overlook Dr 75033
Overwood Dr 75034
Oxford Pl 75035
Oyster Bay Dr 75034
Pacific St 75035
Pacific Dunes Dr 75034
Pacific Way Dr 75034
Pack Saddle Way 75034
Packard Dr 75033
Paducah Dr 75035
Page Rd 75034
Pagewynne Dr 75035
Pagosa Springs Dr 75034
Painted Rock Ct 75033
Paisano Dr 75035
Palace Pl 75033
Palazzo Dr 75035
Palisades Dr 75034
Palm Desert Ln 75035
Palm Springs Ln 75035
Palmdale Dr 75035
Palmer Ct 75034
Palmetto Dr 75035
Palo Duro Dr 75033
Palo Pinto Dr 75035
Palomino Dr 75034
Paloverde Ln 75034
Panorama Dr 75035
Panther Creek Pkwy
2600-2698 75033
9201-9499 75035
Panther Creek Rd 75033
Park Ln 75034
Park Garden Dr 75035
Park Ridge Dr 75034
Parkbrook Dr 75034
Parker Creek Pl 75034
Parkside Dr 75034
Parkview 75033
Parkwood Blvd 75034
Parliment Ln 75035
Parma Ln 75034
Parterre Dr 75033
Pasadena Dr 75033
Pasatiempo Dr 75034
Passatiempo Dr 75034
Patch Grove Dr 75033
Paterno Dr 75035
Patmos Ln 75033
Patriot Dr 75034
Pattison Dr 75035
Paxton Ln 75034
Payne St 75033
Peace Dr 75034
Peace River Dr 75035
Peachtree Ln 75035
Peacock Ln 75035
Peak Cir 75035
Pear Ridge Dr 75035
Pearson Dr 75035
Pebble Beach Dr 75034
Pebble Creek Ct 75033
Pebblebrook Dr 75034
Pebblestone Cv 75035
Pecan St 75034
Pecan Brook Ln 75034
Pecan Chase Ln 75034
Pecan Hollow Ln 75035
Pecos Ct 75033
Pelican Dr 75033
Pendle Forest Dr 75034
Pendleton Ct 75033
Penick Way 75033
Pennywise Dr 75035
Pensham Dr 75035
Penton Pl 75035
Peoria Ln 75035
Pepperbark Dr 75034
Perkins Ln 75035
Perry Dr 75035
Persimmon Ln 75033
Petersburgh Pl 75035
Pewter Dr 75035
Pheasant Run 75034
Philmont Rd 75034
Phinney Dr 75035
Picadilly Park 75034
Pickwick Dr 75035
Pike Lake Dr 75035
Pilgrim Dr 75034
Pine Ln 75034
Pine Bluff Cv 75035
Pine Hills Dr 75034
Pine Valley Dr 75034
Pinecrest Dr 75035
Pinehurst Ct & Dr 75034
Pineview Ln 75035
Pinnacle Dr 75033
Pintail Ln 75034
Pioneer Dr 75033
Piper Dr 75033
Pisa Ln 75034
Pistoia Dr 75034
Pistol Creek Dr 75034
Pitkin Rd 75034
Placid Pond Dr 75034
Plains Cir 75033
Plainsman Ln 75035
Plainview Dr 75035
Plantation Ln 75035
Planters Row Dr 75033
Plateau Trl 75033
Player Ct 75034
Pleasant Grove Dr 75035
Pleasant Hill Ln 75033
Pleasant Valley Ln 75034
Plum Creek Rd 75034
Plum Valley Dr 75033
Plymouth Ln 75034
Point Loma Dr 75034
Point Verda Dr 75034
Pointe Vedra Dr 75034
Polo Heights Dr 75033
Pomegranate Dr 75035
Pompei Pl 75033
Pond Cypress Ln 75035
Pondview Ln 75035
Ponzano Ct 75035
Poppy Hills Dr 75035
Port Rd 75035
Port Edwards Ln 75033
Possum Kingdom Dr 75033
Post N Paddock 75034
Post Oak Dr 75034
Postell Ln 75035
Potomac Ln 75035
Potter Rd 75035
Powder Horn Ln 75033
Powlett Creek Dr 75034
Prairie Bend Ln 75034
Prairie Creek Trl 75033
Prairie Flower Ln 75033
Prairie Hill Dr 75033
Preachers Ln 75035
Prelude Dr 75035
Premier Dr 75033
Prescott Cir & Dr 75033
Preserve Ln 75035
Presidio Dr 75033
Presthope Dr 75035
Prestige Dr 75033
Prestmont Pl 75035
Preston Cir 75034
Preston Rd
1800-2398 75034
2400-8999 75034
9200-16099 75033
16101-17899 75033
Preston Manor Dr 75033
Preston North Dr 75034
Preston Trace Blvd & Rd 75033
Preston Vineyard Dr 75035
Prestwick Dr 75033
Price Cir 75034
Primrose Ln 75035
Prince Edward Ln 75033
Prince William Ln 75034
Princess Ln 75034
Princess Caroline Ct 75034
Printers Way 75033
Pristine Pond Dr 75034
Pritchett Dr 75034
Private Road 3411 75034
Promenade Rd 75035
Promise Land Dr 75035
Promontory Dr 75035
Prospect Dr 75034
Prospero Ln 75034
Providence Dr 75035
Pueblo Ln 75034
Purdue St 75034
Quail Run 75034
Quail Creek Dr 75034
Quail Meadow Ln 75034
Quarry Chop Dr 75035
Queen Anne Cir 75033
Queens Rd 75035
Queens Quarter Dr 75033
Quest Ct & Dr 75035
Quiet Meadow Ln 75033
Quiet Oak Ln 75034
Rachel Dr 75034
Radslow Dr 75035
Raft St 75035
Railswood Dr 75035
Rainbow Falls Dr 75034
Raintree Way 75033
Raleigh Dr 75035
Rambling Trl 75034
Ranch Gate Ln 75034
Ranchero Dr 75033
Randel Rd 75033
Randwick Trl 75034
Ranger Rd 75035
Ranier St 75034
Rankin Dr 75035
Rasor Dr 75034
Ratliff Dr 75035
Raveneaux Dr 75033
Ravenhill Dr 75035
Ravens Cliff Dr 75034
Rawlins Ln 75034
Red Cedar Dr 75035
Red Clover Dr 75033
Red Hawk Dr 75033
Red Hill Ln 75034
Red Rock Canyon Rd 75034
Red Stone Dr 75035
Redbud Ln 75034
Redcreek Trl 75035
Reel St 75035
Reflection Bay Dr 75034
Refugio Rd 75034
Regal Oak Ln 75035
Regello Dr 75034
Regent Ln 75034
Reims Ct 75034
Reisling Dr 75035
Remington Ln 75033
Remuda Rd 75033
Renault Dr 75033
Republic Dr 75034
Resaca Dr 75033
Research Rd 75033
Revalen Ln 75034
Revere Ln 75035
Revolution Way 75033
Reynolds Ln 75033
Rhinelander Dr 75033
Richmond Dr 75035
Ridge Spring Dr 75035
Ridge View Rd 75034
Ridgecrest St 75033
Ridgeland Dr 75034
Ridgetop Cir 75035
Ridgewood Dr 75035
Rifle Gap Rd 75034
Rimrock Cir 75034
Rincon St 75035
Riney Ct 75035
Rio Blanco Dr 75033
Rio Grande Dr 75033
Rio Secco Rd 75035
Ripplewood Rd 75035
Rising Star Blvd 75033
Riva Rdg 75034
River Glen Dr 75035
River Oaks Dr 75035
Riverhill Rd 75033
Riverside Dr 75035
Riverwood Ln 75034
Riviera Rd 75035
Roadster Dr 75033
Roanoke Dr 75035
Roaring Fork Ln 75033
Robert St 75035
Robertson Dr 75034
Robincreek Ln 75035
Robinwoods Dr 75035
Rochdale Ct 75035
Rock Bluff Dr 75033
Rock Brook St 75034
Rock Creek Ln 75034
Rockhill Rd 75035
Rockledge Ct 75034
Rocky Point Dr 75035
Rockyford Dr 75035
Rockyridge Dr 75035
Rodeo Dr 75035
Rogers Rd 75033
Rolater Rd 75035
Rolinda Ct 75035
Rolling Brook Dr 75034
Rolling Hills Dr 75034
Rolling Meadow Rd 75034
Roma Dr 75084
Roosevelt Dr 75034
Rose Ln 75034
Rose Garden Blvd 75035
Rose Hill Ln 75034
Rosedale Dr 75035
Rosedown Ln 75035
Roselawn Ln 75035
Rosini Ct 75035
Rough Riders Trl 75034
Round Mountain Dr 75035
Round Tree Ln 75034
Roundtable Dr & Rd 75035
Royal Acres Trl 75034
Royal Oaks Dr 75034
Royalwood Ln 75035
Ruidosa Ln 75033
Running Brook Dr 75034
Rushing Creek Dr 75035
Rushing Water Dr 75034
Ruskin Cir 75034
Russell Rd 75035
Rustic Ridge Rd 75035
Ruth Borchardt Dr 75035
Ryan Ln 75035
Ryeworth Dr 75035
Sabino Ct 75033
Saddle Dr 75035
Saddle Tree Rd 75034
Saddlebrook Dr 75034
Saddlehorn Dr 75035
Sage Ridge Dr 75034
Sage Valley Ln 75034
Sagebrush Dr 75033
Sagewood Dr 75034
Saguaro St 75033
Sahallee Dr 75033
Sailboat Way 75034
Sailmaker Ln 75035
Saint Andrews Ct 75034
Saint Augustine Dr 75033
Saint Clair St 75034
Saint Croix Dr 75034
Saint James Way 75034
Saint Johns Trl 75034
Saint Laurent Pl 75034
Saint Petersburg Dr 75034
Saint Phils St 75035
Saint Stephens Sq 75035
Salano Creek Dr 75035
Salem Dr 75035
Salisbury Dr 75035
Salmon Dr 75035
Salt Grass Ln 75035
Samantha Dr 75035
San Andres Dr 75033
San Clemente Dr 75034
San Gabriel Ave 75033
San Marcos Way 75034
San Marino Dr 75035
Sanctuary Dr 75033
Sand Castle Dr 75034
Sand Dune Dr 75033
Sand Hill Dr 75033
Sandalwood Ln 75035
Sandia Ln 75033
Sandra Dr 75034
Sandstone Dr 75034
Sandy Creek Dr 75033
Santa Clara Dr 75033
Santa Fe Trl 75033
Santa Rosa Dr 75033
Santee Ln 75033
Sao Paulo Rd 75035
Sara Dr 75035
Saratoga Trl 75034
Sardinia Way 75034
Savannah Cir & Ct 75034
Savannah Ridge Dr 75034
Sawgrass Ct 75034
Saxony Ct 75034
Saxton Ave 75034
Scarborough Ln 75035
Scenic Rd 75035
Scotch Pine Dr 75035
Scott Cir 75034
Scottsdale Way 75034
Sea Eagle Ln 75035
Seagull Way 75034
Seahawk Dr 75034
Sean Dr 75035
Seashore Ln 75034
Seaside Ln 75035
Seastat Dr 75034
Seaton Cir 75033
Seawood Dr 75035
Sebastian Inlt 75035
Secluded Pond Dr 75034
Sedalia Ct & Trl 75034
Seedling Dr 75035
Seguin Dr 75035
Senate Ln 75034
Seneca Dr 75034
Serenity Dr 75035
Settlers Knoll Trl 75035
Sevier Wells Rd 75034
Sewanee Dr 75035
Seymour Dr 75033
Shackelford Dr 75035
Shaddock Creek Ln 75033
Shade Tree Cir 75034
Shadow Brook Ln 75035
Shadow Glen Dr 75035
Shadow Ridge Ct & Dr 75034
Shady Creek Ct 75033
Shady Oaks Dr 75034
Shady Shore Dr 75034
Shadybrook Ln 75033
Shadywood Dr 75035
Shakespeare Ln 75034
Shamrock Dr 75034
Shannon Dr 75034
Sharlis Dr 75034
Sharpshire Dr 75035
Shelby Pl 75035
Sheli Ln 75034
Shell Ridge Dr 75033
Shellwood Ln 75035
Shenandoah Dr 75034
Shepherds Hill Dr & Ln 75035
Sherbrooke Dr 75035
Sherry Ln 75034
Sherwood Dr 75035
Shetland Cir 75034
Shield Rd 75035
Shingle Mill Rd 75034
Ship St 75035
Shiprock Rd 75033
Shire View Dr 75035
Shirland Ln 75035
Shirley Ct 75034
Shoal Creek Dr 75035
Shoal Forest Ln 75033
Shoemaker Rd 75034
Shorehaven Ct 75035
Shoreline Dr 75034
Short St 75034
Shoshone Dr 75034
Shumard Ln 75035
Shy Dr 75034
Sicily Dr 75034
Siena Dr 75033
Sierra Dr 75033
Sigma Ln 75035
Silentbrook Ct 75034
Silver Spur 75034
Silver Dollar Dr 75033
Silver Falls Ln 75034
Silver Horn Dr 75033
Silver Stream Ln 75034
Silverbrook Ln 75034
Silverton Dr 75033
Simon Ave 75035
Sims Way 75035
Singing Brook Rd 75035
Single Creek Trl 75035
Skeeter Dr 75034
Skipper Dr 75035
Sky Ridge Dr 75035
Skyline Dr 75034
Sleepy Creek Dr 75034
Sleepy Hollow Trl 75033
Slick Rock Trl 75033
Smotherman Rd 75033
Snow Lake Dr 75035
Snowberry Dr 75035
Snowdrop Ln 75034
Snowshill Dr 75035
Snug Hbr 75034
Snug Harbor Cir 75034
Snyder Dr 75035
Soaring Star Ln 75034
Soledad Rd 75035
Solitude Creek Ct 75034
Somerset Ln 75033
Sonoma Valley Dr 75035
Sonterra Ln 75033
Sophora Ln 75034
Sorano Dr 75035
Sorrento Dr 75035
Soto Ln 75034
Southbury Ln 75033
Southern Hills Ct & Dr 75034
Southern Pines Ct 75034
Southhampton Dr 75034
Southmark Dr 75035
Southwyck Dr 75033
Sowell Dr 75035
Spanish Moss Trl 75033
Spanish Oaks 75034
Sparkling Brook Dr 75033
Sparks Dr 75034
Sparrows Dr 75034
Spicewood Ln 75034
Spillway Cir 75034
Spindletop Trl 75033
Spirit Falls Dr 75033
Split Rock Ct 75033
Sports Village Rd 75033
Spring Dr 75035
Spring Hill Dr 75035
Spring Lake Rd 75035
Spring Wagon Dr 75035
Springbok Cir 75034
Springflower Dr 75035
Springwood Dr 75035
Spruce Creek Ln 75034
Spyglass Ct 75034
Spyglass Hill Ln 75034
Squaw Creek Dr 75035
Squire Ln 75035
Stacy Cv 75033
Stadium Ln 75033
Stagecoach Way 75033
Staley Dr 75034
Stallion Ranch Rd 75034
Stancil Ln 75035

Stand Rock Ct 75033
Stanhope Dr 75035
Stanmere Dr 75035
Stanton Pl 75033
Stapleton Dr 75033
Star Crk 75033
Star Meadow Dr 75033
Star Mesa Dr 75034
Star Ridge Ln 75034
Star Trail Dr 75034
Starboard St 75035
Stargazer Dr 75033
Stark Rd 75034
Starling Dr 75034
Stars Rd 75035
Starwood Dr 75034
State Highway 121
5000-8698 75034
State Highway 121
9100-15798 75035
Statesman Ln 75034
Steamers Ln 75035
Stephanie St 75033
Stephenville Dr 75035
Stern St 75035
Stetson Way 75034
Stevens Point Dr 75033
Still Hollow Dr 75033
Stillwater Trl 75034
Stockard Dr 75034
Stockton Ln 75034
Stone Canyon Dr 75034
Stone Creek Ln 75035
Stone Crest Rd 75035
Stone Falls Ln 75035
Stone Hearth Dr 75035
Stone House Ln 75033
Stone River Dr 75034
Stonebriar Way 75034
Stonebridge Dr 75035
W Stonebrook Pkwy 75034
Stoneridge Dr 75034
Stoneview Dr 75034
Stonewyck Ln 75033
Story Ln 75035
Stowell Dr 75035
Strattford Dr 75035
Stream Bend Dr 75035
Streamside Ct 75034
Sturgis Dr 75033
Stuttgart Dr 75033
Sugar Mill Ln 75033
Sugarberry Dr 75033
Sugartree Ln 75034
Sulphur Springs Dr 75035
Summer Dr 75035
Summer Springs Dr 75034
Summer Star Ln 75034
Summerwoods Ln 75035
Summit Ct 75034
Summit Run Dr 75035
Sumter Ct 75035
Sun Garden Dr 75033
Sun King Ln 75035
Sundeck St 75035
Sundown Trl 75034
Sunflower Way 75033
Sunland Park Dr 75033
Sunny St 75033
Sunnyvale Cir 75034
Sunrise Dr 75034
Sunrise Ln 75035
Sunset Dr 75033
Superior Dr 75033
Sutton Dr 75035
Swan Lake Dr 75033
Sweeney Trl 75034
Sweet Iron Rd 75034
Sweetwater Dr 75035
Swisher Cir 75034
Sycamore Dr 75034
Sycamore St 75033
Sydney Dr 75033
Sylvan Dale Rd 75034
Sylvan Shores Dr 75034
Taber Trl 75035

Taffy Dr 75034
Taft Powell Rd 75035
Tahoe Ln 75035
Talbot Dr 75033
Tall Grass Trl 75035
Tallahassee Dr 75035
Talley Ln 75033
Tallow Ln 75034
W Talon Dr 75033
Tamarack Trl 75035
Tambra Dr 75033
Tangerine Ln 75033
Tanglerose Dr 75033
Tanglewood Ln 75035
Tanyard Ln 75033
Tappatio Springs Ln 75035
Tara Ln 75033
Tarlton Dr 75035
Tascate Dr 75034
Tate Ln 75033
Tatum Dr 75034
Tavern Creek Ct 75035
Taylor Way 75035
Teakwood Dr 75035
Teal Hollow Dr 75035
Tealsky Dr 75033
Tealwood Ln 75035
Technology Dr 75033
Teel Pkwy
7500-8998 75034
8811-8811 75035
8811-8899 75034
9101-9397 75033
9399-11899 75035
11901-13599 75033
Telemark Trl 75034
Tenison Ln 75033
Terrazzo Ln 75035
Texoma Dr 75033
Thackery Dr 75034
The Landings Ct 75033
Thistletree Ln 75033
Thistlewood Ln 75034
Thomasville Ln 75033
Thompson Cir 75033
Thorncliff Dr 75035
Thorndale Cir 75033
Thornton Dr 75035
Thorntree Dr 75033
Throne Hall Dr 75033
Timber Ln 75034
Timber Bluff Ln 75033
Timber Crest Ct 75035
Timber Ridge Dr 75034
Tisbury Dr 75035
Tivoli Ln 75033
Tobias Ln 75033
Toffenham Dr 75035
Toledo Bend Dr 75033
Tomah Dr 75033
Topiary Hill Ct 75034
Torino Dr 75035
Torrey Pines Ln 75034
Torrington Dr 75035
Toscana Way 75035
Touraine Dr 75034
Tournament Rd 75035
Tower Rd 75035
Town And Country
Blvd 75034
Towne Bridge Dr 75035
Townsend Dr 75033
Trail Glen Dr 75035
Trail View Ln 75034
Trailing Oaks Dr 75034
Trailridge Dr 75035
Trails Pkwy 75033
Trailway Dr 75035
Tranquil Pond Dr 75034
Travis Dr 75034
Tree Shadow Ln 75035
Tree Top Dr 75033
Treehouse Dr 75034
Treemont Pl 75034
Trestles Rd 75035
Trevino Ln 75034

Trinity Blvd 75034
Triple Bar Pl 75034
Triplemark Trl 75034
Trolley Dr 75035
Troon Dr 75034
Trull Brook Ln 75033
Truman Dr 75034
Tucker Ln 75035
Tularosa Ln 75033
Tumbleweed Way 75034
Tumbling Creek Trl 75035
Tumbling River Dr 75034
Tupelo Ln 75035
Turnberry Dr 75034
Turnbridge Dr 75035
Turnstone Trl 75033
Turtle Creek Ln 75035
Twilight Dr 75035
Twin Cove Dr 75035
Twin Harbors Dr 75034
Twisting Trl 75035
Tyler Dr 75035
Tyning Cir 75035
Union Creek Dr 75034
Union Grove Ln 75033
United Ln 75034
Upper Meadow Dr 75034
Valencia Dr 75035
Valhalla Dr 75034
Valley Brook Dr 75035
Valley Mills Dr 75033
Valley Spring Dr 75035
Valverde Ln 75035
Valway Ct 75034
Van Horn Ln 75034
Vandelia St 75035
Vanderbilt Ln 75033
Vanguard Dr 75034
Varese Ct 75035
Vassar Dr 75035
Velasco Dr 75035
Venetian Way 75034
Veneto Dr 75033
Venice Ct 75035
Ventura Ln 75034
Vera Cruz Rd 75035
Veranda Ct 75035
Verbena Ln 75034
Verdant Valley Dr 75034
Verde Ln 75034
Verona Ct 75035
Veronica Ln 75033
Versailles Ave 75034
Via Bello Ct 75035
Vickie Ln 75035
Vicksburg Pl 75035
Victory Dr 75034
View Meadow Ln 75035
Village Blvd 75034
Villandry Ln 75033
Villanova Dr 75035
Vintage Dr 75035
Viola Dr 75033
Vista Terrace Dr 75034
Vistaview Pl 75034
Vistoso Dr 75034
Vita Dolce Ct & Dr 75035
Vizcaya Ln 75033
Voltaire Dr 75033
Voyager Dr 75034
Wade Blvd
8500-8599 75034
8601-8799 75034
9000-9298 75035
9300-9799 75035
9801-9899 75035
Waimea St 75035
Wainhouse Rd 75035
Wake Bridge Dr 75034
Walden Ct 75033
Wales Dr 75035
Wallis Dr 75033
Walnut St 75033
Walnut Grove Ln 75034
Walnut Ridge Dr 75035
Waltham Dr 75035

Warren Pkwy
5301-5497 75034
5499-7800 75034
7802-8598 75034
9100-9199 75035
9201-10299 75035
Warwick Ln 75034
Washakie Rd 75034
Washington Dr 75034
Water Rd 75035
Waterbury Dr 75035
Watercress Ln 75033
Waterford Ln 75035
Waterlily Ln 75033
Waters Edge Ln 75035
Waterslide Way 75034
Waterstone Dr 75034
Waterview Dr 75035
Waverly Ln 75035
Waycross Ln 75033
Wedmore Dr 75035
Weeping Willow Dr 75035
Welch Folly Ln 75035
Wellington Ln 75033
Wellshire Ln 75035
Wendover Dr 75034
Wentworth Dr 75035
Westchester Ln 75034
Western Trl
5600-9599 75034
12400-12498 75035
12500-15899 75035
Western Hills Dr 75033
Westlawn Ln 75033
Westpoint Ln 75033
Westwood Ct 75035
Wetland Dr 75033
Wexford Ln 75033
Wharf St 75035
Wheat Ridge Dr 75033
Whirlwind Dr 75034
Whispering Lake Dr 75034
Whispering Pines Dr 75033
Whistler Dr 75035
Whistling Straits Ln 75035
White Bluff Dr 75034
White Oaks Ln 75035
White Rock Ct 75034
White Spruce Dr 75033
Whitefish Lake Dr 75035
Whitehart St 75035
Whitewing Dr 75034
Whitney Dr 75034
Wichita Trl 75033
Wicklow Dr 75034
Widgeon Way 75034
Wild Creek Dr 75035
Wild Oak Dr 75035
Wild Stream Dr 75033
Wilderness Ct 75033
Wildfire Ln 75033
Wildwood Ln 75033
Wiley Ln 75034
Williams Ave & Pl 75033
Williamsburg Ln 75035
Williford Trl 75033
Willoughby 75033
Willow Bend Dr 75035
Willow Creek Dr 75034
Willowbrook Ln 75035
Wilmington Dr 75035
Wilton Dr 75035
Wimberley Dr 75035
Wimbledon Ct 75034
Winchester Dr 75033
Wind Surf Dr 75034
Windgate Ln 75033
Winding Way 75035
Winding Creek Dr 75035
Winding Hollow Ln 75033
Windjammer Dr 75034
Windmill Pt 75033
Windsong Dr 75035
Windsor Rdg 75034
Windy Hill Dr 75034
Windy Ridge Rd 75033

Wing Point Dr 75033
Winged Foot Dr 75034
Wingfield Ln 75035
Winston Dr 75035
Winter Park Dr 75035
Winterberry Ln 75034
Wishing Well Ct 75035
Wisteria Dr 75035
Witt Rd 75034
Wolf Snare Dr 75035
Wood Ct 75034
Wood Lake Dr 75035
Woodbine Trl 75034
Woodbluff Dr 75035
Woodbury Dr 75033
Woodcreek Ln 75034
Woodland Way 75035
Woodstream Dr 75034
World Cup Way 75033
Wovenedge Ct 75035
Wrangler Dr 75035
Wright Dr 75035
Wyndbrook Dr 75035
Wyoming Dr 75035
Yacht St 75035
Yarmouth Ln 75034
Yarra Ln 75034
Yellow Rose Pl 75035
Yellowstone Dr 75033
Yoakum Dr 75035
York Dr 75035
York Castle Ct 75035
Yorkshire Ln 75033
Yorktown Dr 75035
Yosemite Ln 75033
Yucca Dr 75035
Yuma Dr 75033
Zander Dr 75034
Zinnia Cir 75035
Zumwalt Cir 75034
Zurich Ln 75034

NUMBERED STREETS

1st St 75034
9000-9098 75033
2nd St
8600-8700 75034
8702-8798 75034
8901-9099 75033
3rd St
8601-8697 75034
8901-8997 75033
8999-9499 75033
4th St
8600-8700 75034
8702-8898 75034
8900-9098 75033
9101-9599 75033
5th St
7401-8497 75034
8499-8599 75034
8601-8899 75034
8901-9097 75033
9099-9199 75033
9201-9299 75033
6th St
8500-8698 75034
8701-8899 75034
8901-9199 75033
7th St 75034

GAINESVILLE TX

General Delivery 76240

POST OFFICE BOXES MAIN OFFICE STATIONS AND BRANCHES

Box No.s
All PO Boxes 76241

RURAL ROUTES

01, 02, 04, 05, 06, 07, 08, 09, 11, 12 76240

HIGHWAY CONTRACTS

51 76240

NAMED STREETS

Airport Dr 76240
Alabama Dr 76240
Alakerli 76240
Alice Ln 76240
Andrews St 76240
Anthony St 76240
Apache Cv 76240
Aquadec Ponds Ln 76240
Arend Dr 76240
Arizona St 76240
Arkansas St 76240
Ashland Ct & Dr 76240
Aspen Rd 76240
Aster St 76240
Austin St 76240
B And B Mhp 76240
Barbara Jordan Ave 76240
Baugh Rd 76240
Bayside Cir 76240
Beattie St 76240
Beecher St 76240
Belcher St 76240
Bell St 76240
Bella Vista Dr 76240
Belmont St 76240
Berend St 76240
Bersano Ave 76240
Big Indian Rd 76240
Big Tree Ln 76240
Bird St 76240
Black Hill Dr 76240
Blackfoot Trl 76240
Blackwood St 76240
Blankenship Hill Ln 76240
Blanton St 76240
Bluebird Dr 76240
Bola Dr 76240
Boley St 76240
Bonner Rd 76240
Bowie Cv & Dr 76240
Brenda Ln 76240
Brentwood St 76240
Briarcliff Cir 76240
Bridle Ln 76240
Broadus St 76240
E & W Broadway St 76240
Brookhollow Cir 76240
Buck St 76240
Burns City Rd 76240
S Burris St 76240
Butcher Pt 76240
C A Ward Ln 76240
E California St
100-322 76240
321-321 76241
324-2198 76240
401-2199 76240
W California St 76240
Campbell St 76240
Candlewood Cir 76240
Captains Cutt Rd 76240
Carnes St 76240
Cartwright Hill Ln 76240
Cason Dr 76240
Cayuga Cv & Trl 76240
E Cedar Crst & St 76240
Cedar Hill Rd 76240
Center Hill Rd 76240
Chaparral Dr 76240
Chapman 76240
Cherry St 76240
N & S Chestnut St 76240
Cheyenne Dr 76240
Chippewa Cv 76240

Chism Cv 76240
Choctaw Cv 76240
E & W Church St 76240
Clark Rd 76240
N & S Clements St 76240
E & W Cloud St 76240
Cocopa Cv & Dr 76240
Cole St 76240
College St 76240
College View St 76240
Colorodo St 76240
Colt Dr 76240
Columbine Dr 76240
Columbus St 76240
Comanche Dr 76240
N & S Commerce St 76240
Corporate Dr 76240
County Road 107 76240
County Road 115 76240
County Road 117 76240
County Road 119 76240
County Road 121 76240
County Road 122 76240
County Road 123 76240
County Road 128 76240
County Road 131 76240
County Road 133 76240
County Road 134 76240
County Road 135 76240
County Road 136 76240
County Road 137 76240
County Road 138 76240
County Road 139 76240
County Road 145 76240
County Road 146 76240
County Road 147 76240
County Road 148 76240
County Road 149 76240
County Road 150 76240
County Road 151 76240
County Road 154 76240
County Road 155 76240
County Road 158 76240
County Road 159 76240
County Road 161 76240
County Road 162 76240
County Road 163 76240
County Road 171 76240
County Road 172 76240
County Road 173 76240
County Road 174 76240
County Road 178 76240
County Road 180 76240
County Road 181 76240
County Road 182 76240
County Road 183 76240
County Road 187 76240
County Road 188 76240
County Road 189 76240
County Road 190 76240
County Road 191 76240
County Road 193 76240
County Road 194 76240
County Road 195 76240
County Road 196 76240
County Road 197 76240
County Road 198 76240
County Road 199 76240
County Road 201 76240
County Road 202 76240
County Road 206 76240
County Road 207 76240
County Road 2070 76240
County Road 208 76240
County Road 209 76240
County Road 211 76240
County Road 2112 76240
County Road 2114 76240
County Road 2115 76240
County Road 2116 76240
County Road 2117 76240
County Road 2118 76240
County Road 2119 76240
County Road 212 76240
County Road 2121 76240
County Road 2123 76240

County Road 2124 76240
County Road 2125 76240
County Road 2126 76240
County Road 2127 76240
County Road 2130 76240
County Road 2134 76240
County Road 2135 76240
County Road 2136 76240
County Road 214 76240
County Road 2152 76240
County Road 2156 76240
County Road 218 76240
County Road 2183 76240
County Road 219 76240
County Road 220 76240
County Road 222 76240
County Road 224 76240
County Road 226 76240
County Road 227 76240
County Road 237 76240
County Road 238 76240
County Road 239 76240
County Road 257 76240
County Road 260 76240
County Road 262 76240
County Road 263 76240
County Road 264 76240
County Road 265 76240
County Road 276 76240
County Road 278 76240
County Road 281 76240
County Road 283 76240
County Road 285 76240
County Road 294 76240
County Road 295 76240
County Road 296 76240
County Road 297 76240
County Road 299 76240
County Road 3003 76240
County Road 301 76240
County Road 304 76240
County Road 306 76240
County Road 307 76240
County Road 308 76240
County Road 312 76240
County Road 313 76240
County Road 314 76240
County Road 315 76240
County Road 318 76240
County Road 321 76240
County Road 323 76240
County Road 327 76240
County Road 329 76240
County Road 331 76240
County Road 333 76240
County Road 336 76240
County Road 337 76240
County Road 338 76240
County Road 339 76240
County Road 340 76240
County Road 346 76240
County Road 352 76240
County Road 353 76240
County Road 354 76240
County Road 3628 76240
County Road 3629 76240
County Road 3630 76240
County Road 3631 76240
County Road 3632 76240
County Road 3633 76240
County Road 3634 76240
County Road 365 76240
County Road 366 76240
County Road 367 76240
County Road 377 76240
County Road 380 76240
County Road 381 76240
County Road 393 76240
County Road 397 76240
County Road 401 76240
County Road 402 76240
County Road 403 76240
County Road 404 76240
County Road 405 76240
County Road 406 76240
County Road 407 76240
County Road 408 76240
County Road 409 76240
County Road 410 76240
County Road 411 76240
County Road 412 76240
County Road 418 76240
County Road 420 76240
County Road 422 76240
County Road 434 76240
County Road 437 76240
County Road 440 76240
County Road 444 76240
County Road 446 76240
County Road 451 76240
County Road 452 76240
County Road 453 76240
County Road 455 76240
County Road 460 76240
County Road 463 76240
County Road 464 76240
County Road 466 76240
County Road 473 76240
Court House Sq 76240
Courtney Ln 76240
Crawford St 76240
Crockett Dr 76240
Cross Creek Ln 76240
Cross Timbers Ln 76240
Crossen Ranch Ln 76240
N Culberson St 76240
E & W Cummings St 76240
Cunningham St 76240
Custer City Ln 76240
Cypress Ct & St 76240
Dairy Ln 76240
Daisy Ln 76240
Davis St 76240
Delossantes Ln 76240
Denison St 76240
N & S Denton St 76240
Diamond Cir 76240
Dillard Rd 76240
N & S Dixon St 76240
Dodge St 76240
Dodson St 76240
Doss St 76240
Doty St 76240
Dove Ln 76240
Dover Cir & Dr 76240
Dozier St 76240
Edison Dr 76240
Eldridge St 76240
Elizabeth St 76240
E & W Elm St 76240
Elmwood St 76240
Eternity Ln 76240
Ethan 76240
Everglade Ct & Dr 76240
Fair Ave 76240
Fairfield St 76240
Falls Creek Cir 76240
Faye St 76240
Field St 76240
First St 76240
Fletcher St 76240
Floral Dr 76240
Florida St 76240
Fm 1198 76240
Fm 1199 76240
Fm 1200 76240
Fm 1201 Ext 76240
Fm 1202 76240
Fm 1306 76240
Fm 1630 76240
Fm 2071 76240
Fm 2383 76240
Fm 2896 76240
Fm 3092 76240
Fm 3108 76240
Fm 3164 76240
Fm 3496 76240
Fm 371 76240
S Fm 372 76240
Fm 51 76240
E Fm 678 76240
Fm 902 76240
E Foreline St 76240
Foreman St 76240
Fox Creek Ct & Ln 76240
Fox Hollow St 76240
Fox Land Dr 76240
Frasher St 76240
E & W Garnett St 76240
Gladney St 76240
Gladys St 76240
Glenwood St 76240
Gordon St 76240
E Gorham St 76240
Gossett St 76240
N Grand Ave 76240
Greenbriar Ct & Dr 76240
Gribble St 76240
Gunter St 76240
E & W Haight St 76240
Hall St 76240
Hancock St 76240
Hannah St 76240
Harper Lease Rd 76240
Harrell Rd 76240
Harris St 76240
Harvey St 76240
Hay Ln 76240
Heather Rd 76240
Hemming St 76240
Hickman Trl 76240
High Cliff Dr 76240
Highpoint Church Rd 76240
E & W Highway 82 76240
Hillcrest Blvd 76240
Hillside Dr 76240
Hilltop Dr 76240
E & W Hird St 76240
Hockley Creek Rd 76240
Hogan Dr 76240
Holly Ln 76240
Horseshoe Ln 76240
Horsinaround Ln 76240
Hospital Blvd 76240
Houston Cv & Dr 76240
N & S Howeth St 76240
Huron Trl 76240
Independence Ave 76240
N & S Interstate 35 76240
Ira Ward Ln 76240
Iriquois Dr 76240
Iris St 76240
Island Rd 76240
E & W J M Lindsay Blvd 76240
Jack Aly 76240
Jean St 76240
Jefferson St 76240
Jodi Ln 76240
Joslin 76240
Jrc Rd 76240
Justice Center Blvd 76240
Karok Cv 76240
Kent Cir & Dr 76240
Kiowa Cv & Dr E, N, S & W 76240
Kirby St 76240
Kirk Rd 76240
Laborde Ln 76240
N Lake Ln 76240
Lakeline Dr 76240
Lakeside Ln 76240
Lakeway Ln 76240
Lanius St 76240
Laurel Rd 76240
Lawrence St 76240
Leach St 76240
S Lindsay St 76240
W Line Dr & Rd 76240
Locust St 76240
Lone Star Dr 76240
Longhorn Dr 76240
Luther Ln 76240
Lynch St 76240
Lyndaker Ln 76240
Lynwood St 76240
Magnolia St 76240
E & W Main St 76240
Makah Cv 76240
Manito Cv 76240
Maplewood Ct & Dr 76240
Marlissa Ln 76240
Martin Ln 76240
Martin Luther King Jr Ave 76240
Mary St 76240
Mccary St 76240
Mcclain St 76240
Mccrary St 76240
Mccubbin St 76240
Mcdaniel St 76240
Mcnew Rd 76240
Meadow Dr 76240
Meadowlark Ln 76240
Medal Of Honor Blvd 76240
Melody Ln 76240
Merrywood Way 76240
Mesquite Cir & St 76240
Meyersville Ln 76240
Middle Ln 76240
Mill St 76240
Minnie St 76240
Modoc Trl 76240
Modrall St 76240
Mohave Dr E 76240
Mohawk Cv 76240
Mohican Trl 76240
Molala Cv 76240
Montrose Ave 76240
Mooney St 76240
Moran St 76240
Morningside Dr 76240
N & S Morris St 76240
Morrison Hill Ln 76240
Morrow Bend Ln 76240
Morse Ln 76240
Moss St 76240
Moss Lake Rd 76240
Mule Run 76240
Murphy St 76240
Myrtle St 76240
Natalie Dr 76240
Navajo Trl 76240
Neals Hill Rd 76240
Neely Trl 76240
Never Mind Dr 76240
Newland Dr 76240
Nila Dr 76240
Noel Dr 76240
Northridge Dr 76240
Northshore Dr 76240
Nortman Dr 76240
Noweta Pl 76240
Nowetta Cv 76240
Oak Ridge Dr 76240
Oakview Rd 76240
Old Denton Rd 76240
Old Mill Cir 76240
Old Sivells Bend Rd 76240
Olive St 76240
One Horse Ln 76240
Oneal St 76240
Oscar Cole St 76240
Ottowa Cv 76240
Oxford Dr 76240
Park Ln 76240
Parkside Cir & Ln 76240
Parkview 76240
Parkwood Ct 76240
Patricia Dr 76240
Paul Ln 76240
Pawless Ln 76240
Pawnee Trl 76240
E & W Pecan Dr & St 76240
Pecan Grove Mhp 76240
Pembroke Ranch Ln 76240
Phillips St 76240
Pontiac Cv & Dr 76240
Poole Rd 76240
Potter St 76240
Prairie Grove Rd 76240
Preston St 76240
Prime Outlet Blvd 76240
Pueblo Dr 76240
Quail Run St 76240
N & S Radio Hill Rd 76240
Railroad Ave 76240
Ranch Mart Rd 76240
Reasor Rd 76240
Rebecca Dr 76240
Red Oak 76240
N & S Red River St 76240
Redbud Rd 76240
Refinery Rd 76240
Rice Ave 76240
Riley St 76240
Ritchey St 76240
River Bluff Ln 76240
Robertson Ln 76240
Rocky Ln & Pt 76240
Rocky Ridge Flatts 76240
Rocky Top Dr 76240
Rose Ranch Ln 76240
Rosedale Dr 76240
Roseman Ln 76240
Roy St 76240
Rural Ranch Rd 76240
N & S Rusk St 76240
San Chez Dr 76240
Santa Fe St & Trl 76240
Santee Dr 76240
Sarsi Cv 76240
Savage Ln 76240
Scenic Pt 76240
N & S Schopmeyer St 76240
Scotsmeadow St 76240
E & W Scott St 76240
Seminole Cv & Dr 76240
Sequoya Cv & Dr 76240
Shadowood Ln 76240
Shawnee Dr 76240
Shipley St 76240
Shoreline Dr 76240
Short St 76240
Shoshone Cv & Dr 76240
Silver Oak Dr 76240
Smith St 76240
Southland Dr 76240
Southside Dr 76240
Spanish Oak Ln 76240
E & W Spring Creek Rd 76240
Spur Ln 76240
St Onge Dr 76240
Stanford Dr 76240
E & W Star St 76240
Stone Ridge Cir & Dr 76240
Summa St 76240
Sunset Pl 76240
Sunset Village Mhp 76240
N & S Taylor St 76240
Team Bjr Ln 76240
Teepee Cv 76240
E & W Tennie St 76240
Texas Cv 76240
The Oil Rd 76240
Thomas St 76240
Thompson Rd & St 76240
Thrasher Rd 76240
Throckmorton St 76240
Tomahawk Dr 76240
Tower Hill Ln 76240
Trimbles Ln 76240
Truelove St 76240
Tulane Ave 76240
Turner Ln 76240
Tyler St 76240
E & W University Dr 76240
E & W Us Highway 82 76240
Ute Cv 76240
Vallana Dr 76240
Vintage Ave 76240
Wagon Wheel Rd 76240
Walnut Ln 76240
Walter Rd & St 76240
Wampum Cv 76240
Wasco Cv 76240
Washington Ct 76240
Water Well Ln 76240
N & S Weaver St 76240
Weber Dr 76240
Welch Hill Ln 76240
Wendy Lee 76240
Westaire Dr 76240
Whaley Dr 76240
Wheeler Creek Cir, Ct & Dr 76240
Whisper Pt 76240
Whitleys Ridge Ln 76240
Williams St 76240
Willow Way 76240
Windsor Dr 76240
S Wine St 76240
Witherspoon St 76240
Wolf Run 76240
Woodbine Ct & Ln 76240
Woodbine Estates Rd 76240
Woodland Ct 76240
Woodlawn Ct & St 76240
Woods 76240
Yates St 76240
Young St 76240
Yuma Dr 76240

NUMBERED STREETS

All Street Addresses 76240

GALVESTON TX

General Delivery 77550

POST OFFICE BOXES MAIN OFFICE STATIONS AND BRANCHES

Box No.s
1 - 2670 77553
3001 - 3998 77552
8001 - 9050 77553
16001 - 17265 77552

RURAL ROUTES

01, 02, 04 77554

NAMED STREETS

Adler Cir 77551
Admiral Cir 77554
Airport Blvd 77554
Airways Ln 77554
Al West Dr 77551
Alamo Dr 77551
Alamo Rear Dr 77551
Albacore Ave 77550
Alice St 77554
Amanda Cir 77554
Anderson Way St 77554
Ann Marie Ln 77551
Antigua 77554
Antilles Ave 77551
Ashton Pl 77551
Audubon Pl 77554
Austin Dr 77551
Austin Rear Dr 77551
Avalon Way 77550
Avenue N
1200-4499 77550
4500-5099 77551
Avenue S
3000-3048 77550
3050-4499 77550
4500-5899 77551
Avenue W 77551
Avenue B Rear 77550
Avenue H 77551
Avenue K
500-4499 77550
4500-5699 77551
Avenue K Rear
500-4399 77550
4500-4598 77551
4600-5699 77551
Avenue L
600-4499 77550
4500-6499 77551
Avenue L Rear
700-4499 77550
4500-4998 77551
5000-5699 77551
5701-6299 77551
Avenue M
900-4499 77550
5000-5699 77551
Avenue M 1/2
1000-4299 77550
5000-5699 77551
Avenue M 1/2 Rear
1000-4199 77550
5000-5698 77551
Avenue M Rear
900-4499 77550
5000-5699 77551
Avenue N 1/2
1200-4499 77550
4500-7299 77551
Avenue N 1/2 Rear
1500-4499 77550
4500-4698 77551
4700-5199 77551
5201-5599 77551
Avenue N Rear
1200-4099 77550
4701-5099 77551
Avenue O
1500-4499 77550
4500-7099 77551
Avenue O 1/2
1800-4499 77550
4500-6999 77551
Avenue O 1/2 Rear
1800-4399 77550
4401-4499 77550
4500-5599 77551
Avenue O Rear
1500-4399 77550
4600-5300 77551
5302-5598 77551
Avenue P
1800-4499 77550
4500-6999 77551
Avenue P 1/2
2200-4499 77550
4500-7599 77551
Avenue P 1/2 Rear
2200-4200 77550
4202-4498 77550
4500-6999 77551
Avenue P Rear
1900-4499 77550
4500-5599 77551
5601-5699 77551
Avenue Q
2400-4499 77550
4500-6799 77551
Avenue Q 1/2
2400-4499 77550
4500-7199 77551
Avenue Q 1/2 Rear
2400-4299 77550
4500-6699 77551
Avenue Q Rear
2400-4199 77550
4501-4697 77551
4699-6799 77551
Avenue R
2800-4499 77550
4500-7399 77551
Avenue R 1/2
2800-4499 77550
4500-5699 77551
Avenue R 1/2 Rear
2800-4499 77550
4501-4597 77551
4599-5599 77551
5601-5699 77551

Avenue R Rear
2800-4499 77550
4700-6099 77551
Avenue S 1/2
3500-4499 77550
4500-6099 77551
Avenue S 1/2 Rear 77550
Avenue S 1/4 77551
Avenue S Rear
3000-4499 77550
4501-4597 77551
4599-5200 77551
5202-5598 77551
Avenue T
3700-4499 77550
5100-6099 77551
Avenue T 1/2
4100-4399 77550
5700-6098 77551
Avenue T 1/2 Rear 77550
Avenue T Rear
3700-4499 77550
5701-5797 77551
5799-5999 77551
Avenue U
3900-4499 77550
4500-5699 77551
Avenue U Rear 77551
Avenue V 1/2
5300-5699 77551
9500-9599 77554
Azalea Ct 77551
Back Bay Cir & Dr 77551
Ball St 77550
Ball Rear St 77550
Bamaku Bnd 77554
Bamar Ln 77554
Bamboo Dr 77554
Banintow St 77550
Barometer Close 77554
Barque Ln 77554
Barracuda Ave 77550
W Bay Rd 77554
Bay Breeze Dr 77554
Bay Meadows St 77554
Bay Water Dr 77554
Bayou Cir 77551
Bayou Front Dr 77551
Bayou Homes Dr 77551
Bayou Homes Rear Dr 77551
Bayou Shore Dr 77551
Bayou Shore Rear Dr 77551
Bayside Ave 77554
W Beach 77554
E Beach Dr 77550
Beachside 77554
Beachtown Psge 77550
Beall Ln 77554
Beard Dr 77554
Beaudelaire Cir 77551
Beech St 77554
Belo Pl 77551
Beluche Dr 77551
Bermuda Beach Dr 77554
Bernice Dr 77554
Binnacle Ct & Way 77554
Biovu Dr 77551
Bluebonnet Ct 77551
Bluewing Teal Ct 77554
Blume Dr 77554
Bonanza 77554
Bonita Ave 77550
Bora Bora Dr 77554
Borden Ave 77551
Bowie Dr 77551
Bristow Dr 77554
Broadway St
600-4499 77550
4500-5825 77551
5826-6498 77551
5826-5826 77552
5827-6499 77551
6500-9399 77554
Broadway Rear St
700-998 77550
1000-4199 77550
4600-6299 77551

Bryan St 77554
Buccaneer Blvd 77554
Buena Vista Dr 77554
Burnet Dr 77554
Cadena Ct, Dr & Pl 77554
Caduceus Pl
4300-4499 77550
4500-4799 77551
Caduceus Rear Pl 77551
Camp Dr 77554
Campbell Ln 77551
Campeche Cir & Dr 77554
Campeche Estates Dr 77554
Caravelle Ct 77554
Carmel Ct 77554
Castaway St 77554
Cat Tail Dr 77554
Catamaran Dr 77554
Cedar St 77551
Cedar Lawn Cir & Dr 77551
Central Plz 77550
Central City Blvd 77551
Cessna 77554
Channelview Dr 77554
Chantilly Cir 77551
Charlie St 77554
Chelarai 77551
Christopher Sq 77551
Church St 77550
Church Rear St 77550
Cindy Rd 77554
Clara Barton Ln 77551
Cloud Ln 77551
Coast Guard St 77550
Coconut St 77554
Colony Park Cir & Dr 77551
Comanche Dr 77554
Commander Dr 77554
Commodore Dr 77554
Compass Cir 77554
Copilot Ln 77554
Copra St 77554
Coral Ln 77550
Coral Way 77554
Coronado Ct 77554
County Rd 77554
Courageous Ln 77554
Cove Ln 77554
Cove View Blvd 77554
Cozumel Cir 77554
Cozy Cove Ln 77554
Criolla Ct 77554
Crockett Blvd 77551
Crockett Rear Blvd 77551
Curiosity Ln 77554
Cutwater Pl 77554
Cypress St 77551
Dale St 77554
Dana Dr 77554
E Dansby Dr 77551
Darcy St 77554
David St 77554
Defender Ln 77554
Denver Dr 77551
Diamond Head Dr 77554
Dolphin Ave 77550
Dominique Dr 77551
Driftwood Ln 77551
Driftwood Rear Ln 77551
Duncan Way 77554
Easterly Dr 77554
Eckert Dr 77554
El Cielo 77551
El Lago St 77554
Estuary Dr 77554
Evia Main 77554
Fairway Dr 77551
Fannin Dr 77551
Farris Acres St 77554
S Ferry Rd 77550
Flamingo Dr 77554
Foremast Dr 77554
Fort Bend Dr 77554
Fort Crockett Blvd 77551
Fort Point Rd 77550
Fraser Ave 77551

Fraser Rear Ave 77551
Galleon 77554
Garfield Way 77554
Gentry Ln 77554
Gerol Cir, Ct & Dr 77551
Glei 77554
Glossy Ibs Way 77554
Golf Crest Dr 77551
Grassy Pointe Dr 77554
Great Blue Heron Dr 77554
Green Heron Dr 77554
Greenwing Teal Ct 77554
Grover Ave 77551
Gulf Dr 77554
Gulf Fwy 77554
Gulf Ln 77550
Gulf Palms St 77554
Gull Dr 77551
Hall St 77554
Hammock Trl 77554
Hana Dr 77554
Harbor Cir 77554
Harbor View Cir & Dr 77550
Harborside Dr
200-3799 77550
4500-8299 77554
Harborside Rear Dr 77550
Harris Way 77551
Harris Rear Way 77551
Hawaii Dr 77554
Heards Lane Cir 77551
Heron Ave & Dr 77551
Hershey Bch 77554
N Holiday Dr 77550
Holly Ct 77551
Hollywood Ave 77551
Hollywood Rear Ave 77551
Homer Rd 77554
Homrighaus Rd 77554
Hope Blvd 77554
Houston Dr 77551
Hutchings 77551
Ibis Dr 77551
Intrepid Ln 77554
Island Psge 77554
Isles End Rd 77554
J H Clouser St 77550
Jack Johnson Blvd 77550
Jamaica Bch 77554
Jane Rd 77554
W Jean St 77554
Jeanie Lynn St 77554
Jenkins Rd 77554
Jibstay Ct 77554
John Reynolds Cir &
Rd 77554
Jones Dr
2500-2599 77554
2601-2999 77554
6800-7499 77551
Jones Lake Rd 77554
Kabah Ct 77554
Kahala Dr E 77554
Kameha Dr 77554
King Rail Cir 77554
Kirwin St 77551
Kleinmann Ave 77551
Kona Dr 77554
Lafitte Ave 77551
Lafittes Pt 77554
Lakeview Dr 77551
Lampasas Dr 77554
Lanai St 77554
Lanyard Pl 77554
Larkspur Ct 77551
Las Palmas St 77554
Lasker Dr 77551
Latitude Ln 77554
Lebrun Ct 77551
Leeland Dr 77551
Leeward Dr 77551
Legas Dr 77551
Leilani Dr 77554
Leslie Dr 77551
Lewis Ln 77554
Lillian Ln 77554

E, N, S & W Live Oak
Cir 77550
Lockheed Rd 77554
Lokai St 77554
Long Reach Dr 77554
Lotus Dr 77554
Lyncrest Dr 77550
Mackeral St 77550
Maco St 77551
Magnolia Ct 77551
Magnolia Blossom 77551
Magnolia Homes 77550
Majuro Dr 77554
Makatea St 77554
Mango Dr 77554
Mangrove Dr 77554
Manor Way 77550
Maple Ln 77551
Marina Blvd 77554
Marine Dr 77550
Mariner Pass 77554
Market St 77550
Market Rear St 77550
Marlin Ave 77550
Maui Dr 77554
Mayapan Ct 77554
Mccullough Ave 77551
Mechanic St 77550
Mechanic Rear St 77550
Menard Ave 77551
Menard Rear Ave 77551
Mendocino Dr 77554
Merida Ct 77554
Meridian Way 77554
Milam Dr 77551
Milam Rear Dr 77551
Millies Rd 77554
Miramar Dr 77554
Monterey Ct 77554
Moody Plz 77550
Moody Rear Ave 77550
Moorea St 77554
Moyenne Pl 77554
Mustang Dr 77554
Neptune Cir 77554
Neumann Dr 77551
New Strand St 77550
Oahu Dr 77554
Oak St 77551
Offats Point Cir 77551
Old Port Industrial Rd 77554
Oleander Ave 77551
Oleander Dr 77554
Oleander Homes 77551
Orleans Pl 77551
Ostermeyer Rd 77554
Outrigger St 77554
Pabst Rd 77554
Palm Cir 77551
E Palm Cir 77551
W Palm Cir 77551
Palm Ter
3A-3J 77550
4A-4J 77550
5A-5J 77550
6A-6H 77550
7A-7H 77550
8A-8H 77550
9A-9H 77550
10A-10J 77550
11A-11J 77550
12A-12J 77550
13A-13H 77550
14A-14J 77550
15A-15J 77550
16A-16H 77550
17A-17H 77550
18A-18J 77550
19A-19J 77550
20A-20J 77550
21A-21J 77550
22A-22H 77550
23A-23H 77550
24A-24J 77550
25A-25J 77550
26A-26J 77550

27A-27F 77550
28A-28F 77550
29A-29H 77550
30A-30H 77550
31A-31H 77550
32A-32H 77550
33A-33H 77550
34A-34F 77550
35A-35F 77550
36A-36H 77550
37A-37H 77550
38A-38H 77550
39A-39H 77550
40A-40H 77550
1-99 77550
Palm Cove Ct 77554
Palmdale Ct 77554
Palmetto Dr 77554
Palmira Way 77551
Papeete St 77554
Paradise Dr 77554
Park Ln & St 77551
Pean St 77554
Pelican Is 77554
Pencherl Rd 77554
Pennzoil Rd 77554
Perry Ave 77551
Pier 77550
Pilot Ln 77554
Pine St 77551
Pirates Bch W 77554
Pirates Beach Cir 77554
Pointe West Dr 77554
Pompano Ave 77550
Poplar Dr 77551
Porch St 77554
Port Holiday Mall 77550
Port O Call St 77554
Positano Rd 77550
Post Office St
200-4499 77550
5100-5199 77551
Post Office Rear St 77550
Princeton St 77554
Pruitt Dr 77554
Quayside Dr 77554
Quintana Cir, Ct, Dr &
Pl 77554
Ramsar Rd 77550
Randall Pl 77551
Reagor Way 77554
Rice St 77554
Rosewood Dr 77551
Royal Tern Ln 77554
Saladia St 77551
Sampan Dr 77554
San Fernando Dr 77550
San Jacinto Dr
1-99 77550
3200-4299 77554
San Marino Dr 77550
San Simeon Ct 77554
E & W Sand Hill Ct &
Dr 77554
Sandhill Crane Way 77554
Santa Fe Pl 77550
Sarna Ct 77550
Sausalito Dr 77554
Schaper Rd 77554
Schattel Ln 77554
Schwartz Dr 77554
Sea Isle 77554
Sea Grass Ln 77554
Sea Urchin 77554
Sealy St
600-4499 77550
5000-5399 77551
Sealy Rear St
600-4399 77550
5100-5199 77551
Seashore Dr 77554
Seaside Dr 77550
Seawall Blvd
1-4499 77550
4500-6900 77551
6902-8198 77551
8200-9599 77554

Seawall Rear Blvd 77550
Seawolf Pkwy 77554
Settegast Rd 77554
Shell Rd 77554
Sherman Blvd
4300-4499 77550
4500-5099 77551
Sherman Rear Blvd 77551
Shiraz Psge 77550
S Shore Dr 77551
S Shore Rear Dr 77551
Shores Dr 77554
Short Reach Dr 77554
Sias Dr 77551
E Silver Sands 77554
Skimmer St 77554
Skipper Dr 77554
Skymaster Rd 77554
Snowy Egret Dr 77554
N & S Sonny Ln 77554
Southern Cross 77554
Spanish Grant 77554
Sportsman Rd 77554
Spotted Sandpiper Dr 77554
Stella Mare Ln 77554
Stewart Ave 77551
Stewart Rd
5700-8099 77551
8200-14599 77554
Strand St 77550
Strand Rear St 77550
Sunbather Ln 77554
Sunny Ln 77554
Sunset Cir, Ct & Ln 77554
E Sunset Bay Dr 77554
Surf Dr 77554
Swan Dr 77551
Sycamore Dr 77551
Sydnor Ln 77554
Sylvia Dr 77551
Tahiti Rd 77554
Tamana Dr 77554
Tarpon Ave 77550
Teakwood Dr 77551
Teal Dr 77551
Teichman Rd 77554
Terminal Dr 77554
Termini San Luis Pass
Rd 77554
Tern Dr 77551
Texas Ave 77550
Texas Clipper Rd 77554
Tikal Ct 77554
Tiki Cir & Dr 77554
Todd Rd 77554
Tradewinds Dr 77554
Travel Air 77554
Travis Dr 77551
Travis Rear Dr 77551
Trout St 77550
Tuna St 77550
University Blvd 77550
University Rear Blvd 77550
E & W Ventura Dr 77554
Victory St 77551
Video Ln 77550
Virginia Point Dr 77554
Vista Rd 77554
Vista Bella 77554
Wahini St 77554
Walsh Ln 77554
Water Dr 77550
Weber Ave 77551
Weiss Dr 77551
Wentletrap 77554
Wern Dr 77554
Westerly Dr 77554
Wharf Rd 77550
Wharton Dr 77551
Wharton Rear Dr 77551
Whiting St 77550
Wilknox St 77551
Willet Ln 77554
Williams Dr 77551
Williamsburg Cir 77551
Willow Ln 77551

Wimcrest St 77551
Windlass Cir & Ct 77554
Windsong Way 77554
Windward Way 77554
Winnie St
400-4499 77550
4700-5399 77551
Winnie Rear St 77550
Woodrow Ave 77551
Woodrow Rear Ave 77551
Yale St 77554
Youpon Dr 77551
Yucca Dr 77551
Zingelmann Rd 77554

NUMBERED STREETS

1st St 77550
7 1/2 Mile Rd 77554
7 Mile Rd 77554
7th St 77550
7th Rear St 77550
8 Mile Rd 77554
8th St 77550
9 Mile Rd 77554
9th St 77550
10th St 77550
11th St 77550
12th St 77550
13th St 77550
13th Rear St 77550
14th St 77550
14th Rear St 77550
15th St 77550
15th Rear St 77550
16th St 77550
17th St 77550
18th St 77550
19th St 77550
19th Rear St 77550
20th St 77550
20th Rear St 77550
21st St 77550
21st Rear St 77550
22nd St 77550
22nd Rear St 77550
23rd St 77550
23rd Rear St 77550
24th St 77550
24th Rear St 77550
25th St
100-600 77550
601-2299 77550
601-601 77553
602-2298 77550
25th Rear St 77550
26th St 77550
26th Rear St 77550
27th St 77550
27th Rear St 77550
28th St 77550
28th Rear St 77550
29th St 77550
29th Rear St 77550
30th St 77550
30th Rear St 77550
31st St 77550
31st Rear St 77550
32nd St 77550
32nd Rear St 77550
33rd St 77550
33rd Rear St 77550
34th St 77550
34th Rear St 77550
35th St 77550
35th Rear St 77550
36th St 77550
36th Rear St 77550
37th St 77550
37th Rear St 77550
38th St 77550
38th Rear St 77550
39th St 77550
39th Rear St 77550
40th St 77550
40th Rear St 77550

41st Rear St 77550
42nd St 77550
43rd St 77550
43rd Rear St 77550
44th St 77550
44th Rear St 77550
45th St 77550
45th Rear St 77550
46th St 77551
47th St 77551
47th Rear St 77551
48th St 77551
48th Rear St 77551
49th St 77551
49th Rear St 77551
50th St 77551
51st St 77551
51st Rear St 77551
52nd St 77551
52nd Rear St 77551
53rd St 77551
54th St 77551
54th Rear St 77551
55th St 77551
55th Rear St 77551
56th St 77551
57th St 77551
57th Rear St 77551
59th St 77551
59th Rear St 77551
60th St 77551
61st St 77551
62nd St 77551
62nd Rear St 77551
63rd St 77551
63rd Rear St 77551
64th St 77551
64th Rear St 77551
65th St 77551
67th St 77551
68th St 77551
69th St 77551
71st St 77551
71st Rear St 77551
72nd St 77551
72nd Rear St 77551
73rd St 77551
73rd Rear St 77551
74th St 77551
75th St 77551
77th St 77554
80th St 77551
81st St 77554
3400-3699 77551
83rd St 77554
85th St 77554
87th St 77554
89th St 77554
89th 1/2 St 77554
91st St 77554
93rd St 77554
10 Mile Rd 77554
103rd St 77554
105th St 77554
11 Mile Rd 77554
12 Mile Rd 77554

GARLAND TX

General Delivery 75040

POST OFFICE BOXES MAIN OFFICE STATIONS AND BRANCHES

Box No.s
450001 - 455734 75045
460001 - 469046 75046
472001 - 479510 75047
493501 - 498898 75049

NAMED STREETS

Abbey Ct 75044
Aberdeen Dr 75044
Abingdon Dr 75043
Ablon Trl 75043
Acorn Green Cir & Dr 75043
Action St 75042
Adarlerl Dr 75040
Alamo Ln 75040
Aldenham Dr 75043
Alderney Dr 75043
Alderon Ln 75044
Alderwood Dr 75044
Aldwick Dr 75043
Alec Dr 75043
Alexandria Ave 75040
Allegheny Trail Ln 75043
Allen St 75040
Almeta Dr 75041
Alonsdale Dr 75040
Alta Oaks Dr 75043
Altair Dr 75044
Alto Dr 75040
Alyssum Ct 75040
E & W Amberway Ln 75040
Ambrose Ct 75040
Amelia Ct 75040
Amherst Dr 75042
Amy Ave 75043
Anatole Ct 75043
Anchor Bay Dr 75043
Anchor Cove Cir 75043
Ancilla Dr 75042
Andover Dr 75041
Andrea Ln 75040
Angel Fire Dr 75044
Angelina Dr 75040
Angle Ridge Cir 75043
Anita Dr 75041
Ann St 75040
Annette Ct 75044
Annmarie Ct 75040
Antares Cir 75044
Apache Dr 75043
Apollo Ct 75044
Apollo Rd
102-198 75040
200-1399 75040
1401-1499 75040
1700-1798 75044
1800-2499 75044
2501-3499 75044
E Apollo Rd 75040
Appalachia Dr 75044
Apple Valley Dr 75043
Appollo Villa Rd 75044
Aquarius Cir 75044
Arapaho Rd 75044
Arbor Trl 75043
Arbor Creek Dr 75040
Arbor Gate Dr 75040
Arborview Dr 75043
Arcady Dr 75041
Archery Ln 75044
Arendale Dr 75040
Aries Dr 75044
Armor Cir 75044
Armstrong Dr 75040
Arrow Ln 75042
Arrowcrest Ct & Ln 75044
Arrowhead Cir & Dr 75043
Asbury Park 75044
Ashglen Dr 75043
Ashley Dr 75041
Ashville Dr 75041
Ashwood Dr 75041
Aspen Ln 75044
Asset St 75042
Aster Dr 75043
Atherton Dr 75043
Atlanta Cir & Dr 75041
Auburn St 75041
Audrey Dr 75040
Augusta Dr 75041
Auriga Dr 75044
Austin St 75040
Autumn Trl 75040
Autumnwood Ln 75044
Avalon Dr 75043
E & W Avenue 75040
E & W Avenue A 75040
E Avenue B 75040
W Avenue B
100-999 75040
W Avenue B
1001-1199 75040
1400-1499 75042
1501-1799 75042
W Avenue C 75040
E & W Avenue D 75040
E & W Avenue F 75040
E & W Avenue G 75040
Avon Dr 75041
Axe Dr 75041
Azalea Ln 75043
Azalea St 75040
Baccarat Dr 75043
Bachman Blvd 75043
Bahamas Dr 75044
Baldcypress Ct 75043
Ballinger Dr 75041
Ballybunion Cir 75044
Balsam Fir Dr 75043
Baltusrol Cir 75044
E & W Bancroft Dr 75040
Bandera Ln 75040
Bankhead St 75040
Barcelona Dr & Pl 75043
Barclay Ln 75044
Bard Ct & Dr 75040
Bardfield Ave 75041
Barger St 75040
N & S Barnes Dr 75042
Baron Dr 75040
Barrington Ln 75043
Baruna Cir 75043
Basil St 75040
Baskerville Dr 75043
Bass Pro Dr 75043
Basswood Trl 75040
Bay Vw 75043
Bay Island Dr 75043
Bay Shore Dr 75040
Bay Valley Dr 75043
Bayberry Ln 75043
Bayport Dr 75043
Beacon Hill Ct 75043
Beasley Dr 75041
Beaus Way 75043
Beaver Run 75044
Becket Ct 75044
Becky Ct 75044
Beebalm Ln 75040
Belinda Ct 75040
Belita Dr 75041
Bella Dr 75040
Bellaire Dr 75040
Bellbrook Ln 75040
Bellerive Ct 75044
Bellmeade Dr 75040
Bellwood Dr 75040
Belmont Dr 75040
Belt Line Rd
100-698 75040
700-1399 75040
1400-2345 75044
2346-3098 75044
2346-2346 75045
2347-3499 75044
Ben Davis Rd 75040
Bending Oaks Trl 75044
Bent Bow Dr 75044
Bent Creek Dr 75040
Bentley Dr 75043
Benton St 75042
Bergen Dr 75040
Berkeley Ct 75043
Berkner Dr 75044
Bermuda Dr 75044
N & S Bernice Dr 75042
Berrywood Cir 75040
Beth Ct 75044
Bethany Dr 75042
Betty Jo Ln 75042
Beverly Dr 75040
Big Ben Ln 75044
Big Oaks Dr 75044
Big Springs Rd 75044
Billie Johnson Ln 75044
Birchwood Dr 75043
Biscay Dr 75043
Bishops Bridge Dr 75043
Bison Ct 75044
Bitter Creek Dr 75040
Black Swan Cir 75044
Black Walnut Dr 75044
Blackhawk Ln 75043
Blacksmith Dr 75044
Blair Dr 75040
Blakes Way 75042
Blanco Cir & Ln 75040
Blazing Star Dr 75043
Blenheim Dr 75043
Blossom Cir & Rd 75041
Blue Bonnet Cir 75040
Blue Cove Dr 75043
Blue Creek Dr 75043
Blue Flax Dr 75043
Blue Oak Dr 75043
Blue Sage Ln 75040
Bluebird Ln 75042
Bluebonnet Trl 75043
Blueridge Ln 75042
Bluestem Dr 75044
Bluewood Dr 75043
Bluffview Dr 75043
Bob White Dr 75040
Bobbie Ct & Ln 75042
Bobby Boyd Ln 75044
Bobtown Rd 75043
Boca Raton Dr 75043
Bois D Arc Ct 75042
Boisenberry Dr 75044
Bonanza Ln 75042
Bonita Dr 75041
Bonnie View Dr 75042
Bosque Dr 75040
Bowie St
800-1399 75040
1400-1699 75042
Boxwood Dr 75040
Brackett St 75040
Bradfield Dr 75042
Brae Loch 75044
Branch Dr 75041
Branch Hollow Cir & Dr 75043
Branch Oaks Dr 75043
E Brand Rd
100-299 75040
801-1597 75044
1599-1799 75044
1801-2599 75044
W Brand Rd 75040
Brandon Park Dr 75044
Brazos St 75041
Breanna Way 75040
Breeds Hill Rd 75040
Briar Way 75043
Briar Creek Cir 75044
Briar Hollow Ln 75043
Briar Knoll Cir & Dr 75043
Briarbrook Ln 75040
Briarcliff Dr 75043
Briarcrest Dr 75043
Briarglen Ct 75044
Briarmeadow Dr 75044
Briaroaks Dr 75044
Briarwood Dr 75041
Bridgeport Dr 75043
Bridle Path Ct 75044
Bridlewood Dr 75040
Bright Ct 75043
Brighton Ln 75043
Brightwood Dr 75043
Bristol Ct 75043
Brittany Dr 75040
Broadway Blvd
2500-3099 75041
3100-6499 75043
Broadway Commons 75043
Broken Bow Ln 75044
Bromley Ct 75043
Bromwich St 75040
Bronze St 75042
Brook Glen Dr 75044
Brook Meadow Dr 75043
Brook Tree Dr 75040
Brookcrest Dr & Pl 75040
Brookdale Cir & Dr 75040
Brookfield Dr 75040
Brookhollow Dr 75041
Brookport Dr 75043
Brooks St 75041
Brookshire Cir 75043
Brookside Dr 75042
Brookview Dr 75043
Brookwood Ln 75044
Browne Dr 75041
Bruce Dr 75043
Bryan Dr 75042
Buckboard Way 75044
Buckethorn Ct 75044
E Buckingham Rd 75040
W Buckingham Rd
101-797 75040
799-1299 75040
1301-1399 75040
1400-3500 75042
3502-4598 75042
Bucknell Dr 75042
Buena Vista Ave 75043
Buhler Dr 75040
N & S Bullock Dr 75042
Bungalow Dr 75043
Burdock Dr 75043
Burgundy St 75040
Burke Dr 75040
Burlingame Dr 75043
Burnett Ct 75044
Burning Tree Ln 75042
Buttercup Cir 75040
Butterfly Ln 75041
Buttermilk Way 75044
Butternut Dr 75044
Buttonwood Ln 75043
Cabana Ln 75042
Cactus Ct 75044
Caddys Cir 75043
Caladium Ct 75040
Calaveras Cove Dr 75040
Caldwell Dr 75041
Caledonia Cv 75043
Callejo Rd 75044
Calm Meadow Ct 75044
Calvin Dr 75041
Cambridge Dr 75043
Camden Dr 75041
Cameo Ct 75043
Camilla Ln 75040
E & W Campbell Rd 75044
Candlestick Dr 75043
Candlewood Ln 75041
Canis Cir 75044
Canyon Creek Dr 75042
Capella Cir 75044
Capstone Ln 75043
Captains Pl 75043
Caravaca Dr 75043
Cardigan St 75040
Cardinal Ln 75042
Carlton Ct & Dr 75043
Carmen Dr 75041
Carnaby Ln 75044
Carnation Ct 75040
Carney Dr 75041
Carnoustie Ct 75044
Carolina Ct 75044
E & W Carolyn Dr 75041
Carpenter Dr 75040
Carriage Ln 75043
Carriagehouse Ln 75040
Carrington Dr 75043
Carroll Cir, Dr & Way 75041
Cartman Rd 75040
Caruth Dr 75040
Carver Dr 75040
Carya Trl 75044
Casa Vista Cir & Dr 75043
Casalita Dr 75040
Cascade Dr 75041
Cashmere Dr 75041
Castle Dr 75040
Castle Rock Ln 75044
Castleford Ln 75040
Castleglen Dr 75043
Castleman Cove Dr 75040
Castleview Ln 75044
Castlewood Dr 75040
Catalpa St 75044
Cavalier Dr 75042
Ce Ora Dr 75042
Cedar Dr 75040
Cedar Brook Dr 75040
Cedar Cove Dr 75040
Cedar Creek Dr 75043
Cedar Elm Ln 75043
Cedar Sage Dr 75040
Cedarcrest Dr 75042
Cedarview Dr 75040
Cedarwood Dr 75040
E & W Celeste Dr 75041
Centaurus Dr 75044
Centennial Dr 75042
E Centerville Rd
100-1999 75041
2200-2798 75040
2800-2900 75040
2902-3898 75040
W Centerville Rd 75041
Century Park Dr 75040
Chablis St 75040
Chads Crk 75043
Chadwick Ln 75044
Chaha Rd 75043
Champion Ct 75043
Chandler Dr 75040
Channel Isle Dr 75043
Chariot Ln 75044
Charles Dr 75041
Charleston Dr 75041
Charlotte Dr 75041
Charter Dr 75043
Chelsea Way 75044
Cherryhill Ln 75042
Cherrywood Dr 75040
Chesapeake Dr 75043
Chesterfield Rd 75043
Chestnut Pl 75043
Chevy Chase Dr 75043
Cheyenne Trl 75044
E & W Chico Dr 75041
Chicosa Trl 75043
Chimneyrock Trl 75043
Chinaberry Dr 75043
Chisholm Trl 75042
Christie Cir & Ln 75044
Christina Ln 75043
Chumley Rd 75044
Churchill Way 75044
Citadel Dr 75040
Clack Dr 75044
Clamdigger Way 75043
Clara Barton Blvd 75042
Claridge Ter 75043
Clarissa Pl 75040
Clark St 75040
Classic Dr 75042
Claymore Ave 75043
Clear Creek Dr 75044
Clear Point Dr 75041
Clear Ridge Dr 75044
Clear Springs Cir & Pkwy 75044
Clearfield Dr 75043
Clearhaven Dr 75040
Clearwood Dr 75044
Clemson Dr 75042
Cliff Dr 75042
Cliff View Ln 75044
Cliffwood Dr 75043
Clinton St 75040
Clover Ln 75043
Clover Meadow Dr 75043
Clover Valley Dr 75043
Cloverdale Ln 75043
Club Cir 75043
Club Country Dr 75043
Club Creek Blvd, Cir & Ct 75043
Club Hill Dr 75043
Club Meadow Dr
2200-2599 75041
2600-3199 75043
Club Oaks Ct 75042
Club Town Dr 75044
Clubview Dr 75044
Coastal Dr 75043
Cobblestone Ln 75042
Colbath Dr 75040
Colchester St 75040
Cole St 75040
Coleta Pl 75040
Colgate Cir, Ct & Ln 75042
Colleen Dr 75043
College Ave 75042
Collingwood Dr 75043
Collins Blvd 75044
Colonel Cir & Dr 75043
Colonial Dr 75043
Colony Dr 75040
Columbia Blvd & Cir 75043
Columbine Dr 75043
Comanche Trl 75043
Commerce St 75040
Commercial St 75040
Commonwealth Dr 75043
Concho Dr 75040
Concord Dr 75042
Coneflower Dr 75040
Connie Dr 75043
Copper St 75042
Copperleaf Dr 75040
Coral Ridge Dr 75044
Corley Dr 75040
Cornell Dr 75042
Cornerstone Dr 75043
Corona Dr 75044
Coronado Dr 75043
Cortez Dr 75041
Cotton Gum Rd 75044
Cottonwood Ct 75044
Country Ct 75040
Country Club Cir 75043
Country Club Pkwy
2300-2599 75041
2600-2899 75043
N Country Club Rd 75040
S Country Club Rd
2000-2599 75041
2600-5399 75043
S Country Club Rd E 75040
S Country Club Rd W 75040
Country Dell Dr 75040
Country Hollow Ln 75040
Country Oaks Dr 75040
Country Valley Rd
2200-2599 75041
2600-2899 75043
Country View Ln 75043
Court Pl 75041
Courtenay Pl 75040
Courtland Pl 75040
Courtside Dr 75044
Cove Dr 75040
Covewood Dr 75044
Covington Dr 75040
Coyle St 75040
Crabtree St 75040
Cranbrook Park 75043
Cranford Dr 75041
Crawfish Ln 75043
Creek Ct 75043
Creek Xing 75040
Creek Bend Cv 75044
Creek Meadow Ln 75040
Creek Valley Dr 75040
Creekbend Dr 75044

Creekdale Dr 75044
Creekridge Ct, Ln & Pl 75043
Creekside Ct 75040
Creekview Dr 75043
Creekway Dr 75043
Creekwood Dr 75044
Creighton Dr 75044
Crest Park Dr 75042
Crestcove Dr 75042
Crested Cove Dr 75040
Crestedge Dr 75044
Cresthaven Dr 75040
Cresthill Ln 75043
Crestmeade Dr 75040
Crestmont Dr 75040
Crestpoint Ln 75043
Crestridge Dr 75042
Creststone Dr 75040
Crestview Dr 75042
Crestwood Dr 75043
Cripple Creek Dr 75041
Crist Rd 75040
Crockett St
800-1399 75040
1400-1999 75042
Crooked Crk 75043
Cross Courts Dr 75040
Cross Timbers Ln 75044
Crossbow Ln 75044
Crosslands Dr 75040
Crown Cir 75044
Crystal Ln 75043
Crystal Creek Ln 75040
Crystal Falls Dr 75044
Cuero Dr 75040
Cumberland Cir 75041
Cumberland Dr
1300-1999 75040
2000-2899 75041
Curtis Dr 75040
Cypress Point Dr 75043
Dabney Ct 75040
Dairy Rd
601-897 75040
899-1199 75040
1201-1799 75040
2000-2800 75041
2802-2998 75041
Daisy Ct 75040
Dakota Dr 75043
Dale Dr 75041
Dalewood Trl 75040
Danbury Dr 75040
Dandelion Dr 75043
Dandridge Cir 75040
Daniel Dr 75041
Danville Dr 75042
Dartmoor Ln 75040
Dartmouth St 75043
E & W Daugherty Dr 75041
Daventry Dr 75040
David Dr 75043
Davidson Cir & Dr 75044
Davis Blvd 75042
Dawn Dr 75040
Daytona Dr 75043
Dearborn Ln 75040
Debra Ct 75044
Deep Canyon Dr 75043
Deepwood Dr 75040
Deer Brook Rd 75044
Deer Creek Ct 75040
Deer Meadow Dr 75044
Degge Cir 75040
Delano Dr 75041
Dell Oak Dr 75040
Dellwood Dr 75040
Delmar Dr
1000-1999 75040
2000-2099 75041
Delores Dr 75040
Delray Dr 75043
Denmark Dr 75040
Dent St
800-1399 75040
1400-1699 75042

Denton Dr 75041
Desert Rose St 75040
Deville Cir 75043
Devonshire Dr 75041
Devonwood Dr 75041
Diamond Oaks Dr 75044
Diana Dr 75043
Dillon Dr 75040
Distribution Dr 75041
Dividend Dr 75042
Dixie Dr 75041
Dogwood Dr 75040
Dollye Dr 75041
Don Gomez Ln 75043
Donald Dr 75041
Donegal Ln 75044
Dorado St 75040
Doral Pl 75043
Dorchester Ln 75040
Doss Dr 75042
Douglas Dr 75041
Dove Dr 75040
Dove Meadow Dr 75043
Dover Dr 75043
Downs Way 75040
Drake Ln 75043
Drawbridge Ln 75044
Drexel Dr 75043
Driftwood Cir 75040
Dublin Dr 75044
Duchess Dr 75040
Duck Creek Dr 75043
Duck Creek Pkwy 75044
Duke St 75043
Dukeswood Dr 75040
Dumas Trl 75043
Dunrobin 75044
Durango Dr 75043
Dutch Elm Ct 75044
Eagle Nest Dr 75044
Eagle Pass Dr 75040
Eastern Hills Dr 75043
Eastern Star Dr 75040
Eastgate Dr 75041
Easton Meadows Dr 75043
Eastpark Dr 75044
Eastside St 75040
Eastview Dr 75040
Easy St 75042
Echo Dr 75040
Eden Dr 75043
Eden Crest Dr 75042
Edgebrook Dr 75040
Edgecliff Dr 75043
Edgefield Cir & Dr 75040
Edgemere Cir, Ct &
Dr 75043
Edgemont Dr 75042
Edgewood Dr 75042
Edinburgh Way 75040
Edna Smith Dr 75040
Elderberry Dr 75043
Eldorado Dr 75042
Eleanor Ct 75042
Elizabeth Dr 75042
Ellinced Dr 75042
Elm Creek Dr 75040
Elm Ridge Ln 75044
Elmcrest Cir 75040
Elmhurst Dr 75041
Elmwood Ct, Dr & Pl 75043
Ember Lee Dr 75040
Embercrest Ln 75044
Emberwood Dr 75043
Emerson Dr 75044
Enchanted Cir 75044
Enclave Ct 75040
Enfield Dr 75043
English Cir & Dr 75041
English Oak Dr 75043
Escabosa Dr 75040
Esquire Ln 75044
Eton Pl 75042
Evelyn Dr 75042
Evergreen St
1700-1799 75040
1801-1999 75040
2000-2199 75041
Ewing Dr 75040
Excalibur Cir & Dr 75044
Executive Dr 75041
Exeter Dr 75043
Express Dr 75041
Fair Meadow Dr 75044
Fair Oaks Dr 75040
Fairbanks Dr 75043
Faircove Cir 75043
Faircrest Dr 75040
Fairfax Dr 75041
Fairfield Dr 75043
Fairhaven Dr 75040
Fairlake Dr 75043
Fairlands Dr 75040
Fairview St 75040
Fairway Cir 75043
Fairway Lakes Ct &
Dr 75044
Fairway Meadows Dr 75044
Fairwood Dr 75040
Falcon Ct 75040
Fall Creek Ct 75044
Fallbrook Dr 75043
Farrington Dr 75044
Fawn Ridge Trl 75042
Fern Dr 75040
Fern Glen Dr 75043
Fernwood Dr 75042
Ferris Rd 75044
Field Knoll Dr 75043
Fieldcrest Cir, Ct & Dr 75042
Fieldside Dr 75043
Fieldview Dr 75044
Firecrest Dr 75044
Fireside Ct 75044
Firestone Dr 75044
Firewheel Dr 75044
Firewheel Pkwy 75040
Fitchburg Ave 75044
Fitzgerald Ct 75044
Flagstone Dr 75044
Flameleaf St 75044
Flamingo Ln 75042
Flarity Ln 75044
Fletcher Dr 75044
Flook St 75040
Flores Dr 75041
Foliage Dr 75043
Fondren Dr 75043
Forbes Dr 75040
Ford St 75040
Fordham Dr 75042
Forest Ln S 75042
Forest Bend Ct 75040
Forest Center Plz 75042
Forest Cove Ln 75040
Forest Creek Dr 75043
N & S Forest Crest Dr 75042
Forest Gate Dr 75042
Forest Hills Cir 75044
Forest Park Dr 75040
Forest Point Dr 75043
Forest Ridge Dr 75042
Forestbrook Dr 75040
Forrest Springs Cv 75043
Fountain Hills Dr 75044
Foxboro Dr 75044
Foxcroft Ln 75044
Foxe Basin Dr 75040
Foxglove Ct 75040
Foxtrail Dr 75044
Frances Dr 75042
Francisco Dr 75044
Freeman Dr 75040
Freemont Dr 75040
Freeport Dr 75043
Friar Ln 75040
Frio Cir & Ln 75040
Frontier Rd 75043
Fulton Dr 75044
Galaxie Cir 75041
Galaxie Dr 75041
Galaxie Rd 75044

Gallahad Dr 75044
Galway Dr 75044
Gannet Ln 75043
Garden Dr 75040
Garden Gate Cir 75043
Gardenia Dr 75041
Garfield St 75042
N Garland Ave
100-5499 75040
5800-7598 75044
S Garland Ave
111-197 75040
199-1999 75040
2000-3699 75041
Garret Ct 75043
Garrison Way 75040
Garvon St 75040
Gary Dr 75041
Gate Ridge Cir 75043
Gateway Dr 75040
Gatewood Rd 75043
Gautney St 75040
Gayle Dr 75044
Geary St 75043
Gelene Ct 75040
Gemini Dr 75040
Geneva Ct & Dr 75040
George Brown Dr 75043
Georgetown Dr 75043
Glacier Ln 75042
Gladiola Ct 75040
Glen Abbey Ct 75044
Glen Canyon Dr 75040
Glen Heights Dr 75044
Glen Hollow Dr 75044
Glen Meadow Ct 75044
Glen Vista Dr 75044
Glenbrook Cir 75041
Glenbrook Ct 75041
N Glenbrook Dr 75040
S Glenbrook Dr
101-597 75040
599-699 75040
701-1899 75040
2000-3899 75041
Glenbrook Meadows
Dr 75040
Glencrest Ln 75040
Glendale Dr 75041
Glenfield Dr 75040
Glengarry Dr 75043
Glenhaven Cir & Dr 75042
Glenmoor Dr 75043
Glenrose Dr 75042
Glenshire Dr 75043
Glenview Cir 75040
Glenville Dr 75042
Glenwick Ln 75040
Glenwood Cir 75042
Gloria Dr 75042
Glouchester Dr
1100-1198 75040
1200-1399 75040
1400-1899 75044
Glynn Dr 75040
Gold St 75042
Golden Meadow Dr 75044
Golden Oaks Dr 75044
Goldenrod Dr 75043
Goldfinch Ln 75042
Goliad Cir & Dr 75042
Goodwin Dr 75042
Goose Creek Pkwy 75040
Gorham Dr 75044
Grace Dr 75043
Grader St 75041
Graham Dr 75043
Granada Dr 75043
Grand Oak Dr 75044
Grand Villa Ln 75044
Grant St 75042
Grantham Dr 75043
Grasmere St 75040
Graybar Dr 75040
Graystone Dr 75043
Green Apple Dr 75044

Green Meadow Dr 75044
Green Oaks Dr 75040
Green Pond Dr 75040
Green Valley Dr 75043
Greenbriar Dr 75043
Greenbrook Dr 75043
Greencove Dr 75040
Greenfield Cir 75040
Greenhaven Dr 75043
Greenleaf Ct 75044
Greensboro Cir 75041
Greenspring Cir 75044
Greentree Ln 75042
Greenview Cir & Dr 75044
Greenway Dr 75041
Greenwood Dr 75041
Gregory St 75041
Greyson Dr 75043
Grinnell Dr 75043
Grinstad Dr 75040
Grove Dr 75040
Grovetree Ln 75043
Grovewood Dr 75043
Guildford St
1100-1399 75040
1400-1999 75044
Gulfport Dr 75043
Guthrie Rd 75043
Hackberry Ln 75042
Hamlett Ln 75043
Hampden Dr 75043
Hampshire Dr 75040
Hannah Ln 75040
Hanover Dr 75042
Harbor Town Dr 75044
Hardwick Dr 75044
Hardy Cir, Dr & Way 75041
Harpers Ferry Ln 75043
Harris Dr 75041
Hart St 75040
Hartford Dr 75043
E & W Harvard Dr 75041
Harvest Run 75040
Haskell Dr 75040
Hastings Dr 75042
Hattiesburg Ln 75044
Havencrest Ct 75040
Havenway Dr 75043
Havenwood Ln 75043
Hawaii Dr 75044
Hawk Ct 75040
Hawthorne Dr 75041
Hayman Dr 75043
Hazelwood Dr & Pl 75044
Hearthcrest Dr 75044
Hearthside Ln 75044
Hearthstone Ct 75040
Heather Dr 75042
Heather Glen Dr 75043
Heather Hill Dr 75044
Heather Ridge Ln 75040
Heathercrest Dr 75044
Heathers Moor 75043
Hedgeway Cir 75044
Helen St 75040
Hemlock Dr 75041
Henderson Cir 75040
Herald Dr 75044
Heritage Cir & Dr 75043
Herrmann Dr 75041
Hiawatha Way 75043
Hibiscus Dr 75040
Hickory Trl 75040
Hickory Bend Dr 75044
Hidalgo Ct 75043
Hidden Ct 75043
Hidden Creek Rd 75043
Hidden Springs Ln 75044
High Bluff Dr 75041
High Country Dr 75041
High Grove Dr 75041
High Hill Pl 75041
High Hollow Dr 75041
High Meadow Cir & Dr 75040
High Mesa Dr 75041
High Plateau Dr 75044

High Point Cir 75041
High Star Dr 75041
High Summit Dr 75041
High Valley Dr 75041
Highbrook Ct 75044
Highcrest Dr 75043
Highdale Dr 75041
Highgate Pl 75044
Highland Creek Cir 75040
Highmont Dr & Pl 75041
Highridge Dr 75043
Hightower Dr 75041
Hightrail Ln 75043
Highway 66 75040
Highwood Dr & Pl 75041
Hiland St 75040
Hill Creek Dr 75043
Hillcrest Dr 75040
Hillsdale Ln 75042
Hillside Ct & Ln 75043
Hilltop Dr 75042
Hilton Head Dr 75044
Hockaday Ave 75043
Holbrook Dr 75040
Holden Ct 75044
Holford Rd 75044
Holland Dr 75040
Hollow Way 75041
Hollow Bend Ln 75043
Hollow Creek Ct 75040
Holly Dr 75040
Holly Tree Trl 75044
Hollydale Dr 75044
Holm Dr 75041
Holy Cross Ln 75044
Homer Johnson Ln 75044
Homestead Pl 75044
Honey Hill Dr 75040
Honeysuckle Dr 75041
Hopewell Dr 75043
Hopkins St 75040
Horizon Dr 75043
Horseshoe Dr 75040
Housley Dr 75043
Howard Ln 75044
Hubbard Dr 75040
Hudson Dr 75043
Huntington Dr 75042
Huskey St 75041
Idlewood Dr 75040
Independence Dr 75043
Indian Creek Ct 75040
Indian Hills Dr 75044
Indian School Rd 75044
Indian Trail Ln 75043
Industrial Ln 75041
Innsbrook Dr 75044
N & S International Rd 75042
E & W Interstate 30 75043
Intervale Dr 75043
Intrepid Dr 75043
Inverness Dr 75040
Inwood Blvd 75042
Iroquois Dr 75043
Island Ct 75043
Ivanhoe Ln 75044
Ivanridge Cir & Ln 75044
Ivy Way 75043
Jack Franzen Dr 75043
Jackson Dr 75041
Jacobson Rd 75042
Jacqueline Dr 75042
Jade Ct 75040
Jamaica Pl 75044
James Dr 75042
James Good Ln 75043
Jamestown Dr 75043
Jamie Dr 75040
Janwood Ln 75044
Jarrell Cir 75042
Jasmine Ln 75044
Jennifer Dr 75042
Jenny Ln 75042
Jeremes Lndg 75043
Jessica Dr 75040
Jester Dr 75044

Jo Ann Dr 75042
John Glenn Dr 75040
John Sharp Cir 75044
Jon Boat Dr 75043
Joyce Dr 75040
Julia Ln 75042
June Dr 75040
N Jupiter Rd
100-398 75042
400-1999 75042
2000-7698 75044
S Jupiter Rd
114-198 75042
200-1799 75042
1801-1999 75042
2000-3299 75041
Justice Ln 75042
Kaiser St 75040
Karen St 75043
Kathleen Ct 75044
Katy St 75040
Kazak 75042
Kazak St 75041
Keele Dr 75041
E Keen Dr 75041
Kelly Cir 75044
Kelso Ct, Ln & Pl 75043
Kensington Ct 75040
Kent Brown Rd 75044
Kentcroft Dr 75043
E & W Kenwood Cir, Dr
& Way 75041
Kerry Ln 75043
Kettering Dr 75043
Key Bnd 75043
Key Colony Dr 75043
Key West Dr 75044
Keystone St 75041
Kilchurn 75044
Kilkee Ct 75044
Kimberly Dr 75040
King Ln 75042
King Arthur Dr 75044
Kingfisher Rd 75043
Kings Rd 75042
Kings Row 75043
Kingsbridge Cir 75040
Kingsbridge Ct 75040
Kingsbridge Dr
100-1399 75040
1400-1899 75044
E Kingsbridge Dr 75040
Kingsbury Dr 75040
E & W Kingsley Rd 75041
Kingston Pl 75043
Kingswood Dr 75040
N & S Kirby St 75042
Kirkridge Pl 75044
Kirkwood Dr 75041
Kite Dr 75043
Knight Ln 75042
Knighthood Ln 75044
Knights Haven Ln 75044
Knightsbridge Ct & Ln 75043
Knob Hill Dr 75043
Knoll Point Dr 75043
Knollridge Dr 75043
Kristin Ct 75044
Kynn Dr 75041
La Costa Ct 75044
La Fawn Cir 75043
La Jolla Dr 75043
La Prada Dr 75043
Lacewood Dr 75044
Ladyfern Way 75040
Ladywood Dr 75040
Laguna Dr 75043
Lake Dr 75040
Lake Bluff Dr 75043
Lake Forest Ct 75044
Lake Hollow Cir 75040
Lake Hubbard Pkwy 75043
Lake Shore Dr 75044
Lake Terrace Ct 75043
Lake Valley Dr 75040
Lakebreeze Dr 75043

Lakebrook Dr 75043
Lakecrest Dr 75043
Lakehill Dr 75043
Lakeland Park Dr 75043
Lakemere Dr 75041
Lakeridge Ct 75043
Lakeside Dr
1200-1399 75040
1400-2699 75042
Lakestone Ct 75044
Lakewalk 75040
Lakeway Dr 75043
Lakewood Dr
1300-1399 75040
1400-3299 75042
Lamesa Dr 75041
Lamont Dr 75040
Lancaster St 75044
Lancecrest Dr 75044
Lancelot Pl 75043
Lancer Ln 75044
Landa Dr 75042
Landershire Ln 75044
Lansdowne Dr 75040
Lantana Dr 75040
Larchbrook Dr 75043
Larchfield Dr 75042
Larchwood Cir 75040
Laredo Ln 75043
Largo Trl 75044
Lariat Ln 75042
Larkin Ln 75043
Larkspur Ct 75040
Larry Dr 75041
Las Palmas Ct 75043
Latham Dr 75044
Laura Dr 75040
Laurel Oaks Ct & Dr 75044
Lauren Ln 75043
Lavendale Ln 75040
Lavista Dr 75040
Lavon Dr 75040
Lawler Rd 75042
Lawndale Dr 75044
Lawrence Dr 75044
Lawson Dr 75042
Leameadow Dr 75043
Leatherwood Ln 75042
Lee St 75041
Leeds Ct 75043
Leesburg Dr 75043
Legend Dr 75040
Leicester St
1300-1399 75040
1400-1899 75044
Lemon Tree Ln 75043
Lena Ct & St 75040
Lennox Ln 75043
Leo Dr 75044
Leon Rd 75041
Lesa Ln 75042
Lewis Dr 75041
Lexington Dr 75041
Libra Dr 75044
Lilac Dr 75040
Lillian Ln 75040
Limerick Ln 75044
Limestone Ln 75040
Lincoln Ct 75041
Lincolnshire Dr 75043
E & W Linda Dr 75041
Linden Ln 75040
Lindenwood Ln 75042
Lipscomb St 75040
Lister Dr 75040
Little Ln 75043
Live Oak Dr 75040
Livenshire Dr 75041
Lo Chalmers Ln 75043
Lochmoor Ln 75044
Lochness Ln 75044
Lochwood Ct 75044
Locke Dr 75041
Locust Grove Rd 75043
Loma Dr 75040
Lombard St 75043
Lone Hollow Ct 75040
Lone Oak Trl 75044
Lone Pecan Dr 75040
Long Cv 75044
Longbeach Dr 75043
Longbow Dr 75044
Longcrest Dr 75043
Longhorn Trl 75043
Longleaf Dr 75042
Longridge Rd 75040
Lonnecker Dr 75041
Lookout Dr 75044
Lordsburg Dr 75040
Lore Way 75040
Los Santos Dr 75043
Lourock St 75040
Loving Dr 75043
Low Tide Dr 75043
Lucinda Dr 75040
Luna Ln 75044
Lupine Dr 75043
Lupton Dr 75044
Luther Ln 75043
Lynch Ln 75044
Lyndon B Johnson
Fwy 75041
Lynn Dr 75040
Lynnbrook Ln 75041
Lyons Rd 75043
Lyric Cir & Dr 75040
Macgregor Dr 75043
Mackey St 75040
Madera Dr 75040
Madison Ln 75040
Madrid Dr 75040
Magnolia Dr 75040
Mahogany Trl 75040
Maidstone Dr 75043
Main St 75040
Majestic Ct 75040
Malibu Dr 75043
Mallards Pond 75043
Manchester Dr 75041
Manitoba Dr 75040
Manor Dr 75041
Maple Dr
800-1399 75040
1400-3299 75042
Maple Glen Dr 75043
Mapleleaf Dr 75040
Mapleridge Dr 75044
Mapleview Dr 75042
March Ln 75042
Marcie Ct 75044
E & W Marguerita Dr 75040
Marie Curie Dr 75042
Marigold Dr 75041
Marilee Dr 75043
Marina Cv & Dr 75043
Marion Dr 75042
Maritime Cv 75043
Market St 75041
Marketplace Dr
1301-1897 75041
1899-1900 75041
1902-1998 75041
4800-5499 75043
Marlbourough Ct 75043
Marquis Dr 75042
Marriott Ln 75040
Mars Cir, Ct & Dr 75040
Marsden Ct 75042
Martie Ln 75043
Martin David Way 75042
Martindale Dr 75043
Marvin Loving Dr 75043
Mary Jane Ln 75043
Marydale Rd 75041
Matador Dr 75042
Matterhorn Dr 75044
Mayapple Dr 75043
Maydelle Ln 75042
Mayfield Ave 75041
Mayflower Dr 75043
Mccallum Dr 75042
Mccartney Ln 75043
Mcclary St 75040
Mccormick St 75040
Mccree Rd 75041
Mcdivitt Dr 75040
Mcdonald Cir, Dr &
Way 75041
Mcintosh Dr 75040
Mckenzie Ln 75043
Mckinley St 75042
Mclemore Dr 75040
Meadow Ct 75040
Meadow Ln 75040
Meadow Way 75042
Meadow Flower Ln 75043
Meadow Glen Dr 75044
Meadow Oaks Dr 75043
Meadow Park Dr 75040
Meadow Vista Ln & Pl 75043
Meadowbrook Dr
1200-1399 75040
1400-1699 75042
Meadowcove Cir 75043
Meadowcreek Ct & Ln 75043
Meadowcrest Dr 75042
Meadowdale Cir 75043
Meadowgate Dr 75040
Meadowhill Dr 75043
Meadowood Dr 75040
Meadowridge Dr 75044
Meadowside Cir, Ct &
Dr 75043
Meadowview Cir, Ct &
Dr 75043
Meandering Way 75040
Means Farm Rd 75044
Medical Plaza Dr 75044
Medina Dr 75041
Medio Dr 75040
Melissa Ln 75040
Melody Ln 75042
Melrose Cir 75042
Melrose St
800-1399 75040
1400-1999 75042
Menlo Park Dr 75043
Mercury Dr 75040
Mercy Ct 75043
Meredith Ln 75042
Meridian Way 75040
Merlin Dr 75043
Merrimac Trl 75043
Merritt Dr 75041
Mesa Ct 75040
Metairie Ct 75040
Miami Dr 75043
Michael St 75040
Michael Ann Dr 75042
Middle Glen Dr 75043
Milford Ave 75044
Milky Way 75040
Mill Xing 75040
Mill Branch Dr 75040
Mill Creek Rd 75044
Mill Pond Cir & Rd 75044
Mill River Dr 75043
Mill Spring Dr 75040
Mill Wood Ln 75040
Millay Blvd 75041
Miller Park N 75042
Miller Park S 75042
E Miller Rd 75041
W Miller Rd 75041
Miller Park Dr 75042
Mills Rd 75040
Millwick St 75044
Mimosa Dr 75040
Mint Dr 75043
Mira Dr 75044
Mission Dr 75042
Misty Way 75040
Mobile Dr 75041
Mockingbird Ln 75042
Monarch Dr 75040
Monica Dr 75041
Montclair Dr 75040
Monterrey Dr 75042
Monticello Ct 75043
Montier Dr 75041
Moonglow Dr 75044
Moonlight Dr 75040
Moore St 75040
Morning Star Ln 75043
Morningside Dr
1700-1999 75042
2000-2599 75041
Morris Dr 75040
Morrison Cir, Ct, Dr &
Pl 75040
Moss Trl 75044
Mosswood Cir, Ct, Dr &
Way 75042
Mossy Glen Ct 75040
Moultrie Dr 75040
Mount Vernon Pl 75043
Mountain Ash Ct 75044
E & W Muirfield Rd 75044
Mulberry Dr 75043
Muriel Dr 75042
Murray Dr 75042
Museum Plaza Dr 75040
Mustang Ridge Rd 75044
Myers Dr 75043
Myers Meadows Dr 75043
Naaman Forest Blvd
4801-4999 75040
5401-5497 75044
5499-5700 75044
5702-6698 75044
Naaman School Rd 75040
Nancy Jane Cir 75043
Naples Dr 75040
Nash St
800-1399 75040
1400-1699 75042
National Cir, Ct, Dr &
Pl 75041
Navasota Dr 75040
Neal Dr 75040
Nebulus Dr 75044
Needham Dr 75044
Nesbit Ct & Dr 75041
Nettle Dr 75043
Newburyport Ave 75044
Newcastle Dr 75041
Newfield Ct 75044
Newgate Dr 75041
Newman St 75040
Newport Dr 75043
Niagara St 75041
Nicholson Rd 75042
Nickens Rd 75043
Nicole Ln 75040
Noble Ln 75044
Nona St 75040
Norfolk Ct & Dr 75044
Norma Dr 75042
North Ct 75044
Northlake Dr 75040
Northridge Dr 75043
Northshore Dr 75040
Northumberland Dr 75041
Northview Cir 75044
Northwest Hwy
900-2199 75041
4600-5499 75043
Northwind Ct & Ln 75040
Northwood Dr 75040
Norway Dr 75040
Norwich Dr 75043
Nottingham Dr 75041
Nova Dr 75044
Novel Cir, Ct, Dr & Pl 75040
Nueces Dr 75040
Nutmeg Ln 75044
O Banion Rd 75043
O Henry Dr 75042
O Malley Ct 75044
O Phelan Ln 75044
O Ryans Cir 75044
O Shannon Ln 75044
Oak St 75040
Oak Bend Ln 75040
Oak Creek Ct 75040
Oak Forest Dr 75042
Oak Grove Cir 75040
Oak Hill Dr 75043
Oak Meadow Cir 75040
Oak Point Dr 75044
Oak Springs Dr 75044
Oak Tree Ln 75043
Oakcrest Dr 75044
Oakglen Dr 75040
Oakhurst Trl 75044
Oakland Ave 75041
Oakmont Ln 75043
Oakridge Cir 75040
Oaks Trl 75043
Oakwood Dr 75043
E Oates Rd
100-398 75043
400-500 75043
501-999 75043
501-501 75049
502-1498 75043
W Oates Rd 75043
Oceanport Dr 75043
Old Mill Run
1300-1499 75042
1501-1899 75042
2001-2099 75044
Old North Rd 75044
Old Orchard Rd 75041
Old Pecan Way 75043
Oldgate Ln 75042
Onion Creek Dr 75044
Ontario Dr 75040
Orchard Trl 75040
Orchard Ridge Dr 75043
Oriole Ln 75042
Oslo Dr 75040
Osprey Ln 75044
Overbrook Ct 75043
Overcrest Dr 75043
Overglen Dr 75043
Overhill Dr 75041
Overland Dr 75040
Overview Ln 75044
Oxford Park 75043
Ozark Trail Ln 75043
Palm Desert Dr 75044
Palm Valley Dr 75043
Palo Alto Dr 75043
Palo Duro Dr 75040
Palomino Ln 75043
Pamela Pl 75044
Paradise Cv 75043
Paris Dr 75040
Park Ave 75042
Park Cir 75044
Park East Cir & Dr 75043
Park Forest Dr 75042
Park Hill Rd 75043
Park Meadow Ct 75043
Parkcrest Dr 75041
Parker Cir & Rd 75040
Parkhaven Dr 75043
Parkhurst Dr 75040
Parkmont Dr 75041
Parkrise Ct 75044
Parkside Dr 75040
Parkview Dr 75043
Parkway Dr 75040
Partridge Pl 75044
Patrice Dr 75041
Patricia Ln
1200-1999 75042
2000-2899 75041
Patton Dr
1600-1999 75042
2000-2099 75041
Paul St 75043
Peace Rose Ave 75040
Peaceful Dr 75043
Peaceway Dr 75043
Peach Tree Ln 75041
Peakwood Dr 75044
Pear Tree Ln 75042
Pearl Trl 75044
Pebble Beach Dr 75043
Pebblebrook Ct & Dr 75044
Pebblecreek Dr 75040
Pebblestone Dr 75044
Pecan Ln 75041
Pecan Creek Dr 75044
Pecan Grove Dr 75040
Pecan Meadow Dr 75040
Pecan Valley Dr 75043
Pecan View Dr 75040
Pecos St 75041
Pegasus Dr 75044
Peggy Ln 75042
Pelican Ct 75040
Pembroke St 75040
Pendleton Dr 75041
Peninsula Way 75043
Pensacola Dr 75043
Penshire Pl 75044
Penstemon Ct 75040
Pepperidge Dr 75044
Perdido Dr 75043
Periwinkle Ct 75040
Persimmon Ct 75044
Pheasant Dr 75040
Phillips Dr 75044
Phoebe Ln 75042
Phoenix Dr 75040
Piccadilly Ct 75044
Pickett Pl 75044
Piedmont Dr 75040
Pike Pl 75044
Pilot Way 75040
Pin Oak Ct 75044
Pine Hill Dr 75043
Pine Knot Dr 75044
Pinehurst Dr 75043
Pineridge Dr 75042
Pinewood Dr 75044
Place One Dr & Ln 75042
N & S Plano Rd 75042
Plantation Rd 75044
Platinum St 75042
Plaza Dr 75041
Plaza Park Dr 75042
Pleasant Valley Rd 75040
Plymouth Rd 75043
Point Blvd 75043
Ponderosa Trail Ct 75043
Poplar Trl 75042
Portola Dr 75043
Post Oak Rd 75044
Potomac Dr & Pl 75042
Powderhorn Dr 75044
Prairie Aster Dr 75043
Prairie Clover Dr 75040
Prairie Creek Ct & Trl 75040
Prescott Dr 75041
N President George
Bush Hwy
2901-4797 75040
4799-5199 75040
5201-5399 75040
5300-5398 75044
5400-7199 75044
7201-7299 75044
Presidio Dr 75043
Preston Trl 75043
Prestwick Cir 75044
Primrose Dr 75040
Princeton Dr 75042
Princewood Dr 75040
Proctor St 75041
Profit Dr 75040
Provence Rd 75044
Providence Dr 75043
Pueblo Ct & Dr 75040
Pulsar Dr 75044
Purcell Dr 75040
N & S Purdue Dr 75042
Putman Way 75040
Pyramid Dr 75040
Quail Dr 75040
Quail Crest Dr 75040
Quail Hill Cir 75040
Quail Hollow Cir & Dr 75043
Quail Ridge Dr 75040
Quail Run Dr 75040
Quebec Dr 75040
Queens Ct 75043
Queenswood Ln & Pl 75040
Quincy Cir & Dr 75040
Quintana Dr 75043
Rahall St 75040
Raleigh Dr 75044
Ramblewood Dr 75044
Ranch Dr 75041
Randolph Dr 75041
Random Cir 75043
Range Dr 75040
Ranier Cir 75041
Ravencroft Dr 75043
Ravina Dr 75041
Ravine Xing 75040
Rayburn St 75040
Red Cedar Trl 75040
Red Gum Rd 75044
Red Oak Dr 75043
Red River Dr 75044
Redbrook Dr 75040
Redbud Ln 75042
Redcliff Ct & Ln 75043
Redell St 75040
Redpine Dr 75043
Redridge Pl 75044
Redwood Dr & Pl 75043
Regal Dr 75040
Regency Crest Dr 75041
Regents Park Ct & Ln 75043
Reinosa Dr 75043
Reisen Dr 75040
Remington Dr 75044
Reserve St 75042
Resistol Rd 75042
Rex Ln 75040
Riberry Ln 75043
Rice Dr 75042
Richard Dr 75040
Richbrook Dr 75044
Richcreek Dr 75044
Richfield Dr 75040
Richland Dr 75044
Richmond St 75041
Richoak Dr 75044
Richview Ct 75044
Richwood Dr 75044
Ridge Way 75043
Ridge Oak Ct, Dr & Pl 75044
Ridge Top Ln 75043
Ridgecove Dr 75043
Ridgecrest Dr
1800-1999 75042
2000-2600 75041
2602-2698 75041
Ridgedale Dr 75041
E Ridgegate Dr & Pl 75040
Ridgemeade Dr 75040
Ridgemoor Dr 75044
Ridgestone Dr 75040
Ridgeview Ln 75044
E & W Ridgewood Dr 75041
Riley Dr 75040
Rilla Dr 75041
Rim Fire Dr 75044
Rimes Dr 75044
E & W Rio Grande St 75041
Rio Rita Dr 75040
Ripplewood Dr 75044
Rita Dr 75042
River Birch Trl 75040
River Canyon Ln 75041
River Fern Ave 75040
River Oaks Pkwy 75044
Rivercove Dr 75044
Riviera Ct & Dr 75040
Roan Cir & Rd 75043
Roanoke Dr 75041
Roberta Ct 75040
Robin Ln
1600-1999 75042
2000-2599 75041
Robin Rd 75043

Robin Hill Ln 75044
Robinglen Dr 75043
Rochdale St 75040
Rock Creek Dr 75040
Rockcrest Dr 75044
Rockledge Dr 75043
Rockport Cir 75044
Rocky Trl 75044
Rocky Pointe Ct 75044
Rodando Dr 75042
Rodeo Ct 75044
Rolando Dr
400-1999 75040
2000-2099 75041
Rolling Oak Ln 75044
Rollinghill Cir 75043
Rollingridge Ln 75043
Rollingwood Ct & Dr 75043
Roma Dr 75041
Roman Way 75040
Roosevelt St 75042
Rosehill Rd 75043
Rosewood Hills Dr 75040
Round Rock Cir & Rd 75044
Roundtable Ln 75044
Roundtree Ln 75044
Rowlett Rd 75043
Royal Dr 75041
Royal Birkdale Dr 75044
Royal Coach Way 75044
Royal Crest Cir & Dr 75043
Royal Oaks Cir & Dr 75040
Royalshire Ln 75044
Royalty Dr 75044
Running River Rd 75044
Russell Dr 75040
Russwin Dr 75042
Russwood Ln 75044
Rustic Ln 75040
Rustic Creek Dr 75040
Rustic Glen Dr 75043
Rustic Meadow Dr 75044
Rustic Ridge Dr 75040
Ruth Dr 75042
Rutledge Rd 75044
Saddleback Rd 75043
Saddlebrook Dr 75044
Saddleridge Ct 75043
Sage Cir & Dr 75040
Sage Brush St 75040
Sagebrush Trl 75044
Saharah Dr 75044
Saint Albens Pl 75040
Saint Andrews Ct 75043
Saint George Dr 75044
Saint James Pl 75043
Sairenco Dr 75044
Salazar St 75040
Salem Dr 75043
Sam Houston Dr
1101-1799 75042
2000-2298 75044
2300-2999 75044
San Antonio Dr & Ln 75042
San Bruno Dr 75043
San Carlos Dr 75043
San Clemente Dr 75043
San Gabriel Dr 75043
San Maria Dr 75043
San Mateo Dr 75043
San Pedro Dr 75043
Sandee Ln 75043
Sanderling Dr 75043
Sanders Dr 75042
Sandestin Ct 75044
Sandpiper Ln 75043
Santa Anna Dr 75042
Santa Cruz Dr 75043
Santa Rosa Dr 75043
Santiago Dr 75043
Sara Dunn Dr 75042
Sarasota Dr 75043
Sasaki Way 75043
Saturn Rd
2000-3299 75041
3260-3260 75047
3300-5098 75041
3301-5099 75041
Saturn Springs Dr 75041
Savannah Dr & Pl 75041
Savoy Pl 75043
Sawgrass Ct & Dr 75044
Scenic Cir 75043
Sceptre Cir 75043
School St 75042
E & W Schreiber St 75040
Scorpius Dr 75044
Scotswood Dr 75041
Scottsboro Ln 75044
Sea Sparrow Ln 75043
Sea View Dr 75043
Seaport Dr 75043
Seashell Ln 75043
Security St 75042
Seminary Cir & Rdg 75043
Senada Trl 75040
Sendero Dr 75040
Seneca Dr 75040
Sequoia Dr 75041
Serena Ct 75040
Sevilla Dr 75043
Shadow Trl 75043
Shadow Brook Trl 75043
Shadwell Dr 75041
Shady Ln 75042
Shady Brook Cir 75043
Shady Glen Dr 75043
Shady Hollow Ct 75040
Shady Oaks Ct 75044
Shady Valley Ct 75043
Shadycreek Dr 75042
Shadywood Ln 75043
Shalain Dr 75040
Shalfont Ln 75040
Shalimar Dr 75040
Shamrock Ct 75044
Shannons Pl 75043
Shari Ln 75043
Sharon Dr 75041
Sharp Ct 75044
Shattuck Dr 75044
Shea St 75040
Shearwater Ln 75043
Sheffield Dr 75040
Shelby Ct & St 75041
Shenandoah Dr 75042
Shepherd Dr 75042
Sheridan Dr 75041
Sherwin St 75041
Sherwood Dr 75041
Shield Ln 75044
N Shiloh Rd
100-298 75042
300-1799 75042
1801-1917 75042
2000-2098 75044
2100-6300 75044
6302-7098 75044
S Shiloh Rd
101-197 75042
199-1599 75042
1601-1999 75042
2000-4199 75041
Shinnecock Hills Cir 75044
Shoal Creek Trl 75044
Shorecrest Dr 75040
Shoregate Dr & Sq 75043
Shorehaven Dr 75040
Shoreside Dr 75043
Sicily Ct & Dr 75040
Sierra Trl 75043
Silktree Dr 75043
Silver St 75042
Silver Creek Ct 75040
Silver Maple Ct 75044
Silverado Cir 75044
Silverdale Ln 75044
Silverleaf Ln 75043
Singing Hills Dr 75044
Skillman Dr 75041
Skyline Dr 75043
Sleepy Hollow Dr 75043
Smoke Tree Trl 75040
Snapdragon Ct 75043
Snowdrop Dr 75043
Snowmass Ln 75044
Solitude Dr 75043
Somerset Dr 75040
Sonora Dr 75043
Sotogrande Dr 75044
Southampton Blvd 75043
Southern Dr 75043
Southern Cross Dr 75044
Southgate Cir & Dr 75041
Southwick Dr 75044
Southwood Dr 75040
Spanish Moss Dr 75040
Spicewood Dr 75044
Spindrift Psge 75043
Spinnaker Cv 75043
N Spring Ct 75044
Spring Brook Dr 75044
Spring Creek Dr 75040
Spring Hill Ln 75044
Spring Hollow Ln 75043
Spring Lake Cir & Dr 75043
Spring Meadow Ln 75044
Springbranch Cir & Dr 75043
Springpark Way 75044
Springside Dr 75043
Springview Dr 75040
Springwood Ln 75044
Sprucewood Ln 75044
Spyglass Ln 75043
Stadium Dr 75040
Stagecoach Ln 75043
Stampede Dr 75044
Stanford St 75041
Stanton Dr 75042
Star Trek Ln 75044
Starleaf Trl 75040
E State St 75040
W State St
100-1232 75040
1234-1298 75040
1600-1798 75042
1800-1999 75042
2001-2099 75042
Steamboat Springs Dr 75044
Stephen Ct 75044
Stetson Dr 75043
Stillmeadow Dr 75040
Stillwater Ct 75044
Stirling Dr 75043
Stone Haven Dr 75044
Stone Hill Ct 75044
Stone Mountain Ct 75044
Stonecastle Dr 75044
Stonecreek Ct 75043
Stonehenge Dr 75041
Stoneleigh Dr 75044
Stoneridge Dr 75044
Stonewall St 75043
Stony Brook Ln 75043
Strait Ln 75042
Stratford Dr 75041
Strother Cir & Dr 75044
Stroud Ln 75043
Sugarberry Ln 75044
Sugarbush Dr 75044
Summertree Ct 75043
Summerwood Ln 75044
Summit Ln 75042
Summit Ridge Dr 75043
Sun Valley Dr 75043
Suncrest Dr 75044
Sundown Ln 75043
Sunflower Dr 75041
Sunningdale Cir & Dr 75044
Sunnybrook Ln 75041
Sunridge Dr 75042
Sunrise Dr 75043
Sunscape Way 75043
Sunset Cir & Dr 75040
Surrey Ct 75043
Susan Dr 75040
Sussex Dr 75041
Swallow Ln 75042
Swan Dr 75040
Sweet Gum St 75044
Sweetbriar Dr 75042
Sweetleaf Ln 75043
Sword Dr 75044
Sycamore Dr 75041
Sylvan Dr 75040
Syracuse Dr 75043
Tacoma Dr 75043
Tahoe Dr 75043
Talley Rd 75044
Tampa Dr 75043
Tanager Ln 75042
Tanglewood Ln 75042
Tarry Dr 75043
Tartan Trl 75044
Taurus Dr 75044
Tawakoni Ln 75043
E & W Taylor Dr 75040
Teakwood Dr 75044
Tealwood Cir & Pl 75043
Tearose Dr 75040
Telecom Pkwy 75044
Tennyson Cir 75040
Tennyson Dr 75041
Tensley Dr 75040
Thicket Dr 75043
Thistle Dr 75043
Thomas St 75040
Thomasville 75044
Thornhill Ln 75040
Three Oaks Dr 75040
Thrush Ct 75040
Thunderbrook Rd 75044
Ticonderoga Dr 75043
Tiehack Ln 75044
Tiffany Cir & Ct 75043
Timber Oaks Dr 75040
Timber Ridge Dr 75044
Timbercreek Dr 75042
Timberline Dr 75042
Timberview Cir 75043
Tina Dr 75040
Tobin Trl 75043
Toler Trl 75043
Torrance Dr 75040
Torrey Pines Ln 75044
Tower St 75040
Town Ct & Pl 75041
Town Bluff St 75040
Town Center Blvd 75040
Town Square Blvd 75040
Towngate Blvd & Dr 75041
Townshed Dr 75044
Townshire Rd 75044
Toyah Creek Ln 75040
Trafalas Ct 75044
Trail View Ln 75043
Trailcrest Dr 75043
Trailridge Dr 75043
Trails Ct & Pkwy 75043
Trailwood Ct 75043
Tralee Ln 75044
Tranquility Dr 75043
Travis St
800-1399 75040
1400-1999 75042
Treasure Rd 75041
Tree Line Rd 75040
Tree Top Ln 75044
Treece Trl 75040
Treemont Dr 75043
Trellis Cir, Dr & Way 75040
Trend Dr 75043
Trickling Creek Dr 75041
Trinidad Ln 75040
Trinity St 75041
Troon Cir 75044
Trowbridge St
1300-1399 75040
1400-1899 75044
Tulane Cir, St & Way 75043
Tulip Dr 75041
Turnberry Dr 75044
Turning Leaf Ln 75040
Turtle Cove Rd 75044
Twilight Dr 75040
Twin Court Pl 75044
Twin Oaks Ct 75044
Tynes Cir, Dr & Way 75042
University Dr 75043
Upland Way 75042
Urban Dr 75041
Ursa Cir 75044
Vail Dr 75044
Valarie Ct 75043
Valencia Dr 75041
Valiant Cir 75043
Valley Cove Dr 75043
Valley Creek Dr 75040
Valley Glen Ct 75040
Valley Mills Dr 75043
Valley Oak Ct 75040
Valley Park Dr 75043
Valley View Ln 75043
Van Ness St 75043
Vanderbilt Ct 75043
Vegas Dr 75042
Vera Cruz Cir & Dr 75043
Vicksburg Dr 75041
Vicky Ct 75044
Victoria Dr 75040
Viewside Dr 75043
Villa Pl 75044
Villa Ridge Dr 75043
Village Creek Dr 75040
Village Crest Cir & Dr 75044
Village Green Dr 75044
Villawood Ln 75040
Vine Ct & Dr 75040
Vinecrest Cir 75042
Vineridge Pl 75044
Vinewood Dr 75043
Vineyard Trl 75044
Vintage Way 75042
E & W Vista Dr 75041
Vista Creek Ct 75044
Vista Oaks Dr 75043
Vista Ridge Ct 75044
Wagon Wheel Rd
1200-1399 75040
1400-3100 75044
3102-3498 75044
Waikiki Dr 75043
Waits Cir 75043
Wakefield Dr 75040
Waldorf Dr 75041
Wall St 75041
Wallace Dr 75041
Wallingford Dr 75043
E Walnut Cir 75040
W Walnut Cir 75040
Walnut Pkwy 75042
E Walnut St 75040
W Walnut St
101-197 75040
199-1001 75040
1000-1000 75046
1003-1399 75040
1200-1298 75040
1400-4499 75042
4501-4799 75042
Walnut Creek Trl 75040
Walnut Grove Ln 75044
Walnut Park Cir 75042
Walter Reed Blvd 75042
Waltham Ct 75043
Walton Heath Dr 75044
E & W Wanda Dr 75040
Warbler Ln 75043
Warren Dr 75042
Warwick St
1200-1399 75040
1400-1899 75044
Washington St 75040
Water Oak Dr 75044
Waterbird Ln 75043
Waterbury Ct 75040
Waterford Pl 75044
Waterfront Cir & Dr 75042
Waterhouse Blvd 75043
Waterside Ct 75044
Waterview Ln 75043
Waterway Dr 75043
Watson Dr 75041
Weathered Wood Ln 75040
Wedgecrest Ln 75040
Wedgemere Dr 75040
Wedgewood Dr 75043
Weeping Willow Rd 75044
Welbeck Ct 75043
Wellesley Ave 75044
Wellington Ave 75043
Wembley Dr 75041
Wendell Way 75043
Westbridge Way 75044
Westbrook Dr 75043
Westchester Dr 75041
Westcreek Dr 75042
Western Dr 75042
Westlake Ct & Dr 75043
Westminster Ln 75040
Weston Dr 75043
Westpark Dr 75040
Westshore Dr 75043
Westside St 75040
Westview Dr 75040
Westway Ave 75042
Wexford Dr 75043
Whatley Dr 75043
Wheatfield Rd 75044
Wheelwright Dr & Pl 75044
Whippoorwill Dr 75040
Whispering Cove Cir & Ct 75044
White Dr 75040
White Gum Ln 75044
White Swan Dr 75044
Whitehall Ln 75043
Whitehaven Dr 75043
Whiteoak Dr 75040
Whiterock Trl 75043
Whitney Dr 75040
Wicklow Ln 75044
Wigeon Way 75043
Wiggs Way 75043
Wild Oak Ln 75044
Wildbriar Dr 75043
Wildgrove Dr 75041
Wildhaven Dr 75043
Wildlife Trl 75044
Wildwood Cir 75042
Willett Ln 75043
William A Taylor Dr 75043
Williams Dr 75042
Williamsburg Dr 75043
Willoughby Ct & Dr 75043
Willow Way 75043
Willow Creek Ct 75040
Willow Hollow Dr 75040
Willow Ridge Dr 75044
Willowbrook Ct 75044
Willowcrest Dr 75040
Willowhaven Cir 75043
Willowood Dr 75040
Wills Dr 75043
Wilmington Dr 75040
Wilton Dr 75040
Wiltshire Ct & Dr 75043
Wimbledon Ct 75041
Wind Lake Cir 75040
Wind River Ln 75042
Winding Brook Dr 75044
Winding Creek Trl 75043
Winding Oak Trl 75044
Windmill Ln 75044
Windridge Dr 75043
Windsor Dr 75042
Windward Psge 75043
Windy Dr 75044
Windy Ridge Ln 75044
Winecup Way 75040
Winell Dr 75043
Winged Foot Ln 75044
Winifred Dr 75041
Winnetka Dr 75043
Winter Oak Dr 75044
Winterberry Trl 75040
Winterwood Ct 75044
Wisteria Ct 75040
Woburn Dr 75043
Wolverton Ct 75043
Wood Dr 75041
Wood Creek Ln 75044
Woodbridge Pl 75044
E & W Woodbury Dr 75041
Woodcastle Dr 75040
Woodcrest Dr 75040
Woodglen Dr 75040
Woodhaven Ln 75040
Woodland Dr 75040
Woodland Park Dr 75040
Woodmeadow Ct & Dr 75043
Woodmere Dr 75043
Woodnote Ln 75040
Woodpark Dr 75044
Woods Ct & Ln 75044
Woodside Knoll Dr 75040
Woodsprings Dr 75044
Woodway Dr 75042
Worcester Ln 75040
Wordsworth Ct & Dr 75043
Worthing Dr 75043
Wyatt Dr 75040
Wycliff Dr 75040
Wycombe Dr 75043
Wykes Dr 75043
Wyland Dr 75040
Wymess Dr 75043
Wyndemere Ln 75042
Wyndham Ct 75043
Wynford Dr 75043
Wynn Joyce Rd 75043
Wynne Dr 75044
Wyre Dr 75043
Wyrick Ln 75044
Wyster Dr 75040
Xavier Dr 75043
N & S Yale Dr 75042
Yaupon Dr 75044
Yorkshire Dr 75041
Yorktown Dr 75043
Younger Ct 75044
Yukon Dr 75040
Zion Rd 75043
Zodiac Dr 75044

NUMBERED STREETS

N 1st St 75040
100-1999 75040
2000-3699 75041
S 2nd St 75040
N & S 3rd 75040
N & S 4th 75040
S 5th Cir 75041
N 5th St 75040
S 5th St
201-1497 75040
1499-1800 75040
1802-1998 75040
2000-2921 75041
2923-3099 75041
N & S 6th 75040
N & S 7th 75040
N & S 9th 75040
N & S 10th 75040
N & S 11th 75040
N & S 12th 75040
S 13th St 75040
15th St 75041
16th St 75041
17th St 75041

GEORGETOWN TX

General Delivery 78626

POST OFFICE BOXES MAIN OFFICE STATIONS AND BRANCHES

Box No.s
All PO Boxes 78627

RURAL ROUTES

01, 02, 03 78626

NAMED STREETS

Abilene Ln 78628
Abrams Rd 78633
Acacia Way 78633
Acker Rd 78633
Adams 78628
Addie Ln 78628
Adkins Cv 78626
Admiral Nimitz Ct 78628
Adobe Cv 78633
Adorno Ln 78628
Aero Dr 78628
Agave Ln 78633
Airborn Cir 78626
Airport Rd 78628
Alabaster Caverns Dr 78628
Alamosa Creek Ln 78633
Alberto Dumont Cv 78626
Aldea Cv & St 78633
Algerita Dr 78628
Alhambra Dr 78628
Allen Cir 78633
Alpine Ct 78633
Alyssa Dr 78633
Amberjack Ct 78633
Amiata Cv 78628
Anchor Dr 78633
Andice Rd 78633
Anemone Cir & Way 78633
Angelina Cv 78633
Anika Cv 78628
Animas Dr 78626
Antler Dr 78628
Apache Trl 78633
Apache Mountain Ln 78633
Appaloosa Way 78626
Apple Creek Dr 78626
April Meadows Loop 78626
Aragon Ct 78628
Aransas Cv 78633
Arapahoe Trl 78633
Armstrong Dr 78633
Arrezo Ln 78628
Arrowhead Ln 78628
Arrowhead Rd 78633
Arroyo Dr 78633
Ascot St 78626
Ash St 78626
Ashberry Trl 78626
Ashley Dr 78633
Ashwood Ln 78628
Aspen Trl 78626
Aster Cir 78633
Atlanta Park Dr 78628
Augusta Dr 78628
N & S Austin Ave 78626
Austin Elaine Dr 78633
Autumn Trl 78626
Avalanche Ave 78626
Axis Deer Cv 78628
Azalea Dr 78626
Azul Ct 78628
Bandera Cv 78626
Barberry 78626
Barcelona Ct & Dr 78628
Barcus Dr 78626
Barkridge Ter 78626
Barn Dance Cv 78633
Barrington Farm Ct 78633
Bartlett Peak Dr 78633
Bartley Dr 78628
Bass St 78633
Bastian Ln 78626
Bastrop Dr 78628
Battleship Dr 78628
Bay Hill Ct 78628
Baylor Mountain Cv 78633
Beach Mountain Cv 78633
Bear Creek Ln 78633
Beautybush Cir & Trl 78633
Bedford Ct 78628
Bee Creek Ct 78633
Belaire 78628
Belfalls Dr 78633
Bell Gin Rd 78626
Bella Vis 78633
Bella Risa Dr 78633
Bello Cir 78628
Belmont Dr 78626
Beltorre Dr 78633
Ben Wood Dr 78626
Benchmark St 78626
W Bend Dr 78626
Bent Tree Dr 78628
Bergin Ct 78626
Berry Cv 78628
Berry Ln 78626
Berry Creek Dr 78628
Berrywood Ln 78633
Bethel St 78633
Big Dr 78628
Big Bend Trl 78633
Big Oak Ln 78633
Big Sky Trl 78633
Big Spring St 78633
Big Thicket St 78633
Big Valley Spur 78633
Birch Dr 78628
Bird Stone Ln 78633
Bison Cv 78626
Black Walnut Cir 78633
Blacksmiths Cir & Dr 78633
Blanco Cv 78633
Blazing Star Dr 78633
Blue Heron Ln 78628
Blue Jay Ct 78633
Blue Quail Dr 78628
Blue Ridge Dr 78626
Blue Sky Ct 78633
Blue Springs Blvd 78626
Bluebell Dr 78633
Blueberry Hl 78626
Bluebonnet Trl 78628
Bluebonnet Valley Dr 78626
Bluehaw Dr 78633
Bluestem Dr 78633
Bluff Meadow Cv 78626
Bob White Ln 78628
Bobbys Cv 78633
Bon Winde Rd 78633
Bonham Loop 78633
Bonnett Ln 78633
Bonnie Rose 78633
Booty Rd 78628
Boquilla Trl 78633
Bos Bnd 78633
Bosque Trl 78628
Boulder Run 78626
Bowie Cir 78633
Boxwood 78628
Bradley Ranch Rd 78628
Branding Iron Cv 78633
Brandy Ln 78628
Brangus Rd 78628
Brant Dr 78633
Brantley Lake Ln 78628
Brayden Cv 78633
Brazos Dr 78628
Breckenridge St 78633
Breezeway Ln 78633
Brendon Lee Ln 78626
Brentwood Dr 78626
Brian Cir 78626
Briar Glen Dr 78626
Briar Hill Dr 78626
Briar Park Dr 78626
Briar Patch Cv 78633
Briarcrest Ct & Dr 78628
Briarwood Dr 78626
Bridge St 78626
Bridle Path Ct 78626
Bright Leaf Trl 78633
Briley St 78628
Broad Peak Rd 78633
Broad Vista Ct 78628
Broken Spoke Trl 78628
Bronco Cir & Dr 78633
Brook Meadow Cv 78626
Brookhollow Ter 78626
Brooks Cir 78633
Brushy Ave 78626
Buck Bnd & Ln 78628
Buckmeadow Dr 78628
Buckskin Ct 78628
Buena Vista Ct & Dr 78633
N & S Buffalo Pass 78633
Buffalo Springs Trl 78628
Bumble Bee Dr 78628
Buoy Cir & Dr 78633
E Burnap 78626
Burning Tree Dr 78626
Burr Oak Ln 78633
Burson Ln 78633
Busby Xing 78633
Buttercup Trl 78633
Butterfly Cv 78633
Buttermilk Gap St 78628
Cactus Bend Cv 78633
Caddo Lake Dr 78628
Caddo Lake Trl 78633
Cadiz Ct 78628
Caladium Ct & Dr 78626
Camp Dr 78633
Camp Springs Ln 78633
Candee St 78626
Candle Ridge Trl 78626
Candlelite Cir 78628
Caney Creek Cv 78633
Canterbury Trl 78626
Canyon Rd 78628
Canyon Lookout Ln 78633
Canyon Oak Loop 78633
Canyon Vista Ln 78633
Capote Peak Dr 78633
Caprock Pl 78626
Caprock Canyon Trl 78633
Capstan Ln 78633
Caribou Dr 78626
Carlson Cv 78633
Carmel Bay St 78628
Carol Ct 78626
N & S Carriage Hills Dr 78626
Casa Blanca Dr 78628
Casa Loma Cir 78633
Casa Verde Cv & Dr 78633
Cascada Cv 78633
S Cassidy Ct & Dr 78628
Castle Pines Cv 78628
Cathedral Mountain Pass 78633
Cattle Trail Way 78633
Cavu Rd 78628
Cedar Dr 78628
Cedar Branch Dr 78628
Cedar Breaks Rd
2000-2099 78633
2100-2198 78628
2100-2198 78633
2101-2199 78633
Cedar Elm Ln 78633
Cedar Hill St 78628
Cedar Hollow Rd 78628
Cedar Lake Blvd 78633
Cedar Ridge Dr 78628
E & W Central Dr 78628
Chadwick Dr 78628
Chamber Way 78626
Champions Ct & Dr 78628
Chaparral Rd 78628
Charmstone Ln 78633
Cherokee Trl 78633
Cherokee Rose Cir 78626
Cherry Glade Trl 78628
Cherry Wood Ct 78633
Cherrywood Ln 78633
Chestnut Ct 78633
Chestnut Meadows Bnd 78626
Chi Chi Dr 78633
Chickadee Cv 78633
Choke Canyon Ln 78628
Chuckwagon Trl 78633
N & S Church St 78626
Churchill Farms Dr 78626
Cibolo Creek Dr 78633
Cibolo Ridge Dr 78628
Cider Orchard Cv 78633
Cielo Dr 78628
Cimarron Ln 78628
Cimarron Hills Trl E & W 78628
Citizens Plz 78626
City Lgts 78626
Claiborne Lake Ln 78633
Claris Ln 78626
Clay St 78628
Clear Ridge Cv 78628
Clear Springs Rd 78628
Clearview Rd 78626
Clearwater Ct 78628
Clearwing Cir 78626
Cleburne Pass 78633
Cliffwood Dr 78633
Clover Valley Ln 78626
Cloverdale Ln 78626
Clovis Dr 78633
Cobalt Cv 78633
Cobb Cavern Dr 78633
Cobb Creek Rd 78633
Cody 78626
Coffee St 78626
Coffee Mill Creek Rd 78633
Cold Springs Dr 78633
Coleto Creek Ln 78633
N & S College St 78626
Colonial Dr 78628
Colony Glen Ln 78626
Colorado River Rd 78633
Columbine Ct 78633
Comanche Trl 78633
Commerce St 78626
Concho Trl 78628
Cool Spgs 78633
Cooper Lake Dr 78633
W Cooperative Way 78626
Copano Bay Cv 78633
Copper Breaks Dr 78633
Copper Lake Ln 78633
Copper Leaf Ct 78633
Copper Point Cv 78633
Copperas Creek Cv 78633
E & W Cordoba Cir 78628
Coreopsis Way 78633
Corral Cv 78626
Corsair Dr 78633
Cortona Cv 78628
Cottontail Ln 78626
Cottonwood Dr 78628
Cougar Cv 78633
Council Rd 78633
Country Rd 78633
Country Club Rd 78628
Countryside Ct 78626
County Road 100 78626
County Road 102 78626
County Road 103 78626
County Road 104 78626
County Road 105 78626
County Road 106 78626
County Road 107 78626
County Road 110 78626
County Road 120 78626
County Road 121 78626
County Road 124 78626
County Road 126 78626
County Road 127 78626
County Road 130 78626
County Road 140 78626
County Road 141 78626
County Road 142 78626
County Road 143 78633
County Road 144 78626
County Road 145 78626
County Road 146 78633
County Road 147 78633
County Road 148 78626
County Road 149 78626
County Road 150 78626
County Road 152 78626
County Road 153 78626
County Road 154 78626
County Road 155 78626
County Road 156 78626
County Road 157 78626
County Road 158 78626
County Road 159 78626
County Road 162 78626
County Road 166 78626
County Road 167 78626
County Road 176 78628
County Road 188 78626
County Road 189 78626
County Road 191 78626
County Road 192 78626
County Road 194 78626
County Road 196 78633
County Road 234 78633
County Road 237 78633
County Road 238 78633
County Road 239 78633
County Road 242 78633
County Road 245 78633
County Road 247 78633
County Road 248 78633
County Road 250 78633
County Road 251 78633
County Road 252 78633
County Road 253 78633
County Road 254 78633
County Road 255 78633
County Road 258 78633
County Road 261 78633
County Road 262 78633
County Road 266 78628
County Road 267 78628
County Road 268 78633
County Road 289 78633
County Road 316 78633
County Road 317 78626
County Road 339 78626
County Road 341 78626
Courthouse 78626
Courtnees Way 78626
Courtway Cv 78626
Courtyard Garden Ln 78633
Covey Ln 78626
Covington Cv 78628
Cowan Creek Dr 78633
Coyote Trl 78633
Creek Dr 78628
Creekside Dr & Ln 78626
Creekway Ln N & S 78626
Crepe Myrtle Ln 78633
Crested Butte Way 78626
Crockett Loop 78633
Crockett Garden Rd 78628
Crockett Gardens Rd 78633
Crosby St 78628
Cross Crk 78628
Crossland Dr 78633
Cruden Cv 78628
Crystal Knoll Blvd 78626
Crystal Springs Dr 78633
Cyrus Ave 78626
D B Wood Rd 78628
Daisy Path 78633
Dakota Dr 78633
Dan Moody Trl 78633
Dandelion Dr 78633
Davis Ln 78626
Davis Mountain Cir 78633
Dawana Ln 78628
Dawn Dr 78633
Dawson Trl 78633
Daylily Loop 78626
Debora Ct & Dr 78628
Deck Rd 78633
Deepwood Dr 78628
Deer Trl 78628
Deer Draw St 78628
Deer Field Dr 78633
Deer Meadow Cir 78633
Del Aire Ct 78628
Del Prado Ln 78628
Del Rio Ct 78628
Del Webb Blvd 78633
Delmar Dr 78626
Derby Ln 78626
Dewberry Dr 78633
Diamond Trl 78633
Diamond Dove Trl 78628
Dickens Cir 78633
Dixon Creek Ln 78633
Doe Run 78628
Dogwood Dr 78626
Dome Peak Ln 78633
Double Fire Trl 78633
Dove Hollow Trl 78633
Dove Meadow Cv 78626
Dove Tail Cv & Ln 78628
Dove Valley Dr 78626
Draper Ln 78628
Drifting Meadow Dr 78628
Drovers Cv 78626
Duck Creek Ln 78633
Dunman Dr 78628
Durango Trl 78633
Eagle Mountain Cv 78633
Eagle Trace Dr 78626
East Dr 78626
Eastview Dr 78626
Edgecliff Path 78633
Edgewood Dr 78628
Edwards Dr 78633
Egret Cv 78633
Eisenhower Ct 78633
El Ranchero Rd 78628
Elderberry Cv & St 78633
Elk Dr 78626
S Elm St 78626
Elmwood Dr 78628
Emory Peak Trl 78633
Enchanted Dr 78633
Enchanted Rock Trl 78633
Enclave Trl 78628
Equestrian Way 78626
Escalera Pkwy 78628
Escondido Dr 78633
E & W Esparada Dr 78628
Essex Ln 78633
Estancia Way 78628
Estrella Xing 78633
Eubank St 78626
Evans Rd 78633
Everest Ct 78633
Evergreen Cir 78626
Evergreen Rd 78633
Fair Oaks Dr 78628
Fairfield Ct 78633
Fairmont 78626
Fairview Rd 78628
Fairway Ln 78626
Fairwood Dr 78628
Falcon Cv & St 78633
Falcon Flight Cv 78628
Falling Hills Dr 78626
Falls Cir 78633
Family Cir 78626
Farm Dale Ct 78626
Farm Hill Dr 78633
Farris Ranch Rd 78633
Faubion Dr 78633
Fawn Gln & Ln 78628
Fawnridge St 78628
E Ferlerm Br E 78633
Ferretti Dr 78626
Fieldstone Dr 78633
Finch Ln 78626
Fish Spear 78628
Flintridge Trl 78633
Flintrock Dr 78626
Florenz Ln 78628
Fm 1105 78626
Fm 1460 78626
Fm 1660 78626
Fm 3405 78633
Fm 970 78633
Fm 971 78626
Fm 972 78626
Folsom Ct 78628
Forest St 78626
Fort Boggy Dr 78633
Fort Cobb Way 78633
Fort Davis St 78633
Fort Griffin Trl 78633
Fort Mabry Loop 78628
Fort Park Cv 78633
Fosini Cv 78628
Fossil Rim Cv 78628
Founders Oak Way 78626
Fountainwood Cir & Dr 78633
Four T Ranch Rd 78633
Foust Trl 78633
Fox Chase Cir 78633
Fox Hollow Dr 78628
Fox Home Ln 78633
Freddie Dr 78626
Freedom Dr 78626
Friendly Cir 78633
Friends Camp St 78626
Friendswood Dr 78628
Frontier Trl 78633
Gabriel Vis E & W 78633
Gabriel Forest Rd 78628
Gabriel View Dr 78628
Gabriel Vista Ct 78633
Gabriel Woods Dr 78633
Gabriels Loop 78628
Gaillardia Way 78633
Gann St 78626
Garden Meadow Dr 78628
Garden View Dr 78628
Garden Villa Cir & Dr 78628
Garner Cv 78633
Garner Park Cv & Dr 78628
George St 78626
Georgian Dr 78626
Glass Mountain Cv 78633
Glasscock Bethke Rd 78626
Glean Mdw 78626
Glenwood 78626
Golden Bear Dr 78628
Golden Oaks Dr & Rd 78628
Golden Vista Dr 78633
Goldenrod Way 78633
Goldridge Cir & Dr 78633
Golf View Dr 78633
Goodnight Dr 78628
Goodwater St 78633
Goose Island Dr 78633
Grace Blvd 78633
Granada Dr 78633
Grand Junction Trl 78626
Grand Oaks Ln 78628
Grande Mesa Dr 78626
Granger Rd 78626
Granite Dr 78626
Granite Peak Cv 78633
Grapevine Ln 78633
Grapevine Springs Cv 78628
Grassland Ln 78628
Graystone Ln 78633
Great Frontier Dr 78633
Green Grv 78633
Green Acres 78626
Green Branch Dr 78626
Green Leaf Ln 78628
Green Slope Ln 78626
Greenridge Rd 78628
Greenside Ln 78633
Greenwood Ct & Dr 78628
Grist Mill Loop 78626
Grosseto Ln 78628
Grove Ln 78626
Guadalupe Trl 78633
Guadalupe River Cv & Ln 78628
Gulfstream Dr 78626
Gunn Ranch Rd 78633
Hacienda Ln 78628
Hacienda Heights Cv 78633
Hagen Ct 78628
Hale Ct 78633
Hallie Ct 78633
Halmar Cv 78628

Hamlet Cir 78628
Hammer Stone Cv 78628
Hampton Cir 78633
S Hangar Dr 78628
Hanover Ct 78633
Harbor Cir, Cv & Dr 78633
Harmony Ln 78628
Harness Ln 78633
Harrison Ln 78628
Hart St 78626
Havelka Rd 78626
Haven Ln 78626
Haverland Dr 78626
Hawkeye Point Rd 78626
Hawthorne Cv 78628
Hazeltine Dr 78628
Hedgewood Dr 78628
Heiderosa Run 78633
Helm Ln 78633
Heritage Holw 78626
Heritage Oaks Bnd 78633
Hester Holw 78633
Hickory Ln 78633
Hickory Tree Dr 78626
Hidden Springs Trl 78633
Hideaway Cv 78628
High Point Way 78626
High Tech Dr 78626
High Trail Dr 78633
Highalea Ct 78626
Highland Dr 78626
Highland Ridge Rd 78628
Highland Springs Ln 78633
Highlander 78626
Highview Rd 78628
Hill Country Dr 78633
Hill Valley Cv 78628
Hills Of Texas Trl 78633
Hillstone Trl 78633
N Hillview Dr 78628
Hillvue Rd 78626
Hogg St 78626
S Holly St 78626
Holly Springs Ct 78628
Hollyberry Ln 78633
Honey Creek Trl 78633
Honeysuckle Cv 78633
Hopewell Cir 78628
Horseshoe Trl 78628
Howry Dr 78626
Huisache Ct 78628
Hummingbird Cv 78633
Hunters Glen Dr 78626
Hunters Point Dr 78633
Huntsville Cv 78633
Hutto Rd 78626
Ignacia Dr 78626
Igor Sikorsky 78626
Independence Dr 78633
Independence Creek Ln 78633
Indian Creek Cv & Dr 78626
Indian Lodge St 78633
Indian Meadow Dr 78626
Indian Mound Rd 78633
Indian Springs Rd 78633
Indigo Ln 78628
Industrial Ave 78626
Industrial Park Cir 78626
Inks Lake Dr 78628
NE & SE Inner Loop 78626
Innwood Cir & Dr 78628
N Interstate 35
101-3699 78628
N Interstate 35
2100-8898 78626
4501-7099 78633
7201-7599 78626
S Interstate 35
200-249 78628
250-298 78626
251-299 78628
300-499 78626
501-7999 78626
620-628 78628
650-698 78626
700-3198 78628
4200-5398 78626
Iris Dr 78626
Iron Horse Trl 78626
James St 78626
Jamie Ct 78626
Jan Ln 78626
Janae Ct 78626
E & W Janis Dr 78628
Jasmine Trl 78626
Jasper Ct 78628
Jaydee Ter 78628
Jefferson Ln 78626
Jennifer Cir 78626
Jennings Br 78633
Jib Cir & Ln 78633
Jim Hogg Dr & Rd 78633
Jm Page St 78628
John Thomas 78628
Jonah Loop & Spur 78626
Jonah Mill Rd 78626
Jonathan Cv 78626
Joshua Dr 78633
Judy Dr 78628
Juniper St 78626
Juniper Berry Trl 78633
Kajon Cv 78626
Katherine Ct 78626
Kathi Ln 78628
Katie Marie Cv 78633
Katy Ln & Xing 78626
Kauffman Loop 78628
Keenland Dr 78626
Kempton St 78626
Kendall St 78626
Keystone Cv 78633
Kickapoo Creek Ln 78633
Kieran Cv 78628
Kimberly St 78626
Kimra Cv 78628
King Rea 78633
Kingfisher Dr 78633
Kings Creek Rd 78633
Kingsway Rd 78628
Klein Ct 78626
Klondike Dr 78633
Knight St 78626
Kristina Dr 78633
Kuykendall 78626
Kyle Ln 78633
La Grotta Ln 78628
La Mesa Ln 78628
La Paloma Dr 78628
La Quinta Dr 78628
Lady Bird Cv & Ln 78633
W Lake Pkwy 78628
Lake Creek Ct 78633
Lake Livingston Dr 78633
Lake Mineral Wells Dr 78628
Lake Overlook Dr 78633
Lake Side Cv & Dr 78628
Lake Sommerville Trl 78633
Lake Texana Ct 78628
Lake Theo Ln 78628
Lake Whitney Ct 78628
Lakeview Ln 78633
Lakeway Dr 78628
N & S Lakewood Dr 78633
Lampasas Pass 78633
Lancaster 78628
Landmark Inn Ct 78633
Landons Way 78633
Lantana Dr 78633
Lariat Dr 78633
Larkspur Ln 78633
Las Colinas Dr 78628
Las Plumas Cir & Dr 78628
Laurel St 78626
Lauren Ln 78633
Lavaca Ln 78628
Laverne Ter 78628
Lawhon Ln 78628
Layton Way 78633
Lazy Rd 78626
Leander Rd
100-699 78626
1000-1900 78628
1902-1998 78628
Leander St 78626
Leanne Dr 78633
Ledgemont 78628
Leeds Castle Walk 78628
Legend Oaks Dr 78628
Lesa Ln 78626
Liatris Ln 78633
Lightning Ranch Rd 78628
Lilian Bland Cv 78626
Limestone Dr 78628
Limestone Shoals Ct 78633
Linda Ct 78628
Lindero Pass 78633
Lindsey Ln 78633
Liscio Cv & Loop 78628
Little Bend Dr 78628
Little Cypress Cv 78633
Little Deer Trl 78628
Live Oak Dr 78628
Live Oak Trl 78633
Liz Ln 78633
Llano Cv 78633
Logan Rd 78628
Logan Ranch Rd 78628
London Ln 78626
Lone Star Dr 78633
Lonesome Trl 78628
Long Pt 78628
Long Branch Dr 78626
Long Knife Cir 78626
Long Shadow Ln 78633
Longfield Dr 78628
Longhorn Trl 78633
Longhorn Cavern Cv 78633
Longwedge Ln 78628
Lonnie Thomas Dr 78626
Lookout Rdg 78626
Lost Cedars 78633
Lost Maples Trl 78633
Lost Oak Cv 78628
Lost Peak Path 78633
Lost River Blvd 78628
Louise St 78626
Lovett Cv 78633
Lovie Ln 78628
Lubbock Dr 78633
Lucinda Ter 78626
Luna Trl 78628
Luther Dr 78628
Lynn Cv 78633
Madison Oaks 78628
Madrid Dr 78626
Madrone Dr 78628
Magnolia Ct 78628
Mahogany Ln 78626
S Main St 78626
W Majestic Oak Ln 78633
Major Peak Ln 78633
Malaga Dr 78628
Mallard Ln 78633
Mancos Dr 78626
Manorwood Ct 78633
Manzanita Dr 78628
Maple St 78626
Marbella Way 78633
Marcos Dr 78628
Maria Ct 78628
Mariposa Cir 78628
Mariposa Bonita Cv 78633
Market St 78626
Marquesa Trl 78633
Marshall Ct 78628
Martin Luther King St 78626
Marvin Lewis Ln 78626
Mason Ct 78628
Mason Ranch Rd 78628
Matthew Ln & Rd 78626
May Cv 78626
Mccombs Dr 78626
Mccook Dr 78626
Mccoy Pl 78626
Mckinney Falls Ln 78633
Mckittrick Ridge Rd 78633
Mcshepherd Cv & Rd 78626
Meadow Dr 78633
Meadow Greens Dr 78628
Meadow Park Dr 78626
Meadow Ridge Loop 78626
Meadow Turn 78626
Meadowbrook Dr 78628
Meadowcrest Dr 78626
Meadowlark Cir 78626
Meadows End 78626
Meandering Creek Cv 78626
Meda St 78626
Medina Creek Cv 78633
Melanie Cv 78633
Melanie Ln 78628
Melissa Cir 78626
Melissa Ct 78628
Memorial Dr 78628
Mesa Dr & Spur 78628
Mesquite Ln 78628
Michelle Ct 78633
Mickelson Ln 78628
Midnight Ln 78626
Mill Creek Path 78633
Mill Pond Path 78633
Miller Hill Rd 78626
Mimosa St 78626
Mineral Wells Dr 78628
Miramar Dr 78628
Mission Tejas Dr 78628
Mistflower Ln 78633
Mockingbird Ln 78633
Monahans Dr 78628
Monarch Trl 78633
Montalvo Ln 78626
Montell Dr 78628
Montgomery St 78626
Montley Trl 78633
Monument Hill Trl 78633
Moral Pass 78628
Moreland Dr 78633
Morning Glory Cir 78633
Morris Dr 78628
E & W Morrow St 78626
Morse Cv 78628
Mottey St 78628
Moulins Ln 78626
Mount Lock Ct 78633
Mountain Creek Pass 78633
Mountain Laurel Way 78633
Mourning Dove Ln 78626
Mud Creek Cv 78633
Muir Ct 78633
Mulberry Cir 78633
Mule Deer Cv 78628
Mustang Way 78633
Mustang Island Trl 78633
N & S Myrtle St 78626
Namboca Way 78633
Naranjo Dr 78628
Nasoni Trl 78633
Nassau Cir 78633
Naturita Dr 78626
Navajo Trl 78633
Navasota Cir 78633
Neches Trl 78633
Neil Knl 78633
Newbury St 78626
Nicole Way 78633
Nighthawk Way 78633
Nolan Dr 78633
Northcross Rd 78628
Northwest Blvd 78628
Northwood Dr 78633
Norwood Cv, Dr & St 78628
Nueces Trl 78633
Oak Ln 78628
Oak Bend Ct 78633
Oak Branch Dr 78633
Oak Breeze Cv 78633
Oak Crest Ln 78633
Oak Grove Ln 78633
Oak Haven Cir 78633
N & S Oak Hollow Rd 78628
Oak Meadow Cv, Dr & Ln 78628
Oak Plaza Cv & Dr 78628
Oak Ridge Cir 78628
Oak Trail Dr 78628
Oak Tree Dr 78628
Oak Valley Ct 78633
Oakland Dr 78628
Oakland Rd 78633
Oakland Hills Dr 78633
Oakmont Ct & Dr 78628
Oakridge Rd 78628
Oakview Cv & Pl 78628
Oakwood Dr 78628
N & S Ocatillo Ln 78633
Ocendeld 78626
Old Airport Rd 78626
Old Bishop Rd 78626
Old Blue Mountain Ln 78633
Old Chisholm Trl 78633
Old Peak Rd 78626
Old State Highway 29 E 78626
Olde Oak Dr 78633
Olin Cv 78633
Olive Br 78633
Olive St 78626
Orange Cv 78633
Orange Tree Ln 78626
Orion Rd 78633
Oro Ct 78633
Orville Wright Dr 78626
Osage Ct 78626
Overlook Ct 78628
Owen Cir 78626
Owl Creek Dr 78633
Oxbow Cv 78628
Page Whitney 78626
Paige St 78626
Painted Bunting Ln 78633
Paleface Dr 78626
Palmetto Dr 78633
Palo Duro Ct 78628
Palo Duro Canyon Trl 78633
Paloma Pt 78628
Park Ln 78628
Park Central Blvd 78626
Park Place Dr 78626
Parker Cir & Dr 78628
Parkview Dr 78626
Parkway St 78628
Parque Cir, Ct & Cv 78626
Parque Vista Dr 78626
Patricia Rd 78628
Patriot Way 78626
Patti Dr 78626
Peach Blossom Cir 78633
Peach Tree Ln 78626
Pebble Creek Dr 78628
Pecan Ln 78628
Pecan St 78626
Pecan Vista Cv & Ln 78626
Pecos Ct 78628
Pedernales Falls Dr 78633
Pennington Ln 78626
Penny Ln 78633
Perkins Pl 78626
Persimmon Ln 78633
Piedmont Ln 78633
Pilot Pl 78628
Pimlico Cv 78626
Pin Oak Dr 78628
S Pine St 78626
Pinnacle Dr 78626
Pioneer Trl 78626
Pipe Creek Ln 78633
Pitchstone Cv 78628
Plateau Trl 78626
Pleasant Valley Dr 78626
Plover Pass 78633
Plum Ct 78628
Polo Bnd 78626
Poplar Dr 78628
Poplar Ridge Cv 78628
Poppy Ct 78626
Poppy Hills Cv & Dr 78628
Portafino Ln 78633
Portsmouth Dr 78633
Post Oak Ln 78628
Potter Ln 78633
Potters Peak Way 78626
Powder Creek Cv 78633
Powderhorn Rd 78633
Power Cir & Rd 78628
N & S Prairie Ln 78633
Prairie Creek Trl 78633
Prairie Dunes Dr 78628
Prairie Grass Ln 78633
Prairie Springs Cv, Ln & Loop 78626
Preakness Pl 78626
Precipice Way 78633
Primrose Trl 78628
Pristine Ln 78633
Private Road 902 78633
Private Road 904 78633
Private Road 906 78626
Private Road 909 78633
Private Road 910 78626
Private Road 914 78633
Private Road 915 78626
Private Road 916 78626
Private Road 917 78626
Private Road 946 78626
Prospector Pass 78633
Prosperity Hills Dr 78628
Providence St 78633
Purple Sage Dr 78633
Purtis Creek Ln 78628
Quail Ln 78628
Quail Meadow Dr 78626
Quail Valley Dr 78626
Rabbit Run 78626
Rabbit Hill Rd 78626
Rabbit Hollow Ln 78626
Railroad St 78626
Rain Lily Ln 78633
Raindance Dr 78626
Raintree Dr 78626
Rainwater Cv 78633
Ramada Trl 78628
Ranch Rd 78633
Ranch House Cv 78633
Ranch Road 2243 78628
Ranch Road 2338 78628
Ranch View Rd 78626
Rancho Bueno Dr 78628
Randolph Rd 78628
Randy St 78626
Ranger Peak Ln 78633
Ranier Ln 78633
Rath Dr 78633
Rawhide Ln 78633
Rebecca Rd 78633
Red Bird Trl 78633
E & W Red Bud Mdw 78633
Red Cedar Cir 78633
Red Oak Cir 78633
Red Oak Ct 78628
Red Poppy Trl 78633
Redbird Rd 78626
Reef Ln 78633
Reinhardt Blvd & Ct 78626
Retama Ct & Dr 78626
Richard Rd 78626
Richard Pearce Cv 78626
Richland Ln 78628
Ridge Cir & Ct 78628
Ridge Oak Dr 78628
Ridge Run Ct & Dr 78628
Ridge View Cv & Dr 78628
Ridgecrest Rd 78628
Ridgemont Ct 78628
Ridgewood Cv
100-199 78633
200-299 78628
Ridgewood Dr 78628
E Ridgewood Rd 78633
W Ridgewood Rd 78633
Rifle Bend Dr 78626
Rim Rock Cv & Dr 78628
Ringtail 78633
Rio Azul Dr 78633
Rio Bravo Rd 78628
Rio Concho Cv 78633
Rio Grande Loop 78633
Rio Leon Cv 78633
Rio Vista Cv & Dr 78626
River Rd 78628
River Bend Dr 78628
River Bluff Cir 78626
River Bow Dr 78628
River Chase Blvd & Ct 78628
River Down Rd 78628
River Hills Dr 78628
River Oaks Cv 78626
River Park Cv & Ln 78626
River Ridge Dr 78628
River Rock Dr 78633
River Tree Cv 78628
River Walk Trl 78633
Riverhaven Dr 78626
Riverside Dr 78628
Riverview Cv & Dr 78628
Riverwood Dr 78628
Rivery Blvd 78628
Roberts Cir 78633
Roble Cir 78628
Roble Grande Cir 78628
Roble Roja Dr 78633
S Rock St 78626
Rock Dove Ln 78626
Rock Ledge Dr 78626
Rock Mill Loop 78626
Rock Rose Ct 78633
Rockcrest Dr 78628
Rockmoor Dr 78628
Rockney Rd 78626
Rockride Ln 78626
Rockwood Pass 78633
Rocky Hollow Trl 78628
Rodeo Dr 78633
Rolling Meadow Trl 78633
Ronald Rd 78626
Ronald W Reagan Blvd
17400-17498 78628
17500-18199 78628
18201-21199 78628
26201-33797 78633
33799-35199 78633
Rose Spg 78628
Rosebud Ln 78633
Rosecliff Dr 78633
Rosedale Blvd 78628
Rosemary Cv 78626
Rowan Dr 78628
Royal Dr 78626
Ruby Dr 78633
Rucker St 78626
Ruellia Dr 78633
Running Water St 78633
Rushmore Cv 78633
Rusk Ln 78633
Rustic Cedar Trl 78633
E Rustle Cv 78633
Ryan Ln 78633
Sabinas Ct 78628
Sabine Dr 78628
Sachen St 78626
Saddle Trl 78633
Sage Brush Ct 78628
Saint Andrews Dr 78628
Salado Creek Ln 78633
Salt Creek Ln 78633
San Antonio Rd 78633
San Gabriel Blvd 78628
San Gabriel Overlook E & W 78628
San Gabriel Village Blvd 78626
San Jacinto Creek Cv 78633
San Jose St 78626
San Marino Trl 78633
San Matteo St 78628
San Miniato St 78628
San Saba Dr 78633
Sanaloma Dr 78628
Sand Hills Cv 78628
Sandpiper Cv 78633
Sandy Creek Trl 78633
Santa Anita Way 78626
Santa Maria St 78628

Sarazen Loop N & S 78628
Saw Grass Trl 78628
Scenic Dr
101-697 78626
699-2100 78626
2102-2130 78626
2300-2398 78626
2300-2300 78627
Scenic Lake Dr 78626
Scenic Meadow Cv 78626
Scissortail Trl 78633
Scurlock Farms Rd 78626
Scurry Pass 78633
Sea Rim Cv 78633
Sebastian Ln 78633
Sedro Trl 78633
Segundo Dr 78628
Seminole Canyon Dr 78628
E & W Sequoia Spur & Trl E & W 78628
Serenada Dr 78628
Service Dr 78628
Settlers Path 78626
Sevilla Dr 78628
Shady Grv 78633
Shady Elm 78633
Shady Hollow Dr 78628
Shady Oak Dr 78628
Shannon Ln 78628
Sharon Ln 78626
Shasta Cv 78633
Sheldon Lake Dr 78633
Shell Rd & Spur 78628
Shell Stone Trl 78628
Shepherd Rd 78628
Sherwood Ct 78628
Sheryl Ann Cv 78633
Shinnecock Hills Dr 78628
Shirley Ln 78633
Shoal Dr 78633
Shumard Peak Rd 78633
Sierra Dr 78628
Sierra Blanco Loop 78633
Sierra Rose Loop 78626
Sierra Way St 78626
Silver Bell Cir 78633
Silver Bonnet Dr 78633
Silver Leaf Dr 78633
Silver Leaf St 78628
Silver Valley Ln 78626
Silverado Dr 78633
Silverstone 78633
Sinuso Dr 78628
Six Flags Dr 78633
Skinner Ln 78628
Skyline Rd & Spur 78628
Smith Branch Blvd 78626
Snapper Cv 78628
Snead 78626
Solona Cir 78628
Sonora Trce 78633
Sotol Pass 78633
Southcross Rd 78628
Southwalk St 78626
Southwestern Blvd 78626
Spanish Dove Ct 78628
Spanish Oak Cir & Dr 78628
Sparrow Cv 78626
Spearpoint Cv 78628
Spray Ln 78633
Spring Ct 78633
Spring St 78626
E Spring St 78626
Spring Hollow Dr 78628
Spring Valley Rd 78628
Springwater Ln 78633
Springwood Ln 78628
Spur 155 N 78626
Spyglass Cir 78628
Squirrel Hollow Dr 78628
Stacey Ln 78628
Stadium Dr 78626
Stagecoach Dr 78628
Standing Oak Dr 78633
Star Mountain Ln 78633
Stardust Ln 78633

Starlight Trl 78633
Starview Dr & Ln 78633
State Highway 130 78626
State Highway 195
101-199 78628
State Highway 195
301-499 78633
600-1098 78633
1200-1399 78628
1501-1599 78633
1901-1999 78628
2401-3097 78633
3099-4199 78633
4201-5399 78633
E State Highway 29 78626
W State Highway 29 78628
Stearman Dr 78628
Steeplechase Dr 78626
Stephanie 78626
Stephen Ln 78626
Stetson Cir & Trl 78633
Still Meadow Cv 78626
Stillwater Ct 78628
Stockman Trl 78633
Stone Cir 78626
Stonehedge Blvd 78626
N & S Sumac Cv 78633
Summer Rd 78633
Summer Oak Ct 78628
Summer Ridge Ln 78633
Summer Wood Ct 78628
Summercrest Blvd 78626
Summers Grn 78633
Summit St 78633
Summit Hill Dr 78626
Sun City Blvd 78633
Sunbird Ct 78633
Sundance Ln 78633
Sunflower St 78633
Sunny Creek Dr 78626
Sunny Grove Ln 78633
Sunny Meadows Loop 78626
Sunny Trail Dr 78626
Sunnyside Bnd 78633
Sunnyvale 78626
Sunrise Valley Ln 78626
Sunset Dr 78628
Sunset Rd 78633
Sunset Rdg 78633
Sunshine Dr 78628
Susana Ct & Dr 78628
Sutton Pl 78628
Swallowtail Cir 78633
Sybert Ln 78628
Sycamore St 78633
Tallwood Dr 78628
Tamara Ct & Dr 78628
Tanager Trl 78633
Tanglewood Dr 78628
Tanksley Cir 78628
Tanner Cir 78626
Tanza Ct 78628
Taos Ct 78628
Tascate St 78628
Tasus Way 78628
Taylor Rd 78626
Tea Tree Cv 78633
Teacup Cv 78633
Tejano Ct 78628
Tejas Trl 78633
Ten Oaks Dr 78633
Teri Ct 78633
Terlingua Trl 78628
Terminal Dr & Rd 78628
Terrace View Dr 78628
Terry Ln 78628
Texas Dr 78633
Texas Traditions 78628
Tholdene Dr 78628
Thomas Ln 78626
Thornton Cv & Ln 78628
Thornwood Rd 78628
Thousand Oaks Blvd 78628
Thunder Valley Trl 78626
Thunderbay Dr 78626
Thunderbird Ln 78626

Tiffany Cir & Ln 78628
Tiger Vly 78628
Tiger Woods Dr 78628
Tiller Ln 78633
Timber St 78626
Timber Hitch Ct 78633
Timberline Rd 78633
Tipps Ct 78633
Toledo Trl 78628
Toltec Trl 78626
Tomahawk Trl 78626
Tonkowa Trl 78628
Torrey Pine Cir 78628
Tortoise Ln 78628
Tower Dr 78626
N & S Towns Mill Rd 78626
Tracy Chambers Ln 78626
Trail Driver Cv 78626
Trail Of The Flowers 78633
Trail Rider Way 78633
Trailridge Rd 78633
Trails End Dr 78626
Travis Dr 78633
Trinity Ln 78633
Trotter Dr 78626
Turkey Trl 78628
Turkey Trot Cir 78633
Turnberry Ct 78628
Turtle Bnd & Cv 78628
Tuscany Dr 78628
Tuscany Way 78633
Twin Creek Dr 78626
Twin Springs Rd 78633
E University Ave 78626
W University Ave
100-198 78626
200-999 78626
1000-2299 78628
University Park 78626
V P Ranch Rd 78628
Vail Ct 78633
Val Verde Dr 78628
Valencia Ct 78628
Vallecito Dr 78626
S Valley 78633
Valley Dr 78626
W Valley Spur 78633
E Valley St 78626
Valley Crest Cv 78626
Valley Oaks Loop 78626
Valley View Rd 78626
Valleycrest Loop 78626
Venada Trl 78628
Venezia Cir Ln 78633
Venus Ln 78633
Verbena Dr 78633
Verde Ct 78628
Verde Vis
4100-4399 78628
4601-4699 78633
Verna Spur 78628
Verrena Way 78628
Village Dr 78628
Village Gln 78633
Village Commons Blvd 78633
Village Park Dr 78633
Vinca Dr 78633
Vine St 78626
Virginia St 78626
Vista Ln 78633
Vista Rdg 78626
Vivion Ln 78633
Vortac Ln 78626
Wagon Wheel Trl 78633
Waizel Way 78628
Walburg Heights Dr 78626
Waller Ct 78633
S Walnut St 78626
Walnut Tree Loop 78633
Warbler Way 78628
Warbonnet 78626
Warnock St 78628
Water Stone Cv 78628
Water Valley Dr 78626
Watercrest Dr 78626
Waterford Ln 78628

Waterlily Cir & Ln 78633
Waters Edge Cir 78626
Watersong Ln 78628
Waycross Dr 78628
Weiss Ln 78626
West St 78626
Westbury Ln 78633
Western Trl 78628
Western Hills Dr 78626
Westfield Dr 78628
Westinghouse Rd 78626
Westview Dr 78628
Westwood Ln 78628
Whippoorwill Cv & Way 78633
Whirlabout Way 78626
Whirlwind Cv 78633
Whisper Ln 78628
Whisper Oaks Ln 78628
Whispering Spring Ln 78633
Whispering Wind Dr 78633
White Eagle Pass 78626
Whitestone Dr 78628
Whitetail Dr 78628
Whitewing Way 78633
Whitney Woods Cir 78633
Wichita Trl 78633
Wilbarger Pt 78626
Wilbur Wright Dr 78626
Wilco Way 78626
Wild Horse Way 78633
Wild Plum Cir 78633
Wild Ridge Cv 78633
Wild Rose Dr 78633
Wild Turkey Ln 78633
Wildflower Ln 78626
Wildwood Dr & Xing 78633
Wilkie Ln 78626
Williams Dr
1000-1098 78628
1100-4499 78628
4500-6299 78633
6301-6399 78633
Willis Creek Ct 78633
Willow Run 78633
Winchester Dr 78626
Wind Hollow Dr 78633
Wind Ridge Cv 78628
Windflower Ln 78628
Winding Way Dr 78628
Windmill Cv 78628
Windmill Ranch Rd 78633
Windridge Village Cv 78626
Windy Hill Rd 78626
Windy Hill School Rd 78626
Winecup Way 78633
Wingfoot Cv 78628
Winter Dr 78633
Wisteria Dr 78626
Wolf Rd 78628
Wolf Ranch Pkwy & Rd 78628
Wolverine Cv 78626
Wood Ct 78628
Wood Cv 78633
Wood Ranch Rd 78628
Woodall Dr 78628
Woodbine Cir 78628
Woodcrest Ct 78628
Woodcrest Rd 78633
Woodlake Dr 78633
Woodland Park 78633
Woodland Rd 78628
Woodmont Dr 78628
Woodstock Dr 78633
Woodstone Dr 78628
Woodview Dr 78626
Woodway Dr 78628
Wright Brothers Dr 78628
Yaupon Ln & Vly 78633
Yellow Rose Trl 78633
Yellowstone Rd 78633
Yosemite Rd 78633
Young Ranch Rd 78633
Yucca Cv 78633
Yukon Ter 78633
Zenith Rd 78626

NUMBERED STREETS

All Street Addresses 78626

GILMER TX

General Delivery 75644

POST OFFICE BOXES MAIN OFFICE STATIONS AND BRANCHES

Box No.s
All PO Boxes 75644

RURAL ROUTES

02, 03, 04, 06, 07, 12 75644
01, 05, 08, 09, 10, 11, 13 75645

NAMED STREETS

Abney St 75644
Adelyn Ln 75645
Adkins Ln 75645
Airstrip Rd 75644
N Aligator Rd 75644
Allen St 75644
Amaryllis Rd 75645
Andrews Cir 75644
Ant Rd 75644
Antelope Rd 75644
Apple Tree Rd 75644
Applewood 75645
Apricot Rd 75644
Armadillo Rd 75644
Arrowwood Rd 75644
Ash Rd 75644
Ashley Venn Rd 75644
Ashwood Cir 75645
Aspen Rd & Trl 75644
Aster Rd 75644
Aviation Dr 75645
Avocado Rd 75644
Azalea Rd 75645
Azalea St 75644
Badger Rd 75644
Ballard Rd 75644
Balsam Rd 75645
Barber Rd 75644
Bayberry Rd 75645
Bear Rd 75644
Beaver Rd 75644
Beaver Bend Est & Rd 75645
Beaverwood 75645
Beechnut Rd 75644
Bell St 75644
Binion Rd 75644
Birch St 75644
Bison Rd 75644
Black Gum Rd 75644
Black Hawk Ln 75645
Black Jack Rd 75644
Black Walnut Rd 75644
Blackbird Rd 75645
Blackhaw Rd 75645
N Bledsoe St 75644
Blue Spruce Rd 75644
Bluebell Rd 75644
W Bluebird Rd 75645
Bluebonnet Rd 75644
Bluejay Ave 75645
Bluets Rd 75645
Boar Rd 75644
Bob O Link Rd 75645
Bob White Dr 75645
Bobwhite Rd 75645
Bois D Arc Rd 75644
Boles Rd 75645
Border St 75644

Box Oak Rd 75644
Boxwood Rd 75644
N & S Bradford St 75644
Briarwood St 75644
Brooks Rd 75644
Brooksy St 75644
Bruce St 75645
Buckeye Rd 75645
Buffalo Rd & St 75644
Bullpine Rd 75645
Burro Rd 75644
E & W Butler St 75644
Buttercup Rd 75645
Buttonwood 75645
Cactuswood Trl 75645
Calvert Ln 75645
Camel Rd 75644
Camellia St 75644
Camp Rd 75645
Canary Rd 75645
Canvasback Ct 75645
Capital St 75644
Cardinal Rd 75645
N & S Caribou Rd 75644
Carlock St 75645
Carly Ln 75644
Carnation Rd 75645
E & W Cass St 75644
Cat Rd 75644
Cat Squirrel Rd 75644
Catbird Rd 75645
Cedar Rd 75644
Cedarwood Trl 75645
Chandler St 75644
Chaparral Rd 75645
Cherokee Trce 75644
Cherry St 75644
Cherry Laurel Rd 75645
Cheyenne Trl 75644
Chickasaw Trl 75644
Chinaberry Rd 75645
Chinchilla Rd 75644
Chinkapin Rd 75644
Chipmunk Rd 75644
Chuckar Dr 75645
Circle Dr 75644
Circle Ridge Dr 75645
Clark St 75644
Clematis Rd 75645
Club Dr 75645
Coconut Rd 75645
Collie Rd 75644
Colt Rd 75645
Condor Rd 75645
Coon Hunters Rd 75645
Cottonwood Rd & Trl 75645
Cougar Rd 75644
Coulter Rd 75645
County Road 1250 75644
Cox Trl 75644
Coyle Rd 75645
Coyote Rd 75644
Crabapple Rd 75645
Crane Rd 75645
Crawford St 75644
Crestline St 75644
N & S Cricket Ln 75644
Crocodile Rd 75644
Crocus Rd 75645
Curry Rd 75644
N & S Cypress St 75644
Cypresswood Trl 75645
Daffodil Rd 75645
Dahlia Rd 75644
Davenport Rd 75645
Davis St 75644
Dawn St 75644
Day Lily Rd 75645
Dean St 75644
Deer Rd 75644
Diamond Loch Rd 75644
Dodd Rd 75644
Doe Trl 75645
Dogwood 75645
Dogwood Cir 75645
Dogwood Dr 75645

Dogwood St 75644
Dove Rd 75645
Duncan St 75644
Eagle Rd 75645
Eastwood Dr 75645
Elderberry Rd 75644
Elephant Rd 75644
Elizabeth St 75644
Elk Rd 75644
Elm Rd 75645
Elmwood Trl 75645
Emily St 75644
Emma St 75644
Ermine Rd 75644
Ervin Hls 75645
Eucalyptus Rd 75644
Evergreen Rd 75645
Fairway Dr 75645
Falcon Rd 75645
Fallow Trl 75644
Fannie St 75644
Fawn Crossing Rd 75644
Fern Rd 75645
Fig Rd 75645
Filly Rd 75645
Finch Rd 75645
Firwood Dr & Trl 75645
Flamingo Rd 75645
Flicker Rd 75645
Floy Lee Rd 75645
Floyd Rd 75645
Fluellen Rd 75644
Flying Squirrel Rd 75644
Fm 1404 75645
Fm 1649 75645
Fm 1650 75645
Fm 1795 75644
Fm 1844 75645
Fm 1845 75645
Fm 1972 75645
Fm 1975 75644
Fm 2088 75644
Fm 2263 75644
Fm 2454 75644
Fm 2685 75645
Fm 2796 75644
Fm 3358 75645
Fm 49 75645
Fm 555 75645
Fm 556 75644
Fm 593 75644
Fm 726 N & S 75645
Fm 852 75644
Ford St 75644
Forestwood 75645
Forget Me Not Rd 75644
Fox Rd 75644
Foxglove Rd 75645
Foxtail Ln 75645
Francis St 75644
Frazler St 75644
Frog Rd 75644
Frost St 75644
Fuller Rd 75644
Gannet Rd 75645
Gardenia Rd 75645
Geers Rd 75645
Gilmer Plz 75644
Ginger Rd 75644
Gipson Rd 75644
Giraffe Rd 75644
Glenn Hill Rd 75644
Glenwood Dr 75645
Glenwood Oaks Park 75645
Goat Rd 75644
Gold Leaf 75644
Golden Eagle Rd 75645
Goldenrod Rd 75645
Goldfinch Rd 75645
Golf Rd 75645
Goose Rd 75645
Gopher Rd 75644
Gorilla Rd 75644
Great Dane Rd 75644
Green St 75644
Green Hills Rd 75645

Street	ZIP
Greenridge Rd	75644
Greenway St	75644
Greyhound Rd	75644
Groundhog Rd	75644
Grouse Rd	75645
Guinea Rd	75645
Gull Rd	75645
Gumcreek	75645
Gumwood Trl	75645
H Williams Rd	75645
Hack Berry Rd	75644
Hale Rd	75645
Hall St	75645
Hamilton St	75644
Hare Rd	75644
Harris Rd	75645
E & W Harrison St	75644
Harvey St	75644
Hawthorne Rd	75644
Hemlock Rd	75644
Henchinc Rd	75645
Henderson St	75644
Heron Rd	75645
Hidden Falls Dr	75645
Highland Dr & Rd	75645
Hillcrest Dr	75645
Hilltop Ave	75645
Hollins St	75644
Holly Rd	75644
Hollybrook St	75644
Honeysuckle Rd	75645
Horse Rd	75644
Horton Rd	75644
Huckleberry Ln	75645
Hummingbird Rd	75645
Hunter Rd	75644
Hyacinth Rd	75645
Hyena Rd	75644
Ibex Rd	75644
N & S Impala Rd	75644
Indigo Trl	75645
Industrial Blvd	75644
Iris Ln	75644
Ironwood Rd	75644
Ivy Rd	75645
Jack Rabbit Rd	75644
Jackson Cir	75644
Jacobin Dr	75645
Jaguar Rd	75644
Jasmine Rd	75645
E Jefferson St	75644
John Dean Rd	75644
Jones Loop	75644
Jonquil Rd	75645
June Rd	75645
Kangaroo Rd	75644
Katie Ln	75644
E & W Kaufman St	75644
Kelsey Creek Ln	75644
Kimway St	75644
Kingfisher Rd	75645
Klima Dr	75645
Kola Dr	75644
Lakewood Cir & Dr	75645
Lamb Rd	75644
Lane St	75644
Langford St	75644
Lantana Rd	75645
Lark St	75644
Larkspur Rd	75645
W Latch Rd	75644
Lauren Rd	75645
Lavender Rd	75644
Lawrence St	75644
Lazy Daisy Rd	75645
Lemon Rd	75644
Lilac Ln	75645
Lime Tree Rd	75644
Linda Loop	75645
Live Oak Dr	75645
N Live Oak Rd	75644
S Live Oak Rd	75644
Lizard Rd	75644
Llama Rd	75644
Loblolly Rd	75645
Loch St	75644
Locust Rd	75645
Long St	75645
Lookout Ln	75644
Lupine Rd	75644
Lyles Rd	75644
Lynx Rd	75644
Machen Ln	75644
Mackey Rd N	75645
Madelaine Dr	75644
E & W Madison St	75644
Magnolia	75644
Main St	75645
Maple St	75644
Maplewood	75645
Marable St	75644
Mare Rd	75645
E Marshall St	75644
Martin Ln & St	75645
Mary St	75644
Mayhaw Rd	75645
Medlin Rd	75645
Mell Ave	75644
Merganser Ln	75645
Michiel St	75644
Mildred Rd	75644
Miller St	75644
N & S Mimosa Rd	75644
Mirage St	75645
Mistletoe Rd	75644
Mitchell St	75644
Mockingbird Ln & Rd	75645
Monk Rd	75645
Monroe St	75644
N & S Montgomery St	75644
Mora Rd	75644
Morning Glory Rd	75645
E Mountain N	75645
Mule Deer Rd	75644
Municipal Dr	75645
Muskrat Rd	75644
Mustang Rd	75645
Mynah Bird	75645
Myra St	75644
Myrtlewood Trl	75645
Nandena Rd	75644
Nectarine Rd	75644
New Hope Rd	75645
Newsome St	75645
Newt Rd	75644
Nichols Trl	75645
Nighthawk Rd	75645
Nightingale Rd	75645
Norfolk Rd	75645
North St	75645
Northwood Dr	75645
Nuthatcher Rd	75645
Nutmeg Rd	75645
Oakwood Dr	75645
Oasis St	75645
Ocelot Rd	75644
Old Coffeeville Rd	
201-297	75644
299-499	75644
700-1699	75645
1701-2199	75645
Old Highway 271 N	75644
Olive Rd	75645
Oriole Rd	75645
Osage Ln	75645
Osprey Rd	75645
Ostrich Rd	75645
Owens St	75644
Pacal Rd	75645
Panda Rd	75644
Pansy Rd	75645
Park St	75644
Parkway Ln	75645
Parkwood Dr	75645
Paw Paw Rd	75645
Peach Rd	75644
Peacock Rd	75645
Pecan Dr & St	75644
N & S Pelican Rd	75645
Pencilwood	75645
Penguin Rd	75645
Peony Ln	75644
Pepperwood	75645
Perkins Rd	75645
Pheasant Rd	75645
Phlox Trl	75645
Pigeon Rd	75645
Pignut Rd	75644
Pin Oak Rd	75645
Pine St	75644
Pinecrest St	75644
Pinewood Dr	75645
Pinion Rd	75645
Pintail Pl	75645
Pinto Rd	75645
Pipit Rd	75645
Plum Rd	75644
Poinsettia Rd	75644
Polk St	75644
Pomagranate Rd	75645
Ponderosa Trl	75644
Pony Rd	75644
Poplar Rd	75645
Poppy Rd	75644
Possum Holw	75644
Powell Rd	75644
Primrose Rd	75645
Pritchett Rd	75644
Private Road 1000	75645
Private Road 1001	75645
Private Road 1002	75645
Private Road 1003	75645
Private Road 1004	75645
Private Road 1008	75645
Private Road 1011	75645
Private Road 1052	75645
Private Road 1053	75645
Private Road 1062	75645
Private Road 1118	75645
Private Road 1119	75645
Private Road 1121	75645
Private Road 1125	75645
Private Road 1126	75645
Private Road 1127	75645
Private Road 1128	75645
Private Road 1129	75645
Private Road 1130	75645
Private Road 1131	75645
Private Road 1132	75645
Private Road 1133	75645
Private Road 1134	75645
Private Road 1135	75645
Private Road 1136	75645
Private Road 1142	75645
Private Road 1151	75645
Private Road 1152	75645
Private Road 1171	75645
Private Road 1172	75645
Private Road 1196	75645
Private Road 1197	75645
Private Road 1200	75645
Private Road 1201	75645
Private Road 1202	75645
Private Road 1209	75645
Private Road 1210	75645
Private Road 1211	75645
Private Road 1212	75645
Private Road 1213	75645
Private Road 1214	75645
Private Road 1218	75645
Private Road 1219	75645
Private Road 1220	75645
Private Road 1221	75645
Private Road 1222	75645
Private Road 1223	75645
Private Road 1224	75645
Private Road 1225	75645
Private Road 1226	75645
Private Road 1227	75645
Private Road 1228	75645
Private Road 1229	75645
Private Road 1230	75645
Private Road 1231	75645
Private Road 1234	75645
Private Road 1235	75645
Private Road 1241 N	75645
Private Road 1278	75645
Private Road 1279	75645
Private Road 1280	75645
Private Road 1281	75645
Private Road 1290	75645
Private Road 1501	75645
Private Road 1601	75645
Private Road 2000	75644
Private Road 2010	75645
Private Road 2012	75645
Private Road 2013	75645
Private Road 2014	75645
Private Road 2015	75644
Private Road 2072	75645
Private Road 2090	75645
Private Road 2102	75644
Private Road 2107	75645
Private Road 2108	75645
Private Road 2109	75645
Private Road 2110	75645
Private Road 2111	75645
Private Road 2112	75645
Private Road 2113	75645
Private Road 2114	75645
Private Road 2115	75645
Private Road 2116	75645
Private Road 2117	75645
Private Road 2118	75645
Private Road 2120	75645
Private Road 2121	75645
Private Road 2152	75644
Private Road 2153	75644
Private Road 2161	75644
Private Road 2181	75645
Private Road 2230	75644
Private Road 2231	75644
Private Road 2232	75644
Private Road 2233	75644
Private Road 2234	75644
Private Road 2235	75644
Private Road 2300	75644
Private Road 2301	75644
Private Road 2304	75644
Private Road 2411	75645
Private Road 2413	75645
Private Road 2414	75645
Private Road 2416	75645
Private Road 2417	75645
Private Road 2475	75644
Private Road 2901	75644
Private Road 3030	75644
Private Road 3031	75644
Private Road 3032	75644
Private Road 3033	75644
Private Road 3051	75644
Private Road 3071	75644
Private Road 3076	75644
Private Road 3077	75644
Private Road 3078	75644
Private Road 3079	75644
Private Road 3080	75644
Private Road 3081	75644
Private Road 3082	75644
Private Road 3083	75644
Private Road 3084	75644
Private Road 3085	75644
Private Road 3086	75644
Private Road 3087	75644
Private Road 3088	75645
Private Road 3092	75644
Private Road 3093	75644
Private Road 3094	75644
Private Road 3100	75644
Private Road 3102	75644
Private Road 3103	75644
Private Road 3104	75644
Private Road 3105	75644
Private Road 3111	75644
Private Road 3112	75644
Private Road 3120	75644
Private Road 3124	75645
Private Road 3140	75644
Private Road 3150	75644
Private Road 3151	75644
Private Road 3160	75644
Private Road 3161	75644
Private Road 3162	75644
Private Road 3163	75644
Private Road 3164	75644
Private Road 3165	75644
Private Road 3173	75644
Private Road 3174	75644
Private Road 3207	75645
Private Road 3208	75645
Private Road 3209	75645
Private Road 3210	75645
Private Road 3211	75645
Private Road 3212	75645
Private Road 3213	75645
Private Road 3214	75645
Private Road 3215	75645
Private Road 3220	75645
Private Road 3221	75645
Private Road 3222	75645
Private Road 3223	75645
Private Road 3225	75645
Private Road 3230	75645
Private Road 3240	75645
Private Road 3260	75645
Private Road 3278	75645
Private Road 3279	75645
Private Road 3280	75645
Private Road 3281	75645
Private Road 3282	75645
Private Road 3283	75645
Private Road 3284	75645
Private Road 3285	75645
Private Road 3288	75645
Private Road 3290	75645
Private Road 3291	75645
Private Road 3300	75645
Private Road 3302	75645
Private Road 3303	75645
Private Road 3304	75645
Private Road 3305	75645
Private Road 3350	75645
Private Road 3351	75645
Private Road 3352	75645
Private Road 3353	75645
Private Road 3354	75645
Private Road 3358	75645
Private Road 3361	75645
Private Road 3401	75645
Private Road 3402	75645
Private Road 3430	75645
Private Road 3707	75644
Private Road 3715	75644
Private Road 4001	75644
Private Road 4002	75644
Private Road 4010	75644
Private Road 4011	75644
Private Road 4012	75644
Private Road 4013	75644
Private Road 4015	75644
Private Road 4021	75644
Private Road 4022	75645
Private Road 4024	75644
Private Road 4029	75644
Private Road 4030	75644
Private Road 4040	75644
Private Road 4075	75644
Private Road 4078	75644
Private Road 4079	75644
Private Road 4080	75644
Private Road 4081	75644
Private Road 4082	75644
Private Road 4083	75644
Private Road 4084	75644
Private Road 4085	75644
Private Road 4086	
101-599	75644
Private Road 4086	
1100-1198	75645
Private Road 4087	75645
Private Road 4088	75645
Private Road 4089	75645
Private Road 4090	75644
Private Road 4091	75644
Private Road 4092	75644
Private Road 4093	75644
Private Road 4094	75644
Private Road 4095	75644
Private Road 4096	75644
Private Road 4097	75644
Private Road 4100	75644
Private Road 4101	75644
Private Road 4102	75644
Private Road 4104	75644
Private Road 4124	75644
Private Road 4126	75644
Private Road 4128	75644
Private Road 4131	75644
Private Road 4161	75644
Private Road 4162	75644
Private Road 4200	75644
Private Road 4211	75644
Private Road 4212	75644
Private Road 4214	75644
Private Road 4215	75645
Private Road 4216	75644
Private Road 4217	75644
Private Road 4220	75644
Private Road 4221	75644
Private Road 4222	75644
Private Road 4223	75644
Private Road 4253	75644
Private Road 4254	75644
Private Road 4300	75644
Private Road 4301	75644
Private Road 4302	75644
Private Road 4322	75644
Private Road 4328	75644
Private Road 4334	75644
Private Road 4351	75644
Private Road 4400	75644
Pullen Rd	75644
Purple Martin	75645
Quail Dr	75645
Quiet Oak Dr	75645
Rabbit Rd	75644
Railroad St	75644
Red Hawk Rd	75645
Red Head Ln	75645
Red Oak Rd	75644
Red Pheasant Dr	75645
E & W Redbud St	75644
Redwood Rd & Trl	75645
Reynolds Rd	75645
Ridgeway St	75644
N & S Roberts St	75644
Robertson Rd	75644
Rooster Rd	75645
Rose Trl	75644
Royal St	75645
Ruby St	75644
Salter Ln	75645
Sand St	75644
Sara Rd	75644
Scarlet Oak Rd	75645
Scharant Rd	75644
Schley St	75644
E & W Scott St	75644
Seahorn Trl	75644
Seawood Trl	75645
Serendipity Rd	75644
Shamburger Rd	75645
Shattles Rd	75644
Shaw Rd	75644
Sheep Rd	75644
Shetland Rd	75645
Short Rd & St	75645
Silk Tree Rd	75645
Silk Tree Lake Est	75645
Silver Aly	75644
Silver Spruce Rd	75645
Simpson St	75644
Skylark Rd	75645
Skyview Dr	75644
Smith Ave	75644
Smith Rd	75645
Snider Rd	75645
Sorrell Rd	75645
Sorrells St	75644
Southpark St	75644
Stable Rd	75645
Stallion Rd	75645
State Highway 154 E	75645
State Highway 154 W	75644
State Highway 155 N	75644
State Highway 155 S	75645
State Highway 300	75645
Stevens St	75645
Stocks Rd	75645
Stonebridge Ct	75645
Stoney Ln	75645
Stuart St	75644
Sturrock Rd	75645
Success St	75644
Suffolk Rd	75644
Sugar Pine Rd	75645
Sumac Rd	75644
Summit Dr	75644
Sun Flower Rd	75644
Sunglade St	75644
Swallow Rd	75645
Sweet Pea Rd	75644
Tall Timbers	75645
E & W Taylor St	75644
Teal Ln	75645
Tennison Rd	75645
Texas Ave	75645
Thomas St	75644
Thrush Rd	75645
Timmons St	75644
Titus St	75644
Toad Rd	75644
Tobe St	75644
Todd Rd	75645
Tranquil Dr	75645
N & S Trinity St	75644
Tulip Rd	75644
W Tyler St	75644
N Us Highway 259	75645
Us Highway 271 N	75644
Us Highway 271 S	
200-498	75644
500-1199	75644
1201-1297	75645
1299-8699	75645
8701-8899	75645
Venters Rd	75645
Vfw Rd	75644
Vinewood Trl	75645
Voss Rd	75645
Walker Rd	75645
Walker St	75644
Walnut St	75644
Warren St	75644
N Water Lily Rd	75644
Waters Rd	75644
Waylon St	75644
Waynes Ln	75644
Webb St	75645
Welch Rd	75645
Whale Rd	75644
Whip O Will	75645
White Tail Rd	75644
Whitewood	75645
Widgeon Ln & Rd	75645
Wildwood Dr	75645
Willet Rd	75645
Willowood Trl	75645
Wilson St	75644
Winding Way	75645
Windridge Rd	75645
N & S Wood St	75644
Wood Duck Ln	75645
Woods Ln	75644
Woodway Ln	75644
Yapaco St	75644

NUMBERED STREETS

Street	ZIP
All Street Addresses	75644

GRANBURY TX

Street	ZIP
General Delivery	76048

POST OFFICE BOXES MAIN OFFICE STATIONS AND BRANCHES

Box No.s	ZIP
1 - 2476	76048

5001 - 7390 ... 76049
94801 - 94802 ... 76048
94901 - 94901 ... 76049

RURAL ROUTES

01, 05, 06, 08, 10, 13, 15, 17, 20, 22, 24, 27, 29, 32 ... 76048

HIGHWAY CONTRACTS

51 ... 76048
02, 03, 04, 07, 09, 11, 12, 14, 16, 18, 19, 21, 23, 25, 26, 28, 30, 31, 34, 35 ... 76049

NAMED STREETS

Abby Bend Dr ... 76048
Abes Landing Ct & Dr ... 76049
Ables St ... 76048
Acoma Ct ... 76048
Acorn Run ... 76049
Acton Cir & Hwy ... 76049
Acton Meadows Ct ... 76049
Acton School Rd ... 76049
Ada Ct ... 76048
Adams St ... 76048
Adobe Ct ... 76049
Afton Ct ... 76049
Agate Dr ... 76049
Agua Ct ... 76049
Aguila Trl ... 76048
Ailensor Ct ... 76049
Air Park Dr ... 76049
Ajo Ct ... 76048
Alabama Trl ... 76048
Alamo Ct ... 76049
Alamo Dr ... 76048
Alaska Ct ... 76048
Albatross Dr ... 76049
Alexa Ct ... 76048
Alexandria Dr ... 76048
Allen Ct ... 76048
Alpha Ln ... 76048
Alpine St ... 76048
Alta Vista Ct ... 76049
Ambling Way Ct ... 76049
Amsterdam Ct ... 76048
Anaconda Ct & Trl ... 76048
Andrews Cir & Ct ... 76048
Angel Bluff Ct ... 76048
Angela Ct ... 76048
Angelina Ct N ... 76049
Angelina Ct S ... 76049
Angelina Dr ... 76049
Angelina St ... 76048
Anna Cir ... 76048
Annette Ct ... 76049
Apache Cir ... 76048
Apache Ct ... 76049
E Apache Trl ... 76048
W Apache Trl ... 76048
Apache Ridge Rd ... 76049
Apache Trail Ct ... 76048
Apollo Ct ... 76049
Appletree Ct ... 76048
Aqua Vista Ct & Dr ... 76049
E & W Aquarius Ct ... 76049
Arbor Ct ... 76048
Arbor Bluff Ct ... 76048
Archer Ct ... 76048
Archery Ct ... 76048
Arcola Ct ... 76049
Argyle Ct ... 76049
Arizona Trl ... 76048
Arkansas Trl ... 76048
Arkansas River Dr ... 76048
W Arnold St ... 76048
Arrow Dr ... 76048
Arrow Creek Dr ... 76049
Arrowhead Cir ... 76048
Arrowhead Ct ... 76048
Arrowhead Dr ... 76048
Arrowhead Ln ... 76049
Ary Ct ... 76048
Ash Ct ... 76048
Ashland Ct ... 76049
Ashley Ct ... 76049
Ashwood Dr ... 76048
Ashworth Ct ... 76048
Aspen Ct ... 76048
Asphodel Ct ... 76049
Atasta Dr ... 76048
Atchley Dr ... 76048
Atwood Ct & Rd ... 76049
Auburn Ct ... 76048
Augusta Ct & Dr ... 76049
Aurora Ave ... 76048
Austin Ct & Dr ... 76048
Autumn Ridge Dr ... 76049
N & W Avalon Blvd & Ct ... 76048
Avra Cir ... 76048
Azalea Dr ... 76049
Azalea Trl ... 76048
Aztec Ct ... 76048
Back Forty Ct ... 76049
Bahama Ct ... 76048
E & W Baja Ct ... 76048
N & S Baker St ... 76048
Balboa Ct ... 76048
Bandera Dr ... 76049
Bandera Trl ... 76048
Bandy Rd ... 76049
Bar Harbor Ct ... 76049
Barcelona Ct ... 76048
Barkridge Dr ... 76049
Barnwood Ct ... 76049
E Barton St ... 76048
Basswood Ct ... 76049
Battle Creek Rd ... 76048
Bay Shore Cir ... 76049
Bayshore Dr ... 76049
Bayside Ct ... 76049
Beacon Vista Cir ... 76049
Beau West Ct ... 76049
Beauvoir Ct ... 76049
Beechwood St ... 76048
Belaire Cir ... 76048
Bellechase Rd ... 76049
Bellevue Ct ... 76049
Belvidere Cir ... 76049
Bent Tree Ct ... 76049
Bentwater Ct & Pkwy ... 76049
Berry Rd ... 76049
Berry Patch Ln ... 76049
Beryl Ln ... 76049
Betty Ct ... 76049
Betzel Ranch Ct ... 76049
Beverly Dr ... 76048
Big Horn Dr ... 76048
Big Timber Ln ... 76049
Billy June Rd ... 76049
Birch St ... 76048
Bird Ct ... 76048
Birdsong Ct ... 76049
Bishop Ct ... 76049
Black Ct ... 76049
Black Diamond Ct ... 76049
Black Pine Cir ... 76048
Blackfoot Ct ... 76048
Blackfoot Trl ... 76049
Blackhawk Cir ... 76048
Blackjack Ln ... 76048
N Blanche St ... 76048
Bliss Ct ... 76048
Blue Bird Ct ... 76049
Blue Heron Ct ... 76049
Blue Jay Ct ... 76049
Blue Lake Ct ... 76049
N & S Blue Quail Ct ... 76049
Blue Water Cir & Ct ... 76049
Blueberry Trl ... 76048
E & W Bluebonnet Ct & Dr ... 76048
Bluff Ct ... 76049
E Bluff St ... 76048
W Bluff St ... 76048
Bluff View Ct & Dr ... 76048
Bob White Ct & Dr ... 76049
Bobbie Ann Ct & Dr ... 76048
Bobby Ln ... 76048
Bobcat Trl ... 76048
Boca Bay Ct ... 76048
Boca Vista Ct & Dr ... 76048
Bocage Ct ... 76049
Bolton Rd ... 76049
Bonita Ct & Dr ... 76049
Bontura Ct & Rd ... 76049
Boot Hill Rd ... 76049
Boot Trail Ct ... 76048
Boquillas Cir ... 76048
Boquillas Ct E ... 76049
Boquillas Ct W ... 76049
Bordeaux Dr ... 76048
Bosque River Dr ... 76048
Boston Smith Pkwy ... 76048
Bowie St ... 76049
Boyd Rd ... 76049
Boynton Ave ... 76049
Brad Justin Rd ... 76049
Brandi Ln ... 76048
Branding Iron Trl ... 76049
Brannon Ct ... 76049
Bray St ... 76048
N & S Brazos Ct, Dr & St ... 76048
Brazos Harbor Cir & Dr ... 76048
Brazos River Ct & Dr ... 76048
Brazos View Ct ... 76048
E & W Briarwood St ... 76048
E & W Bridge St ... 76048
Brierfield Rd ... 76049
Bringier Ct ... 76049
Broken Bow Dr ... 76048
Broken Bow Rd ... 76049
Bronco Rd ... 76049
Brook Valley St ... 76048
Brooke Ct ... 76049
Brookhollow Dr ... 76048
Brushy Rd ... 76048
Buckboard Trl ... 76049
Buena Vista Cir, Ct & Dr ... 76049
Bueno Dr ... 76049
Buffalo Trl ... 76049
Bulow Ct ... 76049
Bunky Ct ... 76049
Burn Ct ... 76049
Burroak Dr ... 76049
Business Blvd ... 76049
Buttercup Ct ... 76049
Buzzard Hollow Ct ... 76048
Caballo Ct & Way ... 76049
Cactus Aly & Ct ... 76048
Cactus Hill Ct ... 76048
Cadiz Cir ... 76048
Calhoun St ... 76048
Calico Ct ... 76049
California Ct ... 76048
Calinco Dr ... 76048
Calviton Ct ... 76048
Camp Crucis Ct ... 76048
Camp Paradise Ct ... 76048
Camper Ct ... 76048
Campfire Ln ... 76049
Canadian River Trl ... 76048
Canaveral Ct ... 76049
Canvasback Dr ... 76049
Canyon Rd ... 76049
Canyon Trl ... 76048
Canyon Creek Ct ... 76049
Capricorn Dr ... 76049
Captains Ct ... 76049
Caraway St ... 76048
N & S Cardinal Ct & Dr ... 76049
Carla Ct ... 76049
Carmel Ct ... 76048
Carmichael Ct ... 76049
Carol Ct ... 76048
Caroline Ct ... 76048
Carolyn Ct ... 76049
Carrizo Dr ... 76049
Carruth Rd ... 76048
Carson Ct ... 76048
Carson Trl ... 76049
Carter Ct ... 76049
Carter Rd ... 76048
Casas Del Norte Ct & St ... 76049
Casas Del Sur Ct & St ... 76049
Cash Point Ct ... 76049
Cassidy Ct ... 76049
Catalina Bay Blvd & Ct ... 76048
Catfish Ct ... 76048
Cathy Dr ... 76049
Cattle Barn Ln ... 76049
Cattle Drive Ct ... 76049
Cedar Cir & Dr ... 76049
Cedar Crest Ct & Dr ... 76048
Cedarbrush St ... 76048
Cedarhill St ... 76048
Cedarwood Trl ... 76048
Celina Ct ... 76048
Centaurus Way ... 76048
Centre Ct ... 76049
Chaco Trl ... 76048
Chad Ln ... 76049
Champions Dr ... 76049
Chaparral Ct ... 76049
Chaparral Dr
100-399 ... 76049
1200-1299 ... 76048
N & S Chaparral Estates Ct ... 76049
Charles Ct ... 76049
Charlie Ct ... 76049
Charterhouse Cir ... 76048
Chavez Ct ... 76048
Chelsea Ct ... 76048
Chelsea Bay Ct ... 76048
Cherokee Ct ... 76048
Cherokee Dr ... 76049
Cherokee Trl ... 76048
Cherokee Lake Ct ... 76049
Cherree Ct ... 76049
N & S Cherry Ln ... 76048
Chesapeake Bay Ct ... 76048
Cheyenne Trl ... 76048
Chickasha Cir ... 76048
Chicken Gristle Rd ... 76048
Chief Ct ... 76048
E & W Chippewa Ct & Trl ... 76048
Chisec Ct ... 76048
N & S Chisholm Trl ... 76048
E & W Choctaw Ct & Dr ... 76049
Christa Ct ... 76049
Christine Dr ... 76049
Christopher Ct ... 76049
Christy Dr ... 76049
Chuck Ct ... 76049
Cimmaron Trl ... 76049
Cindy Ct ... 76049
Circo Dr ... 76049
Citation Ct ... 76049
Claiborne Shr ... 76049
Claremont Dr ... 76049
Clark St ... 76048
Clay St ... 76049
Clear View Dr ... 76049
Cleburne Hwy ... 76049
N Cleburne St ... 76048
Cleveland Rd ... 76048
Cliff Swallow Ct & Dr ... 76048
Cliffview Ct ... 76049
E & S Clifton Rd ... 76049
Clover Ln ... 76048
Clovis Trl ... 76048
Club Dr ... 76049
Club Cove Ct ... 76049
Clubhouse Dr ... 76049
Cluster Oak Ct ... 76049
Coates Rd ... 76048
Cobblestone Ct ... 76049
Cochise Trl ... 76048
Cockatoo Rd ... 76048
Cody Ct ... 76049
Coffee Pot Ln ... 76049
Cogdell St ... 76048
Coke Ct ... 76048
Cold Water Ct & Trl ... 76048
Collins Ct ... 76048
Cologne Dr ... 76048
Colonial Dr ... 76049
Colorado River Dr ... 76048
Comal Ct ... 76048
Comanche Ct ... 76048
Comanche Dr ... 76049
Comanche Cove Ct & Dr ... 76048
Comanche Shadow Ct ... 76048
Comanche Vista Ct & Trl ... 76049
Comet Trl ... 76048
Commercial Ln ... 76048
Concho Ct ... 76048
Concord Ct ... 76048
Conejos Ct ... 76048
Conejos Dr ... 76048
Contrary Creek Rd ... 76048
Copper Mountain Ct ... 76048
Coral Sands Ct ... 76048
Cordova Cir ... 76048
Corona Dr ... 76048
Corporate Dr ... 76049
Corral Ct & Dr ... 76048
Cortez Ct ... 76048
Cortez Dr ... 76049
Corto Ct ... 76048
Corto Dr ... 76048
Cottage Ct ... 76049
Cottonwood Ct ... 76049
Cottonwood Dr ... 76048
Cougars Bluff Ct & Trl ... 76048
S Coulston St ... 76048
Country Ln ... 76048
Country Club Dr ... 76049
Country Meadows Cir & Rd ... 76049
Counts Aly ... 76048
County Road 302 ... 76048
County Road 322 ... 76048
County Road 323 ... 76048
County Road 324 ... 76048
Courtney Ct ... 76049
Cove Timber Ave, Cir & Ct ... 76049
Covered Wagon Trl ... 76048
Cowboy Ct ... 76049
Cowboy Ln ... 76049
Cowpoke Rd ... 76049
Coyote Trl ... 76048
Crabb Apple St ... 76048
Crawford Ave & Ct ... 76048
Cree Trl ... 76048
Creek Dr ... 76048
Creekview Ct & Dr ... 76049
Crescent Ct & Dr ... 76049
Crestridge Dr ... 76048
Crestview Dr ... 76048
Crestwood Dr ... 76048
Cripple Creek Ct ... 76048
S Crites St ... 76048
Crockett Dr ... 76048
Crockett St ... 76049
N Crockett St ... 76048
S Crockett St ... 76048
Crook Ct ... 76049
Cross Creek Ct ... 76049
Crossbridge Cir ... 76049
Crossland Rd ... 76049
Crow Ct ... 76048
Crow Creek Dr ... 76049
Crube Ct ... 76048
Crystal Ct ... 76049
Crystal Clear Ct ... 76049
Crystal Lake Dr ... 76049
Cuero Dr ... 76049
Cuilco Ct ... 76048
Cypress St ... 76048
Daisy Dr ... 76049
Dakota Trl ... 76048
Daniels Ct ... 76049
Darby Dan Ct ... 76049
Daugherty Ct ... 76049
Davis Rd ... 76049
Dawn Ct ... 76048
Day Dr ... 76048
Dayla Ct ... 76049
Dcbe Marina Ct ... 76049
De Cordova Ranch Rd ... 76049
Dean Ct ... 76049
Deep Water Ct ... 76048
Deer Trl ... 76048
Deer Hollow Ct ... 76049
Deer Park Ct ... 76048
Deer Run Acres ... 76049
Deer View Cir ... 76049
Del Prado Dr ... 76048
Del Rio Ct ... 76049
Deleon Ct ... 76049
Delmarva Ct ... 76048
Deputy Larry Miller Dr ... 76048
Devils River Dr ... 76048
Devon Ct ... 76048
Diamond Ct ... 76049
Diann Dr ... 76049
Divot Dr ... 76049
Dixie Ct ... 76049
Dog Leg Ct ... 76049
Dogwood Ct ... 76048
Donathan Ct ... 76049
Donna Cir & Ct ... 76049
Dorado Dr ... 76049
Doris Ct ... 76048
Dorthy Ct ... 76048
Dove Ct ... 76049
Dove Trl ... 76048
Dove Hollow Rd ... 76048
Dover Ct ... 76049
W Doyle St ... 76048
Doyle Springs Rd ... 76048
Dresden Dr ... 76049
Drift Ct ... 76049
Driftwood Ct ... 76049
Drury Ct ... 76049
Dry Creek Rd ... 76049
Ducros Ct ... 76049
Dulcito Ct ... 76049
Dunaway Ct ... 76049
Dunleith Ct ... 76049
Dunn Ct ... 76049
Durango Trl ... 76048
Durant Ct ... 76049
Durham Ct ... 76049
Duro Ct ... 76048
Eagle Bluff Ct ... 76048
Eagle Nest Ct ... 76048
East Rd ... 76049
Eastridge Rd ... 76049
Eastview Ct ... 76049
Eastview Ter ... 76049
Eastwood Ct ... 76049
Easy Ct ... 76048
Echo Trl ... 76049
Edgebrook Ct ... 76049
Edgecliff Ct ... 76049
Edgecreek Ct ... 76049
Edgewood Ct ... 76049
El Rancho Ct ... 76048
Elizabeth Blvd & St ... 76048
Elk Trl ... 76048
Elkton Ct & Dr ... 76049
Ellerslie Cir ... 76049
Elliseo Dr ... 76048
Elms Ct ... 76049
Elmwood Ct ... 76049
Elmwood Dr ... 76048
Emerald Ct ... 76048
E & W Emerald Bend Ct ... 76049
Emu Ct ... 76049
Enchanted Ct ... 76049
Enchanted Rd ... 76049
Endsley Rd ... 76049
Equestrian Ct & Dr ... 76049
Esplanade Ct ... 76049
Estate Dr ... 76049
Evening View Dr ... 76048
Evergreen Dr ... 76048
Everidge Ct ... 76049
E Ewell St ... 76048
Fairview Ct & Dr ... 76049
Fairway Cir, Ct & Dr ... 76049
Fairway Place Ct ... 76049
Fall Creek Hwy ... 76049
Fame Ct ... 76048
Farm Land Ct ... 76048
Fawn Cir & Dr ... 76049
Faye St ... 76049
Feather Ct ... 76048
Fencerow Dr ... 76048
E & W Fernwood Ct ... 76049
Ferry Boat Ln ... 76049
Field Ct ... 76048
Fiesta Way ... 76048
E Final Approach Ct ... 76049
Firehouse Ct & Dr ... 76049
Fireside Ct ... 76049
Firewood Trl ... 76048
Flachitt Ct ... 76049
Flagstick Ct & Dr ... 76049
Flagstone Ct ... 76049
Flamingo Rd ... 76049
Flight Plan Dr ... 76049
Flint Ct & Dr ... 76048
Flint Rock Cir ... 76048
Forest Hill Ln ... 76048
Forest Oak Ct ... 76049
Forest Park Dr ... 76049
Fork Ct & Rd ... 76049
Fountain Way ... 76049
Fox Ct ... 76048
Fox Fire Ct ... 76049
Fox Hollow Ct ... 76049
Fox Run Ct ... 76049
Francis Ct ... 76049
Frank Ln ... 76049
French Kingston Ct ... 76049
Frio Ct & Dr ... 76048
Frisco Cir & Ct ... 76048
Frontier Ct & Trl ... 76048
Galaxy St ... 76049
Gallivant Dr ... 76049
Garden Cir & Ct ... 76049
Garden Terrace Ct ... 76049
Garden View Dr ... 76049
Garrett Ct ... 76049
Garrett Ranch Rd ... 76049
Garry Ct ... 76049
N Gate Rd ... 76049
Gateway Ct ... 76049
Gateway Hills Ct & Ln ... 76049
Gauntt Ct & Rd ... 76049
Gee Rd ... 76049
Gemini Ct ... 76049
Gene Ct ... 76048
Geonito Camino Ct ... 76049
Georgia Trl ... 76048
Georgiana Ct ... 76049
Gerry Dr ... 76049
Gibson Ct ... 76049
Gifford Dr ... 76049
Gila Cir ... 76048
Gilliam Ct ... 76049
Gimme Ct ... 76049
Gina Cir ... 76049
Givens Place Ct ... 76049
Gladys Dr ... 76049
Glen Rose Hwy ... 76048
Glenburnie Blvd ... 76049
Gleneagles Cir & Dr ... 76049
Glenwood Ct ... 76049
E Glide Slope Ct ... 76049
Gloria Ct & Dr ... 76049
Godley Rd ... 76049
Gold Mine Ct ... 76048
Golden Oaks Cir ... 76049
Goldeneye Dr ... 76049
Goliad Ct & Dr ... 76049
Goodnight Ct ... 76049
Gooseberry Trl ... 76048

N Gordon St ... 76048
Gran Tera Ct ... 76049
Granada Calle Ct & St ... 76049
Granbury Ct ... 76049
Grand Harbor Ct ... 76049
Grand Point Ct ... 76049
Grande Ct ... 76049
Grande Cove Ct ... 76049
Grandview Dr ... 76049
Granek Ct ... 76049
Granite Blf & Ct ... 76048
Gray Rd ... 76049
Great Plains Ct ... 76048
Green Leaves Dr ... 76049
Green Meadows Ct & Rd ... 76049
Green Oak Dr ... 76048
Green Wing Dr ... 76049
Greenbrook St ... 76048
Gregory Ct ... 76048
E Grove St ... 76048
Guadalupe Ct ... 76048
Guadalupe River Dr ... 76048
Hackberry Ct ... 76048
Halfway Hill Ct ... 76049
Halo Ct ... 76049
S Hampton Dr ... 76049
Hampton South Ct ... 76049
Hanging Moss Dr ... 76049
N & S Hannaford St ... 76048
Hano Trl ... 76048
Hanover Ct ... 76049
N, S & W Harbor Ct & Dr ... 76048
Harbor Lakes Dr ... 76048
Harbor View Ct ... 76048
Harborside Dr ... 76048
Harness Trl ... 76049
Hartwood Dr ... 76049
Haven Ct ... 76048
Hawaiian Ct ... 76048
S Hawthorne St ... 76048
Hayden Ct ... 76048
Hayloft Ln ... 76048
Hayworth Hwy ... 76048
Headquarters Cir ... 76049
Heather Dr ... 76049
Hedge Row St ... 76048
Hedgerow Trl ... 76048
Henard Ln ... 76048
Henslee Ct ... 76049
Hercules Ct & Dr ... 76048
Hereford Ln ... 76049
Heritage Ct & Trl ... 76048
Hermosa Hills Ct ... 76048
Heron Ct ... 76049
Herons Nest Dr ... 76048
Hewitt Ct ... 76049
Hickey Ct ... 76049
Hickory Ct ... 76048
Hickory Hill Dr ... 76049
Hidden Ct ... 76048
Hidden Cove Ct & Trl ... 76049
Hidden Oak Dr ... 76048
Hidden Valley Rd ... 76049
Hideaway Bay Ct ... 76049
Highland Ct ... 76048
Highland Dr ... 76048
N Highland Dr ... 76049
W Highland Dr ... 76049
Highland Oaks Ct ... 76049
Highview Ct ... 76049
Highview Dr ... 76048
N Highway 144 ... 76048
Hike Rd ... 76049
Hill Blvd & Ct ... 76049
Hillcrest Dr ... 76048
Hillside Dr ... 76048
Hilltop Ct & Rd ... 76048
Hitching Post Rd ... 76049
Holiday Ct ... 76048
E & W Holiday Estates Ct ... 76049
Holland Dr ... 76048
Holly Ct ... 76048
Holly Hills Cemetery Rd ... 76048
Holmes Dr ... 76048
Homestead Ct ... 76049
Hondo Dr ... 76049
Hood Ct ... 76048
Hoover Ct ... 76049
Hopi Ct ... 76048
Hoppe Ct ... 76048
Hopper Ct ... 76048
Hopsewee Ct ... 76049
Horizon Ct ... 76049
Horseshoe Trl ... 76048
N Horton St ... 76048
N & S Houston Ct, Dr & St ... 76048
Howard Clemmons Rd ... 76048
Huddleston Rd ... 76048
Hudson Rd ... 76049
Hummingbird Ct ... 76049
Hunters Ct ... 76048
Hunters Glen Ct ... 76048
Hunterview Dr ... 76048
Hunterwood Dr ... 76048
Huntington Cove Ct ... 76048
Huron Ct & Dr ... 76048
Hydra Ct ... 76048
E & W Iberian Ct ... 76048
Ibis Ct ... 76049
Idaho Ct & Trl ... 76048
Illinois Trl ... 76048
Inca Ct ... 76048
Indian Dr ... 76048
Indian Creek Ct ... 76049
Indian Creek Dr ... 76048
Indian Creek Trl ... 76049
Indian Mountain Ct ... 76048
Indian Wells Dr ... 76049
Industrial Ave ... 76049
Inverness Rd ... 76049
Inwood Trl ... 76049
Iowa Ct & Trl ... 76048
Iron Horse Trl ... 76048
Island Village Ct ... 76048
Ivy Ct ... 76049
Izapa Ct ... 76048
Jacinth Ln ... 76049
Jackson Ln ... 76049
Jackson Bend Ct ... 76049
Jackson Heights Ct ... 76049
James Rd ... 76049
Janis St ... 76049
Jason Ln ... 76048
Jasper Ln ... 76049
Jewel Ct ... 76049
Joann Ct ... 76049
John Gee Ct ... 76049
Johnson Ct ... 76048
Johnson Rd ... 76049
N & S Jones St ... 76048
Joseph Dr ... 76049
Josh Ct ... 76049
Joshua Ct & Way ... 76048
June Rose Ct ... 76049
Juniper Ct ... 76048
Jupiter Ave ... 76049
Justine Ct ... 76048
Kailey Ct ... 76049
Karen Way ... 76049
Kathy Ln ... 76049
Katie Ct ... 76048
Kayann Dr ... 76048
Kaywood Dr ... 76048
Keechi Trl ... 76048
N Keith Ct & St ... 76048
Keller Ct ... 76049
Kelly Ct & Dr ... 76048
Kemah Ct ... 76049
Kenilworth Ct ... 76049
E & W Kenwood Ct ... 76049
Kessler Dr ... 76048
Kikaga Rd ... 76048
Killough Rd ... 76049
King Air Ct & Dr ... 76049
Kingdom Ct ... 76048
Kings Plz ... 76049
Kingsley Cir ... 76049
Kinson St ... 76049
Knob Hill Dr ... 76048
Kristenstad Ct ... 76049
Kristy Ct ... 76049
Kruse Ct ... 76049
La Vista Ct ... 76049
Labatut Ct ... 76049
Lady Amber Ct & Ln ... 76049
Laguna Ct ... 76048
Laguna Vista Ct & Dr ... 76048
Laiken Dr ... 76049
Lake Dr ... 76049
Lake Country Dr ... 76049
Lake Granbury Dr & Trl ... 76048
Lake View Dr ... 76049
Lake Village Ct ... 76048
Lake Vista Ct ... 76049
Lakecrest Cir ... 76048
Lakeridge Ct & Dr ... 76048
Lakeshore Dr ... 76048
Lakeside Dr ... 76048
N & S Lakeside Hills Ct ... 76048
Lakeview Ct & Rd ... 76048
Lakewood Ct & Trl ... 76049
Lakota Ct ... 76048
N & S Lambert Ct & St ... 76048
Lamota Ct ... 76048
N & S Lancaster St ... 76048
Landmark Ct ... 76049
Lands End Ct & St ... 76048
Langdon Leake Ct ... 76049
Lansdowne Ct ... 76049
Lantana Dr ... 76049
Laramie Ct ... 76049
Laramie Dr ... 76049
Laramie Trl ... 76049
Laredo Ct ... 76049
Laredo Dr ... 76049
Largo Dr ... 76049
Lark Harbor Ct ... 76049
Larson Ct ... 76049
Lauren Ln ... 76048
Lazy Ct ... 76048
Lazy Hill Ct ... 76049
Le Jeune Ct ... 76049
Leatherwood Ct ... 76049
Leisure Ln ... 76049
Leo Rd ... 76049
Leonard Bend Dr ... 76049
Lewis Ct ... 76049
Liberty Rd ... 76049
Libra Dr ... 76049
Lightning Bar Ct ... 76049
Lilac Dr ... 76049
E & W Limestone Ct ... 76049
Linda Ct ... 76048
Linda Way ... 76049
Linden Ct ... 76049
Lipan Dr & Hwy ... 76049
Little Rd ... 76049
Little Rock Rd ... 76049
Little Valley Ct ... 76049
Live Oak Cir & St ... 76048
Llano St ... 76048
E Localizer Ct ... 76049
Logan Cir ... 76049
Lois Cir ... 76049
Loma Alto Ct ... 76049
Lone Prairie Trl ... 76048
Lone Star Cir ... 76048
Lonesome Creek Rd ... 76049
Long Dr ... 76049
Long Creek Ct ... 76049
Longhorn Trl ... 76049
N & S Longwood Dr ... 76049
Lookout Cove Ct ... 76049
Loon Ct & Dr ... 76049
NE Loop 567 ... 76048
Lost Trl ... 76049
Lottie Ct ... 76049
Louise Dr ... 76049
Louisiana Trl ... 76048
Lowland Dr ... 76048
Lucero Dr ... 76048
Luker Ct ... 76049
Lunar Cir ... 76049
Lusk Branch Ct ... 76049
Lynch Ct ... 76048
Lyndi Ln ... 76049
Lynn Ln ... 76049
Lynnwood Dr ... 76048
M And M Ranch Ct & Rd ... 76049
Mabery Ct & Dr ... 76049
Macaw Dr ... 76049
Mack Gee Ct ... 76049
Madera Ct ... 76048
Madewood Ct ... 76049
Magnolia Vale Dr ... 76049
Maine Trl ... 76048
Malibu Bay Ct ... 76048
Mallard Ct & Way ... 76048
Mallard Pointe Dr ... 76049
Mambrino Hwy ... 76048
Man O War Ct ... 76049
Mandy Dr ... 76049
Maplewood St ... 76048
Marana Dr ... 76048
Marble Ct ... 76049
Marble Bluff Ct ... 76049
Maria Dr ... 76049
Mariana Ct ... 76048
Marie Ct ... 76049
Marigold Ct ... 76049
Marina Ct ... 76049
Mariscal Ct ... 76049
Mark St ... 76048
Mars Ct ... 76049
Marseilles Ct ... 76049
Mary Lou Ct ... 76048
Massey Rd ... 76049
Matlock Rd ... 76049
Matt St ... 76048
Matthew Ct ... 76049
Maynard Ct ... 76049
Mazatan Ct ... 76048
Mccreary Rd ... 76049
Mcsmith Ct ... 76048
Meadow Wood Rd ... 76049
Meadowlark Cir ... 76049
Meadowlark Ln ... 76048
Meadows Dr N ... 76048
Meander Rd ... 76049
Meandering Way ... 76048
Mearlens Ct ... 76048
Medical Plaza Ct ... 76048
Medina St ... 76048
Medinah Ct & Dr ... 76049
Meith St ... 76048
Melmont Ct ... 76049
Melrose Cir ... 76049
Melynn Ct ... 76049
Mercedes Cir & St ... 76048
Mercury Ct ... 76049
Mesa Cir ... 76049
Mesa Loop ... 76048
Mesquite Dr & Trl ... 76048
Meteor Trl ... 76048
Meyer Ct ... 76048
Mid Haven Cir & Ct ... 76048
Midway Ct ... 76049
Mill St ... 76048
Mill Branch Ct ... 76049
Miller Ct ... 76049
Millstream Ct ... 76049
Mimosa Dr ... 76048
Mission Cir & Ct ... 76048
Missouri Trl ... 76048
Mistletoe Ct, St & Trl ... 76048
Misty Ct ... 76048
Misty Meadow Dr ... 76048
Mitchell Dr ... 76048
Mitchell Bend Ct & Hwy ... 76048
Mockingbird Dr ... 76049
Mohawk Ct ... 76049
Mojave Dr ... 76049
Mojave Trl ... 76048
Monarch Ct ... 76048
Monna Ct ... 76049
Monroe Hwy ... 76049
Montana Trl ... 76048
Montego Blvd ... 76049
Montego Bay Ct ... 76049
Monteign Ct ... 76049
Monterrey Ct & Dr ... 76049
Monterrey Bay Ct ... 76048
Montgomery Dr ... 76049
N & S Monticello Cir, Ct & Dr ... 76049
Moon Ct ... 76049
E & W Moore St ... 76048
Moose Dr ... 76048
N & S Morgan St ... 76048
Morning Ct ... 76049
Morningside Dr ... 76048
Moss Rock Trl ... 76048
Mountain Hollow Dr ... 76048
N Mountain View Rd ... 76048
S Mountain View Rd ... 76048
Mountain View Trl ... 76049
Mountain Vista Dr ... 76048
Mountainside Dr ... 76048
Mtm Ct ... 76048
Muirfield Dr ... 76049
Mulberry Dr ... 76048
Murphy Ct ... 76048
Mustang Trl ... 76049
Myrtle Ln ... 76049
Nacogdoches River Dr ... 76048
Nassau Ct ... 76049
Navaho Trl ... 76049
Navarro Trl ... 76048
Navasota St ... 76048
Nebraska Trl ... 76048
Nech Ranch Rd ... 76048
Neches St ... 76048
Neches River Trl ... 76048
Neil Ct ... 76048
Nelson Ct ... 76049
Neptune Ct & Dr ... 76049
Neri Rd ... 76048
Nevada Ct ... 76048
New Jersey Ct ... 76048
New Mexico Trl ... 76048
New York Ct ... 76048
Newlin Ln ... 76048
Newport Bay Ct ... 76049
Nichols Ct ... 76049
Nimmo Ct ... 76048
Nocona Dr ... 76049
Nolan Creek Ct ... 76049
Norfolk Bay Ct ... 76049
Northview Ct ... 76048
Northwood Ct ... 76049
Nottaway Ct ... 76049
Nubbin Ridge Ct ... 76048
Nueces Ct ... 76049
Nutcracker Ct & Dr ... 76049
Nutt Grove Ct ... 76049
E, S & W Oak Ct & Trl ... 76048
Oak Grove Ct ... 76049
Oak Hill Dr ... 76048
Oak Meadow St ... 76048
Oak Trail Dr ... 76048
Oak Wood St ... 76048
Oakland Ct ... 76048
Oakridge Ln ... 76048
Oaks Dr ... 76049
Oakwood Ct ... 76049
Oakwood Lake Ct ... 76049
Oaxaca Ct ... 76048
Ohio Ct ... 76048
Ohio River Trl ... 76048
N & S Oklahoma Trl ... 76048
Old Barn Ct ... 76048
Old Bridge Rd ... 76049
Old Cleburne Rd ... 76048
Old Granbury Rd ... 76049
Oldham Ln ... 76048
Olson Ct ... 76048
Onyx Dr ... 76048
Orange Blossom St ... 76048
Orchard Dr ... 76049
Oregon Trl ... 76048
Oriole Ct ... 76049
Orion Way ... 76048
Ormond Ct ... 76049
Osage Ct ... 76048
Osprey Ct ... 76048
Oto Ct ... 76048
Ottawa Dr ... 76048
Overhill Rd ... 76048
Overlook Ct ... 76049
Overton Ct ... 76049
Overview Rd ... 76048
Paddle Boat Dr ... 76049
Pago Pago Ct ... 76048
Paint Rock Trl ... 76048
Pala Dura Ct ... 76048
Paluxy Hwy, Rd & Trl ... 76048
Paluxy Medical Cir ... 76048
Panama Ct ... 76048
N & S Park Ct, Dr & St ... 76048
Parker Ct & Ln ... 76048
Parkside Ct ... 76048
Parlange Ct ... 76049
Partridge Ct ... 76049
Pathfinder Ct ... 76048
Paul St ... 76048
Paula Ct ... 76049
Pauline St ... 76048
Pawnee Ct & Trl ... 76048
N & S Peaceful Ct ... 76048
Peach St ... 76048
Peachtree Cir, Ct & St ... 76048
Peak Rd ... 76048
Pear Orchard Rd ... 76048
E & W Pearl St ... 76048
Pease River Dr ... 76048
Pebble Dr ... 76048
Pebble Bay Ct ... 76048
Pebble Beach Ct & Dr ... 76049
Pecan Ln ... 76049
Pecan Arbor Ct ... 76049
Pecan Grove Ct ... 76049
Pecan Valley Ct & Dr ... 76048
Peck Rd ... 76049
Pecos Ct ... 76049
Pecos St ... 76048
Pecos River Dr ... 76048
Pecos Trail Ct ... 76048
Pedernales Ct ... 76048
Peninsula Ct ... 76048
Pennsylvania Trl ... 76048
Penny Ct ... 76049
Penrod Dr & St ... 76048
Peppertree Rd ... 76048
Pequeno Ct ... 76049
Perfect View Dr ... 76048
Perkins Ct ... 76048
Peveler Ct & Rd ... 76049
Pheasant Trl ... 76049
Phillips Ct ... 76048
Phoenix Ct ... 76048
Pica Trl ... 76048
Pigeon Ct ... 76049
Pima Ct ... 76048
Pinckard Ct ... 76048
Pine Cir ... 76048
S Pinehurst Ct & Dr ... 76049
Pinnacle Ridge Way ... 76049
Pinoak St ... 76048
Pintail Ct ... 76049
Pinto Ln ... 76049
Pioneer Rd ... 76049
Pirate Dr ... 76048
Pirlie Ct ... 76049
Pisces Dr ... 76049
Plains Ct ... 76048
Plantation Blvd ... 76049
N Plaza Dr ... 76048
Plaza East Ct ... 76049
Pleasant Ct ... 76049
Pleasant Hill Dr ... 76048
Plum Bush St ... 76048
Pluto Ct & St ... 76049
Poco Ct ... 76048
Ponca Dr ... 76048
Poplar Dr ... 76048
E Port Ridglea Ct ... 76049
Portal Dr ... 76049
Porter Ct ... 76048
Ports O Call Ct & Dr ... 76048
Post Oak St ... 76048
Post Oak Ter ... 76049
Power Plant Ct ... 76048
Prairie Ln ... 76048
Presidio Ct ... 76048
Preston Trail Ct ... 76048
Prestwick Ct ... 76048
Prominade Dr ... 76049
Prospect Hill Dr ... 76049
Pueblo Ct ... 76048
Purple K Ct ... 76049
Quail Ct & Run ... 76049
Quail Ridge Ct ... 76049
Quail Run Trl ... 76048
Rainey Ct ... 76049
Raintree Trl ... 76048
Rambling Ct ... 76049
Rance Dr ... 76049
Ranch Rd ... 76049
Ranch House Ln ... 76049
Ranchview Dr ... 76049
Randle Rd ... 76049
Random Ct ... 76049
Randy Ct ... 76049
Rasco Ct ... 76048
Rash Ct ... 76049
Raupe Ln ... 76048
Ravenna Ct ... 76049
Ravenswood Rd ... 76049
Rawhide Ct ... 76049
Red Bird Ln ... 76048
Red Fox Ct ... 76049
Red Oak Dr ... 76048
Redwood Dr ... 76049
Reed Rd ... 76049
Remington Ct ... 76048
Rendezvous Ct ... 76049
Resort Dr ... 76048
Retreat Ct ... 76049
Reunion Ct ... 76048
Rhea Ct, Ln & Rd ... 76049
Rhode Island Trl ... 76048
Richard Ct ... 76049
Richardson Rd ... 76049
Rickabaugh Rd ... 76048
Ricky St ... 76049
Ridgecrest Dr ... 76048
Ridgeview Cir & Trl ... 76048
Rienzi Ct ... 76049
Rifle Rd ... 76049
Riley Ct ... 76048
Rim Rock Ct ... 76049
Rio Vista Dr ... 76049
Rising Star Ct ... 76048
River Rd ... 76048
River Run ... 76049
River Bank Ln ... 76049
River Country Ln ... 76049
River Ridge Ct & St ... 76048
River View Ct & Trl ... 76048
N & S Roadrunner Ct ... 76049
Roam Ct ... 76049
Roaring Springs Ct ... 76048
Rob Dr ... 76049
Roberson Ct ... 76048
Roberts Dr ... 76048
Roberts Bend Ct ... 76048
Robin Ct ... 76049
Robinhood Dr ... 76049
Robins Way ... 76048
Robinson Ct ... 76048
Robinson Creek Dr ... 76048
Rock Harbor Ct & Dr ... 76048
Rock Ridge St ... 76048
Rockcliff Ct ... 76049
Rockview Dr ... 76049
Rockwood Dr ... 76048
Rocky Hill Ct ... 76049
Roe Ct ... 76048
Rollins Rd ... 76049

Rosalie Ct 76049
Rosedown Ct 76049
Rosehill Ln 76048
Rosie Ct 76049
Ross Ln 76048
N & S Rough Creek Ct 76048
Rove Dr 76049
Royal Ln 76049
Ruby Dr 76048
E & W Rucker St 76048
Ruckers Ct 76049
Ruff Country Ct 76048
Running Deer Ct 76049
Ruth Smith Dr 76048
Sabine St 76048
Sabine River Trl 76048
Saddle Rd 76049
Saddle Creek Ct 76048
Saddleview Ct 76048
Sage Ct 76048
N & S Sagecrest Ct 76049
Sagittarius Ln 76049
Saint John Ct 76049
Samoan Ct 76048
San Gabriel Ct & Dr 76048
San Jacinto Dr 76048
San Marcos Ct & Dr 76048
San Mateo Ct 76048
San Saba Ct 76048
Sand Castle Ct 76049
Sandstone Ln 76048
Sandy Beach Dr 76049
Santa Cruz St 76049
Santa Elena Ct 76049
Santa Fe St 76049
Santiago Dr 76048
Sapphire Ln 76049
Sardius Blvd 76049
Satellite Ct 76048
Saturn Dr 76049
Saunter Ln 76049
Savannah Ln 76049
Sawgrass Ct 76049
E & W Scandinavian Ct 76048
Scenic Ct 76048
Scenic Dr 76048
Scenic Way 76049
Scenic Hill Ln 76048
Scenic View Ct 76048
Scissortail Dr 76049
Scorpio Dr 76049
Seattle Slew Ct 76049
Secretariat Ct 76049
Seminole Ct 76049
Seminole Dr 76049
Seminole Trl 76048
E & W Seneca Ct 76048
Setting Sun Ct & Trl 76048
S & W Shadowood St 76048
Shadows Ct 76049
Shady Ln 76049
Shady Bluff Ct 76048
Shady Cove Ct 76048
Shady Grove Cir, Ct & Dr 76049
Shady Haven Rd 76048
Shady Ridge Ct 76049
Shale Bluff Ct 76048
Shallow Creek Ct 76048
Shane Dr 76049
Shannan Cir 76048
Shawnee Trl 76048
Sheila Dr 76049
Sheldon Dr 76049
Shenandoah Ct & Ln 76048
Sherry Ct & Dr 76049
Sherwood Dr 76048
Shorthorn Ct 76049
Sierra Vista Ct & Dr 76048
Siesta Ct 76048
Silver Creek Ct 76048
Sioux Ct 76048
Sioux Dr 76049
Sioux Trl 76048

Six J Ct 76049
N & S Sky Ct & Ln 76049
Sky Harbour Ct & Dr 76049
Skylark Dr 76049
Skyline Dr 76048
Skyview Ct 76048
Sleepy Water Ct & Rd 76048
Smokehouse Rd 76049
Smokerise Trl 76048
Smoky Hill Ct 76049
Snake River Dr 76048
Solar Ct 76049
Song Thrush Dr 76049
Sonora Ct 76049
Sonora Dr 76049
Sonterra Ct 76049
Southaven Ct 76049
Southdown Ct 76049
Southtown Dr 76049
Southwest Pkwy 76049
Space Ct 76049
E & W Spanish Ave & Ct 76048
Spanish Flower Dr 76048
Spanish Moss Dr 76048
W Spanish Oak Dr & St 76048
W Spanish Trail Ct & Dr 76048
Spider Ct 76049
Spring St 76048
Spring Ridge Cir 76048
Spring Willow Ct 76048
Springtime St 76048
Spruce Ct 76048
Spur Ct & Trl 76049
Spyglass Ct 76049
Squaw Ct 76048
Squaw Creek Dr 76049
Stampede Ct 76048
Stanton Ct 76048
Star Ct & Dr 76049
Starlight Ct 76048
Steamers Ct 76048
Steele Trl 76049
Steepleridge Cir & Trl 76048
Stellar Ct 76048
Stembridge Rd 76049
Sterling Rd 76048
Stewarts Oaks Ct 76049
N Stockton St 76048
Stockton Bend Rd 76048
Stone St 76048
Stone Bluff Ct 76048
Stonegate Cir 76048
Stoneridge Dr 76048
Stoneview Dr 76048
Stoney Creek Ct 76049
Stray Rd 76049
Stroll Dr 76049
Stroud Creek Ave 76048
Sumac Dr 76048
Summer Hill Ct 76048
Summercrest Ct 76049
Summerlin Ct & Dr 76048
Summit Rd 76048
Sun Ct 76049
Sun Meadow Cir 76048
Sun Valley Ct 76049
E, N & W Sunchase Ct & Dr 76049
Sundance Ct 76049
Sundance Place Ct 76049
Sundown Trl 76049
Sunflower Ln 76048
Sunrise Ct 76048
Sunrise Dr 76049
Sunrise Bay Ct 76048
Sunset Ct 76049
Sunset Acres Ct 76048
Sunset Bay Ct & Dr 76048
Sunset Cove Ct 76049
Supply Ln 76048
Swaim Dr 76049
Switzer St 76048
Sycamore Cir & Ct 76048

Tahiti Dr 76048
Tahitian Ct 76048
Tahoe Ct 76048
Tahoka Dr 76048
Tall Timber Ct 76049
Tanglewood Dr 76048
Tankersly Rd 76049
Tanton Sound Ct 76049
Taos Ct & St 76048
Tara Ct 76049
Target Ct 76049
Taurus Rd 76049
Taxco Ct 76048
Taxiway Dr 76049
Teal Pl W 76048
Tee Box Ct 76049
Tejas Trl 76048
N & S Teka Ct 76049
Teller Bell Ct & Ln 76049
Temple Hall Hwy 76049
Temple Oaks Ct 76049
Tennessee Trl 76048
Teocalli Ct 76049
Tepee Trl 76048
Teresa Ct
100-199 76049
1000-1099 76048
Terlingua Dr 76048
Terrace Ct 76048
Terri Lee Ln 76048
Terrill Ln 76049
Texas Ave 76049
Texas Trl 76048
Tezcuco Ct 76049
The Briers Ct 76049
The Landing Blvd 76049
The Trees Ct 76049
Thelma Dr 76049
Thicket Ct & Trl 76048
Thomas Rd 76049
Thorp St 76048
Thorpe Springs Rd 76048
N & S Thrash St 76048
Three Creek Ct 76049
Thunderbird Ct & Trl 76049
Timberhaven Ct 76049
Timberline Dr 76048
Timberview Dr 76048
Timberwood Ct 76049
Tin Top Hwy 76048
Tioga Ct 76049
E Tioga Ct 76048
W Tioga Ct 76048
Tomahawk Dr 76048
Tomlinson Rd 76049
Tommie Faye Dr 76049
Topaz Ln 76049
Topeka Ct 76048
W Torrey St 76048
Totem Trl 76048
Tour Ct 76049
Trail Bluff Ct 76048
Trails Edge Ct 76048
Trailwood Ct 76048
Tran Haven Ct 76049
N & S Travis St 76048
N Traylor St 76048
Treaty Oaks Blvd 76048
Tree Dr 76048
Tree Top Ct 76049
Trek Ct 76049
Trinity Ct 76049
Trinity River Trl 76048
Troon Dr 76049
Trotter Ct 76049
Troy Ct 76049
Tulip Dr 76049
Tumbleweed Ln 76049
Turner Cir 76048
Turner Ct 76048
Turquoise Trl 76048
Twin Oak Ct 76048
Twin Sisters Ct 76048
Two Creek Ct 76049
Tyler Ct 76048
Ulua Ct 76048

Umphress Ct 76048
Underwood Ct 76049
Unicorn Ct 76048
Upper Lake Cir 76049
E Us Highway 377
100-1599 76048
E Us Highway 377
1600-6299 76049
W Us Highway 377 76048
Utah Trl 76048
Ute Ct 76048
Uvalde Ct 76048
Valcour Ct 76049
Valhalla Ct & Dr 76049
S Valley Ridge Dr 76048
Valley View St 76048
Van Horn Dr 76048
Vanessa Ct 76048
Vegas Rd 76048
Venus Ct & Dr 76049
Vera Dr 76049
Verde Trl 76048
Verde Hills Trl 76049
Vermont Ct 76048
Victoria Ct 76048
Victorian Ct 76049
Viejo Ct 76049
Vienna Dr 76049
View Point Dr 76048
Villa Ridge Ct 76049
Village Ct & Rd 76049
Vineyard Dr 76048
Virginia Dr 76049
W Virginia Dr 76048
W Virginia Trl 76048
Virgo Ct 76049
Vista Dr 76049
Vista Bluff Ct 76048
Wagon Train Trl 76049
Wagon Wheel Rd 76049
Walker Ct & St 76049
Walnut St 76048
Walnut Creek Cir, Dr & Pkwy 76049
Walnut Place Ct 76049
Walters Dr 76048
Walters Bend Ct 76049
Wandering Ct 76049
Wann Perkins Cir 76048
Waples Dr & Rd 76049
Waples West Ct 76049
Wappoo Ct 76049
War Paint Trl 76048
Warden St 76048
Warnick Ct 76049
Washington St & Trl 76048
Water View Dr 76048
Waterbury Ct 76048
Waterfield Ct & Dr 76048
Waterford Ct 76048
Watermark Blvd 76048
Waterpoint Ct E & W 76048
Waters Edge Dr 76048
Waterview Rd 76048
Waterway Xing 76048
Waterwood Ct & Dr 76048
N & S Waverly Ct 76049
Weatherford Hwy
200-299 76049
1100-2399 76048
2700-6399 76049
Webbs Landing Ct 76048
W Wedgefield Rd 76049
E & W Weems Ct 76049
Weems Estates Ct & Dr 76048
Welham Ct 76049
Wesley St 76049
Western Hills Ct & Trl 76049
Westover Cir, Ct & Dr 76048
Weylene Paseo 76049
Wheeler Ct 76049
Whippoorwill Dr 76049
Whispering Oaks Ct 76049
Whisperview Cir & Dr 76049
Whisperwood Ct 76048

White Cliff Rd 76048
White Horse Ct & Dr 76049
White Oak Trl 76048
White Rock Dr 76048
E White Tail Dr 76049
Whitehead Dr 76048
Whitney Ct 76049
Wichita St 76048
Wigeon St 76049
Wildwood Cir & Ct 76049
Will Walters Rd 76048
Williams Dr 76049
Williamsburg Ct 76048
Williamson Rd 76048
Willow Ct 76048
Willow Ridge Cir 76049
Wills Way Ct & Dr 76049
Wilma Ct 76048
Windcrest Ct & Dr 76049
Winding Rd & Way 76049
Windsor Ct 76049
Windy Heights Ct 76048
Windy Ridge Ct 76049
Winterwood Ct 76048
Winton Terrace Ct 76048
Wisconsin Ct 76048
Wishbone Ct 76049
Wolf Hollow Ct 76048
Wood Ct 76048
N & S Wood Duck Ct & Ln 76049
E, W & N Woodcreek Ct & Dr 76049
Woodcreek Crossing Dr 76049
Woodcrest Ct & Trl 76048
Woodhaven Ct & Dr 76048
Woodlake Dr 76048
Woodland Dr 76048
Woodlawn Dr 76049
Woodmere Trl 76048
Woodview Dr & Trl 76048
Wren Dr 76049
Wren Meadow Ct 76049
Wright Ct 76049
Wyoming Ct 76048
X A Meyer Rd 76049
Yana Ct 76048
Yaqui Trl 76048
Yucatan Dr 76048
Yucca Ct & Dr 76049
Zanzibar Ct 76048
Zuni Ct 76048

NUMBERED STREETS

All Street Addresses 76048

GRAND PRAIRIE TX

General Delivery 75051

POST OFFICE BOXES MAIN OFFICE STATIONS AND BRANCHES

Box No.s
530001 - 539504 75053
540001 - 543540 75054

NAMED STREETS

Abbey Ct 75052
Abbington Ln 75052
Aberdean Trl 75052
Abilene Ct 75052
Acapulco St 75050
Acer Ct 75052
Acosta St 75051
Adam Dr 75052
Aero Dr 75052
Aggie Dr 75051
Airport St 75050
Alamo Ct 75052
Albares 75054
Alcala 75054
Alcott Ln 75052
Alder Trl 75052
Alexander St 75051
Alice Dr 75051
Allegro Ln 75052
Almansa 75054
Alouette Dr 75052
Alspaugh Ln 75052
Altea 75054
Alva Dr 75052
Alyson Way 75052
N American Pl 75051
Amerigo Dr 75051
Amesbury Ln 75052
Amherst Ln 75052
Andante Dr 75052
Andrews Dr 75052
Annalea Ct 75052
Anthony Ln 75052
Antietam Dr 75052
Apache Trce 75051
Appalossa Dr 75052
April Ln 75050
Arabian Dr 75052
N Arbor Rose Dr 75050
Archer Dr 75052
Arenoso 75054
Argus Dr 75052
Arkansas Ln 75052
Arlington Webb Britton Rd 75054
Armed Forces Dr 75051
Armstead Ave 75051
Armstrong Rd 75052
Arrowhead Trce 75051
Arroyo Springs Dr 75052
Ash St 75050
Ashbrook Dr 75052
Ashbury Ct 75050
Ashley Ln 75052
Ashwood Ct 75052
Atlas Ct 75052
Atrium Dr 75052
Augusta Ln 75052
Austin Ave & St 75051
Austrian Rd 75050
Autumn Hl 75052
Autumn Breeze 75052
Autumn View Dr 75050
Avatar Dr 75052
Avenue E 75051
Avenue N 75050
Avenue S 75050
Avenue A 75051
Avenue B 75051
Avenue C 75051
Avenue D 75051
Avenue F 75051
Avenue H 75050
E Avenue J 75050
E Avenue K 75050
Avenue M 75050
Avenue R 75050
Avenue T 75050
Avery Ln 75052
Aviation Pkwy 75052
Axminster Ct & Dr 75050
Babbling Brook Dr 75050
Badbury Ln 75052
N & S Bagdad Rd 75050
Bahamas Ct 75050
Bahia 75054
Baja Dr 75052
Balchen Way 75051
Bald Eagle Way 75052
Baldwin St 75052
Balla Way 75051
Balla Way Ct 75051
Balmoral Ct 75052
Bandera 75054
Barberini Dr 75052
Barcelona Trl 75052

Barco 75054
W Bardin Rd 75052
Barn Owl Trl 75052
Baron Pl 75051
Basswood Dr 75052
Baxter Dr 75052
Bay Shore Ln 75054
Bayfront Dr 75051
Baylor Dr 75051
Bayside Dr 75054
Beach Dr 75051
Beachview Dr 75054
Beacon Dr 75054
Beatty Dr 75052
Beaumont St 75051
Beavers Bend Trl 75052
Becki Dr 75051
Bee Dr 75052
Beechcraft Ave 75051
Beechwood Dr 75052
Belmont Dr 75052
Belt Dr 75052
N Belt Line Rd 75050
S Belt Line Rd
201-597 75051
599-2399 75051
2500-4000 75052
4002-4098 75052
Benissa 75054
Bennie Ln 75051
Bennington Ct 75052
Bent Tree Trl 75052
Bentley Ct & Dr 75052
Bentwood Trl 75052
Berkshire Ln 75052
Bethlehem Dr 75054
Betts Dr 75052
Big Bend Dr 75050
Bigwood Ct 75052
Bill Irwin St 75050
Birch St 75050
Birchbrook St 75052
Birchwood Ln 75050
Birmingham Dr 75052
Biscayne Park Ln 75050
Bishop St 75050
Blackberry Ln 75050
Blackburn St 75050
Blacksmith Ct 75052
Blackstone Dr 75052
Blanco Dr 75052
Bleriot Pl 75051
Bloomfield Dr 75052
Blue Ridge Trl 75052
Blueberry Ln 75052
Bluebonnet Dr 75052
Bluefield Ln 75052
Bluegrass Dr 75052
Bluestone Dr 75052
Boat Ct 75052
Boer Ct 75052
Bogarte Dr 75051
Bois D Arc Ln 75052
Bold Forbes Dr 75052
Bolero 75052
Bonham St 75050
Boots And Saddle Ct 75052
Boscombe Ct 75052
Bosque 75054
Bosswood Ct & Dr 75052
Bowie Ln 75052
Bowles St 75050
Boxwood Dr 75052
Bradford St 75051
Bradley Cir 75052
Bradwood Ave 75052
Brady Ln 75052
Braes Meadow Ct & Dr 75052
Brandon St 75052
Brandy Station Rd 75052
Brannon St 75051
Brave Maxim Ct 75052
Brazoria Dr 75052
Brazos Ct 75052
Brent Ct 75051

Brentwood Dr & Trl 75052
Breton Dr 75052
Brevito Dr 75052
Brewster Ct 75052
Brian Dr 75052
Briar Hill Dr 75052
Briar Oaks Ln 75052
Briarwood Dr 75050
Bridgemarker Dr 75054
Bridgewater Dr 75054
Bridle Path 75050
Bridle Bit Dr 75051
Brim Ct 75052
Bristo Park St 75050
Bristol Cir 75051
British Blvd 75050
Briton Ct 75052
Brittany Ln 75052
Broadsword Ln 75052
Brook Ln 75052
Brookcove Dr 75052
Brookfield Dr 75052
Brookhaven Dr 75052
Brookhurst Dr 75052
Brookvalley Ln 75052
Brookwood Ct 75052
Brown Lee Dr 75052
Browning Ln 75052
Brownwood Ave 75052
Brushcreek St 75052
Bryce Cyn 75052
Bucanero 75054
Buckingham Dr 75052
Buena Dr 75052
Burleson St 75050
Burnet Dr 75052
Burrows Trl 75052
Butterfield Trl 75052
Buxton Dr 75052
Byrd Way 75051
Cabot Dr 75052
Cactus Trl 75052
Calder Dr 75052
Calendar Ct 75050
Caliente Dr 75051
California Trl 75052
Camara Ct 75051
Cambridge Pl 75051
Camden Rd 75051
Camelot St 75050
Cameron Dr 75052
Caminata 75054
Camino Ct 75052
N & S Camino Lagos 75054
W Camp Wisdom Rd 75052
Campfire Dr 75052
Campo St 75051
Campolina Dr 75052
Cana 75054
Canadian Cir 75050
Canal Ct 75054
Cancun St 75051
Candace Dr 75051
Candlelight Ln 75052
Candlestick Dr 75051
Candlewood Pl 75050
Canterbury Ct 75050
Canterbury Park Dr 75050
Cantrell St 75052
Canyon Rd 75052
Canyon Springs Dr 75052
Cap Rock Ln 75052
Cape Cod Dr 75054
Cape Pearl Dr 75054
Capetown Dr 75050
Carcara Ct 75052
Cardiff St 75051
Cardigan Dr 75052
Cardinal Creek Dr 75050
Carlisle Ct 75052
Carlsbad Dr 75051
Carmen Dr 75052
Carmona 75054
Carnation Ct 75052
Carol Dr 75052
Carolina St 75052

Carriage Ct 75050
Carrie Ct 75052
N Carrier Pkwy 75050
S Carrier Pkwy
500-803 75051
802-802 75053
804-2498 75051
805-2499 75051
2500-4799 75052
4801-5099 75052
W Carrier Pkwy 75050
Carrier Pl 75050
Carrington Ln 75052
Carrolls Croft Ct 75050
Carson Trl 75052
Cartgate Ln 75052
Cascade Dr 75050
Caspian Way 75052
Castaway Dr 75051
Castille Dr 75051
Castlecove Dr 75052
Castlerock Cir 75052
Castlewood Cir 75052
Cat Tail Ln 75050
Catamaran Dr 75054
Cathedral Dr 75052
Cavalcade Dr 75052
Cedar Dr 75052
Cedar Glen Ct & Dr 75052
Cedar Ridge Dr 75052
Cedarbrook Dr 75052
Cedro 75054
Celian Dr 75052
Celtic Ash Dr 75052
N Center St 75050
S Center St
101-199 75050
200-1099 75051
Central Ave 75050
Central Park Ln 75050
Cesareo Dr 75052
Chalk Ct 75052
Chamberlain Pl 75051
Champion Hill Dr 75052
Chancellorsville Pkwy 75052
Channing Dr 75052
Chanute Dr 75052
Chaparral Dr 75052
Charon Ct 75052
Chase Ct 75052
Chatham Ct 75052
Chaucer Ct 75052
Cherokee Trce 75051
Cherry Cir & St 75050
Cheshire Way 75052
Chester St 75050
Chestnut Dr 75052
Chickapoo Trce 75051
Chickasaw Trce 75051
Childress Dr 75052
Chipper Ct 75052
Chippewa Ln 75052
Chisholm Trl 75052
Choctaw Trce 75051
Chris Ct 75050
Christina Pl 75051
Christopher Ct & St 75052
Christy St 75051
E & W Church St 75050
Cielo Vista Dr 75052
Cimarron Trce 75051
Cindy Ln 75052
Cladius Dr 75052
Clarebrook Dr 75050
Claremont Dr 75052
Clarice St 75051
Clark Trl 75052
Clay Ct 75052
Clayton St 75052
Clayton Oaks Dr 75052
Clear Brook Cir 75050
Clearlake Dr 75054
Clearwater Dr 75052
Clearwood Dr 75052
Clemente Dr 75052
Cleta Ct 75051

Clifton Ct 75051
Clipper Dr 75054
Club Crest Ct 75052
Clydesdale Dr 75052
Coastline Dr 75054
E & W Cober Dr 75051
Coffeyville Trl 75052
Colca Canyon Rd 75052
Cold Water Trl 75052
College St 75050
Collin Dr 75052
Colosseum Way 75052
Colt Ter 75050
Columbia St 75052
S Columbine Cir & Ln 75052
Columbus 75054
Comal Dr 75052
Comanche Trl 75052
Commodore Dr 75052
Commonwealth Cir 75052
Compas 75054
Compolina Dr 75052
Condor Dr 75051
Condor St 75052
Conover Dr 75051
Conrad Ln 75052
Constantine Ct 75052
Constitution Dr 75052
Cook Dr 75050
Cool Water Ter 75054
Cooper St 75052
Coopers Hawk Ct 75052
E & W Coral Way 75051
Coral Cove Dr 75054
Cordwood Ct 75052
Corn Valley Ct 75052
Corn Valley Rd
2300-2399 75051
2900-3198 75052
3200-3800 75052
3802-4298 75052
Coronado Dr 75052
Corral Rd 75052
Corrida Ct 75052
Cottonwood Ct & St 75050
Cottonwood Valley Ln 75050
Couch Cir 75050
Country Ln 75052
Country Club Cir, Dr & Pl 75052
Courtside Dr 75051
Cove Dr 75054
W Cove Way 75052
Coventry Ct & Dr 75052
Covey Ln 75052
Covington Ct 75052
Coyote Trl 75052
N Cozumel St 75051
Cranbrook Ln 75052
Crane Ct & Dr 75052
E & W Creek Ln 75052
Creekside Way 75050
Creekwood Ln 75052
Crescent Dr 75050
Crescenzio Dr 75052
Crestbrook Ln 75052
Crestview Dr 75052
Crickett Way 75052
Cristin Ln 75051
Crockett St 75051
Croft Creek Cir 75050
Crooks Ct 75051
Crosbyton Ln 75052
Cross Creek Cir 75052
E & W Crossland Blvd 75052
Crow Ct 75051
Crown Dr 75052
Cruise Dr 75054
Crystal Way 75052
Crystal Brook Ct 75052
Cumberland Ln 75052
Curtis Pl 75051
Curtiss St 75050
Curts Cir & Dr 75052
Cypress Ct & Dr 75050
Cypress Glen Dr 75052

Cyrus Ct 75052
Dahlia Dr 75052
Daisy Ln 75052
Daja Ln 75050
Dales Cir 75052
Dallas Ave 75050
NW Dallas St 75050
SE Dallas St 75051
SW Dallas St 75051
Dalway St 75051
Dalworth St 75050
Damon Dr 75052
Danberry Ln 75052
Danish Dr 75050
Danzig Dr 75052
Darbytown Rd 75052
Darsena 75054
Dartmouth Dr 75052
David Dr 75052
David Daniels Dr 75051
Davis St 75050
Dawson Cir 75051
Day Miar Rd 75052
N Day Miar Rd 75054
Dayton Ln 75052
Daywood Ln 75052
Debbie Dr 75052
Deep Lake Dr 75052
Deerbrook Cir 75052
Delollis Dr 75052
Delores Dr 75052
Denali Park Dr 75050
Denmark St 75050
Densman St 75051
Derby Ct 75052
Derek Way 75052
Desco Ln 75051
Desert Sage 75052
Devon Ct 75052
Devonshire Dr 75052
E & W Dickey Dr & Rd 75051
Dillard St 75051
Divot Ct 75052
Dockside Dr 75054
Dodge Trl 75052
Dogwood Ct 75050
Domingo Dr 75051
Donna Dr 75051
Donnie Ln 75052
Doreen St 75050
Dorothy Dr 75051
W Dorris Dr 75051
Doryn Dr 75052
Doubletree Ln 75052
Douglas Pl 75051
Dove Cir 75052
Doy Dr 75051
Duck Pond Dr 75052
Duncan St 75050
Duncan Perry Rd 75050
Durango St 75051
Durham Ct 75052
Durrand Dr 75052
Duval Dr 75052
W E Roberts Dr 75051
Eagle Dr 75052
Earhart Ave 75051
Earle Dr 75052
Earnest Dr 75052
Eastland Dr 75052
Eastwood Ct 75050
Echo Dr 75052
Ector Dr 75052
Ed Smith Ct 75050
S Edelweiss Ct & Dr 75052
Edgeview Ct & Dr 75052
Edgewood Ct & Dr 75052
Edinburgh Ln 75052
Egyptian Way 75050
El Corte St 75050
El Paso St 75051
Elgin Ct 75052
Ellis Ct 75052
Ellis Dr 75050
S Elm Dr 75052

Elmbrook Dr 75052
Embers Trl 75052
Emberwood Dr 75052
Emerald St 75051
Emerson Dr 75052
Enchanted Ct 75050
Endicott Dr 75052
England Pkwy 75054
Enterprise St 75051
Eric St 75052
Erin Ln 75052
Ernie Ln 75052
Escoba Dr 75052
Esplanade 75052
Esquire Pl 75050
Essex Ct & Dr 75052
Estado 75054
Estancio 75054
Estate Dr 75052
Estela 75054
Euclid Dr 75052
Europa Dr 75052
Eva St 75051
Excalibur Dr 75052
Exmoor Ct 75052
Explorador 75054
Eyrie Ct 75052
Fair Oaks Dr 75052
Fairchild St 75051
Fairfax St 75050
Fairfield Dr 75052
Fairhaven Dr 75050
Fairmont Ct & Dr 75052
Fairview Dr 75052
Fairway Dr 75052
Fairway Park St 75050
Falcon Dr 75051
Falcon Trl 75052
Fall Dr 75052
Fall Creek Dr 75052
Fallbrook Dr 75050
Family Cir 75051
Fannin Trl 75052
Fargo Dr 75052
Farmers Rd 75050
Farrier Ct 75052
February Ln 75050
Fenwick St 75052
Ferdinand 75054
Ferncrest Ct 75052
E & W Ferndale Ln 75052
Festival Park Ln 75050
Fieldstone Dr 75052
Fig Tree Ln 75052
Filly Ct 75050
Finland St 75050
Finnhorse Dr 75052
Fishburn St 75050
E Fishcreek Rd 75052
Flamencia 75054
Fleetwood Cove Dr 75052
Florence St 75052
Florida Ct 75050
Fluvia 75054
Foghorn Ln 75054
Fontana 75054
Forest Ct 75052
Forest Lake Dr 75052
Forest Oaks Dr 75052
Forest Park Pl 75052
Forest Trail Dr 75052
Forestedge Dr 75052
Forrest Hill Cir & Ln 75052
Forsyth Ln 75052
Fort Bend Dr 75052
Fort Scott Trl 75052
Fort Worth St 75050
N & S Forum Dr 75052
Fountain Pkwy
500-504 75050
505-1299 75050
505-505 75053
506-1298 75050
Fox Meadow Trl 75052
Foxglove Ct 75052
Frances Dr 75052

Franklin St 75052
Freestone Dr 75052
Freetown Rd 75051
Friars Ln 75052
Frontera 75054
Frontier Dr 75052
Fuente 75054
Furlong Dr 75051
Gaines Mills Rd 75052
Galaway Bay Dr 75052
Gallo 75054
Galveston St 75051
Garden Rd 75052
Garden Grove Ct & Rd 75052
Garden Oaks Pl 75052
Garrett St 75051
Gateway Cir 75051
Gaylewood Ct 75052
Gentry Place Rd 75050
Gifford St 75050
E, S & W Gilbert Cir & Rd 75050
Gildersleeve St 75052
Gillespie Ct & Ln 75052
Glacier Park Ln 75050
Glen Key St 75051
Glenbrook Dr 75052
Glenda Dr 75052
Glendale Dr 75052
Glenwood St 75052
Gloucester Dr 75052
Glynn Cir 75051
Goerte Dr 75051
Golden Eagle Dr 75052
Golf View Ln 75052
Goliad Trl 75052
Goodnight Ct & Trl 75052
Goodwin St 75052
Goshawk St 75052
Gotland Dr 75052
Graham St 75050
Gramley St 75051
Granada St 75051
Grand Central Ctr 75050
N Grand Peninsula Dr 75054
E & W Grand Prairie Rd 75051
Grandview Dr 75052
Grant St 75051
Grason Dr 75052
Grayco Dr 75052
N Great Southwest Pkwy 75050
S Great Southwest Pkwy
401-497 75051
499-2199 75051
2501-3097 75052
3099-4099 75052
4101-4199 75052
Green Branch Dr 75052
Green Hollow Dr 75052
NE Green Oaks Blvd 75050
Green Vista Ct & Trl 75052
Greenbriar Ct 75050
Greenbrook Ln 75052
Greenhill Ln 75052
Greenland Way 75050
Greentree Dr 75052
Greenview Dr 75050
Greenwich Dr 75052
Greenwood Dr 75050
Gregory Ln 75052
E & W Grenoble Dr 75052
W Grove Ln 75052
Guadaloupe 75054
Guilia Dr 75052
Gwyndellons Ln 75052
Hacienda Ct 75052
Halifax St 75050
Hallmark Ct & St 75052
Hamilton Dr 75052
Hammond Dr 75052
Hampshire St 75050
N Hampton Cir & Dr 75052
Hanger Dr 75052

Hanger Lowe Rd 75054
Hanover St 75052
Harbor Lights Dr 75051
Harbour Dr 75054
Harbourtown Dr 75052
Hardrock Rd 75050
Hardwood Ct 75052
Hardy Rd 75051
Harper Ct 75051
Harpers Ferry Dr 75052
Harrell Dr 75052
Harrier St 75052
Harrison St 75051
Hartford Ave 75051
Harvard Dr 75052
Hastings Dr 75052
Hathaway Dr 75052
Hatton Dr 75052
Hawaii Dr 75050
Hawco Dr 75052
Hawthorne Ln 75052
Haymeadow Dr 75052
Haynes St 75050
Haystack Ct & Dr 75052
Hazelwood Dr 75050
Heather Ct & Dr 75052
Heatherbrook Ln 75052
Heinz Way 75051
Hemingway Dr 75052
Hemlock Dr 75052
Hensley Dr 75050
Herboso 75054
Heritage Ct 75050
Hickory St 75050
Hidden Brook Dr 75050
Hidden Cove Dr 75050
Hideaway Dr 75052
High Hawk Blvd 75052
High Prairie Rd 75050
High School Dr 75050
Highland Dr 75051
Highridge Trl 75052
Highvalley Trl 75052
Hill St 75050
Hill Top Ln 75052
Hillcrest Ln 75052
Hilldale Ct 75052
Hillside Dr 75051
Hilton Head Dr 75052
Hinton St 75050
Hobble Ct 75052
Hobbs Dr 75052
Hobby Falcon Trl 75052
Hockley Dr 75052
N & S Holiday Dr 75052
Holland St 75051
Hollow Oak Dr 75052
Holly Hill Dr 75052
Holstein Dr 75052
Homestead Trl 75052
Homewood Ln 75050
Honey Suckle Dr 75052
Hopewell Ct & St 75052
Hopi Trl 75052
Hopkins Dr 75052
Horizon Dr 75054
Horned Owl St 75052
Hospital Blvd 75051
Houston St 75050
Huddleston Dr 75050
Hudson Ave 75052
Hummingbird Dr 75052
W Hunter Ferrell Rd 75050
Huntington Dr 75051
Hunts Pt 75050
Huntwick St 75050
Hyde Park Dr 75050
Idlewild Rd 75051
Independence Ct & Trl 75052
Indian Hills Dr 75051
Industrial St 75050
Ingleside Dr 75050
Inglewood Dr 75051
Ingram Dr 75052
E & W Interstate 20 75052
Inwood Ct 75052

Iris Dr 75052
Ironwood Dr 75052
Isbella Dr 75052
Island Dr 75054
Isuzu Pkwy 75050
Italia Ln 75052
Ivanhoe Cir 75050
Ivy Glen Ct & Dr 75052
Jackson St 75051
Jacob Dr 75052
Jaime Jack Dr 75052
Jamie Dr 75052
Jan Dr 75052
January Ln 75050
Jason Dr 75052
Jasper Dr 75052
E & W Jefferson St 75051
Jelmak St 75050
Jennifer Trl 75052
Jere St 75050
Jerett Dr 75052
Jesse St 75051
Jillian Way 75052
Johnson St 75050
Jon Paul Dr 75052
Jones St 75050
Jordan Dr 75050
Josephine St 75050
Jousting Ln 75052
Joy Dianne Dr 75052
Juneau St 75050
Juniper Dr 75050
Jutland Dr 75052
Kaitlin Way 75052
Kalgary Ln 75052
Kate Ln 75052
Kathryn Dr 75052
Kaylie St 75052
Kelley Dr 75052
Kenedy Ln 75052
Kensington Ct 75052
Kent Dr 75052
Kentshire Dr 75052
Kentucky Ct & Dr 75052
Kenwood Dr 75051
Kessler St 75052
Kestrel St 75052
Kettering Ct 75052
Kiger Dr 75052
Kildeer Ct & Trl 75052
Kimberly Ln 75052
King Arthur St 75050
King Harbor Blvd & Ct 75052
King Richard Dr 75050
Kings Ct 75051
Kingsbridge St 75050
Kingsley Dr 75050
Kingston Dr 75051
Kingsway Dr 75052
Kingswood Blvd 75052
Kirby Creek Dr 75052
N Kirbywood Trl 75052
Kite Rd 75052
Kitty Hawk Ln 75051
Kiwi Ct 75051
Kleberg Dr 75052
Klondike St 75050
Knight Cir 75050
Knights Xing 75052
Knightsbridge St 75050
Knoll Ridge Ct 75050
La Cresta Ct 75052
La Fiesta Dr 75052
La Fontana 75052
La Mancha 75054
La Moda St 75050
La Roche St 75050
La Roda 75054
La Salle Trl 75052
La Sombra St 75050
La Valse St 75052
Lagoon Dr 75054
Lake Dr 75051
Lake Country Dr 75052
Lake Forest Dr 75052
Lake Garden Dr 75052
Lake Grove Dr 75052
Lake Haven Ln 75052
Lake Park Dr 75052
Lake Point Dr 75050
Lake Ridge Pkwy 75052
Lake Way Dr 75052
Lakebend Dr 75054
Lakecrest St 75051
Lakefront Dr 75054
Lakeland Dr 75054
Lakemont Dr 75052
Lakeshore Dr 75051
Lakeview Dr 75051
Lakewood Dr 75054
Lancaster Dr 75052
Lancelot Cir 75050
Landing Dr 75054
Lanshire Ct 75052
Lantern Ln 75052
Laredo Ct & Dr 75052
Largo Dr 75052
Larkspur Ct 75052
Larreta 75054
Las Flores Ct 75052
Las Palmas Dr 75052
Laura Ln 75052
Laurel St 75050
Lavaca Rd 75052
Lavanda 75054
Lazy Creek Dr 75052
Lazybrook Ln 75050
Legendary Ct 75050
Lemart St 75051
Lemon Dr 75052
Leon Dr 75052
Leonard St 75050
Lewis Trl 75052
Lexington Cir 75050
Leyfair Dr 75050
Libby Ln 75050
Liberty Pl 75052
Lida Ct 75050
Limestone Dr 75052
Limousin Ln 75052
Lincoln Park Dr 75050
Lincolnshire Dr 75052
Linda Kay Ln 75052
Lindbergh Ln 75051
Linden Ln 75052
Lindly St 75052
Lindsey Ln 75052
Links View Ct 75052
Lisa St 75051
Lisetta St 75052
Little John Dr 75050
Liverpool Ln 75052
Livingston Ln 75052
Llano Trl 75052
Locksley Dr 75050
Loda Ct 75050
Lodosa 75054
Lone Star Pkwy 75050
Longbow Dr 75052
Longhorn Trl 75052
Lorenzo Dr 75052
Lorraine Ave 75052
Lost Crk 75052
Lost Mesa 75052
Lotus Ct 75052
Louella St 75051
Lovell St 75050
Loving Trl 75052
Lower Tarrant Rd 75050
Lucena Ct 75052
Lusino Ct 75052
Luxor Ct 75052
Lynne Dr 75052
Maberry Ct 75052
Macarthur Blvd 75050
Macaw Ct 75051
Macgregor Dr 75050
Madison Dr 75052
Magellan 75054
Magna Carta Blvd 75052
Magnolia Dr 75052
E & W Main St 75050
Maine Anjou Dr 75052
Malero Dr 75051
Malvern Hill Rd 75052
Manana Dr 75050
Manchester St 75050
Manning St 75051
Manor St 75050
Maple St 75050
Marblearch Dr 75052
March Ln 75050
Marco Dr 75052
Marcy Ct 75052
Marea 75054
Margaret St 75051
Maria Dr 75052
Marian St 75050
Marigold Dr 75052
Marina Dr 75054
Marine Forces Dr 75051
Mark Dr 75052
Marsh Harrier Ave 75052
E & W Marshall Dr &
Plz 75051
Martha St 75050
Martin Pl 75051
Martin Barnes Rd 75052
Mary Pat Dr 75052
Matagorda Ct & Ln 75052
Matamoros St 75051
Matson Dr 75050
Matt Pl 75051
Matthew Rd 75052
Maverick Dr 75052
May Ln 75050
Mayfield Rd 75052
Mckensie Ct & Ln 75052
Meacham Ct 75052
Meade Dr 75052
Meadow Cir 75052
Meadow Ct 75050
Meadow Ln 75050
Meadow Creek Ct 75052
Meadow Lake Dr 75050
Meadow Park Ln 75052
Meadowbrook Dr 75052
Meadows Dr 75052
Meadowside Ct 75052
Medical Row 75051
Melorine Dr 75051
Mercer St 75052
Meriden Ct 75052
Merlin Dr 75052
Merritt St 75052
Mesa Ridge Trl 75052
Mesa Verde 75052
Meseta 75054
Metronome Dr 75052
Michael Dr 75052
Middleton Ave 75051
Midnight Ln 75052
Midpointe Blvd 75050
Mildred Way 75051
Milford St 75051
Miller St 75051
Millpond Ct 75051
Minuet St 75052
Mirabella Blvd
401-2099 75054
6000-6298 75052
6300-6398 75052
Mirada 75054
Mirado 75054
Miramar 75054
Misty Meadow Dr 75052
Misty Mesa Trl 75052
Mobile Rd 75052
Modelli Dr 75052
Montague Ln 75052
Montalbo 75054
Montana Trl 75052
Monteleon St 75051
Moonbeam Ln 75052
Moore St 75050
Moorgate Ct 75052
Morgan Dr 75052
Morning Meadow Ln 75052
Morning Mist Ln 75052
Morning Star Dr 75054
Morningside Dr 75052
Mosaic Ct 75052
Motley St 75051
E & W Mountain Ln 75052
E & W Mountain Creek
Ct & Dr 75052
Mountain Laurel Dr 75052
Music Way 75051
Mustang Ln 75050
Nacogdoches Trl 75052
Nadar 75054
Nadine Ln 75052
Nantucket Way 75054
Naples Ln 75052
Nashwood Dr 75051
Natchez Ct 75052
Nava 75054
Navarro Ln 75052
Navigation Dr 75054
New Forest Dr 75052
New Haven St 75051
Newberry St 75052
Newcastle Ln 75052
Newport St 75052
Nicholas Ct 75052
Nina Cir 75052
Nina Dr 75051
Noric Dr 75052
Normandy Way 75052
North St 75050
Northstar Dr 75054
Northtown Dr 75050
Northview Dr 75051
Northwood Ct 75050
Norway Ln 75052
Norwich Ln 75052
Nottingham Pl 75050
Novus Ct 75052
Nueces Ln 75052
Nueva Tierra St 75052
Nunez Dr 75051
Oak Ln 75051
Oak St 75050
Oak Briar Ln 75052
Oak Crest Dr 75052
Oak Glen Ct & Dr 75052
Oak Hollow Dr 75052
Oak Knoll Way 75050
Oak Meadow Dr 75052
Oak Ridge Pl 75052
Oakbrook Dr 75052
W Oakdale Rd 75050
Oakhaven Dr 75050
Oakland St 75052
Oakmont Dr 75052
Oaknut Cir 75052
Oakview Dr 75050
Oakwood Dr 75050
Ola Ln 75050
Olympia Dr 75052
Olympic Park Dr 75050
Opelousas Ct & Trl 75052
Oregon Ct 75052
Orion Dr 75054
Oryx Ln 75052
Osage Ct & Trl 75052
Osler Dr 75051
Othen Dr 75052
Ouida St 75051
Our Ln 75052
Over Ridge Dr 75052
Overland Trl 75052
Owen Trl 75051
Oxford Cir 75051
Ozark Dr 75052
E Pacific St 75050
Paddington Ln 75052
Paddock Way Dr 75050
Padilla 75054
Padre Ct & Ln 75052
Paducah Ln 75052
Paintbrush Ct 75052
E & W Palace Dr &
Pkwy 75050
Paladium Dr 75052
Palencia 75054
Palmer Trl 75052
Palo Pinto 75052
Palomino Way 75052
Palos Verdes St 75052
Pampa 75054
Pamplona 75054
Pangburn St 75051
Panorama Ln 75052
Paolo Dr 75052
Parham Dr 75052
Paris Dr 75050
Parish Ct 75052
Park Pl 75052
Park Sq E 75050
Park Sq N 75050
Park Place Dr 75052
Park Ridge Dr 75052
Park Springs Dr 75052
Parkcrest Dr 75052
Parker Rd 75050
Parkline Trl 75052
Parkside Dr 75052
Parkvale Ln 75052
Parkview Dr 75052
Parkway Dr 75051
Parkwood Dr 75050
Partridge Ct 75052
Paseo 75054
Peaceful Lake Ct 75054
Peach Tree Bnd 75050
Pearson Dr 75052
Pearwood Ct 75050
Pebblebrook Ct 75050
Pecan Dr 75050
Pecos Way 75052
Peek St 75051
Pegasus Ct 75052
Pendleton Ct 75052
Penny Ln 75052
Peregrine Ct 75052
Performance Pl 75050
Perrine Pl 75052
Persimmon Dr 75052
Pez Dr 75051
Pheasant Run Ct 75052
E & W Phillips Cir &
Ct 75051
Piazza Ct 75054
Pietro Dr 75052
Pigeon Ct 75051
Pine St 75050
Pine Valley Dr 75052
Pinebrook Dr 75052
Pinehill Ln 75052
Pinewood Dr 75051
Piney Meadow Pl 75050
Pinnacle Point Dr 75054
Pino 75054
Pinoak Dr 75052
Pinta Cir 75052
E & W Pioneer Pkwy 75051
Pisces St 75051
Plains Ct 75052
Plattner St 75050
Playa 75054
Pleasant Hill Rd 75052
Plymouth Dr 75052
Pollock Pl 75050
W Polo Rd 75052
Pompi Dr 75052
Ponce De Leon 75054
Pond View Ct 75052
Ponderosa Dr 75052
Ponds Edge Trl 75052
Ponzano 75054
Porma 75054
Portillo 75054
Portside Dr 75054
Post N Paddock St 75050
Post Oak Dr 75050
Postbridge Rd 75050
Potter Ct 75052
Poulin Ave 75050
Prado 75054
Prairie Ln 75052
Prairie Creek Ct & Dr 75052
Prairie Falcon Ct 75052
Prairie Hill Dr 75051
Prairie Oak Blvd 75052
Prairie Ranch Dr 75052
Prairie View Ct 75052
Preakness Dr 75051
Presidio Dr 75052
Presto Cir 75052
Preston Trl 75052
Primrose Ct 75052
Prince Ct 75051
Prince John Ct & Dr 75050
Proctor Dr 75051
Promontory Dr 75054
Pryor Pl 75051
Pueblo Rdg 75052
Purcell St 75050
Putter Ct 75052
Quail Ct & Xing 75052
Quail Creek Dr 75052
Quail Hollow Dr 75051
Quannah Dr 75052
Quarter Horse Dr 75050
Queens Way 75052
Queenston Dr 75050
Queenswood Dr 75052
Racehorse Dr 75050
Rachel St 75052
Racquet Club Dr 75052
Ragland Rd 75052
Rainbow Dr 75052
Raintree Ct 75050
Ralph St 75051
Ranch Rd 75052
Ranchview Dr 75052
Raptor Ct 75052
Ravenwood Dr 75050
Raynes Park Ln 75050
Raywood Dr 75052
Rebecca Ct 75052
Red Hawk Dr 75052
Red Mine Ln 75052
Red Oak Dr 75052
Red River Trl 75052
Redwood Dr 75052
Reforma Dr 75052
Regal Oak Rd 75052
Regatta Dr 75054
Regency Dr 75050
Remmington Dr 75052
Renfro St 75051
Reno Way 75052
Rhapsody St 75052
Rialto Way 75052
Rice St 75050
Richardson Dr 75051
Rickenbacker Pl 75051
Ridge Point Dr 75052
Ridgecrest Rd 75052
Ridgemar Dr 75051
Ridgeway Dr 75052
Ridgewood Dr 75052
Rinehart St 75050
Rio Grande Dr 75052
River Lake Way 75052
River Ridge Blvd 75050
Riverside Pkwy 75050
Riverwood Ln 75052
Roaring Springs Rd 75052
Robertson Rd 75050
Robin Dr 75052
Robinhood Dr 75050
Robinson Ct 75051
Robinson Rd 75051
S Robinson Rd 75052
Roble 75054
Rocco Dr 75052
Rochester Ct 75052
Rock Creek Dr 75050
E & W Rock Island
Rd 75050
Rockwall Dr 75052
Rolling Hills Ln 75052
Roman Rd 75050
Rongway St 75051
Rose Lee Seaton Rd 75050
Rosedale Dr 75052
Rosemont Ave 75052
Rosewood St 75050
Rosina 75054
Roundtable Ct 75050
Roy Orr Blvd 75050
Royal Ave 75051
Royal Valley Rd 75052
Royalwood Ct 75052
Ruby Rd 75050
Ruea St 75050
Rueda 75054
Rugby Ln 75052
Ruggles St 75050
Rustlewind Ln 75052
Ryan Rd 75052
Sabine Ln 75052
Saddle Hill Dr 75050
Saddleridge Ct 75052
Safran Dr 75052
Sagebrush Dr 75052
Saguaro Dr 75052
Sail Away Pl 75054
Saint Andrews Dr 75052
Saint Johns Way 75050
Salem St 75052
Salisbury Dr 75052
Sally Ct 75052
Saloon Dr 75052
Saltillo St 75051
Sampsell Dr & St 75051
San Antonio St 75051
San Augustine Ln 75052
San Carlos St 75051
San Grande Ct 75050
San Jacinto Dr 75052
San Patricio Dr 75052
San Pedro St 75051
San Remo Dr 75052
N & S San Saba St 75052
San Sebastian Cir 75052
Sandalwood Dr 75052
Sanders St 75051
E Sandra Ln 75052
Sandy Ln 75050
Sandy Shoal Ct 75050
Santa Anna Dr 75052
Santa Barbara Dr 75052
Santa Clara Ct 75051
Santa Cruz Ct 75051
Santa Fe Ct & Trl 75052
Santa Margarita St 75052
Santa Maria Ct 75051
Santa Monica Dr 75052
Santa Paula Dr 75052
Santa Rita Dr 75052
Santa Rosa Ct 75051
Santa Sabina Dr 75052
Santerre St 75050
Santiago Cir 75052
Sara Jane Pkwy 75052
Sarria 75054
Sarum Ct 75052
Saugus Dr 75052
Savage Station Dr 75052
Scarborough Dr 75052
Scarlet Ln 75050
Scotland Dr 75052
Screech Owl Ln 75052
Sea Gull Dr 75051
Sea Harbor Dr 75054
Sea Hawk St 75052
Sea Star Dr 75054
Seabreeze Dr
1501-1597 75051
1599-1699 75051
6900-6999 75054
Seacoast Dr 75054
Seascape Dr 75054
Secretariat Dr 75052
Sedgemoor Dr 75052
Sedona Dr 75052
E Seeton Rd 75054
Seider Ln 75052

Senda 75054
Sequoia Dr 75052
Serenade St 75052
Serpis 75054
N & S Serrano 75054
Seven Hills Dr 75052
Seven Pines Dr 75052
Shackleford Trl 75052
Shadow Pass 75050
Shady Ln & Trl 75052
Shady Creek Dr 75052
E & W Shady Grove Rd 75050
Shady Oak Trl 75052
Shalloway Dr 75054
Shalot Cir 75050
Shannon Ln 75052
Sharlis Cir 75050
Sharpsburg Dr 75052
Sharpshire St 75050
Shawnee Trce 75051
Sheffield Dr 75052
Shelby Ln 75052
Sheriff Dr 75051
Sherman St 75051
Sherry Cir 75050
Sherwood Dr 75050
Shield Dr 75052
Shire Way 75052
Shirebrook Ct 75052
Shirecreek Cir 75052
W Shore Dr 75052
Shoreview Dr 75054
Shoreway Dr 75054
Short St 75051
Shorthorn Ct 75052
Show Pl 75051
Showdown Ln 75052
Sicily Ct 75052
Sierra Ct & Dr 75052
Sierra Springs Dr 75052
Siesta Trl 75052
Silver Trl 75052
Silver Horn Ct 75050
Silver Meadow Ln 75052
Silver Sage Ln 75052
Silverado Trl 75052
Singleton Dr 75051
Sir Guy Dr 75050
Sir Roland Dr 75052
Sir Stewart Cir 75052
Skinner Way 75052
Skyline Cir 75050
Skyline Rd 75051
Skyway Dr 75052
Slaton Dr 75052
Sleepy Glen Dr 75052
Small St 75050
Small Hill Dr 75050
Smokewind Ln 75052
Snowy Owl St 75052
Soaring Eagle Ct 75052
Socrates Dr 75052
Somerton Dr 75052
Somervell Trl 75052
Sommerset Dr 75052
Sonora Ct & Ln 75052
Sotogrande St 75051
Southlook Dr 75052
Southridge Ct 75052
Southwood Trl 75052
Spanish Trl 75052
Sparks St 75051
Sparrow Hawk Ct 75052
Spartacus Dr 75052
Spencer Cir 75052
Spikes St 75051
Spinner Ln 75052
Spring Ct 75052
Spring Creek Cir 75054
Spring Lake Dr 75054
Spring Meadow Ln 75052
Springbrook Ave 75050
W & E Springdale Cir & Ln 75052
Springwood Dr 75052
Spur Dr 75052
Spyglass Dr 75052
Squire Ct 75051
Stadium Dr 75050
Stagecoach Way 75052
Stallion Ln 75050
Starbridge Ln 75052
N State Highway 161 75050
S State Highway 161
800-1999 75051
S State Highway 161
2900-2998 75052
N State Highway 360 75050
S State Highway 360 75052
Stearman Pl 75051
Steeple Chase Ct 75052
Stephen St 75052
Stephens Pkwy 75051
Steppington St 75052
Still Meadow Ct 75052
Stinwick Ln 75052
Stockton Trl 75052
Stonebrook Dr 75052
Stonehenge Dr 75052
Stonelake Dr 75050
Stoneridge Dr 75050
Stones River Rd 75052
Stonewall Dr 75052
Stoneway Dr 75052
Stratford Dr 75051
Stream Dr 75052
Stresa Ln 75052
E & W Strong Pkwy 75050
Suffolk Dr 75052
Sugar Creek Ln 75050
Sugar Mill Ln 75050
Summerfield Ln 75052
Summertree Ln 75052
Summervell Trl 75052
Summerview Dr 75052
Summerwood Dr 75052
Summit Ct 75052
Summit View St 75050
Sun Rise Ln 75052
Sunny Meadow Ln 75052
Sunnybrook St 75051
Sunnyvale Rd 75050
Sunset Ln 75052
Sunset Ridge Dr 75050
Sunvalley Dr 75052
Surfside Ln 75054
Surrey Cir 75050
Susanna Dr 75052
Sussex Ave 75052
Sutton Dr 75052
Swainsons Hawk Ln 75052
Swallowtail Ct 75052
Sweet Birch 75052
Sweetbriar Ln 75052
Sweetwater Dr 75050
Swenson Ct 75052
Sword Dancer Way 75052
Talon St 75052
Tamara Ln 75051
Tamarack Dr 75052
Tampico St 75051
Tanbark Ct 75052
Tangle Ridge Dr 75052
Tanglebrook Dr 75052
Tanner Way 75052
Taos Dr 75051
Tapley St 75051
Tarpon Ln 75052
Tarragon Ln 75052
E & W Tarrant Rd 75050
Tawny Owl Rd 75052
Teal Dr 75052
Teodoro Dr 75052
Teresa Ln 75052
E & W Terrace St 75050
Terrell Dr 75052
Terry Dr 75051
Tersk Ct 75052
Texas St 75051
Thames Dr 75052
Thicket Trl 75052
Thornbush Dr 75052
Thornwood Trl 75052
Thoroughbred Ln 75050
Three Tee Ct 75052
Throckmorton Dr 75052
Tiago Dr 75050
Tiber River Ct & Ln 75052
Tiffany Trl 75052
Timber Ct 75052
Timber Creek Dr 75052
Timber Oaks Ln 75051
Timberdale St 75052
Timberleaf Dr 75052
Timberwood Ct 75052
Times St 75052
Tina Dr 75052
Tinto 75054
Tipperary Dr 75052
Tivoli Dr 75052
Toccata 75052
Tokara Ct 75052
Tolosa 75054
Tompkins Dr 75051
Torio 75054
Tormes 75054
Tournament Ct 75050
Town Lake Dr 75054
E & W Townhouse Ln 75052
Trail Lake Dr 75054
Trailerdell St 75051
Trailwood Dr 75052
Tranquilo 75054
Trent Ct 75052
Trevino 75054
Trible Dr 75050
Trigg St 75051
Trilene Dr 75052
Trinidad Dr 75052
Trinity Blvd 75050
Triple Crown Ln 75051
Tripoli Trl 75050
Triton Ct 75052
Turf Ct 75052
Turnberry Ln 75052
Turner Blvd 75050
Turner Pkwy 75051
Tuscany Ln 75052
Tusing St 75050
Tuskegee St 75051
Twilight Dr 75052
Twin Brooks Dr 75052
Twisted Vine Ln 75052
Tyler Dr 75052
Typhon Dr 75052
Tyre St 75051
Val Verde Ct 75052
E Valley Ln 75050
Valley Brook Ln 75052
Valley View Dr 75050
Van Zandt Dr 75052
Varsity Dr 75051
Vega Ct & St 75050
Vela 75054
Velero 75054
Venecia Way 75052
Venice Dr 75054
Vera Cruz Dr 75052
Veranda Ct 75050
E & W Verde Woods St 75052
Vespesian Ln 75052
Vicky Ln 75052
Victoria Dr 75052
Villa Di Lago 75054
Village Green Dr 75052
Vineyard Rd 75052
Vintage Dr 75052
Virginia St 75051
Vista Cir 75052
Vista Heights Ln 75052
Vista Verde Dr 75051
Vivian Cir 75052
Volturno Dr 75052
Vought Pl 75051
Waco Pl 75051
Waggoner St 75051
Wagon Wheel Dr 75052
Wahoo Trce 75051
Walden Place Ct 75052
Wales Ct 75052
Walingford Dr 75052
Walker St 75052
Walnut St 75050
Walsh Ln 75052
Walter Hill Dr 75050
Warder Way 75051
Ware Dr 75051
Warrington Dr 75052
E & W Warrior Trl 75052
Warwick Ave 75052
Water Oak Dr 75052
Waterbridge St 75052
Waterbury St 75051
Watercrest Ln 75054
Waterfield Ct 75052
Waterford Dr 75052
Waterfront Dr 75054
Waters Edge Dr 75054
Waterside Dr 75054
Waterview Dr 75050
Waterway Dr 75054
Waterwheel Ct 75052
Waterwood Dr 75052
Watson St 75051
Wayne Way 75052
Weathered Trl 75052
Web Ct 75052
Webb Britton Rd 75052
Webb Lynn Rd 75052
Wedgewood Dr 75050
Weirgate Ct 75052
Welara Dr 75052
Wellington Dr 75051
Wendy Dr 75052
Wentworth Dr 75052
Wescott Dr 75052
Westbriar Ln 75052
Westbrook Ct 75052
Westchase Dr 75052
E & W Westchester Pkwy 75052
Westchester Glen Dr 75052
Westcliff Rd 75052
Westcrest Ct 75050
Westfield St 75050
Westhoff Dr 75052
Westminster Dr 75050
Westover Dr 75052
Westpark Dr 75050
Westridge St 75050
Wexford Dr 75052
Weyland Dr 75052
Wheathill Dr 75051
Wheeler St 75052
Whispering Breeze Dr 75050
White Oak Dr 75052
Whitehall Dr 75052
Whitman Ln 75052
Wichita Trl 75052
Wild Covey Trl 75052
Wild Valley Trl 75052
Wilderness Trl 75052
Wilderness Way Dr 75054
Wildflower Dr 75052
Wildlife Blvd 75050
Wildwood Dr 75050
Will Point Dr 75052
Willington Dr 75052
Willouby Dr 75052
Willow St 75050
Willow Trl 75052
Willow Glen Ct 75052
Willow Spring Ct 75052
Willowbrook Cir 75052
Willowood Ln 75052
Wilmer Dr 75052
Wilmington Ct & Dr 75052
Wiltshire St 75050
Winchester Ct 75052
Windbrook Dr 75052
Windchime Ct & Dr 75051
Windermere Ln 75052
Windham Dr 75052
Windhurst Dr 75052
Winding Trl 75052
Winding Creek Dr 75052
Winding Forest Ct & Dr 75052
Winding Ridge Trl 75052
Windsor Pl 75051
Windward Dr 75054
Windy Meadow Ln 75052
Windy Point Dr 75052
Winford Dr 75052
Winners Row 75050
Winslow Dr 75052
Winston St 75052
Wintercrest Rd 75052
Wise Rd 75052
Wisteria Dr 75050
Wolcott Ln 75052
Wolfforth Dr 75052
Wood Brook Dr 75052
Wood Lake Trl 75054
Wood Stream Dr 75052
Wood Thrush St 75052
Woodacre Dr 75052
Woodcrest Dr 75052
Wooddale Ct 75052
Woodfield Dr 75052
Woodhaven Ln 75052
Woodland Ct 75052
Woodlawn Dr & Ln 75052
Woodside Dr 75052
Woodsman Ct 75052
Woodstone Trl 75052
Woodview Ct 75050
Woodvine Ct 75052
Woodward Ct 75052
Worthway Dr 75051
Wren Ct 75052
Wright Blvd 75050
Wright Pl 75051
Wuthering Cir 75052
Yale Dr 75052
Yarrow Ct 75052
Yaupon Dr 75052
Yellow Tavern Ct 75052
Yellowleaf Dr 75052
Yeltes 75054
Yorkshire Dr 75050
Young St 75050
Zanes Ct 75052
Zion Hl 75052

NUMBERED STREETS

NE 2nd St 75050
NW 2nd St 75050
SE 2nd St 75051
SW 2nd St
100-108 75050
110-120 75050
200-798 75051
800-999 75051
1001-1099 75051
NE 3rd St 75050
SE 3rd St 75051
SW 3rd St 75051
NE 4th St 75050
NW 4th St 75050
SE 4th St 75051
SW 4th St 75051
NE 5th St 75050
NW 5th St 75050
SE 5th St 75051
SW 5th St 75051
NE 6th St 75050
NW 6th St 75050
SW 6th St 75051
NW 7th St 75050
NW 8th St 75050
SE 8th St 75052
NE 9th St 75050
NW 9th St 75050
SE 9th St 75051
NE 10th St 75050
NW 10th St 75050
SE 10th St 75051
NE 11th St 75050
NW 11th St 75050
SE 11th St
101-109 75050
200-999 75051
NE 12th St 75050
SE 12th St 75051
NE 13th St 75050
NW 13th St 75050
SE 13th St 75051
NW 14th St 75050
SE 14th St
113-199 75050
201-297 75051
299-2599 75051
2601-2699 75052
3200-3498 75052
SW 14th St 75051
NE 15th St 75050
NW 15th St 75050
SE 15th St 75050
SW 15th St 75051
NW 16th St 75050
SE 16th St 75050
SW 16th St 75051
NE 17th St 75050
NW 17th St 75050
SE 17th St 75050
SW 17th St 75051
NE 18th St 75050
NW 18th St 75050
SW 18th St 75051
NE 19th St 75050
NW 19th St 75050
SE 19th St 75050
SW 19th St 75051
NE 20th St 75050
NW 20th St 75050
SW 20th St 75051
NW 21st St 75050
NE & NW 22nd 75050
NE 23rd St 75050
NW 23rd St 75050
SW 23rd St 75051
NW 24th St 75050
NW 25th St 75050
NE & SE 26th 75050
NE 27th St 75050
NE 28th St 75050
NE 29th St 75050
NE 31st St 75050
NE 32nd St 75050
NE 33rd St 75050
NE 35th St 75050
NE 36th St 75050
NE 37th St 75050
NE 38th St 75050
107th St 75050
108th St 75050
109th St 75050
110th St 75050
111th St 75050
112th St 75050
113th St 75050
114th St 75050

GRAPEVINE TX

General Delivery 76099

POST OFFICE BOXES MAIN OFFICE STATIONS AND BRANCHES

Box No.s
All PO Boxes 76099

RURAL ROUTES

01, 04, 05, 06, 08, 11, 12, 14, 15, 19, 23, 27, 28, 37 76051

NAMED STREETS

Abercorn Dr 76051
Ainsworth Cir 76051
Airline Dr 76051
Alamo Trl 76051
Alice Ct 76051
Altacrest Ct & Dr 76051
Amesbury Cir 76051
Anderson Gibson Rd 76051
Anglers Dr & Plz 76051
Appling Dr 76051
Arbor Oak Dr 76051
Asbury Dr 76051
Ashcroft Dr 76051
Ashington Dr 76051
Ashmore Ln 76051
Ashwood Ln 76051
N & S Aspenwood Dr 76051
Austin St 76051
Austin Creek Dr 76051
Austin Oaks Dr 76051
Autumn Dr 76051
Autumn Ridge Ln 76051
Autumndale Dr 76051
Avondale Dr 76051
Avonia Dr 76051
Azalea Dr 76051
S Ball St 76051
Banyan Dr 76051
Barberry Rd 76051
N & S Barton St 76051
Basin Trl 76051
Bass Pro Dr 76051
Bayou Rd 76051
Beacon Hill Ct 76051
Bear Haven Dr 76051
Bear Run Dr 76051
Bellaire Dr 76051
Bennington Ct 76051
Bentley Ct 76051
Bentwood Ct 76051
Berkley Dr 76051
Berkshire Ln 76051
Berry St 76051
Beverly Dr 76051
Big Bend Dr 76051
Birch Ave 76051
Blair Ct 76051
Blair Meadow Dr 76051
Blairstone Pnes 76051
Blevins St 76051
Blueberry Ln 76051
Bluebird Ct 76051
Bluebonnet Dr 76051
Bonham Trl 76051
Bowie Ln 76051
Box Canyon Ct 76051
Boxwood Dr 76051
Boyd Dr 76051
Bradford Dr 76051
Branch Hollow Ln 76051
Branchwood Dr 76051
Brentcove Dr 76051
Brenton Oaks Dr 76051
Brentwood Cir 76051
Brettenmeadow Dr 76051
Brewer St 76051
Brian Ct 76051
Briana Ct 76051
Briar Cv 76051
Briarcrest Dr 76051
Briarcroft Dr 76051
Briarwood Dr 76051
Bridle Ln 76051
Bridlewood Dr 76051
Brighton Cv 76051
Brittany Ln 76051
Brook Meadow Ct 76051
Brookcrest Ln 76051
Brookgate Dr 76051
Brookhill Ln 76051
Brookshire Dr 76051
Brookside Dr 76051
Brookwood Dr 76051
Brownstone Ct & Dr 76051

Buckhorn Ct 76051
Burninglog Dr 76051
Bushong Rd 76051
Butterfield Dr 76051
Cabernet Ct 76051
Cable Creek Ct, Dr & Rd 76051
Cambridge Ct 76051
Camelot Dr 76051
Cameron Xing 76051
Candle Ct 76051
Cannon St 76051
Canyon Dr 76051
Capitol St 76051
Caprock Ct 76051
Cardinal Ct & Dr 76051
Carlsbad Ct 76051
Carly Dr 76051
Carnegie Ln 76051
Casa Loma Ct 76051
Castle Ct 76051
Caviness Dr 76051
Cedar Dr 76051
Cedarpoint Dr 76051
Central Ave 76051
Chadourne Ct 76051
Champagne Blvd 76051
Chaparral Ct 76051
Chase Oak Dr 76051
Chasewood Dr 76051
Chatam Hill St 76051
Chatsworth Dr 76051
Chelsea St 76051
Chesapeake Ct 76051
Cheshire Dr 76051
Choteau Cir 76051
Chris Ln 76051
Chris Craft Dr 76051
Church St 76051
Churchill Loop 76051
Cimarron Ct & Trl 76051
Circle View Ct 76051
Circlewood Ct 76051
Clearfield Dr 76051
Clearwater Ct 76051
Cliffside St 76051
Cliffwood Dr 76051
Cloverdale Ct 76051
Cobblestone Dr 76051
Cobbs Dr 76051
E & W College St 76051
Columbine Dr 76051
Coppell Rd 76051
Copperfield Dr 76051
Corporate Dr 76051
Cory St 76051
Country Ln 76051
Country Forest Ct 76051
Countryside Ct & Dr 76051
Coventry Dr 76051
Coveside 76051
Creekbend Cir 76051
Creekview Cir & Dr 76051
N & S Creekwood Ct & Dr 76051
Cresthaven Ct & Dr 76051
Crestline Dr 76051
Crestridge Ct 76051
Crestview Dr 76051
Crestwood Ct 76051
Cripple Creek Trl 76051
Crockett Ct 76051
Cross Creek Dr 76051
Cross Roads Dr 76051
Crystal Brooke 76051
Cypress Creek Ct 76051
E & W Dallas Rd 76051
Daniel St 76051
Dartmont Dr 76051
Dawn Ln 76051
Deer Crk 76051
Devonshire Ct 76051
Dogwood Dr 76051
N & S Dooley Ct & St 76051
Dorchester Ct 76051
Double Creek Dr 76051

Dove Rd 76051
Dove Creek Cir & Pl 76051
E Dove Loop Rd 76051
Dove Meadow Ct 76051
Dove Pond Dr 76051
Drexel Dr 76051
Dublin Cir & St 76051
Dunn Ct & St 76051
Eagle Cir & Dr 76051
Eagle Crest Dr 76051
Earls Alley St 76051
East Ct 76051
Easy St 76051
Eaton Ln 76051
Echo Cv 76051
Eckley St 76051
Edgehill St 76051
Ellington Dr 76051
Emerald Ct 76051
Enchanted Way 76051
Estill St 76051
Euless Grapevine Rd 76051
Everglade Ct 76051
Evergreen Ct 76051
Evinrude Dr 76051
Fair Field Dr 76051
Fair Oaks Dr 76051
Fairfax Cir 76051
Fairmount Dr 76051
Fairway Dr 76051
Fall Crk & Ct 76051
Fern Ct 76051
Fieldwood St 76051
Flameleaf Dr 76051
Forest St 76051
Forest Hills Rd 76051
Forestdale Dr 76051
Fox Run Dr 76051
Foxchase Ln 76051
E & W Franklin St 76051
Freeport Pkwy 76051
Garden Ct 76051
Gaylord Trl 76051
Glacier Ln 76051
Glade Ln & Rd 76051
Glen Wood Dr 76051
Glenbrook Dr 76051
Glenwych Cv 76051
Goliad Ln 76051
Grace Ln 76051
Grandview Dr 76051
SW Grapevine Pkwy 76051
E, N & W Grapevine Mills Blvd, Cir & Pkwy 76051
Grayson Dr 76051
Great Wolf Dr 76051
Greenbriar Ct 76051
Greenbrook Ct 76051
Greenhaven Ln 76051
Greenwood Ln 76051
W Hall St 76051
Hall Johnson Rd 76051
Hallmont Dr 76051
Hampton Rd 76051
Hanger St 76051
Hanover Dr 76051
Harber Ave 76051
Harmon Dr 76051
Harmony Hill Rd 76051
Hartford Rd 76051
Harvest Gln 76051
Harvest Hill Dr 76051
Harvest Moon Dr 76051
Harvestwood Ct & Dr 76051
Harwell St 76051
Haversham Dr 76051
Hawthorne St 76051
Haydenbend Cir 76051
Hazy Meadow Ln 76051
Hearthside Dr 76051
Heartstone Dr 76051
Heather St 76051
Heather Wood Dr 76051
Heatherbrook Dr 76051
Heatherdale Dr 76051
Heritage Ave & Cv 76051

Heritage Oak Ct 76051
Hidden Lake Cv & Dr 76051
High Dr 76051
High Cliff Dr 76051
High Countryside Dr 76051
High Meadow Dr 76051
High Mesa Ct 76051
High Oaks Dr 76051
High Point Ct & Dr 76051
High Ridge Dr 76051
Highcrest Dr 76051
Hightimber Ct & Dr 76051
Highview Ln 76051
N Highway 121 76051
Hill St 76051
Hill Creek Ln 76051
Hill Meadow Rd 76051
Hillcrest Ct 76051
Hillside Trl 76051
Hilltop Dr 76051
Hillview Dr 76051
Hillwood Way 76051
Holly St 76051
Homestead Ln 76051
Honeysuckle 76051
Hood Ln 76051
Hood Ridge Ct 76051
Horseshoe Dr 76051
Houston Oaks Ct 76051
E & W Hudgins St 76051
Hughes Rd 76051
Hummingbird Trl 76051
Hunters Ridge Dr 76051
Huntington Ct 76051
Hyland Greens Dr 76051
Idlewood Dr 76051
Indian Oak Dr 76051
Industrial Blvd 76051
Inland Dr 76051
Inwood St 76051
Ira E Woods Ave 76051
Ivy Glen Dr 76051
Jean St 76051
Jenkins St 76051
Johnson Ct 76051
Jones St 76051
Joyce Ct & Way 76051
Juniper Ln 76051
Kaitlyn Ln 76051
Kelsey Ct 76051
Kenwood Dr 76051
Killarney St 76051
Kimball Ave & Ct 76051
Kimberly Dr 76051
King St 76051
Kings Canyon Ct & Dr 76051
Kingswood Dr 76051
Knob Oak Dr 76051
Knoll Crest Ct 76051
Labrador Bay 76051
Laguna Vista Way 76051
Lake Forest Ct & Rd 76051
Lake Park Dr 76051
Lakecrest Dr 76051
Lakeridge Dr 76051
Lakeshore Dr 76051
Lakeside Cir & Ct 76051
Lakeview Dr 76051
Lakewood Ln 76051
Lancaster Dr 76051
Landing Ct 76051
Lark Ln 76051
Laurel Ln 76051
Laurel Creek Dr 76051
Leafwood Ct 76051
Lexington Ave 76051
Liberty Park Plz 76051
Lilac Ln 76051
Limerick Ln 76051
Linkside Dr 76051
Lipscomb St 76051
Live Oak Dr 76051
Lone Star Ln 76051
Longhorn Trl 76051
Lookout Ct & Dr 76051
Los Robles St 76051

Lovers Ln 76051
N Lucas Dr 76051
Magnolia Ct, Ln & Trl 76051
Mahan Ct 76051
N & S Main St 76051
Majestic Oak Dr 76051
Manchester Ln 76051
Manor Way St 76051
Mapleridge Dr 76051
Marsh Ln 76051
Martin Ct 76051
Mcpherson Dr 76051
Meadow Dr 76051
Meadow Crest Dr 76051
Meadowbrook Dr 76051
Meadowmere Park 76051
Mercury Dr 76051
Meredith Ln 76051
Meritage Ln 76051
Merlot Ave 76051
Mesa Verde Trl 76051
Mesquite Ln 76051
Michol St 76051
Mill Crossing St 76051
Mill Pond Dr 76051
Minters Chapel Rd 76051
Mockingbird Dr 76051
Monument Butte 76051
Moss Creek Dr & Knls 76051
Mountainview Ct 76051
Mulholland Dr 76051
Municipal Way 76051
Murrell Rd 76051
Mustang Ct & Dr 76051
Myrtle Crk 76051
E & W Nash St 76051
Nestlewood Ln 76051
New Haven Rd 76051
Newcastle Dr 76051
Nolen Dr 76051
Normandy Dr 76051
Northview Dr 76051
E & W Northwest Hwy 76051
Northwood St 76051
Oak Ln 76051
Oak Cliff Dr 76051
Oak Creek Dr 76051
Oak Forest Dr 76051
Oak Grove Loop S 76051
Oak Hurst Dr 76051
Oak Ridge Pt 76051
Oak Tree Ln 76051
Oakmont Ct 76051
Oakwood Dr 76051
October Ct 76051
N & S Odell Ct 76051
Old Mill Run 76051
Overlook Dr 76051
Oxford Ln 76051
Palo Duro Trl 76051
Panhandle Ct & Dr 76051
N & S Park Blvd & Ct 76051
Park Hill Ln 76051
Park View Dr 76051
Parkside Ct 76051
Parkway Dr 76051
Parkwood Dr 76051
Parr Ln & Rd 76051
Patriot Dr 76051
W Peach Ct & St 76051
Pebble Stone 76051
Pebblebrook Dr 76051
Pecan Ln 76051
Pecan Hollow Ct 76051
Pecos Dr 76051
Peninsula Dr 76051
Pheasant Ridge Dr 76051
Pickering Ln 76051
Pilot Pt 76051
Pin Oak Dr 76051
S Pine St 76051
Pine View Dr 76051
Pinehurst Dr 76051
Pinon Ct 76051
Placid Cir 76051
Plared Dr 76051

Pony Pkwy 76051
Pool Rd 76051
N Port Ct 76051
Port America Pl 76051
Post Oak Rd 76051
Premier Pl 76051
Preston Pl 76051
Pritchard Dr 76051
Prospect Pkwy 76051
Quail Ln 76051
Quail Crest St 76051
Quail Hollow Dr 76051
Rainbow Trl 76051
Ravenswood Dr 76051
Red Bird Ln 76051
Redbud Ln 76051
Redwood Trl 76051
Regent Dr 76051
Regional Rd 76051
Rider Cir 76051
Ridge Ct, Ln & Rd 76051
Ridgebend Dr 76051
Ridgerow Dr 76051
Ridgeview Dr 76051
Ridgewood Dr 76051
Rio Bend Ct 76051
River Crest St 76051
E Riverside Dr 76051
Roaring Springs Rd 76051
Roberts Rd 76051
Robin Ct 76051
Robindale Ln 76051
Rock Port Cv 76051
Rolling Hills Ln 76051
Rolling Ridge Dr 76051
Rose Ct 76051
Rosecliff Ter 76051
Rosewood Dr 76051
Roundup Trl 76051
Ruby Ct 76051
Rustic Dr 76051
Ruth St 76051
Ruth Wall Rd 76051
Ryan Ct & Rdg 76051
Sabel Ridge Ln 76051
Saddle Ridge Dr 76051
Sagebrush Trl 76051
San Jacinto Ln 76051
Sandalwood Ln 76051
Sandell Dr 76051
Sandhurst Ct 76051
Sandpiper St 76051
Sandstone Dr 76051
Santa Fe Trl 76051
Satinwood 76051
Savannah Ct 76051
Scarborough Ct 76051
Scenic Dr 76051
N & S Scribner St 76051
Sentinal Butte 76051
Sequoia Ct 76051
Shadow Ct & Rdg 76051
Shadow Glen Dr 76051
Shady Brook Dr 76051
Shady Creek Dr 76051
Shady Glen Dr 76051
Shady Hill Ct 76051
Shady Meadow Dr 76051
Shady Oak Dr 76051
Shannon St 76051
Sheffield St 76051
Shenandoah Ave 76051
Shorewood Dr 76051
Sierra Dr 76051
Silkwood 76051
Silver Leaf Ct 76051
Silver Oak Dr 76051
Silvercrest Ln 76051
Silverlake Dr 76051
Silverside Dr 76051
Skyline Ct 76051
Sleepy Hollow Ct 76051
Smith St 76051
Soft Wind Ct 76051
Somerset Ct 76051
Sonnet Dr 76051

Southridge Ct & Dr 76051
Southshore Dr 76051
Southwood Ct 76051
Sprindeltree Dr 76051
Spring Creek Dr 76051
Spring Willow Dr 76051
Springbranch Ct 76051
Springbrook Ct 76051
Springhill Dr 76051
Spruce Ln 76051
Spur Trl 76051
Squire Ct 76051
Stafford Rd 76051
N Starnes St 76051
Starr Pl 76051
E & W State Highway 114 76051
State Highway 26 76051
State Highway 360 76051
Steeplewood Dr 76051
Sterling Ln 76051
Stone Brooke Dr 76051
Stone Creek Ln 76051
Stone Moss Ln 76051
Stone Myers Pkwy 76051
Stonecrest Dr 76051
Stonehurst Dr 76051
Stoneway Dr 76051
Stratford Chase 76051
Summer Wind Dr 76051
Summerfield Dr 76051
Summit Ct 76051
Summit Ridge St 76051
Sun Meadow Dr 76051
W Sunset St 76051
Sunshine Ln 76051
Surrey Ln 76051
Sweet Briar St 76051
Sweet Gum Ln 76051
Sycamore Ct 76051
Tamarack Ct 76051
Tanglewood Dr 76051
Taylor Ln 76051
Terrace Dr 76051
S Terrell St 76051
Teton Dr 76051
Texan Trl 76051
E & W Texas St 76051
Thatcher Trl 76051
Thistlewood Ct & Ln 76051
Thomas Ct 76051
Thorn Ln 76051
Tiffany Forest Ct & Ln 76051
Timber Crest Ct 76051
Timber Hill Dr 76051
Timber Ridge Pt 76051
Timberline Dr 76051
Tipperary Dr 76051
Trade Center Dr 76051
Tradewind St 76051
Trail Edge Dr 76051
Trail Lake Dr 76051
Travis Ct 76051
Trevor Trl 76051
Trumarc Dr 76051
Trunkwood 76051
Tumbleweed Ct & Trl 76051
Turner Rd 76051
Turtledove Ln 76051
Twelve Oaks Ln 76051
Twilight Trl 76051
Twin Creek Cv 76051
Twin Oaks Cir 76051
Valley Vista Dr 76051
Valleyview Dr 76051
Valleywood Dr 76051
View Mdw 76051
Vine St 76051
Wagon Wheel Dr 76051
Walker Pl 76051
E & W Wall St 76051
E Walnut St 76051
Waltham Dr 76051
Warwick Way 76051
Washington St 76051
Water Oak Dr 76051

Waterford Dr 76051
Wateridge Ct 76051
Weddle Dr 76051
Wedgewood Dr 76051
Wellington Ln 76051
Wentwood Dr 76051
West Ct 76051
Westbrook Dr 76051
Westbury Dr 76051
Westchase Cir 76051
Westgate Plz 76051
Westover Ct 76051
Westport Pkwy 76051
Westwood Ter 76051
Whispering Vine Ct 76051
Whitby Ln 76051
White Oak Dr 76051
Whitney Ln 76051
Wickersham Ct 76051
Wild Oak Trl 76051
Wildflower Trl 76051
Wildwood Cir, Ct & Ln 76051
William D Tate Ave
900-1252 76051
1251-1251 76099
1253-5399 76051
1254-4598 76051
Williams Ct 76051
Willow Bnd & Ct 76051
Willow Creek Dr 76051
Willowood Dr 76051
Wilshire Ave 76051
S & W Winding Creek Dr 76051
Windomere Dr 76051
Windsor Forest Dr 76051
Windswept Ct & Ln 76051
Windview St 76051
Windy Knoll Ct 76051
Winslow Ln 76051
Winter Wood Dr 76051
Wintergreen Ter 76051
Wonder Way 76051
Wood St 76051
Wood Creek Dr 76051
Wood Crest Dr 76051
Wood Meadow Dr 76051
Woodbriar Dr 76051
Wooded Trail Ct 76051
Woodglen Dr 76051
Woodhaven Dr 76051
Woodhill Ct 76051
Woodland Ct 76051
Woodland Hills Dr 76051
Woodmoor Ct 76051
Woodside Knls 76051
E & W Worth St 76051
Wortham Dr 76051
Worthington St 76051
Wren Ridge Dr 76051
Wycliff St 76051
Yellowstone Dr 76051
Yorkshire Ct 76051

GREENVILLE TX

General Delivery 75401

POST OFFICE BOXES MAIN OFFICE STATIONS AND BRANCHES

Box No.s
1 - 7000 75403
8001 - 9358 75404

RURAL ROUTES

01, 02, 03, 09 75401
02, 04, 05, 06, 07, 08, 09 75402

NAMED STREETS

Street	ZIP
Ablowich Dr	75402
Adam Ln	75402
Adams St	75401
Aerobic Ln	75402
Aileen Blvd	75402
Air Park Ave	75402
Albert St	75401
Alpha St	75401
Alpine St	75401
Anderson St	75401
Angela Ln	75402
Arbor Trl	75402
Arrowhead Dr & Way	75402
Ashland Dr	75402
Austin St	75402
Avondale Dr	75402
Axe Trl	75402
Barling St	75401
Baylor Dr	75402
E & W Beach Dr	75402
Bear Ln	75402
Beauchamp St	75401
Beaver Pl	75402
Beecha St	75401
Beer Can Aly	75401
Bell Dr	75401
Belmont Pl	75402
Bent Oak St E & W	75401
Benton Ln	75401
Benton St	75402
Berkshire Ct	75401
Bethel Dr & Rd	75402
Beverly Dr	75402
Blades St	75401
Bliss St	75402
Blueberry Hill Rd	75401
Bluebonnet Trl	75402
Bois D Arc St	75401
Bonham St	75402
Bonnie Lea St	75402
Bonnie View Rd	75402
Bordeaux Ln	75402
Bourland St	75401
Bowie Cir	75402
Bradley Cir	75401
Branch St	75401
Briarwood Cir	75402
Briscoe St	75401
Broadview St	75402
Broken Bow Dr	75402
Brooke St	75402
Brown Rd	75401
Buena Vista Dr	75402
Burgundy Dr	75402
Burnett Dr	75402
Business Highway 69 S	75402
Caddo St	75401
Cambridge Ct	75401
Campbell Dr	75401
Canterbury Way	75401
Canton St	75402
Canvasback Dr	75402
Carol Dr	75402
Carolina Dr	75402
Carradine St	75401
Carver St	75401
Casie Ct	75402
Catfish Cv	75402
Cedar St	75401
Cedar Creek Ln & Rd	75402
Cedar Crest St	75402
Cedar Oaks Trl	75402
Cedar Ridge Rd	75402
Center Point Ln & Rd	75402
Champion Ct	75402
Chaparral Dr	75402
Chapman Dr	75402
Charles St	75402
Charlotte St	75402
Cheltenham Pl	75402
Cherokee St	75402
Cheyenne Dr	75402
Church St	75401
Churchill Ln	75402
Clark St	75401
Claudette Ct	75402
Clearview Ln	75402
Cleveland St	75401
Clubhouse Rd	75402
Coleman St	75401
College St	75401
Colony Dr	75402
Colorado St	75402
Comanchee Dr	75402
Commerce Dr	75401
Coops Ln	75402
Cordell St	75401
Cornelia St	75401
Country Pl	75401
Country Oaks	75401
County Road 1001	75401
County Road 1002	75401
County Road 1003	75401
County Road 1031	75401
County Road 1032	75401
County Road 1033	75401
County Road 1034	75401
County Road 1035	75401
County Road 1036	75401
County Road 1037	75401
County Road 1038	75401
County Road 1040	75401
County Road 1041	75401
County Road 1057	75401
County Road 1059	75401
County Road 1061	75401
County Road 1062	75401
County Road 1063	75401
County Road 1065	75401
County Road 1066	75401
County Road 1067	75401
County Road 1068	75401
County Road 1069	75401
County Road 1070	75401
County Road 1071	75401
County Road 1072	75401
County Road 1073	75401
County Road 1074	75401
County Road 1077	75401
County Road 1079	75401
County Road 1081	75401
County Road 1083	75401
County Road 1084	75401
County Road 1114	75401
County Road 1116	75401
County Road 1118	75401
County Road 1119	75401
County Road 1123	75401
County Road 1151	75401
County Road 1152	75401
County Road 1154	75401
County Road 1155	75401
County Road 1156	75401
County Road 1157	75401
County Road 1158	75401
County Road 1160	75401
County Road 1163	75401
County Road 1178	75401
County Road 2100	75402
County Road 2110	75402
County Road 2112	75402
County Road 2116	75402
County Road 2118	75402
County Road 2120	75402
County Road 2124	75402
County Road 2126	75402
County Road 2130	75402
County Road 2132	75402
County Road 2134	75402
County Road 2146	75402
County Road 2148	75402
County Road 2172	75402
County Road 2173	75402
County Road 2176	75402
County Road 2178	75402
County Road 2180	75402
County Road 2182	75402
County Road 2184	75402
County Road 2186	75402
County Road 2200	75402
County Road 2202	75402
County Road 2204	75402
County Road 2206	75402
County Road 2208	75402
County Road 2234	75402
County Road 2236	75402
County Road 2240	75402
County Road 2241	75402
County Road 2242	75402
County Road 2243	75402
County Road 2244	75402
County Road 2246	75402
County Road 2248	75402
County Road 2250	75402
County Road 2252	75402
County Road 2256	75402
County Road 2260	75402
County Road 2264	75402
County Road 3101	75402
County Road 3102	75402
County Road 3103	75402
County Road 3104	75402
County Road 3110	75402
County Road 3113	75402
County Road 3114	75402
County Road 3115	75402
County Road 3119	75402
County Road 3120	75402
County Road 3121	75402
County Road 3123	75402
County Road 3124	75402
County Road 3125	75402
County Road 3126	75402
County Road 3127	75402
County Road 3128	75402
County Road 3130	75402
County Road 3301	75402
County Road 3302	75402
County Road 3303	75402
County Road 3304	75402
County Road 3305	75402
County Road 3306	75402
County Road 3307	75402
County Road 3308	75402
County Road 3309	75402
County Road 3310	75402
County Road 3311	75402
County Road 3312	75402
County Road 3313	75402
County Road 3314	75402
County Road 3317	75402
County Road 3318	75402
County Road 3320	75402
County Road 3321	75402
County Road 3322	75402
County Road 3323	75402
County Road 3324	75402
County Road 3325	75402
County Road 3326	75402
County Road 3327	75402
County Road 3328	75402
County Road 3343	75402
County Road 3501	75402
County Road 3502	75402
County Road 3514	75402
County Road 3518	75402
County Road 3519	75402
County Road 3521	75402
County Road 3524	75402
County Road 3525	75402
County Road 3552	75402
County Road 4100	75401
County Road 4101	75401
County Road 4102	75401
County Road 4104	75401
County Road 4105	75401
County Road 4106	75401
County Road 4107	75401
County Road 4108	75401
County Road 4109	75401
County Road 4110	75401
County Road 4123	75401
County Road 4200	75401
County Road 4201	75401
County Road 4202	75401
County Road 4214	75401
County Road 4218	75401
County Road 4300	75401
County Road 4301	75401
County Road 4302	75401
County Road 4304	75401
County Road 4305	75401
County Road 4306	75401
County Road 4307	75401
County Road 4308	75401
County Road 4309 E & N	75401
County Road 4311	75401
County Road 4414	75401
County Road 4418	75401
Coyote Xing	75402
Creek Crossing Dr	75402
Creekside Dr	75402
Crockett St	75401
Cross St	75401
Dalton St	75401
Davis Cir	75402
Deer Dr	75402
Del Ra Dr	75402
Dell Dr	75401
Division St	75401
Dixon Cir	75401
Dove Cv	75402
Drew Ct	75402
Eagles Nest	75402
Eastland St	75402
Ed Rutherford Dr & Rd	75402
Edgar St	75401
Edgewood Dr	75402
Edgington Dr	75401
Edmondson St	75401
Egret Ln	75402
Ellis Cir	75401
Elmwood Dr	75402
Enterprise	75402
Erica Cir	75402
Ermine Dr	75402
Esma St	75401
Ethan Dr	75402
Eutopia St	75401
Fairway St	75402
Fannie Jo St	75401
Fannin St	75401
Finch Dr	75402
Flamingo Rd	75402
Fm 118 Spur	75401
Fm 1564 E & W	75402
Fm 1566 E	75401
Fm 1569	75401
Fm 1570 N & W	75402
Fm 1737	75402
Fm 1903	75402
Fm 2101	75402
Fm 2194	75401
Fm 2736	75401
Fm 2874	75401
Fm 2947	75402
Fm 3211	75402
Fm 3427	75401
Fm 36 N	75401
Fm 499	75401
Fm 903	75401
Forrester St	75401
Fox Trl	75402
Frazier St	75401
Fred St	75401
Frontage Rd	75402
Fuller St	75401
Furlong Dr	75402
Gamecock Ct & Dr	75402
Garber Cir	75402
Garden Dr	75402
Gee St	75401
Gibbons St	75401
Gillespie St	75401
Gilstrap St	75402
Glendale St	75401
Glenlivet Pl	75402
Gloucesite Ct	75401
Gold St	75402
Gordon St	75401
Graceland Dr	75401
Grand Oaks Ranch Rd	75401
Granger St	75401
Green Ct	75402
Green Mdws	75401
Greenbriar St	75402
Gussie Nell Davis Dr	75402
Hackberry Cir & Dr	75402
Hale Blvd	75401
Halifax St	75402
Hallmark St	75402
Hamilton Ln	75402
Hare Ln	75402
Harrell St	75402
Harris St	75401
Hayter St	75402
Hemphill St	75401
Henderson Dr	75402
Henderson St	75401
Henry St	75402
Heritage Pl	75402
Highland St	75402
Highland Oak Ct	75402
Highland Oaks Dr	75402
Highmeadow Ln	75402
Highway 224	75401
Highway 34 N	75401
Highway 380 W	75401
Highway 380 Business	75401
Highway 50	75401
Highway 66	75402
Highway 69 N	75401
Hill St	75401
Hillcrest Ave	75402
Hilltop Dr	75402
Holsum Cir	75401
Horne Dr	75402
Horseman S Rd	75401
Horsley St	75401
Houston St	75401
Hunters Run St	75402
Huntington Ct	75401
Ina St	75401
Industrial Dr	
5700-5798	75401
5800-6400	75402
6402-7098	75402
Interstate Highway 30	75402
Jack Finney Blvd	75402
Jackson St	75402
Jacksons Run	75402
Jacquline Blvd	75402
Jamie Way	75402
Jeanette St	75401
Jefferson St	75401
Jeri Ln	75402
Joanne Cir	75402
Joe Ramsey Blvd	75402
Joe Ramsey Blvd E	75401
Joe Ramsey Blvd N	
1501-1597	75401
1599-1699	75401
1701-1949	75401
5900-6400	75402
6402-6898	75402
John St	75402
Johnson St	75401
Jones St	75401
Jordan St	75401
Joyce Ln	75402
Justin Ln	75402
Kari Ln	75402
Katy Dr	75401
Kayway Dr	75402
Kennedy St	75401
Kent Cir	75402
King St	
1200-4900	75401
5300-5398	75402
5400-6099	75402
6101-6399	75402
Kings Ct	75401
Kingston Rd	75401
Kingswood Cir & Dr	75402
Kiowa Dr	75402
La Fontaine Ln	75402
La Rochelle Dr	75402
Lacy Ln	75402
Lafayette Dr	75402
N Lake Dr	75402
Lake St	75401
Lake Side Dr	75402
Lakewood St	75401
Lamar St	75402
Lancer Rd	75401
Laney Dr	75402
Lange St	75402
Langford St	75401
Lark St	75402
Laurel Dr	75402
Leatherwood Ln	75402
Lee St	75401
Legacy Oaks Cir	75402
Linda Ln	75402
Lions Lair Rd	75402
Lipan St	75402
Little Creek Rnch	75402
Live Oak St	75402
Logan St	75401
Long Branch Dr	75402
Long Mile Rd	
100-198	75401
301-399	75402
Loraine Cir	75401
Lou Finney Blvd	75401
Lovell Ln	75402
Luna Dr	75402
Lynn St	75402
Mac Dr	75402
Main St	75401
Majors Rd	75402
Mallard Dr	75402
Mamie Rd	75402
Manor Garden Curv	75401
Maple Ave	75402
Marita Rd	75402
Marshall St	75401
Mary Ln	75401
Mary Morris Dr	75402
Mathew Ln	75402
Mcclean Rd	75402
Mcdougal St	75401
Mckinney St	75402
Meadow Ln	75402
Meadowbrook Dr	75402
Medical Pkwy	75401
Memphis St	75402
Michele Dr	75402
Miles Ln	75401
Mill St	75401
Mills Way	75401
Mineola St	75401
Mink Dr	75402
Mitchell St	75402
Mockingbird Ln	75402
Montana Dr	75402
Monty Stratton Pkwy	75402
Morgan Ln	75402
Morgan St	75401
Morris Ln	75402
Morrison St	75401
Morse St	75401
Moulton St	75401
Mullaney Dr	75402
Muskrat Pl	75402
Mustang Xing	75402
Mustang Crossing Anx	75402
Nashville Ave	75402
Nathan Cir	75402
Neola Rd	75402
Nevada Dr	75402
New Haven St	75402
Nobhill Dr	75402
Norma Cir	75402
Northgate Ct & Trl	75402
Nottingham Dr	75401
Oak St	75401
Oak Trl	75402
Oak Creek Dr	75402
Oak Glen Dr	75402
Oak Village Rd	75402
Oakridge Dr	75402
Oakwood Dr	75402
Old Mill Rd	75402
Oliver Cir & St	75401
Oneal St	75401
Oriole Cir	75402
Osborne St	75401
Otter Trl	75402
Owl Tree Trl	75402
Owls Roost	75402
Oxford Ct	75401
Pace St	75401
Park St	75401
Parkwood Ln	75402
Patterson Dr & Rd	75402
Patti J St	75402
Paul St	75402
Peacock Ln	75402
Pearl St	75402
Pecan Dr	75401
Pecan Ln	75402
Peerless Ranch Rd	75402
Pepperport Dr	75402
Pickett St	75401
Pier Ln	75402
Pine St	75401
W Point Dr	75402
Polk St	75401
Pollard St	75401
Poplar St	75402
Post Oak Cir & Trl	75402
Priscilla Ln	75402
Private Road 1171	75401
Private Road 1172	75401
Private Road 1173	75401
Private Road 1174	75401
Private Road 1176	75401
Private Road 1179	75401
Private Road 1183	75401
Private Road 1198	75401
Private Road 2174	75402
Private Road 2213	75402
Private Road 2249	75402
Private Road 3141	75402
Private Road 3143	75402
Private Road 3329	75402
Private Road 3332	75402
Private Road 3335	75402
Private Road 3336	75402
Private Road 3339	75402
Private Road 3340	75402
Private Road 3341	75402
Private Road 3342	75402
Private Road 3344	75402
Private Road 3345	75402
Private Road 3346	75402
Private Road 3348	75402
Private Road 3349	75402
Private Road 3350	75402
Private Road 3351	75402
Private Road 3548	75402
Private Road 3549	75402
Private Road 3550	75402
Private Road 3551	75402
Private Road 3848	75402
Private Road 4127	75401
Private Road 4128	75401
Private Road 4129	75401
Private Road 4327	75401
Private Road 4328	75401
Private Road 4330	75401
Private Road 4420	75401
Quail Run St	75402
Rabb Dr	75402
Rainey St	75401
Ranchers Ln	75401
Ranchwood Cir & Dr	75402
Red Cedar Trl	75402
Red Cloud Dr	75402
Redbud St	75401
Reed St	75401
Rees St	75401
Regent Ln	75402
Reiger Dr	75402
Richtor Ranch Rd	75402

Ridgecrest Rd 75402
Rienzi Dr 75402
River Oaks Dr 75402
Road Runner Ln 75402
Roberts St
2900-3598 75401
3600-4500 75401
4502-4898 75401
5400-5499 75402
Robin Rd 75402
Robinson St 75401
Rodeo Dr 75402
Rogers Dr 75402
Rolling Hills Dr 75402
Rosemary St 75401
Rosewood Dr 75402
Royal Ln 75402
Royal Oaks Dr 75402
Sabine St 75401
Sabine River Rd 75401
Sahara Dr 75402
Saint John St 75401
Salem St 75401
San Vincente Blvd 75402
Sayle St
900-4199 75401
4201-4799 75401
5000-5198 75402
5200-6600 75402
6602-6998 75402
Seminole Ln 75402
Shady Brook Rd 75402
Shauna Dr 75402
Shawnee St 75402
Shelby Ave 75402
Short St 75401
Shreveport St 75401
Silver St 75401
Simonds St 75401
Simpson St 75401
Skyline Dr 75401
Snider Dr 75402
Snider Ln 75401
Sockwell Blvd 75401
Speedway St 75401
Spencer St 75401
Spoonemore Ln 75401
Stanford St 75401
Star St 75402
State Highway 34 S 75402
State Highway 66 75402
State Highway 69 S 75402
Steeplechase Ln 75402
Stephenson Dr 75401
Stevens St 75401
Stonewall St
1400-4699 75401
4701-4999 75401
5001-5197 75402
5199-6699 75402
6701-6999 75402
Stuart St 75401
Sun Pt 75402
Sundown Rd 75402
Sunhill Dr 75402
Sunset St 75401
Sunset Strip 75402
Tanglewood Dr 75402
Tar Heel Dr 75402
Taylor St 75402
Taylor Plaza Dr 75402
Technology Cir 75402
Templeton St 75401
Terrell Rd 75402
Terry Pl 75402
Texas St 75401
Thibodaux Dr 75402
Thornhill Dr 75401
Timber Creek Ln E 75402
Timberside Dr 75402
Tipps Dr 75402
Toma Hawk Dr 75402
Tracy Ln & St 75402
Traders Cir & Rd 75402
Trafalgar Dr 75402
Travis St 75401
Treehouse Rd 75402
Trego Ln 75402
Tremont St 75401
Trinity St 75402
Tulane St 75401
Turtle Creek Dr 75402
Twilight Peninsula 75402
Up The Grove St 75401
Utah St 75402
Utilis St 75401
Vale St 75402
Vernon St 75402
Villa Fontana St 75402
Village Ct, Dr, Pl & St 75401
Vinnie St 75401
Volunteer Dr 75402
Wade Ln 75402
Walnut St 75401
Walworth St 75401
Wanda Ln 75402
Washington St 75401
Watchill Dr 75402
Webb Ave 75402
Wellington St
1700-4799 75401
4800-5200 75402
5202-5298 75402
Wesley St
1101-1197 75401
1199-2299 75401
2301-4899 75401
2600-4998 75401
2600-2600 75403
5001-6400 75402
6305-6305 75404
6401-10499 75402
6402-9998 75402
Western Cir 75401
Westminster Ln 75402
Whitehall Ln 75402
Whitehurst St 75401
Wiggs Rd 75402
Williams St 75401
Williamsburg Rd 75401
Willow Ridge Rd 75402
Wilson Hill Rd 75401
Wilton Dr 75401
Winding Ln 75402
Windy Hill Rd 75402
Wolf Creek Dr 75402
Wolfe City Dr 75401
Wolverine Ln 75402
Woodchuck Dr 75402
Woodland Dr 75402
Woodrow Blvd 75402
Wren Dr 75402
Wright St 75401
Yellowstone Dr 75401
Zora Dr 75402

NUMBERED STREETS

All Street Addresses 75401

HARLINGEN TX

General Delivery 78550

POST OFFICE BOXES MAIN OFFICE STATIONS AND BRANCHES

Box No.s
1 - 3609 78551
530001 - 534376 78553

RURAL ROUTES

02 78550
01, 03, 05, 06, 07, 09, 10 78552

NAMED STREETS

N & S A St 78550
Abd Rd 78552
Abel Q Pr 78552
Ac Zamora St 78552
Acacia 78552
W Acadia St 78552
E & W Adams Ave 78550
Adams Landing Ave 78550
Adkins Dr 78550
W Adrian St 78552
Ailani Cir 78552
Airport Dr 78550
Al Conway Dr 78550
Alamo Dr 78552
Albatross St 78552
E Alcott Ave 78550
Alexis Ave 78552
Algodon Ct 78552
Alma St 78552
Alonzo Cir 78550
Alonzo Rd 78552
Alta Vista Ct 78550
N & S Altas Palmas Dr & Rd 78552
S Alvarez 78552
American Legion Dr 78550
Amistad Rd 78550
N Anadal St 78550
Angel St 78552
Ann St 78550
W Ann Arbor St 78552
Apple Ct 78550
Aragon Dr 78552
W Arbor St 78552
Arcadia Dr 78550
S Arden St 78552
Armadillo Dr 78552
Arnold Palmer Dr 78552
Arrington Rd 78552
Arroyo Dr 78552
E Arroyo Dr 78550
W Arroyo Dr 78550
Arroyo St 78552
Arroyo Acres 78552
Arroyo Bank Dr 78552
E, N, S & W Arroyo Park Ln 78550
Arroyo Vista Ct 78550
W Arthur St 78550
Ash St 78552
Ashley Ct 78552
Atlanta St 78550
Atrium Place Dr 78550
Augusta Dr 78552
N Augusta National Dr 78550
E Austin Ave 78550
W Austin Ave 78552
Austrian Pine Ct 78550
Autrey Dr 78552
Autumn Ct 78550
Avalon Dr 78552
N & S B St 78550
Bacon Way Rd 78552
Baker Potts Rd 78552
Ball St 78550
W Ballard Ave 78550
Bamboo Cir 78552
Bamboo Palm Ct N & W 78552
Banyon Cir & Dr 78550
E & W Barbara St 78550
W Barcelona Ave 78550
E & W Barger Ct 78552
Barnes Ct 78552
Barton St 78550
Basin Cir & St 78550
Bass Blvd 78552
Bass 3 Ln 78552
Bass Pro Dr 78552
Bay Hill Ct 78550
Bayview Ave 78552
Beaumont St 78550
E & W Beck St 78550
Beckham Rd 78552
Becky Ln 78550
Bell St 78550
Bellino Dr 78552
Ben Hogan Cir 78552
Benwood St 78550
Betty Pl 78552
Betty Bob Dr 78552
Birch St 78552
Blackhawk Dr 78552
N Blake St 78550
Blue Bonnet Dr 78550
N Bluebird Ln 78550
Blum Ln 78550
Boardwalk Ave 78552
Bobby Jones Dr 78552
Bobcat Ln 78550
Bodenhamer Rd 78550
Bonham St 78550
N Bonito Rd 78550
Borchardt St 78552
Boros Ct 78552
Bothwell Rd 78552
Botts Ave 78552
Bougainvillea Dr
5100-5500 78552
5502-5598 78552
21300-21499 78550
Bouldin Rd 78550
Bourbon St 78550
Bowen Rd 78550
E Bowie Ave 78550
W Bowie Ave 78552
Boxwood St 78550
Brazil Rd 78552
Brazilwood Ct 78552
Brazo Cir 78552
N Breedlove St 78550
Brennaman Rd 78552
Brentwood Dr 78550
Briana Cir 78552
Briggs Coleman Rd 78550
Brittany Ct 78552
Brown Ave 78552
Brown Pelican Ln 78552
Brownstone Cir E & N 78552
E & W Buchanan St 78550
W Buena Vista Ave 78550
Burke Ct 78550
Burns Rd 78552
Bush St 78550
N Business 77 78552
W Business 83 78552
Business Highway 77 78552
Buttercup Ct 78552
Byron Nelson Dr 78552
N & S C St 78550
Cactus Dr 78550
S California St 78552
Calle Condesa 78552
S Calle Duquesa 78552
S Calle Princesa 78552
S Calle Reina 78552
Camelot Dr 78550
Camelot Plaza Cir 78550
Candy Ct 78552
Cardinal Dr 78550
Carlos St 78552
Caro Cir 78552
S Carolina St 78550
E & W Carrol St 78550
Carter St 78550
Carver Rd 78552
Casper Ct 78552
Catlin Ct 78552
E Cenizo St 78550
Century Ct 78552
Cesar Menchaca Ct 78550
Challenger 78552
Champions Dr 78552
Chaparral St 78550
Chapote Ave 78552
Charger 78552
Charles St 78550
Cherry Ct 78550
W Chester Circle St 78552
Chester Park Rd 78552
Chico Blvd & Cir 78552
Chinaberry Rd 78552
Christians Cir 78550
Chuparosa Ct 78550
Citronia Ave 78552
Citrus Dr 78552
Citrus Ter 78550
Clark St 78550
E & W Cleveland Ave 78550
Clifford St 78550
E & W Cobblestone Creek Dr 78550
Coco Palm Dr 78552
Coconut Dr 78552
Colony Ct 78552
W Colorado Ave 78550
Colorado St 78552
N & S Commerce St 78550
Cook Ln 78552
E & W Coolidge Ave 78550
E Cora St 78550
W Cora St
201-397 78550
399-599 78550
3200-18299 78552
Cottonwood St 78550
Country Dr 78550
Country Dr N 78550
Country Ln 78552
N Country Club Ct 78552
Countryside Ln 78552
Court Pl 78550
Cowart St 78550
Cragon Rd 78552
E Crockett Ave 78550
Crockett Ct 78552
Crockett Rd 78552
Crossett Rd 78550
Crystal Ln 78550
Curlew St 78552
Curtis St 78550
Cypress Dr 78550
Cypress Gardens Dr 78550
N & S D St 78550
S Dakota St 78552
Dalton St 78550
Daniel Cir 78550
Daniella Ct 78552
Darrell St 78550
E & W Darrell Wayne Shipp St 78550
Date Dr 78552
Davis Rd 78552
E Davis St 78550
W Davis St 78550
Daytona 78552
Del Rio Cir 78552
N Dennis St 78550
Diamond Cir 78552
N & S Dilworth Rd 78552
Dixieland Rd 78552
Doane Rd 78552
Dogwood 78550
Dolores St 78552
E & W Dominion Dr 78550
Doral Ave 78552
Doral Ct 78550
E Dove Ave 78550
Dracaena Dr 78552
Drury Ln & Rd 78552
E Dunkin Cir 78550
Duval Ave 78552
N & S E St 78550
Eagle Dr 78552
W Ebano Ct 78550
Ebony Dr & Rd 78550
Ed Carey Dr 78552
N Ed Carey Dr 78550
S Ed Carey Dr 78552
El Camino Real 78552
El Campo Rd 78552
El Cielo Cir 78552
El Cielo Lindo Ct 78552
El Jardin Cir 78552
El Paso Cir & Dr 78552
El Rancho Dr 78552
Ella St 78550
Ellie Ln 78552
Elm St 78552
Elmwood Dr 78550
Elsworth Ln 78550
Emerald Dr 78550
Emerald Lake Dr 78550
Encino St 78550
Esperanza 78552
Estates Dr 78550
S Estrellita Ave 78552
E Euna Ct 78550
Evergreen Ct 78550
Ewing Dr 78552
Executive Dr 78552
N Expressway 77
200-298 78552
N Expressway 77
201-299 78550
301-2999 78552
400-1198 78550
2800-2898 78552
3700-4198 78550
17101-20999 78550
S Expressway 77
101-5599 78550
3900-4106 78552
4108-4110 78550
4200-4498 78552
S Expressway 83
401-997 78550
999-1099 78550
1100-1298 78552
1101-5699 78550
1500-1598 78550
2000-5498 78552
W Expressway 83 78552
N & S Eye St 78550
N F St 78550
S F St
100-198 78550
200-1799 78550
2200-2300 78552
2302-2898 78552
Fair Park Blvd 78550
Fairfield Ct 78550
Fairway 78552
Falcon Dr 78550
Fan Palm Dr E 78552
Fannin St 78550
Farley St 78550
Ferguson Dr 78550
Ferree St 78550
Fiesta Dr 78552
E & W Filmore Ave 78550
Findley St 78550
Firestone Dr 78552
N Flamingo Ln 78550
Flores Ave 78552
Flores Rd 78550
E & W Flynn Ave & Ct 78550
Fm 106 78550
Fm 1420 78550
Fm 1595 78550
Fm 1599 78550
Fm 3195 78552
Fm 507 78550
Fm 508 78550
N Fm 509 78550
Fountain View Ct 78550
Foxtail Palm Dr 78552
Frances St 78550
N & S G St 78550
Gabriels Lndg 78550
Gann 78552
W Garfield St 78550
Garrett Rd 78552
E, N, S & W Gartuck Cir 78552
Gary Player Cir 78552
Garza Rd 78552
Gayle Ave 78550
Georgia Ct 78552
Glasscock Ave 78550
Glenn Way Dr 78552
Godwin Rd 78550
Gold Rush Cir 78552
Goldenrod Ln 78552
Golf Course Dr 78552
Gomez Rd
2700-2899 78552
24601-25699 78550
Gonzales St 78552
Gonzalez Rd 78550
Grace Ave 78550
Graham Rd 78552
Grande Cir 78552
W Grant Ave 78550
Grapefruit Ave 78552
Green Ln 78552
Green Jay 78552
Greenbriar Dr 78550
Greenway St 78550
E Grimes Rd & St 78550
Groves Ave 78552
Guava Cir & Dr 78552
Gutierrez Rd 78550
N & S H St 78550
Hacienda Cir & Rd 78552
Hackberry St 78552
Haine Dr 78550
Hale Ave 78550
Halpin Rd 78552
Hamilton St 78550
Hancock Dr 78552
Hand Rd 78552
Hangar Way 78550
Hanmore Industrial Pkwy 78550
W Hanson St 78550
E & W Hapner Ct & St 78550
Hara Ct 78552
E & W Harding Ave 78550
Harris Rd 78550
E Harrison Ave 78550
W Harrison Ave
101-197 78550
199-1899 78550
1901-1999 78550
2001-2099 78552
Hatchett Rd 78552
Haverford Blvd 78552
Hawk Dr 78552
Hawthorne Ln 78550
Hayden St 78550
W Hayes St 78550
Heather Dr & Ln 78552
Helena Dr 78552
Henderson St 78550
Heritage Way 78550
Hermie Ln 78552
W Hick Hill Rd 78552
Hickory Ct 78550
Hidalgo Ave 78552
Hidden Dr 78552
High St 78550
Highland Dr 78552
Hitching Post Blvd 78552
Hodes Ave 78552
Hoening Rd 78550
Hollowell Way 78552
E & W Hoogland Ave 78550
Horseshoe Cir 78552
Hoss Ln 78552
Hossway Rd 78552
S Houston Dr 78550
Hughes Rd 78552
Hummingbird Ln N 78552
Hunter Dr 78550
Hunters Crossing St 78550
Hurd Ct 78552
E & W Hurst St 78550
S Idaho St 78552
Indian Wells Dr 78550
W Indiana Cir 78550
Indiana St 78552
Industrial Way 78550
Inverary Dr 78552
W Iowa Ave
100-799 78552

1900-2099 78550
Ironwood Ct 78552
Ivory Cir 78552
Iwo Jima Blvd 78550
N & S J St 78550
S J 1/2 St 78550
Jacaranda Dr 78550
Jack Nicklaus Dr 78552
E & W Jackson St 78550
Jacob Ct 78552
N & S Jade Dr 78550
Jeff St 78550
E & W Jefferson Ave 78550
Jenn Cir 78552
Jennifer Ct 78550
Jessica Ln 78552
E Jim Hogg Ave 78550
W Johnson St 78550
Johnston Ln 78552
Jones St 78550
Jordan St 78552
Julia Marie Dr 78552
N & S K St 78550
Ka Mar Rd 78550
N Kansas St 78550
Karime Ave 78552
Karis Ct 78550
Kayla Ln 78552
Kelly Dr 78552
N Kelly St 78550
W Kennedy Ave 78550
E Kent Ave 78552
Kermie Ave 78552
Kerr Ave 78552
Kika De La Garza St 78552
Kilborne Rd 78552
Kilbourn Rd 78550
Kilgore Dr 78550
W Kimble Ave 78550
King Ave 78552
King Arthur Dr 78550
King Palm Dr 78552
Kingbird Dr 78552
W Knox Ave 78550
Kratzer 78550
Kristine Dr 78552
Kroger Ave 78552
Krupla Rd 78550
N & S L St 78550
S L 1/2 St 78550
La Cana Cir & Dr 78552
La Canada 78552
La Cantera Dr 78552
La Costa Ct 78550
La Estrella Cir 78552
La Luna Cir 78552
La Paloma Ave 78550
La Plaza Cir 78552
W La Salle Ave 78550
La Sombra Dr 78552
La Vista Cir 78552
Lafayette 78550
W Lafayette Ave 78550
W Lafayette St 78552
Lago Dr 78552
Lake Dr 78550
Lake Shore Dr 78552
Lakewood 78550
Lamar St 78550
W Lamb Ave 78552
Lamon Rd 78552
Lantana Dr 78552
E Lantana Dr 78550
Larlenw Ave 78550
Las Palmas Cir & Dr E,
N, S & W 78550
Laurel Dr 78550
Laurie St 78550
Lazy Lake Dr 78550
Lazy Palm Dr N & S 78552
E & W Lee St 78550
Legacy Ln 78552
E Leggett Rd 78550
W Lela St 78550
Lemon Ave & Dr 78552
Leo Araguz St 78552
Leon Cir 78550
Levens Way 78552
S Lewis Ln 78552
Lexington Ave 78552
Liberty Ave & St 78552
Lime Ave & Dr 78552
Lincoln Ave 78552
E Lincoln Ave 78550
W Lincoln Ave 78550
W Lincoln St 78552
E & W Linda St 78550
Linda Vista Ave 78552
Lisa Ann Ave 78550
E Little Creek Dr 78550
Live Oak Cir 78550
Llewelyn 78552
Lodestar St 78550
E, N, S & W Loop 499
N 78550
Loquat Dr 78552
Loretta Dr 78550
E Lori Ln 78550
Los Alamos 78552
Los Amigos 78552
Los Amigos Dr 78550
W Los Arboles Cir 78550
Los Arroyos Ct 78550
Los Ranchitos 78552
Lotus St 78550
Lou Ann Ln 78550
Louis Pl 78550
W Louisiana St 78552
W Lozano St 78550
Lubbock St 78550
Lupita Cir 78552
S M St
500-1499 78550
2600-2698 78552
Macbeth Ct 78552
Macfarlane Ct 78552
Maco Dr 78550
E & W Madison Ave 78550
Maggie Ln 78552
Magnolia Ct 78550
Magnolia Pt 78552
Manana Cir 78552
Mandarin Ave 78552
Mango Cir 78552
Mangrove Palm Dr 78552
Maple Ct 78550
Maple Dr 78552
Marchita Ave 78550
Marie Pl 78552
Marine Dr 78550
Mariposa Ln 78550
W Marjory Ave 78550
E, N, S & W Mark Cir 78550
Markowsky Ave 78550
Marshall St 78550
Martha St 78550
Massachusetts 78552
Masters Blvd 78552
E & W Matz Ave 78550
Mayfield Rd 78552
Mccarver 78552
Mcduff Ct 78552
Mcfetridge St 78550
Mcgee Ct 78552
Mcgregor St 78550
Mckenzie Ln 78552
E & W Mckinley Ave 78550
Mclelland Dr 78552
Mcleod Rd 78550
Meadow Ct 78550
Melissa Dr & Ln W 78552
Memorial Ln 78552
W Memphis St 78550
Mendez St 78550
Merion Ct 78550
E Mesquite Dr 78550
W Michigan Dr 78550
Midlane Dr 78552
Mill Dr 78552
Millenium Dr 78550
Minnesota Dr 78552
N Minnesota St 78550
Mississippi St 78550
N Missouri St 78550
Mitchell St 78550
N Mockingbird Ln 78550
E & W Monroe Ave 78550
W Montana Ave 78550
Montana Dr 78552
Monte Alto Ct 78550
Monte Cristo Ct 78550
Monte Vista Ct 78550
Montezuma Rd 78550
Morgan Blvd 78550
Morris Rd 78552
Morrison Ave 78552
Mourning Dove Cir 78550
Mulberry 78552
Murphy Dr 78552
Murrah St 78550
Mustang Cir 78552
Myers Ln 78552
Nacahuita Ln 78552
Nantucket Dr 78550
N Nebraska St 78550
Nesmith St 78550
Nevada Ave 78550
New Combes Hwy
1101-1397 78550
1399-1599 78550
1502-1502 78553
1601-22999 78550
2800-22998 78550
E New Hampshire St 78550
W New Hampshire St 78552
W New Orleans Ave 78550
Nixon Rd
2900-2999 78552
20401-20897 78550
20899-23899 78550
Norma Rd 78552
November Dr 78552
Nueces Dr 78550
N & S Nueces Park
Ln 78552
N & S O St 78550
Oak Ct 78550
Oak St 78552
Oak Hollow Ln 78550
Oakmont Dr 78550
Oakmount Cir 78552
Odom Ln 78552
Ohio 78552
Oklahoma St
100-500 78550
502-598 78552
1300-1399 78550
1401-1499 78550
Olive Wood Dr 78552
W Ona St 78550
Orange Dr & Ln 78552
Orange Grove Dr 78550
Orange Heights Dr 78550
Oregon St 78552
Osborn Ave 78552
N & S Oscar St 78552
Osprey St 78552
N & S P St 78550
Pacific Ave 78552
Palis Dr 78552
N & S Palm Ave &
Blvd 78552
S Palm Court Dr 78552
Palm Tree Dr 78552
Palm Valley Cir & Dr E,
N, S & W 78552
Palm Vista Dr & Est 78552
Palmetto Dr 78552
E Palmetto Dr 78550
W Palmetto Dr 78550
Palmetto Palm Dr 78552
Paloma Cir, Ct & Ln E,
N & S 78552
Paloma Blanca Ct 78550
Paloma Celeste Ct 78550
Palomino Cir 78552
Papaya Cir 78552
Paradise Ave 78552
Park Bnd & Ln E, N, S &
W 78552
Parker Ave 78552
Parkview Cir 78550
E Parkwood Dr 78550
Pat Neff Ave 78550
Peach Tree Ct 78550
Pease St 78550
Pebble Beach Dr
600-699 78552
3200-3298 78550
3300-3599 78550
Pecan Ct & St 78550
E Pendleton St 78550
Perk Ln 78552
Perkins Rd 78552
Perry Rd 78550
Pheasant Dr 78550
W Pickens Ave 78550
E & W Pierce Ave 78550
Pine Ct 78550
Pine St 78552
Pine Valley Dr 78550
Pinehurst Dr
600-699 78552
2700-3199 78550
Pineridge Ave 78552
Pink Flamingo St 78552
Pittman St 78550
Plantation Dr 78550
Plumeria Ln 78552
Plumosa Ct 78552
Pocahontas Dr 78552
Poinciana St 78550
Polara 78552
E & W Polk St 78550
Polo Cir 78552
Ponderosa Dr 78552
Poplar St 78550
Port Rd 78550
E Porte Ct 78550
Post Oak Rd 78552
Postage Due St 78550
Powell Pl 78550
Preston Trl 78552
Price Ln 78552
Primavera Dr 78552
Primera Rd 78552
Primrose Ln 78552
Progress Dr 78550
Pummelo Ave 78552
Purple Ln 78552
N Q St 78550
Quail Run St 78552
Queen Sago Dr 78552
N R St 78550
W Railroad St 78552
Rainbow Cir 78550
Ralphs Pl 78550
Ramsey Rd 78552
S Rangerville Rd 78552
Ravenwood Ln 78550
Reagan St 78550
Rebel Dr 78550
Red Ln 78552
Red Oak 78552
N Redbird Ln 78550
Regency Ct 78550
Regina Dr 78552
Remington Dr 78552
Retama Pl & Rd 78550
Revere Ln 78550
Richmond Cir, Ct & Dr 78552
Rico Cir 78552
Rio Conchos Cir 78552
Rio Grande Cir 78552
Rio Hondo Rd 78552
Rio Panuco Ave 78552
Rio Rancho Rd 78552
Rio Red 78552
River Dr & Ln 78552
River Oaks Dr 78552
Riverside Dr 78550
Riverview Cir 78550
Road 434 78552
Road 554 78550
Road 607 78550
Road 684 78552
Road 728 78552
Road 827 78552
Road 839 78550
Road 926 78550
Roberts Ave 78552
E Robin Ave 78550
Robusta Ct 78552
Rock Cir 78550
Rodeo Dr 78552
Rodriguez St 78552
E Roosevelt Ave 78550
W Roosevelt Ave 78550
Roosevelt Rd 78552
Rose Cir 78552
N Rose St 78550
Royal Palm Dr 78552
Ruby Red Cir 78552
Runnels St 78550
Russell Ct & Ln 78552
Rusty Ln 78552
Ryan Rd 78552
N S St 78550
Sabal Dr 78550
Sabal Palm Dr 78552
Sago Palm Dr 78552
Sam Houston Dr 78550
Sam Snead Dr 78552
San Miguel St 78552
Sapphire Cir 78552
Scarlett Cir 78552
Scenic Ln 78552
Schmoker Rd 78550
Scotch St 78550
Scotch Pine Ct 78550
Seagull Ln 78552
Searcy Ranch Rd 78550
Sebastian Cir 78552
W Second St 78552
Seminole Ct 78550
Sendero E 78552
E, W & S Sesame Dr &
Sq 78550
Shadowbrook Cir 78550
E & W Shelley Dr 78552
Sherwood Way 78550
N Shirley St 78550
Shofner Ln 78552
Sid Jones Rd 78552
Skyview Cir 78550
S Somerset St 78552
Sonesta Ct & Dr 78552
Southfork Cir & Dr 78552
Southgate Dr 78552
Spangler Ln 78552
Sparrow 78552
Spc Eric D Salinas St 78552
W Spencer Ct 78550
Spicewood 78552
Spoonbill St 78552
Spring Ct 78550
Spring Meadow Ln 78550
Spruce Dr 78552
W Spur 54 78552
Spyglass Hill Dr 78550
N Stack Cir 78550
E Star Cir 78550
N Star Circle Dr 78550
Starbuck Rd 78552
State Highway 107 78552
Sterling Ave 78550
Stone Dr 78550
Stone Creek Dr 78550
Stone Pine Ct 78550
Stonebriar Rd 78552
Stonechase Rd 78552
Stonegate Dr 78552
Stonehaven Dr 78552
Straus Ln 78550
N & S Stuart Place
Rd 78552
Sugar Ct 78552
Sugar Pine Ct 78550
E Sul Ross Ave 78550
Sumatra Cir 78552
Summer Ct 78550
Summer View Ct 78552
Summerfield Ln N 78550
Sun Dr 78552
Sun Chase Cir & Dr 78552
Sun Country Dr 78552
Sun Crest Dr 78552
Sun Down Dr 78552
Sundance Cir 78552
Sunny Cv 78552
Sunnyside Dr & Ln 78552
Sunrise Blvd 78552
Sunset 78552
Sunset Cir 78550
Sunset Dr 78552
N Sunset Dr 78550
Sunset Ln 78552
Sunshine Dr 78552
Sunwest Blvd 78552
Susan St 78550
Swan Ln 78550
Swiss Pine Ct 78550
N & S T St 78550
E & W Taft Ave 78550
N & S Tamm Ln & St 78552
Tanberg Ct 78552
Tangelo Ave, Cir & Dr 78552
Tangerine Ave & Dr 78552
Taos Blvd 78552
Taylor Rd 78552
E Taylor St 78550
W Taylor St 78552
Ted Cir 78550
W Teege Ave 78550
Teege Rd 78552
N Teege St 78550
Templeton Ave 78552
Templeton Rd 78550
Templeton St 78552
Tennessee St 78550
Terrace Cir & Ln 78550
Terry Ln 78552
The Dell Ave 78552
Theresa St 78550
Thieme Rd 78552
Thomae Ln 78552
Thomas Ln 78550
Throckmorton St 78550
Times Sq 78552
Todd St 78552
Topaz Dr 78552
Tovar Rd 78550
Town Lane Dr 78552
Travis St 78550
Traxler Way 78552
Treasure Haven Dr 78550
Treasure Hills Blvd &
Ct 78550
Treasure Oaks Dr 78550
Trimpe Ln 78552
Tromon Ct 78552
Troywood Cir 78552
Tucker Rd 78552
Tumbleweed Dr 78550
E & W Tyler Ave 78550
N U St 78550
Us 77 Expy 78552
Us 83 Expy 78552
N Us Expressway 77 78552
Us Highway 77 78550
Us Highway 83 78552
N V St 78550
E, N, S & W Valencia
Cir 78552
E Van Buren Ave
100-300 78550
221-221 78551
301-2499 78550
302-2498 78550
W Van Buren Ave 78550
Vanessa Cir 78550
Vangie Ln 78552
W Velvet Oaks Ave 78550
Venado 78552
Venturi Dr 78552
Verde Cir 78552
Vermont 78550
Veterans Dr 78550
Victoria Ln 78550
E & W Vinson Ave 78550
Violet Ln 78552
Virginia Pine Ct 78550
Viriole Ln 78552
Vista Dr 78550
N & S Vista Del Sol
Dr 78552
Vista Verde Cir E 78552
Wagon Trl 78552
Walianc Rd 78552
Walnut Ct 78550
Warren St 78550
E & W Washington Ave
& Cir 78550
Washington Palm Dr 78552
Washingtonian 78552
Washmon Ave 78552
Water Edge 78552
S Watson Ln 78552
Wayne Pl 78552
Weighost Dr 78552
S West St 78550
S Westbrook Ln 78552
Westchester Ln 78550
Westfield Dr 78550
Weston Way Dr 78552
Westway Dr 78552
Westwood 78552
Whalen Rd 78550
Whipple Ln 78552
White Oak Dr W 78552
White Tail Dr 78550
E, N, S & W Whitehouse
Cir 78550
Whitewing Dr 78550
W Wichita Ave 78550
Wilcox Rd 78552
Wild Laurel 78552
Wild Oak 78552
Wild Olive 78552
Wild Orchid 78552
Wild Persimmon 78552
Wildwood Dr 78550
S Williams Ln 78552
E & W Williamson Ave 78550
Willow Tree Way 78552
Willowicke St 78550
E Wilson Ave 78550
W Wilson Ave 78550
Wilson Rd 78552
E Wilson Rd 78552
Windcrest Ln 78550
Winddrift St 78550
Windfield Dr 78550
S Winston Ln 78552
W Wisconsin Ave 78550
Wood Ave 78552
Woodall 78550
Woodhollow Ln 78550
E Woodland Dr 78550
Woods Rd 78552
W Wright St 78550
Wright Ranch Rd 78552
Wyoming Dr 78552
Wyrick 78552
Young Rd 78552
Zoy St 78552

NUMBERED STREETS

N & S 1st 78550
N & S 2nd 78550
N 3rd St 78550
S 3rd St 78550
W 3rd St 78552
N & S 4th 78550
S 5 1/2 St 78550
N & S 5th 78550
N & S 6th 78550
7th St 78550
N & S 8th 78550
N & S 9th 78550
N & S 10th 78550

N & S 11th 78550
S 12th St 78550
N & S 13th 78550
S 16th St 78550
N & S 17th 78550
N & S 21st 78550
S 23rd St 78550
S 24th St 78550
N & S 25th 78550
N & S 26th 78550
N & S 27th 78550
N 28th St 78550
N 29th St 78550
S 54th St 78550
N 20 1/2 St 78550
76 Dr 78550
N & S 77 Sunshine Strip 78550

HENDERSON TX

General Delivery 75652

POST OFFICE BOXES MAIN OFFICE STATIONS AND BRANCHES

Box No.s
All PO Boxes 75653

RURAL ROUTES

01, 04, 08 75652
03, 06 75654

NAMED STREETS

Adaway Ln 75652
Adelyn Ln 75654
Alabama St 75652
Alberta Ave 75654
Allen Dr 75652
N Alta Vista Ave 75652
S Alta Vista Ave 75654
Amy Rd 75652
Angela Ln 75654
Annie St 75654
Arnold St 75652
Ashby Ln 75652
Aspin St 75652
Atlesta N 75652
Austin St 75652
Bahia Rd 75654
Baker St 75652
Ballow St 75654
Bell St 75652
Bellaire St 75654
Belvedere Dr 75652
Bermuda Rd 75654
Beverly Ave 75654
Biggers St 75652
Biloxi St 75652
Birch St 75652
Blacknall Dr 75652
Boren St 75654
Brachfield Rd 75654
Bradford Dr 75652
Brenda Ln 75652
Briarwood Trl 75654
Brick Plant Rd 75652
Broadway St 75652
Brown St 75652
Bryanhurst St 75654
Buck Run 75654
Buford Ln 75652
Bunyon St 75652
Burnett St 75654
Caddo St 75652
N & S Calhoun St 75652
Camp St 75654
Campus Ave 75654
Carol St 75652
Carver St 75652
Castlegate Dr 75654
Cedar St 75652
Centre Ct 75654
Charles St 75652
E & W Charlevoix St 75652
Charlotte St 75654
Chase Creek Dr S 75654
Cherokee Trl 75652
Cherry St 75652
Choctaw Trl 75652
Christian St 75652
Church St 75652
Cindy Lou Ave 75654
Clay St 75652
Clayton Ln 75652
Clearbrook Cir 75652
Cleaver St 75652
College Ave 75654
Collins St 75654
Colonial Dr 75652
Country Road Dr 75652
County Roa 266a N 75652
County Road 102 W 75652
County Road 103 N 75652
County Road 104d 75652
County Road 105d 75652
County Road 107 W 75652
County Road 110d 75652
County Road 201 75652
County Road 202 E 75652
County Road 203 N 75652
County Road 204d 75652
County Road 205 N 75652
County Road 206d 75652
County Road 207 W 75652
County Road 208 N 75652
County Road 209d 75654
County Road 209d E 75652
County Road 2108d 75652
County Road 2109d 75652
County Road 210d 75652
County Road 2110d 75652
County Road 2111d 75652
County Road 2112d 75652
County Road 2113d 75652
County Road 2114d 75652
County Road 2116 75652
County Road 2117 E 75652
County Road 2119d 75652
County Road 211d 75652
County Road 212 E 75652
County Road 2125 N 75652
County Road 2125a 75652
County Road 2125b 75652
County Road 2126 N 75652
County Road 2127 N 75652
County Road 2128 N 75652
County Road 2129d 75652
County Road 2130d 75652
County Road 2131 E 75652
County Road 2135d 75652
County Road 2136 N 75652
County Road 2137 75652
County Road 2138 N 75652
County Road 2139 75652
County Road 2139d 75652
County Road 2141d 75652
County Road 2143 N 75652
County Road 2147d 75652
County Road 2157d 75652
County Road 215d 75652
County Road 216 N 75652
County Road 2160d 75652
County Road 2164 N 75652
County Road 2165d N 75652
County Road 2166 N 75652
County Road 2169d 75652
County Road 217 E 75652
County Road 2173 E 75652
County Road 218d 75654
County Road 222 N 75652
County Road 223 N 75652
County Road 223d 75652
County Road 226d 75652
County Road 227d 75652
County Road 228d 75652
County Road 229d 75652
County Road 231 N 75652
County Road 231a 75652
County Road 232 N 75652
County Road 234d 75652
County Road 235 N 75652
County Road 236 E 75652
County Road 237 E 75652
County Road 238 E 75652
County Road 239d 75652
County Road 240 N 75652
County Road 241 E 75652
County Road 243 N 75652
County Road 243a 75652
County Road 243d 75652
County Road 245 E 75652
County Road 246 N 75652
County Road 247 E 75652
County Road 248d 75652
County Road 251 E 75652
County Road 255d 75652
County Road 258 N 75652
County Road 261d 75652
County Road 262 N 75652
County Road 262d 75652
County Road 263 N 75652
County Road 264d 75652
County Road 265 N 75652
County Road 266 N 75652
County Road 266a 75652
County Road 268 E 75652
County Road 269d 75652
County Road 270 E 75652
County Road 271 N 75652
County Road 272 N 75652
County Road 272a 75652
County Road 273 N 75652
County Road 275d 75652
County Road 276d 75652
County Road 2810 75652
County Road 2811 75652
County Road 301 S 75654
County Road 302d 75654
County Road 303 E 75654
County Road 304 S 75654
County Road 306a 75654
County Road 306d 75654
County Road 307d 75654
County Road 308 E & W 75654
County Road 309 W 75652
County Road 3101d 75652
County Road 3102 N 75652
County Road 3103 N & S 75652
County Road 3104 E 75654
County Road 3105 N 75652
County Road 3106 S 75654
County Road 3107 S 75654
County Road 3108 E 75654
County Road 3109d 75654
County Road 310d 75652
County Road 311 75654
County Road 3111 E 75654
County Road 3113 S 75654
County Road 3114 S 75654
County Road 3115d 75654
County Road 3116 S 75654
County Road 3117d 75654
County Road 3118d 75654
County Road 3125 S 75654
County Road 312d 75654
County Road 313 S 75654
County Road 314 S 75654
County Road 316d 75654
County Road 317 S 75654
County Road 318 75654
County Road 319d 75654
County Road 320d 75654
County Road 321d 75652
County Road 324 N 75652
County Road 329d 75652
County Road 332 N 75652
County Road 333 N 75652
County Road 334 E 75652
County Road 335d 75652
County Road 336 N 75652
County Road 337d 75652
County Road 338d 75652
County Road 339d 75652
County Road 340d 75652
County Road 341 N 75652
County Road 342 S 75654
County Road 343 E 75654
County Road 345 S 75654
County Road 346 E 75654
County Road 347 S 75654
County Road 351 S 75654
County Road 352 E 75654
County Road 353 S 75654
County Road 354d 75654
County Road 355 S 75654
County Road 357 75654
County Road 358 E 75654
County Road 359d 75654
County Road 361 S 75654
County Road 362 E 75654
County Road 363 S 75654
County Road 364 S 75654
County Road 365 E & S 75654
County Road 366 E 75654
County Road 367 E 75654
County Road 368 E 75654
County Road 369d 75654
County Road 371d 75654
County Road 372d 75654
County Road 373d 75654
County Road 374 S 75654
County Road 375 E 75654
County Road 376 E & W 75654
County Road 377 W 75654
County Road 382 W 75654
County Road 382a 75654
County Road 383 S 75654
County Road 389d 75652
County Road 392 E 75652
County Road 393d 75654
County Road 394 N 75652
County Road 395d 75652
County Road 396d 75652
County Road 397 E 75652
County Road 398 E 75652
County Road 399d 75652
County Road 401 S 75654
County Road 401a 75654
County Road 402 W 75654
County Road 405d 75654
County Road 406 S 75654
County Road 406a 75654
County Road 407 S 75654
County Road 409d 75654
County Road 4101 75654
County Road 4103 S 75654
County Road 4104 W 75654
County Road 4105 N 75652
County Road 4107 S 75654
County Road 4108 W 75654
County Road 4109d 75654
County Road 410d 75652
County Road 4110d 75654
County Road 4111 W 75654
County Road 4112 S 75654
County Road 4113 S 75654
County Road 4113a 75654
County Road 4113b 75654
County Road 4114 S & W 75654
County Road 4115 W 75654
County Road 4116 W 75654
County Road 4117 S 75654
County Road 4118d 75654
County Road 4119d 75654
County Road 411d 75654
County Road 4120d 75652
County Road 4121 75654
County Road 4126d 75654
County Road 412d 75654
County Road 413 W 75654
County Road 4131 N 75652
County Road 4132 W 75652
County Road 4133a 75652
County Road 4133d 75652
County Road 4134d 75652
County Road 414 W 75654
County Road 415 W 75654
County Road 416 S 75654
County Road 416a 75654
County Road 4171d 75654
County Road 417d 75654
County Road 4182 W 75654
County Road 4183 S 75654
County Road 4185 W 75654
County Road 4186 W 75654
County Road 4187 S 75654
County Road 4188 S 75654
County Road 418d 75652
County Road 4191d 75654
County Road 4192d 75654
County Road 4193d 75654
County Road 4194 W 75654
County Road 4195d 75654
County Road 4196d 75654
County Road 4199d 75654
County Road 419d 75652
County Road 420 75654
County Road 4201d 75654
County Road 420d 75654
County Road 421 N 75652
County Road 4221 W 75654
County Road 422d 75652
County Road 423 N 75652
County Road 424 W 75652
County Road 424a 75654
County Road 4252d 75654
County Road 4253d 75654
County Road 4254 S 75654
County Road 4255 S 75654
County Road 4256 S 75654
County Road 4257d 75654
County Road 425d 75654
County Road 426 N 75652
County Road 4260d 75654
County Road 426a 75652
County Road 427d 75652
County Road 429d 75652
County Road 430 W 75652
County Road 431d 75652
County Road 433 S 75654
County Road 434d N 75652
County Road 438 W 75654
County Road 439d 75652
County Road 441 75654
County Road 442d 75654
County Road 444d 75654
County Road 445 W 75654
County Road 446d 75654
County Road 447 W 75654
County Road 454 S 75654
County Road 455 S 75654
County Road 456 S 75654
County Road 459 W 75654
County Road 460d 75654
County Road 462 S 75654
County Road 463d 75654
County Road 464d 75654
County Road 465d 75654
County Road 466d 75654
County Road 468 W 75654
County Road 468a 75654
County Road 469d 75654
County Road 471 W 75654
County Road 472 W 75654
County Road 473a 75654
County Road 474 W 75654
County Road 475 S 75654
County Road 476 S 75654
County Road 477 W 75654
County Road 478 S 75654
County Road 481 W 75654
County Road 483 S 75654
County Road 484 W 75654
County Road 486d 75654
County Road 487 S 75654
County Road 488d 75654
County Road 491 S 75654
County Road 492d 75654
County Road 493d 75654
County Road 494 W 75654
County Road 495 S 75654
County Road 496 W 75654
County Road 497 S 75654
County Road 498d 75654
County Road 499 S 75654
Crim St 75652
Crosby Dr 75652
Cross Park 75654
Cumberland Ln 75652
Cypress St 75652
Dallas St 75652
Dean St 75654
Deer Trl 75654
Delia St 75654
E & W Depot St 75652
Dobbs St 75652
Doe Run 75654
Dogwood Dr 75654
Dogwood St 75652
Duncan Dr 75654
Eastwood Dr 75652
Edgebrook St 75652
Elaine St 75654
Elizabeth Dr 75654
E & W Elk St 75654
Elm St 75652
Emma St 75652
N & S Estates Cir & Ln 75652
Evans St 75654
N Evenside Ave 75652
S Evenside Ave 75654
Evergreen Dr 75652
Fair Park Ave & Dr 75654
Fawn Cir 75654
Fm 1251 E 75652
Fm 13 W 75654
Fm 1662 W 75654
Fm 1716 E 75652
Fm 1798 E & W 75654
Fm 2011 E 75652
Fm 225 S 75654
Fm 2276 N 75652
Fm 2658 N 75652
Fm 2867 E 75652
Fm 3135 E 75652
Fm 3231 N 75652
Fm 3310 S 75654
Fm 348 E & S 75654
Fm 782 N 75652
Fm 782a E 75652
Fm 839 S 75654
Fm 839a 75654
Fm 840 E 75654
Fm 850 E 75654
Foley St 75654
E & W Fordall St 75652
Forrest St 75654
S Frisco Ave 75654
N Frisco St 75652
Garden Ln 75652
Gene St 75652
Gerald St 75654
Glendale Ave 75654
Golden Eagle Rd 75654
Grant St 75652
Gray St 75652
Hamlett St 75652
Hardy Rd 75654
Harkless St 75652
N Harriett St 75652
S Harriett St 75654
Hays St 75652
Heangto S 75654
N & W Heights St 75652
Hickory St 75652
N High St 75652
S High St 75654
Highland Dr 75654
Hill St 75654
Hillcrest St 75652
Hillview St 75652
Hodge St 75652
Holliman St 75652
Hollister St 75654
E Holly St 75652
Hollycreek Rd 75654
Honeysuckle St 75652
Hubbard Dr 75652
Industrial Dr 75652
Inglewood St 75654
Inwood Oaks Dr 75652
Isaac St 75652
Isaiah St 75652
Ivy St 75652
N Jackson Rd & St 75652
Jacksonville Dr 75654
James St 75652
Jan St 75654
Jenkins St 75652
Johnson Dr 75654
Jola Ave 75654
Jonell St 75654
Jones St 75654
Joseph Ave 75654
Julie St 75654
Katherine St 75652
Katy St 75654
Kaylee Ln 75654
Kaynell Dr 75654
Kellifield Dr 75654
Kenneth Dr 75652
Kenswick St 75654
Kickapoo Trl 75652
Kilgore Dr 75652
W Lake Rd & St 75652
Lake Cherokee 75652
Lake Forest Pkwy 75652
E & W Lakeview St 75652
Lancaster Dr 75652
Larkwood Trl 75654
Laurinda St 75654
Laylon Ave 75652
Lee St 75652
Lewis St 75652
Linco Rd 75652
Lion St 75654
Lobb St 75654
Lock Haven St 75654
Lone Oak St 75654
Lone Star St 75654
Lone Star Church Rd 75654
Longview Dr 75652
Loop 571 75652
W Loop 571 75652
W Loop 571 S 75654
Lowrie Dr 75652
Magnolia St 75654
E Main St 75652
N Main St 75652
S Main St 75654
W Main St 75652
Maple St 75654
Margaret Ave 75654
Marie St 75652
Marilyn Ave 75652
N Marshall St 75652
S Marshall St 75654
Mary St 75652
Mcallen St 75654
Mcclarty St 75652
Mcmurray Rd 75654
Mcnee Dr 75654
Meadowbriar St 75654
Meadowbrook Dr 75652
Meadowwood Rd 75654
Melanie Ln 75654
N Mill St 75652
S Mill St 75654
Millard Dr 75652
Millville Dr 75652
E & W Minden St 75654
Mockingbird Ln 75652
Monroe St 75652
Montgomery Dr 75654
Morningside Ave 75652
Morris Ave 75652
Neal St 75652
N Oak St 75652

S Oak St 75654
Oaklawn Dr 75652
Ohio St 75652
Old Jacksonville Rd 75654
Old Longview Rd 75652
Old Nacogdoches Rd 75654
Oliver St 75652
Overton St 75652
Paige St 75652
Palmer St 75652
Pamela St 75654
Parkview Dr 75652
Parnell Dr 75654
Peach St 75652
Pecan Creek Dr 75654
Penbrook St 75654
Penn St 75654
Peterson Ln 75654
Pine St 75654
Pinecrest Dr 75654
Pinedale Ave 75654
Pinehill Rd 75654
Plum St 75652
Pope St 75652
Preston Rd 75652
Price St 75654
Private Road 2101 75652
Private Road 2904d 75652
Private Road 3803 E 75652
Private Road 681 75652
Private Road 6812 75652
Pruitt St 75652
Quail Run 75654
E & W Ragley St 75654
Ramblewood Dr 75652
Ravenwood St 75654
Rayford Rd 75654
Raymond St 75652
Red Oak St 75654
Redbud St 75652
Reedy St 75652
Regan St 75654
Regent St 75652
Richardson Dr 75654
Ridgewood Rd 75654
Ridglea Ln 75652
Roberts St 75652
Robertson Blvd 75652
Rogers Ave 75654
Rook Plz 75654
Rosebrook St 75654
Ruby St 75654
Russell St 75654
Saint Paul St 75654
Sand Ave 75652
Sandy Ln 75652
Shady Creek Cir 75652
Shady Lake Cir 75652
Sharon Sue Dr 75652
Shawnee St & Trl 75654
Silvey Dr 75652
N Sioux St 75652
Slaydon St 75654
Smith St 75654
Southfork Acres 75654
Southview Dr 75654
Southwind Dr 75654
Southwood Dr 75654
Spring Valley Rd 75652
Stadium St 75654
S Standish St 75654
State Highway 322 N 75652
State Highway 323 W 75652
State Highway 42 S 75654
State Highway 43 E 75652
State Highway 64 W 75652
Stone St 75654
Stone Brook Dr 75654
Summer St 75652
Sundown Trl 75654
Sunset Ave 75654
Suzy Ln 75652
Sweet Gum St 75652
Tate St 75654
Tatum St 75652
Taylor St 75652
Texas St 75654
Theron St 75652
Thomas Rd 75654
Thompson St 75652
Timberline Dr 75654
Timothy St 75654
Tipps St 75654
Town East Rd 75654
Traffic Cir 75652
Travis St 75654
Truman Dr 75652
Us Highway 259 N 75652
Us Highway 259 S 75654
Us Highway 79 E 75652
Us Highway 79 N 75652
Us Highway 79 S
100-7112 75654
7114-7120 75654
7148-7148 75652
7150-7199 75652
7200-7226 75654
7201-7299 75652
7280-7298 75652
7300-15000 75654
15002-15198 75654
N Van Buren St 75652
S Van Buren St 75654
E Van Sickle St 75652
Village St 75654
Waggoner Ln 75654
Waldrop Ln 75652
Walnut St 75654
Waskom St 75652
Watson St 75652
Webb St 75654
Webster Dr 75652
Wellborn Dr 75652
Westview St 75654
Westwood Dr 75654
Whatley St 75652
Whippoorwill Ave 75652
Williams St 75652
Willowbrook Dr 75652
Wilson St 75652
Windy Ln 75654
Winter St 75652
Winterbrook Dr 75652
Wood St 75652
Woodbox Dr 75652
Woodhaven Cir 75654
Woodhaven Dr 75652
Woodlawn St 75652
Woody Ln 75652
Worth St 75654
Wylie St 75652
Yale St 75654
Yandle Dr 75652
Young St 75654
Zeid Blvd 75652
Zion St 75652

HOUSTON TX

General Delivery 77052

POST OFFICE BOXES MAIN OFFICE STATIONS AND BRANCHES

Box No.s
3607C - 3607C 77273
EXXON3 - EXXON3 77267
FIRST - FIRST 77267
1 - 992 77001
1 - 20 77056
1001 - 1992 77251
1903 - 1905 77248
2001 - 2992 77252
3000 - 3992 77253
4001 - 4999 77210
5001 - 5998 77262
6501 - 6996 77265
7001 - 7499 77248
7305 - 7305 77273
7501 - 7994 77270
8001 - 8494 77288
8501 - 8998 77249
9001 - 9592 77261
9601 - 9998 77213
10001 - 10997 77206
11001 - 11998 77293
12601 - 12990 77217
14001 - 14999 77221
15000 - 15999 77220
16001 - 16990 77222
18001 - 18074 77206
19001 - 19999 77224
20001 - 20999 77225
21001 - 21700 77226
22001 - 22979 77227
23000 - 23999 77228
24001 - 24816 77229
25001 - 25998 77265
27001 - 27992 77227
30001 - 30619 77249
31001 - 31999 77231
34001 - 34999 77234
35001 - 35999 77235
36001 - 36996 77236
37001 - 37476 77237
38001 - 38994 77238
40001 - 40999 77240
41000 - 41995 77241
42001 - 42959 77242
46011 - 47084 77210
52001 - 53995 77052
55001 - 55992 77255
56001 - 56794 77256
58001 - 58980 77258
60001 - 60999 77205
61001 - 61998 77208
62001 - 62996 77205
66001 - 66999 77266
70001 - 70996 77270
73001 - 73905 77273
75001 - 75420 77234
79000 - 79974 77279
87001 - 87910 77287
88001 - 88602 77288
90001 - 90999 77290
91001 - 91810 77291
92001 - 92005 77290
92998 - 92998 77206
96001 - 96905 77213
99001 - 99119 77261
111101 - 112145 77293
130001 - 135500 77219
202000 - 202138 77220
218000 - 219998 77218
230001 - 233913 77223
250001 - 250001 77202
262001 - 269998 77207
270001 - 273998 77277
280001 - 280538 77228
300001 - 301446 77230
310001 - 311440 77231
321000 - 321477 77221
330000 - 332099 77233
350001 - 350001 77203
420001 - 422360 77242
430001 - 437010 77243
440001 - 442168 77244
450001 - 451997 77245
460001 - 461998 77056
524001 - 526299 77052
540001 - 542348 77254
550001 - 550999 77255
570001 - 573959 77257
580001 - 580694 77258
590001 - 592012 77259
610001 - 610158 77208
630001 - 632082 77263
667001 - 667656 77266
670001 - 674441 77267
680001 - 684016 77268
690001 - 692496 77269
701001 - 701296 77270
710001 - 711506 77271
720001 - 722929 77272
740001 - 744951 77274
750001 - 753902 77275
770001 - 773998 77215
790049 - 790049 77279
800001 - 809085 77280
820001 - 822035 77282
840001 - 843510 77284
882000 - 886005 77288
890001 - 894010 77289
920501 - 926398 77292
940001 - 941920 77094
944929 - 944930 77274
980001 - 982960 77098

NAMED STREETS

Aarons Way Dr 77066
Abalone Way 77044
Abana Ln 77090
Abbey Chase Ct & Ln 77095
Abbey Oak Cir & Dr 77073
Abbey Point Ln 77049
Abbeydale Dr 77031
Abbeywood Dr 77058
Abbotshall Ln 77044
Abbott St 77007
Abby Glen Way 77084
Abby Ridge Way 77044
Aber Trail Ct 77095
Abercrombie Dr 77084
Aberdeen Ct 77095
Aberdeen Way 77025
Aberdeen Forest Dr 77095
Aberdeen Green Dr 77095
Aberdeen Lake Dr 77095
Aberdeen Meadow Ln 77053
Aberdeen Oaks Dr 77095
Aberdeen Palms Dr 77095
Aberdeen Park Dr 77095
Aberdeen Trails Dr 77095
Abergreen Trl 77095
Aberham Dr 77066
Abernathy St 77026
Abernathy Glen Ct 77014
Aberton Forest Dr 77084
Abide Dr 77085
Abigail Grace Ct 77025
Abilene St 77020
Abinger Ln 77088
Abington Way 77008
Abloom Way 77066
Abney Dr 77060
Abruzzo Dr 77085
Abundant Life Ln 77048
Acacia Arbor Ln 77041
Acacia Forest Trl 77089
Acaciawood Way 77051
Academy St
5000-5799 77005
5801-6799 77005
6800-8499 77025
Acadian Dr 77099
Acanthus Ln 77095
Acapulco Dr 77040
Ace St 77063
Acer Ct 77075
Achgill St 77040
Acme Ct 77022
Acoma Dr 77076
Acorn St 77092
Acorn Clearing Path 77044
Acorn Forest Dr 77088
Acorn Meadow St 77067
Acorn Wood Way 77059
S Acres Dr
3700-4399 77047
4700-6699 77048
Acuna Ln 77045
Adagio Ave & Ln 77040
Adair St 77004
Adam Ln 77003
N Adams St 77011
Adams Walk Ct 77077
Adamsborough Dr 77099
Addenmoor Ct 77014
Addicks Clodine Rd
3300-4099 77082
6400-8099 77083
Addicks Howell Rd
200-400 77079
315-315 77094
401-599 77079
402-598 77079
Addicks Satsuma Rd 77084
Addicks Stone Dr 77082
Addison Rd 77030
Ade St 77063
Adel Rd 77067
Adelbert St 77093
Adele St 77009
Adelia Ct 77015
Adelia St 77026
Adeline Ln 77054
Adella Dr 77049
Adelle St 77093
Aden Dr 77003
Aden Mist Dr 77003
Adina Springs Ln 77095
Adirondack Dr 77089
Adkins Rd 77055
Adler Dr 77047
Adler Lake Dr 77083
Adobe Cir & Dr 77095
Adobe Pines Ln 77084
Adobe Ridge Ln 77089
Adobe Trace Ln 77084
Adolph Dr 77091
Adrian St 77012
Adriana Ln 77049
Advance Dr 77065
Aeropark Dr 77032
Aerospace Ave 77034
Afsar Ave 77014
Aft Valley Dr 77073
Afton St 77055
Afton Meadow Ln 77072
Afton Ridge Ln 77084
Afton Woods Dr 77055
Aftonshire Dr 77027
Agar Ln 77043
Agarita Ln 77083
Agate Canyon Way 77095
Agate Praire Dr 77095
Agave Ridge Ln 77089
Aggie Ln 77076
Agnes St 77087
Agua Vista Dr 77084
Aguila St 77013
Ahrens St 77017
Aiden Cir 77048
Aiken Ln 77032
Aimua Ct 77083
Ainsdale Dr 77077
Ainsworth Dr 77099
Air Center Blvd 77032
Airedarn Rd 77047
Airfoil Rd 77032
Airline Dr
4000A-4000K 77022
5610B-5610C 77076
1400-2899 77009
2901-2999 77009
3000-5399 77022
5400-7499 77076
7500-12000 77037
12002-12098 77037
Airmail Rd 77032
Airport Blvd
1900-3699 77051
4000-4299 77047
4700-6689 77048
6691-6699 77048
6700-9299 77061
W Airport Blvd
3400-4398 77045
4400-4499 77045
5300-6699 77035
6700-9099 77071
9300-10099 77031
Airstream Loop 77044
Airtex Dr 77090
E Airtex Dr 77073
Airway Dr 77037
Airybrook Ln 77094
Ajax St 77022
Akard St
3000-3199 77051
4100-4298 77047
4300-4499 77047
Akron St 77029
Akron Oak St 77070
Akumal Ln 77073
Alabama Ct 77027
Alabama St 77004
W Alabama St
100-199 77002
200-1699 77006
1700-3399 77098
3400-4799 77027
4900-5499 77056
Alabaster Ct & Dr 77083
Alabonson Rd 77088
Alakerli Dr 77044
Alaman Dr 77090
Alamar Dr 77095
Alameda Point Ln 77041
Alametos Dr 77083
Alamo St 77007
Alannah Lagoon Ct & Dr 77083
Alanneil Dr 77081
Alanwood St 77061
Alaska St 77017
Alba Rd
3400-5199 77018
5300-5499 77091
Alba St 77088
Albacore Dr 77074
Albans Rd & St 77005
Albany St 77006
Albany Springs Ln 77044
Albelia Meadows Dr 77083
Albemarle Ln 77021
Alber St 77009
Alberene Dr 77074
Alberta St 77021
Albin Ln 77071
Albright Dr 77017
Albury Dr
8900-8999 77074
9400-11299 77096
Alcala Ct 77078
Alcanterra Dr 77078
Alchester Ln 77079
Alcomita Dr 77083
Alconbury Ln 77021
Alcorn St 77093
Alcott Dr
8500-9699 77080
10400-10899 77043
Alcove Ln 77090
Aldates Dr 77015
Alden St 77084
Alden Ridge Dr 77053
Aldenwick Ln 77073
Alder Dr 77081
Alderete Dr 77068
Alderfer St 77047
Alderfield Ct 77084
Alderford Ct 77070
Alderney Dr 77055
Alderson St
5900-7599 77020
13700-14699 77015
Aldine Bender Rd
1-799 77060
800-5799 77032
Aldine Mail Rd
710RR-710RS 77037
100-1099 77037
1100-5499 77039
Aldine Meadows Rd 77032
Aldine Park Ln 77093
Aldine Western Rd 77038
Aldine Westfield Rd
2300-12399 77093
12400-14799 77039
14800-16999 77032
17000-19699 77073
14625-1-14625-2 77039
Aldis St 77075
Aldon St 77093
Aldrich St 77055
Aldsworth Dr 77088
Aldwell Ct 77064
Aledo St 77051
Aleen St 77029
Alegria Dr 77083
Alejo Dr 77088
Alenzo Dr 77032
Aletha Ln 77081
Alex Ln 77071
Alex Springs Ln 77044
Alexander St
800-899 77007
900-1599 77008
Alexis Cir 77014
Alfano St
6301-6597 77076
6599-6699 77076
7700-7899 77037
Alfred Ln 77041
Algerian Way 77098
Algiers Rd 77041
Algonquin Dr 77089
Algregg St
600-899 77008
900-1199 77009
Alice Ln 77015
Alice St 77021
Alief Clodine Rd
11600-11700 77082
11701-11799 77072
11702-17398 77082
11901-17399 77082
Alief Place Dr 77072
Alief Village Dr 77072
Aline St 77087
Alisa Ln 77084
Aliso Bend Ln 77041
Aliso Canyon Ln 77083
Aliso Shadow Ct 77089
Alkay St
14400-14699 77045
15100-15199 77053
All Oak Trl 77084
Allbritton Dr 77093
Allday Dr 77036
Allegheny St 77021
Allegro Ct 77040
Allegro Dr 77040
E Allegro St 77080
N Allegro St 77080
S Allegro St 77080
Allen Pkwy 77019
Allen St 77007
Allen Genoa Rd
100-1300 77017
1302-2398 77017
5300-5599 77034
Allendale Rd 77017
Allens Landing Dr 77065
Allensby St 77022
Allenwick Ln 77084
Allerton St 77084
S Alley Ct 77082
Alliant Dr 77032
Allington Ct & Dr 77014
Allison Ln 77054
Allison Rd 77048
Allison Bend Ct 77086
Allston St
500-899 77007
900-1599 77008
4000-4299 77018
Allsup St 77061
Allum Rd 77045
Allview Ln 77094
Allwood St
7900-10299 77016
11200-11399 77093
Alma St 77009
Almeda Mall 77075

Almeda Rd
12112A-2-12112B-2 .. 77045
12112A-3-12112B-3 .. 77045
12112A-1-12112B-1 .. 77045
12112B-4-12112B-5 .. 77045
3500-4199 77004
4110-4110 77288
4200-6098 77004
4201-6099 77004
6100-6799 77021
6801-6999 77021
6900-6998 77030
7000-7300 77054
7205-7205 77230
7301-9299 77054
7302-9298 77054
10500-13399 77045
13400-15299 77053
E Almeda St
8800-9599 77054
10500-10699 77051
Almeda Bend Ct 77075
Almeda Forest Ct 77045
Almeda Genoa Rd
100-4099 77047
4100-6699 77048
6700-9899 77075
9898-9898 77275
9900-10298 77075
9901-10299 77075
10500-11000 77034
10935-10935 77234
11001-13199 77034
11002-13198 77034
Almeda Meadows Dr ... 77048
Almeda Oaks Dr 77075
Almeda Park Dr 77045
Almeda Pines Dr 77075
Almeda Plaza Dr 77045
Almeda School Rd 77047
Almeece St
14400-14699 77045
15100-15199 77053
Almenar Cir 77038
Almington Ln 77088
Almond Bay Ln 77083
Almond Brook Ln 77062
Almond Creek Dr 77059
Almond Glen Ct 77044
Almond Grove Ct & Dr . 77077
Almond Lake Ct & Dr .. 77047
Almond Springs Dr 77095
Almont Dr 77016
Aloe St 77007
Aloha Trail Dr 77044
Alon Ct & Ln 77014
Alpena Ln 77095
Alperton Dr 77088
Alpha St
3600-3699 77019
12100-12299 77072
E Alpine Dr 77061
Alpine Ridge Way 77089
Alpine Vale Ct 77038
Alrover St
14400-14699 77045
15000-15199 77053
Alsace St 77021
Alseth Cir 77086
Alstead Dr 77041
Alsuma St 77029
Alta Loma Way 77075
Alta Mar Dr 77083
Alta Mesa Dr 77083
Alta Vista St 77023
Altamont Dr 77074
Althea Dr 77018
Altic St
1-599 77011
600-1098 77023
1100-1199 77023
Altic Lane Ct 77066
Altmor Ln 77075
Alto St 77060
Alto Lake Dr 77067
Alton St 77012
Altonbury Ln 77031
Altoona St 77026
Altus Dr 77051
Alvar Dr 77014
Alvarado Dr 77035
Alvin St
3700-4699 77051
4700-4999 77033
Aly Trace Ct 77064
Alzaada Ln 77070
Amado Dr 77065
Amadwe St 77051
Amalie St 77093
Amanda Ln 77063
Amanda Mdws 77089
Amanda Pines Dr 77089
Amani Ln 77095
Amapola Dr 77083
Amaranth Dr 77084
Amaranth Meadow Ln .. 77085
Amargos Dr 77083
Amarillo St
6900-7699 77020
8100-8199 77029
Amarose Dr 77090
Amasa St 77022
Ambassador Way 77056
Amber Ct 77069
Amber St 77022
Amber Way 77049
Amber Bough Ct 77062
Amber Canyon Dr 77095
Amber Creek Ct 77095
Amber Dale Ct 77059
Amber Forest Dr 77068
Amber Grove Ct 77083
Amber Knoll Ct 77062
Amber Lake Dr 77084
Amber Lodge Ln 77083
Amber Mist Ln 77095
Amber Queen Ct & Ln . 77041
Amber Rose Ln 77039
Amber Valley Ct 77066
Ambergate Dr 77077
Amberly Ct 77063
Ambermist Ln 77095
Ambern Dr 77053
Ambershadow Dr 77015
Amberton Ln 77024
Amberwick Dr 77031
Amble Ln 77085
Amble Oak Ct 77059
Amblewood Dr
8300-8599 77072
8600-10699 77099
Amboy St
1100-1199 77020
2500-3499 77026
Ambrosa Dr 77044
Ambrose St 77045
Ambursen St 77034
Amcreek Rd 77068
Amelia Dr 77045
Amelia Rd 77055
American Beauty Ct 77041
American Fork Ct 77090
Ames Cir 77024
Amesbury Dr 77084
Amesbury Manor Ln 77094
Ameswood Rd 77095
Amherst St 77005
Amir St 77072
Amira Dr 77065
Ammi Trl 77060
Amoor St 77029
Amos St 77021
Amsterdam Dr 77089
Amundsen St 77009
Amy St 77028
Amy Ridge Rd 77053
Anabel Ln 77076
Anacortes St 77061
Anadarko Ln 77095
Anadell St 77055
Anagnost Rd 77047
Analisa Cir 77084
Anaqua Dr 77092
Anchick St 77076
Anchor St 77088
Anchorage Ln 77079
Andante Dr 77040
Ander Oak Ln 77070
Anderson Rd
3100-5799 77053
6200-6599 77085
E Anderson Rd 77047
Anderson St 77081
Anderson Oaks Ct &
St 77053
Anderson Woods Dr 77070
Anderwoods Ct 77070
Andiron Cir 77041
Andisour St 77091
Andorra Ln 77015
Andover Woods Ct 77095
Andrea St 77021
Andrea Way Ln 77083
Andrew Way 77082
Andrews St 77019
Andwood St 77087
Andy Dr 77091
Angel Ln 77045
Angel Falls Ln 77041
Angel Fire Ln 77070
Angel Island Ln 77053
Angel Shores Ln 77041
Angelas Meadow Ln 77095
Angeline St 77009
Angelique Dr 77065
Angelo St 77009
Angie Ln 77038
Angler Bend Dr 77044
Angler Leaf Ct 77044
Anglerbend Lndg 77095
Angleton St 77033
Angus St 77028
Anice St 77039
Anita St
300-899 77006
1000-4199 77004
Ann Ln 77064
Ann St 77003
Ann Arbor Dr 77063
Ann Louise Rd 77086
Anna Green St 77084
Anna Held St 77048
Annapolis Ct & St 77005
Anne Dr 77058
Anne St 77055
Annette Ln 77076
Anniston Dr 77080
Annunciation St 77016
Anoka Ct 77015
Ansbury Dr 77018
Ansdell Ct 77084
Anselm St 77045
Anson Point Ln 77040
Antean Way Ct 77065
Antelope Dr 77063
Antha St
4400-4599 77093
4600-6299 77016
Anthonette Ln 77015
Anthony Pine Ln 77088
Antibes Ln 77082
Antietam Ln 77083
Antigua Ln 77058
Antilles Ln 77058
Antoine Dr
2884A-2884D 77092
700-999 77024
1000-2199 77055
2800-5299 77092
5300-6999 77091
7000-9099 77088
9200-11099 77086
11200-12299 77066
12300-12599 77067
2884-1-2884-4 77092
Antoinette St 77087
E & W Antone Cir 77071
Antonio St 77045
Antwerp Cv 77070
Anvil Cir, Ct & Dr 77090
Anwar Dr 77083
Anza Cir 77012
Anzac St 77020
Anzio Rd 77033
Apache St
500-1499 77022
6900-7499 77028
Apache Plume Dr 77071
Apache Way Dr 77095
Apala Dr 77032
Apgar St 77032
Apollo St
800-900 77058
902-998 77058
4100-5099 77018
5301-6497 77091
6499-6999 77091
Apothecary Ln 77064
Appaloosa Ave 77084
Appelt Dr 77015
Appian Way 77015
Appin Ct 77095
Apple Bend Cir 77044
Apple Bough Cir 77067
Apple Creek Rd 77017
Apple Dale Dr 77084
Apple Forest Trl 77065
Apple Glen Ln 77072
Apple Hill St 77084
Apple Knoll Ct 77059
Apple Mill Dr 77095
Apple Seed Ct 77082
Apple Tree Rd 77079
Apple Valley Ln 77069
Appleby Dr 77031
Applecross Ln 77084
Appleridge Dr 77070
Appleton St 77022
Appletree Hill Ln 77084
Appletree Ridge Rd 77084
Applewood St 77024
April Ln 77092
April Way 77024
April Arbor Ct 77031
April Creek Ln 77095
April Falls Trl 77083
April Glen Ct 77084
April Hill St 77095
April Ridge Dr 77083
April Wind Dr 77014
Aqua Ln 77072
Aqueduct Rd 77044
Arabella St 77091
Arabelle Crst 77007
Arabelle Grv 77007
Arabelle St
2100-2799 77007
8700-8799 77088
Arabelle Lake St 77007
Arabian Cir 77084
Aragon Dr 77083
Aragon Meadow Ln 77049
Aramis Dr 77073
Aransas Dr 77088
Arapahoe St 77020
Arberry St 77012
Arboles Dr 77035
S Arbor Dr 77089
Arbor St 77004
Arbor Bend Dr 77070
Arbor Falls Ln 77084
Arbor Field Ln 77044
Arbor Garden Ln 77066
Arbor Glen Rd 77071
Arbor Ivy Ln 77044
Arbor Meadow Dr 77071
Arbor Mill Ct 77059
Arbor Mist 77094
Arbor Oak Dr 77088
Arbor Park Ct 77095
Arbor Ridge Dr 77071
Arbor Trellis Dr 77066
Arbor Vitae Dr 77092
Arbor Wood Dr 77040
Arborcrest St 77062
Arbordale Ln 77024
Arborway St 77057
Arbuckle St 77005
Arc St 77063
Arcadia St 77026
Arcadia Bend Ct & Ln .. 77041
Arcadian Shores Dr 77084
Archduke Dr 77032
Arched Oak Dr 77095
Archer St 77009
Archer Glen Dr 77073
Archley Dr 77055
Archmont Dr 77070
Archway Dr 77082
Archwood St 77049
Archwood Trl 77007
Arcidian Forest Dr 77088
Arcola Ridge Ct & Dr ... 77083
Arcridge Cir 77053
Arden Ct 77033
Arden Glen Ln 77044
Arden Ridge Ln 77014
Ardennes St 77033
Ardent Oak Cir 77059
Ardfield Dr 77070
Ardley Cir 77088
Ardmore St
5500-6699 77021
6800-7599 77054
Areba St 77091
Arendale St 77075
Argentina St 77040
Argonne St
2000-2199 77019
2800-3299 77098
Argyle Rd 77049
Ariel St
5200-5799 77096
5800-8899 77074
Arista Dr 77083
Arizona St 77017
Arkansas St 77026
N Arkansas St 77093
Arledge St 77075
Arletta St 77061
Arlicious St 77020
Arlington St
300-899 77007
900-2899 77008
3000-3499 77018
4200-4799 77022
5500-5699 77076
Arlington Forest Dr 77088
Arlington Square Dr 77034
Arlon Trl 77082
Armada Dr 77091
Armand Shore Dr 77058
Armatta Ct 77075
Armour Dr 77020
Armstead St 77009
Armstrong St 77029
Arnage Ln 77085
Arncliffe Dr 77088
Arndt Rd 77044
Arnell Dr 77018
Arnett Ln 77037
Arnim St 77087
Arnold St
100-199 77007
3700-4099 77005
Arnot St 77007
Arp St 77085
Arranmore Ln 77095
Arrondi Cir 77065
Arrow Flint Cv 77084
Arrow Hill Rd 77077
Arrow Ridge Ct & Dr ... 77067
N & S Arrowana Ln 77036
W Arrowdale Dr 77037
Arrowgrass Dr 77064
Arrowhead Ln 77075
Arrowhead Glen Dr 77071
Arrowhead Trace Ln 77089
Arrowpoint Dr 77022
Arrowrock Trl 77050
Arrows Peak Ln 77095
Arrowwood Cir N 77063
Arroyo Verde Ln 77041
Arroyo Vista Ct & Ln ... 77067
Art St 77076
Artdale St 77063
Artem Ct 77051
Artesian Pl 77002
Arthington St 77053
Arthur St 77019
Arto St 77093
Aruba Dr 77080
Arvana St 77034
Arvilla Ln 77021
Arvin St
9100-9499 77028
9600-9899 77078
Arvonshire Ct 77049
Asbury Pl, St & Ter 77007
Ascalon Cir 77069
Ascot Ln 77092
Ascot Glen Ln 77082
Ash Pl 77007
Ash St 77044
Ash Butte Dr 77090
Ash Creek Dr 77043
Ash Fork Dr 77064
Ash Garden Ct 77083
Ash Hollow Dr 77082
Ash Meadow Dr 77090
Ash Oak Dr 77091
Ash Tree Ln 77073
Asharair Dr 77035
Ashbloom Ln 77080
Ashbournne Springs
Ln 77095
Ashbrook Dr 77081
Ashburn Spur 77061
Ashburn St
5600-5699 77033
6900-7599 77061
Ashburnham Dr 77082
Ashburton Dr 77040
Ashbury Park Ct & Dr .. 77077
Ashby St 77005
Ashclift Dr 77082
Ashcott Dr 77072
Ashcroft Dr
6301-6597 77081
6599-7499 77081
8300-11199 77096
11400-12699 77035
Ashdale Ln 77083
Ashentree Way 77083
Ashfield Dr 77082
Ashford Pkwy 77077
Ashford Riv 77072
Ashford Arbor Dr 77082
Ashford Bend Dr 77082
Ashford Brook Dr 77082
Ashford Chase Dr 77082
Ashford Creek Dr 77082
Ashford Forest Dr 77079
Ashford Green Ln 77072
Ashford Hills Dr 77077
Ashford Hollow Ln 77077
Ashford Knoll Dr 77082
Ashford Meadow Dr 77082
Ashford Oak Dr 77082
Ashford Park Dr 77082
Ashford Pine Dr 77082
Ashford Point Dr 77082
Ashford Trail Dr 77082
E, N, S & W Ashford
Villa Ln 77082
Ashgrove Dr 77077
Ashington Dr 77067
Ashkirk Dr 77099
Ashland St
700-899 77007
900-2899 77008
Ashland Brook Ct 77084
Ashland Forest Dr 77088
Ashlawn Dr 77083
Ashlee Ln 77014
Ashlen Dr 77073
Ashley Ct 77041
Ashley Ln 77089
Ashley Rd
14500-14699 77034
18800-18999 77084
Ashley Run 77077
Ashley St 77017
Ashley Circle Dr E 77071
Ashley Cove Ct 77094
Ashley Glen Cir 77073
Ashley Grove Dr 77084
Ashley Hall Ct 77084
Ashlock Dr 77082
Ashmead Dr 77077
Ashmole Ln 77088
Ashmoor Ct & Way 77058
Ashmore Dr 77069
Ashoglen Ln 77077
Ashton Dr 77095
Ashton St 77091
Ashton Lake Ln 77041
Ashton Park Dr 77082
Ashurst Dr 77077
Ashville Dr 77051
Ashwood St 77025
Ashwood Valley Dr 77095
Ashworth St
11500-11699 77016
11700-11899 77050
Askew St 77087
Askins Ln
4800-5199 77093
5300-5499 77016
Aspen St 77081
Aspen Bend Dr 77068
Aspen Bough Cir 77065
Aspen Cove Ct & Dr ... 77077
Aspen Grove Dr 77077
Aspen Hills Dr 77062
Aspen Hollow Ln 77082
Aspen Knoll Ct 77059
Aspen Meadow Dr 77071
Aspen Park Ln 77084
Aspen Place Dr 77071
Aspen River Ln 77062
Aspen Star Ct 77053
Aspen Tree Ct 77014
Aspen View Ct 77088
Aspen Wood Dr 77040
Aspenglen Dr 77084
Aspenglenn Dr 77084
Aspenway Dr 77070
Aspley Ct 77094
Aste Ln 77065
Asterbend St 77083
Aston St 77040
Astonshire Ln 77014
Astoria Blvd 77089
Astwood Ct 77068
Atherton Ln 77094
Atherton Canyon Ln 77014
Athlone Ct & Dr 77088
Athos St 77012
Atlantic St 77009
Atlasridge Dr 77048
Atlasta Ln 77037
Atlaw Dr 77071
Atlerank St 77033
Atmore Place Dr 77082
Atrium Pl 77084
Attar St 77007
Attingham Dr 77024
Attlee Dr 77077
Attridge Rd 77018
Attucks St 77004
Attwater St 77028
Atwell Dr
6300-7299 77081
8900-11199 77096
11300-12499 77035
Atwood Ln 77076
Atwood Glen Ct & Ln .. 77014
Atwood Grove Ln 77086
Aubert St 77017
Aubreywood Ln 77070
Auburn Pl 77005
Auburn St 77017

Auburn Falls Ln 77084
Auburn Glen Ln 77095
Auburn Grove Ln 77041
Auburn Knoll Ave 77049
Auburn Meadows Dr 77094
Auburn Shores Ct 77041
Auburn Woods Dr 77084
Auburndale St 77023
Aucuba Ln 77095
Auden St 77005
Audley St 77098
Audra Ln 77083
Audrey Ln 77015
Audubon Pl 77006
Audubon Hill Ct 77038
Audubon Springs Dr 77040
Augusta Ct
1-99 77064
5800-5899 77057
Augusta Dr 77057
Augusta St 77007
Augustine Dr 77036
Auguswood Ln 77073
Auline Ln 77055
Auronia Dr 77067
Aurora St
100-699 77008
700-1299 77009
Aurora Falls Ln 77083
Aurora Mist Ln 77053
Austin St
100-799 77002
800-1199 77010
1200-2299 77002
2300-5799 77004
Austin Hollow Ct 77044
Australia St 77040
Autauga St 77080
Auto Park Way 77083
Autrey St 77006
Autum Berry Ln 77049
S Autumn Dr 77089
Autumn Ln 77016
Autumn Arbor Dr 77092
Autumn Blossom Ct 77095
Autumn Bridge Ln 77084
Autumn Canyon Trce 77062
Autumn Chase Dr 77065
Autumn Creek Dr 77070
Autumn Dawn Way 77084
Autumn Falls Ln 77095
Autumn Field Ct 77095
Autumn Forest Dr
5000-5199 77091
5800-6399 77092
Autumn Grove Dr 77072
Autumn Harvest Dr 77064
Autumn Hills Dr 77084
Autumn Hollow Ln 77041
Autumn Laurel Trl 77095
Autumn Leaf Ln 77072
Autumn Leigh Dr 77083
Autumn Meadow Ln 77064
Autumn Mill Dr 77070
Autumn Oaks Dr 77079
Autumn Park Dr 77084
Autumn Pine Ln 77084
Autumn Pines Trl 77084
Autumn Ridge Trail Dr 77048
Autumn Sky Ct & Ln 77095
Autumn Sun Dr 77083
Autumn Trace Ct 77083
Autumn Trails Ln 77084
Autumn View Dr 77048
Autumn Way Ct & Dr 77064
Autumn Wind Dr
8300-8399 77040
16200-16399 77090
Autumnbrook Dr 77068
Autumnsong Dr 77064
Autumnwood Dr 77013
Avalon Ct 77044
Avalon Pl 77019
Avalon Ter 77057
Avalon Way 77057
Avenel Iron Dr 77064

Avenell Rd 77034
Avenida De Las
Americas 77010
Avenida La Quinta St 77077
Avenida Vaquero St 77077
Avenue E
6601-6613 77011
Avenue E
6615-7409 77011
7411-7499 77011
7511-7517 77012
7519-8099 77012
Avenue N
6949 1/2A-6949 1/
2B 77011
6501-6599 77011
6601-7435 77011
7500-7612 77012
7614-7698 77012
Avenue S 77011
Avenue W 77011
E Avenue N 77012
E Avenue S 77012
Avenue B
6500-7399 77011
7500-8099 77012
Avenue C
6400-7399 77011
7501-7597 77012
7599-8099 77012
Avenue F
6500-7499 77011
7500-8099 77012
Avenue H
4700-7499 77011
7500-7999 77012
11400-11499 77034
E Avenue H 77012
Avenue I
4700-7499 77011
7600-7899 77012
E Avenue I 77012
Avenue J
5300-7499 77011
7501-7597 77012
7599-7799 77012
E Avenue J 77012
Avenue K
6500-7499 77011
7500-7799 77012
E Avenue K 77012
Avenue L
6600-7499 77011
7500-7799 77012
E Avenue L 77012
Avenue O
6600-7499 77011
7500-7699 77012
E Avenue O 77012
Avenue Of Oaks St
100-1099 77009
2400-2599 77026
Avenue P
6600-7499 77011
Avenue P
7500-7699 77012
E Avenue P 77012
Avenue Q 77011
E Avenue Q 77012
Avenue R 77011
E Avenue R 77012
Avenue T 77011
Avenue U 77011
Avenue V 77011
Averill St 77009
Avernus St 77022
Averrenc St 77051
Avert Ct 77088
Avery Trace Ct 77065
Avery Vale Ct & Ln 77014
Aves St 77034
Avie St 77007
Avignon Ct 77082
Avila Dr 77038
Avila Bend Dr 77095
Avion St 77044
Aviva Ln 77083

Avocet Ln 77040
Avon Pl 77066
Avon Brook Ln 77034
Avon Park Ln 77083
Avondale St 77006
Avonelle Ln 77045
Avongate Ln 77082
Avonmoor Dr 77049
Avonshire Dr 77083
Awty School Ln 77055
Axilda St 77017
Aycliff Dr 77039
Ayesha Park Dr 77099
Ayrshire Pl 77089
Azalea Ct 77017
Azalea Park 77008
Azalea St
800-899 77018
7400-7799 77023
Azalea Vlg 77088
Azalea Brook Way 77084
Azalea Creek Trl 77065
Azalea Garden Dr 77038
Azalea Glen Ct 77084
Azalea Shores Ct 77044
Azalea Shores Dr 77070
Azalea Trace Dr 77066
Azalea Walk Ln 77044
Azaleadell Dr 77018
Azeem Ave 77099
Aztec Ln 77049
Aztec Wood Dr 77084
Azure Brook Dr 77089
B St 77072
Babbitt Ct & St 77034
Baber Ct & Dr 77095
Baber Run Cir 77095
Baca St
1-899 77013
1000-1299 77029
Bacard Ln 77099
Bacchus St 77022
Bace Ct 77007
Bace Dr 77055
Bach Elm St 77070
Bach Orchard Trl 77038
Bacher St 77028
Bachwood Dr 77040
Back Bay Ct 77058
Back Bay Brook Trl 77045
Back Bay Ridge Way 77089
Backcove Ct 77064
Backen Ln 77084
Backgate Dr 77034
Bacon St 77021
Bacons Castle Ln 77084
Bacor Rd 77084
Bade St 77055
Baden St 77009
Badger Ct 77084
Badger Canyon Dr 77095
Badger Forest Dr 77088
Badgerwood Dr 77013
Baer St 77020
Baffin Ln 77090
Bafing Dr
13100-13199 77099
13200-13499 77083
Bagby St
100-298 77002
300-2299 77002
2300-3199 77006
Baggett Ln 77055
Bagpipe Ln 77084
Baiamonte St 77085
Baikal Ct 77044
Bailey St
900-1899 77019
1900-2099 77006
Bain St 77026
Bainbridge St 77016
Bainbridge Trl 77065
Bainbridge Hill Ln 77047
Baird Ct 77041
Baird St 77023
Bairnsdale Ln 77070

Baker Dr 77017
Baker Rd 77094
Baker St 77002
Baker Trl 77094
Baker Cove St 77024
Bakerwood Dr 77064
Bal Harbour Dr 77058
Balarama Dr 77099
Balbo St 77091
Balcones Dr 77034
Balcrest Dr 77070
Bald Eagle Ct 77044
Bald Mountain Cir 77067
Bald Ridge Ln 77095
Baldinger St 77011
Baldwin St
1900-2299 77002
2300-3199 77006
Baldwin Hill Ct 77044
Baldwin Square Dr &
Ln 77077
Balfour St 77028
Balkin St 77021
Ball St 77003
Ballantine St 77075
Ballantrae Ct & Ln 77015
Ballardvale Ln 77067
Ballast Rd 77044
Ballfour Park Ln 77047
Ballina Canyon Ct &
Ln 77041
Ballina Ridge Ct 77083
Ballinger Cir & Dr 77064
Bally Castle Dr 77070
Balmforth Ln 77096
Balmoral Ln 77024
Balmore Cir 77069
Balmorhea Ave 77039
Balsam Ln 77078
Baltic Ln 77090
Baltimore St 77012
Baltrusol Dr 77095
Balvenie Ct 77095
Balzy Rd 77018
Bamboo Rd 77041
Bamboo Forest Trl 77044
Bambriar Dr 77090
Bambridge Dr 77090
Bambrook Ln 77090
Bamcrest Dr 77090
Bammel Ln 77098
Bammel Rd
100-300 77090
302-348 77090
350-1599 77073
Bammel Fields Ct 77014
Bammel North Houston
Rd
9800-10999 77086
11000-13999 77066
14000-15599 77014
Bammel Oaks Ct 77014
Bammel Timbers Ln 77068
Bammel Village Dr 77014
Bammel Westfield Rd 77090
Bammelwood Dr 77014
Bamwick Dr 77090
Bamwood Dr 77090
Banbury Pl 77027
Banchester Ct 77070
Bancroft St 77027
Bandelier Dr 77080
Bandell Dr 77045
Bandera St 77015
Bandera Hollow Ln 77082
Bandera Valley Ct 77089
Bandit Trail Dr 77095
Bandlon Dr 77072
Bandon Ln 77073
Baneway Dr 77072
Banff St 77062
Banff Mountain Trl 77038
Banfield Ct 77075
Bangle St 77012
Bangs Rd 77076
Banjo St 77088

Banks St
1000-1098 77006
1100-1699 77006
1700-2199 77098
Bankside Dr
5500-6499 77096
7600-7899 77071
9101-9197 77031
9199-9499 77031
Banna Dr 77090
Banner Dr 77013
Banning Dr 77027
Bannister Ln 77076
Bannowsky Ln 77049
Bantam Brook Ln 77066
Bantam Ridge Ct 77053
Banter Trails Ct & Dr 77049
Banting St 77078
Bantry Meadow Dr 77060
Bantum St 77093
Banty Falls Ct 77068
Banyan St 77028
Banzer St 77055
Barada St 77034
Barajas Ln 77039
Barazi Oaks Ct 77024
Barbados Dr 77088
E Barbara Cir 77071
W Barbara Cir 77071
Barbara Ln 77005
Barbara Mae St 77015
Barbarella Ct 77088
Barbarossa Dr 77083
Barbee St 77004
Barber St 77007
Barber Grove Ln 77095
Barberry Dr 77051
Barberton Dr 77036
Barbizon Dr 77089
Barbstone Dr 77044
Barbuda Ln 77058
Barcus Ln 77015
Bardwall Lake Ct 77044
Bardwell St 77009
Bare Oak St 77082
Barely Ln 77070
Barger Rd 77074
Bark Ln 77015
Bark Ridge Ln 77095
Barkdull St 77006
Barker Dr 77044
N Barker St 77084
Barker Clodine Rd 77094
Barker Cypress Rd
300-499 77094
1000-6999 77084
Barker Oaks Dr 77077
Barker Springs Rd
16600-16899 77084
16830-16830 77218
16900-16998 77084
16901-16999 77084
Barkers Cv 77079
Barkers Crest Dr 77084
Barkers Crossing Ave 77084
Barkers Forest Ln 77084
Barkers Green Way 77084
N & S Barkers Landing
Ct & Rd 77079
Barkers Point Ln 77079
Barkers Wood Ln 77084
Barkerview Ct 77084
Barkley St
400-1299 77022
4900-8500 77017
8502-8598 77017
Barkley Bend Ln 77044
Barksdale Dr 77093
Barleton Way 77058
Barley Mill Ct 77095
Barlow St 77028
Barnes St 77007
Barnes Ridge Ln 77072
Barnesworth Dr 77049
Barnett St 77017
Barney Rd 77092

Barnham St 77016
Barnhart Blvd 77077
Barnhart Ln 77065
Barnsley Ln 77088
Barnston St 77026
Barnwell Dr 77082
Baron St 77020
Baron Creek Ln 77044
Baron Hollow Ct 77014
Baron Oaks Ct & Dr 77069
Baronbrook Ln 77044
Barons Cv 77041
Barons Bridge Dr 77069
Baronshire Dr 77070
Baronshire Round 77070
Baronsmede Dr 77083
Barr Cir & St 77080
Barr Lake Dr 77095
Barracuda Ct 77024
Barranca Dr 77083
Barremore St 77023
Barren Way 77064
Barren Springs Dr 77090
Barrett St
5200-5399 77022
5401-5499 77076
Barrett Brae Dr 77072
Barrett Post Ln 77095
Barrett Ridge Ln 77044
Barretts Glen Ct 77065
Barrington Gdn 77069
Barrington Grn 77069
Barrington Rd 77056
Barrington Fairway 77069
Barron Wood Cir 77083
Barrow Ln 77065
Barrow Creek Ln 77089
Barrow Downs Way 77034
Barrow Point Ln 77014
Barrow Ridge Ln 77082
Barrowhollow Dr 77083
Barry Tree Ct 77070
Barrycliff Ct 77070
Barryknoll Ct 77079
Barryknoll Ln
11800-12799 77024
13100-14799 77079
Barrytree Dr 77070
Bart Ln 77040
S & W Bartell Dr 77054
Bartlett St
900-1299 77006
2100-2599 77098
Bartlett Cove Dr 77067
Bartlett Pear Ct 77049
Bartletts Harbor Ct 77040
Barton Fls 77041
Barton St
5600-5699 77028
8800-9299 77075
Barton Hills Ct 77014
Barton Oaks Ct & Dr 77095
Barton River Ln 77044
Barwood Dr 77043
Barwood Bend Dr 77065
Barziza St 77011
Basalt Ln 77077
Bascom Ln 77080
Bash Pl 77027
Basil Ln 77036
Basil St 77003
Basilan Ln 77058
N Basildon Ct 77073
Basilica St 77099
Baskove Dr 77088
Bass Ct & St 77007
Bass Pro Dr 77047
Bassdale Dr 77070
Basselford Dr 77083
Bassetdale Ln 77084
Bassett St 77051
Bassford Dr
13000-13199 77099
13200-13399 77083
Bassoon Dr 77025
Basswood St 77022

Basswood Dale Dr 77084
Basswood Forest Ct 77095
Basswood Springs Ct 77062
Bastogne Rd 77033
Bastrop St
300-2299 77003
2300-4399 77004
Bataan Rd 77033
Bateman Ln 77088
Bates Ave 77030
Bateswood Dr 77079
Bathgate Ln 77084
Bathurst Dr
14201-14299 77045
14800-15199 77053
Baton Rouge St 77028
Batterson St 77026
Battle Hills Dr 77040
Battle Plains Dr 77040
Battlecreek Dr
7600-7999 77040
16300-16599 77095
Battleoak Dr 77040
Battlepine Ct & Dr 77040
Battlewood Dr 77040
Bauer Dr 77080
Bauer Elm St 77044
Bauer Oaks Dr 77095
Bauerle Ct 77024
Bauerlein Dr 77086
Bauman Rd
6900-9399 77022
9400-12099 77076
12401-12697 77037
12699-13199 77037
Bavaria Dr 77070
Baxter Ave 77084
Baxter Hills Ln 77070
Bay St 77026
Bay Area Blvd 77058
Bay Bridge Dr 77064
Bay Cedar Ct & Dr 77048
Bay Cliff Ct 77077
Bay Cove Ct 77059
Bay Forest Dr 77062
Bay Front Dr 77077
Bay Green Ct 77059
Bay Isle Ct 77059
Bay Lodge Ln 77086
Bay Oaks Blvd 77059
Bay Oaks Rd 77008
Bay Pointe Ct 77062
Bay Winds Ct 77059
Bayard Ln
4900-5299 77006
5300-5399 77005
Bayberry Dr 77045
E Bayberry Bend Circle
Dr 77072
Baybrook Dr 77062
Baychester Ln 77073
Baycrest Dr 77058
Bayfield Dr 77033
Bayfield Glen Ln 77047
Bayglen Ct 77068
Bayhurst Dr 77024
Bayland Ave 77009
Bayless Dr 77017
Baylor Plz 77030
Baylor St 77009
Baymeadow Dr 77062
Baynard Dr 77072
Bayou Dr 77022
N Bayou Dr 77017
Bayou Pkwy 77077
Bayou St 77020
Bayou Bend Ct 77004
Bayou Branch Dr 77084
Bayou Bridge Dr 77096
Bayou Brook St 77063
Bayou Cove Ct 77042
Bayou Crest Dr 77088
Bayou Forest Dr 77088
Bayou Glen Rd
5200-5699 77056
5700-6699 77057

10000-10799 ... 77042
Bayou Island Dr ... 77063
Bayou Knoll Dr ... 77079
S Bayou Knoll Dr ... 77072
Bayou Lake Ln ... 77040
Bayou Manor Ln ... 77064
Bayou Meadow Ln ... 77007
Bayou Mist Ct ... 77077
Bayou Oaks Dr ... 77088
Bayou Oaks Vista Dr ... 77019
Bayou Parkway Ct ... 77077
Bayou Pine Ct ... 77040
Bayou Place Ct, Dr &
Ln ... 77099
Bayou Pointe Dr ... 77063
Bayou River Ct & Dr ... 77079
Bayou Shadows St ... 77024
Bayou Timber Ln ... 77056
Bayou Trail Ct & Ln ... 77064
Bayou View Dr ... 77091
Bayou Vista Dr ... 77091
Bayou Woods Dr ... 77088
Bayram Dr ... 77055
Bayswater Dr ... 77047
Baythorne Dr ... 77041
Baytree Dr ... 77070
Bayview Cove Dr ... 77054
Baywood St ... 77011
Baywood Park Dr ... 77068
Bazin St ... 77089
Beacave Bend Ct ... 77086
Beach St ... 77044
Beach Bay Dr ... 77044
Beacham Dr ... 77070
Beachcomber Ln ... 77062
Beachton St ... 77007
Beachwood St ... 77021
Beacon St ... 77015
Beacon Manor Ln ... 77041
Beaconridge Dr ... 77053
Beacons Trace Ct ... 77069
Beaconsfield Dr ... 77015
Beaconshire Rd ... 77077
Beadwass Rd ... 77050
Bealey Ln ... 77047
Beall St
1300-2599 ... 77008
5500-6299 ... 77091
Beall Landing Ct ... 77008
Beamer Rd ... 77089
Bean St
9200-9499 ... 77028
9600-9799 ... 77078
Bear Creek Dr ... 77084
Bear Creek Meadows
Ln ... 77043
Bear Hill Dr ... 77084
Bear Lodge Ct ... 77084
Bear Mist Dr ... 77095
Bear Oaks Dr ... 77083
Bear Valley Dr ... 77072
Bearcove Cir ... 77064
Beard Ct ... 77007
Beard Rd ... 77044
Bearden Place Ln ... 77082
Bearmon Rd ... 77072
Bearwood Rd ... 77038
Beasley Hills Ln ... 77008
Beatrice St ... 77076
Beatty St ... 77023
Beau Ln ... 77039
Beau Geste Dr ... 77088
Beau Harp Ct & Dr ... 77049
Beau Monde Dr ... 77099
Beauchamp St ... 77009
Beaudry Dr ... 77035
Beaufort Sea Dr ... 77067
Beaujolais Ln ... 77077
Beaumont Hwy
9800-11500 ... 77078
11502-11598 ... 77078
11600-12398 ... 77049
12400-19599 ... 77049
12210-1-12210-2 ... 77049
15315-1-15315-2 ... 77049
Beaumont Pl ... 77049

E & W Beaupre Point
Dr ... 77015
Beauregard Dr ... 77024
Beauvoir Dr ... 77065
Beaver Dr ... 77029
Beaver Bend Ct ... 77037
Beaver Bend Rd
200-498 ... 77037
500-699 ... 77037
800-2299 ... 77088
Beaver Creek Dr ... 77090
Beaver Pond Cir ... 77084
Beaver Springs Cir, Ct &
Dr ... 77090
Beaver Tail Pt ... 77024
Beaver Trail Dr ... 77086
Beaverbrook Dr ... 77084
Beaverhill Dr ... 77084
Beaverhollow Dr ... 77084
Beawood Dr ... 77083
N Becca Ln ... 77092
Becca Crossing Way ... 77067
Beck Ridge Dr ... 77053
Beckenham Dr ... 77099
Becker St ... 77012
Becketts Oak Ct ... 77083
Beckfield Ct & Dr ... 77099
Beckford Dr ... 77099
Beckland Ln ... 77084
Beckledge Ln ... 77047
Beckley St ... 77088
Becklin Ln ... 77099
Beckman St ... 77076
Beckwith Dr ... 77014
Beckwood Cir ... 77014
Beckwood Post Dr ... 77095
Bedford St
100-199 ... 77012
10600-12599 ... 77031
Bedford Pass Dr ... 77095
Bedworth Ln ... 77088
Bee Ln ... 77067
Bee Line Ct ... 77073
Beebe Ln ... 77024
Beech Bend Dr ... 77077
Beech Cove Ln ... 77072
Beech Crossing Dr ... 77083
Beech Glen Dr ... 77083
Beech Hollow Ln ... 77082
Beech Meadow Dr &
Ln ... 77083
Beech Park Dr & Ln ... 77083
Beech Ridge Ln ... 77083
Beecham Cir & Dr ... 77068
Beechaven St ... 77053
Beechcrest St ... 77083
Beechdale Ct ... 77014
Beechgate Ln ... 77083
Beechglen Ln ... 77083
Beechgrove Dr ... 77058
Beechmont Rd ... 77024
Beechmoor Dr ... 77095
Beechnut St
4200-5699 ... 77096
5700-7899 ... 77074
7901-7999 ... 77074
8000-9999 ... 77036
10000-11704 ... 77072
11703-11703 ... 77272
11705-13199 ... 77072
11706-13198 ... 77072
13200-17199 ... 77083
Beechurst Ct & Dr ... 77062
N & S Beechwood Ct ... 77059
Beekman Rd ... 77021
Beekman Place Dr ... 77043
Beela Rd ... 77048
Beeman Way ... 77040
Beeston Ln ... 77084
Beeville Dr ... 77064
Befaye Rd ... 77076
Beggs St ... 77009
Beinhorn Dr ... 77065
Beinhorn Rd ... 77024
Belarbor St
5600-6199 ... 77033

6200-6599 ... 77087
Belasco Ln ... 77099
Belaya Ln ... 77090
Belbay St ... 77033
Belcamp Ct ... 77075
Belcourt St ... 77065
Belcrest St
5600-6199 ... 77033
6200-6599 ... 77087
Beldart Ct ... 77033
Beldart St
5600-6199 ... 77033
6200-6699 ... 77087
Belgard St ... 77033
Belgian Beauty Ct ... 77044
Belgold St ... 77066
Belgrade Dr ... 77045
Belhaven Dr ... 77069
Belin Dr ... 77029
Belin Manor Dr ... 77024
Belinda Ct ... 77069
Belk St ... 77087
Bell St
623-797 ... 77002
799-1499 ... 77002
1501-1599 ... 77002
1601-1797 ... 77003
1799-3799 ... 77003
4100-5600 ... 77023
5602-5698 ... 77023
W Bell St ... 77019
Bell Gardens Dr ... 77041
Bell Manor Ct ... 77047
Bell Shadow Ln ... 77038
Bella Pine Ct ... 77078
Bella Vista St ... 77022
Bellaire Blvd
3500-4299 ... 77025
5500-6299 ... 77081
6301-6397 ... 77074
6399-7299 ... 77074
7300-9999 ... 77036
10000-13199 ... 77072
13200-16599 ... 77083
N & S Bellaire Estates
Dr ... 77072
Bellaire Gardens Dr ... 77072
Bellamy Ln ... 77083
Bellario Ln ... 77041
Bellavista Ct ... 77041
Bellbrook Dr ... 77096
Belle Glade Dr ... 77018
Belle Glen Dr
6800-7100 ... 77072
7102-8098 ... 77072
8700-9399 ... 77099
Belle Haven Dr ... 77065
Belle Hollow Dr ... 77084
Belle Park Dr
3900-8199 ... 77072
8601-8997 ... 77099
8999-9399 ... 77099
Belle River Ln ... 77077
Belleclaire Ln ... 77044
Bellefontaine St
2200-2599 ... 77030
2600-4199 ... 77025
Bellerive Dr
7100-7899 ... 77036
11000-11599 ... 77072
Bellerose Ln ... 77070
Belleshire Ln ... 77084
Belleshire Glen Ln ... 77084
Bellevue St ... 77017
Bellewood Dr ... 77055
Bellfair Dr ... 77072
Bellfall Ct ... 77082
Bellfield Manor Ln ... 77084
Bellflora Ct ... 77083
Bellflower St ... 77063
Bellforest Ct ... 77044
W Bellfort Ave
1600-3199 ... 77054
3900-4199 ... 77025
12300-13398 ... 77099
Bellfort Ct ... 77033

Bellfort St
2300-4699 ... 77051
4801-4997 ... 77033
4999-6169 ... 77033
6170-7499 ... 77087
7500-7999 ... 77061
W Bellfort St
4300-6605 ... 77035
6607-6699 ... 77035
7500-8599 ... 77071
8600-10599 ... 77031
10600-11699 ... 77099
Bellfort Chase Dr ... 77031
Bellfort Village Dr ... 77031
Bellgreen Dr ... 77030
Bellgreen Ln ... 77062
Bellingham Dr ... 77028
Bellknap Rd ... 77040
Bellmar Dr ... 77037
Bellmeade St ... 77019
Bellmoor Ln ... 77084
Bellnole Dr ... 77017
Bellows Ln ... 77030
Bellport Dr ... 77084
Bellspring Dr ... 77072
Bellville Dr ... 77038
Bellwood Ln ... 77036
Belmark St
5600-6199 ... 77033
6200-6599 ... 77087
Belmont Cir ... 77065
N Belmont Ct ... 77065
S Belmont Ct ... 77065
Belmont St ... 77005
Belmont Legend Ct ... 77047
Belneath St ... 77033
Belridge St ... 77016
Beloit St ... 77028
Belrose Dr ... 77035
Belshear Ct ... 77073
Belterraza Ct & Dr ... 77083
Beltwood Dr ... 77038
Belvedere St ... 77021
Belvedere Park Ct ... 77047
Ben Dr ... 77022
Ben Hur Dr ... 77055
Ben Ledi Dr ... 77084
Ben Nevis Dr ... 77084
Benbow Way ... 77080
Benbrook Dr ... 77076
Benchfield Dr ... 77091
Benchley Dr ... 77099
Benchmark Dr ... 77053
N Bend Ct ... 77073
N Bend Dr ... 77073
W Bend Dr ... 77082
E Bend Ln ... 77007
W Bend St ... 77085
Bend Rock Way ... 77044
Bendell Dr ... 77017
Bending Oaks Ln ... 77024
Bending Oaks St ... 77050
Bending Pecan Ct ... 77040
Bending Post Dr ... 77095
Bending Willow Ln ... 77064
Bendwood Dr ... 77024
Benfer Rd ... 77069
Benfield Dr ... 77082
Benford Dr
13000-13199 ... 77099
13200-13399 ... 77083
Benignus Rd ... 77024
Benita St ... 77085
Benmar Dr
200-799 ... 77060
800-1099 ... 77032
Benmore Dr ... 77099
Benne Ct ... 77014
Bennett St ... 77029
Bennie St ... 77022
Benning Dr
4300-5299 ... 77035
5500-6099 ... 77096
8800-9499 ... 77031
Benningcrest Ln ... 77047
Benningfield Ln ... 77064

Bennington St
100-1199 ... 77022
1700-3499 ... 77093
3700-4899 ... 77016
4900-7099 ... 77028
Benson St ... 77020
Bent Bough Ln ... 77088
Bent Branch Dr ... 77088
Bent Oak Dr ... 77040
Bent Spur Ct & Ln ... 77064
Bent Trail Ct ... 77066
Bentana Ct ... 77095
Bentcrest Ct ... 77072
Bentfield Ct & Way ... 77058
Benthos Dr ... 77083
Bentley St ... 77093
Bentley Park Ct ... 77070
Bently Green Ln ... 77008
Bentondale Ln ... 77075
Bentongrove Ln ... 77044
Bentpath Ct & Dr ... 77014
Bentridge Dr ... 77044
Bentshire Way ... 77058
Bentvine Cir & Dr ... 77084
Bentworth Dr ... 77077
Benwich Cir ... 77095
Beran Dr ... 77045
Berclair Dr ... 77038
Berendo St ... 77092
Beresford St ... 77015
Bergin St ... 77026
Bergstrom St ... 77091
Bering Cir ... 77057
Bering Dr ... 77057
Bering St ... 77003
Beringwood Dr ... 77083
Berkeley Lake Ln ... 77062
Berkley St
1200-2899 ... 77012
2900-3499 ... 77017
3600-3699 ... 77087
Berkley Park Ct ... 77058
Berkridge Dr ... 77053
Berkshire St ... 77093
Berkshire Forest Dr ... 77095
Berkshire Green Dr ... 77083
Berkshire Manor Ln ... 77084
Berkshire Park Dr ... 77084
Berkway Trl ... 77065
Berkwood Ct ... 77038
Berlin Ct ... 77070
Bermuda Dunes Ct &
Dr ... 77069
Bernadette Ln ... 77043
Bernard Way ... 77058
Berncrest Ln ... 77049
Berndale St ... 77029
Bernice St ... 77087
Bernina Ln ... 77044
Berridge House Ct ... 77086
Berrington Dr ... 77083
Berry Ct ... 77004
Berry Rd
1-1499 ... 77022
1500-3599 ... 77093
Berry St ... 77004
Berry Branch Dr ... 77084
Berry Brook Dr ... 77017
Berry Creek Dr ... 77017
Berry Laurel Ln ... 77014
Berry Leaf Ct ... 77084
Berry Limb Dr ... 77099
Berry Meadow Dr ... 77071
Berry Place Dr ... 77071
Berry Springs Dr ... 77070
Berry Tree Dr ... 77064
Berrydale St ... 77017
Berryfield Dr ... 77077
Berryhill Ct ... 77017
Berrywood Ln ... 77077
Bersey Ln ... 77091
Bertasz Dr ... 77049
Bertellis Ln ... 77091
Bertha St ... 77026
Berthas Ln ... 77015
Berthea St ... 77006

Bertner Ave ... 77030
Bertrand St ... 77093
W Bertrand St
400-599 ... 77037
900-1099 ... 77088
Bertwood St ... 77016
N Berwick Dr ... 77095
Berwick St ... 77015
Berwyn Dr ... 77037
Beryl St ... 77074
Bessemer St ... 77034
Bessie Swindle Way ... 77047
Bestin Ln ... 77065
Betanna Dr ... 77095
Bethan Glen Ln ... 77084
Bethany Ln ... 77039
Bethel Blvd ... 77092
Bethje St ... 77007
Bethlehem St ... 77018
Bethnal Green Dr ... 77066
Bethune Dr ... 77091
Bethune Way ... 77085
Betral St ... 77022
Betsy Ln ... 77027
Bettencourt Ln ... 77073
Bettina Ct ... 77024
Bettis Dr ... 77027
Betty Ln ... 77084
Betty Boop St ... 77028
Betty Jane Ln ... 77055
Betty Sue Ln ... 77047
Beulah St ... 77004
Beutel Dr ... 77055
Beverly Dr ... 77065
Beverly St
700-799 ... 77007
801-899 ... 77007
900-1799 ... 77008
Beverly Gardens Ct ... 77057
Beverly Hills Walk ... 77057
Beverlyhill St
5300-5599 ... 77056
5600-6599 ... 77057
7900-8799 ... 77063
8728-8728 ... 77263
8801-9699 ... 77063
9000-9698 ... 77063
Beversbrook Dr ... 77031
Bevis St ... 77008
Bevlyn Dr ... 77025
Bexar Dr ... 77064
Bexhill Dr ... 77065
Bexley Dr ... 77099
Bianca Ct ... 77078
Biarritz Ct ... 77082
Bibb Dr ... 77069
Bicentennial Ct ... 77066
Bichester Ln ... 77039
Bickwood Ct & Dr ... 77089
Bideford Ln ... 77070
Bienville Ln ... 77015
Big Bend Dr ... 77055
Big Branch Ct ... 77064
Big Creek Dr ... 77064
Big Hollow Ln ... 77042
Big Horn Dr ... 77090
Big John St ... 77038
Big Lake Dr ... 77077
Big Oak Trail Dr ... 77040
Big Oaks Dr ... 77050
Big Stone Dr ... 77066
Big Sur Dr ... 77095
Big Valley Dr ... 77095
Big Willow Ln ... 77064
Bigelow St ... 77009
Biggs Ct ... 77061
Bigwood St
7300-7799 ... 77016
8000-8499 ... 77078
Bihia Forest Dr ... 77088
Billikin Dr ... 77086
Billings Dr ... 77055
Billingsley St ... 77009
Billington St ... 77084
Billit Way Dr ... 77094
Billy St ... 77020

Biloxi St ... 77017
Bingham St ... 77007
Bingham Manor Ln ... 77056
Binghampton Dr ... 77089
Bingle Rd
1000-3399 ... 77055
3401-3599 ... 77055
4000-4098 ... 77092
4100-6899 ... 77092
Bink Ct ... 77014
Binley Ct & Dr ... 77077
Bintliff Dr
5600-5700 ... 77036
5702-5798 ... 77036
6601-6797 ... 77074
6799-9399 ... 77074
Binz St ... 77004
Birch Ave ... 77044
Birch Cv ... 77084
Birch Bend Cir ... 77067
Birch Canyon Ct & Dr ... 77041
Birch Falls Rd ... 77065
Birch Grove Dr
13000-13199 ... 77099
13300-13399 ... 77083
Birch Hollow Ln ... 77082
Birch Knoll Ln ... 77047
Birch Meadow Dr ... 77071
Birch Park Ln ... 77073
Birch River Dr ... 77082
Birch Run Ct & Ln ... 77067
Birch Springs Dr ... 77095
Birch Vale Dr ... 77084
Birchaven Ln ... 77072
Birchcroft Dr ... 77088
Birchglen Ln ... 77070
Birchmont Ct ... 77092
Birchmont Dr
5000-5699 ... 77091
5800-6199 ... 77092
Birchton St ... 77080
Birchtree Forest Dr ... 77088
Birchwood St ... 77093
Bird Creek Dr ... 77084
Bird Forest Dr ... 77088
Birdhill Cir ... 77064
Birdie Ln ... 77015
Birds Eye Maple Ln ... 77064
Birdsall St ... 77007
Birdsall Market Pl ... 77007
Birdwing Ln ... 77067
Birdwood Ct ... 77096
Birdwood Rd
5100-5799 ... 77096
5800-8899 ... 77074
Birmingham St ... 77028
Birnam Garden Ln ... 77086
Birney Point Ln ... 77044
Bisbane Dr ... 77014
Bisbee St
1200-1599 ... 77012
2500-2699 ... 77017
Biscayne Way ... 77076
Biscayne Ridge Ln ... 77095
Bishop St ... 77009
Bishop Bend Ln ... 77047
Bishop Knoll Ln ... 77084
Bishop Way Dr ... 77083
Bishops Glen Ct & Ln ... 77084
Bishops Manor Ln ... 77070
Bishopvale Dr ... 77037
Bisley Ln ... 77088
Bismark St ... 77007
Bison Dr ... 77079
Bissonnet St
1000-4299 ... 77005
5401-5497 ... 77081
5499-6299 ... 77081
6300-9399 ... 77074
9500-10299 ... 77036
10300-13199 ... 77099
13200-16599 ... 77083
16601-16799 ... 77083
Bistro Ln ... 77082
Biton Dr ... 77083
Bitridge Cir ... 77053

Bittercreek Dr 77042
Bitternut Dr 77092
Bivens Brook Dr 77067
Bizerte St 77022
Black St 77023
Black Cliff Ln 77075
Black Fin Ln 77072
Black Gold Ct 77073
Black Gum Dr 77092
Black Locust Dr 77088
Black Maple Ln 77088
Black Oak Dr 77092
Black Pearl Ct 77073
Black Rock Rd 77015
Black Sands Dr 77095
Black Tern Ln 77040
Black Walnut Dr 77015
Blackamore Cir 77065
Blackberry Hollow Dr 77073
Blackbrook Ln 77041
Blackburn St 77012
Blackcastle Dr 77068
Blackhaw St 77079
Blackhawk Blvd
8400-9899 77075
10000-11999 77089
Blackhawk Cir 77075
Blackjack Ct & Ln 77088
Blackpool Ln 77066
Blackridge Rd 77067
Blackshear St 77018
Blacksmith Ct & Dr 77064
Blackstock Ln 77083
Blackstone Ct 77077
Blackthorne Dr 77094
Blackwater Ln 77015
Blackwood Ave 77032
Blade Borough Ct 77089
Blades St 77016
Blaffer St 77026
Blaine Lake Dr 77086
Blair St 77008
Blair Hill Ln 77044
Blaire Ct 77095
Blairmont Ln 77062
Blairstone 77084
Blairwood Dr 77049
Blake Bend Cir 77095
Blake Way St 77032
Blakewood Ct 77068
Blalock Cir 77024
Blalock Ln 77024
Blalock Rd
200-799 77024
1000-1499 77055
1500-4199 77080
4300-5199 77041
Blalock Forest St 77024
Blalock Pines Ct 77024
Blalock Woods St 77024
Blanchard Hill Ln 77047
Blanchard Springs Dr 77095
Blanche St 77011
Blanchmont Ln 77058
Blanco St 77063
Blanco Terrace Ln 77041
Bland St 77091
Blandford Ln 77055
Blanding Dr 77015
Blankenship Dr
7700-8299 77055
8400-9799 77080
Blanton Blvd 77092
Blarney Dr 77047
Blazey Cir 77095
Blazey Dr
13301-13999 77041
14000-14299 77095
Bleker St
2000-2999 77026
6700-7199 77016
Blend Stone 77084
Blenheim Palace Ct & Ln 77095
Bligh St 77045
Blindlake Dr 77084
Blinnwood Ln 77070
Bliss St 77017
Bliss Trl 77084
Blisswood Dr 77044
Blodgett St 77004
Bloom Dr 77076
Bloom Mist Ct 77072
Bloombury Ln 77064
Bloomfield St 77051
Blooming Grove Ln 77077
Blooming Ivy Ln 77089
Blossom St 77007
Blossom Bay Ct & Dr 77059
Blossom Field Ct 77044
Blossom Walk Ln 77041
Blount St 77008
Blue St 77028
Blue Ash Dr 77090
Blue Bell Rd
922A-922E 77038
Blue Bird Rd 77028
Blue Bonnet Blvd
2300-2599 77030
3000-4199 77025
Blue Bonnet Dr 77053
Blue Bonnet Run Ct 77095
Blue Castle Ct & Ln 77015
Blue Creek Ranch Dr 77086
Blue Cromis Ln 77045
Blue Feather Dr 77064
Blue Gama Dr 77095
Blue Glen Ln 77073
Blue Grass Ln 77044
Blue Haven Rd 77039
Blue Heron Ln 77048
Blue Hills Rd 77069
Blue Iris Trl 77079
Blue Island Dr 77044
Blue Jasmine Ct 77059
Blue Lily Ln 77095
Blue Marlin Ln 77083
Blue Meadow Ln 77039
Blue Morning Dr 77086
Blue Mound Ter 77095
Blue Mountain Dr 77067
Blue Oak Dr 77065
Blue Orchid Ct 77044
Blue Ridge Dr 77087
Blue River Dr 77050
Blue Rock Ct 77060
Blue Rock Springs Dr 77073
Blue Sky St 77088
Blue Spring Dr 77068
Blue Spruce St 77066
Blue Spruce Vale Way 77089
Blue Stream Ct 77041
Blue Swallow Dr 77086
Blue Timbers Ct 77044
Blue Vista Dr 77095
Blue Water Ln 77018
Blue Willow Dr 77042
Blue Wind Ct 77084
Blueberry St
100-499 77018
8800-9199 77049
Blueberry Hill Ct & Dr 77084
Bluebird Ln 77079
Bluebonnet Dr 77053
Bluebonnet Meadows Ln 77084
Bluebonnet Place Cir 77019
Bluegate Ct & St 77025
Bluegrass St 77018
Bluejay St
6601-6699 77048
7400-7499 77075
Bluerock St 77039
Bluestem St 77045
Bluestone Dr 77016
Bluestone Edge Ln 77089
Bluff Point Dr 77086
Bluff Springs Dr 77095
Bluffdale Dr 77084
Bluffridge Cir 77095
Blume Ave 77034
Blushing Pear Ct 77084
Blythe St 77015
Blythewood St 77021
Bo Jack Dr 77040
Boardwalk St 77042
Bob St 77011
Bob White Dr
8100-8900 77074
8902-9098 77074
9400-11099 77096
11500-12399 77035
Bobbie St 77086
Bobbitt Ln 77055
Bobbitt Manor Ln 77055
Bobbitt Place Ln 77055
Bobby Burns St 77028
Bobcat Rd 77064
Bobolink St 77017
Boca Ct 77099
Boca Grande Ln 77044
Boca Raton Dr 77069
Bodart Cir, Ct & Dr 77090
Bodega Bay Dr 77053
Boeneman Dr 77091
Bogan Flats Ct & Dr 77095
Bogey Way 77089
Boggess Rd 77016
Boheme Dr
12000-12999 77024
13000-13199 77079
Bohnhof Strasse St 77070
Boicewood St 77016
Bois D Arc St 77087
Boise St 77015
Bold Forest Dr 77088
Bolden St 77029
Boldere Ln 77049
Bolero Dr 77049
Bolero Point Ct & Ln 77041
Bolero Point Circle Ct 77041
Boles St 77011
Bolin Rd 77092
Bolington Dr 77083
Bolivia Blvd
3700-4099 77092
5100-5999 77091
Bolling Ln 77076
Bollingbrook Dr 77083
Bollinger Park Ct 77047
Bolsa Chica Ln 77041
Bolsover St 77005
Bolt St 77051
Bolton Pl 77024
Bolton Gardens Ct & Dr 77066
Bomar St 77006
Bomford St 77015
Bomoseen Lake Rd 77044
Bonaire St 77028
Bonann Dr 77070
Bonanza Rd 77062
Bonaventure Dr 77065
Bonazzi St 77088
Bond St 77026
Bondale St 77040
Bondi Ct 77094
Bonham St
6900-7699 77020
13700-14699 77015
Bonham Oaks Ln 77047
Bonhomme Rd
5600-5799 77036
5801-6399 77036
8101-8797 77074
8799-9399 77074
Bonilla Ln 77083
Bonita St 77016
Bonita Springs Dr 77083
Bonn Echo Ln 77017
Bonnabel Ln 77070
Bonnebridge Way Blvd 77082
Bonner Dr 77017
Bonner St 77007
E Bonner St 77007
Bonner View Ln 77007
Bonnercrest Dr 77083
Bonnet Creek Dr 77095
Bonney Brier Dr 77069
Bonnie Brae St 77006
Bonnie Park Ct 77068
Bonniefield Ln 77077
Bonnington Dr 77034
Bonno Pl 77020
Bonny Loch Ln 77084
Bonny Ridge Ct 77053
Bonnyton Ln 77014
Bonnyview Dr 77095
Bonover St 77007
Bonsrell St 77023
Bonway Dr & Ln 77045
Booker St 77028
Boone Rd
3900-8499 77072
8500-10199 77099
Boone Loop Rd 77099
Boonridge Ct & Rd 77053
Boonway Dr 77045
Boot Ridge Rd 77053
Booth St
700-1099 77009
15000-15099 77053
Boothbay Ln 77058
Boots Rd 77091
Borden St 77029
Borden Bluff Ln 77095
Borden Manor Dr 77090
Border Lake Ln 77044
Borderwood Dr 77013
Bordley Dr
5300-5699 77056
6100-6199 77057
9900-9998 77042
10000-10799 77042
Boreas Dr 77039
Boridge Cir 77053
Boris Cove Trl 77047
Boros Dr 77024
Bosley Ln 77084
Bosque St 77056
Bossingham Ln 77049
Bostic St
1700-3799 77093
4700-4999 77016
2619-1-2619-2 77093
Boston St 77006
Boswell St 77009
Bosworth St 77017
Botany Ln
3700-4499 77047
5300-5398 77048
5400-5499 77048
8000-8499 77075
Bothwell Way 77024
Bottlebrush Ct & Ln 77095
Bough Ct 77092
W Bough Ln 77024
Boulder St 77012
Boulder Bluff Dr 77073
Boulder Falls Ct 77062
Boulder Field Ln 77044
Boulder Oaks Dr 77084
Boulder Point Ct 77059
Boulder Ridge Ct 77095
Boulder Springs Dr 77083
Boulder Springs Ln 77077
Bouldercrest Dr 77062
Boulderwoods Dr 77062
Bouldgreen 77084
N Boulevard Park 77098
Boundary St 77009
Bourgeois Rd 77066
Bourgeois Forest Dr 77066
Bova Rd 77064
Boveda Dr 77083
Bow Ln 77053
Bow String Cv 77079
Bowen St 77051
Bowfin Rd 77070
Bowhead Dr 77013
Bowie St 77012
Bowie Ridge Ln 77053
Bowlan Ln 77035
Bowline Rd 77062
Bowling Green St 77021
Bowman St 77022
Bowmore Ct 77095
Bowridge Ln 77053
Bowsprit Ln 77062
Bowtrail 77084
Boxelder Dr 77082
Boxelder St 77066
Boxhill Dr 77066
Boxwood Brg 77041
Boxwood Terrace Dr 77083
Boxwood Way Ln 77041
Boy St 77028
Boyce St 77020
Boyce Springs Dr 77066
Boyd St 77022
Boyer Ln 77015
Boykin St 77034
Boyles St 77020
Boylston Dr 77015
Boynton Dr 77045
Boysenberry Ln 77095
Brabant Ct 77088
Brace St 77061
Bracher St 77055
Brackenhurst Ln 77049
Brackenridge St 77026
Bracket Ct 77065
Brackley Ln 77088
Bracknell St 77017
Bracrest Ln 77044
Bradbridge Ln 77082
Bradburn Hill Ln 77014
Braden Dr E & N 77047
Bradenway Ln 77089
Bradfield Ct 77024
Bradfield Rd 77060
Bradford St
3400-3599 77025
7400-7899 77087
Bradford Colony Dr 77084
Bradford Way Dr 77075
Bradley St 77009
Bradmar St 77088
Bradmore Dr 77077
Bradney Dr 77077
Bradshaw St 77008
Bradstone Ct & Dr 77084
Bradwell Dr 77062
Brady St 77011
Brae Acres Ct & Rd 77074
Braeburn Bend Dr 77031
Braeburn Glen Blvd 77074
Braeburn Valley Dr 77074
Braemar Crescent St 77095
Braes Blvd 77025
Braes Bayou Dr
9101-9497 77074
9499-9600 77074
9602-9698 77074
10700-10900 77071
10902-10998 77071
Braes Bend Dr 77071
Braes Forest Dr 77071
Braes Meadow Dr 77071
Braes Park Dr 77071
Braes River Dr 77074
Braesdale Ln 77071
Braesglen Dr 77071
Braesheather Cir, Ct & Dr 77096
Braesmain Dr
8000-8300 77025
8205-8205 77225
8301-8399 77025
8302-8398 77025
Braesmont Dr 77096
Braesridge Ct & Dr 77071
Braesvalley Dr 77096
Braesview Ln 77071
Braeswest Dr 77082
Braeswood Blvd 77030
N Braeswood Blvd
1900-2298 77030
2300-2499 77030
2800-4199 77025
4400-5799 77096
5900-6298 77074
S Braeswood Blvd
1000-2499 77030
2500-4099 77025
4101-4199 77025
4200-6699 77096
7501-7797 77071
7799-8599 77071
8600-8698 77031
8700-8899 77031
8900-9099 77074
Braeswood Ct 77030
Braeswood Sq 77096
Braeswood Park Dr 77030
Braewick Dr
8000-8098 77074
8100-8400 77074
8402-8998 77074
9400-11199 77096
11400-12399 77035
Braewin Ct 77068
Braewood Glen Ln 77072
Bragg St 77009
Brahms Ct & Ln 77040
Brailsfort St 77004
Bramble St 77003
Bramble Crest Ct 77095
Bramble Hill Ct 77059
Bramblewood Dr 77079
Brambling Dr 77059
Bramford Ct 77070
Bramford Point Ln 77070
Bramshaw Glen Ct 77049
Branard St
300-1699 77006
1700-3399 77098
3400-4099 77027
Branch St 77021
Branch Bend Cir 77024
Branch Canyon Ct 77095
Branch Forest Dr 77082
Branch Lake Dr 77066
Branch Point Dr 77095
Branchport Dr 77095
Branchwest Dr 77082
Branchwood Ct 77040
Brandemere Way St 77066
Branding Iron Ln 77060
Brandon St 77051
Brandon Way 77024
Brandon Gate 77095
Brandon Rock Ln 77044
Brandonwood Ct & Pl 77069
Brandt St 77006
Brandy Ln 77044
Brandy Mill Rd 77067
Brandywine Ln 77024
Brandywyne Ct & Dr 77077
Branford St 77091
Branford Greens Dr 77083
Branford Manor Dr 77083
Branham Dr 77083
Braniff St 77061
Brannon St 77093
Brannon Field Ln 77041
Brant Grove Ln 77044
Brant Rock Dr 77082
Brantfield Ct 77095
Brantly Ave 77034
Brants Way Ct 77065
Branum St 77017
Brashear St 77007
Brasil Ln 77095
Brass Hammer Ct 77065
Braunston Ln 77088
Braxton Dr
3900-3999 77063
5600-5799 77036
Braxtonshire Ct 77069
Braydon Bend Dr 77041
Brayford Place Ct & Dr 77014
Brays St 77012
Braysworth Dr 77072
Brayton Ct 77065
Brazil St 77093
Brazoria St 77019
Brazos St
900-2299 77002
2300-3199 77006
Brea Crest St
200-1299 77037
2100-3699 77093
Breakwater Path Dr & Loop 77044
Breakwood Dr
4000-4199 77025
4300-4499 77096
Breanna Ln 77049
Breccia Dr 77041
Brechin Ct & Ln 77095
Breck St 77066
Breckenridge Dr 77066
Brecon Hall Dr 77077
Breeds Hill Ct 77024
Breen Dr
4800-7599 77086
7800-8599 77064
S Breeze Dr 77071
Breeze Park Dr 77015
Breezeway St
7400-8100 77040
8102-8198 77040
12900-13199 77037
Breezewood Dr 77082
Breezy Knoll Dr 77064
Breezy Meadow Ct & Ln 77044
Breland St 77016
Breman Crest Ln 77040
Bremen Dr 77066
Bremond St
200-599 77006
1000-1199 77002
1400-3799 77004
W Brenda St 77076
Brendam Ln 77072
Brenford Dr 77047
Brenham Ct 77064
Brenhaven Dr 77038
Brenner St 77022
Brenner Creek Ct 77079
Brenner Ridge Ln 77047
Brent Dr 77085
Brentford Ct & Dr 77083
Brentlawn Ct 77045
Brentleywood Ct & Ln 77070
Brenton St 77093
Brentonwood Ln 77077
Brentshire Ln 77069
Brentway Dr 77070
Brentwood Dr 77019
Brentwood Park Dr 77045
Bresslyn Ct 77044
Bretagne Dr 77015
Bretford Ct 77065
Breton Ridge St 77070
Bretshire Dr 77016
Bretton Dr 77016
Brettwood Cir, Ct & Dr 77089
Brewster St
1700-1899 77020
1900-3599 77026
6800-6899 77093
Brian Haven Dr
4700-4999 77018
5400-5499 77091
Briar Dr
5200-5699 77056
10000-10399 77042
Briar Trl 77056
Briar Way 77027
Briar Arbor 77094
Briar Bayou Dr 77077
S Briar Bayou Dr 77072
Briar Branch Dr 77042
Briar Branch Ln 77024
Briar Cross Ct 77084
Briar Dale Ct 77027
Briar Falls Ct 77059
Briar Forest Ct 77059

Briar Forest Dr
8900-9299 77024
9300-9699 77063
9700-11299 77042
11300-14799 77077
Briar Glade Dr 77072
Briar Heath Dr 77077
Briar Hill Dr 77042
E & S Briar Hollow Ln & Pl 77027
Briar Knoll Dr 77079
S Briar Knoll Dr
3200-3499 77082
6200-6299 77072
Briar Oaks Cv 77056
Briar Oaks Ln 77027
Briar Patch Rd 77077
Briar Path Dr 77079
Briar Place Dr 77077
Briar Ridge Dr 77057
Briar River Dr 77042
Briar Rose Dr
6100-6399 77057
7500-7599 77063
10000-10299 77042
11300-11699 77077
Briar Terrace Dr 77072
Briar Town Ln 77057
Briarbend Dr
4300-5223 77035
5258-5260 77096
5262-5699 77096
Briarbrook Dr
800-2699 77042
14000-14299 77039
Briarchase Ct & Dr 77014
Briarcliff Dr 77076
Briarcreek Blvd 77073
Briarcrest Dr 77077
Briarglen Dr 77027
Briargreen Dr 77077
Briargrove Dr 77057
Briarhills Pkwy 77077
Briarhurst Dr & Park 77057
Briarleaf Ct 77083
Briarlee Dr 77077
Briarloch Ln 77073
Briarmead Dr 77057
Briarmoor Ct 77062
Briarpark Dr 77042
Briarpark Trail Ln 77064
Briarpine Ct 77041
Briarport Dr 77077
Briarsage Ct 77077
Briarstem Dr 77077
Briartrace Ct 77044
Briarturn Dr 77077
Briarview Dr 77077
Briarwest Blvd & Cir 77077
Briarwick Ln
2900-3099 77093
5200-5400 77016
5402-5898 77016
Briarwild Ln 77080
Briarwood Ct 77019
Briarwood Forest Dr 77088
Briarworth Dr 77077
Briceland Springs Dr 77082
Brick Village Dr 77095
Bricker St
4500-4699 77051
4700-5099 77033
Brickhaven Ln 77083
Brickman Ct 77084
Brickyard Ct 77041
Bridge Crest Blvd & Ct 77082
Bridge Cross Ln 77067
Bridge Down Dr 77065
Bridge Falls Way 77084
Bridge Forest Dr 77088
Bridge Hollow Ct 77062
Bridge Park Dr 77064
Bridgeberry Ln 77082
Bridgedale Dr 77039
Bridgefoot Ln 77064

Bridgeland Ln 77041
Bridgepath Ct, Cv & Ln 77041
Bridgeport Rd 77047
Bridges Fairway Ln 77068
Bridgewalk Cv & Ln 77041
Bridgewood St 77024
Bridle Ct 77044
Bridle Bend Dr 77084
Bridle Path Dr 77044
Bridle Ridge Loop 77073
Bridle Springs Ln 77044
Bridle Spur Ln 77055
Bridlechase Ln 77014
Bridledon Ln 77014
Bridlepark Cir 77016
Bridleway Cir 77016
Bridlewood St 77024
Bridlington St 77085
Briefway St 77087
Brier Gardens Dr 77082
Brierley Ln 77084
Brig O Doon Cir 77096
N Bright Dr 77073
Bright Ember Ct 77062
Bright Grove Ct 77095
Bright Penny Ln 77015
Bright View Ln 77034
Bright Willow Ln 77044
Brightbrook Dr 77095
Brightling Ln 77090
Brighton Ln 77031
Brighton Lake Ln 77095
Brighton Park Dr 77044
Brighton Place Ct 77095
Brighton Trace Ln 77044
Brightonfern Ln 77049
Brightwood Dr 77068
Briley St 77004
Brill St 77026
Brillock Ave 77032
Brim St 77028
Brimberry St 77018
Brimfield Dr 77082
Brimhurst Dr 77077
Brimmage Dr 77067
Brimridge Ln 77048
Brimwood Cir 77068
Brindle Trl 77044
Bringate Ct 77066
Bringhurst St
1-1999 77020
2000-3099 77026
1411 1/2-1411 3/4 77020
Brinkley St
4100-4699 77051
4700-4999 77033
Brinkman Ct 77091
Brinkman St
2500-2599 77008
3400-5099 77018
5201-5297 77091
5299-6099 77091
Brinkwood Dr 77090
Brinkwurth Ln 77070
Brinton Ct 77095
Brinwood Dr 77043
Brisbane Dr 77048
Brisbane St
200-899 77061
3000-3299 77051
4100-4200 77047
4202-4498 77047
6900-6999 77061
Briscoe St
4500-4699 77051
4700-5399 77033
Bristle Creek Dr 77095
Bristlebrook Dr 77083
Bristol St 77009
Bristol Bank Ct 77041
E & S Bristol Harbour Cir 77084
Bristol Lake Dr 77070
Bristol Lane Ct 77066
Bristol Ridge Dr 77095

Britford 77084
British Knoll Ct 77014
Britoak Ln 77079
Briton Centre Ct 77069
Briton Cove Dr 77084
Britt Way 77043
Brittan Leaf Ln 77034
Brittania Dr 77094
Brittany Ferry Ln 77049
Brittany Knoll Dr 77095
Brittany Park Ln 77066
Britterige St 77084
Brittmoore Rd
600-999 77079
1000-4299 77043
4300-7299 77041
Brittmoore Park Dr 77041
Broad St 77087
Broad Haven Dr 77067
E & W Broad Oaks Cir, Ct, Dr, Ln, Park & Trl 77056
Broad Oaks Estates Ln 77056
Broad Ridge Rd 77053
Broadelm Dr 77095
Broadfield Blvd 77084
Broadglen Ct 77082
Broadgreen Dr 77079
Broadhurst Dr 77047
Broadlawn Dr 77058
Broadmead Dr 77025
Broadmeadow Ln 77077
Broadmoor St 77023
Broadstairs St 77013
Broadsweep Dr 77064
Broadview Dr 77061
Broadway Ave 77064
Broadway St
8326A-1-8326A-2 77061
100-2699 77012
2700-3899 77017
3900-4199 77087
8100-8999 77061
N Broadway St 77034
Brock St 77023
Brock Park Blvd 77078
Brockhampton St 77013
Brockley Ln 77087
Brockton St 77017
Brockwood Dr 77047
Brody Ln 77083
Brody Falls Ct 77044
Brogden Rd 77024
Broken Arrow St 77024
Broken Bough Cir & Dr 77024
Broken Bridge Dr 77085
Broken Cypress Cir 77049
Broken Ridge Dr 77095
Broken Sky Ct & Dr 77064
Broken Stone 77084
Broken Timber Cir & Way 77095
Brollier St 77054
Bromel Station St 77070
Bromley St 77055
Brompton Ct 77024
Brompton Rd 77005
Brompton St 77025
Brompton Place Dr 77083
Brompton Square Dr 77025
Bron Holly Dr 77018
Bronco Dr 77055
Broncroft Ct 77044
Bronson St 77034
Bronton St 77092
Bronwynn Ln 77047
Bronze Bay Ct 77059
Brooding Oak Cir 77096
Brook Arbor Ct 77062
Brook Forest Dr 77059
Brook Lea St 77087
Brook Meadow Cir, Ct, Dr & Ln 77089
Brook Mill Ct 77065
Brook Park Way 77062

Brook Pine Ln 77082
Brook Run Ln 77040
Brook Springs Dr 77095
Brook Stone Dr 77040
Brook Trail Cir 77040
Brook Village Rd 77084
Brookbank Dr 77068
Brookbend Dr 77035
Brookbluff Ln 77077
Brookcrest Cir 77072
Brooke Vista Ln 77034
Brookes Bnd 77094
Brookfalls Dr 77070
Brookfield Dr
3200-5499 77045
5500-6599 77085
Brookfield Park 77041
Brookfir Ln 77040
Brookford Ct & Dr 77059
Brookglade Cir 77099
Brookglen Dr 77017
Brookhaven St 77051
Brookhaven Park Cir & Dr 77065
Brookhead Trl 77066
Brookhill Dr 77087
Brookhollow Court Dr 77084
Brookhollow Grove Ct 77084
Brookhollow Mist Ct 77084
Brookhollow Oaks Trl 77084
Brookhollow Pine Trl 77084
Brookhollow Pines Ct 77084
Brookhollow Trace Ct 77084
Brookhollow West Dr
6900-7099 77040
7050-7050 77240
7050-7050 77241
Brookings Dr 77084
W & E Brooklake Ct & Dr 77077
Brooklawn Dr
4700-5099 77066
6200-6298 77085
6300-6499 77085
Brookleaf Dr 77041
Brookledge Dr 77099
Brooklet Dr 77099
Brooklet View Ct 77059
Brooklyn St 77093
Brookmeade Dr 77045
Brookmere Dr 77008
Brookmont Ln 77044
Brooknoll Dr 77084
Brookpoint Dr 77062
Brookren Cir 77072
Brookridge Ln 77053
Brookriver Dr 77040
Brooks St
500-1699 77009
1700-2699 77026
2700-2799 77020
Brookshire Ln & St 77041
Brookside Dr 77023
Brookside Forest Dr 77040
Brookspring Dr 77077
Brookston St 77045
Brooksure Cir 77072
Brooktondale Ct 77084
Brooktree Dr
2000-2599 77008
10200-10299 77043
Brookvale Dr 77038
Brookvalley Dr 77071
Brookvilla Dr 77059
Brookville Ln 77083
Brookway Dr 77084
Brookwoods Dr 77092
Brookwulf Dr
8400-8616 77072
8617-9099 77099
Broom St 77091
Broomsedge Dr 77084
Brora Ct 77084
Brou Ln 77074
Brower St 77017
Brown Bark Dr 77092

Brown Leaf Cir 77096
Brown Saddle St 77057
Browncroft St 77021
Brownfields Ct & Dr 77066
Brownie Campbell Rd
2700-3199 77038
3200-6699 77086
Browning St 77005
Brownstone Ln 77053
Brownstone Ridge Ln 77084
Brownsville St
6500-7599 77020
13700-14699 77015
Brownway St 77056
Brownwood St
6900-7599 77020
13700-14699 77015
Broyles St 77026
Bruce St 77009
Brumbley St 77012
Brummel Dr 77099
Brun St 77019
Brundage Dr 77090
Brunswick St 77039
Brunswick Meadows Dr 77047
Brunswick Place Dr 77047
Brunswick Point Ln 77047
Brush Hollow Rd 77067
Brush Wood Dr 77088
Brushfield Rd 77064
Brushy Ct 77088
Brushy Canyon Dr 77073
Brushy Creek Cir 77084
Brushy Glen Dr 77073
Brushy Ranch Trl 77049
Brushy River Ct 77095
Brutus St 77012
Brutus Hill Ln 77072
N Bryan St 77011
Bryan Creek Ct 77044
Bryant St 77075
Bryant Park Ct 77086
Bryant Pond Dr 77041
Bryant Ridge Rd 77053
Bryce Meadow Ln 77047
Brykerwoods Dr 77055
Bryn Mawr Cir 77024
Bryn Mawr Ln 77027
Bryngrove Ln 77084
Bryonston Dr 77066
Bryonwood Dr 77055
Brystone Dr 77041
Bryton Park Dr 77083
Bubbling Brooks Ln 77095
Bubbling Spring Ln 77086
Bucan St 77076
Buccaneer Ln
15700-16699 77062
16800-16999 77058
Buchanan St 77029
Buchanan Oaks Ln 77044
Buck St 77020
Buckboard Dr 77060
Buckeye Ridge Way 77084
Buckhaven Dr 77089
Buckhurst Dr 77066
Buckingham Ct & Dr 77024
Buckland Ln 77039
Buckle Ln 77060
Buckleridge Rd 77053
Buckmann Ct 77043
Bucknell Rd 77016
Buckner Ct 77073
Buckner St 77019
Bucroft St 77029
Buell Ct 77006
Buelow Ave 77023
Buena Park Ct & Dr 77089
Buena Vista St 77087
Buescher Dr 77043
Buffalo Ter 77019
Buffalo Bend Dr 77064
Buffalo Bend Ln 77089
Buffalo Pass Dr 77095
Buffalo Ridge Cir 77056

Buffalo River Way 77084
Buffalo Run Cir 77067
Buffalo Speedway
2700-3899 77098
Buffalo Speedway
5100-6799 77005
6800-9899 77025
9900-10099 77054
10101-10299 77054
13800-14699 77045
16500-16799 77047
Buffington St 77060
Buffkin Ln 77069
Bufflehead Ct 77044
Buffum St 77051
Buford St 77023
Bugle Rd 77072
Bull Creek Rd 77095
Bullfinch St 77087
Bullock Ln 77055
Bunche Dr 77091
Bundick Dr 77091
Bundy Ln 77080
Bungalow Ln
4300-4599 77047
5100-5499 77048
Bunker Hill Cir 77024
Bunker Hill Rd
200-999 77024
1000-1399 77055
Bunker Ridge Rd 77053
Bunker Wood Ln 77086
Bunningham Ln 77055
Bunny Run Dr 77088
Bunte St 77026
Bunton St 77009
Bunzel St 77088
Buoy Rd 77062
Buras Pass Ln 77045
Burbank St 77076
Burberry Cir 77044
Burch St 77003
Burden St 77093
Burdine Ct 77085
Burdine St
9100-11199 77096
11500-12199 77035
12500-12598 77085
12600-12999 77085
Burford Ln 77088
Burg St 77088
Burger Ln 77040
Burgess St 77021
Burgoyne Dr 77077
Burgoyne Rd
5800-6499 77057
7500-8099 77063
10000-10999 77042
13700-14499 77077
Burgundy Ln 77023
Burke Forest Dr 77070
Burkehall Ln 77084
Burkes Garden Dr 77065
Burkett St
2300-5599 77004
6600-7099 77021
Burkhart Cir, Ct & Rd 77055
Burkhart Forest Ct 77055
Burkhart Ridge Dr 77095
Burkridge Dr 77041
Burl St 77028
Burlcreek 77084
Burleson Ct 77064
Burleson St 77091
Burleson Bend Dr 77049
Burlingame Dr 77099
Burlinghall Dr 77035
N Burlington Dr 77092
Burlington St 77006
Burlwood Dr 77089
Burma Rd 77033
Burman St 77029
Burnaby Trail Ct 77073
Burnell Oaks Ln 77090
Burnett Ct 77020
Burnett St
601-697 77009

699-899 77009
901-1299 77009
1700-1999 77026
2700-2799 77020
Burnham St 77053
Burning Hills Dr 77071
Burning Palms Ct 77042
Burning Tree Dr 77036
Burningbush Ln 77016
Burnley St 77037
Burnside Ln 77041
Burnt Amber Ln 77073
Burntfork St 77064
Burnwood Ln 77073
N Burr St 77011
Burr Oak Dr 77092
E Burress St 77022
Burrowdale Ct 77084
Burt St
5100-5198 77018
5800-6299 77091
7500-7599 77088
Burtcliff St 77060
Burton St 77049
Burwell St 77023
Burwood Ct & Way 77058
Busch St 77060
Buschong St
500-799 77060
800-1999 77039
Bushy Creek Dr 77070
Busiek St 77022
Business Center Dr 77043
Business Park Dr 77041
Bute St
3800-4099 77006
4200-4299 77002
Butler Blvd 77030
Butler St 77007
Butlercrest St 77080
W Butte Canyon Rd 77038
Butte Creek Rd 77090
Butte Meadows Ln 77047
Butter Mill Ln 77067
Buttercup St 77063
Butterfield Rd 77090
Butterfly Ct 77079
Butterfly Ln
12800-12999 77024
13300-13799 77079
Buttergrove Dr 77041
Butternut Ct 77088
Buxley St
13001-13197 77045
13199-14699 77045
14700-15198 77053
Buxton St 77017
W By Northwest Blvd 77040
Bycreek Dr 77068
Bylake Ct 77077
Bylane Dr 77024
Byrne St 77009
Byron St 77005
Byronstone Dr 77066
Bywater Dr 77077
Byway St 77007
Bywood St 77028
C St 77072
C E King Pkwy 77044
Caballero Dr 77078
Cabell St 77022
Cabernet Ln 77055
Cabildo Dr 77083
Cabin Creek Dr 77064
Cabin Wood Way 77084
Cabo Blanco Ct 77041
Cabot St
7400-7799 77016
7900-8499 77078
Cabot Creek Cir 77070
Cabot Hill St 77044
Cabots Landing Dr 77084
Cabrera Ct & Ln 77083
Cabrina Ln 77083
Cabrini Trace Ct 77073
Cactus St 77026

Cactus Flower Dr 77086
Cactus Forest Dr 77088
Cactus Point Ct 77095
Cactus Valley Ct 77089
Cadawac Rd 77074
Cadbury Dr 77084
Caddo Rd
7300-7799 77016
8000-9599 77078
Caddo Creek Ln 77089
Caddo Lake Ln 77083
Caddo Point Ct 77041
Caddo Terrace Ln 77041
Cade Ct & Dr 77095
Cadenhorn Ln 77084
Cadenza Ct 77040
Cades Creek Ct 77089
Cadillac St 77021
Cadiz Cir 77038
Cadman Ct 77096
Cadmus St 77022
Cady Ct 77077
Caffrey St 77075
Cage St 77020
Cain Cir 77015
Cairngale St 77084
Cairngorm Ave 77095
Cairngorm Dr 77084
Cairngrove Ln 77084
Cairnladdie St 77084
Cairnlassie St 77084
Cairnleigh Ct & Dr 77084
Cairnloch St 77084
Cairnlomond St 77084
Cairnsean St 77084
Cairntosh St 77084
Cairnvillage St 77084
Cairnway Dr
16000-16100 77084
16015-16015 77284
16101-16699 77084
16102-16698 77084
Caitlyn Ct 77094
Cal Dr 77065
Caladero Dr 77083
Calais Rd 77033
Calaway Cove Ct 77041
Calcutta Spring Dr 77083
Calder St 77007
Caldera Ct 77066
Caldera Canyon Ct & Dr 77095
Caldermont Ct 77084
Calderwood Dr 77073
Caldwell Canyon Ln 77014
Calendar St 77009
Calgary Ln 77016
Calhoun Ct 77003
Calhoun Rd
4700-5099 77004
5100-6999 77021
7300-8399 77033
Cali Dr 77090
Calico Ln 77024
Calico Falls Ln 77041
Calico Glen Ln 77084
Calico Hills Cir 77094
N & W Calico Rock Ln 77073
Calico Woods Ln 77041
California St 77006
Calistoga Ct 77053
Calix Ln 77083
Callahan Dr 77049
Callan Ln 77049
Calle Cadiz Pl 77007
Calle Catalina Pl 77007
Calle Cordoba Pl 77007
Calle Lozano Dr 77041
Calle Montilla Pl 77007
Calle Ronda Pl 77007
Calle Sevilla Pl 77007
Callery Creek Dr 77053
Calles St 77020
Callie Ct 77024
Callie St 77004
Calloway St 77029
Calm Ct 77084
Calm Brook Ct 77095
Calm Lagoon Ct 77095
Calm Wind Way 77045
Calmont Dr 77070
Calton Cove Cir 77086
Calumet St 77004
Calverton Pines Ln 77095
Calvin Ave 77088
Calvin Rd 77090
Cam Ct 77055
Camara Ln 77079
Camargo Ct 77074
Camay Dr 77016
Camber Brook Ct & Dr 77089
Camberwell Green Ct & Ln 77070
Camborne Ln 77070
Cambridge St
1400-1506 77030
1508-7399 77030
7400-8599 77054
Cambridge Eagle Dr 77044
Cambridge Glen Ln 77035
Cambridge Oaks Cir 77094
Cambury Dr 77014
Camby Park Dr 77047
Camden Dr 77021
N Camden Pkwy 77067
S Camden Pkwy 77067
Camden Cove Ln 77044
Camden Hill Ln 77089
Camden Row Ct 77095
Camelback Ct 77079
Camelia Crest Ln 77064
Camellia St 77007
Camellia Dale Trl 77084
Camellia Knoll Trl 77084
Camelot Ln 77024
Camelot Centre Ct 77069
Cameo Dr 77080
Cameron St 77098
Camillo Ct 77094
Camino Del Sol Dr 77083
Camino Oaks Dr 77064
Camino Rancho Dr 77083
Camino South Shopping Ctr 77062
Camino Verde Dr 77083
Campbell Ct 77055
Campbell Rd
900-999 77024
1000-1600 77055
1602-1698 77055
1700-4299 77080
4300-5799 77041
9200-9499 77080
Campbell St
1200-1599 77009
1601-1699 77009
1700-4199 77026
Campbellton Dr 77083
Campden Hill Rd
14401-14597 77045
14599-14699 77045
15201-15699 77053
Campeachy Cir & Ln 77083
Campeche Dr 77045
Camphor Dr 77082
Camphorwood Dr 77089
Camporee Ln 77083
Campos Dr 77065
Campton Ct 77055
Camptown Cir 77069
Camrose Cir 77085
Camrose Ct 77086
Camway St 77028
Camwood St 77087
Canaan Bridge Dr 77041
Canada Dry St 77023
Canadian St 77009
Canady Park Ln 77075
Canal Ct 77011
Canal St
2000-4399 77003
4400-7499 77011
7500-7999 77012
Canaridge Dr 77053
Canario Dr 77083
Canary Grass Ln 77059
Canarywood Dr 77089
Canasta Ln 77083
Cancence Dr 77086
N Cancun Dr 77045
Canda Ln 77083
Candace St 77055
Candela Ct & Dr 77083
Candle Ln 77071
Candle Ridge Park 77073
Candlecrest Dr
4900-4999 77018
5400-5499 77091
Candleglow Dr 77018
Candlegreen Ln 77071
Candleleaf Dr 77018
Candlelight Ln 77018
Candlelight Place Dr 77018
Candlemist Dr
4900-4999 77018
5400-5499 77091
W Candler Dr 77037
Candlerock Ct 77095
Candleshade Ln 77045
Candleshine Cir 77095
Candletree Dr
4900-5099 77018
5400-5499 77091
Candlewick St 77015
Candlewood Dr
5400-5699 77056
10000-11199 77042
Candlewood Ln 77057
Candlewood Glen Ln 77014
Candy St 77029
Candyridge Ct 77053
Candytuft Ct & St 77038
Cane Creek Ct & Dr 77070
Cane Grove Ln 77075
Cane Valley Ct 77044
Canebrake Ln 77083
Canemont St 77035
Caneridge Dr 77053
Caney Springs Ln 77044
Canfield St 77004
Canino Rd 77076
E Canino Rd 77037
W Canino Rd 77037
Canmere Ct 77070
Cannady Ct 77069
Cannata Dr 77045
Canniff St
8700-8799 77061
9100-9399 77017
Cannock Rd 77074
Cannock Chase Ct & Dr 77065
Cannon Knls 77084
Cannon St
7700-7799 77021
7900-8499 77051
Cannon Falls Ln 77044
Cannonway Dr 77032
Cannonwood Ln 77070
Canoga Ln 77080
Canongate Dr 77056
Canova Hill Ln 77044
Cantata Ct 77040
Canterbury Dr 77014
Canterbury St 77030
Canterbury Way 77069
Canterdale St 77047
Canterhurst Cir & Way 77065
Canterlane Dr 77047
E & W Canterra Cir, Ct & Way 77095
Canterview Dr 77047
Canterville Rd 77047
Canterway Dr 77048
Canterwell Rd 77047
Canterwood Dr 77068
Canton St 77012
Canton Bluff Ln 77073
Canton Oaks Ct 77068
Canton Park Ln 77095
Canton Spring Ln 77044
Cantonwood Ct 77044
Cantor Cir 77084
Cantrell St 77074
Cantwell Dr 77014
Canvasback Ln 77047
S Canyon Dr 77089
Canyon St 77051
Canyon Arbor Way 77095
Canyon Blanco Dr 77045
Canyon Bluff Ct 77059
Canyon Brook Ct
4000-4099 77059
11100-11199 77065
Canyon Chase Dr 77095
Canyon Cliff Ct 77041
Canyon Creek Rd 77090
Canyon Creek Sq 77084
Canyon Echo Dr 77065
Canyon Forest Dr 77088
Canyon Glen Dr 77095
Canyon Green Dr 77095
Canyon Hill Dr 77083
Canyon Hollow Dr 77084
Canyon Hollow Loop 77083
Canyon Knoll Dr 77095
Canyon Mills Ct & Dr 77095
Canyon Oak Ct 77068
Canyon River Ln 77084
Canyon Rose Ln 77070
Canyon Springs Dr 77090
Canyon Stream Ct 77095
E Canyon Trace Dr 77095
Canyon Trail Dr 77066
Canyon Way Dr 77086
Canyoncrest Ln 77086
Cape Bahamas Ln 77058
Cape Breeze Dr
9700-9799 77095
9800-9899 77070
Cape Charles Ln 77058
Cape Cod Ln 77024
Cape Coral Ct 77095
Cape Forward Dr 77083
Cape Hatteras Dr 77041
Cape Henry Ln 77084
Cape Hyannis Dr 77048
Cape Laurel 77014
Cape Province Dr 77083
Cape Rise Trl 77044
Capello Dr 77035
Caperton St 77022
Capetown Dr 77058
Capewalk Dr 77054
Capistrano St 77015
Capital Park Dr 77041
Capitol St
300-1599 77002
1601-1697 77003
1699-3499 77003
3900-4000 77023
4002-4398 77023
4700-7499 77011
7500-7698 77012
7700-7999 77012
8001-8099 77012
N Capitol St 77011
S Capitol St 77023
Capitol Heights Dr 77065
Caplin St
100-1599 77022
1800-5599 77026
Cappamore St 77013
Capri Cir 77095
Capri Dr 77040
Capri St 77024
Capri Isle Ct 77077
Caprice Ct 77044
Caprice Ln 77058
Capridge Dr 77048
Capron St 77020
Capshaw Ct 77065
Capstan Rd 77062
Captain Dr 77036
Captains Walk 77079
Caracara Dr 77040
Caracas Dr 77083
Caradine St 77085
Caravan Dr 77031
Caraway Ln 77036
Carbide Cir 77040
Carbridge Dr 77084
Carby Rd 77037
Cardenia Bend Dr 77053
Cardiff Rd
11700-11899 77076
12200-12300 77037
12302-12898 77037
Cardiff Cliff Ln 77053
Cardiff Park Ln 77094
Cardinal Ln 77079
Cardinal Bay 77041
Cardinal Bend Ln 77070
Cardinal Creek Ct 77062
Cardwell Ct, Dr, Ln & St 77055
Caren Ct 77031
Carew St
5000-5699 77096
5700-7699 77074
Carey Pl 77073
Carey St 77028
Carey Ridge Ct 77094
Careywood Dr 77040
Cargill St 77029
Caribbean Ln 77089
Caribe Ln 77047
Caridas Rd 77085
Carillo Dr 77091
Carino Dr 77091
Caris St 77091
Caritas Cir 77065
Carl St 77009
Carla St 77076
Carlaris Ct 77041
Carleen Rd
2300-2399 77018
4600-4799 77092
Carlford Cir 77018
Carlin Bend Ln 77095
Carlingford Ln 77079
Carlington Dr 77093
Carlingwood Dr 77070
Carlisle St 77017
Carlisle Park Ln 77084
Carlon St 77005
Carlos St 77029
Carlota Ct
1-9099 77074
10600-10799 77096
Carlsbad Ct & St 77085
Carlson Ln 77047
Carlton Dr 77047
Carlton Park Ct 77024
Carly Park Way 77084
Carmalee St 77075
Carmel Cir 77095
Carmel Grv 77073
Carmel St 77091
Carmel Cove Ct 77041
Carmel Dale Ln 77089
Carmen St
4600-4699 77051
4700-5399 77033
Carmilenda St 77037
Carmine Glen Dr 77049
Carnarvon Dr 77024
Carnation St 77022
Carnegie St 77005
Carnegie Park Ct 77058
Carnelian Ct & Dr 77072
Carola Forest Dr 77044
Carolane Trl 77024
Carolcrest Cir & Dr 77079
N Carolina St 77029
Carolina Way 77005
Carolina Grove Ln 77073
Carolina Hollow Ln 77044
Caroline St
201-297 77002
299-800 77002
801-897 77010
802-898 77002
899-1099 77010
1100-1198 77002
1101-1199 77010
1200-2299 77002
2300-5599 77004
5800-5899 77030
Caroline Shore Way 77089
Caroline Way Ct 77073
Carols Way Cir & Dr 77070
Carolton Way 77073
Carolwood Dr 77028
Carothers St
3300-3799 77087
6800-7699 77028
Carousel Ct 77041
Carousel Ln 77080
Carpenters Cove Ln 77049
Carpenters Hollow Ct 77049
Carr St
1200-1499 77020
1600-3399 77026
Carriage Ct
13600-13699 77044
18600-18699 77058
Carriage Ln 77058
Carriage Brook Way 77062
Carriage Creek Dr 77064
Carriage Hill Dr 77077
Carriage Lake Dr 77065
Carriage Point Dr 77073
Carriage Ridge Ct 77070
Carriage Walk Ln 77077
Carrick St 77022
Carrie St 77047
Carrigan Pl 77083
Carrige Ridge Dr 77070
Carrizo Fall Ct 77041
Carrollton Creek Ct & Ln 77084
Carrolton St 77023
Carrswold Dr 77071
Carruth Ln 77083
Carsa Ln 77014
Carsen Bend Dr 77049
Carsey Ln 77024
Carshalton Ct 77084
Carson Ct 77004
Carson Rd 77048
Carson Hill Ln 77092
Carsondale St 77017
Carsonmont Ln 77070
Carstairs Dr 77070
Cart Gate Ct & Dr 77095
Cartagena St 77035
Carter Rd 77070
Carter St 77008
Cartersville St 77029
Carthage Dr 77089
Caruso Forest Dr 77088
Caruthers Ln 77024
Carved Rock Dr 77085
Carvel Cir 77072
Carvel Ln
6700-7199 77074
7901-7997 77036
7999-9499 77036
10700-13199 77072
13200-13499 77083
Carver Rd
6200-6999 77091
7000-8499 77088
Cary St 77003
Casa Del Monte Dr 77083
Casa Grande Dr 77060
Casa Loma Dr 77041
Casablanca Dr 77088
Cascade Cir 77095
Cascade Caverns Ct & Ln 77044
Cascade Falls Dr 77062
Cascade Hills Dr 77064
Cascade Oaks Ct 77084
Cascade Pines Dr 77049
Cascade Point Dr 77084
Cascadera Dr 77086
Cascadia Dr 77082
Case St 77005
Caseta Dr 77082
N Cashel Cir 77069
Cashel Castle Dr 77069
Cashel Forest Dr 77069
Cashel Glen Dr 77069
N & S Cashel Oak Dr 77069
Cashel Park Ln 77084
Cashel Point Ln 77084
Cashel Spring Dr 77069
Cashel Wood Dr 77069
Cason St 77005
Caspersen Dr 77029
Caspian Ln 77090
Cassandra Ln 77064
Cassia Cir 77065
Cassidy Pl 77066
Cassidy Creek Ct 77095
Castilian Dr 77015
Castille Ln 77082
Castle Ct 77006
Castle Court Pl 77006
Castle Cove Ln 77044
Castle Crest Ct & Dr 77083
Castle Fraser Dr 77084
Castle Gate Ct & Dr 77083
Castle Glen Dr 77015
Castle Heath Ln 77084
Castle Hills Ct 77070
Castle Knoll Dr 77066
Castle Lane Dr 77066
Castle Peak Dr 77095
Castle Pond Ct 77095
Castle Ridge Dr 77077
Castle Way Dr 77083
Castle Way Ln 77015
Castlebar Ct 77015
Castlebay Dr 77092
Castlebridge Dr 77065
Castlecombe Dr 77044
Castlecreek Ln 77053
Castledale Dr
900-1299 77037
2600-4399 77093
Castleford St 77040
Castlegory Ct 77015
Castlegory Rd 77015
N Castlegory Rd 77049
Castlereagh Dr 77045
Castlerock Dr 77090
Castlestone Dr 77065
Castleton St 77016
Castlewood St 77025
Castolan Dr 77038
Castor St 77022
Cat Tail Spring Ct 77095
Cataldo Ct 77040
Catalina Ln 77075
Catalina Shores Dr 77041
Catalina Village Dr 77083
Catalpa Cir 77065
Catamore St 77076
Catarina Cir 77084
Catawissa Dr 77095
Catford St 77075
Cathcart Dr 77091
Cathedral Dr 77051
Cathedral Grove Ln 77040
Cather St 77076
Catherine St 77009
Catherwood Ln 77084
Catherwood Pl 77015
Cathey Ln 77080
Cathy Dr 77065
Catina Ln 77045
Catskill Bluff Ln 77095
Cattails Ln 77035
Caudle Dr 77055
Causeway Dr 77083
Cavalcade St
101-2099 77009

2400-6499 77026
6900-7199 77028
W Cavalcade St
100-116 77009
118-699 77009
634-634 77249
700-1198 77009
701-1199 77009
Cavalier St 77087
Cavanaugh St 77021
Cavehill Ct 77047
Cavell Ct, Ln & St 77055
Cavendish Ct & Dr 77059
Caversham Dr 77096
Cawdor Way 77024
Caxton St 77016
Cay Sol Ct 77044
Cayey St 77016
Caylor St 77011
Cayman Mist Dr 77075
Cayton St 77061
Cayuga St 77054
Caywood Ln 77055
Cebra St 77091
Cecil Loop Ln 77075
Cecil Ridge St 77075
Cecil Summers Ct & Way 77089
Cedar Brg 77075
Cedar St 77044
Cedar Bend Crk 77041
Cedar Bluff Dr 77064
Cedar Creek Ct 77077
Cedar Creek Dr
5000-5699 77056
6100-6299 77057
10000-10899 77042
11300-11699 77077
Cedar Crest St 77087
Cedar Field Way 77084
Cedar Gap Ln 77072
Cedar Gardens Dr 77082
Cedar Hill Ct 77093
Cedar Hill Ln
2800-5299 77093
5400-5699 77016
Cedar Isle Dr 77084
Cedar Mesa Dr 77034
Cedar Mound Ln 77083
Cedar Park Ln 77086
Cedar Pass Ct & Dr 77077
Cedar Placid Cir & Ln 77068
Cedar Point Cir, Ct & Dr 77070
Cedar Post Ln 77055
Cedar Ridge Ct 77082
Cedar Ridge Dr 77082
Cedar Ridge Trl 77059
Cedar Sage Dr 77095
Cedar Shoals Rd 77062
Cedar Shores Ln 77044
Cedar Top Dr 77088
Cedar Woods Pl 77068
Cedarbrake Dr 77055
Cedarbrook Dr 77055
Cedarburg Dr 77048
Cedarcliff Ct & Dr 77070
Cedardale Dr 77055
Cedaredge Dr 77064
Cedarhurst Dr 77096
Cedarmoor Ct 77082
Cedarspur Dr 77055
Cedarview Ln 77041
Cedel Dr 77055
Celeste River Ct 77095
Celestial Ln 77039
Celestite Dr 77072
Celia Dr 77015
Celina Ln 77040
Celtis St 77029
Cendiank Dr 77071
Cendonde St 77006
Ceneradi Rd 77039
Centenary St 77005
Centennial Dr 77055
Center St 77007
Center Hill Dr 77079
Center Point Dr 77054
Centerfield Dr 77070
Centerplaza Dr 77007
Centerwood Dr 77013
NW Central Dr 77092
Central Pkwy 77092
Central St
300-1599 77012
1700-2299 77017
Central Falls Dr 77041
Central Green Blvd 77032
Central Park Cir 77059
Centralcrest St 77092
Centre Ct 77072
Centre Pkwy 77036
Centre Grove Ct & Dr 77069
Centre Oaks Dr 77069
Centrepark Dr 77043
Century Ln 77015
Century Plaza Dr 77073
Cerca Ct 77086
Cerca Blanca Dr 77083
Cereza Dr 77083
Cerritos Dr 77035
N & S Cesar Chavez Blvd 77011
Cetin Ct 77073
Cetti St 77009
Cettipark St 77009
Chaco St 77004
Chadbourne Ct & Dr 77079
Chadbrook Ln 77099
Chadwell Dr 77031
Chadwell Glen Ln 77082
Chadwick St 77029
Chaffin St 77087
Chain St 77033
Chalcos Dr 77017
Chalet Rd 77038
Chaletford Dr 77044
Chalfield Cir & Ct 77044
Chalfont Ct 77066
Chalfont Dr
3200-3399 77066
11500-11510 77065
Chalford Dr 77083
Chalk Maple Ct & Ln 77095
Chalk Rock Dr 77067
Challenger 7 Dr 77029
Challie Ln 77088
Challis Park Ct 77040
Chalmette St 77015
Chamberlain Dr
12800-12899 77077
17400-17499 77095
Chamberlain St 77093
Chamberlain Park Ln 77047
Chambers St 77034
Chambler Ct 77069
Chambly Dr 77015
Chamboard Ln 77018
Chamomile Ct 77083
Chamomile Green Ct 77070
Champaign St 77039
Champion Ln 77091
Champion Forest Dr
11300-12999 77066
13000-14699 77069
Champion Villa Dr 77069
Champion Village Ct & Dr 77069
Champions Dr 77069
Champions Bend Cir 77069
Champions Centre Ct & Dr 77069
Champions Centre Estate Dr 77069
Champions Colony E & W 77069
Champions Colony Iii 77069
Champions Court Pl, Trl & Way 77069
Champions Glen Dr 77069
Champions Green Dr 77066
Champions Grove Ct & Ln 77066
Champions Hamlet Ct 77069
Champions Park Dr 77069
Champions Plaza Dr 77069
Champions Valley Dr 77066
Champions Walk Ln 77066
Champions Way Ln 77066
Championship Ln 77069
Champlain Bend St 77056
Chancel Dr 77071
Chancellorsville Ln 77083
Chancery Rd 77034
Chandler St 77007
Chandler Chase Ct 77044
Chandler Hollow Ln 77049
Chandlers Way Dr 77041
Changing Oak Ridge Ct 77082
Channelside St 77012
Chanteloup Dr 77047
Chantilly Cir 77018
Chantilly Ln
900-2399 77018
4800-5799 77092
Chantry Dr 77084
Chanute Rd 77032
Chapal Gate Ln 77044
Chaparral Dr 77043
Chapel Belle Ln 77024
Chapel Bend Dr 77068
Chapel Brook Dr 77069
Chapel Creek Ct 77067
Chapel Hill Dr 77099
Chapel Oaks Dr 77067
Chapel Park Ct & Way 77059
Chapelbrook Ln 77095
Chapelfield Ln 77049
Chapelle Ct 77077
Chapelstone Ct 77044
Chapelwood Ct & Ln 77024
Chapis St 77093
Chaplin St 77032
Chapman St
900-1299 77002
1500-5799 77009
5801-5899 77009
6100-6399 77022
17800-18099 77044
Chapman Lake Ct 77044
Charade Dr 77066
Chardonnay Dr 77077
Charidges Ct & Dr 77034
Charing Way 77045
Charing Cross Dr 77031
Charles Rd
300-1199 77076
1500-2699 77093
7000-7099 77041
11200-11899 77041
Charles St 77088
Charlesmont St
7600-7799 77016
8000-8399 77078
Charleston St 77021
Charleston Park Dr 77025
Charlestown Colony Ct & Dr 77084
Charlie St 77088
Charlie Voix St 77015
Charlmont Dr 77083
Charlotte St 77005
Charlton Park Dr 77077
Charlton Way Dr 77077
Charlynn Oaks Dr 77070
Charney Ln 77088
Charnwick Ct 77069
Charnwood St 77022
Charrin Dr 77032
Charriton Dr 77039
Charriton St 77060
Chart House Ct 77044
Charter Oaks Dr 77093
Charter Pine St 77070
Charter Ridge Dr 77070
Charter Rock Dr 77070
Charterlawn Cir 77070
Chartermoss Cir 77070
Charterstone Dr 77070
Charterwood Dr 77070
Chartley Falls Dr 77044
Chartres St
1-399 77002
601-2099 77003
2800-5699 77004
Chartreuse Ct & Way 77082
Chartwell Ct 77024
Chartwell Dr 77031
Charwell Crossing Ln 77069
Charwon St 77093
Charwood Ct 77068
Chas Ln 77091
Chase Hbr 77041
Chase St
1500-2399 77026
7400-7899 77093
Chase Lake Dr 77077
Chaseland Ln 77077
Chasewick Cir 77014
Chasewood Park Dr 77070
Chason Ct 77084
Chaston Dr 77041
Chasworth Dr 77041
Chatam Ln 77024
Chatburn Dr 77077
Chateau St 77028
Chateau Forest Dr 77088
Chateau Point Ln 77041
Chateaucrest Ct 77047
Chatfield St 77025
Chatford Hollow Ln 77014
Chatham Ln 77027
Chatham Creek Ct 77077
Chatham Hill Ln 77084
Chatham Island Ln 77035
Chatham Way Dr 77084
Chatham Woods Dr 77084
Chatsworth Dr 77024
Chatten Way 77024
Chatterton Dr 77043
Chatwood Dr 77078
Chaucer Dr 77005
Chaucer Oaks Ct 77082
Chaumont Dr 77089
Chazen Dr 77029
Chazenwood Dr 77064
Cheadint St 77078
Cheam Cir 77015
Cheaney Ct & Dr 77066
Cheatham Ln 77015
Checkerboard St 77096
Chedworth Dr 77062
Cheena Dr
4000-4099 77025
4300-6299 77096
Cheer St 77063
Cheeves Dr 77016
Chelsea Blvd
1-799 77006
800-899 77002
Chelsea Bend Ct 77083
Chelsea Brook Ct & Ln 77089
Chelsea Elm Ct 77038
Chelsea Knoll Ln 77067
Chelsea Oak St 77065
Chelsea Walk Dr 77066
Chelseahurst Ln 77047
Chelsworth Dr 77083
Cheltenham Dr 77096
Chelton St 77015
Chelwood Pl 77069
Chenevert St
1-97 77002
99-399 77002
600-700 77003
702-798 77003
800-1199 77010
1200-2299 77003
2300-5699 77004
N Chenevert St 77002
Chennault Rd 77033
Cher Ct 77040
Cherbourg Rd 77033
Cherie Cove Dr 77088
Cherie Crest Ct 77088
Cherie Grove Cir 77088
Cherokee St 77005
Cherokee Lake Ln 77044
Cherry Run 77084
Cherry St 77026
Cherry Bend Dr 77077
Cherry Creek Dr 77017
Cherry Creek Bend Ct & Ln 77041
Cherry Forest Dr 77088
Cherry Fork Dr 77065
Cherry Grove Ct 77059
Cherry Hills Dr 77064
Cherry Hills Rd 77069
Cherry Hollow Ln 77082
Cherry Limb Dr 77099
Cherry Meadow Dr 77039
Cherry Mill Ct 77059
Cherry Mound Rd 77077
Cherry Oak Cir & Ln 77088
Cherry Park Dr 77095
Cherry Ridge Dr 77077
Cherry Spring Dr 77038
Cherrybark Ln 77079
Cherrybark Oak Dr 77082
Cherrydale Dr 77087
Cherryglade Ct 77044
Cherryhill St 77087
Cherryhurst St 77006
Cherryknoll Dr 77077
Cherryshire Ct & Dr 77083
Cherrytree St 77092
Cherrytree Grove Dr 77084
Cherrytree Park Cir 77062
Cherrytree Ridge Ln 77062
Cherryville Dr 77038
Cherton Ct 77045
Cheryl St 77085
Cheryl Lynne Ln 77045
Chesapeake Way 77056
Chesapeake Bay Ct 77084
Chesham Ct 77031
Cheshire Ln
1000-2399 77018
5500-5699 77092
Cheshire Bend Ln 77084
Cheshire Grove Ln 77090
Cheshire Oaks Dr 77054
Cheshire Park Rd 77088
Cheshire Place Dr 77083
Cheshire Vale St 77024
N & S Cheska Ln 77024
Chesney Downs Dr 77083
Chessington Dr 77031
Chesswood Dr 77072
Chester St
4201-4297 77007
4299-4399 77007
4401-4499 77007
17800-18099 77044
Chester Gables Ct & Dr 77083
Chester Oak Dr 77083
Chester Park Dr 77064
Chesterbrook Dr 77031
Chesterfield Dr 77051
Chestnut Pl 77094
Chestnut St 77009
Chestnut Bluff Dr 77095
Chestnut Brook Ct 77084
Chestnut Forest Dr 77088
Chestnut Mills Rd 77067
Chestnut Springs Ln 77062
Chestnut Tree Ln 77067
Chestnut Woods Trl 77065
Chestnutfield Ct 77094
Cheston Dr 77029
N & S Chestwood Dr 77024
Cheswick Dr 77037
Cheswood St 77087
Chetland Place Dr 77095
Chetman Dr 77065
Chetwood Dr 77081
Cheviot Cir 77099
Chevy Chase Dr
2900-3899 77019
5100-5699 77056
6100-6399 77057
7500-7999 77063
10000-11099 77042
11300-14499 77077
Chew St 77020
Chia St 77017
Chia Valley Ct 77089
Chicago St 77017
Chichester Ln 77040
Chickadee Ln 77048
Chickamauga Ln 77083
Chickasaw Ln 77041
Chickering St 77026
Chickfield Ct 77075
Chickory Woods Ln 77083
Chickwood Dr 77089
Chicory Dr 77084
Childress St 77005
Chilton Rd 77019
Chimes Dr 77077
Chimira Ln 77051
Chimney Brook Ln 77068
Chimney Hill Cir 77095
Chimney Ridge Rd 77053
Chimney Rock Rd
200-299 77024
500-3599 77056
5300-7499 77081
8601-8797 77096
8799-11199 77096
11300-11900 77035
11805-11805 77231
11805-11805 77235
11901-12499 77035
11902-12498 77035
16100-16799 77053
Chimney Rose Ct 77047
Chimney Sweep Dr 77041
Chimneystone Dr 77095
China Doll Ct 77041
Chinaberry Dr 77092
Chinn Ridge Ln 77083
Chinni Cir & Ct 77094
Chinon Cir 77071
Chinquapin Pl 77094
Chipman Ln 77060
Chipman Glen Dr 77082
Chippendale Rd 77018
Chippewa Blvd 77086
Chippewa Ridge Ct 77089
Chipping Ln 77088
Chisel Point Dr 77094
Chiselhurst Dr & Way 77065
Chiselhurst Way Ct 77065
Chisholm Trl 77060
Chisholm Wood Ln 77075
Chisum St 77020
Chiswell St 77025
Chiswick Rd 77047
Chitwood Ct 77094
Choate Cir 77017
Choate Rd 77034
Cholla Hill Ct 77064
Cholla Walk Ln 77064
Chorale Ct 77040
Chowning Rd 77024
Chris Dr 77063
Chrisman Rd 77039
Christensen St 77003
Christian Dr 77044
Christie St 77026
Christine St 77017
Christmas Fern St 77064
Christopher Pl 77066
Christopher Glen Pl 77073
Christophers Walk Ct & Trl 77089
Christy Glen Ct 77089
Christy Mill Ct 77070
Christy Park Cir 77084
Chronicle Dr 77084
Chrysanthemum Dr 77085
Chrystell Ln 77092
Chuckanut Ln 77024
Chuckberry St 77080
Chuckson Dr 77065
Chuckwood Rd 77038
Church Ln 77043
Church Rd 77013
Church Light Ln 77064
Churchill Ct 77024
Churchill St 77009
Churchill Gardens Ln 77066
Churchill Way Cir & Dr 77065
Churchville Dr 77080
Chute Forest Dr 77014
Cibola Park Ln 77041
Cibolo St 77013
Cicada Ln 77039
Cicero Rd 77095
Ciceter Rd 77039
Cielio Bay Ct & Ln 77041
Cienna Dr 77040
Cimarron St 77015
Cinder Cone Trl 77044
Cinderella St 77028
Cinderwood Ct 77015
Cindy Ln 77008
Cindywood Cir & Dr 77079
Cinnabar Dr 77072
Cinnamon Ln 77072
Cinnamon Creek Cir 77084
Cinnamon Fern Ct 77059
Cinnamon Fern St 77064
Cinnamon Glen Dr 77073
Cinnamon Oak Ln 77079
Cinnamon Scent St S 77064
Cira Ct 77044
Circle Dr
1-99 77013
10600-10699 77034
E Circle Dr 77071
N Circle Dr 77071
S Circle Dr 77071
Circle Cove Ct 77088
Circlewood Way 77062
Circling Hawk Ct 77095
Citadel Ln 77092
Citadel Plaza Dr 77008
Citation Ct 77088
Citruswood Ln 77089
City Ct 77014
City Club Dr 77046
City Park Central Ln 77047
City View Pl 77060
Citypark Loop 77013
Citywest Blvd 77042
Clabury Ct 77070
Claiborne St
7400-7799 77016
7900-8499 77078
Claire Ln 77015
Clairy Ct 77076
Clan Macgregor Dr 77084
Clan Macintosh Dr 77084
Clanton St 77080
Clara Rd
5300-6499 77041
10800-11099 77013
Clara Hills Ln 77044
Claradeen Ct 77047
Clarblak Ln 77080
Clarborough Pl 77043
Clarehouse Ln 77047
Claremont Ln 77019
Claremont St 77023
Claremont Garden Cir 77047
Clarence St 77093
Clarendon Ln 77024
Clarewood Dr
5300-6199 77081
7100-9799 77036
12000-13199 77072
13400-13599 77083

Clarewood Oak Estates Ln 77081
Claridge Dr
5700-6299 77096
7600-7799 77071
9200-9499 77031
Clarington St 77016
Clarion Way 77040
Clark Ct 77020
Clark Rd
4200-4499 77040
9700-11199 77076
Clark St
400-1399 77020
10000-10099 77064
Clark Grove Ln 77075
Clark Wheeler St 77049
Clarkcrest St 77063
Clarkdale Ct 77094
Clarkdon Ct 77066
Clarke Springs Dr 77053
Clarks Fork Ct & Dr 77086
Clarkson Ln 77055
Claudia Dr
1-99 77013
12400-12498 77015
Claverton Dr 77066
Clawson St 77055
Claxton St 77087
Clay Rd
8700-10199 77080
10300-11499 77041
11500-11999 77043
12000-12999 77041
13000-19099 77084
17608-1-17608-2 77084
Clay St
300-1500 77002
1502-1598 77002
2001-2097 77003
2099-3399 77003
3401-3599 77003
3900-5400 77023
5402-5698 77023
W Clay St 77019
Clay Hill Dr 77084
Clay Point Ct 77024
Clayberry St 77080
Claybrook Dr 77089
Claycliff Ct 77034
Claygate Dr 77047
Claymoore Park Dr 77043
Claymore Ct & Rd 77024
Claypool St 77032
Clayridge Dr 77053
Clayton Bend Ct & Dr 77082
Clayton Gate Dr 77082
Clayton Green Dr 77082
Clayton Greens Ct 77082
Clayton Hill Dr 77041
Clayton Lake Ln 77044
Clayton Ridge Ct 77082
Clayton Trace Trl 77082
Clayton Woods Dr 77082
Claywood St 77024
Clear Arbor Ln 77034
Clear Brook Oak St 77089
Clear Cape Ln 77085
Clear Cove Ln 77041
Clear Hollow Ln 77089
Clear Lake City Blvd
1000-2399 77062
4400-4499 77059
Clear Meadow Ln 77089
Clear Oak Way 77058
Clear River Dr 77050
Clear Spring Dr 77079
Clear Trail Ln 77034
Clear Valley Dr
1201-1353 77014
1355-1899 77014
15400-15599 77095
Clear Villa Ln 77034
Clearbourne Ln 77075
Clearbrook Ln 77057
Clearcrest Dr 77059
Clearfield Dr 77044
Clearfork Dr 77077
Cleargrove Ln 77075
Clearmont Dr 77053
Clearsable Ln 77034
Clearsmoke Cir 77095
Clearview Cir 77025
Clearview St 77033
Clearview Villa Pl & Way 77025
Clearwater St 77029
Clearway Dr 77033
Clearwood Dr 77075
Clearwood Crossing Blvd 77075
Clearwood Landing Blvd 77075
Cleburne St 77004
Cleft Stone Dr 77084
Clematis Ln 77035
Clement St 77026
Clementine St
2100-2399 77020
2800-2999 77026
Clementshire St 77087
Clemson St 77092
Cleneres Dr 77073
Cleobrook Dr 77070
Clerkenwell Dr 77084
Clermont Harbor Ct 77045
Clerradi Dr 77082
Clevedon Ln 77040
Cleveland St 77019
Cleveland Bay Ct 77065
Clevera Walk Ln 77084
Cliff Ct 77076
S Cliff Dr 77089
Cliff Haven Ct & Dr 77095
Cliff Park Dr 77065
Cliffbrook Ct 77095
Cliffdale St 77091
Cliffgate Dr 77072
Cliffmarshall St 77088
Cliffrose Ct 77089
Cliffrose Ln 77062
Cliffshire Ct 77083
Cliffside Dr 77076
Cliffton Forge Dr 77065
Cliffwood Dr
9000-9700 77096
9702-9998 77096
10000-11399 77035
Clift Haven Dr
4700-4999 77018
5400-5499 77091
Clifton St 77011
Clifton Oaks Dr 77099
Clifton Park Dr 77099
Climber Ct 77041
Climbing Branch Ct & Dr 77068
Climbing Ivy Cir 77084
Cline Rd 77050
Cline St 77020
Clinton Dr
100-198 77015
2700-7499 77020
7800-9899 77029
9901-9999 77029
12501-12599 77015
Clinton Park St 77029
Clintridge Dr 77084
Clintway Dr 77014
Clio St 77009
Clipper Winds Way 77084
Clippers Sq 77058
Clippers Cove Dr 77058
Clipperwood Pl 77083
Cliveden Dr 77066
Clodine Rd 77083
Clodine Reddick Rd 77083
Cloud Cliff Ln 77077
Cloud Swept Ln 77086
Cloudcap Ct 77044
Cloudmount Dr 77084
Clove Cir 77078
Clover Hl 77094
Clover St
4100-4699 77051
4700-5199 77033
Clover Canyon Cir 77095
Clover Crest Dr 77095
Clover Gardens Dr 77095
Clover Glen Ln 77084
Clover Green Ln 77067
Clover Grove Ct 77084
Clover Knoll Ct 77095
Clover Lane Ct 77066
Clover Ridge St 77087
Clover Trail Ln 77067
Clover Walk Ln 77041
Cloverbrook Dr 77045
Cloverdale St 77025
Cloverlake Ct 77040
Cloverleaf St 77015
Clovermill Dr 77066
Clovermist Dr 77064
Cloverstone Ct 77094
Cloverwalk Ln 77072
Clovis Rd 77008
Clow Rd 77068
W Club Ln 77099
Club Creek Dr 77036
Club Green Ct 77034
Club Lake Dr 77095
Club Valley Dr 77082
Cluett St 77028
Cluster Dr 77055
Cluster Pines Ct 77066
Clyde St 77007
Clydesdale Dr 77084
Coach Rd 77060
Coach Lamp Ct & Ln 77060
Coachcreek Dr 77085
Coachfield Ln 77035
Coachlight Dr 77077
Coachman Ln 77024
Coachwood Dr
6300-6499 77035
7500-7799 77071
Coahuila St 77013
Coal St 77026
Coalport Ct 77073
Coan St 77093
S Coast Dr 77047
Coast Bridge St 77095
Coastal Way 77085
Coastal Greens Dr 77054
Coastal Oak Ct & Dr 77059
Coastway Ln 77075
Coba Ct 77073
Cobalt St 77016
Cobalt Creek Ln 77095
Cobalt Falls Dr 77095
Cobb St 77004
Cobbdale Ln 77014
Cobble Creek Dr 77073
Cobble Falls Ct 77095
Cobble Grove Ln 77084
Cobble Hill Rd 77050
Cobblefield Ln 77071
Cobbleshire Ct & Dr 77037
Cobblestone Dr 77024
Cobblestone Path 77084
Cobblestone Creek Way 77084
Cobbleton Dr 77034
Cobbs Cove Ln 77044
Cobbs Creek Ct & Rd 77067
Cobden Ct 77034
Cobles Cor 77069
Cobleskill Ln 77099
Cobre Valley Dr 77062
Cochran St
1900-5999 77009
6100-7699 77022
Cockburn St 77078
Cockerel St 77018
Cockrum Blvd 77066
Coco Shores Ct 77044
Cocona Ln 77073
Cody St 77009
Coe Ct 77088
Coffee St 77033
Coffee Creek Ct 77044
Cogburn Park Dr 77047
Cohen Green Ln 77094
Cohn Gdn 77007
Cohn Mdw 77007
Cohn St
700-798 77007
800-2799 77007
6500-6899 77091
Cohn Ter 77007
Cohn Trl 77007
Cohn Arbor 77007
Coho Ln 77045
Cohutta Ln 77093
Coke St 77020
Cola St 77088
Colby St 77003
Colchester St 77018
Cold Harbor Ln 77083
Cold Lake Dr 77088
Cold Spring Dr 77043
Coldstream Rd 77055
Cole Creek Dr
6900-7299 77092
9200-9399 77040
Colebrook Dr 77072
Coleburn Dr 77095
Colemans Way 77089
Colendale Dr 77037
Coleridge St 77005
Colfax St 77020
Colgate St
3700-4199 77087
8000-8299 77061
4019-1-4019-2 77087
Colima Dr 77083
Colleen Rd 77080
Colleen Meadows Cir 77080
Colleen Woods Cir 77080
College St
1700-1799 77017
5900-6699 77005
E College St 77005
W College St 77005
College Green Dr 77058
Colley St 77093
Collier St 77023
Collin Park 77075
Collina Springs Ct 77041
Collingsworth St
600-2099 77009
2400-6299 77026
Collins Pl 77002
Collins Rd
1400-5199 77093
5500-5899 77016
Colmar Way 77084
Cologne Dr 77065
Coloma Ln 77024
Colomba St 77045
Colonel Fischer Rd 77032
Colonial Ln 77051
Colonial Bridge Ln 77073
Colonial Trail Dr 77066
Colonnade Dr 77030
Colony Ct 77041
Colony Ln 77076
Colony St 77036
Colony Crest Ct 77082
Colony Glen Ct 77062
Colony Heath Ln 77085
Colony Hill Ln 77014
Colony Point Ct 77095
Colorado St 77007
Colquitt St
200-399 77002
400-1699 77006
1700-3399 77098
3700-4099 77027
Colt Canyon Ln 77089
Colton St 77016
Colton Cove Dr 77095
Colton Hollow Dr 77067
Colton Mining Ct 77040
Columbia St
300-899 77007
900-2899 77008
3000-3499 77018
Columbine Ln 77049
Columbus St 77019
Colvin St 77013
Colwell Rd 77068
Colwyn Ln 77040
Coma St 77051
Comal St 77051
Comanche Ln 77041
Comanche Peak Ln 77089
Comanche Springs Ct 77095
Combine Ln 77049
Comely Ln 77079
Comet Dr 77086
Comfort Glen Ct 77047
Comile St 77022
Cominsky Dr 77049
Commerce St
800-898 77002
900-2299 77002
2300-2398 77003
2301-2399 77002
2400-3899 77003
Commerce Creek Dr 77040
Commerce Park Dr 77036
Commodore Way 77079
Common St 77009
Common Crest Dr 77095
Common Park Dr 77009
Commons Ct 77095
Commonwealth St 77006
Community Dr 77005
Community College Dr 77013
Compaq Center West Dr 77070
Compton St 77016
Comstock Cir 77090
Comstock Meadows Dr 77095
Concert Dr 77030
Concerto Cir 77040
Concho Mtn 77069
Concho St
6800-7099 77074
8000-9199 77036
10700-11499 77072
Concho Bay Ct & Dr 77041
Concord Cir 77024
Concord Grv 77084
Concord Ln 77064
Concord St 77017
Concord Bridge Dr 77041
Concord Meadow Ln 77047
Concord Park Dr 77040
Concourse Dr 77036
Concrete St 77012
Condessa Dr 77083
Condon Ln 77053
Cone Creek Dr 77090
Conecrest Ct 77088
Conestoga Lane Ct 77066
Confederate Rd 77055
Conger St 77075
Congo Ln 77040
Congress St
600-698 77002
700-2199 77002
2200-2399 77003
Conifer Rd 77079
Conifer Bay Ct 77059
Conifer Springs Ct & Ln 77067
Conklin Ln 77034
Conklin St 77088
Conlan Bay Dr 77041
Conley St 77021
Conlon St 77061
Connaught Way 77015
Connaught Garden Dr 77083
Connecticut St 77029
Conner Creek Ln 77044
Connie St 77076
Connor St 77039
Connorvale Ct 77060
Connorvale Ln 77060
Connorvale Rd 77039
Conoly St 77009
Conover Ct 77015
Conrad Sauer Dr 77043
Conroy St 77026
Constance Dr 77024
Constellation Ln 77075
Consuela Dr 77074
Consulate Plaza Dr 77032
Conti St
1300-1500 77002
1502-1598 77002
2600-2899 77020
Continental Dr 77072
Contour Pl 77096
Convention Center Blvd 77010
Converse St 77006
Conward Dr 77066
Conway St 77025
Cook Rd
4100-8599 77072
8600-10699 77099
Cook St 77006
Cookglass Dr 77072
Cookridge Ln 77014
Cooksteel Dr 77072
Cookwind Dr 77072
Cookwood Dr 77072
Cool Mist Dr 77013
Cool River Ln 77067
Cool Spring Dr
301-497 77037
499-599 77037
1400-1499 77088
Coolgreen St 77013
Coolgrove Dr 77049
Coolidge St 77012
Coolridge Ct 77062
Coolshire Ln 77070
Coolwood Dr 77013
Cooper Rd 77076
Coopers Hawk Ct & Dr 77044
Cooperstown Dr 77089
Copeland Dr 77070
Copeland St 77020
Copeland Mill Ln 77047
Copley Ln 77093
Coppage St 77007
Copper Branch Ln 77095
Copper Cove Dr 77095
Copper Creek Ct 77044
Copper Crossing Ct 77084
Copper Grove Blvd 77095
Copper Harbor Ct 77095
Copper Hollow Ln 77044
E & W Copper Lakes Ct & Dr 77095
Copper Mill Dr 77070
Copper Mist Ln 77095
Copper Shore Cir & Dr 77095
Copper Valley Ct 77067
E & W Copper Village Dr 77095
Copperas Cv 77077
Copperas Bend Ct 77095
Copperbrook Dr 77095
Copperdale Ln 77064
Copperfield Dr 77031
Coppermeade Ct & Dr 77067
Coppertree Ln 77035
Coppervine Ln 77084
Copperwillow Ct 77044
Copperwood Dr 77040
Copra Ln 77073
Cora St 77088
Coral St
501-597 77023
599-699 77023
701-799 77023
1000-2399 77012
Coral Bell Ln 77049
Coral Cove Ct 77095
Coral Creek Dr 77017
Coral Crest Ct 77041
Coral Gables Dr 77069
Coral Garden Ln
10800-10899 77075
13901-13999 77044
Coral Glen Ct 77062
Coral Oak Ct 77059
Coral Pointe Dr 77041
Coral Reef Dr 77044
Coral Ridge Ct & Rd 77069
Coral Sands Dr 77062
Coralbend Dr 77095
Coralstone Rd 77086
Coralville Ct 77041
Corbel Ln 77083
Corbin St 77055
Corbindale Rd 77024
Cordell St 77009
Corder St
2800-3199 77054
3401-3497 77021
3499-4099 77021
Cordoba Dr
10601-10797 77088
10799-11000 77088
11002-11098 77088
11200-11899 77038
Cordoba Pines Dr 77088
Cordon St 77026
Corey Woods Ct 77095
Corinth St 77051
Corinthian Pointe Dr 77095
Cork Dr 77047
Corken Way Ct 77034
Corksie St 77051
Corkwood Ct & Dr 77089
Corl St 77087
Cornell St
2500-2999 77009
3100-4399 77022
Cornell Park Ct 77058
Corner Crk 77084
Corner Oaks Ln 77036
Cornerstone Park Dr 77014
Cornerstone Village Dr 77014
Cornett Dr 77064
Corning Dr 77089
Cornish St 77007
Cornwall St 77040
Cornwall Bridge Ln 77041
Cornwell St 77086
Corola Trail Dr 77066
Corona Ln 77072
Corona Del Mar Dr 77083
Coronado St 77009
Coronation Dr 77034
Corondo Ct 77005
Corporate Dr 77036
Corporate Centre Dr 77041
Corpus Christi St
6300-7599 77020
12800-14699 77015
Corral Dr 77090
Corral Corner Ct & Ln 77064
Corral Path Ct 77064
Corrales Dr 77083
Corrian Park Cir 77040
Corrigan Ct & Dr 77014
Corsair Rd 77053
Corsica St 77015
Corsicana St 77020
Corta Calle Dr 77083
Cortelyou Ln 77021
Cortes Dr 77083
Cortina Dr 77083
Cortlandt St
200-899 77007
900-2899 77008
3000-4399 77018
5500-5600 77076
5602-5798 77076
Corto St 77016
Corum St 77089
Corvallis Dr 77095
Corvette Ct & Ln 77060
Corwin Pl 77024

Corwin St 77076
Cory Hollow Ct 77040
Corza Ct 77045
Corzatt Dr 77065
Cosby St 77021
Cosmos St 77009
Cossey Rd 77070
Costa Del Rey Ct 77041
Costa Mesa Dr 77053
Costa Rica Rd 77092
Costa Sienna Ln 77041
Costero Dr 77083
Cote Ct 77064
Cotillion Dr 77060
Cotorra Cove Ct 77041
Cotswold St 77009
W Cottage St 77009
Cottage Elm Ct 77089
Cottage Field Rd 77041
Cottage Gate Ln 77088
Cottage Landing Ln 77077
Cottage Oak Ln 77091
Cottage Park Cir & Dr 77094
Cottage Timbers Ct & Ln 77044
Cottingham St 77048
Cotton Dr 77092
Cotton Grove Ln 77044
Cotton Meadows Ln 77047
Cotton Ridge Trl 77053
Cotton Run Ct 77040
Cottonglen Ct 77041
Cottontop Ct 77086
Cottonwood St 77087
Cottonwood Way 77059
Cottonwood Bend Ct 77064
Cottonwood Canyon Dr 77095
Cottonwood Heights Ln 77090
Cottonwood Park Ln 77041
Cottonwood Trail Ct & Ln 77095
Cottrell Ct 77077
Couch St
2100-2699 77008
3400-3499 77018
6500-6899 77091
Cougar Pl 77004
Coulcrest Dr 77055
Coulson Cir & St 77015
Council Grove Ct & Ln 77088
Counselor St 77065
Count St 77028
Count Eric Dr 77084
Counter Point Dr 77055
Country Ct, Ld & Way 77024
Country Arbor Ln 77041
Country Bend Rd 77095
Country Bridge Rd 77095
Country Brook Ct & Ln 77095
Country Club Ct 77040
Country Club Dr 77023
Country Creek Dr 77036
Country Green Ct 77059
Country Haven Ct 77044
Country Knoll Dr 77086
Country Orchard Ln 77089
Country Path Way 77038
Country Place Dr 77079
Country Ridge Dr 77062
Country Spring Rd 77084
Country Square Dr 77084
N & S Country Squire St 77024
Country View Dr 77040
Country Wind Ct & Ln 77040
Countrywood Ln 77039
County Cress Dr 77047
County Fair Dr 77060
Courben Cir & Ln 77078
Courrege Ln 77037
Cours St 77093
N Course Dr 77072
S Course Dr
8300-8499 77072
8500-9399 77099
S Court Dr 77099
W Court Dr 77017
Court Rd 77053
Court St 77007
Court Glen Dr 77099
Court Of Lions St 77069
Court Of Lords 77069
Court Of Regents 77069
Court Of York 77069
Courtcliff Dr 77066
Courtesy Rd 77032
Courtlandt Pl 77006
Courtley St 77065
Courtney St 77026
Courtney Bend Cir 77086
Courtney Greens Rd 77089
Courtney Lane Dr 77042
Courtshire Rd 77076
Cove Creek Ln 77042
Covenant Springs Ct 77044
Coveney Dr 77090
Covens Forest Dr 77044
Covent Garden St 77031
Coventry Fls 77084
Coventry Field Ln 77084
Coventry Oaks Dr 77084
Coventry Park Dr 77084
Coventry Square Dr 77099
Coventry Squire Dr 77084
Covered Bridge St 77075
Covern St 77061
Covey Ct & Ln 77099
Coveywood Ct 77084
Covington Dr
5100-5199 77018
6600-6999 77091
7700-7798 77095
E & W Cowan Dr 77007
Cowart St
7200-7399 77020
7900-8899 77029
Cowling St 77011
Coyle St
3400-4099 77003
4300-4499 77023
Coyote Creek Dr 77095
Coyotillo Ln 77095
Coyridge Ln 77053
Coz Ct 77049
Cozy Hollow Ln 77044
Cozy Terrace Ln 77084
Crab Orchard Rd 77057
Crabapple Cv 77084
Craddock Dr 77099
Cradianc Dr 77080
Cradle St 77053
Cradle Cove Ct 77095
Craftmade Ln 77044
Craig St 77023
Craighead Dr 77025
Craighurst Ct & Dr 77059
Craigmont St 77023
Crakston St 77084
Crammond St 77064
Cranberry Hill Ct & Dr 77079
Cranbourne Dr 77062
Cranbrook Rd
5500-5599 77056
10600-11199 77042
Cranbrook Creek Ln 77044
Cranbrook Hollow Ln 77095
Crandon St 77026
Crane St 77026
Cranhurst Ln 77053
Cranleigh Ct 77096
Cransley Dr 77084
Cranston Ct 77008
Cranswick Rd 77041
Cranway Dr 77055
Cravenridge Dr 77083
Cravens St 77076
Crawford Rd 77041
Crawford St
100-799 77002
800-1199 77010
1200-2299 77002
2300-5599 77004
16000-16400 77040
16402-16498 77040
N Crawford St 77002
Crawford Crest Ln 77053
Crayford Ct & Dr 77065
Crazy Horse Trl 77064
Creager St 77034
Creede Dr 77040
Creegan Park Ct 77047
E Creek Cir 77086
NW Creek Cir 77086
Creek Dr
1700-1799 77055
1800-1899 77080
S Creek Dr 77084
S Creek Ln 77073
Creek Trl 77084
Creek Arbor Cir 77084
Creek Bend Trl 77084
Creek Crest Dr 77095
Creek Glen Dr 77095
Creek Grove Ct & Dr 77066
Creek Meadow Dr 77084
Creek Mountain Dr 77084
Creek Springs Dr 77083
Creek Vine Dr 77040
Creek Wood Way 77024
Creekbend Dr
4300-5199 77035
5200-6499 77096
7500-7698 77071
7700-8399 77071
Creekbriar Ct & Dr 77068
Creekdale Dr 77068
Creekhaven Ct & Dr 77084
Creekhickory Rd 77068
Creekhurst Dr 77099
Creeklea Rd 77068
Creekleaf Rd 77068
Creekmont Dr 77091
Creekmont Trace Ln 77091
Creekside Cir 77024
N Creekside Ct 77055
S Creekside Ct 77055
E Creekside Dr 77024
W Creekside Dr 77024
Creekside Ln
1-99 77055
700-799 77024
Creekside Acres Ct 77008
Creekside Park Dr 77082
Creeksouth Rd 77068
Creekstone Cir 77055
Creekstone Lake Dr 77054
Creektree Dr 77070
Creekview Park Dr 77082
Creekwind Cir 77084
Creekwood Dr 77063
N Creekwood Hills Ln 77070
Creeping Vine Ln 77088
Creighton Ct 77065
Crenchrus Ct 77086
Crenshaw Rd
300-399 77034
12500-12599 77044
Crenshaw St 77017
Crepe Myrtle Ct 77017
Crescendo Ct 77040
Crescent Sq 77084
Crescent Bay Dr 77094
Crescent Bluff Ln 77070
Crescent Canyon Ct & Dr 77095
Crescent Forest Ct 77062
Crescent Gate Ct & Ln 77024
Crescent Green Ct & Dr 77094
Crescent Landing Dr 77062
Crescent Manor Ln 77072
Crescent Mills Dr 77083
Crescent Moon Dr 77064
Crescent Park Dr
2300-2399 77077
12000-12099 77067
N Crescent Park Dr 77067
S Crescent Park Dr 77067
Crescent Parkway Ct 77094
Crescent Peak Dr 77067
Crescent Plaza Dr 77077
Cresent Oaks Ct 77068
Cresent Palm Ct & Ln 77077
Cresline St
300-1199 77076
1500-2599 77093
Cressida Glen Ln 77072
Crest Ct & St 77033
Crest Gate 77082
Crest Hill Ln 77007
Crest Lake Dr 77072
Crest Park Dr 77082
Crestbend Dr 77042
Crestbourne Ct 77014
Crestbrook Dr
900-1099 77038
15700-15899 77059
Crestdale Cir & Dr 77080
Crested Butte Ct 77067
Crested Green Dr 77082
Crestfield Ct 77070
Crestford Park Ln 77084
Cresthaven Cir 77048
Cresthill St 77033
Cresthollow Ln 77082
Crestmont St 77033
Crestmoon Ct 77089
Crestmoor Way 77082
Crestmore St 77096
Creston Dr 77026
Crestridge St 77033
Crestvale Dr 77038
Crestview Dr
7800-8299 77028
8800-9699 77078
Crestview Trl 77082
Crestville St 77033
Crestwater Ct & Trl 77082
Crestwick Dr 77083
Crestwood Dr 77007
Crestwood Estates Dr 77024
Creswell Ct 77084
Crete St 77020
Cribbage Ct 77083
Cricket Ln 77093
Cricket Wood Cir 77082
Cricketbriar Ct 77084
Crickett Hollow Dr 77069
Cricklewood Creek Ln 77083
Crieffe Rd 77039
Crim Ct & Rd 77049
Crimson Trl 77084
Crimson Canyon Dr 77095
Crimson Meadows Dr 77048
Crimson Oak Ct 77059
Crimson Sky Dr 77083
Crinkleawn Dr 77086
Cripple Brook Ct 77017
Cripple Creek Ct & Dr 77017
Crisp Wood Ln 77086
Crispin Ln 77080
Crites St
4100-4499 77003
4600-4699 77011
Crittenden St 77026
Crocker St
1000-1599 77019
1800-2799 77006
Crockett St 77007
Croes Dr 77055
Croft Ct 77065
Crofton St
7400-7699 77028
9400-9799 77016
Croftwood Dr 77068
Croker Ridge Rd 77053
Cromarty Ct 77084
Cromwell St
1001-1299 77037
1400-3399 77093
Crooked Ln 77084
N & S Crooked Creek Dr 77017
Crooked Wood Ln 77086
Crooks Way Ct 77065
Crooms St 77007
Croquet Ln 77085
Crosby Fwy
11500-11599 77013
14000-14998 77049
15000-17099 77049
17101-17299 77049
Crosby St 77019
Crosby Field Ln 77034
N Cross Dr 77073
Cross Continents Dr 77032
Cross Draw Dr 77067
Cross Glade Ct 77044
Cross Junction St 77084
Cross Plains Ct 77095
Cross Springs Ct & Dr 77095
Cross Stone Ct 77089
Cross Valley Dr 77066
Crossbranch Dr 77094
Crosscove Ct 77095
Crossfield Dr 77095
Crosshaven Ct & Dr 77015
Crosspark Pl 77007
Crosspoint Ave 77054
Crossriver Ln 77095
Crossroads Dr 77079
Crossroads Park Dr 77065
Crosstimbers St
200-211 77018
213-299 77018
301-1399 77022
E Crosstimbers St
1-1399 77022
1700-3799 77093
4000-5099 77016
W Crosstimbers St 77018
Crosston St 77018
Crossvale Ln 77047
Crossview Dr 77063
Crossway Dr 77084
Crosswell St 77087
Crosswinds Dr 77032
Crosswood Rd 77038
Croteau Dr 77044
Croton Rd 77036
Crow Valley Ln 77099
Crown St 77020
Crown Brook Ct 77083
Crown Colony 77069
Crown Glen Ct 77062
Crown Hill Ln 77084
Crown Meadow Ct 77095
Crown Park Dr 77067
Crown Point Dr 77099
Crown Ridge Ct 77059
Crownover Rd 77080
Crownwest St 77072
Croxton Dr 77015
Croydon Ct 77008
Cruse Rd 77016
Crystal Ct 77008
Crystal Way 77036
Crystal Bay Dr 77084
Crystal Brook Dr 77068
Crystal Cove Cir
8600-8613 77044
9300-9499 77070
Crystal Cove Ct 77044
Crystal Cove Dr 77044
Crystal Grove Dr 77082
Crystal Hills Dr 77077
Crystal Moon Dr 77040
Crystal Rock Ct 77072
Crystal View Cir & Ct 77095
Crystalglen Ln 77095
Crystalwood Dr 77013
Cub Ln 77075
Cucklebur Cir 77095
Culberson St 77021
Culebra St 77013
Cullen Blvd
700-1999 77023
2100-4999 77004
5400-7299 77021
7300-9443 77051
9444-10198 77051
9444-9444 77233
9445-10199 77051
10200-15299 77047
W Cullen St 77030
Cullen Meadow Ct 77047
Culmore Dr
4800-4999 77021
6300-7299 77087
Culver St 77051
Cumberland St 77023
Cummins St 77027
Cuney Dr 77004
Cunningham Rd 77041
Curly Oaks Dr 77053
Currency St 77013
Currie St 77034
Currin Forest Dr 77044
Curry Rd 77093
Curry Creek Ln 77090
Curry Landing Dr 77095
Curt Ln 77041
Curtin St
700-1499 77018
4900-5099 77023
Curtis St 77020
Curvey Ln 77047
Cushing St
1100-1899 77019
2900-3599 77026
Cushman Pl 77002
Custer St 77009
Cuta Ct 77039
Cutler Ridge Ln 77044
Cutten Pkwy 77069
Cutten Rd
10600-13099 77066
13100-14899 77069
15000-16399 77070
Cutting Horse Ln 77064
Cyberonics Blvd 77058
Cymbal Ct 77040
Cynthia Ann Ct 77025
Cypress Ct 77065
Cypress Run 77094
Cypress St
5800-6299 77074
7900-8599 77012
Cypress Trl 77065
Cypress Vis 77094
Cypress Bay Dr 77084
Cypress Corner Ln 77065
Cypress Cove St 77090
Cypress Creek Pkwy
1-2299 77090
2301-4499 77068
7300-10999 77070
E & W Cypress Forest Dr 77070
Cypress Garden Dr
8600-8699 77095
15300-15699 77069
Cypress Grove Ln 77088
Cypress Island Dr 77073
Cypress Knee Ln 77039
Cypress Landing Dr 77090
Cypress Laurel St 77095
Cypress Meadows Dr 77047
Cypress N Houston Rd 77065
Cypress Park Dr & Spur 77065
Cypress Place Dr 77065
Cypress Point Dr 77069
Cypress Pond Ct 77059
Cypress Shadow Dr 77065
Cypress Station Dr 77090
Cypress Trace Rd 77090
Cypress Way Dr 77065
Cypressbrook Dr 77095
Cypressvine Dr 77084
Cypresswood Dr 77070
Cypresswood Crossing Blvd 77070
Cypresswood Medical Dr 77014
Cypresswood Place Dr 77070
Cypresswood Trail Dr 77070
Cyprus Fld 77070
Cyrl Ln 77044
E & W Cyrus Dr 77064
D St 77072
D S Bailey Ln 77091
Dabney St 77026
Dacca Dr
3000-3199 77051
4100-4499 77047
Dacoma St 77092
Dacus Dr 77029
Dadebrook Ct 77041
Daehne Dr 77014
Daffodil St 77063
Dagg Rd 77048
Dahlia St 77012
Dahlia Field Way 77082
Dahlia Green Way 77038
Dahlia Vale Walk 77044
Dairy Ashford Rd 77079
N Dairy Ashford Rd 77079
S Dairy Ashford Rd
1000-2599 77077
2600-4099 77082
6100-8607 77072
8608-12799 77099
Dairy Brook Dr 77099
Dairy View Ln
7800-8699 77072
9100-9399 77099
Daisey Bell Ln 77067
Daisie Mae Dr 77032
Daisy St 77012
Daisy Clover Ct 77089
Daisy Cove Ln 77064
Daisy Meadow Ct 77041
Daisy Mist Ln 77038
Daisyetta St 77085
Dakar Dr 77065
Dakota Ridge Ct & Dr 77095
Dakton Dr 77039
Dalby St 77034
Dale St 77060
Dale Carnegie Ln 77036
Dale Oak Way 77058
Dale Ridge Trl 77084
Dale Spring Ct 77045
Dalebrook Dr 77016
Daleburg Dr 77032
Dalebury Ct 77066
Dalecrest Dr 77080
Daleford Ln 77049
Dalehurst Ct 77075
Dalerose Ct 77062
Daleside Dr 77099
Dalewood Dr 77060
Dalkey Dr 77051
Dallam Ct & Ln 77064
Dallas Ave 77040
Dallas St
200-1200 77002
1201-1999 77010
1202-1498 77002
1600-1998 77003
2000-3499 77003
3900-4499 77023
7100-7499 77011
W Dallas St
100-699 77002
700-3699 77019
Dallas Acorn St 77078
Dalmatian Dr 77045
Dalmore Ct 77095
Dalstrom St 77047
Dalton St 77017
Dalview St 77091
Daly Dr 77077
Daly Pl 77009

Street	ZIP
Damascon Ct	77014
Damascus Dr	77088
Damico St	77019
Damon Ct	77006
Dan St	77020
W Dana Ln	77024
Dana Leigh Dr	77066
Danbury Rd	77055
Danbury Bridge Dr	77095
Danbury Hollow Ln	77075
Danbury Park Ln	77073
Danbury Run Dr	77041
Danby Heath Ln	77073
Dancy Rd	77041
Dandelion Ln	77071
Dandy St	77016
Dandy Park Ct	77047
Dane St	77093
Danebridge Dr	77084
Danfield Dr	
101-197	77047
199-499	77047
4800-5499	77053
Danford Dr	77053
Danford Ln	77016
Danforth Dr	77062
Danforth Way	77083
Daniella Dr	77034
Danielle Ct	77099
Daninced St	77098
Danna Ln	77009
Dano Ct	77090
Danshire Ct & Dr	77049
Dante Dr	77053
Dantintr St	77012
Danton Falls Dr	77041
Danube St	77051
Danvers Dr	
11800-11899	77044
12600-12799	77049
Daphne St	77021
Dapple Ln	77065
Darby Cv	77077
Darby Mill Ln	77095
Darby Rose Ln	77044
Darby Square Trl	77084
Darbydale Dr	77090
Darbydale Crossing Ln	77090
Darcus St	77005
Dardanelles Ct	77084
Darden St	77093
Darfield Ct	77014
Daria Ct & Dr	77079
Darien St	77028
Darjean St	77039
Dark Cavern Ct	77095
Darkento St	77025
Darkwood Dr	77088
Darla Ln	77038
Darling St	77007
Darlinghurst Dr	
3500-5399	77045
5700-6499	77085
Darlington Dr	77028
Darlington Oak St	77016
Darnay Dr	77033
Darnell Cir	77074
Darnell St	
5000-5799	77096
5800-7499	77074
Darnley Ln	77077
Darrah Dr	77090
Darrian Ln	77049
Darrington Ln	77069
Darschelle Ct & Dr	77069
Dart St	77007
Darter St	77009
Dartmoor Ridge Trl	77066
Dartmouth Ave	77005
Darton St	77053
Dartwood Dr	77049
Darwin St	77093
Darwood Ct	77083
Daryns Landing Dr	77038
Dashwood Dr	
5300-5498	77081
5500-6299	77081
7600-8599	77036
11800-12099	77072
12101-12299	77072
Date St	
3500-3599	77026
17400-17599	77044
Dattner Rd	77013
Daugherty St	77029
Daun St	77039
Dauntless Dr	77066
Dauphin Ct	77058
Davenport St	77051
Davenridge Ln	77047
Daventry Ln	77039
Davenway Dr	77084
Davenwood Cir, Ct & Dr	77089
S David St	77054
Davidson St	77091
Davis St	77026
Davon Ln	77058
Dawkins Ln	77014
Dawn Rd	77067
Dawn St	77025
Dawn Canyon Rd	77084
N & S Dawn Cypress Ct	77059
Dawn Harvest Ct & Dr	77064
Dawn Haven Ct	77095
Dawn Hollow Ln	77072
Dawn Meadows Dr	77068
Dawn Point Ct	77065
Dawn Vale Dr	77062
Dawnblush Ct & Ln	77095
Dawnbrook Dr	77068
Dawnchase Ct	77069
Dawnfields Dr	77064
Dawnridge Dr	
5500-6499	77035
7600-8999	77071
Dawnridge Ln	77099
Dawnview St	77087
Dawnwood Dr	77013
Dawson Ln	77051
Dawson Hill Ln	77044
Dawson Mill Ct	77095
Day Rd	77043
Day Hollow Ln	77070
Day Lily Way	77067
Dayco St	77092
Daycoach Ln	77064
Daylight Ln	77095
Daylilly Creek Dr	77083
Dayport St	77091
Dayridge Ln	77048
Dayton St	77012
Daywood Dr	77038
De Boll St	77022
De Forrest St	77066
De George St	77009
De Haven St	77029
De Koven St	77011
De Lange Ln	77092
De Leon St	
3600-4199	77087
8000-8199	77061
De Lozier St	77040
De Milo Dr	
1700-2299	77018
4300-6199	77092
De Moss Dr	
5900-6199	77081
6500-6799	77074
6500-6500	77236
6500-6500	77274
7600-8599	77036
De Priest St	
6200-7299	77091
7300-9000	77088
9002-9098	77088
De Soto St	77091
Deadwood Dr	77040
Deal St	77025
Deams St	77093
Dean St	77039
Deanmont Dr	77053
Deanwood St	77040
Dearborn St	77055
Deaton Mill Dr	77095
Deauville Plaza Dr	77092
Debbie Ln	
1100-1199	77055
9700-9799	77038
Debbie Gay Dr	77040
Debbielou Gardens Dr	77034
Debeney Dr	77039
Debes Rd	77044
Deborah Ln	77092
Deborah St	
7100-7199	77087
8100-8599	77064
Deborah Ann Way	77073
Debra Rd	77013
Debra Terrace Ct	77077
Decatur St	77007
Deckard St	77061
Deeda Dr	77017
Deeds Rd	77084
Deep Forest Cir	77092
Deep Forest Dr	
5300-5400	77092
5402-5598	77092
7000-7599	77088
Deep Meadow Dr	77064
Deep Oak Ct	77059
Deep Prairie Dr	77095
Deep Spring Ln	77077
Deep Valley Dr	77044
Deepcreek Ln	77091
W Deepgrove Dr	77037
Deepwell Ln	77024
Deepwood Dr	77023
Deer Gln	77068
Deer Chase Dr	77082
Deer Cove Ln	77041
Deer Grass Ct	77059
Deer Grass Ln	77044
Deer Key Cir	77084
Deer Leap Dr	77084
Deer Lick Dr	77090
Deer Lodge Dr	77018
N Deer Meadow Dr	77071
Deer Ridge Ln	77086
Deer Sage Ct	77041
Deer Shadow Ct	77041
Deer Track Ct	77064
Deer Trail Dr	
8900-9099	77088
9101-9399	77088
9500-10299	77038
Deerbriar Run Dr	77048
Deerfield St	77022
Deerfield Village Dr	77084
Deergrove St	77039
Deerhurst Ln	77088
Deering Dr	77036
Deerwood Rd	
5900-5998	77057
6000-6399	77057
10300-10799	77042
Defender St	77029
Degas Ln	77016
Deihl Rd	77092
Deirdre Anne Dr	77088
Del Glen Ln	77072
Del Monte Dr	
2100-3999	77019
5100-5699	77056
6100-6599	77057
7500-7999	77063
10000-10799	77042
11300-11599	77077
Del Norte St	77018
Del Papa St	77047
Del Rey Ln	77071
Del Rio St	77021
Del Sur St	77018
Delafield St	77023
Delaney St	77009
Delano St	
100-698	77003
700-1800	77003
1802-1898	77003
2400-5199	77004
N Delano St	77003
Delavan Dr	77028
Delaware St	77029
Delbarton Dr	77083
Delbury St	77085
Delery Dr	77055
Delgado Dr	77083
Delhi St	77022
Delia St	77026
Delilah St	77033
Dell Ct	77009
Dell St	77007
Dell Hollow Dr	77066
Della St	77093
Dellbridge Ln	77073
Dellbrook Dr	77038
Dellfern Ct & Dr	77035
Dellwild Ct	77049
Dellwood Springs Dr	77095
Delmack St	77032
Delman St	77093
Delmar St	
1-300	77011
302-598	77011
600-799	77023
801-999	77023
N Delmar St	77011
Delmas St	77087
Delmont Park Ln	77075
Delphi Ln	77067
Delsanto St	77045
Delta Springs Ln	77084
Delta Wood Ct	77059
Deluxe St	77047
Delwin St	77034
Delwood St	77087
Delwood Springs Ln	77044
E Delz Dr	77022
Delz St	77018
Demarco Ct	77045
Demaree Ln	77029
Demaret Ln	77055
Demontrond St	77090
Demp Nash Ln	77086
Dempley Dr	77041
Den Oak Dr	77065
Denbridge Ct & Dr	77083
Denbury Way	77025
Denby St	77012
Denfield Ct	77070
Denio Dr	77082
Denise Dr	77024
Denise Dale Ln	77084
Denison St	77020
Denman St	77019
Denmark St	
3200-3399	77093
4000-5299	77016
5400-5699	77028
Denning Dr	77078
Dennis St	
1-899	77006
1000-1099	77002
1100-4199	77004
Dennis Way Ln	77044
Denny	77040
Denoron Dr	77048
Denridge Dr	77038
Denslow Cir	77076
Densmore Dr	77035
Dentantr St	77087
Denton St	77028
Dentwood Dr	77014
Denver St	77003
Denver Arbor Ct	77053
Denver Oaks Dr	77065
Depelchin St	77007
Derby Dr	77067
Derbyhall Dr	77066
Derbyshire Dr	77034
Derham Parc St	77024
Dermott Dr	77065
Derrik Dr	77080
Derril Ln	77082
Derrington Rd	77064
Derwent Ln	77064
Des Chaumes St	
1600-1799	77020
1800-4099	77026
Des Jardines St	77023
Desert Canyon Ct & Dr	77041
Desert Cloud Ct & Ln	77040
Desert Flower Ln	77086
Desert Ivy Dr	77094
Desert Maize Ln	77095
Desert Marigold Dr	77073
Desert Rose Ln	77086
Desert Springs Cir	77095
Desert Trace Ct	77044
Desota Glen Ct	77049
Destin Shore Dr	77084
Detering St	77007
Determined Dr	77039
Detric Ln	77053
Detroit St	77017
Deussen Pkwy	77044
Deutser St	77093
Devencrest Dr	77066
Deveron Ln	77090
Devin Ct	77073
Devon St	77027
Devon Glen Dr	77077
Devon Lee Ct	77040
Devoncroft Dr	77031
Devonshire St	77019
Devonshire Crescent Dr	77030
Devonwood Ln	77070
Dew Arbor St	77067
Dew Drop Ln	77095
Dew Mist Ln	77095
Dewalt St	77088
Dewberry St	77021
Dewberry Blossom Ln	77064
Dewberry Crescent Dr	77095
Dewey St	77015
Dewey Eve Ct	77070
Dewgrass Dr	77060
Dewitt Rd	77028
Dewmont Ln	77070
Dewville Ln	
6600-6799	77076
7600-7899	77037
Dexter St	77075
Diakovic Dr	77015
Diamond St	77018
Diamond Bay Ct	77041
Diamond Brook Dr	77062
Diamond Grove Ct	77059
Diamond Lake Ct & Ln	77083
Diamond Leaf Ln	77079
Diamond Ridge Dr	77053
Diamond Springs Dr	77077
Diamond Star Dr	77082
Dian St	77008
Diana Ct	77062
Diana Ln	
15001-15097	77062
15099-16799	77062
16800-17099	77058
Diane Ln	77067
Dickens Rd	77021
Dickey Pl	77019
Dickinson Rd	77089
Dickson St	77007
Dickson Way	77085
Dieppe St	77033
Dierker Dr	77041
Diez St	77023
Dijon Ct & Dr	77015
Dillard Dr	77040
Dillard St	77091
Dillon St	77061
Dillon Hill Cir	77086
Dincans St	77005
Dinorah Ct	77094
Dionne Dr	77076
Diplomat Ct & Way	77088
Diplomatic Plaza Dr	77032
Dipping Ln	77076
Dirby St	77075
Directors Row	77092
Discipline Ave	77014
Discovery Ln	77084
Dismuke St	77023
Distant Rock Ln	77095
Distant Woods Ct & Dr	77095
Distribution Blvd	77018
Ditmas Ln	77021
Dittmans Ct	77020
Dividend St	77013
Division St	77004
Dixie Dr	
2400-4599	77021
6100-8199	77087
Dixie Farm Rd	77089
Doak Ln	77075
Dobbin Stream Ln	77084
Dobson Dr	77032
Dockal Rd	77028
Dockens Forest Ln	77049
Dodd Ln	77077
Dodiewood Ln	77086
Dodson St	77093
Dogwood St	77022
Dogwood Blossom Trl	77065
Dogwood Brook Trl	77062
Dogwood Falls Rd	77095
Dogwood Mountain Rd	77066
Dogwood Springs Dr	77073
Dogwood Tree St	77060
Dogwood View Ln	77064
Dolbeau Dr	77015
Dolben Ct	77088
Doliver Dr	
5000-5699	77056
5700-6299	77057
9400-9699	77063
10000-10099	77042
Dolly Wright St	77088
Dolores St	
5500-5599	77056
5600-5999	77057
Dolphin Ct	77024
Dominic Ln	77049
Dominion Park Dr	77090
Domino Ln	77076
Don Alejandro	77091
Don Gil St	77075
Donald Dr	77076
Doncaster Rd	77024
Donegal Way	77047
Donellan Dr	77088
Doney St	77023
Donforth Dr	77053
Dongered St	77010
Dongerle Dr	77068
Donlen St	77022
Donley Dr	77088
Donna Dr	
10800-10891	77041
10893-10899	77041
12400-12599	77067
Donna Bell Ln	77018
Donna Lynn Ct & Dr	77092
Donnacorey Dr	77013
Donnet Ln	77032
Donoho St	77033
W Donovan St	77091
Donrel Way	77067
Donwhite Ln	77088
Donys Ct & Dr	77040
Doolittle Blvd	77033
Dora St	77005
Doral Ln	77073
Doraldale Ct	77040
Doran Ln	77032
Dorbrandt St	77023
Dorchester St	
100-1199	77022
3700-4199	77016
Dorchester Forest Dr	77070
Doris Oaks Cir	77028
Dorita Ln	77038
Dormstom Ln	77088
Dornoch Dr	77070
Dorothy St	
700-899	77007
900-1599	77008
Dorothy Ann Dr	77076
Dorrance Rd	77031
Dorray Ln	77082
Dorrcrest Ln	77070
Dorrington St	77030
Dorsetshire Dr	77040
Dorsett St	77029
Dorwayne Ct	77015
Dorywood Rd	77038
Dosia St	77051
Doskocil Dr	77044
Dotson Rd	77070
Double Ave	77088
Double Lilly Dr	77095
Double Pine Dr	77015
Double Shoals Cir	77090
Double Tree Dr	77070
Doubleday Dr	77089
Doubletree Glen Dr	77073
Doubletree Park Dr	77073
Doud St	77035
Douglas St	77018
Douglas Fir St	77066
Douglas Lake Rd	77044
Doulton Dr	77033
Dounreay Dr	77084
Dove St	77015
Dove Way	77075
Dove Brook Ct	77041
Dove Creek Cir	77086
Dove Fern Ct	77041
Dove Oaks Ct	77041
Dove Park Ct	77075
Dove Point Ln	77041
Dove Prairie Ct	77041
Dove Ridge Ln	77041
Dove Shores Ct	77044
Dove Springs Dr	77066
Dovecott Ln	77083
Dovedale Ct	77067
Dover Mdw	77070
Dover St	
2800-3699	77017
3700-4199	77087
8100-8899	77061
8901-8999	77061
11300-12399	77031
W Doverfield Dr	77037
Doverside St	77022
Doverwood Way	77058
Doves Nest Ct	77090
Dow Rd	77040
Dowber Rd	77076
Dowling St	
300-2299	77003
2300-5399	77004
5401-5499	77004
Dowlwood Dr	77032
Downey St	77076
Downey Violet Ln	77044
Downgate Dr	77084
Downheath Ln	77073
Downing St	77020
Downs Ln	77093
Downwood Forest Dr	77088
Doyle St	77093
Dracaena Ct	77070
Dragonwick Dr	77045
Dragonwood Trl	77083
Drake St	77005
Drakeford Ct	77047
Drakemill Dr	77077
Drakestone Blvd	77053
Drane Ct	77008
Draper Rd	77014
Drava Ln	77090
Draycott Ln	77045
Drayton Ln	77088
Dream Ct	77085

Dreamscape Cir ... 77047
N Drennan St ... 77003
Drenner Park Ln ... 77086
Dresden St ... 77012
Dresden Ridge Ln ... 77070
Drew St
98A-98D ... 77006
1-899 ... 77006
1011-1049 ... 77002
1051-1099 ... 77002
1101-1129 ... 77004
1131-4199 ... 77004
W Drew St ... 77006
Drewberry St ... 77080
Drexel Cir & Dr ... 77027
Drexel Hill Dr ... 77077
Drexelbrook Dr ... 77077
Dreyfus St
1000-1199 ... 77030
3500-4499 ... 77021
Drifting Oaks Ct & Dr ... 77095
Drifting Pine Ct ... 77066
Drifting Winds Dr ... 77044
Driftwood St ... 77021
Driftwood Oak Ct ... 77059
Driftwood Park Dr ... 77095
Driftwood Prairie Ln ... 77095
Dripping Springs Dr ... 77083
Driscoll St
1500-2599 ... 77019
3800-4299 ... 77098
Droddy St ... 77091
Drouet St ... 77061
Drowsy Pine Dr ... 77092
Droxford Dr ... 77008
Druid St ... 77091
Drum Roll Dr ... 77064
Drumcliffe Ct ... 77015
Drummond St ... 77025
Drummond Cliff Ln ... 77064
Drummond Park Dr ... 77044
Drury Ln ... 77055
Dryad Dr ... 77035
Dryberry Ct ... 77083
Dryden Rd ... 77030
Dryden Mills Ln ... 77070
Drysdale Ln ... 77041
Drystone Ln ... 77095
Du Barry Ln ... 77018
Du Bois St ... 77051
Du Boise Rd ... 77091
Du Lock Ln ... 77055
Duan St ... 77022
Duane Ct ... 77047
Duane St
8600-9199 ... 77051
10600-12199 ... 77047
Duart Dr ... 77024
Dublin St ... 77085
Duchamp Dr ... 77036
Duchess Ct ... 77024
Duchess Ln ... 77070
Duckett Park Dr ... 77086
Ducklake Ln ... 77084
Duckwater Cv ... 77095
Dude Rd ... 77064
Dudley St ... 77021
Duff Ln ... 77022
Duffer Ln ... 77034
Duffield Ln ... 77071
Duke St ... 77005
Duke Of York Ct & Ln ... 77070
Dulaney Rd ... 77084
Dulcimer St ... 77051
Dulcrest St ... 77051
Duller Ln ... 77017
Duluth St ... 77015
Dumas St ... 77034
Dumbarton St ... 77025
Dumble St
400-599 ... 77011
601-697 ... 77023
699-2099 ... 77023
6300-7099 ... 77021
Dumfries Dr ... 77096
Dumore Dr ... 77048

Dunain Park Ct ... 77095
Dunaway St ... 77015
Dunbar St ... 77009
Dunbeath Dr ... 77024
Dunbrook Dr ... 77070
Duncan Rd ... 77066
Duncan St ... 77093
Duncannon Dr ... 77015
Duncansby Vale Rd ... 77095
Duncaster Dr ... 77079
Duncum St
10300-10899 ... 77013
13700-14699 ... 77015
Dune Brook Dr ... 77089
Dunfield Ln ... 77099
Dunham Dr ... 77076
Dunhaven Ct ... 77062
Dunhurst Ln ... 77047
Dunkirk Rd ... 77033
Dunkley Dr ... 77076
Dunlap St
6500-6598 ... 77074
6600-9099 ... 77074
9101-9199 ... 77074
10600-11199 ... 77096
11400-12699 ... 77035
12800-13399 ... 77085
Dunlavy St
700-1499 ... 77019
1500-5299 ... 77006
Dunlop St ... 77009
Dunman Ln ... 77044
Dunmoor Dr ... 77059
Dunmore Ct ... 77069
Dunnam Ln ... 77024
Dunnethead Dr ... 77084
Dunraven Ln ... 77019
Dunsford Ct ... 77083
Dunsinane St ... 77024
Dunsmere St
4600-4999 ... 77018
5400-5499 ... 77091
Dunson Glen Dr ... 77090
Dunstan Rd ... 77005
Duntriv St ... 77019
Dunvale Rd ... 77063
Dunvegan Way ... 77013
Dunwick St ... 77048
Dunwoody Dr ... 77076
Duoto St ... 77091
Dupont St ... 77021
Dupree St ... 77054
Dural Dr ... 77094
Duran Canyon Ct & Ln ... 77067
Duran Falls Ct ... 77044
Durango Dr ... 77055
Durango Bay Ln ... 77041
Durango Point Ln ... 77070
Durango Way Dr ... 77040
Durban Dr
2600-3099 ... 77043
4400-4499 ... 77041
Durbridge Ct ... 77065
Durbridge Trail Dr ... 77065
Durford St ... 77007
Durham Dr ... 77007
N Durham Dr
700-2799 ... 77008
3000-3099 ... 77018
Durham Chase Ln ... 77095
Durham Manor Ln ... 77075
Durhill St ... 77025
Durklyn Ln ... 77070
Durley Dr ... 77079
Durness Way ... 77025
Durrette Dr ... 77024
Durwood St ... 77093
Dusk Haven Ln ... 77095
Dusty Dawn Dr ... 77086
Dusty Hollow Ln ... 77089
Dusty Ridge Ln ... 77044
Dusty Trail Dr ... 77086
Dutton Trace Ln ... 77082
Duval St ... 77087
Duxbury St ... 77035

Dwarf Honey Suckle Ct ... 77084
Dwight St ... 77015
Dwinnell St ... 77023
Dwyer Rd ... 77090
Dyer Gln ... 77070
Dyer St ... 77088
Dyer Brook Dr ... 77041
Dyer Lake Ln ... 77008
Dylans Crossing Dr ... 77038
Dylans Point Ct ... 77084
Dyna Dr ... 77060
W Dyna Dr ... 77037
Dyson Ln ... 77041
E St ... 77072
Each Elm Way ... 77084
Eagan Mill Dr ... 77077
Eagle Lndg ... 77085
Eagle St
1001-1099 ... 77002
1100-3799 ... 77004
Eagle Bluff Ct ... 77082
Eagle Creek Ln ... 77036
Eagle Falls Ct & St ... 77077
Eagle Fork Dr ... 77084
Eagle Glen Dr ... 77041
Eagle Island Ln ... 77034
Eagle Pass St
6300-7599 ... 77020
13700-14699 ... 77015
Eagle Ridge Way ... 77084
Eagle Trail Dr ... 77084
Eagle View Ln ... 77067
Eagle Vista Dr ... 77077
Eaglecove Dr ... 77064
Eaglerock Dr ... 77080
Eagles Glide Dr ... 77090
Eaglewood Dr ... 77089
Eaglewood Glen Trl ... 77083
Eaglewood Shadow Ct & Dr ... 77083
Eaglewood Spring Ct & Dr ... 77083
Earhart St ... 77028
Earl St ... 77098
Earle St ... 77030
Earline St ... 77016
Earlswood Dr ... 77083
Early Ln ... 77055
Early Dew Ct ... 77045
E Early Dusk Cir ... 77044
Early Elm Ct ... 77049
Early Forest Ln ... 77043
Early Green Trl ... 77084
Early Harvest Cir ... 77064
Early Mist Ct ... 77064
Early Spring Cir & Dr ... 77064
Early Square Ct ... 77070
Earnestwood Dr ... 77083
Easingwold Dr ... 77015
East Fwy
1100-1199 ... 77002
1600-7799 ... 77020
7800-12199 ... 77029
12201-12297 ... 77015
12299-14724 ... 77015
14726-14798 ... 77015
East Ln ... 77026
East Loop N ... 77029
East Rd ... 77054
East St ... 77007
Eastbourne Dr ... 77034
Eastbrook Dr ... 77013
Eastcove Cir ... 77064
Easten St ... 77014
Easter St
5900-5999 ... 77091
7000-8699 ... 77088
Easterling Dr ... 77065
Eastern Redbud Ln ... 77044
Eastern Run Trl ... 77038
Eastex Fwy
1300-1598 ... 77020
1600-1699 ... 77020
1801-1897 ... 77026
1899-6499 ... 77026
6600-11699 ... 77093
11700-13599 ... 77039
13901-14399 ... 77032
Eastgate St ... 77012
Eastgrove Ln ... 77027
Easthampton Dr ... 77039
Easthaven Blvd
6800-6998 ... 77017
7000-7899 ... 77017
8000-8199 ... 77034
8400-8598 ... 77075
8600-10099 ... 77075
Eastheimer St ... 77064
Eastlake St ... 77034
Eastland St ... 77028
Eastleigh Ln ... 77049
Eastman St
2400-2899 ... 77009
3000-3299 ... 77022
Eastmoore Ct ... 77014
Easton St ... 77017
Easton Commons Dr ... 77095
Easton Park Dr ... 77095
Eastover St ... 77028
Eastpark Dr ... 77028
Eastside St
2500-2599 ... 77019
3000-3899 ... 77098
Eastwood Cir ... 77095
Eastwood St
1-324 ... 77011
326-506 ... 77011
600-1999 ... 77023
5800-7199 ... 77021
N Eastwood St ... 77011
Easy St ... 77026
Eaton Ct ... 77024
Eaton Sq ... 77027
Eaton St ... 77030
Eavesdown Ct ... 77095
Ebb St ... 77089
Ebbtide Dr ... 77045
Eberhard St ... 77019
Eblen Dr ... 77040
Ebony Ln ... 77018
Ebury Dr ... 77066
Echo Ln ... 77024
Echo Brook Dr
6600-6699 ... 77076
7600-7899 ... 77037
Echo Canyon Dr ... 77084
Echo Falls Ln ... 77095
Echo Glade Ct ... 77064
E & W Echo Glen Dr ... 77076
Echo Grove Ln ... 77043
Echo Hill Dr ... 77059
Echo Hollow St ... 77024
Echo Lake Ln ... 77069
Echo Landing Dr ... 77070
Echo Ledge St ... 77067
Echo Lodge Dr ... 77095
Echo Mar Ln ... 77084
Echo Point Ln ... 77095
Echo Spring Ln ... 77065
Echo Valley Dr ... 77055
Echo Wood St ... 77024
Eclipse St ... 77018
Ector ... 77056
Eddie St ... 77026
Eddington St ... 77023
Eddlemont Dr ... 77049
Eddlewood Ct ... 77049
Eddyrock St ... 77089
Eddys Edge Ct ... 77089
Eddystone Dr ... 77043
Edell St ... 77093
Eden St ... 77012
Eden Falls Cir & Ct ... 77095
Eden Manor Ln ... 77044
Eden Park Ln ... 77018
Eden Springs Ln ... 77041
Eden Trails Ln ... 77094
Edena Dr ... 77049
Edenglen Ct & Dr ... 77049
Edenhollow Ct ... 77049
Edenport Ct ... 77049

Edenway Ct ... 77049
Edfield St
4500-4599 ... 77051
4600-5099 ... 77033
Edgar Rd ... 77039
Edgar St
8700-9199 ... 77051
10600-11999 ... 77047
Edge Branch Ln ... 77044
Edgebaston Ct ... 77073
Edgeboro St ... 77049
Edgebrook Dr ... 77034
E Edgebrook Dr ... 77034
Edgebrook St ... 77075
Edgebrook Forest Ct & Dr ... 77088
Edgecreek Dr ... 77066
Edgefield Lakes Dr ... 77054
Edgegrove Ct ... 77014
Edgehill Dr ... 77049
Edgemont Dr ... 77053
Edgemoor Dr
5501-5597 ... 77081
5599-6199 ... 77081
6300-7299 ... 77074
7800-8899 ... 77036
Edgeton Ct ... 77015
Edgevale Ct ... 77095
Edgeview Rd ... 77084
Edgewater Dr
4800-5099 ... 77093
14500-14699 ... 77047
Edgeway Dr ... 77055
Edgewick Ct ... 77069
Edgewood Dr ... 77059
Edgewood St
2-98 ... 77011
100-322 ... 77011
324-398 ... 77011
600-699 ... 77023
N Edgewood St ... 77011
Edgewood Park Dr ... 77038
Edgewood Village Trl ... 77049
Edgeworth St ... 77093
Edgware Dr ... 77084
Edinburg St ... 77087
Edinburgh Ct ... 77077
Edison St ... 77009
Edison Park Ln ... 77081
Edisto Ct ... 77084
Edith St
5300-5499 ... 77096
5500-5699 ... 77081
Edloe St
2600-3499 ... 77027
5135-5197 ... 77005
5199-6799 ... 77005
7200-7299 ... 77025
Edmont Ln ... 77088
Edmund St ... 77020
Edmundson St
1300-1999 ... 77003
2200-2299 ... 77004
Edna St ... 77087
Edo Cir ... 77083
Edsee St ... 77009
Edward Dr ... 77032
Edwards St
1000-2399 ... 77007
10100-10199 ... 77086
Edwina Blvd ... 77045
Effingham Dr ... 77035
Egan St ... 77020
Egbert St ... 77007
Egret Bay Blvd ... 77058
Egret Field Ln ... 77049
Egret Hill Ct ... 77089
Egret Meadow Ln ... 77084
Egret Oaks Ln ... 77058
Egypt St ... 77009
Eichler Dr ... 77036
Eichwurzel Ln ... 77009
Eigel St ... 77007
Eisenhower Rd ... 77033
El Buey Rd ... 77034
El Buey Way ... 77017

El Camino St ... 77054
El Camino Del Rey St ... 77081
El Camino Real
14000-14918 ... 77062
El Camino Real
14917-14917 ... 77259
14917-14917 ... 77289
14919-16799 ... 77062
14920-16798 ... 77062
16800-18099 ... 77058
El Camino Village Dr ... 77058
El Capitan Dr ... 77083
El Centro St ... 77018
El Cresta Dr ... 77083
El Diamante Dr ... 77048
El Dorado Blvd
600-1999 ... 77062
3101-3199 ... 77059
El Dorado Oaks Ct & Dr ... 77059
El Granate Dr ... 77048
El Grande Dr ... 77083
El Miranda Dr ... 77095
El Mundo St ... 77054
El Oro Dr ... 77048
El Padre Dr ... 77083
El Paseo St ... 77054
El Paso St ... 77020
El Pico Dr ... 77083
El Rancho St ... 77087
El Rio St ... 77054
El Salvador Dr ... 77066
El Sereno Dr ... 77083
El Tesoro Dr ... 77083
El Toro Ln ... 77062
Elaine Rd ... 77047
Elbeck Dr ... 77035
Elbert St
3000-3099 ... 77098
6800-9199 ... 77028
Elberta St
1000-1299 ... 77051
5700-5899 ... 77050
Elder St
900-999 ... 77002
1100-1299 ... 77007
Elderberry Ln ... 77049
Elderwood Dr ... 77058
Eldon St ... 77060
Eldora Dr ... 77080
Eldora Springs Ct ... 77070
Eldorado Centre Ln ... 77069
Eldoro Canyon Ln ... 77095
Eldridge Pkwy
1001-2299 ... 77077
2500-3999 ... 77082
6900-7599 ... 77083
Eldridge Pkwy S ... 77077
N Eldridge Pkwy
600-999 ... 77079
4000-4099 ... 77084
5600-8699 ... 77041
9600-12199 ... 77065
13800-14999 ... 77070
Eldridge Chase Ct ... 77041
Eldridge Garden Cir ... 77083
Eldridge Glen Dr ... 77041
Eldridge Meadow Ct & Dr ... 77041
Eldridge Place Dr ... 77041
Eldridge Springs Way ... 77083
Eldridge Trace Dr ... 77083
Eldridge Valley Dr ... 77083
Eldridge View Dr ... 77083
Eleanor St ... 77009
Eleanor Tinsley Way ... 77023
Electra Dr
100-299 ... 77079
300-599 ... 77024
600-799 ... 77079
Elegant Way ... 77066
Elegia Dr ... 77080
Elfwood Ct ... 77015
Elgin Ct ... 77004
Elgin St
400-899 ... 77006
1000-3599 ... 77004
3601-4399 ... 77004
Eli St ... 77007
Elia Ct ... 77044
Elias Peak Ct ... 77073
Elise Dr ... 77047
Elizabeth Ct ... 77025
Elizabeth Rd ... 77055
Elizabeth Rose Ct & Dr ... 77089
Elk Hill Ct ... 77062
Elk Park Ln ... 77062
Elk Point Ln ... 77064
Elk River Cir & Rd ... 77090
Elk Run Cir ... 77079
Elk Springs Dr ... 77067
Elk Valley Cir ... 77090
Elkdale Dr ... 77082
Elkhart St ... 77091
Elkington Ct ... 77071
Elkins Rd ... 77060
Elkins Creek Ct ... 77044
Elkwood Dr ... 77038
Elkwood Forest Dr ... 77088
Ell Rd ... 77093
Ella Blvd ... 77038
N & S Ella Creek Dr ... 77067
Ella Lee Ln
2300-3399 ... 77019
3400-4099 ... 77027
5600-5699 ... 77056
6100-6499 ... 77057
7800-9599 ... 77063
10000-11099 ... 77042
11300-14399 ... 77077
Ella Ridge Ln ... 77067
Ella View Ln ... 77067
Ellen Ln ... 77015
Ellena Rd ... 77076
Ellenville Dr ... 77089
Ellerton Ln ... 77090
Ellesmere Dr ... 77015
Ellinger Ln ... 77040
Ellington Fld ... 77034
Ellington St ... 77088
Elliott St ... 77023
Ellis Ct ... 77020
Ellis Sands Ln ... 77044
Elliston St ... 77023
Elm Ave ... 77044
Elm St
5100-5298 ... 77081
5300-6200 ... 77081
6202-6298 ... 77081
7400-7799 ... 77023
E Elm St ... 77012
Elm Bayou Ct ... 77064
Elm Bluff Ct ... 77064
Elm Bough Ct ... 77065
Elm Bridge Ct ... 77065
Elm Crest Trl ... 77059
Elm Edge Way ... 77084
Elm Estates Dr ... 77077
Elm Heights Ln ... 77081
Elm Hill Ct ... 77084
Elm Knoll Ct & Trl ... 77064
Elm Lake Dr ... 77083
Elm Meadow Trl ... 77064
Elm Park Way ... 77058
Elm Point Ct ... 77095
Elm Shores Dr ... 77044
Elm Springs Dr ... 77048
Elm Trail Ln ... 77014
Elm Tree Dr ... 77048
Elm View Cir ... 77084
Elmbank Dr ... 77095
Elmcrest Dr ... 77088
Elmcroft Dr ... 77099
Elmdale Dr ... 77070
Elmdon Dr ... 77084
Elmen St ... 77019
Elmfield St ... 77047
Elmgate Dr ... 77080
Elmhurst St ... 77075
Elmlawn Dr ... 77033
Elmont Dr ... 77095
Elmora St ... 77005

Elmpark Ct 77014
Elmridge St 77025
Elmsford Ct 77083
Elmsgrove Ln 77070
Elmside Dr 77042
Elmsworth Dr 77099
Elmview Dr & Pl 77080
Elmview Trace Ln 77080
Elmwood St 77051
Elmwood Glen Ct 77095
Elmwood Park Ct 77059
Elpyco St 77051
Elrod St 77017
Elroy St 77009
Elsbury St 77006
Elser St 77009
Elsie Ln 77064
Elsies Ln 77015
Elstree Dr 77015
Elton St 77034
Elvera St 77012
Elwood Dr 77040
Elwood St 77012
Elysian St
1100-1299 77020
1400-2399 77026
2400-5899 77009
Embarcadero Dr 77082
Embassy Plaza Dr 77032
Ember Glen Ct 77095
Ember Isles Ln 77041
Ember Lake Rd 77066
Ember Sky Ct 77094
Ember Trails Ct & Dr 77094
Emberwood Dr 77070
Emberwood View Ln 77075
Embla Dr 77049
Embry St 77009
Embry Hills Dr 77073
Embry Stone Ln 77047
Emeashi Dr 77060
Emeashil St 77004
Emerald Brk 77041
Emerald Ct
100-199 77009
1900-1999 77094
Emerald Cv 77077
Emerald Dr 77074
Emerald Bluff Ct 77095
Emerald Briar Ln 77084
Emerald Creek Dr 77070
Emerald Falls Ct & Dr 77059
Emerald Garden Ln 77084
Emerald Glen Ln 77070
Emerald Green Dr & Ln 77094
Emerald Heights Ct & Ln 77083
Emerald Hill Dr 77070
Emerald Isle Dr 77095
Emerald Lake Ct 77062
Emerald Leaf Dr 77094
Emerald Oaks Dr 77070
Emerald Park Dr 77070
Emerald Pine Dr 77070
Emerald Ridge Ln 77094
Emerald Shire Ln 77041
Emerald Shore Ct 77095
Emerald Springs Ct & Dr 77094
Emerald Stone Ln 77094
Emerald Trail Dr 77070
Emerald Tree Cir 77084
Emerald Valley Ct 77095
Emerald Wood Dr 77070
Emerson St 77006
Emery Dr 77099
N Emile St 77020
Emite Ct 77011
Emma Lou St 77088
Emmett Rd 77041
Emmott Rd 77040
Emnora Ln
8500-8598 77080
8600-9321 77080
9320-9320 77243
9320-9320 77280
9322-10198 77080
9323-10199 77080
10200-10699 77043
Emory Ave 77005
Empanada Dr 77083
Emperor Ln 77072
Empire Central Dr 77040
Emporia St 77015
Empress Dr 77034
Empress Oaks Ct 77082
Empson Dr 77032
Emsworth Cir 77077
Enchanted Forest Dr 77088
Enchanted Isle Dr 77062
Enchanted Path Dr 77044
Enchanted Rock Dr 77073
Enchanted Stone Ct & Dr 77070
Encinita Dr 77083
Encino Cove Ct 77064
Encino Pass Trl 77064
Enclave Ln, Pkwy, Sq & Trl E, N, S & W 77077
Enclave At Shady Acres Ct 77008
Enclave Fountains Ln 77091
Enclave Lake Dr 77077
Enclave Waters Ln 77091
Encreek Rd 77068
Endicott Ln
8600-9499 77096
10600-11599 77035
Endor St 77012
Enero Dr 77083
Engel St 77011
Engelke St 77003
Engelmohr St 77054
England Ct & St 77021
Englebrook Dr 77095
Engleford St 77026
Englewood St 77026
English St 77009
English Elm St 77067
English Rose Ln 77082
Enid St
200-5799 77009
6500-6699 77022
Enmore Ct 77095
Ennis St
304-1899 77003
3000-5599 77004
N Ennis St 77003
Ennsbury Dr 77084
Enoch St 77054
Enos St 77086
Enridge Ln 77048
Ensbrook Dr 77099
Ensemble Ct & Dr 77040
Ensenada Dr 77083
Ensenada Canyon Ln 77041
Ensley Wood Dr 77082
Ensworth Dr 77016
Enterprise St 77088
Envoy St 77016
Enyart St 77021
Eola Creek Ln 77049
Epernay Pl 77040
Eppes St
4700-4999 77021
6300-7299 77087
Eppingdale Dr 77066
Epsom Rd 77093
Equador St 77040
Equity Dr 77041
Erastus St
1900-2499 77020
2800-3699 77026
Erath St 77023
E Erath St 77012
Erby St
3600-3899 77023
3900-4199 77087
Erica Ln 77051
Ericston Dr 77070
Erie St
3700-3799 77017
3900-4199 77087
8000-8099 77061
Erin Ct 77071
Erin St 77009
Erin Cove Ct 77095
Erin Creek Ct 77062
Erin Dale Ct 77083
Erin Knoll Ct 77059
Erin Way Ct 77095
Ernestine St 77023
Ernie Rd 77016
Errington Dr 77049
Erskine Ct 77070
Ertel Ln 77040
Erwin Rd 77039
Escondido Cir & Dr 77083
Eskridge St 77023
Esperanza St 77023
Esperson St 77011
Espinosa Dr 77083
Esplanade Blvd 77060
Essenbruk Dr 77066
Essendine Ln 77045
Essex Ln & Ter 77027
Essex Green St 77027
Essie Rd 77086
Essman Ln 77073
Estaril Cir 77038
Estella Ln 77090
N Estelle St 77003
Esterbrook Dr 77082
Estes Glen Ln 77040
Estes Park Ln 77067
Esther Dr 77088
Estrada Dr 77083
Estrella Ct 77045
Estrellita Dr 77060
Ethel St 77028
Etheline Dr 77039
Etheridge St 77087
Eton St 77087
Eton Brook Ln 77073
Etta St 77093
Ettrick Dr 77035
Eubanks St
400-1299 77022
1700-2099 77093
Euclaire Dr 77086
Euclid St 77009
Euel St 77009
Eugene St 77093
Eunice St
3100-3199 77009
17800-18099 77044
Eureka St 77008
Europa St 77022
Eva St 77093
Evangeline Dr 77013
Evans St 77061
Evanston St 77015
Eve St 77013
Evella St 77026
N Evelyn Cir 77071
S Evelyn Cir 77071
Evelyn St 77009
Evendale Ct 77094
Evening Shore Ct & Dr 77041
Everest Ln 77073
Everett St 77009
Everett Oaks Ln 77095
Everglade Dr 77078
Evergreen Dr
700-899 77023
1000-4933 77087
4935-4999 77087
Evergreen St 77081
Evergreen Bay Ct 77059
Evergreen Brook Way 77095
Evergreen Canyon Rd 77066
Evergreen Elm Ct & Way 77059
Evergreen Falls Dr 77084
Evergreen Grove Dr 77083
Evergreen Haven Ct 77084
Evergreen Oak Dr 77068
Evergreen Place Dr 77083
Evergreen Ridge Way 77062
Evergreen Terrace Ln 77040
Everhart Ln 77040
Evermore Manor Ln 77073
N & S Evers Park Dr 77024
Everseen Ln 77040
N Everton St 77003
Everwood Ln 77024
Evesborough Dr 77099
Evesham Dr 77015
Evonne St 77017
Ewing St 77004
Exbury Way 77056
Excalibur Ct 77094
Exchange St 77020
Exeter St 77093
Explorer Dr 77044
Export Plaza Dr 77032
Express Ln 77078
Exton Ln 77070
Ezzard Charles Ln 77091
F St 77072
Faber St 77037
Fabiola Dr 77075
Faculty Ln 77004
Fadeway Ln 77045
N Fair Ct 77073
Fair St 77088
Fair Acres St 77072
Fair Elm Ct 77082
Fair Forest Dr 77088
E & W Fair Harbor Ln 77079
Fair Knoll Way 77062
Fair Oaks Rd 77023
Fair Park Dr 77014
Fairbanks St
200-1799 77009
2400-4499 77026
Fairbanks N Houston Rd
5600-7999 77040
8000-10299 77064
Fairbanks White Oak Rd 77040
Fairbend St 77055
Fairbloom Ln 77040
Fairbuff Ln 77014
Fairbury Dr 77089
Fairchild St 77028
Faircrest Ln 77076
Faircroft Dr
9200-9299 77033
10600-10999 77048
Fairdale Ln
5300-5599 77056
5600-6599 77057
7600-9699 77063
Fairdale Oaks E & W 77057
Fairday Ln 77076
Fairfax St 77029
Fairfield St 77023
Fairgate Dr 77094
Fairgate Ln 77075
Fairgrange Key Ln 77073
Fairgreen Ln
4100-4399 77047
4700-5499 77048
Fairgrove Park Ct & Dr 77095
Fairgrove Ridge Dr 77045
Fairhill Dr 77063
N & S Fairhollow Ln 77043
Fairhope Pl & St 77025
Fairhope Oak Ct & St 77084
Fairland Dr 77051
Fairlane Dr 77024
Fairlane Oaks Dr 77070
Fairlawn St 77087
Fairmeadow Dr 77071
Fairmont St
5000-5200 77005
5202-5498 77005
11300-11899 77035
Fairplum Dr 77099
Fairpoint Dr 77099
Fairport Ln 77079
Fairstone Dr 77064
Fairvalley Dr 77068
Fairview St
100-1899 77006
1900-2299 77019
7000-7999 77041
Fairview Forest Dr 77088
Fairview Valley Ct 77084
Fairway Ct 77088
Fairway Dr
6300-7499 77087
11100-11199 77064
Fairway Estates Dr 77068
Fairway Park Dr 77092
Fairway Square Dr 77084
Fairwind Dr 77062
Fairwood Dr 77088
Fairwood Meadow Ct 77084
Faith Pl 77085
Falba Rd 77070
Falcon Rd 77064
Falcon St 77015
Falcon Pass Dr 77062
Falcon Reach Dr 77080
Falcons Cove Dr 77095
Falkirk Ln 77025
Fall St 77054
Fall Breeze Dr 77064
Fall Chase Ct 77044
E Fall Fern Cir 77044
Fall Glen Dr 77040
Fall Grove Ct 77059
Fall Hollow Dr 77041
Fall Meadow Ln 77039
Fall Point Dr 77065
Fall River Cir 77090
Fall River Ct 77024
Fall River Rd 77024
Fall Shadows Ct 77059
Fall Valley Dr 77077
Fallbrook Dr
100-3199 77038
4400-4499 77018
6300-7899 77086
7900-11099 77064
11100-12199 77065
Fallcrest Dr 77065
Falleadw Dr 77014
E & N Fallen Bough Dr 77041
Fallen Leaf Way 77058
Fallen Oak Rd 77038
Fallen Oaks Dr 77091
Fallen Palms Ct 77042
Fallen Pine Ln 77088
Fallen Woods Dr 77080
Falling Cherry Pl 77049
Falling Creek Dr
14500-14599 77014
14600-15799 77068
Falling Elm Ln 77015
Falling Leaf Ln 77024
Falling Limb Ct 77049
Falling Oaks Rd 77038
Falling Rapids Ct 77070
Falling River Dr 77095
Falling Tree Ct 77015
Fallmont Cir, Ct & Dr 77086
Falloon Ln 77013
Fallow Ln 77049
Falls St 77026
S Falls Ter 77095
Falls At Fairdale 77057
Falls Church Dr 77067
Falls Coppice Ln 77089
Fallsbridge Dr 77065
Fallstone Rd 77099
Fallsview Ln 77077
Fallwood Dr 77065
Falmouth Ave 77084
Falmouth Dr 77059
Falvey St 77017
Falworth Dr 77060
Famcamp Rd 77034
Family Cir 77085
Fana Ct 77032
Fannette St 77029
Fannin St
2-98 77002
100-900 77002
901-999 77010
902-2998 77002
1001-2999 77002
3000-5799 77004
6400-7399 77030
7400-9299 77054
9400-10099 77045
Fannin Sta 77045
Fannin Sta E 77045
Fannin Sta N 77045
Fannin Sta S 77045
Fannin Sta W 77045
Fantasy Dr 77039
Fantasy Woods Dr 77094
Far Point Ct 77095
Faraday Dr 77047
Farb Dr 77016
Farber St 77005
Fargo St 77006
Fargo Woods Cir & Dr 77015
Farhills Ct 77090
Faring Rd 77049
Farish Cir 77024
Fariss St 77054
Farlan Ln 77014
Farley Dr 77032
Farley Rd 77034
Farley Pass Dr 77095
Farlington Cir 77077
Farmer St 77020
Farmingham Dr 77099
Farmington St 77080
Farndale Dr 77062
Farnham St 77098
Farnham Park Dr 77024
Farnington Dr 77084
Farnsfield Dr 77084
Farnsworth St 77022
Farqueson St 77029
Farragut St 77078
Farrell Dr 77070
Farrell Rd 77073
Farrell St 77022
Farther Pt 77024
Farwell Dr 77035
Farwood St 77009
Fashion St 77023
Fashion Hill Dr 77088
Fastgreen Cir 77089
Fathom Ln 77062
Fatima Ln 77091
Fatima Lake Dr 77099
Faucette St 77023
Faulkey Gully Cir & Ct 77070
Faulkner St 77021
Fauna St 77061
Fauna Woods Ct 77044
Faust Ln 77024
Favian Ct 77083
Fawcett Dr 77069
Fawn Ct 77015
Fawn Dr 77015
Fawn Vis 77068
Fawn Run Ln 77084
Fawn Terrace Dr 77071
Fawn Villa Dr 77068
Fawn Wind Ct 77040
Fawncliff Dr 77069
Fawncrest Dr 77038
Fawndale Ln 77040
Fawngrove Dr 77048
Fawnhope Dr 77008
Fawnlake Dr 77079
Fawnridge Dr 77028
Fawnshadow Ct 77064
Fawnview Dr 77070
Fawnway Dr 77048
Fay St 77023
Fayette St 77056
Fayridge Dr 77048
Faywood Dr 77060
Feagan St 77007
Feamster Dr 77022
Feather Craft Ln 77058
Feather Creek Dr 77086
Feather Fall Ln 77095
Feather Springs Dr 77095
Featherstar Ln 77067
Featherstone St 77020
N Featherwood Dr 77034
Federal Rd 77015
Feland St 77028
Feld Dr 77053
Feldman St 77045
Feldspar St 77092
Felecia St 77091
Felgate Creek Ct & Dr 77084
Felice Dr 77081
Felicia Oaks Trl 77064
Fellows Rd 77047
Felt Cir 77011
Fenland Field Ln 77047
Fenn St 77018
Fennell St 77012
Fennemore St 77086
Fenton Pl 77073
Fenwick St 77009
Fenwood Rd 77005
Ferdinand St 77051
Fergus Park Ct 77047
Ferguson Way 77088
Feridald Dr 77077
Ferieriv Dr 77059
Fern Dr 77079
Fern Basin Dr 77084
Fern Forest Dr 77044
Fern Grove Ln 77059
Fern Meadow Ln 77039
Fern Mill Ct 77041
Fern Ridge Dr 77084
Fern Shadows Ct 77084
Fern Springs Ct 77062
Fern Terrace Dr 77075
Fern Trail Ct 77084
Fern Vale Ct 77065
Fern Valley Dr 77044
Fern Walk Ct 77089
Fern Wood Frst 77040
Fernbank Dr 77049
Fernbrook Ln 77070
Fernbush Dr 77073
Fernchase Cir & Ct 77095
Ferncliff Ln 77095
Ferncrest Ct 77070
Ferndale 77017
Ferndale St 77098
N Ferndale Place Dr 77064
Ferndale View Dr 77064
Ferndale Way Dr 77064
Ferndell St 77016
Fernglade Dr 77068
Fernlake Dr 77049
Fernlea St 77016
Fernspray Ln 77084
Fernstone Ln 77070
Fernway Ln 77049
Fernwood Dr 77021
Fernwood Way 77058
Ferol Rd 77016
Ferrara Dr 77083
Ferraro Ln 77037
Ferris Dr
6300-6598 77081
8500-9099 77096
Ferry Hill Ln 77015
Festival Dr 77062
Fetlock Dr 77065
Feuhs Ln 77022
Fichter St 77022
Fiddlers Green Dr 77082
Fidelia Ct 77024
Fidelity St 77029
Field Brook Ct 77089
Field Manor Ln 77047
Field Ridge Dr 77095
Field Run Ct 77049
Field Springs Ln 77059
Field Stone Dr 77041

Field View Ct 77075
Fieldbrook Dr 77077
Fieldcliff Ct 77041
Fieldcross Ln 77047
Fieldglen Dr 77084
Fielding Ln 77049
Fieldmont Ln 77073
Fields St 77028
Fieldsboro Dr 77031
Fieldstone Ct 77095
Fieldstone Dr 77041
Fieldwood Dr 77056
Fieldworth Dr 77037
Fiesta Ln 77004
Figaro Dr 77024
Filaree Trl 77044
Filaree Ridge Ln 77089
Filey Ct & Ln 77013
Fillmont Ln 77044
Fillmore St 77029
Filltop St 77028
N Finch Cir 77028
S Finch Cir 77028
Finch St
1100-1799 77009
5500-7499 77028
Finch Grove Ln 77090
Finchley Dr 77082
Finchwood Ln 77036
Find Horn Ct 77095
Findlay St 77017
Finesse Dr 77032
Finewood Way 77058
Finn St 77022
Finn Grove Ln 77094
Finnigan Park Place Ct 77020
Finnigans Cir 77044
Fintona Way 77015
Finwood Ln 77044
Fir St
7100-7199 77087
7300-7899 77012
Fir Canyon Trl 77049
Fire Creek Dr 77043
Fire Hills Dr 77038
Firebird Dr 77099
Firebrick Dr 77041
Firecreek Ridge Dr 77095
Firedel St 77016
Firefly Ave 77017
Firenza Dr 77035
Firerock Dr 77085
Firestone Dr 77035
Firhill Dr 77077
Firnat St
500-1499 77022
2000-3399 77093
4500-9499 77016
Firth Ln 77084
Firtree Way 77062
Fishel St 77093
Fisher Rd 77041
Fisher St 77018
Fisher Glen Ln 77072
Fisk St 77009
Fitch St 77016
Fitzgerald St 77091
Fitzhugh St 77028
Fitzroy Ct 77083
Five Iron Dr 77089
Fjord Ct 77066
Flack Dr 77081
Flag Stone Pass Ln 77089
Flaghoist Ln 77079
Flagler St 77071
Flagridge Ln 77066
Flagship Dr 77029
Flagstaff Ln 77049
Flagstone Dr 77041
Flagstone Ter 77017
Flagstone Creek Rd 77084
Flagstone Walk Way 77049
Flair Cir & Dr 77049
Flair Oaks Dr 77040
Flamingo Dr
5400-5899 77033
6200-7199 77087
Flamingo Lakes Ct 77065
Flannery Park Ln 77094
Flannery Ridge Ln 77047
Flansour Dr 77072
Flatridge Ct 77083
Flatrock Trl 77050
Flatrock Creek Dr 77067
Flax Dr 77071
Flaxen Dr 77065
Flaxman St 77029
Fleethaven Ct & Ln 77084
Fleetway Dr 77024
Fleetwell Dr 77045
Fleetwood St 77093
Fleetwood Oaks Dr 77079
Fleetwood Place Dr 77079
Fleming Ct & Dr 77013
Flemington Ave 77084
Fleta Dr 77028
Fletcher St 77009
Fletcher Way Dr 77073
Fleur Dr 77065
Flint St 77029
Flint Cove Ct 77095
Flint Forest Ln 77024
Flint Point Dr 77024
Flint River Dr 77024
Flintdale Rd 77024
Flintgate Ct 77014
Flintlock Rd 77040
Flintridge Dr 77028
Flintrock Cir 77067
Flintstone Dr 77070
Flintwood Ct & Dr 77024
Fliser Dr 77041
Flora St 77006
Flora Mae Meadows Rd 77089
Floradora Ln 77076
Floral St 77087
Floral Crest Dr 77083
Floral Park Ct 77095
Floralgate Ln 77095
Floramorgan Ln 77089
Florence St 77009
Floria Ct 77044
Florida St 77026
Florida View Ln 77044
Florinda St 77021
Florine St 77087
Flossie Mae St 77029
Flossmoor St 77044
Flower Creek Ln 77077
Flower Garden Ln 77077
Flower Mist Ln 77095
Flower Path St 77044
Flowerdale St 77055
Flowerfield Ln 77060
Flowers St 77087
Flowerwood Ct & Dr 77062
Floyd St 77007
Flushing Meadows Dr 77089
Flying Eagle Ct 77083
Fm 1464 77083
Fm 1959 Rd 77034
Fm 1960 Rd
100-3099 77073
4500-7299 77069
11000-13499 77065
5506-1-5506-2 77069
Fm 518 Rd 77047
Fm 529 Rd
10900-14399 77041
11400-12198 77041
14401-14597 77095
14599-17999 77095
Fogle St 77026
Foley St 77055
Folger St 77093
Folkglen Ct 77034
Folkstone Ln 77075
Folkway Dr 77060
Followfield Ln 77085
Folsom Dr 77049
Folwell Ln 77024
Fonda St 77035
E Fondren Cir 77071
W Fondren Cir 77071
Fondren Rd
2400-4099 77063
5600-7399 77036
7400-9199 77074
9201-9523 77074
9600-11299 77096
11300-13099 77035
13100-13699 77085
Fondren Bend Dr 77071
Fondren Lake Dr 77071
Fondren Meadow Dr 77071
Fondren Place Dr 77071
Fondren Village Dr 77071
Fonmeadow Dr 77035
Fontainbleu St 77024
Fontana Dr 77043
Fontenelle Dr 77035
Fontinot St
2100-2399 77020
2800-3299 77026
Fonvilla St 77074
Fonville Dr 77075
Foote St 77020
Foothill St 77092
Forbes Rd 77075
Forbesbury Dr 77084
Force St
6200-7599 77020
13100-14699 77015
Ford St 77012
Fordham St 77005
Fordham Park Ct 77058
Fordshire Dr 77025
Foredale St 77075
Foreland Ct & Dr 77077
Foreman St 77017
N Forest Blvd 77090
W Forest Dr
500-999 77079
1200-1399 77043
E Forest Ln 77015
Forest St 77011
Forest Acres Dr 77050
Forest Arbor Ct 77095
Forest Bark Ln 77067
Forest Bay Ct 77062
Forest Birch Ct 77059
Forest Bloom Ln 77044
Forest Branch Blvd 77014
Forest Bridge Way 77066
Forest Cedars Dr 77084
Forest Commons Ct 77095
Forest Dale Ln 77078
Forest Dawn Way 77095
Forest Deer Rd 77084
Forest Enclave Ln 77068
Forest Estates Dr 77066
Forest Falls Ct 77065
Forest Fir 77084
Forest Glen St 77024
Forest Grove Dr 77080
Forest Gully 77067
Forest Heights Dr 77095
Forest Hill Blvd
100-499 77011
1501-1697 77023
1699-2099 77023
Forest Hillside Ln 77067
Forest Hollow St 77078
Forest Home Dr 77077
Forest Ivy Ln 77067
Forest Knoll Dr 77049
Forest Land Dr 77084
Forest Lodge Cir, Ct & Dr 77070
Forest Mews Ct 77049
Forest Moss Ct 77084
Forest Nook Ct 77018
Forest Oaks Blvd & Dr 77017
Forest Pines Village Ln 77067
Forest Plaza Ct 77066
Forest Ranch Dr 77049
Forest Ridge Lndg & Pt 77084
Forest Star 77067
Forest Thicket Ln 77067
Forest Town Dr 77084
Forest Trails Dr
5400-5899 77084
14700-15499 77095
Forest View St 77078
Forest Way Dr 77090
Forest Willow Ln 77068
Forest Wind Ln 77066
Forestburg Dr 77038
Foresthaven Dr 77066
Forestside Ln 77095
Forestwood Dr 77015
Forge Creek Rd 77067
S Fork Blvd 77089
Fork Creek Dr 77065
Forked Bough Dr 77042
Forked Lake Dr 77044
Forkland Ln 77077
Forney Dr 77036
Forney Ridge Ln 77047
Forrest Valley Dr 77065
Forrestal St 77033
Forstall Dr 77014
Forsythe Ln 77073
Fort Nelson Dr 77083
Fort Royal Dr 77038
Fort Sumter Ct & Ln 77084
Forthbridge Ct & Dr 77084
Forthloch Ct 77084
Fortrose Ct 77070
Fortune St 77088
Fortune Park Dr 77047
Forum Dr 77055
Forum Park Dr 77036
Forum Place Dr 77036
Forum West Dr 77036
Fosbak St 77022
Fossil Rock Ln 77034
Foster St 77021
Foster Point Ln 77095
Foster Springs Ln 77095
Fostoria Ln 77076
Founders Way Ct 77091
Fountain St 77051
Fountain Hills Ct 77086
Fountain Shores Dr 77065
Fountain Spring Dr 77066
Fountain View Dr 77057
Fountainbridge Ln 77069
Fountaincrest Ct & Dr 77041
Fountaine St 77028
Fountainhead Dr 77066
Four Leaf Dr 77084
Four Oaks Dr 77073
Four Rivers Ct 77091
Four Season Dr 77084
Fourcade St 77023
Fowler St 77007
Fowlie St 77028
Fox Rd 77064
Fox St 77003
Fox Arrow Ln 77041
Fox Brush Ln 77041
Fox Chase Ct 77041
Fox Creek Park Dr 77083
Fox Prairie Ln 77084
Fox Springs Dr 77084
Fox Trace Ln 77066
Fox Wind Ct 77041
Foxburo Dr 77065
Foxdale Dr 77084
Foxfern Cir & St 77049
Foxford Way 77015
Foxgate Ct & Rd 77079
Foxglove Ln 77076
Foxhill St 77093
Foxhunter Rd 77049
Foxlake Dr 77084
Foxleigh Ct & Rd 77049
Foxmoor Ln 77069
Foxridge Dr 77037
Foxrow Ln 77064
Foxrun Ct 77080
Foxshire Ln 77047
W Foxshire Ln 77053
Foxtail Lily Cir 77084
Foxton Rd 77048
Foxton Place Ct 77095
Foxtree Ln 77094
Foxville Dr 77067
Foxwood Rd 77008
Foy Ln 77093
Foyce St 77022
Fragrant Cloud Ct 77041
Fragrant Pine Ln 77049
Frail Ln 77076
Francine Ln 77016
Francis Ct 77004
Francis St
600-999 77002
1000-3499 77004
Francis Marion Dr 77091
Francitas Dr 77038
Francoise Blvd 77042
Frandora Ln 77024
Frank Rd 77032
Frankford Ct 77048
Frankie St 77015
Franklin Rd 77070
Franklin St
1-297 77002
299-399 77002
401-499 77201
401-401 77001
401-401 77251
401-401 77252
401-401 77253
401-401 77210
501-697 77002
699-2299 77002
Frankton Way 77073
Frankway Dr 77096
Franz Rd 77084
Fraser Lake Ln 77083
Frasier St 77007
Frawley St 77009
Frazer Ln
400-699 77037
800-899 77038
Frazier River Dr 77050
Fred St 77088
Fredericksburg Ln 77083
Fredonia Dr 77073
Freecrest St 77034
Freedonia Dr 77055
Freehill St 77034
Freeland St
8500-8549 77061
8550-9399 77075
Freeman St 77009
Freemont St 77009
Freemont Fair Ct 77075
Freeport St 77015
Freestone St 77034
Freestone Plum Ct 77049
Freeton St 77034
Freewood St 77034
Frels Ln 77076
French Rd 77084
French Chateau Dr 77088
French Creek Dr 77017
French Oak Ln 77082
French Village Dr 77055
Frensham Cir 77041
Fresh Air Ct 77084
Freshmeadows Dr 77063
Fresno Dr 77083
Freund St 77003
Frey Rd 77034
Friar Point Rd
3000-3199 77051
4100-4499 77047
E & W Friar Tuck Ln 77024
Friarcreek Ln 77055
Friars Hl 77070
Frick Rd
2300-3199 77038
3200-3499 77086
Friendly Rd 77093
Friendship Rd 77080
Fries Ct & Rd 77055
Fringewood Dr 77028
Frio St 77012
Friobend Ln 77040
Frisco St 77022
Fritz Oaks Pl 77068
Frontenac Dr 77071
Frontier Dr 77041
Frostdale Ln 77047
Frostwood Dr 77024
Frostwood Valley Ct 77095
Frosty Brook Dr 77085
Fruge Rd 77047
Fruitvale Dr 77038
Fruitwood Dr 77089
Fry Rd 77084
Fuel Storage Rd 77073
Fuerte Dr 77083
Fugate St 77009
Fulham Ct 77063
Fuller St 77084
Fullerton Dr 77043
Fulton St
4306A1-4306A1 77009
1400-5999 77009
6100-7900 77022
7825-7825 77222
7901-9399 77022
7902-9398 77022
9500-10699 77076
Fulton Meadows Ln 77092
Funston St 77012
Fuqua Ct 77075
Fuqua St
2900-4039 77047
4041-4099 77047
4100-6299 77048
7600-9999 77075
10000-11499 77089
11500-11552 77034
11554-13099 77034
W Fuqua St
2900-3099 77045
3030-3030 77245
3100-4898 77045
3101-4899 77045
5700-5799 77085
Fuqua Breeze Dr 77075
Fuqua Gardens Dr 77075
Fuqua Gardens Vw 77045
Fuqua Glen Ln 77075
Fuqua Oaks Ln 77075
Fuqua Ridge Ln 77075
Fuqua Villas Ln 77075
Fur Market Dr 77064
Furay Rd 77016
Furlong Ln 77071
Furman Rd 77047
Furray Rd 77028
G St 77072
Gable Ln 77066
Gable Glen Ln 77095
Gable Hill Ln 77067
Gable Lodge Ct 77024
Gable Point Dr 77095
Gable Wind Ct 77095
Gable Wind Mill Ln 77044
Gablewinn Ct 77070
Gabriel St 77063
Gabriella Bluff Ln 77047
Gaby Virbo Dr 77083
Gadshill Cir 77044
Gadwall Ct 77044
Gaeldom Dr & Ln 77084
Gaelic Ct & Ln 77084
Gaelic Green St 77045
Gaelicglen Ln 77084
Gaffney Ln 77084
Gage Ct 77024
Gagelake Ln 77084
Gager St 77093
Gagne St 77020
Gailey Ln 77040
Gaines St 77009
Gaines Meadow Ct & Dr 77083
Gainesville St
6200-7599 77020
13700-14699 77015
Gainsborough Ct & Dr 77031
Gairloch Ln 77025
Galaxy St 77078
N Galayda St 77086
Galbreath Dr 77066
Gale St 77009
Galena Creek Dr 77086
Galesburg St 77051
Galewood Ln 77073
Galewood Way 77058
Gallagher Dr 77045
Gallahad St 77078
Gallant Ct 77082
Gallant Forest Dr 77088
Gallant Glen Ln 77095
Gallant Ridge Ln 77082
Galleon Dr 77036
Gallery Ct 77053
Gallinule Ln 77048
Galveston Rd
1900-2399 77012
2401-2497 77017
2499-5303 77017
5302-5302 77217
5302-5302 77287
5304-6098 77017
5305-6099 77017
7201-7397 77034
7399-11999 77034
E Galwan Cir 77070
Galway Ln 77080
Game Cove Ln 77044
Gamebird Ln 77034
Gamlin Bend Dr 77082
Gammage St
4900-4999 77021
6300-7299 77087
Gammon Dr 77022
Gammon Oaks Dr 77095
Gander Bay Ln 77040
Gander Bayshore Ln 77040
Ganderwood Dr 77089
Gannett St 77025
Gano St 77009
Gans St 77029
Gant Rd 77066
Ganyard Dr 77043
Garapan St 77091
Garber Ln
10500-10899 77029
13700-14699 77015
Garcroft St 77029
Garden Grv 77082
Garden St
7000-7199 77087
7200-7899 77012
N Garden St 77071
S Garden St 77071
Garden Breeze Dr 77075
Garden Bridge St 77075
Garden City Dr 77088
Garden Creek Way 77059
Garden Crest Ln 77018
Garden Estate St 77072
Garden Fern Ct 77062
Garden Gale Ln 77044
Garden Gate Way 77059
Garden Glade Ct 77095
Garden Grove Ct 77082
Garden Grove Dr 77066
Garden Hill Ln 77095
Garden Land Ct 77073
Garden Laurel Ln 77014
Garden Manor Dr 77084
Garden Oaks Blvd, Ter, Trce & Vw 77018
Garden Parks Dr 77075
Garden Path Ct 77059
Garden Rose Ln 77018
Garden Run Ct 77084

Garden Shadow Ln 77018
Garden Springs Dr 77083
Garden Stream Ct 77062
Garden Trace Ln 77018
Garden Trail Ct 77072
Garden View Dr 77067
Gardencrest Ln 77077
Gardendale Dr
 1000-1199 77018
 3700-6299 77092
Gardenglen Dr 77070
Gardenia Dr 77018
Gardenia Bend Dr 77053
Gardenia Mist Ln 77044
Gardentree Dr 77044
Gardenview Dr 77014
W Gardner St 77009
Gardners Brk 77049
Gardnerville St 77034
Garett Green Cir 77095
Garfield St
 2400-2799 77088
 7900-8299 77029
Garfield Park Ln 77075
Gargan St 77009
Garland St
 1300-2599 77087
 8000-8499 77017
Garlenda Ln 77034
Garner Mill Ln 77089
Garnercrest Dr 77095
Garnet St 77005
Garralde St 77002
Garrett Rd 77044
Garrett Pine Ln 77044
Garrettson Ln 77056
Garrick Ct & Ln 77013
Garrison Ct 77014
Garrison Point Dr 77040
Garrotsville St 77022
Garrott St
 3400-4299 77006
 4300-4399 77002
Garrow St
 2500-4399 77003
 4400-6099 77011
Garsee Dr 77040
Garvin Ave 77064
Garwood Dr 77091
Gary St 77055
Gas Light Village Dr 77095
Gaslamp Dr 77095
Gasmer Dr 77035
Gasser Ln 77085
Gaston St
 4400-5499 77093
 5501-5599 77093
 5600-6399 77016
N & S Gate Stone 77007
Gate View Dr 77073
Gatecrest Dr 77032
Gatehouse Dr 77040
Gatemont Ct 77066
Gatepoint Dr 77073
Gateridge Dr 77041
Gates St 77028
Gatesbury Ct & Dr 77082
Gatesbury North Dr 77082
Gateship Dr 77073
Gateside Dr 77032
Gateway Dr 77093
Gatewood Ave 77053
Gatlinburg Dr 77031
Gatton Park Dr 77066
Gaucho Dr 77083
Gauguin Dr 77088
Gault Rd 77039
Gautier Ct & Dr 77065
Gavin Ln 77049
Gavin Place Dr 77088
Gawain Ln 77024
Gay St 77022
Gaylawood Dr 77066
Gaylord Dr 77024
Gaylyn Cir 77073
Gaymoor Dr 77035

E & W Gaywood Dr 77079
Gazania St 77065
Gazin St 77020
Gears Loop & Rd 77067
Gehring St 77021
Gellhorn Dr
 200-399 77013
 500-1600 77029
 1602-1798 77029
Gembrook Ln 77089
Gemini St 77058
Gena Ct 77064
N & S Gena Lee Dr 77064
Genadena St 77034
Genard Rd 77041
Gendley Dr 77041
Genemaury St 77088
Genesee St
 1000-1899 77019
 1900-2599 77006
Geneva Dr 77066
Genoa Red Bluff Rd 77034
Genova St 77009
Gens Ct 77055
Gentilly Pl 77024
Gentle Bend Dr 77069
Gentle Brook Ct 77062
Gentle Cove Ct 77084
Gentle Slope Ln 77044
Gentle Stone Ct & Dr 77095
Gentle Water Dr 77044
Gentlewood Ct 77095
Gentry St 77009
Gentryside Ct & Dr 77077
N George St 77026
Georgetown St 77005
Georgetown Colony Dr 77084
Georgetown Park Ct 77058
Georgi Ln 77092
Georgia St 77029
Georgibelle Dr 77043
Geral Ln 77084
Gerhart Dr 77045
Gerlach St 77034
Gerngross Ln 77044
Geronimo Lake Ct & Dr 77047
Gerrards Cross Dr 77082
Gershwin Dr 77079
Gershwin Oak St 77089
Gertin St 77004
Gessner Rd
 2038A-2038D 77080
 1-999 77024
 1000-1399 77055
 1400-3099 77080
 4300-6399 77041
 6500-8099 77040
N Gessner Rd 77064
S Gessner Rd
 3730-A-3730-D 77063
 9299A-9299B 77074
 1000-3899 77063
 3836-3836 77215
 3900-3998 77063
 3901-3999 77063
 5700-8399 77036
 8400-8498 77074
 8500-9599 77074
 9600-10999 77071
 10910-10910 77271
 11000-12698 77071
 11001-12699 77071
Getty Rd 77086
Gianna Ct 77083
Gianna Way 77073
Gibbons St 77012
Gibbs St 77009
Gibraltar Cir 77038
Gibson St 77007
Gibson Crossing Way 77067
Giddings Ln 77064
Gil Jr Ln 77075
Gil Rodriguez Loop 77075
Gilder Rd 77064
Gill St 77044

Gillen St 77087
Gillespie St 77020
Gillette St
 700-1899 77019
 1900-2199 77006
Gilliom Dr 77084
Gillman Park 77073
Gillman St 77078
Gilman Trace Ln 77092
Gilpin St 77034
Gilson Ln 77086
Gina Ln 77037
Gineridge Dr 77053
Ginger Ln 77040
Ginger St 77091
Ginger Bell Dr 77084
Ginger Cove Ln 77086
Ginger Lei Ln 77044
Gingerleaf Ln 77055
Gingham Dr 77024
Girard St 77007
Girnigoe Dr 77084
Gironde Dr 77071
Givens St 77007
Glacier Dr 77067
Glacier Brook Ct 77059
Glacier Creek Ln 77083
Glacier Hill Dr 77077
Gladden Dr 77049
N Glade Dr 77073
Glade Hollow Dr 77014
Glade Park Ct 77084
Gladebrook Ct & Dr 77068
Gladebrook Glen Ln 77095
Gladefield Dr 77099
Gladeridge Dr 77068
Gladewell Dr 77072
Gladewick Dr 77077
Gladewood Dr 77041
Gladewood Ln 77071
Gladstone St 77051
Gladys St 77009
Glamis Ln 77084
Glamorgan Dr 77040
Glascock Ln 77064
Glascow Grn 77089
Glaser Dr
 1700-1899 77009
 11200-11499 77076
Glasgow Pl 77077
Glasgow St 77026
Glasholm Dr 77073
Glass Cir, Ct & St 77016
Glassblower Ln 77064
Glassford Dr 77089
Glazebrook Dr 77060
Gleason Rd 77016
Glebe Rd 77018
Glee Ln 77032
Glen Ave 77088
S Glen Dr 77099
Glen Allen Ln 77069
Glen Arbor Dr 77025
Glen Bay Ct 77089
Glen Briar Ln 77084
Glen Canon Ln 77069
Glen Chase Ct & Dr 77095
Glen Cove Ct & Dr 77021
Glen Dell Ct 77061
Glen Echo Dr 77088
Glen Echo Ln 77024
Glen Erica Dr 77069
Glen Falls St 77049
Glen Green Ln 77069
Glen Haven Blvd
 2100-2599 77030
 2600-3799 77025
E Glen Haven Blvd 77025
S Glen Haven Blvd 77025
W Glen Haven Blvd 77025
Glen Knoll Ct & Dr 77077
Glen Lane Ct 77066
Glen Manor Dr 77028
Glen Mar Dr 77082
Glen Mist Ct 77038
Glen Mist Ln 77069

Glen Nook Dr 77016
Glen Oaks St 77008
Glen Park St 77009
Glen Pines Dr 77069
Glen Prairie St 77061
Glen Riley Dr 77083
Glen Rio St 77045
Glen Rock Dr 77087
Glen Shadow Dr 77088
Glen Turret Ct 77095
Glen Valley Dr 77061
Glenaire St 77061
Glenalbyn St 77015
Glenalta St 77061
Glenarm St 77020
Glenbank Way 77095
Glenborough Dr 77067
Glenbrae St 77061
Glenbrook Ct 77087
Glenbrook Dr 77017
Glenbrook Knoll Ln 77095
Glenburnie Dr 77022
Glenbury Dr 77037
Glenchase Ln 77014
Glenchester Dr 77079
Glenclan Ln 77084
Glencliffe Ln 77070
Glencoe St 77087
Glencove St 77007
Glencrest St 77061
Glencroft St 77078
Glencross St 77061
Glenda St 77037
Glenda Kay Dr 77065
Glendale St 77012
Glendaven Way 77082
Glendenning Ln 77024
Glendora St 77012
Glendown Ln 77070
Gleneagles Ct & Dr 77084
Gleneviss Dr 77084
Glenfield Ct
 1-99 77074
 9400-10799 77096
Glenfield Manor Ln 77014
Glenfield Park Ln 77070
Glenforest Ct 77061
Glengarry Rd 77048
Glengate Ln 77036
Glenhagen Ct & Dr 77084
Glenheath St 77061
Glenheather Dr 77068
Glenhilshire Dr 77055
Glenhollow Dr
 8100-8199 77033
 10900-10998 77048
 11000-12999 77048
Glenhouse Ct & Dr 77088
Glenhurst Dr 77033
Glenkirk Dr 77089
Glenlea St 77061
Glenledi Dr 77084
Glenleigh Dr 77014
Glenloch Dr 77061
Glenmark Dr 77084
Glenmawr Dr 77075
Glenmeade Dr 77059
Glenmeadow Dr 77096
Glenmont Dr
 4500-5098 77081
 5100-6199 77081
 8600-8999 77036
Glenmore Dr 77023
Glenmore Forest St 77055
Glenmorin Ct 77049
Glenmorris Ct & Dr 77084
Glenn Cliff Dr 77064
Glenn Lakes Dr 77069
Glenn Ricki Dr 77045
Glenn River Dr 77050
Glennale Ct & Dr 77084
Glenneyre Ln 77084
Glennlast Ln 77037
Glennville Ct 77024
Glenora Dr 77065
Glenpatti Dr 77084

Glenpine Dr 77068
Glenray Dr 77084
Glenridge Ct 77053
Glenridge Frst 77094
Glenridge Ln 77053
Glenrose St 77051
Glens Ferry Ln 77073
Glenscott St 77061
Glenshadow Way 77038
Glenshannon Dr 77059
Glenshire St 77025
Glenside St 77033
Glenstein Dr 77084
Glenstone St 77013
Glentide Cir 77045
Glentworth Ct 77084
Glenvale Dr 77060
Glenview Dr
 7600-7999 77061
 8000-8198 77017
 8200-8599 77017
Glenvillage St 77084
Glenvista St 77061
Glenwater Ct 77044
Glenway Dr 77070
Glenwolde Dr 77099
Glenwolf Dr 77084
Glenwood Dr 77007
Glenwood Canyon Ln 77077
Glenwood Forest Dr 77078
Glenwood Park Dr 77095
Glenwyck St 77045
Glesby St 77029
Globe St 77034
Gloger St 77039
Gloria Dr 77013
Glorieta Dr 77083
Glorietta Turn 77068
Glorywhite Ct 77034
Glosridge Dr 77055
Glouchester Ln 77073
Glourie Cir & Dr 77055
Glover St 77012
Glover Meadows Ln 77047
Gloyna St 77088
Glynn Way Dr 77056
Gnarled Chestnut Ct 77075
Gnarlwood Dr 77089
Goar Rd 77077
Gober St 77017
Godsey Ct 77024
Godwin St 77023
Goettee Cir 77091
Goforth St 77021
Gold St 77026
Gold Bridge Ct 77053
Gold Creek Dr 77080
Gold Cup Way 77065
Gold Dust Ln 77064
Gold Medal Cir 77041
Gold Mesa Ct & Trl 77062
Gold Point Dr 77064
Gold Ridge Ln 77053
Gold Star Dr 77082
Gold Tee Ct & Dr 77036
Goldcrest St
 9100-9299 77022
 9600-10299 77076
Golden Pass 77067
Golden Appaloosa Cir 77044
Golden Bluff Ln 77044
Golden Brook Dr 77085
Golden Chord Cir 77040
Golden Circle Way 77083
Golden Fern Ct 77075
Golden Field Ct & Dr 77059
Golden Flame Ct 77094
Golden Forest Dr
 4800-5199 77091
 5700-6299 77092
Golden Gate Dr 77041
Golden Glade Ln 77095
Golden Glen Dr 77099
Golden Grain Dr 77064
Golden Lodge Ln 77066
Golden Meadow Dr 77064

Golden Morning Cir 77084
Golden Park Ln 77088
Golden Pine Dr 77070
Golden Pond Dr 77084
Golden Prairie Ln 77086
Golden Ridge Dr 77084
Golden River Ln 77083
Golden Sands Dr 77095
Golden Spike Ln 77086
Golden Star Dr 77083
Golden Stream Dr 77066
Golden Sunshine Dr 77064
Golden Tee Ct & Ln 77099
Golden Thistle 77058
Golden Trace Ct 77083
Golden View Ct & Dr 77083
Golden Water Ct 77044
Golden Wings Ct 77041
Golden Wood Ln 77086
Goldenglade Cir & Dr 77064
Goldenrod St 77009
Golders Green Dr 77082
Goldfield Ln 77064
Goldfinch St 77035
Goldsmith St 77030
Goldspier St
 5400-5498 77091
 5500-6699 77091
 6701-6799 77091
 7000-7199 77088
Goldwater Ct 77044
Golf Dr
 3400-5199 77018
 5400-5499 77091
Golf Green Cir 77036
Golf View Trl 77059
Golfcrest Blvd 77087
Golfcrest Dr 77089
Golfridge Cir 77089
Golfway St 77087
Goliad St
 1000-1199 77002
 1200-2199 77007
Gollacks Dr 77083
Golondrina Dr 77083
Gonzales St 77020
Good Spring Dr 77067
Goode St 77012
Goodhope St 77021
Goodloe St 77093
Goodman St 77084
Goodmeadow Dr 77064
Goodnight Trl 77060
Goodridge Dr 77048
Goodrum Rd 77041
Goodson Dr 77060
Goodspring Dr 77064
Goodyear Dr 77017
Gooselake Ln 77084
Gore Dr 77016
Gorham Dr 77084
Gorham Park Cir 77067
Gorman Dr 77049
Gorman Brook Dr 77095
Gospel Way 77085
Gostic St 77008
Goswami Way St 77018
Gotham Dr 77089
Goulburn Dr 77045
Gould Pl 77026
Gould St 77023
E & W Governors Cir 77092
Gowland St 77045
Grab Rd 77032
Grace Ln 77021
Grace St 77003
Grace Hall Dr 77065
Grace Point Ln 77048
Gracechurch Dr 77066
Gracefield Ct 77047
Graceland St 77009
Gracia St
 7100-7400 77076
 7402-7498 77076
 7500-7798 77037
Graduate Cir 77004

Grady St 77016
Grafton St 77017
Grafton Bridge Ln 77047
Graftondale Ct 77084
Graham Spring Ln 77044
Graham Springs Ct 77044
Grahamcrest Dr 77061
Grahamwood Ln 77047
Gramercy St
 2300-2699 77030
 2700-4199 77025
Grammar Rd 77047
Grampin Dr 77084
Gran Vista Dr 77083
Granada St 77015
Granberry St 77007
Grand Ave 77064
Grand Blvd
 6100-6899 77021
 6900-7299 77054
Grand Brook Ct & Dr 77089
Grand Canyon Dr 77067
Grand Chateau Ln 77084
Grand Cross Ln 77072
Grand Elm Cir 77068
Grand Estates Dr 77065
Grand Flora Ct 77041
Grand Floral Blvd & Ct 77041
Grand Forest Dr 77084
Grand Haven Dr 77088
Grand Heights Ct 77062
Grand Isle Ct 77044
Grand Knolls Dr 77083
Grand Lake St 77081
Grand Masterpiece Ct & Ln 77041
Grand Mountain Ct 77095
Grand Noble Cir 77068
Grand Nugget Ct & Ln 77062
Grand Oaks Blvd & Dr 77015
Grand Plains Dr 77090
Grand Plaza Dr 77067
Grand Point Rd 77090
Grand Prince Ln 77073
Grand Terrace Ct 77095
Grand Teton Dr 77067
Grand Valley Cir & Dr 77090
Grand View Ter 77007
Grand Winds Ln 77084
Grandridge Dr 77049
Grandriver Dr 77078
Grandvale Dr 77072
Grandview St 77051
Grandville St 77028
Granger St 77020
Granite St 77092
Granite Isle Ct 77089
Granite Mountain Trl 77049
Granite Ridge Ln 77095
Granite Vale Rd 77084
Graniteville Dr 77078
Grannis St 77075
Grant Rd 77070
Grant St 77006
Grantley Dr 77099
Grantmoor Ln 77045
Granton St 77026
Grantwood St 77004
Granvia Dr 77083
Granville Dr 77091
Grape St
 5000-5799 77096
 5800-7699 77074
 8800-9199 77036
 17200-17599 77044
Grapevine St
 3700-5499 77045
 5500-6699 77085
Grapewood Cir, Ct & Dr 77089
Grasilla Dr 77045
Grass Valley St 77018
Grasshopper Ln 77079
Grassland Cir 77070
Grassmere St 77051

Grassy Briar Ln 77085
Grassy Cove Dr 77070
Grassy Creek Dr 77082
Grassy Fields Ct 77060
Grassy Meadow Dr 77064
Grassy View Dr 77073
Grassyglen Dr 77064
Graustark St 77006
Gray Ct 77004
Gray St
100-1400 77002
1402-1502 77002
1700-2699 77003
2700-3199 77004
W Gray St
100-1599 77019
1601-2099 77019
1900-2098 77019
1900-1900 77219
Gray Falls Dr 77077
Gray Jay Ct & Dr 77040
Gray Moss Ln 77055
Gray Ridge Ct, Dr & Ln 77082
Graycliff Dr 77049
Grayford Ct 77073
Grayling Ln 77067
Grayson Rd 77034
Grayson St 77020
Graystone Ln 77069
Grayton Ln 77041
Graywood Ct & Dr 77089
Graywood Grove Ln 77062
Great Bridge Dr 77065
Great Easton Ln 77073
Great Glen Dr 77084
Great Hawk Ln 77075
Great Hill Ct 77083
Great Oaks Dr 77050
Great Oaks Glen Dr 77083
Great Oaks Hollow Dr 77083
Great Oaks Shadow Dr 77083
Great Plains Ln 77064
Great Ridge Ct 77083
Great River Ct 77089
Great Salt Dr 77044
Greatwood Dr 77013
Grecian Way 77024
Greeley St 77006
S Green Dr 77034
Green Ln 77066
Green St 77020
Green Vis 77068
Green Arbor Dr 77089
Green Ash Dr 77081
Green Aspen Ln 77047
Green Bluff Ct 77044
Green Butte Ct 77044
Green Castle Way 77095
Green Cedar Dr 77083
Green Chase Ln 77073
Green Colling Park Dr 77047
Green Coral Dr 77044
Green Cove Bend Ln 77041
Green Crest Dr 77082
Green Devon Dr 77095
Green Dolphin St 77013
Green Falls Dr 77088
Green Feather Dr 77049
Green Forest Pass 77084
Green Garden Ln 77084
Green Glade Dr 77099
Green Glen St 77032
Green Hazel Ct & Dr 77084
Green Heather Ln 77085
Green Hill Dr 77032
Green Island Dr 77032
Green Isle Dr 77044
Green Ivy Ct 77059
Green Knoll Dr 77067
Green Land Way 77084
Green Lawn Dr 77088
Green Meadow Ln 77091
Green Mills Dr 77070
Green Mountain Dr 77032
Green Oak Meadow Ln 77060
Green Oaks Dr
11500-11599 77024
16100-16199 77032
Green Oaks St 77024
Green Pear Ln 77049
Green Pines Cir 77066
Green Pines Dr 77066
Green Pines Frst 77067
Green Plaza Dr 77038
Green Point Ct 77024
Green Ray Dr 77095
Green River Dr
7800-8639 77028
8641-8699 77028
11700-13199 77044
N Green River Dr
8636-8698 77028
8701-8799 77028
8800-9499 77078
Green Rock Rd 77032
Green Sage Dr 77064
Green Shade Dr 77090
Green Shadow Dr 77032
W Green Shoals Ln 77066
Green Smoke Dr 77095
Green Springs Dr 77066
Green Spur St 77032
Green Stone Ct
400-499 77094
6700-6799 77084
Green Stone Dr 77084
Green Teal Ln 77039
Green Terrace Ln 77088
Green Top Ct 77084
Green Trail Dr
1101-1899 77038
4600-4899 77084
Green Tree Dr 77032
Green Tree Park 77007
Green Tree Rd
5000-5699 77056
5900-6099 77057
10000-10399 77042
Green Vale Dr 77024
Green Valley Dr
1100-1199 77055
2200-2499 77032
8700-8799 77055
Green Valley Ln 77064
Greenbank Ln 77095
Greenbay Cir, Dr & St 77024
Greenbelt Dr 77079
Greenbend Blvd 77067
Greenbriar St
2600-3741 77098
3740-3740 77254
3742-4498 77098
3743-4499 77098
4500-5699 77005
5700-7999 77030
8000-8199 77054
Greenbriar Colony Dr 77032
Greenbriar Park Dr 77060
Greenbriar Plaza Dr 77060
Greenbriar Point Ln 77095
Greenbriar Springs Dr 77073
Greenbrook Dr 77073
Greenbush St 77025
Greencanyon Dr 77044
Greencourt Dr 77062
Greencove St 77024
Greencraig Dr 77035
Greencreek Cir & Dr 77070
Greendale Dr 77032
Greendowns St 77087
Greenedge Dr 77040
Greenfield Ln 77064
Greenfork Dr 77036
Greenglen Dr 77044
Greengrass Ct & Dr 77008
Greenhaven Ln 77092
Greenhill Forest Dr 77088
Greenhood St 77091
Greenhouse Rd 77084
Greenhurst St 77091
Greenleaf Ln 77062
Greenleaf St 77009
Greenleaf Lake Dr 77095
Greenloch Ln 77044
Greenmesa Dr 77044
Greenmont Dr 77092
Greenoak Dr 77032
Greenpark Dr 77079
S Greenpark Dr
3200-3399 77082
6100-6299 77072
Greenpark Trl 77007
Greenpark Manor Ln 77085
Greenport Ln 77084
Greenranch Dr 77039
Greenrich Dr 77060
Greenridge Dr 77057
Greenrock Ln 77044
Greens Ct 77067
Greens Pkwy 77067
Greens Rd
1-1199 77060
1200-1248 77032
1250-5799 77032
W Greens Rd
100-2999 77067
3100-6799 77066
7200-7499 77064
Greens Bayou St 77015
Greens Cove Way 77059
Greens Crossing Blvd
10400-10799 77038
11200-11400 77067
11402-11498 77067
Greens Landing Dr 77038
Greens Manor Ln 77044
Greens Orchard Dr 77066
Greensboro Dr 77021
Greensbrook Forest Dr 77044
Greensbrook Garden Dr 77044
Greensford Ct 77049
Greenshire Dr 77048
Greenside Dr 77083
Greensmark Dr
1500-1599 77067
1530-1530 77267
Greenspark Ln 77044
Greenspoint Dr & Mall 77060
Greenspoint Park Dr 77060
Greenstone St 77087
Greenstone Park Ln 77089
Greensward Rd 77080
Greenswarth Ln 77075
Greenvale Ln 77066
Greenview Dr 77032
Greenville St
6900-7499 77020
13700-14699 77015
Greenway Ct 77087
Greenway Plz 77046
Greenway Chase Ct & St 77072
Greenway Forest Ln 77088
Greenwich St 77078
Greenwich Place Dr 77019
Greenwich Terrace Dr 77019
Greenwichwood Ln 77073
N, E, S & W Greenwick Ct, Ln & Loop 77085
Greenwillow St
9000-9999 77096
10000-11399 77035
Greenwind Chase Dr 77094
Greenwood Ln S 77044
Greenwood St 77011
N Greenwood St 77011
Greenwood Estates St 77066
Greenwood Forest Dr 77066
Greenwood Lakes Ln 77044
Greenwood Oaks Dr 77062
Greenwood Pines Dr 77062
Greenyard Dr 77086
Gregdale Rd 77049
Gregg St
100-1936 77020
1937-2999 77026
Gregory St 77026
Gregory Crossing Way 77067
Greiner Dr 77080
Gren St 77021
Grenada Ln 77058
Grenada Falls Dr 77095
Grenadier Dr 77089
W Grenfell Ln 77076
Grennoch Ln 77025
Grenshaw St 77088
Gretel Dr 77024
Gretna Green Dr 77084
Grey Mills Dr 77070
Grey Oaks Dr 77050
Greyburn Ln 77080
Greyfield Ln 77047
Greyfriar Dr 77037
Greylog Dr 77048
Greymoss Ln 77073
Greys Ln 77095
Greyton Ln 77024
Griffin St 77009
Griggs Rd
3500-5299 77021
5210-5210 77221
5300-5798 77021
5301-5799 77021
5900-7199 77023
Grigsby St 77026
Grimes St 77087
Gripper Way 77073
Grisby Rd 77079
Groeschke Rd 77084
Gros Ventre Ln 77095
Grosbeak Dr 77048
Gross St 77019
Grossmount Dr 77066
Grosvenor Sq 77069
Grosvenor St 77034
Grota St 77009
Grothe Ln 77022
Groton Dr
3000-3199 77051
4100-4499 77047
Grouse Ct 77084
Grouse Moor Dr 77084
Grove Pt 77066
Grove St 77020
Grove Canyon Ct 77049
Grove Fair Ct 77084
Grove Field Ln 77084
Grove Gardens Dr 77082
Grove Glen Dr 77099
Grove Haven Dr 77083
Grove Hollow Ct 77065
Grove Park Dr 77095
Grove Ridge Dr 77061
Grove Valley Trl 77084
Grovecrest St 77092
Grovedale Dr 77073
Grovehill St 77092
Groveland Ln 77019
Grovemill Dr 77045
Grovemist Ln 77082
Groven St 77092
Grover Ln 77041
Groveside Dr 77039
Grovespring Dr 77068
Groveton St 77033
Groveton Ridge Ln 77094
Groveway Dr 77087
Grovewood Ln 77008
Grovey St 77026
Grow Ln 77040
Grumbach St 77020
Gruss Dr 77060
Guadalcanal Rd 77033
Guadalupe St 77016
Guadalupe River Dr 77067
Guese Rd
1300-1799 77008
3001-3497 77018
3499-3599 77018
Guessena St 77013
Guest St
9400-9499 77028
9600-9899 77078
Guhn Rd 77040
Guildford Rd 77074
Guinea Dr 77055
Guiness Ct 77095
Guinevere St 77029
Guinn St 77044
Guiton St 77027
Gulf Fwy
2501-4099 77003
2700-4298 77004
4101-4497 77023
4499-6599 77023
6600-7199 77087
7200-7298 77017
7300-9399 77017
9800-15599 77034
Gulf St
3700-3899 77017
4000-4099 77087
Gulf Bank Rd 77037
W Gulf Bank Rd
302A-302C 77037
331A-331E 77037
100-699 77037
700-6399 77088
7000-10499 77040
Gulf Bridge Cir, Ct & St 77075
Gulf Central Dr 77023
Gulf Creek Dr 77012
Gulf Isle Ct 77095
Gulf Meadows Dr 77075
Gulf Palms 77034
Gulf Pines Dr 77090
Gulf Pointe Dr 77089
Gulf Spring Ln 77075
Gulf Terminal Dr 77023
Gulf Tree Ln 77075
Gulf Valley St 77075
Gulfcrest St 77023
Gulfdale Dr 77075
Gulfgate Mall 77087
Gulfgate Center Mall 77087
Gulfton St
5100-6499 77081
7601-7697 77036
7699-7999 77036
Gulfwind Ct & Dr 77094
Gulfwood Ln 77075
Gulick Ln 77075
Gullwood Dr 77089
Gum Grove Ln 77088
Gum Valley Dr 77088
Gumas St 77053
Gundle Rd 77073
Gunnison St 77053
Gunter St 77020
Gunwale Rd 77062
Gurney Ln 77037
Guse St 77076
Gustav St 77023
Gustine Ct & Ln 77031
Gusty Trail Ln 77041
Gusty Winds Ct & Dr 77064
Guywood St 77040
Gwen St 77093
Gypsum Ct 77041
H St 77072
H And R Rd 77073
H Mark Crosswell Jr St 77021
Habersham Ln 77024
Hablo Dr 77083
Hacienda Ln 77024
Hackamore Hollow Ln 77014
Hackberry Ln 77027
Hackett Dr 77008
Hackmatack Way 77066
Hackney St 77023
Hadden Hollow Dr 77067
Haddick St
9200-9499 77028
9600-10199 77078
Haddington Dr
10000-10099 77080
10100-10799 77043
Haddock Ct 77041
Haddon St
1400-1799 77006
1800-2099 77019
Haddonfield Ln 77070
Hade Falls Ln 77073
Hade Meadow Ln 77073
Haden Rd 77015
Hadley St
300-1599 77002
1600-2699 77003
2700-3699 77004
Hadley Falls Ct 77067
Hafer Rd 77090
Hafner Dr 77055
Hage St 77093
N Hagerman St 77011
Hahl Dr 77040
Hahlo St 77020
Hahn Rd 77040
Hahns Peak Dr 77095
Haight St 77028
Haile St 77093
Hailey St
1600-1899 77020
1900-2499 77026
Hain St 77009
Halbert St 77087
Halcyon Time Trl 77045
Haldane Dr 77055
Halerres St 77074
Halewood Dr 77062
Haley Falls Ln 77095
Haley Woods Ct 77095
Haleys Landing Ln 77095
Halfpenny Rd 77095
Halifax St 77015
Halifax Brook St 77089
Hall Pl 77008
Hall Rd
7700-8399 77075
9400-11499 77089
S Hall St 77028
Hall Forest Dr 77075
Hall Greens Ct 77075
Hall Lake Dr 77075
Hall Meadows Ct 77075
Hall Oak Dr 77075
Hall Pines Ct 77075
Hall Ranch Ct 77075
Hall Ridge Ct 77075
Hall Ridge Trace Ln 77067
Hall Shepperd Rd 77049
Hall Terrace Ct 77075
Hall View Dr 77075
Hallcroft Ln 77073
Halldale Dr 77083
Halle Trace Ln 77047
Hallfield Dr 77014
Hallie Dr 77024
Halliford Dr 77031
Hallmark Dr 77056
Hallmark Fair Ct 77059
Hallowing Point Rd 77067
Hallowyck Ct 77045
Hallshire Dr 77016
Hallsleigh Ln 77090
Halmart St 77087
Halpern St 77009
Halsey St 77015
Halstead Meadows Cir 77086
Hambledon Village Dr 77014
Hamblen St 77009
Hambleton Cir 77069
Hambleton Dr 77069
Hambleton Way 77065
Hambleton Way Cir 77065
Hambrick Ct 77060
Hambrick Rd 77060
W Hambrick Rd 77037
Hamill Rd 77039
Hamill Ranch Ln 77066
Hamillcrest Dr 77014
Hamilton Cir 77040
Hamilton St
1-499 77002
600-799 77003
800-1199 77010
1200-2299 77003
2300-3898 77004
3900-4099 77004
E Hamilton St 77076
N Hamilton St 77002
W Hamilton St
100-299 77076
300-300 77091
302-399 77091
Hamilton Grove Ln 77047
Hamilwood Dr 77095
Hamlet St 77078
Hamlet Vale Ct 77070
Hamlin Valley Dr 77090
Hamman St 77007
Hammerly Blvd
7400-7498 77055
7500-8599 77055
8600-10199 77080
10200-10498 77043
10500-11099 77043
Hammermill Ln 77044
Hammill Path Dr 77066
Hammock St 77009
Hammond Dr 77065
Hammond Hills Ct & Ln 77044
Hampden Point Ct 77040
E Hampton Cir 77071
W Hampton Cir 77071
Hampton Ct 77024
W Hampton Dr 77082
Hampton St 77088
Hampton Bend Ln 77070
Hampton Cove Dr 77077
Hampton Falls Ct & Dr 77041
Hampton Glen Ct 77083
Hampton Green Ln 77044
Hampton Oaks Cir 77094
Hampton Ridge Ln 77069
Hampton Villa Ln 77047
Hamstead Park Dr 77084
Hanby Creek Ct 77094
Hancock St 77004
Handbrook Dr 77069
Hanford St 77078
Hanfro Ln 77088
Hanging Moss Trl 77064
Hanka Dr
10000-10099 77080
10100-10199 77043
Hankla St 77076
Hanley Ln
4200-5299 77093
6300-6899 77016
Hanley St 77040
Hanlon Ct 77083
Hanna St 77028
Hanning Ln 77041
Hannon Dr 77040
Hanover St 77012
Hanover Mill Ln 77040
Hansel Ln 77024
Hansen Rd
7600-8099 77061
8100-8599 77075
Hansford St 77023
Hansom Rd 77038
Hansons Creek Ct 77044
Hanston Ct 77094
Hanus Cir 77040
N & S Hanworth Dr 77031
Happy Hollow St 77018
Haralson Rd 77071
Harbin Dr 77065
Harbor St 77020
Harbor Glen Ln 77084
Harbor Hills Dr 77054
Harbor Key Cir 77084
Harbor Point Dr 77071

Harbor Town Dr 77036
Harbour Dr 77058
E & S Harbour Bend Ln 77044
Harbour Light Dr 77044
Harbour Sands Dr 77094
Harbrook Dr 77087
Harby St 77023
Harcourt Dr 77016
Harcourt Bridge Ct & Dr 77084
Harcroft St 77029
Hard Rock Dr 77084
Hardeman Ct 77064
Hardie St 77026
Harding St 77012
Hardison Ln 77041
Hardway St 77092
Hardwick Oaks Dr 77073
Hardwicke Rd 77060
Hardwood Ln 77093
Hardwood Forest Dr 77088
E Hardy Rd
7600-11098 77093
11100-11200 77093
11202-11698 77093
11900-12398 77039
12400-14100 77039
14102-14998 77039
15200-16998 77032
17000-21100 77073
21102-21498 77073
W Hardy Rd
6101-6297 77022
6299-9399 77022
10101-11999 77076
12101-12797 77037
12799-13099 77037
13101-14797 77060
14799-16799 77060
19300-21999 77073
Hardy St
800-1299 77020
1300-2399 77026
2400-5899 77009
Hardy Stone Dr 77073
Hare St 77020
Harford Mills Dr 77083
Hargrave Rd
7400-14499 77070
14500-14699 77069
Harkness St 77076
Harland Dr
1800-2199 77055
3800-3999 77092
Harlem St 77020
Harmon St
4900-5299 77093
6301-6599 77016
Harmony Cv 77036
Harmony Rd 77049
Harmony Springs Dr 77095
Harms Rd 77041
Harness Creek Ln 77024
Harness Oaks Ct 77077
Harold St
600-1699 77006
1700-2199 77098
Haroldson Forest Dr 77044
Harper St 77005
Harper Forest Dr 77088
Harpers Bridge Dr 77041
Harpers Glen Ln 77072
Harpswell Ln 77073
Harrell St 77093
Harriet St 77023
Harriman St 77026
Harrington St
300-398 77009
400-1699 77009
1700-2799 77026
Harris Ct 77009
Harris St 77020
Harrisburg Blvd
2700-4399 77003
4400-7499 77011
7500-8099 77012

Harristown Dr 77047
W Harrow Dr 77084
Harrow St 77093
Harrow Hill Ct & Dr 77084
Harrowgate Dr 77031
Hart St 77029
Hartford St 77017
Hartington Dr 77066
Hartland St 77055
Hartland Lake Ln 77044
Hartlepool Ln 77066
Hartley Rd 77093
Hartman Rd 77049
Hartman St 77007
Hartman Ridge Ct 77053
Hartridge Dr 77090
Harts Garden Ln 77075
Hartsdale Dr
3900-3999 77063
5600-5799 77036
Hartshill Ct & Dr 77044
Hartsook St 77034
Hartsville Rd
3000-3199 77051
4101-4197 77047
4199-4599 77047
Hartt St 77025
Hartwell Dr 77084
W Hartwick Ln 77037
Hartwick Rd
200-1299 77037
1300-5499 77093
5500-6699 77016
Hartwood Way 77058
Harvard St
1-899 77007
900-2799 77008
3600-3698 77018
3700-4499 77018
5600-5699 77076
Harvest Ln 77004
Harvest Bend Blvd 77064
Harvest Brook Ct 77059
Harvest Dale Ave 77065
Harvest Dawn Ct 77095
Harvest Glen Ct 77062
Harvest Hill Ln 77073
Harvest Moon Ln 77077
Harvest Ridge Rd 77062
Harvest Run Ln 77044
Harvest Star Ct 77084
Harvest Stream Way 77084
Harvest Summer Ct 77059
Harvest Sun Dr 77064
Harvest Time Ln 77060
Harvest Wind Ct 77064
Harvester St 77095
Harvey Ln 77013
Harvey Wilson Dr 77020
Harwell Dr 77023
Harwin Dr
6600-10699 77036
10800-13099 77072
Harwood Dr 77055
Harwood Springs Dr 77080
Hasbrook St 77087
Hasie Dr 77032
Haskell St 77007
Hastings St 77017
Hastings Green Dr 77065
Hastingwood Dr 77084
Hat St 77099
Hathorn Way Dr 77094
Hattie St 77088
Hatton St 77025
Hatwell St 77023
Hauser St 77023
Havant Cir 77077
Havard Oaks Dr 77095
Havel St 77092
N Haven Dr 77040
Haven Crossing Ct 77065
Haven Hills Dr 77084
Haven Lock Dr 77077
Haven Oaks Dr 77068
Haven Point Dr 77084

Havencrest Dr
2100-2499 77038
9000-9299 77083
Havendale Dr 77072
Havengate Cir 77015
Havenhurst Dr 77059
Havenpark Ct & Dr 77059
Havenridge Dr 77083
Havenrock Dr 77038
Havens St 77076
Havenvale Ln 77049
Havenview Dr 77041
Havenway Ln 77064
Havenwoods Dr 77066
Haver St 77006
Haverdown Dr 77065
Haverhill Dr 77008
Haversham Dr 77024
Havershire Ln 77079
Haverstock Dr 77031
Haverton Dr 77016
Haverty Dr 77032
Haviland St 77035
Havner Ct 77037
Havner Ln
200-1299 77037
1700-3599 77093
W Havner Ln 77037
Hawaii Ln 77040
Hawick Dr 77084
Hawkeye Ct 77049
Hawkins Ave 77037
Hawkins Bnd 77044
Hawkins St 77003
Hawks Nest Dr 77067
Hawley Ln 77040
Hawthorne St
100-1699 77006
1700-1999 77098
Hawthorne Falls Ln 77049
Hawthorne Shores Dr 77044
Hay Meadow Ln 77039
Haybrook Dr 77089
Hayes Rd
1400-2599 77077
2800-3199 77082
Haygood St 77022
Haymarket Ln 77015
Haynes Dr 77069
Haynes Rd 77066
Haynes St 77088
Haynesworth Ln 77034
Hays St 77009
Hayslip Ln 77041
Hayward Ct 77095
Haywood Dr 77061
N Haywood Dr 77061
S Haywood Dr 77061
Haywood St
4200-4899 77093
5000-5699 77016
Haywood Oaks Dr 77095
Hazard St
1500-2599 77019
2600-3498 77098
3500-5299 77098
5300-5799 77005
Hazel St
1400-1599 77019
1600-1699 77006
Hazel Cove Dr 77095
Hazel Creek Cir 77095
Hazel Glade Ct 77059
Hazel Park Dr 77082
Hazel Ridge Ct 77062
Hazelgrove Dr 77084
Hazelhurst Dr
10000-10099 77080
10100-11199 77043
Hazelton St 77035
Hazelwood Ln 77077
Hazen St
5600-5699 77081
6800-7099 77074
8000-9100 77036
9102-9198 77036

10600-11799 77072
Hazlitt Dr 77032
Hazy Creek Dr 77084
Hazy Hill Dr 77044
Hazy Meadow Ln 77040
Hazy Park Dr 77082
Hazy Pines Ct 77059
Hazy Valley Ln 77086
Hazyglen Dr 77082
Hazyknoll Ln 77067
Headelak Dr 77088
Heaney Dr
200-299 77076
1600-2199 77093
Hearth Dr 77054
Hearth Hollow Ln 77047
N, S & W Hearthstone Green Ct & Dr 77095
Hearthstone Meadows Dr 77095
Hearthwood Dr 77040
Heartwind Ct 77095
Heath Ct & St 77016
Heath Cote Ln 77073
Heath Hollow Way 77058
Heath Park Trl 77089
Heath Spring Ct 77044
Heathbrook Ln 77094
Heathcliff Ct 77024
Heather Cir 77055
Heather Ct 77024
Heather Run 77041
Heather Bend Ct 77059
Heather Bluff Ct & Ln 77075
Heather Cove Ct 77062
Heather Falls Dr 77065
Heather Falls Way 77062
Heather Green Dr 77062
Heather Heights Way 77095
Heather Hill Dr 77086
Heather Landing Ln 77072
Heather Meadow Ct 77059
Heather Row Ln 77044
Heather Spring Ln 77008
Heather Trail Dr 77075
Heather Valley Way 77062
Heatherbank Dr 77095
Heatherbloom Dr
3700-5399 77045
5700-6499 77085
Heatherbrook Dr
3700-5499 77045
5600-6499 77085
Heathercliff Ln 77075
Heathercrest St 77045
Heatherdale Dr 77059
Heatherfield Dr 77079
Heatherford Ct & Dr 77041
Heatherglen Dr 77096
Heathergold Dr 77084
Heatherhill Pl 77077
Heatherly Dr 77083
Heathermill Dr 77066
Heathersage Dr 77084
Heatherside St 77016
Heatherton Hill Ln 77047
Heatherview Dr 77099
Heatherwind Ln 77047
Heatherwood Dr 77076
Heatherwood Park Cir 77094
Heathfield Ct 77084
Heathford Ln 77053
Heathgate Ct & Dr 77062
Heathglen Ln 77075
Heathmoor Ln 77084
Heathrow Forest Pkwy 77032
Heathton Dr 77099
Heathwick Ln 77043
Heathwood Ct & Dr 77077
Heaton Dr 77084
Heaven Leigh Trl 77064
Hebert St 77012
Hebert Trail Dr 77082
Hector St 77093
Hedge Way Dr 77065
Hedgecroft Dr 77060

Hedgedown Dr 77065
Hedgegate Dr 77065
Hedgewick Dr 77084
Hedgewood St 77016
Hedgley Pl 77069
E & W Hedrick St 77011
Hedwig Cir, Ct, Ln, Rd & Way 77024
Hedwig Green St 77024
Hedwig Shadows Dr 77024
Heffernan St 77087
Heflin Ln 77095
Heidelberg Ct 77070
Heidrich St 77018
Heights Blvd
1-899 77007
900-1999 77008
S Heights Blvd 77007
E, N, S & W Heights Hollow Ln 77007
Heilig Rd 77074
Heiner St 77002
Heiser St 77087
Heite St 77022
Helberg Rd 77092
Helen St 77009
Helena St
2000-2099 77002
2300-3199 77006
Helios Way 77079
Helmers St
4901-4999 77009
5800-5898 77009
6100-9299 77022
Helms Rd 77088
E Helms Rd 77037
W Helms Rd 77037
Helmsbrook Dr 77089
Helmsdale St 77043
Helvick Blvd 77051
Helvick Crescent Ave 77051
Hemlock St
6800-7199 77087
7200-7899 77012
Hemlock Hill Dr 77083
Hemlock Park Dr 77073
Hemphill St 77007
Hempstead Rd
12922C-1-12922C-1 77040
8000-9399 77008
9400-12899 77092
12900-16199 77040
15700-15798 77040
19800-20299 77065
Hempstead Villa Dr & Ln 77008
Hemwick Cove Dr 77083
Hemwood Ct 77039
Henderson Ave 77058
Henderson St 77007
Hendon Ln
6700-7199 77074
8700-8798 77036
8800-9699 77036
11200-12099 77072
Hendrix St 77093
Henke St 77020
Henley Dr 77064
Henniker Ct & Dr 77041
Henninger St 77023
Heno St 77051
Henrietta St 77088
Henry Rd 77060
Henry St 77009
Hensen Creek Dr 77086
Henson St 77028
Hepburn St 77054
Heradere St 77007
Herald St 77029
Herald Square Dr 77099
Herbrand Dr 77034
Hercules Ave 77058
Herdsman Dr 77079
Hereford Ln 77058
Hereford St 77087
Hereliso Dr 77094

Heritage Ct 77024
Heritage Ln
11900-11999 77024
18100-18200 77058
18202-18298 77058
Heritage Shr 77094
Heritage Creek Park, Ter & Vlg 77008
Heritage Creek Oaks 77008
Heritage Crown Ct 77047
Heritage Elm Ct 77084
Heritage Grove Dr 77066
Heritage Oaks Ln 77024
Heritage Trail Dr 77047
Heritage West Ln 77024
Heritage Wood Dr 77082
Heritagestone Dr 77066
Herkimer St
700-899 77007
900-1599 77008
Herlerle Dr 77049
Hermann Dr 77004
Hermann Rd 77050
Hermann Circle Dr 77030
Hermann Lake Dr 77021
Hermann Museum Circle Dr 77004
Hermann Park Ct 77021
Hermann Park Dr 77030
Hermann Pressler Dr 77030
Hermitage Ln 77079
Hermosa Ct 77024
Herngrif St 77032
Heron Dr
5400-5899 77033
6200-7199 77087
Heron Cove Ct 77084
Heron Field Ct 77059
Heron Flight St 77064
Heron Lakes Dr 77064
Heron Meadows Dr 77095
Heron Nest Dr & St 77064
Heron View St 77064
Heron Village Dr 77064
Heron Walk St 77064
Herongate Dr 77084
Herridge St 77022
Herschell St 77028
Herschelwood St 77033
Hershe St
4200-7799 77020
7900-8100 77029
8102-8198 77029
13700-14699 77015
Hertford St 77048
Hertford Park Dr 77084
Heslep St 77009
Hesta Ln 77016
Hewitt Dr
1300-2399 77018
5500-5999 77092
Hewrick St 77020
Heysham St 77013
Hezekiah Ln 77088
Hiacintas Way 77073
Hialeah Dr
2200-2399 77018
4900-5699 77092
Hiawatha Dr 77036
Hibernia Dr 77088
Hibiscus Point Dr 77095
Hibury Ct & Dr 77024
Hickman St 77026
Hickok Ln
3800-4399 77047
8000-8999 77075
Hickory St 77007
Hickory Bend Ct 77084
Hickory Bend Dr 77070
Hickory Cove Dr 77095
Hickory Downs Dr 77084
Hickory Forest Dr 77088
Hickory Grove Dr 77084
Hickory Hollow St 77024
Hickory Knoll Dr 77059
Hickory Lawn Dr 77077

Hickory Meadow Ct 77044
Hickory Meadow Ln 77084
Hickory Mill Ct 77095
Hickory Point Ct & Rd 77095
Hickory Post Ln 77079
Hickory Ridge Dr 77024
Hickory Shadows Dr 77055
Hickory Trail Ln 77064
Hickory Tree Ct 77065
Hickorywood Ln 77024
Hicks St 77007
Hidalgo St 77056
Hidalgo Valley Ln 77090
Hidden Cv 77079
Hidden Hvn 77095
Hidden Rdg E 77073
Hidden Rdg W 77073
Hidden Acres Dr 77084
Hidden Arbor Ln
6300-6499 77088
7000-7099 77040
Hidden Bend Dr 77064
Hidden Breeze Dr 77049
Hidden Bridle Ct 77073
Hidden Castle Dr 77015
Hidden Chase Dr 77049
Hidden Chestnut Ln 77084
Hidden Crest Dr 77049
Hidden Dell Ct 77059
Hidden Harbor St 77079
Hidden Key Ct 77090
Hidden Leaf Dr 77049
Hidden Manor Dr 77049
Hidden Moon Dr 77064
Hidden Nest Ct 77084
Hidden Oaks Ln 77095
Hidden Park Dr 77049
Hidden Port Ln 77089
Hidden Springs Dr 77084
Hidden Terrace Dr 77049
Hidden Trace Ct 77066
Hidden Valley Dr
500-699 77037
700-1899 77088
Hiddenwood Dr 77070
N & S Hide Ct 77073
Hideaway Cir 77074
N Hideaway Bend Ln 77044
Hiensley St 77009
Hiford Dr 77047
Higgins St 77033
High St 77007
High Banks Ln 77034
High Bridge Ct 77065
High Castle Ct 77059
High Cotton Ln 77072
High Haven Dr 77083
High Hollow Ln 77070
High Knob Dr 77065
High Knoll Ln 77095
High Level Rd 77029
High Life Dr 77066
High Mesa Ct 77059
High Mountain Dr 77088
High Point Ln 77053
High Sierra Ln 77084
High Star Dr
5800-6099 77081
6400-6499 77074
7700-7899 77036
10900-13199 77072
13200-13399 77083
High Tree Trl 77089
High Village Dr 77095
Highbury Ct 77084
Highbury View Ct 77047
Highcliff Ct 77049
Highcrest Dr
7500-8599 77055
9100-9199 77080
Highcroft Dr 77077
Highfalls Dr 77068
Highfield Dr 77095
Highgrove Dr 77077
Highgrove Park 77024
Highland St 77009

Highland Trl 77084
Highland Arbor Dr 77070
Highland Brook Dr 77083
Highland Canyon Dr 77095
Highland Castle Ln 77015
Highland Cove Dr 77070
Highland Cross Dr 77073
Highland Farms Rd 77095
Highland Glen Dr 77070
Highland Green Ct 77070
Highland Hollow Ln 77073
Highland Lodge Ln 77044
Highland Meadow Dr 77089
Highland Meadow Vlg
Dr 77089
Highland Mist Cir 77015
Highland Park Ct & Dr 77070
Highlander Dr 77082
Highlands View Ct 77084
Highlawn St 77022
Highmanor Dr 77038
Highmeadow Dr 77063
Highpines Dr 77068
Highridge St 77013
Highrock Rd 77092
Highsprings Dr 77068
Highview Dr 77039
Highway 6 N 77084
Highwood Rd 77079
Hilary St 77026
Hilda St 77033
Hilda Oaks Dr 77028
S Hill Dr 77089
S Hill Ln 77089
Hill Rd
100-1299 77037
1300-1799 77039
Hill St 77020
Hill Branch Dr 77082
Hill Canyon Ln 77072
Hill Oak Dr 77092
Hillard Green Ln 77047
Hillbarn Dr 77040
Hillbrook Ct & Dr 77070
Hillcrest Rd 77040
Hillcroft St
2700-3999 77057
5600-5999 77036
6000-8299 77081
8300-11199 77096
11300-12699 77035
12700-14499 77085
Hilldale St 77055
Hillenberg Ln 77034
Hillendahl Blvd 77055
Hiller St 77015
Hillglen Ct 77062
Hilliard St 77034
Hillingdale Ln 77070
Hillingworth Ct 77084
Hillis St
9200-9499 77028
9600-9799 77078
Hillman St 77023
Hillman Glen Cir 77086
Hillmere 77070
Hillmont St 77040
Hillock Bluff Cir 77073
Hillsboro St
5700-7699 77020
7900-8199 77029
13700-14699 77015
Hillsgrove Ct 77088
Hillside Dr 77039
Hillside Bayou Dr 77080
Hillside Elm St 77062
Hillside Falls Trl 77062
Hillside Glen Trl 77065
Hillside Hickory Ct 77062
Hillside Oak Ln 77062
Hillside Springs Cir 77084
Hillside Woods Ct 77049
Hillstar St 77009
Hillstone Dr 77049
Hillvale Dr 77077
Hilshire Glen Ct 77080

Hilshire Green Dr 77055
Hilshire Grove Ln 77055
Hilshire Lake Dr 77080
Hilshire Oaks Ct 77055
E Hilshire Park Dr 77055
Hilshire Terrace Ct 77080
Hilshire Trail Dr 77080
Hilton St 77093
Hilton Hollow Ct & Dr 77084
Hiltoncrest St 77064
Hiltonview Rd 77086
Hinds St 77034
Hinesburg Ct 77075
Hinman St 77061
Hinsdale Ct 77084
Hinsdale Springs Ln 77053
Hinton Blvd 77022
Hira Lake Dr 77099
Hiram Clarke Rd
12300-14699 77045
14700-16799 77053
Hiridge St 77055
Hirondel Ct 77087
Hirondel St
5400-5698 77033
5700-5899 77033
6200-6699 77087
Hirsch Rd
1-499 77020
4000-6699 77026
6700-11699 77016
11700-12099 77050
Hitchcock St 77093
Hobbs Reach Ln 77008
Hobby St 77053
Hockley St 77012
Hockley Garden Ln 77049
Hodgefield Ln 77090
Hodges St 77085
Hodges Bend Dr 77083
Hodgkins St 77032
Hoffer St
10800-10999 77075
11000-11099 77089
Hoffman St
100-1199 77020
3800-5199 77026
6000-7499 77028
7700-8799 77016
Hogan St 77009
Hogg St 77026
Hogue St 77087
Hohen Cir 77091
Hohl St
700-899 77022
2800-3199 77093
Hohldale St
100-299 77022
300-599 77091
Holborn Dr 77034
Holbrook St 77093
Holcombe Blvd
1000-2272 77030
2274-2292 77030
2401-2431 77021
2433-3299 77021
W Holcombe Blvd
2100-2599 77030
2600-3600 77025
3602-3698 77025
Holder Forest Cir, Ct &
Dr 77088
Holford Ct 77070
Holidan Way 77024
Holiday Ln 77075
Holland St 77029
Holland Fields Cir 77095
Hollandale Dr 77082
Hollandbridge Ln 77073
Holley Ct 77044
Hollins Way 77058
Hollis St 77093
Hollisbrook Ln 77044
Hollister Dr 77086
Hollister Rdg 77040
Hollister Spg 77040

Hollister St
1500-1799 77055
1800-4199 77080
4400-5198 77040
5200-9999 77040
14000-16799 77066
Hollister Cole 77040
Hollister Woods 77040
Hollock St 77075
Hollow Dr 77024
Hollow Ash Ct 77015
Hollow Banks Ln 77095
Hollow Bay Ln 77095
Hollow Bend Ct 77018
Hollow Brook Dr 77082
Hollow Cedar Dr 77049
Hollow Creek Ct & Dr 77082
Hollow Cypress Ct 77049
Hollow Glen Ln 77072
Hollow Hearth Dr 77084
Hollow Hook Rd
1600-1698 77080
1700-2699 77080
4300-5299 77041
Hollow Oaks Dr 77050
Hollow Pines Ct & Dr 77049
Hollow Quill Dr 77088
Hollow Ridge Dr 77095
Hollow Ridge Rd 77053
Hollow Rock Dr 77070
Hollow Sands Ct 77084
Hollow Tree Ln 77090
Hollow Wood Dr 77090
Holloway Ct 77048
Holloway Dr
4101-4297 77047
4299-4399 77047
4401-4499 77047
4700-4898 77048
4900-5099 77048
Hollowcreek Park Dr 77082
Hollowgreen Ct & Dr 77082
Hollowhaven Ct 77095
Hollowmill Ln 77082
Holly St
1201-1297 77007
1299-1899 77007
1901-1999 77007
5500-5599 77081
5700-5999 77074
Holly Way 77084
Holly Bend Ct & Dr 77084
Holly Chase Dr 77042
Holly Court Est 77095
Holly Crossing Dr 77042
Holly Falls Ct 77095
Holly Forest Dr 77084
Holly Green Dr 77084
Holly Hall St
2000-2098 77054
2100-3299 77054
3300-3399 77021
Holly Hill Ln 77041
Holly Knoll St 77077
Holly Lynn Ln 77077
Holly Meadow Dr 77042
Holly Oak Ct 77068
Holly Path Dr 77042
Holly Ridge Dr 77024
Holly River Dr 77077
Holly Shores Dr 77042
Holly Springs Dr
5300-5699 77056
6100-6299 77057
10000-11199 77042
Holly Stone Dr 77070
Holly Terrace Dr 77056
Holly Thicket Dr 77042
Holly Trail Dr 77058
Holly View Cir & Dr 77091
Holly Vista Dr 77070
Hollyberry Dr 77073
Hollybrook Ln 77039
Hollydale Dr 77062
Hollyglen Dr 77016
Hollygrove Dr 77061

Hollyhurst Ln 77056
Hollymist Dr 77084
Hollyoak Dr 77084
Hollypark Dr 77015
Hollytree Dr 77068
Hollyvale Dr 77060
Hollyvine Ln 77089
Hollywell Dr 77084
Hollywind Cir 77094
Hollywood Ct 77020
Hollywood St 77015
Holman St
700-999 77002
1000-3899 77004
Holmes Rd
1-2299 77045
2300-4499 77051
4500-4699 77033
4701-4799 77033
Holmsley Ln 77040
Holmwood Dr 77040
Holston Hills Ct & Dr 77069
Holt St 77054
Holtcamp St 77011
Holtman St 77060
Holworth Dr 77072
Holy Rood Ln 77024
Holyhead Dr 77015
Hombly Ct & Rd 77066
Home St 77007
Home Point Dr 77091
Homebrook Dr 77038
Homeland Dr 77083
Homer St 77091
Homestead Ct 77028
Homestead Rd
4000-8300 77028
8302-8498 77028
8700-11699 77016
11700-12299 77050
12800-13899 77039
Homette St 77044
Homeview Dr 77049
Homewood Ln
7800-8699 77028
8800-9399 77078
11900-12099 77024
Homewood Row Ln 77056
Hondo St 77051
Hondo Hill Rd 77064
Honey Cir 77004
Honey Ln 77085
Honey Bee Ct 77039
Honey Creek Dr 77082
Honey Creek Ln 77095
Honey Grove Ln 77065
Honey Hill Dr 77077
Honeysuckle Dr 77087
Honeyvine Dr 77048
Honeywell St 77074
Honeywood Ct 77059
Honeywood Trl 77077
Honolulu St 77040
Honor Ct & Dr 77041
Honor Park Dr 77065
Honsinger St 77007
Hood St 77023
Hook St 77064
Hook Left Dr 77089
Hooker St 77060
Hooks Creek Ct 77095
Hooper Rd 77047
Hoot Owl Rd 77064
Hooton St 77081
Hoover St 77092
Hoover Gardens Dr 77095
Hopetown Dr 77049
Hopewell Ln 77071
Hopkins St 77006
Hopkins Park Dr 77094
Hopper Cir 77037
Hopper Rd
1200-1299 77037
1300-5399 77093
5400-7099 77016
Hopson St 77019

Horace St 77026
Horatio St 77029
Horencot Dr 77081
Hornbeam Dr 77082
Hornberger Rd 77044
Hornbrook Dr 77099
Horne St 77088
Hornpipe Ln 77080
Hornwood Dr
5800-6099 77081
6500-6698 77074
6700-6899 77074
7500-7698 77036
7700-8599 77036
Horse Ln 77053
Horsepen Bayou Dr 77084
Horseshoe Bend Dr 77064
Horseshoe Lake Ln 77084
Horseshoe Springs Ln 77090
Horsetooth Canyon Dr 77095
Horton St 77026
Hosanna Way 77066
Hoskins Dr 77080
Hot Springs Dr 77095
Hotchkiss St 77012
Housman St 77055
Houston Ave
501-697 77007
699-2399 77007
2500-2698 77009
2700-3399 77009
3401-3599 77009
6900-6999 77040
E Houston Rd 77028
W Houston Center
Blvd 77082
Houston National Blvd 77095
Houston Oaks Dr 77064
N Houston Rosslyn Rd
5800-6699 77091
7200-11599 77088
11600-12899 77086
Howard Dr 77017
Howcher St
4100-4599 77047
5100-5199 77048
Howell St 77032
Howell Grove Ln 77095
Howell Sugar Land Rd 77083
Howland Ct & St 77084
Howth Ave 77051
N Howton St 77028
Hoya Ct 77070
Hoyte Dr 77031
Hub St 77023
Huckleberry Cir & Ln 77056
Huddler St 77074
Hudson Cir 77024
Hudson Ct 77024
Hudson St
7800-7999 77012
10000-10199 77064
Hudson Bend Cir 77095
Hudson Oaks Dr 77095
Hudson River Trl 77075
Huey St 77087
Huff Dr 77031
Huffmeister Rd
6900-6999 77084
7000-9899 77095
10000-11999 77065
Hufsmith Kohrville Rd 77070
Huge Oaks St 77055
Huggins Dr 77035
Hugh Rd 77067
Hughes Rd 77089
Hughes St
100-299 77011
300-1599 77023
1601-1699 77023
Hughes Ranch Rd 77089
Huisache St 77081
Huldy St
1700-2599 77019
2600-3099 77098
Hull St 77021
Hullsmith Dr 77063

Humble Westfield Rd 77073
Hummingbird Ln 77060
Hummingbird St
4300-5299 77035
5400-6299 77096
7800-7899 77071
Hummingbird Point Ln 77090
Humphreys Dr 77083
Hunkler Dr 77047
Hunt St 77003
Hunt Lake Ln 77084
Hunter St 77029
Hunters Branch Dr 77024
E, N, S & W Hunters
Court Dr 77055
Hunters Cove Ct 77039
Hunters Creek Dr & Pl 77024
E, N, S & W Hunters
Creekway Dr 77055
Hunters Den Dr 77079
Hunters Field Ln 77044
Hunters Forest Dr 77024
Hunters Grove Ln 77024
Hunters Lake Ct &
Way 77044
Hunters Lake Way Ct 77044
Hunters Park Dr 77024
Hunters Park Ln 77024
Hunters Park Way 77055
Hunters Ridge Ct 77024
Hunters Trace St 77042
Hunters Trail St 77024
Hunters Way Ct 77024
Hunterstone Ct 77084
Hunterwood Dr 77024
Huntford Ln 77044
W Hunting St 77026
Hunting Briar Dr 77099
Hunting Brook Dr 77099
Hunting Path Ct 77065
Huntingdon Pl 77019
Huntington Cv 77063
Huntington Crest Dr 77099
Huntington Dale Dr 77099
Huntington Estates Dr 77099
Huntington Field Dr 77099
Huntington Hill Dr 77099
Huntington Park Cir 77024
Huntington Park Ct 77024
Huntington Park Dr 77099
Huntington Place Dr 77099
Huntington Point Dr 77099
Huntington Valley Dr 77099
Huntington Venture Dr 77099
Huntington View Dr 77099
Huntington Way Dr 77099
Huntington Wick Dr 77099
Huntington Willow Ln 77090
Huntington Wood Dr 77099
Huntingwick Dr 77024
Huntley Dr 77056
Huntress Ln 77062
Huntwick Parc Ct 77069
Huntwyck Dr 77024
Hurfus Dr 77092
Hurley St
600-899 77022
2800-4099 77093
Hurlingham St 77093
Hurlplan St 77093
Hurst St 77008
Hurst Hill Ln 77075
Hurst Point Ln 77049
Hurtgen Forest Rd 77033
Huse St 77039
Hussion St 77003
N Hutcheson St 77003
Hutchins St
1-299 77002
300-2299 77003
2300-4199 77004
E & W Hutchinson Cir 77071
Hutton St 77026
Hyacinth St 77009
Hyacinth Path Way 77049
Hycohen Rd 77047

Hyde Park Blvd 77006
Hyde Park Pl 77069
Hydethorpe Dr 77083
Hydroville Ct 77078
Hyland Park 77014
Hylander Dr 77070
Hyta St 77018
Iberia Dr 77065
Ibex Ln 77049
Ida Bell St 77007
Ida Wells Forest Dr 77016
Idaho St 77021
Ideal St 77009
Idle Water Ln 77044
Idlebrook Dr 77070
Idylwild St 77009
Idylwood Dr 77023
Igloo Rd 77032
Ilex St
6700-7199 77087
7201-7297 77012
7299-7699 77012
Illene Dr 77093
Illinois St 77021
Ilona Ln 77025
Imani Ln 77085
Imogene St
4700-5499 77096
5800-8899 77074
8900-9292 77036
9294-9298 77036
Imperial St 77093
Imperial Bend Dr 77073
Imperial Brook Dr 77073
Imperial Crown Dr 77043
Imperial Falls Ct 77095
Imperial Forest Ln 77073
Imperial Grove Dr 77066
Imperial Lake Dr 77073
Imperial Manor Ln 77073
Imperial Point St 77072
Imperial Stone Dr 77073
Imperial Valley Ct 77060
Imperial Valley Dr
14900-18399 77060
18601-20297 77073
20299-22999 77073
Ina St 77028
Ince Ln 77040
Inch Rd 77055
Incline Dr 77066
Independence St 77051
India St 77047
Indian Blf 77057
Indian Byu 77057
Indian Cir
5600-5699 77056
5700-5799 77057
Indian Trl 77057
Indian Autumn Trce 77062
Indian Blanket Ln 77083
Indian Creek Rd 77079
Indian Field Ct 77084
Indian Hawthorn Ct &
Dr 77094
Indian Ledge Dr 77064
Indian Mill Dr 77082
Indian Oaks Ln 77044
Indian Paintbrush Ln 77095
Indian Quail Cir 77095
Indian River Dr 77088
Indian Shores Ln 77041
Indian Spring Trl 77050
Indian Sunrise Ct 77059
Indian Vista Dr 77064
Indian Wells Dr
11900-12999 77066
14100-14299 77069
Indiana St
1400-1799 77006
1800-2099 77019
Indianapolis St 77015
Indianola Dr 77032
W Indies Ct 77058
Indigo Lk 77077
Indigo St
5000-5799 77096

5800-6499 77074
Indigo Brook Ct 77089
Indigo Cove Ln 77041
Indigo Isles Ln 77041
Indigo Mist Ct 77084
Indigo Trace Ct 77070
Indigo Villa Ln 77083
Indindi Dr 77013
Indus St 77089
Industrial Dr 77029
Industrial Rd 77015
Industrial Way 77011
Industry St 77053
Inez St 77023
Inga Ln 77064
Ingersoll St 77027
Ingle Oak Ct & Dr 77041
Inglebrook Ln 77083
Ingold St 77005
Ingomar Way 77053
Inkberry Dr 77092
Inkberry Valley Ln 77045
Inker St 77007
Inland Hill St 77045
Inland Spring Ct 77059
Inlane St 77012
Inman St 77020
Innisbrook Dr 77095
Innisfree St 77024
Innsbruk Ct & Dr 77066
Innsbury Dr 77093
Innsdale Dr 77076
Innshire Ln 77045
Insley St
14400-14699 77045
15100-15199 77053
Institute Ln 77005
Interchange Dr 77054
Interdrive E & W 77032
International Blvd 77024
International Plaza Dr 77032
Intervale St 77075
Interwood N Pkwy 77032
Interwood S Pkwy 77032
Intrepid St 77072
Intrepid Elm St 77084
Intrepid Oak Ln 77073
Inverness Dr 77019
Inverness Forest Blvd 77073
Inverness Park Cir & Way 77055
Inverness Path Ln 77053
Inverrary Ct & Dr 77095
Invierno St 77029
Inwood Dr
2100-3899 77019
5300-5699 77056
5800-6299 77057
7500-7599 77063
10000-10899 77042
11300-11699 77077
Inwood Hollow Ln 77088
Inwood North Dr 77088
Inwood Oaks Dr 77024
Inwood Park Ct 77057
Inwood Park Dr 77088
Inwood Shadows St 77088
Inwood West Dr 77088
Iola St 77017
Ipswich Rd 77061
Ira St 77011
Irby St
6200-6299 77091
9300-9799 77088
Ireland St
4300-4499 77093
4500-5299 77016
Irene St
100-198 77009
14800-14899 77085
Iris Arbor Ln 77095
Iris Crossing Ln 77049
Iris Garden Ln 77044
Iris Hollow Way 77089
Iris Lake Ct 77070
Iris Lee Ln 77024

Iris Park Ct 77094
Iris Valley Way 77038
Irish Hill Dr 77053
Irish Oaks Ct 77083
Irish Spring Dr 77067
Iriswood Dr 77089
Iron Bridge Dr 77066
Iron Crown Cir 77068
Iron Horseshoe Ln 77044
Iron Lake Dr 77084
Iron Liege Ct 77088
Iron River Dr 77064
Iron Rock St 77087
Iron Springs Dr 77034
Iron Weed Dr 77095
Ironfork Dr 77053
Ironside Creek Dr 77053
Ironside Hill Dr 77053
Ironside Turn Dr 77053
Ironstone Ct 77067
Ironwood Blvd 77015
Iroquois St 77037
Irving Way 77087
Irvington Blvd
3400-6000 77009
6002-6098 77009
6100-9399 77022
9400-10299 77076
Isabella St
800-899 77002
1000-3199 77004
Isabella Way 77089
Isadore Cts 77026
Isetta Ln 77060
Isfall Park Pl 77053
Ishmeal St
100-299 77076
300-399 77091
Isla Vista Ct 77041
Islamorada Ct & Dr 77044
Island Breeze Dr 77041
Island Falls Ct 77041
Island Grove Ct 77079
Island Hills Dr 77059
Island Meadow Ct 77062
Island Oak St 77062
Island Palm Ct 77059
Island Shore Cir, Ct & Dr 77095
Island Song Dr 77044
Islandwoods Dr 77095
Isle Of Pines Ct 77049
Isle Vista Dr 77041
Isolde Dr 77024
Isom St 77039
Ithaca St 77017
Ivan Reid Dr 77040
Ivanhoe St 77027
Ivanhoe Springs Dr 77083
Ivory Brook Dr 77094
Ivory Falls Ct 77095
Ivory Meadows Ln 77084
Ivory Mills Ln 77094
Ivory Mist Ln 77041
Ivory Ridge Ln 77094
N Ivy Cir 77084
S Ivy Cir 77084
Ivy Park 77075
Ivy St 77026
Ivy Arbor Ln 77070
Ivy Bluff Ct 77062
Ivy Bridge Ln 77095
Ivy Brook Ct 77095
Ivy Creek Ln 77060
Ivy Crest Ct 77077
Ivy Dell Ct 77059
Ivy Falls Ct 77040
Ivy Falls Dr 77068
Ivy Field Ct 77070
Ivy Glen Dr 77077
Ivy Green Dr 77082
Ivy Grove Dr 77058
Ivy Heath Ln 77041
Ivy Leaf St 77016
Ivy Oaks Ln 77041
Ivy Parkway Dr 77077

Ivy Path Ct 77095
Ivy Point Ct & Dr 77083
Ivy Spring Ln 77088
Ivy Stream Dr 77095
Ivy Trail Ct 77095
Ivy Wall Ct & Dr 77079
Ivy Wild Ln 77095
Ivydale Dr 77049
Ivyhurst Ln 77082
Ivyknoll Dr 77035
Ivymist Ct 77044
Ivyridge Rd 77043
Ivyside Dr 77077
Iwo Jima Rd 77033
J St 77072
J C Oaks Cir 77028
J L Reaux St 77016
J Star Ct 77024
J W Peavy Dr 77011
Jachinge St 77023
Jacinth Ct 77066
E & W Jacinto Dr 77044
Jacintoport Blvd 77015
Jack St 77006
Jackrabbit Rd 77095
Jackson Blvd 77006
Jackson St
100-102 77002
104-299 77002
600-799 77003
800-1199 77010
1200-2299 77003
2300-5799 77004
N Jackson St 77002
Jackson Hill St 77007
Jackson Manor Ln 77047
Jackson Pines Dr 77090
Jackstone Dr 77049
Jackwood St
4800-4898 77096
4900-5799 77096
5800-7600 77074
7602-7698 77074
8800-9199 77036
Jacob Field Ln 77047
Jacobs Trace Ct 77066
Jacquelyn Dr 77055
Jade Ct 77076
Jade Cove Dr 77077
Jade Falls Ct 77095
Jade Green Ct 77059
Jade Hollow Ln 77077
Jade Meadow Ct 77062
Jade Ridge Ln 77095
Jade Springs Dr 77095
Jade Star Dr 77082
Jade Treasure Dr 77072
Jademont Ln 77070
Jadestone Terrace Ln 77044
Jadewood Dr 77088
Jaimes Ct 77094
Jalna St 77055
Jamaica St 77012
Jamail Dr 77023
Jamals Way 77073
Jamara Cir & Ln 77077
E Jambenti Plz 77046
Jameel Rd 77040
Jamels Way 77073
Jamerria Dr 77040
James Pl 77085
James St 77009
James Franklin St 77088
James River Ln 77084
Jamestown Mall 77057
Jamestown Rd 77024
Jamestown Colony Dr 77084
Jamie Ln 77048
Jamie Lee Ct & Dr 77095
Jan Glen Ln 77070
Jan Kelly Ln 77024
Janak Dr 77055
Janbar Rd 77047
Jane Austen St 77005
Jane Lynn Ln 77070
Janet St 77055

Janey St 77015
Janisch Rd 77018
E Janisch Rd 77022
Jansells Crossing Dr 77065
Japhet St 77020
Japonica St
6600-7199 77087
7300-7699 77012
Jardin St 77005
Jarmese St 77033
Jarrard St 77005
Jarvis St 77063
Jasamine Path Dr 77044
Jasmine Fld 77066
Jasmine Trl 77084
Jasmine Arbor Ct & Ln 77088
Jasmine Brook Ln 77089
Jasmine Creek Ct 77095
Jasmine Hollow Ln 77041
Jasmine Landing Ln 77044
Jasmine Park Ln 77044
Jasmine Ridge Ct 77062
Jasmine Stone Dr 77072
Jasmine Terrace Ln 77047
Jasmine Tree Ln 77049
Jason Dr 77014
Jason St
4700-5799 77096
5800-8899 77074
Jay St 77028
Jaycee Ln 77024
Jaycreek Ct & Dr 77070
Jaycrest Dr 77037
E & W Jayhawk St 77044
Jaywood Dr 77040
Jean St 77023
Jeanetta St 77063
Jeanna Ridge Ct 77083
Jeannine Dr 77008
Jeff St 77091
Jeffers Cir 77032
Jeffers Ct 77024
Jefferson St
400-1699 77002
1700-3999 77003
4200-4298 77023
4300-6499 77023
Jeffery St 77028
Jelicoe Dr 77047
Jengo Dr 77083
Jenikay St 77084
N Jenkins St 77003
Jenkins Park Ct 77047
Jennifer Ln 77029
E & W Jennifer Way Dr 77075
Jennings St 77017
Jenny Anne Ln 77070
Jennys Park Pl 77053
Jensen Dr
7900A1-7900A2 77093
1-1699 77020
1700-3599 77026
3520-3520 77226
3600-6598 77026
3601-6599 77026
6600-10499 77093
S Jensen Dr 77003
E & W Jerad Dr 77018
Jerek Dr 77053
Jericho Ct 77091
Jerome St 77009
Jerry St 77022
Jersey Dr 77040
Jersey Hollow Dr 77040
Jersey Shore Dr 77047
Jessamine St
200-299 77009
5400-6199 77081
6201-6299 77081
Jessica Ln 77069
Jessica Falls Cir 77044
Jessie Anne Ln 77041
Jester St 77051
Jet Pilot St 77075

Jethro St 77033
Jetty Ln 77072
Jewel St 77026
Jewel Ann St 77082
N Jewel Bend Ln 77075
Jewel Meadow Dr 77053
Jewel Park Ln 77094
Jewett St
500-1099 77009
1101-1199 77009
4001-4099 77026
Jezebel St 77033
Jillana Kaye Dr 77086
Jillian Crossing Dr 77067
Jim St 77092
Jipsie Ln 77051
Joan St 77085
Joan Of Arc Dr 77024
Joanel St 77027
Jocelyn St 77023
Jockey Club Ct & Dr 77065
Jody Ct 77099
Joe Annie St 77019
Joe Louis Ln 77091
Joel Wheaton Rd
2100-2499 77077
2500-2699 77082
Johanna Dr 77055
John St 77012
John Alber Rd 77076
E John Alber Rd 77037
John Dillon St 77044
John Dreaper Dr 77056
John F Kennedy Blvd
12300-13299 77039
14000-18799 77032
John Freeman Blvd & St 77030
John Ralston Rd
1900-1998 77013
2000-2799 77013
6400-6899 77049
6900-11099 77044
Johns Rd 77049
Johnsbury Dr 77067
Johnson St
1000-1298 77007
1300-2100 77007
2102-2398 77007
14500-14599 77034
Johnston St 77022
Joliet St 77015
Jolly Wood Ct 77086
Jonathan Ln 77011
Jones Ct 77004
Jones Rd
8000-8898 77065
8001-8899 77065
8900-10999 77065
11000-15299 77070
Jones Rd W 77065
Jones St
2500-2999 77026
4700-5099 77016
Joplin St
7300-7899 77087
7901-7999 77087
8000-8199 77017
8201-8299 77017
E Jordan Cv 77055
N Jordan Cv 77055
S Jordan Cv 77055
Jordan St 77017
Jordan Falls Dr 77085
Jordan Heights Dr 77016
Jordan Oaks St 77053
Jordens Rd 77084
Jorent Dr 77088
Jorine Dr 77036
Jorns St 77045
Joseph Pine Ln 77088
Josephine St 77026
Joshua Cir 77014
Joshua Ln 77055
Joshua Tree Ln 77073
Josie St 77029

Jove St 77060
Joy Cir 77060
Joy St 77028
Joy Oaks Ln 77073
Joyce Blvd 77084
Joyce St 77009
Joycedale Ln 77044
Joyner St 77087
Jubilee Ct & Dr 77083
Jubilee Park Ct 77065
Jubilo Ln 77049
Judalon Ln
5300-5599 77056
9500-9699 77063
Judia Ln 77099
Judiway St
800-2500 77018
2499-2499 77292
2501-2599 77018
2502-2598 77018
Judiwood St 77090
Judson Ave 77005
Judwin St 77075
Judy Ct 77015
Judyleigh Dr 77084
Juella Dr 77039
Julia St 77022
Juliabora St 77017
Julian St 77009
Julie Ln 77042
Juliet St 77087
Julius Ln 77021
Julliane Ct 77099
July St 77093
Jumada Cir 77091
Junco Dr 77040
Junction Dr 77045
Junction Place Dr 77045
June St 77016
Juneau Ln 77040
Junell St 77088
Junior St 77012
Juniper St 77087
Juniper Xing 77041
Juniper Canyon Ln 77062
Juniper Dale Ct 77049
Juniper Forest Ln 77062
Juniper Glen Dr 77041
Juniper Grove Dr 77084
Juniper Meadows Ln 77053
Juniper Park Ct 77066
Juniper Place Ct 77075
Juniper Point Dr 77083
Juniper Shores Dr 77044
Juniper Vale Cir 77084
Junius St 77012
Jupiter Dr 77053
Jupiter Hills Dr 77069
Jura Dr 77084
Justice Park Dr 77092
Justin St
4600-4899 77093
5700-5899 77016
Justin Trl 77070
Jutland Rd
7300-9300 77033
9302-9498 77033
10900-12899 77048
K St 77072
Kabee St 77020
Kacee Dr 77084
Kaeling Meadow Ct 77075
Kaeling Park Ct 77075
Kahlden Ct 77079
Kainer Meadows Ln 77047
Kaiser St 77040
Kaitlyn Dr 77049
Kakerglen Ct 77084
Kale Ct 77066
Kaler Rd 77060
Kalewood Dr 77099
Kaliste Meadow Dr 77090
Kaltenbrun Rd 77086
Kamala Dr 77049
Kamiah Ct 77040
Kamren Dr 77049

Kanah Ln 77090
Kandarian St 77093
Kane St 77007
Kansack Ln 77086
Kansas St 77007
Kappa Dr 77051
Kapri Ln 77025
Karalas Ln 77047
Karbach St 77092
Karbo Ln 77073
Karcher St 77009
Karelian Dr 77091
Karen St
7100-7299 77076
7901-8397 77037
8399-8599 77037
8601-8699 77037
Karen Rose St 77075
Karenbeth Dr 77084
Kari Ct
400-499 77024
8500-8699 77040
Kari Springs Ct 77040
Karissa Ct 77049
Karlanda Ln 77073
Karlow Trail Ln 77060
Karlwood Ln 77099
Karnauch Dr 77028
Karnes St
200-299 77009
7200-7399 77020
Karos Ln 77024
Karsen Dr 77049
Karter Ct 77064
Kashmere St 77026
Kassarine Pass 77033
Kassikay Dr 77084
Katelyn Manor Ln 77073
Katherine Ct 77089
Kathi Ann Ln 77038
Kathleen Haney Dr 77086
Kathryn St 77015
N & S Kathy Ave 77071
Katrina Ct 77089
Katy Fwy
2401-3197 77007
3199-5600 77007
5602-5898 77007
7400-9099 77024
9100-10098 77055
9101-10699 77024
10100-11698 77043
10701-11697 77079
11699-14699 77079
14701-14799 77079
14800-19999 77094
Katy St 77007
Katy Knoll Ct 77082
Katya Gillian Dr 77034
Kay Cir 77051
Kay Ln 77064
Kay St 77093
Kay Jo Ln 77044
Kayla Ln 77015
Kaylyn St 77060
Kearny Dr 77076
Keating St 77003
Keatley Dr 77077
Keats St 77085
Keegan Rd 77099
Keegan Run Dr 77084
Keegans Forest Ln 77031
Keegans Glen Dr 77031
Keegans Ridge Rd 77031
Keegans Ridge Way Dr 77083
Keegans Wood Dr 77083
Keel St 77076
Keeland St
3801 1/2A-3801 1/2B 77093
2400-3899 77093
4700-5099 77016
Keelby Dr 77015
Keely St 77045
Keenan Cv 77084

Keene St 77009
Keene Mill Ct 77067
Keeneland Ln 77038
Keenen Ct 77077
Keese Dr 77089
Keira Ct 77069
Keith St 77093
Kelbrook Dr 77062
Kelburn Dr 77016
Kelford St 77028
Kell Cir & Dr 77040
Kellaken Dr 77037
Keller St
6600-7199 77087
7200-8099 77012
Kellerwood Dr 77086
Kellett St
8200-8699 77028
8800-8999 77078
Kelley Crk 77094
Kelley St
101-197 77009
199-1299 77009
2000-5899 77026
Kelling St 77045
Kellogg St 77012
Kellway Dr 77015
Kellwood Dr 77040
Kelly Ln 77066
Kelly Brook Trl 77038
Kelly Hill Ct 77034
Kelly Lake Trl 77089
Kellywood Ln 77079
Kelsey Meadows Ct 77040
Kelsey Rae Ct 77069
Kelsey Trail Ln 77047
Kelso St 77021
Kelton St 77021
Kelvin Dr
4500-5699 77005
6600-6799 77030
Kelving St 77030
Kemberton Dr 77062
Kemble Creek Dr 77084
Kemerton Dr 77099
Kemp St 77023
Kemp Forest Dr 77080
Kemp Hollow Ln 77043
Kempridge St 77080
Kempsey Ln 77040
Kempwood Dr
7600-8199 77055
8201-8399 77055
8400-10199 77080
10200-10899 77043
Kemrock Cir, Ct & Dr 77049
Kemton St 77012
Kemwood Dr 77024
Kenbridge Dr 77067
Kenchester Dr 77073
Kenco St 77093
Kendale Dr 77083
Kendalia Dr 77036
N Kendall St 77003
Kendall Ridge Ln 77095
Kendallbrook Dr 77095
Kendalls Path Ct 77053
Kendrick Plaza Dr 77032
Kenilwood Dr 77033
Kenilworth St 77024
Kenlea Ln 77060
Kenmore St 77023
Kennard Dr 77074
Kennebeck Pl 77077
Kennedy St 77003
Kennedy Commerce
Dr 77032
Kennedy Heights Blvd 77048
Kennedy Oaks St 77053
Kennewick Dr 77064
Kennon St 77009
Kennonview Dr 77068
Kenny St 77015
Kenrick Dr
600-799 77060
800-1099 77032
Kenross St 77043
Kensico Rd 77036
Kensington Ct 77024
N Kensington Dr 77031
S Kensington Dr 77031
Kensington Pl 77034
Kensley Dr 77082
Kenswick Key Ln 77047
Kent St 77005
Kent Oak Dr 77077
Kentfield Dr 77093
Kentford Dr 77062
Kentland Ct & Dr 77067
Kenton St 77028
Kenton Hills Ct 77089
Kentshire Dr 77078
Kentstead Ln 77047
Kentucky St 77026
Kentwalk Dr 77041
Kentwater Ct 77095
Kentwick Dr 77084
Kenwell Dr 77083
Kenwood Ln 77013
Keough Rd 77040
Kerbey St 77029
Kermit St 77009
Kern St 77009
Kernel St
6400-7199 77087
7200-7699 77012
Kerr St 77029
Kerrwood Ln 77080
Kerry Glen Cir & Ln 77078
Kershaw St 77037
Kersten Dr 77043
Kess Way Ln 77075
Kessington Ln 77094
Kessler Park Ct 77047
Kestrel Ct 77069
Keswick Pines Ln 77066
Ketchwood Dr 77099
Kettering Dr 77027
Kettle Mar Dr 77084
Kettlebrook Ln 77049
Kevin Ln 77043
Kevindale Ct 77040
Kevinkay Dr 77084
Kew Garden Dr 77047
Kewalo Basin Ln 77034
Kewanee St 77051
Key St 77009
Key Biscayne Ct 77065
Keyhole Ln 77084
Keyko St 77041
Keymill Dr 77064
Keyport Ln 77015
Keystone St 77021
Keystone Fairway Ct &
Dr 77095
Keystone Oak St 77084
Keystone Ridge Ln 77070
Keystone Spring Way 77089
Keyworth Dr 77014
Kiam St 77007
Kiamesha Ct 77069
Kian Ct 77081
Kiber Dr 77031
Kickerillo Ct & Dr 77079
Kidlington Ct 77039
Keith Harrow Blvd 77084
Kiev Hills Ln 77047
Kilburn Rd 77055
Kildare Dr 77047
Kiley Dr 77073
Kiley Park Ct 77089
Kilgore St 77021
Kilkenny Dr
3501-3697 77047
3699-4099 77047
4601-5399 77048
Killarney Ct 77074
Killene St 77029
Killiney Ct 77051
Killough St
5200-5299 77038
5300-7299 77086
Kilmory Ct 77014
Kilroy St
601-797 77013
799-899 77013
1300-1899 77029
Kilts Dr 77024
Kilwinning Dr 77084
Kimball St 77026
Kimberlee St 77049
Kimberley Ct 77079
Kimberley Ln
11900-12899 77024
12900-14999 77079
Kimberly Loch Ln 77089
Kimble St 77017
Kimbleton Ct 77082
Kimwood Dr 77080
Kinbrook Dr 77077
Kinder Ln 77051
Kindinde Dr 77043
Kindletree Cir & Dr 77040
Kindlewood Dr 77099
Kindred St 77049
King St
100-1299 77022
1800-4199 77026
7700-7899 77028
King Post Dr 77088
Kingdom Come Pl 77048
Kingfield Dr 77084
Kingfisher Dr
4300-5299 77035
5400-5499 77096
Kinghaven St 77083
Kinghurst St 77099
Kinglet St
4300-5299 77035
5400-5599 77096
Kings Row
1-99 77069
18000-18699 77058
Kings Way 77069
Kings Canyon Ct 77067
Kings Chase Dr 77044
Kings Cross Sta 77045
Kings Garden Ct 77044
Kings Gate Cir 77074
Kings Grove Dr 77044
Kings Head Dr 77044
Kings Lynn St 77058
Kings Meadow Dr 77044
Kings Park Ln 77058
Kings Path Ln 77044
Kings Ransom Ct 77041
Kings Ridge Rd 77053
Kings Walk Ln 77070
Kings Walk Round 77070
Kingsbridge Ln 77077
Kingsbridge Rd 77073
Kingsbridge Way 77083
Kingsbridge Meadow
Dr 77083
Kingsbrook Rd 77024
Kingsbury St 77021
Kingscourt Dr 77015
Kingsflower Cir 77075
Kingsford Dr
800-899 77094
12700-12899 77060
Kingsgate Ln 77058
Kingslake Forest Dr 77044
Kingsland Blvd 77094
Kingsley St
7300-7999 77087
8000-8199 77017
Kingsman Dr 77082
Kingsmark Dr 77094
Kingspass St 77075
Kingspoint Rd 77075
Kingsride Ln
12100-12298 77024
12300-12799 77024
13300-14199 77079
Kingsrose Ln 77075
Kingston St 77019
Kingston Cove Ln 77077
Kingston Green Ln 77073
Kingston Manor Ln 77089
Kingston Point Ln 77047
Kingston River Bnd &
Ln 77044
Kingston Vale Dr 77082
Kingstown Ct 77058
Kingstree Ln 77058
Kingsvalley St 77075
Kingsville St 77063
Kingsville Park Dr 77083
Kingsway Dr 77087
Kingswick Ct 77069
Kingswood St 77092
Kingsworthy Ln 77024
Kingussie Dr 77084
Kinkaid St 77093
Kinkaid School Dr 77024
Kinley Ln 77018
Kinloch Dr 77084
Kinney Rd 77099
Kinney St 77087
Kinney Point Ln 77073
Kinrush Ct 77095
Kinsale Valley Ln 77060
Kinsbourne Ct & Ln 77014
Kinsdale Ct 77067
Kinsdale Crossing Ln 77075
Kinslowe Ct 77064
Kinsman Rd 77049
Kintyre Dr 77084
Kintyre Point Rd 77095
Kiowa River Ln 77095
Kiplands Ct 77014
Kiplands Bend Dr 77014
Kiplands Way Dr 77014
Kipling St
600-1699 77006
1700-2999 77098
3500-3699 77027
Kipp Way Dr 77099
Kippers Dr 77014
Kirby Dr
800-2599 77019
2600-5299 77098
5300-6699 77005
6800-7899 77030
7900-9499 77054
12100-12299 77045
14600-15099 77047
Kirbyville St 77033
Kirk Ave 77034
Kirk St 77026
Kirkaldy Dr 77015
Kirkaspen Dr 77089
Kirkbend Dr 77089
Kirkbluff Dr 77089
Kirkbriar Dr 77089
Kirkbrook Dr 77089
Kirkbrush Dr 77089
Kirkbud Dr 77089
Kirkby Dr 77083
Kirkdale Dr 77089
Kirkfair Dr 77089
Kirkfalls Dr 77089
Kirkfield Ln 77060
Kirkgard Dr 77045
Kirkglade Ct 77095
Kirkglen Dr 77089
Kirkgreen Dr 77089
Kirkhall Dr 77089
Kirkhill Dr 77089
Kirkhollow Dr 77089
Kirkholm Dr 77089
Kirkland Dr 77089
Kirkland Oaks Ln 77095
Kirkland Woods Dr 77095
Kirklane Dr 77089
Kirkmead Dr 77089
Kirkmeadow Dr 77089
Kirkmont Dr 77089
Kirknoll Dr 77089
Kirkpark Dr 77089
Kirkpatrick Blvd 77028
Kirkplum Dr 77089
Kirkridge Dr 77089
Kirksage Ct & Dr 77089
Kirkshire Dr 77089
Kirkside Dr 77096
Kirkstall Dr 77090
Kirkton Dr 77095
Kirktown Dr 77089
Kirkvale Dr 77089
Kirkvalley Dr 77089
Kirkville Dr 77089
Kirkway Dr 77089
Kirkwell Dr 77089
N Kirkwood Rd
400-799 77079
1000-1199 77043
S Kirkwood Rd
1200-2799 77077
2800-2899 77082
4100-8199 77072
8201-8299 77072
8300-10899 77099
Kirkwood St 77022
Kirkwren Ct & Dr 77089
Kirkwyn Dr 77089
Kirwick Dr 77024
Kirwin Ln 77041
Kiskadee Ln 77058
Kisling St 77021
Kismet Ln 77043
Kit St 77096
Kitchener St 77093
Kite Hill Dr 77041
N Kitmore Dr 77099
Kittrell St 77034
Kittridge St 77028
Kitty Ln 77015
Kitty Brook Dr & Ln 77071
Kittycrest Ln 77032
Klamath Ln 77090
Klamath Falls Ct & Dr 77041
Kleberg St 77056
Kleberg Place Dr 77064
Kleckley Dr 77075
Kleewood Dr 77064
N & S Klein Circle Dr 77088
Kleinbrook Ct & Dr 77066
Kleindale Ct & Dr 77066
Kleinfields Ct & Dr 77066
Kleingate Ln 77066
Kleinmeadow Ct & Dr 77066
Kleinway Dr 77066
Klimer Way 77077
Klondike St 77075
Knickerbocker St 77035
Knight Rd
7500-9399 77054
9400-9699 77045
Knight St
800-1499 77022
2200-2399 77093
Knighton Cir 77034
Knights Dr 77065
Knights Bridge Ln 77058
Knights Crest Dr 77083
Knights Hill Ct 77065
Knightsland Trl 77083
Knightsridge Ln 77094
Knightsway Dr 77083
Knightwick Dr 77008
Knightwood Ct & St 77016
Knightwood Forest Dr 77088
Knipp Ct & Rd 77024
Knipp Forest St 77024
Knipp Oaks St 77024
Knippwood Ln 77024
Knob Creek Ct 77062
Knob Mountain Trl 77016
Knobbley Oak Ct 77065
Knobby Knoll Dr 77092
Knobcrest Ct 77060
Knobcrest Dr
100-399 77060
11600-12499 77070
Knoblock St 77023
Knoboak Cir 77080
Knoboak Dr
9800-10199 77080
10200-10699 77043
Knockomie Ct 77095
Knodell St 77026
Knoll St 77080
W Knoll St 77028
Knoll Arbor Ct 77049
Knoll Bend Ct & Ln 77070
Knoll Cliff Ct 77095
Knoll Glen Dr 77082
Knoll Lake Dr 77095
Knoll West Dr 77082
Knollcrest St 77015
Knollridge Ct 77053
Knolls Lodge Ct & Dr 77095
Knollwest Dr 77072
Knollwick Ct 77053
Knollwood St 77019
Knotty Elmwood Trl 77062
Knotty Glen Ln 77072
Knotty Green Dr 77084
Knotty Oaks Trl 77045
Knotty Pine Trl 77050
Knotty Wood Dr 77092
Knottynold Ln 77053
Knox St
100-1699 77007
5600-7199 77091
7200-8799 77088
Knoxdale Ln 77047
Knoxville St 77051
Knoxwood St 77016
Knute St 77028
Koala Dr 77061
Kobi Ct 77068
Kodiak Ct 77067
Kody Ridge Ct 77034
Koehler St 77007
Koenig St 77034
Koester St 77040
Koinm Rd 77032
Kokomo St 77015
Kolb Rd 77017
Kolb St 77007
Kolfahl St 77023
Koloa River Ct 77040
Kona Cay Dr 77044
Kopman Dr 77061
Korenek St 77039
Korff Dr 77037
Kowis St 77093
E Kowis St 77037
Kransbury Ln 77095
Kress St
100-1899 77020
3900-4899 77026
Krisdale Ct 77084
Krist Dr 77055
Krista Ct 77049
Kristin Dr 77031
Kristin Lee Ct & Ln 77014
Kristina Ct 77089
Kriswood Dr 77014
Krueger Rd 77033
Kube Ct 77040
Kuester St 77006
Kuhlman Rd 77024
Kuldell Dr
5400-5799 77096
5800-6199 77074
Kulkarni St 77045
Kurland Dr 77034
Kury Ln 77008
Kuykendahl Rd
12000-12099 77067
12400-15799 77090
15800-17199 77068
Kyle St 77006
Kylewick Dr 77085
Kylie Springs Ln 77066
L St 77072
La Avenida Dr 77062
La Branch St
100-799 77002
800-1199 77010
1200-2299 77002
2300-5799 77004
La Brea Dr 77083
La Cabana Dr 77062
La Casa Ln 77062
La Concha Ln
1300-1699 77054
13500-13699 77083
La Costa Ln 77079
La Crosse St 77029
La Entrada Ct & Dr 77083
La Estancia Ln 77093
La Fonda Dr 77060
La Fontaine 77014
La Fonte St 77024
La Gloria Dr 77083
La Granada Dr 77083
La Grove Ln 77015
La Jolla Cir & Ln 77060
La Loma Dr 77083
La Luna Dr 77083
La Mancha Dr 77083
La Mesa Dr 77083
La Mirada Dr 77083
La Mora Dr 77083
La Noche Dr 77083
La Paloma Dr 77083
La Paseo St 77087
La Perla Dr 77048
La Place Ct & Dr 77083
La Porte Fwy
7900-8098 77012
8201-8213 77012
9300-9698 77017
9700-10200 77017
10202-10250 77017
La Porte Rd 77012
La Puente Dr 77083
La Quinta Ln 77079
La Rana Dr 77083
La Retama Dr 77013
La Riviera Cir & Dr 77015
La Roche Ln 77036
La Rochelle Cir 77071
La Rochelle Dr 77015
La Rue St 77019
La Salette St 77021
La Salle St 77027
La Sombra Dr 77083
La Terra Dr 77083
La Violetta Dr 77083
La Vista Dr 77041
Labco St 77029
Labelle Ln 77015
Labrador Dr 77047
Lacewing Ln 77067
Lacewood Ln 77024
Lacey Crest Dr 77070
Lacy St 77007
Lacy Cove Ct 77034
Lacy Hill Dr 77036
Lacyberry St 77080
Ladbroke Ln 77039
Ladera Dr 77083
Ladin Dr 77039
Lady St 77021
Lady Anne Dr 77044
N Lady Fern Ln 77073
W Lady Fern Ln 77073
Lady Fern St 77064
Lady Jane Ct 77044
Lady Slipper Rd 77038
Ladybug Dr 77064
Lafayette St 77005
Lafferty Oaks St 77013
Lago Bend Ln 77041
Lago Crest Dr 77054
Lago Royale Ln 77041
Laguna Cir 77095
Laguna St 77015
Laguna Bay Ct 77041
Laguna Beach Ln 77036
Laguna Del Rey Dr 77041
Laguna Falls Ct 77041
Laguna Meadows Ct &
Ln 77094
Laguna Pointe Ln 77041

Laguna Springs Ct & Dr 77095
Laguna Terrace Dr 77041
Laguna Trail Dr 77095
Laguna Villas 77036
Laguna Vista Ln 77044
Laird St 77008
NW Lake Dr 77095
Lake Ln 77040
Lake Rd 77070
Lake St
3000-3899 77098
5800-6299 77005
Lake Ter 77041
Lake Aquilla Ln 77044
Lake Arlington Ln & Rd 77044
Lake Barkley Ln 77044
Lake Benbrook Dr 77044
Lake Bend Dr 77084
N Lake Branch Ln 77044
Lake Center Run Ct 77041
Lake Champlain Dr 77044
Lake Chesdin Rd 77044
Lake Crystal Dr 77095
Lake Edge Ct 77071
Lake Excursion Ct 77044
Lake Falls Ct 77059
Lake Forest Blvd & Cir 77078
Lake Geneva Ct 77084
Lake Harbor Way 77084
Lake Harbor Way Cir 77084
Lake Hollow Ln 77084
N Lake Houston Pkwy 77044
S Lake Houston Pkwy
5000-7399 77049
12900-12999 77044
7010-1-7010-2 77049
W Lake Houston Pkwy 77044
Lake Iris Dr 77070
Lake Limestone Ln 77044
Lake Livingston Dr 77044
Lake Lodge Dr 77062
Lake Manor Dr 77084
Lake Meadows Ct 77077
Lake Medina Way 77044
Lake Michigan Ave 77044
Lake Orange Ct 77044
Lake Park Dr 77078
Lake Passage Ln 77044
Lake Place Dr 77041
Lake Prince Ln 77044
Lake Ridge Ct 77071
Lake Scene Trl 77059
Lake Sophie Ct 77044
Lake Tahoe Ct 77044
Lake Terrace Dr 77041
Lake White Rock Dr 77044
Lake Willoughby Ln 77044
Lake Willowby Ln 77044
Lakebrook Ct & Dr 77038
Lakecliff Dr 77077
Lakecliffe Dr 77095
Lakedale Dr 77095
Lakefield Dr 77033
Lakehurst Dr 77087
Lakeland Dr 77025
Lakemere St 77079
Lakemont Dr
2400-2699 77039
6500-6999 77050
Lakes At 610 Dr 77054
Lakes Of Pine Forest Ct & Dr 77084
Lakeshore Rdg 77041
Lakeshore Way 77077
Lakeshore Bend Dr 77080
Lakeshore Edge Dr 77080
W Lakeshore Landing Dr 77044
Lakeshore Ridge Ct 77041
Lakeshore Terrace Dr 77080
Lakeshore Way Ct & Cv 77077
Lakeside Cv 77094
Lakeside Dr 77050
Lakeside Ln 77058
Lakeside Trl 77077
Lakeside Bend Ct & Dr 77077
Lakeside Enclave Dr 77077
Lakeside Estates Dr 77042
Lakeside Forest Dr 77088
Lakeside Forest Ln 77042
Lakeside Gables Dr 77065
Lakeside Oaks Dr 77042
Lakeside Park Dr 77077
Lakeside Place Dr 77077
Lakeside Terrace Dr 77044
Lakeside Valley Dr 77042
Lakeview Cir 77084
Lakeview Dr 77040
Lakeview Pl 77070
Lakeview Haven Dr
6800-6999 77084
7000-7099 77095
Lakeway Ct 77071
Lakewind St 77061
Lakewood Cv 77070
Lakewood Dr
3000-3999 77093
7200-7799 77016
Lakewood Ests 77070
Lakewood Pl 77070
Lakewood St 77078
Lakewood Xing 77070
Lakewood Crossing Blvd 77070
Lakewood Forest Dr 77070
Lakeworth Dr 77088
Lakin St 77007
Laleu Ln 77071
Lamar St
400-798 77002
800-1199 77002
1201-1297 77010
1299-1999 77010
2000-3599 77003
3800-4299 77023
7300-7499 77011
W Lamar St 77019
Lamar Fleming St 77030
Lamar Park Ln 77049
Lamb St 77019
Lambert St 77044
Lambeth Palace Dr 77066
Lambright Rd 77075
Lamina Ln 77017
Lamkin Rd 77049
Lamond Ln 77095
Lamonte Ln
800-2399 77018
4800-5411 77092
5413-5499 77092
Lampasas St 77056
Lamppost Ct & Ln 77064
Lamprey St 77099
Lampson Manor Ct 77044
Lana Ln 77027
Lana Lee Ct 77084
Lanark Ln 77025
Lancashire 77027
Lancaster St 77087
Lancaster Lake Dr 77073
Lancaster Place Dr 77083
Lancaster Walk Dr 77066
Lance Cir 77053
Lancelot Dr 77031
Lanceoak Ct 77039
Land Rd 77047
Land View Dr 77073
Landa Ln 77023
Landcross Dr 77099
Lander Ln 77057
Landfair St 77060
Landfall Ln 77087
Landing Pines Trl 77084
Landmark St 77045
Landon Ln 77024
Landon Oaks Dr 77095
Landor St 77028
Landover Ln 77099
Landry Blvd 77070
Lands End Cir & Dr 77099
Landsbury Cir, Ct & Dr 77099
Landsdowne Dr
9000-10799 77096
11400-12399 77035
12401-12499 77035
Landshire Bend Dr 77048
Landswalk Dr 77099
Landward Ln 77066
Landwood Dr 77040
N Lane Cir 77086
W Lane Dr 77027
Lane St 77029
Lanecrest Ln 77024
Lanell Ln 77055
Lanesborough Dr 77084
Laneview Dr 77070
Lanewell St 77029
Lanewood Dr 77016
Lang Rd 77092
Langbourne Dr 77077
Langbrook Ct 77084
Langdale Rd 77076
Langdon Ln
6601-6697 77074
6699-7199 77074
7900-9600 77036
9602-9698 77036
10700-12099 77072
Langfield Ct 77040
Langfield Rd
4400-5399 77040
5800-7399 77092
8800-8898 77040
8900-9099 77040
Langham Dr & Way 77084
Langham Creek Dr 77084
Langham Crossing Ln 77084
Langham Dawn Ln 77084
Langham Heights Ln 77084
Langham Mist Ln 77084
Langham Way Dr 77084
Langhamwood Ln 77084
Langley Rd
2300-4999 77093
5000-7999 77016
Langley Springs Ct & Dr 77095
Langsbury Ct & Dr 77084
Langston St 77007
Langtry Ln 77041
Langtry St 77040
Langwick Dr 77060
Langwood Dr 77079
Lanham Ln 77075
Lani Blue Ln 77040
Lanibeth St 77032
Lanier Dr 77030
Lanier Shore Ln 77047
Lanny Ln 77077
Lansbury Dr 77099
Lansdale Dr 77036
Lansdown Dr 77049
Lansing St 77023
Lansing Crest Cir & Dr 77015
Lansing Field Ln 77073
Lanswick Dr 77062
Lantana St 77017
Lantern Ln 77015
Lantern Bend Dr 77090
Lantern Creek Ln 77068
Lantern Point Dr 77054
Lantry Way 77038
Lapas Dr 77023
Lapstone Dr 77082
Lar Ree Oaks Cir 77028
E & W Larah Ln 77094
Laralint St 77026
Larchbrook Dr 77049
Larchmont Rd 77019
Laredo St
6300-7599 77020
8100-8199 77029
13700-14699 77015
Larenerl Dr 77058
Lariat Dr 77055
Larimer St 77020
Lark Ln 77025
Lark Rdg 77070
Lark Brook Ln 77065
Lark Fair Ln 77089
Lark Haven Ln 77085
Lark Meadow Dr 77040
Lark Mountain Dr 77064
Lark Point Ct 77044
Larkdale Dr 77099
Larkfield Ct & Dr 77059
Larkhall Ln 77014
Larkin St 77007
Larknolls Ln 77092
Larks Trace Ln 77090
Larkspur St
4100-4699 77051
4700-5199 77033
Larkstone St 77028
Larkwood Dr
6700-6899 77074
6901-8599 77074
9800-11099 77096
Larrali Rd 77032
Larry St 77093
Larson St 77061
Larston St
8800-10099 77055
10200-10399 77043
Larwood Ct & Ln 77038
Las Brisas Dr 77083
Las Cruces Cir & St 77078
Las Flores Dr 77083
Las Palmas St 77027
Las Terrazas Dr 77075
Lasaber Ct 77038
Lasbury Dr 77083
Lashbrook Dr 77077
Laskey St 77034
Lasso Ln 77079
Last Arrow Dr 77079
Lasting Light Ct & Ln 77095
Lasting Shadow Cir 77095
Latch Ln 77038
Latchmore Ln 77049
Lateen Cir 77015
Laterna Ln 77083
Latexo Dr 77018
N Latham St 77011
Lathrop St 77020
Lathy St 77044
Latma Ct & Dr 77025
Latson St 77069
Lattimer Dr 77035
Lattimore Creek Dr 77084
Lauder Rd 77039
Lauderdale St 77030
Laughing Wood Ct 77086
Laughton Ln 77084
Laura Anne Dr 77049
Laura Koppe Rd
2800-4199 77093
4200-6699 77016
7100-8499 77028
8800-9500 77078
9502-9598 77078
Laurajean Ln 77084
Laurel Dr 77021
Laurel Run 77084
Laurel Trce 77040
Laurel Arbor Dr 77014
Laurel Bank Way 77014
Laurel Bay Dr 77014
Laurel Bend Ln 77014
Laurel Birch Dr 77014
Laurel Bough Ln 77014
N Laurel Branch Dr 77064
S Laurel Branch Dr 77064
Laurel Branch Way 77014
Laurel Briar Ln 77044
Laurel Brook Ln 77014
Laurel Chase Trl 77073
Laurel Creek Ct 77040
Laurel Creek Dr 77014
Laurel Creek Way 77017
Laurel Falls Ct & Ln 77014
Laurel Forest Way 77014
Laurel Gate Ter 77094
Laurel Haven Way 77014
Laurel Heights Ct & Dr 77084
Laurel Land Ln 77014
Laurel Meadow Way 77014
Laurel Mist Way 77014
Laurel Nook Way 77014
Laurel Oaks Dr 77014
Laurel Park Ln 77094
Laurel River Bnd 77014
Laurel River Dr 77083
Laurel Rose Ln 77014
Laurel Rustic Oaks 77014
Laurel Shadows Ct 77062
Laurel Stone Ln 77040
Laurel Terrace Way 77014
Laurel Trails Dr 77095
Laurel Vale Way 77014
Laurel Valley Dr 77062
Laurel Wind Ct 77040
E & N Laureldale Ct, Dr & Rd 77041
Laurelfield Dr 77059
Laurelwood Dr 77058
Lauren Ln 77082
Lauren Forest Ln 77044
Lauren Veronica Dr 77034
Laurenhurst Ct 77043
Laurentide St 77029
Laurie Ln 77024
Lausanne Dr 77070
Lautrec Dr 77088
Lavaca St 77012
Lavell Dr 77018
Lavender St
2900-6299 77026
6500-6899 77028
7000-9499 77016
Lavender Shade Ct 77073
Laverne Cres & St 77080
Laverne Park Ln 77080
Lavon Lake Ln 77044
Law 77005
Lawford Ln 77040
Lawler Rdg 77055
Lawler St 77051
Lawn Ln & St 77088
Lawn Arbor Dr 77066
Lawn Wood Ln 77086
Lawncliff Ln 77040
Lawndale Plz 77023
Lawndale St
5100-5500 77023
5415-5415 77223
5415-5415 77261
5501-7183 77023
5502-7198 77023
7200-9499 77012
9500-9798 77017
9800-14099 77017
14101-15099 77017
Lawngate Dr 77080
Lawnhaven Dr 77045
Lawnridge St 77016
Lawrence St
700-899 77007
900-2899 77008
3000-3399 77018
Lawson St 77023
Lawsons Creek Ln 77072
Layhill Ct 77077
Layton St 77012
Lazaras St 77022
Lazee Trl 77024
Lazy Creek Ln 77017
Lazy Elm Ct 77095
Lazy Hollow Dr 77063
Lazy Lagoon 77065
Lazy Lake Dr 77058
Lazy Lane Blvd 77019
Lazy Meadows Dr 77064
Lazy Nook St 77076
Lazy Oaks St 77080
Lazy Pines St 77093
Lazy Ravine Ln 77073
S Lazy Ridge Rd 77053
Lazy River Ln 77088
Lazy Spring Dr 77080
Lazy Wood Ln 77024
Lazybrook Dr 77008
Lazydale Ln 77078
Lazywood Ln 77023
Le Badie St 77026
Le Chateau Dr 77015
Le Green St
700-899 77008
1000-1099 77009
1101-1199 77009
Le Harv Ct 77014
Le Havre Rd 77033
Lea St 77048
Lea Valley Dr 77049
Leacrest Cir, Ct & Dr 77049
Leader St
6300-7299 77074
7700-9499 77036
11500-13199 77072
Leader Trl 77072
Leaders Crossing Dr 77072
Leading Cir 77072
Leading Point Dr 77091
Leadore Dr 77040
Leaf Arbor Dr 77092
Leaf Glen Ln 77072
Leaf Oak Dr 77065
Leaf Point Ct 77095
Leafmore Ct 77083
Leafwood Ln 77084
Leafy Ln 77055
Leafy Arbor Dr 77070
Leafy Brook Ct 77084
Leafy Elm Ct 77062
Leafy Glen Dr 77059
Leafy Hollow Ct 77018
Leafy Shores Dr 77044
Leafy Tree Dr 77090
Leago St
200-299 77022
600-699 77091
Leahbelle St 77088
Leaholm Ln 77090
Leal Dr 77069
Leamington Dr 77070
Leamington Ln 77095
Leamont Dr
7900-8499 77072
8600-9199 77099
Leander St 77012
Leandra Dr 77083
Leaning Ash Ln 77079
Leaning Magnolia Ct 77049
Leaning Oak Dr 77088
Leaning Pine Dr 77070
Leaning Tree Ln 77064
Lear St 77015
Leath St 77093
Leather Market St 77064
Leather Saddle Ct 77044
Leaton Park Ct 77077
Leawood Blvd
8300-8599 77072
8600-10799 77099
Lebate St 77028
Leben St 77028
Leclerc Ln 77077
Ledbetter St 77087
Ledford Ln 77016
Ledge St 77075
Ledgecrest Dr 77038
Ledger Ln 77015
Ledgestone Dr 77059
Ledgewood Dr 77049
Ledla Ln 77032
Ledwicke St 77029
Lee Rd 77032
Lee St
1200-1699 77009
1700-3999 77026
4400-5499 77020
Lee Otis St 77051
Lee Shore Ln 77079
Leedale St 77016
Leeds Ln
15300-15499 77040
15600-15699 77083
Leedswell Ln 77084
Leedwick Dr 77041
Leek St 77004
Leeland St
700-1599 77002
1600-3999 77003
4000-5699 77023
Leemont Ct 77070
Leeshire Dr 77025
Leeward Ln 77058
Leffingwell St 77026
Legacy Park Dr 77064
Legare Ct 77084
Legend Ln 77024
Legend Cove Ct 77095
Legend Falls Ct 77083
Legend Grove Ct 77062
Legend Manor Dr 77082
Leghorn St 77040
Legion St 77026
Lehall St
1000-1199 77030
3600-3899 77021
Lehigh Ave 77005
Lehman St 77018
Leicester Ln 77034
Leighann Lane Dr 77047
Leighton St 77016
Leila Bend Ct & Dr 77082
Leila Oaks Cir, Ct, Dr & Ln 77082
Leinad Dr 77090
Leisure Ln 77024
Leitrim Way 77047
Leitz Rd 77075
W Leland Anderson St 77021
Lelay Cir 77022
Lelda Ln 77071
Lelia St 77026
Lemac Dr
4000-4199 77025
4300-4499 77096
Lemay St 77015
Leming Ct 77015
Lemma Dr 77041
Lemoine Ln 77049
Lemon Ridge Ln 77035
Lemon Tree Cir & Ln 77088
Lemond Dr 77016
Lemonwood Ln 77038
Lempira Ct 77069
Lena Dr 77022
Lenard St 77009
Lenclaire Dr 77053
Lendown Ln 77070
Lennington Ln 77064
Lennox Gardens Dr 77066
Lenore St 77017
Lenox St
1-499 77011
701-797 77023
799-899 77023
901-999 77023
N Lenox St 77011
Leon St 77009
Leona St 77026
Leonard Rd 77049
Leonard St 77023
Leonidas St 77019
Leonora St 77061
Leopold Dr 77021
Leprechaun St 77017
Lera St 77016
Lerner Dr 77015
Lerwick Dr 77084
Leslie St 77020

Leslie Ann Ave 77076
Lester St 77007
Letcher St 77028
Letein St 77008
Letica Dr 77040
Leto Rd 77080
Lettie Ave, Ct & St 77075
Levering Ln 77028
Leverkuhn St 77007
Levonshire Dr 77025
Lew Briggs Rd 77047
Lewis Dr 77099
Lewis St
1800-1899 77009
16200-16399 77040
Lewiston Ct & St 77049
Lexford Ln 77080
Lexham Dr 77083
Lexi Ln 77084
Lexington St 77098
Ley Rd
7100-8799 77028
8800-9499 77078
Leycrest Rd
8700-8799 77028
8800-9099 77078
Leywood Cir 77099
Libbey Dr 77018
Libbey Ln 77092
Libby Brook Ct 77044
Liberty Rd
2800-6399 77026
6501-6997 77028
6999-9199 77028
Liberty Bell Cir 77024
Liberty Bluff Dr 77049
Liberty Canyon Trl 77049
Liberty Creek Trl 77049
Liberty Cypress Ct 77049
Liberty Falls Ct 77049
Liberty Hall Dr 77049
Liberty Isle Ct 77049
Liberty Lakes Dr 77049
Liberty Maple Dr 77049
Liberty Mesa Ln 77049
Liberty Oak Ct 77049
Liberty Pine Ln 77049
Liberty Prairie Ct 77049
Liberty Ridge Ln 77049
Liberty River Dr 77049
Liberty Tree Ln 77049
Liberty Vista Trl 77049
Libson Falls Dr 77095
Lido Ln 77092
Lidstone St 77023
Lieder Dr 77065
Light Fall Cir 77095
Lightcliffe Dr 77031
Lighthouse Dr 77058
Lightstar Dr 77045
Lila Ln 77015
Lila St 77026
Lilac Spgs 77095
Lilac St 77009
Lilac Glen Ct 77095
Lilac Manor Ct 77065
Lilac Mist Ln 77038
Lilac Stone Ct 77044
Lilac Vale Ct 77084
Lilleux Rd 77067
Lillian St 77007
Lillja Rd
13800-13999 77037
14000-15999 77060
Lillus 77093
Lilly Mist Ln 77038
Lily Park Ln 77085
Lilygate Ct 77047
Lima Dr 77099
Limber Oak St 77082
Lime Springs Dr 77095
Limerick Ln 77024
Limestone St 77092
Lina St 77087
Linares Dr 77078
Linbrook Dr 77089

Lincoln Dr 77038
Lincoln St 77006
Lincoln Ridge Ln 77085
Lincolnshire Rd 77048
Lincrest Ln 77056
Linda St 77087
Linda Mesa Dr 77083
Linda Vista Rd
7800-8299 77028
8800-9399 77078
Lindale St 77022
Lindbergh St 77087
Linden St
6400-7199 77087
7200-7699 77012
Linden Chase Ln 77066
Linden Creek Ln 77017
Linden Gate Dr 77075
Linden Glen Ln 77039
Linden Knoll Ln 77085
Linden Springs Ct & Dr 77095
Lindenbrook Ln 77095
Lindencrest St 77061
Lindencroft Ct
9500-9599 77044
14100-14199 77070
Lindenloch Ln 77085
Lindenwood Dr 77024
Linder St 77026
Lindfield Ln 77073
Lindita Dr 77083
Lindsay Ln 77011
Lindsay St 77023
Lindy Ln 77023
Lindyann Ln 77008
Line St 77009
Line Camp Ct 77064
Linea Del Pino St 77077
Linecamp Dr 77064
Liner Ln 77095
Linfield Way 77058
Lingard Park Ct 77047
Lingonberry St 77033
Link Ct 77025
Link Rd
200-2800 77009
2802-2898 77009
3200-3499 77022
Link Valley Dr 77025
Linkfair Ln 77025
Linklea Dr 77025
Linkmeadow Ln 77025
Linkpass Ln 77025
Linkshire Dr 77062
Linkterrace Ln 77025
Linkview Dr 77025
Linkwood Dr 77025
Linn St 77026
Linnet Ln 77048
Linnhaven Dr 77072
E, N, S & W Linpar Ct 77040
Linsley Ln 77034
Linton Rd 77008
Linvale Dr 77016
Linwood St 77011
Lipan Rd 77063
Lipizzan Ln 77044
Lipps Ln 77041
Lipscomb St 77023
Lisa Ln 77021
Lisa Dawn Ln 77049
Liscomb Dr 77084
Litancor Dr 77024
Litchfield Ln 77024
Little Ct 77077
Little St
7900-7999 77028
14500-14599 77045
Little Ashlee Ct 77014
Little Barley Ct 77086
Little Branch Ct 77082
Little Fawn Dr 77084
Little Fox Ln 77060
N Little John Cir 77071
S Little John Cir 77071

Little John Ln 77024
Little John Way 77043
Little Leaf Ct 77082
Little Lisa Ln 77024
Little Pinto Ct 77095
Little Riata Dr 77095
Little River Rd 77064
Little Willow Walk 77062
Little York Rd
100-999 77076
1400-4205 77093
4206-4208 77016
4207-4999 77093
4210-4998 77093
5000-8199 77016
8600-9799 77078
13700-13899 77044
E Little York Rd 77076
W Little York Rd
330B1-330B2 77076
100-499 77076
500-6499 77091
6500-10299 77040
10300-13399 77041
14900-17999 77084
Littleberry Rd 77088
Littleborne Birdwell Ln 77047
Littlecrest Rd 77093
Littleford St 77045
Littleglen Ln 77084
Littleneviss Dr 77084
Littleton St 77022
Littonwood Ct 77094
Live Oak Aly 77003
Live Oak Frst 77049
Live Oak St
5515A-5515B 77004
5527A-5527B 77004
5543A-5543B 77004
500-598 77003
600-2199 77003
2201-2299 77003
2300-5599 77004
N Live Oak St 77003
Live Oak Green Ct 77049
Live Oak Hill St 77067
Lively Ln 77080
Livernois Rd 77080
Liverpool St 77021
Livings St 77028
Livingston St 77051
Livorno Way 77021
Lizette Ct 77075
Lloyd St 77022
Lloydmore St 77093
Lobera Dr 77083
Loblolly Bay Ct 77059
Loblolly Pines Way 77082
Lobo Trl 77084
Loch Bend Ct 77086
Loch Bruceray Dr 77084
Loch Courtney Ln 77089
Loch Creek Ct 77062
Loch Dane Dr 77070
Loch Glen Ct 77059
Loch Katrine Ct & Ln 77084
Loch Langham Ct & Dr 77084
Loch Lomond Ct & Dr 77096
Loch Maree Ln 77084
Loch Raven Ln 77060
Lochland Ln 77088
Lochmire Ln 77039
Lochnell Dr 77062
Lochshin Cir & Dr 77084
Lochshire St 77077
Lochstone Dr 77073
Lochtyne Cir & Way 77024
Lockbourne Dr 77038
Lockcrest St 77047
Locke Ln
2300-3299 77019
3400-3799 77027
5600-5699 77056
6200-6299 77057
7800-7999 77063
10000-10099 77042

13700-14499 77077
Locke Haven Dr 77059
Lockern St 77016
Lockett St 77021
Lockfield St 77092
Lockford Ln 77073
Lockgate Ln 77048
Lockhart St 77051
Lockhaven Dr 77073
Lockheed Ave 77061
Locksford St 77008
Locksley Rd 77078
Locksley Trace Ct 77094
Lockway Dr 77045
Lockwood Dr
211-397 77011
399-699 77011
700-2599 77020
3401-3403 77026
3405-6299 77026
6300-6999 77028
7000-9700 77016
9702-9798 77016
E Lockwood Dr 77026
S Lockwood Dr
1-332 77011
334-398 77011
1101-1199 77023
Lockwood Rd 77044
Locust Grove Dr 77095
Locust Springs Dr 77095
Lodenbriar Dr 77072
Lodestar Rd 77032
Lodestone Ct 77095
Lodge St 77092
Lodge Creek Dr 77066
Lodge Hollow Ct 77024
Lodge Run Ln 77065
Lodge Wood Ct 77086
Lodgehill Ln 77090
Lodgepole Rd 77049
Loeser Dr 77055
Lofland Dr 77055
Lofting Wedge Dr 77089
Lofty Elm St 77038
Lofty Mountain Trl 77062
Lofty Oak Ct 77059
Lofty Peak Ln 77062
Lofty Pines Dr 77065
Lofty Ridge Ct 77059
Log Cradle Dr 77041
Log Hollow Dr
6500-6999 77088
7000-8199 77040
Log View Dr 77040
Logan Ln 77007
Logan Mill Dr 77070
Logan Ridge Dr 77072
Loganberry Park Ln 77014
Logancrest Ln 77086
Logandale Ln 77032
Logans Run Ln 77075
Logger Pine Trl 77088
Loggers Trail Ct 77040
Logwood Dr 77088
Loire Ln 77090
Lolly Ln 77084
Loma Alta Dr 77083
Loma Linda St 77085
Loma Paseo Dr 77083
Loma Verde Dr 77083
Loma Vista St 77085
Lomax St 77093
Lombardy St 77023
Lomcrest St 77085
Lomitas St 77098
Lonallen St 77088
London Ln 77083
London St 77021
London Bridge Sta 77045
Londonderry Dr 77043
Londres Dr 77083
Lone Brook Dr 77041
Lone Dove Ct 77082
Lone Hickory Ct 77059
Lone Maple Dr 77083

Lone Meadow Ct 77095
Lone Oak Rd 77093
Lone River Ct 77095
Lone Shadow Trl 77050
Lone Star Dr 77055
Lone Tree Dr 77084
Lone Wolf Pass 77095
Lonesome Bayou Ln 77088
Lonesome Dove Ct & Trl 77095
Long Dr 77087
Long Rd 77044
Long Barrel Ln 77040
Long Bay Ct 77059
Long Bough Ct 77059
Long Branch Ln 77055
Long Creek Ct & Ln 77088
Long Gate Dr 77047
Long Glen Dr 77039
Long Lake Dr 77084
Long Leaf Dr 77088
Long Look Dr 77053
Long Meadow Dr 77047
Long Oak Ct & Dr 77070
Long Pine Dr 77077
Long Play Ln 77044
Long Point Rd
6400-7999 77055
8000-10098 77055
8000-8000 77255
8001-10099 77055
10100-10199 77043
Long Shadow Dr 77015
Long Shadow Ln 77024
Long Timbers Ln & Trl 77024
Longacre Dr 77055
Longbow Ln 77024
Longbrook Dr 77099
Longbury Ct 77084
Longcliffe Dr 77084
Longcommon Dr 77099
Longenbaugh Dr 77095
Longfellow Ln 77005
Longfield Cir 77063
Longford Dr 77049
Longforest Dr 77088
Longhorn Cir 77041
Longhorn Dr
1400-2199 77080
3300-3599 77084
Longhorn Ln 77041
Longlane Dr 77084
Longleaf Ln 77024
Longmeadow St 77033
Longmont Dr
5000-5699 77056
6100-6299 77057
9400-9799 77063
10000-10799 77042
Longmont Ln 77057
Longmont Place Ct 77056
Longmoor Dr 77084
Longren St 77089
Longridge Dr 77055
Longshire Ln 77040
Longstaff Dr 77031
Longtom Ct 77086
Longvale Dr 77059
Longview St
6200-7599 77020
13700-14699 77015
Longvine Ct & Dr 77072
Longwood Ct 77024
Longwood Garden Way 77047
Longwoods Ln 77024
Longworth Ln 77024
Lonnie Ln 77091
Lonniewood Dr 77059
Lonsford Dr 77086
Lonzo St 77063
Lookout Ct 77025
Lookout Mountain Ct & Dr 77069
S Loop W 77054
N Loop Rd 77070

Loop Central Dr 77081
Looscan Ln 77019
Loper St 77017
Loramie Creek Ct 77044
Lord St 77029
Loren Ln 77040
Lorena Spring Ln 77073
Loretto Dr 77006
Lori Ln 77040
Lori Brook Ln 77065
Lori Falls Ct 77065
Lorinda Dr 77018
E & W Lorino St 77037
Lorinowoods Dr 77066
Lorna St 77037
Lorne Dr 77049
Lornmead Dr 77024
Loro Linda Dr 77083
Lorraine St
1200-1699 77009
1700-2799 77026
Lorrie Dr 77025
Lorrielake Ln 77024
Lorton Dr 77070
Los Altos Dr 77083
Los Angeles St
3400-6399 77026
6700-7499 77016
Los Tios Dr 77083
Los Tres Ranchos Dr 77014
Losa Dr 77032
Lost Anchor Way Ln 77044
Lost Eagle Dr 77064
Lost Fable Ln 77095
Lost Forest Dr 77092
Lost Meadow Ln 77079
Lost Mill Ln 77095
Lost Pines Bnd 77049
Lost Pines Bend Ct 77049
Lost Spring Dr 77084
Lost Thicket Dr 77085
Lost Timber Ln 77066
Lost Trail St 77088
Lottman St 77003
Lotus St
4700-5399 77045
5400-5799 77085
Lotusbriar Ln 77077
N & S Lou Al Dr 77024
Lou Anna St 77040
Lou Anne Ln 77092
Lou Edd Rd 77070
Lou Ellen Ln 77018
Louetta Rd 77070
W Louise Rd 77037
Louise St 77009
Louisiana St
200-2299 77002
2300-3399 77006
3400-3599 77002
4900-5099 77006
Louisville St 77015
Lourdes Dr 77049
Louvre Ct & Ln 77082
Love Plz & St 77026
Lovebird Ln 77067
Lovejoy St 77003
Loveland Pass Dr 77067
Lovers Ln 77091
Lovers Wood Ln 77014
Lovett Blvd 77006
Loving St 77034
Lovington Dr 77088
Lowden St 77051
Lowden Crest Ln 77070
Lowellberg Ln 77084
Lower Arrow Dr 77086
Lower Ridgeway 77075
Lower Valley Dr 77067
Lowercove Cir 77064
Lowrie St 77093
Loxley Dr 77014
Loxley Meadows Dr 77082
Loyal Ln 77016
Loyel Pointe Dr 77064
Lozier St 77021

Lubbock St
1400-1499 77002
1500-2399 77007
Luca St 77021
Lucario Dr 77037
Lucas St 77026
Lucas Trace Ct 77066
Luce St 77087
Lucerne St 77016
Lucille St 77026
Lucinda St 77004
Lucky St 77088
Lucky Star Dr 77082
Lucore St 77017
Ludgate Pass 77034
Ludington Dr
5600-6699 77035
7500-7698 77071
7700-7899 77071
Luell St 77093
Luetta St 77076
Lufborough Dr 77066
Lufkin St 77026
Lugary Dr
5801-6997 77036
6999-7399 77036
8101-8197 77074
8199-9399 77074
Luke St 77091
Lula St 77009
Lum Ln 77078
Lumber Ln 77016
Lumber Jack Dr 77040
Lumber Ridge Trl 77034
Lumberdale Rd 77092
Lumpkin Rd 77043
Luna St 77076
Lundwood Ln 77084
Lundy Rd 77093
Lunia Ln 77021
Luns Ln 77073
Lupton Ct & Ln 77055
Lure Ct & Dr 77065
Lurlene St 77017
Luthe Ln 77032
Luthe Rd 77039
Luther St 77076
Luton Park Dr 77082
Luxembourg Dr 77070
Luzerne Dr 77070
Luzon St 77009
Lybert Rd 77041
Lycomb Dr 77053
Lyden Ridge Dr 77053
Lydia St 77021
Lyerly St 77022
Lylewood Ct 77040
Lymbar Dr
4100-4199 77025
4400-6299 77096
Lynbrook Dr
5300-5699 77056
5800-6299 77057
10000-11299 77042
Lynbrook Hollow St 77042
Lynchester Dr 77083
Lynda Dr 77038
Lyndhurst Dr
5100-6199 77033
6200-6899 77087
Lyndon St 77030
Lyndon Meadows Dr 77095
Lyndonnille Falls Ln 77078
Lyndonville Dr 77041
Lynette St 77028
Lynette Falls Dr 77095
Lynford Crest Dr 77083
Lyngrove Dr 77038
Lynkat Ln 77083
Lynn St 77017
Lynn Crest Ct 77083
Lynnfield St
1900-2799 77093
3600-4199 77016
5300-5499 77028
Lynnview Dr 77055

Lynnville Dr 77065
Lynwood Banks Ln 77092
Lynx Ct & Dr 77014
Lyons Ave
1600-7799 77020
7800-8499 77029
M D Anderson Blvd 77030
Maack Ln 77037
Mable St 77023
Mabry Mill Rd 77062
Macarthur St 77030
Macclesby Ln 77049
Macgregor Way 77004
N Macgregor Way
1301-1397 77023
1399-1400 77023
1402-1998 77023
2101-3197 77004
3199-3417 77004
3419-4499 77004
S Macgregor Way 77021
Machala Ln 77040
Mackenzie Dr 77086
Mackinaw St 77053
Mackinson St 77023
Mackmiller St 77049
Macleish Dr 77084
Macleish Ln 77032
Macmillan Ln 77083
Macnaughton Dr 77039
Macon Place Ct 77082
Maconda Ln 77027
Macridge Blvd 77053
Madalyn Ln 77021
Madden Ln
3900-4499 77047
5100-6799 77048
Maddox St 77078
Madeley St 77093
Madeline Alyssa Ct 77025
Madeline Grove Dr 77008
Madera Rd 77078
Madge St 77039
Madie Dr 77022
Mading Ln 77037
Madison St 77091
Madison Trl 77084
Madison Kendall Ln 77066
Madison Oak St 77038
Madrid St 77021
Madrone Ct 77095
Mae Dr 77015
Maeline St 77039
Maete Ln 77039
Maffitt St 77026
N & S Magazine Cir 77084
Magdalene Dr 77024
Magee Rd 77032
Magenta Oaks Dr 77072
Maggie Ln 77063
Maggie St
4100-4699 77051
4700-4899 77033
Magic Dr 77039
Magna St 77093
Magnet St 77054
Magnolia Cir 77024
Magnolia Cyn 77099
Magnolia St
5700-5899 77050
7400-7799 77023
E Magnolia St 77012
Magnolia Trl 77084
Magnolia Vw 77099
Magnolia Way 77070
Magnolia Bend Dr 77024
Magnolia Bloom Trl 77073
Magnolia Creek Rd 77084
Magnolia Crest Ln & Pl 77070
Magnolia Grove Ln 77049
Magnolia Hill Trl 77038
Magnolia Lake Ln 77083
Magnolia Leaf St 77065
Magnolia Ridge Dr 77070
Magnolia Shadows Ln 77095

Magnolia Shores Ln 77044
Magnolia Springs Dr 77066
Magnus Ln 77083
Mahan Rd 77068
Mahoning Dr 77074
Maiden Ln 77053
Maidencane Ct 77086
Maidstone Ln 77095
Maile Park Dr 77034
Main St
1-5299 77002
5300-5599 77004
5600-5800 77005
5802-6498 77005
6201-6497 77030
6499-7899 77030
7900-11699 77025
11700-15499 77035
N Main St
100-399 77002
401-499 77002
1500-6999 77009
7000-9099 77022
W Main St
404-406 77006
408-1699 77006
1701-3399 77098
3900-3900 77027
3902-4099 77027
Main Plaza Dr 77025
Mainbluff Ln 77040
Mainer St 77021
Mainford St 77009
Mainstay Place Ln 77044
Maisemore Rd 77015
Maize Ln 77041
Maize Field Way 77049
Majave Cove Ct 77089
Majestic St
500-1199 77020
3800-4899 77026
Majestic Trl 77059
Majestic Canyon Ln 77070
Majestic Glen Ln 77073
Majestic Oaks Dr 77040
Majestic Place Ct 77047
Majestic Ridge Dr 77049
Majesticbrook Dr 77095
Majesty Ln 77085
Major St 77061
Major Blizzard Dr 77089
Majorca Dr 77076
Makaha Cir 77095
Makalu St 77051
Makayla Dr 77049
Makeig St 77026
Makenna Ct & Ln 77049
Mal Paso Ct & Dr 77082
Maladi Dr 77053
Malcolm Dr 77076
Malcomboro Dr 77041
Malcomson Rd 77070
Malden Dr 77075
Maldon Ct 77016
Maleashi Dr 77090
Malfrey Ln 77084
Malibu Dr 77092
Malin Ct 77083
Mallard Dr 77043
Mallard Way 77044
Mallard Lake Ln 77084
Mallard Landing Ct 77066
Mallard Stream St 77038
Mallie Ct 77055
Mallorca Cir 77038
Mallory St 77051
Mallory Bridge Dr 77095
Mallow St
4100-4699 77051
4700-5199 77033
Malmedy Rd 77033
Malone St 77007
Maltby St 77011
Malvern St 77009
Mammoth Springs Ct & Dr 77095

Manacor Cir 77038
Manassas Ln 77083
Manatee Ln 77090
Manboro Ct 77067
Mance Ct 77094
Manchester St
7100-7199 77023
7400-10099 77012
Mancos Park Dr 77073
Mandalay Way 77045
Mandate Dr 77049
Mandavilla Dr 77095
Mandell St
2400-5199 77006
5300-5399 77005
Manderly Dr 77077
Mandolin Ct & Dr 77070
Mandrake Ct 77085
Mandrill Ln 77067
Manet Ct 77082
Manfield Dr 77082
Mango St
9600-9999 77075
10000-10699 77089
Mangum Rd
1700-5099 77092
5300-5499 77091
Manhattan Dr 77096
Manila Ln 77043
Manitou Dr 77013
Mankay Ln 77070
Mann St 77093
Manning Ln 77075
Mano St 77076
Manor Ct 77072
Manor St 77015
Manor Bridge Ct 77095
Manor Creek Ln 77092
Manor Green Dr 77077
Manor Park Dr 77077
Manor Point Dr 77095
Manor Square Dr 77062
Manor Tree Ct & Ln 77068
Manordale Dr 77082
Manorford Ct 77095
Manorgate Dr 77031
Manorhaven Ln 77084
Manorhill Dr 77062
Manorhouse Ln 77082
Manorstone Ct 77044
Mansard St 77054
Mansas Park Dr 77065
Mansfield St 77091
Mansfield Glen Ct 77014
Mansfield Point Ln 77070
Mansor Dr 77041
Mantle Ct 77065
Manton St 77028
Mantova Dr 77073
Manus St 77093
Manville St 77008
Manx St 77083
Manzano Dr 77083
Maple St
5301-5499 77096
5700-6199 77074
Maple Way 77015
Maple Acres Ct & Dr 77095
Maple Bend Ct 77084
Maple Bough Ln 77067
Maple Brook Ln 77095
Maple Chase Ln 77094
Maple Gate Way 77095
Maple Green Ln 77044
Maple Grove Ln 77092
Maple Hill Dr 77088
Maple Leaf Dr 77064
Maple Leaf St 77016
Maple Manor Dr 77095
Maple Rock Dr 77077
Maple Shores Dr 77044
Maple Springs Dr 77043
Maple Trace Dr 77070
Maple Tree Dr 77088
Maple Valley Rd 77056
Maplecreek Dr 77084

Maplecrest Dr
8100-8199 77072
8500-9399 77099
Maplemont Dr 77095
Mapleridge St 77081
Mapleton Dr 77043
Mapletrail Dr 77084
Mapletwist St 77083
N Maplewood St 77011
Maplewood Falls Ct 77062
Mar Vista Dr 77083
Marable Dr 77022
Maranon Ln 77090
Marathon St 77018
Marbella Cir 77083
Marble Dr 77070
Marble Bluff Ln 77049
Marble Canyon Way 77044
Marble Creek Ct 77077
Marble Crest Dr 77095
Marble Gate Ln 77069
Marble Glen Ln 77095
Marbledale Ct 77059
Marblemount Dr 77064
Marbrook Ct 77077
Marburg Ct & Dr 77066
Marbury Ct 77014
Marceau Dr 77065
Marcelia Dr 77049
Marcella St 77091
Marchant Rd 77047
Marchmont Dr 77024
Marchwood Manor Dr 77090
N Marcia Cir 77071
S Marcia Cir 77071
Marcia Dr 77065
Marcia St 77039
Marcolin St 77088
Marconi St 77019
Marcrest Ct 77070
Marcus St 77026
Marcy Dr 77033
Mardale Dr 77016
Mardel Ct 77077
Mardi Ln 77055
Mardi Gras Dr 77014
Marek Dr 77038
Margaret St 77093
Margarita St 77020
Margate Dr 77099
Margeson St 77084
Margie Ln 77037
Maria Edna St 77037
Mariah St 77051
N & S Marianne Cir 77071
Maribelle Way 77055
Maricella Cir 77084
Maricopa Ln 77015
Marie St 77009
Marietta Ln 77021
Marigny Dr 77014
Marigold St 77009
Marigold Bloom Ln 77044
Marigold Glen Way 77034
Marilane St 77007
Marilee Ln 77057
Marilyn Ln
2900-3399 77093
7200-7499 77016
Marina St 77007
Marina Vista Ln 77041
Mariner Grv 77084
Mariners Hbr 77041
Mariners Bay Dr 77095
Marinette Dr
6100-6198 77036
6200-6300 77036
6302-6798 77036
7400-7500 77074
7502-9098 77074
Marinwood Dr 77053
Marion St 77009
Mariosa St 77028
Mariposa St 77025
Mariposa Bend Ln 77089
Marisa Alexis Dr 77075

Marisol Dr 77083
Maritime Dr 77044
Marjorie St 77088
Mark Rd 77073
Mark St 77039
Market St
3000-5600 77020
5602-7798 77020
5901-7799 77020
5901-5901 77220
Market Garden Ln 77084
Market Street Rd
7800-11799 77029
11801-11999 77029
12200-14799 77015
14801-14999 77015
Markham St 77027
Markley St 77087
Marks Rd 77084
Markscott Dr 77082
Markwood Ct & Ln 77053
Marlberry Ln 77084
Marlborough Dr 77092
Marlebone Ct 77069
Marleen St 77034
Marlin St 77023
Marlink 77025
Marlive Ln 77025
Marlo St 77023
Marlowe St 77005
Marlstone Ct & Dr 77094
Marne Ln 77090
Marnel Rd 77055
Marners Ct 77014
Marnie Ln 77076
Maroby St 77017
Maroneal St
2100-2599 77030
3000-3799 77025
Maroon Ln 77077
Marquart St 77027
Marquette St 77005
Marquita Ln 77039
Marrs Dr 77065
Marsden St 77011
Marseilles Ln 77082
Marsha Ln 77024
Marshall St
200-1699 77006
1700-2099 77098
E & W Marsham Cir & Ln 77066
Marshfield Dr 77065
Marshhay Ct 77086
Marshwood Rd 77038
Marston St 77019
Marston Park Ln 77084
Marston River Ln 77066
Marta Dr 77083
Martell St 77051
Martha Ln 77032
Martha St 77026
Martha Springs Ct & Dr 77070
Martin Ct 77055
Martin Ln 77055
Martin St 77018
Martin Heights Dr 77031
Martin Luther King Blvd
4800-6399 77021
6400-9699 77033
10601-10897 77048
10899-12999 77048
Martin Wood Ct & Ln 77086
Martindale Rd 77048
Martineau St 77032
Martinique Dr 77058
Martinshire Dr 77025
Martinville Dr 77017
Marvell Dr 77032
Marwick Ct 77095
Marwood St 77015
Marwood Falls Ct 77070
Mary St
1000-1099 77020
1500-2399 77026

Mary Bates Blvd 77036
Mary Francis Dr 77039
Mary Jan Rd 77041
Mary Kay Ln 77048
Mary Lou Dr 77092
Mary Mount Way 77058
Marydel St 77076
Maryknoll Dr 77015
Maryland St
1400-1899 77006
1900-1999 77019
Marylebone Dr 77034
Marywood Chase 77079
Marzelle St 77093
Mascot St 77029
Mason Ct 77012
Mason St
200-299 77006
1300-1899 77019
1900-2899 77006
Mason Oaks 77085
Masonridge Dr 77095
Masonwood Ln 77070
Massachusetts St 77029
Massie St 77026
Masters Dr 77069
Masters Point Dr 77091
Masterson St 77029
Matamoras St 77023
Mateo Park Dr 77047
Mathewson Ln 77043
Mathis St 77009
Mathis Church Rd 77090
Matilda Dr 77032
Matilda St 77039
Matisse Dr 77079
Matson St 77078
Mattby St 77061
Matthews St 77019
Matthias Trl 77083
Mattina Dr 77042
Mattingham Dr 77066
Mattison Dr 77088
Maud St 77007
Maudlin St 77087
Maufferd St 77009
Mauna Kai Dr 77095
Mauna Loa Ct & Ln 77040
Maurine St 77039
Mauritz Dr 77032
Maury St
900-1399 77020
1400-2399 77026
2600-2698 77009
2700-5899 77009
Mauvewood Dr 77040
Maux Dr 77043
Maxey Rd
1-899 77013
900-1299 77015
Maxfield Dr 77082
Maxie St 77007
Maxim Dr 77065
Maximilian St
2100-2299 77039
2600-2799 77032
Maximos Dr 77083
Maxine Ln 77068
Maxine St 77029
Maxroy St
2500-2699 77007
3000-3299 77008
5900-6899 77091
7400-9899 77088
E Maxroy St 77088
Maxwell Ln & St 77023
May St 77076
May Laurel Dr 77014
May Showers Cir & Ct 77095
Mayard Rd 77041
Maybank Dr 77055
Maybank Shores Ct 77045
Maybell St 77091
Mayberry St
9400-9499 77028
9600-10499 77078

Maybrook Dr 77015
Maybrook Hollow Ln 77047
Mayde Creek Farms Ln 77084
Mayde Park Ln 77084
Mayerling Dr 77024
Mayfair St 77087
Mayfield Rd 77043
Mayfield Oaks Ln 77088
Mayflower St
4000-4500 77051
4502-4598 77051
4600-4798 77033
4800-5099 77033
Mayford St 77076
Mayhaw Ln 77044
Mayle St 77016
Maymount Ln 77093
Maynard Pl 77064
Mayo Ave 77017
Maypine Ln 77085
Mayport Ln 77077
Mayridge Cir 77099
Maysel St 77080
Mayside Ln 77040
Mayview Dr 77091
Maywood Dr 77053
Maywood Falls Cir 77084
Maywood Forest Dr 77088
Mazefield Ct 77070
Mcafee Ct & Dr 77031
Mcallister Rd 77092
Mcalpine St 77003
Mcashan St 77003
Mcaulty Rd 77032
Mcavoy Dr 77074
Mccabe St 77076
Mccadden St 77045
Mccall St 77020
Mccarty St 77029
N Mccarty St
3300-3899 77029
3900-5599 77013
Mccharen Ct 77086
Mcclearen Dr
10800-10899 77096
11900-11998 77035
Mcclelland St 77093
Mcclendon St 77030
Mcclosky St 77037
Mccomb St 77022
Mcconnell Place Ln 77070
Mccormick Ct 77095
Mccormick Dr 77095
Mccormick St 77023
Mccormick Mill Ct 77095
Mccracken Rd 77032
Mccrarey Dr 77088
Mccue Rd 77056
Mcculloch Cir 77056
Mcdade St 77080
Mcdaniel St
600-1199 77022
1700-2899 77093
Mcdermed Dr
4000-4199 77025
4300-4899 77035
Mcdermott Dr 77032
Mcdonald St 77007
Mcdoyle Rd 77048
Mcduffie St
1100-2599 77019
2700-4299 77098
1614-1-1614-2 77019
Mcewen St 77009
Mcfarland Rd 77060
Mcfarland St 77011
Mcgallion Rd
8500-9399 77022
9600-11899 77076
Mcgee Ln 77071
Mcgee St 77026
Mcginty Dr 77041
Mcgowan St 77034
Mcgowen St
1-899 7700

1000-1099 77002
1100-4099 77004
Mcgrath Rd 77047
Mcgrew St 77087
Mchard Rd 77053
Mchenry St 77087
Mcilhenny St
300-899 77006
1000-1299 77002
1300-3899 77004
Mcintosh St 77009
Mcintyre Ln 77053
Mckamy Ct & Dr 77067
Mckaughan Rd 77032
Mckean Dr 77080
Mckee St
100-1299 77002
1500-2599 77009
Mckinley Ln 77088
Mckinley St
3800-4499 77051
11500-11799 77038
Mckinney St
500-798 77002
800-1100 77002
1102-1198 77002
1200-1999 77010
2000-3599 77003
3600-5099 77023
7400-7499 77011
W Mckinney St 77019
Mckinney Creek Ln 77044
Mckinney Park Ln 77003
Mckinstry Blvd 77085
Mcknight St 77035
Mclain Blvd 77071
Mclean St 77051
Mcleary St 77020
Mcleod Dr 77060
Mcleods Ln 77024
Mcloughlin St 77034
Mcmeans Dr 77073
Mcmillan St 77007
Mcnair St 77015
Mcnee Rd 77054
Mcneil St 77009
Mcwilliams Dr 77091
N Meadow Dr 77073
Meadow St 77020
Meadow Bend Ln 77065
Meadow Branch Ct 77095
Meadow Butte Dr 77090
Meadow Cove Ln 77084
Meadow Creek Ln 77017
Meadow Crest St 77071
Meadow Crossing Ln 77095
Meadow Frost Ln 77044
Meadow Gardens Dr 77062
Meadow Glen Dr 77071
Meadow Grove Trl 77059
Meadow Hawk Ct 77041
Meadow Hawk Dr 77089
Meadow Heights Dr 77095
Meadow Joy Ct & Dr 77089
Meadow Lake Dr 77077
Meadow Lake Ln
3400-4099 77027
5200-5699 77056
6100-6299 77057
7800-7999 77063
10000-10999 77042
Meadow Lea Dr 77022
Meadow Leaf Ln 77039
Meadow Manor Ct 77062
Meadow Mill Forest Ln 77044
Meadow Mist Ct 77041
Meadow Oak Dr 77068
Meadow Park Dr 77048
Meadow Place Ct 77071
Meadow Place Dr
3700-3899 77082
11800-12199 77071
Meadow Point Ct 77095
Meadow Run Ct 77066
Meadow Village Dr 77095
Meadow Vista Blvd 77064

Meadow Walk Ln 77067
Meadoway Dr 77089
Meadowbriar Ln 77063
Meadowbrook Dr 77017
Meadowbrook Sq 77084
Meadowbrook Farm
Rd 77082
Meadowchase Ct 77065
Meadowchase Dr 77065
Meadowchase Ln 77014
Meadowcroft Dr 77063
Meadowfair St 77076
Meadowfern Dr 77067
Meadowglen Crst 77082
Meadowglen Cv 77082
Meadowglen Ln
7600-9699 77063
9700-10999 77042
11100-11899 77082
Meadowgrass Ln 77082
Meadowgreen St 77076
Meadowgrove Dr 77037
Meadowick Dr 77024
Meadowlake Ct 77044
Meadowland Dr 77063
Meadowlark St 77017
Meadowlawn St 77023
Meadowline Dr 77082
Meadowlink St 77037
Meadowmoor Dr 77037
Meadowpass St 77076
Meadowridge Dr 77037
Meadows Edge Ln 77084
Meadows Way Dr 77084
Meadowshire St 77037
Meadowside Dr 77062
Meadowvale Dr 77063
Meadowview Ct 77040
Meadowview Dr 77037
Meadowvine Dr 77044
Meadowyork St 77037
Meadville St 77061
Meadway Ct 77082
Meadway Dr
3000-3599 77082
6100-6299 77072
Meandering Meadow
Ln 77084
Meaux Dr 77031
Mecom Rd 77032
Medani Ct 77095
Medfield Dr 77082
Medford Dr 77033
Medicine Bow Cir 77067
Medina St 77012
Medina Bend Ln 77041
Medio Dr 77083
Medora St 77049
Meek St 77002
Meer Dr 77015
Meeting Ln 77084
Megan Place Dr 77095
Megan Woods Loop 77089
Megginson St 77048
Meiko Dr 77045
Meineke St 77087
Meisterwood Dr 77065
Melanie St 77016
Melanite St 77053
Melba Ln 77041
Melbourne St
1-1399 77022
1800-4199 77026
Melbrook Dr 77041
Melcher Dr 77045
Meldrum Ln 77075
Melford Dr 77077
Melissa St 77039
Melissa Lea Ln 77040
Mellariv St 77015
Mellenbrook Ln 77075
Mellon St 77098
Mellow Brook Dr 77099
Mellville Dr 77089
Melody Cir 77040
Melody Ln 77024

Melody Park 77066
Melody Glen Ln 77014
Melody Park Ln 77044
Melon St 77091
Melrose St 77022
Melting Shadows Ln 77095
Melva St 77020
Melvern Ct 77041
Melvin Oaks Ct & Dr 77095
W Melwood St 77009
Members Dr 77089
Memel St 77026
Memorial Cir 77024
Memorial Ct 77007
Memorial Cv 77024
Memorial Dr
1500-1798 77007
1800-6299 77007
6301-6599 77007
8500-12899 77024
12900-16099 77079
E Memorial Loop 77007
N Memorial Way 77007
Memorial Brook Blvd 77084
Memorial Chase Rd 77070
Memorial City Way 77024
Memorial Crest Blvd 77007
Memorial Heights Dr 77007
Memorial Mews St 77079
Memorial Point Ln 77024
Memorial Village Dr 77024
Memorial Woods Dr 77024
Memory Ln 77037
Memphis St 77011
Menard St 77003
Menasco Ct 77077
Mendez St 77029
Mendocino Dr 77083
Mendota Ln 77032
Menking Ct 77024
Menlo Dr 77083
Menwood Cir 77088
Meraldo Dr 77078
Mercado Dr 77083
Mercedes Ln 77022
Mercer St
3200-3499 77027
5300-6799 77005
Merchant Springs Ln 77084
Mercury Dr
301-397 77013
399-899 77013
900-1799 77029
17200-17399 77058
Mercury Cove Ct 77075
Meredith Elise Ct 77025
Meredith Gate Cir &
Ct 77044
Merenerm Dr 77079
Merewood Ln 77071
Merganser Dr 77047
Meria Coves Dr 77095
Meriburr Ln 77021
Merida Dr 77047
Meriden Dr 77084
Meridian St 77017
Meridian Lakes Dr 77095
Meridian Springs Ln 77077
Meris Ln 77015
Merit Way Ct 77065
Merkel St 77003
Merle St 77033
Merlin Ct & Dr 77055
Merlot Ln 77055
Mermaid Ln 77062
Merna Dr 77040
Merona Ln 77041
Merrick St 77025
Merridel Rd 77024
Merrie Way Ln 77024
Merrill St 77009
Merrimac St 77093
Merrimont Ln 77085
Merritt Ln 77060
Merriwood Ln 77076
Merry Ln 77023

Merry Meadow Dr 77049
Mersey Dr 77014
Mersmann Ct 77014
Merton Ct & Dr 77015
Merwin St 77027
Mesa Dr
3400-3799 77013
5400-9499 77028
9500-11299 77078
11800-12109 77016
12111-12199 77016
Mesa Mtn 77069
Mesa Brook Ln 77041
Mesa Gardens Dr 77095
Mesa Point Ct & Dr 77095
Mesa Ridge Rd 77043
Mesa Springs Ct 77095
Mesa Verde Dr 77059
Mesa Village Dr 77053
Mesa Vista Ct & Dr 77083
Mescalero Canyon Ct &
Ln 77095
Mesenbrink Ln 77049
Mesita Dr 77083
Mesones Dr 77083
Mesquite St 77093
Mesquite Brush Ln 77095
Mesquite Canyon Dr 77095
Mesquite Ridge Dr 77073
Mestina St 77028
Meta St 77022
Metcalf St
2600-2699 77012
2900-2999 77017
Meters St 77020
Metro Blvd 77083
Metrodale Dr 77040
Metronome Dr
10100-10199 77080
10200-11099 77043
Metz St 77034
Mews Cir 77082
Meyer Rd 77073
Meyer St 77087
Meyer Forest Dr 77096
Meyerland Plaza Mall 77096
Meyersville Dr 77049
Meyerwood Dr
4100-4199 77025
4300-4499 77096
Mi Castillo Ct 77045
Mi Estado Ct 77045
Mica Dr 77082
N Michael Cir 77071
S Michael Cir 77071
Michael Dr 77017
Michaux St 77009
Micheline Cir 77071
Michelle Ct 77040
Michigan St 77006
Michulka Ln 77093
Mickey Way 77055
Mickle Creek Dr 77049
Mickler St 77025
Mickleton Dr 77088
Mickwayne Ct 77069
Micliff Blvd 77068
Micollet St 77016
Mid Ln 77027
Mid Pines Dr 77069
Mid Pines St 77049
Middle St 77003
Middle Dale Ln 77047
Middle Forest Dr 77059
Middle Oaks Blvd 77082
Middlebrook Dr
14200-15299 77058
16100-17198 77059
17200-17299 77059
Middlebury Ln 77070
Middleglen Ln 77034
Middlerose Ln 77070
Middlesbrough Ln 77066
Middleton St 77003
Middleton Oaks Cir 77028
Middlewood St 77063

Midernew Rd 77048
Midfield Dr 77092
Midfield Glen Ct 77059
Midforest Dr 77068
Midgeley St 77091
Midhurst Dr 77072
Midland Ct 77060
Midland Dr 77037
Midland Fields Dr 77083
Midland Forest Dr 77088
Midnight Ln 77047
Midridge Dr 77084
Midvale St 77087
Midway Blvd 77029
Midway St 77028
Midwood Ct 77067
Mierianne St 77093
W Mierianne St
400-599 77037
900-1099 77088
Mighty Falls Ct 77095
Mighty Oak Dr 77066
Mighty Redwood Ct &
Dr 77059
Mignon Ln 77024
Mikado St 77011
Milam St
100-2299 77002
2300-3399 77006
3400-3799 77002
3800-5099 77006
Milan Dr 77047
Milan Ests 77056
Milart St 77021
Milbrad St 77026
Milburn St 77021
Milby St
100-422 77003
424-534 77003
700-1213 77023
1215-1297 77003
1299-2099 77003
2300-3100 77004
3102-3198 77004
N Milby St 77003
Milda Dr 77088
Mildenhall Ct 77084
Mildoge St 77048
Mile Dr 77065
Miles St 77015
Miley Falls Dr 77028
Milfoil Ln 77083
Milford Pl 77014
Milford St
900-1699 77006
1700-2299 77098
Mill Ct 77070
Mill Creek Dr 77008
Mill Garden Ct 77059
Mill Hedge Dr 77070
Mill Hollow Dr 77084
Mill Lane Dr 77070
Mill Oaks Dr 77084
Mill Path Ct 77084
Mill Point Dr 77059
Mill Shadow Dr 77070
Mill Stream Ln 77060
Mill Stream Way 77041
Mill Trail Ln 77070
Mill Valley Rd 77048
E & W Mill Village Cir 77095
Mill Wheel Dr & Ln 77070
Millard St 77028
Millbanks Dr 77031
Millbrae Ln 77041
Millbridge Dr 77059
Millbrook Dr 77095
Millbrook St 77024
Millbury Dr 77096
Millcrest Ln 77083
Miller St
1400-1999 77003
10000-10199 77086
Miller Glen Ln 77072
Miller House Ln 77086
Miller Road 1 77049

Miller Road 2 77049
Miller Road 3 77049
Miller Valley Dr 77066
Millers Way 77095
Millers Chestnut St 77049
Millers Landing Ln 77049
Millerview Dr 77091
Millet St 77012
Millford Ct 77049
Millgrove Ln 77024
Millhouse Cir, Ct & Rd 77073
Millicent St 77093
Milliken St 77016
Millport St 77092
Millridge Ln 77095
Millridge Bend Dr 77070
Millridge Forest Ct 77070
Millridge North Dr 77070
Millridge Pines Ct 77070
Millrun Dr 77095
Mills Cir 77070
Mills Ln 77065
Mills Rd
8000-8999 77064
9000-10999 77070
Mills St 77026
Mills Way 77070
Mills Bend St 77070
Mills Breeze Dr 77070
Mills Cove St 77070
Mills Crossing Ln 77070
Mills Cut St 77070
Mills Flat St 77070
Mills Landing St 77070
Mills Meadow Ln 77094
Mills Pass Dr 77070
Mills Point Dr 77070
Mills Prairie St 77070
Mills Rapids St 77070
Mills River St 77070
Mills Run Dr 77070
Mills Trail Ln 77070
Mills Walk Dr 77070
Mills Wharf St 77070
Millscott Dr 77070
Millshaw Dr 77070
Millshire Way 77095
Millsite Rd 77050
Millspring Dr 77080
Millstead Ct 77084
Millstone Dr 77073
Millsview Rd 77070
Millvan Dr 77070
Millville Dr 77091
Millway Dr 77070
Millwood Dr 77008
Milner Rd 77032
Milners Point Dr 77066
Milredge St 77017
Milroy Ln 77066
Milton St 77005
Milwaukee St
200-1099 77009
2400-2799 77026
Milwee St 77092
Mimbrough St 77029
Mimosa Dr 77019
Mimosa View Ln 77086
Mina Way 77081
Minden St 77026
Mindy Park Ct & Ln 77069
Mindywood Ct 77068
Mineral Haven Dr 77048
Miners Bnd 77095
Minetta St 77035
Minglewood Blvd 77023
Minimax St 77008
Minnesota St
2100-2500 77034
2502-8398 77034
9500-9598 77075
Minola St 77007
Minola Oaks Dr 77064
Minor St 77085
Mint Fld & Trl 77066
Mint Arbor 77066

Mint Teal Ct 77066
Mintglade Ln 77014
Minto Ct 77053
Minturn Ln 77064
Mintz Ln 77014
Minutemen Ct 77067
Mira Monte Cir, Ct &
Dr 77083
Mira Vista Dr 77083
Miracle Ln 77085
Miraglen St 77023
Miramar St 77006
Miramar Shores Dr 77065
Miramichi Ct 77053
Miranda St 77039
Mirawood St 77078
Miriam Ln 77071
Mirkwood Ln 77014
Mischire Dr 77025
Mission Ln 77011
Mission Rd 77065
Mission Bay Dr 77083
Mission Bell Dr 77083
Mission Bridge Ct 77083
Mission Chase Dr 77077
Mission Court Dr 77083
Mission Creek Cir &
Dr 77084
Mission Crest Ct 77083
Mission Estates Ct &
Dr 77083
Mission Falls Dr 77095
Mission Forest Dr 77083
Mission Gate Ct 77083
Mission Glen Dr 77083
Mission Grove Dr 77068
Mission Hills Dr 77083
Mission Mill Cir & Ln 77084
Mission Oak Dr 77083
Mission Ridge Ln 77073
Mission Terrace Ct &
Dr 77083
Mission Valley Dr 77069
Mission View Ct 77083
Mission Village Dr 77083
Missionary Ridge Ln 77083
Mississippi St 77029
Missouri St
1000-1899 77006
1900-1999 77019
Missy Falls Dr 77065
N Mist Ct 77073
N Mist Dr 77073
Mist Ln 77070
Mistic Meadows Ct 77064
Mistic Moon Ct 77064
Mistissin Ln 77053
Misty Mnr 77094
Misty Trl 77088
Misty Arbor Dr 77085
Misty Bluff Dr 77085
Misty Bridge St 77075
Misty Brook Ln 77084
Misty Chase Ln 77053
Misty Cross Dr 77084
Misty Fern Ct 77095
Misty Forest Ct 77068
Misty Glen Ln 77099
Misty Grove Ct 77062
Misty Heath Ln
2700-2899 77082
15700-15999 77084
Misty Heather Ct 77059
Misty Hollow Dr 77068
Misty Knoll Ct 77062
Misty Lantern Ln 77044
Misty Laurel Dr 77014
Misty Lea Ln 77090
Misty Leaf Ct & Ln 77044
Misty Loch Ln 77084
Misty Meadow Ln 77079
Misty Mill Dr 77041
Misty Moss Ln 77070
Misty Paloma Dr 77049
Misty Park Dr 77082
Misty Ridge Ln 77071

Misty River Dr 77086
Misty Sands Ln 77034
Misty Shadow Ct & Dr 77041
Misty Shadows Dr 77041
Misty Stone Ct 77044
Misty Summit Dr 77086
Misty Trail Dr 77095
Misty Vale Dr & Ln 77075
Misty Valley Dr 77066
Misty Vine Ct 77088
Misty Willow Dr 77070
Mistymont Dr 77070
Mistywood Dr 77090
Mitchell Ln 77066
Mitchell Rd 77037
E Mitchell Rd 77037
W Mitchell Rd 77037
Mitchelldale St 77092
Mittlestedt Rd 77069
Mittlestedt Champions Dr 77069
Moary Firth Dr 77084
Mobile St
7500-7599 77011
13300-13599 77015
Mobud Dr
6300-7299 77074
7900-8999 77036
Mockingbird Cir 77074
Mockingbird Ln 77024
Modesto Dr 77083
Modiste St 77055
Modley Ct 77088
Moers Rd 77075
Mohave Hls 77069
Mohawk St
2800-5299 77093
5500-6699 77016
Mohlerbruk Dr 77066
Moline St 77087
Molly St 77039
Moltere Dr 77065
Mona St 77093
Mona Lee Ln 77080
Mona Vista Dr 77083
Monaco Rd 77070
Monarch Rd 77047
Monarch Gardens Ct 77089
Monarch Mist Ln 77070
Monarch Oaks St 77055
Monarda Ct 77069
Moncur Dr 77095
Mondrian Dr 77083
Monet St 77093
Monica St 77024
Monique Dr 77065
Monitor St 77093
Monrad Dr
14600-14699 77045
14700-15499 77053
Monroe Rd
6800-6899 77017
7000-9199 77061
9200-11399 77075
W Monroe Rd 77061
Monroe St 77023
Monsanta St 77087
Monsey Dr 77063
Montague Manor Ln 77072
Montaigne Dr 77065
Montana St 77007
Montana Ridge Ct 77041
Montauk Dr 77084
Montbrook Dr 77099
Montclair Dr 77030
Montclair Point Ct 77047
Montcliff Ct 77066
Monte Bello Ridge Ln 77041
Monte Carlo Ct & Ln 77053
Monte Cello St 77024
Monte Vista Dr 77083
Montebello Ct 77024
N Montenero Way 77021
Monterrey St 77078
Monterrey Springs Dr 77041
Montesa Ct & Dr 77083

Montford Dr 77099
Montglen Ct & St 77061
W Montgomery Rd
5600-7699 77091
7700-11599 77088
11600-11899 77086
Monticello Dr 77045
Montilla Ct 77083
Montimarte Blvd 77082
Montour Dr 77062
Montridge Dr
8000-8198 77055
8200-8599 77055
9300-9499 77080
Montrose Blvd
1000-1599 77019
1600-5200 77006
5202-5298 77006
5300-5399 77005
Montvale Dr 77059
Montverde Ln 77099
Montwood Ct & Dr 77062
Monument Valley Dr 77067
Monza Dr 77014
Moody St 77009
Moon Beam St 77088
Moon Rock Dr
15900-16299 77062
16300-16499 77058
Mooncrest Dr 77089
Moondance Ln 77071
Mooney Rd
1536A-1536B 77093
1100-1299 77037
1300-4699 77093
Moonglow Dr
11500-12199 77038
16300-16399 77090
Moonhollow Dr 77084
Moonlight Dr 77096
Moonlight Creek Ct 77095
Moonlight Forest Dr 77088
Moonlight Shadow Ct 77059
Moonlit Fields Ct 77064
Moonlit Meadows Ct 77064
Moonlit Pond Ct 77084
Moonmist Dr
5800-6099 77081
7600-7899 77036
11500-12099 77072
Moonridge Dr 77015
Moonrise Ln 77049
Moonset Ln 77016
Moonstone Cir 77018
Moorberry Ln
9500-10199 77080
10200-10599 77043
Moorcreek Dr 77070
Moore Rd 77049
Moore St 77009
Mooredale Ln 77024
Mooreknoll Ln 77024
Mooremeadow Ln 77024
Mooreview Ln 77014
Moorfield Ct & Dr 77083
Moorhead Dr 77055
Mooring Ridge Ln 77075
Moorpark Ln 77064
Moorwick Ln 77043
Moosehead Ln 77064
Mopan Springs Ln 77044
Mopan Valley Ln 77066
Morales Rd 77032
Moray Ln 77016
Moreau St 77093
Morehouse Ln 77088
Moreno Ave 77045
Morewood Ct & Dr 77038
Morgan Crk 77077
E Morgan Dr 77065
W Morgan Dr 77065
Morgan St 77006
Morgan Stable Ct 77044
Morgans Turn 77095
Morgensen Dr 77088
Morgood St 77026

Morin Pl 77002
Morinscott Ct & Dr 77049
Moritz Ct, Dr, Gln, Grn, Park & Walk 77055
Morley St 77061
Morley Lake Dr 77095
Morning Blossom Pl 77084
Morning Breeze 77041
Morning Brook Ln 77094
Morning Dawn Ct & Dr 77095
Morning Dew Ln 77067
Morning Gate Ct 77082
Morning Glen Ln 77083
Morning Lodge Ln 77044
Morning Mist Dr 77090
Morning Pine Ln 77068
Morning Rose Ln 77095
Morninglight Dr 77084
Morningsage Ln 77088
Morningshade Dr 77090
Morningshire Ln 77084
Morningside Dr
3400-4499 77098
4500-5699 77005
5700-7599 77030
Morningside View Dr 77047
Morningview Dr 77080
Morocco Rd 77041
Morris St
100-1799 77009
2500-2699 77026
Morris Hill Ln 77095
Morrisfield Ct 77094
Morrisglen Ct 77084
Morrison St 77009
Morrisville Ct 77078
Morrisway Ct 77084
Morrocastle St 77075
Morrow St 77091
Morse St 77019
Mortimer Dr 77066
Morton Ct 77084
Morwood St 77026
Mosa Creek Ct 77017
Mosby Cir 77007
Moses St 77020
Mosewood St 77040
Mosher Ln
600-699 77037
800-2299 77088
Mosielee St 77086
Mosley Ct 77004
Mosley Rd
7601-7697 77017
7699-7799 77017
7900-7998 77061
8100-8699 77075
Mosman Ct 77094
Moss St 77009
Moss Boulder Ct & Dr 77084
Moss Branch Rd 77043
Moss Glenn Ln 77088
Moss Green Ct 77059
Moss Hill Dr 77080
Moss Hollow Ct 77018
Moss Oaks Dr 77050
Moss Ridge Rd 77043
Moss Rose St
6500-7199 77087
7200-7699 77012
Moss Spring Ln 77024
Moss Tree Rd 77043
Mossbriar Ct & Ln 77095
Mosscrest Dr 77048
Mossford Dr 77087
Mossforest Dr 77090
Mosshang Ct 77040
Mosside St 77021
Mosspine Ct 77084
Mossridge Dr 77069
Mossville Ct 77068
Mosswood Dr 77028
Mossy Bark Ln 77041
Mossy Branch St 77073
Mossy Elm Ct 77059

Mossy Gate Ln 77082
Mossy Hollow Ln 77075
Mossy Lake Cir 77084
Mossy Log Ct 77084
Mossy Meadow Ln 77085
Mossy Ridge Cv 77041
Mossy Ridge Ln 77095
Mossy Shores Ct 77044
Mossy Stone Dr 77077
Mossy Tree Ln 77064
Mossycup Dr 77024
Mott Ln 77024
Moultrie Ln 77084
Mount St
7000-7099 77091
7100-7699 77088
Mount Carmel St 77087
Mount Crest Ct 77095
Mount Houston Rd
4200-5699 77093
5700-9599 77050
W Mount Houston Rd
100-699 77037
700-2999 77038
4700-6199 77088
Mount Pleasant St 77021
Mount Royal Cir 77069
Mount Vernon St 77006
Mountain Cliff Ln 77044
Mountain Daisy Rd 77038
Mountain Flower Ct 77059
Mountain Heights Dr 77049
Mountain Mist Trl 77049
Mountain Oak Ct 77068
Mountain Park Dr 77086
Mountain Ranch Dr 77049
Mountain Ridge Rd 77043
Mountain Rose Ln 77043
Mountain Shadows Dr 77084
Mountain Valley Dr 77095
Mountainhead Dr 77049
Mountbatten Rd 77033
Mountfield Dr 77084
Mountwood St
4400-4599 77018
5500-5999 77091
Moursund St 77030
Mowery Rd
2400-2999 77045
4100-4599 77047
Moy St 77007
Mt Andrew Dr 77089
Muckelroy St 77076
Muddy Spring Dr 77095
Muirfield Cir 77095
Muirfield Ln 77095
Muirfield Pl 77055
Muirfield Valley Dr 77095
Muirfield Village Dr 77069
Muirwood Ln 77041
Mulberry St 77006
Mulberry Hill Ln 77084
Mulberry Meadows Dr 77084
Mulberry Ridge Way 77062
Mule Springs Dr 77034
Muleshoe Ct 77095
Mulford St 77023
Mullins Dr
6700-8199 77081
8400-10999 77096
11400-12499 77035
Mullins Ln 77032
Mulvey St 77020
Mum Ln 77034
Mundare Ln 77086
Munford St 77008
Munger St 77023
Munn St 77029
Munson Ln 77053
Murdock St 77047
Murley St 77038
Murphy St 77033
Murr Way 77048
Murray Rd 77044
Murray Bay St 77080
Murray Brook Dr 77071

Murrayhill Dr 77043
Murworth Dr
2500-2799 77054
3000-3899 77025
Muscatine St
10101-10297 77029
10299-11299 77029
13700-14699 77015
Musgrove Ln 77041
Musical Ct 77040
Muskegon St 77032
Musket Ln 77024
Musket Groves St 77067
Muskingum Ln 77053
Mustang Mountain Ct 77070
Mustang Ridge Rd 77067
Myers Dr 77090
Mykawa Rd
5600-7098 77033
7100-7500 77033
7502-7998 77033
8300-9898 77048
9900-10999 77048
Mylla St 77015
Mynor Woods Ln 77060
Myra St 77039
Myrna Ln 77015
Myrtle Ln 77015
Myrtle St
300-399 77009
2800-2999 77054
6400-7399 77087
Myrtle Field Ln 77044
Myrtle Oak St 77016
Myrtlea Dr & Ln 77079
Myrtlewood St 77033
E Mystic Mdw 77021
N Mystic Mdw 77021
S Mystic Mdw 77021
W Mystic Mdw 77021
Mystic St 77020
Mystic Arbor Ln 77077
Mystic Bridge Dr 77021
Mystic Crossing Ct 77065
Mystic Harbor Ln 77095
Mystic Ridge Ct 77089
Mystic Water Ln 77044
Mystic Wood Dr 77038
Nachita Dr 77049
Nadala Dr 77065
Nadine St 77009
Nadolney St 77015
Nagle St
100-1900 77003
1902-2298 77003
2300-3799 77004
N Nagle St 77003
Nagra Dr 77065
Nairn St 77074
Nalle St 77004
Namora Ct & Ln 77080
Nan St 77092
E, N, S & W Nanaksar Dr 77041
Nance St
1200-1599 77002
1700-3699 77020
Nancet Dr 77041
Nancy Ann St 77009
Nancy Rose St 77015
Nandina Cir 77065
Nanes Dr & Rd 77090
Nanette Dr 77050
Nantucket Dr 77057
Nantucketwood Ln 77057
Naomi St 77054
Naomi Hollow Ln 77082
Napa Vine Dr 77053
Napawood Ct 77088
Napier Ct & Ln 77069
Naples Grove Ln 77047
Naples Park Ct & Ln 77070
Napoleon St
1700-1999 77003
2200-3699 77004
Napoleonic Ct 77014

Napoli Dr 77070
Narcissus St
6500-7199 77087
7200-7999 77012
Narcissus View Trl 77089
Narnia Springs Ct 77075
Narrow Brook Way 77016
Narrow Gate Dr 77095
Nasa Pkwy 77058
Nash St 77019
Nashua St 77008
Nashville St 77028
Nashwood Ct 77040
Nassau Ct & Rd 77021
Nassau Bay Dr 77058
Nat St 77085
Nat Turner Dr 77085
Natalias Ct 77082
Natalie St 77053
Natalie Rose Dr 77090
Natasha Ln 77015
Natasha Run Ln 77066
Natchez St 77021
Natchez Brook Ln 77073
Natchez Hill Trl 77084
Nathan St 77066
Nathaniel St 77075
Nathaniel Brown St 77021
Nathans Cv 77089
Nathans Park Pl 77053
National St 77007
N Native Ln 77022
Nature Trl 77044
Naughton St 77024
Nautical Pointe Ln 77095
Nautique Way 77047
Nauts Ct 77008
Navarro St 77056
Navasota St 77016
Navidad Rd 77083
Navigate Point Ln 77044
Navigation Blvd
2200-4399 77003
4400-7499 77011
7500-7799 77012
E Navigation Blvd 77012
Nayland Rock St 77066
Naylor St 77002
Neal St 77017
Neches St 77026
Neconidge Dr 77053
Nectar Ct 77082
Nectar Grove Ct 77089
Nedwald St 77029
Neece Dr 77041
Needham St 77013
Needles Nest Rd 77038
Needles Throw Ln 77038
Neeley Dr 77055
Neeshaw Dr 77065
Neff St
6300-7299 77074
7900-9500 77036
9502-9598 77036
11500-12199 77072
Neils Branch Dr 77077
Neiman Ln 77091
W Nelda Rd
400-699 77037
900-1100 77088
1102-1198 77088
Nelkins Ct 77026
Nell St 77034
Nellie St 77022
W Nellis Rd 77037
Nellsfield Ln 77075
Nelms St 77061
Nelson St 77045
Nelson Falls Ln 77008
Nelwood Dr 77038
Nelwyn St 77009
Nemard Ln 77049
Nenana Dr
4000-4099 77025
4300-4799 77035
Nentwich Ln 77049

Neon St 77047
Neptune Ln 77062
Nesmith Dr 77035
Nest Ln 77022
Neston Dr 77041
Netherfield St 77087
Nett St 77007
Nettleton St 77004
Neuens Rd
9400-10099 77080
10200-10398 77043
Neuhaus St 77061
Neumann Dr 77058
Neurath St 77003
Nevada St 77006
Nevisway St 77084
New Brunswick Dr 77089
New Cedars Dr 77062
New Field Dr 77082
New Forest Pkwy 77049
New Garden View Ln 77018
New Hampshire St 77029
New Hastings Dr 77095
New Haven Dr 77076
New Leaf Ct 77073
New Market Ln 77083
New Meadow Dr 77064
New Mexico St 77029
New Orleans St
2401-2699 77026
3000-5499 77020
New Rochelle Ct & Dr 77089
New Vista Ln 77067
New York St 77021
Newberry St 77051
Newborough Dr 77099
Newbridge St 77092
Newbrook Cir & Dr 77072
Newburgh Dr 77095
Newcastle Dr
3100-3899 77027
8400-8499 77096
Newcastle St 77081
Newcomb Way 77058
Newcomen Dr 77066
Newcrest Dr 77060
Newdale Dr 77099
Newel Elm St 77038
Newglen Ln 77084
Newhall St 77093
Newhoff St 77026
Newhouse St 77019
Newkirk Ln 77021
Newlight Bend Dr 77095
Newly Dr 77084
Newman St 77098
Newmark Dr 77014
Newpark Dr 77041
Newport St 77023
Newport Shore Dr 77065
Newquay St 77085
Newshire Dr 77025
Newsome Glenn Dr 77090
Newton St
10800-10999 77075
11200-11499 77089
Nexus Rd 77053
Ney St 77034
Neyland St 77022
Nia Pl 77085
Niagara St 77051
Nible Ln 77049
Nicar St 77037
Nice Ct 77015
Nicholas St 77085
Nichole Woods Ct & Dr 77047
Nichols St 77020
Nicholson St
700-899 77007
900-2799 77008
Nickel Grove Dr 77095
Nickel Plank Rd 77049
Nickelwood Ct 77070
Nickerson Ln 77060
Nicole Cir & Ln 77084

Nicoles Place Trl 77089
Nielan St 77028
Nigh Way 77034
Night Star Ln 77077
Nighthaven Ct 77095
Nightingale Dr
5400-5699 77017
13500-14199 77050
Nightshade Crest Ln 77085
Niles St 77017
Nimitz St 77015
Nimrod St 77020
Nina Lee Ln
1700-2299 77018
4400-6199 77092
Nine Iron Ct 77089
Nita St 77051
Nitida St 77045
Nix St 77003
Noah Lndg 77064
Noah St 77021
Noah Arbor Ln 77094
Noahs Landing Ln 77047
Nobility Dr 77099
Noble St
1100-1699 77009
1700-3699 77026
3900-5299 77020
Noble Brook Ct 77049
Noble Cypress Ct 77059
Noble Energy Way 77070
Noble Lakes Ln 77082
Noble Meadow Ln 77073
Noble Oak Ct 77095
Noble Oak Trl 77059
Noble Pass Ln 77095
Noble Pine Dr 77059
Noble Sage Ct 77059
Noble Springs Rd 77062
Noblecrest Dr 77041
Noblewood Bnd & Way 77082
Noblewood Crest Ln 77082
Nocturne Ln 77043
Nodaway Creek Ct 77085
Nodding Pines Ln 77044
Noel St 77033
Noisy Waters Dr 77095
Nola Ct 77013
Nolan St 77003
Nold Dr 77016
Nolda St 77007
Noldale Dr 77016
Nolridge Dr 77016
Nook Ct 77040
Noonday Ct & Ln 77060
Noras Ln 77022
Norborne Ln 77069
Norchester Village Dr 77070
Norcrest Dr 77055
Nordic Dr 77049
Nordling Rd
5400-7499 77076
7501-7597 77037
7599-8100 77037
8102-8298 77037
Nordway Dr 77084
Norfolk St
1600-1699 77006
1700-3399 77098
3700-3999 77046
4000-4199 77027
Norford Ln 77083
Norgrove Ct 77070
Norham Ct 77083
Norham Dr 77083
Norham St 77022
Norhill Blvd 77009
Norhill Pointe Dr 77044
Norkey St 77086
Norland St 77022
Norlinda St 77093
N Norma St 77009
Normandale St 77029
Normandy St 77015
Normandy Way 77021

Normandy Crossing Dr 77015
Normans Woods St 77077
Normeadow Ln 77076
Norments St 77039
Normont Dr 77070
Norris Dr 77025
Norstand Ln 77084
North Blvd
1300-1699 77006
1700-2799 77098
North Fwy
3898A-3898F 77022
3910A-3910L 77022
5598A-5598B 77076
1301-2197 77009
2199-3599 77009
3800-3898 77022
3900-5399 77022
5400-7499 77076
7500-11399 77037
11400-13699 77060
13700-18499 77090
North Ln 77088
North Loop
100-598 77008
101-105 77018
115-117 77008
201-307 77018
309-309 77008
311-319 77018
405-405 77008
507-535 77018
600-1698 77009
613-1599 77022
307 1/2-503 1/2 77018
North Loop E
2-1698 77009
319-1209 77022
2000-6499 77026
6700-8099 77028
8100-10399 77029
North Loop W
200-204 77018
219-299 77008
301-409 77008
411-2999 77008
700-716 77018
904-910 77008
1502-2298 77018
2500-3098 77092
North St 77009
Northacre Dr 77073
Northaire Dr 77073
E Northampton Pl 77098
W Northampton Pl 77098
Northampton Way 77055
Northborough Dr 77067
Northbriar Dr 77073
Northbrook Dr 77043
Northchase Dr 77060
Northchase Ridge Ln 77044
Northcliffe Manor Dr 77066
Northcourt Rd 77040
Northcreek Ln 77073
Northdale St 77087
Northern St 77071
Northern Oak St 77016
Northern Star Dr 77084
Northew St 77091
Northfalk Dr 77084
Northfield Ln 77092
Northfleet Ct & Dr 77082
Northgate Forest Cir & Dr 77068
Northgate Village Dr 77068
Northgreen Blvd 77032
Northhagen Dr 77084
Northington St 77039
Northlake Dr 77049
Northland Dr 77084
Northlawn Dr 77073
Northleaf Ct & Dr 77086
Northline Dr
6200-7499 77076
7501-7697 77037
7699-8299 77037
Northline Lake Dr 77044

Northmark Dr
6300-6399 77084
16000-16099 77073
Northoaks Dr 77073
Northpark Central Dr 77073
Northpoint Dr 77060
Northport Dr 77049
Northpost St 77093
Northridge Dr 77033
Northridge Park Dr 77073
Northrup Dr 77092
Northside Dr 77073
Northton St 77029
Northtrace Dr 77073
Northumb Rd 77047
Northumberland Dr 77095
Northvale Dr 77014
Northvalley Dr 77073
Northview Dr 77086
Northville St
400-699 77037
700-1599 77038
Northway Ct & Dr 77084
Northwest Fwy
9800-10098 77092
10100-12799 77092
12800-15399 77040
15400-17500 77040
17501-17501 77065
17503-18999 77065
19000-19098 77065
19100-20699 77065
Northwest Mall 77092
Northwestern St 77005
Northwind Dr 77064
Northwind Ln 77014
Northwinds Dr 77041
Northwood St 77009
Northwood Forest Dr 77039
Norton Dr
8500-9299 77080
10400-10699 77043
Norvell Ct 77024
Norvic St
7200-7399 77020
7900-10799 77029
Norview Dr 77022
Norville Ln 77047
Norway St 77047
Norwich St 77028
N Norwood St 77011
N Nottingham Cir 77071
S Nottingham Cir 77071
Nottingham St 77005
Nottingham Oaks Trl 77079
Nova Ct & Dr 77077
Novato Dr 77053
Nrg Park 77054
Nuben St 77091
Nubenbrook Lake Dr 77044
Nubia St 77093
Nueces St 77012
Nuggent St 77093
Nulake West Ct 77044
Numid Lake Ct 77044
Nunn St 77087
Nuttall Oak Dr 77082
Nuwood Ln 77053
Nyack Dr 77089
Nyoka St 77041
Nyssa St 77078
Nystrom Cir 77060
O Donnell Dr 77076
O Mally Dr 77067
E & W O S T Dr 77013
Oahu Ct 77040
S Oak Cir 77089
Oak Ct 77006
S Oak Ct 77089
N Oak Dr 77073
S Oak Dr 77089
W Oak Dr 77056
Oak Ln 77024
W Oak Mews 77056
Oak Pl 77006
Oak St 77018

Oak Acres Dr 77065
Oak Arbor Dr 77088
Oak Bay Dr 77091
Oak Bayou Ln 77064
Oak Bend Dr 77079
Oak Bend Forest Dr 77083
Oak Blossom Ct 77059
Oak Bluff Ct & Dr 77070
Oak Bough Dr 77088
Oak Breeze Dr 77084
Oak Brook Dr 77013
Oak Chase Dr 77062
Oak Cove Dr 77091
Oak Creek Dr 77017
Oak Creek St 77024
Oak Falls Dr 77066
Oak Fern 77040
Oak Forest Dr 77018
Oak Gate Dr 77070
Oak Glen Ct
8700-8799 77088
11600-11699 77024
Oak Glen Dr 77076
Oak Glen Meadows Ln 77095
Oak Grove Church St 77028
Oak Harbor Dr 77062
Oak Hedge St 77044
Oak Hill Dr 77087
Oak Hollow St 77024
Oak Knoll Ln
7800-8299 77028
8800-9399 77078
Oak Laurel Ln 77092
Oak Leaf Ln 77015
Oak Ledge Dr 77065
Oak Limb Dr 77065
Oak Links Ave 77059
Oak Meadows St 77017
Oak Mesa Ct 77070
Oak Mountain Dr 77095
Oak Park Cir 77070
Oak Park Ct 77070
Oak Park Dr 77070
Oak Park St 77032
Oak Parkway Dr 77077
Oak Pass Dr 77091
Oak Pines Dr 77040
Oak Place Dr 77006
Oak Point Dr
9700-9899 77055
10200-10300 77043
10302-10398 77043
Oak Ridge St 77009
Oak Ridge Park Dr 77084
Oak Shadows Dr 77091
Oak Shadows Ln 77024
Oak Spring Dr 77043
Oak Stream Dr 77043
Oak Terrace Ct & Dr 77082
Oak Thicket Dr 77040
Oak Trail Ln 77091
Oak Tree Dr
1100-1398 77055
1400-1499 77055
1501-1597 77080
1599-1799 77080
Oak Valley Dr
800-999 77024
11500-11799 77065
Oak View Ter 77094
Oak Vista St 77087
Oak West Dr 77073
Oakberry St 77042
Oakcenter Dr 77072
Oakcliff St 77023
Oakcroft Dr 77070
Oakdale St
1-199 77006
1000-3599 77004
Oakendell Dr 77084
Oakengates Dr 77015
Oakerann St 77028
Oakford Ct & Dr 77024
Oakgrove Dr 77058
Oakhall Dr 77066

Oakham St 77085
Oakhampton Dr 77084
Oakhaven Ln 77091
Oakhurst St 77023
Oakington Dr 77071
Oaklake Pointe Ln 77040
Oakland Bnd 77064
Oakland Cir 77064
Oakland Ct 77064
Oakland Dr 77064
Oakland Hl 77064
Oakland Ln 77064
Oakland St 77023
Oakland Way 77064
Oakland Brook St 77038
Oakland Hills Dr 77069
Oaklawn Dr 77024
Oaklawn Park Dr 77069
Oakleaf Forest Dr 77088
Oaklet St 77044
Oakley St 77006
Oakmantle Dr 77085
Oakmont Ct 77064
Oakmont St 77021
Oakmont Club Ct 77059
Oakmoor Pkwy 77051
Oaknut Dr 77088
W Oaks Mall 77082
Oaks Crossing Ln
14600-14799 77070
16900-16999 77083
W Oaks Plaza St 77082
Oakshire Dr 77027
Oakside Dr 77053
Oakstone St 77015
Oakview Creek Ln 77048
Oakville St 77093
Oakwick Ln 77044
Oakwilde Ct 77043
E Oakwood Ct 77040
W Oakwood Ct 77040
Oakwood Grv 77040
Oakwood Park 77040
Oakwood Pl 77040
Oakwood St 77025
Oakwood Trce 77040
Oakwood Trl 77040
Oakwood Bend Dr 77040
Oakwood Falls Trl 77084
Oakwood Forest Dr 77040
Oakwood Garden St 77040
Oakwood Hollow Ct & St 77040
Oakwood Lakes Dr 77095
Oakwood Place Ct E 77040
Oakwood Trace Ct 77040
Oakworth Dr 77084
Oarman Ct 77079
Oasis Dr 77096
Oasis Park 77021
Oasis Palm 77021
Oasis View Ln 77034
Oat Harvest Ct 77038
Oat Meadow Trl 77049
Oat Mill Dr 77095
Oates Ln 77015
Oates Rd
1-799 77013
1000-1299 77029
3600-5699 77013
5700-5799 77078
Oats St 77020
Oban St 77085
Oberlin St 77005
Obion Rd 77076
W Obion Rd
200-299 77076
300-599 77091
Oboe Dr 77025
Obra Ln 77045
Observatory St 77088
Obsidian Dr 77095
Ocean Laurel Ln 77014
Oceania Ct 77094
Oceanside Dr 77095
Oceanview St 77071

Ocee St 77063
Ocelot Ln 77034
Ocotillo Dr 77095
Octavia St 77026
Octavia Way 77073
Oddo St 77022
Oder Ln 77090
Odessa Ct 77060
Odet Ct 77088
Odin Ct 77021
Odinglen Dr 77095
Odom Blvd 77054
Odyssey Ct 77099
Offer Dr 77031
Office City Dr
7000-7199 77087
7500-7699 77012
Office Park Dr 77070
Offshore Dr 77044
Ogden St 77017
Ogden Forest Dr 77088
Ogilvie St 77017
Oglesby St 77029
Oglethorpe Dr 77031
Ohara St 77085
Ohio St 77047
Ohsfeldt St 77008
Oil Center Blvd & Ct 77073
Ojeman Rd
1500-1799 77055
1800-3399 77080
Okachobee Dr 77044
Okanella St 77041
Okay St 77016
Okinawa Rd 77033
Oklahoma St 77093
Ola Dr 77032
Olana Dr 77032
Oland Way 77073
Olathe St 77055
Old Bammel Rd 77090
Old Bammel N Houston Rd 77086
Old Barngate Ln 77073
Old Brickhouse Dr 77041
Old Bridge Lk 77069
Old Brook Dr 77071
Old Chatham Ln 77035
Old Chocolate Bayou Rd 77048
Old Clinton Rd 77020
Old Coach Ln 77024
Old Creek Rd 77060
Old Dock Ln 77090
Old Fairbanks N Houston Rd 77086
Old Farm Rd 77063
Old Foltin Rd 77086
Old Forest Ln 77084
Old Genoa Red Bluff Rd 77034
Old Greenhouse Rd 77084
Old Greens Rd 77032
Old Hearth Dr 77084
Old Katy Rd
6800-7399 77024
14511-14515 77079
14517-14524 77079
14526-14532 77079
Old Lake Rd 77057
Old Ledge Ln 77088
Old Lighthouse Ln 77084
Old Lodge Dr 77066
Old Main Street Loop Rd 77025
Old Meadow Ln 77064
Old Mill Ln 77073
Old Mission Rd 77095
Old Oaks Dr 77024
Old Pine Ln 77015
Old Post Rd 77082
Old Ranch Rd 77073
Old Richmond Rd
12900-13199 77099
13200-13599 77083
Old Saybrook Dr 77084

Old Spanish Trl
1000-3199 77054
3200-5399 77021
5400-6099 77023
Old Spring Ln 77015
Old Stone Trl 77079
Old Telegraph Rd 77067
Old Trail Dr 77040
Old Tybee Rd 77084
Old Valley Way 77094
Old Walters Rd 77014
Old Woods Ln 77073
Old Yale St 77018
Oldband Ln 77040
Oldcastle St 77013
Olde Manor Ln 77068
Olde Tavern Ct 77068
Oldenburg Ln 77065
Oldham St 77011
Oldhaven St 77074
Oldridge Dr 77084
Oleander Ct 77017
Oleander St 77009
Oleander Grove Way 77049
Oleander Point Dr 77095
Olentangy St 77075
Oleoke Ln 77015
Olga Ln 77041
Olinda Dr 77041
Olive Gdn 77077
Olive Park 77077
Olive Pl 77077
Olive St 77007
Olive Trce 77077
Olive Trl 77077
Olive Branch Ct 77083
Olive Brook Ln 77095
Olive Glen Dr 77082
Olive Green Ct 77059
Olive Leaf Dr 77084
Olive Oak Ct 77059
Olive Springs Ct 77062
Olive Wood Ct 77089
Oliver St 77007
Olivewood Dr 77089
Olney Oak Dr 77079
Olster Dr 77084
Olympia Dr
1900-3899 77019
5600-5699 77056
6100-6499 77057
7500-7699 77063
10000-11299 77042
11300-12599 77077
Olympia Fields Ln 77069
Olympiad Dr 77041
Olympus Dr 77084
Omar St
400-1199 77009
1200-1399 77008
Omeara Dr
3500-4100 77025
4102-4198 77025
4300-4899 77035
Omega St 77022
One Token Dr 77065
Oneil St 77019
Oneness Ave 77014
Onslow St 77016
Opal Ct 77009
Opal Glen Ln 77075
Opal Meadow Dr 77095
Opal Ridge Dr 77095
Opatrny Meadows Ln 77064
Opelika St 77080
Opelousas St 77020
Open Sea Dr 77044
Opper Ln 77064
Opus Ct 77040
Ora St 77092
Oradiand Dr 77057
Oralia Dr 77065
Orandend Dr 77089
Orange Dr 77050
Orange St 77020
Orange Brook Ct 77089

Orange Grove Dr 77039
Orange Jasmine Ct 77059
Orange Leaf Ct 77059
Oratorio Ct 77040
Orchard Ct 77054
Orchard Dr 77054
S Orchard Dr 77089
Orchard Blossom Way ... 77084
Orchard Country Ln 77062
Orchard Farms Ln 77062
Orchard Garden Way ... 77066
Orchard Glen Ct 77062
Orchard Hill St 77077
Orchard Hollow Way 77065
Orchard Mountain Dr ... 77059
Orchard Park Dr 77077
Orchard Peak Ct 77062
Orchard Springs Dr 77067
Orchard Vale Dr 77084
Orchard Valley Ct 77084
Orchid St 77017
Orchid Trl 77041
Orchid Creek Ln 77084
Orchid Spring Ln 77044
Orchid Trace Ln 77047
Orean St 77034
Orebo St 77088
Oregano Cir 77036
Oregold Dr 77041
Oreilly St 77007
Orem Dr 77047
E Orem Dr
4401-4499 77047
4900-5898 77048
5900-6899 77048
6900-7699 77075
W Orem Dr
1200-1299 77047
2900-5499 77045
5500-8299 77085
Oriole St
200-499 77018
4900-5799 77017
Oriole Lake Way 77089
Oriole Wood Ct 77038
Orion St 77088
Orlando St
3100-3499 77093
7200-7399 77016
Orleans St 77015
Ormandy St
11600-11899 77035
12100-12499 77085
Ormel St
14700-14999 77039
15000-15099 77032
Ormond Ct 77095
Orr St 77009
Ortega Ln 77083
Orville St 77028
Oryan Ct 77015
Osage St
3700-4099 77063
4100-5999 77036
6001-7499 77036
8801-8899 77074
Osage Park Dr 77065
Osakwe St 77075
Osborn St 77033
Osby Dr
4000-4199 77025
4300-4499 77096
Osiris Core Ln 77095
Osprey Dr 77048
Oswego St 77029
Othello St 77029
Otis St 77026
Ottawa Ln 77043
Otterbury Dr 77039
Otto St 77093
Ouachita St 77039
Our Lane Pl & Trl 77024
Ouray Dr 77040
Ourlane Cir, Ct & Cv ... 77024
Out Dr 77045
Outlaw Ridge Rd 77095

Outlook Dr 77034
Outpost Dr 77041
Outview Ct 77040
Ovenesta Dr
16900-16998 77096
31300-31398 77065
Overbrook Ln
3400-4099 77027
5600-5699 77056
6200-6299 77057
7800-7899 77063
10000-11099 77042
11300-14399 77077
Overcross Dr 77045
Overcup Dr 77024
Overdale St
5600-5899 77033
6200-6499 77087
Overglen Ct 77072
Overhill St 77018
Overland Trl 77090
Overland Park Dr 77049
Overlea Dr 77089
Overlook Dr 77041
Overmann St 77091
Overmead Dr 77065
Overmyer Dr 77008
Overton Cir 77065
Overton Ct 77004
Overture Dr 77082
Ovid St 77007
Owen Lake Ct 77095
Owendale Dr 77015
Owens Rd 77095
Owens St 77029
Owens Cross Dr 77067
Owens Park Dr 77094
Owl Echo Ct 77082
Owl Forest Ct 77084
Owl Roost Ln 77016
Oxberg Trl 77073
Oxford St
300-899 77007
900-2699 77008
3400-4799 77022
Oxford Way 77069
Oxford Grove Dr 77095
Oxford Oak St 77082
Oxford Park Dr 77082
Oxford Point Ln 77014
Oxham St 77029
Oxham Falls Ct 77044
Oxwick Cir 77044
Oyster Tree Dr 77084
Ozark St 77021
Pachiney St 77020
Pachitt St 77034
Pacific St 77006
S Pacific St 77049
Pacific Pearl St 77072
Pacific Ridge Ct 77095
Packard St 77040
Packard Bend Trl 77089
Packard Elm St 77038
Packerton Ct 77094
Paddington St 77085
Paddington Place Dr ... 77083
Paddock Ct & Way 77065
Paddock Brook Ln 77038
Paddock Park Dr 77065
Paddock Way Ct 77065
Padfield St 77055
Pado St 77055
Padok Rd 77044
Pagehurst Dr 77084
Pagett Place Ct 77044
E & N Pagewick Dr 77041
Pagewood Ln
5300-5599 77056
7500-9699 77063
9700-9899 77042
Pago Ln 77041
Pagosa Springs Dr 77040
Paige St
300-1599 77003
2900-5099 77004

N Paige St 77003
Paige Place Dr 77089
Paigetree Ln 77014
Paine St 77022
Paintbrush Ledge Ln ... 77089
Painted Mesa Cir 77038
Painted Trail Dr 77084
Paisley St 77096
Paiter St 77053
Palace Oaks Ct & Dr ... 77082
Palacios Ct 77064
Paladora Dr 77083
Paladora Park Ln 77083
Paladora Point Ct 77041
Palazzo Dr 77070
Palcio Real Dr 77047
Pale Ivy Ln 77072
Pale Star Dr 77064
Palermo Dr 77084
Palestine St
6900-7399 77020
10100-11099 77029
Palisade Dr 77048
Palisade Lakes Ct &
Dr 77095
Palisades Heights Ct &
Dr 77095
Palisades Point Dr 77059
Pallaral Dr 77084
Pallet Rd 77032
Palm St 77004
Palm Brook Ct 77095
Palm Desert Ln 77099
Palm Falls Ct 77095
Palm Forest Ln 77077
Palm Grass Ct 77059
Palm Island St 77034
E, N, S & W Palm Lake
Dr 77034
Palm Leaf Ct 77044
Palm Shadows St 77075
Palm Valley Ct 77083
Palma Grv 77073
Palmbeach St 77034
Palmcrest St
1-99 77085
12000-12399 77034
Palmcroft St 77034
Palmdale St 77034
Palmdate St 77034
Palmer St
100-1500 77003
1502-1598 77003
3500-5499 77004
N Palmer St 77003
Palmer Glen Ln 77044
Palmer Park Ct 77086
Palmer Springs Dr 77070
Palmerton Dr 77064
Palmetto Pnes 77032
Palmetto St
5300-5399 77081
6800-7199 77087
Palmetto Shores Dr 77065
Palmfield St 77034
Palmfree St 77034
Palmhill St 77034
Palmlake St 77034
Palmonari Dr 77049
Palmsprings Dr 77034
Palmton St 77034
Palmway St
12000-12499 77034
15400-15499 77071
Palmyra St 77022
Palo Alto St
2000-2099 77023
7900-7999 77078
Palo Blanco Rd 77078
Palo Lake Ln 77044
Palo Pinto Dr
2500-2799 77080
4300-4699 77041
Palo Verde Dr 77044
Palo Vista Dr 77044
Paloma Park Ct & Ln ... 77041

Palomino Trails Ct 77095
Palston Bend Ln 77014
Palton Springs Dr 77082
Pama Cir 77024
Pambrooke Ln 77094
Pamela Dr 77075
Pamela Holly Trl 77089
Pampass Pass 77095
Panagard Dr
2400-2499 77077
2500-2899 77082
Panair St 77061
Panama St 77009
Panatella Dr 77055
Panay Dr
8100-8199 77033
10900-12899 77048
Panay Park Dr 77048
Panay Village Dr 77048
Pandora Dr 77013
Panicum Ct 77086
Pannell St
1200-2099 77020
2100-2499 77026
Pano Ln 77070
Panola Way 77065
Panorama View Ln 77089
Pantano Dr 77065
Panther Ct 77099
Panther Place Dr 77099
Panther Point Dr 77099
Panther Villa Ct 77099
Papadosa St 77053
Papalote St 77041
Par Four Dr 77088
Paradise Ln 77048
Paradise Valley Ct 77069
Paradise Valley Dr
12000-12099 77066
13000-14499 77069
Parakeet St 77034
Paralinc St 77022
Paramount Ln 77067
Parana Dr 77080
Parasol Ln 77064
Pardee St
4000-5999 77026
7700-8099 77028
Pardoe Dr 77032
Pardue Ct 77088
Parfield Ln 77084
Paril Creek Dr 77073
Paris St 77021
Park Ave 77053
E Park Ct 77082
W Park Ct 77082
Park Dr 77023
NW Park Dr 77086
S Park Grv 77007
Park Ln
6600-6799 77023
10600-10699 77093
Park Row
14200-14499 77084
14700-14799 77079
14800-19899 77084
Park St 77019
Park Ter 77017
Park Trl 77024
Park Almeda Dr 77047
E & W Park At Beverly
Hls 77057
E Park At Fairdale 77057
E & W Park At Shady
Villa 77055
Park Bank Ct 77068
Park Bayou Dr 77077
Park Center Ct, Dr &
Way 77059
Park Centre Ct 77069
Park Circle Dr 77057
Park Circle Way 77059
Park Creek Ct & Dr 77070
Park Cypress St 77094
Park Douglas Dr 77084
Park Entry Dr 77041

Park Estates Ln 77062
Park Falls Dr 77095
Park Firth Dr 77084
Park Gate Ct 77018
Park Grand Rd 77062
Park Green Way 77058
Park Harbor Ct & Dr ... 77084
Park Harbor Estates
Dr 77084
Park Harbor Oaks Ct ... 77084
Park Haven Dr 77077
Park Heath Ln 77088
Park Hollow Ct 77095
Park Key Cir 77084
Park Laureate Dr 77024
Park Lodge Ct 77062
Park Lorne Dr 77084
Park Manor St 77053
Park Meadow Ct & Dr .. 77089
Park Oaks Dr 77017
Park Place Blvd
7400-8099 77087
8100-8699 77017
8701-8799 77017
NW Park Place Dr 77086
Park Plaza Dr
4900-5099 77018
5300-5398 77091
5400-5499 77091
Park Royal Dr 77077
Park Saddle Brook Ln .. 77024
Park Scot Dr 77084
Park Shadows Trl
11800-11898 77059
12400-12499 77058
Park Shore Dr 77084
Park South Vw 77051
Park Talon Dr 77067
Park Ten Blvd & Pl 77084
Park Thicket 77058
Park Trail Dr
9400-9499 77044
19000-19099 77094
Park Trail Ln 77007
Park Trail Run 77019
Park Trail Vis 77019
Park Trail Way 77019
Park View Ct 77084
Park Village Dr 77048
Park Vista Dr 77072
Park West Dr 77063
E Park West Dr 77072
W Park West Dr 77072
Parkborough Dr 77041
Parkchase Timber Ct &
Dr 77070
Parkchester Dr 77062
Parkcrest Dr 77034
Parkcrest Forest Dr 77088
Parker Rd
1-1299 77076
1500-4899 77093
5000-7799 77016
8000-8499 77078
E Parker Rd 77076
W Parker Rd
100-199 77076
201-299 77076
400-699 77091
Parker St 77007
Parkerhaven Ct 77008
Parkers Cove Ct 77044
Parkers Hideaway Dr ... 77089
Parkersburg Dr 77036
Parkes St
7100-7198 77091
7300-7399 77088
Parkesgate Dr 77083
Parkette Dr
8500-8599 77028
8800-9199 77078
Parkey Ln 77015
Parkfront Dr 77036
Parkglen Dr 77049
Parkhaven Ln 77077
Parkhill Forest Dr 77088

Parkhollow Dr 77082
Parkhurst Dr 77028
Parkland Ct 77055
Parkmore Dr 77095
Parkridge Ct & Dr 77053
Parkridge Glen Dr 77082
Parkriver Dr 77070
Parksley Dr 77059
Parkstone Dr 77076
Parkstone View Cir 77083
Parkvale Dr 77099
S Parkview Dr 77084
Parkview St
101-197 77009
199-399 77009
15401-15499 77071
Parkville Dr 77068
Parkway Ct 77077
Parkway Pl 77040
Parkway Forest Dr 77044
Parkway Plaza Dr 77077
Parkway Vista Dr 77019
Parkwood Dr 77021
N Parkwood Dr 77021
S Parkwood Dr 77021
Parkwood Way 77059
Parkwood Circle Dr 77036
Parliament Dr
100-399 77034
16600-16899 77083
Parlin Ridge Dr 77040
Parmer Ct 77064
Parnell St
7700-7899 77021
7900-8499 77051
Parramatta Ln 77073
Parryville Dr 77041
Parsley Hawthorne Ct .. 77059
Parsley Path Ln 77064
Parsons St 77012
Parsons Glen Dr 77044
Partage Ln 77069
Partha Way 77073
Partlow Ln 77040
Partridge Ln 77060
Partridge Green Ct &
Dr 77084
Partridge Run Dr 77094
Partridgeberry Ct 77059
Parwill St 77081
Pasa Robles Ln 77083
Pasadena St 77023
Pasadero Dr 77083
Paschall St 77009
Paseo Arboles Ave 77076
Paseo Caceres Dr 77007
Paseo Del Rey Dr 77083
Pasha Dr 77040
Pasket Ln 77092
Paso Del Flores Dr 77045
Paso Del Sol Dr 77083
Paso Dobble Dr 77083
Paso Hondo Dr 77083
Paso Real Dr 77083
Paso Rello Dr 77077
S Pass Ln 77064
Pastel Dawn Trce 77049
Pastoria Dr 77083
Pasture View Ln 77024
Patchester Dr 77079
Pate Rd 77016
Patel Ln 77039
Paterno Dr 77064
Path Green Dr 77095
Pathenso Dr 77069
Pathfield Dr 77084
Patience Ave 77014
Patio Dr 77017
Patio Glen Dr 77071
Patricia Ln 77012
Patricia Manor Pl 77012
Patrick Ct 77024
Patrick St 77076
Patrick Palace 77089
Patridge Dr 77070
Patterson St 77007

Patti Lane Ct 77073
Patti Lynn Ln 77024
Pattibob St 77029
Pattiglen Dr 77084
W Patton St 77009
Paul B Koonce St 77061
Paul Quinn St 77091
Paul Revere Dr 77024
Paula St 77033
Paulus Dr 77041
Paulwood Dr 77071
Pauma Dr 77069
Pavilion Dr & Pt 77083
Pavona Ridge Ln 77040
Pavonia Ct & Dr 77095
Pawley Dr 77065
Pawnee St 77054
Paxston Point Ln 77095
Paxton Dr 77014
Payette Dr 77040
Payne St 77009
Payson St 77021
Peabody St 77028
Peace Ct 77041
Peacedale Ct 77015
Peaceful Ln 77016
Peaceful Way 77085
Peach St 77093
Peach Blossom St 77075
Peach Bough Ln 77095
Peach Brook Ct 77062
Peach Country Ct 77059
Peach Creek Dr 77017
Peach Forest Ct 77095
Peach Grove Dr 77099
Peach Hollow Ln 77082
Peach Leaf St 77039
Peach Limb Dr 77099
Peach Spring Dr
500-699 77037
800-1499 77088
Peach Tree Ct 77064
Peach Valley Cir 77084
E, N, S & W Peachfield
Cir 77014
Peachford Ln 77062
Peachridge Dr 77070
Peachtree St
6200-7399 77028
7400-10599 77016
Peachwood Ct 77077
Peachwood Bend Dr ... 77077
Peacock St 77033
Peacock Hills Dr 77035
Peadonda Dr
16000-16098 77036
33101-33199 77095
Peakwood Dr 77090
Pear St
800-899 77060
2800-2899 77026
Pear Brook Trl 77062
Pear Creek Cir 77084
Pear Knoll Ct 77062
Pear Limb Dr 77099
Pear Meadow Ln 77039
Pear Oak Dr 77065
Pear Tree Ln 77073
Pear Woods Ct 77059
Pearhaven Dr 77062
Pearl Dr 77064
Pearl St 77029
Pearl Bluff Ln 77047
Pearl Lake Dr 77095
Pearl Point St 77044
Pearl Shadow Ln 77044
Pearland Pkwy 77089
Pearsall Dr 77064
Pearson St 77023
Pearwood Dr 77038
Pease St
800-1599 77002
1600-3999 77003
4300-5499 77023
Peatwood Rd 77038
Peavine Cir 77080

Pebble Ln 77087
Pebble Mdws 77041
Pebble Path 77070
Pebble Bank Ln 77041
Pebble Beach Ct 77064
Pebble Beach Dr 77069
Pebble Bend Dr 77068
Pebble Crest Ct & Ln 77083
Pebble Falls Dr 77095
Pebble Hill Dr 77024
Pebble Lake Dr 77095
Pebble Mesa Cir 77088
Pebble Park Ln 77036
Pebble Rock Ct & Dr 77077
Pebble Run Ct 77095
Pebble Springs Dr 77066
Pebble Trace Dr 77068
Pebble Way Ct & Ln 77041
Pebblebrook Dr
12100-12799 77024
13000-14099 77079
Pebbledowne Dr 77064
Pebbleglen Dr 77095
Pebblemill Ln 77086
Pebbleshire Dr 77062
Pebblestone St 77072
Pebbleton Dr 77070
Pebblewalk Cir N & S 77041
Pecan Ct 77013
Pecan Grv 77077
Pecan St 77087
Pecan Creek Dr 77043
Pecan Gap Dr 77065
Pecan Glen Ct 77040
Pecan Green Way 77073
Pecan Grove Ln 77086
Pecan Grove St 77013
Pecan Meadow Dr 77071
Pecan Oak Dr 77065
Pecan Park Cir 77018
Pecan Place Dr 77071
Pecan Shores Dr 77044
Pecan Springs Dr 77040
Pecan Trail Ln 77055
Pecan Villas Dr 77061
Pecan Wood Dr 77088
Pecanwood Ln 77024
Pech Rd 77055
Peckham St
2100-2399 77019
2600-2699 77098
Pecore St 77009
Pecos St 77055
Peddie St
600-899 77008
1000-1199 77009
Peden St
301-301 77006
303-1699 77006
1700-2099 77019
Pederson St 77033
Peebles Dr 77084
Peekskill Ln 77075
Peer Dr 77043
Peerless St 77021
Peermont St 77062
Peg St 77092
Peggy St 77022
Peggys Ct & Ln 77015
Pelham Dr 77019
Pelican Beach Ln 77044
Pelican Way Rd 77084
Pella Dr 77036
Pelsey St 77029
Pemberton Dr 77005
Pemberton Rdg 77025
Pemberton Trce 77025
Pemberton Walk 77025
E, N, S & W Pemberton Circle Dr 77025
Pemberton Crescent Dr 77025
Pemberwick Park Ln 77070
Pembridge Dr 77071
Pembroke St 77048
Pembroke Ridge Dr 77065
Pembrook St 77016
Penchenw Dr 77062
Penconde Dr 77041
Penelope Dr 77013
Penfield Ln 77021
Penhurst St 77093
Peninsula St 77015
Peninsula Park Dr 77041
Penn St 77093
Penn City Rd 77015
Penn Hills Ln 77062
Penn Manor Ct 77055
Pennant Park Ct 77044
Pennbright Dr 77090
Pennbury Dr 77094
Penner St 77055
Penner Crest St 77055
Pennington St
700-999 77022
2300-2599 77093
Pennsylvania St 77029
Pennworth Ln 77084
Penny Ct & Ln 77069
Penny Park Trl 77089
Pennybrook Ct 77066
Pennyroyal Ct 77073
Pennywood Ct 77070
Penrod St 77028
Penrose Dr 77049
Penrose Point Dr 77095
Pensdale St 77033
Pensgate St 77062
Penshore Park Ln 77044
Pentacle Ln 77085
Pentonshire Ln 77090
Penway St 77022
Penwood Way 77023
Peoria St 77015
Pepper Ln 77079
Pepper Hill Way 77058
Pepper Knoll Dr 77065
Pepper Landing Ln 77089
Pepperbrook Dr 77041
Pepperbush Ct 77070
Pepperdine Ln 77071
Peppergate Ln 77044
Peppermill Rd 77080
Pepperstone Ct 77053
Pepperstone Ln 77044
Peppertree Ln 77015
Pepperweed Dr 77084
Pepperwood Ln 77084
Perch Creek Dr 77049
Percussion Pl 77040
Percy Rd 77093
Pereida St 77028
Perfidia Dr 77015
Peridot Cv 77095
Perigrine Dr 77065
Perimeter Rd 77034
Perimeter Park Dr 77041
Periwinkle St 77038
Perkins St 77020
Perrington Cir 77082
Perrington Heights Ln 77056
N Perry Ave 77071
S Perry Ave 77071
Perry Rd
10800-11999 77064
12000-13999 77070
Perry St 77021
Perryman St 77044
Perryton Ln 77073
Persa St
2000-2399 77019
2600-2699 77098
Pershing St 77033
Persian Dr 77014
Persimmon St 77093
Perth St 77048
Perthshire Rd
12100-12599 77024
13000-14999 77079
Petal Ct 77038
Petaluma Dr 77053
Petersburg Ln 77083
Petersham Dr 77031
Petra Dr 77083
Petre Dr 77076
S Petro Ln 77045
Petropark Dr 77041
Pettibone St 77093
Pettit St 77009
Petty St 77007
Petworth Dr 77072
Peveto St 77019
Peyton Rd 77032
Peyton St 77028
Peyton Circle Ct 77049
Peyton Ridge Cir 77049
Peyton Stone Cir 77049
Pfeiffer Dr 77082
Pheasant St 77018
Pheasant Hill Dr 77014
Pheasant Lake Ct 77041
Pheasant Oak Dr 77083
Pheasant Ridge Ln 77041
Pheasant Trace Ct 77064
Phil St 77012
Phil Halstead Dr 77086
Philco Dr 77080
Philfall St 77098
Philibert Ln 77028
Philippine St 77040
Phillips St
5800-6699 77091
7000-8099 77088
Philmont Dr 77080
Phlox St 77051
Phoenix Dr 77030
Pica St 77007
Picador Dr 77083
Picardy Ln 77044
Picasso Pl 77096
Piccadilly Dr 77061
Pickens St 77007
Pickering St 77091
Pickfair St 77026
Pickford Knolls Ct & Dr 77041
Pickrell Ct 77073
Picton Dr 77032
Piedmont St 77016
Piedmont Creek Trl 77073
Pier Pointe Way 77044
Pierce St
100-1599 77002
1600-2699 77003
W Pierce St 77019
Piermain Dr 77035
Pierre Ct 77089
Pierrepont Dr 77040
Pierwood Ct 77041
Pifer Rd & Way 77024
Pifer Green Cir 77024
Pigeon Bluff Dr 77065
Pigeonwood Dr 77089
Pillar Park Cir 77041
Pillot St 77029
Pilot Point Dr 77038
Pimlico Ct 77038
Pin Oak Park 77081
Pin Oak Ridge St 77073
Pinacle Pt 77085
Pinafore Ln 77039
Pincay Oaks Ct & St 77088
Pinckney St 77009
Pincourn Dr 77066
Pinderfield Ct 77083
Pine St 77081
Pine Arbor Dr 77066
Pine Bank Ct & Dr 77095
Pine Bark Dr 77092
Pine Bayou St 77024
Pine Blossom Trl 77059
Pine Briar Cir 77056
S, E, N & W Pine Brook Cv & Way 77059
Pine Burr Ln 77040
Pine Bush Dr 77070
Pine Castle Dr 77095
Pine Center Dr 77095
Pine Chase Dr 77055
Pine Cliff Dr 77084
Pine Cone Ln 77041
Pine Cove Dr 77092
Pine Creek Ct 77017
Pine Creek Ln 77055
Pine Crescent Ct 77024
Pine Crest St 77020
Pine Crest Trl 77059
Pine Cut 77032
Pine Desert Ln 77088
Pine Falls Dr 77095
Pine Flats Dr 77095
Pine Forest Cir 77056
Pine Forest Ln 77084
Pine Forest Rd
5200-5699 77056
5900-6099 77057
10000-10399 77042
Pine Forest Green Blvd 77084
Pine Forest Hollow Trl 77084
Pine Fork Ct 77062
Pine Gap Dr 77090
Pine Green Trl 77059
Pine Grove Cir 77024
Pine Grove Dr 77092
Pine Gulch Ct 77049
Pine Gully Blvd 77017
Pine Heather Ct 77059
Pine Hollow Ln 77056
Pine Hollow Trce 77084
Pine Hollow Landing Ct 77084
Pine Island Dr 77050
Pine Knoll Dr 77099
Pine Lake Dr 77055
Pine Lake Trl 77068
Pine Landing Dr 77088
Pine Laurel Ct 77082
Pine Lodge Dr 77090
Pine Meadow Dr 77071
Pine Meadow Ln 77039
Pine Moss Dr 77040
Pine Mountain Ct & Dr 77084
Pine Pass Ct & Dr 77070
Pine Point Ct 77070
Pine Ridge Ln 77088
Pine Ridge Terrace Rd 77081
Pine Row St 77049
Pine Shadows Dr 77056
Pine Straw Ct 77088
Pine Stream Ct 77083
Pine Thicket Ln 77085
Pine Thorn Dr 77095
Pine Timbers St 77041
Pine Tree Dr 77093
Pine Tree Gln 77049
Pine Tree Ln 77024
Pine Tree Spg 77049
Pine Tree Forest Trl 77049
Pine Vale Ln 77037
Pine Valley Ct & Dr 77019
Pine Village Dr 77080
Pine Vista Ln 77092
Pinebrook Ln 77053
Pinechester Dr 77066
Pinecreek Holw Ln 77095
Pinecrest Holw 77084
Pinedale St 77006
Pinefield Ln 77063
Pinegate Dr 77008
Pinehall Ln 77044
Pinehaven Dr 77024
Pinehill Ln
1-99 77019
9000-9099 77041
Pinehook Ln 77016
Pinehurst Ct 77064
Pinehurst Dr 77023
Pinelake Canyon Ct 77084
Pineland Dr 77024
Pineland Rd 77044
Pineleaf Dr 77068
Pineloch Dr
700-898 77062
900-1099 77062
1101-2299 77062
2500-2599 77059
Pinemont Dr
3545RR-3545RS 77018
700-4699 77018
4700-6999 77092
7000-8299 77040
S Pinemont Dr 77041
Pinemoor Way 77058
Pineneedle Dr 77024
Pinenut Bay Ct 77059
Pineridge St 77009
Pinerock Ln
12100-12699 77024
13300-14199 77079
Pinesage Dr 77045
Pinesap Dr 77079
S Pinesap Dr 77072
Pinesbury Dr 77084
Pineshade Ln 77008
Pineview Dr 77012
Pineway Blvd 77023
Pinewest Ct & Dr 77049
Pinewilde Dr 77066
Pinewold Cir, Ct & Dr 77056
Pinewood Cir 77024
Pinewood Grn 77084
Pinewood Cove Dr 77062
Pinewood Springs Dr 77066
Pinewood Trace Ln 77041
Piney Forest Ct & Dr 77084
Piney Lake Ct 77038
Piney Links 77068
Piney Meadow Ct 77041
Piney Oaks Dr 77065
Piney Place Ct 77094
Piney Point Cir 77024
Piney Point Rd 77024
S Piney Point Rd 77063
Piney Run Ct 77066
Piney View Ln 77044
Piney Woods Ct 77077
Piney Woods Dr 77018
Pink Azalea Trl 77079
Pinky Way 77015
Pinnacle Pl 77069
Pinnacle Run Dr 77073
Pinole Ln 77086
Pinole Forest Dr 77088
Pinole Lane Ct 77066
Pinon Dr 77092
Pinon Vista Dr 77095
Pintan Ln 77014
Pinto Cir 77090
Pinto Pony Trl 77044
Pinto Springs Ln 77073
Pinyon Creek Ct & Dr 77095
Pipers Gap Ct 77090
Pipestone St 77074
Piping Rock Dr 77077
Piping Rock Ln
3400-4099 77027
5200-5699 77056
6100-6299 77057
7800-7899 77063
10000-10999 77042
13700-14599 77077
Pipingwood Dr 77084
Pirates Cv 77058
Pirtlewood Cir 77088
Pitch Pine Dr 77070
Pitching Wedge Ct 77089
Pitkin Iron Ct 77077
Pitner Rd 77080
Pittman St 77009
Pittsburgh St 77005
Pittswood Ln 77016
Pitzlin St 77023
Pizer St 77009
Pizzito Ln 77065
Pizzitola St 77034
Plaag St
3600-3799 77093
4100-4799 77016
N Place Dr 77073
Place Rebecca Ln 77090
Place Royale Way 77056
Placid St 77022
Placid Bayou Trl 77045
Placid Brook Ct 77059
Placid Stream Ct 77059
Plainfield St
9600-9698 77036
9700-9799 77036
10500-11999 77031
Plainview St 77087
Plainwood Dr 77079
Plaistow Ct 77084
Plantation Rd 77024
Plantation Glen Park 77049
Plantation Oak Dr 77068
Plantation Valley Dr 77083
Plarallo Dr 77067
Plastics Ave 77020
Platzer Dr 77045
Playa Ct 77034
Playa Lucia Ct 77044
Player St 77045
SW Plaza Ct 77074
Plaza Dr 77050
SW Plaza Dr 77074
Plaza Dale Dr 77045
Plaza Del Sol Dr 77083
Plaza Del Sol Park 77020
N Plaza East Blvd 77073
Plaza Libre Dr 77083
Plaza Verde Dr 77038
Pleadwal St 77021
Pleani Dr 77064
Pleasant Colony Dr 77065
Pleasant Cove Ct 77059
Pleasant Lily Ct 77084
Pleasant Ridge Dr 77095
Pleasant Ridge Ln 77041
Pleasant Trace Ct & Dr 77059
Pleasant Valley Rd 77062
Pleasant Villas Ln 77075
Pleasantbrook Dr 77095
Pleasanton Dr 77038
Pleasantville Dr 77029
Plens Dr 77070
Plum Dr 77087
Plum Bough Ct 77084
Plum Creek Dr 77012
Plum Creek Ln 77087
Plum Creek Forest Ln 77087
Plum Creek Meadow Ct 77087
Plum Creek Terrace Ln 77087
Plum Creek Trail Ln 77087
Plum Dale Way 77034
Plum Falls Ct 77062
Plum Forest Rd 77084
Plum Glen Ct 77059
Plum Grove Ln 77088
Plum Hollow Dr 77059
Plum Knoll Ct 77084
Plum Lake Dr
8201-8297 77095
8299-8723 77095
10600-10699 77065
Plum Meadow Ln 77039
Plum Orchard Cir 77049
Plum Ridge Dr 77064
Plum Tree Ter 77077
Plum Vale Ct 77065
Plumb St 77005
Plumbrook Dr 77099
Plumbwood Way 77058
Plummer St 77029
Plumpoint Dr 77099
Plumtree Forest Cir & Ct 77095
Plumwood Dr 77014
Plymouth St 77022
Poco Ct 77073
Poco Rd 77080
Poe Rd 77051
Poinciana Dr
2300-2399 77018
4900-5499 77092
E Point Dr 77054
S Point Dr 77054
W Point Dr 77005
Point Blank Dr 77038
Point Broad Oak 77056
Point Clear Dr 77069
Point Lookout Dr 77058
Point Northwest Blvd 77095
Point Park Dr 77095
Point Six Cir 77095
Point West Dr 77036
Pointer St 77016
Poitiers Dr 77071
Polarstone Ct 77044
Polished Stone Cir 77095
Polk St
600-1599 77002
1700-1998 77003
2000-3799 77003
3801-3899 77003
3900-5799 77023
6500-6799 77011
W Polk St 77019
Pollard St 77020
Polly St 77016
Polo St 77085
Pom Ct 77055
Pomander Rd 77021
Pomeran Dr 77080
Pompano Ln 77072
Pompton Dr 77089
Ponce Dr 77016
Poncha Springs Ct 77040
Ponder Ln 77039
Ponderate Ct 77065
Ponderosa Ln
9200-9299 77074
9301-9499 77074
9500-9599 77036
Ponderosa Pines Dr 77090
Poneal Ct 77084
Ponnel Ln 77088
Pontchartrain Trl 77044
Pontiac Dr 77096
Pony Express Rd 77064
Pool Creek Dr 77095
Poolview St 77071
Popes Creek Ln 77044
Poplar Blf 77095
Poplar St 77087
Poplar Creek Dr 77077
Poplar Glen Ln 77082
Poplar Grove Dr 77068
Poplar Hill St 77095
Poplar Run Ct 77059
Poplar Springs Ln 77062
Poplarwood Ct & Dr 77089
Poppy St 77092
Poppy Trails Ln 77084
Porchlight Ct 77073
Porichin St 77009
Porindin St 77076
Port NW 77041
Port St 77020
Port Alexander Way 77083
Port Angeles Dr 77086
Port Erroll Dr 77095
Port Houston St 77029
Port Royal Dr 77058
Portal Dr
5600-6399 77096
7600-7899 77071
7901-8099 77071
9200-9499 77031
Porter St
2600-2899 77026
3900-4499 77021
Porter Meadow Ln 77014
Porter Ridge Dr 77053
Porterway Dr 77084
Portland St
1-99 77002

100-399 77006
Portman Glen Ln 77047
Portmanshire Ln 77084
Porto Rico Rd 77041
Portobello Dr 77083
Portofino Rd 77082
Portree Dr 77067
Portsmouth Ave 77027
Portsmouth St 77098
Portwall St 77029
Portway Dr 77024
Portwest Dr 77024
Portwood St 77011
Posey St 77009
Possum Creek Rd 77017
Possum Hollow Ln 77065
Possumwood Dr 77084
Post St 77022
Post Oak Blvd
515-515 77027
520-598 77027
700-700 77056
702-3199 77056
N Post Oak Ln 77024
S Post Oak Ln 77056
Post Oak Pkwy 77027
N Post Oak Rd
400-999 77024
1000-1599 77055
S Post Oak Rd
9500-10299 77096
10300-11599 77035
12400-14899 77045
14900-16999 77053
Post Oak Green Ln 77055
Post Oak Manor Dr 77085
Post Oak Park Dr 77027
Post Oak Place Dr 77027
Post Oak Timber Dr 77056
Posthorn Ln 77015
Postwick Ct 77095
Potomac Dr 77057
Potomac Enclave Dr 77057
Pottinger Dr 77083
Poulson Dr 77031
Poundbury Ct 77047
Pouter Dr 77083
Powder Springs Ln 77070
Powderhorn St 77024
Powell Ln 77015
Power St 77012
Poynes Dr 77065
Pradera Dr 77083
Prado Ln 77070
Prague St 77007
Prairie Dr 77064
Prairie St
600-1599 77002
2200-2399 77003
Prairie Brook Ct 77062
Prairie Creek Dr 77084
Prairie Dale Ct 77075
Prairie Dunes Dr 77069
Prairie Grove Dr 77077
Prairie Hawk Dr 77064
Prairie Hill Ct 77059
Prairie Knoll Ct 77059
Prairie Larkspur Dr 77073
Prairie Mark Ln 77077
Prairie Mist St 77088
Prairie Oak Dr 77086
Prairie Oaks Dr 77083
Prairie Ridge Rd 77053
Prairie Rose Dr 77070
Prairie View Dr 77088
Prairie Wind Ln 77040
Praise Ct 77048
Praliani Dr 77038
Prallara St 77093
Prantriv St 77030
Prattsford Ln 77090
Preakness Way 77071
Predgert Dr 77055
Prelude Ct 77040
Premier St 77040
Prentiss Dr 77061

Presa St 77078
Prescott St 77025
Preserve Ln 77089
Presidents Ct & Dr 77047
Presidio Dr 77053
Presidio Square Blvd 77083
Presley St 77093
Press St 77020
Pressler St 77030
Prestige Row 77065
Preston St
2-98 77002
100-2100 77002
2102-2198 77002
2200-3799 77003
Preston Cliff Ct 77077
Preston Field Ln 77095
Preston Park Dr 77095
Preston Springs Ct & Dr 77095
Preston Trail Dr 77069
Prestonwood Forest Dr 77070
Prestwick Ct 77057
Prestwick St 77025
Prestwood Dr
6400-6499 77081
7701-7897 77036
7899-7999 77036
Previn Ct 77088
Price St 77088
Price Grove Ln 77095
Prichett Dr 77096
Prickly Pear Ct 77090
Prides Crossing Rd 77067
Priest Dr 77093
Prillerman Trails Dr 77016
Prima St 77083
Prima Vera Dr 77045
Primrose St 77017
Primrose Acres Ln 77031
Primrose Meadow Ln 77095
Primwood Dr 77070
Prince St 77008
Prince Pine Ct & Trl 77059
Prince William Ln 77058
Princess Dr 77034
Princess Garden Way 77047
Princeton St 77009
Princeton Park Ct 77058
Princeton Point Ct 77047
Prior Park Dr 77047
Priscilla Ct 77015
Prism Ln 77043
Pristine Park Ct & Dr 77041
Privada Saratoga Ave 77076
Proctor St 77038
Produce Row 77023
Profet St 77013
Progreso Dr 77038
Prospect St 77004
Prospect Hill Dr 77064
Prospect Meadows Dr 77095
Prospect Ridge Ln 77094
Prosper St 77088
Prosperity Cir 77018
Prosperity Point Dr 77048
Prosperity Ridge Dr 77048
Prosperity River Ct 77072
Proswimmer St 77088
Provence Ln 77095
Providence Park 77024
Providence St
1100-1599 77002
1600-4999 77020
Providence Oak St 77084
Providence Pine Trl 77062
Providence View Ln 77049
Provident Oaks Ln 77077
Province Point Dr 77015
Prudence Dr 77045
Puebla Rd 77045
Puerta Vallaea Dr 77083
Puerta Vallarta Dr 77083
Puerta Vista Ln 77083
Pulford Ct 77094

Purdue St 77005
Purdy Ct 77084
Purple Plum Ln 77062
Purple Rose Ct 77094
Purple Sage Rd 77049
Purplemartin St 77083
Purpleridge Ct 77053
Purston Ct 77083
Pyron Way 77036
Quail St 77017
Quail Cove Ln 77053
Quail Creek Ct
100-199 77024
14600-14699 77070
Quail Creek Dr 77070
Quail Field Dr 77095
Quail Grove Ln 77079
Quail Hawk Dr 77014
Quail Hollow Ln 77024
Quail Meadow Dr
6200-6499 77035
7500-7999 77071
Quail Oak Dr 77014
Quail Rock Cir 77095
Quail Village Dr 77053
Quailwood St 77014
Quanah St 77026
Quander Ln 77067
Que Manor Dr 77090
Quebec Dr 77096
Queen St 77028
Queen Annes Rd 77024
Queenbury Hills Dr 77073
Queens St 77017
Queens Retreat Dr 77066
Queens River Dr 77044
Queens Way Cir 77044
Queensbury Ln
11900-12899 77024
12900-14199 77079
Queensclub Dr 77069
Queensdale Dr 77082
Queensgate Dr 77066
Queensland St 77028
Queensland Way 77083
Queensloch Dr 77096
Queensmill Ct 77079
Queensride Ln 77070
Queenston Blvd
5500-6799 77084
7100-12399 77095
Queenstown Rd 77015
Queenswood Ln 77008
Quenby Ave & St 77005
Quennell Cir 77032
Quention Dr 77045
Quercus Cir 77075
Querida Ct 77045
Quetzal Ln 77083
Quicksilver Ct 77067
Quiet Ln 77016
Quiet Bay Ct 77095
Quiet Bluff Ln 77077
Quiet Brook Dr 77084
Quiet Creek Dr 77095
Quiet Dale Ct 77095
Quiet Dawn Ct 77095
Quiet Forest Dr 77040
Quiet Green Ct 77062
Quiet Knoll Ct 77059
Quiet Loch Ct & Ln 77084
Quiet Meadows Dr 77067
Quiet Place Dr 77082
Quiet Prairie Trl 77049
Quiet Spring Ln 77062
Quiet Stream Ct 77095
Quiet Summer Ct & Ln 77044
Quiet Valley Ln 77075
Quiet Village Ct 77053
Quiet Villas Ln 77075
Quiet Water Ct 77065
Quiet Wood Ct 77038
Quill Dr 77070
Quill Garden Ln 77075
Quincannon Ln 77043

Quince St 77087
Quincewood Dr 77089
Quinn St 77009
Quinn Ridge Way 77038
Quintero Dr 77083
Quitman Ct 77026
Quitman St
100-198 77009
200-1699 77009
1700-1798 77026
1800-4499 77026
Quiver Ln 77067
R V Mayfield Dr 77088
Rabbit Oak Dr 77065
Rachel St 77091
E Rachlin Cir 77071
Racine St 77029
Rack St 77051
Racquet Ct 77069
Radbrook Ln 77079
Radcliffe St
1700-2599 77007
6400-6498 77091
6500-6999 77091
Radenz Rd 77066
Radford Ln 77099
Radford Park Cir 77062
Radha Ln 77018
Radial St 77021
Radio Rd 77075
Radney Cir & Rd 77024
Radney Road Est 77024
Radstock Dr 77062
Radwell Ct 77062
Radworthy Dr 77084
Rafael St 77013
Ragland Dr 77067
Raia Ln 77071
Raider Cir E 77080
Railey St 77009
Railhead Ln 77086
Railspur St 77078
Railton Ct & St 77080
Railwood Dr 77078
Rain Cloud Dr 77095
Rain Dance Dr 77090
Rain Hollow Pl 77024
Rain Lily Ln 77083
Rain Shadow Ct 77070
Rain Valley Ct 77044
Rain Willow Ct 77053
Raina Ln 77024
Rainbow Dr 77023
Rainbow Falls St 77083
Rainbow Glen Dr 77064
Rainbow Lake Rd 77095
Raincove Dr 77016
Raindrop Hollow Dr 77041
Rainesville Ln 77075
Rainglen Ln 77044
Rainhollow Dr 77070
Rainier Dr 77024
Rainlily Dr 77084
Rains Way 77007
Raintree Cir 77024
Rainwood Dr 77079
Rainy Meadow Ln 77013
Rainy River Dr
500-699 77037
801-897 77088
899-2299 77088
Rainy Sun Cir 77049
Raleigh St 77021
Ralfallen St 77008
Ralph St 77006
Ralph Culver Rd 77086
Ralphcrest Dr 77039
Ralston St
2500-3199 77026
6700-6899 77016
Ralstons Ridge Dr 77083
Ram Ct 77072
Ramada Dr 77062
Rambler Dr 77044
Rambleridge Dr 77053
Ramblewood Park 77094

Ramblewood Rd 77079
Rambling Trl 77089
Ramey Cir 77075
Ramin St 77093
Ramla Place Trl 77089
Rampart St
5400-8199 77081
10700-10999 77096
11600-12399 77035
Rampchester Ln 77015
Ramsay Way 77051
Ramus St 77092
Rana Ct 77068
Ranch St 77026
Ranch View Trl 77073
Rancheria Dr 77083
Ranchester Dr 77036
Rancho Bauer Dr 77079
Rancho Blanco Ct & Dr 77083
Rancho Grande Dr 77049
Rancho Mirage Dr 77069
Rancho Mission Dr 77083
Rancho Paloma Blvd 77049
Rancho Verde Way 77095
Rancho Vista Dr 77083
Ranchstone Dr 77064
Rand St
4100-6299 77026
7700-8099 77028
Randall St 77018
Randolph St
900-998 77088
1000-1099 77088
8900-9099 77061
9300-10100 77075
10102-10498 77075
Randon Rd
4200-5099 77092
5300-5799 77091
Randwick Dr 77092
Randy Dr 77055
Range Haven Ct 77073
Rangely Dr 77055
Ranger St
600-699 77029
4500-5099 77028
Rangewood Ct 77062
Ranic Dr 77064
Ranier Dr 77031
Rankin Cir E 77073
Rankin Cir N 77073
Rankin Cir W 77073
Rankin Rd
100-2099 77073
2100-5599 77032
W Rankin Rd
100-399 77090
600-1099 77067
Rankin Park Dr 77073
Rannie Rd 77080
Ransom St 77087
Rantrang St
7701-7799 77018
17800-17898 77075
Rapid River Ln 77086
Rapidcreek Dr 77053
Rapido Rd 77033
Raritan Dr
10000-10099 77080
10200-10599 77043
Rasmus Dr 77063
Ratama St 77017
Ratama Creek Ln 77064
Rathbone Dr 77031
Raton St 77055
Rauch Ct 77040
Rauch St 77029
Raul Hector 77075
Raven Canyon Ln 77095
Raven Crossing Ln 77089
Raven Ridge Dr 77053
Raven River Dr 77059
Raven View Dr 77067
Ravena Ct 77089
Ravenfield Ct & Dr 77084

Ravenhead Dr 77034
Ravenhurst Ln 77070
Ravenmoor Dr 77077
Ravens Nest Ct 77083
Ravens Nest Ln 77089
Ravenscroft Way 77083
Ravensworth Dr 77031
Ravenwind Rd 77067
Ravenwood Cir 77055
Ravenwood View Ln 77075
Rawley St
3200-3299 77026
3400-4700 77020
4702-4898 77020
Rawls St 77008
Ray St 77093
Ray Brook Ln 77089
Raybluff Ln 77040
Raydell Dr 77031
Raydon Ln 77024
Raylin Dr 77055
Raymac St 77037
Raymond St
3200-3799 77007
7100-7199 77021
Raymondville Rd 77093
Raymont Cir 77065
Rayson Rd 77080
Raywood Blvd 77040
Reads Ct 77015
Readsland Ln 77084
Reagan St 77009
Reagan Meadow Ct 77064
Real St 77087
Reality Rd 77039
Reamer St
5600-5799 77096
5800-8999 77074
Reba Dr 77019
Rebecca St
100-299 77022
3400-3899 77021
Rebecca Pines Ct 77024
Rebel Rd 77016
Record St 77028
Red Alder Cir 77073
Red Bay Ct 77062
E, N, S & W Red Birch Cir 77038
Red Bud Ln 77060
Red Carriage Ct 77062
Red Cloud Rd 77064
Red Coat Ln 77024
Red Coral Ct 77059
Red Falls Cir 77095
Red Fern Ct 77095
Red Fir Dr 77088
Red Haw Ln 77022
Red Hawk Cir 77064
Red Hill Trl 77095
Red Hummingbird Dr 77047
Red Lodge Dr 77084
Red Maple Dr 77064
Red Mesa Ct & Dr 77095
Red Mulberry Ln 77044
Red Oak Dr
16800-17118 77090
17119-18199 77090
17119-17119 77273
17119-17119 77290
17120-18198 77090
Red Oak St 77009
Red Oak Leaf Trl 77084
Red Pheasant Ct 77040
Red Pine Ridge Way 77049
Red Ripple Rd
100-299 77076
300-499 77091
Red River Trl 77095
Red Robin Ln 77075
Red Rugossa Dr 77095
Red Slate Ln 77095
Red Springs Dr 77082
Red Spruce Ln 77040
Red Tailed Hawk Ct & Ln 77044

Red Valley Dr 77049
Red Willow Dr 77084
Red Wolf Ct 77084
Red Wolf Dr 77084
Red Wolf Ln 77064
Redan St 77009
Redberry Glen Ln 77041
Redbird Ln 77044
Redbridge Ct 77059
Redbrook Dr 77089
Redbud St
3300-3698 77051
3700-4699 77051
4700-4798 77033
4800-5099 77033
Redbud Xing 77077
Redbud Brook Trl 77089
Redbud Point Ln 77049
Redbud Shores Ln 77044
Redbud Valley Trl 77062
Redbud Villa Ln 77086
Redcedar Ln 77094
Redcliff Rd 77064
Redcrest Dr 77095
Redcrest Springs Ct 77073
Redding Rd 77036
Redding Oak Ct 77088
Redding Springs Ln 77086
Reddingford Ln 77084
Reddleshire Ln 77043
Reddy Ln 77053
Redemption Cir 77018
Redfern Dr
8100-8199 77033
12100-12899 77048
Redford St
1200-1499 77034
9300-9499 77075
Redgate Cir 77071
Redgate Dr 77015
Redhaven Ct 77065
Redhaw St 77079
Redhead Ct 77044
Redland Woods Dr 77040
Redlands Dr 77040
Redleaf Ln 77090
Redleaf Hollow Ct & Ln 77095
Redmond St 77015
Redoak Pass Ln 77064
Redoak Ridge Ln 77064
Redondo Dr 77015
Redrock St 77088
Redroot Dr 77084
Redstart St
4500-5299 77035
5300-5599 77096
Redway Ln 77062
Redwicke Ln 77084
Redwin Cir 77047
Redwing Dr 77049
Redwing Bluff Dr 77009
Redwing Cove Dr 77009
Redwing Grove Way 77038
Redwing Haven Dr 77009
Redwing Park Dr 77009
Redwing Pines Dr 77009
Redwing Place Dr 77009
Redwing Ridge Dr 77009
Redwood St
900-999 77023
1300-1999 77087
Redwood Bend Trl 77062
Redwood Bough Ln 77062
Redwood Cove Ct 77062
Redwood Falls Dr 77082
Redwood Place Dr 77079
Redwood Run Ct 77062
Redwood Shadows Ct 77084
Redwood Shores Dr 77044
Reed Ct 77087
Reed Rd
1900-4699 77051
4700-5899 77033
6200-7199 77087
Reed Hollow Ln 77008

- Reedcrest St 77085
- Reedpoint Dr 77090
- Reeds Ferry Dr 77041
- Reedwood Ln 77036
- Reedwood Ridge Rd 77065
- Reese St 77012
- Reeves St 77004
- Reeveston Rd 77039
- Refugio Ct 77064
- Regal Row 77040
- Regal St 77034
- Regal Hollow Ln 77073
- Regal Manor Ln 77075
- Regal Oaks Bend Ln 77047
- Regal Pine Ln 77070
- Regal Pine Trl 77059
- Regal Ridge Ln 77053
- Regal Spruce Ct 77095
- Regal Trace Ln 77073
- Regal Wood Dr 77038
- Regalbrook Ct & Dr 77095
- Regalshire Ct 77047
- Regena St 77039
- Regency Dr 77045
- Regency Ln 77088
- Regency Square Blvd & Ct 77036
- Regency Villa Dr 77084
- Regents Cove Ct 77099
- Regents Park Dr 77058
- Regentview Dr 77079
- Regg Dr 77045
- Regina Dr 77084
- Regional Park Dr 77060
- Regnal St 77039
- Reichert Farms 77024
- Reid St
  - 1-1499 77022
  - 1900-4199 77026
- Reid Lake Dr 77064
- Reims Rd
  - 5900-6200 77036
  - 6202-6298 77036
  - 8400-8499 77074
  - 8501-8599 77074
- Rein St 77009
- Reinald Rd 77014
- Reinerman St 77007
- Reinicke St 77007
- Reissen Ln 77069
- Remegan Rd 77033
- Remington Ln 77005
- Remington Bend Ct & Dr 77073
- Remington Bridge Dr 77073
- Remington Chase Ct 77073
- Remington Creek Dr 77073
- Remington Crest Ct & Dr 77094
- Remington Cross Dr 77073
- Remington Glen Ct 77073
- Remington Green Ct & Dr 77073
- Remington Harbor Ct 77073
- Remington Heights Dr 77073
- Remington Lodge Ct 77073
- Remington Martin Dr 77073
- Remington Mill Dr 77073
- Remington Park Ct & Dr 77073
- Remington Point Ct 77073
- Remington Prairie Dr 77073
- Remington Ridge Dr 77073
- Remington Run Ln 77066
- Remington Springs Dr 77073
- Remington Walk Ct 77073
- Remington Wick Dr 77073
- Remlap St 77055
- Remme Ridge Ln 77047
- Remus Dr 77053
- Remwick Dr 77073
- Remy St 77045
- Rena St 77092
- Renaissance Ln 77071
- Renata Cir 77084
- Renault St 77015
- Renmark Ln 77070
- Renn Rd 77083
- Renners Ct 77007
- Renoir Dr 77079
- Renshaw St 77023
- Rental Car Ave 77032
- Renton Rd 77032
- Rentur Dr 77031
- Renwick Dr
  - 5301-5397 77081
  - 5399-7400 77081
  - 7402-7798 77081
  - 9000-11099 77096
  - 11101-11199 77096
  - 11500-12499 77035
- Renwood Dr 77080
- Renwood Frst 77084
- Reo St 77040
- Repa Ln 77014
- Reseda Cir & Dr 77062
- Reservoir St 77049
- Resica Falls Ln 77094
- Resource Pkwy 77089
- Restaurant Row 77084
- Reston Glen Ln 77073
- Reston Grove Ct & Ln 77095
- Restover Ln 77064
- Restridge Dr 77055
- Retherford Dr 77086
- Retlin Ct 77041
- Retreat Ridge Ln 77095
- Retta St 77026
- Reveille St 77087
- Revelstoke Dr 77086
- Revere St
  - 1900-2099 77019
  - 2600-3799 77098
- Reverend B J Lewis Dr 77088
- Reverse St 77055
- Rexton Dr 77084
- Reynolds St 77009
- Rhapsody Ln 77040
- Rhea St 77034
- Rhema Ln 77048
- Rhett Dr 77024
- Rhine Ln 77090
- Rhinebeck Dr 77089
- Rhiney Ct 77089
- Rhobell St
  - 7200-7799 77016
  - 8000-8299 77078
- Rhode Pl 77019
- Rhode Island St 77029
- Rhyme Court Rd 77067
- Rhythm Ln 77040
- Rial Ct 77069
- Riana Dr 77065
- Riane Ln 77049
- Riata Ln 77043
- Ribbonwood St 77078
- Ribstone Cir & Dr 77016
- Ricaby Dr 77064
- S Rice Ave
  - 3010-3131 77056
  - 3133-3399 77056
  - 5201-5297 77081
  - 5299-5700 77081
  - 5702-6298 77081
  - 8800-9799 77096
- Rice Blvd 77005
- Ricecrest St 77035
- Ricefield Dr 77084
- Ricelake Ln 77084
- Riceville School Rd 77031
- Rich Ct 77077
- Richard Arms Cir 77099
- Richards St 77029
- Richardson Rd 77069
- Richardson St 77020
- Richcrest Dr 77060
- Richcroft St 77029
- Richelieu Ln 77018
- Richey Rd 77090
- E Richey Rd 77073
- W Richey Rd 77066
- Richey St 77002
- S Richey St 77017
- Richfield Ln 77048
- Richland Dr
  - 7800-8299 77028
  - 8800-9499 77078
- Richland Springs Dr 77073
- Richmeadow Dr 77048
- Richmond Ave
  - 102-298 77002
  - 300-399 77002
  - 401-499 77002
  - 500-1318 77006
  - 1319-1699 77006
  - 1319-1319 77266
  - 1320-1698 77006
  - 1700-3399 77098
  - 3400-3799 77046
  - 3800-4999 77027
  - 5000-5599 77056
  - 5600-6499 77057
  - 7500-9699 77063
  - 9700-11100 77042
  - 11101-11197 77082
  - 11102-11198 77042
  - 11199-15199 77082
- S Richmond Ave 77082
- Richmond Hill Dr 77041
- Richton St 77098
- Richvale Ln 77062
- Richview Ct & Dr 77060
- Richwood Rd 77087
- Ricky St 77033
- Riddlelink 77025
- Riddlewood Ln 77025
- Riderdale Park Ln 77070
- Riderwood Dr 77099
- Ridge Dr 77073
- E Ridge Dr 77040
- S Ridge Rd 77090
- Ridge St 77009
- Ridge Bank Ln 77041
- E & W Ridge Creek Cir & Dr 77053
- Ridge Forest Dr 77088
- Ridge Glen Ct 77073
- Ridge Harbor Dr 77053
- Ridge Hill Ct & Ln 77084
- Ridge Hollow Dr 77067
- Ridge Lake Dr 77082
- Ridge Manor Dr 77053
- Ridge Maple St 77038
- Ridge Oak Dr 77088
- Ridge Park Dr 77095
- Ridge Row Ct 77041
- Ridge Run Dr 77064
- Ridge Scene Way 77084
- Ridge Top Dr 77090
- Ridge Trail Ln 77084
- Ridge Turn Dr 77053
- Ridge Wind Ln 77053
- Ridgebar Cir 77053
- Ridgeberry Dr 77095
- Ridgebriar Dr 77014
- Ridgebriar Ln 77085
- Ridgeburg Ct 77077
- Ridgebury Cir 77095
- Ridgechase Ln 77014
- Ridgecoral Dr 77038
- Ridgecreek Cir & Dr 77053
- Ridgecrest Dr 77055
- Ridgecroft Rd 77053
- Ridgecrossing Ln 77077
- Ridgedale Dr 77039
- Ridgegate Rd 77053
- Ridgeglen Ln 77082
- Ridgegreen Dr 77082
- Ridgehaven Dr 77053
- Ridgeland Ave 77039
- Ridgeland Ct 77060
- Ridgeley Dr 77055
- Ridgelow Ln 77070
- Ridgemar Cir 77053
- Ridgemeadow Ct 77083
- Ridgemont Pl 77053
- Ridgemont St 77087
- Ridgemore Dr 77055
- Ridgepoint Dr 77055
- Ridgerod Ln 77053
- Ridgeroe Ln 77053
- Ridgeside Dr 77072
- Ridgestone St 77053
- Ridgeton Dr 77053
- Ridgevan St 77053
- Ridgeview Dr
  - 7900-8099 77055
  - 10900-10999 77043
- E & S Ridgewalk Dr 77053
- Ridgeway Dr
  - 5000-6199 77033
  - 6200-7399 77087
- Ridgewell Dr 77062
- Ridgewest St 77053
- N Ridgewood Cir 77071
- S Ridgewood Cir 77071
- Ridgewood Pl 77055
- Ridgewood St 77006
- Ridgewood Canyon Dr 77059
- Ridgewood Knoll Ln 77047
- Ridgewood Lake Ct 77062
- Ridgewood Reef 77041
- Riedel Dr 77024
- Riesner St 77002
- Rietta St 77016
- Rigdale St 77084
- Rigel Rd 77088
- Rigger Ln 77062
- Riggs Rd 77022
- Rika Pt 77077
- Riley Ln 77003
- Riley Rd 77047
- W Riley Rd 77053
- Riley St 77005
- Rileybrook Cir 77094
- Rill Ln 77062
- N Rim Dr 77067
- Rim Rock Dr 77088
- Rimwood Rd 77049
- Rincon Dr 77077
- Riner St 77093
- Ringfield Dr 77084
- Ringford Ct 77084
- Ringold St 77088
- Rinn St 77078
- Rio Blanco Dr 77083
- Rio Bonito Rd 77083
- Rio Bravo Rd 77064
- Rio Crystal Cir & Dr 77095
- Rio Del Sol Dr 77083
- Rio Dell Dr 77083
- Rio Grande Dr 77064
- Rio Grande St 77040
- Rio Oaks Ct 77068
- Rio Pinar Cir & Dr 77095
- Rio Plaza Dr 77083
- Rio Quatro Dr 77045
- Rio Rancho Ct 77064
- Rio Ridge Ln 77041
- Rio Verde Ln 77044
- Rio Villa Dr 77049
- Rio Vista St 77021
- Rip Van Winkle Dr & Ln 77024
- Ripple Creek Dr
  - 300-599 77024
  - 1200-1299 77057
- S Ripple Creek Dr 77057
- Ripple Glen Dr 77071
- Ripple Lake Dr 77065
- N & W Ripple Ridge Dr 77053
- Ripplebrook Dr 77045
- E Rippleridge Dr 77053
- Ripplestream St 77068
- Ripplewind Ln 77068
- Ripplewood Ln 77015
- Rippling Creek Way 77062
- Rippling Fields Ct & Dr 77064
- Rippling Meadows Dr 77064
- Rippling Water Dr 77084
- Riptide Dr 77072
- Rising Springs Ln 77073
- Ristina Cir 77048
- Rita Ln 77015
- Ritow St 77089
- Rittenberg Ct 77084
- W Rittenhouse Rd 77091
- Rittenhouse St 77076
- E Rittenhouse St 77076
- W Rittenhouse St 77076
- Rittenhouse Village Ct & Rd 77076
- E & W Ritter Cir 77071
- Ritz St 77028
- Riva Ridge Ln 77071
- River Cir 77063
- River Dr 77017
- River Basin Ct 77089
- River Bend Dr 77063
- River Birch Way 77059
- River Bluff Dr 77085
- River Cliff Ln 77095
- River Fern Dr 77040
- River Forest Ct & Dr 77079
- River Garden Dr 77095
- River Glynn Dr 77063
- River Hollow Ln 77027
- River Keg Dr 77083
- River Laurel Dr 77014
- River Maple Ln 77062
- River Meadows Rd 77084
- River Oaks Blvd 77019
- River Park Ct & Dr 77070
- River Point Dr 77063
- River Ridge Ct 77068
- River Roads Dr 77079
- River Sage Dr 77084
- River Springs Dr 77050
- River Trail Dr 77050
- Riverbank Ridge Ct & Ln 77089
- Riverbend Canyon Ct & Ln 77089
- Riverchase Ln 77014
- E & W Rivercrest Dr 77042
- Rivercroft Ln 77089
- Rivercross Rd 77064
- Riverglade Dr 77095
- Rivergrove Dr
  - 400-599 77015
  - 14200-14299 77070
- Riverhill Ct 77014
- Riverine Ct 77055
- Riverlace Dr 77079
- Riverland Ln 77040
- Riverridge Park Ln 77089
- Rivershire Ln 77073
- Riverside Dr 77004
- Riverside St 77044
- Riverside Grove Dr 77083
- Riverside Lodge Dr 77083
- Riverside Walk Ln 77064
- Riverstone Lake Ln 77089
- Riverstone Ranch Rd 77089
- Riverview Cir 77077
- Riverview Ct 77077
- Riverview Dr
  - 10600-11111 77042
  - 11300-12099 77077
- Riverview Way
  - 5900-6399 77057
  - 7500-7599 77063
  - 11100-11299 77042
- Riverway Dr 77056
- Riverwell Cir E & W 77083
- E & W Riverwood Dr 77076
- Roan Dr 77065
- Roandale Dr 77048
- Roane St 77028
- Roanoke St 77028
- Roanwood Ct & Dr 77090
- Roaring Brook Ln 77024
- Roaring Fork Ln 77095
- Roaring Point Dr 77088
- Roaring Rapids Dr 77059
- Roaring Springs Dr 77064
- Roark Rd
  - 10800-11199 77099
  - 11301-11597 77031
  - 11599-11699 77031
- Robbie St 77009
- Robbins Dr 77024
- Roberson St 77085
- Robert E Lee Rd 77044
- Robert James St 77038
- Robert Lee Rd 77009
- Robertcrest St 77039
- Roberts St
  - 201-397 77003
  - 399-1399 77003
  - 1401-1599 77003
  - 2000-2399 77004
- N Roberts St 77003
- Roberts Trl 77037
- Robertson St 77009
- Robertsvale Rd 77037
- Robin Blvd 77045
- Robin St
  - 300-399 77002
  - 700-1699 77019
- Robin Hill Ct 77059
- Robin Hood Ct 77043
- Robindell Dr 77074
- Robinglen Dr 77083
- Robinhood St 77005
- Robinlake Ln 77024
- Robinwood Ln 77024
- Robita St 77019
- Roble Ct 77045
- Robmore St 77076
- Rochdale St 77025
- Rochelle Dr 77032
- Rochester St 77015
- Rochow St 77019
- Rock Cv 77079
- N Rock Dr 77073
- Rock Arbor Ln 77095
- Rock Dove Ln 77044
- Rock East Dr 77073
- Rock Falls Ct 77095
- Rock Falls Way 77041
- Rock House Rd 77060
- Rock Knoll Dr 77083
- Rock Maple Ln 77040
- Rock Pass Dr 77064
- Rock Ridge Dr 77049
- Rock Rose St 77051
- Rock West Dr 77073
- Rockampton Dr 77031
- Rockarbor Dr 77063
- Rockaway Dr 77016
- Rockbend 77084
- Rockbridge Ln 77023
- Rockbridge Meadow Ln 77085
- Rockbrook Dr 77015
- Rockby Dr 77085
- Rockcliff Dr 77037
- Rockcreek Ln 77049
- Rockcrest Dr & Rd 77041
- Rockford Dr
  - 8100-8699 77033
  - 11101-11397 77048
  - 11399-12999 77048
- Rockfowl Dr 77049
- Rockglen St 77015
- Rockharbor Ln 77070
- Rockhaven Dr 77062
- Rockhill St 77061
- Rockhurst Dr 77080
- Rockin Dr 77077
- Rockingham St 77051
- Rockland Dr 77064
- Rockleigh Pl 77017
- Rockley Rd 77099
- Rockmore Dr 77064
- Rockrill Dr 77045
- Rockshire Dr 77039
- Rockstone 77084
- Rocktree Dr 77040
- Rockville Dr 77064
- Rockwell Blvd 77085
- Rockwood Dr 77004
- Rocky Ln 77040
- Rocky Bend Dr 77077
- Rocky Bluff Dr 77085
- Rocky Cliff Ct 77095
- E & W Rocky Creek Rd 77076
- Rocky Hill Dr 77066
- Rocky Knoll Dr 77077
- Rocky Lake Ct & Dr 77070
- Rocky Meadow Dr 77024
- Rocky Mount Dr 77088
- Rocky Mountain Dr 77037
- Rocky Oak Ct 77059
- Rocky River Rd 77056
- Rocky Springs Trl 77045
- Rocky Valley Dr 77083
- Rockyridge Dr 77063
- Rockytop Cir 77067
- Rodale Dr 77049
- Rodeo Square Dr 77072
- Rodgers Rd 77070
- Rodney St 77034
- Rodney Ray Blvd 77040
- Rodrigo St 77007
- Roe Dr 77087
- Roebourne Ln 77070
- Roehampton Ct 77084
- Rogerdale Rd
  - 2400-3000 77042
  - 2909-2909 77242
  - 3001-3999 77042
  - 3002-3998 77042
  - 5800-6699 77072
- E Rogers St 77022
- Rogue River Dr 77086
- Roland St 77026
- Rolbury Ln 77066
- Rolff Ln 77084
- Rolgom Place Ct 77021
- Rolido Dr 77063
- Rolk Rd 77077
- Rolke Rd 77099
- Rolla St 77055
- Rolland St 77091
- Rolleston Ln 77034
- Rolling Creek Dr 77090
- Rolling Fork Ln 77040
- Rolling Mill Dr 77088
- Rolling Oaks Dr 77070
- Rolling Pine Dr 77049
- Rolling Ridge Dr 77072
- Rolling River Ct & Ln 77044
- Rolling Rock St 77040
- Rolling Run Ct 77062
- Rolling Timbers Ct & Dr 77084
- Rolling Water Ct & Dr 77069
- Rollingbrook Dr
  - 6100-6299 77096
  - 7600-7899 77071
- Rollingwood Dr 77080
- Rollins St 77091
- Roma St 77080
- Romaine Ln 77090
- Roman Hills Ct & Ln 77070
- Romano Park Ln 77090
- Romans St 77012
- Romea St 77028
- Romney Rd 77036
- Romona Blvd 77086
- Romsley Ln 77049
- Ronald St 77093
- Ronaldsay Mews St 77095
- Ronan Rd 77060
- Ronan Park Pl 77060
- Ronda Ln 77074
- Rondo Ct 77040
- Ronson Rd 77055
- Rook Blvd 77087
- Rookin St 77074
- Roos Rd
  - 6300-6398 77074
  - 6400-7299 77074
  - 7900-9499 77036
  - 11600-11899 77072

Roosevelt St 77012
Roper St 77034
Rosa Allen St 77017
Rosa Ridge Ln 77041
Rosalie St
400-999 77006
1000-3899 77004
Rosalind Ln 77053
Rosalinda Ln 77073
Rosamond St
100-599 77076
2400-2699 77098
W Rosamond St 77076
Rosastone Trl 77024
Rosbrook Dr 77038
Rose Ct 77004
Rose St 77007
Rose Way 77025
Rose Arbor Ln 77060
Rose Cottage Dr 77069
Rose Garden Dr 77083
Rose Landing Dr 77070
Rose Manor Dr 77095
Rose Mist Ln 77038
Rose Petal Ln 77038
Rose Shadow Ln 77038
Rose Valley Dr 77070
Rosebank Dr 77084
Rosebay Dr 77018
Rosebranch Ct 77059
Rosebrier Park Ln 77082
Rosebud Dr 77053
Rosebud Dale Ct 77084
Rosebury Dr 77039
Rosecrest Dr 77045
Rosecroft Dr 77048
Rosedale Cir 77004
Rosedale St
700-899 77006
900-999 77002
1000-3899 77004
Rosefield Dr 77080
Roseglen Meadow Ln 77085
Rosehaven Dr 77051
Roseheath Ln 77073
Rosehedge Ct 77047
Rosehill Ct, Dr & Ln 77070
Roseland St 77006
Roselane St 77037
E Roselane St 77076
Rosemary Ln
2800-5299 77093
6300-6799 77016
Rosemary Bend Ln 77044
Rosemary Park Ln 77082
Rosemeadow Ct & Dr 77094
Rosemont St 77051
Rosemont Park Ln 77044
N Roseneath Dr 77021
Rosenridge Dr 77053
Rosepoint St 77018
Roseridge Ln 77053
Rosethorn Dr 77049
Rosewell Ct 77095
Rosewick St 77015
Rosewin Cir 77047
Rosewood St
1300-3799 77004
13600-13698 77083
Rosewood Way Ln 77041
Rosie St 77091
Rosillion Ct 77095
Rosine St 77019
Roslyn Ct 77081
Rosprim St 77040
Ross Rd 77034
Ross Sterling St 77030
Rossette Dr 77080
Rossiter Ln 77049
Rosslare Dr 77066
Rosslyn Rd
4300-5199 77018
5200-5399 77091
Rosston Cir 77082
Rosstown Way 77080
Roswell St 77022

Rotan Dr 77032
Roth Dr 77076
Rothbury St 77043
Rothchilde Ct 77069
Rothermel Rd 77093
Rothesay Chase Rd 77095
Rothglen St 77070
Rothmoore Ln 77066
Rothway St 77040
Rothwell St
900-1200 77002
1202-1598 77002
1700-2499 77020
Rotman St 77003
Roufa Rd 77003
Rouge Cir 77063
Roughlock St 77016
Round Bank Ct & Dr 77064
Round Dale Ln 77075
Round Grove Ln 77095
Round Lake Dr 77077
Round Mountain Dr 77090
Round Oak Ct 77059
Round Rock Dr 77049
Round Up Ln 77064
Roundabout Way 77049
Roundbluff Ln 77075
Roundhouse Ln 77078
Roundstone Ln 77015
Roundtree St 77015
Rouse St 77020
Roush Rd 77077
Rousseau Dr 77065
Rowan Ln
6300-6899 77074
7900-9499 77036
11500-11899 77072
Rowan Oak Ln 77095
Rowboat Way 77044
Rowe Ln 77075
Rowena Ln 77041
Rowlett Rd 77075
Rowlock Ln 77079
Rowlock Vine Dr 77084
Rowood Dr 77070
Roxburgh Dr 77041
Roxbury Rd 77087
Roxdale Ridge Dr 77044
Roxella St
700-1399 77076
1500-1999 77093
Roxton Dr 77077
Roy Cir & St 77007
Roy Bean Dr 77041
Royal Walk 77069
Royal Way 77083
Royal Arbor Ln 77084
E & W Royal Arch Dr 77077
Royal Ascot Ct 77065
Royal Bell Ct 77047
Royal Birkdale St 77095
Royal Blue Dr 77088
Royal Cape Ct 77095
Royal Chase Dr 77047
Royal Chateau Ln 77082
Royal Crest Dr 77058
Royal Crest Way 77083
Royal Fern Ct 77062
Royal Fort Ln 77073
Royal Garden Dr 77095
Royal George Ln 77047
Royal Grove Ct 77083
Royal Hill Dr 77083
Royal Lake Dr 77050
Royal Manor Dr 77082
Royal Mile Ln 77084
Royal Mountain Dr 77090
Royal Oak Dr 77050
Royal Oak St 77083
Royal Oaks Crst 77082
Royal Oaks Dr 77016
Royal Oaks Grn 77082
Royal Oaks Grv 77082
Royal Oaks Trce 77082
Royal Oaks Vw 77082
Royal Oaks Xing 77082

Royal Oaks Club Dr 77082
Royal Palms St 77021
Royal Park Dr 77083
Royal Pine Dr 77093
Royal Place Ct 77088
Royal River Dr 77042
Royal Rock Ct 77088
Royal Rose Dr 77082
Royal Royce Dr 77042
Royal Sage Dr 77088
Royal Sands Ct 77088
Royal Shadows Dr 77082
Royal Spring Ct 77077
Royal Stone Ln 77073
Royal Thistle Ct & Dr 77088
Royal Village Dr 77088
Royalbrook Dr 77095
Royall St 77022
Royalton St 77081
Royalwood Dr 77049
Royan Dr 77071
Royce Ln 77013
Royce Palms Dr 77042
Royder St 77009
Roydon Dr 77034
Rubenstein St 77076
Rubin St
8500-8699 77051
10600-12599 77047
Ruble Dr 77084
Ruby Canyon Ln 77095
Ruby Meadow Dr 77095
Ruby Red Ct 77073
Ruby Rose St 77093
Ruby Star Dr 77082
Rue St 77033
Rue Cambon St 77074
Rue Carre St 77074
Rue Chablis St 77074
Rue Crillon St 77074
Rue De La Paix Way 77056
Rue Fontaine Ln 77015
Rue Saint Cyr St 77074
Ruell St 77017
Ruellen Ln 77038
Ruffino Rd 77031
Rufus St 77091
Rugley St 77004
Ruidosa Ct 77053
Ruiz St 77002
Ruland Rd 77055
Rumar Ln 77029
Rumbling Wood Ct & Ln 77086
Rumford Ln 77084
Rummel Creek Rd 77079
Runbell Pl 77095
Runnels St 77003
Running Arabian Ln 77044
Runnymeade Dr 77096
Runswick Dr 77062
Runyan St 77039
Rupert St 77026
Rupley Cir 77087
Rural St 77009
Rural Oak St 77034
Rush Mill Ct 77095
Rush Trace Ct 77095
Rushbrook Dr 77077
Rushcreek Dr 77067
Rushcroft Dr 77082
Rushwood Cir 77067
Rushworth Dr 77014
Rusk St
300-398 77002
400-1299 77002
1300-1998 77010
1301-1599 77002
1601-1997 77003
1999-3599 77003
3801-3897 77023
3899-5099 77023
6500-7499 77011
Rusk Landing Ct 77049
Ruskin St 77005
Russ Dr 77039

Russelfern Ln 77049
Russelfield Ln 77049
Russell St 77026
Russelville Rd 77048
Russet Field Ct 77070
Russett Dr
5500-5599 77056
10600-10799 77042
Russett Fields Ct 77044
Rustic St 77087
Rustic Bend Ct 77064
Rustic Canyon Trl 77090
Rustic Falls Ct 77083
Rustic Garden Dr 77083
Rustic Glen Ct 77095
Rustic Harbor Ct 77062
Rustic Park Ct 77083
Rustic Pecan Ln 77049
Rustic Pine Trl 77090
Rustic Sands Dr 77084
Rusting Willow Ln 77084
Rustler Ridge Ln 77089
Rustlers Way Ct 77064
Rustling Aspen Ln 77095
Rustling Brook Ln 77094
Rustling Leaves Rd 77083
Rustling Lvs Dr 77083
Rustling Maple Dr 77064
Rustling Moss Dr 77068
Rustling Villas Ln 77075
Rustling Winds Dr 77064
Rustling Woods Ct 77059
Ruston Oaks Ct & Dr 77088
Rustralm Dr 77031
Rusty St 77093
Rustyleaf Ln 77090
Rutgers Ave & Pl 77005
Rutgers Park Ct 77058
Ruth St 77004
Ruthby St 77061
Rutherford Ln 77088
Rutherglenn Dr 77096
Ruthven St 77019
Rutland Pl 77007
Rutland St
600-899 77007
900-2899 77008
4000-4299 77018
E & W Rutledge Ct 77084
Ryan Landing Dr 77065
Ryan Oaks Dr 77065
Ryan Park Dr 77095
Ryan Ridge Ln 77044
Ryan Trails Dr 77065
Ryaneagles Cir, Ct & Dr 77044
Ryans Park Ln 77089
Ryans Path Ln 77073
Ryanwood Dr 77065
Rye St 77029
Ryegate Dr 77041
Ryewater Dr 77089
Ryland Rd 77066
E Rylander Cir 77071
Rylis St 77019
Ryoaks Dr 77095
Ryon St 77009
Ryson St 77080
Ryton Ln 77088
Saba Rd 77045
Sabastian Dr 77083
Saber Ct 77038
Sabine St 77007
N Sabine St 77009
Sabine Brook Way 77073
Sable Ct & Ln 77014
Sable Meadow Ct & Ln 77064
Sable Mills Dr 77095
Sable Pines Ln 77014
Sable Terrace Ln 77044
Sable Trail Ct & Ln 77064
Sable Tree Dr 77084
Sablebend Ln 77014
Sablebrook Ln 77095

N & S Sablechase Ct, Dr & Ln 77014
Sablecliff Ln 77075
Sablecrest St 77014
Sablegarden Ln 77014
Sableglen St 77014
Sablegrove Ct & Ln 77014
Sablemist Ct 77014
N & S Sableridge Cir, Ct, Dr & Ln 77014
Sablerun Ct & Ln 77014
Sablesprings Ln 77014
Sablewood Ln 77014
Sabo Rd 77089
Sabra Ct 77048
Sabrina Dr 77066
Sabrooke Ln 77073
Sacaton Dr 77086
Sachar St 77039
Sackett St 77098
Saco River Way 77044
Sacramento St 77015
Saddle Crk 77024
Saddle Ln 77080
Saddle Back Pass 77095
Saddle Bred Dr 77084
Saddle Brush Trl 77095
Saddle Horn Dr 77060
Saddle Rock Dr
500-699 77037
800-1899 77088
Saddlebend Dr 77070
Saddlebough Dr 77065
Saddlebranch Ct 77024
Saddlebrook Ln 77024
Saddlecreek Dr 77090
Saddlehorn Ln 77024
Saddlehorn Trl 77064
Saddlewood Ln 77024
Saddlewood Estates Dr 77024
Sadler St
1100-1399 77022
1700-3499 77093
4800-4999 77016
Safebuy St 77028
Safeguard St
8400-8599 77051
10600-12599 77047
Saffolk Punch Dr 77065
Sagamore St 77096
Sagamore Hills Dr 77082
Sage Rd 77056
Sage St 77009
Sage August Ln 77089
Sage Deck Ln 77089
Sage Dock Ct 77089
Sage Gale Dr 77089
Sage Lee Dr 77089
Sage Linda Ln 77089
Sage Manor Dr 77084
Sage Marie Ln 77089
Sage Place Dr 77071
Sagearbor Dr 77089
Sageaspen Ln 77089
Sagebark Dr 77089
Sagebend Ln 77089
Sageberry Dr 77089
Sageblossom Dr 77089
Sagebluff Dr 77089
Sagebriar Dr 77089
Sagebrook Dr 77089
Sagebrush Dr 77093
Sagebud Ln 77089
Sageburrow Dr 77089
Sagecanyon Dr 77089
Sagecastle Ln 77089
Sagecherry Dr 77089
Sagecircle St E 77056
Sagecliff Dr 77089
Sagecountry Dr 77089
Sagecourt Dr 77089
Sagecreek Dr 77089
Sagecrest Ln 77089
Sagecroft Dr 77084
Sagedale Dr 77089

Sagedowne Ln 77089
Sageelm Ln 77089
Sageforest Dr 77089
Sagegate Dr 77089
Sageglen Dr 77089
Sageglow Dr 77089
Sagegreen Ct & Dr 77089
Sagegrove Ln 77089
Sagegulf Ln 77089
Sagehaven Dr 77089
Sageheather Dr 77089
Sagehill Dr 77089
Sagehollow Ln 77089
Sageholly Cir 77089
Sagehurst Ln 77089
Sagekaron Dr 77089
Sageking Dr 77089
Sageknight Dr 77089
Sageknoll Ln 77089
Sagelake Ln 77089
Sageland Dr 77089
Sagelea Ln 77089
Sageleaf Ln 77089
Sagelink Cir, Ct & Dr 77089
Sagemark Dr 77089
Sagemeadow Ct & Ln 77089
Sagemill Dr 77089
Sagemist Ct & Ln 77089
Sagemorgan Dr 77089
Sagemoss Ln 77089
Sageoak Dr 77089
Sageorchard Cir, Ct & Ln 77089
Sagepark Ln 77089
Sageperry Dr 77089
Sagepike Cir & Dr 77089
Sagepine Ln 77089
Sageplum Dr 77089
Sagequeen Dr 77089
Sager Dr 77096
Sageridge Cir 77089
Sageriver Ct & Dr 77089
Sagerock Dr 77089
Sageroyal Ln 77089
Sagesquare St 77056
Sagestanley Dr 77089
Sagestar Ln 77089
Sagestone Ct 77095
Sagetown Dr 77089
Sagetrail Dr 77089
Sagetree Dr 77089
Sagevale Ct & Ln 77089
Sagevalley Dr 77089
Sageview Dr 77089
Sageville Dr 77089
Sageway Dr 77089
Sagewell Dr 77089
Sagewhite Dr 77089
Sagewick Dr 77089
Sagewillow Ln 77089
Sagewind Cir, Ct & Dr 77089
Sagewood Dr 77089
Sagewoods Hills Dr 77072
Sageyork Dr 77089
Saginaw Dr 77076
Sago Ln 77084
Sai Baba Dr 77038
Saibaba Dr 77038
Sailboat Dr 77058
Saint St 77027
Saint Agnes St 77030
Saint Alban Ct 77015
Saint Anne Forest Dr 77088
Saint Augustine St
700-999 77023
5800-7399 77021
Saint Benedict St 77021
Saint Charles St
201-697 77003
699-2199 77003
2300-3799 77004
N Saint Charles St 77003
Saint Clair St 77088
Saint Claude Ct 77015
Saint Cloud Dr 77062

Saint Edwards Green Dr 77015
Saint Elmo St 77020
Saint Finans Way 77015
Saint Francis Ln 77079
Saint George Ln 77079
Saint George Place St 77056
Saint George Square Ln 77056
Saint Helena Way 77053
Saint Helier St 77040
Saint James Pl 77056
Saint John Ct
10700-10799 77071
16000-16099 77040
Saint John Dr 77058
Saint Johns Woods St 77077
Saint Joseph St 77023
Saint Louis St 77028
Saint Marys Ln 77079
Saint Michel Dr 77015
Saint Thomas Ct 77070
Saint William Ln 77084
Saintes Cir 77071
Sakowitz St
700-2799 77020
3300-3899 77026
Salama Fls 77089
Salerno Ln 77076
Salford Dr 77008
Salge Dr 77040
Salida De Sol Dr 77083
Salina St
4500-6199 77026
7600-7799 77020
Salinas Ln 77095
Salisbury St 77019
Salma Ct 77073
Salmon Crk 77041
Salta Dr 77083
Salter Dr 77032
Saltillo St 77013
Saltus St 77003
Saluda Creek Ln 77085
Sam St 77091
E Sam Houston Pkwy N
1500-5799 77015
5800-8199 77049
8200-13999 77044
14001-14299 77044
E Sam Houston Pkwy S 77034
N Sam Houston Pkwy E
416A1-416A2 77060
6-162 77060
164-799 77060
800-5799 77032
N Sam Houston Pkwy W
500-798 77067
501-1097 77038
1099-3399 77038
3400-5899 77086
6100-6199 77066
6600-10919 77064
10921-10953 77064
S Sam Houston Pkwy E
600-2798 77047
2800-4099 77047
4400-5999 77048
7700-8499 77075
8501-8599 77075
10800-11999 77089
S Sam Houston Pkwy W
1700-1716 77047
1718-2699 77047
3700-4200 77053
4202-5598 77053
6200-8599 77085
9500-10699 77071
10700-12499 77031
W Sam Houston Pkwy N
100-999 77024
1000-4399 77043
4400-6999 77041
7100-8900 77040
8902-8998 77040
9000-10999 77064

W Sam Houston Pkwy S
400-4099 77042
5800-8599 77072
8800-10799 77099
Sam Houston St 77016
Sam Houston Center Dr 77064
Sam Houston Park Dr 77064
Sam Wilson St 77020
Samantha Suzanne Ct 77025
Sammies Ct 77020
Samoa Way 77053
Sampley Way 77092
Sampson St
100-1899 77003
2100-5599 77004
N Sampson St 77003
Samrose Dr 77091
Samsarah Cir 77084
Samuel Ln 77015
N & S San Cir 77044
San Alberto 77017
San Angelo St 77020
San Antonio St
700-999 77012
6900-6998 77040
7000-7299 77040
San Benito Dr 77083
San Bernadino St 77066
San Blas 77017
San Bonifacio 77017
San Carlos St 77013
San Clemente St 77066
San Dario Dr 77083
San Dimas Dr 77083
San Felipe St
2100-3399 77019
3700-4699 77027
4700-5699 77056
5700-6699 77057
7500-7899 77063
8300-8599 77024
San Fernando Dr 77060
San Gabriel Dr 77084
San Ignacio 77075
San Jacinto St
1-700 77002
701-899 77002
701-701 77052
702-798 77002
900-999 77010
1001-1099 77010
1012-1098 77002
1100-2599 77002
2600-5699 77004
11900-12099 77044
N San Jacinto St 77002
San Jose St 77020
San Juan St 77020
San Julio Dr 77091
San Lorenzo 77017
San Lucas Dr 77083
San Lucia River Dr 77050
San Luis Rey Dr 77083
San Marcos St 77012
San Martin Ln 77083
San Mateo Dr 77053
San Miguel Ln 77060
San Milo Dr 77068
San Morino Dr 77083
San Pablo Dr 77083
San Pablo Gardens Dr 77045
San Patrico Ct 77064
San Pedro St 77013
San Pietro Dr 77070
San Rafael Ln 77083
San Ramon Dr 77083
San Remo Dr 77083
San Rio Dr 77083
San Saba St 77012
San Sebastian Ct & Ln 77058
San Simeon Dr 77083
Sanborn Dr 77092
Sanbow Ln 77044
Sanchez St 77012

Sand Dollar Dr 77065
Sand Lodge Ln 77089
Sand Mountain Ct & Ln 77044
Sand Myrtle Dr 77059
Sand Pass Ln 77064
Sand Prairie Dr 77095
Sand Tracks Ct 77064
Sandalfoot St 77095
Sandalwood Dr 77024
Sandbrook Dr 77066
Sandbur Valley Way 77045
Sandcastle Ln 77057
Sanderford Ln 77083
Sanders St 77004
Sanders Rose Ln 77044
Sandestine Ct & Dr 77095
Sandfield Dr 77077
Sandford Lodge Dr 77073
Sandgate Rd 77061
Sandgate Falls Ct 77062
Sandhill Crane Dr 77044
Sandhill Park Ln 77044
Sandhurst Dr
8100-8199 77033
11300-12899 77048
Sandia Cove Ct 77041
Sandia Lake Ln 77041
Sandisfield Ln 77084
Sandle St 77088
Sandle Crest Ct 77041
Sandlewood Trail Ln 77014
Sandman St 77007
S Sandman St 77098
Sandover Dr 77014
Sandpebble Chase 77077
Sandpiper Dr
7001-7297 77074
7299-7399 77074
7401-9099 77074
10300-10999 77096
11800-12699 77035
Sandra St
6100-7499 77028
7500-9999 77016
Sandra Ann Ct 77025
Sandradale St 77016
Sandri Ln 77077
Sandridge Ct 77049
Sandringham Dr 77024
Sandrock Dr 77048
Sands Point Dr
6400-6498 77074
6500-6800 77074
6802-6898 77074
7700-8600 77036
8602-8698 77036
11000-11599 77072
Sands Trail Ct 77064
Sandstone St
6600-6699 77074
8800-9699 77036
10700-12399 77072
Sandswept Ln 77086
Sandtown Cir & Ln 77064
Sandwood Ct 77089
Sandy Blf 77079
Sandy Cv 77058
Sandy St 77028
Sandy Bend Ct 77044
Sandy Bottom Pond Ln 77044
Sandy Cliffs Dr 77090
Sandy Creek Dr 77070
Sandy Falls Ct 77044
Sandy Glen Ln 77071
Sandy Hill Dr 77084
Sandy Hook Dr 77089
Sandy Meadow Ln 77039
Sandy Oaks Dr 77050
Sandy Path Ln 77084
Sandy Plains Ln 77062
Sandy Point Ln 77066
Sandy Port St 77079
Sandy Shoals Dr 77071
Sandy Springs Rd 77042

Sandydale Ln 77039
Sandygate Ln 77095
Sanford Rd
4300-5299 77035
5400-6699 77096
7600-7699 77071
9200-9499 77031
Sangamon Ln 77074
Sangerbrook Dr 77038
Sanguine Sound Ln 77089
Sanibel Falls Ct 77095
Sanspereil Dr 77047
Santa Bernadetta 77017
Santa Cecilia Ln 77017
Santa Christi Dr 77053
Santa Cruz St 77013
Santa Elena St 77061
S Santa Fe Dr 77061
Santa Fe Springs Ct & Dr 77041
Santa Lucia Ct & Dr 77083
Santa Maria St 77023
Santa Monica Blvd 77089
Santa Rita Dr 77083
Santa Rosa St 77023
Santa Teresa Rd 77045
Santee St 77018
Santiago St 77023
Santiago Cove Ln 77041
Santo Domingo 77017
Santone Ln 77076
Santrey Dr 77084
Sapling Way 77031
Sapling Oak Ct & Dr 77082
Sapphire Bay Ct 77094
Sapphire Mist Ct 77073
Sapphire Star Dr 77082
Sapphire Valley Rd 77095
Sapphire Vista Ln 77041
Sara Jo Ln 77086
Sara Rose St 77018
Saragosa Crossing Ln 77066
Sarah St
2000-2299 77054
3400-3599 77026
Sarah Lake Dr 77099
Sarahs Ln 77015
Saranac Dr 77089
Saratoga Dr 77088
Saratoga Forest Dr 77088
Saratoga Springs Ln 77041
Sardis Ln 77088
Sarita St 77012
Sarong Dr
4100-4199 77025
4300-4499 77096
Sarti St 77066
Sashay Dr 77099
Satchel Ct 77038
Satin Tail Ln 77095
Satsuma Dr
6600-12599 77041
15000-15099 77084
Satsuma St 77023
Satsuma Point Ct 77049
Satterfield Ln 77084
Sattler Park Dr 77086
Saturn Ln
16600-16698 77062
16800-18199 77058
Sauer St 77004
W Saulnier Cir & St 77019
Saulsworth St 77099
Saums Rd 77084
Saunders Rd
3800-4999 77093
7200-7499 77016
Sauris Ct 77038
Sauve Ln 77056
Savannah Trl 77095
E & W Savile Cir 77065
Saville Ct 77083
Savoy Dr 77036
Sawgrass Ridge Ln 77073
Sawmill Trl 77040
Sawmill Run Ln 77044

Sawmill Stream Cir 77067
Sawtooth Oak Dr 77082
W Sawyer St 77007
Sawyer Heights St 77007
Sawyer Knoll Ln 77044
Saxet St 77055
Saxon Dr
6205A-6205D 77092
1600-2399 77018
4900-6399 77092
17400-17599 77095
Saxon Hollow Ct & Ln 77084
Saxony Ln 77058
Sayan Glen Ln 77070
Saybrook Ln 77024
Sayers St
3300-6499 77026
6700-7999 77016
Saylynn Ln 77075
Scanlock St 77012
Scarab Dr 77041
Scarborough Fair St 77077
Scarlet Dr 77048
Scarlet Glen Ct 77077
Scarlet River Dr 77044
Scarsdale Blvd
10000-10098 77089
10100-12999 77089
13100-14099 77034
Scaup Dr 77040
Scenic Dr 77048
Scenic Canyon Ln 77095
Scenic Elm St 77059
Scenic Glade Dr 77059
Scenic Green Dr 77088
Scenic Haven Dr 77083
Scenic Lakes Way 77095
Scenic Peaks Ct 77059
Scenic Ridge Dr 77043
Scenic River Dr 77044
Scenic View Dr 77062
Scenic Water Dr 77044
Scent Fern St 77064
Sceptre Cir 77072
Schade Ln 77037
Schaffer Ln 77070
Schalker Dr 77026
Schambray St 77085
Scharpe St 77023
Scherzo Ln 77040
Schevers St
5600-5899 77033
6200-6499 77087
Schilder Dr 77093
Schiller Rd 77082
Schiller St 77055
Schiller Park Ln 77014
Schintri St 77008
Schley St 77087
Schlumberger St 77023
Schneider St 77093
Scholl St 77034
Schooley Dr 77071
Schroeder Rd
5800-6099 77021
12900-14799 77070
Schroeder St 77011
Schroeder Oak Ct 77070
Schuler St 77007
Schuller Rd 77093
Schuller Place Ct 77093
Schumacher Ln
5300-5599 77056
5600-5999 77057
8600-8799 77063
Schumann Ct & Ln 77083
Schurmier Rd
600-4099 77047
4200-6699 77048
Schutz St 77032
Schwab Ln 77055
Schwartz St 77020
Schweikhardt St
400-2399 77020
2800-3399 77026
Scofield Ln 77096

Scone St 77084
Scoregga Ln 77037
Scotch Grove Ct 77014
Scotch Hollow Ln 77083
Scotch Pine Dr 77049
Scotland St 77007
Scotney Castle St 77095
Scotsbrook Dr 77038
Scott St
1300-1999 77003
2200-5399 77004
5400-7699 77021
7700-10599 77051
10800-13000 77047
13002-13898 77047
Scottcrest Dr 77021
Scotter Dr 77015
Scranton St
8400-8499 77061
8500-9499 77075
Scribner Rd 77074
Scyrus Ln 77066
Sea Biscuit Ln 77071
Sea Branch Dr 77084
Sea Cove Ct 77058
Sea Island Dr 77069
Sea King St 77008
Sea Lark Rd 77062
Sea Liner Dr 77062
Sea Myrtle Dr 77095
Sea Queen Ct 77008
Sea Shore Dr 77072
Sea Smoke Ln 77079
Seaboard Loop 77099
Seabrook St 77021
Seacliff Dr 77062
Seafoam Rd 77062
Seaford Dr 77089
Seagate Ln 77062
Seagler Rd 77042
Seagler Park Ln 77047
Seagler Pond Ln 77073
Seagler Springs Ln 77044
Seagram St 77029
Seagrove Ct 77041
Seagull St 77017
Seahorse Dr 77062
Seakale Ln 77062
Sealey St
6500-6999 77091
7700-8299 77088
Seamaster Dr 77062
Seamist Ct & Dr 77008
Sean Park Ct 77095
Searle Dr 77009
Searrank St 77029
Searston Dr 77084
Seaside Ln 77062
Seaspray Ct 77008
Seastone Ln 77068
Seaswept Dr 77071
Seaton Gln 77094
Seattle St 77040
Seattle Slew Dr 77065
Seavale Rd 77062
Seawolf Dr 77062
Seawood Dr 77089
Seclusion Dr 77049
Secret Canyon Dr 77095
Secret Falls Ct 77089
Secretariat Ct 77071
Secretariat Dr 77065
Secretariat Ln 77071
Security Ln 77049
Security Rd 77032
Security Way 77040
Sedalia Springs Ct 77077
Sedge Wren Ct 77083
Sedgeborough Dr 77084
Sedgie Dr 77080
Sedgwick Dr 77076
Sedona Ct 77083
Sedona Hls 77069
Sedona Woods Ln 77082
Seedling Dr 77032
Seegers Trail Dr 77066

Seeker St
8100-9499 77028
9600-9799 77078
Segrest Dr 77047
Seine Ct 77014
Seinfeld Ct 77069
Sela Ln 77072
Selinsky Rd 77048
Sellers Rd 77060
Selma St 77030
Selwyn Dr 77015
Seminar Dr 77060
Seminary Ridge Ln 77083
Seminole Spring Ln 77089
Semmes St
800-1399 77020
1600-2399 77026
6900-7299 77093
Senate Ave 77040
Senca Park Dr 77077
Seneca St 77016
Senegal St 77016
Senior St 77016
Senna St 77028
Senna Ledge Ct 77089
Sentinel Dr 77053
Sentinel Pines Ct 77059
Sentry Ct 77065
Sentry Park Ct & Ln 77084
Sequoia Dr 77041
Sequoia Bend Blvd 77032
Sequoia Pass Ct 77095
Serena Vista Way 77068
Serenade Ln 77040
Serene Elm St 77089
Serene Waters Ln 77084
Sereniah Cir 77084
Serenity Ct 77025
Serpentine Dr 77029
Serrano Terrace Ln 77041
Service St 77009
Sesame St 77048
Seton Lake Dr 77086
Settemont Rd 77085
Settle Dr 77071
Seuss Dr 77025
Seven Mile Ln 77093
Seven Pines Ln 77083
Seven Springs Dr 77084
Sevenhampton Ln 77015
Seville St 77016
Sewalk St 77047
Sewanee Ave 77005
Sewanee St 77025
Sexton St 77028
Seyborn St 77027
Seymour Dr 77032
Shadder Way 77019
Shaddock Dr 77041
Shadeland Dr 77043
Shadewood Ct 77015
Shadow Ln 77080
Shadow Trl 77084
Shadow Bayou Ct 77082
Shadow Bend Dr 77043
Shadow Bluff Ct 77082
Shadow Branch Ln 77077
Shadow Briar Ln 77073
N & S Shadow Cove Ct, Dr & Ln 77082
Shadow Creek Dr 77017
Shadow Crest St
5500-5599 77096
6100-8899 77074
Shadow Dust Ct 77082
Shadow Edge Cir 77095
Shadow Falls Ct 77059
Shadow Fork Ct 77082
Shadow Garden Ln 77077
Shadow Gate Ct & Ln 77040
Shadow Green Dr 77082
Shadow Hill Ln 77072
Shadow Island Dr 77082
Shadow Isle Ln 77084
Shadow Knoll Ct 77082
Shadow Lawn St 77005

Shadow Lawn Way 77095
Shadow Ledge Dr 77095
Shadow Oaks Dr 77043
Shadow Path Dr 77059
Shadow Pine Dr 77070
Shadow Royal Dr 77082
Shadow Run Dr 77082
Shadow Spring Ct 77082
Shadow Trace Cir 77082
Shadow Trail Dr 77082
Shadow Tree Dr 77035
Shadow View Ln 77077
Shadow Villa Ln 77044
Shadow Way Ct & St 77024
Shadow Wick Ln 77082
Shadow Wind Dr 77040
Shadow Wood Dr
9800-9999 77080
10100-10198 77043
10200-10999 77043
Shadowbark Dr 77082
Shadowbriar Dr
2000-2899 77077
2900-3099 77082
Shadowchase Ct & Dr 77082
Shadowdale Dr
1100-3099 77043
4400-5099 77041
N Shadowdale Dr 77041
Shadowfern Ct & Dr 77082
Shadowfield Dr 77064
Shadowglade Ct 77064
Shadowhollow Dr 77082
Shadowknoll Dr 77082
Shadowleaf Dr 77082
Shadowmeadows Dr 77082
Shadowmist Dr 77082
Shadowood Ct 77024
Shadowpoint Dr 77082
Shadowridge Dr 77053
Shadowside Ct 77082
Shadowvale Dr 77082
Shadowvista Ct & Dr 77082
Shadowwalk Dr 77082
Shadrack St 77013
Shadway Dr 77084
Shadwell Dr 77062
Shady Cyn 77070
Shady Dr 77016
Shady Ln 77093
E Shady Ln 77063
W Shady Ln 77063
Shady Acres Ct & Lndg 77008
Shady Arbor Ct & Ln 77040
Shady Bend Dr 77070
Shady Bough Dr 77070
Shady Breeze Dr 77082
Shady Bridge Ct 77095
Shady Brook Dr 77084
Shady Canyon Ct & Dr 77095
Shady Corners Ln 77040
N & S Shady Creek Ct & Dr 77017
Shady Downs Dr 77082
Shady Elms Dr 77059
Shady Fern Ct 77065
Shady Glade Dr 77090
Shady Green Mdws 77083
Shady Grove Ct 77040
Shady Grove Ln
1-99 77024
7300-8199 77040
11600-11699 77024
Shady Harbor Dr 77082
Shady Hollow St 77056
Shady Lane Cir & Ct 77063
Shady Meadow St 77039
Shady Mill Dr 77040
Shady Moss Ln 77040
Shady Nook Ct 77018
Shady Palms Dr 77095
Shady Park Dr 77017
Shady River Dr
5200-5699 77056

5700-5999 77057
10100-10799 77042
Shady Rock Ln 77015
Shady Square Ct 77095
Shady Stream Dr 77090
Shady Timbers Dr 77016
Shady Trail Ln 77038
Shady Tree Ln 77086
Shady Vale Ln 77040
Shady Villa Cv, Gdn, Hvn, Mdw, Pne & Walk 77055
Shady Villa Fern 77055
Shady Villa Manner 77055
Shady Woods Ln 77008
Shadybriar Dr 77077
Shadybrook Dr 77094
Shadycrest Dr 77082
Shadydale Ln 77016
Shadymist Dr 77082
Shadyview St 77011
Shadyvilla Ln 77055
Shadywind Dr 77082
Shadywood Rd 77057
Shaftsbury Dr 77031
Shagbark Dr 77078
Shagwood Dr 77049
Shakespeare St 77030
Shallow Lake Ln 77095
Shallow Oaks Dr 77065
Shallow Ridge Blvd 77095
Shallowbrook Ln 77024
Shallowlake Ct 77095
Shaman Ln 77083
Shamrock Dr 77030
Shamrock St 77017
Shane St 77037
Shanemoss Ct 77068
Shanghai St 77040
Shango Ln 77095
Shangrila Ln 77095
Shannon Cir 77024
Shannon St 77027
Shannon Glen Ln 77084
Shannon Hills Ct & Dr 77099
Shannon Marie Ln 77077
Shannon Mills Ln 77075
Shannon Ridge Rd 77062
Shannon Valley Dr 77077
Shapiro Springs Ln 77095
Shar Mist Ln 77066
Sharman St 77009
Sharmon Rd 77038
Sharon St 77020
Sharondale Dr 77033
Sharp Pl 77019
Sharpbill Dr 77083
Sharpcrest St
6700-7199 77074
7900-9999 77036
11200-12099 77072
Sharpstown Ctr 77036
Sharpstown Green Cir 77036
Sharpton Dr 77038
Sharpview Dr
6301-6397 77074
6399-7299 77074
7900-9699 77036
10600-12599 77072
Shartle Cir 77024
Shasta Dr 77024
Shasta Sq 77084
Shasta Leaf Ct 77044
Shasta Springs Dr 77034
Shatner Dr 77066
Shatnerwood Dr 77095
Shavelson St 77055
S Shaver St 77034
Shawna Dr & St 77084
Shawnbrook Dr 77071
Shawnee St 77034
Shawnway Ln 77094
Shawood Ln 77089
Shawwood Ct 77070
Shayan Ct 77037
Shea Pl & St 77002
Shearn St 77007
Sheer Water Dr 77082
Sheffield Blvd 77015
Sheffield Bend Ct & Dr 77095
Sheffield Falls Ct 77095
Sheffield Knoll Ln 77095
Sheffield Pines Ln 77095
Sheffield Run Dr 77084
Shekel Ln 77015
Shelbourne Xing 77073
Shelbourne Meadows Dr 77095
Shelbourne Park Ln 77084
Shelburne Rd 77049
Shelby Cir 77051
Shelby St 77009
Sheldon Rd
10315-A-10317-A 77049
6300-10499 77049
10500-11399 77044
S Sheldon Rd 77015
Sheldon St 77008
Sheldon Ridge Way 77044
Shell Creek Ct 77064
Shellans St 77027
Shelley St 77009
Shellhorn Ct 77014
Shellville Ct 77040
Shelmer Dr 77080
Shelterwood Dr 77008
Shelton Ct 77099
Shelton Rd 77093
Shelton Grove Dr 77070
Sheltons Bend Ct 77077
Shelwick Dr 77031
Shenandoah St 77021
Shepherd Dr 77007
N Shepherd Dr
3938A-3938D 77018
500-799 77007
800-2999 77008
3000-3899 77018
3816-3816 77206
3900-5198 77018
3901-5199 77018
5200-7499 77091
7500-7600 77088
7511-7511 77238
7511-7511 77291
7511-7511 77222
7601-7999 77088
7602-7998 77088
S Shepherd Dr
900-2599 77019
2600-5299 77098
5300-5399 77005
Shepherd Falls Ln 77075
Shepherds Way 77066
Shepherds Ridge Dr 77077
Shepperton Ct 77065
Sheraton St 77039
Sheraton Oaks Dr 77091
Sherbourne St 77016
Sherbrooke Rd 77056
Sherbrooke Canyon Ln 77047
Sherburne Dr 77072
Sheree St 77049
Sheri Hollow Ln 77082
Sheridan Rd
11200-11699 77016
11700-11899 77050
Sheridan St 77030
Sherina Park Dr 77095
Sheringham St 77085
Sherman St
2900-4399 77003
4400-7499 77011
7500-8099 77012
Sherman Oaks Dr 77085
Sherman Ridge Ln 77083
Shermons Pond 77041
Sherrill Dr 77089
Sherry Ln 77041
Sherrywood Dr 77044
Sherway Dr 77016
Sherwick St 77093
Sherwin St 77007
Sherwood Dr 77021
Sherwood Grv 77043
Sherwood Ln 77092
Sherwood Run 77043
Sherwood Trl 77043
Sherwood Bend Dr 77068
Sherwood Forest St 77043
Sherwood Forest Glen Ct & Dr 77043
Sherwood Garden Dr 77043
Sherwood Mills Ln 77043
Sherwood Oaks Dr 77015
Sherwood Park Cir 77043
Sherwood Point Ln 77043
Sherwood Ridge Dr 77043
Sherwood Springs Ln 77043
Sheryl St 77029
Shetland Ln 77027
Shield St 77017
Shillington Dr 77094
Shilo Dr 77032
Shiloh St 77020
Shiloh Church Rd 77066
Shimmering Maple Dr 77064
Shindins St 77017
Shindler Cir 77064
Shiner Ln 77072
Shingle Oak Ln 77088
Shining Brook Ct 77044
Shining Rock Ln 77095
Shining Sumac Ave 77084
Shinnecock Hills Dr 77069
Shire Wood Ln 77082
Shireoak Dr 77084
Shirkmere Rd 77008
Shirley Ln
1400-1499 77015
5600-5799 77032
Shirley Mae Ln 77091
Shiro Dr 77014
Shive Dr 77078
Shiveley Cir 77032
Shoal Creek Dr 77064
Shoal Lake Ln 77095
Shoalwater Ln 77070
Shoppe St 77034
Shorebrook Dr 77095
Shorecrest Dr 77095
Shoreham St 77093
Shorehaven Cir 77048
Shoreline Terrace Dr 77044
Shorewood Lakes Dr 77095
Short St 77021
Short Bridge St 77075
Short Brook Ln 77041
Shorthorn Cir & Ln 77041
Shortpoint St 77055
Shoshone Rd 77055
Shottery Dr 77015
Shotwell St
1-1299 77020
6000-7499 77028
7600-8799 77016
Shreveport Blvd 77028
Shumard Oak Ct 77065
Shurmard Dr 77092
Sibelius Ln 77079
Siberian Elm Ln 77073
Sibley St 77023
Sicklepod Dr 77084
Sidney St
1-411 77003
413-499 77003
700-1899 77023
1901-1999 77023
5800-7199 77021
N Sidney St 77003
Sidonie Dr 77053
Sieber Dr 77017
Siebinthaler Ln 77084
Siegel St 77009
Siena Vista Dr 77083
Sienna Arbor Ln 77041
Sienna Bay Ct 77041
E, N, S & W Sienna Cove Ln 77083
Sienna Hill Dr 77077
Sienna Rosa Ln 77041
Sienna Trace Ct 77083
Sierra Dr
9300-10599 77051
15700-15799 77040
Sierra Blanca Dr 77083
Sierra Breeze 77094
Sierra Grande Ct & Dr 77083
Sierra Hill Ct 77083
Sierra Pines Ct & Dr 77068
Sierra Skies Dr 77083
Sierra Trails Dr 77083
Sierra Valle Cir & Dr 77083
Sierra Vista Dr 77083
Siesta Ln 77029
Signal Creek Dr 77095
Signal Point Ln 77064
Signat Dr 77041
Signet St 77029
Sikes St 77018
Silber Rd
900-999 77024
1000-2199 77055
Silent Cedars Dr 77095
Silent Elm St 77044
Silent Shore Ln 77041
Silent Spruce Ct 77084
Silent Star Ct 77095
Silent Wood Ln 77086
Silkleaf Ln 77094
Silkwood Dr 77031
Silky Leaf Dr 77073
Silky Moss Dr 77064
Silo Ln 77071
Silsbee St 77033
Silvan Wind Ln 77040
Silver St 77007
Silver Ash Ln & Way 77095
Silver Aspen Ct 77059
Silver Bank Ct 77058
Silver Bay Ct 77095
Silver Bell Dr 77038
Silver Bell St 77045
Silver Birch Dr 77073
Silver Bough Cir 77059
Silver Canyon Ct & Ln 77067
Silver Chalice Dr 77088
Silver Charm 77014
Silver City Dr 77064
Silver Cloud Ln 77086
Silver Creek Dr
5100-5199 77017
12100-12199 77070
Silver Crescent Dr 77064
Silver Crossing Ct 77084
Silver Cup 77014
Silver Fir Dr 77095
Silver Forest Dr 77092
Silver Fox Dr 77066
Silver Frost Dr 77066
S Silver Green Dr 77015
Silver Hollow Ln 77082
Silver Island Cir 77067
Silver Knight Ct 77062
Silver Lace Ln 77070
Silver Lake St 77025
Silver Leaf Ln 77088
Silver Maple St 77064
Silver Meadow Ct 77041
Silver Oak Ln 77038
Silver Poplar Ln 77084
Silver Ridge Dr 77090
Silver Rod Ln 77041
Silver Rush Dr 77095
Silver Sage Dr 77077
Silver Sands Cir & St 77095
Silver Shade Dr 77064
Silver Sky Ct 77062
Silver Sky Ln 77095
Silver Spring Ln 77025
Silver Star Dr 77086
Silver Stone St 77048
Silver Tree 77014
Silver Valley Dr 77084
Silverado Dr 77077
Silverado Trace Dr 77095
Silverbonnet St 77055
Silvercrest St 77076
Silverdale St 77029
Silverfield Ln 77014
Silvergate Dr 77079
Silverglen Estates Dr 77014
Silvermeadow Dr 77014
Silverpark 77041
Silverpines Rd 77062
Silversand Ct 77044
Silversmine Dr 77014
Silverstag Trail Ln 77073
Silverstream Ct 77014
Silverton Creek Ln 77040
Silverton Star Ln 77070
Silverwood Dr
4000-4099 77025
4300-4599 77035
Silverwood Way 77070
Silverwyck Dr 77014
Simmans St 77032
Simmons 77005
Simmons Ct 77004
Simmons St
3000-3599 77004
9100-9199 77093
Simpson St 77020
Sims Dr 77061
Simsbrook Dr 77045
Simsbury St 77022
Simsdale St
5600-5699 77033
6200-6399 77087
Simsview Dr 77045
Simswood Ct 77045
Sinaloa Dr 77083
Sinea Dr 77073
Sinfonia Dr 77040
Singapore Ln 77040
Singing Bird Cir 77084
Singing Bird Ct 77053
Singing Sonnet Ln 77072
Singing Trees Ln 77016
Singleton St 77008
Siril Dr 77073
Sivley St 77055
Six Flags Dr 77040
Six Oaks Ln 77065
Sixpence Ln 77073
Skelton Dr 77067
Skene Way 77024
Skinner Rd 77093
Skipping Stone Ct & Ln 77064
Sky Ct & Dr 77073
Sky Blue Ln & Pl 77095
Sky Brook Ct & Ln 77044
Sky Hawk Dr 77064
Sky Land Dr 77073
Sky Lark Ln 77056
Skybird Dr 77064
Skybright Ln 77095
Skycountry Ln 77094
Skye St 77084
Skygaze St 77090
Skyknoll Ln 77082
Skylight Ln 77095
Skyline Dr
6000-6499 77057
7600-9599 77063
Skyline Trl 77019
Skyline Vis 77019
Skyline Arbor Ter 77094
Skyline Village Dr, Park & Trl 77057
Skymeadow Dr 77082
Skypark Dr 77082
Skytrain Rd 77032
Skyview Dr
1600-1699 77043
6200-6699 77041
Skyview Bend Dr 77047
Skyview Chase Ln 77047
Skyview Cove Ct 77047
Skyview Creek Ct 77047
Skyview Crescent Ct 77047
Skyview Crest Ct 77047
Skyview Downs Dr 77047
Skyview Forest Dr 77047
Skyview Glen Ct 77047
Skyview Green Dr 77047
Skyview Grove Ct 77047
Skyview Knoll Ct 77047
Skyview Landing Dr 77047
Skyview Manor Dr 77047
Skyview Mill Dr 77047
Skyview Moon Dr 77047
Skyview Point Dr 77047
Skyview Ridge Ct 77047
Skyview Shadows Ct 77047
Skyview Star Ct 77047
Skyview Trace Ct 77047
Skywood Dr 77090
Slate Creek Ln 77077
Slate Field Dr 77064
Slate Mountain Ln 77044
Slate River Ln 77089
Slate Stone Ct 77064
Slate Stone Ln 77084
Slater Ln 77039
Sledge St 77009
Sleepy Creek Dr 77017
Sleepy Creek Mdws 77083
Sleepy Hollow Ct 77019
Sleepy Hollow Trail Ln 77089
Sleepy Meadow Ln 77039
Sleepy Oaks Cir 77024
Sleepy Pines Dr 77066
Sleepyvale Ln 77018
Slice Right Cir 77089
Slippery Elm Ln 77095
Sloan St 77087
Sloandale Ct 77073
Slumber Ln 77023
Slumberwood Dr 77013
Small Leaf Cir 77063
Smallwood Ln 77023
Smart St 77037
Smilax St 77088
Smiling Wood Ln 77086
Smincha Dr 77045
Smith Ln 77050
Smith St
600-699 77002
700-2298 77002
700-700 77208
701-2299 77002
2300-3399 77006
16200-16399 77040
16401-16499 77040
Smith Lake Ln 77044
Smithdale Ct & Rd 77024
Smithdale Estates Dr 77024
Smitherman Rd 77044
Smokehollow Ct & Dr 77064
Smokerock Ln 77040
Smokey Dr 77064
Smokey Hollow Dr 77068
Smokey Pass Cir 77038
Smokey Ridge Ln 77075
Smokey Trail Dr 77041
Smokey Wood Ln 77086
Smooth Oak Ln 77053
Snail Hollow Dr 77064
Sneider 77034
Snover St 77007
Snow Bay Dr 77067
Snowbank Dr 77064
Snowden St 77028
Snowdrop Ln 77067
Snowflake Ct 77053
Snowmass Dr 77070
Soaring Eagle Dr 77083
Soaring Forest Dr 77059
Soboda Ct 77079
Society Ln 77084
Sockeye Dr 77045
Soft Breeze Dr 77095
Soft Pines Dr 77066
Soft Shadows Ln 77013
Sol St 77029
Solana Dr 77083
E & W Solano Bay Ln 77041
Solar Point Ln 77041
Solara Bnd 77083
Solara Bend Ct 77083
Soldiers Creek Cir 77024
Soledad Dr 77083
Solera Ln 77040
Solero Ridge Ln 77089
Solitaire Cir 77070
Solo St
700-2399 77020
2900-3899 77026
Solomon St 77040
Solon Rd 77064
Solvista Hill Ct 77044
Solvista Pass Ln 77070
Solway Ln 77025
Soma Dr 77083
Somerford Dr 77072
Somerland Way 77024
Somerset Knls 77094
Somerset Ln 77093
Somerset Grove Dr 77084
Somerset Knolls Ct 77094
Somersworth Dr 77041
Sommerall Dr
6700-6999 77084
7200-7299 77095
Sommermeyer St 77041
Sommerville Ave 77041
Somonas Ln 77086
Sonata Ct
7900-8099 77040
16700-16799 77053
Sonata Canyon Ln 77041
Sondick Ct 77020
Sonesta Point Ln 77083
Soneto St 77083
Song Ridge Ct 77041
Songbrook Dr 77083
Songwood St 77023
Sonnet Glen Ln 77095
Sonnet Meadow Ct 77047
Sonneville Dr 77080
Sonnier St 77044
Sonoma Dr & Way 77053
Sonoma Breeze Dr 77049
Sonoma Del Norte Dr 77095
Sonoma Oak Dr 77041
Sonoma Park Dr 77049
Sonoma Trace Ln 77049
Sonoma Trail Dr 77049
Sonora St 77020
Sonora Canyon Cir & Ln 77041
Sonoran Blue Way 77045
Sophia Dr 77090
Sophia Springs Ln 77094
Sopris Dr 77077
Sorbete Dr 77083
Sorella Ct 77024
Soren Ln 77076
Sorrel Dr 77064
Sorrel Grove Ct 77047
Sorsby Dr & Way 77047
Soto Cir 77012
Souninti St 77085
Souris Valley Ct & Ln 77085
South Blvd
1300-1699 77006
1700-2599 77098
South Dr
3600-4499 77053
10300-12499 77099
South Fwy
4301-4397 77004
4399-4899 77004
7500-7699 77021
8100-10999 77051
11900-14399 77047
South Ln 77088
South Loop E
3200-3899 77021

4300-4399 77051
4400-6050 77033
6051-6097 77087
6052-6098 77033
6099-7499 77087
7701-8099 77012
7800-8498 77017
8500-8600 77017
8602-8698 77017
South Loop W 77025
South St 77009
Southampton Est 77005
Southaven Dr 77084
Southbank St 77033
Southbelt Industrial Dr 77047
Southbluff Blvd 77089
Southbridge Rd 77047
Southbrook Cir 77060
Southbrook Dr
5600-5699 77033
6200-6699 77087
Southchase Ln 77014
Southchester Ln 77079
Southcrest St 77033
Southdown Trace Trl 77034
Southerland Rd 77092
Southern St 77087
Southern Breeze Ct 77049
Southern Hills Dr 77069
Southern Magnolia Cir 77044
Southern Maple Ln 77094
Southern Oaks Dr 77068
Southern Pass Ct 77062
Southern Spring Ln 77044
S Southern Stone Dr 77095
Southfield Ct & Dr 77045
Southford St 77033
Southgate Blvd 77030
Southgood St 77033
Southhook Ct 77073
Southington St 77033
Southlake Dr 77077
Southlark St 77033
Southlawn St 77021
Southlea St 77033
Southmeadow Dr 77071
Southminster Dr 77035
Southmont St 77033
Southmore Blvd & Cir 77004
Southmund St 77033
Southover Ct 77075
Southpoint Ln 77034
Southpoint Wind Ln 77040
Southport Dr 77089
Southridge St 77033
Southseas St 77033
Southship Ct 77073
Southspring Dr 77047
Southtown St 77033
Southurst St 77033
Southview St
8200-8999 77051
10700-11100 77047
11102-12098 77047
Southville St 77033
Southvine Ct 77073
Southwark St 77028
Southway Dr 77087
Southway Bend Ln 77034
Southwell St 77033
Southwest Fwy
400-499 77002
1900-3199 77098
3200-4799 77027
5000-5599 77056
5600-6199 77057
6200-11099 77074
11100-11899 77031
Southwestern St 77005
Southwick St 77080
Southwind St 77033
Southwold Ln 77096
Southwood Ct N & S 77035
Southwood Trace Ln 77049
Soutine St 77021
Sovereign Dr 77036
Soway St 77080
Sowden Rd
12000-12099 77055
12101-12499 77080
Space Center Blvd
11300-11698 77059
11700-13199 77059
14000-16299 77062
16300-19299 77058
Space Park Dr 77058
Spaniel St 77013
Spanish Mill Dr & Rd 77064
Spanish Moss Ln 77077
Spanish Needle Dr 77084
Spanish Oak Dr 77066
Spann St 77019
Sparkling Bay Ln 77062
Sparkling Springs Dr 77095
Sparks St 77093
Sparks Valley Ct & Dr 77084
Sparrow St 77051
Sparrow Way Ct 77095
Sparta St 77028
Spartan Ct & Dr 77041
Spaulding St 77016
Spear Point Cv 77079
Spearman Dr 77040
Spears Rd
1200-3499 77067
3500-3699 77066
11400-12199 77067
Spectrum Blvd 77047
Speer Landing Dr 77064
Spell St 77022
Spellbrook Dr 77084
Spellman Rd
4300-5299 77035
5300-6499 77096
9100-9499 77031
Spelman St 77005
Spence Rd 77060
Spence St 77093
Spencer Ct 77089
Spencer Rd 77095
Spencer St 77007
Spenwick Dr 77055
Sperber Ln 77003
Sperry Gardens Dr 77095
Sperry Landing Dr 77095
Speyburn Ct 77095
Spice Ln 77072
Spicewood Ln 77044
Spikewood Dr 77078
Spillers Ln 77043
Spindle Dr 77086
Spindlewood Dr 77083
Spinet St 77016
Spiralwood Ln 77086
Spirit Lake Ct & Ln 77044
Splintered Oak Dr 77065
Split Branch Ct 77077
Split Branch Ln 77095
Split Cedar Dr 77015
Split Cypress Ln 77041
Split Oak Ct & Dr 77040
Split Pine Dr 77040
Split Rail Ln 77071
Split Ridge Ln 77075
Split Willow Dr 77083
Spode St 77078
Sporan Ln 77075
Spotslyvania Ln 77083
Spotted Horse Dr 77064
Spottswood Dr 77016
Sprads Rd 77037
Sprangletop Ct 77086
E & W Spreading Oak
Dr 77076
Sprey Dr 77084
Spriggs Way 77024
Spring Crk 77084
Spring St 77007
Spring Trl 77095
Spring Apple Ct 77073
Spring Branch Dr 77080
Spring Brook Ct & Dr 77041
Spring Canyon Ct 77067
Spring Cedar Ln 77077
Spring City Ct 77090
Spring Creek Ln 77017
Spring Cypress Rd 77070
Spring Fern Ln 77040
Spring Field Rd 77062
Spring Forest Ct 77059
Spring Forest Dr
5000-5199 77091
15700-16099 77059
Spring Glen Dr 77070
Spring Green Dr 77095
Spring Grove Dr 77099
Spring Harvest Dr 77064
Spring Hollow St 77024
Spring Lake Dr 77070
Spring Line Ct 77086
Spring Maple Ln 77062
Spring Miller Dr 77070
Spring Mountain Ct &
Ln 77044
Spring Music Dr 77065
Spring Oaks Cir 77055
Spring Park St 77056
Spring Place Dr 77070
Spring Point Vw 77083
Spring Sage Ct 77094
Spring Shadows Dr 77064
Spring Showers Ct 77084
Spring Trace Ct 77094
Spring Valley Rd
3300-3399 77080
4300-4699 77041
Spring Villa Dr 77070
Spring Wind Dr & Ln 77040
Springbank Dr 77095
Springbridge Dr 77073
Springbrook Dr 77041
Springcourt Dr 77062
Springcrest Dr 77072
Springcross Ct 77077
Springdale St 77028
Springer St 77087
Springhill St 77021
Springhope Ct 77049
Springland Ct & Dr 77065
Springmeadows St 77080
Springmere Ct 77095
Springmont Dr 77080
Springridge Rd 77053
Springrock Ln
1100-1398 77055
1400-1499 77055
1900-3499 77080
Springshire Dr 77066
Springside Ln 77040
Springsong Dr 77064
Springtail Ln 77067
Springtime Ln 77075
Springview Ln 77080
Springville Dr 77095
Springwell Dr 77043
Springwood Dr 77055
Springwood Forest Dr 77080
Sprite St 77040
Spruce St 77003
Spruce Cove Dr 77095
Spruce Creek Dr 77084
Spruce Forest Dr
5000-5199 77091
5800-6399 77092
Spruce Haven Dr 77095
Spruce Hill Dr 77077
Spruce Hollow Ct 77059
Spruce Knoll Cir 77065
Spruce Manor Ln 77085
Spruce Mill Dr 77095
Spruce Mountain Dr 77067
Spruce Needle Dr 77082
Spruce Park St 77082
Spruce Point Cir & Dr 77084
Sprucedale Ct 77070
Sprucewood Ln 77024
Spur Ln 77080
Spurflower Path Ln 77075
Spyglass Ct 77064
Spyglass Dr 77095
Squiredale Dr 77070
Squirehill Ct 77070
Squires Place Dr 77083
Ssgt Macario Garcia Dr
100-2399 77011
2500-2699 77020
St Emanuel St
100-499 77002
600-2299 77003
2300-3699 77004
St Germain Way 77082
St Ives Ct 77079
St Joseph Pkwy
300-1599 77002
1600-2399 77003
St Laurent Ln 77082
St Lo Rd 77033
St Simon Manor Dr 77047
St Tropez Way 77082
Stable Ln 77024
Stable Crest Blvd & Ct 77024
Stable Side Ct 77073
Stabledon Dr 77014
Stableford Ct 77014
Stabler Ln 77076
Stableridge Ct & Dr 77014
Stableton Ln 77049
Stableway Cir, Ct &
Dr 77065
Stablewood Blvd & Ct 77024
Stacey Rd 77084
Stacy Crst, Fls, Gln &
Knl 77008
N Stadium Dr
7800-7999 77030
8000-8399 77054
Stafford Dr 77093
Stafford St 77079
Stafford Springs Dr 77077
Staffordale Manor Ln 77047
Staffordshire Cres &
St 77030
Stage Run Dr 77090
Stage Stop Cir 77024
Stagecoach Dr 77041
Staghill Dr 77064
Staghorn Coral Ln 77045
Stallings Dr 77088
Stallion Ln 77071
Stallion Ridge Way 77089
Stally St 77092
Stalynn Ln 77027
Stamen Dr 77041
Stamp St 77026
Stampede Canyon Ln 77089
Stampede Pass Dr 77095
Stamper Way 77056
Stampford Dr 77077
Stan Brook Dr 77089
Stanbridge Dr 77083
Stancliff Rd 77099
Stancliff St 77045
Standing Oaks St 77050
Standing Rock Ct 77089
Stanford Ct 77041
Stanford St
500-1599 77019
1600-4599 77006
Stanhope Ct & Dr 77084
Stanmore Dr 77019
Stansberg Dr 77066
Stanton St 77025
Stanwick Dr 77087
Stanwood Dr 77031
Staples St
1800-1920 77020
1921-3099 77026
Staples Way 77056
Star Ln 77057
N Star St 77088
Star Hollow Ln 77095
Star Peak Dr 77088
Star Shadow Ln 77066
Starboard Dr 77058
Starboard Point Dr 77054
Starbridge Dr 77095
Starcreek Ln 77044
Stardust Ln 77041
Starfield Dr 77084
Starfire Ln 77036
Starfish Ln 77072
Stargate Ct 77068
Starhill Ct 77077
Starkridge Dr 77035
Starksboro Ct 77073
Starlamp Ln 77095
Starlight Rd 77049
Starlight Harbour Ct 77077
Starling St 77017
Starlit Meadows Ct 77064
N & S Starpoint Dr 77032
Stars Hollow Dr 77073
Starshadow Pl 77015
Starway St 77023
Starwood Dr 77024
Stassen St 77051
State St 77007
State Highway 249
21155A-21155B 77070
State Highway 249
11500-16299 77086
16300-17899 77064
17900-22599 77070
State Walk Cir 77064
Stately Ave 77034
N Station Ct 77073
Station Dr 77061
Staunton St 77027
Stayton Cir 77024
Steadmont Dr 77040
Steamboat Ln 77079
Steamboat Springs Dr 77067
Stearns St 77021
Stebbins Cir & Dr 77043
Stedman St 77029
Steel St 77098
Steelhead Dr 77045
Steelman St 77017
Steeple Ln 77039
Steeple Way Blvd 77065
Steeplecrest Dr 77065
Steeplepark Dr 77065
Steepletop Dr 77065
Steffani Ln 77041
Steinbergs Ct 77020
Stella Link Rd
9121A-9121C 77025
6700-6799 77005
6800-10799 77025
Stemply Ct 77094
E Stephanshire St 77077
Stephens Ln 77044
Stephenson Rd 77032
Stepney Green Dr 77070
Steppingstone Ln 77024
Stepwood Dr 77038
Sterling Brk 77041
Sterling St 77051
Sterling Green Blvd &
Ct 77015
Sterling Heights Ln 77094
Sterling Lake Dr 77095
Sterling Point Ln 77044
Sterling Stone Dr 77073
Sterling Wood Way 77059
Sterlingame Dr 77031
Sterlingcrest Rd 77049
Sterlingshire St
7300-7799 77016
7900-9499 77078
Sterlingstone Dr 77066
Stern St 77044
Stern Creek Ln 77044
Sterrett St 77002
Stetson Ln 77043
Stevens St 77026
Stieler Dr 77049
N Stiles St 77011
Stilesboro Ct 77062
Still Bay Ct 77077
Still Cove Ln 77089
Still Harbour Dr 77041
Still Meadow Dr 77079
Still River Dr 77088
Stillbrooke Dr
4300-5215 77035
5216-5799 77096
Stillcreek Dr 77070
Stillforest St 77024
Stillhollow Ln 77094
Stillhouse Lake Ct 77044
Stillington Dr 77015
Stillman St 77007
Stillstone Dr 77073
Stillview Dr 77068
Stillwater Dr 77070
Stillwell St
6300-6599 77023
6600-6699 77087
Stillwood Dr 77080
Stilson Branch Ln 77092
Stimson St 77023
Stirring Winds Ln 77086
Stirrup Dr 77039
Stockwell Dr 77083
Stockwood Dr 77064
Stoerner Dr 77032
Stokes St 77022
Stokesmount Dr 77077
Stone St 77061
Stone Bluff Dr 77073
Stone Bridge Dr 77064
Stone Brook Ln 77040
Stone Cactus Dr 77095
Stone Castle Dr 77064
Stone Cottage Ln 77047
Stone Creek Model Ct 77084
Stone East Dr 77035
Stone Gables Ln 77044
Stone Haven Way 77085
Stone Mallow Dr 77095
Stone Meadows Ln 77094
Stone Mesa Dr 77073
Stone Mountain Ln 77073
Stone Oak Ct 77070
Stone Peaks Dr 77095
Stone Pine Ln 77041
Stone Porch Ln 77064
Stone Post Cir 77064
Stone Prairie Dr 77095
Stone Terrace Ct 77089
Stone Valley Dr 77095
Stone Village Ln 77040
Stone Way Dr 77082
Stone West Dr 77035
Stonebelt Dr 77073
Stonebridge Trl 77095
Stonebury Trail Ln 77044
Stonechase 77084
Stonecreek Ln 77036
Stonecrest Dr 77018
Stonecross Bend Dr 77070
Stonefair Ln 77075
Stonefield Dr 77014
Stonefield Manor Ct &
Dr 77044
Stonefir Ct 77040
Stonegate Dr
1-99 77024
7200-7299 77040
Stonehaven Dr 77059
Stonehearth Ln 77040
Stonehedge Dr 77073
Stonehedge Bend Dr 77073
Stonehenge Ln 77015
Stonehenge Trl 77066
Stonehill Dr 77062
Stonehouse Ln 77025
Stoneleigh Dr 77079
Stoner Ct 77088
Stoneridge Canyon Ct &
Ln 77089
Stonerun 77084
Stones Throw Rd 77057
Stonesdale Dr 77095
Stoneshire St
13800-13999 77037
14000-14299 77060
Stoneside Dr 77095
Stonewalk Dr 77056
Stonewall Dr 77023
Stonewall St 77020
Stonewater 77084
Stonewick Dr 77068
Stonewood St 77078
Stonewood Pointe Ln 77066
Stoney Brook Dr
1800-3999 77063
6001-6199 77036
Stoney Creek Dr 77024
Stoney Falls Dr 77095
Stoney Fork Dr 77084
Stoney Glade Ct 77095
Stoney Hill Dr 77077
Stoney Lake Dr 77064
Stoney Meadow Dr 77095
Stoney Oak Dr 77068
Stoney Point St 77056
Stoney Ridge Ln 77024
Stoney Wood Dr 77082
E & S Stoneygrove
Loop 77084
Stoneyvale Dr 77083
Stoneyview Dr 77083
Stoneyway Dr 77040
Stonham St
3500-3699 77047
5900-5999 77048
Stonington St 77040
Stony Dell Ct 77061
Storm Creek Ct & Dr 77088
Storm Meadow Dr 77064
Storm Wood St 77040
Stormy Sky Dr 77064
Story St 77055
Storywood Dr 77024
Stoughton Dr 77066
Stover St 77075
Strack Rd 77069
Stradbrook Dr 77062
Straight Creek Dr 77017
Straightfork Dr 77082
Strait Ln 77084
Strand Ct 77034
Strata Way 77070
Stratfield Ln 77075
Stratford St 77006
Stratford Park Dr 77084
Stratford Skies Ln 77072
Stratford Way Ln 77070
Strathclyde Sound Rd 77095
Strathmill Ct 77095
Strathmore Dr 77078
Strathmore Manor Ln 77090
Stratton St 77023
Strawberry Cactus
Loop 77064
Strawbridge Ln 77040
Strawgrass Dr 77064
Strawn Rd 77039
Streamside Dr 77088
Streamwood Dr 77083
Strey Ln 77024
Strick Ln 77015
Strickland St 77093
Strong Creek Dr 77084
Strong Winds Dr 77014
Stroud Dr
6400-6899 77074
7900-9799 77036
10900-12099 77072
Stroudwater Ln 77084
Stuart Mnr 77082
Stuart St
500-899 77006
900-999 77002
1000-2599 77004
Stubbs Dr 77083
Stuckey Ln 77024
Stude St 77007
Studemont St 77007

Studer St 77007
Studewood St
400-899 77007
900-1999 77008
2000-2200 77009
2202-2298 77009
Stuebner Airline Rd
5600-7499 77091
7500-7799 77088
14000-15599 77069
Sturbridge Dr 77056
Stuyvesant Ln 77021
Styers St 77022
Styling Ct & Dr 77016
Suburban Rd
11300-11599 77016
11700-12099 77050
Suburban Oaks Rd 77093
Success Rd 77068
Sudan St 77020
E, N, S & W Suddley Castle St 77095
Sudeley Ln 77039
Sue Ln 77099
Sue St 77009
Sue Barnett Dr 77018
Sue Ellen St 77087
Sue Marie Ln 77091
Suez St 77020
Suffield Ct 77073
Suffolk Dr 77027
Suffolk Bridge Ln 77073
Suffolk Chase Ln 77077
Suffolk Woods Ln 77047
Sugar Branch Dr 77036
Sugar Bush Dr 77048
Sugar Dock Ct 77044
Sugar Grove Ct 77066
Sugar Hill Dr
5300-5699 77056
5700-6299 77057
10000-10899 77042
Sugar Maple St 77064
E & W Sugar Meadow Dr 77090
Sugar Mill Cir 77095
Sugar Pine Cir, Dr & Ln 77090
Sugar Ridge Dr 77095
Sugar Springs Dr 77077
Sugar Tree Ct & Dr 77070
Sugarberry Cir 77024
Sugarbun Ct & Way 77073
Sugarbush Ridge Ln 77089
Sugarplum Ln 77062
Sul Ross St
100-199 77002
200-1699 77006
1700-3399 77098
4000-4099 77027
Sulky Trail Ct & St 77060
Sullins Way 77058
Sulphur St 77034
Sulphur Springs Dr 77067
Sulphur Stream Ct & Dr 77095
Sultan Dr 77078
Sumerlin St 77075
Summer Fls 77041
Summer St 77007
Summer Ash Ln 77044
Summer Breezes Ln 77067
Summer Crossing Ln 77084
Summer Dawn Ln & Pl 77095
Summer Dew Ln 77095
Summer Forest Dr 77091
Summer Garden Dr 77083
Summer Glen Ln 77072
Summer Heath Ct 77044
Summer Knoll Ln 77044
Summer Lake Ranch Dr 77044
Summer Laurel Ln 77088
Summer Meadows Ct 77064
Summer Mill Dr 77070
Summer Reef Dr 77095
Summer Rose Ln 77077
Summer Run Dr 77064
Summer Snow Cir & Dr 77041
Summer Trail Dr 77040
Summer Villa Ct & Ln 77044
Summer Wind Dr 77090
Summerbell Ln 77074
Summerblossom Ln 77077
Summerbrook Ct
10300-10399 77038
12200-12299 77066
Summerbrook Dr 77038
Summerdale St 77077
Summerfair Ct 77044
Summerhill Dr 77070
Summerhill Ln 77024
Summerland Ridge Ct & Ln 77041
Summerleaf Ln 77077
Summerlyn Point Ln 77053
Summerset Way 77094
Summerset Meadow Ct 77075
Summertime Dr 77045
Summertree Dr 77040
Summerville Ln
6100-6299 77041
14200-14299 77084
Summerway Ln 77014
Summerwood Gln 77041
Summerwood Ln 77013
Summerwood Lakes Ct & Dr 77044
Summit Pl 77071
Summit St 77018
Summit Bridge Ln 77070
S & E Summit Canyon Ct & Dr 77095
Summit Hollow Dr 77084
Summit Mist Ct 77044
Summit Ridge Ct & Dr 77085
Summit Valley Dr 77082
Sumner Dr 77018
Sumpter St
1800-3399 77026
3600-4699 77020
Sun City Ct 77099
Sun Harbor Dr 77062
Sun Kiss Ln 77082
Sun Lodge Ct & Dr 77073
Sun Meadow Dr 77072
Sun Prairie Dr 77090
Sun Rise Ln 77072
Sun Terrace Ln 77095
Sun Valley Dr 77025
Sun Village Dr 77083
Sunbeam St
2900-3699 77051
4700-5499 77033
Sunbeam River Dr 77084
Sunbird Dr 77084
Sunbonnet Ln 77064
Sunbriar Ln 77095
Sunbridge Ln 77094
Sunbright Ct & Dr 77041
Sunburst Meadow Dr 77083
Sunbury Ln 77095
Sunbury St 77028
Sundale Rd 77038
Sunderland Rd 77028
Sundew Cir, Ct & Dr 77070
Sundew Cove Ct 77041
Sundown Dr
7300-7699 77028
9200-9499 77016
Sundowner Ct & Dr 77041
Sundrop Ln 77084
Sunfish Ln 77067
Sunflare Ln 77041
Sunflower St
4000-4699 77051
4801-4997 77033
4999-5099 77033
Sunflower Bluff Ln 77064
Sunflower Prairie Ct 77049
Sunflower Ridge Ln 77064
W Sunforest Dr 77092
Sungate Ln 77071
Sungold Ct 77095
Sunlamp Ct 77095
Sunland Gardens Ln 77044
Sunlight Ln 77095
Sunlight Way 77058
Sunlight Oak Ln 77070
Sunlit Leaf Ct 77038
Sunlit Orchard Dr 77072
Sunlit Wood Way 77082
Sunmoore Ct 77088
Sunmount Pines Dr 77083
Sunny Dr
1000-1299 77037
1700-2499 77093
Sunny Creek Dr 77066
Sunny Field Dr 77099
Sunny Grove Dr 77070
Sunny Heath Ln 77044
Sunny Oaks Way 77095
Sunny Ridge Dr 77095
Sunnycove Dr 77084
Sunnycrest St 77087
Sunnydale Dr 77051
Sunnyhill St 77088
Sunnyland St 77023
Sunnynook St 77076
Sunnyside St 77076
E Sunnyside Gln 77076
W Sunnyside St
100-199 77076
300-599 77091
Sunnyvale Forest Dr 77088
Sunnywood Dr
8700-8898 77088
8900-9399 77088
9400-9999 77038
Sunridge Way 77087
Sunrise Rd 77021
Sunrise Way 77065
Sunrise Chase Way 77084
Sunrise Knoll Way 77062
Sunrise Manor Ct 77082
Sunrise Meadow Ln 77095
Sunrise Valley Ln 77083
Sunrose Ln 77045
Sunset Blvd 77005
Sunset Bluff Dr 77095
Sunset Dune Dr 77082
Sunset Garden Dr 77083
Sunset Lake Ct 77065
Sunset Meadow Ln 77035
Sunset Place Dr 77071
Sunset River Ln 77084
Sunset Rock Dr 77084
Sunset View Dr 77083
Sunshine St 77049
Sunshine Bay Ct & Dr 77060
Sunstone Dr 77068
Sunstream Ct 77082
Sunswept Way 77082
Sunswept Fields Ln 77064
Suntanti Dr 77092
Sunturf Ln 77044
Sunview Ct 77095
Sunview Dr 77084
Sunwick St 77060
Sunwood Dr
2801-2999 77038
10200-10299 77041
N Super St 77011
Superior Way 77039
Supply Row 77011
Sur Ct 77033
Surf Ct 77058
Surles Dr 77032
Surratt Dr 77091
Surrey Ln 77024
Surrey Meadow Ct 77049
Surrey Oaks Ln 77024
Surrey Square St 77017
Surreydon Dr 77014
Surry St 77028
Susan St 77034
Susan Ann Ct 77004
Susan Forest Ln 77089
Susanna Ln 77072
Suspiro Dr 77083
Sussex Dr 77083
Sussex Ln 77041
Sutherland Sq 77081
Sutherland St 77023
Sutter Glen Ln 77075
Sutter Park Ln
6300-6799 77066
9400-9599 77086
Sutter Ranch Cir & Dr 77064
Sutters Field Dr 77072
Sutton Ct 77027
Sutton St 77006
Sutton Glen Ln 77047
Sutton Meadows Ct & Dr 77086
Suttonford Dr 77066
Suwanee Ln 77090
Swallow St 77087
Swallowfield Dr 77077
Swan Ct 77058
Swan Creek Dr
11900-12199 77065
15300-15599 77095
Swan Glen Dr 77099
Swan Green Ln 77095
Swan Hollow Ct & Ln 77041
Swan River Dr 77050
Swandale Ln 77095
Swanfield Ct & Dr 77083
Swank St 77021
Swanley Ct 77062
Swanpond Ct 77075
Swansea St 77048
Swansea Harbor Ln 77053
Swansfield Ln 77073
Swanson St
1000-1199 77030
10100-10199 77064
Swarthmore St 77005
Sway St 77085
Sweeney Rd 77060
Sweeney Park Ct & Ln 77084
Sweet Birch Ln 77041
Sweet Cicely Ct 77059
Sweet Fern St 77070
Sweet Flower Dr 77073
Sweet Grass Trl 77090
Sweet Hall Ln 77067
Sweet Maple Ct 77049
Sweet Surrender Ct 77041
Sweet Willow Ct 77031
Sweetbay Ln 77041
Sweetbriar St 77017
Sweetbrook Dr 77038
Sweetbrush Dr 77064
Sweetgum Shores Dr 77044
Sweetgum Trace Dr 77040
Sweetrose Pl 77095
Sweetwater Ln 77037
Sweetwater Creek Dr 77095
Sweetwater View Dr 77047
Sweetwood Dr 77070
Sweno Ct 77084
Swift Blvd 77030
Swift Falls Ct 77094
Swiftwater Ln 77075
Swinbrook Ln 77039
Swinden Dr 77066
Swingle Rd
3500-4099 77047
4400-4599 77048
4601-4699 77048
Swirling Winds Dr 77086
Swisher St 77064
Swiss Ln 77075
Swiss Hill Dr 77077
Switchgrass Ln 77095
Switzer St
600-798 77013
1300-1799 77029
Swonke Ln 77040
Swords Creek Rd 77067
Sycamore St 77012
Sycamore Grove Dr 77062
Sycamore Heights St 77065
Sycamore Lake Rd 77062
Sycamore Park Ct 77094
Sycamore Ridge Ln 77073
Sycamore Trace Ct 77073
Sycamore Wind Ct 77073
Sycamore Wood Dr 77073
Sydnor St 77020
Sylmar Rd
5500-5699 77081
6700-6799 77074
Sylvan Rd 77023
Sylvan Glen Dr 77084
Sylvan Lake Dr 77062
Sylvanfield Dr 77014
Sylvania St 77023
Sylvester Rd 77009
Symbol St 77093
Symphonic Ln 77040
Synott Rd
2400-4099 77082
6100-9999 77083
Syracuse St 77005
T Bar M Blvd 77069
T C Jester Blvd
100-599 77007
700-999 77008
3700-4099 77018
4100-4599 77018
4700-6099 77091
7200-7399 77088
11200-12299 77067
13100-13699 77038
14400-14499 77014
14700-15999 77068
E T C Jester Blvd
1000-1598 77008
1600-2699 77008
3300-3598 77018
3681-3699 77018
W T C Jester Blvd
1000-2699 77008
2700-2798 77018
2800-3721 77018
3723-3799 77018
6500-6999 77091
Tab Ln 77070
Tabernash Dr 77040
Tabitha Ct 77090
Tablerock Dr 77064
Tabor St 77009
Tackaberry St 77009
Tacoma Dr 77041
Tadlock Ln 77085
Tadworth Ct & Dr 77062
Taffaine Dr 77090
Taft St
500-1599 77019
1700-3399 77006
Taftsberry Ct & Dr 77095
Taggart St 77007
N Tahoe Dr 77040
Tahoe Canyon Ln 77084
Tahoe Crossing Ln 77066
Tahoe Lake Ln 77073
Tain Dr 77084
Tain Round Ct 77084
Tainson Dr 77041
Taintor St 77045
Tal Ct 77055
Tala St 77093
Talbott St 77005
Talbrook Dr 77038
Talcott Ln 77049
Talcott St 77015
Tali Dr 77032
Talina Way
2500-2699 77080
4300-5099 77041
Talisman Ct 77076
Tall Elm Ct 77059
Tall Firs Ln 77095
Tall Hill Cir 77044
Tall Maple Ct 77095
Tall Meadow Ct & Ln 77088
Tall Oaks St 77024
Tall Pine Dr 77059
Tall Pines Dr 77088
Tall Timbers Dr 77065
Tall Willow Dr 77088
Tallant St 77076
Talley Ln 77041
Tallheath Ct 77044
Tallow Ln 77021
Tallow Briar 77075
Tallow Forest Ct 77062
Tallow Point Ct 77062
Tallow Tree Cir & Dr 77070
Tallowbend Ct 77064
Tallowood Rd 77024
Tallshadows Dr 77032
Tallulah Ct & Ln 77077
Tallwood Crossing Ln 77041
Tallyho Rd
8700-9099 77061
9300-9399 77017
Taloncrest Ct & Dr 77083
Talton St
7900-8799 77028
8800-9499 77078
Talton Oaks Dr 77064
Tam Ct 77055
Tam O Shanter Ln 77036
Tamara Ln 77038
Tamarack Pl 77082
Tamarack Way 77094
Tamayo Dr 77083
Tambento St 77011
Tamerisk Centre Ct 77069
Tamerlaine Dr 77024
Tamfield Dr 77066
Tami Renee Ln 77040
Tammany Ln 77082
Tammarack Dr 77013
Tammy Ct 77026
Tampa St 77021
Tampico St 77016
Tamworth Dr 77016
Tamworth St 77015
Tamy Ln 77055
Tanager St
6200-7699 77074
8800-9199 77036
9201-9499 77036
11900-12099 77072
Tanberry Ln 77044
Tancah Ln 77073
Tandy Park Way 77047
Tangerine St 77051
Tangiers Rd 77041
Tangle Ln 77056
Tangle Circle Ln 77057
Tangle Pines Ct 77062
Tangle Tree Ln 77084
Tanglehead Ct 77086
Tanglerose Ct 77084
Tanglewilde St
2100-4099 77063
7701-7799 77036
Tanglewood Rd 77056
Tanglewood Cove St 77057
Tanglewood Park St 77057
Tangley Rd & St 77005
Tannehill Dr 77008
Tanner Rd 77041
Tanner Meadow Ln 77047
Tanner Park Ct 77075
Tanvern Ct & Ln 77014
Tanwood Dr 77065
Tanya Cir 77079
Taos Ln 77070
Tappenbeck Dr 77055
Tappengate Ln 77073
Tar Oaks Ct 77082
Tara Dr 77024
Tara Gables Ct 77082
Tara Hills Ct 77034
Tara Oak Dr 77065
Tara Ridge Oak Ct 77082
Taranto Ln 77015
Tarawa Rd 77033
Tarbell Rd 77034
Tarberry Rd 77088
Tareyton Ln
4100-4499 77047
8000-8499 77075
Target Ct & Dr 77043
Tarik Dr 77083
Tarleton Dr 77024
Tarley St 77009
Tarna Ln 77074
Tarnbrook Dr 77084
Tarnef Dr 77074
Tarpon Ln 77049
Tarpon Springs Ct & Ln 77095
Tarragon Ln 77036
Tarrant Ct 77064
Tarrington Ct & Dr 77024
Tarrytown Mall 77057
Tartan Ln 77025
Tartan Walk Ln 77075
Tarton Way Ct 77065
Tarver St 77009
Tascosa Ln 77064
Tasia Dr 77085
Tassel Brook Dr 77070
Tassell St 77076
Tasselwood Ln 77014
Tassia Ln 77058
Tate St 77028
Tatefield St 77028
Tatom St 77093
Tattenhall Dr 77008
Tatteridge Dr 77069
Taub Loop 77030
Taub Rd 77064
Tautenhahn Rd 77016
Tavenor Ln
3900-4499 77047
4700-5499 77048
8000-9799 77075
Tavern St 77040
Taverns Corner Ct & Ln 77084
Taverns Crossing Ln 77084
Tavistock Dr 77031
Tawinee St 77065
Tawny Ct 77089
Tawny Trace Ct 77044
Taylor Ct 77020
Taylor Rd
8000-8099 77086
12000-12599 77041
Taylor St
700-2399 77007
7900-8099 77064
Taylor Brook Ct 77094
Taylor Leigh Ln 77066
Taylorcrest Ct 77024
Taylorcrest Rd
11400-12799 77024
12900-14099 77079
Taylorwood Ln 77070
Taymouth Dr 77084
Teaberry Hl 77044
Teaberry Breeze Ct 77044
Teague Rd
2000-3099 77080
5400-6099 77041
Teak Forest Trl 77084
Teakwood Ln 77024
Teal Ln 77047
Teal St 77029
Teal Bay Ln 77070
Teal Cove Ln 77077
Teal Fern Ct 77059
Teal Glen Ct 77062
Teal Oaks Ln 77041
Teal Run Dr
6300-6499 77035
7500-7799 77071
Teal Shore Ct 77077
Teal Sky Ct 77089
Tealcrest Ln 77047

Tealmeadow Ct 77024
Tealstone Falls Ct 77044
Tealwood Dr 77024
Tealwood North Dr 77024
Teanaway Ln 77029
Teaneck Dr 77089
Teaside Dr 77066
Teawick Ct 77068
Tebo St 77076
Tebroc Ct 77094
Teck Ct 77047
Tecumseh Cir & Ln 77057
Ted St 77040
Teesdale Dr 77028
Teetshorn St 77009
Telean St 77075
Telephone Rd
5307-A-5307-D 77087
100-3999 77023
4000-6399 77087
6400-8999 77061
9000-11899 77075
5312-1-5312-4 77087
Televista Dr 77037
Telfair Ct 77084
Telge Rd 77095
Telge St 77054
Tellepsen St 77023
Telluride Dr 77040
Teluco St 77055
N & W Tempe Cir & Ct 77095
Tempera Ct 77038
Temple Ct 77095
Temple Dr 77019
S Temple Dr 77095
W Temple Dr 77095
Temple St 77009
W Temple St 77009
Templegate Dr 77066
Templeridge Ln 77075
Tenaha Dr 77014
Tenbury St 77040
Tenbury Glen Dr 77066
Tenderwood Dr 77041
Teneha Dr 77033
Tenleyton Ln 77075
Tenneco Dr 77099
Tennessee St 77029
Tenneta Dr 77099
Tennis Ct & Dr 77099
Tennyson St 77005
Tenton Park Ln 77092
Tepee Trl 77064
Tercel Trl 77034
Teresa Dr 77055
Teriwood Cir 77068
Terlin St 77039
Terlizzi Way 77070
N Terminal Rd 77032
S Terminal Rd 77032
W Terminal Rd 77032
Terminal St
300-799 77020
900-1300 77011
1302-2198 77011
3300-3499 77020
Ternerne Dr 77056
Terra Cotta Dr 77040
Terrace Dr 77007
Terrace Brook Ct & Dr 77040
E Terrace Creek Cir 77014
Terrace Glade Ct 77070
Terrace Glen Dr 77095
Terrace Hills Ln 77007
Terrace Manor Dr 77041
Terrace Oaks Dr 77068
Terrace Park Dr 77095
Terrace Run Ln 77044
Terrace Wind Dr 77040
Terrace Wood Ct 77070
Terrance St 77085
Terranova Ln 77090
Terravita Hls 77069
Terraza Cove Ln 77041
Terrell St 77093

Territory Ln 77064
Terry St 77009
Terry Court Pl 77073
Terrydale Ct & Dr 77037
Terwilliger Way
5600-5699 77056
6200-6299 77057
Tessa Ct 77040
Tetela Dr 77083
Teton St
4500-4699 77051
4700-5099 77033
Teton Peak Way 77089
Tewantin Dr 77061
W Tex Dr 77055
Texaco Rd 77013
Texarkana St
6200-7599 77020
13700-14699 77015
Texas St
500-1599 77002
1600-1698 77003
1700-3699 77003
4700-7499 77011
Texas Acorn Ave 77078
Thackery Ln 77016
Thamer Cir & Ln 77024
Thames Ln 77083
Tharp St 77003
Thatcher Dr 77077
Theall Rd 77066
Thelma Dr 77009
Thelma Ann Ln 77048
Theresa St 77051
Thermon St 77075
Theron St 77022
Therrell Dr 77064
Theta St 77034
Thetford Ln 77070
Theysen Cir & Dr 77080
Thicket Ln 77079
Thicket Mdws 77083
Thicket Green Ln 77035
Thicket Grove Rd 77084
Thicket Hill Ct 77073
Thicket Ridge Ln 77077
Thistle St 77047
Thistle Creek Ct 77044
Thistle Down St 77069
Thistle Trail Dr 77070
Thistlecroft Dr 77084
Thistledew Dr 77082
Thistleglen Cir & Dr 77095
Thistlemeade Dr 77094
Thistlemont Dr 77042
Thistlemoor Ln 77044
Thistlewood Dr 77079
Thomas Rd 77041
Thomas St 77009
Thomasville Dr 77064
Thompson St 77007
Thompson Creek Dr 77067
Thonig Rd
1800-2199 77055
3800-3999 77092
Thorn St 77078
W Thorn Way 77015
Thornbranch Dr 77079
Thornbrook Dr 77084
Thornburg Ln 77067
Thorncreek Way 77095
Thorne Creek Ln 77073
Thorne Haven Dr 77073
Thornhampton Ct 77014
Thornhill Oaks Dr 77015
Thornhollow Dr 77014
Thornhurn Ct 77065
Thornlea Dr 77089
Thornleaf Ln 77070
Thornmont Ln 77070
Thornoak Ln 77070
Thornton Cir 77018
Thornton Rd 77018
E Thornton Rd 77022
N & S Thorntree Dr 77015
Thornville Ln 77070

Thornvine Ln 77079
Thornwall St 77092
Thornwell Ct 77070
Thornwick Dr 77079
Thornwilde Park Ln 77073
Thornwood Ln 77062
Thorough Good Ln 77084
Thoroughbred Dr 77065
Thoroughbred Trails Ln 77044
Thousand Oaks Cir 77092
Threadall Park Dr 77077
Threadleaf Dr 77066
Threadneedle St 77079
Three Corners Dr 77024
Three Oaks Cir 77069
Three Sisters St 77093
Three Wood Dr 77089
Threeawn Ct 77086
Threlkeld St 77007
Throckmorton Ln 77064
Thrush Dr
5400-5899 77033
6200-7199 77087
Thrustmaster Dr 77041
Thunderbay Dr 77062
Thunderbird Rd 77041
Thunderhaven Dr 77064
Thunderhead Ct 77064
Thurleigh St 77031
Thurmon St 77034
Thurow St 77087
Tiara Ln 77043
Tiber St 77024
Tiburon Way 77053
Tickner St 77055
Tico Dr 77083
Ticonderoga Rd 77044
Tideswept Ct 77095
Tidewater Dr
2600-5399 77045
5400-5899 77085
Tidford St 77093
Tidwell Ln 77093
Tidwell Rd
1-1499 77022
1500-4499 77093
4500-7599 77016
7800-7832 77028
7834-8799 77028
8814-8822 77078
8824-10119 77078
10121-10199 77078
11700-11898 77044
11900-13699 77044
E Tidwell Rd 77022
W Tidwell Rd
100-299 77022
300-5699 77091
5700-7299 77092
7306-7598 77040
7600-8800 77040
8802-8898 77040
9500-9699 77041
Tidwell Estates Ln 77091
Tiel Way 77019
Tierra Park 77034
Tierra Lake Ct 77041
Tierra Mountain Ct 77034
Tierra Palms Ct 77034
Tierra Ridge Ct 77034
Tierra Verde Dr 77083
Tierwester St
2100-5499 77004
6100-7899 77021
Tierwood Ct 77068
Tiff Trail Dr 77095
Tiffany Ct 77058
Tiffany Dr
3700-5499 77045
5600-6499 77085
Tiffany Pl 77025
Tiffin St 77026
Tifway Ln 77044
Tiger Ln 77040
Tiger Trl 77043

Tiger Lilly Way 77085
Tiger Trace Ct & Ln 77066
Tigris Ln 77090
Tilbrook Ct & Dr 77038
Tilbury Dr 77056
Tilbury Estates Dr 77056
Tilden St 77025
Tilfer St 77087
Tilgham St
7200-7399 77020
7800-8799 77029
Tilia St 77029
Tilley St 77084
Tillison St 77088
Tilson Ln
2700-4299 77080
4300-4799 77041
Tiltree St 77075
Tiltrum Ln 77086
Tim St 77093
Tim Allen Ct 77014
Timber Cir 77079
Timber Cor 77082
Timber Holw
11600-11799 77065
12300-12499 77058
Timber Ln 77027
Timber Briar Cir & Ct 77059
Timber Bright Ct 77044
Timber Chase Dr 77082
Timber Court Holw 77084
Timber Creek Dr 77017
Timber Creek Place Ct, Dr & Ln 77084
Timber Crest Dr 77065
Timber Falls Ct 77082
Timber Forest Blvd 77044
Timber Green Cir 77094
Timber Hill Dr 77024
Timber Park Trl 77070
Timber Rock Ct & Dr 77082
Timber Run Dr 77082
Timber Strand Dr 77084
Timber Terrace Rd 77024
Timber Valley Dr 77070
Timber View Ct 77070
Timber Village Dr 77068
Timbercraft Dr 77095
Timbercreek Falls Dr 77095
Timberdale Ln 77090
Timberglen Dr 77024
Timbergrove Ln 77008
Timberhaven Dr 77066
Timberknoll St 77024
Timberland Ct 77062
Timberland Trce 77065
Timberlark Dr 77070
Timberline Rd 77043
Timberline Run Ln 77095
Timberloch Dr 77070
Timbermeadow Dr 77070
Timberoak Dr
10000-10099 77080
10200-10999 77043
Timberside Dr 77025
Timberside Circle Dr 77025
Timbertree Ln 77070
Timberway Ln 77072
Timberwilde Ln 77024
Timberwind Ln 77094
Timberwood Dr
10001-10099 77080
10400-10599 77043
Timbo Ln 77041
Times Blvd 77005
Timmons Ln
2600-2899 77027
2802-2802 77227
2802-2802 77256
2901-3599 77027
3100-3698 77027
Timor Ln 77090
Timsbury Dr 77084
Timur Way 77047
Tina Ln 77037
Tina Oaks Ct 77082

Tinas Terrace Dr 77038
Tinker St 77084
Tinsley Ct 77014
Tinway Ct 77073
Tiny Trl 77024
Tipper Ct 77067
Tipperary Ln 77061
Tippett St
6600-6799 77091
7200-7399 77088
Tipps St 77023
Tirrell St 77019
Tish Ct 77040
Titan Dr 77058
Tite St 77029
Titus Pt 77085
Tivoli Dr 77077
Toast Hollow Ct & Ln 77073
Tobar Falls Cir 77064
Tobasa Ct 77086
Tobruk Ln 77033
Tocatta Blvd 77040
Todd St 77055
Todwick Ln 77082
Toho Ct & Dr 77032
Tokeneke Trl 77024
Tolar Ave 77093
Toledo St 77008
Toliver St 77093
E Toliver St 77016
Tollis St 77055
Tolman St 77034
Tolnay St 77021
Tomahawk Trl 77050
Tomkins Cove Dr 77083
Tomlin Rd 77037
Tomlinson Trail Dr 77067
Tommye St 77028
Tomsbrook Dr 77067
Tonawanda Dr 77035
Toni Ave 77017
Tonnochy Ct & Dr 77083
Tonya Dr 77060
Tooke St 77023
Tooley Dr 77031
Top St 77002
Top Gallant Ct 77065
Topaz St 77063
Topeka St 77015
Topham Cir 77018
Topping St 77093
Torchlight Dr 77035
Tornado 77091
Torquay Ln 77074
Torreon St 77026
N & S Torrey Chase Blvd & Ct 77014
Torrey Creek Ln 77014
Torrey Forest Dr 77014
Torrey Village Dr 77014
Torrey Vista Dr 77014
Torridon Ct 77095
Torrington Ln 77075
Torry Pines Rd 77062
Torry View Cir & Ter 77095
Tosca Ln
12800-12999 77024
13000-13799 77079
Totem Trl 77064
Tottenham Dr 77031
Toucan Ln 77067
Touche St 77015
Touchstone St
7100-7699 77028
8600-8699 77016
Toulouse St 77015
Tourmaline Ct 77095
Tournament Dr 77069
Tours St 77036
Tower St 77088
Tower Bridge St 77075
Tower Hill Ln 77066
Tower Oaks Blvd
10600-10999 77070
11000-11399 77065
Tower River Ct 77062

E & N Towerglen Ct & Loop 77084
Towering Oak Ct 77059
Towering Oak St 77082
Town And Country Blvd 77024
Town And Country Ln 77024
Town And Country Vlg 77024
Town And Country Way
10401-10497 77024
10499-10506 77024
10505-10505 77224
10505-10505 77279
10508-10698 77024
10601-10699 77024
Town Creek Dr 77095
Town Elm Ct 77065
Town Green Dr 77083
Town Hill Dr 77062
Town Lake Ct 77059
Town Oaks Dr 77062
Town Park Dr
8701-8797 77036
8799-9999 77036
10300-10499 77072
Town Plaza Dr 77045
Townboro Dr 77062
Townhurst Dr 77043
Townplace St 77057
Townsend Mill Ct 77094
Township Dale Ct 77038
Township Grove Ln 77082
Township Meadows Ct 77095
Townshire Dr 77077
Townwood Dr 77045
Toyah Ave 77039
Trabajo Dr 77083
Trace Dr 77077
S Trace Dr 77066
Trace Glen Ln 77083
Trace Mill Ct 77066
Tracelynn Ln 77066
Tracemeadow Dr 77066
N Tracewood Bnd 77077
S Tracewood Bnd 77077
Tracewood Cv 77077
Tracewood Gln 77077
Tracewood Ln 77066
Trade Winds Dr 77086
Trademark Pl 77079
Trading Post Dr 77064
E & W Traditions Blvd & Ct 77082
Trafalgar Dr
5403-A-5403-B 77045
4100-5499 77045
5500-5799 77085
N Trail Dr 77073
Trail Bend Ln 77084
Trail Blazer Dr 77040
Trail Creek Dr 77017
Trail Hollow Dr
12600-12799 77024
12900-13200 77079
13202-13398 77079
Trail Lake Dr 77045
Trail Ridge Ct & Dr 77064
Trail Side Dr 77040
Trail Valley Way 77086
Trail Wind Ct 77049
Trailblazer Ln 77064
Trailbrook Dr 77095
Trailing Clover Ct 77084
Trailing Moss Ct & Dr 77064
Trailmobile Dr 77013
Trailmont Dr 77077
Trailridge Forest Dr 77088
Trails Ct 77024
Trails End St 77024
Trailside Dr 77095
Trailview Dr 77049
Trailville Dr
13700-13899 77077
15700-15799 77079
Trailwood Dr 77023
Train Ct 77041

Tralle St 77020
Tramonto Dr 77042
Tramore Dr 77083
Tranquil Frst 77084
Tranquil View Dr 77084
Transcentral Ct 77032
Trapper Ln 77065
Trapper Hill Dr 77077
Trappers Forest Dr 77088
Travelair St 77061
E & W Travelers Way Cir & Ln 77065
Traviata Dr 77024
Travick Ln 77073
Travis St
2-98 77002
100-2299 77002
2300-3399 77006
3400-5299 77002
6500-6799 77030
Travis Court Pl 77073
Travis Point Ln 77084
Traweek St 77055
Treadslow Ln 77067
Treasure Dr 77076
Treaty Oaks St 77053
Trebeau Ct 77031
Treborway Dr 77014
Tree Branch Dr 77064
Tree Bridge St 77075
Tree Frog Dr 77074
Tree Path Ln 77013
Tree Sparrow Ln 77083
Treebank Ln 77070
Treebark Ln 77018
Treefork Ln 77094
Treemont Lndg 77084
Treesey Way 77066
Treewater Dr 77072
Tregarnon Dr 77015
Treichel Rd 77041
Trellis Ln 77073
Trembling Forest Ln 77092
Tremendo Dr 77083
Trementina Dr 77088
Tremont St 77028
Tremont Springs Ln 77089
Tremout Hollow Ln 77044
Tremper St 77020
Trendale St 77087
Trendwest Dr 77084
Trenton Rd 77093
Trenton Lake Ln 77041
Trentway St 77040
Trenwood Ln 77022
Tres Lagunas Dr 77083
Trescon Dr 77048
Trevlig Trl 77073
Trevor Hill Dr 77066
Trey Dr 77084
W Tri Oaks Ln 77043
Trianon St 77024
Trica Ct 77040
Trickey Rd 77067
Tridens Ct 77086
Trierier Dr 77063
Trigg St 77093
Trimble St 77009
Trinidad St 77003
Trinity St 77007
Trinity Glen Ln 77047
Trinity Mist Ln 77073
Triola Ln
6701-6897 77074
6899-7299 77074
8000-9699 77036
10700-11899 77072
Triple Crown Dr 77071
Triple Oak Ct 77077
Trippell St 77093
Tristan St 77021
Triway Ln
1700-3099 77043
5400-5699 77041
Trixie Ln 77042
Trogon Ln 77083

Trompilla Ln 77083
Tronewood St
4300-4399 77093
4500-5299 77016
Troon Rd 77019
Troost St 77026
Trophy Club Rd 77095
Trophy Deer Ct 77084
Tropical Way 77087
Tropicana Dr 77041
Troulon Dr
7100-7799 77074
8700-8798 77036
8800-9199 77036
11900-12299 77072
Trout St 77093
Trowbridge Ct & Dr 77062
Troy Rd 77076
W Troy Rd
100-299 77076
300-599 77091
Truckee Dr 77082
Trudeau Dr 77065
Truesdell Dr 77071
Truett St 77023
Trulley St 77004
Truman St 77018
Trumbull St 77022
Trumpet St 77078
Trumpetvine St 77083
Truro St 77007
Truscon Dr 77080
Truxillo St
900-999 77002
1000-3399 77004
Tryon Dr 77065
Tuam St
1-799 77006
900-1099 77002
1100-3999 77004
Tuck St 77020
Tucker St 77087
Tucker Cypress Dr 77095
Tuckerton Rd 77095
Tucumcari Dr 77090
Tudor Mnr 77082
Tudor Point Ct 77082
Tuely Ct 77049
Tufa Ct 77072
Tuffly St 77029
Tulane St
700-899 77007
900-1599 77008
3900-4399 77018
Tulip Dale St 77084
Tulip Garden Ct 77065
Tulip Trails Ct 77075
Tuliptree Ln 77090
Tully Rd 77079
Tully St 77016
Tulsa St 77092
Tulum Ln 77073
Tumbleweed Trl 77095
Tumbling Falls Ct 77062
Tumbling Rapids Dr 77084
Tunbridge Ln 77024
Tunbury Ln 77095
Tunell Ln 77032
Tunham Trl 77073
Tupper Lake Dr
5400-5699 77056
10600-11199 77042
Tupperglenn Dr 77070
Tura Blvd 77044
Turchin Dr 77014
Turf Ct 77039
Turf Valley Dr 77084
Turfwood Ln 77088
Turkey Trl 77079
Turkey Creek Dr 77079
Turkey Trail Ct 77079
Turlock Ct 77041
Turn St 77093
Turn Point Ct 77044
Turnberry Cir 77025
Turnbow St 77029
Turnbridge Trl 77065
Turnbury Oak Ln & St 77055
Turner Dr
1-1099 77076
1101-1199 77076
1500-3899 77093
Turner Oaks 77085
Turner Place Rd 77037
Turner Point Cir 77095
Turney Dr
400-699 77037
700-1199 77038
Turning Basin Dr 77029
Turning Point Ct 77015
Turning Spring Ln 77044
Turnpike Rd 77008
Turnstone Ct 77083
Turquoise Ln 77055
Turquoise Stream Dr 77095
Turrett Point Ln 77064
Turriff St 77055
Turtle Bay Dr 77062
Turtle Beach Ln 77036
Turtle Creek Rd 77017
Turtle Gate Dr 77070
Turtle Lagoon Row 77036
Turtle Lake Dr 77064
Turtle Log Trl 77064
Turtle Oak Ct 77059
Turtlewood Ct 77072
Turtlewood Dr 77072
Turtlewood St 77049
Tuscon St 77026
Tuskegee St 77091
Tussendo Dr 77083
Tustin Dr 77095
Tutbury Cir 77044
Tutor Ln 77077
Tutson Pl 77085
Tuttle Point Dr 77082
Tweed Dr 77061
Twelve Oaks Dr
4200-4299 77027
10600-10699 77024
E & W Twickenham Trl 77076
Twig Dr 77089
Twig Leaf Ln 77084
Twila Springs Ct & Dr 77095
Twilight Falls Ln 77084
Twilight Manor Ct 77044
Twilight Moon Dr 77064
Twilight Sky Ct 77059
Twillingate Ln 77040
Twin Aspens Ln 77073
Twin Candle Dr 77018
Twin Circle Dr 77042
Twin Elm Ln 77073
Twin Falls Rd 77088
Twin Fountains Dr 77068
Twin Hills Ct 77031
Twin Hills Dr
7600-8599 77071
9100-9399 77031
Twin Lakes Blvd 77041
Twin Lamps Ln 77064
Twin Maple St 77082
Twin Oaks St 77076
Twin Tree Ln 77071
Twinbrooke Dr
500-699 77037
800-2299 77088
Twinkle Ct 77072
Twinridge Ln 77099
Twinwalker Dr 77049
Twisted Ash Ct 77015
Twisted Brook Dr 77053
Twisted Cedar Ct 77015
Twisted Elm Ct 77038
Twisted Oak Ln 77079
Twisted Pecan Ct 77015
Twisted Pine Ct 77039
Twisted Rattan Ln 77015
Twisted Spruce Ct 77015
Twisted Trunk Ct 77015
Twisting Rd 77084
Twisting Oak St 77082
Twisting Vine Ln 77040
Two Oaks Cir 77065
Twopenny Ln 77015
Tybor Dr 77074
Tyler St
1900-2000 77009
2002-2098 77009
3400-3499 77053
Tyler Point Ln 77089
Tyne Ct 77024
Tyne St 77007
Tynebridge Ln 77024
Tynebrook Ln 77024
Tyneland Ct 77070
Tynewood Dr 77024
Tysor Park Ln 77095
Ubuntu Ct 77091
Umber Ct 77099
Umber Cove Ct 77048
Umiak Dr 77045
Una St 77022
Underhill St 77092
Underwood St
2300-2599 77030
3000-4199 77025
Underwood Creek Way 77062
N Union Ct 77073
Union St 77007
Union Mill Rd 77067
Unique Cir 77044
United Dr 77036
United St 77093
Unity Dr
2900-2999 77057
2950-2950 77237
2950-2950 77257
3001-3499 77057
3200-3498 77057
Universal Dr 77072
University Blvd
1900-2201 77030
2203-2299 77030
2300-4299 77005
University Dr 77004
University Oaks Blvd 77004
Upas St 77006
Upfield Dr 77082
Uphall Ct 77095
Upland Dr, Lks & Park 77043
Upland Elm St 77084
Upland Forest Dr 77043
Upland Oak Dr 77043
Upland Rapids Dr 77089
Upland River Dr 77043
Upland Sky Ln 77043
Upper Bay Rd
18000-18215 77058
18214-18214 77258
18216-18898 77058
18217-18899 77058
Upper Hollow Rd 77067
Upperbrook St 77064
Uppercove Cir 77064
Upperway Ln 77056
Upshur Ln 77064
Upton St 77020
Uptown Dr 77045
Uptown Park Blvd 77056
Upward Ct 77073
Urban Dr 77050
Urban Dale Ct 77082
Urban Glen Ct 77038
Urban Woods Trl 77008
Ursa St 77020
Usener St 77009
Utah St
1100-1899 77007
6500-6899 77091
Utica St 77015
Uvalde Rd
1-1299 77015
5600-8199 77049
Vaiden Falls Ct 77083
Vailrun Dr 77070
Vailview Dr 77016
Val Lena Dr 77024
Val Verde Ct 77057
Val Verde Dr 77083
Val Verde Park 77057
Val Verde St
5300-5599 77056
5600-5999 77057
9300-9699 77063
Val Vista Dr 77083
Valarno Dr 77066
Vale Scene Ct 77073
Valechase Ln 77014
Valedon Ct & Ln 77014
Valemist Ct 77084
Valencia Dr 77013
Valentine St & Way 77019
Valera Ln 77083
Valerie St 77081
Valeta Dr 77083
Valeview Dr 77072
Valhallah Way 77095
Valiant Dr 77044
Valiant Scene Ct 77038
Valinda Ct & Dr 77083
Valkeith Dr 77096
Vallejo Ct & Dr 77053
Vallen Dr 77041
Valleta Dr 77008
N Valley Ct 77073
S Valley Ln 77089
Valley Acres Rd 77062
Valley Bend Dr 77068
Valley Breeze Dr 77078
Valley Club Dr 77078
Valley Cove Ln 77085
Valley Creek Dr 77095
Valley Crest Ln 77075
Valley Dale Ct 77062
Valley Elm Ln 77040
Valley Estates Dr 77082
Valley Falls Ct 77078
Valley Flag Dr 77078
Valley Forest Dr 77078
Valley Forge Dr
1-99 77024
5800-6299 77057
10000-10799 77042
6010-1-6010-2 77057
Valley Glen Dr 77077
Valley Gold Ct 77078
Valley Green Ct 77059
Valley Grove Dr 77066
Valley Hills Dr 77071
Valley Hollow Dr 77078
Valley Kings Dr 77089
Valley Knoll Dr 77084
Valley Lake Dr 77078
Valley Laurel Ct 77095
Valley Ledge Dr 77078
Valley Meadow Dr 77078
Valley Mill Ct 77078
Valley Park Dr 77078
Valley Pond Ct 77078
Valley Rock Dr 77078
Valley Side Dr 77078
Valley Song Dr 77078
Valley South Dr 77078
Valley Spring Dr 77043
Valley Star Dr 77024
Valley Stream Dr 77043
Valley Stream St 77037
Valley Sun Dr 77078
Valley Tree Ln 77089
Valley View Ln 77074
Valley Vista Ct & Dr 77077
Valley West Ct 77078
Valley Wind Dr 77078
Valleyfield Dr 77080
Valleygate Ln 77072
Valleywood Dr 77041
Valmont Dr 77016
Valor St 77093
Valwood Ct 77088
Van Rd 77049
Van Brook Ln 77095
Van Buren St
1000-1299 77019
1600-2599 77006
12200-12399 77064
Van Cleve St 77047
Van Etten St 77021
Van Fleet St 77033
Van Hut Ln 77044
Van Meter St 77047
Van Molan St 77022
Van Ness St 77037
Van Wall St 77040
Van Zandt St
4900-5099 77093
5400-6199 77016
Vanbury Dr 77084
Vance St
1900-2799 77093
3800-4199 77016
Vancouver Ln 77064
Vandalia Way 77053
Vandel St 77022
Vandeman St 77087
Vander Rock Dr 77095
Vanderbilt St 77005
Vanderbilt Park Dr 77058
Vandercroft Ct 77070
Vanderford Dr 77099
Vanderheath Dr 77031
Vanderpool Ln 77024
Vanessa Cir 77069
Vanilla Cir 77044
Vanilla Circle Ct 77044
Vanilla Ridge Ct 77044
Vanlynn Ln 77084
Vantage Pkwy E & W 77032
Vanwood St 77040
Vaquero Way 77095
Vardon Ct 77094
Varick Ct 77064
Varla Ln 77014
Varnell St 77039
Varner Rd 77080
Varsity Ln 77004
W Vashti Dr 77037
Vassar St
1300-1699 77006
1700-1999 77098
Vasser Rd 77033
Vatani Dr 77034
Vaughn St
1800-2799 77093
3900-4199 77016
Vaughnville Dr 77084
Vaulted Oak St 77008
Vauxhall Dr S 77047
Veenstra St 77022
Vega St 77088
Velasco St
100-198 77003
200-499 77003
501-1799 77003
2200-3399 77004
3401-3599 77004
N Velasco St 77003
Veller Dr 77032
Velvet Grass Ln 77095
Vena Dr 77087
Vendi Dr 77085
Venice St 77007
Venida St 77028
Vennard Rd 77034
Ventura Ln 77021
Venus St 77088
Venus Park Ln 77082
Ver Lee Ct 77037
Vera Jean Ct & Dr 77088
Vera Lou St 77051
Veramarion St 77070
Verano St 77029
Verbena Ln 77083
Verdant Way 77069
Verdant Brook Dr 77085
Verdant Willow Ct & Way 77095
Verde Glen Ln 77071
Verde Mar Ln 77095
Verde Meadow Ct 77041
Verde Trails Dr 77073
Verdenbruk Dr 77066
Verdi Way Ct 77044
Verdome Ln 77092
Verdun Dr 77049
Verhalen Ave 77039
Veridian Grove Dr 77072
Verlaine Dr 77065
Vermont St
1400-1899 77006
1900-2099 77019
Vermont Green Trl 77075
Vernage Rd 77047
Vernlake Cir 77084
Vernon St 77020
Vernwood St 77040
Verret Ln 77090
Versailles Ct & Dr 77015
Versailles Lakes Ln 77082
Versante Ct 77070
Vest Ct 77073
Vestavia Ct & Dr 77069
Veterans Memorial Dr
10625A-10625Z 77038
7901-7997 77088
7999-9399 77088
9500-10799 77038
10800-12299 77067
12300-13999 77014
Veyblum St 77029
Via Bella Dr 77083
Via Del Norte Dr 77083
Via Espana Dr 77083
Via Real Dr 77083
Via Verde Dr 77083
Via Vista Dr 77083
Vialinda Dr 77083
Vicdale Dr 77031
Viceroy Dr 77034
Vicheash Dr 77053
Vickers Cir 77077
Vickery Dr 77032
Vickery St
11400-11699 77093
11700-13199 77039
Vicki Ln 77015
Vicki John Dr 77096
Vickie Springs Ln 77086
Vickijohn Cir 77071
Vickijohn Ct 77071
Vickijohn Dr
7601-7697 77071
7699-7899 77071
9100-9198 77031
9200-9499 77031
Vickita Dr 77032
Vicksburg St 77015
Vickston Ln 77014
Victor Aly 77019
Victor Ln 77077
Victor St 77019
Victoria Dr 77022
Victoria St
6300-7599 77020
13700-14699 77015
Victoria Chase Ln 77075
Victoria Crest Ln 77075
Victoria Falls Ln 77075
Victoria Forest Dr 77088
Victoria Grove Ln 77075
Victoria Heights Ln 77075
Victoria Park Ln 77075
Victoria Point Ln 77075
Victoria Ridge Ln 77075
Victoria Wood Way 77089
Victorian Manor Ln 77047
Victorian Village Dr 77071
E & W Victorson St 77015
Victory Dr 77088
Vienna Trails Ln 77095
Vieta St 77049
Vieux Carre Dr 77009
View Glen Ct 77034
N & W View Meadow Ln & Loop 77034
View Park Ln 77095
View Pointe Ln 77034
Viewfield Ct 77059
Viking Dr
1600-2299 77018
4300-6099 77092
Vikram Dr 77038
Villa Dr 77061
N Villa Dr 77064
W Villa Dr 77064
E Villa St 77017
Villa Arbor Dr 77070
Villa Bend Dr 77069
Villa Bergamo Ct & Ln 77094
Villa De Matel Rd 77023
Villa De Norte St 77070
Villa Del Norte Dr 77073
Villa Del Sol Dr 77083
Villa Fontana Way 77068
Villa Glen Dr 77088
Villa Heights Dr 77066
Villa Hills Dr 77066
Villa Lago Ln 77070
Villa Lake Dr 77095
Villa Lea Ln 77071
Villa Palms Dr 77095
Villa Ridge Dr 77068
Villa Rose Dr 77062
Villa Verde Dr 77064
Village Dr 77040
W Village Dr
12339A-12339D 77039
12343A-12343D 77039
12407A-12407D 77039
12419A-12419D 77039
12435A-12435D 77039
12200-12499 77039
12339-1-12339-2 77039
12343-1-12343-2 77039
12407-1-12407-4 77039
12419-3-12419-4 77039
12435-3-12435-4 77039
Village Pkwy 77005
Village Ter 77040
Village Way 77087
Village Bell Dr & Ln 77038
Village Bend Ln 77072
Village Birch St 77062
Village Center Ct 77064
Village Chase Dr 77084
Village Corner Ct & Dr 77059
Village Dale Ave 77059
Village Dogwood Ct 77084
Village Elm St 77062
Village Evergreen Trl 77062
Village Forest Ct 77092
Village Gate Dr 77082
Village Green Ct 77077
Village Green Dr 77040
Village Hollow Ln 77072
Village Maple Ct 77084
Village Oaks Ln 77055
Village Of Fondren Dr 77071
Village Of Kings Lake Blvd 77044
Village Park Cir 77024
Village Place Dr 77077
Village Rose Ln 77072
Village Square Dr 77077
Village Trace Dr 77053
Village Trail Dr 77065
Village Tree Way 77084
Village Way Dr 77041
Villagrove Dr 77049
Villanova St 77005
Villaret Dr 77083
Villas Palmas Dr 77070
Villawood Ln 77072
Villita St 77013
Villmont Ln 77077
Vilven Ln 77080
Vincent St 77009
Vindale Dr 77044
Vindon Dr 77024

Vine St 77002
Vinearbor St 77033
Vinecrest Dr 77086
Vinedale Dr 77099
Vinemont Ln 77084
Vinetree Ln 77040
Vinett St 77017
Vinewood Cir 77088
Vinewood Dr 77088
Vinewood Ln 77072
Viney Creek Dr 77095
Vineyard Dr 77082
Vineyard Falls Dr 77083
Vinita St 77034
Vinkins Ct & Rd 77071
Vinland Dr 77058
Vinson St 77088
Vintage St 77026
Vintage Centre Dr 77069
Vintage Leaf Cir 77070
Vintage Park Blvd 77070
Vintage Preserve Pkwy 77070
Vintage Springs Ln 77070
Vintage Valley Dr 77082
Vintage Villa Dr 77070
Vinton Ct 77040
Vinvale Rd 77066
Viny Ridge Dr 77083
Violet Path Ln 77085
Vira Ct & Ln 77014
Virgil St 77088
Virginia Ct 77005
Virginia St 77098
W Virginia St 77076
Virginia Fern Way 77059
Virginia Water Ln 77095
Virline Ln 77067
Viscount Rd 77032
Vision Ln 77048
N Vista Dr 77073
Vista Bay Ln 77041
Vista Bend Dr 77073
Vista Brook Dr 77041
Vista Camino Dr 77083
Vista De Oro St 77070
Vista Del Mar Dr 77083
Vista Del Rancho Dr 77083
Vista Del Sol Dr 77083
Vista Grande St 77083
Vista Grove Cir 77073
Vista Mar Cir 77095
Vista Norte Ct 77076
Vista Oak Dr 77073
Vista Oaks Mnr 77028
Vista Oro Dr 77041
Vista Trace Dr 77073
Vista Trail Ct 77073
Vista Verde St 77087
Vista Village Ln 77092
Vista Woods Dr 77028
S & W Vistaglen Loop 77084
Vistamont Dr 77083
W & E Vistawood Ct & Dr 77077
Vistrist St 77005
E Vita Cir 77070
Vitry Ln 77071
Vivian Rd 77093
Vivian Point Ln 77095
Vogel Rd 77088
Vogue Ln
8200-8599 77055
9000-9999 77080
Voight St 77009
Volley St 77022
Vollmer Rd 77092
Voltaire Dr 77065
Volute Ct 77038
Voss Rd
200-999 77024
1000-1299 77055
1301-1399 77055
S Voss Rd 77057
Voss Park Dr 77024
Voss Village Mall 77057

Vossdale Rd 77027
Votaw Ln 77088
Voyager Dr 77062
Vrana Dr 77049
Wabash Elm St 77073
Waco St 77020
Wade Hampton Dr 77024
Wadebridge Way 77015
Wadlington Dr 77044
Wadsworth St 77015
Wages St 77093
Wagg Way Rd 77041
Wagner St
500-1499 77007
14700-14799 77034
Wagon Rd 77060
Wagon Boss Rd 77049
Wagon Gap Trl 77090
Wagon Point Dr 77090
Wagon Trail Rd 77064
Wagonwheel Cir & Ln 77088
Wahl Manor Ct 77083
Wainfleet Ln 77096
Wainscot Ct 77038
Wainwright St 77022
Waiting Spring Cir & Ln 77095
Wakefield Dr 77018
Wakefield Village Dr 77095
Wakeforest Ave 77005
Wakeforest St
3600-3899 77098
5000-5299 77005
Walbrook Dr 77062
Walcott Ln 77088
Wald Rd 77034
Waldemar Dr 77077
Waldemere Dr 77077
Walden Ln 77024
Walden Hill Ct 77077
Walden Park Ct 77049
Waldens Pond Ct 77044
Waldine St 77015
Waldo St 77063
Waldron Cir & Dr 77084
Walford Mill Ln 77095
Walhalla Dr 77066
Walk Dr 77076
Walker St
601-697 77002
699-1099 77002
1100-1298 77010
1101-1299 77002
1300-1999 77010
2000-2399 77003
3800-5199 77023
7300-7499 77011
10000-10199 77064
W Walker St 77019
Walkers Forest Dr 77088
Walksew St 77047
Walkup Way 77044
Walkway St 77036
Walkwood Cir, Ct & Dr 77079
Wall St
800-2599 77088
16000-16499 77040
Wall Fern Way 77034
Walla Ln 77037
Wallace St 77022
Wallboard Ct 77038
Waller St 77012
Waller Park Ln 77064
Walling St 77009
Wallingford Dr, Pl & Pnes 77042
Wallington Dr 77096
Wallis Trail Ct 77049
Wallisville Rd
5500A-5500C 77020
5500-7799 77020
7800-9199 77029
9200-12999 77013
13300-19399 77049
Walnut St 77002

Walnut Bend Ln 77042
Walnut Bridge Ct 77062
Walnut Brook Ct 77040
Walnut Cove Dr 77084
Walnut Creek Dr 77017
Walnut Dale Ct 77038
Walnut Glen Dr 77064
Walnut Green Dr 77062
Walnut Hollow Ln 77082
Walnut Knoll Way 77084
Walnut Lake Rd 77065
Walnut Meadow Dr 77066
Walnut Pond Ct & Dr 77059
Walnut Shores Dr 77044
Walnut View Ct 77038
Walnut Wood Dr 77084
Walston Ln 77060
Walters Rd
11300-12199 77067
12200-12202 77014
12204-14404 77014
14403-14403 77268
14405-14599 77014
14406-14598 77014
14600-15399 77068
Walterville Rd 77080
Walthall Dr 77022
Walton Rd 77044
Walton St 77009
Walton Heath Dr 77069
Waltrip St 77087
Waltway Dr 77008
Walwick Dr 77024
Walworth Ct & Dr 77088
Wanakah Dr 77069
Wanda Ln
6501-7599 77074
7800-7999 77044
Wandering Wood Dr 77015
Wanita Pl 77007
Wann Park Dr 77073
War Memorial Dr 77084
Warantra St 77003
Warath Oak Ct 77065
Ward St
3100-3199 77053
3500-5099 77021
Wardmont St
1100-1299 77037
2100-3699 77093
Wardville St 77093
Warelarr St 77054
Warfield Ln 77084
Waring St 77027
Warkerli St 77016
Warkworth Dr 77085
Warm Springs Rd 77035
Warner St 77022
Warradi Dr 77042
Warren Rd 77040
Warrenford Dr 77083
Warrenton Dr 77024
Warrenwood Dr 77066
Warwana Rd
9700-10099 77080
10800-10899 77043
Warwick Rd 77093
Warwickshire Ct & Dr 77077
Waseca St 77055
Washam Rd 77075
Washburne Ln 77095
Washelin Dr 77099
Washforde Ln 77049
Washington Ave
300-1499 77002
1500-8299 77007
Washington Dr 77038
Washington St 77093
Wateka Cir & Dr 77074
Water Canyon Ct 77077
Water Elm Ct & Way 77059
N & S Water Iris Ct 77059
Water Leaf Ln 77088
Water Park Ct & Ln 77086
Waterbury Dr 77055
Watercastle Ct 77077

Watercress Cir 77064
Watercress Park 77041
Watercrest Dr 77008
Waterdance Ln 77095
Waterelm Dr 77084
Waterfern Ct 77064
Waterford Cv 77094
Waterford Dr 77033
Waterfowl Ct 77014
Waterhaven Ln 77084
Watering Oaks Ln 77083
Waterloo Dr
12900-14699 77045
14700-15399 77053
Watermist Ln 77041
Waters Edge Pl 77041
Waterside Dr 77015
Waterside Way 77041
Waterstone Dr 77042
Watertown Mall 77057
Waterville Way 77015
Waterwall Dr 77056
Watkin Way 77015
Watonga Blvd 77092
Watson St 77009
Watson Crossing Way 77067
Watts St 77030
Waugh Dr
1-199 77007
500-1599 77019
1600-2799 77006
Waughcrest St 77006
Waughford St 77007
Wavecrest Ln 77062
Waveland Dr 77072
Wavell St 77088
Waverdale Ct 77094
Waverly Ct 77005
Waverly Dr 77032
Waverly St
601-697 77007
699-899 77007
900-1599 77008
Waverly Grove Dr 77084
Waving Fields Dr 77064
Wax Mallow Ct & Dr 77095
Wax Myrtle Ln 77079
Waxahachie St
6900-7799 77020
7900-8199 77029
13700-14699 77015
Waxwing St 77035
Waxwood Dr 77089
Way St 77028
Way Out West Dr 77092
Waybridge Dr 77062
Waybridge Glen Ln 77095
Waycreek Rd 77068
Waycross Dr 77035
Wayfarer Ln 77075
Wayforest Dr 77060
Wayland St 77021
Waylord Dr 77041
Wayne St
1400-1499 77020
2300-6399 77026
Waynemer Way 77040
Waynesboro Dr 77035
Waypark Dr 77082
Wayside Dr 77011
N Wayside Dr
200-2899 77020
4600-9599 77028
9700-9799 77078
S Wayside Dr
100-619 77011
621-699 77011
700-3799 77023
4300-5899 77087
8000-8099 77033
13000-14499 77048
Wayside Stream Ln 77048
Wayward Rd 77064
Wayward Wind Ct & Ln 77064
Weatherhill Ln 77041

Weathering Oaks Dr 77066
Weatherly Way 77022
Weathersby St 77091
Weathersfield Trace Cir 77014
Weatherwood Dr 77080
Weaver Rd
3600-3799 77093
4100-5899 77016
6600-7099 77028
Weaver St 77023
Webb Dr 77017
Weber St 77007
Webercrest Rd 77048
Webster St
200-1599 77002
1600-2699 77003
2700-3499 77004
W Webster St 77019
Weckford Blvd 77044
Wedgefield St 77028
Wedgeford Ct 77044
Wedgehill Ln 77077
Wedgewood Ln 77055
Wedgewood St 77093
Wednesbury Ln 77074
Wee Laddie Ln 77084
Wee Lassie Ln 77084
Weedy Ln 77093
Weems St 77009
Weeping Cedar Ln 77084
Weeping Willow Rd 77092
Weil Pl 77060
Weiland Manor Ln 77073
Weiman Rd 77041
Weingarten St 77021
Weisenberger Dr 77022
Weiss St 77009
Welch St
100-1899 77006
1900-2399 77019
Welcome Ln 77014
Weldon Dr
1700-1999 77073
2000-15641 77032
15643-15699 77032
Welk St 77034
Welland Dr 77031
Wellers Way 77095
Wellesley Dr 77024
Wellford St 77022
Wellford Point Dr 77095
N Wellington Ct 77055
S Wellington Ct 77055
Wellington Pkwy 77014
Wellington Pt 77094
Wellington St
1-1299 77076
1500-2299 77093
E Wellington St 77076
W Wellington St 77076
Wellington Way
1600-1698 77055
1700-1799 77055
4800-4999 77069
Wellington Bend Ln 77073
Wellington Park Dr 77072
Wellman Ln 77060
Wellness Landing Ln 77072
Wells Fargo Dr 77090
Wells River Dr 77041
Wellsworth Dr 77083
Wellwood Ct 77083
Welsh Stone Ln 77049
Welshpool Glen Dr 77066
Welwyn Dr 77040
Wembley Dr 77031
Wemyss Bay Rd 77095
Wenda St
4600-4699 77051
4700-5799 77033
Wendel St 77009
Wendelyn Ln 77069
Wendemere St 77088
Wendover Ln 77024
Wendy Hill Way 77058

Wenlock Dr 77048
Wennington Dr 77099
Wentworth Ct 77055
Wentworth St 77004
Wentworth Park Dr 77015
Wenwood Cir 77040
Werlein Ave 77005
Werner St
4500-5399 77022
5401-5597 77076
5599-7499 77076
7500-8600 77037
8602-8698 77037
N Werrington Way 77073
Wertz St 77034
Wesco Way 77041
Weslayan St
2600-4999 77027
5100-5399 77005
5340-5340 77277
5340-5340 77265
5400-6698 77005
5401-6799 77005
Wesley St 77023
Wesley Oaks Dr 77085
Weslow St 77087
Wessex Dr 77089
West Ct 77082
West Dr 77053
West Ln 77019
West Loop N
300-399 77024
1000-1452 77055
1454-1498 77055
1500-1798 77008
West Loop S
1001-1097 77027
1099-3199 77027
5201-5699 77081
8500-8899 77096
8901-9099 77096
West Rd
101-199 77037
200-1299 77038
6300-7399 77086
7800-10999 77064
11100-11599 77065
12101-12197 77065
12199-12299 77065
12600-14499 77041
14500-17899 77095
E West Rd 77060
West St
900-1499 77020
1500-2400 77026
2402-2498 77026
7600-8599 77093
N & S West Oak Dr 77056
Westacre Pl 77083
Westbank Ave 77064
Westbay Ln 77044
Westbluff Dr 77084
Westbrae Pkwy 77031
Westbrae Gardens Ct 77031
Westbrae Manor Dr 77031
Westbrae Meadows Dr 77031
Westbrae Oaks Ln 77031
Westbrae Park Ct & Ln 77031
Westbrae Village Dr 77031
Westbranch Ct 77072
Westbranch Dr
1600-1799 77077
6100-7399 77072
Westbranch Meadows Ct 77041
Westbriar Ln 77056
Westbrook Dr 77037
Westbrook Rd 77016
Westbrook Bridge Dr 77041
Westbury Ct 77084
Westbury Sq 77035
Westcenter Dr 77042
Westchase Dr 77042
Westchester Ave 77005
Westchester Ct 77005

Westchester Cts
6711-6799 77005
6726-6798 77025
Westchester St
5252-5298 77005
6900-6999 77025
Westcott Rd 77016
Westcott St 77007
Westcove Cir 77064
Westcreek Ln 77027
Westcrest Dr 77055
Westcross St 77018
Westdale St 77087
Westella Dr 77077
Westerfield Ln 77084
Westerham Pl 77069
Westerland Dr 77063
Westerley Ln 77077
Westerloch Dr 77077
Westerman St 77005
Westermill Dr 77082
Western Dr
8200-8599 77055
9100-9199 77080
Western Branch Ct 77066
Western Oak Ln 77040
Western Pass Ln 77095
Western Saddle Ct 77044
Western Skies Dr 77086
Western Trail Dr 77040
Western Village Ln 77043
Westfair East Dr 77041
Westfair West Dr 77041
Westfield St
100-1299 77022
6600-6699 77085
Westfield Loop Rd 77073
Westfield Place Dr 77090
Westfield Ridge Dr 77073
Westford St
500-1199 77022
1700-1899 77093
Westgard Blvd 77044
Westgate Dr 77019
Westgate St 77098
Westglen Dr 77063
Westgrove Ln 77027
Westhampton Dr 77045
Westhaven Dr 77084
Westheimer Ct 77056
Westheimer Pkwy 77082
Westheimer Rd
5868A-1-5868A-1 77057
1756A-1756C 77098
8401A-8401B 77063
100-1699 77006
1700-3399 77098
3400-4799 77027
4901-4997 77056
4999-5699 77056
5700-6599 77057
7500-9699 77063
9700-11299 77042
11300-14599 77077
14600-17999 77082
Westheimer Place Dr 77082
Westhill Ln 77077
Westhollow Dr & Pkwy 77082
Westhollow Park Dr 77082
Westholme Dr 77063
Westhorpe Dr 77077
Westhurst Ln 77077
Westington Ln 77040
Westknoll Ln 77072
Westlake Rd 77062
Westlake Way 77084
Westlake Park Blvd 77079
Westlake Place Dr 77084
Westland East Blvd 77041
Westland West Blvd 77041
Westleigh Dr 77077
Westline Dr 77036
Westmart Dr 77042
Westmead Dr 77077
Westmeadow Dr
1700-1898 77084

3700-4099 77082
Westmere Ct & Dr 77077
Westminister Ct 77069
Westminster Dr 77024
Westminster Glen Ln 77049
Westminster Plaza Dr 77082
Westminster Village Ct & Dr 77084
Westmont Dr 77015
Westmoreland St 77006
Westnut Ln 77040
Westoffice Dr 77042
Weston St 77021
Westover St
5100-5598 77033
5600-6199 77033
6200-7599 77087
Westover Ridge Dr 77072
Westpark Dr
2600-2799 77098
2900-3399 77005
3700-4799 77027
5000-5599 77056
5600-6499 77057
7700-9999 77063
10000-11299 77042
11300-16299 77082
Westplace Dr 77071
Westplain Dr 77041
Westport Ln 77079
Westport Shore Dr 77094
Westray St 77043
Westridge Pl 77041
Westridge St
2400-2999 77054
3200-3519 77025
3521-3599 77025
Westshire Dr 77013
Westshore Dr 77094
Westside Forest Dr 77094
Weststar Ln 77072
Westview Dr
5800-10099 77055
10100-10899 77043
S Westview Circle Dr 77043
Westward St 77081
Westway 77093
Westway Ln 77077
Westway Park Blvd 77041
Westwick Dr
1600-1699 77077
3000-3399 77082
6200-6799 77072
Westwick Forest Ln 77043
Westwillow Dr 77064
Westwind Ct & Ln 77071
E Westwood Cir 77071
W Westwood Cir 77071
Westwood Dr 77055
Westwood Glen Ln 77047
Westwood Manor Ln 77047
Westwood Place Dr 77036
Westwood Village Dr 77036
Wetherby Ln 77075
Wetherill St 77093
Wexford Ct 77024
Wexford Park Dr 77088
Weybridge Dr 77031
Weyburn St 77028
Weyburn Grove Dr 77088
Weymouth Dr 77031
Wharf St 77012
Wharton St 77055
Wheat St
3100-3199 77038
3200-3499 77086
Wheat Cross Dr 77095
Wheat Mill Ln 77095
Wheatbridge Dr 77041
Wheatfield Dr 77095
Wheatland Dr 77064
Wheatley St
5400-6999 77091
7200-9399 77088
Wheatmill Ct 77095
Wheaton Dr 77089

Wheaton Creek Ct 77073
Wheaton Edge Ln 77095
Wheaton Forest Ln 77095
Wheatridge Dr 77064
Wheeler St
1000-1098 77002
1100-4899 77004
5900-6299 77023
Whetstone Ln 77064
Whidbey Island Dr 77086
Whimsey Ct 77084
Whipple Tree Dr 77070
Whippoorwill Rd 77024
Whisper Pass 77094
Whisper Point Dr 77040
Whispering Breeze Ln 77094
Whispering Creek Way 77017
Whispering Falls Ct & Dr 77084
Whispering Meadows Trl 77064
Whispering Palms Dr 77066
Whispering Pines Dr 77055
Whispering Ridge Ter 77094
Whispering Sands Ct 77041
Whispering Star Ct 77095
Whispering Wood Ln 77086
Whispertrail Ct 77014
Whistlers Cottage Ct 77088
Whistling Pines Dr 77090
Whitaker Creek Dr 77095
Whitbourne Dr 77084
Whitbourne Meadow Ln 77040
Whitchurch Dr 77066
Whitchurch Way 77015
White Rd 77047
White St 77007
White Birch Ln 77095
White Canyon Ln 77044
White Cap Ln 77072
White Cedar St 77015
White Chapel Ln 77074
White Cliff Dr 77065
White Clover Dr 77089
White Fawn Dr 77041
White Fir Dr 77088
White Gate Ln 77067
White Hart Run 77084
White Heather Dr 77045
White Ibis Dr 77044
White Jasmine Trl 77079
White Maple St 77064
White Mills Dr 77041
White Oak Cir 77040
White Oak Dr
1500-2398 77009
2400-2699 77009
2700-3699 77007
White Oak Ln 77040
White Oak Pl 77040
White Oak Bend Dr 77064
White Oak Landing Blvd 77065
White Oak Ridge Dr 77095
White Oak Trail Ln 77064
White Pillars Ln 77024
White Pine Ln 77016
White Plains Dr 77089
White Rock St
4500-4699 77051
4800-4899 77033
White Star Dr 77062
White Summit Ct 77044
N & S White Tail Ct 77084
White Thorn St 77016
White Water Trl 77013
White Wing Ln 77079
Whiteback Dr 77084
S Whiteback Dr 77094
Whitebrook Dr 77038
Whitebud Dr 77082
Whitecastle Ln 77088
Whitecross Dr 77083
Whitefriars Dr 77087
Whiteglade Ln 77084

Whitehall Dr 77060
Whitehall Ln 77058
Whitehead St 77088
Whitelock Dr 77095
Whitepost Ln 77086
Whitesage Ct 77082
Whiteside Ln
10000-10099 77080
10100-10199 77043
Whitestone Ln 77073
Whitewater Ln 77079
Whitewater Falls Ct 77059
Whitewind Dr 77094
Whithorn Dr 77095
Whitinham Dr 77067
Whitlock Dr 77062
Whitman St 77027
Whitmire St 77012
Whitmore Ln 77083
Whitney St 77006
E Whitney St 77022
W Whitney St 77018
Whitter Forest Dr 77088
Whittier Dr 77032
Whittingham Ln 77099
Whittington Ct N 77077
Whittington Ct S 77077
Whittington Dr
12000-12654 77077
12655-13399 77077
12655-12655 77244
12655-12655 77282
12656-13398 77077
Whittington Park Ln 77095
Whitton Dr 77085
Whitty St 77026
Wichita St 77004
Wichman St 77007
Wickbriar Dr 77053
Wickchester Ln
11501-11697 77043
11699-11999 77043
12000-12199 77079
Wickdale Dr 77024
Wickdale Garden Ln 77044
Wickenburg Dr 77031
Wickerbay St 77080
Wickersham Ln
3400-4099 77027
5600-5699 77056
6200-6299 77057
7800-7899 77063
10000-11099 77042
11300-14399 77077
N & S Wickerwood St 77080
Wickford Dr 77024
Wickhamford Way 77015
Wickhollow Ln 77043
Wickley Dr 77085
Wickline Dr 77024
Wicklow Meadow Ln 77060
Wicklowe St 77016
Wickmere Dr 77062
Wickover Ln 77086
Wickshire Ln 77043
Wickstone Ln 77014
Wickview Ln 77053
Wickway Dr 77024
Wickwild St 77024
Wickwood Dr 77024
Widcombe Dr 77084
Widdicomb Ct 77008
Widley Cir 77077
Wier Dr 77017
Wigeon Ridge Ln 77047
Wiggins St
7200-7299 77020
7900-11199 77029
Wightman Ct 77069
Wigton Dr 77096
Wilbarger Cir 77064
Wilburforce St 77091
Wilbury Park 77041
Wilchester Blvd 77079
Wilcrest Dr
100-3899 77042
6000-8499 77072
8500-9599 77099
11800-12099 77031
N Wilcrest Dr 77079
S Wilcrest Dr 77099
Wilcrest Green Dr 77042
Wild Basin Dr 77088
Wild Bluebonnet Way 77084
Wild Columbine Rd 77038
Wild Hollow Ln 77088
Wild Indigo St 77027
Wild Mustang Ln 77044
Wild Oak Cir 77055
Wild Oak Dr 77090
Wild Oak Run 77094
Wild Orchid Dr 77084
Wild Pecan Trl 77084
Wild Pine Dr 77039
Wild Plum St 77013
Wild Rose St 77083
Wild Strawberry Rd 77038
Wild Stream Ct 77095
Wild Valley Rd 77057
Wild Willow Ln 77084
Wild Wind Ln 77013
Wildacres Dr 77072
Wildbrook Dr 77038
Wilde Glen Ln 77072
Wilde Laurel Ln 77014
Wilde Rock Way 77018
Wilder St 77008
Wilderness Cliff Ct 77062
Wildforest Dr 77088
Wilding Ln 77024
Wildmoor Ct 77094
Wildspruce Ct & Dr 77088
Wildwood Way 77023
Wildwood Brook Ct 77095
Wildwood Glen Dr 77083
Wildwood Lake Dr 77083
Wildwood Park Ln 77070
Wildwood Springs Ct & Ln 77044
Wiley Rd
3400-4899 77093
5000-7499 77016
Wileyvale Rd
6300-6999 77028
7200-8799 77016
Wileywood Dr 77049
Wilken St 77008
Wilkenberg Dr 77066
Wilkenburg Dr 77086
Wilkenson St 77019
Wilkes St 77009
Wilkie Ln 77076
Wilkins St 77030
Wilkins Oaks Dr 77028
Wilkshire Ct 77069
Will Clayton Pkwy 77032
Willacy Ct 77064
Willancy Ct & Ln 77095
Willard St 77006
Willemette St 77049
Willers Way
5200-5699 77056
6100-6299 77057
Willgus Trail Ln 77066
Willia St 77007
William St 77002
William Tell St 77093
Williamcrest Ln 77071
Williamhurst Ln 77090
Williams St 77040
Williams Court Ln 77081
Williams Field Dr 77064
Williamsburg Dr & Ln 77024
Williamsdell St 77088
Williamstown Dr 77084
Willie St 77093
Williford St 77012
Willingham Way 77095
Willington Ln 77049
Willis St
14700-14999 77039
15000-15199 77032

Williston Dr 77065
Williwaw Dr 77083
Willomine Way 77045
N Willow Cir 77071
S Willow Cir 77071
N Willow Dr 77073
S Willow Dr 77035
Willow St 77088
Willow Trl 77035
Willow Beach Dr 77072
Willow Branch Ct & Dr 77070
Willow Bridge Cir 77095
Willow Brook Park 77066
Willow Centre Dr 77066
Willow Chase Blvd & Dr 77070
Willow Creek Way 77017
Willow Crossing Ct & Dr 77064
Willow Dale St 77087
Willow Fairway Dr 77095
Willow Glen Dr 77033
Willow Hearth Dr 77084
Willow Heights Ct 77059
Willow Lake Dr 77077
Willow Landing Ln 77085
Willow Lodge Ct 77064
Willow Meadow Dr 77031
Willow Mint Ln 77086
Willow Mountain Ln 77047
Willow Oak Dr 77092
Willow Park Grn 77070
Willow Park Ln 77064
Willow Park Vw 77070
Willow Place Dr N 77070
Willow Place Dr S 77070
Willow Place Dr W
12900-12999 77070
12955-12955 77269
Willow Quill Ct & Dr 77088
Willow Ranch Dr 77095
Willow River Dr 77095
Willow Rock Rd 77088
Willow Shores Dr 77062
Willow Springs Ln 77080
Willow Trace Ct 77064
Willow Tree Dr 77066
Willow View Ct 77070
Willow Walk St 77069
Willow Wand Ct 77070
Willow West Dr 77073
Willow Wind Ln 77083
Willow Wood Ln 77086
Willow Wood Way 77070
Willowbend Blvd
3500-3699 77054
4000-4199 77025
4300-5199 77035
5200-6599 77096
Willowbridge Park Blvd 77064
Willowbrook Blvd 77021
Willowbrook Mall 77070
Willowby Dr 77008
Willowcrossing Cir 77064
N & S Willowdale Cir 77071
Willowend Dr 77024
Willowford Ct 77082
Willowgren Dr 77024
Willowgrove Dr 77035
Willowick Cir 77024
Willowick Rd
2100-2599 77027
3600-4099 77019
Willowilde Dr 77035
Willowisp Dr 77035
Willowlake Dr 77077
Willowlake Park Dr 77064
Willowmist Dr 77064
Willowmoss Ct 77008
Willowood Ln 77023
Willowron Dr 77024
Willowshire Ln 77014
Willowtwist St 77083
Willowview Ln 77080
E & W Willowwind Cir 77071
Willwood Dr 77072

Wilma Way 77073
Wilmer St 77003
Wilmerdean St 77061
Wilmington St
3000-4699 77051
4700-5499 77033
Wilmington Park Ln 77084
Wilo Dr 77032
Wiloak St
9200-9499 77028
9700-10199 77078
Wilomill Dr 77040
Wilona Way 77073
Wiloway St 77016
Wilshire Lks 77040
Wilshire Rdg 77040
Wilshire St 77023
Wilshire Fern 77040
Wilshire Park Dr 77038
Wilshire Place Dr 77040
Wilson St
1000-1899 77019
1900-1999 77006
Wilson Pines Ct 77031
Wilson Reid Dr 77040
Wilsons Creek Ln 77083
Wilston Ct 77077
Wilstone Dr 77084
Wilthorne Gardens Ct 77084
Wilton St
5100-5198 77098
5300-5399 77005
Wiltshire Way 77089
Wiltshire Downs Ln 77049
Wimberley Hollow Ln 77053
Wimberly St 77093
Wimberly Canyon Ct 77075
Wimberly Knoll Ct & Ln 77084
Wimberly Park Dr 77049
Wimbledon Ln 77070
Wimbledon Oaks Dr 77065
Winbern St
800-999 77002
1000-3399 77004
Winchell St 77022
Winchester Village Ct 77064
Wincroft Ct 77069
Wind Brook St 77040
Wind Cave Ln 77040
Wind Chimes Dr 77066
Wind Dale St 77040
Wind Flower Ln 77086
Wind Forest Ct & Dr 77040
Wind Free Dr 77040
Wind Hollow Cir 77040
Wind Lawn Dr 77040
Wind Lock Cir 77040
Wind Rock Ct & St 77040
Wind Side Dr 77040
Wind Stream Dr 77040
Wind Trail St 77040
Wind Veil Dr 77040
Wind Walker Trl 77095
Wind Willow Dr 77040
Windamere Lakes Blvd 77065
Windbreak Trl 77079
Windbriar Ct 77068
Windchase Blvd & Ct 77082
Windcrest Ct 77064
Windell Ln 77040
Windemere St 77033
Windermere Ln 77063
Winderwick Ln 77066
Windfall Ct & Ln 77040
Windfern Rd
4300-5899 77041
6000-8399 77040
8400-13499 77064
Windfern Forest Dr 77040
Windfern Lakes St 77064
Windfern Trace Dr 77064
Windgrove Ct 77083
Windham Springs Ct 77041
Windhaven St 77049

Winding Brook Ln 77024
Winding Canyon Ln 77083
Winding Creek Vw 77072
Winding Creek Way 77017
Winding Manor Dr 77044
Winding Meadow Ct 77040
Winding Moss Dr 77068
Winding River Dr 77088
Winding Stream Ln
2800-2899 77089
18900-19099 77084
Winding Trace Dr 77086
Winding Valley Dr 77095
Winding Walk Dr 77095
Winding Way Dr 77091
Winding Wood Ct & Dr 77038
Windjammer St 77072
Windlake Ct & Dr 77070
Windlea Ln 77040
Windmark Dr, Ln & Pl 77099
Windmill Elm St 77008
Windmill Forest Dr 77082
Windmill Lakes Blvd 77075
Windmill Meadows Ct 77082
Windmill Park Ln 77064
Windmill Village Dr 77082
Windmist Cir 77084
Windoak Ln 77040
Windrift Dr 77066
Windriver Cir & Dr 77070
Windrose Ct 77064
Windrow Ln 77072
Windsong Trl 77084
Windsor Ct 77055
Windsor Ln 77031
Windsor Mnr 77069
Windsor Pl 77055
Windsor St 77006
Windsor Crest Dr 77094
Windsor Forest Dr 77088
Windsor Garden Ln 77044
Windsor Grove Ln 77084
Windsor Lake Xing 77094
Windsor Lakes Ct & Dr 77094
Windsor Locks Dr 77065
Windsor Oaks Ln 77062
Windsor Palms Dr 77094
Windsor Park Dr 77094
Windsor Sails Dr 77094
Windsor Valley Ln 77049
Windsor Village Dr 77071
Windswept Ln
5300-5500 77056
5502-5598 77056
6100-6599 77057
7600-9699 77063
6410-1-6410-2 77057
Windswept Grove Dr 77083
Windvine Dr 77072
Windward Ln 77058
Windward Passage St 77072
Windwater Dr 77075
Windwater Pkwy N 77036
Windwater Pkwy S 77036
Windwater Lagoon 77036
Windwater Pointe 77036
Windwood Dr 77035
Windy Ln 77024
Windy Acres Dr 77040
Windy Canyon Ln 77084
Windy Cove Ct & Dr 77095
Windy Creek Dr 77040
Windy Dunes Dr 77071
Windy Glen Dr 77095
Windy Heath Ln 77085
Windy Knoll Dr 77084
Windy Meadow Dr 77084
Windy Nook Dr 77084
Windy Oaks Dr 77040
Windy Orchard Ln 77084
Windy Peaks Ct 77067
Windy Ridge Ln 77062
Windy Royal Dr 77045
Windy Spring Ct & Ln 77089

Windy Stone Dr 77084
Windy Stream Ln 77044
Windy Summer Ln 77044
Windy Thicket Ln 77082
Windy Trail Dr 77040
Windy Wisp Ln 77071
Wine Rock Dr 77070
Winecup Ln 77047
Winehill Ln 77040
Winewood Dr 77044
Winfield Rd
4600-5799 77039
5900-9799 77050
Winfree Dr
4700-4999 77021
6300-7299 77087
Winfrey Ln 77076
Wingate Park 77082
Wingate St 77011
Wingdale Ct & Dr 77082
Winged Foot Dr 77069
W Wingfoot Rd 77041
Wingleaf Dr 77084
Wingtip Dr
9000-9099 77061
9100-10699 77075
Wink Rd 77024
Winkbow Dr 77040
Winkle Wood Ln 77086
Winkleman Rd 77083
Winkler Dr
100-499 77087
8300-9399 77017
9401-9599 77017
Winmont Ct 77082
Winmoss Ct 77068
Winner Cir 77024
Winnetka St 77021
Winnie St 77009
Winningham Ln 77055
Winnsboro Dr 77088
Winnwood Ct 77070
Winrock Blvd 77057
Winsford Dr 77084
Winship St 77028
Winshire Cir 77024
Winslow St 77025
Winslow Forest Ln 77047
Winsome Ln
5600-6199 77057
9300-9699 77063
Winston St 77009
Winston Point Ln 77084
Winston Woods Dr 77024
Winter St 77007
Winter Bay Ln 77088
Winter Bloom Ln 77088
Winter Brook Dr 77066
Winter Creek Ct 77077
Winter Garden Ct 77083
Winter Glen Ln 77072
Winter Harvest Ct 77059
Winter Knoll Way 77062
Winter Oaks Dr 77079
Winter Park Ct & St 77067
Winter Rose Way 77083
Winter Run Dr 77064
Winter Stone 77084
Wintercove Ct 77082
Winterfair Dr 77082
Wintergrove Ct 77049
Winterhaven Dr 77087
N & S Wintersage Ln 77066
Winterwood Way 77013
Winthorne Ln 77066
Winthorpe Ct 77047
Winthrop St
3700-3899 77047
8000-8499 77075
Winthrop Bend Dr 77084
Winton St 77021
Winwood Ln 77024
Wipprecht St
1400-2399 77020
2900-6299 77026
Wirevine Ln 77072

Wirksworth Dr 77066
Wirt Rd
800-999 77024
1000-2499 77055
Wirtcrest Ln 77055
Wisdom Woods Ct & Way 77094
Wiseman Rd 77053
Wishing Well Ln 77088
Wisner Cir 77014
Wister Ct & Ln 77008
Wisteria Hill St 77073
Wisteria Hollow Ln 77062
Wisteria Park Dr 77072
Wisteria Ridge Ct 77095
Wisteria Run Ct 77062
Wisterwood Dr 77043
E Witcher Ln 77076
Witham Ct 77095
Withers Way Cir 77065
Withersdale Dr 77077
Witt Rd 77034
Witte Rd
1000-1399 77055
1400-1899 77080
Wittershaw Dr 77090
Woerner Rd 77090
Wolbrook St 77016
Wolcott Park Ln 77075
Wolf Ct 77024
Wolf Creek Pass 77067
Wolf Hollow Dr 77084
Wolf Run Ln 77065
Wolfboro Dr 77041
Wolfe Rd 77064
Wolfield Ln 77071
Wolfs Knl 77094
Wolheb Way 77089
Wolsley Ct 77065
Wonder Land Way 77084
Wood Ln 77024
Wood St 77002
Wood Bayou Dr 77013
Wood Bend Dr 77049
Wood Bluff Blvd 77040
Wood Branch Park Dr 77079
Wood Canyon Dr 77040
Wood Circle Ln 77015
Wood Creek Ct & Way 77017
Wood Dawn Ln 77015
Wood Downe Ln 77040
Wood Fall Ct 77014
Wood Forest Blvd & Dr 77013
Wood Glen Ln 77084
Wood Grove Ct 77040
Wood Heather Ln 77040
Wood Hollow Dr 77057
Wood Hollow Ln 77043
Wood Leaf Ct 77013
Wood Lodge Dr 77077
Wood Loop St 77015
Wood Mist Dr 77013
Wood Orchard Dr 77040
Wood River Dr 77085
Wood Shadows Dr 77013
Wood Smoke Dr 77013
Wood Spring Ln 77013
Wood Stone Walk Dr 77084
Wood Stork Ct & Ln 77044
Wood Terrace Dr 77038
Wood Trail Dr 77038
Wood Village Ln 77084
Wood Vista Dr 77013
Woodacre Dr 77049
Woodard St
200-1799 77009
2400-2999 77026
Woodbend Ln 77079
Woodbend Park N 77055
Woodbend Park S 77055
Woodbend Park W 77055
Woodbend Oaks Dr 77070
Woodbend Trail Dr 77070
Woodbend Village Ct 77055

Woodbine St 77017
Woodbough Ct & Dr 77038
Woodbourne Dr 77062
Woodbriar Dr 77068
Woodbrook Ln 77008
Woodbrook Way 77081
Woodbuck Trl 77013
Woodburn Dr 77049
Woodbury St 77030
Woodcamp Dr 77088
Woodcastle Bnd 77094
Woodchase Dr 77042
Woodchurch Ln 77073
Woodcliff Dr 77013
Woodcluster Ln 77073
Woodcombe Dr 77062
Woodcote Ct 77062
Woodcourt St 77076
Woodcraft St 77025
Woodcreek Ln 77073
Woodcreek Glen Ln 77073
Woodcreek Meadows Ln 77073
Woodcrest Dr 77018
Woodcroft Ct & Dr 77095
Wooddove Cir 77089
Wooded Pine Dr 77073
Wooded Valley Dr 77095
Woodedge Dr
9800-10999 77070
11000-11399 77065
Wooden Oak Ct 77059
Woodfair Dr 77036
Woodfern Dr 77040
Woodfield Ln 77073
Woodfin St 77025
Woodford Dr 77015
Woodforest Blvd & Ct 77015
Woodfox St 77025
Woodgate St 77039
Woodglen Dr 77084
Woodgreen St 77033
Woodham Dr 77073
Woodhaven St 77025
Woodhead St
1300-2599 77019
2600-5299 77098
Woodhill Rd 77008
Woodhorn Ct & Dr 77062
Woodhurst St 77013
Woodico Dr 77038
Wooding St 77011
Woodington Dr 77038
Woodkerr St 77045
Woodknoll Ln 77071
Woodknot Dr 77089
Woodlake Sq 77063
E Woodland St 77009
Woodland Creek Ln 77095
Woodland Forest Dr 77088
Woodland Gate Dr 77040
Woodland Glade Dr 77066
Woodland Haven Rd 77062
Woodland Oaks Ct & Dr 77040
Woodland Park Dr
1700-2699 77077
2700-3299 77082
Woodland Pine Dr 77040
Woodland Plaza Dr 77084
Woodland Springs St 77077
Woodland Trails Dr
6400-6499 77088
7100-7199 77040
Woodland West Dr 77040
Woodland Willows Dr 77083
Woodlark St 77017
Woodleigh Dr 77083
Woodleigh St 77023
Woodlett Ct 77095
Woodline Dr 77015
Woodlite Ln 77015
Woodlong Dr 77088
Woodlyn Rd
7800-8699 77028
8800-9399 77078

Woodmaple Ct 77015
Woodmeadow St 77025
Woodmill Pl 77082
Woodmont Dr 77045
Woodmoss Dr 77037
Woodnettle Ct & Ln 77086
Woodnook Dr 77077
Woodoak Dr 77040
Woodpath Ln 77075
Woodpecker St 77035
Woodport Ln 77090
Woodridge Dr
2800-7199 77087
7200-7299 77012
Woodridge Pl 77055
Woodridge Cove Dr 77087
Woodridge Manor Dr 77087
Woodridge Row Dr 77087
Woodridge Square Dr 77087
Woodring Ct & Dr 77045
Woodrow St 77006
Woodruff St 77012
Woods Bridge Way 77007
Woods Edge Ln 77024
Woodsage Dr 77024
Woodsborough Cir 77055
Woodsdale Blvd & Ct 77038
Woodshaver Dr 77013
Woodshire St 77025
Woodside Dr 77062
Woodside St 77023
Woodsman Trl 77040
Woodson Rd 77060
Woodson Park Dr 77044
Woodson Valley Ct & Dr 77016
Woodsorrel Dr 77084
Woodspire Dr 77085
Woodstone St 77024
Woodthorpe Ln
12300-12599 77024
13800-14999 77079
Woodtown Dr 77038
Woodtrek Ln 77015
Woodvale St 77012
Woodvalley Dr
3500-3719 77025
3721-3899 77025
4300-4499 77096
Woodville Gardens Dr 77077
Woodvine Dr 77055
Woodvine Trl 77072
Woodvine Place Ct 77055
Woodviolet Dr 77089
Woodward St 77051
Woodward Gardens Dr 77082
Woodway Dr
4500-4599 77024
4800-5699 77056
5700-6599 77057
7500-8899 77063
Woodway Oaks Ln 77056
Woodway Place Ct 77057
Woodwick St
7600-8899 77028
9900-10699 77016
Woodwild Dr 77038
Woodwind Dr & Ln N & S 77025
Woodwind Lakes Dr 77040
Woodwolf Ct 77015
Woody Ln 77093
Woody Oaks Dr 77095
Woodyard Dr 77073
Woolford Dr 77065
Woolwich Dr 77032
Woolworth St
100-1199 77020
3800-4899 77026
Wordsworth St 77030
World Houston Pkwy 77032
Worms St 77020
Worrell Dr 77045
Wortham Blvd 77065
Wortham Ct 77065
Wortham Way 77033

Wortham Brook Ln 77065
Wortham Center Dr 77065
Wortham Falls Blvd 77065
Wortham Gate Dr 77065
Wortham Grove Blvd 77065
Wortham Landing Dr 77065
Worthington Dr 77083
Worthington St 77093
Worthshire St 77008
Wortley Dr 77084
Wovenwood Ln 77041
Wray Ct 77088
Wren Ln 77079
Wren Crossing Dr 77038
Wren Forest Ln 77084
Wrencrest Ln 77073
Wrenstone Dr 77068
Wrenthorpe Dr 77031
Wrenwood Cir 77099
Wrenwood Lks 77043
Wrenwood Mnr 77043
Wrenwood Park 77043
Wressell Cir & Dr 77044
Wright Rd
3500-5499 77032
7000-7999 77041
Wright Oaks Dr 77014
Wrightwood St 77009
Wrigley St 77045
Wroxton Ct & Rd 77005
Wunder Ln 77091
Wunderlich Dr 77069
Wuthering Heights Dr 77045
Ww Thorne Blvd 77073
Wyandott Blvd 77040
Wyatt St 77023
Wyatt Oak Ln 77044
Wycliffe Dr
300-999 77079
1200-2299 77043
Wycomb Dr & Ln 77070
Wylie St 77026
Wynberry Dr 77041
Wynbourn Ct & Way 77083
Wynbrook St 77061
Wyndale St 77030
N & S Wynden Ct & Dr 77056
Wynden Commons Ln 77056
Wynden Creek Dr 77056
Wynden Crescent Ct 77056
N Wynden Estates Ct 77056
Wynden Oaks Ct & Dr 77056
Wynden Oaks Garden Dr 77056
Wynden Place Ln 77056
Wynden Trace Ln 77056
Wynden Villa Dr 77056
Wyndham Ct 77040
Wyndham Ln 77083
Wyndham Village Dr 77040
Wyne St 77017
Wynell St 77022
Wynlea St 77061
Wynmeadow Dr 77061
Wynne St 77009
Wynnewood St 77013
Wynnpark Dr 77008
Wynnwood Ln 77008
Wynona St 77087
Wynrun Ct 77038
Wyoming St 77021
Wyrick St 77026
Wysall Cliff Ct 77064
Wyte Ln 77093
Xenophon Dr 77082
Yale St
2-98 77007
100-899 77007
900-1099 77008
1050-1050 77248
1050-1050 77270
1100-2898 77008
1101-2899 77008
3000-5199 77018
5200-5599 77091

5600-6400 77076
6402-7098 77076
7900-8599 77037
Yampa Ln 77040
Yancy Dr 77015
Yarberry St
14600-14999 77039
15000-15299 77032
Yarbo Creek Dr 77082
Yardmaster Trl 77034
Yarmouth St 77028
Yarrow Crest Ct 77085
Yarwell Dr 77096
Yates St 77020
Yaupon Holly Ln 77044
Yaupon Square Ln 77008
Yearling Cir 77065
Yearling Ct 77065
Yearling Dr 77065
Yearling Mdws 77094
Yearling Branch Dr 77075
Yearling Colt Ct 77038
Yeatmah Ln 77067
Yellow Pine Dr 77040
Yellow Rail Dr 77044
Yellow Tulip Trl 77079
Yellowstone Blvd
3000-3216 77054
3217-3297 77021
3218-3298 77054
3299-5200 77021
5202-6998 77021
Yellowstone Way Dr 77054
Yestereve Ct 77084
Yoakum Blvd 77006
Yoe St
7200-7799 77016
8000-8099 77078
Yolandita 77075
Yore Ln 77044
Yorenern St 77061
York Mdws 77084
York St 77003
N York St 77003
York Bend Ln 77044
York Creek Dr
1300-1399 77090
1400-1799 77014
York Hollow Ln 77044
Yorkchester Dr 77079
Yorkdale Dr 77091
Yorkfield St 77040
N & S Yorkglen Dr 77084
Yorkglen Manor Ln 77084
Yorkhampton Dr 77084
Yorkingham Dr 77066
Yorklyn Dr 77066
Yorkpoint Dr 77084
Yorkshire St
500-1299 77022
3200-3399 77093
4000-4199 77016
Yorkshire Oaks Dr 77065
Yorkstone Dr 77024
Yorktown St 77056
Yorktown Colony Dr 77084
Yorktown Crossing Pkwy 77084
Yorktown Meadow Ln 77084
Yorktown Plaza Dr 77040
Yorkwood St
2900-2999 77093
5200-5899 77016
Yosemite St 77021
Yosemite Glen Trl 77038
Young St 77034
N Young Elm Cir 77073
Youngberry St 77044
Younglake Blvd 77084
Youngtree Cir 77084
N & S Youngwood Ln 77043
Youpon St 77044
Youpon Hill Ct 77084
Youpon Lake Ct 77084
Youpon Leaf Way 77084
Youpon Valley Ct & Dr 77073

Youpon Wood Ct 77062
Yucca Mountain Dr 77090
Yucca Tip Ln 77073
Yuma St 77029
Yupon St 77006
Yupon Ridge Dr 77072
Yupondale Dr 77080
Yvonne Dr 77044
Zachary St 77029
Zada Park Ln 77088
Zagar Ln 77090
Zaka Rd 77064
Zapata Dr 77083
Zarroll Dr 77099
Zarzana Aly 77020
Zavalla St 77085
Zedan Way Dr 77044
Zelma Dr 77076
Zenith St 77045
Zephyr St 77021
Zephyr Glen Way 77084
Zilonis Ct 77040
Zimmermann Dr 77088
Zinnia Dr 77095
Zircon Ct 77099
Zoch Ln 77092
Zoe St 77020
Zoemark Ln 77021
Zola Rd 77076
Zoltowski St 77020
Zoo Circle Dr 77030
Zora St 77055
Zuinn St 77086
Zume St 77088
Zurich Ct 77070

NUMBERED STREETS

1st St 77044
2nd St 77044
E 2nd St 77007
3rd St 77044
E & W 4th 77007
E 4th 1/2 St 77007
5th St 77064
11600-11699 77044
11900-12299 77072
E 5th St 77007
W 5th St 77007
E 5th 1/2 St 77007
6th St
10100-10199 77064
11900-12299 77072
W 6th St 77007
E 6th 1/2 St
600-799 77007
1000-1199 77009
7th St
11800-11900 77044
11901-11911 77072
11902-11912 77044
11913-12299 77072
E 7th St
200-398 77007
400-799 77007
1000-1199 77009
W 7th St 77007
7th 1/2 St 77044
E 7th 1/2 St
601-607 77007
609-799 77007
1000-1199 77009
W 7th 1/2 St 77007
8th St 77044
E 8th St 77007
W 8th St 77007
E 8th 1/2 St 77007
9th St 77044
E 9th St 77007
W 9th St 77007
10th St 77044
E 10th St 77008
W 10th St 77008
E & W 10th 1/2 77008
W 11th Pl 77005
11th St 77044

E 11th St
100-799 77008
1000-1199 77009
W 11th St
200-3699 77008
3800-4099 77055
E 11th 1/2 St 77008
E 12th St 77008
100-3699 77008
3700-4499 77055
E 12th 1/2 St 77008
E & W 13th 77008
E 13th 1/2 St 77008
E 14th St
100-799 77008
800-1199 77009
W 14th St 77008
W 14th 1/2 St 77008
E & W 15th 77008
W 15th 1/2 St 77008
E 16th St
100-799 77008
1000-1199 77009
W 16th St 77008
E & W 17th 77008
E 18th St 77008
100-2799 77008
4400-4799 77092
E & W 19th 77008
E & W 20th 77008
E & W 21st 77008
E & W 22nd 77008
E 23rd St
100-799 77008
800-1299 77009
W 23rd St 77008
E 24th St
100-799 77008
800-1299 77009
W 24th St 77008
E 25th St
100-799 77008
800-1199 77009
W 25th St 77008
E 26th St
100-699 77008
700-1299 77009
W 26th St 77008
E 27th St
100-629 77008
631-699 77008
700-1399 77009
628 1/2-628 1/2 77008
W 27th St 77008
E 28th St
100-699 77008
700-1400 77009
W 28th St 77008
E 29th St
300-699 77008
700-1399 77009
E & W 30th 77018
E 31st St
200-212 77018
214-509 77018
511-523 77018
600-1599 77022
W 31st St 77018
E 31st 1/2 St 77018
E 32nd St
100-599 77018
600-1299 77022
W 32nd St 77018
E 32nd 1/2 St 77022
E 33rd St
100-599 77018
600-1599 77022
W 33rd St 77018
E 34th St
200-599 77018
600-1499 77022
W 34th St
200-2499 77018
3400-6399 77092
W 34th 1/2 St 77018
E 35th St
200-499 77018
500-1499 77022
W 35th St 77018
E 36th St
200-499 77018
500-1499 77022
E 37th St
100-499 77018
500-1199 77022
E 38th St
100-499 77018
500-1199 77022
W 38th St 77018
E 39th St
100-399 77018
500-1099 77022
W 39th St 77018
E 40th St
300-399 77018
400-1499 77022
E 40th 1/2 St
100-499 77018
500-1399 77022
E 41st St
100-199 77018
300-799 77022
W 41st St 77018
E 42nd St
100-299 77018
300-899 77022
W 42nd St 77018
E 42nd 1/2 St 77018
E 43rd St
100-299 77018
300-899 77022
W 43rd St
700-2299 77018
4300-7299 77092
1820-1-1820-9 77018
E & W 44th 77018
E 45th St 77018
S 65th 77011
S 66th 77011
S 69th St 77011
70th St 77011
71st St 77011
S 72nd 77011
73rd St 77011
S 74th 77011
S 74th 1/2 St 77011
75th St 77011
S 75th St
100-300 77011
302-398 77011
501-597 77023
599-999 77023
76th St 77012
S 77th 77012
S 78th 77012
S 79th 77012
S 80th 77012
92nd St 77012
93rd St 77012
95th St 77012
96th St 77012
97th St 77012
NW 100 Dr 77092

HUMBLE TX

General Delivery 77338

POST OFFICE BOXES MAIN OFFICE STATIONS AND BRANCHES

Box No.s
All PO Boxes 77347

RURAL ROUTES

03, 17, 26, 32, 36, 52 77338
07, 10, 54 77396

NAMED STREETS

Abidie Gardens Dr 77396
Acapulco Cove Ct & Dr 77346
Acapulco Village Dr 77338
Ackley Dr 77396
Adams Ridge Ln 77346
Admiral Oak Ct 77346
Adobe Rose Dr 77396
Adobe Stone Dr 77396
Aerobic Ave 77346
Agile Pines Dr 77346
Alabaster Oaks Ln 77396
Alan Thai Ln 77396
Albert Dr 77396
Aldercy 77338
Aldine Bender Rd 77396
Aldine Westfield Rd 77338
Aleutian Bay Ct & Ln 77346
Alex Landing Dr 77396
Alinawood Ct & Dr 77346
Alisa Bend Ct 77396
Allegro Shores Ln 77346
Allenham Ct & Ln 77338
Allison Dr 77396
Almond Grv 77396
Alpine Brook Ln 77396
Alsea Bay Ct 77346
Alyssa Ct 77396
Alyssa Gardens Ln 77396
Amber Ash Ct 77346
Amber Cove Dr 77346
Amber Pine Ct 77346
Ambergate Dr 77396
Ambergris Ct 77338
Amy Brook Ct 77396
Anchor Bay Ln 77346
Ancient Forest Dr 77346
Ancient Oaks Dr 77346
Andeldel Dr 77346
Andrews Ridge Ln 77396
Angler Dr 77346
Anne Ave 77338
Antler Ln 77338
Apache Point Dr 77396
Appaloosa Ridge Dr 77338
Apple Hollow Ct & Ln 77396
Aquatic Dr 77346
Arapaho Hill Ln 77346
Arbolada Green Ct 77346
Arbor Bend Ct 77346
Arbor Grove Ln 77338
Arbor Knoll Ct 77346
Arbor Pines Ln 77346
Arbor Trace Ln 77396
Arbor Walk Dr 77338
Arbury Ln 77396
Arbury Glen Ln 77338
Arcadia Park Ln 77338
Arcadia Point Ln 77346
Arcaro Glen Ct 77346
Arenas Timbers Dr 77346
Arizona Sky Ct 77396
Arkansas Post Ln 77346
Armbull Ct 77346
Arnette Park Ln 77346
Arrington Forest Ln 77338
Arrow Cove Ct & Dr 77346
Arrowhead Terrace Ln 77396
Arrowsmith Dr 77338
Artesian Way 77346
Artesian Plaza Dr 77338
Ashe Park Ct 77346
Ashford Springs Ln 77396
Ashland Pines Ln 77396
Ashley Creek Ct 77396
Ashtex Dr 77396
Ashton Grove Ct 77396
Ashwood Dr 77338
Aspen Chase Ln 77396
Aspen Haze Ln 77396
Aspen Leaf Ln 77396
Aspen Trace Ln 77338
Atasca Creek Dr 77346
Atasca Oaks Dr 77346
Atasca South Ct & Dr 77346
Atasca Villas Dr 77346
Atasca Woods Trce & Way 77346
Atascocita Rd
100-3999 77396
4000-4048 77346
4050-7299 77346
Atascocita Trl 77346
Atascocita Way 77396
Atascocita Bend Dr 77396
Atascocita Forest Dr 77346
Atascocita Lake Dr & Way 77346
Atascocita Meadows Dr 77346
Atascocita Park Dr 77346
Atascocita Pines Dr 77346
Atascocita Place Dr 77346
Atascocita Point Dr 77346
Atascocita Shores Dr 77346
Atascocita Timbers N 77346
Atascocita Trace Dr 77346
Atascocita West Trl 77346
Atlanta St 77396
Atwood Hills Ln 77338
Auburn Ash Cir 77346
Auburn Oak Trl 77346
Auburn Pine Ct 77346
Audubon Forest Dr 77396
August Sunset Dr 77396
Aurelia Mist Ln 77396
Aurora Park Ln 77338
Autumn Creek Ln 77346
Aveleigh Ln 77396
N & S Avenue 77338
N & S Avenue A 77338
N & S Avenue B 77338
N & S Avenue C 77338
N & S Avenue D 77338
N & S Avenue F 77338
N & S Avenue G 77338
N & S Avenue H 77338
Avonlake Ln 77396
Badlands Bend Ln 77346
Bailey Hills Ln 77346
Baileys Town Ct 77346
Bainbrook Ln 77396
Baird Mount Ct 77346
Baker Rd 77338
Balie Ln 77338
Bambiwoods Ct & Dr 77346
Bandera Creek Ln 77346
Banff Springs Ct 77346
Banks St 77338
Banner Ridge Ln 77396
Barlow Springs Ln 77396
Barnhill Dr 77338
Barr Spring Dr 77396
Barry Ln 77346
Barton Grove Ln 77396
Bass Point Way 77396
Baton Pass 77346
Baumgartner Dr 77338
E Bay Crest Cir 77346
Bayou Mead Ct & Trl 77346
Bayou Ridge Dr 77338
Beacon Tree Ct 77346
Bear River Ln 77346
Bearden Creek Ln 77396
Bearden Falls Ln 77396
Beatty Dr 77396
Beaver Lake Ct 77346
Beckett Creek Ln 77396
Beckett Ridge Dr 77346
Bedell Bridge Ln 77346
Bedford Peak Ct 77346
Beigewood Dr & Ln 77338
Bell Timbers St 77346
Bellaw Woods Dr 77338
Belle Way Dr 77396
Belleau Wood Dr 77338
Bellows Falls Ln 77396
N Bender Ave 77338
S Bender Ave 77338
Bender Ct 77396
Bender Rd 77396
Bent Pine Dr 77346
Bent Tree Ct 77346
Beretta Bend Dr 77396
Bering Bridge Ln 77346
Big Basin Ln 77346
Big Spring Trl 77346
Big Timber Ct & Dr 77346
Bighorn River Ln 77346
Biltmore St 77396
Birch Arbor Ct 77396
Birchbark Dr 77338
Birchridge Dr 77338
Birchwood Dr 77338
Birnam Wood Blvd 77338
Biscayne Pass Ln 77346
Bishops Gate Ln 77338
Bison Back Dr 77346
Black Crickett Ct 77396
Black Tooth Way 77396
Blackmyrtle Dr 77396
Blackstone River Dr 77346
Blackstone Trails Dr 77396
Bladon Dr 77396
Blanca Springs Ct & Way 77346
Blanca Terrace Dr 77396
Blanco Pines Dr 77346
Blue Cedar Ln 77338
Blue Forest Dr 77346
Blue Jay Cir 77396
Blue Lake Dr 77338
Blue Lake View Ln 77338
Blue Mist Ct 77338
Blue Spruce Hill St 77346
Bluebird Bnd 77396
Bluebird Park Ln 77338
Bluejay Twin Cir 77396
Bluewater Cove Dr 77346
Bluff Trail Dr 77338
Bolton Bridge Ln 77346
Boness Rd 77396
Bonham Lakes Ln 77396
Bonham Park Ln 77338
Bonhamford Ct 77396
Booners Cove Ct 77346
Borders Dr 77338
Bordersville Church Rd 77338
Boughton Ln 77396
Boulder Bay Ln 77346
E Boulder Cliff Ln 77396
Bower Rd 77338
Boxster Ct 77396
Boysen Ct 77346
Brandy Creek Ct & Ln 77338
Brannon Hill Ln 77346
Brannon Point Ln 77396
Branson Park Ln 77338
Brayden Rock Ln 77346
Brazos Bend Trl 77346
Brenda Ln 77338
Brewer Ln 77338
Brian St 77396
Briar Oak Dr 77338
Bridgedale Ln 77338
Bridger Bend Ln 77346
Brightstone Dr 77338
Brilliant Lake Dr 77396
Bristol Bay Ct 77346
Broad Vale Cir 77346
Broadmark Ln 77338
Broken Trace Ct 77338
Bronze Trail Dr 77346
Broze Rd 77338
Brushy Arbor Ln 77396
Bryce Manor Ct & Ln 77346
Bryce Mill Ct 77346
Buck Island Ct 77346
Buckeye Glen Ln 77338
Buckow Dr 77396
Buffalo Peak Ct 77346
Bunker Bend Ct & Dr 77346
Bunting Ct 77396
Burle Oak Dr 77346
Burle Oaks Ct 77346
Burnt Ash Dr 77338
Butano Springs Ln 77346
Butterfly Path Dr 77396
Bytrail Ct 77346
Cabin Green Ct 77346
Caddy Cir 77346
Caelwood Dr 77346
Caitlyn Falls Ln 77396
Caldicote St 77346
Caldwalder Ln 77396
Caldwell Pointe Ct 77346
Cambridge Village Dr 77338
Camden Hollow Ln 77396
Caminito Trl 77346
Camp Lillie Rd 77346
Campers Crest Dr 77346
Canary Ln 77396
Cane River Ln 77346
Canoe Crest Ct 77346
Canterbury Dr 77338
Cantertrot Dr 77338
Canton Trce 77338
Canton Cliff Ct 77346
Canton Hills Ct 77346
Canyon Ln 77346
Canyon Lakes Trace Dr 77396
Canyon Shore Dr 77396
Cape Lookout Way 77346
Cape Sable Ct 77346
Capewood Dr 77396
N & S Caprock Way 77346
Caprock Cove Ln 77396
Cardinal Ln 77396
Carina Forest Ct 77396
Carisbrook Ln 77338
Carmelwood Ct & Ln 77338
Carmine Oak Ct 77346
Caroline Ridge Dr 77396
Caroling Oaks Ct 77346
Carolyn Ct 77338
Carpenter Rd 77396
Carr Creek Ln 77346
Carriage Oak Cir 77346
Carriage Park Dr 77396
Carrington Ridge Ln 77346
Carver Ave 77338
Cascade House Ct & Dr 77396
Cascadia Knoll Ct 77346
Cascading Springs Ln 77346
Castle Rain Dr 77346
Catamaran Dr 77346
Catbird Ct 77396
Cattail Gate Ct 77396
Cave Creek Ct & Dr 77346
Caven St 77396
Cedar Cir & Ln 77396
Cedar Breaks Ct 77346
Cedar Grove Ct 77346
Cedar Jump Dr 77346
Cedar Key Trl 77346
Cedar Pond Dr 77396
Cedarwood Dr 77338
Chalkstone Ln 77396
Chamisal Ct 77396
Chancewood Ln 77338
Chaplin Place Dr 77396
Charles St 77338
Charleston Sq 77338
Charpiot Ln 77396
Chaste Tree Ln 77338
Chateau Gate Ct 77396
Chatsworth Sky Ct 77346
Cheeca Lodge Ln 77346
Cherry Oaks Ln 77346
Cherry Place Ct 77346
Chestnut Crest Dr 77346
Chestnut Hollow Ct 77346
Chipplegate Ln 77338
Clairfield Ln 77338
Clanton Pines Dr 77396
Clara Vista Dr 77396
Claretfield Ct 77338
Clear Dale Dr 77346
Clear Fork Dr 77396
Clear Glen Dr 77346
Clear Sky Dr 77346
Clearwater Xing 77396
Cleburn Lakes Dr 77396
Cleeve Close 77346
Cliff Ln 77338
Climbing Oaks Dr 77346
Clover Creek Point Ln 77346
Clover Land Ct 77338
Clover Park Dr 77346
Cloyanna Ln 77346
Club Point Dr 77346
Cluster Oaks Dr 77346
Clydesdale Ridge Dr 77338
Cold River Ct & Dr 77396
Cold Spring St 77396
Coldwater Meadow Ln 77338
Cole Point Dr 77396
Colonial Falls Ln 77396
Colony Ln 77396
Colorado Dr 77396
Colt Creek Ct 77346
Comet View Ct 77396
Commons Cove Ct 77396
Commons Walk Ln 77396
Conifer Ridge Way 77346
Continental Pkwy 77346
Coon Tree Ct 77346
Cooper Breaks Dr 77346
Coral Rose Ct 77396
Corburt Bend Ct 77346
Cordell Falls Ct 77346
Cordoba Ct 77346
Cormorant Ct 77396
Coronado Park Ln 77346
Cottonglade Ln 77338
Cottonwood Cir 77396
Country Side Ln 77338
Country Village Blvd 77338
Craighill Pl 77338
Crater Lake Ct 77346
Creek Water Ln 77396
Crescent Bridge Ct 77396
Crescent Mountain Ln 77346
Crescent Royale Way 77346
Crescent Valley Ln 77346
Crestline Rd 77396
Cricket Mill Dr 77346
Crimson Oak Cir & Trl 77346
Criswell Dr 77396
Crockett Bend Ct & Ln 77346
Crockett Canyon Ct 77346
Cross Country Dr 77346
Crosstrees Ln 77396
Crystal Isle Ln 77396
Culross Ct 77346
Culross Close 77346
Cumberland Park Ln 77346
Cypress Cir & Dr 77396
Cypresswood Dr 77338
Cypresswood Point Ave 77338
Cyril Dr 77396
Dain Place Dr 77338
Dale Forest Ct 77346
Dalegrove Ct 77346
Danalyn Ct 77346
Dappled Trl 77346
Dappled Grove Trl 77346
Dappled Ridge Way 77338
Darthouth Chase Dr 77396
Davenport Hills Ln 77346
Davis St 77338
Dawn Mist Ct & Dr 77346
Dawn Shadows Dr 77346
Dawn Star Dr 77346
Dawn Timbers Ct 77338
Dawnburst Dr 77346
Dawnmist Ct 77346
De Lorean Ct 77396
Deaton Dr 77346
Decathalon Ct 77346
Dee Oaks Dr 77346
Dee Woods Dr 77346
Deep Dale Dr 77338
Deep Shade Ct 77346

Deer Crossing Dr 77346
Deer Run Dr 77338
Deer Timbers Trl 77346
Deerbrook Park Blvd 77338
Deerwood Lake Dr 77346
Defee St 77338
Delfan Cir 77396
Delicado Dr 77396
Deloache Ave 77338
Delta Wood Trl 77346
Dempsey Oaks Dr 77346
Denali Ln 77346
Dennis St 77338
Derrick Dr 77338
Desco Dr 77338
Devlin Dr 77346
Dewberry Shores Ln 77396
Diamond M Dr 77346
Diamond Peak Ct 77346
Diane Manor Ln 77396
Dinero Dr 77346
Discus Dr 77346
Dockside Hill Ln 77346
Dogwood Dr 77338
Dogwood Trail Dr 77346
Dolphin Arc Dr 77346
N Dominion Falls Ln 77396
Donata Cir 77338
Dorylee Ln 77396
Dove Cove Cir 77396
Dove Forest Ln 77346
Dover Falls Ct 77338
Dragonfly Meadow Ct 77396
Drake Field Ln 77338
Drakeland Dr 77396
Drawbridge Dr 77396
Drew Forest Ln 77346
Droitwich Dr 77346
Droxshire Dr 77338
Dry Ridge Ct 77346
Dunbar Ave 77338
Dunbar Cave Ct 77346
Duncan Ln 77338
Dune Gate Ct 77396
Duneberry Trl 77346
Durham Ridge Ln 77346
Dutch Harbor Ln 77346
Dwyer Dr 77396
Eagle Hollow Dr 77338
Eagle Mills Ct 77338
Eagle Nest Ln 77396
Eagle Pass Falls Ct 77346
Eagle Springs Pkwy 77346
Eagles Ledge Ct 77338
Early Autumn Ct 77396
Early Fall Dr 77338
Eastern Bluebird Dr 77396
Eastway Village Dr 77338
Ebeys Landing Ln 77346
Echo Peak Ln 77396
Echo Pines Ct & Dr 77346
Eddie Dr 77396
Eddy St 77338
Edward Dr 77396
Egret Lake Way 77346
El Dorado Dr 77396
Elk Lake Ct 77346
Elkfield Ln 77338
Elkgrove Ln 77338
Elkhorn Ln 77338
Elkway Ln 77338
Ellenberger Ave 77396
Ellis Springs Ln 77396
Elm Cir 77396
Elm Drake Ln 77338
Elm Fork Dr 77396
Elm Valley Ct 77346
Elmbend Ct 77338
Elmtex Dr 77396
Elmwood Ave 77338
Emerald Ash Ct 77346
Emerald Glade Ln 77396
Emerald Meadow Ln 77396
Emerald Spruce Ct 77346
Emery Mills Ln 77338
Emily Springs Ct 77396
Emory Brook Ct 77346
Encenada Green Trl 77346
Enchanted Mist Dr 77346
Enchanted Rock Trl 77346
Enchanted Timbers Dr 77346
Engle Forest Cir 77346
English Brook Cir 77346
Entrada Ct 77346
Escala Dr 77338
Evening Shades Ct 77346
Evergreen Trace Ln 77346
Everhart Brook Ln 77346
Everhart Key Ln 77338
Fair Oak Dale Ln 77346
Fair Park Ct 77346
Fairway Island Dr 77346
Faith Mills Stream Dr 77338
Falcon Crest Dr 77346
Falcon Forest Ct & Dr 77346
Falcon Hill St 77338
Falcon Ridge Dr 77396
Falcongate Ct 77338
Falcons Talon Cove Ln 77396
Fall Creek Bnd & Xing 77396
Fall Creek Bend Ct 77396
Fall Creek Preserve Dr 77396
Fall Creek View Dr 77396
Fall Foliage Dr 77338
Fall River Pass Ct & Ln 77346
Fall Springs Ln 77396
Farm Ridge Ln 77338
Farmingham Rd 77346
Farrell Rd 77338
Favor Bend Ct & Dr 77396
Fawn Hollow Ct 77346
Fawn Park Ct 77396
Fawn Trail Ln 77346
Faye Oaks Ct & Dr 77346
Fenham Ln 77338
W Ferguson St 77338
Fern Creek Trl 77346
Fernwood Cir 77338
Ferrari Dr 77396
Field Cottage Ln 77338
Field House Ct 77338
Fieldtree Dr 77338
Fieldwick Ln 77338
Finch Landing Ln 77338
Finn Way Dr 77396
Fiorella Way 77346
Fir Hollow Cir 77346
Fire Sage Ct & Dr 77396
Firesign Dr 77346
Fisher Rd 77338
Fisher Grove Ln 77346
Fisher River Ln 77346
Flamingo Park 77396
Flax Bourton St 77346
Flax Bourton Close 77346
Flaxwood Dr 77346
Fleming Springs Ct & Dr 77396
Flower Bridge Ct 77396
Fm 1960 Rd E
2100-4099 77338
4100-8730 77346
8732-8778 77346
Fm 1960 Rd W
3101-3107 77338
3109-7300 77338
7231-7231 77205
7302-10010 77338
7371-10099 77338
4701-1-4701-2 77338
Fm 1960 Bypass Rd E & W 77338
Forest Fern Ct & Dr 77346
Forest Glade Dr 77338
Forest Glen Dr 77338
Forest Light Ct 77338
Forest Magic Ln 77338
Forest Point Dr 77338
Forest Rain Ln 77346
Forest Shadows Dr 77338
Forest Stream Dr 77346
Forest Timbers Cir, Ct & Dr 77346
Forest Trace Dr 77346
Forest Vista Dr 77338
Fort Dupont Ln 77346
Fossil Canyon Dr 77396
Fossil Point Ct & Ln 77346
Fossil Ridge Ln 77346
Fosters Run Ln 77396
Fountain Lilly Dr 77346
Fountain Stone Ln 77396
Fox Cliff Ln 77338
Fox Cove Trl 77338
Fox Cub Ln 77338
Fox Forest Trl 77338
Fox Glen Ln 77338
Fox Grove Ct & Ln 77338
Fox Hall Ln 77338
Fox Haven Ln 77338
Fox Hillside Way 77338
Fox Hound Ln 77338
Fox Knoll Ln 77338
Fox Manor Ln 77338
Fox Mesa Ln 77338
Fox Scene Dr 77338
Fox Star Ln 77338
Fox Stone Ln 77338
Fox Swift Ct 77338
Fox Trail Ln 77338
Fox Trot Ct 77338
Fox Walk Trl 77338
Foxbend Ln 77338
Foxbrick Ln 77338
Foxbrook Dr 77338
Foxchester Ln 77338
Foxcrest Ct & Ln 77338
Foxcroft Ln 77338
Foxfield Ln 77338
Foxglen Ln 77338
Foxhound Ln 77338
Foxhurst Ln 77338
Foxlodge Ln 77338
Foxmar Ln 77338
Foxmont Ln 77338
Foxport Ln 77338
Foxshadows Ln 77338
Foxside Ln 77338
Foxvalley Ln 77338
Foxvista Ln 77338
Foxwaithe Ln 77338
Foxwalk Ln 77338
Foxway Ln 77338
Foxwick Ln 77338
Foxwood Fair Ln 77338
Foxwood Forest Blvd, Ct & Trl 77338
Foxwood Garden Dr 77338
Foxwood Glen Ln 77338
Freedom River Dr 77338
Freemont Peak Ln 77346
Friesian Trl 77338
Friesian Meadow Ln 77338
Frost St 77396
Fuchsia Ln 77346
Gadsen St 77396
Gamble Oak Dr 77346
Garden Knoll Ln 77396
Garden Mist Ln 77346
Garnet Falls Ln 77396
Garnet Hill Ln 77346
Garretts Cove Ct 77396
Gaslight Knoll Dr 77396
Gastonbury Ln 77338
Gentry Shadows Ln 77396
Gerber Ln 77396
German Bend Dr 77396
Gianna Springs Ct 77396
Gila Cliff Ln 77346
Glacier Bay Ct 77346
Glacier Point Ct 77346
Gladewick Dr 77396
Glen Breeze Ct 77346
Glen Burn Ct 77346
Glen Crossing Cir 77346
Glen Grove St 77346
Glen Hollow Dr 77338
Glen Lee Dr 77396
Glen Valley Dr 77338
Glendo Ct 77346
Glenhew Rd 77396
Glenvine Dr 77396
Gnarled Oaks Ct 77346
Golden Bough Ln 77396
Golden Eagle Dr 77396
Golden Foliage Trl 77338
Golden Hawthorn Ct 77346
Golden Kings Ct 77346
Goldfinch Dr 77396
Grace Ln 77338
Graceful Bend Ln 77396
Grackle Run Ln 77338
Granberry St 77338
Grand Arches Ln 77346
Grand Field Ct 77338
Grand Linden Ct 77338
Grand Manor Ln 77396
Grand Portage Ln 77346
Grand Prairie Dr 77396
Grand Prix Dr 77396
Grandin Wood Ct 77338
Grandy St 77396
Granger St 77338
Granite Park Way 77396
Granite Woods Ct 77346
Grants Creek Ct 77346
Grayton Edge Ct 77346
Great Frst 77346
Great Basin Ct 77346
Great Forest Ct 77346
Great Laurel Ct 77346
Great Sands Ct & Dr 77346
Green Manor Dr 77396
Green Summer Ln 77338
Green Timbers Dr 77346
Greenbranch Dr 77338
Greencape Ct 77396
Greenfield Trl 77346
Greens Rd 77396
Greenstill Dr 77346
Guadalupe Trail Ct & Ln 77346
Guildwick Cir 77338
Gypsy Forest Dr 77346
Hagilbert Ct 77338
Hailey Springs Ln 77396
Halcyon Days Dr 77338
Half Moon Ct & Trl 77346
Half Volley Cir 77346
Hamblen Dr 77396
Hamill House Dr 77396
Hampton Hills Dr 77338
Hannah Oaks Ln 77396
Hapsburg St 77396
Harbor Canyon Dr 77396
Harbour Lake Ct 77396
Hardwood Dale Way 77338
Harmony Hall Ln 77346
Harvest Glen Dr 77346
Harveys Way 77396
Haven Meadows Ln 77396
Havens Edge Ct 77338
Haverhill Dr 77338
Haviland Falls Dr 77396
Hawes 77396
Hawk Park 77396
Hawthorne Hill Cir 77346
Hayden Springs Ct 77396
Haylee Way 77338
Hayley Springs Ct 77396
Hazy Brook Ln 77346
Heart Grove Dr 77346
Heartland Ct 77346
Heather Grove Ct 77346
Heaton Hall St 77338
Heavy Anchor Ln 77396
Hedge Maple Ct 77346
Heidi Oaks Ln 77396
Heritage Pines Dr 77346
Heritage Water Ct 77396
Herman St 77338
Heron Forest Ln 77346
Heron Park Ct & Dr 77396
Heronwood Dr 77346
Hickory Ashe Dr 77346
Hickory Branch Ln 77338
Hickory Canyon Ct 77396
Hickory Wind Dr 77346
Hickorytex Dr 77396
W Higgins St 77338
Highdale Ct 77346
Highland Branch Dr 77346
Highland Villa Ln 77396
Highmore Dr 77396
Hightower Ln 77338
Highway 59 N
14200-14398 77396
Highway 59 N
14400-18099 77396
18100-20999 77338
21001-21099 77338
Hikers Trail Dr 77346
Hill School Rd 77338
Hill Timbers Dr 77346
Hirsch Rd 77338
Hobby Forest Ln 77346
Hodges Run Ln 77396
Hollow Cir & Dr 77396
Homestead Rd 77396
Honey Creek Trl 77346
Honeysuckle Ln 77396
Honeysuckle Springs Rd 77346
Horizon Falls Ln 77396
Horton Landing Ln 77396
Hot Creek Ct & Trce 77346
N Houston Ave 77338
S Houston Ave
100-112 77338
114-1520 77338
1522-1598 77338
1600-1602 77396
1604-3199 77396
Howard St 77338
Huffman Ln 77338
Humble Pkwy 77338
Humble Brook Dr 77338
Humble Place Dr 77338
Humble Westfield Rd 77338
Hummingbird Ln 77396
Huntermoor Cir 77338
Hunters Village Dr 77346
Huntersglen Cir 77396
Huron Park Trl 77346
Hurst Forest Dr 77346
Hurst Wood Dr 77346
Ibis Pond Ln 77338
Imber Forest Ln 77346
Indian Cove Ct 77346
Indian Gardens Way 77396
Indian Lodge Ln 77396
Indian Maple Dr 77338
Indian Mountain Ln 77346
Indiana St 77396
International Vlg 77338
Inverloch Way 77338
Inverness Lake Dr 77346
Inwood Elm Cir 77346
Iris Creek Way 77338
Isaacks Rd 77338
Island Lake Loop E & W 77338
Isle Royale Ct 77346
Ivory Ash Ct 77346
Ivy Point Cir 77346
Ivy Wood Ct 77396
J M Hester St 77338
Jackson Creek Bend Ln 77396
Jade View Ct 77338
James Lndg 77396
Jamestown Crossing Ln 77346
January Dr 77346
Jarratt Sq 77338
Jasmine Leaf Trl 77338
Jasmine Meadows Ln 77346
Jasperwood Dr & Ln 77338
Jayci Park Ln 77396
Jeffrey Trl 77396
Jennings Rd 77396
Jetton Park Ln 77346
Jodywood Dr 77346
Joggers Ln 77338
Jones St 77338
Jordan Branch Ln 77396
Julie Meadows Ln 77396
Juliedale Dr 77396
June Forest Dr 77346
Juniper Green Trl 77346
Juniper Springs Dr 77338
Juniper Tree Ct 77346
Kacey Lane Ct 77346
Kathy St 77338
Kaybull Dr 77346
Kayla Springs Ln 77396
Keats Ct 77338
Keeling Trl 77346
Keely Woods Ct 77396
Keller Forest Ct 77346
Kelly Mill Ln 77346
Kelly Oaks Ct 77346
Kelly Pines Ct 77346
Kelly Timbers Dr 77346
Kemble Rd 77346
Ken St 77338
Kennemer Dr 77338
Kennesaw Mountain Ln 77346
Kens Ct & Run 77396
Kenswick Dr 77338
Kenswick Meadows Ct 77338
Kentington Oak Dr 77396
Kentucky Derby Cir 77346
Kenya Manor Dr 77396
Kerrybrook Ln 77396
Keyturn Ln 77346
Kildee Park 77396
Killdeer Ct & Ln 77396
Kimball Way Ln 77396
Kingfisher Ct & Dr 77396
Kings Pkwy 77346
Kings Clover Ct 77346
Kings Crown Ct 77346
Kings Hill Ln 77346
Kings Lake Estates Blvd 77346
Kings Oaks Ln 77346
Kings River Ct, Dr, Ln & Pt 77346
Kingsland Bay Ln 77346
Kingsriver Cir 77346
Kingston Falls Ln 77396
Kingwood Glen Dr 77346
Kinkaid Meadows Ln 77346
Kiowa Timbers Dr 77346
Kirk Forest Ct 77346
Kirkham Ln 77338
Kittydale Dr 77396
Kiwi Pl 77338
Knob Hill Lake Ln 77346
Knoll Forest Dr 77338
Kobuk Valley Cir 77346
Kracher Springs Dr 77396
Kristen Oaks Ct 77346
Kristen Park Ct & Ln 77346
Kristen Pine Dr 77346
Krone Ct 77396
Kurt Dr 77396
Kyack Ct 77346
Lafayette Hollow Ln 77346
Lago Forest Dr 77346
Lagovista Ct 77346
Lake Chelan Ln 77346
Lake Clark Ln 77346
W Lake Houston Pkwy 77346
Lake Malone Ct 77346
Lake Mead Ln 77346
Lake Mist Ct 77346
Lake Park Trl 77346
Lakeland Dr 77338
Lakelane Dr W 77338
Lakeshire St 77346
Lakeshore Villa Dr 77346
Lakeside View Ln 77396
Lakeview Dr 77338
Lakeway View Ln 77396
Landing Brook Dr 77346
Landsdown Ridge Way 77346
Landshire Dr 77338
Lansing Meadows Dr 77396
Lantana Branch Ln 77396
Laramie St 77396
Larchwood Dr 77396
Lark Ln 77396
Lark Hill St 77338
Lassen Forest Ln 77346
Laurel Leaf Ln 77346
Laurelton Ct & Dr 77396
Lauren Oaks Ln 77396
Laurenwood Ct 77396
Layton Ridge Dr 77396
Lazy Shadow Ct 77346
Lazy Timbers Dr 77346
Le Conte Ln 77338
Leafdale Ct & Dr 77338
Leafpark Ln 77338
Leaftex Dr 77396
Leaning Timbers Dr 77346
Lee Rd
14300-18098 77396
18100-21699 77338
Lee Oaks Ct 77338
Leens Lodge Ln 77346
Leewood Ct 77346
Legend Oak Dr 77346
Leighwood Creek Ct & Ln 77396
Leisure Place Dr 77346
Leo Creek Ln 77396
Level Pond Ln 77338
Lexington Sq 77338
Lexus Dr 77396
Liberty Point Ln 77338
Liberty Sky Ln 77346
Lido Park Ct 77396
Lighthouse Lake Ln 77346
Liles Ct & Ln 77396
Limber Bough Dr 77346
Lindale Rose Ln 77396
Linden Hills Ln 77338
Linden Hollow Dr 77396
Linden House Ct 77338
Lions Gate Ct & Dr 77338
Lionsgate Ln 77338
Little Fans Dr 77396
Little Shoe Ln 77396
Live Oak Dr
7500-7699 77396
20100-20299 77338
Lockhart Reach Ln 77396
Logan Falls Ln 77396
Loggia Ln 77396
Logging Trail Dr 77346
Lone Bridge Ln 77338
Lonesome Woods Trl 77346
Long Climb Cyn 77396
Long Hunter Ct 77346
Long Timber Dr 77346
Long Trace Dr 77346
Longs Peak Ln 77346
Lost Maples Ct 77346
Louie Welch Dr 77338
Lovis Way 77338
Lowell Lake Ln 77346
Loys Coves Ct 77396
Lucia Ln 77346
Lynn Ln 77338
Lynnbrook Falls Ln 77396
Mabels Island Ct 77346
Machaelas Way 77396
Macondray Dr 77346
Madison Boulder Ln 77346
Magenta Springs Dr 77346
Magnolia Cir 77396
Magnolia Bend Dr 77346
Magnolia Cove Ct 77346
Magnolia Glen Dr 77346

Mahan Wood Dr 77346
Main St 77338
Maize Clearing Trl 77338
Majestic Spring Ln 77396
Major Glen Cir 77346
Malardcrest Dr 77346
Malibu Creek Ln 77346
Malletia Dr 77338
Mallory Creek Dr 77396
Manasses Springs Ln 77346
Mango Ridge Ct 77396
Manning Rd 77338
Manor Way 77396
Maple Dr 77338
Maple Ln 77396
Maple Fox Dr 77338
Maple Gables Ln 77396
Maple Harvest Ln 77338
Maple Leaf Ln 77396
Maple Rapids Ct & Ln 77338
Maple Rock Dr 77396
Maple Spring Pl 77346
Maple Walk Dr 77346
Maples Perch Ct 77346
Marble Arch Ct 77338
Marblehead Ct & Dr 77338
Maria Amore St 77338
Marine Rd 77396
Mariner Pl 77346
Mariner Reef Way 77396
Mariposa Grove Ln 77346
Maris Way 77396
Marker Ridge Dr 77338
Marlin Waters Dr 77346
Marquette Point Ln 77346
Marsh Hawk St 77396
Martha Ln 77396
Martin Grove Ct 77338
Martin Luther King Dr 77338
Marvel Oak Ct 77346
Marwood Dr 77396
Mason Grove Ct 77346
Masterwood Ct 77346
Matagorda Lakes Dr 77396
Match Play Dr 77346
Match Point Cir 77346
Matt Cir & Rd 77346
Matthews Crest Ct 77396
Maywater Crest Ct 77346
Mcdannald Park Ln 77396
Mcdugald Rd 77338
Mckay Dr 77338
Mcknight Ln 77338
Meadow Belle Ct 77346
Meadow Ford Ct 77396
Meadow Rose Ct 77346
Medicine Bow Ct & Dr 77346
Meek Rd 77338
Megans Falls Ct 77396
N & S Memorial Blvd & Dr 77338
Memorial Glen Dr 77338
Memphis St 77396
Mercedes Benz Ct 77396
Merganser Ct 77396
Meridian Park Ln 77396
Merrillwood Dr 77346
Mesa Blvd & Dr 77396
Miami St 77396
Micheala Way 77338
Mile Run Rd 77346
Mill Rd 77396
Mill View Ln 77396
Milloak Dr 77346
Milloak Station Ct 77346
Millwood Cove Dr 77396
Mineral Bluff Ln 77346
Mineral Spring Cir & Ln 77396
Mira Blossom Dr 77346
Mist Creek Ln 77396
Misty Cove Ct 77346
Misty Lace Dr 77396
Misty Landing Ct 77396
Misty Meadow Creek Ln 77338
Misty Moon Dr 77346
Misty Morning Dr 77346
Misty Peak Ln 77346
Misty Pines Ct & Dr 77346
Misty Ridge Dr 77396
Misty Sage Ct 77396
Mitchell Pass Ln 77346
Mobile St 77396
Monarch Springs Ln 77396
Montgomery Ln 77338
Moonlight Ridge Dr 77396
Moonriver Dr 77338
Moonscape Vw 77396
Moonshadows Dr 77346
Moonshine Hill Loop & Rd 77338
Moosewood Ct 77346
Morgan Ranch Trl 77338
Morning Dove Dr 77396
Morning Shadows Way 77346
Morningdale St 77396
Mosaic Canyon Ct 77396
Moss Cove Ct 77346
Moss Park Ct 77346
Mossey Pines Ct 77338
Mosstex Dr 77396
Mossy Grv 77346
Mossy Grove Ct & Dr 77346
Mossy Timbers Dr 77346
Mount Loretto Ct 77346
Mountain Wood Way 77338
Muir Woods Trl 77338
Murrelet Ct 77396
Muscory Dr 77396
Mustang Corral Dr 77338
Mustang Park Ct 77396
Mystic Falls Ln 77396
Mystic Forest Ln 77396
Mystic Springs Dr 77396
Nashua Pines Ct 77346
Natchez Park Ln 77346
Natural Way 77338
Nautica Cir 77346
Neath St 77346
Neelie Ct 77338
Nehoc Ln 77346
Nella Cir 77338
Neva Ct 77338
New Kings Trl 77346
New Oak Ct & Trl 77346
Noble Run 77346
Noble Forest Dr 77346
Noelle Ct 77338
Normand Meadows Ln 77338
North St 77338
E North Belt 77396
Norwood Trails Dr 77396
Nueces Forest Dr 77396
Nueces Garden Dr 77396
Nueces Glen Dr 77396
Nueces Hollow Dr 77396
Nueces Lake Dr 77396
Nueces Moss Dr 77396
Nueces Park Rd 77396
Nueces Shore Dr 77396
Nutcracker Ct 77396
Nyad Ln 77346
Oak Cir 77396
Oak Bower Dr 77346
Oak Branch Ct 77346
Oak Briar Dr 77346
Oak Center Ct 77346
Oak Cove Ln 77346
Oak Green Ct 77346
Oak Limb Ct & Ln 77338
Oak Station Dr 77346
Oak Timbers Dr 77346
Oak Village Dr 77396
Oak Walk Dr 77338
Oaken Gate Way 77338
Oakhall Dr 77346
Oakland Wood Ct 77346
Oakrun Dr 77396
Oaktrace Ct & Dr 77396
Oakway Dr 77346
Oakwell Station Ct 77346
Oakwood Ct 77338
Ohio Canal Ct 77346
Old Arbor Way 77346
Old Humble Rd 77396
Old Maple Ln 77338
Old North Belt Dr 77396
Old Pine Grove Dr 77346
Oldridge St 77338
Olympic Cir 77346
Olympic Park Ln 77346
Opal Hill Ln 77396
Opalwood Ct & Ln 77338
Open Oak Way 77346
Oradongt Dr 77396
Orange Siren Dr 77338
Orchard Ridge Ln 77338
Oriole Ln 77396
Oriole Trl 77338
Oriskany Ct 77396
Ornella Cir 77338
Otter Creek Trl 77346
Otter Crest Ct 77346
Outback Lakes Trl 77346
Overlook Park Ct 77346
Owen Oak Dr 77346
Owl St 77396
Owl Crossing Ln 77338
Pablo Trl 77396
Pacific Crest Ct 77346
Pagemill Point Ln 77346
Palamino Ct 77346
Palestine Cove Ln 77396
Palmer Place Ln 77346
Paloma Glen Ln 77396
Palomino Ridge Dr 77338
Par Five Dr 77396
Par Two Cir 77346
Park Square Ln 77396
Paso Fino Dr 77338
Passing Pine Ct 77346
Patricia Haven Ln 77396
Peach Orchard Dr 77346
Peach Run Dr 77396
Peachtex Dr 77396
Peacock Park 77396
Pear Ridge Pl 77396
Pearson Ln 77346
Pebble Farms Ct 77346
Pecan Ln 77396
Pecantex Dr 77396
Pecos Bluff Ct 77346
Pecos Park Ln 77346
Peeble Trail Ct 77338
Pelican Cove Ct 77346
Peninsula Garden Way 77396
Pennymill Dr 77396
Percheron Trl 77338
Perdido Key Ln 77346
Pergola Pl 77396
Perryoak Dr 77346
Pheasant Run 77396
Pheasant Field Dr 77346
Pheasant Run Ln 77396
Phillips Ln 77338
Picket Hills Ln 77346
Pickwick Pines Dr 77396
Pilgrim Ln 77396
Pin Oak Dr 77396
Pine Ln 77396
Pine Arrow Ct 77346
Pine Bower Cir & Ct 77346
Pine Cluster Ln 77346
Pine Cone Dr 77338
Pine Crest Dr 77338
Pine Croft Dr 77396
Pine Cup Cir & Dr 77346
Pine Echo Dr 77346
Pine Green Ln 77346
Pine Heath Ct 77346
Pine Hollow Dr 77396
Pine Shores Dr 77346
Pine Trace Ct 77346
Pine Trail Ln 77346
Pine Wind Ct & Dr 77346
Pinefield Ct & Ln 77338
Pinehurst Dr 77346
Pinehurst Bend Dr 77346
Pinehurst Grove Ct 77346
Pinehurst Place Dr 77346
Pinehurst Shadows Dr 77346
Pinehurst Trail Cir & Dr 77346
Pinelands Park Ln 77346
Pinemill Rd 77338
Pines Place Dr 77346
Pinetex Dr 77396
Pinewood Park 77346
Pinewood Bluff Ln 77346
Pinewood Canyon Ln 77346
Pinewood Crest Ln 77346
Pinewood Mist Ln 77346
Pinion Ct 77346
Pinson Mound Ct 77346
Pintail Park Ct 77396
Pinto Ridge Dr 77338
Pioneer Ct 77346
Pipestone Point Ct 77346
Pippin Glen Dr 77396
Placid Pt 77396
Placid Point Ct 77396
Plantation Pass Dr 77346
Player Park Dr 77346
Plover Ct 77396
Plume Tree Dr 77338
Plummers Lodge Ln 77346
Plumtex Dr 77396
Pocito Ct 77346
Polo Meadow Dr 77346
Pond St 77338
Poplar Ridge Ln 77346
Porsche Dr 77396
Possum Park Rd 77338
Possums Run Dr 77396
Post Oak View Ct 77346
Potts Rd 77338
Powerscourt Dr 77346
Prairie Oak Trl 77346
Preakness Palm Cir 77346
Prescott Green Cir 77396
Prince Edward Ct 77338
Puddle Duck Ct 77396
Putting Green Dr 77346
Quail Brock Dr 77346
Quail Run Dr 77396
Quail Tree Ln 77396
Quaker Ln 77396
Quartz Creek Ln 77338
Quartz Lake Dr 77346
Quiet Grove Ct & Ln 77346
Quiet Trail Dr 77396
Quincy Ct 77338
Rackingham Pl 77338
Racquet Ridge Rd 77346
Racquet Sports Way 77346
N & S Railroad Ave 77338
Rain Leaf Ct 77338
Rainbow Bridge Ln 77346
Rainer Valley Ln 77346
Raingold Dr 77338
Rally Run Cir 77346
Ralston Rd 77396
Ramblebrook Ct 77396
Ramblewood Dr 77338
Rankin Rd 77396
Raven Hollow Ln 77396
Ravendale Rd 77396
Rawlings St 77396
Rayford Rd 77338
Rebawood Dr 77346
Rebecca Ln 77338
Red Canna Vis 77396
Red Castle Ln 77396
Red Cedar Ct 77346
Red Creek Ct 77396
Red Creek Cove Ln 77396
Red Eagle Ct 77346
Red Finch Ct 77396
Red River Canyon Dr 77346
Red Sails Pass 77346
Red Tail Way 77396
Redbird Ridge Dr 77396
Redbud Trl 77346
Redwing Ln 77396
Reflections Path Way 77396
Regatta Rd 77346
Relay Rd 77346
Rezanof Rd 77338
Riata River Ln 77346
Ribbon Meadow Ct 77346
Rich Mountain Ct 77396
E Richey Rd 77338
Richland Chambers Ln 77396
Ridgeworth Ln 77396
Rigby Ct 77346
Rising Star Dr 77338
River Brook Ct & Dr 77346
River Crest Dr 77338
River Dale Canyon Ln 77338
River Ridge View Ln 77338
Rivermoss Ln 77396
Riverside Pines Dr 77346
Riviera Ln 77338
Roach Rd 77396
Roadrunner Ln 77396
N & S Roaring River Ct 77346
Robbie Creek Ln 77396
Roberta Ln 77396
Robin Ridge Dr 77396
Roble Green Trl 77346
Roche Rock Dr 77396
Rock Creek Ct 77346
Rock Forest Ln 77396
Rockbourne Dr 77396
Rockwall Trail Dr 77346
Rocky Nook Dr 77396
Rolling Acres Dr 77396
Rolling Rapids Rd 77346
Rolling Shores Ct 77346
Rolls Royce Ct 77396
Rose Village Dr 77346
Rosebud Bend Dr 77346
Rosemarie Ln 77338
Ross Lake Ct 77346
Rotary Dr 77338
Rough Neck Dr 77338
Rough River Ct 77346
Roxette Ct 77338
Royal St 77396
Rubilee Ave 77396
Runners Ln 77346
Rushire Sq 77338
Rushmore Ln 77346
Rustic Oar Way 77346
Rustlewood Dr 77338
Ruston St 77396
Rustwood Ct & Ln 77338
Rusty Anchor Ct 77346
Ruthann Dr 77338
Ryan Ct 77396
Rye Harbor Ct 77346
Sackville Close 77346
Saddle Mountain Ln 77346
Saddle Ranch Dr 77338
Sage Flower Ct 77338
Sage Tree Trl 77346
Sailfish Cove Dr 77346
Sailing Dr 77346
Salina Cir, Ct & Ln 77396
Salt River Valley Cir & Ln 77346
Salzburg Ct & Ln 77338
N Sam Houston Pkwy E 77396
Sammon Dr 77338
Sand Trap Ct 77346
Sanders Forest Ct 77338
Sanders Glen Ln 77338
Sanders Hill Ln 77396
Sandia Pines Dr 77396
Sandpiper Cir & St 77396
Sandstone Canyon Dr 77396
Sandy Shore Ln 77346
Sarah Ann Ct 77346
Saratoga Woods Ln 77346
Satinwood Trl 77346
Saxon Creek Dr 77338
Saybrook St 77396
Scarlet Tanager Dr 77396
Scenic Cv & Vis 77396
Scenic Bluff Ln 77338
Scenic Cove Ct 77396
Scotts Bluff Ct 77346
Sculptured Rock Ln 77346
Sean Ct 77346
Sears Dr 77338
Season Ct 77346
Sebastian Cir 77346
Seco Creek Ln 77396
Secretariat Ridge Dr 77338
Senda Ct 77346
Sentry Pine Ct 77346
Sequoia Valley Ln 77346
Sequoia View Ln 77346
Serena Ln 77338
Serenata Ct & Ln 77396
Serene Ave 77338
Serrano Creek Ln 77396
Set Point Ln 77346
Settlement Ln 77396
Shaded Pines Dr 77396
Shady Ace Ln 77346
Shady Cove Ln 77346
Shallow Dr 77338
Shannon Ct & Ln 77396
Sharon Dr 77338
Shay Ln 77346
Shearwater Bend Dr 77396
Shelburne St 77396
Sheldonham Dr 77338
Shelton Shadows Ct 77346
Shiloh Valley Ln 77346
Shinwood Dr 77346
Shire Ridge Ln 77338
Shire Trail Ct 77338
Shirley Ln 77396
Shoregrove Dr 77346
Shoreview Cir, Ct & Ln 77346
Shrub Oak Dr 77396
Shumaring Dr 77338
Siano Pines Dr 77396
Sierra Creek Ln 77346
Sierra Ridge Dr 77396
Sierra Sunset Dr 77396
Silent Oaks Dr 77346
Silhouette Ridge Dr 77396
Silver Bend Dr 77346
Silver Lure Dr 77346
Silver Oak Trl 77346
Silver Yacht Dr 77346
Silverwood Trl 77346
Singing Woods Dr 77346
Sinks Canyon Ln 77346
Skewen St 77346
Skippers Helm 77346
Skyla Cir 77338
Sleepy Rose Ct 77396
Small Pebble Way 77396
Smith Rd 77396
Smokey Mountain Ct 77346
Snapping Turtle Dr 77338
Snead Ct 77346
Songbird Ln 77338
Sorrento Ct 77396
Southern Leaf Ln 77338
Southshore Dr 77338
Southwick Dr 77338
Spears Dr 77396
Spinner Court Dr 77346
Spirit Falls Ct 77346
Spirit Mound Ln 77346
Spoonwood Ct & Dr 77346
Sports Haven Dr 77346
Spring Creek Cir E & W 77338
Spring Sun Ct & Dr 77346
Springhaven Ct & Dr 77396
Springtree Dr 77396
Sprinters Dr 77346
Sprintwood Ct 77346
Sprouse Cir 77338
Spruce Bough Ct & Ln 77346
Squire Place Dr 77338
St Michaels Crest Ln 77396
Stag Brook Ct 77338
Stagewood Dr 77338
Staitti St 77338
Stallion Trail Dr 77338
Standifer St 77338
Stapley Dr 77396
Star Lake Ct & Dr 77396
Stark Point Ct 77346
Steamboat Inn Dr 77346
Steel Meadows Ln 77346
Steeple Chase Glen Dr 77346
Stellas Point Ct 77396
Still Springs Ct & Dr 77346
Stillwater Place Dr 77346
Stimpson Park Dr 77396
Stone Angel Dr 77346
Stone Trail Manor Dr 77346
Stonebridge Creek Ln 77396
Stonemount Ct 77338
Stones River Ln 77346
Stoney Rise Ln 77346
Storey Dr 77396
Storm Cove Vw 77396
Straight Arrow Dr 77346
Suffield Glen Ln 77338
Sugar Wood Ct 77338
Summer Anne Dr 77346
Summer Oaks Dr 77346
Summer Place Dr 77338
Summer Range Dr 77346
Summer Sunset Dr 77396
Summit Pines Dr 77346
Sun Rd 77396
Sun Glaze Ct & Dr 77346
Sun Point Ct 77396
Sun Trail Ct 77346
Sunburst Falls Dr 77396
Suncove Ln 77346
Sundance Dr 77346
Sundown Peak Ct 77346
Sunfall Creek Ln 77396
Sunfield Dr 77396
Sunflower Grove Ct & Dr 77346
Sunlight Peak Cir & Ln 77346
Sunlit Park Dr 77396
Sunlit Pass Loop 77396
Sunny Shores Dr 77346
Sunset Bay Ct 77396
Sunset Creek Dr 77396
Sunset Range Dr 77346
Sunset Villa Ct 77396
Sunstone Terrace Ln 77396
Sutter Creek Ln 77396
Swallow Park Dr 77396
Swan Meadow Ln 77338
Swanmore Dr 77396
Sweet Blue Jasmine Ln 77338
Sweet Forest Ln 77346
Sweet Magnolia Pl 77338
Sweet Violet Ct & Trl 77346
Sweetgum Dr 77396
Sweetgum Forest Ct & Dr 77346
Swiftbrook Dr 77346
Sycamore Cir 77396
Sycamore Shoals Ln 77346
Sylvan Dale Dr 77346
Tabor Brook Dr 77346
Tahoe Pines Ln 77346
Tahoe Shores Ct 77346
Tallgrass Prairie Ln 77346
Tamarack Bend Ln 77346
Tamarron Ct & Dr 77346
Tanner Woods Ln 77338
Tapper Ridge Ln 77346
Tassel Field Ln 77338
Tattershall Cir 77338
Tawny Wood Ct 77338
Teal Creek Dr 77346

Teal Park Ct & Dr 77396
Telico Junction Ln 77346
Texas Laurel Loop & Trl 77346
Texian Forest Trl 77346
Theiss Rd 77338
Thelma Dr 77338
Thicket Trail Dr 77346
Thom Rd 77346
Thomas Dr 77338
Thomastone Ln 77346
Thorncliff Dr 77396
Timber Edge Ln 77346
Timber Forest Dr 77346
Timber Oaks Rdg 77346
Timber Path Dr 77346
Timber Pines Dr 77346
Timber Post Ln 77346
Timber Quail Dr 77346
Timber Rail Ct & Dr 77396
Timber Shores Ln 77346
Timber Spring Ct & Dr 77346
Timber Trace Dr 77346
Timber Tree Ct 77346
Timber Twist Dr 77346
Timber View Dr 77346
Timber Way Dr 77346
Timbers Dr 77346
Timbers Edge Dr 77346
Timbers Quail Dr 77346
Timbers Trace Dr 77346
Timbers Trail Dr 77346
Tiny Turtle Pt 77396
Toddington Rd 77346
Tom Thumb Ln 77396
Topsfield Point Dr 77346
Torregon Ln 77396
Tournament Trails Dr 77346
Tower Falls Ct & Ln 77346
Town Center Blvd 77346
Towne Vue Ct 77338
Townsan Rd 77396
Townsen Blvd 77338
Trace Ct 77396
Tracelawn Ct 77396
Trail Cir 77346
Trail Mountain Ct 77346
Trail Timbers Dr 77346
Tranquility Dr 77346
Treaschwig Rd 77338
Treble Dr 77338
Tree Mist Ct 77346
Tree Moss Ct & Pl 77346
Tree Oaks Ct 77346
Tree Trail Ct 77346
Treeline Dr 77346
Treewood Dr 77346
Trent Oaks Ln 77396
Trevino Trl 77346
Trilby Way 77338
Trinity Hills Ln 77396
Trinity Joe Ln 77396
Trinity Knoll Way 77346
Trophy Place Dr 77346
Truxton St 77396
Tumbling Rd 77346
Tupelo Garden Cir 77346
Turkey Dr 77338
Turtle Cove Ct 77346
Turtle Manor Dr 77346
Twain Mark Ln 77338
Twigsworth Ln 77346
Two Creeks Rd 77338
Tyler Creek Ln 77396
Tyler Springs Ln 77346
Umber Oak Ct 77346
Upper Green St 77338
Upper Lake Dr
3200-3599 77338
5400-5898 77346
5900-6599 77346
Upper Ridge Ln 77346
Upshaw Dr 77396
Upwood Dr 77338
Valiant Brook Ct 77346
Vallecito Ln 77396

Valley Lodge Pkwy 77346
Vandergrift Dr 77396
Vantage View Ln 77346
Vaulted Pine Dr 77346
Vegas St 77396
Velma Ln 77396
Vera Dr 77396
Veranda Green Trl 77346
Verde Valley Dr 77396
Veredger Dr 77338
Vermejo Park Ln 77346
Vesper Lake Ct 77396
Victoria Rose Ln 77396
Village Bridge Dr 77346
Village Grove Dr 77396
Village Well Dr 77396
Villandry Ln 77338
Viola Dale Ct 77338
Viscaro Ln 77396
Vistadale Ct & Dr 77338
Volley Vale Ct 77346
Volvo Ct 77396
Walden Forest Dr 77346
Walden Glen Cir 77346
Walden Terrace Ln 77396
Walnut Ridge Dr 77338
Warbler Ln 77396
Warehouse Center Dr 77338
Water Edge Pt 77396
Water Edge Point Ln 77396
Water Point Ct & Trl 77346
Water Wood Trl 77346
Water Works Way 77396
Waterbury Edge Ln 77346
Watergroove Ct 77396
Waterpine Dr 77338
Watson Ln 77338
Waveland Bend Ln 77346
Wax Bill Ct 77396
Waxleaf Dr 77338
Waxwing Park Dr 77396
Welch St 77338
Wellesley Dr 77338
Wellington Chase Ln 77396
Wells Mark Dr
3600-4099 77396
4100-4299 77346
Wellswood Ct 77346
Westerbrook Ln 77396
Westerlake Ct 77396
Western Briar Ln 77396
Westminster Dr 77338
Whirlaway Elm Dr 77346
Whisper Bluff Dr 77396
Whispering Pnes 77338
Whistling Springs Dr 77346
Whitaker Dr 77338
White Arbor Ct 77338
White Berry Ct 77346
White Blossom Ln 77338
White Deer Ln 77338
White Swan Dr 77396
Whitman Mission Ln 77346
Wickerhill Falls Ct 77346
Wickton Ln 77338
Wide Brim Ct 77346
Wide River Ln 77346
Wigeon Way Dr 77396
Wild Basin Trl 77346
Wild Lilac Trl 77346
Wild Rye Trl 77346
Wild Violet Dr 77346
Wildbird Ln 77338
Will Clayton Pkwy
5700-10899 77338
10900-10999 77396
11200-13699 77346
13701-13799 77346
Willow Dr & St 77338
Willowtex Dr 77396
Wilson Rd
40AA-40AD 77338
1-1700 77338
1701-6899 77396
Wilson Park Ct 77396
Wilson Road Ct 77396

Winberry Hill Dr 77396
Wind Cove Place Ct 77346
Windemere Ct 77338
Winding Green Dr 77338
Winding Timbers Cir, Ct & Ln 77346
Winding View Ln 77346
Windley Key Ct 77346
Windswept Dr 77338
Windwood Falls Ln 77396
Windy Crossing Ln 77396
Winstead Ln 77396
Winston Falls Ct & Ln 77396
Winter Blossom Dr 77346
Winterberry Ct 77346
Wintercress Ln 77396
Wintergreen Dr 77396
Wisteria Chase Pl 77346
Wolf Creek Ct & Trl 77346
Wood Arbor Ct 77346
Wood Duck Park 77396
Wood Thorn Ct 77396
Wood Walk Ln 77346
Woodbreeze Dr 77346
Wooded Acres Dr 77396
Wooded Oaks Dr 77396
Wooded Terrace Ln 77338
Woodglen Shadows Dr 77346
Woodhall Ct & Ln 77338
Woodlace Dr 77396
Woodland Hills Dr
14800-15299 77396
17300-18699 77346
Woodland Meadows Ln 77346
Woodland Oak Trl 77346
Woodmancote Dr 77346
Woodpecker Bnd 77396
Woodside Crossing Ln 77396
Woodsong Ct 77346
Woodview Dr 77396
Woolsey Ct 77396
Wortham Oaks Dr 77338
Wortham Stream Ct 77396
Wren Park 77396
Wren Dale Ln 77346
Wren Hollow Way 77338
Yaupon Trl 77346
Yellow Birch Trl 77346
Yellowstone Trl 77346
York St 77396
Youngstown Pl 77396
Yukon Pass Dr 77346
Yukon Ridge Trl 77346
Yukon Valley Ln 77346

NUMBERED STREETS

1st St 77338
1st St E
200-1299 77338
1202-1202 77347
1300-2198 77338
1301-2199 77338
1st St W 77338
2nd St 77338
3rd St 77338
4th St 77338
5th St 77338
6th St 77338
7th St 77338
12th Fairway Ln 77346
17th Green Ct & Dr 77346
18th Fairway Dr 77346

HUNTSVILLE TX

General Delivery 77340

POST OFFICE BOXES MAIN OFFICE STATIONS AND BRANCHES

Box No.s
A - A 77342
1 - 1980 77342
2100 - 2100 77340
4001 - 7580 77342
8001 - 11910 77340

NAMED STREETS

A O Reeves Ln 77320
Abbey Rd 77340
Aberdeen Dr 77340
Acorn Hill Dr 77320
Adams Dr 77320
Airport Dr 77320
Akridge Dr 77320
Alabama Ave 77320
Allbritton Rd 77320
Allen Dr & Rd 77320
Alta Vis 77340
Amber Dr 77320
American Bank St 77320
Anders Ln 77320
Andrew St 77320
Angier Rd 77340
Annie Ln 77320
Apache St 77320
Archer St 77320
Archie Rd 77320
Arizona Ln 77320
Armadillo Dr 77320
Armadillo Ranch Rd 77320
Arnell Kelly Rd 77320
Arrowhead Dr & Ln 77320
Ashley Ln 77320
Ashworth Rd 77320
Atakapa Cir 77320
Audry Ln 77320
Autumn Way 77320
Avenue E
1320A-1320B 77340
200-399 77320
1100-1499 77340
Avenue N
1913A-1913B 77340
700-1099 77320
1100-2199 77340
Avenue S 77340
Avenue B 77340
Avenue C
800-1099 77320
1100-1599 77340
Avenue D 77320
Avenue G
600-799 77320
1100-1299 77340
1301-1399 77340
Avenue H
400-1099 77320
1100-1199 77340
Avenue I
900-1099 77320
1200-1398 77340
1400-2499 77340
Avenue J
300-1099 77320
1100-2399 77340
Avenue L 1/2 77340
Avenue M
100-999 77320
1000-2399 77340
Avenue N 1/2 77340
Avenue O
900-1099 77320
1100-2299 77340
Avenue P
801-897 77320
899-999 77320
1300-2499 77340
Avenue P 1/2 77340
Avenue Q 77340
Avenue R 77340
Avenue T 77340
Badger Ln 77320
Bagwell St 77320
Baker St 77340
Bakers Ln & Rd 77340
Ball Rd 77340

Ballew Rd 77340
Barbara Rd 77320
Barre Ln 77320
Bass Ln 77320
Bath Ln & Rd 77340
Bawden Rd 77320
Bear Scott Rd 77340
Bearkat Blvd 77340
Beaver Ln 77320
Bedias 77320
Bent Bough Park 77340
Bernice Dr 77320
Beth Cir 77320
Beto St 77340
Betty Ct 77320
Big Lake Cir & Ln 77320
Bird Farm Rd 77320
Birmingham St 77320
Bishop Rd 77320
Black Jack Rd 77340
Blalock St 77320
Blossom Ln 77320
Bluebird Dr & Ln 77320
Bluegill Ln 77320
Blythe Ranch Rd 77320
Bob O Link Rd 77320
Bobby K Marks Dr 77340
Boettcher Dr 77340
Boettcher Mill Rd 77340
Bois D Arc St 77320
Bolero Way 77340
Booker Rd & Spur 77320
Bowden Rd 77340
Bowers Blvd 77340
Bracewell Dr 77320
Branch Ln 77320
Brandenburg Ln 77340
Brandon Rd 77320
Brazil Blvd 77340
Brazos Dr 77320
Briana Way 77320
Briar Mdw 77320
Briarwood Dr 77320
Brittany Ln 77320
Broad Leaf Ln 77320
Brook Dr 77340
Brookside Dr 77320
Brookview Dr 77320
Brown Rd 77320
Browning 77320
Brumley Rd 77320
Brunch Ave 77320
Buckthorn Acres Dr 77340
Bullard St 77320
Burnett Rd 77340
Bush Dr 77320
Bybee Cir 77320
Caddo Dr & St 77320
Calvary Rd 77320
Caney Ct 77320
Caney Creek Dr 77320
Canyon Run Blvd 77320
Carolina Way 77320
Carolyn St 77320
Carranza Loop 77340
Carter Rd 77340
Catalina Rd 77340
Catechis Rd 77320
Cauthen Dr 77320
Cedar Ct 77340
Cedar Dr 77320
Cedar Ln 77320
Cedar Rdg 77320
Cedar Hill Dr 77320
Champion Woodyard Rd 77340
Chandler Ln & Rd 77320
Chandlers Way 77320
Charlotte St 77320
Cherokee Dr 77320
Chestnut Bnd 77320
Chimney Rock Rd 77320
Circle Dr 77340
Clansong Rd 77320
Clay Cir 77340
Cliff Swallow 77320

Cline St 77340
Cogans Grv 77320
Col Etheredge Blvd 77340
Collard Rd 77340
Colonial Dr 77320
Comanche Rd 77320
Conner Rd 77340
Connor Ln 77320
Coonville Rd 77320
Copeland Rd 77320
Cotton Rd 77340
Cotton Creek Cemetary Rd 77340
Cottonwood Ln & St 77320
Countz Spur 77320
Cozy Cv 77320
Crawford St 77340
Creek Pt & Rd 77320
Creek Site Ct 77320
Creendis Rd 77340
Cresthill St 77340
Crooks Dr
1-99 77340
400-1099 77320
Crosstimbers St 77320
Crossway 77320
Crute Dr 77320
Cyntolyn Rd 77320
Cypress Bnd 77340
Cypress Cir 77320
Cypress Glenn 77320
Dahlia Rd 77320
Daisey Ln 77340
Dale Ln 77320
Dallas Young Rd 77320
Daniels St 77320
Darrell White Rd 77340
Davidson Rd 77320
Davis Ln 77340
Davis Rd 77320
Davis Hall Rd 77320
Deborah St 77340
Dee Ln 77320
Deepwood Ln 77320
Deer Track Park Ln 77340
Deerfield Rd 77340
Delaware 77320
Desirable Cir 77340
Didlake Rd 77340
Dodge Oakhurst Rd 77320
Dogwood Ave 77340
Dogwood Cir 77340
Dogwood Dr 77340
Dogwood Ln 77320
Dogwood Rd 77320
Dogwood Trl 77320
Dorothy St 77320
Dorrell Rd 77340
Duerer Rd 77320
Duke Ln & Way 77320
Dustin Ln 77320
Dusty Rd 77320
Earl Rd 77320
Easley Cir 77320
East Ave & Spur 77320
Echo Ln 77320
Ed Kelly Rd 77320
Edgewood 77320
Eisenhower Ln 77320
El Rd 77320
El Toro Dr 77340
Elkins Lk & Rd 77340
Elks Dr 77340
Elkwood Cir 77340
Ellen Ln 77320
Ellisor Rd 77320
Elm Ave 77320
Elmina Rd 77340
Elmwood St 77320
Emerald Pt & Way 77320
Emerald Oaks Ct 77320
Emily Rd 77320
Enchanted Oaks Ct 77320
Enfield Ct 77320
Erin Dr 77320
Essex Blvd 77320

Eucalyptus Rd 77320
Evans Ln 77320
Evelyn Ln 77340
Fairchild Ln 77320
Falls View Ct 77320
Far Hills Ln 77320
Financial Plz 77340
Firewood Rd 77340
Fish Hatchery Rd 77320
Fishermans Trl 77320
Flynt Rd 77320
Fm 1374 Rd 77340
Fm 1375 Rd E 77320
Fm 1696 Rd E & W 77320
Fm 1791 N 77320
Fm 1791 Rd 77340
Fm 2296 Rd 77340
Fm 247 Rd 77320
Fm 2550 Rd 77320
Fm 2628 Rd 77320
Fm 2793 Rd 77340
Fm 2821 Rd E & W 77320
Fm 2929 Rd 77340
Fm 2989 Rd 77320
Fm 3179 Rd 77340
Fm 3454 Rd 77320
Fm 3478 Rd 77320
Fm 405 Rd 77320
Fm 980 Rd 77320
Forest Dr 77320
N Forest Dr 77340
Forest Gln 77340
Forest Ln 77340
Forest Creek Dr 77320
Forest Service 200 Rd 77340
Forest Service 207 Rd 77340
N Fork Ln 77320
Four Notch Rd 77340
Frank Cloud Rd 77320
Fraser St 77320
Frazier Ln 77320
Front St 77320
Frostwood St 77340
Gail Ln 77340
Gainous St 77320
Gambrell Rd 77320
Garden Acres 77320
Garvey Rd 77340
Gatlin Rd 77320
Gazebo St 77340
Geneva Rd 77320
George Wilson Rd 77320
Gerome Dr 77320
Gibbs St 77320
Gibbs Hightower Rd 77340
Ginsel Ln 77320
Glen Ct 77340
Golden Oaks 77320
Golden Rod St 77340
Goodrich Dr 77320
Goree Cir 77340
Gospel Hl 77320
Gospel Hill Rd 77320
Gourd Creek Dr 77340
Gourd Creek Cemetary Rd 77340
Grace Ln W 77320
Graham Rd 77340
Grant Colony Cemetary Rd 77320
Grapevine Cir 77320
Gray St 77320
Green Leaf St 77340
Green Rich Shrs 77320
Grossie Ln 77320
Guerrant Rd 77320
Gus Randel Rd 77340
Haas Rd 77320
Hadley Creek Bnd 77320
Hall Rd 77320
Hall Ranch Rd 77320
Hank Benge Rd 77320
Harding Rd & St 77340
Hardy Ln 77320
Hardy St 77340
Hardy Bottom Rd 77340

- Harlow Ln ... 77320
- Harmon Creek Dr ... 77320
- Harold Cir ... 77320
- Hartley Ln ... 77320
- Hayman St ... 77340
- Haynes Rd ... 77320
- Haywood St ... 77320
- Hazel Ave ... 77320
- Heather Hl ... 77340
- Heaton Ave ... 77320
- Heatonville Dr ... 77320
- Helen St ... 77340
- Heritage Oak Dr ... 77320
- Hickory Bnd ... 77320
- Hickory Holw ... 77320
- Hickory Ln ... 77340
- Hickory St ... 77320
- Hickory Lake Dr ... 77320
- Hidden Creek Dr ... 77320
- Hidden Valley Cir ... 77340
- High Oak ... 77340
- Highland Crk, Dr & Ln ... 77320
- Highway 190 E ... 77340
- Highway 30 E ... 77320
- Highway 30 W ... 77340
- Highway 75 S ... 77320
- Highway 980 N ... 77320
- Hill St ... 77320
- W Hill Park Cir ... 77320
- Hill Top Ln & Rd ... 77320
- Hillpine St ... 77340
- Hillsborough Dr ... 77340
- Hilltop Dr
  - 1-99 ... 77340
  - 500-1099 ... 77320
- Hilltop View Ct ... 77320
- Holly Dr & Ln ... 77340
- Holly Springs Dr ... 77320
- Hoot Owl Rd ... 77340
- Hopewell Rd ... 77320
- Horace Smith Rd ... 77320
- Horseshoe Lake Dr & Rd ... 77320
- Houston Dr ... 77320
- Houston Rd ... 77340
- Hoyt Ln ... 77320
- Hummingbird Ln ... 77320
- Hunters Creek Dr ... 77340
- Hutson Ln ... 77340
- Ida Olivia Rd ... 77320
- Industrial Dr ... 77320
- Interstate 45 N ... 77320
- Interstate 45 S ... 77340
- Island Pt ... 77340
- Issac Ln ... 77320
- J D Edwards Rd ... 77340
- J H Massey Ln ... 77320
- Jackson Rd ... 77320
- Jacob St ... 77320
- Jameson Rd ... 77320
- January Ln ... 77340
- Jeffrey St ... 77320
- Jeffro St ... 77320
- Jenkins Dr ... 77340
- Jenkins Rd ... 77320
- Jenkins Spur ... 77320
- Jessica St ... 77320
- Jester Dr ... 77340
- Jim Benson Rd ... 77320
- Joe Novak Rd ... 77320
- Joe Smith Rd ... 77320
- Joe Werner Ln & Way ... 77320
- John And Doris Dr ... 77320
- John Kay Rd ... 77320
- Johnson Rd & St ... 77320
- Jones View Dr ... 77320
- Jordan Dr ... 77320
- Jordy Rd ... 77320
- Josey St ... 77340
- Joshua St ... 77320
- Julia St ... 77320
- Julia Justice Rd ... 77320
- Julie Beth St ... 77320
- Kalyn Rd ... 77340
- N & S Kamper Dr ... 77320
- Kathryn Dr ... 77320
- Kathy Ln ... 77320
- Kay Ter ... 77340
- Kelly Rd ... 77320
- Kenle Ln ... 77340
- Kevin Williams Memorial Dr ... 77320
- Kickapoo Dr ... 77320
- Kingston Dr ... 77340
- Kiser Rd ... 77340
- Knapp Rd ... 77320
- Knight Ln ... 77320
- Knob Oaks Dr ... 77340
- Knotty Pine Ln ... 77340
- Knox Cir ... 77320
- Koehl Rd ... 77320
- Kornegay Ln ... 77320
- Kristin Cir ... 77320
- Kuykendall Rd ... 77320
- Kyle Dr ... 77320
- Lacee Ln ... 77320
- Lake Ct ... 77320
- Lake Dr ... 77320
- S Lake Dr ... 77320
- Lake Rd
  - 1-299 ... 77320
  - 2300-3199 ... 77340
  - 4900-5999 ... 77320
- E Lake Rd ... 77340
- W Lake Rd ... 77340
- Lake Falls Ln & Rd ... 77320
- Lake Shore Dr & Ln ... 77320
- Lake View Dr ... 77320
- Lake View Ln ... 77340
- Lake View Trl ... 77320
- Lake View Way ... 77320
- Lake Wood Cir ... 77320
- Lakeland Rd ... 77320
- Lakeridge St ... 77340
- Lakeshore Dr ... 77340
- N, S & W Lakeside Dr & Vlg ... 77320
- Lakeview Cir & Ct ... 77320
- Landis Lake Rd ... 77320
- Langley Rd ... 77320
- Lawrence Ln ... 77320
- Lazy Bend Dr ... 77320
- Lee Dr ... 77320
- Lee Hightower Rd ... 77340
- Lee Wood Rd ... 77320
- Leigh Anne St ... 77320
- Lessa Ln ... 77340
- Lily Cv ... 77340
- Lincoln Dr ... 77320
- Linda Ln ... 77320
- Little Lake Cir ... 77320
- Live Oak Ct ... 77320
- Long Point Rd ... 77320
- Lookout Rdg ... 77340
- Lost Indian Camp Rd ... 77320
- Lost Oak Ct ... 77320
- Louis Davis Dr ... 77320
- Louis Grant ... 77320
- Louis Voan Rd ... 77320
- Lowery Ln ... 77320
- Lsv Dogwood Ln ... 77320
- Lsv Hilltop Dr ... 77320
- Lsv Oak Ln ... 77320
- Lula Dr ... 77320
- Lynell Dr ... 77320
- Lynne Ln ... 77320
- M Williams Rd ... 77340
- Magnolia Dr ... 77340
- Magnolia Ln ... 77340
- Magnolia Way ... 77340
- Main Ave & St ... 77340
- Majestic Dr ... 77340
- Mann Rd ... 77320
- Manor Ln ... 77340
- Maple Ln ... 77320
- Marigold Ln ... 77340
- Marina Pt ... 77320
- Marjorie Ln ... 77320
- Marla Cir ... 77320
- Mars Dr ... 77320
- Martha Ln ... 77320
- Martin Luther King Blvd ... 77340
- Martin Luther King Dr ... 77320
- Mary Ave & Dr ... 77320
- Mary Lake Ct ... 77320
- Mathis Dairy Rd ... 77340
- Mcadams Ln ... 77320
- Mcbee Ln ... 77320
- Mccaffety Ln ... 77320
- Mccollum Dr ... 77340
- Mccrory Dr ... 77320
- Mcdougal St ... 77340
- Mcfaddin Rd ... 77340
- Mcgilberry Rd ... 77320
- Mcguire Ln ... 77340
- Mcleod Dr ... 77320
- Mcmillan Rd ... 77320
- Mcshane St ... 77320
- Mcshore Dr ... 77320
- Meadow Ln ... 77340
- Meadow Link Rd ... 77320
- Medical Center Pkwy ... 77340
- Medical Park Ln ... 77340
- Melody Ln ... 77320
- Memorial Hospital Dr ... 77340
- Merchant St ... 77320
- Merino Rd ... 77340
- Merlin Spur ... 77320
- Mesquite St ... 77320
- Methodist Church Rd ... 77340
- Michael St ... 77320
- Michaels Ln ... 77320
- Mike Beth Cir ... 77320
- Milam St ... 77340
- Mill Cir ... 77340
- Mimosa Ln ... 77320
- Mize St ... 77320
- Mock Rd ... 77320
- Mockingbird Ln ... 77320
- Moffett Springs Rd ... 77320
- Mohawk Spur ... 77320
- Molly Dr ... 77340
- Monaco Way ... 77320
- Montgomery Rd ... 77340
- Morgan Ln ... 77340
- Morris Ln ... 77320
- Mosley Dr ... 77320
- Mosley Ln ... 77320
- E Mosley Ln ... 77340
- Mossback St ... 77320
- Mott Ln ... 77320
- Mt Zion Church Rd ... 77320
- Mulberry Cir ... 77320
- Murphy Farm Rd ... 77320
- Murray Ln ... 77340
- Mutt Young Rd & Spur ... 77320
- Nanway St ... 77340
- Natures Way Rd ... 77340
- Neiderhoffer Subdivision Rd ... 77340
- Nelwyn Dr ... 77320
- Nestor Rd ... 77340
- Newport Lndg & Way ... 77320
- Newport Village Dr ... 77320
- Nita Dr ... 77320
- Nixon Rd ... 77340
- Normal Park Dr
  - 1-97 ... 77320
  - 99-1099 ... 77320
  - 1500-2399 ... 77340
- North Park ... 77320
- Nottingham St ... 77340
- Oak Dr ... 77320
- W Oak Dr ... 77320
- Oak Gln ... 77320
- Oak Ln ... 77340
- Oak Rdg ... 77340
- Oak Bend Dr ... 77320
- Oak Creek Dr ... 77340
- Oak Forest St ... 77320
- Oak Hill Dr ... 77320
- Oak Lawn St ... 77340
- Oak Trail Rd ... 77320
- Oakbend St ... 77340
- Oakdale Dr ... 77320
- Oakland Ct ... 77340
- Oakview Cir ... 77340
- Oakwood Ct & Dr ... 77320
- Obannon Dr ... 77320
- Obannon Ranch Rd ... 77320
- Old Cincinnati Rd ... 77320
- Old Colony Rd ... 77320
- Old Houston Rd ... 77340
- Old Madisonville Rd ... 77320
- Old Phelps Rd ... 77340
- Old Sycamore ... 77340
- Old Tram Rd ... 77320
- Olde Oaks Dr ... 77320
- Olive St ... 77340
- Owv Park Ln ... 77320
- Oxbow Ln ... 77340
- Paisano Ln ... 77340
- Palisade Cir ... 77320
- Palm St ... 77340
- Park Dr & Ln ... 77320
- Park Hill St ... 77340
- Parker Creek Rd ... 77320
- Parkwood Pl ... 77340
- Parr Dr ... 77320
- Pat Henry Cemetery Rd ... 77320
- Pat Kelly Rd ... 77320
- Patrick St ... 77320
- Paul Bruno Rd ... 77320
- Paul Dixon Rd ... 77320
- Paul Knox St ... 77320
- Paula Ln ... 77320
- Peaceful Dr ... 77340
- Peach Tree St ... 77320
- Pear Dr ... 77320
- Peavy Rd ... 77320
- Pebble Ct ... 77340
- Pecan Ln & St ... 77320
- Pecan Tree Ln ... 77320
- Pegoda Rd ... 77340
- Peninsula Pt ... 77340
- Perch Ln ... 77320
- Percy Howard Rd ... 77320
- Persimmon Dr ... 77340
- Phelps Creek Dr ... 77340
- Phelps Slab Rd ... 77340
- Phil Wood Rd ... 77320
- Pierce Rd ... 77320
- Pine Ave ... 77340
- Pine Blvd ... 77340
- Pine Cir ... 77320
- Pine Dr ... 77340
- Pine St ... 77320
- Pine Breeze St ... 77340
- Pine Crest Dr ... 77320
- Pine Grove Dr ... 77340
- Pine Hill Rd ... 77340
- Pine Hollow Dr ... 77340
- Pine Hollow Ln ... 77340
- Pine Knot Sq ... 77320
- Pine Lake Dr ... 77340
- Pine Lake Ln ... 77340
- Pine Meadows St ... 77340
- Pine Needle Dr ... 77340
- Pine Oak Ln ... 77340
- Pine Prairie School Rd ... 77340
- Pine Ridge Ln ... 77340
- Pine Shadows Dr ... 77320
- Pine Tree Rd ... 77320
- Pine Valley St ... 77340
- Pine Wood Dr ... 77340
- Pinedale Rd ... 77320
- Pinedale Subdivision Rd ... 77320
- Pinewood Dr ... 77340
- Piney Bough Dr ... 77340
- Piney Point Ln ... 77340
- Piney Point Rd ... 77340
- Pinoak Dr ... 77340
- Pipkin Rd ... 77340
- Pleasant St ... 77320
- Pleasant Valley Dr ... 77340
- Plum Creek St ... 77320
- Plum Ridge Rd ... 77320
- Point Loop ... 77320
- Pool Rd ... 77340
- Poppy Ln ... 77340
- Possum Walk Loop ... 77340
- Post Oak Dr & Rd ... 77320
- Pot Of Gold ... 77320
- Powell Rd ... 77340
- Pratt St ... 77320
- Prentice St ... 77340
- Preston Ln ... 77320
- Price Ln ... 77320
- Purple Martin St ... 77320
- Quality Blvd ... 77320
- Quiet Pine Way ... 77340
- R Williams Ln ... 77320
- Rainbow Dr ... 77320
- Raintree St ... 77320
- Ranch Acres Dr ... 77340
- Ranchview Dr ... 77320
- Randall St ... 77320
- Raven Hill Dr ... 77340
- Raven Terrace Dr ... 77320
- Raven Wood St ... 77320
- Rawlinson Rd ... 77320
- Red Bud Ln ... 77340
- Red Oak ... 77320
- Redbird Ln ... 77320
- Reece Ln ... 77340
- Renfro Valley Dr ... 77320
- Rhodes Dr ... 77320
- Rice Ln ... 77320
- Ridge Run ... 77320
- Ridge Top Dr ... 77320
- Ridge View Ln ... 77340
- Rigby Ln ... 77320
- Rigsby Rd ... 77320
- Ripple Creek Dr ... 77320
- Riverside Ln ... 77320
- Riverwood Dr, Ln & Vlg ... 77320
- Roark Rd & St ... 77320
- Roberts Rd & Spur ... 77320
- Robin St ... 77320
- Robinson Rd ... 77320
- Robinson Spur ... 77320
- Robinson Way ... 77340
- Robinson Creek Pkwy & Rd ... 77340
- Rocky Point Ln ... 77320
- Rogers Ln ... 77320
- Roosevelt St ... 77320
- Rose Hill Ct ... 77320
- Rose Ranch Rd ... 77320
- Rosenwall Rd ... 77320
- Rosewood Ln ... 77340
- Ross St ... 77320
- Ross Mcbride Ln ... 77340
- Round Prairie Rd ... 77320
- Roundabout Ln & Rd ... 77320
- Roy Webb Rd ... 77320
- Royal Oaks St ... 77320
- Running Deer Ln ... 77320
- Rushing Oak Ct ... 77320
- Rwv Hilltop Ln ... 77320
- Ryans Ferry Rd ... 77320
- Sabine St ... 77320
- Sabrina Ln ... 77340
- Sage St ... 77340
- Sam Houston Ave
  - 100-1099 ... 77320
  - 1100-5099 ... 77320
- Samantha Ln ... 77340
- San Jacinto St ... 77320
- Sand Dr ... 77340
- Sandel Rd ... 77340
- Sandhill Ln ... 77340
- Sandra Dr ... 77320
- Sandra Rogers Rd ... 77320
- Sandy Creek Dr ... 77340
- Sandy Creek Nursery Rd ... 77340
- Sara Ln ... 77320
- Scales Ranch Rd ... 77320
- Scattered Oaks Dr ... 77320
- School Rd ... 77340
- Scott Rd & St ... 77320
- Sendero Dr ... 77340
- Settlers Way ... 77320
- Shady Ln ... 77320
- Shady Oak Ln ... 77320
- Shady Oaks Dr ... 77320
- Shannon Dr
  - 1600-2199 ... 77340
  - 2200-2299 ... 77320
- Shannon St ... 77320
- Shaw Ln ... 77320
- Shepard Dr ... 77340
- Shepard Rd ... 77320
- Shiloh Ln ... 77320
- Shoreline Dr ... 77320
- Shorewood Dr ... 77320
- Shotwell Rd ... 77320
- Simmons St ... 77320
- Sims Ln ... 77320
- Sleepy Hollow Cir ... 77320
- Smith Hill Rd ... 77320
- Smither Dr ... 77340
- South Park ... 77340
- Southwood Dr ... 77320
- Southwood Forest Rd ... 77340
- Sowell Dr & Ln ... 77320
- Spriggs Rd ... 77320
- Spring Dr
  - 1-99 ... 77320
  - 3700-3899 ... 77340
- Spring Circle Dr & Loop ... 77320
- Spring Creek Cir ... 77320
- Sprott St ... 77320
- Spur Ln ... 77320
- St Marys Rd ... 77320
- St Olive Cemetery Rd ... 77320
- Stallings Ln ... 77320
- Starlite Dr ... 77320
- State Highway 19
  - 100-599 ... 77340
- State Highway 19
  - 600-3799 ... 77320
- State Highway 30 W ... 77340
- State Highway 75 N ... 77320
- State Highway 75 S
  - 7130B2-7130B6 ... 77340
  - 7130D1-7130D2 ... 77340
  - 7405C1-7405C3 ... 77340
  - 7405D1-7405D2 ... 77340
  - 7405E1-7405E3 ... 77340
  - 7405F1-7405F2 ... 77340
  - 7405G1-7405G2 ... 77340
  - 7405H1-7405H2 ... 77340
  - 7130A1-7130A4 ... 77340
  - 7130C2-7130C7 ... 77340
  - 7130E1-7130E6 ... 77340
  - 6000-9099 ... 77340
- Steamboat Rd ... 77320
- Sterling Chapel Rd ... 77320
- Stockton Dr ... 77320
- Strawberry Ln ... 77320
- Stubblefield Lake Rd ... 77340
- Sugar Hill Rd ... 77320
- Sumac Rd ... 77340
- Summer Ln & Pl ... 77320
- Sunfish Ln ... 77320
- Sunny Hill Dr ... 77340
- Sunnyside St ... 77320
- Sunrise Loop ... 77320
- Sunset Lake Rd ... 77320
- Sutterfield Ln ... 77320
- Swearingen Rd ... 77340
- Sweetgum Ave ... 77340
- Sycamore Ave ... 77340
- Sycamore Dr ... 77320
- T Carter Rd ... 77340
- Tall Timbers ... 77320
- Tall Timbers Dr ... 77320
- Tall Timbers Ln ... 77340
- Tall Timbers St ... 77320
- Tall Timbers Way ... 77320
- Tam Rd ... 77320
- Tanglewood Dr ... 77320
- Tara Ln ... 77320
- Teal Ln ... 77320
- Tejas Dr & St ... 77320
- Tenolia Ln ... 77340
- Terry Rd ... 77340
- Thamsher Ln ... 77320
- Thomas Spur ... 77320
- Thomas Lake Rd ... 77320
- Thomason St ... 77320
- Thompson Rd & St ... 77320
- Thornwood Way ... 77340
- Three Notch Rd ... 77340
- Thurman Dr ... 77340
- Timber Ln ... 77320
- Timberline Cir & Dr ... 77320
- Timberwilde Dr ... 77320
- Timberwood Ln ... 77340
- Tinker Ln ... 77320
- Tomahawk Cir & St ... 77320
- Tonkawas Rd ... 77320
- Tony Ln ... 77320
- Town And Country Dr ... 77320
- Townley Ranch Dr ... 77320
- Tracy St ... 77320
- Trail Ridge Rd ... 77320
- Trailwood Dr ... 77340
- Trinity Cut Off ... 77320
- Turner Rd ... 77320
- Turner St ... 77340
- Turtle Creek Cir ... 77340
- Twin Creek Dr ... 77320
- Twin Oaks Ln ... 77340
- Underwood Dr ... 77340
- University Ave
  - 100-1099 ... 77320
  - 1100-1699 ... 77340
- Us Highway 190 ... 77340
- Utility St ... 77320
- Utley Rd ... 77320
- Valley Dr ... 77320
- Valley View Ct ... 77320
- Varsity Dr ... 77340
- Vela Rd ... 77340
- Venice Way ... 77320
- Venus Dr ... 77320
- Veronica Ln ... 77340
- Veterans Memorial Pkwy
  - 900-999 ... 77320
  - 1400-2399 ... 77340
- Vick Spring Rd ... 77340
- Vicki Dr ... 77340
- Victoria Way ... 77320
- Villa Cir, Ln & Way ... 77320
- Violet St ... 77340
- Vista Way ... 77340
- Walker ... 77320
- Walker Ln ... 77320
- Walker Loop ... 77340
- Walker Trl ... 77320
- Wallace Rd ... 77320
- S Walnut Bnd, Ct, Cv, Dr, Ln & Rd ... 77320
- E & W Walnut Lake Dr ... 77320
- Walnut Ridge Dr ... 77320
- Wanza Rd ... 77320
- Warbonnet ... 77320
- Ward Ranch Rd ... 77320
- Waterwood ... 77320
- Watkins St ... 77320
- Watson Lake Rd ... 77340
- Wendy Ln ... 77340
- Westberry Cir ... 77340
- Westridge Dr ... 77340
- Westwood Dr ... 77320
- Whatley Ln ... 77320
- Whippoorwill Dr ... 77340
- Whippoorwill St ... 77320
- Whispering Pne ... 77320
- Whistler Ln ... 77320
- White Rd ... 77320
- White Oak Dr ... 77320
- White Tail Ln ... 77320
- Wichita Cir ... 77320
- Wickham ... 77320
- Wild Iris Ct ... 77340
- Wildflower ... 77320
- Wildwood St ... 77340
- Wildwood Lake Dr N ... 77340
- Wilkerson Ln ... 77320
- Williams Rd ... 77340

Willis Wood Rd 77340
Willow St 77340
Willow Creek Dr 77340
Willow Oak Ct 77320
Willowbend St 77320
Wimberly Ln 77320
Winding Rdg 77320
Winding Way 77340
Windridge Ln 77340
Windsor St 77340
Windwood St 77340
Windy Oaks 77320
Winkler Dr 77340
Winter Way 77340
Wire Rd 77320
Wire Road Loop 77320
Wm Thomas Rd 77320
Woelfley Ln 77320
Wolverton St 77340
Wood St 77320
Wood Farm Rd 77320
Wood Farm Estates Rd 77320
Wood Forest Ln 77340
Wood Lodge Dr 77320
Woodhaven Dr 77320
Woodland Dr 77320
Woodland Ln 77340
Woodland Hills Dr 77320
Woodridge Dr 77320
Woodview Dr 77320
Woodward Dr 77340
Wunderlich Rd 77320
Yates Ln 77320
Yegua Cir 77340
Yolanda St 77320
Young Rd & St 77320
Youpon St 77340

NUMBERED STREETS

1st St 77320
2nd St 77320
3rd St 77320
6th St 77320
7th St 77320
8th St 77320
9th St 77320
10th St 77320
11th St
1-99 77320
400-2999 77340
12th St 77340
13th St 77340
14th St 77340
15th St 77340
16th St 77340
17th St 77340
18th St 77340
19th St 77340
20th St 77340
21st St 77340
22nd St 77340
23rd St 77340
25th St 77340
13 1/2 St 77340
19 1/2 St 77340
20 1/2 St 77340
21 1/2 St 77340

HURST TX

General Delivery 76053

POST OFFICE BOXES MAIN OFFICE STATIONS AND BRANCHES

Box No.s
1 - 2177 76053
54001 - 55716 76054
93000 - 95310 76053
95401 - 95401 76054

RURAL ROUTES

01, 03 76053
02 76054

NAMED STREETS

Acapulco Dr 76053
Acorn Ln 76054
Airport Fwy
601-1099 76053
700-1098 76054
8600-8798 76053
Anderson Dr 76053
Antwerp Dr 76054
Apple Blossom Ln 76054
Arcadia St 76053
Arthur Dr 76053
Arwine Dr 76053
Arwine Cemetery Rd 76053
Ascension Dr 76053
Ashley Dr 76054
Aspen Ct 76054
Austin Ct 76054
Autumn Dr 76054
Baker Ct & Dr 76054
Barbara Ann Dr 76053
Barber St 76053
Bear Creek Dr 76054
Bedford Ct E & W 76053
Bedford Euless Rd 76053
Bell Dr 76053
Bell Helicopter Blvd 76053
Bellaire Dr 76053
Belmont St 76053
Bent Tree Ct & Dr 76054
Betty Ct & Ln 76053
Billie Ruth Ln 76053
Billy Creek Cir & Dr 76053
Birch St 76053
Black St 76053
Blossom Ln 76053
Bluebonnet Dr 76053
Bob St 76053
N & S Booth Calloway Rd 76053
Bordeaux Ln 76054
Bowles Ct & Dr 76053
Bowspirit Cir & Ln 76053
Bradford Ct & Dr 76053
Brandi Ct 76054
Brazil Ct & Dr 76054
Brazos Dr 76054
Bremen Ct & Dr 76054
Briar Trl 76054
Briargrove Dr 76054
Briarwood Ln 76053
Bridget Way 76054
Brook Forest Ln 76053
Brookfield Dr 76053
Brookridge Ct & Dr 76054
Brookside Dr 76053
Brookview Dr 76054
Brown Trl
100-799 76053
1515-1597 76054
1599-1899 76054
Brown Trail Ct 76053
Buena Vista Dr 76053
Burford Ct 76053
Cactus Dr 76054
Caduceus Ct & Ln 76053
Calcutta St 76053
Calloway Ct & Dr 76053
Cambridge Dr 76054
Campus Dr 76054
Cannon Dr 76054
Cardinal Rd 76053
Carnation Ln 76053
Carolyn Dr 76054
Castle Dr 76053
Cavender Ct 76054
Cavender Dr
900-1499 76053
1500-2099 76054
W Cedar St 76053
Central Park Dr 76053
Chadwick Ct 76054
Chantilly Ct 76054
Charlene Dr 76053
Charles Ct 76054
Charleston Ct & Pl 76054
Chase Cir 76053
Chateaux Ln 76054
Cherry Ct 76053
E & W Cheryl Ave 76053
Chisholm Trl 76054
Cimarron Trl
1300-1499 76053
1500-2099 76054
Circleview Dr N & S 76054
Clear Fork Dr 76054
Comanche Trl 76054
Concord Dr 76054
Cooper Dr 76053
Corinna Ct 76053
Cottonwood Ln 76054
W Creek Dr 76053
Creekside Dr 76053
Crestline Dr 76053
Crestview Dr 76053
Crestwood Ter 76053
Crosstimber Ct & Dr 76053
Crystal Ln 76054
Crystal Glenn Cir 76054
Cullum Ave & Ct 76053
Cumberland Dr 76054
Cynthia Ln 76054
Daisy Ct 76053
Dalton Dr 76054
Daly Dr 76053
David Dr 76054
Debra Dr 76053
Desiree Ln 76053
Devin Ln 76053
Dianna Ave 76053
Dillon Ct 76054
Donald Ct & Dr 76053
Donna Dr 76053
Dorothy Ln 76053
Dorris St 76053
Dustin Trl 76054
Eastridge Ct 76054
Edgehill Dr 76053
Edgepoint Trl 76053
El Camino Real St 76053
Elizabeth St 76053
E & W Ellen Ave 76053
Elm St 76053
Elmview Dr 76053
Encino Dr 76053
Englewood Ln 76053
Eunice St 76053
Evan Dr 76054
Evergreen Dr 76054
Fairhaven Ct & Dr 76054
Fairlane Ct 76054
Fall Crest Dr 76054
Fanning Dr 76053
Farrington Ln 76054
Fieldwood Ter 76054
Fleming Dr 76053
Foothill Dr 76053
Forest Ln 76053
Forest Crossing Dr 76053
Forest Hollow Dr 76053
Forest Oaks Ln 76053
Forest View Ct 76054
Fountain Pkwy 76053
Fountainview Ter 76053
Fox Glenn Ct 76054
Frazier Dr 76053
Garden Oaks Dr 76053
W Glade Rd 76054
Glade Creek Dr 76054
Glade Pointe Ct 76054
Glenhaven Dr 76054
Glenn Dr 76053
Glenwood Ter 76053
Grace Cir 76053
Grapevine Hwy 76054
Grayson Ct 76054
Green Tree Dr 76054
Greenbelt Rd 76053
Greenway Dr 76053
Greenwood Cir, Ct & Dr 76053
Hardie St 76053
Harmon Rd 76053
Harris Ave 76053
Harrison Ln 76053
E & W Harwood Ct & Rd 76054
Hat Creek Dr 76054
W Hayes Ln 76053
Heather Ln 76054
Heneretta Dr 76054
Henson Dr 76053
Heritage Cir & Way 76053
Herman Dr 76054
Hickory Ct 76054
Highland Crest Ct & Dr 76054
Highland Park Ct & Dr 76054
Highstar Ct 76054
Highview Ct & Ln 76054
Hill Ct 76053
Hill Crest Ct & Dr 76053
N Hills Blvd 76053
Hillview Ct & Dr 76054
Holder Dr 76053
Holiday Ln 76053
W Holloway Ct & Dr 76053
Holly Hill Ct & Dr 76053
Huey Trl 76053
E & W Hurst Blvd 76053
Hurst Town Center Dr 76054
Hurstview Ct 76054
Hurstview Dr
100-1499 76053
1500-3299 76054
Indian Trl 76054
Inwood Dr 76053
Irwin Dr 76053
Jane Ln 76053
Jeannie Ct & Ln 76054
Jetranger Rd 76053
Joanna Dr 76053
John Ct N & S 76054
Josephine Dr 76054
Julia Dr 76054
Juliet Pl 76054
Karla Dr 76053
Kathryn Ct & St 76053
Kay Ct 76054
Kayla Ct 76053
Keith Dr 76053
Keren Pl 76053
Knight Cir 76053
Lake Ter 76053
Lake Bend Trl 76053
Lake Brook Dr 76053
Lake Crest Ln 76053
Lake Hill Ln 76053
Lake Knoll Ct 76053
Lake Meadows Ln 76053
Lake Park Dr 76053
Lake Springs Trl 76053
Letha Ct 76053
Lewis Dr 76054
Liberty Cir 76053
Livingston Dr 76053
Liz Ln 76054
Lonesome Dove Trl 76054
Longranger Dr 76053
Lookout Ct & Trl 76054
NE & S Loop 820 76053
Lorean Ct 76054
E & W Louella Ct & Dr 76054
Ludo Cir 76054
Lynda Ct 76053
Lynn Ct & Dr 76053
Lynndale Ct 76054
Lynwood Ct 76053
Madison Ave 76054
Madrid Ct & St 76053
Magnolia Ct 76053
NE Mall Blvd 76053
Marseille Dr 76054
Martin Rd 76054
Mary Dr 76053
Marynell St 76054
Mason Dr 76053
Mayfair Ct & Dr 76054
Melbourne Ct & Rd 76053
Mesa Ct 76054
Mesquite Trl 76054
Michael Blvd 76053
Mid Cities Blvd 76054
Mill Haven Dr 76053
Mill Ridge Dr 76053
Monterrey Blvd 76053
Montreal Ct & Dr 76054
Moore Creek Rd 76053
Mountain Ter 76053
Mountainview Dr 76054
Municipal Dr 76054
Myrtle Ct & Dr 76053
Naples Dr 76054
Natchez Ct 76054
Normandy Dr 76054
Northglen Dr 76054
Northridge Dr 76054
Norwich Dr 76054
Norwood Dr
100-1499 76053
1500-2599 76054
S Norwood Dr 76053
Norwood Plz 76054
Oak Dr 76053
Oak Creek Dr 76054
Oak Park Dr 76053
Oak Ridge Dr 76053
Oakdale Ct & Dr 76054
Oakhurst Ct & Dr 76053
Oakview Ct & Dr 76054
Oakwood Ave & Dr 76053
Olive St 76053
Overhill Ct & Dr 76053
P C Wynne Ln 76053
Page Ct & St 76053
Palo Duro Ct & Dr 76054
Pamela St 76053
Paridelm Dr 76053
Park Forest Ct & Dr 76053
Park Place Blvd 76053
Parkland Ct 76053
Parkridge Ct & Dr 76054
Parkview Ct & Dr 76053
Patricia Rd 76053
Paul Dr 76054
E & W Pecan St 76053
Phillip Dr 76054
Piccadilly Cir 76053
Pine St 76053
E, S & W Pipeline Ct & Rd 76053
Plainview Ct & Dr 76054
E Plaza Blvd 76053
E & W Pleasantview Ct & Dr 76054
Ponderosa Dr 76053
Post Oak Cir & Dr 76053
Powers St 76053
Precinct Line Rd
100-1499 76053
1500-2200 76054
2202-7798 76054
S Precinct Line Rd 76053
Prestondale Dr 76054
Princess Ln 76053
Quail Cove Ct 76054
Raider Dr 76053
Reaves Ln 76053
E & W Redbud Dr 76053
Reed St 76053
Reese Ln 76054
Regency Dr 76054
Renee Dr 76054
Rickel Park Dr 76053
Rickle Park 76053
Ridgecrest Dr 76053
Ridgeline Dr 76053
Ridgeview Ct 76053
Ridgewood Cir & Dr 76054
N & S Riley Ct & Pl 76054
River Bend Dr 76054
Riverlakes Dr 76053
Riversprings Dr 76053
Rock Ridge Ct 76053
Ronald Ct 76053
Royal Ln & Ter 76053
Ruth Ln 76053
Sabine Ct 76054
Sage Trl 76054
Salem Dr 76054
Scott Dr 76053
Sean Ct 76053
Seashal Dr 76054
Shade Tree Cir & Ct 76054
Shadow Wood Ln 76054
Shadowbrook Ln 76053
Shady Ln 76053
Shady Lake Ct & Dr 76054
Sheppard Ct 76053
Sheri Ln 76053
Shoreside Pkwy 76053
Silent Creek Trl 76053
Simmons Dr 76053
Simpson Dr 76053
Sotogrande Blvd 76053
Souder Dr 76053
Southridge Ct 76053
Spanish Cir 76053
Spring Crest Ct 76053
Spring Valley Dr 76054
Springbrooke Dr 76054
Springhill Ct & Dr 76054
Springwood Dr 76054
Steeplechase Ct 76054
Stephan Dr 76054
Stephanie Ln 76054
Steve Dr 76054
Stonehenge Dr 76054
Stratford Ct & Dr 76054
Summerdale Dr 76054
Sunnyvale Ter 76053
Sunset Ct & Dr 76054
Sylvan Dr 76053
Tally Ho Dr 76054
Tanglewood Dr 76053
Taylor Ct 76054
Terrace Trl 76053
Terry Rd 76053
Texas Trl 76054
Texas Trail Ct 76054
Thomas Ave 76053
Thousand Oaks Ct & Dr 76054
Timbercreek Dr 76053
Timberhill Dr 76053
Timberline Dr 76053
Toni Ct & Dr 76054
Tradonna Ln 76054
Trails End Cir & Ct 76054
Trailwood Dr 76053
Treadwell Ct & Dr 76053
Trinity Blvd 76053
Trinity Lakes Dr 76053
Trinity Vista Trl 76053
Tube Dr 76053
Tumbleweed Dr 76054
Twin Creek Dr 76053
Val Oaks Ct 76053
Valencia Dr 76053
Valentine St 76053
Valley View Ct & Dr 76053
Valley Vista Dr 76053
Van Ct 76053
Vendome Ct 76054
Venice St 76053
Vicki Pl 76053
Walker Dr 76053
Walnut Ln 76054
Wanda Way 76053
Wedgeview Dr 76053
Well Springs Dr 76053
Westover Ct 76054
Westridge Ct & Dr 76054
Weyland Dr 76053
Wheelwood Dr 76053
Whitney Way 76054
Willow St 76053
Wingate Ct 76054
Winter Falls Trl 76053
Winterhaven Dr 76054
Womack Ct 76054
Wondol Ct 76053
Woodbridge Dr 76054
Woodcrest Dr 76053
Wooded Trl 76053
Woodland Ct 76053
Woodland Park Dr 76053
Woodridge Dr 76054
Woodside Dr 76053
Woodview Ter 76053
Woodway Dr 76053
Wreyhill Dr 76053
Yates Dr
1300-1499 76053
1600-1799 76054
Yucca Trl 76054
Zelda Dr 76053

IRVING TX

General Delivery 75015

POST OFFICE BOXES MAIN OFFICE STATIONS AND BRANCHES

Box No.s
140001 - 143608 75014
152007 - 158999 75015
162000 - 169382 75016
170001 - 177866 75017
630001 - 639595 75063

RURAL ROUTES

03, 05 75038

NAMED STREETS

Aaron St 75061
Abbey Rd 75063
Abbott Dr 75060
Abelia St 75061
Abraham Ct 75060
Acapulco Ct & St 75062
Ackers Ln 75061
Ada St 75061
Adah Ln 75062
Adams Ct 75061
Addington St 75062
Admirality Way 75061
E & W Airport Fwy 75062
Al Piano Ct 75060
Al Razi St 75062
Alan A Dl 75061
Alcazar Ct 75062
Alden St 75061
Alexander Ct & St 75061
Alhambra Dr 75062
Alice Ct 75061
Allen St 75060
Allison Ct 75062
Almanzor Ave 75062
Almeria Ct 75062
Alpine Ct 75060
Altman Dr 75062
Alto Vista Dr 75062
Alvis St 75060
Amber Dr 75061
Amherst Ct 75038
Anchor Ter 75063

Andalusia St 75062
Anderson St 75062
Andover Ln 75060
Andre Dr 75063
Andrea St 75060
Angelina Dr 75039
Angie Ln 75060
Anita St 75060
Anna Dr 75061
Annesley Ln 75062
Annette Dr 75061
Apache Trl 75060
Apple Way 75063
Apple Tree Ct 75061
Aransas Dr 75039
Arapaho Trl 75060
Arawe Cir E & W 75060
Arbol 75039
Arbor Ct 75060
Arcady Ln 75061
Aristocrat Dr 75063
Arlington Dr 75061
Armeda Ave 75061
Armour Dr 75038
Arrowhead Dr 75060
Arthur Ct 75060
Ash St 75060
Ashcroft Ct 75062
Aspen Dr 75060
Astoria St 75062
Atkinson St 75060
Atlanta Dr 75062
Augustine Rd 75063
Austin St 75061
Autumn Leaves Trl 75060
Avalon Ave 75061
Avenida Loop 75062
Avicenna Ct 75062
Azalea Trl 75063
Backbay Dr 75063
Bailey Ct 75063
Balboa Ct & St 75062
Bald Cypress Cir 75063
Balleywood Rd 75060
Balta Ct 75063
Bangor Ct E & W 75062
Barbara Dr 75060
Barcelona 75039
Barton St 75060
Bay Meadows Dr 75063
Bay Side Dr 75060
Bay View Dr 75060
Beacon Hill Dr 75061
Bear Creek Ct 75061
Bel Aire Crst 75061
Belclaire Ln 75060
Belew St 75061
Bell Ln 75060
Bella Vis 75039
Bellah Ct & Dr 75062
Belltower Dr 75061
Bellview 75060
Belmead Ln 75061
Belmont Ct 75060
N Belt Line Rd
100-198 75061
200-1999 75061
2200-2398 75062
2400-3699 75062
3700-5000 75038
5002-5198 75038
6200-8499 75063
S Belt Line Rd 75060
Ben Dr 75061
W Bend Dr 75063
Benjamin Rd 75060
Bent Branch Dr 75063
Bent Tree Ct 75061
Beranger Dr 75039
Berkley Plz 75061
Betsy Ln 75061
Beverly Pkwy & St 75061
Billings Ct 75062
Biltmore Ln 75063
Birch Dr 75060
Biruni St 75062
Biscayne Dr E & W 75060
Black Jack Dr 75060
Black Rock Ct 75063
Blackwell Dr 75061
Blanco Dr 75039
Blaylock Cir N & S 75061
Block Dr 75038
Blue Jay Way 75063
Blue Oak Dr 75060
Blue Sage Ct 75063
Bluebird Dr 75061
Bluebonnet Dr 75060
Bluelake Ct 75060
Bluewater Ter 75063
Bob O Link Dr 75062
Boise Ct 75062
Bolden Rd 75060
Bonanza 75060
Bond St 75038
Bonham Ct 75038
Borama Dr 75062
Bordeaux Sq 75038
Boston Dr 75061
Bottlebrush Ln 75063
Boundbrook Ln 75060
Bower Dr 75061
Bowling Green St 75060
Bowman St 75060
Boxwood Ct & Dr 75063
Boyd Dr 75061
Bradford St 75061
Bradford Pear Dr 75063
Brady Dr 75061
Brandon Ct 75060
Brangus Dr 75038
Branscome Dr 75060
Breakers Point Ct 75063
Bremerton Ct & St 75062
Brenda Dr 75060
Brenton St 75062
Brentwood Ct & Dr 75061
Briar Oaks Dr 75060
Briarcliff Cir, Ct & Dr N & S 75062
Briarcrest Ct & Dr 75063
Briarwood Ln 75061
Briarwylde Dr 75060
Bridge Lake Dr 75060
Bridlewood Ct 75063
N Briery Rd 75061
S Briery Rd 75060
Brighton Downs 75060
Brim Dr 75062
Bristol Ct N & S 75062
Britain Cir 75062
Britain Ct 75062
N Britain Rd
200-2099 75061
2201-2497 75062
2499-3399 75062
S Britain Rd 75060
Broadmoor Ln 75061
Brockbank Dr 75062
Broken Point Dr 75063
Brookhaven Dr 75061
Brookhollow Dr 75061
Brookhurst St 75061
Brookside Dr 75063
Brookstone Dr 75039
Brookview Ct 75063
Brown Dr & St 75061
Brownwood Ct 75060
Bruce 75061
Brushwood Dr 75063
Bryan Ct 75060
Bryan Pkwy 75061
Bryant St 75061
Bryn Mawr Dr 75062
Bryson 75063
Buckingham Dr 75038
Bunker Hill Dr 75061
Bunn Dr 75061
Bur Oak Dr 75060
Burning Tree Ln 75062
Burnwood Dr 75062
Burris Price Ct 75061
Button Willow Ct 75063
Byron Cir & Ct 75038
Cabell Dr 75063
Cabeza De Vaca Cir 75062
Cabrillo 75039
Cache Ct 75039
Cactus Ct 75060
Cactus Flower Ct 75063
Caddo Dr 75060
Caesar Ln 75038
Caleta 75038
Calgary Ct E & W 75062
Calle Del Sol 75062
Calli Ct 75060
Calvin Rd 75063
Cambridge Dr 75061
Camden Ct 75061
Camelia Ct 75060
Camelot Dr 75060
Cameron Ct & Pl 75060
Camilla 75039
Camino Lago 75039
Camino Rio 75039
Campana Ct 75061
Campbell Ct 75061
Campus Circle Dr E & W 75063
Canadian Dr 75039
Canal St 75063
Canary Dr 75062
Candlewood Trl 75063
Caneel Ct 75060
Canterbury St 75062
Cantrell St 75062
Canyon Ln 75063
Canyon Crest Cir & Dr 75063
Canyon Oaks Dr 75061
Canyon Side Way 75063
Capistrano St 75039
Capitol Ct 75060
Carano Ct 75063
Carbon Rd 75038
Cardinal Ln 75062
Carl Rd
1500-1598 75061
1600-2199 75061
2200-2698 75062
2700-2731 75062
2733-2799 75062
Carlisle St 75062
Carlton Way 75038
Carnaby St 75038
Carolyn St 75061
Carriage Dr 75062
Carrington Ct 75060
Carroll Ave 75061
Carter Cir 75060
Cartha Valley Ct 75063
Cartwright St 75062
Carver Ct, Ln & Pl 75061
Casa Dr 75063
Casa Bello Ct 75062
Casa Grande Ct 75061
Casa Oaks Cluster St 75060
Cascade Dr 75061
E & W Cason St 75061
Castillo St 75039
Castle Ct & St 75038
Castle Rock Ct 75038
Catalina Way 75039
Catalpa Cir 75063
Causey Ln 75061
Cavalier Ct 75062
Cay Ct 75060
Cecilia Ct 75060
Cedar Dr 75061
Cedar Elm Ct & Dr 75063
Cedar Valley Dr 75063
Central Ave 75062
Century Cir 75062
Century Center Blvd 75062
Century Lake Dr 75062
Chamberlain St 75060
Champagne Dr 75038
Chandelle Dr 75060
Chandler Ct 75060
Channel St 75061
Chaparral 75060
Charles Dr 75060
Charleston St 75063
Chase Ln 75063
Chaucer Hill Ln 75063
Chemsearch Blvd 75062
Cherokee Trl 75060
Cherry Laurel Ln 75063
Cherrywood Ct 75060
Chestnut St 75060
Chevy Chase Dr 75062
Cheyenne Ct N 75062
Cheyenne Ct S 75062
Cheyenne St
2201-2297 75062
2299-3499 75062
3501-3699 75062
3700-3798 75038
3800-3899 75038
Chime Cir, Ct, Pl & St 75062
Chinook Ct 75062
Chisholm Trl 75062
Choctaw Ct 75060
Christie Ct 75060
Christopher Ct 75060
Churchill Dr & Way 75060
Churchill Downs 75060
Chuy Ct 75063
Cibola Dr 75062
Cimarron Trl & Way 75063
Circle Dr 75060
Cistercian Rd 75039
Clark St 75060
Clay Ave 75061
Clearbrook Dr 75062
Clearspring Dr N & S 75063
Clearwater Dr 75039
Cliffside Ct & Dr 75063
Cloverleaf Ln 75061
Club House Cir & Pl 75038
Cobb 75061
Cochran St 75062
Cody Ct & St 75062
Coker St 75062
Colby Ct 75060
Colgate Ln 75062
Collier St 75060
Collins Dr 75060
Colony Ct & Dr 75061
Colony Ridge Ct 75061
Colony View Ln 75061
Colorado Dr 75039
Columbia Cir 75062
Colwell Blvd 75039
Comal Dr 75039
Comanche Trl 75060
Comano Dr 75061
Commerce Dr 75063
Commonwealth St 75062
Compass Link 75039
Compton Ave & Ct 75061
Concho Dr 75039
Concord Dr 75061
Condor Dr 75060
Conflans Rd 75061
Connection Dr 75039
Connor Ct 75060
Cooper Dr 75061
Coral Ct 75060
Coral Rock Ct 75060
Corbeau Dr 75038
Cordova Bnd 75060
Cornell Cir 75062
Coronado Ct & St 75062
Coronet St 75062
Corporate Ct & Dr 75038
Corral Dr 75063
Cortez Ct E & W 75062
Cortina Dr 75038
Cosbie Ct & Dr 75063
Cotoneaster Ct 75063
Cottonwood Ln 75038
Cottonwood Valley Cir, Ct, Dr & Pkwy N & S 75038
Coulee St 75062
Country Club Ct 75038
Country Club Dr W 75038
Country Club Rd N
3400-3699 75062
3701-3913 75038
4000-4098 75038
Countryside Dr 75062
County Line Rd 75061
Courtside Dr 75038
Cove Holw 75060
Coventry Ct 75061
Covey Ct 75060
Cowboys Pkwy 75063
Cox Dr 75062
Cozy St 75060
Crabapple Ln 75063
Craig St 75060
Crandall Rd 75060
Cranston Ct E & W 75062
Crape Myrtle Cir 75063
Crater Lake Ct 75062
Creek Dr 75060
Creek Ridge Ct 75060
Creek Wood Ct 75060
Creekside Cir & Ct 75063
Creekway Dr 75039
Crescent Ct 75063
Crest Ridge Ct & Dr 75061
Crestview Cir 75062
Cripple Creek Dr 75061
Crisp Dr 75061
Crockett Cir & Ct 75038
Cross Bnd 75061
Cross Bend Ct 75061
Cross Country Trl 75061
Cross Timbers Dr 75060
Crosswood Ln 75063
Crowberry Ln 75063
Crown Ct 75038
Crown Point Cir 75063
Croydon St 75062
Crystal Ct 75060
Cuesta Dr 75038
Cumberland Cir, Dr & Pl 75063
Cunningham St 75062
Currency St 75063
Custer Ct 75062
Customer Way 75039
Cypress Dr 75061
Cypress Waters Blvd 75063
Daisy Ln 75061
Dakota Trl 75063
Dale Pl 75061
Dames Ln 75039
Dana Ct 75060
Danfield Ct 75062
Daradown Dr 75061
Darr St 75061
Darrell Ct 75060
Dartmouth Dr 75062
Davis Dr 75061
Daywood Ln 75061
Decker Ct & Dr 75062
Deeplake Ct 75060
Del Mar Dr 75060
Del Rancho Dr 75061
Del Rio Ct 75062
N Delaware St 75061
S Delaware St 75060
Deleon St 75039
Dennis St 75062
Deseo 75039
Devonshire Ct E & W 75062
Dewey Ct 75060
Dewitt St 75062
Diamond Oak Dr 75060
Diana Ln 75061
Dillon Trl 75063
Dixon Dr 75061
Dobbins Ln 75063
Dogwood Ln 75063
Dominion Blvd 75038
Doncaster St 75062
Donley Dr 75063
Dorris Rd 75038
Dorsett Ct & Dr 75063
Dory Ln 75061
Double Oak Ln 75061
Double Tree Trl 75061
Douglas Ave & Cir 75062
Dover Rd 75060
Dowling Dr 75038
Drake St 75062
Drayton Dr 75063
Drexel Dr 75061
Driskill Dr 75038
Druid Dr 75060
Dulles Dr 75063
Dumas 75061
Dunbar St 75062
Duncan St 75060
Dunning St 75061
Dupree St 75062
N & S Durango Cir & Ct 75062
Durham St 75062
Dyer St 75061
Eagle Nest 75063
Eastside Dr 75061
Easy St 75060
Edgestone Dr 75063
Edgewood Dr 75060
Edinburgh St 75062
Edith St 75061
Edmondson Dr 75060
Edwards Ct N & S 75062
Elaine Dr 75060
Elby St 75061
Elder Ct 75060
Elizabeth St 75060
Elkhorn Path 75063
Ellen St 75062
Elm Valley Dr 75063
Elms Rd 75060
Elwood Rd 75061
Emerald Dr 75060
Emerson Park Ln 75063
Emmit Dr 75061
Empire Way 75038
Encanto Cir 75062
Encina 75038
Endres St 75061
English St 75061
Entrada Blvd 75038
Erikson Trl 75060
Escena Blvd 75039
Escondido St 75039
Esplendor Ave 75062
Esters Blvd 75063
Esters Ct 75062
Esters Rd
200-2099 75061
2101-2199 75061
2401-3399 75062
3600-3698 75062
3701-3797 75038
3799-4299 75038
Estrada Pkwy 75061
Estrella 75039
Etain Rd 75060
Ethan Dr 75060
Eugene Ct N & S 75062
Evening Star Ct 75063
Evergreen St 75061
Evergreen Oak Cir 75063
Executive Cir & Dr 75038
Exeter St 75062
F A A Blvd 75061
Fair Ct 75060
Fair Oaks Dr 75060
Fairbanks Ct 75062
Fairbrook St 75062
Fairdale St 75062
Fairfax Dr 75060
Fairfield St 75062
Fairmont St 75062
Falcon Dr 75060
Fallen Leaf Ct 75063
Falls Rd 75063
Familia Ct 75061
Fannin Dr 75038
Farine Dr 75062
Farnham Ct E & W 75062
Faulkner Pt 75063
Fenimore Ave 75060
Ferguson Ct 75062
Fiesta Cir 75063
Finley Rd 75062
Fireside Way 75060
Flagstone Dr 75039
Flamingo Ln 75062
Fleming Ave 75060
Flintridge Ct & Dr 75038
Florence Dr 75038
Fluor Dr 75039
Ford St 75061
Forest Cir 75062
Forest Dr 75061
Forest Glen Dr 75063
Forest Hills Dr 75063
W Fork 75039
Fountain Dr 75039
Fountainview Dr 75039
Fouts Dr 75061
Fowler St 75061
Fox Glen Cir & Dr 75062
Fox Hollow Trl 75063
Fox Horn Dr 75063
Fox Run Dr 75063
Foxcroft St 75062
Francine Dr 75060
Frank St 75061
Franklin St 75060
Freeport Pkwy 75063
French St 75061
Friar Tuck 75060
Frio Dr 75039
Frisco Ave 75061
Frye Rd 75061
Fuente 75039
Fuller Dr 75038
Fulton Dr 75060
Furlong Ct 75060
Gail Ct 75060
Galle St 75062
Game Lake Dr 75060
Garden Isle Dr 75060
Garden Oaks Dr 75061
Garden Terrace Dr 75060
Gardenia St 75063
Garrett Dr 75062
Gates Dr 75061
Gateway Dr
1901-1999 75038
2001-2199 75038
2300-2398 75063
2400-3099 75063
Gaywood 75061
Geneva Rd 75061
Gent Ct 75063
Gentry Rd 75062
George Ct 75061
Ghazali Ct 75062
Gibraltar St 75062
Gilbert Rd 75061
Gilbreath Cir 75061
Ginkgo Cir 75063
Glacier St 75062
Glavica Dr 75062
Glen Ct 75062
N Glen Dr 75063
Glen Alta Dr 75061
Glen Cove Dr 75062
Glen Dell Dr 75061
Glen Lea Dr 75062
Glen Loch Dr 75062
Glen Valley Dr 75061
Glen Vista Dr N & S 75061
Glenbrook Dr 75061
Glencrest Ct 75061
Glenhaven Ct 75061
Glenmore St 75060
Glenview Dr 75061
Glenwick Ln 75060
Glenwood Dr 75060
Gloucester Ct & St N & S 75062

Street	ZIP
Gold Oaks Dr	75060
Goodyear St	75062
Gorbet	75039
Grace Ln	75061
Granada Dr	75060
Grand Teton Ct	75062
Grand Turk Ct	75060
Grande Bulevar	75062
Grant St	75061
E & W Grauwyler Rd	75061
Great Falls Ct	75062
Green Ct	75063
Green Oaks Dr	75061
Green Park Dr	75038
Greenbrier Dr	75060
Greene St	75062
Greenhills Ct E & W	75038
Greenview Dr N & S	75062
Greenway Cir & Dr	75038
Greenwood St	75061
Greg Ct	75060
Griffiths Dr	75061
Grimes Rd	75061
Grosse Pt	75061
Grove St	75060
Guadalajara Cir & Ct	75062
Guadalupe Dr	75039
Guava Ct	75063
Guthrie St	75061
Hacienda Cir	75062
Hackmore Loop	75061
Hadrian Ct & St	75062
Haley St	75060
Hampshire St	75062
Hampton Cir	75061
Hancock St	75061
Hanover Ln	75062
Hanson Dr	75038
Hapsburg Ct	75062
Harbor Trl	75060
Harbor Dune Ct	75063
Hard Rock Rd	75061
Harlan St	75060
Harris Ct	75063
Harrison Ct	75061
Hartin Cir	75061
Harvard Cir N	75062
Harvard Cir S	75062
Harvard St N	75062
Harvard St S	75061
Harvest Lake Dr	75060
S Hastings St	75060
Hawn Ct	75038
Hawthorne St	75061
Heather Ridge Ct	75063
Heatherstone Dr	75063
Heatherwood Dr	75063
Heathrow Dr	75063
Helmet St	75060
Hemingway Ln	75063
Henderson Ct	75061
Hendrix Dr	75061
Henry Dr	
2000-2099	75061
2700-2799	75062
Hereford Dr	75038
Herring Ave	75061
Hickory St	75060
Hickory Hollow Ln	75063
Hidalgo St	75062
Hidden Rdg	75038
High Crest Ct & Dr	75061
High Point Dr	75038
High School Ln	75060
Highfield Trl	75063
E & W Highland Dr	75062
Highland Park Ct & Dr	75061
Hilburn Ct	75060
E Hill Dr	75038
Hill N Dale Dr	75038
Hillcrest Ct & Dr	75062
Hillshire Ln	75063
Hillside Ln	75062
Hilltop Dr & Pt	75060
Himes St	75060
Hinton Dr	75061
Hodges St	75061
Hogan Dr	75038
E & W Holland Dr	75062
Holly St	75061
Holly Tree Ct	75063
Hollywood Dr	75039
Home Depot Rd	75063
Homeplex Ct	75060
Homestead Ct	75061
Honeylocust Dr	75063
Honfleur Ct	75038
Hope Ln	75061
Horizon Way	75063
Horseshoe Bnd	75061
Hosanna Ct	75061
Houston St	75061
Howard Ct	75060
Howley Ct	75063
Hudson St	75060
Hughes Dr	75062
Hunt Dr	75062
E & W Hunter Ferrell Rd	75060
Huntersridge Ct & Dr	75063
Huntingdon Ct & Dr	75061
Hurd Dr	75038
Hux Ct	75060
Ichabod Ct	75061
Imperial Dr	75062
Indian Creek Dr	75060
Indiana Ct	75060
Indy Ct	75060
Inner Cir	75060
Innisbrook Dr N & S	75038
International Pl	75062
Iowa St	75060
Irby Ln	75061
E & W Ireland Dr	75062
Irene Dr	75061
Iris Dr	75061
Iron Horse Dr	75063
Irongate Cir	75060
Ironwood Dr	75063
Irvin Rd	75060
E Irving Blvd	75060
W Irving Blvd	
100-503	75060
505-899	75060
1300-2600	75061
2602-3498	75061
2701-2701	75015
2701-2701	75017
2701-3499	75061
Irving Mall	75062
E Irving Heights Dr	75060
N Irving Heights Dr	75061
S Irving Heights Dr	75060
Island Ct	75060
Iva St	75060
Jackson St	75061
James St	75061
Jamestown Dr	75061
Jan Ct	75060
Janell Dr	75062
Jardin St	75038
Jasmine Ln	75063
Jaynes Ct	75060
Jeff Ct	75060
N Jefferson St	75061
S Jefferson St	75060
Jeffery Trl	75062
Jennifer Cir	75060
Jenny Kay Ln	75060
Jetstar Dr	75063
Jill Ave	75061
Jim Dr	75061
Jimmydee Dr	75060
Jody Ln	75061
Joffre Dr	75061
E John Carpenter Fwy	75062
W John Carpenter Fwy	
100-298	75039
300-1199	75039
1201-1599	75039
1900-4600	75063
4602-5198	75063
John Smith Dr	75061
Johnson Rd	75061
Jordan Ct	75061
Joslin St	75060
Julia Ln	75060
Katelyn Ct	75060
Katherine Cir	75061
Kathy Ln	75060
Katy Dr	75061
Keathley Dr	75060
Keats Cir	75061
Keeler Dr	75060
Keisa Ln	75060
Kellywood Ct E & W	75038
Kendall Ln	75062
Kennedy Ct	75061
Kent Dr	75062
Kevin Ct	75060
Keyhole Cir & St	75062
Kim Dr	75061
Kimbrough Dr	75038
Kimili Ct	75060
King Ave	75060
King Richard St	75061
Kings Country Dr	75038
Kingston Dr	75061
Kinwest Pkwy	75063
Kirby	75061
Knight Ln	75060
Knob Oak Ct	75060
Knox St	75063
Konet St	75060
Kosstre Ct	75061
Kris St	75060
Krohn Ct	75038
La Chona St	75061
La Cima	75039
La Costa Ct	75038
La Jolla	75039
La Nita	75060
La Paz Ct	75062
La Reunion Ct	75060
La Vida Ct	75062
La Villita Blvd	75039
Lacebark Dr	75063
Lackey Ct	75060
Ladner Ln	75063
Lady Tiger Way	75061
Lago Vista Loop	75062
Laguna	75039
Lake Ct	75063
Lake Bend Dr	75060
Lake By Dr	75060
Lake Carolyn Pkwy	75039
Lake Gardens Dr	75060
Lake Haven Dr	75060
Lake Isle Cir	75060
Lake Point Dr	75039
Lake Tahoe Dr	75062
Lakebreeze Rd	75063
Lakecrest Cir & Ct	75063
Lakemont Dr	75039
Lakeridge Ct & Ln	75063
Lakeshore Ct & Dr	75060
Lakeside	75061
Lakeside Dr	75062
Lakeview	75061
Lakeway Dr	75060
Lakewood Dr	75063
Lamar Ct	75038
Lamesa Ct	75063
Landmark Ct & Rd	75060
Landover Pl	75063
Landry Ct	75063
Lane St	75061
Lantana Ln	75063
Laramie St	75062
Laredo Dr	75063
Larindel St	75062
Lark Ct & Ln	75062
Larriat St	75060
Larry Dr	75060
Las Brisas Ct & Dr	75038
Las Colinas Blvd	
5301-5997	75039
5999-6492	75039
6494-6798	75039
7401-7497	75063
7499-7599	75063
Las Colinas Blvd E	75039
Las Colinas Blvd W	75039
Las Colinas Rdg	75063
Las Cruces Dr	75063
Lasalle Dr	75062
Laurel Canyon Rd	75063
Laurel Oaks Dr	75060
Lavaca Dr	75039
Lawndale Dr	75063
Lawrence St	75061
Lawson St	75062
Lazy St	75060
Leann Ln	75061
Ledbetter Ct	75063
Lee St	75060
Lee Park Dr	75062
Legacy Trl	75063
Leisure Ln	75063
Lela St	75061
Lena Ln	75038
Lennox Ln	75060
Leslie Ln	75060
Lewis	75061
Lexington Dr	75061
Liberty Dr	75061
Lilac Ln	75060
Lilly Ct	75063
Limetree Ln	75061
Lincoln St	75061
Lincolnshire Ct & Dr	75061
Linda Ln	75062
Linden Lea	75061
Lindenwood Ln	75063
Lindhurst St	75061
Lindy Ct & Ln	75060
Linwood Ln	75061
Lismore Ln	75063
Little John Dr	75061
Live Oak Dr	75061
Lively St	75061
Liverpool Ln	75063
Llano Trce	75063
Lloyd Ct	75060
Locksley Chase	75061
Locust St	75063
Logan Ct & St	75062
Lohr Valley Rd	75063
Loma Alta Rd	75063
Loma Linda Dr	75063
Long Acre St	75060
Longhorn Dr	75063
Longmeadow Hill Dr	75063
Longview Rd	75063
Longwood Ct	75038
Lookout Cir	75060
N Loop 12	75061
S Loop 12	75060
Los Alamos Trl	75063
Lost Canyon Rd	75063
Louise St	75060
Love Dr	75039
Lowell Dr	75062
Lucille St	75060
Luckenbach Ln	75063
Luke St	75061
Luper Rd	75060
Luther Rd	75063
Luxor Dr	75062
Luzon Rd	75060
Lydia Cir	75060
Lydia Ct	75061
W Lyndon B Johnson Fwy	75063
Lynn Dr E & W	75062
N Macarthur Blvd	
100-2199	75061
2200-3600	75062
3602-3798	75062
4000-4198	75038
4200-5699	75038
5900-6700	75039
6702-7098	75039
7300-10399	75063
10401-10799	75063
S Macarthur Blvd	75060
Macarthur Ct	75061
Macarthur Park	75063
Maceta St	75039
Madera Rd	75038
Magenta Ct	75039
Magnolia Dr	75062
N Main St	75061
S Main St	75060
Malaga	75039
Maltby Rd	75061
Mandalay Canal	75039
Manders Ct	75063
Manesh Dr	75062
Manion St	75062
Maple St	75060
Marbella	75039
Marble Canyon Cir	75063
Marchant Ln	75063
Marcillia Cir	75038
Marie Ln	75060
Marigold Dr	75063
Marina Dr	75063
Mariposa Dr	75038
Mark St	75061
Market Pl	75063
Market Place Blvd	75063
Markland St	75060
Marlynn St	75061
Marshall Ct	75060
Marta Dr	75060
Marvel Dr	75060
Mary Lee Cir	75060
Maryland Dr	75061
Matador Dr	75039
Mateo Trl	75063
Mather Cir & St	75061
Maupin Ln	75061
Maverick	75060
Mavis St	75061
Maxwell Ave	75061
Mayflower Dr	75061
Maykus Ct	75061
Mayleaf Dr	75060
Mayo St	75060
Mccarthy St	75062
Mcclendon St	75061
Mcclure Cir & St	75062
Mccollum St	75061
Mccoy Dr	75062
Mcdermott St	75061
Mcham St	75062
Meadow Crst	75060
Meadow Dl	75060
Meadow Dr	75063
Meadow Gln	75060
Meadow Vly	75060
Meadow Creek Dr	75038
Meadow Lark	75060
Meadowbrook Ln	75061
Meadowview	75061
Meandering Dr	75060
Medina St	75061
Melrose Ave	75039
Mercy Ln	75061
Meredith Ct & Dr	75063
Merlot Sq	75038
Mesa St	75062
Mesquite Bend Dr	75063
Metker St	75062
Meyers Rd	75060
Michael Ct	75061
Michener Way	75063
Midcrest Dr	75063
Middlefork	75063
Midland	75061
Milam Ct	75038
Milan Dr	75038
Mill Creek Rd	75063
Mills Ln	75062
Millswood Dr	75062
Milner Rd	75061
Mimosa St	75061
Minto Dr	75063
Mission Cir	75063
Missoula St	75062
Missy Ln	75060
Mistletoe Dr	75060
Mitchell Rd	75060
Mohawk Dr	75061
Mojave Pl	75061
Monroe Ct	75061
Montego Bay Dr	75038
Monticello Dr	75061
Moonlight Way	75063
Morgan St	75062
Morning Star Ct	75063
Morris Ave	75061
Morton Ct	75063
Morven Park	75063
Mosley Dr	75060
Moss Hill Rd	75063
Moss Rose Cir	75061
Mosswood Ln	75061
Mossy Oak Dr	75063
Mount Vernon Dr	75061
Mountain Ct	75062
Mulberry Way	75063
Mulholland Dr	75039
Mullicane Ln	75061
Mullins St	75061
Muret St	75062
Murl Dr	75062
Mustang Dr	75063
Nancy Dr	75060
Naples Dr	75039
Napoli Way	75038
Nathan Dollar Ln	75060
National Dr	75060
Native Oak Ln	75063
Navajo Pl	75061
Navidad Ct	75063
Neece Dr	75060
Nellore St	75062
Nelson Dr	75038
New Haven St	75062
Newcastle Bnd	75063
Newton Cir E & W	75062
Nia Dr	75038
Nichols St	75060
Nocona Dr	75063
Nonesuch Pl	75061
Norma Dr	75061
Norman Ct	75063
Normandy Dr	75060
North Shr	75038
Northern Oak Cir	75063
E & W Northgate Dr	75062
Northlake Ct	75038
Northridge Ct & Dr	75038
Northview Dr	75038
Northwest Hwy	75039
Notre Dame Dr	75039
Nottingham Dr	75061
Novin Dr	75062
Nueces Dr	75039
N Nursery Rd	75061
S Nursery Rd	75060
N O Connor Blvd	75039
O Connor Ct	75062
N O Connor Rd	
100-110	75060
200-2199	75061
2201-2697	75062
2699-4999	75062
5001-5099	75062
S O Connor Rd	75060
O Connor Ridge Blvd	75038
Oak Lake Dr	75060
Oak Lea Dr	75061
Oak Meadow Dr	75061
Oak Ridge Ln	75061
Oak Valley Ct	75063
Oak Vista Dr	75060
E & W Oakdale Rd	75060
Oakhurst Dr	75061
Oakland Dr	75060
E Oaks Ln	75063
Oakwood Dr	75061
Oceanview St	75062
Oeste Dr	75039
Offshore Dr	75063
Ogden Pl	75061
Ohio St	75060
Old Faithful Ct	75062
Old Hickory Dr	75060
Old Mill Cir	75061
Old North Rd	75060
Old Oak Dr	75063
Old Orchard Dr	75061
Old Tree Walk St	75060
Old York Rd	75063
Olde Towne Dr	75061
Oleander Way	75063
Olympia St	75062
Onetta Dr	75061
Osage Ct	75060
Ouida Rd	75061
Owen Dr	75061
Owenwood Dr	75061
Oxbow Dr	75038
Oxer Dr	75063
Pacific Ct	75062
Palacio St	75039
Palm Oak Dr	75060
Paluxy Dr	75039
Pam Ct	75060
Pamela Dr	75062
W Park Dr	75061
S Park Ln	75060
Park Pl	75061
Park Crest Ct	75060
Park Grove Dr	75060
Park Place Ct	75061
Park Square Dr	75060
Parker St	75062
Parkridge Blvd	75063
Parkrow Pl	75060
Parkside Ave	75061
Parkway Dr	75061
Parkwood Pl	75060
Parliament St	75062
Parma Ct	75060
Partridge Ln	75062
Patricia St	75060
Patrick St	75060
Paula St	75060
Peach Tree Ln	75062
Pearl Ln	75060
Pearson St	75061
Pebblebrook Trl	75060
Pecan Dr	75061
Pecan Grove Ct	75060
Pecan Valley Dr	75063
Pecos Trl	75063
Pedernales Trl	75063
Pembroke St	75060
Pendleton Ct	75062
Penn St	75061
Pennington St	75062
Penny Ln	75063
Perkins Dr	75063
Perry St	75060
Persimmon St	75063
Peters Rd	75061
Peveto Dr	75060
Phelps Dr	75038
Phillip Ct	75060
Phyllis Ct	75060
Pic Dr	75061
Piccadilly	75060
Pickwick Cir & Ln	75060
Piedmont St	75061
Piedras	75038
Pilgrim Dr	75061
Pin Oak Dr	75060
Pine St	75063
Pioneer Dr	75061
Pistachio Cir & Dr	75063
Plantation Dr	75062
Plaza Dr	75063
Plaza Via	75039
Pleasant Oaks Dr	75060
Pleasant Run Rd	
3301-3397	75062
3399-3699	75062
3700-3898	75038

3900-3999 75038
4001-4399 75038
Plover Ln 75060
Plum Dr 75063
Plymouth Dr & Park 75061
Pocatello St 75062
Polaris Dr 75038
Ponce Dr 75061
Ponderosa Trl 75063
Poplar Ln E 75063
Portales Ln 75061
Portland St
3500-3600 75062
3602-3698 75062
3700-3798 75038
3800-3999 75038
4000-4199 75062
Posey Dr 75062
Post Oak Dr 75061
Postwood Ct 75060
Preakness Dr 75060
Premier Dr 75063
Preston Trl 75063
Primrose Dr 75063
Princeton Dr 75062
Priscilla Ln 75061
Pritchett Dr 75061
Proctor St 75061
Province Pl 75038
Pueblo Pl 75061
Puget St 75062
Puritan Dr 75061
Quail Crk 75063
Quail Rdg 75060
Quail Vly 75060
Quail Hollow Ln 75063
Quail Meadow Dr 75063
Quanah St 75060
Rainier St 75062
Raintree Dr 75063
Raleigh Cir 75061
Ranch Trl 75063
Ranch Hill Dr 75063
Ranch Vista Dr 75063
Ranchero Cir 75062
Rancho Cir 75063
Ranchview Dr 75063
Randy Dr 75060
Raton Pass 75063
Raven Ln 75063
Rawhide 75060
Rawls Cir 75061
Reale Dr 75039
Recognition Point Dr 75061
Red Oak Dr 75060
Red River Trl & Way 75063
Redbird Dr 75061
Redbud Ln 75061
Redondo 75039
Redwood Ct 75038
Reef Ct 75060
Reese Dr 75063
Regal Ridge Pkwy 75061
Regency Dr 75062
Regent Blvd 75063
Regina Ct N & S 75062
Reid Dr 75061
Renee Dr 75061
Renfro Ct 75063
Reserve Way 75038
Revere Dr 75061
Ricci Ct & Ln 75062
Richard Ct 75061
Richland St 75061
Richmond Ct & St 75063
Ricker Ct 75061
Rider Cir 75061
Ridge Hollow Trl 75063
Ridgecrest Dr 75060
Ridgedale St 75062
Ridgefield St 75062
Ridgehaven St 75062
Ridgemont St 75062
Ridgepoint Dr 75063
Ridgeview Cir & Ln 75062
Ridgeway St 75062
Ridgewood St 75062
Rindie St 75060
Rio Grande Dr 75039
Rita Ct 75060
River Hill Rd 75061
River Oaks Dr 75060
Riverlake Ct 75060
Riverside Dr 75039
Riverview Dr 75060
Riverwalk Ln 75063
Riviera Dr 75039
Roanoke Dr 75061
Robbie Dr 75061
Roberts Ave 75060
Robin Rd 75061
Robinhood Ct & Dr 75061
Robinson St 75060
Rochelle Blvd
204-1022 75062
1024-1300 75062
1400-1698 75039
Rochelle Pt 75062
E Rochelle Rd 75062
W Rochelle Rd 75062
Rock Island Rd 75060
W Rock Island Rd 75061
Rockingham Dr 75063
Rocklake Ct 75060
Rocky Cv & Ln 75060
Rodeo Dr 75063
Roger Williams Dr 75061
Rogers Pl 75060
N Rogers Rd 75061
S Rogers Rd 75060
Rolling Fork Bnd 75039
Rolston Rd 75060
Rome Ct 75038
Ronne Dr 75060
Rose Ct 75060
Rose St 75061
Rosebud Dr 75060
Rosedale St 75060
Rosita St 75062
Ross Dr 75061
E Royal Ln 75039
N Royal Ln 75063
W Royal Ln
501-797 75039
799-899 75039
901-1099 75039
1501-2197 75063
2199-4399 75063
4401-5099 75063
Royal Coach Ln 75060
Royal Oaks Dr 75060
Royal Ridge Pkwy 75063
Royalty Row 75062
Ruby Rd 75060
Rue De Vl 75038
Ruff Trl 75063
Rugby Dr 75063
Ruidosa Trl 75063
Runge Ct E & W 75038
Runstone Dr 75060
Rusdell Dr 75060
Russ Ct 75060
Rustic Ct & Dr 75060
Ruston Ln 75063
Rutgers Dr 75062
Rutherford St 75062
Ryan St 75061
Sabine Ct 75063
Saddle Rock Ct 75063
Saddle Tree Trl 75063
Saddlehorn Dr 75063
Sadge Ln 75063
Sagebrush 75060
Saint Andrews Blvd 75038
Saint Clair Dr E 75061
Saint Croix Grn 75038
Saint Durney Ct 75038
Saint Emelion Ct 75038
Saint Francis Ct 75039
Saint James Rd 75063
Saint Lo Dr 75060
Saint Monet Dr 75038
Saint Regis Dr 75038
Salem St 75061
Salida St 75062
Salinas Ct 75062
Salmon St 75062
Sam Hill St 75062
San Benito 75039
San Bernard Dr 75039
San Carlos Ct 75062
San Clemente 75039
San Felipe Dr 75039
San Fernando 75039
San Gabriel Dr 75039
San Jacinto Dr 75063
San Jose St 75062
San Juan Ct 75062
San Marcos Dr 75039
San Mateo Ct 75062
San Miguel Ct 75062
San Pedro Dr 75039
San Roque 75039
San Saba 75039
San Villa Dr 75061
Sandbar Dr 75063
Sanders Pl 75062
Sandra Dr 75060
Sandy Cir & Ln 75060
Sandy Shore Ct & Rd 75063
Santa Anita Blvd 75060
Santa Clara St 75062
Santa Fe Cir & Trl 75063
Santa Rosa Way 75062
Santiago Ct 75062
Savannah Dr 75062
Scarlet Oaks Dr 75060
Scenic Dr 75039
Schukar Ct 75061
Schulze Dr 75060
E & W Scotland Dr 75062
Scott Ct 75060
Sea Ter 75060
Sea Isle Dr 75060
Seabeach St 75062
Seagull Ct 75060
Seaside St 75062
Secretariat Ln 75060
Segundo Dr 75060
Senda 75039
Senter Rd 75060
Senter Valley Rd 75060
Sequoya Trl 75060
Seva Ct 75061
Sewell Ct 75038
Shadow Ln 75060
Shadow Rdg 75061
Shadowbrook Ln 75063
Shady Ln 75061
E & W Shady Grove
Rd 75060
Shady Spring Ct E &
W 75060
Shadylake Ct 75060
Shalamar Pl 75061
Shana Ln 75061
Sharon St 75061
Sheffield St 75062
Shelby Ct 75061
Shelly Cir 75061
Shepherd St 75060
Shere Cir & Ln 75060
Sheridan Trl 75063
Sherwood Ct 75061
Sherwood Dr 75060
Shinoak Vly 75063
Shirley Ln 75060
Shoaf Dr 75061
Shore Line St 75061
Shoreside Bnd & Dr 75039
Shrum Ct 75060
Shufford Ct & St 75060
Shumard Cir & Ct 75063
Shumard Oak Ln 75063
Shupe Ct 75060
Sicily St 75038
Sierra Dr 75039
Sierra Blanca Pass 75063
Silver Maple Dr 75063
Silver Oaks Cluster St 75060
Silverdollar Trl 75063
Silverstone Ln 75063
Silverton Dr 75063
Single Tree Trl 75061
Singleton Blvd 75060
Skylake Ct 75060
Skyline Dr 75038
Skyview Dr 75060
Skyway Cir N & S 75038
Sleepy Hollow Dr N &
S 75061
Smith Ave 75061
Soapberry Cir 75063
Socorro Ln 75061
Soledad Dr 75062
Somerset Dr 75061
Sonoma 75039
Sonora Ct 75062
Southcourt Cir 75038
Southern Oak Dr 75063
Southfork Bnd 75039
Southlake Ct 75038
Southridge Way 75063
Southstone Ln 75060
Southtrees St 75060
N Sowers Rd 75061
Spanish Trl 75060
Spear Ct 75039
Spicewood Ct 75063
Spinnaker Ct 75063
Spokane St 75062
Spring Canyon Dr 75063
Springlake Ct 75060
Springwood Dr 75063
Spur 482 75062
Spyglass Hill Ln 75038
Squire St 75062
Stafford St 75062
Staffordshire Dr 75061
Stagecoach Trl 75061
Stallion Xing 75060
Standish Dr 75061
Stanford Dr 75062
N Star Dr 75038
Starlake Ct 75060
Starlite Ln 75061
State Highway 161
3001-3199 75062
State Highway 161
6500-7400 75039
7402-7598 75039
N State Highway 161 75038
E State Highway 356 75060
Statesman Dr 75063
Staubach Dr 75063
Steeplechase Dr 75062
Steinbeck Ct & Ln 75063
Stella St 75060
Sterling St 75063
Steven St 75062
Stewart Dr 75061
Still Meadow Rd 75060
Stokes Ln 75063
Stone Dr 75061
Stone Canyon Dr 75063
Stone Gate Dr 75063
Stone Harbor Way 75063
Stonebrook St 75062
Stonecreek Dr 75063
Stonecrest Dr 75063
Stonehaven Ct 75038
Stoneledge 75063
Story Rd W
2300-3299 75038
2300-2300 75016
N Story Rd
100-1941 75061
1943-2199 75061
2200-3799 75062
3801-3897 75038
3899-4099 75038
4101-4199 75038
S Story Rd 75060
Story Vlg 75062
Storyglen St 75062
Stovall St 75061
Strait St 75062
Strawberry Cir 75060
Strickland Plz 75060
Sugar Maple Dr 75063
Sumac Rd 75063
Summer Moon Ct 75063
Summer Place Cir &
Dr 75062
Summit Dr 75062
Summitview Dr 75063
Sun Valley Ct & St 75062
Sundance Cir & Trl 75063
Sunny Ln 75060
Sunnybrook Dr 75061
Sunrise Ct 75063
Sunset Dr 75061
Sunstone Dr 75060
Supreme Ct 75061
Surrey Ln 75060
Surry Cir 75061
Sutton Ct 75062
Swallow Ln 75062
Swan Ln 75062
Sweetgum Dr 75063
Swiss Ln 75038
Sycamore Dr 75063
Syracuse Dr 75062
Tacoma St 75062
Tall Tree Dr 75060
Tallow Dr 75063
Tally Ho Dr 75062
Tameria Dr 75060
Tampico St 75062
Tangier St 75062
Tanglewood Dr E 75061
Taos Trl 75063
Tarango Ln 75061
Tejas Trl 75060
Teleport Blvd
3800-3898 75039
3900-3900 75014
3900-3998 75039
Tenneyson Ridge Dr 75063
Terraza 75039
Terry Way 75060
Teton Ct 75062
Texas Dr 75062
Texas Ash Dr 75063
Thad Dr 75061
Thames St 75062
Thistle Sage Ct 75063
Thomas St 75061
Thompson Ln & St 75061
Thorncliff Trl 75063
Thrush Dr 75062
Tienda 75039
Tierra 75038
Timberidge Dr 75038
Timberlake Dr 75062
Timberline Dr 75060
Timbers Dr 75061
Timberview Dr 75060
Time St 75061
Tioga Dr 75063
Tipton Rd 75060
Toler Ln 75062
Tom 75061
Tophill Ln 75038
Touchdown Dr 75063
Towne Cv 75061
Towne Colony Dr 75061
Towne Lake Ct 75061
Townsell Ct 75061
Tracey Cir 75060
Trae St 75060
Trailwood Ln 75061
Tranquilo 75039
Travis Cir & Ct 75038
Trent St 75061
Trinity St 75062
Trinity View St 75060
Tristar Dr 75063
Trotter St 75061
Truax Dr 75063
Trula Ln 75060
Truman Ln 75060
Tucasa Dr 75061
Tucker St 75060
Tudor Ln 75060
Turnberry Ct 75063
Turtle Cv 75060
Turtle Lake Blvd 75060
Tuscan Dr 75039
Tuscany Ct 75062
Twin Falls St 75062
Twinpost Ct 75062
E, N & W Union Bower
Ct & Rd 75061
University Park Ln 75062
Upton Pl 75060
Valencia Blvd 75039
Valley Trl 75063
Valley Lake Ct & Ln 75063
Valley Oaks Ct 75061
Valley Ranch Pkwy E 75063
Valley Ridge Dr 75062
Valley View Ln
100-1899 75061
1901-2199 75061
2200-3998 75062
4100-6098 75038
Valley Vista Dr 75063
Van Horn Dr 75060
Vance Dr 75061
Vanco Dr 75061
Vancouver St 75062
Vanetta St 75061
Vassar Dr 75062
Venice Dr 75038
Ventura Park 75061
Vera Ct 75060
Verde 75039
Via Amalfi 75039
Via Positano 75039
Via Ravello 75039
Vickie Dr 75060
Victoria St 75062
Victory Ct 75063
Vienna St 75038
E & W Vilbig St 75060
Village Ctr 75061
Village Creek Dr 75060
Village Green Dr 75038
Vince Hagan St 75062
Vine St 75039
Vinson Ct 75060
Virginia St 75061
Vista Cir 75063
Vivion St 75060
Voirin Rd 75061
Wade St 75060
Wagonwheel Ct 75061
Wahl St E 75060
Waldrop St 75061
Wales Pl 75062
Wallin Dr 75062
Walnut St 75060
E Walnut Hill Ln 75039
W Walnut Hill Ln 75038
Walnut Ridge Dr 75038
Walton Blvd 75063
Wanda Dr 75060
Wandering Brk 75060
Warren Cir 75062
Waterbrook Dr 75039
Waterford Dr 75063
Waters Ct & Dr 75063
Waters Edge Dr 75039
Waterside Dr 75063
Waterview Dr 75039
Weathered Cir & St 75062
Wellesley Dr 75062
Wellington Rd 75063
Wellington Point Dr 75063
Wells Rd 75061
Wendy Ct & St 75060
Wentwood Dr 75061
Wesleyan Dr 75062
Westbrook Dr 75060
Western Trl 75063
Westminster Dr 75038
Westmont Dr 75063
Westridge Cir & Dr N 75038
Westshore Ct 75060
Westside Dr 75061
Westwood Dr 75060
Whippoorwill Ln 75062
Whispering Trl 75060
White Ln 75063
White Hall 75038
White Lake Dr 75060
White Oaks Dr 75060
White Sands Trl 75063
Whitham St 75060
N Wildwood Dr 75061
S Wildwood Dr 75060
Wilesta Dr 75061
William Brewster Dr 75062
William Brewster St 75061
William Dehaes Dr 75038
Williams Rd 75060
Williamsburg Rd 75061
Willow Ln
500-699 75061
2400-2599 75060
Willow Creek Dr 75061
Willow Oak Dr 75060
Willow Wood Ct 75060
Willowdale Ln 75063
Wilshire Ct & Dr 75061
Wilson St 75061
Wilton Ter 75060
Wind River Ct 75062
Windmere Ct 75063
Windmill Ln 75061
Windsong Ln 75060
Windsor St 75062
Windsor Ridge Dr 75038
Windsor View Dr 75038
Windy Hollow Dr 75063
Wingren Dr
3400-3498 75062
3500-4299 75062
4300-4398 75039
Wingren Rd 75062
Winners Dr 75063
Winslow St 75062
Winston 75060
Winthrop St 75061
Witton St 75062
Wolf Creek Dr 75063
Woodbrook Ct 75061
Woodcreek Dr 75063
Woodenrail Ln 75061
Woodford Cv 75060
Woodland Dr 75060
Woodleigh Dr 75061
Woodoak Ct & Dr 75060
Woodway Dr 75063
World Cup Way 75038
Wrangler 75060
Wyche Dr 75061
Yale St 75061
Yaupon Dr 75063
Yellowstone Ct & St 75062
Yogi Way 75038
Yorkshire St 75061
Yorktown Dr 75061

NUMBERED STREETS

All Street Addresses 75060

KATY TX

General Delivery 77449

POST OFFICE BOXES MAIN OFFICE STATIONS AND BRANCHES

Box No.s
B - P 77492

OO - OO 77492
1 - 2001 77492
5001 - 6958 77491
9998 - 9998 77492

NAMED STREETS

A St 77493
Abbey Springs Ln 77494
Abbotglen Ln 77494
Abbotshire Ct 77494
Abbotswood Ct 77450
Abbutsford Ln 77450
Abby Ct 77493
Abby Aldrich Ln 77449
Abersham Ct 77450
Abigail Reese Way 77449
Acacia Glen Ln 77494
Acacia Wood Way 77449
Acadia Pine Ln 77494
Acorn Oaks Dr 77493
Acorn Square Ct 77493
Ada St 77494
Addison Forest Trl 77494
Addison Hills Ln 77494
Addlestone Ridge Ln 77494
Adelaide Meadows Ct & Dr 77449
Admiral Bay Ln 77494
Adwick Ct 77450
Afton Forest Ln 77449
Agave Dr 77494
Airline Dr 77493
Alabama St 77494
Alana Springs Dr 77450
Albee Dr 77449
Albion Cresent Dr 77449
Alden Manor Ln 77494
Aldenshire Ct 77494
Alder Pass Ct 77449
Alder Springs Ct & Ln 77494
Alderfield Manor Ln 77494
Aldersgate Ct 77450
Alexander Crossing Ln 77494
Alicia Way Ln 77493
Allenford Ct 77494
Allingham Ln 77494
Allister Ct 77494
Almond Park 77450
Almond Orchard Ln 77494
Alpine Crest Ln 77494
Alpine Rose Ln 77494
Alpine Trail Ln 77494
Alta Peak Ct & Way 77449
Alverstone Dr 77494
E & W Amber Bluff Ln 77494
Amber Chase 77450
Amber Cliff Dr 77449
Amber Glade Ct 77494
Amber Glen Ln 77494
Amber Meadow Dr 77449
Amber Springs Dr 77450
Amberfield Ln 77449
Amberleaf Ct 77494
Amberlight Ln 77450
Ambervine Cir 77450
Ambrosia Springs Ct & Ln 77494
Amela Plantation Dr 77449
Amelia Plantation Dr 77449
Amethyst Arbor Ln 77494
Amy Shores Ct 77494
Anchor Lake Ln 77494
Andrew Ln 77449
Angel Gate Ct 77494
Anson Falls Ct 77450
Antelope Creek Ln 77494
Anthem Cv 77494
Anthony Hay Ct & Ln 77449
Anthurium Ct 77449
Apache Falls Dr 77450
Apache Gardens Ln 77449
Apache Lake Dr 77449
Apache Meadow Dr 77449
Apple Park Dr 77450
Applewhite Dr 77450
Applewood Forest Dr 77494
April Springs Ln 77494
Arbor Cv 77494
Arbor Breeze Ct 77450
Arbor Creek Dr 77449
Arbor Pine Ln 77494
Arbor Point Ct 77450
Arbor Rose Ln 77494
Arbor Stream Dr 77450
Arbury Crest Ct 77494
Arcadia Glen Ct & Ln 77494
Arcadia Ridge Ln 77449
Archdale Ct 77494
Archibald Blair Ln 77449
Aristata Dr 77494
Armillary Dr 77449
Armstrong Ln 77494
Arrow Field Ln 77450
Arrow Lake Dr 77450
Arrow Star Ct & Dr 77493
Arrowbrook Ct 77494
Arrowchase Ct 77449
Arrowhead Bay Ln 77449
Arrowwood Trl 77494
Arroyo Hill Ct 77450
Artesian Springs Ct 77494
Ash Ln 77493
Ash Forest Dr 77450
Ash Haven Ln 77449
Asheboro Dr 77450
Ashford Grv 77450
Ashford Ridge Ln 77450
Ashford Sky Ln 77494
Ashfork Dr 77449
Ashland Hollow Ln 77494
Ashland Meadow Ln 77494
Ashley St 77494
Ashley Hope Dr 77494
Ashley Ridge Ln 77494
Ashley Spring Ct 77494
Ashmore Park Dr 77494
Ashwood Creek Ln 77494
Aspen Canyon Dr 77450
Aspen Hollow Ct 77494
Aspen Mist Ln 77449
Aspen Point Dr 77449
Aspen Ranch Ct 77449
Aspen Shores Ct 77449
Aspen Trails Dr 77449
Aspenfield Ln 77450
Aspenlodge Ln 77494
Aster Dr 77493
Asterglen Ct 77449
Astoria Brook Ln 77494
Athea Glen Cir 77450
Atwater Canyon Ln 77494
Aubrey Falls Ct 77450
Aubrey Hills Ln 77494
Auburn Dr 77493
Auburn Hollow Ln 77450
Auburn Trace Ct 77450
Auburn Vale St 77493
Augusta Breeze Ln 77494
Augusta Mist Ln 77449
Augusta Pointe Ct 77494
Austinville Dr 77449
Australia Reef Dr 77449
Autumn Branch Ct 77494
Autumn Fern Dr 77450
Autumn Flowers Dr 77449
Autumn Glade Pl 77449
Autumn Hills Dr 77449
Autumn Knoll Cir 77449
Autumn Lake Dr 77450
Autumn Meadow Dr 77449
Autumn Mist Ct 77450
Autumn Orchard Ct & Ln 77494
Autumn Shore Cir & Dr 77450
Autumn Terrace Ln 77450
Autumn Thistle Dr 77449
Autumn Trails Ln 77449
Autumnglow Ct 77494
Autumnwind Ct 77494
Avalon Bay Ln 77494
Avalon Canyon Ct 77450
Avalon Garden Ln 77494
Avebury Ct 77450
Aventine Plantation Dr 77449
Avenue A 77493
Avenue B
700-799 77494
800-1999 77493
Avenue C 77493
Avenue D 77493
Avery Cove Ln 77450
Avery Point Dr 77449
Avonbury Ln 77494
Aylesworth Ct 77494
Ayscough Ln 77493
Azalea Leaf Ct 77449
Azalea Meadow Ln 77494
Azalea Ranch Dr 77494
Azalea Valley Ct & Dr 77449
Azure Lake Ct 77494
Azure Pass Dr 77494
Baby Blue Ln 77494
Baden Oaks Ct 77494
Bagley Garden Ct 77449
Bailey Springs Ct 77450
Baileys Run Ln 77494
Bainford Ct 77494
Baird Ave 77493
Balch Springs Ln 77449
Baldridge Ln 77494
Baldwin Oaks St 77449
Ballina Meadows Ct & Dr 77449
Ballstonefield Ln 77494
Balmoral Glen Ln 77494
Balsa Rock Ct 77494
Balsam Brook Ln 77450
Balsam Creek Ln 77494
Bandera Branch Ln 77494
Bandera Glen Ln 77494
Bandera Ranch Ln 77449
Bandera Run Ln 77494
Banister Cv 77494
Bankers House Dr 77449
Banks Ridge Ln 77494
Banks Run Ct & Ln 77449
Banksfield Ct
3200-3299 77494
21700-21799 77449
Banning Park Ct & Ln 77494
Banning Point Ct 77494
Banning Springs Ln 77493
Banter Point Ln 77494
Banyan Crest Ln 77449
Barany Ct 77449
Barbons Heath Ct 77449
Barcan Cir 77450
Bare Meadow Ln 77494
Barker Bend Ct & Ln 77449
Barker Canyon Ln 77450
Barker Hollow Dr 77494
Barker Village Ct 77449
Barkermist Ln 77450
Barkston Ct & Dr 77450
Barley St 77494
Barleycorn Ln 77494
Barlow Bend Ln 77450
Baron Bend Ln 77449
Baron Cove Ln 77450
Baron Ridge Ln 77494
Baron Trace Ln 77449
Baronsledge Ln 77449
Barossa Valley Ln 77494
Barraud Ct 77449
Barrington Hills Ln 77450
Barrington Lodge Ln 77494
Barrow Glen Dr 77494
Barry Estate Ct & Dr 77493
Barstow Bend Ln 77449
Bartlett Rd & St 77493
Barton Creek Ct & Trl 77450
Barton Hollow Ln 77449
Barton Meadow Ln 77494
Barton Park Ln 77450
Basil Brook Ct 77494
Basil Clear Trl 77494
Basil Field Ct 77494
Basil View Ln 77494
Baslow Dr 77449
Bass Cove Ct 77493
Bassett Hall Ln 77493
Bassfield Ln 77494
Battle Dr 77494
Baughman Ridge Dr 77494
Bauxhall Ct 77450
Baxters Ct 77494
Bay Bower Ln 77449
Bay Hill Blvd 77494
Bay Hollow Ct & Dr 77450
Bay Mist Ridge Ln 77494
Bay Palms Dr 77449
Bay Pines Dr 77449
Bay Spring Dr 77450
Bay Wind Ct 77494
Bayliss Valley Ln 77449
Baylor Dr 77493
Baymist Ct 77450
Bayou Arbor Ln 77494
Bayou Vista Cir & Ct 77494
Beachgrove Ln 77494
Beachwater Dr 77450
Beachy Ct 77449
Beacon Brook Ln 77494
Beacon Cove Ct 77450
Beacon Springs Ln 77449
Bear Canyon Ct 77450
Bear Cave Ln 77449
Bear Hunters Dr 77449
Bear Meadow Ct & Ln 77449
Bear Pass Ct 77449
Bear Paw Cir 77449
Bear Run Ln 77449
Bear Springs Dr 77449
Bear Trail Ln 77449
Bear Tree Trl 77449
Beauford Dr 77494
Beaver Pass Ln 77449
Beckendorff Rd
22100-22999 77449
25000-29999 77493
Becker Pines Ln 77494
Becketts Knoll Ct 77494
Beech Canyon Dr 77494
Beech Landing Ln 77450
Beech Tree Ct & Dr 77449
Beechknoll Ln 77449
Beechview Ln 77449
Beeston Hill Dr 77449
Belfry Ct 77450
Belham Creek Dr 77494
Bell Canyon Ln 77494
Bell Hollow Ln 77494
Bell Mare Dr 77494
Bell Mountain Dr 77494
Bell Patna Dr 77449
Bella Meda Ln 77494
Bellefrost Ln 77450
Bellfield Ct 77494
Bellow Glen Dr 77449
Bellows Bend Ct & Dr 77450
Bellows View Dr 77494
Bellwood Pines Dr 77494
Belmont Bnd 77450
Belmont River Ln 77494
Belmont Spring Ln 77449
Belt Rose Ct 77494
Beltone Dr 77450
Belvoir Park Dr 77450
Belwin Dr 77450
Benbrook Springs Ln 77449
Benbury Dr 77450
Bend Willow Ct & Ln 77450
Bending Green Way 77450
Bending Pines Ct & Ln 77494
Bendstone Cir 77450
Bennington Spgs Dr 77494
Benson Arbor Ln 77494
Bent Arbor Ct & Ln 77450
Bent Brook Way 77449
Bent Hollow Ln 77494
Bent Lake Dr 77449
Bent Meadow Ct 77494
Bent Sage Ct 77494
Bent Spring Ct 77449
Bent Springs Ln 77449
Bentgrass Ct & Dr 77450
Bentgreen Chase Ct 77494
Bentley Glen Ln 77494
Bentridge Park Ln 77494
Bergenfield Ct 77450
Bering Crossing Dr 77494
Berkshire Elm St 77493
Berzin Ct 77493
Bethal Green Dr 77450
Betonica Ln 77449
Bevington Oaks Cir & Ct 77450
Bhandara Ct 77493
Bianca Spring Ln 77494
Bickford Ct 77494
Big Canyon Dr 77450
Big Meadow Ln 77494
Big Sky Dr 77450
Big Wells Dr 77449
Big Wood Springs Dr 77450
Billineys Park Dr 77449
Billingford Dr 77450
Billingsgate Dr 77449
Binalong Dr 77449
Birch Bay Ct 77449
Birch Manor Ln 77494
Birch Maple Dr 77493
Birch Point Dr 77450
Birch Rain Ct 77449
Birch Valley Ct & Dr 77450
Birchbank Ln 77449
Birchfield Oak Ct 77494
Birchleaf Dr 77449
Birchmere Ct 77450
Birkdale Ct 77494
Biscayne Pond Ct 77494
Biscayne Valley Ln 77449
Bitterroot Ranch Dr 77449
Black Bamboo Ln 77494
Black Canyon Dr 77450
Black Cherry Xing 77494
Black Eagle Dr 77494
Black Hickory Ct 77449
Black Mesa Ct 77494
Black Mountain Way 77449
Blackbluff Ct 77449
Blackheath Ct 77494
Blacksburg Ct 77450
Blacktip Dr 77449
Bladesdale Ct 77494
Blair Manor Ct & Ln 77449
Blairmore Ct 77450
Blaisefield Ct 77450
Blanchard Grove Dr 77494
Blane Dr 77493
Bleham Creek Dr 77494
Blenfield 77450
Blinkwood Park 77494
Bliss Canyon Ct 77494
Blissfield Ln 77450
Blooming Park Ln 77450
Blooming Sage Ct 77449
Bloomridge Cir 77450
Blossom Brook Ln 77450
Blossom Meadow Ct 77494
Blossombury Ct 77449
Blue Beech Dr 77449
Blue Canyon Dr 77450
Blue Caspian Ct 77494
Blue Dawn Dr 77449
Blue Finch Ct 77449
Blue Heather Ct 77494
Blue Holly Ln 77494
Blue Jay Ln 77494
Blue Juniper Dr 77449
Blue Lake Creek Trl 77494
Blue Mills Ct 77449
Blue Mountain Park Ln 77493
Blue Oasis Ct 77494
Blue Opal Ln 77494
Blue Reef Dr 77449
Blue Sage Dr 77494
Blue Water Bay Dr 77494
Bluebonnet Ln 77493
Bluebottle Ln 77449
Bluecreek Rdg 77449
Bluehaw Mdw Ln 77449
Bluff Canyon Way 77450
Bluffton Ln 77450
Bluma Ranch Dr 77494
Blushing Hollow Dr 77494
Boaters Crossing Dr 77493
Bob White Ave 77493
Bobby Jones Rd 77494
Bogden Village Cir 77449
Bollinger Ct 77494
Bolsover Sky Ct 77449
Bolton Trails Ln 77494
Bonnamere Ln 77494
Bonners Park Cir & Ct 77449
Bonnie Bend Ln 77494
Bonnie Bray Dr 77494
Bonnie Chase Ln 77449
Borah Peak Way 77449
Boren Dr 77493
Botany Bay Ln 77450
Botetourt Ct 77493
Boulder Hl 77494
Boulder Xing 77493
Boulder Bend Ln 77494
Boulder Cove Ct 77494
Boulder Lakes Ct 77494
Boulder Meadow Ln 77449
Boulder Trace Ln 77449
Boulder Valley Dr 77449
N Boundary Peak Way 77449
Bowcreek Ln 77449
Bowie Bend Ln 77494
Boxridge Ln 77449
Boxthorn Ct 77494
Boyden Knoll Dr 77494
Bracken Hurst Dr 77494
Brackenfern Rd 77449
Brad Hurst Ct 77494
Bradford Ridge Dr 77494
Bradgate Ct 77494
Bradly Ln 77493
Bradworthy Dr 77449
Brae Point Ct 77449
Braer Ridge Dr 77494
Brafferton Ln 77449
Braidwood Dr 77450
Braken Carter Ln 77449
Braken Manor Ln 77449
Braleybrook Ct 77494
Bramblefern Pl 77449
Branchmead Ct 77450
Brandon Oaks Way 77449
Brandyshire Dr 77494
Branford Hills Ln 77450
Brant St 77493
Brant Crossing Dr 77494
Brasstown Mountain Way 77449
Brattle Dr 77494
Braybend Ln 77450
Braypark Ln 77450
Breezeway Bend Ln 77494
Breezy Bend Dr 77494
Breezy Birch Ct 77494
Breezy Hill Dr 77449
Breezy Hollow Ln 77450
Brennan Ridge Ln 77450
Brentsprings Run Ln 77494
Brenwick Ct 77450
S Brenwood Cir & Dr 77449
Brenwood Glen Trl 77449
Brenwood Manor Dr 77449
Brenwood Trails Ln 77449
Breton Shore Ln 77494
Bretonwood Ln 77494
Briar Canyon Ct 77450
Briar Landing Ln 77450
Briar Moss Ln 77449
Briarchester Dr 77450
Briarsedge Ct 77449
Brickarbor Dr 77449
Bridge Creek Ln 77494
Bridge Falls Ct 77449
Bridge Light Ln 77449
Bridge Springs Ln 77449
Bridgebay Ln 77449
Bridgebluff Ln 77449
Bridgehaven Ct & Dr 77494
Bridgemeadows Ln 77449
Bridgewater Pt 77449
Bridgewater Manor Ln 77449
Bridgewater Village Dr 77449
Bridle Bluff Ct 77494
Brigade Trails Dr 77449
Bright Dawn Ct 77494
Bright Falls Ln 77449
Bright Hollow Ln 77494
Bright Sky Ct 77494
Brighton Hill Ln 77450
Brighton Hollow Ln 77449
Brighton Sky Ln 77494
Brighton Springs Ln 77449
Brightspring Ct 77449
Brigstone Park Dr 77450
Brinmont Place Ct & Ln 77494
Brinton Oaks Ct 77450
Brinton Trails Ln 77494
Brisbane Meadows Dr 77449
Bristlecone Dr 77449
Bristleleaf Dr 77449
Bristlestar Dr 77449
Bristol Band Ln 77450
Bristol Bend Ln 77450
Bristolwood Ct 77494
Britannia Dr 77450
British Manor Ln 77494
Britton Hill Way 77449
Britton Ridge Dr 77494
Broadcrest Ct 77494
Broadsky Dr 77449
Broadstone Dr 77449
Broadwind Ln 77449
Brockington Dr 77494
Brodie Ln 77449
Broken Branch Ct 77494
Broken Pebble Ct 77450
Bronco Bluff Ct 77450
Brondesbury Dr 77450
Bronze Bluff Dr 77449
Bronze Loquate Ct 77449
Brook Garden Ln 77449
Brook Grove Dr 77450
Brook Mills Ct 77494
Brookchester Dr 77450
Brookgreen Falls Dr 77450
Brookline 77494
Brookmall Dr 77449
Brookrock Cir 77449
Broughwood Cir 77449
Brown Meadow Ct 77449
Browndale Ct 77494
Brunson Grove Dr 77494
Brush Park Trl 77494
Brushmeade Ln 77449
Brushy Meadow Ct 77494
Bryan Garden St 77493
Bryan Pond Ct 77449
Bryce Canyon Dr 77450
Bryce Landing Ln 77494
Bryce Summit Ln 77494
Brynn Branch Ln 77494
Buchanan Hill Ln 77494
Buckeye Dr 77450
Buckland Park Dr 77449
Buckskin Ln 77493
Buckskin Trail Ct 77450
Buckthorn Dr 77494
Bucktrout Ln 77449
Buffalo Cove Ln 77493
Bugle Run Dr 77449
Bulrush Canyon Trl 77494
Bunker Bluff Ct 77494
Bunting Meadow Ct & Dr 77449
Burgess Heights Ln 77494

Burwood Cir 77449
Butler Springs Ct & Ln 77494
Byron Meadows Dr 77449
Cabin Line Ln 77494
Cable Brook Ln 77449
Cable Terrace Dr 77494
Cabra Ct 77449
Cabrera Trails Ln 77494
Cabrillo Landing Ct 77494
Cactus Bloom Ln 77494
Cactus Field Ln 77449
Cactus Finch 77494
Cactus Rose Dr 77449
Cactus Sage Trl 77494
Caddo Passway 77494
Cadencrest Ct 77494
Cadogan Ct & Ln 77450
Cairns Dr 77449
Cajon Canyon Ct 77450
Calaway Falls Ln 77494
Calaway Oaks Ln 77494
Calder Field Dr 77494
Calderbrook Dr 77449
Calderstone Ct 77494
Caledonia Dr 77449
Calgary Woods Ln 77494
Calico Crossing Ln 77450
Calico Trace Ln 77494
Calico Woods Ln 77494
Calthorte Ct 77450
Calvary Ln 77449
Calvert Crossing Ct 77449
Calvert Forest Dr 77494
Calveryman Ln 77449
Cambridge Dale Ct 77493
Cambridgeport Ct 77494
Cambry Park 77450
Cambry Crossing Ct 77494
Camden Bend Ct & Ln 77450
Camden Brook Ln 77494
Camden Garden Ln 77494
Cameron Bluff Ln 77494
Cameron Cove Ln 77450
Camillia Ct 77493
Camillia Ridge Way 77493
Camirillo Creek Ln 77494
Campfield Ct & Dr 77449
Camphor Tree Dr 77449
Camron Point Cir 77449
Canadian St 77493
Canaras Ct 77449
Canary Isle Ct 77450
Candle Gate Ln 77494
Candle Stick Ln 77494
Candleston Ln 77450
Candlewood Park Ln 77494
Candover Ct 77450
Cane Fields Rd 77493
Caney Fork Ct 77494
Caneybrook Ct 77449
Canfield Oaks Ln 77450
Cannon Fire Dr 77449
Cannondale Ln 77450
Cansfield Ct & Way 77494
Cantigny Ct & Ln 77450
Canton Crest Dr 77494
Canton Pass Ln 77450
Canvasback St 77493
Canyon Chase Dr 77450
Canyon Cypress Ct & Ln 77449
Canyon Dew Ln 77494
Canyon Forest Ct 77450
Canyon Fork Ct 77450
Canyon Garden Dr 77450
Canyon Gate Blvd & Ct 77450
Canyon Heights Ct 77494
Canyon Links Ct & Dr 77450
Canyon Park Dr 77450
Canyon Pass Dr 77494
Canyon Peak Ln 77450
Canyon Reach Dr 77494
Canyon Ridge Ct 77450
Canyon Rock Way 77450
Canyon Run Ct 77450
Canyon Sage Ln 77494
Canyon Shadow Dr 77450
Canyon Terrace Ct & Ln 77450
Canyon Top Ct 77450
Canyon Trace Ct 77450
Canyon Wren Dr 77494
Canyonview Ct 77450
Cape Meadow Ct 77494
Caper Meadow Ln 77494
Capesbrook Ct 77494
Capilano Ct 77494
Capitan Falls Ln 77494
Capitol Landing Ln 77449
Caponi Falls Ln 77494
Caravelle Ct 77494
Cardiff Mist Dr 77494
Cardiff Rocks Dr 77494
Cardinal Ln 77493
Cardona Dr 77449
Careybrook Ln 77449
Carlson Manor Ct & Dr 77494
Carlton Springs Ln 77494
Carmel Falls Ln 77494
Carmel Valley Dr 77449
Carmelite Ct 77450
Carnation St 77493
Carnoustie Ct 77494
Carol Collier Ct 77494
Carolina St
700-799 77494
6800-6898 77493
Caroline Chase Ct 77494
Caroline Cove Ln 77450
Carpet Bagger Dr 77449
Carriage Bend Dr 77450
Carrizo Springs Ct 77449
Carsen Spring Ct 77449
Carson Dr 77493
Carstone Ct 77450
Carter Moir Ln 77449
Carters Grove Ln 77449
Carver Pines Dr 77494
Cascade Rdg 77494
Cascade Creek Dr 77450
Cascade Glen Dr 77494
Cascade Springs Dr
6200-6299 77450
22100-22799 77494
Cascet Ct 77450
Cash Dr 77493
Casper Cliff Ct 77494
Cassidy Park Ln 77450
Castell Manor Dr 77494
Castle Bend Dr 77450
Castle Falls Ct 77494
Castle Gardens Ct & Ln 77449
Castle Peak Ct 77494
Castle Springs Dr 77450
Castleheath Ct 77494
Castlemills Ct 77450
Castleton Creek Ct 77450
Castlewind Cir, Ct & Dr 77450
Caswell Ct 77450
Cat Springs Ct 77449
Catalina Harbor Ct 77494
Catalina Island Dr 77494
Catron Xing 77493
Cattle Call Way 77494
Cavendale Ct 77494
Cayman Point Dr 77450
Cedar Ln
2000-2299 77494
6500-6899 77493
25500-25599 77494
Cedar Cove Ct & Dr 77450
Cedar Pine Dr 77494
Cedar Point Pl 77449
Cedar Rain Dr 77449
Cedar Shade Rd 77494
E Cedar Sun Trl 77449
Cedar Village Ct 77450
Cedardale Falls Dr 77494
Cedardale Pines Dr 77494
Cedarfield Rd 77494
Cedarsham Ln 77494
Celtic Terrace Dr 77494
Cenizo Park Ct 77494
Centennial Glen Dr 77450
Center Village Dr 77494
Centerbrook Ln 77450
Century Plant Dr 77494
Chablis Ridge Ct 77449
Chadbury Park Dr 77450
Chadell Point Ln 77449
Chalet Knolls Ln 77494
Chalet Park Dr 77494
Chalet Ridge Dr 77494
Chamberlin Cv 77494
Chamomile Meadow Trl 77494
Chandon Mist Dr 77449
Channelwood Ln 77450
Chantalle Dr 77449
Chantel Way 77494
Chapel Cone Ln 77494
Chapel Glen Ct 77450
Chapel Rock 77494
Charlenes Way Dr 77494
Charlisa Springs Dr 77449
Charlton House Ln 77493
Charlton Oaks Ct 77494
Charter Lake Cir & Ln 77494
Chasestone Ct 77450
Chateau Bend Ct & Dr 77450
Chatfield Pond Way 77449
Chaus Ct 77494
Cheddington Dr 77450
Chelsea Canyon Ct 77450
Chelsea Park Ct 77450
Chelsea Ridge Ct 77450
Chelsen Bridge Ln 77450
Cheltenham Dr 77450
Cherish Trl 77494
Cherokee St 77494
Cherokee Hollow Dr 77450
Cherrington Ct & Dr 77450
Cherry Haven Cir 77449
Cherry Orchard Ct & Ln 77449
Cherry Quartz Ct 77494
Cherry Ranch Dr 77494
Chesapeake Bend Ln 77449
Chesley Park Ct & Dr 77494
Chessgate Ct 77450
Chesterton Ct 77494
Chesterwick Dr 77450
Chestnut Hills Ct & Dr 77450
Chestnut Pines Dr 77494
Cheyenne Crest Ln 77494
Cheyenne Meadows Dr 77450
Chickasaw Plum Way 77494
Chickory Trl 77450
Chicory Chase Ct 77494
Chicory Star Ln 77494
Chilton Ln 77493
China Lake Ct 77494
Chippenham Dr 77450
Chislestone Ln 77449
Chisolm Creek Ct 77449
Christopher Ln 77493
Churchill Gate Ln 77494
Cimarron Pkwy 77450
Cinco Blvd 77450
Cinco Falls Dr 77494
Cinco Forest Trl 77494
Cinco Lakes Ct & Dr 77450
Cinco Manor Ln 77494
Cinco Park Pl 77450
Cinco Park Rd 77450
Cinco Park Place Ct 77494
Cinco Ranch Blvd
21900-23099 77450
23100-27299 77494
Cinco Ridge Dr 77494
Cinco Terrace Dr 77494
Cinco Village Center Blvd 77494
Cinnamon Dr 77450
Circle Lake Dr 77494
Cisco Hill Ct 77450
Cisco Terrace Ct 77449
Citrus Field Ln 77449
City Shores Ln 77494
Claradon Point Ln 77450
Claremore Ct 77449
Claridge Park Ct & Ln 77494
Clarissa Ct 77494
Clay Rd
19200-21499 77449
21501-21799 77449
23200-28799 77493
Clay Canyon Dr 77450
Clay Landing Ln 77449
Claybeck Ln 77494
Claymill Ct 77449
Claysprings Ln 77450
Clear Bend Ln 77450
Clear Canyon Dr 77450
Clear Mill Ln 77494
Clear Water Park Dr 77450
Clemson Dr 77493
Cliff Park Dr 77450
Cliff Pointe Ln 77494
Cliffhill Ct 77494
Cliffpoint Ct 77449
Cliffstone Ln 77449
Cloud Lake Ct 77450
Cloudbrook Ln 77449
Cloudcliff Ln 77494
Cloudcraft Ct 77494
Cloudhaven Ct 77449
Clover Trl 77494
Clover Ranch Cir & Dr 77494
Cloverfield Dr 77494
Clubhollow 77450
Clydehurst Grove Ct 77494
Coastal Mdw 77494
Coastal Grove Ln 77494
Coastal Prairie Ln 77493
Coats Creek Ln 77449
Cobble Canyon Ln 77494
Cobia Dr 77494
Cocoplum Dr 77449
Coffee Mill Ct 77449
Colbury Ct 77450
Colby Bend Dr 77450
Colby Lodge Dr 77450
Cold Spring Trce 77494
Coldfield Dr 77449
Coldwater Canyon Ln 77449
Cole Park Cir 77450
Cole Trace Ln 77494
Coleman Creek Ct 77449
Colesberry Ct 77450
Colliford Creek Ct 77494
Collinford Ct 77494
Colonial Pkwy
22601-22699 77449
23400-24899 77493
Colonial Bend Ln 77450
Colonial Birch Ln 77493
Colonial Crest Dr 77493
Colonial Elm Dr 77493
Colonial Manor Dr 77493
Colonial Maple Dr 77493
Colonial Park Ln 77494
Colonial Point Dr 77494
Colony Green Dr 77494
Colony Grove Ln 77449
Colony Trail Ln 77449
Colt Bluff Ct 77494
Colt Sky Ct 77494
Columbia Falls Ct & Ln 77450
Commerce Pkwy 77494
Commercial Center Blvd 77494
Community Cir 77494
Comstock Springs Dr 77450
Conant Ct 77494
Concho Springs Dr 77449
Concord Run Ct 77493
Concordia Dr 77450
Condors Nest 77494
Conestoga Cir 77450
Connor Grove Ct 77493
Conrad Ln 77449
Conroy Pointe Ln 77494
Conway Meadows Ct 77494
Cook Point Ct & Ln 77494
Coopers Gulch Trl 77449
Copinsay Dr 77449
Copper Cliff Dr 77449
Copper Creek Dr & Ln 77450
Copper Manor Ct 77494
Copper Sky Ct & Ln 77494
Coppersmith Dr 77450
Coquina Dr 77494
Coral Chase Ct 77494
Coral Meadow Ct 77449
Coral Shadows Dr 77449
Coral Springs Ct 77494
Corcoran Dr 77449
Corditt St 77494
Cordova Brook Ln 77494
Corey Cove Ln 77494
Coriander Dr 77450
Corianne Ct & St 77493
Corinne Ct 77449
Corinth Meadow Ct 77449
Cornell Park Ln 77494
Cornerstone Place Dr 77450
Cornflower Ln 77494
Corral Gate Ct 77450
Corry Crest Cir 77493
Cottage Cove Ln 77450
Cottage Manor Ln 77494
Cottage Oak Ln 77494
Cottage Pines Dr 77449
Cottage Point Dr 77494
Cottage Ridge Ln 77494
Cottage Sky Ln 77493
Cottage Springs Ct 77494
Cottage Stone Ln 77449
Cottage Wind Ln 77494
Cottage Wood Ct 77494
Cotton Bay Ln 77449
Cotton Field Ln 77449
Cotton Gin Dr 77449
Cotton Ranch Dr 77494
Cottondale Ct 77450
Cottonwood Dr 77493
Cougar Bend Ln 77449
Country Corner Ct 77494
Country Cove Ln 77494
Country Park Ct & Dr 77450
County Down Ct 77494
Courtland Oaks St 77494
Courtney Manor Ln 77494
Cove Hollow Dr 77450
Cove Lake Dr 77449
Coyote Call Ct 77449
Coyote Echo Dr 77449
Coyote Ridge Ln 77449
Cozy Cabbin Dr 77449
Cramer Ct 77450
Cranes Creek Ct 77494
Cranfield Ct & Dr 77450
Cranford Sage Ln 77494
Crazy Horse Circle Dr 77449
Creek Bridge Ln 77449
Creek Edge Ct 77449
Creek Landing Ct 77449
Creek Ledge Dr 77494
Creek Village Dr 77449
Creekmist Ct 77494
Creekshore Dr 77449
Creektrace Ln 77449
Crescent Common Dr 77494
Crescent Cove Ct 77494
Crescent Creek Ln 77449
Crescent Point Cir & Dr 77494
Crescent Star Ct 77450
Cresent Cove Ct & Ln 77494
Cresent Creek Dr 77449
Cresent Point Dr 77450
Crest Peak Ct & Way 77449
Crestbrook Bend Ln 77449
Crested Butte Dr 77494
Crested Lark Ct 77450
Crestford Park Ln 77494
Creston Cliff Ct 77494
Creston Woods Dr 77494
Crestwind Run Ln 77494
Crestworth Ln 77449
Crimson Clover Xing 77449
Crimson Star Ter 77494
Crisfield Ct 77450
Crispy Canyon Ct 77494
Crongtow Dr 77449
Crosby Sky Ct 77494
Cross Hollow Ln 77494
Crossbend Dr 77494
Crossbrook Ct & Dr 77450
Crosscoach Ln 77449
Crossfield Dr 77450
Crossing Nexus Ln 77450
Crossmill Ln 77450
Crossover Rd 77494
Crossprairie Dr 77494
Crossvale Ridge Ln 77494
Crownfield Ln 77450
Crutchfield Ln 77449
Crystal Bay Dr 77450
Crystal Downs Ct & Dr 77450
Crystal Forest Ct & Trl 77493
Crystal Greens Dr 77450
Crystal Leaf Ln 77494
Crystal Meadow Pl 77494
Crystal Pass Ct 77449
Crystal Point Dr 77449
Crystal Springs Ln 77494
Crystal Stone Ln 77494
Crystal Wind Ln 77494
Cumberland Brook Ln 77494
Custard Apple Trl 77494
Cypress Ln 77493
Cypress Arbor Ct & Dr 77449
Cypress Bay Ct & Dr 77449
Cypress Bough Dr 77449
Cypress Canyon Dr 77449
Cypress Cliff Dr 77449
Cypress Colony Ln 77449
Cypress Dawn Ln 77449
Cypress Flower Dr 77449
Cypress Glades Cir, Ct & Dr 77449
Cypress Harbor Dr 77449
Cypress Harrow Dr 77449
Cypress Moss Dr 77449
Cypress Peak Ln 77449
Cypress Rain Ln 77449
Cypress River Dr 77449
Cypress Rose Ct 77449
Cypress Royal Dr 77449
Cypress View Cv 77494
Cypress Willow Dr 77449
Cypressbluff Ln 77449
Cypressthorn Ln 77449
Cyrus Hill Dr 77449
Dabney Manor Ct & Ln 77449
Dahlia Ln 77493
Daisy Meadow Dr 77449
Dakota Run Ln 77493
Dalton Bluff Ct 77494
Dalton Spring Ln 77449
Dan Cox Ave 77493
Dan River Dr 77493
Danbridge Gulch Ln 77494
Danbridge Hills Ln 77494
Dandelion Meadow Ln 77494
Daniel Falls Ln 77449
Danover St 77494
Dapplewood Ln 77449
Dark Canyon Ct 77449
Darmouth Hill Ct 77493
Dartford Springs Ln 77494
Dartmouth St 77493
Davenmoor Ct 77494
Davenport Dr 77494
Davids Crest Ct 77450
Dawn Sq 77449
Dawn Hollow Ln 77494
Dayflower Dr 77449
Daystrom Ln 77494
Debras Trace Ln 77450
Decker Dr 77494
Decker Ridge Ct & Dr 77449
Deep Canyon Dr 77450
Deep Cliff Dr 77494
Deep Coral Ct 77494
Deep Glen Ln 77449
Deep Hollow Dr 77494
Deep South Ct & Dr 77449
Deer Meadow Ln 77493
Deer Run Ct 77493
Deercreek Cir 77493
N Deerfield Ct & Dr 77493
Deermeadow Falls Ln 77494
Deermoss Dr 77449
Deerwood Ct 77493
Defoe Dr 77449
Deforest Ridge Cir & Ln 77494
Delfren Ln 77493
Delta Queen Dr 77449
Delta Spring Ln 77450
Denali Range Ct 77449
Denford Ct 77450
Denison Oaks Dr 77494
Dennington Dr 77449
Densberry Ln 77494
Denton Meadows Ct 77449
Dentredg Rd 77493
Derbybrook Ct 77494
Derbyshire Dr 77493
Derbywood Glen Ln 77494
Dering Ct 77450
Desert Cliff Ct 77494
Desert Gold Dr 77494
Desert Oasis Ln 77494
Desert Sage Dr 77449
Desert Willow Dr 77449
Destiny Park Ct 77449
Devereaux Ct 77450
Deville Dr 77450
Devon Green Dr 77449
Devonberry Ln 77450
Devonport Dr 77449
Dewberry Ln 77494
Dewberry Creek Ln 77494
Dewcrest Dr 77449
Dewflower Dr 77494
Diamond Hills Ln 77449
Diamond Hollow Ct 77450
Diamond Knoll Ct 77494
Diamond Ranch Dr 77494
Diamond Rock Ct & Dr 77449
Diamond Run Ct 77494
Diamond Shore Ct 77450
Diamondale Ct 77450
Diamondcliff Ct 77494
Dill Canyon Ln 77494
Dillon Creek Ln 77494
Dillon Wood Ct 77449
Dillsbury Ct 77449
Dinner Creek Ct & Dr 77449
Dockside Terrace Ct & Ln 77494
Dogwood Ln 77493
Dogwood Park Ct & Ln 77449
Doherty Cir & Pl 77449
Dolan Fall Ln 77450
Dolan Hills Ct 77494
Dollins St 77493
Domineco Ln 77450
Dominion Dr 77450
Doonside Dr 77449
Doral Rose Ln 77449
Dorman Ct 77494
Douglas Park Ct 77450
Dove Ln 77493
Dove Glen Dr 77449
Dover Creek Ln 77494

Dover Harbor Ln ... 77494
Dover Mist Ln ... 77449
Dover Park Ln ... 77450
Dover Springs Ct ... 77494
Doves Gate Ct ... 77494
Doveshire Ct ... 77449
Downdale Cir ... 77450
Downing Park Blvd ... 77494
Drake Ct ... 77493
Drake Falls Ct ... 77450
Drakefield Ct ... 77494
Drakewood Dr ... 77449
Draycutt Dr ... 77494
Drennanburg Ct ... 77449
Drewlaine Fields Ln ... 77449
Drews Manor Ct ... 77494
Drexel Dr ... 77493
Driftwood Springs Dr ... 77449
Dripping Point Ln ... 77494
Driver Green Ln ... 77493
Dry Canyon Ct ... 77449
Drybank Dr ... 77449
Drybank Creek Ln ... 77494
Dryfalls Ct ... 77449
Dunbrook Park Ln ... 77449
Dunhill Ct ... 77494
Dunhill Park Ln ... 77494
Dunlap Meadows Ln ... 77494
Dunlin Terrace Dr ... 77494
Dunsley Dr ... 77449
Durango Canyon Ln ... 77494
Durango Creek Ln ... 77449
Durango Falls Ln ... 77494
Durango Mist Ln ... 77449
Durban Oaks Dr ... 77494
Durfey Ln ... 77449
Durham Chase Ln ... 77449
Dusty Creek Dr ... 77449
Dusty Heath Ct ... 77450
Dusty Hollow Ln ... 77494
Dusty Manor Ln ... 77494
Dusty Meadow Ct ... 77449
Dusty Terrace Ln ... 77449
Dutton Point Ct & Dr ... 77493
Dylan Springs Ln ... 77450
Eagle Bnd ... 77450
Eagle Canyon Way ... 77450
Eagle Haven Dr ... 77494
Eagle Meadow Dr ... 77450
Eagle Nest Fls ... 77449
Eagle Park Ln ... 77494
Eagle Peak Ct ... 77494
Eagle Point Trail Dr ... 77449
Eagle Ridge Dr ... 77449
Eagle Sky Blvd ... 77449
Eagle Talon Ct ... 77494
Eagle Watch Ct ... 77450
Eaglebend Ln ... 77494
Eagles Walk ... 77450
Eagles Knoll Ct ... 77494
Earl Of Dunmore Ln ... 77449
Earls Court Dr ... 77450
Earthstone Dr ... 77494
East Ave ... 77493
Eastman Pl ... 77449
Eastonwood Ct ... 77494
Eatons Creek Ct & Trl ... 77449
Eberhart Star Ct ... 77494
Echo Falls Dr ... 77450
Eden Point Ct & Ln ... 77494
Edendale Cir ... 77450
Edensborough Dr ... 77449
Edgecliff Falls Ct ... 77449
Eldarica Way ... 77494
Elden Hills Ct & Way ... 77494
Elder Rd ... 77493
Elder Park Ct ... 77449
Elenas Bend Ct ... 77494
Elizabeth Place Ct ... 77494
Elk Bluff Ln ... 77494
Elk Ridge Ln ... 77494
Elk Vista Ct ... 77494
Elkana Deane Ln ... 77449
Elks Dr ... 77494
Ellerbe Springs Ln ... 77494
Ellingham Dr ... 77450
Ellis Hill Ct ... 77494
E & W Elm Cir ... 77493
Elm Chase Ct ... 77494
Elm Hurst Ln ... 77450
Elm Wing Ln ... 77450
Elmsbury Ct ... 77449
Elmtree Estates Dr ... 77449
Elsberry Park Ln ... 77450
Elsinore Dr ... 77450
Elton Knolls St ... 77449
Ember Canyon Ln ... 77449
Ember Falls Ln ... 77449
Emberwood Falls Dr ... 77494
Emerald Bay Cir ... 77449
Emerald Branch Ln ... 77450
Emerald Canyon Rd ... 77450
Emerald Loft Cir ... 77450
Emerald Meadow Ct ... 77494
Emerald Ridge Cir ... 77450
Emerald River Dr ... 77494
Emery Heights Ln ... 77494
Emily Ln ... 77449
Emily Forest Trl ... 77494
Emily Park Ln ... 77494
Emily Trace Ln ... 77494
Emory Green St ... 77493
Empire Oaks Ln ... 77494
Emporia Chase Ct ... 77494
Emporia Point Ct ... 77494
Empty Saddle Ct ... 77450
Enchanted Mdw & Xing ... 77494
Enchanted Cactus Dr ... 77494
Enchanted Crest Ct & Dr ... 77449
Enchanted Landing Ct & Ln ... 77494
Enchanted Meadow Ln ... 77450
Enchanted Park Ln ... 77450
Endell Ct ... 77450
Enford Ct ... 77450
Englefield Ct ... 77449
Englewood Point Ct ... 77494
English Turn Dr ... 77494
Ensbrook Meadow Ln ... 77449
Erica Lee Ct ... 77450
Erika Way Dr ... 77450
Erin Ashley Ln ... 77494
Erincrest Ct ... 77450
Ernstes Rd ... 77494
Estes Lake Ln ... 77494
Eula Morgan Rd ... 77493
Eule Dr ... 77493
Eva Ln ... 77493
Evan Ln ... 77449
Evangeline Springs Ln ... 77494
Evanmill Ln ... 77494
Evans Grove Ln ... 77494
Evening Cloud Ct ... 77450
Evening Moon Ct & Ln ... 77449
Evening Rose Ln ... 77449
Everett Glen Dr ... 77494
Everett Knolls Dr ... 77494
Evergreen Meadow Ct ... 77449
Everhart Manor Ln ... 77494
Everhill Cir ... 77450
Everington Cir & Dr ... 77450
Exeter Cir ... 77493
Ezra Hill Dr ... 77494
Faded Trl ... 77494
Fair Chase Ct & Dr ... 77494
Fair Dawn Ct ... 77450
Fair Meadow Ln ... 77494
Fair Walnut Way ... 77494
Fairbay Dr ... 77450
Fairbranch Ct & Dr ... 77494
Fairbreeze Dr ... 77494
Faircliff Ln ... 77449
Faircreek Ln ... 77450
Fairgrange Place Ln ... 77494
Fairhope Grove Cir ... 77449
Fairleaf Cir ... 77494
Fairmont Hills Ln ... 77494
Fairmont Ridge Ln ... 77494
Fairvine Park Dr ... 77494
Fairwater Dr ... 77450
Fairway Bnd ... 77450
Fairway Valley Ln ... 77494
Fairweather Ct ... 77450
Fairwick Ct ... 77450
Falcon Hollow Ln ... 77494
Falcon Knoll Ln ... 77494
Falcon Landing Blvd ... 77494
Falcon Meadow Dr ... 77449
Falcon Park Dr ... 77494
Falcon Point Dr ... 77494
Falcon Talon Ct ... 77494
Falcon View Dr ... 77494
Falcongrove Ln ... 77494
Fall Branch Dr ... 77450
Fall Ridge Cir ... 77494
Fall Wind Ct ... 77494
Fallen Branch Dr ... 77494
Falling Rock Ln ... 77494
Falling Water Ln ... 77494
Falling Water Estates Ln ... 77494
Fallmist Cir & Ct ... 77494
Fallridge Ct ... 77494
Falls Canyon Ct ... 77494
Fantail Dr ... 77494
Far Hills Dr ... 77494
Far West Trl ... 77494
Farrier Run Dr ... 77494
Faulkner Ridge Dr ... 77450
Fawnbrook Ct ... 77450
N & S Fawnlake Cir & Dr ... 77493
Feather Glen Ct ... 77494
Fenton Rock Ln ... 77494
Fergis Dr ... 77449
Fermandi Dr ... 77494
Fern Ln ... 77493
Fern Bend Ln ... 77494
Fern Hollow Ct ... 77449
Fern Mist Ct & Ln ... 77449
Fern Pine Ct ... 77449
Ferndale Meadows Dr ... 77494
Fernglen Dr ... 77449
Fernhaven Dr ... 77449
E Fernhurst Dr ... 77450
W Fernhurst Dr ... 77494
Ferry Boat Dr ... 77449
Field Briar Dr ... 77450
Field Manor Ln ... 77450
Field Meadow Ct & Dr ... 77449
Fieldbluff Ln ... 77449
Fielder Dr ... 77450
Fielder Brook Ln ... 77494
Fielder Village Ln ... 77494
Fieldshire ... 77494
Fieldshire Cir ... 77449
Fieldthorne Ct ... 77450
Fieldvine Ct ... 77450
Fiesta Flower ... 77494
Figurine Ct ... 77450
Finbury Ln ... 77494
Finbury Oaks Ln ... 77449
Fincastle Dr ... 77450
Finch Springs Ln ... 77494
Finchgrove Ln ... 77494
Finsbury Field Dr ... 77493
Fiona Pines Trl ... 77494
Fiona Sky Ln ... 77494
Firecrest Ct & Dr ... 77494
N & S Firethorne Rd ... 77494
Firewalk Trce ... 77494
Fish Creek Dr ... 77450
Flagmore Ct & Dr ... 77450
Flannery Ct ... 77450
Flat Creek Ln ... 77450
Flatwood Dr ... 77449
Flint Hill Dr ... 77449
Flint Valley Ln ... 77494
Flintlock Dr ... 77449
Flintoff Ln ... 77449
Flintside Dr ... 77449
Floral Glen Ln ... 77449
Floral Valley Ln & Way ... 77449
Florina Ranch Dr ... 77494
Flower Bud ... 77494
Flower Creek Ct ... 77494
Flower Crest Cir ... 77449
Flower Ridge Ct ... 77494
Flowering Ash Xing ... 77494
Fm 1463 Rd ... 77494
Fm 2855 Rd ... 77493
Fm 529 ... 77449
Folkstone Cir ... 77494
Fordham Cir ... 77493
Forest Dew Dr ... 77449
Forest Lake Trl ... 77493
Forest Pine Ln ... 77494
Forest Sage Ln ... 77494
Fork Ct & Dr ... 77450
Forrester Trl ... 77449
Fort Bowie Ct ... 77449
Fort Bridger Dr ... 77449
Fort Custer Ct ... 77449
Fort Davis Ct ... 77449
Fort Dodge Dr ... 77449
Fort Laramie Dr ... 77449
Fort Stanton Dr ... 77449
Fort Stockton Dr ... 77449
Forthlin Cir ... 77494
Fortuna Dr ... 77493
Fossil Creek Cir ... 77450
Fossil Park Dr ... 77494
Foster Bridge Ln ... 77494
Foster Gardens Ln ... 77449
Foundary Dr ... 77493
Founding Dr ... 77449
Fountain Mdw ... 77494
Fountain Arbor Ln ... 77449
Fountain Spray ... 77494
Fox Path ... 77494
Fox Arbor Ln ... 77449
Fox Path Ct ... 77494
Fox Ridge Ln ... 77494
Foxbend Dr ... 77449
Foxberry Glen Ln ... 77494
Foxcrest Dr ... 77494
Foxrun Vista Dr ... 77494
Foxtail Pine Ln ... 77450
Franklin Park Dr ... 77494
Franz Rd
5100-6499 ... 77493
19800-23099 ... 77449
23100-26099 ... 77493
Frasier Knolls Ct ... 77494
Fred St ... 77494
Freeman Ave & Rd ... 77493
Freeridge Ct ... 77449
Fremont Manor Ln ... 77494
Fresco Dr ... 77449
Fresco Wells Dr ... 77449
Fresh Canyon Ct ... 77449
Friar Tuck Dr ... 77493
Frost Gate Ct ... 77449
Frostmeadow Ct ... 77450
Fry Ct ... 77450
N Fry Rd ... 77449
S Fry Rd
200-6099 ... 77450
6100-10699 ... 77494
Fulford Ct ... 77450
Fulford Point Ln ... 77494
Fullgarden Ct ... 77449
Gable Creek Ct ... 77494
Gable Grove Ln ... 77494
Gable Hollow Ln ... 77450
Gable Landing Ln ... 77494
Gable Lodge Dr ... 77494
Gable Ridge Dr ... 77450
Gablepoint Dr ... 77450
Gablestone Ln ... 77450
Gabrielle Canyon Ct ... 77450
Gadwall Dr ... 77494
Gail Meadow Ct ... 77494
Galapagos Ct ... 77449
Galena Stone Ln ... 77494
Galleon Oaks Dr ... 77450
Ganado Creek Ct ... 77449
Gannet Peak Way ... 77449
Ganton Dr ... 77450
Garden Branch Ct ... 77450
Garden Canyon Ct ... 77450
Garden Canyon Dr
6400-6799 ... 77449
22700-22999 ... 77450
Garden Chase Ct & Dr ... 77494
Garden Cove Ct ... 77494
Garden Field Ln ... 77450
Garden Flower Ct ... 77449
Garden Green Trl ... 77449
Garden Heath Ln ... 77449
Garden Meadow Dr ... 77449
Garden Terrace Dr ... 77494
Gardenia Ln ... 77493
Gardenia Ranch Dr ... 77494
Gardenlily Ct ... 77494
Gardensage Ln ... 77494
Garnet Grove Ct ... 77494
Garnet Shadow Ln ... 77494
Garnet Stone Ln ... 77494
Garnetfield Ln ... 77494
Gaston Rd ... 77494
Gate Creek Ct ... 77494
Gatemere Ct ... 77450
Gatewood Manor Dr ... 77494
Gatling Ct ... 77449
Gemstone Cove Ct ... 77494
Genet Dr ... 77494
Gentilly Dr ... 77450
Gentle Moss Ln ... 77494
Gentle Willow Ln ... 77494
George Bush Dr ... 77493
Georgetown St ... 77493
Gerald Glen Ct ... 77450
Geronimo Ct ... 77450
Gettysburg Valley Ct & Dr ... 77449
Gibbons Crest Ln ... 77449
Gilford Ln ... 77494
Gillian Park Dr ... 77449
Gillside Manor Dr ... 77494
Ginger Bluff Trl ... 77494
Ginger Branch Ct ... 77494
Ginger Creek Trl ... 77450
Ginger Gables Ln ... 77494
Ginger Hill Ln ... 77449
Ginger Lily Ln ... 77494
Ginger Ranch Dr ... 77494
Gingham Check Ct ... 77449
Ginter Ln ... 77494
Glacier Creek Dr ... 77494
Glade Shadow Ct ... 77494
Gladesdale Park Ln ... 77450
Gladeside Dr ... 77449
Gladestone Ridge Ct ... 77494
Gladway Manor Dr ... 77494
Glen Abbey Dr ... 77494
Glen Arden Ln ... 77450
Glen Burrow Ct ... 77494
Glen Canyon Ct ... 77450
Glen Cypress Ct ... 77449
Glen Holly Ln ... 77494
Glen Landing Dr ... 77449
Glen Rosa Dr ... 77494
Glenburn Manor Ln ... 77449
Glendale Hills Ln ... 77494
Glendavon Ln ... 77450
Glenhope Dr ... 77449
Glenirish Dr ... 77494
Glenlevan Ln ... 77494
Glenover Dr ... 77450
N & S Glenrock Hills Ct & Dr ... 77494
Glenthorpe Ct & Ln ... 77494
Glenway Falls Dr ... 77449
Glenwood Dr ... 77493
Godfrey Cove Ct ... 77494
Golden Brook Ln ... 77450
Golden Eye ... 77493
Golden Fork Dr ... 77494
Golden Larch Dr ... 77494
Golden Mesa Dr ... 77494
Golden Mews Ln ... 77494
Golden Nugget Ct ... 77450
Golden Raintree Dr ... 77449
Golden Terrace Ct ... 77494
Golden Wave Ct ... 77494
Golden Wave Dr ... 77449
Golden West Dr ... 77450
Golden Willow Ct & Dr ... 77449
Goldenport Ln ... 77494
Goldlake Dr ... 77449
Goldstone Dr ... 77450
Goodwin Dr ... 77493
Gorki Park Dr ... 77449
Gorton Dr ... 77449
Gosforth Dr ... 77449
Goss Hollow Ln ... 77449
Governors Place Dr ... 77450
Governorshire Dr ... 77450
Goynes Rd ... 77493
Grace Hills Ln ... 77494
Gracefield Manor Ct ... 77450
Graceful Oak Xing ... 77494
Gracys Landing Ln ... 77494
Graham Park Ln ... 77449
N Grand Pkwy ... 77449
W Grand Pkwy N ... 77493
W Grand Pkwy S ... 77494
Grand Bay Ln ... 77449
Grand Canyon Gate Dr ... 77450
N Grand Circle Blvd ... 77449
Grand Colony Ct & Dr ... 77449
Grand Corner Dr ... 77494
Grand Cove Ct ... 77450
Grand Creek Ct & Ln ... 77450
Grand Cypress Ln ... 77449
Grand Forks Dr ... 77450
Grand Glen Ct ... 77494
Grand Harbor Dr ... 77494
Grand Hollow Ln ... 77450
Grand Junction Dr ... 77450
Grand Meadows Ct & Dr ... 77494
Grand Pass Ct & Ln ... 77494
Grand Pebble Ln ... 77494
Grand Phillips Ln ... 77450
Grand Shores Ct ... 77494
Grand Springs Dr ... 77494
Grand Terrane Ln ... 77449
Grand Vista Ln ... 77494
Grandmill Ln ... 77494
Grandwood Ln ... 77450
Granger Oaks Ct ... 77494
Granite Bluff Ln ... 77494
Granite Brook Ln ... 77494
Granite Creek Ct ... 77449
Granite Meadow Dr ... 77494
Granite Springs Ln ... 77449
Grassy Haven Ln ... 77494
Gray Hawk Ln ... 77449
Grayson Bend Dr ... 77494
Grayson Lakes Blvd ... 77494
Grayson Point Ln ... 77449
Graystone Crossing Dr ... 77494
Great Creek Ln ... 77450
Great Meadows Dr ... 77493
Great Prairie Ln ... 77494
Great Springs Ct ... 77494
Green Emerald Ct ... 77494
Green Forest Bluff Trl ... 77494
Green Hedge Dr ... 77494
Green Heron Dr ... 77494
Green Leaf Spring Ln ... 77494
Green Meadows Ln ... 77493
Green Oasis Ct ... 77449
Green Stem Path ... 77494
Greenbrae Ln ... 77494
Greenbusch Rd ... 77494
Greenhead St ... 77493
Greenheath Ln ... 77450
Greenhouse Rd ... 77449
Greenough Dr ... 77494
Greenrush Dr ... 77494
Greenside Hill Ct & Ln ... 77449
Greenvalley Trail Dr ... 77449
Greenvine Cir ... 77494
Greenwade Cir ... 77449
Greenway Park Cir ... 77494
Greenway Village Ct & Dr ... 77494
Greenwell Springs Ln ... 77494
Greenwood Trace Ln ... 77494
Gregwood Ct ... 77450
Grenoble Ln ... 77450
Grey Peregrine Dr ... 77494
Grey Reef Dr ... 77449
Grey Sparrow Dr ... 77494
Grey Swan Dr ... 77494
Greytip Ct ... 77449
Griffin Ln ... 77493
Griffin House Ln ... 77493
Grove Square Ct ... 77449
Groveton Ct ... 77494
Guardsman Ln ... 77449
Guilford Glen Ln ... 77494
Gulfmont Dr ... 77494
Gummert Rd ... 77449
Guster Dr ... 77494
Guston Hall Ln ... 77449
Guthrie Ridge Ln ... 77494
Hackamore Brook Ct ... 77449
Hackberry Dr ... 77494
Hackberry Ln ... 77493
Hackberry Creek Dr ... 77494
Haden Park Dr ... 77450
Hadley Rock Dr ... 77494
Hadrian Dr ... 77449
Haggard Nest Dr ... 77494
Hailey Grove Ln ... 77449
Halbrook Glen Ln ... 77494
Hall Colony Ct ... 77449
Hall Croft Chase Ln ... 77449
Hall Meadow Ln ... 77494
Hall Pond Ct ... 77449
Hamden Ct ... 77450
Hamilton Mill Ct ... 77494
Hamlet Ridge Ln ... 77449
Hammerhead Ct ... 77449
Hampshire Rocks Dr ... 77450
Hampton Bay Ln ... 77494
Hampton Lakes Ct & Dr ... 77493
Hampton Oak Ct ... 77449
Hamptonshire Ln ... 77494
Hanneck Ct ... 77450
Hanneck Valley Ln ... 77450
Hannington Dr & Ln ... 77450
Hannover Grove Ln ... 77449
Harbor Lakes Ln ... 77494
Harbour Chase Dr ... 77450
Hardwick Hills Ln ... 77494
Hardwidge Ct ... 77450
Harmony Mill Ct ... 77494
Harmony Shores Dr ... 77494
Harper Creek Ln ... 77494
Harper River Ct ... 77494
Harrier Ct ... 77494
Harris Mill Dr ... 77449
Harrison Ct ... 77450
Hartcliff Cir ... 77449
Harte Ct ... 77449
Hartglen Cir ... 77450
Hartwill Dr ... 77494
Harvest Pointe Ln ... 77494
Harvest Trail Ln ... 77449
Harwood Heights Dr ... 77494
Harwood Hts Dr ... 77494
Hatcher Dr ... 77494
Hatfield Glen Dr ... 77449
Haven Cove Ln ... 77449
Haven Creek Dr ... 77449
Haven Field Ct ... 77494
Haven Green Cir ... 77449
Haven Hill Dr ... 77494
Haven Valley Dr ... 77449
Havenmoor Pl ... 77449
Havenport Dr ... 77494
Havenshire Ct ... 77494
Havenwood Canyon Ln ... 77494
Haverbay Ct ... 77449
Hawk Meadow Dr ... 77449
Hawkes Bay Ct ... 77494
Hawkins Creek Ct ... 77494

Hawkins Glen Ln 77449
Hawkins Manor Ln 77449
Hawks Harbor Ct 77494
Hawkstone Ct 77494
Hawthorne Bend Dr 77494
Hawthorne Garden Way 77494
Hayden Park Dr 77494
Hayman Ct & Dr 77449
Haystream Dr 77449
Haywards Crossing Ln 77494
Haywards Crossing South Cir 77449
Hazel Alder Way 77494
Hazel Berry Way 77494
Hazel Field Ct 77494
Hazel Ranch Dr 77494
Hazepoint Dr 77494
Hazy Ln 77449
Hazy Bluff Ct 77449
Heart Pine Way 77494
Heartland Key Ln 77494
Heather Ln 77449
Heather Hollow Dr 77449
Heather Way Ct 77449
Heatherbriar Ln 77494
Heathercroft Dr 77450
Heatherdawn Ct 77494
Heatherwood Ct 77494
Heights Dr 77493
Helding Park Ct 77494
Helmsman Knolls Dr 77494
Hemlock Red Ct 77494
Hendricks Pass Dr 77494
Henson Falls Dr 77494
Heritage Dr 77493
Heritage Grand 77494
Heritage Star Xing 77494
Heritage Stream Dr 77494
Herons Grove Ln 77494
Herons Pointe Ln 77494
Herrick Ct 77450
Hesse Ct 77449
Hickman Manor Ln 77449
Hickory Bay Ct 77450
Hickory Burl Ct 77449
Hickory Chase Ct & Dr 77450
Hickory Farm Dr 77449
Hickory Trail Pl 77450
Hidden Alley Dr 77494
Hidden Brook Ln 77449
Hidden Canyon Rd 77450
Hidden Falls Ct 77450
Hidden Garden Mist Ln 77449
Hidden Knoll Dr 77494
Hidden Ranch Dr 77494
Hidden Shore Cir & Dr 77450
Hidden Timbers Ln 77494
High Bridge Ct 77494
High Canyon Ct 77450
High Desert Ln 77494
High Landing Ln 77494
High Plains Dr 77449
High Stone Ln 77449
Highland Knls 77494
Highland Bay Ct 77450
Highland Falls Ln 77450
Highland Knolls Blvd 77494
Highland Knolls Dr 77450
Highland Stone Ct 77450
Highway Blvd 77494
Highwind Bend Ln 77449
Hikers Bend Dr 77493
Hillgreen Dr 77494
Hillpark Dr 77450
Hillwood Ln 77449
Hockaday Dr 77450
Holbrook Springs Ct 77449
Holiday Bay Ct 77494
Hollingers Is 77450
Hollingsworth Pine Ln 77494
Hollinwell Dr 77450
Hollow Ash Ln 77450
Hollow Bloom Ln 77494
Hollow Branch Dr 77450
Hollow Field Ln 77450
Hollow Harvest Ln 77449
Hollow Lodge Ct 77450
Hollow Pass Ln 77494
Hollow Wind Dr 77450
Hollowback Dr 77494
Hollowlog Dr 77449
Hollowvine Ln 77494
Holly Canyon Ct 77450
Holly Cove Ln 77449
Holly Lake Ct & Dr 77450
Holly Ranch Dr 77494
Hollycrest Dr 77494
Hollydale Ridge Ln 77494
Hollyfare Dr 77494
Hollyfield Ln 77493
Holton Ridge Dr 77494
Hon Ct 77449
Honey Blossom Ln 77494
Honey Glen Ln 77494
Honey Locust Dr 77449
Honey Mesquite Way 77494
Hope Wood Mills Dr 77494
Hopeview Ct 77449
Hopewell Dr 77493
Hoppers Creek Dr 77449
Horizon Grove Ln 77494
Horned Owl Dr 77494
Horse Prairie Dr 77449
Houghton Rd 77450
Hoveden Ct & Dr 77450
Hoyt Ln
100-1499 77494
1600-1799 77449
27000-27299 77494
Hudgens Ave 77493
Hudson Falls Ln 77494
Humboldt Park Ln 77494
Hunstanton Ct 77450
Hunter Ln 77494
Hunterclif Ln 77449
Hunters Rock Ln 77494
Hunters Shore Dr 77494
Hunting Bay Ct 77494
Hunting Meadow Dr 77449
Hunting Valley Ct & Ln 77494
Huntington Ct 77493
Huntland Ct 77450
Huntswell Ct 77494
Huntwood Hills Ln 77494
Hurston Glen Ln 77494
Hurstshire Bnd 77494
Hutton Park Dr 77494
Iberville Glen Dr 77494
Ibis Lake Ct 77449
Ibris Ranch Dr 77494
Ida Rose Ct 77449
Idian Grass Ln 77494
Igloo Rd 77494
Imperial Bend Ln 77493
Imperial Colony Ln 77449
Imperial Landing Ln 77494
Indian Crest Ct 77494
Indian Grass Dr 77449
Indian Grove Ln 77450
Indian Hills Way 77494
Indian Knoll Dr 77450
Indian Ridge Ct & Dr 77450
Indian Stone Ln 77449
Indiangrass Ct & Ln 77494
Indigo Acres Ct 77494
Indigo Bay Ct 77494
Indigo Hill Ln 77450
Indigo Pines Ln 77450
Indigo Pointe Ln 77494
Indigo River Ln 77449
Indigo Stone Ln 77449
Ingham Dr 77449
Inscho Ln 77450
Inwood Dr 77493
Iris Ln 77493
Irish Mist Ct 77450
Iron Castle Ct 77450
Iron Point Ct 77494
Iron Tree Ln 77494
Ironloft Ct 77450
Isthmus Cove Ct 77494
Ivory Creek Ln 77450
Ivory Gate Ln 77449
Ivory Lake Ct 77494
Ivy Cv 77494
Ivy Blossom Ln 77450
Ivy Fair Way 77449
Ivy Meadow Ln 77449
Ivy Run Ct 77450
Ivy Stone Ct
4900-4999 77449
22300-22399 77450
Ivy Terrace Ct 77450
Ivy Trace Ln 77494
Jack Pine Dr 77494
Jackson Bluff Dr 77494
Jackson Park Ln 77494
Jacob Bend Dr 77494
Jacob Canyon Dr 77450
Jacobs Landing Ln 77494
Jade Bloom Ct 77494
Jade Bluff Ln 77450
Jade Brook Ct 77494
Jade Clover Ln 77494
Jade Forest Ln 77494
Jamie Brook Ln 77494
Jamintre Dr 77450
Jan Ct 77493
Jarl Ct 77449
Jasmine Field Way 77494
Jasmine Hills Ct 77494
Jasperwood Cir 77449
Jeanene Ct 77449
Jervis Ln 77449
Jessica Ct 77493
Jessica Ln 77449
Jetty Cove Ct 77494
Jewel Springs Ln 77494
Jocelyn Park Ct 77493
John Clapp Rd 77494
John Clyde Dr 77494
John Crump Ln 77494
John Rolfe Ln 77449
Johndale Ct 77494
Jordan Terrace Ln 77494
Jordanfield Ln 77494
Josey Springs Ln 77494
Joshua Ln 77449
Joshua Kendell Ln 77449
Josslyn Ct 77494
Julie Marie Ln 77494
Junction Bend Ln 77494
Juneberry Ct 77494
Juniper Forest Fall Ln 77494
Juniper Spring Trl 77449
Juniper Stone Ln 77494
Juniper Terrace Ln 77494
Juniper Walk Ln 77494
Justin Ridge Rd 77494
Jutewood Ln 77450
K St 77493
Kadabra Dr 77449
Kale Garden Ct 77494
Kale Ranch Dr 77494
Karankawa Dr 77493
Karen Rd 77494
Katex Blvd 77493
Kathy Ln 77493
Katie Ridge Ln 77450
Katy Fwy
20000-21698 77449
20001-21099 77450
21201-21299 77449
21301-23199 77450
23500-29599 77494
Katy Arbor Ln 77494
Katy Creek Ranch Dr 77494
Katy Flewellen Rd 77494
Katy Fort Bend Rd 77493
S Katy Fort Bend Rd 77494
Katy Fulshear Rd 77494
Katy Gap Rd 77494
Katy Gaston Rd 77494
Katy Hockley Rd 77493
Katy Hockley Cut Off Rd 77493
Katy Hollow Dr 77449
Katy Mills Blvd, Cir, Dr & Pkwy 77494
Katy Mist Dr 77449
Katy Ranch Rd 77494
Katy Shadow Ln 77494
Katy Springs Ln 77494
Katy Town Ln 77493
Katybriar Ln 77449
Katyland Dr 77493
Kayvon Ct 77494
Kearsley Dr 77493
Keiller Cir 77450
Kellicreek Dr 77450
Kelliwood Arbor Ln 77450
Kelliwood Courts Cir 77450
Kelliwood Greens Dr 77450
Kelliwood Grove Ct & Ln 77450
Kelliwood Lakes Ct & Dr 77450
Kelliwood Manor Ln 77450
Kelliwood Oaks Dr 77450
Kelliwood Park Ct & Ln 77450
Kelliwood Trails Ct & Dr 77450
Kelly Rd 77493
Kempsford Ct & Dr 77450
Kendall Rock Ln 77449
Kendall Shay Ct 77450
Kendra Ln 77450
Kendra Forest Trl 77494
Kenlake Dr 77450
Kenneth Way 77494
Kenny St 77493
Kensington Briar Ln 77449
Kent Falls Ct & Dr 77450
Kent Ranch Ct 77494
Kentbury Ct 77450
Kenwich Oaks Ln 77449
Kerryblue Dr 77450
Kessler Cove Ln 77494
Kestrel Vw 77494
Kestrel Trace Ln 77494
Key West Dr 77493
Keystone Trl 77450
Keystone Pine Ct 77449
Keywood Ln 77449
Kieth Harrow Blvd 77449
Kimberly Xing 77494
Kincross Ct 77450
Kindle Oaks Dr 77450
King Hallow Ln 77449
King Richard Dr 77493
Kinglet Pines Dr 77494
Kings Arms Way 77493
Kings Camp Dr 77450
Kings Castle Dr 77450
Kings Landing Ln 77494
Kings Summit Dr 77450
Kingsbriar Ct & Ln 77450
Kingsbrook Sky Ln 77494
Kingsburg Ct 77450
Kingsgate Cir & Ln 77494
Kingsland Blvd
20000-22999 77450
23200-26099 77494
Kingspur Ridge Dr 77494
Kingston Glen Ln 77494
Kingston Heights Ln 77494
Kingston Hill Ln 77494
Kinross Ln 77449
Kinsgate Forest Dr 77494
Kinwicke Ct 77494
Kittansett Cir 77450
Knight Hollow Ct 77494
Knights Hollow Ct 77494
Knightsbrook Ln 77449
Knobby Pines Dr 77494
Knoll Lake Ln 77450
Knoll Shadows Ln 77449
Knolls Spring Trl 77450
Kurz Pointe Ct 77449
Kyla Cir 77493
Kyle Bend Ln 77493
Kyle Cove Dr 77449
Kyler Cove Ln 77494
La Terre De Vin Ct 77449
Lacey Oak Meadow Dr 77494
Laceyland Ln 77449
Lago Vista Ln 77494
Laguna Edge Dr 77494
Laguna Point Cir & Dr 77450
Lake Dr 77494
Lake Chase Ct 77493
Lake Creek Ln 77449
Lake Fountain Dr 77494
Lake Grayson Dr 77494
Lake Path Cir 77493
Lake Sherwood Dr 77450
Lake Sydney Dr 77494
N & S Lake Village Dr 77450
Lakearies Ln 77449
Lakebluff Ct 77450
Lakebriar Dr 77494
Lakecrest Bend Dr 77493
Lakecrest Creek Dr 77493
Lakecrest Forest Dr 77493
Lakecrest Gardens Dr 77493
Lakecrest Glen Dr 77493
Lakecrest Grove Dr 77493
Lakecrest Harbor Dr 77493
Lakecrest Manor Dr 77493
Lakecrest Park Dr 77493
Lakecrest Pass Ct 77493
Lakecrest Ridge Dr 77493
Lakecrest River Dr 77493
Lakecrest Run Dr 77493
Lakecrest Terrace Ct 77493
Lakecrest Town Dr 77493
Lakecrest Village Ct & Dr 77493
Lakecrest Way Dr 77493
Lakefield Trl 77493
Lakeland Gardens Ct & Dr 77449
Lakenshire Falls Ln 77494
Lakes Of Bridgewater Dr 77449
Lakes Of Katy Ln 77493
Lakeside Xing 77494
Lakespire Dr 77449
Lakeview Rd 77494
Lakewood View Ct 77450
Lakota Dr 77449
Lamplight Trail Dr 77450
Lamppost Hill Ct 77449
Lancefield Ct 77494
Landimore Ct 77450
Landon Brook Ct 77450
Landon Creek Ln 77494
Landon Park Dr 77449
Landon Point Cir 77450
Landover Ln 77493
Landover Hills Ln 77494
Langdon Ct 77494
Langhorne Ct 77450
Langmont Ln 77449
Langton Ct 77450
Lanham Dr 77450
Lanning Dr 77493
Lansing Ridge Ln 77449
Lantana Creek Ct 77494
Lantern Bay Ln 77449
Lantern Village Ln 77450
Lantern Walk Ln 77449
Lanville Ln 77449
Lapis Creek Ln 77450
Lara Brook Ct 77494
Laramie Lake Dr 77494
Laramie River Ct & Trl 77449
Lariat Canyon Ct & Dr 77450
Larissa Cir & Dr 77449
Lark Creek Ln 77449
Larkhill Ln 77449
Larkspur Ridge Dr 77494
Lashley Ct 77450
Lasker Brook Ct 77494
Latigo Ln 77494
Latrobe Ln 77450
Latta Creek Dr 77494
Latta Plantation Dr 77449
Lauderwick Ct 77450
Lauderwood Ln 77449
Laura Way Dr 77450
Lauras Glen Ct 77450
Laurel Chase Ln 77494
Laurel Glen Dr 77449
Laurel Lock Dr 77450
Laurel Rain Ct 77449
Laurel Terrace Ct 77450
Laurel Walk Ct 77494
Laurelwick Ct 77494
Lauren Meadow Ln 77494
Laureumont Ct & Ln 77494
Lavaca Ranch Ln 77449
Lavander Quartz Ct 77494
Lavender Bend Ln 77494
Lavender Cove Ct 77449
Lavender Mist Ln 77449
Lavenderwood Dr 77449
Laverton Ct & Dr 77450
Lawton Bend Ln 77494
Lawton Landing Ln 77494
Laxton Ct 77450
Lazy Valley Dr 77494
Le Carpe Plantation Ct 77449
Leachwood Dr 77493
Leaf Crk 77494
Leaf Ridge Dr 77494
Leaflock Ln 77450
Leaning Willow Dr 77494
Leatherwood Dr 77450
Ledgecreek Ln 77449
Ledgeside Ct 77494
Ledgeway Ct 77450
Leedstown Ln 77449
Legacy Oak St 77493
Legend Hill Dr 77494
Legend Spring Ct & Dr 77494
Legendary Lane Dr 77494
Lemonmint Meadow Dr 77494
Lennon Park Ct 77494
Lenora Ct & Dr 77493
Leopard Ct 77449
Lexington Lake Ct 77494
Leyden Ct 77450
Liberty Valley Dr 77494
Lidstone Point Ct 77494
Lightbranch Ct 77494
Lilac St 77493
Lilac Ranch Dr 77494
Lily Glen Ct & Ln 77494
Lily Ranch Dr 77494
Lilywood Springs Dr 77449
Lime Creek Dr 77450
Limestone Crest Ln 77449
Lincoln Green Dr 77493
Lincoln Round Dr 77493
Lincoln Town Dr 77493
Linda Ln 77493
Lindabury Hollow Dr 77494
Linden Belle Dr 77494
Linden Cove Ct 77494
Linden Forest Ln 77449
Linden May Ln 77494
Linden Mill Ct 77494
Linden Rock Dr 77494
Linden Tree Dr 77449
Lindenfield Ct, Dr & Pl 77449
Lindsay Ln 77493
Linfield Bluff Ln 77494
Linksman Ct & Ln 77449
Linmont Ridge Ln 77493
Lisburn Dr 77494
Litchfield Bend Ln 77494
Little Big Horn Dr 77449
Little Harbor Way 77494
Little John Ln 77493
Little Pine Ln 77449
Little Stone Ct 77494
W Little York Rd 77449
Live Meadow Ln 77449
Live Oaks Spring Dr 77450
Livingston Ridge Ct 77449
Llano Creek Dr 77449
Llano Springs Dr 77494
Loch Briar Ct 77494
Lochmere Ln 77450
Lodenberry Ct 77494
Lodenstone Ct 77494
Lodge Meadows Dr 77494
Lodge Stone Ct 77450
Lodgeglen Ct 77494
Lodgemist Ct 77494
Lodgepoint Dr 77494
Logan Saddle Ln 77494
Logancrest Ct 77494
Logans Landing Ln 77494
London Mills Ct 77494
Lone Creek Ct 77449
Lone Creek Hill Ct 77494
Lone Prairie Way 77449
Lone Ridge Ln 77449
Lonerock Cir 77449
Lonestone Cir 77449
Long Arbor Ln 77449
Long Cove Cir 77450
Long Leaf Valley Dr 77494
Long Prairie Dr 77450
Longdraw Cv & Dr 77494
Longenbaugh Rd 77493
Longleaf Valley Dr 77494
Longmont Hills Ln 77494
Longmont Park Ct & Ln 77494
Longspring Dr 77450
Longspur Dr 77494
Longview Creek Dr 77494
Lookout Mountain Ln 77449
Lost Canyon Dr 77450
Lost Creek Cir & Rd 77450
Lost Fall Ln 77449
Lowell Ct 77494
Lower Canyon Ln 77494
Lucas Canyon Ln 77494
Lucinda Meadows Dr 77449
Luckel Dr 77493
Lucky Star Ln 77494
Luke Ridge Ln 77494
Luna Vista Ln 77494
Luong Field Ct 77449
N & S Lyford Dr 77449
Lynden Trace Ct 77493
Lytham Ln 77450
Mabry Stream Ct 77449
Macinac Ct 77450
Macklind Ridge Ln 77494
Macquarie Dr 77494
Madera Creek Ln 77494
Madison Ln 77449
Madison Elm St 77493
Madison Falls Ln 77494
Madrid Hill Ln 77494
Madrone Mdw Ct & Dr 77494
Magnolia St 77493
Magnolia Summit Ln 77494
Mahogany Run Dr 77494
Maily Meadow Ln 77450
Main Mast Ct 77494
Majestic Cove Ct 77494
Malca Manor Dr 77493
Malden Motte Dr 77494
Mallard Dr 77493
Mallard Bay Ln 77494
Mallard Pass Ln 77494
Mallard Run Ct 77494
Malope Ranch Dr 77494
Mandrake Falls Ct 77494
Manette Dr 77450
Manito Cir 77450
Manitou Falls Ln 77449
Manor Ct 77449
Manor Court Dr 77449
Manor Creek Ln 77494
Manor Estates Dr 77449
Manor Hollow Ln 77450

Manor Ridge Ct 77494
Manorcliff Ln 77449
Manorfield Dr 77449
Manorwood Dr 77493
S Maple Dr 77493
Maple Ace Dr 77493
Maple Bluff Dr 77449
Maple Mist Dr 77449
Maple Moss Ct 77450
Maple Pass Ct 77449
Maple Rain Ct 77449
Maple Red Dr 77494
Maplewood Dr 77449
Marble Cove Ct & Ln 77494
Marble Falls Bnd 77494
Marble Hill Dr 77450
Marble Hollow Ln 77450
Marble Manor Ln 77449
Marble Point Ln 77494
Marble Springs Dr & Ln 77494
Marbrook Meadow Ln 77494
Mardell Manor Ct 77494
Mare Shadow Ln 77494
Marian St 77493
Marina Canyon Way 77450
Mariner Point Ln 77494
Market Place Dr 77494
Market Square Ln 77449
Markstone Ct 77494
Marot Dr 77493
Marquette Trl 77494
Marti Rd 77493
Martin Down Ln 77450
Maryvale Dr 77494
N Mason Rd 77449
S Mason Rd 77450
Mason Creek Dr
200-299 77450
19900-20099 77449
Mason Creek Path 77493
Mason Knights Ct & Dr 77493
Mason Park Blvd 77450
Mason Stone Ln 77494
Mason Trail Dr 77493
Mather Dr 77494
Mathis Dr 77493
Maverick Park Ln 77449
Maverick Point Ct & Ln 77494
Maverly Crest Ct 77494
Maybrook Park Cir, Ct & Ln 77450
Mayes Bluff Dr 77494
Mayfly Ct 77449
Maymist Dr 77449
Mcdonough Way 77494
Meadow Ln 77494
Meadow Arbor Ct 77450
Meadow Cross Ln 77494
Meadow Crossing Ct 77449
Meadow Dawn Ct & Ln 77494
Meadow Lilly Ln 77449
Meadow Oaks Dr 77494
Meadow Pond Cir & Dr 77450
Meadow Prairie St 77493
Meadow Stone Ct 77494
Meadowbloom Ln 77449
Meadowbrook Farms Club Dr 77494
Meadowfield St 77493
Meadowivy Ln 77449
Meadowlark Ln 77493
Meadowstream Ct 77450
Meagan Hills Ct 77494
Meandering Spring Dr 77494
Medallion Pointe Ct & Dr 77450
Medical Center Dr 77494
Meeks Bay Ct 77494
Melody Canyon Ct 77494
Melody Oaks Ln 77494
Memorial Pass Dr 77450
Merabrook Dr 77450
Mercantile Pkwy
23300-23399 77449
23600-23699 77493
Merchant Hills Ln 77494
Merchants Way 77449
Merlin Roost Ct 77494
Merrill Hills Cir 77450
Merrimac Trace Ct 77494
Merrymount Ct & Dr 77450
Mersea Dr 77449
Mert Ln 77493
Mesa Canyon Ct 77450
Mesa Terrace Dr 77450
Mesquite Meadow Ln 77494
Mesquite Orchard Ln 77494
Mia Rosa Ct 77494
Michener Falls Ln 77494
Mid Peak Way 77449
Middle Canyon Rd 77494
Middlecrest Hill Ct 77494
Middlelake Ct 77450
Middleoak Grove Ln 77494
Middlesprings Ln 77494
Middlewood Manor Ln 77494
Mill Crossing Ln 77450
Mill Ferry Ln 77449
Millbrook Bend Ln 77493
Millcross Ln 77449
Miller Ave 77493
Millers Ln 77493
Millerton Ln 77450
Mills Lake Ct 77494
Mills Manor Dr 77494
Mills Pass Ct & Way 77494
Mills Trace Ct 77450
Millstone Ridge Ln 77449
Millvale Ridge Dr 77494
Minard Dr 77449
Mission Hills Ct & Ln 77450
Mission Springs Dr 77450
Mist Lake Ct 77494
Misted Jasmine Ct 77449
Mistflower Ln 77449
Misty Bend Dr 77494
Misty Cove Dr 77449
Misty Dale Dr 77449
Misty Fall Ln 77449
Misty Glade Ct 77494
Misty Heath Ln 77494
Misty Island Ct 77494
Misty Isle Ct 77449
Misty Laurel Ct 77494
Misty Mountain Ln 77494
Misty Terrace Ct 77494
Misty Waters Ln 77494
Mizzen Ct 77494
Mockingbird Ln 77493
Mockingbird Valley Dr 77449
Monarch Vly 77494
Monarch Beach Dr 77494
Monarch Glen Ln 77494
Monarch Grove Ln 77494
Monarch Hollow Ln 77449
Monarch Lake Ln 77494
Monarch Meadow Ct & Ln 77494
Monarch Terrace Ct & Dr 77494
Monkswood Dr 77450
Monona Dr 77449
Montbury Ln 77450
Montclair Meadow Ln 77449
Montecola Pine Dr 77494
Monterey Bend Ln 77494
Monticello Hill Dr 77494
Monticello Ter Ln 77449
Montview Ct & Dr 77450
Moon Indigo Ln 77494
Moon Ridge Ct 77494
Moonflower Ln 77449
Mooningate Ct 77449
Moonlit Lake Ct 77450
Moonstone Mist Ln 77494
Moortown Cir 77450
Morfontaine Ln 77450
Morgan Pkwy 77494
Morgan Canyon Ct 77450
Morgan Knoll Ln 77449
Morganfair Ln 77450
Morgans Cove Ct 77494
Morgans Forest Ln 77449
Morgans Pointe Cir 77449
Morley Pointe Ct 77450
Morning Cove Ln 77449
Morning Creek Dr 77450
Morning Gale Ln 77494
Morning Lake Dr 77450
Morning Park Dr 77494
Morning Raven Ln 77494
Morning Sky 77494
Morning Song Dr 77449
Morning Willow Dr 77450
Morninggate Ct 77494
Morningmount Ln 77449
Morningtide Ct & Dr 77449
Mornington Ln 77494
Morrison Blvd & Ln 77493
Morton Rd
5400-6499 77493
19300-23499 77449
24500-29799 77493
27502-1-27502-9 77493
27523-1-27523-1 77493
Morton Cove Ln 77449
Morton Ranch Rd
20100-23299 77449
23300-23399 77493
Moscone Ct 77449
Moss Arbor Ct 77494
Moss Fern Dr 77494
Moss Garden Ln 77494
Moss Meadow Ln 77449
Mossback Pine Rd 77494
Mossy Canyon Ln 77494
Mossy Hedge Ln 77449
Mossy Hill Ln 77449
Mossy Path Ln 77494
Mossy Trail Dr 77450
Mossy Trails Ct & Dr 77494
Mount Auburn Dr 77494
Mountain Creek Ct 77450
Mountain Forest Dr 77449
Mountain Laurel Dr 77449
Mountain Meadows Dr 77450
Mountain Pines Ln 77449
Mt Davis Way 77449
Mt Elbrus Way 77449
Mt Everest Way 77449
Mt Mckinley Way 77449
Mt Vinson Way 77449
Mt Whitney Way 77449
Mulberry Ranch Dr 77494
Munsey Ct 77449
Mustang Draw Ln 77494
Mustang Falls Ct 77450
Mustang Hill Ln 77449
Mustang Retreat Ln 77494
Myrna Ln 77493
Myrtle Lake Ln 77494
Myrtle Rain Ct 77449
Myrtle Ranch Dr 77494
Mystic Berry Dr 77494
Mystic Cypress Dr 77449
Mystic Point Ct 77450
Mystic Port Ct 77494
Mystic Shadow Ln 77494
Naples Ridge Ct 77449
Naples Run Ln 77449
Naples Terrace Ln 77449
Nash Creek Ct 77494
Nashua Falls Ln 77494
Natalie Bend Rd 77449
Natchez Ridge Ct 77449
Nautical Mile Ln 77494
E, N, S & W Navaho Trl 77449
Necklace Tree Ln 77494
Nellie Gail Trail Ln 77450
N Nelson Ave 77493
S Nelson Dr 77493
Nelson Way 77494
Nelva Park Ct & Dr 77449
Nero Lake Dr 77494
Netleaf Gdn Dr 77494
Nettlebrook Ln 77450
New Hope Ln 77494
New South Wales Ct 77450
New World Dr 77449
Newbear Dr 77449
Newbury Dr 77449
Newbury Park Dr 77450
Newhope Terrace Ln 77449
Newmint Ct & Dr 77449
E, N, S & W Newport Bnd 77494
N Newport Bend Cir 77494
Niche Way 77450
Nicholas Ln 77494
Nickleby Ct 77494
Nicks Run Ln 77494
Nicollet Lake Ln 77494
E & W Nightingale Hill Ln 77494
Nightmist Ct 77494
Nobbe Hollow Dr 77494
Noble Grove Ln 77494
Nocturnal Ct 77493
Noel Ln 77493
Nomini Hall Ln 77493
Norfolk Trail Ln 77494
Norhill Crossing Ln 77494
North St 77494
Northern Colony Ct 77449
Northshire Ct & Ln 77494
Norton House Ln 77493
Norwalk Dr 77450
Norwhich Valley Ct 77494
Norwood Hills Dr 77450
Norwood Meadows Ln 77494
Nottingham Dr 77493
Nottingham Bluff Ln 77494
Nueces Canyon Ct 77450
Nullarbor Ct 77449
Oak Ln 77493
Oak Creek Ct & Dr 77450
Oak Hampton Rd 77449
Oak Mist Ln 77494
Oak Motte Dr 77494
Oak Park Trails Ct & Dr 77450
Oak Rain Ct 77449
Oak Rambling Dr 77494
Oak Royal Dr 77450
Oak Sand Dr 77450
Oak Stand Ct 77449
Oakbridge Park Ln 77450
Oakcreek Hollow Ln 77450
Oakfield Village Ln 77449
Oakington Ln 77449
Oakland Valley Dr 77449
Oakthorn Ct 77494
Oakton Springs Dr 77494
Oakwell Ln 77449
Oakwood Knoll Dr 77494
Oakwood Rock Ln 77494
Oasis Pt 77493
Ocean Park Ln 77449
Oceanic Dr 77449
Ocotillo Ct 77494
Old Church Ln 77449
Old Farmhouse Ln 77449
Old Glory Dr 77449
Old Hickory St 77449
Old Railroad St 77493
Oldfield Ct 77494
Olive Ridge Ct 77494
Olympia Springs Ln 77449
Opal Spgs 77450
Opal Cove Ct 77494
Opal Crest Ln 77494
Opal Falls Ln 77494
Opal Sky Dr 77449
Opal Village Ln 77494
Orange Orchard Ln 77493
Orchard Chase Ct 77450
Orchard Creek Ln 77494
Orchard Knoll Ln 77494
Orchard Mill Ln 77449
Orchard Oak Ln 77450
Orchid Spring Ln 77494
Orchid Tree Ln 77449
Oriole Sky Way 77493
Osprey Pass 77494
Osprey Park Dr 77494
Otter Trail Ct 77449
Outback Dr 77493
Outfitter Pt 77493
Overbrook Terrace Ct & Ln 77494
Overby Park Ln 77494
Overland Gap Ct 77494
Overton Park Dr 77450
Owens Trace Ln 77449
Owl Landing Dr & Ln 77494
Oxborough Dr 77450
Oxbow Park Ln 77450
Oxbridge Ct 77449
Oxford Brook Ct 77493
Pacific Grove Ln 77494
Packard Elm Ct 77449
Packwood Dr 77449
Paddle Wheel Dr 77449
Pagosa Falls Ct 77494
Paintbrush Trl 77494
Paintbrush Dawn Ct 77493
Painted Daisy Ln 77494
Painted Meadow Cir 77449
Paintedfern Pl 77449
Palace Green Ct 77449
Palacious Falls Ln 77449
Palamino Bluff Ln 77494
Pale Meadow Ct 77450
Palisade Green Dr 77493
Palm Forest Ct 77494
Palm Rain Ct 77449
Palm Trail Dr 77494
Palmetto Park Ct & Dr 77493
Palmoral Dr 77449
Pantego Ln 77449
Papaya Bend Dr 77494
Paper Rose Ln 77494
Paradise Canyon Ct 77450
Paralee Dr 77494
Parco Verde Cir 77450
Park Ln 77450
Park Bend Dr 77450
Park Birch Ln 77450
Park Bishop Dr 77450
Park Bluff Dr 77450
Park Briar Dr 77450
Park Bridge Dr 77450
Park Brook Dr 77450
Park Brush Cir, Ct & Ln 77450
Park Bud Ln 77450
Park Canyon Dr 77450
Park Downe Ln 77450
Park Forest Dr 77450
Park Green Dr 77450
Park Grove Ln 77450
Park Hills Ct & Dr 77494
Park Holly Ct 77450
Park Ivy Ct & Ln 77494
Park Knoll Ln 77450
Park Landing Ct 77449
Park Leaf Ln 77450
Park Maple Dr 77450
Park Meadow Dr 77450
Park Mill Dr & Ln 77450
Park Mount Dr 77450
Park Orchard Dr 77450
Park Pine Dr 77450
Park Point Dr 77450
Park Point Ln 77494
Park Post Ln 77450
Park Ridge Ct & Dr 77450
Park Rock Ln 77450
Park Row Dr
19800-20199 77449
20180-20180 77491
20200-21598 77449
20201-21599 77449
Park Royale Cir, Ct, Dr & Ln 77450
Park Run Dr 77450
Park Timbers Ln 77450
Park Tree Ln 77450
Park Valley Dr 77450
Park Villa Dr 77450
Park Vine Ct & Ln 77450
Park Wick Ln 77450
Park Willow Dr 77450
Park Wind Ct & Dr 77450
Park York Dr 77450
Parkcanyon Ln 77494
Parkfair Ct 77450
Parkfield Pl 77449
Parklake Vlg 77450
Parks Branch Ln 77494
Parkside Trace Ct 77493
Parkstone Bend Ct & Ln 77449
Parkvine Ln 77450
Parkwalk Ln 77494
Parkwater Cir 77450
Parquetry Ct 77450
Parsley Ridge Ct 77494
Parsons Green Ct 77450
Parsons Landing Dr 77494
Parsonsfield Ln 77494
Path Way Ct 77449
Patna Dr 77493
Patricia Ln 77493
Patriot Park Ln 77449
Patsy Pence St 77494
Pattison Rd 77493
Pavero Pl 77450
Paxton Hills Ln 77494
Payton Chase Ct & Ln 77494
Payton Manor Ln 77449
Peabody Hill Ln 77494
Peach Knoll Ln 77494
Peach Oak Xing 77494
Peach Tree Ct 77449
Peacock Gap Ln 77494
Pear Blossom Ln 77494
Pearl Creek Ln 77494
Pearl Lake Dr 77449
Pebble Bay Dr 77450
Pebble Beach Pl 77494
Pebble Bluff Ln 77494
Pebble Canyon Ct 77450
Pebble Chase Dr 77450
Pebble Garden Ln 77449
Pebble Terrane Ln 77494
Pebblecreek Xing 77494
Pebblepath Ln 77494
Pecan Ln
1300-1399 77494
6100-6299 77493
25100-25199 77494
Pecan St 77494
E, N, S & W Pecos Valley Trl 77449
Pedernales Trails Ln 77450
Pederson Rd 77494
Peek Rd 77494
S Peek Rd 77450
Pelican Hill Ct & Dr 77494
Pembrough Ln 77494
Pence Cliff Ct 77494
Penmark Ln 77450
Pennshore Ct & Ln 77450
Penny Ln 77494
Penny Ranch Ln 77494
Penny Rock Ct 77449
Pennyrile Ln 77450
Pennywell Ln 77494
Penrice Dr 77450
Penshore Place Ln 77450
Penzance Ct & Dr 77449
Pepper Bend Ln 77494
Pepper Hollow Ln 77494
Pepper Sage Ln 77494
Pepperidge Dr 77494
Pepperell Place Ct & St 77493
Peralta Glen Ln 77494
Peralta Preserve Ln 77494
Perdido Bay Dr 77450
Pernod Oaks Dr 77494
Perrington Ct 77450
Perth Meadows Ct 77449
Pewter Ct 77493
Pewter Knolls Dr 77494
Phoebe Trce 77494
Phoenician Dr 77494
Pickford Dr 77450
Piedra Negras Ct 77450
Pierceton Ct 77494
Pierrmont Ct 77494
Pilibos Park Ct 77494
Pimlico Pine Ln 77494
Pin Oak Rd 77494
Pine Trl 77493
Pine Cone Dr 77493
Pine Grove Ct 77494
Pine Lakes Dr 77493
Pine Meadow Dr 77493
Pine Mill Rnch 77494
Pine Monte Ridge Ln 77449
Pine Needle Dr 77493
Pine Rain Ct 77449
Pinebridge Slate Ln 77494
Pinebrook Park Ln 77494
Pinebury Ln 77493
Pinecreek Pass Ln 77449
Pinewood Ct & Ter 77493
Piney Knoll Ct 77494
Piney Ranch Ln 77494
Pinkstone Ct 77494
Pinnacle Ridge Dr 77494
Pinpoint Crossing Dr 77494
Pintail Ct 77494
Pintail St 77493
Pioneer Bend Ct & Ln 77450
E Piper Grove Dr 77449
Piper Shadow Ln 77494
Piper Terrace Ln 77450
Pipestone Glen Ln 77494
Piralta Ridge Ln 77449
Pitts Rd 77493
Pittsford Ct & Dr 77450
Plantain Dr 77449
Plantation Bay Dr 77449
Plantation Bend Ln 77449
Plantation Cove Ln 77449
Plantation Crest Dr 77449
Plantation Field Dr 77449
Plantation Forest Dr 77449
Plantation Grove Trl 77449
Plantation Myrtle 77449
Plantation Tree Ct 77449
Planters Heath 77494
Planters House Ct & Ln 77449
Pleasant Forest Dr 77494
Pleasant Mill Ln 77494
Pleasant Stream Dr 77449
Plum Park Dr 77450
Plum Trails Ct, Ln & Rd 77449
Plumero Meadow Dr 77494
Plumfield Ln 77450
Plympton Dr 77494
N Point Pl 77494
Point Cuero Ct 77494
Pointed Oak Ln 77450
Pointer Ridge Ln 77494
Polly Creek Way 77450
Pomegranate Ln 77449
Ponderosa Hills Ln 77494
Pontius Dr 77493
Pop Oman St 77493
Poplar Terrace Ln 77449
Poppy Trails St 77449
Poppyfield Ct & Dr 77450
Port Mist St 77494
Portage Rock Ln 77450
Porter Rd 77493
Portfield Ct 77494
Porthcawl Ct 77494
Portlick Ct & Dr 77449
Portrush Ct 77494

Posey Ridge Ln 77494
Possum Hill Ct 77494
Postwood Manor Ct 77494
Powder Mist Ln 77449
Powder Ridge Dr 77494
Powder River Dr 77450
Powderhorn Ln 77493
Powell House Ln 77449
Prairie Ln 77494
Prairie Lily Ln 77494
Prairie Meadow Dr 77449
Prairie Pebble Ct 77494
Prairie School Ln 77494
Prairie Trails Dr 77450
Prairie Village Dr 77449
Prairie Wing Pt 77493
Prairiestone Trail Ln 77450
Precious Stone Ln 77494
Prescott Glen Ln 77494
Prescott Hollow Ct 77494
Prescott Run Ln 77494
Presidio Canyon Dr 77450
Preston Cove Ct 77494
Price Plz 77449
Prime West Pkwy 77449
Primrose Bluff Dr 77494
Primrose Springs Ct 77494
Prince Creek Ct & Dr ... 77450
Prince George Ct & St . 77449
Prince Jeffry Ln 77493
Prince Lawrence Ct 77493
Princess Deanna Ln 77493
Princess Snow Cir 77493
Princeton Dr 77493
Promenade Blvd 77450
Prospect Glen Ln 77449
Providence Point Dr 77449
Provident Green Dr 77449
Province Place Dr 77450
Provincial Blvd 77450
Purple Cornflower Trl ... 77494
Purple Sunset Ct 77449
Purslane Dr 77449
Putnam Ct 77494
Quail St 77493
Quail Chase Dr 77450
Quail Springs Ln 77494
Quarry Path Way 77493
Quarry Place Ln 77493
Queens Bay Dr 77494
Queensfield Ct 77494
Quentin Canyon Ct 77450
Quiet Falls Ct 77450
Quiet Heron Ct 77493
Quiet Lake Ct & Dr 77450
Quiet Sage Ln 77494
Rachel Ln 77493
Rachelle Ct 77450
Rachels Ct 77494
Rachels Manor Dr 77494
Radcliff Lake Dr 77494
Radrick Ln 77450
Ragsdale Ct & Ln 77494
Rainbluff Ln 77494
Rainbow Bend Ln 77450
Raincrest Dr 77449
Rainfield Ct 77494
Raingate Ln 77449
Raingreen Dr 77449
Rainhill Ct 77449
Rainmead Dr 77449
E, N & W Rainmill Ct & Dr 77449
Rainmont Ln 77449
Rainpark Ln 77449
Rainport Cir & Dr 77449
Rainshore Dr 77449
Rainstone Ct 77449
Rainterra Dr 77449
Raintree Village Dr 77449
Rainy Heath 77449
Ralston Bend Ln 77494
Ramble Rock Ct 77494
Ranch Hollow Ct 77494
Ranch Lake Ct & Ln ... 77494
Ranch Point Dr 77494

Ranch Prairie Trl 77449
Ranch Riata Ct & Dr ... 77449
Ranchwood Ct 77450
Ranchwood Springs Ln 77494
Randy Ln 77449
Ranger Point Ct 77450
Rangeview Dr 77450
Rathford Ct 77494
Raudabaugh Dr 77494
Ravello Rd 77449
Raven Blf 77494
Raven Forest Ln 77494
Raven Hills Ln 77494
Raven Mist Ct 77449
Raven Oak Ct 77450
Ravenloch Ct 77450
Ravenmeadow Ln 77449
Ravenna Ln 77450
Ravenpass Ln 77449
Ravens Lake Dr 77450
Ravens Landing Ct 77494
Ravens Prairie Dr 77494
Ravenside Dr 77494
Rayburn Ridge Dr 77450
Razorbill Ct 77494
N & S Rebecca Burwell Ln 77449
Rebecca Meadow Fall Ln 77494
Rebel Yell Dr 77449
Red Bluff Ct & Trl 77494
Red Burr Oak Trl 77494
Red Cedar Hollow Dr ... 77494
Red Cliff Rdg 77494
Red Lion St 77449
Red Maple Dr 77494
Red Oak Grove Ct 77494
Red Oak Valley Dr 77494
Red Pine Valley Trl 77494
Red River Ct & Dr 77450
Red Rock Canyon Ct & Dr 77450
Red Rooster Ln 77494
Red Shady Oaks Dr 77494
Red Sun Dr 77449
Red Wren Cir 77494
Red Yucca Dr 77494
Redbay Rd 77449
Redberry Ln 77494
Redberry Juniper Trl ... 77494
Redbud St 77493
Redbud Rain Dr 77449
Redding Ridge Ln 77494
Redgrove Ln 77494
Redgum Dr 77449
Redhead Ln 77493
Redleaf Forest Ln 77494
Redstone Glen Ln 77494
Redwing Brook Trl 77449
Redwood Creek Dr 77450
Reflection Sky Ct 77494
Regal Isle Ct 77494
Regents Corner Dr 77449
Regents Crest Ln 77449
Remington Park & Trl .. 77493
Remington Rise Ln 77494
Remson Hollow Ln 77494
Rennie Dr 77450
Repiton Way 77493
Reston Hill Ln 77494
Reston Landing Ln 77494
Retama Falls Ln 77494
Retreat Creek Ct & Ln . 77494
Rexora Ln 77493
Reynolds Park Dr 77494
Riata Park Ct 77494
Rice St 77493
Rice Mill Ave 77493
Ricewood Way 77449
Ricewood Village Trl 77449
Richland Hills Dr 77494
Richwood Oaks Dr 77494
Ricker Park Cir 77449
Ridgebluff Ln 77449
Ridgetop Pole Ln 77494

Rimcrest Ct 77494
Ringford Ridge Ln 77494
Rioja Bluff Ln 77449
Rippling Shore Ct 77494
Rising Bend Ln 77494
Rising Meadow Ln 77494
Rising Oak Ln 77494
Rising Sun Rd 77449
River Bottom Rd 77449
River Court Dr 77449
River Knoll Ct & Ln 77449
River Mist Ct 77494
River Place Dr 77494
River Pointe Ln 77449
River Rock Ct & Dr 77449
Rivergreen Park Ct 77494
Riverine Crest Dr 77494
Rivermead Ct & Dr 77449
Rivermoss Ln 77494
Riverside Ridge Ln 77449
Roaring Hill Ct 77449
Roaring Hills Ln 77449
Roaring Oaks Ln 77449
Roaring Peaks Ln 77449
Roberts Rd 77494
Roberts Run Ln 77494
Robillard Springs Ln 77494
Robin Ave 77493
Robin Meadow Ct 77449
Robwood Ct 77449
Rochs Hill Ct 77494
Rock Canyon Dr 77450
Rock Green Ct 77494
Rock Harbor Ct 77449
Rock Wren Ct 77494
Rockchester Dr 77450
Rockpoint Dr 77450
Rocky Ter 77449
Rocky Coral Dr 77449
Rocky Crest Dr 77449
Rocky Hollow Ln 77450
Rocky Landing Ln 77494
Rocky Ledge Ln 77494
Rocky Manor Ln 77449
Rocky Walk Ct 77494
Roesner Ln & Rd 77494
Roland Rd 77493
Rollinford Ln 77494
Rolling Knl 77494
Rolling Hills Ln 77449
Rolling Meadow Ln 77450
Rolling Pointe Cir 77449
Rolling Ridge Dr 77494
Rolling Sage Dr 77449
E & W Rolling Silver Ln 77494
Rolling Springs Ln 77449
Rollingwood North Loop 77494
Rollingwood South Loop 77494
Ropers Trail Ct 77450
Rosa Lee Dr 77494
Rose Ln 77494
Rose Bush Trl 77494
Rose Canyon Ln 77494
Rose Fair Ct & Dr 77450
Rose Grove Ln 77494
Rose Hollow Ct, Dr & Ln 77450
Rose Sage 77494
Rosebend Dr 77494
Rosebluff Ct 77494
Rosehearth Ct 77494
Rosemary Hill Ln 77494
Rosemary Knoll Ln 77494
Rosemont Park Ln 77494
Rosetrail Bend Ln 77494
Rosewater Ct 77494
Rosewood Valley Dr 77494
Round Hill Ct 77494
Round Hollow Ct 77494
Round Robin Dr 77449
Round Valley Dr 77450
Roundleaf Ct 77494
Royal Adelaide Dr 77450

Royal Arms Ct 77449
Royal Canyon Ln 77494
Royal Cypress Dr 77449
Royal Downs Dr 77450
Royal Hollow Ct & Ln .. 77450
Royal Meadow Ct 77449
Royal Montreal Dr 77450
Royal Villa Dr 77449
Ruby Red Ln 77494
Rue Canyon Ct 77450
Rum River Ct 77449
Rumbling Canyon Ct ... 77449
Rumbling Rock Ln 77494
Rumson Dr 77494
Rushing Creek Ln 77449
Rushville Ct 77449
Rushwind Ct 77494
Russet Trail Ct 77449
Rustic Cove Ln 77494
Rustic Field Ln 77449
Rustic Hollow Ln 77450
Rustic Knolls Ct & Dr ... 77450
Rustic Meadow Ct 77494
Rustic Ranch Ln 77494
Rustic Shores Ln 77450
Rustic Woods Ln 77494
Rustling Branch Ln 77449
Rustling Gates Ln 77494
Rustling Glen Ln 77494
Rustling Trails Dr 77449
Rusty Hawthorne Dr 77494
Rusty Ridge Ln 77449
Rutherford Place Ct 77494
Ruthin Ct 77449
Ruttand Park Ln 77450
Ryan Hills Ct 77449
Ryans Branch Ln 77450
Ryans Creek Ct 77494
Ryans Ranch Ln 77494
Rye Creek Dr 77449
Ryewood Ct 77450
Sabal Palms Ct, Dr & Park 77449
S Sabinal Dr 77449
Sabine Pass Ct 77450
Sabine Ridge Dr 77494
Sabine Spring Ln 77449
Sable Field Ln 77449
Sable Ridge Ln 77494
Sable Stone Cir 77450
Sabrina Oaks Ln 77449
Saches Ct 77449
N & S Saddlebrook Cir, Ln & Way 77494
Saddlehorn Trl 77494
Saddlespur Ln 77494
Saddlewood Dr 77494
Sage Ter 77450
Sage Mountain Ln 77450
Sage Pointe Ct 77449
Sage Rain Ct 77449
Sagecrest Dr 77494
Sageford Ct 77494
Sagewood Forest Dr ... 77494
Saginaw Point Ct & Ln 77449
Sagrantino Ct 77449
Sahalle Dr 77494
Sail Harbour Ct 77450
Salt Creek Ln 77494
Salt River Ct 77449
Salt Valley Dr 77493
Salta Verde Pt 77494
Sam Creek Ct 77494
Samantha Cove Ct 77494
San Clemente Point Ct 77494
San Marino Dr 77450
San Nicholas Pl 77494
San Salvador Pl 77494
San Vicente Ln 77450
Sancroft Ct 77450
Sanctuary Cv 77450
Sand Pnes 77494
Sand Ter 77450
Sand Bunker Cir 77450

Sand Colony Ln 77449
Sand Creek Ct 77449
Sand Hollow Ln 77450
Sand Plum Dr 77449
Sand Ripple Ln 77449
Sandahl Ct 77494
Sandal Springs Dr 77493
Sandalia Ct 77494
Sandelford Dr 77449
Sanderford Ct 77494
Sandersgate Ln 77494
Sandhill Pine Ct 77494
Sandi Ln 77494
Sandsage Ln 77494
Sandspoint Dr 77449
Sandwith Dr 77449
Sandy Arbor Ct & Ln ... 77494
Sandy Bay Ct & Ln 77449
Sandy Hollow Dr 77449
Sandy Mist Ct 77494
Sandy Sage Ct 77494
Sandy Trace Ct & Ln ... 77494
Sandy Valley Ct & Dr .. 77449
Sandyfields Ln 77494
Sandystone Ln 77449
Sanford St 77493
Sansford Cir 77449
Santa Catalina Ct 77450
Santa Clara Dr 77450
Santa Inez Ct 77450
Santa Isabel Ct 77450
Santiago Mountain Ct .. 77494
Santolina Ln 77449
Sapphire Ct 77449
Sapphire Hill Ln 77494
Sara Ridge Ln 77450
Saratoga Heights Ct 77494
Saums Rd 77449
Saunton Dr 77450
Savannah Creek Ln 77449
Savannah Pines Dr 77449
Savory Springs Ln 77494
Sawgrass Meadow Ln .. 77494
Sawland Dr 77494
Sawleaf Cir 77494
Saxon Glen Ct & Ln 77494
Scarlet Crest Ln 77494
Scarlet Trail Ct 77494
Scarlett Bay Ct 77450
Scarlett Sage Ct & Ln .. 77494
Scenic Falls Ln 77494
Scenic Hollow Ct 77450
Schivener House Ln ... 77493
Schlipf Rd 77493
Scotchwood Dr 77449
Scottsbury Ct 77494
Screech Owl Ct 77494
Scrivener Ln 77493
Sea Meadow Ct 77449
Sea Pine Dr 77450
Seablossom Ln 77449
Seabury Ct 77494
Seabury Path Ct 77449
Seagler Glen Ln 77449
Seahorse Bend Dr 77449
Seal Valley Ln 77450
Seaton Dr 77449
Sebastian Hill Dr 77494
Sebey Ridge Ln 77494
Sedalia Brook Ln 77494
Sedgeborough Cir & Dr 77449
Sedgecreek Dr 77449
Sedgeland Trail Ln 77494
Seguin Valley Dr 77494
Seminole Hill Ln 77494
Seminole Peak Ln 77494
Senca Springs Ct 77450
Seneca Falls Ln 77494
Sentry Park Ln 77494
Sequoia Park Ln 77494
Serrano Trl 77450
Serringdon Dr 77449
Setting Sun 77494
Settlers Lake Cir E 77449
Settlers Square Ln 77449

Settlers Valley Dr 77449
Settlers Village Dr 77449
Seven Meadows Pkwy . 77494
Seventh Heaven 77494
Shadow Breeze Ln 77494
Shadow Canyon Ln 77494
Shadow Creek Ct 77494
Shadow Forest Dr 77494
Shadow Grass Dr 77493
Shadow Line Ct 77449
Shadow Mill Ct 77450
Shadow Mountain Dr ... 77450
Shadow Park Dr 77494
Shadowmere Ln 77494
Shady Dawn Ln 77494
Shady Heath Ln 77494
Shady Manor Dr 77449
Shady Spruce Ct & Ln . 77494
Shady Valley Dr 77450
Shady Walk Ln 77494
Shallow Creek Ct 77449
Shallow Creek Ln 77450
Shallow Glen Ln 77450
Shallow Spring Ct 77494
Shaly Ct 77450
Shambala Way 77494
Shannon Falls Ct 77494
Shannon Forest Ct 77494
Shannon Wood Ct 77494
Sharp Rd 77493
Shaw Perry Ln 77493
Shelby Park Dr 77450
Sheldonwood Ct 77449
Shelford Ct 77449
Sherbrook Park Ln 77449
Sherfield Ridge Dr 77450
Sherry Mist Ln 77449
Sherwood Dr 77493
Shetland Ln 77493
Shillington Ct & Dr 77450
Shiloh Cliff Ln 77494
Shiloh Creek Ct & Ln ... 77449
Shiloh Mist Ln 77449
Shiloh Pine Ln 77494
Shining Creek Ct 77494
Shining Leaf Ct 77449
Shining Rock Ln 77494
Shiremist Ct 77494
Shirley St 77493
Shoal Glen Ln 77494
Shoal Ridge Ct 77449
Shore Castle Ct 77450
Shortfin Mako Ct 77494
Shortleaf Ridge Dr 77494
Sica Hollow Ln 77494
Sidonie Rose Ln 77494
Sienna Terrace Ln 77494
Sierra Lake Ct 77494
Sierra Lake Dr 77450
Sierra Shadows Dr 77450
Sierra Springs Ln 77494
Sierra Woods Ln 77494
Silbury Ct & Dr 77450
Silent Flight Dr 77494
Silent Spring Creek Ct & Dr 77450
Silent Vale Ln 77449
Silhouette Ct & Dr 77493
Silk Oak Ct 77449
Silk Tree Ln 77449
Silkbay Meadow Dr 77494
Silky Ct 77449
Sills Dr 77493
Silver Bridge Ln 77494
Silver Brook Ln 77494
Silver Cedar Trl 77449
Silver Cypress Ct & Dr 77449
Silver Lode Dr 77450
Silver Morning Cir, Ct & Dr 77450
Silver Rock Ct & Dr 77449
Silver Shores Ln 77449
Silver Spring Trl 77449
Silver Spur Dr 77449
Silver Timber Ct 77449

Silver Timbers Ln 77494
Silver Trace Ct 77449
Silver Trumpet Dr 77449
Silverbit Trail Ln 77450
Silverbow Ct 77450
Silverbrook Ln 77449
Silverfield Park Ln 77449
Silverhawk Dr 77449
Silverhorn Dr 77450
Silvermist Ln 77494
Silverpeak Ct 77450
Silverside Dr 77449
Silversmith Ln 77493
Silverton Valley Ln 77494
Singing Spurs Dr 77450
Single Ridge Way 77493
Sinton Ct 77449
Site View Trl 77494
Skiers Crossing Dr 77493
Skipping Falls Ln 77494
Sky Hollow Ln 77450
Sky Timbers Ln 77449
Skye Springs Ln 77494
Skyline Park Dr 77449
Slate Bridge Ct 77449
Slate Crossing Ln 77449
Slate Ridge Ln 77494
Slate River Ln 77494
Slocom Dr 77449
Slover Creek Ln 77494
Smithfield Crossing Ln .. 77449
Smoke House Dr 77449
Smokey Brook Ln 77494
Smokey Hill Dr 77450
Smokey River Dr 77449
Smokey Sage Ct & Dr .. 77450
Smokey Valley Ln 77494
Snake Canyon Dr 77449
Snake River Rd 77449
Snapdragon Mdw 77494
Snow 77493
Snow Finch Ct 77494
Snow Goose Ln 77493
Snowflower Mdw Ln 77494
Snowy Egret Dr 77494
Snug Harbour Ct 77449
Somerset Cove Ct 77494
Somerset Meadows Ct . 77494
Somerset Park Ln 77450
Songbury Cir 77494
Sonny Path Ct & Dr 77493
Sonoma Mission Ct 77449
Sorney Ct 77450
South St 77494
Southbend Park Ct & Ln 77494
Southbriar Ln 77494
Southcott Ct 77450
Southern Colony Ct 77449
Southern Glen Ln 77494
Southford Manor Ln 77494
Sowles Park Dr 77493
Sparrow Creek Ct 77494
Sparrow Crest Dr 77494
Sparrow Knoll Ct 77450
Sparrows Rdg 77450
Spatswood Ln 77449
Spice Leaf Trl 77494
Spice Trail Ct 77494
Spiceberry Dr 77494
Splendora Dr 77449
Spoon Bill St 77493
Spring Ash Ln 77494
Spring Aspen Ct 77494
Spring Blossom Ct 77450
Spring Cove Ln 77494
Spring Green Blvd 77494
Spring Iris Ln 77494
Spring Meadow Ln 77494
Spring Rose Dr 77450
Spring Run Ln 77494
Spring Silver Dr 77449
Spring Tide Ct 77494
Spring Vine Ln 77450
Spring Walk Dr 77494
Springbend Ln 77450

Springbury Ln ... 77494
Springfield Ridge Dr ... 77494
Springhaven Ct ... 77494
Springport Ct ... 77450
Springwood Glen Ln ... 77494
Springwood Lake Dr ... 77494
Spruce Falls Ct ... 77494
Spur Branch Ln ... 77450
Spyglass Hills Dr ... 77450
St Romain Dr ... 77494
Stableview Ct ... 77450
Stackstone Ln ... 77450
Stackwood Ln ... 77449
Stacy Park Cir ... 77449
N & S Stadium Ln ... 77494
Stafford Hill Cv ... 77494
Stamford Brook Ct ... 77449
Stanbury Place Ln ... 77494
Stanford Park Ct ... 77450
Stanville Dr ... 77494
Stanwick Crossing Ln ... 77494
Star Wish Ln ... 77494
Starboard Ct ... 77494
Starbridge Park Ln ... 77449
Starbridge Pointe Ln ... 77449
Starbrook Creek Dr ... 77494
Starflower ... 77494
Starlight Beach Rd ... 77494
Starlight Canyon Ln ... 77494
Starlit Ranch Dr ... 77494
Starry Night ... 77494
Statfield Glen Ct & Ln ... 77450
Steep Forest Cir ... 77494
Stependale Dr ... 77450
Sterling Ct ... 77494
Sterling Canyon Dr ... 77450
Sterling Cloud Ln ... 77494
Sterling Creek Cir ... 77450
Sterling Falls Dr ... 77449
Sterling Hollow Dr ... 77449
Sterling Meadow Ct & Dr ... 77449
Sterling Stone Ln ... 77494
Sterling Vista Blvd ... 77494
Stewart Dr ... 77493
Still Manor Ct ... 77449
Still Meadow Ln ... 77494
Stillwood Meadow Ln ... 77494
Stockbridge Ln ... 77449
Stockdick Rd
5900-5998 ... 77494
29000-29999 ... 77493
29666-1-29666-9 ... 77493
29700-1-29700-9 ... 77493
29902-1-29902-9 ... 77493
Stockdick School Rd
5000-5498 ... 77449
5500-22999 ... 77449
23500-29999 ... 77493
29666-1-29666-9 ... 77493
29700-1-29700-9 ... 77493
29902-1-29902-2 ... 77493
Stockholm Ct ... 77449
S Stone Ln ... 77494
Stone Bush Ct ... 77493
Stone Cross Ct ... 77450
Stone Falcon Ln ... 77494
Stone Harbour Ln ... 77494
Stone Landing Ln ... 77449
Stone Springs Dr ... 77494
Stoneburg Dr ... 77450
Stonecloud Ln ... 77494
Stonecroft Cir ... 77450
Stonecross Creek Ln ... 77449
Stonecross Terrace Ln ... 77449
Stonefort Ct ... 77449
Stonegate Dr ... 77494
Stonehurst Ln ... 77494
Stonelodge Dr ... 77450
Stoneport Ln ... 77449
Stonestead Dr ... 77494
Stoney Bluff Ln ... 77449
Stoney Cloud Dr ... 77494
Stoney Haven Dr ... 77449
Stoney Knoll Ln ... 77494
Stormcroft Cir & Ln ... 77450
Stoughton Ct ... 77494
Stratford House Ln ... 77449
Strathmere Ct ... 77450
Strathmore Place Ct & Ln ... 77449
Stratsborough Dr ... 77494
Strawberry Park Ln ... 77450
Stream Mill Ln ... 77494
Strongs Ct ... 77449
Suffield Glen Ct & Ln ... 77494
Suffolk Creek Ln ... 77494
Suffolk Sky Ct ... 77449
Sugar Field Ln ... 77449
Sugar Harbor Ln ... 77493
Sugarside Glen Dr ... 77494
Sullivan Springs Dr ... 77494
Summer Gardens Ln ... 77493
Summer Park Ln ... 77450
Summer Ranch Dr ... 77494
Summer Savory Ln ... 77494
Summer Walk Ln ... 77494
Summerbend Hollow Ln ... 77494
Summerfield Glade Ln ... 77494
Summerhill Manor Ln ... 77494
Summerlin Dr ... 77449
Summers Glen Ct ... 77449
Summerside Dr ... 77450
Summit Bend Ln ... 77494
Summit Lodge Dr ... 77449
E Summitry Cir ... 77449
Summits Edge Ln ... 77494
Sumners Creek Ct ... 77494
Sun Creek Dr ... 77450
Sun Glen Ct ... 77449
Sun Haven Dr ... 77449
Sunchase Ct & Way ... 77449
Suncoast Dr ... 77449
Suncrest Ct ... 77494
Sundance Hollow Ct & Ln ... 77494
Sundance Summit Ln ... 77494
Sundance Valley Dr ... 77450
Sundown Way ... 77449
Sundown Canyon Ct & Ln ... 77494
Sundown Cove Ln ... 77494
Sundrop Meadows Ln ... 77494
Sunfall Bend Ln ... 77449
Sunflower Chase Ct & Dr ... 77449
Sunny Leaf Ln ... 77449
Sunny Meadows Ln ... 77449
Sunrise Dr ... 77493
Sunrise Pine View Ln ... 77450
Sunrise Ranch Ln ... 77494
Sunrise Springs Ln ... 77494
Sunset Ct ... 77494
Sunset Cove Ln ... 77494
Sunset Knoll Ln ... 77449
Sunset Landing Dr ... 77449
Sunset Manor Ln ... 77450
Sunset Meadow Dr ... 77449
Sunset Park Dr ... 77449
Sunset Pine View Cir ... 77450
Sunset Ranch Dr ... 77449
Sunset Sky ... 77494
Suntree Cir & Ln ... 77450
Sunwood Glenn Ln ... 77494
Surrey Creek Ct ... 77450
Surrey Park Cir & Ln ... 77494
Surrey Stone Ct ... 77450
Surrey Trail Ln ... 77450
Sutherland Springs Ln ... 77494
Sutton Shadow Ln ... 77494
Swallows Cove Ln ... 77494
Sweet Gum St ... 77493
Sweet Juniper Ln ... 77449
Sweet Melissa Dr ... 77494
Sweet Oak Ln ... 77449
Sweet Orchid Ln ... 77494
Sweet Pine Dr ... 77450
Sweetspire Rd ... 77449
Swordfern Pl ... 77449
Sycamore St ... 77493
Sycamore Bluff Dr ... 77494
Sycamore Crest Ln ... 77449
T St ... 77493
Tabana Dr ... 77449
Tahoka Springs Dr ... 77449
Tall Canyon Ct ... 77450
Tall Juniper Hill Dr ... 77494
Tallow Grove Ln ... 77450
Tallowpine Ter ... 77493
Tallowwood Ter ... 77493
Tamara Branch Ln ... 77494
Tamworth Ln ... 77493
Tancy Ranch Ct ... 77494
Tanner Crossing Ln ... 77494
Tapa Springs Ln ... 77494
Tapestry Dr ... 77494
Tara Way Dr ... 77449
Tarpley Ct ... 77493
Tasmania Pl ... 77449
Taswell Dr ... 77494
Tavern Springs Ln ... 77449
Tayloe House Ln ... 77493
Taylor Mill Ct ... 77494
Taylor Park Ln
6600-6799 ... 77449
25200-25299 ... 77494
Taylors Glen Ct ... 77494
Tayman Park Ln ... 77494
Tea Tree Dr ... 77494
Teagarden Ct ... 77450
Teal ... 77493
Teal Lake Ct ... 77494
Teal Point Dr ... 77450
Teal View Ln ... 77494
Tealwater Ct ... 77449
Teasel Ct ... 77450
Telegraph Square Ct & Ln ... 77449
Tembrook Cv ... 77494
Temecula Cv ... 77494
Tenby Dr ... 77450
Teresa Cove Ln ... 77449
Terra Forest Ct ... 77494
Terra Springs Dr ... 77449
Terrace Rdg ... 77494
Terrace Arbor Ln ... 77494
E & W Terrace Gable Cir ... 77494
Terrace Gate Ln ... 77450
Terrace Sage Ln ... 77494
Terrace View Dr ... 77449
Terrance Fall Dr ... 77494
Terrance Springs Ln ... 77494
Terry Ln ... 77449
Texas Laurel Dr ... 77494
Texas Oak Dr ... 77449
Texmati Dr ... 77494
Thaxton Hill Ln ... 77494
Thayer Ct ... 77494
Thicket Path Way ... 77493
Thickey Pines Ct ... 77494
Thistlemoor Ct ... 77494
Thistlewood Park Ct ... 77494
Thomas Ave ... 77494
Thorn Berry Creek Ct & Ln ... 77449
Thornbird Ct & Dr ... 77494
Thorngate Ct ... 77494
Thornsby Ct ... 77494
Thorpeshire Ct ... 77494
Three Forks Dr ... 77450
Thresher Ct ... 77449
Thunder Ridge Ln ... 77449
Thunder Rock Dr ... 77449
E Tide Bay Cir ... 77494
Tiger Shark Ct ... 77494
Tigris Ridge Dr ... 77449
Tigris Springs Cir ... 77449
Tilstock Dr ... 77450
Timber Bay Ct ... 77450
Timberfield Ct & Pl ... 77449
Tina Ln ... 77493
Tinker Round St ... 77493
Tinton Ct ... 77494
Tobacco Rd ... 77449
Tokatee Ct ... 77494
Tolstin Lakes Ln ... 77494
Tonbridge Ln ... 77449
Top Mark Ct ... 77494
Torchlite Ter ... 77494
Torrance Elms Ct ... 77449
Torrence Falls Ct ... 77449
Touhy Dr ... 77494
Touhy Lake Dr ... 77494
Tourney Ln ... 77493
Tower Side Ln ... 77494
Town Park Blvd ... 77493
Townhall Ct & Ln ... 77449
Townsgate Cir & Ct ... 77450
Trace Shadow Ct ... 77494
N & S Trafalgar Ct ... 77449
Trailcliff Ct ... 77494
Trails West Dr ... 77449
Trailstone Ct & Ln ... 77494
Trailwood Manor Ln ... 77449
Tramonte Trl ... 77494
Tranquil Springs Ln ... 77494
Travis Trl ... 77494
Travis House Ln ... 77493
Travis Mill Ct ... 77494
Treasure Oaks Ct & Dr ... 77450
Tree Lark Ln ... 77449
Tree Orchard Dr ... 77494
Treemill Ct ... 77449
Treesdale Ct & Ln ... 77450
Treetoad Dr ... 77449
Tremont Glen Ln ... 77494
Tremont Trail Ln ... 77450
Trent Park Ct ... 77449
Trent Stone Ln ... 77449
Trenton Reach Dr ... 77494
Trenton Valley Ln ... 77449
Tres Sabores Ln ... 77494
Trevors Trace Ln ... 77494
Treyburn Trl ... 77450
Tribeca Ln ... 77493
Trinity Creek Ct ... 77494
Tristan Mill Ln ... 77449
Tristan Ridge Ln ... 77449
Triton Ct ... 77450
Trophy Ln ... 77494
Trotter Dr ... 77493
Trotwood Ln ... 77494
Tucker House Ln ... 77493
Tudor Ranch Ln ... 77449
Tulip Glen Ct ... 77449
Tulip Ranch Dr ... 77449
Tull Dr ... 77449
Tullis Trail Ct ... 77494
Tully Meadows Ct ... 77449
Turncreek Ln ... 77450
Turquoise Springs Ln ... 77494
Turret Crown Dr ... 77494
Tuscola Ln ... 77449
Tustin Ranch Ct ... 77494
Twilight Canyon Rd ... 77449
Twin Canyon Ct ... 77450
Twin Creek Dr ... 77449
Twin Meadow Ln ... 77449
Twin Stone Ln ... 77449
Twinmont Ln ... 77494
Twisted Willow Ct & Ln ... 77450
Two Harbors Glen St ... 77494
Two Rivers Ct & Ln ... 77450
Tyler Park Ln ... 77494
Tynemeadow Ct ... 77449
Umber Elm Ct ... 77493
Unicorns Horn Ln ... 77449
Union Park Ct & Dr ... 77450
Upland Creek Dr ... 77449
Upland Dale Ct ... 77449
Upland Fair Ln ... 77449
Upland Ridge Ln ... 77494
Upland Spring Trce ... 77493
Usher Ct ... 77449
Vadini Shores Ln ... 77494
Valencia Ridge Ln ... 77494
Valerian Ln ... 77449
Valley Blossom Ct ... 77494
Valley Bluff Ln ... 77494
Valley Landing Dr ... 77450
Valley Oaks Ct ... 77450
Valley Ranch Dr ... 77450
Valley Spring Trl ... 77449
Valley Wells Dr ... 77449
Valleylight Dr ... 77494
Valleyside Dr ... 77494
Vallingby Dr ... 77450
Vander Dale Ct ... 77450
Vanderwick Dr ... 77450
Vanderwilt Ct & Ln ... 77449
Vaneta Dr ... 77449
Veneto Hills Ct ... 77449
Ventura Canyon Ct & Dr ... 77494
Veranda Dr ... 77449
Verdant Meadow Ct ... 77449
Verde Canyon Dr ... 77450
Verde Place Ln ... 77493
Vermillion Ct ... 77449
Vermont Glen Ct ... 77493
Victoria Lakes Dr ... 77493
Victory Terrace Ln ... 77450
View Valley Trl ... 77493
Viewpoint Ct ... 77449
Viewridge Dr ... 77494
Village Ct ... 77493
Village Arbour Dr ... 77493
Village Circle Dr ... 77493
Village Green Dr ... 77493
Village Lakes Dr ... 77493
Village Oak Dr ... 77493
Village Park Dr ... 77493
Village Stone Ct ... 77493
Village Way Dr ... 77493
Vinca Ranch Dr ... 77494
Vinemead Ct ... 77450
Vineyard Haven Ct ... 77449
N & S Vineyard Mdw Ln ... 77449
N & S Vineyard Meadow Ln ... 77449
Vining Rose Ct ... 77494
Vinson Ranch Ln ... 77494
Vintage Grove Ct ... 77449
Virginia Fields Dr ... 77494
Vista Valley Dr ... 77450
Vobe Ct ... 77449
Volga River Dr ... 77449
Walden Grove Ln ... 77450
Walden Gulch Ln ... 77494
Walder Ct ... 77449
Walderford Dr ... 77450
Walkabout Way ... 77450
Walker Mist Ln ... 77494
Walker Retreat Ln ... 77494
Waller Springs Ln ... 77494
Walnut Canyon Dr ... 77450
Walnut Springs Dr ... 77494
Walsh Crossing Dr ... 77494
Walter Peak Ln ... 77494
Walworten Ct ... 77450
N & S Warmstone Ct & Way ... 77494
Warren Park Dr ... 77494
Warrington Dr ... 77450
Wassail Way ... 77493
Water Edge Ln ... 77494
Water Hill Ct ... 77494
Waterford Gln ... 77494
Waterline Ln ... 77494
Watermist Glen Ct ... 77494
Waterport Ln ... 77449
Watts Ave ... 77493
Waverly Bnd ... 77450
Waverly Bend Ct ... 77450
Waverly Glend Dr ... 77450
Waverly Key Ct ... 77494
Waynoka Rd ... 77450
Wedgeoak Ct & Dr ... 77494
Wedgewater Crest Ln ... 77494
Weiman Dr ... 77493
Welch House Ln ... 77493
Weld Ct & Dr ... 77494
Wellbrook Ln ... 77450
Wellington Grove Cir & Ln ... 77494
Wellington Meadows Dr ... 77449
Wellsford Glen Dr ... 77449
Wellshire Dr ... 77494
Welwick Ct ... 77449
Wescott Pines Dr ... 77494
Westborough Dr ... 77449
Westbourne Dr ... 77494
Westbrook Cinco Ln ... 77450
Westcliffe Falls Dr ... 77450
Westenfield Ln ... 77450
Western Hills Ct & Dr ... 77450
Western Meadows Dr ... 77450
Western Pine Trl ... 77494
Western Springs Dr ... 77450
Western Valley Dr ... 77449
Westerpine Ln ... 77449
Westfield Pkwy ... 77449
Westfield Estates Dr ... 77449
Westfield Parkway Dr ... 77449
Westfield Village Dr ... 77449
Westfork Ct & Dr ... 77449
Westgreen Blvd ... 77450
N Westgreen Blvd ... 77449
S Westgreen Blvd ... 77450
Westgreen Ct ... 77450
Westheimer Pkwy
20600-22799 ... 77450
22800-27299 ... 77494
Westheimer Lakes North Dr ... 77494
Westland Crk ... 77449
Westwind Garden Pass ... 77494
Westwood Pines Dr ... 77449
Wetherburn Ln ... 77449
Wetherwind ... 77449
Wheat Harvest Ln ... 77494
Wheat Snow Ct & Ln ... 77449
Wheathall Camp Ln ... 77449
Wheeler Peak Way ... 77449
Whisper Trace Ct ... 77494
Whispering Creek Dr ... 77493
Whispering Hollow Ln ... 77449
Whispering Lakes Dr ... 77493
Whispering Oaks Dr ... 77493
Whispering Pines Dr ... 77493
Whispering Wind ... 77494
White Creek Trl ... 77450
White Eagle Ln ... 77450
White Falls Ln ... 77449
White Frye Dr ... 77494
White Pines Dr ... 77494
White Poplar Dr ... 77449
White Sands Rd ... 77450
Whitebranch Ln ... 77450
Whitebridge Ln ... 77449
Whitefield Ln ... 77493
Whitehurst Ct ... 77450
Whitetail Springs Ct ... 77494
Whitetip Ct ... 77449
Whitevine Way ... 77450
Whitewater Creek Cir ... 77450
Whitford Ct ... 77450
Whittmore Fields Dr ... 77494
Whitwell Dr ... 77449
Wickerhill Way ... 77494
Wickfield Dr ... 77450
Wickham Ct ... 77450
Wickman Glen Ln ... 77450
Wide Creek Ct & Dr ... 77449
Wiedner Dr ... 77494
Wigmaker Dr ... 77493
Wild Berry Ct & Dr ... 77449
Wild Dunes Cir ... 77450
Wild Horse Cyn ... 77493
Wild Horse Valley Rd ... 77450
Wild Jasmine Ln ... 77450
Wild Milberry Dr ... 77494
Wild Mustang Canyon Ln ... 77493
Wild Oak Lake Dr ... 77494
Wild Olive Ct ... 77449
Wild Orchard Ct & Ln ... 77494
Wild Palomino Dr ... 77493
Wild Peregrine Cir ... 77494
Wild Plains Dr ... 77449
Wild River Dr ... 77449
Wild View Ct ... 77450
Wild Willow Ln ... 77449
Wildbrook Canyon Ct & Ln ... 77449
Wildbrook Xing Ln ... 77494
Wildcroft Dr ... 77449
Wilderness Glen Ct ... 77449
Wildflower Cir & Ct ... 77494
Wildhawk Dr ... 77449
Wildoak Glen Ln ... 77494
Wildoats Dr ... 77449
Wildwood Ct & Ln ... 77494
Wildwood Grove Dr ... 77450
Willamette Dr ... 77449
Willhanna Dr ... 77449
Williams Cir ... 77449
Williamschase Dr ... 77449
Willow Bnd ... 77494
Willow Ln
6300-6499 ... 77493
26500-26999 ... 77494
E Willow Bluff Rd ... 77449
Willow Canyon Dr ... 77494
Willow Colony Ln ... 77494
Willow Cove Ct & Dr ... 77449
Willow Creek Ln ... 77494
Willow Fork Ct & Dr ... 77450
Willow Glade Dr ... 77450
Willow Lake St ... 77494
Willow Moss Dr ... 77449
Willow Peak Ln ... 77494
Willow Pond Dr ... 77494
Willow Side Ct ... 77450
Willow Stone Ct ... 77449
Willow Trace Ct ... 77450
Willowford Ct ... 77494
Willowford Park Dr ... 77450
Willowgreen St ... 77494
Willowwood Dr ... 77449
Wilrose Haven Dr ... 77494
Wimberly Place Ln ... 77494
N & S Wimbledon Dr ... 77449
Winberie Ct ... 77450
Winberry Ct ... 77449
Winchester Ranch Trl ... 77493
W Wind Canyon Ln ... 77493
Wind Hawk Ct & Dr ... 77494
Wind Trace Dr ... 77449
Windbury Ct ... 77450
Windcliff Ct ... 77449
Windcrest Ct ... 77450
Windcroft Hollow Ln ... 77449
Windcross Ct ... 77449
Windemere Park Ct & Ln ... 77494
Windhurst ... 77494
Winding Branch Dr ... 77449
Winding Canyon Ct ... 77493
Winding Canyon Ln ... 77449
Winding Cove Ln ... 77450
Winding Glen Dr ... 77494
Winding Hollow Dr ... 77450
Winding Knoll Dr ... 77494
Winding Lake Ct & Way ... 77450
Winding Point Ln ... 77494
Winding Run Ln ... 77494
Winding Shore Ct & Ln ... 77450
Winding Trail Ln ... 77449
Windlewood Dr ... 77449
Windmill Bluff Ln ... 77450
Windmont Dr ... 77494
Windmoor Ct, Dr & Pl ... 77450
Windsor Glen Dr ... 77450
Windsor Hollow Ct ... 77449
Windsor Ranch Ln ... 77494
Windsor Woods Ln ... 77494
Windy Bluff Ct ... 77449
Windy Brook Ln ... 77449
Windy Chase Ln ... 77494
Windy Cypress Ct ... 77449
Windy Drift Ln ... 77494
Windy Ridge Dr ... 77450

Windy River Ln 77449
Windy Village Ln 77449
Windys Way 77449
Windystone Dr 77449
Wine Cedar Ln 77450
Wineberry Dr 77450
Winebrook Creek Ln 77494
Winecup 77494
Winford Dr 77449
Wing Elm Dr 77494
Winlock Trace Ct & Dr 77450
Winsor Terrace Cir 77450
Winston Gulch Ct 77493
Winston Hollow Ln 77494
Winstrome Ct 77449
Winter Dale Ct 77493
Wispy Way 77494
Wistful Dr 77494
Withington Dr 77450
Wittman Ct & Ln 77450
Wolf Rock Dr 77449
Wolfs Hill Ln 77494
Wolfs Meadow Ln 77494
Wood Rain Ct 77449
Woodcreek Bend Ln 77494
Woodcreek Cove Ln 77494
Wooded Canyon Dr 77494
Wooded Hollow Ct & Ln 77494
Wooded Trace Ct 77449
Woodglen Dr 77449
Woodhaven Ct 77494
Woodland Green Dr 77449
Woodlark Dr 77494
Woodoak Ct 77450
Woodrose Dr 77450
Woods Ln 77494
Woodseem Ct 77449
Woolongong Dr 77449
Worth Creek Ln 77494
Worth Hills Ln 77449
Wrangler Sky Ct 77494
Wren Brook Ct 77449
Wren Valley Trl 77493
Wrenfield Ct 77449
Wright Dr 77493
Wrights Crossing St 77449
Wylie Valley Ln 77494
Wyndehaven Lakes Dr 77494
Y St 77493
Yale Dr 77493
Yale Square Ct 77449
Yardley Dr 77494
Yasmine Ranch Dr 77494
Yaupon Trace Ct & Dr 77494
Yearling Ridge Ct 77449
Yellow Cornerstone Dr 77494
Yellowwood Ct 77494
Yelverton Glen Dr 77493
Yorkpine Ct 77450
Yorkway Dr 77450
Yosemite Ridge Ct 77493
Young Meadows Way 77449
Young Pine St 77493
Zachary Bend Ln 77494
Zanardo Ct 77449
Zareen Ln 77493
Zion Park Dr 77493
Zoe Fair Ct 77494
Zubin Ln 77493

NUMBERED STREETS

1st St 77493
2nd St 77493
3rd St 77493
4th St 77493
5701-5701 77492
5701-6099 77493
5702-6098 77493
E 5th 77493
10th St 77493
11th St 77493
13th St 77493

KELLER TX

General Delivery 76248

POST OFFICE BOXES MAIN OFFICE STATIONS AND BRANCHES

Box No.s
All PO Boxes 76244

RURAL ROUTES

05, 08, 18, 21, 24, 25, 27, 28, 29, 30, 31, 32, 33, 34, 37, 39, 40, 41, 42, 43, 44, 45, 46, 47, 48, 76244
01, 02, 03, 04, 06, 07, 09, 10, 11, 12, 13, 14, 15, 16, 17, 19, 20, 22, 26, 35, 36, 54, 55 76248

NAMED STREETS

Adalina Dr 76248
Adeline Dr 76248
Adonis Dr 76248
Alma Ct & Dr 76248
Alta Ridge Dr 76248
Amber Ct 76248
Ambiente Ct 76248
Anita Ave 76248
Anson Dr 76248
Apache Trl 76248
Apeldoorn Ln 76248
Applewood Dr 76248
Arabian Ln 76248
Arboledas Ln 76248
Arcadia Ct & Dr 76248
Arden Ln 76248
Asher Dr 76248
Ashmore Ct & Dr 76248
Ashwood Dr 76248
Atascosa Dr 76248
Atlee Dr 76248
Audrey Dr 76248
Austin St 76248
Austin Thomas Dr 76248
Avebury Ct 76248
Avignon Trl 76248
Axton Carter Dr 76248
Bancroft Rd 76248
Bandera Dr 76248
Bandit Trl 76248
Barbara Ln 76248
Bart St 76248
W Bates St 76248
Bayou Ct 76248
Beacon Hill Dr 76248
Bear Holw, Rdg & Run 76248
Bear Creek Pkwy & Rd 76248
Beeding Ln 76248
Belinda Dr 76248
Bellstone Dr 76248
Bennington Ln 76248
Berkshire Hill Dr 76248
Bermail Dr 76248
Beverly Dr 76248
Big Bend Dr 76248
Birch Grove Trl 76248
Birchmont Ln 76248
Blackjack Trl 76248
Blackoak Ct 76248
Blevins Dr 76248
Bloomfield Dr 76248
Blue Quail Rd 76248
Blue Ridge Rd 76248
Blue Spruce Ct 76248
Bluebonnet Dr 76248
Bluestar Dr 76248
Bobbi Ct 76248
Bodega Bay Dr 76248
Bourland Rd 76248
Bradford Ct 76248
Bradford Grove Trl 76248
Bradley Ct & Dr 76248
Bramble Woods 76248
Branchview Ct 76248
Brentwood Trl 76248
Brian Dr 76248
Briar Run 76248
Briar Grove Dr 76248
Briar Meadow Ct & Dr 76248
Briar Ridge Dr 76248
Britney Ct 76248
Broiles Ct & Ln 76244
Bronco Ln 76248
Brook Hill Ct 76248
Brookfield Path 76248
Brushcreek Dr 76248
Buckner Ln 76248
Bur Oak Ct 76248
Burnet Dr 76248
Bursey Rd 76248
Buttercup Dr 76248
Cactus Ct 76248
Cadbury Ln 76248
Calais Dr 76248
California Trl 76248
Calverley Pl 76248
Camberley Ct 76248
Cambridge Ct 76248
Canterbury Ln 76248
Canyon Ct & Dr 76248
Canyon Wren Ln 76244
Cardinal Ln 76248
Carlow Ct 76248
Carmel Dr 76248
Carriage Ln 76248
Castleman Ct 76248
Cat Hollow Ct 76248
Cat Mountain Trl 76248
Cedar Ridge Ct & Dr 76248
Cedarwood Dr 76248
Celeste Ln 76248
Chandler Rd 76248
Charles St 76248
Charleston Ct 76248
Charrington Ct & Dr 76248
Chase Oaks Dr 76248
Chatham Ln 76248
Cherokee Ct & Trl 76248
Cherry Bark Dr 76248
Cherry Blossom Ln 76248
Cherry Blush Ct 76248
Cherry Glow Ct 76248
Cherry Tree Dr 76248
Chestnut Dr 76248
Cheyenne Trl 76248
Chisolm Trl 76248
Cielo Vista Dr 76248
Cindy Ct & St 76248
Clara Ln 76248
Clark Lake Cir 76248
Clark Springs Dr 76248
Clay Hibbins Rd 76248
Clear Brook Dr 76248
Clear Springs Dr 76248
Clearwater Ln 76248
Cliffmoor Dr 76248
Clover Ct & Ln 76248
Cobblestone Parks Dr 76248
Cold Springs Ct 76248
Colin Ct 76248
College Ave & St S 76248
Colt Ct & Ln 76248
Comal Ct 76248
Conchos Cir E & W 76248
Cotswold Ct 76248
Cottonwood Trl 76248
Country Brook Dr 76248
Country Glen Ct & Ln 76248
Country Manor Dr 76248
Countryhill Dr 76248
Countryside Trl 76248
Coyote Ct 76248
Crater Lake Cir 76248
Creek Ct & Rd 76248
Creek Bluff Dr 76248
Creek Crossing Trl 76248
Creek Terrace Dr 76248
Creekbend Dr 76248
Creekhaven Ct 76248
Creekhollow Ct & Dr 76248
Creekridge Dr 76248
Creekside Dr 76248
Creekview Dr 76248
Creekvista Ct & Dr 76248
Creekwood Ct 76248
Crestview Dr 76248
Crestwood Trl 76248
Crimson Ln 76248
Crimson Glory Ct & Ln 76248
Crockett St 76248
Cross Timbers Dr 76248
Crossing Ct 76248
Crown Ct 76248
Crystal Glen Dr 76248
Cumberland Dr 76248
Cutting Horse Ln 76248
Cypress Ct & Dr 76248
Dale Ct 76248
Dalton St 76248
Dana Dr 76248
Danbury Parks Dr 76248
Davis Blvd 76248
Davis Mountain Rd 76244
De Moss Ct 76248
Deep Eddy Trl 76248
Deer Run 76248
Deer Path Ct 76248
Deerwood Ln 76248
Denali Ln 76248
Denise Ct 76248
Devin Cir 76248
Diamond Rim Pass Rd 76248
Diar Ln 76248
Dodge Trl 76248
Dogwood Trl 76248
Doral Ct 76248
Double Springs Ln 76248
Dove Mdws 76248
Doyle Dr 76248
Drake Ct 76248
Dream Dust Ct & Ln 76248
Driftwood Ct 76248
Dripping Springs Dr 76248
Dunmore Ct 76248
Durrand Oak Dr 76248
Dusk Dr 76248
Eagle Ct, Pass & Trl 76248
Eagle Glen Ln 76248
Eastwood Dr 76248
Ed Bourland Rd 76248
Edenderry Dr 76248
Edgebrook Ave & Ct 76248
Edgemere Dr 76248
Edgewood Dr 76248
Edinburgh Ln 76248
Elaine St 76248
N & S Elm St 76248
Elmgrove Ct & Ln 76248
Emerald Green Ln 76248
Emerald Knoll Ct & Dr 76248
Emerald Ridge Dr 76248
Estes Park Ct 76248
Estrellas Dr 76248
Evelyn Ct 76248
Everest Rd 76248
Evergreen Ct 76248
Falcon Cir & Dr 76248
Fall Creek Trl 76248
Farm View Trl 76248
Flanigan Hill Dr 76248
Flint Ct & Trl 76248
Flusche Ct 76244
Flying Trl 76248
Forest Bend Ln 76248
Forest Green Ct 76248
Forest Lakes Ct & Dr 76248
Forest Park Ct & Dr 76248
Fostery King Pl 76248
Fowler St 76248
Fox Meadow Dr 76248
Foxcroft Ct & Ln 76248
Foxford Dr 76248
Frank Ln 76248
Frio Dr 76248
Gatewood Dr 76248
Gentle Wind Dr 76248
Glasgow Ln 76248
Glass Canyon Ct 76244
Glass Mountain Trl 76244
Glen Dr & Holw 76248
Glendale Dr 76248
Glenhurst Rd 76248
Glenmont Rd 76248
Gloria St 76248
Golden Triangle Blvd 76248
Goldenrod Ln 76248
Goliad Dr 76248
Grand Meadows Dr 76248
Granite Falls Dr 76248
Gray Owl Rd 76248
Graystone Ct 76248
Green Trl 76248
Greenbriar Dr 76248
Greenhill Ct 76248
Grey Kingbird Trl 76244
Guadalupe Rd 76248
Haddington Ln 76248
Hallelujah Trl 76248
Hardwick Trl 76248
Harper Ct & Ln 76248
Hayley Dr 76248
Hays Dr 76248
Heather Ln 76248
Helen St 76248
Heritage Ct 76248
Hibiscus Dr 76248
Hidden Cove Ct 76248
Hidden Woods Dr 76248
Hideaway Ct & Dr 76248
Highfield Ln 76248
Highland Lakes Ct & Dr 76248
Highland Oaks Dr 76248
Highway 1709 76248
Hill St 76248
Hillside Dr 76248
Hillview Dr 76248
Holland Ln 76248
Holly Ct 76248
Holly Hills Ct 76248
Holly Ridge Ct & Dr 76248
Homestead Dr 76248
Hovenkamp St 76248
Hudnall Ct 76248
Hudnall Farm Rd 76248
Huffman Blf 76248
Hunter Ct 76248
Hunter Manor Dr 76248
Huxley St 76248
Imperial Pointe Dr 76248
Imperial Springs Dr 76248
India St 76248
Indian Blanket Dr 76248
Indian Creek Ct 76248
Indian Knoll Trl 76248
Ironwood Dr 76248
Ivy Ct 76248
Jacob Ave & Ct 76248
Jessie St 76248
Johnson Ct & Rd 76248
Joshua Ct 76248
Joyner Ln 76248
Justin Ct 76248
Kaitlyn Ct & Ln 76248
Karnes Dr 76248
Kate Ct 76248
W Keller Pkwy 76248
Keller Hicks Rd 76248
Keller Smithfield Rd S 76248
Kelly Green Ct 76248
Kelsey Dr 76248
Kendall Ct 76248
Kerr Ct & Ln 76248
Keystone Way 76248
Kilkenny Ct 76248
King Trl 76248
Kingsmill Ct 76248
Kingwood Dr 76248
Knightsbridge Ln 76248
Krokus Dr 76248
La Fontaine Ln 76248
La Quinta Cir N & S 76248
Lacey Oak Ln 76248
Laguna Trl 76248
Lakepoint Dr 76248
Lakeridge Dr 76248
Lakeview Dr 76248
Lakeway Dr 76248
Lakewood Ct 76248
Lamar St 76248
Landsbury Ct 76248
Lantana Dr 76248
Lark Ct 76248
Lark Haven Ln 76248
Lasalle Dr 76248
Lasater Ct 76248
Latigo Ln 76248
Laurel Valley Dr 76248
Lauren Ct 76248
Lavena Ct & St 76248
Lazy Oaks St 76244
Ledara Ln 76248
Legacy Ct 76248
Lewis Crossing Ct & Dr 76248
Lilac Dr 76248
Limestone Creek Dr 76248
Linda St 76248
Lindsey Dr 76248
Lizzy Ct 76248
Lockwood Dr 76248
Longford Ct 76248
Longhorn Trl 76248
Longview Ct & Dr 76248
Lorine St 76248
Lost Trl 76248
Lost Lake Dr 76248
Luna Dr 76248
Lyndhurst Way 76248
Madera Ct 76248
Maggie Ct 76248
Magnolia Ct 76248
N & S Main St 76248
Majestic Ct 76248
Mallard Ct 76248
Maple Ridge Trl 76244
Maplewood Dr 76248
Marble Pass Dr 76248
Marblewood Dr 76248
Mariposa Dr 76248
Marlin Ln 76248
Marsha St 76248
Marshall Ridge Pkwy 76248
Martha Ct 76248
Mason Ct & Ln 76248
Mcentire Ct 76248
Meadow Cir & Ct 76248
Meadow Creek Dr 76248
Meadow Knoll Ct 76248
Meadow Park Dr 76248
Meadow Ridge Dr 76248
Meadowbrook Ln 76248
Meadowlands Blvd 76248
Meadowlark Dr 76248
Meadowside Dr 76248
Meandering Woods Dr 76248
Medina Ct & Dr 76248
Menton Ln 76248
Meridian Ct 76248
Mesa Trl 76248
Mesquite Dr & Ln 76248
Micah Way 76248
Mineral Springs Ct & Dr 76248
Minnie St 76248
Misty Ct 76248
Misty Oak Ln 76248
Misty Ridge Dr 76248
Mockingbird Ct & Ln 76248
Monarch Ct & Way 76248
Monarch Hill Ct & Rd 76248
Montana Ct N & S 76248
Monte Alto St 76244
Monte Carlo Way 76244
Monterey Dr 76248
Montgomery Dr 76248
Moonlight Ln 76248
Morning Star Ct & Ln 76248
Morris Dr 76248
Mossy Oak Dr 76248
Mossy Rock Dr 76248
Mossycup Ct 76248
Mount Gilead Rd 76248
Mountain Laurel Dr 76248
Muirfield Rd 76248
Mulberry Dr 76248
Navajo Dr 76248
Newton Ranch Rd 76248
Norma Ln 76248
Northern Trce 76248
Northshore Ct 76248
Northwyck Ln 76248
Nottingham Rd 76248
Oak Dr 76248
Oak Bend Ln 76248
Oak Hill Rd 76248
Oak Ridge Ct & Dr 76248
Oak Valley Ct & Dr 76248
Oakbriar Ln 76248
Oakmont Ct 76248
Oakwood Cir & Dr 76248
Old York Dr 76248
W Olive St 76248
Olympic Dr 76248
Opelousas Ct N & S 76248
Osito Ct 76248
Overcup Ln 76248
Overleaf Dr 76248
Overlook Ridge Dr 76248
Oxford Ct 76248
Pacific Grove Dr 76248
Page St 76248
Paint Pony Ln 76248
Paintbrush Dr 76248
Palancar Dr 76244
Palo Duro Trl 76248
Palomino Trl 76248
Park Ct & Dr 76248
Park North Ln 76248
Park Place Ct 76248
Parkside Dr 76248
Parkview Ln 76248
Parma Ln 76244
Pate Orr Rd N & S 76248
Pearl St 76248
N & S Pearson Ln & Xing 76248
Pebblecreek Dr 76248
Pecan St 76248
Pecan Hollow Ct 76248
Pecos Valley Rd 76244
Pembrook Ct 76248
Pendleton Ct 76248
Penny Ln 76248
Pheasant Rdg 76248
Pienza Path 76248
Pimlico Dr 76248
Pin Oak Trl 76248
Pine Hurst Dr 76248
Pine Ridge Ct 76248
Pioneer Dr 76248
Pixie Rose Dr 76248
Placid View Ct 76248
Pleasant Run 76248
Pond Springs Ct 76248
Ponder Path 76248
Ponderosa Dr 76248
Post Oak Rd 76248
Preston Ln 76248
Preston Brook Dr 76248
Prewit St 76248
Promontory Dr 76248
Pryor Ct N & S 76248
Quail Rdg 76248
Quail Ridge Ct 76248

Quail Run Dr 76248
Quarter Horse Ln 76248
Queensgate Dr 76248
Quest Ct 76248
Quiet Path 76248
Ramblewood Ct 76248
Ranch Ct 76248
Rancho Grande Trl 76248
Rancho Serena Dr 76248
Ranger Dr 76248
Rapp Rd 76248
Rawhide Path 76248
Reata Rd 76248
Red Gate Cir 76244
Red Oak Ct 76248
Redbud Dr 76248
Redwood Ct & Dr 76248
Regal Xing 76248
Renaissance Ct 76248
Rhonda Rd 76248
Richmond Ln 76248
N Ridge Ct 76248
Ridge Crest Dr 76248
Ridge Point Pkwy 76248
Ridgecliff Dr 76248
Ridgegate Dr 76248
Ridgeway Dr 76248
Rim Rock Dr 76248
River Trl 76248
N Riverside Dr 76244
Rock Springs Dr 76248
Rockhurst Trl 76248
Rockwood Dr 76248
Rodeo Ct & Dr 76248
Roland Dr 76248
Rolling Bend Ct & Dr 76248
Rolling Ridge Dr 76248
Rolling Wood Ln 76248
Rosebriar Ln 76248
Rosewood Dr 76248
Roxbury Ct & Way 76248
Roy Ct & Ln 76248
Royal Glade Dr 76248
Ruby St 76248
N Rufe Snow Dr 76248
Runnymede Ct & Rd 76248
Rush Creek Ct & Rd 76248
Rustic Ridge Dr 76248
Saddleback Pass Rd 76248
Saddletree Ln 76248
Sagebrush Trl 76248
Sagewood Ct 76248
Saint Andrews Ln 76248
Saint George Ct 76248
Saint James Pl 76248
San Clemente Dr 76248
San Jacinto Ct 76248
Sandy Trl 76248
Santa Barbara Ct & Dr 76248
Santa Cruz Dr 76248
Santa Fe Trl 76248
Sarah Brooks Dr 76248
Sawgrass Ct 76248
Sawtooth Oak Trl 76248
Scot Ln 76248
Seaton St 76248
Sendero Dr 76248
Sequoia Ln 76248
Serene Ct 76248
Settlers Ridge Dr 76248
Shadow Glen Ln 76248
Shadowbrook Dr 76248
Shady Ln N & S 76248
Shady Bridge Ln 76248
Shady Grove Rd 76248
Shady Hollow Ct 76248
Shady Oak Dr 76248
Shannon Ct 76248
Shasta Ln 76248
Shawnee Trl 76248
Shoreline Ct & Dr 76248
N Shropshire Ct & St 76248
Shumard Oak Trl 76248
Sierra Ln 76248
Signet Ct 76248
Silkwood Ct 76248
Silver Chase Dr 76248
Silver Lake Dr 76248
Silver Sage Ct 76248
Silverado Trl 76248
Silverleaf Dr 76248
Silverwood Ct 76248
Simmons Dr 76248
Sioux St 76248
Smethwick Cv 76248
Smoketree Dr 76248
Snow Mountain Cir 76248
Sorano Way 76244
Sorenson Trl 76248
Sorrel Trl 76248
Southern Hills Ct & Dr 76248
Southfork Dr 76248
Spanish Bay Dr 76248
Spicewood Ct 76248
Split Rock Dr 76248
Sports Pkwy 76248
Spring Creek Ct & Dr 76248
Spring Lake Dr 76248
Springbranch Dr 76248
Spyglass Ct 76248
Spyglass Hill Dr 76248
Stallion Ct & Dr 76248
Stansbury Dr 76248
Stanton Ct 76248
Starlight Ct & Dr 76248
Stegall Rd 76248
Sterling Trace Dr 76248
Stillwater Ct 76248
Stone Ct 76248
Stoneridge Dr 76248
Stratford Pl 76248
Stratton Dr 76248
Summertree Dr 76248
Suncrest Dr 76248
Sunlight Ct 76248
Sunrise Ct & Dr 76248
Sunset Ct 76248
Sustrik Ct 76248
Sweet Adeline Ln 76248
Sweetgum Cir 76248
Sycamore Dr 76248
Tahoe Ln 76248
Talbot St 76248
Tall Oak Ln 76248
Tall Pine Ct 76248
Talon Ct & Dr 76248
Tamarron Ct 76248
N Tarrant Pkwy 76248
Taylor St 76248
Teal Ln 76248
Tealcrest Ct 76248
Tealwood Ct & Dr 76248
Templemore Dr 76248
The Lakes Ct 76248
Timberline Ct & Dr 76248
Tipperary Dr 76248
Toulouse Ln 76248
Town Center Ln 76248
Trail Ridge Ct & Dr 76248
Trailwood Ct 76248
Travis St 76248
Trinity Ln 76248
Trowbridge Ct 76248
Tulip Way 76248
Tulla Ct 76248
Twin Creeks Dr 76248
Unbridled Ln 76248
Union Church Rd 76248
Uvalde Dr 76248
Valle Vista Ct & Ln 76248
Valley Ridge Dr 76248
Vasey Oak Dr 76248
Veiled Ct 76248
Verona Way 76248
Versailles Ln 76248
Vicki St 76248
Victoria Dr 76248
Village Trl 76248
E Vine St
100-519 76248
520-520 76244
520-598 76248
521-597 76248
W Vine St 76248
Volterra Way
2800-2899 76248
11400-11499 76244
Wagonwheel Trl 76248
Wales Dr 76248
Waterbury Ct & Way 76248
Watercrest Ct & Dr 76248
Waterford Ln 76248
Waters Edge 76248
Waterwood Dr 76248
Wayside Dr 76248
Wellington Ct & Dr 76248
Western Trl 76248
Westover Trl 76248
Weybridge Ln 76248
Whispering Oaks Dr 76248
Whitley Rd 76248
Wickford Ct 76248
Wickham Ct 76248
Wildcreek Ct & Trl 76248
Williamsburg Ct & Ln 76248
Willis Ln 76248
Willow Ct 76248
Willow Glen Ct 76248
Willowwood Trl 76248
Wilson Ln 76248
Windcrest Dr 76248
Windemere Way 76248
Winding Creek Dr 76248
Windsong Cir 76248
Windy Ridge Dr 76248
Wingate Ct 76248
Winhall Dr 76248
Wise St 76248
Wishing Tree Ln 76248
Wisteria Dr 76248
Woodborough Ln 76248
Woodbury Ct 76248
Woodford Dr 76248
Woodland Trl 76248
Woodridge Dr 76248
Woody Creek Dr 76248
Wyndham Cir 76248
Yosemite Ln 76248
Zavala Rd 76248

KERRVILLE TX

General Delivery 78028

POST OFFICE BOXES MAIN OFFICE STATIONS AND BRANCHES

Box No.s
All PO Boxes 78029

HIGHWAY CONTRACTS

04 78028

NAMED STREETS

A St 78028
Aaron Dr 78028
Ace Ranch Rd 78028
Acorn Aly 78028
Adkins Rd 78028
Afroal Rd 78028
Agarita St 78028
Ahrens Rd 78028
Airport Loop & Rdg 78028
Airport Commerce Pkwy 78028
Al Mooney Rd 78028
Alamo Dr 78028
Alice St 78028
Alpine Dr 78028
Alto Vista St 78028
Alvin Dr 78028
Amelia Ct 78028
Andrew Rd 78028
Ann Ln 78028
Antelope Trl 78028
Antler Dr 78028
Apache Dr 78028
Appaloosa Dr 78028
Aqua Vista Dr 78028
Aransas St 78028
Arcadia Loop 78028
Arizona Ash Dr 78028
Arkansas 78028
Arrow Ln 78028
Arrowhead Dr 78028
Arroyo Dr & Trl 78028
Ashley Dr 78028
Aspen Dr 78028
Athens Ave 78028
Augusta Cir 78028
Aurora Dr 78028
Avery Rd 78028
Avis Pero Rd 78028
B St 78028
Backacre Rd 78028
Bailey Jo Dr S 78028
Baker Ln 78028
Ball Dr 78028
Balmoral Dr 78028
Baltic Ave 78028
Bandera Hwy 78028
Barbara Ann St 78028
Barker St 78028
W Barnett St 78028
Barry Dr 78028
Bayless Rd 78028
Bear Creek Rd 78028
Bear Hollow Trl 78028
Bear Run Ln 78028
Bearskin Trl 78028
Beech St 78028
Begonia St 78028
Bel Aire Dr 78028
Ben Denton Holw 78028
Benson Dr 78028
Bent Oak Ln 78028
Bessie Ln 78028
Beverly Hills Ln 78028
Birch Dr S 78028
Birdo Blvd 78028
Birkdale Ln 78028
Black Jack Aly 78028
Blacksmith Ln 78028
Blanks St 78028
Blessed Ln 78028
Blue Rdg W 78028
Blue Bird Cir 78028
Blue Sage Loop 78028
Blue Sky Ln 78028
Blue Stem Trl 78028
Bluebell Rd 78028
Bluebonnet Dr 78028
W Bluff Dr 78028
Bluff Ridge Dr 78028
Bluffview Cir 78028
Bobcat Trl 78028
Bobwhite Dr 78028
Bonnie Rd 78028
Boot Hill Trl 78028
Bootlegger Ln 78028
Bow Dr & Ln 78028
Bowie Dr 78028
Box Canyon Rd 78028
Box Elder Dr 78028
Box S Dr 78028
Boyington Ln 78028
Braden Cir 78028
Braeburn Cir 78028
Brandis Ln S 78028
S Brandon Rd 78028
Brian Dr 78028
Briarwood Ln 78028
Bridal Path 78028
Brinda 78028
Broadway 78028
Brown Sugar Ln 78028
Browns Dr 78028
Brunos Curv 78028
Buck Creek Rdg 78028
N Buckboard Dr 78028
Buckskin Trl 78028
Buena Vista Dr 78028
Buffalo Dr 78028
Bullard Dr 78028
Bulwer Ave 78028
Burleson Blvd 78028
Burnet Dr 78028
Burney Ln 78028
Burroughs Ln 78028
Bushwhack Rd 78028
Business Dr W 78028
C St 78028
Caddo Ln 78028
Calcote Rd 78028
Caliche Ln 78028
Calle Del Roble 78028
Camelot Dr 78028
Camino Real Rd 78028
Camp Meeting Rd 78028
Candice Dr 78028
Canon Canyon Pl 78028
Canter Ln 78028
Canyon Dr & Rd 78028
Canyon Creek Ln 78028
Canyon Ridge Vw 78028
Canyon View Dr 78028
Cardiff St 78028
Cardinal Dr 78028
Carefree Trl N 78028
Caribou Ln 78028
Carmichael St 78028
Carol Ann Dr 78028
Cartuck St 78028
Caruthers Ln 78028
Castle Pne 78028
Catalina Ct 78028
Cattail Creek Dr 78028
E & W Cedar Dr, Rdg & Way S 78028
Cedar Knoll Rd 78028
Cedar Mill Rd W 78028
Cedar Ridge Rd 78028
Cedar Wood Rd 78028
Cedro Vista Dr 78028
Celia Cir N 78028
Center Ave 78028
Center Point River Rd 78028
Chalet Cir & Trl 78028
Chambliss Way 78028
Chaney Ranch Rd 78028
Chaparral Dr 78028
Chapman Dr 78028
Charles Rd & St 78028
Cherry Ln & Way 78028
Cherry Ridge Rd 78028
Chinaberry Ln 78028
Chole Way 78028
Christian Dr 78028
Chula Vista Dr 78028
Cielo Dr 78028
Cimmaron Rd 78028
Cindy Jacks Dr 78028
Circle Ave 78028
Clairmont Dr 78028
Clara St 78028
Claret Flds 78028
Clay St 78028
Clear Spring Dr 78028
Clearwater Paseo 78028
N Cloud Dr 78028
Clovis Ct 78028
Club House Dr & Rd 78028
Club View Cir & Ct 78028
Cobbler Ln 78028
Codrington Dr 78028
Coker Holw & Rd 78028
Coleman St 78028
Colinas Dr 78028
College St 78028
Colonial Ln 78028
Comanche Spur 78028
Comanche Trace Dr 78028
Commerce St 78028
Concho Dr 78028
Connally Dr 78028
Contour Dr 78028
Corbin Ln 78028
Cordoba Ave 78028
Coronado Cir & Dr 78028
Corral Trl 78028
Cottage St 78028
Cotton Gin Ln 78028
Coultress Rd 78028
Country Ln 78028
Country Club Dr 78028
Covey Ln 78028
Cox Ave 78028
Coyote Ridge Dr 78028
Crawford St 78028
Creek Rd & Run 78028
Creekside Dr 78028
Creekwood Rd 78028
Crescent Dr 78028
Crest Ridge Dr 78028
N Crestline 78028
Crestwood Dr 78028
Creswell Ln 78028
Crider St 78028
Crockett Dr 78028
Crown Ridge Dr 78028
Crown View Dr 78028
Cub Ln 78028
Cully Dr
200-299 78028
244-244 78029
Cummings Ln 78028
Cydney Ln 78028
Cynthia Dr 78028
Cypress Dr & St S 78028
Cypress Creek Rd 78028
D St 78028
Danielle Dr 78028
Dasha Dr S 78028
E & W Davis St 78028
Dawn Dr 78028
Dean Dr 78028
Deer Trl 78028
Deer Haven Ln 78028
Deer Park Ln 78028
Deer Spring Cv 78028
Deerfield 78028
Deerwood Dr 78028
Degrasse Dr 78028
Del Ct 78028
Del Valley Loop 78028
Demasco Rd 78028
Dena Dr 78028
Denise Dr 78028
Denlu Rd 78028
Denton St 78028
Derrek Rd S 78028
Diamond Two Rd 78028
Diana Dr 78028
Dingley View Dr 78028
Docs Ln W 78028
Donna Dr 78028
Donna Kay Dr 78028
Doris Dr 78028
Double Eagle Cir & Dr 78028
Douglas Dr 78028
Dover Dr 78028
Downing Rd 78028
Doyle Rd 78028
Dragonfly Ln 78028
Drew Ln 78028
Drummond Dr 78028
Dry Hollow Cir & Dr 78028
Duffy Dr 78028
Dunks Rd 78028
E St 78028
Eagles Nest 78028
Earl Dr 78028
Earl Garrett St 78028
East Ln 78028
Easy St 78028
Edgar Fiedler Rd 78028
Edinburgh Dr 78028
Editha Dr 78028
Eds Way 78028
El Rancho Grande Rd 78028
Elm Rdg, St & Way 78028
Elm Valley Dr 78028
Elmo Ln 78028
Elmwood 78028
Enchanted Valley Dr 78028
Encino Dr & Loop 78028
Encino Vista Dr 78028
Enderle Ct 78028
Englewood Cir & Dr 78028
Eric St 78028
Erin Dr 78028
Ernest St 78028
Espada Mission St 78028
Estates Dr 78028
Everett St 78028
F St 78028
Fairview Dr 78028
Fairway Ct & Dr 78028
Faith Ln 78028
Fall Creek Rd 78028
Fallow Dr 78028
Faltin Rd 78028
Family Cir 78028
Fannin Dr 78028
Fawn Dr & Run 78028
Fawn Dale Ln 78028
Fawn Ridge Trl 78028
Fawn Valley Ln 78028
Fay Dr 78028
Felix Dr 78028
Fifer St 78028
Firefly Ln 78028
Fitch St 78028
Flanders 78028
Florence St 78028
Florian Dr 78028
Floyd Van Hoozer 78028
Foothills Dr 78028
Foradeli Dr 78028
Ford St 78028
Forest Cir 78028
Forest Hill Ln 78028
Forest Ridge Dr 78028
Four Bears Trl 78028
Francisco Lemos St S 78028
Frederick Dr 78028
Fredericksburg Rd 78028
Freedom Trl 78028
Friar Tuck Way 78028
Frio Rd N 78028
Front St 78028
Fudge Ln 78028
Fuller St 78028
Furr Rd 78028
S G St S & W 78028
Gabe Rd 78028
Galbraith Ave 78028
Gallup Trl 78028
Garden St 78028
Garner Dr 78028
Gary Cross Way 78028
Gasoline Aly 78028
Gay Dr 78028
Genesis Dr 78028
George Ct & St 78028
George Hollow Rd 78028
George Muck Dr 78028
Gibsons Dr 78028
Gilmer St 78028
Ginger Rd 78028
Glen Rd 78028
Glen Oaks Dr 78028
Glen Shadows Dr 78028
Glory Cir 78028
Gloucester Ct & Pt 78028
Goat Creek Pkwy & Rd 78028
Goat Creek Cut Off Rd 78028
Golden Vly 78028
Golf Ave 78028
Goss St 78028
Grace Ln 78028
Grady Ln 78028

Granada Pl 78028
Green Mdws 78028
Green Oak Dr 78028
Green Tree Ln 78028
Greenbriar Cir 78028
Greenleaf Dr 78028
Greenwood Dr 78028
Guadalupe Plz & St 78028
H St 78028
Halston Cir S 78028
Hamilton St 78028
Hancock Dr 78028
Hans Dr 78028
Happy Trl 78028
Harmon Way 78028
Harold St 78028
Harper Rd & St 78028
Hartshorn Dr 78028
Harville Rd 78028
Hays St 78028
Hazelett Dale Rd 78028
Heather Ct 78028
Heidi Ln 78028
Herzog St 78028
Hi Wood Ln 78028
Hiawatha Dr 78028
Hidden Acres Rd 78028
Hidden Hollow Dr 78028
Hidden Pond Trl 78028
Hidden Valley Rd 78028
High Dr 78028
High Pointe Dr 78028
Highlands Dr 78028
Highridge Ct & Dr 78028
Highway 27 78028
Hill Country Dr 78028
Hillcrest Ave 78028
NW Hills Dr 78028
Hillside Dr 78028
Hilltop Dr & Rd 78028
Holdsworth Dr 78028
Holland Ln 78028
Hollomon Rd 78028
Holly Dr 78028
Homer Dr 78028
Homestead 78028
Honeycomb Ln 78028
Honor Dr 78028
Hoofbeat Trl 78028
Hopi Way 78028
Horizon Blvd 78028
Horseshoe Rdg 78028
Hortons Habitat Dr 78028
Hough Rd 78028
Hugo St 78028
Hugo Real Rd 78028
Hummingbird Ln 78028
Hunt St 78028
Hunters Way 78028
Hunters Pointe Dr 78028
Huntsberry Ridge Rd 78028
Indian Trl 78028
Indian Bluff Dr 78028
Indian Creek Loop 78028
Indian Hills Dr 78028
Indian Lake Dr 78028
Indian Oaks Dr 78028
Indian Springs Dr 78028
Indian Wells Dr 78028
Indianhead Trl 78028
Industrial Dr 78028
Irene 78028
Ivy Ln 78028
Jack Dr 78028
Jack Parks Ln 78028
Jacks Dr 78028
Jackson Rd 78028
Jade Loop 78028
Janie Rd 78028
Jasper Ln 78028
Jefferson St W 78028
Jeffery Scott Rd 78028
Jennings Blvd 78028
Jessica Ln 78028
Jody Rd 78028
Johnson Dr 78028

Jonas Dr 78028
Jones Rd 78028
Josephine St 78028
Joshua Dr 78028
Joy Harvest 78028
Judys Pl 78028
Junction Hwy 78028
Juniper Dr & Rdg S 78028
Kally Ln 78028
Kamira 78028
Kara Rdg 78028
Kathy Dr 78028
Kathyleen Ln 78028
Katy Ln 78028
Keeter Rd 78028
Keith Blvd 78028
Kensington Blvd 78028
Kenwood Cir 78028
Kermit Rd 78028
Kerr Canyon Pass 78028
Kerrville Rd 78028
Kerrville Country Dr 78028
Kerrville South Dr 78028
Kimberly Dr 78028
Kings Ct 78028
Kite Ct & Dr 78028
Knapp Rd 78028
Kodiak Trl 78028
La Casa Dr 78028
La Cumbre Cir & Dr 78028
La Reata Rd 78028
E & W Lacey Oak Pkwy 78028
Lafayette St 78028
Laguna Vista Pt 78028
Lake Dr 78028
Lake Dawn Rd 78028
Lake Ridge Rd 78028
Lakeside Ln 78028
Lakeview Cir 78028
Lakeway Dr 78028
Lakewood Dr 78028
Lamar St 78028
Lamb Creek Rd 78028
Lammers St 78028
Landmark Rd 78028
Lane Dr 78028
Lang Dr 78028
Lantana Rd 78028
Lantern Pkwy 78028
Larry Ln 78028
Larry Lee Dr 78028
Las Colinas Dr 78028
Laura Belle Dr 78028
Laurel Hts, St & Way 78028
Lawson St 78028
Lazy Ln 78028
Leaning Tree Ln 78028
Lee St 78028
Legend Ln 78028
Legion Dr 78028
Lehmann Dr 78028
Leland St 78028
Lenard Ln 78028
Leroy Rd 78028
Leslie Dr 78028
Lessie Ln 78028
N & S Lewis Ave 78028
Liggett Ln 78028
Lightning Ln 78028
Lil Bit Ln 78028
Lillian Dr 78028
Lime Creek Rd 78028
Limestone Rdg 78028
Lincoln Ave 78028
Linda Joy 78028
Lindheimer Trl 78028
Lindsey Trl 78028
Link Ln 78028
Linn Rd 78028
Live Oak Dr, Ln & St S 78028
Liz Run 78028
Lloyd Dr 78028
Lochaven Ln 78028
Locust St 78028

Lois St 78028
Loma Linda Dr 78028
Loma Vista Dr 78028
Loma Vuelta Dr 78028
Lone Oak 78028
Lonesome Dove Ln 78028
Longhorn Trl 78028
Loop 13 78028
Loop 534 78028
Los Cedros Loop 78028
Los Encinos 78028
Lost Creek Rd 78028
Lost Valley Rd 78028
Loudair Dr 78028
Lower Turtle Creek Rd 78028
Lowrance Dr 78028
Lowry St 78028
Loyal Valley Rd 78028
Lucille St 78028
Lucky Ridge St 78028
Lucy Rd 78028
Lydick Ln 78028
Lyn Del Dr 78028
Lytle St 78028
Mack Hollimon Dr 78028
Mackay Dr 78028
Madrona Dr 78028
Mae Dr 78028
Magical Ln 78028
Mai Rd 78028
W Main St 78028
Malibu Dr 78028
Manor Dr 78028
Maple Rd & St S 78028
Margaret Dr 78028
Marion Dr 78028
Mark Dr S 78028
Marshall Dr 78028
Mary Frances Dr 78028
Mary Louise 78028
Mary Ruth Rd S 78028
Mathison Dr 78028
Mcallen Dr 78028
Mccullough Rd 78028
Mccullough Ranch Rd 78028
W Mcfarland Dr 78028
Meadow Ridge Dr 78028
Meadowview Ln 78028
Medina Hwy 78028
Medio Vista Dr 78028
Meeker Rd 78028
Melvin Dr 78028
Memorial Blvd 78028
Mesa Trl 78028
Mesa Del Sol 78028
Mesa Park Dr 78028
Mesa Vista Ln 78028
Mesquite St 78028
Methodist Encampment Rd 78028
Mica Ln 78028
Michelle Dr 78028
Michon Dr S 78028
Middle Rd 78028
Middle Forest Dr 78028
Mill Run 78028
Miller St 78028
Milton St 78028
Mimosa St 78028
Mina Dr 78028
Mission Arroya Vis 78028
Misty Ln 78028
Mockingbird Ln 78028
Molina Dr 78028
Monarch Dr 78028
Monroe Dr 78028
Monterrey St 78028
Montibello Ct 78028
Moonwilde 78028
Moore St 78028
Morningside Dr 78028
Morris Rd 78028
Moss Ln 78028
Mosty Ahrens Rd 78028
Mott Dr 78028
Mount Haven Dr 78028

Mountain Dr 78028
Mountain Laurel 78028
Mountain Ridge Spur 78028
Mountain Top Dr 78028
Mountain Way Dr 78028
Mulberry Rd 78028
Muleshoe Dr 78028
Mull Rd 78028
Mulligan Cir & Way 78028
Mustang Trl 78028
Myrta St 78028
Nancy Beth Dr 78028
Neunhoffer Ranch Rd 78028
Newberry Hl 78028
Newton St 78028
Nichols St 78028
Nimitz Dr 78028
Nixon Ln 78028
Nora Dr 78028
Norfolk Ln 78028
North St 78028
Oak Aly, Dr, Ln, St & Way 78028
Oak Hill Dr 78028
Oak Hollow Dr 78028
Oak Park Dr 78028
Oak Valley Dr 78028
Oak Wood Rd 78028
Oakcrest Way 78028
Oakland Hills Ln 78028
Oakridge Dr 78028
Oakview Dr 78028
Ocean Dr 78028
Old Fm 689 78028
Old Harper Hwy 78028
Old Oaks 78028
Old Pasture Rd E 78028
Olmos Vista Dr 78028
Olympia Dr 78028
Olympic Dr 78028
Orange Cir 78028
Oriole Dr 78028
Oso Way 78028
Ottilie 78028
Overhead Dr 78028
Overhill Dr 78028
Overlook Dr 78028
Oxford Pl 78028
Packsaddle Rd 78028
Padre Pio Dr 78028
Painted Rock Dr 78028
Pal Dr 78028
Palmer St 78028
Palo Duro Cir 78028
Palo Verde Dr 78028
Panorama Dr 78028
Paradise Ave 78028
Paragon Pl 78028
Park Ln & St 78028
Paschal St 78028
Paseo Encinal Dr 78028
Pass Creek Rd 78028
Patriot St 78028
Patton Ave 78028
Peace Dr 78028
Peach Ave 78028
Peaks Cv 78028
Pearl St 78028
Pecan Dr, St, Trl & Way S 78028
Peddler Ln 78028
Pershing Ave 78028
Persimmon Dr 78028
Peterson Dr 78028
Peterson Farm Rd 78028
Phoenix Dr 78028
Pikes Peak Rd 78028
Pin Oak Way 78028
Pine Trl S 78028
Pinnacle Vw E 78028
Pinnacle Club Dr 78028
Plaza Dr 78028
Pleasant View Dr 78028
Poco Vista Dr 78028
Point Rdg 78028
Pond Cir 78028

Poplar St 78028
Powell Ave 78028
Powers Pl 78028
Prescott St 78028
Presidio Dr 78028
Preston Trail Loop 78028
Primrose 78028
Prine Ln 78028
Private Road 2085 78028
Purple Sage Dr 78028
Pyracantha Ln 78028
Quail Run 78028
Quail Valley Dr 78028
Quailwood Ln 78028
Quick Draw 78028
Quinlan St 78028
Quinlan Creek Dr 78028
Rabbit Run 78028
Rambling Creek Rd 78028
Ranch House Rd 78028
S Ranch Road 783 78028
Ranch View Ct 78028
Ranchero Rd 78028
Rancho Oaks Dr 78028
Ranger Trl 78028
Rankin Nix Dr 78028
Rawson St 78028
Re Ranch Rd 78028
Real Woods Vw 78028
Red Bud Cyn 78028
Red Rose Rd 78028
Redbud Ln 78028
Redemption Rd 78028
Reed Ln 78028
Rees St 78028
Reid Graham Rd 78028
Remschel Ave 78028
Renee 78028
Rhonda Dr 78028
Rhum Rd 78028
Richards Rd 78028
Richardson St 78028
Ridge Dr & Rd 78028
Ridge Crest Dr 78028
Ridge Grove Rd 78028
Ridge Hollow Ln 78028
Ridge Pointe Dr 78028
Ridge Rock Cv 78028
Ridgemont Ln 78028
Ridgeway Dr E 78028
Rim Rock Rd 78028
Rio Robles Dr 78028
Rio Valle Dr 78028
Rio Vista Dr 78028
Riojas Dr 78028
Ripplewood 78028
Rit Jons Dr 78028
Riveira Canyon Rd 78028
Riverfront Dr S 78028
Riverhill Blvd 78028
Riverhill Club Ln 78028
Riverside Dr 78028
Riverview Rd 78028
Road Less Traveled Ln 78028
Roadrunner Ln 78028
Roanoke Ln 78028
Robb Rd 78028
Robby Ln 78028
Robertson Rd 78028
Robin Hill Vw 78028
Robinson Ave 78028
Rock Barn Dr 78028
Rock Creek Dr & Loop 78028
Rockridge St 78028
Rockwood Cir 78028
Rocky Hill Dr 78028
Rocky Ridge Rd 78028
Rodeo Dr 78028
Rodriguez St 78028
Rogers Cir & Trl 78028
Roland Trl 78028
Rolling Green Dr 78028
Rooster Rdg 78028
Ross St 78028

Roundabout Ln 78028
Roundup Trl 78028
Rowland Ln 78028
Roy St 78028
Royal Oaks Rd 78028
Rugged Trl 78028
Ruth St 78028
Saddle Club Dr 78028
Saddle Mountain Trl 78028
Saddlewood Blvd 78028
Sailing Way N 78028
Saint Andrews Loop 78028
Saint Marks Path 78028
Saint Peter St 78028
Sam Houston Dr 78028
San Antonio Hwy 78028
San Jacinto Dr 78028
S San Jose 78028
San Juan S 78028
Sand Bend Dr 78028
Sandlewood Ln 78028
Sandra Kay Ln 78028
Sandy Ln 78028
Sarahs Barn Rd 78028
Sawgrass Dr 78028
Sb Rees Dr 78028
Scarlet Dr 78028
Scenic Hills Rd 78028
Scenic Valley Rd 78028
Schreiner St 78028
Schwethelm Rd 78028
Scott Rd & St 78028
Scott Ridge Rd 78028
Seabee Highway Rd 78028
Secluded Oaks Ln 78028
Secret Valley Dr 78028
Seefeldt Cir 78028
Sendero Rdg 78028
Serenity Ln 78028
Shadow Ridge Ln 78028
Shady Dr E & W 78028
Shady Oak Ln 78028
Shalako Dr 78028
Shannon Dr S 78028
Shanon Trl 78028
Sharbella Trl 78028
Sheppard Rees Rd 78028
Sherron Ter 78028
Sherwood Ln 78028
Shin Oak Way 78028
Short St 78028
Short Timber Rd 78028
Short Upper St 78028
Sidney Baker St S 78028
Sierra Rd 78028
Sika Dr 78028
Silver Crk 78028
Silver Hills Rd 78028
Silver Saddle Dr 78028
Silver Springs Rd S 78028
Simms Ln 78028
Singing Wind Dr 78028
Six Shooter Cyn 78028
Sky Blue Dr 78028
Skye Dr 78028
Skyline Dr 78028
Skyview Dr 78028
Sleepy Hollow Cir 78028
Sleepy Mountain Rd 78028
Smith Rd 78028
Smokey Mountain Dr 78028
Solar Hill Dr 78028
South St 78028
Southway Dr 78028
N & S Spanish Oak Dr, Ln & Trl 78028
Sparkman Dr 78028
Spence St 78028
Spicer Loop 78028
Spike Dr 78028
Splitrock Rd 78028
Spring Buck Ln N 78028
Spring Creek Ln N 78028
Spring Meadow Ln 78028
Spring Mill Dr 78028
Springbranch Dr 78028

Springwood Ln 78028
Spur 100 78028
Spyglass Cir 78028
Stablewood Ln 78028
Stacy Ln 78028
Stadium Dr 78028
Starkey St 78028
Steepside Ln 78028
Stephanie Dr 78028
Stephen St 78028
Stephen F Austin Dr 78028
Stone Ridge Dr 78028
Stonecreek Cir & Dr 78028
Stonewall St 78028
Stoney Brook Rd 78028
Stringer Dr 78028
Sumack 78028
Summer Loop 78028
Summit Dr & Spur 78028
Summit Crest Cir & Dr 78028
Summit Point Dr 78028
Summit Ridge Dr 78028
Summit Top Dr 78028
Sun Haven Dr 78028
Sun View Ln 78028
Sunny Ln 78028
Sunrise Dr 78028
E Sunset Dr 78028
Sunset Point Dr 78028
Surber St 78028
Susan Dr 78028
Sweetwater 78028
Swigert St 78028
Tall Timber Rd 78028
Tanager St 78028
Tanglewood Ln 78028
Tate Trl 78028
Taylor Rd 78028
Teague Rd 78028
Teddy Bear Trl 78028
Tejas Rd 78028
Temple Dr 78028
Tennis St 78028
Teri Ln 78028
Terrace Ln 78028
Texas Cir & Dr 78028
Texas Troubadour Rd N 78028
Thompson Dr 78028
Thunder Rd 78028
Thurman St 78028
Tierra Grande Rd 78028
Tierra Vista Dr 78028
Timber Ln 78028
Timber Oak Rd 78028
Timber Ridge Dr 78028
Timberway Ln 78028
Timberwood Rd 78028
Tivy St 78028
Tomahawk Trl 78028
Top Dr 78028
Toscano Dr & Way 78028
Town Creek Rd 78028
Trabajo Ln 78028
Trace Cir 78028
Trail Head Dr 78028
Trail Ridge Rd 78028
Trail Wood Cir 78028
Trails End 78028
Travis St 78028
Treasure Hills Rd 78028
Tree Ln 78028
Treehouse Ter 78028
Treetops Ln 78028
Trent Rd 78028
Troulon Dr 78028
Troy Dr 78028
Tuffy Ln 78028
Tumbleweed Dr 78028
Turkey Spur & Vly 78028
Turkey Hollow Ln 78028
Turkey Run Cir 78028
Turkey Trot Dr 78028
Turnberry Cir 78028
Turtle Creek Hill Dr 78028
Turtle Creek View Dr 78028

Twin Peaks Rd ... 78028
Twin Springs Dr & Rd N ... 78028
Twombly Dr S ... 78028
Upala Springs Ranch Rd ... 78028
Upland Run ... 78028
Upper St ... 78028
Upper Scott Rd ... 78028
Upper Turtle Creek Rd . 78028
Ute Trl ... 78028
Uvalde St ... 78028
Valencia Dr N ... 78028
Valle Verde Rd N ... 78028
Valle Vista Dr ... 78028
Valley Dr ... 78028
Valley Oaks Ln ... 78028
Valley Ridge Dr ... 78028
Valley View Dr ... 78028
Van Hoozer Dr ... 78028
Vantage Cir ... 78028
Vesper Dr ... 78028
Vickers Cir ... 78028
Vicksburg Ave ... 78028
Victoria Dr ... 78028
Victory Ln ... 78028
View Dr & Pt ... 78028
Village Dr ... 78028
Vine St ... 78028
Virginia Dr ... 78028
Vista Hills Dr ... 78028
Vista Ridge Dr ... 78028
Vista View Cir ... 78028
Voelkel Ln ... 78028
Voges Ln ... 78028
Von Trl ... 78028
Waggoman Rd ... 78028
Wagner Ln ... 78028
Wagon Trl ... 78028
Wallace St ... 78028
Wallace Canyon Rd ... 78028
Walnut Rdg ... 78028
Walters Way ... 78028
Warbler Dr ... 78028
Ward St ... 78028
Washington St ... 78028
W Water St ... 78028
Water Front Dr ... 78028
Webster Ave ... 78028
Wedgewood Ln ... 78028
Wendy Dr ... 78028
Wesley Dr ... 78028
West Ln ... 78028
Westchester Cir ... 78028
Westcrest Dr ... 78028
Westminster St ... 78028
Weston Loop ... 78028
Westridge Cir ... 78028
Westway Dr ... 78028
Westwood Ln ... 78028
Wharton Rd ... 78028
Wheless Ave ... 78028
Whippoorwill Ln ... 78028
Whiskey Canyon Ranch Rd ... 78028
Whiskey Ridge Trl ... 78028
Whisper Valley Ln ... 78028
Whispering Oaks ... 78028
Whispering Woods Loop ... 78028
White Oak Rd ... 78028
Whitetail Rd ... 78028
Whitewing Dr ... 78028
Wichita Ln ... 78028
Wigwam Ln ... 78028
Wild Cherry Dr ... 78028
Wild Timber Dr ... 78028
Wildcat Loop ... 78028
Wilderness Trl ... 78028
Wildflower Ln ... 78028
Wildridge Ln ... 78028
Wildrose Ln ... 78028
Wildwood Ln ... 78028
Williams Trl ... 78028
Willis Loop ... 78028
Willow Way ... 78028
Windmill Rd ... 78028
Windwood Rd ... 78028
Winged Foot Ln ... 78028
Wisteria ... 78028
Wood Dr & Trl ... 78028
Wood Duck Ln ... 78028
Wood Edge ... 78028
Wood Ridge Dr ... 78028
Woodcreek Dr ... 78028
Woodcrest Dr ... 78028
Wooden Nickel Rd ... 78028
Woodhill Rd ... 78028
Woodland Rd ... 78028
Woodlawn Ave ... 78028
Woodside Dr ... 78028
Woodstone ... 78028
Wren Rd ... 78028
Yaupon Dr ... 78028
Yorktown Blvd ... 78028
Yucca Dr ... 78028
Zenner Ahrens Rd ... 78028
Zysko Ln ... 78028

NUMBERED STREETS

All Street Addresses ... 78028

KILGORE TX

General Delivery ... 75662

POST OFFICE BOXES MAIN OFFICE STATIONS AND BRANCHES

Box No.s
All PO Boxes ... 75663

RURAL ROUTES

01, 02, 03, 04, 05, 07, 08, 09 ... 75662

NAMED STREETS

Access Rd ... 75662
S Ace King Rd ... 75662
Addie St ... 75662
Airport Rd ... 75662
Alexander St ... 75662
Allen St ... 75662
Amanda Ln ... 75662
E & W Amos Ln ... 75662
Anderson Dr ... 75662
Andrews St ... 75662
Angeline St ... 75662
Ann St ... 75662
Apple Dr ... 75662
Arrowwood Rd ... 75662
Ash Ln ... 75662
Aspen St ... 75662
Bagwell St ... 75662
Bailey St ... 75662
Baker Rd & St ... 75662
Bar M Ranch Rd ... 75662
Barber Rd ... 75662
Barnett Rd & St ... 75662
Bass Rd ... 75662
Bates St ... 75662
Baughman Rd ... 75662
Beall St ... 75662
Bean Ave ... 75662
Beckley St ... 75662
Bell Rd & St ... 75662
Bellamy St ... 75662
Bellburn Rd ... 75662
Benton St ... 75662
Bermuda St ... 75662
Bills Dr ... 75662
Birch Ln ... 75662
Birdsong St ... 75662
Bob Rd ... 75662
Boettcher Dr ... 75662
Boisdarc ... 75662
Boone St ... 75662
Bowie St ... 75662
Briar Ln ... 75662
Broadway Blvd ... 75662
Brook Dr ... 75662
Brookview St ... 75662
Browne St ... 75662
Browning St ... 75662
Bryan St ... 75662
Bud Rd ... 75662
Burch Rd ... 75662
Burns St ... 75662
Caddo St ... 75662
Cain Ln, Pl & St ... 75662
Caldwell Rd ... 75662
Camacho Rd ... 75662
Camp St ... 75662
Campbell St ... 75662
Cargill Rd ... 75662
Carlisle Dr ... 75662
Carr Rd ... 75662
Carrie St ... 75662
Carroll Ave ... 75662
Carter Jones St ... 75662
Carver St ... 75662
Casiday Ln ... 75662
Cedar Dr, Ln & St ... 75662
Chad Loop ... 75662
Chandler St ... 75662
Charles Devall Rd ... 75662
Cherokee Trl ... 75662
Cherokee Creek St ... 75662
Chism St ... 75662
Choice St ... 75662
Church Rd ... 75662
Circle Dr ... 75662
Clark Rd & St ... 75662
Clay St ... 75662
Clements Ranch Rd ... 75662
Colt Dr & St ... 75662
N & S Commerce St ... 75662
Cooper St ... 75662
Copperhead Trl ... 75662
Corrigan St ... 75662
Couch St ... 75662
County Rd ... 75662
County Line Rd ... 75662
County Road 1107d ... 75662
County Road 1108d ... 75662
County Road 1109d ... 75662
County Road 1111 N ... 75662
County Road 1112d ... 75662
County Road 1112d1 ... 75662
County Road 1112d2 ... 75662
County Road 1113 N ... 75662
County Road 1114 W ... 75662
County Road 1115 W ... 75662
County Road 1116d ... 75662
County Road 1117 N ... 75662
County Road 1119d N .. 75662
County Road 1120d ... 75662
County Road 1121 ... 75662
County Road 1122 ... 75662
County Road 1123 ... 75662
County Road 1124 ... 75662
County Road 1125d ... 75662
County Road 1127d ... 75662
County Road 1128d ... 75662
County Road 1130 ... 75662
County Road 1131 ... 75662
County Road 1132 ... 75662
County Road 1133 ... 75662
County Road 1134 ... 75662
County Road 138 N ... 75662
County Road 167d ... 75662
County Road 168 W ... 75662
County Road 169d ... 75662
County Road 170d W ... 75662
County Road 171 W ... 75662
County Road 172 ... 75662
County Road 173 N ... 75662
County Road 175 N ... 75662
County Road 176 E & N ... 75662
County Road 177d ... 75662
County Road 178 ... 75662
County Road 179d ... 75662
County Road 180d ... 75662
County Road 185d ... 75662
County Road 186 E ... 75662
County Road 187d ... 75662
County Road 188 E ... 75662
County Road 190d ... 75662
County Road 191 E ... 75662
County Road 192 E ... 75662
County Road 193d ... 75662
County Road 194d ... 75662
County Road 194d1 ... 75662
County Road 195d ... 75662
County Road 198d ... 75662
County Road 199d ... 75662
County Road 2104d E .. 75662
County Road 2105 E ... 75662
County Road 2106d ... 75662
County Road 2106d1 ... 75662
County Road 2107d ... 75662
County Road 243 N ... 75662
County Road 245 N & S ... 75662
County Road 246 N ... 75662
County Road 267d ... 75662
County Road 277d ... 75662
County Road 278d ... 75662
County Road 279d ... 75662
County Road 280d ... 75662
County Road 281 N ... 75662
County Road 281a ... 75662
County Road 282 E ... 75662
County Road 283 N ... 75662
County Road 284 E ... 75662
County Road 285d ... 75662
County Road 286d ... 75662
County Road 287 ... 75662
County Road 287d ... 75662
County Road 288 N ... 75662
County Road 289d ... 75662
County Road 290d E ... 75662
County Road 291 E ... 75662
County Road 292 E ... 75662
County Road 293 N ... 75662
County Road 294 E ... 75662
County Road 295 N ... 75662
County Road 296 E ... 75662
County Road 297 N ... 75662
County Road 298 N ... 75662
County Road 3111 N ... 75662
County Road 3112 N ... 75662
County Road 3113 ... 75662
County Road 3120 N ... 75662
County Road 3137 ... 75662
County Road 3185 N ... 75662
County Road 3200 E ... 75662
Cox Dr ... 75662
Craven Dr & St ... 75662
Crawford Rd ... 75662
Creek St ... 75662
Crescent Dr ... 75662
Crestview Ln & Pl ... 75662
Crestwood Ln ... 75662
Crim Ave ... 75662
Crimwood Ln ... 75662
Cynthia Ln ... 75662
Cypress Dr ... 75662
D Holland Rd ... 75662
Daisy Way ... 75662
Dale Dr ... 75662
S, E & W Danville Dr, Rd & St ... 75662
Darwin St ... 75662
Davis Rd ... 75662
Debbie St ... 75662
Denmon St ... 75662
Diamond J Cir ... 75662
Diana Rd ... 75662
Dick Jones Rd ... 75662
Dickson Ct ... 75662
Dodgen Ln ... 75662
Dogwood St & Trl ... 75662
Donna Rd ... 75662
Douglass St ... 75662
Downs Pl ... 75662
Driftwood St ... 75662
Dudley Dr & Rd ... 75662
Duggin Dr ... 75662
Duncan St ... 75662
Dwain Dr ... 75662
East St ... 75662
Eastridge Rd ... 75662
Echo Ln ... 75662
Ector Rd ... 75662
Eden St ... 75662
Edgewood Rd ... 75662
Elder St ... 75662
Elder Lake Rd ... 75662
Emerson St ... 75662
Emily Ln ... 75662
Emmons St ... 75662
Energy Dr ... 75662
Enterprise St ... 75662
Epworth Rd ... 75662
Everett St ... 75662
Fairmont St ... 75662
Fason Dr ... 75662
Fawn Creek Rd ... 75662
Fette Dr ... 75662
Ffa Rd ... 75662
Florence St ... 75662
Florey Lk & St ... 75662
Floyd Wingo Dr ... 75662
Fm 1249 E ... 75662
Fm 1252 E & W ... 75662
Fm 1639 N ... 75662
Fm 2011 E ... 75662
Fm 2012 N ... 75662
Fm 2087 S ... 75662
Fm 2204 ... 75662
Fm 2207 ... 75662
Fm 2276 N ... 75662
Fm 2767 E ... 75662
Fm 3053 N ... 75662
Fm 349 ... 75662
Forest Ln ... 75662
Forest Hills Dr ... 75662
Forrest St ... 75662
Fortson Rd ... 75662
Four S Industrial Blvd .. 75662
Fox Run ... 75662
Fredonia ... 75662
Fritz Swanson Rd ... 75662
E Gail St ... 75662
Gann Cir ... 75662
Garcia St ... 75662
Garland Rd ... 75662
Gateway Ctr & Dr ... 75662
Gay St ... 75662
Gene St ... 75662
Gene Jones Rd ... 75662
Giles St ... 75662
Gilstrap ... 75662
Gipson Rd ... 75662
Gladewater St ... 75662
Glendale Ln & St ... 75662
Glenwood St ... 75662
W Goforth Rd ... 75662
Goodrich St ... 75662
Gordon St ... 75662
Gray St ... 75662
Green Blackman Rd ... 75662
Greene St ... 75662
Greenhills Dr ... 75662
Greenwood St ... 75662
Greenwood Ranch Rd .. 75662
N & S Griffin St ... 75662
Griffin Davis Rd ... 75662
Gulf Camp Rd ... 75662
Gulf Hercules St ... 75662
Hale St ... 75662
Hardwick Rd ... 75662
Hardy Rd ... 75662
Harris St ... 75662
Hart St ... 75662
Harvey Blvd & Rd ... 75662
Hazel St ... 75662
Helen St ... 75662
N & S Henderson Blvd ... 75662
Herby Rd ... 75662
Hickory St ... 75662
Hidden Cir ... 75662
Higginbotham Rd ... 75662
Highland Dr ... 75662
Highway 135 ... 75662
Highway 42 N ... 75662
Highway 42 N Access Rd ... 75662
Highway 42 W Access Rd ... 75662
Hill Ter ... 75662
Hillburn Rd ... 75662
Hillcrest Rd ... 75662
Hillmont St ... 75662
Hillside St ... 75662
Hillvale St ... 75662
Hollybrook St ... 75662
Hopkins St ... 75662
Horseshoe Dr ... 75662
Horton St ... 75662
Houston St ... 75662
Howell St ... 75662
Hughes Ln ... 75662
Hunter St ... 75662
Idylwood Dr ... 75662
Industrial Blvd ... 75662
Interstate 20 Rd E ... 75662
Interstate 20 North Access Rd ... 75662
Inwood Cir & Rd ... 75662
Ivy St ... 75662
Jackson Rd & St ... 75662
Jacomah St ... 75662
James Rd & St ... 75662
Jane Dr ... 75662
Jill St ... 75662
Jimy Ln ... 75662
Johnson St ... 75662
Jones St ... 75662
Joni Cir & Ln ... 75662
Joy Dr ... 75662
Joy Wright Mountain Rd N ... 75662
Juniper Dr ... 75662
Karen St ... 75662
Karolina St ... 75662
Katherine St ... 75662
Kathleen St ... 75662
Katy St ... 75662
E Kay St ... 75662
Kenny Dr ... 75662
Kilgore Plz ... 75662
N Kilgore St
100-499 ... 75662
500-1398 ... 75662
500-500 ... 75663
501-1399 ... 75662
S Kilgore St ... 75662
Kim St ... 75662
Kimberly St ... 75662
King St ... 75662
King Ranch Rd ... 75662
Kings Hwy & Rd ... 75662
Knowles St ... 75662
Kris St ... 75662
La Salle St ... 75662
Lacy St ... 75662
Laird Ave ... 75662
Lantana Dr ... 75662
E & W Lantrip St ... 75662
Larkspur Ln ... 75662
Laura Lee Ln ... 75662
Laurel St ... 75662
Lawrence St ... 75662
Layton St ... 75662
Leach St ... 75662
Leake St ... 75662
Leanne St ... 75662
Ledbetter St ... 75662
Lee Dr & Rd ... 75662
Lewis St ... 75662
Lexington Pkwy ... 75662
Line Rd ... 75662
Little Ln ... 75662
Littleton Rd ... 75662
Lockhaven St ... 75662
Locust St ... 75662
N & S Longview St ... 75662
Lonnie St ... 75662
Looney Ave ... 75662
Lori Ln ... 75662
Luder St ... 75662
Magnolia Rd & St ... 75662
E & W Main St ... 75662
Maple St ... 75662
Maple Grove St ... 75662
Mark Pl ... 75662
Mark Daniels Rd ... 75662
Marlin Dr ... 75662
N & S Martin St ... 75662
Martin Luther King Jr Dr ... 75662
Marvin A Smith Rd ... 75662
Masters St ... 75662
Maverick Dr ... 75662
Mcentyre St ... 75662
Mckinnon Dr ... 75662
Mcmichael St ... 75662
Mcqueen Rd ... 75662
Meador Rd ... 75662
Meadow Ave ... 75662
Meadowgreen Dr ... 75662
Megason Rd ... 75662
Memorial St ... 75662
Memory Ln ... 75662
Mercer St ... 75662
Mexia St ... 75662
Michael St ... 75662
Midtown Plz ... 75662
Mike Dr ... 75662
Miles Blvd ... 75662
Miller Ln & St ... 75662
Millie Ln ... 75662
Mimosa Pl ... 75662
Mobley St ... 75662
Moccasin Trl ... 75662
Mockingbird Ln ... 75662
Modisette Cir ... 75662
Monroe St ... 75662
Montgomery St ... 75662
Mount Pisgah Rd ... 75662
Mount Pleasant Rd ... 75662
Mustang Dr ... 75662
Myrtle St ... 75662
Neal St ... 75662
New Town Rd ... 75662
Nolen St ... 75662
Norris Rd ... 75662
E & W North Dr & St ... 75662
Northfork Cv ... 75662
S Oak Dr, Rd & St ... 75662
Oakland St ... 75662
Oakwood Dr, Ln & Rd .. 75662
Oehler St ... 75662
Old Highway 135 N & S ... 75662
Old Highway 26 ... 75662
Old Highway 31 ... 75662
Old Longview Rd ... 75662
Old Post Oak Rd ... 75662
Old Stone Rd ... 75662
Oliphant Rd ... 75662
Palmer St ... 75662
Paluxy St ... 75662
Park Ln, Rd & St ... 75662
Parkview Est & St ... 75662
Parkwood St ... 75662
Peach St ... 75662
Pearl St ... 75662
Peavine Rd ... 75662
Pecan St ... 75662
Penny Ln ... 75662
Pentecost Rd ... 75662
Pepper St ... 75662
Perry St ... 75662
Peterson Rd ... 75662
Phillips Dr ... 75662
Pin Oak Rd ... 75662
S Pine St ... 75662

Pine Burr Ln ... 75662
Pine Manor Cir ... 75662
Pinecrest St ... 75662
Pipeline Johnson Rd ... 75662
Pitner St ... 75662
Plaxco Rd ... 75662
Plum St ... 75662
N Point Rd ... 75662
Post Oak Rd ... 75662
Powderhorn Rd ... 75662
Private Road 1902d ... 75662
Private Road 1907d ... 75662
Private Road 2338 ... 75662
Private Road 2430 ... 75662
Private Road 2433 ... 75662
Private Road 2435 ... 75662
Private Road 2441 ... 75662
Private Road 2444 ... 75662
Private Road 2451 ... 75662
Private Road 2457 ... 75662
Private Road 2560 ... 75662
Private Road 2605 ... 75662
Private Road 3322 ... 75662
Private Road 3325 ... 75662
Private Road 3340 ... 75662
Private Road 3350 ... 75662
Private Road 3351 ... 75662
Private Road 3368 ... 75662
Private Road 3370 ... 75662
Private Road 3380 ... 75662
Private Road 3391 ... 75662
Private Road 3437 ... 75662
Private Road 3455 ... 75662
Private Road 3481 ... 75662
Private Road 3487 ... 75662
Private Road 3500 ... 75662
Private Road 3506 ... 75662
Private Road 3514 ... 75662
Private Road 3525 ... 75662
Private Road 3526
Anx ... 75662
Private Road 3531 ... 75662
Private Road 3561 ... 75662
Private Road 3573 ... 75662
Private Road 3576 ... 75662
Private Road 3627 ... 75662
Private Road 3628 ... 75662
Private Road 3636 ... 75662
Private Road 3659 ... 75662
Private Road 3662 ... 75662
Private Road 3694 ... 75662
Private Road 3695 ... 75662
Private Road 3703 ... 75662
Private Road 3711 ... 75662
Private Road 3730 ... 75662
Private Road 3732 ... 75662
Private Road 3737 ... 75662
Private Road 3738 ... 75662
Private Road 3755 ... 75662
Private Road 3756 ... 75662
Private Road 3757 ... 75662
Private Road 3758 ... 75662
Private Road 3790 ... 75662
Private Road 3845 ... 75662
Private Road 3896 ... 75662
Purslane Dr ... 75662
Pyle St ... 75662
Rabbit Creek Cir & Dr ... 75662
Ray Rd ... 75662
Rebecca St ... 75662
Red Oak St ... 75662
Redbud St ... 75662
Regent St ... 75662
Remington Ct ... 75662
Reynolds St ... 75662
S Rice Rd ... 75662
Richards St ... 75662
Richland Dr ... 75662
Rickey St ... 75662
Ridge Ln & Rd ... 75662
Ridgecrest Ln ... 75662
Rim Rd ... 75662
River Rd ... 75662
Riverside Dr ... 75662
Roberson St ... 75662
Roberts St ... 75662
Rockbrook Dr ... 75662
Rocking Chair Rd ... 75662
Rogers St ... 75662
Rogge Dr ... 75662
Ronnie Brown Rd ... 75662
Rosedale St ... 75662
Ross Dr ... 75662
Roy St ... 75662
Roy Austin Rd ... 75662
Royal Dr ... 75662
N & S Rusk St ... 75662
E & W Sabine St ... 75662
Samples Rd ... 75662
Sanders St ... 75662
Sceyne Rd ... 75662
School Rd & St ... 75662
Sequoia Cir ... 75662
Shady Lk ... 75662
Shafer Rd ... 75662
Shawna St ... 75662
Shell Rd ... 75662
Sherry Ln ... 75662
Shirley St ... 75662
Simmons St ... 75662
Sinclair Rd ... 75662
Skeeter Rd ... 75662
Smackover St ... 75662
Smith St ... 75662
E & W South St ... 75662
Southport Rd ... 75662
Spann St ... 75662
Spear St ... 75662
Spell St ... 75662
Spinks Chapman Rd ... 75662
Spradley Rd ... 75662
Spring Lake Dr ... 75662
Spring Tree Ln ... 75662
Spruce St ... 75662
State Highway 135 N &
S ... 75662
State Highway 31 ... 75662
State Highway 322 N ... 75662
State Highway 42 ... 75662
State Highway 42 N W
Access Rd ... 75662
Steele Rd ... 75662
Steven St ... 75662
Still St ... 75662
Stone Rd & St ... 75662
Stonehaven Ct ... 75662
Stoneridge Cir ... 75662
Sun Camp Rd ... 75662
Sun Lease Rd ... 75662
Sunset Dr & Ln ... 75662
Susan Ct & St ... 75662
Suzanne St ... 75662
Swanee Cir ... 75662
Swanson Ln & St ... 75662
Sweetgum Ln ... 75662
Sycamore Dr ... 75662
Synergy Blvd ... 75662
Tami St ... 75662
Templeton Rd ... 75662
Thomas St ... 75662
Thompson Dr & St ... 75662
Tidewater St ... 75662
Tierra Del Sol ... 75662
Timberdale Dr ... 75662
Timberline Rd ... 75662
Timbers Rd ... 75662
Town Oaks Cir & Dr ... 75662
Treeline Rd ... 75662
Triad Ln ... 75662
Tucker Rd ... 75662
Turkey Creek Dr ... 75662
Turner St ... 75662
Typeskie Rd ... 75662
Us Highway 259 N ... 75662
Utzman Rd ... 75662
Valley View Dr ... 75662
Van Meter Rd ... 75662
Velma Dr ... 75662
Verbena Dr ... 75662
Wagon Wheel Rd ... 75662
Walnut St ... 75662
Walton St ... 75662
Watson Rd ... 75662
Wells St ... 75662
Westwood St ... 75662
Whaleda ... 75662
Whipporwill Ln ... 75662
White St ... 75662
Whiteside Ln ... 75662
Whitmore Ave ... 75662
Whittington Rd & St ... 75662
Wicks St ... 75662
Wildflower Hill Rd ... 75662
Wildwood Ln ... 75662
Williams St ... 75662
Willow Bnd & Ln ... 75662
Willow Springs Rd ... 75662
Wilshire Rd ... 75662
Winchester Cir ... 75662
Windingway St ... 75662
Windsor Park Ln ... 75662
Woodbend Dr ... 75662
Woodbine Dr ... 75662
Woodcrest St ... 75662
Woodgate St ... 75662
Woodhaven St ... 75662
W Woodlawn St ... 75662
Woodview Ln ... 75662
Woodway Ct ... 75662
Worm Hill Rd ... 75662
Wright Dr ... 75662
Wrong Rd ... 75662
Wychelm Dr ... 75662
Wynns Creek Rd ... 75662
Yoredall St ... 75662

NUMBERED STREETS

All Street Addresses ... 75662

KILLEEN TX

General Delivery ... 76540

POST OFFICE BOXES MAIN OFFICE STATIONS AND BRANCHES

Box No.s
A - Z ... 76540
AA - AB ... 76540
OO - OO ... 76540
1 - 4540 ... 76540
9997 - 12276 ... 76547
690001 - 692756 ... 76549

RURAL ROUTES

23 ... 76543
03, 10, 20, 24, 37 ... 76549

NAMED STREETS

Aaron St ... 76543
Abigail Dr ... 76549
Abilene Dr ... 76549
Abu Bakar Dr ... 76542
Acorn Ln ... 76542
Acorn Creek Trl ... 76542
Acron Dr ... 76543
Adams Ave ... 76541
Addie Dr ... 76542
Adeel Dr ... 76542
Adela St ... 76541
Adobe Dr ... 76542
Adolph Ave ... 76549
Adrian Barnes Dr ... 76542
Agate Dr ... 76549
Alabaster Dr ... 76542
Alamo Ave ... 76541
Alamocitos Creek Dr ... 76549
Alan Kent Dr ... 76549
Alexander St ... 76541
Alexus Dr ... 76542
Ali Dr ... 76542
Alicante Ct ... 76542
Alleeta Dr ... 76549
Allegany Dr ... 76549
Allstar Ct ... 76543
Alma Dr ... 76549
Almond Dr ... 76542
Alpine St ... 76542
Alta Mira Dr ... 76541
Alta Vista Dr ... 76549
Alvin Dr ... 76542
Amanda Dr ... 76542
Amber Ct & Rd ... 76543
Amber Jill Cv ... 76549
Ambrey Cv ... 76542
Ambrose Dr ... 76549
American Legion Rd ... 76541
Amethyst Dr ... 76549
Ancestor Dr ... 76549
Andalucia St ... 76542
E & W Anderson Ave ... 76541
Andover Dr ... 76542
Angus Cir ... 76542
Anna Lee Dr ... 76549
Antelope Trl ... 76542
Aquamarine Dr ... 76542
Aquarius Dr ... 76542
Arc Cir ... 76543
Ariana Ct ... 76542
Aries Ave ... 76542
Arkansas Ave ... 76541
Arlee St ... 76541
Armadillo Dr ... 76549
Armstrong County Ct ... 76549
Asa Dr ... 76542
Ashlyn Dr ... 76542
Aspen Cir ... 76549
Aspen Dr ... 76542
Athens St ... 76541
Atkinson Ave
2302A-2302A ... 76543
Atlas Ave ... 76542
Attas Ave ... 76541
Auburn Dr ... 76549
August Dr ... 76549
Augustine Dr ... 76549
Aurora Cir ... 76542
E & W Austin Ave ... 76541
Autumn Valley Dr ... 76549
E & W Avenue ... 76541
E & W Avenue A ... 76541
E & W Avenue B ... 76541
E & W Avenue C ... 76541
E & W Avenue D ... 76541
E & W Avenue F ... 76541
E & W Avenue G ... 76541
E Avenue H ... 76541
W Avenue I ... 76541
W Avenue J ... 76541
W Avenue K ... 76541
Azalea Dr ... 76541
Bachelor Button Blvd ... 76549
Bacon Ranch Rd ... 76542
Bade Ct & Dr ... 76549
Bald Eagle Ct ... 76549
Bald Ridge Ct ... 76542
Baldwin Loop ... 76549
Bally Dr ... 76549
Bamboo Ln ... 76549
Barbara Ln ... 76549
Barbed Wire Dr ... 76549
Barcelona Dr ... 76542
Barkey Ct ... 76542
Barrington Trl ... 76549
Barry Dr ... 76543
Basalt Dr ... 76549
Bass Cir ... 76542
Basset Ct & Dr ... 76543
Bastion Loop ... 76542
Baumann Dr ... 76542
Bayberry Dr ... 76542
Bayer Hollow Dr ... 76549
Beach Ball Dr ... 76549
Beagle Ct ... 76543
Bear Br & Riv ... 76542
Becker Dr ... 76543
Becky Dr ... 76543
Bedrock Dr ... 76542
Bell Tower Rd ... 76549
Bellaire Dr ... 76541
Bellgrove Ct ... 76542
Belmont Dr ... 76549
Belo Dr ... 76542
Belt Loop ... 76543
Benchmark Trl ... 76543
Bending Trl ... 76542
Benttree Dr ... 76543
Beretta Dr ... 76543
Bermuda Dr ... 76549
Bertha Dr ... 76542
Beta Cir ... 76543
Biels Loop ... 76542
Big Bend Dr ... 76549
Bigleaf Dr ... 76549
Billy B ... 76542
Binion Trl ... 76549
Birdcreek Dr ... 76543
Birmingham Cir ... 76542
Bishop Dr ... 76541
Black Forest Ln ... 76549
Black Orchid Dr ... 76549
Blackburn Dr ... 76543
Blair St ... 76541
Blake St ... 76541
Blayney Dr ... 76549
Blue Cedar Rd ... 76542
Blue Ridge Dr ... 76543
Blueberry Rd ... 76542
Bluebonnet Dr ... 76549
Blueduck Dr ... 76549
Bluejay Dr ... 76549
Bluestem Ln ... 76542
Bobby Lee Dr ... 76549
Bolivar Dr ... 76549
Bonner Dr
1000-1099 ... 76542
1200-1399 ... 76549
Bonnie Dr & Spur ... 76549
Boot Scootin Ct ... 76542
Boots Dr ... 76549
Boswell Cir & Dr ... 76543
Botanical Dr ... 76542
Bowfield Dr ... 76542
Bowie Ct ... 76541
Bowles Dr ... 76549
Boxelder Trl ... 76542
Boyd Ave ... 76543
Boydstun Loop ... 76549
Bramblewood Dr ... 76542
Brandy Loop ... 76549
Bream Cir ... 76542
Breckenridge Dr ... 76542
Breeder Ln ... 76549
Bremser Ave ... 76541
Bremser Dr ... 76542
Brenda Dr ... 76542
Brewster Ave ... 76541
Brian Dr ... 76542
Briar Ln ... 76543
Briarcroft Ln ... 76542
Bridgewood Dr ... 76549
Bridle Dr ... 76549
Briggs Rd ... 76549
Briscoe Dr ... 76549
Bristol Dr ... 76542
Brock Dr ... 76543
Bronze Dr ... 76542
Brook Dr ... 76541
Brook Haven Cir ... 76542
Brook Hollow Cir ... 76542
Brookbend Dr ... 76543
Brooking Rd ... 76542
Brooklyn Kay Dr ... 76542
Brookside Dr ... 76542
Brookway Dr ... 76542
Brown Cir ... 76543
Browning Dr ... 76542
Brownsville Dr ... 76549
Brushy Creek Dr ... 76549
W & E Bryce Ave &
Dr ... 76541
Buccaneer Dr ... 76549
Buckaroo Pl ... 76542
Buckeye ... 76542
Buckley Dr ... 76549
Buggy Rd ... 76542
Bugle Dr ... 76543
Bull Run Dr ... 76549
Bundrant Dr ... 76543
Bunny Trl ... 76549
Bur Oak Dr ... 76542
Burk Rd ... 76549
Buttercup Cir ... 76542
Cactus Cir ... 76542
Cactus Dr ... 76549
Cactus Spur ... 76542
Calcstone Dr ... 76542
Cambridge Dr ... 76549
Camilla Ct & Rd ... 76549
Camp Cooper Dr ... 76549
Canadian River Loop ... 76549
Candlefly Ln ... 76542
Canine Dr ... 76542
Cantabrian Dr ... 76542
Canterdury Dr ... 76549
Canyon Cir ... 76542
Capri Dr ... 76549
Caprice Dr ... 76543
Capricorn Loop ... 76542
Caprock Cir & Dr ... 76549
Captain Dr ... 76549
Cardinal Ave ... 76541
Carlee Ct ... 76543
Carlisle Ave ... 76541
Carly Dr ... 76542
Carmen St ... 76541
Carnation Dr ... 76542
Carol Way ... 76541
Carolyn Dr ... 76542
Carousel Dr ... 76543
Carpet Ln ... 76549
Carrie Ave & Cir ... 76541
Carrollton Ave & Cir ... 76541
Carter St ... 76541
Cartwright Loop ... 76543
Cascade Dr ... 76549
Casey Dr ... 76543
Castellon Ct ... 76542
Castle Gap Dr ... 76549
Castleton Dr ... 76542
Castlewood Dr ... 76542
Catalina Dr ... 76549
Causeway Ct ... 76549
Cavalry Ln ... 76549
Cedar Cir & Dr ... 76543
Cedar Crest Dr ... 76543
Cedar Ridge Cir ... 76542
Cedarhill Cir & Dr ... 76543
Cedarview Cir & Dr ... 76543
E Central Texas Expy
100-398 ... 76541
400-1800 ... 76541
1801-2197 ... 76543
1802-2098 ... 76541
2199-5700 ... 76543
5702-5798 ... 76543
4400-1-4400-3 ... 76543
W Central Texas Expy
101-197 ... 76541
199-1399 ... 76541
1400-6298 ... 76549
Cessnock Dr ... 76549
Chad Dr ... 76542
Chafin Dr ... 76543
Chameleon Dr ... 76549
Champion Dr ... 76542
Chandler Dr ... 76549
Chantz Dr ... 76542
Chaparral Rd ... 76542
Chaps Ct ... 76549
Charisse St ... 76543
Charleston Ct ... 76542
Charlotte Ln ... 76542
Charolais Dr ... 76542
Chase Cir ... 76543
Chaucer Dr ... 76543
Cheaney Dr & Spur ... 76543
Chelsea Dr ... 76549
Cherry Ln & Rd ... 76543
Chestnut Dr ... 76543
Cheyenne Dr ... 76542
Chico Ct ... 76541
Chimney Rock Rd ... 76542
Chippendale Dr ... 76549
Chips ... 76549
Chisholm Cir & Trl ... 76542
Christie Dr ... 76542
Christina Ln ... 76542
Chuckwagon Cir ... 76542
E & W Church Ave ... 76541
Cimmaron Dr ... 76543
Cinch ... 76549
Cinco Dr ... 76543
Cinnabar Way ... 76542
Cinnamon Stone Dr ... 76542
Circle Dr ... 76542
Circle M Dr ... 76549
Circle Tree Loop ... 76549
Citrine Dr ... 76542
Clairidge Ave ... 76549
Clarawood Dr ... 76549
Claymore St ... 76542
Clear Brook Dr ... 76549
S Clear Creek Rd ... 76549
Clementine Dr ... 76549
Clinkenbeard Dr ... 76543
Cloud Ln ... 76549
Cloud St ... 76541
Coach Dr ... 76543
Coal Oil Dr ... 76549
Cobalt Ln ... 76542
Cobblestone Dr ... 76542
Cody Ln ... 76542
Cody James Dr ... 76542
Cody Poe Rd ... 76549
Coffield St ... 76541
Cojack Ct ... 76549
Cokui Dr ... 76542
Colby Dr ... 76542
Cole St ... 76541
Coley Dr ... 76543
College St ... 76541
Collins Ave ... 76541
Collins Ranch Rd ... 76542
Colonial Ln ... 76543
Colorado Dr ... 76542
Commerce Dr ... 76543
Community Blvd ... 76542
Conder St ... 76541
Connell Dr ... 76543
Conner Ct ... 76542
Constellation Dr ... 76542
Continental Dr ... 76543
Cooke Dr ... 76543
Cool Creek Dr ... 76549
Copper Crk ... 76549
Copperfield Cir ... 76543
Copperhead Dr ... 76549
Coral Bay Ln ... 76549
Cordwood Dr ... 76542
Corona Dr ... 76549
Cosper Creek Dr ... 76542
Cosper Ranch Rd ... 76542
Cotton Ct ... 76542
Cotton Patch Dr ... 76549
Cougar Crk ... 76549
County Rd ... 76543
County Road 219 ... 76549
County Road 220 ... 76549
County Road 221 ... 76549
Courage ... 76542
Courtney Ln ... 76542
Covey Ln ... 76542
Coy Dr ... 76543
Cranford Ave ... 76543
Creek Branch Cv ... 76543
Creek Land Rd ... 76549
Creek Place Dr ... 76549
Creekside Dr ... 76543
Creekwood Ct ... 76542
Creekwood Dr ... 76543
Crescent Dr ... 76543
Crested Butte Dr ... 76542

Street	ZIP
Crestridge Dr	76549
Crestview Dr	76549
Crestwood Dr	76549
Cricket Dr	76542
Cricklewood Dr	76542
Crockett Dr	76541
Crooked Oak Dr	76542
Cross Dr	76543
Cross Bend Dr	76543
Cross Timber Dr	76543
Crosscut Loop	76542
Crossland Dr	76543
Crystal Dr	76541
Culp Ave	76541
Cunningham Rd	76542
Currie Ave	76541
Curtis Dr	76542
Custer Cir	76543
Cypress Dr	76543
Daffodil Dr	76542
Dahlia Ct	76542
Daisy Dr	76542
Dallas St	76541
Dan Dr	76543
Daniel Adam Ct	76543
Daniels Dr	76543
Dannen Ct	76549
Danver Dr	76542
Dartmouth Dr	76542
Daude Ave	76549
David Dr	76542
David Freeze Ln	76542
Davis Dr	76543
Daybreak Cir & Dr	76542
Daytona Dr	76549
E & W Dean Ave	76541
Debra Cir	76543
Deek Dr	76549
Deer Run	76549
Deer Park Rd	76542
Deerwood Loop & Trl	76542
Del Mar Ct	76549
Dell Dr	76541
Deloris Dr	76542
Delta Cir	76543
Delwin Cir	76541
Denia Ct	76542
Denise Dr	76542
Denver Dr	76542
Deorsam Loop	76542
Deputy Dr	76549
Derby Dr	76549
Derik Dr	76542
Desert Willow	76549
Devonshire Ct	76542
Dewitt County Ct	76549
Diamond Cir	76541
Diamond Dr	76542
Diana Dr	76542
Diane Dr	76543
Diaz Dr	76549
Dickens Dr	76543
Dillon Dr	76542
Dimple St	76541
Dirt Rd	76542
Dixon Dr	76542
Dobbs Ave	76543
Docia Ln	76542
Dodge City Dr	76549
Doffy Dr	76549
Dogwood Blvd	76543
Donegal Bay Ct	76549
Donnie Ave	76541
Doraine Ct	76549
Doris Dr	76543
Dorothy Jane Dr	76542
Doubletree Dr	76542
Dover Rd	76543
Draco St	76542
Driftwood Ct	76542
Driftwood Dr	76549
Dripping Springs Dr	76543
Drystone Ln	76542
Dubroc Dr	76541
Dugger Cir	76543
Duke Ln	76549
Dunblane Dr	76542
Duncan Ave	76541
E & W Dunn Ave & Cir	76541
Duran Dr	76543
Durango Dr	76542
Dusk Dr	76543
Dustin Ct	76549
Duvall Dr	76541
Eastside Dr	76543
Eastwood Dr	76549
Easy St	76542
Echo Dr	76549
Eclipse Ct	76542
Edgefield St	76549
Edgewood Dr	76542
Eisenhower Dr	76543
El Dorado Dr	76543
El Paso Dr	76549
Elam Cir	76543
Eldie Ct	76543
Elia St	76541
Elk Ridge Ct	76542
Elkins Cir	76543
Elkins Pl	76541
Ellis Dr	76543
E Elms Rd	76542
W Elms Rd	
100-298	76542
300-799	76542
2301-2999	76549
Elms Run Cir, Ct & Rd	76542
Elyse Dr	76549
Embers Dr	76542
Emerald Dr	76542
Emilie Ln	76542
Encino Loma	76542
Encino Oak Way	76542
English Ln	76549
English Oak Dr	76542
Ennis Dr	76549
Eppinette Dr	76542
Eric Dr	76542
Esta Lee Ave	76549
Estate Dr	76549
Estelle Ave	76541
Estes Dr	76541
Esther Cir	76543
Ethel Ave	76549
Eugene Cir	76541
Eula Bea Ct	76549
Evans St	76541
Evergreen Dr	76541
Evetts Rd	76541
Excel Dr	76542
Fabianna Dr	76549
Fairlane Dr	76549
Fairview Dr	76541
Fairway Dr	76549
Farhills Dr	76549
Fawaz Dr	76542
Fawn Dr	76542
Fay Dr	76542
Featherline Rd	76542
Federal St	76543
Felix Rd	76543
Fergus St	76541
Ferndale Dr	76549
Fieldcrest Dr	76549
Fieldstone Dr	76549
Fiesta Oak Dr	76542
Fire Ln	76542
Fishpond Ln	76542
Flag Stone Dr	76542
Flagstaff Dr	76543
Flamingo Dr	76549
Flanigan Dr	76542
Flat Slate Dr	76542
Fleeta Dr	76549
Fleetwood Dr	76543
Flintstone Cir	76543
Florence Rd	
700-798	76541
800-1799	76541
1801-2099	76541
2200-3599	76542
Fluorite Ct	76542
Flynn St	76543
Fm 2484	76542
Fm 2670	76549
Fm 439 Loop	76543
Forest Hill Dr	76542
Forest Ridge Dr	76543
N Fort Hood St	76541
S Fort Hood St	
100-798	76541
800-1106	76541
1107-1197	76542
1108-1112	76541
1199-6800	76542
6802-6898	76542
Fossil	76542
Foster Ln	76549
E & W Fowler Ave	76541
Fox Creek Dr	76543
Foxglove Ln	76549
Franz Dr	76541
Fratelli Ct	76542
Fred Patrick	76542
Fremont Dr	76549
French St	76541
Frigate Dr	76549
Frisco Dr	76549
Frog Dr	76542
Frontier Trl	76542
Fry Ct	76543
Gaberial Ct	76543
Galaxy Dr	76543
Galderiv Dr	76543
Galereli Dr	76549
Gallop Dr	76549
Gann Branch Rd	76549
Gardenia Ave	76543
Garland Dr	76549
Garner Ave	76541
Garnet Rd	76543
Garrett Dr	76543
Garris	76542
E Garrison Ave	76541
Garth Dr	76541
Gary Loop	76542
Gateway Dr	76542
Gautier Ave	76549
Gaynor Dr	76549
Gazelle Dr	76549
E & W Gemini Ln	76542
Gemstone	76542
Generations Dr	76549
Gilmer St	76541
Ginger Rd	76549
Girard Ct	76542
Glass Mountain Dr	76542
Glen St	76541
Glendale Dr	76549
Glennwood Dr	76542
Glenoak Dr	76542
Glynhill Ct	76542
Godman St	76543
Golden Dr	76542
Golden Eagle Ct & Dr	76549
Golden Gate Dr	76549
Golden Oak Ln	76542
Goode Cir & Dr	76543
Goodhue Dr	76549
Goodnight Dr	76541
Gowen Ct & Dr	76543
Grandon Cir & Dr	76541
Granex Dr	76542
Granite Dr	76549
Graphite Dr	76542
Grasslands Dr	76549
N & S Gray Dr & St	76541
Grazing Ct	76542
Great Divide Rd	76549
E & W Green Ave	76541
Green Meadow St	76549
Green Oaks Dr	76542
Green Valley Dr	76542
Greenbriar Cir & Dr	76543
Greenforest Cir	76543
Greengate Dr	76543
Greenlee Dr	76542
Greenwood Ave	76541
Grey Fox Trl	76543
Greyfriar Dr	76542
Greyhound Dr	76549
Greystone Dr	76549
Grider Cir	76543
Griffin Dr	76543
Griffith Loop	76549
Grove Rd	76542
Gunnison Dr	76542
Gus Dr	76549
Hailie	76542
Halbert St	76541
Hall Ave	76541
E & W Hallmark Ave	76541
Hammerstone Trl	76542
Hammond Dr	76543
Hamza Cir	76542
Hank Dr	76549
Hanson Rd	76543
Hanterre Ave	76541
Happy St	76541
Harbour Ave	76541
Harlan Dr	76542
Harris Ave	76541
E & W Harrison Ave	76541
Hatton	76542
Haven Dr	76543
Haynes Dr	76543
Heath Dr	76543
Heather Ln	76549
Hector Dr	76549
Hedy Dr	76542
Hemlock Dr	76549
Henderson St	76541
Henry Dr	76543
Hercules Ave	76542
Heredity Ln	76549
Hereford Ln	76542
Hermosa Dr	76541
Herndon Ct & Dr	76543
Hezekiah Dr	76542
Hi Ridge Dr	76549
Hickory Dr	76549
Hidden Hill Dr	76543
Hidden Valley Dr	76543
Highland Ave	76543
Highridge Cv	76543
W Highway 190	76549
Hill St	76543
Hillcrest Dr	76541
Hilliard Ave & Loop	76543
Hillside Dr	76543
Hilltop Loop	76549
Hinkle Ave	76549
Hitchrock Dr	76549
Hogg Mountain Rd	76542
Holbert Dr	76543
Hold St	76541
Hollow Rd	76542
Holly St	76543
Holly Oak Ln	76542
Holster Dr	76549
Hondo Dr	76549
Honeystreet Bridge Ln	76549
Honeysuckle Cir	76542
Honeysuckle Dr	
100-1499	76549
3200-3399	76542
Hooper St	76543
Hooten St	76543
E & W Hoover Ave	76541
Hope Dr	76542
Horizon Dr	76549
Horne Dr	76542
Houston St	76541
Hub Dr	76542
Huckleberry Dr	76549
Hudson Dr	76549
Hummingbird Rd	76542
Hunt Cir & Dr	76543
Hunters Ridge Trl	76542
Huntsman Cir	76543
Hydrangea Ave	76549
Ida Dr	76549
Iduma Trl	76549
Illinois Ave	
600-1699	76541
2800-3099	76543
Imperial Dr	76541
Indian Hawthorne Dr	76542
Indigo Dr	76542
Industrial Blvd	76549
Indy Dr	76549
Inspiration Dr	76549
Inwood Cir	76542
Iredell Dr	76543
Iris Ave	76543
Irish Ln	76549
Iron Bridge Ln	76542
Ivory Ln	76549
Jack Barnes Ave	76549
Jackson St	76541
Jacobs Ln	76543
Jacqueline St	76541
Jade Rd	76543
Jake Spoon Dr	76549
James Dr & Loop	76542
Jana Dr	76542
Janelle Ct & Dr	76549
Janis Dr	76549
Jasmine Ln	76549
Jason Cv	76549
E Jasper Dr	76541
W Jasper Dr	
100-198	76542
200-1100	76542
1102-1198	76542
1200-1298	76549
1300-1399	76549
Jaycee Dr	76542
Jeff Scott Dr	76549
Jefferies Ave	76543
Jennifer Dr	76542
Jenny St	76543
Jeremy Dr	76549
Jerome Dr	76543
Jerry Rd	76541
Jim Ave	76549
Jitterbug Ct	76542
Joe Dr	76542
John Rd	76543
John David Dr	76549
John Haedge Dr	76549
John Helen	76549
John Porter Dr	76543
Johnson Dr	76549
Jon Cir	76541
Joseph Dr	76542
Josh Dr	76542
Joshua Dr	76542
Joshua Taylor Dr	76549
Jovana	76542
Joy Dr	76543
Joyce Ln	76549
Joyner Cir	76541
Judson Ave	76549
Julia Ln	76542
Julie Ln	76549
Julie Jacqueline Dr	76542
July Dr	76549
June St	76543
Juniper	76549
Kaitlyn Dr	76542
Kali Dr	76549
Kangaroo Ave	76543
Karen Dr	76549
Kathey Dr	
1000-1199	76542
1200-1399	76542
Katy Creek Ln	76549
Kaydence Ct	76542
Kbs Ct	76549
Keith Ave	76543
Kelley Ln	76542
Kenyon St	76543
Kern Rd	76541
Kerrville Ct	76549
Kevin Shaw Dr	76549
Kilgore Dr	76543
Killeen St	76541
Kilpatrick Dr	76542
Kim Dr	76543
Kimberly Ln	76549
Kingman Rd	76549
Kings Ct	76542
Kingwood Dr	76543
Kirk Ave & Cir	76543
Kit Carson Trl	76542
Knob Ct	76542
Koala Dr	76543
Kyara Dr	76549
Kylie Cir	76549
Lago Cir & Trl	76543
Lain Dr	76543
Lake Rd	76543
Lake Ann Ave	76543
Lake Belton Ave	76543
Lake Charles Ave	76543
Lake Inks Ave	76543
Lake Travis Ave	76543
Lakecrest Dr	76549
Lakeshore Dr	76543
Lakeview Dr	76542
Lakeview Loop	76543
Lakeway	76549
Lampasas Ct	76549
Lampasas Spur	76542
Lampasas River Ln	76542
Lamplight Dr	76543
Lana Ct	76542
Lance Loop	76549
Lansberry Ct	76549
Lantana	76542
Larissa Dr	76549
Larkspur Dr	76549
Latigo Dr	76549
Laura Dr	76549
Laurel Ln	76543
Lauren Lea Dr	76549
Lauren Mackenzie	76549
Lava Ln	76549
Lavender Ln	76549
Lawndale St	76549
Lazy Ridge Dr	76543
Lea Ann Dr	76549
Leader Dr	76549
Leadership Pl	76549
Leadville Dr	76542
Leaning Oak Dr	76542
Leather Dr	76549
Ledgestone Dr	76549
Lee Dr	76541
Leea Ln	76542
Legacy Ln	76549
Leifester Cir	76549
Leisha Dr	76549
Lennox Ave	76549
Leo Ln	76542
Leroy Cir	76542
Leslie Cir	76549
Levy Ln	76542
Lewis St	76543
Lhr Ln	76542
Liberty St	76543
Liberty Bell Loop	76543
E & W Libra Dr	76542
Lightning Rock Trl	76542
Lilac Ct	76542
Lily Dr	76542
Linda Ln & Spur	76542
Lindsey Dr	76542
Line Dance Ct	76542
Lineage Loop	76549
Lions Gate Ln	76549
Lisa Ln	76543
Litang Dr	76542
Little Ave	76541
E & W Little Dipper	76542
Little John Dr	76549
Little Nolan Rd	76542
Little Trimmier Rd	76542
Littleleaf Ct & Dr	76549
Littlepine Dr	76549
Littlerock Dr	76549
Littlewood Dr	76549
Live Oak Dr	76541
Live Oak Cemetery Rd	76542
Llama Rd & Spur	76542
Llano Estacado Ct	76549
Llewellyn Ln	76542
Lloyd Dr	76549
Lobrecht Ct	76542
Lohse Rd	76543
Lolly Loop	76542
Loma Gaile Ln	76549
London Ln	76543
Lone Oak Dr	76542
Lonely Oaks Ln	76542
Lonesome Dove Dr	76549
Long Ave	76541
Longhorn Cir	76542
Longview Dr	76543
Lookout Mountain Ln	76549
Loop Rd	76542
Lorena Dr	76549
Lori Dr	76549
Lorne Dr	76542
Lorraine Cir	76543
Lost Oak Dr	76542
Louise Ln	76549
Love Rd & Spur	76542
Lowes Blvd	76542
Loyal Ln	76549
Lu Cir	76543
Lucille Dr	76549
Luxor Dr	76549
Lydia Dr	76541
Lyna Ct	76543
Lynn Ave	76543
Lyra Dr	76542
Madison Dr	76543
Maedell Dr	76542
Maggie Dr	76549
Magnum Cir	76543
Maid Marian Cir	76549
Malachi Ln	76542
Malakoff St	76541
Malibu Ln	76543
Mallard Ln	76542
Mallow Cir	76542
Malmaison Rd	76542
Mamye Jane Dr	76542
Mandalay	76549
Manganite Dr	76542
Manor Ct	76541
Maple St	76543
Marble Falls Dr	76542
Margarita Dr	76542
Maria Dr	76549
Marigold Dr	76542
Mark Dr	76543
Marlboro Dr	76543
Marlin Dr	76543
Marsh Cv	76542
Marsh Dr	76543
Martin Luther King Jr Blvd	76543
Mary Ln	76543
E & W Mary Jane Cir, Ct & Dr	76541
Mason Dr	76549
Massey St	76541
Mather Dr	76543
Matt Ct & Dr	76549
Mattie Dr	76549
Maxdale Rd	76549
Mcarthur Dr	76541
Mccarthy Ave	76549
Mccreary Ave	76549
Mcdaniel Cir	76543
Meadow Ct	76549
Meadow Dr	76549
Meadow Ln	76542
Meadow Spur	76549
Meadow Glen Dr	76543
Meadow View Dr	76549
Meadowbrook Dr	76543
Medical Dr	76543
Medina Dr	76542
Melanie Dr	76542
Melissa Cir	76543

Menard Dr 76549
Mesa Dr 76542
Metropolitan Dr 76541
Michael Dr 76549
Michele Dr 76542
Middleton St 76541
Mighty Oak Ln 76542
Mikey Dr 76542
Mikulec Dr 76542
Mildred Ave 76549
Miles Cir 76543
Milky Way Ave 76542
Mimosa St 76541
Minthorn Dr 76542
Mirage Dr 76549
Missouri Ave 76541
Misty Cir & Ln 76542
Mockingbird Ln 76541
Modesto Rd 76542
Mohawk Dr 76549
Mona Dr 76549
Money Pit Rd 76542
Monroe Loop 76543
Montague County Dr 76549
Monte Carlo Ln 76543
Montrose Dr 76542
Moonlight Dr 76543
Moonstone Dr 76549
Moose Rdg 76542
Morning Glen Ln 76542
Morning Star Ln 76542
Mosaic Trl 76542
Moss Cir 76542
Moth Rd 76542
Mountain Creek Rd 76542
Mountain View Dr
4200-4499 76543
4501-4599 76543
6201-6497 76549
6499-7199 76549
Muir Dr 76543
Mulberry Dr 76549
Mulford St 76541
Murphy St 76541
Mustang Dr & Ln 76549
Mustang Creek Rd 76549
Nadine Dr 76549
Nancy Dr 76542
Nancy Jane Dr 76542
Napier Dr 76542
Nathan Dr 76541
Natural Ln 76549
Needlepoint Ln 76549
Neel Ct 76543
Nessy Dr 76549
Neta Dr 76549
Newton Dr 76549
Nicholas Cir 76542
Nickelback 76542
Nicole St 76542
Nimitz Cir & Dr 76543
Nina Dr 76549
Nolan Ave 76541
Norman Cir 76541
Norris Ave 76541
Northcrest Cir & Dr 76543
Northside Dr 76541
Northwood Ct 76542
Norton Dr 76542
Nottingham 76549
Nyla Dr 76549
O W Curry Dr 76542
Oak St 76543
Oak Grove Loop 76543
Oak Valley Dr 76542
Oak Vista Cir 76542
Oakalla Loop & Rd 76549
Oakhill Dr 76541
Odelia Dr 76542
Odom Dr 76541
Old Copperas Cove Rd 76549
Old Florence Rd 76542
Old Fm 440 Rd 76549
Old Homestead St 76549
Omar Dr 76542
Omega Cir 76543
Onion Rd 76542
Opal Rd 76543
Orchid Dr 76542
E & W Orion Dr 76542
Orts Dr 76542
Osbaldo Dr 76542
Osman Dr 76542
Oster Dr 76542
Owen Ct 76542
Owl Hollow Cv 76543
Oxford Dr 76542
Paintbrush Dr 76542
Paintrock Dr 76549
Palmtree Ln 76549
Pandos Way 76543
Panhandle Dr 76542
Paragon Dr 76542
N & S Park Ln & St 76541
Parkmill Dr 76542
Parkwood Dr 76542
Parmer Ave 76541
Passion Flower Blvd 76549
Pasture Cir 76542
Patricia Cir 76543
Patriotic St 76543
Patton Dr 76541
Paula Rd 76543
Peaceable Kingdom Rd 76542
Peach Hollow Cv 76543
Peak Ln 76542
Peaks Dr 76543
E & W Pearl St 76541
Pebble Cv & Dr 76542
Pecan Cir 76541
Pecan St 76543
Pecan Creek Rd 76549
Pecos Ct 76549
Peebles Dr 76543
Pennington Ave 76549
People Cir 76542
Pepper Mill Holw 76542
Perch Cv 76542
Perseus 76542
Pershing Dr 76549
Persimmon Dr 76542
Pete Dr 76549
Petunia Cir 76542
Phil Dr 76542
Phoenix Dr 76543
Phyllis Dr 76541
Pickwick Ln 76543
Pilar Spur 76541
Pilgram Dr 76543
Pinckney Ct 76542
Pine Dr & St 76543
Pinyon Cir 76549
Pixton Dr 76543
Plains Dr 76542
Plantation Cir 76542
Plateau Cir 76542
Platinum Dr 76542
Plaza 76542
Pleasing Cir 76542
Plum Hollow Cv 76543
Poage Ave
1500-1999 76541
2001-2099 76541
2200-2298 76543
2300-2699 76543
Poage Cir 76543
Polk St 76543
Polka Pl 76542
Pondview Dr 76542
Poppy Dr 76542
Poppy Wood Cir 76542
Powder Riv 76549
Powell St 76541
Prairie Dr 76543
Prather Dr 76541
Prestige Loop 76549
Price Dr 76542
Priest Dr 76541
Primrose Ln 76543
Progress Dr 76543
Puddo Ln 76543
Purple Martin Dr 76542
Purser Dr 76543
Quail Cir 76549
Quarry Dr 76543
Quenselite Trl 76542
Quinn Ave 76543
Rachael Ave 76543
Raeburn Ct 76542
Rainbow Cir 76543
Rainforest Ln 76549
Rainlily St 76542
Rambling Range Dr 76549
Ramhorn 76542
Rampart Loop 76542
Ranch Meadow St 76549
E Rancier Ave
100-2100 76541
2102-2198 76541
2200-6999 76542
7001-7099 76543
W Rancier Ave 76541
Randall Rd 76541
Raspberry Rd 76542
Raven Dr 76543
Ray Ave 76541
Raymond St 76541
Red Pine Dr 76542
Redondo Dr 76541
Redstone Dr 76543
Redwood St 76543
Reed Cir & Ln 76542
Reese Creek Rd 76549
Regency Dr
3300-3599 76549
4600-4699 76542
Rein Dr 76542
Remington Dr 76543
Renick Ranch Rd 76549
Republic Of Texas Dr 76549
Resident Dr 76549
Rev R A Abercrombie Dr 76543
Rhode Island St 76541
Rhonda St 76541
Rich Dr 76542
Richard Dr 76541
Ricks Rd 76549
Ridgehaven Dr 76543
Ridgemont Dr 76549
Ridgeview Dr 76549
Ridgeway Dr 76549
Ridglea Ct 76543
Rifle Dr 76542
Riley Dr 76542
Rim Dr 76542
Rimes Ct 76549
Rimes Ranch Rd 76549
Rio Blvd 76543
Rio Grande Ct 76542
River Oaks Dr 76543
River Ridge Ranch Rd 76549
Riverrock Dr 76549
Riverside Dr & Spur 76542
E & W Riverwood Ct 76542
Roadrunner Dr 76549
Roadrunner Ln 76542
Robert E Lee Dr 76543
Robert Tyler Dr 76542
Robin Hood Dr 76549
Robindale Dr 76549
Robinett Rd 76549
Rockdale Dr 76542
Rocking C Dr 76549
Rockwall Dr 76549
Rocky Ln
1000-1112 76541
1114-1298 76541
1133-1199 76542
1201-1295 76541
1297-1299 76542
Rocky Rd 76542
Rogano Ct 76542
Rolling Hills Dr 76543
Ronald Dr 76542
Ronnie Ln 76549
Ronstan Dr
1000-1199 76542
1400-1899 76549
Root Ave 76541
Rose Ave 76543
Rose Quartz Dr 76542
Rosebelle Ave 76549
Rosita Oak Dr 76542
Roundrock Dr 76549
Rowdy Dr 76542
Roy J Smith Dr 76543
N & S Roy Reynolds Dr 76543
Royal Crest Cir & Dr 76549
Royal Vista Dr 76549
Rudolph Dr 76549
Ruger Dr 76543
Ruiz Dr 76543
Rusack Dr 76542
Rush Cv 76542
Saddle Dr 76543
Saddle Ridge Dr 76549
Saegert Ct 76542
Saegert Ranch Rd 76542
Safady St 76541
Safari Dr 76542
Sagebrush Dr 76549
Saint Francis St 76543
Salt Fork Dr 76549
San Antonio St 76541
Sand Dollar Dr 76549
Sandra Sue Dr 76542
Sands Ln 76549
Sandstone Dr 76549
Sandyford Dr 76542
Santa Fe Ave 76543
Santa Fe Plaza Dr 76541
Santa Rosa Dr 76541
Sapphire Dr 76542
Saratoga Ave 76543
Sassi Ln 76542
Saul Dr 76542
Savage Dr 76543
Sawtooth Dr 76542
Scarlet Oak Dr 76542
Schneider Dr 76542
Schorn Dr 76542
Schottische Ln 76542
Schrader Rd 76542
Schulze Cir & Dr 76549
Schwald Rd 76543
Schwertner Dr 76543
Scott And White Dr 76543
Scottsdale Dr 76543
Screaming Eagle Dr 76549
Seabiscuit Dr 76549
Seahorse Dr 76549
Searcy Dr 76543
Secretariat Dr 76549
Sedona Cir 76543
Selena Dr 76549
Selenite Ct 76542
Serpentine Dr 76542
Sevilla Dr 76542
Shad Cir 76542
Shady Dr 76543
Shady Loop 76549
Shagbark Dr 76542
Shamrock Dr 76549
Shanarae Cir 76549
Shannon Cir 76542
Sharp Cemetery Rd 76542
Shaw Ln 76542
Shawlande Dr 76542
Shawn Dr 76542
Shellrock Dr 76549
Sherman Dr 76543
Sherwood Forest Dr 76549
Shimla Dr 76542
Shoemaker Dr 76543
Shofner St 76541
Short Ave 76541
Shumard Dr 76542
Sidewinder Dr 76549
Sierra Dr 76543
Siltstone Loop 76542
Silverhill Dr 76543
Silverton Dr 76542
Silverway Dr 76549
Simmons Dr 76543
Simone Dr 76542
Sissom Ct & Rd 76541
Skylark Cir 76549
Skyline Ave 76541
Slate Ct 76542
Slawson Ln 76542
Smith Dr
100-400 76542
402-498 76542
1100-1799 76541
Smoky Quartz Dr 76542
Snapper Cv 76542
Snowy River Dr 76549
Sodalite Ct 76542
Solomon Dr 76542
Sommerville Ln 76542
Sonora Dr 76549
Sorcerer Ct 76549
Soukup Ln 76542
Southbrook Dr 76549
Southern Belle Dr 76542
Southhill Dr 76549
Southport Dr 76542
Southside Dr 76541
Southwood Dr 76549
Sparrow Rd 76542
Spc Laramore Dr 76542
Spicewood Dr 76543
Splawn Ranch Rd 76542
Split Oak Dr 76542
Spoke Dr 76542
Spotted Horse Dr 76542
Spring Dr 76542
Spring Branch Dr 76541
Spring Hollow Cv 76543
Spring Rose Cir 76543
Spring Valley Dr 76542
Springbrook Cir 76543
Springforest Cir 76543
E & W Sprott Ave 76541
Spur 3219 76543
E Stagecoach Rd 76542
Stallion Dr 76549
E Stan Schlueter Loop 76542
W Stan Schlueter Loop
201-397 76542
399-499 76542
501-599 76542
1000-1298 76549
1300-5199 76549
5201-5399 76549
Standridge St 76543
Stanford Dr 76542
Stardust St 76543
Starfish Dr 76549
Starlight Dr 76543
Starling Dr 76549
State Highway 195 76542
Stealth Ln 76549
Steamboat Springs Dr 76542
Stephen St
1000-1099 76542
1200-1599 76549
Sterling Cir 76542
Stetson Ave 76543
Steve Ave 76543
Stewart St 76541
Stillman Valley Rd 76542
Stillwood Cir & Dr 76543
Stirrup Ln 76542
Stone Ave 76541
Stoneham Ln 76542
Stonetree Dr 76543
Stonleigh Dr 76549
Stovall Ave 76541
Stratford Dr 76549
Stringer St 76541
Success Dr 76542
Sue Anne 76542
Suellen Ln 76542
Sulfur Spring Dr 76542
Sumac Dr 76549
Sundown Dr 76543
Sunfish Cir 76542
Sunflower Ct & Dr 76542
Sungate Dr 76549
Sunny Ln
2200-2299 76541
2300-2400 76543
2402-2498 76543
Sunny Beach Ct 76549
Sunrise St 76542
Sunset St 76543
Sunset Ridge Dr 76549
Sunstone Cv 76543
Supt E M Green St 76543
Sutton Dr 76541
Suzie St 76542
Swanner Loop 76543
Swope Dr 76541
Sycamore Dr 76543
Sydney Harbour Ct 76549
Sykes Ln 76542
Sylvia Dr 76549
Taffinder Ln 76549
Taft St 76543
Tahoe Ct 76543
Tallwood Dr 76549
Tally Ho Rd 76542
Tangent Ct 76543
Tanglewood Cir 76543
Tanner Cir 76549
Tanner St 76541
Tanzanite Dr 76542
Tara Dr 76549
Taree Loop 76549
Tarrant County Dr 76549
Tatonka Dr 76549
Taurus Dr 76542
Taylor St 76542
Taylor Renee Dr 76542
Teal Dr 76542
Tecovas Springs Ct 76549
Telluride Dr 76542
Temora Loop 76549
Terrace Dr
100-399 76542
401-499 76542
801-897 76541
899-1599 76541
1601-1799 76541
2200-2298 76543
2300-2899 76543
Terrapin Cv & Dr 76542
Terri Linn 76549
Terry Dr 76543
E & W Texas Ave 76541
Thoroughbred Dr 76549
Thunder Creek Dr 76549
Tidal Wave Dr 76549
Tiffany Cir 76549
Tiger Dr 76549
Timber Oak Dr 76542
Timberline Dr 76543
Timberwood Ct 76542
Titanium Dr 76542
Todd St 76543
Toledo Dr 76542
Toliver St 76541
Tom Lockett Dr 76549
Topaz Rd 76543
Topsey Dr 76542
Tortoise Cir & Ln 76542
Tortuga Ln 76542
Tourmaline Dr 76542
Tower St 76541
Tower Hill Ln 76542
Tracey Ann Ln 76543
Tracy Cir 76543
Traditions Dr 76549
Trail Boss 76549
Trailridge Cir 76549
Trails End Dr 76543
E & W Trailwood Ct 76542
Transit Dr 76543
Traverse Dr 76543
Trey St 76542
Trimmier Rd
700-2299 76541
2500-5400 76542
5402-8098 76542
E Trimmier Rd 76542
W Trimmier Rd 76542
Triple 7 Trl 76542
Tripp Trl 76543
Tropicana Ct & Dr 76549
Trotwood Trl 76543
Trout Cv 76542
Tucker Dr 76543
Tucson Dr 76543
Tudor Dr 76543
Tumbled Stone Dr 76542
Tumbleweed Dr 76542
Tumut Ln 76549
Tungsten 76542
Turkey Trot 76542
Turner Ave 76543
Turquoise 76542
Turtle Back Cv 76542
Turtle Bend Dr 76542
Turtle Creek Dr 76542
Turtle Rock Dr 76542
Twilight Dr 76543
N & S Twin Creek Dr 76543
Twin Oaks Cir 76542
Two Step Pl 76542
Tyler St 76541
Tyrel Dr 76542
U S Grant Dr 76543
Upper Ridge Ct 76542
Utah St 76541
Uvalde Dr 76549
Uvero Alto Dr 76549
Vahrenkamp Dr 76549
Vail Dr 76542
Valencia Dr 76542
Valentine St 76549
Valley Rd 76541
Valley Forge Dr 76542
Valley Vista Dr 76542
Van Zanten Ct & Dr 76541
Vanguard Ln 76549
E & W Vardeman Ave 76541
E & W Vega Ln 76542
Velma Dr 76542
Venetian Ct 76549
Verbena Loop 76542
Vermont St 76541
Vernice Loop 76549
E Veterans Memorial Blvd
100-2199 76541
2200-5900 76543
5902-6298 76543
W Veterans Memorial Blvd 76541
Vicki Dr 76542
Victoria Cir 76543
Viewcrest Dr 76549
Viola Dr 76542
Violet Ave 76543
Virginia St 76541
E & W Voelter Ave 76541
N W S Young Dr 76543
S W S Young Dr
600-2299 76543
2400-2498 76542
2500-3099 76542
3100-3100 76547
3100-5898 76542
3101-4499 76542
Wade Dr 76549
Wagon Gap Rd 76542
Wagon Wheel Dr 76542
Wales Cir & Dr 76549
Walnut Dr 76549
Walton Walker Dr 76542
Waltz Ct 76542
Warfield Dr 76543
Washington St 76541
Water St 76543
Water Oak Dr 76542
Watercrest Rd 76549

Waterfall Dr 76549
Waterford Dr 76542
Waterproof 76549
Waterside Dr 76549
Wayne Ave 76543
Weatherly Dr 76542
Weeping Oak Dr 76542
Weiss Dr 76542
Wells Cir & St 76541
Wells Fargo Rd 76542
Wesley Dr 76549
West Ln
1000-1099 76542
1200-1899 76549
Westcliff Loop & Rd 76543
Westcreek Cir 76543
Western Swing Ct 76542
Westover Dr
1000-1099 76542
1200-1599 76549
Westrim Dr 76549
Westside Church Rd 76549
Westview Dr 76543
Westway Cir & Dr 76549
Westwood Dr 76549
Wheeler Ave & Cir 76549
Whippoorwill Rd 76542
Whispering Forest Cir 76543
Whispering Oak Dr 76542
Whispering Oaks Loop 76549
White Ave 76541
White Castle Ln 76542
White Cedar Trl 76542
White Oak Dr & Way 76549
White Rock Dr 76542
White Willow Ct 76549
Whitlow Dr 76541
Whitmire Dr & Ln 76543
Wickfield Way 76543
N Wild Fire Rd 76542
Wild Horse 76542
Wild Mountain Rd 76542
Wild Ridge Rd 76542
Wildflower Dr 76549
Wiley Dr 76543
Willacy Dr 76549
William Tell Dr 76542
Williamette Ln 76549
Williamson Dr 76541
Willow Springs Rd 76549
Willowbend Dr 76543
Wilshire Cir & Dr 76543
Wilson Branch Rd 76542
Winchester Dr 76543
Wind Ct 76549
Wind Song Dr 76542
Windcrest Dr 76549
Windfield Dr 76549
Windmill Ct & Dr 76549
Windsor Cir 76549
Windward Dr 76543
Windwood Dr 76542
Winkler Ave 76542
Winslow Dr 76542
Wisconsin St 76541
Wisteria Ln 76549
Wolf St 76541
Wolfridge Rd 76549
Wood St 76541
Woodlake Dr 76549
Woodlands Dr 76549
Woodrow Dr 76549
Worth St 76541
Wright Way 76543
Wyoming St 76541
Y S Pak Ct 76542
Yantis St 76543
Yates Rd 76549
Yellow Pine Ct 76542
Yi Dr 76549
York Ave 76541
Yorktown St 76543
E & W Young Ave & Cir 76541
Youngsport Loop & Spur 76542
Yuma Cir 76543
Zayden Dr 76542
Zephyr Rd
1300-2299 76541
2300-4311 76543
4313-4399 76543
Zinc 76542
Zinnia Cir, Ct & Dr 76542

NUMBERED STREETS

N & S 2nd 76541
N & S 4th 76541
S 6th St 76541
N & S 8th 76541
N 10th St 76541
300-300 76540
S 10th St 76541
N 12th St 76541
N 14th St 76541
N & S 16th 76541
N 18th St 76541
N & S 20th 76541
N 22nd St 76541
N & S 24th 76541
S 28th St 76541
N & S 38th 76543
S 40th St 76543
N & S 42nd 76543
N 46th St 76543
S 48th St 76543
S 50th St 76543
N & S 52nd 76543
S 53rd St 76543
S 54th St 76543
S 56th St 76543
S 58th St 76543
N 60th St 76543

KINGSVILLE TX

General Delivery 78363

POST OFFICE BOXES MAIN OFFICE STATIONS AND BRANCHES

Box No.s
WW - WW 78363
XX - XX 78363
YY - YY 78363
A - H 78364
1 - 1847 78364
2001 - 4120 78363
5001 - 6040 78364

RURAL ROUTES

01, 02 78363

NAMED STREETS

All Street Addresses 78363

NUMBERED STREETS

All Street Addresses 78363

KINGWOOD TX

POST OFFICE BOXES MAIN OFFICE STATIONS AND BRANCHES

Box No.s
All PO Boxes 77325

NAMED STREETS

Aldens Oak 77339
Amber Alcove Ct 77345
Amber Holly Ct 77345
Anderson Cir & Rd 77339
Any Way 77339
Appalachian Trl 77345
Apple Forest Ct 77345
Applevale Ct 77345
April Run Ct 77345
Aqua Vista Dr 77339
Arbor Bridge Ct 77345
Arbor Forest Trl 77345
Armor Oaks Dr 77339
Armor Smith Dr 77339
Ash Glade Ct 77345
Ash Park Dr 77339
Ashford Way 77339
Aspen Creek Ct 77345
Aspen Glade Dr 77339
Aspen Lake Ct 77345
Aspen Mountain Trl 77345
Aspen Pass Dr 77345
Aspen Shadows Ln 77345
August Hill Dr 77345
Autumn Alcove Ct 77345
Autumn Dogwood Way 77345
Autumn Garden Ct 77345
Avon Way 77339
Babbling Creek Dr 77345
Baldsprings Trl 77345
Baron Grove Dr 77345
Bassingham Dr 77339
Beacon Falls Dr 77345
Bear Lake Dr 77345
Beaver Falls Dr 77345
Beaver Glen Dr 77339
Beaver Lodge Dr 77345
Beech Point Dr 77345
Belgravia Way 77339
Bellington Ct 77345
Bens Branch Dr 77339
Bens View Ln & Trl 77339
Berkshire Hills Dr 77345
Berry Knoll Ct 77345
Betty Anne Ln 77339
Big Cedar Dr 77345
Big Falls Dr 77345
Big Fir Dr 77345
Big Hickory Dr 77345
Big Meadows Dr 77339
Big Piney Dr 77345
Big River Dr 77345
Big Springs Dr 77339
Big Spruce Dr 77339
Billfish Blvd 77345
Birch Bough Ct 77345
Birch Creek Dr 77339
Birch Haven Dr 77339
Birch Villa Dr 77345
Birchland Ct 77345
Birchmoor Ct 77345
Bishops Mill Ct 77345
Black Opal Ln 77339
Blackstone Creek Ln 77345
Blantyre Way 77339
Blossom Creek Ct, Dr & Trl 77339
Blue Creek Dr 77345
Bluebonnet Pond Ln 77345
Bluff Creek Dr 77345
Bonnie Gln 77339
Boulder Creek Dr 77339
Boulder Lake Ct 77345
Breezy Pines Ct 77345
Breezy Point Dr 77345
Brentford 77339
Broadleaf St 77345
Bronze Sunset Ct 77345
Brook Grove Dr 77345
Brook Shadow Dr 77345
Brook Shore Ct 77345
Brookdale Dr 77339
Brookgreen Dr 77339
Brookside Pine Ln 77345
Brooktrail Dr 77339
Brookvale Ct 77345
Buckeye Creek Rd 77339
Buckingham Way 77339
Burning Tree Rd 77339
Buttercup Ln 77339
Calgary Pointe Dr 77339
Camelot Grove Dr 77339
Canford Ct 77345
Canna Lily Ct 77345
Cape Forest Dr 77345
Cardinal Brook Way 77345
Cardinal Creek Way 77345
Carriage Manor Ln 77339
Cascade Creek Dr 77339
Castle Arch Ct 77339
Castle Combe Way 77339
Castle Hill Trl 77339
Castle Meadow Ln 77339
Castlecliff Ln 77339
Cave Springs Dr 77339
Cedar Bay Dr 77345
Cedar Falls Dr 77345
Cedar Forest Dr 77339
Cedar Knolls Dr 77339
Cedar Lodge Ct 77345
Cedar Mill Ct 77345
Cedar Mills Dr 77345
Cedar Valley Dr 77345
Cedar Village Dr 77345
Cedarville Dr 77345
Chanay Ln 77339
Charing Cross Way 77339
Charming Creek Ct 77345
Chasebrook Trl 77345
Chateau Lake Dr 77339
Chelsea Way 77339
Cherry Glen Ct 77345
Chestnut Grove Ln 77345
Chestnut Isle Ct 77345
Chestnut Peak Ct 77345
Chestnut Ridge Dr & Rd 77339
Chimney Vine Ln 77339
Chivalry Ct 77339
Clear Falls Dr 77339
Clear Ridge Dr 77339
Clemwood Ln 77345
Clover Creek Dr 77345
Clover Spring Dr 77339
Clover Valley Dr 77345
Club Oak Ct 77339
Cobblestone Hill St 77345
Coldwater Ln 77339
Conifer Creek Trl 77345
Cool Creek Ct 77345
Coral Haven Ct 77345
Cornwall Way 77339
N Cotswold Manor Dr & Loop N & S 77339
Cottage Glen Ct 77345
Country Falls Ln 77345
Courtland Manor Ln 77339
Covewood Dr 77339
Cranford Ct 77345
Creek Manor Ct & Dr 77339
Creek Shadows Dr 77339
Crescent Springs Dr 77339
Crichton Ct 77345
Crimson Berry Trl 77345
Crimson Maple Ct 77345
Crimson Valley Ct 77345
Crown Chase Dr 77339
Crown Forest Dr 77345
Crown Haven Ct & Dr 77339
Crown Rock Dr 77339
Crowns Cove Ln 77339
Crystal Falls Dr 77345
Crystal River Dr 77345
Crystal Springs Dr 77345
Cumberland Oak Ct 77345
Cypress Ln 77339
Deep Lake Dr 77345
Deep River Ct 77339
Deer Cove Trl 77339
Deer Falls Ct 77345
Deer Hollow Dr 77345
Deer Mountain Ct 77345
Deer Ridge Estates Blvd 77339
Deer Springs Dr 77339
Deerbrook Dr 77339
Deerland Ct 77345
Denmere Ct 77345
Dewberry Brook Ct 77345
Dobbin Springs Ln 77345
Dogwood Ridge Ln 77345
Dominica Dr 77345
Dristone Dr 77339
Duke Alexander Dr 77345
Eagle Creek Dr 77345
Eastwood Lake Ct 77339
Echo Falls Dr 77345
Echo Mountain Dr 77345
Echo Ridge Ct 77339
Elk Canyon Ct 77345
Elk Creek Dr 77339
Elm Canyon Ct 77345
Elm Glen Dr 77339
Elm Grove Ct 77339
Elmstone Ct 77345
Elmwood Hill Ln 77345
Ember Spring Dr 77339
Emerald Grove Dr 77345
Enchanted Woods Dr 77339
Everest Way 77339
Evergreen Cliff Trl 77345
Evergreen Glade Ct & Dr 77339
Evergreen Valley Dr 77345
Evergreen Village Ct 77345
Eversham Way 77339
Fair Falls Dr 77345
Faircourt Dr 77339
Fairhope Meadow Ln 77339
Fairway Farms Ln 77339
Fairway Green Dr 77339
Fall Orchard Ct 77345
Falling Brook Dr 77345
Fawn Creek Dr 77339
Fawn Glen Dr 77345
Fawnbrook Hollow Ln 77345
Feather Lakes Way
4000-4024 77339
4025-4025 77325
4025-4099 77339
4026-4098 77339
Fern Creek Trl 77345
Fern Garden Ct 77345
Fern Park Dr 77339
Fern River Dr 77345
Fern View Dr 77345
Fir Cv 77339
Fir Grove Dr 77339
Fir Springs Dr 77339
Fir Valley Dr 77345
Flint Creek Dr 77339
Foliage Green Dr 77339
Forest Bluff Dr 77339
Forest Center Dr 77339
Forest City Dr 77339
Forest Course Cir & Way 77339
Forest Cove Dr 77339
Forest Falls Dr 77339
Forest Garden Dr 77345
Forest Green Trl 77339
Forest Holly Dr 77345
Forest Laurel Dr 77339
Forest Manor Dr 77339
Forest Mountain Ct 77345
Forest North Dr 77339
Forest Row Dr 77345
Forest Shores Dr 77345
Forest Springs Dr 77339
Forest Vale Ct 77339
Forest Village Dr 77339
Foster Hill Ct & Dr 77345
Four Pines Dr 77345
Fox Grass Trl 77345
Friarwood Trl 77339
Gallant Knight Ln 77339
Garden Ford Dr 77345
Garden Hills Ln 77345
Garden Hollow Ct 77345
Garden Lake Dr 77339
Garden Point Dr 77345
Garden Springs Dr 77339
Garden Village Dr 77339
Gardenwood Dr 77339
Glade Creek Dr 77339
Glade Estates Dr 77339
Glade Forest Dr 77339
Glade Springs Dr 77345
Glade Valley Dr 77339
Gladehill Dr 77345
Glen Ivy Dr 77345
Glen Spring Dr 77339
Glenburn Dr 77345
Glencastle Ct 77345
Glennwell Ct 77345
Glenroyal Ct 77339
Glenview Dr 77345
Glenwood Springs Ct & Dr 77345
Golden Bear Ln 77339
Golden Cove Ln 77339
Golden Lake Dr 77345
Golden Leaf Dr 77339
Golden Pond Dr 77339
Golden Trails Dr 77345
Golden Willow Dr 77339
Golf Links Ct 77339
Grand Falls Dr 77345
Grand Lancelot Dr 77339
Grand Mesa Dr 77345
Graystone Bluffs Ct 77345
Graystone Creek Ct 77345
Green Oak Dr & Pl 77339
Green Oak Terrace Ct 77339
Green Pine Dr 77339
Green Village Dr 77339
Greenriver Valley Dr 77345
Greens Court Way 77339
Greens Edge Dr 77339
Greenway View Trl 77339
Greenwood Glen Dr 77345
Grove Lake Dr 77339
Grove Manor Dr 77339
Grove Oaks Dr 77339
Grove Terrace Dr 77345
Haileys Mnr 77339
Hallelujah Trl 77339
Halton Ct 77345
Hamblen Rd 77339
Hamlet Way 77339
Hansford Timber Dr 77345
Harvest Creek Ct 77345
Harvest Spring Dr 77345
Haven Glen Dr 77339
Haven Lake Dr 77339
Haven Oaks Dr 77345
Haven Pines Dr 77345
Havenbrook Dr 77339
Hazel Brook Ct 77345
Hazy Hillside Ct 77345
Heartwood Oak Way 77345
Heather Blossom Ln 77345
Heather Lake Ct 77345
Heatherpark Dr 77345
Heathervale Ct 77345
Hemlock Lakes Dr 77345
Hermitage Hollow Ln 77339
Hickory Ln 77339
Hickory Bough Ct 77345
Hickory Brook Ln 77345
Hickory Creek Dr 77339
Hickory Falls Dr 77345
Hickory Glen Ct 77345
Hickory Green Ct 77345
Hickory Knob Dr 77339
Hickory Park Dr 77345
Hickory Springs Dr 77345
Hickory Village Cir, Ct & Dr 77345
Hidden Creek Dr 77339
Hidden Garden Dr 77339
Hidden Glen Dr 77339
Hidden Hill Cir 77339
Hidden Lakes Dr 77345
Hidden Links Ct 77339
Hidden Pines Dr 77339
Hidden Villas Dr 77339
High Glen Ct 77345
High Valley Dr 77345
Highgreen Dr 77339
Highland Fern Ct 77345
Highland Glade Ct 77339
Highland Lakes Dr 77339
Highland Laurels Dr 77345
Highway 59 N 77339
Hill Forest Dr 77345
Hill Springs Dr 77345
Hill Top Ln 77339
Hogans Aly 77339
Holley Ridge Dr 77339
Holly Green Ct & Dr 77339
Honey Brook Dr 77345
Iron Knoll Dr 77339
Iron Manor Ln 77339
Iron Squire Dr 77339
Island Fern Ct 77345
Island Green Ct 77339
Island Heather Ct 77345
Jade Creek Ct 77345
Jasper Grove Ct 77345
Junegrass Ct 77345
Juniper Bluff Ct 77345
Juniper Knoll Ln 77345
Kellington Dr N 77339
Kelso St 77339
Kenlake Grove Dr 77345
Kensington Way 77339
Kingdom Edge Dr 77339
Kings Trl 77339
Kings Bend Dr 77339
Kings Creek Dr 77339
Kings Crescent Dr 77339
Kings Crossing Dr 77345
Kings Forest Dr 77339
Kings Guild Ln 77339
Kings Harbor Ct 77345
Kings Lodge Dr 77345
Kings Manor Dr N & S 77339
Kings March Ct 77339
Kings Mill Ln 77339
Kings Mill Crest Dr 77339
Kings Mill Forest Dr 77339
Kings Mountain Dr 77345
Kings Park Hollow Dr 77339
Kings Retreat Cir 77345
Kings View Dr 77339
Kingshill Dr 77339
Kingsmark Springs Ln 77345
Kingsway Ct 77339
Kingwood Dr
20000A-20000B 77339
500-524 77339
526-4499 77339
4500-5899 77345
19701-19997 77339
19999-20098 77339
Kingwood Greens Dr 77339
Kingwood Medical Dr 77339
Kingwood Place Dr 77339
Kingwood Villas Ct 77339
Knights Cove Dr 77339
Knights Tower Ct & Dr 77339
Knoll Manor Dr 77345
Knoll Terrace Dr 77339
Ladbrook Dr 77339
Lake Creek Dr 77339
E & W Lake Crescent Dr 77339
Lake End Dr 77339
Lake Gardens Ct & Dr 77339
Lake Hills Dr 77339
W Lake Houston Pkwy 77339
Lake Kingwood Trl 77339
Lake Oak Dr 77345
Lake Point Dr 77339
Lake Shade Ct 77345
Lake Stream Dr 77339
Lake Village Dr 77339

Lake Wilderness Ln 77345
Lakehaven Dr 77339
Lakeshore Dr 77339
Lakeside Ct & Ln N 77339
Lakeview Cir 77339
Lakeville Ct & Dr 77339
Lancelot Oaks Dr 77339
Lantern Hills Dr 77339
Lark Valley Ct 77345
Laurel Caverns Dr 77345
Laurel Crest Ct & Dr 77339
Laurel Fork Ct & Dr 77339
Laurel Garden Dr 77339
Laurel Hill Dr 77339
Laurel Lake Dr 77339
Laurel Mist Ct 77345
Laurel Pine Cir & Dr 77339
Laurel Point Ct 77339
Laurel Ridge Dr 77345
Laurel Rock Dr 77345
Laurel Sage Dr 77339
Laurel Springs Ln 77339
Laurel Timbers Dr 77339
Laurelwood Dr 77345
Lavender Jade Ct 77339
Lazy Grove Dr 77339
Leaf Forest Dr 77345
Leafy Aspen Ct 77345
Leafy Pine Ct 77345
Leatherstem Ln 77345
Links Ct 77339
Links Side Ct 77339
Lisa Ln 77339
Little Bear Dr 77345
Little Cedar Dr 77339
Lochmere Way 77345
Lodge Falls Ct 77345
Loft Forest Ct 77339
Lofty Magnolia Ct 77345
Lofty Maple Trl 77345
Lofty Mills Dr 77345
Lone Cedar Dr 77345
Lone Rock Dr 77339
Lonerani Dr 77339
Long Glen Dr 77339
Long Valley Dr 77345
Longflower Ct & Ln 77345
Longleaf Pines Dr 77339
Loop 494 77339
Lost Hollow Dr 77339
Lost Lake Dr 77339
Lost Maple Forest Ct 77345
Lost Maples Trl 77345
Magnolia Ln 77339
Magnolia Cove Dr 77345
Magnolia Falls Ct 77345
Magnolia Woods Dr 77339
Maidens Crossing Dr 77339
N Main St 77339
Majestic Falls Dr 77339
Majestic Hill Ct & Dr 77345
Majestic Pines Ct & Dr 77345
Mandover Ln 77345
Manor Crest Ct 77339
Manor Falls Dr 77339
Manor Forest Dr 77339
Manor Glen Dr 77345
Manor Grove Dr 77345
Manor Oaks Dr 77339
Maple Bend Dr 77345
Maple Brook Ln 77345
Maple Glade Dr 77345
Maple Glen Dr 77345
Maple Heights Dr 77345
Maple Hill Trl 77345
Maple Knob Ct 77345
Maple Knoll Dr 77339
Maple Lakes Dr 77339
Maple Park Ct & Dr 77339
Maple Square Dr 77339
Maple Terrace Dr 77345
Marians Holw 77339
Marina Dr 77339
Markham Woods Ct & Dr 77345
Mast Ct 77339
Master Way Ct 77339
Masters Way 77339
Mayfair Way 77339
Mcclellan Cir & Rd 77339
Meadow Forest Ln 77345
Meadow Glade Cir 77345
Meadow Springs Dr 77339
Meadowgold Ln 77345
Meandering Trl 77339
Merlot River Dr 77339
Mid Way 77339
Middle Creek Dr 77339
Middle Falls Dr 77345
Midlothian Ln 77339
Mighty Elm Ct 77345
Mill Bridge Way 77345
Mill Lake Dr 77339
Millingham Ct 77345
Mills Branch Dr 77345
Mills Creek Ct & Dr 77339
Mills Ridge Ct 77345
Millvale Dr 77345
Mistletoe Ln 77339
Misty Alcove Ct 77345
Misty Gardens Ct 77345
Misty Hill Ln 77345
Misty River Trl 77345
Misty Timbers Way 77345
Monarch Manor Ln 77339
Monarch Wood Dr 77339
Moody Pines Ct 77345
Mossy Rock Ct 77345
Mount Forest Dr 77345
Mountain Aspen Ln 77345
Mountain Bluff Ln 77345
Mountain Green Trl 77345
Mountain Lake Dr 77345
Mountain Maple Ct 77345
Mountain Peak Way 77345
Mountain View Dr 77345
Mulberry Grove Dr 77345
Mulberry Hills Dr 77339
Mulberry Park Ln 77345
Mustang Trl 77339
My Way 77339
Mystic Castle Ln 77345
Mystic Glen Loop 77345
Mystic Trail Loop 77345
Natural Bridge Dr 77345
New Green Ct 77339
Northpark Dr
1715B1-1715B4 77339
101-149 77339
151-3399 77339
3400-4899 77345
22000-22099 77339
Northpark Plaza Dr 77339
Northpines Dr 77339
Northshore Dr 77339
Oak St 77339
Oak Cove Dr 77339
Oak Fair Dr 77345
Oak Gardens Dr 77339
Oak Glade Dr 77339
Oak Lake Dr 77339
Oak Mill Dr 77345
Oak Shores Dr 77339
Oakbank Dr 77339
Oaks Forks Dr 77339
Old Oak Ln 77339
Olive Grove Ct 77345
Orchard Canyon Ct 77345
Orchard Valley Ct 77345
Otter Peak Dr 77339
Palace Pines Ct & Dr 77339
Palisade Falls Trl 77345
Pallavi Woods Dr 77345
Palm Ridge Ct 77345
Palmetto Ln 77339
Palmetto Creek Dr 77339
Palomino Ln 77339
Park Garden Dr 77339
Park Point Dr 77339
Park Royal Dr 77339
Park Sands Ln 77345
Park Springs Ln 77345
Parkdale Dr 77339
Parkwood Manor Dr 77339
Peachtree Hill Ct 77345
Pear Glen Ct 77345
Pebble Stream Ct 77345
Pecan Knoll Dr 77339
Pecan Park Ln 77345
Penmere Ct 77345
Pheasant Run Dr 77339
Pickwick Park Dr 77339
Pin Oak Creek Ln 77345
Pine Rd 77339
Pine Alcove Ct 77345
Pine Arbor Trl 77345
Pine Bend Dr 77339
Pine Blossom Ct 77345
Pine Breeze Dr 77345
Pine Cone Dr 77339
Pine Garden Dr 77339
Pine Prarie Ln 77345
Pine River Dr 77339
Pine Terrace Dr 77339
Pinewood Park Dr 77345
Piney Birch Ct 77339
Pinnacle Dr 77339
Plateau Ct 77339
Players Path 77339
Plaza Pines Dr 77345
Pleasant Creek Dr 77345
Plum Valley Dr 77345
Poplar Park Dr 77339
Poplar Valley Way 77345
Prim Water Ct 77345
Professional Dr 77339
Prost Ct 77339
Purple Meadow Ln 77345
Queens Glen Dr 77345
Quest Brook Ln 77339
Quiet Country Ct 77345
Quiet Glade Ct 77345
Quiet Glen Dr 77339
Rambling Creek Dr 77339
Rambling Pines Dr 77339
Rapid Brook Ct 77345
Rapid Creek Ct 77345
Red Bud Ln 77339
Red Cliff Dr 77339
Red Magnolia Ct 77345
Red Maples Dr 77339
Red Oak Ter 77339
Red Oak Branch Ln 77339
Red Wren Ct 77345
Redwood Bridge Trl 77339
Redwood Grove Ct 77345
Redwood Lake Dr 77345
Redwood Lodge Ct & Dr 77339
Redwood River Dr 77345
Regal Green Ct 77345
Regal Green Ln 77339
Regal Landing Dr 77345
Regal Shores Ct 77345
Regency Pines Dr 77339
Regent Manor Dr 77345
Ridge Green Dr 77345
Ridge Manor Ct 77345
Ridge Pine Dr 77339
Ridge Vista Dr 77339
Ridgedale Dr 77345
Ridgeway Trl 77339
Ridgeway Park Ct & Dr 77339
Right Way 77339
River Bend Dr 77339
River Bend Way 77339
River Blossom Ln 77345
River Branch Dr 77339
River Falls Dr 77345
River Hill Dr 77345
River Lilly Dr 77339
River Manor Dr 77339
River Rock Trl 77345
River Valley Dr 77339
River Village Dr 77339
Riverchase Trl 77345
Riverchase Forest Ct 77345
Riverchase Glen Dr 77345
Riverchase Village Dr 77345
Riverford Dr 77339
Riverglen Forest Dr 77345
Riverlawn Dr 77339
Rivers Edge Trl 77339
Riverside Oaks Dr 77345
Riverway Oak Ct & Dr 77345
Riverwood Park Dr 77345
Rock Springs Dr 77339
Rockmead Dr 77339
Rocky Brook Dr 77345
Rocky Trail Dr 77339
Rocky Woods Dr 77339
Rolling Meadows Dr 77339
Rolling View Ct 77345
Rose Mill Dr 77339
Rose Park Ct 77339
Ross Rd 77339
Round Spring Dr 77339
Royal Frst 77339
Royal Circle Dr 77339
Royal Creek Trl 77345
Royal Crescent Dr 77339
Royal Crossing Dr 77339
Royal Emerald Ln 77339
Royal Glen Dr 77339
Royal Hill Ct 77345
S Royal Point Ct & Dr 77345
Royal Sands Ln 77345
Royal Shores Cir 77345
Royal Timbers Dr 77339
Royal Trail Dr 77339
Running Creek Ct 77345
Running Springs Dr 77339
Rushing Brook Dr 77345
Rushing River Dr 77345
Russell Palmer Rd 77339
Rustic Bridge Ln 77339
Rustic Creek Ln 77345
Rustic Haven Ct 77345
Rustic Park Dr 77339
Rustic Villa Dr 77345
Rustic Woods Dr
2600-2899 77345
3901-3997 77339
3999-4099 77339
4100-4198 77345
Rustling River Dr 77339
Rye Hollow Ln 77345
Saile Ct 77339
Saint Andrews Rd 77339
Same Way 77339
Sandberry Dr 77345
Sandy Cedar Dr 77345
Sandy Forks Dr 77339
Sandy Grove Ct & Dr 77345
Sandy Lake Dr 77339
Sandy Lodge Ct 77345
Sandy Park Dr 77339
Sandy Trail Ct 77339
Santrins Dr 77345
Savell Rd 77339
Scenic Mountain Ct 77345
Scenic Shore Dr 77345
Scenic Valley Dr 77345
Scenic Woods Trl 77345
Seasons Trl 77345
Senour Ct 77339
Seven Maples Dr 77345
Seven Oaks Dr 77339
Sevenleaf Ln 77345
Shadbury Ct 77339
Shadow Rock Dr 77345
Shady Run 77339
Shady Alcove Ct 77345
Shady Birch Holw 77345
Shady Branch Dr 77339
Shady Gardens Ct & Dr 77339
Shady Green Dr 77339
Shady Hills Dr 77339
Shady Maple Ct & Dr 77339
Shady Terrace Dr 77345
Shady Village Dr 77345
Sheltering Oaks Ln 77345
Sherwood St E & W 77339
Sherwood Hollow Ln 77339
Shore Hills Dr 77345
Shorelake Dr 77339
Silver Dawn Ct 77345
Silver Falls Dr 77339
Silver Glade Dr 77345
Silverberry Trl 77345
Soaring Pine Ct 77345
Soft Fern Ct 77345
Southern Hills Rd 77339
Southern Pines Ct & Dr 77339
Splintwood Ct 77345
Spring Arbor Way 77345
Spring Gardens Dr 77339
Spring Lodge Dr 77345
Spring Manor Dr 77345
Spring Palms Ct 77345
Spring Pine Ct 77345
Spruce Bay Dr 77345
Spruce Glen Dr 77339
Spruce Grove Dr 77339
Spruce Knob Ct & Dr 77339
Spruce Lodge Dr 77339
Spruce Park Cir 77345
Spruce Pine Dr 77345
Spruce Ridge Way 77339
Spruce Valley Dr 77345
Squires Park Dr 77339
Stately Oak St 77345
Still Glade Ln 77345
Stillbridge Ln 77339
Stonecrop Ct 77345
Stonehollow Dr 77339
Stoney Glen Dr 77339
Stoney Park Ct & Dr 77339
Straight Way 77339
Stratford Way 77339
N & S Strathford Ln 77345
E & W Summer Rain Ct & Dr 77339
Summit Falls Ct 77345
Summit Lake Dr 77339
Summit Way Ct 77345
Sunny Knoll Ct 77339
Sunny Oaks Ct 77345
Sunny Vale Dr 77345
Sunrise Trl 77339
Sunset Maple Ct 77345
Sunshine Point Dr 77345
Swan Fountain Dr 77345
Sweet Bay Rd 77339
Sweet Gum Ln & Trl 77339
Sweet Orchard Ct 77345
Sweetgum Hill Ln 77345
Sweetstem Ct & Dr 77345
Swift Creek Dr 77339
Sycamore Ln 77339
Sycamore Creek Dr 77345
Sycamore Shadows Dr 77339
Sycamore Springs Ct & Dr 77339
Sycamore Tree Ct 77345
Sycamore Villas Dr 77345
Sylvan Grove Dr 77345
Tall Ridge Ct 77345
Tamarind Trl 77345
Tangle Lake Dr 77339
Tangle River Dr 77339
Tawny Oaks Dr 77345
Teal Arbor Ln 77345
Tern Lake Dr 77345
Terrace Pines Dr 77345
That Way 77339
This Way 77339
Thousand Pines Dr 77339
Three Pines Dr 77339
Threeflower Ct & Ln 77345
Timber Country Way 77345
Timber Glade Ct 77345
Timber Pine Trl 77345
Timber Shade Dr 77345
Timber Shadows Dr 77339
Timberbrook Trl 77345
Timbercreek Trl 77345
Timberlark Dr 77339
Timberline Ct & Dr 77339
Tims Harbor Dr 77339
Tinechester Dr 77339
Towerguard Dr 77339
E & W Town Center Cir & Pl 77339
Town Grove Ct 77345
Trail Forest Ct 77339
Trail Lodge Dr 77339
Trail Oaks Ct 77339
Trail River Dr 77345
Trail Springs Ct 77339
Trail Tree Ln 77339
Trail Water Ct 77339
Trailwood Village Dr 77339
Tranquil Oaks Ct 77345
Treasure Ln 77339
Treasures Ridge Dr 77339
Tree Ln 77339
Tree Manor Ln 77345
Trinity Isle Ct 77345
Tulip River Ct 77345
Twin Greens Ct 77339
Twin Grove Dr 77339
Twin Knolls Dr 77339
Twin Springs Dr 77339
Twisting Pine Ct 77345
Valley Branch Dr 77339
Valley Chase Dr 77345
Valley Fair Dr 77345
Valley Gardens Dr 77345
Valley Glade Dr 77345
Valley Haven Dr 77339
Valley Heather Ct 77345
Valley Lark Ct 77345
Valley Manor Dr 77339
Valley Pines Dr 77345
Valley Rose Dr 77339
Valley Way Dr 77339
Vandermere Ct 77345
Villa Creek Dr 77339
Villa Hill Dr 77345
Villa Park Dr 77339
Villa Pines Dr 77339
Village Falls Ct 77339
Village Manor Dr 77345
Village Oaks Dr 77339
Village Park Dr 77339
Village Pine Dr 77339
Village Springs Ct & Dr 77339
Village Walk Ct 77345
Village Woods Dr 77339
Villagedale Dr 77339
Vine Creek Dr 77339
Vista Manor Dr 77339
Vista Ridge Dr 77339
Waleston Ct 77339
Walham Ct 77345
Walnut Ln & Rd 77339
Walnut Hills Dr 77345
Walnut Knob Ct 77345
Walnut Peak Ct 77345
Walnut Point Dr 77345
Waterview Dr 77339
Waterwell Dr 77339
Welland Way 77339
Wellington Ct 77339
Westwood Lake Ct & Dr 77339
Which Way 77339
Whispering Brook Dr 77345
Whispering Fern Ct 77345
Whispering Forest Dr 77339
Whispering Trails Cir & Dr 77339
Whispering Winds Ln 77339
White Oaks Hills Ln 77339
White Sands Dr 77339
Whitehall Way 77339
Whitney Way 77339
Wild Blackberry Dr 77345
Wild Plum Ct 77345
Wilderness Falls Trl 77339
Wilderness Park Ct 77339
Wilderness Point Dr 77339
Wildridge Dr 77339
Wildwood Ridge Ct & Dr 77339
Wildwood Valley Ct 77345
Willow Knoll Ct 77345
Willow Pass Dr 77339
Willow Point Dr 77339
Willow Ridge Dr 77339
Willow Terrace Dr 77345
Willow Wood Trl 77345
Wind Creek Dr 77345
Windy Gorge Ct & Dr 77345
Windy Green Dr 77345
Windy Haven Dr 77339
Windy Hollow Dr 77345
Windy Lake Dr 77345
Windy Park Dr 77339
Windy Woods Ct 77345
Winter Grape Ln 77345
Wood Dale Dr 77345
Wood Gardens Ct 77339
Woodbridge Dr 77339
Wooded Villas Dr 77345
Woodford Green Dr 77339
Woodland Brook Dr 77345
Woodland Creek Dr 77345
Woodland Falls Dr 77345
Woodland Gardens Dr 77345
Woodland Grove Dr 77339
Woodland Hills Dr 77339
Woodland Ridge Dr 77345
Woodland Valley Dr 77339
Woodland View Dr 77345
Woodland Vista Dr 77339
Woods Estates Dr 77339
Woodsend Ln 77345
Woodspring Acres Ct & Dr 77345
Woodspring Forest Dr 77345
Woodspring Glen Ln 77345
Woodstream Dr 77339
Woodstream Way 77345
N Woodstream Way 77345
S Woodstream Way 77345
Woodstream Village Dr 77345
Woodvale Dr 77345
York Timbers Dr 77339

LA PORTE TX

General Delivery 77571

POST OFFICE BOXES MAIN OFFICE STATIONS AND BRANCHES

Box No.s
All PO Boxes 77572

NAMED STREETS

E A St 77571
W Adams St 77571
Airport Blvd 77571
Alamo Dr 77571
Alvy Dr 77571
Andrews Ct 77571
E Andricks Rd 77571
Antrim Ln 77571
Apple Tree Cir N 77571
Applewood Dr 77571
Appomattox St 77571
Archway Ct & Dr 77571
Arizona St 77571
Ashton Ln 77571
Ashwood Cir 77571
Ashwyne Ct & Ln 77571
Aspen Dr 77571
Avington Rd 77571

Awesome Ln 77571
E & W B St 77571
Bandridge Rd 77571
E & W Barbours Cut Blvd 77571
Barmont Dr 77571
Barracuda Ln 77571
Barry Oaks Ct 77571
Barrybrook Ln 77571
Barton Ct 77571
S Battleground Rd 77571
Battleview Rd 77571
Bay St 77571
Bay Colony Cir & Dr 77571
Bay Forest Dr 77571
Bay Harbor Dr 77571
Bay Oaks Dr 77571
Bay Shore Dr 77571
Bay View Ln 77571
Bayer St 77571
Bayou Dr 77571
Bayou Forest Dr 77571
Bayou Glen Dr 77571
Bayridge Rd 77571
Bayshore Dr 77571
Bayside Dr 77571
Baywood St 77571
Beaver Creek Dr 77571
Beech Cove St 77571
Beechaven Rd 77571
Belfast Rd 77571
Bernard St 77571
Bexar Dr 77571
Birch Dr 77571
Birdie Cir 77571
N & S Blackwell St 77571
Blazing Star Ct & Dr 77571
Blue Bird St 77571
Bogey Cir 77571
Bois D Arc St 77571
Bonita Ln 77571
Bonner St 77571
Bowie Dr 77571
Boyett St 77571
Briar Creek Dr 77571
Briarglen Ln 77571
N & S Broadway St 77571
Brook Meadow Dr 77571
Brookside Dr 77571
Brookview Dr 77571
Brookwind Dr 77571
Brookwood Dr 77571
N & S Brownell St 77571
Browning St 77571
Buchanan St 77571
Bull Run St 77571
Burkett Dr 77571
Byway St 77571
E, N, S & W C St 77571
Caddo Ct 77571
Cammy Ln 77571
Canada Rd 77571
Canyon Springs Dr 77571
Caplan St 77571
Cardinal St 77571
Carlisle St 77571
Carlow Ln 77571
N & S Carroll St 77571
Catlett Ln 77571
Cavalry Rd 77571
Cedar St 77571
Cedar Cove St 77571
Cedarmont Dr 77571
Charmont Rd 77571
Chattanooga St 77571
Cherry Ct 77571
Choctaw Dr 77571
Circle Dr 77571
Clairmont Dr 77571
Clarksville St 77571
Collingdale Rd 77571
Collingswood Dr & Rd 77571
Conifer Dr 77571
Coral Dr 77571
Cottonwood Dr 77571
E, N, S & W Country Club Dr 77571
Coupland Dr 77571
Creekview Dr 77571
Creel Ct 77571
Crescent Dr 77571
Crescent View St 77571
Crestway Dr 77571
Crockett Dr 77571
Cullen Ct 77571
Cypress Ln & St 77571
Cypress Cove St 77571
E, N & W D St 77571
Davis St 77571
Deaf Smith St 77571
Defiance St 77571
E Desert Dr 77571
Desert Run Dr 77571
Desirable Dr 77571
W Dogwood Ct & Dr 77571
Dolphin Ln 77571
Donaldson St 77571
Dover Hill Rd 77571
Dry Desert Way 77571
Dry Sand Dr 77571
Dry Springs Dr 77571
Duane Dr 77571
Dwire Dr 77571
E, N & W E St 77571
Eagle Ln 77571
Eagle Fork Ct 77571
Eagle Nest Ct & Dr 77571
Eagle Rock Ct 77571
Eagle Run St 77571
East Blvd 77571
Eastwick Ln 77571
Easy St 77571
Edgewood St 77571
Elizabeth Ln 77571
Elmhaven Rd 77571
Elmwood Ave 77571
Erin Ct 77571
F St 77571
Fairbrook Ln 77571
Fairfield St 77571
E Fairmont Pkwy 77571
W Fairmont Pkwy
12204A-C-12204A-C 77571
8401-A-8401-B 77571
100-800 77571
801-12299 77571
801-801 77572
802-12298 77571
Fairway Dr 77571
Fairwood Dr 77571
Falcon Pass St 77571
Falk Ave & Ct 77571
N Farrington Blvd 77571
Fern Rock Dr 77571
Fieldcrest Dr 77571
Flintlock Rd 77571
Fondren St 77571
E & W Forest Ave 77571
N Forrest Ave 77571
Fountain Dr 77571
Foxglove Dr 77571
E & W G St 77571
Garden Walk Dr 77571
Garfield St 77571
Gaucho Cir 77571
Gladwyne Ct & Ln 77571
Glenbay Ct 77571
Glencrest Dr 77571
Glenmeadows Dr 77571
Glenpark Dr 77571
Glenvalley Dr 77571
Glenview Ct & Dr 77571
Golden St 77571
Graywood Ct 77571
Green Leaf Ln 77571
Green Meadow Dr 77571
Grove St 77571
E H St 77571
Hackberry St 77571
Hamilton St 77571
Hazel St 77571
Heather Springs St 77571
Hedgestone Ct 77571
Highway 134 77571
Highway 146 N & S 77571
E Highway 225 77571
Hillridge Rd 77571
Hillsdale St 77571
Hollow Tree St 77571
N & S Holmes St 77571
Houston Dr 77571
Howald St 77571
Hummingbird St 77571
Humphreyville St 77571
Huntersfield Ln 77571
S Idaho St 77571
E Idlewood Ct & Dr 77571
Independence Pkwy S 77571
N & S Iowa St 77571
Ivy Dr 77571
Jamie Ct 77571
S Jamison St 77571
Janie Ct 77571
Jefferson St 77571
Josh Way 77571
Juniper Dr 77571
S Kansas St 77571
Kensington Ct 77571
Kevin Ct 77571
King Arthur Ct 77571
King William Dr 77571
N L St 77571
Laura Ln 77571
Layne Ct & St 77571
Lazy Brook Ln 77571
Lazy Pine Ln 77571
Lee St 77571
Lemon Ln 77571
E Linwood Ct & Dr 77571
Littlebrook Rd 77571
S Lobit St 77571
Loc Loma Ln 77571
Lomax Dr 77571
Lomax School Rd 77571
Luella Blvd 77571
S M St 77571
W Madison 77571
Mahan Dr 77571
E & W Main St 77571
Maple St 77571
Maple Creek Dr 77571
Maple Leaf Cir 77571
Maplewood Dr 77571
Marlin Ln 77571
Mary Ln 77571
Mccabe Rd 77571
Mccarty Ln 77571
Meadow Crest St 77571
Meadow Lark Ln 77571
Meadow Park Dr 77571
Meadow Place Dr 77571
Meadowlawn St 77571
Mesquite Dr 77571
Milam Dr 77571
Miller Cut Off Rd 77571
Miramar Dr 77571
Mission Dr 77571
Mocking Bird Ln 77571
Mohawk Dr 77571
Montana St 77571
Montgomery Ln 77571
Monument Cir & Rd 77571
Moore Dr 77571
Mossey Dr 77571
W Mulberry Ct & Dr 77571
Myrtle Creek Dr 77571
N & S Nugent St 77571
S Oak St 77571
Oak Creek Dr 77571
Oak Grove St 77571
Oak Leaf St 77571
Oakdale St 77571
Oaken Ln 77571
Oakhaven Rd 77571
Oakhurst St 77571
Oakmont Dr 77571
Oakshores St 77571
Oakwilde Cir 77571
Oakwood Dr 77571
S Ohio St 77571
Old Desert Rd 77571
Old Hickory Dr 77571
Old La Porte Rd 77571
Old Orchard Rd 77571
Old Underwood Rd 77571
S Oleander Ln & St 77571
Olincol Dr 77571
Orchard Ln 77571
Oregon St 77571
Otter Creek Dr 77571
N P St 77571
Par Cir 77571
Park Dr & Ln 77571
Park Road 1836 77571
Parkcrest Dr 77571
Parkmont Dr 77571
Parkway Dr & St 77571
Patti Ln 77571
Pawnee Dr 77571
Pecan Cir & Dr 77571
Pecan Crossing Ln 77571
Pike Ct 77571
Pine Trl 77571
Pine Bluff St 77571
Pine Creek Dr 77571
Pinewood Ct 77571
Piney Brook Dr 77571
Plainbrook St 77571
E & W Plantation Dr 77571
W Polk St 77571
Poplar Cove St 77571
Porter Rd 77571
Primrose Ln 77571
Quiet Hill Rd 77571
S R St 77571
Redbud Dr 77571
Reynolds Ct 77571
Ridgecrest Dr 77571
Ridgefield Rd 77571
Ridgepark Dr 77571
Ridgevalley Dr 77571
River Creek Dr 77571
Robin St 77571
Robinson Rd 77571
Rock Springs Dr 77571
Rocky Hollow Rd 77571
Roscoe St 77571
Roseberry Dr 77571
Rosemont Dr 77571
Roseway Ln 77571
Rosewood Ct 77571
Rustic Gate Rd 77571
Rustic Rock Rd 77571
Sailfish Ln 77571
San Jacinto Dr & St 77571
San Saba Ct 77571
Sandy Ct & Ln 77571
Santa Anna Ln 77571
Scotch Moss Ln 77571
Seabreeze St 77571
Seagrove St 77571
Seguin Ct 77571
Sens Rd 77571
Shadow Creek Dr 77571
N & S Shady Ln 77571
Shady River Rd 77571
Shady Tree Ct 77571
Shadylawn St 77571
Shell Rock Rd 77571
Shirley Ln 77571
Shore Acres Blvd & Cir 77571
Silver Springs Dr 77571
Sioux Dr 77571
Sky View Ln 77571
Somerton Dr 77571
Southbrook Dr 77571
Sparrow St 77571
Spencer Hwy & Lndg E, N, S & W 77571
Spencer Landing Ln 77571
Springwood Dr 77571
Spruce Dr N & S 77571
Stone Creek Dr 77571
Stonemont Rd 77571
Strang Rd 77571
Stuart Dr 77571
Sugar Creek Dr 77571
Sugar Hill Dr 77571
Sullivan St 77571
Summer Breeze Dr 77571
Summer Winds Dr 77571
Sunrise Dr 77571
Sunset Ridge St 77571
Sycamore Dr N & S 77571
Sylvan St 77571
Tanya Dr 77571
Tara Pl 77571
Tarpon Ln 77571
Teakwood Dr 77571
Tejas Ct 77571
Thornwood Dr 77571
Thrush St 77571
Travis St 77571
Tree Hollow Cir 77571
Twin Cannon Ln 77571
W Tyler St 77571
Underwood Rd 77571
N & S Utah St 77571
Valley Brook Ct & Dr 77571
Valley View Dr 77571
Venture Ln 77571
Vinsonia St 77571
N & S Virginia St 77571
Vista Rd 77571
Wayside Dr 77571
Weatherford St 77571
Westpark Dr 77571
Westview St 77571
Wichita Dr 77571
Willmont Rd 77571
Willow Creek Dr 77571
Willow View St 77571
S Wilson St 77571
Winding Trail Rd 77571
Windleaf Dr 77571
Wood Drift Ct 77571
Woodland Ct 77571
Wren St 77571
E X St 77571
S Y St 77571
Youpon Dr 77571

NUMBERED STREETS

All Street Addresses 77571

LANCASTER TX

General Delivery 75146

POST OFFICE BOXES MAIN OFFICE STATIONS AND BRANCHES

Box No.s
All PO Boxes 75146

RURAL ROUTES

03 75134
01, 02 75146

NAMED STREETS

Aaron St 75146
Abby Ln 75134
Aberdeen Dr 75146
Addison Dr 75134
N & S Alba Rd 75146
Aldridge Dr 75134
Alexander St 75146
Alhambra Dr 75146
Alicia Ln 75134
Allerton Ln 75146
Amber Waves Ln 75134
Ambercrest Dr 75146
Ames Rd 75134
Annette St 75146
Apollo Ln 75134
W Appaloosa Dr 75146
Apple Valley Dr 75134
April Showers Ln 75134
Arbor Ln 75134
Arbordale Ct 75134
Arcady Cir & Ln 75134
Arlington Ln 75134
Artemus Dr 75134
Ash Ln 75146
Ashley Ct 75146
Aspen St 75134
Athena Dr 75134
Atteberry Ln 75146
Augusta St 75146
Babbling Brook Ln 75134
Badger Run 75134
Bahama Dr 75146
Bald Cypress Dr 75146
Balkan Dr 75134
Balomede St 75134
Banyan Ct 75146
Barclay Dr 75146
Barnett St 75146
Barry Ln 75146
Baskin Dr 75134
Bayport Dr 75134
Bear Creek Rd 75146
N Beckley St 75134
Becky Ln 75134
E & W Belt Line Rd 75146
Belvedere Rd 75134
Bermuda Ave 75146
Big Sandy Ln 75146
Birchwood Dr 75146
Birkenhead Ln 75134
Blackberry Trl 75134
Blanco Rd 75134
Blue Sage Dr 75146
N Bluegrove Rd
101-1299 75146
1300-1999 75134
S Bluegrove Rd 75146
Boca Raton Way 75146
Bonnywood Dr 75134
Bordner Dr 75146
Boxwood Dr 75146
Boye St 75146
Branchwood Dr 75146
Brantley Dr 75134
Breezewood Ln 75146
Briarcove Pl 75146
Briarview Dr 75146
Bridle Path Dr 75146
Brook Meadow Cir 75134
Brookhaven Dr 75134
Brooks Dr 75134
Brookview Dr 75146
Bruce Dr 75134
Bumble Bee Dr 75134
Camden Ct 75146
Candace Dr 75146
Candler Dr 75134
Cansler Ln 75134
Canvas Ct 75146
Canyon Oaks Dr 75146
Cardigan Ln 75134
Cardwell Dr 75146
Carol Ave
1201-1299 75146
1400-1599 75134
Carsen Way 75146
Catalina Dr 75146
Cayman Dr 75146
Cayotillo St 75146
E & W Cedar St 75146
Cedar Valley Dr 75134
Cedarbrook Trl 75146
Cedardale Rd 75134
Cedarwood Dr 75134
N Centre Ave 75146
S Centre Ave 75146
Centre Ln 75134
Chapman Dr
600-699 75146
1301-1397 75134
1399-1999 75134
W Chapman Dr 75146
Cherry Hills Dr 75134
Cheshier Rd 75146
Cimarron St 75146
Clear Stream Dr 75134
Clearbranch Dr 75146
Clearbrook St 75134
Cloverleaf Dr 75146
Colgate Ct & Dr 75134
Collier Ct 75146
E Colonial Dr 75134
Concord Ln 75134
Conlin Dr 75134
Copperfield Ln 75146
Coral Dr 75146
Cornell Rd 75134
Cottage Ln 75134
Creekwood Dr 75146
Crepe Myrtle Dr 75146
N Crest St 75146
Cresthaven Dr 75134
Crimson Clover Dr 75134
Criswell St 75134
Cromwell St 75134
Cross Oaks Dr 75146
Cumberland St 75134
Cummings Ln 75146
Cypress Ln 75146
Daisy Dr 75134
N Dallas Ave
100-1299 75146
1300-4299 75134
S Dallas Ave 75146
Dancer St 75146
Daniel Ln 75134
Danieldale Rd 75134
Dasher St 75146
Deep Branch Cir 75146
Delle Ln 75146
Depot St 75146
Devine Dr 75146
Dewberry Blvd 75134
Diamond Ln 75146
Diann Cir & St 75146
Dogwood Trl 75146
Donlee Rd 75134
Doyle Ln 75134
Dyer St 75146
Eagle River Trl 75146
Eastwood Dr 75134
Echo Creek Ln 75146
Edgewater Way 75146
Edgewood Dr 75146
Edwards St 75134
El Camino Real 75146
Elders Dr 75146
Elkins Ave 75134
N & S Ellis St 75146
N Elm St
200-1300 75146
1302-1398 75146
1400-1699 75134
S Elm St 75146
Enchanted Ln 75146
Encino Dr 75146
Everton Dr 75134
Fabrication Dr 75134
Fair Weather Dr 75146
Fairfield Ct 75134
Falerest Dr 75134
Ferris Rd 75146
Fitzhugh Ct & St 75146
Flower Ridge Dr 75134
Fox Glen Cir & Rd 75146
Francis St 75146
Franklin St 75134
Frederick St 75134
Gant Dr 75134
Gentle Rain Dr 75134

Gentry St 75134
Gerry Way St 75134
Ginger Dr 75146
Glen Hollow Dr 75134
Glendover Ct & Dr 75146
Glenwood Dr 75134
Godiva St 75134
Golden Grass Dr 75134
Goldenrod Dr 75134
Graystone Dr 75134
Green Dr 75134
Green Acre Ln 75146
Greenbriar Ln 75146
Greene Rd 75146
Griffin St 75146
Hackberry St 75146
Hall St
500-1199 75146
1201-1299 75146
1300-1399 75134
Halley Ln 75146
E & W Hammond St 75146
Harbor Ct 75134
Hartford Ln 75134
Harvard Ln 75134
Harvest Hill Ln 75146
Hash Rd 75146
Haywood Cir 75146
Hearthstone Dr 75146
Heather Ridge Dr 75146
Henry Rd 75134
N Henry St 75146
S Henry St 75146
High Meadow Ln 75146
High Ridge Dr 75146
Highland St 75134
Hill Rd 75146
Hillview Ln 75134
Hilton Dr 75146
Historic Town Sq 75146
Hogan Run 75146
Hollow Oak Rd 75134
Homestead Dr 75146
Honey Bee Ln 75134
N Houston School Rd
100-298 75146
300-1400 75146
1402-1426 75146
1500-4699 75134
S Houston School Rd 75146
Hullette Ave 75134
Idlewild Ct & Ln 75134
Illinois Ave 75134
Indian Lilac Dr 75146
Industrial St 75134
Inspiration Dr 75146
N Interstate 35 E
100-1398 75146
N Interstate 35 E
1400-3598 75134
S Interstate 35 E 75146
Interurban Rd 75134
Irene Ave 75134
N Jefferson St
400-1299 75146
1301-1897 75134
1899-1999 75134
Jessie Ln 75146
Jewell Ln 75146
Johns Ave 75146
Katrina Ln 75134
Katy St 75146
Kensington Ct & Pl 75134
Kentucky Ave 75134
Kim St 75146
Kings Cross Dr 75134
Kiowa Cir 75146
Lake Trail Dr 75146
N Lancaster Hutchins Rd
301-497 75146
499-1100 75146
1102-1198 75146
1400-3799 75134
S Lancaster Hutchins
Rd 75146
Lancaster Park Dr 75146
Lanwood Ct 75146
Laurel St 75134
Lavender Rd 75146
Lawndale Dr 75134
Lemita Dr 75146
Lentisco Dr 75146
Lexington Dr 75134
Linda Ln 75134
Lindenwood Dr 75134
Linkwood Dr & Ln 75146
Lions Club Park Rd 75146
Loch Wood Dr 75146
Logan Dr 75146
Lomita Dr 75146
Long Branch Dr 75146
N Longhorn Dr 75134
Lotus Ln 75134
Lyle St 75134
Lynnette Ct 75134
Lyon St 75134
Magnolia Ln 75146
E & W Main St 75146
Mallory Ln 75134
Manchester Ln 75134
Maple St 75146
Maplecrest Dr 75146
Margaret Ct 75134
Margeaux Dr 75134
Marimont Ln 75134
Marquis Ln 75134
Marsalis Rd 75134
Marsh Dr 75134
Martin Dr 75146
Martindale Dr 75134
Marvin Dr & Gdns 75146
Mary Wilson Dr 75146
Mason Rd 75146
Mason Way 75134
Masonic Dr 75146
May Ct 75146
Mayfair Ln 75134
Mayflowers Ln 75134
Mcbride Rd 75146
Mccormick Dr 75134
Mcintosh Ct 75134
Mckenzie Ln 75134
Mckinney Dr 75134
Mcneely St 75134
Meadow Gln & Ln 75146
Meadow Creek Ct &
Dr 75146
Meadowgate Ln 75134
Meadowlark Ct & Ln 75146
Melrose Ln 75146
Mercury Ln 75134
Merrimac Ln 75134
Midbury Dr 75134
Midelac Rd 75146
Mill Branch Ln 75146
Mill Creek Cir & Rd 75146
Millbrook Dr 75146
Mimosa Ln 75146
Mink Rd 75146
Mission Ln 75146
Monarch Dr 75146
Montclair St 75146
Monticello Ln 75134
Montrose Ln 75134
Moreland Rd 75146
Mosley Dr 75146
Murphy Dr 75146
Muttick Ln 75146
Myrtle St 75134
Nail Dr 75146
Nancy Ln 75146
Native Cir 75146
Nautilus Dr 75146
Neches Pl 75146
Newport Dr 75146
Nichols Dr 75146
Nicklaus Nook 75146
Nokomis Cir, Pl & Rd 75146
Nolan Rd 75146
Northampton Trl 75134
Norwood Ln 75146
Nottingham Dr 75134
Oak St 75146
Oak Farms Blvd 75134
Oakbluff Dr 75146
Oakbrook Ct & St 75134
Oakmont Dr 75134
Oakwood Dr 75146
Ocean Dr 75146
Old Red Oak Rd 75146
Olympus Dr 75134
Oneal St 75134
Overlook Dr & Ln 75146
Paint Brush Pl 75134
Palm Dr 75146
Palma Pita St 75146
Palmer Cir 75146
N Palomino Dr 75134
Park Circle Dr 75146
E & W Park Place Dr 75134
Parkerville Rd 75146
Parkside Ln 75146
Patman St 75134
Payne Dr 75134
Pebble Beach Dr 75134
E Pecan Grv & St 75146
Pecan Hollow Dr 75146
Pecan Leaf Dr 75146
Pecos Ct 75146
Pegasus Dr 75134
Pennsylvania Ave 75134
E & S Pepperidge Ct &
Dr 75134
Percy St 75134
Pewitt Dr 75134
Picket Fence Dr 75134
Pierson St 75146
Pike Dr 75134
Pin Oak Ln 75146
E Pine St 75146
Pinto Rd 75134
Pioneer Ct, Ln & Way 75146
E & W Pleasant Run
Rd 75146
Poinsettia Dr 75134
S Pointe Dr 75134
Poplar Ln 75146
Poppy Pl 75134
Portwood Dr 75134
Poseidon Dr 75134
Potomac Dr 75134
Prairie Dr 75146
Prairie Aster Dr 75146
Prancer St 75134
Prescott Dr 75134
Princeton Dr 75134
Quail Hollow Dr 75146
Quail Run Ln 75146
Raintree Dr 75146
Randlett St 75146
Ransom Dr 75146
Rawlins Dr
600-899 75146
1300-1398 75134
Rea Ave 75146
Rebecca Ln 75134
Red River Rd 75146
E & W Redbud Ln 75146
E & W Reindeer Rd 75146
Reynolds St 75134
Riley Dr 75134
Rising Crest Dr 75134
River Bend Dr 75134
River Oaks Cir & Dr 75134
Riverdell Ct 75134
Riverway Ln 75134
Roan Dr 75134
Robin Ln 75146
Rockbrook St 75146
Rogers Ave 75134
Rolling Ct 75146
Rolling Hills Pl 75146
Rolling Meadows Dr 75146
Rosa Parks Blvd 75146
Rosewood Ln 75146
Rowe Ln 75146
Rutgers Dr 75134
Ryder Dr 75146
Saddlebrook Dr 75146
Saint Andrews Dr 75146
Saint Charles Pl 75134
Saint Croix Ave 75146
Saint Johns Ave 75146
Saint Martin Dr 75146
Saint Thomas Ln 75146
Sandalwood Trl 75146
Sequoia Dr 75146
Serena Dr 75134
Sewell Dr 75146
Shady Ln 75146
Shadybrook St 75134
Shadygrove Dr 75146
Shanna Dr 75134
Shasta Dr 75134
Shell Ln 75146
Shelton Dr 75146
Sherwood Ave 75134
Sierra Trl 75146
Singing Bird Dr 75134
Sleepy Hollow Ln 75146
Smokey Oak St 75134
Southridge Dr 75146
Southwood Dr 75146
Spring Creek Dr 75146
Spring Hill Ln 75146
Spring Water Dr 75134
E & W Springcrest Cir 75134
Springfield Ave 75134
Springmont Dr 75134
Springtree Cir 75146
Sprucewood Dr 75146
Stacia Ln 75134
Stainback Rd 75146
Stanford Dr 75134
N & S State St 75146
State Highway 342 75146
Stephanie St 75146
N & S Stewart Ave 75146
Stonewall St 75134
Stonewood Dr 75134
Stonycroft Ct & Dr 75134
Strain Ct 75134
Suffolk Ln 75146
Summerview Ln 75146
Sunnymeadow Rd 75134
Sunnyside Dr 75146
N Sunrise Rd 75146
Sunset Dr 75146
Sunshine Ct & Way 75134
Swift Fox Dr 75134
Sycamore Ln 75146
Talco Rd 75146
Tall Grass Dr 75134
Tamerisk Dr 75134
Tanglewood Dr 75134
Tara Cir 75146
Taylor St 75134
Telephone Rd 75134
Ten Mile Rd 75146
Texas St 75146
W Thoroughbred Dr 75146
Tifton Ct 75146
Town North Dr 75134
Tracy Ln 75146
Trevino Trl 75146
Tribute Rd 75146
Trinity Dr 75146
Trippie St 75134
Trojan Dr 75134
Truman Cir 75146
Tulia St 75146
N University Hills Blvd 75134
Valley Cir 75134
Van Rd 75146
Vanderbilt Rd 75134
Vanguard Pl 75146
Venus Dr E & W 75134
Vermont Ave 75146
Verona Rd 75134
Veterans Memorial
Pkwy 75134
Wade Rd 75146
Waldrop Dr 75146
Walnut St 75146
Warwick Dr 75134
Waterfall Cir 75146
Watermill Rd 75146
Waters St 75134
Watson Dr 75146
Waverly Dr 75146
Waynelee Dr 75146
W Welsh Dr 75146
Western Hills Dr 75146
Westin Ct 75134
Westover Dr 75134
Westridge Ave 75146
Westwood Dr 75146
E Wheatland Rd 75134
Wild Grove Ln 75146
Wild Horse Way 75134
Wilderness Pass 75146
Wildwood Trl 75146
Willow Creek Dr 75146
Willowbrook Ct & St 75134
Willowood Ln 75134
Wilson Rd & St 75146
Windsor Dr 75134
E & W Wintergreen
Rd 75134
Witt Rd 75134
Woodcrest Dr 75134
Woodglen Dr 75134
Woodmere Dr 75134
Worthington Ln 75134
Yale Dr 75134
Yellow Rose Ln 75134
Yorkshire Ln 75134
Zeus Dr 75134
Zion Dr 75134
Zollman Ct 75146

NUMBERED STREETS

All Street Addresses 75146

LAREDO TX

General Delivery 78041

POST OFFICE BOXES MAIN OFFICE STATIONS AND BRANCHES

Box No.s
2163LL - 2163LL 78045
5802BBL - 5802BBL 78045
5810SMA - 5810SMA 78045
11905SA - 11905SA 78045
8805LL - 8805LL 78045
1 - 1599 78042
499 - 1005 78045
1600 - 3796 78044
6001 - 420598 78042
430001 - 430640 78043
440001 - 440920 78044
450001 - 452814 78045

RURAL ROUTES

03, 24 78043
02, 07, 11, 22 78045
01, 13, 23 78046

HIGHWAY CONTRACTS

60 78046

NAMED STREETS

Abbeville Dr 78045
Aberdeen Loop 78043
Abigail Dominguez 78043
Acacia St 78045
Acadia Loop 78045
Acapulco 78046
Acerra Ln 78046
Acuna 78046
Ada Dr 78045
Adair 78046
Adelita Rd 78043
Adenia Loop 78043
Adriana Ct 78040
Aduanales Ln 78041
Agate 78046
Agatha Christie Dr 78041
Agave 78041
Aguanieve Dr 78046
Aguascalientes 78046
Aguila Azteca 78043
Aida Ct 78045
Aidin St 78045
Airpark Dr 78041
Alabama Ave & Cir 78041
Alameda Dr 78045
Alamo St 78040
Alan Ln 78045
Alaska Cir 78041
Albany Dr 78045
Aldama St
1001-1199 78040
1701-1797 78043
1799-2899 78043
Alder Ln 78045
Alegria 78046
Alegro Cir 78041
Alejandra 78041
Alemany 78046
Alexandra Ct 78043
Alfonso Ct 78040
Alfonso Ornelas 78046
Alicante Dr 78046
Allarke St 78043
Allegheny 78045
Allen Dr 78045
Allende St 78041
Almeja Dr 78043
Almond St 78046
Aloe Vera Dr 78043
Alpes Ct 78043
Alta Mira Dr 78045
Alta Vista Dr 78041
E Alvarado 78043
W Alvarado 78043
Alvarado Ln 78046
Alvarez 78043
Alysha Ct 78040
Amador Salinas Dr 78045
Amanda Ln 78046
Amanecer Rd 78043
Amazon Ct 78046
Amber Ave 78045
Amethyst Dr 78045
Amhurst Dr 78045
E & W Amiens Pl 78045
Amistad Dr 78041
Amparan Rd 78045
Amy Rd 78043
Andrade Cir 78045
Andrea Ct 78046
Andrew Ave, Cir, Ct &
Ln 78045
Andy Ramos 78043
Anejo Dr 78045
Aneto Dr 78043
Anfield Loop 78045
Angel Fls 78041
Angela Dr 78046
Ann Harbor St 78045
Anna Ave 78040
Ansel 78043
Antelope Ln 78045
Anthony Ln 78046
Antler Crossing Ave 78045
Antonia St 78045
Antonieta Ln 78046
Anylu Ct 78046
Apache Ln 78045
Appaloosa Rd 78045
Appleby Ct 78045
Aransas Pass Dr 78045
Arapahoe Dr 78045
Archer Dr 78045
Arco Iris Rd 78043
Areca Dr 78045
Arena 78041
Arguello Dr 78046
Arias Ct 78046
Arizona Loop 78041
Ark Cts 78046
N Arkansas Ave 78043
S Arkansas Ave
600-698 78043
801-999 78043
1700-3599 78046
Armadillo St 78041
Armando Hinojosa Ln 78046
Arrowhead Cir 78045
Artic Ct 78045
Arzube Ln 78046
E Ash St
200-1099 78040
2100-3499 78043
3501-3599 78043
W Ash St 78040
Ashton Loop 78045
Asis 78043
Aspen Ln 78041
Asturias Ave 78046
Atlanta Dr 78045
Atlee Ave 78040
Auburn Rd 78045
Augusta Loop 78045
E & W Aurora Dr 78041
S Auto Rd 78041
Autumn Cir & Dr 78045
S Aviator Rd 78043
Avila Dr 78046
E & W Avon Ct 78041
Azinger Dr 78045
Aziz St 78045
Azucena Dr 78046
Backwoods Trl 78045
Badajoz 78046
Baffin Bay 78041
Baker St 78045
Balboa St 78043
Balcones Dr 78046
Baltimore St 78041
Bandera Dr 78046
Bannock Ln 78043
W Banyan Ct 78041
Barcelona Ave
3000-3700 78040
3702-3798 78040
3800-3898 78041
3900-4299 78041
Barcelona Cir 78041
Baretta Ct 78043
Barracuda Dr 78043
Barrera Rd 78043
Barrileros Dr 78045
Barrios St 78043
N Bartlett Ave
200-298 78043
300-2700 78043
2702-3798 78043
4000-7598 78041
7600-7699 78041
S Bartlett Ave
800-898 78043
900-1300 78043
1302-1498 78043
1500-3599 78046
Bartolome Ln 78043
Bass Inlt 78041
Basswood Dr 78045
Bayard St 78046
Baycliff Ln 78041
Bayonne Ln 78045
N Beach Ln 78041
Bear Crk 78045
Bear Claw Ln 78043
Bedford Dr 78045
Begay 78045
Begona Ct 78046
Belaire Dr 78041
Belen Cts 78045

Street	ZIP
Belize Dr	78045
Belton Dr	78046
Beltran Loop	78046
Beltway Pkwy	78045
Ben Hur Ranch Rd	78045
Benavides St	78040
Bencha Dr	78043
Bengo Bay	78041
Bennington Dr	78045
Beringer Ct	78041
Berkley Rd	78045
Bermuda Dr	78045
Beverly Dr	78045
Bexar Ct	78046
Birch Loop	78046
Birchwood Ln	78041
Birney Dr	78046
Biscayne Loop	78045
Bismark St	78043
Black Buck Cir	78045
Black Diamond Cir	78045
Black Hawk Cir	78045
Black Hills Ln	78043
Black Kettle Ln	78043
Blackfoot Dr	78045
Blaine St	78043
Blair St	78040
Blancas Dr	78045
Blitzen Dr	78045
Blue Lk	78041
Blue Bonnet Ln	78046
Blue Jay Ln	78045
Blue Sky Cir	78045
Bob Bullock Loop	
2300G-2398G	78043
200-2398	78043
701-799	78045
1001-1999	78043
5000-5098	78041
5100-9499	78041
9501-9899	78041
12801-12899	78045
NE Bob Bullock Loop	78045
W Bob Bullock Loop	78045
Bobwhite Ave	78045
Boise Way	78041
Bonaparte Ln	78046
Boomtown St	78043
Bordeaux Dr	78041
Boros Ct	78045
Borrado Dr	78045
Bosco Ln	78046
Boston St	78041
Bougainvillea St	78046
Boulanger St	78043
Brahea Dr	78045
Braids Dr	78045
Brand Dr	78041
Brazos Ave	78046
Breeze Cir	78041
Breezewood Cir	78045
Brewster Dr	78043
Brighton Dr	78045
Bristol Rd	78045
Brixton Ct	78041
Broadcrest Dr	78045
Brooks Ct	78045
Brown Dr	78045
Browning St	78043
Brumoso Ct	78046
Bruni Ct & St	78040
N Buena Vista Ave	78043
S Buena Vista Ave	
100-499	78043
3001-3097	78046
3099-3499	78046
Buenos Aires Dr	78045
Buffalo Ct	78045
Bull Elk Ln	78045
Bunker Cir	78046
Burgundy Loop	78045
Burke Dr	78045
Burnet Dr	78043
Burnside St	78040
Bush Ct	78046
Business Ave	78045
E & W Bustamante St	78041
Butia Dr	78045
Caballo Dr	78045
Cabezut Dr	78045
Cabo San Lucas St	78046
Cabo Wabo	78045
Cactus Dr	78041
Cadena	78046
E & W Calais Pl	78045
California St	78041
Callaghan St	78040
Calle Bonita Ct	78045
Calle Cancun	78046
Calle Chiapas	78046
Calle Chiquita Ct	78045
Calle Del Norte	78041
Calle Ferraez	78041
Calle Piedra Ln	78045
Calle Puebla	78046
Calle Tuxpan	78046
Calle Vistoso Ln	78045
Callow Ct	78045
Calloways Ct	78041
E & W Calton Rd	78041
Calvery Ct	78045
Camacho Ln	78046
Camargo Dr	78045
Cambridge Loop	78045
Camelia Dr	78041
Camelot	78041
Camino Columbia Toll Rd	
N	78045
Camp St	78040
Campanario Ln	78043
Campeche Dr	78046
Campos Dr	78043
N Canada Ave	78043
S Canada Ave	
500-1099	78043
1101-1399	78043
1500-2000	78046
2002-2898	78046
E & W Canal St	78041
Cancun St	78046
Candela	78043
Candlewood Rd	78045
Canelo Dr	78046
Cannel St	78045
Canones Blvd	78046
Cantera Ct	78045
Canterbury Ln	78041
Canvasback Dr	78045
Canyon Dr	78043
Canyon Bluff Cir	78041
Canyon Creek Cir	78041
Capistran Loop	78045
Capitol Ln	78046
Cardigan Ct	78043
Cardinal Ln	78045
Caroline St	78046
Carreta Ct	78045
Carriers Dr	78045
Carrizo Dr	78045
Carrol Dr	78045
Carter Dr	78046
Casa Blanca Rd	78041
Casa Del Sol Blvd	78043
Casa Verde Rd	78041
Casares Ct	78046
Cascade Dr	78046
Cashew Ave	78046
Casimir Dr	78045
Cassata Ln	78046
Castaneda St	78041
Castellanos Ct	78045
Castilla Cir	78043
Castle Heights Dr	78041
Castro Urdiales Dr	78046
Catalina Dr	78045
Catedral Loop	78043
Cavazos St	78043
Cayman Ct	78045
Cecilia Ln	78046
Cedar Ave	
700-3799	78040
3800-4199	78041
Celita Loop	78041
Ceniso Loop	78046
Centenario Dr	78045
Centennial Ct	78046
Centeno Ln	78046
Center Rd	78045
Century Blvd, Cir & Dr	
E, N, S & W	78046
Cereus Ct	78043
Cerralvo Dr	78045
Cerrito Prieto Ct	78041
Cerros Dr	78046
Chacon St	
800-1298	78040
1300-1599	78040
1600-3199	78043
3201-3299	78043
Chacota St	78046
Chalan Dr	78045
Chambers Ct	78046
Chaparral St	78041
Chardonnay Ct	78045
Charreada Dr	78045
Chateau Lafitte Ct	78041
Chaucer Dr	78041
Cheetah Ln	78045
Cherokee Dr	78045
E Cherry Ln	78041
E Cherry Hill Dr	78041
Chestnut St	78046
Chetumal Dr	78045
Chevy Chase Dr	78041
Chianti Ct	78041
Chibcha Cts	78046
Chicago St	78041
Chickasaw Ln	78043
Chicote Rd	78045
Chihuahua St	
2403-A-2403-C	78043
100-1599	78040
1600-3299	78043
Chimayo Rd	78045
Chiquis Rd	78045
Chris Ln	78045
Christine Ln	78046
Cibola St	78046
Cid	78043
Cielito Lindo	78046
Cielo Dr	78046
Cielo Encantado	78045
Cimarron Dr	78041
Cinnamon Teal Loop	78045
Cipress	78046
Circle Dr	78040
Cirio Ln	78046
Ciruelo	78046
Cisneros St	78043
Citrine	78046
Clark Blvd	
2-98	78040
100-1599	78040
1600-4399	78043
Clark Crossing Dr	78043
Claveles Dr	78041
Cleveland St	78043
Cliff Dr	78045
Clinton Ln	78046
Clubview Dr	78041
Coahuila Loop	78045
Cobble	78046
Cochiti Dr	78045
Cocoa Ln	78046
Cocos Dr	78045
Codorniz Dr	78045
Coke St	78040
Colinas Dr	78046
College Port Dr	78045
Colonia Loop	78046
Colorado Cir & St	78041
Colt Dr	78043
Columbia Dr	78046
Comal Loop	78046
Comales Dr	78046
Comanche Loop	78043
Comet Dr	78045
Comino Nuevo	78043
Commerce Dr	78041
Concord St	78043
Concord Hills Blvd	78046
Conde Dr	78045
Conley Rd	78045
Conrad Dr	78041
Conroe St	78046
Constantinople St	78040
Constitution Ct	78046
Continental Cir	78046
Convent Ave	
100-3499	78040
3500-4499	78041
Coolidge Dr	78046
Coos Bay	78041
Copper Bend Rd	78045
Copper Mine Rd	78045
Copperfield Cir	78045
Coral Hills Dr	78045
Cordova Ln	78043
Cornell Dr	78045
Coronado Ave	78043
Corpus Christi St	
100-1599	78040
1600-3800	78043
3802-3898	78043
Corrada Ave	78046
Corral Dr & Loop	78045
Cortez St	
100-198	78040
200-1599	78040
1600-3399	78043
Coruna Ct	78046
Corvina	78043
Costa Del Sol Dr	78046
Costello Loop	78046
Cottonwood Cir	78041
Country Club Ct	78041
Country Club Dr	
1401-1499	78045
1800-1898	78045
7401-7497	78041
7499-7599	78041
8300-8399	78045
E Country Club Dr	78045
Couples Dr	78045
Coventry	78046
Cowbird Cove Ct	78045
Cozumel Dr	78046
Cpl Rd	78041
Crackle Grove Dr	78045
Crater Lake Dr	78041
Crenshaw Dr	78045
Cresent	78041
Crest Ln	78046
Crest Oak Cir	78045
Crestview Dr	78045
Crestwind	78045
Cross St	78046
Crossbill St	78045
Crosscountry Ln	78045
Crossfield Cir	78045
Crossroads Loop	78045
Crossview Loop	78045
Crossway Dr	78045
Crow Ln	78043
Crownwood Dr	78045
E & W Croydon Pl	78045
Crystal Ct	78045
Cuatro Vientos Dr	78046
Cuellar Ct	78040
Cuencas	78046
Cuernavaca Dr	78046
Cuervo Dr	78045
Culiacan Dr	78046
Cullaton Cir	78045
Cupid Ln	78045
Curly Ln	78045
Cypress Dr	78041
Daffodil Ave	78046
Daisy Ln	78046
E & S Dakota	78041
Dalia Ln	78046
Daly Dr	78045
Dancer Dr	78045
Daniela Loop	78043
Dante Loop	78041
Dasaw Ln	78043
Dasher Dr	78045
Date Palm Dr	78045
Daugherty Ave	78041
David Ln	78046
Davis Ave	
200-3399	78040
3600-4199	78041
De Novo St	78045
De Simone Ct	78046
Deacon	78045
Deane Cir	78046
Declaration Dr	78046
Deer Ln	78045
Deer Ridge Blvd	78045
Del Ct	78041
E Del Mar Blvd	
2-98	78041
100-2394	78041
2395-2395	78045
2396-4698	78041
2501-4599	78041
W Del Mar Blvd	78041
Del Norte Cir	78041
Delaware St	78041
Delfina Dr	78041
Della Falls Dr	78041
Dellwood Dr	78045
Delphina	78043
Delta Dr	78045
Demaret Ct	78045
Denmark Ln	78045
Derby St	78043
Des Perado Rd	78043
Desert Chief Dr	78045
Desert Palm Dr	78045
E & W Devon Pl	78045
Devonshire Ct	78041
Diamond Dr	78045
Diana Dr	78041
Diaz Ave & St	78043
Dickey Ln	78043
Dickinson Dr	78041
Diego Ln	78043
Distribution Ave	78045
Dixie	78046
Doc Adams	78045
Doc Sigi Perez Loop	78046
Doctora Eve Perez Ln	78046
Doe Ct	78045
Dogwood Ave & Rd	78041
Dolphin	78043
Dominique Ct	78041
Don Andres Ct	78045
Don Baldo Ct	78045
Don Beto	78041
Don Jose Dr	78045
Don Pascual Ct & Ln	78045
Don Sergio	78045
Don Tomas Loop	78045
Dona Luz Dr	78045
Doncaster Ln	78045
Doner Rd	78045
Dorado Dr	78046
Dorel Dr	78043
Dos Reales Loop	78045
Dove Trail Ct	78045
Dover Ln	78041
Drake	78043
Drake St	78045
Durango Ave	78046
Dutour Ct	78045
Duval Loop	78045
Eagle Ct	78045
Eagle Crest Loop	78045
Eagle Nest Ln	78043
Eagle Pass Ave	
100-3298	78040
3300-3399	78040
3401-3499	78040
3500-4199	78041
4201-4299	78041
Eagle Ridge Ct	78045
Eagle Trace Dr	78045
East Dr	78041
Eastpoint Dr	78045
Eastwood Dr	78043
Eaton Ln	78041
Ebony Ave	78046
Eden Ln	78041
Edgar Allen Poe Loop	78041
Edgefield Ct	78045
Edward Ln	78046
Eisenhower Dr	78046
E & W Eistetter St	78041
N Ejido Ave	78043
S Ejido Ave	
400-1298	78043
1300-1399	78043
1401-1499	78043
1800-2299	78046
2301-4899	78046
El Gato Rd	78045
El Lucero Rd	78043
El Monte Loop	78045
El Rocio Rd	78043
El Sabinal Ln	78046
Elizabeth	78046
Elizondo Dr	78046
Elk Dr	78045
Elkington Loop	78045
E Elm Loop	78043
E Elm St	
400-1099	78040
2200-3299	78043
W Elm St	78040
Eloy Ct	78045
Els Ct	78045
Elsa Gerardo St	78041
Elva Teresa St	78041
Emerald Lake Dr	78041
Emerald Valley Dr	78043
Emiliano Rd	78043
Emily Ave	78045
Emory Loop	78043
Encino Cir	78041
W End Washington St	78040
Endeavor	78041
Enlace Rd	78043
Enterprise St	78045
Entrada Loop	78045
Escandon Dr	
201-299	78043
11100-11199	78045
Eskimo Dr	78045
Espada	78043
N & S Espana Dr	78043
Espejo Molina Rd	78046
Esperanza Dr	78041
Espino Dr	78046
Espuela Ct	78045
Estate Dr	78045
Estrella	78043
Eucalyptus	78043
Evans Ave	78040
Everest Ct	78043
Evergreen Dr	78041
Exeter Dr	78045
Exodus Dr	78046
Export Rd	78045
Ezra Pound Dr	78041
Fair Oaks Ct	78045
Fairfield Dr	78043
Fairway Ln	78041
Falcete Ct	78045
Falcon Dr	78045
Falcon Ridge Cv	78045
Faldo Dr	78045
Fall Dr	78046
Fallow Ln	78045
False Bay	78041
Farias St	78041
Farragut St	78040
Farrell Rd	78045
Fasken Blvd	78045
Fawn Dr	78045
Feather St	78043
Felipe Ave	78043
Fenwick Dr	
1-99	78045
100-700	78041
702-998	78041
Feria Dr	78043
Fesco	78043
Ficus Cir	78045
Field Crest Cir	78045
E & W Fiesta Loop	78043
Finch	78045
Fishers Hill Loop	78045
Flag St	78043
Flamenco Cir	78041
Flathead	78045
Flathead Lake Dr	78041
Flecha Ln	78045
Fleming Dr	78041
Floral Blvd	78043
Flores Ave	
200-298	78040
300-3499	78040
3500-4499	78041
Florida St	78041
Fm 1472	78045
Fm 3338	78045
Fm 3464	78045
Foggy Loop	78045
Foothills Dr	78043
Ford Ct	78046
Forest Loop	78045
Fort Mcintosh	78040
Foster Ave	78041
Fox Ln	78045
Foxtail Dr	78045
Franc Cigarroa Dr	78046
France Ct	78043
Franciscanos Dr	78043
Frank Sciaraffa Dr	78046
Frankfort St	78040
Franklin St	78041
Franzetta St	78046
Fray Augusto Ln	78043
Free Trade St	78045
Freedom Ln	78046
Frees St	78046
Freight	78041
Fremont St	78043
E Fremont St	78040
W Fremont St	78040
Frida Dr	78046
Frio Plz	78046
E Frost St	
101-197	78040
199-1599	78040
1600-3599	78043
W Frost St	78040
Fuente Ln	78046
Gage Loop	78046
Galardon Dr	78045
Gale Ct & St	78041
Galisteo Dr	78045
Gallagher Ave	78041
Galveston St	
100-1599	78040
1600-3699	78043
Game Creek Blvd	78045
Gandara Dr	78043
Ganges Ct	78046
Garcia St	78040
Garden St	78040
Gardenia Ct	78041
Garfield St	
100-1599	78040
1600-3400	78043
3402-3498	78043
Garland	78045
Garnet Dr	78045
Garza St	78040
Garza Jones Ln	78045
Gates St	
1400-1599	78040
1600-1899	78043
Gaucho Ln	78045
Gavin Rd	78045
Geiberger	78045
General Franco	78046
General Milton	78045
Gentlewind Ct	78045
George Ln	78046

George Read Dr 78046
Georgia St 78041
Geronimo Dr & Loop 78041
Gilbert Rd 78041
Gilberto St 78041
Gilman 78046
Girasol Ct 78043
Glacier Ct 78045
Gladiola Ln 78046
Glen Ln 78045
Glenwood Dr 78045
Goldeneye Ct 78045
Goldfinch St 78045
E Gomez 78043
Gonzalez Ct & St 78040
Graceland Dr 78045
Granada Cir & Dr 78041
Granados St 78045
Grand Central Blvd 78045
Grande Bay 78041
Grant St 78040
Gravas St 78046
Graywood Ct 78045
Great Salt Lk 78041
Green St
1300-1500 78040
1502-1598 78040
1600-3100 78043
3102-3298 78043
Green Jay Ln 78045
Green Meadow Dr 78041
Greenway Ln 78041
Grenville Rd 78045
Grey Fox Cir 78045
Grisell Dr 78041
Grosbeak St 78045
Grove Ave 78045
Guadalajara 78046
Guadalupe St
1-97 78040
99-1599 78040
1600-3700 78043
3702-3798 78043
Guanajuato 78045
Guatemozin St
200-1599 78040
1600-3299 78043
Guaymas Ave 78046
Guerra Dr 78045
Guerrero St 78043
E Guerrero St 78040
W Guerrero St 78040
Gumwood Ln 78041
Gust St 78041
Gustavus St 78043
E Gustavus St 78040
W Gustavus St 78040
Gutierrez Rd 78043
Hachar Ln 78046
Hackberry Ct 78041
Hagen Loop 78045
Hall St 78046
Hallmark Dr 78045
Hampton Ct 78041
Hancock Ct 78046
Harcourt St 78045
Harding Ave 78043
Harlan St 78045
Harrison Ct 78045
Harvard St 78045
Havana 78045
Hawaii Cir 78041
Hawk Ridge Ct 78045
Hawthorne Ln 78041
Haynes Ave 78041
Hayter Rd 78045
Hazelnut Ct 78046
Headen Ave 78040
Heashold St 78046
Hemingway Loop 78041
Hemlock Dr 78041
Hendricks Ave
200-498 78040
500-3600 78040
3602-3698 78040
3800-4599 78041

Heritage Ct 78043
Hermosillo Dr 78046
Hernandez 78046
Herradura Ct 78045
Hewes Ave 78046
Hibiscus Cir & Ln 78041
Hickory Ln 78041
Hidalgo St 78040
Hidden Ln 78041
High Creek Dr 78045
High Ridge Cir 78045
Highland Dr 78045
Hillcrest Cir 78045
Hillplace Dr 78045
E & W Hillside Rd 78041
Hilltop Rd 78045
Hogan Ct 78045
Holguin 78046
E & W Holly Ct 78041
Homer Dr 78041
Honeysuckle Ct 78041
Hopi Dr 78045
Horinest Ave 78041
Horizon Cir & Loop 78046
Hornet Rd 78045
Hortensia Ln 78046
Hospitality Dr 78045
Houston St 78040
Huber St 78045
Huisache Dr 78041
Huisaches Rd 78045
Hunters View Cir 78045
Hutch Ct 78041
W Ibarra St 78043
Idaho Cir & St 78041
Idylwood Ln 78045
Illinois St 78041
Imperial Dr 78045
Import Rd 78045
Independence Dr 78043
N India Ave 78043
S India Ave
401-497 78043
499-999 78043
1001-1499 78043
1600-1898 78046
1900-2599 78046
Indian River Ave 78045
Indiana St 78041
Industrial Blvd 78041
Industry Ave 78045
Interamerica Blvd 78045
International Blvd 78045
N Interstate 35 78045
Inverness Rd 78041
Investment Ave 78045
Invierno Ln 78046
Inwood Rd 78045
Iowa Cir 78041
Irapuato Dr 78046
Ireland St 78046
Iris St 78045
Irwin 78045
Island 78041
Iturbide St 78040
Ivana Ct 78045
Ixtapa Dr 78046
J E F Dr 78045
J.D.Salinger Dr 78041
Jacales Ct 78045
Jacaman Rd 78041
Jacaranda Ct 78041
Jacent Ct 78045
Jackson Cv 78045
Jackson St 78040
Jade St 78045
Jaen Ct 78046
Jaime St 78041
Jaime Zapata Memorial Hwy 78043
Jalapa St 78046
James Ct 78045
James Smith 78046
Jara Dr 78041
N Jarvis Ave
300-3099 78043

3101-3599 78043
4000-4008 78041
4010-4099 78041
4101-4299 78041
S Jarvis Ave
800-1198 78043
1800-1898 78046
1900-3599 78046
Jasmine Ct 78041
Jazmin Dr 78043
Jean St 78046
Jefferies Ln 78045
Jefferson St 78040
Jemez Loop 78046
Jennifer Loop 78045
Jerry Loop 78045
Jessica Ln 78045
Jimenez 78046
Jj Jorge St 78041
John Adams 78046
John Steinbeck Ct 78041
Johnson Dr 78046
Jones Dr 78045
Jordan Dr 78041
Josefina 78041
Juarez Ave
200-3499 78040
3500-4599 78041
4601-4699 78041
Junction Dr 78041
Juniper Ln 78041
Justice Dr 78045
Justo Penn St 78041
Kahlo Loop 78045
Kansas St 78041
Karen 78046
Katiana Dr 78046
Katy Gustavo St 78041
Kay Bailey Rd 78043
E Kearney St
100-1499 78040
1600-3299 78043
W Kearney St 78040
Kennedy Loop 78046
Kentucky St 78041
Key Ave 78041
Kickapoo Dr 78045
Killam Industrial Blvd 78045
Kimberly Dr 78045
King Ln 78045
King Arthurs Ct 78041
King Palm Dr 78045
Kings Cir 78041
Kingston Ln 78043
Kingwood Dr 78045
Kirby Dr 78045
Kite Dr 78045
Knoll Ave 78045
Krone Ln 78041
La Brea Ln 78046
La Cienega Ln 78046
La Herradura Ct 78045
La Joya Ln 78046
La Parra 78046
La Pita Mangana Rd 78046
La Plaza Loop 78041
Lacho Ln 78041
Lady Di Loop 78045
Lafayette St 78041
Lago Del Valle Dr 78046
Lagos Ave 78045
Laguna Del Mar Ct 78041
Lake Carnegie Ct 78041
Lake Chapala Dr 78041
Lake Clark 78041
Lake Como Rd 78041
Lake Geneva Dr 78041
Lake Kariba 78041
Lake Louise Ct 78041
Lake Lugano Rd 78041
Lake Maracaibo Rd 78041
Lake Morraine Loop 78041
Lake Nakuru 78041
Lake Odessa Rd 78041
Lake Powell 78041
Lake Superior Rd 78041

Lake Victoria 78041
Lakeview Blvd 78041
Lakota St 78043
Lamar Dr 78046
N Lamar Dr 78045
Lamrick Cir 78046
Lancer 78041
Lane St 78043
E Lane St 78040
W Lane St 78040
Lantana Dr 78045
Lapis Ln 78045
Lara 78046
Larch Pl 78041
Laredo St
100-1599 78040
1600-3799 78043
Larga Vista Dr 78043
Lariat Loop 78041
Larry Ln 78045
Las Cruces Dr 78045
Las Cuatas St 78041
Las Tiendas Rd 78045
Lasso Ln 78045
Latour Ct 78041
Laura Ct 78040
Laurel Ct 78041
Laurel Dr 78045
Lauren Ln 78045
Leal St 78041
Lee Ave
1600-2199 78040
2201-3299 78040
3501-3599 78041
Lemonwood Dr 78045
Leon Ave 78046
Leonard Ct 78045
Leopoldo Dr 78043
Lexington Ave
700-3500 78040
3502-3798 78040
3800-4099 78041
Liberty Loop 78045
Ligarde St 78043
Lilac Pl 78041
Lily Ln 78046
Lima Loop 78045
Linares Cir 78045
Lincoln St 78040
Linden Ct & Ln 78041
Lindenwood Dr 78045
S Lindenwood Dr 78041
Linvistona Dr 78045
Lipan Dr 78045
Lirios Dr 78046
Little Foot Dr 78045
Little Oak Ln 78043
Littler Ct 78045
Live Oak Ave 78045
Llano 78046
Lobo Loop 78045
E Locust St
300-1099 78040
1101-1399 78040
2200-3299 78043
W Locust St 78040
Logan Ave
301-397 78040
399-3700 78040
3702-3798 78040
3800-4299 78041
Logistics 78045
Lois Ln 78045
Loma Vista Dr 78046
Lomas Del Sur 78046
Longfellow Ct 78041
Longhorn Dr 78045
Longoria Loop 78041
Longshadow Rd 78041
Longspur Ct 78045
Loop 20 78043
Lope De Vega 78046
Lopez 78046
Loreto Dr 78045
Loring Ave 78041
N Loring Ave 78040

S Loring Ave 78040
Loring Cir 78040
Los Altos Dr 78043
Los Botinas Ln 78045
Los Cedros Ln 78046
Los Cerezos 78046
Los Ebanos Dr 78041
Los Fresnos Loop 78046
Los Huisaches Rd 78045
Los Laureles 78046
Los Martinez Dr 78041
Los Minerales Anex Rd 78045
Los Nietos 78043
Los Olivos Ln 78046
Los Pinos 78046
Los Presidentes Ave 78046
Los Reyes Ct 78041
Los Suenos Ct 78045
N & S Lost Creek Loop 78046
Lost Hills Trl 78041
Lost Oak Rd 78041
N Louisiana Ave 78043
S Louisiana Ave
101-197 78043
199-1499 78043
1500-3599 78046
Lourdes Dr 78045
Loverde Ln 78046
Lowry Rd 78045
S Lucy 78046
Lugo Dr 78046
Luka Ln 78046
Lyla Ct 78046
Lyles Loop 78045
Lyman Hall Dr 78046
Lynn Loop 78045
E Lyon St
100-1500 78040
1502-1598 78040
1600-3699 78043
W Lyon St 78040
Madera Ave 78046
Madero Ave 78043
Madison St 78040
Madrid Dr 78043
Magnolia Ln 78041
Magnum Rd 78043
Maguey Dr 78041
Mahara Dr 78045
Maher Ave 78041
Mahin Dr 78045
Mahogany Ct
1401-1499 78041
8400-8599 78045
Maida Ln 78046
Main Ave
200-298 78040
300-3400 78040
3402-3498 78040
3500-3698 78041
3700-4199 78041
S Main Ave 78040
Majestic Palm Dr 78045
Malaga Dr 78046
N Malinche Ave 78043
S Malinche Ave
100-798 78043
800-1400 78043
1402-1498 78043
1500-3599 78046
Mall Del Norte Dr 78041
Mallard Loop 78045
Mallorca Dr 78046
Manchester Loop 78045
Mangana Hein Rd 78046
Mangrum Ct 78045
E & W Mann Cir & Rd 78041
Manor Pl & Rd 78041
Mante Dr 78046
Manzanares Dr 78045
Manzanillo St 78046
W Maple Cir & Loop 78041
Maquila Loop 78045
Marbella Ct 78046

Marble Falls St 78046
Marcella Ave
600-3799 78040
3800-3899 78041
4000-5300 78041
5302-5498 78041
Marcy Loop 78046
Marfa Rd 78045
Margarita Ln 78046
E & W Maria Elena St 78043
Maria Luisa Dr 78043
Marigold Cir 78046
Marina Ct 78046
Marion St
1300-1599 78040
1600-2699 78043
Mark Twain Dr 78041
Market St
100-198 78040
200-1599 78040
1600-3399 78043
Markley Ln 78041
Marla Dr 78046
Marsh Ln 78045
Marshall St 78045
Martens Ct & Rd 78041
Martha Dr 78046
N Martin Ave 78043
S Martin Ave 78046
Martingale 78041
Martinique Dr 78045
Maryland Ave
501-997 78040
999-3699 78040
3701-3799 78040
3800-4300 78041
4302-4698 78041
W Mason Rd 78041
Masterson Rd 78046
Matamoros St
100-1299 78040
1300-2298 78040
1300-1300 78042
1301-2299 78040
Mauricio St 78041
Mauser Ln 78043
Maya Rd 78041
E & W Mayberry St 78041
Mayfair Dr 78045
Mazatlan St 78046
Mccallister 78045
Mcclelland Ave
400-3799 78040
3800-4599 78041
Mcdonald St 78043
Mcdonell Ave
2000-3699 78040
3800-4299 78041
4301-4399 78041
Mcpherson Ave
1-397 78040
399-3100 78040
3102-3798 78040
3801-3805 78041
3807-4399 78041
Mcpherson Dr 78041
Mcpherson Rd
4400-7699 78041
7700-11200 78045
11202-11298 78045
N Meadow Ave
101-197 78040
199-3200 78040
3202-3298 78040
3900-4498 78041
S Meadow Ave 78040
S Meadow St
1100-1399 78043
1401-1499 78043
1500-2000 78046
2002-2198 78046
Meaghan Ct 78046
Medical Loop 78045
Medina 78046
Medio Ct 78046
Mehlhorn Loop 78045
E & W Meir 78043

Melinda Ln 78045
Melville Loop 78041
N & S Mendiola Ave 78043
E Mendoza St 78043
Menta Dr 78046
Mercado Ln 78043
Mercer St
1300-1398 78040
1401-1599 78040
1601-1697 78043
1699-3199 78043
Mercury Dr 78045
Mercury Mine Rd 78045
Merida Dr 78046
N Merida Dr 78043
Merlin Dr 78043
Merlin Rd 78041
Merrimack Loop 78046
Mescalero Dr 78045
Mesquite Ln 78041
Metro Ct 78041
Metropolitan Rd 78045
Mexico Ave 78046
Michigan Ave 78045
Michoacan Loop 78045
Mickelson 78045
Middlecoff Ln 78045
Middlestone Dr 78045
Midland 78045
Mier St
100-1599 78040
1600-3799 78043
Milagro 78043
Milford Ct 78043
Milk St 78043
N Milmo Ave 78043
S Milmo Ave
600-898 78043
900-1499 78043
1600-3599 78046
Milo Rd 78045
Milton Ct 78041
Mims Ave 78041
Mina Verde Rd 78046
Minerales Anex Rd 78045
Mines Rd 78045
Minutemen Dr 78046
Miraflores Ct 78045
Mirasol Dr 78043
Misty Wood Ave 78045
Mize Dr 78045
Mockingbird Ct 78045
Moctezuma St 78040
Modern Ln 78041
Mohawk Dr 78045
Mohican Dr 78045
Molly 78045
Monaco Blvd 78045
Monaguillo Dr 78043
Monarch Dr 78045
Moncayo Rd 78043
Monclova Dr 78046
Montana St 78041
Monterrey Ave
900-998 78040
1000-3699 78040
3800-4400 78041
4402-4498 78041
Monterrey Loop 78041
Monterrey St 78046
Montes 78046
E Montgomery St
100-198 78040
200-1099 78040
2100-3299 78043
W Montgomery St 78040
Monticello Ave 78046
Montjac Deer Ct 78045
Montoya Dr 78045
Montserrat Ct 78046
Montura Rd 78045
Moon Dance Ct 78045
Moon Tract Ln 78046
Moonstone 78046
Morada Ct 78045
Morales 78046

Morelia Ave 78046
Morelos Dr 78046
N Moreno Ave 78043
S Moreno St 78046
Mountain Crk 78045
Mourning Dove Ct 78045
Mulberry Cir 78041
Mule Deer Ct 78045
Muller Blvd 78045
Muller Rd 78041
Munoz St 78045
Murcia Dr 78046
Musgo Dr 78046
Musket Dr 78046
Musser St
401-697 78040
699-1499 78040
1501-1599 78040
1600-3199 78043
3201-3299 78043
E Musser St 78040
W Musser St 78040
Mustang Island Dr 78045
Nacogdoches Rd 78043
Nafta Blvd 78045
Napoleon St 78043
Natalia Dr 78045
Nautla Dr 78046
Navajo Ln 78045
Navarra Cir 78043
Nayarit 78046
Nebraska St 78041
Neches Ave 78046
Nelson Ct 78045
Nevada Cir 78041
Nevera Loop 78043
Nevers Ct 78045
New Castle Dr 78045
New River Dr 78045
N New York Ave 78043
S New York Ave
501-597 78043
599-1199 78043
1201-1499 78043
1600-1798 78046
1800-3500 78046
3502-3598 78046
Newport Ave 78043
Nicholas Ln 78046
Nicklaus Loop N 78045
Niebla Dr 78046
Nightingale Bnd 78045
Nile Ct 78046
Nispola Dr 78046
Nixon Dr 78046
Noel Ln 78045
Nogal Ln 78046
Nogalitos Ln 78046
Nopal Dr 78046
Norman Dr 78045
North Ave 78045
Northcreek Dr 78041
Northcrest Dr 78045
Northgate Ln 78041
Northpoint Dr 78041
Northridge Loop 78045
Northstar Dr 78045
Northview Dr 78041
Northwood Dr 78041
Norton St 78046
Norwich Loop 78045
Nottingham Dr 78043
Nubes 78046
Nueces Plz 78046
Nuevo Leon Dr 78045
Nye Dr 78041
O Henry Dr 78041
Oak Cir 78041
Oakeneri Ave 78040
Oakmont Loop 78045
Oakridge Loop 78045
Obsidian 78046
Ocampo Dr 78046
Ocean Dr 78043
Ohio Cir 78041
Oil Patch Rd 78043

Okane St
100-1599 78040
1600-1698 78043
1700-3400 78043
3402-3498 78043
Oklahoma St 78041
Old Milwaukee Rd 78043
Old Santa Maria Rd 78041
Old Spanish Trl 78046
Oleander St 78046
E & W Olive St 78041
Olmos Dr 78046
Olympia Bay 78041
Omeara Cir 78045
Ontario Loop 78045
Onyx Dr 78046
Opal 78046
Orange Blossom Dr &
Loop 78045
Orchard Ct 78045
Oregon Cir 78041
Orense Ct 78046
Organo Blvd 78046
Orilla Ave 78041
Oriole Ave & Ln 78045
Orleans Loop 78045
Orquidia Ln 78046
Ortiz St 78041
Otanes Ave 78046
Otono Ln 78046
Ovenbird Thicket Dr 78045
Owk Dr 78043
Ozark Dr 78045
Pace St 78041
Padre Island Ct 78045
Palacio Dr 78045
Palafox Dr 78045
Palencia Ave 78046
Palestine Dr 78046
Palm Ave & Cir 78041
Palmer Dr 78045
Palmito Dr 78046
Palo Alto Ln 78046
Palo Blanco St 78046
Paloma Ct & Ln 78041
Palomino Rd 78045
Pamplona Loop 78046
Pan American Blvd 78045
Papalote Rd 78045
Pappas St 78041
Paradise Dr 78046
W Paredes St 78043
Pargo Dr 78043
Park St 78040
Parrera 78043
Partridge Loop 78045
Parula Place Ct 78045
Paseo De Danubio 78046
Paseo De Neva 78046
Paseo De Tiber 78046
Paso De Jacinto Loop 78045
Pasto Ct 78046
Patio Ct & Ln 78041
Patol St 78043
Patricia Ln 78046
Patrick Henry Dr 78046
Patriot Dr 78046
Patron Loop 78045
Paul Revere Dr 78046
Pavin Dr 78045
Pawnee Ct 78043
Paz Ln 78046
Peaceful Meadows Ct 78041
E & W Peach Ln 78041
Peach Tree Ln 78041
Peak Dr 78041
Peanut Cir 78046
Pearl Stone 78046
Pearson Moss Ln 78045
Pebble Trl 78045
Pecan St 78046
Pecan Circle Dr 78043
Pecos Plz 78046
Pedrito Ct 78046
Pedrosa St 78045
Pellegrino Ct 78045

Pena Dr 78046
Peoples Blvd 78045
Perez Ct 78045
Pericles Ln 78046
Persimmon Ct 78045
Peruviana Ct 78045
Peyramale Ct 78045
Pheasant St 78045
Phelps Rd 78045
Philadelphia St 78041
Phoenix Palm Dr 78045
Picard Dr 78045
Pico Rd 78045
Piedmont 78045
Piedra China St
3201B-3299B 78043
1300-1599 78040
1600-2599 78043
2601-3299 78043
Pierce St 78041
Pin Oak St 78043
Pinder Ave
1200-3400 78040
3402-3498 78040
3500-3598 78041
3600-3999 78041
Pindo Dr 78045
Pine St 78046
Pine Sisken St 78045
Pinecrest Cir 78041
Pinos Cir 78043
Pintail St 78045
Pinto Valle 78045
Pinzon Rd 78043
Pipit Pass Dr 78045
Pirul Ct 78046
Pistachio Ct 78046
Pita Dr 78041
Pitaya Dr 78046
Placita Dr 78045
Plantation East Dr 78045
Players Ct 78045
Plaza Ln 78043
E Plum St
201-297 78040
299-1399 78040
1401-1499 78040
1600-3299 78043
W Plum St 78040
Plumas Dr 78045
Plymouth Ln 78041
Poggenpohl St 78040
Poinsetta Dr 78041
Polaris Dr 78041
Pomian Ct 78045
Ponderosa Dr & Pl 78041
Pontevedra Ct 78046
Poplar Ln 78041
Porfirio Dr 78045
Port Dr 78045
Port Bolivar Dr 78045
Port Edward Dr 78045
Port Isabel Dr 78045
Port Lavaca St 78045
Port Miami St 78045
Port San Angelo Dr 78045
Portland St 78045
Portugal 78046
Post Oak Dr 78041
Potomac Ct & Loop 78046
Potranca Ct 78045
Potrero Ct 78045
Poza Rica Dr 78046
Prada Machin Dr 78046
Prancer Rd 78045
Presa Ln 78046
Prescott Loop 78046
Preston Dr 78045
Price Cts 78043
E Price St
100-1599 78040
1600-3299 78043
W Price St 78040
Primavera Ln 78046
Primrose Ln 78041
Princeton St 78045

Proctor Ct 78046
Puerto Alegre 78045
Puerto Amarante 78045
Puerto Angel 78045
Puerto Belo 78045
Puerto Escondido 78045
Puerto Isabel 78045
Puerto Marques 78045
Puerto Vallarta 78045
Puerto Viejo 78045
Puerto Yael 78045
Puig Dr 78045
Purtzer Dr 78045
Puscas Ct 78046
Quadrangle Cir 78041
Quail Ct 78041
Quail Creek Rd 78045
Quail Hollow Loop 78045
Queen Palm Dr 78045
Queens Ct 78045
Queretaro Loop 78046
Quintana Dr 78045
Quintero St 78045
Quito Loop 78045
Quivira Dr 78045
R W Emerson Loop 78041
Raes Creek Dr 78045
Rains 78043
Ramirez Dr 78043
Ranch Rd
100-199 78043
300-699 78045
Ranch Road 6073a 78046
Ranch Road 6073c 78046
Ranch Road 6078a 78041
Ranch Road 6078b 78041
Ranch Road 6086c 78043
Ranch Road 6086d 78043
Ranch Road 6086f 78043
Ranch Road 6086h 78043
Ranch Road 6086j 78043
Ranch Road 6086k 78043
Ranch Road 6176a
Rd 78045
Ranch Road 6176b 78045
Ranch Road 6250b
Rd 78045
Ranch Road 7006b 78043
Ranch Road 7008d 78043
Rancho Grande 78043
Rancho Nopal Rd 78045
Rancho Penitas Rd 78045
Rancho Pila Rd 78045
Rancho Viejo Dr 78045
Ranchway Dr 78045
Rasoul Dr 78045
Reagan Dr 78046
Real Ct 78045
Rebecca Ct 78040
Red Cloud Cir & Dr 78045
Red Fish 78043
Red Oak Cir 78045
Red River Ave 78046
Redford Dr 78045
Redwing Ct 78045
W Redwood Cir 78041
Regal Dr 78041
Regional Dr 78045
Remington Rd 78043
Remuda Ln 78045
Reposado Dr 78045
Reserve Dr 78045
Resource 78045
Retama Dr 78041
Revilla Dr 78045
Revolution Rd 78046
Reyes 78046
Reynolds St
100-1500 78040
1502-1598 78040
1600-3299 78043
Reynosa Cir 78045
Rhine Falls Ct 78041
Rhonda Dr 78041
Rhone Ln 78041
N Riata Rd 78043

Richard Ln 78046
Richard Raymond 78046
Richmond Ct 78045
Richter Dr 78040
Riddle 78046
Ridge Rd 78041
Ridgemore Ln 78041
Rienda Dr 78045
Rio Amur 78046
Rio Bravo Dr 78041
Rio Grande Dr 78041
Rio Hudson 78046
Rio Morava 78046
Rio Nilo 78046
Rio Norte Cir & Ln 78041
Rio Plata 78046
Rio Rojo 78046
Rio Sena 78046
Rio Sur Cir & Ln 78041
Rio Tamesis 78046
Rio Vista Dr 78041
Rio Volga 78046
Rita 78046
River Bend Cir 78045
River Front St 78046
River Lake Dr 78046
Rivera Way 78043
Riverbank Dr 78045
Riverhill Dr & Loop 78046
Riverside Dr 78041
Riverview 78046
Roadrunner 78045
Rob Brogan Ct 78041
Robert Ln 78046
Robert Frost 78041
Robles Ln 78046
Rocio Dr 78041
Rock Creek Cir 78041
Rock Port Rd 78045
Rock Springs Cir 78045
Rocky Ledge Loop 78041
Rodeo Ln 78046
Rodriguez 78046
Rolling Hills Dr 78045
Roosevelt Ave 78043
Roosevelt St 78040
Roque Loop 78046
Rosa 78043
Rosalba 78043
Rosales 78046
Rosales Ct 78041
Rosario St
100-498 78040
500-1599 78040
1600-3299 78043
Rosco 78045
Rosewood Dr 78041
Rosie Ct 78040
Ross St 78043
Rosson Ln 78041
Rotary Dr 78043
Rothchild Dr 78041
Royal Oaks St 78043
Royal Palm 78045
Royale Cir 78041
Rubio Rd 78043
Ruby Rd 78043
Ruger Dr 78043
Ruhlman Dr 78045
Running Doe St 78045
Rutledge Dr 78046
E & W Ryan St 78041
Sabal Loop 78045
Sabine Plz 78046
S Sacred Heart Dr 78046
Saenz 78043
Sage Dr 78041
Sagebrush Cir 78041
Sago Dr 78045
Saguero Ln 78043
Saint Charles Loop 78046
Saint Croix Dr 78045
Saint David 78046
Saint Gerard Ln 78046
Saint Hunna Ct 78046
Saint Iada St 78046

Saint Isaac Loop 78046
Saint James Dr 78041
Saint John Loop 78045
Saint Jude Dr 78041
Saint Julia Ct 78046
Saint Julien Dr 78041
Saint Kathryn Loop 78046
Saint Luke 78046
Saint Margaret Ln 78046
Saint Michael Dr 78045
Saint Patrick Dr 78045
Saint Pierre Ln 78045
Saint Pius Ln 78046
Saint Sylvia Loop 78046
Saint Thomas Ct & Dr 78045
Saint Veran Ct 78041
Sako Ct 78043
Salado Dr 78045
Salamanca Ave 78046
Saldana Ave 78041
Salem Dr 78045
Salinas Ave
100-3499 78040
3500-4599 78041
Saltillo St 78046
Salvia 78043
Sam Bratton 78046
Samlon Cir, Ct & Dr 78041
San Agustin Ave
300-398 78040
400-3499 78040
3500-4000 78041
4002-4498 78041
San Bernardo Ave
200-298 78040
300-3499 78040
3500-5000 78041
5002-7198 78041
E & W San Carlos St 78041
San Dario Ave
7001A-7099A 78041
801-3499 78040
3501-4197 78041
4199-7099 78041
7101-8997 78045
8999-9299 78045
9206-1-9206-5 78045
San Eduardo Ave
500-3499 78040
3500-4099 78041
4101-4699 78041
San Enrique Ave 78040
San Eugenio Ave 78040
San Felipe Ln 78046
San Francisco Ave
100-3499 78040
3500-3798 78041
3501-3699 78040
3800-5200 78041
5202-5298 78041
San Gabriel Dr 78045
San Ignacio Ave
900-1398 78040
1400-3200 78040
3202-3398 78040
3600-3999 78041
San Isidro Pkwy 78045
San Jacinto 78046
San Jorge Ave 78040
E San Jose St
100-198 78040
200-1100 78040
1102-1198 78040
2100-3099 78043
3101-3299 78043
W San Jose St 78040
San Juan Rd 78045
San Leonardo Ave 78040
San Lorenzo Dr 78045
San Luis St 78046
San Mateo Dr 78045
San Miguel Dr 78046
San Nicolas Dr 78046
San Pablo Ave 78040
E & W San Pedro St 78041
San Rafael Ln 78046
San Rio Blvd 78046

San Salvador St 78046
Sanchez St 78040
Sand Creek Ct 78043
Sand Dollar Ct 78041
Sandcliff 78045
Sanderania 78045
Sanders Ave
701-997 78040
999-3799 78040
3800-4499 78041
Sanders Cir 78041
Sandhill 78045
Sandia Ct 78045
Sandman St 78041
Sandpiper Ln 78045
Sandtrap Cir 78041
Sandy Cv & Ln 78045
Santa Anita Loop 78046
Santa Barbara St
2000-2098 78043
2100-3299 78043
3300-3599 78046
Santa Clara St 78046
Santa Claudia 78043
Santa Cleotilde Ave
400-3499 78040
3500-4199 78041
4201-4399 78041
Santa Inez Ln 78046
Santa Isabel Ave
100-198 78040
200-2400 78040
2402-2498 78040
3600-4499 78041
Santa Maria Ave
7101B-7101B 78041
400-898 78040
900-3499 78040
3500-6000 78041
6002-7398 78041
Santa Martha Blvd 78046
Santa Rita Ave
2-98 78040
100-2199 78040
2201-3299 78040
3500-3698 78041
3700-4399 78041
4401-4499 78041
Santa Rosa Dr 78046
Santa Ursula Ave
800-3098 78040
3100-3200 78040
3202-3498 78040
3500-4498 78041
Santander Dr 78046
Santiago Loop 78045
Santo Tomas St 78045
Sao Paulo Dr 78045
Sapphire St 78045
Sara Rd 78045
Sarazen Ct 78045
E Saunders St
100-2399 78041
2401-7299 78041
2700-2700 78044
2700-7298 78041
W Saunders St 78041
Savannah Loop 78046
Savitee Dr 78045
Scissor Trail Cir 78045
Scott St 78040
Segovia Dr 78046
Seminole Cir 78045
Sendero Ct 78045
Senegal Palm Dr 78045
Sepulveda Ln 78046
Sequin Ct 78045
Sequoia Ln 78041
Serene Dr 78045
Sereno 78046
Sergio St 78041
Serrano 78043
Sesame Ln 78045
Severita Ln 78046
Sevilla Loop 78043
N Seymour Ave
200-2600 78040

2602-3098 78040
3900-4499 78041
S Seymour Ave 78040
Seymour Cir 78040
Shahram Dr 78045
Shalom Cir 78045
Shama Cir 78045
Shark Bay 78041
Shasta Dr 78043
Shea St 78040
Sheffield St 78043
Sherman St 78040
Sherwood Dr 78045
Shiloh Dr 78045
Shoke Port St 78045
Sierra Vista Blvd 78046
Sika Deer Ct 78045
Silhouette Dr 78045
Siller Loop 78045
Silver Mine Rd 78045
Silver Palm Dr 78045
Silverwood Dr 78045
Sinaloa Dr 78046
Sinatra Dr 78041
Singh Ct 78045
Sitting Bull 78043
Slowriver Ct 78046
N Smith Ave 78043
S Smith Ave
400-1500 78043
1502-1598 78043
1600-1698 78046
1700-1800 78046
1802-2298 78046
Snake Dr 78045
Snead Ct 78045
Snow Falls Dr 78045
Socrates Ln 78046
Sofia 78046
Soledad Loop 78043
Solis 78046
Somerville St 78046
Songbird Ln 78045
Sonoma Ct 78045
Soria Dr 78046
Soubirous Rd 78045
Southern Oaks Loop 78045
Southlake Dr 78043
Spanish Dagger Dr 78043
Sparks Ct 78045
Spindrift Dr 78045
Spivey Dr 78045
Spring Creek Dr 78045
Spring Valley Cir 78045
Springfield Ave
1201-1397 78040
1399-3799 78040
3800-7400 78041
7402-8098 78041
8400-8498 78045
Spruce Ln 78041
Stadler Ct 78045
Stamford St 78043
Stapelia St 78043
Star Ct 78041
Starla Ct 78045
Starling Creek Loop 78045
Starmount 78045
State Highway 359 78043
Sterling Loop 78045
E Stewart St
100-1599 78040
1600-3299 78043
W Stewart St 78040
Stillmeadow Ct 78045
N Stone Ave
101-397 78040
399-2700 78040
2702-3098 78040
3900-4499 78041
S Stone Ave 78040
Stone Field Ln 78045
Stratford Ln 78041
Sudadero Rd 78045
Sulfur Mine Cir & Rd 78045
Summerwind Blvd 78041

Summit Dr 78045
Sun Dance Loop 78045
Sun Ray Loop 78041
Sunberry Ct 78045
Suncrest Ct 78045
Sunflower Ave 78046
Sunridge Loop 78041
Sunrise Cts 78046
Sunset Dr 78041
Sunset Loop 78046
Sunset Acres Rd 78045
Sunshine Dr 78046
Suntan Ct 78041
Superior Dr 78045
Surrey Rd 78041
Susie Dr 78046
Sutton Ct 78045
Sweden Ln 78045
Sweetwind Dr 78045
Swift Dr 78041
E & W Sycamore Ln & St 78041
Sylvia 78046
T.S. Eliot Dr 78041
Tabasco Dr 78046
Tacuba St 78041
Taft Ct 78046
Taiga Ct 78045
Tamarack Loop 78045
Tamayo Ct 78046
Tanquecitos Rd 78045
N & S Tapeyste Ave 78043
Tara Loop 78045
Tarpon Ln 78043
Taylor St 78041
Tays 78046
Teak Dr 78041
Teakwood Ln 78041
Tejas Loop 78045
Temple 78043
Tempo St 78043
Tepic Dr 78046
Teresita Ln 78046
Teruel Ln 78046
Tesoro Ln & Plz 78041
N Texas Ave 78043
S Texas Ave
2901B-29099B 78046
1200-1499 78043
1600-1898 78046
1900-3599 78046
Texoma St 78046
Theisel Rd 78045
Thomas Ave 78041
Thurman St 78046
Tiara Trl 78045
Tiger Cts 78045
Tilden Ave
500-3799 78040
3800-3898 78041
3900-4599 78041
Timber Ln 78045
Tinaja St 78046
Tlaxcala Dr 78045
Toinette 78045
Toledo Dr 78043
Toluca St 78045
Tomcat Rd 78045
Topaz Ct & Trl 78045
Toribio Dr 78043
Toro Dr & Loop 78045
Torreon St 78046
Totem Pole 78043
Tournament Trail Dr 78041
Tours Ln 78045
Townlake Dr 78041
Trade Center Blvd 78045
Tradewind Cir 78041
Transportation Ave 78045
E Travis St
100-1199 78040
2100-3199 78043
3201-3299 78043
W Travis St 78040
Trent Dr 78046
Trevino Ct 78045

Trey Dr 78041
Trinity Ct 78045
Trinity Plz 78046
Trophy Dr 78045
Truchas 78045
Truman Ln 78046
Tucson Ln 78045
Tulane Dr 78045
Tulip Cir 78046
Tuna Rd 78046
Tundra Ave 78045
Twilight Dr 78045
Tyler 78043
Ugarte St 78041
Union Pacific Blvd 78045
Uniroyal Dr 78045
N & S Unitec Dr 78045
United Ave 78045
University Blvd 78041
Upper Falls Dr 78045
N Urbahn Ave 78043
S Urbahn Ave
100-1200 78043
1202-1298 78043
1501-3097 78046
3099-3499 78046
3501-3599 78046
Us Highway 59 78041
Us Highway 83 78046
Us Highway 83 N 78045
Utah Cir 78041
Valdez 78046
Valdosa 78043
Valencia Ave
2900-3198 78040
3200-3699 78040
3801-3897 78041
3899-4299 78041
Valeria Loop 78046
Valeriana Dr 78043
Valero Ct 78046
Valladolid Ave 78046
Valley View Cir 78045
Valnera Dr 78043
Vanesita 78046
Vaquero Ct 78045
Vaqueta Rd 78045
Vela 78046
Venado Ct 78045
Ventura St 78040
Veracruz Dr 78046
Verano Cts 78046
Vicente St 78046
Victor Hugo 78041
Victoria St 78040
Vidaurri Ave
1-3300 78040
3302-3398 78040
3500-4500 78041
4502-4598 78041
Vientos Rd 78046
Villa Ct & Dr 78045
Villa Hermosa Dr 78045
W Village Blvd 78041
Villastrigo St 78045
N Villaway Ave 78043
Vinewood Oak Ct 78046
Vineyard Loop 78045
Vintage Ln 78041
Violeta Ct 78041
Violette Dr 78043
S Vista 78046
Viviana Ct 78046
Volcan Dr 78046
Waco Ct 78046
Wadkins Dr 78045
Wagner Ct 78045
Walker 78041
E & W Walnut Cir & St 78041
Warehouse Ln 78041
Warren Ave 78046
Washington Dr 78045
Washington St 78040
Washingtonia Dr 78045
Wastralm Dr 78045

Water St 78040
Watson Ct 78045
Watson Lake Dr 78041
Waxwing Cedar Dr 78045
Weathers Dr 78045
Weatherwood Rd 78041
Webb Rd 78045
Wedgewood Dr 78041
Weeping Willow St 78043
Weiskopf Ct 78045
Welby Ct 78041
Welch Rd 78043
Well Ln 78045
West Dr 78041
Westchester 78043
Westgate Cir, Ct & Dr 78041
Westham 78045
Westmont Dr 78041
Westside Ln 78041
Whisper Hill Dr 78045
White Oak Ln 78041
White Rock Cir 78045
White Sands Dr 78046
White Tail Ln 78045
White Wing Loop 78045
Whitewood Dr 78045
Whitney Ave 78046
Widener Ln 78041
Wilcox 78043
Wild Flower Ave 78045
Wildcat 78043
Wildrose Cir & Ln 78041
Wildwood Cv & Ln 78041
Wilfrano Dr 78046
Wilhelm Ave 78040
Williams Ct 78045
Willow St
800-1599 78040
1600-2900 78043
2902-3298 78043
Willow Oak 78043
Wilson Ln 78046
Wilson Rd 78043
Wimberley Rd 78045
Winburn Dr 78045
Wincrest Cir 78045
Windfall Rd 78045
Windmill Rd 78045
Windmill Palm Dr 78045
Windrift Ln 78041
Windsor Ct & Rd 78041
Wingate Ct 78045
Wingfoot Loop 78045
Winrock Dr 78045
Winsome Ct 78045
Winwood 78045
Witherspoon Loop 78046
Wolf Creek Dr 78045
Woodland Cv & Dr 78045
Woodridge 78045
Woods 78041
Woodstone Ct 78045
Wooster St
1300-1599 78040
1600-2700 78043
2702-3098 78043
World Trade Center Loop 78045
Wren Pt 78045
Wright Way 78046
Wye Oak 78043
Wyndum Terrace Trl 78045
Wyoming St 78041
Yale St 78045
Yeary St 78041
Yellow Oak Ave 78045
Yellowstone Lake Dr 78041
Yorkshire St 78043
Yucatan Loop 78045
Yucca Dr 78041
Yukon Ln 78045
Zacatecas St 78046
Zamora Loop 78046
N Zapata Hwy 78043
S Zapata Hwy
100-198 78043

200-1299 78043
1300-5300 78046
5302-7898 78046
2702-1-2702-5 78046
Zaragoza St 78040
Zebra Dr 78045
Zoque Dr 78045
Zulema 78041
Zuni St 78046

LEAGUE CITY TX

General Delivery 77573

POST OFFICE BOXES MAIN OFFICE STATIONS AND BRANCHES

Box No.s
All PO Boxes 77574

NAMED STREETS

Abbey Ln 77573
Aberdeen Dr 77573
Abilene St 77573
Ableside Dr 77573
Acacia Ct & St 77573
Acorn Ct & St 77573
Admiral Dr 77573
Afton Ct 77573
Agave Dr 77573
Aggie Ln 77573
Alabama Ave 77573
Alaska Ave 77573
Aldersby Ln 77573
Alentina Ct 77573
Alessandria Ln 77573
Almond Pointe 77573
Altavilla Ln 77573
Amber Ln 77573
Anchor Way 77573
Anchor Point Ct 77573
Andover Hills Ct 77573
Apache Xing 77573
Apple Ln 77573
Apricot St 77573
Arbor Cir 77573
Arborwood Dr 77573
Arizona Ave 77573
Arkansas Ave 77573
Arlington Pointe Dr 77573
Ash Dr 77573
Ash Pointe 77573
Ashberry Ct 77573
Ashe Creek Dr 77573
Ashland Creek Ln 77573
Ashley Falls Ln 77573
Astoria Ln 77573
Attwater Way 77573
Auburn Creek Ln 77573
Auburn Sky Ct 77573
Audubon St 77573
Augusta Dr 77573
Aurelia Ln 77573
Austin St 77573
Austin Breeze Ln 77573
Autumn Ct 77573
Autumn Brook Ln 77573
Autumn Cove Dr 77573
Autumn Lake Dr 77573
Autumn Mist Ct & Ln 77573
Avery Hollow Ct 77573
Avondale St 77573
Azahar Ct 77573
Azalea Pointe 77573
Aztec Ct 77573
Balearic Island Ct 77573
Balsam Lake Ln 77573
Barbetta Ct 77573
Barcelona Way 77573
Barger St 77573

Barrington Pointe Ct & Dr 77573
Barton Ct 77573
Barton Falls Ct 77573
Barton Springs St 77573
Basswood Dr 77573
Bastrop Glen Ln 77573
Bataan Dr 77573
Bauer Ave 77573
W Bay Area Blvd 77573
Bay Haven Way 77573
Bay Hill Dr 77573
Bay Spring Dr 77573
Baycliff Ct 77573
Baycrest Dr 77573
Bayou Dr 77573
Bayou Bend Dr 77573
Bayou Cove Ln 77573
Bayport Ln 77573
Bayridge Dr 77573
Beacons Hollow Ln 77573
Beaumont St 77573
Bel Riposo Ln 77573
Belcara Vw 77573
Bella Luna Ln 77573
Benbrook Oaks Ln 77573
W Bend Dr 77573
Bend Cove Ct 77573
Bending Shore Ct 77573
Bending Stream Dr 77573
Bennigan St 77573
Bennington Ct 77573
Bent Creek Ln 77573
Bent Sail Ct & Ln 77573
Bent Tree Trl 77573
Bern St 77573
Berwick Ln 77573
Bianco Ln 77573
Big League Dreams Pkwy 77573
Birdsong Dr 77573
Biscayne Bend Ln 77573
Black Duck Dr 77573
Black Skimmer Ct 77573
Blackburn Ct 77573
Blooming Garden Ct 77573
Blossomwood Dr & Ln 77573
Blue Cypress Ln 77573
Boden St 77573
Bolgheri Ln 77573
Bonham Pines Ln 77573
Bonita Way 77573
Bonnie Bay Ct 77573
Booth Bay Ct 77573
Bounty Dr 77573
Boxelder Pointe Ct 77573
Bradford Ln 77573
Bradie Ct 77573
Brae Ln 77573
Brandy Branch Ct 77573
Brazos Ct 77573
Brazzo Ct 77573
Breckenridge Cove Ln 77573
Breezway Bend Ln 77573
Briarglen Dr 77573
Briarwood Ct 77573
Bridgewater Ln 77573
Bright Sail Cir 77573
N Bristol Ct 77573
Bristol Breeze Ln 77573
Brittany Colony Dr 77573
Brittany Lakes Dr 77573
Broad Bay Ct & Ln 77573
Broadmoor Ct & Dr 77573
Brook Haven Dr 77573
Brookdale Dr 77573
Brookstone Ln 77573
Brown Pelican Ln 77573
Bruce Ave 77573
Brunello St 77573
Brunswick Dr 77573
Brushill Ct 77573
Buffalo Springs Ln 77573
Bull Run Dr 77573
Bullhead Dr 77573
Bumblebee Ct 77573

Burgundy Ln 77573
Burham Ln 77573
Butler Rd 77573
Buttercup St 77573
Byron St 77573
Bywater Ct 77573
Cabot Lakes Dr 77573
Cadiz Ct 77573
Caine Hill Ct 77573
Calder Dr 77573
Calypso Ln 77573
Cambria Ct 77573
Cambridge Ct N & S 77573
Camellia Way 77573
Cameo Ct 77573
Cameron Ct 77573
Canary Cir 77573
Candlewood Dr 77573
Canonsburg 77573
Cantabria Ln 77573
Canterbury Dr 77573
Canyon Crest Dr 77573
Canyon Falls Ct 77573
Cape Coral Ct 77573
Capewood Dr 77573
Capri Ct 77573
Caravel Dr 77573
Cardinal Dr 77573
Carefree Cir & Dr 77573
Carina Ct 77573
Carlisle Ln 77573
Carlisle Park Cir 77573
Carmicheal Ct 77573
Carolina Ave 77573
Carolina Shores Ln 77573
Carrera Ct 77573
Casa Grande Dr 77573
Cascade View Ct 77573
Casciano Ct 77573
Castle Dr 77573
Castle Bay Dr 77573
Castle Beach Ct 77573
Castle Cove Ln 77573
Castle Creek Ct 77573
Castle Peak Ln 77573
Castlewind Ct 77573
Casual Ln 77573
Casual Shore Ct 77573
Catalonia Cv 77573
Catamaran Dr 77573
Catania Ln 77573
Cavalry Cir 77573
Cayman Bend Ln 77573
Cecina St 77573
Cedar Ave 77573
Cedar Branch Dr 77573
Cedar Creek Dr 77573
Cedar Fork Dr 77573
Cedar Lake Dr 77573
Cedar Point Dr 7757
Cedar Prairie Dr 77573
Ceole Cir & Ln 77573
Chalmette St 77573
Champions Ct 77573
Chancellorsville Ct 77573
Chapparal Xing 77573
Chariss Glen Dr 7757
Charter Pointe Ct 77573
Cherry Blossom Dr 77573
Cherry Hills Dr 77573
Cherrywood Ct 77573
Chesterfield Ln 77573
Chestnut Grv 77573
Chetwood Cir 7757
Chiara Ct 7757
Chickadee Dr 77573
Chinaberry Park Ln 7757
Cibola Rd 77573
Cinnabar Bay Ct & Dr 7757
Cintola Ln 77573
Civil Dr 77573
Claiborne Dr 77573
Claremont Crossing Dr 77573
Clear Creek Ave 7757
Clear Creek Mdws Dr 77573
Clearsky Ct 7757

Street	ZIP
Clearwood Ct & Dr	77573
Cliffmont Ln	77573
Cloudbridge Ct & Dr	77573
Clover Rdg	77573
Cloverdale Dr	77573
Coastal Ct	77573
Coburn St	77573
Cochise Trl	77573
Coffee Mill Ct	77573
Colchester Ln	77573
Coldwater Bridge Ln	77573
Coleman Boylan Dr	77573
Colonial Ct & Dr	77573
Colorado Ave	77573
Colton Way	77573
Columbia Cir	77573
S Compass Rose Blvd	77573
Concord Cir & Dr	77573
Concordia Ct	77573
Coneflower Rd	77573
Constellation Blvd	77573
N & S Cook Cir	77573
Coral Bay Dr	77573
Coral Cove Ct	77573
Coral Lilly Dr	77573
Coral Ridge Ct & Dr	77573
Cordoba Cv	77573
Cornell Ln	77573
Corniche St	77573
Coronado Way	77573
Coronado Lakes Dr	77573
Cortona Ct	77573
Coryell Ct & St	77573
Costa Brava Park	77573
Costa Mesa Cir	77573
Cottage Bay Ct	77573
Cottage Grove Ct	77573
Cottonwood Ct	77573
Cottonwood Creek Ln	77573
Country Ln & Pl	77573
Country Glen St	77573
Country Green St	77573
Countryaire St	77573
Countryside Dr	77573
County Park Dr	77573
Courageous Dr	77573
Courtland St & Vw	77573
Courtney Ln	77573
Courtside Dr	77573
Cranbrook Ln	77573
Crane Hawk Ln	77573
W Creek Dr	77573
Creek Bend Dr	77573
Creek Gate Dr	77573
Creekhaven Ct	77573
Creekside Ct, Dr & Ln	77573
Creekview St	77573
Crescent Bay Ct & Dr	77573
Crescent Coral Dr	77573
Crescent Pointe Dr	77573
Crescent Shore Dr	77573
Crimson Bay Dr	77573
Crimson Coast Ct & Dr	77573
Crimson Cove Ct	77573
Crimson Lake Ln	77573
Cross Bay Ct	77573
Cross Creek Ct & Ln	77573
Cross Spring Ln	77573
Crossbrook Ct	77573
Crows Nest Dr	77573
Crystal St	77573
Crystal Bay Ln	77573
Crystal Cascade Ln	77573
Crystal Reef Dr	77573
Cumberland Dr	77573
Cumberland Ridge Ct & Ln	77573
Custer Dr	77573
Cutter Dr	77573
Cypress Pointe Dr	77573
Dakota St	77573
Dallas St	77573
Damasco Cv	77573
Danna St	77573
Darlington Ct	77573
Daroca Dr	77573
David Ave	77573
Davis Rd	77573
Davison Ct	77573
Dawn Ct & Dr	77573
Dawn Crest Ct	77573
Dawn Sky Ln	77573
Deer Fern Dr	77573
Deer Ridge Dr	77573
Delaware Ave	77573
Dellore Ln	77573
Derby Ct	77573
Desert Springs Ct	77573
Desert Willow Ct & Dr	77573
Devereux Dr	77573
Diamante Dr	77573
Dickinson Ave	77573
Dinastia View Ct	77573
Dixie Dr	77573
Dogwood St	77573
Domenico Ln	77573
Doral Ct	77573
Dornoch Dr	77573
Dove Haven Ln	77573
Dover Ln	77573
Downing Cir	77573
Drake Ln	77573
Driftwood St	77573
Drummer Dr	77573
Drywood Creek Dr	77573
Dublin Dr	77573
Dunbar Ct	77573
Dunes Dr	77573
Dunes Ridge Way	77573
Dunlavy Ln	77573
Dunrich Ct	77573
Durazno Ct	77573
Eagle Cv & Dr	77573
Eastland Ct & St	77573
Edelweiss Dr	77573
Edens Ave	77573
Edgewood St	77573
Edinburg Ave	77573
Effie St	77573
N & S Egret Bay Blvd	77573
El Toro St	77573
Elderberry St	77573
Eli Way	77573
Elizabeth Ln	77573
Elkins Hollow Ln	77573
Ellen Ave	77573
Ellis Rd	77573
Elm Creek Dr	77573
Elm Pointe	77573
Elmore St	77573
Emerald Brook Ln	77573
Emerald Cloud Ln	77573
Emerald Cove Dr	77573
Emerald Point Ln	77573
Emilia Ct	77573
Empress Ln	77573
Enchanted Lake Dr	77573
Encino Ave	77573
Englewood Dr	77573
Enterprise Ave & Cir	77573
Ervin St	77573
Essex Ct	77573
Estella Ct	77573
Estrada Dr	77573
Evening Bay Ln	77573
Ewell Dr	77573
Exeter Rd	77573
Fair Pointe Dr	77573
Fairbay Cir	77573
Fairfield Ct N & S	77573
Fairtide Ct	77573
Fairwater Park Dr	77573
Fairway Pointe Dr	77573
Falkirk Ct	77573
Falling Springs Ln	77573
Farnworth Cir & Ln	77573
Fawn Ct	77573
Fawn Valley Dr	77573
Fennigan Ct & Ln	77573
Ferndale Dr	77573
Field Glen Ct	77573
Fife Ct	77573
Fir Tree Dr	77573
Firestone Ct & Dr	77573
Flagship Ct	77573
Flagstaff Ln	77573
Flamenco Gdns	77573
Flamingo Dr	77573
Fleetwood Cir	77573
Flint Ct	77573
Florida Ave	77573
Flower Croft Ln	77573
Flower Reef Cir	77573
Floyd Rd	77573
Flycatcher Cove Dr	77573
Fm 518 Rd E	77573
W Fm 646 Rd	77573
Fontana Way	77573
Forest Creek Dr	77573
Forest Hills Dr	77573
Forest Point Dr	77573
W Fork Dr	77573
Formentera Pl	77573
Fountain View Ln	77573
Fox Run Ln	77573
Foxglove St	77573
Foxtail Ct	77573
Fra Mauro Ct	77573
Francesca Ct	77573
Francis Ct	77573
Frederick Ln	77573
Fredericksburg Dr	77573
Freshmeadow St	77573
Gairloch Dr	77573
Galleon Dr	77573
Galloway Ln	77573
E Galveston St	77573
W Galveston St	
100-299	77573
240-240	77574
300-998	77573
301-999	77573
Gastonbury Ct	77573
Georgia Ave	77573
Gerona St	77573
Gettysburg Dr	77573
Gibbons Hill Ln	77573
Gila Ct	77573
Gladewater Ln	77573
Gladstone Dr	77573
S Glen Ln	77573
Glen Haven Ct & Dr	77573
Glen Iris Dr	77573
Gleneagles Dr	77573
Golden Bay Ln	77573
Golden Cape Dr	77573
Golden Sails Dr	77573
Golden Shores Ln	77573
Goldeneye Ln	77573
Goldfinch Ln	77573
Golf Green Ct	77573
Graham Trace Ln	77573
Gran Canary Dr	77573
Grand Creek Ct & Dr	77573
Grand Shore Ct	77573
Granger Ln	77573
Grants Harbour Ln	77573
Green Cedar Dr	77573
Green Meadow Ct	77573
Green Oaks Dr	77573
Greenbriar	77573
Greenridge Cir	77573
Greenshire Dr	77573
Greenthread	77573
Greenville Dr	77573
Grove Park Dr	77573
Gulf Fwy N & S	77573
Halls Brg	77573
Hammersmith Ln	77573
Hampton Ln & Rd	77573
Hannahs Way	77573
Harbour Cir	77573
Harlequin Ct	77573
Haro Ln	77573
Harpers Ferry Dr	77573
Harvard Pointe Dr	77573
Harwood Dr	77573
Hawaii Ave	77573
Hawkins Creek Ln	77573
Hawthorne Pointe	77573
Haysden Ln	77573
Hearthside Cir	77573
Heather St	77573
Heather Springs Ln	77573
Heatherwood Ct	77573
Henderson Ln	77573
Hermosa Arroyo Dr	77573
Hewitt St	77573
Hickory Limb Ct	77573
Hidden Brook Ln	77573
Hidden Cove Ct	77573
Hidden Lake Dr	77573
Hidden Oaks St	77573
Hidden Pines Ct	77573
High Canyon Ct	77573
High Meadow St	77573
Highland Ter	77573
Highstone Ct	77573
Highway 3 N & S	77573
Hill Ave	77573
Hispania View Dr	77573
Hobbs Rd	77573
Holbrook Springs Ln	77573
Holbrook Valley Ln	77573
Hollander Ct	77573
Hollow Ln	77573
Hollow Reef Cir	77573
Holly Ln	77573
Holly Fern Ct & Dr	77573
Hopi Ct & Dr	77573
Houston Ave	77573
Hunter Wood Dr	77573
Hyde Ct	77573
Hyland Ln	77573
Idaho Ave	77573
N & S Illinois Ave	77573
E & W Independence Ave	77573
Indian Blanket Dr	77573
Indianapolis Dr	77573
Indianmeadow Dr	77573
Indigo Cove Ct	77573
Indigo Harbour Ln	77573
Inscho Point Cir	77573
Interurban St	77573
Intrepid Way	77573
Invincible Cir	77573
N & S Iowa Ave	77573
Ironclad Dr	77573
Island Breeze Cir	77573
Island Falls Ct	77573
Island Manor Ln	77573
Island Villas Dr	77573
Itasca Ct	77573
Ivory Pointe Dr	77573
Ivory Stone Ln	77573
Ivy Glen Ct	77573
Ivy Mist Ct	77573
Ivycreek Ct	77573
Jackson Ln	77573
Jag Holw	77573
James River Ct	77573
Jeb Stuart Ct & Dr	77573
Jerome Rd	77573
Jessamine Way	77573
Jordan Creek Ct	77573
N & S Kansas Ave	77573
Kemper Dr	77573
Kendal Ln	77573
Kentucky Ave	77573
Kesslers Xing	77573
Ketch Ct	77573
Kettering Ln	77573
Keva Glen Dr	77573
Kildeer Ct	77573
Kingfisher Ct	77573
Kingsfield Ct	77573
Kingston Cv	77573
Kingsway Dr	77573
Kinston Dr	77573
Kirkham Ln	77573
Knoll Forest Dr	77573
Knoxville Dr	77573
Kofa Dr	77573
Kurth Canyon Ct	77573
La Escalona Dr	77573
La Salle Ln	77573
Laddingford Ln	77573
Lafayette Ln	77573
Laguna Coral Ct	77573
S Laguna Pointe Dr	77573
Laguna Shores Ln	77573
S Lake Dr	77573
Lake Bridge Ln	77573
N & S Lake Front Ct & Dr	77573
S Lake Land Dr	77573
Lake Landing Dr	77573
Lake Park Ln	77573
Lake Point Ct & Dr	77573
Lake Shore Dr	77573
Lake Star Dr	77573
Lakemist Ct	77573
Lakeway Dr	77573
Lakewind Ct & Ln	77573
Lancaster Ln	77573
Landing Blvd	77573
Landrum Ave	77573
Langley Ct	77573
Lanier Dr	77573
Lanyard Pointe Cir	77573
Lapaz Ct	77573
Lark Hollow Ln	77573
Las Palmas Dr	77573
Laughing Gull Ln	77573
Laura Ln	77573
Laurel Ct & St	77573
Laurelglen Ct	77573
Laurelridge Dr	77573
Lauren Lake Dr	77573
Lazy Ln	77573
Lazy Hollow Dr	77573
Le Doux Oaks	77573
Leafwood Cir	77573
League St	77573
E & W League City Pkwy	77573
Lees Ct	77573
Leghrand Ct	77573
Leisure Ln	77573
Leo Ln	77573
Lewis St	77573
Lexington Ct	77573
Liberty St	77573
Lightstone Ln	77573
Lilac Pointe	77573
Lily Ct	77573
Lilyglen Ct	77573
Linda Ln	77573
Livingstone Ln	77573
Loch Lomond Dr	77573
Lockland Ln	77573
Lodge Crest Ct	77573
Lombardia Dr	77573
Lomelina Ln	77573
Lone Oak Dr	77573
Lone Star Ct	77573
Longspur Ln	77573
Longwood Ct	77573
Lost Creek Ln	77573
Louisiana Ave	77573
Lucca Ct	77573
Madison Ave	77573
Magnolia Cir, Rdg, St, Trce, Way & Xing	77573
Magnolia Bend St	77573
Magnolia Blossom	77573
Magnolia Estates Dr	77573
Magnolia Green Ln	77573
E & W Main St	77573
Malaga Ln	77573
Mallorca Pass	77573
Mandy Ln	77573
Mango Ct	77573
Mangrove Bend Dr	77573
Mannington	77573
Manor Bay Ct	77573
Manor Ridge Ln	77573
Mansfield Park Ct	77573
Maple Leaf Dr & St	77573
Maresca Ln	77573
Maria St	77573
Maricopa Ct	77573
Marina Bay Dr	77573
Marina View Way	77573
Mariner Dr	77573
Mariner Cove Ct	77573
Marlin Ct	77573
Marmora Ct	77573
Marshall St	77573
Maryland Ave	77573
Masters Ct & Dr	77573
Mayhaw St	77573
Mccarron Ct	77573
Mcguire Rd	77573
Mckibben Ln	77573
Mcvoy Dr	77573
Meade Ct	77573
Meadow Pkwy N	77573
Meadow Bend St	77573
Meadow Brook Ct & Dr	77573
Meadow Creek Ct	77573
Meadow Forest Dr	77573
Meadow Gate Dr	77573
Meadow Wood Ct	77573
Meadowbriar St	77573
Meadowlark Ln	77573
Meadowpoint Dr	77573
Meadows Blvd	77573
Meadows Pond	77573
Meadowside St	77573
Merion Dr	77573
Merrimac Dr	77573
Mesa Verde Dr	77573
Messina Ct	77573
Metairie St	77573
Mezzomonte Ln	77573
N Michigan Ave	77573
Midway Ct	77573
Milano Ln	77573
Milazzo Ln	77573
Milburn Dr	77573
Millers Water Ln	77573
Millikens Bnd	77573
Mimosa Ct	77573
Miramar Dr	77573
Mist Creek Ct	77573
Misty Brook Ln	77573
Misty Glen Ln	77573
Misty Harbour Cir	77573
Misty Meadow St	77573
Misty Morning	77573
Misty Shore Dr	77573
Misty Trails Ln	77573
Misty Waters Ln	77573
Misty Wind Ct	77573
Mitchell Ct	77573
Modeste Dr	77573
Mojave Trl	77573
Moncrey Ave	77573
Montclair Ct	77573
Monticello Ct	77573
Monticello Pines Ln	77573
Montieri St	77573
Moody Ave	77573
Moonlit Lake Cir	77573
Morley Point Ct	77573
Morning Creek Ln	77573
Morning Lake Dr	77573
Morning Tide Ln	77573
Morningside Dr	77573
Mossy Oak Dr	77573
Mulberry St	77573
Murfield Dr	77573
Muricia Dr	77573
Mystic Port Ln	77573
Napoli Ct	77573
Natchez Ct	77573
Navajo Pass	77573
New London Dr	77573
Newcastle Ln	77573
Newport Blvd	77573
Noah Ln	77573
Noblewood Ct	77573
Nolte Toscano	77573
Northern Dr	77573
Norwalk Dr	77573
N Nottingham Dr	77573
Nottoway Ct	77573
Oak Creek Cir, Ct, Dr & Ln	77573
Oak Estates Ct	77573
Oak Forest Dr	77573
Oak Hill Cir	77573
Oak Hollow Dr	77573
Oak Lodge Ct	77573
Oak Ridge Dr	77573
Oak Shadow Ct	77573
Oakdale Pl	77573
Oaklawn St	77573
Oakleaf Trail Ln	77573
Oakmont Ct	77573
Oakshire Ct	77573
Oakwood St	77573
Oboe Trl	77573
Ocean Way	77573
Ocean Manor Ln	77573
Oceanside Ln	77573
Ocotillo St	77573
Ohio St	77573
Oklahoma Ave	77573
Old Hickory Ln	77573
Old Oaks St	77573
Oleander Ln	77573
Olive St	77573
Olive Pointe	77573
Olympia Springs Dr	77573
Olympic Dr	77573
Oneida Ct	77573
Opal Sky Ct	77573
Oracle Dr	77573
Orange Blossom Ct	77573
Orange Grove St	77573
Oregon Ave	77573
Oriole Dr	77573
Orion Dr	77573
Orleans St	77573
Padova Ct	77573
Paintbrush Ave	77573
Paisley Meadow Dr	77573
Palermo Ct	77573
Pallins Way	77573
Palm Castle Ct & Dr	77573
Palm Island Cir	77573
Palm Lagoon Dr	77573
Palmetto Dr	77573
Palomar Ln	77573
Palomino St	77573
Pampas Ln	77573
Pamplona Ln	77573
N Park Ave	77573
Park Bridge Ln	77573
Park Falls Ct & Ln	77573
Park Trail Ln	77573
Park View Ln	77573
Parker Ct	77573
Pasqua Trl	77573
E Peach St	77573
Pear St	77573
Pearl Dr	77573
Pebble Bay Dr	77573
Pebble Beach Dr	77573
Pebble Brook Dr	77573
Pebblebank Ln	77573
Pecan Dr	77573
Pecan Orchard Rd	77573
Pegasus Ln	77573
Pelago St	77573
Pelican Ct	77573
Pelican Landing Ct	77573
Pembroke Bay Dr	77573
Pergola	77573
Perkins Ave	77573
Persimmon Pointe	77573
Pescara Ct	77573
Piares Ln	77573
Pickett Dr	77573
Pienza Ln	77573
Pilgrim Oaks Ln	77573
Pima Ct	77573

Pine Mills Dr 77573
Pine Point Ct 77573
Pine Pointe 77573
Pinehurst Dr 77573
Pinewood Dr 77573
Pinnacle Dr 77573
Pinnacle Cove Ct 77573
Pinola Ct 77573
Pisana 77573
Plantation St 77573
Pleasant Palm Cir 77573
Pleasant Valley Dr 77573
Plymouth St 77573
Pontchartrain Ct 77573
Ponte Leone Ln 77573
Ponte Rossi 77573
Ponte Serra Dr 77573
Poppy St 77573
Port Bridge Ln 77573
Port Rose Ln 77573
Porta Rosa Ln 77573
Portefino Ln 77573
Portglen Dr 77573
Porto Way 77573
Porto Bianco Ln 77573
Portside Ct 77573
Potenza Ct 77573
Potomac Dr 77573
Power St 77573
Prattwood Ct 77573
Prescott Dr 77573
Preston Ln 77573
Prestwick Dr 77573
Primrose Ln 77573
Pueblo Ct 77573
Purple Horse Dr 77573
Quail Dove Ln 77573
Quiet Falls Ln 77573
Quiet Lake Ct 77573
Quill Meadow Dr 77573
Quivira Trce 77573
Ragusa Ln 77573
Railroad Ave 77573
Rainbow Cir E 77573
Rainflower Cir N & S 77573
Rampart Ct & St 77573
Ramsay Ln 77573
Raven Springs Ln 77573
Ravenknoll Ct 77573
Ravens Lake Cir & Dr 77573
Ravenscreek Ct 77573
Red River St 77573
Red Timber Ct 77573
Redbridge Ln 77573
Redbud Cir 77573
Reef Dr 77573
Reynolds Ave 77573
Rincon Dr 77573
Rio Bella Ct 77573
Rio Grande St 77573
Rippling Spgs 77573
Rising Tide Ln 77573
River Ct 77573
Riverside Dr 77573
Riviera Dr 77573
Rock Brook Falls Ln 77573
Rock Harbor Ln 77573
Rockpoint Cir 77573
Rocky Hollow Ln 77573
Romano Ln 77573
Rose Hill Dr 77573
Rosemist Dr 77573
Rosswood Dr 77573
Royal Dr 77573
Royal Bay Ct 77573
Royal Creek Ct 77573
Royal Oaks Dr 77573
Royal Palm Ct 77573
Royal Terns Ct 77573
Ruby Falls Ct 77573
Rufina St 77573
Running Pine Ct & Dr 77573
Rushton Cir 77573
Rustic Oaks Dr 77573
Rustic Pier Ln 77573
Rustling Wind Ln 77573

Ryder Ct 77573
Sabal Park Ct & Ln 77573
Saber Ct 77573
Sabero Ln 77573
Saffron St 77573
Saguaro Dr 77573
Sailaway Dr 77573
Saint Andrews Pl 77573
Saint Charles St 77573
Salamanca Way 77573
Salerno Ct 77573
Salinas Ln 77573
Salt Marsh Ct 77573
San Benedetto 77573
San Marco Ln 77573
San Mateo Ct 77573
San Nicolo Ln 77573
San Remo Ln 77573
San Sebastian Ct 77573
Sand Mist Cir 77573
Sand Reef Ct & Ln 77573
Sand Shadow Ct & Dr 77573
Sandcove Ct 77573
Sandpiper Ln 77573
Sandvalley Ct & Way 77573
Sandwell Ct 77573
Sandy Coast Cir 77573
Sandy Meadow Ln 77573
Sandy Ridge Dr 77573
Sandy Schoals Dr 77573
Sandy Shore Dr 77573
Santa Cruz Ln 77573
Santa Luz Path 77573
Santiago Ln 77573
Santo Domingo Dr 77573
Sara Ln 77573
Saratoga Dr 77573
Satsuma St 77573
Saturnia Ln 77573
E & W Saunders St 77573
Savanna Ct N & S 77573
Sawgrass Ct 77573
Scarborough Ln 77573
Scarlet Sage Dr 77573
School St 77573
Schooner Cove Ln 77573
Scottsdale Ct 77573
Sea Bright Ct 77573
Sea Mist Dr 77573
Sea Pines Pl 77573
Seaborough Ln 77573
Seabreeze Dr 77573
Seacrest Blvd 77573
Seahurst Ct 77573
Sedona Ct & Dr 77573
Segovia Dr 77573
Seneca Ct 77573
Senna Ave 77573
Serenity Ln 77573
Serrano Dr 77573
Shadecrest Ln 77573
Shadow Cir 77573
Shadow Bay Cir 77573
Shadow Point Dr 77573
Shadowcliff Ct 77573
Shady Knoll Ln 77573
Shallow Springs Ln 77573
Shaly Breeze Ln 77573
Sharnoll Cir 77573
Shear Water Ct 77573
Sheffield Ln 77573
Sherl St 77573
Sherwood Forest Cir 77573
Shoal Creek Dr 77573
Shoal Lake Ct 77573
Shoal Pointe Ct & Ln 77573
S Shore Blvd 77573
Shore Breeze Ln 77573
Shore Brook Cir & Ct 77573
Shore Meadow Dr 77573
Shore Pointe Dr 77573
S Shores Blvd 77573
Shrub Oak Dr 77573
Sierra Brook Ln 77573
Signature Cv 77573
Signature Point Dr 77573

Silent Shore Ct 77573
Silent Springs Ct 77573
Silver Leaf Dr 77573
Siskin Trl 77573
Skyspring Ln 77573
Slider Ct 77573
Small Cedar Dr 77573
Smith Ln 77573
Snyders Blf 77573
Soffiano Ln 77573
Somerset Landing Ln 77573
Somerset Pointe Dr 77573
Sonora Dr 77573
Sorrelwood Dr 77573
Southchase Ln 77573
Southern Hills Dr 77573
Southwell Ln 77573
Spellbrook Ct 77573
Spinnaker Dr 77573
Spoonbill Dr 77573
Sportsplex 77573
Spring Breeze St 77573
Spring Haven Ct 77573
Spring Hill Ln 77573
Spring Iris Ct 77573
Spring Moss Dr 77573
Springbrook Ct 77573
Springstone Ct 77573
Spyglass Dr 77573
St Christopher Ave 77573
Stanford Ct 77573
Starborrough Dr 77573
Starcroft Ct 77573
Stargrass Ct 77573
Steddum Dr 77573
Sterling Creek Ct 77573
Sterling Pointe Ct 77573
Stillwater Bay Ct 77573
Stone Bridge St 77573
Stoneridge Terrace Ln 77573
Stonewall Dr 77573
Strawberry St 77573
Sugar Wood Dr 77573
Sugarvine Ct 77573
Summer Pl 77573
Summer Cape Cir & Ct 77573
Summer Haven Cir, Ct & Dr 77573
Summer Manor Dr 77573
Summer Place Ct 77573
Summer Reef Dr 77573
Summer Shore Dr 77573
Summerstorm Ln 77573
Summit Pass Ln 77573
Sumpter Ct 77573
Sunny Bay Ct 77573
Sunny Isle Ln 77573
Sunset Cir & Ct 77573
Sunset Ridge Ct & Dr 77573
Sunset Terrace Dr 77573
Sutherland Ln 77573
Suzanne St 77573
Swan Meadow Ct 77573
Sweetgum St 77573
Swift Creek Dr 77573
Sycamore Pointe 77573
Tahoe Ct 77573
Tallowood Dr 77573
Tarpon Dr 77573
Teal Bay Bend Ln 77573
Teal Shore Ct 77573
Ted Pickett Ln 77573
Tempe St 77573
Terranova Ln 77573
Terrell Cove Ln 77573
Texas Ave 77573
Thistledown Dr 77573
Thistlewood Ct 77573
Thorndon Park Ct 77573
Tiegs St 77573
Timbermoss Ct 77573
Toledo Ct 77573
Toluca Dr 77573
Tonto Dr 77573
Torano 77573

Torrance Dr 77573
Torrey Ct 77573
Township Dr 77573
Trailbrook Ct 77573
Tranquility Ln 77573
Travellers St 77573
Tree Bark Ln 77573
Trent Ct 77573
Trinity St 77573
Triple Mast Cir 77573
Troon Dr 77573
Tucker Rd 77573
Turnberry Dr 77573
Turner St 77573
Turtlewood Dr 77573
Tuscan Lakes Blvd 77573
Tuscan Village Dr 77573
Tuscania Ln 77573
Tuscarora Ct 77573
Twinleaf Dr 77573
Umbria Ln 77573
Valencia Cv 77573
Valley Blossum Ln 77573
Vance St 77573
Vantage Pointe Cir 77573
Varuna Ct 77573
Vega Ct 77573
Velvet St 77573
Veneto Ct 77573
Ventura Dr 77573
Verona Ct 77573
Via Montesano 77573
Via Roma 77573
Victoria Ct 77573
Viejo Rd 77573
Villa Bella Ct 77573
Villa Pisa Ln 77573
Village Way 77573
Vincench Dr 77573
Vinewood Ln 77573
Viola Dr 77573
Virginia Ave 77573
Virtue Ct 77573
Volterra Ln 77573
Waco Ave 77573
Wakefield Dr 77573
E & W Walker St 77573
Walnut Creek Dr 77573
Walnut Pointe 77573
Warrington Ln 77573
Warwick Dr 77573
Washington St 77573
Water Oak Dr 77573
Waterborough Ct 77573
Watercastle Ct 77573
Watercrest Harbor Ln 77573
Waterfall Cove Ct 77573
Waterglen Ct 77573
Waters Edge Ln 77573
Waterside Dr 77573
Wavecrest St 77573
Waverly Dr 77573
Waverly Canyon Ln 77573
Waxwing Dr 77573
Weathersfield Ct 77573
Webster St 77573
Weeks St 77573
Well Brook Ln 77573
Wentworth Oaks Ct 77573
N Wesley Dr 77573
Westminster Dr 77573
Westover Park Ave 77573
Westshore Ct 77573
Westwind Ct 77573
Westwood Dr 77573
Weyer St 77573
White Dove Ct 77573
White Ibis Ct 77573
White Oak Pointe 77573
White Sands Way 77573
Whitehall Cir & Ln 77573
Whitesail Dr 77573
Wickford Ct 77573
Wilburn St 77573
Wild Plum Dr 77573
Wildfire St 77573

Wildflower Pl 77573
E & W Wilkins St 77573
Williamhurst Ln 77573
Williams St 77573
Williamsburg Ct N & S 77573
Williamsport St 77573
Willow Ln 77573
Willow Branch Dr 77573
Willow Creek Ct & Dr 77573
Willow Pointe Dr 77573
Willow Springs Ct 77573
Willowood Dr 77573
Windgate Ct 77573
Windhollow Cir 77573
Winding Oak Ln 77573
Winding Springs Dr 77573
Windsor Chase Ln 77573
Windward Ct & Dr 77573
Windy Briar Ln 77573
Windy Brook Ln 77573
Windy Cape Ln 77573
Windy Cove Ct 77573
Winecup Ln 77573
Winged Dove Dr 77573
Winged Foot Dr 77573
Winslow Ln 77573
Winterwood Dr 77573
N & S Wisconsin Ave 77573
Wood Creek Ln 77573
Wood Hollow Dr 77573
Woodcrest Dr 77573
Woodhall Ct 77573
Woodvale Dr 77573
Woodwind Way 77573
Woodwren Ct 77573
Wren Dr 77573
Yacht Harbor Ln 77573
York Harbour Ct 77573
Yorktown Ct N & S 77573
Yucca Ct 77573
Yuma Ct 77573

NUMBERED STREETS

All Street Addresses 77573

LEANDER TX

General Delivery 78641

POST OFFICE BOXES MAIN OFFICE STATIONS AND BRANCHES

Box No.s
91 - 2398 78646
4200 - 7258 78645

RURAL ROUTES

02, 08, 10, 12 78645

NAMED STREETS

Acacia Dr 78641
Adena Ln 78641
Admiral Park Dr 78645
Adobe Trl 78645
Adrian Blvd 78645
Adrian Dr 78641
Adrian Way 78645
Agua Frio Dr 78645
Aiken Dr 78641
Alamo Cv 78645
Alamo Bound 78641
Alexander Dr 78641
Alfalfa Dr 78645
Allegiance Ave 78645
Alpine Mountain Dr 78641
Alta Vista Dr 78641
Alvarado Pass 78645

Amandas Way 78641
Amarone Dr 78641
Amazon Lilly Cv 78641
Amber Valley Ln 78641
Ambush Cyn 78641
American Cir, Cv & Dr 78645
Amos Dr 78641
Anderson Trl 78641
Angel Mountain Dr 78641
Angel Side Dr 78641
Angel Springs Dr 78641
Angel Valley Dr 78641
Angelique Ct 78641
Annapolis Cv 78645
Antlers Trl 78641
Apache Cv 78645
Apache Trl 78641
Apple Springs Cir, Dr & Holw 78641
Applerock 78641
Aqua Bell Cv 78641
Arlington Cv 78645
Armstrong Dr 78641
Arren Ter 78641
Arrowhead Dr
4801-4897 78645
4899-5699 78645
14700-16599 78641
Arrowhead Pt 78645
Arroyo Ave 78645
Arroyo Cir 78641
Arroyo Grande 78641
Arthur Cir 78641
Arvada Dr 78641
Ashbury Dr 78641
Aspen Meadow Rd 78641
Atkins St 78641
August Jake 78641
N Augusta Cir, Cv & Dr
N 78645
Austin Blvd, Cv & Dr 78645
Autrey Dr 78641
Avenida Ann St 78645
Bachelor Gulch 78641
N & S Bagdad Rd & St 78641
N & S Baker Cir & Ln 78641
Banner Ave 78641
Bar K Ranch Rd 78645
Bar Ryder Trl 78641
Baranco Way 78641
Barberry Dr 78645
Barclay Dr 78641
Bardolino Ln 78641
Barley Rd 78641
Barn Owl Loop 78641
Barnard Ln 78641
Battlecreek Ln 78641
Beach Rd
4000-4099 78645
10700-11399 78641
Beacon Point Cv 78645
Bear Rd 78645
Bear Claw 78641
Bearcreek Dr 78641
Beauregard Dr 78641
Bee St 78645
Bell Ln 78645
Belladoma Cv 78641
Bello Dr 78641
Benetton Way 78641
Bent Oak Cv 78641
Bentwood Dr 78641
Bernard St 78641
Bertram St 78645
Beverly Cv & Ln 78641
Big Falls Dr 78641
Big Oak Cir 78641
Big Sandy Cv & Dr 78645
Bighorn 78641
Billy Pat Rd 78641
Bingham Creek Rd 78641
Birch Brook Dr 78641
Bison 78645
Black Kettle Dr 78641
Blackfoot Cv 78645

Blanco Cir & Dr 78645
Blended Tree Ranch Dr 78641
Block House Dr 78641
Blue Canyon Cv 78645
Blue Heron Cv 78641
Blue Sky Ln 78645
Blueberry Cir 78645
Bluebonnet Cir 78645
Bluebonnet Ct 78641
Bluebonnet Trl 78641
Bluejay Blvd 78645
Blueline Rd 78641
Bluff Rdg 78645
Bluffwater Way 78645
Boat Dock Rd 78645
Boggy Ford Rd 78645
Bold Sundown Dr 78641
Bonanza St 78645
Bonita Ct 78641
Bonita Verde Dr 78641
Boone Dr 78645
Booth Cir 78641
Bordeaux Dr 78641
Borho 78641
Bottle Springs Ln 78641
Bowen St 78641
Bradley Cv 78645
Bramble Bush Cir 78645
Branding Iron 78645
Branding Iron Ln 78641
Breakwater Dr 78645
Breeds Cv 78645
Breeze Way 78645
Brentwood Dr 78645
Brewer Ln 78645
Briarwood Cir 78645
Briarwood Dr 78641
Bridle Path Rd 78645
W Broade St 78641
Broken Arrow St 78645
Broken Bow Cv 78645
Bronco Ln 78645
Bronco Buster Trl 78645
Bronze Ln 78641
S Brook Dr 78641
Brown Bluff Cir 78641
N & S Brushy St 78641
Bryan Cv 78645
Buchanan Cv 78645
Buckeye Dr 78645
Buckhorn Cir & Dr 78645
Buckskin Rdg 78645
Buddy Ln 78641
Buena Vis 78645
Buffalo Trl 78645
Buffalo Gap 78641
Buffalo Speedway 78641
Buffalo Thunder 78641
Bufflehead 78641
Bunker Cv 78645
Bunyan Cir 78645
Burba 78641
Burgess Dr 78641
Burning Tree Cir 78645
Burnside Cir 78645
Buttercup Ct 78641
Byrd Ave 78645
Byron Cir 78641
Caballero Rd 78641
Caballo Ranch Blvd 78641
Cabernet Way 78641
Cactus Mound Dr 78641
Cactus Valley Dr 78641
Calcutta Run Dr 78645
Calhoun Ave 78645
Calhoun Ln 78641
Calistoga Dr 78641
Calla Lily Blvd & Cv 78641
Calming Ct 78645
Camel Back St 78645
Camelback 78641
Camille Ct 78645
Camino Alemeda 78641
Camino Alto Dr 78641
Camino Real Dr 78641

Canadian Cv 78641
Candlelight Dr 78641
Cannery Cv 78641
Cantina Sky 78641
Canyon Vw 78641
Canyon Oaks Dr 78645
Capitol Ave 78645
Cardinal Ave 78645
Carol Ave 78641
Cartier Cv 78645
Carto St 78641
Cascade Cir 78645
Casitas Ct 78641
Castlewood Trl 78641
Catalina 78641
Catlin Cv 78641
Cedar Blf 78645
Cedar Cir 78645
Cedar Dr 78645
Cedar Gln 78645
Cedar Rdg 78641
Cedar St 78645
Cedar Lime Rd 78641
Cedar Ridge Cir & Dr 78645
Cedar Sage Ct 78645
Cedarridge Ct 78641
Center St 78645
Cerezo Dr 78641
Cerrito Cv 78641
Cerro Ct 78641
Chalet Cir 78641
Chalk Bluff Ct 78641
Champagne Ct 78641
Champions Cir & Cv 78645
Champions Corner Ct & Dr 78641
Chandler Branch Dr 78641
Chantilly Trl 78645
Chaparral Dr 78641
Chardonnay Xing 78641
Charley Harley Dr 78641
Cherry Ln 78645
Cherry Hollow Ct, Cv, Dr & Xing 78641
Chestnut Cv 78645
Cheyenne Cv 78645
Cheyenne St 78641
Chickadee Ln 78641
Chickory Ct 78641
Chimney Dr 78641
Chimney Rock Rd 78641
Chippewa Cir 78645
Choctaw Cv 78645
Christopher Ln 78641
Cimarron Cv 78641
Cimmaron Trl 78645
Cindy Ln 78641
Circulo Dr 78645
Cisco Trl 78641
Civic Dr 78645
Claudia Dr 78641
Clay Ln 78645
Clayton Dr 78641
Clear Lake Ln 78641
Clear Spring Ln 78641
Clear Springs Ct 78641
Clearcreek Dr 78641
Clearview Dr 78645
Clinton Ln 78645
Clubhouse Dr 78645
Cody Ave 78645
Cold Spring Dr 78641
Colina Dr 78645
Colinas Verdas Rd 78641
Collier Ln 78645
Colonial Ln 78645
Colt Cv 78645
Columbine Ln 78641
Columbus Ln 78645
Comanche 78645
Comanche Ln 78645
Comanche Pt 78645
Comanche Trl 78641
Commelina Dr 78641
Comstock Cv 78645
Concord Cir 78645
Conestoga Cv 78645
Congress Ave 78645
Constitution Cv, Dr & Sq 78645
Continental Dr 78645
Coolidge Ln 78645
Cooper Cir & Ln 78645
Copper Ln 78641
Copper Leaf Ln 78641
Coral Valley Dr 78641
Cornell Cv 78645
Coronado 78641
Costa Azul Cv 78641
Cottage Ln 78645
Cottontail Dr 78641
Cottonwood Dr 78641
Country Club Dr 78645
County Cork Ln 78641
County Glen St 78641
County Road 175 78641
County Road 177 78641
County Road 179 78641
County Road 180 78641
County Road 264 78641
County Road 269 78641
County Road 270 78641
County Road 271 78641
County Road 272 78641
County Road 274 78641
County Road 276 78641
County Road 279 78641
County Road 280 78641
County Road 281 78641
County Road 282 78641
County Road 283 78641
County Road 290 78641
Courageous 78641
Cowboy Cv 78645
Cowpoke Trl 78645
Coyote Ln 78641
Coyote Trl 78645
Cree Lake Ct 78641
Creek Bluff Cv 78641
Creek Meadow Cv 78641
Creek Run Dr 78641
Creekside Dr 78641
Creekview Cir 78645
Crestview Dr 78645
Crockett Ave 78645
Cross St 78645
Cross Draw Trl 78641
Crossbow Trl 78645
Crossland Cv 78641
Crossover Ln 78641
Crumley Creek Rd 78645
Crystal Cv & Way 78645
E Crystal Falls Pkwy 78641
Cumberland Cv 78645
Cynthia Ct 78641
Dakota Cir 78645
Darby Ln 78641
E, N & W Darleen Dr & Ext 78641
Davenport Cv 78645
Davis Cv 78645
Davy Dr 78641
Dawn Dr 78645
Dayna Cv 78641
Deadend Rd 78645
Debbie Dr 78641
Debbie Ann Dr 78641
Deckhouse Dr 78645
Declaration Cir 78645
Deede Dr 78645
Deep Crk 78645
Deepwood Dr 78645
Deepwoods Trl 78641
Deer Run
6500-6598 78645
7600-7899 78645
Deer Canyon Cv & Rd 78645
Deercreek Ln 78641
Del Paso 78641
Demarett Dr 78645
Destination Way 78641
Dew Drop Ln 78641
Dewberry Holw 78641
Dews 78641
Dexter Dr 78641
Diamond Cv & Trl 78645
Digby Ct 78641
Dillon Lake Bnd 78641
District Ln 78645
Diversion Cir 78645
Divide Dr 78641
Dodd St 78641
Dodge Trl 78645
Doolittle Cv 78645
Dormax Cir 78641
Dos Amigo Dr 78645
Double Canyon Dr 78645
Douglas Cv 78645
Dove Rd 78641
Dove Ridge Trl 78641
Dove Song Dr 78641
Downing Ln 78641
Downridge Dr 78641
Drake Cv
1000-1299 78641
3000-3099 78645
Draper Mountain Cv 78645
Drapers Cv 78645
Drapers Mountain Trl 78645
Dream Catcher Dr 78641
Dublin Dr 78641
Durango Cv 78645
Dusk Ct 78645
Eagle Owl Loop 78641
Eaglecreek Dr 78641
Eagles Way 78641
N East St 78641
Easy St 78645
Echo Bay Ct 78645
Edgewood Cv 78645
Edgewood Way 78645
Edna Rd 78645
Edson Ct 78641
Eisenhower Ave 78645
El Cielo 78641
El Dorado St 78645
Elaina Loop 78641
Elkhorn Ranch Rd 78641
Ellason Dr 78645
Elm Crst 78641
Elm St 78645
Elm Ridge Dr 78641
Emerald Rd 78645
Emerald Isle Dr 78641
Emerson Cv 78645
Emma Rose 78641
Encanto Dr 78641
Encinita Dr 78641
Encino Dr 78641
English River Loop 78645
Ericanna Ln 78641
Erin Cir 78641
Escondido Dr 78641
Estancia Way 78641
E Evans St 78641
Evans Oaks 78645
Evergreen St 78645
Fair Oaks St 78641
Fairfield Loop 78641
Fairlawn Dr 78641
Fairway Dr 78645
Falcon Ln
100-899 78641
20600-21699 78645
Falcon Oaks Dr 78641
Fall Creek Dr 78641
Fandango 78641
Farragret Cv 78645
Farview Cir 78641
Faubion Trl 78641
Faustino Cv 78645
Fawn Cir 78645
Fawn Dr 78641
Fawn Park 78645
N Fawn Rdg 78641
Fawn Ridge Dr 78645
Fawnridge Cir 78645
Feather Reed Dr 78641
Fillmore Cv 78645
Firemans Trl 78645
Fireplace Ct 78641
Firestone Cir 78645
First Vw 78645
Fisher Hollow Trl 78641
Fishermans Way 78645
Flagship Park Dr 78645
Flanagan Dr 78641
Flightline Rd 78645
Flintlock Cir 78645
Flintlock Dr 78641
Fm 1431
17300-18199 78641
Fm 1431
18245-19699 78645
19801-20497 78641
20499-21600 78645
21602-21698 78645
Fm 2769 78641
Foothills 78641
Ford Cv 78645
Forest Trl 78641
Fossil Trl 78641
Franklin Cv 78645
Friendship Cv 78641
Frio Ln 78641
Friuli Cir 78641
Frontier Cv 78645
Fulkes Ln & Rd 78641
N & S Gabriel Dr & St 78641
Gabriel Mills Dr 78641
Garnet Ridge Dr 78641
Garrison Dr 78641
Gaviota Ln 78641
Genessee Cv 78645
Gentry Dr 78641
Georgetown Dr 78645
Geronimo 78641
Getaway Dr 78645
Gift Horse Pass 78641
Gilbert Cv 78645
Gillum Creek Dr 78641
Glass Dr 78641
Glen Oak Ln 78641
Glen Valley Ln 78641
Glendale Rd 78645
Glerindo Dr 78645
Glory Ln 78641
Golden Bridle Trl 78641
Golden Butterfly Dr 78641
Golden Eagle 78645
Golden Gate Dr 78641
Golfview Cir 78645
Goodnight Trl 78641
Government Cv 78645
Grand Lake Pkwy 78641
Grandview Dr 78645
Granite Creek Dr 78641
Granite Hill Cv & Dr 78641
Granite Springs Rd 78641
Grant Ct 78641
Grant Ln 78641
Grapevine Canyon Trl 78641
Grassland Dr 78641
Great Oaks Blvd 78641
Greeley Cv 78645
Green Cv 78645
Green Park Dr 78641
Green Shore Cir 78645
Green Valley Dr 78641
Greener Dr 78641
Greening Way 78641
Greenlee Dr 78641
Gregg Bluff Rd 78645
Haleys Cv 78641
Hamilton Ave 78645
Hancock Ave 78645
Haneman Cv 78641
Harandow Dr 78641
Harbor Dr 78645
Harding Cv 78645
Harkey Cv 78641
Harrison Cv 78645
Hartman Dr 78641
Harvard Cv 78645
Harvest Dance Dr 78641
Hawkins Dr 78641
Hayes Cv 78645
Hazlewood St 78641
Heather Dr 78645
Hedder Cir 78641
Helmway Cir 78645
Henderson Dr 78641
Henry Ave 78645
Hensley Dr 78641
Heritage Grove Rd 78641
Hernandos Loop 78641
Hero Way 78641
Herradura Dr 78641
Herrero Path 78641
Hiawatha 78641
Hidden Trce 78641
Hidden Mesa 78641
Hidden Ridge Pl 78645
Hideaway Ln 78645
Hideout Cv 78641
High Dr 78645
High Chaparral Dr 78641
High Gabriel Dr E 78641
High Horse 78641
High Lonesome Trl 78641
High Mountain Cir & Dr 78645
Highclimb Ct 78641
Highland Trl 78641
Highland Lake Dr & Loop 78645
Highlander 78641
Highline Dr 78645
Highway 183 78641
N Highway 183 78641
S Highway 183
101-597 78641
599-699 78641
701-799 78641
801-2799 78641
801-801 78646
Hill Cir & Dr 78641
Hill Country Dr 78641
Hillsborough Cv 78641
Hillside Cir & Dr 78645
Hilltop Dr 78641
Hilltop Climb Dr 78641
Hilltop Divide Ln 78641
Hitching Post 78645
Hobby Ln 78645
Hogan Cir 78645
Holly Hill Dr 78641
Homecoming 78641
Homes Cv 78645
Homestead Cv 78645
Honeybee Ln 78641
Honeycomb Cir, Ct, Dr, Holw & Ln 78641
Honeycomb Mesa 78641
Honeysuckle Dr 78641
Hoot Owl Ct & Ln 78641
Hoover Cv 78645
Hopewell Ct 78641
Hopkins Cv 78645
Horizon Cv 78645
Horizon Park Blvd 78641
Horseshoe Dr 78641
Horseshoe Loop 78645
Horseshoe Ranch Dr 78641
House Creek Dr 78641
Housefinch Loop 78641
Houston Cv 78645
Howe Mountain Rd 78645
Huaco Cv 78645
Hummingbird Ln 78641
Hunt Cir 78641
Hunters Point Ct 78641
Hutton Ct & Ln 78641
Hyde Cv 78641
Inca Dove 78641
Indian Trl & Wls 78641
Indigo Bunting Cv 78641
Inspiration Cir 78645
Inverness St 78641
Ireland Dr 78641
Iron Horse 78641
Irving Cv 78645
Ivean Pearson Rd 78645
Jackpot Run 78641
Jackson Ave 78645
Jackson St 78641
Jacqueline Dr 78641
Jadestone Dr 78641
Jake Pickle Pass 78641
Jennifer Ln 78641
Jess Maynard 78641
Jewel Park Rd 78645
Joe Bates Dr 78641
Joes Cv 78641
Johnathan Way 78641
Johnson Rd 78641
Jonestown St 78645
Joppa Rd 78641
Jordan Cv 78641
Journey Pkwy 78641
Joy Rd 78641
Joyce Dr 78641
Juniper Ct & Trl 78641
Juniper Rim Rd 78641
Katherine Way 78641
Kathleen Cv & Ln 78641
Katie Cv 78641
Kelly Cv & Dr 78645
Key Cv 78645
Kicking Bird Dr 78641
Killarney Dr 78641
Killdeer 78641
King Ln 78641
King Elder Ln 78641
Kingfisher Ln 78641
Kingfisher Ridge Cv & Dr 78645
Kiowa Cv 78645
Kwai Cv 78645
La Cantera 78641
La Costa 78641
La Crema Ct 78641
La Mesa St 78645
La Paloma Dr & Ln 78645
Lacy Dr 78641
Ladera Trl 78645
Lafayette Park Rd 78645
Lafayette Square Dr 78645
Lago Vista Way 78645
Lajitas 78641
Lake Crest Dr 78645
Lake Mountain Ln 78641
Lake Oaks Dr 78645
Lake Park Cv & Dr 78645
W Lake Terrace Dr 78645
Lakefront Cir, Cv & Dr 78645
Lakehead Cir 78645
Lakeland Cir & Dr 78645
Lakeline Blvd 78641
Lakepoint Cv 78645
Lakeridge Dr 78645
Lakeshore Blvd, Cir, Dr & Pt 78645
Lakeside Dr 78645
Lakeview Ave 78645
E Lakeview Dr 78645
N Lakeview Dr 78645
W Lakeview Dr 78645
Lakeview St 78641
Lakewood Trl 78641
Lambrusco Ln 78641
Lantana Ct & Ln 78641
Lantern View Dr 78645
Lark St 78641
Las Colinas Dr 78641
Laughing Dog Ct 78641
Laurel Ln
1700-1999 78641
10700-10799 78645
Laurel Glen Blvd 78641
Lauren Loop 78641
Layne Loop 78641
Leaders Ln 78641
Leander Dr 78641
Leaning Oak Dr 78645
Leatherman Ln 78641
Ledge St 78645
Lee Dr 78641
Lee Ln 78645
Legend Trl 78641
Legend Hill Dr 78641
Leisure Ln 78645
Len Bar Ct & Ln 78641
Les Cv 78641
Lighthouse Ln 78645
Lily Pad 78641
Lime Creek Rd 78641
Limerick Ln 78641
Limestone Creek Rd 78641
Lincoln Cv 78645
Lindeman Ln & Loop 78641
Lindo Dr 78641
Link Rd 78645
Lion Dr 78641
Lions Den 78641
Lions Lair 78641
Lit Candle Cv 78641
Little Ln & Loop 78645
Little Oak Cir 78645
Little Valley Rd 78641
Live Oak 78645
Live Oak Cir 78645
Live Oak Dr 78641
Live Oak Rd 78641
Live Oak St 78641
Livenza Pl 78641
Logan Dr 78641
Loggerhead Cv 78641
Logue Cv 78641
Lohmans Ford Rd 78645
Loma Cedro Bnd 78641
Lombard Dr 78641
Lomita Dr 78641
Londonderry Dr 78641
Lone Mountain Pass 78641
Lone Oak Dr 78641
Lone Wolf Dr 78641
Lonesome Ct & Cv 78641
Long Bow Dr 78641
Long Hill Cv & Dr 78641
Long Hollow Loop & Trl 78641
Lookout Pt 78645
Lookout Knoll Dr 78641
Lookout Range Dr 78641
Los Robles Dr 78641
Los Vista Dr 78641
Lost Mine Trl 78641
Lost Ridge Cir 78641
Lotus Flower Loop 78641
Lucky Hit Rd 78641
Luke Ln 78641
Lupe Ln 78645
Lura Ln 78645
Lyla Ln 78641
Lyme Ridge Dr 78641
Lynn Ln 78645
Ma Draper Cv 78645
Mackenzie Way 78641
Mackinaw Xing 78645
Macks Canyon Rd 78641
Madeira Cv 78641
Madisina Dr 78641
Madison Cv 78645
Madrone Trl 78641
Magellan Cv 78645
Magpie Goose 78641
Main St 78645
Mallard Ln 78641
Mallard Lake Trl 78641
Manada Trl 78641
Mandana St 78641
Mann Cv 78645
Maplecreek Dr 78641
Mapleridge Cir 78641
Maplewood Dr 78645
Marble Slab Ln 78645
Marcheeta Way 78641
Marin Cv 78641
Marina Vista Cir 78641
Mariners Pt 78645
Maritime Pass 78645

Maritime Point Dr 78645
Marsala Cir 78641
Marshall Point Dr 78645
Mary St 78641
Mary Ella Dr 78641
Mason St 78641
Mason Creek Blvd 78641
Masters Cir & Cv 78645
Matheson Dr 78641
Matisse Point Dr 78645
Mayflower Cv 78645
Mcarthur Ave 78645
Mccarthur Dr 78641
Mccormick Cv 78645
Mcdowell Bnd 78641
Mckinley Cv 78645
Meadow View Dr 78641
Media Dr 78641
Medicine Hat 78641
Medina Vista Ln 78645
Mercury Cv 78641
Merlot Cv 78641
Mesa Dr, Rdg & Trl 78641
Mesa Grande 78641
Mesa Oaks 78641
Mesa Vista Dr 78641
Mica Ln 78641
Michael Cv 78641
Middle Brook Dr 78641
Middle Darleen 78641
Mikes Way 78641
Millbrook Loop 78641
Millcreek Ln 78641
Milton Cv 78641
Mimosa Ln 78641
Mir Woods Dr 78641
Mira Vis 78641
Mira Lago 78645
Mirador 78641
Mission Hls 78641
Misty Bnd 78641
Misty Ridge Dr 78641
Misty Valley Rd 78641
Mixtli Cv 78641
Mockingbird Ln 78641
Mockingbird St 78645
Mockingbird Hill St 78641
Mohawk St 78645
Mojave Bnd 78641
Molly Ln 78641
Molson Lake Dr 78641
Mones Ln 78641
Monet Pt 78645
Monroe Cv 78645
Montana Ct 78641
Montebelluna Pl 78641
Montello Ct 78641
Moon Glow Dr 78641
Moon Rise Cv & Trl 78645
Moorhen Cv & Ln 78641
Morgan Dr 78641
Morgan Ln 78645
Moser River Dr 78641
Moss Pt 78645
Moss Creek Dr 78641
Mount Laurel Dr & Rd 78645
Mount Vernon 78645
Mount View Dr 78645
Mountain Ridge Dr 78645
Mountain Side 78645
Mountain Springs Ln 78641
Mountain Top Cir 78645
Mourning Dove Ln 78641
Muledeer Run 78641
Municipal Dr 78641
Municipal Complex Way 78645
Mustang Rd 78641
Muzzie Ln 78641
Nakota Ct 78641
Nameless Rd 78641
Nantucket 78645
Napa Cv 78641
Napa Valley Bnd 78641
Nashville Cv 78645
National Dr 78645
Natures Way 78645
Navajo Cv 78645
Navajo Pass 78641
Navigation Ln 78645
Needles Cv 78645
Nettie 78641
Nettle Ln 78645
Nevins Cv 78645
E New Hope Dr 78641
Newcastle Ln 78641
Newhaven Cv 78645
Newport Cv 78645
Newton Dr 78645
Nightshade Ln 78641
Nimitz Ave 78645
Nobel Cir 78645
Nocona Cv 78645
Nogales Ln 78641
North Bnd 78641
North St 78645
Northcreek Blvd 78641
Northern Trl 78641
Northlake Hills Dr 78645
Northland Cir & Dr 78645
Norton Ave 78645
Norwood 78641
Nuttall Bluff Cv 78641
Oak Gln, Rdg & St 78645
Oak Canyon St 78641
Oak Creek Rd 78641
Oak Dale Dr 78645
Oak Forest Dr 78645
Oak Grove Rd 78641
Oak Hill Ln 78645
Oak Hollow Dr 78641
Oak Ridge Trl 78641
Oakland Cv 78641
Oakridge Cv 78641
Oaks Pl 78645
Oakville Cv 78641
Oakwood Dr & Trl 78641
Ocotillo 78641
Old 2243 W 78641
Old Anderson Mill Rd 78641
Old Bagdad Rd 78641
Old Burnet Rd 78645
E & S Old County Road 180 78641
Old Fm 1431 78645
Old Pecan Ln 78641
Old Quarry Rd 78641
Olmos Dr 78641
One House Rd 78645
Orchard Cv & Dr 78641
Osage Dr 78641
Osprey Dr 78641
Osprey Ridge Loop 78645
Outer Ave 78641
Outlook Ridge Loop 78641
Outpost Trce 78645
Overland Dr 78641
Overlook Bnd 78641
Oveta St 78645
Oxford Dr 78645
Pa Draper Ln 78645
Packsaddle Rd & Trl 78645
Paddock Cv 78645
Paine Ave 78645
Painted Bunting Cv 78641
Palo Alto 78641
Palo Duro Dr 78645
Palomino Cv 78645
Palomino Ranch Dr 78641
Palominos Pass 78641
Palos Verdes 78641
Pampas Ricas Dr 78641
Panhandle Cv 78645
Panorama Rdg 78645
Panoramic Vw 78645
Panther Hall 78641
N Park Dr 78645
Park Strip St 78645
Parkhurst Dr 78641
Parkwood Dr 78641
Parliament Cv 78645
Pasa Tiempo 78641
Paseo De Charros 78641
Paseo De Rancheros 78641
Paseo De Vaca Cir & Dr 78645
Paseo Verde Dr 78641
Patriot Dr 78645
Patton Ave 78645
Patty Dr 78645
Paw Print 78641
Pawnee 78641
Pawnee Trl 78645
Peacemaker Trl 78645
Pecan Dr 78645
Pecan Holw 78641
Pecan Grove Dr 78641
Pecan Valley Dr 78641
Peckham Dr 78645
Pecos Cv 78641
Pecos Dr 78645
Penn Cv 78645
Peoria Dr 78641
Peregrine Way 78641
Perry Cv 78645
Perry Mayfield 78641
Pershing Ave 78645
Phantom Horse 78641
Phillip Cv 78641
Picton Ct 78641
Piedmont Ct 78641
Pine Portage Loop 78641
Pinehurst Cir 78645
Pinewood Cv 78641
Pinnacle Cv 78645
Pinot Noir St 78641
Pinto Cv 78645
Pitkin Dr 78641
N Place St 78645
Plateau Cv 78645
Plazaway St 78645
Plume Cv 78641
Pocohontas Trl 78641
Poe Cv 78645
Point Cv 78645
Pokalong Path 78645
Port Anne Way 78641
Port Daniel Dr 78641
Port Hood Dr 78641
Porter Ln 78641
Posse Trl 78641
Post Oak Dr 78645
Pow Wow 78641
Powell Dr 78641
Pradera Cv & Path 78641
Presidio Dr 78641
Prickly Pear Cv 78641
Primrose Ln 78641
Privacy Hedge St 78641
Private Road 911 78641
Private Road 918 78641
Private Road 919 78641
Private Road 920 78641
Private Road 921 78641
Private Road 949 78641
Prosperity 78641
Pueblo Cv 78645
Pumpkin Rdg 78641
Purple Martin Cv 78641
Purple Moor Cv & Pass 78641
Purple Sage Cir 78641
Quail Ct 78641
Quail Run Cv 78645
Quail Valley Ct, Cv & Dr 78641
Quarry Loop 78641
Quick Fort Dr 78641
Quiet Brook St 78645
Rabbits Tail Dr 78641
Raider Way 78641
Railroad Rd 78641
Rainbow Hollow Dr 78645
Raindance 78641
Rainy River Dr 78641
Raleigh Cv 78645
Ramrod Trl 78645
Ran Rd 78641
Ranch Rd 78641
Ranch House Cv 78641
Ranch Road 2243 78641
Ranchero Rd 78641
Ranchland Hill Vis 78645
Ranchland Hills Blvd 78645
Rancho Cielo Ct 78645
Rancho Mirage 78641
Rancho Verde Dr 78641
Rancho Viejo 78641
Randolph St 78641
Rattan Cir 78641
Rawhide Trl 78645
Ray Vista St 78641
Red Bird Cv, Dr & Trl 78645
Red Bud Cv 78641
Red Bud Ln 78645
Red Hawk Dr 78641
Red Heron Dr 78641
Red Oak Ln 78641
Red River Ln 78641
Red Wagon Ln 78641
Redbud Ln 78641
Reed Dr 78641
Reed Park Rd 78645
Reedy Ct 78645
Regatta Cv 78645
Regatta View Dr 78645
Remington Dr 78641
Republic Trail Blvd 78641
Revere Cv 78645
Rich Trl 78641
N Ridge Cir 78641
S Ridge Cir 78641
Ridge Rd 78645
N Ridge St 78645
S Ridge St 78645
Ridge Crest Dr 78641
Ridge Rim Dr 78641
Ridge View Dr 78641
Ridgebluff Cir 78641
Ridgeline Rd 78641
Ridgemont Cir 78641
Ridgerock Cv 78641
Ridgeview Loop & Rd 78645
Ridgeway Cv & St 78645
Ridgewood Dr 78641
Ridgmar Rd 78641
N Rim Dr 78641
W Rim Dr 78645
Rim Rock Dr 78641
Rimrock Cir, Ct & Dr 78645
Rio Azul Cv 78641
Rio Bravo Loop 78641
Rio Seco 78641
Rio Verde Dr 78641
Riva Rdg 78641
River Crst & Run 78645
River Fern Ct 78641
River Oak Dr 78641
Riverchase Dr 78645
Riverway Ln 78641
Riviera Estates Dr 78641
Roaring Frk 78641
Robin Hood Rd 78645
Rock Cliff Cv 78641
Rock Cliff Dr
8300-8398 78645
8400-8599 78645
13901-13903 78641
13905-14899 78641
Rock Park Cir & Ln 78645
Rock Terrace Dr 78645
Rockdale Dr 78645
Rockefeller Cv 78645
Rockhill Dr 78645
Rockrose Ct 78641
Rockwood Dr 78645
Rolling Hills Trl 78645
Rolls Rd 78641
Ronald W Reagan Blvd 78641
Roosevelt Cv 78645
Rosemont Ct 78641
Ross Ln 78645
Rossport Bnd 78641
Round Mountain Cir & Rd 78641
Roundrock Rd 78645
Roundup Trl & Way 78645
Rubles Ct 78641
Ruby Isle Dr 78641
Running Wyld 78641
Rural Space Rd 78641
Rusty Spur 78641
Rutherford Dr 78641
Saddle Blanket Pl 78641
Sage Dr 78645
Sagebrush Trl 78645
Saint Genevieve Dr 78641
Saint Helena Dr 78641
Salvia Ct 78641
San Gabriel Pkwy 78641
San Vicente Dr 78641
Sand Piper Cv 78641
Sandy Ln 78645
Sandy Rdg 78641
Sandy St 78645
Sandy Meadow Cir 78641
Sangiovese St 78641
Santa Ana Cv 78645
Santa Carlo Ave 78645
Santa Elena Cir 78645
Santa Madrina 78645
Santa Monica Ave 78645
Santa Rosa Ave 78645
Sawyer Trl 78641
Scenic Dr & Path 78641
Scottsdale Dr 78641
Sedona 78641
Seminole Rd 78641
Sendero Ln 78641
Sequoia Cv & Dr 78641
Seward View Rd 78641
Shady Ln 78645
Shady Mountain Rd 78641
Shady Rock Cv 78645
Shamitas Ct 78641
Shamrock Dr 78641
Shannon Cir 78641
Sharon Rd 78641
Shawnee 78641
Sheep Hollow Trl 78641
Sheila Dr 78641
Shell Hill Cv 78641
Sherman St 78641
Sherry Dr 78641
Shipshaw River Cv & Dr 78641
Shoreline Ranch Rd 78645
Short Rd 78641
Shumard Bluff Dr 78641
Sidewinder 78641
Sidewinder Cv 78645
Sierra Trl 78645
Sierra Vista Dr 78645
Signal Hill Dr 78641
Signature Ln 78641
Sil Cv 78641
Silver Creek Dr 78641
Silver Fountain Dr 78641
Silver Leaf Cv 78641
Silver Spur Cv & Ln 78641
Silverhill Cir & Dr 78645
Singing Hls 78641
Sioux 78645
Sioux Trl 78641
Sky Kiss 78641
Skyview Ter 78641
Sleepy Hollow Dr & Ln 78645
Snelling Cv & Dr 78641
Snow Goose 78641
Snowy Egret 78641
Socorro Bnd 78641
Solano Cv 78641
Sonny Dr 78641
Sonoma Cv 78641
Sorrel Ct 78641
E & W South St 78641
Southbend St 78645
Southcreek Dr 78641
Southwind Rd 78645
Spanish Oak Cir 78645
Spanish Oak Dr 78645
Spanish Oak Trl 78641
Spanish Oaks 78641
Sparkling Brook Ln 78641
Sparrow Hawk 78641
Speaking Rock 78641
Spivey Rd 78641
Spotted Eagle Dr 78641
Spreading Oaks Dr 78641
Spring Ln 78645
Spring Hollow Dr 78641
Springbrook Ln 78641
Spumanti Ln 78641
Spy Cv 78641
Spyglass Hl 78641
Squaw Vly 78641
Stacey Ln 78645
Stage Coach Cv 78645
Stagecoach Bnd & Cv 78641
Staghorn Dr 78645
Stampede Trl 78645
Stanford Dr 78641
Starboard Cv 78645
Starr Pass 78641
Still Meadow Dr 78641
Stillwood Ct 78645
Stirrup Cv 78641
Stirup Cv 78645
Stockton Dr 78641
N & S Stuart Cv 78641
Summit Ridge Dr N 78645
Summit View Dr 78641
Sun Dance Cv 78645
Sun Mountain Dr 78641
Sundancer Ln 78645
Sundown St 78645
Sunflower Ct 78641
Sunny Ln 78645
Sunny Brook Dr 78645
Sunny Oak Ln 78645
Sunset Holw 78641
Sunset Ln 78645
Sunset Strip St 78645
Sunswept Dr 78645
Surrey Ln 78645
Susan Ln 78645
Swallow Cv 78641
Sweet Spring Ct 78641
Sydnee Dr 78641
Sylvester Ford Rd 78645
Tabernash Dr 78641
Tablerock Cir 78641
Talking Stick 78641
Tall Chief 78641
Tallahassee Ave 78645
Talon Cir 78645
Talon Grasp Trl 78641
Tamarac Trl 78641
Tammye Ln 78645
Tanager Pass 78641
Tanglewood Dr 78645
Tarantula Ct 78641
Teal Ln 78645
Tejas Trl 78641
Tempe Dr 78641
Tenderfoot Cv 78645
Terrace Dr
900-1099 78641
18201-18299 78645
Terrace Mountain Dr 78645
Terry Ln 78641
Thomas Cv
200-299 78641
21600-21698 78645
Thorpe Cv 78645
Thrush Dr 78641
Thunder Horse 78641
Thunderbird St 78645
Thurman Rd 78645
Ticonderoga Ave & Cv 78645
Tierra Alto St 78641
Timarron 78641
Timber Trl 78645
Tip Top Dr 78645
Tipperary Dr 78641
Tomahawk St 78645
Topaz Ln 78641
Tracy Cv 78641
Tradewind View Dr 78645
Traditions Ct 78641
Trails End Cv & Rd 78641
Trapper Ln 78645
Travis Cir, Dr & St 78645
Travista 78641
N & S Treasure Oaks Dr 78641
Treat Trl 78645
Tribal Way 78641
Trident Ln 78645
Trimaran Cv 78645
Trinity Woods St 78641
Trolley Cv 78641
Truman Cv 78645
Trustworthy Ct 78641
Tulip Lotus Cv 78641
Tumbling River Dr 78641
Tumlinson Fort Dr 78641
Turkey Bend Dr 78645
Turnback St 78645
Turtle River Dr 78641
Twain Cv 78645
Twin Cedars 78641
Twin Peaks Cv 78641
Twisted Oak Dr 78641
Twisting Trl 78645
Tyler Trl 78645
Tyrone Dr 78641
Union St 78641
Unity Dr 78641
Valle Verde Dr 78641
Valley Forge Cv 78645
Valley Hill Dr 78645
Valley View Cir, Dr & Rd 78641
Valleyview St 78645
Van Allen Cv 78645
Vance Circle Rd 78645
Vassar Rd 78645
Veneto Cir 78641
Venezia Vw 78641
Ventana Cyn 78641
Venture Blvd & Dr 78645
Verbena Ct 78641
Verde Ranch Loop 78641
Verde Vista Dr 78645
Verdura Way 78641
Victoria Chase Rd 78645
Villa Hill Dr 78641
Vineyard Cv 78641
Vintage Dr 78641
Vista Corta 78645
Vista Heights Dr 78641
Vista Oaks Dr 78641
Vista Ridge Dr 78641
Vista Rock Dr 78641
Wagon Wheel 78645
N & S Walker Dr 78645
Warfield 78641
Warren Cv 78645
Washburn Dr 78641
Washington Square Dr 78641
Water Hyacinth Cv & Loop 78641
Water Hyssop 78641
Watercliff Dr 78645
Waterfall Ave 78641
Waterside Dr 78645
Wedgescale Pass 78641
West Dr 78641
Western Justice 78641
Westwater Ct 78645
Wharf Cv 78641
Whippoorwill Cir 78641
Whippoorwill Trl 78645
Whiskey Ct 78641
Whispering Holw 78645
Whispering Hollow Cir 78645
White Oak Dr 78645
White Rim Ter & Trl 78645
White Stallion Way 78641

Whiterock Dr 78645
Whitewing Dr 78641
Whitley Dr 78641
Whittier Cv 78645
Wicklow Dr 78641
Wigwam 78641
Wildcatter 78641
Wildfire 78641
E & W Willis St 78641
Willow Creek Dr 78641
Windemere E & W 78641
Winding Oak Dr 78641
Windmill Cir 78641
Windy Valley Rd 78641
Winecup Ct 78641
Winners Ct 78641
Winslow Cv 78645
Winslow Dr 78641
Winthrop Cv & Dr 78645
Wire Rd 78641
Wishbone Dr 78645
Wolf Dancer 78641
Womack Dr 78641
Woodland Trl 78641
Woodley Rd 78641
E Woodview Dr 78641
Woodway Dr 78641
Yaupon Trl 78641
Yellow Iris Rd 78641
Yenawine Way 78641
Yountville Dr 78641
Yucca Dr 78645
Zieschang Ln 78645
Zinfandel Ln 78641
Zurga Ln 78641
Zyanya Cv 78641

NUMBERED STREETS

1st St 78645
W 1st St 78641
2nd St 78645
3rd St 78645
4th St 78645
5th St 78645
6th St 78645
183a Toll Rd 78641

LEVELLAND TX

General Delivery 79336

POST OFFICE BOXES MAIN OFFICE STATIONS AND BRANCHES

Box No.s
1 - 2000 79336
8001 - 8840 79338
93601 - 93601 79336

RURAL ROUTES

01, 02, 03, 06 79336

HIGHWAY CONTRACTS

04, 05 79336

NAMED STREETS

All Street Addresses 79336

NUMBERED STREETS

All Street Addresses 79336

LEWISVILLE TX

General Delivery 75067

POST OFFICE BOXES MAIN OFFICE STATIONS AND BRANCHES

Box No.s
1 - 1775 75067
292001 - 299217 75029

NAMED STREETS

Aaron Dr 75067
Aberdeen Dr 75077
Abigail Dr 75077
Abilene Dr
500-599 75067
600-799 75077
Ace Ln 75067
Acorn Dr 75067
Acosta Ln 75067
Adams Ave 75077
Addison Dr 75077
Adventurous Shield Dr 75056
Ajax Pl 75077
Alice Ln 75067
Almsbury Ln 75056
Alpine Pass 75077
Altstatten Ln 75067
Amber Ct 75067
Amherst Dr 75067
Amhurst Dr 75077
Andrea Ct 75067
Andrew Ct 75056
Angela Dr 75067
Angis Ln 75056
Anna Ave 75056
Annalea Cove Dr 75056
Antler Ct & Trl 75067
Apenzell Ln 75067
Appalachian Trl 75077
Applegate Dr 75067
Arbor Ct 75077
Archer Ave 75077
Arena Dr 75067
Argyle Ln 75067
Arron Ct 75077
Ash St 75057
Ashby Dr 75067
Ashley Ct 75077
Ashwood Dr 75067
Aspen Dr & Pl 75077
Aspermont Way 75067
Auburn Dr 75067
Austin Ln 75067
Autumn Trl 75067
Autumn Breeze Ln 75077
Avalon Dr 75056
Azalia Bnd & Dr 75067
Babbling Brook Dr 75067
Baird Cir 75077
Balleybrooke Dr 75077
Balleyduff Dr 75077
Bans Crown Blvd 75056
Barbara Dr 75067
Barfknecht Ln 75056
Barge Rd 75057
Barksdale Dr 75077
Barley Ct & Dr 75077
Barnett Dr 75077
Barrington Ln 75067
Bart Ln 75067
Barton Crk 75077
Bay De Vieux Dr 75056
Baythorne Dr 75077
Beasley Dr 75057
Bedford Ln 75077
Beechwood Dr & Pl 75067
Bellaire Blvd 75067
Belltower Ct, Dr & Pl 75067
Belmont Ct 75067
Belvedere Dr 75067
Benjamins Way 75057
Bennett Ln 75057
Bentley Ct 75077
Bentwood Dr 75067
Benwick Way 75056
Berne Ln 75067
N & S Berry Trail Ct 75077
Beverly Ct 75067
Bexar Dr
200-299 75077
201-229 75067
231-299 75067
Bierstadt Dr 75077
Big Bend Dr 75077
Big Elm St 75077
Big Sky Dr 75077
Birch St 75057
Birchwood Ct 75067
Birkshire Dr 75077
Biscayne Dr 75067
Black Castle Dr 75056
Black Jack Ln 75077
Blair Dr 75057
Blair Oak Dr 75067
Blue Jay Dr 75077
Blue Oak Dr 75067
Bluebonnet Dr 75077
Blueridge Dr 75067
Bluff Cir 75077
Bluffview Dr 75067
Bobing Dr 75067
Bogard Ln 75077
Bowling Green Cir & Dr 75067
Boxwood Dr 75067
Brady Dr 75057
Braemar Ln 75077
Brandon Dr 75056
Brazos Blvd 75077
Breezewood Dr 75077
Bregenz Ln 75067
Brent Dr 75057
Briar Grove Ct 75077
Briarcliff Rd 75067
Briarhill Blvd 75077
Briarwick Ln 75077
Briarwood Dr 75067
Briary Trace Ct 75077
Brighton Ct 75077
Bristol Ln 75077
Brittany Ct 75067
Brittany Dr 75067
Brittany Pl 75077
Broken Sword Dr 75056
Brook Cove Ln 75067
Brookdale Dr 75077
Brose Dr 75067
Brown Cliff Ct 75077
Brown Knight Ln 75056
Brownwood Dr 75067
Brutus Blvd 75056
Bryce Ln 75077
Buckingham Ln 75077
Buehler Ct & Pl 75067
Buffalo Bend Dr 75067
Bunker Hill Ln 75056
Burr Oak Dr 75067
Busher Dr 75067
Butterfield Stage Rd 75077
Cactus Cir 75067
Cain Dr 75077
Caitlin Dr 75067
Calgary Ct 75077
Calstone Cir 75077
Calvert Ct 75067
Cambridge Dr 75077
Camden Dr
200-299 75077
900-999 75067
Camelia Dr 75067
Camelot Ct 75067
Camelot Dr 75067
Cameo Dr 75067
Cameron Bay Dr 75056
Camille Dr 75056
Campbell Ct 75077
Campbell Dr 75057
Campbellcroft Dr 75077
Campfire Ct 75067
Canberra Ct 75077
Candlewood Cir 75067
Cannon Ln 75077
Canterbury Dr 75077
Canterbury Ln 75067
Canyon Creek Dr 75077
Cardinal Cir 75067
Cardinal Ln 75077
Carl Ct 75057
Carnation Dr 75067
Carrington Ln 75067
Carroll Ln 75067
E Carruth Ln 75067
Carver Cir 75077
Cascade Falls Dr 75067
Cascade Range 75077
Cascades Ct 75056
Case Castle Ct 75056
Casey Trl 75077
Cassion Dr 75067
Castle Rock Ct & Dr 75077
Castlewood Blvd 75077
Catalina Dr 75067
Catesby Pl 75077
Catlin Cir & Ter 75077
Caymus Ct 75067
Cedar Dr 75077
Cedar Keys Dr 75077
Cedar Ridge Dr 75067
Cedarcrest Ln 75077
Centennial Dr 75067
Century Oaks Dr 75077
Chaleur Bay Dr 75056
Chambers Dr 75067
Chaparral Ct 75077
Chapel Hl 75077
Chapel Springs Dr 75077
Chapelwood Dr 75077
Chariot Castle Dr 75056
N Charles St 75057
S Charles St
100-321 75057
320-320 75067
323-899 75057
400-1098 75057
Chelsea Ct 75067
Chelsea Bay 75067
Cherry Hill Ln 75067
Chester Dr 75056
Cheyenne Rd 75077
Chinaberry Dr 75077
Chinn Chapel Rd 75077
Chinns Chapel Ln 75077
Chisolm Trl 75077
Choctaw Ridge Dr 75067
Christopher Ln 75077
E & W Church St 75057
Cimmaron Strip 75077
Cimmaron Strip Ln 75067
Cindy Ln 75067
Circle Creek Dr 75067
Civic Cir
100-199 75067
194-194 75029
1000-1098 75067
Clarendon Dr 75067
Clary Rd 75056
Clear Creek Dr 75067
Clear Lake Ln 75077
Clear Water Dr 75056
Clearview Ct 75057
N & S Clearwater Dr 75077
Cliff View Dr 75077
Cliffrose Ln 75067
Clifton Dr 75077
Cloudy Sky Ln 75067
Club Ridge Dr 75067
Clydesdale Dr 75067
Cobblestone Dr 75067
Cody Ln 75067
Colby Dr 75067
Cole Castle Dr 75056
Colgate Dr 75077
College Pkwy 75077
E College St 75057
W College St 75057
Collin Dr 75077
Colonial Ct 75077
Colt Ln 75067
Columbia Dr 75067
Community Ctr 75077
Conner Plz 75057
Continental Dr 75067
S Copper Woods Ln 75077
Copperas Trl 75077
Copperas Branch Ct 75077
Cordero Dr 75077
Corners St 75056
Corporate Ct 75067
Corporate Dr 75067
E Corporate Dr
101-331 75067
333-357 75067
401-457 75057
459-699 75057
W Corporate Dr 75067
Cottonwood Crk 75077
Country Rdg 75067
Country Glen Ct 75077
E Country Ridge Rd 75067
Courtney Ln 75077
N & S Cowan Ave 75057
Craig Cir 75077
Creek Ct 75067
Creek Pl 75077
Creek Haven Dr 75077
Creekbank Dr 75067
Creekbend Dr 75067
Creekmeadow Ln 75067
Creekpoint Dr 75067
Creekside Ct 75077
Creekside Dr
100-199 75077
800-999 75067
Creekside Way 75077
Creekview Dr 75067
Creekway Dr 75067
Creekwood Ct, Dr & Ln 75067
Crescent Ave 75057
Crescent Dr 75077
Crest Hollow Cir 75067
Crested Butte Dr 75077
Crestview Dr 75067
Crestview Point Dr 75067
Crestwood Cir 75067
Crestwood Ln 75077
Cripple Creek Ln 75077
Crockett 75057
Cross Timbers Dr 75077
Crosshaven Dr 75077
Crown Ct 75077
Crown Of Gold Dr 75056
Crutchfield Ln 75077
Crystal Bay 75067
Cuero Pl 75077
Cypress Dr 75067
Daffodil Ln 75077
Dallas Ln 75067
Dame Brisen Dr 75056
Dame Laurel Ln 75056
Dame Susan Ln 75056
Damsel Caroline Dr 75056
Damsel Cherry Ln 75056
Damsel Ginger Ln 75056
Damsel Katie Dr 75056
Danielle Ln 75067
Dark Forest Dr 75067
Darlington Dr 75077
Dartmouth Dr 75067
Deanna Ct 75077
Decker Ln 75057
Deer Crk 75077
Deer Path 75077
Deer Run 75067
Deer Park Dr 75067
Deerhurst Dr 75077
Deering Dr 75067
Degan Ave 75057
Delano Dr 75077
Denise Ct 75067
Denton Tap Rd 75067
Desiree Ln 75077
Devin Ln 75067
Devron Ct 75077
Dewberry Dr 75067
Di Orio Dr 75067
Diamond Creek Ct 75067
Diane Cir 75067
Dickinson Dr 75077
Dogwood Trl 75067
Donna Cir 75077
Double Oaks Dr 75077
Doubletree Dr 75077
Dove Cir 75067
Dove Trl 75077
Dove Creek Ct 75077
Dover Dr 75056
Downey Dr 75067
Drake Ln 75077
Drexel Dr 75067
Dublin St 75067
Duke Saxony Dr 75056
Dumas Ct 75067
Dundee Dr 75077
Duvall Blvd 75077
Eagle Ct 75057
Eagle Nest Pass & Pl 75077
Eagle Point Rd 75077
Eagles Peak Ln 75077
Eastland Dr 75056
Eastwood Dr & Pl 75067
Ebenezer Dr 75077
N Edgewater Dr 75077
Edgewood Dr
100-199 75067
200-299 75077
Edinburgh Ct 75077
S Edmonds Ln 75067
Edmondson Dr 75077
Edmonton Dr 75077
N & S Edna Ave 75057
Edwards 75057
El Paso St 75077
Elam Dr 75067
Elika Ct 75067
Elizabeth Dr 75067
Elm St 75057
Elm Creek Dr 75056
Elmtree Dr 75077
Elmwood Dr
100-199 75077
900-1299 75067
Embleton Dr 75067
English Channel Ln 75056
Enid Dr 75056
Erec Dr 75056
Eringlen Ln 75077
Estates Dr 75077
Evelake Ct 75056
Evergreen Dr 75067
Excalibur Blvd 75056
Excalibur Dr 75077
Fagg Dr 75057
Fairfield Ct & Ln 75077
Fairland Dr 75077
Fairway Dr 75057
Falcon Dr 75077
Falken Ct 75077
Falling Water Dr 75067
Feather Ln 75077
Fenimore Dr 75077
Ferguson Dr 75057
Fern Ct 75067
Ferndale Dr 75077
Fernwood Ct 75077
Fernwood Dr 75077
Fernwood Pl 75067
Ferris Ln 75077
Firewater Cir & Pl 75067
Firewood Pl 75067
Flamingo Dr 75077
Florence Dr 75056
Florence Way 75067
Fm 2281 75056
Foggy Gln 75077
N & S Forest Ln 75077
Forest Creek Dr 75067
Forest Hill Cir 75067
Forest Oak Ct 75077
Forest Park Dr
100-220 75077
1000-1099 75057
Forest Shores Ln 75077
Forestbrook Dr 75067
Forestglen Dr 75067
Forestmeadow Dr 75067
Foster Ln 75067
Fountain Dr 75067
Fox Ave
300-688 75057
690-1099 75067
Fox Hill Ct 75077
Fox Trot Ln 75077
Foxmoor Ct & Dr 75077
Foxwood Pl 75067
Frankie Ln 75057
Franklin 75057
Frontier Trl 75067
N Garden Ridge Blvd
100-198 75067
343-577 75067
900-1700 75077
1702-2298 75077
S Garden Ridge Blvd 75067
Gareths Sword Dr 75056
Garrett Dr 75077
Gayle Ln 75077
Glasgow Ct 75077
Glen Haven Ct 75077
Glen Hollow Cir 75067
Glen Ridge Dr 75077
Glencairn Ln 75067
Glencastle Ct 75077
Glenhaven Dr 75067
Glenhill Ln 75077
Glenmere Dr 75077
Glenmore Dr 75077
Golden Grove Dr 75067
Goldfinch Dr 75077
Grail Castle Dr 75056
Grail Maiden Ct & Ln 75056
Granada Ln 75067
Grand Canyon Dr 75077
Grandys Ln 75077
Granview Dr 75067
Green Hollow Ct 75077
Green Oak Ct 75077
Green Oak Dr 75067
Green Ridge Dr 75077
Greenbriar Ln 75077
Greenland Rd 75057
Greenleaf St 75077
Greenslopes Dr 75077
Greensprings St 75077
Greenvalley Ln 75077
Greenway Ct 75077
Greenwood Ln 75067
Grove Ct & Dr 75077
Gunnison Trl 75077
Hamilton St 75067
S Hampton Ct 75056
Happy Pass Dr 75077
Harbor Dr 75057
Hardrock Castle Dr 75056
Hardy St 75057
Harn Dr 75057
Harpes Castle Ct 75056
Harris Plz 75056
Harris St 75057
Harvard Ave 75077
Harvest Knls 75077
Harvest Hill St 75067
N & S Hatcher St 75057
Haven Wood Ct 75077
Havencreek Cv 75067
Hawk Rd 75022
Hawk Crest Ln 75077
Hawse Dr 75077
Hawthorn Cir 75077
Hawthorne Ct & Dr 75077

Hayden Dr 75067
Heather Glen Dr 75067
Heatherglen Ct 75077
Hebron Pkwy 75057
Hedgerow Ln 75057
Helen Ln 75067
Hembry St 75057
Hemlock Ct 75067
Henrietta St 75057
Hereford Dr 75056
Heritage Hill Dr 75067
Herod St 75057
Hershey Ln 75077
Hickory St 75057
Hickory Ridge Dr 75077
Hidden Oak Ct 75077
Hidden Trail Dr 75067
High Chapel Ct 75077
High Meadow Ct & Pl 75077
High Oak Dr 75077
High School Dr 75057
Highgate Dr 75067
Highland Ct 75077
Highland Dr 75067
Highland Knls 75077
Highland Forest Dr 75077
Highland Hills Ln 75077
Highland Lake Dr 75077
Highland Meadows Dr 75077
Highland Shores Blvd 75077
Highland Village Rd 75077
Highpoint Dr 75077
Highpoint Oaks Dr 75067
Highview Dr 75077
N Hill Ct 75077
Hill Dl 75077
W Hill Ln 75056
Hillcrest Dr 75077
Hilldale Dr 75067
E Hillpark Rd 75056
Hillshire Dr 75067
Hillside Ct 75077
Hillside Dr
100-899 75057
900-3199 75077
Hilltop Ct & Dr 75077
Hillview Dr 75067
Hillwood Dr 75067
Hobart Ln 75067
Hobie Point Dr 75056
Holfords Prairie Rd 75056
Hollow Hill Ln 75056
Hollow Oak Ct 75077
Holly Ln 75067
Holly Oak Dr 75067
Holy Grail Dr 75056
Honeysuckle Ln 75077
Hoover Dr 75067
Horseshoe Dr 75077
Houston St 75057
Huddersfield Crst 75077
Hudson Bay Ct 75077
Huffines Blvd 75056
Huffines Plz 75057
Hummingbird Cir 75067
Hundred Knights Dr 75056
Hunt Dr 75067
Hunters Glen St 75067
Huntington Dr 75067
Hyatt Dr 75077
Idlewild Ct 75077
Idlewilde Dr 75067
Inca Pl 75077
Indian Paint Trl 75067
Inverness Cir 75077
Inverness Dr 75067
Iris Ln 75067
Ivan Dr 75067
Ivyglen Ct 75067
Jackson Dr 75067
Jacobson Dr 75067
Janwood Pl 75067
Jasmine Dr 75077
Javelin Way 75077
Jefferson Ave 75077
Jenkins Ln 75067
Jennifer Ct & Pl 75077
Jernigan Rd 75077
Jewels Way 75067
E Jones St 75057
Jubilee Ln 75056
Julia Ct 75067
Juniper Ln & Pl 75077
Justin Rd 75077
Kamla Rd 75067
Karen Renee Ct 75077
Kathryn Dr 75067
Kathy Ln 75067
Kay Ln 75057
N & S Kealy Ave 75057
Keeson Trl 75077
Kelda Ln 75067
Kelly Ln 75077
Kemper Ct 75067
Kenny Ct 75067
Kent Dr 75067
Kielder Dr 75067
Kimberlee Ln 75077
King Cir 75067
King Arthur Blvd 75056
King Ban Dr 75056
King Bors Ln 75056
King Galloway Dr 75056
King Lionel Ln 75056
King Lot Ln 75056
King Mark Dr 75056
Kingfisher Dr 75057
E Kings Rd 75077
Kingston Dr 75067
Kingwood Cir & Ct 75077
Kirkwood Dr 75067
Knob Hill Ln 75077
Knobb Hill Ct 75067
Knoll Ct & Rd 75077
Knollridge Dr 75077
Knorain Dr 75057
Krista Ct 75056
Kyle Ct 75077
Kyle Ln 75067
La Vista Ln 75077
Lady Amide Ln 75056
Lady Carol Dr 75056
Lady Cornwall Dr 75056
Lady De Vance Ln 75056
Lady Lore Dr 75056
Lady Of The Lake
Blvd 75056
Lady Rule Ln 75056
Lady Viviane Ln 75056
Laguna Bay 75067
Lake Cv & Vis E, N, S &
W 75077
Lake Breeze Dr 75077
Lake Brook Ct 75077
Lake City Dr 75056
Lake Creek Dr 75077
Lake Crest Ln 75057
Lake Haven Ct 75077
Lake Haven Dr 75057
Lake Heights Ct 75077
Lake Highlands Dr 75077
Lake Hollow Ct 75077
W Lake Park Rd 75057
Lake Ridge Rd 75056
Lake Shore Dr 75057
Lake Trail Ct & Dr 75077
Lake Vista Dr 75067
Lakeland Dr
100-399 75077
900-1099 75067
Lakepointe Dr 75057
Lakeside Cir 75057
Lakeside Dr 75077
Lakeview Cir 75057
Lakeway Dr 75057
Lakewood Ct 75077
Lambeth Ln 75056
Lamesa Dr 75077
Lamiterl Dr 75067
Landoine Ln 75056
Lanier Pl 75077
Lansbury Dr 75077
Laramie Dr & Pl 75077
Lark Ln 75077
Laurel Ln 75067
Lea Meadow Dr 75077
League Rd 75067
Lees Ct 75067
Legends Dr 75057
Leigh Ct 75077
Len Mar Dr 75077
Leonard St 75057
Leslie Ln 75077
Lester St 75057
Lewisville Plz 75067
Lincoln Ct 75077
Lincolnshire Ln 75056
Lindsey Trl 75077
Linlee Ln 75067
Liones Ln 75056
Little Den Dr 75067
Little Fawn Ct 75067
Live Oak Ct 75067
Live Oak Dr 75067
Live Oak Ln 75077
Lochmoor Ln 75077
Logan Dr 75077
Lone Oak St 75057
Lonesome Dove Ln 75077
Long Isles Ln 75056
Longfellow Dr 75077
Longhorn Dr 75067
Louis Ln 75056
Louise Ln 75077
Louise St 75057
Lusk Ln 75077
Lynn Ave 75057
Lynnwood Pl 75067
Macarthur Blvd 75067
Madison Ave 75077
Madison Cir 75067
Madison Dr 75067
Magic Mantle Dr 75056
Magnolia Dr 75067
Mahogany Ln 75077
Maidens Castle Dr 75056
Main St 75077
E Main St 75057
W Main St
100-607 75057
609-647 75057
701-719 75067
721-1799 75067
1801-1899 75067
Malibu Dr 75077
Mallard Ct & Dr 75077
Manchester Rd 75077
Manco Rd 75067
Mandalay Bay Dr 75056
Maple Dr 75057
Maple Leaf 75077
Maplewood Dr 75067
Marblecrest Dr 75067
Marblehead Dr 75067
Marchant Pl 75067
Marchwood Dr 75077
Marcus Dr 75057
Marina Ct 75067
Marina Vista Dr 75056
Market Pl 75077
Martin St 75057
Marys Ct 75057
Massey Dr 75067
Matterhorn Way 75077
Mauve Dr 75067
Maxwell Dr 75077
Mayberry Ct 75077
Mayfair Ct & Ln 75077
Mayflower Ln 75077
Mcdonnell St 75057
Mcgee Ln 75077
Mckenzie St 75057
Mcmahan Dr 75077
Mcmakin Rd 75077
N Meadow Ct 75077
Meadow Dr 75077
Meadow Pl 75067
Meadow Rd 75077
Meadow Bend Ct 75077
Meadow Knoll Rd 75077
Meadow Lake Ct 75077
Meadow Oak Ct 75077
Meadowbrook Dr 75077
Meadowcrest Dr 75077
Meadowglen Dr 75067
Meadowlark Dr 75067
Meadowlark Ln 75077
Medina Dr 75077
Memory Ct 75077
Meriwood Dr 75067
Merlin Dr 75056
Merlins Rock Ln 75056
Merriman Dr 75077
Merryvale Ct 75067
Metro Business Park 75057
Metro Park Blvd & Cir 75057
Michael Ave 75077
Midway Cir 75057
Midway Rd 75056
Milan St 75067
Milestone Rdg 75067
N & S Mill St 75057
Millican Dr 75057
Millington Dr 75077
Millwood Dr 75077
Milton St 75057
Mimosa Ln 75077
Misty Ln 75077
Misty Oak Dr 75077
Mobile Dr 75077
Moccassin Trl 75077
Mockingbird Cir 75067
Mockingbird Dr 75067
Mockingbird Ln 75077
Modesto Ct 75067
Monaco Dr 75067
Monarch Dr 75067
Monday Haus Ln 75077
Montclair Ln 75067
Montego Bay Cir 75067
Monti Dr 75057
Moran Dr 75077
Mordred Ln 75056
Morgan Lefay Ln 75056
Morningside Ave 75057
Mosswood Dr 75077
Muirfield Dr 75067
Mulberry Dr 75067
Mulholland St 75077
Mullins 75057
Mustang Ct & Dr 75067
Mystic Hollow Dr 75067
Napoli Cir 75077
Nelson Pkwy 75077
Newhaven Dr 75077
Niagara Blvd & Ct 75077
Nightingale Dr 75077
North St 75057
Northfork Cir 75057
Northside Ave 75057
Northwood Dr 75077
Nowlin Dr 75077
Oak St 75077
Oak Creek Dr 75077
Oak Creek Estates Dr 75067
Oak Forest Dr 75077
Oak Grove Cir 75077
Oak Hill Cir 75067
Oak Hollow Ln 75077
Oak Knoll Cir 75067
Oak Leaf Ct 75077
Oak Trail Dr 75077
Oak View Pl 75067
Oakbend Dr 75067
Oakbrook Dr 75057
Oakridge Blvd 75057
Oakridge Cir 75057
Oakridge Trl 75077
Oaktree Dr 75077
Oakview Dr 75077
Oakwood Ct 75077
Oakwood Ln 75067
Office Park Cir 75057
Old Barn Ln 75067
Old Mill Cir 75057
N Old Orchard Ln
101-499 75067
600-698 75077
700-799 75077
801-899 75077
S Old Orchard Ln 75067
Olivia Dr 75067
Olympic Ct 75077
Ontzlake Dr 75056
Orchard Dr 75067
Orchid Dr 75067
Oriole Dr 75077
Ottawa Ln 75077
Overlook Cir 75077
Overlook Dr 75067
Oxford Ct 75056
Palermo Trl 75077
Palisades Dr 75067
Palmert Trl 75077
Park Ln & Vw 75077
Park Lane Dr 75067
Parker Rd 75056
Parkhurst Cir 75077
Parkside Ct & Trl 75077
Parkway Dr 75057
Parkwood Pl 75067
Parma Dr 75077
Patricia Ln 75077
Peachtree Ln 75067
Peacock Ct 75077
Pebble Knl 75077
Pebble Beach Dr 75067
Pebble Ridge Dr 75067
Pebblebrook Dr 75067
Pecan Ln 75067
Pecan St 75077
Pecos St 75077
Pelham Ln 75077
Pendragon Dr 75056
Penjay Ln 75077
Peregrine Ct & St 75077
Perro Pl 75077
Perry Ave 75057
Pheasant Dr 75077
Pickett St 75057
Piedmont Dr 75067
Pilot Ln 75077
Pine Dr & St 75057
Pine Ridge Dr 75067
Pinebluff Dr 75067
Pinehurst Ct & Dr 75077
Pinewood Pl 75067
Pinnacle Cir 75077
Pinto Ln 75067
Plantation Dr 75067
Pleasant Run 75067
Pleasant Oaks Dr 75067
Point Rd 75057
Porter Rd 75022
Post Oak Dr 75077
Post Oak St 75057
N & S Poydras St 75057
Prairie Dr 75067
Prairie Dell St 75067
Preserve Pl 75067
Preston Ln 75077
Preston Oaks Dr 75067
Prestwick Ln 75067
Price Dr 75067
Primrose Ln 75077
Purdue Dr 75067
Purgatory Pass 75077
E Purnell Rd 75057
W Purnell Rd
101-133 75057
135-525 75057
527-595 75057
600-799 75067
Quail Cir 75067
Quail Cove Dr 75077
Quail Ridge Ct 75077
Quaker Ln 75077
Queen Elaine Dr 75056
Queen Elizabeth Blvd 75056
Queen Guinevere Dr 75056
Queen Margaret Dr 75056
Queen Morgan Ln 75056
Queen Peggy Ln 75056
Queens Ct 75077
Rachels Ct 75067
N & S Railroad St 75057
Rain Tree Ln 75056
Raintree Dr 75077
Raldon St 75067
Raleigh Dr 75077
Ramblewood Dr 75067
Rancho Vista Dr 75077
Ranier Ct 75077
Ranney Dr 75077
Raven Ln 75077
Red Bud St 75057
Red Castle Dr 75056
Red Hawk Rd 75056
Red Oak Dr 75067
Red River Dr 75077
Red Wing Dr 75067
Redbird Cir 75067
Redbird Ln 75077
Redwood Dr 75077
Redwood Pl 75067
Regal Ct 75077
Regency Dr 75067
Rembert Ct 75077
Remington Dr & Ter 75077
Reno Run & St 75077
Richland St 75057
Ridge Cove Dr 75067
Ridge Haven Dr 75067
Ridge Meade Dr 75067
Ridge Point Dr 75067
Ridge Stone Dr 75067
Ridgebriar Dr 75077
Ridgecreek Dr 75067
Ridgecrest Dr 75067
Ridgedale Dr 75067
Ridgeview 75057
Ridgeway Cir 75067
Rivercrest Dr 75067
Riverside Dr 75067
Robertson 75057
Robin Rd 75077
Robincreek Cv 75067
Rockbrook Dr 75067
Rockland Dr 75077
Rocky Point Dr 75077
Rolling Acres Dr 75077
Rolling Ridge Dr 75067
Rolling View Ct 75077
Roma Cir 75077
Roma Dr 75067
Rose Cir 75077
Rosedale St 75077
Ross Dr 75067
E & W Round Grove
Rd 75067
Round Mountain Cir 75056
Round Table Blvd 75056
Royal Oaks Dr
100-198 75077
900-999 75067
Ruidoso Run 75077
Runge Dr 75057
Rushmore Ct 75067
Russell Dr 75077
Saddle Brook Dr 75077
Saddleback Ln 75067
Safe Harbor Dr 75056
Sage Ct 75077
Sailmaker Ct & Dr 75067
Sailors Ave 75056
Saint Andrew Dr 75077
Saint Andrews Dr 75067
Saint Gallen Ln 75067
Saint James Ct 75077
Salado Dr 75067
Salem Ct & Trl 75067
Salisbury Ct 75056
Sam Dennis Dr 75077
Samuel St 75057
San Antone Ln 75077
San Jacinto Dr 75067
Sandberg Pl 75077
Sandero Dr 75077
Sandra Dr 75057
Sandy Beach Rd 75057
Sandy Hook 75077
Santa Fe 75077
Sante Fe Dr 75077
Santiago Bay 75067
Savage Ln 75057
Savanna Dr 75077
Scenic Dr 75077
Scotti St 75056
Scottish Mist Trl 75077
Seige Ct 75056
Sellmeyer Ln 75077
Sendero Trl 75067
Seneca Pl & Way 75067
Sequoia Grove Ln 75067
Settlers Way 75067
Seven Shields Ln 75056
Shade Tree St 75077
Shaded Place Dr 75077
Shadow Ridge Dr 75077
Shadow Vale Ct 75077
Shadow Wood Cir 75077
Shadow Wood Ln 75067
Shadowridge Cir 75067
Shady Bend Ct 75077
Shady Creek Dr 75067
Shady Elm Ln 75067
Shady Hill Ln 75077
Shady Lane Ct 75077
Shady Meadow Ct &
Dr 75077
Shady Oaks Ln 75077
Shannon Dr & Ln 75077
Shasta Ct 75077
Sheldon Ct 75077
Sherbourne St 75067
Sherwood Ln 75077
Shetland Dr 75077
Shoal Crk 75077
E Shore 75057
W Shore 75057
N Shore Dr 75077
N Shore Pl 75077
S Shore Pl 75067
Shore View Dr 75077
Shoreham Cir 75056
Shoreline Way 75056
Shufords Ct 75067
Sicily Way 75067
Sides Ct 75057
Sienna Trl 75067
Sierra Dr & Pl 75077
Silver Cloud Cir 75067
Silver Oak Ln 75067
Silver Table Dr 75056
Silverstone Dr 75067
Silverthorne Ct & Trl 75077
Simmons Ave 75057
Simmons Rd 75077
Simpson Ct 75067
Sinclair Ct 75067
Singletree St 75077
Sir Alexander Ln 75056
Sir Amant Dr 75056
Sir Andred Ln 75056
Sir Bedivere Ln 75056
Sir Belin Dr 75056
Sir Brine Dr 75056
Sir Castor Ct 75056
Sir Constantine Dr 75056
Sir Ector Ln 75056
Sir Galahad Ln 75056
Sir Gawain Ln 75056
Sir Kay Dr 75056
Sir Lancelot Blvd &
Cir 75056
Sir Lovel Ln 75056
Sir Malory Ln 75056
Sir Patrice Ln 75056
Sir Percival Ln 75056
Sir Torin Ln 75056
Sir Tristram Ln 75056
Sir Turquin Ln 75056

Sir Wade Way 75056
Sleepy Holw 75077
Smith St 75057
Smokey Hill Dr 75067
Snow Trl 75077
Snow Bird Trl 75077
Snowdon Ct 75077
Snowmass Pl 75077
Solway Dr 75067
Somerset Rd 75067
Sorrento Ln 75077
Southfork Dr 75057
E & W Southwest Pkwy 75067
Southwood Ct 75067
Southwood Dr 75077
Sparks Ct 75077
Sparrow Ct 75077
Spence Dr 75067
Spenrock Ct 75077
Spring Creek Ct 75077
Spring Creek Ln 75067
Spring Glen Dr 75067
Spring Hill Ln 75077
Spring Hollow Ct 75077
Spring Lake Ct 75077
Spring Oaks Dr 75077
Spring Park Ct 75077
Spring Water Ct 75077
Springaire Ln 75077
Springway Dr 75077
Springwood Dr 75067
Spruce Dr 75077
Stanford Ln 75067
Starling Ln 75077
State Highway 121 75056
E State Highway 121
200-358 75057
E State Highway 121
360-1199 75057
1550-2298 75056
2300-2699 75056
2701-2799 75056
S State Highway 121 75067
State Highway 121 Byp 75067
S State Highway 121 Bus 75067
Steamboat Trl 75077
Stella Dr 75067
N Stemmons Fwy
100-1258 75067
1260-1850 75067
2131-2897 75077
2899-3000 75077
3002-3098 75077
S Stemmons Fwy 75067
Sterling Ln 75067
Stillwater Pl 75067
Stone Canyon Dr 75077
Stone Canyon Way 75067
Stone Circle Ln 75056
Stone Creek Dr 75056
Stonehenge Ln 75056
Stonewall 75056
Stony Brook Dr 75067
Stony Passage Ln 75056
Stover Dr 75067
Strathmore Dr 75077
Stuart St 75057
Sugarloaf Ct 75077
Summercreek Dr 75067
Summertime Trl 75067
Summertrail Ct 75077
Summerwind Cir, Ct & Ln 75077
Summit Ave 75077
N Summit Ave 75067
Summit Dr 75077
Summit Park 75077
Summit Rdg 75077
Summit Run 75077
Summit Way 75077
Summit Peak 75077
Summit Pointe 75077
Sundance Ct 75067
Sunday Haus Ln 75077
Sunderland Ln 75067
Sunflower Ln 75077
Sunny Grove Dr 75067
Sunny Haven Ct 75077
Sunny Point Ct 75077
Sunnydale 75067
Sunrise Trl 75067
Sunset Ln & Path 75067
Sunswept Ter 75077
Surf St 75067
Surrey Ln 75077
Swallow Cir & Ln 75077
Swan Ct 75077
Swan Lake Dr 75077
Sweet Gum Dr 75067
Sweet Spring Ct 75067
Sweetbriar Dr 75067
Sword Bridge Dr 75056
Sylvan Creek Bnd & Dr 75067
Tablerock Way 75077
Tahoe Dr 75067
Talon Dr 75077
Tanglewood Ln 75077
Tanner Dr 75077
Tara Ct 75067
Tartan Trl 75077
Taylor Ln 75077
Teague Dr 75067
Teakwood Ct & Ln 75077
Teal Ct 75077
Temple Dr 75057
Tennie Dr 75057
Terence Ln 75067
Terracotta Ct 75067
Teton Trl 75077
Texas St 75057
Tharp Dr 75077
The Lakes Blvd 75056
Thistle Ct 75077
Thomas St 75057
Thompson Dr 75067
Thornberry Trl 75077
Thornhill Cir 75077
Thrush Ct 75077
Tiburon Bnd 75067
Tiffany Ln 75067
Timber Bnd & Way 75077
Timber Creek Dr 75067
Timber Crest Ln 75077
Timber Way Dr 75067
Timberbrook Dr 75077
Timbercrest Cir 75077
Timberlake Ln 75067
Timberleaf Ct & Dr 75077
Timberline Dr 75077
Timberview Dr 75077
Toronto Dr 75077
Tower Bay 75077
Trail Ridge Dr 75077
Trailing Oaks Dr 75077
Trails End 75077
Treasure Cove Dr 75056
Tree Crest Dr 75077
Tree Haven Ct 75077
Tucson Dr 75077
Tuesday Haus Ln 75077
Turman Ct 75077
Turnberry Ln 75067
Turpin Dr 75077
Tuscany Way 75067
Twilight Dr 75056
Twin Coves Dr 75077
Twin Lakes Ct & Dr 75077
Twin Point Dr 75056
E & S Uecker Dr & Ln 75067
N Umberland Dr 75056
Union Station Pkwy 75057
University Pl 75067
Utica Ln 75077
Vagon Castle Ln 75056
Vail Pl 75077
Valencia Ln 75067
N Valley Pkwy
101-177 75067
179-599 75067
601-697 75077
699-1699 75077
S Valley Pkwy 75067
Valley Oaks Dr 75067
Valley Ridge Blvd
100-600 75057
602-838 75057
850-858 75077
870-898 75057
900-1300 75077
1302-1498 75077
Valley Ridge Cir 75057
Valley Ridge Ct 75077
Valley View Dr 75067
Valley View Trl 75077
Valley Wood Ct 75077
Valleybrook Dr 75067
Vancouver Dr 75077
Venice Trl 75067
Via Italia Dr 75067
Victoria Dr 75077
Victory Ln 75077
E View Ct 75077
Villa Creek Dr 75077
Villa Park Dr 75077
Village Dr 75067
Village Pkwy 75077
Village Estates Dr 75077
Village Tree Dr 75077
Vista Ct & Dr 75067
Vista Bluff Blvd 75067
Vista Heights Ln 75077
Vista Noche Dr 75067
Vista Ridge Mall 75067
E Vista Ridge Mall Dr 75067
Vista Trail Dr 75067
Vista View Ct & Dr 75067
Waite Dr 75077
Wake Forest Dr 75077
Waketon Rd 75077
Wales Way 75056
Wallbrook Dr 75067
Waller Crk 75077
Wallingford Ln 75056
Wallington Way 75067
Walnut Dr 75067
E & W Walters St 75057
Wanderlust Dr 75067
Warrior Dr 75067
Washington Ave 75077
Water Bridge Dr 75056
Water Oak Dr 75067
Waterford Dr 75077
Waters Ridge Dr 75057
Wellesley Dr 75067
Wellington Dr 75067
Wentworth Dr 75067
Wentworth Way 75077
West Way 75057
Westminster Dr 75056
Westwood Dr & Pl 75067
Whatley Ave 75057
Whispering Cv 75067
Whispering Oaks Dr 75077
Whispering Trail Cir 75067
Whistling Duck Ln 75077
White Rock Dr 75056
White Stag Way 75056
Whitehorse Dr 75077
Whitmore Ln 75057
Whittier Ct & St 75077
Wild Forest Cir 75056
Wild Horse Corral 75067
Wildfire Dr 75067
Wildvalley Dr 75067
Willow Brk 75067
Willow Cv 75077
Willow St 75057
Willow Way 75077
Willow Creek Est 75077
Willow Grove Dr 75067
Willow Oak Ct 75077
Willow Oak Dr 75067
Willow Springs Dr 75067
Willowridge Cir 75067
Willowross Dr 75077
Wimbledon Dr 75077
Winchester Dr 75056
Wind Wood Dr 75067
Windcrest Ct 75077
Windhaven Cir 75067
Winding Bend Cir 75077
Winding Creek Dr 75077
Windsor Ct 75077
Windsor Castle Way 75056
Windy Ct 75077
Winnipeg Dr 75077
Winston Dr 75077
Winter Park Ln 75077
Winterstone Dr 75067
Winterwood Dr 75067
Witherby Ln 75067
Wolf Creek Pass 75077
Wood Heights Dr 75067
Woodbend Dr 75067
Wooded Creek Cir 75067
E & W Woodglen Dr 75077
Woodhaven Ct & Dr 75077
Woodhill Dr 75067
Woodhollow Ct & Dr 75077
Woodlake Ct 75077
N & S Woodland Dr & Trl 75077
Woodmere Dr 75067
Woodrow Dr 75067
Woodside Ct & Dr 75077
Woven Trl 75067
Wren Ct & Ln 75077
Yacht Club Dr 75056
Yale Ave 75057
Yates St 75057
Yellowstone Ave 75077
York Ct 75056
Yorkshire Cir & Ter 75067
Yosemite Dr 75077
Yukon Dr 75077

LONGVIEW TX

General Delivery 75606

POST OFFICE BOXES MAIN OFFICE STATIONS AND BRANCHES

Box No.s
1 - 4759 75606
5002 - 6964 75608
7001 - 8940 75607
9001 - 10314 75608
12001 - 14003 75607
150001 - 151394 75615

RURAL ROUTES

07 75601
01, 13, 17 75602
03, 06, 11, 16 75603
04, 08, 19 75604
02, 05, 09, 10, 12, 14, 15 75605

NAMED STREETS

Aaron St 75602
Aars St 75601
Abe St 75601
N Access Rd 75602
S Access Rd
100-198 75603
500-598 75602
700-799 75603
800-2999 75602
Acorn Dr 75604
Adams Rd 75604
Adams St 75601
Aden Dr 75602
Adrian Rd 75605
Agness Dr 75602
Airline Rd 75605
Airpark Dr 75603
Akin Dr 75605
Alberta St 75605
Aledo St 75604
Alexander Rd & St 75604
Alexis Dr 75605
Alice Cir 75605
Alice Dr 75605
Alice St 75603
Alicia Dr 75605
Alicia Dawn Dr 75605
Allen Rd 75605
Alley St 75602
Alma St 75605
Alpine Rd 75601
Alpine St 75605
Alta St 75604
Alvarez St 75604
Ambassador Row 75604
Amber St 75604
Amberwood Dr 75605
America Dr 75604
American Legion Blvd 75601
Amesbury Cir 75605
Amherst Cir & St 75601
Amos Rd 75602
Amy St 75605
Amy Scott Ct 75605
Anderson Rd 75604
Andrea St 75604
Andrews St 75602
Angelina Ct 75604
Anita St 75603
E & W Ann Dr 75601
Annette Dr 75604
Anniversary St 75604
Antler 75605
Apache Ct 75605
Apple Rd & St 75605
April Ct 75604
Arapaho St 75605
E Arden Dr 75602
Arkansas St 75601
Arland Dr 75604
Armond Dr 75602
Arno St 75604
Arnold St 75602
Arrow Ln 75604
Arthur Dr 75604
Arvern St 75602
Asaff St 75602
Ash St 75605
Ashbourne Ln 75605
Ashbriar Ln 75605
Ashcraft Ln 75604
Ashford Ln 75605
Aspen St 75605
Aster Ct 75604
Astronaut Dr 75603
Atlanta Ct 75604
Atoka St 75604
Auburn Dr 75601
Audrey St 75601
Augusta St 75601
E Aurel Ave 75602
Autumn Ln 75604
E & W Avalon Ave 75602
N & S Avenue A 75604
Avenue B 75604
Avenue C 75604
Avenue D 75604
Avondale St 75601
Awalt St 75604
Azalea Cir & Dr 75601
Aztec Aly 75604
Bacle Rd 75604
Balsam St 75605
Bancroft Cir 75605
Bandera Trl 75604
E & W Bank St 75601
Bar Chase Trl 75605
Bar K Ranch Rd 75605
Barainti Rd 75605
Barbara Dr 75604
Barton St 75603
Bass Dr 75604
Bassett St 75602
Bates St 75602
Batman St 75605
Baxley Ln 75604
Baxter Ave 75602
Bay St 75604
Baylee Dr 75605
Baylor Dr 75601
Bazzell Dr 75604
Beall Rd 75604
Beall Mountain Rd 75604
Beasley St 75602
Beaty Rd 75605
Beaumont St 75602
Beaver Run 75603
Becky Dr 75605
Bedford Cir 75601
Belclaire Cir 75605
Bell St 75602
Bell Meadows Dr 75605
Bella Terra Dr 75605
Bellengrath Dr 75605
Ben Hogan Dr 75605
Ben Mitchell Rd 75603
Benbrook Ln 75604
Bend St 75601
Bennington Ct 75601
Benny St 75604
Bent Tree Ln 75605
Benton St 75602
E & W Berkley St 75604
Berkshire Dr 75605
Bermuda Ln 75605
Bernice St 75604
Berry Ln 75602
Bertha Ave 75602
Berts St 75604
Beth Dr 75605
Bethel St 75601
Betty Dr 75602
Betty Jo Dr 75605
Beverly St 75601
Big Rd 75603
Big Bend Dr 75605
Big Oak Blvd 75602
Big Woods Rd 75605
Bill Harris Rd 75604
Bill Owens Pkwy
100-2699 75604
2700-4399 75605
Bill Wright Rd 75604
Birch St 75604
Birdie Pl 75604
E & W Birdsong St 75602
Birdwell Ln 75605
Biscayne Ct & Dr 75604
Bishop St 75602
Bison Trl 75601
Bivins Ct 75601
Blackberry Cir 75603
Blackstone Rd 75604
Blaine Trl 75604
Blake Dr 75604
Blake Rd 75602
Blount St 75602
Bluebird Dr 75601
Bluebonnett Ln 75604
Blueridge Pkwy 75605
Bob White Rd 75605
Bobby St 75602
Bobolink Ln & St 75603
Bodie St 75601
Bogie St 75604
Bois D Arc St 75604
Boliver St 75601
Bolton St 75602
Bonnell Dr 75601
Bonner St 75602
Bonner Norris Ln 75604
Bonnie St 75605
Bonnita St 75604
Booker St 75602
Booth St 75601
Borders Rd 75603
S Boring St 75601
Borman Rd & St 75605
Bostic Dr 75602
Boston Dr 75601
Boyd Rd 75604
W Boyd St 75601
Bradley St 75602
Bramlette Ln & Pl 75601
E & W Branch St 75604
E Brandon St 75604
Brandywine Dr 75601
Braniff Ln 75605
Brassie Way 75605
Breland Rd 75604
Brenner 75603
Brent Rd 75604
E & W Brentwood St 75604
Bretta Cir 75605
Brewton St 75602
Briarmeadow Dr 75604
Briarwood Ln 75604
Bridgers Hill Rd 75604
Bridle Path 75605
Brisbane Dr 75605
W & E Broadway Ct & St 75604
Bromlett Ln 75601
Bronco St 75602
Brookhaven Dr 75602
Brooks St 75602
Brookside Cir 75604
Brookside Dr 75602
Brookway Ln 75604
Brown Rd 75605
Brown St 75601
Brownwood Dr 75602
Bruce Ln 75604
Bryant St 75605
Bryn Mawr St 75604
Buccaneer Dr 75604
E Buchanan Ave 75602
Buckner Dr 75604
S Budd Pl 75602
Bull Run Trl 75604
Bundrick Ln 75604
Bunker Hill Ct 75601
Burks Rd 75605
Burnam Rd 75605
Burton St 75603
Butler Dr 75602
Cabec Dr 75605
Cactus St 75601
Caddo St 75602
Cadillac Cir 75602
Cain Cemetery Rd 75602
Cairy Ln 75604
Caldwell St 75602
Callahan Rd 75602
Calvin Blvd 75602
Cambridge Ln 75601
Camden Ct 75601
Camellia Ln 75601
Camelot Ct 75605
Cameron St 75604
Camille Dr
500-799 75604
800-1199 75605
1201-1299 75605
Camp Rd 75605
W Camp Switch Rd 75604
Campbell Rd 75605
Campbell St 75604
Candace 75605
Cannon St 75604
Canterbury Blvd 75605
Canyon Ridge Ct 75604
Capacity Dr 75604
Capp St 75601
Caprock Dr 75605
Captains Cor 75605
Cardinal Ln 75605
Cardinal St 75601
Carnegie Dr 75601
Carrie Dr 75605
E Carrie Dr 75605

Carrie Ln 75602
S Carter St 75601
Carver St 75602
Casandra Dr 75605
Casey Ct 75604
Castle St 75604
Castle Ridge Dr 75605
Castleberry St 75605
Castlegate St 75604
Castlemaine Cir 75605
Cattail Ln 75604
Cedar Ave 75602
Cedar Crest St 75602
Cedar Hill Rd 75601
Cedar Ranch Rd 75605
Cedar Ridge Rd 75602
Cedar Springs Rd 75605
Celebration Way 75605
Celess Ave 75602
Cendenwo Rd 75604
Centenary Cir & Dr 75601
N & S Center St 75601
Central Rd 75603
W & N Cerliano Dr & Rd 75605
Chad St 75604
Chaffin Cir 75605
Champion Way 75604
Chapparal St 75603
Chappell Ave 75602
Charlene St 75604
Charlotte Dr 75601
Charron Ave 75601
Chase Ct 75605
Chase Creek Pl 75605
Chase Crest Cir 75605
Chase Ridge Dr 75605
Chase Wood Way 75605
Chateau Ct 75604
Cherie Ln 75604
Cherokee St 75604
Cherokee Trce
1-99 75603
2100-2199 75604
Cherokee Trl 75603
Cherrywood Cir 75604
Cheryl St 75604
E Cheryl St 75605
Chestnut Ln 75604
Chickasaw St 75605
Chigger Rdg 75604
Chippewa St 75605
Chisolm Pl 75605
Chisom Rd 75605
Choctaw St 75605
Chris Dr 75605
Christal Dr 75601
Christian Rd 75604
Christie St 75605
Christine St 75605
Christopher Dr 75604
E Church Dr 75601
Church St
400-599 75605
1000-1298 75603
1501-1599 75603
Cielo Way 75604
Cindi Ct 75605
Cippele Dr 75605
Circle Rd 75602
City Center Way 75605
Claire Ln 75605
Clarence Ct 75605
Clarendon St 75601
Clark St 75601
Clarkway Pl 75605
Claudia Cir 75605
Clay Dr 75605
Clayton St 75605
Clear Lake Dr 75605
Cleardale Dr 75604
Clearwood Dr 75604
Clemens Rd 75605
Clendenen Ln 75605
Cliffwood St 75603
Clingman Dr 75602

Clinic Dr 75605
Clinton St 75604
Cloud Rd 75604
Clover Ln 75602
N & S Club Dr 75602
Clyatt St 75605
Clyde St 75604
Cobb Dr 75604
Cochise St 75603
Cole Dr 75602
Coleman Dr 75605
Colgate Dr 75601
E & W College St 75601
Collins Ave 75605
Colonial Dr 75605
Colony Cir 75604
Colt St 75604
Columbia Dr 75601
Comanche St 75605
Commander Dr 75605
Commerce St 75604
Common St 75601
Community Blvd 75605
Concord St 75604
Conrad St 75604
Conroe St 75604
Conway St 75601
Cook Ln 75604
Coolant Ln 75604
Cordoba Trl 75605
Cornell Cir & St 75601
Corporate Rd 75603
Cortland Cir 75605
E Cotton St
100-599 75601
600-798 75602
800-2999 75602
W Cotton St
100-298 75601
300-399 75601
401-499 75601
600-1899 75604
Country Pl 75605
Country Club Dr & Rd 75602
Country Villa Ln 75602
County Road 2115d 75603
County Road 2118 75603
County Road 2118a 75603
County Road 2121 75603
County Road 2121a 75603
County Road 2122d 75603
County Road 2123 N 75603
County Road 2123a 75603
County Road 2124d 75603
County Road 2146d 75603
County Road 2152d 75603
County Road 2158d 75603
County Road 2161 N 75603
N & S Court St 75601
Courthouse Dr 75605
Coushatta Ct & Trl 75605
Cove Pl 75604
Covehaven Cir 75605
Covington Dr 75602
Cox Ln 75605
Cox Dairy Rd 75604
Craig St 75602
Creek Ln 75605
Creek Bend St 75604
Creekmont Ln 75605
Creekside Dr 75604
Creekwood Cir & Ln 75602
Crenshaw St 75605
Crepe Myrtle Ln 75604
Crescent Dr 75602
Crestview Dr 75604
Crestwood Dr 75601
Crockett St 75604
Cross Creek Rd 75602
Crossroads Dr 75605
Crowder Ln 75603
Crown Dr 75602
Crystal Dr 75604
E & W Culver St 75602
Cumberland Dr 75601
Cummins St 75602

Cunyus St 75604
Cupit Dr & Rd 75604
Curtis St 75603
Cynthia Dr 75605
Cypress St 75604
D K Ellis Rd 75602
Daffodil Ln 75604
Daisy Ct 75604
Dale St 75601
Dallas St 75602
S Dalston Ave 75602
Dana Way 75602
Dancer Dr 75604
Danville Ct 75605
Darney St 75604
Dartmouth St 75601
Davis St 75602
Dawn Cir 75605
Dawn St 75604
E Dean Ave 75602
Debra Dr 75604
Dee Cir 75604
Dee Dee St 75602
Dee Scott Rd 75605
Deer Park Ct 75604
Deer Run Trl 75605
Deerfield Rd N 75605
Deerfield Lake Cir 75605
Deerwood Dr 75604
Del Roy Ln 75603
Delano St 75604
Delia Dr 75601
Dell St 75602
Della Ln 75602
Dellbrook Dr 75604
Delmar St 75604
Delmonte Ln 75605
Delmora Dr & St 75605
Delta Ln 75605
Delta St 75604
Delwood Dr 75605
Dennard Dr & St 75605
Dennis Dr 75605
Denson Dr 75604
Diamond St 75601
Diane Dr 75602
Dianna Dr 75602
Dickard Trl 75605
Dixon St 75602
Doctor Cir 75605
Doctors Rd E & W 75602
E Dodd St 75603
Dogwood Cir & Ln 75605
Dollahite Ln 75604
Dollins Ave 75604
Don Koble Ln 75605
Donald Dr 75604
Doral Dr 75605
Dorchester Cir 75605
Dortch Dr 75605
Dossey St 75601
Doublewood Dr 75604
Douglas St 75602
Dovee Jo St 75603
Dovel Rd 75603
Dowden Pl 75605
Dowell Dr 75604
Doyle St 75601
Drake Blvd 75605
Dreamers Ln 75605
Dudley St 75602
Dumas Rd 75604
Dunbar St 75602
Duncan St 75604
Dundee Rd 75604
Dylan Ln 75604
Eagle Hill Trl 75605
Ealine St 75604
S East St 75602
N Eastman Rd
100-2199 75601
2200-3299 75605
S Eastman Rd 75602
Easton Rd 75603
Eastside Rd 75603
Eastside Airport Rd 75601

Eastwood St 75604
W Eckman St 75601
Eddie St 75602
Eden Dr
100-1899 75605
1900-2299 75601
E & W Edgefield Ave 75602
Edgewood St 75604
N Edith St 75601
Edmond St 75602
Edna Ln 75602
Edward St 75604
Edwards St 75602
Edwin St 75602
Eitelman Ln 75605
El Paso St 75602
Elderville Rd 75602
Elderville Peatown Rd 75603
Electra St 75602
Elgin St 75604
Elm St 75605
W Elm Creek Dr 75605
Elmira Dr 75605
Elmwood St 75604
Emerald Dr 75605
Emily Dr 75601
Emily Ln 75605
Emmanuel Ln 75602
Enchanted Ln 75604
Encore Cir 75605
Englewood St 75601
English Ln 75605
Enterprise St 75604
Envy Ln 75604
Eric Ln 75605
Erskine Dr 75601
Estates Ct 75605
Estes Dr 75602
Estes Pkwy
2400-2598 75602
2600-3199 75602
3600-5699 75603
5701-8299 75603
Estesville Rd 75602
Ethel St 75602
Etheredge Rd 75602
Eubanks St 75602
Eugene St 75602
Eugenia Dr 75605
Eva Cir 75602
Eva Dr 75605
Evangeline St 75605
Evelyn Dr 75602
Everett St 75604
Evergreen St
100-1299 75604
1300-1499 75605
E Ewing St 75602
Expert Dr 75604
Fagan St 75601
Fair St 75601
Faircreek Ln 75604
Fairhaven St 75605
E & W Fairlane Dr 75604
E Fairmont St
500-1399 75601
1400-1699 75604
W Fairmont St 75604
Fairview Dr 75604
Fairway Dr 75604
Fairway Oaks Ln 75605
Falcon Way 75605
Falls Crk 75605
Falls Creek Dr 75605
Farmer St 75605
Farmview Cir 75602
Fastener Ln 75604
Fawn Trl 75604
Fenton Rd 75604
Ferndale St 75604
Fernridge Dr 75605
Fernwood Dr 75605
Finch Dr 75605
Fir Ct 75604
First St 75603
Fisher Rd 75604

Flagstick Park 75602
Flagstone Dr 75605
Flanagan Dr 75602
Fleetwood Dr 75605
E & W Fleming St 75604
Fm 1844 75605
Fm 1845
1600-7299 75604
Fm 1845 S
100-298 75602
300-399 75602
700-1198 75603
1200-1599 75603
Fm 2011 E 75603
N & S Fm 2087 75603
Fm 2204 75603
Fm 2206 75604
Fm 2208 S 75605
Fm 2751 75605
Fm 2879 75605
Fm 2906 St 75603
Fm 2963 75603
Fm 349 S 75603
Fm 449 75605
Fm 968 W 75602
Ford Ln 75602
Forest Lk & Sq E, S & W 75605
Forest Hill Church Rd 75605
Forest Park Dr 75604
Forget Me Not Ln 75605
Fort Dr 75604
Foster St 75602
Foundry Dr 75604
Fountain Ln 75604
Fountain Bleau Ave 75605
Fountain Place Blvd 75605
Fountain Valley Ct 75605
Fountainview Cir 75605
Fowler St 75602
Fox Ln 75601
Fox Glove Ln 75605
S Frances St 75603
Francis Dr 75602
Frank Adams Rd 75603
Frank Lucy Rd 75603
Franklin Dr 75601
Freda St 75604
Frederick Dr 75604
N Fredonia St 75601
S Fredonia St
100-599 75601
600-1299 75602
Fredrick Ct 75605
Freedom St 75604
French Dr 75604
Friendswood Dr 75605
Frj Dr 75602
Fuller Dr 75602
N Fuller Rd 75605
S Fuller Rd 75605
Fulton St 75604
Gamel Ln & Rd 75604
Garden Dr 75603
Gardenia Ln 75601
Gardiner Mitchell Pkwy 75603
W Garfield Dr 75602
Garland Dr 75602
Garmon Ln 75602
Garner Ln 75605
Garrett Rd 75603
Garrett St 75602
W Gates Ave 75601
Gay St 75602
Gayle Dr 75604
Gayle Ln 75605
Gemi Dr 75604
Gene Dr 75604
Geneva St 75605
E George Richey Rd 75604
Georgia Ln 75604
Gibson Rd 75602
Gilmer Rd 75604
Gladewater Rd 75604
Gladstone Way 75604
Glencrest Ln 75601

Glenda Dr 75602
Glenhaven Dr 75601
E & W Glenn St 75602
Glenrose St 75604
Glover Dr 75601
Godfrey Rd 75603
Golden Hill Church Rd 75602
Golf Ave 75602
Golfcrest Dr 75604
Good Shepherd Way 75605
Goodnight Trl 75604
Gordon St 75602
Grace Ave 75602
Graham Dr 75602
Graham Rd 75604
Grammer Rd 75605
E & W Grand Blvd & St 75604
Grand Cypress Dr 75605
Granite Rd 75604
S Grant St 75601
Grape Dr & Rd 75605
Graves Ct 75605
Gray St 75602
Grayson Ct & Dr 75604
Graystone Rd 75605
Great Woods 75605
N Green St 75601
S Green St
100-398 75601
400-499 75601
501-599 75601
600-2899 75602
Green Hills Rd 75605
Green Oak Dr 75604
Greenbriar Dr 75604
Greenbriar Rd 75603
Greenhill Rd 75605
Greenleaf St 75605
Greenridge Dr 75605
Greenwood Cir 75602
Greenwood St 75603
Gregg St 75601
Gregg Tex Rd 75604
Grey Hawk Ln 75605
Griffin St 75602
Grigsby St 75601
Grove Ct & St 75601
Groveland Ave 75601
S Gum St 75601
Gum Springs Rd E 75602
Gum Valley Cir 75602
H G Mosley Pkwy
1-2399 75604
2401-2997 75605
2999-3199 75605
Habitat Ct 75601
Hackney St 75602
Hailey Dr 75602
Hale St 75604
Hall Dr 75605
Hall Rd 75603
Hallie Dr 75605
Hallsville Hts 75602
Hamby Rd 75605
Hampshire St 75605
Hampton Ct 75605
Hancock Blvd 75605
Happiness St 75601
Happy Hollow Dr 75603
Hardy St 75604
Harlem Ave 75601
Harley Ridge Rd 75604
Harmon Dr 75602
Harrell Ave 75601
Harriett St 75605
Harris Cv 75605
Harris St 75602
E Harrison Rd 75604
W Harrison Rd 75604
S Harrison St 75601
Harroun Ct & Dr 75604
Harvard St 75601
Harvest Ln 75604
N Haven Ln 75605
E & W Hawkins Pkwy 75605

Hawthorne St 75602
Hayden Rd 75603
Hearn Rd 75603
Hearne St 75603
Heather Ln
100-199 75605
1100-1399 75604
Heights Park Dr 75601
Helane Ln 75604
Henderson Ln 75605
E Henderson St 75601
Henry Lee Dr 75605
Heritage Blvd 75605
Hesser Ln 75602
Heston St 75604
Hiawatha St 75603
Hickory St 75602
Hickory Creek Ln 75605
Hickory Hill Rd 75605
Hickory Stick Ct 75605
Hidden Frst N, S & W 75605
Hidden Lake Dr 75604
Hiett Ln 75605
N High St 75601
S High St
100-599 75601
900-2499 75602
E & W Highland St 75602
Hill St 75605
Hillcrest Dr 75601
Hillmont Ave 75601
Hillsdale Dr 75605
Hillshore Cir, Dr & St E, N, S & W 75605
Hillside Dr & Ln 75605
Hilltop Dr 75604
Hiltzman St 75605
Hines 75603
Hitching Post Ln 75604
Hobson St 75605
Hoffman St 75602
S Holland St 75602
Hollers St 75601
Holliday St 75601
S Holly St 75602
Holly Trl 75605
Holly Ridge Dr 75605
Hollybrook Dr 75605
Holyfield Ln 75605
Home St 75601
Homewood Dr 75605
Honey St 75605
Honey Creek Ln 75605
Honeysuckle Ln 75605
Honeysuckle St 75604
E & W Hope Dr 75604
Hopkins St 75601
N Horaney St 75601
Hornsby Dr 75604
Horseshoe Ln 75605
Horton St 75602
Hoskins St 75601
Hotel Way 75605
S Houston St 75602
Howard St 75602
E & W Hoyt Dr 75601
Hubbard Dr 75602
Huckaby Rd 75605
Hudson Ave 75601
W Hughes St 75602
Hughey Dr 75601
Humble Ave 75602
Hummingbird Cir 75601
Hunt Rd 75604
Hunter Rd 75605
Hunters Cir 75605
Hunters Creek Dr 75605
Huntington Cir & St 75601
Huntsman Way 75602
Hurst Pl 75601
S Hutchings Blvd 75602
Hutchins Dodd St 75603
Hyacinth Dr 75601
E & W I 20 Access Rd 75603
Ida Rd 75604

Ida St 75605
Idylwood Dr 75602
Imperial Cir 75604
Independence Dr 75604
Industrial Dr 75602
Ingram St 75601
Innovation Cir 75605
Institute Dr 75602
Interstate 20 Service Rd 75602
Inverness St 75601
Inwood Rd 75601
Ira Dr 75602
Irene St 75605
Iris Cir 75601
Irving St 75605
Isgren Dr 75602
Ithaca Dr 75604
Ivory Ln 75602
Ivy Ln 75605
Iwana Cir 75603
Jack Ct 75601
Jackson Rd 75604
S Jackson St 75602
Jacobs St 75602
Jahan Trl 75604
Jamaica St 75604
Jamerson Rd 75604
James Dr 75605
Jamie Ct 75605
Jana St 75605
Jane Dr & St 75601
Janet St 75601
Janet Kay Dr 75605
S Jarvis St 75601
Jasmine Ln 75604
Jasper Ct 75604
Jay Dr
200-299 75603
2600-2999 75605
Jaycee Dr 75604
N & S Jean Dr 75602
Jefferson Dr 75603
Jefferson St 75601
Jenny St 75604
Jerome St 75602
Jerry Lucy Rd 75603
Jessica Ln 75605
Jester Cir 75604
Jet Dr 75603
W Jewell Dr 75602
Jill St 75604
Joan Ln 75605
Joanie St 75605
Joaquin Ct 75604
Joe Bitner Dr 75605
Joe Burl Ln 75603
John St 75602
John Robert Ct 75604
Johnny Clark Rd 75603
Johnson Rd 75605
Johnson St 75602
Johnston St 75601
Jones Rd 75603
Jones St 75601
W Jones St 75602
Jonquil Dr 75601
Joplin Dr 75601
Jordan St 75602
Jordan Trl 75605
Jordan Valley Rd 75604
Joseph Cir 75601
Joshua Tree Ln 75604
N Journal St 75602
Joyce St 75601
Juanita Dr 75605
E Juanita Rd 75605
N Juanita Rd 75605
W Juanita Rd 75605
Juanita St 75604
Judson Rd
900-1799 75601
1800-6899 75605
Julia St 75601
Julieanna Dr 75604
Juniper St 75604

Kanzeta Dr 75603
Karen Blvd 75602
Karnes Rd 75604
Kate St 75605
Kathleen Dr 75604
Katie Lee Ln 75601
Katy St 75605
Kay Ct & Dr 75601
Kayla Ln 75602
Keasler Rd 75605
Keiffer Rd 75605
Keighley Dr 75605
Kelly Ct 75605
Kelly Lynn Ln 75605
Kelso Trak 75604
Kennedy Blvd 75603
Kennedy Trl 75605
Kensington Ct 75605
Kent St 75604
Kentucky Dr 75605
Kenwood Ln 75604
Kerri Ct 75605
Keystone St 75605
Kieffer Rd 75605
Killingworth 75604
Kim St 75602
Kimberly Ln 75604
Kimbrell Dr 75605
Kincaid Pl 75604
King St 75602
Kingbird Cir 75603
Kings Ln 75605
Kings Mountain Dr 75605
Kingsbury Ct 75604
Kingston Dr 75604
Kiowa Ct 75605
Knobcrest Dr 75604
Knox Lee 75603
Kodak Blvd 75602
Kriss Dr 75604
Krissy Dr 75605
Krista St 75604
Kyla St 75604
Kyle St 75602
Kyle Wilson Rd 75602
L Lee St 75605
La Vista St 75601
Lacebark Ln 75605
Lacy St 75602
Ladd Ln 75604
Lafamo Rd 75604
Lafayette Dr 75601
Lafoy Ln 75604
Lago Trl 75604
Lake Dr 75601
Lake Rd 75603
Lake Cherokee 75603
E & W Lake Devernia Rd 75604
Lake Estates Trl 75605
Lake Harris Rd 75604
Lake Lamond Rd 75604
Lakeshore Dr 75605
Lakeside Dr 75604
Lakeview St 75604
Lakeway Ln 75604
Lakewood Dr 75604
S Lakewood St 75603
Lambert Ln 75602
Lancaster St 75601
Lancer St 75605
Landondo St 75602
N & S Lane Wells Dr 75604
Laney Dr 75605
Lansford St 75604
Lansing Ln & Loop 75605
Lansing Switch Rd 75602
Larissa St 75604
Larriat Ln 75604
Larry Dr
200-299 75605
400-499 75602
Lassiter Rd 75602
Lasso Loop 75604
Latham Ln 75602
Latigo Trce 75604

Latonia Ct & St 75605
Laura Ln 75601
Laurel St 75601
Lauren Ct 75604
Lavelle Ct 75605
Lavender Ln 75605
Lavender Leaf 75604
Lawndale Ave 75604
Lawrence Dr 75604
Lawrence Rd 75605
Lawrence St 75601
Lawson St 75601
Lazy Ln 75604
Le Duke Blvd 75601
Ledger St 75602
Lee St 75604
Lehigh St 75601
Leisure Ln 75605
Lemmons Dr 75602
Leona St 75601
Leonard Dr 75602
Leota St 75601
Lesley Ln 75604
Letourneau Dr 75602
Lettie St 75601
E Level St 75602
Lewan Cir 75604
Lewis St 75605
Lexington Ct 75601
Libby Ln 75602
Liberty Ct 75604
Lilac Dr 75601
Lilac Ln 75605
Lilly St 75602
Limestone Pl 75605
Linco Rd 75604
Lincoln Dr 75604
Lincoln Way 75603
Linda Ct & Ln 75601
Linda Kaye Dr 75604
Lindsey Ln 75601
Lindsey Brook Ln 75605
Liner St 75603
Lismore Ln 75605
Little St 75604
Live Oak Dr 75601
Livingston St 75601
Lloyd Cir 75605
N Lloyd Cir 75605
Lloyd Ct 75605
Lloyd St
1-99 75605
200-499 75602
Loblolly Ln 75605
Locklear Ave 75605
Lois Dr 75605
E & W Lomax Dr 75603
Lomond Ave 75601
London Ln & Way 75604
Lonesome Deer Ct 75604
Lonesome Pine Rd 75605
Longmorn Ln 75604
Longview Pkwy 75601
Lookout Ct 75605
Loop Cir S 75603
Loop Dr 75604
E Loop Dr 75602
S Loop Dr 75603
E Loop 281 75605
E Loop 281 S
4200-4499 75605
E Loop 281 S
5500-5799 75602
5801-5899 75602
5900-6099 75605
SE Loop 281 75602
W Loop 281
100-499 75605
500-4700 75604
4702-4798 75604
5500-5599 75602
W Loop 281 S 75603
Lopez Ct 75605
Loraine Ct 75604
Lori Ln
100-199 75602

2600-2999 75605
Lori Small Ln 75605
Lorin Dr 75602
Loring Ln 75604
Lotus Ln 75604
Louie Bryan Rd 75603
Louise St 75601
Louisiana St 75601
Lovers Ln 75604
Ltr Park Dr 75603
W Luckett St 75601
Lucy Rd 75602
Lula St 75605
Lura St 75603
Lynn Rd 75604
E & W Lynnwood Ln 75604
Macarthur St 75602
Mack Smelley Rd 75605
Mackey Rd 75605
Macy Grace Ln 75605
Maddi Dr 75604
Madison Ct 75601
Madison Dr 75603
Magnolia Ln 75605
Magnolia St 75602
E Magrill St 75601
Mahaffey Ln 75605
Mahlow Dr 75601
Mahon St 75603
Main St 75603
S Main St
400-499 75601
2000-3000 75603
3002-3098 75603
Maisie Ct & Ln 75604
Majestic Pace St 75604
Maledon St 75602
Mamon Dr 75604
Maple St 75602
Maple Springs Rd 75602
Marc Ct 75601
Margo St 75602
Marguerite Dr 75601
Marigold Ln 75604
Marion Dr 75602
Mark Dr 75604
Market St 75604
Markhaven Dr 75605
Marlboro St 75605
Marlin St 75604
E Marshall Ave 75601
W Marshall Ave
100-899 75601
900-6099 75604
Martha Dr 75601
Martin Ln 75605
Martin Rd 75605
Martin St 75602
S Martin Luther King Jr Blvd 75602
Marty Dr 75604
Martz St 75604
Mary Ellen Dr 75605
Mary Jane Dr 75601
Mary Lawson Rd 75604
Mary Lee Ln 75601
Mary Lou Ave 75602
Mason Springs Church Rd 75602
Massey Rock Rd 75603
Massingill Dr 75601
Matt Dr 75605
Mattox Rd 75605
Maxey Rd 75605
Mayes Ln 75605
Maywood Dr 75604
Mcbride Rd 75604
Mccann Rd
600-798 75601
800-2300 75601
2302-2398 75601
2400-4500 75605
4501-6799 75605
4501-4501 75608
4501-4501 75615
4502-7098 75605

Mccann Creek Rd 75605
Mccarver St 75602
Mcclendon Ln 75605
Mccord St 75605
Mcdade Pl 75605
Mcgrede St 75605
Mckay Dr 75604
Mckesson Dr 75604
Mckinley Ln 75604
Meadow Ln 75601
Meadow Lake Dr 75604
Meadowbrook Dr 75601
Meadowchase Trl 75605
Meadowlark Ln & St 75603
Meadows Ln 75603
Meadowview Cir, Dr & Rd 75604
Meandering Way 75604
Medical Dr 75605
Medlock St 75602
Megan Cir & Dr 75605
Melanie Ct, Dr & Ln 75603
Melany Ln 75605
Melba St 75602
Melinda Ln 75604
Melissa St 75605
E Melrose St 75604
E & W Melton St 75602
Melvin St 75604
Memphis St 75604
Merrill Lake Rd 75604
Meshach Dr 75601
E Methvin St
100-200 75601
201-201 75606
201-899 75601
202-898 75601
W Methvin St 75601
Meyers Rd 75604
Miami Cir & Dr 75601
Michael St
1-99 75605
200-299 75603
Michelle Dr 75605
Milam Rd 75603
Miles Dr & St 75605
Mill Creek Dr 75604
Mill Creek Rd 75605
Mill Run Dr 75604
Miller St 75603
Millie St 75602
Milligan Dr 75604
Millpond Dr 75604
Millstone Ln 75604
Milton Ln 75602
E Minnie Jones Dr 75604
Miria Ct 75601
Miriam Ct 75605
Mission Creek Dr 75601
Mistletoe St 75604
Misty Ln 75605
Misty Glen Ct 75604
Mitchell St 75601
Mitzi St 75604
S Mobberly Ave
101-197 75602
199-2399 75602
2336-2336 75607
2400-2498 75602
2401-2499 75602
Mobil Rd 75604
Mobile Dr 75604
Mockingbird Ln 75601
Mohawk St 75605
S Molton St 75601
Mona Dr 75601
Monica St 75602
Monroe St 75602
Montague Way 75604
Montclair Cir & St 75601
Montie St 75604
Montreal Dr 75601
Montrose Ln 75605
Monty Dr 75603
Moore St 75601
Mopac Rd 75602

Morgan St 75602
Morning Glory Ln 75605
Morningstar Pl 75605
Morris Dr 75602
Morrison St 75602
Mosley Cir N & S 75605
Moss Dr 75602
Mountain Rd S 75604
Mumford Dr 75604
Mundy Ln 75604
Myers Rd
100-199 75604
2100-2199 75605
Myra St 75601
Myra Lynn Ln 75605
E Myrle Ave 75602
Myrtle St 75604
Nancy Cir 75601
Nandina St 75605
Navajo Trl 75605
Neal St 75602
Ned Williams Rd 75603
Neiman Marcus Pkwy 75602
Nell St 75604
E & W Nelson St 75601
New Forest Dr 75601
E & W Niblick St 75604
Nikki Ct & Dr 75604
Nimitz St 75602
Nimrod Trl 75604
Nixon Ln 75604
Nixson Dr 75602
Noble Dr 75601
Noel Dr 75602
Nolan St 75602
Noonday Rd 75605
Norcross St 75604
Norma Dr 75604
Norma Lee Ln 75602
Normandy Cir 75601
Northbrook Dr 75605
Northcastle St 75604
Northcrest Chase 75605
Northcutt Ave 75601
Northgate Blvd 75605
Northglen Ct 75605
Northhaven Dr 75605
Northhill Ct 75605
Northknoll Cir 75601
Northpark Cir 75605
Northridge Cir, Dr & Rd 75605
Northview Dr 75605
Northwest Dr 75604
Northwood Ct 75605
Norton Dr 75602
Nowlin St 75602
Nueces Trl 75604
Oak St 75605
Oak Creek Ridge Dr 75605
Oak Forest Dr 75605
Oak Forest Country Club Dr 75605
Oak Hollow St 75604
Oak Isle Dr 75605
Oak Knoll Cir 75605
Oak Valley Dr 75605
Oakdale Ave 75602
Oakland Dr 75605
Oakleigh St 75605
Oakmont Cir 75605
Oakridge Ln 75605
Oakview 75603
Oakwood Dr 75604
Oasis Dr 75601
Oden Rd 75603
Oden St 75602
Old Easton Rd 75603
Old Fm 2879 75605
Old Highway 80 75604
Old Magnolia Rd 75604
Old Maple Springs Rd 75602
E Olive St 75601
Oliver Ave 75605
Olympic Dr 75605
Omega St 75601

Omie Dr 75605
S Oneal St 75602
Oraleark St 75601
Orange Ct 75604
Orange St 75602
Orchard St 75605
Osborne St 75602
Ouida Cir 75603
Overlook Dr 75604
Owens Rd 75604
Owings Ave 75602
Oxford Ln 75601
E Pacific Ave 75602
Padon St 75601
Page Rd
500-3199 75601
3200-4899 75605
N Page Rd 75605
Page St 75604
Page 1 Rd 75605
Palisades Blvd 75605
Palmer St 75605
Palms Ln 75601
Pals Pkwy 75604
Pam St 75602
Panola Ct 75604
Panther Creek Ranch Rd 75605
Par Ct 75605
Paradise Pt 75605
Paris St 75604
Park Dr 75601
E Park Ln 75601
Park Pl 75605
S Park St 75601
Parkview St 75601
Pat Dr 75601
Patio St 75605
Patricia Ave 75602
Patriot Cir 75604
Patton Dr 75605
Patty Ct 75605
Paul St 75605
Paul Blakely Ct 75601
Paverstone Ln 75605
Payne Rd 75604
Peach Orchard Rd 75603
Peanut Cir 75605
W Pearl St 75601
Pearson Ln 75604
Peatown Church Rd 75603
Pebble Beach Ct 75605
Pebble Creek Dr N & S 75605
W Pecan St 75601
Pecan Ridge Xing 75605
Pecos St 75604
Peggy Ruth Dr 75605
Pegues Pl 75601
Pegues Rd 75603
Pelphrey Dr 75604
Penny St 75605
Peoples Rd 75605
Perry St
300-399 75602
1300-1499 75601
S Perry St 75602
W Perry St 75601
Person Rd 75604
Peterson Pl 75602
Pickett St 75605
Pin Oak Trl 75604
Pine Rd 75603
Pine St
100-199 75603
600-698 75601
700-1217 75601
1219-1299 75601
Pine Bluff Dr 75604
Pine Hill Ln 75605
Pine Trail Ln 75605
Pine Tree Pkwy & Rd 75604
Pinebrook Pl 75601
Pinecrest Dr 75602
Pinegrove Ln 75604
Pineland St 75604

Pineridge St 75604
Pinnacle 75605
E & W Pirate St 75604
Pittman St 75602
Plainview St 75604
Player Dr 75605
Pleas Cocke Rd 75603
Pleasant Dr 75602
Pleasant Green Rd 75603
E & W Pliler St 75602
E & W Pliler Precise Rd 75605
Plum Creek Rd 75605
Polk St 75603
Pony Dr 75605
Poppy Ln 75604
Porter Ln
1-299 75604
400-499 75605
E & W Potter St 75601
Powers Ct 75605
Prairie Ln 75605
Pratt Dr 75604
Premier Rd 75604
Preston Dr 75604
Price Ln 75605
E & W Primrose Ln 75604
Prince Ave 75601
Prince Rd 75604
Princess Ln 75604
Princeton Dr 75601
Private Road 1230 75605
Private Road 1232 75605
Private Road 1233 75605
Private Road 1236 75605
Private Road 1237 75605
Private Road 1239 75605
Private Road 1253 75605
Private Road 1282 75605
Private Road 1324 75605
Private Road 1425 75605
Private Road 1490 75605
Private Road 1518 75605
Private Road 1542 75605
Private Road 1612 75605
Private Road 1643 75605
Private Road 1665 75605
Private Road 1780 75605
Private Road 1789 75605
Private Road 1825 75605
Private Road 2095 75604
Private Road 2096 75604
Private Road 2146 75604
Private Road 2150 75604
Private Road 2161 75604
Private Road 2173 75604
Private Road 2221 75604
Private Road 2297 75604
Private Road 2317 75603
Private Road 2336 75603
Private Road 2409 75603
Private Road 2432 75603
Private Road 2446 75603
Private Road 2454 75603
Private Road 2459 75603
Private Road 2531 75603
Private Road 2533 75603
Private Road 256 75603
Private Road 2598 75603
Private Road 2668 75603
Private Road 2672 75603
Private Road 2704 75603
Private Road 2705 75603
Private Road 2710 75603
Private Road 2728 75603
Private Road 2769 75603
Private Road 2771 75603
Private Road 2802 75603
Private Road 2816 75603
Private Road 2823 75603
Private Road 3333 75604
Private Road 3435 75602
Private Road 3436 75602
Private Road 3437 75602
Private Road 3439 75602
Private Road 3443 75602
Private Road 3445 75602
Private Road 3449 75602
Private Road 3454 75602
Private Road 3455 75602
Private Road 3456 75602
Private Road 3457 75602
Private Road 3470 75602
Private Road 3552 75605
Private Road 3558 75605
Private Road 3559 75605
Private Road 3637 75605
Private Road 3654 75605
Private Road 3655 75605
Private Road 3661 75605
Private Road 4331 75604
Private Road 4335 75604
Private Road 4358 75604
Private Road 4359 75604
Private Road 4374 75604
Private Road 4392 75604
Private Road 4434 75605
Private Road 4612 75604
Private Road 4613 75604
Private Road 4614 75604
Private Road 4617 75604
Private Road 4620 75604
Private Road 4686 75604
Progress Blvd 75604
Prospect Rd 75603
Prowler St 75604
Pruitt St 75605
Purdue Dr 75601
Putter Dr 75604
Quail Ln 75602
Quail Run 75603
Queens Ct 75604
Quietshadows St 75604
Quince Way 75605
Rabbit Run Trl 75603
Radar Rd 75603
E & W Radio St 75602
Railroad Rd 75604
Rainbow Dr 75604
Ralph St 75605
Ramblewood Cir, Ct, Dr & Pl 75605
Rambling Dr & Rd 75604
Ramo Rd 75604
Randall St 75602
Rande St 75605
Raney St 75602
Ranier Dr 75604
Rash Rd 75604
Ravena St 75603
Ravencrest Cir & Dr 75605
Rawley Ct & St 75601
Ray St 75602
Ray Bussey Rd 75605
Ray Creek Dr 75605
Rayburn Dr 75602
Rayna Dr 75605
Rebecca Cir 75605
Red City St 75601
Red Gum Gap St 75605
Red Mason Rd 75605
Red Oak Cir 75605
Red Oak Trl 75604
Red Rock Rd 75604
Redbud Ln 75604
Redmon Rd 75602
Reel Rd
100-1299 75604
1300-1399 75605
Reese St 75603
Reeves Rd 75605
Reeves St 75604
Regal Oak Dr 75604
Regency Dr 75604
Regina St 75605
Remington Trl 75605
Restoration Rd 75604
Restview St 75605
Reva St 75605
Revelon St 75602
Revelyn Ave 75602
Rex Ln 75602
Rice Rd 75605
W Richardson Dr & St 75602
Richfield St 75605
Richwood St 75604
Rick Dr 75605
Ridgecrest Dr 75602
Ridgelea Ave 75602
Ridgeview Ln 75604
Ridgewood Dr 75605
Riley Ln 75604
Rimrock 75605
Ringo Cir 75604
Rita St 75602
W River Oaks Dr 75604
Riverstone 75605
Riverwood 75603
Riverwood Dr 75604
Riviera Dr 75605
Robbinwood Ct & Ln 75601
Robert Wilson Rd 75602
Robyn Ln 75605
Rockdale Dr 75604
Rocket St 75603
Rocking B Ranch Rd 75604
Rockrose Dr 75605
Rockwall Ct & Dr 75604
Rockwood Ln 75604
Rodden St 75604
Roenia Cir 75604
Rolling Hills Dr 75604
Rollingwood Dr 75604
Rollins St 75602
Ron St 75604
Roosevelt St 75601
Rose Ln 75604
Rose St 75601
Rose Mount Dr 75601
Rosedale St 75604
Rosedown St 75604
Rosewood Ct 75604
Rosewood Ln 75605
Rothrock Dr 75602
Rouncival Dr 75605
E Rowe Ave 75605
Rowland Dr 75602
Roy Green Rd 75602
Royal Ln 75604
Ruby Ln 75604
Rue Du Soleil 75605
Ruidosa St 75605
Rupe Huffman Rd 75605
Russell Dr 75602
Russell Rd 75602
Russell St 75601
Rustic Oak Dr 75604
Ruth Dr 75601
Ruth St 75602
Ruthlynn Dr 75605
Ryan Dr 75602
Ryder Dr 75602
Ryder Ln 75604
W Sabine St
100-999 75601
1000-1899 75604
Safari Pl 75605
Sage Rd 75604
Sago Ct 75601
Saint Andrews Dr 75605
Saint Clair Dr 75605
Saint Thomas Dr 75602
Salem Ct 75601
Sally St 75603
Sam Page Rd 75605
San Antonio St 75602
San Augustine Ln 75604
San Jacinto Way 75604
San Jose Dr 75601
San Salvador Dr 75602
Sandal Stone Pl 75605
Sandefur St 75601
Sanders Rd 75603
Sandhill Ave 75603
Sandlin St 75602
Sandstone Dr 75605
Sandy Ln 75605
Sandy Creek Dr 75605
Santa Cruz 75601
Sapphire St 75602
E & W Sarah Ave 75604
Saratoga Dr 75601
Sawmill Rd 75603
Scenic Dr 75604
School Dr 75601
Seabiscuit Trce 75604
Secluded Ln 75604
Secretariat Trce 75604
Seminole Ln 75605
Sequoyah Ln 75605
Serenada Trl 75605
Serendipity Ln 75605
Serenity Ln 75604
Service Dr 75604
Settlers Rd 75605
Seven Pines Cut Off Rd 75605
Sexton 75603
Sha Ct 75605
Shadow Crk 75605
Shady Ln
1-99 75604
100-399 75605
1800-1899 75604
Shady Trl 75604
Shady Brook Ln 75602
Shamrock Dr 75604
Shannon Ln 75604
Sharon Kay Dr 75604
Shawn Dr 75605
Shawnee Dr 75605
Sheffield Dr 75605
Shelton St 75601
Shely St 75604
Shenandoah Ct & Dr 75605
Sheppard St 75604
Sherwood Dr 75605
Sheryl Ln 75604
Shiloh Rd 75604
Shirley Dr 75604
E & W Shofner Dr 75604
Shoreview Cir & Dr 75605
Short St 75601
Short Davis St 75602
Short El Paso St 75602
Short Harlem St 75601
Short White City St 75601
Short Young St 75602
Sibley St 75602
Sidney St 75602
Sierra Vista Ln 75605
Signal Hill Dr 75602
Silver Spur 75604
Silver Falls Rd 75604
Simmons St 75605
Simms St 75604
Simon Ln 75603
Simpson St 75605
Sinclair Rd 75604
Singing J Cir 75605
Sioux Ct 75605
Sioux Ln 75603
Skelly St 75602
Skinner Ln 75605
Skogee Cir 75605
Skyline Dr 75605
Skyway 75603
Sleepy Hollow Ln 75604
Small Rd 75605
Smallwood Dr 75601
Smelley Rd 75605
Smith Dr 75605
Smith Rd 75604
Snoddy Rd 75604
Solaris Pl 75604
Solti St 75605
E & W South St 75601
Southcastle St 75604
Southcrest Ct 75605
Sovereign Dr 75604
Sparks Rd 75605
Spillway Dr 75604
Spoonbill Rd 75605
Spring St 75604
Spring Creek Pl 75604
Spring Creek Rd 75603
Spring Hill Rd 75605
Spring Valley Cir & Ct 75605
Springdale St 75604
N & S Spur 63 75601
Spyglass Dr 75605
Stacy St 75604
Stadium Dr 75605
N & S Standard St 75604
Stanford Dr 75601
Stanley Dr 75605
Stanley Rd 75603
Stanolind St 75604
Stardust Dr 75604
Starling St 75603
Starwood Dr 75605
State Highway 149 75603
State Highway 300 75604
State Highway 31 N 75603
E State Highway 31 75604
State Highway 322 N 75603
State Highway 42 75604
Steeplechase Trl 75605
Stevens Dr 75603
Stevens St 75604
Stewart St 75604
Stewart Chandler Rd 75604
Stillmeadow Ln 75604
Stone Lake Rd 75605
Stone Trail St 75604
Stonecreek Ct 75604
N & S Stonegate Ct & Dr 75601
Stonehaven St 75604
Stoneridge Trl 75605
Stonewall Ct & Dr 75604
Stonewood Rd 75604
Stracener Rd 75605
Strait Ln 75604
Strickland Hills Rd 75605
Stuart St 75603
Stuckey Dr 75601
Sue Dr 75605
Sue St 75602
Sugar Creek Cir & Ln 75605
Summer Creek Way 75604
Summerfield Rd 75605
Summerset Ct 75605
Summit St 75601
Sunbeam Dr 75604
Sunnybrook Dr 75605
Sunnyside Dr 75605
Sunrise Dr 75605
Sunset Dr 75601
Sunshine Sq 75601
Supply St 75604
Surratt Rd 75604
Suzanne Dr 75604
Swan Dr 75604
Swancy St 75602
Sweetbriar St 75604
Sweetheart Ln 75605
Sweetwater Trl 75605
Swinging Bridge Rd 75604
Syble Ln 75605
E & W Sycamore Ln 75604
Syfrett Dr 75604
Sylvan Dr 75602
Sylvia St 75604
Tad Williams Rd 75605
Tall Pines Ave 75605
Talley Rd 75602
Tallwood Ln
1-99 75605
700-799 75604
Tammy Lynn Dr 75604
Tanglewood Ct & Dr 75604
Taylor St 75604
Taylor George Rd 75605
Taylor Moore St 75603
N Teague St 75601
Teakwood Dr 75605
Tealwood Dr 75605
Technology Ctr 75605
Teer Ln 75604
Temple St 75604
Tennery Ln 75604
Tenneryville Rd 75604
Tennessee St 75605
Terese Dr 75605
Terilynn Dr 75604
Terminal Cir 75603
Terra Ln 75605
Terra Pl 75604
W Terrace Dr 75601
Tevey Rd 75605
Tex Pack St 75604
W Texaco Rd 75604
Texas St 75601
Thelma Ct & St 75604
Thislebrook Ln 75604
Thomas Rd & St 75605
Thompson Rd 75604
Thornton St 75605
Thorntree 75601
Tiffany Ln 75604
Tiffany St 75605
Timber Trl 75605
N Timber Falls Dr 75605
Timberbrook Park 75601
Timberbrook Rd 75605
Timberlake St 75603
Timberline Dr 75604
Timberwood Trl 75605
E Timpson St 75602
Toler Ct 75604
Toler Rd
800-1999 75604
2000-2199 75605
Tomlinson Pkwy 75605
Tooke Rd 75604
Tower Rd 75603
Towering Oaks Hvn, Ln & Mdws 75602
Towhee Dr 75603
Town Lake Dr 75601
Traci Lynn St 75604
Tracy Dr
100-298 75603
500-699 75602
Tradinch 75603
Trailwood Ln 75605
Travis Ave 75602
Treetop Ln 75604
Trenton Ct 75601
Trevino St 75605
Triple Creek Dr 75601
Tristan Ln 75604
Tryon Rd
1700-2200 75601
2202-2298 75601
2500-7599 75605
Tubbs Rd 75604
Tulane Ave 75601
Tulip Ln 75601
Tullie Cir & Dr 75601
Tumble Weed Trl 75604
Tupelo Dr 75601
Turk St 75601
Turner Dr 75601
Turtle Creek Bnd & Dr 75605
Tuttle Blvd & Cir 75605
E & W Twilight Ct & Dr 75604
Twin Creeks Dr 75602
Twin Oaks Ln 75605
E & W Tyler St 75601
Tyra Ct 75604
Union St 75603
University Blvd 75605
Us Highway 259 N 75605
Us Highway 80 75604
E Us Highway 80 75605
Valentine Ln 75604
Valley Dr 75601
Valley Brook Ln 75605
Valley Ranch Rd 75602
Van St 75602
Vanderbilt Dr 75601
Vanderslice Rd 75602
Velma St 75602
Venus Rd 75604
Veranda Pl 75604
Vesta St 75602
Vicksburg Ct 75601
Vicky Dr 75604
Victor Dr 75601
Victoria Dr 75604
Victorian Oaks 75603
Victory St 75602
Viewcrest Dr 75604
Villa Ln 75604
Village Dr 75605
Village Green Dr 75605
Vine St 75605
Vinewood Ln 75604
Vintage Trl 75605
Virgie St 75605
Virginia St 75602
Wade Rd 75603
Waggoner St 75604
Wagster St 75602
Wain Dr 75604
Wainwright Ct 75605
Wal St 75605
Walnut Ln 75605
N Walnut Ln 75605
W Walnut St 75601
Walnut Hill Dr 75605
Walter St 75605
Walters St 75603
N & S Ward Dr 75604
Ware St 75601
Warren St 75602
Warwick Cir E & W 75601
W Washington St 75601
Waskom Ct 75604
Water View Dr 75605
Waterchase Ct 75605
Waterlily Ln 75604
Waters Edge 75605
Watkins Cir 75603
Watkins St 75604
Watson Rd 75604
Weaver Ln 75605
Webb St 75605
Webster St 75602
Wedgewood Ln 75604
Welch Ln 75601
Welch Rd 75603
Weldon Ln 75605
Wellington Cir, Dr & Ln 75605
Wells St 75602
Wendy Dr 75605
Wendy Acres Ave 75602
Wesley St 75605
West St 75602
Westchester St 75601
Westmoreland Dr & Rd 75604
Weston Ct 75604
Westover Ave 75601
Westwood Dr 75604
E & W Whaley St 75601
Whatley Rd 75604
Whiffle Tree Dr 75604
Whispering Pines Blvd 75604
Whitaker Cir 75605
Whitaker St 75602
White Rd 75603
White City St 75601
Whitehurst Dr 75602
Whitney Dr 75603
Whitney St 75602
Whitney Jo St 75603
Wilbert St 75604
Wilcrest Pl 75604
Wilderness Way 75604
Wildflower Dr 75604
Wildwood Ct & St 75604
Wiley Page Rd 75605
Wilkes Dr 75605
Will Way 75604
Willellen St 75601
Williams 75603
Williams St 75601

Willie Smith Rd 75602
Willis Dr 75601
Willow Dr 75602
Willow Bend Dr 75602
Willow Oak Dr 75601
Willow Springs Dr 75604
Willowood St 75604
Willowview St 75604
Wilson St 75601
Wimberly St 75601
S Winchester Ln 75602
Windemere Cir 75601
Winding Way 75605
Winding Run Ln 75605
Windland Pkwy 75601
Windmill Ln 75601
Windrush Blvd 75604
Windsock Ln 75605
Windsong Ln 75604
Windsor Dr 75604
Windy Ln 75602
Wingate St 75602
Wintergreen St 75604
Wisteria Ln 75604
N Wood Ln 75605
Wood Pl 75601
Wood Chuck Ln 75604
Woodbine Pl 75601
Woodbrook Ct 75604
Woodcock Rd 75604
Woodcreek Dr 75605
Woodcrest 75603
Woodcrest Ln 75601
Wooded Trl 75605
Wooded Way 75602
Woodgrove Ln 75605
Woodhaven Ct 75605
Woodhaven St 75604
Woodhollow Ct 75604
Woodland Dr 75605
Woodland Rd 75602
Woodland St 75602
Woodlawn Dr 75604
Woodmark Dr 75605
Woodridge Cir 75601
Woodridge Est 75602
Woodridge St 75602
Woodvine St 75604
Woodway Ct & Ln 75605
Wylie Cir & Dr 75602
Yale Ave 75601
Yarborough Rd 75604
Yates Dr 75601
Yates Rd 75605
Yellow Throat Rd 75604
Yellowstone Dr 75605
Yorktown Ct 75601
Yosemite Way 75605
E Young St 75602
Younger St 75603
Zeola St 75604

NUMBERED STREETS

1st St 75605
N 1st St 75601
N & S 2nd 75601
N & S 3rd 75601
N 4th St
300-398 75601
2200-3499 75605
N 5th Ave & St 75601
N 6th St 75601
N 7th St 75601
N 8th St 75601
N 9th St 75601
S 9th St 75602
N 10th St 75601
S 11th St 75602
S 12th St 75602
S 13th St 75602
S 14th St 75602
S 15th St 75602

LUBBOCK TX

General Delivery 79408

POST OFFICE BOXES MAIN OFFICE STATIONS AND BRANCHES

Box No.s
CALLER - CALLER 79408
1 - 2982 79408
3001 - 3996 79452
4001 - 4840 79409
5001 - 5980 79408
6001 - 6999 79493
10101 - 11720 79408
12001 - 12440 79452
15941 - 16999 79490
41008 - 45891 79409
53001 - 54560 79453
64001 - 65858 79464
79491 - 79491 79452
90801 - 90803 79408
91601 - 91608 79490
93001 - 94896 79493
95204 - 95204 79452
96402 - 96402 79464
98001 - 99180 79499
99001 - 99007 79490

RURAL ROUTES

01, 03, 07, 25 79403
10, 21 79404
05, 11, 16, 19 79407
02, 15, 28 79415
41 79416
06, 09, 20, 22, 27, 32, 36, 42 79423
04, 12, 13, 17, 18, 24, 29, 31, 33, 35, 37, 38, 39 79424

NAMED STREETS

Abbeville Ave 79424
Aberdeen Ave
1800-1899 79416
1900-3199 79407
5100-5399 79414
5401-5699 79414
6701-7097 79424
7099-9799 79424
Acuff Rd 79403
Addison Ave 79407
Adrian St
200-1699 79403
4100-4399 79415
Akron Ave
100-198 79415
1200-1299 79409
2000-3299 79410
3301-3399 79410
4100-4199 79413
7401-7497 79423
7499-11199 79423
11201-11299 79423
N Akron Ave 79415
Albany Ave
1800-1898 79416
1900-2099 79407
2101-2299 79407
4701-5199 79414
6400-6498 79424
6500-9699 79424
Alcove Ave
1201-1899 79416
1900-2098 79407
2100-8099 79407
8201-9199 79424
Alligator Rd 79407
Alma St 79415
Amarillo Rd 79403
Amherst Pl 79416
Amherst St
2500-3399 79415
4700-7399 79416
E Amherst St 79403
Anderson Rd 79403
Arkansas Rd 79407
Armadillo Rd 79407
Ash Ave 79404
N Ash Ave 79403
Ash Dr 79404
Aspen Ave 79404
N Aspen Ave 79403
S Aspen Ave 79403
Atlanta Ave 79416
S Auburn Ave 79403
Auburn Dr 79416
Auburn St
1200-1300 79401
1302-1598 79401
2201-2497 79415
2499-3199 79415
3201-3399 79415
4700-7499 79416
E Auburn St 79403
Ave P 79423
Ave Q 79423
Avenue E
401-497 79401
Avenue E
499-1300 79401
1302-1798 79401
1901-2197 79404
2199-3799 79404
Avenue N
100-1700 79401
1702-1798 79401
1900-3399 79411
3400-6599 79412
7900-7999 79423
Avenue S
100-399 79415
400-498 79401
500-1899 79401
1900-2699 79411
3400-7199 79412
8100-9899 79423
Avenue W
100-399 79415
400-1899 79401
1901-1997 79411
1999-3199 79411
3400-6599 79412
6601-6999 79412
7200-9899 79423
9901-16999 79423
N Avenue N
100-299 79401
301-399 79401
601-1197 79403
1199-2100 79403
2102-2298 79403
N Avenue S 79415
Avenue A
500-1198 79401
1200-1800 79401
1802-1898 79401
1900-2298 79404
2300-6099 79404
6101-6199 79404
N Avenue A 79403
Avenue B
600-1800 79401
1802-1898 79401
2301-2897 79404
2899-5699 79404
Avenue C
1800-1899 79401
1900-1998 79404
2000-4799 79404
Avenue D 79404
Avenue F
300-398 79401
400-1799 79401
1801-1899 79401
1900-2298 79404
2300-8499 79404
Avenue G
101-297 79401
299-600 79401
602-898 79401
2701-3097 79404
3099-5899 79404
Avenue H 79423
Avenue J
100-498 79401
500-1899 79401
1900-1998 79411
2000-2400 79411
2402-3398 79411
3400-4500 79412
4502-4598 79412
7700-12799 79423
N Avenue J 79403
Avenue K
100-1699 79401
1701-1899 79401
1900-2699 79411
3400-3799 79412
N Avenue K 79401
Avenue L
100-1799 79401
1900-2900 79411
2902-3398 79411
4200-5400 79412
5402-5498 79412
9000-13899 79423
N Avenue L
100-299 79401
1201-1299 79403
Avenue M
100-1899 79401
1900-3099 79411
3101-3399 79411
9000-9199 79423
N Avenue M
100-299 79401
2201-2299 79403
Avenue O
101-297 79401
299-1899 79401
1900-2200 79411
2202-2308 79411
6500-6599 79412
7901-7999 79423
N Avenue O 79401
Avenue P
100-200 79401
202-398 79401
1900-2999 79411
3001-3099 79411
3400-6500 79412
6502-6598 79412
7500-9699 79423
N Avenue P
100-299 79401
801-2999 79403
Avenue Q
200-399 79415
400-1899 79401
1900-3399 79411
3400-7099 79412
9000-11099 79423
N Avenue Q
201-399 79415
600-798 79403
800-3199 79403
Avenue Q South Dr 79412
Avenue R
201-297 79415
299-399 79415
500-1899 79401
1901-1997 79411
1999-2099 79411
3400-6599 79412
N Avenue R 79415
Avenue T
100-399 79415
500-598 79401
600-1799 79401
1901-1997 79411
1999-3199 79411
4201-4497 79412
4499-6599 79412
8900-9899 79423
N Avenue T 79415
Avenue U
100-399 79415
401-497 79401
499-1599 79401
2100-2198 79411
2200-3199 79411
3400-6700 79412
6702-6998 79412
7500-9799 79423
N Avenue U 79415
Avenue V
100-399 79415
401-497 79401
499-1899 79401
2000-2098 79411
2100-2799 79411
2801-3199 79411
3500-4000 79412
4002-6098 79412
7500-7698 79423
7700-9799 79423
N Avenue V 79415
Avenue X
100-199 79415
201-399 79415
400-1700 79401
1702-1898 79401
2001-2197 79411
2199-2699 79411
2701-3399 79411
3400-4899 79412
7300-10099 79423
N Avenue X 79415
Avenue Y 79401
N Avenue Y 79415
Bangor Ave
400-1899 79416
2901-3399 79407
3800-5299 79414
6600-9899 79424
N Bangor Ave 79416
Bangor Dr 79407
Barry St 79415
Basin St 79424
Bates St
1500-1599 79401
1701-1797 79415
1799-3399 79415
4701-4799 79416
E Bates St 79403
Baylor Dr 79415
Baylor St
1500-1699 79401
1700-1898 79415
1900-3399 79415
7600-7699 79416
E Baylor St 79403
Bear Rd 79407
Bearcat Rd 79407
Beaufort Ave
600-699 79416
8000-9899 79424
N Beaufort Ave 79416
Beech Ave
100-1699 79403
1701-1899 79403
2900-2999 79404
E Belarthe St 79404
Belmont Ave
3400-3499 79407
4300-4999 79414
6600-16899 79424
N Belmont Ave 79416
Belton Ave
4600-4899 79413
9100-10999 79423
Belton Dr 79423
Birch Ave 79404
N Birch St 79403
S Birch St 79403
Blandon Ave 79423
Bledsoe Ttu 79406
Bluefield Rd 79403
Boston Ave
101-199 79415
1803-1803 79406
1901-2097 79410
2099-2800 79410
2802-3098 79410
4100-6399 79413
8200-10699 79423
N Boston Ave 79415
Boston Ttu 79406
Bourbon St 79424
Bradley St
900-1699 79403
4500-4699 79415
E Bradley St 79403
Breldelm St 79401
Brentwood Ave
100-199 79416
6600-16299 79424
N Brentwood Ave 79416
Brentwood Cir 79407
Briercroft Office Park 79412
Broadway 79401
E Broadway 79403
Broadway Ave 79406
E Brown St 79403
Brownfield Dr
4400-4599 79410
5600-5799 79414
Buddy Holly Ave
200-1899 79401
1900-2400 79404
2402-2498 79404
Bull Rider Rd 79404
Canton Ave
2001-2297 79410
2299-3000 79410
3002-3198 79410
3700-7099 79413
7200-11200 79423
11202-11298 79423
N Canton Ave 79415
Canyon Rd 79403
Canyon Lake Dr
1500-1799 79403
2400-2498 79415
Caprock Dr 79412
Carpenter Wells Ttu 79406
Cat Rd 79407
Cedar Ave 79404
N Cedar Ave 79403
Cesar E Chavez Dr
1201-1599 79401
1700-1800 79403
1802-1998 79403
2000-2698 79415
Cherry Ave 79403
N Chester Ave 79415
Cheyenne Ln 79404
Chicago Ave
101-597 79416
599-700 79416
702-1498 79416
2900-3700 79407
3702-3898 79407
4000-5099 79414
5101-5499 79414
6100-16699 79424
N Chicago Ave 79416
Chippewa Trl 79404
Chitwood Ttu 79406
Chuck Wagon Rd 79404
Cimarron Dr 79403
City Bank Pkwy 79407
Clement Ttu 79406
Clemson Dr & St 79403
Clinton Ave 79424
N Clinton Ave 79416
Clovis Rd 79415
Coleman Ttu 79406
Colgate Dr 79416
Colgate St
2100-3299 79415
3301-3399 79415
5700-5800 79416
5802-5898 79416
E Colgate St 79403
Colorado Rd 79407
Colton Ave 79424
N Colton Ave 79416
Comanche Dr 79404
Compress Ave 79403
Cornell St
2000-2098 79415
2100-3399 79415
5600-5798 79416
5800-5899 79416
E Cornell St 79403
Country Club Dr 79403
County Road 1030 79407
County Road 1100 79407
County Road 1150 79407
County Road 1160 79407
County Road 1170 79407
County Road 1200 79407
County Road 1240 79407
County Road 1250 79407
County Road 1260 79407
County Road 1300 79407
N County Road 1300 79416
N County Road 1330 79416
County Road 1340 79407
N County Road 1340 79416
N County Road 1350 79416
N County Road 1370 79416
County Road 1420 79407
County Road 1425 79407
County Road 1430 79407
N County Road 1430 79416
County Road 1435 79407
County Road 1440 79407
N County Road 1440 79416
County Road 1450 79407
N County Road 1450 79416
N County Road 1460 79416
County Road 1470 79407
County Road 1500 79407
N County Road 1500 79416
County Road 1570 79407
N County Road 1600 79416
N County Road 1610 79416
N County Road 1640 79416
N County Road 1650 79416
N County Road 1660 79416
N County Road 1670 79416
County Road 1700
11600-12799 79424
County Road 1700
13101-14099 79415
N County Road 1700 79416
County Road 1715 79424
County Road 1735 79424
County Road 1740 79424
N County Road 1740 79415
County Road 1760 79424
N County Road 1770 79415
County Road 1800 79424
County Road 1810 79424
County Road 1820 79424
N County Road 1820 79415
County Road 1830 79424
County Road 1835 79424
County Road 1840 79424
County Road 1850 79424
County Road 1860 79424
County Road 1865 79424
County Road 1870 79424
N County Road 1900 79415
County Road 1910 79424
County Road 1920 79424
County Road 1940 79423
County Road 1950 79424
N County Road 1950 79415
N County Road 1960 79415
County Road 2 79423
County Road 2000 79424
N County Road 2000 79415
County Road 2040 79423
County Road 2100 79423
N County Road 2100 79415
County Road 2110 79423
County Road 2120 79423
County Road 2130 79423
County Road 2140 79423
County Road 2150 79423

N County Road 2150 ... 79415
County Road 2160 79423
N County Road 2160 ... 79415
County Road 2165 79423
County Road 2170 79423
County Road 2200 79423
N County Road 2200 ... 79415
County Road 2220 79423
County Road 2240 79423
County Road 2270 79423
County Road 2300 79423
N County Road 2300 ... 79403
County Road 2330 79423
County Road 2340 79423
County Road 2360 79404
County Road 2400 79423
N County Road 2400 ... 79403
County Road 2420 79404
County Road 2430 79404
County Road 2500
8400-12700 79404
12702-12898 79404
13000-17299 79423
County Road 2540
8300-8700 79404
8702-8998 79404
16600-19299 79423
County Road 2600 79404
N County Road 2600 ... 79403
N County Road 2700 ... 79403
N County Road 2740 ... 79403
N County Road 2750 ... 79403
N County Road 2755 ... 79403
N County Road 2760 ... 79403
N County Road 2770 ... 79403
N County Road 2775 ... 79403
N County Road 2800 ... 79403
N County Road 2810 ... 79403
N County Road 2811 ... 79403
N County Road 2820 ... 79403
N County Road 2830 ... 79403
County Road 2840 79404
N County Road 2840 ... 79403
N County Road 2850 ... 79403
N County Road 2860 ... 79403
N County Road 2900 ... 79403
N County Road 2930 ... 79403
N County Road 2960 ... 79403
N County Road 2970 ... 79403
County Road 3 79423
N County Road 3000 ... 79403
N County Road 3010 ... 79403
County Road 3020 79403
County Road 3030 79403
County Road 3040 79403
N County Road 3100 ... 79403
N County Road 3200 ... 79403
N County Road 3240 ... 79403
N County Road 3300 ... 79403
N County Road 3500 ... 79403
N County Road 3640 ... 79403
County Road 5300 79415
E County Road 5300 ... 79403
County Road 5400
300-498 79403
500-2099 79403
2700-2898 79415
2900-6999 79415
E County Road 5400 ... 79403
County Road 5500
1900-2098 79403
3000-7099 79415
E County Road 5500 ... 79403
E County Road 5640 ... 79403
County Road 5700 79415
E County Road 5700 ... 79403
County Road 5800 79415
E County Road 5800 ... 79403
County Road 5825 79415
County Road 5830 79415
County Road 5850 79415
E County Road 5920 ... 79403
County Road 6000 79415
E County Road 6000 ... 79403
County Road 6100 79415
E County Road 6100 ... 79403

County Road 6140 79415
County Road 6150 79415
E County Road 6160 ... 79403
County Road 6170 79415
E County Road 6170 ... 79403
E County Road 6171 ... 79403
E County Road 6200 ... 79403
County Road 6220 79415
County Road 6300
4500-4598 79415
4600-5199 79415
5500-7299 79416
E County Road 6300 ... 79403
E County Road 6350 ... 79403
County Road 6400 79416
E County Road 6400 ... 79403
County Road 6410 79416
E County Road 6410 ... 79403
County Road 6420 79416
E County Road 6420 ... 79403
County Road 6430 79416
E County Road 6430 ... 79403
County Road 6440 79416
E County Road 6440 ... 79403
E County Road 6450 ... 79403
E County Road 6460 ... 79403
E County Road 6470 ... 79403
County Road 6500 79416
E County Road 6500 ... 79403
County Road 6520 79416
E County Road 6520 ... 79403
E County Road 6540 ... 79403
E County Road 6550 ... 79403
E County Road 6560 ... 79403
E County Road 6570 ... 79403
E County Road 6610 ... 79403
E County Road 6640 ... 79403
E County Road 6650 ... 79403
E County Road 6660 ... 79403
County Road 6700 79407
E County Road 6700 ... 79403
E County Road 6710 ... 79403
County Road 6740
6100-6199 79403
9900-10299 79407
County Road 6800 79407
County Road 6830 79407
County Road 6840 79407
E County Road 6840 ... 79403
County Road 6860 79407
County Road 6870 79407
County Road 6875 79407
County Road 6900 79407
E County Road 6900
7300-7499 79403
8000-8099 79404
County Road 6910 79407
County Road 6915 79407
County Road 6920 79407
County Road 6930 79407
County Road 6935 79407
County Road 6940 79407
County Road 6945 79407
County Road 6950 79407
County Road 6960 79407
County Road 6965 79407
County Road 7000 79407
E County Road 7000 ... 79403
County Road 7050 79407
E County Road 7110 ... 79404
E County Road 7130 ... 79404
E County Road 7160 ... 79404
County Road 7200 79424
E County Road 7200 ... 79404
County Road 7220 79423
County Road 7230 79423
County Road 7240 79423
County Road 7245 79423
County Road 7250 79423
E County Road 7250 ... 79404
E County Road 7260 ... 79404
E County Road 7270 ... 79404
County Road 7300
200-699 79404
1101-1599 79423
E County Road 7300 ... 79404

County Road 7320 79424
County Road 7330 79424
County Road 7340
1600-1999 79423
4400-5499 79424
County Road 7350
2300-2398 79423
4400-5699 79424
County Road 7360
900-1599 79423
5200-5499 79424
County Road 7365 79423
County Road 7370 79423
County Road 7405 79424
County Road 7410 79424
County Road 7415 79424
County Road 7420 79424
County Road 7425 79424
County Road 7430 79424
County Road 7435 79424
County Road 7440 79424
County Road 7445 79424
County Road 7450
2500-2999 79423
6300-6499 79424
County Road 7460 79424
County Road 7470 79424
County Road 7475 79424
County Road 7500
200-3899 79423
4900-5899 79424
E County Road 7500 ... 79423
County Road 7505 79423
County Road 7510
3000-3099 79423
3101-3399 79423
5500-5599 79424
County Road 7520
3000-3399 79423
5400-5599 79424
County Road 7530
3000-3399 79423
5400-5599 79424
County Road 7540
2501-2997 79423
2999-3399 79423
5300-5699 79424
County Road 7545
3300-3399 79423
5100-5199 79424
County Road 7550
3000-3399 79423
5300-5799 79424
County Road 7560
3000-3198 79423
3200-3300 79423
3302-3398 79423
5300-5599 79424
County Road 7570
1700-2999 79423
5300-5398 79424
5400-5500 79424
5502-5698 79424
County Road 7600 79423
County Road 7610 79423
County Road 7620
2300-2499 79423
5800-6799 79424
County Road 7630 79423
County Road 7640 79424
County Road 7650 79423
County Road 7670 79423
County Road 7700
100-3499 79423
4700-5798 79424
5800-6799 79424
E County Road 7700 ... 79423
County Road 7710 79423
County Road 7720 79423
County Road 7730 79423
County Road 7760 79423
County Road 7820 79423
County Road 7825 79423
County Road 7830 79423
County Road 7835 79423
County Road 7900
900-1699 79423

4800-4998 79424
County Road 7910 79424
County Road 7920 79424
County Road 7930 79424
County Road 7940 79424
County Road7820 79423
County Road7825 79423
County Road7830 79423
County Road7835 79423
Cowboy Ln 79404
Crescent Pl 79416
Crickets Ave
1201-1297 79401
1299-1500 79401
1502-1898 79401
1601-1601 79402
1603-1899 79401
1900-1999 79404
Cypress Rd 79403
Dana St 79415
Dartmouth Dr 79416
Dartmouth St
2100-3399 79415
5500-5900 79416
5902-8498 79416
E Dartmouth St 79403
Date Ave 79404
N David Ave 79403
Davis Dr 79416
Deer Rd 79407
Detroit Ave
301-399 79415
1900-1998 79410
2000-2099 79410
4600-6899 79413
7600-11199 79423
N Detroit Ave 79415
Dixie Dr 79411
Dixon Ave 79423
N Dixon Ave 79415
Doak Ttu 79406
Dover Ave
700-900 79416
902-1298 79416
2000-3699 79407
4600-4698 79414
6600-10699 79424
N Dover Ave 79416
E Drew St 79403
E Dubuque St 79403
Duke St
2100-3399 79415
5600-6399 79416
E Duke St 79403
Dupage Ave 79416
N Durant Ave 79416
Durham Ave 79424
N Durham Ave 79416
E Dr 79404
Eashort St 79416
E Edinboro Ave 79403
Elder Ave 79404
Elephant Rd 79407
Elgin Ave
1901-2097 79410
2099-2399 79410
2401-3399 79410
3400-6999 79413
7400-10699 79423
10701-10899 79423
N Elgin Ave 79415
Elk Rd 79407
Elkhart Ave
1400-1899 79416
3400-3799 79407
4400-4499 79414
6100-10799 79424
N Elkhart Ave 79416
Elkridge Ave
6900-6999 79413
8100-10699 79423
Elleadon St 79412
E Ellis St 79407
Elm 79404
Elm Ave
1200-1298 79403
2000-7499 79404

N Elm Ave 79403
Elmwood Ave
3400-3799 79407
6100-10199 79424
N Elmwood Ave 79416
Emory St
2100-3399 79415
4900-6399 79416
E Emory St 79403
Emporia St 79415
Englewood Ave
3400-4099 79407
4400-4899 79414
5300-10199 79424
N Englewood Ave 79416
Englewood St 79424
Erskine St
101-397 79403
399-1699 79403
1800-3800 79415
3802-3898 79415
4600-5598 79416
5600-8699 79416
E Erskine St 79403
Essex Ave 79407
N Essex Ave 79416
N Essex Dr 79416
Evanston Ave
3400-3499 79407
6100-15499 79424
N Evanston Ave 79416
Everett Ave 79424
Fig Ave 79403
Filly Rd 79407
Fir Ave 79404
E Flarling St 79403
Flint Ave
401-499 79415
909-909 79406
1802-1802 79406
2000-3398 79410
3400-6999 79413
8100-19399 79423
N Flint Ave 79415
N Fm 1264 79415
Fm 1294
200-2400 79403
Fm 1294
2402-2498 79403
2600-6699 79415
E Fm 1294 79403
Fm 1585
100-4099 79423
4400-7299 79424
E Fm 1585
100-1699 79423
2300-3299 79404
Fm 1729
102-2399 79403
2401-2603 79403
2617-2897 79415
2899-2900 79415
2902-3498 79415
2905-2999 79403
3401-3403 79415
4200-4299 79403
4500-4504 79415
4506-6499 79415
E Fm 1729 79403
N Fm 1729 79403
W Fm 1729 79403
Fm 1730 79424
Fm 179 79407
N Fm 179 79416
N Fm 2378 79407
N Fm 2528 79415
Fm 2641 79415
E Fm 2641 79403
E Fm 3020 79404
Fm 3431 79404
E Fm 3523 79403
E Fm 40 79403
N Fm 400 79403
Fm 41
100-598 79423
600-5099 79423
5100-6499 79424

E Fm 41 79423
Fm 835
5900-6599 79403
6600-7099 79404
E Fm 835 79403
Fordham St
801-1199 79403
2300-2698 79415
2700-3499 79415
4600-5799 79416
5801-6599 79416
E Fordham St 79403
Fox Rd 79407
Fraillar St 79424
Frankford Ave
100-1099 79416
2400-2608 79407
2610-3699 79407
3701-4299 79407
4800-12299 79424
N Frankford Ave 79416
Frankford Ct 79416
Freeport Ave 79424
Fremont Ave
6900-6999 79413
8100-10999 79423
French Quarter Ct 79424
Fulton Ave
200-700 79416
702-798 79416
2400-2499 79407
6401-6697 79424
6699-9299 79424
9301-10199 79424
N Fulton Ave 79416
Gannon St 79415
Gardner Ave 79424
N Gardner Ave 79416
Garfield Dr 79416
Gary Ave
1900-2100 79410
2102-2698 79410
3400-5015 79413
5014-5014 79493
5016-6998 79413
5017-6999 79413
8100-10599 79423
N Gary Ave 79415
Gaston Ttu 79406
Gates Ttu 79406
Geneva Ave
5600-7099 79413
8200-12599 79423
Geneva Dr 79423
Genoa Ave
200-1199 79416
2700-2799 79407
5700-11099 79424
N Genoa Ave 79416
Gerald Ave 79403
S Gilbert Dr 79416
Glenna Goodacre Blvd . 79401
Globe Ave 79404
N Globe Ave 79403
Gordon Ttu 79406
N Granby Ave 79416
Greek Cir 79416
Grinnell St
1101-1199 79403
1300-1398 79403
2400-2798 79415
2800-3399 79415
3401-3599 79415
4600-5799 79416
Grover Ave
200-1299 79416
6600-6898 79424
6900-9899 79424
N Grover Ave 79416
N Guava Ave 79403
Halearri St 79423
Hanover Dr & St 79416
E & W Hardin St 79403
Hartford Ave
201-299 79415
1900-1999 79410
3500-7099 79413

8100-12599 79423
N Hartford Ave 79415
Hartford Dr 79423
Harvard Dr 79416
Harvard St
1300-1399 79403
1900-3699 79415
4600-6799 79416
E Harvard St 79403
Hazelwood Ave 79403
Hickory Ave 79404
High Meadow Rd 79404
Highway 114 Ests 79407
Highway 62 79407
E Highway 62 79403
Highway 84
4401-5999 79416
Highway 84
4700-5198 79415
E Highway 84 79404
Highway 87 79423
Hillside Dr 79415
N Holly St 79403
Homestead Ave
200-1199 79416
6300-10300 79424
10302-11898 79424
N Homestead Ave 79416
Homestead Dr 79416
Hoover Dr 79416
Hope Ave 79424
Horn Ttu 79406
Horse Rd 79407
Hudson Ave 79423
N Hudson Ave 79415
Hulen Ttu 79406
E Hunter St 79403
Huron Ave
200-1299 79416
4300-4399 79407
6600-10300 79424
10302-10498 79424
N Huron Ave 79416
Hyden Ave
400-1299 79416
3400-3499 79407
6800-9199 79424
9201-9399 79424
N Hyden Ave 79416
Idalou Rd 79403
Immaculata St 79415
W Imperial St 79403
Indian Trl 79404
Indiana Ave
201-299 79415
600-1298 79415
2100-3198 79410
3400-7099 79413
7200-14899 79423
14901-18999 79423
N Indiana Ave 79415
Indiana Dr 79423
Inler Ave
100-899 79416
901-1599 79416
1900-2699 79407
N Inler Ave 79416
Insurance Rd 79403
Interstate 27
2200-3699 79404
Interstate 27
3701-8399 79404
3800-3898 79412
5000-8398 79404
N Interstate 27 79403
N Inverness Ave 79416
Iola Ave
400-1699 79416
1900-4399 79407
6200-11699 79424
N Iola Ave 79416
Iola Dr 79416
Iona St 79415
Ironton Ave
400-1199 79416
3400-4400 79407
4402-4598 79407

7000-7298 ... 79424
7300-9999 ... 79424
Ironton Dr ... 79416
N Ironwood Ave ... 79403
Itasca St
1301-1399 ... 79403
3100-3699 ... 79415
4400-6799 ... 79416
E Itasca St ... 79403
Ithaca Ave
2200-2298 ... 79410
2301-2399 ... 79410
8200-8298 ... 79423
8200-8298 ... 79453
8201-8299 ... 79423
8201-8299 ... 79453
9600-9699 ... 79423
N Ithaca Ave ... 79415
Ivory Ave ... 79404
N Ivory Ave ... 79403
E Jamestown St ... 79403
W Jarrell St ... 79403
Jarvis St
1200-1298 ... 79403
1300-1399 ... 79403
3100-3699 ... 79415
4400-5499 ... 79416
E Jarvis St ... 79403
Jason Ave ... 79407
Joliet Ave
2200-2398 ... 79410
2400-3299 ... 79410
3400-6499 ... 79413
7200-15299 ... 79423
Joliet Dr ... 79413
Jordan Ave & Dr ... 79423
Juneau Ave
400-1199 ... 79416
1900-3499 ... 79407
7300-10000 ... 79424
10002-11398 ... 79424
N Juneau Ave ... 79416
Juniper Ave ... 79404
Justice Ave
400-1199 ... 79416
3400-3499 ... 79407
7300-10799 ... 79424
W Justin St ... 79403
N Keel Ave ... 79403
Kelsey Ave ... 79407
Kemper St
1101-1399 ... 79403
3600-3699 ... 79415
4400-5499 ... 79416
E Kemper St ... 79403
Kenosha Ave
2500-2599 ... 79410
5000-5398 ... 79413
7700-7798 ... 79423
7800-10999 ... 79423
Kenosha Dr
6100-6299 ... 79413
8500-8699 ... 79423
Kent St
700-2499 ... 79403
2500-4498 ... 79415
4500-4899 ... 79415
4901-4999 ... 79415
5400-5499 ... 79416
E Kent St ... 79403
Keuka St ... 79403
Kewanee Ave
400-1199 ... 79416
1900-3499 ... 79407
7001-7297 ... 79424
7299-9199 ... 79424
Kimberly Dr ... 79403
King Ave ... 79404
N King Ave ... 79403
Kirby Ave
400-1799 ... 79416
2900-2999 ... 79407
7300-7698 ... 79424
7700-11299 ... 79424
N Kirby Ave ... 79416
Kit Carson Ln ... 79404

Kline Ave
400-1199 ... 79416
2900-2999 ... 79407
7301-11097 ... 79424
11099-11199 ... 79424
N Kline Ave ... 79416
Knapp Ttu ... 79406
Knoxville Ave
2500-2600 ... 79410
2602-3398 ... 79410
3400-5099 ... 79413
7900-10799 ... 79423
N Knoxville Ave ... 79415
Knoxville Dr
3500-3699 ... 79423
6100-6399 ... 79413
7700-7799 ... 79423
7801-8639 ... 79423
Knoxville Pl ... 79423
W Krum St ... 79403
La Salle Ave ... 79407
Lakeridge Dr ... 79424
Landmark Ln ... 79415
Langford Ave ... 79407
Lariat Loop ... 79404
Lasalle Ave
1100-1199 ... 79416
7700-7799 ... 79424
Lehigh St
3600-3699 ... 79415
4400-6599 ... 79416
E Lehigh St ... 79403
W Leming St ... 79403
Leon Rd ... 79407
Liberty Ave
1100-1199 ... 79416
2900-2999 ... 79407
Linden Ave ... 79403
E Llano Ave ... 79407
Locust Ave ... 79404
E Loop 289 ... 79403
N Loop 289
300-398 ... 79403
N Loop 289
400-500 ... 79403
502-1698 ... 79403
1701-2797 ... 79415
2799-2899 ... 79415
2901-4399 ... 79415
4600-4898 ... 79416
NE Loop 289 ... 79403
S Loop 289
101-199 ... 79404
1300-1398 ... 79412
1400-1500 ... 79412
1501-4399 ... 79423
1502-1598 ... 79412
4300-4398 ... 79413
4400-4998 ... 79414
4401-4899 ... 79424
4901-4901 ... 79464
4903-5399 ... 79424
SE Loop 289 ... 79404
W Loop 289
100-128 ... 79416
130-1199 ... 79416
1201-1699 ... 79416
1900-4399 ... 79407
4501-5899 ... 79414
4900-5998 ... 79424
Loop 493 ... 79423
Louisville Ave
2500-2800 ... 79410
2802-2998 ... 79410
3600-3698 ... 79413
3700-4899 ... 79413
4901-5399 ... 79413
7200-15300 ... 79423
15302-16498 ... 79423
Louisville Dr
6100-6299 ... 79413
8500-8599 ... 79423
Loyola St ... 79415
E Loyola St ... 79403
Lubbock Business Park
Blvd ... 79403
Lynnhaven Ave ... 79423

Lynnhaven Dr
6100-6299 ... 79413
6301-6999 ... 79413
9400-9499 ... 79423
Lynnhaven Pl ... 79423
Mac Davis Ln ... 79401
Madison St ... 79415
E Madison St ... 79403
Magnolia Ave ... 79404
N Magnolia Ave ... 79403
Main St
300-498 ... 79401
500-2499 ... 79401
3211-3211 ... 79406
E Main St ... 79403
Mallard Rd ... 79407
Manhattan Dr ... 79404
Manioca Rd ... 79403
Mardi Gras ... 79424
Marlboro St
400-498 ... 79403
2500-2699 ... 79415
2701-2799 ... 79415
E Marlboro St ... 79403
Marsha Sharp Fwy
501-597 ... 79401
599-1699 ... 79401
1700-2500 ... 79415
2502-2598 ... 79415
4100-7299 ... 79407
Marshall St
1600-1699 ... 79403
1900-3699 ... 79415
4400-5499 ... 79416
W Marshall St ... 79416
Martin L King Blvd ... 79404
N Martin Luther King
Blvd ... 79403
Mason Rd ... 79407
Mcguire St ... 79416
N Meadow Dr ... 79403
Memphis Ave
2200-2798 ... 79410
4901-6397 ... 79413
6399-7099 ... 79413
7200-9899 ... 79423
N Memphis Ave ... 79415
Memphis Dr ... 79423
Mesa Dr ... 79404
Mesa Rd ... 79403
Miami Ave
1900-2099 ... 79410
7000-7099 ... 79413
8501-8597 ... 79423
8599-10899 ... 79423
W Miles St ... 79403
Mill Rd ... 79403
Milwaukee Ave
900-1899 ... 79416
1900-5099 ... 79407
6200-11800 ... 79424
11802-12398 ... 79424
N Milwaukee Ave ... 79416
Mindelde St ... 79407
Mobile Ave ... 79416
Mockingbird Hl ... 79404
S Monroe Ave ... 79403
Monticello Ave ... 79416
N Mulberry Ave ... 79403
E Municipal Dr ... 79403
Murdough Ttu ... 79406
Murray Ttu ... 79406
Nashville Ave
1900-1999 ... 79410
2001-2499 ... 79410
3400-6899 ... 79413
8200-10999 ... 79423
N Nashville Ave ... 79415
Nashville Dr ... 79413
Natchez Trce ... 79424
Ncr 1900 ... 79415
Newcomb St
400-599 ... 79403
2500-2699 ... 79415
E Newcomb St ... 79403
Nightingale Rd ... 79407
N Niter Ave ... 79403

W Noble St ... 79403
Noradwas St ... 79410
Norfolk Ave
1601-1697 ... 79416
1699-1799 ... 79416
5600-7099 ... 79413
7500-12599 ... 79423
Norwich Ave
1700-1799 ... 79416
2100-2599 ... 79407
N Norwich Ave ... 79416
Norwood Ave
6600-6699 ... 79413
9800-12599 ... 79423
Oak Ave
1300-1498 ... 79403
1801-1899 ... 79403
2300-4998 ... 79404
5000-8099 ... 79404
Oak Dr ... 79404
Oak Ridge Ave ... 79407
Oakridge Ave
300-1099 ... 79416
6600-7999 ... 79424
N Oakridge Ave ... 79416
Oberlin St ... 79415
Olive Ave
100-5998 ... 79403
6000-6199 ... 79403
7800-7899 ... 79404
N Olive Ave ... 79403
Orlando Ave
1400-1899 ... 79416
3600-7099 ... 79413
7800-12599 ... 79423
Oshkosh Ave ... 79416
E Owen St ... 79403
Owl Rd ... 79407
Oxford Ave
2000-2098 ... 79410
2100-2199 ... 79410
2201-2299 ... 79410
3500-7099 ... 79413
8400-12299 ... 79423
12301-12599 ... 79423
Palamino Dr ... 79404
Paris Ave
200-399 ... 79401
3600-3700 ... 79412
3702-3798 ... 79412
7500-11100 ... 79423
11102-11198 ... 79423
N Paris Ave ... 79403
Parkway Dr ... 79403
Peach Ave
200-299 ... 79403
8300-8698 ... 79404
Peoria Ave
1701-1799 ... 79416
2801-3097 ... 79410
3099-3199 ... 79410
3201-3399 ... 79410
3500-6099 ... 79413
6101-7099 ... 79413
10000-13499 ... 79423
Pheasant Rd ... 79407
Pontiac Ave
400-1799 ... 79416
3400-3700 ... 79407
3702-3798 ... 79407
6800-9399 ... 79424
N Pontiac Ave ... 79416
Pony Express Trl ... 79404
Prennert St ... 79411
Prentiss Ave
400-1099 ... 79416
3600-3799 ... 79407
7501-7597 ... 79424
7599-7699 ... 79424
7701-7899 ... 79424
Primrose Ave
400-1199 ... 79416
9300-9399 ... 79424
Princeton St
2401-4297 ... 79415
4299-4399 ... 79415
5800-5899 ... 79416

E Princeton St ... 79403
Private Road 1040 ... 79407
Private Road 1150 ... 79407
Private Road 1250 ... 79407
Private Road 1305 ... 79407
Private Road 1740 ... 79424
Private Road 1760 ... 79424
Private Road 1970 ... 79415
Private Road 2000 ... 79424
Private Road 2240 ... 79423
Private Road 2270 ... 79423
Private Road 2370 ... 79423
Private Road 2410 ... 79423
N Private Road 2420 ... 79403
Private Road 2450 ... 79404
Private Road 2500 ... 79423
Private Road 2570 ... 79404
Private Road 2760 ... 79403
N Private Road 2940 ... 79403
Private Road 3140 ... 79403
E Private Road 6040 ... 79403
E Private Road 6200 ... 79403
E Private Road 6250 ... 79403
Private Road 6260 ... 79415
Private Road 6310 ... 79415
Private Road 6470 ... 79416
Private Road 6500 ... 79416
E Private Road 6605 ... 79403
Private Road 6655 ... 79416
Private Road 6850 ... 79407
Private Road 6855 ... 79407
Private Road 6860 ... 79407
Private Road 6935 ... 79407
E Private Road 7130 ... 79404
Private Road 7150 ... 79423
E Private Road 7150 ... 79404
E Private Road 7160 ... 79404
Private Road 7305 ... 79423
Private Road 7310 ... 79423
Private Road 7320
2300-2499 ... 79423
Private Road 7320
5800-6099 ... 79424
Private Road 7325 ... 79423
Private Road 7330 ... 79423
Private Road 7340 ... 79423
E Private Road 7340 ... 79404
Private Road 7350 ... 79423
Private Road 7355 ... 79423
Private Road 7360 ... 79423
Private Road 7365 ... 79423
Private Road 7630 ... 79423
E Private Road 7640 ... 79423
Private Road 7670 ... 79423
Private Road 7675 ... 79423
Private Road 7730 ... 79424
Private Road 7945 ... 79424
Prondint ... 79409
Prospect Ave ... 79416
Purdue St ... 79415
E Purdue St ... 79403
Quail Rd ... 79407
Quaker Ave
400-499 ... 79416
501-1799 ... 79416
1900-1998 ... 79407
2301-2397 ... 79410
2399-3399 ... 79410
3401-3497 ... 79413
3499-6699 ... 79413
6701-6999 ... 79413
7000-12999 ... 79424
13200-13300 ... 79423
13302-13698 ... 79423
N Quaker Ave
801-2299 ... 79416
1200-1298 ... 79415
1400-1998 ... 79416
2801-4300 ... 79415
4302-4428 ... 79415
Quanah Ave ... 79423
Queens St ... 79415
E Queens St ... 79403
Quetzel Ave ... 79403
Quincy Ave
3400-3498 ... 79407

6600-12199 ... 79424
N Quincy Ave ... 79416
Quinlan St ... 79403
E Quinn St ... 79403
Quinton Ave
2401-2499 ... 79410
8000-10999 ... 79424
N Quinton Ave ... 79416
Quinton Pl ... 79424
Quitman Ave ... 79424
Quitsna Ave ... 79416
Raleigh Ave
1800-1898 ... 79416
1901-2199 ... 79407
2600-2698 ... 79410
3400-4099 ... 79414
7400-10999 ... 79424
Raleigh Dr ... 79414
Red Springs Ave ... 79423
Redbud Ave
200-1399 ... 79403
2200-2398 ... 79404
2400-2900 ... 79404
2902-6898 ... 79404
N Redbud Ave ... 79403
N Redwood Ave ... 79403
Reese Blvd N ... 79416
Regis St
200-299 ... 79403
301-799 ... 79403
2700-2799 ... 79415
E Regis St ... 79403
Remington Ave
3400-3499 ... 79407
9100-9799 ... 79424
Research Blvd ... 79407
Rhodes Cir ... 79423
Rice St ... 79415
E Rice St ... 79403
Richard Ave ... 79403
Richmond Ave
5501-5797 ... 79414
5799-5900 ... 79414
5902-5998 ... 79414
7400-11099 ... 79424
Ridge Rd ... 79403
Ridgely Ave ... 79424
Rochester Ave
3401-3497 ... 79407
3499-3599 ... 79407
6600-9399 ... 79424
Ross Ave ... 79424
Runway Dr ... 79416
Salem Ave
2600-2698 ... 79410
3900-6699 ... 79414
7000-7398 ... 79424
7400-11199 ... 79424
Salem Dr ... 79424
Salisbury Ave
3100-3398 ... 79410
8501-8697 ... 79424
8699-9999 ... 79424
Salisbury Blvd ... 79424
San Jose Dr ... 79415
Santa Fe Dr
2500-2598 ... 79415
5100-7199 ... 79407
Saratoga Ave
2600-3299 ... 79407
6800-9299 ... 79424
Savannah Ave ... 79424
E Seaton ... 79404
Seguin Ave ... 79423
Shallowater Dr ... 79415
Sherman Ave
100-399 ... 79415
6100-6699 ... 79412
8100-9899 ... 79423
N Sherman Ave ... 79415
Simmons St ... 79403
E Slaton Rd ... 79404
Slide Rd
200-1300 ... 79416
1302-1798 ... 79416
1900-2198 ... 79407
2200-3099 ... 79407

3400-6299 ... 79414
6500-6698 ... 79424
6700-12500 ... 79424
12502-12898 ... 79424
N Slide Rd ... 79416
Sneed Ttu ... 79406
Southeast Dr ... 79404
N Spruce Ave ... 79403
Spur 327 ... 79424
Spur 331 ... 79404
Stanford St ... 79415
E Stanford St ... 79403
Stangel Ttu ... 79406
E State Road 114 ... 79407
N & S State Road 168 ... 79407
State Road 2130 ... 79407
Strelles St ... 79415
Student Union Bldg ... 79409
N Sumac Ave ... 79403
Sunset Ln ... 79403
Suntranc St ... 79414
Sycamore Park ... 79403
Talkington Ttu ... 79406
Teak Ave
400-1799 ... 79403
2600-3299 ... 79404
N Teak Ave ... 79403
Temple Ave
100-399 ... 79415
5401-6197 ... 79412
6199-6799 ... 79412
8100-8999 ... 79423
N Temple Ave ... 79415
Terrell Ave ... 79423
Texas Ave
200-598 ... 79401
600-1899 ... 79401
1900-2600 ... 79411
2602-2998 ... 79411
Texas Tech University ... 79409
Toledo Ave
301-303 ... 79416
305-399 ... 79416
3301-3399 ... 79410
3401-3497 ... 79414
3499-4799 ... 79414
7400-10700 ... 79424
10702-11098 ... 79424
N Toledo Ave ... 79416
Tommy Fisher Dr ... 79404
Topeka Ave
400-499 ... 79416
2100-2498 ... 79407
7400-12199 ... 79424
N Topeka Ave ... 79416
Trafalgar Ave ... 79424
Trenton Ave
3000-3299 ... 79407
7600-8599 ... 79424
Triverne ... 79406
Troy Ave
100-499 ... 79416
10600-11299 ... 79424
N Troy Ave ... 79416
Ttu ... 79409
E Tulane St ... 79403
N Tulip Ave ... 79403
N Turmeric Ave ... 79403
Tuscan Villa Cir ... 79423
N Twinberry Ave ... 79403
University Ave
100-321 ... 79415
323-399 ... 79415
401-1699 ... 79401
1901-3399 ... 79410
3400-7099 ... 79413
7300-12299 ... 79423
N University Ave ... 79415
Upland Ave
500-1698 ... 79416
1700-1799 ... 79416
2000-6799 ... 79407
6900-10799 ... 79424
Urbana Ave
2200-5999 ... 79407
8200-8899 ... 79424
8901-9399 ... 79424

Urbana Pl 79407
Ursuline St
700-899 79403
3900-3999 79415
4001-4399 79415
5501-5599 79416
E Ursuline St 79403
Us Highway 87 79423
Ute Ave
400-1799 79403
2900-4899 79404
4901-4999 79404
Utica Ave
100-306 79416
308-398 79416
2400-2599 79407
3800-4899 79414
4901-6699 79414
7000-10999 79424
11001-11799 79424
N Utica Ave 79416
Utica Dr
400-499 79416
9300-10599 79424
Utica Pl 79424
Uvalde Ave
100-399 79415
3900-7099 79412
7800-9799 79423
N Uvalde Ave 79415
Uxbridge Ave 79424
N Vale Ave 79416
Valencia Ave
500-598 79416
5900-6099 79407
8200-8899 79424
Valley View Dr 79403
Vanda Ave
400-1799 79403
2800-4799 79404
Vardo Ln 79403
N Varnish Ave 79403
Vassar St 79403
Vega Ln 79403
Venita Ave
100-398 79416
5900-5999 79407
8000-9399 79424
N Venita Ave 79416
Vernon Ave
100-399 79415
6000-6099 79412
7700-9899 79423
Vicksburg Ave
300-1699 79416
1900-2000 79407
2002-2198 79407
2600-2698 79410
2700-3199 79410
3201-3399 79410
3400-3699 79414
7000-10699 79424
N Vicksburg Ave 79416
Victoria St 79415
Villa Dr 79412
Vinton Ave 79424
N Vinton Ave 79416
Viola Ave
1800-1899 79416
3200-3299 79407
8100-9699 79424
Virginia Ave 79424
Vistrenc St 79413
Wabash St 79403
Waco Ave
100-399 79415
7400-9799 79423
9801-9899 79423
Wall Ttu 79406
Walnut Ave
201-299 79403
400-898 79403
2800-2899 79404
N Walnut Ave 79403
Wausau Ave
1800-1899 79416
2100-2599 79407
9000-9100 79424
9102-9298 79424
Wayne Ave
300-399 79416
2200-2299 79407
3400-5599 79414
6800-10699 79424
10701-12699 79424
N Wayne Ave 79416
Weatherford Ave 79423
Weber Dr 79404
Weeks Ttu 79406
Wells St 79415
Western Dr 79403
Weymouth Ttu 79406
Wheelock St 79403
Whisperwood Blvd & Cir 79416
Wiggins Ttu 79406
Wilshire Blvd 79416
Windsor Ct 79416
Winston Ave 79424
N Winston Ave 79416
N Wood Ave 79403
Woodrow Rd
101-113 79423
115-4399 79423
4400-6799 79424
E Woodrow Rd 79423
Xavier St 79403
N Xenia Ave 79416
Yale St 79403
York Ave
300-399 79416
2300-2899 79407
3600-3700 79414
3702-5798 79414
7000-10699 79424
10701-12899 79424
N York Ave 79416
York Dr 79414
York Pl 79424
Yucca Ave & Ln 79403
Yuma Ave 79407
N Yuma Ave 79416
Zadar Ave 79424
Zeeland Ave 79407
N Zenith Ave 79403
Zoar Ave
200-299 79416
7001-7097 79424
7099-7899 79424

NUMBERED STREETS

1st Pl
1001-1099 79401
2500-3399 79415
4800-5799 79416
E 1st Pl 79403
1st St
1300-1400 79401
1900-2499 79415
4800-7399 79416
E 1st St 79403
2nd Dr 79416
2nd Pl
700-798 79401
2101-2197 79415
5500-5799 79416
E 2nd Pl 79403
2nd St
1000-1300 79401
1901-2097 79415
4701-4797 79416
E 2nd St 79403
2nd Place Dr 79416
3rd Dr 79416
3rd Pl
700-899 79401
2400-2500 79415
E 3rd Pl 79403
3rd St
301-499 79401
1700-2298 79415
5500-7399 79416
E 3rd St 79403
4th Dr 79416
4th St
2800-2904 79415
3121-3121 79409
3801-3899 79415
4400-5499 79416
5400-5498 79499
5500-9498 79416
E 4th St 79403
5th St
1600-1698 79401
4600-7499 79416
E 5th St 79403
6th Pl 79416
6th St
900-1099 79401
4400-8699 79416
E 6th St 79403
7th Dr 79416
7th St
900-1698 79401
1700-2499 79401
4400-7699 79416
E 7th St 79403
8th Dr 79416
8th Pl 79416
8th St
800-898 79401
1101-1799 79401
4400-8699 79416
E 8th St 79403
9th Dr 79416
9th St
1300-1398 79401
1400-2499 79401
3502-3598 79415
4400-8899 79416
E 9th St 79403
10th Dr 79416
10th Pl 79416
10th St
200-698 79401
700-2400 79401
2402-2498 79401
3401-3599 79415
4400-8899 79416
E 10th St 79403
11th Pl & St 79416
12th St 79416
13th St
500-698 79401
4400-8899 79416
E 13th St 79403
14th St
701-1097 79401
4400-8899 79416
E 14th St 79403
15th Dr 79416
E 15th Pl 79403
15th St
600-998 79401
1000-2499 79401
2519-2519 79406
2600-2699 79409
4000-8899 79416
E 15th St 79403
16th Pl 79416
16th St
900-1098 79401
1100-2499 79401
4000-8899 79416
E 16th St 79403
17th Pl 79416
17th St
600-898 79401
900-2399 79401
4100-8899 79416
E 17th St 79403
18th Pl 79416
18th St
200-598 79401
600-2399 79401
2803-3115 79406
4400-8899 79416
E 18th St 79403
19th St
300-2499 79401
2501-3797 79410
3799-3899 79410
3901-4105 79410
4100-4106 79407
4108-9612 79407
9614-9698 79407
E 19th St 79403
20th St
1300-1898 79411
2500-3899 79410
4400-9499 79407
21st St
1300-2499 79411
2500-4099 79410
4400-9499 79407
22nd Pl
2400-2499 79411
3401-3407 79410
4500-6599 79407
22nd St
1500-2499 79411
2500-4099 79410
4400-9499 79407
23rd St
200-599 79404
601-699 79404
1001-1097 79411
1099-2499 79411
2500-4399 79410
4500-6599 79407
E 23rd St 79404
24th Pl 79411
24th St
1101-1297 79411
1299-2499 79411
2500-4100 79410
4102-4398 79410
4800-7399 79407
E 24th St 79404
25th St
1001-1097 79411
1099-2499 79411
2500-4099 79410
5200-8999 79407
E 25th St 79404
26th St
100-799 79404
1300-2499 79411
2500-4499 79410
5200-7599 79407
E 26th St 79404
27th St
400-799 79404
1300-2499 79411
2500-4799 79410
5000-6499 79407
E 27th St 79404
28th St
600-899 79404
1300-2499 79411
2500-4799 79410
5200-6499 79407
E 28th St 79404
29th Dr
4900-4940 79410
5100-5199 79407
29th Pl 79411
29th St
600-899 79404
1000-1098 79411
1100-2499 79411
2500-4899 79410
5200-6399 79407
E 29th St 79404
30th St
200-799 79404
1100-1298 79411
1300-2499 79411
2500-4699 79410
5200-7299 79407
E 30th St 79404
31st St
200-598 79404
600-899 79404
901-1297 79411
1299-2499 79411
2500-4700 79410
4702-4798 79410
5300-6499 79407
E 31st St 79404
32nd St
500-899 79404
900-2499 79411
2500-4699 79410
5300-7199 79407
33rd St
901-1097 79411
1099-2499 79411
2500-4699 79410
5300-6499 79407
E 33rd St 79404
34th Pl 79407
34th St
100-899 79404
900-1098 79411
1100-2499 79411
2500-5199 79410
5400-8799 79407
E 34th St 79404
35th St
1100-2499 79412
2500-4299 79413
4400-5199 79414
5400-6999 79407
7001-7099 79407
E 35th St 79404
36th St
200-799 79404
1100-2499 79412
2500-4399 79413
4400-5199 79414
5400-6999 79407
E 36th St 79404
37th St
200-799 79404
1100-2499 79412
2500-4299 79413
4400-5199 79414
5500-6700 79407
6702-6998 79407
E 37th St 79404
38th St
200-699 79404
900-2499 79412
2500-4399 79413
4400-5499 79414
5500-6499 79407
E 38th St 79404
39th Dr 79414
39th St
200-699 79404
1300-2499 79412
2500-4399 79413
4400-5399 79414
5401-5499 79414
6100-6199 79407
40th St
200-700 79404
702-898 79404
900-2200 79412
2202-2498 79412
2500-4399 79413
4400-5499 79414
5700-5799 79407
E 40th St 79404
41st St
500-599 79404
900-2099 79412
2500-4399 79413
4800-5499 79414
5700-5799 79407
42nd St
200-699 79404
900-2099 79412
2500-4399 79413
4400-5599 79414
6000-6099 79407
E 42nd St 79404
43rd St
200-699 79404
701-799 79404
1100-2099 79412
2500-4399 79413
4400-5699 79414
6000-6999 79407
44th St
200-599 79404
900-2499 79412
2500-4399 79413
4400-5699 79414
E 44th St 79404
45th St
200-599 79404
900-2499 79412
2500-4399 79413
4400-5799 79414
6000-6199 79407
46th Pl 79412
46th St
200-899 79404
900-2499 79412
2500-4399 79413
4400-5799 79414
E 46th St 79404
47th St
500-799 79404
1200-2499 79412
2500-4399 79413
4400-5799 79414
E 47th St 79404
48th St
300-899 79404
900-2499 79412
2500-4399 79413
4400-5799 79414
10300-10699 79407
E 48th St 79404
49th Pl 79413
49th St
500-599 79404
1200-2399 79412
2600-4399 79413
4400-5500 79414
5502-5598 79414
5800-5899 79424
E 49th St 79404
50th St
200-899 79404
900-2499 79412
2500-4399 79413
4400-5731 79414
5732-5999 79424
7000-7599 79407
E 50th St 79404
51st St
200-599 79404
1300-2399 79412
3800-4299 79413
4401-5399 79414
E 51st St 79404
52nd St
200-899 79404
1000-2499 79412
2500-4399 79413
4400-5099 79414
E 52nd St 79404
53rd St
200-599 79404
1000-2399 79412
2500-4399 79413
4400-5599 79414
E 53rd St 79404
54th St
200-599 79404
900-2399 79412
2500-4399 79413
4400-5599 79414
E 54th St 79404
55th Dr 79414
55th St
500-599 79404
1600-2399 79412
2500-4399 79413
4400-5199 79414
E 55th St 79404
56th St
500-599 79404
1600-2399 79412
2500-4399 79413
4400-5699 79414
E 56th St 79404
57th St
900-2399 79412
2500-4399 79413
4400-5299 79414
58th Pl 79412
58th St
800-899 79404
900-2399 79412
2500-4399 79413
4400-5599 79414
5600-5899 79424
E 58th St 79404
59th St
1300-2399 79412
2500-4399 79413
4400-5199 79414
6800-7399 79407
60th St
1300-2399 79412
2500-4399 79413
4400-5199 79414
7300-7399 79407
7401-7499 79407
E 60th St 79403
61st St
1300-2399 79412
2500-4399 79413
4400-5099 79414
5700-5799 79424
7000-7299 79407
E 61st St 79403
62nd Dr 79413
62nd St
1300-2399 79412
2500-4399 79413
4400-5199 79414
5700-5799 79424
E 62nd St 79403
63rd Dr 79413
63rd St
1900-2099 79412
2500-4399 79413
4500-4999 79414
5700-5899 79424
5901-6099 79424
7100-7299 79407
E 63rd St 79403
64th Dr 79413
64th St
1900-2199 79412
2500-4300 79413
4302-4398 79413
4500-4999 79414
5700-5899 79424
E 64th St
500-599 79404
4200-4399 79403
65th Dr
1100-1341 79412
1343-1349 79412
3400-3498 79413
65th Pl 79412
65th St
900-2199 79412
2700-4299 79413
4500-4999 79414
5500-5599 79424
E 65th St 79403
66th Dr 79413
66th St
900-2399 79412
2500-4299 79413
4400-4999 79414
5300-6999 79424
7200-7299 79407
E 66th St 79404
67th St
1900-2199 79412
2800-3899 79413
4600-4799 79414
5500-5899 79424
5901-5999 79424
68th Dr 79413
68th St
1600-2199 79412

2700-4299 79413
5200-7099 79424
69th Dr 79413
69th Pl 79424
69th St
1600-2199 79412
2500-4099 79413
5100-5899 79424
70th Dr 79413
70th Pl
1600-1699 79412
5400-5799 79424
70th St
1100-2399 79412
2500-4299 79413
5000-6599 79424
6601-7199 79424
E 70th St 79404
71st St
1600-2199 79412
2500-2599 79413
4401-4497 79424
4499-6599 79424
72nd Pl & St 79424
73rd St
1900-3799 79423
4800-6200 79424
E 73rd St 79404
74th Pl 79423
74th St
100-199 79404
1601-1897 79423
1899-3799 79423
4400-7399 79424
7401-7499 79424
E 74th St 79404
75th Dr 79424
75th Pl
3800-4099 79423
6000-6399 79424
75th St
1600-4099 79423
4900-6399 79424
6401-8399 79424
E 75th St 79404
76th Pl 79424
76th St
100-799 79404
1600-4099 79423
4400-7499 79424
E 76th St 79404
77th Dr 79423
77th Pl 79423
77th St
100-799 79404
1100-3999 79423
4400-7299 79424
E 77th St 79404
78th Dr 79423
78th St
300-799 79404
1100-4298 79423
4400-7499 79424
E 78th St 79404
79th Dr 79424
79th Pl 79423
79th St
100-799 79404
1400-1598 79423
1600-3599 79423
4400-7199 79424
E 79th St 79404
80th St
6-98 79404
100-799 79404
900-3399 79423
4400-7499 79424
E 80th St 79404
81st Pl 79424
81st St
100-799 79404
900-3399 79423
4500-6099 79424
6101-6399 79424
E 81st St 79404
82nd Ln 79424
82nd Pl 79424
82nd St
100-799 79404
900-4399 79423
4400-7899 79424
E 82nd St 79404
83rd Dr 79423
83rd Ln 79424
83rd St
900-3399 79423
4500-7499 79424
E 83rd St 79404
84th St
500-598 79404
900-4299 79423
4500-7699 79424
E 84th St 79404
85th Pl 79424
85th St
500-599 79404
2200-4299 79423
4400-4598 79424
4600-7899 79424
86th Dr 79423
86th St
2000-4199 79423
4400-7599 79424
7601-7699 79424
E 86th St 79404
87th Pl 79424
87th St
2000-4299 79423
4400-7499 79424
88th Dr 79423
88th Pl
4000-4299 79423
4400-6199 79424
88th St
2000-4299 79423
4400-6999 79424
E 88th St 79404
89th St
2000-4399 79423
4400-6999 79424
90th St
1700-3699 79423
5200-6999 79424
91st Ln 79424
91st Pl 79424
91st St
900-3599 79423
4600-6999 79424
92nd St
1300-4399 79423
4600-6999 79424
93rd Dr 79424
93rd Pl 79423
93rd St
2100-4399 79423
4600-7499 79424
94th Pl 79423
94th St
1100-4399 79423
4600-7499 79424
95th St
2100-4399 79423
4800-7499 79424
96th St
1300-4399 79423
4600-4706 79424
97th Pl 79423
97th St
2100-4399 79423
4900-6200 79424
98th St
1300-4299 79423
4400-7700 79424
99th Pl 79423
99th St
1900-4099 79423
4500-6200 79424
100th Pl 79423
100th St
1700-4099 79423
4400-6899 79424
101st Pl 79424
101st St
2100-4199 79423
4400-6299 79424
102nd Pl 79424
102nd St
2301-3097 79423
4400-6299 79424
103rd St
3000-4199 79423
4400-6100 79424
104th St
3000-4399 79423
4700-6899 79424
105th Pl 79424
105th St
3000-3098 79423
3100-4399 79423
4400-5599 79424
5601-6299 79424
106th St
2500-4399 79423
4400-5799 79424
107th Dr 79423
107th St
2800-4399 79423
5300-5799 79424
108th Dr 79423
108th Pl 79423
108th St
2700-4399 79423
4400-5799 79424
5801-6299 79424
E 108th St 79404
109th Pl 79424
109th St
2100-4399 79423
4400-7299 79424
110th St
1700-4099 79423
4400-6899 79424
111th Dr 79424
111th St
1600-4099 79423
4600-6499 79424
112th Dr 79424
112th St
1600-4099 79423
4500-6399 79424
E 112th St 79404
113th St
3800-4099 79423
4700-6299 79424
114th St
1101-1499 79423
1501-4299 79423
4301-4399 79423
4400-7599 79424
115th St 79424
116th St
901-1097 79423
4400-6099 79424
117th St
900-998 79423
4400-5200 79424
118th St
2300-2499 79423
4400-5199 79424
119th St 79424
120th Blvd 79424
120th Pl 79424
120th St
2300-2400 79423
2402-2498 79423
6400-6499 79424
121st Pl & St 79424
122nd St
1600-3499 79423
4401-5497 79424
123rd St 79423
124th St
1600-4199 79423
4400-4699 79424
125th St 79423
126th St
1600-4099 79423
4601-5497 79424
127th St 79423
128th St 79423
130th St
1500-1598 79423
4500-6200 79424
132nd St 79423
133rd St 79423
134th St
901-997 79423
999-4300 79423
4302-4398 79423
5500-5799 79424
135th St 79423
136th St 79423
138th St
1000-1599 79423
5500-5799 79424
140th St 79423
142nd St 79423
146th St 79423
147th St 79424
148th St
3400-3599 79423
5700-5799 79424
149th St 79424
150th St
3400-3599 79423
5100-5799 79424
152nd St 79423
154th St
3400-3899 79423
5700-5799 79424
156th St 79423
158th St 79423
164th St 79424
165th St 79424
166th St 79424
168th St 79424
170th St 79424
173rd 79423
175th St 79423
184th St 79423

LUFKIN TX

General Delivery 75901

POST OFFICE BOXES MAIN OFFICE STATIONS AND BRANCHES

Box No.s
A - H 75902
1 - 2660 75902
3001 - 3960 75903
150101 - 156854 75915

RURAL ROUTES

01, 02, 03, 06, 09, 13, 15, 16 75901
04, 05, 07, 08, 10, 11, 12, 14, 17, 18 75904

NAMED STREETS

A K Dr 75904
A M Jones Rd 75901
Abby Rd 75904
Abert Rd 75901
Abney Ave 75904
Acorn Dr 75904
Adams St 75901
Addie Ave 75901
Ae Burgess Rd 75904
Airport Ave 75904
Albritton Ln 75901
Alco Church Rd 75901
Allen Dr 75904
Allendale Dr 75904
Allentown Loop 75904
Alta St 75901
Alton St 75901
Alvie Ln 75904
Amber Wood 75904
Amey St 75904
Anderson St 75904
Andrews Ave 75901
N & S Angelina Ave 75904
Ann St 75904
Annette St 75904
Anthony Dr & Pl 75901
Antique Ln 75901
April Dr 75904
Arena St 75901
Arizona Ave 75904
Arkansas Ave 75901
Armory Dr 75901
Asa Read Rd 75901
Ashley Ave & Ln 75904
Ashwood Bnd 75904
Aspen St 75901
Atkinson Dr 75901
Atoyac Ave 75901
Attaberry Rd 75901
Audubon Ln 75904
August Ln 75904
Augusta Dr 75901
Austin St 75904
Autumn Ln 75904
Autumn Lake Dr 75904
Avalon Dr 75901
Aviranches St 75901
Avondale St 75904
Azalea Dr 75904
Bailey Dr 75901
Baird Ln 75904
Baker Ln & Rd 75904
Ballard Rd 75904
Baltusrol Ct 75901
N Banks St 75904
Bar B Q Rd 75904
Barberry Ct 75904
Barclay St 75901
Bartmess Dr 75901
Barto Dr 75904
Bates Rd 75901
Bear Creek Dr 75901
Beasley Rd 75904
Beechmont Cir 75904
Beechnut Cir 75904
Bell St 75901
Ben Dunn Rd 75904
Ben Weeks Rd 75901
Bending Brook Cir 75904
Bending Oak St 75904
Bennett St 75904
Bennie St 75901
Bent Tree Ct 75901
Benton Dr 75901
Bernier Ln 75901
Berry Rd & St 75904
Bethlehem Rd 75904
Bette Cir & St 75901
Betty Dr 75901
Bill Jones Rd 75901
Billie St 75904
Billingsley St 75901
Birch St 75904
Birdsong St 75901
Blachers Dr 75901
Blackburn Switch Rd 75904
Blake Ln & Rd 75901
Blanco River Rd 75901
Bledsoe St 75904
Bloomer Mccall Dr 75904
Blue Bonnet St 75904
Blue Rock Ln 75904
Bluebird Ln 75904
Bluejay Cir 75904
Blythe Rd 75901
Boardwalk Pl 75901
Bob St 75904
Bobbitt Rd 75904
Bobwhite Dr 75904
Boggy Slough Trl 75904
Bois D Arc St 75904
Boles St 75901
Bonita St 75904
N Bonner St 75904
Booker St 75904
Bostick Pl 75901
Bougainvillaea Ct 75901
Boulware Rd 75901
Bowers St 75904
Box Car Rd 75904
Boxwood Ct 75904
Brady St 75901
Branch St 75904
Branchwood St 75904
Brandy Ln 75904
Brasell St 75901
Brashear Rd 75901
Brazil Rd 75901
Brazos Blvd 75901
E Bremond Ave 75901
Brenda St 75901
Brenda Kay St 75901
Brenkie St 75904
N Brentwood 75904
Brentwood Dr 75901
Briar Village St 75904
Briarhill Rd 75904
Briarwood Dr 75901
Bridges Dr & St 75901
Bridle Path 75904
Broaddus St 75901
N & S Broadmoor Dr 75904
Broadway Rd 75901
Brock St 75904
Brook Hollow Dr 75904
Brooks St 75904
Brooks Henry Rd 75904
Brookwood Pl 75904
Broussard Ave 75901
Brown Dr 75904
Brown Rd 75901
Browning Pl 75904
Bruce St 75901
Bryce Rd 75904
Buddy St 75904
E Burke Ave 75901
W Burke Ave 75904
Burton Ave 75904
Burton Rd 75901
Butler St 75904
Buttermilk Rd 75901
Bw Ln 75904
N & S Bynum St 75904
C M Ln 75904
Cain St 75904
Cairo St 75904
Calhoun Loop & Rd 75901
California Blvd 75904
Callaway Ln 75901
Calvary St 75904
Calvert Dr 75904
Calvert St 75901
Calvin St 75904
Camelot Cir 75904
Cameron St 75904
Camp St 75904
Canadian Ave 75901
Canal Ave 75901
Canary Cir 75904
Candy St 75904
Canyon Creek Rd 75904
Card Dr 75901
Carolyn Dr 75904
Carr Rd 75901
Carrell Rd 75901
Carriage Dr 75904
Carrol Ave 75904
Carter Ln 75901
Carver Ave 75904
Cascade Ct 75901
Casey Rd 75901
Casper St 75904
Caspers Cove Rd 75904
Castle Ct 75901
Castle Oaks St 75904
Castle Pines Ct 75901
Castlewood Cir 75904
Catherine St 75901
Cavaso Rd 75904
Caver Rd 75901
Cc Dubose 75901
Cd Rd 75904
Cedar Bend St 75904
Cedaridge St 75904
Centralia Ave 75904
Chambers St 75901
Chambliss Rd 75901
Champions Dr 75901
Champions Hill Dr 75901
Chaparral Ln 75904
Charles Rd 75901
Charlie Hall Rd 75901
Charlotte Dr 75901
Charlton Rd 75904
Charlton St 75901
Cherokee Trl 75904
Cherry St 75901
Cherry Hill Dr 75904
Chester St 75901
Chester Allen Rd 75904
N & S Chestnut St 75901
Chevron Usa St 75904
Chimney Rock St 75904
Christie Dr 75904
Christopher Dr 75904
Church St 75901
Cicero Hill Rd 75904
Cimmaron Dr 75901
Cimmarron St 75904
Circle Dr 75901
Clark Ave 75901
Clay Ave 75901
Clem Rd 75904
Clingman St 75901
Clinton Dr 75901
Cm Mayes Rd 75904
Coach Redd Rd 75901
Cody Ln 75904
College Dr
400-698 75904
700-800 75904
802-3498 75904
3900-4198 75901
Collins St 75904
Colonial Ct 75901
Colonial Hill Dr 75901
Colorado Ct 75901
Columbia Ct 75901
Columbine Dr 75904
Columbus St 75901
Conditt Rd 75904
Condon Ave 75901
Conn Ave 75901
Connie Ln 75904
Cooper St 75904
Copeland St 75904
Copperfield Loop 75904
Copperwood Loop 75901
Cordelia St 75904
N & S Cotton Sq 75904
Cotton Thompson Rd 75901
Cotton Valley St 75901
Cottonbelt St 75904
Country Craft Rd 75904
Counts Rd 75904
County Barn Rd 75904
Courtney Ln 75901
Cousart St 75901
Covey Ln 75904
Covington Dr 75904
Cox Rd 75904
Cozy Cove St 75901
Craft Fenley Loop 75904
W Creek St 75904
Cripple Creek Rd 75904
Cris Rd 75901
Crockett St 75904
Crooked Creek Dr 75904
Cross Timbers St 75901
Crosscut Dr 75901
Crosswood St 75904
Crown Colony Dr 75901
Culverhouse St 75904
Cumming St 75904
Cunningham Dr 75901
Curry St 75901

Cypress St 75901
Cypress Point Ct 75901
Dale St 75901
Dan St 75901
Daniel Mccall Dr 75904
Daniels St 75904
Darceille St 75901
Darlington St 75901
Dave Johnson Rd 75901
David Massingill Rd 75901
Davidson Rd 75901
Davis St 75904
N Davisville Rd 75901
Dawnwood St 75901
Dawson Dr 75901
Dc Lawson Rd 75904
Deans Ln 75901
Deans Way 75904
Deer Ln, Rdg, Run & Trl 75901
Deer Pond Rd 75904
Deer Trace Cir 75901
Deerbrook Ln 75901
Deerfield Dr 75901
Deerwood Cir 75901
Della Russell Rd 75904
Delmas Dr 75901
E Denman Ave 75901
W Denman Ave 75904
Denver Ave 75901
Derek Rd 75904
Desert Willow Dr 75901
Dexter St 75904
Diana St 75901
Dickerson Dr 75901
Dixon Ln & St 75904
Doda St 75904
Dogwood Cir 75904
Dogwood Dr 75901
Dogwood Trl 75904
Dominy St 75901
Don Boyd Ln 75901
Don Willmon Rd 75904
Donna Dr 75904
Doral Cir 75901
Doris St 75901
Dorsett Rd 75901
Doss Ave 75904
Double Creek Ln 75901
Doubletree St 75904
N Douglas St 75901
Doyle Edwards Rd 75904
Doyle Renfro Rd 75901
Doyles Rd 75904
Dudley Rd 75901
Duke St 75904
Duncan Ave 75901
Duncan Slough Rd 75901
Dunlap Ave 75901
Durango 75904
Durant Rd 75904
Duren St 75904
Dusty Creek Ln 75904
Eagle Creek Dr 75901
Earl Largent Rd 75904
Earline Booker Rd 75901
Earnest Landrum Rd 75901
Eason Lake Rd 75904
Eastwego Rd 75901
Eastwood Pl 75901
Echo Ln 75904
Ed Smith Rd 75904
Eddings Ln 75904
Edgewood Cir 75904
Edith St 75901
Edwards Ave 75901
Egg Farm Rd 75904
Elbys Place Rd 75901
Eleanor St 75901
Elhew Pl 75904
Elk Run Rd 75901
Ellen St 75904
Ellen Trout Dr 75904
Ellington Dr 75901
Ellis Ave 75904
Ellis Ln 75901

Elm St 75904
Elsie St 75901
Elwyn Gipson 75904
Englewood Dr 75901
Enkema St 75901
Epley St 75904
Erwin St 75904
Esther St 75901
Etex Dr 75904
Ethel St 75901
Ethel Lewis Rd 75904
Evans Dr & Rd 75904
Evans Gann Rd 75904
Evergreen St 75904
Everitt St 75901
Fair St 75904
Fair Oaks Cir 75901
Faires Ln 75904
Fairfield St 75904
Fairy St 75904
Falcon Ave 75904
Falvey St 75904
Fargo St 75901
Farmer St 75904
Farrell Ln 75901
Feagin Dr 75904
February Ln 75904
Felton Rd 75904
Ferguson Rd 75901
Fielder Cemetery Rd 75901
Finley Ave 75901
S First St 75901
Fish Rd 75901
Flowers Path 75904
Floyd Dr 75901
N & S Fm 1194 75904
Fm 1475 75901
Fm 1818 75901
Fm 2021
200-298 75901
Fm 2021
300-3799 75901
3801-3897 75904
3899-12299 75904
Fm 2108 75901
Fm 2251 75904
Fm 2497 75904
Fm 2680 75904
Fm 3150 75904
Fm 324 75904
Fm 325 75901
Fm 3258 75904
Fm 326 75901
Fm 3521 75901
Fm 58 75901
S Fm 706 75904
Fm 819 75901
Fm 841 75901
Fm 842 75901
Fm 843 75904
Ford St 75904
Ford Chapel Rd 75901
Forest Creek Dr 75901
Forest Park Blvd 75904
E & W Forest View Rd 75904
Forsythe Rd 75901
N Forty Cir 75901
Foster Rd 75901
Foundry Ave 75904
Foy Dr 75904
E Frank Ave 75901
W Frank Ave 75904
Frank Jones Rd 75901
N & S Franklin Ave 75904
Fred Ave 75901
Fredonia Ave 75904
Free Rd 75901
Freeman St 75901
Freeman Cemetery Rd 75904
Frio Ln 75901
Fritz Ln 75904
Fuller Springs Dr 75901
Gainer Rd 75901
Garden Walk Ln 75901
Garner Ave & Rd 75904

Garrison Dr 75901
N & S Garvin St 75901
Garvis St 75904
Gary Rd 75901
Gaslight Blvd 75904
Gaslight Medical Pkwy 75904
Gatewood Ln 75904
Gayle St 75904
Gaylon Wallace Rd 75901
Gene Samford Dr 75904
Generic Ln 75904
Georgia Walker Ln 75901
Gesford Rd 75901
Gibson Dr 75904
Gilbert Rd 75901
Ginn Way 75901
Gipson St 75904
Glade St 75901
Gladstone Pl 75904
Glass Ave 75901
Glengary Rd 75901
Glenn Ave 75901
Glenn Massingill Rd 75901
Glenn Nerren Rd 75901
Glenview Ct 75901
Glenwood 75904
Gobblers Knob Rd 75904
Golden Rd 75904
Golden Rod Ct 75904
Golf Course Rd 75901
Gordon Way 75904
Grace St 75901
Graham St 75904
Grant Ave 75901
Green Mdws 75904
Green Acres Dr 75904
Greenbriar Dr 75901
Greenridge Blvd & Cir 75904
Greer Ave 75901
Greg Rudd Rd 75901
Grimes Cemetary Rd 75901
Grisham Rd 75904
E Groesbeck Ave 75901
E & W Grove Ave 75904
Guadalupe St 75901
Guy York Rd 75901
Haag St 75904
Hackney Ave 75904
Hadaway Rd 75901
Hageon Rd 75904
Hall St 75901
Hanks St 75904
Harbuck Ave 75901
Harley Golden Rd 75901
Harmony Hill Ct & Dr 75901
Harnett Rd 75901
Harper Rd 75901
Harris Ln & St 75904
Harvey Ln 75901
Harvey Walker Rd 75901
Havard Dr 75901
Hawthorne 75904
Hayes Rd 75904
Haylie Way 75901
Hayswood Dr 75904
Heather St 75904
Heatherwood St 75904
Helen St 75901
Hemlock Rd 75901
Henderson St 75904
Henry St 75901
Herman St 75904
Herndon St 75904
Herty St 75901
Hh Allen Rd 75904
Hickory St 75901
Hickory Hill Dr 75901
Hickory Hollow Rd 75904
Hidden Holw 75904
Hidden Lake Rd 75901
Hidden Valley Ranch Rd 75901
Higgins Ave 75901
Hightower Rd 75901
Hill St 75904
Hillside Dr 75904

Hilltop Loop 75904
Hodge St 75901
Hogan Evans Rd 75904
Hogue Rd 75904
Holcombe Rd 75904
Holland St 75901
Holly St 75901
Holmes Rd 75904
Home Ave 75901
Homeplace Rd 75901
Homer Cir & St 75901
Homer Alto Hwy & Rd 75904
Homer Cemetery Rd 75901
Homewood Dr 75901
Honeysuckle Ct 75904
Hoo Hoo Ave 75904
Hopkins St 75901
Hornet Ln 75904
Horseshoe Cir 75904
Horton Glen Rd 75904
Hortons Hollow Rd 75904
Hosea Dolphus Sr Ave 75904
Hoshall Dr 75904
Hoshall Garden Rd 75904
Hoskins Ave 75901
House St 75904
Houston St 75904
Howard Ave 75901
E Howe Ave 75901
W Howe Ave 75904
Hubbard St 75901
Hubert Carroll Rd 75901
Hudson Place Dr 75904
Hughes Rd 75901
Hulsman Rd 75904
Humason Ave 75901
Hummingbird Ln 75904
Hunters Run 75904
Hunters Creek Dr 75901
Hunters Glen Dr 75904
Hyde Ln & Rd 75901
Hylane St 75904
I D Henderson Jr Rd 75904
Ida Duncan Rd 75904
Idylwood Dr 75904
Indigo Ct 75904
Industrial Blvd 75904
Innisbrook Dr 75901
Inwood St 75901
Irving St 75901
Ithica Pl 75904
Ivey Rd 75904
Ivy Terrace St 75901
Iwo Jima St 75901
Jack St 75901
Jack Creek Rd 75904
Jack Nerren Rd 75901
Jackson Ave & Rd 75904
Jacobo Rd 75901
James Ave 75904
James Oates Rd 75904
Jana Dr 75904
Jane Ave 75901
Janeway Ave 75904
January Ln 75904
Jasmine Ct 75901
Jayroe St 75904
Jeanne Ave 75901
Jefferson Ave 75904
Jerri St 75904
Jerry Vann Rd 75901
Jessica Ln 75904
Jewel Rd 75904
Jhb Cir 75901
Jim Fenley Loop 75901
Jim Nelson Rd 75904
Jim Stephens Rd 75904
Jimmie St 75904
Jo Ann Ave 75904
E Jodie Ave 75901
Joe Rd 75904
Joe Bynum Rd 75901
Joe C Ln 75901
Joe Goins Dr 75901
Joe Kelley Rd 75904

Joe Nick Rd 75904
Joe Trevathan Cir 75904
John Brown Rd 75904
John James Rd 75901
John Kolb Rd 75901
John Lucy Ln 75904
N John Redditt Dr 75904
S John Redditt Dr
100-102 75904
104-799 75904
800-3298 75904
800-800 75915
801-3099 75904
Johnnaville Ave 75904
Johnny Grimes Rd 75901
Johnson Ave 75904
Johnson Ln 75901
Jones St 75901
Joplin St 75904
Jordan Ave & Ln 75904
Joshua Ln 75904
Joshua P Ln 75904
Journeys End 75904
Joyce Ln 75901
Jr Childers Rd 75901
Judith St 75901
Judson Dr 75901
Julius Rd 75904
July Ct 75904
June Dr 75904
Junge Rd 75901
Juniper Ln 75904
K Morgan Ave 75901
Karen Dr 75901
Karla St 75901
Karnes Rd 75904
Keathley Rd 75904
N & S Kelley St 75904
Kelly Field St 75904
Keltys St 75904
Kemp Ave 75901
Kendrick Ln 75904
Kenner Rd 75904
Kenneth Carrell Rd 75901
Kenneth Koon Rd 75901
Kenneth Pinner Rd 75901
Kent St 75901
Kentwood Dr 75901
E Kerr Ave 75901
W Kerr Ave 75904
Key Largo Ln 75904
Keys St 75901
Kiawah Ct 75901
Kilgore Dr 75901
Kiln St 75904
Kim Ann St 75901
Kimberly Ln 75904
Kimmey St 75901
King Rd 75901
Kings Forest Dr 75904
Kings River Rd 75901
Kingston St 75901
Kingwood Cir 75901
Kirkland Rd 75904
Kirksey Dr 75904
Kiwanis Park Dr 75901
Knight Ave 75901
Knollwood St 75904
Kurth Dr 75904
Kye St 75901
L L Ln 75904
La Costa Cir 75901
La Madera St 75901
Lacey Cir 75901
Ladd Ln 75904
Lafayette St 75904
Lake Aly 75904
Lake Dr 75901
Lakeview St 75904
Lakewind Dr 75901
Lakewood Ct 75904
Lance St 75901
Lancewood Cir & Dr 75904
Landrum Rd 75904
Lane Dr 75904
Lang Dr 75904

Largent St 75904
Lariat Ln 75904
Lark St 75904
Larkspur Cir 75904
E Laurel Ave 75901
W Laurel Ave 75904
Lavan St 75904
Lawnview St 75901
Lazy Ln 75904
Lazy Oaks St 75901
Leach St 75904
Lee Ave 75901
Lee Ln 75904
Lela St 75904
Lemans Dr 75901
Lennox Rd 75904
Leon Ln & St 75901
Leon Tillman Rd 75901
Leslie Ln 75901
Lewellin Pl 75904
Lewis Rd 75904
Lightfoot Rd 75901
Lilac Ave 75901
Liles Ln 75904
Lincoln Dr 75901
Linden St 75901
Lindsey Ln 75904
Lining St 75901
Linkwood Dr 75901
Linton Rd 75901
Little Hollow Dr 75904
Live Oak Ln 75904
Llano Ln 75901
Lloyd St 75901
Loblolly Ln 75904
Locke Aly & St 75901
Loftin St 75904
Lola Nerren Rd 75901
Lone Oaks Dr 75901
Lone Star Ln 75904
Lone Star Rd 75901
Lonesome Pine Rd 75901
Long Ave 75904
Long Leaf Cir 75904
Loop Ln 75904
Lost Pines Cir 75901
Lost Site Ln 75901
Lotus Ln 75904
Lou Ln 75904
Louis Lambert Rd 75904
Lovelady Ln 75904
Loving Rd 75901
Lowe St 75901
Lowery St 75901
Lubbock St 75901
E Lufkin Ave 75901
W Lufkin Ave 75904
E Lufkin Rd 75902
Lynn Ave 75904
Maas St 75904
Madison St 75901
Magnolia Ave & Bnd 75904
Malone Rd 75901
Mamie St 75904
Manley Ln 75904
Mantooth Ave 75904
Maple St 75904
Maplewood Dr 75901
March Ct 75904
Margaret St 75901
Marion St 75904
Mark St 75904
Markus Ave 75904
Martha St 75901
Martin Luther King Jr Blvd 75904
Mary Ave 75904
Mary Ann St 75901
Mary L Evans Rd 75904
Massingill Rd 75901
Master Crafted Rd 75904
Mathews St 75901
Maurine Ln 75901
Maxwell St 75901
May St 75901
Mayberry St 75901

Mayo Pl 75904
Mcadams Dr 75901
Mccall St 75901
Mccarty Rd 75904
Mcclendon Rd 75904
Mccoy 75901
Mcdonald St 75904
Mcgaughey Rd 75904
Mcgregor Dr 75904
Mcguire Rd 75901
Mchale St 75901
Mckeever Rd 75901
Mckindree Rd 75901
Mckinney St 75901
Mcknight Ln 75901
Mcmullen St 75904
Mcshane Cir 75901
Meadow Ln 75901
Meadow Brook Dr 75904
Meadowview St 75904
Mearrint St 75904
N & S Medford Dr 75901
Medical Center Blvd 75904
Medical Park Dr 75904
Medina St 75901
Melvin Ave 75904
E Menefee St 75901
W Menefee St 75904
Metz Dr 75901
Michaels Loop 75901
Mickey Ave 75901
Milam St 75901
Miles Rd & Way 75901
Mill St 75904
Miller St 75901
Milner St 75901
Mimosa Ln 75901
Mimosa St 75904
Minnie Lou St 75904
Miranda Ln 75901
Mirtie Smith Rd 75901
Mission Hills Dr 75901
Mistywood Cir 75904
Mitchell Ave & Rd 75901
Mize Ave 75904
Mockingbird Ln 75904
Mockingbird Trl 75901
Modisette Loop 75904
Moffett Rd 75901
Molasses Ln 75901
Monday Dr 75904
Montclair St 75901
Montrose St 75901
Moody St 75901
Moore Ave 75904
Morningside Dr 75904
Morris Ln 75904
Morrison Ave 75904
Morrow St 75904
Mosely Rd 75901
Moss Dr 75904
Mossfield Rd 75904
Mossy Creek Rd 75904
Mount Carmel Rd 75904
Mount Pleasant Rd 75904
Mountain Vw 75904
Muirfield Dr 75901
Mulberry Ct 75904
Murphy Ave 75904
Muscadine Cir 75904
Myria St 75901
Myrna Ave 75901
Myrtie St 75901
Nada St 75904
Narraway Loop 75904
Nash Ct & Rd 75901
Nathan St 75904
Neal Rd 75904
Neches Blvd & St 75901
Nerren Ave 75901
Nerren Cemetery Rd 75901
Nesbitt Ave 75901
New Bethel Rd 75904
Newman St 75904
Newsom Ave 75904
Neyland Rd 75904

Nile St 75904
Nobia Rd 75901
Norman St 75904
Normandy Dr 75901
Norris St 75904
North Ave 75904
Northwood St 75901
Norwood Dr 75904
Nye Lee St 75904
Oak Ave 75904
Oak Crest Dr 75901
Oak Hill Pl 75904
Oak Hollow St 75901
Oak Meadow Ln 75904
Oak Shadows St 75901
Oak Trace Dr 75901
Oak Valley St 75904
Oak View St 75904
Oakland Cir 75904
Oakmont Ct 75901
Oakridge Cir 75904
Oakwood Dr 75901
Oates Ln 75901
Odell Mills Rd 75904
Old Beulah School Rd 75901
Old Bonner Rd 75904
Old Diboll Hwy 75904
Old Ewing Rd 75901
Old Gobblers Knob Rd 75904
Old Highway 59 75904
Old Highway 69 75901
Old Homer Alto Rd 75901
Old Mill Rd 75904
Old Moffett Rd 75901
Old Orchard Dr 75901
Old Pond Rd 75901
Old Schoolhouse Rd 75901
Old Union Rd 75904
Oleta Ave 75901
Oliver Rd 75901
Opal Ln 75901
Oquinn Ave 75904
Oscar Berry Rd 75904
Oscar Bridges Rd 75901
Otis Edwards Rd 75904
Otteson Ln 75901
Packer St 75904
Pahal Rd 75901
Paint Brush Cir 75904
Palmetto Ct 75901
Palmore Rd 75904
Pamela Ln 75904
E Park Ave 75901
Park Ln 75904
Park Pl 75901
Parker Dr 75901
Parker Ln 75904
Parkman St 75901
Parks Cir 75904
Parkview Cir 75904
Parkway Plz 75904
Parnell Rd 75901
Parrish Rd 75904
Patton St 75904
Paul Ave 75901
Paul Hawkins Rd 75901
Payton St 75901
Pd Selman Rd 75901
Peace Ave 75901
Peachtree St 75901
Peavy Switch Rd 75904
Pebble Creek St 75904
Pecan St 75901
Pee Wee Smith Rd 75901
Peggy Ln 75904
N Pendarne 75903
Penn Bonner Rd 75904
Penn Farm Rd 75904
Penson St 75904
Percy Simond St 75904
Periers Ave 75901
Permenter Rd 75901
Perry Dr 75904
Pershing Ave 75904
Persimmon Ave 75904
Phelps St 75904
Picardy Ln 75904
Pickwick Pl 75901
Pierce St 75904
Pine Burr St 75901
Pine Cone Ln 75901
Pine Forrest Dr 75901
Pine Hill St 75904
Pine Island Rd 75904
Pine Valley Dr 75901
Pinecrest Ct 75901
Pinehurst Dr 75904
Pinemont Pl 75904
Pinetree Ln 75904
Pinewood Park Dr 75904
Piney Hollow Pl 75904
Pipeline Rd 75901
Plantation Dr 75901
Platt Rd 75901
Pleasant Dr 75904
Plez Rd 75904
Plum Rdg 75904
E Polk Ave 75901
W Polk Ave 75904
Ponderosa Dr 75901
Porter Rd 75904
Possum Trl 75901
Post Oak Rd 75904
Potsy Ln 75904
Powder River Rd 75901
Prairie Ave 75901
Preston St 75901
Primrose Ct 75904
Providence Rd 75904
Quail Creek Dr 75904
Quail Hollow Cir 75901
Quarles Rd 75901
Rabe Rd 75901
N Raguet 75903
N Raguet St 75904
S Raguet St 75904
Rain Drop Dr 75901
Raintree Ct 75901
Rainwood Dr 75901
Ralph Ave 75901
Ramsey Rd 75904
Rancher St 75904
Rancho Mirage Ct 75901
Randall Palmore Ln 75904
N & S Randolph Ave 75904
Randybrook Dr 75901
Ransom Brown Rd 75904
Ratcliff Ave 75904
Ray St 75901
Ray Fisher Rd 75901
Raymond Rd 75904
Rebecca Ln 75904
Red Ln 75901
Red Barn Hl 75904
Red Bud Ln & Trl 75904
Red Hill Rd 75904
Red Loving Rd 75901
Red Oak Ln 75904
Red Town Rd 75904
Redbird Cir 75904
Redland Church Rd 75904
Redland Theatre Rd 75901
Redwood Cir 75904
Reece Ln 75904
Reed Rd 75904
Reen Dr 75901
Reeves Rd 75901
Regal Row 75904
Register Ct 75901
Remington Pl 75904
Renfro Dr 75901
Reynolds Rd 75901
E Rhodes Ave 75901
Rice Dr 75901
Richard Hill Rd 75904
Richard Martin Rd 75904
Richardson Rd 75904
Richey St 75904
Ricks Rd 75901
Ridge St 75901
Ridgecrest St 75901
Ridgewood St 75904
River Oak St 75901
Rivercrest Dr & Rd 75901
Riviera Dr 75901
Rl Smith Rd 75904
Road Runner Ct &
Pass 75901
Robdelk St 75904
Robert Massingill Dr 75901
Robin St 75901
Robinhood Ln 75904
Robinson Rd 75904
Robinwood Dr 75904
Rocky St 75901
Roger St 75904
Roger Nerren Rd 75901
Rolling Meadows Dr 75904
Rollingwood Dr 75904
Ronnies Loop 75904
Roper Rd 75904
Rosebrook Dr 75901
Rosedale Dr 75901
Roseneath St 75904
Rosewood Cir 75901
Ross Ave 75901
Ross Nash Ln 75904
Rowe Ave 75901
Roy Christie Rd 75904
Royal Pnes 75904
Royce Ave 75904
Royce Oliver Rd 75904
Royle St 75901
Rudd Ln 75901
Ruel St 75901
Runyan Ct 75901
Rushwood Dr 75904
Russell Ave 75904
Rustwood St 75904
Ruth Ln & St 75904
Sabine Cir 75904
Saddle Brook Dr 75904
Saddle Creek Dr 75904
Saddle Ridge Dr 75904
Saddle Trail Dr 75904
Sadie Freeman Dr 75901
Sage Ln 75904
Saint Andrews Cir 75901
Saint Clair St 75901
Saint Lo St 75901
Sam Baird Rd 75901
Sanches Rd 75901
Sand Rd 75904
Sand Hills Dr 75904
Sandalwood St 75904
Sandy Ln 75901
Sandy Brook St 75901
Sandyland Dr 75904
Sapphire Rd 75904
Sarah Ln 75901
Sarah Anna Rd 75904
Sawgrass Cir 75901
Sawmill Ln 75904
Sayers St 75904
Scarbrough St 75901
Schoolcraft Rd 75901
Schuller St 75904
Scogins Dr 75904
Scott St 75904
Scotty Beard Rd 75901
Sea Pines Ct 75901
Seales Rd 75904
Seaman Rd 75901
Sedgefield Pl 75904
Self Rd 75901
Sellers St 75904
Seminole Ct 75901
Setliff St 75904
Shady Ln 75904
Shady Bend Dr 75901
Shady Grove Loop 75904
Shady Oak Ct 75901
Shady Pine St 75901
Shady Springs Bnd 75901
Shadybrook Ln 75904
Shadywood Dr 75904
Shands Dr 75904
Shangri La Ct 75904
Shelly Dr 75904
E Shepherd Ave 75901
W Shepherd Ave 75904
Shermell St 75901
Sherwood Rd 75904
Shirey Ln 75904
Shoemaker Ln 75904
Shorty Pounds Rd 75901
Sid Love Rd 75901
Silverton St 75904
Simon St 75901
Singleton Ave 75904
Singletree St 75904
Sips Ln 75904
Skeetwood St 75904
Skip St 75904
Slack St 75901
Sleepy Hollow Dr 75904
Sloan Ln 75901
Smallwood Rd 75904
Smith St 75901
Smith Farm Rd 75904
Solly Dr 75904
Sonterra Dr 75901
Southbend Dr 75901
Southend Blvd 75901
Southern Dr 75901
Southern Hills Dr 75901
Southern Trace Dr 75901
Southpark Dr 75904
Southwood Dr 75904
Spain Rd 75901
Spanish Moss Dr 75904
Sparrow Ln 75904
Spence St 75904
Spikes St 75904
Spivey Rd 75904
Spring St 75904
Spring Branch St 75904
Spring Creek Rd 75904
Spring Lake Dr 75904
Spring Meadow Dr 75901
Springwood Cir 75901
Spruce St 75901
Sprucewood Dr 75904
Spyglass Dr 75901
Squyres Loop 75901
Stacey St 75901
Stanley Ln 75901
Stardust Ln 75904
Stark St 75901
State Highway 103 W 75904
E State Highway 103 75901
N State Highway 94 75904
Stephenson Brown Rd 75904
Steptoe Rd 75901
Steve Rd 75901
Stone Dr 75904
Stonewood Dr 75901
Stubblefield Dr 75904
Studewood St 75901
Sue Dr 75901
Sugar Ln 75904
Sulser St 75904
Summerset Dr 75901
Sun Meadow St 75904
Sundale St 75901
Sunrise Ave 75901
Sunset Blvd & Dr 75901
Suntory Way 75901
Surrey Ln 75901
Susan St 75901
Susie St 75904
Sybil St 75901
Sycamore Dr 75901
T And K Ln 75901
Tanglewood Ct 75904
Tarver Hill Rd 75904
Taylor Ave 75904
Ted Trout Dr 75904
Teer St 75901
Temple Blvd 75901
Templewood Ln 75904
Terry St 75901
Texas Blvd 75904
E Texas Rd 75901
Texas Forest Service
Loop 75904
Thompson St 75904
Thornton Cor 75904
Thornton Rd 75901
Tillman Rd 75901
Timber Creek Dr 75901
N & S Timberland Dr 75901
Timberwood St 75904
Toby St 75901
Tom Baty Rd 75904
Tom Hampton Rd 75904
Tom Holland Rd 75904
Tom Taylor Ave 75901
Tom Temple Dr 75904
Toney Ln 75904
Toran Rd 75904
Torres Ln 75901
Torrey Pines Dr 75901
Tower Ln 75901
Townwood Dr 75904
Trailwood Blvd, Cir, Crk
& Ct 75904
Travis St 75904
Travis Jordan St 75904
Traylor St 75901
Treadwell Ave 75904
Trenton St 75901
Trevathan 75904
Trimble Ln 75904
Trinidad 75904
Triple Crk 75904
Tripletree St 75904
Trout St 75904
Troy Johnson Rd 75901
W Tulane Dr 75901
Tullos Ln 75901
Turner St 75904
Turtle Creek Dr 75904
Twin Creek St 75904
Twin Oaks Rd 75901
Two Jima St 75901
Tynes St 75904
Us Highway 59 N 75901
Us Highway 69 N 75904
S Us Highway 69 75901
Valley Ave 75901
Van St 75901
Verna St 75901
Vincent St 75901
Vine Dr 75904
Virgie Rd 75904
Virgil Ave 75901
Virginia Rd & St 75904
Vivion St 75904
Voyle St 75901
Wade St 75904
Walden Ct 75901
Walker Loop 75904
Wallace St 75901
Walnut Bend St 75904
Walnut Hill Rd 75904
Walters St 75901
Ward St 75901
Ware Rd 75901
N & S Warren St 75901
Warren Hughes Rd 75901
Washington St 75904
Water Well Rd 75904
E Wathesto Rd 75902
Watson Ln 75904
Watson Loggins Ln 75901
Wayland Dr 75904
Wayne St 75901
Weaver Ave 75904
Webber St 75904
Weeks St 75904
Weiner St 75904
Weisinger Rd 75904
Welchs Hill Top Rd 75901
Wesch Dr 75904
Westbury Dr 75901
Westchester St 75901
Westerholm Ct 75901
Western Dr 75904
Westfield Loop 75904
Westlake Dr 75904
Westly Rd 75904
Westmont Ln 75904
Westmoreland St 75904
Westridge St 75904
Westwood Dr 75904
Westwood Loop 75904
Westwood Pl 75901
Westwood Lake Dr 75904
Wf Anderson Rd 75904
Wheeler St 75901
Whippoorwill Dr 75901
Whisenant Rd 75904
Whisper Ln 75904
Whispering Pine Ln 75901
Whistle Hollow St 75904
White Ave 75904
White Dove Dr 75901
White Oak Dr 75904
White Oak Loop 75901
White Rock Dr 75904
Whitehead Rd 75901
Whitehouse Dr & St 75901
Whitehouse Hill Ct 75901
Whitehouse Oaks St 75901
Whitworth Ln 75904
Wilcox Ln 75904
Wildbriar Dr 75904
Wildlife Ln 75904
Wildwood Cir 75904
Wilkerson Rd 75901
Willa Ln 75901
Williams St 75904
Willie Nerren Rd 75901
Williford Ln 75901
Williford House Pl 75901
Willis Ln 75901
Willis Rd 75904
Willow Bay Dr 75901
Willow Bend Dr 75901
Willow Brook Dr 75901
Willow Oak Dr
100-199 75904
500-700 75901
702-798 75901
Willow Ridge Dr 75901
Wilma St 75904
Wilson Aly & Ave 75904
Wilton St 75901
Winchester Pl 75904
Wind Drift Dr 75901
Windsor Ct 75901
Windy Ln 75904
Winged Foot Ct & Dr 75901
Winston 8 Ranch Rd 75904
Wise Rd 75904
Wisteria Way 75901
Wj Harbuck Rd 75901
Wood Ave 75901
Woodberry Dr 75904
Woodhaven Ct 75904
Woodhue Ct 75904
Woodland Dr 75904
Woodlawn Cir 75904
Woodmont 75901
Woods Rd 75901
Woodstock Dr 75904
Woodward Rd 75901
Wortham Cir 75904
Wr Blake Rd 75901
Wursthaus Dr 75904
Yancey Dr 75904
Yellowood Rd 75901
York Dr 75901
Yount Rd 75901
Zeagler Ave 75904
Zed Creek Rd 75904
Zoo Cir 75904

NUMBERED STREETS

N 1st St
100-1399 75901
1401-1499 75901
1501-1597 75904
1599-1699 75904
1701-1799 75904
S 1st St 75901
N & S 2nd 75901
N & S 3rd 75901
N & S 4th 75901
N 5th St 75901
N 6th St 75901
N 7th St 75901

MABANK TX

General Delivery 75147

POST OFFICE BOXES MAIN OFFICE STATIONS AND BRANCHES

Box No.s
All PO Boxes 75147

RURAL ROUTES

01, 03, 09, 16, 19 75147
04, 05, 06, 07, 08, 10,
11, 12, 13, 14, 15 75156

NAMED STREETS

A B Woodlands St 75147
Abrams Rd 75156
Acorn Est 75147
E, S & W Acres Loop &
Rd 75156
Addison Ln 75156
Adelia Dr 75156
Admiral Dr 75156
Alamosa St 75156
Albacore Dr 75156
Albany Dr 75156
Alder Dr 75156
S & W Alene Dr 75147
Allen St 75156
Anchor Ln 75156
Anderson Ln 75156
S Andrea Dr 75147
W Andrew Dr 75147
Andrews Ln 75147
Annie Ln 75156
Apache Cir & Dr 75156
Arapaho Trl 75156
Arbolado Blvd 75156
Archer Dr 75156
Armada Loop 75156
Arrow Way 75156
Arrowhead St 75156
Ash Ln 75156
Ashley Ln 75156
Autry Way 75147
Autumn Wood Trl 75156
Avco Cir 75147
Avery Ln 75156
Aztec Dr 75156
Backlash Dr 75156
Baff Bay Dr 75156
Baker Dr 75156
Bandera Cir & St 75156
Bar 10 Ln 75147
E & W Bar H Dr 75156
Barcelona St 75156
Barrett Dr 75156
N, S & W Bay Cir, Ct &
Dr 75156
Bay Tree Trl 75156
E & W Bayside Dr 75156
Bayview St 75156
Baywood Blvd, Cir &
Plz 75156
Beachwood Cir & Dr 75156
Bear Creek Dr 75156
Beautiful Hills Dr 75156
Beaver Brush Trl 75156
Bedfords Bnd 75156

Beechwood Cir ... 75156
Belmar Dr ... 75156
Ben Lacy Dr ... 75156
Bennett Pt ... 75156
S Bettie St ... 75147
Beverly Dr ... 75156
E Bexar St ... 75147
Big Chief Dr ... 75156
Birch Cir & Rd ... 75156
Birchwood Cir ... 75156
Blackfoot Dr ... 75156
Blackhawk Dr ... 75156
Blake St ... 75147
Blue Bird Loop ... 75156
Blue Jay Ln ... 75156
Blue Stone Cir ... 75147
Bluebonnet Dr ... 75156
Bluewater Cir ... 75156
Bluff View Dr ... 75156
Bobbie St ... 75147
Bonita Point Dr ... 75156
Boshart Way ... 75156
Bounding Main St ... 75156
Bowie St ... 75156
Box Rd ... 75156
Boyce Dr ... 75156
Brett Dr ... 75156
Briarwood Dr ... 75156
Bridges Ln ... 75147
Brokenbow Dr ... 75156
Brook Valley St ... 75156
Buena Vista St ... 75156
Buffalo Springs Rd ... 75156
Burden Ln ... 75156
Bushwhacker Dr ... 75156
Butler Trl ... 75156
Butte Dr ... 75156
Butterfly Ln ... 75156
Caddo St ... 75156
Calle Colleen St ... 75156
Callie Ln ... 75156
E Cambridge Ct ... 75147
Camelot Dr ... 75156
Camino Robles St ... 75156
Canal St ... 75156
Canoe Ct ... 75156
N & S Canton St ... 75147
Canyon Cv ... 75156
Cardinal Ln ... 75156
Carly Ln ... 75147
Carmel Pl ... 75156
Carolynn Rd ... 75156
Carr Cir ... 75147
Carribean Cir ... 75156
Carson Rd ... 75156
N Casteel St ... 75147
Castlewood Rd ... 75156
Causeway Ct ... 75156
Cawthon Dr ... 75156
Cayuga Dr ... 75156
Cedar Dr, St & Trl ... 75156
Cedar Acres Loop ... 75147
Cedar Oaks Dr ... 75156
Cedar Trail Dr ... 75156
Cedarglen St ... 75156
Cedarview Dr ... 75156
Cedarwood Dr ... 75156
Channel Dr ... 75156
Channel View Dr ... 75156
Chapperall Dr ... 75156
Cherokee Ln & Trl ... 75156
N & S Cherokee Shores Dr ... 75156
Cherry Ln ... 75156
Cherrywood St ... 75156
Cheryl Cir ... 75156
E & W Chestnut St ... 75147
Cheyenne Trl ... 75156
Chickasaw Dr ... 75156
Chico Ct ... 75156
Chicota St ... 75156
Chillacothe Trl ... 75156
Chisholm Trl ... 75156
Choctaw Dr ... 75156
Christi Dale Cir ... 75156
Church St ... 75156

Circle Dr ... 75156
Circulito Cir ... 75156
City Lake Rd ... 75147
Clear Frk ... 75156
Clear Creek Rd ... 75156
Clover Dr ... 75156
Club Cir ... 75156
Club View Dr ... 75156
Coahoma St ... 75156
Cody Austin St ... 75156
Cold Duck Hook St ... 75156
N & S Coleman St ... 75147
Colonial Dr ... 75156
Colt Cir ... 75156
Comanche Dr ... 75156
Commander Dr ... 75156
Commodore Dr ... 75156
Coral Reef St ... 75156
Cordoba St ... 75156
Cortez St ... 75156
Cottonwood Trl ... 75156
Countryman Estates Rd ... 75156
County Line Rd ... 75147
County Road 116 ... 75147
County Road 117 ... 75147
County Road 2529 Rd ... 75156
County Road 2530 ... 75156
County Road 2533 ... 75156
County Road 2701 ... 75156
County Road 2829 ... 75156
County Road 2830 ... 75156
County Road 2831 ... 75156
County Road 2832 ... 75156
County Road 2837 ... 75156
County Road 2851 ... 75156
County Road 2925 ... 75156
County Road 2928 ... 75156
County Road 2930 ... 75156
County Road 2938 ... 75156
County Road 4001 ... 75147
County Road 4002 ... 75147
County Road 4003 ... 75147
County Road 4004 ... 75147
County Road 4005 ... 75147
County Road 4006 ... 75147
County Road 4007 ... 75147
County Road 4008 ... 75147
County Road 4009 ... 75147
County Road 4010 ... 75147
County Road 4011 ... 75147
County Road 4011a ... 75147
County Road 4012 ... 75147
County Road 4013 ... 75147
County Road 4013a ... 75147
County Road 4014 ... 75147
County Road 4015 ... 75147
County Road 4017 ... 75147
Craft Rd ... 75156
Cree St ... 75156
Creek Dr ... 75156
Creekside ... 75147
Creekwood Dr ... 75156
Crest View Dr ... 75156
Crestwood Cir & Dr ... 75156
Cross Road Dr ... 75156
Crow St ... 75156
Custer Rd ... 75156
Cutter Cir ... 75156
Daisy Cir ... 75156
Dakota Dr ... 75156
Daniel Dr ... 75156
Dardenwood Way ... 75156
Deep Harbor Dr ... 75156
Deep Hill Cir ... 75156
S Deer Cove Dr ... 75156
Deer Island Rd ... 75156
Deer Landing Trl ... 75156
Deer Park Loop ... 75156
Deer Path Dr ... 75156
Deer Run Ln ... 75156
Deer Valley Dr ... 75147
Deer Walk Ln ... 75156
Deer Wood Dr ... 75156
Desota Cir ... 75156
Diamond Cir ... 75156

Diamond Oaks Dr ... 75156
Diamond Point Dr ... 75156
Diann Dr ... 75156
Diaz St ... 75156
S Dink St ... 75147
Doe Trl ... 75156
Doe Run Rd ... 75156
Doering Bay Cir ... 75156
Dogwood Cir, Loop & Trl ... 75156
Dolly Dr ... 75156
Don Ct ... 75147
Donna Dr ... 75156
Double Bridge Rd ... 75156
Douglas Dr ... 75156
Dove Ln ... 75156
Dowdy Ln ... 75156
Driftwood Ln ... 75156
Drydock Ln ... 75156
Dunaway Ave ... 75156
Dune Ln ... 75156
Dyer Cir ... 75156
Eagle Dr ... 75156
Eagle Pkwy ... 75147
Eagle Nest St ... 75156
S Easley Pkwy ... 75147
Eastern Hills Dr ... 75156
Eastexas Rd ... 75156
Eastshore Dr ... 75156
Eastwood Cir ... 75156
Easy St ... 75156
Edgewood Cir ... 75156
Edythe Dee Ln ... 75156
El Groom Pkwy ... 75147
Elaine Dr ... 75156
Elk Cove Dr ... 75156
Ellen Ln ... 75156
Elm Cir & St ... 75156
W Emerton ... 75147
Empire Dr ... 75147
Enchanted Dr ... 75156
Enchanted Isles Cir & Dr ... 75156
Enchanted Oak Dr & Rd ... 75156
Erie St ... 75156
Eskota St ... 75156
Esquire Estates Rd ... 75156
E & W Eubank St ... 75147
Evergreen Dr ... 75156
Excalibur Cir ... 75156
Fairhill Ln ... 75156
Fairwood Cir ... 75156
Fall Ln ... 75156
Fargo Rd ... 75156
Fate St ... 75156
Fawn Trl ... 75156
Ferdinand St ... 75156
Fernwood Dr ... 75156
Finch Ln ... 75156
Flagship Ln ... 75156
Flanagan Fairway ... 75156
Fleetwood Cir ... 75156
Flying Bridge Dr ... 75156
Fm 1256 ... 75147
Fm 1836 ... 75147
Fm 3080 ... 75147
Fm 316
400-3299 ... 75147
5500-6199 ... 75156
Fm 47 ... 75147
Fm 85 ... 75156
Fm 90 ... 75147
Folsom Dr ... 75156
Ford Cir ... 75156
Forest Gln & Ln ... 75156
Forest Lane Dr ... 75156
Forgotten Ln ... 75156
Forrest Oaks Dr ... 75156
Frazier Ln ... 75156
Friar Tuck Cir ... 75156
Frolic Rd ... 75156
G G Cir ... 75147
Gale Dr ... 75156
Garden Ct ... 75147
Garden Ln ... 75156

Gardendale ... 75147
Garner Dr ... 75156
Garrett Ln ... 75156
Gateway Dr ... 75156
Gawayne Dr ... 75156
Geronimo Trl ... 75156
Glen Cove Rd ... 75156
Glen Oaks Rd ... 75156
Glenn Rd ... 75156
E Glenwood St ... 75147
E Golden Oaks Dr ... 75156
Gordon Ln ... 75147
Granada St ... 75156
N & S Grand Ave ... 75147
Grande Ln ... 75156
Green Acres Rd ... 75156
Greenwood Cir ... 75156
Greer Rd ... 75147
Griffith Bend Rd ... 75156
Grissom Dr ... 75156
Grubbs Ln ... 75156
Guadalupe Dr & St ... 75156
Guinevere Cir ... 75156
Gull Cove Dr ... 75156
N & S Gun Barrel Ln ... 75156
Halibut Ln ... 75156
Hammer Rd ... 75156
Happy Trl ... 75156
Happy Hill Trl ... 75156
Harbor Dr ... 75156
Harbor Haven St ... 75156
Harbor Point Rd ... 75156
Harbour Light Dr ... 75156
Harmon Rd ... 75156
Harrell St ... 75156
Havenwood Dr ... 75156
Hawthorne Cir ... 75147
Helen St ... 75156
Henderson Ln ... 75156
Henderson Harbor Cir ... 75156
Henry Iv Trce ... 75156
Heritage Pkwy ... 75156
Hi Stirrup ... 75147
Hiawatha St ... 75156
Hickory Dr, Ln, Rd, St, Trce & Trl ... 75156
Hickory Creek Cir ... 75156
Hickory Tree Rd ... 75156
Hidalgo Loop ... 75156
Hidden Cir ... 75156
Hidden Hills Dr ... 75156
Hidden Valley Dr ... 75156
Hide A Way Dr ... 75156
High Point Dr ... 75156
Hillcrest Dr & St ... 75156
Hillside Blvd & Dr ... 75156
Hilltop Dr, Rd & St ... 75156
Hilton Head Island Dr ... 75156
Hob O The Hill St ... 75156
Holiday Dr ... 75156
Holly Hill Dr ... 75156
Hollyglen St ... 75156
Homestead Pl ... 75156
Hopi Trl ... 75156
Huntoon Trl ... 75156
Hyde Away Ln ... 75147
Idlewood Rd ... 75156
Imperial Dr ... 75156
Inca Dr & Trl ... 75156
Independence Dr ... 75156
Indian Gap Dr ... 75156
Indian Harbor Dr ... 75156
Inwood Cir ... 75156
Island Dr ... 75156
Island Beach Rd ... 75156
Island Park Dr ... 75156
Ivy Ln ... 75156
E Jack St ... 75147
W James St ... 75147
Janice Ln ... 75156
Jeff Acres Rd ... 75156
Jeffery Cir ... 75156
E & W Jeter St ... 75147
Jib Dr ... 75156
Jim St ... 75156
Johnson Rd ... 75156

Jolly Cir & Dr ... 75156
Joy Ln ... 75156
Joyce Cir ... 75156
Jr Scott Dr ... 75156
Judy Ln ... 75156
Jurassic Cir ... 75147
K J Cir ... 75147
Kaci Jo Dr ... 75147
Kanawka Rd ... 75156
Karen Ln ... 75156
Karla Ln ... 75156
Kathy Cir ... 75156
E Kaufman St ... 75147
Kayak Dr ... 75156
N & S Kemp St ... 75147
E Kempner St ... 75147
Kevin Cir ... 75156
Kickapoo Trl ... 75156
Kim Ln ... 75156
King Arthur Rd ... 75156
Kingswood Dr ... 75156
Kiowa Dr & Trl ... 75156
Kokomo Dr ... 75156
La Jolla St ... 75156
La Salle St ... 75156
Ladybug Ln ... 75156
Lago Dr & Ln ... 75156
Lagoon Dr ... 75156
Lake Dr ... 75156
Lake Arrowhead Dr ... 75156
Lake Creek Dr ... 75156
Lake Forest Dr ... 75156
Lake Front Dr ... 75156
Lake Shadows Cir ... 75156
Lake Terrace Dr ... 75156
Lakeland Rd ... 75156
Lakeport Dr ... 75156
Lakeshore Dr ... 75156
Lakeside Dr & Ln ... 75156
Lakeview Blvd, Ct, Dr & St ... 75156
Lakeway Ln ... 75156
Lakewood Dr ... 75156
Lancelot Dr ... 75156
Lark Dr & Pl ... 75156
Larry Dr & Ln ... 75156
Las Brisas St ... 75156
Launch Ln ... 75156
Lazy Launch Ln ... 75156
Legendary Ln ... 75156
Leisureland Rd ... 75156
E Letava Dr ... 75147
Levee Dr ... 75156
Lighthouse Dr ... 75156
Lilac Ln ... 75156
Lindy Lee Ln ... 75156
Lisa Layne St ... 75156
Little Feather Rd ... 75156
Little John St ... 75156
Little River Bnd ... 75156
Live Oak Ln ... 75156
Longhorn Rd ... 75156
Longleaf St ... 75156
Loon Bay Ct & Dr ... 75156
Los Arboles St ... 75156
Los Peces St ... 75156
Lost Forest Rd ... 75156
Loving Ln ... 75156
Lowe Dr ... 75156
Luann Way ... 75156
Lundy Ln ... 75156
Luther Ln ... 75156
Lynn Creek Cir, Cv & Dr ... 75156
Lynne Cir & St ... 75156
Mabelle Ln ... 75156
E Mae Dr ... 75147
Magellan Loop ... 75156
E & W Main St ... 75156
Maple St ... 75156
Maple Leaf St ... 75156
Maple Valley St ... 75156
Maples Trl ... 75156
Marencou ... 75156
Marina Dr ... 75156
Mariner Cir ... 75156

E & W Market St ... 75147
E & W Mason St ... 75147
Masthead Rd ... 75156
Matex Cir ... 75147
W Mcafee Dr ... 75147
Mcalister St ... 75156
Mcanally Dr ... 75147
Mcdonald Dr ... 75156
Meadow Heath St ... 75156
Meadow Lake Dr ... 75156
Meadowlark Ln ... 75156
Meadowood Rd ... 75156
Meandering Way ... 75156
Memorial Dr ... 75156
Memory Ln ... 75147
N & S Merlin Dr ... 75156
Merlyn Cir ... 75156
Merry Way ... 75156
Mesa Dr ... 75156
Misty Glen Cir ... 75156
Moccasin Dr ... 75156
Mockingbird Dr ... 75156
Mohican Trl ... 75156
Mona Lisa Cir ... 75156
Mosely Ln ... 75156
E & W Mount Vernon St ... 75147
Mulberry Ln ... 75156
Municipal Dr ... 75156
Mustang Dr ... 75156
Mutiny Dr ... 75156
Nancy Dr ... 75156
Natchez Trl ... 75156
Nautical Rd ... 75156
Navajo Dr ... 75156
Navarro Dr ... 75156
Neches Dr ... 75156
Newton Ln ... 75156
Nina St ... 75156
Nob Hill Cir & Rd ... 75156
Norma Leigh Ln ... 75156
E North Park Plz ... 75147
Northern Shore Cir ... 75156
Northwood Pl ... 75156
Nuevo Leon St ... 75156
Oak Dr & St ... 75156
Oak Harbor Dr ... 75156
Oak Haven Dr ... 75156
Oak Hills Dr ... 75156
Oak Ridge Rd ... 75156
Oak Shore Rd ... 75156
Oak Trail St ... 75156
Oakview Trl ... 75156
Oakwood Cir & Pl ... 75156
Ocean Dr ... 75156
Old Highway 85 ... 75156
Old Highway 90 ... 75147
Oliver Rd ... 75156
Osage St ... 75156
Ottawa Dr & Trl ... 75156
Outboard Dr ... 75156
Overlook Trl ... 75156
Owens Cir ... 75156
Oxbow St ... 75156
Oxford Dr ... 75156
Paddock Dr ... 75156
Pakuna Dr ... 75156
Palisade Cir, Dr, Loop & Pl ... 75156
Palo Blanco St ... 75156
Palo Pinto Pass ... 75156
S Park Blvd ... 75147
Park Dr ... 75156
Park St ... 75156
Park Crest Dr ... 75156
Park View St ... 75156
Paschall Blvd ... 75147
Paseo Patricia St ... 75156
Pauline Rd ... 75156
Pawnee Trl ... 75156
Payne Springs Pl ... 75156
Peach Tree Rd ... 75156
Pebble Beach Dr ... 75156
Pecan Rd ... 75156
Pecos Dr ... 75156
Peninsula Point Ter ... 75156

Pennant Cir ... 75156
Peyton Dr ... 75156
Pierce Dr ... 75156
Pin Oak Cir & Dr ... 75156
E Pine St ... 75147
Pine Bloom Blvd ... 75156
Pinehurst Dr ... 75156
Pinnacle Club Ct, Dr & Pl ... 75156
Pinta St ... 75156
Plantation Dr ... 75156
Pleasant Dr & Trl ... 75156
Pleasure Hills Cir ... 75147
Pleasure Land Rd ... 75156
Plum St ... 75156
Po Pines Rd ... 75156
Pocahontas St ... 75156
Point O View St ... 75156
Point Tara St ... 75156
Polly Ln ... 75156
Pollyanna Dr ... 75156
Port Dr ... 75156
Porthville Dr ... 75156
Post Oak Dr & Ln ... 75156
Prairie Dr ... 75156
Prewitt St ... 75156
Private Road 2607 ... 75147
Private Road 6080 ... 75147
Private Road 6198 ... 75147
Private Road 6501 ... 75156
Private Road 6605 ... 75147
Private Road 6606 ... 75147
Private Road 6607 ... 75147
Private Road 6710 ... 75147
Private Road 6718 ... 75147
Private Road 6815 ... 75147
Private Road 6816 ... 75147
Pueblo St ... 75156
Punto Pescader St ... 75156
Quail Creek Pl ... 75156
Quail Run St ... 75156
E & W Quanah Rd ... 75156
Queenswood Dr ... 75156
Railroad Dr ... 75147
Railroad St ... 75156
Raintree St ... 75156
Ranch Rd ... 75156
Randall Dr ... 75156
Randy St ... 75156
Ravenwood Dr ... 75156
Red Bird Ln ... 75156
Red Bluff Loop ... 75156
Red Bud Rd ... 75156
Red Oak Dr & Ln ... 75156
Red Robin Rd ... 75156
Red Water Rd ... 75156
Redondo Dr ... 75156
Remington Cir ... 75156
Rickey Rd ... 75156
Rickrod Dr ... 75147
Ridgecrest Dr ... 75156
Rising Star Trl ... 75156
Robby Pop Rd ... 75147
Robin Hood Way ... 75156
Rock And Roll Ln ... 75156
Rocky Point Run ... 75156
Rodney Dr ... 75156
Rolling Hills Dr ... 75156
Royalwood Dr ... 75156
Rudder Rd ... 75156
Rueda Encina St ... 75156
Running Bear Dr ... 75156
Running Brook Rd ... 75156
Running Deer Rd ... 75156
Rush Rd ... 75156
N & S Rye Blvd & Pl ... 75156
Sage Cir ... 75147
Sailboat Dr ... 75156
Sailfish Dr ... 75156
Saint Andrews Dr E ... 75156
Saint Annes Dr ... 75156
Saint Francis Ln ... 75156
E Salenert Blvd ... 75147
Salmon Ln ... 75156
San Felipe Dr ... 75156
Santa Maria St ... 75156

Santa Monica Dr 75156
Scenic Dr 75156
Schooner Rd 75156
Scott Ln 75156
Seabreeze Dr 75156
Seacraft Dr 75156
Seaside Dr 75156
Seminole Loop 75156
E & W Shadowwood St 75156
Shady Trl 75156
Shady Acres Rd 75147
Shady Grove Rd 75156
Shady Shores Dr 75156
Shadywood Pl 75156
Shallowater Rd 75156
Sharpe Dr 75156
Shawnee Cir & Dr 75156
Sherie Ln 75156
Sherwood Shore Dr 75156
Shoreline Dr 75156
Sierra Madre St 75156
Silveroaks St 75156
Sioux Trl 75156
Sj Cir 75147
Skiff Dr 75156
Skylark Dr 75156
Snapper Ln 75156
Softwind St 75156
Solar Turbine Way 75147
Sonjon Cir 75147
E South Way Dr 75147
Southern Pine Pl 75156
Southlake Dr 75156
Southland Dr 75156
Sowards Cir 75156
Spanish Trl 75156
Spearman St 75156
Spring Ln 75156
Spring Valley St 75156
Springwood Rd 75156
Spruce Trl 75156
Squaw Dr 75156
Stan Woods Cir 75156
Starboard Dr 75156
Starfish Dr 75156
State Highway 198
6200-9799 75156
9801-9999 75156
10400-10828 75147
10830-10834 75147
10851-10999 75156
11000-11014 75147
11001-11035 75156
11016-11024 75156
11050-11054 75147
11100-11348 75156
11155-11165 75147
11201-11211 75156
11215-11233 75147
11235-11799 75156
11350-11398 75147
11400-11548 75156
11550-11558 75147
11600-11898 75156
11801-11899 75147
11901-11963 75156
11965-11997 75147
11999-12000 75147
12001-12031 75156
12002-12098 75147
12051-12055 75147
12059-12099 75156
12200-12740 75156
12201-12249 75147
12251-12899 75156
12750-12760 75147
12778-12848 75156
12850-12898 75147
12900-13398 75156
12901-12999 75147
13001-13157 75156
13159-13199 75147
13201-13257 75156
13259-13299 75147
13301-13349 75156
13351-13497 75147
13499-16500 75147
16502-16798 75147
State Highway 334 75156
Stephens Dr 75156
Still Water St 75156
Sudan Cir 75156
Summer Ln 75156
Summerall Dr 75156
Summit Ridge Dr 75156
Sun Vly 75147
Sun Down Trl 75156
Sundrift Dr 75156
Sunfish Dr 75156
Sunflower Rd 75156
Sunny Glen St 75156
Sunnymeadow St 75156
Sunray St 75156
Sunset Dr & Pt 75156
N & S Sunset Acres Dr 75147
Sunset Bay Dr 75156
Surferview St 75156
Surls Dr 75156
S Sutton St 75147
Sycamore Cir 75156
Tahoka Rd 75156
Tamarack Dr & Trl 75156
Tanglewood Dr, Fwy, Loop, Pl & St 75156
Taos Dr 75156
Tara Trace Cir & Dr 75156
Tarlton Rd 75147
Tarno Ln 75156
Tarpon Dr 75156
N Taylor St 75147
Teague Ln 75147
Tejas Bnd & Dr 75156
That Way 75147
The Lee Way 75156
This Way 75147
Thornton Cir 75156
Thrush Rd 75156
Thunderbird Dr 75156
Timber Rd & Trl 75156
Timbercrest Dr 75156
Timberglen Pl 75156
Timberview Dr 75156
Timberwood Cir 75156
Tioga Cir 75156
Totem Pole St 75156
Trails End St 75156
Trailwind St 75156
Trailwood Rd 75156
Tree Line Dr 75156
Tres Lagos Blvd & Cir 75156
E & W Troupe St 75147
Tupelo Cir 75156
Turners Cir 75156
Twin Creek Ln 75147
Us Highway 175 W 75147
Ute Trl 75156
Valleyview Dr & St 75156
Van Horn Dr 75156
Vaughn St 75156
Veterans Ln 75156
Victor Ln 75156
Victory Dr 75156
Vistaridge Cir, Dr & Pl 75156
Vz County Road 2311 75147
Vz County Road 2312 75147
Vz County Road 2417 75147
Vz County Road 2420 75147
Vz County Road 2422 75147
Vz County Road 2430 75147
Vz County Road 2431 75147
Vz County Road 2436 75147
Vz County Road 2602 75147
Vz County Road 2603 75147
Vz County Road 2604 75147
Vz County Road 2606 75147
Vz County Road 2607 75147
Vz County Road 2701 75147
Vz County Road 2702 75147
Vz County Road 2703 75147
Vz County Road 2704 75147
Vz County Road 2705 75147
Vz County Road 2706 75147
Vz County Road 2707 75147
Vz County Road 2708 75147
Vz County Road 2709 75147
Vz County Road 2710 75147
Vz County Road 2711 75147
Vz County Road 2712 75147
Vz County Road 2713 75147
Vz County Road 2714 75147
Vz County Road 2715 75147
Vz County Road 2716 75147
Vz County Road 2717 75147
Vz County Road 2718 75147
Vz County Road 2719 75147
Vz County Road 2721 75147
Vz County Road 2722 75147
Vz County Road 2723 75147
Vz County Road 2724 75147
Vz County Road 2725 75147
Vz County Road 2801 75147
Vz County Road 2802 75147
Vz County Road 2803 75147
Vz County Road 2804 75147
Vz County Road 2805 75147
Vz County Road 2806 75147
Vz County Road 2807 75147
Vz County Road 2808 75147
Vz County Road 2809 75147
Vz County Road 2810 75147
Vz County Road 2811 75147
Vz County Road 2812 75147
Vz County Road 2813 75147
Vz County Road 2814 75147
Vz County Road 2815 75147
Vz County Road 2816 75147
Vz County Road 2908 75147
Vz County Road 2909 75147
Vz County Road 2912 75147
Vz County Road 2923 75147
S Wade St 75147
Waldman Dr 75156
E & W Walnut St 75147
Waterfront Dr 75156
Waurika St 75156
Wayne Dr 75156
Wedgewood Dr, Loop & Pl 75156
Welch Ln 75156
Wells Cir 75147
Westshore Dr 75156
Westview Dr 75156
Westwood Cir 75156
Whispering Pt & Trl 75156
Whispering Oaks Trl 75156
White Cap Ln 75156
White Deer Run 75156
White Dove Trl 75156
White Oak Dr 75156
Whiteface Dr 75156
Whiterock Rd 75147
Wildflower Dr 75156
Wildgrove Dr 75156
Wildwind St 75156
Wildwood Crossover St 75156
N & S Wilks Way Dr 75147
Will Scarlet Ct 75156
Willow Run 75156
Willowood Dr 75156
Wilson Way 75156
Winchester Cir 75156
Windjammer Rd 75156
Windward 75156
Winter Ln 75156
Wood Ln 75156
Woodcanyon Pl 75156
Woodcreek Cir & Rd 75147
E Woodland St 75147
W Woodland St 75147
Woodland Trl 75156
Woodside Dr 75156
Woodwind St 75156
Woody Dr 75156
Wren Ln 75156
Yankee Cir 75156
Yuma Dr 75156
Zuni St 75156

NUMBERED STREETS

N & S 1st 75147
1st Mate St 75156
1st Oak Dr 75156
N & S 2nd 75147
N & S 3rd 75147
N & S 4th 75147
N & S 5th 75147
6th St 75147
S 7th St 75147
S 8th St 75147
S 9th St 75147
N 10th St 75147
N 11th St 75147
12 Oaks Cir 75156

MAGNOLIA TX

General Delivery 77355

POST OFFICE BOXES MAIN OFFICE STATIONS AND BRANCHES

Box No.s
All PO Boxes 77353

NAMED STREETS

Abel Ln 77355
Aberdeen Dr 77354
Abilene Dr & St 77354
Abney Ln 77355
Acacia Ct & Dr 77355
Acker St 77354
Acorn Ct 77354
Adams Way 77355
Aden 77354
Agassi Ct 77354
Aggie St 77354
Alamoway 77355
Albert Miller Ln 77354
Alford Rd 77355
Allene Dr 77355
Allyson Rd 77354
N & S Almondell Cir, Ct & Way 77354
Alton Wright Dr 77355
Amarillo Dr & St 77354
Ambie Ln 77355
Amici St 77355
Anchor Way 77354
Anderson Rd 77354
Andy Ln 77354
Angel Oaks Cir & Dr 77355
Angela Dr 77355
Ann Cir 77355
Ansley Rd 77355
Antelope Ln 77355
Apache Trl 77354
April Vista St 77354
Arlene Dr & St 77355
Arndt Ln 77355
Arrow Head Trl 77355
Ascot Farms Rd 77354
Ashbrook Ln 77355
Ashlyn Timbers Ct & Ln 77355
Ashvale 77354
Atlantic Ave 77354
Autumn Day Ct 77354
Autumn Forest Ct 77354
S Autumn Leaf Cir 77354
Autumn Mist Cv 77354
Autumncrest Ct 77354
Autumnwood Dr 77354
Azalea Ct & Trl 77354
Azure Lake Dr 77354
Badger Hollow Dr 77355
Baker Cemetery Rd 77355
Baltic Ave 77354
Bancock Ct 77355
Bandera Trl 77355
Baneberry Rd 77355
Bar R Blvd 77355
Barbara Ln & St 77355
Barksdale Dr & Rd 77354
N & S Barnett St 77355
Barrymore Ln 77354
Bastrop Ln 77355
Bayberry Creek Dr 77355
Bayou Tesch Dr 77354
Beaconsfield Ct 77355
Bear Branch Ln 77354
Bearclaw Ct 77355
Beaumont Dr 77354
Beaver Ln & St 77355
Beaverwood 77354
Becky Ln 77354
Beisert Cir 77355
Bent Horn Ln 77355
Bent Oak Ln 77354
Bergman Dr 77355
Bermar St 77355
Beth Ln 77354
Beth Marie 77355
Beyette Rd 77355
Big Horn Ln 77355
Big Oak Cir 77355
Big Oak Ln 77354
Big River Dr 77355
Black Cherry St 77354
Black Forest Dr 77354
Black Jack Ln 77354
Black Oak Dr 77354
Black Swan Ct & Pl 77354
Blackgum Dr 77355
Bloomhill Pl 77354
Blue Jack Ln 77354
E Blue Lake Dr 77354
Blue Wildflower Pl 77354
Bluebonnet Ln 77354
E & W Bluff Dr 77354
Bluff View Ct 77354
E & W Boardwalk Dr 77354
Bob Link St 77355
Bobcat Ln 77355
Boothill Rd 77355
E & W Border Oak Ct, Dr & Park 77354
Bourelle Cir 77355
Bowerbank Ct 77354
Box Elder Dr 77354
Bradbury Rd 77355
Brady St 77355
Bramble Rose Ln 77354
Bramblevine Dr 77355
Branding Iron Ln 77355
Brantley Ln 77354
Brasswood Ct 77355
Brautigam Rd 77355
Breckenridge Dr 77354
Breezy Ct 77355
E, N, S & W Brenda Ln 77354
Briar Grv & Ln 77354
Bridge Ln 77354
Bridgewater Dr 77355
Bridle Cyn & Fls 77355
Bridle Creek Dr N & S 77355
Bridleway Cir 77355
Broadford 77355
Brookefield Cir 77355
Brown Bark 77354
Brown Cone Ln 77354
Brownsville St 77354
Brownwood Ct & Dr 77354
Bryan St 77355
Buck Ct & Rd 77355
Buckhorn Ln 77354
Buckshot Ln 77354
Buddy Riley Blvd 77354
Bumble Bee Ct 77355
Burklin Ln 77355
Burlington 77355
Burr Oak Trce 77354
Bushy Oaks Trl 77355
Butera Rd 77355
Butter Cove Ln 77354
Buttercup Ln 77354
Caddo Trl 77354
Calvary Charge 77355
Camden Cir 77354
Camelia Ct 77354
Campwood Cir & Dr 77354
Camwood St 77355
Candleridge Ct 77355
Candy Ln 77355
Canterbury Ranch Rd 77354
Canyon Vw 77355
Canyon Ranch Cir, Ct & Rd 77355
Canyon View Ct 77355
Carlene Rd 77355
N Carolina Ave 77354
Carolton Ct 77355
Carraway Ln 77354
Carriage Ct 77354
Carrie Ln 77355
Carrington Dr 77354
N & S Carroll Ln 77355
Carson Dr 77354
Carter Rd 77354
Cascade Ct 77354
Casita Dr 77354
Catamaran Way 77354
Cattle Dr 77354
Cecilia Cir 77355
Cedar Ct 77355
Cedar Ln 77355
Cedar Vw 77354
Cedar Ridge St 77355
Cedardale St 77355
Century Oaks Ct 77355
Chad Ct 77355
Chalet St 77355
Champion Way 77355
Champion Oaks Dr 77354
Champions Dr 77355
Champions Ridge Rd 77354
Chance Ct 77354
Chandlers Way 77355
Charlie Ln 77355
Charlie St 77354
Charlotte Ln 77355
Charred Pine Dr 77354
Chelsie Pl 77355
Cherokee Ln 77354
Cherokee Rose Ln 77354
Chipwood Dr 77355
Chris Ct 77355
Christiana Dr 77355
Chuckwagon Trl 77355
Cimarron Way 77354
Cimmaron Dr 77355
Cindy Lynn Ln 77355
Clare Point Dr 77354
Clearbrook Ln 77355
Clearwater Ct 77354
Clepper St 77355
Clint Neidgk Rd 77354
Clouds Rst 77355
Clover Creek Blvd 77355
Cloverleaf Dr 77355
Cloverwood Dr 77355
Cloyd Dr 77355
Clubhouse Cir 77354
Clubhouse Ln 77355
Cluster Oaks Dr 77355
Cobblestone Ct 77354
Coe Ln 77355
Coe Loop 77355
Cole Valley Dr 77354
Colette St 77355
Colfax Rd 77355
Collier Smith Rd 77354
Colt Ct 77354
Comanche Trl 77355
Commerce St 77355
Community Rd 77354
Concho Trl 77355
Connecticut Ave 77354
Connie St 77355
Conroe Huffsmith Rd 77354
Cool Springs Ct 77354
N & S Cooter Ct & St 77355
Corbin Dr 77354
Coriander Ct & Dr 77355
Corolla Rd 77354
Corporate Wood Dr 77354
Corpus Dr 77354
Cottonwood Bnd 77354
Cottonwood Ln 77355
Cotulla Trl 77355
Cougar St 77355
Country Bnd 77355
Country Ct 77354
Country Flds 77355
Country Grv 77355
Country Ln 77354
Country Mdw 77355
Country Birch 77355
Country Cedar 77355
Country Creek Ct 77354
Country Crest St 77355
Country Crosing Cir 77354
Country Elm 77355
Country Forest Dr 77354
Country Heights St 77355
Country Hollow St 77355
Country Lake Dr 77355
Country Oak 77355
Country Oak Ct 77354
Country Pines Ct & Rd 77355
Country Place Rd 77355
Country Redbud 77355
Country Ridge Ln 77355
Country Timbers 77355
Country Woods Trl 77355
Couples Ct 77354
Craven Park Ct 77354
N Creek Dr 77354
S Creek Dr 77354
Creek Xing 77355
Creekside Dr 77354
Crestlake Blvd 77354
Crestwater Cir 77354
N Cripple Creek Dr 77354
Croger Dr 77354
Cross Way Oaks 77354
Crown Point Ct 77354
Crystal Cove Dr 77354
Cullen 77354
Cypress Way Dr 77354
Dallas St 77355
Damon Ct 77354
Dan Dr 77355
Dan Rd 77354
Daniel St 77354
Davis St 77355
Dawn Mist Ct 77354
De Sota Rd 77354
Debbi Ln 77355
N, S & W Decker Dr 77355
Decker Forrest Blvd 77354
Decker Hills Dr 77355
Decker Pines St 77355
Decker Prairie Rd 77355
Decker Prairie Rosehl Rd 77355
Decker Woods Dr 77354
Deepwood Dr 77355
Deer Crk & Vly 77355
Deer Creek Way 77355
Deer Lodge Rd 77354
Deer Path Ln 77355
Deer Run St 77355
Del Rio Trl E & W 77355
Denton St 77354
Deringer Ln 77354
Desert Willow Ct & Dr 77355
Deveron 77354
Dewdrop Ct 77355
Dewlight Pl 77354
Diamante Dr 77354
Diamond Ct 77355

Diamond Creek Dr 77355
Diamond Oaks Dr 77355
Dillon Dr 77354
Dobbin Huffsmith Rd 77354
Doe Ct, Dr & Trl 77355
Doerner Ln 77354
Dogwood Dr 77355
N Dogwood Ln 77355
S Dogwood Ln 77355
Dogwood Trl
200-1099 77354
32500-32799 77355
Donna Ana Rd 77354
Donterre Rd 77355
Dorris Dr 77355
Dorsey Dr 77354
Douglas Fir Dr 77354
Dove Lake Dr 77354
Dry Creek Rd 77354
Dundee Dr 77354
Dunlevy St 77355
Durango Dr 77354
Durango Creek Dr 77354
Dustin Ln 77354
Eagle Cv 77355
Eagle Ridge Dr 77355
Eagles Lndg 77354
Eagles Wing 77354
Eastwood St 77354
Easy St 77355
Echo Holw 77355
Ed Dr 77355
Edendale Cir 77355
Edgewater Dr 77354
Edwards Dr 77354
Egypt Ln 77354
Eileen St 77355
El Paso St 77354
Elgin 77354
Elm Ln 77354
Elm St 77355
Elm Trace Dr 77355
Emerald Way 77355
Emerald Oaks 77355
Enderli St 77354
Equestrian Blvd 77354
Eric St 77355
Ernest Cir 77355
Estherwood Pl 77354
Eureka Rd 77354
Evergreen St 77354
Evergreen Timbers 77355
Fairbanks Dr 77354
Fairhope Ln 77355
Fairlee Ct 77354
Fallen Leaf Pl 77354
Fantail St 77355
Fawn Ln 77354
Fawnwood St 77355
Fern Rose Ct 77355
Fish Rd 77355
Fitz Ln 77355
Flower Mound Ln 77354
Fm 1486 Rd 77354
Fm 1488 Rd
4001-4997 77354
4999-18699 77354
18700-25499 77355
12747-1-12747-5 77354
14535-1-14535-5 77354
14605-1-14605-5 77354
18106-1-18106-4 77354
19520-1-19520-6 77355
5412-1-5412-6 77354
5416-1-5416-4 77354
5420-1-5420-4 77354
2000-2299 77355
Fm 149 Rd 77354
Fm 1774 Rd
38927-4A-38927-4A 77355
36000-40099 77355
40900-43699 77354
37215-217-37215-221 77355
37223-1-37223-5 77355
38927-1-38927-4 77355

Fm 2978 Rd 77354
Forest Mdw 77354
Forest Green Dr 77355
Forest Hill Dr 77355
Forest Ridge Dr 77355
Forest West St 77354
Forestvale 77354
Forestview Dr 77355
Frances Ln 77355
Frank Cir & Ln 77354
Freemont Rd 77354
Friar Way 77354
Friendship Dr 77355
Frontier Rd 77355
Gable Cir 77354
Gaff Rd 77355
Galleria Oaks Ct & Ln 77354
Gardenia Ct 77354
Garland Rd 77355
Garrett Dr 77354
Garwood Ct & Dr 77354
Geronimo St 77355
Giant Hickory 77355
Glasgow 77354
Glenda Dr 77354
Glenmont Estates Blvd 77355
Glynwood Dr 77354
Gold Panning Ct 77355
Golden Floral Ct 77354
Golden Orchard Pl 77354
Goldenrod Ln 77354
Golf Club Trl 77355
Goodnight Trl 77355
Goodson Rd
600-900 77355
815-815 77353
901-1499 77355
902-1498 77355
Gossamer Ln 77355
Grand Oaks Blvd 77355
Grant Dr 77354
Grapevine St 77355
Great Oak Ct 77354
Green Bend Ct 77354
Green Forest Dr 77354
Green Meadow St 77355
Green Oak Cir & St 77355
Green Persimmon Ln 77354
Green Tree Rd & St 77354
Green Willow St 77355
Greenbriar Dr 77355
Greenfield Forest Dr 77354
Greenwood St 77355
Greylake Pl 77354
Gromwell Dr 77355
Guang Ming Way 77354
Gunnison 77354
Hackberry St 77354
Hallowed Oaks 77354
Hanks Rd 77355
Harbor Way 77354
Hardin Store Rd 77354
Hartman Rd 77355
N Hawkhurst Cir & Ct 77354
Hawkin Ct 77354
Hayden Dr 77354
Hazy Hollow Rd 77354
Hazy Meadow Dr 77354
Hearthshire Cir & Ct 77354
N & S Heaton Ct & Ln 77355
Heflin St 77355
Heidler Rd 77354
Heightmont Est 77354
Helga 77355
Hennelly Dr 77354
Heritage Cir, Dr, Ln, Pl & Trl 77354
Heritage Point Blvd 77355
Heron Ct 77355
Hickory Ct & Ln 77355
Hickory Ridge Rd 77354
Hidden Ct 77354
Hidden Cv 77354
Hidden Lk E 77354
Hidden Lk W 77354

Hidden Cove Dr & Park 77354
Hidden Hill Ln 77354
Hidden Lake Cir & Ct 77354
High Chaparral 77355
N High Meadow Cir 77355
S High Meadow Cir 77355
High Meadow Dr 77354
High Meadow Ranch Dr 77355
High Point Dr 77355
Highland Blvd & Ct 77354
Hillandale Ct 77354
Hillhouse 77355
Hilltop Ln 77355
Hinsdale 77354
Hitching Post Ct 77355
Hitching Rack Ln 77355
Holly Ct 77355
Holly Lord 77355
N & S Holly Oaks Cir & Ct 77355
Hondo Cir 77355
Honea Egypt Rd 77354
Honeysuckle Ln 77354
Hooten Ln 77355
Hope Ln 77354
Horseshoe Trl 77355
Hosford Rd 77354
Hufsmith Conroe Rd 77354
Hughes Ln 77355
Hunters Grv & Rd 77354
Hunting Trl 77355
Idle Dr 77355
Imperial Oak Dr 77355
Indian Falls Ct 77355
Indian Springs Trl 77355
Indiana Ave 77354
Indigo Ct 77355
Indigo Hills Dr 77355
Indigo Lake Ct & Dr 77355
Industrial Dr 77355
Inverness Dr 77354
Ithaca Ln 77355
Ivy Ct 77354
J B Fleming St 77355
Jacana Ct & Dr 77355
James Ct 77354
Jeter St 77355
Joanna Ct 77355
Johlke Rd 77355
Johnson Aly 77355
Jui Ln 77355
Julia Ln 77355
Julie Ln 77355
Karen Dr 77355
Karen Switch Rd 77354
Kate Dr 77355
Katherine St 77354
Kathy Ln 77355
Katy Lee Ln 77354
Kayla Ct 77355
Keehan St 77355
Kelcey Cir 77355
Kelly Rd 77354
Ken Lake Dr 77354
Kentucky Ave 77354
Kilkenny Dr 77354
Kingern Rd 77355
Kingsley Ct 77355
Kinley Ann Ct 77355
Klein Dr 77355
Knobby Oaks Pl 77355
Knotty Oaks Trl 77355
Kotlan Ct 77355
Lacey Wood Ct 77354
Lafitte Ct 77355
Lago Dr 77354
Lago Vista Real St 77354
Lake Cir 77355
E Lake Dr 77355
Lake Trl 77355
Lake Circle Ln 77355
Lake Edge Ln 77355
Lake Park Ct 77355
Lake Side Dr 77354

Lake Tahoe Ln 77355
Lake Windcrest Blvd 77354
Lakefield Blvd 77355
E & W Lakeshore Dr 77355
E Lakeside Dr 77354
Lakeside Grn 77355
Lakeside Trl 77355
Langtry Dr 77355
E Lantana Dr 77355
Laredo Dr 77354
Larue St 77355
Laurel Ct 77355
Laurel Ln 77354
Lawrence Rd 77354
Lazee Oaks St 77355
Lazy Ln 77355
Lazy Brook Ln 77355
Lazy Summer Ct 77354
Leafton Ln 77354
Leafy Dr 77354
Leafy Oak Ct & Way 77354
Leaman St 77355
Lee St 77354
Leeward Ln 77354
Legacy Ct 77355
Legend Oaks Dr 77355
Leisure Ln 77355
Levee Ln 77354
Levi Bnd 77354
Lily Ct 77354
Limber Pines Ct & Dr 77355
Linden Ln 77355
Ling Rd 77354
Linn Ln 77354
N & S Lite St 77355
Little Bough Ln 77354
Little Brook Ln 77355
Little Thorn Ln 77355
Little Trail Ln 77354
Little Twig Ln 77354
Little Wren Ln 77354
Live Oak Dr & Park 77354
Loafers Ln 77354
Logger Ln 77355
Lois Ln 77354
Lone Oak St 77355
Lone Shadow Trl 77355
Lonesome Pine St 77355
Long Branch Ln 77354
Long Neck Dr 77355
Long Pines Ln 77354
Long Trail Ln 77355
Longbow Cir & St 77354
Lookout Lake Ln 77354
Lopez Ct 77354
Lori Ln 77355
Los Encinos Ct & Dr 77354
E, N, S & W Lost Creek Blvd 77355
Lost Path Ln 77354
Lotus Cir 77354
Lotus Lake Dr 77354
Lower Lake Ln 77354
Lynnwood Ct 77354
Macduff 77354
Mackintosh Dr 77354
Magnolia Blvd 77355
S Magnolia Blvd 77354
Magnolia Cir 77355
Magnolia Pkwy 77355
Magnolia Business Park Dr 77354
Magnolia Colony Ct 77354
Magnolia Hills Dr 77354
Magnolia Pines Dr 77355
Mahogany Way 77354
Mahogany Ridge Dr 77355
Maitland Ct 77354
Majestic Oaks 77354
Mallard Cv 77354
Manor Dr 77354
Maple Ct 77355
Mapleleaf St 77354
N & S Marek Ln 77355
Marias Way 77354
Marlin Ct 77354

Marlin Ln 77354
Marlin St 77355
Marshall Ct & Dr 77354
Marvin Gdns 77354
Masters Cir 77355
Matthews Ln 77354
Maurice Rd 77354
Maury Ln 77354
Maverick Ranch Rd E 77355
Maya Rd 77354
Mcbee Pl 77355
Mccall Park & Trce 77355
Mccall Sound Blvd 77355
Mcdaniel Dr 77354
Mcintosh Cir & Rd 77355
Mckinley Cir 77354
Meadow Fls, Frst & Xing 77355
Meadow Creek Ct 77355
Meadow Edge Dr 77354
Meadow Falls Ct 77355
Meadow Lake Dr 77355
Meadow Wood Dr 77355
Meadowsweet Dr 77355
Meadowwood Grn 77355
Medina Cir 77355
Mellow Brew Ct, Pl & St 77355
Melton St 77354
E, N, S & W Memory Ln 77355
Mercado Rd 77355
Merry Merchant St 77354
Mesa Oaks 77355
Mesa Verde Dr 77354
Mesquite Dr 77355
Michael Dr 77355
Michael St
29600-29699 77354
31700-31999 77355
Middle Trl 77354
Midland St 77354
N Mill Cir & Dr 77354
Mill Bend Ct 77355
Mill Creek Rd 77354
Miller Rd 77354
Mink Cir 77355
Mink Creek Ct 77355
Mink Lake Dr 77355
Miranda Ln 77355
Missouri Pacific St 77355
Mistletoe Trl 77354
Misty Meadow Dr
30000-30499 77355
30500-31199 77354
30503-1-30503-7 77354
Mockingbird Ln 77355
Mohawk Trl 77354
Monarch Oak Dr 77354
Montano Ct 77354
Moore Rd 77354
Morgan St 77355
Morris Rd 77354
Mostyn Ct & Dr 77354
Mulberry Ct
25900-25999 77354
28600-28699 77355
Mulligan Trl 77354
Mustang Ct 77354
Mustang Trail Dr 77355
Mystic Cv 77354
Naomi St 77355
Napa View Valley Dr 77354
Natures Way 77354
Navajo Rd 77355
Neidigk Sawmill Rd 77355
New York Ave 77354
Newfane Ct 77354
Newgrove Ct 77354
Nichols Sawmill Rd 77355
Nickaburr Creek Dr 77355
Noack Rd 77355
Noble View Ct 77355
Nueces Trl 77355
Oak Holw 77355
Oak Hvn E 77354

Oak Hvn W 77354
Oak Ln
17400-17499 77355
29700-30299 77354
Oak Run 77355
Oak Xing 77355
Oak Bluff Dr 77354
Oak Cluster E & W 77354
Oak Creek Dr 77354
Oak Crest Cir 77354
Oak Hills Ct 77354
Oak Hollow Blvd 77355
Oak Lace Ln 77355
Oakdale Ct 77355
Oaklane Trl 77355
Oakview St 77355
Oakwood Dr & Ln 77354
Octavia Dr 77354
Odell 77354
Odessa Dr 77354
Old Coach Rd 77355
Old Fm 1488 Rd 77354
Old Hardin Store Rd 77354
Old Hempstead Rd 77355
Old Hockley Rd 77355
Omar Dr 77354
Oneal Ln 77354
Otero Rd 77354
Pacco Ln 77354
Pacific Ave 77354
Palmer Ct 77354
Palmetto Rd 77355
Palo Duro 77355
Palo Pinto Trl 77355
Park Dr 77354
Park Loop 77355
Park Meadow Pass 77355
Park Place Blvd 77354
Parker Rd 77354
Parkway St 77355
Parkway Oaks Ln 77355
Pathfinder Dr 77355
Patricia Ln 77355
Pattys Lndg 77354
Pebble Bend Way 77354
Pebble Lake Dr 77354
Pecan Dr 77355
Pecan Gap St 77355
Pecan Grove Cir 77354
Pecan Hollow Rd 77354
Pecos Rnch 77355
Peden Rd 77355
Pelican St 77355
Penguin St 77355
Pennsylvania Ave 77354
Perth Cir 77354
Pickford Rd 77354
Pierce Hill Ln 77355
Pin Oak Dr 77354
Pin Oak Ln 77354
Pin Oak St 77355
Pin Rose Ln 77354
Pine Dr 77355
Pine Ln 77354
Pine Trl 77355
Pine Xing 77355
Pine Bark Ln 77354
Pine Creek Way 77355
Pine Forest Dr 77355
Pine Knot Rd 77354
Pine Needle Ln 77355
Pine Top 77355
Pinehurst Ln 77354
Pinehurst Loop 77355
Piney Pathway 77355
Piney Wood Ln 77354
Pinion Creek Cir & Rd 77355
Pinter 77354
Pinwood Ct 77354
Pipestem Dr 77355
Pipestone Rd 77355
Placid Lake Ln 77354
Pleasant Frst 77355
Pleasant Oaks Dr 77355
Pleasant Valley Rd 77354
Ponderosa Dr 77354

Portsoy Dr 77354
Possum Trl 77354
Post Oak 77355
Post Oak Cir 77355
Post Oak Ct
100-199 77355
12300-12399 77354
Post Oak Run 77355
Post Oak St 77354
Post Oak Forest Dr 77354
Presley Dr 77354
Pretty Woods Ln 77355
Primrose Ln 77354
Prine Ln 77354
Pryor Rd 77354
Purvis St 77355
Quiet Frst & Way 77355
Quillwood Pl 77354
R L Butler 77355
R R Herring Blvd 77354
Raccoon Bnd 77354
Rachelle Ln 77355
Rain Lily St 77355
Rainfern Dr 77355
Rainy Oaks Dr & Park 77354
Ralph Cir 77355
Ramblewood Dr 77354
Ranch Creek Ct & Way 77354
Ranch Hill Dr 77354
Ranch Lake Dr 77354
Ranch Park Dr 77354
Ranch Trail Ct 77354
Ranchcrest Dr 77355
Rancho Bauer 77355
N & S Ravenswood Dr 77354
Red Adler Cir & Ct 77355
Red Bay Cir 77354
Red Bluff Cir 77355
Red Oak Ct 77354
Red Oak Dr 77355
Red Oak Holw 77355
Red Oak Ln 77355
Red Oak Rd 77354
Red Oak St 77355
Red Rock 77355
Redwood Ct 77355
Remington Frst E 77355
Remington Ln 77354
Remmington Frst E 77355
Remmington Forest Blvd 77355
Renaissance Ct 77354
Research Forest Dr 77354
Restful Holw 77355
Revelwood Dr 77354
Rhode Island St 77355
Riata Dr 77354
Rickett Ln & Rd 77355
S Ridge Park Dr 77354
Ridgecrest St 77354
Ridgewood 77354
Ridgewood Dr 77355
Rimwick Forest Dr 77354
River Park Dr 77355
Riverwood Dr 77354
Roadie Pass 77355
Robbie Lee Rd 77354
Roberts Trl 77355
Robin Ln 77355
Robin George Trl 77354
Rockchapel 77355
Rolling Forest Dr 77354
Rolling Hills Dr 77354
Rolling Timbers St 77355
Romero Ln 77355
Rose Cir 77355
Rose Pine Ct 77355
Rosebud St 77354
Rosie Ln 77355
Roundup Rd 77354
Roy Ln & St 77354
Ruby Ln 77354
Ruby Terrace Ln 77355
Ruel Rd 77355

Running Wood Ct 77354
Russell St 77355
Rustic Ln 77355
Rustic Oaks Dr 77354
Rustling Oaks St 77355
Ryder Cup 77354
Sabinal Trl 77355
Sagebrush Ln 77354
Saint Charles Pl 77354
Saint James Pl 77354
Samantha Ln 77354
Sampras Ct 77354
San Angelo Dr 77354
San Patricio Calle 77354
Sand End 77354
Sanders Rd
8700-8899 77354
20200-20499 77355
Sanders Cemetery Rd
23000-24799 77355
42900-43999 77354
Sanders Ranch Rd 77355
Sandy Crk 77355
Santa Fe Dr 77355
E Sapling Oaks Pl 77355
Sapphire Cir & Ct 77354
Sarah Ln 77355
Satin Clover Ct 77355
Satterwhite Ln 77354
Saw Oaks Dr 77355
Sawgrass Ct 77354
Sawmill Dr 77355
Scenic Green Dr 77354
Scotty St 77355
Sea Mist 77354
Sea Turtle Ct & Ln 77355
Seahorse Ln 77355
Seascape Run 77354
Selman Ln 77355
Seminole St 77354
Sendera Dr 77354
Sendera Ranch Dr 77354
Seneca Trl 77354
Serenity Sound 77354
Settlers Ml 77355
Shadberry Dr 77355
Shadow Ln 77355
Shadow Springs Trl 77354
Shady Bnd 77355
Shady Dr 77355
Shady Ln
8900-9499 77354
19400-19499 77355
Shady Brook Ln 77355
Shady Oaks Dr 77355
Shady Villa St 77355
Shag Bark St 77355
Shalamar Dr 77354
Shannon Cir 77355
Sharon Louise 77355
Sharps Ln 77354
Sheephorn Ct 77354
Sherrie Ln 77355
Shire Glen Pl 77354
Shirley Ct & Mdws 77355
Short Leaf 77354
Short Line Rd 77354
Side Saddle Way 77355
Sienna Ridge Ln 77355
Silver Spur 77355
Silver Elms Pl 77355
Silver Leaf St 77355
Singletree Dr & Ln 77355
Sioux Dr 77354
Sky Frst 77355
Sky Forest Cir 77355
Skylark St 77355
Skylight Ln 77354
Sleepy Brook Ln 77355
Sleepy Hollow Ln 77355
Slumber Ln 77355
Smith Rd 77354
Sonoma Valley Dr 77355
Sonora Trl 77355
Spencer Blvd 77355
Spencer Ct 77354
Spencer Ter 77355
Spinnaker Run 77354
Spotted Lily Way 77354
Spotted Pony Ct 77355
Spring Lake Dr 77354
Springfield Ln 77354
Springwood Dr 77354
Spruce Ln 77355
Spur Trl 77355
Spur 149 Rd 77354
Squires Way 77354
Squirrel Oaks Dr 77355
Stagecoach Rd 77355
Stagecoach Crossing Dr 77355
Stallion Ct 77354
Stallion Run 77355
Standard Rd 77355
Stapleton 77354
States Ave 77354
Stegar Ln 77355
Stetson Cir 77355
Stone Creek Dr 77354
Stonehaven Dr 77354
Strathdon 77354
Stubbs Rd 77354
Stubby Ln 77354
Sugar Bend Dr 77355
Sugar Bush Dr 77354
N & S Sugar Maple Cir & Ct 77355
Sugar Oaks Ct & St 77355
Sugar Wood Dr 77355
Sulphur Branch Bnd 77355
E, N, S & W Sulphur Creek Dr 77355
Summer Lake Dr 77354
Sun Fisher Ct 77355
Sunblaze Ct 77355
Sunburst St 77354
Sundew Ct 77355
Sunflower Ln 77355
Sunrise Dr 77355
Sunrise Frst 77355
Sunrise Way 77354
Sunset Ave 77354
Sunset Ln 77355
Superior Ln & Rd 77354
Surrey Ln 77355
Susan Ct & St 77355
Sweetbay Cir 77354
Sweetbriar Ln 77354
Sweetgum Ln & Rd 77354
Sweetwater Cir 77355
N Sweetwater Cir 77355
Sweetwater St 77354
Swiney Rd 77355
Sycamore Cir 77355
Sycamore Ct 77355
Sycamore Hl 77355
Sylvan Pl 77355
Tadpole Trl 77355
Tall Pnes 77355
Tall Oaks Way 77355
Tall Pines Ct 77355
Tall Pines Dr 77354
Tamina Rd 77354
Tanglewood St 77354
Taylor Rd 77355
Tea Rose Ln 77355
Teakwood Ln 77354
Teal Ct 77355
Temple St 77354
Teneya Cyn 77355
Terri Ln 77355
Texarkana Dr 77355
Thistle Down Ln 77354
Thomas Ln 77355
Thomas Rd 77355
Thomas Ter 77354
Thousand Oaks Blvd 77355
Thousand Oaks Ct 77355
Three Forks Rd 77354
Tiffany Ln 77354
Tilbury Ct 77354
Timber Cir 77354
Timber Vlg 77355
Timber Oaks Ct 77355
Timber Ranch Dr 77355
Timber Ridge Ct & Dr 77355
Timber Village Ct 77355
Timberbranch Ct 77355
Timberbreeze Ct 77355
Timberbriar Ct 77355
Timbergreen Cir & Dr 77355
Timberknob Ct 77355
Timberleaf Dr 77355
Timberline Trl 77355
E & W Timberloch Ct & Trl 77355
Timbershade Ct & Xing 77355
Timbershire Ct 77355
Timberway Ct 77355
Todd Rd 77355
Tomahawk Trl 77355
Topaz Rdg 77355
Tory Ann Dr 77354
Tournament Ln 77355
Towering Oaks Dr, St & Trl 77355
S Trace Dr 77355
Trailwood 77355
Trailwood Estates Dr 77354
Tranquility Ln 77355
Tree Farm Rd 77354
Tudor Way 77355
Turner Rd 77355
Turriff Cir 77354
Turtle Creek Ln & Way 77355
Turtle Dove Ln 77355
Twin Oaks Dr 77355
Unity Park Dr 77355
Valley Oaks Dr 77355
Vaught Rd 77354
Ventnor Ave 77355
Vershire Cir 77354
Vesta Ct 77355
Veterans Rd 77355
Vickie Ln 77354
Village Bnd, Crk & Trl 77355
Village Oaks Ct 77355
Village Ridge Ct 77355
Village Trail Ct 77355
Vinton Ln 77355
Violet Ct 77354
Virgie Community Rd 77354
Virginia Pl 77355
Wagon Wheel Ct & Rd 77355
Wagonwheel Way 77355
Walnut Ln & Xing 77355
Walnut Creek Ct & Rd 77355
Walnut Grove Ln 77355
Walnut Springs Ln 77355
Wanda Ln 77354
Water Front Ct 77354
Water Oak Ct & Dr 77354
Wedgewood Dr 77354
Weeping Willow Way 77354
Weir Way 77355
Weisinger Dr 77354
Wellesly Ct 77355
West Ln 77354
Westmoreland 77354
Westward Ho St 77355
Westwood North Dr 77354
Westwood Square East Dr 77354
Westwood Square West Dr 77354
Whipstock Rd 77354
Whispering Mdw & Pne 77355
Whispering Pines St
1-99 77354
200-699 77355
White Oak Ct
100-199 77355
33300-33399 77354
White Oak Dr 77354
Whitekirk Pl 77354
Wichita Falls St 77354
Wide Oak Cir 77355
S Wiggins St 77355
Wild Oaks 77355
Wilderness Ln & Trl 77355
Wildflower Dr 77354
Wildforest 77355
Wildwood Cir, Pt & Trce 77354
Wiley Dr 77354
Willow Way 77355
Willow City Rd 77355
Winchell Place Rd 77355
Winchester Ct 77354
Wind Song Trce 77355
Windcrest Cir & Dr 77354
Windcrest Estates Blvd & Ct 77354
Winding Crk 77355
Winding Brook Ln 77355
Winding Creek Ct & Ln 77355
Winding Hill Dr 77354
Winding Way Ct 77354
Windward Ln 77354
Windy Ridge Trl 77355
Winhall Pl 77354
Winter Song Dr 77354
Wintergreen Dr 77355
Wisteria Rd 77355
Wood Song Trl 77355
Woodbine Ct 77355
Woodbury Ct 77355
Woodland Oaks 77354
Woodlane Blvd & Cir 77354
Woodmoor Pl 77354
Woods Edge Dr 77354
Woodway Dr 77355
Woodway St 77354
Wright Rd 77355
Yancey Dr 77355
Yellow Rose Ln 77354
Zahn St 77355

NUMBERED STREETS

1st St 77354
2nd St 77354
3rd St 77354
4th St 77354
5th St 77355
6th St 77355
N 6th St 77354
7th St 77355
8th St 77355
9th St 77355
10th St 77355

MARSHALL TX

General Delivery 75670

POST OFFICE BOXES MAIN OFFICE STATIONS AND BRANCHES

Box No.s
All PO Boxes 75671

RURAL ROUTES

05, 07, 09, 10 75670
03, 04, 06, 08, 11, 12 75672

NAMED STREETS

Abbie Ln 75672
Abel St 75670
Acadia St 75672
Achte St 75672
Acie Rhodes Rd 75672
Acorn Dr 75670
Adair St 75670
Adams Rd & St 75672
Addiebelle St 75672
Adkins St 75670
Airline Dr 75672
Airlite Rd 75670
S Airport Rd 75672
N & S Alamo Blvd 75670
Albemarle Rd 75672
Albert St 75670
Alex St 75670
Alexander St 75670
Alice Calloway Rd 75672
Alice Hope Rd 75672
Alice Wilder Rd 75672
N & S Allen Blvd 75670
Alpine Dr 75672
Alvin St 75670
Ambassador Blvd 75672
Anderson Ln 75672
Angelo St 75672
Ann Dr 75672
Annette St 75672
Argyle St 75670
Ark St 75672
Arkansas St 75670
Arlington Rd 75672
Arrowhead Cv 75672
Arthur Epps Rd 75670
Ashwood Ter 75672
Atkins Blvd 75670
Aubry St 75672
E Austin St
100-1099 75670
2200-2399 75672
W Austin St 75670
Avenue D 75670
Azalea Way 75672
B L Pyle Rd 75672
Baffo Rd 75672
Bailey Cutoff 75670
Baker St 75670
Baker Bridge Rd 75670
Barnes St 75670
Barrett Gibson Rd 75672
Barry Dr 75672
Bausley Rd 75672
Bays Rd 75672
Beachum St 75670
Bean St 75670
Beauregard St 75670
Beauty Shop Rd 75672
Beaver St 75670
Beavers Bnd 75672
Beckie Cir 75672
Bel Air Dr 75672
Bell St 75672
Bell Cut Off Rd 75672
Belle Ct 75672
Belmont Dr 75672
Benita Dr 75672
Bennett St 75670
Bergstrom Pl 75672
Berry Ln 75670
Bertha Jackson Rd 75670
Beth Ann Dr 75672
Beverly Cir 75672
Bill Davis Rd 75672
Billups St 75670
Billy Ray Rd 75672
Binotti Rd 75670
Bird St 75670
Birmingham Rd 75672
N & S Bishop St 75670
Black St 75670
Blackburn St 75670
Bledsoe St 75670
Block St 75670
Blocker Rd 75670
Blue Fox Rd 75670
Bluebonnet Ln 75672
Boards Ferry Rd 75672
Bogue Rd 75670
Bois D Arc Dr 75672
Bolding Rd 75670
N & S Bolivar St 75670
Bomar St 75670
Booker St 75672
Boone St 75672
Bostick Dr 75672
E Bowie St
100-1799 75670
2200-2299 75672
W Bowie St 75670
Branch St 75670
Brandy Dr 75672
Brassell Dr 75672
Brenda Dr 75672
Briarwood Ter & Trce 75672
Bridger Way 75672
Bridle Path 75672
Brimm St 75672
Britton St 75670
Brook St 75670
Brown Rd 75672
Brown St 75670
Brownrigg Ave 75672
Bruckmuller St 75670
Brumley St 75672
Bryan St 75670
Buck Sherrod Rd 75672
Buena Vista Ct & Dr 75670
Buffo St 75670
E & W Burleson St 75670
Bussey Rd 75670
Byrnes St 75670
Byron Terry Rd 75672
Caddo St 75672
Cade St 75672
Cain St 75670
Calloway Rd & St 75672
N & S Callum St 75670
Calvert Dr 75672
Camp Rd 75672
Canaan Church Rd 75672
Carey Rd 75670
Cargill Rd E 75672
Carlile Cir 75672
E & W Carolanne Blvd 75672
Carrol Dr 75672
Carson St 75672
Carter Rd 75672
S Carter St 75670
Carters Ferry Rd 75670
Carthage St 75670
Cass St 75670
Cassey Ln 75672
Cave Springs Rd 75670
Cedar Cir 75672
Cedar Loop 75672
Cedar St 75670
Cedarcrest Dr 75672
Center St 75670
Center Hill Rd 75670
Central St 75672
Chapparal Dr 75672
Chapparal Ranch Rd 75670
Charleston St 75670
Charlotte St 75670
Chatham St 75672
Cherrywood Cir 75672
Chestnut St 75672
Chico Ln 75670
Circle Dr 75670
Clara Pl 75670
Cobb St 75670
Coffee St 75670
Cole Rd 75672
N & S College St 75670
Color Aly 75670
N & S Columbus St 75670
Commerce St 75672
Compress St 75670
Cook St 75670
Cooks Rd 75670
Cooper St 75670
Corti St 75670
Cotton Ct 75672
Country Ln 75672
Country Club Dr 75672
County Road 312 75672
County Road 3122 75672
County Road 3123 75672
County Road 3133 75672
Cox Rd 75672
Coxy St 75672
Craig Rd 75670
Crawford St 75670
Creek Dr 75672
Creekside Dr 75672
Crestwood Dr 75672
E & W Crockett St 75670
Cross St 75670
Cypress St 75670
Dallas St 75670
Daniels Rd 75670
Darco Rd 75670
Darco Cutoff W 75670
David St 75670
Davidge Dr 75672
Davis St 75670
Dean Dr 75672
Decatur St 75670
Decker Dr 75672
Dee Mullikin Rd 75672
Dell Dr 75672
Denise Dr 75672
Denton St 75672
Deveroe Rd 75672
Dial St 75670
Dickson St 75670
Dixie Ct 75672
Dogan St 75670
Dogwood Dr & Ln 75672
Dolores Dr 75672
Donna Dr 75672
Dorchester Rd 75670
Dorothy Ct 75672
Doty St 75670
Draw St 75672
Duncan Rd 75672
Durel St 75670
East Ave 75670
Eastmoor Dr 75672
Eddie Butler Rd 75672
Eddington Rd 75672
S Edwards St 75670
Elaine Dr 75672
Elbert Wells St 75670
Eldridge St 75670
Elliott St 75670
Elm St 75670
Elmer Robertson Rd 75670
Elmore St 75670
Elmwood St 75672
Elsie St 75670
Elysian Fields Ave
600-1799 75670
1801-1897 75672
1899-4400 75672
4402-4608 75672
Elysian Fields Rd 75672
Elysian Fields Cut-Off 75672
E & W Emory St 75670
E End Blvd N 75670
E End Blvd S
100-2299 75670
2300-6999 75672
Enfield Dr 75672
Enola Mae Dr 75670
Epps Rd 75670
Erma Dr 75670
Ernest Dr 75670
Esplanade St 75670
Estes St 75670
Esther St 75672
Evans St 75670
Evergreen Dr 75672
Everitt Rd 75670
Exomet Rd 75670
Fair St 75670
Fairfield St 75672
Fairview St 75672
Fairway Ln 75672
E & W Fannin St 75670
Farmer St 75672

Fern Lake Rd 75672
Fern Lake Cutoff 75672
Fernbrook Ln & Ter 75672
Ferrell St 75670
Field St 75670
Fields Estate Rd 75672
Findley St 75670
Fir Trl 75672
Fire Ln 75672
Fisher Dr 75670
Fitzgerald St 75672
Five Notch Rd
900-1599 75670
2300-3198 75672
3200-10100 75672
10102-10298 75672
Fleetwood Dr 75672
Fletcher St 75670
Floyd Evans Rd 75672
Fm 1186 75672
Fm 1793 75672
Fm 1997 N & W 75670
Fm 1998 75672
Fm 2199 N & S 75672
Fm 2625 E 75672
Fm 2625 W
100-198 75672
Fm 2625 W
200-5699 75672
6000-6799 75670
Fm 2983 75672
Fm 3001 75670
Fm 31 75672
Fm 3251 75670
Fm 3379 75670
Fm 449 W 75670
Fm 451 75672
Fm 968 W 75670
Foreman Rd 75672
Forest Dr & Trl 75672
Forrest Ter 75670
Foster Dr 75672
Frances St 75670
W Francis St 75670
Frank St 75670
N & S Franklin Rd & St 75670
Frazier St 75670
Frierson Rd 75672
Fry St 75670
N & S Fulton St 75672
Furrh St 75672
Futrell Rd 75672
Fyffe Rd 75672
Fyffe Cutoff 75672
Gail Cir & Dr 75670
Gainsville Rd 75672
Garber Aly & St 75670
Garcia Ln 75670
Garden Ct 75672
Garden Oaks 75672
Garden Vista Dr 75672
Garland St 75672
Garrett Aly 75670
N Garrett St 75670
S Garrett St
500-2099 75670
2101-2199 75670
2200-3999 75672
S Garrett Ter 75672
Gatewood St 75670
Gehlan St 75670
Genevieve St 75670
George St 75670
George Gregg St 75672
George Ives Rd 75672
Georgetown St 75670
Gill Store Cutoff 75672
Ginocchio St 75670
Glenbrook Cir 75672
Goforth Rd 75670
Gooch Rd 75670
Goodwin St 75670
Gordon St 75670
Grace St 75672
Grafton St 75670
E Grand Ave
100-1799 75670
1800-2099 75672
W Grand Ave 75670
S Grangeway Rd & St 75672
Gray Cir & Rd 75672
Gray Fox Rd 75670
Green Dr 75670
Greenwood Ave 75670
Grimes Rd 75672
Grismore St 75672
Griss St 75670
N & S Grove St 75670
Guimon Rd 75672
Gunbarrell Rd 75672
Haggerty St 75672
Hall Rd 75670
Hank St 75670
Hanover Ter 75672
Hargrove St 75670
Harkins Ln 75672
Harleton Rd 75670
Harmon Rd 75672
Harper Dr 75672
Harrington Rd 75670
Harris Rd 75672
Harris House Rd 75672
Harris Lake Rd 75672
Harrison St 75670
Harry Sneed Rd 75672
Harvey St 75670
Hatley Rd 75670
Hawley St 75670
Hayes St 75670
Haynes Rd 75670
Hays Rd 75672
N & S Hazelwood St 75670
Henderson St 75670
Henderson Schoolhouse 75670
Henley Perry Dr 75670
Henrietta St 75672
Henry St 75670
Henry Everitt Rd 75672
Herbert St 75670
Heritage Rd 75672
Herndon St 75670
Hester St 75670
Hezzie Cook Rd 75672
Hickory St 75670
Hidden Lake Rd 75672
Hideaway Ln 75672
Higgins Aly & St 75670
High St 75670
Highbridge St 75670
Highland St 75670
Highland Lake Rd 75672
Hillcrest Ter 75672
Holcomb Rd 75672
Holcomb St 75670
Holland St 75670
Hollins St 75670
Hollis Rd 75672
Holmes Rd 75672
N Holmes Rd 75670
Homer Cooper Rd 75672
Hood St 75670
Hope Cir 75670
Horseshoe Rd 75672
E Houston St
1-1799 75670
1800-2699 75672
W Houston St 75670
Howard St 75670
Hudson St 75670
Hugh St 75670
Hughes St 75672
Hunt St 75670
Hynson St 75670
Hynson Springs Rd 75672
I H 20 N Service Rd W 75670
Ida St 75670
Idylwild Ter 75672
Indian Springs Dr & Rd 75672
Inman St 75670
N & S Interstate 20 Rd E & W 75672
Irvin Mcclelland Rd 75672
Ivy St 75670
Jack Futrell Rd 75672
James St 75670
James Farmer St 75670
James Marshall Rd 75670
Jamincou Rd 75672
Janice Ln & St 75672
Jasper Dr 75672
Jean Dr 75672
Jeff Davis St 75672
Jefferson Ave 75670
Jewell Gooch Rd 75670
Jim Davis Ln 75672
Joe Rd 75672
John Jeff Rd 75672
John Reagan St 75672
John Sanders Rd 75672
John Wilson Rd 75670
Johnson Rd 75672
Johnson St 75670
Jones Rd 75670
Joyce St 75672
Judge Furrh Rd 75672
Julie St 75670
Julius Davis Ln 75672
Justin Rd 75672
Kahn St 75670
Karen Ln 75672
Karis Ln 75672
Karnack Hwy 75672
Katherine St 75670
Kathy St 75670
Kay Dr 75672
Kelly Ct 75672
Key St 75670
Key Farm Rd 75672
Key Farm Cutoff 75672
King Rd 75672
Kingfish St 75670
Kings Rd 75672
N & S Lafayette St 75670
Lake St 75670
N Lakeview Dr & St S 75672
Lancaster St 75670
Lane Rd & St 75670
Lane Lewis St 75672
Lansdowne St 75672
Larry Dr 75672
Larry Woodley Rd 75672
Laurel Ln 75672
Lavernia Dr 75672
Lawson St 75670
Lee St 75670
Lee Island Rd 75672
Leigh Ln 75672
Leland St 75672
Leona St 75670
Leslie St 75672
Levin St 75670
Liberty Church Rd 75672
Liberty Cutoff 75672
Lighting St 75670
Linda Ln 75672
Lindsey Dr 75670
Linwood Dr 75670
Lisa Ln 75672
Locust St 75670
Loden Rd 75670
Log Rd 75670
Lon St 75670
Lona Ln 75670
Long John Rd 75672
Longview Rd 75670
Lonnie Williams Rd 75672
Loop 390 W 75670
E Loop 390 75672
E Loop 390 N 75672
W Loop 390 N 75672
Lothrop St 75670
Louis Waskom Rd 75672
Louise Cir 75670
Louisiana St 75670
E Lovely Rd 75672
Lower Port Caddo Rd 75672
Lucille St 75672
Ludolph St 75672
Lynoak St 75672
Macedonia Rd 75670
Madam Queen St 75670
Madewood Rd 75672
Madison St 75670
Mae Dr 75672
Magnolia St 75670
Mahone St 75672
Main St 75670
Manes St 75670
Manning Rd 75672
Marcella Ln 75670
Margaret Dr 75670
Marianne St 75670
Marigold Ave 75670
N & S Marion St 75670
Mark Dr 75672
Marks Hill Rd 75672
Marshall St
100-198 75670
200-334 75670
336-398 75670
365-365 75672
N Marshall Industrial Ave 75670
Marshall Leigh Rd 75672
Martha St 75670
Martin Aly, Pl & St 75670
Martin Luther King Jr Blvd 75670
E & W Martindale Dr 75672
Mary Mack Dr 75672
Maryland Dr 75670
Massey St 75670
Mastercraft Ave 75670
Matthewson Dr 75670
S Maulding St 75670
Maverick Dr 75670
May St 75670
Mcalpine St 75672
Mccauley Rd 75672
Mclendon St 75670
Meadow Ln & St 75670
Meadowbrook Ter 75672
Medco Dr 75672
Medill St 75670
Melanie St 75670
Memorial Dr 75670
S Memory Ln 75670
Mercer Rd 75672
Meredith St 75670
Merrill St 75672
E & W Merritt St 75670
S Merzbacher St 75670
Middle St 75670
Middle Roseborough Spg Rd 75672
Milam St 75670
Mildred Lee Ave 75670
Mill St 75670
Miller Dr 75672
Milton St 75670
Minden St 75670
Mission St 75670
Mitchell Rd 75670
Mobile St 75670
Mockingbird Ln 75670
Mollie Ln 75672
Molly Maye Dr 75672
Monigold Rd 75672
Moore St 75670
Morris Rd 75672
Morrison St 75670
Morton St 75672
Munden Dance Hall 75672
Muntz Cutoff 75670
Murphey Dr 75672
Murray St 75672
Myrtlewood Dr 75672
Nathan St 75672
Navajo Trl 75672
Nesbitt Rd & St 75670
Nesbitt Cemetery Rd 75670
Nesbitt Cutoff 75670
Newman St 75672
Newton Loop & Rd 75672
Nolan St 75670
North Dr 75670
Norwood St 75670
Oak Dr 75672
Oak St 75670
Oak Lawn Ter 75670
Oakley Dr 75672
Oakwood Dr 75672
Oakwood Estates Blvd 75672
Old Calloway Loop 75672
Old East Highway 154 75670
Old Elysian Fields Rd 75672
Old Elysian Fields Road 1 75672
Old Elysian Fields Road 2 75672
Old Elysian Fields Road 3 75672
Old Epps Rd 75670
Old Leigh Island Rd 75670
Old Longview Rd 75670
Old Town Rd 75670
Old Woodley Rd 75672
Olive St 75670
Oris St 75670
Oscar Moore Rd 75672
Pacific Dr 75672
Page St 75670
Palato Dr 75672
Palestine St 75670
Palm Plz 75672
Pamela Dr 75672
Park Dr 75670
Park Pl 75672
Park School Rd 75670
Parker St 75670
Paula St 75670
Peach Orchard Rd 75672
Peach Tree Springs Rd 75670
Pecan St 75670
Pemberton St 75670
Pennsylvania Ave 75672
Penny Ln 75672
Person Rd 75672
Peter Whetstone Sq 75670
Phillips St 75670
Pierce St 75670
Pine Burr Cir & Ter 75672
Pine Cove St 75672
Pine Island Dr 75672
Pine Tree Dr & Ter 75670
Pine Valley Dr 75672
E & W Pinecrest Dr 75670
Pinehurst Dr & St 75670
Pinewood Dr 75672
Piney Loop 75672
Piney Grove School Rd 75672
Pitts Ave 75672
Plantation Ln 75672
Poag St 75670
Pocono St 75672
Pond Dr & St 75672
Pondorosa Rd 75672
Pope St 75670
Poplar St
100-1899 75670
2100-4300 75672
4302-4498 75672
Portland Ave 75670
Positive Pl 75670
Post Oak Dr 75672
Preston St 75670
Price St 75670
Private Road 1032 75672
Private Road 1128 75672
Private Road 1147 75672
Private Road 1149 75672
Private Road 1150 75672
Private Road 1228 75672
Private Road 1229 75672
Private Road 1239 75672
Private Road 1329 75672
Private Road 1330 75672
Private Road 1331 75672
Private Road 1332 75672
Private Road 1335 75672
Private Road 1336 75672
Private Road 1337 75672
Private Road 1338 75672
Private Road 1339 75672
Private Road 1340 75672
Private Road 2124 75672
Private Road 2125 75672
Private Road 2126 75672
Private Road 2127 75672
Private Road 2134 75672
Private Road 2135 75672
Private Road 2136 75672
Private Road 2137 75672
Private Road 2220 75672
Private Road 3053 75672
Private Road 3055 75672
Private Road 3056 75672
Private Road 3057 75672
Private Road 3058 75670
Private Road 3327 75670
Private Road 3824 75670
Private Road 4002 75670
Private Road 4027 E & W 75670
Private Road 4028 75670
Private Road 4031 75670
Private Road 4032 75670
Private Road 4035 75670
Private Road 4318 75670
Private Road 4320 75670
Private Road 4333 75670
Private Road 7133 75670
Private Road 916 75672
Pumpkin Center Rd 75672
Pyle Rd 75672
Quail Dr 75672
Rainey St 75670
Ralph St 75670
Randall Cir 75672
Randarne St 75670
Randle St 75670
Randolph St 75670
Ray St 75670
Reba Ln 75672
Rebel Ln 75672
Red Fox Rd 75670
Red Oak Rd 75672
Redwood Trl 75672
Regency Rd 75672
Repose Ln 75670
Richmond Dr 75672
Ridgeway 75672
Riggs Cir 75670
Riptoe St 75670
Rock Springs Church Rd 75670
Rogers St 75670
Rolliegh St 75670
Rollingwood Dr 75672
Roosevelt Taylor Rd 75670
Rosborough St 75670
Rosborough Springs Rd
1200-2099 75670
2100-9900 75672
9902-10098 75672
Rose Blvd 75670
Rosebud Dr 75672
Rosewood Cir 75672
Ross St 75672
Ruby Ct 75672
Rudd St 75670
Runnels Rd 75670
Rural Aly 75670
Rusk Ave 75672
E Rusk St
100-1500 75670
1502-1598 75670
2200-2299 75672
W Rusk St 75670
Saint Francis St 75670
Saint James Rd 75670
Sallie Sue Dr 75672
Samuel St 75672
Sanders St 75672
Sandrock Dr 75672
Sanford St 75670
Scenic Loop 75672
Scheuber St 75670
Schmidt Dr 75672
Scotts Quarter Rd 75670
Scottsville Rd & Xing 75672
Scottsville Crossing Loop 75672
Sedberry St 75670
Serenity Ln 75672
Shadowood Dr 75672
Shady Dr 75672
Shady Grove St 75672
Shadywood Dr 75672
Shaw Rd 75672
Shaw St 75670
Sherman Dr 75672
Sherry Dr 75672
Shiloh St 75672
Shirley St 75670
Silver Fox Rd 75670
Singleton St 75672
Skinner Rd 75672
Sledge St 75670
Slone Dr 75672
Small St 75670
Smoke Rd 75670
South Dr & St 75670
Southfield Ln 75672
Southside Dr 75670
Southwest Rd 75670
Speed St 75670
Spellings Rd 75670
Spring Dr 75672
Spring St 75670
Spring Hill Rd 75670
Spruce St 75670
Stagecoach Rd 75672
Standpipe Rd E & W 75670
Starkey Creek Trl 75672
Starr St
1600-1799 75670
1800-1899 75672
State St 75670
State Highway 154 75670
State Highway 43 N 75672
State Highway 43 S 75670
Steelman Rd 75672
Stephens St 75670
Stonecreek Dr 75672
Stonewall Dr 75672
Strickland Springs Rd 75672
Strong Rd 75670
Stuart Ln 75672
Suburban Acres Rd 75672
Sue Dr 75672
Sue Belle Lake Rd 75670
Sugar Creek Dr 75672
Summit St 75670
Sun Pl 75672
Sunset Dr & Loop 75672
Sylvester Dr 75670
Taft St 75670
Talley St 75670
Tanglewood St 75670
Taylor Rd 75672
Taylor St 75670
Teddy St 75672
Ten Vote Rd 75672
Terrapin Neck Rd 75672
Terry St 75672
Texas St 75670
Thomas St 75670
Thompson Rd 75670
Tiger Dr 75670
Timber Dr 75672
Timberland Dr 75672
Tolivar Rd 75670
Tom Daniels Rd 75670
Tom Woodley Rd 75672
Tower Dr 75672

Town Oaks Dr 75672
Tracy Rd 75672
Trammels Trce 75672
Tranquility Ln 75672
E Travis St
100-299 75670
202-202 75671
300-1798 75670
301-1699 75670
1800-3199 75672
W Travis St 75670
Turtle Creek Dr 75670
Twyman St 75670
Underwood Rd 75672
United Flight 93 Blvd 75670
University Ave 75670
Us Highway 59 N 75670
Us Highway 59 S 75672
Us Highway 80 E 75672
Us Highway 80 W 75670
Vale St 75670
Valerie St 75672
Valleloma St 75670
Valley Vw 75672
Van Zandt Ave 75670
Veterans Ave 75672
Victory Dr 75672
Virginia St 75670
Walker Rd 75672
Wall St 75670
Walnut St 75670
Walnut Hill Ln 75670
Walter Dr 75670
Walters Ln 75672
Wanda Ct 75670
Ward St 75670
Warren Dr 75672
S Washington 75672
N Washington Ave 75670
S Washington Ave
101-297 75670
299-2199 75670
2300-5799 75672
Washington Pl E 75670
Washington Pl N 75670
Washington Pl S 75670
Washington Rd 75672
Water St 75670
Waubun St 75672
Wausau St 75670
Waverly St 75672
Weaver St 75670
N & S Wellington St 75670
Wesson St 75670
West Rd 75672
West St 75670
Whaley Ave 75672
Wheeler St 75672
Whetstone St 75670
White Fox Rd 75670
Wildwood Ter 75672
Wiley Ave 75670
Williams Rd 75672
S Williams St 75670
Willie Hall Rd 75672
Willie Knighten Rd 75672
Willow St 75670
Wilson St 75670
Wingwood Dr & Ter 75670
Winn St 75672
Winston St 75670
Wood Aly & St 75670
Woodall St 75672
E & W Woodland Rd 75672
Woodlawn Ests 75670
Woodley Rd 75672
Woodrow St 75670
Woodworth St 75670
Wrandott St 75670
E & W Wright St 75670
Yaney St 75670
Yates St 75672
York Rd 75672
Young St 75670
Youngsdale Cir 75670
Yvonne Ln 75672

NUMBERED STREETS

1st St 75670
3rd St 75670
4th Ave 75672
5th St 75670
6th Ave 75672
6th St 75670

MCALLEN TX

General Delivery 78501

POST OFFICE BOXES MAIN OFFICE STATIONS AND BRANCHES

Box No.s
1 - 2172 78505
2211 - 9710 78502
52201 - 52980 78505
720001 - 721056 78504

RURAL ROUTES

01 78503

HIGHWAY CONTRACTS

01 78503
07, 16, 30 78504

NAMED STREETS

Academy 78503
Acapulco Ave 78503
E & W Agusta Ave 78503
Alarradi Ave 78503
Amherst Ave 78504
Arroyo Ave 78504
Ash Ave 78501
Auburn Ave & St 78504
NE, NW, SE & SW
Augusta Sq 78503
Austin Ave 78501
E Avocet Ave 78504
Azteca Ave 78503
E Balboa Ave 78503
Bales Rd 78503
Baylor Ave 78504
Baywood Ave 78501
Bc Ave 78501
E Beaumont Ave 78501
E Beech Ave 78501
Ben Hogan Ave 78503
N Bentsen Rd
100-198 78501
200-3999 78501
4001-4197 78504
4199-10999 78504
11001-11599 78504
S Bentsen Rd
100-1300 78501
1302-1398 78501
1600-2098 78503
2100-7499 78503
7501-7599 78503
N Bicentennial Blvd 78501
S Bicentennial Blvd
100-799 78501
801-1399 78501
1801-2497 78503
2499-2599 78503
N Bicentennial Dr 78504
Blachent Ave 78501
E Bluebird Ave 78504
Booker T Ave 78501
Brand Dr 78504
N Brandon 78504
Brazos Ave & Ct 78504
Broadway Cir 78504
N Broadway St
2-98 78501
100-2000 78501
2002-2298 78501
5600-5999 78504
S Broadway St 78501
Buddy Owens Ave 78504
E & S Burns Ct & Dr 78503
Burns South Dr 78503
W Business Highway
83 78501
Byron Nelson St 78503
N C St
800-2299 78501
2301-3599 78501
4300-4400 78504
4402-5598 78504
E & W Camellia Ave, Cir
& Ct 78501
Canal St 78501
Canary Ave 78504
E Cardinal Ave 78504
Carnation Ave, Cir &
Ct 78501
S Casa Linda St
400-599 78501
2900-3399 78503
W Cd Ave 78501
E Cedar Ave & St 78501
E Chicago Ave 78501
Chris Ln 78503
Chula Vista St 78501
Col Rowe Blvd 78504
N Col Rowe Blvd 78501
S Col Rowe Blvd
2-98 78501
100-200 78501
202-1298 78501
1800-1800 78503
1802-2200 78503
2202-3698 78503
Colbath Ave 78503
Colorado Ave 78504
N Commerce Ctr 78501
Condor Ave 78504
Convention Center
Blvd 78501
E Cornell Ave 78504
Cortez Ave 78503
Cottonwood Ave 78501
Country Club Ln 78503
E Covina Ave 78503
N Cynthia Cir 78501
N Cynthia Ct 78504
N Cynthia Ln 78501
N Cynthia St
501-597 78501
599-3899 78501
4501-4897 78504
4899-7900 78504
7902-8298 78504
S Cynthia St
100-1399 78501
1801-1997 78503
1999-2600 78503
2602-2798 78503
N D St 78504
S D St 78503
E & W Daffodil Ave 78501
E Dallas Ave 78501
Dartmouth Ave 78504
Date Palm Ave 78501
Daytona Ave 78503
Denton Creek Ave 78504
Dianthus Ave 78501
Diaz Ave 78503
Dora Ln 78504
E & W Dove Ave 78504
E Duke Ave 78504
Dunlin Ave 78504
Durango Ave 78503
N E St
3400-3598 78501
4800-5198 78504
S E St
100-198 78501
1001-1199 78501
3800-3899 78503
Eagle Ave 78504
E Ebony Ave 78501
El Rancho Ave 78503
Elliot Dr 78504
Elliott Dr 78504
Ellis Dr 78504
Elm Ave 78504
Elmira Ave 78503
E Emory Ave & Ct 78504
Erie Ave 78501
E & W Esperanza Ave &
Ln 78501
Eucaliptus Ave 78501
Eugenia Cir 78501
E Expressway 83
300-1498 78503
E Expressway 83
701-1399 78501
2900-3698 78501
SW Expressway 83 78503
W Expressway 83
2-4098 78501
101-4097 78503
4099-4199 78503
4200-4998 78501
4201-5099 78503
5000-5098 78503
5100-5199 78501
S F St 78503
Fairmont Ave 78504
Falcon Ave 78504
Fern Ave 78501
E Fir Ave 78501
W Flamingo Ave, Cir &
Ct 78504
Fordham Ave 78504
Formosa Ave 78503
Fox Dr 78504
E Francisca Ave 78503
Freddy Gonzales Rd 78504
E Fresno Ave 78501
Frio Ave 78504
Frontera Rd 78504
Fuerte Ave 78504
Fullerton Ave 78504
S G Ln 78503
N G St
301-499 78501
5501-5599 78504
S G St
300-698 78501
700-799 78501
3000-3899 78503
Galveston Ave 78501
E & W Gardenia Ave &
Cir 78501
George Mcvay Dr 78503
E Geranium Ave 78501
Gloria Ave 78503
Goldcrest Ave 78504
E Goldenrod Ave 78501
Gonzalez Ln 78504
Grambling Ave 78504
Grayson Ave 78504
NE, NW, SE & SW
Greenbriar Sq 78503
Guadalupe 78504
Gull Ave 78504
Gumwood Ave & Cir 78501
S H Ln 78503
N H St 78501
S H St
700-799 78501
2901-3097 78503
3099-4499 78503
E & W Hackberry Ave 78501
Hangar Ln 78503
Harvard Ave 78504
E & W Harvey Cir &
St 78501
E & W Hawk Ave, Cir &
Ct 78504
E Helena Ave 78503
Heron Ave & Ct 78504
Hibiscus Ave 78501
Hickory Ave 78501
W Highland Ave & Ct 78501
Hildreth Ln 78504
Hondo Ave 78504
E & W Houston Ave 78501
Howard Dr 78503
Hummingbird Ave 78504
N I St 78501
S I St 78503
Ibis Ave 78504
Idela Ave 78503
Ij St 78501
Incarnate Word Ave 78504
Indian Hl 78504
Indian Creek Ave 78504
Industrial Dr 78504
S International Pkwy 78503
E & W Iris Ave 78501
Ithica Ave 78501
W Ivy Ave 78501
N J Ct 78501
N J St 78501
S J St
201-697 78501
699-799 78501
2900-4499 78503
4501-4599 78503
E Jackson Ave
101-597 78501
599-999 78501
1001-1099 78501
1100-1298 78503
1300-1499 78503
W Jackson Ave 78501
N Jackson Rd
501-3999 78501
4601-5199 78504
S Jackson Rd 78503
Japonica Ave 78501
E & W Jasmine Ave &
Ct 78501
E Jay Ave & Ct 78504
Jefferson Ave 78504
Jk St 78501
E & W Jonquil Ave 78501
Jordan Ave 78503
Judith Ave 78503
Juniper Ave 78501
N K Ctr 78501
S K Ln 78503
S K St 78503
S K Center St
200-298 78501
301-699 78501
3000-4499 78503
Katrina Ave 78503
Keeton Ave 78503
Kendlewood Ave &
Cts 78501
Kennedy Ave & Cir 78501
Kent Ln 78503
Kerria Ave 78501
Kerry Ln 78501
Kilgore Ave 78504
Kingdom Ave 78504
Kingsborough Ave 78504
E Kiwi Ave & St 78504
L Ln & St 78503
La Cantera Ave 78503
N La Lomita Rd 78504
E & W La Vista Ave &
St 78501
Lafferty Ln 78504
E Lakeview Dr 78501
E Lark Ave & Ct 78504
W Larkspur Ave 78501
Las Palmas 78504
E Laurel Ave 78501
Leczinska Dr 78504
Lindberg Ave & Cir 78501
Longoria Ln 78504
Loras Ln 78501
Los Padres Rd 78504
Loyola Ave 78504
Lucille Ave 78503
M Ln & St 78503
N Main St
100-3100 78501
3102-3898 78501
4200-4998 78504
5000-8500 78504
8502-8698 78504
S Main St
1-1399 78501
1401-1699 78501
1800-2298 78503
2300-2399 78503
Malaga Ln 78504
Manor Cir 78501
E & W Maple Ave 78501
Marigold Ave 78501
E Martin Ave 78504
Martz Ln 78504
N Mccoll Cir 78501
S Mccoll Cir 78501
N Mccoll Rd
100-3900 78501
3902-3998 78501
4100-4198 78504
4200-5599 78504
S Mccoll Rd
101-197 78501
199-1199 78501
1801-1997 78503
1999-2599 78503
2601-3599 78503
Melba Ave 78503
Mile 6 Rd 78504
Mile 6 1/2 Rd 78504
Mile 7 Rd 78504
W Military Hwy 78503
Mobile St 78501
Mockingbird Ln 78501
S Mockingbird St 78503
Mona Ave 78504
Mynah Ave 78504
Myrtle Beach Ave 78503
E Nassau Ave 78503
Neuhaus Dr 78503
Newport Ln & St 78501
Nightingale Ave & Ct 78504
Nightshade Ave 78504
E & W Nolana Ave 78504
Nopal 78504
Norma Ave 78503
Northgate Ln 78504
Northwestern Ave &
St 78504
Notre Dame Ave 78504
E Nyssa Ave 78501
Oakland Ave 78501
E Oakland Ave 78503
Old Orchard Rd 78503
Olga Ave 78503
E Olympia Ave 78503
Orange Ave & St 78501
Orchid Ave 78504
Oriole Ave & Ct 78504
Oxford Ave 78504
Ozark Ave 78504
Palenque Dr 78504
Park Cir & Vly 78501
Parker Ln 78503
Paula Ave 78503
Peach Ave 78501
Pecan Ave 78501
Pecan Blvd 78501
E Pecan Blvd
100-699 78501
620-620 78502
701-1399 78501
1000-1098 78501
N Peking St 78504
S Peking St 78501
E Pelican Ave 78504
Periwinkle Ave 78504
Petunia Ave 78504
E & W Pineridge Ave &
Ln 78503
Plerlist Ave 78504
Portland St 78503
Postage Due St 78501
Primrose Ave 78504
Princeton Ave 78504
Providence Ave 78504
Quail Ave & Ct 78504
E Quamasia Ave 78504
E Quebec Ave 78503
Queens Rd 78504
Queta Ave 78503
E Quince Ave, Cir &
Ln 78501
Raquel Ave 78503
Redbird Ave 78504
E Redbud Ave 78504
E Redwood Ave 78501
Rice Ave 78504
Richland 78503
Richmond Ave 78503
E Ridge Rd 78503
E Ridgeland Ave 78503
Robin Ave 78504
Rogers Ln 78504
N Rooth Rd 78504
Rosalva Ave 78503
S Rose Ellen Blvd 78501
N Rose Ellen Cir 78501
S Rose Ellen Cir 78501
Rose Ellen Dr 78503
Royal Palm Cir 78501
Rutgers Ave 78504
Saint George Ave 78503
Sandpiper Ave 78504
Sandy Ln 78503
E Sandyhills Ave 78503
Sarah Ave 78503
E Savannah Ave 78503
Scenic Way Ave 78503
Selinda Dr 78504
Shasta Ave 78504
Sims Ln 78504
Sonora Ave 78503
W Sprague St 78504
Stanford 78504
W State Highway 107 78504
Sun Bow 78504
Sundown Ct & Dr 78503
E Sunflower Ave 78504
Sunset Dr 78503
Swallow Ave 78504
Sweetwater Ave 78503
Sycamore Ave 78501
Tamarack Ave 78501
Tanya Ave 78503
N Taylor Rd
200-3398 78501
4000-5998 78504
6000-11500 78504
11502-11598 78504
S Taylor Rd
201-1499 78501
1901-2199 78503
Teal Ave 78504
E & W Tearose Ave 78504
Teresa Ave 78503
E Thornhill Ave 78503
Thunderbird Ave 78504
E Toronto Ave 78503
Toucan Ave 78504
W Trenton Rd 78504
Trophy Dr 78504
E Tulip Ave & Cir 78504
Tyler Ave 78503
E Ulex Ave 78504
Umar Ave & Ct 78504
Umbrellabird Ave 78504
E & W Upas Ave, Ln &
St 78501
E Uphall Ave 78503
W Ursula Ave 78503
E Us Highway 281 78503
E & W Us Highway 83 78501
Uvalde Ave 78503
Vanessa Ave 78503
E Verdin Ave 78504
E Vermont Ave 78503
Victoria Ave 78503
Villas Jardin Dr 78503

Vine Ave 78501
E Violet Ave 78504
Vw Ave 78501
W Vw Ave 78501
Vw Ct 78504
E & W Walnut Ave & St 78501
Wanda Ave 78503
Warbler Ave 78504
N Ware Rd
101-497 78501
499-3099 78501
3101-3999 78501
4100-11500 78504
11502-11698 78504
S Ware Rd
100-400 78501
402-1598 78501
1800-2698 78503
2700-6300 78503
6302-6898 78503
Ware Del Norte 78504
Warrior Dr 78501
E Water Lilly Ave 78504
Well Spring Rd 78504
E & W Westway Ave & Ct 78501
Whitewing Ave 78501
Wichita Ave 78503
E Willow Ave 78501
Winterhaven Ave 78501
E Wisteria Ave 78504
Worthington Ave 78503
E Xanthisma Ave 78504
Xavier 78504
E Xenops Ave & Ct 78504
Yale Ave 78504
E Yarrow Ave 78504
Yellowhammer Ave & Ct 78504
York Ave 78504
E Yucca Ave 78504
E Yuma Ave 78503
Yz Ave 78504
Zelda Ave 78503
Zenaida Ave 78504
Zinnia Ave 78504
Zurich Ave 78504

NUMBERED STREETS

N 1st Ln
2900-3199 78501
4500-7199 78504
N 1st Ln E 78504
N 1st Ln W 78501
S 1st Ln 78501
N 1st St
100-1698 78501
5100-7899 78504
S 1st St
100-1299 78501
1900-2000 78503
S 1st 1/2 St 78501
N 1st Lane Ct 78504
N 2 1/2 St
800-999 78501
4901-4999 78504
N 2nd Ln 78504
N 2nd St 78504
S 2nd St 78503
N 3rd Ln 78504
N 3rd St
300-1199 78501
4200-4498 78504
4500-7599 78504
S 3rd St 78503
S 4th Cir 78501
N 4th Ct 78504
N 4th Ln 78504
N 4th St
200-1999 78501
2001-2399 78501
4100-4498 78504
4500-7900 78504
7902-7998 78504
S 4th St 78501
N & S 5 1/2 78501
N 5th Ct 78504
N 5th Ln 78504
S 5th Ln
900-999 78501
3100-3298 78503
N 5th St
200-798 78501
4301-4497 78504
S 5th St
1-899 78501
1700-1798 78503
N 6th Ln 78504
S 6th Ln 78503
N 6th St
200-3999 78501
4401-4597 78504
4599-4800 78504
4802-5498 78504
S 6th St
600-1499 78501
2100-2299 78503
2301-3099 78503
N 7 1/2 St 78501
N 7th Ct
3800-3899 78501
6700-6899 78504
N 7th St
300-2799 78501
4400-4598 78504
4600-6900 78504
6902-7198 78504
S 7th St 78501
N 8th Ct 78501
N 8th St
200-2799 78501
4401-4597 78504
S 8th St
201-297 78501
1901-1999 78503
N 9th Ct 78504
N 9th St
101-197 78501
199-1000 78501
1002-2398 78501
4600-5199 78504
S 9th St 78501
N 10th St
100-3999 78501
4000-11599 78504
11601-11699 78504
8517-1-8517-5 78504
S 10th St
200-1399 78501
1401-1599 78501
1700-8599 78503
N 11th Ln 78504
N 11th St
100-1699 78501
1701-3299 78501
4500-6300 78504
6302-6398 78504
S 11th St
1-799 78501
1801-1899 78503
6300-6498 78503
N 11th 1/2 St 78501
N 12th Ln 78504
N 12th St
2-298 78501
4100-4698 78504
S 12th St
100-298 78501
406-406 78505
500-998 78501
6200-6599 78503
N 13th St 78501
N 13th 1/2 St 78501
N 14th Ln 78504
S 14th 1/2 St 78501
N 15th Ln 78504
N 15th St
101-297 78501
299-1399 78501
1401-1499 78501
4900-9399 78504
S 15th St 78501
N 16th Ln 78504
N 16th St
100-2199 78501
2201-3999 78501
4801-4997 78504
4999-7199 78504
S 16th St
100-1400 78501
1402-1598 78501
1800-1898 78503
S 16th 1/2 St 78501
N 17th St
1-2199 78501
2201-2699 78501
5301-5997 78504
5999-7700 78504
7702-9698 78504
S 17th St 78501
S 17th 1/2 St 78501
N 18th Ln 78504
S 18th St 78503
N 19th Ln 78504
N 19th St
500-1099 78501
6300-8999 78504
20th St 78504
N 20th St
100-3399 78501
6300-8799 78504
S 20th St 78501
N 21st Ln 78504
N 21st St
101-197 78501
199-3400 78501
3402-3798 78501
4100-7298 78504
7300-8900 78504
8902-8998 78504
S 21st St 78501
N 21st 1/2 St 78501
N 22nd Ct 78504
22nd Ln 78504
N 22nd Ln 78504
N 22nd St
300-3700 78501
4000-4098 78504
S 22nd St
1-297 78501
2601-2697 78503
N 23rd Cir 78504
N 23rd Ln
3500-3599 78501
5700-10799 78504
N 23rd St
100-3800 78501
4001-4097 78504
S 23rd St
2-98 78501
1600-6599 78503
N 24th Cir 78504
N 24th Ln 78504
N 24th St
800-1098 78501
1100-2999 78501
5700-10799 78504
S 24th St
2-98 78501
100-899 78501
4100-4199 78503
4201-5199 78503
N 24th 1/2 St 78501
N 25th Ln
3501-3799 78501
4100-10799 78504
N 25th St
1200-1798 78501
1800-3199 78501
4100-10700 78504
10702-10798 78504
S 25th St
1-899 78501
5000-5098 78503
N 25th 1/2 St 78501
N 26th Ct 78504
N 26th Ln
2700-2799 78501
4300-10399 78504
S 26th Ln 78503
N 26th St
100-198 78501
5200-5998 78504
S 26th St
1-1100 78501
1900-2298 78503
N 27th Cir 78501
N 27th Ln
2200-2999 78501
4300-10399 78504
S 27th Ln 78503
N 27th St
500-898 78501
4300-9299 78504
S 27th St
1-1199 78501
2200-2298 78503
N & S 27th 1/2 78501
N 28th Ln
2400-2599 78501
4300-10399 78504
S 28th Ln 78503
N 28th St
201-697 78501
699-2900 78501
2902-3398 78501
4300-10699 78504
S 28th St
200-699 78501
2200-6699 78503
N 29th Ln
2300-2398 78501
4201-4797 78504
S 29th Ln 78503
N 29th St
200-598 78501
4201-4997 78504
S 29th St
1-699 78501
1600-5199 78503
N 30th Ct 78504
N 30th Ln 78504
N 30th St
500-698 78501
700-3699 78501
5400-10999 78504
S 30th St 78503
N 31st Ln
2400-2498 78501
2500-2599 78501
10700-10898 78504
10900-10999 78504
S 31st Ln 78503
N 31st St
501-697 78501
699-3699 78501
5400-10999 78504
S 31st St 78503
N 32nd Ln
500-3699 78501
7200-11099 78504
11101-11299 78504
N 32nd St
700-2098 78501
2100-3699 78501
5301-5397 78504
5399-9299 78504
S 32nd St 78503
N 33rd Ln 78504
N 33rd St
3000-3699 78501
4601-5997 78504
5999-7599 78504
7601-7699 78504
S 33rd St
400-499 78501
1900-7099 78503
N 34th Ln
3500-3699 78501
8800-8899 78504
8901-9499 78504
N 34th St
501-1697 78501
1699-3699 78501
4100-4498 78504
4500-8899 78504
S 34th St 78503
N 35th Ln
300-2399 78501
8800-8899 78504
N 35th St
500-2399 78501
5400-6900 78504
S 35th St
1-197 78501
1900-6100 78503
N 36th Ln
300-3499 78501
5400-8999 78504
N 36th St
500-3399 78501
4901-5397 78504
5399-6900 78504
6902-9298 78504
S 36th St 78503
N 37th Ln
2700-2899 78501
7200-7398 78504
S 37th St 78503
N 38th Ln 78504
N 38th St
200-3699 78501
5100-5698 78504
5700-5899 78504
5901-10999 78504
S 38th St 78503
N 39th St
200-3699 78501
5600-5698 78504
S 39th St 78503
N 40th Ln 78501
N 40th St
200-499 78501
501-1199 78501
1900-2099 78503
2601-2697 78501
2699-3699 78501
5600-5699 78504
5701-7699 78504
S 40th St 78503
N 41st Ct 78501
41st Ln 78501
N 41st Ln
3400-3699 78501
6400-6498 78504
N 41st St
200-2799 78501
5301-5597 78504
S 41st St
701-899 78501
1900-2099 78503
N 42nd Ct 78501
N 42nd Ln
2900-2999 78501
4000-4199 78504
S 42nd Ln 78503
42nd St 78501
N 42nd St
600-1499 78501
2300-2399 78503
2800-2999 78501
4001-5597 78504
S 42nd St
700-798 78501
1900-2500 78503
N 43rd Ln 78504
N 43rd St
600-699 78501
2000-2499 78503
2701-2797 78501
2799-3800 78501
3802-3998 78501
4000-4198 78504
S 43rd St 78503
N 44th Ln
1900-2999 78501
5300-7000 78504
N 45th Ln 78504
45th St 78504
N 45th St 78501
S 45th St 78503
N 46th Ln 78504
N 46th St
300-3199 78501
5300-6300 78504
6302-6798 78504
S 46th St 78503
N 47th Ln
1000-1299 78501
4800-5399 78504
N 47th St
800-2499 78501
4600-5399 78504
S 47th St 78503
N 48th Ln
2100-2199 78501
6000-6398 78504
S 48th Ln 78501
N 48th St 78501
S 48th St 78503
N 49th Ln 78501
S 49th Ln 78503
N 49th St 78501
S 49th St
100-499 78501
2100-2399 78503
N 50th St 78501
N 51st Cir 78501
N 51st St
900-999 78501
6001-6199 78504
N 14 1/2 St 78504
N & S 19 1/2 78501
S 20 1/2 St 78501
N 22 1/2 St E 78501
N 25 1/2 St 78501
S 25 1/2 St 78503
S 25 1/2 St E 78501
S 25 1/2 St W 78501
S 26 1/2 St
200-1199 78501
1900-2799 78503
N 28 1/2 St 78501
N 29 1/2 St 78501
S 29 1/2 St 78503
S 30 1/2 St 78503
N 37 1/2 St 78501
N 38 1/2 St 78501

MCKINNEY TX

General Delivery 75070

POST OFFICE BOXES MAIN OFFICE STATIONS AND BRANCHES

Box No.s
1 - 3816 75070
6001 - 6878 75071
8000 - 8095 75070

NAMED STREETS

Abbey Rd 75070
Abbeygale Dr 75071
Abbot Ct 75070
Aberdeen Ave 75070
Abernathy Cir 75071
Abilene Way 75070
Abraham Lincoln Dr 75070
Acorn Ln 75070
Adams Ct 75071
Addie Ln 75071
Addison St 75071
Adonis Cir 75070
Adriatic Pkwy 75070
Aero Country Rd 75071
Aerobic Way 75070
Aeronca Ln 75071
Affirmed Ln 75069
N & S Airport Dr 75069
Akela Way 75071
Albany Dr 75070
Alder Dr 75071
Alex Ct 75070
Alexandria Dr 75071
Alfalfa Dr 75070
Allegiance Dr 75071
Allison Rd 75071
Alma Rd 75070
Almeta Ln 75069
Almond Ln 75070
Aloe Dr 75070
Alpine Ct 75071
Alpine Meadows Dr 75071
Altair Ln 75070
Alto Vista St 75069
Amanda Way 75070
Amber Way 75070
Amber Downs Dr 75070
Ambrym Dr 75069
N American Ln 75071
Amherst Cir 75070
Amon Carter Dr 75070
Amscott St 75069
Anderson St 75069
Andrews St 75069
Angeles Ave 75070
Angola Dr 75070
Anita Dr 75070
Anna Dr 75071
Annalea Dr 75071
Annie St 75069
Anthem Ct 75071
Anthony St 75069
Antique Rose Trl 75069
Aplamado Dr 75070
Appalachian Way 75071
Apple Way 75071
Apple Blossom Ln 75070
Applewood Ct 75071
April Sound 75071
Arbor Creek Ln 75070
Arbor Glen Dr 75070
Arbor Hollow Dr 75070
Arbury Dr 75071
Archer Way 75070
Ardmore St 75071
Ariel Cv 75070
Arledge Ct 75070
Armadillo Rdg 75071
Armstrong St 75069
Arrow Dr 75070
Arrowhead Way 75070
Arrowwood Ct 75070
Arroyo Trl 75070
Arroyo Blanco St 75069
Arthur St 75071
Ash Ln 75070
Ashburn Dr 75070
Ashcroft Dr 75069
Ashford Ln 75070
Ashhurst Ln 75071
Ashton Way 75071
Ashwood Dr 75071
Ashwood Ln 75069
Aspen Dr 75070
Assembly Dr 75070
Atwood Dr 75070
Atworth Ln 75070
Auburn Dr 75070
Audelia Ln 75070
Audi Dr 75071
Audubon Dr 75070
Auger Pl 75070
Augusta 75070
Aura Ct 75070
Austin Ln 75071
Autumn Ct & Way 75070
Autumn Point Cir & Dr 75070
Autumn Ridge Cir & Dr 75070
Avalon Creek Way 75071
Avalon Woods Dr 75070
Avenel Rd 75070
Avery Ln 75070
Aviary Dr 75070
Avondale Dr 75070
Aylesbury Ct 75070

Street	ZIP
Azalea Ln	75069
Bachman Creek Dr	75070
Bahnman Dr	75070
Baker St	75069
Bald Cypress Ln	75071
Bald Eagle Dr	75071
Baldwin Pl	75071
S Ballantrae Dr	75070
Balsam Dr	75071
Baltic Ave	75070
Baltusrol Dr	75070
Bandera St	75070
Bankhead Pl	75070
Bardmore Pl	75070
Barkley Dr	75071
Barkridge Dr	75069
Barkwood Dr	75071
Barnes St	75069
Barranca Way	75069
Barre Meadow Ln	75071
Barton Springs Dr	75069
Basil Dr	75070
Basilica Ln	75071
N & S Bass St	75069
Basswood Dr	75071
Bastille Ct	75070
Baxter Well Rd	75071
Bayberry Ct	75070
Beacon Ln	75071
Beacon Hill Rd	75070
Bear Creek Dr	75070
Bear Valley Dr	75071
Beaver Creek Ln	75070
Beaver Run Dr	75070
Bedford Ln	75071
Bedrock Dr	75070
Beech Ln	75070
Beechwood Ln	75069
Belaire Dr	75069
Belden Cir	75069
Belew Dr	75071
Belford Pl	75071
Bellcrest Dr	75070
Belle Ct	75070
Bellegrove Dr	75071
Bellemeade Ln	75071
Belmont Ct	75070
Belton Ln	75070
Belvoir Cir	75070
Benbrook	75071
Bending Oak Trl	75069
N & S Benge St	75069
Bennington	75070
Bent Creek Rd	75071
Bent Tree Dr	75070
Bentley Ct	75070
Benton Ave	75069
Bentrose Dr	75070
Bentwood Way	75071
Benwick Dr	75070
Berkley Dr	75070
Berkshire Rd	75070
Berkshire Way	75069
Berry Hl	75069
Bertram Rd	75071
Berwick Dr	75070
Bethpage Ct	75069
Bevoe St	75069
Big Bend Dr	75069
Big Creek Dr	75071
Big Fork Trl	75070
Big Pine Dr	75070
Billy Ln	75071
Billy Mitchell	75071
Biltmore Ln	75071
Binbranch Ln	75071
Birchwood Dr	75071
Biscayne Dr	75070
Bitterroot Trl	75070
Black Bear Dr	75071
Black Canyon Dr	75070
Black Diamond Ct	75069
Black Gold Dr	75070
Blackberry St	75070
Blackelm Dr	75071
Blackjack Oak Dr	75070
Blackstone Dr	75070
Blacktail Trl	75070
Blackwater Creek Trl	75070
Blackwood Dr	75071
Blanco Ln	75071
Blanco Creek Trl	75070
Bloomdale Rd	75071
Blossom Ct	75070
Blue Bonnet St	75069
Blue Hole Ct	75070
Blue Jay Ct	75070
Blue Quail Dr	75070
Blue Ridge St	75070
Blue Sage Dr	75071
Blue Skies Dr	75070
Blue Spring Dr	75070
Blue Spruce Ln	75070
Bluebird Ln	75069
Bluebonnet Ct	75070
Bluewood Dr	75071
Bluff Creek Ln	75071
Bluffs Ct	75071
Bluffview Dr	75071
Bluffwood Ave	75070
Board St	75069
Bobcat Ln	75070
Boerne St	75070
Bois D Arc Cir	75069
Bois D Arc Pl	75071
Bois D Arc Rd	75071
Bolin Rd	75069
Bolivar Dr	75070
Bolton Ct	75070
Bomar Ln	75071
Bonanza Ln	75071
Bonifay Ct	75071
Bonner St	75069
Boone Dr	75070
Borchard Trl	75071
Bordeaux Dr	75070
Boston Ln	75070
Boulder Creek Dr	75070
Boulder Lake Rd	75070
Boulder River Trl	75070
Bountiful Grove Dr	75070
Bowie Ct	75070
Boxwood Ln	75070
Boyd Creek Rd	75071
Braddock Dr	75069
Bradford Oaks Dr	75071
N & S Bradley St	75069
Braemar Ter	75071
Braewood Dr	75070
Brakebill Hill Dr	75071
Bramble Branch Cir & Ln	75069
Branch Oaks Dr	75070
Brand Dr	75070
Branding Iron Way	75069
Brandywine	75070
Brasstown Dr	75070
Braxton Ct	75071
Bray Central Dr	75069
Brayford Way	75071
Breaker Ct	75070
Breckenridge Ct	75070
Brenden Dr	75070
Brenham Dr	75070
Brent Way	75070
Brentwood Dr	75070
Briar Trl	75069
Briar Brush Dr	75071
N & S Briar Ridge Cir	75070
Briardale Ct	75069
Briargrove Ln	75070
Briarwood Dr	75071
Bridge Point Cir & Dr	75070
S Bridgefarmer Rd	75069
Bridgeport Rd	75071
Bridgewater Dr	75070
Bridle Ct	75069
Bridlegate Dr	75069
Brighton Dr	75070
Brimwood Dr	75070
Brinlee Branch Ln	75071
Bristlewood Dr	75070
Bristol Dr	75071
Brittany Ln	75070
Broad St	75069
Broad Leaf Ln	75070
Broad Meadow Ln	75071
Broadmoor Dr	75070
Broadview Ct	75071
Broadwing Dr	75069
Broken Pt & Spur	75070
Broken Arrow Ln	75071
Broken Bend Dr	75070
Broken Spoke Ln	75070
N Brook Dr	75070
Brook Ln	75069
Brook Hill Rd	75070
Brook Hollow Dr	75070
Brook Wood Dr	75071
Brookfield Way	75070
Brookgreen Ct	75071
Brookridge Ave	75071
Brookside Ct & Ln	75070
Brookview Dr	75070
Brookwater Dr	75071
Brown St	75069
Brownstone Dr	75070
Brush Creek Trl	75070
Bryce Canyon Dr	75070
Bryn Mawr Dr	75070
Buchanan St	75071
Bucker Ln	75071
Buckeye Dr	75071
Buckhill Dr	75070
Buckingham St	75070
Buckland Dr	75070
Buckleigh Point Ct	75071
Buckskin Dr	75071
Buckthorn Dr	75071
Buena Vista Ln	75070
Buffalo Creek Dr	75070
Bull Creek Dr	75071
Bumpas St	75069
Bunker Hl	75070
Burgundy Ct	75070
Burnett Dr	75070
Burnham Dr	75070
Burning Tree	75070
Burr Ferry Dr	75071
Burton Ln	75070
Bush Dr	75070
Buttercup Ln	75070
Butterfield Trl	75070
Butterfly Way	75069
Butternut Ln	75070
Byrne St	75069
Byron Nelson Dr	75070
Cabellero Ct	75069
Cabernet Ct	75069
Cabot Ln	75070
Cactus Dr	75070
Cactus Ln	75069
Caddo Cv	75071
Cades Cv	75070
Cadet Ln	75070
Caelan Ct	75071
Calais Cir	75070
Caliente Dr	75070
Calloway Dr	75070
Camberton Dr	75071
Cambridge Dr	75069
Camden	75070
Camellia Ln	75069
Camino Trl	75070
Camino Real	75069
Campbell Dr	75071
Canal St	75069
Candide Ln	75070
Candletree Ln	75070
Caney Creek Ln	75071
Cannock Dr	75070
Canterbury Ter	75070
Canvasback Blvd	75070
Canyon Pt	75071
Canyon Bay	75070
Canyon Creek Dr	75070
Canyon Crest Dr	75071
Canyon Lake Vw	75070
Canyon Valley Dr	75071
Canyon View Ct	75071
Canyon Wren Dr	75071
Capri Dr	75070
Caprock Rd	75071
Cardinal Way	75070
Caribou Trl	75070
Carlisle St	75071
Carlton Ct	75070
Carmel Falls Ct	75070
Carmel Mountain Dr	75070
Carnoustie Dr	75070
Carol St	75069
Carolina Cir	75071
Carpenter Ln	75069
Carriage Trl	75070
Carrington St	75069
Carson Cir	75070
Carter Dr	75070
Cartier Ct	75070
Carver St	75069
Casa Loma Trl	75070
Cascade Dr	75069
Cascades Dr	75070
Caseys Trl	75071
Casmir Dr	75070
Cason Falls Rd	75071
Castine Dr	75071
Castle Pines Cir	75070
Castle Ridge Dr	75071
Castle Rock Cir	75071
Castlewood Dr	75071
Catherine Ln	75071
Cattle Baron Ct & Rd	75069
Cattleman Dr	75071
Cayenne Dr	75070
Cedar Ln, Rdg & St	75069
Cedar Bluff Dr	75070
Cedar Breaks Vw	75070
Cedar Crest Dr	75070
Cedar Elm Dr	75070
Cedar Mountain Dr	75071
Cedar Ridge Dr	75070
Cedar View Ln	75070
Cedardale Dr	75070
Cedarwood Ct	75070
Center St	75069
Centeridge Ln	75071
Central Cir	75069
N Central Expy	
200-2200	75070
2202-2398	75070
2400-2498	75071
2500-3600	75071
3602-3798	75071
S Central Expy	
100-3700	75070
3702-3998	75070
5000-5798	75069
Chadwick Dr	75070
Challenger Dr	75070
Challis Trl	75070
Chamberlain Pl	75071
Champion Ln	75071
Champlain Way	75070
Chancellor Ln	75070
Chaparral Dr	75070
Chapel Ln	75069
Chapel Hill Ln	75069
Chapel View Dr	75070
Chardonnay Dr	75069
Charles Trl	75070
Charleston St	75069
Charlotte Dr	75071
Chatburn Ln	75070
Cheatham Ct	75071
Chelsea Dr	75070
Cheltenham Ave	75071
Cherokee Dr	
100-199	75071
4000-4599	75070
Cherry Ln	75071
Cherry Pt	75069
Cherry Blossom Ln	75070
Cherry Hill Ln	75070
Cherry Spring Dr	75070
Cherrywood Way	75071
Chesapeake Ln	75071
Chessington Ln	75070
Chesterfield Dr	75071
N & S Chestnut St	75069
Cheverny Dr	75070
Cheyenne Dr	75069
Chickasaw Trl	75070
Chico Rd	75070
Chief Spotted Tail Dr	75070
China Berry Dr	75070
Chippendale Dr	75071
Chisholm Trl	75070
Choctaw Ln	75070
Christian St	75069
Chuck Wagon Ln	75070
Chukar Dr	75070
N & S Church St	75069
Cimarron Rd	75070
Cinnamon Cir	75071
Circle In The Woods	75069
Citabria Dr	75070
Clara Ave	75069
Claridge Ln	75070
Clark St	75069
Clear Bay	75070
Clear Brook Dr	75071
Clear Springs Ct	75070
Clearview Dr	75070
Clearwater Dr	75071
Clematis Ct	75070
Cliffview Dr	75071
Clifton Ln	75070
Clinton Dr	75070
Cloister Way	75069
Clopper Ln	75071
Cloudcroft Ct	75070
Clouds Creek Ct	75070
Clove Ct	75070
Clover Hill Ct	75071
Clover Leaf Ln	75070
Cloyd St	75069
Club Oaks Ct	75070
Clublake Trl	75070
Coastal Dr	75071
Cobblestone Ct	75070
Cochron Dr	75070
Cockrell St	75069
Cockrill Dr	75070
Cojimar Dr	75070
Cold Stream Dr	75069
Coldwater Dr	75071
Cole St	75069
Coleman St	75069
Colesher St	75069
Colfax Dr	75070
N & S College St	75069
Collier Dr	75071
Collin Mckinney Pkwy	75070
Collinwood Dr	75069
Colmena Rd	75071
Coloma Dr	75070
Colonial Cir	75070
Colony Dr	75070
Colonywood Dr	75070
Colorado St	75069
Columbia Falls Dr	75070
Columbus Dr	75070
Comal River Trce	75071
Comanche Way	75070
Comanche Wells Dr	75071
Commerce Dr	75069
Community Ave	75071
Conch Train Rd	75070
Concho Ln	75070
Concord Ct	75070
Conestoga Dr	75069
Conner Ct	75071
Connestee Dr	75070
Constitution Dr	75071
Convention Dr	75070
Coolidge Dr	75070
Copper Ct & Xing	75070
Copper Mountain Ln	75070
Copper Ridge Dr	75070
Copperhead Ln	75071
Coralberry Dr	75070
Cordova Ln	75070
Corinth Dr	75071
Cornerstone Dr	75070
Coronado Dr	75070
Corporate	75069
Corral Ct	75070
Corral Creek Dr	75070
Cortez Ln	75070
Corys Cir	75071
Cotton Mill Dr	75070
N Cotton Ridge Rd	75070
Cotton Seed Dr	75070
Cottonwood Pl	75069
Couch Dr	75069
Country Ln & Trl	75069
Country Club Dr	75070
Country Club Rd	75069
Country Ridge Ln	75071
Country View Ln	75069
Country Walk Dr	75071
Countryside Dr	75069
County Road 1001	75071
County Road 1006	75071
County Road 1007	75071
County Road 1029	75071
County Road 1038	75071
County Road 1060	75071
County Road 1084	75071
County Road 115	75070
County Road 1200	75071
County Road 1205	75071
County Road 121	75071
County Road 1218	75071
County Road 123	75071
County Road 124	75071
County Road 125	75071
County Road 147	75070
County Road 161	75071
County Road 163	75071
County Road 164	75071
County Road 165	75071
County Road 166	75071
County Road 167	75071
County Road 168	75071
County Road 201	75071
County Road 202	75071
County Road 203	75071
County Road 205	75071
County Road 206	75071
County Road 22	75070
County Road 228	75071
County Road 281	75071
County Road 282	75071
County Road 317	75069
County Road 318	75069
County Road 324	75069
County Road 325	75069
County Road 326	75069
County Road 329	75071
County Road 330	75071
County Road 331	75071
County Road 332	75071
County Road 335	75071
County Road 336	75071
County Road 337	75071
County Road 338	75071
County Road 340	75071
County Road 341	75071
County Road 342	75071
County Road 403	
101-397	75069
County Road 403	
399-600	75069
602-898	75069
3800-4299	75071
County Road 405	75071
County Road 406	75071
County Road 407	75071
County Road 408	75071
County Road 409	75071
County Road 410	75071
County Road 411	75071
County Road 412	75071
County Road 465	75071
County Road 468	75071
County Road 469	75071
County Road 470	75071
County Road 471	75071
County Road 722	75069
County Road 852	75071
County Road 853	75071
County Road 854	75071
County Road 855	75071
County Road 856	75071
County Road 857	75071
County Road 858	75071
County Road 859	75071
County Road 860	75071
County Road 862	75071
County Road 943	75071
County Road 972	75071
County Road 988	75071
County Road 995	75071
County Road 997	75071
Courtland Ln	75069
Courtney Ln	75071
Courtside Dr	75070
Courtyards Dr	75070
Cove Cir	75071
Cove Meadow Ct	75071
Coventry Ln	75069
Covey Ln	75071
Covey Glen Rd	75070
Cowan Ln	75071
Crabapple Way	75070
Craftsbury Ln	75071
Craig Dr	75070
Cranberry Ln	75071
Cranbrook Ln	75070
Crane Ct	75070
Crator Dr	75070
Crawford St	75070
Creek Bend Ct & Dr	75070
Creek Canyon Ln	75071
Creek Crest Dr	75071
Creek Crossing Dr	75070
Creek Ridge Dr	75070
Creek Ridge Est	75071
Creekline Way	75070
Creekside Ct & Dr	75071
Creekstone Ct	75071
Creekview Cir	75069
Creekview Ct	75071
Creekwood Cir & Dr	75069
Crestcreek Ct	75071
Cresthaven Dr	75071
Crestview Dr	75071
Crestway Ct	75071
Crimson Dr	75070
Crockett Ct	75070
Crooked Cat Dr	75070
Cross Creek Ln	75070
Cross Fence Dr	75069
Cross Point Rd	75070
Cross Post Ln	75069
Cross Timbers Dr	75069
Cross Trail Ln	75069
Crossridge Dr	75071
Crossvine Ln	75070
Crown Point Rd	75070
Crutcher Xing	75070
Crystal Ct	75070
Crystal Falls Dr	75071
Cuesta Ln	75070
Culross Ln	75070
Cumberland Ct	75070
Cunningham Rd	75071
N Custer Rd	75071
S Custer Rd	75070
Cypress Ct	75070
Cypress Hill Dr	75071
Cypress Point Dr	75070
Cypress Springs Trl	75070
Daffodil Ln	75070
Daisy Ct	75070
Dale Dr	75071
Dalhart Trl	75070
Dalmatia Dr	75070
Dalton Dr	75070
Daniels Dr	75069
Dapper Dr	75070

Dara Dr 75071
Dark Forest Dr 75070
Darrow Dr 75071
Dartford Ct 75070
Datewood Ln 75071
E Dave Brown Rd 75071
E & W Davis St 75069
Dawson Creek Dr 75071
Dean Pl 75071
Deep Valley Dr 75071
Deer Path 75069
Deer Trl 75071
Deer Crossing Dr 75071
Deer Lake Dr 75071
Deer Ridge Trl 75070
Deer Run Dr 75070
Deerhurst Pl 75070
Delaware Dr 75070
Delta Wood Bnd 75071
Denali Dr 75070
Denton Creek Dr 75070
Denver Dr 75070
Derbyshire Dr 75070
Desert Dunes Trl 75070
Desert Falls Dr 75070
Desert Palms Dr 75070
Deshan Trl 75071
Desoto Dr 75070
Desperado Dr 75070
Devils River Dr 75071
Devon Dr 75070
Devonshire Ct 75071
Dewberry Ln 75069
Dewland Dr 75070
Dexter Ct 75071
Diamond Dr 75070
Diamond Peak Ct 75071
Dickinson Dr 75071
Dimebox Dr 75070
Doe Run 75070
Dog Leg Trl 75069
Dogwood Trl 75070
Dolomite Dr 75070
Dolores St 75070
Donelson Dr 75071
Doolittle 75071
Doral Cir 75069
Dorothy 75069
Dorsey Ave 75069
Double Diamond Trl 75070
Double Eagle Dr 75070
Douglas Dr 75071
Dove Crk 75071
Dove Ct 75070
Dove Tail Dr 75070
Dover Ct & Dr 75069
Dowdy Rd 75069
Dowell St 75071
Downhill Ln 75070
Drake Ct 75070
Drake Rd 75071
Drake Hill Dr 75069
Drayton Dr 75070
Drew Ct 75071
Drexel St 75069
Drift Dr 75071
Drip Rock Dr 75070
Dripping Springs Ln 75070
Dryden Dr 75070
Duclair Ct & Dr 75071
Dudperkins St 75069
Dumas Dr 75070
Dumont Ct 75069
Dun Loggin Dr 75070
Dunaway Xing 75069
Dunbar Dr 75070
Dunes Dr 75070
Dunn 75069
Dunster Dr 75070
Dupree Dr 75069
Durango Ln 75070
Durst Haven Ln 75071
Duskview Dr 75071
Duttons Meadow Ln 75071
Duvall St 75069
Eagle Dr 75071
Eagle Pt 75070
Eagle Creek Trl 75070
Eagle Ridge Ct 75071
Eaglestone Dr 75070
Earlston Ct 75071
Eastbrook Dr 75071
Easy Ln 75071
Eaton Dr 75070
Echo Canyon Dr 75070
Echo Valley Trl 75069
Eden Dr 75070
Edgarton Way 75071
Edgestone Dr 75070
Edgewater Dr 75070
Edgewood Dr 75070
Edward Dr 75071
Eider Dr 75070
Eisenhower Dr 75071
Elderberry Ct 75070
Eldorado Pkwy
200-1598 75069
1600-1999 75069
2001-2097 75070
2099-7800 75070
7802-8398 75070
Elisabeth Way 75069
Eliska Ln 75071
Elite Rd 75071
Elk Rdg 75069
Elk Mountain Trl 75070
Elk Run Rd 75070
Elk Springs Dr 75071
Ellington Ct 75070
Elm St 75069
Elm Creek Dr
400-599 75071
1001-1099 75069
Elm Fork Dr 75071
Elm Grove Ct & St 75071
Elmbrook Dr 75069
Elmwood Ct 75071
Emerald Ln 75071
Emerson Ct & Way 75069
Enchanted Rock Trl 75070
Enclave Ct 75070
Engle Nook Ct 75069
English Ivy Dr 75070
Enloe Rd 75069
Enterprise Dr 75069
E & W Erwin Ave &
Pl 75069
Escalante Trl 75070
Essex Ct 75069
Essex Dr 75071
Estates Way 75070
Estes Park Ln 75070
Eureka Bnd 75070
Eutaw Spgs 75070
Evanshire Way 75070
Evelyn St 75069
Evening Shade Ln 75070
Evergreen Ct & Dr 75070
Evers Dr 75071
Excalibur Dr 75071
Ez St 75071
Fair Oaks Dr 75071
Fair Timber Way 75071
Faircloud Ln 75070
Fairfax Ct 75070
Fairfield Ct 75070
Fairlanding Ave 75069
Fairview Pkwy 75069
Fairview Station Pkwy 75069
Fairway Hill Ln 75070
Fairway Ridge Dr 75070
Fairway Vista Dr 75070
Falcon Ln 75071
Falcon Creek Dr 75070
Falcon Crest Dr 75070
Falcon Hollow Rd 75071
Falcon Ridge Ln 75071
Falcon View Dr 75070
Falconet Cir 75070
Falcons Fire Dr 75070
Fallen Branch Dr 75070
Fallen Leaf Ln 75070
Falling Water Dr 75070
Faraday Ln 75071
Farms Rd 75071
Farmstead St 75069
Farringdon Ln 75070
Fawn Holw 75070
Feather Crst 75070
Felicia Ct 75070
Fenet St 75069
Fenway Dr 75070
Fern Ct 75070
Fern Creek Trl 75071
Fern Valley Ln 75070
Ferndale Dr 75071
Ferrule Dr 75069
Fieldcrest Dr 75071
Fieldstone Ct 75070
Fife Hills Dr 75070
Fillmore Dr 75070
Finch Ave 75069
Fir Ct 75070
Firewheel Pl 75069
Fisher Rd 75071
Fisk Ln 75070
Fitzgerald Ave 75071
Fitzhugh St 75069
Fitzhugh Mill Rd 75069
Flagstone Dr 75070
Flat Bluff Ct 75070
Flat Creek Trl 75070
Fleming Dr 75070
Florence St 75069
Flowerwood Ln 75070
Flying A Trl 75070
Fm 1461 75071
Fm 1827 75071
Fm 2478 75071
Fm 2933 75071
Fm 543 75071
Fm 546 75069
Fm 720 75070
Foot Hill Rd 75070
Foote St 75069
Fordham Dr 75069
Forest Crk 75070
Forest Ct 75070
Forest Hls 75070
Forest Ln 75069
Forest Cove Dr 75071
Forest Hills Ct 75070
Forest Lake Cir 75070
Forest Lawn Dr 75071
Forest Oaks Ct & Dr 75069
E & W Fork Ln 75071
Formby Dr 75070
Forsythia Dr 75070
Fort Buckner Dr 75070
Fortinbras Dr 75071
Fountain Ct 75069
Fowler St 75069
Fownes Link Dr 75070
Fox Run 75070
Fox Chase Ln 75071
Fox Ridge Ln 75071
Fox Trail Ln 75070
Fox Wood Dr 75071
Foxboro 75070
Foxdale 75069
Foxfield Trl 75071
Foxglove Trl 75069
Francis St 75069
Franklin Ave 75069
Franklin Branch Rd 75071
Freedom Dr 75071
Freeport Dr 75070
Fringetree Dr 75071
Frio River Trl 75070
Frisco Rd 75069
Frontier Ln 75071
Fruitwood Dr 75070
Fuchia Ct 75070
Furrow Dr 75070
Gabriel Dr 75071
Gadwall Ct 75070
Gallatin St 75070
Gallery Way 75070
Garcia St 75069
Garden Grove Dr 75070
Gardenia Ln 75070
Garfield Dr 75070
Garnet Way 75070
Garreth Ln 75071
Gary Dr 75071
Gate Haven Ct 75071
Gateway Blvd 75070
General Bond Ct 75071
Geneva Ln 75070
Gentle Creek Dr 75070
Geode Ln 75070
George Bush Dr 75070
George Washington Dr 75070
Geranium Ct 75070
Geren Trl 75071
Germantown 75070
Gerrish St 75069
Gershwin Way 75070
Gillespie Rd 75070
Ginger Ct 75070
Gingerwood Dr 75071
Glade Valley Dr 75071
Glen Garden Dr 75070
Glen Hollow Ct & Dr 75070
Glen Oaks Dr 75070
Glendale Way 75071
Glendevon Dr 75071
Gleneagles Ct 75070
Glenhaven Dr 75071
Glenn Ln 75070
Glenshire Ct 75070
Glenwood Cir 75069
Glenwood Ct 75071
Glenwood Springs Ln 75070
Gold Rush Dr 75070
Golden Bear Ln 75070
Golden Eagle Dr 75071
Golden Leaf Ln 75070
Golden Meadow Ct 75069
Golden Nugget Dr 75069
Golden Wheat Ln 75070
Goldeneyes Ln 75070
Goldenrod Ct 75070
Goldfinch Dr 75070
Goldstone Dr 75070
Golfview Dr 75069
Goose Meadow Ln 75071
Gough St 75069
Grace Ranch Trl 75071
Gracewood Dr 75070
Graham Ln 75071
E Graham St 75069
W Graham St 75069
Grampian Way 75071
Granada Dr 75071
Grand Canyon Ct 75070
Grand Cypress Ln 75069
Grand Haven Ln 75071
Grand Mesa Pkwy 75070
Grant St 75071
Grapevine Cv 75071
Grassland Dr 75070
Grassmere Ln 75071
N & S Graves St 75069
Gray Branch Rd 75071
Grayson Rd 75070
Great Divide Ln 75070
Great Worth Way 75070
Greatstone Ln 75070
Grecian Dr 75070
Green St 75069
Green Apple Ln 75069
Green Ash Dr 75071
Green Hill Dr 75070
Green Leaf Ct 75070
Green Meadow Dr 75070
Green Moss Hl 75071
Green Mountain Pl 75070
Green Tree 75070
Greenbriar Ln 75069
Greenview Dr 75070
Greenville Rd 75069
Greenway Dr 75070
Greenwood Rd 75069
Greer St 75069
Gregory Dr 75071
Greystone Ct 75070
Greywalls Dr 75070
Griffen Ct 75070
Griffin St 75069
Grove Cove Dr 75071
Grover Cleveland Dr 75070
Grovewood Dr 75071
Grumman Ln 75071
Guadalupe Way 75071
Guildford Ln 75070
Guthrie Ln 75069
Gwendola Dr 75071
Habersham Way 75071
Hackberry Dr 75069
Hackberry Ridge Dr 75070
Hackett Creek Dr 75070
Haddington Ln 75071
Haddock St 75069
Half Moon Dr 75070
Halifax Ct 75070
Hall St 75069
Hall Meadow Ln 75071
Hamilton St 75069
Hammerly Dr 75069
Hampshire Dr 75070
Hampstead Ct 75071
Hampton Ct
200-399 75069
9000-9099 75071
Hamptonbrook Dr 75071
Haney Cir 75070
Harbor Town Dr 75070
Harcourt Ave 75070
S Hardin Blvd 75070
Hardin Rd
901-999 75070
1301-1399 75071
Hardwood Dr 75069
Harlequin Dr 75070
Harlow Ct 75070
Harmony Dr 75070
Harrell Dr 75070
Harrisburg Ln 75071
Harrison St 75069
Harroun Ave 75069
Harry St 75071
Hart Ct & Rd 75069
Hartford Ct 75070
Harvest Dr 75070
Harvest Hill Ln 75071
Hastings Blf 75070
Havasu Ln 75070
Havenridge Rd 75071
Haverford Way 75071
Hawk Hill Dr 75071
Hawkins Dr 75070
Hawks Nest 75070
Hawkswood Dr 75069
Hawthorne Ln 75071
Hayes St 75071
Headington Ct 75071
Heads And Tails Ln 75071
Healy St 75069
Heard St 75069
Hearthstone Way 75070
Heather Ct 75070
Heather Glen Trl 75070
Heatherwood Dr 75071
Hedge Bell Dr 75070
Helena Way 75070
Hell Cat Ln 75071
Hemlock Ln 75070
Henneman Way 75070
W Henry St 75069
Heritage Dr 75069
Heritage Palms Trl 75070
Herndon 75069
Herns Meadow Ln 75071
Heron Bay Ln 75070
Hickory Bend Trl 75071
Hickory Hill Ln 75071
Hickory Stick Ln 75070
Hicks Holw 75071
Hidden Trl 75069
Hidden Creek Ln 75070
Hidden Forest Dr 75070
Hidden Have Dr 75070
Hidden Knolls Dr 75071
Hidden Meadow Rd 75070
Hidden Pine Ln 75070
Hidden Springs Ct 75071
Hidden Valley Dr 75071
Hideaway Rd 75070
High Crst 75070
High Meadow Dr 75070
High Pointe Blvd 75071
Highgate Dr 75070
Highlands Dr 75070
Highridge Cir 75069
Highridge Dr 75071
Highridge Ln 75069
Highridge Trl 75069
Highridge Farms Rd 75069
Hight St 75069
Highview Ct 75070
Higier Ct 75071
Hill St 75069
Hill Lockwoods Dr 75070
Hillcrest Ct 75070
Hills Creek Dr 75070
Hillside Dr 75071
Hillview Ct 75070
Hilton Head Dr 75070
Hitch Wagon Dr 75071
Hitching Trl 75070
Hitching Post Dr 75069
Hobkirks Hl 75070
Hobson Ave 75069
Hogans Hl 75070
Holburn Dr 75070
Holder Trl 75071
Holley Ridge Way 75071
Hollow Knoll Dr 75071
Hollowbrook Cir 75070
Holly Dr 75070
Home Pl 75069
Honey Creek Dr 75070
Honey Creek Farms 75071
Honeysuckle Dr 75070
Hook Bill Dr 75070
Hoover Dr 75071
Hope Cir 75071
Hopewell Dr 75071
Hopkins Dr 75070
Horizon Trl 75071
Horizon Ridge Dr 75071
Horseshoe Bnd 75069
Horseshoe Ln 75070
Horseshoe Trl 75069
Howard St 75069
Howell St 75069
Hudson Xing 75070
Hummingbird Ct 75070
Hummingbird Ln 75069
E & W Hunt St 75069
Hunter Chase Dr 75070
Hunters Ct 75070
Hunters Creek Dr 75070
Huntington Ct 75071
Hyde Park Ct & Dr 75069
Ida St 75069
Illinois Ave 75070
S Independence Pkwy 75070
Indian Knoll Dr 75070
Indian Oak Dr 75071
Indian Palms Trl 75070
Indigo Dr 75070
Industrial Blvd 75069
Inland Ln 75070
Inspiration Ln 75071
Interchange St 75071
Inverness Cir 75070
Inverness Dr 75069
Inwood Dr 75069
Irene Dr 75070
Iris Ct 75070
Ironhorse Dr 75071
Irons Ct 75070
Ironstone Ln 75070
Ironwood Dr 75070
Irwin Ct 75070
Isaac Ln 75071
Isleworth Ln 75070
Istina Dr 75070
Itasca Dr 75070
Ivy Ct 75070
Ivy Ln 75071
Ivy Glen Dr 75071
Ivyleaf Ln 75070
Ivyridge Ln 75071
Jackson Dr 75070
Jacobs Dr 75070
Jacques Ln 75070
James Herndon Trl 75071
James Pitt Rd 75071
Jameson Xing 75069
Jamestown Ln 75071
Jasmine Ct 75070
Jasper Ln 75071
Jeanette Ln 75071
Jeans Creek Dr 75071
Jefferson St 75069
Jennie St 75069
Jerico Dr 75070
Jewel Dr 75070
Jocelyn Way 75071
N & S Johnson St 75069
Joliet Pl 75070
Jones St 75069
Joplin Dr 75071
N Jordan Rd 75071
S Jordan Rd 75070
E & W Josephine St 75069
Joshua Tree Trl 75070
Joyce Way 75069
Jubilee Dr 75070
Julian Dr 75071
Juliette Dr 75071
June Dr 75070
Jungmeister Ln 75071
Juniper Dr 75070
Juno Springs Way 75071
Kappa Way 75071
Kathryn Way 75070
Katie Cir 75071
Katie Loop 75069
Keechie Dr 75070
Kelly Dr 75070
Kempton Park Ln 75069
Kennedy Dr 75070
Kensington Ln 75070
Kenswick Dr 75071
Kentmere Ln 75070
N & S Kentucky Ln &
St 75069
Kentwood Dr 75070
Kerrville Way 75070
Kestrel Ct 75070
Keystone Dr 75070
Kickapoo Dr 75070
Killarney Dr 75070
Kimbrough Ln 75071
Kincaid St 75069
King Forest Ln 75071
Kings Row 75069
Kings Lake Dr 75070
Kingsbrook Cir 75070
Kingsbury Dr 75069
Kingsdale Ct 75071
Kingsland Trl 75070
Kingsway Ln 75070
Kinner Dr 75071
Kiowa Dr 75071
Kirkwood Dr 75071
Knightsbridge Dr 75070
Knoll Park Ct 75070
Knollwood Dr 75070
Kristen Ct 75071
Kyle Dr 75070
La Cima Dr 75071
La Cumbre Dr 75070
La Paloma Ln 75070
La Quinta Ln 75070
La Tierra Linda Trl 75070
Lacewing Dr 75070
Lacrosse Ln 75071

Laguna St 75071
Lake Trl 75069
Lake Bend Dr 75071
Lake Bluff Dr 75071
Lake Breeze Dr 75071
Lake Creek Dr 75070
Lake Crest Dr 75071
Lake Forest Dr 75070
N Lake Forest Dr 75071
S Lake Forest Dr 75070
Lake Meadow Dr 75071
Lake Point Cir 75070
Lake Ridge Ln 75071
Lake Shore Dr 75071
Lake Trails Cir 75069
Lake Village Dr 75071
Lake Worth Cv 75071
Lakefront Ct 75071
Lakehill Ln 75071
Lakeridge Dr 75069
Lakesedge Dr 75070
Lakeshore Ct 75070
Lakeside Dr 75070
Lakeview Cir 75070
Lakeview Dr 75071
Lakeway Trl 75069
Lakewood Dr
400-599 75069
800-1499 75070
Lakota Trl 75070
E & W Lamar St 75069
Lambeau Ct 75070
Lampassas Trl 75070
Landmark Dr 75070
Landon Ln 75071
Landreth Dr 75070
Lands End Dr 75071
Landsdowne Dr 75070
Langmuir Dr 75071
Langston Ln 75069
Langtry Way 75071
Lanners Dr 75070
Lansdale Dr 75070
Lanshire Dr 75070
Largent St 75069
Lariat Trial Dr 75070
Lark Cir 75071
Larrow Ct 75070
Lasalle Ln 75070
Lassen Ln 75069
Lasso Ln 75070
Latham Dr 75069
Latigo Trl 75070
Laughing Waters Trl 75070
Laura Ln 75070
Laurel Cherry Dr 75070
Laurel Fork Dr 75070
Laurel Oak Dr 75071
Lauren Dr 75070
Lava Dr 75070
Lavaca River Dr 75071
Lavon Dr 75069
Lawndale Ct 75070
Lawnview Dr 75070
Lawrence Ln 75071
Lazy Ln 75070
Lea Ln 75071
Leaf Ct 75070
Learjet Ln 75071
Ledgenest Dr 75070
Lee St 75069
Leeds Dr 75070
Leesa Dr 75070
Leesburg Ct 75071
Legend Dr 75070
Leisure Ln 75070
Lela St 75069
E & W Leland Ave 75069
Lenox Dr 75071
Leven Ln 75070
Lewis Canyon Ln 75071
Lexington Pl 75070
Lighthouse Ln 75071
Lilac Cir 75071
Lily Ct 75070
Lincoln St 75069

Lindale Dr 75070
Lindsey St 75069
Linehan Ln 75071
Linhurst Ct 75069
Linkside Point Dr 75071
Linksview Dr 75070
Linley Ct 75070
Lisburn Dr 75071
Litchfield Dr 75071
Littleport Rd 75070
Littrell Ln 75071
Lively Hl & St 75069
Livingston Ln 75070
Llano Falls Dr 75071
Llano River Trl 75070
Lloyd Stearman Dr 75071
Loblolly Ln 75070
Loch Haven Ct 75070
Lochwood Cir 75070
Lock Rdg 75069
Lockhart Dr 75070
Locust Dr 75070
Lodgestone Dr 75070
Log Run Ct 75070
E Logan St 75069
Loma Alta Trl 75070
Lombardy Ln 75071
Lomeria Way 75070
Lone Mountain Trl 75070
Lone Oak Ct 75071
Lone Star Cir 75071
Lonesome Spur Trl 75070
Long Cove Dr 75069
Long Hill Ct 75071
Longfellow Ln 75069
Longhorn Dr 75071
Longleaf Dr 75070
Longneedle Ln 75070
Longwood Dr 75071
Lookout Dr 75071
Los Alamos Ln 75070
Los Padres Pl 75070
Los Rios Dr 75070
Lost Creek Trl 75069
Lost Pines Dr 75071
E & W Louisiana St 75069
Love Ct 75071
Lullaby Ln 75070
Lupton Dr 75070
Luscombe Ln 75071
Luzerne Dr 75070
Lynnwood Ln 75070
Maddie Ln 75071
Maddock Dr 75070
Madeleine 75070
Madison Ct 75070
Madrid Falls Dr 75071
Madrone Way 75070
Magnolia Dr 75070
Maidstone Way 75070
Main St 75069
Maize Ct 75070
Majestic Grove Ln 75069
Mallard Lakes Dr 75070
Malone Dr 75070
Man O War Ln 75069
Manassas Rdg 75071
Mandarin Ct 75070
Mandina Ct 75070
Maple Ln 75069
Maple Creek Dr 75069
Maple Leaf Ln 75071
Maples Ave 75069
Mapleshade Dr 75070
Maplewood Dr 75071
Marble Ln 75070
Margaret Dr 75071
Mariner St 75070
Marion Dr 75070
Mariposa Dr 75070
Marquette Cir 75070
Marquise Ct 75070
Marquita Way 75071
Marshbrook Dr 75071
Martina Dr 75070
Marvin Gdns 75070

Mason Dr 75070
Masters Ct 75070
Masterson Dr 75070
Matador Dr 75070
Matilda Dr 75071
Maudsley Dr 75071
Maverick Ct 75069
Maverick Trl 75070
Max Dr 75069
May Trl 75069
Maybach Ct 75071
Mayberry Dr 75071
Mayfair Ln 75071
Maywood Ln 75070
Mccarley Pl 75071
Mccauley St 75069
Mcclintick Rd 75070
N Mcdonald St
100-1099 75069
1330-1428 75071
1430-4499 75071
S Mcdonald St 75069
Mcintire Rd 75071
Mckinney Ave 75069
Mckinney Pkwy 75071
Mckinney Meadows Dr 75071
Mckinney Place Dr 75070
Mckinney Ranch Pkwy 75070
Mcmakin St 75069
N Meadow Cir 75069
Meadow Dr 75069
Meadow Hl 75070
Meadow Ln 75071
Meadow Crossing Dr 75071
Meadow Glen Dr 75070
Meadow Ranch Cir & Rd 75071
N & S Meadow Ridge Cir 75070
Meadow Rue Dr 75070
Meadow View Dr 75071
Meadowbrook Dr 75069
Meadowlark Dr 75070
Meadows Dr 75071
Meadowside Dr 75071
Meadowview Ct 75071
Meandering Way
400-498 75069
500-699 75069
1900-2399 75071
Meandro Ria Ln 75069
Medical Center Dr 75069
Medina Way 75071
Medinah Dr 75069
Mediterranean Dr 75070
Melrose Dr 75070
Memory Ln 75070
Mendocino Trl 75070
Meramac Dr 75071
Mercury Cir 75071
Meredith Ct 75071
Mereta Dr 75070
Meridian Dr 75070
Merion Ct 75069
Merlin Ct 75070
Merlot Ct 75069
Mesa Dr 75070
Mesa Valley Dr 75071
Mesa Verde Dr 75070
Mesquite Dr 75070
Mesquite Trl 75071
Metro Park Dr 75071
Michael Ct 75071
Midcrest Ct 75070
Midland Cir 75070
E & W Midway St 75069
Milano Dr 75071
Mile High Ln 75070
Mill Brg 75070
Mill Run Dr 75070
Millard Pond Dr 75070
Millbend Dr 75070
Miller St 75069
Millerd Pond Dr 75071
Millie Way 75070
Millwood Rd 75069

Milsap Rd 75070
Minturn Ln 75071
Mission Rdg 75070
Misty Way 75070
Mitas Hl 75071
Mockingbird Ln 75070
Monroe Dr 75070
Montclair Cir 75071
Monte Vista Ln 75070
Monterey St 75069
Monticello Dr 75070
Mooney Dr 75071
Moongold Ct 75069
Moonlight Dr 75071
Moore St 75069
Morning Dove 75070
Morning Glory Way 75070
Morningside Dr 75071
Mornington Dr 75070
N & S Morris St 75069
Moss Cliff Cir 75071
Moss Creek Ct 75070
Moss Glen Ct 75070
Mosswood Dr 75071
Mount Olive Ave 75070
Mountain Creek Dr 75070
Mountain Pointe Dr 75071
Mountain Ridge Ln 75071
Mountain View Dr 75071
Mozart Way 75070
Mulligan Dr 75070
N & S Murray Ct, Pl, Rd & St 75069
Murray Farm Dr 75069
Muscovy Dr 75070
Mustang Dr 75069
Mystic Dunes Dr 75070
Nabors Ln 75071
Nacogdoches Trl 75071
Nandina St 75071
Naphill Rd 75070
Naples Cir 75070
Natalie Dr 75071
National Pines Dr 75070
Nature Pl 75069
Nature Nate Farms 75071
Navajo Dr 75070
Navasota Trl 75071
Neches River Dr 75071
Needlewood Ln 75070
Neilson St 75069
Nelson St 75069
Neveda Ct 75070
New St 75069
New Castle Ct 75070
New Glen Dr 75070
New Hope Rd E & W 75071
New Hope Farms 75071
New York Ave 75071
Newbridge Dr 75070
Newbury St 75070
Newchester Dr 75069
Newhaven Ct 75071
Newmarket Ct 75071
Newport Ln 75071
Niblick Ct 75070
Nicklaus Ct 75070
Nicolet Ln 75070
Nightingale Dr 75070
Nixon Dr 75070
Nob Hill Pl 75071
Nocona Dr 75071
Norfolk Ln 75071
Norman Rockwell Ln 75071
Normandy Dr 75070
North St 75069
Northgate Dr 75070
Northview Dr 75070
Northwood Dr 75071
Norwich Dr 75071
Nottingham Dr 75070
Nueces Cv 75070
Nutmeg Dr 75070
Oak Blf 75069
Oak Cir 75071
Oak Gln 75069

Oak St 75069
Oak Creek Ct & Dr 75071
Oak Falls Dr 75070
Oak Hill Ct 75071
Oak Hollow Ln 75070
Oak Leaf Dr 75070
Oak Point Dr 75071
Oak Ridge Dr 75069
Oak Valley Ct 75071
Oakbury Ln 75071
Oakcrest Dr 75070
Oakdale Cir 75069
Oakfield Dr 75071
Oakhurst Ln 75070
Oakland Way 75071
Oakland Hills Dr 75069
Oakley Rd 75070
Oakmont Ct 75069
Oakmont Dr 75070
Oakridge Ct 75070
Oakwood Cir 75069
Oakwood Ct 75070
Oakwood Trl 75069
Ocala Ln 75070
Ocean Dr 75069
Odell St 75069
Old Bridge Ct 75070
Old Course Cir 75070
Old Eagle River Ln 75070
Old Field Dr 75070
Old Glory Ct 75071
Old Hickory Ln 75070
Old Lake Cir 75069
Old Mcgarrah Rd 75070
Old Mill Rd 75069
Old Oak Dr 75071
Old Salado Rd 75071
Old South Ct 75071
Old York Rd 75070
Oldham Dr 75070
Oleander Way 75071
Olivia Dr 75070
Olympia Dr 75071
Ontario Dr 75070
Oosty Ct 75070
Opal Ct 75070
Orchard Pkwy 75069
Orchard Hill Trl 75071
Orchard Park Ct & Dr 75071
Orchid Dr 75070
Osage Dr 75071
Ottawa Dr 75071
Overland Dr 75069
Overlook Ct 75070
Owl Creek Ln 75070
Oxbow Dr 75070
Oxford Ct 75070
Oxten Cir 75070
Ozark Cv 75070
Pacific Ave 75070
Packhorse Dr 75070
Paddock Trl 75069
Paint Horse Trl 75071
Palermo Way 75071
Palm Valley Dr 75071
Palmdale Dr 75070
Palmer Ct 75070
Palmtree Dr 75070
Palo Duro Canyon Dr 75070
Paloma Dr 75069
Palomino Ct 75071
Palomino Way 75069
Paluxy Ln 75071
Pamilla Ln 75071
Pandale Valley Dr 75071
Papa Trl 75070
Paradise Dr 75070
Paradise Ranch Trl 75071
Parish Ave 75071
Park Cir 75069
Park Row 75070
Park Central 75069
Park Hill Ln 75069
Park Lake Dr 75070
Park Meadow Ln 75071
Park Place Ln 75071

Park Row Cir 75070
Park Springs St 75071
Park View Ave 75070
Park Village Loop 75069
Parkdale Dr 75069
Parker St 75069
Parkhaven Dr 75071
Parkside Ln 75070
Parkvillage Ave 75069
Parkwood Ct 75070
Parnell Dr 75070
Partridge Ln 75070
Patrician Ct 75069
Patriotic Ln 75071
Patton Dr 75070
Paul Revere Way 75070
Paula Rd 75069
Peacham Ct 75071
Peachtree Ln 75070
Peacock Trl 75071
Peak Dr 75071
Pear Valley Rd 75070
Pearl St 75071
Pearson Ave 75069
Pebble Ct 75070
Pebble Beach Pl 75070
Pebble Ridge Dr 75070
Pecan Cir 75071
Pecan Dr 75069
Pecan Bend Ln 75070
Pecan Creek Farms 75071
Pecan Hill Rd 75070
Pecan Hollow Trl 75070
Pecan Knoll Dr 75070
Pecan Meadow Dr 75071
Pecan Park Ln 75071
Pecan Place Dr 75071
Pecan Point Dr 75070
Pecan Ridge Ln 75070
Pecan Trail Dr 75070
Pecan Tree Cir 75070
Pecan Valley Dr 75071
Pecos Trl 75070
Pelican Hills Dr 75069
Pembroke Ln 75070
Penny Ln 75070
Penobscot Ln 75071
Pepper Tree Cir 75070
Peradent Dr 75070
Percy Dr 75071
Peregrine Dr 75070
Periwinkle Ln 75071
Perry Meadow Ln 75071
Persimmon Ct 75070
Peterhouse Dr 75071
Petrified Tree Ln 75070
Petunia Dr 75070
Phantom Ln 75071
Pharr Dr 75070
Pheasant Knls 75070
Pheasant Run Dr 75070
Piedmont Dr 75071
Pierce Dr 75070
Piersall Dr 75070
Pikes Peak Ct 75070
Pilar Way 75070
Pillar Bluff Way 75070
Pin Oak Dr 75070
Pine St 75069
Pine Hollow Dr 75070
Pine Meadow Ln 75070
Pine Needle Dr 75070
Pine Ridge Blvd 75070
Pine Valley Ct & Dr 75069
Pinecone Dr 75070
Pinecrest Ct 75070
Pinetree Dr 75070
Pinewood Dr 75071
Ping St 75069
Pinnacle Dr 75071
Pintail Dr 75070
Pinyon Dr 75070
Pioneer Dr 75069
Piper Cub Dr 75071
Pitchstone Dr 75070
Placid Dr 75070

Planters Row Dr 75070
Plateau Dr 75069
Pleasant Valley Trl 75070
Plum Ln 75070
Plumas Pl 75070
Plumwood Way 75069
Plymouth Dr 75070
W Point 75070
Pond Bluff Way 75069
Pond Crest Trl 75069
Pond Spring Cir 75069
Pond View Ln 75069
Ponderosa Dr 75070
Pope St 75069
Popes Creek Ct 75071
Poplar Dr 75070
Poppy Ln 75070
Port Royal Ln 75070
Post Oak Ln 75070
Powder Horn Ln 75070
Powerhouse 75071
Prairie Rd 75069
Prairie Creek Dr 75071
Predarth St 75069
Prentiss Dr 75071
Presario Rd 75071
Prescotte Pointe 75071
Preservation Ln 75069
Preston Ln 75071
Preston Creek Dr 75070
Preston Wood Dr 75070
Prestwick Dr 75070
Pride Ct 75069
Priest Meadow Ct 75071
Primrose 75071
Primrose Dr 75070
Priscilla Cir 75071
Prism Ln 75070
Private Road 5079 75071
Private Road 5091 75071
Private Road 5307 75071
Private Road 5312 75071
Private Road 5334 75071
Private Road 5343 75071
Private Road 5344 75071
Private Road 5434 75071
Private Road 5436 75071
Private Road 5441 75071
Private Road 5461 75069
Private Road 5480 75071
Private Road 5492 75071
Private Road 5499 75071
Private Road 5612 75071
Private Road 5613 75069
Promenade Ter 75070
Promised Land Dr 75071
Pronghorn Rd 75070
Province St 75071
Provine Ct & Rd 75070
Pueblo Dr 75070
Purple Martin Dr 75071
Purple Martin Way 75070
Quail Holw 75070
Quail Run 75071
Quail Creek Dr 75070
Quail Ridge Dr 75070
Quail Rise 75069
Quail View Dr 75071
Quaker Dr 75069
Quarry Ln 75070
Quarry Oaks Dr 75069
Quartz Dr 75070
Queen Anne Dr 75070
Quicksilver Dr 75070
Quisenberry St 75069
Radio Flyer Dr 75071
Railhead Cir 75069
N & S Railroad St 75069
Rain Fern Dr 75070
Rain Forest Dr 75070
Raincrest Dr 75071
Raines St 75069
Raintree Dr 75071
Ranch House Dr 75069
Rancho Ln 75070
Rancho Bernardo Trl 75070

Street	ZIP
Rancho De La Osa Trl	75070
Rancho Del Norte Trl	75070
Rancho Vista Dr	75070
Rand Creek Trl	75070
Randy Lee Ln	75071
Ransom Ridge Rd	75070
Raspberry Rd	75070
Raven Ct	75071
Ravencliff Dr	75070
Ravenwood Dr	75070
Rayburn Ln	75070
Reagan Dr	75070
Rearwin Ln	75071
Red Bluff Dr	75070
Red Cedar Dr	75071
Red Feather Trl	75070
Red Hawk Pl	75071
Red Oak Cir N	75071
Red Oak Cir S	75071
Red Oak Cir W	75071
Red Oak Ln	75071
Red Oak Trl	75069
Red Oaks Dr	75070
Red Rock Dr	75070
Red Wood Cir N	75071
Redbud Blvd	75069
Redbud Dr	75070
Redbud Trl	75069
Redhawk Pl	75071
Redhead Ct	75070
Redondo Dr	75071
Redwood Dr	75070
Reed Dr	75070
Regal Rd	75070
Regal Oaks Dr	75070
Regency Trl	75070
Regents Park Dr	75070
Releigh Ct	75070
Remembrance Hill Ln	75071
Remington Ct & Park	75069
Renault Way	75071
Republic Dr	75071
Reston Dr	75070
Revere Dr	75071
Rice St	75069
Richmond Dr	75071
Ridge Cir	75071
Ridge Rd	75070
N Ridge Rd	
500-598	75071
1701-1799	75071
2300-2399	75070
S Ridge Rd	75070
Ridge Lily Ln	75071
Ridge Point Ct	75070
Ridge Run Dr	75071
Ridgeback Dr	75071
Ridgecrest Dr	75069
Ridgemoor Dr	75069
Ridgepass Ln	75071
Ridgeson Dr	75071
Ridgevalley Dr	75071
Ridgeview Trl	75071
Ridgeway Ct	75069
Ridgeway Dr	75071
Ridgewood Dr	75071
Rike St	75069
Rio Bravo Dr	75069
Rio Concho Trl	75071
Ripley St	75071
River Xing	75070
River Highlands Dr	75070
River Hills Ct	75069
River Oaks Cir & Dr	75069
River Rock Ln	75070
Riverbirch Dr	75070
Riverstone Way	75070
Riverview Dr	75071
Riverwalk Trl	75070
Riviera Dr	75070
Roanoke Ct	75071
Robbin Cir	75070
Roberts Ave	75069
Robilyn Dr	75069
Rochelle Dr	75070
Rock Canyon Ln	75071
Rock Falls Dr	75071
Rock Ridge Way	75070
Rock Springs Dr	75070
Rock Wood Ln	75070
Rockcrest Rd	75071
Rockdale Rd	75071
Rockhill Rd	
1601-1697	75069
1699-1700	75069
1702-1798	75069
2100-2298	75070
2300-2600	75070
2602-2998	75070
Rockledge Dr	75071
Rockport Dr	75071
Rockwall St	75069
Rocky Mountain Ln	75070
Rocky Springs Dr	75071
Roger Graves Cir	75070
Roland Dr	75070
Rolling Hills Dr	75071
Rolling Meadows Dr	75070
Rolling Rock Dr	75070
Rollins St	75069
Rookery Ct	75070
Roosevelt St	75069
Rose Ct	75070
Rose Bud Ct	75070
Rose Garden Ct & Dr	75070
Rosebury Cir	75071
Rosemary Ct	75071
Rosemont Ln	75069
Rosewood Blvd	75071
Rossmore Ln	75070
Rottino Dr	75070
Rouen Dr	75070
Rough Way	75069
Rough Creek Dr	75071
Round Hill Rd	75070
Round Up Ln	75070
Roundrock	75070
Rowlett Creek Way	75070
Rowley Mile	75069
Roxboro Ln	75071
Royal Aberdeen Way	75070
Royal Crest Ct	75070
Royal Glen Trl	75069
Royal Gorge Ln	75070
Royal Oaks Dr	75070
Royal Troon Ct	75070
Rubblestone Dr	75070
Ruby Ct	75070
Rudder Ln	75071
Ruidoso Ln	75070
Runford Ct	75071
Running Brook Ln	75071
Rush Creek Rd	75070
Rushden Rd	75070
Rushing Water Ct	75069
Rustic Ridge Dr	75071
Ryan Ct	75070
Ryan Trl	75071
Ryder Ct	75070
Sabine Dr	75071
Sacred Way	75069
Saddle Rd	75071
Saddle Club Trl	75070
Saddleback Dr	75069
Saddlebrook Dr	75070
Saddlehorn Dr	75071
Sadie Ln	75069
Sadler Dr	75070
Sage Dr	75070
Sagebrook Dr	75069
Sailboard Dr	75070
Saint Albans Dr	75071
Saint Andrews	75070
Saint Armond Ct	75070
Saint Clair Dr	75071
Saint Gabriel Way	75070
Saint Germain Dr	75070
Saint James Ct	75069
Saint James Dr	75069
Saint James Pl	75070
Saint Michael Dr	75070
Saint Michelle Ln	75070
Saint Pierre	75070
Saint Remy Dr	75070
Saint Tropez Ct	75070
Salado Pass	75070
San Fernando Ln	75070
San Jacinto Trl	75071
San Juan Trl	75070
San Marcos Dr	75071
San Mateo Ln	75070
Sand Trap Dr	75070
Sandalwood Dr	75070
Sanden Dr	75070
Sandlin Dr	75070
Sandstone Ln	75070
Sandy Ct	75070
Sandy Rdg	75069
Sandy Creek Way	75070
Sandy Mountain Dr	75070
Sandy Point Rd	75070
Santa Cruz Ln	75070
Santa Fe Ln	75070
Sapphire Dr	75070
Sara Cv	75071
Sarasota Ln	75070
Saratoga	75070
Sassafras Ct	75070
Savannah Dr	75070
Saw Dust Dr	75070
Sawgrass Dr	75070
Sawmill Rd	75070
Scarlet Dr	75070
Scenic Hills Dr	75071
Scenic Ranch Cir	75069
Scoter Ln	75070
Scott Pl	75070
Sea Breeze Ct	75069
Sea Pines Pl	75069
Sea Side Ln	75070
Seattle Slew Ln	75069
Seclusion Cove Dr	75070
Secretariat Ln	75069
Sedalia Dr	75070
Sedona Ln	75070
Seneca Blvd	75069
Serenity Ln	75069
Serenity Trl	75071
Setting Sun Trl	75069
Settlement Ln & Way	75070
Settlers Bnd & Trl	75069
Seville Ln	75070
Sexton Dr	75070
Shadow Creek Dr	75069
Shadow Lane Dr	75070
Shadow Ridge Dr	75070
Shady Bend Dr	75071
Shady Brook Ln	75069
Shady Grove Ln	75071
Shady Oaks Cir	75070
Shadywood	75070
Shaker Run	75069
Shallowford Ln	75070
Shannon Dr	75070
Sharon Ln	75069
Sharps Dr	75070
Shasta Dr	75071
Shasta Ranch Ln	75069
Shawnee Rd	75071
Sheldon Dr	75070
Shelley St	75069
Shenandoah Dr	75071
Shenfield Dr	75071
Sherbrooke Ln	75070
Sherman St	75069
Shetland Rd	75070
Shinnecock Ct	75069
Shire Ln	75071
Shoal Creek Ct & Dr	75069
Shooting Star Dr	75071
Shoreview Dr	75070
Short St	75069
Shumate Dr	75071
Sidney Ln	75070
Sienna Ct	75070
Sierra Dr	75071
Silver Spur	75070
Silver Buckle Dr	75070
Silver Leaf Dr	75070
Silver Oak Ct	75070
Silver Run Dr	75070
Silverado Trl	75070
Silverlake Rd	75070
Silverstone Ln	75070
Silverton Ave	75070
Silverweed Dr	75070
Singletree Ct	75070
Sioux Dr	75071
Six Gun Ln	75070
Ski Lift Ct	75070
Skyline Dr	75071
Skywagon Ln	75071
Slalom Dr	75071
Sleepy Hollow Dr	75070
Sleepy Hollow Rd	75071
Sliding Rock Dr	75070
Sloan Xing	75069
Sloan Creek Pkwy	75069
Smallwood Ave	75070
Smith St	75069
Smoke Tree Ln	75070
Snapdragon Ln	75070
Snowmass Ln	75070
Snyder Dr	75070
Soapberry Dr	75070
Soccer Dr	75070
Soda Springs Dr	75071
Soldiers Home Ln	75070
Solitude Canyon Dr	75071
Somerset Dr	75070
Songbird Ln	75071
Sonnet Dr	75071
Sonoma Dr	75070
Sorrell Rd	75070
Southern Hills Dr	75069
Southgate Dr	75070
Southwind Ln	
301-399	75069
5800-6400	75070
6402-6498	75070
Spanishmoss Dr	75070
Sparr Surveys	75069
Sparrow Pt	75071
Sparrow Hawk	75070
Spectrum Dr	75070
Spencer Pl	75071
Spicewood Dr	75070
Spring Dr	75070
Spring Blossom Ct	75070
Spring Falls Dr	75071
Spring Hill Dr	75070
Spring Meadow Dr	75069
Spring Wagon Dr	75071
Springcress Dr	75070
Spruce Cir	75071
Spruce Meadow Ln	75071
Sprucewood Dr	75071
Spur Ln	75071
Spur 399	75069
Squeezepenny Ln	75070
St Johns Dr	75070
Stacy Rd	
101-897	75069
899-1899	75069
4101-6997	75070
6999-8999	75070
Stafford Ct	
500-599	75069
2800-2899	75070
Stagecoach Dr	75069
Staghorn Ct	75071
Stags Leap Dr	75071
Stallion Dr	75069
E & W Standifer St	75069
Stanford Ct	75070
Stapleton Dr	75071
Starfire Dr	75070
Stargazer Dr	75070
Stars Ave	75070
State Blvd	75071
State Highway 121	75070
S State Highway 5	75069
Steamboat Dr	75070
Stearman Ln	75071
Steeple Ridge Ct	75069
Steepleview Ln	75069
Sterling Trl	75071
Sterling Gate Dr	75070
Stewart Rd	75069
Stickhorse Ln	75071
Still Canyon Dr	75071
Stirrup Ln	75071
Stoddard Rd	75069
Stone Brooke Ct & Xing	75070
Stone Canyon Ct	75070
Stone Cliff Ct	75071
Stone Cottage Ln	75069
Stone Creek Dr	
1100-1199	75069
2100-2198	75070
2200-2399	75070
Stone Forest Cir	75070
Stone Gate Trl	75070
Stone Hinge Dr	75069
Stone Hollow Dr	75070
N Stonebridge Dr	75071
S Stonebridge Dr	75070
Stonebrook Dr	75069
Stonecrest Dr	75071
Stonehaven Ct	75070
Stoneleigh Pl	75071
Stonemoss Dr	75070
Stoneoak Dr	75070
Stonepark Pl	75071
Stonepointe	75070
Stonewood Dr	75070
Stoney Trl	75070
Stonington Dr	75071
Stony Hill Rd	75070
Stover Creek Dr	75071
Straightaway Dr	75070
Stratford Pl	75071
Strathmore Dr	75070
Stray Creek Ln	75070
Stream Crest Way	75069
Streams Edge Trl	75069
Studebaker Dr	75071
Sugar Pine Dr	75070
Sugar Valley Rd	75070
Sugarberry Dr	75071
Summer Glen Dr	75070
Summer Hill Ct	75070
Summer Hill Ln	75069
Summer Point Dr	75070
Summer Sweet Dr	75070
Summer Tree Ln	75071
Summercrest Ln	75069
Summerfield Ct	75069
Summerside Ln	75070
Summerwood Ct	75070
Summit Ct	75069
Summit Dr	75071
Summit View Dr	75071
Sundance Dr	75071
Sundown Cir	75069
Sunflower Dr	75070
Sunglow Trl	75070
Sunlight Ter	75071
Sunny Mdws	75070
Sunnyside Dr	75070
Sunridge Ln	75069
Sunrise Dr & Trl	75071
Sunset Cir	75069
Sunset Rdg	75070
Sunset Trl	75071
Surrey Ln	75070
Surrey Estates Rd	75071
Sussex Dr	75071
Sutherland Dr	75071
Sutton Cir	75070
Swallow Ct	75071
Swan Dr	75070
Sweet Harmony Ct	75069
Sweetbriar Dr	75070
Sweetgum Ct	75071
Sycamore Ct	75069
Sycamore Trce	75070
Sylvan Way	75070
Synergy Dr	75070
Tablestone Dr	75070
Talbot Ln	75070
Talia Cir	75069
Talon Ct	75070
Tangle Ridge Dr	75071
Tanglebrush Dr	75070
Tanglewood Dr	75070
Tanner Sq	75070
Tansy Ct	75070
Taprock Dr	75070
Tarvin Rd	75071
Tatum Dr	75071
Taylor Ln	75071
Taylor Burk Dr	75071
Taylorcraft Dr	75071
Teakwood Dr	75070
Teal Ln	75070
Teddy Roosevelt Dr	75070
Tee Dr	75069
Tejas Ct	75071
Telluride Dr	75070
Temecula Creek Trl	75070
Templegate Dr	75070
Tenison Ln	75069
N & S Tennessee St	75069
Terra Verde Ln	75069
Terrace Dr	75071
Terrace View Dr	75071
Terry Ln	75071
Texian Trl	75070
The Crossings Ct, Dr & Pl	75069
Therrell Way	75070
Thicket Dr	75071
Thimbleberry Dr	75071
Thistledown Dr	75071
Thomas Jefferson Dr	75070
Thompson Ln & Rd	75071
Thornapple Dr	75071
Thornberry Dr	75071
Thornbird Dr	75071
Thornfield	75071
Thorntree Dr	75070
Throckmorton Pl & St	75069
Thunder Ln	75071
Ticonderoga	75070
Tiercels Dr	75070
Tilbury Ct	75071
Timarron Ln	75070
Timber Ln	75069
Timber Circle Dr	75070
Timber Creek Dr	75070
Timber Edge Dr	75070
Timber Glen Ln	75070
Timber Ridge Trl	75070
Timber Wagon Dr	75070
Timberbrook Trl	75070
Timberland Dr	75070
Timberline Dr	75070
Timberview	75070
Timberwood Cir & Ln	75069
Timothy Dr	75071
Tina Dr	75070
Tipperary Dr	75070
Titus St	75069
Tobosa Cir	75071
Todd Cir	75070
Tonkawa Trl	75070
Topaz Dr	75071
Torrey Pines Way	75070
Torreya Dr	75071
Touchstone Dr	75070
Tour Dr	75070
Tourette Ct	75070
Tourmalin Dr	75071
Tower Ln	75069
Town Pl	75069
Townsend Blvd	75071
Tpc Dr	75070
Trading Post Dr	75070
Trail Dr	75071
Trail Ridge Dr	75070
Traildust Dr	75069
Trailwood Dr	75070
Tralee Cir	75070
Tranquility Dr	75069
Travis Dr	75070
Traxxas Way	75070
Tree Hill Ct	75070
Treeline Dr	75070
Tremont Blvd	75071
Trenton	75070
Trickling Crk	75071
Trinity Ln	75070
Trinity Oak Cir	75071
Trinity View Dr	75071
Trixie Trail Dr	75070
Trolley Trl	75070
Troon Rd	75070
Troutt Dr	75070
Truett St	75069
Truman St	75071
Truro Dr	75071
Tucker St	75069
Tulip Dr	75070
Tully Ct	75071
Turnberry Cir	75070
Turnbridge Ct	75070
Turquoise Dr	75070
Turtle Ct & Way	75070
Turtle Creek Dr	75070
Turtleback Ct	75070
Tuscan Oaks Dr	75071
Tuscany Ct	75071
Twilight Dr	75071
Twin Cities Ln	75070
Twin Grove Rd	75071
Twin Knoll Dr	75071
Twin Mallets Ln	75071
Twin Oaks Dr	75070
Ty Cir	75071
Tyler Dr	75070
Union Ct	75071
E University Dr	75069
W University Dr	
100-1899	75069
2000-10800	75071
10802-11698	75071
University Business Dr	75071
Uvalde Way	75071
Vail Dr	75070
Val Verde Dr	75071
Valcour Bay	75070
W Valley Cir	75071
Valley Frg	75070
Valley St	75069
Valley Creek Trl	75070
Valley Crest Dr	75070
Valley Oak Ct	75071
Valley Ridge Ln	75071
Valley View Dr	75071
Van Landingham Dr	75071
Vanderbilt Dr	75070
Varnum Way	75069
Varsity Ln	75071
Vatican Dr	75071
Ventanna Ct	75070
Verdi Way	75070
Vermont Ave	75070
Vernon Ct	75071
Verona Dr	75071
Versailles Ct	75070
Victoria Cir	75070
E View Ct	75070
N Village Dr	75071
S Village Dr	75070
Vinechase Rd	75071
Vineyard Hl	75071
Vineyard Ln	75070
Vintage Ct	75070
Violet Ct	75070
Virginia Pkwy	75071
E Virginia St	75069
W Virginia St	75069
S Virginia Hills Dr	75071
Virginia Woods Dr	75071
Vista Oaks Dr	75070
Vista Verde Trl	75070
Voltaire Blvd	75070
Vought Ln	75071
Waco Ln	75071
N & S Waddill St	75069

Wade Haven Ct 75071
Wadkins Ct 75070
Wakefield Dr 75070
Wales Dr 75070
E & W Walker St 75069
Wallace St 75070
Walnut St 75069
Warbler Ln 75070
Wareham Dr 75071
Warren Dr 75071
Warrington Dr 75070
Warwick Cir 75070
Washington Ave 75069
Water Tree Dr 75070
Waterbrook Dr 75070
Waterbury Ct 75070
Waterfall Dr 75070
Waterford Ln 75071
Waterfront Dr 75071
Watersedge Dr 75070
Waterside Dr 75070
Waterstone Way 75070
Waterstone Estates Dr 75071
Watertower Way 75069
Waterview Ct 75071
Watson Dr 75070
Watt St 75069
Wayside Trl 75071
Weatherford Trce 75071
Webb Dr 75070
Wedge Hill Rd 75070
Wedgewood Dr 75070
Weeping Willow Ct 75070
Well Meadow Ln 75071
S Wellington Point Rd 75070
Wells Ln 75070
Welty St 75071
Wembley Ct 75070
Wentworth Dr 75070
West St & Way 75069
Westchester Ct 75070
Westgate Ctr 75070
Westminster Ct 75070
Westmont Dr 75070
Westmoreland Dr 75069
Weston Dr
 1-199 75069
 5900-5999 75070
Westpark Dr N 75071
Westpark Dr S 75070
Westport Dr 75070
Westridge 75070
Westview Dr 75070
Westwood Cir 75070
Wethington Ct 75071
Wheat Field Dr 75070
Whetstone Dr 75070
Whippoorwill Dr 75070
Whisper Ln 75070
Whisper Willow Dr 75070
Whispering Oaks 75071
Whistlestop Way 75069
W White Ave
 100-298 75069
 300-2199 75069
 2200-3699 75071
White Cir 75069
White Way 75069
White Oak Rd 75070
White Owl Dr 75070
White Pine Dr 75070
White Rock Creek Dr 75070
White Spruce Dr 75071
White Stallion Trl 75070
White Water Ln 75070
White Wing Ln 75070
Whitehall Ct 75070
Whitehead St 75070
Whitestone Dr 75070
Whitetail Ct 75070
Whitney Ln 75070
Wichita Trl 75071
Widgeon Ct 75070
Wilcox St 75069
Wild Ginger Dr 75070
Wild Ridge Dr 75070
Wild Rose Ct 75070
Wilderness Ct 75069
Wildwood Dr 75070
Wilford Dr 75070
Willard Dr 75070
Willie St 75069
Willow Ct 75069
Willow Ln 75070
Willow Creek Trl 75071
Willow Crest Dr 75070
Willow Grove Blvd 75070
Willow Springs Dr 75070
Willow Tree Dr 75071
Willow Way Dr 75070
Willowbend Dr 75071
Willowdale Ct 75070
Wilmeth Rd
 700-1598 75069
 1600-1700 75069
 1702-1798 75069
 2000-2599 75071
Wilshire Ct 75070
Wilson St 75069
Wilson Creek Blvd & Pkwy 75069
Winchester St 75070
Wind Rdg 75070
Wind Chime Trl 75069
Wind Crest Ct 75071
Wind Flower Ln 75070
Wind Row Dr 75070
Wind Song Dr 75071
Windhaven Dr 75071
Winding Ln 75070
Winding Hollow Ln 75070
Windleaf Way 75071
Windmill Dr 75071
Windmill Est 75071
Windmill Ln 75069
Windsor Cir 75069
Windsor Dr 75070
Windwood Ct 75070
Windy Hill Dr 75071
Windy Ridge Rd 75071
Windymeadow Ln 75069
Wingate Ln 75070
Winged Foot Dr 75069
Winsley Cir 75071
Winstanley Ln 75071
Winston Dr 75070
Winter Haven Ln 75071
Wiregrass Dr 75071
Wisteria Way 75071
Witten Park Way 75070
Wolf Ct & Run 75071
Wolfe St 75069
Wolford St 75071
N Wood St 75069
Wood Duck Ln 75070
Wood Ridge Dr 75071
Woodberry Ln 75071
Woodbluff Ln 75071
Woodbridge Dr 75070
Woodcliff Dr 75070
N & S Woodcreek Cir 75071
Woodcrest Dr 75071
Wooded Creek Ln 75071
Wooded Trail Dr 75071
Woodglen Dr 75071
Woodhaven Dr 75070
Woodheath Cir 75070
Woodhurst Dr 75070
Woodland Ct 75070
Woodlawn Rd 75071
Woodleigh Dr 75069
Woodrow Wilson Dr 75070
Woodside Cir 75070
Woodson Dr 75070
Woodstream Ln 75070
Woodway Dr 75071
Woody Crest Cir 75069
Wootson St 75069
Worchester Ln 75070
Wrangler Dr 75069
Wren Cv 75070
Wrexham Dr 75071
Wurlitzer Ct 75071
Wyndham Ct 75069
Wynford Ct 75069
Wysong Dr 75069
Yellowstone Dr 75070
York Pl 75071
Yorkshire Rd 75070
Yorktown St 75071
Yosemite Pl 75069
Young Trl 75069
Youpon Dr 75071
Yukon Dr 75071
Zaharias Dr 75070

NUMBERED STREETS

1st Ave 75069
4 Seasons Ln 75071

MESQUITE TX

General Delivery 75149

POST OFFICE BOXES MAIN OFFICE STATIONS AND BRANCHES

Box No.s
850001 - 853075 75185
870001 - 872634 75187

RURAL ROUTES

05, 06, 10, 11, 16 75149
15 75150
01, 03, 07, 08, 09, 12, 13, 14, 20, 21, 25 75181

NAMED STREETS

Abbey Ln 75181
Abilene Dr 75150
Abston Dr 75150
Acorn Grv 75181
Action Dr 75150
Adelaide Dr 75149
Adrian Ct 75150
Agnew St 75149
Airport Blvd 75181
Alameda Dr 75150
Albany Dr 75150
Alexander Rd 75181
Alexandria St 75149
Allegheny Dr 75149
Allen Dr 75149
Almond Dr 75149
Aloha Cir & Dr 75150
Alta Mesa Ct 75150
Alta Vista St 75149
Amber Spgs 75181
Americana Ln 75150
Amesbury Dr 75150
Amur St 75150
Amy Dr 75150
Anchor Dr 75150
Anders Dr 75150
Andover Dr 75149
Andrew St 75149
Anita Dr 75149
Antelope Dr 75181
Anthony Dr 75150
Antietam Ct & Way 75149
Antilles Dr 75150
Apache Trl 75149
Apollo Way 75150
Appalachia Dr 75149
Appleblossom Ln 75149
Appomattox Dr 75149
Aqueduct Ct 75181
Aralia St 75150
Arapaho Trl 75149
Arbor Ct & Dr 75150
Arborside Dr 75150
Ariel Dr 75181
Arrowwood St 75150
Ash Crk 75181
Ashcrest St 75150
Ashland Dr 75149
Ashley Pl 75181
Ashwood Dr 75150
Aspen Dr 75150
Astor Rd 75150
Athel Dr 75149
Athens Dr 75149
Austin Dr 75181
Autumndale Dr 75150
Avis Cir & St 75149
Avocet Dr 75181
Baccus Dr 75150
Bahamas Cir & Dr 75150
Baker Dr 75150
Bamboo St 75150
Banbury Ct 75181
Bandera Pl 75181
Barbara St 75149
Barcelona Cir 75150
Barclay Dr 75149
Baretta Dr 75181
Barnes Bridge Rd 75150
Barnhart Dr 75181
Barton Dr 75149
Bayberry Dr 75149
Bear Dr 75181
Beau Dr 75181
Becard Dr 75181
Bedford Dr 75150
Beeman Dr 75181
Belhaven Dr 75150
Belmont St 75149
N Belt Line Rd
 900-1899 75149
 1900-2499 75150
 2501-4899 75150
S Belt Line Rd
 1000-1599 75149
 1700-1898 75181
 1900-1999 75181
Bent Brook Dr 75181
Bent Oak Dr 75181
Bent Tree Ln 75181
Benwynd Dr 75149
Berkshire Dr 75150
Berry Rd 75181
Berrywood Ct 75181
Beth Dr 75150
Bette Ct & Dr 75149
Beverly Hills Ln 75150
Big Bend Dr 75150
Big Lake Dr 75181
Big Thicket Trl 75149
Big Town Blvd
 1200-1498 75149
 1500-2299 75149
 2301-2399 75150
 2500-3099 75150
Big Town Shopping Ctr 75149
Bill Shaw Dr 75149
Biloxi Ln 75150
Binbrook Dr 75150
Binkley Ct 75181
Birch Bnd 75181
Birch Dr 75150
Birchwood Cir & Dr 75149
Bitter Creek Dr 75181
Bitter Root Dr 75181
Black Coral Dr 75149
Blackfoot Trl 75149
Blackwillow Dr 75150
Blair Dr 75150
Blanco Dr 75150
Blue Heron Dr 75181
Blue Mesa Ln 75150
Blue Ridge Dr 75150
Bluebird Ln 75149
Bluebonnet Ln 75149
Bluecap Ct 75181
Bluefield Rd 75149
Bluejay Blvd 75181
Bluffview Dr 75150
Boardwalk Dr 75181
Bobwhite Blvd 75149
Boca Raton 75150
Bodine St 75149
Bois D Arc Cir 75149
Bonita Vista Cir 75150
Bonnywood Dr 75150
Borchardt St 75149
Borman Ave 75150
Bowie Dr 75181
Bowles Ln 75181
Boxwood Dr 75150
Braden St 75149
Bradford Pl 75149
Braewick Ct 75181
Branch Hollow Cir & Dr 75150
Brandy Station Dr 75181
Brazoria Dr 75150
Brazos Dr 75150
Brenda Dr 75149
Brenwood Dr 75181
Briar Ln 75181
Briarcliff Dr 75181
Briargate Ln 75181
Briargrove Dr 75181
Briarwood Ct & Dr 75149
Bridger Dr 75149
Bridgewater Ln 75181
Bristol Ct 75149
Brittany Dr 75150
N & S Broad St 75149
Broadmoor Dr 75149
Brockden Dr 75149
Brook Crest Dr 75150
Brook Hollow Ct & Ln 75150
Brook Meadow Dr 75150
Brookchase Dr 75181
Brookhaven Dr 75150
Brooks Dr 75149
Brookside Dr 75181
Brookstone Dr 75181
Brookway Dr 75181
Brownfield Dr 75150
Browning Dr 75181
Brunswick Ln 75149
Brushwood Ln 75150
Brushy Creek Trl 75181
W Bruton Ln & Rd E & W 75149
N & S Bryan Ave, Cir, Pl, St & Way 75149
N & S Bryan Belt Line Rd 75149
Buck Dr 75181
Buckeye Dr 75181
Buena Vista St 75149
Burnet Dr 75181
Buttercup Trl 75149
Butterfield Dr 75150
Button Dr 75150
Byrd Dr 75150
Cade Ct 75149
Caladium Dr 75149
Calle Hanby 75149
Calle Real 75149
Calle Williams 75149
Cambridge Dr 75149
Cameron Way 75181
Camino Dr 75149
Camp David St 75149
Canary Cir, Ct & Pl 75149
Candise Ct 75149
Candleberry Dr 75149
Cantura Dr 75181
Caracas Dr 75150
Caraway Dr 75149
Cardinal Ct 75149
Caribbean Dr 75150
Caribou Ct 75181
Carissa Ct & Dr 75150
Carlsbad Dr 75149
N & S Carmack St 75149
Carmody Dr 75149
Carnation Dr 75149
Carriage Ave 75181
Carson Ct & Dr 75149
E Cartwright Rd
 101-297 75149
 299-1799 75149
 1800-4999 75181
W Cartwright Rd 75149
Carver St 75149
Cary Dr 75150
Casa Dr 75149
Casa Ridge Dr 75150
Cascade St 75149
Case Dr 75181
Catalina Dr 75150
Catskill Dr 75149
Cavern Dr 75181
Cedar Dr 75149
Cedar Trl 75181
Cedar Ridge Dr 75181
Cedar Vista Dr 75181
Cedarbriar Dr 75181
Cedarbrook Dr 75181
Cedarcrest Cir & Dr 75149
Chancellorsville Dr 75149
Chandlers Lndg 75181
Chapman Dr 75149
Chappell St 75149
Charles Dr 75150
Charleston Cv 75149
Charter Creek Ct 75181
Chase Rd 75149
Chasepark Dr 75181
Chattanooga Dr 75149
Chelsea Cir, Ct & Dr 75149
Cherrywood Ct & Trl 75149
Cheshire Ct 75181
Cheshire Creek Pl 75181
Chestnut Dr 75150
Childress Ave 75150
Chimney Ct 75181
Chippewa Trl 75149
Chisolm Trl 75150
Choctaw Dr 75149
Christa Dr 75149
Cielo Ct 75181
Clary Dr 75149
Clay Mathis Rd 75181
Clear Creek Dr 75181
Clear Lake Ln 75150
Clear Springs Dr 75150
Clearmeadow Dr 75181
Clearview Dr 75181
Clearwater Dr 75181
Clifton Dr 75149
Clover Dr 75150
Club Crest Dr 75150
Club Estate Pl 75150
Club View Cir 75150
Cochran Dr 75149
Cochran St 75181
Colborne Dr 75149
Colby Cir 75149
Colchester Dr 75149
Cold Spring Ct 75181
E & W College St 75149
Colonial 75150
Colony Dr 75149
Columbia Pkwy 75150
Comanche Dr 75181
Comfort Dr 75181
Commerce Way 75149
Como Dr 75149
Comstock Ln 75181
Concord Dr 75150
Conger Dr 75149
Cool Springs Cir & Dr 75181
Coolwood Ct & Ln 75149
Copper Meadow Dr 75150
Corbett Dr 75149
Cordia Dr 75149
Cordova Dr 75150
Corkwood Dr 75150
Corta Dr 75149
Coryell Way 75150
Cottage Ln 75181
Cottonwood Dr 75150
Country Cir 75181
Country Club Dr 75150
Courtland Dr & Pl 75150
Courtney Dr 75150
Covey Ln 75150
Covington Dr 75149
Craig Dr 75181
Cranberry Ct 75181
Cranston Dr 75150
Crawford Dr 75149
Creek Bluff Cir 75149
Creek Crossing Rd 75181
Creek Royal Dr 75181
Creek Valley Rd 75181
Creekbend Ct & Dr 75149
Creekside Dr 75181
Creekview Ct & Dr 75181
Creekwood Ln 75149
Creighton Ct & Dr 75150
Crest Hill Dr 75149
Crest Meadow Ln 75181
Crest Park Dr 75149
Cresthaven Dr 75149
Crestover Dr 75150
Crestridge Dr 75149
Crockett Pl 75181
Crooked Crk 75181
Crooked Ln 75149
Cross Timber Dr 75181
Crossbow Ct 75149
Crosscreek Ln 75181
Crystal Falls Dr 75181
Crystalwood Dr 75149
Culberson Dr 75150
Cumberland Dr 75150
Curlew Ct 75181
Cutler Dr 75149
Cypress Dr 75149
Daffodil Cir & Dr 75149
Dalworth Dr 75150
Danbury Dr 75149
Dandelion Dr 75149
Daniel Crk 75181
Darien Dr 75149
Darnel Dr 75149
E & W Davis St 75149
Dawson Way 75181
Daybreak Trl 75181
Debra Dr 75149
Decoy Dr 75181
Deepwood St 75181
Deerhollow Dr 75181
Del Oak Dr 75149
Del Rio Dr 75149
Demaret Dr 75150
Denmark Dr 75149
Derby Ln 75149
Desco Dr 75149
Develon Dr 75149
Devonshire Ln 75150
Diane Dr 75149
Dinalynn St 75149
Dixon St 75181
Doe Meadow Ln 75181
Dogwood Dr 75150
Don Cobler Dr 75150
Doral 75150
Doris Dr 75149
Doubletree Dr & Pl 75149
Douglas Dr 75149
Dove Ln 75181
Dovetail Ln 75181
Downing Way 75150
Dranguet Cir & Dr 75150
Driftwood Dr 75150
Dublin Trl 75149
Dumont Dr 75150
Duncan Dr 75149
Dunning Dr 75150
Duvall Dr 75149
Eagle Pass 75150
Eagle Mountain Dr 75181
Eastbrook Cir & Dr 75150
Eastern Heights Dr 75149

Street	ZIP
Eastgate Dr	75181
Eastglen Blvd	
1300-2099	75149
2100-3399	75181
Eastover Cir & Dr	75149
Eastridge Dr	75150
Eastside Dr	75149
Eastview Ct	75150
N & S Ebrite St	75149
Ector Cir	75150
Edgebrook Dr	75150
Edgemont Dr	75149
Edinburg St	75150
Edith Dr	75149
Edwards Church Rd	75181
Egret St	75181
El Paso Way	75150
El Rio Dr	75150
Elder Dr	75150
Elderwood Loop	75181
Elkridge Dr	75181
Ellington Dr	75150
Elm Cir	75149
Elm Falls Pl	75181
Elmwood Dr	75181
Embassy St	75149
Ember Ln	75149
Emerald Dr	75150
Emerald Oaks	75181
Emily Dr	75150
E & W Emporium Cir	75150
Ervin Ln	75149
Essex Dr	75149
Eulane Dr	75149
Evans Dr	75149
Evergreen Dr	75149
Executive Blvd	75149
Fairview Ct	75181
Faithon P Lucas Sr Blvd	75181
Fallen Wood Dr	75181
Falls Church Ln	75149
Fantail Dr	75181
Farley Dr	75149
Farrington St	75150
Fawn Meadow Ln	75181
Feathercrest Ln	75150
Fernwood Dr	75150
Field Trail Dr	75150
Fielding Dr	75149
Fieldwood Dr	75150
Finch Dr	75181
Flamingo Cir, Ct & Way	75150
Fleet Cir	75149
N & S Florence St	75149
Forest Creek Cir	75149
Forestbrook Dr	75181
Forney Rd	75149
Fountain Dr	75181
Fowler Ct	75181
Foxboro Ln	75150
Foxglen Dr	75150
Foxwood Dr	75181
Franklin Dr	75150
Fredricksburg Dr	75181
Freeman St	75149
Front St	75149
Frontier Blvd	75150
Fulmar Ln	75181
Fulton Dr	75150
Futrelle St	75149
Gageway Ct & Dr	75150
N Galloway Ave	
100-2099	75149
2100-5699	75150
S Galloway Ave	75149
Gannet Dr	75181
Garden Trl	75149
Garnet Dr	75150
Gate Lane Dr	75149
Gayle Dr	75150
Gerber Dr	75181
Gettysburg St	75149
Gibson St	75149
Gillette Dr	75149
Ginger Cir	75149
Glacier Ct	75150
Glen Meadows Dr	75150
Gleneagle St	75150
Glenhaven Dr	75149
Glenmore Dr	75150
Glenn Cir	75149
Glenridge Dr	75149
Golden Grove Dr	75149
Golden Meadow Ave	75181
Goldfinch Dr	75181
Gonzales Dr	75150
Goodwin Dr	75149
Granada Dr	75181
Granbury Dr	75150
Grand Cayman Way	75149
Grand Junction Blvd	75149
Grande Dr	75149
Gray Dr	75150
Grayson Ave	75181
Green Canyon Dr	75150
Greenbrier Dr	75149
Greenfield Ct & Dr	75181
Greenhill Dr	75150
Greenland Dr	75150
Greenleaf Dr	75149
Greenway Dr	75149
Greenwood Dr	75181
Gregory Dr	75150
Greywood Dr	75149
Grinnel Dr	75150
E & W Gross Rd & St	75149
Grove Cir	75149
Grubb Cir	75149
E Grubb Dr	
100-121	75149
120-120	75185
123-1099	75149
200-1098	75149
W Grubb Dr	75149
Guadalupe Dr	75181
Gus Thomasson Rd	
2100-3502	75150
3501-3501	75187
3503-5299	75150
3504-5298	75150
Hackamore St	75149
Hackberry Crk	75181
Haddock Dr	75149
Hamden Ln	75149
Hampstead Dr	75181
Hancock Dr	75149
Haney Ln	75149
Harbinger Dr	75150
Hardeman St	75150
Hardwood Trl	75150
Harlan Dr	75150
Harper Dr	75150
Harpers Ferry Ct	75181
Harrier Dr	75181
Harvard St	75149
Harvester Ln	75150
Harvey Dr	75150
Hastings St	75149
Haverstraw Pl	75149
Hawk Dr	75181
Hazel Ct	75149
Hearthstone Dr	75150
Heath Ln	75150
Heather Glen Dr	75150
Heatherdale Dr	75150
Helen Ln	75181
Hermitage St	75149
Hickory Ridge Dr	75181
Hickory Tree Rd	75149
Hidden Ridge Dr	75181
Hidden Springs Dr	75181
Hideaway Cir	75149
High Meadow Dr	75181
High Plains Dr	75181
High Point Dr	75149
Highbank Dr	75181
Highland St	75149
Highland Village Dr	75149
Highway 352	75149
Highwood St	75181
Hillcrest St	75149
Hillrise Dr	75149
Hillside Dr	75149
Hilltop Ct	75149
Hillview St	75149
Hillwood Dr	75149
Hilton Dr	75150
Hockley Cir	75150
Hogan Dr	75150
E Holley St	75149
Holley Park Dr	75149
Holloman Rd	75181
Hollow Bnd	75150
Homestead Dr	75181
Hoops Ln	75149
Horse Shoe Bnd	75149
Houston Dr	75149
Howard Dr	75150
Hugh Walker Dr	75149
Hula Dr	75150
Hummingbird Way	75181
Hunters Trl	75150
Hunters Creek Dr	75150
Hunters Glen Dr	75150
Huntington Dr	75149
Hutchinson St	75150
Hyacinth Dr	75181
Hyde Park Dr	75150
Idlewyld Dr	75149
Independence Dr	75150
Indianpaint Dr	75149
Indigo Ct	75150
Ingram Cir	75181
Innovative Way	75149
Interstate 20	75181
Interstate 30	75150
Irene Dr	75149
Island View Ct & Dr	75149
Island Wren Dr	75181
Ithaca Dr	75181
Ivy Dr	75150
Jacksonhole Ln	75149
Jade Dr	75150
Jamaica Way	75150
James Edwards Dr	75149
Jamestown Dr	75150
Jamilia Ct	75150
Jane St	75149
Janice St	75149
Jardin Dr	75149
Jasanda Way	75149
Jasper Dr	75181
Jeanette Dr	75149
Jeremy Dr	75181
Jessica Dr & Ln	75149
John Glenn Pkwy	75150
John Peter Ct & Way	75149
John West Rd	75150
Johnson Dr	75181
Juanita St	75149
Judy Dr	75149
Julian Dr	75150
Junction Run	75181
Juniper Ln	75149
Karla Dr	75150
Karnes Dr	75150
Kathy Dr	75149
E & W Kearney St	75149
Kedy St	75149
Kenneth Hopper Dr	75149
Kensington Dr	75150
Kent Dr	75149
Kerrville Dr	75181
Kestrel Dr	75181
Keswick Ln	75150
Kevin Cir	75149
Keystone St	75149
Kiamesha Way	75150
Kim Ln	75149
Kimbell St	75149
Kimberly Dr	75149
E & W Kimbrough St	75149
Kingfisher Ln	75181
Kirkwood St	75149
Kiwi Ln	75181
Knollcrest Ln	75181
Knollview Ln	75150
Kory Dr	75149
La Costa	75150
La Paz	75150
La Prada Dr & Pkwy	75150
Lacy Ln	75181
Lagoon Cir & Dr	75150
Lakedale Ct	75181
Lakefield Dr	75181
Lakehurst Dr	75181
Lakeland Dr	75149
Lakeshore Dr	75149
Lakeside Dr	75149
Lakeside Rd	75181
Lakeview Dr	75149
Lambert Dr	75150
Lancaster Ave	75149
Lane St	75149
Lanemar Dr	75149
Lanshire Ct	75149
Laramie Dr	75149
Larchmont Dr	75150
Laredo Ln	75150
Laridald Dr	75150
Las Brisas Dr	75149
Las Hadas	75150
Las Lomas Dr	75150
Lasater Rd	75181
Laurel	75149
Laurel Ln	75150
Lawrence Dr	75181
Lawrence St	75149
Lawson Rd	75181
Lee St	75149
Lemonwood Cir	75149
Lesley Ln	75181
Leta Way	75150
Leyenda Dr	75149
Liberty Ln	75149
Lilac Ln	75149
Liles Ln	75181
Lindale Ln	75149
Lindo Dr	75149
Lindsey Ave	75149
Linfield Ct	75150
Linhaven Dr	75150
Lisa Ln	75150
Little Bnd	75150
Live Oak Dr	75150
Liverpool Dr	75149
Lochwood Dr	75181
N & S Locust St	75149
Loma Alta Dr	75150
Lometa Ct	75181
Lone Pecan Dr	75181
Lone Star Ct	75181
Long Canyon Dr	75150
Long Creek Rd	75149
Longcourt Cir	75150
Longshadow Ln	75150
Longview St	75149
Lookout Mountain Trl	75149
Lorraine Ln	75149
Los Altos Dr	75150
Los Rios Dr	75150
Los Robles Ln	75150
Lou Ann Dr	75150
Lovell Dr	75150
Loyce Dr	75149
Luau Cir & St	75150
Lucille Dr	75149
Lumley Rd	75181
Lyndon B Johnson Fwy	
15300-19200	75150
19202-19898	75150
19900-21899	75149
Magnolia Dr	75149
Mahan Cir	75149
E & W Main St	75149
Majors Cir & Dr	75149
Manchester Dr	75150
Manorview Ln	75150
Maple Dr	75150
Maple Ridge Dr	75149
Maplewood Ct	75181
Margo Dr	75150
Marigold Trl	75150
Mariposa Dr	75150
Mark Dr	75150
Marlin Dr	75149
Mason Dr	75150
Mastrani Rd	75181
Matador Ln	75149
Matthew Dr	75149
Mayda St	75150
Mayfair Dr	75149
Mcconnell St	75150
Mckenzie Rd	75181
Mckinney St	75149
Mclead Dr	75149
Meadow Ln	75150
Meadow Ridge Dr	75150
Meadowbrook Dr	75149
Meadowcreek Dr	75150
Meadowcrest Dr	75149
Meadowdale Dr	75150
Meadowglen Ln	75150
Meadowlark Dr	75149
E Meadows Blvd	75150
Meadowview Dr	75150
Meandering Way	75150
Medina Dr	75150
Melanie Ln	75149
Melinda Dr	75149
Melton Ln	75149
Memorial Blvd	75149
Menlo Dr	75149
Mercury Pl	75181
Meriden Ln	75149
Mesa Ct	75181
Mesa View Dr	75150
N Mesquite Dr	75150
Mesquite Valley Rd	
1400-2699	75149
2700-3199	75181
Micarta Dr	75181
Michelle Way	75149
Midstream Ct	75181
Midway St	75149
Milam Rd	75181
Military Pkwy	75149
Miller Pl	75150
Millie St	75149
Millridge Dr	75150
E & W Mimosa Ln	75149
Miranda Dr	75149
Mistletoe Way	75150
Mockingbird Trl	75149
Modlin St	75150
Monarch Ct & Dr	75181
Monica Ct & Ln	75149
Montclair Ln	75150
Montego Dr	75149
Monterrey Trl	75149
Monticello Dr	75149
Moon Dr	75150
Moore Dr	75149
Moreland Dr	75150
Morgan Cir & Dr	75150
Morningside Ct & Dr	75150
Morrison Dr	75150
Mossberg Ln	75181
Motley Dr	75150
Mount Pleasant Dr	75149
Mount Vernon Dr	75149
Mulberry Ln	75149
Municipal Way	75149
Myers Crk	75181
Nabholtz Ln	75150
Narcissus Ln	75149
Narobi Pl	75181
Natchez Trce	75149
Nathan Ln	75149
Neal Gay Dr	75149
Nectar Dr	75149
Nehrmeyer St	75150
Nelson Dr	75150
Neville Ct	75150
New Market Rd	75149
Newbury Dr	75150
Newcastle Rd	75181
Newport Dr & Pl	75149
Newsom Rd	75181
Newsome Rd	75149
Nighthawk Dr	75181
Nimitz Way	75181
Norcross Dr	75149
Norma Dr	75149
North Pkwy	75149
Northview Dr & Pl	75150
Northwest Ct & Dr	75150
Norton Cir & Dr	75149
Norwich Ln	75149
Norwood St	75149
O Hare Dr	75150
Oak Blf	75150
Oak Crk	75181
Oak Dr	75149
Oates Ct & Dr	75150
Ocean Reef	75150
Old Barn Ln	75149
Old Lawson Rd	75181
Old London Ln	75149
Oleander Trl	75150
Olympia Dr	75150
Omar Dr	75150
Onyx Ct	75149
Opal Ln	75149
Orange Ln	75149
Orchard Dr	75181
Orchid Ave	75149
Orian Dr	75181
Oriole St	75149
Osage Trl	75149
Osprey Ct	75181
Overland Trl	75149
Owen Ln	75150
Oxbow St	75149
Oxford Pl	75149
Paddy St	75149
Paintbrush St	75149
Paldao Dr	75149
Palisades Pl	75181
Palm Dr	75150
Palo Alto Dr	75150
Palos Verdes Dr	75150
Pampa Dr	75149
Pandale Dr	75181
Panola Dr	75150
Park Dr & Ln	75149
Park Run Dr	75150
Park Valley Dr	75181
Parkchase Cir	75181
Parkdale Dr	75149
Parker Dr	75181
Parkhaven Dr	75149
Parkhurst Dr	75150
Parkmont St	75150
Parkside Dr	75150
Parkwood Trl	75149
Partridge Dr	75181
S Pass Rd	75181
Patria Dr	75149
Paula Ct & Ln	75149
Pavillion Ct	75150
Paza Dr	75149
Peabody Ct	75181
N & S Peachtree Rd	75149
Peacock Pl	75181
Pear Trl	75150
Pearl Ct	75149
Pebble Creek Ln	75149
Pecan Dr	75149
Pecan Xing	75181
Pecan Creek Dr	75181
Pecan Shadow Way	75181
Pecos St	75150
Penrose Dr	75150
Perkins St	75149
Pheasant Dr	75150
Phillip St	75149
Picadilly Blvd	75149
Picketts Dr	75149
Pikes Peak	75149
Pinecrest Ct	75181
Pinehurst Ln	75150
Pinenut Dr	75181
Pioneer Rd	
200-298	75149
300-1999	75149
2000-2899	75181
Pittsburg Lndg	75181
Placid Dr	75150
Plantation St	75150
Planters Rd	75149
Point East Dr	75150
Poplar Cir, Dr & Pl	75149
Portsmouth Dr	75149
Post Rd	75181
Poteet Dr	75150
Potomac Ave	75149
Potter Ln	75149
Powell Cir & Rd	75149
Prairie Ln	75150
Presidential Row	75149
Preston Crk	75181
Preston Trail Dr	75150
Primrose St	75149
Purple Sage Trl	75149
Pyramid Dr	75149
Quail Hollow Dr	75150
Quail Run Dr	75149
Quapaw Trl	75149
Rancho Dr	75149
Range Dr	75149
Raven Ct	75181
Rayburn Ave	75149
Red Ash Cir	75150
Red Mill Ln	75149
Red River Pt & St	75150
Red Start Dr	75181
Redfield Dr	75181
Redman Ave & Ct	75149
Redstart Dr	75181
Redwolf Dr	75150
Redwood St	75181
Reesling Dr	75150
Regal Ave	75149
Regal Blf	75150
Regent St	75149
Remington Trl	75181
Republic Pkwy	75150
Retriever Ln	75150
Rhonda St	75149
Richard St	75149
Richman Dr	75150
Ridge Ranch Rd	75181
Ridgebrook Ct	75181
Ridgecrest St	75149
Ridgedale Dr	75150
Ridgefield Cir	75149
Ridgeview Plz & St	75149
Riggs Cir	75149
Rimrock Trl	75181
Rio Grande Pass	75150
Ripplewood Dr	75150
River Oaks Ln	75150
Riverbrook Cir	75181
Rivercrest Dr	75181
Riverport Dr	75150
Riverview Dr	75181
Riverway Ct	75181
Roanoke Cir	75150
Robert Jones Dr	75150
Robin Ln	75149
Robinhood Blvd	75149
Robinlynn St	75149
Rockcliff Dr	75150
Rockcrest Dr	75150
Rockne Ln	75150
Rocky Dr	75149
Rodeo Dr	75149
Rodeo Center Blvd	75149
Rolling Vis	75150
Rollingwood Dr	75150
Rosbury Ct	75181
Rose Ln	75149
Rose Marie Dr	75149
Rosebluff Ter	75149
Rosedown Ln	75150
Rosemont St	75149
Rosewood Dr	75150
Rosinweed	75149

Roundrock Trl 75149
Roundtree Dr 75150
Royal Crest Dr 75149
Ruby Dr 75150
Rue Cir 75149
Rugel St 75149
Running Brook Ln 75149
Rupard St 75149
Rusk Dr 75149
Rustown Dr 75150
Rutherford Dr 75149
Ryan Dr 75149
Sabine Pass 75150
Sabrina Ct & Dr 75149
Saddlehorn Dr 75181
Saffron Cir 75149
Sage Ct 75181
Sagebrush Dr 75181
Saint James Ct 75150
Sako Ln 75181
Salem Dr 75150
Salerno Dr 75150
N & S Sam Houston Rd 75149
Samuell Blvd 75149
San Marcus Dr 75150
San Mateo Dr 75150
San Saba St 75150
San Simeon Dr 75181
Sandalwood Dr 75181
Sandcastle Trl 75149
Sandhurst Dr 75181
Sandpiper Ln 75149
Sandra Lynn Dr 75150
Sandy Ln 75149
Santa Maria Dr 75149
Santiago Dr 75150
Sara Dr 75149
Sarazen Dr 75150
Savage Dr 75149
Savannah St 75149
Schirra Way 75150
Schrade Trl 75181
Scottsdale Dr 75150
E Scyene Rd
900-1999 75149
2000-5099 75181
W Scyene Rd 75149
Sea Pnes 75150
Sea Shell Dr 75149
Seabreeze Dr 75150
Seaton St 75149
Seedling Ln 75150
Seminary Rdg 75149
Seminole Trl 75149
Sesame Dr & Pl 75149
Sessom Dr 75149
Shackelford Dr 75150
Shadow Crk 75181
Shadwell St 75149
Shady Creek Trl 75150
Shadywood Ct 75150
Shands Dr 75150
Shannon Rd 75181
Shearwater Dr 75181
Sheffield Ct 75149
Shelduck Dr 75181
Shenandoah St 75150
Sherwood Dr 75150
Sheryl Dr 75150
Shiloh Ln 75181
Shoe Dr 75149
Shoreline Dr 75149
Shorewood Dr 75150
Sidney Dr 75150
Siebold Ct 75150
Sierra Dr 75149
Silver Creek Dr 75181
Silver Leaf Dr 75181
Silverado Dr 75181
Silversprings Dr 75181
Silverthorn Ct & Dr 75150
Siskin Dr 75181
Skylark St 75149
Skyline Dr 75149
Smokehouse St 75149

Smokey Mountain Trl 75149
Snapdragon Trl 75149
Snow Dr 75150
Snowy Owl Dr 75181
Sonora Ln 75181
Sorrento Dr 75150
South Pkwy 75149
Southerland Ave 75150
Southern Hills Ln 75181
Southwynd St 75150
Spiceberry Ln 75149
Spicewood Dr 75181
Spoonbill Ct 75181
Spring Branch Rd 75181
Spring Lake Dr 75149
Spring Meadow Dr 75150
Spring Mills Rd 75181
Spring Rain Dr 75181
Spring Ridge Dr 75149
Springbrook St 75149
Springcrest Dr 75149
Springfield Dr 75181
Springhaven Dr 75181
Springleaf Dr 75181
Springmont Dr 75181
Springview Ln 75181
Springwell Dr 75181
Springwood Dr 75181
Stafford Ln 75150
Stallcup Dr 75150
Stanfield St 75181
Staple Dr 75149
Starling Dr 75149
Statler Dr 75150
Stephens Green Dr 75150
Stephenson Dr 75149
Sterling Ln 75181
Stewart Dr 75181
Stillmeadow Dr 75181
Stillwater Dr 75181
Stonebrook Ln 75181
Stoneridge Dr 75149
Stonewall Ct & Way 75149
Stoney Glen Dr 75150
Stratford Dr 75150
Strayhorn Dr 75150
Stream Bend Ave 75150
Stream Side Ct 75181
Stroud Ln 75150
Sue Cir 75149
Sugarberry Dr 75150
Summit St 75149
Sumner Dr 75149
Sunset Ct 75150
Surrey Pl 75149
Susan Dr 75150
Sutters Way 75181
Swallow Dr 75181
Sweetbriar Ct 75150
Sybil Cir & Dr 75149
Sycamore Dr 75149
Tam O Shanter Dr 75150
Tamarix Ct 75150
Tanager Dr 75181
Tanglewood St 75181
Tansey Cir 75149
Taylor Dr 75149
Taylor Creek Dr 75181
Teakwood St 75149
Tealridge Dr 75181
Tealwood Dr 75181
Tedlow Trl 75150
Terrace Dr 75150
Teton Dr 75150
E & W Texas St 75149
Thistle Dr 75149
Thrush Dr 75181
Tierra Dr 75149
Tiffany Ln 75149
Tigris Trl 75181
Tiki Cir 75150
Timber Ridge Ln 75181
Timberland Dr 75181
Timbertrace Ln 75181
Timberview Dr 75149
Toler Dr 75149

Tonka Cir 75149
Topaz Dr 75150
Tosch Ln 75149
N Town East Blvd 75150
S Town East Blvd 75149
Town East Cir 75150
Town East Mall 75150
Town East Shopping Ctr 75150
Town Park Dr 75150
Towne Centre Dr 75150
Towne Crossing Blvd 75150
Tradewind Dr 75150
Travis St 75181
Trenton Cir & Dr 75150
Trinidad Dr 75150
Trinity Hl 75181
Tripp Rd 75150
Tulip Trl 75149
Turnestr Dr 75149
Turnstone Dr 75181
Turtle Dove Ln 75181
Twin Oaks Dr 75181
Upland Ln 75149
Us Highway 80 E
100-4498 75149
Us Highway 80 E
101-4799 75150
Uvalde St 75150
Val Verde Way 75181
Valley Trl 75149
Valley Falls Ave 75181
Valley View St 75149
Valleycreek Rd 75181
Vanderbilt Ln 75181
Vena Rd 75181
Ventanna Dr 75181
Versailles St 75149
Via Altos 75150
Via Avenida 75150
Via Balboa 75150
Via Ballena 75150
Via Barcelona 75150
Via Bravo 75150
Via Corona 75150
Via Coronado 75150
Via Del Mar 75150
Via Del Norte 75150
Via Del Rey 75150
Via Del Sur 75150
Via La Paloma 75150
Via Madonna 75150
Via Miramonte 75150
Via Plata 75150
Via Sevilla 75150
Via Sonoma 75150
Via Valencia 75150
Via Ventura 75150
Vickie St 75149
Vicksburg Dr 75181
Villa Siete 75181
Village Green Dr 75150
Vineyard Trl 75150
Violet Ct 75150
Virgie Joe Dr 75149
Virginia Dr 75150
Vista Dr 75149
Viva Dr 75150
Wagoner St 75149
Walden Pl 75181
N & S Walker St 75149
Walnut Dr 75149
Walnut Creek Dr 75181
Walnut Ridge Ln 75181
Wanda Dr 75149
Warm Springs Rd 75149
Warren St 75149
Warwick Dr 75150
Waterford Dr 75150
Waterloo Ln 75181
Waterside Ct 75181
Waterway Dr 75181
Waterwood Ln 75181
Wayfaring St 75150
Weatherby Dr 75181
Wedgewood Dr 75150

Welch Ave 75149
Weldon Dr 75149
Wellington Dr 75149
Wesley Dr 75149
Westview Dr 75150
Westwood Dr 75150
Wheatfield Ct & Dr 75149
Wheatridge St 75150
Whippoorwill Dr 75149
Whit Dr 75150
Whitehurst St 75149
Whitetail Dr 75181
Whitewing Dr 75150
Whitson Way 75150
Wichita Dr 75149
Widgeon Way 75181
Wiggins Pkwy 75150
Wilderness Trl 75149
Wildflower Ln 75149
Wildwood Dr 75149
Wilkinson Dr 75149
Wilkinson Rd 75181
Williams Crk 75181
Willow Crk 75181
Willow Way 75150
Willow Ridge Dr 75150
Willowbrook Dr 75149
Willowglen Dr 75150
Wimberly Ct 75181
Winchester Ln 75181
Windbell Cir & St 75149
Winding Creek Dr 75149
Windmill Ln 75149
Windmire Dr 75181
Windsong 75149
Windsor Ct 75149
Windsor Dr
1600-1799 75149
1800-1999 75181
Windswept Ln 75181
Wise Dr 75150
Wisteria Way 75149
Wood Crk 75181
Wood Pigeon Dr 75181
Woodbluff Dr 75150
Woodbridge Way 75149
Woodcrest Dr 75149
Wooded Lake Dr 75150
Woodglen Dr 75149
Woodgrove St 75181
Woodhaven Ln 75181
Woodhill St 75181
Woodhollow Ave 75150
Woodlawn Pkwy 75149
Woodshire Ave 75181
Woodside Dr 75150
Woodstream Pl 75149
Woodthorpe Dr 75181
Yellowstone Dr 75150
Yorkshire Dr 75149
Yorktown Rd 75149
Yosemite Trl 75149
Zavala Ct 75150

MIDLAND TX

General Delivery 79701

POST OFFICE BOXES MAIN OFFICE STATIONS AND BRANCHES

Box No.s
1 - 3903 79702
4001 - 6056 79704
7001 - 9952 79708
10001 - 11412 79702
12723 - 15200 79711
30001 - 30939 79712
50001 - 53896 79710
60001 - 62900 79711
80061 - 908002 79708

HIGHWAY CONTRACTS

34 79706

NAMED STREETS

N A St
300-498 79701
500-900 79701
902-1598 79701
1700-1998 79705
2000-5199 79705
S A St 79701
Abbey Pl 79707
Abell Hanger Cir 79707
Aberdeen Dr 79703
Acklen Dr 79703
N & S Adams St 79701
Adobe Dr 79707
Adonia St 79706
Advance Ave 79701
Affirmed Ave 79705
Ainslee St 79701
Alamo Dr 79703
Alcove Ct 79703
Alford St 79705
Alicia Ct 79707
Alkan St 79706
Allandale Ct 79707
Allorenw Dr 79705
Almey Ct 79707
Almont Pl 79705
Alpine St 79703
Alta Ave 79705
Alta Vista Dr 79706
Alysheba Ln 79705
Amelia Dr 79703
Amhurst Ct 79705
Amigo Dr 79703
Amistad Dr 79707
Andover Ave 79705
Andrews Hwy
100-198 79701
200-3299 79701
3300-5199 79703
5401-5899 79706
Anetta Dr 79703
Angelina Dr 79707
Ann Dr 79705
Apache Dr 79703
Apollo Ct 79707
Apperson Dr 79705
Apple Creek Rd 79707
Arapahoe 79705
Arbor Cir 79707
Arrowhead Trl 79705
Arroyo Dr 79707
Arthur Ct 79703
Ashdown Pl 79705
Ashlin Dr 79705
Ashwood Ct 79707
Aspen Dr 79707
Aster Ave 79707
Atlanta St 79701
Auburn Ct 79705
Auburn Dr 79705
Auburn Pl 79705
E Auburn St 79707
Audie Ct 79703
Augusta Dr 79705
Aurora Ln 79707
Austin St 79703
Avondale Dr 79703
Azalea Ct 79707
N B St
601-1699 79701
2000-2099 79705
S B St 79701
N & S Baird St 79701
Baldwin St 79701
Balfour Ct 79707
Baltic Ave 79705
Bandera Dr 79707
Bankhead Hwy 79701
Barkley Ave 79701
Barton Crk 79707

Barton Springs Ct 79707
Basin St 79703
Basswood Cir 79707
Bates St 79707
Baumann Ave
3200-3299 79701
3300-3699 79703
Bay Meadows Ln 79705
Bayberry Pkwy 79705
Baybridge Ct 79705
Baybrook Ct, Dr & Pl 79707
Beachwood St 79706
Beal Pkwy 79703
Beckley Dr 79703
Bedford Ave 79703
Bedford Dr 79701
Beechwood Ct 79707
Belaire Dr 79703
Belfield Ct 79705
Bella Pl 79707
Belle Grove Ct 79705
Bellechasse Ct 79705
Belmont St 79701
Belton Pl 79707
Bent Tree Trl 79707
Bentley Ct 79705
N Benton St 79705
S Benton St 79701
N & S Bentwood Dr 79703
Bermuda Ct 79707
N Big Spring St
100-1799 79701
1800-5300 79705
5302-5498 79705
S Big Spring St 79701
Billingsley Blvd 79705
Bishops Castle Dr 79705
Blackberry Cir & Ct 79705
Blackwood 79707
Blakemore Ct 79707
Blue Bonnet Ave 79707
Blue Haven Dr 79703
Bluebird Ln
2100-3299 79705
3300-3899 79707
Bluebird Branch Ct 79705
Boardwalk 79705
Boeing Dr
1401-1499 79701
2600-2699 79705
Bonham St 79703
Boulder Dr 79707
Bowie Dr 79703
Bowman Cir 79705
Boyd Ave
700-3299 79705
3400-3699 79707
Bradford Ct 79705
Brazos Ave & Ct 79707
Breckenridge Dr 79705
Breezeway Ct 79707
W Brennest Ave 79701
Brentwood Dr 79707
Briarpath Dr 79707
Briarwood Ave 79707
Bridgewater Cir 79707
Brighton Pl 79705
Brinson 79703
Bristol Ct 79705
E & W Broadway St 79701
Bromegrass St 79706
Bromley Pl 79705
Brookdale Dr 79703
Brooks Dr 79703
E Brown 79707
Brown Heart Ln 79707
Brownwood Dr 79703
Brunson Ave 79701
Brunswick Cir 79705
Bryant St
1700-1799 79701
1801-1899 79701
1901-2099 79705
Buchanan Pl 79707
Bunche St 79701
Burchill Dr 79703

Burleson St 79701
Butler Ave 79701
Butternut Ln 79705
N C St
100-1699 79701
2000-2099 79705
S C St 79701
Cactus Trl 79707
Caldera Blvd
2800-3199 79705
3201-3299 79705
3300-3699 79707
3900-3998 79705
Caldera Dr 79705
Calen Ct 79707
N & S Calhoun St 79701
E & W California Ave 79701
Callaway Dr 79707
Calumet St 79706
Camarie Ave
2300-3299 79705
3300-3599 79707
Cambridge Ct 79705
Camden 79707
Camino Reale 79707
Camp Dr & St 79701
Canadian Ave 79707
Candle Tree Cv 79705
Candlestick Dr 79706
Canemont Dr 79707
Canonero St 79705
Canterbury Dr 79705
Canyon Dr 79703
Cape Cod Ln 79707
Cardinal Ln
1700-1798 79705
3300-4599 79707
Carlton St 79701
Carmel Ct 79707
Carnation Ave 79707
Carol Ln 79705
Caroline Ct 79705
Carrington Ct 79707
N Carrizo St 79701
Carter Ave 79701
Carver St 79705
N Carver St
101-297 79701
299-599 79701
601-699 79701
1801-1899 79705
S Carver St 79701
Casady Ct 79707
Cascade Ct 79703
Casper Ct 79705
Castle Pine Rd 79707
Castle Rock Ct 79705
Castleford Rd 79705
Cedar Ave 79705
Cedar Creek Rd 79705
Cedar Spring Dr 79703
Centerview 79707
Century Dr 79703
Cerrillos Ave 79705
Cessna Dr 79705
Chadwick Ct 79707
Challenger Dr 79706
Champions Dr 79706
Chaparral St 79706
Chapel Hill Dr 79705
Charismatic Dr 79705
Chatham Ct 79705
Checotah 79705
Chelsea Pl 79705
Cherokee Dr 79703
Cherry Ln 79701
E & W Cherrywood Ct & Dr 79707
Chesley Ct 79707
Chestnut Ave 79701
Cheyenne St 79706
Chickasaw 79705
Chisos Dr 79707
Choate Pl 79707
Choctaw 79705
Chon Cv 79707

Chretien Pl ... 79705
Chukar Ln ... 79706
Churchill Way ... 79705
Cimmaron Ave
2300-2498 ... 79705
2500-3299 ... 79705
3300-4599 ... 79707
Cimmaron Dr ... 79705
Cindy Pl ... 79707
E Circle Dr ... 79701
Cisco ... 79705
Citation ... 79705
City View Rd ... 79701
Claremont Dr ... 79707
Clarewood Dr ... 79707
Clark St ... 79701
N & S Clay St ... 79701
Clayton Ct ... 79707
Clemente Ct ... 79706
Cloud Ave ... 79705
Cloudcroft Ct ... 79707
Cloverdale Rd ... 79701
Club Dr
100-1599 ... 79701
2100-2198 ... 79705
Coleman Ct ... 79705
E Colgate St ... 79707
Coliseum Ct ... 79706
College Ave ... 79701
Collins Ave ... 79701
Colonial Oaks ... 79705
N & S Colorado St ... 79701
Colt Ct ... 79706
Comanche Dr ... 79703
E Comiskey ... 79706
Commerce Dr ... 79703
Commercial Dr ... 79701
Common Electric ... 79706
Community Ln ... 79701
Compton Dr ... 79707
Concho Dr ... 79707
Concord Ave ... 79705
Connell St ... 79701
Conroe Ct ... 79707
Copus St ... 79705
Coquina Ct & Ln ... 79707
Cord Dr ... 79705
Corporate Dr ... 79705
Corsair ... 79707
Cotton Flt ... 79706
Cotton Flat Rd
1200-1298 ... 79701
1300-1899 ... 79701
1901-2399 ... 79701
3900-4099 ... 79706
Cottonwood Ave ... 79705
E Cottonwood Rd ... 79707
Country Club Dr
900-2699 ... 79701
4300-4899 ... 79703
E County Road 101 ... 79706
E County Road 102 ... 79706
E County Road 103 ... 79706
E & W County Road 104 ... 79706
S County Road 1040 ... 79706
E County Road 105 ... 79706
N County Road 1050 ... 79706
S County Road 1058 ... 79706
E County Road 106 ... 79706
S County Road 1060 ... 79706
N County Road 1061 ... 79706
S County Road 1063 ... 79706
S County Road 1065 ... 79706
S County Road 1066 ... 79706
S County Road 1067 ... 79706
N & S County Road 1068 ... 79706
S County Road 1069 ... 79706
E County Road 107 ... 79706
N & S County Road 1070 ... 79706
S County Road 1071 ... 79706
S County Road 1072 ... 79706
E County Road 108 ... 79706
N County Road 1081 ... 79706
S County Road 1082 ... 79706
S County Road 1083 ... 79706
N & S County Road 1084 ... 79706
S County Road 1084 1/2 ... 79706
S County Road 1085 ... 79706
N & S County Road 1086 ... 79706
N & S County Road 1087 ... 79706
S County Road 1089 ... 79706
E County Road 109 ... 79706
N & S County Road 1090 ... 79706
S County Road 1096 ... 79706
E & W County Road 110 ... 79706
S County Road 1101 ... 79706
N & S County Road 1105 ... 79706
E & W County Road 111 ... 79706
N & S County Road 1110 ... 79706
S County Road 1114 ... 79706
S County Road 1115 ... 79706
N County Road 1117 ... 79705
S County Road 1117 ... 79706
N County Road 1118 ... 79705
S County Road 1118 ... 79706
N County Road 1119 ... 79705
S County Road 1119 ... 79706
W County Road 112 ... 79706
N County Road 1120
1000-2499 ... 79706
N County Road 1120
4600-5399 ... 79705
S County Road 1120 ... 79706
S County Road 1121 ... 79706
S County Road 1122 ... 79706
N County Road 1123 ... 79705
N County Road 1125
2301-2399 ... 79706
4200-5399 ... 79705
S County Road 1126 ... 79706
N County Road 1127
1400-2298 ... 79706
2300-2499 ... 79706
4000-4399 ... 79705
S County Road 1127 ... 79706
N County Road 1128 ... 79705
S County Road 1128 ... 79706
N County Road 1129 ... 79705
S County Road 1129 ... 79706
E & W County Road 113 ... 79706
N County Road 1130
1000-1999 ... 79706
2200-2298 ... 79705
2300-5899 ... 79705
S County Road 1130 ... 79706
S County Road 1131 ... 79706
N County Road 1133 ... 79705
S County Road 1133 ... 79706
N County Road 1134 ... 79705
S County Road 1134 ... 79706
N County Road 1134 1/2 ... 79705
N County Road 1135 ... 79705
S County Road 1135 ... 79706
N County Road 1135 1/2 ... 79705
N & S County Road 1136 ... 79706
N County Road 1137 ... 79705
S County Road 1137 ... 79706
N County Road 1137 1/2 ... 79705
N County Road 1138 ... 79705
S County Road 1138 ... 79706
N County Road 1138 1/2 ... 79705
N County Road 1139 ... 79705
N County Road 1139 1/2 ... 79705
E & W County Road 114 ... 79706
W County Road 114 1/2 ... 79706
N County Road 1140
1400-1698 ... 79706
2000-4399 ... 79705
S County Road 1140 ... 79706
S County Road 1142 ... 79706
N County Road 1144 ... 79705
N County Road 1147 ... 79705
N County Road 1148 ... 79705
E & W County Road 115 ... 79706
W County Road 115 1/2 ... 79706
N County Road 1150 ... 79705
S County Road 1150 ... 79706
N & S County Road 1151 ... 79706
S County Road 1152 ... 79706
S County Road 1154 ... 79706
S County Road 1156 ... 79706
S County Road 1157 ... 79706
S County Road 1159 ... 79706
W County Road 116 ... 79706
W County Road 116 1/2 ... 79706
S County Road 1160 ... 79706
S County Road 1161 ... 79706
N County Road 1162 ... 79705
S County Road 1165 ... 79706
S County Road 1167 ... 79706
S County Road 1168 ... 79706
S County Road 1169 ... 79706
E & W County Road 117 ... 79706
S County Road 1172 ... 79706
S County Road 1173 ... 79706
S County Road 1175 ... 79706
S County Road 1178 ... 79706
W County Road 118 ... 79706
S County Road 1180 ... 79706
S County Road 1182 ... 79706
S County Road 1183 ... 79706
S County Road 1183 1/2 ... 79706
S County Road 1184 ... 79706
S County Road 1185 ... 79706
S County Road 1187 ... 79706
S County Road 1189 ... 79706
E & W County Road 119 ... 79706
S County Road 1191 ... 79706
S County Road 1191a ... 79706
S County Road 1192 ... 79706
S County Road 1193 ... 79706
S County Road 1194 ... 79706
S County Road 1195 ... 79706
S County Road 1196 ... 79706
S County Road 1197 ... 79706
S County Road 1198 ... 79706
S County Road 1199 ... 79706
E & W County Road 120 ... 79706
S County Road 1200 ... 79706
S County Road 1201 ... 79706
S County Road 1202 ... 79706
S County Road 1204 ... 79706
S County Road 1205 ... 79706
S County Road 1206 ... 79706
S County Road 1207 ... 79706
S County Road 1208 ... 79706
E & W County Road 121 ... 79706
S County Road 1210 ... 79706
S County Road 1211 ... 79706
S County Road 1212 ... 79706
S County Road 1213 ... 79706
S County Road 1214 ... 79706
S County Road 1215 ... 79706
S County Road 1216 ... 79706
S County Road 1217 ... 79706
S County Road 1218 ... 79706
S County Road 1220 ... 79706
S County Road 1221 ... 79706
S County Road 1222 ... 79706
S County Road 1223 ... 79706
S County Road 1223 1/2 ... 79706
S County Road 1224 ... 79706
S County Road 1225 ... 79706
S County Road 1226 ... 79706
S County Road 1227 ... 79706
E & W County Road 123 ... 79706
S County Road 1230 ... 79706
E & W County Road 124 ... 79706
N County Road 1241 ... 79707
S County Road 1242 ... 79706
N County Road 1243 ... 79707
N County Road 1244 ... 79707
N County Road 1246 ... 79707
N County Road 1247 ... 79707
S County Road 1247 ... 79706
E & W County Road 125 ... 79706
N County Road 1250 ... 79707
S County Road 1250 ... 79706
N County Road 1255 ... 79707
S County Road 1255 ... 79706
S County Road 1257 ... 79706
E & W County Road 126 ... 79706
N County Road 1260 ... 79707
S County Road 1260 ... 79706
S County Road 1262 ... 79706
S County Road 1264 ... 79706
S County Road 1265 ... 79706
E & W County Road 127 ... 79706
S County Road 1270 ... 79706
N County Road 1273 ... 79707
N County Road 1275 ... 79707
S County Road 1276 ... 79706
N County Road 1278 ... 79707
S County Road 1278 ... 79706
E County Road 128 ... 79706
N County Road 1283 ... 79707
N County Road 1284 ... 79707
S County Road 1285 ... 79706
S County Road 1288 ... 79706
S County Road 1289 ... 79706
E County Road 129 ... 79706
N County Road 1294 ... 79707
N County Road 1297 ... 79707
N County Road 1298 ... 79707
County Road 130 ... 79706
S County Road 1302 ... 79707
S County Road 1309 ... 79707
E & W County Road 132 ... 79706
E & W County Road 133 ... 79706
W County Road 134 ... 79706
E & W County Road 135 ... 79706
E & W County Road 136 ... 79706
E County Road 136 1/2 ... 79706
E & W County Road 137 ... 79706
E & W County Road 138 ... 79706
E & W County Road 139 ... 79706
E & W County Road 140 ... 79706
E County Road 141 ... 79706
E & W County Road 142 ... 79706
E & W County Road 143 ... 79706
W County Road 143 1/2 ... 79706
E & W County Road 144 ... 79706
E & W County Road 145 ... 79706
E County Road 146 ... 79706
E & W County Road 148 ... 79706
E & W County Road 149 ... 79706
E & W County Road 150 ... 79706
E County Road 151 ... 79706
W County Road 152 ... 79706
E County Road 153 ... 79706
E & W County Road 154 ... 79706
W County Road 155 ... 79706
E County Road 156 ... 79706
E County Road 157 ... 79706
E County Road 158 ... 79706
E County Road 159 ... 79706
E & W County Road 160 ... 79706
W County Road 162 ... 79706
W County Road 166 ... 79706
W County Road 170 ... 79706
W County Road 174 ... 79706
W County Road 180 ... 79706
W County Road 181 ... 79706
W County Road 182 ... 79706
W County Road 183 ... 79706
W County Road 184 ... 79706
W County Road 185 ... 79706
W County Road 186 ... 79706
E County Road 190 ... 79706
E County Road 230 ... 79706
W County Road 270 ... 79706
W County Road 30 ... 79707
E County Road 300 ... 79706
W County Road 302 ... 79706
E County Road 320 ... 79706
W County Road 33 ... 79707
W County Road 330 ... 79706
W County Road 35 ... 79707
W County Road 39 ... 79707
E County Road 40 ... 79705
W County Road 40 ... 79707
W County Road 41 ... 79707
E & W County Road 44 ... 79707
W County Road 45 ... 79707
W County Road 46 ... 79707
W County Road 48 ... 79707
E County Road 50 ... 79705
W County Road 50 ... 79707
W County Road 51 ... 79707
E County Road 52 ... 79705
W County Road 52 ... 79707
E County Road 53 ... 79705
W County Road 53 ... 79707
W County Road 54 ... 79707
E County Road 55 ... 79705
W County Road 55 ... 79707
W County Road 56 ... 79707
E County Road 57 ... 79705
W County Road 57 ... 79707
E County Road 58 ... 79705
W County Road 58 ... 79707
E County Road 59 ... 79705
W County Road 59 ... 79707
E County Road 60 ... 79705
W County Road 60 ... 79707
E County Road 61 ... 79705
E County Road 62 ... 79705
E County Road 63 ... 79705
E County Road 64 ... 79705
E County Road 65 ... 79705
E County Road 66 ... 79705
E County Road 67 ... 79705
W County Road 67 ... 79707
W County Road 68 ... 79707
W County Road 69 ... 79707
E County Road 71 ... 79705
E County Road 72 ... 79705
W County Road 72 ... 79707
E County Road 73 ... 79705
E County Road 75
5000-5499 ... 79705
6300-6499 ... 79706
W County Road 75 ... 79707
E County Road 75 1/2 ... 79705
E County Road 76 ... 79705
E County Road 76 1/2 ... 79705
E County Road 77 ... 79705
W County Road 77 ... 79707
E County Road 78 ... 79705
E County Road 79 ... 79705
E County Road 81
4000-4299 ... 79705
12500-12698 ... 79706
12700-12799 ... 79706
E County Road 83 ... 79706
E County Road 84 ... 79706
E County Road 85 ... 79706
E County Road 86 ... 79706
E County Road 89 ... 79706
E County Road 90 ... 79706
E County Road 91 ... 79706
W County Road 91 ... 79707
E County Road 92 ... 79706
E County Road 93 ... 79706
E County Road 94 ... 79706
E County Road 95 ... 79706
E County Road 96 ... 79706
E County Road 97 ... 79706
E County Road 98 ... 79706
County Road C2300 ... 79705
Courtney Ct ... 79707
Courtyard Dr ... 79705
Coventry Ln ... 79705
E & W Cowden Ave ... 79701
Coyote Trl ... 79707
Cranston Pl ... 79707
Crenshaw Dr ... 79705
Crescent Pl ... 79705
Crested Butte Ct ... 79705
Crestgate Ave ... 79707
Crestline Ave ... 79707
Crestmont Dr ... 79707
Crestridge Dr ... 79707
N & S Crestview Rd ... 79701
Crestwood Ave ... 79707
Crista Ln ... 79707
Crockett Ave ... 79703
Crosley Dr ... 79706
Crowley Blvd ... 79707
Crump St ... 79701
Culpeper Dr ... 79705
Culver Dr ... 79705
Cunningham Dr ... 79703
E Cuthbert Ave ... 79701
W Cuthbert Ave
100-3299 ... 79701
3300-4899 ... 79703
Cynthia Dr ... 79705
Cypress Ct ... 79707
N D St
400-498 ... 79701
500-1699 ... 79701
1700-1798 ... 79705
1800-2299 ... 79705
S D St ... 79701
Dahlia Ave ... 79707
E & W Dakota Ave ... 79701
N & S Dallas St ... 79701
Dalton Dr ... 79705
Dartmouth Dr ... 79705
Daventry Pl ... 79705
Davis Ave & St ... 79701
Dawn Cir ... 79707
Dayton Rd ... 79706
Deauville ... 79706
Debbie Cv ... 79707
Deeanna Ln ... 79707
Deer Run Ave ... 79707
Deerfield Dr ... 79705
Delano Ave
2500-2598 ... 79701
2600-3299 ... 79701
3300-3399 ... 79703
Dellwood St ... 79703
Delmar Dr & St ... 79703
E Dengar Ave ... 79705
W Dengar Ave
100-3299 ... 79705
3300-4799 ... 79707
Dentcrest Dr ... 79707
Denton St ... 79703
Desert Wind ... 79707
Desta Dr ... 79705
Devlin Pl ... 79707
Devonian Dr ... 79703
Devonshire Ct ... 79705
N & S Dewberry Dr ... 79703
Diamond Dr ... 79707
Dimaggio Ct ... 79706
Dodson St ... 79701
Dogwood Ct ... 79707
Donald St ... 79701
Dora Pl ... 79707
Doral Ct ... 79705
E & W Dormard Ave ... 79705
Douglas Ave
700-898 ... 79701
900-2099 ... 79701
3300-4399 ... 79703
Douglas Dr ... 79701
Downing Ave ... 79707
E Drake St ... 79707
Drexel Ct ... 79707
Driftwood Dr ... 79707
Dukes Dr ... 79705
Dunbar St ... 79703
Dunbarton Oaks Blvd ... 79705
Dunblane Dr ... 79707
Dunkirk St ... 79707
Dunraven Ct ... 79707
Durant Dr ... 79705
Dyer Cir ... 79707
S E St ... 79701
Eagle Cv ... 79707
Eastwood Dr ... 79703
Ebbets ... 79707
Edgebrook Ct, Dr & Pl ... 79707
Edgemont Dr ... 79707
Edgewood Dr ... 79703
Edinburgh Dr ... 79707
Edwards St ... 79701
N Edwards St ... 79705
N & S Eisenhower Dr ... 79703
Eldorado Dr ... 79707
Elizabeth Ave ... 79701
Elk Ave ... 79701
Elkins Rd ... 79705
Ellen Jayne Way ... 79707
Elm Ave ... 79705
Elma Dr ... 79707
Elwyn ... 79701
Emerson Ct ... 79705
Emerson Dr ... 79705
Emerson Ln ... 79705
Emerson Pl ... 79705
E Emerson St ... 79707
Empresa Dr ... 79706
English Dr ... 79705
Erie Dr ... 79703
E & W Estes Ave ... 79701
Eugene Ave ... 79705
Evans ... 79701
Evans Ln ... 79705
Evening Star ... 79707
Evergreen Ave ... 79707
Executive Ct ... 79707
Exeter Ave ... 79705
N & S F St ... 79701
Fairbanks Dr ... 79707
Faircircle ... 79707
Fairfax Ct ... 79705
Fairfield Ln ... 79705
Fairgate Dr ... 79707
Fairgreen Ct ... 79707
N Fairgrounds Rd
800-1799 ... 79706
1901-1999 ... 79705
2200-4398 ... 79705
S Fairgrounds Rd
300-1198 ... 79701
1200-1600 ... 79701
1602-2098 ... 79701
2100-2199 ... 79706
Fairhaven Ct ... 79707
Fairmount Dr ... 79703
Fairpark Rd ... 79701

Fairview Ln 79705
Fairwood Ct & Dr 79707
Falcon Pl 79707
Fannin Ave
2301-2397 79705
2399-3299 79705
3300-4599 79707
Faulkner Dr 79705
Feldspar Ln 79707
Fenway 79707
Fern Ave 79707
Ferncliff Ave 79707
Fielder St 79707
Fields Pl 79705
Fiesta Ave 79705
Fir Dr 79707
Fisher St 79701
Flare Ct 79705
E & W Florida Ave 79701
Floyd Ct 79705
Flynt 79701
Fm 1208 79706
Fm 1213 79706
Fm 1357 79706
E Fm 1379 79706
W Fm 1787 79706
N Fm 1788 79707
S Fm 1788 79706
E Fm 2401 79706
Fm 307 79706
Fm 715 79706
E Fordham St 79707
N & S Fort Worth St 79701
Fox Hollow Ct 79707
Foxboro Ct 79705
E & W Francis Ave 79701
Franklin Ave 79701
Fredna Pl 79707
Freeport Ln 79707
Friar Tuck Ct 79707
Fringewood Dr 79707
E & W Front St 79701
Frontier Dr 79705
Frost Pl 79705
N & S G St 79701
Garden Ln 79701
Garden City Hwy 79701
N Garfield 79701
N Garfield St
501-1597 79701
1599-1700 79701
1701-2099 79705
1702-2398 79701
2301-2399 79701
2600-2798 79705
2800-5199 79705
S Garfield St 79701
Gaston Dr 79703
Gateway Ct & St 79707
Gehrig Ave 79706
Genchil Dr 79707
George Ave 79705
Geraldine St 79707
E & W Gist Ave 79701
Gladewood Dr 79707
Gladiola Ave 79707
Glasgow Dr 79707
Gleneagles Ct & Dr 79707
N & S Glenwood Dr 79703
Goddard Ct, Dr & Pl 79705
Godfrey Ct 79707
Godfrey St
300-1399 79703
1401-1499 79703
2901-3897 79707
3899-4199 79707
Golden Gate Dr 79707
Golf Course Rd 79705
E Golf Course Rd
101-397 79701
399-1800 79701
1802-1998 79701
2100-2699 79706
W Golf Course Rd
800-3299 79701
3300-3500 79703
3502-3598 79703
Goliad Dr 79703
S Goode St 79701
Graceland Dr 79703
Graham Dr 79705
Granite Ln 79707
Grassland Blvd & Ct 79707
Greathouse Ave 79707
Green Hill Ct 79707
Green Tree Blvd 79707
Greenbriar Dr 79707
Greenridge 79707
Greenville Dr 79707
Greenwich Dr 79705
W Griffin Ave 79701
Griffith Ct 79706
Guadalupe 79707
Gulf Ave
800-3199 79705
3500-4699 79707
N H St
1600-1699 79701
1700-2200 79705
2202-2298 79705
S H St 79701
Hackberry Ct 79707
Half Moon Cir 79707
E & W Hamby Ave 79701
Hanover Dr 79705
Harlowe Dr 79703
Harmony Dr 79703
Harris Ave 79701
Harrison St 79701
Hart Ave 79701
Harvard Ave
800-898 79701
900-2700 79701
2702-3198 79701
4300-4899 79703
Hathaway Ct 79707
Hawthorne Dr 79705
Haynes Ave 79707
Haynes Dr 79705
Haywood Dr 79707
Heartland Ct 79707
Heather Rd 79705
Heidelberg Ln 79707
Helen Greathouse Cir 79707
S Henderson Blvd 79701
Hereford Blvd 79707
Heritage Blvd 79707
Hermitage Ct 79705
Hialeah Dr 79705
Hickory Ave 79705
E & W Hicks Ave 79701
Highland Blvd & Ct 79707
Highsky Dr 79707
E & W Highway 80 79706
Hill Ave
3200-3299 79701
3300-3499 79703
Hillcrest Ct & Pl 79707
Hillsboro Ct 79705
Hilltop Dr 79707
Hodges St
1600-1699 79701
2600-2699 79705
Hogan Ct 79705
N Holiday Hill Rd 79707
Hollendale 79705
Holloway Ave 79701
Holly Dr 79703
Holmsley Ave 79701
Homestead Blvd 79707
Hopi Ct 79705
Houston Ave 79701
Howard Dr 79703
Hoya Dr 79707
Hudson Ave 79705
Hughes St 79705
Humble Ave
201-1097 79705
1099-3199 79705
3400-4699 79707
Hummingbird Ct 79705
Hunter St 79701
Huntington St 79705
Hyde Park Ave 79707
N I St
201-1597 79701
1599-1699 79701
1701-1797 79705
1799-3299 79705
S I St 79701
Idlewilde Dr
400-1699 79703
1700-2398 79707
2400-2699 79707
E Illinois Ave 79701
W Illinois Ave
200-998 79701
1000-3299 79701
3300-5200 79703
5202-5298 79703
Imperial Ave 79707
E & W Indiana Ave 79701
E Industrial Ave 79701
W Industrial Ave
101-3299 79701
3401-5299 79703
5401-6297 79706
6299-6499 79706
6501-9999 79706
E Industrial Loop 79701
S Industrial Loop 79701
W Industrial Loop 79701
E Interstate 20
301-2699 79701
E Interstate 20
2600-6399 79706
W Interstate 20
200-798 79701
800-3299 79701
3301-3399 79701
4400-4899 79706
4901-10199 79706
5100-5298 79703
6300-10098 79706
Inwood Ct 79705
Ironwood 79707
Irvin Dr 79705
Irwin Ct 79705
Island Cir & Dr 79707
N & S J St 79701
N Jackson St
100-198 79701
200-799 79701
1900-2199 79705
S Jackson St 79701
Jacotte Cir 79705
Jadewood Dr 79707
Jasmine Dr 79706
E & W Jax Ave 79701
S Jefferson St 79701
Jesse St 79701
Johnston St 79701
Jordan Ave 79707
Joy Dr 79703
Juniper Ct 79707
N & S K St 79701
Kanawha 79705
E Kansas Ave 79701
W Kansas Ave
100-598 79701
600-3299 79701
3300-3598 79703
3600-3899 79703
Keenland Dr 79707
Keith St
1201-1297 79701
1299-1400 79701
1402-1798 79701
1900-2099 79705
Kensington Ln 79705
Kent St 79701
E & W Kentucky Ave 79701
Keri Ct 79705
Kerth St 79703
Kessler Ave 79701
Keswick Cv & Rd 79705
Keystone Ct 79705
Kimsey Way 79705
King St 79701
King Richards Row 79707
Kingsboro Ct 79705
Kingston Dr 79705
Kingwood Ct 79707
Kiowa Dr 79703
Kniffen Dr 79705
Knights Pl 79705
Koufax Ct 79706
N L St
300-1598 79701
1600-1699 79701
1701-1897 79705
1899-2799 79705
S L St 79701
La Jolla Cv 79707
La Salle Cir 79707
Lafayette Pl 79705
Laforce Blvd 79706
Lajitas Dr 79707
Lakes Dr 79705
N Lamesa Rd
101-397 79701
399-1799 79701
1900-3298 79705
3300-5199 79705
S Lamesa Rd 79701
Lancashire Rd 79705
Lanham St
700-1499 79701
3300-4699 79705
Lantana Ln 79705
Latta St 79701
Laura Dr 79703
Lavaca Ave & Ct 79707
Lawson Ave 79701
Lazywood Ln 79705
Learmont Dr 79705
Leddy Dr 79703
N & S Lee St 79701
Legacy Oaks 79705
Legends Blvd 79706
Lehigh Dr 79707
Leisure Dr 79703
Lemonwood Ct & Dr 79707
Lennox Dr 79707
Lexington St 79705
Liberator Ln 79706
Liberty 79706
Liddon Ave 79705
Limestone Ln 79707
Lincoln Grn 79707
N Lincoln St 79701
S Lincoln St 79701
Linda Ct 79705
Lindora Way 79707
Little John Ln 79707
Live Oak Dr 79705
Livingston St 79707
Llano Ct 79707
Lockheed Ave 79703
Lockheed Dr 79701
Locksley 79707
Loma Dr 79705
Loma Vista St 79701
London Pl 79707
Longhorn Ln 79707
E & W Longview Ave 79701
Lonoke Ave 79707
E Loop 250 N 79705
N Loop 250 W
301-497 79703
N Loop 250 W
499-1000 79703
1002-1598 79703
1301-1399 79706
1701-1897 79707
1899-3399 79707
3401-3499 79707
S Loop 250 W 79703
W Loop 250 N
500-2298 79705
2300-3199 79705
3300-4498 79707
4500-5399 79707
Loop 40 79711
N & S Loraine St 79701
Los Alamitos Ct & Dr 79705
Los Conchos Ln 79705
Los Patios Dr 79707
E Louisiana Ave 79701
W Louisiana Ave
100-2316 79701
2315-2315 79704
2318-3298 79701
2401-3299 79701
3300-3799 79703
N Loyola Ave 79707
Lynn Ave 79705
N & S M St 79701
Ma Mar Ave 79705
Ma Mar Ct 79707
Maberry St
1400-1498 79701
1700-1899 79705
N & S Madison St 79701
Magnolia Ave 79705
Maid Marian Ct 79707
N Main St
100-1799 79701
1800-2399 79705
2401-3199 79705
S Main St 79701
Mann St 79701
Manor Ct & St 79703
Manor Village Cir 79707
Mantle Ct 79706
S Mantrai 79706
Maple Ave 79705
Maranatha Pl 79707
Marble Ln 79707
Marchelle Ct 79705
Marcie Ct & Ln 79707
Mariana Ave
300-3299 79701
3300-3399 79703
Marie Dr 79705
N Marienfeld St
100-398 79701
400-1399 79701
1401-1699 79701
1701-1897 79705
1899-1900 79705
1902-1998 79705
S Marienfeld St 79701
Marinor Ct 79705
Mark Ln 79707
Market St 79703
Marlin St 79701
Marmon Dr 79705
N & S Marshall St 79701
Mathis St 79707
Maxwell Dr
2300-3299 79705
3300-3399 79707
Mays Dr 79706
Mcclintic St
1600-1699 79701
2600-2699 79705
Mcdonald St
100-1699 79703
1700-2999 79707
Mckenzie St 79701
Mckittrick Dr 79707
Meadow Dr 79703
Meadowbrook Dr 79705
Meadowlark Ln 79707
Meadowpark Dr 79705
Meadowridge Ln 79707
Meadowview Ln 79707
Meadowwood Ct 79705
Medina Dr 79707
Melton Aly 79705
Melville Dr 79705
Memorial 79706
Mercedes Dr 79703
Meredith Pl 79707
Merrill Ct & Dr 79707
Mesquite Ln 79701
Meta Dr 79701
Metz Ct, Dr & Pl 79705
E Michigan Ave 79701
W Michigan Ave
712-798 79701
800-3299 79701
3300-3799 79703
N Midkiff Rd
200-1299 79701
1301-1699 79701
1901-2597 79705
2599-5599 79705
S Midkiff Rd
700-2500 79701
2502-2598 79701
2700-2899 79706
N Midland Dr
300-1799 79703
1800-5699 79707
5701-6099 79707
S Midland Dr 79703
Midway 79707
Mile High 79706
Millbrook Pl 79707
Miller Ct & Dr 79705
Milltown Rd 79705
Mimosa Ct 79707
N & S Mineola St 79701
Mira Vista Cir 79705
Mission Ct 79703
Mississippi Ave 79701
E & W Missouri Ave 79701
Mitchell St 79701
Mockingbird 79705
Mockingbird Ln
100-599 79705
3300-6599 79707
Mogford St
600-698 79701
700-1499 79701
2800-3198 79705
Monclave Dr 79703
Monterrey Dr 79703
E & W Montgomery
Ave 79701
Monticello Ct 79705
Monty Dr 79703
Moran St 79701
Morgan Way 79705
Moss Ave 79705
Moss Ct 79707
Mosswood Dr 79707
Mount Vernon Ct 79705
Mulberry Ln
1101-1899 79701
2100-2399 79706
Murray St 79701
Mustang Dr 79707
N N St
100-1699 79701
2000-2598 79705
2600-2699 79705
S N St 79701
Nash Ave 79705
Nassau Dr 79707
Nasworthy Pl 79707
Navajo 79705
Navarrado 79707
Neely Ave
400-2699 79705
2701-3099 79705
3300-4799 79707
4801-4899 79707
Neely Ct 79707
Neill Ave 79701
Nelson Rd 79707
Network Dr 79703
E & W New Jersey
Ave 79701
E & W New York Ave 79701
Newcastle Dr 79705
Nicklaus St 79705
E & W Nobles Ave 79701
Noel Ave 79705
Nolan Ryan Dr 79706
Norden Dr 79706
Normandy Ln 79705
Northcrest Dr 79707
Northfield Ct & Dr 79707
Northrup Dr 79705
Northtown Ct & Pl 79705
Norwood St 79707
Nottingham Ln 79707
N O St 79701
E & W Oak Ave 79705
Oak Creek Dr 79707
Oak Valley Dr 79707
Oaklawn Dr & Park 79705
Oakmont Dr 79707
Oakridge Ct & Dr 79707
Oakwood Ct 79707
E Ohio Ave 79701
W Ohio Ave
100-298 79701
300-3299 79701
3300-3600 79703
3602-3798 79703
Ojibwa 79705
Oliver St 79701
Olympic Ct 79706
Onyx Dr 79706
Opal Ct 79707
Orchard Ln 79701
Oriental Ave 79705
Oriole Dr 79707
Osage 79705
Oxford St 79703
Pacific Ave 79705
Pagewood Dr 79707
Palmer Dr 79705
Palo Duro Dr 79707
Palo Verde Gln 79705
Palomino 79705
Paradise Ln 79707
Park Ln
3200-3299 79701
3300-3599 79703
Parkdale Dr 79703
E & W Parker Ave 79701
Parkhurst Dr 79707
Parkwood Dr 79703
Parsley 79701
Parton Way 79705
Pasadena Dr 79703
Passage Way 79705
Patman Pl 79707
Patrick Pl 79705
Peach St 79701
Pebble Ct 79707
E & W Pecan Ave &
Ct 79705
E Peck Ave 79701
Pecon Tree 79706
N Pecos St
400-1198 79701
1200-1400 79701
1402-1498 79701
1900-2098 79705
2100-3099 79705
3101-3299 79705
S Pecos St 79701
Pedernales Dr 79707
E & W Pennsylvania
Ave 79701
Permian Ct 79703
Permit Number 79701
Perry St 79705
Peve House Pkwy 79707
Phillip Pl 79707
Pilot Ave 79706
Pimlico Dr 79707
E & W Pine Ave & Ct 79705
Pine Meadow Dr 79705
Pinehurst Dr 79705
Pinemont Dr 79707
Pinewood Ct 79705
Pinion Ct 79707
Placid Ct 79703
Player Ct 79705
Plaza St 79701
Pleasant Ct & Dr 79703
Polo Pkwy 79706
Polo Club Rd 79705
Porterfield Rd 79705
Portico Way 79707
Powell St 79701
Prairie Ridge Dr 79707
Pratt St 79701

Preston Dr 79707
Princeton Ave
900-3299 79701
3300-5100 79703
5102-5298 79703
Private Road C2100 79705
Private Road C2133 79705
Private Road C2153 79705
Private Road C2161 79705
Private Road C2193 79705
Private Road C2200 79705
Private Road C2205 79705
Private Road C2232 79705
Private Road C2234 79705
Private Road C2240 79705
Private Road C2300 79705
Providence Dr 79707
Pueblo 79705
Purple Sage Cv & Trl 79705
Pylant St 79703
Quail Pt 79705
Quail Run 79707
Quail Ridge Rd 79706
Quartz Ln 79707
Queens Ct 79707
Quicksand Cv & Dr 79707
Racquet Club Dr 79705
Radcliff Ct 79707
Rainbow Cir & Rd 79707
Raleigh Ct 79707
Ranchland Dr 79705
Ranger St 79707
Rangers Ct 79706
Rangewood 79707
Rankin Hwy 79701
Raymond Rd 79703
Reading Ave 79707
Rebel Dr 79707
Reeves Cir 79703
Regal Pl 79707
Regency Oaks 79705
Reo Ct & Dr 79705
Rhode Island Ave 79701
Ric Dr 79703
N Rice Ave 79707
Richmond Ct & Dr 79705
Ridgeboro Ct 79707
Ridgefield Ct 79707
Ridgemont Ct & Pl 79707
Ridglea Dr 79701
Ridgmar Ct 79707
Rio Grande Ave 79707
Riverfront Dr 79706
Riviera Ct 79705
Roadrunner Trl 79707
Robin Ln 79707
Robin Hood Ct 79707
Rocky Lane Dr 79703
Roosevelt Ave 79701
Roosevelt Dr 79703
Rosalind Redfern Grover Pkwy 79701
Rosemont Dr 79707
Rosewood Dr 79707
Rosita Dr 79707
Ruby Dr 79703
Ruidoso Ct 79707
Russell Ct & Dr 79707
Rustic Trl 79707
Sabine Dr 79707
Saddle Club Dr 79705
Saddle Horn Ln 79707
Sage St 79705
Sagemont Dr 79707
Saint Andrews Ct & Dr 79707
Salisbury Pl 79707
San Andres 79706
San Angelo St 79701
San Antonio Ave & Ct 79707
San Saba Ave & Ct 79707
Sandelwood Dr 79703
Sandhill Cir 79705
Sands St 79705
Santa Anita Ln 79705
Saratoga Dr 79707
Savoy Pl 79705
E & W Scharbauer Dr 79705
Scottsboro Ln 79707
Seaboard Ave
1500-3299 79705
3500-3599 79707
Seattle Slew Trl 79705
Secor St 79701
Secretariat St 79705
Seminole Dr 79703
Semper Fidelis 79705
Sentinel Ave 79703
Sentinel Dr 79701
Sequoia Dr 79707
Shady Bend Ct 79707
Shady Oak Ct 79707
Shadylane Dr 79703
Shadyview Pl 79707
E Shandon Ave 79705
W Shandon Ave
100-3299 79705
3300-3699 79707
Shanks Dr 79705
Shawnee 79705
Shea Ln 79706
Shell Ave
700-3299 79705
3400-3700 79707
3702-3898 79707
Sherwood Dr 79707
Shirley Ct & Ln 79705
Siesta Ln 79705
Silverton Dr 79705
Sinclair Ave
700-3299 79705
3301-3397 79707
3399-5299 79707
5301-5399 79707
Sioux Ct 79705
Sir Barton Pkwy 79705
Skyline Dr 79707
Skywood 79705
Smith Rd 79705
E Solomon Ln 79705
Sonora Dr 79707
E & W Sorrell Ln 79705
South St 79701
Southampton Ln 79705
Southridge Ct 79705
Sparks St
1100-1699 79701
1700-1998 79705
Spartan Dr 79705
Spence Dr 79707
Spraberry Dr 79703
Spring Meadow Ct & Ln 79705
Spring Park Dr 79705
Springfield Ct 79707
Springmont Dr 79707
Springwood Ct 79705
E & W Spruce Ave 79705
Spy Glass 79705
Stanolind Ave
800-3299 79705
3400-4499 79707
Stanolind Ct 79707
State St 79703
E State Highway 158 79706
W State Highway 158 79707
State Highway 191 79707
N State Highway 349
6100-7099 79705
N State Highway 349
24700-29499 79706
S State Highway 349 79706
Stellar Pl 79707
Sterling Ct & Pl 79707
Stewart Ave 79707
Stillmeadow Dr 79707
E & W Stokes Ave 79701
Stonecrest 79707
Stoneleigh Dr 79705
S Stonewall St 79701
Stoneybrook Dr 79703
Storey Ave
500-2699 79701
2701-3299 79701
3300-5299 79703
E Stratford 79707
Stratford Ct 79705
Stratton Dr 79707
Stutz Ct, Dr & Pl 79705
Suffolk Dr 79705
E Summit Ave 79701
Sunburst Dr 79707
Suncrest Ave 79707
Sundance Ct & Pl 79707
Sundown Cir 79705
Sunmore Cir 79707
Sunnyside Dr 79703
Sunrise Ct 79707
Sunset St 79701
Sunshine Pkwy 79707
Sweetbriar Dr 79703
Sycamore Ave
3200-3299 79701
3300-3499 79703
Tamarind Dr 79705
Tammy Cv 79707
Tampico Dr 79703
Tanforan Ave 79707
Tanglewood Dr 79703
Tank Farm 79706
Tanner Dr 79703
Tarleton St
1000-1099 79703
1101-1299 79703
1901-1997 79707
1999-2199 79707
Tattenham Cor 79707
E & W Taylor Ave 79701
Teakwood Trce 79707
Tealwood Pl 79707
Technology Cir 79703
Tejas 79705
Telluride Ct & Dr 79705
E & W Tennessee Ave 79701
Terra Ct 79705
Terrace Ave
2300-2699 79705
3300-3399 79707
N & S Terrell St 79701
E & W Texas Ave 79701
Texland Cir 79705
Thames Ct 79705
Thomas Ave
3100-3299 79701
3300-3599 79703
Thomas St 79703
Thomason Dr 79703
Thornberry Dr 79707
Thornridge Dr 79703
Three Rivers 79706
N & S Tilden St 79701
Timber Ct & Ln 79707
Timberglen Cir & Pl 79707
Timberwolf Trl 79705
Todd Dr
900-1699 79706
1800-4399 79705
Trade Dr 79706
Tradewinds Blvd 79706
Traillak Dr 79703
Travis Ave
3000-3299 79701
3300-3699 79703
Tremont Ave 79707
Trenton Dr 79707
Trevino St 79705
Trinidad Pl 79705
Trinity Ct & Dr 79707
Trinity Meadows Dr & Pl 79707
Trobaugh Blvd 79707
Tumbleweed Trl 79707
N Tyler St
100-699 79701
701-899 79701
1900-2100 79705
2102-2498 79705
S Tyler St 79701
Unbridled Trl 79705
Upland St
300-1399 79703
2000-2099 79707
Valley Dr 79707
Valley Frg 79705
Ventnor Ave 79705
Ventura Ave 79705
Verde Glen Ct 79707
Vermont Ave 79705
Versailles Dr 79703
Veterans Airpark Ln
301-497 79705
499-699 79705
612-612 79710
701-999 79705
Village Cir 79701
Virginia Ave 79705
Vista West Pkwy 79705
E Wadley Ave 79705
W Wadley Ave
100-3299 79705
3300-3399 79707
3304-3304 79708
3401-6199 79707
3500-6198 79707
Wagner Dr & St 79706
Walcott St 79701
Walker Ct & St 79701
E Wall St
100-1999 79701
100-100 79702
W Wall St
101-197 79701
199-3699 79701
3700-4100 79703
4102-5398 79703
Wallace Cir 79707
Walnut Ln 79701
Walton Ave 79705
Ward St
1000-1099 79701
1700-3400 79705
3402-4498 79705
Warehouse Rd 79703
Warwick Pl 79705
E & W Washington Ave 79701
Washita 79705
Watson Ct 79705
Watson St 79701
Waukomis Pl 79705
Waurika Pl 79705
Waverly Dr 79703
Wayside Dr 79701
N & S Weatherford St 79701
N Webster St 79705
S Webster St 79701
Wedgwood Ct & St 79707
Weeping Willow Ln 79705
Wellington Ct 79705
Westar Rd 79706
Westcliff Dr 79703
Western Dr 79705
Westminister Dr 79707
Westmont Ct 79707
Westwind Ct & Dr 79707
Wewoka Pl 79705
Whitaker St 79701
Whitman Dr 79705
Whitmire Blvd 79705
Whitney Dr
1200-1298 79701
2000-2098 79705
2100-2700 79705
2702-4098 79705
Whittle Way 79707
Widener Strip 79707
Willeys Ave 79701
Willingham Dr 79703
Willow Ct 79705
Willowood Dr 79703
Wilshire Dr 79703
Wimberley Spring Ct 79707
Winchester Ct 79705
Wind Chase 79707
Windecker St 79706
Windridge Cir 79705
Windrift 79707
Windsor Dr 79707
Winfield Rd 79705
E & W Wolcott Ave 79701
Wolfcamp Cir 79706
Wood Dr 79707
Woodbar Ct 79707
Woodcrest Dr 79703
Woodhaven Ct & Dr 79707
Woodhollow Dr 79707
Woodland Park Ave 79705
Woodlawn Dr 79705
Wright Dr 79706
Wrigley 79707
Wydewood Dr 79707
Wylea Cv 79707
Yearwood Dr 79707
Yorkshire Dr 79707
Younger Rd 79706

MINERAL WELLS TX

General Delivery 76068

POST OFFICE BOXES MAIN OFFICE STATIONS AND BRANCHES

Box No.s
All PO Boxes 76068

RURAL ROUTES

01, 02, 03, 04, 05, 06 76067

HIGHWAY CONTRACTS

51, 52 76067

NAMED STREETS

All Street Addresses 76067

NUMBERED STREETS

All Street Addresses 76067

MISSION TX

General Delivery 78572

POST OFFICE BOXES MAIN OFFICE STATIONS AND BRANCHES

Box No.s
1 - 5540 78573
8001 - 8131 78572

RURAL ROUTES

07, 09, 16, 17, 22, 28, 29, 39, 43, 90 78572
71, 72, 73, 74, 75, 76, 77, 78, 79, 80, 82 78573
04, 05, 06, 20, 21, 26, 30, 36, 38, 40, 45, 46 78574

NAMED STREETS

W A St 78572
Aarons Dr 78574
Abbott Ave 78574
Abilene Ave 78574
Abraham St 78573
Abram Blvd 78574
Abram Rd 78574
N Abram Rd
100-2299 78572
2301-2499 78572
2500-3599 78572
3601-3699 78572
4000-4998 78574
5000-11199 78574
S Abram Rd 78572
Acapulco Ave 78574
Acevedo Ln 78572
Acosta Cir E 78573
E Adams Ave 78573
W Adams Ave 78573
Adams Dr 78573
Adams St 78572
E Adams St 78573
Agua Ln 78572
Agua Dulce St 78572
Ahijada St 78574
Ala Blanca Ave 78572
N Ala Moana St 78573
Aladdin Villas W 78572
Alameda Cir & Dr 78574
N Alamo St 78573
N Alaska St 78574
Alberto Trevino St 78572
Alcala Ave 78573
Alcalca Ct 78572
Alcantar Ave 78573
Aldea St 78572
Aldo Dr 78574
Alegre Cir 78574
Alejandra St
800-1199 78573
2900-3200 78574
3202-3298 78574
Alejandro St 78573
Aleli 78573
Alex Dr 78572
Alexander Dr 78572
Alicia Ln 78572
Allende Ave 78573
Alma Ave 78572
Alona Ave 78574
Alpine Ave 78574
N Alton Ave 78573
N Alton Blvd 78573
S Alton Blvd 78573
Alton St 78574
Alton Springs St 78574
N Alvarado St 78573
Alyne 78572
Alyssa Dr 78574
Amanecer St 78572
Amargosa St 78574
Amber St 78574
Americana Ln 78572
Amethyst Ave
2301-2499 78574
3201-3499 78573
Amigo St 78573
Amy St 78572
Andresito Dr 78574
E Andrew Ave 78573
W Andrews St 78573
Angus St 78572
Anita Ave 78572
Anita St 78573
Ann Blvd 78573
Ann Marie St 78572
Ann Richards Rd 78572
Anna Cir & Dr 78574
Antigua Dr 78572
Apache St 78572
Aquarius St 78572
N Aransas 78573
Arco Iris St 78574
Ariana St 78574
Ariel Dr 78572
Ariel St 78574
Aries St 78572
S Arizona 78573
Arrow Point St 78572
Arroyo Claro Dr 78572
Arturo Ln 78574
Ash Dr 78572
Ashley Ave & Way 78574
Aspen Ave 78574
Astrid St 78574
Astro Dr 78574
Audrey Dr 78572
Augusta Dr
2200-2298 78572
2501-2599 78574
Aurora Private Rd 78572
N Austin Cir 78574
S Austin Cir 78574
N Austin St 78573
S Austin St 78573
Avenida Del Paseo St 78572
Avenue A 78574
Avenue B 78574
Avery Ave 78574
Avita St 78574
Azalea St 78573
Azucenas St 78572
Azul St 78574
Azuzena St 78573
W B St 78572
Bagley Dr 78574
Bahia St 78572
Bailey St 78574
Barbara St 78572
Barcelona St 78572
Barnes St 78572
Barnett Dr 78573
Barney Grove Dr 78574
Barnick St 78574
Basham Rd 78573
Bazan Ct 78574
Beatty St 78572
Bella Vista Ave 78572
W Bella Vista Ave 78573
W Bella Vista Ln 78573
Benjamin St 78573
N Bentsen Palm Dr
101-399 78572
400-499 78572
401-497 78574
499-600 78574
601-703 78572
602-698 78574
704-710 78574
705-711 78574
712-714 78574
715-807 78572
716-808 78574
809-820 78572
822-898 78574
901-1297 78574
1299-11799 78574
11801-11999 78574
S Bentsen Palm Dr
101-197 78572
199-305 78572
306-398 78574
307-1399 78572
400-2898 78572
Berlin Ln 78573
Berry St 78572
Bertha Ave 78572
Bertha Blvd 78573
Beto Dr 78574
Betty Dr 78572
Birdie Dr 78572
Black Oak Ln 78573
Blake St 78572
Blanca Cir 78574
Blanca Estela Dr 78574
Blue Jay Dr 78572
Blue Rock Rd 78573
Bluebird Ln 78572
E, N & S Bluebonnet Ln & St 78573
Bluegrass Way 78573
Bml Ln 78574
W Boca Chica Ave 78573
Bogamillia 78572
Bogey Dr 78572

Bougainvillea Dr 78573
Bouganvilla St 78572
Bowen St 78572
Bracey St 78572
Brandi Ct 78574
Brandy Dr 78574
Brazos Ave 78573
Brazos Cir 78572
Brazos Ct 78572
Brazos St 78572
Brentwood Dr 78572
N Breyfogle 78574
N Breyfogle Rd 78572
S Breyfogle Rd 78572
Brian Ave 78573
Briarway St 78574
Briarwood Ct & Dr 78574
S Brier St 78573
Brock St 78572
Broken Tee Dr 78572
Brooks Dr 78572
N Brushline Rd 78574
Brushy Ln 78574
N Bryan Blvd 78573
S Bryan Blvd 78573
N Bryan Rd
100-198 78572
200-2299 78572
2300-3299 78574
3300-12299 78573
4601-4797 78573
4799-5299 78573
11001-11199 78573
S Bryan Rd 78572
Bryce Dr 78572
E Buchanan Ave 78573
W Buchanan Ave
400-2199 78573
3500-3899 78574
Buckhorn Dr 78572
Buddy Owens Cir 78574
Buena Fe St 78574
Buena Suerte St 78574
Buena Vida St 78574
Buena Vista Dr 78572
N Buena Vista St 78573
Bunker Dr 78572
S Bunny St 78573
Bunting Ln 78572
Burney St 78572
Burrus St 78572
Business Center Dr 78572
E & W Business
Highway 83 78572
Business Park Dr 78572
Butchs Dr 78572
Butterfly Park 78572
N California St 78574
Callanan Cir 78572
Calle Cenizo 78574
Calle Marisol 78574
Cambell Dr 78573
Camelot Ct & Dr 78572
Cameron Dr 78574
Camino Escondido St 78574
Camino Grande 78572
Camino Real 78572
Campbell St 78572
E Campeche Ave 78573
W Campeche Ave
401-799 78573
3500-3598 78574
E Campeche St 78573
Canadiana Ln 78572
N & S Canal Ave 78572
Cando Mungia 78572
Canterbury Dr 78573
Cantu Rd 78572
Capri Ct 78572
Capricorn St 78572
Cardenas St 78572
Cardinal Ave 78574
Cardinal Ln 78573
Cardinal St 78572
Cardinal Delta St 78574
Cardinal Valley St 78574

Carianna Ave 78572
Carioca Dr 78572
Carla St 78574
Carlos Cir
601-997 78572
999-1299 78572
3300-3799 78574
Carlos St 78572
Carlotta St 78572
Carol Ave 78573
Carol Dr 78574
Carolina Ave 78572
Carrol Rd 78574
Casados Dr 78574
Casino Dr 78572
Cassandra St 78572
Castillos Y Diamantes
St 78572
Cavazos St 78573
Cedar Rapids St 78574
Celso St 78574
Cemetery Rd 78572
Cenizo St 78574
Center St 78574
Cerda St 78573
E Champion Ln 78574
Charles Dr & St 78572
Charro St 78574
Chelsea Dr 78573
Cheril Rd 78573
Chester St 78572
N & S Chicago St 78573
Chico Ln 78573
Chihuahua Rd & St 78572
E Chimney Rd 78572
Chiquita Cir 78574
Chris Dr 78574
Christen Cir 78574
Christina Ave 78572
Cimarron Ct & Dr 78572
Cipres St 78572
Circle Cir 78573
Circle Dr 78572
Circle Creek Dr 78572
Circle Lake Dr 78572
Ciruelos St 78572
Citraland Dr 78572
Citriana St 78572
Citrus Ln, Loop & St 78574
Citrus Groves St 78574
Citrus Spring St 78574
Claborne St 78572
Claraboya Ln 78572
Claudia St 78574
Clavel Dr 78573
Claveles St 78572
Clay Tolle St 78572
E Clinton Ave 78573
Clinton St 78572
Coby Dr 78574
Cody Ave 78574
Colonial Ave 78572
Colorado Ct 78572
Colorado St 78572
S Colorado St 78573
Colosios 78572
Comanche St 78572
E & W Combes Ave 78572
Commerce Dr 78572
Commercial Plaza Dr 78574
Compton Dr 78573
Concepcion Ave 78574
Concho Ct 78572
Continental Dr 78572
N Conway Ave
100-2299 78572
2300-3099 78574
3101-3199 78574
3200-15100 78573
4100-4198 78573
15102-15698 78573
S Conway Ave 78572
N Conway Blvd 78573
S Conway Levy 78572
Copper Ave 78572
Corales St 78573

Costa Azul Ln 78574
Cottonwood St 78574
Country Cir 78574
Country Ln 78573
Country Club Dr 78572
County Road 4107 78573
Couples Cir 78572
Cowboy Ln 78572
E Cowboy Ln 78574
S Cowboy Ln 78574
W Cowboy Ln 78574
Cowboys Cir 78574
Coyote Cir 78574
Crimson Ave
2300-2498 78574
3200-3399 78573
Crisantema Ave 78572
Crisantema St
2900-3099 78574
3101-3199 78574
3200-4000 78573
4002-4298 78573
Crown Pointe Blvd 78572
Crystal Dr
1900-2098 78572
2100-2199 78572
6900-7099 78574
Cuchilla Cir 78572
Cuesta Del Sol St 78572
E Cuevas St 78572
N Cummings Ave
100-2299 78572
3000-3199 78574
S Cummings Ave 78572
Cyndy Ave 78574
Cynthia Ln 78573
Cynthia St 78572
Daisy Dr 78574
Daisy Ln
301-399 78572
1800-1899 78572
5600-5799 78574
Daisy Ridge Ln 78574
N & S Dakota St 78573
Dalia St 78573
Dallas Cir 78574
N Dallas St 78573
S Dallas St 78573
Dalobo Blvd 78572
Dana Dr 78574
Daniel Ave 78574
Daniel Dr
1401-1599 78573
7701-7899 78574
Daniel Rd 78572
Danielle Dr 78574
Danny Dr 78574
Dario St 78572
Date Ln 78572
Datil Ave 78572
Dave St 78572
David Ave & St 78574
Davina St 78572
Davis Ln 78574
W Dawes Ave 78573
Dawna Ct 78574
E Dawson Ln 78574
E Daytona Dr 78572
De Anda Dr 78572
De Asis Cir 78572
De La Plata 78572
Debby Ln 78572
Del Cobre 78572
Del Mar St 78572
Del Norte 78574
Del Oro Dr 78572
Delaila St 78574
S Delaware St 78573
Deldie Ln 78572
Deleon Rd 78572
Delinda Lou Dr 78572
Delissa Dr 78574
Denia Ct 78572
Dennise Ct 78572
Devan Dr 78573
Devries Ln 78573

Diamond Ave & Dr 78574
W Diamond Head Ave 78573
Diane Dr 78572
Dinastia Dorado St 78572
Dinos Dr 78574
Diosa Ln 78573
N Doffing Ln & Rd 78574
Doherty Ave 78572
Dolores Del Rio Ave 78572
Domingo Trevino Dr 78572
Donahue Ln 78572
Donna Ave & Rd 78572
Dons Dr 78572
Dora Jeanne 78574
Dora Jeanne Dr 78572
Dorado Dr 78573
Double Eagle Dr 78572
Dove Ave 78574
Dove St 78572
Dove Weed St 78574
Driftwood Ct 78574
Driftwood Dr
200-2299 78572
2800-2898 78574
2900-2999 78574
Driftwood Ln 78574
Dudley Ave 78574
N & S Dunlap Ave 78572
Durango Dr
2400-2499 78573
2600-2698 78574
Durango St
800-1099 78572
7400-7699 78574
Dusty Trail Ln 78572
W E St 78572
Eagle Dr 78572
N & S Eagle Pass St 78573
Earth Ln 78573
Eastview Cir 78574
Ebano Ave 78572
Ebony Cir & Ln 78572
Ebony Highlands Dr 78573
Eclipse St 78574
Edgar St 78574
Edgewood St 78573
Edith Dr 78574
Eduardo St 78574
E & W Eisenhower
Ave 78573
El Barquito Dr 78572
El Camino Real 78572
El Cunado St 78574
El Descanso Ln 78572
El Dorado St 78572
El Encino Dr 78573
El Jardin 78572
El Jardin Ct 78572
El Jardin Dr 78574
El Jrdin 78572
El Lucero Ln 78572
El Manantial Dr 78574
El Mileno Dr 78573
E El Ranchito 78572
El Ranchito Cir 78574
E El Rancho Rd 78572
El Sendero Ct 78574
Elfy Trail Cir 78574
Elida St 78573
Elisa St 78574
Elise Dr 78574
Elizabeth Dr 78572
Elizabeth St 78572
Ellie Dr 78574
Elm Dr & St 78574
Elsa Dr 78572
Eman Dr 78573
Emerald Ln 78572
Emily Ave 78573
Enamorados Dr 78574
Encantado Cir 78572
Encanto Blvd 78574
Encino Ave 78572
Encke Rd 78574
E Ephraim Ave 78573
Erdahl Ave 78572

Erin Dr & St 78574
Erma Ave 78572
Escondido St 78573
Escuela Dr 78574
Esperanza Ave 78574
Esteban St 78574
Estella Ct 78572
Esther Dr 78572
Esther St 78574
Eugene Ct 78574
Eunice St 78574
Evan Dr 78573
Evergreen Ave 78572
Executive Business
Ctr 78572
E & W Expressway 83 78572
N & S Ezequiel Loop 78574
W F St 78572
Fair Oaks Dr 78574
Fairview Dr 78574
Fairway Cir, Ct & Dr 78572
Falcon Dr 78572
Farmosa Ave 78574
Feliz St 78574
Field Dr 78574
Fiesta Dr 78574
E Filmore Ave 78573
Finch Ln 78572
Fincher St 78572
Flamingo Ave
1200-1299 78572
2500-3199 78574
Flor Ln 78572
Florencia Ct 78572
Flores Dr
201-799 78572
2300-2499 78574
Flores Dr N 78572
Flores Dr S 78572
Flores Rd 78572
N Florida St 78573
Floyd Dr 78572
E & S Fm 1016 78572
N Fm 492
100-198 78572
N Fm 492
200-300 78572
302-398 78572
400-1800 78574
610-3398 78574
1802-1998 78574
3400-4199 78574
S Fm 492 78572
S Fm 494 78572
Ford St 78572
Forest Cir & Ct 78574
Fortuna 78572
Foshee 78572
Fox Run St 78574
Frances St 78572
Francisco Ave 78573
N Francisco Ave
100-900 78572
901-1699 78572
901-901 78573
902-1598 78572
2800-2898 78574
S Francisco Ave 78572
Franklin Ave 78574
E Franklin Ave 78573
W Franklin Ave 78573
Freedom 78574
Fresa Dr 78574
Frio St 78572
Frontage Rd 78572
Frontier Dr 78574
Fuentes Dr 78574
W G St 78572
Gabriel St 78574
Garcia St 78572
Garden Dr 78572
Garden View Dr 78574
W Garfield Ave 78573
Garland Dr 78573
Garza St 78572
E, N, S & W Gastel Cir
& Dr 78572

Gemini St 78572
N Georgia St 78573
Girasol St 78574
Giselle St 78574
Gladiola 78572
N Glasscock Blvd 78573
S Glasscock Blvd 78573
N Glasscock Rd
200-1899 78572
1901-1999 78572
2300-2398 78574
2400-3199 78574
3201-12499 78573
4400-4498 78573
4500-4599 78573
4601-5199 78573
S Glasscock Rd 78572
Glennwood St 78572
Glenwood Ave 78572
Gold Ave 78574
Golf Dr 78572
N Gooch Rd & St 78574
E Goodwin Rd 78574
N Goodwin Rd 78574
S Goodwin Rd 78572
Goodwin Acres Rd 78574
Gracie Ave & Ln 78574
Graham Ave
2000-2099 78573
2601-2697 78574
2699-2999 78574
Granada Ct 78572
Grand Canal Dr 78572
Grandview Dr 78574
Granite Ave 78572
Granite Dr 78574
Granja Ct 78574
Granjeno St 78572
Grapefruit 78572
Grapefruit Ln 78574
Green Jay Dr & Ln 78572
Green Meadow Dr 78572
Green Valley Cir & Dr 78572
Greenbriar Ave & St 78572
S Greene Rd 78572
Greenfield Ave 78572
Greenland Cir E 78572
Greenlawn Dr & St 78572
Greenway Ave 78572
Gregorio Garza St 78574
Gregory Ln 78574
E Griffin Pkwy 78572
W Griffin Pkwy
101-297 78572
299-1999 78572
2100-2199 78572
2200-2298 78574
2201-2799 78572
Grindelia St 78574
Grove Ln 78574
Grovewood Ave 78572
Grovewood Rd 78573
Guadalajara St 78572
Guadalupe St 78572
Guayabo St 78572
Gus 78572
W H St 78572
Hackberry 78572
Hackberry Ave
400-798 78572
2900-2998 78574
3000-3199 78574
Hackberry St 78574
Hailley Dr 78574
Hanna St 78574
Happy St 78573
E Harding Ave 78573
Harmony Ct & Ln 78574
Harms Way St 78572
W Harrison Ave 78573
Harvest Time Rd 78574
Havana Spring St 78574
Haven Dr 78574
N & S Hawaii St 78573
W Hayes Ave 78573
Helen Ave 78572

Heritage Ln 78572
Hermenegildo Garza 78574
E Hermosillo Ave 78573
Heron Way 78572
Hidalgo St 78572
Hidden Pond Dr 78573
Highland Dr 78574
Highland Park Ave
1001-1697 78572
1699-1799 78572
1801-1899 78572
2500-2798 78574
2800-2900 78574
2902-3198 78574
S Highland Park Ave 78572
W Highway 83 78572
Hilda Ave 78572
Hilda St
800-898 78572
2200-2298 78574
2300-2399 78574
Hill Dr 78572
Hill Crest Dr 78573
Hill View Dr 78573
Hillcrest Dr 78574
Hoerner Rd 78572
Hole In One Dr 78572
N Holland Ave
100-2100 78572
2102-2298 78574
2300-2498 78574
S Holland Ave 78572
Holland St 78574
Hollis St 78574
Hollow Ln 78572
Hollyfield St 78572
E Honolulu Ave 78573
W Honolulu Ave
400-799 78573
2800-3199 78574
Horseshoe St 78572
Hound Dr 78574
Huisache St 78572
Humberto Garza Jr St 78572
Hummingbird Ln 78572
Hunt Valley Rd 78572
Hunter St 78572
W I St 78572
Ibiza Ct 78572
Ida Dr 78572
N Idaho St 78573
Idelma St 78574
W Ignacio Ave 78573
Industrial Way 78572
Inez St 78574
Ingrid St 78574
N Inspiration Blvd 78573
S Inspiration Blvd 78573
Inspiration Rd 78572
N Inspiration Rd
200-498 78572
500-900 78572
902-1098 78572
2500-2698 78574
2700-2999 78574
3001-3199 78574
3201-3297 78573
3299-12900 78573
12902-13998 78573
S Inspiration Rd 78572
International Blvd 78572
Iowa Rd 78574
Iowa St 78572
N Iowa St 78573
S Iowa St 78573
Ira Rd 78574
Irma Garza Cir 78574
Irma Linda St 78574
Iron 78572
S Irving Ln & St 78573
Isaac Dr 78573
Isidro Cir 78574
W Israel Ave 78573
J And A Dr 78574
Jacaranda 78574
E Jackson Ave 78573

Jacob 78572
Jade Dr 78574
Jakob St 78574
James Patrick St 78574
Jamie Cir, Ln & St 78574
Jana Dr 78574
Janice Dr 78574
Janie St 78574
Jarrett Dr 78574
Javier St 78574
Jay Ave 78572
S Jay Ave 78572
Jay Dr N 78573
Jay Dr S 78573
Jaykeith St 78574
E Jefferson Ave 78573
W Jefferson Ave 78573
Jefferson St 78572
Jenna Cir 78573
Jennifer Ln 78574
Jerry Ave 78573
Jessica Ave & Dr 78574
Jewel Dr 78574
Jim Schroder Dr 78573
Jimenez Dr 78572
Jimmy Garza Dr 78572
Jj Dr 78574
N Jo Beth St 78573
Joanna Ave 78572
John St 78574
John Mark Ct 78574
Johnson St 78572
Jonathan Edwards Ct 78574
Jonathon Dr 78572
Jones St 78572
Jonquil Ave 78572
Jorgeanna St 78572
Jose Angel Ave 78574
Jose De La Cruz Rd 78574
Joseph Ave 78574
E & S Joshua Ave & Dr 78574
Jovita St 78574
Joycee Dr 78573
E Juarez Ave 78573
Judy Ave 78572
Julio St 78574
Jupiter St 78574
Justin St 78574
Kansas St 78573
E Kantunil Ave 78573
Karen St 78574
Karime Dr 78574
Karina Dr 78572
Katrina 78573
Katrina Dr 78574
Kayleen Dr 78574
Kelly Cir 78574
Kelly Dr 78572
Kelly St 78572
Ken Dr 78574
Kennedy 78573
E Kennedy Ave 78573
W Kennedy Ave 78573
Kennedy St 78572
N & S Kentucky St 78573
Keralum Ave 78573
E Keralum Ave 78572
N Keralum Ave
100-1399 78572
2300-2399 78574
S Keralum Ave 78572
Keralum St 78574
Kerria Ave 78572
Keystone Dr & St 78574
Kickapoo Crk 78574
E & W Kika De La Garza St 78572
Kim Marie Ave 78574
Kimberly St 78572
Kingfisher Ln 78572
Kings Dr 78574
S Kingsville St 78573
Kirk Ave
2000-2298 78572
2300-2499 78574

Kiskadee Ln 78572
W Kohala Ave 78573
N & S Kountry Loop 78574
Kristi Ln 78574
Kristin Ave 78573
La Camelia 78572
La Estrella St 78572
La Fe Dr 78574
N La Homa Dr 78574
La Homa Rd 78574
N La Homa Rd
100-398 78572
500-598 78574
600-1799 78574
1801-4697 78574
2100-2198 78572
2900-4698 78574
4700-11099 78574
11101-11299 78574
S La Homa Rd
100-1199 78572
201-299 78574
La Joya St 78574
La Loma Dr 78572
La Lomita 78574
La Mancha Dr 78574
La Palma Dr 78572
La Paloma Dr 78572
E La Pointe Ave 78573
La Reina Dr 78574
La Suegra St 78574
La Vista Cir & Dr 78574
Lago Ct 78572
Lake Front Dr 78572
Lake Point Dr 78572
Lake View Dr 78572
Lakeside Dr 78572
Lakeview Dr 78574
N & S Lalos Dr 78572
Lambeth Way 78572
Lanford Rd 78574
Lantana Ln 78574
Laredo Blvd & St 78572
Lark Dr 78572
Las Aves Ln 78572
Las Brisas Dr 78574
Las Colinas Ln
3000-3199 78574
3600-3699 78573
Las Comadres St 78574
Las Palmas Dr 78574
Las Primas St 78574
Laura St 78574
Lauren Ln 78572
Lawndale Rd 78572
Leal Dr 78572
Leal Ln 78573
Leal St
100-899 78572
11000-11199 78573
Leandro St 78574
Leanna Denae Ave 78572
Lee St 78572
Leilahni Dr 78574
Lemon Ln 78574
Leo St 78572
E & W Leo Najo St 78572
Leon Tiger Zamora 78572
Leonor St 78572
Levelland Dr 78574
Liberty Dr 78574
Liberty St 78573
Libra St 78572
Lila Beth Ln 78572
Lilac Ave 78574
Lilly Cove Dr 78572
Lily Dr 78574
Lima Ln 78574
Lime Ct 78574
Limon Dr 78574
Limoneros St 78572
N Linares Dr & St 78573
E Lincoln 78573
Lincoln Ave
2500-2699 78574
3700-3899 78573

E Lincoln Cir 78573
Lincoln St 78572
Linda Ave 78573
S Linda Ln 78573
Linda St 78572
N Linda St 78573
Linda Vista St 78572
Lindberg St 78573
Live Oak St 78574
Liz Dr 78574
Loker St 78572
E, N, S & W Loma Linda Cir & St 78572
Lomita Dr 78572
Lone Grove Ct 78574
Long Dr 78572
Longhorn Dr 78574
Longview Dr 78573
E & W Loop 374 78572
Lopez St
400-698 78573
700-799 78573
3700-4299 78572
Lords Ln 78572
Loriemark Dr 78573
E Los Charcos Dr 78572
Los Compadres 78574
N Los Ebanos Blvd 78573
S Los Ebanos Blvd 78573
Los Ebanos Rd
2501-2897 78574
2899-3000 78574
3002-3098 78574
3201-3297 78573
3299-4000 78573
4002-4098 78573
N Los Ebanos Rd
400-1700 78572
1702-1798 78572
1901-15499 78573
15501-15699 78573
S Los Ebanos Rd
200-222 78572
201-203 78573
205-399 78572
800-898 78573
1201-1299 78573
E Los Indios Pkwy & St 78572
Los Jardines Dr 78574
Los Milagros 78574
Los Ninos St 78574
Los Vecinos St 78574
Lost Greens Dr 78572
N Louisiana St 78573
Loya St 78574
Lucero Ct 78572
Lucksinger Rd 78572
Lucky I St 78573
Lucky J St 78574
Lucy Dr 78574
Lusby St 78574
Lynn Rd 78574
E Madison Ave 78573
Madison St 78572
Madison Hope Dr 78572
Madrid Dr 78574
Magdalena Ave 78572
Magdalena St 78573
Magnolia St
200-399 78572
1700-1898 78573
1900-2199 78573
Magnum Rd 78573
E & W Mahala Ave 78573
E Main Ave 78573
W Main Ave
100-798 78573
401-997 78573
999-1499 78573
1501-2799 78573
3001-3097 78574
3099-3599 78574
3601-3699 78574
W Main St 78573
Mallard Dr 78572
Mango Dr 78574

Mangum St 78572
Manzanos St 78572
N Maple St 78573
Mar St 78572
Mar Verde 78574
Marble Ct 78572
Marc Dr 78574
Maren Dr 78574
Margaret Dr 78574
Margot Dr 78574
Mari Lee Ave 78574
Maria Ave 78573
Maricela St 78572
Marienela St 78574
Marigold St 78572
Marinel Ln 78572
Marisol St 78574
Marissa Dr 78574
Marivel Ortiz Ave 78574
Mark Pl 78572
Marla Dr 78572
Mars Ln 78574
Marshall St 78574
Martha Dr 78574
Martina St 78574
S Maryland St 78573
Mata Blvd 78572
Matamoros St 78572
Mauren St 78574
Mauve Dr 78572
Maxine Dr 78574
May Ave 78574
N Mayberry Ave 78573
N Mayberry Blvd 78573
S Mayberry Blvd 78573
N Mayberry Rd 78573
N Mayberry St
100-2299 78572
2300-2900 78574
2902-3198 78574
S Mayberry St 78572
Mazatlan St 78572
Mckinley Ave 78573
Meadow View Dr 78572
Meadow Way Dr 78572
Megan Dr 78574
Melanie St 78574
Melba Carter St 78572
Melinda Dr
1400-2199 78572
2500-2599 78574
Melissa Cir 78574
Melissa Dr 78573
Melissa Ln 78574
Melissa Rae Dr 78572
Melissa Rea Dr 78574
Melody Ct & Ln 78574
Melos Ln 78574
Mendez Ln 78573
Mercado St 78573
Mercury St 78572
Merlin Dr 78572
Mesquite Dr 78572
Mesquite Ln 78574
Mesquite Loop 78574
Mesquite St 78572
N Mexico St 78573
Mi Sueno St 78574
Mi Suerte Dr 78574
Mianeh 78574
S Michigan St 78573
Midland Dr 78574
Mieke Cir 78574
Mignet Court St 78572
Mike Barrera St 78572
Mikels St 78572
Milagro Ln 78572
Milagro St 78572
Milan Dr 78574
S Mile Rd 78572
Mile 1 1/4 North Dr N 78574
Mile 1 South Rd 78572
W Mile 10 Rd 78574
E & W Mile 2 Rd 78574
E Mile 3 Rd 78573

W Mile 3 Rd
101-397 78573
399-2199 78573
2200-6200 78574
6202-7898 78574
E Mile 4 Rd 78573
W Mile 4 Rd
901-1899 78573
2901-4697 78574
4699-6899 78574
6901-8099 78574
Mile 5 Cir 78574
E Mile 5 Rd 78573
W Mile 5 Rd 78574
Mile 6 Rd 78573
E Mile 6 Rd 78573
N Mile 6 Rd 78573
W Mile 6 Rd 78574
W Mile 6 1/2 Rd
1500-1699 78573
2200-3799 78574
Mile 7 Rd 78573
W Mile 7 Rd
1622-1698 78573
1700-1999 78573
2001-2099 78573
2200-7899 78574
7901-8199 78574
10000-10198 78573
10200-12299 78573
36700-36898 78574
36900-37899 78574
Mile 7 1/2 Rd 78573
W Mile 7 1/2 Rd 78573
Mile 8 Rd 78573
W Mile 8 Rd
1801-1999 78573
2500-3299 78574
5301-5397 78573
5399-6700 78573
6702-7398 78573
7101-7497 78574
7499-8100 78574
8102-8198 78573
8901-8997 78573
8999-9429 78573
9430-9498 78574
9431-12199 78573
10200-12298 78573
36700-37099 78574
W Mile 8 1/2 Rd 78573
W Mile 9 Rd
1800-1899 78573
7201-7299 78574
7600-7798 78574
10801-12399 78573
W Mile 9 1/2 Rd
2500-3299 78574
10001-10997 78573
10999-11999 78573
12001-12399 78573
W & E Military Hwy & Rd 78572
Miller Ave
100-1999 78572
2701-2799 78574
Mimosa St 78574
S Mina De Oro St 78572
Minerva Rd 78572
N Minnesota Rd
200-299 78572
301-399 78572
401-697 78574
699-1400 78574
1402-1498 78572
2200-2299 78572
4401-10500 78574
6300-11399 78574
10502-10798 78574
S Minnesota Rd 78572
S Minnesota St 78573
Mirabel St 78574
Miracle Ln 78572
Miroslava Ave 78573
Mission Springs Ln & St 78574
N & S Mississippi St 78573

N Missouri St 78573
Mistflower St 78574
N Mockingbird Ave & Ln 78572
Molly Dr 78574
Monaco Dr 78573
Monica Ave 78573
Monica Cir 78574
Monica St 78573
E Monroe Ave 78573
Monroe St 78572
N Montana St 78573
Monte Cruz St 78574
N Montemorelos Dr 78573
Moody Ave 78573
N Moore Ln 78573
Moorefield Rd
123-399 78572
401-2299 78572
1000-3498 78574
3500-5300 78574
5302-5698 78574
N Moorefield Rd
100-399 78572
401-1999 78572
500-598 78574
600-2298 78572
2401-2497 78574
2499-4499 78574
4501-11299 78574
4600-4698 78573
4800-4898 78574
5100-5100 78573
5102-11298 78574
S Moorefield Rd 78572
Morales Dr 78573
Moreno St 78573
Morgan St 78574
Morning Ln 78572
Morwil St 78572
Mountain Rd 78573
Mourning Dove Ln 78572
Myra Dr 78574
Nabors Rd 78574
N & S Nacogdoches St 78573
Nacona St 78574
Nadia St 78574
Nappa Valley Dr 78573
Naranja Dr 78574
Naranjo Dr 78574
Naranjo St 78572
Navaho St 78572
Naval Dr 78574
Navel Ln 78574
S Nebraska St 78573
Nevada St
1100-1410 78573
1412-1498 78573
5500-5700 78574
5702-5798 78574
S Nevada St 78573
S New Jersey St 78573
S New Mexico St 78573
New Orleans St 78572
Newport 78574
Nicholson 78574
N Nicholson Ave 78572
S Nicholson Ave 78572
Nickel Ave 78574
Nicklaus Dr 78572
Nicole Dr & St 78574
E Nixon Ave 78573
Noe St 78572
Noel Dr 78574
Nogal St 78572
Nogales St 78572
N Nogales St 78573
W Nopales Ave 78574
Nora Ln 78573
Norma Dr & St 78574
Norman Dr 78572
North St 78572
S North Carolina St 78573
Northpoint Blvd 78574
Nouios Dr 78574

Nueces St 78572
Nuevo Amanecer Dr 78574
Oak Dr 78572
Oak St 78572
N Oak St 78573
Oak Ridge Ln 78573
Oakland Dr 78573
Oakwood Ln 78573
Oasis Ave 78572
Oaxaca 78572
N Oaxaca St 78573
S Oaxaca St 78573
Oblate Ave
100-1699 78572
2400-2798 78574
2800-2899 78574
Obra Dorado 78572
Ocaso Rd 78572
N Ohio St 78573
Ojo De Agua St 78572
Oklahoma St 78572
N Oklahoma St 78573
Old Highway 107 78573
Oleander Dr 78573
Oleander St 78574
Olmo St 78572
Orallind 78573
Orange St 78574
S Orange St 78573
E & W Orange Grove Rd 78574
Ordaz Dr 78574
Oriole Dr & Ln 78572
Orquidea St 78573
Oslo Dr 78574
Osprey Ln 78572
Ottumwa St 78572
S P V Greene Rd 78572
Paisaje Rd 78573
Paisano St 78572
Palazzo 78572
E & W Palm Cir, Dr & St 78574
Palm Creek Blvd 78574
Palm Grove Dr 78573
N & S Palm Leaf Cir 78574
S Palma St 78572
E & W Palma Vista Dr 78572
Palmarina St 78574
Palmas Del Norte Ln & St 78574
Palmer Dr 78572
Palmeras Dr 78573
Palmetto Dr 78574
Palmetto Palm Dr 78573
Palmhurst Dr 78573
Palmview Dr
101-197 78572
199-299 78572
301-399 78572
600-698 78574
N Palmview Dr 78572
Palmview Commercial Dr 78574
Palo Blanco Dr & St 78572
Paloma St 78574
Pam Dr 78574
Pamela Dr 78572
Pammy Cir 78572
Par Dr 78572
Paradise Cir
800-1099 78572
1900-1999 78573
Paris Ln 78573
Paris St 78574
Park Ln 78572
Paseo De La Tranquilidad St 78572
Paseo Del Lago 78573
Paseo Del Rey St 78572
Paseo Encantado St 78572
Patricia St 78572
Patriot St 78572
Paul St 78572
Paula St 78574

Peace Ave
1800-2099 78572
2401-2499 78574
2600-3098 78574
E Pebble Dr & St 78574
Pecan Ave 78572
Pecos St 78572
S Pedro Ave & Rd 78572
Pelican Way 78572
Pena Cir 78574
Pena St
2000-4099 78572
7001-7799 78574
Pena Blanca North Rd 78574
N Pennsylvania St 78573
Pepe Dr 78574
Perez Rd & St 78572
Periwinkle St 78572
Perkins Ave
401-497 78572
499-2299 78572
3000-3099 78574
Persimmon Dr 78573
Pinal St 78572
N & S Pine St 78573
Pino St 78572
Pisces St 78572
Plano Ln 78573
Plantation Grove Blvd 78572
Plaza Dr 78572
Pleasant Ln 78572
Poinsetta 78574
Poinsettia St 78572
Pola St 78574
E Polk Ave 78573
Polk St 78572
Pond Cir 78573
Ponderosa Dr 78572
Ponds Edge Dr & Rd 78573
Ponerail St 78572
Pradera Ln 78572
Pradera St 78574
Primrose Ave 78572
Princess Lea 78572
Princeton Dr & St 78572
Prosperidad Dr 78574
Ptj Dr 78572
Pueblo St 78572
Pueblo Del Norte Ct 78574
Puesta Del Sol Ave 78572
Putter Dr 78572
Q Rd 78574
Quail Ln 78572
Quail Crest Dr 78574
Quale Dr 78574
Quality Dr 78574
Quebec St 78572
Quita Cir 78572
R St 78574
E & W Rabbit Run Ave & Way 78573
Rachel Dr 78574
Rachel Diann Ln 78574
Ragland St 78572
Ram Ave 78572
Ramirez Ln & St 78573
Ramon Ave 78573
Ramon Private Rd 78572
Ramona Blvd 78572
Ramsey Dr 78574
Ranch Rd 78574
S Rancho Del Rey St 78572
Rankin St 78572
Rattler Ln 78573
Raul Aguilar Dr 78572
E & W Ray Cir 78572
Reagan St 78572
E Rebecca St 78574
Red River Dr & St 78572
Redbird Ln 78572
Redstone Dr 78572
Regina Dr 78574
Rene Ave 78573
N & S Resplandor St 78572
Retama Ave 78572
Rey Dr 78574
Reynosa St 78572
N Rhode Island St 78573
Ricardo Ave & Dr 78574
Richardson Ln 78573
Richmond St 78573
Ridge Loop 78574
Rio Dr
1700-1799 78572
5001-5599 78574
Rio St 78572
Rio Balsas 78572
Rio Concho 78574
Rio Grande Ct, Dr & Ln 78572
River Bend Dr 78572
Robert Michaels St 78574
Robin Ln 78572
Robyn Ln 78572
Rocio Dr 78574
N Rockport St 78573
Rolando Dr 78574
Roman St 78573
E Roosevelt 78573
E Roosevelt Ave 78573
Roosevelt St 78572
Roque Salinas Rd 78572
Rosa Ave 78572
Rosa St 78574
Rosalinda Ct & St 78572
Rose Marie St 78574
Rosebud 78574
Rosewood Dr 78573
Royal Dr 78574
Royal Palm St 78572
Royola St 78572
Ruby Cir 78573
Ruby Dr 78574
Ruiz St 78572
Rumorosa Ln 78572
Rush Dr 78573
Russell Cir 78574
Ruth St 78572
Ryan Andrews Ct 78574
Sabinal St 78572
Sabine Ct & St 78572
Saddle Club Cir 78572
Sagittarius St 78572
Saigo Palm Dr 78573
E & W Saint Francis Ave 78573
Saint George 78574
E & W Saint Jude Ave 78573
N & S Saint Marie St 78572
Salinas Dr & St 78572
Samantha St 78574
San Alejandro 78572
San Alejo St 78572
San Andres Ct & St 78572
San Angel St 78572
San Angelo St 78572
San Antonio Ave 78573
San Antonio St 78572
N San Antonio St 78573
San Armando 78572
San Benito St 78572
San Blas St 78572
San Carlos Ct 78572
San Cenovio St 78572
San Clemente 78572
San Daniel 78572
San Delfino St 78572
San Diego 78572
San Eduardo St 78572
San Efrain 78572
San Efren St 78572
San Esteban Ct & St 78572
San Eugenio 78572
San Fabian St 78572
San Federico 78572
San Feliciano St 78572
San Felipe Dr 78572
San Francisco St 78572
San Gabriel St 78572
San Gerardo 78572
San Isidro 78574
San Jacinto St 78572
San Jose 78572
San Lorena 78572
San Lorenzo 78572
San Lucas 78572
San Lucas Ave 78574
San Luis Cir 78573
San Mateo Pkwy 78572
San Miguel 78572
San Monica 78572
San Nicolas St 78573
San Pablo St 78573
San Patricio St 78572
San Rafael St 78572
San Reynaldo St 78572
San Ricardo St 78572
San Rocio St 78572
San Rodrigo 78572
San Roman St 78572
San Saba St 78572
San Sebastian St 78572
E Sandstone Dr 78574
Santa Alejandra 78572
Santa Ana 78572
Santa Clara 78572
Santa Engracia 78572
Santa Erica St 78572
Santa Esperanza 78572
Santa Fabiola St 78572
Santa Fe St
1300-1699 78573
1701-6799 78573
2901-4299 78572
N Santa Fe St 78573
Santa Helena 78572
Santa Idalia Cir 78572
Santa Iliana 78572
Santa Inez Cir & St 78572
Santa Laura 78572
Santa Lorena 78572
Santa Lucia Cir & St 78572
Santa Lydia St 78572
Santa Maria St 78572
Santa Marina St 78572
Santa Monica 78572
Santa Monica Blvd 78574
Santa Olivia St 78572
Santa Paula 78572
Santa Rita 78572
Santa Rocio St 78572
Santa Sofia Ct & St 78572
Santa Susana St 78572
Santa Teresa 78572
Santa Veronica St 78572
Santo Tomas 78572
Saturn St 78572
Sauz St 78572
School Ln 78572
S Schuerbach Blvd 78574
N Schuerbach Rd
701-899 78572
3400-6499 78574
S Schuerbach Rd 78572
Scorpio St 78572
N & S Scott Ln 78572
Scout Ln 78572
Seagull Ln 78572
Sebastian St 78572
Seitz Rd 78574
Seitz St 78572
Selena Dr 78574
Selena St 78572
Sendero Ave 78573
Senecio St 78574
Sequoia Dr 78572
Serendipity Dr 78573
Serenidad Ave 78574
N Shary Blvd 78573
S Shary Blvd 78573
N Shary Rd
101-297 78572
299-2299 78572
2301-2597 78574
2599-2800 78574
2802-3298 78574
3300-13099 78573
4300-4499 78573
4501-5299 78573
S Shary Rd
100-908 78572
910-2198 78572
1001-1099 78573
1101-4499 78572
Sheri Lee Dr 78572
Sherwood Dr 78572
Shirley St 78574
Showers Rd 78572
N Side Dr 78574
Sierra Ct 78574
Sierra Dr 78573
Siesta Dr 78574
Silver Ave 78574
Silver Oak Ave 78574
Silver Spur Ln 78572
Silverado N 78573
Silverado S 78573
Silverado Cir E 78574
Silverado Cir N 78574
Silverado Cir S 78574
E Silverado Dr 78572
S Silverado Dr 78572
W Silverado Dr 78572
E Silverbell St 78573
N & S Slabaugh St 78572
Smirnoff Ln 78574
Sno Bird Ln 78572
Sofia Dr 78574
S Sol Dorado St 78572
Solar Dr 78574
Soleado St 78572
Solera 78572
Sondra St 78574
Sonora St 78572
Sotira St 78572
W South Dakota St 78573
Sparrow Ln 78572
Spring Glen Dr 78574
Spring Glen St 78572
Squire Ln 78572
St Claire Blvd 78572
Stacie Ln 78574
Stadler Dr 78572
State Highway 107 78573
E Stevenson Ave 78573
W Stevenson Ave 78574
N Stewart Blvd 78573
S Stewart Blvd 78573
N Stewart Rd
200-2000 78572
2002-2098 78572
2300-3000 78574
3002-3198 78574
3300-12199 78573
3600-3798 78573
3800-5100 78573
5102-5298 78573
12201-12499 78573
S Stewart Rd 78572
Stone Ridge Ln 78574
E Stonegate Dr 78574
Story Ln 78573
Sue Ellen Dr 78574
Sugar Ln 78572
Summer Breeze Ave & Rd 78572
Sun St 78572
Sun Chase Cir 78572
Sun Valley St 78572
Sundance Cir 78572
Sundance St 78573
Sundrop Ave 78574
Sunni St 78572
Sunny Cir & Dr 78574
Sunny Haven St 78572
Sunrise Ln
100-2199 78574
1600-1799 78573
2201-2399 78574
Sunset Blvd 78574
Sunset Ln
1601-1699 78573
2100-2499 78572
Susana St 78574
Swiss Ln E 78573
Sycamore Ave
401-799 78572
2301-2999 78574
W Sycamore Ave 78573
Tamarindo St 78572
Tampico Ave 78574
Tampico St 78572
Tangelo Ln 78574
Tangelo St 78572
Tangerine Ave 78574
Tangerine Dr 78573
Tanglewood St 78574
Tanner Ct 78574
Taurus Ln 78574
Taurus St 78572
Taylor Rd 78573
N Taylor Rd
101-797 78572
799-899 78572
901-1799 78572
2301-2999 78574
3301-5197 78573
4601-4999 78573
5199-11000 78573
11002-12798 78573
S Taylor Rd 78572
W Taylor Rd 78574
Tecate Dr 78572
Templo Dorado St 78572
Tencha St 78572
Teofilo Dr 78574
Teresa St 78574
Terrace Dr 78572
Texacana Ln 78572
N Texan Rd 78574
Thicket Ln 78574
Thompson Rd
1500-1899 78573
3400-3799 78574
Thornton St 78572
Thornwood Dr & St 78574
Thorton 78574
Thrasher Dr 78572
Tierra Alta Dr 78574
Tierra Dorada Blvd 78572
Tierra Linda Blvd 78572
Tierra Linda Cir E 78572
Tierra Linda Cir W 78572
Tierra Linda Ln 78574
Tiffany Ave 78574
Tiffany Dr 78574
Tiffany St 78573
Tillie Ln 78572
Timberwood Ave
2400-2699 78574
4100-4298 78573
Time Dr 78574
Toledo Ave 78572
E & W Tom Landry St 78572
Toni Dr 78573
Toni Ln 78572
Tornillo St 78574
Toronja Ln 78574
Toronjales St 78572
Torrie Ln 78572
Toucan Ave 78573
Towers St 78572
Tranquilidad Cir 78574
Travis St 78572
Travis Neal 78574
Tray Dr 78574
Trevino Dr 78572
Trey Leal Ave 78574
Trinidad Ln 78573
Trinity St
100-1999 78572
3300-3398 78573
Triple D Dr 78572
Triple J Dr 78572
Triple L Ln 78574
N Trosper Blvd 78573
S Trosper Blvd 78573
Trosper Rd
3000-3199 78574
3200-3298 78573
3300-3500 78573
3502-3598 78573
N Trosper Rd 78573
S Trosper Rd 78573
E Truman Ave 78573
W Truman Ave 78574
Truman St
900-1000 78572
1002-2298 78572
3200-3299 78573
Tuesday Ave 78574
Tula St 78574
Tulip Ave 78574
Tulipan Ave
1601-1897 78572
1899-2099 78572
2101-2199 78572
2301-2399 78574
Tulipan St
200-399 78572
2801-2897 78574
2899-3199 78574
3200-3999 78573
E Turista St 78573
N & S Turtle Ct, Dr & Ln 78572
Tyler St 78572
Umbel St
2201-2299 78572
2300-2399 78574
Union Ave, Ct & St 78572
Ursula St 78572
N Uvalde St 78573
Valencia Ave, Cir & Ln 78574
Valle Bella Dr 78572
Valley Rancheros St 78574
Vanessa Dr 78574
Vaquero Ave 78574
Vatia Blvd 78572
S Vega St 78573
Venecia Dr 78574
Venus St 78572
Veracruz 78572
Vernon St 78572
E & W Veterans Blvd 78572
Victoria Ave & St 78572
E Victory St 78573
Viejo Ln 78572
Viena Dr 78574
Viento Dorado St 78572
Viento Tropical St 78572
E View Cir 78574
N View Ln 78573
S View Ln 78573
Villa Rama Cir 78572
Villa Rama East St 78572
Villa Rama North St 78572
Villa Rama South St 78572
Village Dr & Sq 78572
Vintage Ln 78572
Viola Dr & St 78574
Violet St 78574
Virginia Cir 78574
Virgo St 78572
Vista Del Viento St 78572
Viva Carrol Cir 78574
Volz Ln 78572
Wagner Ct 78574
Wagner Ln 78572
Wagon Trail Dr 78572
Wagon Trail Rd 78573
Walsh Ave 78572
Walton Dr 78574
Ward Rd 78574
Warjebo Trl 78574
Washington Ave
2500-2699 78574
3200-3299 78573
Washington St 78572
S Watson Rd 78572
N Waxahachie St 78573
Wednesday Ave 78574
Wernecke Ave 78574
Wescan Ln 78572
Western Rd
2000-2298 78572
4400-11099 78574
11101-11299 78574
Western St 78572
Western Palm Dr 78574
Western View Dr 78572
Western Village Blvd 78574
Westside Ln 78573
Wharton Rd 78574
White St 78572
White Oak St 78573
Whitney Cir 78574
Wildwood St 78572
W Willacy Ave 78573
Willow St 78574
Wilson Rd 78574
Wilson St 78572
Windcrest Ln 78573
Windsor Glen Dr 78572
Wintex Ln 78572
Wisteria Ave & Dr 78574
Wolf Creek Ave 78573
Wolsey Dr 78572
Wood Fair Ct 78574
Woodland Dr 78574
Woodrow St
1800-1999 78572
2401-2497 78574
2499-2899 78574
Woods St 78572
Wysteria St 78574
S Xanthia St 78573
Xanthisma St 78574
Yarrow St 78574
Yolanda St 78572
Yoli Cir 78574
Yosemite Dr 78572
Yukon Ave 78573
Zarkana St 78574
Zavala Dr 78574
N Zavala St 78573
E Zinnia Ave 78573
W Zinnia Ave 78573
Zinnia St 78574
Zulley St 78573
Zurich Ave 78573

NUMBERED STREETS

E & W 1st Blvd, Ln & St 78572
W 1st 1/2 St 78572
E & W 2nd Blvd, Ln & St 78572
E 2nd 1/2 St 78572
2nd Lane Cir 78572
E 3 Mile Rd 78573
101-199 78573
4400-4498 78574
E, N & W 3rd Blvd, Ln & St 78572
3rd Lane Cir 78572
W 4 Mile Rd 78574
E & W 4th Blvd & St 78572
E & W 5th Blvd & St 78572
E & W 6th Ave & St 78572
W 7 1/2 St 78574
E & W 7th Ave & St 78572
E & W 8th Ave & St 78572
E & W 9th 78572
W 10th St 78572
E & W 11th 78572
E & W 12th 78572
E & W 13th 78572
E & W 14th 78572
E & W 15th 78572
W 16th St 78572
W 17th St 78572
W 18th St 78572
E & W 19th 78572
E & W 19th 78572
E & W 20th 78572
E & W 20th 78572
W 20th 1/2 St 78572
E & W 21st 78572
E & W 21st 78572
E & W 22nd 78572

E & W 22nd 78572
W 22nd 1/2 St 78572
E 23rd Pl 78574
W 23rd Pl 78574
E 23rd St
1700-1800 78574
1802-1998 78574
2200-2400 78572
2402-2498 78572
W 23rd St 78574
E 23rd 1/2 St 78574
E & W 24th Pl & St 78574
E 24th 1/2 St 78574
E & W 25th 78574
E 25th 1/2 St 78574
W 26th St 78574
W 26th 1/2 St 78574
E & W 27th 78574
E & W 28th 78574
E & W 29th 78574
W 29th 1/2 St 78574
E & W 30th 78574
W 30th 1/2 St 78574
E & W 31st 78574
W 31st 1/2 St 78574
E 35th St 78574
W 40th St 78573
W 41st St 78573
W 42nd St
1900-2199 78573
5400-5699 78574
W 45th St 78574
W 46th St 78574
N 56th St 78573
N 57th St 78573
N 58th St 78573
N 59th St 78573
N 65th St 78573
W 65th St 78574
N 66th St 78573
W 66th St 78574
N 67th St 78573
N 85th Ave 78573
N 87th Ave 78573
N 101 St 78573
N 102nd St 78573
N 103rd St 78573
N 105th St 78573
N 106th St 78573
W 15 1/2 St 78572
W 19 1/2 St 78572
W 41 1/2 St 78573
W 42 1/2 St 78573

MISSOURI CITY TX

General Delivery 77489

POST OFFICE BOXES MAIN OFFICE STATIONS AND BRANCHES

Box No.s
All PO Boxes 77459

NAMED STREETS

Abalone Cv 77459
Acacia Pl 77459
Acorn Ct 77489
Acorn Rdg 77459
Acosta Valley Dr 77459
Adams St 77489
Admiral Ct 77459
Adrianna Path Dr 77459
Aegean Dr 77459
Alassio Isle Ct 77459
Alderwood Dr 77489
Aldridge Dr 77459
Alexis Tate Cir 77459
Alger Dr 77489
Aliano Ct 77459
Allerton Dr 77489
Allison Ct 77459
Alpine Cir 77459
Alstead Cir 77489
Alyssa Ave 77489
Amaifi Dr 77459
Amalfi Shores Ct 77459
Ambassador Ct 77459
Americana Dr 77459
Anchor Point Ct 77459
Andrews Ln 77489
Angel Fls 77459
Antelope Aly 77459
Antelope Hills Dr 77459
Antler Way 77459
Apple Dr 77459
Apple Branch Ct 77459
Apple Valley Ln 77459
Appleridge Ct & Dr 77489
Appleton Dr 77489
E & W April Rain Ct 77459
Aqua Fls 77459
Aquilla Ct 77459
Arbor Mill Ln 77459
Ardea Way Dr 77459
Argos Ct & Dr 77459
Arrowhead Ct 77459
Arrowhead Lake Dr 77459
Artesian Park 77459
Artwood Ln 77489
Arum 77489
Ascot Gdn 77459
Ash Creek Dr 77459
Ash Oak Dr 77489
Ashley Ct 77459
Ashmont Ct 77489
Ashmont Dr
2300-2328 77489
2330-2425 77489
2426-2498 77459
2500-2999 77459
Ashmont Ln 77459
Ashmore Ct & Dr 77489
Aspen Ct 77459
Assisi Way Ln 77459
Aster Rd 77489
Athena Ct 77459
Atlas Dr 77459
Aubrey Oaks Ct 77459
Auburn Grove Cir 77459
E, N, S & W Auden
Cir 77459
Augusto Ct 77459
Austin Dr 77459
N & S Autrey Ct 77459
Autumn Lks 77459
Autumn Dawn Ct 77459
Autumn Green Dr 77459
Autumn Springs Dr 77459
Autumn Village Ct &
Dr 77459
Avebury Stone Cir 77459
Aviano Cir 77459
Bahia Ct 77459
Bahia Ln 77489
Bailey Ct & Ln 77459
Bain Dr 77459
Baitland Dr 77459
Bal Harbour Dr 77459
Balsam Gap 77459
Bank Ct & Way 77459
Banta Dr 77489
Barbers Ct 77489
Barcelona Ct 77459
N & S Barnett Way 77459
W Baron Ln 77459
Barrington Cir 77459
Barron Ln 77489
Bassett Ct 77459
Battle Creek Dr 77459
Bay Leaf Ct 77489
Bay Shore Dr 77459
Baybriar Dr 77489
Bayview Ct 77459
Bazel Brook Dr 77489
Bazelbriar Ln 77489
Beacon Hts 77459
Bear Grove Dr 77459
Bears Path Ln 77459
Beauregard Ct 77459
Bedford Forrest Ct &
Dr 77459
Bee Cave Dr 77459
Bee Hollow Ct 77459
Bee Meadow Ln 77489
Beechbend Dr 77459
Beekman Dr 77459
Bees Creek Ct, Knl &
Rd 77459
Bellinger Ct & Way 77459
Bellis Ln 77489
Bellmead Dr 77459
Belmont Shore Ct &
Ln 77459
Belmont Turn 77459
Belnap Ct & Way 77459
Belt Ln 77489
Ben E Keith Way 77489
S Bend Cir 77459
Bending Branch Dr 77459
Benjamin Franklin Ln 77459
Bent Oak Dr 77489
Bentlake Cir 77459
Bentwood Dr 77489
Beretta Ct 77489
Bermuda Dunes Dr 77459
Bermuda Palms Dr 77459
Bermuda Shores Dr 77459
Berrystone Trl 77459
Berryvine Dr 77489
Bethany Bay Dr 77459
Betsy Ross Ct 77459
Big Spg & Trl 77459
Big Cedar Cir 77459
Big Elm Cir 77459
Big Leaf Ct 77459
Big Sky Pass 77459
Big Trail Cir & Ct 77459
E & W Birchdale Dr 77459
Birchstone Dr 77459
Bird Dog Dr 77489
Bird Meadow Ln 77459
Bird Run Dr 77489
Birdhaven Ln 77489
Birdsong Ln 77459
Birkenhead Cir 77459
Bison Blf 77459
Black Creek Ct 77459
Black Horse Cv 77459
Blackberry Cir 77459
Blazing Gap 77459
Blocker Ln 77489
Bloomfield Turn 77459
Blossom Bell Ln 77459
Blue Diamond Dr 77489
Blue Gap 77459
Blue Hills Dr 77459
Blue Iron Dr 77489
Blue Lagoon Ct 77459
Blue Lakes Ln 77459
Blue Quail Dr 77489
Blue Rose Cir & Dr 77459
Blue Sky Ct 77459
Blue Spruce Ct 77459
Bluebird Ln 77459
Bluegrass Ct 77459
Blueridge Ct & Rd 77489
Bluestone Ct & Dr 77459
Bluewater Dr 77459
Bobcat Bnd 77459
Bobolink Cir 77459
Boca Ct 77459
Boca Raton Dr 77459
Bolton Dr 77489
Bonita Crk 77459
Bonney Briar Dr 77459
Border Ct 77459
Bowden Ct 77459
Bradford Dr 77489
Branch View Ln 77459
Brandon Bend Dr 77489
Brazos Bend Dr 77459
Breaker Ct 77459
Breckinridge Ct & Ln 77459
Bremerton Falls Dr 77459
Breton Bay Pass 77459
Brewster Ln 77459
Briar Run Ct 77489
Briar Seasons Dr 77489
Briar Spring Ct 77489
Briarcraft Dr 77489
Briargate Ct, Dr & Trl 77489
Briarstead Dr 77489
Bridgeside Ln 77459
Bright Meadows Dr 77489
Brightlake Way 77459
Brighton Ct 77459
Brights Bnd 77459
Brightwater Dr 77459
Brightwood St 77459
Brindisi Ct 77459
Bristol Ln 77489
Broadgreen Dr 77489
Broadmoor Cir 77459
Broken Arrow 77459
Broken Bough Dr 77459
Bromley Bend Dr 77459
Brookford Dr 77489
Brookline Dr 77459
Brookside Ct 77459
Brown St 77489
Brushy Lake Dr 77459
Buckeye Pl 77459
Buckley Ln 77459
Buckner Ct 77459
Buffalo Run 77489
Buffalo Gap 77459
Bull Ln 77489
Bull Run Ct 77459
Burning Tree Ln 77459
Butler Ct 77459
Buttonhill Dr 77489
Calabria Bay Ct 77459
Caleb Ln & Way 77459
Calender Lake Dr 77459
Calgary Cir 77459
Caloway Ct 77459
Cambridge Ln 77459
Cambridge Cove Cir 77459
Camelot Ln 77459
Camp Sienna Trl 77459
Candace Ct 77489
Canefield Ct 77459
Cangelosi Rd 77489
Canton Hills Ln 77459
Canyon Ct 77459
Canyon Meadows Dr 77489
Cape Blanco 77459
Cape Hatteras Way 77459
Cape Henry 77459
Captains Ct 77459
Caravel Cir, Ct & Ln 77459
Cardono Ln 77489
Caribou Ct & Cv 77459
Caribou Cove Ct 77459
Carlton Sq 77459
Carmel Valley Dr 77459
Carmine Gln 77459
Camden Ln 77459
Carnoustie Dr 77459
Carol Chase Cir 77489
Carol Lynn Dr 77489
Carriage Park Row 77459
Carrollton Ct 77459
Carson Cir 77489
Cartwright Rd
1400-2200 77489
2202-2448 77489
2451-2997 77489
2999-4599 77459
4601-4799 77459
Casa Del Lago Dr 77459
Cashenso Dr 77459
Castello Ln 77459
Castle Creek Dr 77489
Castleview Ln 77489
Cat Springs Ln 77459
Catalpa Pl 77459
Catskill Dr 77459
N & S Caulder Way 77459
Cave Run Dr 77459
Caymus Creek Ct 77459
Cedar Bend Dr 77459
Cedar Hill Ct 77459
Cedar Spring Dr 77459
Cedar Valley Dr 77459
Cedar Wing Ct 77489
Celina Knl 77459
Cèzanne Cir 77459
Chalk Hl 77459
Chambers Cir & Ct 77459
Champions Dr 77459
Chandler Hollow Ln 77459
Chang An Dr 77459
Chapel Ct 77459
Chapel Creek Way 77459
Chapparal Ct 77459
Chappel Hill Dr 77459
Chappell Ln 77459
Charlston Ct 77459
Chase Village Dr 77489
Chasecreek Dr 77489
Chasefield Dr 77489
Chasehill Dr 77489
Chasemont Dr 77489
Chasepoint Dr 77489
Chaseridge Dr 77489
Chaseview Dr 77489
Chaseway Dr 77489
Chasewind Dr 77489
Chasewood Dr 77489
Chatham Cv 77459
Cherry Creek Ct & Dr 77459
Cherry Hills Dr 77459
Cherry Laurel Ln 77459
Cherry Springs Ct &
Dr 77459
Cheryl Ct 77489
Chesham Mews 77459
Chesterdale Dr 77459
Chestnut Bnd 77459
Chestnut Ridge Ct 77459
Chiara Ct 77459
Chimera Ln 77459
Chimney Gap 77459
Chimney Rock Rd 77489
Chinaberry Grv 77459
Chino Valley Ct 77459
Chippenham Ct 77459
Chriesman Ln & Way 77459
Christina Ct 77489
Churchlake Cir 77459
Cicada Dr 77459
Cimmaron Cir 77459
Cinque Terre Dr 77459
Circle Bend Dr 77489
Circlechase Dr 77489
Clark Mnr 77459
Clay Pigeon Ct 77489
Clayton Terrace Dr 77459
Clear Lake Ct 77459
Clearbrook Dr 77489
Clearwater Ct 77459
Cliffdale Dr 77489
Climbing Rose Ct 77459
Cline Way 77459
Cloud Brook Dr 77459
Clyburn Ct 77459
Clymer Mdw 77459
Cobblecreek Way 77459
Cobleskill Ct 77459
Colchester Way 77459
Cold Hollow Ln 77459
Collington Ct 77459
Colonial Ct 77459
Colonial Lakes Dr 77459
Colony Bend Ln 77459
Colony Knolls Ct 77459
Colony View Ln 77459
Columbia Blue Dr 77489
Combwell Gdn 77459
Commanders Cv & Pt 77459
Concord Pl 77459
Condor Way 77489
Confederate Ct & Dr 77459
Confederate South Dr 77459
Connies Court Ln 77459
Continental Dr 77459
Copin Lake Ln 77459
Copper Canyon Ln 77459
Copper Creek Ln 77459
Coral Rocks Ct 77459
Coral Tree Pl 77459
Corbett Ct 77459
Cornwall Ct & Ln 77459
Corona Del Mar Dr 77459
Cory Ln 77459
Cotter Lake Cir & Dr 77459
Cotton Cir 77489
Cotton Iron Dr 77459
Cottonwood Ct 77459
Court Rd 77489
Courtney Ct 77459
Courtside Place Dr 77489
Covenant Way 77459
Covey Cir 77459
Covey Run Ct 77489
Covey Trail Dr 77459
Cowden Ct 77489
Coyote Trail Dr 77459
S Cravens Rd 77489
Creek Bluff Ln 77459
E & W Creek Club Dr 77459
Creek Crossing Ct 77459
Creek Hollow Ln 77459
Creek Meadows Dr 77459
Creek Point Ln 77459
Creek Ridge Ln 77459
Creek Terrace Dr 77459
Creekview Dr 77459
Creekway Cir 77459
Creighton Dr 77489
Crescent Oak Dr 77459
Cresswell Ct 77459
Crestmont Cir 77459
Crestmont Place Loop 77489
Crestmont Trail Dr 77489
Crestview Ct 77459
Crestwood Ln 77489
E Crosby Cmn, Gdn, Ln,
Lndg & Way 77459
Crosscreek Ct 77459
Crow Valley Dr 77459
Cruit Isle 77459
Crystal Pt 77459
Crystal Falls Dr 77459
Crystal Ridge St 77459
Cumberland Ct & Dr 77459
Curtis Xing 77489
Custer Creek Dr 77459
Cypress Point Dr 77459
Cypress Spring Dr 77459
Daffodil Rd 77489
Dakota Ct 77459
Dalewood Dr 77489
Dali Ln 77459
Dancing Creek Ln 77459
Darnell Ct 77459
Dawn Quail Ct 77489
Dawn Star Dr 77489
Dawnbriar Ct 77489
Declaration Dr 77459
Deer Br, Ldg & Xing 77459
Deer Lodge Ct 77459
Deer Meadow Dr 77489
Deerhill Walk 77459
Deerwood Ln 77489
Del Clair Cir 77489
Del Monte Ct 77459
Delacorte Ln 77459
Dell Cir, Ct, Ln & Park 77459
Della Creek Way 77459
Denard Ln 77489
Denoa Ln 77459
Derby Ln 77489
Desert Rose Ct & Pl 77459
Dewalt Ct, Mnr & Way 77459
Diamond Crest Dr 77489
Diamond Springs Dr 77459
Diamondleaf Ct 77459
Dickson Way 77489
Discovery Ln 77459
Dock Ct 77459
Dock View Ln 77459
Dockside Ct 77459
Doe Run Rd 77489
Dogwood Dr 77489
Doliver Cir 77489
N & S Doral Dr 77459
Doris Ct 77489
Double Lake Dr 77459
Double Ridge Xing 77459
Double Trail Ct 77459
Douglas Ln 77489
Doverglen Dr 77489
Doves Yard 77459
Doyle Ct 77459
Drayton Hall 77459
Dream Ct 77489
Dulles Ave 77459
Duncaster Ct & Dr 77459
Durango Bnd 77459
Dusty Rdg 77459
Dusty Ridge Ct 77459
Eagle Ct 77489
Eaglerock Cir 77489
Eastfield Cir & Dr 77459
Eastiner Dr 77489
Eastmont Ln 77489
Eastshore St 77459
S Echo Br 77459
Echo Chase Dr 77489
Echo Creek Dr 77489
Echo Lakes Cir & Ln 77459
Edenderry Ct & Ln 77459
Edgecraft Dr 77489
Edgedale Dr 77489
Edgehaven Dr 77489
Edgewood Dr 77459
Edinburgh Ln 77459
Edison Brook Ln 77459
Edmonson Ct 77459
Eight Willows Rd 77489
El Dorado Blvd 77459
Elk Mountain Ct 77459
Elkwood Dr 77489
Ellis Dr 77489
Elm Glen Dr 77459
Elm Shadow Dr 77489
Elms Ct 77459
Ember Branch Dr 77459
Emerald Lake Dr 77459
Emperors Pass 77459
Enchanted Rock Ln 77459
Enclave Ct 77459
English Rose Trl 77459
Erin Ct 77459
Eros Ln 77459
Evans Rd 77489
Evening Shade Ct 77459
Fairgreen Dr 77489
Fairway Pines Dr 77489
Fairwind Ln 77459
Fall Briar Dr 77489
Fall Creek Ln 77459
Fall Meadow Dr 77459
Fallbrook Dr 77459
Fallen Leaf 77459
Falls Cir 77459
Farley Ct 77459
Farmersville Frk 77459
Fawn Ct 77459
Fawnwood Dr 77489
Feather Ridge Dr 77489
Federal Ln 77459
Feldman Fls 77459
Fern Meadow Dr 77459
Ficus Ct 77459
Fiddlers Green Dr 77459
Fielder Cir 77459
Fieldlark Ln 77489
Fieldstone Dr 77489
Fishermans Cv 77459
N & S Fitzgerald Ct &
Way 77459

Five Oaks Ct, Dr, Ln & Xing 77459
N & S Flamingo Dr 77459
Flamingo Bay Dr 77459
Flamingo Estates Dr 77459
Flamingo Island Ct & Dr 77459
Flamingo Landing Dr 77459
Flat Rock Run 77459
Flicker Dr 77489
Florence Way Dr 77459
Fm 1092 Rd 77459
Foggy Heights Ln 77459
Fondren Rd 77489
Fondren Grove Cir & Dr 77489
Forest Trl 77459
Forest Creek Dr 77459
Forest Hollow Dr 77459
Forest Home Dr 77459
Forest Isle Ln 77459
Forest Leaf Cir 77459
Forest Ridge Dr 77459
Fort Arbor Ln 77459
Fort Graham Ct 77459
Fort Ridge Way 77459
Founders Ct 77459
Fountain Hills Dr 77459
N & S Fountain Valley Dr 77459
Four Winds Dr
2801-2997 77459
2999-3099 77459
14901-14997 77489
14999-15199 77489
Fowler Ct 77459
Foxborrough Ln 77489
Foxfield Dr 77489
Foxfire Cir 77459
Foxglove Dr 77489
Foxhill Dr 77489
Foxwood Ct 77489
Foyer Cir 77459
Francis Ln 77489
Franciscan Ct 77459
Freedom Ct 77459
Freedom Tree Ct & Dr 77459
French Quarter Ln 77459
Fresh Meadow Dr 77489
Frost Lake Ct 77459
Frostview Ln 77489
W Fuqua Dr 77489
Gallaher Ct 77459
Galling Dr 77489
Garden Gln & Way 77459
Garden Crossing Ln 77459
Garner Lake Ln 77459
Gatebriar Ct & Dr 77489
Gatecraft Dr 77489
Gateview Ln 77489
Gauguin Ln 77459
Gazebo Ln 77459
Geddes Grv 77459
Genova Way Ln 77459
Gentle Bend Dr 77489
George Washington Ln 77459
S Gessner Rd 77489
Gilmar Dr 77459
Ginger Gln 77459
Glade Park Dr 77459
Glasgow Dr 77459
Glen Cove Cir 77459
Glen Echo Ln 77459
Glen Park Dr 77489
S & E Glen Willow Ln & Rd 77489
Glenbriar Pl 77489
Glenford Dr 77489
Glengreen Dr 77489
Glenn Lakes Ln 77459
Glenwild Dr 77489
N & S Gold River Cir 77459
Golden Hbr 77459
Golden Hills Ln 77459
Golden Shores Dr 77459
Golden Tee Ct & Ln 77459
Goldenrod Ln 77459
Goldleaf Ct 77459
Good Day Dr 77489
Goodman Ridge Dr 77459
Goudin Dr 77489
Grand Falls Dr 77459
Grand Mesa Pass 77459
Grand Oak Ct 77459
Grand Park Dr 77489
Grand Plantation Ct & Ln 77459
Granite Falls Ln 77459
Granite Lake Ct & Dr 77459
Gray Slate Dr 77459
Gray Thrush 77459
Grayson Ct & Ln 77459
Great Oaks Dr 77459
Green St 77489
Green Cottage Ln 77459
Green Creek Dr 77459
Green Hollow Ct 77489
Green Mansions Ct 77489
Green Meadow Ct 77489
Green Moss Ct 77489
Green Quail Dr 77489
Green Spring Ct 77489
Green Star Ct & Dr 77489
Green Tree Ct 77459
Greenbriar Dr 77459
Greencourt Dr 77489
Greencrest Dr 77489
Greendale Dr 77489
Greenridge Dr 77459
Greenwest Dr 77489
Gregway Ln 77459
Griffin Ln 77459
Griffin Willow Rd 77459
Grove Court Dr 77489
Grove Park Dr 77489
Gulfbriar Pl 77489
Habersham Ct 77459
N & S Halls Point Ct 77459
Halls Retreat Ct 77459
Halstead St 77489
Hammerwood Dr 77489
Hampshire Ln 77459
Hampton Dr 77459
Happy Holw 77459
Harbor Mist 77459
Harbor Point Dr 77459
Harbour Cir & Pl 77459
Harbour Cove Cir 77459
Harbour Gateway Ln 77459
Harbourside Ln 77459
Harbourview Ct 77459
Harrison Ln 77459
Hart Cir 77459
Harvest Moon Dr 77489
Harwich Ln 77459
Havershire Dr 77459
Haviland Ln 77459
Hawk Crk & Rdg 77459
Hawkins Cir, Ct & Ln 77459
Hawks Rd 77489
Hawthorn Pl 77459
Heathcliff Dr 77489
Heatherwood Dr 77489
Heights Creek Dr 77459
Heights Knoll Dr 77459
Helena Bnd 77459
Hera Dr 77459
Herb Appel Cir 77459
Heritage Colony Dr 77459
Heritage Trail Ct 77459
Hernshead Ln 77459
Herringbone Dr 77489
Hewes Point Ln 77459
Hickory Glen Dr 77459
Hidden Cv 77459
Hidden Fort Ln 77459
Hidden Heights Dr 77459
Hidden Hollow Ct 77459
High Bank Dr 77459
High Pine Ct 77459
High Sienna Ct 77459
Highcrest Dr 77489
Highland Lakes Dr 77459
Highway 6 77459
Highway 90 A 77489
Hill Family Ln 77459
Hillcroft St 77489
Hilton Head Ct & Dr 77459
Hoatzin Ct 77459
Hollow Cir 77459
Hollowood Ln 77489
Holly Ct 77459
Hollyridge Dr 77489
Homebriar Ct 77489
Honeysuckle Dr 77489
Honors Ct 77459
Hope Farm Rd 77459
Horseshoe Fls 77459
House Lake Dr 77459
Hubers Ct 77489
Huckleberry St 77459
Hummingbird Ln 77459
Hunters Ct 77489
Hunters Glen Dr 77459
Hunters Park Dr 77459
Hunterwood Dr 77489
Hunting Dog Ct 77489
Hurricane Ln 77459
Hyacinth Pl 77459
Hycliff Ct 77459
Independence Blvd
1500-1699 77489
3400-3499 77489
8200-8300 77489
8302-9298 77489
Indian Crk & Pt 77459
Indian Falls Dr 77489
Indian Lake Dr 77489
Indian Trail Ct & Dr 77459
Indian Wells Ct & Dr 77459
Indian Woods Dr 77489
Indigo Ln 77459
Industrial Dr 77489
Inglewood Cir 77459
Inwood Ln 77489
Iris Ln 77459
Iron Horse 77459
Iron Rise Ct 77459
Island Blvd 77459
Ithaca Dr 77459
Ivy Fls 77459
Ivy Mill Ct & Ln 77459
Jade Pt 77459
Jadwin Ct 77459
James Madison Dr 77459
Jasper Cv 77459
Jennings Ct 77459
Jetty Terrace Cir 77459
Jewel Lndg 77459
John Hancock Ln 77459
John Locke Ln 77459
Johnson Dr 77459
Jonathon Ct 77489
Judy Ter 77489
Kellyway Ln 77459
Kelsey Pass 77459
Kenbriar Dr 77489
Kenbrook Dr 77489
Kenforest Dr 77489
Kenn Ct 77459
Kennesaw Dr 77459
Kenston Pl 77459
Kent Knl 77459
Kenwood 77459
Kenworthy Dr 77459
Kerala St 77459
Key Ct 77459
Key Largo Ct 77459
Kiamesha Dr 77459
Killian Ct 77459
Kilmarnoch Way 77459
N & S Kimball Ct 77459
Kimberly Ln 77489
King Cotton Ln 77459
King Harbour Ln 77459
Kingman Dr 77489
Kings Creek Trl 77459
Kingsbrook Ln 77459
Kingston Ct 77459
Kirkwood St 77489
Kissing Camel Ct 77459
Kitty Hawk Dr 77489
Kitty Hollow Dr 77459
Knights Ct 77459
Kottayam Dr 77489
Krause Dr 77489
Kueben Ln 77489
La Costa Rd 77459
La Crema 77459
La Quinta Dr 77459
Lacey Ln 77489
Ladera Ln 77459
Lady Atwell Ct 77459
Laguna Cir 77459
Laguna Point Ln 77459
Lake Ct & Dr 77459
Lake Colony Dr 77459
Lake Como Dr 77459
Lake Creek Cir 77459
Lake Estate Ct 77459
Lake Garda Dr 77459
Lake Olympia Pkwy 77459
Lake Run Dr 77459
Lake Shore Harbour Blvd & Dr 77459
Lake Terrace Ct 77459
Lake Villa Dr 77459
Lake Vista Cir 77459
Lake Walk Ct 77459
Lake Winds Dr 77459
Lakebrook Dr 77459
Lakecrest Dr 77459
Lakefront Ct & Dr 77459
Lakeshore Forest Ct & Dr 77459
Lakeside Estate Dr 77459
Lakeside Meadow Ct & Dr 77459
Lakeside Village Dr 77459
Lakeview Ct & Dr 77459
Lakewood Ct & Dr 77459
Lamar Dr 77459
Lamb Crk 77459
Lamplighter Cir 77459
Landmark Dr 77459
Landrum Ln 77489
Lanesborough Dr 77459
Lantern Ln 77459
Laughlin Dr 77489
Laurel Creek Ct 77459
Laurel Green Ct & Rd 77459
Laurel Oak Dr 77489
Laurel Woods Cir 77459
Lauren Pl 77489
Lawn Crest Dr 77489
Lazy Ln 77489
Lazy Hollow Ct 77459
Lazy Spring Ct & Dr 77489
Lazy Willow Ct & Ln 77489
Le Moyne Pass Ln 77459
Lead Point Dr 77459
Ledger Ln 77459
Legends Ln 77459
Leicester Way 77459
Lennox Woods 77459
Leslie Ln 77489
Lexington Blvd
1100-1498 77489
3400-4799 77459
Lexington Cmn 77459
Lexington Ct 77489
Lexington Green Dr 77459
Lexington Grove Ct & Dr 77459
Lexington Lake Dr 77459
Lexington Manor Ct 77459
Liberty Ct 77459
Lighthouse Ln 77459
Lily Pond Ct 77459
Linwood Dr 77459
Lisha Ln 77489
Little Trl 77459
Little Leaf Ct 77459
Little Rise Dr 77459
Live Oak Ct 77489
Liverpool Ct 77459
Lodge Ct 77489
Logan Rock Rd 77459
London Ln 77459
Lone Quail Ct & Dr 77459
Lone Willow Ct & Ln 77489
Lonesome Quail Dr 77489
Long Barrel Ln 77459
Long Barrow Ln 77459
Long Bay Ln 77459
Long Rock Dr 77489
Longmont Cir 77489
Lost Hollow Ln 77459
Lost Oak Ct 77459
Lost Quail Dr 77489
Louisiana St 77489
Loupe Ct & Ln 77459
Loutre Pass 77459
Love Crk 77459
Lucy Ln 77489
Lynnwood Dr 77489
Mackenze Way 77489
Maczali Ct & Dr 77459
Mad River Ln 77459
Madewood Dr 77459
Magnolia Bnd 77459
Magnolia Brook Ct 77459
Mahogany Dr 77489
Mainsail Cir 77459
Manchester Cir & Cv 77459
Mangia Tower Ct 77459
Manion Dr 77489
Manorglen Dr 77489
Maplecrest Dr 77489
Maplegate Dr 77489
Marino Dr 77459
Marion Cir & Ct 77459
Marthoman Dr 77489
Martin Ln 77489
Masters Ln 77459
Maverick Bend Ln 77459
Mcallister Dr 77459
Mccreary Way 77459
Mccullum Rd 77489
Mchard Rd 77489
Mckeever Ln & Rd 77459
Mckinney Ln 77459
Mcmahon Ct, Ln & Way 77459
E, N, S & W Meadow Bird Cir 77489
Meadow Green Dr 77489
Meadow Park Cir 77459
Meadow Pond Dr 77459
Meadow Vista Ct & Dr 77459
Meadow Way Dr 77459
Meadowcreek Dr 77459
Meadowview Dr 77459
Medici Ct 77459
Megan Way 77489
Melon Creek Ln 77459
Mercer Ct 77459
Mesa Verde Dr 77489
Middlesbrough Ln 77459
Midmont Dr 77489
Midnight Pass 77459
Midstream Dr 77459
Mill Holw, Ln & Pt 77459
Mill Garden Cir 77459
Mill House Run 77459
Millbrook Ln 77459
Millbury Dr 77489
Millwood Lake Dr 77459
Mimosa Rd 77489
Mission Valley Dr 77459
Misty Crk 77459
Misty Crest Dr 77459
Misty Hollow Dr 77459
Misty Morning Ct 77459
Mockingbird Ln 77489
Moffitt Ln 77489
Montego Bay Ct 77459
Moon Beam Cir 77459
Moonlight Ct 77459
Mooring Point Ct 77459
Moreleigh Branch Dr 77459
Morgan Run 77489
Morning Dew Pl 77459
Morning Glory Ct 77459
Morning Meadow Dr 77489
Morning Quail Ct 77489
Moss Run Dr 77459
Moss Trail Dr 77459
Mossridge Dr 77489
Mountain Frk 77459
Mountain Creek Ln 77459
Mountain Lake Dr 77459
Mountshire Dr 77489
Mulberry Cir 77459
Mullingar Walk 77459
Murray Ct & Lndg 77459
Musselburgh Ct 77459
Mustang Xing 77459
Mustang Crossing Ct 77459
Mustang Springs Dr 77459
Myers Mill Dr 77489
Myrtle Ln 77459
Mystic Frst 77459
Nancy Bell Ln 77459
Naples Point Ln 77459
Napoli Way Dr 77459
Neal Ridge Dr 77489
Neuces Crk 77459
New Tree Ln 77489
Nickel Dr 77489
Nicole Ct 77489
Nine Mile Ln 77459
Noblebriar Ct 77489
Northshore Ct & Dr 77459
Northwinds Dr 77459
Norwich Way 77459
Nottingham Ln 77459
Oak Ct & Walk 77459
Oak Bay Cir 77459
Oak Bough 77459
Oak Cliff Ln 77459
Oak Forest Dr 77459
Oak Hill Dr 77489
Oak Hollow Ct 77489
Oak Leaf Ct 77459
Oak Mill Way 77459
Oak Park Ln 77459
Oak Pointe Blvd 77459
Oak Valley Dr 77459
Oak Vista Dr 77459
Oakbury Ct & Dr 77489
Oakland Cir & Ct 77459
Oakland Falls Dr 77459
Oakland Lake Cir & Way 77459
Oaklawn Oval 77459
Oaklawn Place Dr 77459
Oakley Bnd 77459
Oakmont Ln 77459
Oakview Dr 77459
Oakwick Forest Dr 77459
Oconnor Ln 77459
Ohara Dr 77489
Old Settlement Ct 77459
Old Woods Psge 77459
Olympia Dr 77459
Orchard St 77489
Orchid Dr 77489
Orkney Dr 77459
Otter Creek Way 77459
Outer Banks Ln 77459
Overbrook Ln 77459
Oyster Cove Dr 77459
Oyster Creek Dr 77459
Oyster Creek Village Dr 77459
Oyster Shell Ct 77459
Padons Trace Ct 77489
Painted Grove Ct 77459
Palm Blvd 77459
Palm Desert Ln 77459
Palm Grove Dr 77459
Palm Harbour Dr 77459
Palmer Plantation Dr 77459
Palmera Ct 77459
Palo Pinto Ct 77459
Paluxy Cir 77459
Pamela Ln 77489
Panorama Dr 77459
Parade Ct 77459
Paradise River Dr 77459
N Park Dr 77459
Parkcraft Dr 77489
Parkside 77459
Parkview Ct & Ln 77459
Parsonage Cv 77459
Patricia Ln 77489
Patriot Ct 77459
Patterson Dr 77459
Pawnee Pass 77459
Peach Tree Ln 77459
Peachwood Dr 77489
Pebble Brk 77459
E Pebble Beach Dr 77459
Pebblestone Ct & Dr 77459
Pecan Ct 77459
Pecan Estates Dr 77459
Pecan Field Dr 77459
Pecan Forest Dr 77459
Pecan Glen Dr 77489
Pecan Hollow Dr 77459
Pecan Leaf Dr 77459
Pecan Ridge Dr 77459
Pecan Valley Ct & Dr 77459
Pecan Wood Dr 77459
Pelican Cv 77459
Penhallow Ln 77459
Peninsula Pl 77459
Peninsulas Dr 77459
Pennington Ct & Ln 77459
Penrose Ct 77459
Pepperglen Ct 77489
Peregrine Way 77459
Phantom Hill Ln 77459
Pheasant Valley Dr 77489
Phoenix Ct 77459
Pickett Pl 77459
Pigeon Cove Cir 77459
Pike Rd 77489
Pillar Cove Ln 77459
Pimlico Pt 77459
Pin Oak Cir 77459
Pine Ct 77459
Pine Hollow Dr 77489
Pine Landing Dr 77459
Pine Meadow Dr 77489
Pine Top Ln 77459
Pinehurst Ln 77459
Pinewood Park Dr 77489
Pinwood Dr 77489
Piper Glen Ln 77459
Pipers Landing Ct 77489
Placido Way Ct 77459
Plagens Ln 77489
Plantation Colony Dr 77459
Plantation Creek Ct & Dr 77459
Plantation Hollow Ct 77459
Plantation Lakes Dr 77459
Plantation Mill Pl 77459
Plantation Wood Ln 77459
Planters View Ln 77459
Pleasant Valley Dr 77459
Plum Brook Ln 77459
Plum Creek Ln 77489
Plum Hill Ln 77459
Plymouth Way 77459
Plymouth Pointe Ln 77459
Poco Dr 77489
Poets Corner Ct 77459
Point Clear Ct & Dr 77459
Pointe Ln 77459
Pointed Leaf Dr 77459
Pomme Bay Pass 77459
Pond Brook Pl 77459
Pontchartrain Psge 77459
Pony Crk 77459
Poplar Isle 77459
Poplar Springs Dr 77459
Portofino Ct 77459

Portuguese Bend Ct & Dr 77459
Powell Way 77459
Powell Springs Ct 77459
Prato Park Dr 77459
Pravia Path Dr 77459
Present St 77489
Preserve Ln 77459
Prestwick Sq 77459
Prichard Ct 77459
Princess Ln 77459
Pryor Dr 77489
Purple Finch 77459
Quail Bend Dr 77489
Quail Briar Dr 77489
Quail Burg Ct & Ln 77489
Quail Call Dr 77489
Quail Creek Dr 77459
Quail Crest Ct & Dr 77489
Quail Croft Dr 77489
Quail Dale Dr 77489
Quail Echo Dr 77489
Quail Feather Ct & Dr 77489
Quail Glen Dr 77489
Quail Green Ct 77489
Quail Grove Ln 77459
Quail Gully Dr 77489
Quail Hills Dr 77489
Quail Hollow Dr 77459
Quail Hunt Dr 77489
Quail Meadow Ct 77489
Quail Meadow Dr
3400-3899 77459
16501-16597 77489
16599-16799 77489
Quail Nest Ct 77489
Quail Park Dr 77489
Quail Place Ct & Dr 77489
Quail Prairie Dr 77489
Quail Run Ct & Dr 77489
Quail Shot Dr 77489
Quail Trace Dr 77489
Quail Valley Dr 77459
Quail Valley East Dr
1800-2599 77459
2601-2697 77489
2699-3199 77459
Quail View Ct & Dr 77489
Quail Village Dr 77459
Quail Vista Dr 77489
Quailmont Dr 77489
Quailynn Ct & Dr 77489
Quiet Bend Dr 77489
Quiet Covey Ct 77489
Quiet Quail Dr 77489
Rabbitt Rdg 77459
Rachels Way 77459
Rainbow Valley Ct 77459
Raintree Dr 77459
Raleigh Row 77459
Ramble Ln 77459
Ramble Creek Dr 77459
Rambling Rose Ct 77459
Randon Ln 77459
Raoul Wallenberg Ln 77459
Raven Trl 77489
Ravens Roost 77459
Ravenswood 77459
Raynor Ct 77489
Red Bluff Turn 77459
Red Cardinal Ln 77489
Red Oak Dr 77489
Red Stag Pass 77459
Redcliff Dr 77489
Redcoat Ln 77489
Redland Ct 77459
Redstone Ct 77459
Reecewood Ln 77489
Reedwood Dr 77489
Reefton Ln 77459
Reflection Ct 77459
Reiden Dr 77489
Reindeer Cres & Run 77459
Retriever Ln 77489
Revolution Way 77459
Rhodes Ct 77459
W Ridgecreek Dr 77489
Ridgemont Dr 77489
Ridgerock Rd 77489
Ridgeview Dr 77459
Ridgewood Ln 77459
Ridingwood Dr 77459
Riflewood Cir 77459
Rimina Way Dr 77459
Rimrock Dr 77459
Ring Ct 77459
Ringrose Ct & Dr 77459
Ripple Creek Ct & Dr 77489
N & S Ripples Ct 77459
Rising Walk Ln 77459
Rita Elliott Ct 77459
Rittenmore Dr 77489
Riva Del Lago Dr 77459
River Peak 77459
River Rock Dr 77489
River Valley Dr 77489
Riverstone Blvd 77459
Road Runner Walk 77459
Roarks Psge 77459
Robcrest Way 77489
Roberson Rd 77489
Robinson Rd 77489
Robinson Road Ct 77489
Rockergate Dr 77489
Rockmont Ct 77489
Rocky Creek Dr 77459
Rogers Row 77459
Rolling Green Ln 77459
Roma Ridge Dr 77459
Rory Ct 77459
Rose Ridge Ct 77489
Rosebriar Dr 77459
Rosebud Ln 77489
Roth Dr 77459
Round Meadow Ln 77459
Roundtree Ln 77459
Rowell Ct 77489
Royal Colony Ln 77459
Royal Plantation Ln 77459
Rudolph Ct 77459
Rue Bourbon 77459
Rue De Maison 77459
Rue Orleans 77459
Running Bird Ln 77489
Running Quail Ct 77489
Ruppstock Ct & Dr 77459
Rushbrook Dr 77459
Rustic Crest Dr 77459
Ryon Way 77459
Saberwood Dr 77489
Sabine Cir 77459
Sabine Point Way 77459
Sable River Ct & Dr 77459
Sacred Rdg 77459
Sage Ct 77489
Sage Stone Ln 77459
Sagewood Ct 77489
Sailors Way 77459
Saint Charles Ct 77459
Saint Elmos Ct 77459
Saint James Ct 77459
Salt River Ct 77459
Samuel Adams Ln 77459
Sanctuary Trl 77459
Sandstone Ridge Dr 77459
N & S Sandy Ct 77459
Sandy Knoll Dr 77489
Sandy Oaks Ln 77459
Saratoga Sq 77459
Savannah Ln 77459
Scanlan Rd & Trce 77459
Scanlin Rd 77489
Schooner Cv 77459
Scottsdale Palms Dr 77459
Sea Breeze Ct 77459
Seabold Dr 77459
Secondwind Ct 77459
Secret Forest Ln 77459
Sedona Creek Dr 77489
Senebe Way 77459
Senior Rd 77489
Sentinel Fls 77459
Serenade Terrace Dr 77459
Serina Ln 77459
Serrano Valley Ln 77459
Settemont Rd 77489
Setter Ct 77459
Shadow Briar Ln 77459
Shadow Wind Dr 77489
Shady Riv 77459
Shady Bay Ln 77459
Shady Glen Ln 77459
Shady Oaks Ct 77489
Shady Village Ct 77489
Shadyside Cir 77459
Shapiro Ct 77459
Sheffield Dr 77459
Sherwood Green Ct 77459
Shiloh Ct & Dr 77459
Shindler Ct 77459
Shipmans Landing Dr 77459
Shire Valley Dr 77459
Shiremeadow Dr 77489
Shorelake Dr 77459
Shoreline Dr 77459
Shoreview Ct & Ln 77459
Shotwell Ct 77459
Shreve Ln 77459
Sienna Cir & Pkwy 77459
Sienna Christus Dr 77459
Sienna Ranch Rd 77459
Sienna Springs Blvd & Way 77459
Sign St 77489
Silver Birch Ct 77459
Silver Leaf Dr 77489
Silver Oak 77459
Silver Ridge Blvd 77459
Silver Run Ln 77459
Silver Springs Ct 77459
Six Rivers Ln 77459
Skeet Ct 77489
Skipwood Dr 77489
Skyline Ct 77459
Slate Valley Ct 77459
Sleepy Gap Way 77459
Smithers Ln 77459
Snow Star Ct 77459
Snowy Owl Loop 77459
Sonoma Rdg 77459
Sorrento Way Dr 77459
Southern Bnd 77459
Southern Hills Dr 77459
Southhampton Ct & Rd 77459
Spanish Bay Ct 77459
Sparta Dr 77459
Spencer Ct 77459
Spice Ridge Row 77459
Spirit Hollow Ct 77459
Split Elm Dr 77459
Spring Lks 77459
Spring Bank Cir 77459
Spring Creek Ct 77459
Spring Green Ct 77459
Spring Moss Dr 77459
Spring Place Ct & Dr 77489
Springhill Dr 77459
Spyglass Ln 77459
Stafford Rd 77489
Staffordshire Rd 77489
Standing Stone Ct 77459
Star Lake Ct & Dr 77459
Starboard Shores Ct & Dr 77459
Steele Creek Ln 77459
Steep Bank Psge & Trce 77459
Steeple Chase Rd 77489
Stefano Way 77459
Stellas Psge 77459
Stephanie Dr 77489
Stepping Stone Ln 77459
Sterling Vw 77459
Steve Fuqua Pl 77459
Stevenson Dr 77459
Stiller Dr 77489
Stillmeadow Dr 77489
Stillwater Dr 77459
Stillwell St 77489
Stinson Dr 77459
Stone Lake Dr 77489
Stone Oak Ct 77459
Stone Park Rd 77489
Stonebridge Ct & Dr 77459
Stonebrook Ln 77459
Stones Throw Ln 77459
Stonewall Ct 77459
Stonewood Ln 77489
Stoney Brook Ln 77459
Stony Crst 77459
Story Book Trl 77459
Stowe Creek Ln 77459
Strong Bank 77459
Sugarbush Ln 77459
Sullivans Ct, Ln, Lndg & Way 77459
Summer Lks 77459
Summer Briar Ct 77489
Summer Place Dr 77489
Summer Quail Dr 77489
Summer Ridge Ct & Dr 77489
Summerlee Ct 77459
Summers Dr 77489
Summit Dr 77459
Summit Meadow Dr 77489
Summit Rock Way 77459
Sun City Ct 77459
Sundown Ct 77459
Sunningdale Ln 77459
Sunrise Bnd & Dr 77459
Sunset Field Ln 77459
Sunshine Ct & Ln 77459
Surfside Cir & Ln 77459
Sutters Creek Trl 77459
Swan Isle Blvd 77459
Sweetbrook Cir 77459
Swift Fox Cor 77459
Swinton Ct 77459
Sycamore Ct 77489
Syrian St 77489
T Huxley Ln 77459
Tahoe Basin 77459
Tall Cir & Trl 77459
Tall Trail Ct 77459
Tall Tree Ct 77459
Tallow Ct 77459
Talons Way 77459
Tam O Shanter Ln 77459
Tamarisk Ln 77459
Tanager Ct 77459
Tangier Turn 77459
Tattershall Ln 77459
Taylorcrest 77459
Tayside Trak 77459
Teak Dr 77489
Teal Grove Ln 77459
Tecumseh Ct 77459
Ten Acre Walk 77459
Ten Mile Lk 77459
Ten Point Ln 77459
Texas Pkwy
200-1999 77489
1902-1902 77459
2000-4198 77489
2001-4199 77489
Thebes Ct 77459
Thomas Jefferson Way 77459
Thomas Paine Dr 77459
Thompson Cir 77459
Thompson Lake Dr 77459
Thornberry Hollow Ct 77459
Thornbrook Dr 77459
Thornton Dr 77459
Thornwild Rd 77489
Thunder Ridge Way 77459
Thunderbird St 77459
Timber Creek Ct & Dr 77459
Timberlea Dr 77459
Tiny Tree Dr 77459
Toad Holw 77459
Tommy Ln 77489
Tower Bell Ln 77489
Tower Grove Ct 77489
Towerview Ln 77489
Town Gate Ct 77459
Townhome Ln 77489
Townpark Ln 77459
Townsville Cir 77459
Tradewinds Dr 77459
Trail Bnd & Holw 77459
Trailridge Ct 77459
Trammel Fresno Rd 77459
Tramwood Dr 77489
Travis Ct 77459
Trento Turn Dr 77459
Trigate Dr 77489
Trinity Meadow Dr 77459
Trinity Oaks 77459
Troy Dr 77459
Truesdale Dr 77459
Turin Turn Dr 77459
Turkey Crk 77459
Turning Row Ln 77459
Turtle Beach Ln 77459
Turtle Creek Dr
700-1399 77489
1600-2599 77489
Turtle Pond Ln 77459
Tuscan Shores Dr 77459
Twelve Oaks Ln 77459
Twin Crk 77459
Twin Forks Cir 77459
Twin Twist Ct 77489
Twining Oaks Ln 77489
Two Sisters Ct 77459
Underwood Dr 77489
S University Blvd 77459
Vail Ct 77459
Val Desa Ct 77459
Vale View Cir 77459
E & W Valley Dr 77459
Valley Bend Dr 77489
Valley Forest Dr 77489
Valley Manor Ct & Dr 77489
Valley Stone Ct 77459
Van Gogh Ln 77459
Velasco Ct 77459
Velvet Willow Dr 77459
Veneto Ln 77459
Verado Way 77459
Verdi Bnd 77459
Vermillion Dr 77459
Verona Way Ct 77459
Vesuvius Ln 77459
Via San Carlo Dr 77459
Vicksburg Blvd 77459
Victoria Ct 77459
Vieux Carre Ct 77459
Villa Ln 77459
Villa Del Lago Dr 77459
Village Cir & Ct 77459
Village Garden Dr 77489
Village Lake Ct & Dr 77459
Village Park Dr 77459
Village Square Dr 77489
Village View Dr 77459
Villarreal Dr 77489
N & S Virkus Ct 77459
Volerran Path Ln 77459
Walkabout Cir 77459
Walking Stick Trl 77459
Wallingford Dr 77459
Walnut Bend Ct 77489
Walnut Ridge Dr 77489
Wandering Lake Ln 77459
Warwick Ln 77459
Water Pt 77459
Water Oak Dr 77489
Water Shoal Ln 77459
Water Way Bnd 77459
Waterchase Dr 77489
Waterfall Dr 77489
Waterford Bnd, Ct & Ln 77459
Waterford Park St 77459
Waterford Village Blvd 77459
Waterlily Ct 77459
Waters Lake Blvd, Bnd, Ct & Ln 77459
Waterside Ct & Dr 77459
Waterstone St 77459
Waterview Ct 77459
Waterwood Ct 77459
Watts Plantation Dr 77459
Wavertree Dr 77459
Wedgewood Ct 77489
Weeping Willow Pl 77459
Welborn Ct & Dr 77459
Wellington Ct 77459
Wenona Walk 77459
Westall Ln 77459
Westpoint Dr 77459
Westray Ct & Dr 77459
Westshore Ct & Dr 77459
Whippoorwill Cir 77459
Whippoorwill Dr 77489
Whispering Pine Ct & Dr 77489
Wickson Mnr, Sq & Way 77459
Wild Trl 77459
Wild Peach Pl 77459
Wildhorse Ct 77459
Wildwood Ridge Dr 77489
Willbriar Ln 77489
Williams Bend Ct 77459
Williamsburg Ln 77459
Willmore Ln 77489
Willow Bay Dr 77459
Willow Green Dr 77489
Willow Mill Dr 77489
Willow Oak Dr 77489
Willow Tree Ct 77459
Willow Wisp Dr 77489
Willowcraft Dr 77489
Willowsong Ct 77489
Willview Rd 77489
Windsail Ct 77459
Windshire 77459
Windsor Ct 77459
Windy Willow Ct & Dr 77489
Windysage Ct 77459
Winged Foot Dr 77459
Winter Lks 77459
Winter Briar Dr 77489
Winter Creek Ct 77459
Winter Green Ct 77459
Winterview Dr 77489
Wolfpen Ridge Ln 77459
Wolverhampton Way 77459
Wood Duck Ct 77459
Wood Orchard Ct & Dr 77489
Wood Shadows Dr 77489
Wood Stork Ln 77459
Wood Trails Ct 77489
Woodglen Dr 77489
Woodlake Ln 77459
Woodland Hills Dr 77489
Woods Canyon Ct 77459
Woodsmith Ct 77489
Woodvale Dr 77489
Wrenway Dr 77489
Yankee Ct 77459
Yorktown Ln 77459
Zabaco 77459
Zinnia Rd 77489

NUMBERED STREETS

2nd St 77489
3rd St 77489
5th St 77489
3600-3799 77459

MONTGOMERY TX

General Delivery 77356

POST OFFICE BOXES MAIN OFFICE STATIONS AND BRANCHES

Box No.s
All PO Boxes 77356

RURAL ROUTES

02, 13, 29 77316
04, 05, 08, 09, 10, 11, 12, 14, 15, 16, 17, 18, 20, 21, 22 77356

NAMED STREETS

Aberdeen Ct 77316
Adams Rd 77356
Adela Dr 77316
Adobe Ter N & S 77316
Adoue Rd 77316
Alamo Ct 77316
Alba Rd 77356
Alcott Dr 77356
E & W Alderson 77316
Allison Ct 77316
Aloha Ln 77356
Alvin Aly 77316
Amber Ln 77316
Amber Jack 77356
Amberwood Dr & Rd 77356
Amelia Ct 77356
Amherst Glade Rd 77316
Angie Ln 77316
Angler Rd 77316
Anna Ln 77356
Anna Springs Ln 77356
Apache Bnd, Dr & Ln 77316
April Ct, Cv, Hl & Vlg 77356
April Breeze St 77356
April Harbour Dr 77356
April Park Dr 77356
April Point Dr & Pl 77356
April Sound Blvd 77356
April Villas W 77356
April Waters Dr N & W 77356
April Wind Ct & Dr E, N & S 77356
Arapahoe Dr 77316
Arbor Way Ct 77316
Argosy Ln 77316
Armada Ct 77316
Armadillo Rd 77356
Arnsworth Rd 77356
Arrowhead Dr 77316
Askew Ct & Rd 77356
Aspen Dr & Ln 77356
Austin Mccomb Rd 77316
Autumn Wood 77356
Ava Ln 77316
Avenue E 77356
Bailey Grove Rd 77356
Baja St 77356
Balboa Cir & Rd 77356
Balmoral 77316
Barbara Ln 77356
Bass Way Ct 77316
Bay Point Ln 77356
Bayshore Dr 77356
Bear Canyon Dr 77356
Beautyberry Ct 77316
Beaver Run Rd 77356
Beech Dr 77316
Beechnut Dr 77356
Bellingham Ct 77356
Ben Smith Rd 77316
Bent Tree Ln 77356
Benthaven Ct & Isle 77356
Bentwater Dr 77356
Bentwater Bay Cir, Ct, Dr & Ln 77356
Bentwater Harbor Dr 77356
Bentwood Ct & Dr 77356
Berkley Dr 77356
Bermuda Cir 77356
Berwick Ln 77316
Bessie Price Owens Dr 77356
Bethel Rd 77356
Bethlem Rd 77356
Beulah Ln 77316
Big Oak Dr 77356

Bilsing Cv 77356
Birch Dr 77356
Black Oak Dr & Ln 77316
Blacktail Pl 77316
Blue Gilia Ct 77316
Blue Goose Dr 77316
N, S & E Blue Heron Cir, Ct & Dr 77316
Blue Hill Dr 77356
Bluegill Pl 77316
Bluewater Rd 77356
Boars Head Pl 77316
Bobville Rd 77316
Boca Raton Cir 77356
Bois D Arc Bend Rd 77356
Bolin Rd 77356
Bonanza Dr 77316
Bonnie Alice Dr 77316
Bowie Ct 77316
Brassie Bay Cir 77356
Breckenridge Dr 77356
Breezy Dr 77316
Briarwood Ln 77356
Bridgeview Ln 77356
Brightwood Dr 77356
Brinway Ln 77316
Bristol Ct 77356
Broad Cove Dr & Ln 77356
Broken Wheel Cir 77316
Brontton Ct 77356
Brooke Addison Ct & Way 77316
Brookes Dr 77316
Brookgreen Cir N & S 77356
Brookhaven Dr & Pt 77356
Brookwood Ct 77356
Browning Dr 77356
Bryan Ln 77316
Buccaneer Dr 77356
Buck Ridge Rd 77316
Buckingham Ln 77356
Buckland Ct 77316
Buffalo Spgs 77356
Buffalo Ridge Rd 77356
Burning Tree Dr 77356
Cabanna Way 77316
Calm Harbor Xing 77356
Calmwater Dr & St 77356
Camden Ct & Hls 77356
Camden Hills Dr 77356
Camden Oaks Ln 77356
Canadian River Cir 77316
Candlewood Ct, Ln & Pl 77356
Cannondale Loop 77316
Canterbury Ct & Ln 77356
Canterbury Green Dr 77356
Cape Conroe Dr 77356
Capetown Cir, Ln & Way 77356
Capetown Slip 77356
Capitol Hill Rd 77316
Carapace Cove Pl 77316
Carmel Ct 77356
Carnoustie Ct 77316
Caroline St 77356
Caroline Corner Ct 77316
Carols Ct 77356
Carpenter Rd 77356
Carriage Trl 77316
Cartwright Rd 77316
Case Cove Ct & Ln 77356
Castlebrook Ct 77316
Catamaran Way 77356
Catpaw Trl 77316
Cb Stewart Dr 77356
Cecala Dr 77356
Cedar Ln
1-99 77356
1100-1199 77316
20500-20699 77356
Cedar Hill Dr 77356
Cedar Ridge Ln 77356
E & W Cedar River Rd 77316
Cedargrove Ln 77356
Central Trace Dr 77316
Cessna Dr 77316
Chapel Rd 77316
Chapparal Rd 77356
Chaucer Dr 77356
Checkerbloom Ct 77316
Cherokee Dr 77316
Cherry Bark Pl 77316
Cherry Hill Dr 77356
Cherry Oak Ln 77316
Chestnut Ct 77316
Chestnut Dr 77356
Cheyenne Loop & Rd 77316
Chick Ln 77356
Chickasaw Dr 77316
Chipmunk Dr 77316
Chippers Xing 77356
Churchhill Downs 77356
Circle Dr 77356
Circle Vw 77356
Circle View Dr & Trl 77316
Cissys Ln 77316
Claremont Ct 77356
Claret Cup Ln 77316
Clark Rd 77316
Clear Springs Dr 77356
Clear Water Blvd, Cir & St E & W 77356
Clearmont Pl 77356
Clepper 77356
Cloverdale Ct 77356
Club Dr 77316
Club Creek Dr 77356
Club Island Ct & Way 77356
Colina Vista Way 77316
College St 77356
Collier Ct & Rd 77316
Collier Cemetery Rd 77316
Colony Pl 77356
Colton Ct 77316
Columbia River Rd 77316
Commanche Rd 77316
Commerce Row 77356
Community Center Rd 77356
Compass Point Ct 77356
Concord Cir 77356
Congress Ave 77316
Connie Ln 77316
Continental Quarters 77316
Contraband Dr 77356
Cool Cv 77356
E & W Cool Breeze Ln 77356
Coop Ave 77356
Copelan Chapel Rd 77356
Copper Mtn 77316
Cordova Ct 77356
Corsair Ct 77316
Cottonwood Dr 77356
Country Rd 77316
Country Club Blvd 77356
Country Oaks Blvd 77356
Country Squire Ln 77356
Cove Cir, Pl, Pt & Way W 77356
Cove Place Ct 77356
Cranberry Ln 77356
Crawford Cir 77356
Creekwood Dr 77356
Creightons Ct 77356
Crescent Ct 77356
Crescent Dr 77316
Crestmont 77316
Crestwood Ct 77356
Crestwood Farms Dr 77356
Cripple Creek Cir 77356
Crockett Ct 77316
Crown Ct 77316
E & W Crown Crossing Dr 77316
Crown Lake Ct 77356
Crown Oaks Dr 77356
Crown Ranch Blvd 77316
Crystal River Rd 77316
Cushing Rd 77316
Cypress Point Cir 77356
Dalton Willis Dr 77316
Dans Pl 77316
Dapplegray Ln E & W 77356
Darien Ct 77356
Darton Rd 77316
Dawns Edge Dr 77356
Dean Rd 77316
Debbie Ln 77356
Debonaire Ln 77316
Deep Forest Ln 77316
Deep Water Dr 77356
Deepwater Dr 77356
Deer Creek Ln 77316
Deer Hill Dr 77316
Deer Lake Lodge Rd 77316
Deer Run St 77356
Del Monte Pines Ct & Dr 77316
Del Rey Oaks Pl 77316
Del Sol Villa 77356
Delaware Dr 77316
Denn Ct, Ln & Rd 77356
Desert Inn Cir & Dr 77356
Devlin Downs Ln 77356
Dewberry Pl 77316
Diamondhead Rd 77356
Doe Hill Rd 77316
Dogwood Ln 77316
Dogwood Loop 77316
Dogwood Trl 77316
Doral Cir 77356
Doretta Dr 77316
E & W Dounreay 77316
Dover Dr 77356
Dr Martin Luther King Dr 77356
Drake Rd 77316
Druids Ct 77316
Duchess Ct 77316
Duchess River Cir 77316
Dunes Cir 77356
Eagle Pointe 77316
Eastchase 77316
Eastwood Dr 77316
Eastwood Ln 77316
Ebner Lake Dr 77316
Ebner Lake Front Dr 77316
Echo Ln 77356
Edgemar Rd 77316
Edgewater Ct 77356
Edgewood Cir, Ct & Dr W 77356
Edinburgh Ct 77316
Edwards Rd 77316
Ehler Ln 77356
El Wanda Ln 77316
Elderberry Trl 77316
Elk Trace Pkwy 77316
Ella Brown Rd 77316
Elm Dr 77316
Eloise Dr 77316
Emerson Dr 77356
Emmett Dr 77316
Enchanted 77356
Enchanted Way Dr 77356
Englewood Ct 77356
English Oak Dr 77356
Enzos Way 77316
Erin Dr 77316
Estelle Cir 77356
Ethans Xing 77316
Eva St 77356
Evans Ter 77316
Evergreen Ln & Way 77356
Fair Oak St 77356
Fairfield Dr 77356
Fairhaven Ln 77356
Fairwater Dr 77356
Fairway Park 77356
Fairway View Ct & Ln 77356
Falcon Ct 77356
Falcon Landing Dr 77356
Falcon Sound Dr 77356
Fallin Rd 77356
Fantasy Ln 77356
Fathom Dr & St 77356
Fawn Frst 77356
Fawn Forest Rd 77356
Finchfield Pl 77316
Finwick Dr 77316
Firepine Ln 77316
First Lgt 77356
Fish Creek Ct & Ln 77316
Fish Creek Thoroughfare 77316
Fisher Lake Ct 77316
Fitzgerald Dr 77356
Flamingo Lakes Rd 77356
Fm 1097 Rd 77356
Fm 1375 Rd 77356
Fm 1486 Rd 77356
N Fm 1486 Rd 77356
S Fm 1486 Rd 77316
Fm 149 Rd
6500-13299 77316
13301-14899 77316
15000-21299 77356
22100-22199 77316
22200-23299 77356
22700-23099 77356
Fm 2854 Rd 77356
Forest Blvd 77356
Forest Cir 77356
Forest Cir E 77356
Forest Ct 77356
Forest Dr
4600-4799 77316
15300-20699 77356
Forest Ln 77356
Forest Elk Pl 77316
Forest Glenn St 77316
Forest Heights Ct, Ln & Way 77316
Forest Hills Dr 77316
Forest Lake Ct & Dr 77316
Forest Peak Way 77316
Forest River Cir 77316
Forest Wind Cir & Ct 77316
Forest Woods Ln 77356
E & W Forrestal Ct 77316
Fountainview Dr 77356
Fox Rindle Rd 77356
Foxridge Dr 77316
Franconia Dr 77316
Freedonia St 77316
Freeport Dr 77356
French Kingston Ct 77356
French River Cir 77316
Friartuck Dr 77316
Galley Way 77316
Gary Player Rd 77316
Gay Lake Rd 77316
Gemstone Dr 77356
Giles Rd 77356
Gingham Rd S 77356
Glenforest Dr & Rd 77356
Glenheath 77316
Glenview Dr 77316
Goldfinch Ln 77356
Golfcrest Dr 77356
Golfview Ct & Dr 77356
Grand Harbor Blvd & Pt 77356
Grand Lake Estates Dr 77316
Grand Marion Ct & Way 77316
E & W Grand Pine Cir & Dr 77356
Grand Pines Dr 77356
E & W Grand Pond Ct & Dr 77356
Grand View Ct & Dr 77356
Grandview Blvd, Ct, Dr & Pt 77356
Green Cove Dr 77356
Green Isle Bch 77356
Green Oak St 77316
Green River Rd 77316
Greenbriar Dr & Rd 77356
Greenview St 77316
Grey Moss Ln 77356
Greypine E & W 77356
Grove Clover Ln 77316
Guinevere Ln 77316
Guyton Ln 77316
Haileys Run 77316
Hall Dr N & S 77316
E & W Hammon 77316
Hampton Glen Rd 77356
Happy Hollow Ln 77356
Harbor Cir & Dr 77356
Harbor Breeze Dr 77356
Harbor Court Dr 77356
Harbor Mist 77356
Harbor Side Blvd & Ct 77356
Harbor View Villa 77356
Harbour Town Cir, Ct, Dr, Ln & Way 77356
Hardy Oak 77316
Harley Dr 77356
Harris Ln 77316
Havenshire Dr 77316
Hawkins Ct 77316
Hawkwatch Dr 77316
Hawthorne Dr 77356
Heatherglen Rd 77356
Heatherwood 77356
Hemingway Dr 77356
Henson Rd 77356
Hermitage Dr 77356
Hickory Dr 77356
Hickory Hill Ln 77356
Hickory Hills Dr 77316
Hickory Ridge Loop 77316
Hidden Creek Ln 77356
Hidden Glen Cv 77356
Hidden Valley Dr 77356
High Fire Rd 77356
High Meadow Estates Dr 77316
High Oaks Dr 77356
Highland Lks, Pass, Rdg & Spgs 77316
Highland Point Dr 77356
Highland Ranch Dr 77316
Highline Dr 77316
Highpoint Ln 77356
Highway 105 W 77356
Highwood Ct & Rd 77356
Hill Creek Rd 77316
Hills Pkwy 77316
Hills Lake Ct 77356
Hillsborough Dr E & W 77356
Hillside Ct & Dr 77356
Hilltop Cir & Dr 77316
Hilltop Ranch Ct & Dr 77316
Hillwood Ln 77356
Hilton Head Dr 77356
Hodge Archibald Rd 77316
Holly Dr
15100-15599 77316
15600-15899 77356
Holly Est 77316
Holly Ln E 77316
Holly Ln S 77316
Holly Ln W 77316
Holly Park 77316
Holly St 77356
Honea Rd W 77316
Honea Egypt Rd 77316
Hope Rd 77316
Horseshoe Bnd 77316
Houston St
300-499 77316
500-599 77356
Howelarl Dr 77356
Huckleberry Ln 77316
Huffman St 77316
Huffsmith Rd 77316
Hunters Cir, Ct, Gln, Lndg, Pt, Run & Trl 77356
Hunters Glen Way 77356
E & N Hunting Tower Run 77316
Huntsworth Ln 77316
Imperial Ln 77316
Indian Fls N & S 77316
Inlet Cir & Dr 77356
Intervale Dr 77316
Intrigue St 77356
Inverness Dr & Way 77356
Inwood Forest Dr 77356
Isleworth Manor Pl 77316
E & W Ivanhoe 77316
Jackson Rd & Run 77316
Jakes Lndg 77316
Jaxxon Pointe Dr 77316
Jefferson River Cir 77316
Jenny Ln 77356
Joe Ln 77316
Joe Adams Rd 77356
John A Butler 77356
Johnson Rd
9800-10499 77316
24700-27299 77356
Jordan Pl 77316
Joshua Ct 77316
Joshuas Pl 77316
Julie Ln 77356
E & W Juneau Ct 77316
Juniper Ln 77356
Kaden Creek Ct & Pl 77316
Kate Place Ct 77316
Keaton Ct 77316
Keenan Cut Off Rd 77316
Kempwood 77356
Kentucky Derby 77316
Key Harbor Dr 77356
Kinderwood Trl 77316
King Arthurs Ct 77316
King Edward Ct 77316
King George Ct 77316
King Richards Ct 77316
Kingford Ct & Dr 77316
Kingridge Ct & Dr 77316
Kings Ln 77356
Kings Point St 77356
Kings View Ct 77316
Kinkaid Rd E & W 77316
Kirsten Ct 77316
Knollbrook Cir 77316
Knollcrest Dr 77356
Kohen Ct 77316
E & W Kristina Cir 77316
Kuhn Ct 77316
Kyle Corner Pl 77316
L And M Rd 77316
La Costa Dr 77356
La Jolla Cir 77356
La Mirada Dr 77356
La Torretta Blvd 77356
Laguna Rd 77356
Lake Blf 77356
W Lake Pt 77356
N Lake Rd 77356
S Lake Rd 77356
W Lake St 77356
Lake Ter 77356
N Lake Vw 77316
Lake Conroe Village Blvd 77316
Lake Creek Cir 77356
Lake Estates Ct & Dr 77356
Lake Forest Dr 77356
Lake Island Cir & Dr 77356
Lake Meadows Dr 77316
Lake Mount Pleasant Rd 77356
Lake Oak Dr 77356
Lake Pines Dr 77356
Lake Point Blvd 77356
Lake Shore Dr
9800-10199 77316
12300-12999 77356
Lake View Cir 77356
Lake View Dr 77356
N Lake View Rd 77316
S Lake View Rd 77316
Lake Walden Cv 77356
Lakecrest Dr 77356
Lakeland Dr 77356
Lakeshore Dr 77316
Lakeside Cir 77316
Lakeside Dr 77356
Lakeside Hills Dr 77316
Laketree Dr 77356
Lakeview Dr
1100-1199 77316
12400-12599 77356
Lakeview Ter
102A-202A 77356
102B-206B 77356
102C-204C 77356
102D-314D 77356
102E-204E 77356
102F-204F 77356
102G-208G 77356
102H-204H 77356
101A-203A 77356
101B-205B 77356
101C-203C 77356
101D-315D 77356
101E-203E 77356
101F-203F 77356
101G-207G 77356
101H-203H 77356
Lakeview Vlg 77356
Lakeview Way 77316
Lakeview Forest Dr 77316
Lakeway Dr 77316
Lakeway Ln 77356
Lakewood Dr 77356
W Lakewood Dr 77316
Landrum Ln 77356
Landrum Village Dr & Ln 77316
Laramie Trl 77316
Larson Ln 77316
Lauren Ln 77356
Laurens Ct & Way 77316
Lawrence Dr 77356
Lawson St 77356
Lazy Ln
200-499 77356
4900-9299 77316
Lazy Riv 77316
Lazy Trl 77316
Lazy Hollow Ln 77356
Lazy Lake Ln 77356
Lazy Springs Dr 77356
Leafy Arbor Dr 77356
Leah Dr 77316
Leandro Ct 77356
Leisure Ln 77356
Lewis Ln 77316
Liberty St
100-399 77356
400-14199 77316
14200-15399 77356
N Liberty St 77356
Linda Ln 77316
Lindas Pl 77316
Little John St 77316
Little River Dr 77316
N Log Cabin Rd 77356
Logans Trl 77356
Logansport Ct 77356
Lois Ln 77316
Lone Star Bnd 77356
Lone Star Ct 77316
Lone Star Pkwy 77356
Longfellow Cir & Dr 77356
Looking Glass Blvd 77356
Lorna Rd 77316
Louisa 77356
Lovers Ln 77356
Lowell 77316
Lucky Ln 77356
Lukes Place Ln 77316
Lullabye Ln 77356
Lure Cv 77356
E & W Lynbrook 77316
Lyndsey Dr 77316
Maddys Ct 77316
Madeley Rd 77356
Madeley Ranch Rd 77356
Madeline Ct & Ln 77316
Madison Riv 77316

Mail Route Rd 77316
Majestic Dr 77316
Majestic Lake Ct 77316
Majestic Oak Ct 77316
Majestic Oaks Ct 77316
Mann Ln 77316
Marian Ln 77316
Marietta Ct 77356
Marina Dr & Way 77356
Marina View Dr 77356
Marseille 77356
Martha Rd 77316
Martha Williams Rd 77356
Martin Rd 77316
Mary Ln 77316
Marys Ct 77316
Mason St 77356
Masters Dr 77356
Mccaleb Rd 77316
Mccaleb Rd N
1-1199 77356
200-299 77356
Mccowan St 77356
Mcginnis Ln 77356
Meadow Ct 77356
Meadowcroft 77316
Meadowlark Ln 77316
Meadowview Ct 77316
Meads Mdw 77356
Melbourne Ct 77356
Melissa Lynns 77316
Melrose Dr 77356
Melville Dr 77356
Mesa Vw 77316
Mesquite 77316
Meyers Rd 77356
Mia Lago Dr 77356
Michals Run 77316
Middleton Dr 77356
Millies Run Rd 77316
Milton Whatley Dr 77356
Misty Hbr E & W 77356
Misty Harbor Dr 77356
Misty Manor Ln 77316
Misty Moss 77356
Mitchell Rd 77316
Mizzenmast Ct 77316
Mock Ln & Rd 77356
Mocking Bird Ln 77356
Mohawk Bnd & Dr 77316
Monarch Park Ct & Dr 77316
Monarchs Way 77316
Monk Ln 77316
Monterrey Bnd 77316
Monterrey Ct 77356
Monterrey Cv 77356
Monterrey Rd 77356
Monterrey Rd E 77356
Monterrey Rd W 77356
Monterrey Pines Dr 77316
Moody Dr 77316
Moon Camp Rd 77316
Moonmist Ln 77356
Moonspinner 77356
Moonwalk St 77356
Moore Ln 77356
Morning Mist 77316
Morningside Ct 77356
N Mount Mariah Rd 77356
S Mount Mariah Rd 77316
Mount Mariah Cut Off Rd 77356
Mount Moriah Rd 77356
Mount Pleasant Rd & Vlg 77356
Mountain Laurel Dr 77316
Mountain View Dr 77356
Muirfield Pointe Way 77316
Mulberry Dr 77316
Mulberry Ln 77356
Mulligan Dr 77316
Myers Rd 77356
Mystic Cir & Pt 77356
Mystic Pond Trl 77356
Mystric Rd 77356
Naples Ln 77356
Naples Siding 77356
Natchez River Cir 77316
Nathanael Ct 77356
Nautica Ln 77316
Navajo St 77316
Navigation Cir 77316
Neptunes Cv 77316
Newberry Ct 77356
Nicholas Ct 77316
Nicholson Rd 77316
Northlawn 77316
Northmont Dr & Rd 77356
Northshore Dr 77356
Nottingham Ln 77356
Nubby Bnd 77356
O Henry Dr 77356
Oak Ct 77356
Oak Dr 77356
Oak Ln 77316
Oak Knoll Ct 77356
Oak Knoll Dr 77316
Oak Knoll Ln 77356
Oak Knoll Rd 77356
Oak Village Dr 77356
W Oaks Ct 77356
Oaks On The Water 77356
Oaktree Ct 77356
Ocean Mist Ct 77356
Old Aqua Lndg 77356
Old Dobbin Rd 77316
Old Dobbin Plantersvil Rd 77316
Old Highway 105 W 77316
Old Montgomery Rd 77316
Old Plantersville Rd 77316
Old River Ct & Rd 77356
Omeara 77356
Osage Dr 77316
Osborn Rd 77356
Overland Trce 77316
Oxon Run 77316
Palais Verde Rd 77356
Palm Blvd, Dr & St 77356
Palm Beach Blvd 77356
Palmdate 77316
Pamela Way 77316
Papoose Trl 77316
Paradise Ln 77356
Paradise Oak Dr 77356
Park Cir 77356
E Park Dr 77316
S Park Dr 77316
Park Ln 77316
E Park Ln 77316
W Park Ln 77316
Park Way 77356
Park Ridge Ct 77356
Parkhaven Cir 77316
Parkside Blvd 77356
Parkway Ln 77356
Parrish Trl 77316
N & W Patterson Rd 77356
Patton Ln 77316
Pawnee Dr 77316
Peace Pipe Trl 77316
Pearl River Dr 77316
Pearson Ln & Rd 77356
Pebble Beach Blvd & Cir 77356
Pecan Cv & Dr 77356
Pecan Tree Ln 77316
Peel Rd 77356
Peggy Dr 77316
Penninsula Pt 77356
Pennsylvania Ave 77316
Pepperhill Dr 77356
Perfection Dr 77316
Peterson Rd 77356
Pickerel Pt 77316
Pike Mill Pl 77316
Pimmit Hill Run 77316
Pin Oak St 77316
Pine Dr 77356
Pine Dr N
19000-19099 77356
1-299 77356
S Pine Dr 77356
Pine Hvn 77356
Pine Ln 77356
Pine Rdg 77356
Pine Arbor Dr 77356
Pine Bluff Dr 77356
Pine Bough Ln 77356
Pine Branch Dr 77356
Pine Brook Dr 77356
Pine Bush Dr 77356
Pine Chase Dr 77356
Pine Crest Cir 77316
Pine Hill Ln 77356
Pine Hollow Cir & Ln 77356
E, W & S Pine Lake Cir & Rd 77316
Pine Point Dr 77316
Pine Tree Rd 77356
Pine View Cir 77356
Pinehurst Dr 77316
Pineneedle Dr 77356
Pinerock Ln 77356
Pines Ct & Dr 77356
Pinetrail Ln 77356
Pinewood Trl 77356
Pinnacle Ridge Ct & Dr 77316
Piper Ln 77316
Piping Rock Dr 77356
Platte River Dr 77316
Playmoor Pl 77316
Pleasant Dr 77356
Pleasantview Ct 77316
Pleasure Ct 77316
Poe Dr 77356
Poets Ct 77356
Pond St 77356
Ponderosa Dr & Trl 77356
Pooles Rd 77356
Poppy Hills Dr 77316
Port Au Prince Ct 77316
Porter Rd 77316
Possum Hollow Rd 77316
Post Oak Ln & Way 77316
Post Oak Cemetary Rd 77356
Powder River Cir 77316
Powell Cir 77316
Powell Dr 77356
Powers Ct 77316
Prairie St 77356
Presidio Rd 77356
Preston Ct 77316
Prestwick Ct 77316
Price Rd 77316
Prince Andrew 77316
Prince Charles Ct 77316
Prince Henry Ct 77316
Prince Phillip Ct 77316
Prince William Ct 77316
Princess Ann Ct 77316
Princess Diana Ln 77316
Princess Margaret Ct 77316
Promenade St E 77356
Pronghorn Pl 77316
Quail Ridge Pl 77316
Queen Elizabeth Ct 77316
Queen Victoria Ct 77316
Queensboro Ct 77316
Queenswood 77356
Quiet Hollow Rd 77356
Quiet Water Ln & Way 77356
Quiet Wind Dr 77356
Quintana Ct 77316
Rabon Chapel Rd 77316
Rainforest Ln 77356
Raintree Dr 77356
Ramblewood Ct & Rd 77356
Ranch Top Ct 77356
Ranchette Rd 77356
Rankin St 77356
S Reach 77356
Rebecca Ln 77316
Red Deer Pl 77316
Red Oak Dr 77316
Red Wing Ln 77316
Redbird Ln 77356
Redwing Cir 77356
Reed Rd 77316
Reese Run Ct & St 77316
Regal Hill Ct 77316
Regatta Ct 77316
Regency Pt 77356
Regent Ct 77356
Renaissance Dr 77356
Renee Ln 77356
Retriever Run 77316
Reveille Ln 77316
Rhonda Ln 77316
Ridge Lake Dr 77316
Ridge Lake Ln 77356
Ridgelake Ct 77316
Ridgelake Scenic Dr 77316
Ridgeshore Ct 77316
Ridgeside 77316
Ridgewood Dr 77316
Rimrock Pass 77316
Ripplewind Ct & Dr 77356
River Rd 77356
Riverbend Ct & Way 77316
Riverbend Crossing Dr 77316
Robin Dr 77356
Robin Hood Dr 77356
Robins Nest Rd 77356
Rock River Dr 77316
Rolling Creek Dr 77316
Rolling Oak Ct & Dr 77316
Rolling Oaks Dr 77356
Rolling Springs Dr 77356
Rollingwood 77356
Roman Hills Blvd 77356
Rosalea Way 77356
Rosemont Dr 77356
Royal Haven Ln 77356
Royal Hill Ct 77316
Royal Navigator Rd 77316
Royal Oak Ct 77356
Rubye Ln 77316
Rue Ann St 77356
Ruskin Dr E & W 77356
Rustling Wind Dr 77356
Sabine River Rd 77316
Saddle Oak Dr 77356
Sagestone Ct 77316
Sail View St 77356
Saint Beulah Chapel Rd 77316
Saint Lawrence River Rd 77316
Salem Cir 77356
Sallas Ranch Rd 77316
Sandy Hill Rd 77316
Sanibel Crest Pl 77316
Sarah Ln 77356
Sarasota Cir & Ct 77356
Scenic Dr 77356
Scenic Lake Ct 77316
Scotts Ridge Rd 77356
Sea Island Dr 77356
Seale 77316
Seashell Cir 77356
Season Ln 77316
Sebastians Run 77316
Seibel Ln 77356
Seminole Dr 77316
Serene Water Ct & Dr 77356
E Settlers Bnd 77356
Shadow Ln 77316
Shadowcrest Ct 77356
Shady Glen Dr 77356
Shady Grove Ln 77356
Shady Oaks Blvd 77356
Shady Woods Ct 77356
Shadyside Ln 77356
Shadywater Dr & St 77356
Shamrock Cir 77356
Shane St 77356
Shannon Cir 77316
Sharon Cir 77316
Sharp Rd 77356
Shawnee Dr 77316
Shelleys Run 77316
Sherwood Forest St 77316
Shields Ln 77356
Shirlington Rd 77316
S, W & N Shore Blvd, Ct, Dr & Ln 77316
Shoreline Dr 77356
Short Mill Run 77316
N & S Silver Manor Cir 77316
Silver Minnow Pl 77316
Silver River Dr 77316
Simmons Ln 77356
Simonton Rd & St 77356
Sinclair Dr 77316
Singleton Dr & Rd 77356
Sioux River Rd 77316
Skipper Ln 77316
Skipper Jack 77316
Skylane Dr 77316
Sleepy Holw 77356
Smillann Rd 77316
Smith Rd 77356
Smokey River Bnd 77316
Snug Harbor Dr 77356
Soaring Pines Pl 77316
Somerset Rd 77356
Somerton Dr 77356
Spanish Bay Pl 77316
Spokane River Rd 77316
Spreading Oaks Ct 77316
Spring Branch Rd & Trl 77316
Spring Branch Cemetery Rd 77316
Spring Lake Dr 77356
Spring Stream Bnd 77316
Spring Woods Dr 77316
Springcrest 77356
Springer Rd 77356
Springs Edge Dr 77356
Springshed Pl 77316
Springtime Dr 77356
Spruce Dr & Ln 77356
Spy Glass Hill Dr 77356
Spyglass Park Ln & Loop 77316
Stacy Diane Dr 77316
Stanford Ct 77356
Stanhart Rd 77356
Stanlart Dr 77356
Steamboat Spgs 77356
Steede Rd 77356
Sternway Ct 77316
Stevin Stratt 77356
Stewart St 77316
Stewart Creek Rd 77356
Stewart Hill Dr 77316
Stillwater Blvd & Ct 77316
Stinson Ln 77316
Stone Ct & Xing 77316
Stone Creek Ln 77316
Stone Oak Ct & Dr 77316
Stone Ranch Blvd 77316
Stonefield 77316
Stonehedge Pl 77316
Stonehenge Dr 77356
Stones Edge Dr 77356
Stratford Dr 77316
Strawberry Ln 77356
Strawberry River Dr 77316
Stuart Dr 77356
Stubblefield Lake Rd 77356
Stubby Cir 77356
Summer Hill Dr 77356
Summers Wind St 77356
Sun Valley Ct 77356
Sunburst Ln 77356
Sunnyfield Farm Rd 77316
Sunnyvale E & W 77356
Sunridge Ct 77356
Sunrise Maple Dr 77316
Sunrise Oaks Ct 77316
Sunrise Pines Dr 77316
Sunrise Ranch Ct 77356
Sunset Cir 77356
Sunset Ln 77316
Sunset Path N 77316
Sunset Path S 77316
Sunset Hill Ln 77316
Sunset Ranch Dr 77316
Sunset Terrace Ct 77316
Sweetgum Dr 77356
Sycamore Dr 77356
Tacker Rd 77316
Taylor St 77356
Taylors Ct 77356
Teel Rd 77356
Teewood Ct 77356
Tejas Blvd 77316
Tempo Villa 77356
Texas Trce 77316
Texian Trl 77316
Thames Cir 77356
The Cliffs Blvd & Ct 77356
Thoreau Dr 77356
Thousand Oaks Loop 77316
Tiffanys Ct 77316
Tiki Way 77356
Timberglen Ct 77316
Timberlane Dr 77356
Tisdel Rd 77316
Tobacco Rd 77316
Torrey Pines Dr 77356
Tower Ln 77356
Trace Ct 77316
Trace Way Dr 77316
Trade Winds Ct 77316
Trail Hollow Dr 77316
Trailway Dr 77316
Tranquility View Ct 77316
Treasure Island Dr 77356
Tree Bark Ln 77316
Trelawney Pl 77316
Tri Lakes Rd 77316
Tudor Cir 77356
Turnberry Ct 77356
Turtlecreek Cove Ct 77316
Twain Dr 77356
Twin Circles Dr 77356
Twin Lakes Rd 77316
Upper Beacon Pl 77356
Vail Ct & Dr 77356
Valley Rd 77356
Victoria Ct 77356
Victoria Dr E 77356
Victoria Dr W 77356
Victoria Trce 77356
Victoria Regina Dr 77356
Victorias Way Dr 77316
Villa Valentino 77356
Village Forest Dr 77356
Villas Ways Dr 77356
Vineyard Ln 77356
Vintage Oaks Ct & Dr 77356
Virginia Ave 77316
Virginia Ct 77356
Virginia St 77316
Von Hagge Hollow Ln 77356
Wade Pointe Dr 77316
Waikiki Ln 77356
Wakefield Rd 77316
Walden Rd 77356
Walden Estates Dr 77356
Walding Rd 77356
Walding Woods Dr 77356
Walnut Dr 77356
Walnut Turn St 77356
Wanda Ln 77316
Warwick Glen Dr 77356
Washington Ave 77316
Water Crest Ct & Dr 77356
Waterberry Ct & Way 77356
Waterford Way 77356
Waterfront Dr 77356
N & S Waterhaven Cir 77316
Waters Edge St 77356
Watersound Ct 77356
Waterstone Ct
1-99 77356
300-399 77316
Waterstone Dr 77356
N Waterstone Dr 77356
Waterview Cir & Dr 77356
Watson Ranch Rd 77356
Wedgewood Cir, Ct & Dr W 77356
Wee Creek Ln 77356
Weeren Rd 77316
Wesleys Ct 77316
Westchase 77316
Western Trails Blvd 77316
Westlyn Ct & Ln 77356
Westway Cir & Dr 77356
Whisper Walk 77356
Whispering Pines Ln 77356
Whistling Oak Dr 77356
White Oak Ln, Loop & St 77316
White River Rd 77316
Whitman Dr 77356
Whittier 77356
Wick Willow Dr & Rd 77356
Wickwild Cir 77356
Wilderness Way 77316
Wildwind Way 77356
Will Scarlett St 77316
Willow Ln 77356
Willowbend Rd 77356
Willowrun Dr 77356
Willowside Ct 77356
Wilmington Rd 77356
Wilson Cv 77316
S Wind Dr 77356
Wind Jammer Ln 77316
Windermere Ln 77316
Windfair Loop 77316
Windhill Ln 77356
Windjammer Ln 77356
Windmill Ln 77316
Windsor Ct 77356
Windswept Dr 77356
Windward Ct 77316
Wingate Dr 77356
Winners Cir 77356
Winslow Hill Pl 77316
Wintercrest Dr 77356
Winterhaven Ln 77356
Winthrop Harbor Ct & St N & S 77356
Womack Cemetery Rd 77316
Wood Harbour Dr 77356
Wood Haven Dr 77316
Wood Hollow Ln 77356
Wood Rock Ln 77356
Woodchuck Rd 77356
Woodcreek Rd 77356
Wooddale Ln 77356
Woodlake Trl 77316
Woodland Ln 77356
Woodmont Dr 77356
Woodshay Ct & Dr 77356
Woodside Dr & Ln 77356
Woodwick 77356
Woodwind Cir & Dr 77356
Worsham St 77316
Wyatt Rd 77356
Wycliffe Dr 77356
Wyndemere Dr 77356
Yacht Hbr 77356
Yaupon Ln 77356
Yazoo River Cir 77316
Yellowstone River Rd 77316
Youpon Dr 77316
Youpon Ln
9900-10099 77316
20400-20599 77356
Zoe Loop Dr 77316

NUMBERED STREETS

All Street Addresses 77316

MOUNT PLEASANT TX

General Delivery ... 75455

POST OFFICE BOXES MAIN OFFICE STATIONS AND BRANCHES

Box No.s
All PO Boxes ... 75456

RURAL ROUTES

01, 02, 03, 04, 06, 07, 08, 09, 10 ... 75455

NAMED STREETS

E Alabama St ... 75455
W Alabama St
100-398 ... 75455
201-399 ... 75455
201-201 ... 75456
Alan Dr ... 75455
Alexander Rd ... 75455
Alvis Ln ... 75455
Amy Dr ... 75455
Anita St ... 75455
E & W Arizona St ... 75455
E & W Arkansas St ... 75455
Austin Ave ... 75455
Azalea Ln ... 75455
Baker Ave ... 75455
Bass Creek Trl ... 75455
Beechman Ave ... 75455
N Belmont Ave ... 75455
Bluebird St ... 75455
Boatman St ... 75455
Bob O Link Ave ... 75455
Booker Ave ... 75455
Branch St ... 75455
Brenda Dr ... 75455
W Brestrad St ... 75455
Briarwood Ln ... 75455
Brookmeadow ... 75455
Brookside Cir ... 75455
Brookwood Dr ... 75455
N Bryan Ave ... 75455
E Burton Rd ... 75455
Buster Holcomb Dr ... 75455
Caddo Trl ... 75455
Capers St ... 75455
Carolyn St ... 75455
Carr Dr ... 75455
Cash St ... 75455
N & S Cecelia Dr ... 75455
Cedar Hl & St ... 75455
Cedar Creek Dr ... 75455
Chambers St ... 75455
Chester St ... 75455
Choctaw St ... 75455
N & S Church Ave ... 75455
E & W Circle Dr ... 75455
Clayton Ave ... 75455
Codee Ct ... 75455
Commerce ... 75455
Country Club Dr ... 75455
County Road 1020 ... 75455
County Road 1030 ... 75455
County Road 1035 ... 75455
County Road 1038 ... 75455
County Road 1040 ... 75455
County Road 1042 ... 75455
County Road 1044 ... 75455
County Road 1046 ... 75455
County Road 1048 ... 75455
County Road 1065 ... 75455
County Road 1070 ... 75455
County Road 1118 ... 75455
County Road 1120 ... 75455
County Road 1123 ... 75455
County Road 1125 ... 75455
County Road 1130 ... 75455
County Road 1132 ... 75455
County Road 1135 ... 75455
County Road 1140 ... 75455
County Road 1143 ... 75455
County Road 1150 ... 75455
County Road 1153 ... 75455
County Road 1155 ... 75455
County Road 1165 ... 75455
County Road 1170 ... 75455
NW County Road 12 W ... 75455
County Road 1200 ... 75455
County Road 1220 ... 75455
County Road 1222 ... 75455
County Road 1224 ... 75455
County Road 1230 ... 75455
County Road 1240 ... 75455
County Road 1243 ... 75455
County Road 1245 ... 75455
County Road 1250 ... 75455
County Road 1255 ... 75455
County Road 1257 ... 75455
County Road 1312 ... 75455
County Road 1314 ... 75455
County Road 1315 ... 75455
County Road 1317 ... 75455
County Road 1325 ... 75455
County Road 1330 ... 75455
County Road 1332 ... 75455
County Road 1333 ... 75455
County Road 1334 ... 75455
County Road 1335 ... 75455
County Road 1340 ... 75455
County Road 1342 ... 75455
County Road 1345 ... 75455
County Road 1350 ... 75455
County Road 1355 ... 75455
County Road 1357 ... 75455
County Road 1360 ... 75455
County Road 1362 ... 75455
County Road 1363 ... 75455
County Road 1411 ... 75455
County Road 1430 ... 75455
County Road 1432 ... 75455
County Road 1435 ... 75455
County Road 1440 ... 75455
County Road 1450 ... 75455
County Road 1452 ... 75455
County Road 1455 ... 75455
County Road 1465 ... 75455
County Road 1468 ... 75455
County Road 1475 ... 75455
County Road 1482 ... 75455
County Road 1485 ... 75455
County Road 1487 ... 75455
County Road 1490 ... 75455
County Road 1520 ... 75455
County Road 1535 ... 75455
County Road 1536 ... 75455
County Road 1538 ... 75455
County Road 1540 ... 75455
County Road 1546 ... 75455
County Road 1550 ... 75455
County Road 1601 ... 75455
County Road 1602 ... 75455
County Road 1603 ... 75455
County Road 1604 ... 75455
County Road 1606 ... 75455
County Road 1607 ... 75455
County Road 1608 ... 75455
County Road 1609 ... 75455
County Road 1612 ... 75455
County Road 1614 ... 75455
County Road 1616 ... 75455
County Road 1620 ... 75455
County Road 1635 ... 75455
County Road 1655 ... 75455
County Road 1660 ... 75455
County Road 1662 ... 75455
County Road 1664 ... 75455
County Road 1670 ... 75455
County Road 1673 ... 75455
County Road 1675 ... 75455
County Road 1680 ... 75455
County Road 1683 ... 75455
County Road 1685 ... 75455
County Road 1690 ... 75455
County Road 1695 ... 75455
County Road 1697 ... 75455
County Road 1720 ... 75455
County Road 1725 ... 75455
County Road 1740 ... 75455
County Road 1745 ... 75455
County Road 1749 ... 75455
County Road 1750 ... 75455
County Road 1755 ... 75455
County Road 1765 ... 75455
County Road 1770 ... 75455
County Road 1771 ... 75455
County Road 1773 ... 75455
County Road 1775 ... 75455
County Road 1780 ... 75455
County Road 1787 ... 75455
County Road 1905 ... 75455
County Road 1910 ... 75455
County Road 1915 ... 75455
County Road 1925 ... 75455
County Road 1927 ... 75455
County Road 1933 ... 75455
County Road 1935 ... 75455
County Road 1940 ... 75455
County Road 2010 ... 75455
County Road 2015 ... 75455
County Road 2040 ... 75455
County Road 2042 ... 75455
County Road 2120 ... 75455
County Road 2125 ... 75455
County Road 2140 ... 75455
NE County Road 2200 ... 75455
County Road 2220 ... 75455
County Road 2222 ... 75455
County Road 2225 ... 75455
County Road 2260 ... 75455
County Road 2265 ... 75455
County Road 2300 ... 75455
County Road 2315 ... 75455
County Road 2325 ... 75455
County Road 2330 ... 75455
County Road 2335 ... 75455
County Road 2340 ... 75455
County Road 2355 ... 75455
County Road 2360 ... 75455
County Road 2363 ... 75455
County Road 2365 ... 75455
County Road 2375 ... 75455
County Road 2400 ... 75455
County Road 2415 ... 75455
County Road 2430 ... 75455
County Road 2470 ... 75455
County Road 2512 ... 75455
County Road 2600 ... 75455
County Road 2630 ... 75455
County Road 2640 ... 75455
County Road 2650 ... 75455
County Road 2670 ... 75455
County Road 2675 ... 75455
County Road 2710 ... 75455
County Road 2715 ... 75455
County Road 2718 ... 75455
County Road 2720 ... 75455
County Road 2750 ... 75455
County Road 2810 ... 75455
County Road 3008 S ... 75455
N & S County Road 3010 ... 75455
County Road 3020 ... 75455
County Road 3030 ... 75455
County Road 3032 ... 75455
County Road 3035 ... 75455
County Road 3045 ... 75455
County Road 3050 ... 75455
County Road 3053 ... 75455
County Road 3055 ... 75455
County Road 3060 ... 75455
County Road 3065 ... 75455
County Road 3070 ... 75455
County Road 3080 ... 75455
County Road 3205 ... 75455
County Road 3207 ... 75455
County Road 3210 ... 75455
County Road 3215 ... 75455
County Road 3218 ... 75455
County Road 3220 ... 75455
County Road 3225 ... 75455
County Road 3227 ... 75455
County Road 3230 ... 75455
County Road 3232 ... 75455
County Road 3240 ... 75455
County Road 3241 ... 75455
County Road 3243 ... 75455
County Road 3244 ... 75455
County Road 3245 ... 75455
County Road 3246 ... 75455
County Road 3249 ... 75455
County Road 3250 ... 75455
County Road 3260 ... 75455
County Road 3263 ... 75455
County Road 3265 ... 75455
County Road 3268 ... 75455
County Road 3270 ... 75455
County Road 3275 ... 75455
County Road 3280 ... 75455
County Road 3283 ... 75455
County Road 3285 ... 75455
County Road 3290 ... 75455
County Road 3292 ... 75455
County Road 3310 ... 75455
County Road 3320 ... 75455
County Road 3322 ... 75455
County Road 3325 ... 75455
County Road 3330 ... 75455
County Road 3337 ... 75455
County Road 3345 ... 75455
County Road 3355 ... 75455
County Road 3910 ... 75455
County Road 3913 ... 75455
County Road 3920 ... 75455
County Road 3925 ... 75455
County Road 3930 ... 75455
County Road 3935 ... 75455
County Road 3945 ... 75455
County Road 4015 ... 75455
County Road 4020 ... 75455
County Road 4025 ... 75455
County Road 4030 ... 75455
County Road 4040 ... 75455
County Road 4210 ... 75455
County Road 4215 ... 75455
County Road 4218 ... 75455
County Road 4220 ... 75455
County Road 4221 ... 75455
County Road 4222 ... 75455
County Road 4224 ... 75455
County Road 4226 ... 75455
County Road 4230 ... 75455
County Road 4231 ... 75455
County Road 4235 ... 75455
County Road 4240 ... 75455
County Road 4245 ... 75455
County Road 4250 ... 75455
County Road 4260 ... 75455
County Road 4265 ... 75455
County Road 4270 ... 75455
County Road 4275 ... 75455
County Road 4330 ... 75455
County Road 4340 ... 75455
County Road 4355 ... 75455
County Road 4360 ... 75455
County Road 4365 ... 75455
County Road 4370 ... 75455
County Road 4410 ... 75455
County Road 4415 ... 75455
County Road 4420 ... 75455
County Road 4425 ... 75455
County Road 4426 ... 75455
County Road 4440 ... 75455
County Road 4510 ... 75455
County Road 4520 ... 75455
County Road 4530 ... 75455
County Road 4540 ... 75455
County Road 4550 ... 75455
County Road 4560 ... 75455
County Road 4565 ... 75455
County Road 4610 ... 75455
County Road 4640 ... 75455
County Road 4650 ... 75455
County Road 4660 ... 75455
County Road 4663 ... 75455
County Road 4665 ... 75455
County Road 4705 ... 75455
County Road 4710 ... 75455
County Road 4715 ... 75455
County Road 4720 ... 75455
County Road 4730 ... 75455
County Road 4735 ... 75455
County Road 4740 ... 75455
County Road 4745 ... 75455
County Road 4754 ... 75455
County Road 4755 ... 75455
County Road 4757 ... 75455
County Road 4765 ... 75455
County Road 4805 ... 75455
County Road 4810 ... 75455
County Road 4815 ... 75455
County Road 4825 ... 75455
County Road 4840 ... 75455
County Road 4842 ... 75455
County Road 4844 ... 75455
County Road 4846 ... 75455
County Road 4850 ... 75455
County Road 4855 ... 75455
County Road 4857 ... 75455
County Road 4885 ... 75455
County Road Ne 2010 ... 75455
County Road Ne 2170 ... 75455
County Road Ne 2190 ... 75455
County Road Se 4145 ... 75455
County Road Se 4150 ... 75455
County Road Se 4205 ... 75455
N Crockett Ave ... 75455
Crooks Ln ... 75455
E & W Cross St ... 75455
Deanna Ave ... 75455
Deer Trail Ln ... 75455
Delafield St ... 75455
Dellwood Dr ... 75455
Denman Dr ... 75455
N & S Dessie Dr ... 75455
Devonshire St ... 75455
Diane Ln ... 75455
Dogwood Ln ... 75455
Dove Ave ... 75455
Dunn Ave ... 75455
Eagle Dr ... 75455
Earnest St ... 75455
Eastpoint Dr ... 75455
Eastwood Dr ... 75455
Edgewood St ... 75455
N & S Edwards Ave ... 75455
N & S Ellis Ave ... 75455
Elsye Ave ... 75455
Fairway N ... 75455
Fareway Ln ... 75455
Farm Road 1000 ... 75455
Farm Road 1001 ... 75455
Farm Road 127 ... 75455
Farm Road 1402 ... 75455
N Farm Road 144 ... 75455
Farm Road 1734 ... 75455
Farm Road 1735 ... 75455
Farm Road 1896 ... 75455
Farm Road 21 ... 75455
Farm Road 2152 ... 75455
Farm Road 2348 ... 75455
Farm Road 2882 ... 75455
Farm Road 3007 ... 75455
Farm Road 3133 ... 75455
Farm Road 3417 ... 75455
E & W Farm Road 71 ... 75455
Farm Road 899 ... 75455
E & W Ferguson Rd ... 75455
Fleming Dr ... 75455
N & S Florey Ave ... 75455
Ford Dr ... 75455
Forrest Ave ... 75455
Fort Sherman Dam Rd ... 75455
Fortner Ln ... 75455
Foster Ln ... 75455
Fricke St ... 75455
Friendly Ave ... 75455
N & S Frontage Rd ... 75455
Gale St ... 75455
Garden Ave ... 75455
Gene Dr ... 75455
Gibson Ave ... 75455
Gilmore Ave ... 75455
Glen Eagles Dr ... 75455
Green Hollow Ln ... 75455
Greenbriar Ln ... 75455
Greenhill Rd ... 75455
Greenhill Park Ave ... 75455
Haggard Ave ... 75455
Happy St ... 75455
Harkrider Ln ... 75455
Harts Bluff Rd ... 75455
Hays Ave ... 75455
Henderson St ... 75455
Hickory St ... 75455
Hogan Ln ... 75455
E & W Holland St ... 75455
Holly Hill Ln ... 75455
Houston Ave ... 75455
Hubbard Ave ... 75455
Industrial Rd ... 75455
Interstate 30 South Access Rd ... 75455
Interstate Highway 30 E ... 75455
Ivory St ... 75455
N & S Jefferson Ave ... 75455
Jeffery Ave ... 75455
Joel Rd ... 75455
N & S Johnson Ave ... 75455
Joseph St ... 75455
Julia St ... 75455
Kathryns Ct ... 75455
Keith Ave ... 75455
Kingfisher Ln ... 75455
Lakeside Dr ... 75455
Lakewood Dr ... 75455
Lamar Dr ... 75455
Larkin Ave ... 75455
N Lawn Ave ... 75455
S Lee Ave ... 75455
N & S Lide Ave ... 75455
Linda Dr ... 75455
Links Dr ... 75455
Lisa St ... 75455
Lively Ave ... 75455
Louis Ave ... 75455
N & S Madison Ave ... 75455
E & W Magnolia Dr ... 75455
Margaret Dr ... 75455
Mark Ln ... 75455
Martin St ... 75455
Martin Luther King St ... 75455
Masters Dr ... 75455
Matthew Dr ... 75455
Mckellar Rd ... 75455
Mckinnon St ... 75455
Mclean Ave ... 75455
Mcminn Ave ... 75455
Memorial Ave ... 75455
Merritt Ave ... 75455
Michah Dr ... 75455
Mike Hall Pkwy ... 75455
N & S Miller Ave ... 75455
Millsap Ave ... 75455
Mockingbird St ... 75455
Mollie Ave ... 75455
Monticello Rd ... 75455
Moore Ave ... 75455
Morgan St ... 75455
Morris Ave ... 75455
Mulberry Ave ... 75455
Nevills Rd ... 75455
Nichole Ln ... 75455
Nicholson Ave ... 75455
Oak View Dr ... 75455
Oakwood Dr ... 75455
Old St ... 75455
Old Paris Rd ... 75455
N & S Otyson St ... 75455
Park Dr ... 75455
Patrick St ... 75455
E & W Pecan St ... 75455
Peel Ave ... 75455
Pennye Cir ... 75455
Pleasant St ... 75455
N Pounders Ave ... 75455
Private Road 1050 ... 75455
Private Road 1167 ... 75455
Private Road 1311 ... 75455
Private Road 1344 ... 75455
Private Road 1364 ... 75455
Private Road 1537 ... 75455
Private Road 1608 ... 75455
Private Road 1613 ... 75455
Private Road 1614 ... 75455
Private Road 1617 ... 75455
Private Road 1622 ... 75455
Private Road 1625 ... 75455
Private Road 1629 ... 75455
Private Road 1688 ... 75455
Private Road 1760 ... 75455
Private Road 1917 ... 75455
Private Road 1932 ... 75455
Private Road 1945 ... 75455
Private Road 2010 ... 75455
Private Road 2012 ... 75455
Private Road 2050 ... 75455
Private Road 2305 ... 75455
Private Road 2317 ... 75455
Private Road 2319 ... 75455
Private Road 2321 ... 75455
Private Road 2352 ... 75455
Private Road 2355 ... 75455
Private Road 2357 ... 75455
Private Road 2362 ... 75455
Private Road 2367 ... 75455
Private Road 2376 ... 75455
Private Road 2402 ... 75455
Private Road 2653 ... 75455
Private Road 2655 ... 75455
Private Road 2711 ... 75455
Private Road 2712 ... 75455
Private Road 2713 ... 75455
Private Road 2722 ... 75455
Private Road 2724 ... 75455
Private Road 3012 ... 75455
Private Road 3015 ... 75455
Private Road 3043 ... 75455
Private Road 3061 ... 75455
Private Road 3081 ... 75455
Private Road 3082 ... 75455
Private Road 3234 ... 75455
Private Road 3235 ... 75455
Private Road 3236 ... 75455
Private Road 3328 ... 75455
Private Road 3940 ... 75455
Private Road 3943 ... 75455
Private Road 4032 ... 75455
Private Road 4206 ... 75455
Private Road 4208 ... 75455
Private Road 4266 ... 75455
Private Road 4353 ... 75455
Private Road 4357 ... 75455
Private Road 4515 ... 75455
Private Road 4551 ... 75455
Private Road 4552 ... 75455
Private Road 4570 ... 75455
Private Road 4612 ... 75455
Private Road 4615 ... 75455
Private Road 4630 ... 75455
Private Road 4635 ... 75455
Private Road 4638 ... 75455
Private Road 4644 ... 75455
Private Road 4645 ... 75455
Private Road 4648 ... 75455
Private Road 4721 ... 75455
Private Road 4742 ... 75455
Private Road 4835 ... 75455
Proctor Ave ... 75455
Quail Crk & Run ... 75455
N & S Quillie Ave ... 75455
Red Springs Ave ... 75455
Redbud Ln ... 75455
Redfearn Ct ... 75455
Rhambeau St ... 75455
Richardson Rd ... 75455
N & S Riddle Ave ... 75455
Rikkity Ln ... 75455
Robert Nance Rd ... 75455
Rocky Trl ... 75455
Rogers Ave ... 75455

Rosewood St 75455
Rotan Rd 75455
Rych Oak Ln 75455
Saint Andrews Ct 75455
Samuel Ln 75455
Sanders Ave 75455
Sandlin Ave 75455
Sanford Rd 75455
School St 75455
Searcy Ave 75455
Shady Hollow Dr 75455
Shadywood Ln 75455
Silver Creek Trl 75455
Silver Leaf St 75455
Silver Maple St 75455
Silver Oak St 75455
Silver Spring Trl 75455
Silver Spur Trl 75455
Silverlake Cir 75455
Sleepy Hollow Dr 75455
Sneads Cir 75455
Southgate Dr 75455
Southhill Dr 75455
Stacie St 75455
Stark St 75455
State Spur 134 75455
Stella St 75455
Stephens Ave 75455
Stone Bridge St 75455
Stone Hedge St 75455
Stone Shore St 75455
Stone Wall St 75455
Sunny Ln 75455
Sweet Pea Ct 75455
Tabb St 75455
Tankersley Rd 75455
Taylor St 75455
Tennison Rd 75455
Texas Ave 75455
Texas Highway 49 75455
Therese Ct 75455
Turnberry Cir 75455
Turtle Creek Dr 75455
N & S Us Highway 271 75455
E & W Us Highway 67 75455
N & S Van Buren Ave 75455
Village Rd 75455
Wallace Ave 75455
Walnut St 75455
N Washington Ave 75455
Wentwood Dr 75455
White St 75455
Wildwood Dr 75455
S Williams Ave 75455
Willow Bnd 75455
Wilson Dr 75455
Wolfe Ave 75455
Woodberry Rd 75455
Woodland Rd 75455
Yorke St 75455

NUMBERED STREETS

All Street Addresses 75455

NACOGDOCHES TX

General Delivery 75961

POST OFFICE BOXES MAIN OFFICE STATIONS AND BRANCHES

Box No.s
All PO Boxes 75963

RURAL ROUTES

01, 02, 11, 15, 16, 19 75961
03, 04, 05, 12, 14, 17, 18 75964
06, 07, 08, 10, 13 75965

NAMED STREETS

A St 75961
E Access Rd 75965
Acorn Dr 75961
Airport Rd 75964
Allen Branch Rd 75961
Allen Thurston Rd 75961
Ammons St 75964
Anders Kelly Rd 75964
Anderson Dr 75965
Anderson Trl 75961
Andy Ln 75965
Angela St 75961
Angelina Ln 75961
Apple Blvd 75961
Apple Creek Dr 75965
Appleby Cir 75965
Appleby Sand Rd 75965
Arbor Oak Dr 75964
Armory Dr 75964
Arnold St 75961
Arthur Dr 75965
Arthur Weaver St 75961
Ashbury Ct & Ln 75965
Ashcreek Cir 75965
Ashton Way 75965
Augustine Rd 75964
E Austin St 75965
W Austin St
100-299 75965
1601-3899 75964
Austin Hollow Cir 75965
Austin Woods Dr 75964
Azalea St 75965
Bailey Ave 75961
Baker St 75965
Balch Ln 75961
Banita St 75965
Bark St 75964
Barker St 75964
Barkley Rd 75964
Bass St 75961
Bates Ln 75965
Baxter Ln 75964
Baxter Duncan St 75961
Baywood Dr 75965
Beall St 75965
Beard St 75964
Belle Pointe Dr 75965
Bennett Clark Rd 75961
Berger St 75964
Bermuda Dune Rd 75964
Bermuda Dunes Dr 75964
Berry Dr 75964
Berryhill Rd 75965
Bethel Dr & Rd 75965
Beverly Dr 75964
Big Oak Rd 75964
Big Tanks Rd 75964
Blake Rd 75965
Blanton Dr 75964
Blount St 75965
Blue Lake Dr 75964
Blueberry Valley Rd 75964
Bluebonnett Bnd 75965
Bluff Oak St 75964
Boatman Rd 75965
Bogg Rd 75965
Bois D Arc St 75961
Boney St 75961
Boozer St 75961
Borrego Springs Rd 75964
Bostwick St 75965
Boulder Ln 75965
Bowie St 75965
Bradshaw Ranch Ln 75964
Bremond St 75964
Brewer St 75961
Briargrove Dr 75965
Brixwood Pl 75965
Broadmoor Blvd 75965
Brogan Ln 75961
Bronco Rd 75964
Brook Ln 75964
Brooke Ln 75964
Brookhollow Dr 75964
Brookshire Dr 75965
Brother John Rd 75961
Brown St 75961
Bryan St 75965
Buck Strode Rd 75965
Buckingham Dr 75965
Burgin 75961
Burk St 75964
Burl Dr 75961
Burrows St 75965
Burt Dr 75965
Butcher Rd 75965
Butler St 75961
Cabin Rd 75965
E & W California St 75965
Cambridge Cir 75965
Cambridge Bay Est 75964
Camino Real Dr 75965
Camp Powers Rd 75964
Camp Tonkawa Rd 75965
Canterbury Dr 75965
Canyon St 75964
Cardinal St 75961
Cargal Ln 75965
Cariker St 75961
Carla St 75965
Carole St 75965
Carolyn St 75965
Carrie Lyn St 75964
Carrizo Creek Dr & Est 75965
Case Rd 75965
Cason St 75961
Castleberry St 75961
Cecil Jones St 75961
Cedar St 75961
Cedar Way 75964
Cedar Bluff Rd 75965
Cedar Crest Dr 75964
Cedar View Dr 75965
Cedarwood Dr 75965
Center Ln & Rd 75961
Central Heights Rd 75965
Chalon St 75965
Chambers Ln 75965
Champion Cir 75964
Chandler St 75961
Chaparral Dr 75965
Chapman Rd 75964
Charles Cherry Ln 75965
Chateau Ln 75965
Chelsea Cir 75965
Cherry St 75961
Cherrybrook St 75965
Chestnut St 75965
Chevy Chase Dr 75965
Cheyene Ln 75964
Cheyenne Rd 75964
Chimney Rock Dr 75965
Chris Haney Rd 75961
N & S Church Aly & St 75961
Churchill Dr 75965
Circle Park Dr 75964
Cl Simon St 75961
Clabe Allen Rd 75965
Clarice St 75964
Clay St 75964
Clear Meadow Ter 75961
Cleaver Dr 75961
Clevenger St 75964
Clifton Cemetery Rd 75965
Clinton Rd 75965
Coats Rd 75965
Cobblestone St 75965
Cody Ln 75964
Cole Cir 75961
Coleman St 75961
E & W College St 75965
Collins St 75964
Colonial Dr 75965
Colony Creek Dr 75965
Colston St 75961
Commerce St 75961
Community Rd 75961
Community Estates Dr 75961
E & W Conda Muckleroy St 75965
Consford Ln 75961
Coon Hunters Rd 75964
Cooper St 75964
Coral Gables Dr 75964
Cordell Ln 75965
Cotton St 75964
Cottonwood St 75964
County Road 101 75965
County Road 1011 75965
County Road 102 75965
County Road 103 75965
County Road 104
200-398 75965
County Road 104
400-1999 75965
2001-2699 75965
2100-2198 75961
2200-2898 75965
County Road 105 75965
County Road 106 75965
County Road 107 75965
County Road 109 75965
County Road 111 75965
County Road 112 75965
County Road 113 75965
County Road 114 75965
County Road 115 75965
County Road 116 75965
County Road 117 75965
County Road 1171 75965
County Road 118 75965
County Road 120 75965
County Road 121 75965
County Road 122 E 75965
W County Road 122 75964
County Road 123 75965
County Road 124 75965
County Road 125 75965
County Road 126 75965
County Road 1291 75965
County Road 136 75965
County Road 140 75965
County Road 141 75965
County Road 143 75965
County Road 144 75965
County Road 145 75965
County Road 146 75965
County Road 149 75965
County Road 151 75965
County Road 152 75965
County Road 153 75965
County Road 154 75965
County Road 155 75965
County Road 156 75965
County Road 198 75965
County Road 199 75965
County Road 200 75965
County Road 2011 75965
County Road 202 75965
County Road 2031 75961
County Road 2032 75961
County Road 2041 75965
County Road 205 75965
County Road 2051 75965
County Road 2052 75965
County Road 2053 75965
County Road 2054 75965
County Road 2055 75965
County Road 2056 75965
County Road 206 75965
County Road 2061 75961
County Road 207 75961
County Road 208 75965
County Road 2081 75965
County Road 2082 75965
County Road 2091 75965
County Road 2092 75965
County Road 2093 75965
County Road 2094 75965
County Road 210 75965
County Road 211 75965
County Road 212 75965
County Road 213 75965
County Road 2131 75965
County Road 214 75965
County Road 215 75965
County Road 2151 75965
County Road 2152 75965
County Road 2153 75965
County Road 216 75965
County Road 217 75965
County Road 218 75965
County Road 219 75961
County Road 220 75961
County Road 221 75961
County Road 222 75965
County Road 2221 75965
County Road 2222 75965
County Road 226 75961
County Road 227 75961
County Road 228 75961
County Road 230 75961
County Road 231 75961
County Road 232 75961
County Road 2321 75961
County Road 2322 75961
County Road 233 75961
County Road 234 75961
County Road 235 75961
County Road 236 75961
County Road 2361 75961
County Road 237 75961
County Road 238 75961
County Road 239 75961
County Road 240 75961
County Road 241 75961
County Road 242 75961
County Road 243 75961
County Road 244 75961
County Road 246 75961
County Road 2471 75965
County Road 250 75965
County Road 252 75965
County Road 253 75965
County Road 254 75965
County Road 255 75965
County Road 256 75965
County Road 257 75965
County Road 260 75965
County Road 262 75965
County Road 263 75965
County Road 264 75965
County Road 265 75965
County Road 266 75965
County Road 268 75961
County Road 273 75961
County Road 275 75961
County Road 276 75961
County Road 277 75961
County Road 278 75961
County Road 279 75961
County Road 280 75961
County Road 301 75961
County Road 302 75961
County Road 303 75961
County Road 305 75961
County Road 307 75961
County Road 311 75961
County Road 313 75961
County Road 317 75961
County Road 319 75961
County Road 330 75961
County Road 331 75961
County Road 333 75961
County Road 335 75961
County Road 3351 75961
County Road 336 75961
County Road 337 75961
County Road 338 75961
County Road 341 75961
County Road 342 75961
County Road 344 75961
County Road 345 75961
County Road 349 75961
County Road 350 75961
County Road 353 75961
County Road 381 75961
County Road 384 75961
County Road 387 75961
County Road 388 75961
County Road 389 75961
County Road 392 75961
County Road 404 75961
County Road 4041 75961
County Road 405 75961
County Road 406 75961
County Road 407 75961
County Road 408 75961
County Road 409 75961
County Road 410 75961
County Road 411 75961
County Road 412 75961
County Road 413 75961
County Road 415 75961
County Road 419 75961
County Road 4191 75961
County Road 4192 75961
County Road 4193 75961
County Road 4194 75961
County Road 420 75961
County Road 5011 75961
County Road 5021 75964
County Road 5022 75964
County Road 5023 75964
County Road 5024 75964
County Road 5025 75964
County Road 5026 75964
County Road 503 75961
County Road 504 75961
County Road 505 75961
County Road 5051 75961
County Road 506 75961
County Road 507 75961
County Road 508 75961
County Road 5081 75961
County Road 5082 75961
County Road 5084 75961
County Road 509 75961
County Road 511 75961
County Road 513 75961
County Road 514 75961
County Road 520 75961
County Road 521 75964
County Road 522 75964
County Road 523 75964
County Road 524 75964
County Road 525
200-1799 75964
1800-3100 75961
3102-4198 75961
4901-4999 75964
County Road 526 75961
County Road 527 75961
County Road 528 75961
County Road 532 75964
County Road 534 75961
County Road 5341 75961
County Road 535 75961
County Road 536 75961
County Road 537 75961
County Road 538 75961
County Road 540 75961
County Road 544 75961
County Road 545 75961
County Road 546 75961
County Road 547 75961
County Road 551 75961
County Road 552 75961
County Road 553 75961
County Road 554 75961
County Road 555 75961
County Road 557 75961
County Road 563 75961
County Road 564 75961
County Road 565 75961
County Road 566 75961
County Road 567 75961
County Road 6101 75964
County Road 6102 75964
County Road 6103 75964
County Road 6104 75964
County Road 6105 75964
County Road 6106 75964
County Road 6107 75964
County Road 6108 75964
County Road 612 75964
County Road 613 75964
County Road 615 75964
County Road 617 75964
County Road 618 75964
County Road 620 75964
County Road 621 75964
County Road 627 75964
County Road 628 75964
County Road 629 75964
County Road 630 75964
County Road 631 75964
County Road 635 75964
County Road 641 75964
County Road 659 75964
County Road 701 75964
County Road 702 75964
County Road 703 75964
County Road 705 75964
County Road 706 75964
County Road 707 75964
County Road 709 75964
County Road 710 75964
County Road 711 75964
County Road 712 75964
County Road 713 75964
County Road 714 75964
County Road 715 75964
County Road 716 75964
County Road 717 75964
County Road 718 75964
County Road 719 75964
County Road 720 75964
County Road 721 75964
County Road 722 75964
County Road 723 75964
County Road 724 75964
County Road 7241 75964
County Road 725 75964
County Road 727 75964
County Road 728 75964
County Road 731 75964
County Road 732 75964
County Road 735 75964
County Road 741 75964
County Road 747 75964
County Road 751 75964
County Road 752 75964
County Road 753 75964
County Road 754 75964
County Road 7542 75964
County Road 755 75964
County Road 761 75964
County Road 765 75964
County Road 767 75964
County Road 768 75964
County Road 7681 75964
County Road 7682 75964
County Road 7683 75964
County Road 769 75964
County Road 770 75964
County Road 7701 75964
County Road 771 75964
County Road 801 75964
County Road 802 75964
County Road 803 75964
County Road 804 75964
County Road 805 75964
County Road 806 75964
County Road 807 75964
County Road 808 75964
County Road 809 75964
County Road 810 75964
County Road 811 75964
County Road 8111 75964
County Road 8112 75964
County Road 8113 75964
County Road 812 75964
County Road 813 75964
County Road 814 75964
County Road 815 75964
County Road 8152 75964
County Road 816 75964
County Road 817 75964

County Road 818 75964
County Road 820 75964
County Road 8201 75964
County Road 821 75964
County Road 8211 75964
County Road 822 75964
County Road 823 75964
County Road 8231 75964
County Road 824 75964
County Road 8241 75964
County Road 8242 75964
County Road 825 75964
County Road 826 75964
County Road 8261 75964
County Road 829 75964
County Road 831 75964
County Road 832 75964
County Road 833 75964
County Road 834 75964
County Road 8341 75964
County Road 835 75964
County Road 836 75964
County Road 837 75964
County Road 838 75964
County Road 839 75964
County Road 841 75964
County Road 854 75964
County Road 857 75964
County Road 910 75964
County Road 912 75964
County Road 913 75964
County Road 914 75964
County Road 915 75964
County Road 9151 75964
County Road 9152 75964
County Road 916 75964
County Road 918 75964
County Road 920 75964
County Road 925 75964
County Road 929 75964
County Road 935 75964
County Road 940 75964
W Cox St 75964
Craven St 75961
E Craven St 75964
W Craven St 75964
Crawford St 75965
Creekbend Blvd 75965
Creekside Ln 75964
Creekview Bnd 75965
Creekway Dr 75965
Crestview Dr 75965
Crestwood St 75961
Crisp Rd 75961
Crooked Creek Dr 75965
Cross St 75961
Cumberland Dr 75965
Cureton Rd 75961
Curl St 75961
Curlew St 75964
Dallas St 75965
Dalmont Rd 75964
Dan St 75965
Daniel St 75964
Danna Ln 75961
Davidson Dr 75964
Davis St 75965
Daybreak Dr 75961
Decker St 75965
Deen St 75965
Deer Creek Dr 75965
Deer Run Rd 75964
Deerfield 75965
Dempsey Rd 75964
Denman St 75964
Dennis St 75964
Devereaux St 75961
Devon St 75965
Dewberry Ln 75964
Dianne Dr 75961
Dogwood Dr 75965
Dolph St 75964
Doris Dr 75961
Dorothy Ln 75961
Dorr Creek St 75961
Douglass Rd 75964

Drewery Dr 75964
Duffin Ln 75961
Durrett Rd 75965
Durst St 75964
Dutch St 75961
Dutton Ln 75961
Dyes Rd 75964
Echo Ln 75964
Edgar Rd 75961
Edgewood Ln 75961
Egret Dr 75964
Ej Campbell Blvd 75961
Elbow Rdg 75965
Eliza St 75961
Elizabeth St 75964
Ella St 75961
Ellington St 75965
Ellis St 75964
Elm St 75965
Elm Grove Rd 75961
Eloise St 75961
Emerald Dr 75965
Emily Ct 75964
Emporia Ln 75961
Englewood Dr 75964
Eric Dr 75964
Ernest Aly 75961
Ernest Mclain Rd 75964
Essex St 75965
Esther Blvd 75964
Evans Rd 75964
Evelyn St 75964
Everetts Ln 75964
Everwood Trl 75964
F R Lewis Rd 75964
Faires Rd 75964
Fairview Rd 75961
Fairview Acres Dr 75961
Fairway Dr 75964
Farrell Rd 75961
Faulkner Rd 75965
Faye St 75964
Feazell St 75965
Feeder Access Rd 75964
Felix St 75961
Fellowship Cemetery Rd 75961
Ferguson St 75961
Ferndale St 75964
Fernwood Dr 75964
Fields St 75961
Fire Dept Rd 75961
Fire Tower Rd 75964
Fitts Rd 75964
Flora St 75964
Floyd Harvin 75964
Flying M Ln 75961
Fm 1087 75965
Fm 1275 75961
Fm 1638 75964
Fm 1878 75961
Fm 2112 75961
S Fm 225 75964
Fm 2259 75961
Fm 226 75961
Fm 2609 75965
Fm 2664 75965
Fm 2713 75961
Fm 2782 75964
Fm 2863 75965
Fm 2864 75965
Fm 3228 75961
Fm 3276 75961
Fm 3314 75964
Fm 343 75964
Fm 698 75964
Fm 941 75965
N Fm 95 75961
Fogle Rd 75964
Forbes St 75964
Ford St 75964
Fore St 75964
Forest Ln 75965
Forest Ridge Dr 75961
Fox St 75961
Fox Run Dr 75965

Fox Trot St 75964
Frances Ln 75961
Francis St 75964
Frank St 75964
Frank Hall Rd 75961
Franklin St 75964
Frazier Rd 75965
Fred St 75964
N Fredonia St 75961
S Fredonia St
100-899 75961
900-3899 75964
Friar Tuck Dr 75965
Frost St 75961
Fulgham St 75961
Fussell St 75964
Gardenbrook St 75965
Garner St 75961
Gasaway Rd 75964
Gator Dr 75965
Gayline Dr 75961
E Gaylon Brooks St 75964
Gene Aly 75961
George St 75961
George Arriola Rd 75964
George Sterns Rd 75961
Georgewood Dr 75964
Georgia Oak St 75964
Gidget Dr 75961
Gilbreath St 75961
Glass St 75961
Glen Hollow Dr 75965
Glenbrook Cir 75964
Glenbrook St 75965
Goldsberry St 75964
Goodman Rd 75964
Gound St 75961
Grandview Dr 75964
Granite Hill St 75965
Green Mountain Dr 75964
Greenbrier Dr 75961
Greenwood St 75961
S Greer St 75961
Grove Ln 75961
Guy St 75961
Guy Blount Rd 75964
Guy Blount Ext Rd 75964
Hackberry St 75964
Hall Rd 75964
Haltom St 75961
Handy St 75961
Hanson Cir & Dr 75961
Happy Land Rd
400-3999 75965
4001-4099 75964
Harborview Dr 75964
Hardcastle Rd 75961
Harris Ln 75961
Harris St 75964
Hasley St 75961
Hawthorne St 75964
Hayter St 75965
Hayward St 75961
Hazel St 75964
Hazen Ln 75964
Heartwood Dr 75965
Heather St 75965
Helen Dr 75961
Helpenstell Rd 75965
Henderson Ln 75964
Herbert St 75964
Heron Ct 75964
Herrin St 75961
Hicheld Dr 75965
Hickory Pl & St 75965
Hidden Leaf Trl 75965
Hidden Meadows Dr 75964
High Meadow St 75965
Highland Dr 75965
Hill Ave 75964
Hillencamp St 75964
Hillsview Rd 75964
Hilltop St 75961
Hillview Dr & Rd 75964
Hiram St 75964
Holly Lake Dr 75965

Holly Oak St 75964
Hollyberry Dr 75961
Hollybrook Dr 75965
Hollywood St 75964
Home Ave 75964
Homer Dr 75965
Hope Ln 75961
Hornbuckle Ln 75964
Horsepen Crk 75961
E & W Hospital St 75961
Houston St 75961
Hudson St 75961
Hugh Weatherly Rd 75964
Hughes St 75961
Humble Camp Rd 75964
Humphrey Rd & St 75961
Hunt St 75965
Hunter St 75964
Hunters Ridge Dr 75965
Huntington Cir 75965
Hurst Cir 75964
Hurst Dr 75961
Hurst Rd 75964
Idylwood St 75965
Ila St 75961
Industrial Dr 75964
Infinity Ln 75961
Inwood Ln 75965
Iron Ore Rd 75965
Ivy Strode Rd 75965
J And H Ln 75964
Jack Birdwell Rd 75964
Jack Lock St 75965
Jackson St 75964
Jacobs St 75961
Jade St 75965
Jans Rd 75964
Jeane St 75965
Jefferson 75961
Jeffries St 75964
Jeri Ann Ln 75964
Jim Rd 75964
John St 75965
John C Collins Ln 75964
John Hall Rd 75961
John Richardson Rd 75961
Johnnys Park Dr 75964
Johnson Dr & Way 75964
Jonah St 75965
Jordan St 75964
Joyce Ave 75964
Justice Rd 75961
Justin St 75965
K Jo Lyn Ln 75964
Karle St 75965
Katy Dr 75961
Kemah Dr 75964
Kenbrook Dr 75965
Kenneth St 75964
Kent St 75961
Kerry St 75965
Kevin St 75961
Kilgore Ln 75965
King St 75961
Kings Row Dr 75965
Kirsten Ln 75964
Kolb Ln 75964
Koonce Rd 75964
Kourtney Ln 75961
L And D Dr 75961
La Bega St 75964
Lady Diane Dr 75965
Lady Elaine Dr 75965
Lady Jennifer Dr 75965
Lake Est, Rd & St 75964
Lake Forest Dr 75964
Lake Park Dr 75964
Lakeland Rd 75965
Lakeview Dr 75964
S Lakeview Dr 75964
Lakeview Ln 75965
E & W Lakewood St 75965
Lamar St 75961
Lambert Rd 75961
Lampkin St 75964
Lamplite Ln 75964

N & S Lanana St 75961
E & W Lane Dr 75964
E Laura St 75961
Laurel Ln 75964
Laurel Oak St 75964
Lawson Pkwy 75965
Lazy Brook Dr 75961
Lazy J Ln 75965
Leak St 75964
Lee Ln & Rd 75964
Leita Ln 75965
Lelia St 75961
Lenwood Dr 75964
Leon St 75964
Leroy St 75961
Leroy Weaver Rd 75964
Lewis St 75961
Libby Dr 75961
Liles Blvd 75964
Lilly St 75964
Linda Ln 75964
Linn Flat Church Rd 75964
Little Joe Rd 75964
Live Oak Dr 75965
Lloyd St 75965
Lock St 75964
Logan Cir 75961
Logansport Rd & St 75961
Lola St 75964
Lone Pine Rd 75965
Lone Star Rd 75964
Loni Dr 75964
Looneyville Rd 75964
Loren Rd 75961
Lovaire St 75961
Loveless Ln 75965
Lujan Ln 75964
Lydia St 75964
Lynn St 75964
Mac Rd 75964
Macedonia Rd 75964
Mackechney St 75965
Macon Dr 75965
Madison Ln 75965
Mae St 75964
Magnolia St 75961
Maid Marion Ln 75965
E Main St 75961
W Main St
100-599 75961
600-1699 75964
Majestic Ln 75961
Maness Rd 75961
Maple St 75961
Margaret St 75964
Marilyn St 75961
Mark St 75964
Markham St 75964
Maroney Dr 75965
Martha St 75961
Martin Luther King Jr Blvd 75961
Martinsville St 75961
Marty St 75964
Mary Dr 75961
Mary Evelyn St 75964
Mashie Dr 75964
Mast Aly 75961
Matlock Rd 75964
Matthew St 75964
Maybell St 75961
Mayo Rd
1300-1399 75965
1600-1699 75964
Mccain Ln 75964
E & W Mccrainie St 75961
Mcguire Ln 75964
Mckewen Dr 75965
E & W Mclemore Ct 75964
W Meadow St 75965
Meadowbrook Dr 75964
Meadowview Dr 75965
Meazell Rd 75964
Meisenheimer St 75961
Melody Ln 75964
Melrose East Rd 75961

Melrose South Cir 75961
Melrose Swift Rd 75961
Melwood Cir 75964
Memory Ln 75965
Michael St 75965
Mickersi St 75961
Millard Dr 75965
Mimms Ave 75961
Mimosa St 75964
Mini Dr 75964
Mission Vly 75964
Mission Valley Dr 75964
Mitchell St 75965
Mockingbird Ln 75964
Moody Rd 75961
Moore St 75961
Mora St 75965
Moreland Dr 75965
Morrow Rd 75964
N & S Mound St 75961
Mr Henrys Dr 75965
Mt Moriah Rd 75961
Muckleroy St 75961
Mulberry St 75965
Muller St 75961
Murphy Ln 75964
Murray St 75961
Myrl Rd 75964
Myrtle St 75965
Mystic Ln 75965
Nannie St 75961
Nash St 75964
Nazareth Way 75964
Neal Ln 75965
Neill Rd 75964
Nelson St 75965
Nelson D Carter Rd 75961
New Press Rd 75964
Newman St 75965
Norma St 75965
North St
100-1499 75961
1500-8399 75965
Northern Oak St 75964
Northgate St 75965
Northridge Dr 75965
Northway Dr 75965
Northwood Cir 75965
Norvell St 75961
Nottingham St 75961
E Oak Ln 75961
Oak Creek Dr 75965
Oak Hill Plz 75964
Oakview Dr 75965
Ochiltree St 75961
Ocie J Ln 75964
Ola Aly 75961
Old Douglass Rd 75964
Old Fire Tower Rd 75964
Old Line Dr 75965
Old Lufkin Rd 75964
Old Mills Run 75965
Old North Church Rd 75965
Old Post Oak Rd 75965
Old Runway Rd 75964
Old Shady Grove Rd 75961
Old Tyler Rd
100-499 75961
500-7899 75964
Olds Rd 75961
Oldsmobile Rd 75965
Oliver 75961
Orton St 75961
Oscar Patton Rd 75961
Oso Rd 75964
Otis St 75961
Paluxy St 75964
Pamelia St 75964
Paradise Dr & Rd 75964
Park Pl & St 75961
E & W Parker Rd 75965
Parkwood St 75965
Parmley Dr 75965
Parrott Dr 75965
Pat St 75964
Patricia Dr 75961

Patti Ann St 75964
Patton St 75964
Paul St 75964
Paul Bunyon St 75961
Paula St 75964
Peach St 75961
Pearl St
100-1499 75961
1500-3799 75965
3801-4999 75965
Pebble Ln 75964
Pebble Beach Dr 75964
Pebble Creek St 75965
N Pecan St
100-199 75961
2200-3699 75965
S Pecan St 75961
Pecan Grove St 75961
Pecan Hill Ln 75965
Peck Reynolds Rd 75965
Peoples Ln 75964
Pepper Mill Ln 75965
Perkins Dr 75961
Perry Dr 75964
Pete Aiken Ln 75961
Pete Duke Rd 75961
Pete Strahan Rd 75961
Pettit St 75964
Phillips Rd 75964
Phoenix Ter 75961
Piccadilly Cir 75965
E & W Pilar St 75961
Pilot St 75964
Pin Oak St 75965
Pine St 75965
Pine Creek Rd 75964
Pine Shadows Dr 75965
Pinecrest Dr 75965
Piping Rock St 75965
Pisgah Rd 75965
Pitman St 75961
Pleasant Ln 75964
Ponderosa St 75964
N & S Popp St 75964
Porter St 75961
Poskey Rd 75964
Post Oak Rd 75965
Powers St
100-499 75961
600-1900 75964
1902-1998 75964
Prairie Grove Rd 75961
Press Rd 75964
Price St 75961
Princess Ln 75961
Private Road 6824 75965
Proadenw St 75964
Prosperie Rd 75961
Pruitt Hill Cir & Dr 75961
Quail Run & Way 75965
Quail Ridge Dr 75961
Quarry Ln 75965
Queen St 75964
Queens Row 75965
Raguet St
900-1499 75961
2101-2197 75965
2199-4499 75965
Railroad St 75961
Randall St 75964
Randolph St 75964
Randy Ln 75964
Rangel Rd 75964
Rankin Rd 75961
Rapsilver Ln 75961
Rawlinson Rd 75964
Ray St 75961
Rayburn Dr 75961
Red Bird Ln 75965
Red Creek Ln 75961
Red Oak Dr 75965
Red Rock Cir 75964
Red Rock Ranch Rd 75964
Red Tip Ln 75961
Redbud St 75965

N Redland Community Rd 75965
Redwood Dr 75965
Reedy St 75964
Rho St 75964
Richardson St 75961
Richmond St 75964
Ridge View Dr 75961
Ridgebrook Dr 75965
Ridgecrest Dr 75961
Ridgeview Dr 75964
Ridgewood Dr 75964
Rigby Rd 75964
Ritchie St 75964
Roadrunner Ln 75961
Roark Dr 75964
Rob Ln 75961
Roberts St 75964
Robertson Dr 75965
Robinhood Dr 75961
Rock Oak St 75964
Rock Ridge St 75965
Rockcreek Ct 75965
Rocky Ln 75964
Roddy Brewer Ln 75964
Rodessa St 75964
Roland Dr 75961
Rolling Hills St 75965
Rosa Ln 75965
Rosebud Ln 75961
Roselake Dr 75965
Rosewood Dr 75961
Ross Hardeman Rd 75961
Roweena Ln 75961
Rowlett Dr & Ln 75964
Royal Ln 75965
Rubio Ln 75961
Ruby St 75961
Rudolph St 75964
Rulfs St 75961
Rusche Ln 75965
Rusk St 75965
Russell Blvd & Trl 75965
Russellville Rd 75964
Ruth Williams Ln 75965
Sadler St 75961
Saint Charles Pl 75961
Saint James Pl 75961
Saint Loop 495 75965
Sam Barrett Rd 75965
Sandalwood Cir 75965
N & S Sanders St 75964
Sandia St 75964
Sandra Jean St 75964
Sandstone Ln 75965
Sandy Ln 75961
Sandy Ridge Rd 75965
Sandyland Cir 75964
Sante Fe Pl 75961
Sarah Anne St 75965
Saratoga St 75964
Scarborough Rd 75961
Scarlet Oak St 75964
Scenic Dr 75965
Scott Ln & St 75961
Scroggins Hill Rd 75965
E & W Seale St 75964
Sebren Ln 75965
Seelbach Rd 75965
Shadow Brook Dr 75965
Shady Ln & Trl 75964
Shady Acres Dr & St 75965
Shadybrook St 75965
Shalom Way 75964
Sharon Dr 75961
S Shawnee St 75961
Shebb Rd 75964
Sheffield Dr 75965
Sheina St 75961
Shelton Dr 75965
Shepherd Dr 75964
Shepherd Rd 75965
Sherwood Dr 75965
Shields St 75964
Shiller Dr 75964
Shinn Rd 75964
Shirley St 75965
Shoreline Dr 75964
Shumard Oak St 75964
Shumway Ln 75964
Sidney St 75961
Simmons Ln 75965
Simpson St 75961
Sir Galahad Dr 75965
Sir Gawain Dr 75965
Skyline Dr 75965
Smith Rd 75961
Solomon Rd 75965
Sophie Ln 75964
South St
100-299 75961
700-6000 75964
6002-6898 75964
Southern Oak St 75964
Spanish Bluff Rd 75964
Spanish Trace Rd 75964
Spokane St 75964
E & W Spradley St 75964
Spring Ln 75964
Spring Creek Dr 75965
Spring Valley Dr 75964
Springbrook St 75965
Spurrier Rd 75965
St George Cir 75965
N Stallings Dr
100-698 75965
700-799 75965
1901-1997 75964
1999-2600 75964
2602-2698 75964
NE Stallings Dr
100-2000 75961
2002-2698 75961
2701-2797 75965
2799-4999 75965
NW Stallings Dr 75964
SE Stallings Dr
100-1299 75964
1300-5299 75961
SW Stallings Dr 75964
Stanmark Rd 75961
E & W Starr Ave 75961
State Highway 204 75964
State Highway 21 E 75961
W State Highway 21 75964
E State Highway 7 75961
W State Highway 7 75964
N Steen Dr 75965
Stephens St 75964
Stewart St 75961
Stinson Ln 75964
Stoddard Dr 75965
Stokes Rd 75965
N & S Stone St 75964
Stone Creek Ct 75965
Stonecreek Ln 75961
Stones Throw St 75965
Stratford Cir 75965
Stringer Rd 75964
Sugar Fae Ln 75965
Sullivan Dr 75964
Sumac Dr 75964
Summer Hill Cir 75965
Summit St 75961
Sundown Dr 75964
Sunnybrook St 75965
Sunset Ave 75964
Surrey St 75965
Susan St 75964
Sutton St 75961
Swann Dr 75964
Sweat Cir 75964
Sweetgum St 75961
Sweetser Dr 75964
Swift St 75961
Tall Oak St 75965
Tangleberry Dr 75961
Tanglewood Cir 75961
Tara Ln 75965
Teague Ln 75961
Ted Hill St 75965
Tejas St 75961
Terracewood St 75965
Terry St 75964
Terry Crawford Dr 75964
Texas St 75961
Texas Oak St 75964
Thomas St 75964
Thompson Ln 75961
Till St 75965
Timber Ridge Dr 75961
Timberidge St 75961
Timberlake St 75961
Timberwood Dr 75965
Tindale Rd 75961
Tindall St 75964
Tipps Dr 75964
Tower Rd 75961
Townsend Ave 75964
Tp Richardson Dr 75965
Trailwood Dr 75965
Tran St 75964
Travis St 75965
Tree Line Dr 75961
Tucker Ln 75965
Tudor Dr 75965
Turner Rd 75965
Twinoaks Dr 75965
S Tyler Rd 75961
N University Dr
100-2599 75961
2600-3100 75965
3007-3007 75963
3102-4898 75965
3201-4899 75965
S University Dr 75961
S University St 75961
Upper Melrose Rd 75961
Upton St 75965
Us Highway 259
8600-11899 75965
Us Highway 259
11900-11998 75961
11901-19099 75965
12100-19098 75965
Us Highway 59 N
4100-4798 75964
8201-8297 75965
S Us Highway 59 75964
Valley View Dr & St 75964
Vernell Ln 75964
Vesta Faulkner Gas Unit Rd 75961
Victoria Dr 75965
Vigilante Rd 75961
N Village Blvd 75965
Village Dr 75965
N Village Ln 75964
Village Gate Cir 75961
Virginia Ave 75964
Wade Rd & St 75964
Wages Ln 75964
Walker Aly & Ave 75961
Wallace Ln 75965
Walnut Dr 75965
Walton Rd 75964
Wankan St 75964
Ward St 75961
Warr Cir 75964
Warren Dr 75964
Warwick Ln 75965
Water Oak St 75965
Waterford Cir, Ct & Dr 75965
Waterford Muse 75965
Waters Rd 75961
Weaver St 75964
Wedgewood St 75961
Weldon Dr 75964
Wellington Pt 75965
Wells St 75964
Wesley Cloudy Rd 75964
Western Oak St 75964
Westview Dr 75964
Westward Dr 75964
Wettermark St 75965
Wheeler Ln 75964
Whisper Dr 75964
White Oak St
100-799 75961
4400-4499 75965
Wicker Dr 75964
Wildhurst St 75964
Wildwood Dr 75961
Williams St 75964
Williamsburg Dr 75965
Willie Cox Rd 75961
Willow Oak St 75964
Wilma Ln 75961
Wilson Dr 75964
Wilson Loop 75961
Windsor Dr 75965
Wingate Ln 75964
Woden Rd 75961
Woden West Cir 75961
Woodbine St 75964
Woodcreek Dr 75965
Woodcrest Dr 75965
Woodcrest Vw 75964
Woodhaven Ct & St 75965
Woodland St 75961
Woodland Acres 75964
Woodland Hills Dr 75964
Woods St 75961
Woods Edge 75965
Woods View Dr 75964
Woodway Ln 75965
Woody Ln 75961
Worley Dr 75961
Wortham Dr 75965
Wright Dr 75964
Yolunda Dr 75961
York Dr 75965
Yseleta Creek Rd 75964
Z St 75964
Zavala Dr 75961
Zelpha Way 75961
Zeno St 75965
Zula St 75961

NUMBERED STREETS

1st St 75961
2nd St 75961
3rd St 75961
4th St 75961
31st St 75964
33rd St 75964
34th St 75964
35th St 75964
3h Dr 75964

NEW BRAUNFELS TX

General Delivery 78130

POST OFFICE BOXES MAIN OFFICE STATIONS AND BRANCHES

Box No.s
310001 - 312660 78131
310200 - 312382 78135
315289 - 350050 78131
350050 - 351010 78135
351000 - 351010 78131
351050 - 351070 78135
351050 - 351060 78131
351100 - 351280 78135
351130 - 351200 78131

RURAL ROUTES

06, 12 78132

NAMED STREETS

Aaron Ln 78130
S Abbey Loop 78130
Abbey Rd 78132
Abels Way 78133
N & S Academy Ave 78130
S Access Rd 78133
Acme Rd 78130
Acorn Dr 78130
Acorn Cove Dr 78130
Acquedotto 78132
Adam St 78130
Adams Way 78133
Addstine 78130
Adolph Cir 78130
Advantage Dr 78130
Agarita Trl 78132
Aguayo Dr 78133
Airline Dr 78133
Airport Rd 78130
Albert St 78130
Allemania Dr 78132
Allen Ave 78130
Allen View Dr 78132
Allens Bend Dr 78130
Allison Dr 78130
Alta Vista Ln 78133
Alton Loop 78130
Altwein Ln 78130
Alves Ln 78130
Alysia Cir 78130
Alyssa Way 78132
Amanda 78133
Amaryllis 78132
Amber Arc 78130
American Blvd 78130
Amulet Dr 78132
Amy Ave 78130
Andora Dr 78130
Andrew Run 78133
Angeles Ct 78133
Angelica Vis 78133
Angelina Dr 78130
Angolo 78132
Anhalt Cv & Dr 78130
S Ann St 78130
Anna Lee 78130
Anne Louise Dr 78130
Antigua Cv 78132
Antonia 78132
Apache Dr 78130
Apex Ave 78132
Apg Ln 78132
Apollo Dr 78133
Appalachian Trl 78132
Appellation 78132
April Dr 78133
Aquatic Cir 78130
Aragon Ct 78133
Aransas Pass 78133
Arbor Cir 78130
Arcadia Dr 78133
Archer Blvd 78132
Arendes Dr 78132
Armadillo Ln 78133
Arndt Rd 78130
Arnold Dr 78133
Arrow Ln 78130
Arrowhead Dr 78133
Arroyo Way 78133
Artillery Dr 78133
Asbury Ct 78130
Ash Juniper Dr 78132
Ashberry Ave 78130
Ashland 78132
Ashley Cir 78132
Ashley Ln 78133
Ashmore St 78130
Ashton Oaks 78132
Assiniboia Dr 78133
Astor Crk 78130
Atlentr Dr 78132
E & W Austin St 78130
Autumn Chase 78132
Autumn Oak 78132
Avenue A 78130
Avery Pkwy 78130
Axis Trl 78132
Azalea Ln 78130
Azalea Way 78132
Baden Aly 78130
Bading Ln 78130
Bailey Dr 78133
Balcones Ave 78130
Bald Eagle 78133
Baldy Mountain Ct 78133
Balsa 78133
Bambi Ln 78133
Bamc Dr 78133
Bandera Cir 78130
Bandit Bay Vw 78130
Bandit Beach Rd 78130
Banister 78133
Barbara Dr 78133
Barbarosa Rd 78130
Barbarossa Rd 78130
Barcelona Dr 78130
Barn Swallow 78130
Barolo Ct 78132
Bartels Ct 78130
Barwood Dr 78130
Basel St 78130
Bass Ln 78130
Bass Farms Rd 78132
Bastrop Dr 78130
Bateman Ln 78133
Bavarian Dr 78130
Bear Creek Dr & Trl 78132
Beaty St 78130
Beaver Crk 78130
Beaver Ln 78132
Becker St 78130
Bell St 78130
Bella Vis 78133
Bellaire Dr 78130
Bellewood Ln 78133
Belmead Dr 78130
Belmont Dr 78130
Belvedere Ct 78130
Bendel Ranch Rd 78133
Bending Oak 78132
Benelli Dr 78130
Bent Blf 78132
Bentwood Dr 78130
Bergfeld Ave 78130
Bess St 78130
Beverly Ln 78130
Big Spg 78133
Big Bend Dr 78133
Big Hawk 78130
Big John Ln 78133
Big Oak 78132
Big Sky Dr 78132
Big Wampum 78133
Billabong Ave 78132
Birch Bnd 78130
Birch St 78132
Birdsong Ln 78130
Black Frst 78130
Black Bear Dr 78132
Black Buck Rdg 78132
Black Hawk Trl 78130
Black Oak Dr 78133
Blackjack Oak 78132
Blair Pl 78130
Blazewood Dr 78130
Blend Way 78132
Blue Pt 78132
Blue Bonnet Breeze 78133
Blue Goose 78130
Blue Jay Ct 78133
Blue Jay Dr 78130
Blue Rock 78132
Blue Spruce 78130
Blue Water Dr 78133
Bluebird Dr 78132
Bluebird Rdg 78130
Bluebonnet Ave 78130
Blueridge Dr 78133
Bluff Creek Cir 78130
Bluff End Rd 78132
Bluff Ridge Ct 78132
Bluffside Dr 78130
Blush 78132
Bobby Clark Dr 78133
Bobcat Run 7813
Bobolink Dr 7813
Bobwhite Ln 7813
Boenig Dr 7813
Bogen Rd 7813
Bogi St 7813
Bonner Blvd 7813
Bonnies Way 7813
Bonnyview Dr 7813
Booker Ave 7813
Boomerang 7813
Booneville Ave 7813
Bordeaux 7813
Bordeaux Blanc 7813
Bormann Dr 7813
Bottle Ct 7813
Boulder Oak Dr 7813
Bradfield Cir 7813
Brads Flight 7813
Bradstreet 7813
Branch Rd 7813
Brandenburg Ln 7813
Braunfels East Dr 7813
Bravo Rd 7813
Bremer 7813
Brenda Ln 7813
Brenham Cir 7813
Brentwood Dr 7813
Bretzke Ln 7813
Breve Cir 7813
Brian 7813
Briarbend Dr 7813
Briarwood Dr 7813
E & W Bridge St 7813
Bridget Dr 7813
Bridlewood 7813
Briggs Dr 7813
Brighten Dr 7813
Brinkley Dr 7813
Briscoe Dr 7813
Brittany Grace 7813
Broadmoor Dr 7813
Broadway 7813
Brock St 7813
Brockton Dr 7813
Broken Ski Cir 7813
Broken Spoke 7813
Broken Star Dr 7813
Broken Wheel Ln 7813
Brook Valley Dr 7813
Brookhollow 7813
Brooklynn Ln 7813
Brown Rock Dr 7813
Buch Ln 7813
Buck Trl 7813
Buck Run Pass 7813
Buckhaven Dr 7813
Buckhorn Dr 7813
Buckingham Dr 7813
Buckskin St 7813
Buffalo Crk 7813
Buffalo Springs Rd, Spur & Xing 7813
Bunker St 7813
Burleson Dr 7813
Burr Oak Ln 7813
Bushtail Dr 7813
N & S Business Ih 35 7813
Butcher St 7813
Buttercup 7813
Button Ball 7813
Caballo Trl 7813
Cabernet 7813
Cactus Breeze 7813
Cactus Flower 7813
Cactus Wren Loop 7813
Caddell Ln 7813
Cadillac Canyon Dr 7813
Calhoon Ct 7813
Calhoun Dr 7813
Calico Pass 7813
California Blvd 7813
Callalily 7813
Calm Breeze 7813
Calm Water 7813
Calvin Loop 7813

Street	ZIP
ambridge Dr	78132
ambridge Way	78130
amel Trl	78132
amel Back Dr	78130
amellia Ln	78130
ameron Dr	78130
amino Real	78133
Camp St	78130
amp Joy Rd	78130
amp Porter Rd	78130
amp Willow Rd	78130
ampbell Dr	78133
anal Ln	78130
andlelight Dr	78133
andlewood Cir	78130
ane St	78130
aney Creek Rd	78130
annan Rd	78133
anteen	78133
anterberry Dr	78132
anyon Bnd	78133
anyon Crk	78133
anyon Dr	
100-199	78133
900-1199	78130
anyon Shrs	78133
anyon Trce	78133
anyon Way	78132
anyon Acres	78133
anyon Circle Dr	78133
anyon Edge	78133
anyon Lake Dr	78133
anyon Lake Forest	
r	78133
anyon Oaks Dr	78133
anyon Park Rd	78133
anyon Ranch Dr	78133
anyon Ridge Dr	78133
anyon Springs Dr	78133
ap Ridge Peak	78130
ap Rock Hl	78132
ap Stone Rdg	78130
ara Ln	78130
ardinal Dr & Mnr	78130
arl Dr	78130
arlisle Castle Dr	78130
arlton Dr	78133
arnation Ln	78130
arolyn Cv	78130
arpenter Dr	78133
arson Crk	78133
arson Loop	78130
asa Sierra	78133
ash Ln	78133
& S Castell Ave	78130
astin Ln	78130
astle Hl	78130
astleberry Rdg	78130
astles Dr	78133
astleway Rd	78132
astlewood Dr	78130
attail	78133
aveside Dr	78133
edar Bnd	78133
edar Dr	78133
edar Fls	78133
edar Park	78132
edar Rdg	78132
edar Run	78133
edar Shrs	78133
edar Trl	78130
edar Vly	78133
edar Creek Dr	78132
edar Crest Dr	78133
edar Elm St	78132
edar Grove St	78132
edar Lane Dr	78133
edar Rise Dr	78133
edar Tree Ln	78133
edar Winds Dr	78132
entennial Bnd & Cv	78130
enter St	78130
& S Central Ave	78130
entre Ct	78132
entury Ranch Rd	78130
hablis	78132
Chad St	78130
Chamberlain Way	78133
Chaparral Dr	78132
Chapel Bnd	78130
Chapman Pkwy	78133
Charm Dr	78132
Charter Oak Dr	78133
Chartwell Ave	78130
Chase Oaks	78132
Chelsea St	78130
Chensour Dr	78130
Cherokee Blvd	78132
Cherry Hl	78130
Cherry St	78132
N Chestnut Ave	78130
S Chestnut Ave	78130
Chestnut Fls	78133
Chicago Ave	78130
Chickadee	78133
Chimney Rock	78133
Chinaberry Ln	78130
Churchill Dr	78130
Cielo Vis	78133
Cima Vis	78133
Cindy Dr	78133
Cindy Sue	78133
Cinnamon Teal	78130
Circle Dr & Hvn	78133
Circle Dot Rd	78132
Circleview Dr	78133
Citori Path	78130
E & W Clark Dr	78133
Clay Rdg	78133
Clear Lk & Rdg	78132
Clear Springs Dr	78130
Clearcreek Dr	78133
Clearfield Dr	78130
Clearview Cyn & Dr	78133
Clearwater Ct	78133
Clearwater Dr	78130
Clemens Ave	78130
Cliffview	78133
Cliffwood	78133
Cloud Ln	78130
Cloud Top	78133
Clover Cir	78130
Club Xing	78130
Club House Loop	78133
Cobblestone Dr	78132
Coco Dr	78130
Cody Ct	78133
Coe Rd	78130
Coenen Ln	78130
Cold Spring Dr	78133
Cole Ave	78130
E & W Coll St	78130
Collanade Dr	78132
Colleen Dr	78133
Cologne Cv & Dr	78133
Colvin St	78130
Comal Ave	78130
Comal Cir	78130
Comal Spgs	78133
Comal Park Rd	78133
Comanche Rdg	78132
Comanche St	78130
Comfort	78133
E Commerce St	78130
Common St	78130
Community Dr	78132
Compass Rose	78133
Concepcion Ave	78130
Concho Loop	78130
Conner Dr	78133
Connettere	78132
Connie Dr	78133
Conrads Ln	78130
Contour Dr	78133
Conway Castle Dr	78130
Coolabah Ave	78133
Copper Crk	78132
Copper Crst	78132
Copper Frst	78132
Copper Mtn	78130
Copper Trce	78132
Copper Vly	78132
Copper Bluff Dr	78130
Copper Glen Dr	78130
Copper Hill Dr	78130
Copper Path Dr	78130
Copper Point Dr	78130
Copper Ridge Dr	78132
Copper View Dr	78130
Copper Wood Dr	78130
Copperfield St	78130
Cora Cir & St	78130
Cordoba Dr	78130
Cordova Bnd	78133
Cornerstone Dr	78130
Corona Rnch	78132
Corto Cir	78132
Cotton Blvd & Xing	78130
Cotton Gin	78130
Cottontail Ln	78130
Cougar Dr	78133
Country Dr	78132
Country Ln	78130
Country Pike	78133
Country Club Cir	78130
Country Grace S	78130
Country Ledge Dr	78132
Country Ridge Dr	78132
Country View Cir	78132
Countryside Dr	78132
E & W County Line	
Rd	78130
Courtyard Dr	78130
Covers Cv	78132
Coyote Run	78132
Crane Crest Dr	78130
Cranes Mill Rd	78133
N Cranes Mill Rd	78133
S Cranes Mill Rd	78133
Crazy Horse Trl	78133
Creek Cyn	78132
Creek Dr	78130
Creekside Cir	78130
Creekside Dr	78130
Creekside Way	78130
Creekside Xing	78130
Creekview Dr	78133
Creekview Way	78130
Crest Ln	78130
Crest Rdg	78132
Crested Creek Dr	78130
Crestview Dr	78133
Crockett Ct	78130
Cross St	78130
Cross Oak	78132
Cross River St	78130
Crossbow Dr	78133
NW Crossing Dr	78130
Crosspoint Dr	78133
Crown Cir	78130
Crown Rdg	78132
Crystal Brk	78132
Crystal Springs Rd	78130
Cutler Bay	78130
Cylamen	78132
Cypress Dr	78133
Cypress Bend Cv	78130
Cypress Rapids Dr	78130
Daffodil	78130
Daisy Ln	78130
Dakota Cir	78130
Dallas St	78130
Dalton St	78130
Damar Dr	78133
Dammann Ln	78130
Danchina Dr	78133
Daniel Dr	78132
Darion St	78133
Dauer Ln	78130
Dauer Ranch Rd	78130
David Jonas Dr	78132
Dawnridge Dr	78130
Deborah Dr	78133
Decanter Dr	78132
Decker Dr	78132
Dedeke Dr	78132
Deepwell	78133
Deer Dr	78133
Deer Holw	78130
Deer Ln	78130
Deer Path	78133
Deer Meadows Dr	78133
Deer Oak St	78133
Deer Run Pass	78133
Deer Run Rdg	78132
Deer Run Way	78132
Deer Trot St	78130
Deer Valley St	78133
Deerwood Dr	78133
Delafield Dr	78132
Delaney Rae	78132
Delanoy Dr	78133
Delia Cir	78130
Demi John Bend Rd	78133
Denise Dr	78130
Denver Dr	78130
Desert Rose	78132
Desiree St	78133
Detex Dr	78133
Deveraux	78132
Devin Dr	78133
Dewberry Ln	78132
Diamond Trl	78132
Diamond Oak	78132
Diamondback Trl	78132
Diamondhead Dr	78133
Dickinson Ln	78133
Didgeridoo Trl	78132
Dietert Ln	78133
Dime Box Cir	78130
Dimmitt Dr	78133
Diretto	78132
Dittlinger St	78130
Divine Way	78130
Dodge Dr	78130
Doe Cir & Ln	78133
Doehne Oaks	78132
Doeppenschmidt Rd	78132
Dogwood Dr	78133
Dollar Dr	78133
Donald Ross Pl	78130
Donna Dr	78133
Donnelly Dr	78133
Doris St	78133
Dorman Dr	78133
Dorothy Dr	78133
Double Tree Ln	78133
Douglas Fir Dr	78130
Dove St	78130
Dove Crest Loop	78130
Dove Crossing Dr	78130
Dover Grace	78130
Downda Rd	78133
Dragon Trl	78133
Dreamland Dr	78130
Drew Ln	78133
Driftwind Dr	78133
Dripping Spgs	78130
Dry Crk	78133
Dry Bear Crk	78132
Dry Stack Rd	78132
Duck Mountain Ln	78133
Duke Bnd	78133
Dunbar Dr	78130
Dundee Grace	78130
Dunlap Dr & Loop	78130
Durango Dr	78132
Durham	78133
Dustin Cade Dr	78130
Dusty Ln	78132
Dusty Saddle	78133
Duval Dr	78130
Eagle Mtn	78133
Eagle Flight Dr	78133
Eagle Pass Dr	78133
Eagles Nest	78130
Earl Dr	78130
N & S East Ave	78130
Eastern Finch	78133
Eastlawn Dr	78130
Eastman Ave	78130
Eastside Dr	78133
Eastview Dr	78133
Echo Pt	78133
Echo Hills Dr	78130
Echoing Oak	78132
Eckhardt Rd	78132
Eden Dr	78130
Eden Estates Dr	78132
Eden Ranch Dr	
100-599	78133
100-199	78132
Edenwald Rd	78133
Edgar	78133
Edge Hill Dr	78133
Edgegrove	78133
Edgewater Fls	78133
E Edgewater Ter	78130
W Edgewater Ter	78130
Edwards Blvd	78132
Eiche Cir	78132
Eichen Rd	78130
Eichen Baum Rd	78132
Eikel St	78130
El Capitan Trl	78133
El Rincon	78132
Elf Owl	78130
Elizabeth Ave & Ct	78130
Elk Rdg	78133
Ellen St	78130
Elley Ln	78130
Elm St & Trl	78130
Elm Cedar Dr	78132
Elm Creek Rd	78132
Elmgrove Ave	78133
Elmwood Cv & Dr	78130
Elvira	78133
Emerald Frst	78132
Emiline Ln	78130
Emory Ct	78133
Emu Parade	78132
Enchanted Oak	78132
Enchantment Ln	78130
Encino Dr	78130
Enclave Trl	78133
Engel Rd	78132
Ensenada Dr	78133
Entrance Dr	78130
Entre Rios Blvd	78132
Erika Crst	78133
Ervenberg Ave	78130
Ervendberg Ave	78130
Escarpment Oak	78130
Espada	78132
Essex Grace	78130
Estate Dr	78132
Estrellita Ranch Rd	78133
Evaleen Cir	78133
Evergreen Ln	78130
Eves Way	78133
Eves Spring Dr	78133
Ewald Rd	78130
Ewelling Ln	78130
Ewing Cir	78133
Executive Dr	78130
Fair Ln	78133
Fairmont St	78130
Fairview Dr	78133
Fairway Dr	78133
Fairwood Dr	78133
Falcon Grv	78133
Falcon Ridge Dr	78130
Fallen Oak	78132
Falling Hls	78132
Fannin Dr	78130
E & W Faust St	78130
Fawn Dr, Mdws & Trl	78133
Fawn Valley Dr	78133
Fawnwood Dr	78133
Fayette Dr	78130
Feather Ln	78130
Feldspar Cir	78132
Feldstein Rd	78132
Felger Rd	78130
Fels Mauer Blvd	78132
Felsblock Ln	78132
Felsig Bnd	78132
Felswand Pkwy	78132
Ferguson St	78130
Fern Ave	78130
Fernhill Dr	78130
Ferry Ln	78130
Ferryboat Ln	78130
Fieldcrest	78130
Fieldstone	78132
Fire Field Rd	78130
Firefly Dr	78133
First St	78132
Fitch Dr	78130
Five Oaks Cir	78133
Flaman Rd	78133
Flaming Oak Dr	78132
Flamingo Ct	78133
Flat Crk	78133
Flat Land Pass	78130
Flatrock Dr	78133
Fleetwood Dr	78130
Flint Cir	78133
Flintrock	78133
Flintstone Dr	78133
Floating Star	78130
Flora St	78130
Floral Ave & Cir	78130
Flushing	78130
Fm 1044	78130
Fm 1101	78130
Fm 1102	
2001-4497	78132
Fm 1102	
4499-8700	78132
8702-8998	78132
9101-10199	78130
Fm 1103	78132
Fm 1863	78132
Fm 2252	78132
Fm 2439	78132
Fm 2673	78133
Fm 2722	78133
Fm 3009	78132
Fm 306	
100-1199	78130
1201-1299	78130
1401-1497	78132
1401-12097	78133
1499-11600	78132
11602-11898	78132
12099-23700	78133
23702-23898	78133
Fm 311	
4700-4998	78132
5000-5399	78132
5300-5699	78133
5701-5799	78133
Fm 3159	
35800-36600	78132
36602-39098	78132
39800-39898	78133
39900-42399	78133
Fm 3424	78133
Fm 482	78132
Fm 483	78130
Fm 484	78133
Fm 725	78130
Fm 758	78133
Foot Hill Dr	78130
Forest Crst	78133
Forest Rdg	78130
Forest Trl	78132
Forest Glen Ln	78130
Forest Hill St	78133
Forest Link	78132
Forest Mist	78133
Foresthaven Dr	78132
Fork Crk	78133
Four Winds Dr	78133
Fox Rdg	78133
Fox Glen Rd	78130
Fox Run Cir	78130
Foxwood	78132
Francis Harris Ln	78130
Francisco Pass	78133
Franks Rd	78130
Fredericksburg Rd	78130
Friendly Path	78132
Friendlywood Dr	78133
Friesenhahn Rd	78132
Frio Cir	78130
Froboese Ln	78132
Frostwood Dr	78130
Fuller Dr	78133
Gaines	78130
Gallagher Cres & Dr	78133
Galway Gate	78133
E & W Garden St	78130
Garden Gate Cir	78130
Garden Sun Pl	78130
Gardenia Dr	78130
Garrett Way	78133
E & W Garza St	78130
Gateway Cir	78130
Gatewood Cir	78130
Gelowitz Pl	78133
Gemini Dr	78133
Geneseo Oaks	78132
Gentle Breeze	78130
Genway Pl	78133
George Pass	78133
George Ranch Rd	78133
George Strait	78133
Georgia Pl	78130
S Gilbert Ave	78130
Ginko Cir	78130
Gladstone Pl	78130
Glen Hvn	78132
Glen Shrs	78133
Glen Oaks Dr	78133
Glen Wood Dr	78132
Glenbrook Dr E	78130
Glenn Dr	78133
Glenworth St	78133
Global Dr	78130
Gloria Ave	78130
Gode Ln	78130
Gold Way	78130
Golden Mdw	78132
Golden Eagle Loop	78133
Golf Course Rd	78130
Goliad Dr	78130
Goodwin Ln	
2200-2434	78130
2435-2435	78135
2436-3298	78130
2437-3299	78130
Granada Dr	78130
Granada Hls	78132
Grand Pass	78133
Grandview Ave	78130
Grandview Bnd	78133
Grandview Frst	78133
Granite Cv	78130
Granite Run Dr	78130
N & S Grant Ave	78130
N & S Grape Ave	78130
Graun Wald Ct	78132
Grays Peak Dr	78133
Great Cloud	78130
Great Oaks Dr	78130
Green Vly	78132
Green Castle Pl	78133
Green Hill Dr	78133
Green Mountain Dr	78130
Green Pastures St	78130
Green Valley St	78130
Greenbriar Dr	78133
Greenwood St	78133
Grenache	78132
Greta St	78132
Grey Fawn Dr	78133
Greylock	78132
Greystone Dr	78132
Grooms Ests	78133
Grove Ln	78130
Gruene Cv	78130
Gruene Ests	78130
Gruene Hvn	78132
Gruene Rd	78130
Gruene Spg	78130
Gruene Vis	78132
Gruene Lake Dr	78130
Gruene Leaf Dr	78130
Gruene Park Dr	78130
Gruene River Dr	78132

Gruene Valley Cir 78130
Gruene Vine Ct 78130
Gruene Vineyard Xing 78130
Gruene Vintage 78130
Gruene Wald 78130
Guada Coma 78130
Guadalupe 78132
N & S Guenther Ave 78130
Guenther Ranch Rd 78133
Gumnut Grv 78132
Guna Dr 78130
Gunner Crk 78133
Habersang Ln 78132
N & S Hackberry Ave 78130
Haley Dr 78132
Hall Isle 78133
Hallmark 78133
Halm Dr 78133
Hamburg Ave 78132
Hammermill 78133
Hampe St 78130
Hampshire St 78130
Hampton 78133
Hancock Ln 78130
Hancock Rd 78133
Hannahs Run 78130
Hanover 78132
Hanz Dr 78130
Happy Hollow Dr 78132
Harbor Dr 78130
Harcourt 78133
Hardy Rd 78130
Harriet 78133
Harris Cir 78130
Harris Ranch Rd 78133
Harrison Rd 78132
Harry Colt Pl 78130
Hartley Rdg 78132
Harvest Oak 78132
Haven Pt 78132
Haven Bluff Ct 78132
Havenwood Blvd 78132
Haynes Rd 78132
Hayselton Ave 78130
Hazelwood 78130
Heather Ln 78130
Heaton Hall Dr 78132
Hedgestone 78133
Heidrich Ct 78132
Heimer Ln 78133
Heinen Ln 78130
Helen Dr & St 78130
Henry Hts 78130
Herauf Dr 78133
Herbelin Rd 78132
Herber 78130
Heritage Hl 78133
Heritage Oaks 78132
Herry Ct & Pl 78130
Heynis N & S 78130
N & S Hickory Ave 78130
N & S Hidalgo Ave 78130
Hidden Dr 78133
Hidden Hls 78132
Hidden Holw 78132
Hidden Mdw 78130
Hidden Pt 78132
Hidden Cave Dr 78132
Hidden Fawn 78133
Hidden Meadows Dr 78132
Hidden Peak Cir 78130
Hideaway Cir 78130
Hideaway Hts 78132
High Dr 78132
High Chaparral 78132
High Cloud 78130
High Creek Rd 78132
High Forest Dr 78132
High Hills Dr 78133
High Low Dr 78132
High Oaks Rd 78133
High Track Rd 78133
High Valley Dr 78132
Highland Blvd 78133
Highland Hts 78133
Highland Spgs 78133

Highland Vis 78130
Highland Terrace Dr 78133
Highview St 78133
Highwater Ln 78130
N & S Hill Ave 78130
Hill Haven Dr 78132
Hill Top Dr 78133
Hillclimb 78133
Hillcrest Dr 78130
Hillcrest Frst 78130
Hillrock Dr 78130
Hillside Cir 78132
Hillside Loop 78133
Hilltop Rdg 78132
Hilltop Oaks 78132
Hillview Ave 78130
Hinch Dr 78132
Hitching Post Dr 78133
Hoffmann Ln 78132
Holiday Loop 78132
Holland Spgs 78133
Hollow Oak 78132
Holly Ln 78132
Holly St 78130
Hollyhock Ln 78130
Homestead Rdg 78132
Hondo Dr 78130
Honeysuckle Ln 78130
Horned Lark 78130
Horseshoe Ct & Trl 78132
Horseshoe Falls Dr 78133
House St 78132
N & S Houston Ave 78130
Howard St 78130
Hubertus Rd 78132
Hueco Dr 78130
Hueco Rdg 78132
Hueco Springs Loop
Rd 78132
Huisache Ave 78130
Hummingbird 78133
Hummingbird Dr 78130
Hummingbird Hl 78133
Hunt St 78130
Hunter Rd
1600-1800 78130
1802-1998 78130
2000-2098 78130
2100-4199 78132
Hunter Hills Dr 78132
Hunters Cv, Path, Run,
Trce, Trl, Vlg, Way &
Xing 78132
Hunters Chase 78132
Hunters Creek Dr 78132
Hunters Hideaway 78132
Hunters Point Dr 78132
Hunters Trophy 78132
Ibis Ave 78130
Ibis Falls Dr 78130
Imbuto 78132
Imhoff Ln 78132
Imperial Dr 78132
Incrociato 78132
Independence Dr 78132
Indian Path & Rdg 78132
Indian Chief Trl 78132
Indian Grass Dr 78130
Indian Moon Cv 78132
Industrial Dr 78130
Inglewood Dr 78133
Inspiration Dr 78130
Inspiring Vw 78133
N Interstate 35
101-197 78130
N Interstate 35
199-9099 78130
9101-9599 78130
18900-19198 78132
19200-25399 78132
S Interstate 35
100-3199 78130
3200-6499 78132
Irene Dr 78133
Iris Ln 78130
Iris Run 78132

Iron Horse 78132
Isaac Creek Cir 78132
Island Vw 78133
Ivy St 78130
J W Ln 78130
Jacks Ln 78130
Jackson Crk 78133
Jackson St 78130
Jacobs Ct 78130
Jacobs Creek Park Rd 78133
E & W Jahn St 78130
Jamie Ln 78130
Janet Dr 78133
Janets Way 78130
Janine 78130
Jarratt 78132
Jasmine Breeze 78130
Jasons North Ct 78130
Jasons South Ct 78130
Jasons West Ct 78130
Jaylee 78133
Jc Riley St 78132
Jdj Dr 78132
Jeanette Cir 78133
Jeffrey Ln 78130
Jennings Ct 78133
Jenny 78133
Jerad St 78130
Jericho Rdg 78130
Jesses Cir 78132
Jester Rdg 78130
Jo Lynn 78130
Joheit Ave 78130
Johnson Rd 78133
Johnston St 78130
Jolie Ct 78130
Jonas Dr 78133
Jordan Xing 78130
Josephine St 78130
Joshua Hl 78130
Joy Spg 78130
Joyce 78133
Julia St 78130
Julius Dr 78133
Jung St 78130
Kaleigh Way 78133
Kalksteine Loop 78132
Kalli Jo Ln 78133
Kangaroo Ct 78132
Kanz Dr 78132
Karah 78133
Karbach Ave 78130
Karbach Dr 78132
Kathleen Dr 78133
Katy St 78130
Kays Pl 78133
Keith Foster Dr 78133
Keller Rdg 78132
Kelly Ct & Ln 78130
Kellys Way 78130
Kendra 78133
Kensington Way 78130
Kentucky Blvd 78130
Kerlick Ln 78130
Kessler St 78130
Key Rd 78132
Keystone 78133
Keystone Dr 78133
Kight Rd 78133
Kimberly Dawn Dr 78130
Kindersley St 78133
King Edward 78133
King William 78133
Kingbird Pl 78130
Kingdom Path 78130
Kinglet Ct 78130
Kings Dr & Row 78133
Kings Cove Dr 78133
Kings Crown 78133
Kings Point Dr 78133
Kingsbury 78133
Kingswood Cir 78130
Kirkwood Cv 78130
Kite Cor 78130
Klein Ct 78132
Klein Mdws 78130

E Klein Rd 78130
W Klein Rd 78130
Klein Way 78130
Klemm St 78132
Klingemann 78130
Koala Ct 78132
Koeln St 78132
Kohlenberg Rd 78130
Kolton 78130
Kopplin Rd 78132
N & S Kowald Ln 78130
Kraft Ln 78130
Kramer St 78130
Krause Ln 78130
Krebs 78133
Krippie Kove 78132
Kristina Ln 78132
Kroesche Ln 78130
Krona Ct 78132
N Krueger Ave 78130
S Krueger Ave 78130
Krueger Cyn 78132
Kuehler Ave 78130
Kuntry Ln 78132
La Bahia Loop 78132
La Cresta Dr 78133
La Mesa Dr 78130
La Paloma Dr 78133
Labor Ave 78130
Lackey Ranch Rd 78132
Ladera Vis 78133
Lady Sheryl St 78130
Lago Vista Dr 78133
Lahn Rd 78130
Lake Blf & Frst 78133
Lake Front Ave 78130
Lake Island Dr 78133
Lake Park Loop 78133
Lake Pettit Dr 78133
Lake Ridge Blvd 78133
Lakebreeze Dr 78133
Lakecreek Dr 78133
Lakefield 78133
Lakeland Dr 78133
Lakeline Dr 78130
Lakeshore Dr 78133
Lakeside Dr E 78133
Lakeside Dr W 78133
Lakeside Pass 78130
Lakeview Blvd 78130
Lakeview Cir 78130
Lakeview Dr 78133
Lakeview Loop 78133
Lakeview Ter 78130
Lakewinds Cir 78130
Lakewood Ct 78133
Lamar Draw 78133
Lance Cir 78130
Lancharic Way 78132
Landa St
100-952 78130
954-1198 78130
1300-1398 78132
Landa Park Dr 78130
Landing Ln 78130
Lantana Cir 78130
Laredo Ln 78133
Lariat Rdg 78132
Lark Ln 78130
Larkspur 78130
Larson Dr 78133
Las Brisas Dr 78133
Lashell Ln 78130
Lasso Loop 78130
Laurel Cir, Ln & Trl 78130
Laurel Cliff Dr 78132
Laurel Wood 78132
Lauren St 78130
Laurie Dr 78133
Lavaca 78133
Lazy Frst 78132
Lazy Trl 78130
Lazy Bluff Ln 78130
Lazy Diamond 78133
Lazy Oaks Dr 78133
Leaf Ln 78130

Ledge Path 78133
Ledgerock Dr 78133
Ledgeview Dr 78133
Lee St 78130
Legacy Dr 78130
Legacy Hls 78132
Legend Hl 78130
Legend Pond 78130
Leisure Run 78133
Leisure Village Dr 78130
Lemon Tree 78133
Lewis Ranch Rd 78132
Lexington Pass 78133
N & S Liberty Ave 78130
Lifehaus Industrial Dr 78130
Lightfoot 78133
Lighthouse 78133
Lighthouse Dr 78130
Lilac Wind 78130
Lime Rock 78133
Limerick Ln 78133
Limestone Crk 78130
E & W Lincoln St 78130
Lincolnshire Dr 78130
Linda Dr 78133
Linde St 78130
Lindheimer St 78130
Lindsey Cir 78132
Link Rd 78130
Lions Den 78132
Lipan Dr 78130
Litties Way 78132
Little Bear Creek Rd 78132
Little Ponderosa Dr E &
W 78132
Live Fls 78133
N Live Oak Ave 78130
S Live Oak Ave 78130
Live Oak Dr 78133
Lockener Ave 78130
Lodge Creek Dr 78132
Lodgepole Ln 78130
Loeffler Ln 78132
Logan Trl 78130
Logans Pass 78130
Lois Ln 78133
Loma Verde Dr 78130
Loma Vista St 78130
Lone Mtn 78132
Lone Creek Cir 78132
Lone Oak Rd 78132
N & S Lone Star Ave &
Dr 78130
Lonesome 78133
Lonesome Creek Trl 78130
Long Ln 78130
Long Creek Blvd 78130
Long Gate 78130
Long Hollow Dr 78133
Longhorn Flts 78133
Longhorn Industrial Dr 78130
Longs Peak 78133
Longwood 78132
Lookout Dr 78133
Lookout Rdg 78132
Loop 337 78130
Lorelei Ln 78133
Lori Ln 78132
Lorikeet Ln 78132
Lorine Dr 78133
Lorne Rd 78133
Lost Trl 78132
Lost Antler Dr 78133
Lost Elms 78133
Lost Fawn 78132
Lost Mine 78133
Lost Oak 78133
Lou Ann Dr 78130
Louella Dr 78132
Louisiana Ave 78130
Lower Forty 78130
Lowman 78132
Lubbock Ln 78132
Lucinda Dr 78130
Luckenbach 78130
Luckett Dr 78130

Lucy Ln 78130
Luehlfing Dr 78133
Lullwood Dr 78130
Lupin Cir 78132
Mabel Jones Dr 78133
Mackenzie Dr 78130
Madeline St 78132
Madison Ave 78130
Madrid Dr 78130
Madrona Dr & Pass 78132
Magazine Ave 78130
Magdalena Ln 78132
Magnolia Ave 78130
Magnolia Wind 78130
Mahan Cir 78130
E Main Plz & St 78130
Majestic Oak Dr 78132
Malaga Ct 78133
Mallard Cor 78130
Mallinckrodt 78132
Malone St 78132
Manhattan 78130
Maple Ter & Way 78132
Maple Tree Rd 78130
Maplewood 78132
Marble Dr 78130
Marcia Pl 78130
Marguerite St 78130
Maria Ln 78130
Maricopa Dr 78133
Marigold Dr 78130
Marina 78133
Marine Cir 78133
Mariposa Loop 78132
Market Hts 78132
N Market St 78130
S Market St 78130
Marlin Cir 78130
Marlys Ave 78133
Marquette 78132
Marsh Oval 78130
Mary Blvd 78130
Mary Ann Dr 78133
Mary Preiss Dr 78132
Marymont Dr 78130
Marys Cv 78130
Matagorda Cir 78130
Mather St 78130
Maverick 78132
Mayberry Ml 78130
Mccartney Blvd 78133
Mcgar St 78130
Mcgaugh Ave 78130
Mciver 78133
Mckenna Ave & Vlg 78130
Mckinley St 78130
Mcqueeney Rd 78130
Meadow Ave, Crst &
Park 78130
Meadow Breeze 78132
Meadow Link 78132
Meckel Dr 78133
Meckel Hl 78132
Medina Dr 78130
Megan 78130
Melissa Ln 78130
Mellow Breeze 78130
Melody Ln 78132
Melody Wind 78130
Memorial Cir 78130
Mercury Dr 78133
Meridian Ct & Dr 78132
E & W Merriweather
St 78130
N Mesquite Ave 78130
S Mesquite Ave 78130
Mesquite Fls 78133
Meusebach St 78130
Meyer St 78130
Michelson Ln 78133
Michigan St 78130
Mickesch Ln 78132
N & S Middle Ln 78133
Mikula Pl 78130
Military Dr 78133
Mill Run 78132

E Mill St 7813
W Mill St 7813
Millies Ln 7813
Mills Hl 7813
Minnesota Dr 7813
Mira Loma 7813
Missile Dr 7813
Mission Dr 7813
Mission Hts 7813
Mission Trce 7813
Mission Trl 7813
Mission Way 7813
Mission Hill Run 7813
Mission Hills Dr 7813
Mission Valley Rd 7813
Mission View Ct 7813
Mistletoe Ave 7813
Misty Gln 7813
Misty Holw 7813
Misty Acres Dr 7813
Misty Glen Dr 7813
Misty Hills Dr 7813
Mittmann Cir 7813
Mobile Dr 7813
Mockingbird Dr 7813
Mockingbird Hl 7813
Moeller Ranch Rd 7813
Moerike Rd 7813
Monarch 7813
Monsoon Path 7813
Montanio Dr 7813
Montview St 7813
Moon View Dr 7813
Mooncrest 7813
Moonglow Ave 7813
Moonlight Cir 7813
Moonlight Dr 7813
Moore Trl 7813
Morales Ct 7813
Morning Glory Cir 7813
Morning Moon 7813
Morning Quail 7813
Morning Star 7813
Morning View Dr 7813
Morningside Dr
2201-2397 7813
2399-2999 7813
3201-3297 7813
3299-4099 7813
4101-4111 7813
Morningside Way 7813
Morris Ln 7813
Moss Oak Rd 7813
Moss Rock Dr 7813
Moss Rose Ln 7813
Mount Bear 7813
Mount Breeze Cp 7813
Mount Joy Dr 7813
Mount Lookout Dr 7813
Mountain Spgs & Vis 7813
Mountain Breeze 7813
Mountain Laurel Dr 7813
Mountain Oaks Dr 7813
Mountain Top Loop 7813
Mountain View Dr 7813
Mountain Wood 7813
Mountainview Dr 7813
Mourning Dove 7813
Mulberry Ave 7813
Murango Ln 7813
Muskogee Bnd 7813
Myrtle Run 7813
Mystic Oak 7813
E & W Nacogdoches
St 7813
Nafta Cir 7813
Naked Indian Trl 7813
Nancy Dr 7813
Napoleon St 7813
Narcissus Blvd 7813
Natural Brg 7813
Naumann Way 7813
Navaho Cir 7813
Neal Ln 7813
Nelson Dr 7813
Neuse St 781

New Spgs 78133
New Braunfels St 78130
New York Ave 78130
Newport 78133
Nicholas Cv 78130
Nickel Crk 78130
Nicolai Ave 78130
Nighthawk Ct & Ln 78133
Nor Tex Dr 78132
Normandy Grace 78130
E & W North St 78130
Northcrest Dr 78130
Northern Lgts 78130
Northgap Dr 78130
Northgate Cir 78130
Northhill Cir 78133
Northlake Dr 78130
Northpark Rdg 78130
Northridge 78132
Northstar Loop 78130
Northview Dr 78130
Northway Dr 78130
Northwest Blvd 78130
Northwoods Dr 78132
Nowotny Ln 78130
Nuhn Way 78132
Oak Blf 78132
Oak Bnd 78132
Oak Brk 78132
Oak Crst 78133
Oak Ct 78132
Oak Cv 78132
Oak Dr 78132
Oak Gln 78132
Oak Grv 78132
Oak Ln 78130
Oak Mdws 78133
Oak Path 78132
Oak Smt 78133
Oak Trce 78132
Oak Vis 78132
Oak Xing 78132
Oak Bluff Trl 78132
Oak Brush 78132
Oak Canopy Ct 78132
Oak Cascade 78132
Oak Creek Dr 78132
Oak Crest Cir 78133
Oak Forest Dr & Way 78132
Oak Hideaway Dr 78133
Oak Hill Dr 78132
Oak Hollow Dr 78132
Oak Hollow Way 78133
Oak Knoll Dr 78133
Oak Leaf 78132
Oak Leaf Dr 78133
Oak Mist 78132
Oak Moss 78132
Oak Pass Way 78132
Oak Pebble 78132
Oak Pointe 78132
Oak Post 78132
Oak Ridge Dr 78132
Oak Rock 78132
Oak Run Pkwy & Pt 78132
Oak Shore Dr 78133
Oak Sprawl 78132
Oak Springs Dr 78133
Oak Trail Dr 78133
Oak Tree Ln 78130
Oak Turn 78132
Oak Valley Dr 78132
Oak View Ct 78132
Oak Villa Rd 78133
Oak Willow 78132
Oak Wind 78132
Oakbranch Rdg 78130
Oakcreek Way 78130
Oakcrest Dr 78130
Oakdell Trl 78130
Oaklane St 78133
Oaklawn Dr 78132
Oakmont Cir 78132
Oakridge Ln & St 78133
Oakwood Blvd 78130
Oakwood Holw 78132
Oasis St 78130
Oblate Dr 78133
Oc Trout Dr 78133
Odin Dr 78133
Oelkers Dr 78130
Ogden Ln 78130
Ohio St 78130
Ohlrich Ranch Rd 78132
Oklahoma Ave 78130
Olandi Dr 78132
Olas Path 78130
Old Trl 78130
Old Bastrop Rd 78130
Old Bear Creek Rd 78132
Old Coach Dr 78130
Old Cranes Mill Rd 78133
Old Engel Rd 78132
Old Fm 306 78130
Old Hancock Rd 78133
Old Highway 81 78132
Old Marion Rd 78130
Old Nacogdoches Rd 78132
Old Sattler Rd
2601B-2699B 78133
Old Windmill Rd 78132
Ole Dutchman Rd 78133
Oleander Dr 78130
Olive Hl 78133
Olive Tree 78133
Oliver 78133
Olympic Dr 78132
Orange Ave 78130
Orbit Dr 78133
Orchid Cir 78130
Oriole Dr 78130
Oriole Trl 78133
Orion Dr
600-699 78130
1000-1098 78132
Osage Dr 78133
Oso Arroyo 78132
Osprey Ln 78130
Other Place Dr 78130
Otter Way 78132
E & W Outer Dr 78133
Overcup Ct 78133
Overhill St 78133
Overlook Cir 78132
W Overlook Dr 78133
Overview Dr 78132
Owen 78133
Owl Br & Spgs 78133
Oyster Spgs 78133
Pahmeyer Path & Rd 78130
Paint Rock 78130
Paintbrush Path 78132
Paisano St 78130
Palace Dr 78130
Palisades Vw 78132
Palo Crest Dr 78130
Paloma Dr 78133
Pams Path 78130
Panarama Pl 78132
Panorama Pt 78133
Pantermuehl Rd 78132
Paradise Aly 78130
Paradise Dr 78133
Paradise Hls 78132
Parakeet Ln 78132
Park Pl 78130
Park Rd 78132
N Park Rd 78133
Park Shrs 78133
Park Bend Dr 78132
Park Loop Rd 78132
Park View Loop 78133
Parkdale Dr 78130
Parkview Blvd 78130
Parkview Dr 78133
Parkview Pl 78133
Parkweg Loop 78132
Parsley 78133
Parton Rd 78133
Pathfinder 78132
Patio Dr 78130
Patricia Cir 78130
Patriot Path 78133
Patty Dr 78133
Pavillion Ln 78130
Peace Ave 78130
N & S Peach Ave 78130
Peach Tree 78132
Peacock Ln 78130
Pearl 78132
Pebble Brook Dr 78130
Pecan Bnd 78130
Pecan Cir 78133
Pecan Cor 78130
Pecan Crk 78132
Pecan Ests 78130
Pecan Fls 78133
Pecan Frst 78130
Pecan Hvn 78130
Pecan Mdws 78130
Pecan Pt 78130
Pecan Rdg 78130
Pecan Row 78132
Pecan Spgs 78130
Pecan St
400-498 78133
500-900 78130
902-998 78133
2301-2399 78132
Pecan Arbor 78130
Pecan Farms 78130
Pecan Gable 78130
Pecan Gap 78130
Pecan Leaf 78130
Pecan Way Path 78130
Pecos Cir 78130
Pegg Rnch 78133
Peggs Pl 78133
Pelican Pl 78130
Pennsylvania Blvd 78130
Penny Dr 78133
Perry Maxwell Ct 78130
Perryman St 78130
Petite Verdot 78132
Pfeiffer Ln 78130
Pfeiffer Ranch Rd 78132
Pfeil High Acres Rd 78133
Pheasant Ln 78130
Pieper Rd 78130
Pig Aly 78132
Pin Oak Trl 78132
Pine St 78130
Pine Valley Dr 78130
Pinehurst Dr 78133
Pinnacle Dr 78133
Pinnacle Pkwy 78132
Pinot Blanc 78132
Pintale Pt 78130
Placid Mdw 78130
Placid Cove Dr 78130
Plateau Rdg 78133
Pleasant Ln 78132
N & S Plum Ave 78130
Point Creek Dr 78133
Polly Dr 78133
Ponderosa Dr 78132
Pool Ln 78130
Poolside Dr 78133
Poppy Ln 78130
Port Charles Ave 78130
Porter St 78130
Porto Pt 78132
Posey Pass 78132
Post Rd 78130
Post Vw 78130
Post Oak Dr & Ln 78133
Potters Creek Rd 78133
Potthast Dr 78130
Prado Verde 78130
Prairie Park Dr 78130
Prairie Rock 78130
Prairie Tea 78133
Prairie View Rd 78130
Preston Holw 78132
Preston Wood 78133
Prickly Pear Dr 78130
Pride Dr 78132
Primrose Cir 78130
Primrose Path 78133
Primrose Way 78132
Prince Dr 78130
Provence Pl 78132
Providence Pl 78133
Pueblo Cir 78130
Purgatory Rd 78132
Purple Sage 78133
Qappuella Dr 78133
Quail Crk 78132
Quail Dr 78133
Quail Pass 78132
Quail Ridge Dr 78130
Quail Run St 78133
Quarry Crst & Pt 78132
Queen Anne Cir 78133
Queen Victoria Dr 78130
Queens Dr 78130
Quiet Cv 78133
Quinn Cir 78133
Rachel Dr 78130
Rainbow Rdg 78133
Ramble Hls 78133
Ramblewood Dr 78133
Rambling Dr 78133
Ranch Crk 78132
Ranch Pkwy 78130
N Ranch Estates Blvd 78130
Ranch Loop Dr 78132
Rancho Rd 78130
Range Rd 78132
Ranger Rdg 78132
Rapids Rd 78130
Raven Ct 78133
Raven Rdg 78130
Raysbad Ct 78130
Real Ln 78133
Rebecca Spgs 78133
Rebecca St 78132
Rebecca Way 78133
Rebecca Creek Rd 78133
Rebecca Ranch Rd 78133
Red Bird St 78133
Red Bud Way 78132
Red Cloud Peak 78133
Red Oak Ln 78133
Red Oak Woods 78133
Red Robin Dr 78130
Redbud Ln 78130
Redrock 78132
Regal Dr 78133
Regent Pass 78132
Regina Dr 78133
Remuda Ranch Rd 78133
Research 78133
Resource Dr 78132
Rhine Rd & Ter 78130
Rhinestone 78133
Rhodes Dr 78133
Riada Dr 78132
Richter Ln 78130
Ridge Dr 78130
Ridge Run 78132
Ridge Country 78132
Ridge Hill Dr 78130
Ridge Rock 78130
Ridge Wind 78130
Ridgecliff Dr 78130
Ridgecrest 78130
Ridgehaven St 78133
Ridgeline Rd 78132
Ridgeroad Dr 78130
Ridgerock Dr 78133
Ridgeview Dr 78133
Ridgewood Ave 78130
Ridgewood Bnd 78133
Rieber Rd 78132
Riedel Ln 78133
Rimrock Pass 78133
Rinder Farm Ct 78132
Ringtail 78133
Rio Dr 78130
Rio Verde 78130
Rip Jay Cir 78133
River Hl 78130
River Rd
1200-1299 78130
1300-14499 78132
River Run 78132
River Ter 78130
River Acres Dr 78130
River Bank 78130
River Bend Dr 78130
River Chase Dr &
Way 78132
River Cliff Dr 78133
River Club Dr 78133
River Enclave 78133
River Oaks Blvd 78133
River Oaks Dr 78132
River Park Dr 78130
River Rock 78130
River Star Dr 78132
Rivera 78133
Rivercrest Dr 78130
Riverforest Dr 78132
Rivers Peak 78133
Riverside Dr 78130
Riverside Path 78133
Rivertree Dr 78133
Riviera Dr 78130
Roadrunner Ave 78130
Roadrunner Ln 78133
Roadrunner Spur 78133
Roadside Dr 78133
Roan St 78130
Robert Lee Ln 78133
Robin Ln 78132
Robin Hood Dr 78133
Robin Nest 78133
Robinhood Ln 78132
Rock Grv 78132
Rock Run 78132
Rock St 78130
Rock Castle 78133
Rock Hill Trl 78132
Rock Rose W 78132
Rock Springs Dr 78130
Rockland Dr 78132
Rockmoor 78133
Rockport Dr 78133
Rockwall Pkwy 78132
Rocky Riv & Rnch 78133
Rocky Creek Dr 78133
Rocky Ridge Dr 78133
Rocky Ridge Loop 78133
Rodney Ln 78133
Rodriguez St 78130
Rolling Path, Rdg &
Vly 78130
Rolling Fork Dr 78130
Rolling Hills Dr 78130
Rolling Oaks Dr 78132
Rolling Rapids Dr 78130
Rolling View Ct 78133
Ronda Ct 78133
Roosevelt St 78130
Rosa Parks Dr 78130
Rosalie Dr 78130
Rosario Ln 78132
Rose Ln
1000-1299 78132
1000-1499 78133
1501-1599 78133
Rosedale Ave 78130
Roselawn Cir 78130
Rosemary Dr & Loop 78130
Rosewood Ave 78130
Rosewood Ter 78132
Ross 78133
Rosss Rdg 78133
Rothe Loop 78133
Rotherman 78130
Round Table 78130
Rousey Dr 78130
Roxie Ln 78130
Royal Ave & Crst 78130
Royal Gate Dr 78132
Royal Oak Dr 78133
Royal Troon Ln 78133
Royalwood 78132
Ruddy Duck 78130
S Rueckle Rd 78130
Ruger Path 78130
Running Riv 78130
Rusch Ln 78132
Rush Crk 78133
Rusk St 78130
Russell St 78130
Rustler 78133
Ruth St 78130
Sable Cir 78130
Saddle Tree Dr 78130
Saengerhalle Rd 78130
Safari Dr 78132
Sage Rd 78133
Sagebrook Dr 78130
Sagebrush Dr 78133
Sahm Pass 78132
Saint Mary St 78130
Saint Thomas Dr 78133
Salado Dr 78130
Samuels St 78130
E & W San Antonio St 78130
San Augustine Blvd 78132
San Felipe 78133
San Fernando Ln 78132
San Gabriel Loop 78132
San Ignacio 78132
San Jacinto Dr 78130
San Jose Way 78133
San Juan 78133
San Luis 78132
San Marcos Trl 78132
San Mateo 78132
San Miguel 78132
San Patricio 78132
San Pedro 78132
San Saba 78130
San Salvadore 78133
Sanchez Trl 78130
Sand Bar 78133
Sandalwood Dr 78130
Sandhill Crane 78130
Sandpiper Dr 78130
Sanger Ave 78130
N & S Santa Clara
Ave 78130
Santa Cruz 78132
Santa Maria Ct 78133
Santa Rosa Ct 78133
Santiago St 78133
Sapling Spg 78132
Sarah 78133
Satterfield Rd 78130
Sattler Rd
700-2000 78132
2002-2198 78132
2500-2598 78133
Sauder Dr 78130
Sauder Farms Rd 78130
Saur Ln 78130
Savannah Hill Cir 78133
Sawmill Ln 78130
Scarbourough 78133
Scarlet Ct 78133
Scarlet Tanger 78130
Scenic Dr 78133
N Scenic Loop 78133
S Scenic Loop 78133
Scenic Mdw 78130
Scenic Run 78133
Scenic Hills Dr 78133
Scenic Terrace Dr 78133
Scenic View Dr 78133
Schirmer Pl 78132
Schlamp Bay 78133
Schmidt Ave 78130
Schmucks Rd 78132
Schoenthal Rd 78132
Schoggins Ln 78133
Scholl Rd 78133
School Ave 78130
School House 78132
Schuetz Dr 78132
Schumacher Dr 78133
Schumans Beach Rd 78130
Schwab Rd 78132
Schwarzlose Rd 78130
Scissortail 78133
Scott Way 78133
Sea Breeze 78130
Sean 78130
Seascape Ln 78130
Seay Ln 78132
Secluded Holw 78133
Seele St 78130
Segovia Cir 78133
N Seguin Ave 78130
S Seguin Ave
100-699 78130
686-686 78131
700-1998 78130
701-1899 78130
Sehaco St 78130
Seidel St 78130
Seminole Dr 78130
Sendera Way 78133
Senora Rdg 78133
Sequoia Trl 78133
Serene Mdw 78130
Serene Woods Cir 78133
Serna Dr 78130
Seth Raynor Dr 78130
Seville Dr 78130
Shadow Cir 78130
Shadow Ln 78132
Shady Holw 78132
Shady Oaks Ln 78133
Shady Ridge Dr 78133
Shadyview Dr 78133
Shangrila Ln 78130
Shannon Cir 78130
Shannon Lee 78132
Shayla Ln 78133
Shelly Dr 78133
Shennandoah 78130
Shepherd Hl 78133
Sheridan Dr 78133
Sherwood Dr 78133
Shield Dr 78130
Shiner Cir 78130
Shore Point Dr 78133
Short Cut Rd 78130
Shortcut Pass 78133
Sierra Dr
1-99 78130
28000-28799 78132
Sierra Rdg 78133
Sierra Way 78133
Sierra Blanca 78133
Sierra Madre 78133
Silver Spur Dr 78130
Silver Star Ln 78133
Silverado 78132
Simon Crst 78133
Simon Rdg 78133
Simon St 78130
Sinclair Dr 78130
Singing Hills Dr 78133
Sir Arthur Way 78133
Sir Galahad 78133
Sir Winston Dr 78133
Sitting Bull Trl 78133
Ski Shrs 78133
Sky Cv 78132
Sky Country Dr 78132
Skycliff Dr 78130
Skycrest Cir 78130
Skyforest Dr 78130
Skylark Dr 78133
Skylark St 78130
Skyline Dr & Hls 78133
Skyridge Cir 78130
Skytrail Dr 78130
Skyview Ave 78130
Skyvue Ave 78132
Sleepy Riv 78130
Sleepy Hollow Ln 78130
Slocum Dr 78133
Small Town Dr 78130
Smith Hollow Ct 78133
Snowberry 78130

Street	ZIP
Snowy Egret	78130
Soechting Ln	78130
Soft Wind	78133
Soledad Ln	78132
Solitaire Path	78130
N & S Solms Rd	78132
Somerset	78133
Songbird Dr	78133
Sonnyland Dr	78133
Sorrel Creek Dr	78133
E South St	78130
Southbank Blvd	78130
Southeast Ter	78130
Southland St	78130
Southstar Ln	78130
Southwind Dr	78130
Spanish Trl	78132
Spanish Oak Dr	78133
Spanish Oak Esplanade	78133
Sparrow	78130
Sparrow View Ct	78130
Spectrum Dr	78130
Spike Buck Run	78133
Spire Ln	78132
Spitz Kegel View Dr	78133
Split Mtn	78133
Spotted Owl	78130
Sprecken Isle	78133
Spring Holw	78132
Spring Mdw	78130
Spring Rdg	78133
Spring Mountain Dr	78133
Spring View Dr	78133
Springhill Dr	78130
Springs Nursery	78130
Springwater	78130
Spur St	78130
Spyglass Dr	78130
Squire Cir	78130
Squires Row	78133
Stadtbach St	78130
Stagecoach Dr & Way	78133
Starcrest	78130
Stardust Dr	78133
Starfire	78133
Starkey	78132
Starling Crk	78130
Startz Rd	78133
S State Highway 46	78130
W State Highway 46	78132
Steamboat	78133
Steeple Run	78132
Steeple Chase Run	78132
Stein Ct	78130
Steinig Link	78132
Stenen Dr	78133
Stephens Pl	78130
Sterling Cir	78130
Steubing Cir	78132
Stevens Ranch Rd	78133
Stoeger Dr	78130
Stoepler Rnch	78132
Stolte Rd	78130
Stone Blf	78130
Stone Br	78130
Stone Cyn	78132
Stone Gdn	78130
Stone Holw	78130
Stone Park	78130
Stone Path	78130
Stone Pt	78130
Stone Trl	78130
Stone Way	78130
Stone Xing	78132
Stone Arch	78130
Stone Gate Dr	78130
Stonebrook Rdg	78132
Stonecrest Cir	78132
Stonecrest Path	78130
Stonehaven	78130
Stoneleigh Dr	78130
Stonewall St	78130
Stoney Ridge Dr	78133
Strada Curva	78132
Stradina	78132
Strateman Ln	78130
Stratford Grace	78132
Stratus Path	78130
Strawberry Fld	78130
Strawcove	78130
Sugar Spgs	78133
Sugar Land Dr	78130
Sumac Cir	78130
Summer Hl	78132
Summer Spgs	78133
Summer Glen Ln	78132
Summerside Dr	78132
Summerwood Dr	78132
Summit Blf	78133
Summit Cir	78132
Summit Dr	78132
Summit Skwy	78132
Summit Hurst Dr	78132
Summit Oak Dr	78132
Summit Ridge Dr	78132
Sumner Cir	78130
Sun Riv	78132
Sun Trl	78130
Sun Beam	78133
Sun Chase Blvd	78130
Sun Flower Cir	78130
Sun Ledge Way	78130
Sun Pebble Way	78130
Sun Tree	78130
Sunblossom Cir	78130
Sunburst Ln	78133
Suncrest Dr	78132
Sundance Pkwy	78130
Sundown Trl	78133
Sunfire Cir	78130
Sunflower Blf	78130
Sungate Dr	78130
Sunglow	78133
Sunny Crk	78132
Sunny Side Dr	78130
Sunnybrook Dr	78130
Sunnycrest Cir	78130
Sunrise	78130
Sunrise Dr	78133
Sunset Bnd	78132
Sunset Cv	78132
Sunset Dr	78130
Sunset Rdg	78133
Sunshadow Dr	78130
Sunshine Ln	78130
Sunshine Peak	78130
Sunspur Dr & Rd	78130
Sunstone Cir	78130
Sunview Cir	78130
Surnad Pl	78132
Survista Ln	78132
Susie Dr	78133
Swallow Ct	78133
Swallow Pointe	78130
Swan Dr	78132
Sweet Pea Ln	78133
Sweetwater	78133
N Sycamore Ave	78130
S Sycamore Ave	78130
Sycamore Fls	78133
Sydney Cir	78130
Syrah	78133
T Bar M Dr	78132
T9c Dr	78133
Tadmore Rd	78133
Tag Ln	78130
Talisman Dr	78132
Tamarack Dr	78133
Tanager Dr	78130
Tanger Ter	78130
E & W Tanglewood Dr	78130
Tarrant Trl	78132
Teal Dr	78130
Teal Rdg	78133
Tealwood Ct	78130
Teich Loop	78132
Terra Vista Ct	78133
Terrace Ct	78130
Terrace Pt	78132
Texas Ave	78130
Texas Spgs	78132
Texas Country Dr	78132
Thistle	78132
Thomas	78133
Thompson St	78130
Thrasher Trl	78130
Three Mile Crk	78130
Three Rivers Cir	78133
Thumper Ln	78133
Thunder Canyon Rd	78133
Thunderbolt Rd	78133
Tiara Dr	78133
Tilden Trl	78132
Tillinghast Pl	78130
Timber Dr	78130
Timber Holw	78132
Timber Ln	78132
Timber Mdw	78132
Timber Pt	78132
Timber Rdg	78132
Timber Tap	78132
Timber Wild	78132
Timberdell Dr	78133
Timberhill Dr	78132
Timberlane Dr	78133
Timberline Trl	78133
Timberwood Trl	78132
Tolle St	78130
Tom Creek Ln	78133
Tom Kemp Dr	78133
Tom Tom Trl	78132
Tomah Dr	78133
Tommy Dr	78133
Tonkawa Cir	78133
Tonne Dr E & W	78132
E & W Torrey St	78130
Tower Line	78130
Town Vw	78133
Town Center Dr	78133
Toye Blvd	78133
Tracys Xing	78130
Trade Center Dr	78132
Trail Rdg	78132
Trail Vw	78130
Trail Bluff Dr	78132
Trail Crest Dr	78133
Trail Driver	78132
Trail Pass Dr	78133
Trail Wood	78130
Trailridge Dr	78133
Trauer St	78133
Treasure Way	78133
Tree Top Ln	78132
Trinity Trl	78132
Triple Peak Dr	78133
Tripp Ln	78130
Trophy Ln & Pt	78132
Tropical Dr	78133
Tulip Ln	78130
Tumbleweed Dr	78130
Turkey Cv	78132
Turkey Dr	78130
Turtle Trl	78130
Tuscan Rdg	78130
Twilight Dr	78133
Twin Riv	78133
Twin Deer Ln	78133
Twin Elm Dr	78133
Twin Oaks Cir	78133
Twin Oaks Dr	78133
Twinwood	78132
Twisted Riv	78130
Twisted Oak Ct	78133
Twisted Oaks Ln	78133
Uluru Ave	78130
Unicorn Ave	78130
N & S Union Ave	78130
Union Wine Rd	78130
Upland Ct	78133
Upper Forty	78133
Val Verde Dr	78133
Valero Dr	78133
Valiant	78133
Valley Br	78132
Valley Dr	78133
Valley Frg	78133
Valley Frst	78133
Valley Hvn	78133
Valley Ldg	78132
Valley Rdg	78133
Valley Smt	78133
Valley Vis	78130
Valley Acres Dr	78130
Valley Oaks Dr	78133
Valley Star Dr	78133
Valley View Ln	78130
Valley View St	78133
Vanin Pl	78133
Vantage Pt	78130
Ventura Dr	78130
N & S Veramendi Ave	78130
Vesper	78133
Via Principale	78132
Viewcrest	78130
Viewpoint	78133
Village Dr	78133
Village Path	78130
Village Way	78133
Village Oak	78133
Village Shore Dr	78133
Village Top	78133
Village View Dr	78133
Vineyard Way	78130
Vino Cir	78132
Vintage Way	78132
Vip Dr	78133
Vista Pkwy	78130
Vista Rdg	78133
Vista Vw	78133
Vista Bonita	78133
Vista Del Rio	78130
Vista Verde Dr	78130
Viuzza	78132
Voges	78132
Volunteer Way	78132
Wagon Wheel Dr	78133
Wald Rd & Trce	78132
Walker Cir	78130
Wall St	78130
Wallaby Cir	78132
Wallhalla	78130
N Walnut Ave	78130
S Walnut Ave	78130
Walnut Fls	78133
Walnut Vly	78130
Walnut Heights Blvd	78130
Walts Ln	78130
Walzem Mission Rd	78132
Warwick Pl	78130
N & S Washington Ave	78130
N & S Water Ln & Way	78130
Water Hole Ln	78130
Water Oak Ln	78133
Water Spray Ln	78130
Waterbury	78132
Waterford Grace	78132
Waterfront Park Dr	78133
Waterloo Dr	78130
Waterway Pass	78130
Watson Ln E & W	78130
Watts Ln	78130
Wauford Way	78132
Waverly St	78133
Wegner Rd	78132
Weil Rd	78130
Weiss Rd	78130
Weiss Fels	78132
Well St	78130
Welsch Ln	78132
Weltner Rd	78130
West St	78130
N & S West End Ave	78132
Western Oaks	78132
Western Pecan	78130
Westfield	78132
Westhaven Dr	78133
Westin Hls	78132
Westmeyer Rd	78130
Westminister Sq	78132
Westover Loop	78130
Westpointe Dr	78132
Westshire Ln	78132
Westside Cir	78133
Westview Dr	78133
Westview Court Dr	78133
Westwood	78132
Whippoorwill Dr	78133
Whispering Way	78130
Whispering Breeze Dr	78133
Whispering Hills Dr	78133
Whispering Woods Trl	78132
White Cedar Ln	78132
White Cloud	78130
White Oak Dr	78133
White River Rd	78133
White Tail Ln	78133
White Water Rd	78132
White Wing Way	78130
Whitell Bay	78133
Whooping Crane	78130
Wickford Way	78133
Wicklow Way	78133
Wigeon Way	78130
Wild Cat Roost	78132
Wild Cherry Ln	78133
Wild Oak Dr	78133
Wild Turkey Run	78132
Wilderness Crk	78133
Wilderness Trl	78132
Wilderness Way	78132
Wilderness Oaks	78132
Wildflower Trl	78130
Wildwood Ln	78133
Wildwood Trl	78130
Willer Way	78133
Williams Way	78130
Willie Ct	78133
Willow Ave	78130
Willow Crk	78132
Willow Dr	78133
Willow Xing	78130
Wiltshire Dr	78130
Wind Crest Dr	78133
Wind Gust	78130
Wind Haven Dr	78130
Wind Murmur	78130
Wind Song Ln	78130
Windcliff Dr & Way	78132
Windgate Dr	78130
Winding Vw & Way	78132
Winding Oak Dr	78132
Windmere	78133
Windrush	78133
Windsor Ln	78132
Windsor Pl	78130
Windstar Ln	78133
Winston Ave	78130
Winterberry Cv	78132
Wisdom Ct	78130
Wisteria Ln	78130
Wolf Lair	78132
Wolfeton Way	78130
Wombat Grv	78132
Wooby Way	78130
Wood Mdws & Rd	78130
Woodall Cir	78130
Woodcock Ln	78133
Woodcrest Cir	78130
Woodcrest Dr	78133
Woodland Ave	78130
Woodland Oaks	78132
Woodlane Dr	78132
Woodpecker Run	78130
Woodridge	78133
Woodrow Cir	78133
Woods End	78130
Woodwind Dr	78133
Wray St	78133
Wren Ln	78132
Wren Brook Dr	78133
Wright Ave	78130
Wunderlich Ln	78130
Yacht Clb	78133
Yard Arm Dr	78133
Yellow Wood	78130
York Creek Rd	78130
Yorktown Dr	78133
Youngsford Rd	78130
Yu Dr	78130
Zapata Cir	78130
Zedernholz Run	78132
Zenith Ln	78132
E & W Zink St	78130
E & W Zipp Rd	78130

NUMBERED STREETS

Street	ZIP
All Street Addresses	78130

NORTH RICHLAND HILLS TX

POST OFFICE BOXES MAIN OFFICE STATIONS AND BRANCHES

Box No.s	ZIP
All PO Boxes	76182

RURAL ROUTES

Route	ZIP
123, 67	76180
19, 34, 35, 41, 46, 49, 59, 61, 98	76182

NAMED STREETS

Street	ZIP
Abbott Ave	76180
Abby Rd	76180
Aberdeen Dr	76180
Acapulco Dr	76180
Acorn Dr	76182
Acts Ct	76182
Airport Fwy	76180
Alamo Ct	76180
Amhurst Ct	76182
Amundson Dr & Rd	76182
Amy Ln	76182
Andrea Ct	76182
April Ct & Ln	76182
Arbor Rd	76180
Arborbrook Dr	76182
Arlie Ln	76182
Arnold Ter	76180
Arthur Dr	76182
Ash St	76180
Ashbury St	76180
Ashcraft Dr	76182
Ashley Ct	76182
Ashmore Dr	76180
Ashworth Dr	76182
Aspen Cir	76182
Aston Dr	76182
Aubrey Ln	76182
Autumn Run Ln	76182
Avalon St	76180
Azalea Ct	76182
Bahama Ct	76180
Barbados Dr	76180
Barfields Way	76182
Bartay Dr	76180
Barton Springs Dr	76180
Baywood Ct & Dr	76182
Bedford Euless Rd	76180
Beetle Nut Ln	76180
Belaire Ct & Dr	76182
Belfast Ln	76180
Bella Ct & Ln	76182
Bellhurst Ct	76117
Belmont Ct	76182
Belshire Dr	76182
Bentley Dr	76182
Berkshire Dr	76182
Bermuda Ct & Dr	76180
Beverly Dr	76182
Bewley St	76117
Billie Faye Dr	76180
Birchwood Dr	76180
Biscayne Ct	76182
Blackhawk Ct	76180
Blackman Rd	76180
Blake Ct	76182
Blaney Ave	76180
Blende St	76180
Bluebonnet Ct	76182
Blythe Ct	76182
Bob Dr	76180
Bobwhite Dr	76182
Boca Raton Ct & Dr	76182
Bogart Dr	76180
Bogota Dr	76180
Bonzer St	76180
Booth Calloway Rd	76180
Bosque River Ct	76180
Boulder Ct & Rd	76180
Boulevard 26	76180
Bradley Dr	76182
Brandi Ln & Pl	76182
Brandon Ct	76182
Brandonwood Dr	76182
Brazos Bend Dr	76182
Brentwood Ct	76182
Briarcliff Ct	76182
Briardale Ct & Dr	76182
Briarridge Ct	76182
Briarwood Dr	76182
Bridge St	76180
Bridlewood Ct & Dr	76182
Brighton Ct	76180
Briley Dr	76180
Brittany Park Ct	76182
Brixham Dr	76182
Brockwood Ct	76182
Brookhaven Ct & Dr	76182
Brookridge Dr	76182
Brookshire Trl	76182
Brookview Dr	76182
Browning Ct & Dr	76180
Brynwyck Ln	76182
Buck St	76182
Buckingham Trl	76182
Bud Jenson Dr	76180
Buenos Aires Dr	76180
Bursey Ct & Rd	76182
Cachelle Ct	76182
Caddo Ct	76182
Caladium Dr	76180
Calvert Ln	76182
Camelot Ct	76180
Camino Dr	76182
Cancun Dr	76180
Canoe Ridge Dr	76182
Cantrank Dr	76180
Canyon Oak Dr	76182
Caracas Dr	76180
Cardinal Ct	76180
Cardinal Ln	
8200-8699	76182
8700-9399	76180
Carlisle Ct	76180
Carma Dr	76180
Carol Ct	76180
Carolenna Ct	76182
Carolyn Ct & Dr	76180
Carson St	76117
Carston Ct	76180
Castle Combe Pl	76180
Castle Creek Ct & Rd	76182
Catalina Ct	76180
Catchin Dr	76180
Cato Dr	76180
Caton Dr	76180
Cedar Way	76182
Cedar Bluffs Dr	76182
Cedar Breaks Dr	76182
Cedar Crest Dr	76182
Cedar Grove Dr	76182
Cedar Park Ave	76182
Center St	76182
Central Ave	76182
Century Dr	76182
Chaddington Ct & Dr	76182
Chandler Ct	76182
Chapel Ct	76180

Chapel Park Dr 76180
Chapelwood Dr 76182
Chapman Dr 76182
Charles St 76180
Chartwell St 76180
Chase St 76182
Chasewood Dr 76182
Chatham Rd 76182
Chelmsford Pl 76182
Cherokee Trl 76182
Cherry Glow Ln 76180
Cherrybark Ln 76182
Chestnut Dr 76182
Cheswick Dr 76182
Chilton Ct & Dr 76182
Chimney Creek Dr 76182
Chisholm Trl 76182
Christopher Ct 76180
Christy Ct 76182
Chuck Dr 76182
Cimarron Dr 76182
Cindy Ct 76182
Circle Dr N 76180
Circleview Ct & Dr E & W 76180
Circular Dr 76117
Citadel Ct 76182
City Point Dr 76180
Clark St 76180
Clay Hibbins Rd 76182
Claymore Ct 76180
Clenis Ln 76180
Cliffbrook Dr 76180
Cliffside Dr 76180
Clift St 76182
Clover Leaf Dr 76182
Cloyce Ct 76180
Club House Dr 76148
Coldshire Ct 76182
Collard Ct 76182
N & S College Cir 76180
Colorado Blvd & Ct 76180
Comis Dr 76182
Commercial Dr 76180
Conn Dr 76180
Connie Ct & Ln 76182
Continental Trl 76182
Cook Cir 76182
Copper Canyon Rd 76182
Cork Ln 76180
Corona Dr 76180
Coronet Ave 76180
Cortland Dr 76182
Cottonwood Ct 76182
Country Meadow Dr 76182
Country Oak Dr 76182
Country Place Dr 76182
Country Ridge Dr 76182
Courtenay St 76180
Coventry Cir & Ct 76182
Cox Ln 76182
Crabtree Ln 76182
Crane Rd 76182
Creek View Dr 76180
Creekside Dr 76180
Crescent St 76180
S Crest Dr 76182
Crestview Dr 76182
Crestwood Cir E 76180
Cripple Creek Trl 76180
Cross Dr 76182
Cross St 76180
Cross Keys Dr 76182
Crosstimbers Ln 76182
Crystal Ln 76182
Cummings Dr 76180
Cylinda Sue Cir 76180
Cynthia Cir 76117
Cypress Ct 76182
Daleview Trl 76182
Daley Ave 76180
Dana Ln 76182
Daniel Ct & Dr 76182
Darin St 76180
David Ct & Dr 76180
Davis Blvd
4800-6052 76180
6051-6051 76182
6053-6345 76180
6054-6350 76180
6360-6398 76182
6400-8699 76182
Davis Ln 76182
Dawn Dr 76180
Daytona Dr 76180
Deaver Dr 76180
Delta Ct 76180
Dent Rd 76117
Denton Hwy 76117
Derby Run Dr 76182
Deville Dr 76180
Devonshire Dr 76180
Dewsbury St 76182
Diamond Loch E 76180
Diamond Ridge Dr 76180
Dick Fisher Dr 76180
Dick Lewis Dr 76180
Dogwood Ct & Ln 76182
Donegal Ln 76180
Donna Dr 76182
Dorchester Trl 76182
Doris Ct 76182
Dory Ct 76180
Douglas Ln 76182
Dream Dust Dr 76180
Driffield Cir 76182
Driftwood Ct 76182
Dripping Springs Ct 76180
Dublin Ct & Ln 76180
Dude Ct 76180
Duncan Ct 76180
Dustin Ct 76182
Eagle Dr 76148
Eagle Crest Dr 76180
Eden Rd 76182
Edenborough Ct 76180
Edgemont Ct & Dr 76182
Edinburg Dr 76182
Eldorado Dr 76180
Ellis Dr 76182
Elm Ct 76182
Elm Wood Dr 76182
Ember Oaks Dr 76182
Emerald Cir & Ct 76180
Emerald Hills Way 76180
Euclid Ave 76180
Everglade Dr 76182
Evergreen Ave 76182
Fair Meadows Dr 76182
Fair Oaks Dr 76182
Fairway Ct 76180
Fairwest Ct 76182
Falcon Ct 76180
Fallen Oak Dr 76182
Fenwick Dr 76182
Fern Leaf Ct 76182
Field Stone Ct & Dr 76180
Fin Wood Ct 76182
Finch Dr 76182
Finian Ln 76180
Fireside Dr 76182
Flat Rock Ct 76182
Flory St 76180
Flying H Ranch Rd 76182
Ford Dr 76182
Forest Glenn Ct 76182
Forest Hills Ct 76182
Forest Lakes Ct 76182
Forest Point Ct 76182
Forest Ridge Ct 76182
Forest View Ct 76182
S Fork Dr 76182
Forrest Ct & Ln 76182
Forrest Oak Dr 76182
N Forty Rd 76182
Fountain St 76180
Four Sixes Ranch Rd 76182
Foxwood Dr 76182
Frances Ct 76182
Frankie B St 76182
Franklin Ct 76182
Frawley Dr 76180
Freda Ln 76180
Freedom Way 76182
Friar Dr 76180
Frost St 76180
Galway Ln 76180
Garden Park Dr 76180
Garwood Dr 76117
Gary Ct 76182
Gayle Dr 76180
Gentling Pl 76180
Gentling Place Ct 76180
Georgia Ave 76180
Gibbons Ct & Dr 76180
Gifford Ln 76182
Gillis Ct 76182
Glenann Dr 76182
Glenbrook Dr 76182
Glendale Dr 76182
Glendara Dr 76182
Glengarry Ct 76180
Glenhaven Ct 76182
Glenhurst Dr 76182
Glenmont Dr 76182
Glenview Ct & Dr 76180
Glenwood Dr 76182
Glenwyck Dr 76180
Goodnight Ranch Rd 76182
Grace Ct & Dr 76182
Grand Ave 76180
Grand View Dr 76182
Green Castle Ct 76180
Green Meadow Dr 76180
Green Ridge Trl 76182
Green Valley Dr 76182
Greenacres Dr 76182
Greendale Ct 76182
Greenhill Trl 76182
Greenleaf Ct & Dr 76182
Greenview Ct 76148
Greenway Ct 76180
Greenwood Way 76180
Gregg Ct 76182
Grove St 76180
Guadalajara Dr 76180
Hadley Dr 76182
Hailey Ct 76182
Hallmark Dr 76182
Hanging Cliff Pl 76182
Hanover Ln 76182
Harmonson Ct & Rd 76180
Harrell St 76180
Harvest Hill Rd 76182
Harwick Ln 76182
Harwood Rd 76180
Havana Dr 76180
Havenwood Dr 76182
Hawk Ave 76180
Hazel Pl 76182
Heatherbrook Ct & Dr 76182
Hedge Row Ct 76182
Heidelburg Ct 76180
Herman Jared Dr 76182
Hewitt St 76182
Hialeah Cir N 76182
Hickory Hollow Ln 76182
Hickory Place Ct 76182
Hidden Oaks Dr 76182
High Oaks Dr 76182
High Point Ct 76182
Highland Dr 76182
Hightower Dr 76182
Hilary Ct 76182
Hillcrest Ct 76182
Hills Ct & Dr 76117
Hillside Ct & Dr 76180
Hilltop Dr 76180
Hilton Head Dr 76180
Holiday Ct 76180
Holiday Ln
4800-6200 76180
6202-6298 76180
6300-7399 76180
Holiday Ln E 76180
Holiday Ln W 76180
Holland Dr 76180
Honey Ln 76180
Howard St 76180
Hudson St 76180
Hummingbird Ct 76180
Hunt Dr 76182
Hunter Ln 76182
Huntington Sq 76182
Ice House Dr 76180
India Trl 76180
Inverness Dr 76180
Inwood Dr 76182
Irish Dr 76180
Irish Spring Ln 76180
Iron Horse Blvd 76180
Iron Horse Dr 76148
Irongate Dr 76182
Jackie Lee St 76180
Jade Cir 76180
Jamaica Cir & Way 76180
Jamie Renee Ln 76182
Janetta Dr 76180
Jannie St 76180
Jason Ct 76182
Jean Ann Dr 76180
Jeffrey St 76182
Jennifer Ln 76182
Jennings Dr 76180
Jerrell St 76180
Jerrie Jo Dr 76180
Jerry Ct 76182
Jessica Ct 76182
Jester Ct 76182
Jill Ct 76182
John Autry Rd 76182
Johns Way 76180
Johnson Ave & Ct 76180
Joreen Dr 76180
Joshua Ct 76182
Juniper Dr 76182
Kandy Ln 76182
Kara Pl 76182
Karen Dr 76180
Katherine Dr 76180
Keeter Dr 76180
Ken Michael Ct 76180
Kendra Ln 76182
Keno Ln 76182
Kensington Ct & Ln 76182
Kentwood Dr 76182
Kerry Ave 76180
Killarney Ct 76180
Kilmer Ct 76180
Kimberly Ct 76182
King Arthur Ct 76180
King Ranch Rd 76182
Kingston Ct 76182
Kingswood Ct 76182
Kirk Ct, Ln & Rd 76182
Kris St 76180
Kristina Ln 76182
La Fontaine Dr 76182
Lake Way 76180
Lake Side Cir 76180
Lake View Cir 76180
Lake Way Mews 76180
Lancashire Dr 76182
Lantana Dr 76180
Lariat Trl 76180
Larue Cir 76180
Laura St 76180
Laurel Ln 76180
Layna Ct 76182
Lazy Lane Rd 76180
Leaning Oak Dr 76182
Lewis Ct 76180
Lewis Ln 76182
Limerick Ln 76180
Lincoln Dr 76182
Lincolnshire Ln 76182
Lindwall Ct 76182
Little Ranch Rd 76182
Live Oak Dr 76182
Lochridge Ct 76180
Lola Dr 76180
Londonderry Dr 76182
Lone Oak Dr 76182
Lonesome Oaks Dr 76182
Long Trail Dr 76182
E & NE Loop 820 N 76180
Lost Maple Dr 76182
Loving Trl 76182
Lowery Ln 76182
Lucas Ln 76182
Lucian Dr 76182
Luther Ct 76180
Lynda Ct & Ln 76180
Lynn Ter 76180
Mabell St 76182
Mackey Dr 76180
Madison Dr 76182
Main St 76182
Manor Dr 76180
Maple Dr & St 76182
Mapleleaf Dr 76182
Maplewood Ave & Ct 76180
Marble Falls Dr 76180
Marie St 76180
Marilyn Ln 76180
Mark Ct 76182
Market Ct 76182
Marlette Ct 76182
Marti Ln 76182
Martin Dr 76182
Mary Ct & Dr 76180
Mary Frances Ln 76180
Mary Grace Ct 76182
Maryanna Way 76180
Massey Ct 76182
Matador Ranch Rd 76182
Matson St 76117
Matt Dr 76182
Meadow Ct 76180
Meadow Park N 76180
Meadow Park S 76180
Meadow Rd 76182
Meadow Creek Rd 76182
Meadow Crest Dr 76180
Meadow Lakes Ct & Dr 76180
Meadow Oak St 76180
Meadowbrook Dr 76182
Meadowridge Ct 76180
Meadows Way 76180
Meadowview Ter 76182
Meandering Ct & Dr 76182
Megan Ln 76182
Melissa Ct 76182
Mesa Dr 76182
Mesa Verde Trl 76182
Michael Dr 76182
Mickey Ct & St 76182
Mid Cities Blvd
6700-9298 76180
6701-9299 76182
Mike Ct & Dr 76180
Mimosa Dr 76180
Miracle Ct & Ln 76182
Misty Meadow Dr 76180
Mockingbird Ln 76180
Moody Ct 76180
Morgan Cir 76180
Morning Cloak Rd 76180
Moss Ct & Ln 76182
Mossycup Ln 76182
Mountain Spring Dr 76180
Nancy Ln 76180
Neal St 76180
Neil Ct 76182
Nevada Trl 76180
Newcastle Pl 76182
Newman Dr 76180
Nichols Way 76180
Nicole Ct 76182
Nob Hill Ct & Dr 76182
Noneman Dr 76182
Noreast Dr 76180
Northcut Dr 76117
Northeast Pkwy 76182
Northfield Dr 76182
Northridge Blvd 76180
Nottinghill Ct 76182
O Brian Way 76180
Oak Ct 76182
Oak Hills Ct 76182
Oak Knoll Dr 76182
Oak Leaf Dr 76182
Oak Park Dr 76182
Oak Ridge Dr 76182
Oak View Ave 76182
Oakfield Corner Ct 76182
Oakland Ln 76180
N Oaks Dr 76182
Odell St 76182
Old Hickory Dr 76182
Old Mill Ct & Rd 76182
Oldham Pl 76182
Oliver Dr 76180
Olmstead Ter 76180
Onyx Dr N & S 76180
N Orallind Pkwy 76182
Orange Valley Dr 76182
Orchard Ct 76182
Orient Dr 76117
Oriole Ln 76182
Overton Park 76182
Owen Dr 76180
Paintbrush Ct 76182
Palomar Dr 76180
Paramount St 76117
Parchman St 76180
N Park Dr 76182
Park Brook Ct & Dr 76182
Park Oaks Ct 76180
Park Place Dr 76182
Parkdale Dr 76182
Parker Blvd 76180
Parkridge Dr 76180
Parkview Ln 76182
Parkway Ave & Dr 76182
Parkwood Dr 76182
Passionvine St 76180
Paula Ct 76182
Payte Ln 76182
Peachtree Trl 76182
Pearl Dr & St 76180
Pebble Ct 76180
Pebble Beach Ct 76180
Pebble Creek Dr 76180
Pecan Ridge Dr 76182
Pedernales Rdg 76180
Perkins Dr 76182
Pinehurst Dr 76180
Pleasant Dream St 76180
Pleasant Meadow Dr 76180
Pleasant Ridge Dr 76180
Plumwood Dr 76182
Post Oak Dr 76182
Prairie Dawn Ln 76180
Precinct Line Rd
6000-6299 76180
6301-6397 76180
6401-8197 76182
8199-8299 76182
8301-8599 76182
Price Dr 76180
Puerto Vallarta Dr 76180
Quail Ridge Dr 76180
Quartering Dr 76182
Randle Dr 76180
Randol Dr 76180
Randy Dr 76182
Reatta Ct 76182
Red Oak St 76182
Red River Run 76180
Red Rose Trl 76182
Redhawk Ct 76180
Redondo St 76180
Redwood Ct 76182
Reeves St 76117
Regency Dr 76182
Revenue Way 76182
Reynolds Rd 76180
Richfield Dr 76182
Richland Blvd & Ct 76180
Richland Plaza Dr 76180
Riddle Dr 76182
Ridge Crest Dr 76182
Ridge Line Dr 76182
Ridge Peak Dr 76182
Ridge Run Dr 76182
Ridgeside Dr 76180
Ridgetop Rd 76182
Ridgeview Ct 76180
Ridgeway Ave & Ct 76182
Ridgewood Dr 76182
Rio Bend Ct 76182
Rio De Janeiro Cir 76180
Rio Vista Ct 76182
Rita Beth Ln 76180
Riverdale Dr 76180
Riverview Dr 76180
Riviera Ct & Dr 76180
Road To The Mall 76180
Roaring Springs Dr 76180
Roberta Dr 76180
Roberts Ct 76182
Robin Cir 76180
Robins Way 76180
Rock Springs Dr 76182
Rockdale Ct & Dr 76182
Rogan Dr 76180
Rogene St 76180
Rogers Dr 76182
Rolling Hills Dr 76182
Rolling Ridge Ct & Dr 76182
Romford Way 76182
Rosewood Dr 76180
Ross Rd 76180
Royal Ct 76180
Royal Oaks Dr 76182
Royal Ridge Dr 76182
Rufe Snow Dr 76180
Rumfield Rd 76182
Rushing Spring Dr 76182
Ruthette Ct & Dr 76182
Sable Dr & Ln 76182
Saddle Ridge Trl 76182
Sagebrush Ct N & S 76182
Saint Andrews Dr 76180
Saint Patrick St 76180
San Jacinto Ct 76180
Sandhurst Ln E 76182
Sandy Ct 76182
Santiago Ct 76180
Sao Paulo Ct 76180
Sawgrass Ct 76180
Sayers Ln 76182
Scarborough Pl 76182
Schiller Dr 76180
Scott Dr 76180
Scruggs Dr 76180
Sean Dr 76182
Seville Dr 76182
Shadow Wood Dr 76182
Shady Cove Ct 76180
Shady Grove Rd 76180
Shady Hollow Ct & Ln 76182
Shady Lake Dr 76180
Shady Meadow St 76180
Shady Oaks Dr 76182
Shadybrooke Ct & Dr 76182
Shadydale Ct & Dr 76182
Shadywood Ln 76182
Shamrock Ct 76180
Shane Ct 76182
Shannon Ln 76180
Shauna Dr 76180
Sheffield Ct 76182
Sherbert Dr 76180
Sheridon Ct & Dr 76117
Sherri Ln 76182
Shirley Dr 76180
Short St 76180
Sierra Dr 76180
Silverleaf Dr 76182
Simmons Rd 76182
Skylark Cir & Ct 76180
Smith Dr 76182
Smithfield Rd
6100-6299 76180
6300-8599 76182
Snider St 76182
Southampton Dr 76182
Southern Hills Dr 76180

Southgate Dr 76182
Southmoor Ct 76182
Southridge Ct 76182
Souththorn Dr 76182
Spanish Oaks Dr 76182
Spence Ct & Dr 76182
Spring Run 76182
Spring Lea Way 76182
Spring Meadow Dr 76180
Spring Oak Dr 76182
Spring River Ln 76180
Springbrook Ct 76182
Springdale Ln 76182
Springhill Ct 76182
Spruce Ct 76182
Spurgeon Ct 76180
Squire Ct 76180
Staci Ct 76182
Stamp Dr 76182
Standley St 76180
Stardust Dr 76180
Starnes Rd 76182
Steeple Ridge Dr 76182
Steeplewood Dr 76180
Stephanie Ct & Dr 76182
Steven St 76180
Steward Ln 76182
Stewart Dr 76182
Stillmeadows Cir N & S 76182
Stone Dr 76180
Stone Creek Dr 76182
Stone Villa Cir 76182
Stonecrest Dr & Trl 76182
Stonedale Ct 76182
Stoneridge Dr 76182
Stonewall Ct 76182
Stonybrooke Ct & Dr 76182
Stratford Dr 76182
Strummer Dr 76180
Sudbury Way 76182
Summer Tree Ln 76180
Suncrest Ct 76180
Sunnybrook Dr 76182
Sunrise Dr 76182
Sunset Rd 76182
Surrey Ct 76180
Susan Ct 76180
Susan Lee Ln 76180
Swallow Ln 76182
Sweetbriar Ct 76182
Swenson Ranch Rd 76182
Sybil Dr 76180
Tabor St 76180
Tamarron Ct 76182
Tamiami Ct 76182
Tamra Ct 76180
Tanglewood Ct 76182
N Tarrant Pkwy 76182
Teakwood Ct 76182
Teresa Ct 76182
Terrell Dr 76182
Terry Ct & Dr 76180
Tessa Dr 76182
Texas Dr 76180
Thaxton Pkwy 76180
Thistle Ct 76182
Thornberry Dr 76182
Thornbird Dr 76182
Thornbridge Dr 76182
Thornbrook Ct 76182
Thornbush Dr 76182
Thorncrest Ct 76182
Thorndale Ct 76182
Thorndyke Dr 76182
Thornhaven Ct 76182
Thornhill Dr 76182
Thornmeadow Ct 76182
Thornridge Dr 76182
Thornway Ct & Dr 76182
Thornwood Dr 76182
Thousand Oaks Dr 76180
Tiffin Dr 76180
Timber Dr 76182
Timberhill Ct & Dr 76182
Timberidge Dr 76182
Timberlane Ct & Dr 76182
Timberline Ct 76182
Tipperary Ct 76182
Topper Ct & Dr 76180
Torrey Pines Dr 76180
Tourist Dr 76117
Town Walk Dr 76182
Towne Park Dr 76180
Tradonna Ln 76182
Trail Wood Dr 76182
Trails Edge Dr 76182
Trinidad Dr 76180
Tunbridge Dr 76182
Turner Dr 76182
W Turner St 76182
Turner Ter 76180
Turtle Creek Ct 76180
Twisted Oaks Ct & Way 76182
Uici Dr 76180
Ulster Dr 76180
Vale Ct 76182
Valhalla Dr 76180
Valley Dr 76182
Valley Oaks Dr 76182
Valleyview Dr 76182
Vance Rd 76180
Venice Dr 76180
Victoria Ave & Dr 76180
Vine Wood Dr 76182
Vineyard Ct 76182
Waggoner Ranch Rd 76182
Wakefield Rd 76182
Walker Blvd 76180
Walter St 76182
Wanda Way 76182
Warbler Ln 76182
Waterford Ct 76180
Waterford Ln 76180
Wavyleaf Ln 76182
Weeping Willow Dr 76182
Wendell Ct & Dr 76117
Wentwood Ct 76182
Wentworth Dr 76182
Wesley Ct 76180
Westchase Dr 76180
Westcliff St 76182
Western Oaks Dr 76182
Westgate Dr 76182
Westminster Way 76180
Westover Way 76182
Westwind Ct & Ln 76182
Wexford Ct 76182
Weyland Dr 76180
Whippoorwill Ct 76180
Whispering Woods Ln 76182
Whitfield Ct 76180
Whitney Ct 76182
Wild Horse Dr 76182
Wilhite Ln 76180
Willowcrest Ct & Dr 76117
Winchester Rd 76182
Wind River Dr 76182
Windcrest Ct & Ln E & N 76182
Winder Ct 76180
Windhaven Ct & Rd 76182
Windsor Ct 76180
Winnell Way 76180
Winslow Ct 76182
Winter Park Dr 76180
Wishing Tree Ln 76182
Wood Ridge Dr 76182
Wood View St 76180
Woodbend Park Rd 76182
Woodcreek Ct & Ln 76180
Woodhaven Dr 76182
Woodland Dr 76182
Woodland Hills Dr 76182
Woods Ln 76182
Woodstair Dr 76182
Worthshire Dr 76182
Wren Ln 76182
Wuliger Way 76180
Wyoming Trl 76180
Yarmouth Ave 76182
Yorkshire Ct 76180

ODESSA TX

General Delivery 79761

POST OFFICE BOXES MAIN OFFICE STATIONS AND BRANCHES

Box No.s
1 - 11480 79760
12001 - 15156 79768
69001 - 70996 79769
960003 - 960003 79760

NAMED STREETS

Academy Ave 79764
S Acapulco Ave 79766
N Acts Ave 79763
E Ada St 79761
W Ada St
100-699 79761
700-1399 79763
Adams Ave
200-298 79761
300-2599 79761
2700-3699 79762
N Adams Ave 79761
W Addis St 79763
W Adobe St 79766
S Agate Ave 79766
Airway Dr 79764
Alabama St 79764
Alameda Ave & Ct 79763
Alamosa St 79763
Alareenn Ave 79761
Alaska Ave 79764
W Albert Dr 79764
S Alcario Dr 79766
Alcove Ct & St 79762
Alderfer Ave 79762
Aldridge Ave 79763
N Alexander Ave 79764
Alice St
100-399 79766
2200-2300 79764
2302-2899 79764
N Alleghaney Ave
300-498 79761
500-1999 79761
2700-3099 79764
S Alleghaney Ave 79761
Allionia Ln 79765
Allred Ave 79761
Almond Ave & St 79763
Aloha Dr 79762
Alpine St 79762
Alta Vista Rd 79762
S Alto Ave 79766
N Alturas Ave
1600-2699 79763
2700-3899 79764
N Ambassador Ave 79764
Amber Dr 79762
Amburgey Ave 79763
Amethyst Cv 79762
Amherst Ave 79762
S Amistad Ave 79766
W Amoco St 79764
Anderson Ave 79761
S Andincon Ave 79766
Andrews Hwy
1800-2599 79761
2700-6799 79762
7000-9299 79765
9301-9499 79765
Angel Trl 79766
W Angel Fire St 79763
Angus Rd 79764
Anice St 79762
Ann St 79761
Antebellum Ct 79762
Antietam 79766
E Antigua Dr 79766
S Apache Ave 79763
W Apache Point St 79766
Apollo St 79764
W Apple St 79766
Applewood Dr 79761
Apricot Ave 79763
W April St 79764
Aranda 79764
Arapaho 79763
Arbor Ct 79762
W Arcadia St 79764
Archuleta St 79763
Arkansas St 79764
S Arrowhead Ave 79766
Arroyo Santiago 79762
Arthur Ave 79764
W Artie St 79763
Aspenwood Ln 79761
Atlantic St 79761
S Atwood Ave 79766
Augustine Ct 79765
Austin Ave 79762
Autumn Ave 79763
Avenida De Mexico 79761
N Avenue E 79763
Avenue A Cir 79763
Avenue B 79763
Avenue C 79763
N Avenue D 79763
N Avenue F 79763
N Avenue G 79763
N Avenue H 79763
N Avenue I 79763
N Avenue J 79763
N Avenue K 79763
N Avenue L 79763
N Avery Ave 79763
W Avocado St 79766
N Aztec Ave 79763
Baca Dr 79763
Badger Trl 79766
Bagley Ave 79764
Bainbridge Dr 79762
W Baldwin St 79764
S Bandera Ave 79766
Banff 79765
Bankhead Ave 79763
Bankhead Hwy 79765
W Barbara Dr 79764
Barcelona 79766
Barksdale Ln 79765
N Barrel Ct 79763
Barrett Ave 79761
Barrow Dr 79764
Bass St 79766
Bastrop Ave 79765
Bay Oaks Dr 79762
W Beadendi St 79763
Beal St 79761
Beaty Ave
2600-2698 79763
5701-5797 79764
5799-6499 79764
Beckwood Pl 79763
Bedford Dr 79764
Beechwood St 79761
Beeson Ave 79764
W Bell St 79766
Bella Ct 79763
Bellaire Dr 79762
Bellini St 79765
N Belmont Ave 79763
Ben Brush Dr 79763
Benefield Ave 79762
Benton St 79766
Bernice Ave 79763
W Berry St 79766
Berryhill St 79763
S Beryl Ave 79766
Betty Lou Dr 79766
Beverly St 79761
N Big Dipper Ave 79764
Big Valley Cir 79763
W Bighorn Dr 79764
W Bill St 79763
Billy Hext Rd 79765
S Blackfoot Ave 79763
W Blackgold Dr 79763
Blackshear St 79761
Blackstone Ave 79763
W Blair St 79764
N Blalock Ave 79764
Blossom Ln 79762
Blue Dr 79762
E Blue Diamond St 79766
Blue Jay Trl 79765
Bluebird St 79761
Bluebonnet Ave 79761
Boatwright St 79763
Bobwhite Dr 79761
Boles Rd 79763
S Bonanza Ave 79766
W Bonerive 79765
Bonham Ave
1201-1297 79761
1299-1800 79761
1802-2598 79761
2700-2898 79762
2900-4700 79762
4702-5198 79762
Bonita Fay Dr 79763
Bookins Ave & Ct 79764
E Borman St 79766
Botticelli Ave 79765
Boulder Ave 79762
N Bovina Ave 79763
Bowden St 79763
Bowie Ave 79762
Bracy St 79761
W Bradley Dr 79764
Brahma Rd 79764
S Branding Iron Cir 79766
Brandon 79762
Brazos Ave 79764
N Breckenridge Ave 79763
Brentwood Dr 79762
Briarwood Ln 79762
N Bridle Path 79763
Bristol Ct 79762
Brittany Ln 79761
N Broken Bow Cir 79763
W Bronze St 79766
Brookhaven Ln 79762
Brookover 79763
Broughton Ave 79761
Brown Ave 79762
Brownstone Rd 79765
Bruce Ave 79761
Bruck Ave 79763
S Brunswick Rd 79763
Bryan Rd 79764
Buchanan Ave 79763
Buck Pl 79762
W Buckeye St 79763
N Bucknell Ave 79764
Buffalo Ave 79762
Bull Run St 79766
N Bullard Ave 79764
Bunche Ave 79761
Burchfield St 79766
Burgess St 79764
Burke St 79764
W Burkett St 79763
S Burma Ave 79766
E Business 20
2701-2897 79761
E Business 20
2899-2999 79761
3001-5099 79761
6101-6697 79762
6699-6899 79762
6901-6999 79762
8000-8099 79765
N Butterfield Ave 79764
Byron Ave
1400-1799 79761
2700-3199 79762
Cabrall Ct 79765
Cabrillo Dr 79765
Cabrito Dr 79765
Cagle Ln 79762
E Calcutta St 79766
California Ave 79762
Calle Norte 79762
Cambridge St 79761
W Camino Del Sol 79764
W Cananero Ct 79763
W Candace St 79764
Candlelight Dr 79765
Candy Ln 79762
N Canterbury Ave 79764
Canterbury St 79765
N Canyon Ave 79763
Capistrano Ct 79765
Caprock Dr 79766
Carachic 79763
Cargo Rd 79762
Carl Ave 79763
Carolyn Dr 79764
S Carpenter Ave 79766
S Carrizo Ave 79766
N Carter Ave 79764
Carver Ave 79761
Casa Blanca Dr 79762
Casa Grande Dr 79763
Casa Loma 79765
Cascade Ct 79762
Cassia Rd 79765
Cassie Way 79762
Castle Rd 79762
Castle Oaks Dr 79765
Catalina Dr
2200-2398 79763
2400-2499 79763
2700-2999 79764
W Catalpa St 79763
Catclaw Dr 79764
W Catlin St 79766
S Cattle Dr 79766
W Cavalry St 79763
W Cavazos St 79763
N Cedar Creek Ave 79763
Center Ave
300-798 79761
800-2599 79761
2700-3199 79762
W Centergate St 79764
Central Dr 79761
E & N Century Ave 79762
Cessna Ave 79764
Cevallia Dr 79762
Chambord Dr 79765
W Chaparral Dr 79764
Charles St
701-799 79761
1401-1599 79763
Charles Walker Rd 79765
Chateau Ln 79765
Cherrywood Cir 79761
Chesnut Playa 79762
Chestnut Ave 79762
Chimney Holw 79762
W Chisolm Trl 79763
Chisum Ave 79762
W Cholla Cir 79763
W Choya Dr 79766
Chris Ave 79766
Christo Ln 79762
Christopher Ln 79762
Chukar Run 79761
Churchill Rd 79764
Cibola Ct 79765
W Cielo Alto St 79763
Cielo Vista Pl 79761
Cimarron Ave 79761
Circle Ln 79762
W Citation Dr 79763
W Claire St 79764
N Clay St 79764
Claymoor Dr 79764
Clayton Pl 79762
Clearmont Ave 79762
N Clearview Ave 79763
E Clements St 79761
W Clements St
100-799 79761
800-1400 79763
1402-1698 79763
N Clendenen Ave 79763
Clifford St
300-699 79761
800-1399 79763
Clinton Ave 79762
W Cloudcroft St 79763
Clover Ave 79762
N Clovis Ave 79763
Club Dr
7100-7199 79762
7200-7299 79765
Coahuila Rd 79763
Cobblestone Ln 79765
Cody Ct & Pl 79762
Coen 79766
W Cole 79766
Cole Dr 79762
Coleman Ave 79761
Colima Ln 79765
College Ave 79761
N & S Colonial Dr 79762
Colorado Ave & Ct 79762
Commandra Ave 79762
E Commerce St 79762
Concord Cir 79764
W Conestoga Ln 79766
Conet Dr 79763
Conley Ave & Pl 79762
Conover Ave 79763
Constitution Ave 79762
Cook Rd 79766
Coombs Ave 79764
Cooper St 79763
Copus Ave & Cir 79763
Coral Dr 79764
Cord St 79762
Cordova St 79762
Cornell Ave 79765
Corona Cir 79762
Coronado Ave 79763
Country Club Dr 79762
N County Rd W
200-2699 79763
2700-9100 79764
9102-9598 79764
S County Rd W
200-1399 79763
2200-5199 79766
W County Road 122 79765
W County Road 123 79765
W County Road 124 79765
W County Road 125 79765
W County Road 127 79765
W County Road 128 79765
S County Road 1282 79765
S County Road 1283 79765
S County Road 1285 79765
S County Road 1286 79765
W County Road 129 79765
S County Road 1290 79765
S County Road 1292 79765
S County Road 1293 79765
S County Road 1294 79765
S County Road 1295 79765
S County Road 1296 79765
S County Road 1297 79765
S County Road 1298 79765
S County Road 1300 79765
S County Road 1303 79765
S County Road 1305 79765
S County Road 1305 1/ 2 79765
S County Road 1306 79765
S County Road 1307 79765
S County Road 1307 1/ 2 79765
S County Road 1308 79765
S County Road 1309 79765
S County Road 1310
4500-4899 79765
S County Road 1310
9000-9099 79766

S County Road 1311 79765
S County Road 1312
3500-3599 79765
8700-9099 79766
S County Road 1313 79765
S County Road 1314 79765
S County Road 1315
3700-3799 79765
9000-9099 79766
S County Road 1316 79765
S County Road 1317 79765
W County Road 132 79765
W County Road 133 79765
S County Road 1357 79766
W County Road 172 79766
W County Road 174 79766
W County Road 176 79766
W County Road 177 79766
W County Road 178 79766
W County Road 179 79766
W County Road 272 79766
Courtland Ave 79763
Covey Dr 79762
Covington Ave 79763
W Cowden St 79764
Coyochic 79763
Crane 79766
N Crane Ave 79763
S Crane Ave 79763
S Crazy Horse Ave 79763
E & W Crescent Dr 79761
Crestview Dr 79762
Cristobal Ct 79765
Crockett St 79762
Cromwell Ter 79764
W Cross St 79763
E Crossroad St 79766
N Crosswood Ln 79764
Crown Ave 79761
S Crownover Ave 79766
S Crystal Ave 79766
Cumberland Rd
1400-2699 79761
2700-2799 79762
Cummings Dr 79764
S Cunningham Ave 79766
S Cuspid Ave 79766
Custer Ave
901-1397 79761
1399-2699 79761
2700-2799 79762
N Cynthia Dr 79763
N Cypress Ave 79764
Da Vinci Ct 79765
Daisy Ln 79763
Dakota Ave 79762
Dale St 79761
N & S Damascus Ave 79763
Dania St 79762
Daniel Ave 79764
Dartmouth Cir 79764
Dawn Ave 79762
De Vaca Ct 79765
W Debbie Rd 79763
N Deborah Ave 79764
Deering Dr 79762
Del Rio Dr 79761
Delwood Ave 79762
Denis Ln 79762
Dennard St 79764
Desert Flower 79763
Desert Willow Ct 79763
Desoto Dr 79762
Devonian Ave 79762
Diais Cir 79762
S Diamond 79766
Diana Ave 79764
Disney St 79761
Divine Ave 79763
N Dixie Blvd
100-2599 79761
2700-6799 79762
S Dixie Blvd 79761
Dobbs Ave 79761
S Dock Rd 79762
Doctor Emmitt Headlee
St 79765
Doe Ln 79762
Dolores Ct 79765
Donatello St 79765
S Donna Kay Ave 79763
Doonmore St 79765
Dorado Dr 79765
Doran Dr 79761
W Doris Dr 79764
Dornoch Ln 79765
N Dorothy Ave 79764
Dotsy Ave 79763
Douglas Dr 79762
Dove Dr 79766
Dover Dr 79762
Driver Ave 79761
W Drivers Hall Of Fame
St 79763
Drury Ln
300-699 79761
700-1399 79763
Dublin Ave 79765
Duke Ave 79765
Dumont Dr 79762
Dunbar Dr 79762
W Dunn St 79763
Durango Ave 79762
Dustin Dr 79762
Dwayne St 79763
N Eagle Nest Ave 79764
East Ave 79764
Eastland Ave 79764
Eastover Dr
1600-2499 79761
2700-3299 79762
Eastridge Rd
6000-6599 79762
6601-6799 79762
6900-7399 79765
Eastview 79766
N Eastview Ave 79764
N Easy Ave 79764
Ector Ave 79762
N Eddie Ave 79763
Edgeport Dr 79765
W Edith St 79764
W Edna St 79763
Eidson Ave 79763
S Einstein Ave 79766
E Eisele St 79766
Eisenhower Rd
1801-2599 79761
2700-3899 79762
El Paso Ave 79762
Elderica Ct 79765
Electric St 79761
W Elida St 79764
W Elizabeth Ln 79764
Elliott Ave 79763
Ellis Dr 79764
Elm Dr 79763
Elmwood Ave 79763
Emerald Ave 79761
Emerald Forest Ct &
Dr 79762
Emerald Gardens Dr 79762
Englewood Cir 79762
Englewood Ln
1400-1699 79761
2700-2800 79762
2802-3898 79762
W Eric St 79766
Erron Ave 79764
Escalante 79763
Esmond Dr 79763
Esperanza Ave 79763
N Essex Ave 79763
N Estacado Dr 79763
Estates Dr 79765
S Eva St 79763
W Everett St 79766
E & N Everglade Ave 79762
W Evergreen Cir 79764
Express Way 79761
N Exxon St 79764
Fair Oaks Cir 79762
Fair Palms Pl 79762
Fairbrook Dr 79762
Fairlane Ave 79762
Fairmont Dr 79762
Fairway Dr 79765
Falcon Dr 79762
Falcons Nest Ct 79762
Fall Ave 79763
Fargo Ave 79761
W Farice Dr 79764
S Faudree Rd 79765
Femmer Ct 79762
N Ferguson Ave 79764
Fern Cir 79762
Fernwood St 79762
Field St 79761
W Fig St 79766
Firenze St 79765
W Firewater Trl 79763
Fitch Ave 79761
W Flagstone St 79766
N Flamingo Ave
1600-2699 79763
2700-6699 79764
Flamingo Cir 79763
S Fletchers Trl 79763
Florence Dr 79765
Florida Ave 79764
E & W Fm 1787 79766
N Fm 1936
100-2699 79763
N Fm 1936
2700-4099 79764
S Fm 1936 79763
S Fm 3503 79766
Fontana St 79763
Foote Ct 79762
W Ford Dr 79766
S Forest Park Ave 79766
Fort Worth Ave 79762
Fortune 500 79763
Foster Ave 79763
Fountain Ct & Ln 79761
Fox River Ridge St 79765
Fox Run Rd 79763
N Francis Ave 79764
N Fremont Ave 79764
French Ave 79761
W Frontier Rd 79764
N Frost Ave 79763
S Fulton Ave 79766
Gage Ave 79762
N Galahad Ave 79764
W Galaxie St 79764
S Gallant Fox Ave 79763
Garden Ln 79761
W Garland St 79764
Garnet Ave 79761
W Garrett Dr 79764
Gary Pl 79762
Gary Ter 79764
N Gaston Ave 79763
Gemini St 79764
Gene Ave 79764
Geneva Ave 79763
Georgia St 79764
Gerron St 79761
Gettysburg 79766
Giavanna Dr 79765
Gila Rd 79763
E Gillespie Ln 79765
Giotto St 79765
Gist Ave 79764
Glenda Ave 79762
Glendale Ave 79763
Glenhaven Dr 79762
E Glenn St 79766
Glenn Eagles 79765
Glenwood Ave 79761
W Gold St 79766
S Golden Ave 79766
Golder Ave
201-597 79761
599-2699 79761
2700-8699 79764
8701-8799 79764
S Goodnight Trl 79763
Grace Ave 79762
Graham Ave 79763
N Granada Ave 79763
Grand Mesa Dr 79761
N Grandview Ave
200-498 79761
500-2699 79761
2700-5399 79762
7500-7598 79765
7601-7699 79765
S Grandview Ave
100-1299 79761
1301-1599 79761
2200-2799 79766
N Grant Ave 79761
S Grant Ave
101-297 79761
299-1599 79761
1601-1699 79761
1700-1799 79766
Grant Way 79761
Gravensteen 79765
Graves Ct & Dr 79762
Grayson Ave 79761
Green Dr 79763
Green Oaks Cir 79762
W Green River St 79764
N Greenlee Ave 79764
N Greenway Ave 79764
N Greer Ave 79764
W Grey Eagle St 79763
S Grey Wolf Ave 79766
S Grissom Ave 79766
Groening St 79765
Guernsey Rd 79764
Gulf Ave 79761
S Gunsmoke Rd 79763
W Hacienda Dr 79763
W Hackberry St 79766
Hadden Dr 79765
Halifax Ave
1400-2699 79761
2700-2799 79762
N Hall Ave 79764
Halley Ave 79764
N Halter Ave 79763
E Hammett Dr 79766
N Hancock Ave
100-2599 79761
2700-3699 79762
S Hancock Ave 79761
Haner Ct & Dr 79762
Hanley St 79762
Hannah Dr 79762
Hanover Dr 79761
Happy Ln 79766
Harless Ave 79763
Harned Ct 79762
N Harolds Ave 79763
Harris St 79763
E Harrisburg 79766
E & W Harvard Ave &
Cir 79765
S Hasty Ave 79763
Hawaii Cv 79762
Hawthorne Ct 79765
Hays Ave 79763
Haywood Ave 79761
Hazelwood Ave 79762
Headlee Ave 79763
Heather Ln 79764
W Helena Dr 79766
W Helm St 79764
Hemphill Ave 79763
Henderson Ave 79764
Hendley Ave 79761
Hendrick Ave 79762
Hereford Rd 79764
W Heritage St 79766
Hialeah Cir 79761
Hickory Ave 79763
Highland St 79761
E Highway 191
6000-6098 79762
E Highway 191
6100-6499 79762
6501-7799 79762
7000-7798 79765
7800-13499 79765
W Highway 80 79763
W Highway 80 E 79765
Hillcrest Ave 79761
E Hillmont Rd 79765
W Hillmont Rd 79764
Hilltop Dr 79762
Hinkle St 79762
N Hite Ave 79764
W Hoffman Dr 79764
Holiday Dr 79765
Holley Ave 79762
Holloman Ave 79766
Hollywood Dr 79763
Honeysuckle Ave & St 79761
N Horseshoe Bnd 79763
N Howsey Ave 79764
N Huber Ave 79764
W Hubnik Rd 79763
Hudson Ave 79761
Hughes Ln 79764
Humble Ave 79761
Hummingbird Pl 79761
N Huntington Ave
1800-2599 79763
2700-3999 79764
W Hutson Rd 79763
Hyden Dr 79762
Idlewood Ln
801-897 79761
899-2499 79761
2700-2799 79762
Independence Cir &
Dr 79762
W Industrial Ave & Cir 79761
Innsbrook Cir 79761
E Interstate 20 79766
E Interstate 20 E 79765
W Interstate 20
100-198 79761
W Interstate 20
900-1298 79763
1300-1500 79763
1502-12398 79763
1901-2799 79766
5201-12399 79763
W Interstate 20 E 79765
Inwood Dr 79761
Iola Dr 79764
E & W Ivory St 79766
Ivy Ct & Ln 79762
W J Bar Ct 79764
Jackalyn Ave 79764
N Jackson Ave
101-297 79761
299-2599 79761
3100-4699 79762
S Jackson Ave 79761
S Jade Ave 79766
W Jamerend St 79764
Jane Ave 79764
S Jared Ct 79766
Jarrett St 79764
N Jarry Lee Ave 79764
S Jasper Ave 79766
W Jay St 79763
W Jeff Dr 79766
Jefferson Ave 79761
W Jenkins St 79764
N Jensen Ave 79763
Jeter Ave 79761
W Joan Dr 79764
W Jody Cir 79764
John Ave 79764
S John Ben Sheppard 79766
John Ben Shepperd
Pkwy
801-1497 79761
1499-2699 79761
2701-4197 79762
4199-5299 79762
5301-5399 79762
S John Ben Shepperd
Pkwy 79761
Johnson Ave 79763
Johnson Rd 79764
E Jp Teal Dr 79766
N Juanita Ave 79763
Juarez St 79761
N Jude Ave 79763
N Judkins Dr 79764
Judy Ave 79764
E Junction Dr 79766
Kahala 79762
Kalenak Ct 79762
Karen Ave 79764
W Kassnar Dr 79764
Kathryn Ave 79764
Kauai 79762
Kay Ave
2500-2599 79761
2700-2799 79762
N Kaylee Ave 79764
Keeler Ave 79764
Keeling St 79763
N & S Kelly Ave 79763
Kennedy Dr 79764
Kentucky Ave 79764
Kenwood Dr 79762
Kermit Ave 79762
Kermit Hwy
1801-1997 79761
1999-2399 79761
2401-2499 79761
2501-2597 79763
2599-2699 79763
2701-2797 79764
2799-4099 79764
W Kesler St 79764
Kessler 79764
Kevin Cir 79763
Keyhaven St 79765
Keystone Dr
2300-2499 79761
2700-2899 79762
Kincotte Ave 79762
Kinghorn Dr 79765
Kingsland Ct 79762
Kingston Ave 79762
Kirkwood Dr 79762
S Klondyke Ave 79766
Knoll Cir 79762
N Knox Ave
100-2699 79763
3100-6999 79764
S Knox Ave 79763
N Koleta Ave 79763
La Casa Dr 79763
La Paz Cir 79765
La Promesa Cir 79765
Ladue Ln 79762
Lafayette Pl 79762
E & N Lagow Ln 79762
Laguna Pl 79761
Lahaina 79762
Lake Ln 79764
Lakeside Dr 79762
Lakeview Ctr 79765
Lakeview Dr 79762
N Lakewood Ave 79764
Lamar Ave & Ct 79765
Lamesa St 79761
Lamont Ave 79764
Lamplight Dr 79765
Lanai 79762
Lancaster Dr 79762
Lancewood Ln 79762
Langtry Ave 79764
Larchmont Pl 79764
Laredo Dr 79761
S Lark Ave 79762
W Larry Ln 79763
Lasseter Ave 79763
N & S Lauderdale Ave 79763
Laurel Ave
1201-1297 79761
1299-1799 79761
2900-3199 79762
Laurel Valley Dr 79765
W Laverne St 79764
N & S Lee Ave 79761
W Lemon St 79766
Lemonwood Ln 79761
Lennox Ave 79764
N Leslie Ave 79764
Lettie Lee Ave 79761
Liberty Pl 79762
Lightner Ave 79766
N Lillard Dr 79763
W Lime St 79766
Limestone Ave 79761
N & S Lincoln Ave 79761
Linda Ave 79763
Lindberg St
300-699 79761
700-1399 79763
Lindy Ave 79761
Linwood Dr 79762
S Lisa Ave 79763
W Lisa Dr 79764
W Lockwood Ln 79764
Locust Ave 79762
S Lodgepole Ave 79763
Lola Ct 79766
Loma Dr 79762
Lone Star Dr 79766
Lonesome Trl 79766
N Long Ave 79764
Long Champ Ct 79762
S Longbranch Rd 79763
Longhorn Trl 79766
NE Loop 338 79762
NW Loop 338
801-1297 79763
NW Loop 338
1299-1600 79763
1602-2498 79763
2700-4000 79764
4002-8898 79764
SE Loop 338
100-198 79766
101-199 79762
101-199 79766
200-298 79762
300-349 79766
360-499 79766
500-529 79762
530-1899 79766
531-599 79762
W Loop 338 S 79766
N & S Lori Ave 79763
Lorina Ln 79763
Lotteman Dr 79764
W Louise St 79764
Louisiana Cv 79762
W Love Dr 79764
S Lovell Ave 79766
Lovely Ln 79766
Lovers Ln 79761
S Loving Trl 79763
S Lucia St 79766
Lufkin Rd 79765
N Luke Ave 79764
W Luna St 79764
W Luna Vista St 79763
W Lyman Dr 79764
Lynbrook Ave 79762
Lyndale Dr 79762
N Lynn Ave 79763
E Mable St 79761
W Mable St
100-599 79761
801-899 79763
W Macarthur Ave 79763
Madera Ave
2200-2699 79763
2700-3000 79764
3002-3098 79764
Magill St 79764
Magnolia Blvd 79761
Manford Ln 79765
Mankins Ave 79764
Manor Dr 79763
Mansion Oaks Dr 79765

Maple Ave	
800-1199	79761
1201-1499	79761
3100-4999	79762
W Mapp St	79763
Maravilla Cir	79765
N Marco Ave	79762
Marfa Ln	79762
W Maria Dr	79764
N Mark Twain Ave	79764
Market Ave	79761
E Market St	79762
S Market St	79766
Marksburg	79765
Marland St	79761
S Marlin Dr	79763
W Mars St	79764
Marsh Dr	79762
N Martha Ave	79764
Martin Ave	79764
N Marvin Ave	79763
N Mary Francis Ave	79764
Matamoras Ave	79761
Maui Cv	79762
Maurene Ave	79764
Maurice Rd	79763
W Maxwell St	79763
E & W May St	79761
Mayer Dr	79762
Mccall Pl	79761
W Mccormick St	79766
W Mccoy St	79763
Mccraw Ct & Dr	79765
Mcdonald	79761
Mckinley Ave	79761
Mckinney Ave	79763
Mcknight Dr	79762
N & S Meadow Ave	79761
N Meadow Lake Ave	79763
Meadow Ridge Ln	79762
W Meadowcrest Dr	79764
Mecca St	79762
Medford Ct	79762
Melick Cir	79765
Melody Ln	79762
N Mercedes Ave	79764
N Mercury Ave	
1601-1797	79763
1799-2499	79763
2501-2599	79763
2700-4099	79764
Merrill Ave	79764
N Mesa Cir	79764
Mesa St	79761
W Mescalero Dr	79766
Mesquite Ave	79764
S Mexia Rd	79763
Michelle	79766
Michels Dr	79762
W Middleground Dr	79763
E & W Midland St	79761
W Miguel St	79766
Milano Dr	79765
Milburn Ave	79761
W Miles St	79763
N Milkyway Ave	79764
Mimosa Cir	79761
W Mindy	79766
Mission Blvd & Dr	79765
Mission Santiago Dr	79765
W Mitzi Cir	79763
N & W Mockingbird Ln	79763
S Mohawk Ave	79763
E Monahans St	79761
W Monahans St	
300-398	79761
901-997	79763
999-1199	79763
1201-1399	79763
Monclair Ave	79762
Montana Ave	79762
Monterey Ave	79761
Monticello Dr	79763
Moody Ave	79761
Moon Chase	79762
W Morris St	79764
N Moss Ave	
200-2699	79763
2700-6799	79764
S Moss Ave	79763
Muirfield Dr	79762
E & W Mulberry St	79766
W Mundy Dr	79764
Munos St	79763
E Murphy St	79761
S Murphy St	79766
W Murphy St	
101-497	79761
499-599	79761
701-2497	79763
2499-15099	79763
N Muskingum Ave	
100-698	79761
700-2599	79761
2700-3699	79762
S Muskingum Ave	79761
Myers Ave	79761
Myrtle St	79761
Nabors Ln	
1100-1398	79761
1400-2499	79761
2900-2999	79762
Nairn Dr	79765
N Nancy Ave	79763
N Navajo Ave	79763
Neal St	79764
W Nectarine St	79766
W Nelda St	79764
Nelson Ave	79761
N Neptune Ave	79763
Neta Pl	79762
Nevada Ave	79762
New Castle Ct	79764
New Orleans Dr	79762
Newcomb Dr	79764
Newell Rd	79762
W Newport Ave	79764
Nicole St	79766
W Night Wind St	79763
Nimitz Dr	79761
S Nita Sue Ave	79763
W Nixon St	79764
Noble Ave	79764
Nolan St	79764
Norfolk Ct	79765
N Northstar Ave	79764
Notre Dame Ave	79765
Oahu Ln	79762
Oak Ave	79763
N Oakhill Ave	79764
Oakridge Dr	79762
Oakwood Dr	79761
Oasis	79765
N Ocotillo Ave	79763
E & W Odessa St	79761
Office Park	79762
N Ogilvy Ave	79764
Oicd Dr	79766
Oilfield Cir	79764
Ojinaga Ave	79763
N Oklahoma Ave	79763
Old Course Rd	79765
Old Lampasas Trl	79765
Oleander Ln	79763
E & W Olive St	79761
N Oliver Ave	79763
Onyx Ct	79762
Opal Cir & Dr	79762
Oporto St	79765
W Orange St	79766
Orchard Dr	79764
Orchid Ln	79761
Oregon St	79764
Orlando Dr	79763
S Orrex Ave	79766
Overton Ave	79763
Oxford Dr	79764
Pacific Dr	79764
Pagewood Ave	
1101-1297	79761
1299-2199	79761
2700-2799	79762
S Pagewood Ave	79761
Paisano Cir	79765
W Palm Dr	79764
Palo Verde Dr	79762
N Palo Vista Ave	79763
Paloma Trl	79766
Palomar Ln	79763
N Palomino Ave	79763
W Palomino Dr	79764
W Papaw St	79766
Paradise Ave	79764
Park Ave	79761
Park Blvd	79763
Parker Dr	79761
Parks Village Dr	79765
Partridge Park	79761
N Patsy Ave	79762
Patterson Ave	79761
Patton Dr	79761
W Paula Rd	79763
Peach St	79764
N Peachtree Ave	79763
W Peacock St	79763
N Pear Ave	79763
E & W Pearl St	79761
Pebble Ct	79761
Pecan Pl	79764
Pecos St	79761
Penbrook St	79762
Penwell Ave	79763
Pepperidge Pl	79761
Permian Dr	79762
Perry Ave	79764
Perryville Dr	79761
Pershing Ave	79762
N & S Persimmon Ave	79763
Petroleum Dr	79762
Petty Ave	79764
N Pheasant Ave	79764
N Philemon Ave	79763
Phillips St	79761
Pica Ave & Ct	79765
Piedmont St	79762
S Piedras Ct	79763
Pine Ave	79763
Pine Rdg	79762
Pinecrest Ave	79765
Pinon Ct	79765
W Pioneer Rd	79764
Pittsburg Ave	79761
Placer Ave	79763
Placid Ct	79762
Planet Ave & Ct	79764
Plantation Cv	79762
Plaza Blvd	79762
Plaza Pl	79761
Pleasant Ave	79764
N Plum Ave	79763
W Pluto St	79764
N Polaris Ave	79763
Pollard Ave	79766
Ponderosa Dr	79762
E Pondview St	79766
E Pool Rd	79766
W Pool Rd	79761
Poplar Ave	79764
Pradera Dr	79762
Prairie Ave	79761
Preston Oaks Cir	79761
Preston Smith Rd	79762
Prestwick	79762
Primrose St	79765
Princeton St	79764
Proctor Ave	79762
Production St	79761
Pronto Ave	79762
Prospect	79762
Pueblo St	79761
Purdue St	79765
S Quail Rd	79766
Quail Run	79761
Quail Park Pl	79761
S Quartz Ave	79766
W Quince St	79763
W Quinn Dr	79763
Rabb Ct & St	79762
Railroad St	79761
Rainbow Ct & Dr	79765
S Raintree Ave	79763
Ramos St	79761
N Ranch Ave	79764
Ranchland Ave	79764
Raphael St	79765
Rasco Ave	79764
S Rawhide Rd	79763
Reagan Ave	79764
Reata Loop	79766
Rebecca Ave & Rd	79763
Redbud Ave	
1300-2599	79761
2700-5299	79762
N Redland Ave	79764
N Redondo Ave	
300-2699	79763
2700-4199	79764
S Redondo Ave	79763
Redwood Dr	79762
Reed Ave	79761
S Regal Ave	79763
Rembrandt Ave	79765
W Remington Rd	79763
Revere Pl	79762
Reynosa St	79761
Rice Ave	79765
Richardson Dr	79762
Richmond Ct & St	79762
Richwood Rd	79762
Riders Rd	79762
Ridgecrest Ave	79763
Ridgedale Ave	79762
W Riggs Dr	79764
W Rigsbee Dr	79764
Riley St	79761
N Rita Ave	79763
N Roadrunner Ave	79763
Roanoke Dr	79761
Robbie Rd	79765
Robertson Ave	79764
N Robin Ave	79764
Rocky Pl	79762
Rocky Lane Rd	79762
Roger Ave	
2500-2599	79761
2700-3199	79762
W Rolling Hills Rd	79764
Roma St	79765
Roosevelt Ave	79761
Roper St	79761
N Rosamond Ave	79763
Rose Ave	79761
Rosemary St	79764
Rosewood Ave	79761
N Roundup Ave	79763
Rowland Ave	79763
Roxanna Ave	79761
Royal Manor Dr	79765
Royal Place Cir	79762
Royalty Ave	79761
S Ruby Ave	79766
S Ruffian Dr	79763
W Ruidoso Dr	79763
Russell Ave	79764
Ruth St	79761
Ryan Ave	79761
Saddle Dr	79763
Sadie St	79764
N & S Sage	79766
Sahuarchic	79763
Saint Andrews Dr	79762
Saint Louis Ave	79762
Saint Marys Cir & St	79765
Salinas Ave	79763
E Saltgrass St	79766
S Saltillo Ave	79766
N & S Sam Houston Ave	79761
San Andres Dr	79763
San Antonio St	79765
E San Benito Dr	79766
San Carlos Ter	79763
San Clemente Cir	79765
San Diego St	79765
San Fernando Dr	
1600-2699	79763
2800-2999	79764
San Jacinto St	79762
San Jose Dr	79765
San Juan Ct	79765
San Lucas Ct	79765
San Marcos	79765
San Marino Dr	79765
San Martin	79765
San Mateo Ln	79762
San Miguel Sq	79762
San Pedro Dr	79765
San Raphael Ct	79765
San Saba Ct & Dr	79765
San Simon St	79765
San Subia Ct & Dr	79765
Sandalwood Ln	
1400-1699	79761
2701-2797	79762
2799-2899	79762
W Sandell Ct	79764
Sandia Ct	79765
Sandra Ln	79762
Sands	79766
Sandy St	79763
N Sandyland Ave	79764
Sanson Rd	79763
Santa Ana Ct	79765
Santa Barbara Ct	79765
Santa Clara Ave	79763
Santa Cruz Ln	79763
Santa Domingo Ct	79765
Santa Elena Ct	79765
Santa Fe Dr & Pl	79765
Santa Maria Ct	79765
Santa Monica Ave	
1600-2699	79763
2700-2899	79764
Santa Rita Dr	79763
Santa Rosa Ave	
300-2699	79763
2701-2797	79764
2799-3000	79764
3002-3498	79764
Sapphire St	79762
Sardonyx Ln	79762
Sargent	79766
W Saturn St	79764
Scarlet Ave	79762
Schell St	79761
E Schirra Dr	79766
Scott	79766
Scott St	79762
N Secretariat St	79763
Seguin	79765
Seminole St	79761
N Seward Ave	79764
Shady Grove Ave & Ct	79766
Shafer Ave	79761
Shafter Ave	79761
Shakespeare Rd	79761
S Shani	79766
N Sharon Ave	79763
Shaw Ct	79762
S Shawnee Trl	79763
E Sheppard St	79766
Sherbrook Rd	79762
N Shermark Ave	79763
Sherwood St	79763
Shiloh Rd	79762
N Shirley Ave	79764
Sienna Dr	79765
N Sierra Ave	79764
Sierra Blanca St	79763
W Silver St	79766
Simms St	79761
Sioux	79763
S Sir Barton Ave	79763
Sissy Rd	79766
W Sitting Bull St	79763
N Skylark Ave	79764
Skyline Ave	79764
N Slator Ave	79764
N Slavik Ave	79764
Sleepy Hollow St	79762
Slimleaf Ct	79762
Slough Ct	79762
Smith St	79763
S Snow Moon Ave	79766
Snyder St	79761
Solo Rd	79762
Somerset Ln	79761
S Sonora Ave	79766
N Sooner Ave	
1000-2399	79763
3500-3899	79764
E South Fork St	79766
Southbrook Ct	79762
W Southern Trl	79763
S Southfork Ave	79766
N Sparta Ave	79764
W Spartan Dr	79764
W Spearman Ct	79766
N Spiro St	79764
S Spotted Fawn Dr	79763
Sprague Rd	79764
Springbrook Dr	79762
Springdale Dr	79762
Spruce Ave	79762
Spur Ave	
1000-1398	79761
1400-2699	79761
2700-2899	79762
W Stagecoach Dr	79763
Stalcup Ave	79764
Standard Ave	79761
Star Cir	79763
E Steffey Ave	79766
N Stephanie Ave	79763
Steven Rd	79764
Stevenson Ave	79762
Stillwood Ln	79762
W Stinnet Ct	79766
N Stockton Ave	
1800-2699	79763
4200-6499	79764
Stoddard St	79762
Stonegate Dr	79765
Stonehenge Rd	79765
Stoner Rd	79764
Stowe	79764
Summer Ave	79763
Summer Breeze	79762
Sun St	79763
Sundog Dr	79766
W Sundown St	79766
Sunlight St	79763
Sunnygrove Dr	79761
Sunray Dr	79764
N Sunrise Ave	79764
Sunset Blvd & Ln	79763
W Susan St	79764
W Swan Rd	79763
Sweetbriar Cir	79761
W Sycamore Dr	79763
Tammy Dr	79766
Tampico Ave	79766
Tanglewood Ln	
1300-1700	79761
1702-2198	79761
2700-2798	79762
2800-4400	79762
4402-5198	79762
S Tanna Ave	79766
Tashya	79766
Teak Dr	79764
Teakwood Dr	79761
W Teepee Trl	79763
Tennessee Dr	79764
W Teporachic St	79763
Terlingua	79761
Terminal Ln	79765
Terra Way	79762
Terrace Cir	79761
Terry Dr	79764
Texan Trl	79766
N Texas Ave	
100-198	79761
200-1800	79761
200-200	79760
1802-1898	79761
3700-3900	79762
3902-4598	79762
S Texas Ave	79761
The Villas	79765
Thistle Rd	79763
S Thomas Ave	79766
W Tierra Blanca Dr	79763
Tim Tam Cir	79763
N Timberline Ave	79764
N Timothy Dr	79763
W Tisdale Rd	79763
N Titus Ave	79763
Tobosa Ave	79765
W Todd St	79764
Tom Davis	79761
N Tom Green Ave	
2500B-2599B	79761
301-897	79761
899-2599	79761
2700-5799	79762
S Tom Green Ave	79761
Tom Morris Rd	79765
W Tomahawk Trl	79763
Tomochic	79763
Tool St	79764
Toro Ct	79765
N Torrance Ave	
1900-2699	79763
2700-2999	79764
Tower Dr	79761
Trail Dr	79766
Trails End Rd	79762
S Trainer Ave	79763
Travis Ave	79762
N Treadway Ave	79764
Tres Ct	79765
Tres Hermanas Blvd	79765
W Treva Dr	79764
W Trimble St	79764
W Triple Crown Dr	79763
N Tripp Ave	
100-2699	79763
2700-6599	79764
S Tripp Ave	79763
Troon Dr	79762
Tropicana Ave	79764
Truman St	79763
Trunk St	79762
Tuberosa Ct	79765
Tucker Rd	79765
W Tucson Dr	79763
Tulane Ave	79765
Tulip Ln	79761
Tumbleweed Ln	79764
Turnberry Ln	79765
W Turner St	79763
Twilley St	79766
Twin Oaks Cir	79762
Twin Towers Blvd	79762
Tye Ave	79764
E University Blvd	79762
W University Blvd	
200-4999	79764
5001-12999	79764
5200-12998	79764
5200-5200	79769
N Uranus Ave	79764
S Us Highway 385 N	79766
E Valencia St	79766
N Valley Ave	79764
W Valley Meadow Ln	79764
Valleybrook Ln	79761
N Valleyview Ave	79764
Valverde	79765
Van St	79763
Vassar	79761
N Vega Ave	
2600-2699	79763
2700-3799	79764
W Venita St	79763
Ventura Ave	
2200-2299	79763
2800-2999	79764
W Venus St	79764
Veranda Ct	79762

Verde Ave
1400-2699 79761
2700-2799 79762
W Vermont St 79764
Verona Dr 79765
Versailles Cir 79762
E Vfw Ln 79762
Via Del Corso Cir 79762
Via Entrada 79762
Via Playa Dr 79762
Via Saliha 79762
S Viceroy Ave 79763
Vicksburg 79766
Victor St 79762
Village Way 79762
Vine Ave 79763
Vista Pl & Plz 79761
Vista Crest Ct 79762
Vista Del Sol 79765
N Vista Grande Ave 79763
Wabash Ave 79761
S Wagon Wheel Ave 79766
Waimea 79762
Wallbrook Trl 79762
Walmart Ct 79763
Walnut Ave
1700-2499 79761
2700-3899 79762
Walnut St 79764
Walther Rd 79763
Walton Ave 79764
N & S War Admiral Dr 79763
Warbonnet Ave & Trl 79763
S Warpaint Trl 79763
N Warren Ave 79763
Warwick 79765
N Washington Ave
100-2299 79761
2301-2499 79761
2700-5399 79764
S Washington Ave 79761
Washington Ln 79761
Waverly Ave 79762
E Wavyleaf Ct 79762
Wayland Dr 79762
Wayside Ave 79762
Webb Ave 79764
N Webber Ave 79763
Wedgewood Ave 79761
Wendover Ave 79762
N Wentwood Ave 79764
West Ave 79761
W Westbend St 79764
Westbrook Ave 79761
N Westcliff Rd
100-199 79763
4200-6599 79764
S Westcliff Rd 79763
Western St 79766
N Westgate Ave 79764
W Westland Dr 79764
W Westmark St 79764
W Westmoor Rd 79764
Westover Dr 79764
W Westridge Dr 79764
W Westview Dr 79764
S Westwind Ave 79766
Westwood Dr 79763
W Whirlaway Dr 79763
Whitaker Ave 79763
White Ave 79764
Whitney Ln 79766
Whitson Ct 79762
Wicklow Ave 79763
Wildwood Ave 79761
Williams Ave 79763
Willow Dr 79765
Willow Bend St 79762
Wilshire Dr 79761
Wilson St 79763
Wimberley St 79762
Winchester Ave 79762
Windchase St 79762
Windcrest 79763
S Windmill Ave 79766
W Windsong Dr 79764
Windsor Dr
2400-2499 79761
2700-3199 79762
Windway 79763
Winfield Ave 79764
N Wingate Ave 79764
Wink Ave 79761
Winners Cir 79763
N Winston Ave 79764
W Wintergreen St 79763
S Wisteria Ave 79766
W Witcher St 79763
Wood Ct 79762
Woodhaven Dr 79762
Woodlawn Dr 79761
Woodridge Ln 79762
Wren Cv 79765
Wright Ave 79764
Wyoming Ave 79762
Yale Ave 79765
Yancy St 79765
N Yealonda Ave 79763
S Yellow Wolf Ave 79763
Yellowstone Dr 79765
Ysleta Ct 79765
Yucca Ave 79765
E Yukon Rd 79762
W Yukon Rd 79764
N Yuma Ave 79764
Zacate Dr 79765
Zacatecas Ave 79761
Zeneta Ave 79763

NUMBERED STREETS

E 1st St 79761
W 1st St
100-198 79761
200-699 79761
701-899 79761
1301-1399 79763
E 2nd St 79761
W 2nd St
101-297 79761
299-599 79761
601-699 79761
700-3299 79763
3301-3599 79763
E 3rd St 79761
W 3rd St
200-298 79761
301-399 79761
901-997 79763
999-15499 79763
E 4th St 79761
W 4th St
101-197 79761
199-400 79761
402-598 79761
800-3099 79763
E 5th St 79761
W 5th St
100-500 79761
502-698 79761
700-3099 79763
3101-3699 79763
E 6th St 79761
101-199 79761
800-3099 79763
E 7th St 79761
W 7th St
100-198 79761
301-399 79761
800-2300 79763
2302-2398 79763
E 8th St 79761
W 8th St
100-298 79761
700-4499 79763
E 9th St 79761
W 9th St
101-197 79761
199-599 79761
601-699 79761
701-997 79763
999-2499 79763
E 10th St 79761
W 10th St
100-699 79761
700-998 79763
E 11th St 79761
W 11th St
408-698 79761
1300-9899 79763
E 12th St 79761
W 12th St
200-599 79761
701-1097 79763
E 13th St 79761
100-599 79761
1000-10499 79763
E 14th St 79761
W 14th St
200-698 79761
700-998 79763
E 15th St 79761
200-699 79761
700-4399 79763
E 16th St 79761
W 16th St
101-397 79761
399-599 79761
1501-2197 79763
2199-12599 79763
E 17th St 79761
W 17th St
100-198 79761
200-499 79761
501-699 79761
800-1898 79763
1900-6999 79763
E 18th St 79761
W 18th St
200-300 79761
302-698 79761
800-1398 79763
1400-10199 79763
E 19th St 79761
W 19th St
201-297 79761
299-499 79761
501-699 79761
700-9099 79763
W 20th St
400-499 79761
700-11499 79763
E 21st St 79761
W 21st St
101-199 79761
700-7499 79763
W 22nd St
400-698 79761
800-7199 79763
E 23rd St 79761
W 23rd St
200-300 79761
800-11699 79763
E 24th St 79761
500-599 79761
800-8599 79763
E 25th St 79761
500-599 79761
800-10799 79763
W 26th St 79763
W 28th St 79764
E 29th St 79762
W 29th St 79764
E 30th St 79762
W 30th St 79764
E 31st St 79762
W 31st St 79764
W 32nd St 79764
W 33rd St 79764
W 34th St 79764
E 35th St 79762
W 35th St 79764
E 36th St 79762
W 36th St 79764
E 37th St 79762
W 37th St 79764
E 38th St 79762
W 38th St 79764
W 39th St 79764
W 40th St 79764
W 41st St 79764
E 42nd St 79762
W 42nd St 79764
E 43rd St 79762
W 43rd St 79764
E 44th St 79762
W 44th St 79764
E 45th St 79762
E 46th St 79762
W 46th St 79764
E 47th St 79762
W 47th St 79764
E 48th St 79762
W 48th St 79764
E 49th St 79762
W 49th St 79764
E 50th St 79762
W 50th St 79764
E 51st St 79762
E 52nd St
100-4600 79762
4551-4551 79768
4602-4998 79762
4701-5099 79762
W 52nd St 79764
E 53rd St 79762
W 53rd St 79764
E 54th St 79762
W 54th St 79764
E 55th St 79762
W 55th St 79764
E 56th St 79762
W 56th St 79764
E 57th St 79762
W 57th St 79764
W 58th St 79764
W 59th St 79764
E 60th St 79762
W 60th St 79764
E 61st St 79762
W 61st St 79764
W 62nd St 79764
W 63rd St 79764
W 64th St 79764
W 65th St 79764
E 67th St 79762
W 67th St 79764
W 68th St 79764
W 69th St 79764
W 81st St 79764
W 83rd St 79764
E 86th St 79765
E 87th St 79765
W 87th St 79764
E 88th St 79765
E 89th St 79765
E 91st St 79765
E 92nd St 79765
E 93rd St 79765
E 94th Ct & St 79765
E 95th St 79765
E 96th Ct & St 79765
E 97th St 79765
E 98th St 79765
99th Ct & St 79765
E 100th St 79765

ORANGE TX

General Delivery 77631

POST OFFICE BOXES MAIN OFFICE STATIONS AND BRANCHES

Box No.s
All PO Boxes 77631

RURAL ROUTES

05 77630
12, 15 77632

NAMED STREETS

Abes Dr 77632
Abigail Dr 77630
W Ada Dr 77632
Adam Cir 77630
W Adams St 77630
Admiral St 77630
Akers Rd 77630
Alabama St 77630
Alamo St 77630
Albany St 77630
Albert Dr 77630
Alden St 77630
Alder St 77630
Alice St 77632
Allie Payne Rd 77632
Alvin St 77632
Amaryliss Ave 77630
Amrock Rd 77632
Amsterdam Ave 77632
Ancar St 77630
Anderson St 77632
Anderson Villa 77630
Andy Ln 77632
Angie Ln 77632
Ann Dr 77632
Arabie Rd 77632
Arbor Dr 77630
Arkansas Ave 77630
Arledge Rd 77632
Armitage Dr 77632
Arrow Ln 77632
E & W Ashford Park 77630
Ashford Chase Dr 77630
Ashford Knoll Dr 77630
Ashland Dr 77632
Ashton Dr 77632
Aster St 77632
Atkinson Cir 77630
Audry Ln 77630
Augusta Dr 77630
Austin St 77630
Autumn Oak Ln 77632
Avenue A 77630
Avenue B 77630
Avenue C 77630
Ayrshire Dr 77632
Azalea Ave 77630
Bancroft Rd 77632
W Bancroft St 77630
Barbara St 77632
Barkins Ave & St 77630
Barrett St 77630
Bassett St 77632
Battlin Bear Dr 77632
Bay St 77630
Bayou Bnd 77630
Bayou Pines Ln 77630
Beadle Rd 77630
Beagle Rd 77630
Bean Rd 77632
Bear Trl 77632
Bear Path Dr 77632
Bearfoot Rd 77632
Beechwood Dr 77632
Bellcrest Ave 77630
Ben Mac Rd 77632
Benson Rd 77632
Bentwater Dr 77632
Bentwood Dr 77630
Bessie Heights Rd 77630
Betsy Ln 77632
Beverly Ave 77632
Beverly Dr 77630
Big Oak St 77632
N Bilbo Rd 77632
S Bilbo Rd 77632
W Bilbo St 77630
Bill Ln 77632
Birdie Reed St 77630
Bishop St 77630
Black Oak Dr 77632
Blackberry St 77632
Bland Ln 77632
Bland Rd 77632
W Bland St 77630
Blue Bird Ln 77632
Bluebird St 77630
Bluebonnet Dr 77630
Bluewing Ct 77630
W Bluff Rd 77632
Bob Hall Rd
2500-2600 77630
2602-3398 77630
3400-4798 77632
4800-4900 77632
4902-5598 77632
Bobcat Cir 77632
Boilermaker Dr 77630
Bolton Rd 77630
Bonham St 77630
Bonnie St 77630
Border St 77630
Boston St 77630
Bourque Cir & Ln 77630
Bowie St 77630
Bowling Ln 77630
Boxelder 77630
W Brackinwood St 77632
Bradford St 77630
Brandy Ln 77632
Breckinwood St 77632
Brent Dr 77632
Brevell Ln 77632
Brewer Rd 77632
Briarhill Ave 77632
Bridal Wreath Ave 77630
E & W Bridgefield Dr 77630
Briggs Dr & Rd 77630
Broad St 77630
Broke Rd 77632
Brookshire Dr 77630
Broussard Ave 77630
Broussard Cir 77632
Brown Rd 77632
Brown St 77630
Browning Rd 77630
Bruce Ln 77630
Bubba Rd 77632
Buckingham Dr 77632
Buffalo Ave & St 77630
Buller Ln 77630
Burdine St 77632
Burn Cir 77630
Burnet St 77630
Burr Oak Dr 77632
Burton Ave 77630
N Burton Rd 77632
S Burton Rd 77630
Business Row 77632
Buster Rd 77632
Butler Dr 77630
Byley Blvd 77630
Byron Rd 77630
C St 77632
C J K Ranch Rd 77630
Cajun Way 77630
E & W California St 77630
Callie Ln 77632
Cambridge 77632
Camellia Ave 77630
Camelot St 77630
Campbell Rd 77632
Campus St 77630
Canal St 77632
Canary St 77630
Candlewick Dr 77632
Canter St 77632
Canterbury Dr 77632
Canvasback Ct 77630
Cardinal St 77630
Caribou Dr & Ext 77630
Carlene 77632
Carlton St 77632
Carlyle Dr 77632
Carol St 77630
Carolyn Dr 77632
Carpenter Cir, Ext & Rd 77630
Carpenters Place Dr 77630
Carrie Dr 77632
Carter St 77630
Cedar Ln & Rdg 77632
Center St 77630
Champion Dr 77632
Chapman Ln 77632
Chapman St 77630
Charlotte St 77632
Chasse Gdns & Knl 77632
Chasse Bend St 77632
Chasse Ridge Dr 77632
Chasse Stone Dr 77632
Chaucer Dr 77632
Chauncy St 77632
Chelseas Cir 77632
Cherokee Trl 77632
W Cherry Aly & Ave 77630
Cheryl Ln 77632
Chester St 77630
Chestnut Dr 77632
Chevron St 77630
S Childers Dr & Rd 77630
Chimney Rock Dr 77630
Chisholm Rd 77632
Church St
1500-1899 77630
5100-5499 77632
Church House Rd 77630
Circle E & S 77630
Circle 1 77632
Circle 10 77632
Circle 2 77632
Circle 3 77632
Circle 4 77632
Circle 5 77632
Circle 6 77632
Circle 7 77632
Circle 8 77632
Circle 9 77632
Circle C St 77630
Circle C Ranch Rd 77630
Circle D 77630
Circle F 77630
Circle G 77630
Circle P 77630
Circle Q 77630
Circle R 77630
Claire Dr 77630
Clairmont Dr 77630
Clarence Dr 77630
Clark Cir 77632
Clark Ln 77632
Clark St 77630
Claudia Dr 77632
Cleo St 77632
Clewis Rd 77630
Cobb Ln 77632
Cochran St 77630
Coggins Ln 77630
Cohenour Rd 77632
Coke St 77630
Colburn Ave 77630
College St 77630
S College St 77632
Collins St 77630
Colman Ln 77632
Colonial Dr 77630
Colony Dr & Ln 77632
Colt Cir 77632
Concord St 77630
Cooper Dr 77630
Cooper St 77632
Cordrey Ave & St 77630
Cordwood Cir 77630
Cormier Rd 77630
Coronado Pl 77630
Cortim Cir 77630
Cosmos St 77632
Cottonwood Ln 77632
Country Club Dr 77630
County Road 3125 77632
County Road 3126 77632
County Road 3127 77632
County Road 3128 77632
County Road 3129 77632

Street	ZIP
County Road 3130	77632
County Road 3131	77632
County Road 3134	77630
County Road 3139	77632
County Road 3140	77632
County Road 3141	77632
County Road 3142	77632
County Road 3144	77632
County Road 3145	77632
County Road 3146	77632
County Road 3147	77632
County Road 3148	77632
County Road 3149	77632
County Road 3175	77632
County Road 4128	77632
County Road 4129	77632
County Road 4130	77632
County Road 4131	77632
County Road 4134	77632
County Road 4135	77632
County Road 4138	77632
County Road 4164	77632
County Road 4170	77632
County Road 4171	77632
County Road 4173	77632
County Road 4174	77632
County Road 4175	77632
County Road 4176	77632
County Road 4177	77632
County Road 4179	77632
County Road 4181	77632
County Road 4182	77632
County Road 4183	77632
County Road 4184	77632
County Road 4185	77632
County Road 4186	77632
County Road 4187	77632
County Road 4188	77632
County Road 4189	77632
County Road 4190	77632
County Road 4191	77632
County Road 4192	77632
County Road 4199	77632
County Road 4201	77632
County Road 4202	77632
County Road 4203	77632
County Road 4204	77632
County Road 4205	77632
County Road 4206	77632
County Road 4209	77632
County Road 4211	77632
County Road 4212 S	77632
County Road 4213	77632
County Road 4214	77632
County Road 4215	77632
County Road 4216	77632
County Road 4217	77632
County Road 4218	77632
County Road 4219	77632
County Road 4220	77632
County Road 4221	77632
County Road 4222	77632
County Road 4223	77632
County Road 4224	77632
County Road 4225	77632
County Road 4227	77632
County Road 4228	77632
County Road 4229	77632
County Road 4230	77632
County Road 4231	77632
County Road 4232	77632
County Road 4233	77632
County Road 4234	77632
County Road 4235	77632
County Road 4238	77632
County Road 4950	77632
County Road 4960	77632
County Road 4970	77632
County Road 4995	77632
County Road 7077	77632
County Road 824	77632
County Road 825	77632
County Road 8974	77632
County Road 8990	77632
Courtland St	77630
Cove Dr	77630
Cowboy Trl	77632
Cowpen Rd	77632
Crabtree St	77630
Craft Ln	77632
Craig St	77630
Crater Rd	77630
Creek Rd	77630
Crepe Myrtle Ave	77630
Crockett St	77630
Cross Ln	77630
Crosstimber Dr	77632
Cub Trl	77632
W Curtis Ave	77630
W Cypress Ave	77630
Cypress Mdw	77632
Cypress Wood Dr	77630
Cypresswood Dr	77630
Dahlia St	77630
Dailey Rd	77632
Daisey Ln	77632
Dakota St	77630
Dal Sasso Dr	77630
N & S Dana	77632
Daniel Cir	77630
Darlene	77630
Dartez Rd	77632
Davis St	77630
Dawnwood	77632
Day Farm Rd	77632
Dayton St	77630
Dearing Rd	77630
Debra Ln	77630
E & W Decatur Ave	77630
W Decker Ave	77630
Delaney Dr	77632
Delano St	77630
Dempsey Dr	77630
Dennis St	77632
Devin St	77632
W Dewey Ave	77630
Dewitt Dr	77630
Dickens Dr	77632
Dikeman Ln	77630
W Division Ave	77630
Dogwood St	77632
W Dogwood St	77630
Dolley Dr	77632
Dolores St	77632
Donna Ln	77632
Donnell St	77630
Dorman Rd	77630
Dorman Cemetary Rd	77630
Dougharty Rd	77632
Dowling St	77632
Dronett St	77630
Duhon St	
2000-2299	77632
6300-6599	77630
E Duhon St	77632
S Duhon St	77632
W Duhon St	77632
Duncan Woods Ln	77630
Dunn Ln, Loop & Rd	77632
Dunromin Rd	77632
Dupont Dr	77630
Durso Rd	77632
W Eads Ave	77630
Earsel Rd	77632
Eastway Dr	77630
Eastwood	77632
Echo Ave & Loop	77632
Ector St	77630
Eddie St	77632
Eddleman Rd	77632
W Edgar Dr & St	77630
Edgar Brown Dr	77630
Edgemont Dr	77630
Edinburgh Dr	77632
Egan Dr	77630
Eight Gate Rd	77632
Elizabeth Ln & St	77632
Elk Dr	77630
Elkport St	77630
Ellis Ln & St	77632
Elm St	77632
W Elm St	77630
Elma Dr	77630
Emerson Rd	77630
Enchanted Oaks St	77630
Encore Cir	77630
Englewood Dr	77632
Enner Rd	
2700-2899	77630
2900-3099	77632
Erie St	77630
Essence Ln	77630
Ester St	77630
Eva St	77630
Evergreen Dr	77632
Evergreen St	77630
Ewing Dr	77632
Express Ln	77632
Exxon St	77630
Fairview Dr	77630
Fairway Dr	77630
E Farragut Ave	77630
Fawn	77632
Fernbrook	77632
Fernwood	77632
Finch Rd	77632
Finwick Dr	77632
Firelight	77630
Fish Farm Rd	77632
Flamingo St	77630
Flicker St	77630
Flint St	77630
Flintport Cir	77630
Florence St	
100-299	77630
1400-2699	77632
E & W Florida St	77630
Fm 1006	77630
Fm 105	77630
Fm 1078	77630
Fm 1130	77632
Fm 1135	77630
Fm 1136	77632
Fm 1442	
900-11999	77630
Fm 1442	
12000-17999	77632
Fm 2802	77632
Fm 3247	77632
Fm 408	77630
Fm 736	77632
Ford Ln	77632
Foreman Rd	77630
Foreman Cutoff	77630
Forest Dr	77630
E & W Fox Rd	77632
Foxtrot Dr	77632
Frederick Ln & Rd	77632
Friartuck Dr	77632
W Front St	77630
Frost Pl	77630
Frostwood Dr	77632
Furlough Loop & Rd	77632
Gail St	77632
Galveston St	77630
Gandy St	77630
Gans Ave	77630
Garden Ln	77632
Gardenia Ave	77630
Garner Rd	77632
Garrison Dr, Ln & Rd	77630
Gaylynn Dr	77632
Gentry St	77630
Georgia Ave	77630
Gilbert Dr	77632
Gladys Ave	77630
Glenda Dr	77630
Glenhurst St	77632
Glenwood Dr	77630
Glidden St	77632
Gloria Dr & St	77630
Godfrey St	77632
Godwin Cir & Rd	77630
Golden Oak Dr	77632
Gordan Ln	77632
Goss Rd	77632
Gracie Ln	77632
Grand Ct	77630
W Granger Ln	77630
Grapevine Dr	77630
Gratis Ln	77632
Green Ave	77630
Green Brier Dr	77630
Green Wing Ln	77630
Greenbriar Ave	77632
Greenbriar St	77630
Greenhead Pt	77630
E & S Greenwood Dr	77630
Gregory Cir	77630
Guillory Rd	77632
Gulf Rd	77630
Gull St	77630
Gunn Dr	77630
Gunstream Ln	77630
Gus Ln	77632
Guy Ln	77632
Gypsy	77632
H P Dr	77632
Hada Ln	77630
Hager Dr	77630
Hall Rd	77630
Happy Home Dr	77632
E Harding Cir	77630
W Harding Cir	77632
N Harding St	77632
S Harding St	77632
W Harding St	77632
Harmon Rd	77630
Harris Rd	77632
N Hart Ave	77630
Hartzog Rd	77632
Hawthorne St	77630
Hazelwood	77632
Head St	77632
Hearthside Dr	77630
Hemlock Ln	77630
Henderson Ave	77630
Henrietta St	77630
Henry St	77630
Heron St	77630
Herrington Rd	77630
Hibiscus Dr	77632
W Hickory Ave	77630
Hickory Dr	77630
Hickory Rd	77630
Hickory Trl	77630
Hickory Bend Dr	77632
Hidden Meadows Dr	77632
Hidden Oak Dr	77630
Highland Ave	77632
Highland Park Dr	77632
Highlander	77630
Highline Rd	77632
Highway 12	77632
Highway 62 N	77632
Highway 62 S	77630
Highway 87 N	77632
Highway 87 S	77630
Hiler Rd	77632
Hillbrook Dr	77632
Hillcrest	77632
Hilltop St	77630
Hilton Ave	77630
N Hird St	77630
Hoffpauir Rd	77632
Hogg St	77630
Holcomb Rd	77632
Holiman Cir	77632
Holland St	77630
Holley Ln	77630
Hollis Ln	
4300-8999	77630
11000-11699	77632
Hollis Rd	77630
Holly Dr	77630
N Holly Ln	77632
Holly Rdg	77630
Holly St	77630
Honey Bear Dr	77632
Honeysuckle Dr	77632
Honeywood Rd	77632
E & W Hoo Hoo Rd	77630
Horseshoe Bnd	77632
Houston St	77630
Hudnall Rd	77632
Hudson Rd	77632
Huey Dr	77632
Huff Dr	77632
Humble St	77630
Huntsman St	77632
Huntwick Dr	77632
Hydrangea Ave	77630
Inez Ave & Rd	77630
Inland Rd	77632
International Ave	77632
Interstate 10 E	77630
Interstate 10 W	77632
W Inwood Dr	77630
Inwood Circle A	77630
Inwood Circle B	77630
Irene St	77630
Ironwood Dr	77632
Irving St	77630
Isabell Dr	77632
Ivy Ln	
2000-2399	77632
4800-4999	77630
J B Arrington Rd	77630
Jackie St	77630
Jackson Ave	77630
Jackson Dr	77632
Jacob Cir	77630
Japanese Ln	77630
Jason Ln	77630
Jasper St	77630
Jayway St	77630
Jedry	77632
Jeffery Ln	77632
Jenkins Rd	77632
Jerry St	77630
Jetry P St	77632
Jewel Dr	77630
Jim Brown Rd	77630
Joan Cir	77630
Joe Ln	77632
Joel St	77630
W John Ave	77630
John Baker Cir	77630
Johnnie St	77630
Johnson Rd	77632
Jones Rd	77630
Jordan Ln	77630
Joshua Cir	77630
Joyce St	77630
Juanita St	77630
June St	77630
Juniper St	77630
Kagle Ln	77632
Kaiyute Rd	77632
Karen Rd	77632
Karr Rd	77630
Katherine St	77630
Kathleen St	77630
Kathy St	77632
Kayla St	77632
Kayleigh Rd	77632
Kelly St	77630
Kennedy Cir	77630
Kenneth Dr	77632
E & W Kentucky St	77630
Kenwood St	77630
Kestrel East Rd	77632
Kestrel West Rd	77632
Kibodeaux Rd	77630
Killian Rd	77632
Kinard Ln	77632
Kinder Steel Loop	77630
Kindling Cir	77630
King St	77630
King Arthur Ct	77630
Kings Ct	77630
Kippers Ct	77632
W & N Kirby Ave & St	77632
Kirk Dr	77630
Kisatchia Ln	77632
Kitty Chapin Ave	77632
Knolderl Rd	77632
Knotty Pine Ln	77630
Knox Ave	77630
Koala Rd	77632
Kobs Korner	77632
Kountze St	77630
Kristi Ln	77630
Kusnir Loop	77632
Kyle Rd	77630
La Fleur Rd	77630
Lakeshore Dr	77632
Lakeside Dr	77630
Lamar St	77630
Lamurel Willey Rd	77632
Lancaster Dr	77632
Lancelot St	77630
E & W Landon Ln	77632
Landsbury Ln	77630
Lane Of The Oaks	77630
Langford Forest Blvd	77630
Langham Forest Blvd	77630
Langham West Rd	77630
Lansing St	77630
N & S Lantana	77632
Lariat Loop	77632
Lark St	77630
Laura Dr & Ln	77630
Laurel St	77630
Lauren Dr	77630
Lawanda Ln	77632
Lawn Oak Dr	77632
Lawndale Ave	77630
Lawrence Rd	77630
Lazy Ln	77632
Lazy L Ln	77632
Lazy Pines Dr	77632
Lea St	77632
Leblanc St	77630
Ledoux Rd	77630
Lee Dr	77630
Lemonville Ln	77632
Len Dr	77630
Leonard Rd	77632
Lesleigh Cir	77632
Levingston St	77630
N Lewis Dr	77632
S Lewis Rd	77632
Lexington Dr	77630
Lilac Ave	77630
Lincoln Dr	77630
Linda Ln	77630
Linda St	
100-299	77630
2200-2599	77632
Lindenwood Dr	77630
Link Ave	77630
Linscomb Rd	
2500-3499	77630
7700-9399	77632
Liprie St	77630
Lisa Ln	77630
Liston Rd	77630
Liston Cut Off Rd	77630
Little Cypress Dr	77632
Live Oak Rd	77630
Loblolly Rd	77632
Lois	77632
Lola St	77632
London Cir	77632
Lone Star Trl	77630
Long Spur Dr	77630
Longfellow Rd	77630
Longhorn Ave	77630
Longleaf	77630
Longleaf Ln	77632
Loop 3247	77630
Loring Ln	77630
Louisiana St	77630
Love Ln	77632
E Lutcher Ave	77630
W Lutcher Ave	77630
Lutcher Dr	
100-500	77632
502-4698	77632
511-699	77630
701-799	77632
801-1899	77630
2001-2099	77632
2201-2899	77630
4601-4699	77632
E Lutcher Dr	77632
Lutcher Circle A	77630
Lutcher Circle B	77630
W Luther Dr	77632
Lydia St	77632
Lynne Cir	77630
Lyre St	77630
Macarthur Cir & Dr	77630
Magnolia Cir, Dr, Ln & St	77632
Mahogany St	77632
Main Ave	77630
Mandi Rd	77630
Manley Cir	77630
S Mansfield Ferry Rd	77630
Maple Ave & St	77632
Maplewood	77632
Margaret St	77632
Marguarite Dr	77632
Marilyn Cir & Ct	77630
Market St	77630
Martha Dr	77632
Marthas Ln	77630
Martin St	77630
Martin Luther King Jr Dr	
2498A-2498C	77630
Maryland St	77630
Mason Rd	77632
Masonic Dr	77630
E & W Massachusetts St	77630
Maxwell Cir	77630
May Haw Dr	77632
Mccabe	77632
Mccartney Dr	77632
Mcclelland Rd	77632
Mcfarland Cir	77632
Mcgill Rd	77630
Mcguire Ln	77632
Mckee Dr	77630
N & S Meadow Dr	77630
Meadow Mist St	77632
Meadowlark Dr	77632
Med Davis Rd	77632
Medford Dr	77632
Meeks Dr	77632
Melani Ln	77632
Melcer Dr	77632
Melwood Dr	77630
Memorial Dr	77632
Memphis St	77630
Mesquite Dr	77632
Meyers Rd	77632
Mica Cir	77630
Michael Dr	77632
Michell Rd	77630
Michell St	77632
Michelle Rd	77632
Mickler Dr	77632
Middle St	77630
Midway Dr	77630
E Milam St	77630
Mill St	77630
W Miller St	77630
N Mimosa Ln	77632
S Mimosa Ln	77630
Mimosa Loop	77630
Mississippi St	77630
Missouri St	77630
Mistletoe Dr	77630
Mitchell Dr	77632
Moak Ln	77632
Mockingbird St	77630
Montclair	77632
Monterrey Dr	77630
Montrose St	77632
Moore St	77630
Moose Ln	77630
Morgan Ln	77632
Morrell Blvd	77630
Morris Ln	77632
Morris Rd	77632
Morris St	77630
Morrison Cir	77630
Mortar St	77632
Morvant Rd	77632

Mosier Rd 77632
Moss Ave 77630
Moss Ln 77632
Mouton Ln 77630
Mulberry St
  100-299 77630
  8800-8899 77632
E Murf St 77632
Mustang Ave 77630
Myers St 77630
Myrtle St 77630
Nan Dr 77632
S Naquin Rd 77630
Nash St 77630
Nat Ln 77630
Natalie St 77632
Neches St 77630
Nell St 77632
Nelson St 77630
E & W New Jersey St 77630
E & W New York St 77630
Newton St 77630
Nightingale St 77630
Noah Dr 77630
Nobles Rd 77630
Nora Cir 77630
E & W Norman Cir 77630
Norris Ln 77632
North St 77630
Northbend Rd 77632
Northmont Dr 77632
Northridge Dr 77632
Norwood Dr & St 77630
Not Possum 77632
Nottingham Dr 77632
Oak Gln 77630
Oak Ln 77632
Oak Rd 77630
Oak Vis 77630
Oak Crest Dr 77632
Oak Forest Dr 77632
Oak Glen Dr 77632
Oak Leaf Dr 77632
Oak Shadows 77630
Oak Valley Dr 77632
Oakmont Dr 77630
Oakwood Cir 77630
E & W Ohio St 77630
Oil Patch Rd 77630
Oilla Rd 77630
Old Castle Ln 77630
Old Cattle Xing 77630
Old Champion Rd 77632
Old Highway 62 77632
Old Highway 87 77632
Old Highway 90 77630
Old Oak Dr 77632
Old Peveto Rd 77632
Old Timers Rd 77630
Oleander Dr 77632
Oliver Rd 77632
Optimist Way 77630
W Orange Ave 77630
Orangefield Rd 77630
E & W Oregon St 77630
Osage St 77630
Ospray St 77630
Owens Rd 77632
Owens Illinois Rd 77632
Oxford Dr 77632
Pacific Cir & St 77630
Paige Dr 77630
Palm Dr 77630
Palmer Dr 77632
Paloma St 77632
Pampa St 77630
Panda Rd 77632
Panther Run & Xing 77632
Paris Dr 77632
Parish Rd 77632
Parish Cemetery Rd 77632
W Park Aly, Ave & Pl 77630
Parkland Dr 77632
Parkwood 77630
Pat Dr 77630
S Patillo Cir & Rd 77630

Patricia Ln 77632
Pea Farm Rd 77632
Peach St 77630
Peacock St 77630
Pearson St 77630
Pebble Beach Ln 77630
Pecamp Rd 77632
Pecan Dr 77632
Peet Tree Rd 77632
Pelican St 77630
Pepper Rd 77630
Periwinkle Dr 77630
Perry Rd 77632
Peru Rd 77632
N Peveto Cir 77630
S Peveto Cir 77630
Peveto Ln 77632
Peveto Rd 77630
Pheasant St 77630
Pier Rd 77630
N Pin Oak 77632
Pin Oak Cir 77630
Pin Oak Dr
  1-99 77630
  500-699 77632
Pine Ave 77630
Pine Rdg 77632
Pine St 77632
Pine Bluff Rd 77632
Pine Grove Dr 77630
Pine Needle Dr 77632
Pine Park Blvd 77632
Pinemont Dr 77632
Pinewood Cir 77630
Pintail Ln 77630
Pinto Cir 77632
Pipeline Rd 77630
Plantation Dr 77630
Plum St 77632
Poe Rd 77630
Polar Rd 77632
Polk Ave 77630
Pontinti St 77630
Post Oak Dr 77632
Power House Rd 77630
Private Road 4220 77632
Private Road 7077 77632
Private Road 7078 77632
Private Road 7079 77632
Private Road 7115 77632
Private Road 8094 77632
Private Road 8096 77632
Private Road 8097 77632
Private Road 8098 77632
Private Road 8100 77632
Private Road 8102 77632
Private Road 8105 77632
Private Road 8107 77632
Private Road 8109 77632
Private Road 8110 77632
Private Road 8111 77632
Private Road 8112 77632
Private Road 8113 77632
Private Road 8114 77632
Private Road 8115 77632
Private Road 8116 77632
Private Road 8117 77632
Private Road 8118 77632
Private Road 8119 77632
Private Road 8135 77632
Private Road 8138 77632
Private Road 8157 77632
Private Road 8160 77632
Private Road 8165 77632
Private Road 8175 77632
Private Road 8185 77632
Private Road 8190 77632
Private Road 8195 77632
Private Road 8200 77632
Private Road 8205 77632
Private Road 8210 77632
Private Road 8215 77632
Private Road 8220 77632
Private Road 8809 77632
Private Road 8940 77632
Private Road 8950 77632

Private Road 8955 77632
Private Road 8974 77632
Private Road 8990 77632
Putnam Ave 77630
Quail Dr
  1100-1599 77630
  2200-2399 77632
  9000-9099 77630
Quail Ridge Rd 77632
Quail Trail Rd 77632
Queen Ln 77632
Queens Ct 77630
Quiet Oaks 77630
Quincy St 77630
Railroad Ave 77632
Rainbow Rd 77632
Raintree Ln 77630
Randall Rd & St 77632
Rash Ln 77632
Raven St 77630
Red Bud Dr 77632
Red Oak Dr 77632
Redbird Cir & St 77630
Redwood Dr 77632
Regency Pl 77630
Rein Ave 77630
Rhode Island St 77630
Richard Dr 77630
Ridgemont Dr 77630
Rio Grande Pl 77630
Risa Ln 77632
Riverside Dr 77630
Roberts St 77630
Robin Ave 77632
Roger St 77632
Rolling Rdg 77632
Rose Ln 77632
Rosebud St 77632
Rosewood Dr 77632
E & W Roundbunch
Rd 77630
Royal Oak Ln 77630
Royal Oaks Cir 77632
Ruby Ln 77630
Rue Des Fleurs 77632
Rugby Dr 77632
Sabine Ave 77630
Sage Rd 77632
Sagebrush Rd 77632
Sand Bar Rd 77632
Sand Pit Rd 77632
Sandalwood Dr
  700-899 77632
  4800-4999 77630
Sandra Ln 77632
Saxon Cir & Ln 77632
Saylor Way 77632
Scales Ln 77630
Schley Ave 77630
W Scott St 77630
Sepulvado St 77630
Shadowdale Ln 77632
Shady Ln 77630
Shaffers Ln 77630
Shakespeare Dr 77632
Shangrila Dr 77630
Share Ln 77630
Sharlane Dr 77632
Sharon St 77632
Sheila Dr 77632
Shelly Dr 77630
Sheppard Rd 77630
Sheridan Dr 77630
Sherrill St 77630
Sherry St 77632
Sherwood Dr 77632
Shirley St 77632
Sholars Ave 77630
Sikes Rd 77632
Silver Leaf Dr 77632
Silver Oaks Dr 77632
Simmons Dr 77630
Simon Dr 77630
Simpson Ave 77630
Sims St 77630
Singletary St 77632

Skeeter Dr 77632
Slaby Rd 77632
Smith St 77630
Soapy Sud Rd 77632
Soaring Forrest Dr 77632
Soileau St 77630
Somerset St 77630
Sonnier Dr 77632
South Ave 77630
Sparks Rd 77632
Sparrow St 77630
Spell St 77630
Spooner 77630
Spring Oak Ln 77632
Stacy St 77630
Stagner Ln 77632
Stakes St 77630
Stallion Rd 77632
Stanton Dr 77630
Stark Aly 77630
Stark Rd 77632
Starling St 77630
State Highway 12 E &
W 77632
State Highway 87 S 77632
Stately Ct 77630
Steeple Chasse Dr 77632
Stephanie Dr 77630
Stephenson Rd 77632
Stevenson St 77630
Stonebriar Cir & Dr 77632
Stoneridge Dr 77632
Stonewood Dr 77632
Stori Ln 77630
Stradford Dr 77632
Stratford Dr 77632
Strickland Dr 77630
Strong Rd 77630
Stuart Dr 77632
Sullivan Ln 77632
Summer Ln 77632
Summer Oak Ln 77632
Summerville Ln 77632
Summerwood Dr 77632
Suncrest Dr 77630
Sunrise Oaks Dr 77630
E & W Sunset Dr 77630
Sunset Circle A 77632
Sunset Circle B 77632
Sunset Oaks Dr 77630
E & W Susan Cir 77630
Swallow St 77630
Sweet Bay 77630
Sweet Gum St 77632
Swisher St 77632
Sycamore Bnd 77630
Sycamore St 77632
Tall Oaks Dr 77632
Tall Pine Ln 77632
Tallant 77630
Tallow Trl 77630
Tammy Cir 77632
Tanager St 77630
E Tanager Trl 77632
W Tanager Trl 77632
Tanglebrush Trl 77632
Tanglewood Dr & St 77630
Taylor Cir 77630
Teal Dr 77630
Teal Rd 77632
N Teal Rd 77632
S Teal Rd 77632
Tejas Pkwy 77632
Tenneil Dr 77630
E & W Tennessee St 77630
Tennyson Dr 77632
Terrace Cir 77630
Terri Ln 77632
Terry Rd & St 77630
Terry Estates Dr 77630
Texas Ave 77630
Thames Dr 77632
Theriot Rd 77632
Thomas Rd 77632
Thousand Oaks Dr 77632
Thunderbird Dr 77630

Tick Ln 77630
Tilley Cir 77630
Tillie Smith 77630
Timberland Dr 77632
Timberlane Cir 77630
Timco Dr 77630
Tin Top Arena Rd 77632
Tomcat Trl 77632
Tootie Rd 77630
Tower Rd 77630
Trace Pt 77632
Trailwood 77632
Tranquility Rd 77632
Travis St 77630
Treeline Rd 77632
Treemont Ln 77630
Trinity Rd 77630
Trophy Ln 77632
Tulane Rd 77630
Tupelo 77630
Turner Rd 77630
W Turrett Rd 77630
Turtle Rd 77632
Twin Acres 77632
Twin Lakes Dr 77632
Twin Oaks
  2300-2499 77630
Twin Oaks
  2501-2599 77630
  5100-5199 77632
Tyler Dr 77630
Utopia St 77630
Valda Dr 77630
Valhalla Ln 77630
Valley Oak Dr 77632
Vayon 77630
W Veazy St 77630
Velma Jeter Dr 77632
Vergie Ln 77632
Verrett Rd 77630
Victory Cir & Ln 77630
Victpar Dr 77630
Vincent St 77630
Vireo St 77630
Wade Rd 77632
Wagner Dr & Ln 77632
Waldrep 77630
Walea Dr 77632
Walles Ln 77630
Walnut Ave 77632
Warbler Ln & St 77630
Warren St 77630
Washateria Rd 77632
Water St 77630
Waterford Dr
  1-99 77630
  1400-1499 77632
Waterwood Dr 77630
Wayne Rd 77632
Wendi Ln 77632
Westbend 77632
Westbury St 77630
Westchester Dr 77630
Western Ave 77630
Westmore Ave 77630
Westway St 77630
Westwood Dr 77630
N & S Wheaton St 77632
Whippoorwill St 77630
Whisper Ln 77630
White Cedar Ln 77632
White Oak Rd 77632
Whitman Rd 77630
Wickard Dr 77630
Wicklow Dr 77632
Widgeon Dr 77630
Wildwood Ave 77632
Wilhite Ln 77632
Wilkinson Ln & Rd 77632
Will Ln 77630
Williams St 77630
Williamson Rd 77632
Willougby St 77630
Willow St 77632
Willowglen St 77632
Wilson Ave 77632

Windham Cir 77630
Windham Rd 77632
Windsor St 77632
W Windy Ln 77630
Winfree Rd 77630
Winlin Dr 77632
Womack Rd 77632
W Wood Dr 77632
Wood Thrush 77630
Woodcock St 77630
E & W Woodfern 77630
Woodland Cir 77630
Woodland Dr 77632
Woodland Trl 77630
Woodland Ridge Dr 77632
Woodlark St 77630
Woodmont Dr 77632
Woodpark Cir 77630
Woodridge Dr 77632
Woodway Dr 77630
E & W Wooten 77632
Wren St 77630
Wrenway 77630
E Wyatt Paul Ln 77632
E Wynne Rd 77632
Yaupon St 77630
Yeary Rd 77632
Yorkshire Dr 77632
Young Ln 77630
Young Riders Rd 77632
Yupon Rd 77630
Zavalla Rd 77632
Zeto Dr 77630
Zinnia St 77630
Zurich Dr 77632

NUMBERED STREETS

1st Ave 77630
1st St
  200-1899 77630
  2200-2299 77632
2nd Ave & St 77630
3rd Ave 77630
3rd St
  200-2225 77630
  2227-2239 77632
  2301-2305 77630
  2324-2398 77632
  2325-2599 77630
4th Aly, Ave & St 77630
5th St 77630
6th St 77630
7th St 77630
8th St 77630
9th St 77630
10th St 77630
11th St 77630
12th St 77630
13th St 77630
14th St 77630
N 15th 77630
16th St 77632
  200-3299 77630
  3700-4599 77632
N 16th St Aly 77630
17th St 77630
18th St 77630
19th St 77630
20th St 77630
21st St 77630
23rd St 77630
24th St 77630
26th St 77630
27th St 77632
28th St 77630
29th St 77630
30th St 77630
31st St 77630
33rd St 77630
34th St 77630
35th St 77630
N 37th 77630
39th St 77630
40th St 77630
41st St 77630

N 41st St 77632
43rd St 77630
S 44th St 77630

PALESTINE TX

General Delivery 75801

POST OFFICE BOXES MAIN OFFICE STATIONS AND BRANCHES

Box No.s
All PO Boxes 75802

RURAL ROUTES

01, 05, 08, 11, 14 75801
02, 03, 04, 06, 07, 09,
10, 12, 13 75803

NAMED STREETS

Academy Dr 75801
Alabama St 75803
Aleta Dr 75801
Alpine St 75801
Alta Vista St 75803
An County Road 1100 75801
An County Road 1231 75801
An County Road 1232 75801
An County Road 1233 75801
An County Road 137 75801
An County Road 1370 75801
An County Road 1371 75801
An County Road 1372 75801
An County Road 139 75801
An County Road 140 75801
An County Road 1400 75801
An County Road 1405 75801
An County Road 142 75801
An County Road 144 75801
An County Road 145 75801
An County Road 146 75801
An County Road 147 75801
An County Road 148 75801
An County Road 149 75801
An County Road 150
  101-797 75801
  799-1700 75801
  1702-1898 75801
  4700-4799 75803
An County Road 151 75801
An County Road 1516 75801
An County Road 152 75801
An County Road 153 75801
An County Road 154 75801
An County Road 1553 75801
An County Road 156 75801
An County Road 157 75801
An County Road 159 75801
An County Road 160 75801
An County Road 1612 75801
An County Road 163 75801
An County Road 1635 75801
An County Road 197 75801
An County Road 198 75801
An County Road 199 75801
An County Road 2101 75801
An County Road 2103 75801
An County Road 2104 75801
An County Road 2105 75801
An County Road 2106 75801
An County Road 2107 75801
An County Road 2108 75801
An County Road 2116 75801
An County Road 2117 75801
An County Road 2120 75801
An County Road 2121 75801
An County Road 2122 75801
An County Road 2123 75801
An County Road 2124 75801

An County Road 2125 ... 75801
An County Road 2126 ... 75801
An County Road 2127 ... 75801
An County Road 2128 ... 75801
An County Road 2129 ... 75801
An County Road 2130 ... 75801
An County Road 2133 ... 75801
An County Road 2134 ... 75801
An County Road 2135 ... 75801
An County Road 2136 ... 75801
An County Road 2137 ... 75801
An County Road 2138 ... 75801
An County Road 2139 ... 75801
An County Road 2140 ... 75801
An County Road 2141 ... 75801
An County Road 2142 ... 75801
An County Road 2143 ... 75801
An County Road 2144 ... 75801
An County Road 2145 ... 75801
An County Road 2146 ... 75801
An County Road 2147 ... 75801
An County Road 2148 ... 75801
An County Road 2150 ... 75801
An County Road 2151 ... 75801
An County Road 2201 ... 75803
An County Road 2202 ... 75803
An County Road 2203 ... 75803
An County Road 2204 ... 75803
An County Road 2205 ... 75803
An County Road 2206 ... 75803
An County Road 2207 ... 75803
An County Road 2208 ... 75803
An County Road 2209 ... 75803
An County Road 2210 ... 75803
An County Road 2211 ... 75803
An County Road 2212 ... 75803
An County Road 2213 ... 75803
An County Road 2215 ... 75803
An County Road 2232 ... 75803
An County Road 2233 ... 75803
An County Road 2234 ... 75803
An County Road 2703 ... 75803
An County Road 2811 ... 75803
An County Road 2812 ... 75803
An County Road 2901 ... 75803
An County Road 2902 ... 75803
An County Road 2903 ... 75803
An County Road 2904 ... 75803
An County Road 2905 ... 75803
An County Road 2906 ... 75803
An County Road 2907 ... 75803
An County Road 2908 ... 75803
An County Road 2909 ... 75803
An County Road 2910 ... 75803
An County Road 2911 ... 75803
An County Road 2912 ... 75803
An County Road 2914 ... 75803
An County Road 2915 ... 75803
An County Road 2916 ... 75803
An County Road 2920 ... 75803
An County Road 2921 ... 75803
An County Road 2933 ... 75803
An County Road 3143 ... 75803
An County Road 321 ... 75803
An County Road 3213 ... 75803
An County Road 323 ... 75803
An County Road 328 ... 75803
An County Road 331 ... 75803
An County Road 333 ... 75803
An County Road 3334 ... 75803
An County Road 334 ... 75803
An County Road 335 ... 75803
An County Road 336 ... 75803
An County Road 337 ... 75803
An County Road 338 ... 75803
An County Road 340 ... 75803
An County Road 341 ... 75803
An County Road 342 ... 75803
An County Road 344 ... 75803
An County Road 346
100-898 ... 75803
900-1699 ... 75803
1701-1999 ... 75803
1800-1998 ... 75801
2000-2600 ... 75801
2602-2698 ... 75801
An County Road 3471 ... 75803
An County Road 348 ... 75803
An County Road 349 ... 75803
An County Road 3491 ... 75803
An County Road 350
601-699 ... 75803
900-1398 ... 75801
An County Road 352 ... 75803
An County Road 353 ... 75801
An County Road 354
200-299 ... 75803
2200-4800 ... 75801
4802-5198 ... 75801
An County Road 355 ... 75801
An County Road 3552 ... 75801
An County Road 356 ... 75801
An County Road 358 ... 75803
An County Road 3581 ... 75803
An County Road 3582 ... 75803
An County Road 3585 ... 75803
An County Road 359 ... 75803
An County Road 3592 ... 75803
An County Road 3593 ... 75803
An County Road 3594 ... 75803
An County Road 3595 ... 75803
An County Road 3596 ... 75803
An County Road 360 ... 75803
An County Road 362 ... 75803
An County Road 3621 ... 75803
An County Road 363 ... 75803
An County Road 3631 ... 75803
An County Road 364 ... 75803
An County Road 3641 ... 75803
An County Road 366 ... 75803
An County Road 3665 ... 75803
An County Road 367 ... 75801
An County Road 3681 ... 75801
An County Road 3682 ... 75803
An County Road 369 ... 75803
An County Road 3694 ... 75803
An County Road 3695 ... 75801
An County Road 370 ... 75801
An County Road 3701 ... 75801
An County Road 3702 ... 75801
An County Road 3703 ... 75801
An County Road 3704 ... 75801
An County Road 3705 ... 75803
An County Road 371 ... 75801
An County Road 372 ... 75803
An County Road 3721 ... 75803
An County Road 3722 ... 75801
An County Road 3723 ... 75803
An County Road 3724 ... 75803
An County Road 373 ... 75801
An County Road 3731 ... 75801
An County Road 3732 ... 75801
An County Road 3733 ... 75801
An County Road 374 ... 75801
An County Road 375 ... 75801
An County Road 376 ... 75801
An County Road 3764 ... 75801
An County Road 377 ... 75801
An County Road 378 ... 75801
An County Road 379 ... 75801
An County Road 3792 ... 75801
An County Road 3794 ... 75801
An County Road 380 ... 75801
An County Road 383 ... 75801
An County Road 384 ... 75801
An County Road 385 ... 75801
An County Road 3850 ... 75801
An County Road 3852 ... 75801
An County Road 3854 ... 75801
An County Road 3855 ... 75801
An County Road 386 ... 75801
An County Road 387 ... 75801
An County Road 389 ... 75801
An County Road 391 ... 75801
An County Road 3912 ... 75801
An County Road 3914 ... 75801
An County Road 3951 ... 75801
An County Road 396 ... 75801
An County Road 3961 ... 75801
An County Road 397 ... 75801
An County Road 3971 ... 75801
An County Road 3972 ... 75801
An County Road 398 ... 75801
An County Road 399 ... 75801
An County Road 3992 ... 75801
An County Road 400 ... 75803
An County Road 401 ... 75803
An County Road 4013 ... 75803
An County Road 4014 ... 75803
An County Road 4015 ... 75803
An County Road 402 ... 75803
An County Road 4020 ... 75803
An County Road 403 ... 75803
An County Road 4031 ... 75803
An County Road 4032 ... 75803
An County Road 4033 ... 75803
An County Road 4034 ... 75803
An County Road 4035 ... 75803
An County Road 4036 ... 75803
An County Road 404 ... 75803
An County Road 4040 ... 75803
An County Road 4041 ... 75803
An County Road 4049 ... 75803
An County Road 405 ... 75803
An County Road 406 ... 75803
An County Road 407 ... 75803
An County Road 408 ... 75803
An County Road 409 ... 75803
An County Road 410 ... 75803
An County Road 411 ... 75803
An County Road 412 ... 75803
An County Road 4120 ... 75803
An County Road 4122 ... 75803
An County Road 413 ... 75803
An County Road 414 ... 75803
An County Road 4140 ... 75803
An County Road 415 ... 75803
An County Road 4152 ... 75803
An County Road 416 ... 75803
An County Road 417 ... 75803
An County Road 4170 ... 75803
An County Road 4171 ... 75803
An County Road 418 ... 75803
An County Road 4181 ... 75803
An County Road 419 ... 75803
An County Road 420 ... 75803
An County Road 421 ... 75803
An County Road 422 ... 75803
An County Road 4221 ... 75803
An County Road 423 ... 75803
An County Road 424 ... 75803
An County Road 425 ... 75803
An County Road 4250 ... 75803
An County Road 4251 ... 75803
An County Road 4252 ... 75803
An County Road 4253 ... 75803
An County Road 4254 ... 75803
An County Road 4255 ... 75803
An County Road 4256 ... 75803
An County Road 4257 ... 75803
An County Road 4258 ... 75803
An County Road 4259 ... 75803
An County Road 426 ... 75803
An County Road 427 ... 75803
An County Road 4271 ... 75803
An County Road 4274 ... 75803
An County Road 428 ... 75803
An County Road 4282 ... 75803
An County Road 4283 ... 75803
An County Road 4284 ... 75803
An County Road 4285 ... 75803
An County Road 4286 ... 75803
An County Road 4287 ... 75803
An County Road 429 ... 75803
An County Road 430 ... 75803
An County Road 4301 ... 75803
An County Road 4302 ... 75803
An County Road 4303 ... 75803
An County Road 432 ... 75803
An County Road 433 ... 75803
An County Road 4334 ... 75803
An County Road 434 ... 75803
An County Road 438 ... 75803
W An County Road
441 ... 75803
An County Road 4413 ... 75803
An County Road 4415 ... 75803
An County Road 4416 ... 75803
An County Road 442 ... 75803
An County Road 4420 ... 75803
An County Road 4423 ... 75803
An County Road 443 ... 75803
An County Road 4430 ... 75803
An County Road 4431 ... 75803
An County Road 4433 ... 75803
An County Road 444 ... 75803
An County Road 4441 ... 75803
An County Road 445 ... 75803
An County Road 4451 ... 75803
An County Road 4452 ... 75803
An County Road 4453 ... 75803
An County Road 446 ... 75803
An County Road 447 ... 75803
An County Road 448 ... 75803
An County Road 4480 ... 75803
An County Road 449 ... 75803
An County Road 4493 ... 75803
An County Road 450 ... 75803
An County Road 451 ... 75803
An County Road 452 ... 75803
An County Road 453 ... 75803
An County Road 456 ... 75803
An County Road 458 ... 75803
An County Road 459 ... 75803
An County Road 4591 ... 75803
An County Road 4593 ... 75803
An County Road 4594 ... 75803
An County Road 460 ... 75803
An County Road 4601 ... 75803
An County Road 461 ... 75803
An County Road 465 ... 75803
An County Road 4651 ... 75803
An County Road 466 ... 75803
An County Road 467 ... 75803
An County Road 468 ... 75803
An County Road 469 ... 75803
An County Road 470 ... 75803
An County Road 477 ... 75803
An County Road 4775 ... 75803
An County Road 478 ... 75803
An County Road 480 ... 75803
An County Road 4801 ... 75803
An County Road 481 ... 75803
An County Road 4813 ... 75803
An County Road 482 ... 75803
An County Road 483 ... 75803
An County Road 484 ... 75803
An County Road 4841 ... 75803
An County Road 485 ... 75803
An County Road 486 ... 75803
An County Road 4861 ... 75803
An County Road 487 ... 75803
An County Road 5514 ... 75801
An County Road 7376 ... 75801
Anderson Dr ... 75801
Anderson St ... 75803
E & W Angelina St ... 75801
Angle St ... 75801
Apache Pl ... 75801
Armory Rd ... 75803
Arrowhead Rd ... 75801
Arthur Ct ... 75801
N Ash St ... 75801
Aspen Ct ... 75803
Aurora Ln ... 75803
Austin St ... 75803
Avenue A St ... 75801
Avenue B ... 75803
Avenue C ... 75803
Avenue D ... 75803
Back Gate Rd ... 75803
Bassett Rd ... 75803
Beaver Pond Rd ... 75803
Belfast St ... 75803
Bellview Dr ... 75803
Ben Milam Dr ... 75801
Benbrook Dr ... 75801
Bent Tree Dr ... 75801
Bentwood Dr ... 75803
Berkley Dr ... 75801
Bermuda Ln ... 75803
Beverly Dr ... 75801
Birch St ... 75801
Blackjack Dr ... 75803
Blanton Rd ... 75803
Blue Lake Rd ... 75803
Booker St ... 75803
Boulder Ct ... 75803
Bowen Dr ... 75801
W Bowers St ... 75801
S Bowie St ... 75801
Boyd Dr ... 75803
Brakenridge St ... 75801
E & W Brazos St ... 75801
Bridges Dr ... 75801
Brierwood Dr ... 75801
Bristol Rd ... 75803
Bronco Dr ... 75801
Brookhaven Dr ... 75801
Brookhollow Dr ... 75801
Brooklyn Ave ... 75803
Brookview Ln ... 75803
W Broyles St ... 75801
Brushy Creek Rd ... 75803
Buckhorn St ... 75801
Bullard Dr ... 75801
Burke St ... 75803
Burkitt St ... 75801
Buttermilk Dr ... 75803
Caddo Dr ... 75803
E Calhoun St ... 75801
Callier St ... 75803
E & W Camden St ... 75801
Campbell St ... 75801
Cannon St ... 75803
Caplin Dr ... 75801
Cardinal Dr ... 75801
W Carolina St ... 75803
Carver Dr ... 75801
Catalpa St ... 75803
N Cedar St
500-698 ... 75801
700-1199 ... 75801
1200-1299 ... 75803
Cedar Heights Dr ... 75803
Cedarvale St ... 75801
Cedarview Dr ... 75803
Chamboard St ... 75801
Chancellor Dr ... 75803
Chelsea St ... 75803
W Cherokee St ... 75803
Chestnut Dr ... 75803
Chism Dr ... 75803
N & S Church St ... 75801
Circle Dr ... 75801
Circle R Lake Rd ... 75801
Clara Dr ... 75803
Clay St ... 75801
Clearview Dr ... 75803
Clover Ln ... 75803
Coffee St ... 75803
Colley Dr ... 75803
E & W Colorado St ... 75801
Columbia St ... 75803
Comanche Dr ... 75803
Commerce St ... 75803
N Conrad St
900-998 ... 75801
1000-1399 ... 75803
Conway St
901-999 ... 75801
1200-1499 ... 75803
E & W Cook St ... 75801
E & W Coronaca St ... 75803
N Cottage Ave ... 75801
Cottonwood Ln ... 75803
Country Club Rd ... 75803
County Road 350 ... 75803
County Road 4221 ... 75803
County Road 4528 ... 75803
County Road 4529 ... 75803
Court Dr ... 75803
Covert St ... 75801
Covey Dr ... 75803
Craig Dr ... 75803
E & W Crawford St ... 75801
Creekwood Rd ... 75803
Crescent Dr ... 75801
Crest Dr ... 75801
Crestline Dr ... 75801
Crestwood Dr ... 75803
Crockett Rd ... 75801
Crow Lake Rd ... 75803
Cummings St ... 75801
Cypress Dr ... 75801
Daily St ... 75801
Daisy Ln ... 75801
E & W Dallas St ... 75801
Daniels St ... 75803
David Dr ... 75803
E Davis St ... 75801
W Debard St ... 75801
N Dechard St ... 75801
Dee Ann St ... 75803
Deer Run St ... 75801
Della Dr ... 75801
Delmar St ... 75803
Devonshire Ln ... 75803
Dogwood St ... 75801
Donniebrook St ... 75803
S Dorrance St ... 75801
Douglas St ... 75803
Dove Ridge St ... 75801
S Dowling St ... 75801
Drexel St ... 75803
Durham St ... 75801
W Dye St ... 75801
Easy St ... 75801
Edgewood Cir ... 75803
Edna Dr ... 75803
Eilenstein St
700-1599 ... 75801
1600-1799 ... 75803
N Elm St ... 75801
Elmwood Ct ... 75801
Emerald Ln ... 75803
Erwin St ... 75801
N Esplanade St
500-698 ... 75801
700-941 ... 75801
943-1099 ... 75801
1200-1599 ... 75803
Ethel St ... 75803
Evergreen St ... 75803
Ezell St ... 75801
Falcon Hill Rd ... 75803
N Fannin St ... 75801
Fawn Dr ... 75801
Fay Way Dr ... 75801
Ferguson Rd ... 75803
Fernwood St ... 75803
Field St ... 75801
Fig St ... 75801
Fitzhugh St ... 75803
Fleetwood Ln ... 75803
Florence St ... 75803
Fm 1137 ... 75801
Fm 1817 ... 75801
Fm 19 ... 75803
Fm 1990 ... 75801
Fm 2267 ... 75803
Fm 2419 ... 75801
Fm 2574 ... 75803
Fm 315 ... 75803
W Fm 320 ... 75803
E Fm 321 ... 75803
Fm 322 ... 75801
Fm 3224 ... 75803
E Fm 323 ... 75801
Fm 3266 ... 75801
Fm 3328 ... 75803
Fm 3372 ... 75803
Fm 3452 ... 75803
Fm 645 ... 75803
E Fm 837 ... 75803
Fm 860 ... 75803
Forest Dr ... 75801
N Fort St
300-899 ... 75801
901-1099 ... 75801
1100-1199 ... 75801
Fort Houston Dr ... 75801
N Fowler St ... 75801
Foxwood Rd ... 75801
Front St ... 75803
Front Gate Rd ... 75803
S Fulton St ... 75801
Future St ... 75801
Gambrell St ... 75803
Gardner Dr ... 75803
Garland St ... 75801
Gay Ave ... 75801
Georgia St ... 75803
Gilbert St ... 75801
Giles Rd ... 75803
E Gillespie St ... 75801
Gillis St ... 75803
Giraud St ... 75801
Givens St ... 75803
Glenhaven Rd ... 75801
Glenwood Dr ... 75801
Golfcrest Dr ... 75803
E & W Gooch St ... 75801
Grandberry St ... 75803
Grant St ... 75801
W Green St ... 75801
Greever St ... 75803
Griggs St ... 75803
S Grove St ... 75801
Hamilton Rd ... 75801
W Hamlett St
1-397 ... 75801
399-699 ... 75801
700-1099 ... 75803
Happy Acres Dr ... 75803
Happy Glen Ln ... 75803
Happy Oaks Dr ... 75803
Happy Springs Dr ... 75803
Happy Valley Ln ... 75803
Harcrow Rd ... 75801
Hardin St ... 75803
Harrison St ... 75803
Hays St ... 75801
Head St ... 75801
Hickory St ... 75801
Hickory Ridge Ln ... 75803
Highland Dr ... 75801
N & S Hillcrest Dr ... 75801
Hillside Ln ... 75801
Hilltop Dr ... 75801
E Hodges St ... 75801
Holly Ln ... 75803
Holmes St ... 75803
Homestead Dr ... 75801
Honey Tree Trl ... 75801
S Hood St ... 75801
Hospital Dr ... 75801
N Houston St ... 75801
N Howard St
400-498 ... 75801
500-1099 ... 75801
1200-1499 ... 75803
E & W Hoxie St ... 75801
Huffman Dr ... 75803
E & W Huffsmith St ... 75801
Hunter Dr ... 75801
Hurley St ... 75803
Hurst St ... 75801
Ike St ... 75803
W Illinois St ... 75801
Imperial Valley Est ... 75803
Indian Creek Dr ... 75801
Industrial Blvd ... 75801
Inwood Dr ... 75801
N Jackson St
600-1099 ... 75801
1101-1199 ... 75801
1200-3299 ... 75803
S Jackson St ... 75801
Jamison St ... 75803
Joe Louis St ... 75803
N John St
200-498 ... 75801
500-1199 ... 75801
1200-1599 ... 75803
Johnson St ... 75801
E & W Jolly St ... 75801
Juniper Dr ... 75803
Kent Ave ... 75803
Kentucky St ... 75801
Kenwood Dr ... 75801
Kerwood Pl ... 75801

Kickapoo St 75803
King Blvd 75803
Knox St 75801
E & W Kolstad St 75801
E Lacy St 75801
W Lacy St
100-206 75801
208-1399 75801
1401-1499 75801
1500-1699 75803
Lake Dr 75803
Lakeshore Dr 75801
Lakeside Dr 75801
Lakeview Ave 75801
E Lamar St 75801
Langham Ln 75801
Larkspur Ln 75803
Larry St 75803
Laura St 75803
Laurel St 75803
Lazy Ln 75803
Lazy Day 75801
Lelia St 75803
Leram St 75803
Lincoln St 75803
Linden Dr 75803
N Line St
100-199 75801
1000-1099 75803
N Link St
900-1199 75801
1200-1210 75803
1212-2298 75803
1213-1213 75802
1213-2299 75803
Lipsey Ave 75803
Lisa Ln 75803
Lone Oak Dr 75803
Longhorn Dr 75801
Lookout Dr 75801
N Loop 256
100-4999 75803
N Loop 256
5002-5598 75801
5600-6199 75801
6201-6999 75801
S Loop 256
1000-1198 75801
1200-4299 75801
4301-6999 75801
5000-5098 75803
SE Loop 256 75803
Lori Ln 75803
Lorraine Pl 75801
W Louisiana St 75801
Lowe St 75803
Ludolph St 75803
Lynch St 75803
M L Cary St 75801
E & W Maffitt St 75803
N & S Magnolia St 75801
E & W Main St 75801
N Mallard St 75801
Maple St 75801
Marion St 75803
E Market St 75801
Marsh Ln 75801
Martin Luther King Blvd
1400-1499 75801
1500-2199 75803
Maverick Dr 75801
May St 75801
Mcclellan St 75801
Mccollough St 75801
Mcmeans St 75801
Mcneil St 75801
Meadow Dr 75801
Meadow Bend Rd 75803
Meadowbrook Dr 75803
Medical Dr 75801
Melissa Dr 75803
Memory Ln 75801
S Micheaux St 75801
Middleton St 75803
S Milam St 75801
Miller St 75801
Mills Dr 75803
Mimosa Dr 75803
Missouri St 75803
Mitzie Ln 75803
Mizell 75801
Monica Ln 75803
Montana St 75801
Moody St 75801
Moore Dr 75801
Morestri 75803
Morning Star Ln 75803
Moser Rd 75803
Mound Prairie Dr 75803
Mulberry St 75803
E Murchison St 75801
Mustang Dr 75801
Nannie Ln 75801
E Neches St 75801
W Neches St 75801
Neches Trce 75803
E Newman St 75801
Nixon St 75803
North St 75801
E & W Oak St 75801
Oak Hill Dr 75803
Oak Lawn St 75803
Oakcrest Dr 75803
Oakdale Dr 75801
Oakhurst Dr 75801
Oakland Dr 75801
Oakwood Ct 75801
Odom St 75803
Ohio St 75801
Old Brushy Creek Rd 75803
Old Elkhart Rd 75801
Old Highway 79 75801
Old Neches Hwy 75801
Old Tucker Trl 75801
Overhill Dr 75801
Oxford Rd 75803
Pagosa Dr 75803
Palamino Dr 75801
E & W Palestine Ave 75801
Palm Dr 75801
Palmer Rd 75803
Palmetto Dr 75803
E & W Park Ave 75801
Parkcrest Dr 75803
Peach Tree Dr 75803
Pearl St 75803
Pecan St 75801
Penny St 75803
Perlang Est 75803
N Perry St 75801
Perry Tap Rd 75803
Pershing St 75801
Pillar St 75801
Pine St 75801
Pinetree Dr 75803
Pinewood St 75801
W Point Tap Rd
101-199 75801
200-2399 75803
E Poplar St 75801
Post Oak Ln 75801
Post Oak St 75803
Prantric 75801
Private Road 2205 75803
Private Road 2609 75803
Private Road 2906 75803
Private Road 4181 75803
Private Road 5109 75801
Private Road 5123 75801
Private Road 5137 75801
Private Road 5147 75801
Private Road 5199 75801
Private Road 5227 75801
Private Road 5231 75801
Private Road 5232 75801
Private Road 5301 75801
Private Road 5322 75801
Private Road 5355 75801
Private Road 5396 75801
Private Road 5411 75801
Private Road 5419 75801
Private Road 5514 75801
Private Road 5515 75801
Private Road 5516 75801
Private Road 556 75801
Private Road 5561 75801
Private Road 557 75801
Private Road 6001 75801
Private Road 6002 75803
Private Road 6005 75803
Private Road 6010 75801
Private Road 6022 75803
Private Road 6029 75801
Private Road 6030 75801
Private Road 6031 75801
Private Road 6036 75801
Private Road 6041 75801
Private Road 6042 75801
Private Road 6045 75803
Private Road 6079 75803
Private Road 6094 75803
Private Road 6101 75801
Private Road 6102 75801
Private Road 6103 75801
Private Road 6107 75801
Private Road 6121 75801
Private Road 6129 75801
Private Road 6139 75801
Private Road 6140 75801
Private Road 6141 75801
Private Road 6142 75801
Private Road 6153 75801
Private Road 6202 75803
Private Road 6203 75803
Private Road 6205 75803
Private Road 6206 75803
Private Road 6222 75803
Private Road 6223 75803
Private Road 6224 75803
Private Road 6231 75803
Private Road 6232 75803
Private Road 6233 75803
Private Road 6234 75803
Private Road 6235 75803
Private Road 6294 75801
Private Road 6320 75803
Private Road 6321 75803
Private Road 6322 75801
Private Road 6419 75803
Private Road 6420 75803
Private Road 6421 75803
Private Road 6424 75803
Private Road 6425 75803
Private Road 6426 75803
Private Road 6451 75803
Private Road 6452 75803
Private Road 6453 75803
Private Road 6553 75803
Private Road 6811 75803
Private Road 6900 75801
Private Road 6902 75803
Private Road 6903 75803
Private Road 6904 75803
Private Road 6907 75803
Private Road 6909 75801
Private Road 6912 75801
Private Road 6921 75803
Private Road 6933 75801
Private Road 6990 75801
Private Road 6991 75801
Private Road 7235 75803
Private Road 7321 75803
Private Road 7347 75803
Private Road 7348 75803
Private Road 7349 75803
Private Road 7353 75801
Private Road 7358 75803
Private Road 7370 75801
Private Road 7371 75801
Private Road 7376 75801
Private Road 7383 75801
Private Road 7389 75801
Private Road 7486 75803
Private Road 7705 75801
Private Road 8111 75803
Private Road 8315 75803
Private Road 8320 75803
Private Road 8322 75801
Private Road 8344 75803
Private Road 8400 75803
Private Road 8401 75803
Private Road 8402 75803
Private Road 8403 75803
Private Road 8404 75803
Private Road 8414 75803
Private Road 8416 75803
Private Road 8417 75803
Private Road 8418 75803
Private Road 8419 75803
Private Road 8420 75803
Private Road 8421 75803
Private Road 8422 75803
Private Road 8423 75803
Private Road 8427 75803
Private Road 8441 75803
Private Road 8444 75803
Private Road 8469 75803
Private Road 8485 75803
Private Road 8777 75803
Quail Ridge Rd 75801
N Queen St
200-498 75801
500-1199 75801
1201-1299 75801
1300-1899 75803
S Queen St 75801
Ragland St 75803
Railroad Ave 75801
N Rainey St 75801
Rambling Rd 75801
Rampart St 75801
Randolph St 75803
Range Rd 75801
Ravenwood Dr 75803
Ravine Dr 75801
E & W Reagan Ct & St 75801
Red Oak Ln 75801
Redbud St 75801
Redland Ln 75801
Redus St 75803
Redwood Dr 75801
Reese Rd 75803
Renner St 75801
Reynolds Rd 75803
Richard Cir 75803
Richland Dr 75801
Ricky Dr 75803
Ridgecrest Dr 75801
Ridgewood Dr 75803
Roberts St 75803
Robinson St 75803
S Rogers St 75801
Rolling Hills Dr 75803
Romallen Dr 75801
Rosebud St 75803
Rosewood Dr 75801
Ross St 75801
S Royall St 75801
Rugged Rd 75801
Russell St 75801
Ruth St 75801
Sagebrush Dr 75801
Saint Andrews Dr 75803
Salt Works Rd
100-299 75801
300-2399 75803
Sams Ln 75803
San Diego St 75803
San Jacinto St 75801
Sanderson Farms Pkwy 75803
Sandflat Pl 75803
Sandra St 75803
Sandy Ln 75801
Selden St 75801
Selkirk Ave 75803
Seminole Dr 75801
Sequoia Dr 75803
Settlers Ct 75801
Shadow Wood Dr 75801
Shady Oaks Dr 75803
Shadycreek Dr 75801
Shamrock Dr 75803
Sheridan Dr 75801
Sherry Ln 75803
Sherwood St 75801
Sierra Dr 75801
Sleepy Hollow Ln 75803
W South St 75801
Southhill Rd 75801
Southview St 75801
Spencer St 75801
E Spring St 75801
W Spring St
101-797 75801
799-900 75801
902-1198 75801
1601-1797 75803
1799-1999 75803
Springcreek Dr 75803
Springdale 75803
Springhill Dr 75801
Spruce St 75803
N State Highway 155 75803
N State Highway 19 75803
S State Highway 19 75801
W State Highway 294 75801
Stephanie Dr 75803
Stephen Cir 75803
Stewart St 75803
Stone St 75803
Stryker Blvd 75801
Sugar Ln 75801
Summit Dr 75801
Sunset Rd 75801
Surrey Cir 75801
Swanson Dr 75801
Swantz St 75801
Sweetwood Ln 75803
E Swift St 75801
N Sycamore St
200-298 75801
300-1200 75801
1202-1298 75801
1300-1699 75803
S Sycamore St 75801
S Sylvan Ave 75801
Tanglewood Dr 75803
Tate St 75801
Tejas Rd 75803
N Tennessee St
200-398 75801
400-899 75801
901-999 75801
1000-1399 75803
Terrance St 75801
E Terry St 75801
N Texas Ave
201-201 75801
203-799 75801
801-899 75801
1500-1599 75803
Thomas Rd 75803
Thornwood Dr 75801
Threll St 75803
Tile Factory Rd
1700-1899 75803
1900-1998 75801
2000-2099 75801
Timber Dr 75801
Timberline Trl 75803
Tipp St 75803
Town Creek Dr 75803
Trailhollow Ln 75801
Travis St 75801
Trimble St 75803
Trinity Ct 75801
S Turner Dr 75803
Tyler St 75803
University Dr 75803
Upper Lake Rd 75803
N Us Highway 287 75803
N & S Us Highway 79 75801
E Us Highway 84 75801
Us Park Road 70 75801
Valley View Rd 75803
Van Fleet St 75801
Variah St
100-199 75801
200-899 75803
E Vaughn St 75801
Ventureview St 75803
Victory St 75803
Village St 75801
Virginia Ave 75803
Vista Rdg 75801
Wagon Trl 75801
Wall Dr 75803
E Walnut St 75801
Walton Dr & St 75801
Wanda St 75801
Washington St 75803
Wells St 75801
Wesley Dr 75801
West St 75801
Westbrook St 75803
Westview St 75803
Westwood Rd 75803
Wigwam St 75801
Willow Dr 75801
Willow Creek Pkwy 75801
Willowbrook Way 75803
Winchester Dr 75803
Windridge Rd 75801
Witness Tree Ln 75803
Wolf Creek Rd 75803
Wolf Creek Trail Rd 75803
Woodbine Dr 75803
Woodgate Dr 75801
Woodland Dr 75801
Woodridge Rd 75801
Woodside Dr 75803
Woodway St 75801
Wright Dr 75801
Wynnwood Dr 75801
Yeager St 75801
Yorkshire Blvd 75803
Youpon Dr 75801

NUMBERED STREETS

All Street Addresses 75803

PAMPA TX

General Delivery 79065

POST OFFICE BOXES MAIN OFFICE STATIONS AND BRANCHES

Box No.s
All PO Boxes 79066

RURAL ROUTES

01, 02, 02 79065

HIGHWAY CONTRACTS

02, 02, 03, 04 79065
02, 02, 03, 04 79065
02, 02, 03, 04 79065

NAMED STREETS

All Street Addresses 79065

NUMBERED STREETS

All Street Addresses 79065

PARIS TX

General Delivery 75460

POST OFFICE BOXES MAIN OFFICE STATIONS AND BRANCHES

Box No.s
All PO Boxes 75461

RURAL ROUTES

01, 05, 08, 11 75460
02, 03, 04, 06, 07, 09, 10, 12, 14 75462

NAMED STREETS

Abbott Ln 75460
Abby Ln 75462
Abrams Aly 75460
Aikin Dr 75460
Airport Rd 75462
Allen St 75460
Alpine St 75462
Amherst Ct & Rd 75462
Anderson Rd 75462
Ash St 75460
Ashton Ln 75462
Askins Rd 75462
Aspen 75462
Audubon Rd 75460
E & W Austin St 75460
Balianti Rd 75462
Ballard Dr 75460
Barnes Dr 75462
Bella Vista Dr 75460
Belmont St 75460
Bent Trail Ln 75462
Bentwood Cir & Trl 75462
Beverly Dr 75460
Birch St 75462
Bitter Root Cir 75462
Blackburn St 75462
Blossom Auto Ln 75462
Boardwalk 75462
Bolton Ct 75460
Bonham St 75460
Booker T Washington 75460
E & W Booth Ln, Pl & St 75460
Boulder Ln 75462
E & W Brame St 75460
Brandi Ln 75462
Brandyn Pl 75462
Braydan 75462
Briana Dr 75462
Briar Oak Dr 75462
Briarwood Dr 75460
Brittany Ln 75462
Brooke Ln 75462
Brookes Way 75462
Brown Ave 75460
Brownwood Cir & Dr 75462
Bunker St 75460
Burress Ln 75462
Butler Ln 75460
Bybee St 75462
Campbell St 75460
Cannon Pl 75462
Cardinal Ln 75460
Carr Aly 75460
Carson Ln 75460
Castlegate Dr 75462
Cedar Crk 75462
Cedar St 75460
E & W Center St 75460
Cerwenski Rd 75460
Charles Aly 75460
E & W Cherry Aly & St 75460
Chestnut Ln 75462
Chisholm Trl 75462
Chism St 75460
Choctaw Ln 75460
S Church St
1-2799 75460
2800-3299 75462
Cimarron Cir 75462
Cindy Ln 75462
Clark Ln 75460
Clarksville St
1-499 75460
500-3798 75460
500-500 75461
501-3799 75460

4001-4197 75462
4199-5699 75462
5701-6099 75462
Clement Rd
201-297 75460
299-1699 75460
3200-3799 75462
Cleveland St 75460
Cobb Ranch Rd 75462
Colbie 75462
College St 75460
N Collegiate Dr
100-1399 75460
1700-2099 75462
S Collegiate Dr 75460
Collier Dr 75462
W Collin 75462
Colvin St 75460
Comanche Cir 75462
Connor Ave 75460
Cooper St
1100-1299 75460
5200-5299 75462
Cope Dr 75462
Cornell Dr 75462
County Road 11300 75462
County Road 11320 75462
County Road 11400 75462
County Road 1184 75462
County Road 12000 75462
County Road 12010 75462
County Road 12020 75462
County Road 12050 75462
County Road 12100 75462
County Road 12140 75462
County Road 12200 75462
County Road 12390 75462
County Road 12500 75462
County Road 12510 75462
County Road 12530 75462
County Road 12550 75462
County Road 12600 75462
County Road 12620 75462
County Road 12650 75462
County Road 13100 75462
County Road 13300 75462
County Road 13400 75462
County Road 13420 75462
County Road 13500 E & W 75462
County Road 13600 75462
County Road 13620 75462
County Road 13630 75462
County Road 13650 75462
County Road 13680 75462
County Road 13685 75462
County Road 13700 75462
County Road 13750 75462
County Road 13800 75462
County Road 13850 75462
County Road 13900 S 75462
County Road 13950 75462
County Road 14650 75462
County Road 14655 75462
County Road 14660 75462
County Road 14665 75462
County Road 14680 75462
County Road 14690 75462
County Road 14700 75462
County Road 14720 75462
County Road 14750 75462
County Road 14760 75462
County Road 14790 75462
County Road 14800 75462
County Road 14820 75462
County Road 14850 75462
County Road 14870 75462
County Road 14880 75462
County Road 14900 75462
County Road 15500 75462
County Road 15520 75462
County Road 15560 75462
County Road 15570 75462
County Road 15580 75462
County Road 15600 75462
County Road 15700 75462
County Road 15800 75462
County Road 15900 75462
County Road 15950 75462
County Road 21000 75462
County Road 21400 75462
County Road 22500 75460
County Road 22800 75460
County Road 22820 75460
County Road 22850 75462
County Road 22880 75460
County Road 22900 75460
County Road 22910 75460
County Road 22920 75460
County Road 22950 75460
County Road 22990 75460
County Road 23000 75462
County Road 23070 75462
County Road 23080 75462
County Road 23100 75462
County Road 23110 75460
County Road 23140 75460
County Road 23200 75460
County Road 24050 75460
County Road 24100 75460
County Road 24120 75460
County Road 24130 75460
County Road 24132 75460
County Road 24134 75460
County Road 24136 75460
County Road 24140 75460
County Road 24200 75460
County Road 24240 75460
County Road 31100 75460
County Road 31300 75460
County Road 31700 75460
County Road 32500 75460
County Road 32505 75460
County Road 32900 75460
County Road 33620 75460
County Road 33630 75460
County Road 33640 75460
County Road 33715 75460
County Road 33800 75460
County Road 33810 75460
County Road 33820 75460
County Road 33830 75460
County Road 33840 75460
County Road 33850 75460
County Road 33855 75460
County Road 34710 75460
County Road 34715 75460
County Road 34720 75460
County Road 34721 75460
County Road 34726 75460
County Road 34730 75460
County Road 34731 75460
County Road 34740 75460
County Road 34750 75460
County Road 34760 75460
County Road 34770 75460
County Road 34775 75460
County Road 34778 75460
County Road 34780 75460
County Road 41100 75462
County Road 42000 75460
County Road 42200 75462
County Road 42230 75462
County Road 42250 75462
County Road 4230 75462
County Road 42300 75462
County Road 42310 75462
County Road 42320 75462
County Road 42330 75462
County Road 42370 75462
County Road 42400 75462
County Road 42410 75462
County Road 42440 75462
County Road 42450 75462
County Road 42460 75462
County Road 42500 75462
County Road 42510 75462
County Road 42520 75462
County Road 42530 75462
County Road 42540 75462
County Road 42550 75462
County Road 42560 75462
County Road 42570 75462
County Road 42600 75462
County Road 42604 75462
County Road 42606 75462
County Road 42608 75462
County Road 42610 75462
County Road 42615 75462
County Road 42620 75462
County Road 42625 75462
County Road 42640 75462
County Road 42642 75462
County Road 42700 75462
County Road 42900 75462
County Road 43250 75462
County Road 43300 75462
County Road 43310 75462
County Road 43330 75462
County Road 43340 75462
County Road 43350 75462
County Road 43351 75462
County Road 43360 75462
County Road 43380 75462
County Road 43390 75462
County Road 43400 75462
County Road 43420 75462
County Road 43500 75462
County Road 43600 75462
County Road 43800 75462
County Road 43830 75462
County Road 43850 75462
County Road 43900 75462
County Road 43950 75462
County Road 44105 75462
County Road 44110 75462
County Road 44430 75462
County Road 44450 75462
County Road 44460 75462
County Road 44480 75462
County Road 44550 75462
County Road 44555 75462
County Road 44560 75462
County Road 45400 75462
County Road 45430 75462
County Road 45450 75462
County Road 45480 75462
County Road 45500 75462
County Road 46500 75462
County Road 46540 75462
County Road 46550 75462
County Road 46650 75462
County Road 46700 75462
Cozy Ln 75462
Craigo Aly 75460
Crescent Dr 75460
Cripple Creek Dr 75462
Crockett Cir 75460
Croyhill Rd 75462
Culbertson St 75460
Cypress Dr 75460
Darnell Dr & Rd 75462
Davis St 75462
Dawn Dr 75462
Deer Haven Ln 75462
Del Roy Dr 75460
Deshong Dr 75460
Dickson Ave 75460
Dixon Aly 75460
Dogwood Ln 75460
Dove Holw 75462
Dragon Dr 75460
Drive In Ave 75460
Durango Dr 75460
Eagle Bnd 75462
Eashande St 75460
East Plz 75460
Eastgate Ln 75460
Eastridge Dr 75462
Elm Dr 75462
Enchanted Dr 75462
Evergreen St 75460
Fair Oaks 75462
Fairfax St 75460
Fairway St 75460
Fargo Dr 75462
Farm Road 1184
2-298 75462
Farm Road 1184
300-2699 75462
3101-3397 75460
3399-5599 75460
5601-6499 75460
Farm Road 137 75460
Farm Road 1497 75462
Farm Road 1498 75462
Farm Road 1499 75460
Farm Road 1500 75460
Farm Road 1502 75462
Farm Road 1506 75460
Farm Road 1508 75462
Farm Road 1510 75460
Farm Road 195 75462
Farm Road 196 N 75462
Farm Road 2121 75462
Farm Road 2648 75462
Farm Road 3426 75462
Farm Road 79 75460
Farm Road 905 75462
Farm Road 906 E 75462
Fitzhugh Ave 75460
Fort St 75460
Franklin St 75460
Frisco Ave 75460
Funston Ter 75462
E & W Garrett St 75460
George Wright Homes 75460
Glenwood Dr 75462
Gordon Country Club Rd 75460
Graham St 75460
Grand Ave 75460
Greenwood Ln 75462
Grove St 75460
Hampton Rd 75462
Haning Dr 75462
Harrison Ave 75460
Harvard Dr 75462
Hay Barn Rd 75462
E & W Hearne Ave 75460
Hearon St 75462
Heather Ln 75462
E & W Henderson St 75460
E & W Hickory St 75460
Highland Rd 75460
Hillard St 75460
Hodges Ln 75460
Hogans Bluff St 75462
Holbrook St 75462
Holcomb Dr 75462
E & W Houston St 75460
Hubbard St 75460
Hunnel Dairy Rd 75462
Hyde St 75460
Independence St 75460
Inwood Dr 75462
E Jackson Ct, Ln & St 75460
Jamar Rd 75462
Jana St 75462
Jasmine St 75462
Jefferson Rd
600-3699 75460
3700-4099 75462
Johnson St 75460
Johnson Woods Dr 75460
Jojo Rd 75462
Jordan Hill Ln 75462
E & W Kaufman St 75460
Kessler Dr 75460
Key West Rd 75462
Kimberly St 75460
Kirkland Ln 75462
Knollwood Dr 75462
Kyle Dr 75460
Lake Crook Rd 75460
Lakeshore Dr 75462
Lakeview Dr 75462
Lamar Ave
1-3599 75460
3601-3799 75460
3700-3798 75462
3800-9799 75462
Lamar Rd 75462
Lane Rd 75462
Laredo Dr 75462
Laura Ln 75462
Laurel Ln 75460
Lawrence Dr 75462
Lee Cir 75462
Leigh Dr 75462
Levi Ln 75462
Lewis Ln
100-298 75462
2800-3199 75460
3201-3299 75460
Libby Ln 75462
Linn Dr 75462
Lombardy St 75462
E & W Long Ave & St 75460
NE, NW, SE & SW Loop 286 75460
Maddox Dr 75462
Madewell St 75462
Mahaffey Ln 75460
N & S Main St 75460
Majestic Dr 75460
Mansfield Rd 75462
Maple Ave 75460
Margaret St 75460
Martin Luther King Jr Dr 75460
Meadow Ln 75462
Meadow Park Dr 75460
Meadowbriar Dr 75462
Meadowcrest Ln 75462
Meadowlark Ln 75462
Meadowview Dr 75462
Meandering Way 75462
Medalist St 75460
Methven Ln 75462
Michelle Ln 75462
Miller Pl 75462
Miranda Dr 75462
Misty Gln & Ln 75462
Mockingbird Ln 75462
Morgan Ave 75462
Morningside Dr 75462
Mount Olive Rd 75462
E & W Neagle Ave 75460
Neathery St 75460
Nevada Dr 75462
New Jefferson Rd 75460
Nichols St 75462
Nicole Dr & Ln 75462
North Plz 75460
E Oak Ave 75460
W Oak Ave 75460
Oak Ln 75462
Oak St 75460
Oak Creek Dr 75462
Oakwood Ln 75462
Old Bonham Rd 75460
Old Clarksville Rd 75462
Old Jefferson Rd 75460
Oleander St 75462
Orange St 75460
Paradise Dr 75462
Parc Pl 75460
Parc Ouest Dr 75460
Paris Blvd 75460
Paris Drag Strip Rd 75462
Park Pl 75462
W Park St 75460
Parr Ave 75460
Pecan Pl 75462
Pine Bluff St 75460
Pine Mill Rd
2000-2098 75462
2800-3499 75460
3600-5099 75462
5100-9999 75462
Pine Valley Dr 75462
Pirtle Hall Dr 75460
Plum St 75460
E Polk St 75460
N Post Oak Ln & Rd 75462
Pratt Rd 75462
Preston Dr 75462
E & W Price Cir & St 75460
Pride Cir 75460
Primrose Ln 75462
Private Road 12150 75462
Private Road 24105 75462
Private Road 24110 75462
Private Road 31150 75460
Private Road 33717 75460
Private Road 34995 75460
Private Road 42201 75462
Private Road 42490 75462
Private Road 42495 75462
Private Road 43240 75462
Private Road 43301 75462
Private Road 43375 75462
Private Road 45445 75462
E & W Provine Aly & St 75460
Quail Dr 75462
Quest Ct 75460
Redwood Cir 75462
Reno Dr 75462
Ridgeview Rd 75460
Ripplewood St 75462
Robin Rd 75460
Royal Ln 75462
Rue Calle Dr 75460
Sage Trail Dr 75460
Sandy Ln 75462
Schillinger 75462
Sesame St 75460
Shady Grove Rd 75462
Shady Oaks Ln 75460
Shannon Dr 75462
Shelton Hill Rd 75462
E & W Sherman St 75460
Sherwood Dr 75462
Shiloh St 75460
Silverleaf Dr 75462
Simpson St 75460
Sleepy Holw 75462
Smallwood Rd 75462
South Plz 75460
Sperry Ave 75460
Spruce Dr 75462
Spur 139 75462
Stacy Ln 75460
Stephens Ln 75462
Stillhouse Rd
2000-2299 75460
2300-7099 75462
Stone Ave 75460
Sugar Hill Rd 75462
Summerhill Dr 75462
Sunrise Ave & Dr 75462
Sunset Vw 75462
Sycamore St 75460
Tates Trl 75462
Teubner Ln 75462
Texas Highway 24 75462
Thomas Dr 75462
Thompson Rd 75462
Tiger Town Rd 75460
Timber Brook Dr 75462
Town East Dr 75462
Trails End 75462
E Tudor St 75460
Turtle Creek Dr 75462
Twin Oaks Pl 75460
Twin Pines Dr 75462
Upchurch Ln 75462
Us Highway 271 N 75460
Us Highway 271 S 75462
Us Highway 82 E 75462
Us Highway 82 W 75460
Vagas Dr 75462
Van Zandt St 75460
Village Bnd 75462
Waggoner St 75462
Walker St 75460
Walnut Hill Dr 75462
E & W Washington St 75460
Welch Cir 75462
Wendy Dr 75462
West Plz 75460
Whippoorwill Dr & Ln 75462
Wilburn Dr 75460
Wilderness Trl 75462
Wildwood Ln 75462
Williams Dr 75462
Williams St 75460
Willow Bnd & Cv 75462
Willowcrest Dr 75462
Wood Holw 75462
Wood St 75460
Wood Creek Dr 75462
Woodland Ln 75462
Woodlawn Ave 75460
Yale Dr 75462
Yoder Rd 75460
York St 75460

NUMBERED STREETS

1st St NE 75460
2nd St NE 75460
3rd St NE 75460
3rd St NW 75460
3rd St SE
1-2799 75460
2801-2899 75462
3rd St SW 75460
4th St NE 75460
5th St NE 75460
6th St NE 75460
7 1/2 St NE 75460
7th St NE 75460
8th St NE 75460
9th St NE 75460
10th St NE
1-1899 75460
2800-2899 75462
10th St NW 75460
10th St SE 75460
10th St SW 75460
11th St NE
100-1599 75460
2800-2898 75462
11th St NW 75460
12th St NE 75460
13th St NE 75460
14th St NE 75460
15th St NE 75460
16th St NE 75460
17th St NE 75460
18th St NE 75460
19th St NE 75460
20th St NE
1-1599 75460
1600-1699 75462
20th St NW 75460
20th St SE 75460
21st St NE 75460
22nd St NE 75460
23rd St NE 75460
24th St NE 75460
25th St NE 75460
26th St NE 75460
27th St NE 75460
28th St NE 75460
29th St NE 75460
30th St NE
1-499 75460
1700-1999 75462
30th St NW 75460
30th St SW 75460
31st St NE 75460
32nd St NE 75460
33rd St NE
300-899 75460
3001-3197 75462
3199-3399 75462
33rd St NW 75460
33rd St SE 75460
33rd St SW 75460
34th St NE
100-899 75460
900-1899 75462
34th St NW 75460
34th St SE 75460
34th St SW 75460
35th St NE
1-499 75460
1000-1399 75462

35th St SE 75460
36th St NE 75462
36th St NW 75460
36th St SE 75460
37th St NE 75462
38th NE & SE 75462
39th St SE 75462
39th St SW 75460
40th St NE 75462
40th St SE
800-899 75462
2100-2499 75460
2500-2999 75462
40th St SW 75460
41st St NE 75462
41st St SE 75462
41st St SW 75460
42nd St NE 75462
42nd St SE 75462
42nd St SW 75460
44th St SW 75460
45th St SW 75460
46th St NE 75462
46th St SW 75460
47th NE & SE 75462
48th NE & SE 75462
49th NE & SE 75462
11 1/2 St NW 75460
12 1/2 St NW 75460
14 1/2 St NW 75460

PASADENA TX

General Delivery 77501

POST OFFICE BOXES MAIN OFFICE STATIONS AND BRANCHES

Box No.s
1 - 3488 77501
4000 - 4274 77502
4261 - 4261 77501
4301 - 4999 77502
5001 - 5998 77508
6001 - 6552 77506
7001 - 8250 77508

NAMED STREETS

Aberdeen Rd 77502
Acacia Dr 77502
Affirmed Dr 77503
Alabama St 77503
Alastair Dr 77506
Albemarle Dr 77503
Alecia Dr 77503
Alice Ave 77506
Allen Genoa Rd
1301-2397 77502
2399-2799 77502
3700-5299 77504
Allendale Rd 77502
Almendares Ave 77506
Alpha Dr 77506
Alta Vista Dr 77502
Alvin St 77506
Alydar Dr 77503
Amanda Mellissa Ln 77505
Anacacho St 77504
Anderson St 77506
Andrea Ln 77502
Andrea Sophia Ln 77505
Angelina Ave 77506
Ann St 77506
Anson Cir 77503
Anthony Ct 77506
Anthony Ln 77505
Apache Dr 77503
Arapajo St 77504
Arbor Ln 77505
Arbor Brook Ct 77505
Arboretum Dr 77505
Arcadia Dr 77505
Argentina Cir 77504
Arion Ln 77502
Arlington Ct 77502
Armand View Dr 77505
Armor Ave 77502
Arno St 77502
Aspen Dr 77505
Athens Dr 77505
Augusta Dr 77505
W Austin Ave 77502
Avalon Ct 77505
Avenel Dr 77505
Azalea Ct 77506
Aztec St 77504
Bandera Run Ct 77505
Barbara Ln 77502
Barton Creek Dr 77505
Basket St 77502
Bastrop Ave 77506
Bay Area Blvd 77507
Bay Hill Ln 77505
Bay Oaks Dr 77505
Bayfair St 77505
Bayou Blvd 77506
Baypark Rd 77507
Bayport Blvd 77507
Bayshore Blvd
3000-3099 77502
3100-3299 77504
3301-3399 77504
Baywood Dr 77505
Bear Track Ln 77505
Bearle St 77506
Bee Hive Dr 77505
Belgium Dr 77505
Belmont 77504
Belmont St 77506
W Belmont St 77506
Belshire Rd 77502
Beltway Green Blvd 77503
Benard Ct 77503
Benjamin Ln 77505
Bennett Dr 77503
Bennington Dr 77503
Benton Dr 77504
Bermuda Dr 77503
Bernard St 77506
Bertloma St 77502
Beta Cir 77503
Betty Ln 77502
Beusch Dr 77502
Beverly Ave 77506
Beverly Rd 77503
Bidias St 77504
Birch Dr 77503
Birchwood Dr 77502
W Bird Rd 77502
Birdie Way 77505
Birnham Woods Blvd 77503
Blackberry Dr 77506
Blackburn Dr 77502
N Blackwell St 77506
Blake Ave 77502
Blind River Dr 77504
Bliss Meadows Dr 77505
Blue Bonnet St 77505
Blue Water Ct 77505
Blueberry Ln 77502
Bluebird Ln 77502
Bluefield Dr 77503
Blueridge Ave 77502
Bob St 77502
Bogie Way 77505
Bogota Dr 77505
Bolivia Dr 77504
Bond St 77503
Bournemouth Dr 77504
Boyd Ct 77506
Bramley Dr 77503
Brandon Ct 77506
Bravo Ave 77502
Brazil Cir 77504
Brenda Ln 77502
Briar Dr 77503
Briargreen St 77503
Briarway St 77503
Briarwood Dr 77502
Broadmoor Dr 77505
W Broadway Ave 77506
Brockman St 77506
Brook Ln 77502
Brookhaven Ave 77504
Brower Crest Dr 77504
Brown Dr 77506
Bryan Ave 77506
Buchanan St 77502
Buckingham Dr 77504
Budd St 77502
Bur Oak Dr 77505
Burke Rd
100-1299 77506
1300-3099 77502
3100-5299 77504
Burke Ridge Dr 77504
Busse Cir 77503
Butler Dr 77502
Butterfly Cir 77505
Bystreet Rd 77504
Cactus St 77506
Cadena Dr 77504
Calvin St 77506
Camarosa Dr 77504
Cambridge Ct 77504
Camden Ln 77504
Camden Rd 77502
Camellia Ave 77505
Camille St 77506
Campbell Ave 77502
Canada Dr 77505
Canary Cir 77502
Cann Dr 77503
Cannonade Dr 77503
Cantwell Dr 77505
Canyon Gate Dr 77505
Capital St 77502
Cara Cir 77505
Cardinal Cir 77502
Carl St 77506
Carmel Cir 77505
Carmel Ridge Way 77503
Carmella Dr 77506
Carpenter Ave 77502
Carroll Dr 77506
Carter St 77503
Cascade Ave 77502
Catalina Dr 77503
Cavalier Ln 77502
Cedar Lawn Cir 77505
Cedar Point Dr 77505
Cedarcrest Dr 77503
Cedarwood Dr 77502
Center St
200-1299 77506
5100-5899 77505
Central Ave 77502
Chandler Cv 77504
N Charles St 77506
Chemical Rd 77507
Cherokee Dr 77506
Cherry Ln 77502
Cherry Hills Ln 77505
Cherrybrook Ln 77502
Chestershire Dr 77503
Chestnut Ln 77502
Cheyenne Ave 77505
Chile Dr 77504
Chipley Dr 77505
Chippawa Ln 77504
Choate Rd 77507
N Circle Park St 77504
Citation Dr 77503
Claremont Ave 77502
Cleveland St 77502
Clover Meadows St 77505
Coapites St 77504
Cocoa Ln 77502
Coffee Dr 77505
Cog Hill Dr 77505
Colchester Way 77504
Coldstream Dr 77505
Coleman Ave 77506
Colombia Dr
4200-4399 77504
4800-5099 77505
Colonial Ct 77505
Comal Ave 77506
Comanche St 77503
Commander St 77502
Community Dr 77506
Concord Rd 77502
Conner Ct 77504
N Conrad St 77506
Corinth Dr 77505
Cornoustie St 77505
Cottonwood Dr 77502
Country Rd 77505
Coventry Ct 77502
Cowan St 77506
Cranbrook Way 77502
Crawford Dr 77503
Creekside Ln 77505
Crenshaw Rd
400-4699 77504
5000-6099 77505
Crepe Myrtle Ln 77505
Crescent Dr 77506
Cresta Place Dr 77505
Cresterrace Dr 77505
Crestford Ln 77505
Crestgrove Dr 77505
Crestlea Ct 77505
Crestmeadow Dr 77505
Crestside Dr 77505
Crestwood Ln 77502
Cruse Dr 77506
Crystal Dowels Dr 77505
Cujanes St 77504
Culver St 77502
W Curtis Ave 77502
Cypress St
2600-2799 77502
5200-5399 77503
Dabney Dr 77502
Dade St 77502
Daisy St 77505
Dallas St 77502
Dandridge Ave 77502
Danielle Dr 77505
Danpree St 77504
Darling Ave 77503
Darrel St 77502
Dartmouth Dr 77503
Davis St 77506
Dawson Creek Dr 77503
Dedman St 77503
Dee Dr 77505
Deepwater Ave 77503
Deer Trail Dr 77505
Del Monte Dr 77503
Del Paso Cir 77505
Delta St 77506
Denham Ave 77506
Denkman St 77503
Denmark Dr 77505
Dewberry Ln 77502
Diamante Dr 77504
Dogwood Dr 77506
Dogwood Hill St 77503
Don St 77506
Donerail Dr 77503
Doral Dr 77505
Dorene St 77502
Doris Ave 77502
Dorothy St 77502
Dorsetshire Dr 77504
Double Eagle Dr 77505
Dow Way 77505
Doyle Ct 77503
Dry Creek Dr 77505
Dryden Ln 77505
Dumbarton Rd 77503
Dunhill Ln 77506
Dunstan Rd 77502
Dunwick Ln 77502
Dupont St 77503
Duquesne Ln 77505
Dusky Rose Ln 77502
Eagle Ave 77506
Earl St 77503
Easthaven Dr 77506
Eastman St 77506
Easy St 77502
Ecuador Dr 77504
Edgefield Dr 77503
Edgehill Rd 77502
Edmond Ave 77506
Edmonton Dr 77503
Effie Ln 77502
Egypt Dr 77505
W Ellaine Ave 77506
Ellsworth Dr 77506
Elm Ave 77506
Elmscott Dr 77505
Elmwood Ln 77502
Elsa St 77502
Embe St 77502
Emerald Dr 77505
Emerald Field Dr 77503
Epsilon St 77504
Estate St 77503
Estella Rd 77504
Esther Ave 77502
Eula Ave 77505
Eva Ave 77502
Everbear St 77504
Everglade Dr 77502
Fair Dr 77507
Fairbourne Dr 77505
Faircrest St 77505
Fairdale St 77505
Fairfax Ln 77502
Fairglen St 77505
Fairhaven St 77505
Fairhill St 77505
Fairhope Oak St 77503
Fairmont Pkwy
100-4799 77504
4800-7599 77505
7600-9000 77507
9002-9898 77507
Fairmoor St 77505
Fairshire St 77505
Fairvent St 77505
Fairview St 77504
Fairway St 77505
Fairway Plaza Dr 77505
Fairwood St 77505
Falling Oak Ct 77505
Federal Rd 77504
Fenwood Dr 77502
Fern St 77503
Fern Creek Ct 77503
Fernside Dr 77505
Findlay Dr 77505
Finfrock St 77506
Firwood Cir & Dr 77502
N & S Fisher Ct 77502
Flagler Ave 77505
Flamborough Dr 77503
Flora Dr 77505
Florence Ave 77502
Flowers St 77503
Flynn Dr 77502
Foster Ave 77506
Fountain Creek Ct 77505
Fox Trl 77504
Fox Hollow Ln 77504
Fox Meadow Ln 77504
Fraleri Blvd 77507
France Ln & Way 77505
Francis Dr 77506
Freedom Ln 77504
Fresa Rd 77502
Gallant Fox Dr 77503
Gamma St 77504
Garden Way Ln 77503
Gardenia Trl 77505
Garfield Ave 77506
Garner Rd 77502
Garrett St 77506
Garvey Dr 77506
Gary Ave 77502
Genoa Red Bluff Rd
801-1699 77504
1701-3797 77505
3799-5599 77505
5600-6699 77507
George St 77502
Georgianna Dr 77503
Gerald St 77503
Geronimo Ln 77505
Ghana Ln 77505
Gilbert St 77506
Gillingham Way 77504
Glasgow St 77506
Glen Avon Dr 77505
Glencrest Dr 77502
Gleneagles Dr 77505
Glenmore Dr 77503
Glenn Ave 77506
Glowing Horizon Rd 77503
Golden Villas St 77503
Goldenrod St 77503
Gore St 77506
Grant St 77503
Grape Ln 77502
Green Meadows St 77505
Green Shadow Dr 77503
Green Trail Ct 77503
Green Tree Ct 77505
Greenbriar Ave 77502
Griffin St 77506
Grunewald Dr 77502
Gulf St 77502
Guthrie Dr 77503
Gypsy Pops Dr 77503
Haiti Ln 77505
Halkies Rd 77502
Hamilton Ln 77506
Hamon Dr 77506
Hampton Ct 77504
Hancock Ave 77502
Handell Ln 77502
Hankamer St 77506
Harding St 77502
Hargrave St 77506
Harper Dr 77502
Harriette St 77502
W Harris Ave 77506
Harrison Ct 77503
Harrop Ave 77506
W Hart Ave 77506
Harvard St 77502
Hawthorne Ave 77506
Hays St 77503
Hazeltine Dr 77505
Hearne Dr 77502
Heather Park Dr 77505
Heathfield Dr 77505
Hector Ave 77502
Heights St 77503
Helen St 77502
Hemlock Dr 77502
Hempstead Ave 77506
Hendarr Dr 77505
Herbert Ave 77506
Hernandez Rd 77504
Heron Ln 77502
Hertholi St 77504
Hialeah Dr 77503
Hiawatha Ln 77505
Hickory Ln 77502
Holly Ave
2400-2699 77502
4700-5399 77503
Holly Bay Ct 77505
Holly Park Dr 77505
Holly Terrace Ct 77505
Honduras Dr 77504
Honey Ln 77505
Honeysuckle Ln 77505
House St 77502
S & W Houston Ave & Rd 77502
Howard St 77506
Huckleberry Ln 77502
Hummingbird Ct 77502
Huntington Dr 77506
Imber St 77506
Inca Dr 77503
Indigo Pass Ct 77505
Ingersol Ave 77506
Inglewood Dr 77505
Inverness Way 77505
Inwood Ln 77502
Ireland Ln 77505
Iroquois Dr 77504
Irving Ln 77506
Isaac Ct 77503
Italy Ln 77505
Ivy St 77505
Ivy Green Ct 77503
Jack St 77502
W Jackson Ave 77506
Jacquelyn Cir 77503
Jamaica Ln 77505
James St 77506
Jana Ln 77503
Jane Dr 77502
Jasmine Dr 77503
Jean St 77502
Jeff Ginn Memorial Dr 77506
Jefferson 77506
Jefferson Ave 77502
Jenkins Rd 77506
Jensen Dr 77506
Jessie Ln 77502
Jewel St 77506
Joe St 77502
John St 77502
John David Ln 77505
Johnson St
100-198 77506
200-1299 77506
1700-1799 77502
N Johnson St 77506
Joseph St 77506
Juanita Dr 77502
Judy Ln 77502
Julia Ct 77505
Juliet St 77502
Kalmer St 77502
Kansas St 77506
Kaplan Dr 77503
Kappa St 77504
Karankawas St 77504
Karen Ln 77503
Kathryn Cir 77503
Kathy St 77504
Kay Ave 77506
Keeler Ct 77503
Keith Ave
500-799 77504
5100-5299 77505
Kemp St 77506
Kemper Dr 77505
Kensington Ct 77502
Kent Dr 77505
Kenwick Pl 77504
Kenya Ln 77505
Kerry Dr 77506
Killearn Dr 77505
Kings Court Dr 77502
Kingsdale St 77503
Kinrose Dr 77505
Kinsley Dr 77505
Kiowa St 77504
Kipper Cir 77505
Knob Hill Ave 77505
Knox St 77504
Kolb Rd 77502
La Fleur Pine Ln 77503
La Paz St 77504
Lacey Oak Dr 77505
Lafayette Ave 77502
Lafferty Rd
1100-3099 77502
3100-3499 77504
Laird St 77506
Lakeside Ct 77504
Lakewood Dr 77504
Lakin Ave 77506
Lamar Dr 77502
Lamesa Ave 77506

Lancaster Ln 77506
Lance Ave 77505
Lark Dr 77503
Laura Lee Ln 77504
Laurynnbrook Dr 77505
Lausanne Ave 77505
Laverne Ave 77502
Lavonia Ln 77502
Lawrence Ave 77506
Lee Ave 77506
Leesa Ln 77507
Leisure Ct 77504
Leneva Ln 77502
Lenny Ln 77502
Leonard St 77506
Leora Ave 77506
Leroy Dr 77502
Leslie St 77502
Lewis St 77502
Light Company Rd 77506
Lilac St
2400-2999 77503
3200-3499 77505
Lillian St 77502
Lily St
2400-3099 77503
3100-4399 77505
Linda Ln 77502
Line Dr 77505
Linwood Cir 77502
Little Redwood Dr 77505
Little Willow Dr 77505
Littlejohn Ct 77502
Live Oak St 77506
Llano St 77504
Locklaine Dr 77502
Locust St 77502
London St
1100-1298 77506
1300-1499 77502
Longwood Dr 77503
Lorraine Ct 77506
Los Coyotes Dr 77505
Los Verdes Dr 77504
Lucy Ln 77505
Lynn Cir 77502
Lyric Ln 77503
Mackinac Ln 77505
Madison Ave 77502
Madison Lee Ln 77504
Magnolia Dr 77503
Maid Stone Dr 77505
Maidenhead Dr 77504
Main St
100-1099 77506
1101-1299 77506
1300-1600 77502
1602-1698 77502
N Main St 77506
Malderm St 77506
Malone Dr
3700-3899 77503
4200-4299 77507
Malvern Ave 77503
Manordale Dr 77505
Maple Ave 77506
Maple Cross Dr 77505
Maplewood Ln 77502
Marguerite Ln 77502
Maria St 77506
Marlen Ave 77502
Marlock Ln 77502
Mars Dr 77504
Marsh Grass Ln 77503
Marshall St 77506
E & W Martha Ln 77504
Martin St 77502
Marvick Dr 77506
Mattye Maye Dr 77503
Mavis Ln 77505
Maywood Ln 77503
Mcmasters Ave 77506
Mcnay Dr 77506
N & S Meadow Ct, Dr
& Loop E & W 77505
Meadow Wood Dr 77503

Meadowlake Rd 77503
Mease Ct 77503
Medellin St 77506
Melinda Ln 77505
N & S Memorial Ct 77502
Memorial Park Dr 77506
Merion Cir 77505
Merle St 77502
Miami Rd 77502
Michael Dr 77506
Middle Park St 77504
Middlefield Dr 77505
Midway Ln 77504
Mill Creek Dr 77503
Mill River Ct 77505
Mimosa Ave 77506
Mintiner Ln 77502
Mistletoe Rd 77505
Mistra Dr 77505
Misty Ln 77505
Mize Rd 77504
Mobile Dr 77506
Mockingbird Ln 77502
Mohegan Cir 77504
Monaco Ln 77505
Monmouth Ln 77505
Monroe Dr 77502
Montevideo Cir 77504
Moon Ct 77504
Moonlite Dr 77505
Morning Glory Dr 77503
Morningside Ln 77506
Mulberry Ln 77502
N Munger St 77506
Murphy Ln 77504
Muscadine Ln 77502
Nancy St 77502
Nantucket St 77503
Natchez Ave 77506
National St 77502
Nations Dr 77505
Navajo St 77504
Nell St 77506
New Century Dr 77507
New Decade Dr 77507
New West Rd 77507
Newton Cir & Dr 77503
Nicole Dr 77503
Norman St 77506
North Ave 77506
Northwood Ln 77502
Nottingham St 77502
Oak Ave 77503
W Oak Ave 77502
Oakdale St 77506
Oakmont Cir 77505
Oaks Dr
1200-1299 77506
1300-2799 77502
Old Highway 146 77507
Old Vista Rd 77505
Oleander Dr 77503
Olive Ave 77506
Ollia Cir 77503
Olson Ln 77505
Olympia Dr 77505
Omega Cir 77503
Oneida St 77504
Orange Tree Dr 77505
Oriole Ln 77502
Orrel Dr 77503
Overcrest Ln 77505
N & S Palm Ct 77502
Palmetto Dr 77506
Palmwood Dr 77502
Palos Verdes Dr 77504
Pampa St 77504
Panama St 77504
Pansy St
2100-2198 77503
2200-3099 77503
3100-4099 77505
Paraguay Cir 77504
W & N Park Ln & St 77506
Park Bend Ln 77505
Park Meadow Ct 77504

Park Ridge Dr 77504
Park Trail Ln 77505
Parkland St 77504
Parkside Dr 77502
Parkwood Dr 77503
Parry Sound 77504
Pasadena Blvd
100-1000 77506
1002-1298 77506
1101-1199 77501
1199-1199 77506
1300-2799 77502
2900-4599 77503
N Pasadena Blvd 77506
Pasadena Fwy
115-697 77506
699-2300 77506
2302-2998 77506
3000-4399 77503
4401-4499 77503
W Pasadena Fwy 77506
Pasadena Town Square
Mall 77506
Patras Dr 77505
Patricia Ln 77502
Patrick St 77506
Paul St 77506
Paulette Dr 77504
Pauline Ave 77502
Pawnee Ln 77504
Peach Ln 77502
Peachwood Cir & Dr 77502
Pebble Bay Ct 77505
Pecan Dr 77502
Pendleton St 77506
Penfield St 77506
Perez Rd 77502
Perla Rd 77502
Persimmon St 77502
Peru Cir 77504
Pi Cir 77504
Piedmont St 77504
Pimlico Ln 77503
Pin Oak Dr 77505
Pine Ave 77503
Pine Cone Trl 77505
Pine Needle Ln 77505
Pine Valley St 77505
Pinehurst St 77505
Pineswept Dr 77503
Pinewood Ln 77502
Pinnacle Way 77504
W Pitts Ave 77506
Plainview St 77504
Plaza Blvd 77506
Plymouth St 77502
Pocahontas Dr 77505
Polk Ave 77506
Pomeroy Ave 77506
Pomona Dr 77506
Ponca St 77504
Pont La Salle Ln 77503
Port Rd 77507
Potomac Ave 77502
Prairie Ave 77506
Prairie Shadows Way 77503
Preston Ave
100-3099 77503
3100-5199 77505
N Preston Ave 77503
Preston Trails Ln 77505
Primrose Dr 77502
Providence Ln 77505
Purdue St 77502
Queens Rd 77502
Quiet Meadow Ct 77505
Quitman Dr 77505
Rachelle Ridge Ct 77505
Rainbow Bend Dr 77505
Raindrops Rd 77505
Rainfall Dr 77505
Rainforest Trail Ct &
Dr 77505
Rainier St 77504
Raintree Ct 77505
Rainwater Dr 77505

Rainy River Dr 77504
Ramsey Dr 77503
Rancho Vista Dr 77504
N Randall St 77506
Randolph Rd 77503
Raspberry Ln 77502
Ray Dr & Rd 77505
N & S Rayburn Ct 77502
Raymond St 77506
Rebecca Dr 77506
Red Bluff Ct 77506
Red Bluff Rd
100-2700 77506
2702-2722 77506
2723-5499 77503
5500-6699 77505
7600-11000 77507
11002-12498 77507
Red Coral Dr 77505
Red Oak Ct 77505
Redbud Cir 77502
Redfield Dr 77503
Redman St 77506
Redwinn Dr 77502
Redwood Ln 77502
Redwood Falls Dr 77505
Rena Jane Ln 77503
Reno Dr 77505
Revere Dr 77502
Rex St 77506
Rhodes Dr 77505
Richard Ave 77506
Richey St
101-1299 77506
1300-2199 77502
N Richey St 77506
W Richey Access St 77506
Ridgecrest Dr 77504
Ridgeway Dr 77504
River Oaks Dr 77505
River Ranch Dr 77505
Roaring Springs Rd 77505
Robert St 77502
Robin Cir 77502
Robinhood St 77502
Robinson Dr 77506
Robley St 77502
Rockfield Dr 77505
Romeo St 77502
Rose St 77503
Rosemead Dr 77506
Ross Ave 77506
Royal Dornoch Dr 77505
Royal Knoll Ct 77505
Royal Manor Dr 77505
Ruella Ln 77502
Rustic Dr 77502
Ryann Ct 77505
Sachnik Dr 77502
Sage Brush Ln 77503
Saint Andrews Dr 77505
Saint James St 77502
Saint Jude Dr 77505
Salvador St 77504
Sam St 77502
E Sam Houston Pkwy S
100-3099 77503
3100-5199 77505
Samuels Dr 77505
San Augustine Ave 77503
San Jacinto Dr 77502
Sandlehurst Dr 77504
Sandlewood Dr 77504
Sands Dr 77505
Sandy Ln 77505
Santa Anita Ln 77503
Santiago St 77504
Sao Paulo St 77504
Satsuma St 77506
Savannah Ave 77506
Sawmill Ln 77505
Scarborough Ln
400-1299 77506
1300-1999 77502
Scott St 77506
Scottline Dr 77505

Sea Oak Ct 77505
Secretariat Dr 77503
Selva St 77504
Seminole St 77504
Senate St 77502
Seneca St 77504
Sequoia Ln 77502
Seymour St 77506
Sha Cir 77504
Shadow Ln 77506
Shady Arbour Ct & Dr 77505
Shanna Ln 77504
Sharon St 77502
Shaun Dr 77504
Shaver St
100-1200 77506
1202-1298 77506
1300-3099 77502
3101-3197 77504
3199-3399 77504
3401-4499 77504
N Shaver St 77506
W Shaw Ave 77506
Sheffield Ct 77504
Shenandoah Dr 77502
Sherbrooke Ct & Rd 77503
Sheridan Rd 77502
Sherman Ave 77503
Sherwood Dr 77502
Shoppe Rd 77504
Sienna Heights Ct &
Ln 77505
Sigma St 77504
Silver Grove Ct 77505
Silver Oak Dr 77505
Simmons Blvd 77506
Sinclair St
2400-3099 77503
3100-3499 77505
Sioux Dr 77503
Skylark Rd 77502
Smith Ave 77504
Somerset Ct 77504
Sophie Ann Dr 77503
N South St 77503
Southampton Ct 77504
Southmore Ave
107-2799 77502
2800-2999 77503
W Southmore Ave 77502
Space Center Blvd 77505
Spanish Oak Dr 77505
Spencer Hwy
2200-4699 77504
4700-6099 77505
6100-8298 77505
6100-6100 77508
6101-8599 77505
Spooner St
101-107 77506
109-1299 77506
1500-1599 77502
N Spooner St 77506
Sprague Ave 77505
Spring Dr 77504
Spring Oak Dr 77505
Stanford St 77502
Starkey St 77503
Starlite Dr 77505
Steep Rock Dr 77504
Still Creek Rd 77505
Stone Briar Dr 77505
Stoney Creek Dr 77503
Stoney View Dr 77505
Stratford Ave 77506
Strawberry Rd
900-1099 77506
1101-1299 77506
1300-3099 77502
3100-4999 77504
Stridarn Dr 77503
Sudbury Dr 77504
Suiter Way 77503
Sullivan Ave 77506
Summer Oak Dr 77505
Sunray Ln 77503

Sunset Dr 77506
Sunshine Ln 77505
Surecrop Ln 77504
Susan St 77506
Sweetbriar Dr 77505
Sweetgum St 77502
Sycamore Ave 77503
Tabor St 77506
Taft Ave 77502
Tamar Dr 77503
Tamora Ln 77505
Tanglebriar Dr 77503
Tascott St 77506
Taylor Ave 77506
Teabury Ave 77503
Teakwood Dr 77502
Tealway Dr 77504
Tejas Dr 77503
Terlingua St 77504
Terreno Vista Blvd 77504
W Texas Ave 77506
Thelma Ln 77502
Theresa St 77506
Thistledown Dr 77504
Thistlewood Dr 77504
W Thomas Ave 77506
Thornwood Dr 77503
Thunder Bay Dr 77504
Tidewater Ct 77505
Tiguas St 77504
Tilden Dr 77506
Tiller St 77502
Timber Ct 77505
Timberline Dr 77505
Tiny Hur Dr 77503
Tolima Dr 77505
Tonkawa St 77504
Topango Dr 77504
Townhouse Ln 77502
Tranquil River Dr 77505
Trebor St 77505
Tree Line Dr 77505
Tree Top Dr 77505
Tresa Dr 77504
Trichelle St 77506
Trimm Ave 77502
Trimstone Dr 77505
Trinity Ln 77506
Tripoli Dr 77505
Troon Cir 77505
Truxton Dr 77503
Tulip St
2800-3099 77502
3200-3599 77504
Tupelo Ave 77506
Turnberry Ct 77505
Turtle Cove Dr 77505
Turtle Creek Dr 77505
Tuscarora St 77504
Tynemouth Dr 77504
Underwood Rd 77507
Uraguay Dr 77504
Ute St 77504
Valerie Ave 77502
Valley Forge Dr 77502
Valparaiso Cir 77504
Van Buren Cir 77502
Venetian Way 77503
Vermillion Dr 77506
Verona 77504
Vienna Pl 77502
View St 77502
Village Cir 77504
E Village Ct 77506
W Village Ct 77506
Village Way 77502
Village Heights Ct 77505
Village Park Dr 77504
Village Townhome Dr 77504
Vince St
200-1299 77506
2000-2099 77502
Vineyard Ln 77504
Violet St 77503
Virginia Ln 77502

Vista Rd
100-4699 77504
4701-4703 77505
4705-5499 77505
Vista Park Dr 77504
Vista Pointe Dr 77504
Vivian Ave 77506
Wafer St
100-1299 77506
1300-1599 77502
N Wafer St 77506
Waialae Cir 77505
Wallis St 77502
Walnut Ln 77502
N Walter St 77506
War Admiral Dr 77503
Warwick Dr 77504
Washington St 77503
Water Oak Dr 77505
Watercolor Cv 77505
Waterfall Cv 77505
Watters Rd
2800-3099 77502
3100-4099 77504
Way Fair Dr 77505
Wayne St 77502
Wedgewood Cir 77502
Weiser Dr 77503
Wentwood Dr 77504
Wentworth Ln 77506
West Ave 77502
West Ln 77506
Westbrook Cir 77503
Westchester St 77505
Westfall Ave 77506
Westside Ct 77502
Westside Dr
2700-3099 77502
3100-3699 77504
Whelton Cir & Dr 77503
Whirlaway Dr 77503
Whispering Pines Dr 77503
Whitaker Ave 77506
White Cloud Ln 77504
White Manor Dr 77505
White River Dr 77504
White Water Ct 77505
Whitney Ct 77505
Wichita St 77502
Wilbury Heights Dr 77505
Wildgrove Dr 77504
Williams St 77506
Williamsburg Dr 77502
Willow St 77506
Willow Oaks Cir 77506
Willowind Dr 77504
Willowview Dr 77504
Wilma Lois Ave 77502
Wilson Creek Ln 77503
Winding Rd 77504
Windsor Ln 77506
Windy Way 77505
Winona Dr 77506
Winterborne Dr 77505
N Witter St 77506
Woodhampton Dr 77505
Woodhollow Ln 77504
Woodlawn Ave 77504
Woodlock Dr 77506
Woodridge Ln 77502
Wren Ln 77502
Wyatt St 77503
Wynd Ave 77503
Yale St 77502
Yaupon Ave 77506
Yellowstone Dr
4100-4799 77504
4800-4899 77505
Yepez Rd 77504
Yorkshire Ave 77503
Yosemite Dr 77504
Young St 77504
Yuma Trl 77505
Zapp Ln 77502
Zarate Ave 77506
Zephyr Dr 77506

Zuni Trl 77505

NUMBERED STREETS

All Street Addresses 77504

PEARLAND TX

General Delivery 77581

POST OFFICE BOXES MAIN OFFICE STATIONS AND BRANCHES

Box No.s
1 - 3488 77588
84101 - 842517 77584

NAMED STREETS

Abbey Field Dr 77584
Abbeywood Dr 77584
Abbott Dr 77584
Acorn Ct 77584
Adamo Ln 77581
Adams St 77584
Addison Dr 77584
Adella Ct 77584
Ainsley Way Dr 77581
Airfield Ln 77581
Alamanni Dr 77581
Alberton Ln 77584
Alder Glen Ln 77584
Alexander Ln 77581
Alexander Parc Dr 77581
Alexandros Ct 77584
Alice St 77581
Allen Rd 77584
Almond Cove Ct 77584
Amanda Lee Dr 77581
Amber Creek Ct & Dr 77584
Amber Hill Trl 77581
Amberly Ct 77584
Ameno Dr 77581
Amerson Ct & Dr 77584
Ames St 77584
Amesbury Cir 77584
Amie Ln 77584
Amoco St 77584
Anacacho Ln 77584
Anchor Bay Ct 77584
Andover Dr 77584
Ann Ln 77584
Anthony Ln 77581
Antrim St 77581
Apache Trl 77584
Appian Way 77584
Apple Blossom Dr 77584
Apple Springs Dr 77584
Appleton Dr 77584
April St 77581
Arbor Ct & Dr 77584
Arbor Brook Ln 77584
Arbor Hill Ln 77584
Armstrong Ln 77584
Arnold Dr 77584
Arrowhead Creek Ln 77581
Arrowsmith Ct 77584
Asbury Ct 77581
Ash Rd 77584
Ash Run Ct 77581
Ashbrook Ln 77584
Ashton Park Dr 77584
Ashwood Dr 77584
Aspen Ln 77584
Aspen Sky Ln 77584
Aspenbrook Ct 77581
Aubrell Rd 77584
Auburn Dr 77584
Auburn Creek Dr 77584
Auburn Shores Ct & Dr 77584
Auburn Trail Ln 77584
Auburn Woods Dr 77581
Audubon Pl 77584
Augusta Dr 77581
N & S Austin Ave 77581
Austin Lake Ct 77581
Autumn Ct 77584
Autumn Falls Dr 77584
Autumn Forest Dr 77584
Autumn Lake Trl 77584
Autumnbrook Ln 77584
Autumnjoy Dr 77584
Avalon Cove Ln 77581
Avalon Lake Ln 77581
Avalon Trace Ln 77581
Avanti Ct & Dr 77584
Avey Ct 77584
Avilion Ct 77584
Avory Ridge Ln 77581
E & S Baden Oaks Dr 77581
Bagnoli Rose Ln 77584
Bailey Rd 77584
E & W Bainbridge Cir 77584
Balmoral Ln 77584
Balmorhea Dr 77584
Balsam Breeze Ln 77584
Balsam Lake Ct & Ln 77584
Banks Run Dr 77584
Banyan Wood Way 77584
Barberry Ct 77581
Bardet St 77584
Barkly Ct 77581
Barons Cove Ct & Ln 77584
Barretts Glen Dr 77581
Barrington Ct 77584
Barry Moore Dr 77581
Barry Rose Rd 77581
Barton Ct & Dr 77584
Barton Creek Dr 77584
Barton Shore Dr 77584
Basil Ct 77584
Baughman Dr 77584
Bay Crossing Dr 77584
Bay Ledge Dr 77584
Bay Manor St 77584
Bay Spring St 77584
Baycliff Ct 77584
Bayfront Ct & Dr 77584
Baymeadow Ct & Dr 77584
Bayport Dr 77584
Baywater Canyon Dr 77584
Beacon Bend Ct & Ln 77584
Beacon Green Ln 77581
Beacon Hill Dr 77584
Beacon Pointe 77584
Beacon View Ct 77584
Becket St 77584
Becket Bluff Ct 77584
Beckton Ln 77584
Becky Ln 77584
Beechcraft St 77581
Beechwood Dr 77584
E, N, S & W Belgravia Dr 77584
Bell Creek Ct & Dr 77584
Bend Creek Ln 77584
E & S Bending Oaks Ln 77584
Bending Spring Dr 77584
Benrus Ct 77584
Bent Creek Dr 77584
Bentlake Ln 77581
Bentley Ct & Dr 77584
Berkshire Trce 77584
Berlinetta Dr 77584
Berlino Dr 77581
Berry Rd 77584
Berryfield Ln 77581
Bethany Bay Dr 77584
Betty Ln 77584
Big Spring Dr 77584
Bigallo Dr 77584
Birch St 77581
Birch Bough St 77581
Birch Landing Ct 77584
Birchview Ct 77584
Birdie Ct 77581
Biscayne Lake Dr 77584
Biscayne Springs Ln 77584
Bishopton Cir & St 77581
Black Ln 77584
Black Canyon Ln 77584
Black Rock Ln 77581
Blaesser Dr 77584
Blake Ct 77584
Blakely Grove Ln 77581
Blanco Dr 77584
Blossom Ct 77584
Blossom Walk Ct 77584
Blue Creek Dr 77584
Blue Heron Dr 77581
Blue Sage Dr 77584
Blue Spruce Trl 77581
Bluebird Way 77581
Bluebonnet St 77584
Bobby St 77581
Bodine Dr 77584
Bogey Way 77581
Boulder Dr 77584
Boulder Rdg 77581
Boulder Creek Ct & Dr 77584
Bounds Dr 77584
Boxwood Ct & St 77581
Boxwood Gate Trl 77584
Bracket Ct & Dr 77581
Braesview Dr 77584
Branch Hill Dr 77581
Brandemere Dr 77584
Brantly Cove Ct 77584
Brazos Bend Dr 77584
Breckonridge Cir 77581
Breezeport Ct 77584
Breezeway Ln 77581
Breezeway Bend Dr 77584
Breezy Pines Ln 77584
Brentwood Ln 77581
Brett Dr 77584
Brian St 77584
Briar Cir & Ct 77581
Briar Crest Ct 77584
Briar Rose Ct & Dr 77584
Briar View Dr 77581
Briarglen Dr 77584
Briarsage Ln 77581
Bright Glen Dr 77581
Bright Landing Ct & Ln 77584
Brightlake Way Ln 77584
Brighton Ln 77584
Brighton Brook Ln 77581
Brinton Spring Ln 77581
Briscoe Ct & Ln 77584
Bristol Way 77584
Bristol Banks Ct 77584
Bristol Water Dr 77584
Britt Rd 77581
Broad Bay Ln 77584
Broadway St
1000-2641 77581
2642-2698 77584
2643-4009 77581
2700-8398 77584
4011-4099 77584
4101-8401 77581
8400-8426 77584
8428-13099 77584
Broadway Bend Dr 77584
Broken Bridge Ln 77581
Broken Creek Ct & Ln 77584
Brom Bones Blvd 77581
E, N, S & W Brompton Dr 77584
Brook Arbor Ct 77584
Brook Hollow Dr 77581
Brookhaven Ct 77581
Brookney St 77584
Brookren Ct 77584
Brooks Ct 77584
Brookshore Ln 77584
Brookside Rd 77581
Brookstone Ct 77584
Brookview Dr 77584
Brookwood Ln 77584
Brownstone Pl 77584
Bruno Way 77584
Bryan St 77584
Brymoor Ct 77584
Btist View Dr 77581
Buchanan Way 77584
Buckeye Ct & Ln 77584
Buckholt St 77581
Buescher Ct 77584
Bui Dr 77581
Bunker Hill Ct 77581
Burgess Hill Ct 77584
Burwood Ct 77584
Business Center Dr 77584
Butler Rd 77581
Byron Ave 77581
Cactus Heights Ln 77581
Calico Canyon Ln 77581
Calico Creek Ln 77584
Caloway Cir 77581
Calypso Bay Ct & Dr 77584
Cambridge Cir 77581
Cambridge Bay Dr 77584
Cambridge Shores Ct & Ln 77584
Camden Ln 77584
Camelia Crest Ct 77581
Camelot Ln 77581
Camelots Ct 77584
Campbell Dr 77584
Caneshaw Dr 77584
Canterbury Dr 77584
Canterbury Park Dr & Ln 77584
Canton Dr 77584
Cantu Rd 77584
Canyon Dr 77584
Canyon Creek Ct 77581
Canyon Lake Dr 77581
Canyon Springs Dr 77584
Cape Landing Dr 77584
Capecrest Dr 77584
Capital Ct 77584
E & S Capri Ct & Dr 77581
Capri Place Ln 77581
Caprock Dr 77584
Carmel Hill Ln 77584
Carmona Ln 77584
Carrie Ln 77584
Carrington Ct 77584
Carroll Dr 77581
Carson Ave & Ct 77584
Cartagena Dr 77581
Casey Ct 77581
Cashmere Way 77584
Castle Ct 77581
Castle Oaks Dr 77581
Castle Pond Ct 77584
Castlebay Ct 77584
Castlerock Ct & Dr 77584
Castleton Bay Ln 77584
Castlewind Ln 77584
Catalina Shores Dr 77584
Catalpa Rock Ct 77584
Catamaran Cove Dr 77584
Cayman Bend Ln 77584
Cedar St 77581
Cedar Creek Dr 77584
Cedar Hill Ct & Dr 77584
E & S Cedar Hollow Ct & Dr 77584
E & W Cedar Trail Ct 77584
Cedarwood Dr 77584
Centennial Pl 77584
Centennial Village Dr 77584
Centerbrook Ct & Ln 77584
Champion Dr 77581
Chance Ct 77584
Chaperel Dr 77584
Chappelwood Dr 77584
Charles Ave 77584
Charter Oaks Ct 77584
Chase Harbor Ln 77584
Chatwood Dr 77584
Chelsea Ln 77581
Cherry St 77581
Cheryl Dr 77581
Chesapeake Ct 77584
Chester Dr 77584
Chesterwood Dr 77581
Chestnut Cir 77584
Chestnut Creek Way 77584
Chickory Field Ln 77584
Chickory Wood Ct 77584
Chief Dr 77584
Chisel Rdg 77584
Chrissie Dr 77584
Churchill St 77581
Cimarron Valley Ln 77584
E & W Circle Dr 77581
Clarestone Dr 77584
Clay Creek Ct 77584
Claymill Ln 77581
Clear Creek Rd 77581
Clearfield Springs Ct 77584
Cleburne Dr 77584
Cleo St 77581
W Cliff Stone Rd 77581
Cloudburst Ln 77584
Clover Ln 77584
Clover Creek Ln 77584
Cloverfield Ct & Dr 77584
Clovermist Ln 77581
Clubhouse Dr 77584
Coastwood Ln 77584
Cobble Springs Dr & Ln 77584
Coleberry Ct 77584
Colebrook Ct 77584
Colleen Dr 77581
Colmesneil St 77584
Colonial Dr 77584
Colonial Glen Ct 77584
Colony Ln 77581
Columbus Ct 77584
Comal St 77581
Concord Knoll Dr 77581
Coneley Dr 77584
Confederate Dr 77584
Conroe Lake Ct 77581
Consular Ct 77584
Copper Sky Dr 77584
Coral Cove Ct & Dr 77584
Cork Cir 77581
Cornerstone St 77584
Cotswald Trl 77584
Cottage St 77584
Cottage Creek Dr 77584
Cottage Springs Dr 77584
Cottonwood St 77584
Country Club Dr 77581
E & W Country Grove Cir 77584
S & W Country Meadows Ct, Dr & Ln 77584
Country Place Blvd & Pkwy 77584
County Road 100 77584
County Road 102 77584
County Road 102a 77584
County Road 102b 77584
County Road 102c 77584
County Road 116 77584
County Road 117 77584
County Road 118 77584
County Road 119 77584
County Road 120 77584
County Road 124 77581
County Road 125 77581
County Road 127 77581
County Road 129 77581
County Road 130 77581
County Road 132 77581
County Road 151 77584
County Road 162 77584
County Road 391 77581
County Road 403 77581
County Road 48 77584
County Road 554 77584
County Road 560 77581
County Road 562 77584
County Road 563 77584
County Road 59 77584
County Road 666 77584
County Road 827 77584
County Road 831 77584
County Road 865 77581
County Road 880 77584
County Road 90 77584
County Road 91 77584
County Road 922 77584
County Road 93 77584
County Road 94 77584
Courtyard Ln 77584
Covebrook Ct & Dr 77584
Covey Ln 77584
Covington Ct & Way 77584
Crane Dr 77581
W Creek Dr 77581
Creek Bank Ln 77581
Creek Falls Ct 77581
Creek Run Dr 77584
Creek Shore Ln 77581
Creekridge Dr 77581
Creeks Edge Dr 77581
Creekstone Dr 77584
Crepe Myrtle Ln 77584
Crescent Dr 77584
Crescent Bluff Dr 77584
Crescent Cove Dr 77584
Creston Hls 77581
Crestwind Ct & Dr 77584
Cripple Creek Ln 77581
Crooked Creek Ln 77581
Cross Spring Ct & Dr 77584
Crossbranch Ct 77581
Crossroads Plaza Dr 77584
Crystal Falls Ct & Dr 77584
Crystal Lake Cir E 77584
Crystal Reef Ct, Ln & Pl 77584
Cullen Blvd
100-2699 77581
2700-2702 77584
2701-2799 77581
2704-2798 77581
2900-3099 77584
Cunningham Dr 77581
Curley Maple Dr 77584
Cutler Springs Ct 77584
Cypress Bend Ct 77584
Cypress Hollow St 77581
Cypress Springs Ct & Dr 77584
Cypress Village Ct & Dr 77584
Da Vinci Dr 77581
Daisy St 77581
Dana Lynn Ln 77584
Danbury Ct 77581
Danielle Ln 77581
Dappled Ridge Way 77581
Darby Ct 77584
Dare Rd 77584
Daughtery Rd 77584
Davey Oaks St 77584
David St 77584
Dawn Brook Ct & Dr 77584
Dawn Mist Ct 77584
Dawn River Ln 77581
Dawnridge Dr 77584
Dawson Dr 77581
Dawson Rd 77584
Day Dr 77584
De Leon Ln 77581
Debbie Dr 77584
Decker Field Ln 77584
Dee Rd 77581
Deepbrook Dr 77581
Deer Ct 77581
Deerbrook Ct 77584
Deerwood Ct 77581
Delta Bridge Ct & Dr 77584
Devonshire Dr 77584
Diamond Springs Dr 77584
Diamond Way Ct 77584
Discovery Bay 77584
Dixie Farm Rd 77581
Dixie Hill Ct 77581
Dixie Hollow St 77581
Dixie Woods Dr 77581
Dixon Ct & Dr 77584
Doby Ln 77584
Dogwood Dr 77584
Dogwood Blossom Ct & Trl 77581
Donegal St 77581
Dorothy Ln 77581
Dorsey Ln 77584
Douglas St 77581
Dove Ct 77581
Dove Shores Ln 77584
Dover Mist Ln 77581
Downing St 77581
Drake Falls Dr 77584
Drake Springs Ln 77584
Drifter Ct 77584
Dry Bank Ln 77584
Dublin Cir & Ln 77581
Duesenberg Ct & Dr 77584
Dunlavy Ct & Dr 77581
Dunsmere Ct 77584
Durango Dr 77581
Durango Pass Dr 77584
Eagle Lake Dr 77581
Eagles Way 77581
Eaglet Trl 77584
Eaglewood Ct & Dr 77584
Earlwood Ct 77584
Eastbourne Ln 77584
Easton Springs Ct & Dr 77584
Echo Harbor Dr 77584
Eden Cove Ln 77584
Eden Creek Dr 77584
Eden Glen Ln 77581
Edgewater Bend Ct & Ln 77584
Edgewood Dr 77584
Edith Dr 77584
Edwards Ave 77584
Eiker Rd 77581
N Elder Grove Ct & Dr 77584
Elderberry Ln 77584
Elkmont Ct 77584
Elkton Ct 77584
Ella St 77581
Ellen Dr 77584
Ellis Dr 77581
Elm St 77581
Elm Forest Dr 77584
Elm Hollow St 77581
Elms Dr W 77584
Elmwood Dr 77584
Elsbury Ln 77584
Emerald Brook Ln 77584
Emerald Springs Ct & Dr 77584
Emerald Stone Ct 77581
Emma Dr 77584
Emory Oak Ln 77584
Enchanted Lake Dr 77584
Enclave Lake Ln 77584
Endicott Ln 77584
Englewood Dr 77584
English Oaks Blvd 77584
Erin Dr 77581
Erin Glen Way 77584
Ethel St 77581
Eton Dr 77584
Eucalyptus Ln 77584
Evening Bay Dr 77584
Evening Shore Ln 77584
Evening Star Dr 77584
Evening Wind Dr 77584
Evergreen Dr 77581
Ewing Ln 77584
Excaliburs Ct 77584
Exter Trl 77584
Fair Breeze Ln 77584
Fair Brook Way 77584
Fair Oak St 77584

Fairgrove Ct 77584
Fairlane Dr 77581
Fairway Cir 77581
Fairwood St 77581
Falcon Ridge St 77584
Fall Branch Ln 77584
Fallbrook Ct & Dr 77584
Fallen Oak Ct 77581
Fallscreek Ct 77584
Farmers Field St 77581
Farnham Cir 77584
Fastwater Creek Ct & Dr 77584
February St 77581
Fern Ct 77584
Fern Creek Ln 77581
Fernwood Dr 77584
Ferry Cove Ln 77584
Field Ct 77581
Field Hollow Dr 77584
Fifi St 77581
Figland St 77584
Fir Hollow Way 77581
Firefly Rd 77581
Fite Rd 77584
Flamingo Ct 77584
Flat Creek Dr 77584
Flatwood Ct 77584
Flintrock Dr 77584
Floral Park Ln 77584
Flower Field Ct & Ln 77584
Fm 1128 Rd 77584
Fm 865 Rd 77581
Fontaine Dr 77584
Forest Bank Ln 77581
Forest Creek Ln 77584
Forest Oaks Ln 77581
Forest Sage Ln 77584
Forest Spring Ln 77584
Forrest Ln 77581
Forrester Dr 77584
Fortuna Bella Dr 77581
Founders Green Cir 77581
Fountain Brook Ct & Dr 77584
Fountain Mist Dr 77584
Fox Ct 77581
Fox Run St 77584
Foxden Dr 77584
Foxglove Dr 77584
Foxglove Oaks Ct 77581
Francis Dr 77581
Frank Shore Dr 77584
Frazier Ln 77584
Freedom Dr 77581
Freestone Ave 77584
Frost Creek Dr 77584
Frostwood Dr 77584
Gable Park Ct & Ln 77581
Gable Stone Ln 77581
Galleon Point Ct & Dr 77584
Galloway Dr 77581
N & S Galveston Ave 77581
Garden Rd 77581
Garden Field Ln 77584
Garden Glen Ln 77581
Garden Ivy Ln 77581
Gardenia St 77581
Gardina St 77581
Garner Ct 77584
Garner Park Dr 77584
Garnet Ct 77584
Garrettsville Dr 77584
Gatecreek Dr 77581
Gazelle Ln 77584
Gentlebrook Dr 77584
George Ct & St 77581
Gerda St 77581
Gilbert Dr 77584
Ginger Ln 77581
Ginger Cove Ct & Ln 77584
Glade St 77581
Gladewater Dr 77584
Glastonbury Dr 77581
Glen Cullen Ln 77584
Glen Falls Ln 77581
Glenda St 77584
Glendale Dr 77584
Glenhill Ct & Dr 77584
Glenn Ln 77584
Glenoak Dr 77581
Glenview Dr 77581
Glenwood Dr 77584
Glosson Rd 77584
Golden Creek Ln 77584
Golfcrest Dr 77581
Goodrich St 77581
Gorom Ct 77584
Grace Ln 77584
Gramercy Ct 77584
Grand Blvd 77581
Grand Shore Ct & Dr 77584
Grandoak Dr 77581
Granite Ct 77581
Granite Shoals Ct 77584
Great Creek Dr 77584
Green Apple Dr 77581
Green Falls Dr 77584
Green Forest Ln 77581
Green Mountain Dr 77584
Green Tee Dr 77581
Green Thicket Dr 77584
Greenblade Ct & Dr 77584
Greenhill Rd 77581
Greenwood Dr 77584
Griffin Ln 77584
Griggs Ct 77584
Grimes Ave 77584
Grovesnor Ct & St 77584
Groveton Ln 77584
Grovewood Ct 77581
Gulfton Dr 77581
Gun Powder Ln 77581
Halbert Dr 77584
Haley Ct 77584
Halik St 77584
Hallmark Ln 77584
Hamilton Dr 77584
Hamm Rd 77581
Hammerwood Cir 77581
Hampshire St 77581
E & N Hampton Ct & Dr 77584
Hampton Bay Dr 77584
Hanberry Ln 77584
Hanover Cir 77584
Hans St 77584
Hansford Pl 77584
Hanston Ct 77584
Harbor Chase Ct & Dr 77584
Harbor Pass Dr 77584
Harborside Ln 77584
Harbour Breeze Ln 77584
Harbrook Dr 77584
Hardwood Cir 77584
Harewood Ct 77584
Harkey Rd 77584
Harmony Hall Ct 77584
Harrington Dr 77584
Harris Ave 77584
Harvest Moon Ln 77584
Hastings Cannon Rd 77584
Hastings Friendswood Rd 77581
Hatfield Rd
  1400-2599 77581
  2900-3399 77584
  12400-14899 77581
Haven Brook Ln 77581
Havencrest Ct & Dr 77584
Haverling Dr 77584
Hawk Mdws 77584
Hawk Rd 77584
Hazel St 77581
Hazelwood Dr 77584
Hazystone Ln 77581
Heather Ln 77581
Heatherbend Dr 77581
Helen Dr 77584
Helen Ln 77581
Helena St 77581
Helmsley Dr 77584
Herbert Dr 77584
Heritage Green Dr 77581
Heritage Landing St 77581
Heron Ln 77584
Herridge Rd 77584
Hewn Rock Way 77584
Hickory Ct 77581
Hickory Bend Ct & Ln 77581
Hickory Creek Dr 77581
Hickory Grove Ln 77584
Hickory Hollow Dr 77581
Hickory Knoll Dr 77581
Hickory Springs Ln 77584
Hidden Riv 77584
Hidden Bay Ct & Dr 77584
Hidden Creek Dr 77581
Hidden Falls Dr 77584
Hidden Landing Dr 77584
Hidden Mist Ct 77584
Hidden River Ln 77584
High Falls Ln 77581
High Tide Ln 77584
Highland Glen Ln 77581
Highland Lake Ct & Ln 77584
Highland Point Ct & Ln 77581
S Highway 288 77584
Highway 35 77581
Hillbrook Dr 77584
Hillhouse Rd 77584
Hillock Ln 77584
Hollingsworth Dr 77584
Hollow Mist Ln 77584
Hollow Shore St 77584
Holly Ct 77581
Holly Springs Dr 77584
Honey Creek Ct 77584
Honey Locust Ln 77584
Honeysuckle Ln 77584
Horncastle Ct 77584
Hot Springs Dr 77584
Houston Ave 77581
Houston Lake Dr 77581
Hubbell Dr 77584
Hubstone Way 77581
Huggins Way St 77584
Hughes Ranch Rd
  4500-4599 77584
  7800-8499 77581
  8500-15099 77584
Huisache Blvd & Ct 77581
Huntington Dr & Way 77581
Imperial Shore Dr 77584
Indigo Dr 77584
Indigo Bay Ct 77584
Indigo Creek Ln 77584
Indigo Sands Dr 77584
Industrial Dr
  3300-3399 77581
  8000-8899 77584
Inglewood Ln 77584
Inland Dr 77584
Inverness Ct & Ln 77581
Iris Ct 77584
Iris View Ln 77584
Irish Shores Ln 77584
Iron Landing Ct 77584
Irvington Dr 77584
Isla Dr & St 77581
Island Breeze St 77584
Island Manor St 77584
Ivory Creek Dr 77584
Ivy Arbor Ct & Ln 77584
Ivy Bend Dr 77584
Ivy Run Ln 77584
Ivydale Rd 77581
Ivywood Dr 77584
Jack St 77581
Jacquelyn Dr 77581
James St
  1301-1399 77581
  7700-7999 77584
Jamison Landing Dr 77584
Jamison Oak Dr 77581
Jamison Pine Dr 77581
Janet Ct & Ln 77581
Janice St 77581
Jarred Ct 77584
E & W Jasmine St 77581
Jasmine Hollow Ln 77581
Jasmine Peak Ct 77584
Jasper Rd 77581
Jefferson St 77584
Jenkins Rd 77584
Jerrycrest Dr 77584
Joe Dr 77584
John Ct & St 77581
John Lizer Rd 77581
Johns St 77581
Johnston St 77581
Jolie Dr 77584
Jordan Dr 77584
Josephine St 77584
Julie St 77581
Julie Ann Dr 77584
Juniper Dr 77581
Juniper Springs Dr 77584
Kale Ct & St 77584
Karrywood Ct 77584
Kathy Dr 77584
Katy St 77581
Kaufman Ave 77584
Kay Ave 77581
Kay Ln 77584
Keis Rd 77584
Keithwood Cir & Dr E, S & W 77584
Kelly Dr & Ln 77581
Kendall St 77584
Kennedy Dr 77584
Kensington Dr 77584
Kensington Park 77581
Kerr Ln 77581
Kerry Cir 77581
Keswick Ct & Dr 77581
Kevincrest Dr 77584
Keystone Trl 77584
Kildare Dr 77581
Kilkenny Dr 77581
Killarney Dr 77581
Kimball Dr & Pl W 77584
Kimberly Dr 77581
Kincaid Rd 77584
King Authors Ct 77584
Kingfisher Ct N & S 77584
Kingsley Dr 77584
Kinnerton St 77584
Kirby Dr & St 77584
Kirby Springs Ct 77584
Kleberg Ct 77584
Knapp Rd 77581
Knob Hill St 77581
Knoll Hill St 77584
Knollcrest Ln 77584
Knotty Pine Cir 77581
Kristi Ln 77584
Kyle Ct 77584
La Paloma Blvd 77581
Lacewood Ct 77584
Lack Rd 77581
Lady Leslie Ln 77581
N & S Lago Vista Ct & Dr 77581
Laguna Pointe Dr 77584
Laguna Shores Dr 77584
Lake Dr 77581
Lake Crest Ct 77584
Lake Edge Dr 77581
Lake Hollow Dr 77584
Lake Hurst Dr 77584
Lake Point Ct 77584
Lake Shore Dr 77581
Lake View Dr 77581
Lake Wind Dr 77584
Lakecrest Dr 77584
Lakefront Terrace Ct & Dr 77584
Lakehill Dr 77584
Lakeside Dr 77584
Lakeside Manor Ln 77581
Lakewater Dr 77584
Lakeway Ct & Ln 77584
Lamb Brook Ln 77584
Lambeth Dr 77584
Lamppost Pl 77584
Land St 77584
Landera Ct 77584
Landon Lake Dr 77584
Landsdowne Ct 77584
Lansing Cir & Ct 77584
Lantana Spring Ln 77581
Lantern Lake Ct 77584
Larkdale Dr 77584
E Larkspur Cir 77584
Larrycrest Dr 77584
Laura Ln 77581
Laurel Brook Ln 77584
Laurel Creek Way 77581
Laurel Grove Ln 77584
Laurel Leaf Ln 77581
Laurel Loch Ct & Ln 77584
Laurel Wood Ln 77584
Lauren Ln 77584
Lauren Trl 77581
Lauren Rose Ln 77581
Laurie St 77581
Lavender Hill Ct 77581
Lawrence Ct 77584
Lawson Ct & Dr 77584
Lawton Dr 77584
Layton Place Dr 77581
Lazy Bend St 77581
Lazy Creek Ln 77581
Lazy Hollow Ct & Ln 77581
Leafstone Ln 77581
Leafwood Ln 77584
Leanett Way 77584
Leanett Way Ct 77584
Lee Cir 77581
Lee Ln 77581
Lee Rd 77581
Lee Circle Ct 77581
Leggett Ln 77584
Leisure Ln 77584
Leona Ct 77584
Leroy St 77581
Lesiker Rd 77584
Lester St 77584
Lethbridge St 77581
Letrim St 77581
Lewis Dr 77581
Leyland Ct & Dr 77584
Libby Ln 77584
Liberty Dr 77581
Lila St 77581
Lilac Breeze Ln 77584
Lilac View Ct 77584
Lily Canyon Ln 77584
Limrick Dr 77581
Linda Dr & Ln 77584
Linden Pl 77584
Linden Rose Ct 77584
Linden Walk Ln 77584
Lindenwood Clf 77581
Lindhaven Dr 77584
Linkwood Dr 77584
Linwood St 77581
E Linwood Oaks St 77581
Little Grove Dr 77581
Littleton Cir 77581
Live Oak Ln 77581
Live Oak Hollow St 77581
Livingston Dr 77581
Livingston Lake Ct 77581
Lochman Ct & Ln 77584
Lochmoor Ln 77581
Lockhart Dr 77581
Lockheed St 77581
London Ct 77581
Londonderry Dr 77581
Lone Creek Ln 77584
Long Cove Ct 77584
Long Meadow Ct 77584
Long View Dr 77581
Longherridge Dr 77581
Longlake Dr 77584
Longleaf Dr 77581
Longwood Dr 77581
Loomis Rd 77581
Lost Bridge Ln 77584
Lost Creek Dr 77584
Lost Lake Pl 77581
Lost Maples Dr 77584
Lotus Dr & Ln 77584
Louise Ln 77584
Lucas St 77581
Lynn Dr 77581
Lynn Ln 77584
Macoma Ave 77581
Madewood Pl 77584
Madison Ct & Dr 77584
Magnolia St 77584
E & S Magnolia Elms Dr N & W 77584
Magnolia Oaks Dr 77584
Magnolia Palms Dr 77584
Magnolia Pines Dr 77584
Mahejan Ct & Dr 77584
Mahogany Trl 77584
N & S Main St 77581
Majestic Oak Ct & Dr 77581
Malon St 77581
Manchester Ln 77581
Mandalay Ct 77584
Manor Dr 77581
Manor Lake Ln 77584
Manry Ave 77581
Manvel Rd 77584
Maple Ln 77584
Maple Branch Ln 77584
Maple Leaf Ct 77581
Maple Wood Dr 77581
Marble Brook Ln 77584
Marble Creek Dr 77581
Marble Falls Dr 77584
March St 77581
Margate Ct & Dr 77584
E, N & W Marsala Ct & Dr 77581
Marsha Ln 77581
Martin Ln 77581
Martinec Dr 77584
Mary Ave 77581
Maryfield Ln 77581
E & W Marys Creek Ct & Ln W 77581
Marys Village Dr 77581
Mason Grove Ln 77584
Masters Rd 77584
Matilde Ct 77584
Max Rd 77581
May St 77581
Maybrook Ct 77584
Mcdermott Ct 77581
Mcdonald Dr 77581
Mcdonald Park 77584
Mcginnis Dr 77581
Mchard Rd
  2600-2898 77584
  2900-2999 77584
  3500-3599 77581
Mckeever Rd 77584
Mckinley Ct 77584
Mcknight Rd 77584
Mclean Rd 77584
Meade Rd 77584
Meadow Ln 77584
Meadow Creek Dr 77581
Meadow Green Dr 77581
Meadow Springs Dr 77584
Meadow Wood Dr 77584
Meadowglen Dr 77584
Meadowhurst Dr 77584
Meadowlark Way 77584
Meadowmist Ct 77584
Meadows Pond Ln 77584
Meadowville Dr 77581
Medina Ct 77584
Megan St 77581
Megellan Point Ln 77584
Melanie Ln 77581
Melford Ave 77584
Melody Peak Ln 77581
Melony Hill Ln 77584
Memorial Hermann Dr 77584
Meridian Park Dr 77584
Merlet Dr 77584
Merribrook Ln 77581
Messina Ct & Dr 77581
Michael Ln 77581
Midlane Dr 77581
Millbrook Dr 77584
Miller Ranch Rd 77584
Mimosa Ln 77584
Minnie Ln 77584
Miraglen Dr 77584
Misting Falls Ln 77584
Mistwood Ct 77584
Misty Ln 77581
Misty Bay Ln 77584
Misty Harbor Dr 77584
Misty Lake Ln 77581
Misty Morning Ct & St 77584
Misty Shadow Ln 77584
Misty Shore Ln 77584
W Mockingbird Ln 77584
Modena Ct & Dr 77581
Mona St 77584
Monaldo Ct, Dr & Pl 77581
Monarch Meadow Ln 77581
Montview Dr 77581
Moonlit Lake Ct & Ln 77584
Moore Ct 77581
Moore Dr 77581
Moore Rd 77584
Mooring Pointe Dr 77584
Morenci St 77584
Morgan Bay Ct 77584
Morning Bay Dr 77584
Morning Brook Dr & Way 77584
Morning Cloud Ct & Dr 77584
Morning Dawn Dr 77584
Morris Ct, Dr & St 77584
Morrison St 77584
Moss Creek Ln 77581
Mossy Bend Ln 77581
Mossy Trail Ct & Ln 77584
Mountain Creek St 77584
Mountain Sage Ct & Dr 77584
Mulberry Ct 77581
Mustang Rd 77584
Mykawa Rd 77581
Myrtle Crest Ct 77584
Myrtlewood St 77581
Mystic Arbor Ln 77584
Mystic Cove Ln 77584
Nahas Ct 77584
Nancy St 77584
Nantucket Ct 77584
Narvarro Rd 77584
Neches River Dr 77584
Nelson Rd 77584
Nemes Ln 77581
Netherwood Ct 77584
Newbridge Ct 77584
Newbrook Dr 77584
Newbury Ct 77584
Newhaven Trl 77584
Newport Ln 77584
Nicholas Dr 77581
Night Song Dr 77584
Noblewood Ct 77584
Noel Ct 77584
N & S Nolan Ct, Dr & Pl 77584
Norfolk Dr 77584
Norma Ln 77584
Northfork Ct & Dr 77584
Northgrove Ct 77581
Northwick Dr 77584
Northwood Ct 77581
Norwich St 77584
Nottingham St 77581
Nutwood Dr 77584
Oak Rd 77584
Oak Bark Ct 77581

Oak Bent Dr 77581
Oak Brook Dr 77581
Oak Chase Ct 77581
Oak Cluster Cir 77581
Oak Creek Dr 77581
Oak Crossing Dr 77581
Oak Dale Dr 77581
Oak Fork Cir 77581
Oak Gate Cir 77581
Oak Hollow Dr E 77581
Oak Lake Cir 77581
Oak Lodge Dr 77581
Oak Place Ct 77581
Oak Point Ct & Dr 77581
Oak Ridge Dr 77581
Oak Shire Dr 77581
Oak Top Dr 77581
Oak Trace Ct 77581
Oak Tree Cir 77581
Oak Wood Dr E & N 77581
Oakbranch Dr 77581
Oakbrook Cir 77581
Oakedge Dr 77581
Oakland Cir 77581
Oakleaf Cir 77581
Oakline Dr 77581
Oaks Blvd & Cir 77584
Ocean Point Ct & Dr 77584
Ochoa Rd 77584
Oday Rd 77581
Old Alvin Rd 77581
Old Chocolate Bayou Rd 77584
Old Holly Dr 77584
Old Oaks Blvd 77584
Olive Mount St 77584
Opal Creek Dr 77584
E & W Orange Cir & St E, N & S 77581
Orange Wood Trl 77581
Orchard St 77581
Orchard Briar Ln 77584
Orchard Frost Dr 77581
Orchard Mill Ln 77584
Orchard Spring Ct & Dr 77581
Orchard Trail Dr 77581
Orchard View Ln 77584
Orchard Wind Ln 77584
Orchid Creek Dr 77584
Orchid Trace Dr 77584
Over St 77584
E & W Overdale Dr 77584
Owney Ct 77581
Oxford Dr 77584
Oxhill Ct 77584
Ozark Trl 77584
Page Crest Ln 77584
Paigetree Ln 77584
Paigewood Dr 77584
Palermo Dr 77581
Palm Ct 77584
Palm Bay Ct & St 77584
S & W Palmcrest Ct 77584
Palo Duro Dr 77584
Paradise Canyon Dr 77584
Park Ave 77581
Park Falls Ct & Dr 77584
Park Springs Dr 77584
Parkbriar Ln 77584
Parkshire Dr 77584
Parkside Dr 77584
Parkview Dr 77581
Parry Ct & Dr 77584
Parry Field Ct 77584
Pastureview Dr 77584
Patricia Ln 77581
Patridge Dr 77584
Paul St 77581
Paxton Hill Ct 77584
Peach Ct 77581
Peach Blossom Dr 77584
E, N, S & W Peach Hollow Cir & Ct 77584
Peachtree Ct 77581
E & W Pear Ct & St 77581
Pearl Bay Ct 77584
Pearland Ave & Pkwy 77581
Pearland Sites Rd 77584
Pebble Beach Ln 77584
Pebble Brook Dr 77584
Pebble Creek Dr 77581
Pebble Pointe Dr 77584
Pebble Shores Ln 77584
Pecan Grove Ct & Dr 77584
Pecan Hollow St 77581
Peden Bay Dr 77584
Pedernales Falls Dr 77584
Peekskill Ct 77584
Peggy Ln 77584
Pemberton Dr 77584
Pembrook Ct 77584
Pennyoak Dr 77581
Peonies Ct 77581
Pepper Creek Ln 77584
Perdido Bay Ln 77584
Pheasant Ln 77581
Piccadilly Circus St 77581
Pickering Ct & Ln 77584
Pickwood Dr 77584
Pierwood Creek Ct 77584
Pilgrims Point Ln 77581
Pimlico Dr 77584
Pin Oak Dr E 77581
Pinced Rd 77581
Pinder Ln 77584
Pine Bark Ct 77581
W Pine Branch Dr 77581
Pine Chase Dr 77581
Pine Colony Ln 77581
Pine Cone Ln 77581
Pine Creek Dr 77581
Pine Crest Dr 77581
Pine Field Ct 77581
Pine Forest Dr & Pl 77581
Pine Glen Ct 77581
Pine Grove Ln 77581
E Pine Hill Dr 77581
Pine Hollow Dr 77581
Pine Knot Ct 77581
Pine Lake Dr 77581
Pine Lawn Dr 77581
Pine Meadow Ct 77581
Pine Mill Ct 77584
Pine Moss Ct 77581
Pine Needle Ln 77581
N & W Pine Orchard Dr 77581
Pine Ridge Ln 77581
Pine Sap Ct 77581
Pine Stream Dr S 77581
Pine Tree Ct & Dr 77581
Pine Valley Dr 77581
Pine View Ct 77581
Pine Walk Dr 77581
Pineash Ct 77581
Pinebend Dr 77584
Pinehurst Dr 77581
Pineland Dr 77581
Pinewood Ct 77581
Piney Woods Dr 77581
Piper Rd 77581
Pisa Ct 77581
Plantain Lily Ct 77581
Plantation Ct & Dr 77584
Playa Dr 77584
E & W Plum St 77581
Plum Falls Ln 77581
Plum Grove Ln 77581
Plum Lake Dr 77581
Plymouth Landing Cir 77581
Pompton Ct 77584
Poplar Creek Ln 77584
Poranney Dr 77584
Portsmouth Dr 77584
Postwood Ln 77581
Prairie Creek Dr 77581
Pregeant Ln 77584
Preston Dr 77581
Price Cir 77581
Prickley Ash Way 77584
N & S Primavera Dr 77581
Primrose St 77584
E Primrose Meadows Cir 77584
Primwood Ct 77584
Princess Bay Ct 77584
Princeton Dr 77584
Promenade Ln 77584
Quail Creek Dr 77584
Quail Run Dr 77584
Queen Victoria St 77581
Quiet Arbor Ln 77581
Quiet Bay St 77584
Quiet Lake Ct & Ln 77584
Quiet River Ln 77581
Quiet Trace Ln 77581
Quinn Rd 77581
N Rachel Ct 77581
Raffaello Dr 77581
Rain Lily Ct 77581
Rainbow Ct 77584
Raintree Dr 77584
Rainwater Ct & Dr 77584
Rainwood Dr 77584
Randall St 77581
Rashell Way 77584
Raven Ridge Dr 77584
Ravencrest Ct 77584
Ravenlake Ct & Dr 77584
Ravens Creek Ct & Dr 77584
Ravensport Dr 77584
Ravensway Ct 77584
Ravenwood Ct & Dr 77584
Ray St 77581
Rayburn Ln 77581
Rayburn Lake Ct 77584
Rayleine Dr 77584
Raza Rd 77581
Red Acorn Trl 77581
Red Bud Ct 77581
Red Oak Ln 77581
Redwood Bend Ln 77584
Redwood Grove St 77584
Reflection Bay Dr 77584
Regal Crest Ln 77584
Regal Oaks Dr 77584
Reid Blvd 77581
Reiser Ct 77581
Rest Home Rd 77584
Restless Bay Ln 77584
Rice Rd 77581
Rice Drier Rd 77581
Richard Dr 77581
Richfield Ct 77584
Ridgebrook Ln 77584
Ridgepoint Ct & Dr 77584
Rip Van Winkle Dr 77581
Ripple Bend Ct & Ln 77581
Rippling Creek Ln 77581
Rippling Rock Ct 77584
Rising Bay Ln 77584
River Birch Dr 77581
River Glen Ct 77584
Riverside Dr 77581
N & S Riviera Cir & Ct 77581
Roaring Springs Ct & Dr 77584
Robert St 77581
Robin Spur 77581
Robin Meadow St 77581
Robin Sound St 77581
Robinhood Cir 77581
Robinson Dr 77581
Rock Shoals Way 77584
Rockland Dr 77584
Rocky Cove Ct & Dr 77584
Rocky Creek Ln 77581
Rocky Meadow Ln 77581
Rocky Springs Ct & Dr 77584
Rogers Rd 77581
Roland Rue St 77581
Rolling Fog Dr 77581
Rolling Meadow Ct 77581
Romayor Ct 77581
Rome Dr 77581
Romero Dr 77581
Rose Rd 77581
Rose Bay Ct & Dr 77584
Rosebud Dr 77581
Rosefield Ct 77584
Rosemary Ct 77584
Rosemont Ln 77584
Rothbury Dr 77584
Roy Ct & Rd 77581
Roy Acres Rd 77584
Royal Creek Ct 77584
Royal Ridge Dr 77584
Ruby Dr 77581
Running Brook Ln 77584
Rushing Spring Dr 77584
Russett Pl N 77584
Rustic Ln 77581
Rustic Meadow Ct 77584
Rusting Creek Dr 77584
Ryan Acres Dr 77584
Sabal Palm Ln 77584
Sabine Ct 77584
Sable Ct & Dr 77584
N & S Sacramento Ave 77581
Sage Ct 77584
Sage Forest Ln 77584
Sagewood Ct 77584
Sail Port St 77584
Sailwind Dr 77584
Sailwing Creek Ct 77584
Saint James Pl 77581
Saint John Dr 77584
Salado Dr 77584
San Antonio St 77581
San Conero Dr 77581
San Marino Dr 77581
Sandal Walk 77584
Sandlebrook St 77584
Sandpiper Ct N & S 77584
Sandra St 77581
Sandstone Ct 77584
Sandstone Creek Dr 77581
Sandy Bank Ct & Ln 77581
Sawyer Dr 77581
Sawyer Crossing Ln 77581
Saxton Ct 77581
Scarlatti Dr 77581
Scarsdale Blvd 77581
Scenic Meadow Ct 77581
Schleider Dr 77581
Scott Rd 77581
Sea Cove Ln 77584
Sea Shadow Bnd 77584
Seabreeze Ln 77584
Seabrough Dr 77584
Seagrove Dr 77584
Seagull Ln 77584
Sebago Ct & Dr 77584
Sebastopol Dr 77584
Seddon Rd 77581
Seminole Dr 77584
Seneca Landing Ln 77584
Senova Ct & Dr 77584
Sentore Ct & Dr 77584
Sentry Woods Ln 77581
Sequoia Lake Trl 77581
Shade Ct & Ln 77584
Shadow Bay Dr 77584
Shadow Canyon Ct & Ln 77584
Shadow Creek Pkwy 77584
Shadow Falls Ln 77584
Shadowbend St 77581
Shady Breeze Ct 77584
Shady Brook Dr 77584
Shady Cove Ct 77584
Shady Creek Dr 77581
Shady Falls Ln 77584
Shady Run Ln 77584
Shady Sands Pl 77584
Shady Springs Ct & Dr 77584
Shadybend Dr 77581
Shadycrest Dr 77581
Shakespeare St 77581
Shallow Falls Ct & Ln 77584
Shaly Cove Ln 77584
Shank Rd 77581
Sharon Dr 77581
Sharondale St 77584
Shasta Ct 77584
Shauntel St 77581
Shelby Dr 77584
Sheldon Dr 77584
Shelia St 77581
Shell Island Ct 77584
Shelton Rd 77581
Sherborne St 77584
Shoal Ct 77584
Shoal Creek Ct & Dr 77584
Shoal Lake Ct 77584
Shoal Landing St 77584
Shoalwater Ln 77584
Shore Breeze Dr 77584
Shore Creek Ct & Dr 77584
Shore Pointe Dr 77584
Shorebrook Dr 77584
Shoreside Dr 77584
Short Springs Ct & Dr 77584
Shriner Ct 77584
Siena Ct & Dr 77581
Sienna Springs Dr 77584
Signal Hill Ct & Dr 77584
Silent Creek Dr 77584
Silent Walk Ct & Dr 77584
Silhouette Bay Ct & Dr 77584
Silsbee Dr 77584
Silver Dr 77581
Silver Bay Ct & Dr 77584
Silver Dollar Ct 77584
Silver Leaf Ct 77584
Silver Maple Ln
1300-1599 77581
7800-7899 77584
Silver Star Ct 77584
Silverbrook Ln 77584
Silverlake Pkwy 77584
Silverlake Village Dr 77584
Sky Springs Ln 77584
Skylark Way 77584
Sleepy Creek Way 77581
Sleepy Hollow Dr 77581
Smith Rd 77584
Smith Miller Rd 77584
Smith Ranch Rd 77584
Smith Ranch Road 1 77584
Smith Ranch Road 2 77584
Snowblossom Ct 77581
Softbreeze Ct 77584
Soho Dr 77584
Somerville Lake Ct 77581
Sorenson Dr 77584
Sorrell Ridge Ct 77584
South Fwy 77584
Southbay Dr 77584
Southdown Dr 77584
Southern Ln 77584
Southern Brook Ct 77584
Southern Chase Dr 77584
Southern Creek Dr 77584
Southern Green Dr 77584
Southern Grove Ln 77584
Southern Knoll Ln 77584
Southern Manor Ct & Dr 77584
Southern Mill Ct 77584
Southern Ridge Dr 77584
Southern Trails Ct 77584
Southern Valley Dr 77584
Southern Way Ln 77584
Southgate Dr 77584
Southmere Ln 77584
Southport Dr 77584
Southsand Dr 77584
Southwyck Pkwy 77584
Sparkling Brook Ct 77584
Sparrow Dr 77584
Spill Creek Dr 77584
Spinnaker Bay Ln 77584
Split Creek Ln 77584
Spring Arbor Ct 77584
Spring Branch Dr 77584
Spring Brook Ct 77584
Spring Circle Dr 77584
Spring Creek Ln 77581
Spring Crest Ct 77584
Spring Forest Dr 77584
Spring Garden Dr 77584
Spring Glen Ln 77581
Spring Grove Ct 77584
Spring Landing Dr & Ln 77584
Spring Meadow Dr 77584
Spring Oak Dr 77581
Spring River Dr 77584
Springdale Ct & Dr 77584
Springview Ln 77584
Sprite Ln 77581
Stable Stone Ln 77581
Stacy Dr 77581
Stanton Ct 77584
Starcroft Dr 77584
Starleaf Ln 77584
Starlight Bay Ct & St 77584
Starwreath Dr 77584
W Sterling Dr & Xing 77584
Sterling Brook St 77584
Sterling Fields Dr 77584
Stevens Dr 77581
Stevenson Rd 77581
Still Bay St 77584
Stillwater Dr 77584
Stone Rd 77581
Stone Arbor Ln 77581
Stonebridge Dr 77584
Stonebrook Dr 77584
Stonecrest Ct, St & Way 77581
Stonegate Cir 77584
Stonegrove Ct 77581
Stonehollow Ct 77581
Stonehurst Ct & Dr 77584
Stonelick Ct 77584
Stoneriver Ct 77581
Stonesthrow Ln 77581
Stonewood Heights Ct 77581
Stoney Creek Dr 77584
Stratford St 77581
Suburban Garden Rd 77581
S Sumac Dr 77584
Summer Ln 77584
Summer Breeze Dr 77584
Summer Brook Ct 77584
Summer Cloud Ln 77584
Summer Creek Dr 77584
Summer Moon Dr 77584
Summer Springs Dr 77584
Summer Sun Ln 77584
Summercrest Dr 77584
Summerfield Ct & Dr 77584
Summerwind Ct 77584
Summerwood Ln 77584
Summit Dr 77584
Summit Spgs 77581
Summit Bay Dr 77584
Sun Beam Ct 77584
Sun Cove Ln 77584
Sun Flare Ln 77584
Sun Glen Ct & Dr 77584
Sun Haven Ln 77584
Sun King Dr 77584
Sun Spot Ln 77584
Sun Valley Ct 77584
Sunbird Ct 77584
Sunbonnet Dr 77584
Sunbrook Dr 77581
Sunburst Ln 77584
Suncreek Ln 77584
Sundance Dr 77584
Sunday House Ct & Dr 77584
Sundown Dr 77584
Sunfire Ln 77584
Sunfish Dr 77584
Sunflower St 77584
Sunforest Ln 77584
Sungate Dr 77584
Sunhill Ct 77584
Sunlake Dr 77584
Sunlight Ct & Ln 77584
Sunlit Bay Dr 77584
Sunny Brook Ln 77584
Sunny Shores Dr 77584
Sunnycoast Ln 77584
Sunnycreek Ln 77584
Sunnyside Ln 77584
Sunnyview Ct 77584
Sunperch Ct 77584
Sunray Ct 77584
Sunridge Ct 77584
Sunrise Blvd 77584
Sunrise Dr 77581
Sunrise Trl 77584
Sunrise Harbor Ln 77584
Sunrise Run Ln 77584
N Sunset Dr 77581
Sunset Bay Ln 77584
Sunset Harbor Dr 77584
Sunset Lakes Dr 77581
Sunset Meadows Dr 77581
Sunset Springs Dr 77584
Sunshade Ct 77584
Sunshadow Ct 77584
Sunshape Ct 77584
Sunstone Ln 77584
Sussex Trl 77584
Sweet Wind Ct & Dr 77584
Sweetgum Ct 77581
Swensen Rd 77581
Sycamore Dr 77581
Tall Timbers Ln 77581
Tamara Creek Ln 77584
Tara Pl 77584
Tarrytown Ln 77581
Tawakon Dr 77584
Taylor Ln 77581
Taylorcrest Dr 77584
Teakwood Dr 77584
Teal Ct N & S 77584
Teal Glen St 77584
Tennyson Dr 77584
Terrell Dr 77584
Terrie Ln 77581
Texas St 77581
Thelma St 77581
Thomson St 77581
Thornbriar Dr 77581
Thornton Lake Ln 77584
Thornwood Ct 77584
Three Sister Cir 77581
Thurlow Dr 77581
Tide Rock Ln 77584
Tidenhaven Ct & Dr 77584
Timber Bluff Dr 77584
Timber Creek Dr 77581
E & W Timber Cut Ct 77584
Timber Ridge Dr 77584
Timberwood Dr 77584
Timothy St 77584
Tipperary Dr 77581
Tower Bridge Ct & Rd 77581
W Trail Dr 77584
Trail Creek Ct 77584
Trail Hollow Ct & Dr 77584
Trail Manor Dr 77584
Trail Ridge Dr 77584
Tran Ln 77584
Tranquility Trl 77584
Tranquility Lake Blvd 77584
Travis Lake Ct 77581
Treasure Ln 77584
Tree Top Ln 77584
Trelawney Dr 77581
Trent Cove Ln 77584
Trinity Dr 77584
Trout Ct 77581
Tuscany Ct & Pl 77581
E & W Tuschman Dr 77581
Tweed Way 77584
Twin Lakes Trl 77584
Tye Ln 77584
Tyler St 77581

Union Valley Dr 77581
Valentine Ln 77584
Vanity Dr 77584
Varese Dr 77581
Vatican Ct 77581
Venezia Dr 77581
N & S Venice Dr 77581
Verona Dr 77581
Veterans Dr 77584
Veva Dr 77584
Village Dr 77581
Village Brook Ln 77584
Village Grove Dr 77581
Village Mills Dr 77584
Vinecrest Dr 77584
Vineyard Bend Ct & Dr 77581
Vineyard Hill Ct & Dr 77581
Vista Ln 77584
Wagon Trail Rd 77584
Wakefield Ct 77584
Walden Dr 77584
Walden Creek Ct & Ln 77581
Walker Ct & Dr 77581
E Walnut St
3300-3600 77581
3519-3519 77588
3601-3999 77581
3602-3998 77581
W Walnut St 77581
Walnut Cove Ln 77584
Walnut Grove Ct 77584
Walnut Hollow St 77581
Warren Rd 77584
Washington St 77581
Washington Irving Dr 77581
Water Fern Ln 77581
Water Oak Dr 77581
Water Willow Ln 77581
Watercastle Ct 77584
Waterlilly Ln 77581
Waterloo Rd 77581
Watermist Dr 77584
Waters Edge Ct 77584
Waterside Trl 77584
Waterwood Ct 77584
Watzek Way 77581
N Wayne Ln 77584
Weatherford Ct & Dr 77584
S, E & N Webber Ct & Dr 77584
Wedgewater Ln 77584
Weeping Willow Ln 77584
Wellborne Rd
12400-12899 77581
16800-17799 77584
17715-1-17715-3 77584
Wellbrook Ct 77581
Wellesley Ct 77584
Wellington Dr 77584
Wells Ct & Dr 77584
N & S Wellsford Dr 77584
Wendy Ln 77584
Wentworth Dr 77584
Westchester Cir 77584
Westcreek Dr 77581
Westerlake Dr 77584
Westfield St 77581
Westgate Dr 77581
Westlea Ln 77584
Westminister St 77581
Wheatfield Blvd & Ct 77581
Wheatmeadow Ct & Ln 77581
Wheatridge St 77581
Wheatstalk Ln 77581
Whirlwind St 77581
Whispering Oaks St 77581
Whispering Winds Dr 77581
White Ln 77584
White Cloud Ct 77584
White Falls Dr 77584
White Lane Ct 77584
White Oak Ln 77584
White Water Bay Dr 77584
White Willow Ln 77581
Whitestone Dr 77584
Whitlam Ct & Dr 77584
Wicklow Dr 77581
Wickshire Ct 77584
Wickwood Ct & Dr 77584
Wild Lilac Ct & Dr 77584
Wild Oak Dr 77581
Wild Turkey Ln 77581
Wildwood St 77581
Wilke Rd 77581
Williams Rd & St 77584
Willits St 77581
Willow Blvd 77581
Willow Dr 77584
Willow Brook Ct & Ln 77584
Willow Creek Ln 77581
Willow Lake Dr 77581
Willowyck Cir 77581
Wilshire Cir 77581
Wilton Ct & St 77584
Wimbleton Ct 77581
Windchester St 77581
Windcrest Ct 77581
Windemere Dr 77584
Windfern Dr 77581
Winding Creek Dr 77581
Winding Forest Dr 77581
Winding Shores Dr 77584
Windsor St 77581
Windswept St 77581
Windwood St 77581
Windy Bank Ln 77581
Windy Creek Dr 77584
Windy Dawn Dr 77584
Windy Shores Dr 77584
Windy Way Ln 77584
Winebrook Ct & Dr 77584
Wingtail Way 77584
Winston Ct 77584
Winter Berry Ct 77581
Winter Oak St 77584
Winter Springs Dr 77584
Wolf Ct 77584
Wonard Dr 77581
Wood Creek Dr 77581
Woodbine Pl 77584
Woodbridge Ave 77584
Woodbury St 77584
Woodchase Dr 77581
Woodfern Glen Ln 77584
Woodglen Ct 77581
Woodhaven St 77584
Woodland Ct 77581
Woodoak Ct 77584
Woods Ct 77581
Woodville Ln 77584
Woody Rd 77581
Wooten Rd 77584
Worthington Dr 77584
Wyckchester Dr 77584
Yellowstone Cir 77584
Ymca Dr 77581
Yoakum St 77584
Yorkshire Ct 77581
Yorkshire Creek Ct 77581
Yost Blvd & Rd 77581
Yupon Cir 77581
Zapalac Rd 77581
Zelko Dr 77584

NUMBERED STREETS

All Street Addresses 77581

PFLUGERVILLE TX

General Delivery 78660

POST OFFICE BOXES MAIN OFFICE STATIONS AND BRANCHES

Box No.s
All PO Boxes 78691

NAMED STREETS

A W Grimes Blvd 78660
Abbey Glen Castle Dr 78660
Acanthus St 78660
Alderminster Ln 78660
Alexis Cv 78660
Algreg St 78660
Alison Ann Ct 78660
Alnwick Castle Dr 78660
Amarylis Dr 78660
Amber Day Dr 78660
Ambling Trl 78660
Ambrose Dr 78660
Amen Corner Rd 78660
American Robin Path 78660
Anna Kate Ct 78660
Antique Finish Dr 78660
Antique Heritage Dr 78660
Apache Cv 78660
Apache Plum Ln 78660
Apple Cross Dr 78660
Apple Vista Cir 78660
Applewood Dr 78660
Ardisia Dr 78660
Ascent Cv 78660
Auburn Chestnut Ln 78660
Auk Rd 78660
Autumn Sage Way 78660
Avena Valley Dr 78660
Aviation Dr 78660
Azores Dr 78660
Bach Dr 78660
Balmoral Castle Ct 78660
Bandice Ln 78660
Barbergale St 78660
Barley Field Pass 78660
Bassington Ct 78660
Batavia Dr 78660
Bates Cv 78660
Battenburg Trl 78660
Beach Plum Cv 78660
Beauty Berry Cv 78660
Becker Farm Rd 78660
Bell Rock Cir 78660
Bellaire Oaks Dr 78660
Bellemeade Blvd 78660
Bellerive Dr 78660
Bergamont Dr 78660
Berol Dr 78660
Bethel Way 78660
Bethesda Ct 78660
Betterman Cv & Dr 78660
Betty Baker Cv 78660
Bidermann Way 78660
Bishopsgate Dr 78660
Black Canyon St 78660
Black Isle Dr 78660
Black Locust Dr E 78660
Black Willow St 78660
Blackthorn Dr 78660
Blair Castle Ct 78660
Blue Flax Ln 78660
Blue Pond Dr 78660
Blue Willow Ct 78660
Boca Chica Cir 78660
Boca Rio Ct 78660
Boecher Ln 78660
Botany Bay Cir 78660
Boulder Crest Dr 78660
Boysenberry Ln 78660
Brandon Keller Ct 78660
Brean Down 78660
Brent Knoll Dr 78660
Brewer Blackbird Dr 78660
Bridgefarmer Blvd 78660
Bridie Path 78660
Broken Feather Trl 78660
Brookhollow Dr 78660
Brophy Dr 78660
Brown Dr 78660
Brue St 78660
Bruno Cir 78660
Bumblebee Dr 78660
Bunratty Cir 78660
Burnsall Gates Dr 78660
Bushmills Ct & Rd 78660
Busleigh Castle Way 78660
Buteo St 78660
Butler National Dr 78660
Buttercup Rd 78660
Byerly Turk Dr 78660
Cabriole Dr 78660
Cactus Bend Dr 78660
Cactus Blossom Dr 78660
Cahir Glen Cv 78660
Caisteal Castle Path 78660
Cajuiles Ct & Dr 78660
Callaway Garden Ct 78660
Calm Harbor Dr 78660
Calming Stream Cv 78660
Camargo Ct 78660
Cambourne Dr 78660
Cameron Rd 78660
Camille Ct 78660
Camp Fire Trl 78660
Campanula Ct 78660
Candace Loop 78660
Candleberry Cir 78660
Canna Lily Ln 78660
Cantarra Dr 78660
Canterwood Ln 78660
Canyon Bend Rd 78660
Canyon Maple Rd 78660
Canyon Sage Ln 78660
Canyon Valley Run 78660
Caras Cv 78660
Caribou Ridge Trl 78660
Carlisle Castle Ct 78660
N Cascades Ave 78660
Castleton Dr 78660
Catumet Cv & Dr 78660
Cedar Cv & Ln 78660
Cedar Ridge Dr 78660
Cele Rd 78660
Celestial Ln 78660
Central Commerce Cir & Dr 78660
Century St 78660
Cerridwen Dr 78660
Ceylon Tea Cir 78660
Chamomile Cv 78660
Champions Pt 78660
Charles Dickens Dr 78660
Chayton Cir 78660
Cherokee Run 78660
Cherry Laurel Cir 78660
Chicadee Cir 78660
Chincho Dr 78660
Choice Pl 78660
Chrighton Castle Bnd 78660
Chris Ln 78660
Cistern Cv 78660
Citron Cv 78660
City Park Rd 78660
Clancy Way 78660
Clare Morris Ln 78660
Clarence Bohls Ln 78660
Clems Cv 78660
Clemson Cv 78660
Club Chase Dr 78660
Clyde Bank Cv 78660
Coaches Xing 78660
Colonial Manor Ln 78660
Colorado Sands Dr 78660
Columbine St 78660
Colwyn Bay Cv 78660
Commons Pkwy 78660
Coneflower Cv 78660
Connemara Ln 78660
Conner Downs Dr 78660
Coomer Path 78660
Coopers Hawk Path 78660
Copper Point Cv & Ln 78660
Cora Marie Cv & Dr 78660
Cormac Ct 78660
Cornell Dr 78660
Coronation Way 78660
Cosmos Way 78660
Cottonwood Ln 78660
County Road 170 78660
Craigs Crest Path 78660
Grane Creek Loop 78660
Crater Lake Dr 78660
Craters Of The Moon Blvd 78660
Creekbend Cv & Dr 78660
Creeping Vine Ct 78660
Cresswell Dr 78660
Crete Ln 78660
Crieff Cross Dr 78660
Crimson Apple Way 78660
Crispin Hall Ln 78660
Crooked Creek Dr 78660
Crooked Stick Dr 78660
Crossvine Way 78660
Crystal Bend Dr 78660
Cumulus Dr 78660
E & W Custers Creek Bnd 78660
Cypress Dr 78660
Dahlia Ct 78660
Dakota Dunes Ct 78660
Dalshank St 78660
Damrich Ct 78660
Dansworth Cv & Dr 78660
Darjeeling Dr 78660
Darley Arabian Dr 78660
Dartmouth Cv 78660
Dashwood Creek Ct & Dr 78660
Dawlish Dr 78660
Dawson Crk 78660
Daylily Cv 78660
Deep Water Dr 78660
Defendorf Dr 78660
Delahunty Ln 78660
Demaret St 78660
Dennis Ln 78660
Denny Ln 78660
Derby Day Ave 78660
Derby Hill Ln 78660
Deren Cv & Ln 78660
Dessau Rd 78660
Dewberry Dr 78660
Diablo Ct & Dr 78660
Dillon Pond Ln 78660
Disraeli Cir 78660
Donna Jane Loop 78660
Doras Dr 78660
Dornach Ct & Dr 78660
Dornick Hills Ln 78660
Douglas Maple Way 78660
Dove Haven Dr 78660
Dover Castle Ln 78660
Dovetail St 78660
Drake Elm Dr 78660
Dreamtime Ln 78660
Drifting Meadows Dr 78660
Drusillas Dr 78660
Dry Brook Loop & Xing 78660
Dry Lake Ln 78660
Dry Pond Dr 78660
Duke Cv 78660
Dundalk Bay Cv 78660
Dunes Dr 78660
Dusty Chisolm Trl 78660
Dusty Leather Ct 78660
Eagle Fledge Ter 78660
Eagle Ridge Ln 78660
Earl Bradford Ct 78660
Earl Grey Ln 78660
Edgemere Dr 78660
Edgerly Ct & Ln 78660
Edinburgh Castle Rd 78660
Edwards Plateau 78660
El Malino Dr 78660
Elderberry Tea Cv 78660
Elm Dr 78660
Emblem Ct & Dr 78660
Emily Dickenson Dr 78660
Emmaleighs Ln 78660
Endless Shore Dr 78660
English Rose Dr 78660
Essex Cv 78660
Evening Breeze Way 78660
Evening Grosbeak Dr 78660
Evening Mist Ln 78660
Faber Dr 78660
Fairland Dr 78660
Falcon Pointe Blvd 78660
Falconers Way 78660
Falling Stone Ln 78660
Falsterbo Dr 78660
Fargo Ter 78660
Farm Pond Ln 78660
Fast Filly Ave 78660
Felsmere Dr 78660
Fenway Park 78660
Fern Ridge Ln 78660
Fire Island Dr 78660
Firebush Dr 78660
Firoj Dr 78660
Fitchburg Cir 78660
Flatters Way 78660
Fm 1825 78660
Fm 685 78660
Foothill Farms Loop 78660
Four Hills Ct 78660
Fox Sparrow Cv 78660
Framingham Cir 78660
Frankie Ln 78660
Freestone Dr 78660
Friendship Hill Dr 78660
Friendship Quilt Ln 78660
Fritz Falls Xing 78660
Frost Cir 78660
Fyvie Castle Ct 78660
Gale Meadow Dr 78660
Galway Bay Cv 78660
Ganton Ct 78660
Gantry Dr 78660
Gardena Canyon Dr 78660
Gate Dancer Ln 78660
Gatlinburg Dr 78660
Gavin Trl 78660
Gazania Dr 78660
Gelding Ln 78660
Geyser Ave 78660
Gila Cliff Dr 78660
Ginger Spice Ln 78660
Ginseng Cv 78660
Glacier Bay St 78660
Gladstone Castle Trl 78660
Glastonbury Trl 78660
Glen Rose Chase 78660
Glendalough Dr 78660
Glorious Ln 78660
Godolphin Ct 78660
Gold Dust Pass 78660
Golden Eagle St 78660
Golden Flax Trl 78660
Golden Sunrise Ln 78660
Goodspeed Pkwy 78660
Gower St 78660
Grafton Ln 78660
Grafton Glen Cv 78660
Grail Holw 78660
Grand St 78660
Grand Avenue Pkwy 78660
Grand Banks 78660
Grand Mission Way 78660
Grand National Ave 78660
Grant St 78660
Gravesend Rd 78660
Great Basin Ave 78660
Great Sand Dunes 78660
Green Mdws 78660
Green Field Cv 78660
Green Valley Cv 78660
Greenbrook Pkwy 78660
Greenhill Dr 78660
Greenslope Cir 78660
Greenway Dr 78660
Gregory Cv 78660
Greinert Dr 78660
Grener Cv 78660
Grey Castle Dr 78660
Gypsum Ct 78660
Hackberry Dr 78660
Haig Point Cv 78660
Haley Gray Dr 78660
E & W Hall St 78660
Hallbrook Ln 78660
Halo Dr 78660
Handsome Dr 78660
Hanging Rock Dr 78660
Harbor Point Dr 78660
Harcourt House Ln 78660
Harness Raceway 78660
Harrier Flight Trl 78660
Harrier Hunt Rd 78660
Harris Ridge Blvd 78660
Harvard Dr 78660
Havant Way 78660
Hawk Hood Dr 78660
Hawks Swoop Trl 78660
Hayfield Sq 78660
Hayworth Cv 78660
N Heatherwilde Blvd 78660
S Heatherwilde Blvd
301-397 78660
301-301 78691
399-1299 78660
Hebbe Ln 78660
Hees Ct & Ln 78660
Helios Way 78660
Heritage Well Ln 78660
Heron Call Trl 78660
Heron Roost Pass 78660
Hickory Bark Ct 78660
Hickory Ridge Trl 78660
Hidden Harbor Dr 78660
Hidden Lake Xing 78660
Hidden Park Dr 78660
Hill Top Canyon Cv 78660
Hilltop Commercial Dr 78660
Hodde Ln 78660
Holderness Ln 78660
Holly Ct 78660
Hollyhock Ct 78660
Holsten Hill Dr 78660
Honey Cv 78660
Honey Blossom Dr 78660
Honeysuckle Ln 78660
E & W Hoopes Ave 78660
Horborne Ln 78660
Horned Owl Trl 78660
House Wren Loop 78660
E Howard Ln 78660
Howeth Cv & Dr 78660
Howlin Wolf Trl 78660
Huckabee Bnd 78660
Hughmont Dr 78660
Huntingtower Castle Blvd 78660
Hymill Dr 78660
Hyson Xing 78660
Hytop Dr 78660
Ice Age Trails St 78660
Idaho Falls Cv & Ln 78660
Immanuel Rd 78660
Impact Way 78660
Indian Run Dr 78660
Ingrids Iris Dr 78660
Inks Lake Dr 78660
Interstate 35 78660
Investment Dr 78660
Isle Of Man Ct & Rd 78660
Ivy Dr 78660
Ivybridge Dr 78660
Jackies Ranch Rd 78660
Jan Dr 78660
Jana Patrice Dr 78660
Jane Austen Trl 78660
Jasmine Ct 78660
Jasmine Tea Trl 78660
Jesse Bohls Dr 78660
Jill Sue Cir 78660
Joshua Tree Cir 78660
Julies Walk 78660
Jumpers Delight Ln 78660
Justeford Dr 78660
Kapalua Pl 78660
Katie Lynch Dr 78660
Katies Corner Ln 78660
Kay Ln 78660
Kearney Hill Rd 78660
Keeli Ln 78660

Keilman Ln ... 78660
Kelly Ln ... 78660
Kenai Fjords Dr ... 78660
Kennemer Dr ... 78660
Kensington Castle Trl ... 78660
Kentra Dr ... 78660
Kerbey Heights Ct ... 78660
Kermit Ct ... 78660
Kessler Cv & Dr ... 78660
Kestrel Lore Ct ... 78660
Kickapoo Cavern Dr ... 78660
Kilkenny Dr ... 78660
Killingsworth Ln ... 78660
Kingston Lacy Blvd ... 78660
Kirtomy Loop ... 78660
Knottingham Dr ... 78660
Kodiak Ln ... 78660
Lady Elizabeth Ln ... 78660
Lady Grey Ave ... 78660
Lady Lauras Xing ... 78660
Lafayette Ln ... 78660
Lake Edge Ct & Way ... 78660
Lake Victor Dr ... 78660
Lampting Dr ... 78660
Lanark Loop ... 78660
Langland Rd ... 78660
Lantern Dr ... 78660
Laurel Oak Trl ... 78660
Laurelleaf Dr ... 78660
Lava Bed Dr ... 78660
Lavender Cv ... 78660
Lazyridge Dr ... 78660
Leigh Ln ... 78660
Lemongrass Ln ... 78660
Letti Ln ... 78660
Lewis Carroll Ln ... 78660
Liffey Cv & Dr ... 78660
Limestone Commercial Dr ... 78660
Lincoln St ... 78660
Lincoln Sparrow Cv ... 78660
Linville Ridge Ln ... 78660
Lipton Ln ... 78660
Lismore Ln ... 78660
Loch Linnhe Cv & Loop ... 78660
Lochaline Loop ... 78660
Lonesome Lilly Way ... 78660
Long Meadow Dr ... 78660
Lothian Dr ... 78660
Low Brim Cv ... 78660
Loyola Dr ... 78660
Luedtke Ln ... 78660
Lydia Springs Dr ... 78660
Lynde Cv ... 78660
Lynn Cv ... 78660
Lynx Ct ... 78660
Madden Dr ... 78660
Magic Hill Dr ... 78660
Magnolia Ranch Cv ... 78660
Mahomet Dr ... 78660
Maiden Grass Dr ... 78660
E & W Main St ... 78660
Maize Cv ... 78660
Malden Cv & Dr ... 78660
Mallard Pond Trl ... 78660
Mammoth Cave Blvd ... 78660
Mandarin Xing ... 78660
Mandrake Dr ... 78660
Mangan Way ... 78660
Mangrum St ... 78660
Manish Ct & Dr ... 78660
Maple Vista Dr ... 78660
Maplewood Cir & Dr ... 78660
Marble Glen Ln ... 78660
Maricella Ln ... 78660
Marigold Way ... 78660
Marigold Heights Ct ... 78660
Martin Ln ... 78660
Mashburn St ... 78660
Masi Loop ... 78660
Mason Bend Dr ... 78660
Massengale St ... 78660
Mattapan Dr ... 78660
Maxines Cv ... 78660
Mayapple St ... 78660
Mead Bnd ... 78660
Meadow Ln ... 78660
Meadow Creek Dr ... 78660
Meandering Meadows Ln ... 78660
Meister Ln ... 78660
Melanies Walk ... 78660
Melted Candle Cv ... 78660
Melwas Way ... 78660
Mendips Ln ... 78660
Meridian Blvd ... 78660
Merlin Falcon Trl ... 78660
Merseyside Dr ... 78660
Mexican Heather Ct ... 78660
Middleway Rd ... 78660
Mildura Cv ... 78660
Mill Creek Rd ... 78660
Millhouse Dr ... 78660
Milton Cv ... 78660
Miss Adriennes Path ... 78660
Miss Allisons Way ... 78660
Miss Kimberlys Ln ... 78660
Mission Tejas Dr ... 78660
Mist Flower Dr ... 78660
Misty Harbor Dr ... 78660
Misty Heights Cv ... 78660
Misty Shore Ln ... 78660
Moorlynch Ave ... 78660
Morgana Dr ... 78660
Morgans Choice Ln ... 78660
Morning Mist Ln ... 78660
Mountain View Cv & Dr ... 78660
Moura Cv ... 78660
Moving Waters ... 78660
Muddy Waters Dr ... 78660
Murrelet Way ... 78660
Mustang Grape Ct ... 78660
Mustang Island Cir ... 78660
Narsitin Ln ... 78660
Naruna Way ... 78660
Natural Bridge Ln ... 78660
Nestle Ct ... 78660
New Meister Ln ... 78660
Newgrange Dr ... 78660
Nicole Ln ... 78660
Nightjar View Ter ... 78660
Nightview Dr ... 78660
Nimbus Dr ... 78660
Niobrara River Dr ... 78660
Noatak Trl ... 78660
Northavens Cv ... 78660
Norwell Ln ... 78660
E & W Noton Ct & St ... 78660
Oak Ridge Cv & Dr ... 78660
Oak Vista Dr ... 78660
Oakdale Cir & Ln ... 78660
Oat Meadow Dr ... 78660
Oatmeal Dr ... 78660
Obed River Dr ... 78660
Ocotillo Dr ... 78660
Old Austin Hutto Rd ... 78660
Old Austin Pflugerville Rd ... 78660
Old Gregg Ln ... 78660
Old Tract Rd ... 78660
Oldwick Castle Way ... 78660
E Olympic Dr ... 78660
Oolong Ln ... 78660
Open Plain Dr ... 78660
Option Ave ... 78660
Ora Ln ... 78660
Orange Pekoe Trl ... 78660
Orange Spice Ct ... 78660
Orchard Park Cir ... 78660
Orourke Dr ... 78660
Ortman Dr ... 78660
Orts Ln ... 78660
Oxford Dr ... 78660
Pacers Gait Ln ... 78660
Palitine Ln ... 78660
Palm Vista Dr ... 78660
Palmwood Trl ... 78660
Panther Dr & Loop ... 78660
Parco Path ... 78660
Park Springs Loop ... 78660
Parkcrest Ct ... 78660
Parkview Cv & Dr ... 78660
Parkway Dr ... 78660
Pasqueflower Pass ... 78660
Passion Vine Cv ... 78660
Patterson Industrial Dr ... 78660
Paul St ... 78660
Pauma Valley Way ... 78660
Pawtucket Ct ... 78660
Peach Vista Dr ... 78660
Pear Ct ... 78660
Pearlman Dr ... 78660
Peat Moors Cv ... 78660
Pecan St E ... 78660
Pecan Creek Dr ... 78660
Pedernales Falls Dr ... 78660
Pencil Cactus Dr ... 78660
Pendragon Castle Dr ... 78660
Penny Royal Dr ... 78660
Peppermint Trl ... 78660
Peridot Rd ... 78660
Perth Pass ... 78660
Petunia Ln ... 78660
E Pfennig Ln ... 78660
E & W Pfluger Ln & St ... 78660
Pflugerville Pkwy ... 78660
Picadilly Dr ... 78660
Pigeon Forge Dr & Rd ... 78660
Pin Clover Ct ... 78660
Pine Creek Dr ... 78660
Pine Vista Dr ... 78660
Pinon Hills Ct ... 78660
Pinon Pine Dr ... 78660
Pioneer Bend Dr ... 78660
Pitcairn Dr ... 78660
Plainfield Ct ... 78660
Pleasant Valley Dr ... 78660
Plover Run Trl ... 78660
Plowshare Dr ... 78660
Plumbago Dr ... 78660
Poe Cir ... 78660
Point Run Cv & Dr ... 78660
Polished Stone Cv ... 78660
Poppy Pass ... 78660
Portchester Castle Path ... 78660
Prairie Ridge Trl ... 78660
Priem Ln ... 78660
Princeton Cv & Dr ... 78660
Pumpkin Ridge Ct ... 78660
Purple Iris Cv ... 78660
Purple Martin Ct & Dr ... 78660
Purple Thistle Dr ... 78660
Quail Run Rd ... 78660
Quantico Ct ... 78660
Quiet Meadows Cv ... 78660
Quiet Water Pass ... 78660
Quincy Dr ... 78660
Racers Ford Ln ... 78660
Raglan Castle Path ... 78660
N & S Railroad Ave ... 78660
Ramble Creek Dr ... 78660
Rambling Creek Ln ... 78660
Ramsgate Ct ... 78660
Randalstone Dr ... 78660
Randig Ln ... 78660
Rannoch Dr ... 78660
Ransom St ... 78660
Raptor Roost Rd ... 78660
Raven Caw Pass ... 78660
Ravensbrook Ct ... 78660
Red Ivy Cv ... 78660
Red Tailed Hawk Dr ... 78660
Redwood Ln ... 78660
Regis Dr ... 78660
Rendova Ln ... 78660
Rex Kerwin Ct ... 78660
Richelle Cv ... 78660
Richfield Lndg ... 78660
Ripley Castle Cv ... 78660
Rita Blanca Cir ... 78660
River Birch Way ... 78660
Rochester Castle Way ... 78660
Rocking Spur Cv ... 78660
Rocky Creek Dr ... 78660
Rocky Shore Ln ... 78660
Rolling Meadow Dr ... 78660
Rolling Water Dr ... 78660
Rosehip Ln ... 78660
Rough Berry Rd ... 78660
Rowe Ln & Loop ... 78660
Roxannes Run ... 78660
Royal Ascot Dr ... 78660
Royal Pointe Dr ... 78660
Ruffed Grouse Cv ... 78660
Ruggio Rd ... 78660
Runners Rdg ... 78660
Russell St ... 78660
Rutgers Dr ... 78660
Saddlegirth Ln ... 78660
Sage Ct ... 78660
Sage Boot Dr ... 78660
Saint Croix Ln ... 78660
Saint John Ct ... 78660
Saint Leger St ... 78660
Sally Lunn Way ... 78660
Salt River Bay Dr ... 78660
Samoa Ct ... 78660
Sandpiper Perch Ct ... 78660
Sandpiper Spot Ct & Trl ... 78660
Sandwick Dr ... 78660
Sandy Bottom Dr ... 78660
Sandy Shore Dr ... 78660
Sangremon Way ... 78660
Santolina Ct ... 78660
Sarahs Creek Dr ... 78660
Sassafras Trl ... 78660
Savin Rise Ct ... 78660
Schultz Ln ... 78660
Sea Island Dr ... 78660
Sebastian Bnd ... 78660
Secluded Willow Cv ... 78660
Secretariat Ridge Ln ... 78660
Segovia Way ... 78660
Serenity Dr ... 78660
Seton Hall Ln ... 78660
Setting Sun Ct ... 78660
Settlers Valley Cv & Dr ... 78660
Seven Bridges Ct ... 78660
Shallow Pond Trl ... 78660
Shallow Pool Dr ... 78660
Shanty Creek Pl ... 78660
Shire St ... 78660
Shoreless Dr ... 78660
Shotgun Ct ... 78660
Silene Ct ... 78660
Silent Harbor Loop ... 78660
Silent Water Way ... 78660
Silverbell Ln ... 78660
Simsbrook Dr ... 78660
Sixpence Ln ... 78660
Skylark Hill Ln ... 78660
Sleepy Daisy Cv ... 78660
Sleepy Hollow Dr ... 78660
Sleepytime Trl ... 78660
Smith Ave ... 78660
Smoke Signal Pass ... 78660
Smoothing Iron Dr ... 78660
Snowberry St ... 78660
Sophie Ct ... 78660
Sotogrande Dr ... 78660
Spanish Ridge Cv ... 78660
Sparrow Trl ... 78660
Spearmint Tea Trl ... 78660
Speidel Dr ... 78660
Spinel Rd ... 78660
Split Oak Cv & Dr ... 78660
Spoonemore Dr ... 78660
Spotted Owl Cir & Ln ... 78660
Spring Heath Dr & Rd ... 78660
Spring Hill Ln ... 78660
Spring Peony Ct ... 78660
Springbrook Dr ... 78660
Stacias Way ... 78660
Stage Line Trl ... 78660
Stanley Robin Ln ... 78660
Stansted Manor Dr ... 78660
Staple Cv ... 78660
Star Flower Way ... 78660
Star Gazer Way ... 78660
N State Highway 45 E ... 78660
Statler Bend Dr ... 78660
Steeds Xing ... 78660
Stephens St ... 78660
Stevenage Dr ... 78660
Stevie Ray Dr ... 78660
Still Pond Rd ... 78660
Stirling Castle Ct ... 78660
Stirrat St ... 78660
Stokes Ln ... 78660
Stokesay Castle Path ... 78660
Stone Hill Dr ... 78660
Stoneham Cir ... 78660
Stonepath Way ... 78660
Stonewall Bend Cv ... 78660
Strickling Dr ... 78660
Strontian Pass ... 78660
Sullivan St ... 78660
Sumatra Ln ... 78660
Summit Heights Ct ... 78660
Sunflower Dr ... 78660
Sunken Creek Pass ... 78660
Sunny Oaks Ct ... 78660
Sutton Leighs Ln ... 78660
Suzi Cv & Ln ... 78660
Suzzane Rd ... 78660
Swallow Ridge Cv ... 78660
Sweet Caddies Dr ... 78660
Sweet Leaf Ln ... 78660
Sweet Melissa Dr ... 78660
Sweet William Ln ... 78660
Sweetwood Song Dr ... 78660
Swenson Farms Blvd ... 78660
Sykes Ct ... 78660
Sylvia Ln ... 78660
Tacon Ln ... 78660
Talamore Rd ... 78660
Tanner Trl ... 78660
Tapestry Cv ... 78660
Taylor St ... 78660
Taylor Falls Dr ... 78660
Tayside Dr ... 78660
Tea Leaf Dr ... 78660
Tea Room Cv ... 78660
Teacup Ln ... 78660
Teakwood Trl ... 78660
Teapot Dr ... 78660
Terradyne Dr ... 78660
Texas Meadows Dr ... 78660
Thackeray Ln ... 78660
Thayer Cv ... 78660
The Lakes Blvd ... 78660
Thornblade Ct ... 78660
Three Points Rd ... 78660
Tiddle Ln ... 78660
Timber Bend Dr ... 78660
Timothy John Dr ... 78660
Tobermory Dr ... 78660
Topaz Rd ... 78660
Tophill Cir ... 78660
Town Center Dr ... 78660
Traci Michelle Dr ... 78660
Tralagon Trl ... 78660
Tranquility Ln ... 78660
Treyburn Ln ... 78660
Trickling Springs Way ... 78660
Trotters Ln ... 78660
Tudor House Rd ... 78660
Turning Stream Ln ... 78660
Twin Creek Dr ... 78660
Twisted Fence Dr ... 78660
Valerian Tea Dr ... 78660
Valeries Cv ... 78660
Valjean Dr ... 78660
Valley Glen Cv & Rd ... 78660
Valley Meadow Dr ... 78660
Valley View Dr ... 78660
Vanderbilt Cir ... 78660
Vanilla Bean Dr ... 78660
Vapor Dr ... 78660
Veiled Falls Dr ... 78660
Velias Way ... 78660
Ventana Ct ... 78660
Victoria Ridge Dr ... 78660
Viki Lynn Ct & Pl ... 78660
Vilamoura St ... 78660
Village Glen Cv & Rd ... 78660
Village View Loop ... 78660
Vincent Pl ... 78660
Vision Dr ... 78660
Vogue Cv ... 78660
Wagon Wheel Trl ... 78660
Wakonda Ct ... 78660
W Walnut St ... 78660
Walnut Canyon Blvd ... 78660
Walt Whitman Trl ... 78660
E & W Walter Ave & Ct ... 78660
Wandering Vine Cv ... 78660
Watson Way ... 78660
Waukesha Dr ... 78660
Wayzata Ct ... 78660
Wearyall Hill Ln ... 78660
Weiss Ln ... 78660
E & W Wells Branch Pkwy ... 78660
Westgate Way ... 78660
White Water Cv & Way ... 78660
Whitehall Dr ... 78660
Whittard Of Chelsea Ln ... 78660
E & W Wilbarger St ... 78660
Wild Orchard Dr ... 78660
Wild Petunia Way ... 78660
Wild Senna Dr W ... 78660
Wilke Ln ... 78660
Wilke Ridge Ln ... 78660
William Anderson Dr ... 78660
Willie Dr ... 78660
Willow St ... 78660
Willow Bluff Dr ... 78660
Willow Vista Dr ... 78660
Willow Walk Dr ... 78660
Willow Wood Dr ... 78660
Willowwick Cir ... 78660
Wind Valley Way ... 78660
Wind Vane W ... 78660
Windermere Dr ... 78660
Winding Shore Ln ... 78660
Windless Way ... 78660
Windmill Cir ... 78660
Windmill Ranch Ave ... 78660
Windmill Ridge St ... 78660
Windsor Castle Dr ... 78660
Windsor Hill Dr ... 78660
Windview Ln ... 78660
Windy Vane Dr ... 78660
Winners Ribbon Cir ... 78660
Wiseman Dr ... 78660
Woodlawn Dr ... 78660
Worley Dr ... 78660
Wren Ave ... 78660
Yale Dr ... 78660
Yellow Sage St ... 78660
York Castle Dr ... 78660
Yorkshire St ... 78660
Yucca House Dr ... 78660
Zanzibar Ln ... 78660
Zircon Ct ... 78660

NUMBERED STREETS

All Street Addresses ... 78660

PLAINVIEW TX

General Delivery ... 79072

POST OFFICE BOXES MAIN OFFICE STATIONS AND BRANCHES

Box No.s
All PO Boxes ... 79073

RURAL ROUTES

01, 01, 01, 02, 02 ... 79072

HIGHWAY CONTRACTS

01, 01, 01, 02, 02 ... 79072
01, 01, 01, 02, 02 ... 79072
01, 01, 01, 02, 02 ... 79072
01, 01, 01, 02, 02 ... 79072
01, 01, 01, 02, 02 ... 79072

NAMED STREETS

Aileen St ... 79072
Airport Rd ... 79072
NE, NW, SE & SW
Alpine Dr ... 79072
Amarillo St ... 79072
Andy Taylor Rd ... 79072
Arbor Ave ... 79072
Ash St
100-726 ... 79072
725-725 ... 79073
728-1798 ... 79072
801-1799 ... 79072
S Ash St ... 79072
N & S Austin St ... 79072
Avenida Godsey ... 79072
Aylesworth St ... 79072
S Baltimore St ... 79072
S Beech St ... 79072
Borger St ... 79072
Bravo St ... 79072
E & W Brazier St ... 79072
S Broadway St ... 79072
Bryan St ... 79072
Bullock St ... 79072
S Business I H 27 ... 79072
Calle Martinez ... 79072
Calle Soto ... 79072
E & W Campbell St ... 79072
Canyon St ... 79072
E & W Carver St ... 79072
Castro St ... 79072
S Cedar St ... 79072
College Ave ... 79072
N & S Columbia St ... 79072
Cottonwood Ln ... 79072
Country Ln ... 79072
County Road 10 ... 79072
County Road 100 ... 79072
County Road 102 ... 79072
County Road 105 ... 79072
County Road 110 ... 79072
County Road 115 ... 79072
County Road 120 ... 79072
County Road 125 ... 79072
County Road 130 ... 79072
County Road 135 ... 79072
County Road 145 ... 79072
County Road 15 ... 79072
County Road 150 ... 79072
County Road 155 ... 79072
County Road 170 ... 79072
County Road 175 ... 79072
County Road 195 ... 79072
County Road 20 ... 79072
County Road 215 ... 79072
County Road 225 ... 79072
County Road 25 ... 79072
County Road 35 ... 79072
County Road 40 ... 79072
County Road 50 ... 79072
County Road 55 ... 79072
County Road 60 ... 79072
County Road 62 ... 79072
County Road 65 ... 79072
County Road 68 ... 79072
County Road 70 ... 79072
County Road 80 ... 79072
County Road 85 ... 79072
County Road 90 ... 79072
County Road 92 ... 79072
County Road 95 ... 79072
County Road Aa ... 79072
County Road Bb ... 79072
County Road Cc ... 79072
County Road Dd ... 79072
County Road Ee ... 79072

County Road G 79072
County Road H 79072
County Road K 79072
County Road L 79072
County Road M 79072
County Road O 79072
County Road P 79072
County Road Q 79072
County Road R 79072
County Road T 79072
County Road U 79072
County Road V 79072
County Road X 79072
County Road Y 79072
County Road Z 79072
E & W Crestway St 79072
Dallas St 79072
N & S Date St 79072
Davidson St 79072
Denver St 79072
Dimmitt Rd 79072
Ebeling Dr 79072
Edgemere Dr 79072
El Camino St 79072
El Paso St 79072
Elm St 79072
S Ennis Rd & St 79072
Faulkner St 79072
Ferrell Ave 79072
Fir St 79072
Fisher St 79072
S Floydada St 79072
Fm 1070 79072
Fm 1424 79072
Fm 1612 79072
Fm 179 79072
Fm 1914 79072
Fm 2284 79072
Fm 2286 79072
Fm 2288 79072
Fm 2883 79072
Fm 3183 79072
Fm 37 79072
Fm 400 79072
Fm 784 79072
Fm 788 79072
Fm 789 79072
Fresno St 79072
Frisco St 79072
Galveston St 79072
S Garland St 79072
E & W Givens St 79072
Gladney St 79072
Grandview St 79072
Gray St 79072
Grove St 79072
Hastey Dr 79072
Henry St 79072
Hickory St 79072
S Holliday St 79072
Horseshoe Bnd 79072
Houston St 79072
Howard St 79072
Hoyle St 79072
Independence St 79072
Industrial Blvd 79072
Interstate 27 79072
Irene St 79072
S Itasca St 79072
Ivy St 79072
S Jefferson St 79072
Joliet St 79072
S Juanita St 79072
Juniper St 79072
Kermit St 79072
Kings Row 79072
Kirchwood St 79072
Kirchwood 1 Pl 79072
Kirchwood 2 Pl 79072
Kokomo St 79072
Lancaster St 79072
Lexington St 79072
Lindburg St 79072
Lometa Dr 79072
Magan St 79072
Mann St 79072
Maplewood Ln 79072
Mckinley St 79072
Mesa Cir & Dr 79072
Milwaukee St 79072
S Milwee St 79072
Mulberry Ln 79072
Nassau St 79072
Navajo Trl 79072
S Navasota Dr 79072
Nix Rd 79072
Nixon St 79072
Norma St 79072
Oak St 79072
Oakland St 79072
Oakridge Ln 79072
Olton Rd 79072
Owen St 79072
Park Pl 79072
Parkway St 79072
Pecos Pl 79072
Pioneer Rd 79072
Pleasant Hill Cir 79072
Portland St 79072
Quincy St 79072
Raleigh St 79072
Red Oak Ln 79072
Ridgeway Dr 79072
Rochelle St 79072
Rock Island St 79072
Roselawn St 79072
Sabine St 79072
Saint Louis St 79072
Sam Hearn St 79072
Santa Rosa Cir 79072
Sherwood Rd 79072
Sides St 79072
W Smith St 79072
Smythe St 79072
State Highway 194 79072
Stevens St 79072
Sun Rd 79072
Thomas Blvd 79072
Thunderbird Dr & Way 79072
Travis St 79072
Trinity St 79072
Tumbleweed Rd 79072
Upchurch St 79072
E & W Us Highway 70 79072
Utica St 79072
Vermont St 79072
Vernon St 79072
Villa Dr 79072
Walter Griffin St 79072
Walter Jackson St 79072
Way Rd 79072
Wayland St 79072
Well Rd 79072
N & S Westridge Rd & Sq 79072
Willow Bnd 79072
Wilson St 79072
Wood St 79072
Xenia St 79072
Xray Rd 79072
Yoakum St 79072
Yonkers St 79072
Yucca Ter 79072
Zephyr St 79072

NUMBERED STREETS

All Street Addresses 79072

PLANO TX

General Delivery 75074

POST OFFICE BOXES MAIN OFFICE STATIONS AND BRANCHES

Box No.s
250001 - 259410 75025
260001 - 269035 75026
860000 - 869414 75086
940001 - 942232 75094

RURAL ROUTES

17, 18 75024
16, 22, 24, 31, 59, 82 75025
01, 03, 07, 90 75074
52 75093
02, 105, 56, 92, 94 75094

NAMED STREETS

Aaron Cir 75025
Abbey Rd 75074
Abbotsford Dr 75074
Aberdeen Dr 75093
Abernathy St 75074
Abilene Ct 75023
Ables Dr 75093
Abrams Dr 75074
Academy Ln 75074
Acadia Dr 75023
Accent Dr 75075
Acklin Dr 75025
Acme Cir 75074
Acropolis Way 75074
Adair Ln 75024
Adams Cir 75023
Adavale Dr 75025
Adderberry Ln 75075
Admirals Cove Ct 75093
Adrian Way 75024
Afton Ridge Dr 75025
Afton Villa Ct 75025
Aimpoint Dr 75023
Ainsley Dr 75024
Airpark Ln 75093
Alabama Ct & Rd 75094
Alabaster Rd 75074
Aladdin Dr 75093
Alameda Ct 75074
Alamo Ct 75023
Alamosa Dr 75023
Alandale Dr 75025
Albany Dr 75093
Alcove Ln 75024
Aldenham Dr 75024
Alderwood Dr & Pl 75025
Aldridge Dr 75075
Alexa Ct 75075
Alexander Ct 75074
Aliso Rd 75074
All Saints Ln 75025
Allamore Dr 75093
Allegheny Trl 75023
Allegro Ln 75025
Allende Ct 75074
Alliance Blvd 75093
Allied Dr 75093
Alma Dr
501-697 75075
699-3299 75075
3300-5500 75023
5502-6998 75023
7001-7297 75025
7299-7399 75025
7401-7899 75025
Almont 75024
Alsten Ln 75093
Altessa Dr 75093
Altrick Dr 75093
Amanda Ct
200-299 75094
4600-4699 75024
Amaretto Ct 75024
Amazon Dr 75075
Amber Ln
800-898 75094
1600-1799 75075
Ambiance Way 75024
Ambrose Dr 75094
Ambrosia Ln 75093
Amelia Ct 75075
American Dr 75075
Amesbury Dr
1000-1099 75094
2800-3199 75093
Amethyst Ln
6700-6800 75023
6802-6998 75023
7000-7199 75025
7201-7299 75025
Amherst Dr 75075
Amore Dr 75074
Amy Ln 75074
Anatole Ct 75075
Anchor Dr 75023
Anders Ln 75093
Andora Dr 75093
Andover Dr 75023
Andre Ct 75023
Angel Fire Dr 75025
Angelgate Ln 75074
Angelina Dr 75074
Angels Dr 75024
Angle Ridge Dr 75094
Anglebluff Ln & Pl 75093
Angus Dr 75025
Annabel Ln 75093
Anns Way 75025
Anson Ct 75024
Anthony Ln 75024
Antlers Ct 75025
Antoine Dr 75023
Antwerp Ave 75025
Apache Ct 75023
Apache Trl 75094
Appalachian Ct & Way 75075
Apple Tree Dr 75093
Apple Valley Pl & Rd 75023
Appomattox Cir 75023
Apricot Ln 75074
April Way Cir 75023
Aqua Springs Dr 75025
Aqua Vista Dr 75025
Aransas Dr 75025
Arbor Downs Dr 75023
Arbor Glen Trl 75024
Arbor Vista Dr 75093
Arborcove Dr 75075
Arborcrest Dr 75074
Arbuckle Dr 75075
Arcady Pl 75093
Archerwood St 75074
Archgate Dr 75024
Arcola Dr 75074
Arena Dr 75025
Argentine Way 75024
Argyle Cir & Dr 75023
Arizona Pl 75023
Arlen Ct & Dr 75093
Armstrong Dr 75074
Arnold Pl 75074
Arrow Point Dr 75093
Arrowhead Ln 75093
Arroyo Ct 75074
Arthur Ct 75025
Artist Dr 75023
Arvida Dr 75023
Asaro Pl 75025
Asbury Ln 75025
Ash Creek Ln 75093
Ashburn Pl 75075
Ashby Ct 75025
Ashcroft Ln 75025
Ashdon Ln 75094
Ashford Dr 75023
Ashglen Pl 75023
Ashington Cir, Ct & Ln 75023
Ashley Pl 75094
Ashley Park Dr 75074
Ashmont Dr 75023
Ashwood Cir 75075
Aspen Ct 75094
E Aspen Ct 75075
W Aspen Ct 75075
Aspen Glen Rd 75024
Aspermont Dr 75024
Atherton Dr 75093
Atlanta Dr 75093
Atrium Dr 75075
Attica Ln 75094
Atwater Ct 75093
Auburn Pl 75093
Audubon St 75023
Augusta Cir 75025
Aurora Dr 75093
Austin Dr 75025
Autumn Hl 75094
Autumn Meadows Dr 75024
Autumn Ridge Trl 75093
Autumnwood Trl 75024
Avalanche Dr 75094
Avalon Dr 75025
Avebury Dr 75024
Avon Dr 75093
Avondale Dr 75094
Avondale Ln 75025
Avonshire Ln 75093
Axis Dr 75094
Aylesbury Ln 75075
Azalea Ln 75074
Azinger Dr 75025
Azurite Trl 75075
Bachman Ct 75075
Baffin Bay Ct & Dr 75075
Bagley Dr 75025
Bahama Dr 75074
Bailey Ct 75093
Bainbridge Ct 75023
Baird Dr 75024
Bakersfield St 75074
Balboa Cir & Way 75075
Balcones Dr 75093
Baldwin Ln 75024
Ballet Ct 75023
Ballinger Ct & Dr 75093
Ballycastle Dr 75074
Ballymote Ln 75074
Baltic Blvd 75024
Bamboo Ct 75074
Bamburgh Dr 75075
Banbury Dr 75094
Bandera Dr 75074
Bandolino Ln
2901-2997 75075
2999-3299 75075
3300-3399 75023
3401-3499 75023
Banff Ct 75093
Banister Ct 75093
Bankhead Ln 75074
Banks Cir 75025
Banner Elk Cir 75025
Bantry Ct 75025
Banyon Dr 75023
Barber Oak Dr 75025
Barbican Dr
6800-6999 75023
7000-7198 75025
Barksdale Dr 75025
Barkwood Ct 75074
Barlow Ct 75025
Barnett Dr 75024
Barnsley Dr 75093
Barouche Ct 75023
Barrington Dr 75093
Barrister Cir 75094
Barrymoore Ln 75025
Bartley Cir 75025
Barwyn Ct & Ln 75093
Basalt Dr 75024
Bashful Dr 75093
Bass Dr 75025
Bassinghall Ln 75093
Basswood Ln 75074
Bastille Dr 75024
Bastrop Ct 75023
Bates Rd 75093
Baxter Dr 75025
Bay Hill Dr 75023
Bayberry Ct 75093
Bayham Dr 75024
Bayview Dr 75093
Baywater Dr 75093
Beacon Crest Dr 75093
Beacon Hill Dr 75093
Bear Creek Blvd 75025
Bear Creek Dr 75094
Bear Run Dr 75093
Beatton Ct 75025
Beauchamp Dr 75093
Beaumont Ln 75023
Beauregard Ln 75024
Beaver Bend Dr 75025
Beaver Creek Dr
700-799 75094
1400-1499 75093
1501-1599 75093
Beck Dr 75025
Becket Cir 75025
Beckham Ct 75075
Beckworth Ln 75024
Bedell Ln 75094
Bedfordshire Ln 75075
Bedrock Dr 75093
Beech St 75093
Beechcraft St 75025
Beechmont Ct 75074
Beechwood Dr 75094
Beechwood Pl 75075
Beeman Dr 75023
Belcamp Dr 75023
Belcrest Dr 75024
Belgium Dr 75025
Belgrade Dr 75023
Belinda Ln 75024
Bella Vista Dr 75074
Belladonna Dr 75093
Bellaire Dr 75093
Bellehaven Dr 75023
Bellerive Dr 75025
Bellflower Dr 75075
Bellwood Cir 75074
Belmont Pl 75023
Belvedere Dr 75093
Benchmark Dr 75023
Bender Trl 75075
Bending Oak Trl 75024
Benelux Ct 75025
Bengal Ln 75023
Bennington Ct 75075
Benoit Dr 75024
Bent Horn Ct & Dr 75025
Bent Ridge Dr 75074
Bent Tree Springs Dr 75025
Bentley Ct & Dr 75093
Benton Elm Dr 75024
Berkeley Ct 75023
Berks Ct 75093
Berkshire Dr 75094
Berkwood Dr 75025
Bermuda Dunes Dr 75093
Bernay Ln 75024
Berretta Dr 75023
Bertrand Dr 75094
Berwick Dr 75025
Berwyn Dr 75093
Beth Dr
5900-5999 75093
6000-6099 75024
Betsy Ln 75094
Bettye Haun Dr 75024
Beverly Dr 75093
Bexhill Dr 75025
Bianca Ln 75093
Bierstadt Cir 75023
Big Bend Dr 75023
Big Creek Ct 75093
Big Foot Dr 75025
Big Horn Trl 75075
Big Sky Dr 75024
Bigelow Dr 75024
Billings Ct 75024
Biloxi Cir 75075
Bilsen Ct 75025
Biltmore Pl 75023
Birchmont Dr 75093
Birchwood Ln 75074
Birdsong Ln 75093
Birkdale Dr 75093
Birkshire Ln 75024
Birmingham Ct 75093
Biscayne Cir & Dr 75075
Bishop Rd 75024
Bitterroot Ct 75025
Bixby Dr 75023
Black Canyon Dr 75025
Black Sage Dr 75093
Blackberry Crk 75023
Blackburn Ln 75025
Blackhawk Dr 75093
Blackjack Oak Ln 75074
Blackpool Dr 75093
Blackshear Trl 75093
Blacktree Dr 75093
Blain Dr 75024
Blake Dr 75093
Blanco Ct 75023
Blaylock Pl 75025
Blazer Dr 75025
Blenheim Ct 75025
Bloomfield Ct 75093
Blossom Trl 75074
Blue Flumar Ct 75094
Blue Jay Dr 75094
Blue Mesa Dr 75025
Blue Ridge Trl 75023
Blue Water Dr 75025
Blueberry Ct 75074
Bluebonnet Dr 75023
Bluegrass Dr 75074
Bluesky Ln 75094
Bluffcreek Ln 75024
Bluffmeadow Trl 75023
Bluffton Dr 75075
Blystone Ln 75093
Bob O Link Ct 75093
Boedeker Dr 75074
Bolivar Ct 75023
Bonita Dr
3500-3899 75025
3901-3999 75025
4000-4199 75024
Bonnie Ct 75094
Bonniebrook Dr 75075
Bonsai Dr 75093
Boone Ct 75023
Booth Dr 75093
Boren Ct 75023
Bosque Dr 75074
Boston Dr 75093
Boulder Dr 75023
Boulton Ct 75025
Boundary Creek Cir 75024
Bow Crk 75025
Bowie Dr 75025
Bowling Green Cir 75075
Boxwood Ln 75074
Boysenberry Ln 75074
Bozeman Dr 75024
Brabant Dr 75025
Bradbury Ct 75093
Braden Cv 75074
Bradford Dr 75025
Bradley Ln 75023
Bradshaw Dr 75074
Brady Dr 75024
Braemar Dr 75093
Braewood Cir 75093
Bragg Pl 75024
Bramley Way 75093
Branch Hollow Dr 75023
Branchwood Dr 75093
Branding Green Trl 75093
Brandon Ct 75093
Brandon Ln 75094
Brantford Ct 75093
Brassington Ln 75075
Bravura Dr 75074
Braxton Ln 75025
Brazos Trl 75075
Breakers Ln 75025
Breakwater Ln 75093
Breanna Way 75024
Breckenridge Dr 75025
Brees St 75075

Brennan Ct & Dr 75075
Brentdale Ln 75025
Brentwick Cir 75024
Brentwood Dr
900-1099 75094
1100-1499 75075
Breton Dr 75025
Brewer Dr 75024
Brewster Dr 75025
Brewton Dr 75074
Brian Ln 75023
Briar Bluff Ter 75024
Briar Hollow Dr 75093
Briar Oak Dr 75094
Briar Ridge Ln 75024
Briarcliff Dr 75025
Briarcove Dr 75074
Briarcreek Ct & Ln 75074
Briarcrest Dr 75023
Briarpatch Cir 75074
Briarwood Dr 75074
Bridespring Dr 75025
Bridge Creek Dr 75093
Bridge View Ln 75093
Bridgend Ct 75024
Bridgeport Dr 75093
Bridle Bend Ct & Trl 75093
Brigade Ct 75024
Bright Star Way 75074
Brighton Dr 75094
Brighton Ln 75075
Brimwood Dr 75093
Brinker Ct 75024
Brisbane Ln 75075
Bristol Cv 75074
Broadmeade Dr 75093
Broadmoor Dr 75093
Broadstone Dr 75025
Broadwell Dr 75093
Brodick Way 75025
Broken Bow Cir & Way 75093
Broken Wood Ct 75093
Brompton Dr 75024
Bronco Ln 75023
Bronze Ln 75023
Bronze Leaf Dr 75023
Brook Forest Cir 75024
Brook Meadow Ln 75093
Brookdale Dr 75024
Brookfield Dr 75025
Brookhaven Dr 75093
Brookhollow Dr 75093
Brookmere Ln 75094
Brookmount St 75024
Brooksby Dr 75024
Brookshire Dr 75075
Brookview Dr 75074
Brookwood Dr 75094
Brouette Ct 75023
Brougham Ln 75023
Brown Deer Trl 75023
Browning Dr 75093
Brownley Pl 75025
Brox Ct 75093
Brugge Ct 75025
Brunchberry Ln 75023
Brunswick Dr 75024
Brushfield Dr 75025
Brushy Creek Dr 75025
Bryce Canyon Dr 75025
Brycewood Ln 75025
Bryers Cir 75025
Buchanan Dr 75024
Buck Hill Dr 75025
Buckboard Dr 75074
Buckhorn Ct 75074
Buckingham Ln 75074
Buckle Ln 75023
Buckshot Ct 75094
Buena Vista Dr 75025
Buffalo Bnd 75023
Buffalo Bend Ct 75094
Bull Creek Dr 75025
Bull Run Dr 75093
Bullock Dr 75023

Bulrush Dr 75025
Bunker Hill Cir 75075
Bunny Run 75094
Burgandy St 75093
Burke Cir 75025
Burleson Dr 75074
Burlington Dr 75025
Burlwood Ct 75074
Burnet Dr 75025
Burnham Dr 75093
Burnhill Dr 75024
Burning Tree Cir & Ln 75093
Burnley Dr 75093
Burr Oak Dr 75023
Burrows Ct 75023
Bush Dr 75093
Bushnell Dr 75024
Buttercup Way 75093
Butterfield Ct 75023
Buxton Ct 75025
Cabana Ln 75023
Cabbot Ct 75024
Cabriolet Ct 75023
Cactus Path Dr 75094
Cadbury Ct 75024
Caddo Ct 75023
Cadence Ln 75024
Cadillac Dr 75024
Calaveras Way 75074
Caldwell Ln 75025
Caleche Ct 75023
Caledonia Creek Ln 75024
Caleo Ct 75025
Calhoun Ln 75025
California Trl 75023
Calistoga Springs Way 75024
Callaway Dr 75075
Calumet Dr 75023
Cambria Ct 75025
Cambridge Dr 75023
Camden Ct 75075
Camelia Dr 75074
Camelot Cv 75074
Camino Dr 75074
Camp Wood Ct 75025
Campstone Dr 75023
Campus Ct 75093
Camrose Dr 75024
Camrose Ln 75094
Canadian Trl 75023
Canal St 75024
Candelaria Dr 75023
Candlecreek Ln 75024
Candlepath Trl 75023
Candlewood Trl
600-699 75094
3200-3399 75023
Candlewyck Dr 75024
Cannes Dr 75025
Cannon Falls Dr 75024
Canoe Ln 75023
Canoncita Ln 75023
Canterbury Ct & Dr 75075
Canyon Oaks Cir 75024
Canyon Valley Trl
2100-2399 75023
2800-2900 75075
2902-3298 75075
3300-3399 75023
Canyonbrook Dr 75074
Canyongate Dr 75093
Canyonlands Dr 75025
Cap Rock Dr 75025
Cape Charles Dr 75024
Capella Ct 75025
Capilano Dr 75025
Capital Ave 75074
Capricorn Ct 75023
Capstone Ln 75074
Captiva Dr 75093
Caravan Dr 75025
Cardiff Cir 75025
Cardigan Dr 75093
Cardinal Ct 75094
Cardinal Dr 75023
Carlsbad Dr 75023

Carlton Ln 75025
Carlyle Dr 75025
Carmel Cv & Dr 75075
Carmichael Dr 75024
Carnegie Ln 75093
Caroline Ct 75093
Carolwood Dr 75024
Carolyn Ln 75094
Carousel Ln 75023
Carpenter Dr 75074
Carriage Ln 75023
Carrier Ln 75024
Carrington Dr 75023
Carrington Ln 75094
Carrizo Dr 75074
Carroll Cir 75023
Carta Valley Dr 75024
Carter Hall Ct 75025
Carver Court Ln 75074
Casa Grande Dr 75025
Cascade Dr 75025
Case Dr 75025
Casper Dr 75025
Cassandra Ln 75093
Cassidy Dr 75023
Castille Ct 75023
Castle Dr 75074
Castle Creek Ct & Ln 75093
Castle Pines Dr 75093
Castlebar Ln 75093
Castleglen Dr 75093
Castlemaine Ln 75093
Castlemere Dr 75093
Castlewood Dr 75025
Catalina Pl 75074
Catalpa Trl 75023
Catamaran Dr 75093
Cathedral Dr 75023
Catskill Ct 75025
Cavalier Dr 75024
Cavalry Dr 75023
Cave River Dr
300-599 75094
5900-6099 75093
Cavender Dr 75093
Cavendish Ct 75093
Cayman Cir 75025
Cecile Rd 75024
Cedar Breaks Dr 75025
Cedar Elm Ln 75075
Cedar Falls Ln 75093
Cedar Grove Cir 75093
Cedar Ridge Ct 75093
Cedar Valley Dr 75024
Cedarbird Trl 75094
Cedardale Dr 75025
Celadine Dr 75093
Centenary Dr 75093
N Central Expy
400-6498 75074
601-2999 75075
3301-6099 75023
7201-7299 75025
Central Pkwy E 75074
Century Cir 75023
Chace Ct 75023
Chadbourne Dr 75023
Chadwick Dr 75075
Chalfont Ln 75023
Chalice Dr 75024
Chalk Ct 75025
Chalk Hill Ln 75094
Chalton Dr 75024
Chamberlain Cir & Dr 75023
Chambers Ln 75093
Chambray Ct 75025
Champions Dr 75093
Chancellor Dr 75074
Chandler Dr 75024
Chaney Ct & Ln 75093
Channel Isle Dr 75093
Chantilly Dr 75025
Chanute Dr 75025
Chaparral Rd 75074
Chapel Creek Dr 75024
Chapel Hill Blvd 75093

Chapman Rd 75093
Charlemagne Dr 75093
Charlene Dr 75074
Charles Pl 75093
Charlestown Ln 75024
Charring Cross 75025
Charter Oak Dr 75074
Chase Oaks Blvd
6100-6398 75023
6400-6600 75023
6602-6698 75023
7001-7097 75025
7099-7300 75025
7302-7398 75025
Chasefield Dr 75023
Chateau Ln 75023
Chatsworth Ln 75075
Chattham Ct 75025
Chaucer Ct 75093
Chelsea Ln 75074
Cherbourg Dr 75075
Cherokee Dr 75094
Cherokee Trl 75023
Cherry Creek Dr 75025
Cherry Spring Ct 75025
Cherrywood Ln 75074
Chesapeake Dr 75093
Cheshire Dr 75075
Chester Dr 75025
Chesterfield Dr 75094
Chesterwood Dr 75093
Chestnut Ct 75094
Cheyenne Trl 75023
Chicota Dr 75023
Childrens Way 75025
Chimneyrock Dr 75023
Chinaberry Trl 75023
Chippenham Dr 75093
Chippewa Dr 75093
Chisholm Pl 75075
Chisholm Trl 75094
Chiswick Lake Dr 75093
Choctaw Dr 75093
Christian Ct 75025
Christopher Cir 75094
Christopher Way 75024
Chula Vista Dr 75023
Churchill Ct & Ln 75075
Cielo Dr 75074
Cima Hill Dr 75025
Cimmaron Dr 75025
Circleview Ct 75025
Citadel Dr 75023
Citris Dr 75074
Cityview Dr 75093
Cladding Dr 75075
Clara Dr 75024
Clarendon Dr 75093
Claridge Cir 75075
Clarinet Ln 75074
Clark Pkwy 75093
Clark Springs Dr 75025
Claude Dr 75024
Clay Dr 75094
Claymore Dr 75075
Clayton Dr 75025
Clear Creek Dr 75074
Clear Field Dr 75025
Clear Sky Dr 75025
Clear Springs Dr 75075
Clearview Ct 75025
Clearwater Ct 75025
Clearwell Ln 75024
Clemson Ct 75093
Clermont Cir 75023
Cleveland Dr 75093
Cliffbrook Dr 75075
Cliffside Dr 75023
Cliffview Dr 75093
Clinton Dr 75075
Clipper Ct 75023
Clocktower Ct 75093
Cloister Way 75075
Cloudcrest Dr 75074
Clover Ln 75074
Cloverhaven Way 75074

Cloverleaf Dr 75074
Club Ridge Cir 75074
E & W Clubview Cir & Ct 75094
Clymer Dr 75025
Coach House Ln 75023
Coachlight Ct 75093
Coachman Ct 75023
Coastline Dr 75093
Cobalt Springs Dr 75025
Cobble Brook Ln 75074
Cobblestone Ct 75093
Cobre Valle Ln 75023
Cody Ct 75024
Coffeyville Ct & Trl 75023
Cognac St 75024
Coit Rd
200-2999 75075
3001-3199 75075
3300-3398 75023
3301-5999 75093
3400-3400 75075
3400-3400 75026
3404-6998 75023
6201-9699 75024
7000-9798 75025
Colborne Dr 75025
Colby Dr 75094
Cold Springs Ct 75094
Coldcreek Ct 75093
Coldwater Creek Ln 75074
Coleshire Dr 75075
Coleto Dr 75025
N & S Colfax Cir 75075
Collin Ct
100-199 75094
3000-3099 75075
Colmar Dr 75023
Colonial Dr 75093
Colonnade Dr 75024
Colt Dr 75074
Columbine Way 75093
Colwick Ct 75023
Comanche Trl
500-699 75094
3100-3298 75074
Commerce Dr 75093
Commonsgate Blvd 75024
Commonwealth Ct 75093
Communication Pkwy 75024
Communications Pkwy 75093
Compton Dr 75025
Concho Dr 75074
Concord Cir 75074
Condor Dr 75094
Conecuh Dr 75074
Conestoga Dr 75074
Congress Ave 75025
Congressional Dr 75025
Connell Farm Dr 75024
Conner Cir 75093
Constitution Dr 75025
Coolidge St 75094
Coolwater Dr 75025
Cooper Pl 75093
Copeland Dr 75024
Copper Creek Dr 75075
Copper Ridge Dr 75093
Copperfield Ln 75023
Coral Cove Ct 75093
Corby Dr 75025
Cordoba Ct 75074
Corinthian Bay Dr 75093
Cornell Dr 75093
Cornerstone Dr 75025
Cornflower Dr 75075
Corning Dr 75023
Cornish Pl 75093
Cornwall St 75093
Coronado Dr 75074
Corporate Dr 75024
Corral Ct 75094
Corsica Way 75024
Cortez Dr 75074
Cosa Loma Ct 75074
Cotillion Dr 75074

Cottage Cir 75093
Cotton Ct 75093
Cottonwood Pl 75075
Council Dr 75023
Countess Dr 75074
Country Club Dr 75074
Country Glen Xing 75024
Country Meadow Dr 75094
Country Oak Ct 75093
Country Place Dr
2900-3000 75075
3002-3198 75075
3600-3698 75023
4001-5099 75023
Country Ridge Ln 75024
Couples Dr 75025
Court Meadow Dr 75093
Courtland Dr 75093
Courtney Pl 75075
Courtside Ln 75093
Courtyard Trl 75024
Cousteau Ct 75024
Coventry Ln 75093
Coverack Dr 75025
Coverdale Dr 75024
Covered Wagon Dr 75074
Covey Pl 75093
Covington Ct 75094
Covinton Ln 75023
Cowan Cir 75024
Cowboy Ct 75094
Coyote Way 75074
Crabapple Dr 75074
Cradlerock Cir 75093
Craig Dr 75023
Cranston Pl 75025
Cranwood Dr 75024
Crater Ln 75023
Crawley Dr 75093
Creek Crossing Dr 75093
Creek Hollow Ct 75023
Creekbend Dr 75075
Creekcove Dr 75074
Creekfield Dr 75075
Creekpoint Dr 75093
Creekside Dr 75094
Creekside Ln 75023
Creekstone Dr 75093
Creekview Dr 75093
Creekway Ct 75024
Crenshaw Dr 75025
Crepe Myrtle Ln 75094
Crescent Ct 75093
Crescent Creek Ln 75025
Crested Butte Dr 75025
Crested Cove Ct 75025
Crestfield Cir 75025
Crestforest Cir 75074
Crestridge Dr 75075
Crestview Dr 75024
Crestwick Dr 75094
Creswick Dr 75093
Crickett Dr 75023
Crockett Ct 75023
Cromwell Ct & St 75075
Crooked Ln 75023
Crooked Stick Dr 75093
Cross Bend Rd 75023
Cross Plains Dr 75025
Crosstimber Dr 75093
Crosswind Dr 75094
Croston Dr 75075
Crow Valley Trl 75023
Crowley Dr 75093
Crown Forest Dr 75024
Crown Knoll Ln 75093
Crown Ridge Dr 75024
Crowndale Dr 75093
Crownhill Dr 75093
Crownover Ct 75093
Crystal Way 75074
Crystal Creek Dr 75024
Crystal Falls Dr 75024
Culberson Dr 75025
Cultivator Ct 75075
Cumberland Dr 75094

Cumberland Trl 75023
Cup Dr 75074
Curbstone Way 75074
Curtis St 75093
Custer Rd
701-1297 75075
1299-3200 75075
3202-3298 75075
3300-3398 75023
3400-6999 75023
7900-9799 75025
9801-10599 75025
Cutter Springs Ct 75024
N & S Cypress Cir 75075
Cypress Creek Dr 75025
Cypress Point Dr 75093
Daden Oaks Dr 75093
Daffodil Trl 75093
Dagan Dr 75023
Dakota Dr
300-398 75094
400-499 75094
6300-6499 75024
Dale Dr 75074
Daleport Dr 75094
Dalewood Dr 75074
Dalgreen Ct & Dr 75075
Dallas Pkwy
1400-1498 75093
1500-5999 75093
6701-6797 75024
6799-7400 75024
7402-8298 75024
Dalmation Cir 75023
Dalrock Dr 75024
Dalston Ln 75023
Daly Dr 75025
Dampton Dr 75025
Danbury Dr 75094
Danbury Ln 75074
Danby Dr 75093
Dancing Waters Rd 75024
Dandelion Dr 75093
Dane Ct 75093
Daniel Dr 75094
Daniel Rd 75024
Danmire Ct 75093
Danmire Dr 75094
Danube Ln 75075
Darion Ln 75093
Dark Forest Dr 75025
Darlington Dr 75093
Dartbrook Dr 75075
Dartmouth Cir
1200-1299 75094
3600-3699 75075
Dartmouth Dr 75075
Darton Dr 75023
Data Dr 75075
Davenhill Ct & Dr 75093
Davidson Dr 75025
Davis Cir 75023
Dawson Dr 75025
Daybreak Trl 75093
Daystar Dr 75025
De Grey Ln 75093
De Loach Dr 75025
De Vinci Dr 75074
Deandra Ln 75093
Debbie Dr 75074
Debon Dr 75075
Decator Dr 75093
Decoy Ct 75025
Deep Springs Dr 75025
Deep Valley Ct 75023
Deep Valley Trl
2400-2899 75023
2900-3199 75075
3201-3299 75075
3300-3825 75023
Deer Run 75024
Deer Horn Dr 75025
Deer Park Ln 75093
Deerfield Dr 75023
Deerhurst Dr 75093
Deering Ct 75093

Del Rio Dr 75024
Delaware Ln 75024
Deleon Dr 75025
Delmar Dr 75075
Delmonte Cir 75075
Delta Pl 75094
Democracy Dr 75024
Denham Way
  3800-3999 75023
  4001-4499 75024
Dentelle Dr 75023
Denver Dr 75093
Derwent Dr 75025
Desco Dr 75075
Desert Garden Dr 75093
Desert Mountain Dr 75093
Desert Willow Ln 75094
Desiderata Ct 75023
Desperado Dr 75094
Development Dr 75074
Devenshire Dr 75094
Devlin Ridge Dr 75025
Devonshire Dr 75075
Dewberry Ct 75025
Dexter Dr 75093
Diablo Ct 75074
Diamondhead Dr 75075
Diane Dr 75074
Dibrell Dr 75023
Dickens Dr 75023
Dickerson Ct 75093
Digby Dr 75025
Digital Dr 75075
Dillon Ct 75024
Director Ave 75074
Discovery St 75094
Dividend Ave 75074
Dobbins Dr 75025
Dobie Dr 75074
Dockside Ct 75093
Dodge Ct 75023
Dogwood Dr 75094
Dogwood Pl 75075
Dolente Dr 75074
Domingo Dr 75024
Dominion Pkwy 75024
Donna Dr 75074
Donnington Dr 75093
Donovan Dr 75025
Doral Cir 75093
Dorchester Dr 75075
Dorset Dr 75093
Dottie Dr 75074
Doubletree Ct 75023
Douglas Crk 75023
Douglas St 75093
Dove Cove Ct 75094
Dove Creek Ln 75093
Dove Tail Ct 75094
Dover Dr 75075
Dover Ln 75094
Downing Dr 75023
Drake Dr 75075
Drawbridge Ln 75024
Drexel Dr 75075
Driftwood Dr
  701-797 75094
  799-899 75094
  4300-4399 75074
Dripping Springs Dr 75025
Druid Dr 75075
Dry Creek Dr 75025
Dryden Ln 75025
Dublin Rd 75094
Duchess Trl 75074
Duck Bay Dr 75094
Duke Ct 75093
Dumond Pl 75025
Duncan Dr
  600-699 75094
  8800-8899 75025
Dundee Ln 75093
Dunlap Ct 75093
Dunmoor Dr 75093
Dunster Pl 75025
Dunwick Dr 75023

Dupont Dr 75024
Durango Dr 75023
Durban Park Dr 75024
Durham Dr 75093
Durwood Dr 75025
Dutton Dr 75023
Duval Dr 75025
Dyers Oak Dr 75074
E Ave 75074
Eagle Pass 75023
Eagle Way 75094
Eagle Point Ct 75024
Eagle Vail Dr 75093
Earlshire Pl 75075
Early Morn Ct & Dr 75093
Eastbourne Dr 75093
Eastcreek Pl 75074
Eastglen Pl 75074
Eastlane Pl 75074
Eastleigh Dr 75024
Eastman Dr 75093
Eastport Pl 75074
Eastvale Pl 75074
Eastwick Cir 75094
Eastwick Ln 75093
Eaton Ct 75093
Ebony Ct 75024
N & S Echo Trl 75023
Echo Bluff Dr 75024
Echo Ridge Ln 75094
Echomont Ln 75093
Eddie Dr 75025
Eden Valley Ln 75093
Edgefield Dr 75075
Edgemere Ct 75094
Edgestone Dr 75093
Edgewater Dr 75075
Edgewood Dr 75025
Edinburgh Dr 75093
Edith St 75024
Edmonton Dr 75075
Edna Ct 75024
Edwards Dr 75025
Eggenhufer Cir 75023
Eiffel Dr 75023
Eisenhower Ln 75023
Elam Ct 75093
Elderwood Pl 75075
Eldger Dr 75025
Eldorado Dr 75093
Elganza Ct 75023
Elgin Dr 75025
Elissa Ct 75025
Elizabeth Pl 75025
Elizabeth Trl 75094
Elk Trl 75025
Elkhurst Dr 75023
Ellery Ave 75025
Ellington Dr 75093
Elliot Dr 75024
Ellis Ct 75075
Elm Leaf Ln 75025
Elmcrest Cir 75075
Elmcrest Dr 75094
Elmer Dr 75025
Elmhill Dr 75024
Elmhurst Dr 75093
Elmswood Ln 75025
Ember Ct 75023
Embercrest Dr 75094
Emerald Coast Dr 75074
Emerson Ct & Dr 75093
Emily Dr 75093
Emory Cir 75093
Empire Blvd 75024
Encanto Ct 75023
Enchanted Ridge Dr 75025
Enclave Trl 75074
Endicott Dr 75025
England Dr 75025
Englenook Ct 75023
Englewood Dr 75094
Englewood Ln 75025
English Oak Dr 75024
Enid Dr 75093
Epworth Ln 75024

Erwin Dr 75074
Esquire Ct & Dr 75023
Essex Ln 75024
Estacado Ln 75025
Estrella Dr 75074
Ethridge Dr 75024
Eucalyptus Dr 75075
Eva Pl 75093
Evans Ct & Dr 75075
Evening Sun Dr 75093
Everett Ln 75025
Everglades Dr 75023
Evergreen Dr 75075
Evesham Dr 75025
Exeter Dr 75093
Ezekial Way 75074
F Ave 75074
Fair Meadows Dr 75024
Fair Valley Way 75024
Fairbourne Cir 75093
Fairchild Ct & St 75093
Fairfax Hill Dr 75024
Fairfield Dr 75074
Fairglen Dr 75093
Fairmount Dr 75093
Fairview Dr 75075
Fairwood Ct 75025
Falcon Dr 75025
Falcon Trl 75094
Faldo Ct 75025
Fall Dale Cir 75075
Fall Wheat Dr
  600-699 75094
  3700-3999 75075
Fallbrook Dr 75094
Falling Brook Dr 75023
Falling Water Ln 75024
Fallkirk Dr 75025
Fallmeadow Cir 75024
Fallon Ct 75093
Falmouth Dr 75025
Family Farm 75024
Fandango Ln 75025
Fannin Cir 75025
Fargo Dr 75093
Faringdon Dr 75075
Farmland Dr 75093
Farr Oak Dr 75093
Faulkner Dr 75024
Fawn Hollow Dr 75074
Fawnwood Dr 75093
Faxon Dr 75025
Feathering Way 75074
Featherwood Dr 75094
Fechin Cir 75023
Federal Hall St 75023
Felicia Dr 75074
Felix Dr 75074
Fenwick Ln 75093
Fern Glen Dr 75024
Ferncrest Dr 75024
Ferndale Dr 75025
Fernridge Dr 75025
Fernwood Dr 75075
Field Cove Dr 75023
Fieldlark Dr 75074
Figtree Ln 75074
Filmore Dr 75025
Finch Ct 75094
Finch Dr 75024
Finley Dr 75074
Finsbury Dr 75025
Firebrook Dr 75074
Fireside Dr 75074
Firethorn Cir 75093
Firewheel Dr 75024
Firwood Pl 75075
Fiser Pl 75093
Fitzgerald Dr 75074
Flagstone Dr 75075
Flamingo Ct 75094
Flamingo Ln 75074
Flanders Ln 75025
Flat Creek Dr 75025
Fleetwood Dr 75025
Fletcher Trl 75025

Flicker Ln 75074
Flint Cove Cir 75023
Flintstone Dr 75074
Flora Dr 75074
Florence Dr 75093
Flowing Way 75074
Floyd Dr 75025
E & W Fm 544 75094
Fontaine St 75075
Foothill Dr 75024
Forbes Dr 75093
Fordham Rd 75025
Forest Ln 75094
Forest Bend Dr 75025
Forest Grove Ln 75093
Forest Highlands Dr 75024
Forest Hill Dr 75094
Forest Hills Dr 75023
Forest Park Rd 75024
Forestcrest Dr 75074
Forester Way 75075
Forman Ct 75074
Fort Laramie Dr 75025
Fort Scott Ct 75023
Fossil Ridge Dr 75093
Fountain Dr 75094
Fountain Grove Dr 75024
Fountain Head Dr 75023
Fountain Ridge Dr 75025
Fountain Springs Dr 75025
Fowler Cir 75024
Fox Chase Ln 75024
Fox Hollow Dr 75023
Fox Run Ct 75094
Foxborough Ln 75093
Foxtail Ln 75024
Francesca Ln 75024
Francis Ln 75074
Frazier Dr 75024
Fredman Ln 75023
Fredrick Ct 75093
Freedom Ln 75025
Freeland Dr 75025
Fremont Ln 75093
Fresno Rd 75074
Frontier Ln 75023
Frost Hollow Dr 75093
Frosted Green Ln 75025
Fulgham Rd 75093
Fullerton Dr 75024
Funston Dr 75025
Furneaux Dr 75093
G Ave 75074
Gables Ct 75075
Galaxy Ln 75024
Gallant Fox Ln 75093
Galleria Ct 75075
Galloway Ct 75024
Galsford Dr 75024
Gambel Ln 75025
Gannon Dr 75025
Gansett Dr 75075
Garda Cir 75093
Garden Gate Dr 75024
Garden Laurel Ct 75024
Garden Laurel Dr 75094
Garden Ridge Ct 75025
Gardenbrook Way 75074
Gardengrove Ct 75075
Gardenia Way 75093
Garfield Dr 75023
Garner Ln
  3000-3298 75075
  3300-3499 75023
Garrett Dr 75093
Garrison Pl 75023
Gary Dr 75023
Gastonia Ln 75023
Gateway Dr 75025
Gatewood Ln 75074
Gatlin Pl 75023
Geiberger Dr 75025
Gemini Dr 75025
Gemstone Pl 75093
Gene Autry Ln 75094
Geneseo Cir 75023

Geneva Ln 75075
Genoa Ct 75093
Gent Dr 75025
Gentle Way 75024
Gentry Dr 75024
Geomap Ln 75074
Georgette Dr 75024
Gerber Ter 75094
Germantown Ct 75075
Gerrards Cross 75025
Gettysburg Cir 75023
Gibralter St 75074
Gibsland Dr 75025
Gifford Dr 75025
Gila Ct 75023
Gillespie Dr 75025
Gillingham Dr 75093
Gillum Dr 75093
Ginger Ct 75075
Giovanni Dr 75024
Girvan Dr 75025
Glacier Dr 75023
Gladewood Pl 75075
Gladys Ct 75093
Glasgow Dr 75025
Glastonbury Dr 75075
Glen Canyon Dr 75025
Glen Cove Ct 75075
Glen Echo Dr 75024
Glen Forest Ln 75023
Glen Heather Dr 75093
Glen Meadow Dr 75025
Glen Ridge Dr 75094
Glen Springs Dr 75093
Glenbrook Cir 75093
Glenbrook Dr 75094
Glencliff Dr & Pl 75075
Glencove Dr 75075
Glendale Dr 75023
Glendenny Ln 75024
Glendower Ln 75093
Gleneagles Ct & Dr 75093
Glenhaven Dr 75023
Glenhollow Dr 75093
Glenhome Dr 75025
Glenhurst Ct 75093
Glenmont Dr 75023
Glenrose Way 75093
Glenshire Dr 75093
Glenview Ct 75093
Glenville Dr 75093
Glenwick Dr 75075
Glenwood Dr 75094
Glenwood Ln 75074
Glory Ln 75025
Glover Dr 75074
Glyndon Dr 75023
Goff Dr 75025
Gold Ln 75023
Gold Hills Dr 75025
Golden Gate Dr 75025
Golden Leaf Ct 75093
Golden Springs Dr 75025
Goldenrod Dr 75025
Goodwin Dr 75023
Gooseberry Dr 75074
Gordon Oaks Dr 75023
Grace Ave 75024
Granada Pl 75023
Grand Canyon Dr 75025
Grand Falls Cir 75024
Grand Hollow Dr 75024
Grand Mesa Dr 75025
Grand Teton Dr 75023
Grandbrook Ln 75074
Grandview Dr 75075
Grange Rd 75024
Granite Pkwy 75024
Grant Ln 75024
Grantham Ln 75094
Grapevine Ln 75074
Graphic Pl 75075
Grasmere Dr 75093
Gratitude Trl 75024
Gray Wolf Dr 75024
Grayson Dr 75025

Great Southwest Dr 75025
Grecian Ct 75074
Green Ct 75023
Green Acres Dr 75094
Green Oaks Dr 75023
Greenbriar Cir, Ct &
Ln 75074
Greencastle Ln 75075
Greenfield Dr
  300-499 75094
  1300-1498 75025
Greenhill Dr 75093
Greenleaf Cir 75025
Greenpark Dr 75075
Greensboro Dr 75025
Greenview Dr 75024
Greenway Dr 75075
Greenwood Dr 75025
Greenwyck Dr 75093
Grenada Dr 75074
Grenoble Ct 75023
Greyhawk Cir 75024
Greylyn Dr 75075
Greystone Ct
  600-608 75094
  8400-8499 75025
Greywood Ln 75075
Grifbrick Dr 75075
Grimsby Ct 75025
Grinelle Dr 75025
Grovewood Dr 75023
Guilder Dr 75074
Guinevere Dr 75074
Gulf Breeze Ct 75074
Gull Lake Dr 75025
Gunnison Dr 75025
Gurney Dr 75024
Guston Hall Ct 75025
Guthrie Dr 75024
Gwinn Ct 75025
H Ave & Pl 75074
Hacienda Ct 75023
Hackamore Ct 75023
Hackberry Dr 75094
Hackberry Pl 75025
Haddock Dr 75025
Haddon Way 75025
Hagen Dr 75025
Hagerman Dr 75094
Haggard St 75074
Hague Ct 75025
Halifax Dr 75023
Halkin Ct 75024
Halliford Ct & Dr 75024
Hallmark Ct & Dr 75024
Hallsey Ln 75074
Hallwell Dr 75093
Halverstick Ln 75074
Hamburg Ct 75025
Hamner Ln 75024
Hampshire St 75093
Hampstead Dr 75094
Hampton Ln 75075
Hamptondale Rd 75093
Hancock Pl 75023
Haning Dr 75025
Hannah St 75025
Hanover Ct 75093
Hansell Rd 75024
Harbor Ln 75074
Hardwick Ct 75025
Harkness Dr 75093
Harpers Pl 75075
Harrington Dr 75075
Harris Pl 75025
Harrisburg Ln 75025
Harrods Ct 75024
Hartford Dr 75093
Hartline Ct 75023
Hartsfield Dr 75025
Harvard Ct 75093
Harvest Glen Dr 75023
Harvest Hill Dr 75094
Harvey Ln
  6900-6999 75023
  7000-7299 75025

Harwood Dr 75074
Hasselt Ct 75025
Hastings Ct 75023
Hathaway Pkwy 75024
Hatherly Dr 75023
Haun Trl 75075
Havant Ln 75024
Havard Oak Dr 75074
Havencrest Ct 75074
Havenwood Dr 75094
Havenwood Trl 75024
Haversham Dr 75023
Hawken Dr 75023
Hawkhurst Dr 75024
Hawthorne Dr 75094
Hawthorne Ln 75074
Hayfield Dr 75023
Hayloft Way 75075
Haystack Dr 75025
Hazeltine Dr 75025
Headquarters Dr 75024
Hearst Castle Way 75025
Hearthlight Ct 75024
Hearthstone Dr 75023
Heath Ct 75024
Heather Glen Dr 75025
Heather Hill Ct & Ln 75075
Heather Ridge Dr 75024
Heatherbrook Dr
  300-398 75094
  3200-3399 75074
Heatherton Pl 75023
Heathrow Dr 75025
Hedgcoxe Rd
  800-898 75025
  900-2199 75025
  2201-3905 75025
  4000-4498 75024
  4500-5000 75024
  5002-5298 75024
Hedgerow Dr 75024
Heidi Dr 75025
Helen Ct 75023
Helmsley Ln 75093
Helston Dr 75024
Hemlock Ct 75023
Hempstead Dr 75093
Hendrick Dr 75074
Henley Dr 75093
Henri Ct 75023
Henry Cook Blvd 75024
Heritage Pkwy 75094
Herkimer Ct 75074
Hershey Ln 75024
Hibbs St 75025
Hickory Crk 75023
Hickory Dr 75094
Hickory Hill Dr 75074
Hickory Ridge Dr 75093
Hidalgo Dr 75074
Hidden Cove Dr 75075
Hidden Creek Ct 75024
Hidden Valley Dr 75074
Hideaway Ct 75094
Hideaway Ln 75093
Higgins Ln 75024
High Country Way 75025
High Field Trl 75023
High Gate Rd 75024
High Meadows Dr 75025
High Mesa Dr 75093
High Plains Dr
  701-799 75094
  7200-7298 75024
High Point Dr 75094
Highcourt Dr 75093
Highedge Dr 75075
Highland Dr 75093
Highland Shores Dr 75024
Highlight Pl 75074
Highmount Dr 75093
Highview Dr 75024
N & S Hillbrier Cir 75075
Hillcrest Dr
  100-199 75094
  1800-1999 75074

Hillendale Dr 75025
Hillglen Dr 75094
Hillhaven Dr 75024
Hillridge Dr 75074
Hillsborough Dr 75093
Hillsdale Ct 75093
Hillshire Ct 75093
Hillside Cir & Dr 75074
Hillswick Dr 75093
Hilltop Dr 75094
Hilltop Ln
2900-3299 75075
3300-3699 75023
Hillview Dr 75025
Hilton St 75093
Hinton Dr 75024
Hitching Post Ln 75024
Hobart Cir 75025
Hoffman Dr 75025
Hogan Manor Dr 75025
Hollander Way 75074
Hollingsworth Dr 75025
Holloway Ln 75025
Holly Ct 75094
Holly Berry Dr 75093
Hollypoint Dr 75093
Home Pl 75024
Homestead Ln 75025
Homewood Dr 75025
Hondo Dr 75074
Honey Creek Ln 75023
Honey Locust Dr 75023
Hook Dr 75025
Hope Cir 75094
Hopi Ct 75074
Hopkins Dr 75025
Horizon Ct 75094
Horizon Dr 75094
Horizon Pl 75023
Hornbeam Ct 75023
Horseman Dr 75025
Horseshoe Dr 75074
Hosington Dr 75094
Houlton Ln 75025
Hove Ct 75025
Hudson Dr 75093
Huffman Ct 75093
Hughes Dr 75024
Hulings Ct 75023
Hummingbird Ct 75094
Hummingbird Ln 75093
Hunter Ln 75093
Hunters Gln 75094
Hunters Creek Dr & Pl 75075
Hunters Run Dr 75025
Hunters Trace Ln 75024
Huntington Dr
300-499 75094
2000-2098 75075
2100-2400 75075
2402-2498 75075
Huntly Dr 75023
Huntwick Dr 75024
Huron Trl 75075
Hurstwood Dr 75074
Hutch Dr 75074
Hyannis St 75094
I Ave 75074
Idaho Ct 75094
Idaho Dr 75093
Idaho Ln 75094
Idyllwild Ct & Dr 75075
Imperial Ct 75093
Independence Pkwy
400-1398 75075
1400-3199 75075
3201-3295 75075
3300-5298 75023
5300-6999 75023
7000-9800 75025
9802-10298 75025
Indian Trl 75024
Indian Canyon Dr 75025
Indian Hills Dr 75075
Indian Paint Dr 75025
Indigo Dr 75075
Industrial Blvd 75074
Ingleside Dr 75075
Interlaken Dr 75075
International Pkwy 75093
Inverness Ln 75075
Inverrary Dr 75093
Iola Dr 75025
Iowa Dr 75093
Iowa Rd 75094
Ipswich Dr 75025
Ironside Dr 75075
Ironstone Dr 75074
Irvine Dr 75075
Isaac St 75024
Ishnala Trl 75023
Isle Royale Dr 75025
Ithaca Ct 75025
Ivanhoe Dr 75024
Ivory Ct 75024
J Ave & Pl 75074
Jabbet Cir & Dr 75025
Jackson Dr 75075
Jacobson Dr 75025
Jacqueline Dr 75024
Jagged Way 75074
Jaguar Dr 75024
Jamestown Pl 75023
Jamilia Ct 75093
Janet Ct & Way 75074
Janice Dr 75074
January Dr 75025
Janwood Cir & Dr 75075
Japonica Ln 75074
Jasmine Ct 75074
Jasmine Dr 75094
Jasmine Ln 75074
Jason Cir 75094
Jasper Dr 75074
Jazz St 75024
Jefferson Cir 75023
Jeker Dr 75074
Jenkins Dr 75024
Jennifer Ct 75025
Jenning Ct & Dr 75093
Jeremes Lndg 75075
Jerome Dr 75025
Jessup Ct 75074
Jesters Ct 75074
John Close 75094
John Muir Ct 75025
Johns Wood Dr 75093
Johnson Dr 75023
Jojoba Ct 75023
Jomar Dr 75075
Jones St 75024
Jordan Dr 75025
Josephine St 75024
Joshua Tree Dr 75023
Jowett Dr 75025
Jubilee Rd 75093
Judge Holland Ln 75025
Judy Dr 75074
Julienne Dr 75023
Junction Dr 75093
Jupiter Rd
400-498 75074
500-1199 75074
1200-7198 75074
1200-1200 75094
1201-3799 75074
Justin Dr 75024
Justin Rd 75094
K Ave 75074
Kalgan Cir 75025
Kali Ct 75094
Kansas Trl 75094
Karen Ct 75074
Karen Pass 75094
Karlovich Dr 75025
Kasko Dr 75024
Kate Ave 75024
Kathryn Ln 75025
Kathy Ct 75074
Katrina Path 75023
Kaufman Pl 75025
Keathly Cir 75094
Keats Dr 75093
Keenan Cir 75075
Kellner Pl 75093
Kelly Ln 75093
Kelsey Ct & Dr 75075
Kemerton 75025
Kemper Dr 75023
Kendall Dr 75025
Kennemer Dr 75025
Kenning Ct 75024
Kennison Ct 75093
Kenosha Rd 75024
Kensington Dr 75093
Kenswick Dr 75024
Kent Ct 75093
Kentfield Dr 75074
Kentshire Cir 75025
Kentucky Dr 75024
Kentwood Dr 75094
Kesser Dr 75025
Kettle River Ct 75025
Kettlewood Ct 75025
Keystone Dr 75075
Khyber Pass 75075
Kidwell Cir 75075
Kiestwood Cir 75025
Kildare Dr 75024
Kimberly Ct & Ln 75075
Kimble Dr 75025
Kimbrough Ln 75025
Kincaid Rd 75024
King William Ct & Dr 75093
Kings Way 75074
Kings Canyon Dr 75025
Kings Isle Dr 75093
Kingsborough Dr 75093
Kingsbridge Dr 75075
Kingsbrook Dr 75093
Kingsbury Dr 75093
Kingsfield Dr 75094
Kingsgate Cir 75024
Kingsmill Dr 75025
Kingston Dr 75074
Kinlock Ct 75074
Kinman Ln 75024
Kinney Dr 75094
Kinross Dr 75093
Kinsley Cir 75093
Kiowa Ct 75023
Kipling Dr 75023
Kirby Dr 75075
Kirkland Ct 75093
Kirkwall St 75093
Kirnwood Dr 75075
Kit Ln 75023
Kite Ct 75025
Kite Landing Ln 75074
Kite Meadow Dr 75074
Kittery Dr 75093
Kittyhawk Dr 75025
Klein Rd 75074
Knob Hill Dr 75023
Knoll Hollow Trl 75024
Knollview Dr 75024
Knollwood Ct & Dr 75075
Knox Dr 75024
Kobelco Dr 75024
Kodak Dr 75025
Kristen Ct 75094
Krona Dr 75074
Kyle Dr 75075
L Ave 75074
La Guardia Dr 75025
La Paz Ct & Dr 75074
La Quinta Dr 75023
La Vida Pl 75023
Labelle Ct 75024
Ladbrook Ct 75024
Ladyfern Way 75024
Lafayette Dr 75075
Laguna Ct & Dr 75023
Lake Crest Ln 75023
Lake Falls Dr 75093
Lake Forest Dr 75024
Lake Hill Ln 75023
Lake Hollow Way 75093
Lake Ridge Dr 75075
Lake Shore Ln 75023
Lake Side Ln 75023
Lakebluff Way 75093
Lakebrook Dr 75093
Lakecreek Ct 75093
Lakedale Dr
400-499 75094
3800-3899 75025
Lakefield Dr 75094
Lakefront Trl 75093
Lakehurst Dr 75094
Lakeside Cir 75094
Lakestream Dr 75075
Lakeview Trl 75075
Lakeway Dr 75075
Lakewood Dr 75093
Lambert Ct 75075
Lamorna Dr 75093
Lanarc Dr 75023
Lancaster Ln 75024
Lancelot Dr 75024
Lancome Dr 75025
Land Dr 75093
Landau Ct 75023
Landershire Ln 75023
Langdon Ct 75025
Langley Cir & Dr 75025
Langston Dr 75025
Lansbury Ln 75093
Lantana Ln 75093
Lantern Light Dr 75093
Lantz Cir 75025
Laramie Dr 75023
Larchmont Dr 75074
Laredo Dr 75094
Lark Cir 75075
Larkel St 75093
Las Brisas Dr 75074
Las Palmas Ln 75075
Lasalle Dr 75025
Laser Ln 75023
Latham Dr 75023
Lattice Ct 75075
Laurel Ln 75074
Laurel Hill Ln 75094
Lauren Ln 75094
Lavaca Dr 75074
Lavenham Dr 75025
Lavery Dr 75025
Lawndale Dr & Pl 75023
Lawrence Ln 75093
Lawson Ct 75093
Lawton Ln 75093
Lazy Maple Dr 75074
Lazy Oak Ln 75024
Leafy Glade Rd 75024
Leameadow Dr 75075
Leathertop Dr 75075
Leblanc Dr 75024
Ledgemont Dr 75025
Leeds Dr 75025
Leeward Dr 75094
Leeward Ln 75093
Leflore Dr 75074
Legacy Cir 75024
Legacy Dr
100-3999 75023
4000-4498 75024
4500-7799 75024
Legendary Ln 75023
Leigh Ct & Dr 75025
Leighton Ridge Dr 75025
Lemans Ct 75024
Lemmontree Ln 75074
Lennox Hill Dr 75093
Leon Dr 75074
Leonardo Ct 75025
Leoti Ln 75094
Leslie Ct 75023
Levant Ln 75094
Lexington Dr 75075
Libby Rd 75024
Liberty Dr 75025
Liebert Dr 75024
Lightcatcher Dr 75025
Lighthouse Dr 75074
Lilac Ln 75074
Lincoln Dr 75023
Linda Ln 75075
Linden Dr 75075
Lindfield Ct 75093
Lindsey Dr 75093
Linhurst Dr 75094
Links Dr 75093
Linkwood Ct 75025
Linmore Ln 75093
Little Oak Ln 75074
Live Oak Ln 75075
Liverpool Dr 75025
Livingston Dr 75093
Llano Dr 75074
Loch Haven Dr 75023
Loch Lomond Dr 75093
Loch Maree Dr 75093
Lochridge Dr 75093
Lochwood Dr
500-599 75094
6801-6899 75024
Lockhart Dr 75023
Lockheed St 75093
Locklear Ct 75093
Locksley Cir 75023
Lodengreen Ct 75023
Lodestone Dr 75093
Loftsmoor Ln 75025
Lofty Ln 75093
Logan Dr 75094
Lois Ln 75024
Lombardy Dr 75023
Lomita Cir 75023
Lomo Alto 75024
London Dr 75025
Lone Grove Ln 75093
Lone Ridge Way 75094
Lone Rock Ct 75024
Lone Star Dr 75024
Lone Tree Dr 75093
Lonesome Trl 75023
Lonesome Dove Trl 75094
Long Meadow Ct 75074
Longbow Ln 75023
Longfellow Dr 75093
Longhill Dr 75025
Longhorn Dr 75023
Longtown Dr 75093
Longview Dr 75025
Longwood Ct 75093
Longworth Dr 75075
Lookout Ln 75094
Lookout Trl 75023
Loomis Dr 75024
Lorenzo Dr 75074
Lorimar Dr 75093
Lorraine Dr 75074
Los Altos Dr 75024
Los Rios Blvd 75074
Los Robles Ct & Dr 75074
Lost Arbor Ct 75024
Lost Creek Dr 75074
Lost River Ct 75025
Lottie Ln 75074
Lotus Dr 75075
Lougheed Plz 75025
Louis Dr 75023
Louisville Dr 75093
Love Bird Ln 75094
Lowrey Way 75025
Lucas Ter 75074
Lucient Cir 75024
Ludwig Castle Way 75025
Lufkin Dr 75093
Lukenbach Dr 75074
Lumberton Ct 75025
Lunsford Rd 75024
Luther Dr 75093
Luxborough Dr 75024
Lynbridge 75025
Lynbrook Dr 75075
Lynchburg Dr 75025
Lyndhurst Ln 75025
Lynores Way 75025
Lyon Ct 75093
M Ave & Pl 75074
Mabray Dr 75025
Macao Ct & Pl 75075
Macgregor Dr 75093
Macintosh Dr 75023
Mackenzie Way 75025
Mackey Ct 75024
Macon Dr 75075
Maddox Rd 75024
Madera Ct 75024
Madewood Ln 75025
Madison Cir 75023
Madrone Ct 75074
Magnolia Ln 75074
Magnum Dr 75024
Mahaney Rd 75094
Mahogany Run Ct 75093
Maitland Ln 75025
Maize Dr 75093
Maize Rd 75094
Majestic Dr 75074
Malden Ct 75025
Malibu Cir & Pl 75023
Mallard Trl 75094
Mallow Ct 75093
Malone Dr 75093
Maltby Ct 75024
Malton Dr 75025
Malvern Dr 75093
Manchester Cir 75023
Mandevilla Dr 75024
Mandeville Dr 75094
Mandrake Ct 75093
Manga Dr 75025
Manhattan Ave 75024
Manitowoc Dr 75023
Manor Ln 75093
Manor Lane Ct 75093
Mantissa Dr 75023
Maple Leaf Dr 75075
Maple Ridge Way 75094
Maple Sugar Dr 75094
Maplelawn Dr 75075
Mapleridge Dr 75024
Mapleshade 75093
Mapleshade Ln 75075
Marathon Dr 75024
Marble Canyon Dr 75074
Marble Falls Ln 75093
Marblewood Dr 75093
Marcedonia Dr 75025
Marchman Way 75025
Marcy Ct 75023
Margo Ct 75024
Marigold Ct 75074
Mariners Dr 75093
Mariposa Cir 75075
Marissa Ln 75024
Markham Dr 75075
Marks Pl 75025
Marlborough Ct & Dr 75075
Marlin Dr 75023
Marquette Dr 75093
Marsalis Ln 75074
Marsh Ln 75093
Marshall Ct 75093
Martello Ln 75074
Martin Rd 75024
Martina Ct 75093
Martingale Dr 75023
Martinique St 75024
Marwick Dr 75075
Maryanne Ln 75074
Mason Dr 75025
Mason Ln 75094
Masters Cir 75093
Masterson Dr 75093
Matagorda Springs Dr 75025
Matilda Dr 75025
Matterhorn Dr 75075
Matthew Way 75094
Maumelle Dr 75023
Maverick Dr 75074
Maxwell Dr 75025
Maxwell Ln 75094
N & S Maxwell Creek Rd 75094
Maybrook Ct 75024
Mayfield Dr 75094
Mayflower Ln 75024
Maywood Ct 75023
Mcalice Ct & Dr 75093
Mcbee Dr 75025
Mccall Dr 75093
Mccarran Dr 75025
Mcclary Dr 75093
Mccormick Ranch Ct 75023
Mcdaniel Cir 75075
Mcdermott Rd
2200-3999 75025
4000-5298 75024
Mcdonald Ln 75023
Mcfarland Ct & Dr 75093
Mckamy Trl 75024
Mckavett Dr 75024
Mckinley Dr 75023
Mcmillen Dr 75094
Mcmullen Dr 75025
Mcwilliams Ct 75093
Mead Dr 75024
Meadow Creek Dr 75094
Meadow Hills Ln 75093
Meadow Ridge Dr 75093
Meadowbrook Ct & Dr 75075
Meadowcreek Dr 75074
Meadowcrest Dr 75075
Meadowhaven Dr 75093
Meadowlark Dr
700-899 75094
5100-5199 75093
Meadows Dr 75074
Meadowside Ln 75093
Meadowview Ct 75024
Meandering Way 75074
Means Dr 75024
E, N, S & W Medalist Cir 75023
Medallion Dr 75024
Medical Ave 75075
Medina Dr 75074
Mediterranean Dr 75093
Melanie Ln 75023
Melbourne Dr 75093
Mellville Dr 75075
Melrose Dr 75075
Memorial Ln 75024
Memorial Hill Way 75094
Memphis Dr 75024
Mendocino Cir 75093
Mendota Dr 75024
Mercedes Pl 75075
Meredith Ln 75093
Merideth Dr 75094
Meridian Ct 75023
Merksem Ct 75025
Merrimac Dr 75075
Merriman Dr 75074
Mesa Dr 75074
Mesa Oak Trl 75025
Mesa Verde Dr 75025
Mesquite Ct 75094
Mesquite Trl 75023
Messina Dr 75093
Metropolitan Dr 75023
Metz St 75024
Meyers Canyon Dr 75025
Miami Dr 75093
Micarta Dr 75025
Michael Dr
400-499 75094
501-599 75094
3400-3599 75023
Mid Pines Dr 75025
Midcrest Dr 75075
Middle Cove Dr 75023
Middle Gate Ln 75093
Middleburg Dr 75074
Midnight Cir & Dr 75093
Midpark Ln
1100-1198 75094
4200-4299 75074

Midway Rd 75093
Milano Dr 75093
Mildenhall Dr 75093
Miles Blvd 75023
Milford Dr 75025
Mill Haven Ct 75093
Mill Ridge Dr 75025
Mill Valley Dr 75075
Millard Dr 75074
Millington Dr 75093
Mills Branch Cir 75024
Millsap Ln 75074
Millstream Dr 75075
Milton Ln 75025
Mimosa Dr 75094
Mimosa Ln 75074
Mineral Springs Ct 75025
Minter Rd 75023
Mira Vista Blvd 75093
Mission Ridge Rd
2600-2798 75075
3300-3398 75023
3400-6499 75093
6501-6599 75023
Misted Breeze Dr 75093
Mistletoe Ct 75023
Misty Glen Ln 75094
Misty Haven Ln 75093
Misty Hollow Dr 75024
Mistyglen Dr 75025
Mitchell Dr 75025
Mobley Ct 75093
Moccasin Dr 75023
Mockingbird Dr
500-799 75094
1400-1599 75093
1601-1699 75093
Mockingbird Hill Ct 75094
Moffett Ct 75093
Mollimar Dr 75075
Molly Ln 75074
Monahans Ct 75023
Monarch Ct & Dr 75074
Monastery Dr 75025
Monette Ln 75025
Monford Dr 75074
Monica Cir 75025
Monmouth Ct 75075
Montana Trl
300-399 75094
1600-1899 75023
1901-1999 75023
Montclair Dr 75075
Monte Cristo Ln 75024
Montego Pl 75023
Montell Ct 75025
Monterey Cir 75075
Monticello Cir 75075
Montreal Dr 75023
Montrose Dr 75025
Monument Cir 75093
Moody Dr 75025
Moonbeam Ct 75074
Moonlight Dr 75094
Moore Dr 75074
Moortown Dr 75025
Moregate Ln 75024
Morgan Ct 75093
Morning Dove Dr 75025
Morning Glory Ln 75093
Morning Star Rd 75024
Morning View Way 75094
Morningdew Dr 75025
Morningside Dr 75093
Morningside Trl 75094
Morton Vale Rd 75074
Mossberg Dr 75023
Mossvine Dr 75023
Mosswood Dr 75074
Mossycup Oak Dr 75025
Mott St 75025
Mount Pleasant Ln 75025
Mount Rainier Dr 75025
Mount Vernon Way 75025
Mountain Laurel Ln 75093
Mountain Pass Dr 75023
Mountain Ridge Dr 75025
Mountview Pl 75023
Muirfield Cir 75093
Mulberry Ln 75074
Mulchin S Way 75024
Mulholland Dr 75074
Mulhouse Ct 75024
Mullins Dr 75025
Mulvane Dr 75094
Munich Ct 75025
Municipal Ave 75074
Munnings Pl 75093
Mura Dr 75025
N & S Murphy Rd 75094
Mustang Trl 75093
Mustang Ridge Dr 75094
Myrtle Beach Dr 75093
Myrtle Springs Dr 75025
Myrtleridge Dr 75074
Myrtlewood Ln 75074
Mystery Cir 75023
N Ave & Pl 75074
Nancy Ct 75023
Nantucket Dr 75023
Naomi St 75024
Naperton Dr 75025
Naples Dr 75093
Napolean Ct 75023
Narberth Dr 75024
Nash Ln 75025
Nasmyth Dr 75093
Natalie Dr 75074
Natchez Dr 75023
Nathan Way 75025
Neiman Rd 75025
Nellore St 75074
Nelson Ct 75025
Nest Pl 75093
Netch Dr 75074
Netherlands Ln 75025
Nettle Dr 75025
Nevada Dr 75093
Nevada Trl 75094
New Britton Dr 75093
New College Ln 75025
New Forest Dr 75093
New Haven Dr 75093
New Heart Dr 75024
New Hope Ct 75024
New Orleans Dr 75093
Newbury Ln
300-399 75094
1300-1499 75025
Newcastle Cir 75075
Newcastle Ln 75094
Newcombe Dr 75093
Newell Ave 75023
Newgate Ln 75093
Newhall Dr 75023
Newkirk Dr 75075
Newport Cir 75075
Newport Ct 75094
Nice Dr 75023
Nickel Creek Dr 75025
Nickerson Ln 75094
Nicklaus Dr 75025
Nightfall Dr 75093
Nighthawk Dr
700-820 75094
822-998 75094
2500-2799 75025
Nightingale Ct 75093
Nightland Dr 75024
Noble Ct 75094
Noble Oaks Dr 75074
Nocona Dr 75024
Noel Trl 75023
Nolan Ct & Dr 75025
Norcross Dr 75024
Norfolk Dr 75023
Norman Dr 75025
Normandy Ln 75093
Northbrook Dr 75093
Northcrest Dr 75075
Northern Lights Ct 75074
Northgate Dr 75093
Northridge Dr 75075
Northwood Ln 75074
Norway Ct 75023
Norwich Ln 75025
Norwood Ln 75074
Notre Dame Dr 75093
Nottingham Ln 75074
Nottoway Ln 75074
Nova Trl 75023
Novaro Dr 75025
Nunnley Dr 75024
Nutwood Ln 75074
O Ave & Pl 75074
O Malley Ct 75023
Oak Cir 75075
Oak Arbor Dr 75093
Oak Glen Dr 75094
Oak Grove Ct & Dr 75074
Oak Hill Ln 75094
Oak Hollow Dr 75093
Oak Knoll Dr 75093
Oak Park Ln 75023
Oak Ridge Dr 75025
Oak Shores Dr 75024
Oak Springs Dr 75025
Oak Tree Dr 75025
Oak Vista Dr 75074
Oakbluff Dr 75094
Oakbrook Dr 75025
Oakcrest Dr 75025
Oakdale Dr 75025
Oakdale Ln 75094
Oakhaven Dr 75093
Oakhill Dr 75075
Oakhurst Dr 75094
Oakland Hills Dr 75025
Oakley Dr 75094
Oakmeadow Dr 75093
Oakmont Ct 75093
Oakstone Dr 75025
Oakwood 75024
Oates Dr 75093
Observation 75024
Ocala Ct 75025
Occidental Rd 75025
Oceanview 75074
Odessa Cir & Dr 75093
Ohare Ct 75025
Ohio Dr
600-798 75093
800-3800 75093
3802-6098 75093
6100-8899 75024
Okaloosa Cir 75074
Oklahoma Ave 75074
Old Alma Rd 75025
Old Course Dr 75093
Old Gate Rd 75024
Old Manse Ct 75025
Old Orchard Ct & Dr 75023
Old Pond Dr 75024
Old Shepard Pl 75093
Old Veranda Rd 75024
Old York Dr 75093
Oldfield Dr 75093
Oleander Dr 75074
Olive Branch Ct 75025
Olivia Ln 75024
Olympic Ct 75093
Omar Ln 75023
Opal Ln 75075
Opelousas Ct 75023
Orange Blossom Ct 75025
Orchard Gate Dr 75024
Orchard Hill Dr 75025
Oregon Ct 75023
Oriole Dr 75094
Orlando Cir & Dr 75075
Orly Ct 75025
Orvale Rd 75024
Orwell Dr 75093
Osage Trl 75023
Osborn Pkwy 75024
Osceola Dr 75074
Oswego Dr 75074
Outland Dr 75023
Overdowns Dr 75023
Overglen Dr 75074
Overlake Dr 75023
Overland Dr
1300-1399 75094
3200-3399 75023
Overlook Ct 75024
Overton Dr 75074
Owl Creek Dr
700-899 75094
2600-2699 75025
Oxbow Creek Ln 75074
Oxford Ct 75075
Oxlea Dr 75024
Ozark Dr 75074
P Ave 75074
Paddington Dr 75093
Padre Ct 75075
Pagewynne Dr 75093
Pagoda Oak Dr 75074
Paige Ct 75094
Paint Brush Trl 75024
Paint Creek Ct & Rd 75094
Paisano Trl 75093
Palacios Cv 75025
Palm Valley Dr 75024
Palmdale Dr 75024
Palmer Trl 75023
Palmwood Ct 75074
Palo Alto Cir 75074
Palo Duro Dr 75074
Palomino Dr 75024
Pam St 75024
Panorama Dr 75023
Pantheon Ct 75024
Panther Ridge Ln 75074
Pantigo Dr 75075
Papeete Dr 75075
Paradise Valley Dr 75025
Paris Ave 75025
E Park Blvd 75074
W Park Blvd
501-997 75075
999-3999 75075
4000-6399 75093
6401-6899 75093
Park Creek Dr 75075
Park Meadow Ln 75093
Park Vista Rd 75094
E Parker Rd 75074
W Parker Rd
100-3398 75075
101-2899 75023
2901-3999 75023
2901-2901 75086
4001-4197 75093
4199-6399 75093
6401-7099 75093
Parkhaven Ct & Dr 75075
Parkhurst Ct 75093
Parkmont Dr 75023
Parkridge Dr 75024
Parkshire Dr 75094
Parkside Ct 75094
Parkside Dr 75075
Parkview Ln
1100-1199 75075
1201-1299 75075
1300-1400 75094
1402-1498 75094
Parkwood Blvd
2801-2899 75093
3200-3298 75093
6700-6798 75024
6800-8100 75024
8102-8498 75024
Parliament Ln 75093
Parma Ln 75093
Parnell Ln 75024
Partney Ct 75024
Pasteur Ln 75023
Patagonia Ln 75025
Pataula Ln 75074
Pathfinder Dr & Trl 75093
Patricia Ave 75023
Patrick Ln 75024
Patriot Dr 75025
Paul Calle Ct & Dr 75025
Pauline St 75024
Pavillion Ct 75024
Pawnee Cir 75023
Peabody Pl 75024
Peaceful Trl 75074
Peach Blossom Dr 75025
Peach Tree Dr 75094
Peachtree Ln 75074
Peacock Dr 75094
Pearl Ct 75024
Pebble Beach Dr 75093
Pebble Brook Ln 75093
Pebble Creek Ct 75023
Pebble Vale Dr 75075
Pebblestone Ln 75093
E Pecan Ln 75074
Pecan Valley Dr 75093
Pecos Path Dr 75094
Peek Dr 75075
Peggy Ln 75074
Pelican Bay Ct & Dr 75093
Penbrook Ct 75024
Penelope Ln 75024
Penland St 75023
Pennington Ct 75025
Pennsylvania Ln 75075
Penny Pl 75024
Pensacola Dr 75074
Pentridge Dr 75024
Penzance Dr 75093
Peppertree Pl 75074
Percey Ln 75025
Persimmons Ct 75074
Perthshire Ct 75024
Petersburg Dr 75074
Petticoat Dr 75024
Phaeton Ct 75023
Pheasant Run Dr 75094
Pheasant Run Rd 75023
Phillip Dr 75024
Phoenix Pl 75023
Phyllis Ln 75074
Picato Dr 75074
Pickett Dr 75024
Pickwick Ln 75093
Piedmont Ct & Dr 75075
Piedra Ct & Dr 75023
Pierre Ln 75023
Pike Ct 75093
Pillar Dr 75025
Pilot Dr 75025
Pimernel Ln 75075
Pin Oak Ln 75075
Pine Brook Dr 75024
Pine Lakes Dr 75025
Pine Springs Dr 75093
Pine Top Dr 75094
Pine Valley Dr 75025
Pinebluff Dr 75074
Pinecrest Dr 75024
Pinehurst Ct & Dr 75075
Pinewood Dr 75093
Pinion Dr 75023
Pinkerton Ct 75025
Pinnacle Ct 75093
Pintail Ct 75024
Pinto Cir & Ct 75023
Pioneer Ln 75023
Pioneer Path Dr 75094
Pipe Stone Dr 75025
Piper St 75093
Pirates Cove Dr 75025
Pittner Ln 75025
Placid Ave 75074
Placid Springs Ln 75025
Plains Ct 75074
E Plano Pkwy 75074
W Plano Pkwy
100-298 75075
300-3800 75075
3802-3998 75075
4000-7099 75093
Plantation Cir & Ln 75093
Plateau Dr 75075
Platt Dr 75023
Player Dr 75025
Pleasant Run 75094
Pleasant Hill Dr 75025
Pleasant Valley Dr 75023
Pleasanton Dr 75094
Plentywood Dr 75025
Plumtree Ln 75074
Plymouth Dr 75023
Pocono Dr 75025
Poinciana Ln 75075
Poindexter Ln 75094
Polo Ln 75093
Polstar Dr 75093
Pompeii Way 75093
Ponderosa Crk 75023
Ponderosa Trl 75094
Pondview Dr 75074
Pony Dr 75074
Pool Ln 75074
Poplar Ct 75074
Porsche Ct 75023
Port Royal Ct 75093
Portage Ln 75024
Porter Creek Dr 75025
Porto Fino Dr 75093
Portobello Dr 75024
Portrait Ln 75024
Ports O Call Ct & Dr 75075
Portside Ln 75023
Portsmouth Cir 75023
Post Crest Dr 75094
Post Oak Dr 75025
Post Oak Trl 75094
Postbridge Dr 75024
Potomac Dr 75075
Powderhorn Dr 75025
Prager Port Ln 75025
Prairie Creek Ct 75075
Prairie Creek Dr 75075
Prairie Creek Trl 75094
Prairie Hill Ln 75094
Prairie View Dr 75094
Prairie View Ln 75024
Preakness Ln 75093
Precision Dr 75074
Premier Dr
2301-3299 75075
3300-3318 75023
3320-3500 75023
3502-4098 75023
Prescott Dr
1300-1399 75094
7701-7897 75025
7899-7999 75025
E President George Bush Hwy 75074
W President George Bush Hwy 75075
Presley Ave 75024
Preston Rd
1000-5900 75093
5902-5998 75093
6100-6298 75024
6300-8300 75024
8302-8798 75024
Preston Creek Dr 75024
Preston Meadow Dr
3100-3999 75093
4001-4699 75093
6500-6900 75024
6902-6998 75024
Preston Park Blvd 75093
Prestonwood Dr 75093
Price Dr 75074
Primavera Dr 75074
Prince George Dr 75075
Prince Wales Ct 75025
Princess Ln 75074
Princeton Dr & Pl 75075
Pritchard Ln 75024
Professional Dr 75074
Progress St 75074
Promenade Dr 75023
Promontory Pt 75075
Prospect Ln 75093
Province Pl 75075
Pueblo Ct 75074
Pullam Cir 75024
Puma Rd 75074
Purbrook Dr 75024
Purcell Dr 75025
Purdue Cir 75093
Putnam Dr 75024
Pyramid Dr 75093
Quail Creek Dr 75094
Quail Hollow Ct 75094
Quail Run Dr
501-597 75094
599-699 75094
2600-2699 75075
Quarry Chase Trl 75025
Quebec Ln 75024
Queens Way 75074
Quiet Cir 75024
Quill Dr 75075
Quincy Ln 75024
Quinton Point Dr 75025
R Ave 75074
Rabbit Trl 75074
Racheal Ct 75024
Racquet Ct 75023
Radcliffe Dr 75093
Radford Cir 75025
Rain Forest Trl 75093
Rainbow Cir 75075
Rainforest Ct 75094
Rainhurst Ln 75094
Rainier Rd 75023
Raintree Ct 75074
Raintree Dr
300-398 75094
2400-3399 75074
Rainwood Dr 75024
Ramblewood Way 75023
Rambling Way 75093
Rampart Dr 75074
Ramsgate Cir 75093
Ranch Estates Cir & Dr 75074
Ranchero Rd 75093
Randa Dr 75074
Randall Way 75025
Ranger Ct 75075
Ranger Rd 75094
Raphael Dr 75093
Rapids Ln 75025
Rasor Blvd 75024
Raspberry Ct 75074
Rattle Run Dr 75025
Raven Dr 75094
Ravenhurst Dr 75025
Rawhide Ct 75023
Raywood Cir 75075
Reading Dr 75093
Red Bluff Ct 75093
Red Deer Ct 75093
Red Lion Dr 75025
Red Oak Cir 75075
Red Oak Dr 75094
Red Oak Ln 75075
Red River Dr 75025
Red Wolf Ln 75093
Redbud Ln 75074
Redding Dr 75093
Redfield Dr 75025
Redondo Cir 75075
Redstone Ln 75024
Regal Rd 75075
Regatta Dr 75093
Regency Ct 75024
Regent Dr & Pl 75075
Rembrandt Dr 75093
Remington Cir 75023
Remington Dr
300-398 75094
400-499 75094
3300-3400 75023
3402-3598 75023
Renaissance Dr 75023
Renault Ln 75023
Renee Dr 75023

Renewal Rd 75074
Republic Dr 75074
Research Dr 75074
Resource Dr 75074
Reunion Dr 75024
Revere Cir 75075
Rice Dr 75074
Richmond Dr 75074
Rickmansworth Dr 75025
Rickshaw Ln 75094
Ridge Gate Dr 75074
Ridge Hollow Dr 75023
Ridge Meadow Dr 75074
Ridge Park Way 75024
Ridge Point Ln 75024
Ridge Rock Dr 75074
Ridgecrest Dr 75074
Ridgedale Dr 75024
Ridgefield Dr 75075
Ridgeglen Cir 75074
Ridgehaven Dr 75093
Ridgelake Ln 75074
Ridgemoor Ln 75025
Ridgestone Dr 75094
Ridgetop Ln 75074
Ridgeview Ct 75094
Ridgeview Dr
100-600 75094
602-698 75094
2201-2999 75025
Ridgeway Dr 75074
Ridgewood Cir & Dr 75074
S Rigsbee Dr 75074
Riley Dr 75025
Ringgold Ln 75093
Rio Grande Dr 75075
Riptide Ln 75024
Risborough Dr 75093
Rising Star Ct 75075
Risinghill Dr 75024
River Branch Trl 75024
River Rock Ln 75093
Riverchase Dr 75025
Riveredge Dr 75024
Riverhill Dr 75024
Riverside Dr 75024
Riverton Ct 75093
Riverview Dr 75023
Riviera Dr 75093
Roaring Ridge Dr 75025
Robbie Rd 75024
Roberta Dr 75025
Roberts Dr 75093
Robin Pl & Rd 75075
Robinson Rd 75024
Rochelle Dr
6800-6999 75023
7000-7198 75025
Rochester Way 75094
Rock Trl 75074
Rock Springs Dr 75024
Rockbluff Cir 75024
Rockbrook Ct & Dr 75074
Rockcliff St 75093
Rockcreek Ln 75024
Rockford Dr 75023
Rockingham Way 75093
Rockshire Dr 75074
Rockwall Rd 75025
Rockwood Dr 75074
Rocky Cove Cir 75023
Rocky Glen Cir 75094
Rocky Mountain Dr 75025
Rodeo Dr 75094
Roland Dr 75093
Rolling Hills Dr 75025
Rolling Meadow Dr 75025
Rolling Oak Dr 75094
Rollingridge Cir 75074
Roman Ct 75023
Roper Dr 75025
Rosebriar Ln 75024
Rosehill Ln 75093
Rosemont Dr 75025
Rosewood Ct 75093
Rosewood Dr 75094

Rosita Ct 75074
Rossi Dr 75023
Roswell Dr 75093
Rothland Ln 75023
Rothschild Ln 75094
Round Springs Ln 75024
Round Tree Way 75025
Roundbluff Rd 75025
Roundrock Trl
2000-2398 75075
2400-2999 75075
3001-3299 75075
5200-6599 75023
Roxbury Ln 75025
Roy Rogers Ln 75094
Royal Cir 75075
Royal Ashdown Ct 75093
Royal Birkdale Dr 75025
Royal Creek Ln 75093
Royal Crest Ln 75025
Royal Glen Dr 75094
Royal Lytham Dr 75025
Royal Melbourne Dr 75093
Royal Oak Dr 75094
Royal Oaks Dr 75074
Royal Palm Dr 75093
Royal Sydney Ct 75093
Royal Troon Dr 75025
Ruby St 75094
Rufford Ct 75024
Ruger Ct & Dr 75023
Ruidosa Cir 75023
Runabout Ct 75023
Runnin River Dr 75093
Rushden Ct 75025
Rushing Creek Ct 75093
Rushmore Ln 75025
Russeau Dr 75023
Russell Cir 75023
Russell Creek Dr 75025
Russwood Ln 75075
Rustic Cir & Dr 75075
Rutgers Ct 75093
Rutherford Rd 75023
Ruthridge Dr 75074
Ryan Ct 75094
Ryan Dr 75025
Ryder Ct 75093
Saber Ct 75024
Sabetha Way 75094
Sacramento Ter 75075
Sacred Path Rd 75093
Saddlebrook Dr 75094
Saddlehead Dr 75075
Saddletree Trl 75023
Safari Cir 75025
Sagamore Hill Ct 75025
Sage Brush Trl 75023
Sage Meadow Way 75024
Sagebrush Trl 75094
Sagewood Ct 75025
Saginaw Ct 75024
Sahara Ln 75093
Sail Creek Dr 75093
Sailmaker Ln 75023
Saint Agnes Dr 75093
Saint Albans Dr 75093
Saint Andrews Ct 75093
Saint Annes Dr 75025
Saint Bridges Dr 75093
Saint Charles Dr 75074
Saint Georges Dr 75093
Saint Ives Ct 75075
Saint James Dr 75024
Saint John Ct 75023
Saint Lawrence St 75024
Saint Mark Dr 75094
Saint Marks Dr 75093
Saint Nicholas Ct 75075
Saint Patrick Dr 75074
Saint Peter Dr
901-1099 75094
5600-5699 75093
Saint Regas Dr 75093
Saint Thomas Dr 75094
Sako Dr 75023

Salado Springs Dr 75025
Salem Ct 75023
Salerno Cir 75093
Salford Dr 75025
Salsbury Cir & Dr 75094
Saltburn Dr 75093
San Antonio Ct 75023
San Bernard St 75024
San Gabriel Dr 75074
San Isabel Dr 75025
San Jacinto Pl 75024
San Juan Cir 75023
San Mateo Dr
3300-3999 75023
4000-4199 75093
San Miguel Dr 75074
San Patricio Dr 75025
San Saba Ct 75074
San Simeon Way 75023
Sand Ridge Dr 75025
Sandalfoot Cir 75093
Sanders Ln 75025
Sandhills Cir 75093
Sandhurst Dr 75025
Sandia Dr 75023
Sandlewood Dr 75023
Sandpiper Cir & Ln 75075
Sandray Ct 75093
Sandtrap Ct 75093
Sandy Trail Ct & Ln 75023
Sandy Water Ln 75024
Sanibel Ct 75093
Santa Fe Trl 75023
Santa Rosa Dr 75024
Santana Ln 75023
Santiago Dr 75023
Saragosa Creek Dr 75025
Sarah Way 75094
Saratoga Dr 75075
Sarazen Dr 75025
Sargent Dr 75094
Sassafras Dr 75023
Savage Dr 75023
Savannah Dr 75093
Savino Dr 75093
Savoy 75025
Sawgradd Ct 75093
Sawtooth Dr 75023
Saxon Dr 75093
Scarborough Ln 75075
Scarlet Dr 75023
Scenic Dr 75025
Schofield Ct 75093
Schooner Dr 75074
Scotland Ct 75024
Scottish Way 75093
Scottsdale Dr 75023
Scout Dr 75025
Scruggs Way 75024
Seabrook Dr 75023
Seaham Ct 75025
Seapines Dr 75093
Seascape Ct & Ln 75093
Seaton Ct 75025
Sebago Trl 75023
Sebring Dr 75023
Sedgehill Ct 75024
Sedgewick Ave 75025
Sedona Ln 75025
Segundo Ln 75074
Seleta Dr 75094
Seltzer Dr 75023
Seminary Dr 75075
Seminole Ct 75074
Seminole Trl 75094
Sendero Trl 75024
Seneca Dr 75094
Senna Hills Ln 75025
Sennen Ct 75025
Sequoia Dr 75023
Serenade Cir 75075
Serene Pl 75075
Severn Ct 75024
Seville Ct 75093
Sewanee Dr 75075
Seward Dr 75025

Shaddock Blvd 75093
Shadow Trl 75075
Shadow Crest Dr 75093
Shadow Hill Ln 75093
Shadow Rock Dr
500-599 75094
6600-6698 75024
Shadowlawn Ct 75025
Shady Ln 75024
Shady Bend Ln 75024
Shady Creek Cir 75024
Shady Elm Cir 75093
Shady Oaks Dr 75094
Shady Oaks Ln 75093
Shady Point Dr 75024
Shady Timbers Ln 75094
Shady Valley Rd 75025
Shadybrook Dr 75094
Shadycove Pl 75075
Shadywood Ln 75023
Shalimar Dr 75023
Shallow Creek Ln 75025
Shamrock Ln 75093
Shanandoah Ln 75094
Shannon Dr 75025
Shantara Ln 75093
Sharon Cir 75074
Sharps Dr
6800-6999 75023
7000-7399 75025
Shasta Dr 75025
Sheffield Cir 75075
Sheila Ave 75094
Sheila Dr 75023
Shelbourne Cir 75024
Shelby Trce 75094
Shell Ct 75093
Shelton Way 75093
Shenandoah Dr 75023
Shepard Dr 75025
Sheraton Dr 75075
Sherrye Dr & Pl 75074
Sherwood Dr
100-299 75094
3301-3399 75074
Shetland Rd 75093
Shiloh Rd 75074
Shingle Ln 75093
Shinnery Oak Dr 75074
Shiprock Dr 75025
Shirehurst Dr 75094
Shoal Creek Cir 75093
Shoal Forest Ct 75024
Shorecrest Dr 75074
Shreveport Trl 75023
Shrewsbury Pl 75074
Shumard Oak Dr 75074
Sicilian Cir 75093
Sierra Ln 75075
Sierra Blanca Ct 75025
Silas Ct 75093
Silent Oak Ln 75074
Silkwood Ct 75074
Silver Ln 75023
Silver Creek Dr 75093
Silver Falls Ct 75093
Silver Lake Dr 75093
Silver Ridge Dr 75094
Silver Springs Ln
400-499 75094
3000-3099 75025
Silverglen Dr 75075
Silverstone Dr 75023
Silverwood Ln 75075
Simon Dr 75025
Simpkins Pl 75025
Simsbury Dr 75025
Sinclair Ln 75093
Singletree Trl 75023
Skiles Dr 75075
Skipwith Dr 75023
Sky Harbor Dr 75025
Sky Lake Dr 75093
Sky Park Dr 75093
Skyline Dr
100-200 75094
202-498 75094
3700-3899 75025
Skyridge Dr 75025
Slater Trl 75025
Sleepy Hollow Ct 75094
Sleepy Hollow Dr 75093
Sleepy Spring Dr 75024
Slickrock Dr 75074
Slide St 75025
Sloan Cir 75025
Smith Dr 75023
Smoke Tree Dr 75094
Smokey Dr 75025
Smokey Canyon Way 75024
Smoothstone Dr 75074
Snapdragon Ln 75075
Snead Dr 75025
Snidow Ct & Dr 75025
Snowmass Dr 75025
Socorro Dr 75025
Solarium Pl 75075
Somerville Way 75025
Sonato Cir 75025
Sonnet Trl 75023
Sonora Dr 75074
Sonya Dr 75074
Sora Dr 75094
Soren Dr 75094
Sota Grande Dr 75025
Southern Hills Dr 75025
Southgate Dr 75024
Southport Dr 75025
Southwestern Ave 75074
Southwick Dr 75093
Sowell Dr 75093
Sowerby Dr 75093
Spalding 75024
Spanish Trl 75023
Spanish Moss Dr 75024
Sparkling Dr 75074
Sparrow Dr 75094
Sparrows Point Ct & Dr 75023
Spencer Dr 75024
Spicewood Dr 75025
Spire Ln 75025
Split Trail Rd 75074
Spokane Pl 75023
Spotted Ct 75074
Sprague Dr 75094
E Spring Creek Pkwy 75074
W Spring Creek Pkwy
100-3999 75023
4000-5499 75024
5501-5899 75024
Spring Glade Ct 75093
Spring Grove Dr 75025
Spring Hill Ln 75025
Spring Mountain Dr 75025
Spring Peaks Dr 75025
Spring Ridge Dr
100-199 75094
8200-8399 75025
Spring Valley Ln 75025
Spring View Ln 75075
Springbridge Ln 75025
Springbrook Cir & Dr 75075
Springfellow Dr 75025
Springfield Dr 75025
Springfire Dr 75025
Springhaven Dr 75093
Springleaf Dr 75025
Springmoss Dr 75025
Spruce Ct 75075
Spur Ranch Ct 75023
Spyglass Cv 75075
Stable Glen Dr 75025
Stacia Ct & Dr 75025
Stadium Dr 75023
Stagecoach Trl 75023
Stain Glass Dr 75075
Standish Cir 75025
Stanford Dr
801-899 75094
3000-3399 75075
Stanmore Ln 75025

Stanton Blvd 75093
Stapleton Dr 75025
Star Ct 75074
N Star Ct 75094
N Star Rd 75074
Stargazer Dr 75024
Starlight Trl 75023
Starlite Dr 75094
State Highway 121
2200-3798 75025
State Highway 121
4400-6498 75024
Staten Island Ct & Dr 75024
Statler Dr 75075
Steamboat Dr 75025
Steeplechase Dr 75093
Steinway Ct 75023
Steppington Dr 75025
Sterling Ln 75093
Steven Dr 75023
Stewart Dr 75074
Still Springs Dr 75025
Stillwater Ln 75024
Stilwell Rd 75023
Stinnett Dr 75024
Stinson Dr 75025
Stinson St 75093
Stockport Dr 75025
Stockton Trl 75023
Stoddard Ln 75025
Stone Canyon Dr 75024
Stone Creek Dr 75075
Stone Glen Dr 75074
Stone Meadow Dr 75093
Stone Mountain Ct 75025
Stone Ridge Dr 75025
Stone Trail Dr 75023
Stonebrook Cir 75093
Stonecrest Cir 75074
Stonehaven Dr 75025
Stonehill Dr 75025
Stonehurst Dr 75094
Stonemoss Dr 75075
Stoneview Ct 75093
Stoneway Dr 75025
Stonewick Ct 75093
Stonewood Dr 75024
Stoney Point Dr 75025
Stonington Dr 75093
Stranz Ln 75093
Straw Harvest Dr 75075
Streamwood Ln 75093
Strecker Ln 75025
Stroll Rd 75025
Stromboli Dr 75093
Sudbury Rd 75024
Suffolk Ln 75023
Sugar Maple Crk 75023
Sugar Valley Rd 75094
Sugarplum Dr 75074
Sumac Ct 75094
Summer Pl 75094
Summerfield Dr
601-697 75094
699-799 75094
3500-3599 75074
Summertree Cir 75025
Summit Ave 75074
Summit View Dr 75025
Sun Creek Ct 75093
Sun Meadows St 75024
Sundance Dr 75024
Sundew Ct 75093
Sundown Cir 75023
Sundown Dr 75023
Sundown Way 75094
Sunflower Ln
3800-3999 75025
4000-4199 75024
Sunkist Ln 75025
Sunningdale Ct 75093
Sunny Crest Dr 75094
Sunnybrook Dr 75093
Sunrise Ct 75094
Sunset Cir 75093
Sunset Dr 75094

Sunswept Ter 75075
Suntree Ln 75025
Surrey Ln 75075
Susan Cir 75074
Sussex Dr 75075
Sutherland Ln 75025
Sutton Pl 75093
Swallow Branch Ln 75025
Swan Ct 75094
Swanson Dr 75025
Sweetgum Crk 75023
Sweetgum Dr 75094
Sweetwater Dr 75023
Swiss Ct 75023
Switzerland Ave 75025
Sycamore Dr
300-399 75094
4500-4598 75024
Sylvan Dr 75074
Syracuse Cir 75075
Tabernacle Dr 75024
Tablerock Dr 75094
Tabor Cir 75025
Tahoe Pl 75023
Talisman Trl 75023
Tall Oak Ln 75074
Tall Tree Dr 75094
Tallahassee Ct 75074
Tallgrass Ln 75023
Tallowood Ct 75074
Tamarisk Ln 75023
Tamarron Ln 75024
Tampico Dr 75075
Tanen Dr 75025
Tangerine Ln 75074
Tanglewood Dr 75075
Tanner Trl 75093
Tansy Pl 75025
Tapestry Ct 75075
Tara Ct 75025
Tarkio Rd 75074
Tarrant Ln 75025
Tate Ave 75093
Tavaros Dr 75024
Tawakoni Ln 75075
Tawny Oak Dr 75024
Taylor Dr 75074
Taylor Trl 75094
Teaberry Ct 75093
Teagarden Ct 75094
Teakwood Cir & Ln 75025
Teal Ct 75024
Teal Crest Dr 75024
Tealwood Dr 75094
Tearose Dr 75074
Technology Dr 75074
Teddington Park Dr 75023
Tellford Ln 75025
Tempest Cir 75024
Temple Dr 75093
Templehill Dr 75075
Templin Way 75093
Tennis Pl 75075
Tennyson Pkwy 75024
Tensley Dr 75025
Teresa St 75094
Terping Pl 75025
Terrace Mill Dr 75094
Terrace Mill Ln 75024
Terrace View Ln 75093
Terry Dr 75023
Testament Trl 75074
Texana Way 75074
Texas Trl 75094
Thackery Dr 75093
Thames Dr 75075
Thanksgiving Ln 75024
Therondunn Ct & Dr 75023
Thistledown Dr 75093
Thomas Dr 75094
Thompson Rd 75024
Thornbranch Dr 75093
Thornbury Dr 75024
Thorncliff Trl 75023
Thorndale Cir 75074
Thorneywood Rd 75024

Thorntree Dr 75024
Thornwood Dr 75094
Thorp Springs Dr 75025
Throwbridge Ln 75023
Thunderbird Ln
3200-3298 75075
3301-3399 75023
3800-3898 75023
Thyme Ct 75075
Tiburon Dr 75093
Tidewater Dr 75025
Tidworth Dr 75093
Tiger Dr 75025
Tilden Dr 75074
Timber Brook Dr 75074
Timber Cove Ln 75093
Timber Ridge Dr 75094
Timber Wolf Trl 75093
Timberbluff Ln 75094
Timbercreek Cir & Dr 75075
Timberlake Dr 75023
Timberline Dr 75074
Timberview Dr 75093
Timothy Dr 75023
Tipperary Dr 75093
Tisinger Pl 75075
Tobenjay Trl 75025
Todd Dr 75023
Toddville Cir & Dr 75025
Toledo St 75094
Tom Clevenger Dr 75094
Tomahawk Dr 75023
Topaz Way 75023
Topeka Ct 75074
Toppingham St 75093
Torino Pl 75093
Torrey Mnr & Pl 75023
Tory Hill Ct 75024
Tours Ln 75023
Towanda Dr 75074
Tower Ct 75074
Townbluff Dr
2700-2798 75075
2800-3200 75075
3202-3298 75075
3500-3798 75023
3800-3899 75023
Townbluff Pl 75023
Towne Main Dr 75024
Towne Square Dr 75024
Townsend Ln 75024
W Trace Dr 75093
Traceland Dr 75024
Tradition Trl 75093
Trail Bluff Dr 75024
Trail Lake Dr 75093
Trail Walker Dr 75074
Trailridge Dr 75074
Trailview Dr 75074
Trailwest Ln 75025
Trailwood Dr 75024
Travis Dr 75093
Tree Farm Dr 75093
Tree Shadow Trl 75074
Treehouse Ln
1600-2399 75023
3100-3299 75075
3300-3399 75023
Treeline Dr 75025
Trelady Ct 75024
Trellis Ln 75075
Trenton Ct 75075
Trevino Dr 75025
Treyburn Ct 75075
Tribal Rd 75023
Tribeca Ln 75024
Tribune Way 75094
Trillium Dr 75093
Trilogy Dr 75075
Trinity Ln 75075
Triple Crown Ln 75093
Trophy Dr 75025
Tucson Ct 75023
Tudor Dr 75023
Tumbleweed Ct & Dr 75023
Tumbril Ln 75023

Tupelo Dr 75024
Turnberry Ct 75024
Turner Ln 75094
Turning Leaf Ln 75074
Turquoise Ln 75074
Turtle Creek Dr 75093
Turtle Point Dr 75023
Tuscany Dr 75093
Tuxford Ct 75093
Tweedsgate Dr 75024
Twelve Oaks Cir 75025
Twilight Cir & Trl 75093
Twin Diamond Ct 75023
Twin Knoll Dr 75094
Twin Knoll Ln 75024
Twin Lakes Way 75093
Twin Oaks Dr 75024
Twin Ponds Dr 75074
Twin Valley Dr 75094
Twinfalls Dr 75093
Twist Trl 75093
Tyler Ct 75023
Ulster Ln 75093
Underwood Dr 75024
United Ln 75024
University Dr 75075
Uplands Dr 75025
Upshire Ct 75075
Urbana Cir 75025
Ursula Ct 75075
Usa Dr 75025
Ute Ct 75023
Uxbridge Ln 75025
Vail Dr 75025
Val Verde Dr 75025
Valcourt Dr 75023
Valdez Ct 75074
Valencia Dr 75074
Vallarte Ct 75074
Valleen Dr 75024
Valley Bend Way 75024
Valley Creek Dr 75075
Valley Falls Dr 75025
Valley Forge Dr 75075
Valley Spring Dr 75025
Valleybrook Dr 75093
Van Buren Dr 75074
Van Gogh Dr 75093
Vancouver Dr 75024
Vanderbilt Dr 75023
Vanderpool Dr 75024
Vantage Ct & Dr 75075
Vasque Ct 75024
Vassor Cir 75075
Veloce Dr 75074
Venice Ct 75093
Ventura Dr 75093
Vera Cruz Dr 75074
Verbena Dr 75075
Vermillion Dr 75093
Vernon Ct 75025
Vero Dr 75023
Verona Ct 75093
Versailles Ln 75093
Vetchling Cir 75025
Vickers Dr 75075
Vicki Ln 75093
Vicksburg Ct 75023
Vidalia Ln 75025
Vienna Dr 75025
Villa Downs Dr 75023
Village Dr 75094
Village Creek Dr 75093
Village Springs Dr 75024
Vineyard Dr 75025
Vinson Ln 75093
Vintage Ln 75024
Virginia Ct & Dr 75093
Virgo Dr 75074
Vista Trl 75024
Vista Court Dr 75074
Vista Grande 75024
Vista Knoll Dr 75093
Vista Point Dr 75093
Vista View Dr 75094
Vitex Dr 75094

Voltaire Dr 75023
Vontress St 75074
Waasland Dr 75025
Waddell Dr 75025
Wagner Way 75023
Wagonwheel Ct & Dr 75023
Wake Forest Dr 75093
Wakefield Dr 75093
Walden Dr 75093
Wales Dr 75024
Walington Dr 75093
Walling Ln 75093
Walnut Dr 75094
Walnut Ln 75075
Walnut Ridge Ln 75074
Walnut Square Dr 75025
Walsingham Dr 75093
Walters Dr 75023
Waltham Dr 75093
Wamego Ln 75094
Wandering Trl 75075
Wareham Dr 75024
Warm Springs Cir 75024
Warminster Dr 75093
Warren Ct 75075
Warrington Dr 75093
Warwick Dr 75023
Washburn Dr 75025
Waskom Dr 75024
Watch Hill Cir & Dr 75093
Water Haven Ln 75093
Water Oak Dr 75025
Waterbury Ct 75025
Watercrest Dr 75093
Waterford Dr 75024
Watermill Ct 75093
Waters Edge Way 75094
Watersedge Dr 75093
Waterside Dr 75093
Waterton Dr 75023
Waterway Ct 75093
Watson Dr 75025
Wavertree Ln 75093
Waxleaf Ct 75074
Wayfarer Dr 75093
Weatherby Ln 75093
Weatherstone Dr 75024
Weber Dr 75025
Webley Dr 75023
Webster Ct & Dr 75075
Wedgegate Dr 75023
Wedgestone Dr 75023
Weeping Willow Dr 75094
Weinberg Ct 75074
Weiss Ave 75025
Wellesley Dr 75024
Wellington Ln 75094
Wellington Pl 75075
Wells Dr 75093
Wellshire Ct 75093
Wembley Ct 75024
Wendy Ln 75025
Wentwood Dr 75094
Wentworth Ln 75094
Wentworth Pl 75075
Wentworth St 75075
Wesson Dr 75023
Westblanc Dr 75093
Westbrook Dr 75075
Westchester Ln 75093
Westclarke Dr 75093
Westcreek Pl 75074
Westerley Dr 75093
Westfield Dr 75093
Westglen Pl 75074
Westlake Dr 75075
Westlane Pl 75074
Westminister Ave 75094
Westminster Ave 75094
Westminster Dr 75074
Westmont Dr 75093
Westmoreland Dr 75093
Westover Dr 75093
Westport Pl 75074
Westridge Dr 75075
Westside Dr 75075

Westvale Pl 75074
Westview Ln 75075
Westway Ct 75093
Westwind Dr 75093
Westwood Dr
100-200 75094
202-298 75094
900-1199 75075
Wexford Dr 75093
Weyburn Pl 75023
Wheatfield Dr 75074
Wheatland Ln 75025
Wheeler Bnd 75025
Whiffletree Ct & Dr 75023
Whippoorwill Ln 75093
Whisperfield Dr
301-397 75094
399-499 75094
6900-7199 75024
Whispering Cir 75023
Whispering Tree Ln 75024
Whispering Woods Ct 75024
Whistler Dr 75093
White Castle Ln 75025
White Dove Dr 75093
White Oak Ct & Dr 75074
White Porch Rd 75024
White River Dr 75025
White Rock Ln 75024
White Sands Dr 75025
White Wing Ln 75094
Whitecliff Cir 75093
Whitehall Dr 75023
Whitehaven Dr 75093
Whitestone Dr 75094
Whitestone Ln 75024
Whitlock Ct 75024
Whitney Ct 75023
Whittier Dr 75093
Whittingdon Pl 75093
Wichita Dr 75025
Wickersham Dr 75093
Wickham Ct 75093
Wickliff Trl 75023
Widgeon Dr 75024
Wight St 75093
Wild Oak Cir 75074
Wild Ridge Ct 75024
Wildcreek Dr 75025
Wildflower Dr 75024
Wildwood Cir 75074
Wildwood Dr 75094
Wildwood Pl 75074
Wilkins Way 75025
Williams Way 75075
Williamsburg Dr 75074
Willomet Dr 75025
Willow Ln 75074
Willow Bend Ct 75093
Willow Bend Dr
400-499 75094
2000-3598 75093
Willow Creek Dr 75093
Willow Hills Ct 75024
Willow Point Dr 75094
Willow Wood St 75094
Willowbrook Way 75075
Willowdale Dr 75093
Willowross Way 75093
Wilma Ln 75074
Wilshire Ct & Dr 75023
Wilson Dr 75075
Wilts Ct 75093
Wimbledon Ln 75075
Winchester Dr 75075
Wind Cave Cir 75023
Wind Dance Cir 75024
Windburn Dr 75025
Windcom Ct 75093
Windcrest Dr 75024
Windermere Dr 75093
Windford Dr 75025
Windhaven Dr 75094
Windhaven Pkwy 75093
Winding Brook Dr 75093
Winding Creek Dr 75023

Winding Hollow Ln 75093
Winding Wood Trl 75024
Windjammer Rd 75093
Windmill Ct & Ln 75074
Window Rock Dr 75093
Windsor Dr 75094
Windsor Pl 75075
Windstone Dr 75023
Windward Dr 75094
Windy Knoll Dr 75094
Windy Meadow Dr 75023
Windy Ridge Ct 75025
Winfield Dr 75023
Wing Point Ln 75093
Winged Foot Way 75093
Wingren Dr 75093
Winnsboro Ct 75075
Winona Dr 75074
Winscott Dr 75024
Winslow Dr 75023
Winstead Dr 75024
Winter Wood Ct 75024
Wintergreen Dr 75074
Winterplace Cir 75075
Winterstone Dr 75023
Wishing Well Ln 75093
Wittmore Pl 75093
Wolcott Ln 75074
Wolf Creek Trl 75093
Wolf Ridge Dr 75024
Wolf Run Dr 75024
Wolfe Cir & Ct 75025
Wolfemont Ln 75025
Wolford Ln 75074
Wonderland Dr 75093
Wood Hollow Ct 75024
Wood Lake Dr 75093
Wood Rail Dr 75074
Woodburn Cors 75075
Woodcrest Cir 75094
Wooded Cove Dr 75025
Woodglen Dr 75094
Woodhaven Ct 75093
Woodheights Ct 75074
Woodlake Dr 75094
Woodland Creek Dr 75024
Woodland Hills Ln 75024
Woodland Meadow
Ter 75024
Woodlawn Ln 75025
Woodmill Dr 75025
Woodmont Ct 75093
Woodmoor Dr 75093
Woods Dr 75025
Woodsboro Ln 75024
Woodspring Dr 75093
Woodway Ln 75093
Woodwind Dr 75093
Woody Trl 75093
Wooster Ln 75074
Wooten Pl 75025
Wordsworth Dr 75093
Wornsaddle Ln 75025
Worthington Way 75023
Wrangler Rd 75074
Wyeth Dr 75023
Wyman Dr 75093
Wyngate Blvd 75074
Wynnpage Ln 75075
Wynwood Dr 75074
Wyoming Dr 75094
Wyvonnes Way 75024
Yale Cir 75075
Yancey Ct 75025
Yardley Ln 75024
Yarnell Pl 75094
Yaupon Dr 75074
Yeary Rd 75093
Yellow Flower Way 75024
Yellowstone Dr 75023
York Ln 75093
Yorkdale Dr 75093
Yorkshire Trl 75093
Yorktown Dr 75074
Yosemite Dr 75023
Young Ct 75025

Zachary Walk 75094
Zanes Ct 75023
Zelphia Cir 75025
Zembriski Dr 75025
Zinnia Ct 75075
Zoeller Dr 75025
Zurich Dr 75025

NUMBERED STREETS

10th St 75074
11th St 75074
12th Pl & St 75074
13th St 75074
13th 14th Connector 75074
14th Pl 75074
14th St
500-898 75074
900-4902 75074
4904-5198 75074
5301-5397 75094
5399-5500 75094
5502-5598 75094
15th Pl 75074
E 15th St 75074
W 15th St
100-598 75075
600-3999 75075
4000-4199 75093
16th Pl 75074
E 16th St 75074
W 16th St 75075
17th St 75074
18th Pl 75074
18th St
601-697 75074
699-1199 75074
1112-1112 75086
1201-4099 75074
2100-4098 75074
19th St 75074
20th St 75074
21st St 75074
22nd St 75074

PORT ARTHUR TX

General Delivery 77640

POST OFFICE BOXES MAIN OFFICE STATIONS AND BRANCHES

Box No.s
5000A - 5000B 77640
5100A - 5100D 77640
5200A - 5200D 77640
5700B - 5700B 77640
A - H 77641
1 - 1672 77641
2001 - 3941 77643
4001 - 4282 77641
5000 - 5719 77640

NAMED STREETS

Abe Lincoln Ave 77640
Acres Ave 77640
Aero Dr 77640
Alabama Ave 77640
Alamo Ave 77642
Alamosa St 77642
Alice Ave 77640
Allien Pl 77642
Amherst St 77642
Amino St 77640
Amy St 77640
Anchor Dr 77642
Angel Fire Cv 77642
Angelle Dr 77642
Anne St 77640
Aqua St 77640

Asbury St 77642
Ash Ave 77640
Ashland Dr 77642
Aspen Ln 77642
Atlanta Ave 77640
Atlantic Rd 77642
Augusta Ave 77640
Austin Ave 77640
Ava Ln 77640
Avalon Ave 77642
Avant Ln 77642
Avenue A 77642
Avenue B 77642
Barbara Ln 77640
Barryknoll Ln 77642
Bay St 77642
Bayou Dr 77640
Beaumont Ave 77640
Becker Pl 77642
Beech Ave 77642
Beldon Dr 77642
Bell St 77640
Bernhardt Dr 77642
Bethany St 77642
Big Bend Ave 77642
Birch St 77640
Birchwood Triangle 77642
Bitternut Ct 77642
Blackberry Ln 77642
Bledsoe Pl 77640
Bluebonnet Ave 77640
Bob Hope Way 77642
Bobby St 77640
Bondarid Ave 77642
Booker T Washington
Ave 77640
Boulder Ave 77640
Brai Dr 77640
Brazos Ave 77642
Breckenridge Ct 77642
Briarwood Ln 77642
Bridle Path Dr 77640
Brinkman Dr 77642
Brittani 77642
Brittany Ave 77642
Bryce Ave 77642
Buckner Dr 77640
S Business Park 77640
Cambridge St 77640
Canal St 77640
Candlelight Cir 77642
Carolina Ave 77642
Carroll Ave 77642
Carver Ter 77640
Cashmere Ave 77640
Catalina Ct 77642
Cedar St 77640
Cedar Bend Ct 77642
Cedar Springs Ln 77640
Center Ave 77640
Central Mall Dr 77642
Champions Ct 77642
Chandelle Ln 77642
Channelview Dr 77640
Charles Ave 77640
Charleston Ave 77640
Charlotte Dr 77642
Cherry Ave 77640
Chevy Chase Ln 77642
Chimney Rock Ct &
Ln 77642
Clifford Ave 77642
Cobblestone Ln 77642
Coke Rd 77642
Colorado Ave 77642
Commerce St 77640
Cox St 77640
Crown Meadows Dr 77642
Cultural Center Dr 77642
Daisy Ave 77640
Dallas Ave 77640
Danny St 77640
Darnell Ave 77640
Date St 77642
Davis Ave 77640
Delaware Dr 77642

Delta Dr 77642
Dequeen Blvd 77640
Dewalt Ave 77640
Diamond Ave 77640
Diane Ave 77640
Dixie Dr 77642
Doctors Dr 77642
Dodge Pl 77642
Dominion Ct 77640
Dominion Ranch Dr 77640
Donald St 77642
Dorsey St 77640
Drexel Ave 77642
Drummond St 77640
Dryden Pl & Rd 77642
Duane St 77640
Duff Dr 77642
Dunbar Ave 77640
Easy Ave 77640
Ebony Ln 77640
Eddingston Ct 77642
El Paso Ave 77640
Ellias St 77640
Emory Ln 77640
Eunice Ave 77640
Evelyn St 77640
Everglades Ave 77642
Evergreen Dr 77642
Eyre St 77640
Fairway Ct 77642
Fairway Meadows Dr 77642
Ferndale Dr 77642
Flint Ave 77640
Florida Ave 77640
W Fm 365 Rd 77640
Foley Ave 77640
Forest Ave & Dr 77642
Fort Worth Ave 77640
Fredrick St 77640
Friar Point Dr 77642
Front Ave 77640
Galveston Ave 77640
Garnet Ave 77640
Gates Blvd 77642
George Ln 77642
Gifford Pond Ln 77642
Gilham Cir 77640
Gizelle St 77640
Glacier Dr 77640
Glenwood Dr 77642
Golden St 77640
Golden Meadows Dr 77642
Golfhill Dr 77642
Grand Ave 77642
Grandview Ave 77642
Grannis Ave 77640
Grant Ave 77640
Green Ave 77642
Greenbriar Ln 77642
Greenhill Dr 77642
Greenway Meadows Dr 77642
Greenway Pointe Dr 77642
Griffing Dr 77642
Gulf Ave 77642
Gulfway Dr
100-2899 77640
2900-7199 77642
W Gulfway Dr 77640
Guzman Dr 77640
Hall St 77640
Harding Ave 77640
Hazel Ave 77640
Heatherbrook Ct & Trl 77642
Henry St 77642
Henry O Mills Blvd 77640
Herget Ave 77640
Hickory St 77640
Hickory Cove Ln 77640
High Seas 77640
Highland Ave 77642
Highway 365
100-2899 77640
Highway 365
2900-8598 77642
2901-2999 77640
8600-8699 77642
W Highway 365 77640
Highway 73
1900-3099 77640
3300-4999 77642
Highway 87 77642
Hogaboom Rd 77642
Hollow Bend Ct & Ln 77642
Holly St 77642
Hollywood Dr 77642
Honeywood Trl 77642
Houston Ave 77640
Howell Dr 77642
Imhoff Ave 77642
Indian Fall Dr 77642
Indian River Dr 77642
Indian Valley Cir 77642
Industrial Cir 77640
Intral Coast Rd 77642
Island Way 77640
Jack Ave 77640
Jade Ave 77640
James Ave 77642
Jasonwood Ct 77642
Jean Ave 77642
Jefferson Dr 77642
Jimmy Johnson Blvd
2500-2899 77640
2900-4899 77642
Joe Louis Ave 77640
John St 77642
Julian Dr 77640
Kandywood Dr 77642
Katy Ave 77640
Kelliwood Dr 77642
Kent Ave 77640
Kerry Twin Thomas Dr 77640
Keystone Ave 77640
Kings Ct 77642
Kramer Pl 77642
Kylewood Ct 77642
Lake Arthur Dr 77642
Lake Charles Ave 77640
Lakecrest Dr 77642
Lakeshore Dr
100-2899 77640
3100-5399 77642
Lakeside Dr 77642
Lakeside Plz 77640
Lakeview Ave 77642
Lamplighter Ln 77642
Landry Dr 77642
Lansing Ave 77642
Las Palmas Dr 77642
Laura Ln 77640
Lavender St 77640
Lawn St 77642
Lee Ave 77640
Lemon Tree St 77642
Lewis Dr 77642
Lexington Ave 77642
Liberty Ave 77640
Linda Dr 77642
Linkwood St 77640
Linn St 77642
Lisa Ln 77640
Lisa Wood Ct 77642
Live Oak Ln 77642
Locust Ave 77642
Lombardy Dr 77642
Louisiana Ave 77640
Lynwood Ln 77642
Main Ave 77640
Manning St 77640
Maple Ave 77640
Maple Falls Ln 77642
Marian Anderson Ave 77640
Markwood Ct & Dr 77642
Marshall Ave 77640
Martin Dr 77642
Martin Luther King Jr Dr 77640
Mauve Ave 77640
Meadow St 77642
Medical Center Blvd 77640
Medical Triangle St 77642
Melody Dr 77642
Memorial Blvd
2100-5999 77640
6001-10699 77640
6900-8698 77642
8700-10698 77640
Memphis Ave 77640
Mills Ave 77642
Mimosa St 77640
Minnie St 77640
Mississippi Ave 77640
Mobile Ave 77640
Mockingbird Ln 77642
Moonstone St 77640
Mulberry St 77640
Nashville Ave 77640
Nathan St 77642
Neches Ave 77642
Nederland Ave 77640
New Orleans Ave 77640
Nick Ave 77640
Norma St 77640
Normandy Dr 77642
Northwind 77640
Oak Ave 77640
Oak Hill Ln 77640
Oaklawn Ave 77642
Oakmont Dr 77642
Old Ferry Rd 77642
Old Hebert Rd 77640
Old Yacht Club Rd 77642
Oleander St 77640
Olympic Dr 77642
Orange Ave 77640
Orchid St 77640
Oxford Dr 77640
Ozark Ave 77640
N, S & W Park Cir, Dr & Ln 77642
Park Plaza Cir & Ln 77642
Parks And Wildlife Dr 77640
Pastel Ave 77640
Pat Ave 77640
Pecos Ave 77642
Peek Ave 77640
Philmont Ave 77642
Phyllis Ave 77640
Pine Ave 77640
Pine Ridge Ln 77640
Pine Top Rd 77642
Platt Ave 77640
Plaza Cv & Sq 77642
Pleasant Hill Ct 77642
Pleasure Island Blvd 77640
Pleasure Islet Dr 77642
Poole Ave 77642
W Port Arthur Rd 77640
Portland St 77640
Prairie Knoll Ct 77640
Procter Ext 77642
Procter St
100-2899 77640
2900-5599 77642
W Procter St 77640
Professional Dr 77642
Prospect St 77640
Purdue Ave 77642
Queens Ct 77642
Queens Dr 77640
Quiet Corral Ln 77640
Rachel Ave 77640
Radiance St 77642
Railroad Ave 77640
Rainbow Ln 77642
Ranch Valley Ln 77640
Ray Ave 77640
Reba Dr 77640
Redbird St 77642
Redbud Ave 77642
Regency Dr 77642
Regional Dr 77642
W Rev Dr Ransom Howard St 77640
Rev Raymond Scott Ave 77640
Reyna Ave 77640
Rice Farm Rd 77642
Richard Wycoff 77640
Richmond Ave 77640
Ridgewood Ave 77642
Riley St 77640
Rio Grande Ave 77642
Roanoke Ave 77640
Roberts St 77640
Robinhood Ave 77640
Rolling Rock Dr 77642
Roosevelt Ave 77640
Rosedale Dr 77642
Roshan Ct 77642
Roya Ct 77642
Royal Meadows Blvd, Cir & St 77642
Russell St 77640
Rutgers Ave 77642
Sabine Ave 77642
Saint Augustine Ave 77640
Salisbury Dr 77640
Sam Ave 77640
San Antonio Ave 77640
San Jacinto Ave 77640
Sassine Ave 77640
Savannah Ave 77640
Scenic Park Ct 77640
Schuh Pl 77642
Sequoia Ave 77642
Sgt Lucien Adams Blvd 77642
Shadow Bend Ln 77642
Shady Cove Ln 77642
Shady Ranch Ln 77640
Sharon Dr 77640
Sheppard Ave 77642
Sheridan Ln 77640
Sherylwood Dr 77642
Shirley St 77640
Shortline Ave 77640
Shreveport Ave 77640
Sillered Ave 77640
Silver Ave 77640
Sleepy Hollow Ln 77642
Smith St 77640
Snider Ave 77642
Solomon St 77640
South St 77642
Southwind 77640
Spinel St 77640
S Spoil Levee 77640
Springdale St 77642
Springmeadow Ln 77642
Stable Gate Ln 77640
Stadium Rd 77642
Stanley Blvd 77642
Stevewood Dr 77642
Stilwell Blvd 77640
Stonegate Ct 77642
Stoney Brook Ln 77642
Sugarhill Ct 77642
Sunken Ct 77642
Sunset Dr 77642
Susie Dr 77640
Sycamore Ave 77640
T B Ellison Pkwy 77640
Taft Ave 77642
Tanglewood Ln 77642
Tara Ln 77642
Tartan St 77640
Terminal Rd 77640
Terrace Ave 77640
Terrell St 77642
Terry Ave 77640
Texas Blvd 77640
Thomas Blvd
100-2899 77640
2900-3699 77642
W Thomas Blvd 77640
Thomas Jefferson Dr 77642
Timber Leaf Ct 77642
Tom Dr 77642
Topaz St 77640
Touraine Ave 77642
Trinity Ave & Dr 77642
Tulane St 77642
Turtle Creek Dr 77642
N Twin City Hwy 77642
Tyler Ave 77640
Tyrrell Dr & Pkwy 77642
Upton Dr 77642
Valley Frg 77642
Vassar St 77642
Vera Dr 77642
Vicksburg Ave 77640
Village East Blvd 77642
Waco Ave 77640
Warren Way 77640
Waverly Cir 77640
Weaver Dr 77642
Weaver St 77640
Welford Ave 77640
Wentworth Ave 77642
Wheatley Ave 77640
Wignall Ave 77642
Williams Ave 77642
Willow Ave 77640
Willow Bend Ct & Ln 77642
Willowick Dr 77640
Willowood Ln 77642
Wilson Ave 77640
Windy Hill Ct 77642
Woodfern Ct 77642
Woodland Ave 77642
Woodlawn St 77642
Woodrow Dr 77642
Woodworth Blvd 77640
Yacht Club Rd 77642
Zion St 77642
Zwolle Blvd 77640

NUMBERED STREETS

1st Ave 77640
2nd Ave 77642
3rd Ave & St 77642
4th Ave 77642
4th St
100-2899 77640
3700-5299 77642
W 4th St 77640
5th Ave 77642
5th St
100-2899 77640
2900-5299 77642
W 5th St 77640
6th Ave 77642
6th St
100-2899 77640
2900-5299 77642
W 6th St 77640
7th Ave & St 77642
8th Ave 77642
8th St
100-2899 77640
2900-5299 77642
W 8th St 77640
9th Ave 77642
9th St
100-2899 77640
2900-5299 77642
W 9th St 77640
10th Ave 77642
10th St
100-2899 77640
2900-5299 77642
W 10th St 77640
11th Ave 77642
11th St
100-2899 77640
2900-4499 77642
W 11th St 77640
12th Ave 77642
12th St
100-2899 77640
2900-6199 77642
W 12th St 77640
13th Ave 77642
13th St
100-2899 77640
2900-6299 77642
W 13th St 77640
14th St
100-2899 77640
2900-5299 77642
W 14th St 77640
15th St
100-2899 77640
2900-6099 77642
W 15th St 77640
16th St 77642
17th St
100-2899 77640
2900-6299 77642
W 17th St 77640
18th St
100-2899 77640
2900-3499 77642
W 18th St 77640
19th St
200-2899 77640
2900-3499 77642
W 19th St 77640
20th St 77642
21st St 77640
22nd St
2600-2899 77640
2900-3599 77642
23rd St
2600-2899 77640
2900-4999 77642
24th St
2800-2899 77640
2900-3599 77642
25th St
2600-2899 77640
2900-5499 77642
26th St
2600-2899 77640
2900-3999 77642
27th St
2600-2899 77640
2900-3999 77642
28th St 77642
29th St
2600-2899 77640
2900-3999 77642
30th St 77642
31st St
2600-2899 77640
2900-4099 77642
32nd St 77642
33rd St 77640
34th St
2600-2899 77640
2900-3999 77642
35th St
2600-2899 77640
3300-3999 77642
36th St
2600-2899 77640
2900-4599 77642
37th St 77642
38th St 77642
39th St 77642
40th St 77642
41st St 77642
42nd St 77642
46th St 77642
47th St 77640
48th St 77640
49th St 77640
50th St 77640
53rd St
400-1099 77640
4700-4999 77642
57th St
3000-3099 77640
3300-3699 77642
3800-3899 77640
58th St 77640
59th St 77640
60th St
1100-3899 77640
4000-4999 77642
61st St 77640
62nd St 77640
63rd St 77640
64th St 77640
65th St 77640
66th St 77640
67th St 77640
76th St 77642
77th St 77642
80th St 77642
90th St 77640
95th St 77640

RICHARDSON TX

General Delivery 75080

POST OFFICE BOXES MAIN OFFICE STATIONS AND BRANCHES

Box No.s
830001 - 837321 75083
850001 - 853939 75085
8328244 - 8330099 75083

RURAL ROUTES

04 75082

NAMED STREETS

Aberdeen Ct & Dr 75082
Abingdon Dr 75082
Abrams Rd 75081
Acacia St 75082
Alamdre Ln 75082
Alamo Rd 75080
Albany Pl 75080
Alcatel Way 75081
Alexandra Ave 75081
Allegheny Cir, Ct, Dr, Pl & Way 75080
Allison Dr 75081
Alma Rd
1000-1799 75081
3400-3699 75080
Alpha Dr 75081
Alto Dr 75081
Ambleside Ln 75082
American Pkwy 75081
Amesbury Dr 75082
Amherst Ave 75081
Analog Dr 75081
Andover Ln 75082
Angel Fire Dr 75082
Angelica Trl 75080
Anglewood Dr 75081
Annapolis Dr 75081
Apache Dr 75080
Apollo Ct 75081
Apollo Rd
300-1207 75081
1206-1206 75085
1209-2199 75081
1500-2198 75081
Appleridge Dr 75082
Araf Ave 75081
E Arapaho Rd 75081
W Arapaho Rd 75080
Arbor Ct 75082
Arborcrest Dr 75080
Armstrong Pkwy 75080
Arrowhead Dr 75080
Arvada Dr 75081
Ascot Dr 75081
Ash Cir 75082
Ashbury Dr 75082
Ashfield 75081
Ashland Dr 75080
Ashwood Ct 75082
Aspen St 75082
Aspenwood Dr 75080
Aster Dr 75082
Aston Dr 75081
Auburn Dr 75081

Street	ZIP
Audelia Rd	75081
Aurora Dr	75081
Autumn Ct	75082
Azure Pointe	75080
Balmoral	75082
Baltimore Dr	75081
Banbury Ct	75082
Barclay Dr & Pl	75081
Barley Ct	75082
Barrington Dr	75082
Baskerville Dr	75082
Baylor Dr	75081
Beck Dr	75082
Bedford Dr	75080
Beechwood Dr	75080
Belaire Dr	75080
Belle Grove Dr	
400-434	75080
433-433	75083
435-499	75080
436-498	75080
Belleview Ct	75082
Belt Line Cv	75080
Belt Line Plz	75080
E Belt Line Rd	75081
W Belt Line Rd	75080
E Berkeley Dr & Pl	75081
Berkner Dr	75081
Berrywood Ct	75082
Betty Dr	75081
Beverly Dr	75080
Big Horn Ln	75080
Big Sky Ct	75082
Binley Dr	75082
Birch Ln	75081
Birchwood Ln	75082
Birkshire Ln	75082
Bishop Ave	75081
Bitternut Dr	75082
Blackberry Dr	75082
Blackfield Dr	75082
Blackwood Ct	75082
Blake Dr	75081
Blossom Ln	75081
Blue Bell Pl	75082
Blue Cypress Dr	75082
Blue Lake Cir	75080
Blue Ridge Pl	75080
Bluebonnet Dr	75082
Boulder Trl	75080
N & S Bowser Rd	75081
Box Canyon Ct	75080
Bradford Dr	75082
Braeburn Dr	75082
Brand Rd	75082
Brandeis Dr	75082
Brandy Sta	75080
Brantford Dr	75082
Breckenridge Blvd	75082
Breckinridge Blvd & Ct	75082
Breiton Ln	75082
Brentwood Ln	75080
Briarcove Dr	75081
N & S Briarcrest Ct & Dr	75081
Briarfield Dr	75080
Briarwick Ct	75082
Briarwood Cir	75080
Brick Row Dr	75081
Bridge Canyon Ct	75080
Bridgewater Dr	75082
Bridle Dr	75081
Bristol Ct	75080
Brittany Way Dr	75082
Broadmoor Dr	75082
Brook Glen Dr & Pl	75080
Brookhurst Dr	75080
Brookridge Dr	75082
Brookshire Ln	75080
Brookside Dr	75082
Brookvale Dr	75082
Brookwood Dr	75080
Brush Creek Dr	75081
Bruton Bends Dr	75081
Bryn Mawr Cir	75081
E & W Buckingham Pl & Rd	75081
Bull Run	75080
Bunker Hl	75080
Business Pkwy	75081
Buttercup Dr	75082
Caladium Ave	75080
Calloway Ct	75082
Calstone Ct	75082
Cambridge Cir & Dr	75080
Campbell Ct	75080
Campbell Pkwy	75082
Campbell Rd	75082
E Campbell Rd	75081
W Campbell Rd	75080
Campbell Trl	75082
Campbell Creek Blvd	75082
Candlewood Pl	75081
Cantera Ct & Ln	75082
Canterbury Ct	75082
Canyon Brook Dr	75080
Canyon Creek Dr, Plz, Sq & Vlg	75080
Canyon Ridge Dr	75080
Canyon Valley Dr	75080
Cap Rock Cir & Dr	75080
Cardinal Ln	75080
Carleton Dr	75081
Carnation Dr	75082
Carol Ct	75081
Carol Stream Dr	75081
Carolyn Way	75081
Carriage Ct	75082
Carrington Ct & Dr	75082
Cascada Dr	75081
W Caspia Ln	75080
Cavalier Ct, Dr & Plz	75080
Cedar Ln	75080
Cedar Elm Cir	75082
Cedar Ridge Dr	75082
Cedarbrook Cir	75082
Centenary Dr	75081
Centennial Blvd	75081
N & S Central Expy	75080
Chadwick Dr & Pl	75080
Chainhurst Dr	75082
Champion Ct	75082
Champlin Ct	75082
Chaparral Dr	75080
Chapel Creek Ct	75080
Charleston Dr	75082
Chelsey Cir & Ln	75082
Cherlin Pl	75080
Cherokee Dr & Pl	75080
Cherry Ct	75082
Cherrywood Dr	75080
Chesterton Dr	75080
Chestnut Ln	75082
Chestnut Hill Ln	75082
Cheyenne Dr & Pl	75080
Chickasaw Dr	75080
Chippewa Dr	75080
Christopher Ln	75082
Civic Center Dr	75080
Clear Creek Ct	75082
Clear Lake Cir	75080
Clear Springs Ct & Dr	75082
Clearfield Cir	75081
Clearwater Dr	75080
Clearwood Dr	75081
Clemson Dr	75081
Cliff Ln	75081
N Cliffe	75082
Cliffside Dr	75080
Clifton Dr	75082
Clipper Ct	75082
Clover Trl	75081
Cloverdale Dr	75080
N Coit Rd	
100-400	75080
400-400	75083
418-2298	75080
S Coit Rd	75080
Coleshire Dr	75082
Colfax Cir & Dr	75080
Colgate Dr	75081
College Park Blvd	75081
E Collins Blvd	75081
N Collins Blvd	75080
Collins Ct	75081
Colonial Ct	75082
Columbia Dr	75081
Comanche Dr	75080
Commerce Dr	75081
Compton Dr	75082
Concord Dr	75081
Copper Mountain Ln	75082
Copper Ridge Dr	75080
Copperwood Dr	75082
Coral Cir	75081
Cornell Dr	75081
Cotswolds Ct	75081
Cotters Cir	75082
N & S Cottonwood Dr	75080
Country Meadow Ln	75081
Country Side Ln	75081
Courtney Ln	75082
Coventry Dr	75082
Cramptons Gap Dr	75080
Creekbend Cir	75082
Creekdale Dr	75080
Creekmere Dr	75082
Creekside Dr	75081
Creekview Ct	75081
Creekwood Cir	75080
Cresside Ln	75081
Crested Butte Dr	75082
Crestfield Ct & Dr	75082
Crestover Cir & Dr	75080
Crestview Dr	75080
Crooked Creek Dr	75080
Crossroads Ctr	75081
Crown Pl	75080
Crystal Ct	75081
Crystal Mountain Dr	75082
Crystal Springs Ln	75082
Cullum St	75080
Cumberland Pl	75080
Custer Cv, Pkwy, Plz & Rd	75080
Cypress Dr	75080
Cypress Grove Ct	75082
Daffodil Dr	75082
Dahlia Way	75080
Daisy Cir & Ln	75082
Dal Rich Vlg	75080
Dalhart Dr	75080
Damian Way	75081
Daniel St	75080
Danmire Dr	75080
Danville Dr	75080
Dartmouth Ln	75081
Dawn Cir	75081
Dearborn Cir & Dr	75080
Decca Dr	75080
Deep Valley Dr & Pl	75080
Deer Park Cir	75081
Deer Valley Ln	75082
Deerwood Ct	75082
Delmont Dr	75080
Denise Dr	75082
Derby Dr	75080
Devonshire Dr	75080
Digital Dr	75081
Dogwood Dr	75080
Donna Dr	75080
Doral Pl	75080
N & S Dorothy Dr	75081
Dove Creek Ln	75082
Dover Dr	75080
Downing Dr	75080
Drake Dr	75081
Drew Ln	75082
Drexel Dr	75081
Dublin Dr	75080
Duke Dr	75081
Dumont Dr	75080
Dunbarton Dr	75081
Dunrobin	75082
Dunwich Dr	75082
Durango Ct	75082
Dusty Trl	75082
Eaglebend Dr	75082
Eastfield Dr	75081
Eastpark Dr	75081
Eastview Cir	75081
Eastwood Dr	75080
Edgefield Dr	75080
Edgehill Blvd	75081
Edgeview Ct	75082
Edgewater Ct	75082
Edgewood Dr	75081
Edinburg Dr	75082
Edith Cir	75080
Edmonton Ct	75082
Eldora Ct	75081
Elizabeth Ln	75080
Elk Grove Dr	75081
Elk Springs Trl	75082
Elleandi Dr	75081
Elmsted Dr	75082
Elmwood Dr	75080
Emerald Glen Trl	75080
Enfield Dr	75082
Englecrest Dr	75081
Essex Dr	75082
Eton Dr	75080
Evergreen Dr	75080
Excalibur Ct	75082
Exchange Dr	75081
Executive Dr E & W	75081
Exeter Dr	75082
Fair Oaks Dr	75081
Fairfax Cir	75082
Fairfield Dr	75082
Fairlands Dr	75082
Fairmeadow Dr	75080
Fairview Dr	75081
Fairway Cir & Dr	75080
Fall Creek Dr	75080
W Falls Ct	75080
Farmington Dr	75082
Faversham Dr	75082
Fernhurst Dr	75082
Fernwood Dr	75080
Fieldwood Cir & Dr	75081
Fireside Dr	75081
Firestone Ln	75080
Firman Dr	75081
Flat Creek Dr & Pl	75080
Fleming Trl	75081
Flintwood Dr	75081
N Floyd Rd	75080
S Floyd Rd	
100-799	75080
900-1299	75081
Fontana Ave	75080
Forest Grove Dr	75080
Forest Hills Ln	75080
Forest Meadow Ln	75081
Forest Park Dr	75080
Forestbrook Dr	75082
Forestdale Dr	75081
Forestwood Dr	75081
Forreston Dr	75080
Forsythe Dr	75081
Foxboro Dr	75082
Foxcreek Dr	75082
Frances Way	75081
Freesia Way	75080
Galahad Ln	75082
Galatyn Pkwy	75082
Garden Park Ct	75080
Garden Springs Dr	75082
Garden View Ln	75080
Gardenia Way	75080
Gateway Blvd	75080
Gaylewood Dr	75080
Geneva Dr	75081
N & S Gentle Dr	75080
Georgetown Dr	75081
Gettysburg Ln	75080
Glen Cove Dr	75080
Glen Heather Dr	75082
Glen Meadow Ct	75081
Glenbrook Dr	75082
Glenfield Ct	75080
N Glenville Dr	
100-398	75081
400-1999	75081
2000-2999	75082
S Glenville Dr	75081
Glenwick Ct	75082
Glenwood Springs Ct	75082
Gold Finch Dr	75081
Golden Willow Ln	75082
Goldenrod Dr	75081
Goodwin Dr	75081
Grace Dr	75081
Grandview Dr	75080
Grant Cir & Dr	75081
Grantham Ct & Dr	75082
Grassmere Dr	75080
Gray Stone Ln	75081
Green Meadow Dr	75081
Green View Cir	75081
Greenbriar Ln	75080
Greencove Ln	75081
Greenfield Ct & Dr	75082
Greenhaven Dr	75080
Greenleaf Dr	75080
Greenpark Dr	75082
Greenside Dr	75080
N Greenville Ave	
100-1999	75081
2000-2098	75082
2100-2299	75082
2301-2399	75082
S Greenville Ave	75081
Greenway Dr	75080
Grinnell Dr	75081
N & S Grove Rd	75081
Grove Park Ln	75080
Gun Club Cir	75081
Gunnison Dr	75082
Hackberry Ln	75082
Hamilton Dr	75080
Hampshire Ln	75080
Hampton Ct	75082
Hanbee St	75080
Hanbury Ct	75082
Hanover Dr	75081
Harlington Ln	75082
Harness Ln	75081
Harolds Cir	75081
Harpers Ferry Dr	75080
Hartford Dr	75082
Harvard Dr	75081
Harvest Glen Dr	75081
Harvest Knoll Dr	75082
Hattington Ln	75082
Hayley Ct	75082
Haynes Dr	75081
Heather Way	75081
Heather Glen Ct	75081
Heatherbrook Ln	75082
Hemlock Dr	75081
Heritage Square Sc	75081
Hibiscus Ave	75080
Hidden Cir	75081
High Brook Dr	75080
High Canyon Ct	75080
High Mesa Pl	75080
High Vista Ln	75080
Highland Blvd & Pl	75081
Hill Haven Cir	75081
Hillcrest Ave	75081
Hillingdon Dr	75082
Hillrose Dr	75082
Hillsdale Dr	75081
Hillside Ave	75081
Hilltop Ave	75081
Hilton Dr	75081
Hindsdale Dr	75081
Holford Rd	75082
Hollowridge Ct	75082
Holly Dr	75080
Honeysuckle Dr	75082
Horizon Trl	75081
Horseshoe Bnd	75081
Huffhines St	75081
Hunters Glen Ct	75081
Huntington Dr	75080
Hyde Park Dr	75080
Indintri Dr	75080
Industrial Dr	75081
Infocom Ln	75082
Inge Dr	75080
Inglewood Dr	75080
Insight Pl	75081
International Pkwy	75081
N & S Interurban St	75081
Iris Ct	75082
Island Dr	75081
Ivy Ln	75080
J J Pearce Dr	75081
Jackson St	75081
James Dr	75080
Jasmine Ln	75082
Jay Ell Dr	75081
Jennifer St	75082
Jolee St	75080
Jonsson Blvd	75080
N Jupiter Rd	
101-1797	75081
1799-1999	75081
2001-2597	75082
2599-3699	75082
S Jupiter Rd	75081
Jupiter Sc	75081
Justin Ct	75081
Kas Dr	75081
E & W Kaufman St	75081
Keating Ct	75082
Kelly Dr	75082
Kenshire Ln	75081
Kensington Dr	75082
Keswick Ct	75082
Kettering Ct	75082
Kildonan	75082
Killarney	75081
Kindred Ln	75080
Kingsbury Dr	75082
Kingston Ct & Dr	75082
Kingswood Ave	75080
Kirby Ln	75080
Kyndra Cir	75082
La Mesa Dr	75080
La Salle Dr	75081
Laguna Dr	75080
Lahinch Cir	75081
Lake Park Blvd & Way	75080
Lake Pointe Way	75080
Lake Ridge Dr	75081
Lake Vista Ln	75080
Lakeside Blvd	75082
Laketrail Dr	75081
Lakeview Dr	75080
Lamp Post Ln	75080
Lancelot Ln	75082
Laney Ct	75082
Larchmont Dr	75082
Larkspur Dr	75081
Lartan Trl	75082
Laurel Ln	75080
Lawndale Dr	75080
Lawnmeadow Dr	75080
Lawnview Dr	75082
Ledgestone Ct	75082
Lester Dr	75082
Lexington Ln	75080
Lilac Ct	75082
Lilly Ln	75082
Limestone Ct	75082
Lincolnshire Dr	75082
Linda Ln	75081
N & S Lindale Ln	75080
Lingco Dr	75081
Linhurst Ct	75082
Little Creek Dr	75080
Lochleven	75082
Lockwood Dr	75080
Loganwood Ave	75080
N & S Lois Ln	75081
Lomita Dr	75080
Long Canyon Ct	75080
Longmont Pl	75081
E Lookout Dr	75082
W Lookout Dr	75080
Loop Rd	75080
Lorrie Dr	75080
Lost Canyon Ct	75080
Lotus Dr	75081
Lowell Ln	75080
Lucerne Cv	75080
Lundys Ln	75080
Lynn St	75080
Mackenzie Ln	75082
Mackie Dr	75081
Madison Ct	75082
Magnolia Dr	75080
Maidstone Dr	75082
E & W Main St	75081
Malden Dr	75080
Manchester Dr	75082
Mansfield Dr	75082
Maple St	75081
Mapleleaf Ln	75082
Marchwood Dr	75082
Margate Ln	75082
Mariana Dr	75082
Marilu St	75080
Marlboro Ln	75082
Marlow Ln	75082
Marquette Dr	75081
Marshfield Dr	75082
Martha Mnr	75081
Maryland Dr	75080
Matrix Dr	75082
Matthew Pl	75081
Maycraft Ct & Dr	75082
Mayflower Dr	75081
Mckenzie Dr	75082
Mckinley Ln	75082
N & S Mckinney St	75081
Meadow Cir	75082
Meadow Glen St	75081
Meadow View Cir & Dr	75080
Meadow Wood Dr	75082
Meadowcove Dr	75081
Meadowcrest Dr	75080
Meadowgate Dr	75081
Meadowlark Dr	75080
Melody Ln	75081
Melrose Cir & Dr	75080
Meredith Ln	75081
Meridian Way	75080
Merita Dr	75082
Merrie Cir	75081
Mesa Dr	75080
Midway Cir & Dr	75081
Mill Spgs	75080
Miller Ln	75082
Millwood Dr	75082
Mimosa Dr	75080
Mistletoe Dr	75081
Moffett St	75081
Mohawk Trl	75080
Monmouth Ct	75082
Montclair Dr	75081
Monte Blaine Ln	75080
Morning Glory Dr & Way	75082
Morningstar Trl	75081
Moroney Dr	75082
Mossbrook Dr	75081
Mount Vernon Dr	75081
Mum Dr	75082
Municipal Dr	75080
Murphy Rd	75082
Murray Ln	75080
Nantucket Cir & Dr	75080
Napier Dr	75081
Naples Dr	75080
Navaho Trl	75080
New Castle Ct & Dr	75082
Newberry Dr	75080
Newhaven Dr	75082
Nicole Dr	75082
Normandy Dr	75082
Northill Dr	75082
Northlake Dr	75080
Northpark Dr	75081
Northridge Dr	75082

Northstar Rd 75082
Northview Dr 75080
Norwich Dr 75082
Norwood Cir 75082
Nottingham Dr 75080
Oak Brook Dr 75081
Oakcrest Dr 75080
Oakleaf Ln 75082
Oakmont Dr & Pl 75081
Oakway Ct 75081
Oakwood Ct & Dr 75082
Ocean Dr 75081
Odessa Dr 75080
Old Campbell Rd 75080
Olympic 75081
Omni Dr 75080
Opal Ln 75080
Orchid Dr 75080
Osage Dr 75080
Ottawa Cir & Dr 75080
Overcreek Dr 75080
Overlake Dr 75080
Owens Blvd
1900-1999 75081
2000-2198 75082
2200-3399 75082
Oxford Dr 75080
Pacific Cir & Dr 75081
Palace Dr 75082
Palisades Blvd 75080
Palisades Creek Dr 75080
Palm Cir 75081
Palmer Pl 75080
Palomar Ln 75081
Park Ln & Pl 75081
Park Bend Dr 75081
Park Garden Pl 75082
Park Meadow Ln 75081
Park Vista Rd 75082
Parkhaven Dr 75080
Parkhurst Cir & Ln 75082
Parkside Dr 75080
Parkview Cir & Ln 75080
Pauline Dr 75081
Pawnee Dr 75080
Pebble Beach Ct 75082
Pebblebrook Cir 75080
Peck Pl 75082
Pepperridge Dr 75082
Performance Dr 75082
Periwinkle Ct 75080
E & W Phillips St 75081
Pickwick Ln 75082
Pin Oak Ln 75082
Pine Vly 75081
Pinecrest Dr 75080
Pinehurst Dr 75080
Pinery Ct & Ln 75080
Pinon Canyon Ln 75082
Piper Ct 75081
Pittman St 75081
Pittsburg Lndg 75080
N Plano Rd
100-1999 75081
2000-2498 75082
2500-3599 75082
S Plano Rd 75081
Plaza Ln & Way 75080
Pleasant Valley Ln 75080
Plymouth Rock Dr 75081
Poinsettia Dr 75082
E & W Polk St 75081
Pond View Dr 75082
Ponderosa Dr 75081
Poppy Ln 75081
Portsmouth Dr 75082
Potomac Dr 75081
E & W Prairie Creek
Dr 75080
Prairie Dog Run 75080
E President George Bush
Hwy 75082
W President George
Bush Hwy 75080
Presidential Dr 75081
Prestonwood Dr 75081

Prestwick Ln 75080
Primrose Dr 75082
Prince Albert Ct 75081
Princeton Dr 75081
Profit Dr 75082
Promenade Ctr 75080
Prospect Dr 75081
Provencial Ln 75080
Provincetown Ln 75080
Pueblo Dr 75080
Purdue Cir 75081
Quail Ln 75080
Quality Way 75081
Queen Victoria Ct 75081
Raford Hill Ln 75081
Rainbow Dr 75081
Rams Ct 75081
Ranchview Dr 75082
Ravendale Dr 75082
Rayeed Ave 75081
Rayflex Dr 75081
Red Barn 75082
Red Oak Ln 75082
Redcliff Ct 75082
Redwood Dr 75080
Reflection Pointe 75080
Regal Ct & Dr 75080
Regency Ct & Dr 75080
Renner Pkwy 75080
E Renner Rd 75082
W Renner Rd
100-199 75082
201-257 75080
259-1299 75080
Research Dr 75082
Reston Dr 75081
Richardson Dr 75080
Richardson Square
Mall 75081
Richforest Dr 75081
Richland Dr 75081
Richland Oaks Dr 75081
Richland Park Dr 75081
Ridge Creek Dr 75082
Ridge Crest Dr 75081
Ridgebriar Dr & Pl 75080
Ridgedale Dr 75080
Ridgehaven Pl 75080
Ridgemoor Ln 75082
Ridgeview Cir & Dr 75080
Ridgeway Cir & Dr 75080
Ridgewood Dr 75080
River Oaks Ln 75081
Robert Dr 75082
Robin Way 75080
Rockingham Dr 75080
Rollingwood Dr 75081
Rorary Dr 75081
Roundrock Cir 75080
Roxton Ct 75081
Royal Crest Dr 75081
Rusk Dr 75081
Rustic Cir 75080
Rutford Ave 75080
Rutgers Dr 75081
Ryan Ln 75082
Sage Valley Dr 75080
Sagebrush Trl 75080
N Saint Andrews Dr 75082
Saint Cloud Ln 75080
Saint Croix Ct 75082
Saint George 75081
N Saint Johns Dr 75081
Saint Lukes Dr 75080
Saint Paul Ct & Dr 75080
Salem Ct & Dr 75080
Sallie Cir 75081
Samia Ln 75081
Sandalwood Ave 75080
Sanderosa Ln 75082
Sandhill Dr 75080
Sandy Trl 75080
Sara Ln 75081
Savoy Ln 75080
Scarlet Oak Dr 75081
Scottsboro Ln 75082

Scottsdale Dr 75080
Security Row 75081
Seminole Dr 75080
Serenade Ln 75081
Shadow Bend Dr 75081
Shady Cv & Vis 75080
Shady Brook Dr & Pl 75080
Shady Creek Dr 75080
Shady Hill Dr 75080
Shadyglen Cir 75081
Shadywood Ln & Pl 75080
Shamrock Pl 75081
Shannon Ct & Ln 75082
Sharp Ln 75082
Sheffield Dr 75081
Shenandoah Pl 75080
Sherbrook Dr 75080
S Sherman St 75081
Sherrill Park Ct & Dr 75082
Sherwood Dr 75080
N Shiloh Rd 75082
Shire Blvd 75082
Shirley Ct 75081
Shore Dr & Pl 75080
Sierra Pl 75080
Silver Holly Ln 75082
Silver Springs Ln 75082
Silverstone Dr 75080
Silverthorne St 75082
Sky Ridge Crk 75082
Skyview Dr 75080
Snowden Dr 75080
Snowmass Ct 75082
Somerset Pl 75081
Somerville Dr 75080
Sonoma Creek Ln 75081
Southampton Dr 75082
Southpointe Dr 75082
Southwestern Dr 75081
Sowerby Dr 75082
Spectrum Blvd 75082
N Spring Dr 75082
N & S Spring Creek
Dr 75081
Spring Lake Dr 75082
Spring Meadow Ln 75081
Spring Valley Ct 75081
Spring Valley Plz 75080
E Spring Valley Rd 75081
W Spring Valley Rd
100-499 75081
500-698 75080
700-888 75080
890-1498 75080
Springbranch Dr 75082
Springhill Ln 75082
Springpark Way 75082
Springtree Cir 75082
Springwood Ln 75082
Spruce Dr 75080
Stacey Ct 75081
Stagecoach Dr 75080
Star Crest Ln 75082
Stardust Ln 75080
Starshadow Dr 75081
Sterling Dr 75081
Stewart Dr 75080
Stillmeadow Dr 75081
Stone Canyon Ct 75080
Stoneboro Ln 75082
Stonebridge Dr 75080
Stonebrook Dr 75082
Stonecrest Dr 75081
Stoneham Pl 75081
Stonehenge Dr 75082
Stoneleigh Cir 75082
Stratford Dr 75080
Summerfield Dr 75082
Summertree Ct 75082
Summerwood Ln 75081
Summit Dr 75081
Sundial Dr 75081
Sunningdale 75081
Sunrise Trl 75081
Sunvalley Dr 75082
Surf Cir 75081

Sutton Pl 75080
Sweetbriar Dr 75082
Sweetwater Dr 75082
Synergy Park Blvd 75080
Syracuse Dr & Pl 75081
Tabernash 75082
Tall Oaks Ln 75081
Talon Dr 75082
Tam O Shanter Ln 75080
Tanner Ln 75082
Taos Ct 75082
Taylor Ln 75082
Teakwood Dr & Pl 75080
Tearose Dr 75082
Tejas Trl 75081
Telecom Pkwy 75082
Telluride Ln 75082
Terrace Dr 75081
Terrace Village Ctr 75081
Terryland Dr 75080
N & S Texas St 75081
Thompson Dr 75080
Thorne Hill Ct 75082
Ti Blvd 75081
Tiffany Trl 75081
Timberlake Cir 75080
Timberview Ln 75080
Timberway Dr 75082
Token Dr 75082
Towne House Ln 75081
Trail Lake Dr 75081
Trailridge Dr 75081
Trailwood Dr 75082
Tree Trunk Trl 75082
Trellis Pl 75081
Troon Cir 75081
Tulane Dr 75081
Tulip Dr 75082
Twilight Cir & Trl 75080
Two Creek Plz 75080
E Tyler St 75081
University Dr 75081
University Village Ctr &
Dr 75081
Valcourt Dr 75081
Valley Frg 75080
Valley Brook Dr 75082
Valley Cove Dr 75080
Valley Creek Pl 75080
Valley Glen Dr & Pl 75080
Valley Ridge Dr 75080
Vassar Dr 75081
Vernet St 75080
Versailles Dr 75081
Vickie Dr 75081
Vicksburg Ln 75080
Victoria Ln 75082
Village Grn 75081
Village North Dr 75081
Villanova Dr 75081
Vinecrest Ln 75080
Violet Cir 75080
Vista Cliff Dr & Pl 75080
Wagon Wheel Ct 75082
Wake Dr 75081
Wake Forest Dr 75081
Walker Dr 75082
Walnut St 75081
Walnut Creek Pl 75080
Waltham Dr 75082
Walton St 75081
Wareham Cir 75082
Warfield Way 75080
Warlet Dr 75082
Warm Springs Ln 75082
Warren Way 75080
Warwick Ln 75082
Wateka Way 75080
Waterfall Way 75080
Waterford Ln 75082
N & S Waterview Cir, Dr,
Pkwy & Pl 75080
Waterwood Dr 75082
Waverly Ct 75082
Wayside Way 75080
Weanne Dr 75082

N & S Weatherred Dr 75080
Wedgewood Way 75080
Wellington Dr 75082
Wembley Ct 75082
Wendover Ct 75082
Wendy Way 75081
Wentworth Dr 75081
Wessex Cir 75082
Westbury Ln 75082
Westgate Ln 75082
Westminster Dr 75081
Weston Way 75080
Westover Dr 75080
Westwood Dr 75080
Wheaton Dr 75081
Whispering Oaks Ln 75081
White Cliff Dr 75080
White Oak Dr 75082
Whitemarsh Cir 75080
Whitney Dr 75082
Wilderness Cir & Trl 75080
Wildflower Ct 75081
Wildwood Ln 75080
Williams Way 75080
Willingham Dr 75081
Willow Creek Pl 75080
Willow Crest Dr 75081
Willowbrook Dr 75082
Wilmington Ct 75082
Winchester Dr 75080
Winding Brook Ln 75081
Windsong Trl 75081
Windsor Dr 75082
Winter Park Dr 75082
Wista Vista Dr 75081
Wisteria Way 75080
Wolcott Pl 75082
Woodall Dr 75081
Woodbury Pl 75082
Woodcreek Dr 75082
Woodcrest Dr 75080
Wooded Canyon Ct 75080
Woodglen Dr 75082
Woodhaven Pl 75081
Woodhill Cir 75081
Woodland Way 75080
Woodoak Dr 75082
Woodpile Trl 75082
Woodway Ln 75081
Worcester Way 75080
Wren Ln 75082
Wyndcliff Dr 75082
Wyndham Ln 75082
Wyndmere Dr 75082
Xavier Pl 75082
N & S Yale Blvd, Cir &
Pl 75081
Yorkshire Ct & Dr 75082
Yvonne Pl 75081

RICHMOND TX

General Delivery 77469

POST OFFICE BOXES MAIN OFFICE STATIONS AND BRANCHES

Box No.s
All PO Boxes 77406

NAMED STREETS

A Meyer Rd 77469
Aberdeenshire Dr 77407
Abriola Ct 77406
Acacia Falls Ct 77407
Acacia Rose Ct 77407
Acorn Valley Ln 77469
Adallewo Dr 77469
Adelaide Dr 77407
Adobe Arch Ct 77406

Adoquin Ln 77469
Afton Hollow Ln 77407
Agnes Rd 77469
Alamo Ave 77469
Albany Ct 77406
Alcott Manor Ln 77407
Aldenwilds Ln 77407
Alder Bend Ln 77469
Alexandria Ct 77406
N Aliana Rd 77407
Aliana Lakes Ct 77407
E Aliana Trace Dr 77407
Alief Clodine Rd 77407
Allegro Dr 77406
Allpoint Ct 77407
Alma Ct 77406
Almond Place Ln 77407
Alps Peak Ct 77407
Alta Pine Ln 77407
Amber Crossing Dr 77406
Amber Trail Ln 77469
Amber Village Cir &
Ln 77407
Amoroso St 77406
Amy Point Ln 77407
Anaquitas Creek Ct 77407
Anchor Cv 77469
Anderson Cir 77469
Andes Ridge Ln 77407
Andrea Park Dr 77406
Andrew Oaks Ct 77469
Angel Lake Dr 77406
Angel Oaks Ct 77407
Anilu Dr 77406
Anna Mills Ct & Ln 77469
Ansel Ln 77469
Anthonia Ln 77406
Antonia Manor Ct 77406
Anvil Iron Ln 77406
Anvil Rock Ln 77469
Apple Oak Ct 77407
Apple Orchard Dr 77406
Aqua Vista Ln 77469
Aquarius St 77469
Arabian Ct 77406
Arapahoe Pass Ln 77407
Arbor Bend Ln 77469
Arbor Cove Ct & Ln 77407
Arbor Gate Ct 77469
Arbor Green Ln 77469
Arbor Ranch Dr 77469
Arborvine Ct 77469
Arbury Hill Ln 77469
Ardkinglas Dr 77407
Arlington Ln 77469
Arrow Falls Ln 77407
Arrow Grand Ct 77407
Ascot Dew Ct 77469
Ashland Terrace Ln 77469
Aspen Ridge Ct 77407
Aspenwood Dr 77406
Astrachan Rd 77407
Atlanta Dr 77406
Atlantic Breeze Ln 77407
Atwood Manor Ct 77407
Atwood Preserve Ct 77469
Atwood Ridge Ln 77469
Aubrey Ln 77469
Auburn Canyon Ln 77469
Auburn Shores Ct 77469
Audubon Ct 77406
Augrae Park Ct 77407
August Green Dr 77469
Augusta Dr 77406
Aurora Park Dr 77406
E Austin St 77469
Austin Colony Dr 77406
Austin Oak Ln 77407
Autumn Aspen Ln 77407
Autumn Bluff Ln 77407
Autumn Creek Ln 77406
Autumn Crest Ln 77407
Autumn Field Ln 77469
Autumn Manor Dr 77406
Autumn Stone Dr 77406
Avalon Ct 77406

Avalon Trce 77407
Avellino Ct 77406
Avenida Monterey Pl 77406
Avenue A 77406
Avenue C 77406
Avery Oaks Ln 77406
Avoncrest Ln 77407
Ayala Ct 77469
Azalea Chase Dr 77406
Azzuro Ct 77406
Bahama Blue Dr 77407
Bahia Vista Dr 77406
Bain Bridge Hl 77469
Baldwin Elm St 77407
Ballinger Ridge Ct &
Ln 77407
Balmano Pl 77407
Balvano Dr 77406
Bandera Lake Ln 77407
Bandrock Ter 77407
Banfield Ct 77469
Bannermans Way 77407
Bannon Field Ln 77407
Banyan Oak Ct 77407
Barchan Point Way 77407
Bardwell Lake Ct 77407
Baristone Ln 77407
Barn Course Dr 77407
Baron Sky Ln 77469
Barrett St 77469
Barrett Creek Ln 77407
Barrett Knolls Dr 77406
Barrett Spur Ct 77406
Barrett Woods Dr 77407
Barrowfield Ln 77407
Barton Hollow Ln 77407
Barton Lake Ct 77407
Barton Point Ln 77407
Barton Ridge Ln 77407
Barton River Ct 77469
Basin Ridge Ln 77407
Baudet Dr 77406
Bay Springs View Ct 77406
W Bayou Dr 77469
Baytide Ct 77407
Bedias Creek Ct & Dr 77407
Beech Fern Dr 77407
Beech Trail Ct 77469
Beecham Lake Ct &
Ln 77407
Beechnut St 77407
Belford Park Ln 77407
Bell Castle Ct 77406
Bella Florence Dr 77406
Bella Veneza Dr 77406
Bella Vista Dr 77406
Bellaforte Ct 77406
Bellago Ln 77407
Bellaire Blvd
17300-22499 77407
22600-23298 77406
23300-23899 77406
23901-24199 77406
Belle Cove Ct 77407
Belle Grove Dr 77406
Belle Meadow Ln 77469
Bellflower Glen Dr 77407
W Bellfort
16700-20899 77407
W Bellfort
20900-21599 77406
Bellwood Lake Dr 77406
N & S Belmont Dr 77469
Belshill St 77407
Belvamera Rd 77407
Bent Bridge Ln 77469
Bent Creek Ct 77406
Bent Ray Ct 77469
Bentford Park St 77406
Benton Rd 77469
Benton Springs Ln 77407
Bergamo Dr 77406
Bering Chase Way 77406
Beringer Dr 77469
Berkley Ct 77406
Bernalda Cir 77406

Berry Glen Ct 77469
Beverly Chase Dr 77406
Big Oak Canyon Dr 77469
Big Oaks Grv 77407
Big Thicket Dr 77469
Birch Glen St 77406
Birmingham Ct 77469
Birthisel Bend Ln 77469
Bishop Oaks Dr 77406
Bittersweet Ct & Dr 77406
Bivins Lake Cir 77406
Black Spur Ct 77406
Black Walnut Ct 77469
Blackberry Cove Ln 77469
Blackstone Ct 77469
Blaisdale Rd 77406
Bland Mills Ln 77407
Blidel Rd 77469
Bloommist Ct 77469
Blossom Breeze Ln 77469
Blossom Terrace Ct & Ln 77469
Blossommist Ln 77407
Blue Flagstone Ln 77407
Blue Glade Dr 77406
Blue Grass Dr 77406
Blue Lake Dr 77469
Blue Leaf Dr 77469
Blue Pearl Dr 77407
Blue Ridge Dr 77469
Blue Topaz Dr 77406
Bluefield Ln 77407
Bluestem Cv 77469
Bluff Hollow Ln 77469
Bobwhite Dr 77406
Boerne Ct 77407
Boerne Creek Dr 77407
Bois D Arc Ln 77406
Bonbrook Bend Ln 77469
Bonham Cir 77469
Bonham Oaks Ct 77407
Bonner Landing Ln 77469
Bonnyton Dr 77407
Booth Rd 77469
Boothline Rd 77469
Borax Bend Ct 77407
Bordens Blf 77406
Bosque Hills Ct 77469
Bossut Dr 77407
Boxwood Ridge Ln 77407
Brackstone Ct 77407
Brady Creek Ln 77406
Braeberry Ct 77407
Braecove Cir 77407
Bragg Ct 77469
Branch Ave 77469
Branchgrove Ln 77407
Branching Oak Ct 77407
Brandon Chase Ln 77407
Brandt Rd 77406
Branford Park Ln 77407
Brazos St 77469
Brazos Crossing Dr 77406
Brazos Gardens Dr 77469
Brazos Gate Dr 77469
Brazos Glen Ln 77469
Brazos Lakes Dr 77469
Brazos Meadow Ln 77469
Brazos Traces Ct & Dr 77469
Brazos Wood Dr 77469
Brazoswood Pl 77406
Breezy Shore Ln 77407
Brett Fork Dr 77406
Briar Ln 77469
Briar Green Ct 77406
Briar Trace Ln 77469
Briarmead Dr 77406
Bridal Wreath Dr 77406
Bridge Manor Ln 77407
N & S Bridlewood Ct & Dr 77469
Bright Lake Bend Ct & Ln 77407
Bright Night Dr 77407
Brighton Brook Ln 77407
Brighton Gardens Dr 77406
Brighton Glen Ln 77407
Brighton Knolls Ln 77407
Brightwood Park Ln 77407
Briscoe Rd 77406
Bristlecone Ln 77469
Bristol Bluff Ln 77407
Briza Del Mar Ct 77406
Broad Knoll Ln 77407
Broad Oaks Dr 77406
Broad Run Ln 77407
Broad Springs Ct 77407
Broken Elm Dr 77406
Bronte Springs Ct 77407
Brookwood Holw 77407
Brown School Ct 77406
Browning Trace Ln 77407
Brunson Falls Dr 77407
Bryan Rd 77469
Brynmawr Dr 77406
Buchanan Dr 77469
Buckeye Pass 77407
Buffalo Clover Cir 77406
Buffalo Creek Dr 77406
Buffalo Lake Ct 77406
Bur Oak Ct 77469
Burnet St 77469
Burning Oak Ln 77407
Butler Lakes Ct 77469
Butterfly Ln 77469
Butterstone Ridge Ln 77407
Button Bush Dr 77469
Cactus Garden Cir 77406
Cactus Lake Ln 77407
Caddo Heights St 77407
Caddo Park Ct 77406
Caden Mills Ln 77407
Cadence Ct 77469
Caleta Cir 77406
Calhoun St
100-399 77406
600-1399 77469
Calico Point Ct 77407
Calle Escondido 77469
Calvin Rd 77469
Camden Fields Ln 77407
Camden Oaks Ln 77407
Camelia Evergreen Ln 77407
Camerons Camp Dr 77406
Campaign Cir 77406
Campione Ct 77406
Canal Rd
12200-22098 77407
22100-22299 77406
22500-23699 77406
Canary Point Dr 77406
Candle Point Ln 77407
Candlecreek Dr 77469
Cane Lake Dr 77406
Canella Ct 77406
Caney Creek Ct 77406
Cannon Farm Hills Ln 77406
Cannon Hills Ln 77407
Cannon Ridge Dr 77406
Cannonbury Ln 77406
Cannons Hall Ct 77406
Cantiano Ct 77406
Canton Frst 77407
Canyon Bloom Ln 77407
Canyon Chase Dr 77469
Canyon Crossing Ct, Dr & Ln 77406
Canyon Estates Ln 77469
Canyon Ferry Ln 77407
Canyon Fields Dr 77406
Canyon Pointe Ln 77469
Canyon Sands Ln 77406
Canyon Tree Ct 77406
Canyonwood Park Ct & Ln 77469
Cape Clover Trl 77407
Capeview Cove Ln 77407
Caprile Ct 77406
Cardinal Dr 77469
Cardinal Flower Dr 77469
Cardinal Trail Ct 77469
Carino Strada Dr 77406
Carisio Ct 77406
Carlisle Terrace Ct 77406
Carlton Oaks St 77406
Carmel Grove Ln 77407
Carmen Ln 77469
Carmoyle 77407
Carnation Grove Ln 77469
Carnstonhill Ct 77407
Carolina Way 77406
Carolina Cove Dr 77469
Caroline Dr 77469
Carolyn Ln 77406
Carolyndale Dr 77407
Carriage Ct & Dr 77406
Carriage House Dr 77406
Carriagewood Ct 77469
Carrington Woods Ln 77407
Carroll Rd 77469
Carroll Place Ln 77407
Carta Valley Ln 77469
Carters Lake Dr 77406
Cartwright Ct 77469
Carved Stone Ln 77407
Carver Ave 77469
Cascade Cross Ln 77407
Cascade Oaks Ln 77406
Cascadera Ct 77406
Casey Creek Ct 77407
Cassini Ct 77407
Castle Cliff Ln 77407
Castle Hawk Trl 77407
Castlebury Ln 77407
Catalina Breeze Ct 77406
Catalina Grove Ln 77407
Catalpa Dr 77469
Catapla Ct 77406
Cattail Xing 77407
Cattle Ranch Dr 77469
Cattleman Cv 77469
Cavalier Ln 77469
Cavallo Pass 77406
Cedar Crk 77406
Cedar Dr 77469
Cedar Lk 77406
Cedar Path 77407
Cedar Cove Ct 77407
Cedar Hawk Ln 77469
Celano Dr 77406
Center St 77469
Cerro Puente Way 77406
Certosa Dr 77406
Chaco Hill Ln 77407
Chadbourne Trace Ct & Ln 77407
Chalmers Close Ct 77407
Chambering Ct 77407
Champion Creek Ln 77407
Chapel Bay Rd 77469
Chapel Meadow Ln 77407
Chapelwood Ln 77406
Chapman Falls Dr 77406
Chasegrove Ln 77407
Chaste Ct 77469
Chateau Pl 77469
Chatham Lake Ln 77407
Chathan Glen Ln 77407
Cheridan Cir 77406
Cherry Hill Ct 77469
Cherry Ridge Rd 77469
Chesley Cir 77406
Chessgate Falls Ln 77469
Chestnut Ln 77469
Chestnut Trl 77407
Chevall Ct 77469
Childersburg Ct 77407
Chimney Wood Ct 77406
Chinaberry Sky Ln 77407
Christen Canyon Ln 77406
Christine Crossing Dr 77407
Churchills Fry 77406
Cielo Ct 77406
Cimmaron Oak Ln 77406
Claire Brook Dr 77407
Clara Lake Ct 77406
Clarendon Bend Ln 77407
Clark St 77469
Clay St 77469
Clayhead Rd 77406
Clayhorn Ct 77407
Claythorne Ct 77407
Clear Point Ct 77406
Clearwater Ranch Ln 77407
Cleeves Dr 77407
Cleistes Ln 77469
Clodine Rd 77407
Cloud Croft Ln 77469
Cloudbluff Ln 77469
Clovenstone Path 77407
Clover Leaf Ct & Dr 77469
Clover Walk Ln 77469
Clustering Oak Ct 77407
Cobble Meadow Ln 77469
Cobble Tree Ct 77407
Cobblestone Ct 77406
Cochise Dr 77469
Colby Run Ct 77407
Coldale Glen Ln 77407
Coldstone Ct 77469
Coldstone Creek Ct 77407
Coleridge Ct 77469
Coleridge Ln 77407
Coleto Creek Ct 77406
Colinton Dr 77407
Collins Rd & St 77469
Collins Rose Ct 77469
Colonel Dr 77469
Colonel Court Dr 77406
Colonial Heights Dr 77406
Colonial Rose Ln 77407
Colony Ct 77406
Colony West Dr 77406
Columbia Ct 77406
Comeaux Ln 77469
Compass Rose Dr 77407
Conchola Ln 77469
Concord St 77469
Concordia Park Ln 77407
Cone Flower Dr 77469
Confederate Ct 77406
Conner Cv 77407
Contour Ct 77407
Convento Dr 77406
Cook Landing Dr 77407
Cooks Walk Ct 77406
Cooling Breeze Dr 77406
Copper Ct 77406
Copper Cave Ln 77407
Copper Point Ln 77407
Copper Stream Ln 77406
Copperfield Ct 77406
Copperwood Ct & Ln 77406
Coral Berry Ct 77469
Coral Petal Ln 77469
Corbit Grove Ct 77407
Corbridge Dr 77469
Cordell Landing Dr 77407
Coreybend Ct 77407
Cortez Rd 77469
Cottage Ct 77406
Cottage Creek Ln 77469
Cottage Heath Ln 77407
Cotton Cir 77469
Cotton Ct 77406
Cotton Dr 77469
Cotton Gin Ct 77469
Cotton Lake Ct 77407
Cotton Mill Ct 77469
Country Ln 77469
Country Ln N 77406
Country Club Dr 77469
Country Creek Way 77406
Country Mile Ct & Ln 77406
Country Place Dr 77406
Country Ridge Dr 77469
Country Squire Dr 77406
Countryshire Ln 77406
County Seat Ln 77469
Courtney Dr 77469
Cove Royale Ln 77407
Cowboy Way 77406
Coyote Hills Ln 77469
Cozy Hollow Ln 77469
Cozy Trail Ct 77469
Crabb River Rd 77469
Crainfeld Dr 77407
Cranbrook Retreat Ln 77407
Cranbrook Square Ct 77407
Cranstonhill Ct 77407
Crawford Cir 77406
Creek Colony Dr 77406
Creeks End Blvd & Ct 77407
Creeks Gate Ct 77407
Creekside Dr 77406
Creektrail Ln 77406
Cremona Ct 77406
Crescent Knolls Dr 77406
Crescent Lake Ct 77469
Crescent Spur Dr 77406
Crescent Village Ln 77407
Crestglen Ct 77407
Cresting Knolls Cir 77407
Cresting Ridge Dr 77406
Cresting Sun Dr 77406
Crestline Bay Ln 77406
Creston Meadow Dr 77406
Crestview Cv 77469
Crestwind Ln 77407
Crestwood Dr 77469
Cristelia Cir 77406
Crockett Ridge Dr 77406
Crossbridge Ln 77469
Crown Jewel Dr 77469
Crown Oak Ct 77469
Crownstone Dr 77469
Crystal Blue Ln 77407
Crystal Bluff Ct 77407
Crystal Cascade Ln 77406
Crystal Cove Ln 77406
Crystal Lake Ct 77406
Crystal Oaks Ct & Dr 77406
Crystal Water Ct & Dr 77406
Cub Ln 77469
Culloden Ct 77407
Culpepper Dr 77469
Cypress Dr 77469
Cypress Creek Ln 77469
Cypress Green Ln 77406
Dademount Ct 77407
Dahlia Brook Way 77469
Damon St 77469
Daniels Ln 77469
Darby Park Ln 77407
Dawn Ln 77406
Dawn Bloom Ln 77469
Dawnglen Ct 77469
Dawson Springs Dr 77406
Daylilly Ct 77469
De Palma Ln 77406
Deaf Smith Dr 77469
Debbie St 77469
Decker Park Ct 77406
Decros Pt 77406
Deep Green Dr 77469
Deep River Dr 77469
Deer Rd 77469
Deerfield Ct & Rd 77406
Deerwood Dr 77406
Del Web Blvd 77469
Dellrose Crossing Dr 77406
Delta Lake Dr 77406
Den Oak Dr 77406
Denfield Ct 77469
Dermott Ridge Dr 77406
Descartes Dr 77407
Desert Bluff Ln 77407
Desert Calico Ln 77406
Desert Oaks Ct 77407
Desoto Dr 77406
Devivo Ct 77407
Dewberry Ln 77406
Dewey Lake Dr 77406
Diamond Vase Ct 77469
Dog Leg Ct 77469
Dogwood Trl 77406
Dogwood Creek Ct 77407
Dolan Bluff Ln 77469
Dolci Ln 77406
Domina St 77406
Douglas St 77469
Douglas Spur Ct & Dr 77406
Dove Hollow Ct 77407
Dove Pass Ct 77407
Dovecoft Ln 77469
Dover Ln 77406
Dover Mist Ct 77469
Dovetail Ln 77407
Dowling Dr 77469
Dracena Ct 77406
Dragonfly Dr 77469
Drewfalls Ct & Dr 77407
Driftstone Ct 77469
Drs Dr 77406
Drumlin Field Way 77407
Dudley St 77469
Duncan Ranch Ln 77407
Dunlap Field Ln 77407
Durango Lodge Ln 77407
Durango Ridge Ct 77469
Durham Run Ln 77407
Dusty Canyon Ln 77407
Dusty Patty Ct 77407
Dutch John Cir 77469
Eagle Mountain Ct 77406
Easterleaf Ct 77407
Eastland Lake Dr 77406
Easton Ramsey Way 77406
Eastwood Lake Ln 77407
Eddie Kirk Ct 77469
Eden Crest Ct 77407
Eden Crossing Ln 77407
Eden Park Ct 77406
Eden Praire Dr 77407
Eden Trails Ln 77406
Edge Brook Ct 77406
Edge Manor Ln 77407
Edge Rose Ct 77406
Edgewood Dr 77406
Elderberry Arbor 77407
Eldergrove Ln 77407
Elderhedge Rd 77407
Elderwood Terrace Dr 77406
Elim Ct 77469
Elizabeth Brook Dr 77406
Ellison Ridge Dr 77406
Elm St 77469
Elmcreek Ct 77469
Emerald Cliff Ln 77407
Emerald Loch Ln 77469
Emerald Mountain Dr 77407
Emerald Run Ln 77469
Emerybrook Ct 77407
Emily Morgan Cir 77406
Emmott Dr 77406
Emory Mill Rd 77407
Empress Ln 77406
Enchanted Path Ct 77406
Enclave Hill Ln 77469
Enclave Mist Ln 77469
Endel Way 77407
Erin Hollow Ct 77407
Escambia Way Dr 77406
Esperanza 77406
Esperia St 77406
Esslemont Ct 77407
Estes Ct 77406
Eton Ridge Ct 77407
Euclid Loop 77469
Eugene Heimann Cir 77469
Evening Place Ln 77469
Evening Run Ln 77407
Evening Sun Ct 77469
Evergreen Ct 77469
Everhart Trace Dr 77407
Fair Oaks Dr 77469
Fair Oaks Ln 77406
Fairchild Blvd & Rd 77469
Fairdale Ct 77406
Fairport Harbor Ln 77407
Fairway Dr 77469
Fairwood Springs Ln 77406
Falcon Creek Ct 77406
Falling Dawn Dr 77406
Falling Forest Ct 77406
Falling Trace Ln 77469
Fannin St 77469
Farfalla Ln 77406
Farmer Rd 77406
Farmers Ln 77469
Farmers Creek Ct & Dr 77406
Farrier Dr 77406
Farris Retreat Ct 77407
Fasig Tipton Ln 77407
Fawn Meadow Ln 77406
Fawn Way Ct 77406
Feather Grass Way 77469
Featherfield Ln 77407
Fechser Ln 77407
Felton Mills Ct 77406
Fermill Ct 77407
Fern River Ct 77469
Ferndale Ln 77406
Ferndale Lake Ct 77406
Fernglade Dr 77406
Ferry St 77469
Field Cottage Ln 77407
Fieldcrest Ln 77469
Fielder Green Ln 77469
Fieldrose Ct 77407
Fields St 77469
Fieldstone Ter 77407
Fiesta Ln 77469
Figure Four Lake Ct & Ln 77406
First Oaks St 77406
Fisher Colony Dr 77406
Fisher Lake Ct & Dr 77406
Flagstone Pine Ln 77469
Flathead Range Ct 77407
Flax Flower Dr 77407
Fledgling Trl 77407
Fleming St 77469
Flinton Dr 77406
Floral Bluff Ct 77406
Flower Croft Ct 77407
Flower Grove Ct 77407
Flowering Oak Ct 77407
Fm 1093 Rd
19000-19598 77407
19600-21799 77407
23000-27099 77406
Fm 1464 Rd 77407
Fm 1640 Rd
1700-5500 77469
5502-5598 77469
5560-5560 77406
Fm 2218 Rd 77469
Fm 2759 Rd 77469
Fm 2977 Rd 77469
Fm 359 Rd 77406
Fm 361 Rd 77469
Fm 723 Rd 77406
Fm 762 Rd 77469
Foolish Pleasure Ct 77406
Forenza Ct 77406
Forest Vw 77406
Forest Cross Ln 77407
Forest Glade Dr 77469
Forest Glen Ct 77406
Forest Mill Ln 77407
Fort St 77469
Fort Caney Dr 77406
Fort Hill Ln 77469
Fort Richmond Dr 77406
Fort Sumter Ct 77469
Fossil Stone Ln 77407
Foster Dr 77469
Foster Xing 77406
Foster Brook Ln 77407
Foster Creek Dr 77406
Foster Island Dr 77406
Foster Lake Dr 77406
Foster Leaf Ct & Ln 77406
Foster League 77406
Foster Meadow Dr 77406
Fosters Bend Ln 77407
Fountain Bend Ln 77406
Four River Dr 77469
Fox Trot Cir 77406

Frazer Dr 77469
Front St 77469
Frontera Ct 77406
Frost Lake Dr 77406
Frutteto Ct 77406
Full Moon Ct 77406
Fulshear Gaston Rd 77406
Fulton Springs Ct 77406
Furleson Dr 77469
Futurity Ln 77406
Gable Bridge Ln 77407
Gable Cove Ct 77469
Gable Crossing Dr 77407
Gable Run Ct 77407
Galler Rd 77469
Gallowgate Ln 77407
Gammon St 77469
Garcitas Crk 77406
Garden Arbor Ln 77407
Garden Field Ln 77407
Garden Ridge Cyn 77407
Garden Stream Ct 77406
Garland Mist Ln 77407
Garland Path Bend Ln 77407
Garnet Lake Ct 77407
Garnet Trail Ln 77469
Garrett Green Ln 77407
Garrett Knolls Ln 77407
Gatemound Ct 77407
Gauge Hollow Ct 77407
Gem Dale Ct 77407
Gemstone Park Rd 77407
General Dr 77469
George Ave & Ln 77469
Gettysburg Dr 77469
Gibralter Pl 77407
Giffnock Dr 77407
Gilbert Hollow Dr 77469
Ginger Mint Ct 77406
Gingerstone Ct 77469
Giovanni Ln 77406
Girvan Ln 77407
Glade Hill Ln 77407
Gladys Yoakum Dr 77406
Glasgill Ct 77407
Glen Haven Ln 77406
Glendon Dr 77407
Glenn Ct 77469
Glenridge Ln 77469
Glenrothers Dr 77407
Glenwood Dr 77406
Gneiss Hollow Rd 77407
Gold Haven Dr 77407
Golden Holw 77469
Golden Brandy Ln 77469
Golden Canyon Ln 77407
Golden Creek Ct & Ln 77469
Golden Grain Dr 77469
Golden Heath Ln 77407
Golden Sky Ln 77469
Golfview Dr 77469
Goliad Ave 77469
Goloby Dr 77407
Gonyo Ln 77469
Goodmanville Ct 77407
Gordes Ct 77469
Gracely Park Ln 77407
Grand Blf 77406
W Grand Pkwy S
5200-8198 77406
5701-8099 77407
Grand Bluff Grv 77407
Grand Brook Ct & Ln 77469
Grand Estates Dr 77469
Grand Fir Ct & Ln 77469
Grand Mission Blvd 77407
Grand River Dr 77406
Grand Saline Dr 77469
Grand Villa Ln 77407
Grand Vista Springs
Blvd 77407
Grand Willow Ct & Ln 77469
Grande Gables Dr 77469
Granger Lake Ct 77406
Granger Ridge Ln 77407
Granite Field Ln 77469
Granite Peach Ln 77407
Granite Springs Ln 77469
Granite Trail Ln 77407
Grant Dr 77469
Grants Hollow Ln 77407
Grapevine Trl 77407
Grapevine Lake Ct 77407
Graphite Canyon Ct 77407
Grass Lake Ln 77406
Grasset Ln 77407
Grassy Grove Ln 77407
Grayless St 77406
Green Falls Ct & Ln 77406
Green Trace Ln 77469
N Greens Blvd & Ct 77406
Greens Ferry Ct 77406
Greenwood Dr 77406
Grey Hawk Cv 77469
Grimaldi St 77406
Grove Briar Ln 77407
Grove Chase Ct 77406
Grove Sky Ct 77407
Guldan Dr 77469
Haley Holw 77407
Half Moon Ct 77406
Hamden Valley Dr 77406
Hand Rd 77469
Hankar Way 77407
Hanover Glen Ln 77407
Hanover Springs Ln 77406
Hanoverian Dr 77406
Hard Rock Ln 77469
Harlem Rd
100-1099 77406
7101-9297 77407
9299-10599 77406
11100-257599 77406
Harmony Lake Ln 77469
Harpers Dr 77469
Harvest Hollow Ct 77407
Harvest Mill Ln 77407
Harvest Thistle Dr 77406
S Haven Dr 77469
Haven Bend Ln 77407
Haven Brook Ln 77406
Haven Forest Ln 77469
Haven Springs Ln 77469
Havens Glade Ct 77406
Hawkins Ridge Ln 77469
Hawkley Dr 77406
Hawkspur Cir 77407
Hawkspur Ridge St 77406
Hawthorn Dr 77469
Hayden Falls Dr 77406
Hayward Hill Dr 77469
Hazel Woods Ct 77469
N & S Hearthside Ct &
Dr 77406
Heartland Grove Dr 77406
Heath Grove Ln 77407
Heath Ridge Ln 77469
Heather Springs Ln 77407
Heatherton Hill Dr 77469
Hebron Ln 77406
Hedgepark Dr 77469
Hein Rd 77469
Hellen Rd 77469
Hennessey Rd 77406
Henrico Ln 77469
Herbie Dr 77469
Heritage Ln S 77406
Heritage Haven Ct 77469
Herman Dr 77406
Heron Shadow Ct 77407
Herons Terrace St 77406
Hickory Harvest Dr 77407
Hickory Hollow St 77406
Hidalgo Dr 77469
W Hidden Lake Ln 77406
Hidden Park Ct 77469
Hidden Point Ln 77407
High Ridge Ln 77469
Highland Oak Ct 77407
E Highway 90a 77406
W Highway 90a 77469
Hill Forest Ct 77406
Hillcrest Dr 77469
Hillhaven Ct 77469
Hinkles Fry 77406
Hinkley Glen Ct 77407
Hinson St 77406
Hobson Dr 77406
Hollow Bluff Ln 77407
Hollow Cove Ln 77469
Hollow Hill Ln 77407
Holloway Square Ln 77407
Holly Cir 77469
Holly Hall Dr 77406
Holly Tree Ct 77469
Holly Valley Ln 77406
Holmes Rd 77406
Honey Garden Ct 77469
Honeysuckle Grove Ln 77469
Honeysuckle Vine Dr 77469
Hope Canyon Ln 77469
Hopewell Ct 77406
Hopson Meadow Ln 77406
Hopson Meadows Dr 77406
Horseshoe Ln 77406
Houston St 77469
Houstonian Dr 77407
Hughes Rd 77406
Huisache Dr 77469
Hunterwood Cir 77406
Huntington Ln 77406
Huttons Court Ln 77406
Hyde Cove Ct 77407
Idle Wind Ct & Dr 77406
Idlewood Glen Ct 77406
Imogene Ave 77406
Indigo Field Ln 77407
Indigo Trails Dr 77469
Inland Oaks Dr 77407
Insurance Rd 77469
Inwood Dr 77469
Irby Cobb Blvd 77469
Iris Glen Ln 77407
Iris Rose Ct 77469
Ironwood Ct 77469
Ironwood Dr 77406
Ironwood Ln 77469
Ironwood Forest Dr 77469
Irvin St 77469
Ivy Bush Bend Ln 77407
J Meyer Rd 77469
Jackson St 77469
Jackson Lake Dr 77406
Jacob Crossing Dr 77406
Jacobs Well Ct & Dr 77407
Jade Park Dr 77407
James Long Ct 77406
Janda Rd 77469
Jane Long St 77469
Jane Long League Dr 77406
Jasmine Ct 77469
Jay Thrush Dr 77469
Jeb Stuart Dr 77469
Jeff Davis Dr 77469
Jefferson Ave 77469
Jenny Ln 77469
Jerry Rd & St 77469
Jester Rd 77406
Jewel Ashford Rd 77407
Jewel Brook Ln 77407
Jonathans Lndg 77406
Jones Dr 77406
Jones River Loop &
Rd 77469
Joni Way 77407
Jordans Landing Ln 77407
Jubal Dr 77469
Julia Manor Dr 77406
Juniper Hls 77406
Juniper Berry Dr 77407
Juniper Chase Trl 77407
Juniper Wood Ln 77469
Kainer Springs Ln 77407
Kalissa Ct 77469
N & S Karaugh Dr 77406
Kari Ln 77469
Kaylan Ct 77407
Kearney Dr 77469
Kelistow Dr 77407
Kelly Ln 77469
Kelsey Ln 77406
Kelton Hills Ln 77406
Ken Dr 77406
Kendall Lake Ct & Dr 77407
Kenova Canyon Ct 77407
Kenton Crossing Cir &
Ln 77407
Keplers Ln 77469
Keppie Way 77407
Kern Canyon Ln 77469
Kerry Prairie Ln 77407
Keystone Falls Ct 77407
Kildonan Ct 77407
Kilgarth Dr 77407
Killdeer Ln 77469
Kimisu Ln 77469
Kincaid Falls Ct 77406
King Dr 77469
Kings Forest Ln 77469
Kingsford Trail Ln 77407
Kingsmen Pt 77469
Kingsmill Ln 77469
Kirby Lake Ct 77406
Kirkcaldy Ct 77407
Kirker Ln 77407
Kirkton Moor Dr 77407
E & W Kitty Hawk St 77406
Kneitz Rd 77469
Knight Lake Ct 77406
Knightwood Ct 77469
Knoll Oak Ln 77469
Knollblossom Ln 77469
Knox Estate Dr 77406
Koeblen Rd 77469
Kosler Lane Cir 77406
Kovar Rd 77469
Kurz Point Dr 77406
Kyle Trail Ct 77407
La Hacienda Dr 77406
La Rama 77469
La Salle Ln 77406
Lady Laura Ln 77469
Lago Mirado Way 77406
Lago Verde Dr 77406
Laguna Dr 77406
Laguna Trace Ct & St 77407
Lake Arrowhead Dr 77406
Lake Athens Ct 77406
Lake Ballinger Ln 77406
Lake Bardwell Ct 77406
Lake Brazos Ln 77406
Lake Buchanan Ct 77406
Lake Catherine Ct 77407
Lake Charlotte Ct &
Ln 77406
Lake Commons Dr 77469
Lake Crockett Cir 77406
Lake Dale Ct & Ln 77406
Lake Daniel Ct 77407
Lake Edinburg Ct &
Ln 77406
E Lake Gables Dr 77406
Lake Georgetown Ct 77407
Lake Gladewater Ct 77407
Lake Halbert Ln 77406
Lake Hawkins Ln 77406
Lake Holbrook Ln 77406
Lake Kemp Ct 77406
Lake Lavon Ct 77406
Lake Palestine Ln 77406
Lake Pauline Ct 77406
Lake Pinkston Dr 77406
Lake Point Cir 77469
Lake Quitman Dr 77406
Lake Ridge Dr 77469
Lake Rim Dr 77469
Lake Run Ln 77407
Lake Springs Ct 77406
Lake Wichita Ln 77407
E & W Lakebridge Ln 77407
N & S Lakefair Ct &
Dr 77406
Lakegreen Ct 77407
Lakemont Bend Ln 77407
Lakes Of Mission Grove
Blvd 77406
Lakesage Ln 77407
Lakeshore Point Ln 77469
Lakeshore Vista Dr 77469
Lakeview Meadow Dr 77469
Lakewind Park Ct &
Ln 77407
Lamar Dr 77469
Land Grant Ct & Dr 77406
Landmark Dr 77406
Landscape Way 77406
Lansdowne Dr 77406
Lantana Reach Dr 77406
Lantern Hll Ln 77469
Larch Leaf Ln 77469
Larchmont Ct 77469
Lark Ln 77469
Lark Orchard Way 77407
Larkfield Dr 77469
Larkspur Ln 77469
Larkspur Lndg 77407
Las Botas 77469
Lassiter Hollow Ln 77407
Laurabee Dr 77469
W Laurel Oaks Dr 77469
Lavaca Ln 77406
Lavaerton Wood Ln 77407
Lawson Lake Ln 77407
Laywood Ct 77406
Lazarro Ln 77406
Lea Ln 77406
League Trce 77406
Leaning Oak Trl 77406
Lee Dr 77469
Leecast Ct 77407
Leesway Rd 77406
Legacy Ct 77406
Legendre Rd 77407
Legion Dr 77469
Legion Way Ct 77406
Leirop Dr 77407
Leisure Ln 77406
Lemon Blossom Cir 77407
Leonard Ave 77469
Leonessa Dr 77406
Leroy Rd 77469
Lettie St 77469
Lewis Creek Ct & Dr 77406
Lewisville Dr 77406
Leydenwood Ct 77407
Lian Falls Ln 77407
Liberty St 77469
Libra St 77469
Lilac Manor Ln 77469
Lilac Meadows Ln 77407
Lily Pad Ln 77407
Lincoln Heights Ct &
Ln 77407
Lindemann Cir 77406
Linden Ln 77406
Linden Brook Ln 77469
Linden Meadow Ln 77407
Linden Oaks Ln 77407
Linden Spruce Ln 77407
Linwood Terrace Dr 77407
Lismer Rd 77407
Little Farms Ct 77406
Little Haven Ct 77469
Little Lake Ct 77406
Little River Ct 77406
Little Summer Dr 77469
Little Walnut Dr 77469
Lively Ct 77406
Lochpoint Ct 77407
Lochranza Ln 77407
Lockharton Ct 77407
Lockridge Hill Ln 77469
Lockspur Ct & Dr 77406
Lockwood Byp & Rd 77469
Lodge Ln 77406
Lodgegate Ct 77407
Logan Star Ct 77407
Logstone Dr 77407
Lola Ln 77406
Lombardia Ct 77406
Lone Pine Ct 77469
Lone Star Junction St 77406
Lone Stirrup Dr 77406
Lonely Star Ln 77406
Long Dr 77469
Long Canyon Ln 77469
Long Cross Dr 77406
Long Drive Ct 77469
Long Grove Ln 77469
Long Meadow Farms
Pkwy 77406
Longheath Ct 77407
Longleaf Dr 77469
Longpath Ct 77406
Longvale Dr 77469
Longvale Glen Ct 77469
Los Alamos Ct 77406
Lost Field Ln 77469
Lost Goldenrod Dr 77406
Lost Timber Ln 77469
Lotus Canyon Ct 77407
Lou Edwards Rd 77469
Lubojacky Rd 77469
Lucketts Ln 77406
Luminaire Ln 77407
Lunar Lake Dr 77407
Luray Ct 77469
Lydia St 77469
Mabel St 77469
Mable Pond Ln 77407
Macek Rd 77469
Machall Manor Ct 77406
Madden Rd 77407
Madera Canyon Ct &
Ln 77469
Magellan Manor Dr 77407
Maggie Mist Dr 77406
Magnolia Cir 77407
Magnolia Lk 77406
Magnolia Ln 77469
Magnolia Hollow Ln 77407
Magnolia Sky Dr 77407
Mahogany Trace Ln 77407
Maiden Ln 77469
Main St 77469
Majestic Falls Ln 77469
Majestic Oak 77469
Majestic Vista Ln 77407
Majesty Ln 77469
Malaxis Ln 77469
Mallard Cove Ct 77407
Mallets Bay Ct 77407
Mammoth Springs Ln 77469
Man O War Ct 77406
Manchester Point Ln 77407
Manor Ct & Dr 77406
Manor Lake Ct 77406
Manor Stone Ln 77469
Manor Terrace Ln 77469
Mansfield Bay Ln 77407
Maple Dale Ln 77406
Maravilla Ln 77406
Marble Ravine Dr 77407
Marble Stone Ln 77469
Mardell Crescent Ln 77407
Marie Ln 77406
Mariner Square Ct 77407
Mariposa Edge Ln 77469
Marisa Ln 77406
Market St 77469
Markum Ct 77406
Marsh Creek Ct 77406
Marshall Island St 77469
Marshaven Way 77407
Martin Lake Ct & Dr 77406
Mason Rd 77406
S Mason Rd
7100-9799 77407
9800-9900 77406
9902-9998 77406
Mason Creek Ct 77407
Masonwood Ln 77469
Matthew Glen Ln 77469
Mattwood Dr 77406
Maverick Run Ct 77469
Maybrook Ct 77469
Maybrook Manor Ln 77407
Mayfield Meadow Ln 77407
Mayport Crest Ln 77407
Mayweather Ct & Ln 77406
Mccrary Rd 77406
Mcgee Lake Ct 77407
Mckinnon Rd 77406
W Meadow Ct 77407
Meadow Ln 77469
Meadow Ash Ct 77407
Meadow Forest Dr 77406
Meadow Light Dr 77407
Meadow Way Cir 77406
Meadowbend Cir, Dr &
Ln 77469
Meadowcreek Trl 77407
Meadowlark Ln 77469
Medolla Cir 77406
Medwin Gardens Ave 77407
Mellon St 77469
Melmore Dr 77407
Melody Ln 77406
Menaggio Ct 77406
Menlo Creek Ct 77407
Mercant Mark Ln 77407
Mercy Moss Ln 77406
Mesquite Hill Ln 77469
Mesquite Manor Ln 77407
Mesquite Stone Ln 77407
Messina Ln 77469
Metaphor Way 77406
Mettler Ct & Ln 77469
Middlecrest Ln 77469
Middlegate Ln 77407
Midnight Dawn Dr 77407
Midnight Sky Ct 77407
Midnight Sun Ln 77407
Mier Manor Ct 77406
Milano Ct 77406
Milazzo Dr 77406
Millers Creek Ct 77406
Millers Falls Ct 77406
Millford Hill Ct 77469
Mills Point Ln 77469
Millstead Ct 77469
Millwood Pass Cir 77407
Milrig Ct 77407
Mimosa Cir & Ln 77406
Mineral Falls Ln 77407
Miners Bend Ct & Ln 77469
Mirabella Way 77406
Miraglen Ct 77406
Mirandola Ln 77406
Mirtillo Ct 77406
Mission Bluff Ln 77407
Mission Cove Ln 77407
Mission Fort Ln 77407
Mission Lake Ct 77407
Mission Manor Ln 77407
Mission Olive Cv 77469
Mission Park Dr 77407
Mission Pines Ct & Ln 77407
Mistflower Dr 77469
Mistletoe Cir 77469
Misty Falls Ct & Ln 77406
Misty Lodge Ct 77407
Misty Meadow Ct 77469
Misty Morning Trce 77407
Misty Prairie Ln 77407
Misty River Ln 77406
Mistycreek Dr 77406
Mistyvale Ct 77406
Mitre Peak Ln 77469
Mockingbird Ln 77469
Mohave Ln 77469
Molho Forest Ct 77407
Monarch Falls Ln 77469
Montclair Peak Ln 77469
Monte Rosa Ct 77406
Monterry Oaks Dr 77469
Montgomery Rd 77406
Moreland Ln 77469
Morning Dusk Dr 77407
Morning Glory Trce 77407
Morning News Ln 77407
Morton St 77469

Morton League Ct & Rd 77406
Moss Crk 77406
Moss Bark Trl 77407
Moss Lake Ct 77406
Mossy Creek Ln 77407
Mossy Glen Ct 77406
Mossy Point Ct 77469
Mound Lake Dr 77406
Mountain Mist Ct 77407
Mourning Dove Dr 77469
Mowbray Ct 77407
Mulberry Cir & Dr 77469
Mulberry Farm Ln 77469
Mulligan Ct 77469
Musket Ridge Dr 77406
Muskogee Ln 77469
Mustang Dr 77469
Mustang Lake Ct 77406
Mustang Pointe Ln 77407
Myrtle Flower Ct 77469
Mysterium Ln 77469
Mystic Springs Ln 77407
Naburn Gate 77407
Nandina Knl 77407
Naple Hollow Ln 77469
Natchez Dr 77469
Natchez Crossing St 77406
Nature Ct 77406
Nautical Ln 77469
Neals Rose Ln 77407
Nectarine Ln 77469
Nelders Cv 77469
Nelson Ln 77469
Netherby Ln 77407
Nettle Springs Ct 77469
Newell Dr 77469
Newfalls Ct 77407
Newlin Dr 77406
Newstone Dr 77406
Newton Dr 77469
Nicecrest Dr 77407
Nitshill Ln 77407
Nobel Ct 77469
Noble Ranch Ct 77407
Nogales Bend Dr 77469
Norfolk Ridge Way 77407
Northchase Ln 77469
Northfork Hollow Ln 77407
Norwich Gulch Ln 77407
Norwood Point Ct & Ln 77407
Oak Ln 77406
Oak Canyon Ln 77469
Oak Cottage Ct 77407
Oak Creek Dr 77469
Oak Knoll Dr 77406
Oak Prairie Ct 77407
Oak Run Dr 77407
Oakbranch Manor Ln 77407
Oakbriar Ln 77469
Oakfield Xing 77407
Oakland Mills Dr 77407
Oakleaf Trail Ct & Ln 77407
Oakley Hill Ct 77406
Oakloch Ct 77407
Oakmoss Hill Ct 77407
Oakridge Canyon Ln 77407
W Oaks Village Dr 77407
Oakstone Park Dr 77406
Oakwind Ct 77407
Obsidian Arrowhead Rd 77407
Old Barn Dr 77407
Old Colony Ct & Dr 77406
Old Dixie Dr 77406
Old Needville Fairchild Rd 77469
Old Oak Dr 77406
Old Pecan Dr 77406
Old Prairie Ct 77406
Old River Ln 77406
Old South Dr 77406
Old Windmill Dr 77407
Oleander Way 77469
Oleaster Springs Ln 77469
Olivara Ln 77406
Olive Field Ct 77469
Olive Mill Ct 77406
Onia Ln 77469
Opal Chase Dr 77469
Opul Trails Ct 77407
Orallind Ln 77406
Orange Tree Ln 77469
Orchard Club Dr 77407
Orchard Glen Dr 77407
Orchard Green Dr 77407
Orchard Grove Ln 77407
Orchard Harvest Dr 77407
Orchard Links Dr 77407
Orchard Mill Dr 77407
Orchard Mist Ln 77407
Orchard Shadows Dr 77407
Orchard Sky Dr 77407
Orchard Stables Dr 77407
Oriole Creek Ln 77406
Outback Dr 77469
Ovada Ln 77406
Overland Trail Dr 77406
Owens Rd 77407
Oxford Ct 77469
Oxford Chase Trl 77407
Pacific Spring Ln 77407
Paddle Rock Ln 77469
Pagemill Ln 77406
Palace Way Ct 77407
Palaramo Ct 77407
Palisade Rock Ct 77407
Palm Park Ln 77469
Palmanova Dr 77406
Palmdale Estate Dr 77406
Palmer Pl 77406
Palmetto Bnd 77406
Palmetto Glen Ln 77469
Palmito Ranch Dr 77406
Paloma Ave 77469
Pamunky Ln 77469
Panola Place Ct 77469
Paper Birch Dr 77469
Par Ln 77469
Parabello Ct 77406
Paradise Park Bnd 77407
N Park Dr 77407
Park Place Blvd 77469
Parker Bend Ln 77407
Parkman Grove Dr 77406
Parksun Ct 77407
Parkwater Bridge Ln 77407
Parkway Lake Ct 77407
Parkway Lakes Ln 77407
Parrot Shell Ln 77406
Parsley Mist Ln 77469
Paseo Companario Dr 77406
Paseo Royale Blvd 77406
Payne Ln 77469
Peach Pt 77406
Peach Orchard Ln 77407
Peach Stone Ct 77407
Pear Point Ln 77469
Pearce Lake Ct 77407
Pearl Landing Dr 77407
Pearl Terrace Ln 77469
Pearlstone Ct 77406
Pebble Holw 77407
Pebble Banks Ct 77406
Pebble Grove Ct 77407
Pebble Place Ct 77407
Pecan Ave 77469
Pecan Bend Dr 77406
Pecan Chase Dr 77406
Pecan Cove Ct 77406
Pecan Creek Rd 77406
Pecan Crossing Dr 77406
Pecan Forest Ct 77406
Pecan Lake Cir, Ct & Dr 77406
Pecan Park Dr 77406
Pecan Shadows Dr 77407
S Pecan Trail Dr 77406
Pecan Way Ct 77406
Pecos Pass Dr 77406
Pecos Rose Ln 77407
Pecos Valley Dr 77469
S Peek Rd 77469
Pelham Grove Ln 77407
Pelican Lake Dr 77406
Pemberton Way 77469
Pembrooke Dr & Way 77406
Pemetic Trl 77407
Penn Ln 77406
Pentland Ct 77407
Peonia Ln 77406
Peppermint Hill Ln 77469
Peroni Dr 77406
Persimmon Grv 77469
Persimmon Pass 77407
Petra Ln 77469
Phantom Mist Dr 77406
Phyllis Dr 77406
Piazza Dr 77406
Picacho Ln 77469
Pickett Dr 77469
Pickett Hill Ln 77469
Pico Landing St 77407
Picollo Dr 77406
Pierce Valley Dr 77406
Pilgrim Journey Dr 77406
Pilgrimage Ct 77406
Pine Meadow Dr 77469
Pine Mills Dr 77469
Pineda Cir 77406
Pink Granite Vly 77407
Pioneer Dr 77406
Pipe Creek Ln 77407
Pirtle Rd 77406
Pisces St 77469
Pisklak Rd 77469
Pittman Rd 77469
Pitts Rd 77406
Pladdawa Ln 77407
Plantain Ln 77406
Plantation Dr 77406
Plantation Meadows Dr 77406
Plantation Orchard Ct & Ln 77407
Plantation Springs Dr 77406
Planters Moon Ln 77407
Planters Path Ln 77407
Pleak Rd & Xing 77469
Pleasant Oak Ct 77407
Pleasant Shade Ct 77406
Plum Gate Ct 77407
Plum Springs Ln 77469
Plummer St 77469
Poeta Ln 77406
Point Hollow Ln 77469
Pointe West Cir 77469
Polizzotto Ln 77407
Polley Ct 77407
Pomegranate Pass 77406
Pommel Ln 77407
Pond Arbor Path 77407
Ponder Chase Ct 77407
Ponderosa Dr 77469
Poolman Pl 77469
Poplar Canyon Ct 77407
Poplar Rose Ct 77469
Poppy Crest Ct 77469
Port Bishop Ln 77407
Port Branch Dr 77406
Port Gibson Ct 77469
Port Quintana Ct 77469
Port Toscana Ln 77406
Porte Toscana Ln 77406
Portland Ct & Dr 77406
Powderhorn Pt 77406
Powell St 77469
Power Line Rd 77469
Prade Ranch Ln 77469
Prado Ln 77406
Prairie Crest Dr 77406
Prairie Green Ct 77406
Prairie Lake Ct 77407
Prairie Manor Dr 77406
Prairie Sage Dr 77406
Prarie Run Ct 77406
Preakness Ct 77406
Precinct Line Rd 77406
Preston St 77469
Prestonwood Dr 77407
Primrose Ct 77406
Psencik Rd 77469
Pultar Rd 77469
Pumping Plant Rd 77406
Pureli Ct 77406
Quarry Lakes Ln 77407
Quarry Ridge Rd 77407
Quarterpath Ct & Dr 77406
Quarto Ln 77406
Quartz Cove Ct 77407
Quebec Blvd 77469
Quiet Brook Ln 77406
Quiet Run Trl 77406
Quiet Shores Dr 77407
Quill Rush Way 77407
Rabb Ridge Dr 77469
Rain Barrel Ct 77406
Rain Drop Ct 77407
Rainbow Granite Dr 77407
Rainswept Pass Dr 77469
Ralston Ranch Ct 77469
Rambling Brook Ln 77469
Rambling Stone Dr 77406
Rambling Tree Ln 77407
Rampart Point Dr 77406
Ranch House Ln 77469
Rancho Bella Pkwy 77406
Ranger Spur Way 77406
Ransom Rd 77469
Rappahanook Ln 77469
Rastello Ln 77406
Raven Ln 77469
Ravens Gate Ln 77406
Ravens Point Dr 77406
Ray Allen Rd 77469
Reading Rd 77469
Reata 77469
Rebecca Hill Ct 77406
Red Alder Way 77469
Red Ash Ct 77407
Red Gable Ln 77407
Red Lake Ct & Ln 77406
Red River Dr 77469
Redbird Ln 77406
Redbud Knoll Ct 77469
Redbud Place Ln 77406
Redcrest Manor Dr 77406
Redstaff Ct 77406
Redstone Dr 77407
Redwood Tree St 77407
Reflection View Ln 77407
Regal Pt 77469
Regalside Ct 77469
Renfro Dr 77469
Resada Park Ln 77407
Reston Point Dr 77406
Retreat Blvd 77469
Revalen Ln 77407
Rexford Cove Ct 77407
Ricefield Rd 77469
Richland Park Dr 77406
Richmond Ct & Dr 77406
Richmond Bend Ct 77406
Richmond Ferry Ct 77406
Richmond Foster Rd 77406
Richmond Place Dr 77469
Richmond Vantage Dr 77406
Richter Ln 77469
Richton Falls Dr 77406
Ridgefield Park Ln 77469
Ridgeworth Ln 77469
Riggs Mill Ln 77469
Riley Glen Dr 77406
Rimini Ct 77406
Ripford Ct 77406
Ripley Hills Dr 77406
Rippling Stream Ln 77407
Riva Ridge Dr 77406
E River Dr 77406
W River Dr 77406
River Rd 77469
River Briar Ln 77406
River Cliff Ct 77406
River Delta Ln 77469
River Fern Dr 77469
River Forest Dr 77406
River Look Ct 77406
River Park Dr 77406
Riverchase Dr 77469
Rivercove Ln 77406
Riveredge Dr 77406
Rivergate Ct 77469
Riverine Terrace Dr 77406
Riverknoll Ct 77469
Riverside Creek Dr 77406
Riverview Dr 77469
Riverway Bluff Ln 77406
Riverwood Dr 77469
Rivoli Dr 77406
Roans Prarie Ln 77469
Robertson Rd 77406
Rochelle St 77469
Rock Creek Ct 77469
Rock Fence Dr 77406
Rock Springs Dr 77469
Rockaway Point Ln 77407
Rocky Bar Ln 77469
Rocky Briar Ct 77406
Rocky Falls Pkwy & Rd 77469
Rocky Knoll Ln 77469
Rocky Peak Ln 77407
Rocky Ridge Ln 77407
Rogers Lake Ln 77407
Rohan Rd 77469
Rolling Meadow Dr 77469
Rolling Oaks Dr 77406
Rollingstone Rd 77407
Rollins Bend Ln 77407
Rosa Del Villa Ct 77406
Rosalia Ct 77406
Rose Rock Canyon Dr 77469
Rosebud Hollow Ln 77469
Rosehedge Terrace Way 77406
Rosepath Ln 77407
Rosmarino Ct 77406
Rouken Glen Ct 77407
Round Creek Ct 77407
Round Lake Dr 77469
Roundrock Park Ln 77407
Roundstone Dr 77406
Royal Cliff Ct 77407
Royal Crest Ln 77469
Royal Gate Ln 77407
Royal Lakes Blvd 77469
Royal Lakes Manor Blvd 77469
Royal Retreat 77469
Roycroft Ln 77407
Rozzano Ct 77406
Rubble Ln 77407
Ruby River Ln 77407
Ruby Rock Way 77407
Rufus St 77469
Runaway Scrape Ct 77406
Running Brook Ln 77406
Rush Hollow Ct 77407
Russeff Field Ct & Ln 77469
Rusted Root Ct 77406
Rustic Canyon Ln 77469
Rustic Chase Dr 77407
Rustic Hearth Ct 77407
Rustic Oak Ct & Ln 77469
Rustic Ridge Ct 77406
Rustic Stone Ct 77407
Rustic Trail Ln 77469
Rustling Oaks Dr 77469
Ruston Ridge Ct & Dr 77406
Rutersville College Ln 77406
Ryan Manor Dr 77406
Saber Oaks Dr 77406
Sabinal Creek Dr 77407
Sabine Ln 77406
Sabine Lake Ct 77406
Sable Glen Ct 77469
Saddle Ridge Ct 77406
Saddleback Springs Dr 77469
Saddlebag Way 77469
Sagamore Bay Ln 77469
Sage Bluff Ave 77469
Sage Cove Ln 77407
Sage Creek Ct 77406
Sagebranch Ct 77407
Sagebrush Cv 77407
Sagelaurel Ln 77407
Sagemont Square Ct 77407
Salento Ct 77406
San Jacinto Ave 77469
San Jose St 77469
San Juan St 77469
San Pellino Dr 77406
Sand Ct 77406
Sand Lake Ln 77407
Sand Stone Dr 77406
Sandal Grv 77469
Sandalisle Ln 77407
Sandermeyer Dr 77406
Sandstone Cavern Cir 77407
Sandy Point Dr 77406
Sansbury Blvd 77469
Santa Barbara Way 77406
Sapphire Lake Rd 77407
Saragosa Dr 77469
Saragosa Blue Ln 77407
Sardinia Dr 77406
Sarena Ct 77406
Saronno Dr 77406
Satillo Ln 77469
Sauki Ln 77407
Savannah Dr 77406
Savannah Glen Ln 77469
Savannah Moss Dr 77469
Saxon Hill Ln 77407
Saxonwood Ct 77469
Scarlett Falls Ln 77407
Scenic Oaks Dr 77407
Scenic Orchard Ln 77407
Scoria Rock Dr 77407
Scrub Oak Ct & Dr 77407
Seaglers Point Ln 77406
Sealy Ct 77406
Seco Mines Ln 77469
Seiler Rd 77469
Selwyn Rd 77407
Sendera Ln 77407
Sendero St 77406
Sequoia Trail Ln 77469
Serenity Oaks Dr 77406
Serrato Ln 77469
Settegast Ranch Rd 77406
Settlers Ct 77406
Seven Coves Ct 77407
Shade Crest Dr 77406
Shadow Ln 77406
Shadow Dance Ln 77407
E, N, S & W Shadow Grove Ln 77406
Shadow Hawk Dr 77407
Shadow Terrace Ln 77407
Shady Ln 77406
Shady Isle Ct 77407
Shady Lake Grv 77407
Shady Trail Ct 77406
Shadylane St 77469
Shale Grove Ct 77407
Shallow Bend Ln 77407
Shallow Shaft Ln 77407
Shamrock Ct & Ln 77406
Shane Rd 77469
Shanley Landing Ct 77407
Shanley Trace Ln 77407
Sharpsburg Dr 77469
Shawnee Park Dr 77406
Shelby Meadow Ln 77407
Shelby Oaks Cir & Dr 77407
Shelbyville Dr 77407
Sheldon Bend Dr 77406
Shenandoah Dr 77469
Shenandoah Falls Ln 77469
Shettleston Dr 77407
Shifting Sand Ln 77407
Shiloh Dr 77469
Shiloh Lake Dr 77407
Shining Mist Ln 77469
Shining Stream Ln 77406
Shire Green Ln 77407
N Shore Bnd 77469
Shore Meadows Ln 77407
Shoreside Dr 77469
Sienna Sky Ct 77407
Sierra Bend Dr 77407
Sierra Long Dr 77407
Sierra Night Ct & Dr 77407
Sighting Park Dr 77406
Silent Cedar Cir 77406
Silent Deep Dr 77469
Silent Hills Ln 77407
Silent River Ct & Dr 77406
Silent Shore Ct 77406
Silent Timber Ln 77407
Silktail Ct 77407
Silver Chase Ln 77406
Silver Creek Cir & Ct 77406
Silver Crown Ct 77406
Silver Rawls Ln 77406
Silver Ripple Dr 77469
Silverbelle Ct & Ln 77406
Silverwater Ct 77469
Simon Ct & Ln 77407
Sims Rd 77406
Skinner Ln 77406
Skinner Ridge Ln 77406
Skydale Ln 77469
Skyridge Ln 77469
Slate Ct 77407
Slate Oaks Ln 77469
Slick Rock Dr 77406
Smokey Hill Ct 77469
Snowbell Ct 77469
Snowdrop Ct 77469
Solitude Hill Ln 77407
Solomon Rd 77469
Sombra 77469
Somerset Hill Ct & Ln 77407
Somerset Place Ln 77407
Somervell Ct 77406
Sommerset Branch Ct 77407
Sorrell Hollow Ln 77469
Sorrell Oaks Cir & Ln 77407
Southern Pl 77406
Southwest Fwy 77469
Sovereign Cir 77469
Spacek Rd 77469
Spanish Forest Ln 77406
Sparrows Spur St 77406
Spellbrook Bend Ln 77407
Spreading Bough Ln 77406
Spreading Oak Ln 77406
Spring Meadows Ln 77407
Spring Orchard Ct & Ln 77407
Spring Rock Ct 77469
Spring Run Ln 77407
Spring Sunrise Dr 77407
Spruce View Ct 77407
Spur Canyon Ct 77469
Spur Ridge Ct 77406
Squirrel Rd 77469
Stables Course Ct & Dr 77407
Standing Oak Ct & Ln 77406
Starbridge Lake Ln 77407
Starling Creek Dr 77406
Stetson Heights Ln 77407
Stetson Place Ct 77406
Stevens Creek Ct & Ln 77469
Still Haven Dr 77407
Stillwater Ln 77406
Stock Creek Ln 77406
Stone Chapel Way 77406
Stone Crest Ct 77406
Stone Field Ct 77407
Stone Island Ct 77407
Stone Isle Ct 77407
Stone Leaf Dr 77407
Stone Mission Ln 77407
Stonebriar Ln 77469
Stonebridge Terrace Ct & Dr 77407

Stonegate Cir & Dr 77407
Stonegate Grove Ct 77407
Stonemont Glen Ln 77407
Stoneport Ct 77406
Stoneroses Trl 77407
Stonetrail Rd 77407
Stoneview Dr 77407
Stonewall Dr 77469
Stonewall Ridge Dr 77469
Stormy Orchard Ct 77407
Strange Dr 77406
Streamwood Ln 77469
Strolling Stream Ln 77407
Stubbs Bend Dr 77469
Suffolk Hollow Ln 77407
Sugar Oaks Ct 77407
Summer Acres Ct 77469
Summer Arbor Cir 77469
Summer Breeze Ln 77469
Summer Creek Ln 77469
Summer Crescent Dr 77469
Summer Gate Ct 77469
Summer Haven Ln 77406
Summer Island Way 77407
Summer Lake Pass Ln 77469
Summer Mist Ln 77469
Summer Night Ln 77469
Summer Oaks Ct 77469
Summer Rose Ln 77469
Summer Shore Dr 77469
Summer Trace Ct & Ln 77406
Summer Valley Ln 77407
Summer Wine Dr 77406
Summerall Ct 77406
Summerdale Dr 77469
Summerland Ct & Dr 77406
Summit Cliff Ct 77407
Sun Ranch Dr 77469
Sundance Edge Ct 77407
Sundance Meadows Ln 77407
Sunflower Creek Ln 77469
Sunny Orchard Dr 77407
Sunny River Ln 77406
Sunny Square Ct 77407
Sunnyside Ct 77469
Sunrise Hill Ln 77469
Sunrise Terrace Ln 77407
Sunset Bend Ln 77407
Sunshine Medley Ln 77469
Sunshine Trace Ln 77407
Sunvolt Ct 77407
Supremo St 77406
Surrey Ct 77406
Surrey Ln 77469
Surrey Lake Ln 77407
Swan Ranch Ln 77407
Swanson Dr 77406
Sweeney Brook Ln 77469
Sweeney Lake Ct 77406
Sweetspire Rdg 77407
Swift Hill Ct 77469
Sycamore Rd 77469
Sydney Bay Ct 77407
Tabasco Ct 77406
Talisker Ct & Dr 77407
Talladega Springs Ln 77407
Tallow Knoll Ln 77469
Tanglelane St 77469
Tanglewild Ln 77406
Tara Dr 77469
Tara Blue Ridge Dr 77469
Tara Oaks Ct 77406
Tara Plantation Dr 77469
Taraglen Ct 77407
Tararin Ln 77407
Tarpley Springs Dr 77407
Tarply Springs Dr 77407
Taskwood Dr 77469
Tay Grove Pl 77407
Taylor Lake Ct 77407
Tea Rose Ct 77407
Teakwood St 77469
Terra Hollow Ln 77407
Terrace Creek Ct 77406
Terrell Hills Dr 77469
Terry Ln 77406
Terry Springs Ct 77407
Texana Way 77406
Texas Star Dr 77469
Thaddeus Ct 77406
Thistle Pond Ct 77469
Thompson Rd 77469
Thompson Crossing Dr 77406
Thorncroft Manor Ln 77407
Thorpe Springs Dr 77469
Three River Dr 77469
Thunder Basin Dr 77469
Tierra Amarilla Ln 77406
Tierra Mist Ln 77407
Tilbury Trl 77407
Tilman Dr 77406
Timber Moss Ln 77469
Timber Square Ct 77407
Timerwalk Ln 77407
Timothy Ln 77406
Tipton Oaks Dr 77406
Toledo Bend Ct & Dr 77406
Tolsta Way 77407
Topaz Ln 77469
Tori Rd 77469
Torian Way 77407
E & W Torino Reale Dr 77406
Torriceli Ln 77407
Towering Pine Ln 77469
W Trail Ct 77406
Trail Wood Ln 77406
Tranquil Shores Dr 77407
Traveler Ct 77469
Travertine Pt 77407
Travis St 77469
Travis Brook Dr 77406
Treemont Fair Ct & Dr 77407
Treemont Hollow Ct 77469
Trenton St 77469
Treyfair Ln 77469
Trinity Dr 77469
Trinity Manor Ln 77469
Trinity Meadow Ln 77407
Triple Crown Dr 77406
Tripp Ln 77407
Tulane Dr 77406
Tulip Garden Ct 77469
Tulip Trail Ln 77469
Turnbull Ln 77469
Turnstone Oaks Ct 77406
Turtle Brook Ln 77407
W Twin Cir 77406
N & S Union St 77469
Upland Manor Ct 77406
Upland Mill Ln 77407
Vacanti Dr 77406
Vacek Rd 77469
Valiant Knolls Dr 77406
Valley Ridge Dr 77469
Vancouver Blvd 77469
Venetian Dr 77406
Venture Park Ct & Dr 77406
Verano Dr 77406
Via Capri Ct 77406
Via Fontana Ct 77406
Via Privato Dr 77406
Via Renata Dr 77406
Via Salerno Ct 77406
Via Verdone Dr 77406
Vicki Lynn Ln 77406
Victoria Dr 77469
Victoria Garden Dr 77469
Village Branch Ln 77407
Village Crest Dr 77469
Village Mill Ln 77407
Vintage Cir 77406
Vintage Mill Ct 77407
Virginia Dr 77406
Visconti Ct 77406
Viscount Lndg 77407
Vista Del Rio 77406
Vista Falls Ct 77469
Vista Ridge Ct 77469
Vittorio Ct 77406
Vojt Rd 77469
Waeback Dr 77407
Wakefield Meadow Ct & Ln 77407
Waldridge Dr 77406
Walker Ln 77406
Wall St 77469
Walnut Sq 77407
Walnut Grove Ln 77406
Walters Rd 77469
Wandering Creek Dr 77469
Wandering Willow Dr 77406
Wasatch Valley Ln 77407
Water Bluff Ln 77406
Water Crest Trl 77469
Water Trace Ct 77469
Water Violet Ln 77407
N Waterlake Dr 77406
Waterlilly View Ln 77469
N & S Waterlily Dr 77406
Watermoon 77469
Waters Landing Ln 77469
Waterside Estates Cir & Dr 77406
Waterside Village Ct & Dr 77407
Waterwalk Ct 77469
Wavecrest Ct 77469
Way Saporito 77406
Wearback Dr 77407
Wenzel St 77469
Wessendorf Rd 77406
Westelm Ct 77406
Westford Park Ln 77407
Westmoor Rd 77469
Westspring Ct 77406
Wheatfield Ct & Ln 77469
Wheaton St 77469
Wheaton Hill Ln 77407
Wheatstone Ct 77469
Whighams Pl 77407
Whispering Way Dr 77406
Whispering Woods Ln 77406
Whistle Wood Dr 77406
White Camelia Ct 77407
White Clover Dr 77469
White River Ct 77406
White Willow Ln 77469
Whitehill Ln 77406
Whitewing Dr 77469
Wiergate Ln 77469
Wild Riv 77406
Wild Olive Way 77469
Wild Rose Trce 77407
Wild Rose Hill Ln 77469
Wildbriar Ln 77469
Wildwood Ln 77406
Wildwood Park Rd 77469
Will Point Ln 77469
William Morton Dr 77406
Williams Lake Dr 77469
Williams Way Blvd 77469
Willoughby Ct & Dr 77469
Willow Dr 77469
Willow Way 77406
Willow Bend Ct & Dr 77406
Willow Park Dr 77469
Willowview Dr 77469
Wimberly Knoll Ln 77406
Wimberly Oaks Ln 77407
Winchester Dr 77469
Windham Banks Dr 77469
Winding Path Way 77406
Winding River Dr & Rd 77406
Windloch St 77406
Windmill Dr 77406
Windmill Creek Dr 77407
Windmill Grove Dr 77407
Windmill Hill Cir & Dr 77407
Windmill Links Dr 77407
Windsong Ln 77406
Windsor Trace Ln 77407
Windswept Dr 77406
Windward Ct 77469
Windy Bank Ln 77407
Windy Lea Ln 77407
Windy Orchard Dr 77407
Windy Palms Ct 77407
Windy Port Ln 77407
Winfield Sq 77407
Winford Estate Dr 77406
Winner Foster Rd 77406
Winners Cir 77406
Winnipeg Blvd 77469
Winston Dr 77469
Winston Cove Ct 77407
Winston Homestead Ct, Dr & St 77406
Winston Lake Dr 77406
Winston Ranch Ct & Pkwy 77406
Winter Hedge Ct 77407
Winter Sky Ln 77469
Wisewood Ct 77406
Withers Ridge Dr 77407
Witherspoon Dr 77406
Wixford Trl 77407
Wolny Ln 77406
Wood Thrush Ct 77407
Wooded Lake Ct & Ln 77407
Woodfair Dr 77406
Woodfalls Ln 77407
Woodland Ct & Dr 77406
Woodmere Ln 77406
Woods Edge Dr 77406
Woodvine Ridge Dr 77406
Woodwind Dr 77406
Worthington Lake Dr 77406
Woven Wood Ct & Ln 77406
Wren Meadow Rd 77406
Wyndale Ct 77406
Wynfield Springs Dr 77406
Y U Jones Rd 77469
Yandell Dr 77469
Yaupon Hill Ln 77469
Yaupon Ridge Dr 77469
Yorkhill Ct 77407
Yorktown St 77469
Zieglers Grv 77469
Zillah Wheat Dr 77469

NUMBERED STREETS

All Street Addresses 77469

ROCKPORT TX

General Delivery 78382

POST OFFICE BOXES MAIN OFFICE STATIONS AND BRANCHES

Box No.s
All PO Boxes 78381

NAMED STREETS

Airport Rd 78382
Akin Ln 78382
E & W Alamito St 78382
Albatross Ln 78382
Alexander Dr 78382
N Allen St 78382
Allen M Parks Dr 78382
Alma Ln 78382
Aloha Ln 78382
Alpha St 78382
Amelia St 78382
N & S Ann St 78382
Antler St 78382
N Ashansou St 78382
Astor Cir 78382
Augusta Dr 78382
N & S Austin St 78382
Bahama Dr & St 78382
Balderee Ln 78382
Ball St 78382
Barcelona Dr 78382
E & W Bay Ave, Ct, Rd, St & Vis 78382
Bay Hills Dr 78382
Bay Retreat 78382
Bay Shore Dr 78382
Bayberry Cir 78382
Bayhouse Dr 78382
Bayleaf Ln 78382
Bayshores 78382
Bayview Loop 78382
Baywood Dr 78382
Beach Comber 78382
Beachwood 78382
Bee Rd 78382
Bee Tree Cir 78382
Begonia Cir 78382
Belaire Dr 78382
Bent Tree St 78382
Bentwood Ln 78382
Bermuda Dr 78382
Bernardy 78382
Beta St 78382
Bimini Dr 78382
Bishop Rd 78382
Blue Heron Dr 78382
Bluebird Ln 78382
Boardwalk Ave 78382
Bois D Arc St 78382
Bracht Dr 78382
Breezy St 78382
Broadway St 78382
S Bronte St 78382
Brumley 78382
Buc Dr 78382
Buena Vista Dr 78382
Bufflehead Ln 78382
Burns Rd 78382
N & S Burton St 78382
S Bypass 35 78382
Camellia Cir 78382
Canoe St 78382
Canvasback Ln 78382
Cape Ann St 78382
Cape Charles St 78382
Cape Mccan St 78382
Cape Velero Dr 78382
Captains Cv 78382
Captains Bay Dr 78382
Cardinal St 78382
Carol Ln 78382
Carroll 78382
Cascades 78382
Castle Oak Ln 78382
Catalina Dr 78382
E & W Cedar Rdg & St 78382
Ceilo Vista Dr 78382
Cenizo St 78382
Chachalaca St 78382
Champions Dr 78382
Channelview Rd 78382
Chapparreal 78382
Charlie St 78382
Charlotte Ave & Dr 78382
Cherry Hls & St 78382
China Bay 78382
N & S Church St 78382
Cinnamon Oak 78382
Circle Lake Dr 78382
Clam Dr 78382
Cloberdants St 78382
Club Lake Dr 78382
W Club Oak Ln 78382
Cochran Ln 78382
Colorado St 78382
E & W Concho St 78382
Copano Dr & Pkwy 78382
Copano Cove Rd 78382
Copano Heights Blvd 78382
Copano Point Rd 78382
Copano Ridge Rd 78382
Coral Dr 78382
E & W Cornwall St 78382
E & W Corpus Christi St 78382
Country Club Rd 78382
Cove Hbr N & S 78382
Crescent Ct & Dr 78382
Cruser Dr 78382
Curlew Dr 78382
Cypress Pt 78382
Dallas St 78382
Dana Dr 78382
Davis Loop 78382
De Hausa Dr 78382
Dead Ends Dr 78382
Deer Run Ln 78382
Delta St 78382
Desota Dr 78382
Devaca Dr 78382
Dolphin Dr 78382
Donna Ln 78382
Donnie Dr 78382
Doral Ln 78382
N & S Doughty St 78382
Dove Dr 78382
Driftwood St 78382
Dunes St 78382
Dustin Ln 78382
Edgewater Ct & Ln 78382
Egret Ln 78382
El Cid Dr 78382
Eller Ln 78382
Eloise St 78382
Encina Cir & Dr 78382
Enterprise Blvd 78382
Estates Dr 78382
Estes Dr 78382
Estes Private Rd 78382
Estuary 78382
Fairway Oaks St 78382
Farmers Cir 78382
Finisterre St 78382
Fir 78382
Flamingo Pt & Rd 78382
Flemings Ln 78382
Fm 1069 78382
Fm 1781 78382
Fm 2165
1500-1598 78382
1550-1550 78381
1601-1797 78382
1799-2000 78382
2002-2198 78382
Fm 3036 78382
Forest Hls 78382
Forest Oak Ln 78382
Fort Worth St 78382
Freeze Ln 78382
Friends St 78382
Front St 78382
Ft Worth St 78382
Fulton Ave 78382
N & S Fulton Beach Rd 78382
N & S Fuqua St 78382
N Gagon St 78382
Garnett Rd 78382
Gary Barnum Dr 78382
Georgian Oaks 78382
Glass Ave 78382
W Glen Oak Ln 78382
Grapevine Dr 78382
Green Oak Ln 78382
Greenway Ln 78382
Griffith Dr 78382
E Hackberry St 78382
Hagy Dr 78382
Hailey Rd 78382
Hammer Dr 78382
Harbor Cir, Ct, Cv & Dr 78382
Hardee St 78382
Henderson St 78382
Hermitage Dr 78382
Heron Ln & Way 78382
Heron Oaks 78382
Hewett Dr 78382
Hickory Ave 78382
Highlands St 78382
Highway 35 Byp 78382
Highway 355 78382
Hill St 78382
Hillcrest Dr 78382
Holiday Blvd 78382
Holly Dr 78382
Holly Hock Cir 78382
N & S Hood St 78382
Hooper St 78382
Huckleberry St 78382
Hughes St 78382
Hunter Ave & Ct 78382
Ibis Dr 78382
Ih 35 N 78382
Inverrary 78382
Island Rd 78382
Ivy Ln 78382
Jack Rabbit Rd 78382
Jamaica Dr 78382
E & W James St 78382
Janacek 78382
Jenkins St 78382
John Wendel Rd 78382
Johnson Ave & Dr 78382
Kelly Ln 78382
E & W King Rd & St 78382
Kingfish Dr 78382
Kingfisher Ln 78382
Kluge Trl 78382
N & S Kossuth St 78382
Kresta Ln 78382
Lady Clare St 78382
Lago Vista Dr 78382
Laguna Ln & Vis 78382
S, E & W Lake Dr 78382
Lake Shore Cir 78382
Lakeshore Dr 78382
Lakeside Ct, Dr & Loop 78382
Lakeview Dr & Rd 78382
Lakewood St 78382
W Lamar Dr & St 78382
Lamar Beach Rd 78382
Lands End St 78382
Lanfair Ln 78382
Lantana Ln & St 78382
Lara Garza 78382
Lauderdale Dr 78382
E & W Laurel St 78382
Lazy Ln & Rd 78382
Lee Cir 78382
E & W Liberty St 78382
E & W Linden St 78382
Ling St 78382
N Litron St 78382
E Little Pond Ln 78382
Little San Antonio Rd 78382
W, N & S Live Oak Dr, Ln & St 78382
Long Reach Loop 78382
Lorena St 78382
Lost Acres Ln 78382
Luau Ln 78382
Magnolia St 78382
E & W Main St 78382
Malibu Ln 78382
Mallard Dr 78382
W Maple St 78382
Marion Dr 78382
E & W Market St 78382
S Mathis St 78382
Mazatlan Dr 78382
Mclester Rd 78382
Merinal 78382
W Mesquite 78382
Mesquite Tree Loop 78382
Mills Dr 78382
Milton Harrel 78382
E & W Mimosa St 78382
Miramar Dr 78382
Mission Rd 78382
W Misty Oak Ln 78382
Mockingbird Ln 78382
N Moline St 78382

Monkey Rd ... 78382
Moore St ... 78382
E & W Morgan St ... 78382
Mourning Dove Ln ... 78382
E Murray St ... 78382
Myrtle Ln ... 78382
Nancy Ann St ... 78382
Nassau Dr ... 78382
Navajo Cir ... 78382
Navigation Cir ... 78382
Nell Ave ... 78382
Neptune Dr ... 78382
Newcomb Bend Loop ... 78382
E Nopal St ... 78382
E & W North St ... 78382
Northpointe Dr ... 78382
Northview Dr ... 78382
Northwest Dr ... 78382
Novice St ... 78382
Oak Ave, Rdg, Shr & St ... 78382
Oak Bay St ... 78382
Oakdale Dr ... 78382
Oakmont St ... 78382
Oaktree St ... 78382
Ocean Dr ... 78382
Old Cottage Beach Dr ... 78382
Old Salt Lake Rd ... 78382
Old Schoolhouse ... 78382
Olde Towne Ln ... 78382
Olympic Dr ... 78382
Omohundro St ... 78382
E & W Orleans St ... 78382
Osprey Dr ... 78382
Oyster Cv ... 78382
E, S & W Paisano Dr & Ln ... 78382
Palm Dr & St ... 78382
N & S Palmetto Ave & St ... 78382
Palmetto Point Rd ... 78382
Palo Pinto Dr ... 78382
Park Dr ... 78382
Paso Madera ... 78382
Patton St ... 78382
Peachtree Dr ... 78382
N & S Pearl St ... 78382
Pebble Creek Dr ... 78382
Pecan Harbor St ... 78382
Peets Bend Dr ... 78382
Pelican Dr ... 78382
Perch Ln ... 78382
Percival Ave ... 78382
Perry Jones Ln ... 78382
Picton Ln ... 78382
W Pin Oak Ln ... 78382
Pine Ave ... 78382
Pintail Ln ... 78382
Pirate Dr ... 78382
Plantation Dr ... 78382
Plover Ln ... 78382
Poinciana ... 78382
S & W Point Cir ... 78382
Point Of Woods ... 78382
E & W Pompano Dr ... 78382
E & W Pond ... 78382
Poolside Dr ... 78382
Poquito ... 78382
Port Ave ... 78382
Portia Ave ... 78382
Post Oak Ln ... 78382
Prairie Rd ... 78382
Primrose Cir & Dr ... 78382
Pueblo Dr ... 78382
Quail Dr ... 78382
Rachelle St ... 78382
N Racine St ... 78382
Rattlesnake Point Rd ... 78382
Raven Dr ... 78382
W Red Oak Ln ... 78382
Redbird Dr & Trl ... 78382
Redfish Dr ... 78382
Redfish Point Dr ... 78382
Redhead Rd ... 78382
Redwood Ave ... 78382
Resaca Ln ... 78382
Reserve Ln ... 78382
Retama Ln ... 78382
Ridge Harbor Dr ... 78382
Riviera Dr ... 78382
Rob Cir ... 78382
Rose St ... 78382
Rowan St ... 78382
Rowe St ... 78382
Royal Ave ... 78382
Royal Oak Ln ... 78382
Royal Oaks Dr & Trl ... 78382
Ruby St ... 78382
Ruby Allen St ... 78382
W Rustic Oak Ln ... 78382
E & W Sabinal St ... 78382
E & W Sagebrush St ... 78382
Sailfish Dr ... 78382
Sailhouse Way ... 78382
Saint Andrews Pl & St ... 78382
Saint Charles Loop E ... 78382
Saint Charles Bay Dr ... 78382
Saint Francis Cir ... 78382
Saint Marys St ... 78382
Salt Lake Rd S ... 78382
Sammy Henderson St ... 78382
San Antonio St ... 78382
San Leanna Dr ... 78382
Sanctuary Dr ... 78382
Sandhill Woods ... 78382
Sandollar St ... 78382
Sandpiper Ln ... 78382
Sandra ... 78382
Sandy Cv ... 78382
N & S Santa Clara Dr ... 78382
Santa Fe Dr ... 78382
Scallop Dr ... 78382
Scott St ... 78382
Sea Shell Shores Dr ... 78382
Seagull Ln ... 78382
Seaside Loop ... 78382
Sedona Ct ... 78382
Shady Oak Ln ... 78382
Shadyside Dr ... 78382
Shell Ridge Rd ... 78382
Sherwood Dr ... 78382
Shores Ln ... 78382
Shorewood Ct ... 78382
Sierra Sound St ... 78382
N & S Sierra Woods Dr ... 78382
Silver Leaf Ln ... 78382
Silver Oak Pl ... 78382
Silverado St ... 78382
Sipe St ... 78382
Smith Cove Rd ... 78382
Smithe Dr ... 78382
Smokehouse Rd ... 78382
Sonny Watkins Dr ... 78382
Sorenson Dr ... 78382
Southwind Dr ... 78382
Spanishwoods Dr ... 78382
Sparks Dr ... 78382
Sparks Colony Rd ... 78382
E & W Speckled Trout ... 78382
Spoonbill Ln ... 78382
Spring Ln ... 78382
Spt Cir ... 78382
Spyglass St ... 78382
Square Rigger St ... 78382
Stadium ... 78382
Stanley St ... 78382
Starboard Ave ... 78382
Starfish Dr ... 78382
State Highway 188 ... 78382
State Highway 35 Byp ... 78382
Steart St ... 78382
Steward Ln ... 78382
Sugar Creek Dr ... 78382
Sun Harbor St ... 78382
Sunset Dr ... 78382
Sweet Bay Dr & St ... 78382
Sweetbay Copano Vlg ... 78382
Swordfish Dr ... 78382
Teal Rd & St ... 78382
Tedford Ln ... 78382
Teresa Ln ... 78382
E & W Tern Ln & St ... 78382
W Terrace Blvd ... 78382
N & S Terry St ... 78382
Timber Lane Loop ... 78382
Timothy St ... 78382
Tomahawk Trl ... 78382
Traylor Ave & Blvd ... 78382
Treasure St ... 78382
Tule Park Dr ... 78382
Turkey Neck Cir ... 78382
Turtlebayou ... 78382
Vercie St ... 78382
N & S Verne St ... 78382
Victoria Ave ... 78382
N Walker Rd ... 78382
Walnut ... 78382
Walter Heldenfels ... 78382
Warbler Ln ... 78382
S Water St ... 78382
Water Oak Ln ... 78382
Waterwood St ... 78382
Wayside Ln ... 78382
Weeping Willow ... 78382
Westlake Dr ... 78382
Westpointe Dr ... 78382
E Wharf St ... 78382
Whispering Woods ... 78382
Whistlers Bnd & Cv ... 78382
Whistlers Cove Rd ... 78382
Whitewing Dr ... 78382
Whooping Crane Ln ... 78382
W Wildwood Dr ... 78382
Windcrest Ln ... 78382
Winding Way ... 78382
Windjammer St ... 78382
Wishert Rd ... 78382
N Wood St ... 78382
Woodland St ... 78382
Woods Dr ... 78382
Yaupon St ... 78382
S Young St ... 78382
Yucca Ln ... 78382

NUMBERED STREETS

All Street Addresses ... 78382

ROCKWALL TX

General Delivery ... 75087

POST OFFICE BOXES MAIN OFFICE STATIONS AND BRANCHES

Box No.s
All PO Boxes ... 75087

RURAL ROUTES

03 ... 75032

NAMED STREETS

Abbey Ct & Ln ... 75032
Abby Ln ... 75032
Aberdeen Ln ... 75087
Acacia ... 75032
Acorn Dr ... 75032
Agape St ... 75087
Airport Rd ... 75087
N & S Alamo Rd ... 75087
Alder Ct ... 75032
Alexander St ... 75087
All Angels Hill Ln ... 75087
Alpha Dr ... 75087
Alta Mesa Cir ... 75087
Alta Vista Ct & Dr ... 75087
Althea Rd ... 75032
Aluminum Plant Rd ... 75087
Alvington Ct ... 75032
Amanda Ln ... 75032
Amber Way ... 75032
Amber Knoll Dr ... 75087
Amesbury Ln ... 75087
Amherst Dr ... 75087
Amis Ct ... 75087
Amity Ln ... 75087
Andrew Cv ... 75032
E & N Anna Cade Cir & Rd ... 75087
Antioch Dr ... 75087
Antler Cir ... 75032
Appaloosa ... 75087
W Apple Tree Ln ... 75087
Arbor View Pl ... 75087
Arcadia Way ... 75087
Arden Ct & Dr ... 75087
Argyle Shore Dr ... 75087
Arista Dr ... 75032
Arrowhead Ct ... 75032
Artesia Ln ... 75032
Ashbourne Dr ... 75087
Ashe Bend Dr ... 75087
Ashley Ct & Dr ... 75032
Aspen Ct ... 75087
Audobon Ln ... 75087
Augusta Blvd & Trl ... 75087
Aurora Cir ... 75032
Austin St ... 75087
Austin Corners St ... 75032
Australia Ct ... 75032
Autumn Ct & Trl ... 75032
Avalon Dr ... 75032
Avery ... 75032
Avonlea Dr ... 75087
Azalea Dr ... 75087
Bald Cypress ... 75087
Barksdale Dr ... 75032
Barlass Dr ... 75087
Barnes St ... 75087
Barringer Ct ... 75087
Barrymore Dr ... 75087
Barton Springs Ln ... 75087
Baskerville Dr ... 75087
Bass Rd ... 75032
Bastrop Ct ... 75032
Baxter Trl ... 75087
Bay Ct ... 75032
Bay Crest Trl ... 75032
Bay Line Dr ... 75087
Bay Valley Cir ... 75032
Bay Watch Dr ... 75032
Bayberry Dr ... 75087
Bayhill Dr ... 75087
Bayshore Dr ... 75087
Bayside Dr ... 75087
Beacon Hill Dr ... 75087
Bear Branch Ct ... 75087
Bear Claw Ln ... 75032
Becky Ln ... 75087
Beech Dr ... 75032
Belfort Dr ... 75087
Belfry Ct ... 75087
Bell Haven Ct ... 75032
N Ben Payne Rd ... 75087
Bending Oaks Trl ... 75087
Benton Ct ... 75032
Benton Woods Dr ... 75032
Bentridge Dr ... 75032
Berkdale Ln ... 75087
Berkley Dr ... 75032
Berkshire Ln ... 75032
Bessie St ... 75087
Beta Ct ... 75032
Betty St ... 75087
Bevans Cir ... 75032
Beverly Dr ... 75032
Big Oak Ct ... 75087
Birds Nest Ln ... 75087
Bison Meadow Ln ... 75032
W Black Oak ... 75032
Black Oak Ln ... 75032
Blackhaw Dr ... 75087
Blanchard Dr ... 75032
Blanche Dr ... 75032
Blue Brook Dr ... 75087
Blue Heron Ln ... 75032
Blue Sage Dr ... 75087
Bluebell Ct ... 75032
Bluebonnet Dr ... 75032
Bluffview Dr ... 75087
Bob White Ct ... 75087
Boggs Cir ... 75087
Bost St ... 75087
Bourbon Street Cir ... 75032
E & W Bourn St ... 75087
Bowie Dr ... 75032
E & W Boydstun Ave ... 75087
Bradfield Ln ... 75087
Braewick Dr ... 75032
Brazos Way ... 75032
Bream Dr ... 75032
Breezy Hill Ln ... 75087
Brentwood Dr ... 75032
Briar Gln ... 75032
Briar Oak Dr ... 75087
Briarcrest Cir ... 75032
Bridgecreek Dr ... 75032
Bridle Path Ct ... 75032
Briggs Rd ... 75032
Bright Meadows Rd ... 75032
Brighton Ct ... 75032
Bristlecone Ct ... 75032
Bristol Ln ... 75032
Brittany Way ... 75087
Brockfield Ct ... 75032
Brockway Dr ... 75032
Broken Lance Ln ... 75032
Broken Spoke Ln ... 75032
Brookshore Dr ... 75032
S Brown Ave ... 75087
Bryn Mahr Ln ... 75087
Buck Dr ... 75087
Buckingham Dr ... 75032
Burkwood Dr ... 75032
Burnett Cir & Ln ... 75032
Butternut Dr ... 75032
C B Davidson ... 75087
Cabana Ct ... 75087
Caldwell Ln ... 75087
Calistoga Dr ... 75087
Calling Cir & Ctr ... 75087
Calm Crest Dr ... 75087
Cambria Dr ... 75087
Cambridge Ct & Dr ... 75032
Camden ... 75032
Camelot Ct ... 75087
Camp Creek Rd ... 75087
Canada Ct ... 75087
Candice Cir ... 75032
Candlelite Trl ... 75032
Cannon ... 75087
Canterbury Ct & Dr ... 75032
Canyon Ridge Dr ... 75087
Cape Hatteras Pl ... 75087
Capstone Way ... 75032
Carriage Trl ... 75087
Carriage Hill Ln ... 75032
Carrington Dr ... 75087
Cascade Valley Dr ... 75087
Cauble Dr ... 75087
Cavendish Ct ... 75087
Cedar Ct ... 75032
Cedar Glen Trl ... 75032
Cedar Ridge Rd W ... 75032
Cedar Shore Trl ... 75032
Cedar Tree Ln ... 75032
Cedar View Dr ... 75087
Cedarbluff Dr ... 75087
Cedarwood Trl ... 75032
Cellars Ct ... 75032
Center Ct ... 75032
Chad Way ... 75087
Challenger Ct ... 75032
Chalmers Ct ... 75032
Champions Ct & Dr ... 75087
Chaney Pl ... 75087
Channel Ridge Dr ... 75087
Chantilly Ct ... 75032
Chaparral Ln ... 75032
Chaparral Trot ... 75087
Chapel Hill Ln ... 75032
Chaps Dr ... 75032
Charlotte Ct ... 75032
Chasefield Dr ... 75087
Chatfield Dr ... 75087
Chelsea Ct ... 75032
W Cherry Tree Ln ... 75087
Chesapeake Dr ... 75087
Cheshire Ct ... 75032
Chesterwood Dr ... 75032
Chestnut Ln ... 75087
Chestnut Trl ... 75032
Chilton Pt ... 75032
Chinaberry Ln ... 75087
Chippendale Dr ... 75032
Chisholm Trl ... 75032
Chisholm Ranch Dr ... 75032
Chisholm Ridge Dr ... 75032
Chris Dr ... 75032
Christan Ct ... 75087
Christopher Ct & Rd ... 75032
Chuck Wagon Dr ... 75087
N & S Clark St ... 75087
Clear Creek Dr ... 75032
Clear Meadow Ct ... 75087
Clem Rd ... 75087
Clem Road Ext ... 75087
Clements Ct ... 75032
Cliff View Ct ... 75087
Cliffbrook Dr ... 75032
Clipper Ct ... 75032
Club Lake Cir ... 75087
Clubhill Dr ... 75087
Clubview Dr ... 75087
Clydesdale Dr ... 75087
E Coachlight Trl ... 75087
Coastal Dr ... 75032
Cobblestone Dr ... 75087
Cody Pl ... 75087
Collins Ln ... 75087
Colonial Ct ... 75032
Columbia Dr ... 75032
Commodore Plz ... 75032
Coneflower Dr ... 75087
Connie Ln ... 75032
Conrad Cir ... 75032
Constellation Cir ... 75032
Coolwood Ln ... 75032
Copper Ridge Cir ... 75032
Cornelia St ... 75087
Cornelius Rd ... 75087
Cornell Dr ... 75087
Cornerstone Dr ... 75087
Cornstalk Rd ... 75087
Corporate Xing ... 75032
Cotton Wood Ct ... 75032
N Country Ln ... 75087
Country Pl ... 75032
Country Rdg ... 75087
Country Club Dr ... 75032
County Line Rd ... 75032
County Road 536 ... 75087
County Road 949 ... 75087
County Road 950 ... 75087
Courageous Dr ... 75032
Courtland Way ... 75032
Courtney Cir ... 75032
Cove Creek Ct ... 75032
Cove Ridge Rd W ... 75032
Covey Trl ... 75087
Cox Dr ... 75087
Coyote Run Rd ... 75087
Craig Dr ... 75032
N & S Crawford Dr ... 75087
Creekridge Ct ... 75032
Creekside Dr ... 75087
Creencon Dr ... 75032
Crescent Cove Dr ... 75087
Crestbrook Dr ... 75087
Crestcove Dr ... 75087
Cresthaven Dr ... 75032
Cresthill Dr ... 75032
Crestlake Dr ... 75087
Crestridge Rd ... 75032
Crestview Cir ... 75087
Crestway Dr ... 75087
Crestwood Dr ... 75087
Crisp Rd ... 75032
Crystal Ct ... 75032
Crystal Lake Dr ... 75087
Cullins Rd ... 75032
Cypress Ct ... 75032
Cypress Cv ... 75087
Cypress Ln ... 75087
Daisy Dr ... 75087
Dalton Rd ... 75087
Damascus Rd ... 75087
Dame Pattie Dr ... 75032
Danbury Dr ... 75032
Dancing Waters ... 75032
Danielle Ct ... 75087
Dark Hollow Rd ... 75087
Darr Rd ... 75032
Darrell Dr ... 75032
Darrin Dr ... 75087
Dartbrook ... 75087
Dartmouth Dr ... 75032
Davis Dr ... 75087
Davy Crockett St ... 75087
Daybreak Dr ... 75032
Deaton Dr ... 75087
Deer Ridge Dr ... 75032
Deer Run Ct ... 75032
Deerwood Dr ... 75032
Defender Ct ... 75032
Denison St ... 75087
Desert Falls Ln ... 75087
Deutz Ct ... 75032
Deverson Dr ... 75032
Dhaka Dr ... 75087
Dial Ln ... 75087
Diamond Way Dr ... 75032
Diana Dr ... 75032
Dickie St ... 75087
Discovery Blvd ... 75032
Dogwood Ln ... 75087
Donald Dr ... 75032
Double Oak Dr ... 75032
Dove Hill Cir ... 75032
Dowell Cir & Rd ... 75032
Drew Ln ... 75032
Driftwood St ... 75087
Dunford Dr ... 75032
Durham Dr ... 75087
Dusty Ridge Dr ... 75032
Dwyer Ct ... 75032
Eagle Pass ... 75032
Easterner Pl ... 75032
Eastshore Rd ... 75032
Eastwood Dr ... 75032
Edmondson Trl ... 75087
Eganridge Ln ... 75087
Elgin Ct ... 75032
Elm Dr ... 75032
Elm Crest Dr ... 75087
Elmridge Cir ... 75032
Elvis Presley Ln ... 75032
Emerald Cv ... 75032
Emerald Bay Dr ... 75087
Emma Jane St ... 75087
Endeavor Ct ... 75032
Englewood Dr ... 75032
English Rd ... 75032
Equestrian Ct ... 75087
Equestrian Dr ... 75032
Equestrian Trl ... 75032
Er Ellis ... 75087
Essex Ct ... 75032
Eva Pl ... 75032
Evans Rd ... 75032
Evergreen Dr ... 75032
Faircrest Dr ... 75032
Fairfax Ln ... 75087
Fairfield Dr ... 75032
Fairlakes Ct ... 75087
Fairlakes Pointe Dr ... 75087
Fairview Dr ... 75087
Fairway Cir ... 75032
Faith Trl ... 75032
Falcon Point Dr ... 75032
Falcons View Pass ... 75032
Fallbrook Dr ... 75032
Falls View Dr ... 75087

N & S Fannin St 75087
Farm Ln 75087
E & W Fate Main Pl 75087
Featherstone Dr 75087
Fern Valley Ln 75087
Field Cir 75032
Fieldcrest Dr 75032
Fieldstone Dr 75032
Fireberry Dr 75087
Fireside Ct & Dr 75032
Firewheel Dr 75032
Florence Dr 75087
Fm 1139 75032
Fm 1141 75087
Fm 3097 75032
S Fm 548 75032
S Fm 549 75032
E & W Fm 550 75032
E Fm 552 75087
N Fm 740 75032
Fontana Blvd 75032
Forest Trce 75087
E Fork 75087
Foxborough Ct 75032
Foxchase Ln 75032
Foxwood Ln 75032
France Ct 75032
Freedom Ct 75032
Fremont Dr 75087
Frontier Trl 75032
Gail Ln 75087
Gaines Ct 75087
Garden Crest Dr 75087
Garrett Dr 75087
Garrison Dr 75032
Gatewick Dr 75087
Geary Dr 75087
Genesta Pl 75087
Gentry Ln 75032
Gillon Way 75087
Gleaner Dr 75032
Glen Acres Dr 75032
Glencoe Dr 75087
Glenhurst Dr 75032
Glenmere Ct 75087
Glenn Ave 75087
Glenwick Dr 75032
Gold Coast Ct & Dr 75087
Golden Trl 75032
Goldenwave 75032
N Goliad St 75087
S Goliad St
100-104 75087
106-2099 75087
2101-2397 75032
2399-2700 75032
2702-2898 75032
Gordon Cir 75032
Grace Ln 75087
Grandview 75087
Granger Dr 75032
Granite Ridge Dr 75087
Grant Ct 75032
Grantham Dr 75087
Grass Valley Dr 75087
Graystone Dr 75032
Great Lakes Ct 75087
Green Gables Ct 75087
Greenbriar Ct 75032
Greenbrook Dr 75032
Greencrest Blvd 75087
Greenhill Ln 75087
Greenhollow 75032
Gregory Dr 75032
Gretel Pl 75032
Grisham Dr 75087
Guadalupe Dr 75032
Gullwing Dr 75087
H Wallace Ln 75032
Haciendas Del Lago 75032
Hackberry Dr 75087
Hackberry Creek Rd 75032
Hail Dr 75087
Hainsworth Dr 75087
Halford Dr 75032
Hamilton Ct 75032
Hammack St 75087
Hampshire Ln 75032
Hampstead Dr 75087
Hampton Dr 75087
Hampton Bay Dr 75087
Hanby Ln 75032
Hanover Dr 75087
Harbor Dr 75087
Harbor Cove Dr 75087
Harbor Landing Dr 75032
Harborview Dr 75032
Harker Cir & Trl 75032
Harlan Dr 75087
Harper Dr 75087
Harris Dr 75087
Hartman St 75087
Harvest Hill Dr 75032
Harvest Ridge Cv & Dr 75032
Harvester Dr 75032
Harvey Trl 75087
Haven Hill Ct 75087
Haven Ridge Dr 75032
Hawks Dr 75032
Hawthorn Dr 75032
Hawthorne Trl 75032
Haymaker Dr 75032
Hays Ln 75087
Hayward Dr 75087
Heartstone Ln 75087
E & W Heath St 75087
Heather Glen Dr 75087
Heathland Xing 75032
Hebron Cir 75032
Henry M Chandler Dr 75032
Heritage Pkwy & St 75032
Herron Cir 75032
Hickory Ln 75087
Hickory Creek Ln 75087
Hidden Hls & Vly 75032
Hidden Lakes Way 75032
Hidden Oak Ln 75032
Hideaway Ct 75032
High Cotton Ln 75087
High Meadow Ln 75032
Highbluff Ln 75087
Highcrest Ln 75087
Highland Dr 75087
Highpoint Dr 75087
Highview Ln 75087
Highwater Xing 75032
Hill Ln 75087
Hillcrest Cir 75087
Hillcroft Dr 75087
N Hills Dr 75087
Hillside Dr 75032
Hilltop Cir 75087
Hillview Dr 75087
Hillway Dr 75087
Hodges Lake Dr 75032
Holden Dr 75087
W Holiday 75087
Holli Ln 75087
Holloway Ln 75032
Honey Locust Dr 75087
Hope Dr 75032
Hopkins Dr 75087
Horizon Ct & Rd 75032
Hubbard Dr 75032
Hunt Ln 75087
Huntcliff Dr 75087
Hunters Gln N 75032
Huntington Ct 75032
Huron Dr 75087
Hyer Dr 75087
Independence Pl 75032
Indian Trl 75087
Indian Paintbrush 75087
Industrial Blvd 75087
Innovation Dr 75032
E Interstate 30 75087
E & W Interurban St 75087
Intrepid Cir 75032
Ireland Ct 75087
Iris Dr 75087
Isle Royale Dr 75087
Islemere Dr 75087
Ivey Ln 75087
Ivy Ln 75087
Jackson St 75087
Jacob Xing 75087
James Dr 75032
Jams Ln 75032
Jeff Boyd Rd 75032
Joe White St 75087
John King Blvd 75032
Jordan Ln 75032
Jordan Farm Cir 75032
Julian Dr 75087
Juniper Hills Dr 75032
Justin Rd 75087
Kathryn Dr 75032
E & W Kaufman St 75087
Kay Ln 75087
Kearley Dr 75032
Kelly Ln 75087
Kendal Ct 75032
Kensington Dr 75087
Kenton Ct 75032
Kentwood Cir & Dr 75032
Kenway St 75087
Kerimore Ct 75032
Kernodle St 75087
Kestrel Ct 75032
Keswick Ct 75032
Key Dr 75032
Kimberly Ln 75087
Kinder Way 75032
King Ct 75087
Kings Pass 75032
Kingsbridge Ln 75032
Kingsbury Trl 75032
Kingsford Ct 75032
Kirkhaven Dr 75032
Klutts Dr 75032
Knoll Crest Trl 75032
Knollwood Dr 75087
Kristy Ln 75087
Kuban Rd 75032
Kyle Cir 75032
Kyser Spring Rd 75032
La Costa Dr 75032
La Grande Dr 75087
Lacebark Ln 75087
Lafayette Dr & Lndg 75032
Lago Cir 75032
Lago Vista Ln 75032
Laguna Dr 75087
Lake Ter 75087
Lake Breeze Dr 75087
Lake Brook Cir 75087
Lake Estates Dr 75032
Lake Forest Dr 75087
Lake Glen Cir 75087
Lake Meadows Cir, Ct & Dr 75087
Lakedale Dr 75087
Lakehill Dr 75087
N & S Lakeshore Dr 75087
Lakeside Dr
100-999 75032
3000-3500 75087
3502-3698 75087
Lakeview Dr 75032
Lakeway Dr 75032
Lakewood Ct 75032
Lamar St 75087
Lancashire Dr N & S 75087
Lanshire Dr 75032
Lantana Dr 75087
Lantern Dr 75087
Lariat Dr 75087
Larkspur Dr 75087
Larry Dr 75032
Las Lomas Dr 75032
Laurel Ln 75087
Laurel Crossing Dr 75032
Laurence Dr 75087
Lavender Ct & Way 75032
League Rd 75032
Lee Cir & Dr 75032
Leeward Dr 75087
Legend Dr 75032
Lemley Dr 75032
Leonard Way 75087
Lexington Dr 75087
Liberty Ln 75032
Liechty Ct 75032
Lilac Ln 75087
Lillian St 75087
Limestone Hill Ln 75032
Lincolnshire Ct & Ln 75087
Linda Ln 75032
Lionhart Pl 75032
Livestock Dr 75087
Loch View Ct 75087
Lochness Ct 75087
Lochspring Dr 75032
Lofland Cir 75032
Loma Vis 75087
London Ct 75087
Lone Crest Dr 75087
Lone Rider Ct 75087
Lone Run Dr 75087
Lone Star Trl 75087
Longhorn Ln 75087
Los Altos Dr 75087
Lost Colt Dr 75032
Lost Creek Ct 75032
Lost Valley Ct 75032
Louder Way 75087
Lowe Rd 75032
Lowry Dr 75087
Luchenbach Trl 75032
Luther Ln 75032
Lydia Ln 75087
Lynne Dr 75087
Lyons Ln 75087
Madison Dr 75032
Magnolia Dr 75087
Magnolia Ln 75087
Majestic Ct & Pt 75032
Majestic Point Dr 75032
Mallard Xing 75032
Maltese Cir 75032
Manchester Dr 75032
Mangrove Dr 75087
Manor Ct & Dr 75032
Maple Ct 75032
Mapleridge Dr 75032
Maplewood Dr 75032
Marble Falls Ln 75032
Marcie Ln 75032
Margaret St 75087
Mariah Ct 75032
Mariah Bay Cir & Dr 75032
Marilyn Jayne Dr 75032
Mariner Dr 75032
Mariposa 75087
Market Center Dr 75032
Marty Cir 75087
Marys Gln 75032
Mason Ct 75087
Massey Ln 75032
Mayflower Ct 75032
Maywood 75032
Mccall Dr 75087
Mcclendon Dr 75087
Mccormick Ct 75032
Mcdonald Rd 75032
Mcfarlin Pl 75087
Mckee Ct 75087
Mckenzie Pl 75087
Mckinney Trl 75087
Meadow Dr 75032
Meadowcreek 75032
Meadowdale Dr 75087
Meadowlake Dr & Ln 75032
Meadowlark Cir 75087
Meadowlark Pl 75032
Meadowpark 75032
Meadows Cir & Dr 75087
Meadowview Ct & Rd 75032
Meandering Way 75087
Medical Dr 75087
Mediterranean St 75087
Melrose Ln 75032
Memorial Dr 75087
Merion Dr 75087
Mesquite Ct 75032
Meushaw Dr 75087
Micah Dr 75032
Michael Cir & Dr 75032
Midlake Ln 75032
Midnight Pass 75087
Mims Rd 75032
Mira Vista Ln 75032
Mirage Ln 75087
Miramar Dr 75087
Mischief Ln 75032
Mission Dr 75087
Mistflower Ln 75087
Misty Cv 75087
Misty Ridge Ln 75032
Mockingbird Ln 75032
Mockingbird Hill Ln 75032
Mont Blanc Dr 75032
Mont Cascades Dr 75087
Montclair Dr 75087
Montego Ct 75032
Monterey Dr 75087
Montserrat Cir 75032
Moraine Pl & Way 75032
Morning Cir 75032
Morning Star 75032
Morrish Ln 75032
Mosswood Ln 75032
Mountain Lake Dr 75032
Mulberry Dr 75087
Mulberry Ln 75032
Munson St 75087
Murifield Ave 75087
Murphy Ct & Dr 75032
Mustang Dr 75087
Myers Rd 75032
Mystic St 75032
Napa Dr 75087
Nash St 75087
National Dr 75032
Native Trl 75032
New Forest Dr 75087
New Holland Dr 75032
Newcastle Dr 75032
Newkirk Ct 75032
Newport Dr 75032
Nicole Dr 75087
Nixon Dr 75087
Noah Crest Dr 75087
Noble Ct 75032
Norman Trl 75087
Normandy Ln 75032
Northcrest Cir 75087
Northridge Ln 75087
Norwood Dr 75032
Nova Park Ct 75087
Oak Dr 75087
Oak Bend Dr 75087
Oak Hollow Ln 75032
Oakhurst Ct 75087
Oakridge Dr 75032
Observation Trl 75032
Oconnell St 75087
Odell Ave 75087
Old Millwood Rd 75087
Old Vineyard Ln 75032
Ole West Ln 75087
Olive St 75087
Open Bay Ct 75087
Orchard Ln 75087
Overaler Dr 75087
Overbrook Ct & Dr 75032
Overlook Dr 75032
Oxford Ct & Dr 75032
Pabina Ct 75087
Paddock Ln 75032
Paint Brush Trl 75032
Paintcreek Ct 75032
Painted Pony Ln 75087
Palasades Ct 75087
Palomino Dr 75087
Panhandle Dr 75087
Parade Pt 75032
Park Central Cir & Dr 75087
Park Place Blvd 75087
Park View Dr 75087
Parks Ave 75087
Parkside Cir 75032
Parkway Ct 75032
Parkwood Dr 75032
Partridge Dr 75032
Paul Davis Ln 75032
Payton Way 75087
Pear Dr 75087
Pebble Creek Ln 75032
Pebble Hills Dr 75087
Pecan Dr 75087
Peek Dr 75087
Pelican Cove Dr 75087
Pendleton Dr 75032
Peninsula Ct 75032
Penrith Ct 75032
Peoples Ln 75032
Perch Rd 75032
Peregrine Cir 75032
Petaluma Dr 75087
Peters Colony 75087
Pheasant Hill Dr 75032
Phelps Lake Dr 75087
Phillips Ct 75087
Phyllis Ln 75087
Piatt Ct 75087
Pilgrim 75087
Pin Oaks Cir 75032
Pine Island Cir 75032
Pine Ridge Dr 75032
Pinebluff Ln 75032
Pinehurst Dr 75087
Pinion Ln 75032
Pintail Pt 75032
Pleasant Acres Rd 75087
Pleasant View Dr 75087
Plum Tree Dr 75087
Plummer Dr 75087
Point Royal Dr 75087
Pompei Ct 75087
Pontchartrain Dr 75087
Poplar Point Dr 75032
Portofino Dr 75032
Portside Dr 75087
Portview Pl 75032
Post Oak Dr 75032
Potter Ave 75087
Presidio Dr 75087
Preston Ct & Trl 75087
Price Dr 75087
Primrose Ln 75032
Prince Ln 75087
Princeton Way 75087
Pringle Ln 75087
Private Dr 75032
Promenade Pl 75087
Promontory Ct 75032
Pullen Rd 75032
Puritan Ct 75032
Quail Creek Rd 75032
E & W Quail Run Rd 75087
Rabbit Ridge Ct & Rd 75032
Racheal Dr 75032
Rainbow Cir 75032
Raintree Ct 75087
E & W Ralph Hall Pkwy 75032
Ranch Trl 75032
Ranch House Rd 75032
Random Oaks Dr 75087
Ranger Dr 75032
Rapids Ct 75087
Raven Cir 75032
Ravenhurst Dr 75087
Reba Rd 75032
Red Ridge Dr 75032
Red Valley Run 75087
Red Wolf Dr 75087
Redwood Trl 75087
Reed Dr 75087
Regal Blf 75087
Reliance Ct 75032
Renee Dr 75032
Renfro St 75087
Research Cir 75032
Resolute Ln 75032
Richfield Ct 75032
N Ridge Cir 75087
S Ridge Cir 75087
Ridge Rd
1000-2699 75087
2701-2797 75032
2799-3799 75032
3801-4299 75032
Ridge Rd W 75087
Ridge Crest Pl 75087
Ridge Hollow Rd 75032
Ridge Road Ct 75087
Ridgelake Ln 75032
Ridgetop Ct 75032
Ridgeview Dr 75087
Ridgeway Dr 75087
Riding Club Rd 75087
River Rock Ln 75032
Riverbirch Ln 75032
Riverside Oaks Dr 75087
Robin Dr 75087
Rochdale Dr 75087
Rochell Ct 75032
Rochelle Rd 75032
Rockbrook Dr 75087
Rockhouse Ln 75087
Rockingham Ct 75032
Rockwall Pkwy 75032
Rocky Rd 75032
Rogers Way 75087
Roki Dell Ln 75032
Rolling Meadows Cir & Dr 75087
Roma Ct 75087
Rose Ln 75087
Rose Marie Ln 75032
Rosemary Dr 75032
Rosewood Ln 75087
E Ross St 75087
Ruffian Way 75087
Rush Creek Dr 75032
E & W Rusk St 75087
Russell Dr 75032
Russwood St 75087
Rutherford Dr 75032
Saddle Dr 75087
Saddle Horn Cir 75087
Saddlebrook Ln 75087
Safflower Ct 75087
Saffron Ct 75032
Saint Charles Ct 75087
Saint James Ct 75032
Saint Johns Pl 75087
Saint Mary St 75087
Saint Marys Pl 75087
Saint Michaels Way 75032
Saint Thomas Ct 75087
Salinas Dr 75087
Sam Houston St 75087
San Antonio St 75087
N San Augustine St 75087
N & S San Jacinto St 75087
San Rafael Dr 75087
San Saba Ct 75032
Sandra Dr 75032
Sandstone 75032
Saratoga Dr 75087
Sausalito Dr 75087
Savanah Ct 75087
Savannah Hl 75032
Sawyer Dr 75087
Scarboro Hills Ln 75032
Scenic Dr & Pl 75032
Sceptre Dr 75032
Science Pl 75032
Seascape Ct 75087
Secret Cv 75032
Sequoia Rd 75032
Serene Hvn 75032
Serenity Cv & Ln 75032
Severige Ct 75032
Shadow Oaks Ct 75087
Shady Branch Dr 75087
Shady Creek Ln 75087
Shady Dale Ln 75032

Shady Grove Cir ... 75032
Shady Lane Dr ... 75087
Shamrock Cir ... 75032
Shannon Dr ... 75087
Sharpley ... 75087
Sheffield Ct ... 75032
Shennendoah Ln ... 75087
Shepards Hill Dr ... 75087
Shepherds Way ... 75032
Shepherds Glen Rd ... 75032
Sherman St ... 75087
Shoal Creek Ln ... 75087
Shorecrest Dr ... 75087
Shoreline Trl ... 75032
Shores Blvd, Cir & Ct ... 75087
Shoretrail Cir & Dr ... 75087
Shoreview Dr ... 75087
Sids Rd ... 75032
Sierra Pass ... 75087
Siesta Cir ... 75032
Sigma Ct ... 75087
Signal Ridge Pl ... 75032
Signature Ct ... 75032
Silktree Dr ... 75087
Silver Hawk Ct ... 75032
Silver Lake Dr ... 75087
Silver Leaf Dr ... 75087
Silver Spur Trl ... 75032
Silver View Ln ... 75032
Sinks Rd ... 75032
Skylar Dr ... 75032
Skyline Cir ... 75032
Skyview Ln ... 75087
Sleepy Hollow Ln ... 75032
Smirl Dr ... 75032
Smith Rd ... 75032
N Smith Rd ... 75087
Smoketree Dr ... 75032
Soapberry Ln ... 75032
Somerset Dr & Ln ... 75032
Sonoma Dr ... 75087
Sorita Cir ... 75032
Sourwood Ln ... 75087
Southampton Dr ... 75032
Southern Pnes ... 75087
Southern Cross Dr ... 75032
Southlake Dr ... 75032
Southwestern Dr ... 75087
Southwood Dr ... 75032
Sovereign Ct ... 75032
Sparks Dr ... 75087
Spring Creek Dr ... 75087
Spring Meadow Trl ... 75032
Springer Ln ... 75032
Springs Way ... 75032
Spur Dr ... 75087
Squabble Creek Dr ... 75087
Squaw Vly ... 75032
Stafford Cir ... 75087
Standing Oak Ln ... 75032
Stanford Ct ... 75032
Stanford Dr ... 75087
Star St ... 75087
Starboard Dr ... 75087
Starlight Pass ... 75032
Starlight Pl ... 75087
N State Highway 205 ... 75087
S State Highway 205 ... 75032
State Highway 205 Ext ... 75032
State Highway 276 ... 75032
State Highway 66 ... 75087
Steeple Chase Ct & Ln ... 75032
Steger Towne Rd ... 75032
Sterling Ct ... 75032
Sterling Ridge Ct ... 75032
Stevens Rd ... 75032
Stevenson Dr ... 75087
Stewart Dr ... 75032
Stillwater Dr ... 75087
Stillwaters Dr ... 75032
Stimson St ... 75087
N Stodghill Rd ... 75087
Stonebridge Cir & Dr ... 75087
Stonecrest Dr ... 75087
Stoneleigh Dr ... 75032
Stonewall Trl ... 75032
Stoney Hollow Ln ... 75087
Stoneybrook Dr ... 75087
Storrs St ... 75087
Sugarberry Ln ... 75087
Summer Lee Dr ... 75032
Summer Tanager Ln ... 75032
Summerhill Dr ... 75032
Summit Cir ... 75032
Summit Ridge Dr ... 75087
Sun Dr ... 75032
Sundrop ... 75087
Sunfish Rd ... 75032
Sunflower Trl ... 75032
Sunny Cir ... 75032
Sunpoint Cir ... 75087
Sunset Trl ... 75032
Sunset Hill Dr ... 75087
Sunset Ridge Dr ... 75032
Sutter Dr ... 75087
Sycamore Ln ... 75032
T L Townsend Dr
701-897 ... 75087
899-1199 ... 75087
1201-1299 ... 75087
1501-1899 ... 75032
Taber Ln ... 75087
Tahoe Dr ... 75087
Tall Oaks Pl ... 75087
Tallowtree Dr ... 75087
Tangleglen Dr ... 75032
Tanglevine Ln ... 75032
Tannerson Dr ... 75087
Tanya Dr ... 75087
Tatum Pl ... 75032
Teagle Dr ... 75032
Teakwood Ct & Dr ... 75087
Teal Harbor Ct ... 75032
Tennis Village Dr ... 75032
Terrabella Ln ... 75032
Terry Ln ... 75032
Texas Ave & Rd ... 75032
Thistle Pl ... 75032
Thomas Cir ... 75032
Thorndale Ln ... 75087
Thoroughbred ... 75087
Throckmorton St ... 75087
Timber Creek Dr ... 75032
Timber Ridge Dr ... 75032
Timberline Dr ... 75087
Topside Ln ... 75087
Township Ln ... 75087
Tractor Trl ... 75032
Trail Dr ... 75087
Trail Gln ... 75032
Trailview Dr ... 75032
Travis Ln ... 75032
Trinity Ct ... 75032
Trout St ... 75032
Trumpeter Way ... 75032
Tubbs Rd & St ... 75032
Tucker Rd ... 75032
Tumbleweed Cir ... 75087
Tupelo Dr ... 75087
Turquoise Pt ... 75032
Turtle Cove Blvd ... 75087
Twilight Pt ... 75032
Twin Circle Ct ... 75032
Twin Creek Ln ... 75087
Twin Foal Ct ... 75032
Twin View St ... 75032
Tyler St ... 75087
Urbine Cir ... 75032
Vail Ct ... 75087
Valerie Pl ... 75032
Valiant Dr ... 75032
Valkyrie Pl ... 75032
Vallejo Dr ... 75087
Valley Dr ... 75087
Valley Trl ... 75087
Vance Ct ... 75087
Vaughn Dr ... 75087
Ventura Dr ... 75087
Venus Ct ... 75032
Vernon Dr ... 75087
Versailles Ct & Dr ... 75032
Vervain Dr ... 75087
Victoria Pl ... 75032
Victory Ln ... 75032
Village Dr ... 75087
Village Green Dr ... 75087
Volunteer Pl ... 75032
N W E Crawford ... 75087
Wagon Trl ... 75032
Wagonwheel Dr ... 75032
Wales Dr ... 75087
Waller Dr ... 75087
Walnut Ln ... 75032
Walnut Ridge Dr ... 75032
Warwick Ct ... 75032
Warwick Dr ... 75087
E & W Washington St ... 75087
Water Way ... 75087
Water Way Ct ... 75087
Waterfront Trl ... 75087
Waters Edge Ct ... 75032
Waters Edge Dr ... 75087
Waterside Cir ... 75087
Waterstone Ln ... 75032
Waterview Trl ... 75087
Waterwood Cir ... 75087
Wayne Dr ... 75032
Weatherly Cir ... 75032
Weiskopf Dr ... 75032
Wellington Ln ... 75032
Wells Cir ... 75032
Wembley Way ... 75032
N West St ... 75087
Westbury Dr ... 75032
Westchester Ct ... 75032
Westfield Ln ... 75032
Westminster Dr ... 75032
Weston Ct ... 75032
Westway Cir & Dr ... 75087
Westwood Dr ... 75032
Wheelers Way ... 75032
Whispering Gln ... 75032
Whispering Oaks ... 75087
White Dr ... 75087
White Rd ... 75032
White Buffalo Ln ... 75032
White Hills Dr ... 75087
White Sand Dr ... 75087
White Water Ln ... 75032
Whitmore Dr ... 75087
Whitney Bay Dr ... 75087
Whitney Lakes Dr ... 75087
Whittle Way ... 75087
Wild Geese Ct ... 75032
Wild Oak Ln ... 75032
Wildbriar Ln ... 75087
Wildflower Way ... 75032
Wildrose Dr ... 75032
Wildwood Ln & Ter ... 75087
Wilford Way ... 75032
Williams St ... 75087
Willow Ln ... 75087
Willow Pond Ln ... 75087
Willow Ridge Cir ... 75032
Willow Springs Dr ... 75032
Willowcreek Ln ... 75032
Willowcrest ... 75032
Willowhill Ln ... 75032
Wiltshire Ct ... 75032
Wimberley Ln ... 75032
Wimbledon Ct ... 75032
Wimbledon Dr ... 75087
Wincrest Dr ... 75032
Wind Hill Cir & Rd ... 75087
Windflower Dr ... 75087
Windham Dr ... 75087
Winding Creek Ln ... 75032
Winding Oak Ct ... 75032
Winding Ridge Ln ... 75032
Windjammer Ln ... 75087
Windlake Cir ... 75032
Windmill Ridge Dr ... 75032
Windpointe Dr ... 75032
Windsong Ln ... 75032
Windsor Dr ... 75032
Windsor Way ... 75087
Windward Trl ... 75032
Windy Ln ... 75087
Winecup Ln ... 75032
Winter Park ... 75032
Winterhawk Dr ... 75032
Wisdom Crest Cir ... 75032
Wisperwood Dr ... 75087
Wolf Trl ... 75032
Woodbridge Pl ... 75032
Woodcreek Blvd ... 75087
Woodcreek Dr ... 75032
Wooded Trl ... 75087
Woodhaven Cir ... 75087
Woodland Way ... 75087
Woodmont Cir ... 75032
Woodpark Ln ... 75087
Wright Ave ... 75032
Wurst Rd ... 75032
Wylie Ln ... 75032
Wyndemere Blvd ... 75032
Yacht Club Dr ... 75032
Yankee Ct ... 75032
Yankee Creek Rd ... 75032
E & W Yellowjacket Ln ... 75087
York Dr ... 75087
Yorkshire Dr ... 75032
Yvonne Dr ... 75032
Zeter Dr ... 75087
Zion Hill Cir ... 75087

NUMBERED STREETS

All Street Addresses ... 75087

ROUND ROCK TX

General Delivery ... 78683

POST OFFICE BOXES MAIN OFFICE STATIONS AND BRANCHES

Box No.s
1 - 2585 ... 78680
5001 - 83100 ... 78683

NAMED STREETS

N A W Grimes Blvd ... 78665
S A W Grimes Blvd ... 78664
Aaron Ross Cv & Way ... 78665
Abaco Harbour Cv & Ln ... 78664
Abbey Rd ... 78681
Aberdeen Dr ... 78664
Abyssinian Ln ... 78681
Academy Pl ... 78664
Ada Ln ... 78664
Adagio Pl ... 78681
Adam Cv ... 78681
E & W Adelanta Pl ... 78681
Adelen Ln ... 78664
Adelfa Dr ... 78664
Adler Falls Ln ... 78665
Afghan Path ... 78664
Agarita Trl ... 78665
Agave Loop ... 78681
Alabaster Cv ... 78681
Alazan Cv ... 78664
Albacete Ln ... 78681
Aleman Cv ... 78681
Alexander Ct ... 78665
Alexander Valley Cv ... 78665
Alexandria Way ... 78665
Alexandrite Way ... 78681
Allenscreek Way ... 78664
Almelo Dr ... 78681
Alondra Way ... 78681
Alwin Dr ... 78681
Amanda Cv ... 78681
Amber Skyway Cv ... 78665
Amberglow Ct ... 78665
Ameswood Dr & Pl ... 78664
Amistad Cv ... 78665
Amistad Dr ... 78664
Amistad Way ... 78665
Anacacho Cv ... 78664
Ancona Trl ... 78681
E & W Anderson Ave ... 78664
Andice Path ... 78681
Andover Cv & Dr ... 78664
Andres Way ... 78664
Angelico Cv & Ln ... 78681
Angelina Ct & Dr ... 78665
Angelo Loop & St ... 78665
Anjou Ln ... 78681
Anna Palm Way ... 78665
Ansonia Trl ... 78681
Antonio St ... 78665
Apache Trl ... 78665
Apache Oaks Dr ... 78665
Apollo Cir ... 78664
Applegate Cir ... 78665
Aqua Ln ... 78681
Aqualine Cv ... 78681
Aquamarine Dr ... 78681
Aquila Ct ... 78681
Aransas Cv ... 78664
Arbol Cv ... 78681
Arbor Ct & Dr ... 78681
Arctic Cir ... 78664
Arden Ct ... 78681
Arezzo Dr ... 78665
Aria Cv ... 78681
Arizona Mesa Cv ... 78664
Arnie Ln ... 78664
Arrow Head ... 78681
Arrowhead Cir ... 78681
Arrowood Pl ... 78665
Arroyo Bluff Ln ... 78681
Artesia Bnd ... 78681
Arusha St ... 78664
Asbury Park Dr ... 78665
Ash Glen Ln ... 78681
Ashbury Rd ... 78681
Ashley Dr ... 78665
Ashmere Cv & Loop ... 78681
Ashtree Ct ... 78665
Ashwood Ct ... 78664
Asombra Ln ... 78681
Aspen Trl ... 78664
Aspen Leaf ... 78681
Aster Way ... 78665
Augusta Ct ... 78681
E & W Austin Ave ... 78664
Autumn Run Ln ... 78665
Avaranche Way ... 78681
Avignon Dr ... 78681
Azul Cv ... 78681
Azur Ln ... 78681
Baffin Cv ... 78664
E & W Bagdad Ave ... 78664
Bailey Jean Dr ... 78681
Bainbridge Cv & St ... 78681
Baker St ... 78664
Balanced Rock Pl ... 78681
Balmorhea Ct & Ln ... 78664
Balsam Way ... 78665
Bamfield Cv ... 78665
Bandera Cv & Path ... 78665
Bar Harbor Bnd & Cv ... 78681
Barchetta Dr ... 78665
Barefoot Cv & Ln ... 78665
Barilla Mountain Trl ... 78664
Bark Way ... 78664
Barletta Dr ... 78681
Barlow Dr ... 78681
Barrhall Dr ... 78664
Basalt Cv ... 78681
Bass Loop ... 78665
Bass Pro Dr ... 78665
Bay Ln ... 78664
Bay Hill Ln ... 78664
Bayland St ... 78664
Becca Teal Pl ... 78681
Beckwood Trl ... 78665
Bedouin Ct ... 78664
Belaire Cir ... 78664
Belicia Ln ... 78665
Bellmar Dr ... 78664
Bellview Ave
401-699 ... 78664
701-999 ... 78681
Belvedere Pl ... 78665
Bengal Dr ... 78664
Bent Path ... 78665
Bent Brook Dr ... 78664
Bent Tree Ct, Cv, Dr & Loop ... 78681
Bent Wood Ct & Pl ... 78665
Berry Bend Path ... 78664
Berwick Cv & Dr ... 78681
Beth Ln ... 78664
Bevin Cv ... 78665
Birdhouse Dr ... 78665
N & S Black St ... 78664
Black Rock Bnd ... 78681
Blackburn Pl ... 78665
Blackjack Cv & Dr ... 78681
Blackstone Cv ... 78665
N & S Blair St ... 78664
Blanchard Dr ... 78681
Blessing Ave ... 78681
Blue Bird Ct ... 78681
Blue Cat Way ... 78665
Blue Heron Cv ... 78681
Blue Jay Way ... 78681
Blue Monster Cv ... 78664
Blue Mountain Path ... 78681
Blue Ridge Dr ... 78681
Blue Sky Pl ... 78665
Blue Spring Cir & Cv ... 78681
Blue Sruce Way ... 78664
Bluebell Bend Cv ... 78665
Bluebonnet Dr ... 78664
Bluestone Ln ... 78665
Bluff Dr ... 78681
Bluff Vw ... 78664
Bluffs Landing Way ... 78665
Bluffside Ln ... 78665
Bluffstone Dr ... 78665
Blufftop Cir ... 78681
Bluffwood Pl ... 78665
Bob Estes Cv ... 78664
Bobby Jones Way ... 78664
Bobcat Dr ... 78681
Bobcat Way ... 78665
Bobwhite Ct ... 78681
Bodega Cv ... 78665
Boneset Trl ... 78665
Bonnie Ln ... 78665
Bonwood Dr ... 78681
Boone Valley Dr ... 78664
E & W Bowman Dr & Rd ... 78664
Box Canyon Ter ... 78681
Boxwood Path ... 78664
Bradford Park Dr ... 78664
Bradley Ln ... 78664
Bradmore Dr ... 78664
Braesgreen Dr ... 78664
Bram Cv ... 78681
Brandi Ln ... 78681
Breaux Ln ... 78664
Breezy Ct & Cv ... 78664
Breezy Point Cv ... 78665
Brenda Ln ... 78665
Brentwood St ... 78681
Briar Oak Ln ... 78681
Briarton Ln N & S ... 78665
Briarwood St ... 78681
Brienne Dr ... 78681
Brighton Pl ... 78665
Brisa Bend Way ... 78681
Broken Bow Dr ... 78681
Broken Branch Dr ... 78681
Broken Trace Ct ... 78665
Brokenshoe Cv & Dr ... 78681
Brook View Ct ... 78665
Brookside Ct ... 78681
Brookstone Ct ... 78681
N & S Brown St ... 78664
Brown Juniper Way ... 78664
Brownstone Cv ... 78681
Brunston Ct ... 78681
Brushy Bend Dr ... 78681
Brushy Creek Dr & Rd ... 78664
Bryant Dr ... 78664
Bryco Cv ... 78681
Buckboard Blvd ... 78681
Buckeye Ln ... 78664
Buckley Ln ... 78664
Buckskin Dr ... 78681
Buena Vista Ln ... 78665
Buffalo Pass ... 78681
Bull Horn Loop ... 78665
Burleson Cv ... 78664
Burlwood Ct ... 78664
N & S Burnet St ... 78664
Butler Way ... 78665
Cactus Dr ... 78681
Calcite Cv ... 78681
Caldwell Palm Cir ... 78665
Calico Bush Ln ... 78664
Calima Cv ... 78681
Callabero Cv ... 78681
Calply Dr ... 78664
Cambridge Dr ... 78664
Cameo Dr ... 78664
Cami Path ... 78665
Camino Del Verdes Pl ... 78681
Campanella Cv & Dr ... 78665
Campeche Bay Pl ... 78681
Campus Village Dr ... 78665
Canary Ct ... 78681
Cancelo Cv & Way ... 78681
Candelaria Mesa Dr ... 78664
Cantera Ct & Way ... 78681
Canyon Ledge Cv ... 78681
Canyon Sage Path ... 78665
Canyon Trail Ct ... 78664
Cap Rock Trl ... 78681
Capilano Cv ... 78664
Captain Ladd Ct ... 78665
Cardinal Ln ... 78681
Cargill Dr ... 78681
Caribou Xing ... 78664
Carlin Cv ... 78681
Carmel Dr ... 78681
Carnousty Cv & St ... 78664
Carya Ct ... 78681
Casa Blanca Cv ... 78665
Casa Linda Cv ... 78681
Casa Piedra Pl ... 78664
Cascada Ct & Ln ... 78681
Cascade Cv ... 78664
Casey Ln ... 78664
Casper Cv ... 78664
Caspian Cv ... 78665
Castebar Dr ... 78664
Castellan Ln ... 78665
Castle Crk & Path ... 78681
Castle Creek Cv ... 78681
Castle Rock Cv & Dr ... 78681
Cat Hollow Dr ... 78681
Catalpa Cv ... 78665
Catherine Ct ... 78664
Cave Dome Path ... 78681
Cedar Bend Dr ... 78681
Cedar Creek Cv ... 78681
Cedar Crest Cir & Cv ... 78665
Cedar Elm Ln ... 78681
Cedar Falls St ... 78681
Cedar Grove Cv ... 78681
Cedar Springs Pl ... 78681
Celtic Cv ... 78681
Centerbrook Pl ... 78665
Central Commerce Ct & Dr ... 78664
Cerulean Way ... 78681
Cervinia Dr ... 78665
Chalice Cv & Way ... 78665
Chalk Hill Cv ... 78665
Chalkstone Ln ... 78681
Chamois Knls ... 78664
Chamonix Ter ... 78681
Champion Dr ... 78664
Chancery Ct ... 78681
Chandler Creek Blvd ... 78665

Chandler Crossing Cv & Trl 78665
Chandler Pointe Loop 78665
Chandler View Trl 78665
Chaparral Dr 78681
Charlotte Way 78664
Charolais Ct 78681
Charpiot Dr 78681
Charrington Dr 78664
Chat Ln 78681
Chatelle Dr 78681
Cheetah Cv 78664
Chert Cv & Dr 78681
Chervil Cir 78664
Chestnut Cir 78681
Chestnut Path 78664
Cheyenne St 78665
Cheyenne Valley Cv & Dr 78664
Chi Chi Cv 78664
Chickory Ct 78665
Chinati Mountain Trl 78664
Chincoteague Way 78681
Chino Cv 78665
Chino Valley Trl 78665
Chinquapin Ct 78681
Chippewa 78665
Chiselpoint Cv 78681
Chisholm Trl 78681
Chisholm Trail Cv 78681
Chisholm Valley Dr 78681
Chowan Cv, Pl & Way 78681
Christine Rose Ct 78681
Christopher Ave 78681
Cierne Cv 78681
Cindy Ct 78664
Circle Ave & Dr 78664
Cisco Trl 78665
Cisco Valley Cv & Dr 78664
Citrine Pl 78681
Claremont Ct 78665
Clark St 78681
Clary Sage Loop 78665
Clear Lake Pl 78665
Clear Meadow Ct & Pl 78665
Clear Spring Cv 78665
Clear Vista Path 78665
Clearview Cv & Loop 78664
Clearwater Dr 78681
Clearwater Trl 78664
Cleves St 78681
Cliffside Cv 78665
Clint Cv 78664
Clinton Ct & Pl 78665
Cloud Ct 78681
Cloud Peak Cv & Ln 78681
Cobalt Cv 78681
Cole Cv 78665
Cole Valley Ln 78681
Colina Cv 78681
College Park 78665
College St 78664
Collie Path 78664
Collingwood Cv & Dr 78665
Columbia Falls Cv & Dr 78681
Columbus Loop 78665
Commerce Blvd 78664
Concord Dr 78665
Constantinople Ln 78664
Conway Cv 78665
Cooke St 78664
Cool Canyon Cv 78681
Cool Lake Cv 78665
Cool River Loop 78665
Cooper Way 78681
Copano Cv 78664
Copperhead Cv & Dr 78664
Copperwood Loop 78665
Cora Cv 78664
Coral Cay Ln 78664
Corazon Cv 78681
Cordillera Dr 78681
Corn Hill Ln 78664
Cornerstone St 78681
Coronado Cv 78681
Corral De Tierra Dr 78664
Corrigan Ln 78665
Cortes Ct & Pl 78665
Cortina Ln 78681
Cottonwood Ct 78664
Country Dr 78664
Country Aire Dr 78664
County Road 110 78665
County Road 112 78665
County Road 117 78665
County Road 122 78664
N County Road 122 78665
County Road 123 78664
County Road 170 78664
County Road 172 78681
County Road 186 78665
Courmayeur Ct 78665
Court Del Rey 78681
Courtney Cv 78664
Covered Wagon Trl 78665
Covington Pl 78681
Crabapple Cv 78681
Craig Parry Cv 78664
Crane Canyon Pl 78665
Cranston Cv & Dr 78664
Creek Cv 78664
W Creek Loop 78681
Creek Bend Cir 78681
Creek Crest Way 78664
Creek Ledge Pl 78664
Creek Ridge Blvd & Ln 78664
Creekmont Dr 78681
Creekview Dr 78681
Crenshaw Dr 78664
Crest Cv & Ln 78681
Crestfield Pl 78681
Crestline Ct 78664
Crestridge Dr 78681
Crestview St 78681
Crestwood Cv 78681
Crestwood Ln 78665
Crimson Clover Ct 78665
Crimson Sky Ct 78665
Crosscreek Trl 78681
S Crossing Dr 78664
N Crossing Trl 78665
Crossley Xing 78665
Crystal Cv 78664
Cuero Cv 78681
Curry Loop 78664
Curtis Dr 78681
Cushing Dr 78664
Cushing Park Dr 78664
Cutaway Cv 78681
Cy Young Ct 78665
Cyclone Ridge Cv 78665
Cypress Blvd 78665
Cypress Ln 78664
Cypress Point Cv 78664
Dale Cv 78664
Dalea Blf 78665
Dalea St 78681
Dana Ct 78664
Dark Tree Cv & Ln 78664
Daufuskie Island Rd 78664
David Curry Dr 78664
David Duval Ct & Cv 78664
Dawn Mesa Ct 78665
Dawson Rd 78665
Dayton Dr 78665
Dean Dr 78681
Deep Forest Cv 78665
Deep River Cir 78665
Deepwood Dr 78681
Deer Run 78681
Deer Chase Cv 78681
Deer Creek Trl 78665
Deer Tract St 78681
Deer Trail Cir 78681
Deerfern Ln 78665
Deerfoot Cir & Dr 78664
Deerhound Pl 78665
Del Monte Cv 78664
Dell Way 78664
Dell Center Blvd 78664
Dell City Dr 78664
Denfield Dr 78664
Dennis Dr 78664
Derby Cv & Trl 78681
Desert Candle Dr 78681
Desert Highlands Trl 78665
Desert Willow Cv 78681
Deurne Dr 78681
Diana Dr 78664
Diego Ct & Dr 78665
Dinge Bay 78664
Dixie Ln 78664
Dolomite Trl 78681
Donnell Dr 78664
Donner Path 78681
Doral Ct 78664
Doreen Ct 78664
Doris Ln 78664
Dorman Dr 78681
Double Creek Dr
1100-2299 78664
2250-2250 78683
2300-2598 78664
2301-2599 78664
Double File Cv & Trl 78665
Double Tree St 78681
Dove Creek Dr 78664
Dove Haven St 78664
Dover Ln 78664
Dragon Dr 78681
Dresden Cv 78665
Dry Creek Ct, Cv & Dr 78681
Durban Ct 78664
Durnbury 78664
Dyer Creek Pl 78665
Dyer Crossing Way 78665
Dylan Garrett Cv 78681
Eagle Way 78681
Eagles Nest St 78665
Easton Dr 78664
Eastrock Cv 78664
Eastwood Ln 78664
Echo Wood Pl 78681
Edgecreek Pl 78681
Edville Ln 78664
Edwards Dr 78664
Egger Ave, Ct & Cv 78664
Elder Pl & Way 78664
Elizabeth Anne Ln 78664
Elk Ridge Cv 78665
Ellis Cv 78665
Elm Trl 78681
Elmshade Cv 78665
Emerald Hill Dr 78681
Emilia Ln 78665
Emmanuel St 78681
Emperor Ct 78664
Enchanted Rock Cv 78681
Engadina Pass 78665
Enterprise Dr 78664
Entrada Way 78681
Erika Cv 78664
Esperanza Dr 78665
Estefania Ln 78665
Evans Dr 78681
Evergreen Dr 78664
Fairlane Dr 78664
Fairlawn Cv 78664
Fairmeadow Dr 78665
Fairview Cv & Dr 78665
Fairway Path 78665
Fairway Green Cv 78664
Falcon Dr 78681
Faldo Cv & Ln 78664
Falkirk Cv & Dr 78681
Fallen Leaf Ln 78665
Falling Brook Ct 78665
Fannin Ave 78664
Farali Dr 78681
Farnswood Dr 78664
Farola Cv 78681
Fasher Cv 78681
Favero Cv 78665
Fawn Cv 78681
Fawn Ridge Trl 78681
Fazio Cv 78664
Fenway Park Ct 78665
Fern Bluff Ave 78681
Ferndale Dr 78664
Fernspring Dr 78665
Fernwood Cv 78664
N Field St 78681
Field Lark Dr 78681
Fieldstone Pl 78664
Firethorn Ln & Pl 78664
Fitzgerald Ln 78664
Flameleaf Cv 78664
Flat Stone Ct 78665
Flint Rock Dr 78681
Flintwood Ct & Ln 78665
Flora Vista Loop 78681
Florence St 78664
Flower Hill Dr 78664
Flower Pot Cv 78681
Flowstone Ln 78681
Fm 1431 78681
Fm 1460 78665
Folsom Cv 78681
Foothills Trl 78681
Foppiano Loop 78665
Forest Bluff Trl 78665
Forest Canyon Dr 78665
Forest Creek Dr
2601-2699 78665
3300-3819 78664
3821-3899 78664
Forest Glen Cv 78664
Forest Green Dr 78665
Forest Hill Cv 78665
Forest Meadow Cv & Dr 78665
Forest Mesa 78664
Forest Vista Cv 78665
Fork Ridge Path 78665
Forsman Rd 78664
Fort Grant Cv & Dr 78665
Fort Leaton Dr 78664
Fort Lloyd Pl 78665
Fort Thomas Pl 78664
Fossil Cv 78681
Fossilwood Way 78681
Fountain Grove Cv 78665
Four Cabin Ct 78665
Fox Hollow St 78681
Foxfire Cv & Dr 78681
Frazell Cv 78681
Fred Couples Ct & Dr 78664
Freeland 78664
Freemont Cir, Cv & St 78681
Friarcreek Loop 78664
Frontier Trl 78681
Full Moon Cv & Trl 78681
Gabriel Mills Dr 78664
Gage Cv 78665
Galena Hills Cv, Dr & Loop 78681
Galloping Rd 78681
Garden Ct 78664
Garden Path Cv & Dr 78664
Garden Valley Cv 78664
Gattis School Rd 78664
Geese Rte 78665
Gentle Winds Ln 78681
George St 78681
N & S Georgetown St 78664
Glacier Cv 78664
Gladeview Dr 78681
Glen Cv 78681
Glen Canyon Dr 78681
Glen Eagles Cv 78664
Glen Willow Cv 78681
Glenda Dr 78681
Glenfield Ct 78665
Glenmeadows Dr 78681
Glenn Dr 78664
Glenwood Cv & St 78681
Gnu Gap 78664
Golden Bear Cv & Dr 78664
Golden Creek Cv & Dr 78665
Goldenoak Cir 78681
Goodson Ct & Ln 78664
Grand Isle Dr 78665
Grand Vista Cir 78665
Gray Oak Dr 78681
Grayling Ln 78681
S Great Oaks Cv & Dr 78681
Greatview Ct & Dr 78665
Green Downs Dr 78664
Green Meadow Dr 78664
Green Mountain Cv 78664
Green Oaks Cir 78665
Green Terrace Dr 78664
Green Tree Cv & Dr 78665
Green Valley Cv 78664
Green Vista Ct & Pl 78665
Greenbriar Ct, Cv & Loop 78664
Greenfield Dr 78664
Greenhill Dr
500-698 78665
1803-2399 78664
2401-3099 78664
Greenlawn Blvd 78664
Greenside Dr & Trl 78665
Greenwich Pl 78664
Gregory Ct & Ln 78664
Grey Feather Ct 78665
Greyleaf Path 78665
Greyson Dr 78664
W Grimes St 78664
Grove Dr 78681
Guadalajara St 78665
Guana Cay Dr 78664
Guiterrez Cv 78681
Gulf Way 78665
Gunnison Springs Dr 78681
Gunsight Dr 78665
Haight St 78681
Hailey Ln 78664
Hairy Man Rd 78681
Hal Sutton Cv 78664
Hale Irwin Cv & Dr 78664
Haleys Way 78665
Halfway Cv 78681
Hallie Ln & Way 78664
Hamlet Cir & Cv 78664
Hampton Ln 78664
Hank Aaron 78665
S Harris St 78664
Harvey Penick Cv & Dr 78664
Haselwood Ln 78665
Hawick Dr 78681
Hawk Ct 78681
Hawk Ridge St 78665
Hawk View Cv & St 78665
Hawthorne Ln 78664
Hayden Way 78664
Haynie Bnd 78665
Hearthsong Loop 78665
Heather St 78664
Heathwood Cir 78664
Helada Ct 78681
Henderson Path 78665
Henley Dr 78681
Herbs Cave Cv 78681
Heritage Center Cir 78664
Heritage Springs Trl 78664
Heritage Well Ln 78665
Hermann St 78681
Hermitage Dr 78681
Herrington Cv 78665
Hesters Crossing Rd 78681
Hickok Dr & St 78681
Hickory Ridge Cv 78665
Hickox Dr 78665
Hidden Acres Dr 78665
Hidden Bluff Cv 78665
Hidden Brook Ln 78665
Hidden Glen Cv & Dr 78681
Hidden Oaks Cv 78681
Hidden Springs Path 78665
Hidden Valley Dr 78665
Hidden View Ct & Pl 78665
Hideaway Ln 78664
High Bluff Trl 78681
High Cotton Cv & Way 78664
High Country Blvd 78664
High Point Cv & Dr 78664
Highland Ter 78665
Highland Estates Dr 78664
Highmeadows Cv 78681
Hightower Dr 78681
Hill Cv 78681
Hill St 78664
Hill Street Cv 78664
Hill View Cv 78664
Hillbrook Dr 78681
Hillridge Ct & Dr 78665
Hillrock Cv & Dr 78681
Hillside Cv & Dr 78681
Hilltop St 78681
Hillview Dr 78664
Hilway Dr 78664
Hilton Head 78664
Hogan Ln 78664
Holden Ct 78665
Hollow Trail Ct 78664
Hollow Tree Blvd 78681
Homestead 78664
Homewood Cir 78665
Honey Bear Loop 78681
Honeysuckle Ln 78664
Hoppe Trl 78681
Horseman Cv 78665
Horseshoe Cir 78681
Howell Terrace Pl 78664
Hoyer Cv 78681
Hueco Mountain Rd & Trl 78664
Hummingbird Ct 78681
Hunlac Cv & Trl 78681
Hunters Trl 78681
Hunters Lodge Cv & Dr 78681
Huntington Ct & Trl 78664
Huxley Ln 78664
Hyde Park Dr 78665
Hyridge Cir & St 78664
Ibex Trl 78664
Ikea Way 78665
Indian Camp Trl 78681
Indian Meadows Dr 78665
Indian Oaks 78681
Indian Summer Pass 78665
Indigo Trl 78665
N Industrial Blvd 78681
Inman Ln 78664
N Interstate 35
100-198 78681
N Interstate 35
200-300 78681
302-5198 78681
801-4899 78664
S Interstate 35
1000C5-1000C9 78681
100-2898 78681
501-3399 78664
Inverness Dr 78681
Inwood Cv 78681
Iris Cv 78681
Irishmoss Trl 78665
Ironweed Run 78681
Ivy Ct 78681
Jack Bradley Cv 78665
Jackal Dr 78681
Jacki Dr 78665
Jackie Robinson Pl 78665
Jackrabbit Run 78664
James Pl 78664
James Parker Ln 78665
Jasmine Path 78664
Jazz St 78665
Jeffrey Way 78665
Jennifer Ct 78664
Jennifer Ln 78665
Jerusalem Dr 78664
Jester Farms 78664
Jigsaw Cv 78664
Jigsaw Pathway 78664
Jilbur Dr 78681
Jina Ln 78664
Joe Dimaggio Blvd 78665
Joffa Ct 78664
John Wilson Ln 78664
Johnny Bench 78665
Johnson Rd 78665
Johnson Way 78681
Jordan Ln 78665
Joseph St 78665
Joshua Cv 78665
Joyce Ln 78664
Judy Scholl Way 78681
Julianas Way 78665
Juniper Trl 78664
Justin Leonard Dr 78664
Kafka Cir 78664
Karen Cv 78664
Karolyn Dr 78664
Karstview Cv 78681
Kass Cv 78664
Keeshond Pl 78664
Kelsey Cv 78664
Kempwood Ct & Loop 78665
S Kenney Fort Blvd 78665
Kenneys Way 78665
Kettle Cv 78665
Kim Cv 78665
Kimberly Cv 78665
Kimbrook Dr 78681
King Cotton Ln 78664
Kingsburg Dr 78681
Kinney Fort Trl 78664
Kiphen Rd 78665
Kissatchie Trl 78664
Klamath Falls Dr 78681
Klondike Loop 78665
Knollwood Cir & Cv 78681
Kodiak Dr 78664
Korat Ln 78681
Kristencreek Ln 78681
La Frontera Blvd 78681
Lacey Oak Cv & Loop 78681
Lagoona Dr 78681
Laguna Seca Ln 78664
Lake Cv & Dr 78665
Lake Bluff Cv 78665
Lake Creek Cir 78664
N Lake Creek Dr 78681
S Lake Creek Dr 78681
Lake Forest Cv & Dr 78665
Lake Pines Dr 78681
Lakeside Loop 78665
Lakeview Cv 78681
Lakewood Ln 78681
Lamar Dr 78664
N & S Lampasas St 78664
Lancaster Gate Cv & Dr 78664
Lance Ln 78664
Lantana Dr 78664
Lantern Light Dr 78681
Lara Cv 78665
Larchwood Cv 78681
Las Colinas Way 78681
Lasso Dr 78681
Latigo Trce 78681
Laughing Water Ln 78681
Laura Ct 78681
Laurel Dr & Path 78664
Laurel Bay Loop 78681
Laurel Grove Way 78681
Laurel Oak Loop 78665
Laurel Ridge Dr 78665
Lawmans Ct 78665
Lawnmont Dr 78664
Lazada Ln 78681
Lazy Oak Cv 78681
Leah Ln 78665
Ledbetter St 78681
N Lee St 78664
Lee Trevino Cv 78664
Leghorn Cv 78681
Lenz Dr & St 78681
Lerwick Ln 78681
Leslie Ct 78681
N Lewis St 78664
E & W Liberty St 78664
Liberty Walk Dr 78681

Lightfoot Dr 78681
Lilac Dr 78664
Lime Cv 78664
Lime Rock Dr 78681
Limmer Loop 78665
Limpia Crk 78664
Linda Lee Cv 78665
Lindo Loop 78681
Links Ln 78664
Lisa Rae Dr 78665
Live Oak Cir, Cv & St 78681
Lobo Mountain Ln 78664
Lofty Ln 78681
Logan St 78664
Loncola Ct 78681
London Rd 78664
Lone Oak Trl 78681
Lonesome Cv 78681
Long Cv 78664
Longdraw Dr 78681
Longhorn Dr 78681
Longhorn Trl 78665
Longmeadow Dr 78664
Lookout Tree Ln 78664
Loquat Ln 78664
Lord Byron Cir & Cv 78664
Lorson Loop 78665
Los Alamos Ct & Pass 78665
Lost Spgs 78681
Lost Indigo Trl 78665
Lou Gehrig Ln 78665
Louis Henna Blvd 78664
W Louis Henna Blvd 78681
Loyaga Dr 78681
Luckenwald Cv & Dr 78681
Luminoso Ln E & W 78681
Luther Peterson 78665
Lydia Ln 78665
Lynda Sue St 78681
Madera Ln 78664
Madison Ct 78681
Magellan Way 78665
W Magic Mountain Cv & Ln 78681
Magnolia Dr 78664
Maidstone Cv 78664
E & W Main St 78664
Malaga Hills Dr 78681
Mammouth Ct 78681
S Mandell St 78664
Mangrove Cave Ct 78681
Manjack Cay 78664
Manx Dr 78681
Maple Run 78664
Maple Run Cv 78664
Marcasite Dr 78681
Marfa Lights Trl 78664
Margarita Loop 78665
Mariah Cv 78665
Mark Brooks Cv 78664
Mark Omeara Cv 78664
Marsala Springs Dr 78681
Marsh Harbour Cv & Dr 78664
Marshall Trl 78665
Martin Ave 78681
Mason Cv 78681
Masonwood Way 78681
Massey Way 78681
Mastiff Cv 78665
Matagorda Dr 78664
Mathers Mill Trl 78664
Mayfield Dr 78681
Mayfield Cave Trl 78681
Mayfield Ranch Blvd & Cv 78681
N Mays St
100-2199 78664
2201-2299 78664
2400-2599 78665
2601-3099 78665
S Mays St 78664
Mays Xing 78664
Mckenzie St 78664
Mcneil Rd 78681
Meadow Run & Way 78664
Meadow Bluff Ct & Way 78665
Meadow Brook Dr 78664
Meadow Park Dr 78665
Meadow Vista Ln 78665
Meadowcreek Cir, Cv & Dr 78664
Meadowild Cv & Dr 78664
Meadowrue Cv 78665
Meadows Dr 78681
Meadowside Ln 78665
Meandering Way 78664
Meister Pl 78664
Melbourne Ln 78664
Melinsou Dr 78664
Menlo Park Pl 78681
Mentone 78664
Meredith Ln 78681
Merion Cv 78664
Merrell Cv 78664
E & W Mesa Park Cv & Dr 78664
Mesa Verde Dr 78681
Mesquite Hollow Pl 78665
E & W Messick Loop & Pl 78681
Michelle Lynne Cv 78681
Mickey Mantle Pl 78665
Mid Bark Pass 78664
Midwood Ln 78681
E Milam St 78664
Miller Falls Cv & Dr 78681
Mills Meadow Dr 78664
Mimosa Cv & Trl 78664
Minnow Cv 78665
Mirador Cv 78681
Miramar Cv 78665
Mirasol Dr & Loop 78681
Miraval Cir & Loop 78665
Misty Morning Way 78664
Misty Oaks Way 78665
Misty Woods 78664
Mitchell Cv 78681
Mobil St 78681
Mockingbird Dr 78681
Mohican 78665
Monadale Trl 78664
Monica Ln 78664
Montana Falls Dr 78681
Montclair Dr 78664
Monterey Pines Dr 78664
Monterosa Ln & Loop 78665
Monticello Ct 78665
Monument Dr 78681
Moonmist Cv 78665
Morning Dew Cv 78664
Morning Meadows Cv 78664
Morning View Pl 78665
Morningside Cv 78664
S Morrell St
700-1998 78681
701-999 78664
Moss Hollow Dr 78681
Mount Shasta Cv 78681
Mountain Mist Ln 78681
Mouse Trap Dr 78681
Moye St 78664
Mulligan Dr 78664
E & W Nakoma 78664
Nancy Dr 78664
Napali Ct 78681
E & W Nash St 78664
Nash Ranch Loop 78665
Native Garden Cv 78681
Natural Bridge Ct 78681
Needle Pine Dr 78664
Nelson St 78664
New Cv 78664
Newland Ct, Dr & Pl 78681
Newport Landing Pl 78665
Niagara Falls Ter 78681
Nicholaus Cv 78664
Nick Cv 78664
Nick Faldo Trl 78664
Nick Price Cv & Loop 78664
Nicole Cir & Cv 78664
Nocona Cv 78665
Noe Ln 78665
Nolan Ryan 78665
Nolina Ln 78681
Norman Loop 78664
Normeadows Cir 78681
Northwest Dr 78681
Nottingham Hill Rd 78664
Nueltin Ct 78681
E Oak Dr 78664
W Oak Dr 78664
Oak Pl 78681
Oak Vw 78664
Oak Bend Cv & Dr 78681
Oak Branch Pl 78665
Oak Forest Dr 78681
Oak Haven Dr 78681
Oak Hollow Dr 78681
Oak Meadow Dr 78681
Oak Meadows Cv 78681
Oak Park Dr 78681
Oak Springs Cv 78681
Oak Vista Ln 78681
Oaklands Dr 78681
Oakmont Dr 78665
Oakmoore 78664
Oakridge Dr 78681
Oakview Dr 78681
Oakwood Blvd 78681
Obsidian Ln 78681
Ocelot Cv & Way 78681
Oconnor Dr 78681
Octavia Ln 78681
Ogrin Cv 78664
Old Austin Rock Rd 78681
E & W Old Bowman Rd 78664
Old Meadow Ct 78665
Old Oak Dr 78665
Old Ravine Ct 78665
Old Settlement Rd 78664
Old Settlers Blvd 78681
E Old Settlers Blvd
100-1899 78664
2401-2497 78665
2499-4499 78665
W Old Settlers Blvd 78681
Old West Dr & Pl 78681
Oleander Ln 78664
Olympic Cv 78664
Onion Branch Cv 78681
Onion Creek Village Dr 78664
Orion St 78665
Orwell Ln 78664
Outpost Cv 78665
Overcup Dr 78681
Overland St 78665
Overton St 78665
Overview St 78681
Owl Ct 78681
Oxford Blvd 78664
Pachea Trl 78665
Pack Saddle Pass 78681
Paladen Pl 78664
E Palm Valley Blvd
301-497 78664
499-1999 78664
2000-4000 78665
4002-4798 78665
W Palm Valley Blvd 78664
Palmer Cv & Dr 78664
Palo Duro Loop 78664
Palo Pinto Cv 78665
Paloma Dr 78665
Paloma Lake Blvd 78665
Paola St 78665
Paradise Ridge Cv & Dr 78665
Park Dl 78664
Park Dr 78681
Park Oak Dr 78681
Park Place Cir 78681
Park Valley Dr 78681
Park Vista Trl 78665
Parker Rd 78681
Parkfield Cir & Cv 78664
Parkhill Cv 78664
Parkland Cv 78681
Parkside Cir & Cv 78664
Parkview Dr 78681
Parkway St 78664
Parkwood Cv 78664
Parma St 78665
Parrot Trl 78681
Partridge Ct 78681
Pasada Ln 78681
Pasadera Ln 78664
Pasternak Dr 78664
Pastori Cv 78665
Pathfinder Way 78665
Paul Azinger Ct & Dr 78664
Payne Stewart Dr 78664
Peacemaker St 78681
Peach Tree Cv 78681
Peachtree Valley Dr 78681
Pearl Cv 78681
Pearson Cv & Way 78665
Pebble Ct 78681
Pebble Ridge Cv 78681
Pebblestone Trl 78665
Pecan Ave & Ln 78664
Pecan Crest Cv 78681
Pecos Valley Cv 78665
Pena Cv 78681
Penelope Ct & Way 78665
Penny Ln 78681
Penwood Cv 78664
Perch Trl 78665
Peruga Ln 78681
Pescia St 78665
Peterson St 78664
W Pflugerville Pkwy 78664
Pheasant Holw 78681
Pheasant Rdg 78665
Pheasant Ridge Cv 78665
Phil Mickelson Ct 78664
Phlox Ct 78665
N & S Phoenix Cv & Way 78665
Picadilly Ct & Dr 78664
Picnic Cv 78664
Pigeon View St 78665
Pike Path 78665
Pin Oak Ln 78681
Pine Forest Cir & Cv 78665
Pine Needle Cir, Cv & Ln 78681
Pinehurst Ln 78664
Pioneer Way 78665
Pioneer Crossing Dr 78665
E & W Piper Sonoma Ct & Pl 78665
Placid Creek Ct & Way 78665
Plantation Ct, Cv & Dr 78681
Plateau Vista Blvd 78664
Plume Grass Pl 78665
Pointe Pl 78681
Poker Aly 78681
Pon Ct 78664
Poppy Hills Cv & Trl 78664
Porter Creek Cv 78665
Portulaca Dr 78681
Possum Trot St 78681
Powderhorn Cv & Dr 78681
Prairie Rock Way 78664
Prairie Star Cv & Ln 78664
Preserve Pl 78664
Priest River Cv & Dr 78681
Primrose Trl 78664
Promenade Ct 78664
Provident Ln 78664
Purple Sage Cv & Dr 78681
Putter Cv 78664
Quail Ln 78681
Quail Creek Cir & Dr 78664
Quail Lodge Ct 78664
Quail Ravine 78664
Quail Run Dr 78681
Quanah Dr 78681
Quarry Crk 78681
Quicksilver Cir & St 78665
Quitman Mountain Way 78664
R R 620 78681
Rabbit Run 78664
Rachel Ct & Ln 78664
Radholme Ct 78664
Rainbow Cv 78665
Rainbow Parke Dr 78665
Raintree Path 78664
Rambollet Ter 78681
Rams Horn Way 78665
Ranch Park Trl 78681
Ranier Cv & Ln 78665
Ravenwood Dr 78665
Rawhide Dr & Loop 78681
Ray Berglund Blvd 78664
Red Bud Ln 78664
N Red Bud Ln 78665
Red Bud Trl 78665
Red Cloud Dr 78681
Red Oak Cir 78681
Red Rock Cv & Dr 78665
Red Stag Pl 78665
Redwing Way 78664
Redwood Trce 78664
Regency Ln 78665
Reggie Jackson Trl 78665
Reggio St 78665
Remuda Cir 78681
Renaissance Trl 78665
Resnick Dr 78664
Reston Cv 78665
Reta Cv 78664
Rices Crossing Ln 78664
Ridge Run 78664
Ridge Crest Dr 78664
Ridge Rock Dr 78681
Ridgebend Dr 78665
Ridgefield Loop 78665
Ridgeline Dr 78664
Ridgemeadow Way 78664
Ridgemont St 78664
Ridgetop Dr 78664
Riley Cv 78664
Rimini Cv 78665
Rio Brisas Cv 78681
Risa Ct 78681
Rising Sun Cv 78664
River Crossing Trl 78665
River Forest Cv & Dr 78665
Riverlawn Dr 78681
Robb Ln 78664
Roberto Clemente Ln 78665
Robin Trl 78681
Rock Chalk Ct 78664
Rock Creek Dr 78681
Rock Face Ct 78681
Rock Hill Rd 78681
Rock Midden Ln 78665
Rock Rose Pl 78665
Rock Shelf Ln 78681
Rock Spring Cv 78681
Rocking J Rd 78665
Rockridge St 78681
Rocky Mountain Trl 78681
Rod Carew Dr 78665
Rolling Hl 78681
Rolling Canyon Trl 78681
Rolling Green Dr 78664
Rolling Oak Dr 78664
Rolling Ridge Dr 78665
Rollingway Cv & Dr 78681
Roma St 78665
Ronchamps Dr 78681
Rosalina Loop 78665
Rose May Cv 78681
Rosebud Pl 78681
Rosemary Ln 78664
Rosemount Cv & Dr 78665
Rosenborough Cv & Ln 78665
Rosewood Ct 78664
Ross Cv 78664
Round Rock Ave
2-198 78664
200-599 78664
700-1800 78681
1802-2498 78681
Round Rock Ranch Blvd 78665
Round Rock West Cv & Dr 78681
Roundabout Ln 78664
Roundup Trl 78681
Roundville Ln 78664
Rowland Cv 78665
Royal Burgess Dr 78664
Royal Port Rush Dr 78664
Royal Troon Cv & Dr 78664
Royal Vista Blvd 78681
Royston Ln 78664
Rubio Ave 78664
Rusk Ct & Rd 78665
Russwood Cv 78681
Rustlers Rd 78681
Rusty Nail Loop 78681
Ryders Rdg 78665
Rye St 78664
Ryon Cv & Ln 78681
Sabbia Cv & Dr 78665
Sabertooth Dr 78681
Sable Oaks Dr 78664
Sable Trail Ct 78664
Sacco St 78665
Sagebrush Dr 78681
Saint Andrews Dr 78664
Saint Christina Ct 78665
Saint Christopher Ct 78665
Saint Federico Way 78665
Saint Frances Ct 78665
Saint James Pl 78665
Saint Paul Rivera 78665
Saint Rodrigo Ct 78665
Saint Williams Ave, Loop & St 78681
Salorn Cv & Way 78681
Salt Flat Ln 78664
Salvador Ln 78665
Sam Bass Cir 78681
Sam Bass Rd
701-795 78681
797-797 78680
797-797 78681
799-4599 78681
4601-5499 78681
Sambuco St 78665
San Chisolm Dr 78664
San Fernando Ct 78665
San Michele St 78665
San Milan Pass 78665
San Saba St 78664
Sandy Brook Dr 78665
Sandy Haven Cv 78681
Sandy Koufax Ln 78665
Sandy Lyle Cv 78664
Sanibel Ct 78681
Sansome Ln 78681
Sansone Dr 78665
Santa Ana Ln 78665
Santa Barbara Ct & Loop 78665
Santa Clara Ln 78665
Santa Cruz St 78665
Santa Domingo Dr 78665
Santolina Ln 78664
Sap Cv 78664
Sapphire Ct & Loop 78681
Sara Dr 78664
Sardinia Cv & Dr 78665
Satellite Vw 78665
Saunders Dr 78664
Savannah Ct & Dr 78681
Sawgrass Ln 78681
Scarlet Oak Cv 78665
Scenic Cv 78664
Scenic Loop 78681
Scenic Ter 78681
School Days Ln 78664
Sea Ash Cir 78681
Sebastian Cv 78681
Sedgewick Ln 78664
Seed Cv 78664
Sendero Springs Dr 78681
Senna Ridge Trl 78665
Seton Pkwy 78665
Settlement Dr 78665
Settlers Park Loop 78665
Shaded Way 78664
Shadowbrook Cir 78681
Shadowpoint Cv 78665
Shady Loop 78664
Shady Bluff Cv 78665
Shady Hillside Pass 78665
Shady Oaks Cir 78681
Shady Path Cv 78664
Shady Rock Ct 78665
Shaker Ln 78681
Shark Loop 78664
Sheffield Way 78665
Shellcastle Ln 78681
Sheltie Cv & Ln 78664
N & S Sheppard St 78664
Shiraz Loop 78665
Short Horn Cv & Ln 78665
Shotwell Ln 78664
Shultz Rd 78664
Side Cv 78681
Sierra Cv 78664
Silent Brook Trl 78665
Silk Tree Ln 78664
Silone Cir 78664
Silver Spur 78681
Silver Trl 78664
Silver Lace Ln 78664
Silver Maple Cv 78664
Silver Oak Dr 78664
Silverleaf Cv & Ln 78664
Sinclair St 78681
Sky Ln 78681
Skylers Cir 78665
Skyview Cv & Way 78681
N Smincen St 78665
Smoke Tree Trl 78681
Smyers Ln 78681
Snead Path 78664
Snowdrift Trl 78664
Snowflake Dr 78664
Sofia Pl 78665
Solitaire 78665
Solitude Cv 78665
Somerset Dr 78681
Sophora Ct 78681
Sosa Cv 78665
Southampton Way 78664
Southcreek Dr 78664
Southeastern Trl 78664
Southern Pl 78665
Southwestern Trl 78664
Spanish Bay Ct 78664
Spanish Oak Dr, Ter & Trl 78681
Sparrow Dr 78681
Spindle Top Ter 78681
Splitrock St 78681
Spring Br 78681
Spring St 78664
Spring Breeze Cv & Dr 78664
Spring Canyon Trl 78681
Spring Creek Rd 78681
Spring Hollow Path 78681
Spring Tree St 78681
Springbok Dr 78681
Springfield Gorge Dr 78681
Springridge St 78664
Springwater Dr 78681
Springwillow Ln 78681
Spruce Cv 78664
Spyglass Cv 78664
Stadler Cv 78664
Stagecoach Trl 78681
Starlight Vis 78665
Starling Dr 78681
Steam Way 78665
Stephen St 78665
Stevens Trl 78681
Still Meadow Cv 78681

Stillhouse Spg 78681
Stillmeadow 78664
Stirrup Dr 78681
N & S Stone St 78664
Stone Forest Trl 78681
Stone Oak Dr & Pl 78681
Stone Slope Ct 78665
Stonebridge Dr 78681
Stonecreek Dr & Pl 78681
Stonehaven Ln 78665
Stonehenge Path 78681
Stonewall Dr 78681
Stonewreath Dr 78681
Stoney Brk & Hl 78681
Stoney Point Rd 78665
Stratford Ct, Cv & Dr 78664
Stray Cv 78681
Sugar Berry Cv 78664
Sultana Ct 78664
Sumac Ct 78681
N & S Summercrest Cv & Loop 78681
Summerwalk Pl 78665
Summit St 78664
Sun Lk 78681
Sunbeam Cv 78664
Sunburst Pkwy & Ter 78681
Sundance Dr 78665
Sundance Pkwy 78681
Sundrop Cv & Pl 78665
Sunrise Rd
  1101-1197 78664
  1199-2499 78664
  2600-2698 78665
  2700-4300 78665
  4302-4498 78665
Sunset Dr
  100-400 78664
  402-498 78664
  700-799 78681
Surrey Dr 78664
Sussex Pl & Way 78665
Sweetgum Cv 78664
Sweetgum Ln
  600-799 78664
  900-999 78665
Sweetwater Cv 78681
Sycamore Cv & Trl 78664
Sylvia Ct & Ln 78681
Tad Park Cv 78681
Tailfeather Dr 78681
Tammy Ln 78665
Tamra Ct & Cv 78681
Tandi Trl 78664
Tandi Trail Cv 78664
Tanglewood St 78681
Tapado Canyon Trl 78681
Tarleton Ct & Ln 78681
Taron Cv & Dr 78681
Tassey St 78664
Tate Ln 78665
Tawakoni Loop 78664
Tejas Dr 78681
Tellabs Dr 78665
Tenaza Cv 78664
Teravista Pkwy 78665
Teravista Club Dr 78665
Terra St 78665
Terrier Cv 78664
Texana Ct 78681
Texana Loop 78665
Texas Ave 78664
Texella 78681
Thibodeaux Dr 78664
Thistle Mound Cv 78665
Thompson Trl 78664
Thorn Creek Pl 78664
Thousand Oaks Dr 78681
Tiffany Trl 78681
Tiffany Nicole St 78665
Tiger Trl 78664
Timber Creek Cv 78665
Timberline Dr 78665
Timberwood Dr 78664
Tin Roof Cv 78681
Tiny Trl 78681

Tiny Seed Cv 78664
Todd Trl 78665
Tofino Cv 78665
Tolstoy Cir 78664
Tom Gary Cv 78665
Tom Kite Cv & Dr 78664
Tom Seaver Pl 78665
Tom Watson Cv 78664
Tomcat Cv & Dr 78681
Tomlinson Fort Way 78664
Tonia Loop 78665
Tonkawa Trl 78681
Tonkinese Dr 78681
Tony Dr 78664
Top Rock Ln 78681
Tortoise St 78664
Tourmaline Trl 78681
Tower Dr 78664
Town Centre Dr 78664
Toyahville 78664
Trailing Vine Way 78665
Trailway St 78664
Tree Sap Way 78664
Trevino Dr 78664
Trickle Trace Trl 78681
Trinity Bnd 78664
Troy Ln 78664
Turetella Dr 78681
Twilight Cv 78681
Twin Ridge Dr & Pkwy 78664
Twin Terrace Ct 78665
Twinberry Trl 78681
Two Jacks Trl 78681
Ty Cobb Pl 78665
Tyler Cv 78664
University Blvd 78665
University Oaks 78665
Upper Passage Ln 78681
Valentine Dr 78664
Valerian Trl
  2000-2099 78664
  2100-2399 78665
Valerie Cv 78665
Vallarta Ln 78681
Valley Trl 78664
Valley Vw 78665
Valley Creek Dr 78664
Valley View Cv 78681
Valley View Dr 78664
Valona Dr & Loop 78681
Van Horn Ct & Dr 78664
Vaquera Ct 78681
Vera Way 78664
Verbena Way 78664
Vernell Way 78664
Via Sonoma Dr & Trl 78665
Vibar Cv 78681
Victoria Cv 78664
Villa Cv 78664
Vinson Ct 78664
Vintage Dr 78664
Vinwood Cv 78665
Virginia Dr 78664
Vista Ave 78664
Vista Isle Dr 78681
Vivian Dr 78681
Vonnegut Ct 78665
Wagon Gap Dr 78681
Wagon Wheel Dr 78681
Waimea Bnd & Ct 78681
Walleye Cv & Way 78665
Wallin Loop & Path 78664
Walsh Dr & Ln 78681
Walsh Ranch Blvd & Cv 78681
Wandering Vine Trl 78665
Wapato Cv 78665
War Horse Ln 78664
Warner Ranch Rd 78664
Water Birch 78665
Water Oak Cv 78664
Water Spaniel Way 78664
Wayne Dr 78664
Weddington Dr 78664
Weiskopf Loop 78664
Westcott Dr 78664

Westend Pl 78681
Western Lake Dr 78665
Westhampton Ct 78664
Westinghouse Rd 78681
Westmeadow Trl 78665
Westminster Pl 78664
Westside Ln 78681
Westvalley Pl 78665
Westview Dr 78664
Westwind Ave 78681
Westwood Dr 78681
Whetstone St 78681
Whip O Will St 78681
Whirlwind Trl 78664
Whispering Dr 78664
Whispering Oaks Ln 78681
Whispering Woods Ct 78681
White Fox Cv 78664
White Indigo Trl 78665
White Oak Cir, Cv & Loop 78681
White Wing Way 78664
Whitecrest Cv 78681
Whitehurst Cv & Dr 78681
Whitewater Cv 78681
Whitey Ford Way 78665
Whitlow Cv 78681
Whitworth Ln 78681
Wild Horse Ln 78681
Wilderness Path 78665
Wilderness Way 78664
Wildflower Dr & Trl 78664
Wildvine Cv 78665
Wildwater Way 78681
Wildwood Dr 78681
Willie Mays Ln 78665
Willow Cv, Trl & Way 78664
Willow Oak Ln 78681
Willowbend Cv & Dr 78664
Winchester Dr 78665
Wind Spirit Cv 78681
Windberry Ct & Path 78665
Windcrest Cv & Dr 78664
Windhill Loop 78681
Winding Way 78664
Winding Creek Pl 78665
Winding River Trl 78681
Windrift Way 78664
Windsong Trl 78664
Windsor Rd 78664
Windy Cv 78681
Windy Park Cir, Ct & Dr 78664
Winnsboro Cv 78664
Winsted Ave 78664
Wisteria Way 78664
Witte Cv 78681
Wolf Creek Way 78664
Wolkin Cv 78681
Wonder St 78681
Wood Mesa Ct & Dr 78665
Wood Rock Dr 78681
Wood Sorrel Way 78665
Wood Springs Ln 78681
Wood Vista Pl 78665
Wooded Way 78664
Woodglen Dr 78681
Woodgreen Dr 78681
Woodhaven Ct & Trl 78665
Woodhill Dr 78681
Woodhollow Trl 78665
Woodland Ln & Loop 78664
Woodledge Pl 78665
Woodlief Trl 78664
Woods Blvd & Cv 78681
Woodston Dr 78681
Woodway 78681
Woody Cv 78665
Wren Ct 78681
Wright Cir 78664
Wroxton Way 78664
Wyman Cv 78681
Wyoming Spgs 78681
Yaupon Holw & Trl 78664
Yogi Berra Cv & Way 78665
Yorkshire Ln 78664

Yucca Dr 78681
Zephyr Ln 78664
Zeus Cir 78665
Zimmerman Cv & Ln 78681
Zola Ln 78664
Zunker 78665
Zydeco Dr 78664

ROWLETT TX

General Delivery 75088

POST OFFICE BOXES MAIN OFFICE STATIONS AND BRANCHES

Box No.s
All PO Boxes 75030

RURAL ROUTES

03, 05, 06, 07, 08, 12 75088
01, 02, 09, 10, 13, 25 75089

NAMED STREETS

Abbey Ct 75088
Aberdeen Dr 75089
Acapulco Dr 75089
Ahnee Dr 75089
Ainsdale Ln 75089
Airline Dr 75089
Alazan Bay Dr 75089
Albany Dr 75089
Alexandria Dr 75088
Alissa Dr 75089
Allen Ln 75088
Amanda Ct 75088
Ambassador Ln 75089
Amber Ave 75088
Ambrose Dr 75089
Americas Cup 75089
Amesbury Ln 75089
Amherst Dr 75088
Amy Ave 75088
Andover Ct 75089
Andrea Ln 75088
Anthony Cir 75088
Antioch Dr 75089
Arbor Ct 75088
Arborside Dr 75089
Ardis Dr 75088
Armstrong Ln 75089
Aspen Dr 75088
Aster Ln 75089
Atlantic Dr 75088
Auburn Dr 75088
Augusta Ln 75089
Azalea Dr 75089
Azzurra Dr 75089
Baffin Bay Dr 75089
Ballard Ct 75089
Balsam Dr 75089
Bandalia Dr 75089
Barolo Dr 75088
Barton Creek Cir & Dr 75089
Basswood Dr 75089
Battle Creek Dr 75089
Battlefield Dr 75089
Bayhill Dr 75088
Baylor Dr 75088
Bayonne Dr 75088
Bayport Cir 75088
Bayshore Ln 75088
Baystone Ct 75088
Bayview Dr 75088
Baywatch Dr 75088
Beacon Dr 75089
Beech St 75089
Bellaire Ln 75089
Belmount Rd 75089
Benedict Ct 75088

Bent Tree Dr 75089
Bermuda Cir & Dr 75088
Beverly Dr 75089
Bickers Dr 75089
Big A Rd 75089
Birch Ct 75088
Birchmont Dr 75089
Birdie Ct 75089
Blackfin Dr 75089
Blain Dr 75088
Blair Oak Dr 75089
Blue Quail Ln 75088
Blue Sky Ct 75089
Bluebell Dr 75089
Bluebonnet Dr 75089
Bluewood Dr 75089
Bluffpoint Rd 75088
Bob White Dr 75088
Bobbie Ln 75089
Bois D Arc Ln 75088
Bond St 75088
Bordeaux Ln 75089
Bouvier St 75088
Boyd Blvd 75088
Brandford Rd 75089
Brentwood St 75088
Briarcrest Dr 75089
Briarwood Dr 75088
Bridgewater Dr 75088
Bristol Ct 75089
Brittany Dr 75088
Broadmoor Ln 75089
Brockton Ct 75089
Brookfield Dr 75089
Brookhaven Dr 75089
Brookhollow Dr 75089
Brookline Dr 75089
Brookside Dr 75088
Brownlee Blvd 75088
Bryn Mawr Dr 75089
Buckeye Dr 75089
Buckhorn Dr 75089
Bucknell Dr 75089
Bunker Hill Ct 75089
Burgundy Trl 75088
Cabott Cv 75089
Caleb Dr 75089
Calypso Dr 75089
Cambridge Dr 75088
Camden Ct 75089
Camelot Ln 75089
Canterbury Dr 75089
Canyon Creek Dr 75089
Captains Ct 75088
Caribbean Dr 75088
Carla Dr 75088
Carmel Ln 75089
Carrie Ln 75089
Carroll Ln 75089
Carson Ct 75088
Caruth Dr 75089
Cascade Ct 75088
Castle Dr 75088
Castleroy Ln 75089
Catalina St 75088
Catamaran Rd 75088
Cavalier Dr 75088
Cedar Ln 75088
Cedarbrook Rd 75089
Centenary Dr 75089
Centennial Dr 75088
Century Dr 75088
Chablis Dr 75088
Chaha Rd 75088
Chalkstone Dr 75088
Champion Dr 75089
Chandler Dr 75088
Channel Dr 75088
Chapel Cv 75088
Chapel Hill Dr 75088
Chardonnay Dr 75088
Charleston Dr 75089
Chatsworth Ln 75089
Cherry Hills Ln 75089
Chesham Dr 75088
Chestnut Dr 75089

Cheyenne Dr 75088
Chianti Ct 75088
Chiesa Rd
  1900-5599 75088
  5600-9199 75089
Chimneywood Cir & Dr 75089
Chinkapin Ln 75089
Christine St 75088
Christopher Dr 75088
Churchill Way 75089
Circleview St 75088
Clairmont Ave 75089
Clarendon St 75089
Clay Dr 75088
Clearlake Dr 75088
Clearwood Ln 75089
Clemson Cir 75089
Clubhouse Cir 75089
Clydesdale Ct 75088
Coastway Dr 75088
Colfax Dr 75089
Colgate Ln 75088
College Park Dr 75088
Colonial Dr 75089
Columbia Dr 75089
Columbus Dr 75089
Commerce St 75088
Commodore Dr 75088
Compass Point Dr 75089
Concord Dr 75089
Conestoga Dr 75089
Conley Ct 75089
Conlin Dr 75088
Constitution Dr 75089
Cooke Dr 75088
Copano Bay Dr 75089
Coral Way 75088
Cordelia Rd 75089
Cornell Dr 75089
Cortland Cir 75089
Cottonwood Ct 75088
Country Club Cir 75089
Courageous Dr 75089
Cousteau Dr 75089
Cove Rd 75088
Cove Hollow Ct 75088
Coventry Dr 75089
Covington Dr 75089
Coyle St 75088
Creek Bnd 75089
Creek View Ct & Dr 75089
Creek Wood Ct & Dr 75089
Creekbluff Dr 75088
Creekside Dr 75089
Crestview Ln 75088
Cypress Dr 75089
Daisy Ln 75089
Dalrock Rd
  1600-6399 75088
  6400-10099 75088
Dalton Dr 75089
Dana Dr 75088
Danbury Ct & Dr 75089
Dandelion Ln 75088
Danridge Rd 75089
Dartbrook Dr 75088
Dartmouth Dr 75089
David Cir & Dr 75088
Davis St 75088
Day Farm Ct 75089
Debbie Cir 75089
Deerfield Dr 75089
Deerwood Dr 75089
Defender Ln 75089
Delia St 75088
Delta Dr 75088
Dennis St 75088
Denver St 75088
Dexham Rd
  3700-5599 75088
  5600-6399 75089
Diplomacy Dr 75089
Dockside Dr 75088
Dogwood Trl 75089
Doliver Dr 75088

Dolphin Cir 75088
Donovan Ct 75088
Doral Ct 75089
Dorchester Dr 75088
Douglas Ave 75089
Dove Creek Dr 75088
Dover Dr 75088
Drakestone Ave 75088
Dream Maker Way 75089
Driftwood Ln 75089
Duchess Way 75089
Duck Pond Ln 75088
Duke Cir 75088
Dunhill Pl 75089
Eagle Dr 75088
Eastern Hills Ct 75089
Ebb Tide Dr 75088
Echo Ct 75088
Edenmore Ln 75089
Edgelake Trl 75088
Edgewater Cir 75088
Edgewater Dr
  4800-5299 75088
  5300-5699 75089
Edgeway Cir 75089
Edgewood Dr 75089
Edinburgh Ln 75089
Egret Ct 75088
Elm Grove Rd 75089
Elmhurst St 75089
Enclave Ln 75089
Enterprise Dr
  3300-3499 75088
  3416-3416 75030
Esquire Ln 75089
Essex Dr 75089
Estates Way 75089
Eton Dr 75089
Euclid Dr 75089
Evening Star Dr 75089
Evergreen Dr 75089
Evinrude Dr 75089
Fair Oak Dr 75089
Fairfax Ave 75089
Fairfield Dr 75089
Fairmont Cir, Ct & Dr 75089
Fairway Vista Dr 75089
Falcon St 75089
Falcon Ridge Ct 75088
Faringdon Ln 75089
Faulkner Dr 75089
Fawn Valley Ln & Pl 75089
Fern Hill Ln 75089
Flagstone Ave 75088
Flamingo Ct & Dr 75089
Forainte Dr 75089
Forest Hill Ct 75089
Founders Dr 75089
Foxwood Dr 75089
Francesca Ct 75088
Freedom Ln 75089
Freeman Dr 75089
Freestone Ct 75089
Fuqua Rd 75089
Gardenia Dr 75089
Garner Cir, Ct & Rd 75088
Garrett Dr 75089
Gillon Dr 75089
Glen Hill Dr 75088
Gleneagles Ln 75089
Glenridge Dr 75089
Glenshee Dr 75089
Glenside Dr 75089
Glenstone St 75089
Glenview Way 75089
Glistening Spgs 75088
Gold Rd 75089
Golden Bear Dr 75089
Golden Pond Dr 75089
Gordon Smith Dr
  4800-5299 75088
  5501-5599 75089
Graham Dr 75089
Grant Dr 75088
Greenbriar Ln 75089
Greenhill Dr 75088

Greenlawn St 75088
Greenspoint Dr 75088
Greentree Dr 75088
Greenway Dr 75089
Greenwood Trl 75089
Griffins Pointe Dr 75089
Grisham Dr 75089
Gulf Harbor Dr 75088
Gulfport Dr 75088
Gulfview Dr 75088
Halifax Dr 75089
Hancock Rd 75089
Handen Dr 75089
Hanover Ct 75088
Harbor Dr 75088
Harbor Pointe Dr 75088
Harborview Blvd 75088
Hartford Dr 75089
Harvard Dr 75089
Harvest Hill Dr 75089
Hawkeye Rd 75089
Hawthorne Cv 75089
Hayden Ct 75089
Hewitts Cv 75089
Hickox Rd 75089
Hidden Valley Cir 75088
Highgate Ln 75089
Highlander Dr 75089
Highmeadow Dr 75089
Hillcrest Dr 75089
Hillridge Dr 75089
Hillside Dr 75089
Hogan Dr 75089
Holland Ave 75089
Holly Ln 75089
Homewood Ave 75089
Hominy Rdg 75089
Horizon Dr 75088
Horseshoe Bnd 75089
Hudson Dr 75089
Huffines Dr 75089
Huntington Dr 75089
Independence Ct 75089
Indian Trl 75088
Indian Trail Ct 75088
Industrial St 75088
E Interstate Highway 30 75088
Intrepid Ln 75089
Inverness Dr 75089
Inwood Dr 75089
Iris Dr 75089
Ivy Ln 75089
J A Forster Dr 75089
Jackson St 75088
Jasmine Ln 75089
Jasper Ct 75088
Jennifer Ln 75089
Jessica Way 75089
Joel Ct 75089
Jones Cir & Dr 75088
Jonquil Ln 75089
Journeys End 75089
Joyce St 75088
Juniper Ct 75089
Kallan Dr 75089
Karen Cir 75088
Katherine Dr 75089
Kathlyn Ln 75089
Kearsage Dr 75089
Kensington Dr 75088
Kenwood Ct & Dr 75089
Key Largo Dr 75089
Key West Dr 75088
Killarney Ln 75089
Kings Ct 75089
Kings Link Cir 75089
Kingston Dr 75089
Kirby Rd & St 75088
Kittyhawk Dr 75089
Knight Dr 75089
Knights Bridge Dr 75089
Kyle Rd 75088
La Costa Dr 75088
Lafayette Dr 75088
Lagoon Dr 75088

Lake Bend Dr 75088
Lake Forest Dr 75088
Lake Haven Dr 75088
Lake Highlands Dr 75088
Lake Hill Dr 75089
Lake North Rd 75089
Lake Valley Ct 75088
Lakeland Dr 75088
Lakepointe Ave 75088
Lakeport Dr 75089
Lakeridge Dr 75089
Lakeshore Ct 75089
Lakeshore Dr 75089
Lakeshore Ln 75088
Lakeside Dr 75088
Lakeview Cir 75088
Lakeview Pkwy 75088
Lakeway Dr 75088
Lakewood Dr 75088
Lance Ln 75088
Lansdowne Ln 75089
Larchwood Cir 75088
Larkin Ln 75088
Larkspur Ln 75089
Larry St 75088
Laurel Ct 75089
Lauren Ln 75089
Lawing Ln 75089
Lawton Ln 75089
Leanne St 75088
Leeward Ln 75089
Lexington Ct & Dr 75089
Liberty Ln 75089
Liberty Grove Rd
4800-5199 75088
5500-5598 75089
5600-10500 75089
10502-11498 75089
Lighthouse Dr 75089
Lilac Ln 75089
Lily Ln 75089
Linda Vista Ct & Dr 75088
Lindsey Ct & Dr 75088
Links Fairway Dr 75089
Lisa Dr 75088
Live Oak Dr 75088
Livingstone St 75089
Lochaven Dr 75089
Lochgreen Ln 75089
Locust St 75089
Lofland Ln 75088
Loire Valley Dr 75088
Lois Cir & Ln 75088
Loretta Ln 75088
Luna Cir, Ct & Dr 75088
Lynn Ct & Dr 75088
Lynnwood Dr 75088
Madison Ave 75089
Maggis Meadow Ln 75089
Magnolia Ct & Ln 75089
Main St 75088
Malinda Ln 75089
Mallard Cv & Park 75088
Manchester Dr 75089
Manor Dr 75088
Maple Ct & Ln 75088
Maplewood Dr 75089
Marcella Ln 75089
Marina Cir 75088
Mariner Dr 75088
Mark Ln 75089
Marlin Trl 75088
Marquett Ct & Dr 75088
Martha Ln 75088
Martin Dr 75088
Matagorda Bay Ct 75089
Maui Ln 75089
Mayleaf Ct 75089
Mazy Ln 75089
Mccleery Ln 75089
Mcgee Cove Rd 75089
Mcguire St 75088
Meadowcove Dr 75089
Meadowlark Ln 75089
Meadowview St 75089
Meadowwood Dr 75089

Mediterranean Dr 75088
Melcer Dr 75088
Melton Dr 75089
Mercurys Rd 75088
Merlot Cir 75088
Mermaid Cir 75088
Merritt Rd 75089
Miami Dr 75088
Michaels Pt 75088
Mickelson Dr 75089
Miles Rd 75089
Miller Rd 75088
Miller Heights Dr 75088
Millwood Dr 75088
Mimosa Ln 75089
Miramar Dr 75088
Mistletoe Ln 75088
Misty Ln 75089
Mitchell Ln 75088
Mize Ct 75089
Montego Dr 75089
Monterrey Dr 75088
Mulberry Ln 75089
Munich Dr 75089
Mystic Trl 75088
Nairn St 75089
Nancy Jane Cir 75088
Nantucket Dr 75088
Nassau Dr 75088
Natchez Dr 75088
Navigation Dr 75088
Neptune Cir 75088
New Bury Ct 75089
Newcastleton Ln 75089
Newport Dr 75088
Nicholas Ln 75089
Nita Pearson Dr 75088
Normandy Rd 75089
Northampton Dr 75089
Northpoint Dr 75089
Norwich Ct 75088
Nottingham Ct 75088
Nueces Bay Dr 75088
Oak Ln 75089
Oak Hollow Dr 75088
Oak Trail Dr 75089
Oakmont Ct 75089
Oakridge Dr 75089
October Glory Ln 75089
Onset Bay Dr 75089
Orchard Grove Dr 75089
Orchid Ln 75089
Orlando Cir 75088
Orleans Cir 75088
Osage Dr 75089
Oxford Dr 75089
Pacific Dr 75088
Pacific Pearl Dr 75089
Palisade Fls 75089
Palmer Dr 75089
Palomino Dr 75089
Panama Dr 75088
Panks Ct 75089
Park Ln 75089
Park Lane Ct 75089
Patricia Ln 75088
Patriot Ct 75089
Patty Cir 75089
Paul Pl 75089
Peach Tree Ln 75089
Pebble Beach Dr 75089
Pecan Ln 75089
Pecan Grove Ln 75089
Pecan Ridge Dr 75089
Pendleton Rd 75089
Peninsula Dr 75089
Pennridge Cir 75089
Persimmon Pl 75089
Petersburg Dr 75089
Pheasant Run Dr 75089
Pickard Dr 75089
Pine St 75089
Pine Forest Dr 75089
Pinecreek Dr 75089
Pinehurst Dr 75089
Planetree Dr 75089

Player Dr 75089
Pleraine Dr 75089
Poe Dr 75089
Pointe Loma Dr 75088
Pollard St 75089
Ponder St 75089
Poppy Hill Ct 75088
Port Aransas Dr 75089
Port Isabel Dr 75089
Ports O Call Dr 75089
Portsmouth Dr 75088
Post Oak Dr 75089
Powell Dr 75088
President George Bush Hwy
3600-3798 75088
3800-3900 75088
3902-4798 75088
5500-5598 75089
5600-6099 75089
6101-7299 75089
Prestige Ct 75089
Prestwick Ct 75089
Primrose Ln 75089
Princeton Rd 75089
Providence Dr 75089
Quail Ct 75089
Quail Creek Dr 75089
Quail Glenn Ct 75089
Quail Hollow Ct 75089
Quail Ridge Dr 75089
Radcliffe Dr 75088
Rainbow Dr 75089
Randi Rd 75088
Raney Rd 75089
Red Sky Dr 75089
Red Wing Ct 75089
Redwood Ln 75089
Regatta Dr 75089
Remington Dr 75089
Rice Dr 75089
Richards St 75088
Richmond Ct & Dr 75089
Ridgecove Dr 75088
Ridgecrest Ave 75088
Ridgeview Dr 75089
River Bend Dr 75089
Rock Valley Dr 75089
Rockbluff Ct & Dr 75088
Rosebud Dr 75089
Roseleaf Dr 75089
Rosser Ct 75089
Roughleaf Ln 75089
Rowlett Rd
1100-5299 75088
5300-7800 75088
7802-7898 75088
Royal Bay Dr 75089
Royal Burgess Dr 75089
Royal Montreal Dr 75089
Running Brook Dr 75089
Russell Dr 75089
Rutgers Cir 75089
Ruth Cir 75089
Ryan Rd 75089
Sailors St 75089
Saint Andrews Ln 75089
Saint Annes Dr 75089
Saint Charles Dr 75089
Saint Fillans Ln 75089
Saint Georges Dr 75089
Salem Ct 75089
Salzburg Dr 75089
San Carlos Dr 75088
San Marino Ct & Dr 75089
Sand Pine Dr 75089
Sandra Ln 75088
Sara Dr 75088
Sassafrass Way 75088
Saturn Dr 75088
Sawgrass Ln 75089
Scarlet Oak Dr 75089
Scenic Ct 75088
Scenic Dr
4400-4406 75088
4408-6999 75088

7200-7498 75089
Schrade Rd 75089
Scooner St 75089
Scott Dr 75088
Scottsdale Dr 75089
Seabreeze Dr 75088
Seafield Ln 75089
Seascape Dr 75088
Sequoia Cir 75088
Serenity Ln 75088
Shady Ln 75089
Shadybrook Ln 75088
Shadyoaks Ln 75088
Shawn Dr 75088
Shearer St 75088
Shelley Ln 75088
Sherwood Dr 75088
Shipman St 75088
Shipp Rd 75088
Shoal Creek Dr 75089
Shorecrest Dr 75089
Shoreline Dr 75089
Shorewood Ct 75089
Silver Lake Dr 75089
Silver Springs Way 75089
Silverthorn Dr 75089
Simmons Dr 75089
Singleton St 75088
Skipaway Dr 75088
Skyline Dr 75088
Smartt St 75088
Somerset Dr 75089
Southbay Cir 75089
Southern Hills Ln 75089
Southport Dr 75089
Southridge Dr 75089
Southwick Rd 75089
Spinnaker Cv 75089
Springfield Ln 75088
Springmeadow Ln 75089
Spyglass Hl 75089
Stacy Ct 75089
Stallion Cir 75089
Stamps St 75089
Stanford St 75088
Starboard Trl 75088
Statford Dr 75089
Stone Hollow Dr 75089
Stone Meadow Cir 75088
Stonehaven Ln 75089
Straits Ct & Dr 75089
Sturbridge Dr 75089
Sumac Ln 75089
Summer Hill Ln 75089
Summer Solstice 75088
Sunlight Dr 75089
Sunny Brook Dr 75088
Sunrise Dr 75088
Sunset Hl 75088
Suntide Dr 75088
Suzanne Dr 75089
Sweetgum Ct 75089
Swiss Way 75089
Sycamore St 75088
Tacoma St 75089
Tallowtree Dr 75089
Tangleridge Ln 75088
Teal Cir, Ct & Dr 75088
Terence Dr 75089
Teresa Ln 75089
Tern Harbor Dr 75089
Thistle Ln 75089
Thornhill Way 75088
Tidewater Dr 75089
Timberidge Dr 75089
Timberline Dr 75089
Tobin Trl 75088
Toler Rd 75088
Toscano Dr 75089
Touch Gold Ct 75088
Tracey Trl 75088
Tradewind Cir & Dr 75089
Trail Lake Dr 75089
Trailridge Dr 75089
Travelers Xing 75089
Treasure Cv 75089

Tremont Ave & Ln 75089
Troon Dr 75089
Trophy Ct 75089
Tropic Ln 75088
Trumpet Dr 75089
Tuckers Pl 75089
Tulane Dr 75088
Tulip Ln 75089
Turnberry St 75089
Turrey Pnes 75089
Union St 75089
University Cir & Dr 75088
Vagas Dr 75088
Valencia Dr 75089
Valley Forge Dr 75089
Valleyview Dr 75089
Vanderbilt Ct 75088
Vaughan Dr 75088
Vernon Dr 75088
Victoria Cir & Dr 75088
Victory St 75089
Violet Dr 75089
Virginia Ct 75089
Vista Creek Dr 75088
Walnut Hill Dr 75088
Water Ln 75089
Waterbury Dr 75089
Waterford Dr 75089
Watersedge Ct & Dr 75088
Watersway Dr 75088
Waterview Dr & Pkwy 75089
Waterwheel Dr 75089
Waterwood Dr 75089
Watson Dr 75089
Wayne Cir, Pl & Way 75088
Weatherly Dr 75089
Weems Way 75088
Wellesly Rd 75089
Wentworth Dr 75089
Western Hills Dr 75089
Westfield Dr 75088
Westhaven Dr 75089
Westlake Dr 75088
Westminister Dr 75088
Westover Dr 75089
Westshore Dr 75088
Westview Dr 75088
Westway Dr 75089
Westwood Cir 75088
Wexford Ln 75089
Whispering Brk 75088
White Oak Dr 75089
Whitecedar Ln 75089
Wildhaven Dr 75089
Willard St 75088
Willow Way 75089
Willowbrook Dr 75089
Wills Ct 75089
Wilmington Dr 75089
Wilshire Dr 75089
Wind Drift Ln 75088
Winding Valley Trl 75089
Windjammer Cir & Way 75088
Windridge Ln 75088
Windsor Way 75088
Windward View Dr 75088
Winged Foot Dr 75089
Winterberry Dr 75089
Wolfcreek Ln 75089
Wood Dr 75089
Wood Glen Dr 75088
Woodbridge Dr 75089
Woodbridge Ln 75088
Woodlake Dr 75088
Woodlands Trl 75089
Woodmont Ave 75089
Woodrow Way 75088
Woodside Rd 75088
Yacht Club Dr 75089
Yale Dr 75088
Yeager Rd 75089
Yorkshire Dr 75088
Yorktown Dr 75089

RULE TX

General Delivery 79547

POST OFFICE BOXES MAIN OFFICE STATIONS AND BRANCHES

Box No.s
All PO Boxes 79547

RURAL ROUTES

21, 22 79547

NAMED STREETS

Adams Ave
101-199 79548
600-1199 79547
1201-1699 79547
Amity Ave 79547
Blarenne 79547
Cardiff Ave 79547
Central Ave 79547
County Road 108 79547
County Road 122 79547
County Road 123 79547
County Road 125 79547
County Road 126 79547
County Road 128 79547
County Road 140 79547
County Road 141 79547
County Road 146 79547
County Road 151 79547
County Road 154 79547
County Road 424 79547
County Road 427 79547
County Road 428 79547
County Road 430 79548
County Road 441 79548
County Road 447 79548
County Road 450 79547
County Road 451 79547
County Road 453 79547
County Road 463
3800-4698 79547
County Road 463
4701-4799 79547
5201-5299 79548
5400-5598 79548
County Road 481 79548
County Road 482 79548
County Road 484 79548
County Road 485 79548
County Road 486 79548
County Road 488 79548
County Road 490 79548
County Road 493 79548
Elm Ave 79547
Fm 1225 79548
Fm 1661 79548
Fm 2407 79547
Fm 617 79547
Garfield Ave 79548
Gladstone Ave 79547
Grant Ave 79548
Humble Ave 79547
Jefferson Ave 79548
Loup Ave 79547
Madison Ave 79548
Manteriv 79548
Maple St 79547
Mccarty Ave 79547
Monroe Ave 79548
Pawnee Ave 79547
Robins Ave 79547
State Highway 283 79548
State Highway 6 N 79547
State Highway 6 S
1300-1998 79547
2400-2798 79548
2900-2998 79547
3201-3299 79548

Sunny Ave 79547
Taylor Ave 79547
Union Ave 79547
Us Highway 380 E & W 79547

NUMBERED STREETS

All Street Addresses 79547

SAN ANGELO TX

General Delivery 76902

POST OFFICE BOXES MAIN OFFICE STATIONS AND BRANCHES

Box No.s
1 - 27308 76902
60001 - 63420 76906
90200 - 90299 76902
90602 - 90602 76906

HIGHWAY CONTRACTS

68, 71 76901

RURAL ROUTES

05, 06 76904
02, 03 76905
62, 67, 70 76905

NAMED STREETS

A And M Ave 76904
N A And M Ave 76901
S A And M Ave 76901
A And M Cir 76904
N Abe St
1-1 76902
2-299 76903
S Abe St 76903
Abernathy Rd 76905
Abilene St 76901
Acorn Dr 76903
Ada St 76903
N & S Adams St 76901
Adobe Dr 76903
Adrian St 76903
Akin St 76903
Alamito St 76904
Alamo St 76903
Alexander St 76901
Algerita Dr 76901
Allen St 76903
Allison Cir 76903
E Alma Jo Dr 76905
Almond Cir 76903
Alpha Cir 76903
Alta Loma Cir 76901
Alta Vista Ln 76904
Alto Ln 76904
Alto Grande Rd 76904
Amarillo St 76903
Amberton Pkwy 76901
Amberwood Dr 76903
American Legion Rd 76904
Ames Rd 76905
Amhurst Dr 76901
Amistad Rd 76901
Ancient Ones Trl 76904
Angelo Blvd 76901
Antelope Trl 76901
Anthony Dr 76905
Antonio St 76903
Apache Trl 76901
Apollo Ln 76903
Appaloosa Cir & Trl 76901
April St 76904
Arapahoe Trl 76905
N & S Archer St 76903
Arden Rd 76901
Ardmore St 76905
Arlington St 76905
Armadillo Rd 76904
Armstrong St 76903
Arroyo St 76903
Art St 76903
Arthur Ln 76904
Arthur St 76903
Ashford Dr 76901
Aspen Ave 76904
Aster St 76901
Atlantic Rd 76903
Augusta Dr 76904
Austin St 76903
Autumnwood Trl 76904
W Avenue N
1-899 76903
W Avenue N
900-1499 76901
1500-2999 76904
3000-3199 76901
W Avenue S 76903
W Avenue W 76903
E & W Avenue A 76903
E & W Avenue B 76903
E & W Avenue C 76903
E Avenue D 76903
W Avenue D
1-999 76903
1000-1599 76901
E & W Avenue G 76903
E Avenue H 76903
W Avenue H
1-799 76903
800-1899 76901
E Avenue I 76903
W Avenue I
1-799 76903
800-1999 76901
E Avenue J 76903
W Avenue J
1-799 76903
800-2599 76901
E Avenue K 76903
W Avenue K
1-799 76903
800-2599 76901
E Avenue L 76903
W Avenue L
1-799 76903
800-2599 76901
E Avenue M 76903
W Avenue M
1-899 76903
900-2299 76901
W Avenue O 76903
W Avenue P 76903
W Avenue Q 76903
W Avenue R 76903
W Avenue T 76903
W Avenue U 76903
W Avenue V 76903
W Avenue X 76903
W Avenue Y 76903
W Avenue Z 76903
Averill Way 76901
Avondale Ave 76901
Aztec Ln 76903
Bagpipe Rd 76901
Bailey St 76901
Baker Dr 76905
Baker St 76903
Ballard Rd 76901
Barbara Ave 76904
Barrington Ct 76901
Barton St 76903
Basil Ct 76901
Bass Ln 76904
Baylor Ave 76904
N & S Baze St 76903
Beacon St
923-1197 76903
1199-1599 76903
1600-2099 76905
Bean Rd 76905
Beaty Cir & Rd 76904
E Beauregard Ave 76903
W Beauregard Ave
3-17 76903
19-599 76903
601-699 76903
900-3030 76901
3032-3098 76901
3100-3914 76904
3916-4098 76904
Becaon St 76905
Becker Ln 76904
Belaire Ave
1-99 76903
100-499 76905
N & S Bell St 76903
Belmont St 76901
Ben Ficklin Rd
1800-4299 76903
4801-4897 76904
4899-5800 76904
5802-6198 76904
Benchmark Rd 76904
Benedict Cir & Dr 76903
Bent Grass Ct 76904
Bent Green Ct 76904
Bent Oak Ct 76904
Bent Tree Ct 76904
N Bentwood Ct & Dr 76904
Berkley Rd 76901
Berkshire Rd 76901
Bermuda Dr 76904
Bertha St 76901
Beryl St 76903
Beverly Ct & Dr 76904
Billie Bolin Dr 76904
Billo Dr 76901
Birch Ln 76901
Bird St 76903
Birdie Ct 76904
N & S Bishop St 76901
Bismarck Ct 76904
Bison Trl 76901
Bitner Rd 76905
Black Bear Ln 76901
Blackwood Rd 76905
Blair Ln 76904
Bledsoe Rd 76905
Blue Bird Rd 76901
Blue Grama Cir & Trl 76904
Blue Quail Ln 76901
Blue Ridge Trl 76904
Bluebonnet Ave 76901
Bluebonnet Ln 76904
Bluegrass Cir & Dr 76903
Blum St 76903
Blumentritt Rd 76905
Bob White Ln 76901
Bonham St 76903
Bonita Loop 76904
Bowie St 76903
Boys Ranch Rd 76904
Braden Rd 76905
Bradford St 76903
Bradford Trl 76901
Bramlett Ln 76905
Brazos St 76904
Bremerton Dr 76901
Brewer St 76905
Briant St 76903
Briargrove Ln 76904
Briarwood Cir & Dr 76903
Bright Ave 76904
Bristow Rd 76905
Brodnax Ln 76904
Brook Hollow Ln 76904
Brown Dr 76901
Brown St 76903
N & S Browning St 76903
Bryan St 76903
N Bryant Blvd
1-1 76902
200-298 76903
300-4899 76903
S Bryant Blvd
309-1297 76903
1299-4399 76903
5101-5237 76904
Bryant Ln 76904
E Bryant Ln 76904
S Bryant Ln 76904
W Bryant Ln 76904
Bryant Ranch Rd 76904
N & S Buchanan St 76903
Buck Run 76901
Buckshot Rd S 76904
Buckskin Dr 76904
Buena Vista St 76904
Buffalo Ln 76901
Buick St 76901
Burgess St 76903
Burkett Ln 76901
Burlington Rd 76901
N Burma Rd 76901
Burrell Rd 76901
Butler Dr & Rd 76904
Buttercup Ave 76901
Butterfield Rd 76904
Butterfly Ln 76905
Cactus Ln 76903
Caddo St 76901
Calle Sendera 76904
Callison Rd 76904
Cameron St 76903
Camino Real St 76904
Camper Rd 76904
Campus Blvd 76901
Canadian St 76904
Canal Rd 76904
Canna St 76901
Canyon Rd 76904
Canyon Creek Dr 76904
Canyon Rim Dr 76904
Cardinal Rd 76901
Caribou Trl 76901
Carley St 76903
Carlisle Ln 76901
E & S Carlsbad Loop Rd 76901
Carlton Way 76901
Carnation Ave 76901
Caroline Ln 76904
Carrizo St 76904
Carswell St 76903
Castillo Ln 76905
Cat Tail Ln 76904
Catalina Dr 76901
Cattle Dr 76905
Cauley Ln 76903
N & S Cecil St 76903
Cedar Ln 76901
Cedar Creek Dr & Ln 76904
Cedar Ridge Ln 76904
Cedarhill Dr 76904
Cedarwood Dr 76905
Center St 76905
Century Dr 76903
N Chadbourne St 76903
S Chadbourne St
1-2399 76903
3000-4399 76904
4400-4500 76905
4502-4698 76905
Chalimar Rd 76904
Champion Cir 76904
Chaparral Run 76901
Chapel Hill Dr 76904
Chapman St 76901
Chatterton Dr 76904
Cherokee Rd 76901
Cherry Hill Ln 76904
Chestnut St 76901
Cheyenne Ave 76904
Childress St 76901
Chimney Rock Ln 76904
Chinook Cir 76905
Chisholm Trl 76903
Choate Rd 76901
Choctaw Ave 76904
Christoval Rd
1500-3599 76903
3601-3697 76904
3699-5799 76904
Churchill Blvd 76903
Churchwell Rd 76905
Cielo Vista Plz 76904
Cinnamon Ln 76901
Circle J St 76901
Citation Ct 76904
City Farm Rd 76905
City Hall Plz 76903
Clairmont St 76905
Clare Dr 76904
Clarice Ct 76904
Clark Dr 76904
Classen Blvd 76901
Clayton St
100-199 76905
1500-1599 76903
Clearview Dr 76904
W Clearwater St 76903
Cleo St 76905
Cloud St 76905
Clover Dr 76903
Club House Ln 76904
Club Lake Ct 76904
Club Park Way 76904
Coke St
1200-1599 76903
1600-2499 76905
Coleman St 76901
Coliseum Dr 76903
E & W College Ave 76903
College Hills Blvd & Cir 76904
Colonial Plz 76904
Colorado Ave 76901
Columbia St 76903
Columbine Ln 76904
Comanche Trl 76901
Commissioners Ln 76905
Conchita St 76901
E Concho Ave 76903
W Concho Ave
1-599 76903
1000-2399 76901
Concho Dr 76901
S Concho Dr 76904
S Concho Park Dr 76903
N Concord Loop 76901
W Concord Loop 76901
Concord Rd 76903
N & S Copper Mountain Cir 76901
Copper Rock Rd 76904
Coral Way 76904
Cordell Dr 76901
Cornell Ave & Pl 76904
Cornerstone Dr 76904
Cottonseed Rd 76904
Cottontail Ln 76901
Cottonwood St 76901
S Country Club Rd 76904
Country Club Estates Cir 76904
Countryside Rd 76904
County Road 430 76901
County Road 470 76904
Cove Rd 76904
Coventry Ln 76901
Covington Rd 76905
Cowboy Way 76905
Cox Ln 76903
Coyote Bend Rd 76904
Craft St 76903
Creldel 76902
Crenshaw St 76903
Crescent Rd 76903
Crestwood Dr 76903
Creswell St 76903
Cricket Ln 76905
Crockett St 76903
S Crook Rd 76904
Cross Ranch Rd 76904
S Crossings Ct 76904
Crystal Beach Dr 76904
Crystal Point Dr 76904
Cuero St 76903
Culberson St
1000-1599 76903
1600-1799 76905
Cultus St 76905
Culver Ave 76904
Culwell St 76903
Cumberland Ct & Dr 76904
Cunningham St 76903
Currier St 76903
Cyndi Ln 76903
Cypress Ct 76901
Dahlia Ave 76901
Dailey St 76903
Daisy Ln 76901
Dale Ln 76905
Dallas St 76901
Dan Hanks Ln 76904
Danube Rd 76903
Darlene St 76904
Dartmouth Dr & Pl 76904
Davenport Dr 76901
S David St 76903
Dearborn Rd 76901
Debus Rd
1900-6399 76905
6401-6699 76905
7900-7998 76904
Decoty St 76905
Deer Ln 76904
Deerfield Rd 76904
Delker Dr 76904
Dellwood Ct & Dr 76903
Delong St 76903
Dena Dr 76904
Dennis Ln 76901
Derby Ct 76904
Derringer Dr 76905
Devonian Dr 76903
Devonshire Ln 76901
Diamond Dr 76905
Diana Ln 76904
Dilly Rd 76901
Dominion Rdg 76904
Dominion Ridge Cir 76904
Door Key Rd 76904
Doral Ct & Rd 76904
Dorchester Dr 76901
Dorrance Rd 76904
Doss Ln 76901
Douglas Dr 76904
Dove Creek Dr 76901
Dove Creek Ln 76904
Dove Creek Ln E 76904
Dove Creek Ln W 76904
S Dove Creek Rd 76904
Drexel Dr 76901
Driftwood Ct & Dr 76904
Dry Creek Rd 76901
Duckworth Rd 76905
Ducote Air Park Dr 76904
Duggan St 76903
Duncan Rd 76904
Durham Ct 76901
Dustin Rd 76905
Eagle Ct 76904
Eagle Ln 76901
Eckert St 76905
Edgewood Cir & Dr 76903
Edinburgh Rd 76901
Edmund Blvd 76901
Edwards Rd 76903
El Camino Grande 76904
El Rancho Ln 76905
Elk Run 76901
Ellen St 76903
Ellis St
500-1599 76903
1600-1999 76905
Elm Ln & St 76901
Elmo Ln 76905
N & S Emerick St 76903
N & S Emerson St 76903
Emmitt Ln 76901
Enclave Ct 76904
End St 76905
Equestrian Blvd 76904
Era Ave 76905
Erin St 76903
Erline Dr 76901
Ernest St 76903
Estate Dr 76903
Estella Dr 76903
Eunice Dr 76901
Evans Ave 76901
Evelyn St 76905
Evergreen Ln 76901
Executive Dr 76904
S Fairview School Rd 76904
Fairview School South Rd 76904
Fairway Cir & Dr 76904
Falcon Ln 76901
Fall Creek Dr 76904
N Farr St 76903
Feil Rd 76901
Field St 76901
Fieldstone Dr 76904
Fieldwood Dr 76904
N Fillmore St 76901
S Fillmore St
1-499 76901
1800-1899 76904
Firestone Pl 76904
N & S First Rd 76905
Fish Hatchery Rd 76904
Fisher St 76901
Fishermans Rd 76904
Fitzgerald Dr & Rd W 76904
Flamingo Rd 76901
N & S Florence St 76903
Florida Ave 76904
Floyd Dr 76904
Floyd Ln 76901
Fm 1223 76905
Fm 1692 76905
E Fm 2105
101-299 76903
E Fm 2105
1400-1498 76903
3000-3598 76905
3600-3699 76905
3701-4099 76905
W Fm 2105 76901
Fm 2166 76904
Fm 2288 76901
Fm 2334 76905
S Fm 2335 76904
Fm 380 76905
Fm 388 76905
Fm 584 76904
Fm 765 76905
Foraker St 76903
Ford St 76905
Forest Trl 76904
Forest Hill Dr 76904
Forest Park Ave 76901
Fort Mckavett Rd 76903
Fort Richardson Ct 76903
Foster Rd 76904
Foster St 76903
Fox Hollow St 76905
Freeland Ave 76901
Front St 76901
Fruitland Farm Ct & Rd 76903
Fulton St 76905
Fusselman Dr 76903
Gaelic Rd 76901
Garden Rd 76903
Gardenia Ave 76901
N Garfield St 76901
Garnett Rd 76903
N & S Garrett St 76901
S Gas Plant Rd 76904
Gateway Dr 76905
Gemini Dr 76903
Genchalt St 76901
George Ln & Trl 76905
Gesch Rd 76905

Gilbert St 76905
Gillis St 76903
Gladiola Ave 76901
Glass Rd 76901
Glass Court Rd 76901
Gleneagles Dr 76904
Glenmore Dr 76903
Glenna Dr & St 76901
Glenwood Dr 76901
Golden Ln 76904
Goliad St 76903
Goodfellow Ave 76905
Goodland Loop 76901
Goodnight Trl 76903
Gordon Blvd 76905
Grace Ln 76901
Grand Canal Ct 76904
Grand Court Rd 76901
Grandview Dr 76904
Grape Creek Rd
2900-5799 76903
6400-11799 76901
11801-11899 76901
N Grape Creek Rd 76901
W Grape Creek Rd 76901
Grapevine Ave 76901
Grayburg Dr 76904
Green Rd 76904
Green Meadow Dr 76904
Green Ridge Dr 76904
Green Valley Cir & Trl 76904
Greenbriar St 76904
Greenville St 76903
Greenwood St 76901
Greer St 76903
Gregory Dr 76905
Grey Charles Ct 76904
Grierson St 76901
Grothe St 76903
Grove Cir & Dr 76903
Guadalupe St 76901
Gun Club Rd 76904
Gunter St 76903
Guthrie St 76901
Hackberry Ln 76901
Hagelstein St 76903
Hallye Ct 76904
Hamilton Way 76904
Hangar Rd 76904
Hanover Pl 76901
Hardeman Pass 76903
Harmony Ln 76904
Harriett Rd 76905
E Harris Ave
1-1599 76903
1600-1799 76905
W Harris Ave
1-599 76903
1000-3199 76901
N Harrison St 76901
S Harrison St
400-1799 76901
1801-1815 76904
1817-1899 76904
Harvard Ave & Ct 76904
Harvest Dr 76901
Hassell St 76901
Hatcher St 76901
Hatchery Rd 76903
N Haven Ct 76903
Hawk Ave
2200-4998 76905
5000-6099 76905
8000-11499 76904
11501-11699 76904
Heckaman Rd 76904
Hemlock Dr 76904
Henderson St 76903
Henry Ln 76905
Henry O Flipper St 76903
Herbert Rd 76905
Heslip St 76903
Hickory St 76901
Hickorywood Dr 76904
Hidalgo St 76904
Hidden View Dr 76904
High Butte Dr 76905
High Meadow Dr 76904
High Point Dr 76904
E & W Highland Blvd 76903
S Hill St 76903
Hillary Ct 76901
Hillcrest Dr 76904
Hillside Dr 76904
Hillview Cir 76905
Hilton Head Blvd 76904
Hobbs Rd 76904
Hobbs St 76903
Hoelscher Rd 76905
Hoffman Rd 76905
Hohmann Rd 76905
Holcomb St 76903
Holiday Dr 76903
Holik Rd 76904
Holiman Ln 76905
Homestead Cir & Ct 76905
Honeysuckle Ln 76904
Hopi Trl 76901
Horn St 76901
Houston St 76901
E Houston Harte Expy 76903
W Houston Harte
Expy 76901
Howard St 76901
Howe St 76901
Hudson St 76903
Hudson Oaks Dr 76904
Hughes St 76903
Hugo Ln 76905
Hull St 76903
Humble Rd 76903
Hummingbird Ln 76904
Hunters Glen Rd 76901
Huntington Ln 76904
Idaho Ave 76904
Imperial Ct 76904
Indian Path 76901
W Indian Creek Rd 76901
Industrial Ave 76904
Inglewood Dr 76904
Inwood Dr 76903
Iowa Ave 76904
N & S Irene St 76903
Iris St 76903
Ironwood Ct 76904
Irvindale Rd 76903
N & S Irving St 76903
Jacie Ln 76905
Jack St 76903
Jackrabbit Trl 76904
N Jackson St 76901
S Jackson St
1-1799 76901
1800-3699 76904
3700-5199 76903
Jade Dr 76904
James Ln 76905
Jameson Rd 76904
Janie Ln 76905
Jann Dr 76904
E & S Jarratt Rd 76905
N & S Jefferson St 76901
Jeremiah Ln 76901
Jfk Dr 76903
Jim White Rd 76905
Jody Rd 76904
Johnny Ln 76905
Johnson Ave 76904
Joiner Ave 76905
Jomar St 76901
Jones St 76903
Joseph Ln 76905
Joy Rd 76904
Juanita Ave 76901
Judith Ln 76904
Julian St 76903
June Ln 76905
Juniper Ln 76904
Junius St 76901
Kansas Ave 76904
Kennedy St 76905
Kensington Crk 76904
Kenwood Dr 76903
Keystone Ln 76904
Kildee Trl 76901
Kilt Rd 76901
Kimrey Ln 76904
Kings Rd 76904
Kingsbridge Dr 76901
Kistler Ave 76903
Knickerbocker Rd
600-1199 76903
1201-1397 76904
1399-13500 76904
13502-14498 76904
Koberlin St
200-1599 76903
1600-2199 76905
N & S Koenigheim St 76903
Kristina Rd 76905
Kropala Rd 76905
La Cruz St 76903
La Follette St 76905
La Junta St 76903
La Mesa Ln 76905
La Salle Dr 76903
La Vaca St 76904
La Villa Cir 76904
Lagoon Ln 76904
Laguna Verde St 76904
Lake Dr 76903
Lake Ridge Dr 76904
Lake Shore Blvd 76904
Lake Trail Ct 76904
Lake View Heroes Dr 76903
Lakeside Ave 76901
Lakota Ln 76901
Lanchari St 76903
Landers Rd 76905
Lantana Ct 76904
Larkspur Ave 76901
Las Lomas Ct & Dr 76904
Laura Dr 76905
Laurel Oak Dr 76904
Lawndale Dr 76903
Lbj Dr 76903
Ledbetter Rd 76901
Lehr Rd 76905
Lena Ln 76905
Lester Ln 76903
Lexington Pl 76904
Liberty Ct 76901
Lilac Ave 76901
Lillie St 76903
N Lincoln St 76901
S Lincoln St 76904
Lincoln Park Rd E &
W 76904
Linda Lee Dr 76905
Lindell Ave & Ct 76905
Linden Way 76901
Lindenwood Dr 76904
Line Rd 76904
Link Rd 76904
Lipan Dr 76903
Lipan Creek Rd 76905
Little Barley Trl 76904
Little Sorrel Trl 76904
Live Oak St 76901
Loch Lomond Rd 76901
Loch Ness Rd 76901
Locust St 76901
Log Cabin Trl 76905
Logan St 76903
Loganwood Dr 76904
London Ct 76901
Lone Star Ln 76904
Longhorn Dr 76905
Loop Dr 76904
Loop 306
1301-1397 76904
Loop 306
1399-3202 76904
3201-3201 76906
3203-3999 76904
3204-4198 76904
1200-1598 76905
Lorine Ln 76905
Louis Dr 76903
Louise Dr & St 76901
Love St 76903
Lowrie Ave 76905
Lsu Ave 76904
Lubke Ln 76905
Luna St 76905
Lydian Ct 76904
Lyndhurst Dr 76901
Macann St 76905
Mackenzie St 76901
N & S Madison St 76901
N & S Magdalen St 76903
Magnolia Dr 76901
Magnolia St 76905
Mahon Ave 76904
N & S Main St 76903
Majestic Ct 76904
N & S Malone St 76903
Manchester Ln 76901
Maple Ln 76901
Maplewood Dr 76904
Maravillas St 76904
March Rd 76901
Margaret Ln 76904
N & S Marie St 76905
Marigold Ave 76901
Mariner Ter 76903
Martha Rd 76901
Martin Rd 76905
Martin St 76901
Martin Luther King
Blvd 76903
Marx St 76903
Mary E Lee Park Rd 76904
Maryland St 76905
Mathis St 76903
Maverick Rd 76905
Maxwell St 76905
Mayfair Ln 76901
Mayse St 76903
Mccleary Rd 76904
Mcdevitt St 76905
Mcgill Blvd 76905
Mcglothlin St 76905
Mckee Ln 76904
Meadow Dr 76903
Meadow Creek Trl 76904
Meadow Lark Trl 76901
Meadowbrook Dr 76901
Medina St 76905
Melrose Ave 76901
Mercedes St 76901
Mermaid Rd 76904
Mesquite Ln
2100-2199 76904
8000-8399 76901
Mesquitewood Dr 76905
Metcalf Rd W 76904
Metcalfe St 76903
Michael St 76903
Midget St 76901
Mikulik Rd 76904
Mill Pass Dr 76904
Millbrook Dr 76904
Millspaugh St 76901
N & S Milton St 76901
Mimosa Dr 76903
Mimosa Ln 76901
Mission St 76905
Mockingbird Ln 76901
Mohawk Ave 76904
N & S Monroe St 76901
N Mont Park Dr 76901
Montague Ave 76905
Montecito Dr
300-899 76903
900-1199 76901
Monterrey St 76903
Moon Ln 76901
Moreland Dr 76905
Moritz Cir 76904
Morning Dove Dr 76901
Morris Ave 76903
Motl Rd 76905
Mount Nebo Rd 76901
Mountain View Ln 76901
Muirfield Ave 76904
Mule Creek Rd 76905
Mulecreek Rd 76901
Murphy St 76903
Mustang Rd 76901
Nasworthy Dr 76904
Natalie Ln 76904
Navajo Rd 76901
Neimann Rd 76905
Nelson Ave 76905
Nevada Dr 76904
Nicole Ln 76903
Norma St 76903
Normandy Ln 76901
North St 76901
Northcross Ln 76904
Northgate Dr 76903
Northstar Dr 76903
Norwood Dr 76903
Notre Dame Ave 76904
Nottingham Trl 76901
Nueces Dr 76901
Nutmeg Rd 76901
Oak Ln 76901
Oak Canyon Ln 76904
Oak Creek Dr 76904
Oak Forest Ct & Dr 76904
Oak Grove Blvd & Ct 76904
Oak Hills Trl 76904
Oak Mountain Trl 76904
N & S Oakes St 76903
Oaklawn Blvd 76903
Oakwood St 76903
Oatland Dr 76901
Obryan Ln 76905
Ochoco St 76905
Odell St 76905
Office Park Dr 76904
Ogden Rd 76903
Old Ballinger Hwy
1600-2399 76903
2401-2497 76905
2499-5000 76905
5002-5398 76905
Old Eola Rd 76905
Old Highway 380 76905
Old Knickerbocker Rd 76903
Old Mill Rd 76904
Old Post Cir, Ct & Rd 76904
W Old Sterling City
Hwy 76901
Oleander St N 76901
Olsak Rd 76905
Orchard Dr 76903
Orchid Rd 76901
Oregon Ave 76904
Orient Pass 76905
Orient Rd 76905
Orient St 76903
Oriole Dr 76903
Overhill Dr 76904
Owls Nest Dr 76901
Oxford Ave 76904
Oxford Cir 76904
N Oxford Dr 76901
S Oxford Dr 76904
Pacific Rd 76903
Paint Rock Rd
1-499 76903
500-2800 76905
2802-3698 76905
Paisano Ln 76904
Paisano Pl 76903
Palo Duro Dr 76904
Pansy Ave 76901
Paradise Ln 76901
Paradise Loop Rd 76901
N & S Park St 76901
Parker St 76901
Parkview Dr 76904
E Parkway St 76901
Parkwood Dr 76904
Parsons St 76903
Paseo De Vaca St 76901
Pastrald Dr 76904
Pate Farm Rd 76905
Patrick St 76904
Paul Ann Blvd 76905
Pebble Beach Ct 76904
Pecan Ln 76904
Pecan St 76903
Pecan Creek Ln 76904
Pecan Ridge Dr 76904
Pecan Valley Ln 76904
Pecos St 76901
Penhurst Ct 76901
Penny Ln 76905
Penrose St 76903
Permian Dr 76903
Petite Ln 76905
Petro Dr 76903
Petunia Ave 76901
Pheasant Run 76901
N Pierce St 76901
S Pierce St
1-1799 76901
1800-1899 76904
Pine Ln 76901
Pine Valley St 76904
Pinehurst Ct & Dr 76904
Pinon Ridge Dr 76904
Pinto Path 76901
Plain View Dr 76905
N & S Poe St 76903
Polk St 76901
Ponderosa Ln 76904
N & S Pope St 76903
Poplar Ln 76901
Porter St 76903
Porter Henderson Dr 76905
Possum Hollow Rd 76901
Powell St 76903
Preston Trl 76904
Preston Trail Ct 76904
Preusser St
300-1599 76903
1600-1999 76905
Princeton Ave & Ln 76904
Private Road 403 76904
Private Road 405 76904
Probandt St 76903
Pronghorn Path 76901
Pruitt Dr 76903
Pueblo Pass 76901
Pulliam St
300-1599 76903
1600-3499 76905
Pulliam Ranch Rd 76901
Putter Dr 76904
Pyburn Rd 76901
Quailrun Trl 76901
Queens Ct 76904
Raccoon Rd 76901
Railroad St 76903
Rainey Rd 76905
Ranch Ct & Ln 76904
Ranch Road 853 76901
S Randolph St 76903
Raney St 76901
Ransom Rd 76903
S & W Ratliff Rd 76904
Raven Rd 76901
Ray St 76904
Rebecca Dr 76904
Rebecca Trl 76905
Red Bird Ln 76901
Red Bluff Cir & Rd E &
W 76904
Red Bluff Ramp Rd 76904
N Red Creek Rd 76905
Red Oak Ln 76904
Red Robin Rd 76901
Redwood Ln 76901
Reece Rd 76904
Regent Blvd 76905
Rhine Loop 76903
Ricci Acres Rd 76901
Rice Ave 76904
Richard St 76905
Ricks Ct & Dr 76905
Ridge Rd 76904
Ridgecrest Ln 76904
Ridgemar Dr 76903
Rimrock Cir 76904
Rio Concho Cir & Dr 76903
Rio Grande St 76901
Rio Villa Ln 76904
Rio Vista Cir & St 76904
Ripple Rd 76904
Rita Cir 76905
Rita Blanca St 76904
River Bnd 76903
River Dr
600-699 76901
1500-1599 76903
N River Dr 76903
W River Dr 76903
River Oaks St 76903
River Ridge Ln 76904
River Valley Ln 76904
Rivercrest Ct 76904
Riverfalls Ct & Rd 76903
E Riverside Ave 76905
W Riverside Ave 76903
Riverside Golf Club
Rd 76903
Riverview Ct 76904
Riverwood Dr 76905
Rm Highway 853 76901
Robby Jones Rd 76904
Robert Dr 76905
Robin Hood Trl 76901
Rock Brook Dr 76904
Rock Slough Rd 76904
Rockhouse Rd 76905
Rockwood Dr 76905
Rodeo Dr 76903
N & W Rollin Acres
Rd 76901
Roosevelt St
1300-1599 76903
1600-1799 76905
Rose St 76901
Rosemont Dr 76904
Roundup Rd 76905
Royal Oak Ct & Dr 76904
Royal Troon Dr 76904
Ruby Lee Ln 76904
Runion Rd 76905
Rusk St 76903
Rust Rd 76905
Rust St 76903
Rutgers St 76904
Sac Ave 76904
Saddle Ridge Trl 76904
Saddleside Rd 76904
Sage Rd 76901
Sage Brush Cir 76905
Sage Hen Cir 76905
Saint Andrews Rd 76904
Saint Ann St 76905
Saint Anthony Rd 76905
Saint George Cir & Ct 76904
Saint Johns St 76905
Saint Josephs Pl 76905
Saint Marys St 76904
Sallee Rd 76904
Sam St 76903
Samantha Rd 76905
San Antonio St 76901
San Jacinto St 76903
San Saba St 76904
Sandpiper Way 76901
Sandstone Rd 76904
Sansondo Rd 76905
Santa Fe Park Dr 76903
Santiago Canyon Trl 76904
Sawgrass Dr 76904
Scarlett Oak Ct & Dr 76904
Scenic Vista Dr 76904
School House Dr 76904
N Schroeder Ave 76905
Schwartz Rd 76904
Schwartz St 76903
Schwertner Rd 76903
Scott Ln 76905
Scout St 76903

Sea Island Ct & Rd 76904
Sefcik Rd 76905
Seine Rd 76903
N Sellers St 76903
Selman Ct & Dr 76905
Senisa Trl 76903
Sentinel Cir 76904
Sequoia Cir 76904
Sequoia Ln 76901
Shad Rd 76904
Shadetree Ln 76903
Shady Oaks Dr 76904
Shady Point Circle Dr 76904
Shadyhill Dr 76904
Shafter St 76901
Shahan Rd 76904
Shamrock Dr 76904
Sharp Rd 76901
Sheffield Dr 76901
Shefflera Dr 76904
Shelton St 76903
Sherwood Way
1800-4600 76901
4602-6198 76901
5201-5699 76904
5701-6199 76901
Shiloh St 76901
Shingle Oak Ln 76904
Shirley St 76901
Short St 76903
Side View Rd 76901
Sierra Cir 76904
Sierra Ct 76904
Sierra Dr 76904
Sierra Trl 76905
Silver Spur Dr 76904
Simpson St 76905
Skylark Ln 76901
Sleepy Hollow Rd 76904
Smith Blvd 76905
Smu Ave 76904
E Socha Loop 76905
Southampton Pl 76901
Southern Oak Ln 76904
Southland Blvd 76904
Southridge Dr 76904
Southwest Blvd
2500-2600 76901
2602-2698 76901
2700-5899 76904
Southwestern Ave 76904
Spaulding St
300-1599 76903
1600-2199 76905
Spence St 76903
Spencer St 76903
Spillway Rd 76904
Spraberry Dr 76903
Sprague St 76903
Spring Creek Dr 76901
Spring Creek Ln 76904
Spring Creek Rd 76904
Spring Valley Ln 76904
Spruce Ct 76901
Spy Glass Dr 76904
Stage Coach Trl 76901
Stanford Dr 76904
Stanton St 76901
Star Ln 76901
State Ct & St 76905
State Highway 208
5000-5899 76903
State Highway 208
5900-7699 76905
Stephen St 76905
Stewart Ln 76904
Stokes Rd 76904
Stone Canyon Trl 76904
Stone Garden Dr 76904
Stone Key Ln 76904
Stone Meadow Ln 76904
Stonebridge Dr 76904
Stonegate Ct 76905
Stoneham St 76905
Stonelake Dr 76904
Stonetrail Dr 76904
Stonewall Dr 76905
Stratford Ave 76901
Strawn Rd 76904
Streicher Rd 76904
Sugar Maple Ln 76904
Sul Ross St 76904
Summer Crest Dr 76901
Summit Ave 76903
Summit Ct 76904
Summit Ln 76904
Sun Ln 76901
Sun Lake Dr 76905
Sun Valley Ln 76904
Sunflower Ave 76901
Sunset Ct 76904
Sunset Dr
1600-4299 76904
4300-4499 76901
Sunshine Ave 76903
Surrey Square Ct 76901
Susan Peak Rd 76904
Sussex Pl 76901
Sutters Ave 76901
Sutton Rd 76901
Swain Rd 76905
Sweetbriar Dr 76904
Sykes Cir 76905
Tabosa Dr 76904
Tanglewood Dr 76904
Tartan Rd 76901
Tarver St 76903
N & S Taylor St 76901
Tcu Ave 76904
Tech Ave 76904
Tempe Post Dr 76905
Templin Ct & Rd 76904
Tennis Ct 76905
Terlingua St 76904
Terminal Cir 76904
Terrace Dr 76903
Terry Trl 76903
Texas Ave 76903
Thames Loop 76903
S Third Rd 76905
Threeawn Trl 76904
Timber Ridge Dr 76904
Time Clock Dr 76904
Tlc Way 76901
Toby Ln 76903
Todd Cir & Ln 76903
Tokay Rd 76901
Tomahawk Ln 76901
Town And Country Rd 76903
W Townview Ln 76901
Toyah St 76904
Tracie Trl 76903
Tractor Trl 76905
Travis St 76903
Treece Rd 76905
Tres Rios Cir & Dr 76903
Tridens Trl 76904
Trinity Ave 76904
Truman St 76903
Tulane St 76904
Tulip St 76901
Turkey Run 76901
Turnberry Ct 76904
Turner St 76903
Turtle Dr 76904
Tuscorora Ct 76904
Tweedy Rd 76904
Twin Buttes Marina Park Rd 76904
Twin Lakes Ln 76904
Twin Oaks Dr 76901
E Twohig Ave 76903
W Twohig Ave
1-599 76903
1000-2899 76901
N Tyler St 76901
S Tyler St 76901
Tyler Ter 76905
University Ave 76904
Untermeyer Rd 76904
Upton St
400-1599 76903
1600-1999 76905
N Us Highway 277 76905
S Us Highway 277 76904
Us Highway 67 S 76904
N Us Highway 67 76905
Us Highway 87 N 76901
Us Highway 87 S 76904
Utah Ave 76904
Ute Pass 76901
E & N Valley Dr 76905
Valley Ridge Ln 76904
Valleyview Blvd, Ct & Dr 76904
N Van Buren St 76901
S Van Buren St
1-1799 76901
1800-1899 76904
Van Zandt St 76905
Vance Cir 76903
Vanderventer St 76904
Vaughn St 76903
Veck St
500-1599 76903
1900-1999 76905
Velma St 76903
Venture Dr 76905
Verbena St 76901
Veterans Memorial Dr 76903
Vidler Rd 76905
Village Trl 76904
Village East Cir 76904
Village Park Dr 76904
Villareal Rd 76905
Vines Rd 76905
Violet St 76901
Vista Cir & Ct 76904
Vista Del Arroyo Dr 76904
Voight Blvd 76905
Volney St 76903
Waco St 76901
Wade St 76903
Waldo Cir 76905
Wallace Ln 76905
Walling Pecan Rd 76904
Walnut Ln & St 76901
Walnut Grove Rd 76901
Walnut Hill Ct & Dr 76904
Wanda St 76903
Ward St 76901
Warehouse Rd 76903
Warrior Ave 76904
Warwick Dr 76901
E Washington Dr 76903
W Washington Dr
1-899 76903
900-1099 76901
N Washington St 76901
S Washington St 76901
Watson St 76905
Weaver St 76903
Webb St 76903
Webster St 76901
Welch Rd 76904
Wellington St 76904
Westcliff Cir 76901
Westcross Ln 76904
Western Ct 76904
Westland St 76901
Westminster Ln 76901
Weston Ct & Rd 76901
Westover Ter 76904
Westway Dr 76904
Westwood Dr 76901
Weterans Memorial Dr 76903
Wheatland Dr 76901
Whippoorwill Way 76901
White Ln 76904
White Ash Ln 76904
White Rock Rd 76904
White Tail Ln 76904
White Wing Ln 76905
Whitecastle Ln 76901
Whitney St 76904
Wichita Ave 76901
Wicklow Ct 76901
Wild Rye Trl 76904
Wilde Rd 76905
Wildewood Dr 76904
Wildflower Blvd 76904
Wilds St 76905
Wiley St 76905
Willow Cir 76904
Willow Dr 76904
Willow Ln 76901
Willow St 76901
Willow Brook Dr 76904
Wilma Cir & Ln 76904
Wilshire Pl 76901
Wilson St 76901
Wimberly St 76901
Winchester Dr 76905
Windemere Cir 76901
Windham St 76903
Windmill Dr 76904
Windwood Dr 76904
Winners Cir 76904
Winterberry Ln 76904
Woehl Rd 76904
Wood Cir & Rd 76904
Woodbine Ln 76904
Woodland Cir 76904
Woodlawn Dr 76901
Woodrow St 76903
Woodruff St 76905
Woodstock Ln 76901
Wool St 76903
Wrangler Ln 76904
Wren Rd 76901
Wynne Ave 76905
Wyoming Ave 76904
Yale Ave 76904
Ymca Dr 76904
Yucca Ln 76901
Zinnia Ave 76901
Zuni Ave 76901

NUMBERED STREETS

W 1st St 76903
1st Atlas St 76905
E & W 2nd 76903
E & W 3rd 76903
E & W 4th 76903
5th Rd 76905
E 5th St 76903
W 5th St 76903
E & W 6th 76903
E 7th St 76903
E & W 8th 76903
E & W 9th 76903
E & W 10th 76903
E & W 11th 76903
E & W 12th 76903
E & W 13th 76903
E & W 14th 76903
E & W 15th 76903
E & W 16th 76903
E & W 17th 76903
E & W 18th 76903
E & W 19th 76903
E 19th 1/2 St 76903
E & W 20th 76903
E & W 21st 76903
E & W 22nd 76903
E & W 23rd 76903
E & W 24th 76903
E 24th 1/2 St 76903
E & W 25th 76903
E 25th 1/2 St 76903
E & W 26th 76903
E & W 27th 76903
E & W 28th 76903
E & W 29th 76903
E & W 30th 76903
E & W 31st 76903
E & W 32nd 76903
E & W 33rd 76903
E & W 34th 76903
E 35th St 76903
E & W 36th 76903
E & W 37th 76903
E & W 38th 76903
E & W 39th 76903
E & W 40th 76903
41st Pl & St 76903
E & W 42nd 76903
E & W 43rd 76903
E & W 44th 76903
E 45th St 76903
E & W 46th 76903
E & W 47th 76903
E & W 48th 76903
E & W 49th 76903
E 50th St 76903

SAN ANTONIO TX

General Delivery 78265

POST OFFICE BOXES MAIN OFFICE STATIONS AND BRANCHES

Box No.s
1BB - 1BB 78201
2AA - 2AA 78201
6BB - 6BB 78201
7EE - 7EE 78201
11BB - 11BB 78201
13DD - 13DD 78201
14AA - 14AA 78201
15DD - 15DD 78201
18DD - 18DD 78201
38GG - 38GG 78201
41EE - 41EE 78201
41FF - 41FF 78201
568A - 568A 78292
600A - 600A 78292
5D - 5D 78217
8C - 8C 78217
37BB - 37BB 78201
16AA - 18AA 78201
20AA - 25AA 78201
BH003 - BH003 78201
15CC - 15CC 78201
KENSTV - KENSTV 78299
1C - 1H 78217
1 - 300 78291
301 - 599 78292
601 - 900 78293
901 - 1231 78294
1241 - 1540 78295
1541 - 1839 78296
1841 - 2171 78297
2181 - 2480 78298
2481 - 2967 78299
2951 - 2951 78294
2990 - 2995 78299
5001 - 5999 78201
6000 - 6997 78209
7001 - 7898 78207
8000 - 8695 78208
10001 - 11040 78210
12001 - 12976 78212
13001 - 13743 78213
14000 - 14810 78214
15001 - 15994 78212
17000 - 17994 78217
18001 - 18992 78218
23001 - 23990 78223
27001 - 27807 78227
28001 - 28910 78228
29001 - 29972 78229
33001 - 34992 78265
37001 - 37679 78237
39001 - 39956 78218
40001 - 40600 78229
47001 - 47956 78265
63004 - 63175 78270
65001 - 65280 78265
90001 - 99204 78209
100001 - 101517 78201
120001 - 129913 78212
160001 - 160896 78280
171001 - 171792 78217
190001 - 207916 78220
240001 - 246000 78224
276101 - 276700 78227
290003 - 290653 78280
291001 - 291236 78229
310001 - 310004 78213
380001 - 380858 78268
400001 - 400094 78229
460001 - 469022 78246
591001 - 599706 78259
659400 - 659940 78265
680001 - 682034 78268
690001 - 696999 78269
700001 - 708921 78270
760001 - 769990 78245
780001 - 786099 78278
790000 - 795200 78279
830001 - 839999 78283

RURAL ROUTES

38 78211
162 78221
01, 12, 49 78223
161 78224
135 78252
165, 207, 53 78257

NAMED STREETS

A St 78207
Aaron St 78221
Abacus St 78224
Abbey Cir 78260
Abbey Fls 78249
Abbey Gdn 78249
Abbey Park 78249
Abbey Way 78253
Abbeytown St 78238
Abbotts Pointe 78254
Abbottswood St 78249
Abby Wood 78257
Abdo Ln 78224
Abe Lincoln 78240
Abercorn Dr 78247
Aberdeen Pl 78210
Abilene Trl 78222
Abilene Stage 78245
Abiso Ave 78209
Able Creek Dr 78231
Abrazo 78247
Abshire St 78237
Absolon Farm 78228
Acacia Hl 78244
Acacia St 78209
Acacia Woods 78249
Academic Ct 78204
Academic Post 78250
W Academy St 78226
Academy Oak 78247
Acadian Dr 78245
Acapulco Dr 78237
Acateno 78233
Accolon Dr 78229
Acequia Pass 78237
E Ackard Pl 78221
W Ackard Pl
700-799 78221
1401-1599 78224
Ackerman Rd 78219
N & S Acme Rd 78237
Acorn Cv 78258
Acorn Cyn 78252
Acorn Hl 78217
Acorn St 78207
Acorn Bend Dr 78250
Acorn Creek Dr 78251
Acorn Crossing Dr 78251
Acorn Forest Dr 78251
Acornridge Way 78247
Action Ln 78210
Acuff Sta 78254
Acuna St 78237
Ada St 78223
Ada Mae St 78257
Adaes Ave
100-399 78207
400-500 78201
502-798 78201
Adair Blf 78223
Adair Dr 78238
Adair Post 78250
E Adalerth St 78205
Adalone Cv 78242
Adams Cir 78232
Adams Frst 78252
Adams Pass 78252
Adams Rnch 78245
Adams St 78210
Adams Xing 78255
Adams Hill Dr
8400-8899 78227
9100-9598 78245
9600-9700 78245
9702-9798 78245
Adamston Dr 78220
Addax Dr 78213
Addersly Dr 78254
Addingham 78253
N Addison St 78264
Adelaide 78204
Adelaide Oaks 78249
Adele St 78210
Adelphia Ave 78214
Adena Spgs 78245
Adhinger 78245
Adios 78248
Adkins Rdg 78239
Adkins Trl 78238
Adkins Elmendorf Rd
12400-12599 78263
14500-14799 78223
Adkins Pride 78245
Admiral Dr 78228
Admirals Way 78257
Adobe Crk 78253
Adobe Dr 78213
Adobe Grv 78239
Adobe Run 78232
Adobe Crossing Dr 78232
Adobe Springs Dr 78232
Adobe Square Dr 78232
Adobe Trail St 78232
Adolph St 78211
Adonis Dr 78260
Adrian Dr 78213
Adriana Maria 78253
Adrienne Ct 78240
Advance Dr 78220
Advantage Run 78258
Aero St 78217
Aeromedical Rd 78235
Afcoms Way 78226
Afterglow St 78216
Afterglow Vale 78252
E Afton Oaks Blvd 78232
Agan Ln 78221
Aganier Ave 78212
E Agarita Ave 78212
W Agarita Ave
100-899 78212
900-1599 78201
Agave 78264
Agena Dr 78219
Agency 78247
Agency Pt 78245
Agency Oaks 78249
Agile St 78248
Agin Ct 78258
Agnes Dr 78212
Agnew Rdg 78254
Agoura Hvn 78244
Agua Calientes 78239
Agua Dulce 78249
Ahern Dr 78216
Aids St 78238
Aiken St 78237
Aina Ln 78218
Air Lawn St 78227
Airedale Ln 78260
Airflight Cir & St 78250

Street	ZIP
Airlift Ave	78227
Airlift Dr	78226
Airole Way	78232
Airport Blvd	78216
Ajax Ave	78214
Ajuga	78261
Akin Pl	78261
Akin Doe	78261
Akin Elm	78261
Akin Fawn	78261
Akron St	78237
Alabado	78261
Alabama St	78203
Alameda Cir	78212
Alameda Rdg	78230
Alametos	
500-899	78212
Alametos	
900-1899	78201
Alamito Crk	78254
Alamo Grns	78261
Alamo Pkwy	78253
Alamo Plz	78205
N Alamo St	
101-197	78205
199-400	78205
402-498	78205
500-1999	78215
2001-2199	78215
S Alamo St	
200-999	78205
1000-1400	78210
1402-1498	78210
1500-1698	78204
1700-2000	78204
2002-2098	78204
Alamo Blanco St	78233
Alamo Creek Cir	78230
Alamo Downs Pkwy	78238
Alamo Heights Blvd	78209
Alamo Ranch Pkwy	78253
Alamosa Ave	78210
Alamosa Fls	78255
Alan Bean Dr	78219
Alan Hale St	78240
Alan Shepard Dr	78219
Alanwood Dr	78264
Alarente Dr	78245
Alaskan Trail St	78238
Alaskan Wolf	78245
Alaskian Sunrise	78244
Alazan St	78207
Albany Rdg	78250
Albany St	78209
Albeon Park Dr S	78249
Albert St & Walk	78207
Albert Martin	78253
Albertina Ln	78209
Albin Dr	78209
Albizi Way	78258
Albrecht Ln	78233
Albren Ave	78211
Albright	78247
Alcalde Moreno St	78232
Aldama	78237
Aldebaran Sun	78252
Alder Ln	78202
Alder Creek Dr	78247
Alderton St	78228
Alderwood	78250
Aldon Woods	78250
Aldrich Dr	78227
Aleta	78223
Alexa Pl	78251
Alexander Ave	78201
Alexander Hamilton Dr	78228
Alexandria St	78233
Alfa Dr	78218
Alfonse	78227
Alfred Dr	78220
Algerita Dr	78230
Algo Dulce	78211
Algruth Dr	78220
Alhambra	78201
Alhaven Ave	78210
Ali Ave	78229
Alicante Rd	78257
Alice Aly	78207
Alice Hl	78232
Alice Fay Ave	78237
Alicia Ave	78228
Alida Ln	78260
Alisa Brooke	78254
Alladin Dr	78228
Allard Blf	78254
Allbrook	78244
Allegheny Dr	78229
Allegro	78218
Allegro Crk	78261
Allen St	78209
Allena Dr	78213
Allendale Dr	78226
Allendale Oak	78249
Allendale Peak	78254
Allende Dr	78237
Allenhurst St	78227
Allensworth St	78209
Allentown St	78238
Alling St	78215
Allison Blf	78240
Allison Dr	78212
Allwood St	78233
Alma Dr	78222
Almadin	78258
Almarion Way	78250
Almendra Dr	78247
Almeria Cir	78257
Almond Dr	78247
Almond Park	78249
Almond Crest Dr	78233
Almond Field Dr	78245
Almond Green Dr	78250
Almond Wood	78233
Alms Park Dr	78250
Alnwick St	78228
Aloha Dr	78219
Alovette	78251
Alpha Wolf Bay	78245
Alpine Cir	78248
Alpine Crst	78233
Alpine Ldg	78258
Alpine Rdg	78258
Alpine Run	78255
Alpine Shr	78254
Alpine Vlg	78245
Alpine Aster	78259
Alpine Mist	78258
Alpine Pond	78260
Alpine Trail St	78250
Alpine Valley Dr	78242
Alsace	78232
Alsbrook Dr	78223
Alston St	78228
Alstroemeria	78253
Alsup St	78237
Alta Ave	78209
Alta Day St	78253
Alta Mesa	78258
Alta Sita St	78237
Altadena	78259
Altamirano	78233
Altamonte Oaks	78253
Altgelt Ave	78201
Althea Dr	78238
Altitude St	78227
Altius Pass	78245
Alto St	78207
Alto Cedro	78261
Alto Oaks	78255
Alvarez Pl	78204
Alveda	78233
Alverstone Way	78250
Alwick Ln	78247
Amador	78218
Amalfi Park	78233
Amanda St	
200-1198	78220
1200-1899	78210
Amandas Cv	78247
Amarillo Ave	78225
Amaya	78237
Ambassador Ln	
100-199	78257
1100-1199	78219
Amber Crk	78232
Amber Crst	78249
Amber Cv	78245
Amber Fld	78245
Amber Frst	78232
Amber Gln	78257
Amber Holw	78245
Amber Knl	78251
Amber Rdg	78250
E Amber St	78221
W Amber St	78221
Amber Vis	78254
Amber Vw	78261
Amber Breeze	78245
Amber Chase	78245
Amber Coral	78245
Amber Dusk	78250
Amber Flora Dr	78251
Amber Gap	78245
Amber Glade	78245
Amber Leaf	78245
Amber Ledge	78245
Amber Morning	78245
Amber Oak	78249
Amber Rose	78253
Amber Sky	78260
Amber Star	78253
Amber Tree	78254
Amber Valley St	78227
Amberdale Oak	78249
Ambergris Cv	78223
Amberson Dr	78220
Amberstone Dr	78258
Amberwood Dr	78242
Amble Trl	78249
Amble Coach	78245
Ambleside Ln	78231
Ambling St	78238
Ambridge St	78258
Ambush Crk	78245
Ambush Dr	78240
Ambush Grv	78247
Amelia Pass	78254
Amerada St	78237
Amerson Ln	78213
Ames Ave	78211
Amestoy St	78207
Ameswood Dr	78232
Amethyst Dr	78259
Amethyst Way	78222
Amherst Bay	78249
Amhurst Dr	78213
Amigo Ave	78260
Amigo Dream	78253
Amires Pl	78237
Amistad St	78233
Amity Rd	78210
N & S Amnon Dr	78213
Amor Ln	78207
Amorosa Way	78261
Amos Pollard	78253
Amsterdam	78230
Amy Ln	78233
Amy Frances Dr	78253
Anabella St	78247
Anacacho St	78217
Anaconda Dr	78228
Anaheim St	78211
Anaheim Post	78254
Analissa	78214
Anarbor Fld	78254
Anarbor Post	78245
Anastacia Pl	78212
Ancel Rd	78210
Anchor Dr	78213
Anchorage Hl	78217
Anchorage Bay	78239
Anchors Flt	78245
Anchors Coach	78245
Ancient Bnd	78248
Ancient Anchor	78245
Ancient Coach	78213
Ancient Elm	78247
Ancient Oaks	78255
Ancient Song	78245
Anderson Ave	78203
Andersonville Ln	78240
Andora Rdg	78255
Andover Bay	78258
Andover Creek Dr	78254
Andover Peak	78254
Andrew Pt	78251
Andrews Gdn	78258
Andrews Pass	78254
Andrews St	78209
Andricks Dr	78223
Andros Pl	78227
Andtree Blvd	78250
Andy St	78226
Anemone	78253
Angel Pt	78254
Angel Sergio	78253
Angel Trumpet	78259
Angel Valley St	78227
Angela St	78207
Angeles Dr	78201
Angie Pl	78240
Angora St	78247
Angostura Blvd	78261
Angus St	78247
Aniol St	78219
Anita St	78210
Ann Arbor Dr	78224
Anna Mae Dr	78222
Anna Maria	78214
Annandale	78239
Annapolis Dr	78230
Annarose Ln	78211
Anne Lewis Dr	78216
Annie St	78212
Annuziata	78253
W Ansley Blvd	78224
E Ansley Pl	78221
E Ansley St	78221
W Ansley St	78221
Ansley Bend Dr	78251
Anson Jones	78223
Antares Frst & Park	78239
Antelope Crk	78254
Antelope Dr	78232
Antelope Hl	78261
Antero Dr	78250
Anthurium	78253
Antietam Dr	78239
Antigua	78259
Antioch Dr	78213
Antique Oak St	78233
Antique Rose	78244
Antler Cir	78232
Antler Cyn	78252
Antler Dr	78213
Antler Sta	78251
Antler Creek Dr	78248
Antler Crossing Dr	78248
Antler Post	78245
Antlers Lodge Rd	78251
Antoine Forest Dr	78254
Antoinette Dr	78223
Anton Dr	78223
Antrim Dr	78218
Antsla Sands	78251
Anza St	78223
Apache Cyn	78252
Apache Frst	78266
Apache Rnch	78253
Apache St	78207
Apache Trl	78255
Apache Vlg	78245
Apache Creek Rd	78260
Apache Plume	78258
Apache Springs Dr	78259
Apaloosa Way	78256
Apastron Haze	78252
Aphelion Cv	78252
Apollo St	78214
Appaloosa Run	78244
Appaloosa Bay	78254
Apperson Ave	78207
Apple Grn	78240
Apple Hls	78238
Apple Blossom St	78247
Apple Creek St	78222
Apple Gate Dr	78230
Apple Tree St	78222
Apple Tree Woods	78249
Apple Valley Dr	78242
Apple Way Dr	78240
Applebee St	78211
Appleman	78233
Appler	78215
Appleseed Ct	78238
Appleton Dr	78227
Applewest Cir	78240
Applewhite	78204
Applewhite Rd	
10900-12899	78224
15400-22399	78264
Applewood Rd	78217
Applin Ave	78210
Appomattox St	78245
Apricot Dr	78247
Apricot Bloom	78254
Apricot Field Dr	78245
April Bnd	78250
Aquarius	78214
Arabian	78227
Arabian Bnd	78254
Arabian Crk	78244
Arabian Cv	78244
Arabian Hl	78254
Arabian Isle	78254
Arabian Gate	78254
Arabian Palm	78254
Arabian Sands	78254
Aragon Dr	78211
Aragon Vlg	78250
Aransas Ave	
101-197	78210
199-1499	78210
1800-1898	78203
2100-2598	78220
Aransas Bay	78229
Arapaho Way	78261
Arapahoe Dr	78207
Arbeth Pl	78250
Arbois	78254
Arboleda St	78237
Arboles Verdes	78260
Arbor Blf	78240
Arbor Bnd	78259
Arbor Cir	78231
Arbor Hts	78251
Arbor Pl	
300-398	78207
400-2399	78207
2400-2899	78228
Arbor Bend Dr	78231
Arbor Farm	78239
Arbor Meadow Rd	78256
Arbor Mesa	78249
Arbor Oak	78249
Arbor Ridge Dr	78228
Arbor Springs Dr	78249
Arbor Wood St	78250
Arcade Rdg	78239
Arcadia Crk	78251
Arcadia Park	78247
Arcadia Pl	78209
Arch Blf	78216
Arch Brg	78254
Arch Stone	78258
Archer Pt	78254
Archer St	78212
Archers Grv	78244
Archers Bay	78213
Archers Bow Rd	78232
Archers Coach	78244
Archimedes Dr	78223
Archway Dr	78232
Archwood	78239
Arciniega St	78205
Arcositas	78221
Ardash Ln	78250
Arden Bnd	78250
Arden Gln	78257
Arden Grove St	78215
Ardenwood St	78223
Ardmore St	78237
Argo Ave	78209
Argonne Dr	78220
Argyle Ave	78209
Argyle Pass	78247
Argyle Way	78247
Ariana Dr	78248
Aribe Dr	78216
Ariel Hl	78252
Ariel St	78253
Arion Cir & Pkwy	78216
Aristocrat St	78245
Aristotle Pass	78249
Arizona	78207
Arizona Ash St	78232
Arizona Bay	78244
Arkansas Oak	78223
Arlene Park	78251
Arlene St	78207
Arlington Ct	78210
Arlitt Dr	78222
Armadillo Aly	78202
Armor Arch	78254
Armour Pl	78212
Arms Way St	78233
Armstrong Pl	78202
Armstrong Wl	78249
Army Blvd	78215
Arnaz Dr	78237
Arneson Dr	78219
Arnold	78213
Arnold Palmer	78257
Aronel	78231
Arrid Pass	78238
Arrid Rd	78210
Arriola Ln	78263
Arrow Cyn	78258
Arrow Gln	78258
Arrow Hl	78258
Arrow Rdg	78258
Arrow Spg	78258
Arrow Way	78256
Arrow Bow	78258
Arrow Mound St	78231
Arrow Oaks	78249
Arrow Point Ct	78227
Arrow Stone	78258
Arrow Tree	78258
Arrowhead Dr	78228
E Arrowhead Dr	78228
W Arrowhead Dr	78228
Arrowhead Trl	78245
Arrowhead Pool	78254
Arrowood	78233
Arrowood Pl	78266
Arrowwood Bnd	78261
Arroya Vista Dr	78213
Arroyo Pass	78259
Arroyo Alamo	78253
Arroyo Gold	78232
Arroyo Grande	78253
Arroyo Moss St	78232
Arroyo Oak Dr	78247
Arroyo Verde	78253
E Arsenal	78204
Arteago	78237
Artemis Dr	78218
Artesian Farm	78239
Artesian Oaks St	78232
Arthur St & Walk	78202
Artisan Cv	78245
Artisan Ln	78250
Artisan Way	78260
Artisan Gate	78260
Arts Cir	78247
Arts Crafts Way	78226
Arvie St	78253
Arvin Dr	78209
Asbury Sta	78244
Asbury Vis	78249
Ascend Ter	78249
Ascham Dr	78228
Ascot Ave	78224
Ascot Dr	78238
Ascot Pl	78249
Ash St	78208
Ash Field Dr	78245
Ash Hollow Dr	78245
Ash Village Dr	78245
Ashbel	78223
Ashbourne	78247
Ashbrook	78239
Ashburton	78254
Ashbury Blf	78245
Ashbury Crk	78245
Ashbury Dr	78250
Ashbury Ldg	78247
Ashbury Bay	78258
Ashbury Oaks	78247
E Ashby Pl	78212
W Ashby Pl	
100-1099	78212
1100-2000	78201
2002-2898	78201
2900-3299	78228
3301-3399	78228
Ashby Pt	78233
Ashcroft Pt	78254
Ashdale Rd	78227
Ashe Juniper	78261
Asher Park Dr	78249
Asherton Way	78258
Ashford Dr	78227
Ashford Gln	78232
Ashford Vis	78259
Ashford Point Dr	78240
Ashin Way	78232
Ashington	78247
Ashland Clf	78261
Ashland Dr	78218
Ashleaf Wls	78261
Ashleaf Pecan	78261
Ashley Cir	78232
Ashley Ct	78247
Ashley Grn	78257
Ashley Mnr	78247
Ashley Pl	78247
E Ashley Rd	
200-398	78221
400-1099	78221
1300-2499	78214
Ashley Spgs	78244
Ashley Oaks	78247
Ashley Wilkes	78221
Ashley Wood	78233
Ashling	78260
Ashmont	78258
Ashmont Ter	78233
Ashmore	78245
Ashprington Dr	78251
Ashrock Ct	78230
Ashstone Hl	78254
Ashton Pl	78229
Ashton Audrey	78249
Ashton Oaks	78256
Ashton Village Dr	78248
Ashton Wood	78248
Ashwood Pointe	78254
Asoleado	78261
Aspen Bnd	78238
Aspen Cyn	78253
Aspen Gdn	78238
Aspen Hl	78238
Aspen Hts	78249
Aspen Ln	78232
Aspen Mdw	78238
Aspen Rdg	78248
Aspen Vlg	78245
Aspen Vw	78217
Aspen Creek Dr	78248
Aspen Farm	78244
Aspen Gold	78238
Aspen Oak	78254
Aspen Park Dr	78249
Aspen Valley St	78242
Aspenwood Dr	78219
Aster Cir	78266
Aster Trl	78256
Asteroid St	78217
Astin Pl	78251

Aston Gln 78257
Astor St 78210
Astoria Dr 78220
Astronaut Dr 78217
At And T Center Pkwy 78219
Athel Ave 78237
Athens 78251
Athens Fld 78245
Atherton 78244
Atkins Bay 78245
Atlanta St
400-498 78215
501-599 78215
600-698 78212
700-799 78212
Atlas St 78223
Atlench St 78215
Atoko Way 78256
Atrium Peak 78261
Attleboro St 78217
Attucks Ln 78238
Atwater Crk 78245
Atwater Dr 78213
Atwell Park 78254
Atwood Ln 78228
Aubrey 78204
Aubrey Ct 78216
Auburn Brk 78253
Auburn Gln 78249
Auburn Knls 78249
Auburn Pl 78209
Auburn Rdg 78249
Auburn Way 78249
Auburn Oaks 78247
Auburn Woods 78249
Aucuba Bnd & Fls 78260
Auditorium Cir 78205
Audrey Rdg 78266
Audrey Alene Dr 78216
& S Audubon Dr 78212
Aue Rd 78257
Augsberg 78256
Augusta Cor 78247
Augusta Sq 78247
Augusta St
300-398 78205
600-899 78215
Auldine Dr 78230
Aurelia St
100-498 78220
501-599 78220
1501-1599 78210
Aurora 78228
Aurora Cir 78252
Aurora Crst 78249
Aurora Fld 78245
Austin Hwy
108-398 78209
400-1499 78209
1500-2800 78218
2802-2898 78218
Austin Rd 78209
Austin St
300-498 78215
701-799 78215
800-1499 78208
Austin Vly 78242
Autry Bnd 78254
Autumn Blf 78240
Autumn Cyn 78255
Autumn Gdn 78258
Autumn Grv 78254
Autumn Knl 78258
Autumn Lk 78222
Autumn Ln 78219
Autumn Mdws 78254
Autumn Park 78249
Autumn Pass 78245
Autumn Rdg 78258
Autumn Riv 78245
Autumn Vlg 78245
Autumn Branches 78254
Autumn Breeze 78254
Autumn Chase St 78238
Autumn Cherry 78254
Autumn Dew 78254

Autumn Evening 78254
Autumn Glade 78247
Autumn Gold 78254
Autumn Leaf St 78217
Autumn Mist St 78253
Autumn Moon 78245
Autumn Oaks 78254
Autumn Shade 78254
Autumn Shadows 78254
Autumn Silver 78254
Autumn Skies 78254
Autumn Star 78254
Autumn Storm 78254
Autumn Sun 78254
Autumn Sunrise 78254
Autumn Sunset 78239
Autumn Vista St 78249
Autumn Waters 78254
Autumn Whisper 78254
Autumn Woods St 78232
Autumndale 78254
Ava Way 78253
Avalanche Dr 78238
Avalon Park 78257
Avalon Rdg 78240
Avalon St 78213
Avalon Ter 78239
Avalon Vw 78240
Avalon Star 78240
Avant Ave 78210
Avator Bay 78250
Ave Del Rey 78216
Ave Maria Dr 78216
Avellano 78250
Avellino Blf 78261
Avenida Del Luna 78232
Avenida Del Sol 78232
Avenida Prima St
4100-4698 78233
4101-4199 78217
4201-4699 78233
Avens Arbor 78253
Avenue E
300-399 78205
Avenue E
401-499 78205
500-598 78215
600-699 78215
701-799 78215
Avenue A 78215
Avenue B
701-797 78215
799-2399 78215
3100-3398 78209
3400-3600 78209
3602-3698 78209
Avenue M 78212
Avenue Ventana 78256
Averhoff Cv 78253
Averi Way 78217
Avery Rd 78233
Avery Way 78261
Aviara Gdns 78251
Aviara Golf 78251
Avignon 78258
Avila 78239
Avionics Cir 78226
Avoca Dr 78211
Avocet 78245
Avondale Ave 78223
Axelton Bay 78238
Axis Trl 78232
Axis Xing 78245
Aylesbury Hill St 78209
Aylsbury St 78216
Ayrshire Dr 78217
Azalea Cir 78266
Azalea Sq 78218
Azalea Breeze 78259
Azalea Fern 78253
Azalea Gate 78266
Azalea Pointe 78255
Aztec Msn 78261
Aztec St 78207
Aztec Vlg 78245
Azucena St 78237

Azul Blvd 78211
Azure Oak 78258
Azurite Trl 78222
B St 78207
Babbling Brk 78232
Babcock Rd
100-1299 78201
1301-1499 78201
1500-2899 78229
5400-6399 78240
6400-14800 78249
14802-15398 78249
15501-15897 78255
15899-21400 78255
21402-21898 78255
Babe Ruth St 78240
Babs Dr 78213
Babson St 78249
Bacarro St 78247
Baccarat 78258
Back Nine 78244
Backbay Dr 78230
Backbay Pass 78244
Backdrop 78260
Bacon Rd 78249
Baden 78245
Baden Post 78254
Badger Pt 78250
Badger Pass Dr 78239
Badger Peak 78254
Badger Wolf 78245
Badgers Hls 78238
Baer Trl 78238
E & W Baetz Blvd 78221
Baffin Dr 78222
Baffin Sta 78250
Baffin Oaks 78254
Baffin Peak 78245
Bailey Ave 78210
Bailey Hls 78253
Bainbridge 78240
Bains Landing St 78233
Baird St 78228
Baity Ct 78210
Baja Pt 78242
Bajo Luna 78223
Baker Ave 78211
Baker Hl 78258
Bakersfield St 78228
Bakerswood 78254
Balboa Ave 78237
Balboa Is 78245
Balboa Port Dr 78242
Balcombe 78233
Balcon 78209
Balcon Is 78250
N Balcones Rd 78201
Balcones Gate 78255
Balcones Heights Rd 78201
Bald Mtn 78245
Bald Eagle Way 78245
Baldwin Ave 78210
Baldwin Rdg 78249
Balfour Dr 78239
Balfour Post 78247
Balky St 78240
Ball St 78217
Ballantrae 78239
Ballard Dr 78226
Ballard Peak 78254
Ballerina Ct 78217
Ballet Dr 78216
Ballinger 78244
Ballot Park 78244
Balmoral Pl 78258
Baloc Farm 78244
Balsa Di Prato 78253
Baltic St 78213
Baltic Strm 78251
Baltimore Ave
200-298 78215
300-400 78215
402-498 78215
701-799 78212
Baltzell Ave 78221
Bamburgh Dr 78216

Bammel St
11900-11999 78213
12000-12099 78231
Banbridge Ave 78223
Banbury 78239
Bandberry Bay 78250
Bandbury Oak 78247
Bandera Rd
100-2299 78228
2301-2399 78228
2500-7600 78238
7602-7798 78238
7900-11699 78250
11701-11799 78250
Banditos Rdg 78245
Bane St 78224
Baneberry 78260
Bangor Dr 78228
Banister 78259
Banister Pass 78254
Bank 78204
S Bank Bldg 78205
Bank Of America 78205
Bannocks Dr 78239
Bantry Ct 78240
Bantry Bay 78240
Bar C 78253
Bar Harbor Dr 78228
Bar J 78253
Bar Z Rnch 78245
Baraeswood St 78233
Barbados St 78227
Barbara Dr 78216
Barbe St 78210
Barberry St 78221
Barbet Dr 78213
Barboli 78253
Barbuda St 78227
Barbwire Pass 78254
Barcelona St 78230
Barchester Dr 78216
Barclay Pt 78254
Barclay St 78207
Barcom Ct 78218
Bare Back Trl 78250
Bareback Path 78245
Bargas St 78210
Barhill St 78217
Barhill Bay 78245
Barhill Post 78254
Barilla Pl 78209
Bark Ln 78233
Bark Valley Dr 78242
Barker Bay 78245
Barking Crk 78254
Barking Wolf 78245
Barkley Trl 78250
Barkmeyer St 78223
Barkmore 78258
Barkston Dr 78253
Barlite Blvd 78224
Barlow Ave 78220
Barlow Vlg 78245
Barlow Oak 78213
Barn Owl 78255
Barn Swallow 78255
Barnard Ml 78247
Barnes Aly 78207
Barnes St 78226
Barney Ave 78237
Barneywood St 78238
Barnsbury Sq 78232
Barnsley 78250
Barons Crk 78251
Barons Den 78245
Barons Ridge Dr 78251
Barranca Ave 78221
Barrel Pass 78245
Barrel Pt 78251
Barrel Oak St 78231
Barrel Stage 78244
Barrell Run 78247
Barren Ridge Dr 78239
Barrera St 78210
Barrett Ave 78214

Barrett Pl
100-699 78225
701-799 78225
800-899 78226
Barrett Palms 78224
Barrington Ct 78249
Barrington St 78217
Barron Fld 78245
Barron St 78240
Barrow 78253
Barrow Bay 78258
Barrow Oak 78247
Barrow Peak 78251
Barryhill St 78238
Barsan Rd 78249
Bart Holw 78250
Bart Starr St 78240
Bartell Pt 78254
Bartholomew Ave 78211
Bartlett Fls 78250
Bartlett Pl 78209
Bartlett Bay 78258
Bartmer Ave 78228
Barton Crk 78258
Barton Ct 78225
Barton Holw 78249
Barton Mill St 78233
Barton Rock Ln & Rd 78239
Barton Springs St 78247
Barton Woods 78259
Bascum Blvd 78221
Baseview Dr 78227
Basil Bay 78253
Basil Grass 78245
Basilwood Dr 78213
Basin Dr 78216
Basin Fld 78245
Basin Elm 78239
Basin Oak 78247
Basket Xing 78245
Basket Elm 78254
Basse Rd
800-1399 78212
1500-1598 78213
1600-2499 78213
E Basse Rd 78209
Bassett Ln 78231
Basswood Dr 78213
Bastione 78253
Bastrop 78214
Bastrop Crk 78245
Bat Cyn 78252
Bat Cave Loop & Rd 78266
Battery Ln 78233
Battle Crk 78259
Battle Lk 78260
Battle Pass 78239
Battle Oak 78258
Baum St 78233
Bauman St 78219
Bavaria Ct 78256
Baxter Ave 78220
Baxter Sta 78245
Baxter Peak 78254
Bay St 78237
Bay Vw 78239
Bay Horse Dr 78245
Bay Hurst Dr 78224
Bay Meadows St 78244
Bay Oaks Dr 78240
Bay Orchard Dr 78231
Bayakoa Ct 78245
Bayberry 78240
Bayberry Row 78249
Baybrook 78253
Baycliff 78233
Bayfield 78233
Bayhead Dr 78220
Bayhill Cv 78258
Bayhill Den 78245
Bayliss St 78233
E & W Baylor 78204
Bayonne Dr 78228
Bayou Bnd 78239
Bayou St 78245
Bayport 78239

Bayshore 78259
Bayside Ct 78257
Baytree Dr 78240
Bayville Dr 78226
Baywater Dr 78229
Baywater Stage 78255
Baywave 78233
Baywell Dr 78227
Baywood St 78213
Bda Xing 78235
Beacon Ave 78212
Beacon Crk 78213
Beacon Cv 78245
Beacon Fld 78245
Beacon Pt 78245
Beacon Bay 78239
Beacon Oak 78239
Beacon Park Dr 78249
Beacon Woods 78248
Beadwara 78249
Beal 78201
Beam Blvd 78221
Bear Br 78222
Bear Cyn 78252
Bear Mdw 78222
Bear Mtn 78258
Bear Rdg 78258
Bear Trl 78249
Bear Claw 78258
Bear Creek Dr 78245
Bear Lake Dr 78244
Bear Oak Path 78223
Bear Paw Path 78245
Bear Run St 78247
Bear Springs Dr 78245
Bear Tree Cir 78255
Bear Wood 78238
Bearberry Pass 78254
Beardsly Cv 78258
Beargrass Ct 78258
Bears Crst 78258
Bears Notch 78258
Beartooth Pass 78255
Beartrap Ln 78249
Bearwolf Bay 78245
Beatrice Ave 78214
Beau Brg 78254
Beauchamp St
1500-1599 78213
1600-1699 78231
Beaudine Ave 78250
Beauregard 78204
Beauty Oaks 78251
Beautyberry 78261
Beaver Brk 78260
Beaver Crk 78258
Beaver Ln 78202
Beaver Trl 78249
Beaver Bend Ct 78258
Beaver Elm 78244
Beaver Tree 78249
Beavers Run 78217
Beck Rd 78263
Beckbrook St 78232
Becker Bnd & Fld 78253
Becker Vine 78253
Beckett 78213
Beckington St 78216
Beckley 78250
Beckwith Blvd 78249
Beckwood Dr 78259
Becky Renee 78201
Beconsfield St 78216
Bedazzled 78245
W Bedford Ave 78226
Bedford Crk 78254
Bedford Bay 78239
Bedford Oaks 78254
Bedford Stage 78213
Bee St 78208
Bee Cave St 78231
Bee Tree Cv 78258
Beech Crk 78259
Beech Grv 78245
Beech St
3700-3799 78226

3801-3999 78237
Beech Plain Dr 78245
Beech Trail Dr 78244
Beech Valley St 78242
Beechaven Dr 78207
Beechnut Oak 78223
Beechnut Park Dr 78240
Beechwood Ln 78216
Beethoven St 78210
Beewood St 78233
Before Dawn 78248
Begonia St 78217
Begonia Rock 78245
Belair Dr & Flts 78213
Belclaire 78258
Belcourt Pl 78257
Belcross 78237
Beldelde 78254
Belden Ave 78214
Belen St 78221
Belfast Dr 78209
Belforest 78239
Belga Dr 78240
Belgium Ln 78219
Belgrave Way 78233
Belgravia Frst 78233
Belgreen Dr 78227
Belhaven 78250
Belicena Rd 78253
Belinda Lee St 78220
Belknap Pl 78212
Bell Dr 78217
Bell Flower Dr 78232
Bell Mountain St 78255
Bella Gdn 78256
Bella Crown 78256
Bella Daisy 78260
Bella Donna 78253
Bella Glade 78256
Bella Luna Way 78257
Bella Mist 78256
Bella Rose 78256
Bella Vista Dr 78228
Bella Vista Pl 78253
Bellaire Pt 78249
Bellbrook Dr 78227
Bellcastle 78253
Bellcrest Dr 78217
Belle Vlg 78250
Belle Ellen 78229
Belle Grove St 78230
Belle Vere 78249
Belle Watling 78221
Bellinger St 78220
Bellshire St 78216
Bellview St 78209
Bellwood St 78249
Belmark Ct 78258
Belmont 78202
Belmont Pl 78240
Belmont Stakes 78254
Belmore Cv 78245
Beltran St 78210
Beltway St 78217
Belvidere Dr 78212
Belvin St 78212
Belvoir Dr 78230
Bemis Dr 78237
Ben Ali 78248
Ben Brush St 78248
Ben Casey Dr 78240
Ben Crenshaw Ct 78244
Ben Hogan Ct 78244
Ben Hur St 78229
Ben Milam St 78238
Benava 78204
Benbrook 78250
Bench Oaks 78254
Benchmark Way 78213
Benchwood Cir 78248
Bendell 78250
Bender Dr 78229
Bending Crk 78261
Bending Crst 78239
Bending Dr 78224
Bending Grv 78259

Bending Pt 78247
Bending Trl 78247
Bending Elms 78247
Bending Oak St 78249
Benedetta 78253
Benedict Ct 78258
Benetton Dr 78253
Bengal Brk 78260
Benham Dr 78220
Benhill 78239
Benita St 78210
Benke Farm 78239
Benning Dr 78233
Bennington Dr 78228
Bennington Way 78261
Benrus Blvd 78228
Bent Br 78250
Bent Holw 78259
Bent St 78213
Bent Anchor 78213
Bent Arrow 78258
Bent Bow Dr 78209
Bent Briar 78250
Bent Brook Dr 78266
Bent Elm 78259
Bent Elm Creek Ln 78230
Bent Grass 78261
Bent Hook Ln 78224
Bent Moss St 78232
Bent Oak Dr 78231
Bent Ridge Dr 78249
Bent Waters 78239
Bent Willow 78254
Bentley Dr 78218
Bentley Mnr 78249
Bentoak Holw 78248
Benton St
100-106 78208
108-499 78208
1401-1699 78209
Benton Woods 78258
Bentsen Palm 78254
Bentway St 78217
Bentwood Dr 78230
Bentwood Oaks 78247
Bentwood View Dr 78254
Benward Ln 78250
Benwood Crst 78238
Beowulf St 78254
Berberis 78261
Bercy Ct & Ln 78251
Berean Way 78266
Berg Blvd 78256
Berger Pl 78221
Berkley Sq 78249
Berkley Oak 78230
Berkshire Ave 78210
Berlin Ave 78211
Bermuda 78222
Bermuda Hl 78217
Bermuda Run 78261
Bermuda Trce 78245
Bermuda Trl 78240
Bermuda Palm 78245
Bernadine Dr 78220
Bernard Dr 78221
Bernhardt Rd & Way 78263
Bernice Dr 78228
Berry Br 78233
Berry Grv 78259
Berry Hl 78227
Berrycreek Dr 78218
Berryville Dr 78245
Berrywest Ct & Dr 78240
Bertetti Dr 78227
Berthould Ln 78249
Bertram St 78251
Berwick Dr 78201
Berwick Town 78249
Beryl Cv 78242
Beryl Dr 78213
Besinger Way 78254
Beso Ln 78207
Best Way 78260
Bethany Pl 78201
Bethel Bnd 78247

Bethencourt 78209
Bethlehem Walk 78220
Betsy Ross Dr 78230
Betty St 78224
Betty Jean St 78223
Betty Levy 78227
Betty Lou Dr 78229
Beverly Dr
100-199 78201
200-499 78228
Beverly Ann St 78224
E & W Beverly Mae
Dr 78229
Bexar Dr 78228
Bexar County
Courthouse 78205
Bexar County Justice
Ctr 78205
Bexar Crossing St 78232
Bexar Cty Court
House 78285
Bexley Trl 78259
Bianca 78254
Bible St 78220
Bicentennial St 78219
Bickley St 78221
Blediger Ln 78266
Bienville Dr 78233
Biering Ave 78210
Biering Rd 78249
Biering Peak 78247
Big Bnd 78250
Big Lk 78245
Big Bear 78258
Big Bend Cv 78253
Big Bethel Dr 78240
Big Bluestem 78261
Big Buck Ct 78245
Big Creek Dr 78242
Big Cypress 78261
Big Elk Dr 78245
Big Fawn St 78242
Big Foot
100-499 78204
Big Foot
700-999 78225
Big Geronimo St 78254
Big Horn Bnd 78253
Big Horn Dr 78228
Big John Dr 78224
Big Knife St 78242
Big Leaf Rd 78264
Big Leaf Maple 78227
Big Meadows St 78230
Big Mesa Dr 78245
Big Oak Dr 78264
Big Pond 78261
Big Rock Dr 78227
Big Sky Bnd 78216
Big Sky Dr 78245
Big Spring Ln 78223
Big Trail Dr 78232
Big Tree Dr 78247
Big Valley Dr 78242
Bigbury 78254
Bighorn Cyn 78258
Bigmouth Hook 78224
Bigmouth Rod 78224
Bikeway Ln 78231
Bikini Dr 78218
Bill Anders Dr 78219
Bill Miller Ln 78223
Billings Dr 78245
Billington Dr 78230
Billy Dr 78220
Billy Mitchell Rd 78226
Biltmore Gln 78233
Biltmore Lks 78233
Biltmore St 78213
Bindseil Ln 78266
Bingham Dr 78230
Binham Hts 78249
Binz Engleman Rd
3600-3798 78219
3800-5599 78219
5601-5699 78219

5800-6299 78244
6301-7499 78244
Birch Grv 78259
Birch Hl 78232
Birch St 78210
Birch Way 78254
Birch Field Dr 78245
Birch Stage 78244
Birch Tree St 78247
Birch Valley Dr 78242
Birchbrook 78254
Birchleaf St 78216
Birchwood Dr 78213
Birchwood Bay 78253
Birdhill 78253
Birdie Cv 78221
Birdie Ln 78237
Birdie Rdg 78260
Birdies Grn 78260
E, N, S & W Birdsong 78258
Birdstone Ln 78245
Birnam Oaks 78248
Birnam Wood 78248
Biscay Hbr 78249
Biscay Bay 78249
Biscayne Dr 78227
Biscuit Hl 78253
Bishop 78214
Bishops Grn 78257
Bisley Pass 78245
Bison Cyn 78261
Bison Rd 78232
Bison Run 78251
Bisquet Pt 78233
Bitter Fld 78245
Bitter Creek St 78247
Bitter Crimson 78261
Bitterblue Ln 78218
Bitterlake 78245
Bitternut Woods St 78249
Bitters Rd 78216
E Bitters Rd 78216
W Bitters Rd
100-1200 78216
1202-1298 78216
1400-2100 78248
2102-2398 78248
Black Crk 78257
Black Bass 78224
Black Bear 78253
Black Buck 78266
Black Canyon Trl 78232
Black Drum 78253
Black Elk 78261
Black Fox Dr 78245
Black Gap Dr 78245
Black Hickory Woods
St 78249
Black Oak Pass 78223
Black Oak Woods 78249
Black Powder 78264
Black River Ln 78245
Black Rock 78253
Black Stag 78255
Black Thorn Ln 78240
Black Walnut Woods
St 78249
Black Willow 78264
Black Wolf Bay 78245
Blackberry Dr 78238
Blackbird Ln 78248
Blackbridge 78253
Blackcastle Dr 78254
Blackhawk 78232
Blackhill 78228
Blackjack Bnd, Cir, Pass,
Rd & Vw 78264
Blackjack Oak 78230
Blackmon Cv 78253
Blackoak Bnd 78248
Blacksmith Ln 78238
Blackstone Crk 78254
Blackstone Ct 78259
Blackstone Run 78259
Blackwater Rd 78258
Blaine 78202

Blairstone 78247
Blairwood 78247
Blake Oak Run 78254
Blakeley Dr 78209
Blakeville 78233
Blanche Coker St 78216
Blanco Ky 78247
Blanco Pass 78259
Blanco Rd
101-103 78212
105-4999 78212
5000-5098 78216
5100-14899 78216
15100-16498 78232
16500-18199 78232
18201-19200 78258
19202-20298 78258
21300-23398 78260
23400-28899 78260
28901-30099 78260
23182-1-23182-5 78260
5810-1-5810-5 78216
W Blanco Rd 78232
Blanco Spgs 78258
Blanco Trl 78248
Blanco Oaks 78248
Blanco Park Cv 78248
Blanco Woods St 78248
Blanton Dr 78209
Blazar Way 78252
Blaze Ave 78218
Blazer Pl 78245
Blazewood 78250
Blazing Trl 78249
Blazing Star Trl 78266
Blazing Sunset St 78253
Blazing Tree 78247
Bledsoe Dr 78233
Blenheim 78209
Blenhein Rdg 78231
Blessing St 78228
Blind Ln 78245
Blind Mdw 78222
Blinn St 78249
Bliss Cyn 78260
Blockade Dr 78240
Blocker Rnch 78245
Blocker St 78237
Blocker Way 78223
Blonde Cyn 78252
Bloom Ave 78211
Bloomdale 78218
Bloomfield Dr 78228
Bloomsbury Sq 78218
Bloomwood St 78249
Blossom Bnd 78218
Blossom Cyn 78252
Blossom Dr 78217
Blossom Holw 78247
Blossom Lk 78223
Blossom Tree 78250
Blue Spgs 78260
Blue Ash Dr 78218
Blue Astor Dr 78245
Blue Bonnet Blvd 78209
Blue Bonnet St 78202
Blue Creek St 78232
Blue Crest Ln
1200-1799 78232
1900-1998 78247
Blue Flax Cv 78249
Blue Grass Ln 78239
Blue Heron St 78217
Blue Hill Rd 78229
Blue Jay Dr 78219
Blue Juniper 78253
Blue Lake Dr 78244
Blue Max 78248
Blue Mesa Dr 78245
Blue Oak Ln 78227
Blue Oak Pass 78223
Blue Quail Run 78256
Blue Quail St 78232
Blue Ribbon 78227
Blue Ridge Dr
100-199 78207

400-1799 78228
Blue River Dr 78249
Blue Rock Dr 78232
Blue Sage Trl 78256
Blue Sky Holly 78259
Blue Smoke St 78231
Blue Spruce Dr 78219
Blue Star 78204
Blue Thorn Trl 78256
Blue Topaz 78245
Blue Trinity 78259
Blue Wing Rd
2000-3299 78221
10508-14399 78223
15001-15099 78221
Bluebell Dr 78266
Bluebells Run 78245
Blueberry Hill St 78232
Bluebird Dr 78240
Bluebird Song 78253
Bluebonnet Ln 78223
Bluebonnet Bay 78218
Bluefield St 78230
Bluegrass Crk 78253
Bluegrass Run 78240
Bluegrass Pond 78254
Bluemel Rd
3601-3699 78229
4001-4197 78240
4199-4499 78240
Bluemist Pass 78247
Bluemist Pt 78250
Bluemist Bay 78258
Bluemist Mountain Rd 78255
Bluesage Cv 78249
Bluestone Crk 78254
Bluestone Rd 78249
Bluestone Bay 78250
Bluet Ln 78213
Bluetop Ln 78217
Bluewater Way 78260
Bluewood Dr 78233
Bluff Cyn 78252
Bluff Fld 78245
Bluff Frst 78248
Bluff Holw 78216
Bluff Knls 78216
Bluff Ln 78216
Bluff St 78228
Bluff Trl 78216
Bluff Xing 78244
Bluff Bend Dr 78250
Bluff Breeze 78216
Bluff Cliff Dr 78216
Bluff Garden Cir 78216
Bluff Grove Dr 78216
Bluff Haven Dr 78228
Bluff Ivey Ln 78216
Bluff Line 78266
Bluff Manor Dr 78216
Bluff Park Dr 78216
Bluff Post 78216
Bluff Springs St 78247
Bluff Top Dr 78216
Bluff Villas Ct 78216
Bluff Wind 78216
Bluffcircle 78216
Bluffcourt 78216
Bluffcove 78216
Bluffcrest 78216
Bluffestates 78216
Bluffgate 78216
Bluffhill 78216
Bluffmeadow 78216
Bluffmont 78216
Bluffoak 78216
Bluffridge St 78232
Bluffrock 78216
Bluffside Dr 78227
Bluffton Park 78231
Bluffview St 78232
Bluffwood Dr 78216
Blum St 78205
Blyford Ln 78209
Blythewood St 78249
Boardwalk St 78217

Boatman Rd 78219
Bob Billa St 78223
Bobbi Way 78245
Bobbie Allen Way 78223
Bobbies Ln 78201
Bobbins Rdg 78260
Bobby Lou Dr 78218
Bobcat Blf 78251
Bobcat Bnd 78231
Bobcat Crk 78251
Bobcat Holw 78251
Bobcat Ln 78224
Bobcat Pass 78251
Bobcat Rise 78251
Bobolink Cv 78233
Bobtail St 78250
Bobwhite Dr 78217
Bobwhite Run 78256
Boca Chica St 78224
Boca Del Mar 78258
Boca Raton Dr 78244
Bocawood Dr 78228
Bode Ct 78266
Bodie St 78214
Boehmer 78204
Boerne St 78210
Boerne Stage Rd 78255
Bogart Dr 78240
Bogey Rdg 78260
Bogle St 78207
Bogue Ave 78228
Bohill St 78217
Bois Darc St 78245
Boise Hills Dr 78250
Boland Bnd 78254
Bold Forbes 78245
Bold Ruler St 78248
Bold Venture St 78248
Boldt Rd 78222
Bolero Cir 78230
Boles Way 78207
Boling Brook St 78245
Bolmore Dr 78223
Boltmore Pass 78247
Boltmore Bay 78258
Bolton Hls 78252
Bomar Ln 78233
Bonair Dr 78222
Bonanza Dr 78227
Bonavantura 78245
Boneta Cv 78259
Bonham 78205
Bonham Path 78253
Bonita Spgs 78258
Bonito Park Dr 78249
Bonn Mountain St 78260
Bonnell Dr 78223
E & W Bonner Ave 78214
Bonnet Ln 78263
Bonnie Butler 78221
Bonnieview Ln 78223
Bonny Brg 78240
Bonny Brk 78239
Book Bldg 78205
Booker Aly 78202
Booker Basin 78245
Booker Bay 78244
Booker Palm 78239
Boonsboro Dr 78245
Boot Cyn 78245
Booth Dr 78216
Boquillas St 78233
Borchers Dr 78219
Bordano Ln 78260
Bordeaux Bay 78255
Bordelon Way 78260
Borden Oak St 78233
Border Brk 78238
Border Ln 78232
Border Knoll Dr 78240
Border Mill Dr 78230
Border Mist Dr 78240
Border Pass Dr 78240
Border Ridge Dr 78240
Border Trail Dr 78240
Bordoy St 78225

E & W Borgfeld Dr 78260
Bosal Trl 78245
Bose Cir 78250
Bosque Vis 78258
Bosque Seco 78223
Boston 78202
Boston Farm 78244
Boston Harbor Dr 78242
Bostonian 78218
Boswell 78214
Bottle Brush 7826
Bottomless Lk 78222
Botts St 78217
Boudet Pl 78203
Boughwood 78250
Boulder Ave 78220
Boulder Cyn 78260
Boulder Creek St 78247
Boulder Hill St 78250
Boulder Oaks 78247
Boulder Pass St 78247
Boulder Peak St 78247
Boulder Ridge St 78247
Bouleau 78254
Boundbrook 78254
Bounty Dr 78245
Boutry Hts 78254
Boutwell St 78230
Bouvardia 78253
Bovis Ct 78233
Bow Heights Dr 78230
Bow Willow 78254
Bowden Cross 78230
Bowdoin St 78237
Bowen Br 78254
Bowen Dr 78250
Bowens Crossing St 78250
Bowhill Gln 78233
Bowie Cir 78253
Bowie Ml 78253
Bowie St 78205
Bowline St 78242
Bowman Rdg 78249
Bowood Ct 78218
Bowsprit St 78242
Box Elder Hl 78254
Box Oak 78230
Box T Dr 78253
Boxdale St 78217
Boxelder Ln 78223
Boxer Crk 78245
Boxer Bay 78233
Boxer Palm 78213
Boxing Grv 78244
Boxing Pass 78251
Boxtree Ln 78259
Boxwood Bnd 78254
Boxwood Crk 78254
Boxwood Rd 78222
E & W Boyer Ave 78210
Braburn St 78221
Braches Park 78240
Bracken Crk & Dr 78266
Brackenridge Ave 78209
Brad 78201
Brad Fld 78245
Braddock St 78245
Braden Gate 78244
Bradford Ave 78228
Bradley St 78211
Bradley Creek Cir 78230
Bradley Oak 78223
Brady Blvd
101-397 78207
399-999 78207
1001-1299 78207
1301-1599 78237
Brady Green Comm
Health 78284
Brae Bnd, Gln, Hl, Vis &
Vly 78249
Brae Crest Dr 78249
Brae Moss 78249
Brae Park Dr 78249
Brae Ridge Dr 78249
Braeburn 78264

Braeburn Bnd 78258
Braeburn Oaks 78248
Braefield 78249
Braes Cor 78244
Braes Grv 78254
Braes Run 78254
Braes Stage 78254
Braespoint 78250
Braesview 78213
Braewick Dr 78239
Brahan Blvd 78215
Braidwood St 78249
Bramble Pass 78261
Bramblebush 78231
Brambletree St 78247
Bramblewood 78249
Branch Crst 78245
Branch Rd 78219
Branch Spg 78258
Branch Oak Way 78230
Branch Post 78245
Branch Valley St 78242
Branchfield 78254
Branching Ct 78239
Branching Bay 78259
Branching Elm 78244
Branching Oaks 78247
Branching Peak 78244
Branchwood 78248
Brandeis St 78249
Brandemere Dr 78218
Brandenburg Dr 78232
Branding Fld 78240
Branding Pass 78247
Branding Trl 78244
Branding Bay 78259
Branding Depot 78254
Branding Iron St 78247
E & W Brandon Dr 78209
Brandon Oaks 78253
Brandon Willow 78216
Brandon Yates 78217
Brandyridge 78250
Brandys Farm 78244
Brandywine Ave 78228
Brandywine Cv 78266
Brangus St 78247
Braniff Dr 78216
Brannan Blf 78258
Branson Fls 78255
Branston 78250
Brantley 78233
Branwood 78254
Braswell St 78254
Bratton Dr 78245
Braubach 78214
Braun Bnd 78250
Braun Cir 78250
Braun Crk 78254
Braun Frst 78250
Braun Knl 78254
Braun Mdw 78250
Braun Path 78254
Braun Pl 78254
Braun Pt 78254
Braun Rd 78254
Braun Run 78254
Braun Shr 78250
Braun Sq 78254
Braun Vly 78254
Braun Walk 78250
Braun Way 78250
Braun Falcon 78254
Braun Hill Dr 78254
Braun Oak 78250
Braun Pebble 78254
Braun Willow 78254
Brave Way 78256
Brave Eagle 78251
Bravo Valley St 78227
Brays Frst 78217
Brazoria Park 78254
Brazos Bnd 78245
Brazos Pt 78252
N Brazos St
501-509 78207
511-1499 78207
1501-1599 78207
1800-1998 78201
2000-2099 78201
S Brazos St
201-311 78207
313-2099 78207
2200-2429 78204
2431-2499 78204
Brazos Bay 78259
Brazos Moon 78255
Brazos Stage 78255
Brazoswood 78244
Breakers 78264
Breakers Pt 78238
Breanna Oaks 78254
Breathless View St 78260
Brecon 78239
Breeden Ave
301-497 78212
499-3099 78212
3101-4099 78212
6800-6800 78216
6802-6832 78216
6834-6898 78216
Breeds Hill Dr 78245
Brees Blvd 78209
Breesport St 78216
Breeze Holw 78250
Breeze Rdg 78260
S Breeze St 78258
Breeze Oak 78255
Breeze Valley Dr 78242
Breeze Willow 78254
Breezefield 78240
Breezewood Dr 78209
Breezy Bend Dr 78217
Bremen St 78210
Brenda Ln 78240
Brenda Elaine St 78221
Brendell St 78228
Brenhaven Ave 78210
Brenner St 78237
Brent Ter 78233
Brentcove 78254
Brenton Woods St 78249
Brentridge 78254
Brentshire 78259
Brentwood Oaks 78233
Bresnahan St 78240
Bressani Way 78233
Bret Harte St 78217
Bret Springs St 78233
Bretford Ct 78230
Bretton Rdg 78217
Brettonwood Dr 78218
Brevard 78254
Brewer Dr 78257
Brewster St 78233
Briallen 78253
Brian Clarke St 78240
Brianna Pl 78251
Briar Frst 78217
Briar Pl 78221
Briar Hollow St 78247
Briar Oak St 78216
Briar Patch 78254
Briar Rose 78254
Briarbend St 78247
Briarberry St 78247
Briarbranch St 78247
Briarbrook Way 78261
Briarcircle St 78247
Briarcliff Dr 78213
Briarcrest St 78247
Briarcroft St 78217
Briardale St 78217
Briarfern St 78247
Briarfield Dr 78230
Briargate Dr 78230
Briarglen 78218
Briargrove St 78217
Briarhaven St 78247
Briarhill 78218
Briaridge Dr 78230
Briarknoll St 78247
Briarlake St 78247
Briarlane St 78247
Briarleaf St 78247
Briarledge St 78247
Briarmall St 78247
Briarmeadow St 78217
Briarmist St 78247
Briarmont St 78247
Briarmore St 78247
Briarpath St 78249
Briarpine St 78247
Briarpoint St 78247
Briarstone St 78247
Briarton Pass & Wls 78254
Briartrail St 78247
Briarvalley St 78247
Briarvista St 78247
Briarway Dr 78217
Briarwest St 78247
Briarwick St 78217
Briarwood Dr 78209
Brice St 78220
Brick House 78222
Bricken Cir 78233
Brickwood 78250
Brideman Dr 78219
Bridge Hampton 78251
Bridge Keep 78254
Bridge Oak 78258
Bridge Path St 78233
Bridgefield 78240
Bridgenorth Ln 78218
Bridgeport Way 78244
Bridgeview 78247
Bridgewater Dr 78209
Bridgewood St 78217
Bridington 78239
Bridle Frst 78245
Bridle Path 78240
Bridle Rdg 78227
Bridle Bit 78258
Bridle View Dr 78245
Bridlewood Ln 78240
Bridlington Ct 78218
Brieley 78250
Brierbrook 78238
Brigadoon St 78254
Brigantine Crk 78259
Briggs Rnch 78245
Briggs St
2-98 78224
100-799 78211
Bright Blf 78253
Bright Crk 78240
Bright Pass 78253
Bright Run 78240
Bright Trl 78253
Bright Chase 78253
Bright Star St 78232
Bright Sun St 78217
Bright Valley Dr 78242
Brighton
101-297 78214
Brighton
299-799 78214
800-1599 78211
Brighton Oaks 78231
Brightstone 78250
Brightview St 78217
Brightwater 78254
Brightwood Pl 78209
Briley Elm 78247
Brimhall 78254
Brindley Ct 78245
Brink Ln 78221
Brisa Est 78238
Brisa Royale 78251
Briscoe Aly 78207
Briscoe Ml 78253
Briscoe Trl 78253
Briscoe Leaf 78253
Bristle Oak Dr 78249
Bristlecone St 78240
Bristlewood 78249
Bristol 78214
Bristol Grn 78209
Bristol Riv 78253
Bristol Edge 78259
Bristol Mesa 78259
Briston Park Dr 78249
Bristow Bnd 78250
Bristow Dawn 78217
Britania Ct 78238
Brite Rnch 78245
British Arms St 78251
Britt Ln 78247
Brittany 78212
Brittany Farm 78244
Brittany Oaks 78259
Britton Ave 78225
Brixton 78254
Broad Elk 78253
Broad Forest St 78250
Broad Oak Trl 78255
Broad Plain Dr 78245
Broadbent Ave 78210
Broadmeadow 78240
Broadmoor Bnd 78251
Broadripple St 78230
E & W Broadview Dr 78228
Broadway St
100-499 78205
501-597 78215
599-2699 78215
2700-2798 78209
2800-8499 78209
8500-10400 78217
10402-10598 78217
Broadwick 78239
Broadwood St 78249
Brockman St 78228
Brocks Gap St 78230
Brockthorn Dr 78249
Brockton St 78217
Brogan Dr 78232
Broken Trl 78255
Broken Bough Ln 78231
Broken Elm 78259
Broken Feather Ln 78233
Broken Lance St 78242
Broken Oak St 78232
Broken Tree St 78247
Bromley Pl 78217
Bromwich Ct 78218
Bronco Ln 78227
Bronco Way 78239
Bronco Billy 78222
Bronson Ave 78209
Bronson Crk 78251
Bronte St 78207
Bronze Sand 78253
Bronzeglo Dr 78239
Bronzerock Dr 78244
Brook Blf 78248
Brook Cir 78240
Brook Cv 78240
Brook Fls 78239
Brook Gln 78232
Brook Grn 78250
Brook Mdw 78232
Brook Run 78232
Brook Arbor 78232
Brook Garden Ln 78232
Brook Hollow Blvd 78232
Brook North Dr 78238
Brook Valley Dr 78242
Brooke Pl 78258
Brookfield 78238
Brookglade 78232
Brookhaven St 78217
Brookhill St 78228
Brookhurst Dr 78209
Brooklyn Ave
100-198 78202
200-900 78215
902-1098 78215
1100-1198 78212
1200-1299 78212
Brookport Cir 78238
Brookridge Ct 78249
Brooks St 78208
Brooks A F B 78235
Brooks Lake Dr 78223
Brooksdale Dr 78220
Brookshire Dr 78227
Brookside St 78209
Brookstone 78248
Brooktree Ct 78261
Brookvale 78238
Brookview Dr 78213
Brookway Dr 78240
Brookwood 78248
Brookwood Frst 78258
Broom St 78217
Brothers Ln 78239
Brown Aly 78202
Brown Wl 78254
Brown Oak St 78233
Browning Blf 78245
Browning Dr 78260
Brownleaf Dr 78264
Brownleaf St 78227
S Brownleaf St 78227
Brownstone St 78233
Broxton Dr 78240
Brumby Ln 78260
Bruni St 78224
Brunning Ct 78233
Brunswick Blvd
500-899 78214
900-2000 78211
2002-2098 78211
Brush Creek Dr 78248
Brushy Hl 78217
Brushy Mdw 78254
Brushy Point St 78250
Brusk St 78220
Brussels St 78219
Bryan 78204
Bryanston Ct 78218
Bryce Cyn 78258
Bryker Dr 78209
Bryn Mawr Dr 78209
Bubbling Brk 78260
Bubbling Crk 78259
E & W Buchanan Blvd 78221
Bucher Ln 78232
Buchsbaum Way 78254
Buck Crk 78255
Buck Cyn 78252
Buck Park 78245
Buck Run 78230
Buck Ridge Ln 78232
Buckboard Ln 78227
Buckeye Ave 78201
Buckhaven Dr 78230
Buckhead Ln 78266
Buckhorn Byu 78245
Buckhorn Clf 78233
Buckhorn Parke 78254
Bucking Trl 78254
Buckingham Ave 78210
Buckingham Ct 78257
Buckle Ct 78258
Buckley 78239
Buckmoor St 78217
Bucknell St 78249
Buckner 78226
Buckrail St 78232
Buckskin 78227
Buckskin Bnd 78254
Buckskin Rnch 78254
Buckskin Spur 78254
Buckskin Way 78254
Buckskin Rise 78254
Buckthorn Pass 78261
Buckwheat St 78217
Buda St 78224
Budapest 78230
Budd Dr 78224
Budding Blvd 78247
Budge St 78240
Buena 78201
Buena Lado 78209
Buena Tierra St 78232
Buena Vista St
601-797 78207
799-3499 78207
3501-3599 78207
4200-6599 78237
6600-6799 78227
Buescher Ln 78223
Buescher Path 78245
Buffalo Crk 78238
Buffalo Hls 78256
Buffalo Riv 78253
Buffalo St
101-197 78225
199-200 78225
202-798 78225
1700-1898 78211
1900-2099 78211
2101-2199 78211
2200-2299 78221
Buffalo Trl 78238
Buffalo Bayou Rd 78251
Buffalo Bur 78253
Buffalo Horn 78245
Buffalo Pass Dr 78245
Buffalo Peak 78251
Buffalo Wolf 78245
Buford 78202
Buggywhip Dr 78227
Builder Ln 78237
Bull Creek Dr 78244
Bull Run St 78230
Bullis Hl 78258
Bulverde Grn 78261
Bulverde Pkwy 78259
Bulverde Pt 78247
Bulverde Rd
11500-12100 78217
12102-12298 78217
13600-17199 78247
17201-17399 78247
17600-18198 78259
18200-22199 78259
22200-25398 78261
22201-23799 78259
25400-26200 78261
26202-26498 78261
26600-29200 78260
29202-29398 78260
Bumble Bee 78260
Bumelia Dr 78260
Bundy St 78220
Bunker Dr 78260
Bunker Hill St 78230
Bunsen St 78228
Bunting 78227
Bunyan St 78247
Bur Oak Path & Way 78223
Burbank 78204
Burbank Hl 78256
Burbank Loop 78204
Burcham Ave 78221
E Burcham Ave 78214
Burdick Dr 78227
Burgandy 78240
Burgate Farm 78228
Burgess St 78211
Burgoyne St 78233
Burgundy Pt 78217
Burke Ave 78225
Burkley Springs St 78233
Burleson 78202
Burlington Dr 78245
Burlwood 78249
Burnet Aly & St 78202
Burnham Gln 78257
Burning Crk 78217
Burning Arrow 78258
Burning Bend St 78249
Burning Glade 78247
Burning Hill St 78247
Burning Lamp 78245
Burning Log St 78247
Burning Oak St 78247
Burning Ridge St 78247
Burning Rock St 78247
Burning Sunrise Dr 78244
Burning Trail St
2400-2598 78232
2600-2800 78247
2802-2898 78247
Burning Tree Dr 78240
Burning Wood St 78247
Burnley 78239
Burns Ln, Trl, Way &
Xing 78250
Burnside Dr 78209
Burnt Rdg 78217
Burnt Arrow 78258
Burnt Oak St 78232
Burnwood 78254
Buroak Rdg 78248
Burr Rd 78209
Burr Duval Rd 78209
Burr Hill St 78247
Burr Oak Dr 78230
Burr Press Ln 78245
Burro Bnd 78244
Burrus Pl 78210
Burshard Rd 78263
Burton Ave
100-298 78221
300-400 78221
402-402 78221
403-404 78226
405-2099 78221
Burton Bay 78238
Burton Farm 78244
Burtons Oak 78254
Burwell 78254
Burwick Dr 78230
Burwood Ln
1-99 78216
100-799 78213
Busby Crk 78259
Busby Cyn 78259
Busby Dr 78209
Bushbuck Fld 78245
Bushbuck Path 78258
Bushbuck Way 78251
Bushbuck Chase 78245
Bushbuck Cross 78258
Bushick Dr 78223
Bushnell Ave 78212
Bushwack Pass 78254
Bushy Run Dr 78245
Business Park 78218
Bustillo Dr 78214
Butch Cyn 78252
Butler Bnd 78232
Butler Crk 78232
Butler Dr 78251
Butler Pass 78223
Butler Pt 78251
Butlers Brg 78232
Butte Hl 78258
Butter Fly Pass 78224
Butterfield Dr 78227
Butterfly Flt 78254
Butterfly Walk 78245
Butterfly Bay 78245
Butterfly Bush 78245
Butterfly Palm 78245
Butterfly Peak 78245
Butterfly Ridge St 78260
Butterleigh 78247
Buttermilk Ln 78255
Butternut Blvd 78245
Button Ln 78232
Button Bush 78260
Button Willow Cv 78213
Buxley 78228
Buzz Aldrin Dr 78219
Bynum Ave 78211
Bypass Pt 78247
Bypass Shls 78244
Bypass Trl 78244
Byrnes Dr 78209
Byron St 78247
Byron Nelson 78257
Bywood Dr 78264
C St 78207
Caballero Blvd 78221
Caballero Dr 78224
Caballero Spur 78221
Caballo Cyn 78244

Cabernet 78258
Cabin Rd 78258
Cabin Creek Dr 78238
Cabin Lake Dr 78244
Cabin Path St 78232
Cable Dr 78227
Cable Ranch Rd 78245
Cabot St 78213
Cache Path 78245
Cacias Rd 78222
Cactus Blf 78258
Cactus Cir 78258
Cactus Clf 78258
Cactus Crk 78251
Cactus Fall 78245
Cactus Loop 78258
Cactus Rdg 78258
Cactus St 78203
Cactus Vly 78254
Cactus Crossing Dr 78245
Cactus Flower St 78260
Cactus Gulch 78260
Cactus Meadows Dr 78250
Cactus Oak Rd 78251
Cactus Peak 78258
Cactus Rock 78232
Cactus Star 78260
Cactus Sun 78244
Cactus Thorn 78253
Cactus Wren Dr 78255
Cadara Way 78259
Cadara Woods 78259
Cadbury Dr 78247
Caddo 78211
Caddo Cavern 78254
Caddo Lake Dr 78244
Caden Dr 78214
Cadence Hl 78260
Cades Cv 78238
Cades Cove Cir 78238
Cadillac Dr 78248
Cadiz 78224
Cadley Ct 78258
Cadmus 78214
Cadwallader St 78212
Caen
9200-9298 78250
Caen
9300-9399 78250
9400-9499 78254
Cafe Hl 78260
Cafe Ter 78251
Cagnon 78245
Cagnon Rd 78252
Cahill St 78223
Cahill Oaks 78261
Cailleau Pl 78230
Cairo Dr 78229
Caitlin Ash 78253
Cakebread 78253
Cala Levane 78253
Caladium Dr 78213
Calais Dr 78224
Calais Way 78249
N Calaveras
200-1599 78207
1600-2299 78201
2301-2799 78201
S Calaveras 78207
Calcutta Ln 78260
Calderwood St 78249
Caldwell Crst 78256
Caldwell St 78223
Caldwins Ford St 78233
Caleb Cir 78258
Caledonian Ct 78230
Caleta Bch 78232
Calgary Ave 78226
Calhoun Cv 78253
Calhoun St
300-499 78208
1600-1698 78209
1701-1899 78209
Calico Cor 78245
Calico Crst 78245
Calico Gdn 78260
Calico Pass 78254
Calico Spg 78258
Calico Chase 78260
Calico Creek Dr 78247
Calistoga St 78228
Caliza Dr 78259
Callaghan Ave 78210
Callaghan Rd
100-1298 78228
1300-5799 78228
5801-6199 78228
6300-6498 78229
6500-7999 78229
8000-9299 78230
9301-9599 78230
S Callaghan Rd 78227
Callaway 78260
Calle Aleman 78252
Calle Briseno 78252
Calle Cesar 78252
Calle Cierra 78258
Calle De Cobre 78257
Calle De Luz 78226
Calle Del Sol 78226
Calle Duarte 78252
Calle El Popo 78252
Calle Estrella 78226
Calle Fincias 78252
Calle Rialto 78257
Callen Glen St 78233
Calles St 78207
Calley Cir 78266
Calm Hbr 78253
Calm Spgs 78260
Calm Lake Dr 78244
Calmar Ct 78220
Calmon Park 78249
Calmont Way 78251
Calmwater Cv 78254
Calumet Pl 78209
Calvary Stage 78255
Calypso Dawn 78252
Calzada Trl 78252
Camada St 78207
Camargo St 78210
Camaron St
100-199 78205
800-1698 78212
Camas 78247
Camberwell Dr 78254
Cambie Ct 78233
Camborne 78250
Cambray Dr 78229
Cambria 78258
Cambria Way 78251
Cambridge Dr 78218
Cambridge Oval 78209
Cambridge Wl 78261
Cambridge Bldg 78205
Cambridge Blue 78260
Camden Cv 78258
Camden Hts 78261
Camden Park 78231
Camden St 78215
Camden Vly 78261
Camden Bay 78245
Camden Oaks 78248
Camelback Dr 78209
Camellia Way 78209
Camelot Ct 78226
Camelot Ln 78264
Cameo Ave 78214
Cameron Cir 78258
Cameron Crk 78251
Cameron Ct 78249
Cameron Cv 78253
Cameron Spgs 78244
Camfield 78251
Camier Cv 78218
Camino Grv 78227
Camino Rdg 78258
Camino Vis 78245
Camino Alturas 78257
Camino Bandera 78254
Camino Carlos 78233
Camino De Fe 78228
Camino De Oro 78224
Camino Del Mar 78257
Camino Del Sol 78255
Camino Dorado Dr 78233
Camino Grande 78257
Camino Real 78238
Camino Rey 78245
Camino Rosa 78251
Camino Santa Maria
St 78228
Camino Villa 78254
Cammie Way 78238
Camomile Cv 78249
Camp St 78204
Camp Bullis Rd
4400-6499 78257
6500-6598 78256
6801-7199 78256
Camp Creek Trl 78245
Camp Real Ln 78253
Camp Site Rd 78264
Camp Verde Rio 78255
Campanario 78250
Campanile 78258
Campbellton Rd 78264
Campden Cir & Ct 78218
Campe Verde Dr 78233
Campfire Ln 78227
Camphor Way 78247
Camping Trl 78255
Campion Red 78245
Camplight Day 78245
Campo Dr 78214
Campo Seco 78223
Campobello Dr 78218
Campstool Rd 78239
Campton Farms 78250
Campus Park 78242
W Campus Rd 78247
Campwood St 78233
Camry Spgs 78251
Canaan Cross 78247
Canada Verde St 78232
Canadian 78202
Canadian Goose 78245
Canadian Parke 78254
Canal St 78210
Canary Bnd 78222
Canary Cir 78217
Canary Holw 78222
Canary Ln 78217
Canavan Ave 78221
Canaveral Dr 78217
Candida St 78232
Candle Bnd 78250
Candle Park 78249
Candle Sunrise Dr 78244
Candlearch Cir 78244
Candlebluff Dr 78244
Candlebrite Dr 78244
Candlebrook Ln 78244
Candlecane Cir 78244
Candlecreek Ct 78244
Candlecrest Ct 78244
Candlecrown Ct 78244
Candledim Cir 78244
Candlefire Cir 78244
Candleglade Dr 78244
Candleglenn 78244
Candleglo 78239
Candlehead Ln 78244
Candlehill 78244
Candleknoll Cir 78244
Candlelight Ln 78213
Candlemeadow 78244
Candlemoon Dr 78244
Candlenut 78245
Candleoak Cir 78244
Candlepass Dr 78244
Candler St 78210
Candleridge Dr 78244
Candlerock Cir 78244
Candleside Dr 78244
Candlestone Dr 78244
Candletree 78244
Candleview Ct 78244
Candlewick Ct 78244
Candlewind Ln 78244
Candlewood Ln 78217
Candy Pl 78214
Candytuft Ct 78260
Cane Dr 78233
Cane Rdg 78247
Caney Creek Dr 78245
Canfield Dr 78201
Canham Rnch 78266
Cannes Dr 78228
Cannon Dr 78228
Cannonade St 78233
Canoe Brk 78258
Canoga Park Dr 78245
Canon Perdido 78261
Canonero St 78248
Canopus Bow 78252
Cant Stop 78202
Canteen St 78227
Canteen Creek Dr 78247
Canter Spur 78254
Canter Gait 78231
Canter Horse 78254
Canterbrook 78238
Canterbury Run 78228
Canterbury Hill St 78209
Canterfield Rd 78240
Canterview 78254
Canton 78202
Canton Fld 78245
Cantrell Dr
100-1500 78221
1502-1598 78221
1600-1799 78224
Cantura Crst 78250
Canvas Back 78245
Canyon Brg 78258
Canyon Brk 78248
Canyon Dr 78209
Canyon Frst 78248
Canyon Gln 78260
Canyon Holw 78248
Canyon Lk 78223
Canyon Pkwy 78259
Canyon Row 78260
Canyon Trce 78232
Canyon Vis 78247
Canyon Vlg 78245
Canyon Bay 78253
Canyon Bluff Dr 78227
Canyon Boulder 78248
Canyon Breeze Dr 78248
Canyon Court Dr 78247
Canyon Creek Dr 78232
Canyon Cross 78232
Canyon Edge 78248
Canyon Golf Rd
23500-23698 78258
23700-23799 78258
26100-26198 78260
Canyon Hills Dr 78248
Canyon Ledge St 78232
Canyon Maple 78261
Canyon Mist 78255
Canyon Oaks Dr 78232
Canyon Parke Dr 78232
Canyon Ridge Dr 78227
Canyon Rim 78232
Canyon Rise 78258
Canyon Shadow 78232
Canyon View St 78232
Canyon Wren 78260
Canyonwood Ln 78227
Cap Mountain Dr 78255
Cap Rock Vw 78255
Cap Stone 78258
Cape Blf 78216
Cape Ann St 78242
Cape Cod 78218
Cape Coral 78259
Cape Primrose 78245
Cape Valley St 78227
Capella Crk 78260
Caper St 78232
Capeswood St 78249
Capistrano St 78233
Capital Prt 78249
Capitol Ave 78201
Capotillo St 78233
Caprese Hl & Ln 78253
Capri 78253
Caprock Crk 78254
Caprock Rnch 78245
Caprock St 78230
Capulet Stone 78251
Caracol Pt 78251
Carah Ct 78216
Caramel Way 78244
Caraselle Loop Ct 78253
Caravan Cir 78258
Caravel St 78253
Caraway Bnd 78238
Caraway Cv 78213
Caraway Hl 78245
Carbine Rd 78247
Carbon Path 78250
Cardiff Ave 78220
Cardigan Hl 78232
Cardigan Chase 78260
Cardinal Ave 78209
Cardinal Cv 78254
Cardinal Fls 78239
Cardinal Hl 78260
Cardinal Way 78253
Cardinal Sky 78245
Cardinal Song 78253
Cardita 78259
Carefree Ct 78251
Carefree Ln 78257
Carelin Dr 78233
W Cargo 78216
Caribbean 78260
Caribou Crk 78244
Caribou St 78238
Carina Cyn 78255
Carle Ave 78204
Carleton Ct 78212
Carlisle Ave 78225
Carlota Ave 78228
Carlsbad Rio 78233
Carlton Oaks 78232
Carlton Woods Dr 78254
Carmel Ave 78211
Carmel Hls 78259
Carmel Pl 78201
Carmel Chase 78258
Carmel Oaks 78253
Carmen Pl 78207
Carnaby Creek Dr 78247
Carnahan St 78209
Carnation St 78237
Carney St 78212
Carnot St 78225
Carnoustie Dr 78258
Carol Ann Dr 78223
Carol Crest St 78220
W Carolina St 78210
Carolwood Dr 78213
Carolyn St 78207
Carousel Dr 78227
Carowinds 78251
Carpenter Cir 78260
Carranza St 78225
Carriage Blvd 78249
Carriage Bnd 78249
Carriage Dr 78217
Carriage Fls 78261
Carriage Hls 78257
Carriage Ln 78249
Carriage Pass 78249
Carriage Path 78249
Carriage Run 78249
Carriage Vw 78249
Carriage Bay 78249
Carriage Bush 78261
Carriage Dove 78249
Carriage Elm 78249
Carriage Fern 78249
Carriage Mist 78249
Carriage Moss 78249
Carriage Oaks 78249
Carriage Tree 78249
Carrie Ln 78218
Carrie Louise St 78257
Carrington 78239
Carrizo Spg 78251
Carroll St 78225
Carruthers Oak 78261
Carson Cv 78253
E Carson St 78208
W Carson St 78215
Carswell Bnd 78245
Carswell St 78226
Carswell Peak 78245
Cartegena 78253
Carter 78201
Carters Blf 78239
Carthage Ct 78225
Cartwheel Ln 78227
Cartwright Trl 78253
Cary Grant Dr 78240
Carya 78222
Cas Hills Dr 78213
Casa Alto St 78233
Casa Bella 78249
Casa Bello St 78233
Casa Blanca St 78215
Casa Bonita St 78233
Casa Corona St 78233
Casa Corte St 78233
Casa Del Vista St 78232
Casa Espana St 78233
Casa Grande St 78233
Casa Linda St 78233
Casa Manana St 78233
Casa Nueva St 78233
Casa Oro St 78233
Casa Pinto St 78233
Casa Rica St 78233
Casa Rosa St 78233
Casa Verde St 78233
Casanova St 78207
Casbury 78249
Cascabel Ln 78260
Cascade Cv 78259
Cascade Gln 78232
Cascade Hls 78253
Cascade Pl 78218
Cascade Mist 78261
Cascade Oak Dr 78249
Cascade Ridge Dr 78239
Cascade Valley St 78245
Casco Bay Dr 78245
Cash St 78210
Cashew St 78232
Caspian Bnd 78254
Caspian Fls 78254
Caspian Frst 78254
Caspian Path 78254
Caspian Pt 78245
Caspian Spg 78254
Caspian Ledge 78254
Gass Ave 78204
Cassandra St 78224
Cassia Way St 78232
Cassiano 78204
Cassiano Rd 78223
Cassin Ln & Rd 78211
Cassowary Hl 78247
Castanet St 78230
Castano Ave 78209
Castano Cv 78266
Castellani 78258
Castelluccio 78253
Castile De Oro 78239
Castillo Ave 78210
Castle Brg 78218
Castle Cv 78242
Castle Gln 78218
Castle Grn 78218
Castle Knls 78218
Castle Lk 78218
E Castle Ln 78213
W Castle Ln 78213
Castle Mt 78218
Castle Path 78218
Castle Pnes 78218
Castle Run 78218
Castle Strm 78218
Castle Vw 78218
Castle Walk 78218
Castle Way 78218
Castle Arch 78254
Castle Arms 78218
Castle Bend St 78230
Castle Bow 78218
Castle Brook Dr 78218
Castle Court Dr 78218
Castle Crest St 78230
Castle Cross 78218
Castle Crown 78218
Castle Fawn 78218
Castle Gardens Dr 78213
Castle Gate 78218
Castle George St 78230
Castle Glade 78218
Castle Grove Dr 78231
Castle Guard 78218
Castle Hunt 78218
Castle Inn 78218
Castle Kent 78218
Castle Knight 78218
Castle Lance 78218
Castle Peak 78258
Castle Pond Dr 78218
Castle Prince 78218
Castle Queen 78218
Castle Rock Dr 78218
Castle Rose 78218
Castle Shield 78218
Castle Sword 78218
Castle Throne 78218
Castle Top 78218
Castle Trail Dr 78218
Castle Wood 78218
Castle Yard 78218
Castlebury Dr 78232
Castlecreek Dr 78218
Castledale Dr 78230
Castleoaks Dr 78213
Castlerae 78239
Castleridge St 78227
Castolon Dr 78245
Caston Park Dr 78249
Castroville Rd
100-499 78207
501-697 78237
699-2900 78237
2902-2998 78237
5101-5499 78227
Caswell Cir 78240
Cat Cv 78264
Cat Mtn 78251
Cat Mesa 78251
Catalan Clf 78261
Catalina Ave 78201
Catalina Bay 78242
Catalina Sunrise Dr 78244
Catalpa St 78209
Catanbo Ct 78258
Catchfly 78245
Catclaw 78260
Catfish Holw & Ln 78224
Catfish Pond 78224
Catherine St 78237
Catkin Mdw 78245
Catlin Ct 78258
Cato Blvd 78223
Caton Loop 78261
Cattail Crk 78239
Cattle Bend Ln 78245
Cattle Ranch Dr 78245
Cattleman St 78247
Cavalcade St 78248
Cavalier Ave 78225
Cave Ln 78209
Cavelier Pass 78240
Cavelier Pt 78254
Cavendish Cir 78251
Cavern Hl 78254
Cavern Trl 78245
Cavern Coral 78247
Cavern Oak 78266

Cavern Park Dr 78249
Caversham Pass Ln 78253
Cavewood St 78233
Cayenne Cyn 78245
Cayman Lndg 78255
Cayo Blvd 78224
Cayuga Dr 78228
Caywood Dr 78237
Cazador Trl 78260
Cecelia St 78207
Cecilyann 78253
Cedar Br 78266
Cedar Cv 78249
Cedar Cyn 78231
Cedar Frst 78239
Cedar Ln 78257
Cedar Mdws 78254
Cedar Ml 78231
Cedar Mtn 78249
Cedar Park 78249
Cedar Path 78249
Cedar Rdg 78232
Cedar St 78210
Cedar Trce 78232
Cedar Vlg 78245
Cedar Vw 78213
Cedar Way 78232
Cedar Berry Ln 78255
Cedar Breaks 78255
Cedar Breeze 78244
Cedar Brush 78257
Cedar Cavern 78266
Cedar Corral Dr 78245
Cedar Elm Dr 78230
Cedar Falls St 78232
Cedar Farm 78239
Cedar Fly 78253
Cedar Gap 78266
Cedar Glade Dr 78230
Cedar Glen St 78232
Cedar Grey 78249
Cedar Grove St 78247
Cedar Hill Way 78253
Cedar Knoll Dr 78255
Cedar Moss 78217
Cedar Plain Dr 78245
Cedar Run Dr 78245
Cedar Sound 78244
Cedar Springs Dr 78244
Cedar Tree Way 78247
Cedar Valley Dr 78242
Cedar Vista Dr 78255
Cedarbend Dr 78245
Cedarbrook 78238
Cedarcliff 78245
Cedarcreek Trl 78254
Cedaredge 78263
Cedarhill 78238
Cedarhurst Dr 78227
Cedarmont Dr 78245
Cedarstone Crk 78254
Cedarvale Dr 78245
Cedarwood Ct 78227
Cedro 78260
Cedron Chase 78253
Ceegee St 78217
Celebration Dr 78261
Celestial St 78219
Celestial Vw 78260
Celine Dr 78250
Cellar Crk 78253
Cellini 78258
Celosia 78245
Celtic 78240
Celtic Cor 78244
Celts Cir 78261
Cembalo Blvd 78230
Cemetary Ln 78214
Cenceney 78204
Cenew St 78230
Cenizo 78264
Cenizo Pass 78252
Cenote Dr 78254
Centennial Blvd 78211
N Center 78202
Center Rd 78223
Center Spg 78249
Center Oak Woods St 78249
Center Park Blvd 78218
Center Point Rd 78233
Centergate St 78217
Centergrove Dr 78227
Centerview 78228
Centerville Dr 78245
Centerway Dr 78233
Central Aly 78207
Central Pkwy N 78232
Central Pkwy S 78232
Central Pr 78255
Centralia Dr 78237
Centro Bonito 78245
Centro Grande 78245
Centro Hermosa 78245
Centroloma St 78245
Centrovista Dr 78245
Century Blf 78250
Century Dr 78242
Century Gln 78257
Century Rnch 78251
Century Oak Trl 78232
Ceralvo St
  201-297 78207
  299-1499 78207
  1500-2799 78237
  2801-3299 78237
Cerca Azul Dr 78259
Cerca Madera 78259
Cerca Piedra 78259
Cerca Rojo Dr 78259
Cerca Royale 78251
Ceremonial Rdg 78260
Ceremony Cv 78239
Cerezo 78250
Cerro Alto Dr 78213
Cerro Bajo 78239
Cerro Verde Dr 78224
Cerro Vista St 78233
Cervantes 78228
E Cesar E Chavez Blvd
  401-417 78204
  419-499 78204
  601-697 78206
  699-700 78206
  701-799 78205
  701-799 78206
  702-798 78206
  801-899 78205
  1000-1298 78210
  1300-1499 78210
W Cesar E Chavez Blvd
  100-498 78204
  500-3400 78207
  3402-3798 78207
  4200-5920 78237
  5922-5998 78237
Cessna Dr 78216
E & W Cevallos 78204
Cezanne 78258
Chaco Cyn 78245
Chadbourne St 78232
Chaddsford 78250
Chadwick Dr 78227
Chaffin Lgt & Way 78260
Chagford Ct 78218
Chainfire Cir 78249
Chalet Dr 78232
Chalk Hl 78253
Challedon Cir 78248
Challenger Dr 78235
Chalmers Ave
  400-699 78214
  700-1499 78211
Chamber Bluff Dr 78231
Chamber Oaks 78231
Chambers Cv 78253
Chambers Pkwy 78235
Chambers Rd 78229
Chambord 78257
Chaminade Dr 78224
Chamita St 78211
Chamomile 78245
Champion Clf, Fls, Hvn & Trl 78258
Champion Coach 78254
Champion Oak 78233
Champions Bnd 78258
Champions Ln 78257
Champions Ml 78258
Champions Run 78258
Champions Vw 78258
Champions Way 78258
Champions Hill Dr 78233
Champions Mark 78258
Champlain 78217
Chancellor St 78229
Chandler 78222
Chaney St 78235
Channcy Springs St 78233
Channel Cir & Pass 78232
Channing Ave 78210
Chant St 78248
Chantemar 78250
Chapala Way 78233
Chaparral Ln 78240
Chapel Frst 78239
Chapel St 78217
Chapel Bell St 78230
Chapel Hill Cir 78240
Chapel Oaks 78231
Chapelwood 78254
Chappel Vw 78249
Chaps Dr 78227
Chapultepec 78228
Charben Dr 78237
Charcliff Dr 78220
Chardonnet 78232
Charger Cir 78221
Charing Cross Ln 78227
Chariot Trl 78254
Charles Fld 78238
Charles Rd 78209
Charles Conrad Dr 78219
Charles Williams Pl 78220
Charleston Ln 78240
Charlie Chan Dr 78240
Charline Ln 78254
Charlisas Way 78216
Charlotte St 78225
Charlottesville St 78233
Charolais Dr 78247
Charon Crk 78252
Charreada Trl 78245
Charro Ln 78217
Charter Pt 78250
Charter Bend Dr 78231
Charter Creek Cir 78230
Charter Crest St 78230
Charter Grove St 78230
Charter Oak Dr 78229
Charter Ridge St 78230
Charter Rock St 78230
Charter Trail St 78230
Charter Valley St 78230
Charterwood 78248
Chartres 78240
Chartwell Dr 78230
Charwood St 78233
Chas Windham 78218
Chase Aly 78202
Chase Crk 78260
Chase Cyn 78252
Chase Pt 78251
Chase Hill Blvd
  15601-15697 78256
  15699-15899 78256
  15901-15999 78256
  16001-16097 78255
  16099-16199 78255
  16201-16299 78255
Chase Oak 78232
Chasethorn Dr 78249
Chateau Dr 78219
Chateau Forest Ln 78230
Chatsworth 78250
Chatsworth Way 78209
Chattanooga Dr 78240
Chattington Ct 78213
Chatwood St 78217
Chaucer Ave 78221
Chaucer Hl 78256
Chaucerwood Ct 78249
Chaumont 78257
Chauncey Dr 78216
E Chavaneaux Rd
  600-1299 78221
  1300-1398 78214
  1400-2399 78214
W Chavaneaux Rd
  100-699 78221
  701-899 78221
  1301-1997 78224
  1999-2099 78224
Chavez Cir 78233
Chead Dr 78220
Checkrein St 78240
Chedder Dr 78229
Cheever Blvd 78217
Chelmsford 78239
Chelsea Dr 78213
Chelsea Grn 78257
Chelsea Park 78251
Chelsea Way 78209
Chelsea Wood 78239
Cheltenham Ct 78218
Chenal Pt 78240
Cheney Gln 78254
Chenille St 78232
Chennault Cir 78226
Chennault Path 78235
Cheos Oak 78230
Cherokee Cv 78253
Cherokee Ln 78232
Cherokee Path 78266
Cherokee Hunt 78251
Cherry Spg 78255
N Cherry St 78202
S Cherry St
  100-198 78203
  200-816 78203
  818-898 78203
  900-2800 78210
  2802-3098 78210
Cherry Bark 78230
Cherry Blossom St 78247
Cherry Field Dr 78245
Cherry Hills Ct 78244
Cherry Laurel 78245
Cherry Oak 78230
Cherry Park Dr 78249
Cherry Ridge Dr 78213
Cherry Ridge St 78230
Cherry Way Dr 78240
Cherrybrook St 78238
Cherryleaf St 78238
Cherrywest Cir 78240
Cherrywood Ln 78233
E & W Cheryl Dr 78228
Cheryl Dianne Cir 78257
Chesapeake 78220
Chesham 78254
Cheshire Ct 78218
Cheshire Rdg 78260
Chesley Dr 78226
Chessington Dr 78254
Chesswood Dr 78228
Chester St 78209
Chester Downs 78257
Chesterbrook 78239
Chesterfield Dr 78223
Chesterhill St 78228
Chesterton Dr 78217
Chestnut 78202
Chestnut Bnd 78232
Chestnut Rdg 78230
Chestnut View Dr 78247
Chestnuthill Dr 78218
Cheswick St 78254
Chevening Ct 78231
Cheviot Hts 78254
Chevy Chase Dr 78209
Chevy Oak 78247
Chevy Park St 78209
Cheyenne Ave 78207
Cheyenne Crk 78258
Cheyenne Pass 78254
Cheyenne Star 78253
Chi Chis Cv 78221
Chianti Rdg 78255
Chianti Way 78260
Chicago Blvd 78210
Chichester Pl 78209
Chickasaw 78261
Chickering Ave 78210
Chico Aly 78225
Chihuahua Run 78245
Chihuahua St 78207
Chilliwack Dr 78250
Chilton 78251
Chilton Stage 78255
Chimayo Bnd 78258
Chimney Blf 78250
Chimney Trl 78244
Chimney House Ln 78231
Chimney Nest 78233
Chimney Oak Dr 78249
Chimney Rock Ln 78231
Chimney Springs Dr 78247
Chimney Tops 78260
Chimney Way St 78232
Chimneyhill St 78254
Chinkapin Oak 78223
Chinon 78250
Chinook 78251
Chinook Cor 78261
Chipinque 78237
Chipley Cir 78217
Chipping 78239
Chipping Gln 78257
Chippington Dr 78253
Chiselhurst 78247
Chisholm Trl 78217
Chisom Creek St 78249
Chisos Cyn 78254
Chisos Ln 78261
Chisos Basin 78245
Chisos Oak Dr 78223
Chiswick Ct 78218
Chitterne Sq 78218
Chittim Mdws 78232
Chittim Hollow Dr 78232
Chittim Oak 78232
Chittim Pass Dr 78232
Chittim Trail Dr 78232
Chittim Woods 78232
Chivalry St 78254
Chive Rd 78223
Chloe Hts 78253
Choctaw Trl 78260
Choctaw Pass St 78260
Chrished Bnd 78254
Christian Dr 78222
Christina Path 78247
Christine Dr 78223
Christus Hls 78251
Christy 78214
Chrysanthemum 78253
Chuckwagon 78247
Chula Vis 78232
Chulan Pass 78255
Chulie Dr 78216
Chulita St 78237
N & S Chupaderas St 78207
Church Oak St 78233
Churchill Estates Blvd 78248
Churing Dr 78245
Churubusco Dr 78239
Chuska Way 78256
Cibola Frst 78233
Cibolo Cv 78261
N Cibolo St 78207
S Cibolo St 78207
Cibolo Vis 78261
Cibolo Vw 78266
Cicero Dr 78218
Cielo Ct 78257
Cielo Rnch 78218
Cielo Trce 78261
Cielo Vis 78255
Cielo Way 78253
Cielo Ridge Dr 78256
Cien Dr 78214
Cierra Sur 78258
Cilantro Pl 78238
Cima Linda St 78233
Cimarron Dr 78218
Cimarron Path 78249
Cimarron Rnch 78254
Cimarron Rte 78255
Cinch Dr 78227
Cinch Run 78258
Cinchona Trl 78266
Cincinnati Ave
  100-1700 78201
  1702-1898 78201
  1900-2699 78228
Cinco De Mayo 78252
Cinco Rios 78223
Cinco Woods 78259
Cinder Rdg 78251
Cinderella St 78219
Cindy Lou Dr 78249
Cindy Sue Way 78223
Cinema Rdg 78238
Cinnabar Ct 78266
Cinnabar Cv 78222
Cinnabar Trl 78244
Cinnamon Hl 78240
Cinnamon Ln 78223
Cinnamon Rdg 78251
Cinnamon Creek Dr 78240
Cinnamon Oak 78230
Cinnamon Teal 78253
Cipresso Palco 78253
Cipriani Way 78266
Circle Cyn 78252
Circle St 78209
Circle Carl 78254
Circle Farm 78239
Circle H Dr 78216
Circle Hill Dr 78255
Circle M 78253
Circle Oak St 78232
Circle Path St 78232
Circle Tree St 78247
Ciruela St 78209
Cisco Blvd 78217
Cita Roost 78253
Citadel Plz 78209
Citation St 78248
Citibank Dr 78245
Citizens Pkwy 78229
Citlali Sun 78245
Citron Cir 78260
Citrus Rd 78226
City 78204
City Base Lndg 78235
City View Dr 78228
Civilian 78223
Claggett St 78235
Claiborne Way 78209
Clairmont 78259
Clamp Ave 78221
Clara Ln 78213
Claremont 78209
Clarence St 78212
Clarence Tinker Dr 78226
Clarendon St 78211
Claret 78254
Claret Cup 78253
Claridge 78250
Clarion Dr 78217
Clark Ave
  100-499 78203
  500-1600 78210
  1602-3298 78210
  3300-4699 78223
  4701-5599 78223
Classen Crst 78258
Classen Pass 78258
Classen Rd 78247
Classen Rnch 78266
Classen Spur 78247
Classenoaks 78266
Classic Dr 78251
Classic Oaks Ln 78255
Claude W Black 78203
Claudia Cir 78251
Claudia Grv 78260
Claudia St 78210
Clay 78204
Clay Loop 78227
Clay Oak 78258
Clay Ridge Dr 78239
Claybrook 78254
Claymore Dr 78224
Claypool Dr 78230
Clays Pt 78250
Clayton Crk 78254
Claywell Dr 78209
Clear Ct 78227
Clear Fls 78250
Clear Grv 78247
Clear Pt 78242
Clear Creek St 78232
Clear Crest Dr 78227
Clear Lake Dr 78217
Clear Ridge Dr 78239
Clear Rock Dr 78255
Clear Spring Dr 78217
Clear Springs Park 78261
Clear Valley Dr 78242
Clear Water St 78238
Clearbrook Dr 78238
Cleardrift Dr 78239
Clearfield Dr 78230
Clearstone Dr 78258
Clearview Dr 78228
Clearwater Crk, Mdw & Run 78255
Clearwood St 78233
Clegg Dr 78242
Clematis Trl 78218
Clementine Ct 78254
Clementson Dr 78260
Clemson St 78249
Cleo St 78225
Clermont Ct 78218
Cleveland Ct 78209
Cliff Ave 78214
Cliff Crk 78251
Cliff Cyn 78259
Cliff Park 78258
Cliff Path 78250
Cliff Run 78222
Cliff Vw 78259
Cliff Bank St 78250
Cliff Haven Dr 78250
Cliff Oaks St 78229
Cliff Point Dr 78250
Cliff Ridge Dr 78250
Cliff Rock Dr 78250
Cliff Stone Dr 78250
Cliff Trail Dr 78250
Cliff Valley Dr 78250
Cliff Walk Dr 78250
Cliff Way St 78250
Cliffbrier Dr 78250
Cliffdale Dr 78250
Cliffmont Dr 78250
Cliffmore Dr 78250
Clifford Ct 78210
Cliffside Dr 78231
Clifftop 78232
Cliffvale St 78250
Cliffwood Dr 78213
Clifton Dr 78227
Clifton Forge St 78230
Climbing Rose St 78230
Climbing Vine 78245
Clint Ln 78221
Clints Wls 78245
Clipper Dr 78242
Clipper Pass 78254
Clipper Prt 78239
Clipper Oak Dr 78249
Clistrai Dr 78227
Clock Ln 78207
Clontria Rd 78263
Clorinda 78253
Clornest Ave 78221
Clos Du Bois 78253
Cloud Trl 78250
Cloud Gate 78248

Cloud Top 78248
Cloudcroft Dr 78228
Clouded Crest St 78247
Cloudhaven Dr 78209
Cloudmont Dr 78239
Cloudview 78250
Cloudy Crk 78255
Cloudy Mdw 78222
Cloudy Ridge St 78247
Clovelly Wood 78233
Clover Crk 78245
Clover Dr 78228
Clover Hl 78217
Clover Rdg 78248
Cloverbend St 78238
Cloverbrook St 78245
Cloverdale 78250
Cloverfield Ln 78227
Cloverleaf Ave 78209
Cloverwood St 78249
Clovis Ct 78233
Clovis Pl 78221
Clower
  400-899 78212
Clower
  900-2499 78201
Club Dr 78201
Club Oaks St 78249
Clubhill Dr 78228
Clubhouse 78221
Clubhouse Grn 78257
Cluster Oak 78231
Clutter Ave 78214
Clyde Dent Dr 78250
Clydeville Rd 78216
Clymer 78240
Coach Rd 78216
Coachlight St 78216
Coahuila Way 78253
Coal Mine Rise 78245
Coast Plain Dr 78245
Coastal Ln & Run 78240
Cobas Trl 78256
Cobb St 78217
Cobb Valley Dr 78219
Cobble Dr 78216
Cobble Hl 78217
Cobble Way 78231
Cobble Crest St 78217
Cobble Grove Dr 78231
Cobble Way Cir 78231
Cobblestone Ct 78213
Cobham Way 78218
Coca Cola Pl 78219
Cochise Trl 78260
Cochran Cv 78253
Cockroft Dr 78251
Coconino Dr 78211
Cody 78208
Coe Dr 78251
Coffee Dr 78221
Cogburn 78249
E Coker Loop 78216
Colby Path 78261
Colby St 78237
Colchester 78254
Cold Hbr 78245
Cold Creek Ct 78245
Coldsprings Dr 78244
Coldstream St 78224
Coldwater Dr 78245
Colebrook Dr 78228
Coleman St 78208
Coleridge St 78217
Coleto Crk 78253
Coleus 78261
Colewood St 78233
Colfax Cv 78255
Colfax St 78228
Colgate Ave 78228
Colglazier Ave 78223
Colibries 78261
Colima St 78207
Colita St 78208
Colleen Dr 78228
College Blvd 78209
College Park 78249
College St 78205
College Oak 78249
Collenback Run 78251
Collin Cv 78253
Collingsworth Ave 78225
Collins Ct 78228
Colonia 78254
Colonial Sq 78240
Colonial Sun Dr 78244
Colonialtown St 78233
Colonnade Blvd 78230
Colonneh Trl 78218
Colony Crk 78240
Colony Dr 78230
Colorado Aly 78207
Colorado Bnd 78245
Colorado Cv 78253
N Colorado St
  101-197 78207
  199-1499 78207
  1501-1599 78207
  1600-1799 78201
  1801-1999 78201
S Colorado St 78207
Colorado King 78248
Colosseo Way 78253
Colquitt Dr 78231
Colt Blf 78254
Colt Dr 78227
Colt Isle 78254
Colt Riv 78261
Colt Chase 78254
Colter Rd 78247
Colton Crk 78251
Colton Dr 78209
Colton Wl 78247
Columbia Sq 78227
Columbine St 78209
Colusa Dr 78245
Colwick St 78216
Colwyn Pass 78216
Colzona Rd 78219
N Comal
  200-299 78207
N Comal
  301-1499 78207
  1600-1698 78201
  1700-1899 78212
  1901-1999 78212
S Comal 78207
Comal Cv 78264
Comal Spgs 78253
Comanche Path 78266
Comanche Trl 78245
Comanche Gap 78255
Comanche Sunrise 78244
Comet Mnr 78252
Cometa St 78207
Comfort 78228
Cominsky Park 78250
Command Post St 78233
Commerce Pkwy 78218
E Commerce St
  111-197 78205
  199-1699 78205
  1700-1998 78203
  2000-2900 78203
  2902-2998 78203
  3000-3499 78220
  3501-3699 78220
  3700-3799 78219
W Commerce St
  100-399 78205
  400-4199 78207
  4201-4297 78237
  4299-6399 78237
  6400-9600 78227
  9602-10098 78227
Commerce Bldg 78205
Commerce Plaza Bldg 78205
Commercial Ave
  301-397 78211
  399-1199 78211
  1200-4499 78221
Como St 78220
Compass Rose 78263
Compton Ave 78214
Computer Dr 78229
Comstock 78217
Conbes Dr 78216
Concan St 78251
Conception St 78225
Concerto Dr 78266
Concho Cv 78253
Concho St 78207
Concho Strm 78258
Concio St 78227
Concord Pl 78201
Concord Rdg 78228
Concord Plaza Dr 78216
Concordia Oak 78249
Condalia Ct 78258
Conde Dr 78224
Cone Hill Dr 78245
Conestoga St 78238
Coney St 78223
Congo Ln 78227
Congress Ave 78214
Congressional Blvd 78244
Connelly St 78203
Connemara Bnd, Cv &
Hl 78254
Conner 78204
Connie Mack St 78240
Conrad St 78210
Conroe Ml 78253
Console Dr 78229
Constance St 78210
Constitution St 78233
Consuelo 78228
Contadora 78258
Contessa Dr 78216
Continental 78228
Contour 78264
Contour Dr 78212
Convent St 78205
Conway Dr 78209
Cooke Way 78253
Cooks Pt 78250
Cool Frst 78239
Cool Mdw 78250
Cool Breeze 78245
Cool Creek Dr 78238
Cool Sands St 78233
Cool Valley St 78242
Coolbrook 78250
Coolspring Dr 78254
Coolway Dr 78232
Cooper Cir 78255
Cooper Ml 78255
Cooper Pass 78255
Cooper St 78210
Cooper Vly 78255
Cooper Corral Cir 78255
Cooperbend 78250
Coopers Hawk 78253
Coopwood Ave 78237
Copa Cv 78242
Copano Bay 78229
Copeland 78219
Copinsay Ave 78223
Copper Crst 78260
Copper Ash 78232
Copper Breaks 78247
Copper Cave 78249
Copper Gully 78259
Copper Hill Dr 78232
Copper Point Dr 78259
Copper Pot 78245
Copper Ridge Dr 78259
Copper Rim 78245
Copper Sunset 78232
Copper Trail Dr 78244
Copperas Ln 78260
Copperfield Rd 78251
Copperhead Ln 78222
Coral Ave 78223
Coral Cyn 78252
Coral Hbr 78251
Coral Spgs 78250
Coral Spur 78259
Coral Trl 78244
Coral Vlg 78245
Coral Bay 78251
Coral Elm Dr 78251
Coral Field Dr 78245
Coral Flounder 78244
Coral Glade 78247
Coral Grove Dr 78247
Coral Mist St 78219
Coral Sunrise 78244
Coral Tree Ln 78227
Coral Vine 78261
Coralbean Cv 78249
Coralstone Dr 78254
Coralwood St 78233
Coram Peak St 78248
Corby Ln 78218
Cordelia St 78237
Cordero 78204
Cordoba Crk 78259
Cordoba Mesa 78259
Coreopsis 78261
Corian Creek Dr 78247
Corian Glen Dr 78219
Corian Oak Dr 78219
Corian Park Dr 78249
Corian Springs Dr 78247
Corian Well Dr 78247
Coriander 78261
Coriander Bnd 78253
Corinne Dr 78218
Corita St 78209
Cork Dr 78239
Cork Cove St 78230
Cork Tree Ct 78247
Corkwood Trl 78256
Corliss 78220
Cormorant 78245
Cornelia Ave 78228
Cornell Ave 78201
Corner Pkwy 78219
Cornerway Blvd 78219
Cornflower 78258
Cornish Ave 78223
Cornplanter St 78238
Cornudo Hl & Rdg 78251
Cornwall Dr 78216
Corona Ave 78209
Corona Rdg 78244
Coronado Ave 78237
Coronado Blf 78260
Coronado Cv 78260
Coronado Rdg 78260
Coronet St 78216
Corporate Woods Dr 78259
Corpus Cv 78242
Corral Cir 78247
Corral Gables 78261
Corrilla Dr 78263
Corsicana Ml 78253
Corsini Dr 78258
Cortez Ave 78237
Cortez Cv 78255
Cortland Crk 78233
Cortland Est 78258
Cortland Rdg 78247
Cortland Oak 78254
Corto Cir 78239
Cortona Way 78260
Cortona Mist 78260
Corum Trail Dr 78244
Coryell Cv 78253
Cosgrove St 78210
Cosmic Cor 78255
Costa Leon 78245
Costa Mesa St 78228
Cotillion Dr 78213
Cotoneaster 78261
Cotswold Ln 78257
Cottage Park 78251
Cottesmore Ct 78218
Cotton Crk 78253
Cotton Holw 78251
Cotton Belt Dr 78219
Cotton Cloud 78260
Cotton Tail Ln 78255
Cottonwood Ave
  100-399 78214
  400-999 78225
Cottonwood Way 78253
Cottonwood Bay 78253
Cougar Blf 78258
Cougar Clf 78242
Cougar Crk 78230
Cougar Cv 78242
Cougar Pt 78230
Cougar Rdg 78230
Cougar Run 78258
Cougar Trl 78230
Cougar Vlg 78242
Cougar Chase 78251
Cougar Country 78251
Cougar Gap 78251
Cougar Hunt 78251
Cougar Ledge 78251
Cougar Pass Dr 78230
Cougar Paw 78242
Cougar Rock Dr 78230
Couger Cir 78221
Count Fleet 78248
Count Turf 78248
Countess Adria St 78238
Country Blf 78240
E Country Cir 78247
Country Cor 78245
Country Crk 78216
Country Crst 78216
Country Ct 78216
Country Cv 78249
Country Cyn 78252
Country Frst 78253
Country Grn 78240
Country Hl 78240
Country Hvn 78240
Country Ln 78209
Country Mdws 78253
Country Pass 78216
Country Path 78216
Country Pike 78216
Country Pkwy 78216
Country Rdg 78216
Country Trl 78216
Country Vis 78240
Country Walk 78216
Country Way 78240
Country Breeze 78240
Country Club Ln 78232
Country Cross 78240
Country Dawn 78240
Country Elm 78240
Country Field Dr 78240
Country Flower 78240
Country Glade 78216
Country Hollow St 78209
Country Horn 78240
Country Lawn 78240
Country Ledge 78216
Country Morning St 78247
Country Oaks 78216
Country Rose 78240
Country Shadow 78254
Country Side Dr 78209
Country Sound 78216
Country Springs St 78249
Country Square St 78209
Country Sun Dr 78244
Country Swan 78240
Country Vale 78216
Country View Ln 78240
Country Villa 78231
Country Village St 78209
Country Wood Dr 78216
County Cork Rd 78251
County Line Ln 78223
County Road 150 78223
County Road 281 78253
County Road 282 78253
County Road 283 78253
County Road 350 78223
County Road 374 78253
County Road 375 78253
County Road 381 S 78253
County Road 382 78253
County Road 3820 78253
County Road 3821 78253
County Road 3822 78253
County Road 3823 78253
County Road 3824 78253
County Road 3825 78253
County Road 3826 78253
County Road 3827 78253
County Road 3828 78253
County Road 3829 78253
County Road 3830 78253
County Road 3841 78253
County Road 385 78253
County Road 386 78253
County Road 387 78253
County Road 389 78253
County Sights 78245
Course View Dr 78221
Court Cir 78209
Courtenay Ln 78257
E & W Courtland Pl 78212
Courtside Cir 78216
Courtview 78214
Courtyard 78239
Cove Blf 78216
Cove Hbr 78242
Cove Vw 78258
Cove Creek Dr 78254
Cove End 78255
Cove Meadow Dr 78247
Covel Rd 78252
Covella Ct 78259
Covenant Ct 78233
Covent Gdn 78257
Coventry Ln 78209
Cover Rd 78263
Covina Ave 78218
Covington Rd 78220
Cowhide Dr 78260
Cowsert Ln 78266
Cox Ave 78223
Coxs Aly 78254
Coxwold Ct 78245
Coyanosa Fls 78258
Coyle Pl 78201
Coyol St 78237
Coyote Holw 78253
Coyote Path 78258
Coyote Xing 78245
Coyote Canyon Dr 78232
Cozumel St 78233
Cozy Trl 78249
Cozy Valley Dr 78242
Crab Orch 78240
Craddick Cv 78254
Cradlewood St 78233
Cradwari Dr 78216
E Craig Pl 78212
W Craig Pl
  100-899 78212
  900-2599 78201
  2600-2799 78228
Craigmont Ln 78213
Crainwood St 78233
Cranberry Hl 78254
Cranbrook 78233
Crane Ave 78214
Cranes Ml 78230
Crater St 78222
Crater Lake Dr 78244
Cravens Ave 78223
Crawford Rd 78223
Crazy Crk 78260
Crazy Horse Dr 78260
Creager Cyn 78254
Creath Pl 78221
Cree St 78211
Creek Bnd 78242
Creek Cor 78253
Creek Frst 78230
Creek Holw 78259
Creek Hvn 78253
Creek Knl 78253
Creek Loop 78266
Creek Mdws 78253
Creek Pt 78230
Creek Rdg 78238
Creek Riv 78259
Creek Rnch 78253
Creek Run 78238
Creek Spg 78230
Creek Spur 78253
Creek Xing 78253
Creek Ash 78253
Creek Bluff Dr 78253
Creek Bottom Ct 78245
Creek Bow 78253
Creek Briar 78230
Creek Cabin 78253
Creek Crown 78253
Creek Dawn 78230
Creek Eagle 78245
Creek Farm 78259
Creek Gate 78253
Creek Hill St 78259
Creek Mist 78230
Creek Mountain St 78259
Creek Peak 78253
Creek Pebble 78253
Creek Rock 78230
Creek Stone St 78259
Creek Trail St 78254
Creekline Dr 78251
Creekmoor Dr 78220
Creekrun Path, Trl &
Vw 78249
Creekside Bnd 78259
Creekside Dr 78232
Creekside Pass 78259
Creekview Dr 78219
Creekview Oaks 78266
Creekway St 78247
Creekwood St 78233
Creighton Ave 78211
Crenshaw St 78224
Crepe Myrtle St 78232
Crescent Blf 78257
Crescent Ct 78258
Crescent Fls 78239
Crescent Gln 78258
Crescent Hl 78253
Crescent Park 78257
Crescent Path 78258
Crescent Pl 78258
Crescent Pt 78258
Crescent Run 78258
Crescent St 78209
Crescent Trce 78258
Crescent Vw 78258
Crescent Way 78258
Crescent Chase 78253
Crescent Creek Dr 78231
Crescent Ledge 78257
Crescent Moon 78245
Crescent Oaks 78258
Crescent Peak 78245
Crescent Woods 78258
Cresham Dr 78218
Cressida 78248
Cresswell Cv 78258
Crest Ln 78219
Crest Pl 78233
Crest Trl 78232
Crest Harvest 78233
Crest Noche Dr 78261
Crest View Dr & Way 78261
Cresta Avenida 78256
Cresta Bulivar 78256
Crested Crk, Grv, Land &
Pt 78217
Crested Butte St 78247
Crested Quail 78250
Crested Rise 78217
Crested Rock Dr 78217
Crested Walk Dr 78231
Crestfield St 78227
Cresthill Rd 78220
E Crestline Dr 78201
W Crestline Dr 78228
Crestmont Dr 78217
Creston 78251

Crestpark Dr 78213
Crestridge Dr 78229
Crestview Dr
100-699 78201
700-999 78228
Crestway Dr 78239
Crestwind Dr 78239
Crestwood Ct 78249
Crestwood Hill Dr 78244
Creswell Dr 78220
N Crickett Dr 78226
Crimson Beauty 78260
Crimson Stable 78247
Crimson Star 78261
Crippen St 78233
Cripple Creek St 78209
Cristobal Dr 78266
Criswell Crk 78251
Crittendon St 78211
E Crockett St
100-398 78205
501-897 78202
899-2399 78202
W Crockett St 78205
Crockett Way 78253
Croesus Ave 78213
Croft Trace Ln 78212
Crofton Ave 78210
Cromer 78239
Cromwell Dr
1-99 78201
100-299 78228
Crone Farm 78239
Crooked Trl 78227
Crooked Arrow 78258
Crooked Brook St 78254
Crooked Creek St 78232
Crooked Hill St 78232
Crooked Hollow Dr 78232
Crooked Oaks Dr 78233
Crooked Path St 78254
Crooked Road St 78254
Crooked Sky St 78254
Crooked Stick 78260
Crooked Stream St 78254
Cropsey Ave 78226
Crosby Cv 78253
Crosby St 78208
Cross Cyn
1-61 78247
63-199 78247
14200-15098 78232
Cross Ln 78209
Cross Rdg 78263
Cross Spg 78251
Cross Country St 78247
Cross Key Dr 78245
Cross Mountain Trl 78255
Cross Pond 78249
Cross Trail Rd 78264
Cross Vine 78247
Crossbill Crk 78251
Crossbrook 78253
Crosscreek 78218
Crossette Dr 78228
Crossgate Park 78247
Crossing Oaks 78253
Crossland Rd 78264
Crosspoint 78217
Crossprairie 78258
NW Crossroads 78251
Crossroads Blvd 78201
N Crossroads Blvd 78201
Crosstimber 78258
Crossway St 78219
Crosswell 78218
Crosswind Dr 78239
Crosswinds Way 78233
Crouch Rd 78235
Crow Rd 78263
Crow Vly 78232
Crow Wing Dr 78242
Crown Blf 78216
Crown Brk 78260
Crown Holw 78251
Crown Ln 78219
Crown Mdws 78251
Crown Park 78239
Crown Rdg 78239
Crown Trce 78251
Crown Vw 78239
Crown Way 78239
Crown Xing 78251
Crown Arbor Dr 78251
Crown Gate Dr 78251
Crown Ledge 78251
Crown Silver 78254
Crownhill Blvd 78209
Crownpiece St 78240
Crownpoint Dr 78233
Crowntop St 78217
Crows Ldg 78245
Crows Nest 78233
Croy Hts 78254
Croyden Ave 78226
Cruiseship Bay 78255
Crumpet 78253
Crusade Dr 78218
Crystal
700-798 78214
Crystal
800-1499 78211
Crystal Blf 78258
Crystal Crk 78238
Crystal Cv 78259
Crystal Fld 78254
Crystal Knl 78258
Crystal Path 78259
Crystal Pln 78233
Crystal Pt 78251
Crystal Spg 78258
Crystal Bay 78259
Crystal Bow 78238
Crystal Eagle 78245
Crystal Farm 78244
Crystal Glade 78247
Crystal Moon 78238
Crystal Oak 78258
Crystal Ridge Dr 78259
Crystal Valley St 78242
Cub Cir 78238
Cub Hvn 78251
Cub Lndg 78251
Cub Path 78251
Cub Vly 78251
Cuba Ave 78221
Cuero 78260
Cueva Ln 78232
Cuff St 78224
Culberson Ave 78225
Culberson Ml 78253
Culberson Sta 78258
Culebra Rd
200-2099 78201
2100-5899 78228
5901-6197 78238
6199-7099 78238
7101-7197 78251
7199-10699 78251
10800-11799 78253
Culebra Vly 78254
Cullin Ave 78221
Cullum 78253
Cumberland Rd 78204
Cumbre Dr 78237
Cuney Way 78210
Cunningham Ave 78215
Cup Flower 78245
Cupflower Cv 78249
Cupples Rd
100-1099 78237
1100-1800 78226
1802-2198 78226
Curlew Crk 78223
Curlew Dr 78213
Currency St 78219
Curry Hts 78254
Curtis 78214
Curtis Hl 78254
Cushing 78258
Custer 78214
Custer Pass St 78232
Cutler 78214
Cutter Green Dr 78248
Cutting Crk 78244
Cuyahoga Cir 78260
Cynthia Dr 78266
Cynthia Linn St 78223
Cypress Cir 78240
Cypress Cor 78240
Cypress Cpe 78259
Cypress Crk 78239
Cypress Mdw 78247
Cypress Pass 78240
Cypress Rdg 78255
W Cypress St 78212
Cypress Trl 78256
Cypress Walk 78240
Cypress Bend St 78247
Cypress Crown 78240
Cypress Dawn 78253
Cypress Grove Dr 78227
Cypress Hollow Dr 78232
Cypress Lake Dr 78244
Cypress Mill Dr 78247
Cypress Oaks 78255
Cypress Park St 78247
Cypress Pearl 78232
Cypress Rose 78240
Cypress Vine 78218
Cypress Woods St 78249
Cypressbrook Dr 78245
Cypresscliff Dr 78245
Cypressdale Dr 78245
Cypressfield Dr 78245
Cypressfox Dr 78245
Cypressgarden Dr 78245
Cypressgreen Dr 78245
Cypresshill Dr 78245
Cypresstree Dr 78245
Cypressway Dr 78245
Cyril Dr 78218
Da Vinci 78258
Dabney Ln 78227
Dacus St 78211
Daffodil Ln 78219
Daffodil Way 78245
Dafoste Ave 78220
Dagger Flts 78244
Dagley Dr 78214
Dagmar Dr 78222
Dahlgreen Ave 78237
Dahlia Ter 78218
Daisy Run 78255
Daisy Xing 78245
Dakota Frst 78254
Dakota Pass 78251
Dakota St 78203
Dakota Vly 78254
Dakota Chief 78261
Dakota Sun 78244
Dal Cin Dr 78260
Dale Vly 78227
Dalecrest Dr 78239
Dalehurst Dr 78201
Dalencou St 78237
Dalewood Pl 78209
Dalhart Pass 78245
Dall Trl 78228
Dallari Ct 78216
Dallas St
100-199 78205
400-999 78215
Dallas Coach 78254
Dalton Aly 78202
Dalton Ct 78221
Dan Ct & Rd 78223
Dan Duryea St 78240
Dana Cir 78224
Dana Bible Dr 78240
Danbury St 78217
Dancers Image 78248
Danchenc Dr 78260
Dancing Brk 78254
Dancing Ct 78244
Dancing Bear 78260
Dancing Clouds 78245
Dancing Wolf 78245
Dancove Dr 78250
Dandelion Bnd 78245
Dandelion Ln 78213
Dane Park 78233
Danehill Dr 78253
Danforth Cv 78258
Dani Ln 78213
Daniel Rd 78220
Daniel St 78204
Daniel Boone Dr 78238
Daniel Cloud Dr 78238
Daniel Krug 78253
Danna Marie Dr 78257
Dannelly Fld 78227
Danny Clay Dr 78228
Danny Kaye Dr 78240
Danube Dr 78213
Danvers Dr 78249
Danview Cir 78260
Danville Ave 78201
Dapple Dr 78244
Dapple Gray Ct 78251
Darby Blvd
201-597 78207
599-999 78207
3100-3200 78237
3202-3298 78237
Darby Gln 78257
Dare Ln 78217
Darians Way 78221
Darien Vis 78247
Darien Wing 78247
Dark Horse Ln 78260
Dark Star St 78248
Darkwood 78250
Darlene Dr 78222
Darlington Run 78247
Darlington St 78237
Darlington Gap 78247
Darmondale 78261
Darmstad St 78247
Darson Marie Dr 78226
Dartbrook Dr 78240
Dartford Ln 78257
Dartmoor St 78227
Dartmouth St 78237
Darwin Dr 78228
Dasa Leo St 78210
Dashiell St 78203
Dashing Creek St 78247
Dashmoor Crk 78244
Dashwood 78240
Dason Ledge 78258
Datapoint Dr 78229
Datewest Cir 78240
Dauber 78248
Daughtry Dr 78238
Dauphine Dr 78218
Dave Erwin Dr 78235
Davenport Ln 78257
Daventry Ln 78257
David Dr 78239
David Edward Dr 78233
David Scott Dr 78219
Davis Ct 78209
Davis Cavern 78254
Davy Crockett Dr 78238
Davy Crockett Rd 78226
Dawes Pt 78254
Dawn Crst 78248
Dawn Trl 78254
Dawn Arrow 78258
Dawn Valley Dr 78242
Dawnhaven St 78249
Dawnridge Dr 78213
Dawntree Pl 78251
Dawnview Ln 78213
Dawnwood Dr 78250
Dawson Aly 78202
Dawson Cir 78253
Dawson St 78202
Day Crk 78251
Day Rd 78210
Day Lilly 78260
Day Star St 78248
Daylight Crk, Crst &
Rdg 78230
Daytona Dr 78227
De Chantle Rd 78201
De Chene 78254
De Enclave 78258
De Frene 78254
De Kalb St 78245
De La Vista St 78233
De Leon Dr 78250
De Luna St 78233
De Palma 78239
De Paul St 78249
De Sapin 78254
De Soto St 78225
De Valle 78251
De Vilbiss Ln 78264
De Ville St 78248
De Zavala Pl 78231
De Zavala Rd
3800-3899 78231
4000-4198 78249
4001-4097 78249
4099-4100 78249
4102-4198 78249
4200-5900 78249
5837-5837 78269
5901-6599 78249
5902-6598 78249
Deaf Smith St 78238
Dean St 78212
Dean Martin St 78240
E & W Dean Pannill
Dr 78229
Debbie Dr 78222
Debra St 78224
Decoy Cv 78249
Dede St 78224
Deely Pl 78221
Deendens Dr 78228
Deep Frst 78239
Deep Riv 78253
Deep Bay 78258
Deep Lake Dr 78244
Deep Spring St 78238
Deep Valley Dr 78242
Deepwater Bay 78251
Deepwell Dr 78254
Deepwood St 78232
Deer Blf 78240
Deer Crk 78230
Deer Crst 78248
Deer Frst 78239
Deer Holw 78230
Deer Hvn 78230
Deer Ln 78240
Deer Park 78251
Deer Pt 78253
Deer Rnch 78253
Deer Spgs 78250
Deer Vlg 78250
Deer Blind 78245
Deer Canyon Dr 78266
Deer Country 78253
Deer Creek Run 78254
Deer Cross Ln 78260
Deer Elk Crst 78258
Deer Falls Dr 78249
Deer Garden Cv 78266
Deer Grove Dr 78219
Deer Horn Dr 78238
Deer Lake Dr 78244
Deer Ledge St 78230
Deer Meadow Ln 78253
Deer Mountain St 78232
Deer Oak Run 78254
Deer Pass St 78232
Deer Path St 78232
Deer Ridge St 78232
Deer Run Dr 78264
Deer Run St 78232
Deer Top St 78217
Deer Valley Dr 78242
Deerbrook 78250
Deercliff Pass 78251
Deerfield Dr 78218
Deerfield Wood 78248
Deerhurst 78218
Deeroak 78253
Deerskin St 78238
Deertail Crk 78251
Deerview Ln 78255
Deerwood Dr 78209
Degan Way 78228
Del Lago 78221
Del Lago Ct 78245
Del Mar Cir, Cyn & Trl 78251
Del Oro Cir 78233
Del Pilar Dr 78232
Del Rio Run 78245
Del Rio St 78203
Del Sol Ln 78227
Del Valle Aly 78207
Del Webb Blvd 78253
Delachaise St 78232
Delaware St 78210
Delbert Dr 78245
Delderic 78248
Delfino St 78237
Delflor Way 78210
Delgado St
400-2099 78207
2100-2599 78228
Delight St 78224
Delivery 78247
Dell Pl 78228
Dell Oak Dr 78218
Della Strada 78253
Dellcrest Dr 78220
Dellhaven Dr 78220
Delmar St 78210
Delmont Ct 78258
Delta St 78237
Delta Grove Dr 78247
Dempsey St 78242
Demya Dr 78227
Denae Dr 78233
Denbury Gln 78257
Deneice Dr 78213
Dennler Dr 78238
Dense Star 78245
Denton Dr 78213
Denver Blvd 78210
Depla St 78207
Derby 78239
Derbyshire Ln 78251
Derringer St 78217
Desague St 78214
Descanso Pass 78218
Desert Blf 78258
Desert Cir 78244
Desert Ash 78261
Desert Flower 78258
Desert Glass 78222
Desert Gold Dr 78222
Desert Links 78258
Desert Morning St 78251
Desert Oak 78258
Desert Palm 78253
Desert Poppy 78247
Desert Sands St 78216
Desert Sun St 78238
Desert Trail St 78249
Desert View Dr 78217
Desert Willow 78227
Desilu Dr 78240
Destiny 78216
Destiny Rdg 78260
Deveron 78240
Devin Chase 78253
Devine Rd 78212
Devine St 78210
Devlin Pt 78240
Devon St 78223
Devon Wood 78257
Devonshire Dr 78209
Devoto Ave
900-998 78210
1401-1499 78223
Devout 78247
Dew 78239
E Dewey Pl 78212
W Dewey Pl 78212
Dewey Pt 78251
Dewhurst Rd 78213
Dewitt 78204
Dewitt Ave 78223
Dewitt Cv 78253
Dewitt Way 78253
Dewlap Trl 78245
Dexired Dr 78222
Dexter Dr 78226
Dezarae 78253
Dhaka Vw 78250
Diadem Ln 78219
Diamond Blf 78251
Diamond Cir 78258
Diamond Cv 78242
Diamond Fld 78245
Diamond Fls 78251
Diamond Park 78249
Diamond Pass 78239
Diamond Rdg 78248
Diamond Canyon Dr 78232
Diamond Chase 78259
Diamond Gap 78254
Diamond Hill Dr 78232
Diamond Rock 78251
Diamond Stone 78254
Diamondback Trl 78222
Diamondhead Dr 78218
Diana Fls 78260
Diane Dr 78220
Dick Gordon Dr 78219
Dickens Trl 78253
Dickey Ave 78204
Dickinson Dr 78228
E & W Dickson Ave 78214
Diego Ln 78253
Diego Garcia 78227
Dietrich Rd 78219
Digger Dr 78247
Dignowity Ave 78208
Dijon Ct 78209
Dileen St 78263
Dillons Vis 78251
Dilworth St 78203
Dime St 78249
Dimmit St 78223
Dinn Dr 78218
Dinner Crk 78245
Dion Vlg 78258
Dipper Dr 78216
Director Dr 78219
Dirschell Dr 78245
Disco 78216
Distribution 78218
Diver Pt 78253
Divide Mt 78223
Dividend 78219
Divine Breeze 78251
Division Ave
100-699 78214
700-1499 78225
Dixie Lee 78264
Dixon Plain Dr 78245
Dixon Ridge Dr 78239
Dixon Wood 78245
Dixville St 78219
Doagie 78247
Dobbs Dr 78237
Dodge St 78217
Dodic St 78221
Dodson Trl 78245
Doe Crst 78248
Doe Hvn 78248
Doe Ln 78255
Doe Park 78248
Doefield 78250
Dogleg Right 78221
Dogwood 78213
Dogwood Bnd 78254
Dogwood Path 78259
Dogwood Tree 78245
Dokes Dr 78228
Dolente Rd 78266
Dollarhide Ave 78223
Dolomite Dr 78259

Dolores Ave 78228
Dolorosa
100-398 78205
Dolorosa
400-598 78204
600-999 78207
Domal Ln 78230
Dominic Pl 78247
Dominion Dr 78257
Don January Ct 78244
Don Jose 78237
Don Mills St 78250
Donald Aaron St 78221
Donald Goodrich 78226
Donaldson Ave
100-198 78201
200-724 78201
726-798 78201
900-2099 78228
Donegal St 78254
Donella Dr 78232
Donely Pl 78247
Donerail St 78248
Donley Cv 78253
Donley Pond 78254
Donna Dr 78228
Donna Elaine 78261
Donnek 78233
Donnelly Dr 78228
Donner Lake Dr 78223
Donop Rd 78223
Donore Cir, Pl & Sq 78229
Doolittle St 78211
Doppelt Rd 78235
Dora St 78212
Dorado Pass Dr 78247
Doral Crst & Ct 78260
Dorchester Pl 78209
Dorie St 78220
Dorincha 78285
Dorothy St 78210
Dorothy Louise Dr 78229
Dorris St 78207
Dorset 78216
Dorsetshire St 78254
Dorsey St 78221
Dos Palmas 78221
Dos Verdes 78258
Doss St 78251
Dot Dr 78216
Dotted Palm 78254
Double Fork Rd 78258
Double Rock 78266
Double Tree 78264
Douglas Way St 78210
Doulton Gln 78257
Dounind St 78208
Dove Bnd 78245
Dove Crk 78245
Dove Dr 78223
Dove Mdw 78248
Dove Rnch 78254
Dove Ter 78260
Dove Vly 78242
Dove Circle St 78250
Dove Flight St 78250
Dove Hill Dr 78238
Dove Hollow Dr 78232
Dove Lake St 78244
Dove Mountain St 78209
Dove Nest St 78250
Dove Oak Ln 78254
Dove Park Ln 78253
Dove Shadow 78230
Dove Trail Dr 78244
Dove Wing Cir 78232
Dovefield 78240
Dover Rd 78209
Dover Rdg 78250
Doverbrook 78238
Doverwood 78248
Dovery Way 78249
Dovetail 78253
Dovetree Ln 78251
Dowdy St 78204
Downing Dr 78209

Downshire Dr 78216
Draco Leap 78252
Dragon Crk 78242
Dragon Ln 78252
Dragon St 78254
Dragon Fire 78242
Dragon Tooth 78242
Dragon Weed 78253
Dragway Farm 78239
Drake Ave 78204
Drake Cyn 78254
Drakewood 78247
Draybrook 78253
Drayton Hts 78254
Dream Cv 78249
Dream Valley St 78242
Dreamland Dr 78230
Dreamwood Dr 78233
Dreiss St
100-526 78203
528-598 78203
600-798 78210
800-1000 78210
1002-1098 78210
Dresden Dr 78213
Drew Ave 78220
Drew Gap 78255
E Drexel Ave 78210
W Drexel Ave 78210
Drexel Run 78247
Drifting Sky 78244
Driftwind Dr 78239
Driftwood Hl 78255
Driftwood Pass Dr 78247
Driskill St 78228
Drizzle Run 78240
Drought Way 78207
Drought Cross 78240
Drum Oak 78232
Drury Ln 78221
Dry Run 78253
Dry Canyon Trl 78233
Dry Creek Dr 78245
Dry Creek Pass 78250
Dry Creek Way 78259
Dry Eagle 78245
Dry Moss Way 78224
Dryden Dr 78213
Du Barry Dr 78219
Dubies Dr 78216
Dublin Ave 78223
Dublin Cir 78254
Dublin Ct 78254
Dublin Fld 78254
Dublin Grn 78254
Dublin Hts 78254
Dublin Ldg 78254
Dublin Pl 78254
Dublin Spg 78254
Dublin Sq 78217
Dublin Trce 78254
Dublin Briar 78254
Dublin Moor 78254
Dublin Woods 78254
Dubuque St 78249
Duchess St 78216
Duck Lk 78244
Duck Lndg 78224
Dudleston 78253
Dudley Dr 78230
Dueling Oak 78254
Duerler Cir 78255
Duet Dr 78260
Duffek Dr 78219
Duffield St 78212
Dugas Dr
8800-8998 78251
9000-9299 78251
9400-10599 78245
Duke Ave 78228
Duke Fld 78227
Duke Rd 78264
Dulce Mdw 78252
Dulce St 78228
Dulce Vis 78260
Dulce Creek Dr 78247

Dulcinea Dr 78260
Dull Knife Trl 78255
Dull Knife Way 78239
Dulles 78251
E Dullnig Ct 78223
Dullye Ave 78204
Duluth Dr 78224
Dumaine 78240
Dumas Ln 78228
Dumbarton Dr 78223
Dumont Dr 78227
Dumoulin Ave 78210
Dunaff St 78219
Dunaway St 78211
Duncan Dr 78226
Dundalk 78251
Dundee Ave 78209
Dunes 78264
Dunhill 78239
Dunhill Coach 78255
Dunmore Dr & Hl 78230
Dunn Oak Dr 78223
Dunning Ave 78210
Dunstable 78239
Dunthorte Ln 78250
Dunton St 78226
Dunwoodie Dr 78219
Dupont 78264
Duquesne Dr 78229
Durand Oak 78230
Durango Run & Way 78245
Durango Creek Dr 78247
Durango Eagle 78245
Durant St 78237
Durbin Way 78258
Durette Dr 78224
Durham Bnd, Pl &
Trce 78254
Durham Ledge 78254
Durness St 78231
Durr Rd 78214
Durwood St 78233
Dusky Thrush 78233
Dusseldorf 78230
Dusty Trl 78249
Dusty Diamond 78249
Dusty Run Ln 78254
Dutch Myrtle 78232
Duval St 78208
Duxbury Park 78257
Dwarf Palm 78218
Dwyer Ave 78204
Dwyerbrook 78253
Dyess Ft 78227
Dyewood 78249
Dylan Fern 78253
Dysart St 78220
Eads Ave 78210
Eager St 78210
Eagle Blf 78240
Eagle Cir 78247
Eagle Crk 78222
Eagle Frd 78258
Eagle Gln 78260
Eagle Hls 78249
Eagle Mdw 78248
Eagle Pass 78260
Eagle Pt 78248
Eagle Rdg 78228
Eagle Run 78233
Eagle Trce 78260
Eagle Trl 78227
Eagle Canyon Dr 78247
Eagle Claw St 78242
Eagle Cliff St 78232
Eagle Crest Blvd 78239
Eagle Cross Dr 78247
Eagle Fox 78245
Eagle Gap 78255
Eagle Grove St 78232
Eagle Hollow Dr 78248
Eagle Lake Dr 78244
Eagle Ledge 78249
Eagle Nest 78233
Eagle Park Dr 78250
Eagle Ridge Ct 78258

Eagle Springs Dr 78248
Eagle Star 78248
Eagle Tree 78245
Eagle Vail 78258
Eaglebrook St 78232
Eagleland Dr 78210
Eaglerock Dr 78227
Eagleway St 78247
Eaglewood St 78233
Earl St 78212
Earl Grey 78259
Earl Roberts 78253
Earlston Dr 78253
Early Trl 78228
Earlyway Dr 78233
Earlywood St 78233
Earthstone Dr 78258
Eastbrook Farm 78239
Easterling 78251
Eastern St 78216
Eastgate St 78219
Eastham Ln 78210
Easthill Dr 78201
Eastley Dr 78217
Easton Pass 78244
Easton St 78253
Eastover St 78220
Eastridge Dr 78227
Eastwind 78249
Eastwood Dr 78220
Easy St 78266
Easy Bend Dr 78217
Easy Oak 78258
Easy Valley St 78227
Eaton St 78209
Ebbtide Dr 78227
Ebony 78228
Echo Blf 78245
Echo Frk 78251
Echo Frst 78239
Echo Grv 78259
Echo Hl 78238
Echo Mtn 78260
Echo Spgs 78260
Echo Trl 78244
Echo Bend Cir 78250
Echo Canyon St 78249
Echo Creek Ln 78240
Echo Gap 78254
Echo Glade 78249
Echo Lake Dr 78244
Echo Plain Dr 78245
Echo Port Dr 78242
Echo Sun 78245
Echo Terrace St 78260
Echo Valley Dr 78242
Echo Vista Dr 78247
Echo Willow Dr 78250
Echo Wind St 78250
Echoing Oaks 78255
Echoway St 78247
Eckhert Rd
5500-5898 78240
5900-6200 78240
6202-6598 78240
7000-7300 78238
7302-7398 78238
7500-8399 78240
Ecksminster St 78216
Eclipse Bnd 78252
Eclipse St 78219
Ed White St 78219
Ed Wiseman Trl 78251
Eda 78202
Edalyn St 78219
Eddie Rd 78219
Eddie Wessley St 78207
Eden Ml 78253
Eden Park 78257
Eden Rose Hl 78256
Edens Crk 78233
Edenvale Dr 78224
Edgar St 78208
Edge Ave 78223
Edge Vw 78259
Edge Point Dr 78230

Edgebrook Ln 78213
Edgecreek 78254
Edgecrest Dr 78217
Edgefield Dr 78233
Edgehill Dr 78209
Edgemont St
14400-14499 78217
14600-14798 78247
Edgemoor St 78220
Edgevale Dr 78229
Edgewater 78260
E & W Edgewood Pl 78209
Edie Adams Dr 78240
Edinborough 78238
Edinburg St 78210
Edison Crst 78245
Edison Dr
800-899 78212
900-2399 78201
E & W Edmonds Ave 78214
Edna 78220
Edris Dr 78224
Edward Conrad 78253
Edwards 78204
Edwards Blf 78259
Edwards Ln 78263
Edwards Rd 78252
Edwards Edge 78256
Edwards Oaks 78259
Efron 78228
Egret Ct 78245
Eight Iron 78221
Eisenhauer Rd
2601-2897 78209
2899-3200 78209
3202-3298 78209
3300-3698 78218
3700-5199 78218
5201-5499 78218
El Bosque 78253
El Camino Ct 78254
El Capitan St 78233
El Centro St 78228
El Cerrito Cir 78232
El Chamizal 78261
El Charro St 78233
El Conejo 78264
El Domingo St 78233
El Fledo Ct 78210
El Gusto St 78233
El Jardin Rd 78237
El Largo St 78233
El Marro St 78233
El Matador St 78233
El Matorral 78258
El Medano St 78233
El Mio Dr 78216
El Mirador St 78233
El Montan Ave 78216
El Monte Blvd
100-799 78212
800-2099 78201
El Paisaje 78258
El Palacio St 78233
El Paso St
1-199 78204
300-3799 78207
3800-5499 78237
El Portal Dr 78232
E & W El Prado Dr 78212
El Presidio Dr 78233
El Rancho Way 78209
El Ray Dr 78227
El Riachuelo 78258
El Risco 78258
El Santo Way 78233
El Sendero St 78233
El Sierro 78258
El Simpatico St 78233
El Sonteo St 78233
El Suelo Bueno 78258
El Sueno St 78233
El Tejano St 78233
El Valle 78258
El Vedado St 78233
El Verde Rd 78238

Elaine Rd 78222
Elam Way 78261
Eland Dr 78213
Elbel Ln 78220
Elder Path Pl 78233
Elderberry St 78240
Elderpond 78254
Elderwood 78250
Eldon Rd 78209
Eldon Run 78247
Eldon Rock 78247
Eldorado
500-599 78204
Eldorado
600-1199 78225
Eldridge Ave 78237
Eleanor Ave 78209
Electra Dr 78218
Elegante Way 78266
Elgin Ave 78210
Elijah Stapp 78253
Elisabeth Run 78253
Elise Fls 78255
Elite St 78253
Elizabeth Ct 78240
Elizabeth Rd 78209
Elizabeth Way 78240
Elizabeth Alyn 78237
Elizabeth Ann Ct 78213
Elk Crk 78251
Elk Mtn 78245
Elk Park 78249
Elk Rdg 78249
Elk Trl 78244
Elk Vly 78249
Elk Canyon Dr 78232
Elk Cliff Pass Dr 78247
Elk Glen St 78247
Elk Hollow St 78247
Elk Lake Dr 78244
Elk Runner St 78242
Elkgrove Ct 78260
Elkhorn Dr 78218
Elkhunter Trl 78222
Elkins Dr 78226
Elkins Lk 78260
Elks Dr 78211
Elks Pass Cir & St 78232
Elkton Rd 78232
Elktree Pass 78254
Elkwater 78258
Ella St 78211
Ellana Claire St 78225
Ellerby Pt 78240
Ellerman St 78207
Ellesmere 78257
Ellington Way 78247
Elliott St 78225
Ellis Aly 78202
Ellis Park 78259
Ellis Bean 78204
N Ellison Dr 78251
S Ellison Dr 78245
Ellor Dr 78228
Ellwood St 78209
Elm Blf 78230
Elm Crst 78230
Elm Dr 78266
Elm Gln 78250
Elm Grv 78261
Elm Jct 78249
Elm St 78202
Elm Vis 78230
Elm Country Ln 78230
Elm Creek Pl 78230
Elm Forrest 78253
Elm Gate St 78230
Elm Glade 78251
Elm Hill St 78230
Elm Hollow St 78230
Elm Knoll St 78230
Elm Manor St 78230
Elm Meadow Dr 78251
Elm Park St 78247
Elm Ridge Ct 78258
Elm Ridge Rd 78230

Elm Shadow 78230
Elm Spring Ln 78231
Elm Trail Dr 78244
Elm Tree Park 78259
Elm Valley Dr 78242
Elmbank 78244
Elmbrook 78258
Elmcourt St 78209
Elmcroft 78247
N Elmendorf St
500-598 78207
600-1500 78207
1502-1598 78207
1600-3199 78201
S Elmendorf St 78207
Elmendorf Lavernia Rd 78223
Elmer Blvd 78227
Elmfield Pl 78254
Elmhurst Ave 78209
E & W Elmira St 78212
Elmo Ave 78225
Elmora St 78237
Elmscourt 78230
Elmstone Dr 78254
E & W Elmview Pl 78209
Elmwood Crst 78233
Elmwood Dr 78212
Elsie Ave 78204
E Elsmere Pl 78212
W Elsmere Pl
100-899 78212
900-1599 78201
Elson Ave 78228
Elswood Mist 78251
Elsworthy St 78248
Elusive Pass 78233
Elva Frst 78251
Elvira St 78207
Elwell Pt 78255
Ely St 78221
Elys Path 78230
Embassy Dr 78228
Embassy Row 78216
Embassy Oaks 78216
Emden Holw 78247
Emerald Crk 78230
Emerald Cv 78239
Emerald Pl 78245
Emerald Spg 78250
Emerald St 78204
Emerald Ash 78221
Emerald Bay 78260
Emerald Canyon Dr 78232
Emerald Elm 78251
Emerald Forest Dr 78259
Emerald Glade 78245
Emerald Hill Dr 78231
Emerald Mist 78230
Emerald Oaks Dr 78259
Emerald Port Dr 78242
Emerald Sky Dr 78254
Emerald Stone 78254
Emerald Sun 78245
W Emerson Ave 78226
Emil St 78219
Emilie St 78221
Emilio Guerra Dr 78214
Eminence 78248
Emmaus Trl 78252
Emmett Ave 78221
Emmett Grv 78254
Emory St 78228
Emory Oak Dr 78223
Emory Oak Woods 78249
Emporia Blvd 78209
Empresario Dr 78253
Empress Woods 78249
Encanta St 78233
Encanto Pass 78247
Encanto Rdg 78230
Encanto Creek Dr 78247
Encanto Point Dr 78244
Encanto Vista Dr 78244
Enchanted Bnd 78260
Enchanted Dr 78216
Enchanted Fall 78260

Enchanted Hl 78260
Enchanted Path 78260
Enchanted Vw 78260
Enchanted Way 78260
Enchanted Castle 78247
Enchanted Dawn 78255
Enchanted Draw 78251
Enchanted Eve 78260
Enchanted Flame St 78250
Enchanted Knight Dr 78247
Enchanted Mist 78260
Enchanted Oaks St 78233
Enchanted Rock 78260
Enchanted Springs Dr 78249
Enchanted Sun 78244
Enchanted Sunset St 78253
Enchanted Wind 78260
Enchanted Wood 78248
Enchantment 78218
Encinito St 78232
Encino Ave 78209
Encino Bnd 78259
Encino Crk 78259
Encino Crst 78259
Encino Cv 78259
Encino Frst 78259
Encino Grv 78259
Encino Holw 78259
Encino Lk 78259
Encino Loop 78259
Encino Pt 78259
Encino Riv 78259
Encino Smt 78259
Encino Spg 78259
Encino Vlg 78250
Encino Way 78259
Encino Xing 78259
Encino Alto St 78259
Encino Ash 78259
Encino Belle St 78259
Encino Blanco St 78232
Encino Bluff St 78259
Encino Bow 78259
Encino Breeze 78259
Encino Briar 78259
Encino Brook St 78259
Encino Cabin 78259
Encino Caliza 78259
Encino Cedros 78259
Encino Cliff St 78259
Encino Commons 78259
Encino Crown 78259
Encino Dawn 78259
Encino Dew 78259
Encino Gap 78259
Encino Glen St 78259
Encino Grande St 78232
Encino Knoll St 78259
Encino Ledge 78259
Encino Lookout 78259
Encino Mist 78259
Encino Moss St 78259
Encino Oaks 78259
Encino Park Rd 78240
Encino Pebble 78259
Encino Ridge St 78259
Encino Rio 78259
Encino Robles 78259
Encino Rock 78259
Encino Royale St 78259
Encino Spur St 78259
Encino Stone 78259
Encino Valley Cir & St 78259
Encino Verde St 78232
Encino Viejo St 78232
Encino Vista St 78259
Encino White St 78259
Encino Woods 78259
Encinoso 78261
Enclave Cir, Park & Run 78213
End Gate Ln 78231
Endcliff 78250
Endicott 78214
Enero Park 78230
Enfield Blf 78251
Enfield Park 78232
Enfield Grove Dr 78231
England Dr 78226
Englehart Rd 78264
Engleman 78249
Englewood Dr 78213
English Way 78207
English Saddle 78227
Enid St 78237
Enoch Walk 78220
Enrique St 78237
Ensenda Park 78261
Enterprise 78249
Entex Ln 78228
Entiempo 78261
NE Entrance Rd 78216
Epcot 78260
Epler Dr 78228
Epsilon 78249
Epson 78239
Epworth St 78228
Equinox Hl 78252
Ergill Ln 78227
Erickson Blf 78247
Ericson St 78245
Erie Ave 78215
E Erie Ave 78212
Erin Blvd 78217
Erin Paige 78253
Erline Ave 78237
Ermington 78254
Eross 78202
Errol St 78216
Errol Flynn Dr 78240
Erskine Pl
 100-299 78201
 400-499 78228
Ervin St 78208
Escada 78258
Escada Crst 78254
Escalon Ave 78221
Escondido Ln, Park & Pass 78264
Escort Dr 78233
Escuela 78237
Eskimo St 78225
Esma St 78223
Esmeralda Dr 78228
Espada Bnd 78222
Espada Clf 78222
Espada Rd 78214
Espada Ledge 78222
Espinosa St 78225
Esplanade St 78233
Esquire 78257
Essex Pl 78249
Essex St 78210
Estable St 78233
Estacado 78261
Estancia 78214
Estancia Cir 78260
Estate Dr 78220
Estate Gate Dr 78260
Estate Hill Dr 78258
Estate View Dr 78260
Esterbrook 78238
Estes Ave 78209
Estes Flts 78242
Estes Park 78250
Estin Height St 78260
Estonia Cv 78251
Estonia Gate 78251
Estonia Grey 78251
Estonian Trce 78251
Estrella St 78237
Estrella Noche 78261
Estrid Trl 78244
Estufa Cyn 78245
Eternal 78247
Ethan Allen St 78230
Eton Pl 78249
Eton Green Cir & Dr 78257
Eucalyptus St 78245
E & W Euclid Ave 78212
Eugene Sasser 78260
Eulalee Dr 78220
Eunice St 78219
Eureka Dr 78223
Eva Jane 78261
Evan Cypress 78253
Evandale St 78227
Evans Ave 78209
Evans Rd 78258
E Evans Rd
 2201-2697 78259
 2699-4999 78259
 5600-6798 78266
 6800-8699 78266
 8701-8799 78266
Evans Spgs 78258
Evans Oak Ln 78260
Evanston Ct 78260
Evanswood 78233
Evelina 78253
Evelyn Dr 78228
Even Post Pl 78238
Evening Gln 78258
Evening Dun St 78213
Evening Sun St 78238
Evening Trail Dr 78256
Eveningway Dr 78233
Evenridge Ln 78239
Eventide Dr 78209
Evercrest Ln 78239
Everest St 78209
E & W Evergreen Ct & St 78212
Evers Rd
 4800-5099 78228
 5200-6199 78238
 6201-6699 78238
 6800-6898 78240
Everstone Crk 78251
Evert St 78240
Everton 78245
Evian 78260
Ewald St 78212
Ewing Pl 78201
Ewing Halsell Dr 78229
Exbourne St 78250
Excalibur 78218
Excellence Dr 78252
Excello Path 78247
Exchange Pkwy 78238
Executive Dr 78216
Exeter Rd 78209
Exmoor St 78217
Expedition Crk 78254
Explorer St 78219
Expo Blvd 78230
F St
 100-299 78210
 400-598 78220
 600-999 78220
Fabens 78251
Faber Dr 78245
Fabiana 78253
Fabius 78248
Fabulous Dr
 600-899 78216
 900-1099 78213
Facet Oak 78232
Factory Hill St 78219
Fahrenthold Cir 78257
Fair Ave 78223
Fair Bnd 78250
Fair Cv 78249
Fair Hollow Dr 78249
E & W Fair Oaks Pl 78209
Fair Ridge Dr 78228
Fair Valley St 78227
Fairacres Way 78233
Fairbanks Ave 78210
Fairbrook St 78242
Fairburn St 78228
Faircrest Dr 78239
Faircrown 78242
Fairdale Dr 78218
Fairfax St 78203
Fairfield Bend Dr 78231
Fairfield Farms 78232
Fairford Dr 78228
Fairglen Ct 78258
Fairgreen St 78242
Fairgrounds Pkwy 78238
Fairgrove St 78227
Fairhaven St 78229
Fairhill St 78228
Fairington Dr 78244
Fairlake St 78244
Fairland St 78230
Fairlawn Dr 78223
Fairlee 78217
Fairlong Trl 78254
Fairmeade St 78242
Fairmeadows St 78211
Fairmont 78204
Fairoak Xing 78231
Fairpoint 78250
Fairshire 78242
Fairview Ave 78223
Fairview Cir 78266
Fairview Dr 78266
Fairway Brg 78258
Fairway Cir 78232
Fairway Crst 78217
Fairway Cyn 78258
Fairway Gln 78217
Fairway Spgs 78260
Fairway Vw 78260
Fairway Basin 78217
Fairway Hedge 78217
Fairway Oaks 78217
Fairway Peak 78217
Fairwaycourt 78217
Fairwayhill 78217
Fairwood St 78242
Faith Dr 78228
Faith Rnch 78245
Faithcrest 78253
Faithful Path 78252
Falcon Dr 78228
Falcon Pl 78256
Falcon Trl 78227
Falcon Vw 78257
Falcon Grove Dr 78247
Falcon Hill St 78247
Falcon Ledge 78259
Falcon Oak Dr 78249
Falcon Ridge Dr 78239
Falcon Rock 78244
Falcons Hts 78233
Falcons Nest 78233
Fall Mdw 78222
Fall Bluff Dr 78247
Fall Brook St 78232
Fall Crest Dr 78247
Fall Harvest 78254
Fall Haven Dr 78247
Fall Manor Dr 78247
Fall Mist Dr 78247
Fall Pass St 78251
Fall Place Dr 78247
Fall Ridge Dr 78247
Fall River Dr 78250
Fall Valley Dr 78247
Fall Way Dr 78247
Fallen Grv 78247
Fallen Leaf 78230
Fallen Trail Dr 78244
Fallen Tree Dr 78247
Fallen Willow 78254
Falling Brk 78258
Falling Crk 78259
Falling Quail 78250
Falling Ridge Dr 78239
Falling Star 78242
Falling Timber St 78242
Falling Water 78249
Fallow Run 78248
Fallow Ridge Dr 78248
Falls Church St 78247
Falls Creek Dr 78230
Fallworth St 78254
Familia 78211
Family Tree 78222
Fan Flower 78261
Fanatical Pl 78218
Fancy Saddle 78247
Fannin Post 78240
Fantasia St 78216
Far Niente 78258
Far West Dr 78233
Faraday 78257
Farallon Isle 78245
Farber Dl 78247
Fargo Ave 78220
Fargo Pass 78258
Farhill Ln 78228
Farinon Dr 78249
Farley Rnch 78253
Farlin Park Dr 78249
Farm Rd 78223
Farm House 78253
Farm Wood 78217
Farmsfield 78240
Farmsville Dr 78245
Farne Castle 78249
Farnsworth Dr 78253
Faros Ct 78233
Farr Dr 78242
Farragut Dr
 5800-5899 78228
 5901-5999 78228
 6000-6299 78238
Farrel Dr 78227
Farrow St 78240
Farsight Dr 78233
Farview Ln 78216
Farwell Dr 78213
Faulk Dr 78221
Faust Ave 78237
Fawn Blf 78248
Fawn Crk 78248
Fawn Crst 78248
Fawn Cv 78248
Fawn Dr 78231
Fawn Hvn 78248
Fawn Knl 78258
Fawn Lk 78244
Fawn Mdws 78240
Fawn Brook Dr 78248
Fawn Circle Dr 78248
Fawn Cloud Ln 78248
Fawn Crossing Dr 78248
Fawn Eagle 78248
Fawn Gate 78248
Fawn Glen St 78232
Fawn Mist Ln 78248
Fawn Oak 78232
Fawn Valley Dr 78242
Fawndale Ln 78239
Fawnfield Ln 78248
Fawnridge Dr 78229
Fawnview 78250
Fawnway 78260
Fawnwood St 78233
Faxon Park Dr 78249
Fay Ave 78211
Feather Crest Ln 78233
Feather Nest Ln 78233
Feather Point Dr 78233
Feather Ridge Dr 78233
Featherock 78219
Fedora Dr 78242
Feldtmann Trl 78251
Felisa St 78210
Fellowood St 78238
Felps Blvd 78221
Felton Dr 78226
Fence Xing 78244
Fenfield Ave 78211
Fenimore Ave 78209
Fennel Dr 78213
Fenwick Crst 78258
Fenwick Dr 78239
Fenwood St 78250
Ferdinand Dr 78245
Ferguson Ave 78203
Fermi Dr 78228
Fern Crk 78253
Fern Crst 78250
Fern Ct 78210
Fern Hl 78259
Fern Lk 78244
Fern Orch 78253
Fern Ridge St 78232
Fern Shadow Cv 78258
Fern Valley Dr 78242
Fernbrook 78250
Ferncircle Dr 78224
Ferncroft Dr 78227
Ferndale St 78211
Ferndale Oaks 78249
Fernglen Dr 78240
Fernleaf Ave 78211
Fernmoss St 78238
Fernview 78250
Fernwood Dr 78264
Ferrell Rd 78233
Ferrington Dr 78223
Ferris Ave 78220
Ferris Br 78254
Ferris Crk 78254
Ferrysage Dr 78244
Fess Parker Dr 78254
Fest Rd 78264
E Fest St 78204
W Fest St 78204
Fiat Dr 78218
Ficino 78258
Fickel St 78226
Fiddlers Pass 78260
Fidelia Dr 78224
Field Ct 78249
Field Crest Dr 78209
Field Wood 78251
Fieldcrest Run 78254
Fieldgate Dr 78227
Fielding Ln 78264
Fieldstone Dr 78217
Fieldstone Rd 78232
Fiesta Rnch & Trl 78245
Fiesta Grande 78256
Fig Tree Woods 78249
Figaro 78260
Figaro Cyn 78251
Fillmore Dr 78245
Filly Vly 78254
Finale Ct 78216
Finch 78204
Finch Cir 78253
Finch Knl 78253
Finesilver 78254
Finis Ave 78222
Finland Palm 78251
Finlandia Gap 78251
Finlandia Rock 78251
Finton Ave 78204
Fir St 78210
Fir Valley Dr 78242
Fire Cyn 78252
Fire Cracker 78260
Fire Ring 78245
Fire Sun 78244
Fire Water 78255
Fire Wheel 78245
Firebush 78261
Firefly St 78216
Firefox Den 78245
Firenze Pl 78253
Firestar Trl 78222
Firestone Pkwy 78244
Firethorn Trl 78256
First Colony 78240
First Park Ten Blvd 78213
First View Dr 78217
Firwick Dr 78253
Fischnar Oak 78223
Fish Spgs 78245
Fisher Field Dr 78245
Fisherman Pier 78239
Fisherman Sky 78244
Fishers Cv 78239
Fishers Path 78244
Fishers Bend St 78242
Fishers Glade 78245
Fishers Hill Dr 78240
Fishing Trl 78224
Fishing Stone 78224
Fisk St 78203
Fitch St
 400-498 78214
 500-899 78214
 900-2199 78211
Fite Aly 78207
Fitzhugh Rd 78252
Five Forks St 78245
Five Iron 78221
Five Oaks Dr 78209
Five Palms Dr 78242
Five Spot 78245
Flagle St 78237
Flagship 78247
Flagstaff Dr 78217
Flagstone Cv 78261
Flagstone Dr 78260
Flair Dr 78227
Flair Oak 78258
Flairwood St 78233
Flake Aly 78207
Flame Cir 78221
Flame Tree Cv 78213
Flamewood 78250
Flaming Arrow 78258
Flaming Creek St 78217
Flaming Forest St 78250
Flaming Oak St 78227
Flaming Star 78249
Flamingo Dr 78209
Flamingo Basin 78247
Flanagan St 78249
Flanders Ave
 401-497 78214
 499-799 78214
 800-1599 78211
Flann Aly 78207
Flato 78204
Flatten Rd 78223
Fleet Admiral 78245
Fleethill Dr 78242
Fleetwood Dr 78232
Fleming St 78211
Fleming Surf 78249
Fletcher Way 78207
Fletchers 78254
Flicker St 78217
Flight Nurse 78235
Flint Crk 78255
Flint St 78228
Flint Vw 78244
Flint Arrow 78251
Flint Hill St 78230
Flint Oak 78248
Flint Rock Dr 78238
Flint Valley St 78227
Flintbed 78232
Flintdale Loop 78253
Flintlock 78260
Flintstone Ct & St 78213
Flintwood Cir 78249
Flipper Dr 78238
Flippin Ests 78239
Floating Vw 78255
Floore Holw 78254
Flora Spgs 78253
Flora Mae Dr 78220
Floral Ridge Dr 78247
Floral Way Dr 78247
Florence Ct 78257
Florencia Ave 78228
N Flores St
 101-297 78205
 299-699 78205
 800-898 78212
 900-6499 78212
S Flores St
 100-3699 78204
 3700-6699 78214
 6700-8299 78221
 8301-8699 78221
Florianne 78253
Florida St 78210
Floss Rd 78214
Flourisant Dr 78217
Flower Blf 78240

Flower Bnd 78253
Flower Brk 78232
Flower Frst 78245
Flower Mdw 78222
Flower Pl 78210
Flower Trl 78244
Flowerdale St 78232
Flowing Crk 78261
Flowing Path 78247
Flowing Spg 78247
Flowing Mist 78258
Floyd Ave 78204
Floyd Curl Dr
7700-7700 78229
7702-8399 78229
8401-8499 78229
8517-8897 78240
8899-9299 78240
Flurrywood 78250
Flyer Vis 78261
Flying Arrow 78258
Flying Fury Dr 78254
Flyn Y 78253
Flynn Dr 78228
Fm 1283 78253
Fm 1346
5300-7799 78220
Fm 1346
7800-9599 78263
Fm 1516 S 78263
Fm 1560 N 78254
Fm 1628 78263
Fm 1863 78266
Fm 1937 78221
Fm 1957 78253
Fm 2252 78266
Fm 2537 78221
Fm 3009 78266
Fm 3499 78221
W Fm 471 N 78253
Fm 78
4900-5498 78219
5500-5699 78219
5701-6097 78244
6099-7799 78244
7801-7999 78244
Fog Cyn 78258
Foggy Meadows St 78260
Folonari 78258
Fondren St 78217
Fontaine Dr 78219
Fontana Pt 78240
Fontana Albero 78253
Fontana Colina 78253
Fontenay Park 78251
Fonthill Dr 78254
Fonthill Way 78218
Foothill Pne 78259
Foothill Rd 78210
Foothills Court St 78249
Forcke Ave 78210
Fordham Ave 78228
Forelock St 78240
Forest Bnd 78240
N Forest Bnd 78240
Forest Br 78233
Forest Brg 78233
Forest Brk 78240
Forest Cir 78240
Forest Clfs 78253
Forest Ct 78240
Forest Cv 78240
Forest Cyn 78252
Forest Dr 78264
Forest Grv 78240
Forest Holw 78233
Forest Land 78232
Forest Path 78233
Forest Rdg 78240
Forest Rnch 78233
Forest Run 78233
Forest Smt 78233
Forest Spur 78232
Forest Sq 78233
Forest Strm 78233
Forest Trl 78255
Forest Vlg 78250
Forest Walk 78231
Forest Xing 78233
Forest Arbor 78233
Forest Ash 78233
Forest Bow 78233
Forest Breeze 78233
Forest Briar 78233
Forest Cabin 78233
Forest Country St 78232
Forest Creek St 78230
N Forest Crest St 78240
Forest Crown 78233
Forest Dawn 78233
Forest Deer Ct 78233
Forest Dell St 78240
Forest Dew St 78232
Forest Dream 78233
Forest Echo 78233
Forest Edge 78233
Forest Elf 78233
Forest Farm 78233
Forest Fern 78233
Forest Flame 78239
Forest Fox St 78251
Forest Frost 78247
Forest Glade St 78247
Forest Gleam 78233
Forest Glee 78233
Forest Gnome 78233
Forest Green St 78222
Forest Haven St 78240
Forest Island St 78230
Forest Knoll St 78240
Forest Lagoon 78233
Forest Lake Dr 78264
Forest Lake St 78244
Forest Lawn St 78230
Forest Ledge St 78240
Forest Magic Ct 78233
Forest Meadow St
6800-6899 78238
6901-6997 78240
6999-7299 78240
Forest Mill St 78240
Forest Mist 78232
Forest Mont St 78240
Forest Moon 78233
Forest Moss St 78240
Forest Night 78233
Forest Nook Ct 78233
Forest Oak Dr 78217
Forest Park St 78240
Forest Pass Ct 78233
Forest Peak 78232
Forest Pebble 78232
Forest Pine St 78240
Forest Point Dr 78231
Forest Pond 78233
Forest Rain 78233
Forest Ridge Dr 78239
Forest Rim St 78240
Forest Rock Dr 78231
Forest Rose St 78240
Forest Shade 78250
Forest Shadow St 78240
Forest Shower 78233
Forest Spring St 78232
Forest Stone St 78232
Forest Timber St 78240
Forest Vale 78233
Forest View St 78240
Forest Waters Cir 78266
Forest Way St 78240
Forest Wood St 78240
Forever Amber 78260
S Fork 78255
Fork Crk 78245
N Fork Dr 78250
S Fork Ln 78263
Fork Bend Hl 78261
E & W Formosa Blvd 78221
Forrest Ave 78204
Forrest Vly 78227
Forrest Hill Dr 78209
Forrester Ln 78247
Forrestglen Dr 78209
Forsen Dr 78224
Forsythia 78261
Fort Bnd 78223
Fort Spgs 78255
Fort Allen 78227
Fort Apache 78245
Fort Bliss 78245
Fort Boggy 78253
Fort Chadborne 78245
Fort Clinton St 78233
Fort Concho 78245
Fort Davis Trl 78245
Fort Donelson Dr 78245
Fort Henry St 78245
Fort Laramie 78239
Fort Maddin St 78233
Fort Marcy 78245
Fort Mason 78245
Fort Oswego St 78247
Fort Parker Dr 78211
Fort Pena 78245
Fort Smith 78245
Fort Stanley 78245
Fort Stanwix St 78233
Fort Sumter St 78245
Fort Wyne Dr 78245
Fortaleza 78255
Fortuna Ct, Pl & St 78237
Fortune Dr 78250
Fortune Hl 78258
Forum Cir 78255
Forward Pass 78248
Foss Mdws 78244
Fossel Pass St 78260
Fossil Clf 78261
Fossil Crk 78261
Fossil Cv 78261
Fossil Cyn 78252
Fossil Frst 78261
Fossil Ln 78261
Fossil Park 78261
Fossil Path 78261
Fossil Rdg 78261
Fossil Vly 78245
Fossil Banks 78254
Fossil Fern 78261
Fossil Oak Ln 78255
Fossil Peak 78261
Fossil Rock 78261
Fossil Wood 78261
Foster Mdws 78222
N Foster Rd
100-1198 78219
1800-5699 78244
5701-5799 78244
S Foster Rd
500-2698 78220
2700-2799 78220
3100-3298 78222
3300-9699 78222
9800-10298 78223
10300-11899 78223
Foster Mill Dr 78222
Foster Trail Dr 78222
Fountain Bnd 78250
Fountain Cir 78229
Fountain Dr 78248
Fountain Hl 78244
Fountain Lk 78244
Fountain Way 78248
Fountain Bluff Dr 78248
Fountain Chase 78249
Fountain Mist 78248
Fountain View Dr 78248
Fountainhead Dr 78229
Fountainwood St 78233
Four Colonies 78249
Four Iron Ct 78260
Four Iron Way 78221
Fourmile Crk 78259
Fourwind Pass 78245
Fourwinds Dr 78239
Fowler St 78221
Fox Crst 78233
Fox Cyn 78252
Fox Frst 78253
Fox Holw 78217
Fox Hvn 78248
Fox Knl 78247
Fox Run 78233
Fox St 78223
Fox Creek St 78247
Fox Den 78247
Fox Fire Ln 78231
Fox Glen St 78247
Fox Hall Cv & Ln 78213
Fox Head St 78247
Fox Lair St 78247
Fox Meadow Dr 78251
Fox Oak St 78253
Fox Tree Ln 78248
Foxberry 78248
Foxboro St 78254
Foxcross Dr 78219
Foxford 78253
Foxglove Path 78245
Foxgrove Way 78251
Foxland Dr 78230
Foxmoor Crk 78245
Foxpark Ldg 78261
Foxton Dr 78260
Foxwood St 78238
Foxwood Chase 78254
Foylyn 78214
Fran Fran St 78207
Frances Jean Dr 78223
Francis Drake 78239
E & W Franciscan 78204
Frank St 78208
Frank Borman Dr 78219
Frank Bryant 78219
N & S Frank Luke Dr 78226
Franklin St 78209
Fratt Rd 78218
Fred Haise Dr 78219
Fred May St 78229
Fred Ross Ln 78228
Fredericksburg Rd
1-97 78201
99-4699 78201
4700-8599 78229
8600-10999 78240
E Fredericksburg Rd 78212
Fredonia St 78203
Freedom Dr 78217
Freedom Hls 78242
Freedom Rdg 78242
Freedom Way 78245
Freedom Acres 78242
Freedom Oaks 78242
Freelan Dr 78253
Freeman Dr 78228
Freemans Farm St 78233
Freesia Spg 78253
Freestone St 78222
Freiling 78213
Frelon St 78225
French Ct 78212
E French Pl 78212
W French Pl
100-1099 78212
1100-1899 78201
1901-2799 78201
2800-3299 78228
French Meadow St 78250
French Sea Dr 78219
French Willow 78253
Frenchmans Cv 78253
Frenchton St 78251
Fresno
400-699 78212
Fresno
701-899 78212
900-2399 78201
Friar Tuck Rd 78209
Fridell St 78237
Friesenhahn Ct 78247
Friesenhahn St 78263
Fringe Breeze 78261
Fringetree Woods St 78249
Fringewood 78254
Frio Crk 78245
Frio Run 78245
N Frio St 78207
S Frio St 78207
Frio City Rd
101-1099 78207
1301-1997 78226
1999-2399 78226
2401-2499 78226
Frio Eagle 78245
Frio Valley Dr 78242
Fritas Trl 78252
Frogs Leap 78253
Fromage 78250
Fronda Walk 78207
Front Royal St 78247
Frontier Cv 78239
Frontier Dr 78227
Frontier Pass 78255
Frontier Trl 78251
Frontier Eagle 78245
Frontier Sun 78244
Frost 78201
Frost Trl 78250
Frost Bank Tower 78205
Frost Fire 78245
Frost Plain Dr 78245
Frostwood Dr 78220
Fruitwood St 78238
Fuchsia Vw 78245
Fuego Del Sol 78260
Fuente Aly 78210
Fuller Ln 78237
Fulton Ave
400-799 78212
801-899 78212
900-1699 78201
Fulwood Trl 78239
Funny Cide 78245
Funston Pl 78209
Furman St 78249
Furnish Ave 78204
Furr Dr 78201
Future Dr 78213
G St
100-300 78210
302-398 78210
400-498 78220
500-799 78220
Gable Pt 78251
Gable Oaks 78253
Gable Village Dr 78231
Gablewood 78249
Gabor Dr 78240
Gabriel 78202
Gabrielle Way 78237
Gabriels Pl 78217
Gaddis Blvd 78224
Gaelic 78240
Gage St 78227
Gage Xing 78253
Gaiety Ln 78219
Gailer Dr 78230
Gaines Mill St 78245
Gainesborough Dr 78230
Galacino St 78247
Galahad Dr 78218
Galaway Bay 78240
Galaxy Brk 78252
Galaxy Dr 78227
Galesburg 78250
Galespoint 78250
Galewind Dr 78239
Galewood Ave 78247
Galilee Walk 78220
Galileo Line 78252
Galit Cv 78230
Gallant Frst 78249
Gallant Bloom 78245
Gallant Fox St 78248
Gallant Ridge Dr 78239
Gallatin Dr 78245
Gallaudet Pl 78250
Galleria Dr 78257
Galleria Fair 78232
Gallery Cir 78258
Gallery Ct 78209
Gallery Rdg 78250
Gallery Wls 78261
Gallery Cliff Dr 78249
Gallery Oak St 78227
Gallery Sun Dr 78244
Gallery View St 78249
Galliard 78260
Gallop Dr 78227
Gallop Fls 78254
Gallop Chase 78254
Gallop Leap 78254
Gallorette 78245
Galm Rd 78254
Galo Cyn 78260
Galveston Trl 78253
Galway St 78223
Gambier Dr 78250
Gamble Oak Dr 78223
Ganahl Ct 78216
Gante Walk 78207
Ganton Ln 78260
Gantry Ct 78251
Garcia St 78203
Garden Brk 78245
Garden Ct 78239
Garden Fls 78245
Garden Grv 78250
Garden Hl 78260
Garden Path 78254
Garden Sq 78209
Garden Trce 78260
Garden Way 78260
Garden Arbor 78266
Garden Crest St 78217
Garden Dusk 78245
Garden Gate 78213
Garden Meadow St 78232
Garden North Dr 78266
Garden Oaks Dr 78266
Garden Oaks St 78232
Garden Quarter St 78217
Garden Ridge Dr 78266
Garden Valley St 78227
Gardendale St
4101-4197 78229
4199-4299 78229
4300-4398 78240
4401-4621 78240
Gardenia Pass 78253
Gardenia Bend Dr 78266
S Gardenview 78213
Gardenwood St 78233
Gardina 78201
Gardner Rd 78263
Garfield Aly 78210
Garland St 78225
Garner St 78237
Garnet Pt 78254
Garnet Caverns 78222
Garnett Ave 78221
Garrapata Ln 78232
Garraty Cir, Ct, Hl &
Rd 78209
Garret Grv 78261
Garrett Crk 78254
Garrison Ct 78244
Garston 78253
Garwood Chase 78247
Gary Cooper St 78240
Gary Player St 78240
Garys Park 78247
Gaskin Dr 78212
Gaslamp Ln 78250
Gass Rd 78253
W Gate Rd 78235
Gatecrest 78217
Gateshead 78251
Gateview Dr 78248
Gateway Blvd 78233
Gateway Dr 78210
Gatewood Ct 78209
Gathering Oak
20400-20699 78258
Gathering Oak
20700-21198 78260
21200-21599 78260
Gato Del Sol 78245
Gaucho Ct 78254
Gault Ln 78209
Gavilan Dr 78242
Gavlan Blf 78258
Gavlick Farm 78244
Gawain Dr 78218
Gayle Ave 78223
Gaylord Dr 78224
Gaytan Dr 78254
Gaywood St 78217
Gazania Fld & Hl 78260
Gazel Dr 78213
Gazelle Clf 78245
Gazelle Ct 78259
Gazelle Fld 78258
Gazelle Frd 78251
Gazelle Frst 78251
Gazelle Lk 78245
Gazelle Hunt 78245
Gazelle Leap 78258
Gazelle Range 78259
Geddington 78249
Gelding Hts 78245
Gem Ln 78204
Gem Oak 78232
Gembler Rd 78219
Gemini Dr 78217
Gemsbok Gate 78253
Gemsbuck Ct 78258
Gemsbuck Hl 78259
Gemsbuck Isle 78258
Gemsbuck Ldg 78245
Gemsbuck Chase 78251
Gemsbuck Rise 78258
Gemstone 78232
Gena Rd 78227
Gendarth 78253
Gene Cernan Dr 78219
General Bragg St 78245
General Ent Ct 78226
General Hudnell Dr 78226
General Krueger Blvd 78213
N General Mcmullen Dr
100-499 78237
500-800 78228
802-1398 78228
S General Mcmullen Dr
200-1799 78237
1800-2599 78226
2601-3599 78226
General Store St 78238
Geneseo Rd 78209
Genesis Trl 78252
Genesse Crk 78254
Geneva Frd & Pt 78254
Geneva Moon 78254
Geneva Sound 78254
Geneva Vale 78254
Genevieve Dr 78214
Genova 78237
Gentle Knl 78258
Gentle Pt 78254
Gentle Bend Dr 78250
Gentle Current 78251
Gentle Grove Dr 78251
Gentle Valley Dr 78242
Gentleman Rd 78201
Gentleoak Cv 78258
Gentry Crk 78254
Gentry St 78207
George Rd
12701-12897 78230
12899-13599 78230
13700-14100 78231
14102-14298 78231
George Burns St 78240
George Butler 78253
George Cooper 78247
George Kyle St 78240
George Obrien 78260
Georges Farm 78244
Georgetown Dr 78233
Georgian Oaks St 78230
E Gerald Ave 78214

W Gerald Ave
101-297 78221
299-799 78221
1100-3399 78211
Gerald Ohara 78221
Geraldine St 78224
Geranium 78253
Geranium Path 78218
Germania 78228
Germantown St 78233
Gernander St 78224
Geronimo Dr, Loop & Path 78254
Geronimo Oaks St 78254
Geronimo View St 78254
Gettysburg Rd 78228
N Gevers St 78202
S Gevers St
101-497 78203
499-899 78203
900-3699 78210
4300-4999 78223
Geyser Peak 78253
Ghent Dr 78217
Ghost Dancers 78245
Ghost Hawk St 78242
Gibbens St 78224
Gibbs 78202
Gibbs Sprawl Rd
4700-5199 78219
7101-7799 78239
Gibson 78202
Gideon Rock 78254
Gifford St 78211
Gilbert Ln 78213
Gilder 78233
Gill Brg 78254
Gillcross Way 78250
Gillespie St 78212
Gillette Blvd
100-699 78221
700-1300 78224
1302-1598 78224
E Gillette Blvd 78221
Gillingham Dr 78235
Gillis Dr 78240
Gillmore Ave 78226
Gillum St 78227
Gilmer Ml 78253
Ginger Ln 78209
Ginger Hazel 78253
Ginger Rise 78253
Gingerwood 78231
Gino Park 78247
Girard Oaks 78258
Girasole 78258
Girth Ln 78254
Giselle Ln 78232
Givenchy Hl 78256
Givens Ave 78204
Glacier Lk 78222
Glacier Ln 78209
Glacier Bay St 78242
Glacier Sun Dr 78244
Glad Dr 78223
Glade Xing 78258
Glade Valley St 78242
Gladeview 78250
Gladiator Ln 78260
Gladiola Ln 78213
Gladiolus Way 78253
Gladstone
100-499 78214
Gladstone
500-1599 78225
Gladys Ave 78225
Glamis Ave 78223
Glandore 78260
Glasgow Dr 78223
Glass Ave 78204
Glass Cyn 78260
Glasscock Trl 78253
Glaze St 78249
Gleason Dr 78240
Glen Blf 78239
Glen Brk 78239

Glen Clfs 78239
Glen Crk 78239
Glen Ct 78239
Glen Cv 78266
Glen Cyn 78258
Glen Fls 78239
Glen Grv 78239
Glen Hl 78239
Glen Hts 78239
Glen Hvn 78239
Glen Lk 78239
Glen Mdws 78239
Glen Mnr 78239
Glen Park 78239
Glen Pass 78239
Glen Pt 78239
Glen Ter 78239
Glen Trl 78239
Glen Vis 78239
Glen Vly 78242
Glen Walk 78239
Glen Arbor 78239
Glen Bay 78239
Glen Boro 78239
Glen Breeze 78239
Glen Briar 78239
Glen Castle 78239
Glen Chase 78239
Glen Croft 78239
Glen Cross 78239
Glen Echo 78239
Glen Ellen Bay 78244
Glen Fair 78239
Glen Fox 78239
Glen Gate 78239
Glen Hart 78239
Glen Heather 78240
Glen Hurst 78239
Glen Ivy Dr 78213
Glen Lark 78239
Glen Ledge 78239
Glen Loche Ct 78217
Glen Mist 78239
Glen Mont 78239
Glen Nook 78239
Glen Post 78239
Glen Ridge Dr 78229
Glen Shadow 78239
Glen Shire 78239
Glen Sides 78239
Glen Stone 78239
Glen Tree 78239
Glenarm Pl 78201
Glenbrook 78220
Glenbrook Way 78261
Glencoe Dr 78212
Glencrest Dr
200-298 78201
600-4299 78229
Glendale Ave 78237
Glendale Park 78254
Glendale Wood 78259
Glendalough Ct 78209
Glendora Ave 78218
Glenfield Dr 78227
Glengarden Dr 78224
E Glenn Ave 78204
W Glenn Ave
100-599 78204
600-999 78225
Glenney St 78249
Glenoak Dr 78220
Glenover 78217
Glenrock Dr 78240
S Glenrose Rd 78260
Glentower Dr 78213
E Glenview Dr 78201
W Glenview Dr 78228
Glenwood Ct 78210
Glerinso Rd 78264
Glidden St 78249
Glider Ave 78227
Globe Ave 78228
Globe Willow 78261
Gloria St 78224
Glorietta 78202

Gloxinia Dr 78266
Gnarled Oak Trl 78233
Goat Holw 78232
Goat Creek Run 78232
Goat Peak 78245
Godek Dr 78242
Goeth Rd 78221
Goforth Dr 78233
Gold Hl 78245
Gold Beauty 78245
Gold Canyon Dr
2001-2199 78232
2400-2498 78259
Gold Dust Dr 78245
Gold Holly Pl 78259
Gold Mesa 78259
Gold Mine St 78238
Gold Point Dr 78245
Gold Rush Crk 78245
Gold Spaniard 78253
Gold Stage Rd 78254
Gold Yarrow 78260
Goldcrest Ml 78239
Goldcrest Run 78260
Golden Ave 78211
Golden Bnd 78250
Golden Brk 78250
Golden Frst 78239
Golden Grv 78247
W Golden Ln 78249
Golden Mdws 78250
Golden Pt 78239
Golden Vw 78239
Golden Walk 78227
Golden Bear 78248
Golden Crown Dr 78223
Golden Eye 78245
Golden Gate 78239
Golden Harvest 78250
Golden Maize 78258
Golden Morn 78260
Golden Oak Trl 78233
Golden Pond 78248
Golden Quail 78240
Golden Rush 78253
Golden Spice Dr 78222
Golden Sunset 78250
Golden Trolley 78255
Golden Valley Dr 78242
Golden Wing 78260
Golden Woods St 78249
Golden Wren 78253
Goldenrain Bay 78216
Goldenrod Cir & Ln 78266
Goldfield 78218
Goldfinch Trl 78255
Goldgap Fox 78245
Goldhurst Ln 78251
Goldleaf Dr 78219
Goldsboro St 78230
Goldsmith St 78203
Goldstar Dr 78218
Goldstone Dr 78254
Goldstrike Dr 78254
Golf Bnd 78244
Golf Brg 78258
Golf Cyn 78258
Golf Hts 78244
Golf Way 78244
Golf Ball 78244
Golf Mist 78244
Golf Tee 78244
Golf View Dr 78223
Golf Vista Blvd 78244
Golfcrest Dr 78239
Goliad Rd 78223
Goll St 78266
Golondrina Ave 78204
Gomer Pyle 78240
Goodell Dr 78220
Goodhue Ave 78218
Goodloe Aly 78202
Goodnight Loving 78255
Goodrich
100-399 78207

Goodrich
400-799 78201
801-899 78201
Goodwick Hts 78254
Goodwin Ave 78204
Goodyear Dr 78228
Goolsby Way 78207
Goose Way 78224
Gooseberry 78260
Goosecreek St 78211
Gopher Hl 78263
Gordon Rd 78216
Gordon Cooper Dr 78219
Gordons Hvn & Knl 78253
Gordons Gin 78253
Gordons Mott 78253
Gorham Dr 78226
Gorman 78202
Goshen Grv 78247
Goshen Pass St 78230
Gould St 78207
Government St 78203
Goya 78239
Grabo Dr 78216
Grace Park 78255
Grace Pt 78250
Graceful Oak 78254
Gracie St 78211
Gracies Sky 78260
Graebner Ct 78225
Graf Rd
8600-8698 78223
9100-9199 78214
Graham Walk 78247
Grail Quest 78258
Gramercy Crst 78254
E Gramercy Pl 78212
W Gramercy Pl
100-800 78212
802-898 78212
900-2399 78201
2400-2699 78228
Gran Hts 78259
Gran Cima 78258
Gran Mesa 78259
Gran Palacio 78261
Gran Roble 78258
Gran Vista St 78233
Granada Dr 78216
Granada Hl 78256
Granada Way 78257
Granary St 78245
Granberry 78239
Granburg Cir & Pl 78218
Granby Ct 78217
Grand Aly 78207
Grand Bnd 78250
Grand Cir 78239
Grand Clb 78239
Grand Ct 78239
Grand Hvn 78239
Grand Mdws 78239
Grand Park 78239
Grand Pt 78239
Grand Ter 78257
Grand Xing 78257
Grand Club Dr 78239
Grand Jean 78204
Grand Lake Dr 78244
Grand Oak St 78232
Grand River St 78221
Grand Valley St 78242
Grandioso 78260
Grandstand Dr 78238
Grandstone Ln 78251
Grandview Pl 78209
Grandwood Dr 78239
Granger St 78240
Granger Patch 78247
Granite Clf 78251
Granite Path 78258
Granite Shls 78244
Granite Spg 78258
Granite Bay 78251
Granite Creek Dr 78238
Granite Hill Dr 78255

Granite Stone 78254
Grant Ave
100-299 78209
101-997 78201
999-3799 78201
3801-4099 78201
Grantham Dr 78218
Grantham Gln 78257
Grantilly St 78217
Grants Cyn 78251
Grants Lake Dr 78248
Granville Ct 78212
Granville Way 78231
Grape Blossom St 78247
Grape Creek Ln 78255
Grapeland Ave 78214
Grapeland Dr 78264
Grapevine Hl 78245
Grapevine Lk 78244
Grapevine Pass 78255
Grapevine St 78245
Grasmere Ct 78218
Grass St 78228
Grass Creek Rd 78266
Grass Fight 78253
Grass Hill Dr 78238
Grass Hollow St 78233
Grass Valley Dr 78238
Grassfield Dr 78227
Grassmarket 78259
Grassnook Ct 78251
Grassy Mdws 78258
Grassy Trl 78244
Gravel St 78203
Gravely Point St 78254
Gravetree St 78249
Gray Cyn 78258
Gray Rdg 78233
Gray St 78208
Gray Buffalo St 78242
Gray Cedar 78216
Gray Fox Crk 78245
Gray Mist St 78232
Gray Wing St 78231
Grayling Ln 78259
Grayoak Frst 78248
Grayson Cir 78232
Grayson Cv 78253
E Grayson St
100-124 78215
126-599 78215
601-697 78208
699-900 78208
902-1598 78208
W Grayson St 78212
Grayson Way 78232
Graywood 78258
Great Basin 78251
Great Blueoak 78260
Great Cedar 78249
Great Hills Dr 78238
Great Lakes Dr 78244
Great Navajo 78257
Great Oaks Dr 78232
Great Ridge St 78248
Great Spirit St 78242
Great Tree Dr 78260
Great Wood 78232
Greatfare 78218
Greatland 78218
Greatview St 78230
Grecian Dr 78223
Greco Dr 78222
Gredarad 78259
Greely St 78209
Green 78204
Green Blf 78240
Green Frst 78239
Green Knl 78258
Green Spg 78247
Green St 78225
Green Ter 78255
Green Acres Woods St 78249
Green Apple Dr 78233
Green Arbor St 78223

Green Ash 78227
Green Breeze 78247
Green Brook St 78223
Green Candle 78223
Green Circle Dr 78233
Green Coral 78223
Green Creek St 78232
Green Darner 78253
Green Falls Ct 78258
Green Gate 78264
Green Glade St 78213
Green Glen Dr 78255
Green Grass St 78223
Green Grove St 78223
Green Heights St 78223
Green Hollow St 78223
Green House St 78223
Green Hurst St 78223
Green Jameson 78253
Green Lake St 78223
Green Manor St 78223
Green Meadow Blvd 78213
Green Mesa 78245
Green Mist St 78223
Green Mountain Rd 78247
W Green Mountain Rd 78266
Green Nook St 78223
Green Oak Pl 78221
Green Oaks Woods 78249
Green Park St 78227
Green Plain Dr 78245
Green Post 78223
Green Range Dr 78231
Green River Dr 78260
Green Run Ln 78231
Green Thumb Dr 78233
Green Timber St 78223
Green Top Dr 78233
Green Trail St 78223
Green Valley Rd 78219
Green Vista St 78223
Green Willow Woods 78249
Greenacres St 78230
Greenbay Dr 78230
Greenbelt St 78251
Greenberry Dr 78227
Greenbrier Dr 78209
Greencastle St 78242
Greencrest Dr 78213
Greenham 78239
Greenhaven Dr 78201
Greenhill Pass 78213
Greenjay Dr 78217
Greenlawn Dr 78201
Greenleaf Dr 78218
Greenridge Ave 78213
Greens Clf 78216
Greens Ct 78216
Greens Pt 78250
Greens Shade 78216
Greens Shadow 78216
Greens Whisper 78216
Greensboro Dr 78229
Greenside St 78228
Greenstone 78249
Greensview Ln 78217
Greenthread Dr 78240
Greentree St 78230
W Greenway Ave 78226
Greenwich Blvd 78209
Greenwood 78214
Greenwood Oak 78254
Greenwood Village Dr 78249
Greer St 78210
Gregory Cir 78257
Gregory Ln 78264
Greig St 78226
Grenadier Way 78217
Grenet St 78207
Greta Dr 78248
Grey Bluff Cv 78258
Grey Flint Cv 78258
Grey Fox Ter 78255
Grey Hawk St 78217
Grey Horse Run 78260
Grey Knoll Dr 78230

Grey Oak Dr 78213
Grey Park Dr 78249
Grey Rock Dr 78228
Grey Wolf St 78242
Greycliff Dr 78233
Greyfriars Ln 78257
Greystone Dr 78233
Greystone Rdg 78258
Griffin Ave 78211
Griffin Oaks 78247
Griffin Park Dr 78251
Griffin Ridge Dr 78247
Griggs Ave
1-99 78237
100-599 78228
Griggs Pt 78254
N Grimes 78202
S Grimes 78203
Grimesland 78254
Grissom Br 78251
Grissom Brk 78251
Grissom Cir 78251
Grissom Crst 78251
Grissom Grv 78251
Grissom Park 78251
Grissom Pass 78251
Grissom Pl 78251
Grissom Rd
5400-7199 78238
7300-7398 78251
7400-9199 78251
9201-9255 78251
Grissom Rdg 78251
Grissom Gate 78251
Grissom Mist 78251
Grissom Oaks 78251
Grissom Post 78251
Grissom Woods 78251
Grist Mill St 78238
Grobe Rd 78220
Groff Ave
100-499 78237
700-798 78228
Grogans Mill Dr 78248
Groos Ave 78223
Grosbeak Pass & Way 78253
Grosenbacher Rd 78245
Grosenbacher Rd N 78253
W Grosenbacher Rd 78245
Grosmont Ct 78239
Grosvenor St 78221
Grothues Pl 78207
Grotto Blvd 78216
Grouse 78223
Grove Ave 78210
Grove Bnd 78253
Grove Pl 78209
Grove Pt 78253
Grove Vis 78253
Grove Creek Dr 78256
Grove Ledge 78253
Grove Patch 78247
Grovehill St 78228
Groveland Pl 78209
Groveton St 78210
Grovetree 78247
Grovewoods 78253
Growdon Rd
3601-3699 78227
4407-4499 78237
Grubb St 78219
Gruene Pass 78253
Guadalajara 78221
Guadalajara Dr 78233
Guadalupe St
100-200 78204
202-298 78204
501-697 78207
699-3299 78207
Guadalupe Ybarra St 78207
Guanajuato 78237
E Guenther 78204
W Guenther 78204
E Guenther St 78210
Guernsey St 78247
Guerra Aly 78207

Gugert Ave 78204
Guilbeau Rd 78250
Guilford Ct 78245
N Guilford Dr 78217
S Guilford Dr 78217
Guinevere Dr 78218
Gulf 78202
Gulf Strm 78239
Gulf Shore Blvd 78244
Gulfdale St 78216
Gulfmart St 78217
Gull Lk 78245
Gumtree St 78238
Gunlock Crk 78244
Gunlock Cv 78239
Gunlock Trl 78245
Gunsel Trl 78245
Gunsmoke St 78227
Gunter Ave 78254
Gunter Grv 78231
Gunter Bay 78245
Gunther Blf 78258
Gunther Grv 78266
Gus Eckert Rd 78240
Gus Garcia 78207
Gusty Pln 78244
Guthrie St 78237
Gutierrez St 78207
Gwenda Lea St 78242
Gwendolen Dr 78253
Gypsophila 78253
Gypsy Dr 78228
Gypsy Holw 78261
Gypsy Pt 78245
Gypsy Vw 78261
Gypsy Way 78261
Gypsy Bell 78253
Gypsy Hawk 78261
H St
100-299 78210
301-397 78220
399-1099 78220
Habitat Cv 78258
Haby Dr 78212
Hacienda Dr 78233
Hacienda Acres 78245
Hacienda Trail Dr 78232
Hackamore Ln 78227
N Hackberry
201-213 78202
N Hackberry
215-1327 78202
1329-1399 78202
1400-1899 78208
S Hackberry
100-899 78203
900-2699 78210
2701-3099 78210
3600-4700 78223
4702-4798 78223
Hackberry Hl 78264
Hackberry Loop 78264
Hackberry Pt 78264
Hackley Dr 78207
Hackney Ln 78260
Hada Walk 78207
Hadbury Ln 78248
Hadley Run 78233
Haeli Park 78255
E & W Hafer Ave 78214
Haggin St 78210
Hagy Cir 78216
Halbart Dr 78213
Halcyon Pl 78209
Hale Ave 78204
Half Moon 78218
Halifax Ct 78209
Halifax St 78247
Hall Blvd 78243
Hall Park Dr 78218
Halleck Dr 78228
Halliday Ave 78210
Hallie Ave
200-298 78203
401-499 78203
700-4099 78210

Hallie Cir 78227
Hallie Cv 78227
Hallie Mdw 78227
Hallie Pass 78227
Hallie Pl 78227
Hallie Rdg 78227
Hallie Spirit 78227
Hallmark Dr 78216
Hallmark Path 78264
Hallow Pass 78254
Halm Blvd 78216
Halogen Way 78221
Halsey St 78221
Halstead 78204
Halter Ln 78240
Haltown Dr 78213
Halvern Dr 78228
Hambledon Dr 78250
N Hamilton St
101-297 78207
299-1400 78207
1402-1598 78207
1600-1899 78201
1901-1999 78201
S Hamilton St 78207
Hamilton Pool 78245
Hamilton Wolfe 78240
Hamilton Wolfe Rd 78229
Hamlen Park Dr S 78249
Hamlin Crk 78254
Hammond Ave 78210
Hampshire Ave 78210
Hampstead St 78220
Hampton Dl 78249
Hampton Park 78266
Hampton St
401-599 78220
800-1098 78220
1100-1198 78210
Hampton Way 78249
Hancock Ave 78214
Handley 78214
Handsome Lake Dr 78238
Hanfro Way 78251
Hanging Ledge 78232
Hanging Oak 78266
Hanna St 78210
Hannasch Dr 78213
Hanover Crst 78259
Hansa Hl 78256
Hansen Grns 78260
Hansford St 78210
Hanzi Dr 78223
Happiness St 78219
Happy Trl 78231
Happy Vw 78260
Happy Hollow Dr 78232
Happy Valley Dr 78242
Happys Cor 78258
Harald Dr 78214
Harbison 78261
Harbor Springs St 78245
Harbor View St 78242
Harbour Grey St 78245
Harcourt Ave 78223
Hardee Pass 78253
Hardeman St 78203
Hardesty 78250
E Harding Blvd 78214
W Harding Blvd 78221
Harding Pl 78203
Hardwick Rd 78264
Hardy Rd 78264
Hardy Oak Blvd 78258
Harefield Dr 78228
Harkavy Dr 78213
E Harlan Ave 78214
W Harlan Ave
100-799 78214
800-1599 78211
Harleyhill 78250
Harlow Dr 78218
Harmon Dr 78209
Harmony Ct 78217
Harmony Hls 78260
Harmony Holw 78260

Harness Ln 78227
Harney St 78203
Harper Ct 78259
Harper Oaks 78259
Harper Valley St 78233
Harpers Bnd 78217
Harpers Ferry St 78245
Harpers Ford St 78247
Harriet Dr 78216
Harrigan Ct 78209
Harriman Pl
101-597 78204
599-600 78204
602-698 78204
700-1000 78207
1002-1098 78207
Harris 78219
Harris Hawk 78253
Harrisburg 78223
Harrison Ave 78209
Harrow Dr 78227
Harry Rd 78223
Harry St 78224
Harry Wurzbach Rd 78209
E Hart Ave 78214
W Hart Ave 78214
Hart Clf 78249
Hart Crst 78249
Hart Cv 78249
Hart Fld 78249
Hart Gln 78249
Hart Path 78249
Hart Rnch 78249
Hartford Ave 78223
Hartline Dr 78218
Hartman St 78209
Hartsell St 78211
Hartwick Ln 78259
Harvard Ter 78201
Harvard Oak 78230
Harvest Bnd 78217
Harvest Crk 78244
Harvest Cyn 78258
Harvest Gln 78258
Harvest Grv 78258
Harvest Hls 78258
Harvest Trl 78250
Harvest Meadow St 78250
Harvest Moon 78245
Harvest Oak 78258
Harvest Star 78258
Harvest Time St 78245
Harvest Wood 78258
Harwood Dr 78213
Hasbrook St 78217
Haskin Dr 78209
Hastings 78239
Hatcher Ave 78223
Hatchet Pass Dr 78245
Hatfield St 78227
E & W Hathaway Dr 78209
Hatton St 78237
Hauck Dr 78219
Haufler St 78247
S & W Hausman Rd 78249
Havana Dr 78228
Havasu Hls 78256
Havelock St 78254
Haven Ct 78258
Haven Vly 78242
Haven Farm 78249
Haven For Hope Way 78207
Haven Oak 78249
Havenbrook Dr 78227
Havencrest Dr 78242
Havenhollow 78264
Havenhurst Dr 78232
Havenrock 78259
Havenside 78239
Havenview Dr 78228
Haverford Dr 78217
Haverhill Dr 78228
Haverhill Way 78209
Haversham 78254
Havershan St 78217
Haviland Ct 78251

Hawaiian Cv 78242
Hawaiian Fld 78245
Hawaiian Sun Dr 78244
Hawk Spgs 78249
Hawk Nest St 78250
Hawk Trail St 78250
Hawks Mdw 78248
Hawks Rd 78235
Hawks Rdg 78248
Hawks Tree Ln 78248
Hawksbill Peak 78245
Hawkwolf Crk 78245
Hawkwood 78250
Hawthorn 78261
Hawthorn Woods 78249
Hawthorne
100-399 78214
Hawthorne
400-499 78225
Hayden Dr 78242
Hayden Holw 78251
Hayes 78239
Hayloft Gln 78233
Hayloft Ln 78245
Haymarket St 78217
Haynes Ave 78210
Hays Hl 78256
Hays Pt 78250
Hays St 78202
Haywood Ave 78215
Hazel Cir 78242
Hazel Cv 78242
Hazel St 78207
Hazel Alder 78261
Hazel Valley St 78242
Hazelbury Ln 78253
Hazelton Ln 78251
Hazelwood Ct 78257
Hazy Holw 78255
Headwaters Trl 78254
Heap Cir 78230
Hearne Ave 78225
Hearthglen 78250
Hearthstone 78258
Hearthwood 78248
Heartland Dr 78247
Heath Rd 78250
Heath Circle Dr 78250
Heathcliff 78254
Heather Ave 78223
Heather Blf 78259
Heather Crk 78258
Heather Ct 78221
Heather Frst 78258
Heather Hl 78228
Heather Mdw 78222
Heather Pass 78218
Heather Rdg 78260
Heather Vw 78249
Heather Oaks 78258
Heather Path St 78232
Heatherbrook 78238
Heathers Bnd, Cv, Fld,
Pl, Run & Way 78227
Heathers Farm 78244
Heathers Pond 78227
Heatherwood St 78217
Heathridge 78250
Heavenly Arbor 78254
Heavenly Sky 78260
Heavens Way 78260
Heavens Peak 78258
Hedge Grv 78263
Hedges St 78203
Hedgestone Dr 78258
Hedgewyck St 78217
Hedrick Farm 78239
Hedwig St 78219
Heflin Ct 78210
Heidelberg St 78233
Heidi St 78247
Heights Park, Path &
Way 78230
Heights Hall 78230
Heights Hill Dr 78230
Heights Lane Dr 78230

Heights View Dr 78230
Heimer Rd
100-398 78232
400-699 78232
701-15999 78232
13000-13098 78216
14800-15698 78232
N & W Hein Rd 78220
Helena St 78204
Helios Rise 78252
Heliport Dr 78250
Hematite Rim 78222
Hemisfair Plaza Way 78205
Hemphill Dr 78228
Henderson Pass
14700-15298 78232
15300-15699 78232
15610-15610 78270
15701-17699 78232
16000-17698 78232
Henderson St 78209
Henderson Camp St 78233
Hendon Ln 78257
Henly Ln 78257
Henrietta St 78224
Henry St 78207
Henze Rd 78223
Heraldry St 78254
Herbert Ln 78227
Herbst St 78214
Herder Cir 78251
Hereford 78217
Heritage Grv 78253
Heritage Lk 78244
Heritage St 78216
Heritage Way 78245
Heritage Farm 78245
Heritage Hill Dr 78247
Heritage Park Dr 78240
Heritage Place Dr 78240
Herlinda Dr 78228
Herman Holw 78254
Hermine Blvd
100-599 78212
800-1899 78201
W Hermitage Ct 78223
E Hermosa Dr 78212
W Hermosa Dr
200-599 78212
900-2499 78201
Hermosa Hl 78256
Herron Ct 78217
Hershey Dr 78220
Herweck Dr 78213
Hess St 78212
Hetherington Dr 78240
Hetton Hts 78254
Heuermann Rd 78256
Hi Path St 78232
Hialeah Ave 78218
Hiawatha 78210
Hibiscus Fls 78218
Hibiscus Ln 78213
Hickman
100-300 78212
Hickman
302-398 78212
401-499 78201
Hickory Bnd 78266
Hickory Ct 78264
Hickory Cyn 78252
Hickory Frst 78239
Hickory Holw 78239
Hickory Knl 78264
Hickory Ln 78264
Hickory Mdw 78261
Hickory Pass 78264
Hickory St 78228
Hickory Way 78264
Hickory Arch 78261
Hickory Grove Dr 78227
Hickory Hill Dr 78219
Hickory Legend 78247
Hickory Springs Dr 78249
Hickory Sun 78244
Hickory Tavern 78247

Hickory Trail St 78245
Hickory Well Dr 78247
Hicks Ave 78210
Hidalgo St 78207
Hidden Blf 78218
Hidden Brk 78250
Hidden Cpe 78250
Hidden Crk 78238
Hidden Crst 78250
Hidden Cv 78245
Hidden Cyn 78252
Hidden Dr 78217
Hidden Fld 78250
Hidden Fls 78250
Hidden Hls N 78244
Hidden Holw 78239
Hidden Arrow 78258
Hidden Bay 78250
Hidden Boulder St 78250
Hidden Bow St 78242
Hidden Cross 78250
Hidden Dale St 78250
Hidden Elm 78261
Hidden Elm Woods 78249
Hidden Glade 78250
Hidden Glen St 78232
Hidden Glen Woods 78249
Hidden Haven St 78261
Hidden Iron Cir & St 78250
Hidden Lake St 78222
Hidden Ledge 78250
Hidden Meadow Dr 78230
Hidden Mist Cir 78250
Hidden Oak Trl 78233
Hidden Oak Woods 78248
Hidden Pass St 78232
Hidden Peak St 78247
Hidden Plains St 78250
Hidden Pond 78227
Hidden Rock 78250
Hidden Rose 78250
Hidden Sky St 78250
Hidden Sunrise Dr 78244
Hidden Swan 78250
Hidden Thicket 78240
Hidden Timber Wood 78248
Hidden Valley Dr 78227
Hidden View St 78232
Hidden Well Dr 78247
Hideaway Crk 78254
Hideaway Grn 78261
Hideout Bnd 78254
Hideout Fls 78261
Hideout Rnch 78261
Higbee Ml 78247
Higdon Rd 78223
Higgins Pt 78216
Higgins Rd 78217
E High Ave 78210
W High Ave 78210
High Br 78254
High Cres 78257
High Mdws 78253
High Chapel 78231
High Country Rdg 78260
High Ledge St 78232
High Lonesome 78254
High Mountain Rd 78255
High Noon Way 78254
High Plains Dr 78254
High Quest 78248
High Ridge Cir 78229
High Rise Dr 78232
High Rock St 78232
High Sierra Dr 78228
High Springs Dr 78261
High Stepper Ln 78240
High Timber Pass St 78260
High Vista St 78233
Highcliff Dr 78218
Highcrest Dr 78224
Highfield St 78238
Highgate Dr 78257
Highgrove Ln 78258
Highland Blf 78233
E Highland Blvd 78210

W Highland Blvd 78210
Highland Crk 78245
Highland Hl 78260
Highland Knl 78260
Highland Park 78250
Highland Rdg 78233
Highland Dawn 78254
Highland Farm 78244
Highland Lake Dr 78244
Highland Mist Ln 78251
Highland Oaks St 78227
Highland Peak 78233
Highland Pond 78254
Highland Star 78254
Highline Trl 78261
Highpoint St 78217
Hightree Dr 78217
Highview Dr 78228
Highway Dr 78219
Hilary St 78210
E Hildebrand Ave
101-397 78212
399-900 78212
902-998 78212
2100-2199 78209
W Hildebrand Ave
301-397 78212
399-899 78212
900-1899 78201
1901-1999 78201
Hildebrandt Rd 78222
Hiler Rd 78209
Hill St 78212
Hill Country Ln 78232
Hill Creek Dr 78256
Hill Forest St 78230
Hill Meadow Dr 78256
Hill Mist 78240
Hill Pine Way 78254
Hill Prince St 78248
Hill Ridge St 78250
Hill Trails St 78250
Hillbrook Park 78259
Hillburn Dr 78242
Hillcrest Dr
101-297 78228
299-2799 78228
2800-3399 78201
Hillcroft 78250
Hilldale Pt 78261
Hillgreen Dr 78213
Hillingdon 78209
Hillingway St 78248
Hillje St 78223
Hillman Dr 78218
Hillpoint 78217
Hillrise Dr 78227
Hillrose St 78207
N Hills Village Dr 78249
Hillsboro Dr 78217
Hillsdale Dr 78227
Hillsdale Loop 78249
Hillside Blf 78233
Hillside Ct 78258
Hillside Dr 78212
E Hillside Dr 78249
Hillside Rdg 78233
Hillside Rnch 78254
Hillside Trl 78250
Hillside Vw 78233
Hillside Peak 78233
Hillsong 78258
Hillswind St 78217
Hilltop Crst 78251
Hilltop Crossing Dr 78251
Hilltop Field Dr 78240
Hillview Dr 78209
Hillview Pass Dr 78247
Hillwood Dr 78213
Hilton Ave 78221
Hilton Head St 78217
Hindi St 78224
Hines
100-198 78202
Hines
1300-1399 78208

Hinesville Dr 78240
Hitching Trl 78247
Hitching Post St 78217
Hitchings St 78212
Hobart St 78237
Hobble St 78227
Hobblebush 78260
Hobson St 78223
Hoby 78228
Hodges Dr 78238
Hoefgen Ave
100-200 78205
202-398 78205
800-1600 78210
1602-1698 78210
Hoeneke St 78219
Hof St 78243
Hogan Cv 78221
Hogan Dr 78260
Hogans Trl 78240
Hohen St 78221
Hohmann Ct 78249
Hoke Dr 78254
Holbrook Rd 78218
Holbrook Way 78253
Holder Ave 78211
Hole In One 78221
Holland Ave 78212
Hollenbeck Ave 78211
Hollimon Pkwy 78253
Hollow Bnd 78250
Hollow Brk 78253
Hollow Cir 78227
Hollow Cyn 78252
Hollow Grv 78253
Hollow Hl 78217
Hollow Run 78231
Hollow Trl 78253
Hollow Creek Dr 78231
Hollow Glen St 78233
Hollow Oak St 78233
Hollow Tree St 78230
Hollow View St 78232
Hollow Village Dr 78231
Holly Crst 78260
Holly Mdw 78244
Holly Pl 78254
Holly St 78207
Holly Dale Dr 78250
Holly Mountain St 78250
Hollyberry Ln 78214
Hollyhill Dr 78222
Hollyhock Rd 78240
Hollyridge Dr 78228
Hollyspring Dr 78220
E Hollywood Ave 78212
W Hollywood Ave
100-899 78212
1200-1298 78201
1300-1699 78201
Holm Oaks Dr 78249
Holman Dr 78228
Holmes Ln 78258
Holmgreen Rd 78220
Holy Cross Dr 78228
Home Ave 78212
Homecrest 78204
Homeric Dr 78213
Homestead Dr 78244
Honey Blvd 78220
Honey Hl 78229
Honey Mdw 78222
Honey Bee Ln 78231
Honey Creek Dr 78230
Honey Grove St 78233
Honey Jay Dr 78228
Honey Locust Woods 78249
Honey Mesquite 78258
Honey Oaks 78253
Honey Tree St 78245
Honeycomb St 78230
Honeygold Dr 78222
Honeyridge Ln 78239
Honeysuckle Ln 78213
Honiley St 78254
Honora Ave 78221

Hood St 78208
Hoofs Ln 78240
Hook Dr 78231
Hookberry Trl 78256
Hootananny 78260
Hoover Ave 78225
Hoovers Bnd 78250
Hop Sing Trl 78253
Hop Tree 78260
Hope Dr 78228
Hopecrest St 78230
Hopes Ferry St 78233
Hopeton Dr 78230
Hopewell St 78232
Hopi St 78211
Hopi Dawn 78261
Hopkins St 78221
Hopkins Glade 78249
Hopleaf Trl 78256
Horace St 78212
Horal Dr 78245
Horal St 78227
Horideld St 78224
Horistr Dr 78222
Horizon Blf 78258
Horizon Cir 78258
Horizon Dr 78228
Horizon Lk 78222
Horizon Pt 78242
Horizon Vw 78233
Horizon Way 78258
Horizon Hill Blvd 78229
Horizon Oaks 78244
Horizon Peak 78233
Horizon Star 78252
Hormel Dr 78219
Horn Blvd 78240
Horn Run 78245
Hornet Creek Dr 78247
Hornet Pass Dr 78247
Hornpipe Hls 78260
Horns Cross 78257
Hornsby Bnd 78245
Horse Cres 78254
Horse Holw 78244
Horse Pr 78261
Horse Creek St 78232
Horse Heath 78254
Horse Ranch Rd 78264
Horse Tail Dr 78240
Horse Whip Dr 78240
Horsemint 78247
Horserace 78251
E Horseshoe Bnd 78228
S Horseshoe Bnd 78228
W Horseshoe Bnd 78228
Horseshoe Cyn 78258
Horseshoe Ln 78221
Horseshoe Pass 78254
Hortencia Ave
100-699 78237
700-1399 78228
Horton Pl 78214
Horwich 78239
Hosack Ave 78211
Hot Spgs 78258
Hot Wells Blvd 78223
Hounds Rise St 78248
House Mountain Rd 78255
E Houston St
100-700 78205
601-699 78291
601-699 78292
601-699 78293
601-699 78294
601-699 78295
601-699 78296
601-699 78297
601-699 78298
601-699 78299
701-1399 78205
702-1398 78205
1400-2999 78202
3000-3699 78219
3900-5000 78220
5002-5198 78220

W Houston St
100-298 78205
300-399 78205
400-498 78207
500-4099 78207
4101-4199 78207
Hovingham 78257
Howard St 78212
Howerton Dr 78223
Howle Ave 78223
Howling Wolf 78261
Hoya Ln 78266
Hub Ave 78220
Hubbard Hl 78254
Hubbard St 78209
Hudson 78202
Hudspeth Trl 78253
Huebner Blf 78248
Huebner Crst 78248
Huebner Park 78248
Huebner Rd
6400-6900 78238
6825-6825 78268
6902-6998 78238
7101-7397 78240
7399-10423 78240
10425-10799 78240
11100-11198 78230
11200-13000 78230
12951-12951 78278
12951-12951 78280
13002-14698 78230
13101-14699 78230
14801-15097 78231
15099-15299 78231
15300-16699 78248
16701-16799 78248
16800-20599 78258
20601-20699 78258
Huebner Oak 78258
Huebner Oaks 78230
Huerta St 78207
E & W Huff Ave 78214
Hugo Cir 78224
E Huisache Ave 78212
W Huisache Ave
100-699 78212
900-2399 78201
2400-2600 78228
2602-2798 78228
Huisache Cv 78253
Huisache Daisy 78245
Huizar 78214
Hull St 78223
Humble Ave 78225
Humboldt St 78211
Hume Rd 78264
Hummingbird Hill Ln 78255
Humphrey Ave 78209
Hundred Oaks Dr 78217
Hunnicut Dr 78219
Hunstock Ave 78210
Hunt Est 78253
Hunt Ln
100-198 78245
200-1799 78245
2101-2197 78227
2199-2300 78227
2302-3598 78227
Hunt Xing 78245
Hunter Hl 78217
Hunter St 78224
Hunter Ivy 78253
Hunter Oaks St 78233
Hunters Blf 78250
N Hunters Cir 78230
Hunters Clfs 78230
Hunters Dl 78258
Hunters Frst 78239
Hunters Gln 78218
Hunters Land 78249
Hunters Lk 78249
Hunters Mt 78249
Hunters Trl 78230
Hunters Walk 78230
Hunters Arrow St 78230
Hunters Bay 78230

Hunters Bow St 78230
Hunters Branch St S 78231
Hunters Breeze St 78230
Hunters Brook St 78230
Hunters Chase St 78230
Hunters Circle St 78230
Hunters Creek St 78211
Hunters Crest St 78230
Hunters Dawn St 78230
Hunters Den St 78230
Hunters Dew St 78230
Hunters Dove 78230
Hunters Dream 78230
Hunters Dusk St 78230
Hunters Fern St 78230
Hunters Fox St 78230
Hunters Gate St 78230
Hunters Glade St 78230
Hunters Green St 78231
Hunters Hawk St 78230
Hunters Hideaway St 78230
Hunters Hollow St 78230
Hunters Horn St 78230
Hunters Knoll St 78230
Hunters Lark St 78230
Hunters Ledge 78230
Hunters Meadow St 78230
Hunters Moon 78249
Hunters Moss St 78230
Hunters Peak St 78230
Hunters Pier 78230
Hunters Plane 78245
Hunters Point St 78230
Hunters Pond 78224
Hunters Quail 78230
Hunters Raven 78249
Hunters Ridge St 78230
Hunters Rock 78230
Hunters Run St 78230
Hunters Sound St 78230
Hunters Spring St 78230
Hunters Stand St 78230
Hunters Star St 78230
Hunters Stream St 78230
Hunters Sun Dr 78244
Hunters Tree St 78230
Hunters Vale St 78230
Hunters Valley St 78230
Hunters View St 78230
Hunters Wind St 78230
Hunters Wood St 78230
Hunting Path 78218
Hunting Arrow 78249
Hunting Bear 78249
Hunting Glen St 78247
Hunting Hawk 78249
Hunting Valley St 78247
Huntington Pl 78231
Huntington St 78207
Huntington Woods St 78249
Huntleigh Ln 78209
Huntress Ln 78255
Huntsman Rd 78249
Huntsman Lake Dr 78249
Huntsman Run Dr 78249
Huntsman View Dr 78249
Huntsmoor Ct 78220
Huntwick Ln 78230
Huntwood Cir 78249
Hurley Dr 78238
Huron St 78211
E Hutchins Pl 78221
W Hutchins Pl
100-1500 78221
1502-1598 78221
1601-1797 78224
1799-2100 78224
2102-2898 78224
Huth Dr 78222
Huxley Dr 78218
Hyacinth Ln 78260
Hyatt St 78251
Hyatt Place Dr 78230
Hyatt Resort Dr 78251
Hycroft 78233
Hyde Park 78209

Hyerwood 78259
Hymeadow 78258
Hypoint St 78217
I St
100-199 78210
201-299 78210
601-799 78220
I X L Dr 78253
Ibc Bldg 78205
Iceberg Ln 78238
Icicle Trl 78254
Icicle Bench 78254
Ida Dr & Fls 78222
Ida Spring Dr 78222
Idabel Park 78249
Idaho 78203
Idar Walk 78207
Ideal 78223
Idell Ave 78223
Idle Rdg 78263
Idledale Dr 78249
Idlewood Dr 78242
Idylwild 78258
Igo St 78230
Ike St 78211
Ilene Lynn St 78224
Illg Ave 78211
Ilma St 78220
Ilse Pl 78217
Ima Ruth Pkwy 78257
Imlay St 78209
Imogene Dr 78223
Impala 78258
Impala Bnd 78259
Impala Cir 78259
Impala Park 78251
Impala Spgs 78245
Impala Trce 78258
Impala Way 78258
Impala Peak 78259
Impatiens Vw 78245
Imperial Blvd 78226
Imperial Way 78248
Imperial Oaks 78248
Imperial Topaz 78222
Inca St 78237
Independence Ave 78233
Indian Bnd 78250
Indian Clf 78260
Indian Crk 78230
Indian Crst 78261
Indian Cyn 78252
Indian Holw 78261
Indian Ldg 78253
Indian Run 78233
Indian Wls 78245
Indian Bow 78259
Indian Desert St 78242
Indian Lake Dr 78244
Indian Laurel 78259
Indian Meadows Dr 78230
Indian Mound 78266
Indian Paint Brush Rd 78232
Indian Path St 78247
Indian Peak St 78247
Indian Pipe St 78242
Indian Ridge Cir & Dr 78231
Indian Sky Dr 78242
Indian Summer 78260
Indian Sunrise 78244
Indian Teepee 78260
Indian Valley Dr 78242
Indian Woods 78249
Indiana St 78210
Indianola St 78210
Indigo Bnd 78230
Indigo Crk 78239
Indigo Frst 78239
Indigo Lk 78245
Indigo St 78216
NW Industrial 78238
Industrial Ctr 78217
Industrial Pkwy 78226
Industrial Park Rd 78226
Industry Dr 78217
Industry Park Dr 78218

Inez Ave 78228
Inglenook 78253
Ingleside Dr 78213
Ingleton 78245
Ingram Rd
4900-5799 78228
5801-5999 78228
6000-6800 78238
6802-6898 78238
7300-7498 78251
7500-7799 78251
8601-8699 78245
10700-10798 78245
Iniga 78253
Ink Wells Dr 78250
Inks Farm 78228
Inland Lk 78254
Inne Dr 78216
Inner Cyn 78252
Inner Circle Dr 78235
Inridge 78250
Inslee Ave 78209
Inspiration Dr 78228
Interchange Pkwy 78218
Interloop Rd 78216
Intermezzo Way 78266
International St 78216
International Bldg 78205
Interpark Blvd 78216
Interstate Dr & Way 78219
Interstate 10 E 78219
W Interstate 10
3000-6800 78201
W Interstate 10
6802-6898 78201
6901-6999 78213
7100-7198 78213
7500-7598 78229
7600-7798 78230
7800-11099 78230
11101-12799 78230
11300-11398 78249
11400-12798 78230
12800-15700 78249
15702-15812 78249
15814-17298 78257
17300-25599 78257
Interstate 35 S
6700-8100 78224
N Interstate 35
1401-1497 78208
1499-2800 78208
2802-2998 78208
4200-7900 78218
7902-7998 78218
8200-8498 78239
9400-12299 78233
12301-13099 78233
12500-13098 78233
13100-13300 78233
13302-13998 78233
S Interstate 35
1500-1598 78204
E Interstate Highway
10 78220
Interstate Highway 35
S 78211
Intrigue Dr 78216
Inverness Blvd 78230
Inverrary Dr 78244
Invicta Dr 78218
Invierno 78223
Inview Cv 78248
Invitation Oak 78261
Invitational 78227
Inwood Blf 78248
Inwood Dr 78228
Inwood Frk 78248
Inwood Knls 78248
Inwood Mnr 78248
Inwood Park 78216
Inwood Autumn 78248
Inwood Briar 78248
Inwood Canyon Dr 78248
Inwood Cliffs Dr 78248
Inwood Cove Dr 78248
Inwood Crown 78248

Inwood Elms 78248
Inwood Forest St 78230
S Inwood Heights Dr
N 78248
Inwood Mist 78248
Inwood Moss 78248
Inwood Oaks 78248
Inwood Peak 78248
Inwood Point Dr 78248
Inwood Ridge Dr 78248
Inwood Terrace Dr 78248
Inwood View Dr 78248
Inwood Way Dr 78248
Iota Dr 78217
Iowa St
200-398 78210
400-498 78203
500-2200 78203
2202-2298 78203
Ipswich 78254
Ira Ave 78209
Ira Aldridge Pl 78202
Ira Lee Rd 78218
Irby St 78223
Irene Dr 78222
Iris 78223
Iris Isle 78218
Iris Path 78245
Iris Way 78253
Irish Grv 78247
Irish Elm 78247
Irish Oak 78247
Irma Ave 78237
Irola St 78228
Iron Ml 78230
Iron Horse 78255
Iron Liege 78248
Iron Mesa 78260
Iron Oak Ln 78213
Iron Ridge Ct 78258
Iron Stone Ct & Ln 78230
Irongate Crk 78238
Irongate Pass 78247
Irongate Rd 78213
Irongate Rdg 78253
Irongate Oak 78254
Irongate Rail 78247
Ironside Dr 78230
Ironside Prt 78227
Ironweed 78247
Ironwood Fls 78261
Ironwood Rd 78212
Ironwood Ash 78261
Iroquois St 78211
Irvington Dr 78209
Irwin Dr 78222
Isaac Ryan 78253
Isabel St 78210
Isla Way 78253
Island View St 78242
Isom Rd 78216
Italica Rd 78253
Ithaca Bnd 78239
Ithaca Dr 78227
Ithaca Fls 78239
Ithaca Frst 78239
Ivan Dr 78244
Ivanhoe St 78228
Ivory Crk 78258
Ivory Cyn 78255
Ivory Frst 78239
Ivory Oak St 78233
Ivy Grn 78247
Ivy Ln 78209
Ivy Bend St 78250
Ivy Cadence 78253
Ivy Chase 78253
Ivy Oak St 78231
Ivy Plain Dr 78245
Ivy Ridge Ln 78224
Ivywood Cir 78213
Ivywood Dr 78249
J St
100-199 78210
300-398 78220
400-3399 78220

Jack Bean St 78240
Jack Pine St 78232
Jack White Way St 78205
Jackies Farm 78244
Jackson Ct 78230
Jackson St 78212
Jackson Hole St 78232
Jackson Keller Rd
100-100 78216
102-799 78216
801-899 78216
1000-2199 78213
2200-2398 78230
2400-2599 78230
2601-2699 78230
Jackwood Dr 78238
Jaclyn Park 78250
Jacob Patrick 78240
Jacob Walker 78253
Jacobs St 78210
Jacobs Pond 78253
Jacques St 78233
Jade Cv 78242
Jade Dr 78209
Jade Fld 78240
Jade Gln 78249
Jade Grn 78249
Jade Hl 78251
Jade Hts 78249
Jade Knl 78249
Jade Mdw 78249
Jade Spg 78249
Jade Trl 78249
Jadestone Blvd 78249
Jaenke St 78219
Jalane Park 78255
Jalane Oaks 78255
Jamaica Dr 78227
Jamar St 78226
James Bonham Dr 78238
James Bowie 78253
James Cook 78239
James Gaines 78253
James Lovell Dr 78219
James Vinson 78253
James Webb Dr 78219
Jamestown Dr 78220
Jamie Wynell Cir 78257
Janda Susan Rd 78209
Jandre Pl 78213
Jane Grv 78253
Jane Ellen St 78237
Janet Gale St 78221
Janet Lee Dr 78230
Janice Gail Dr 78224
Janis Rae 78201
Japonica 78260
Jarbet Dr 78220
Jarbo Pass Dr 78245
Jardin Vis 78258
Jardines 78237
Jarrell 78253
Jarve Vly 78251
Jarvis Dr 78253
Jasmine Ln 78237
Jasmine Way 78253
Jason Ave 78255
Jasons Pl 78240
Jasper St 78223
Jasper Leaf 78253
Java Wood 78254
Jay Schellman St 78232
Jay Williams St 78237
Jaylee Dr 78223
Jean St 78207
Jean Verte 78250
Jeanette Dr 78216
Jefferson St 78205
Jeffrey 78201
Jeffs Farm 78244
Jemison St 78203
Jenkins Dr 78247
Jenkins Hl 78255
Jennifer St 78224
Jennifer Nicole 78261
Jennings Ave 78225
Jenny Dr 78239
Jenson Pt 78251
Jenull Ave 78202
Jerome Rd 78227
Jerry Dr 78201
Jersey 78214
Jerusalem Walk 78220
Jess Gdns 78232
Jessamine St 78209
Jesse Ave 78237
Jesse Bowman 78253
Jesus Aly 78207
Jesusita 78237
Jethro Ln 78266
Jetlyn Dr 78249
S & W Jett Rd 78264
Jetty 78239
W Jewell St 78226
Jewett St 78237
Jiggitty Dr 78254
Jim St 78208
Jim Bowie Dr 78238
Jim Seal Dr 78239
Jimmer Cv 78221
Jimmy Foxx St 78240
Jo Marie St 78222
Joan Grona 78238
Joanie Kay 78260
Jockey 78227
Joe Blanks St 78237
Joe Dimaggio St 78240
Joe Lee St 78233
Joe Louis Dr 78220
Joe Newton St 78251
Joes Farm 78244
Jogeva Way 78251
Jogeva Rise 78251
John Adams Dr 78228
John Alden Dr 78230
John Barrett Dr 78240
John Barry St 78233
John Cape Rd 78216
John Chapman 78240
John D Ryan Blvd 78245
John Duncan 78260
John Glenn Dr 78217
John Jay St 78233
John Marshall St 78240
John Miller Ct 78244
John Page Dr 78228
John Rolfe Dr 78230
John Saunders Rd
9201-9397 78216
9399-10099 78216
10101-10299 78216
10250-10250 78246
10250-10250 78279
John Smith 78229
John Speier Dr 78217
John Vance Dr 78216
John Victor Dr 78220
John Wayne St 78240
John Williams 78228
John Young Dr 78219
Johnathan Ave 78223
Johnny Reb Dr 78240
Johns Farm 78228
E & W Johnson 78204
Johnson Grass 78251
Johnstown Dr 78253
Joiner 78238
Jole Cv 78239
E Jolie Ct 78240
Jolie Blossom 78247
Joliet Ave 78209
Joline 78218
Jon Ann 78201
E & W Jones Ave 78215
Jones Fall Dr 78244
Jones Maltsberger Rd
7300-7398 78209
7601-7697 78216
7699-12000 78216
12002-12098 78216
12101-12197 78247
12199-17199 78247
17201-17299 78247
Jonquill St 78233
Jordan Walk 78220
Jordan Xing 78221
Jordans Way 78260
Jordans Wood Cir 78248
Jorwoods Dr 78250
Jose Ln 78227
Joseph Phelps 78253
E Josephine St
100-298 78215
300-600 78215
602-698 78215
700-799 78208
801-899 78208
W Josephine St 78212
N & S Josephine Tobin Dr 78201
Joshua Pt 78251
Joshua Way 78258
Joshua Batton 78217
Joslyn Ln 78227
Joy Dr 78223
Joy St 78212
Juan Seguin Dr 78238
Juanita Ave 78237
Juarez St 78207
Judie Allen 78254
Judivan 78218
Judson Bnd 78261
Judson Rd
12301-12397 78233
12399-12527 78233
12528-12598 78233
12600-14999 78233
15000-16400 78247
16402-17598 78247
19400-19498 78259
Judson St 78212
Judson Lake Dr 78244
Judsonwood 78244
Julia Helen Dr 78222
Julia Ross St 78207
Julians Cv 78244
Julie Dr 78219
Julienne 78232
Juliet Hl 78256
Junction Rdg 78248
June Berry 78260
Jung Rd 78247
Jungman Rd 78252
Junior St 78223
Juniper Cyn 78245
Juniper Flt 78254
Juniper Hl 78245
Juniper Pass 78254
Juniper Rdg 78258
Juniper Spg 78254
Juniper St 78223
Juniper Farm 78244
Juno Hts 78252
Jupe Dr 78222
Jupiter St 78226
Just My Style 78245
Justin Cv 78240
Justin Pt 78251
Justin Ter 78251
Justinian Ln 78257
Justino Trl 78244
Justo St 78227
K St 78220
Kaepa Ct 78218
Kaine St 78214
Kaiser Dr 78222
Kaitlyn Cyn 78258
Kallies Cir 78251
Kallison Bnd 78254
Kalteyer St 78210
Kamary Ln 78247
Kampmann Ave 78209
Kampmann Blvd 78201
Kannesaw 78223
Kansas St 78203
Kapp Cyn 78258
Karat Dr 78232
Kardla Frst 78251
Karen Ln
101-197 78209
199-499 78209
600-899 78218
Karen Skye Cir 78257
Karnes Way 78253
Karnes Leaf 78253
Kashmir Dr 78251
Kashmuir Pl 78223
Kate Schenck Ave 78223
Katharine Gln 78266
Katherine Ct 78209
Katherine Way 78253
Kathy Dr 78223
Katrina Ln 78222
Kauai Bay 78255
Kaufmann Ct 78207
Kava Knl 78253
Kay Ann Dr 78220
Kayla Brk 78251
Kayton Ave 78210
Kazen Cir & Dr 78219
Kearney St 78210
Keats St
600-799 78214
800-1599 78211
Keck 78207
Keegans Blf 78258
Keegans Woods Dr 78254
Keeneland Run 78254
Keila Orch 78251
Keitha Blvd 78227
Keithshire Crk 78245
Kelian Ct 78230
Keller 78204
Kellers Pt 78230
Kelly Dr 78214
Kelsey Ave 78211
Kelsey Rd 78223
Kelso 78248
Kelton Dr 78250
Kemble St 78249
Kemper 78207
Kemper Oaks 78260
Ken Dr 78258
Kenbridge Dr 78250
Kendalia Ave
100-499 78214
500-1099 78221
1100-1899 78224
Kendall St 78212
Kendall Way 78264
Kenedy Leaf 78253
Kenerrad Dr 78213
Kenilworth Blvd 78209
Kenley Pl 78232
Kenmar Dr 78220
Kenna Mist 78247
Kennebec Way 78245
Kennedy Ave 78209
Kennedy Cir 78235
Kennith Ave 78227
Kenrock Rdg 78254
Kenrock St 78227
Kensington Ct 78218
Kensington Run 78228
Kenswick Vw 78223
Kent Frst 78254
Kent Falls Dr 78248
Kentisbury Dr 78251
Kentoaks Dr 78260
Kenton Blf 78240
Kenton Crst 78240
Kenton Ct 78240
Kenton Fls 78240
Kenton Hbr 78240
Kenton Hl 78240
Kenton Knl 78258
Kenton Lk 78240
Kenton Park 78249
Kenton Rpds 78240
Kenton Trce 78240
Kenton Vw 78240
Kenton Ash 78240
Kenton Briar 78240
Kenton Croft 78258
Kenton Mist 78240
Kenton Royalle 78240
Kenton Stone 78240
Kents Store St 78245
Kentsdale 78239
Kentucky Ave
600-1899 78201
1900-1998 78228
2000-2099 78228
Kentucky Trl 78247
Kentucky Oaks 78259
Kenwick St 78238
Kepler Dr 78228
Kernan Dr 78227
Kerr Cir 78264
Kerr St 78215
Kerri Elizabeth 78237
Kerrville St 78251
Kerrybrook Ct 78230
Keslake St 78222
Kestrel Ln 78233
Kettering Dr 78228
Key St 78201
Keystone 78229
Keystone Blf 78258
Keystone Cv 78251
Kiawah Isle Dr 78260
Kicaster Aly 78207
Kicking Bird 78261
Kid Run 78232
Kidneywood 78261
Kiefer Rd 78220
Kihnu Willow 78251
Kildare Ave 78223
Kildoran Ct 78253
Kilkenney 78227
Killarney Dr 78223
Killdee Dr 78223
Kilmarnoch Ln 78251
Kilowatt Rd 78223
Kilrea Dr 78219
Kiltey St 78248
Kim St 78209
Kim Valley St 78242
Kimberly Dr 78227
Kimble Ml 78253
Kimbro Dr 78217
Kimes Park Dr 78249
Kinder Dr 78212
Kinder Pkwy 78260
Kinder Run 78260
Kinderhook 78245
Kindlewood St 78238
Kindred St 78224
King Ave 78211
King Cor 78255
King Albert St 78229
King Arthur Dr 78218
King Birch St 78230
King Davis 78254
King Edward St 78229
King Elm St 78230
King George Dr 78229
King Henry St 78229
King Krest Dr 78219
King Louis Dr 78229
King Maple St 78230
King Oaks Dr 78233
King Richard St 78229
King Roger St 78204
King Walnut St 78230
King William 78204
Kingbard St 78230
Kingbird Cv 78260
Kinghurst 78248
Kinglet Ct 78251
Kingley Dr 78224
Kings Ct 78212
Kings Cyn 78258
Kings Hbr 78242
E Kings Hwy 78212
W Kings Hwy
100-899 78212
900-2399 78201
2400-2699 78228
Kings Mdws 78231
Kings Ml 78257
Kings Mnr 78257
Kings Pt 78217
Kings Spg 78254
Kings Vw 78257
Kings Arms 78218
Kings Castle 78257
Kings Cross St 78254
Kings Crown St 78233
Kings Forest St 78230
Kings Grant Dr 78230
Kings Heath 78257
Kings Lair 78253
Kings Reach 78209
Kings Tower 78257
Kingsbridge 78253
Kingsbury Hl 78217
Kingsbury St 78212
Kingsbury Vw 78240
Kingsbury Way 78240
Kingsbury Wood 78240
Kingsford Ln 78259
Kingsland 78244
Kingston Rnch 78249
Kingsway St 78254
Kingswell Ave 78251
Kingswood St 78228
Kinman Dr 78238
Kinney Bnd 78264
Kinney St 78210
Kinross Dr 78209
Kinsem 78248
Kint Circle St 78247
Kintbury 78253
Kiowa Crk 78255
Kiowa St 78211
Kipling Ave 78223
Kirby Dr 78219
Kirby Heights St 78219
Kirk Ln 78240
Kirk Path 78240
Kirk Pl
100-498 78225
500-699 78225
700-1399 78226
3100-3199 78237
Kirk Way 78240
Kirk Pond 78240
Kirkham 78239
S Kirkner Rd 78263
Kirknewton St 78243
Kirkpatrick Ave 78210
Kirkwood 78214
Kissing Oak St 78247
Kit Cv 78255
Kitchener St 78240
Kleberg 78250
Klein 78204
Klein Cir 78266
Kleir Oak 78232
Kless Dr 78242
Klondike St 78245
Knapwood 78248
Knibbe Ave 78209
Knight Robin Dr 78209
Knighthood 78254
Knights Hvn 78233
Knights Walk 78231
Knights Banner 78258
Knights Cross Dr 78258
Knights Knoll Dr 78254
Knights Peak 78254
Knights Wood 78231
Knob Hl 78258
Knob Oak 78250
Knobsby Way 78253
Knoke St 78237
N Knoll 78240
Knoll Rdg 78263
Knoll Krest St 78242
Knoll Tree St 78247
Knollbend 78247
Knollbluff 78247
Knollbranch 78247
Knollchase 78247
Knollcircle 78247
Knollcliff 78247
Knollcreek 78247
Knollcross 78247
Knolldown 78247
Knollforest 78247
Knollgate 78247
Knollglade 78247
Knollhaven 78247
Knollhill 78247
Knollhollow 78247
Knollmanor 78247
Knollmeadow 78247
Knollpass 78247
Knollpine 78247
Knollplace 78247
Knollpoint 78247
Knollpond 78247
Knollrun 78247
Knollshire 78247
Knollspring 78247
Knollstone 78247
Knollstream 78247
Knolltrail 78247
Knollvalley 78247
Knollvista 78247
Knollwood 78247
Knollwood Dr 78227
Knoriem Ln 78257
Knotty Ln 78233
Knotty Knoll St 78219
Knotty Oak Trl 78220
Knottyash Dr 78230
Knowlton Rd 78263
Knox St 78225
Knute Rockne St 78240
Kodiak Diamond 78245
Koehler Ct 78223
Koenig 78251
Koepke Ave 78214
Kokomo St 78209
Kontiki Pl 78242
Kopplow Pl 78221
Korus Trl 78264
Kosub Ln 78223
Kotzebue St 78217
Kraft St 78220
Krameria Dr 78213
Kramme Cir 78217
Krawietz Ln 78223
Krempen Ave 78233
Krempkau St 78212
Krie Trl 78245
Krie Highlands 78245
Kriewald Rd 78245
Kristen Way 78258
Kristidawn 78253
Krocker Way 78207
Krueger Moore 78250
Krugerrand Dr 78232
Krumm Rnch 78253
Kudu St 78253
Kurre Way 78266
Kyle St
1100-1199 78211
1200-1298 78224
Kyle Rote St 78240
Kyle Seale Pkwy
13000-13399 78249
14801-14897 78255
14899-17899 78255
L B J 78253
La Albada St 78233
La Aventura St 78233
La Bahia 78233
La Bahia Way 78253
La Barca St 78233
La Barranca St 78233
La Bodega St 78233
La Canada 78258
La Cantera Pkwy
15900-15988 78256
16201-17199 78256
17400-17999 78257
La Cantera Ter 78256
La Cascada 78258
La Charca St 78233

Street	ZIP
La Cieniga St	78233
La Cima	78229
La Colonia	78218
La Cresenta St	78228
La Cueva St	78233
La Entrada St	78233
La Escalera	78261
La Falda	78258
La Fleur	78249
La Fonda St	78233
La Fuente St	78233
La Garde St	78223
La Garganta	78258
La Gloria St	78237
La Granja	78253
La Hacienda	78237
La Haya St	78233
La Jara Blvd	78209
La Jolla Dr	78233
La Ladera	78258
La Lira St	78233
La Loma St	78233
La Manana St	78233
La Mancia	78258
La Manda Blvd	
100-599	78212
800-2299	78201
La Marquesa St	78233
La Mesa Pl	78227
La Mesilla	78251
La Noche St	78233
La Parada	78261
La Pena Dr	78258
La Peninsula	78248
La Plata St	78233
La Posada St	78233
La Posita St	78233
La Pradero St	78233
La Puerta	78258
La Quinta St	78233
La Ronda Dr	78224
La Rosa St	78211
La Rue St	78217
La Rue Ann Ct	78213
La Sabre Dr	78218
La Salida St	78233
La Salle	78248
La Santa Rd	78253
La Senda St	78233
La Sierra Blvd	78256
La Sombra Dr	78209
La Tapiceria	78261
La Tierra	78258
La Ventana St	78233
La Verita	78258
La Violeta St	78211
La Vista Dr	78216
Labor St	78210
Laburnum Dr	78209
Lacewood Hl	78244
Lacewood St	78233
Lacey St	78203
Lacey James	78258
Lacey Oak	78230
Lacey Oak Cv	78250
Lacey Oak Path	78223
E & W Lachapelle	78204
Lackell Ave	78226
Laclede Ave	78214
Laddie Pl	78201
Laden Crk	78238
Laden Mdws	78245
Ladera Bnd & Rnch	78261
Lado Bueno	78209
Lady Palm Cv	78213
Lafayette Ave	78209
Lafferty Oaks	78245
Lago Del Mar	78211
Lago Frio	78239
Lagoon Dr	78224
Lagos Ave	78209
Laguna Fls	78251
Laguna Rd	78223
W Laguna Rd	78223
Laguna Norte	78239
Laguna Palm	78254
Laguna Rio	78251
Laguna Verde	78239
Laguna Vista Dr	78216
Laheema Hbr	78251
Lahemaa Fls	78251
Laivita Mist	78251
N Lake	78254
Lake Blvd	78201
Lake Frst	78239
Lake Pt	78245
Lake Rd	78223
Lake Trl	78222
Lake Vis	78227
Lake Vlg	78223
Lake Altair St	78222
Lake Arbor St	78222
Lake Arrowhead St	78222
Lake Bank St	78222
Lake Bluff St	78222
Lake Braunig	78223
Lake Bridge Dr	78248
Lake Brook St	78222
Lake Champlain St	78233
Lake Chap St	78222
Lake Cliff St	78244
Lake Cove St	78222
Lake Crystal St	78222
Lake Emerald St	78222
Lake Falls Dr	78222
Lake Fountain	78217
Lake Glen St	78244
Lake Golden	78244
Lake Granbury	78244
Lake Grande St	78222
Lake Grove Dr	78244
Lake Kemp St	78222
Lake Louise Dr	78228
Lake Lucerne St	78222
Lake Matthew	78223
Lake Meadow St	78222
Lake Mitchell	78223
Lake Mont St	78222
Lake Nacoma St	78222
Lake Oak St	78222
W Lake Oaks	78251
Lake Path Dr	78217
Lake Peipsi	78251
Lake Pines St	78222
Lake Placid	78222
Lake Scarborough St	78222
Lake Shoal St	78222
Lake Sonoma	78253
Lake Sunset Ct	78217
Lake Superior St	78222
Lake Tahoe St	78222
Lake Towne Ct	78217
Lake Valley St	78227
Lake Victoria St	78222
Lake Whitney	78253
Lake Wind St	78222
Lakebend East Dr	78244
Lakebend West Dr	78244
Lakebriar St	78222
Lakebury St	78222
Lakecrest St	78222
Lakedale St	78222
Lakedon St	78222
Lakefield St	78230
Lakefront St	78222
Lakehaven	78222
Lakehills St	78251
Lakeland Dr	78222
Lakeledge St	78222
Lakeloma St	78222
Lakemist St	78222
Lakeplains St	78222
Lakeridge Dr	78229
Lakeshore Dr	78218
Lakeside Dr	78248
Lakeside Pkwy	78245
Laketree	78245
Lakeview Ct	78249
Lakeview Dr	78244
Lakeway Dr	78244
Lakewood Dr	78220
Lakewood Park	78239
Lakota Winter	78261
Lamar	78202
Lamar Brg	78249
Lamb Rd	78240
Lambda Dr	78245
E & W Lambert St	78204
Lambeth Dr	78228
Lame Beaver	78260
Lamerton St	78250
Lamm	78204
Lamm Rd	78221
Lamont Ave	78209
Lampasas Trl	78253
Lampost Rd	78213
Lanark Dr	78218
Lancashire Dr	78230
Lancaster	78214
Lancaster Gap	78247
Lance St	78237
Lancelot Dr	78218
Lancer Blvd	78219
Lancewood Dr	78227
Lancrest Dr	78224
Landa Ave	78237
Landers Farm	78228
Landing Ave	78227
Landis Dr	78219
Landmark Dr	78218
Landmark Hl	78217
Landmark 35 Dr	78233
Lands End	78231
Lands Point St	78250
Lands Pond	78253
Lands Run St	78230
Lands Wake	78247
Lane Dr	78263
Lanerose Pl	78251
Langdon Dr	78260
Langford Pl	78221
Langport	78239
Langton Dr	78216
Langtry St	78248
Lanier Blvd	78221
Lansbury Dr	78250
Lansing Ln	78207
Lantana Bnd	78251
Lantana Cv	78253
Lantana Dr	78217
Lantana Fls	78261
Lantana Rdg	78258
Lantana Way	78258
Lantana Leaf	78253
Lantana Sun	78244
Lantern Crk	78240
Lantern Ln	78248
Laramie Dr	78209
Laramie Hl	78233
Laramie Vly	78253
Larchmont Dr	78209
Larco Way	78230
Larcrest Ln	78251
Laredo Rd	78221
N Laredo St	78207
S Laredo St	
200-298	78207
800-1000	78204
1002-1198	78204
1140-1140	78283
1140-1140	78207
1200-1398	78204
1601-1607	78207
1609-3599	78207
Lari Dawn	78258
Lariat Cv	78260
Lariat Dr	78232
Larimer Sq	78249
Lark Ave	78228
Lark Rdg	78250
Lark Run	78256
Lark Xing	78250
Lark Haven Ln	78263
Lark Valley Dr	78242
Larkabbey St	78233
Larkbrook St	78233
Larkdale Dr	78233
Larkfield Dr	78233
Larkgate Dr	78233
Larkhill	78228
Larkhill Farm	78244
Larkia St	78224
Larklair St	78233
Larkmeadow Dr	78233
Larkplace Dr	78233
Larkshall Ct	78253
Larksong St	78238
Larkspur	78213
Larkstone St	78232
Larkwalk St	78233
Larkway St	78233
Larkwood Dr	78209
Larkyorke St	78233
Larleren Dr	78240
Larmona Cv	78266
Larry	78202
Larson Cavern	78254
Las Aguas	78258
Las Brisas St	78233
Las Campanas St	78233
Las Casitas	78261
Las Cimas Dr	78266
Las Cruces St	78233
Las Gravas	78253
Las Jollas	78245
Las Lomas Blvd	78258
N & S Las Moras St	78207
Las Nubes St	78233
Las Olas Blvd	78250
Las Palmas Dr	78237
Las Puertas	78245
Las Scala St	78233
Las Vegas St	78233
Las Vistas	78258
Lasalle Way	78253
Lasater St	78254
Lasses Blvd	78223
Lassiter Ln	78250
Lasso Bnd	78260
Lasso Dr	78218
Lasswell	78211
Last Run	78260
Latch Dr	78213
Lateleaf Oak	78223
Latigo Bnd	78245
Latigo Plz	78227
Latigo St	78227
Latimer St	78220
Latrobe Post	78240
Lattigo Trl	78245
Lattimer Pond	78254
Laudie Fox	78253
Laura Dr	78239
Laura Ln	78219
Laura Jean St	78220
Laura Lee Way	78223
Lauras Farm	78244
Laureate Dr	78249
E Laurel	78212
W Laurel	
101-197	78212
W Laurel	
199-799	78212
900-2799	78201
3101-3105	78228
3107-3499	78228
Laurel Bnd	78250
Laurel Fld	78260
Laurel Gln	78260
Laurel Grv	78250
Laurel Lk	78245
Laurel Park	78260
Laurel Pass	78260
Laurel Pl	78209
Laurel Pt	78260
Laurel Rdg	78253
Laurel Spgs	78260
Laurel Trl	78240
Laurel Way	78260
Laurel Berry	78260
Laurel Bloom	78260
Laurel Heights Pl	78212
Laurel Hollow Dr	78232
Laurel Meadow St	78253
Laurel Oak Way	78223
Laurel Oaks St	78240
Laurel Pathway	78245
Laurel Sky	78245
Laurel Valley Dr	78242
Laurelbrook	78249
Laurelcrest Pl	78209
Laurelhill Dr	78229
Laurelhurst Dr	78209
Laurelwood Dr	78213
Lauren Ashley	78237
Lauren Mist	78251
Laurens Ct	78250
Laurens Ln	78218
Laurie Michelle Rd	78261
Lavaca Crk	78258
Lavaca St	78210
Lavel Spg	78249
Laven Dr	78228
Lavender Hl	78245
Lavender Ln	78220
Lavenham	78254
Laverne Ave	78237
Lavonia Pl	78214
Law Crk	78254
Lawn Valley Dr	78242
Lawn View St	78220
E & W Lawndale Dr	78209
Lawnwood Dr	78227
Lawrey Dr	78259
Lawton St	78237
Layback Crk	78253
Laza St	78207
Lazy Blf	78216
Lazy Ln	78209
Lazy Trl	78250
Lazy Clover	78261
Lazy Creek St	78242
Lazy Dove	78253
Lazy Forest St	78233
Lazy Fox	78266
Lazy Hollow St	78230
Lazy K	78253
Lazy Nook	78216
Lazy Oaks Dr	78217
Lazy Pebble	78254
Lazyridge Dr	78229
Lazywood Trl	78216
Le Blanc St	78247
Lea Vis	78258
Leading Oaks St	78233
Leafwood Dr	78227
Leafy Ln	78233
Leafy Rdg	78251
Leafy Hollow Ct	78233
Leahy St	
901-999	78221
1000-1099	78211
Leakey	78251
Leal Rd	78264
Leal St	
601-697	78207
699-2799	78207
16100-20099	78221
Leander	78251
Leatherstocking	78260
Leatherwood	78231
Lebanon St	78223
Lecompte Pl	78214
Ledbury	78253
Ledge Holw	78232
Ledge Ln	78212
Ledge Run	78255
Ledge Trl	78232
Ledge Creek St	78232
Ledge Falls St	78232
Ledge Oaks St	78232
Ledge Park St	78232
Ledge Path St	78232
Ledge Point St	78232
Ledge Quail	78250
Ledge Rock St	78232
Ledge Sage St	78232
Ledge View St	78232
Ledge Way St	78232
Ledgebrook Dr	78244
Ledgeside	78251
Ledgestone Dr	78232
Ledgewood St	78233
Lee St	78214
Lee Hall	
800-899	78212
Lee Hall	
900-2499	78201
Lee Trevino	78221
Leesburg St	78220
Leeward Ln	78263
Leewood Dr	78230
Leff Pl	78221
Legacy Park	78257
Legacy Rdg	78260
Legend Crst	78260
Legend Dl	78260
Legend Fls	78253
Legend Gln	78260
Legend Hts	78253
Legend Knl	78260
Legend Ln	78256
Legend Bend Dr	78230
Legend Breeze	78260
Legend Cave Dr	78230
Legend Creek Dr	78230
Legend Elm	78247
Legend Field Dr	78230
Legend Isle Dr	78254
Legend Oaks	78259
Legend Point Dr	
7400-7599	78244
21900-22099	78258
Legend Ranch Dr	78230
Legend Rock	78244
Legend Springs Dr	78247
Legend Well Dr	78247
Legends Ct	78257
Lehman Dr	78219
Leigh St	78210
Leighs Pt	78251
Leisure Dr	78201
Lelani St	78242
Lemans	78258
Leming Dr	78201
Lemon Cv	78258
Lemon Blossom	78247
Lemon Drop	78245
Lemon Tree St	78245
Lemonmint Pkwy	78245
Lemonwood Dr	78213
Lemur Dr	78213
Lenard St	78211
Lendell St	78249
Lennon Ave	78223
Lennox	78218
Lensgrove Ln	78251
Lenten Rose	78259
Leon Creek Dr	78257
Leona Riv	78253
N Leona St	78207
S Leona St	78207
Leonard	78239
Leonhardt Rd	78233
Leonidas Dr	78220
Leopard Holw & Path	78251
Leopard Claw	78251
Leopard Hunt	78251
Leopold St	78210
Leroux St	78207
Les Harrison Dr	78250
Leslie Rd	78254
Leslie Carson	78258
Leslie Nicole	78237
Lester Ave	78211
Lesters Way	78254
Letcombe	78254
Letitia Ln	78217
Levelland	78251
Levi Ln	78260
Lewis Rdg	78245
Lewis St	78212
Lewiston St	78254
Lexi Petal	78253
Lexington Ave	
100-198	78205
201-297	78215
299-400	78215
402-598	78215
700-898	78212
Leyland	78239
Leyte St	78217
Liatris Ln	78259
Liberty	78223
Liberty Fld	78254
Liberty Grn	78245
Liberty Is	78227
Liberty Pt	78254
Liberty Bell St	78233
Liberty Oak St	78232
Liberty Sky Dr	78254
Liberty Stone	78244
Lichen	78214
Lida Rose Dr	78216
Liedecke Rd	78264
Light Bnd	78217
Light Hl	78258
Light House Cv	78242
Light Keeper	78252
Lightning	78238
Lightstone Dr	78258
Lignoso	78261
Liguria Dr	78266
E & W Ligustrum Dr	78228
Lilac Ct	78261
Lilac Ln	78209
Lilac Blossom St	78247
Lilac Dawn	78253
Lilac Mist	78260
Lilac Willow	78253
Lilla Jean Dr	78223
Lillita Ct	78237
Lilly Vly	78254
Lilly Crest Dr	78232
Lilly Flower	78253
Lily Wls	78249
Lily Blair	78253
Lily Pad Ln	78224
Lily Rise	78251
Lima Dr	78213
Lime Blossom St	78247
Lime House	78239
Limelight Dr	78216
Limestone Flt	78251
Limestone Hl	78254
Limestone Rdg	78255
Limestone Trl	78253
Limestone Way	78253
Limestone Creek Rd	78232
Limestone Mill Dr	78244
Limestone Oak	78230
Limestone Pond	78254
Limestone Well Dr	78247
Limpia Crk	78254
Limpio St	78233
Limpkin Ct	78245
Linares St	78225
Linbrooke	78250
Lincoln Crk	78254
Lincoln St	78207
Lincoln Village Dr	78244
Lincolnshire Dr	78220
Linda Dr	78216
Linda Vis	78218
Linda Colonia St	78233
Linda Kay Dr	78222
Linda Lou Dr	78223
Lindal Pointe	78260
Lindaver Ln	78260
Lindbergh Lndg	78235
Lindell Pl	78212
Lindell Wl	78260
Lindeman St	78211
Linden Ave	78211
Lindenwood Dr	78209
Lindquist	78248
Lindseys Cv	78258
N Line Camp St	78255
Linfield St	78238
Link	78213
Linkcrest	78240
Linklea	78240

Street	ZIP
Linkmeadow St	78240
Links Cv	78260
Links Grn	78257
Links Ln	78260
Linkside St	78240
Linkview St	78240
Linkway St	78240
Linkwood St	78240
Linn Rd	78223
Linn Lake Dr	78244
Linus St	78238
Lion Path & Way	78251
Lion Chase	78251
Lion Forrest	78251
Lion Hunt	78251
Lion King	78251
Lion Moon	78251
Lionheart Park	78240
Lirio Dr	78207
Lisa Dr	78228
Lisbon	78213
Liscum Hl	78258
Liser Gln	78257
Lisianthus	78253
Lismore	78260
Litchfield Dr	78230
Little Bnd	78250
Little Brk	78260
Little Ln	78229
Little Angel Cv	78245
Little Bear St	78242
Little Beaver St	78242
Little Brandywine Crk	78233
Little Creek St	78242
Little Fawn St	78238
Little Feather St	78242
Little Geronimo St	78254
Little Joe Trl	78253
Little John	78260
Little John Dr	78209
Little Laurie Dr	78245
Little Leaf Dr	78247
Little Oaks St	78233
Little Squaw St	78242
Little Walnut Dr	78264
Little Wolf St	78242
Little Wren Ln	78255
Littlemill	78259
Littleport	78239
Littlewood St	78238
Live Pt	78250
Live Oak	78202
Live Oak Vis	78250
Live Oak Way Dr	78240
Lively Dr	78213
Liverpool	78251
Livewater Trl	78245
Livingston	78214
Llano St	78223
Llano Ledge	78256
Llano Sound	78258
Lloyd Hughes	78260
Lloyds Park	78266
Lobelia St	78232
Lobo Ln	78240
Lobo Montana	78253
Loch Maree	78240
Lochaven Ln	78213
Lochglen	78240
Lochmoor	78244
Lochshire St	78216
Lock Lomond Ln	78220
Lockberry Ln	78251
Locke St	78208
Lockend St	78238
Locker Ln	78238
Lockhart	78202
Lockhill Rd	78240
Lockhill Selma Rd	
601-799	78216
800-1899	78213
1901-2199	78213
2201-2497	78230
2499-3400	78230
3402-3898	78230
4300-4598	78249
4600-4699	78249
Lockinver Ln	78251
Locknere Ln	78213
Lockridge St	78254
Locksley St	78254
Lockspring	78254
Lockway St	78217
E Locust St	78212
Lodge Arbor	78253
Lodi Rd	78222
Loessberg Ln	78252
Lofty Hts	78232
Logan	78202
Logwood Ave	78221
Logwood Way	78254
Lola Rdg	78252
Loma Vw E & W	78259
Loma Alto Rd	78232
Loma Azul	78233
Loma Blanca	78233
Loma Bonita	78233
Loma Chica	78233
Loma Corona	78233
Loma Grande Dr	78233
Loma Linda Dr	78201
Loma Park Dr	78228
Loma Secca	78233
Loma Sierra	78233
Loma Vallejo	78233
Loma Verde	78264
Loma Viento	78233
Loma Vino	78233
Loma Vista St	78207
Lombard Dr	78226
Lombrano St	
100-198	78207
200-1699	78207
1701-2199	78207
2600-2999	78228
Lomita St	78230
Lomita Creek Dr	78247
Lomita Springs Dr	78247
Lon Chaney Dr	78240
London Hts	78254
Londondary Dr	78260
Londonderry St	78254
Lone Cir	78260
Lone Eagle St	78238
Lone Oak Ave	78220
Lone Shadow Trl	78233
Lone Star Blvd	78204
Lone Star Pass	78264
Lone Star Pkwy	78253
Lone Summit St	78247
Lone Tree St	78247
Lone Valley St	78247
Lone Wolf Trl	78232
Lonehill Ct	78227
Lonesome Pine St	78247
Long Trl	78245
Long Arrow	78258
Long Bow Rd	78231
Long Branch St	78211
Long Creek St	78247
Longacre St	78233
Longbranch Run	78261
Longfellow Blvd	78217
Longfield St	78248
Longhorn Crk	78261
Longhorn Xing	78245
Longhouse Ct	78238
Longing Trl	78244
Longleaf St	78219
Longleaf Coral	78247
Longleaf Palm	78233
Longmeadow Dr	78224
Longmire Trce	78245
Longmont St	78245
Longridge Dr	78228
Longsford	78209
Longvale Dr	78217
Longview Dr	78220
Longwood	78259
Lookout Blf	78258
Lookout Bnd	78233
Lookout Ct	78260
Lookout Cv	78260
Lookout Dr	78228
Lookout Fls	78260
Lookout Frst	78260
Lookout Pt	78260
Lookout Rd	78233
Lookout Rdg	78233
Lookout Run	78233
Lookout Way	78233
Lookout Mesa	78255
Lookout Oaks	78260
Lookover St	78209
Loon Ct	78245
Loop St	78212
Loop 106	78263
E Loop 1604 N	78233
E Loop 1604 S	
9201-9397	78263
E Loop 1604 S	
9399-13299	78263
14000-15399	78223
N Loop 1604 E	
100-2899	78232
3500-3598	78247
3600-6999	78247
7000-7099	78266
7501-7697	78233
7699-7700	78233
7702-7798	78233
N Loop 1604 W	
101-419	78232
421-999	78232
1100-2698	78248
1201-2699	78258
3000-4198	78231
4001-4099	78257
4201-4797	78249
4799-7600	78249
7602-9298	78249
8401-8499	78255
8601-9299	78249
S Loop 1604 E	78264
S Loop 1604 W	78264
W Loop 1604 N	
300-398	78245
400-3200	78251
3202-5798	78251
5301-5699	78253
6101-6497	78254
6499-11499	78254
11501-11899	78254
W Loop 1604 S	
1601-1699	78245
2800-3598	78245
8500-9798	78252
9800-12899	78252
NE Loop 410	
1-400	78216
402-698	78216
700-1699	78209
1701-1797	78217
1799-2799	78217
2800-4200	78218
4202-6298	78218
6800-6898	78219
6900-9500	78219
9502-9598	78219
NW Loop 410	
101-397	78216
399-899	78216
1000-2099	78213
2101-2199	78213
2200-3199	78230
3200-3299	78213
3500-3598	78229
3600-3698	78201
3700-3798	78229
3800-5399	78229
5401-5499	78229
5500-7199	78238
7200-7599	78245
7600-7698	78227
7601-7799	78245
SE Loop 410	
401-997	78220
999-2299	78220
2401-2497	78222
2499-5399	78222
5401-5999	78222
7900-9398	78223
9400-9499	78223
10600-10698	78214
11601-12097	78221
12099-12200	78221
12202-12298	78221
SW Loop 410	
101-399	78245
501-597	78227
599-1531	78227
1533-2899	78227
1538-1598	78224
1600-2098	78227
2300-2404	78224
2410-2426	78227
2428-2432	78224
2434-2898	78227
2900-2998	78224
2901-2999	78211
3101-3299	78227
3700-4498	78227
4700-4799	78211
5201-5497	78227
5499-5599	78227
5601-6899	78227
7200-9400	78242
9402-9498	78242
10700-10799	78211
12501-13999	78224
15101-15399	78221
Loper Bldg	78205
Lord Rd	78220
Lord Curtis	78254
Lordsport	78239
Lorelarb	78252
Lorelei Dr	78229
Lorene Ln	78216
Lorenz Rd	78209
Loretta Pl	78210
Lori Way	78258
Lorimor Ct	78258
Lorita Dr	78214
Lorna Doone St	78254
Lorraine Ave	78214
Los Arboles	78214
Los Campos St	78233
Los Cerdos St	78233
Los Cerros St	78233
Los Espanada St	78233
Los Indios St	78233
Los Palacias St	78233
Los Ranchitos St	78233
Los Reyes St	78233
Los Santos	78214
Loska Grn & Mnr	78251
Losoya St	78205
Lost Blf	78240
Lost Bnd	78240
Lost Crk	78247
Lost Cyn	78258
Lost Ln	78238
Lost Rnch	78254
Lost Trl	78218
Lost Vly	78255
Lost Arbor Cir	78240
Lost Arrow	78258
Lost Cabin St	78232
Lost Forest St	78233
Lost Hilltop St	78230
Lost Holly	78240
Lost Lake Dr	78249
Lost Maples	78253
Lost Mine Trl	78245
Lost Ridge Dr	78233
Lost Spring Dr	78256
Lost Star	78258
Lost Timbers	78248
Lost Tree	78244
Lost Woods	78240
Loststone	78258
Lotus Ave	78210
Lotus Rdg	78253
Lotus Walk	78245
Lotus Blossom St	78247
Lou St	78222
Lou Gehrig St	78240
Lou Jon Cir	78213
Lou Mell Ln	78249
Louis Agusta	78253
Louis Bauer Dr	78235
Louis Pasteur Ct & Dr	78229
Louisa Allen Ct	78240
Louisburg Dr	78245
Louise	78201
Louisiana St	78210
Lovela Bnd	78254
Lovelace Blvd	78217
Lovera Blvd	
100-799	78212
800-1199	78201
Lovetree St	78232
Lovett Ave	78211
Lovett Oaks	78218
Loving Ml	78253
Low Crk	78255
Low Bid Ln	78250
Low Oak St	78232
Lowell St	78210
Lowery Dr	78228
Lowland St	78211
Lowry Peterson	78227
Loy Dr	78228
Loy Morris	78261
Loyal Vly	78251
Loyola St	78249
Lubbers Way	78242
E & W Lubbock St	78204
Lucas Cir	78245
Lucas St	78209
Lucca Mist	78260
Lucerne	78218
Lucinda St	78221
Luckenbach Rd	78251
Luckey Fls, Path, Pne, Run, Smt, Sq, Vis & Vw	78252
Luckey Flower	78252
Luckey Ledge	78252
Luckey Pond	78252
Luckey Tree	78252
Lucky Draw	78250
Lucky Oaks St	78233
Lucky Streak	78227
Lucrezia	78253
Ludgate	78239
Ludlow Ct	78239
Ludlow Trl	78244
Ludtke Ave	78221
Ludwig St	78210
Lugo Way	78253
Luisa	78259
Lula Mae	78219
E Lullwood Ave	78212
W Lullwood Ave	
100-899	78212
900-1699	78201
Luna Ct	78211
Luna Vis	78255
Lunar St	78219
Lunber Sound	78252
Lundblade Ln	78213
Lundys Ln	78239
Lura Ln	78228
Luther Dr	78212
Lux Ln	78210
Luxemburg Dr	78237
Luz Ave	78237
Luz Del Faro	78261
Luzita Ln	78230
Luzon Dr	78217
Lyceum Dr	78229
Lyell St	78211
Lyia Br	78252
Lyman Dr	78209
Lynbrook Manor Dr	78254
Lynda Sue Dr	78257
Lyndell Spgs	78244
Lyndys Farm	78244
Lynette St	78209
Lynfield Ct	78220
Lyngrove St	78249
Lynhaven Dr	78220
Lynhurst Ave	78223
Lynn Anne St	78240
Lynn Batts Ln	78218
Lynn Kaye Cir	78217
Lynn Lake Dr	78244
Lynridge Dr	78260
E Lynwood Ave	78212
W Lynwood Ave	
100-899	78212
900-1599	78201
1601-1699	78201
Lynx Bnd, Mtn & Xing	78251
Lynx Range	78251
Lyons St	78207
Lyric St	78223
Lyster Rd	78235
Lytle Ave	78224
M Bank Alamo Bldg	78205
M G Rd	78251
Mabe Rd	78251
Mabelle Dr	78233
Mabry Dr	78226
Mabuni Dr	78218
Macarthur Vw	78217
Macaw	78218
Macaway Crk	78244
Macdona St	
5700-5799	78211
5801-5899	78211
6100-6499	78221
Mace St	78213
Macey Trl & Way	78253
Macgregor Way	78240
Macias Way	78207
Mack Dr	78263
Mackenzie	78247
Mackey Dr	78213
Macrae Ln	78219
Macro	78218
Maddie Ln	78255
Maddux St	78227
Madeleine Dr	78229
Madero St	78207
Madison	78204
Madison Fls	78245
Madison Park	78260
Madison Oak Dr	78258
Madonna	78216
Madrid St	78237
Madrigal St	78233
Madrona St	78245
Madrugada	78261
Magell St	78207
Magellan	78239
Magendie St	78210
Maggie Ct	78240
Magic Cyn	78252
Magic Dr	78229
Magic Fls	78266
Magic Vw	78260
Magic Oaks	78239
Magna Vista Ct	78258
Magnes St	78227
Magnifico St	78233
E Magnolia Ave	78212
W Magnolia Ave	
100-899	78212
900-2399	78201
2400-2499	78228
Magnolia Blf	78218
Magnolia Bnd	78251
Magnolia Brk	78247
Magnolia Crst	78251
Magnolia Dr	78212
Magnolia Fld	78251
Magnolia Fls	78261
Magnolia Grv	78245
Magnolia Hl	78251
Magnolia Riv	78251
Magnolia Run	78251
Magnolia Smt	78251
Magnolia Spg	78253
Magnolia Blossom	78247
Magnolia Mist	78216
Magnum	78228
Maguey Trl	78245
Mahabo	78218
Mahala Blf	78254
Mahogany Cv	78261
Mahogany Run	78232
Mahogany Chest	78249
Mahogony Trl	78255
Mahota Dr	78227
Mai Kai Dr	78242
Maiden Ln	78228
Maiden Hair	78258
Maidenstone Dr	78250
N Main Ave	
100-298	78205
300-799	78205
801-899	78205
900-908	78212
910-2799	78212
2801-3699	78212
S Main Ave	78204
E Main Plz	78205
W Main Plz	78205
Mainland Blf	78250
Mainland Dr	
7401-7497	78250
7499-8099	78250
8100-8121	78240
8123-8199	78240
8200-8299	78250
Mainland Rdg	78250
Mainland Woods	78250
Maitland	78259
Majestic Dr	78228
Majestic Grv	78258
Majestic Pt	78242
Majestic Vw	78258
Majestic Way	78257
Majestic Oak Cir	78255
Majestic Prince St	78248
Majestic Sage	78261
Malabar Cyn	78245
Malabar Peak	78261
Malacca Dr	78218
Malaga Way	78257
Malapai Park	78249
Malar Ave	78214
Malaya	78218
Malcolm St	78221
Malibu Dr	78239
Malibu Colony	78259
Malim Dr	78222
Malinced	78202
Malintri St	78210
Malkin Pl	78254
Mall View St	78233
Mallard Hvn	78260
Mallard Pt	78239
Mallard St	
100-398	78211
900-998	78224
Mallory Ln	78257
Mallow	78239
Mallow Grv	78253
E Mally Blvd	78221
W Mally Blvd	
100-1099	78221
1200-2299	78224
E Malone Ave	78214
W Malone Ave	
100-198	78214
200-599	78214
600-2100	78225
2102-2298	78225
Maloy Mnr	78250
Malta St	78224
Maltese Gdn & Ln	78260
Maltsberger Ln	78216
Malvern Dr	78250
Man O War	78248
Manassas Dr	78240
Mancero Park	78230
Manchester Dr	78223
Manchester Way	78249
Manda Dr	78239
E & W Mandalay Dr	78212
Mandell	78240

Mandolin Wind 78258
Mandolino Ln 78266
Manes Grv 78247
Mango 78221
Mangrove Dr 78260
Manhattan Dr 78219
Manhattan Way 78261
Manila Dr 78217
Manitou 78228
Manitou Bay 78259
Manning Dr 78228
Mannix Dr 78217
Manor Crk 78245
Manor Dr 78228
Manor Hl 78257
Manor Heights Dr 78231
Manor Ridge Ct 78258
Manoway St 78224
Manoway Bay 78223
Mansfield 78251
Mansions Blfs 78245
Mantle Dr 78258
N & S Manton Ln 78213
Many Oaks St 78232
Manzanita St 78245
Manzano St 78211
Maple Crst 78261
Maple Rnch 78245
W Maple St 78212
Maple Vis 78247
Maple Vly 78227
Maple Brook Dr 78232
Maple Glade 78247
Maple Lake St 78244
Maple Leaf 78254
Maple Park Dr 78249
Maple Ridge Dr 78239
Maple Silver 78254
Maple Springs St 78249
Maplerock St 78230
Mapleton St 78230
Mapletree St 78249
W Maplewood Ln & St 78216
Marancot 78284
Maraval Crk 78245
Marbach Bnd 78245
Marbach Crst 78245
Marbach Cyn 78245
Marbach Ln 78266
Marbach Pass 78245
Marbach Rd
6900-7098 78227
7100-8800 78227
8802-8898 78227
9000-10899 78245
10901-11899 78245
Marbach Oaks 78245
Marbach Woods 78245
Marbauch Ave 78237
Marbella Ct 78257
Marbella Vis 78258
Marble Cv 78242
Marble Lk 78233
Marble Pt 78251
Marble Spg 78258
Marble Spur 78245
Marble Creek Dr 78238
Marble Glade 78245
Marble Tree St 78247
Marblehill Dr 78240
Marceline 78232
March Rd 78214
Marchesi 78258
Marchmont Ln 78213
Marcia Pl 78209
Marco Crst 78233
Marco Polo 78239
Marconi St 78228
Marcum Dr 78227
Marcus Dr 78216
Marcy Rte 78245
Mardell St 78201
Mare Trce 78254
Mare Country 78254
Mare Hunt 78254
Marek St 78224
Marella Dr 78248
Marengo Ln 78254
Mares Mdws 78247
Margaret St 78209
Margate St 78232
Margil St 78225
Margo St 78223
Maria Aly 78207
Maria Elena 78228
Maria Isabell Dr 78211
Marian St
100-198 78204
800-1098 78225
2001-2099 78225
Maribelle 78228
Maricopa 78239
Maricopa Path 78266
Maridel St 78237
Marie Mdw 78266
Marietta St 78237
Marigold Bay 78254
Marigold Trace St 78233
Marilyn Kay St 78238
Marimba Pl 78227
Marin Hls 78259
Marina Dr 78250
Marina Bay 78242
Mariner St 78242
Marion Rd 78209
E Mariposa Dr 78212
W Mariposa Dr
100-599 78212
800-1799 78201
Mariposa Grv 78251
Mariposa Pass 78251
Marisa Pl 78247
Marjorie Dr 78204
Mark Dr 78218
Mark Alan 78261
Mark Osborne St 78255
Mark Wayne 78261
Market Hl 78256
E Market St 78205
W Market St 78205
Markham Gln 78247
Markham Ln 78247
Markham St 78230
Markham Woods 78247
Marlark Pass 78261
Marlay 78204
Marlborough Dr 78230
Marlena Dr 78213
Marley Rock 78253
Marlin Flts & Mdw 78244
Marlinton Way 78230
Marlowe Dr 78226
Marmok Ave 78220
Marne Rd 78257
Marney 78221
Maroon Crk 78260
Marquette Dr 78228
Marquis St 78216
Marriott Dr 78229
Marrogot Run St 78233
Mars St 78226
Marseilles St 78219
Marsh Creek Dr 78250
Marsh Pond 78260
Marshall Blf 78261
Marshall Pass 78240
Marshall Pt 78240
Marshall Rd 78259
Marshall St 78212
Marshall Cross 78214
Marshwood St 78228
Martesia 78259
Martha Rd 78264
Martha Walk 78220
Martha Glynn Ct 78213
E Martin St 78205
W Martin St
301-399 78205
900-4499 78207
4500-4600 78237
4602-4898 78237
Martin Luther King Dr
300-2300 78203
2302-2498 78203
2700-3599 78220
Martinelli 78253
Martinez St
300-398 78205
15400-16399 78221
Martinez Losoya Rd 78221
Martinique Dr 78227
Martins Ferry St 78247
Marty Dr 78217
Marufo Vega 78245
Marwhite St 78227
Mary 78214
Mary Pt 78260
Mary Abbott St 78221
Mary Carolyn St 78240
Mary D Ave 78209
Mary Diane Dr 78220
Mary Helen Dr 78222
Mary Jamison St 78238
Mary Louise Dr 78201
Mary Todd Dr 78240
Maryland St 78203
Marymont Dr & Park 78217
Mas Frio 78223
Mascasa St 78237
Mascota St 78237
Mason Pass 78264
Mason St 78208
Mason Crest Dr 78247
Mason King 78260
Massaro St 78251
Massena Park 78233
Masset Way 78230
Massie Rnch 78253
Masters Ave 78211
Masterson Rd 78252
Matagorda Cv 78223
Matagorda St 78210
Matamoros St 78207
Matchlock Cir 78249
Mateo Ln 78237
Mathews Park 78233
Mathis Cir 78264
Mathis Ln 78264
Mathis Mdw 78251
Mathis Rd 78264
Matthews Ave
100-399 78207
400-899 78237
Matyear St 78237
Mauerman
100-198 78204
Mauerman
600-699 78225
Mauermann Rd 78224
Maui Sands 78255
Mauna Kea St 78213
Maurer Rnch 78253
Maurine Dr 78223
Maury St 78225
Maury Arch 78245
Mauze Dr 78216
Maverick Crk 78247
Maverick Hl 78250
Maverick Pass 78240
Maverick Pt 78240
Maverick Rnch 78254
Maverick St 78212
Maverick Bluff St 78247
Maverick Climb 78250
Maverick Draw 78250
Maverick Gap 78250
Maverick Oak Dr 78240
Maverick Ridge Dr 78240
Maverick Rim 78250
Maverick Trail Dr 78240
Max Rd 78223
Maxine Dr 78228
Maxwell 78214
Maxwell Gln 78257
May 78202
Mayberry Ave 78228
Mayborough Ln 78257
Maybrook Woods St 78249
Maycrest 78250
Mayfair Dr 78217
Mayfair Farm 78244
E Mayfield Blvd 78214
W Mayfield Blvd
100-399 78221
400-2099 78211
Mayflower St 78209
Mayhill Dr 78249
Mayo Dr 78227
Maypole St 78232
Maysey Dr 78227
Mayspring 78217
Maywood Dr 78230
Mazattan Way 78256
Mazzurana St 78207
Mc Bride Dr 78255
Mcadoo Aly 78208
Mcallister Ct 78201
Mcallister Fwy 78216
Mcarthur Ave 78211
Mcaskill 78204
Mcbeath 78239
Mccarty Rd 78216
Mccaskey Rdg 78258
Mccauley Ave 78224
Mccauley Blvd 78221
Mccluskey Ct 78252
Mccormick St 78247
Mccoy Bnd 78245
Mccullough Ave
100-999 78215
1100-5499 78212
5501-5999 78212
7000-7538 78216
7540-10099 78216
10101-10299 78216
Mcdavitt Rd 78227
Mcdermonts Farm St 78233
Mcdonald 78210
Mcdonald Oak 78223
Mcdougal Ave 78223
Mcfaddin 78261
Mcgowen Fld 78227
Mchenry Dr 78239
Mcilvaine
500-699 78212
Mcilvaine
900-1299 78201
Mcinnis Rd 78222
Mcivey Way 78233
Mckay Ave 78204
Mckays Lark 78253
Mckenna Ave 78211
Mckeon Dr 78218
Mckerle 78214
Mckinley Ave 78210
Mcknight Rnch 78245
Mclane St 78212
Mclaughlin Ave 78211
Mclennan Oak 78240
Mcleod 78201
Mcmillan Pl 78210
Mcmonigal Pl 78210
Mcmullen St 78210
Mcnabb Cir 78258
Mcnarney St 78211
Mcneel Rd 78228
Mcnutt St 78222
Mcqueen Pl 78240
Mcwilliams 78257
Meadow Cir 78231
Meadow Cv 78250
Meadow Dr 78251
Meadow Fld 78250
Meadow Gdn 78227
Meadow Grv 78239
Meadow Hl 78251
Meadow Hvn 78239
Meadow Pass 78251
Meadow Plns 78254
Meadow Pt 78239
Meadow Rue 78266
Meadow Run 78251
Meadow Vis 78260
Meadow Wls 78254
Meadow Bea 78251
Meadow Bend Dr 78227
Meadow Breeze Dr 78227
Meadow Briar St 78247
Meadow Cliff St 78251
Meadow Creek St 78251
Meadow Fire St 78251
Meadow Flower St 78251
Meadow Forest St 78251
Meadow Glade Dr 78227
Meadow Glen Dr 78227
Meadow Green St 78251
Meadow Knoll Dr 78227
Meadow Lawn St 78251
Meadow Leaf Dr 78227
Meadow Park St 78227
Meadow Path Dr 78227
Meadow Pond St 78250
Meadow Post St 78251
Meadow Rain St 78251
Meadow Range St 78250
Meadow Ridge St 78210
Meadow Rise St 78250
Meadow River St 78251
Meadow Rose St 78227
Meadow Side Dr 78227
Meadow Star 78227
Meadow Sun St 78251
Meadow Sunrise Dr 78244
Meadow Swan St 78251
Meadow Thrush St 78231
Meadow Trace St 78250
Meadow Trail Dr 78227
Meadow Tree St 78251
Meadow Valley St 78227
Meadow Way Ct & Dr 78227
Meadow Wind 78227
Meadowalk 78253
Meadowbrook Dr 78232
Meadowcrest Dr 78258
Meadowhome St 78230
N & W Meadowlane
Dr 78209
Meadowlark Ave 78210
Meadowlark Bay 78260
Meadowood Ln 78216
Meadowood Oaks 78254
Meadowview Ln 78228
Meandering Cir 78258
Meashori 78250
Mebane St 78223
Mecca Dr 78232
Med Ct 78258
Medallion St 78245
Medaris Ln 78258
Medford Dr 78209
Medical Dr
3600-5200 78229
5202-5298 78229
5300-5398 78240
Medici 78258
Medina Br 78222
Medina Cir 78264
Medina Cv 78245
Medina Ml 78253
N Medina St 78207
S Medina St 78207
Medina Base Rd
5301-5399 78242
5700-5898 78242
6701-6799 78227
7700-7798 78227
Medina Farm 78222
Medio Crk 78245
Medio Dr 78253
Meeks St
3800-4099 78210
4300-4499 78223
Meerscheidt St
400-599 78203
600-699 78210
Meisner Dr 78258
Melanie Cir 78258
Melba Dr 78216
Melbury Frst 78239
Melinda Ct 78240
Melissa Dr 78213
Melissa Ann St 78249
Melissa Sue 78228
Mellbrook St 78230
Melliff Dr 78216
Mello Oak 78258
Melody Ln 78239
Melody Canyon Dr 78239
Melon St 78247
Melrose 78250
E Melrose Dr 78212
Melrose Pl 78212
Melrose Canyon Dr 78232
Melton 78218
Melvin Dr 78220
Memorial Ln 78264
Memorial St 78228
Memory Ln 78216
Memory Trail St 78232
Menarby Ct 78207
Menard 78251
Menard Cir 78245
Menchaca St
400-598 78207
600-2299 78207
2500-2799 78228
Mendelin Dr 78260
Mendocino Park 78261
Mendoza St 78235
Menefee Blvd
200-298 78207
300-699 78207
700-1699 78237
Menger 78259
Menlo Blvd 78223
Mentana Pl 78258
Mentone Way 78253
Mercado Aly 78207
Mercedes St 78207
Mercer Dr 78245
Merchant 78204
Mercury Dr 78219
Mercy Ln 78237
Meredith Dr 78228
Meredith Woods St 78249
Meri Leap 78251
Merida St
100-102 78207
104-1499 78207
1500-1598 78237
Meridian Ave 78201
Meridian Farm 78244
Merkens Dr
5400-5499 78229
5500-5699 78240
Merlin Dr 78218
Merlin Way 78233
Merlot Way 78260
Merrick 78214
Merriford Ln 78209
Merrimac Cv 78249
Merrimac St 78223
Merritime Ct 78217
Merritt St 78227
Merritt Vis 78253
Merrivale Pl 78257
Merriweather 78223
Merry Trl 78232
Merry Ann Dr 78223
Merry Oaks Dr 78242
Merrywood 78250
Merton Ct 78215
Merton Minter St 78229
Mertz Dr 78216
Mesa Blf 78258
Mesa Bnd 78258
Mesa Crk 78258
Mesa Crst 78258
Mesa Cyn 78258
Mesa Hl 78258
Mesa Holw 78258
Mesa Knl 78258
Mesa Ln 78258
Mesa Loop 78258
Mesa Path 78258
Mesa Rdg 78258
Mesa Rnch 78258
Mesa Run 78258
Mesa Trl 78258
Mesa Vis 78224
Mesa Vly 78258
Mesa Vw 78258
Mesa Walk 78258
Mesa Alta St 78232
Mesa Blanca 78248
Mesa Bonita 78218
Mesa Butte 78258
Mesa Draw 78258
Mesa Glade 78239
Mesa Oak Dr 78255
Mesa Point Dr 78232
Mesa Verde St 78249
Mescal Pass 78252
Mescal Trl 78244
S Mesquite 78210
Mesquite Bnd 78264
Mesquite Crk 78244
Mesquite Cv 78264
Mesquite Holw 78255
Mesquite Rdg 78264
N Mesquite St 78202
S Mesquite St 78203
Mesquite Trl 78253
Mesquite Farm 78239
Mesquite Mesa St 78249
Mesquite Smoke St 78217
Mesquite Way Dr 78240
Messenger Crk 78238
Messenger Pass 78245
Messina 78258
Messina Cyn 78255
Metacomet St 78230
Metcalf 78239
Metro Pkwy 78247
Metz Ave 78223
Mexican Alder 78254
Mexican Plum 78253
Mexican Silver 78254
Miami Dr 78218
Micalet Ct 78249
Michael Ave 78223
E Michael Loop 78253
N Michael Loop 78253
S Michael Loop 78253
W Michael Loop 78253
Michael Brian 78237
Michael Collins St 78219
Michelangelo 78258
Michelle Hl 78266
Michelle Way 78239
Michigan Ave 78201
Mickey Rd 78223
Mickey Mantle Dr 78240
Micklejohn St 78207
Micklejohn Walk St 78207
Mico St 78251
Micron Dr 78251
Mid Circle Dr 78230
Mid Hollow Dr 78230
Mid Walk Dr 78230
Midbury 78259
E & W Midcrest Dr 78228
Midcrown Dr
5400-5598 78218
5600-8099 78218
8100-8899 78239
Middle Frk 78258
Middle Ln 78217
Middle Pt 78250
Middle Oaks Dr 78227
Middlebury Dr 78217
Middlefield Dr 78242
Middleground 78245
Middlex Dr 78217
Mider Dr 78216
Midhorizon Dr 78229
Midland Dr 78219
Midnight Dr 78260
Midnight Pass 78245
Midnight Moon 78245
Midnight Stage 78255

Midnight Watch 78260
Midnight Woods St 78249
Midvale Dr 78229
Midway 78204
Midway Crst 78258
Midway Depot 78255
Miho 78223
Mike Nesmith St 78238
Milam 78202
Milam Bldg 78205
Milan 78258
Mildenhall Ln 78218
Mildred 78214
Milestone 78253
Milford Dr 78213
SE Military Dr
700-1799 78214
1900-3799 78223
3801-3999 78223
4200-4298 78222
4301-4399 78222
100-1999 78221
2101-3199 78224
3200-4000 78211
4002-4098 78211
4600-5298 78242
5300-5400 78242
5402-5598 78242
6501-6797 78227
6799-8199 78227
8201-8399 78227
8600-8699 78245
8701-8999 78245
9407-11699 78251
12300-12399 78253
NW Military Hwy
1600-1698 78213
1700-2299 78213
2300-2400 78231
2402-2498 78231
5900-5999 78257
8400-8498 78231
8500-12799 78231
12801-13399 78231
13400-16899 78231
17200-17299 78257
17301-18699 78257
Military Plz
1-199 78205
Milky Way Dawn 78252
Mill Bnd 78217
Mill Ct 78230
Mill Path 78254
Mill Pne 78254
Mill Rdg 78261
Mill Run 78231
Mill Smt 78254
Mill Vlg 78254
Mill Berger 78254
Mill Creek Dr 78231
Mill Love 78254
Mill Meadow Dr 78247
Mill Oak 78258
Mill Peak 78261
Mill Pond St 78230
Mill River Sq 78245
Mill Rock Rd 78230
Mill Stream St 78238
Mill Valley Dr 78242
Mill Wheel St 78238
Millard St 78212
Millbank Dr 78238
Millbrook Dr 78245
Millchase 78218
Milldale St 78230
Miller Ln 78266
Millers Rdg 78239
Millers Trl 78244
Millgrove St 78230
Millhollow 78258
Milling Rd 78219
Millrock Pass 78233
Millset Way 78253
Millset Chase 78253
Millspring 78230
Millstead St 78230
Millstone Dr 78230
Millsway Dr 78253
Millwood Ln 78216
Milojos Rnch 78245
Milsa Dr 78256
Milton St 78209
Milton Favor 78254
Milvid Ave 78211
Mimosa Blf 78245
Mimosa Dr 78213
Mimosa Mnr 78245
Mimosa Way Dr 78240
Mindie Ln 78253
Mindoro Dr 78217
Miner St 78225
Mineral Crk 78259
Mineral Hls 78260
Mineral Bay 78244
Mineral Springs St 78247
Miners Hl 78244
Miners Pt 78252
Miners Gap 78247
Ming Heights Dr 78230
Mingo St 78224
Mink 78213
Minnetonka St 78210
Minnow Ln 78224
Mint St 78247
Mint Julep 78251
Mint Trail Dr 78232
N & S Minter St 78207
Minthill Dr 78230
Minuteman Dr 78233
Mira Vis 78228
Mira Mesa 78259
Miracle Ln 78237
Miranda Hl 78256
Mirar Pass 78255
Mircom Loop St 78233
Mirecourt 78250
Mirepoix 78232
Miro 78253
Mirror Lk 78260
Miss Ellie Dr 78247
Missile Dr 78217
Mission Bnd 78233
Mission Brk 78223
Mission Cir 78223
Mission Crst 78232
Mission Ct 78223
Mission Cv 78223
Mission Fld 78223
Mission Frst 78251
Mission Mdw 78223
Mission Pass 78223
Mission Pkwy 78223
Mission Rd
100-298 78210
300-1199 78210
1201-1599 78210
1801-2797 78214
2799-8999 78214
Mission Rdg 78232
Mission Run 78223
Mission Spgs 78258
Mission St 78210
Mission Strm 78223
Mission Vis 78223
Mission Vly 78233
Mission Vw 78223
Mission Way 78223
Mission Eagle 78223
Mission Gap 78223
Mission Glory 78223
Mission Grande 78221
Mission Hills Dr 78244
Mission Mill Dr 78233
Mission Oaks St 78232
Mission Rose 78223
Mission Sunrise 78244
Mission Top 78223
Mission Trace St 78230
Mission Verde 78223
Mission Viejo 78232
Mission Woods St 78249
Mississippi St 78210
Missouri Bnd 78247
Missy Ct 78240
Mistic Grv 78247
E Mistletoe Ave 78212
W Mistletoe Ave
100-899 78212
900-2399 78201
2400-2899 78228
Misty Blf 78249
Misty Bnd 78217
Misty Brk 78250
Misty Crk 78232
Misty Cv 78250
Misty Cyn 78250
Misty Frst 78239
Misty Gln 78247
Misty Hl 78250
Misty Knl 78258
Misty Pt 78260
Misty Run 78217
Misty Trl 78254
Misty Vw 78245
Misty Arbor 78266
Misty Breeze 78250
Misty Glade 78247
Misty Hollow St 78224
Misty Lake St 78222
Misty Moon 78250
Misty Park St 78250
Misty Peak 78258
Misty Pine Dr 78220
Misty Plain Dr 78245
Misty Spray Dr 78224
Misty Springs Dr 78244
Misty Valley Dr 78242
Misty Water Ln 78260
Misty Way St 78250
Misty Willow St 78250
Mitchel Mdw 78264
Mitchell Blf 78248
E Mitchell St 78210
W Mitchell St 78204
Mitre Peak 78245
N Mittman 78202
S Mittman St
101-697 78203
699-899 78203
900-998 78210
1000-2299 78210
3700-3899 78223
Moana Dr 78218
Mobeetie Trl 78245
Mobile Bay St 78245
Mobud St 78238
Moccasin Lk 78245
Moccasin St 78238
Mockert 78204
Mocking Bird Ln 78229
Model St 78223
Modena Dr 78218
Modena Bay 78253
Modesta Pl 78247
Modred St 78254
Moffitt Dr 78251
Mogford Rd 78264
Mohawk St 78211
Mohawk Valley St 78233
Mohegan Dr 78228
Molino Ct 78247
Mollys Way Dr 78232
Mona Lisa St 78223
Monaco Cir 78263
Monaco Dr 78218
Monahan Park 78254
Monarch 78259
Monarch Pass 78255
Monarchy Row 78255
Moncayo Dr 78232
Monclova Aly 78207
Mondavi 78258
Mondean St 78240
Monet 78258
Monets Gdn 78218
Money Ln 78227
Money Tree 78232
Monica Pl 78228
Monitor Dr 78228
Monmouth 78239
Monroe St 78210
Mont Blanc 78258
Montague Trl 78245
Montaigne 78258
Montana Mdws 78258
Montana St 78203
Montana Bay 78254
Montauk 78251
Montclair St 78209
Monte Cristo 78239
Monte Leon St 78233
Monte Rio St 78233
Monte Seco 78223
Monte Sereno 78213
Monte Verde 78247
Montebello 78259
Montecino 78258
Montecito St 78233
Montego Rd 78250
Monterey Crst 78251
Monterey St
900-998 78207
1000-3499 78207
4200-6599 78237
6600-6799 78227
Monterrey Oak 78230
Montessa Park 78253
Montessori Dr 78217
Montezuma St 78207
Montfort Dr 78216
Montgomery Cir, Pl & Run 78239
Montgomery Oak 78239
Monticello Ct 78223
Montique Ct 78257
Montivillers 78257
Montpelier Dr 78228
Montrose St 78223
Montrose Wood 78259
Montview 78213
N Monumental 78202
S Monumental St 78203
Moody Cavern 78254
Moon 78204
Moon Lgt 78245
Moon Strm 78253
Moon Walk 78250
Moon Dance St 78238
Moon Lake Dr 78244
Moon Mist 78250
Moon Tide 78250
Moon Valley St 78227
Mooncrest 78247
Moondance Hl 78254
Moondance Peak 78251
Moonglow Dr 78216
Moongold Dr 78222
Moongrove Pass 78239
Moonlight Walk 78260
Moonlight Way 78230
Moonlight Terrace St 78233
Moonlit Cyn 78252
Moonlit Grv 78247
Moonlit Park 78249
Moonlit Ridge Dr 78239
Moonrise 78237
Moonstone Dr 78233
Moonwalk Crst 78254
Moore St 78243
Moores Crk 78233
Mooresfield St 78217
Mooreshill Dr 78253
Moorland 78257
Moorside Dr 78239
Moortown Dr 78238
Mopac Dr 78217
Mora St 78207
Moraga St 78217
Moraima St 78237
Morales St
1000-3799 78207
3800-3899 78237
Morelia 78237
Moreshead St 78231
Moreville Farm 78228
Morey Rd 78227
Morey Peak Dr 78213
Morgan Pointe 78260
Morgans Blf 78216
Morgans Cir 78216
Morgans Crk 78230
Morgans Run 78247
Morgans Peak 78258
Morgans Ridge St 78230
Morino Park 78249
Morning Cir 78247
Morning Crk 78247
Morning Ct 78213
Morning Grn 78257
Morning Lgt 78261
Morning Path 78247
Morning Rdg 78247
Morning Spg 78260
Morning Trl 78247
Morning Vis 78253
Morning Brook St 78247
Morning Dove St 78232
Morning Downs 78257
Morning Fog 78258
Morning Glory Dr 78228
Morning Hill St 78232
Morning Mist St 78230
Morning Oak St 78245
Morning Shadow Ln 78256
Morning Star St 78238
Morning Sun 78228
Morning Tree St 78232
Morning Valley St 78227
Morningbluff Dr 78216
Morningfield 78250
Morningside Dr 78209
Morningview Dr 78220
Morocco St 78216
Morrill Ave 78214
Morris Bldg 78205
Morris Lynn 78261
Morris Witt 78226
Morristown St 78233
Morrow 78204
Morse St 78209
Morton St 78209
Mosaly Ave 78214
Moselle Ave 78237
Moss Bnd 78217
Moss Br 78232
Moss Ct 78217
Moss Dr 78213
Moss Gln 78232
Moss Mdws 78222
Moss Pnes 78232
Moss Ter 78232
Moss Vw 78232
Moss Arbor 78232
Moss Arch 78232
Moss Bluff St 78232
Moss Brook Cv & Dr 78255
Moss Cave 78217
Moss Creek Dr 78238
Moss Farm St 78231
Moss Hollow St 78233
Moss Lake St 78244
Moss Mount Dr 78260
Moss Oak Dr 78229
Moss Peak 78232
Moss Pebble 78255
Moss Plain Dr 78245
Moss Spring Dr 78224
Moss Stone 78232
Moss Tree St 78232
Moss Valley St 78227
Moss Way St 78232
Mossbank Ln 78230
Mosscircle Dr 78224
Mossford 78255
Mossgrove Park 78230
Mossledge Dr 78242
Mossoak Cv 78248
Mossrock 78230
Mossy Grv 78253
Mossy Rdg 78227
Mossy Creek Dr 78245
W Mossy Cup St 78231
Motel Dr 78219
Moten Aly 78202
Motes Dr 78237
Motley Trl 78253
Mount Hvn 78250
Mount Arcadia 78255
Mount Baker 78251
Mount Boracho Dr 78213
Mount Calvary 78209
Mount Capote St 78213
Mount Carillon 78260
Mount Crosby 78251
Mount Defiance St 78233
Mount Eagle St 78232
Mount Eden Dr 78213
Mount Erin Pass 78212
Mount Evans 78251
Mount Everest St 78232
Mount Helen 78251
Mount Hood 78251
Mount Hope St 78230
Mount Ida 78213
Mount Kisco Dr 78213
Mount Laurel Dr 78240
Mount Marcy 78213
Mount Mckinley 78251
Mount Mesabi 78213
Mount Meyer 78254
Mount Michelle St 78213
Mount Perkins 78213
Mount Rainier Dr 78213
Mount Rhapsody 78260
Mount Riga 78213
Mount Royal St 78250
Mount Sacred Heart Rd 78216
Mount Serolod Dr 78213
Mount Tipton 78213
Mount Vernon Ct 78223
Mount Vieja Dr 78213
Mountain 78253
Mountain Blf 78240
Mountain Bnd 78258
Mountain Crst 78258
Mountain Cv 78258
Mountain Fall 78258
Mountain Frst 78239
Mountain Grv 78250
Mountain Loop 78261
Mountain Mdw 78222
Mountain Pne 78254
Mountain Pt 78242
Mountain Vw 78251
Mountain Air 78249
Mountain Alder 78216
Mountain Asia 78233
Mountain Blue 78258
Mountain Breeze St 78251
Mountain Brook Dr 78244
Mountain Cloud 78258
Mountain Echo 78260
Mountain Field Dr 78240
Mountain Glen St 78250
Mountain Home 78251
Mountain Laurel Ln 78245
Mountain Mist 78258
Mountain Oak Trl 78233
Mountain Park St 78227
Mountain Quail 78250
Mountain Shadows St 78233
Mountain Spring St 78249
Mountain Star 78251
Mountain Top 78255
Mountain Valley St 78227
Mountain Vista Dr 78247
Mountain Wood St 78232
Mountainside Rdg 78233
Mountjoy St 78232
Mountridge Dr 78228
Moursund Blvd 78221
Mouton 78250
Mozart Ave 78210
Mozley Rise St 78233
Mt Zion Walk 78210
Mud Lake Dr 78245
Muddy Bay 78244
Muddy Peak Dr 78245
Muegge 78202
Muir Glen Dr 78257
Muir Wood Dr 78257
Muirfield St 78229
E Mulberry Ave
100-899 78212
901-999 78212
1001-1097 78209
1099-1399 78209
W Mulberry Ave
100-899 78212
900-2399 78201
2400-2599 78228
2601-2699 78228
Mulberry Path 78251
Mulberry Tree 78251
Mule Train 78255
Mule Tree St 78232
Muleshoe Ln 78227
Muleshoe Pass 78258
Mumford Path 78228
Muncey
100-699 78202
Muncey
900-1399 78208
Munden Dr 78216
Munich Rd 78256
Municipal Pkwy 78266
Muniz 78237
Muriel Ave 78201
Murphy Hts 78254
Murphy Farm 78239
Murray Winn 78239
N & S Murry St 78207
Muscatine 78228
Mushroom Trl 78231
Musket Dr 78224
Muskogee St 78237
Mustang Aly 78207
Mustang Brk 78254
Mustang Cir 78232
Mustang Crk 78240
Mustang Cv 78244
Mustang Cyn 78244
Mustang Isle 78254
Mustang Mdw 78244
Mustang Rnch 78254
Mustang Spg 78254
Mustang Vw 78244
Mustang Walk 78254
Mustang Bay 78254
Mustang Chase 78258
Mustang Farm 78254
Mustang Gate 78254
Mustang Mesa 78254
Mustang Oak Dr 78254
Mustang Point Dr 78240
Mustang Rise 78254
Muster St 78233
Muth St 78208
Muuga Mnr 78251
My Anns Hl 78258
Myda 78237
Myna Bird 78223
Myrick Blvd 78221
Myrna Dr 78218
E Myrtle St 78212
W Myrtle St
701-797 78212
799-1000 78212
1002-1098 78212
1100-1198 78201
Myrtle Trl 78244
Myrtle Oak 78230
Myrtle Valley St 78242
Myrtlewood 78218
Mystery Dr 78216
Mystery Lake St 78222
Mystery Oaks St 78233
Mystic Frst 78239
Mystic Park 78254
Mystic Bend St 78250
Mystic Sunrise Dr 78244
Nabby Cove Rd 78255

Naco Pass 78217
Naco Perrin Blvd
3900-3998 78217
4000-4199 78217
4200-4298 78233
4401-4499 78233
Nacogdoches Loop 78266
Nacogdoches Rd
100-2000 78209
2002-2398 78209
2400-13999 78217
14000-16499 78247
16501-16699 78247
16701-16997 78266
16999-17099 78266
17101-17999 78266
Nadine Rd 78209
Nagel St 78224
E & W Nakoma St 78216
Nakoosa Dr 78260
Nancy 78204
Nancy Carole Way 78223
Nancy Lopez Ct 78244
Nantucket Dr 78230
Napier Ave 78214
Naples Ct 78257
Napoli Valle 78253
Narrow Pass St 78233
Narva Pln 78251
Nash Blvd 78223
Nashville Dr 78245
Nashwa St 78248
Nashwood St 78232
Nassau Dr 78213
Nat White Dr 78240
Natal Plum 78261
Natalen Ave 78209
Natalie Pt 78254
Natchez Trl 78223
Nathan 78204
Nathan Alan 78217
Nathan Hale St 78247
Nathans Peak 78238
Natho St 78222
Nationwide Dr 78251
Native 78222
Native Dancer St 78248
Natural Bridge Caverns Rd 78266
Nature Pass 78249
Nature Oaks 78258
Navajo Lk 78245
Navajo St
2600-2898 78224
2900-3099 78211
Navajo Peace 78261
Navarro St 78205
Navasota Cir 78259
Navato Blvd 78232
N Navidad St
101-197 78207
199-1599 78207
1601-1697 78201
1699-2499 78201
S Navidad St 78207
Navy Rd 78235
Naylor St 78210
Neal Ave 78214
Neal Rd 78264
Nebula Vly 78252
Neches Br 78258
Nectarine 78247
Nedrub Dr 78223
Needle Point St 78260
Needle Rock 78258
Needville 78233
Neer Ave
3600-3698 78201
3700-4098 78213
4100-4300 78213
4302-5598 78213
Neff
100-399 78207
Neff
400-500 78201
502-898 78201

Neil Armstrong Dr 78219
Nellie 78220
Nellina St 78220
Nelson Ave 78210
Nelson Rd 78252
Nemo Aly 78207
Neo Sho Cir 78218
Neptune St 78226
Nesbit St 78212
Nesting Cyn, Gdn & Way 78253
Nesting Tree 78253
Neston 78239
Net Valley Dr 78242
Netherwood Ln 78253
Nettle Brk 78244
Network Blvd 78249
Neulon Dr 78228
Neumann Cv 78249
Nevada St 78203
Neville Rnch 78245
New Aly 78207
New Bond St 78231
S New Braunfels 78235
N New Braunfels Ave
128-198 78202
200-1099 78202
1101-1199 78202
1501-1523 78208
1525-1899 78208
1901-1999 78208
2900-2998 78209
3000-8499 78209
5100-5198 78209
8500-8699 78217
S New Braunfels Ave
100-498 78203
500-899 78203
901-997 78210
999-3100 78210
3102-3198 78210
3500-7100 78223
7102-7498 78223
New Castle Dr 78218
New Dawn 78250
New England Pl 78230
New Forest St 78229
New Fork Dr 78250
New Guilbeau Rd 78250
New Haven Dr 78209
New Kenton 78240
New Laredo Hwy 78211
New London St 78254
New Marne Rd 78257
New Sulphur Springs Rd
5200-6599 78222
6600-11399 78263
11401-11499 78263
New Valley Hi Dr 78227
New World 78239
New York Pl 78214
Newbury Ter 78209
Newcastle Ln 78249
Newcliff 78259
Newcome Dr
4400-5400 78229
5402-5498 78229
5500-5599 78240
Newell Ave
101-199 78212
200-300 78215
302-398 78215
Newoak Park 78230
Newport Dr 78218
Newport Woods St 78249
Newrock Dr 78230
Newson Dr 78201
Newton Trl 78253
Newton Abbot 78257
Niagara St 78224
Nicholas Mnr 78258
Nicia 78253
Nickle St 78249
Night Arrow 78258
Night Bluff Dr 78255
Night Owl 78245
Night Star 78245

Nightfall Pass 78259
Nighthawk Ln 78255
Nightingale St 78226
Nightshade 78260
Nika St 78208
Nikita Dr 78248
Nimitz Dr 78211
Nimrod 78240
Ninas Ct 78254
Nine Iron Way 78221
Niner Ln 78224
Niram Ln 78216
Nix Bldg 78205
Nixon Pt 78254
No Bogie Cv 78221
Noah Park 78249
Nobhill Dr 78228
Noble Ave 78221
Noble Night 78255
Noble Oak Dr 78227
Noblewood 78220
Noche
23400-23499 78261
Noche
26700-26799 78260
Nock Ave 78221
Nocturne Dr 78216
Nogales St 78237
Nogalitos
100-1623 78204
1625-1799 78204
1800-3499 78225
3500-4000 78211
4002-4098 78211
Nolan St 78202
Nona Kay Dr 78217
Noonan Way 78207
Noonday St 78233
Noor 78248
Nopal St 78210
Nopalito 78261
Nora Vista Way 78233
Norfleet St 78208
Norfolk Pl 78201
Norham Hts 78254
Noria St 78207
Noriega St 78227
Norland St 78232
Norman Ln 78240
Normandy Ave 78209
Normangee St 78211
Norse 78240
North Dr 78201
North Holw 78240
North Rd 78235
North Run 78249
E North Loop Rd 78216
Northampton Dr 78230
Northaven St 78229
Northbend St 78239
Northbluff Ct 78227
Northborough Ln 78253
Northbrook Dr 78232
Northchase Blvd 78250
Northcrest Dr 78213
Northcutt Trl 78233
Northeast Pkwy 78218
Northern Blvd 78216
Northern Dancer 78248
Northern Lights St 78238
Northern Oak 78217
Northfield Dr 78228
Northgap St 78239
Northgate Dr 78218
Northglen 78227
Northhill Dr 78201
Northington Rd 78237
Northland Dr 78217
Northledge Dr 78233
Northmont Dr 78239
Northmoor St 78230
Northoak Dr 78232
Northridge Dr 78209
Northstar Dr 78216
Northtowne Dr 78217
Northtrail Dr 78216

Northvalley Dr 78216
Northway Dr 78213
Northwest Pkwy 78249
Northwest Trl 78250
Northwestern 78238
Northwood Ln 78259
Norton St 78226
Norwich Dr 78217
E & W Norwood Ct 78212
Noseler Dr 78228
Notre Dame Dr 78228
Notting Hl 78232
E & W Nottingham Dr 78209
Nova Icaria 78253
Nova Mae Dr 78216
N Nueces 78207
Nueces Cyn 78251
Nueces Spg 78258
S Nueces St 78207
Nueces Parke 78254
E Nueva
126-298 78204
400-498 78205
500-599 78205
W Nueva
100-124 78204
101-127 78205
131-199 78204
200-300 78207
302-498 78207
Nueva Vis 78258
Nuevo Cir 78253
Nufy Rdg 78209
Nugget Ln 78238
Nugget Peak 78259
Null Hts 78254
Nunes St 78225
Nuthatch St 78217
Nutmeg Trl 78238
Nuttall Oak Dr 78223
Nyack Pass St 78260
O Hara Dr 78251
Oak Bnd 78259
Oak Br 78251
Oak Clf 78230
Oak Cyn 78248
Oak Dr 78256
Oak Ml 78251
Oak Pass 78253
Oak Path 78258
Oak Plz 78216
Oak Rnch 78259
Oak Smt 78232
Oak Sq 78216
Oak St 78215
Oak Trl 78228
Oak Arbor St 78232
Oak Ash 78232
Oak Bank St 78230
Oak Blossom 78250
Oak Bluff St 78230
Oak Briar 78232
Oak Cabin 78232
Oak Castle 78232
Oak Cave 78259
Oak Centre Dr 78258
Oak Chase 78239
Oak Cliff Bnd 78259
Oak Climb 78217
Oak Cluster St 78253
Oak Country Way 78247
Oak Court St 78232
Oak Creek St 78232
Oak Cross 78251
Oak Crown 78232
Oak Dew 78232
Oak Downs Dr 78230
E & W Oak Estates Dr 78260
Oak Falls St 78231
Oak Fanfare 78260
Oak Farm 78258
Oak Fence St 78251
Oak Fire St 78247
Oak Flat Rd 78251
Oak Forest St 78233

Oak Glen Dr 78209
Oak Grove Dr 78255
Oak Harbor Dr 78250
Oak Hill Pl 78229
Oak Hollow St 78230
Oak Island Dr
2400-2799 78264
8100-8199 78250
Oak Knoll Dr 78228
Oak Krest 78264
Oak Lake Dr 78244
Oak Ledge Dr 78217
Oak Leigh St 78232
Oak Loft St 78232
Oak Manor Dr 78229
Oak Maple 78254
Oak Marsh St 78233
Oak Meadow Ln 78253
Oak Mist 78232
Oak Mountain St 78232
Oak Nest Ln 78255
Oak Park Dr 78209
Oak Park Gln 78254
Oak Peak 78259
Oak Pebble 78232
Oak Pointe 78254
Oak Post St 78251
Oak Rain 78251
Oak Ridge Ct 78258
Oak Rise 78249
Oak Rock St 78247
Oak Run St 78247
Oak Saddle 78254
Oak Shadows 78232
Oak Sound 78232
Oak Sprawl St 78231
Oak Spring St 78232
Oak Spur St 78232
Oak Star 78229
Oak Terrace Dr 78233
Oak Thicket 78255
Oak Timber St 78251
Oak Top Vw 78255
Oak Trace St 78232
Oak Valley Dr 78227
Oak Village Dr 78253
Oak Vista St 78232
Oak Water 78249
Oak Wild St 78232
Oak Wind St 78217
Oakbrook St 78221
Oakbrooke Hl 78254
Oakcask 78253
Oakcrest Ave 78210
Oakdale Mdw 78254
Oakdale Park 78254
Oakdale St 78229
Oakdell Way 78240
Oakfield Way
4500-4699 78251
4700-4800 78250
4802-4998 78250
Oakfort St 78247
Oakgate Dr 78230
Oakhaven St 78217
Oakheath 78247
Oakhill Rd 78238
Oakhill Way 78231
Oakhill Park Dr 78249
Oakhorne St 78247
Oakhurst Pl 78209
Oakland Bnd 78258
Oakland Clf 78258
Oakland Ct 78258
Oakland Cv 78258
Oakland Holw 78258
Oakland Rd 78240
Oakland Mills St 78231
Oaklawn Dr 78229
Oakleaf Dr 78209
Oakley Farm 78244
Oakline Dr 78232
Oaklyn Pass 78259
Oakmere St 78232
Oakmont Ct 78212
Oakmoss Dr 78260

Oakridge Dr 78229
W Oaks Ct 78213
Oaks Hike 78245
Oakshire St 78232
Oakstead St 78231
Oakstone Pl 78251
Oaktree Park 78249
Oakview Cv 78249
E Oakview Pl 78209
W Oakview Pl 78209
Oakway Dr 78228
Oakwell Ct 78218
Oakwell Farms Pkwy 78218
Oakwood Bnd 78258
Oakwood Crst 78245
Oakwood Ct 78240
Oakwood Dr 78228
Oakwood Gdns 78254
Oakwood Park 78254
Oakwood Pnes 78254
Oakwood Rdg 78254
Oakwood Trl 78249
Oakwood Way 78245
Oasis Crk 78260
Oasis St 78216
Oban Dr 78216
Obbligato Ln 78266
Obera Way 78228
Obispo Cir 78211
Oblate Dr 78216
Obra Dr 78254
Obregon St 78207
Observation Dr 78227
Ocaso Walk 78207
Ocean Spgs 78249
Ocean Gate St 78242
Ocean Glade 78249
Ocean Port St 78242
Ocean Side St 78242
Oceanview Dr 78242
Ocelot Path 78253
Ocenered Dr 78218
Ocenerth St 78238
Ochiltree Trl 78253
Oconee St 78211
Oconnor Cv 78233
Oconnor Rd
10201-10599 78233
10401-11997 78233
10800-11298 78233
11999-13700 78233
13702-13998 78233
14000-17300 78247
17302-17498 78247
Octave 78227
Octavia Pl 78214
Odell St 78212
Odem Dr 78224
Odessa Dr 78220
Odessa Oaks 78251
Odis 78204
Oehler 78239
Oelkers 78204
Offer St 78223
Ogden Ln 78209
Ogden St 78212
Ogelthorpe Oak 78223
Ohio St 78210
Okehampton Ln 78253
Okent Dr 78260
Oklahoma St 78237
Old Lk 78245
Old Path 78260
Old Babcock Rd 78240
Old Bitters Rd 78216
Old Blanco Rd
13300-13398 78216
13400-13999 78216
27518-27598 78260
Old Blue Ln 78230
Old Blue Ridge St 78230
Old Bond St 78217
Old Brook Ln 78230
Old Camp Bullis Rd 78257
Old Campbellton Rd 78264
Old Carriage 78250

Old Castle 78217
Old Chimney 78250
Old Coach Ln 78220
Old Corpus Christi Hwy 78223
Old Corral 78250
Old Creek St 78217
Old Depot 78250
Old Elm Way 78230
Old Farm Rd 78245
Old Federal Courthouse 78205
Old Field Dr 78247
Old Fm 471 W 78253
Old Forge Dr 78230
Old Forrest St 78245
Old Fossil Rd 78261
Old Fredericksburg Rd 78257
Old Galm Rd 78254
Old Gardner Cir 78230
Old Gate Rd 78230
Old Glory Ave 78253
Old Grissom Rd 78251
Old Guilbeau St 78204
Old Hickory Trl 78230
Old Hills Ln 78251
Old Homestead St 78230
Old Lyme 78248
Old Manse St 78230
Old Mesquite 78254
Old Mill Rd 78230
Old Milton Dr 78260
Old Moss Rd 78217
Old Oconnor Rd 78233
Old Orchard Ln 78230
Old Pearsall Rd
5100-6399 78242
6501-6997 78252
6999-8800 78252
8802-8898 78252
Old Perrin Beitel Rd 78217
Old Pleasanton Rd 78264
Old Prue Rd 78249
Old Quarry 78250
Old Ranch Rd 78217
Old Sky Hbr 78242
Old Spanish Trl 78233
Old Stable Rd 78247
Old Stillwater 78254
Old Stone Gate 78249
Old Talley Rd 78253
Old Tezel Rd
6501-7897 78250
7899-7999 78250
8001-8299 78250
9301-9499 78254
Old Theater Rd 78242
Old Thousand Oaks Dr 78247
Old Trail St 78247
Old Tree St 78247
W Old Us Highway 90
100-1199 78237
W Old Us Highway 90
1200-6599 78227
Old Wagon 78245
Old Well Dr 78259
Old Wick Cir & Rd 78230
Olde Village Dr 78250
Oldham 78239
Oldham Cv 78253
Oldoak Park Dr 78247
Oldstead St 78228
Oleander St 78208
Oletha St 78211
Olga St 78237
Olimito St 78224
Olintint Dr 78242
Oliphant Ct 78212
Olive Grn 78260
N Olive St
301-397 78202
399-999 78202
1001-1399 78202
1400-1899 78208
S Olive St
100-799 78203

800-2500 78210
2502-2998 78210
3600-3799 78223
Oliver Rd 78264
Olivia Dl & Vw 78260
E Olmos Dr 78212
W Olmos Dr
100-899 78212
1200-1398 78201
1400-2399 78201
Olmos Creek Dr 78230
Olney Dr
300-799 78209
900-1199 78218
Olney Spgs 78245
Olympia Dr 78201
Olympic Clb 78260
Olympus Bay 78245
Oma Dr 78263
Omaha St 78203
Omega Vale 78252
Omena Ct 78230
Omicron Dr 78245
One Alamo Ctr 78205
One Oak Dr 78228
One Riverwalk Pl 78205
One Ten Bldg 78205
Oneida Dr 78230
Onslow Dr 78202
Ony St 78224
Onyx Way 78222
Oolooteka Dr 78218
Opal Fld 78245
Opal Fls 78222
Opal Creek Dr 78232
Opalstone Crk 78254
Opelousas Trl 78245
Open Cv 78264
Open Pass 78259
Open Meadow St 78230
Open Range Rd 78264
Openforest 78259
Oppenheimer Ave 78221
Oracle Dr 78260
Oraleadw 78256
Orange 78214
Orange Blossom St 78247
Orange Tree 78253
Orbit Dr 78217
Orchard Gln 78266
Orchard Hl 78230
Orchard Path 78245
Orchard Rd 78220
Orchard Acres 78261
Orchard Bend St 78250
Orchard Ridge Dr 78231
Orchard Rim 78259
Orchard Willow 78245
Orchid Grv 78245
Orchid Mdws 78250
Orchid Blossom St 78247
Orchid Star 78218
Ore Terminal 78245
Oregon St 78211
Oriental Ave 78204
Oriental Trl 78244
Oriley St 78251
Oriole Ln 78228
Oriole Hill Dr 78258
Oriskany St 78247
Orkney 78223
Orland Park 78213
Orleans St 78207
Oro Cyn 78254
Oro Rdg 78224
Oro Vis 78224
Oro Viejo Ct 78266
Orphan 78202
Orr Dr 78227
Orsinger Brk, Cpe, Fld,
Fls, Frg, Hl & Ln 78230
Osage Cir 78266
Osage Dr 78207
Osage Trl 78266
Osage Vly 78251
Osage Mesa 78216
Osborn Hl 78209
Osborn Glade 78247
Osburn St 78208
Oscar Dr 78223
Osceola Blf 78261
Osgood St 78233
Osiana Dr 78248
Osnats Pt 78258
Oso Negro 78260
Osprey Hts 78260
Osprey Hvn 78253
Osprey Rdg 78260
Osprey Way 78256
Osprey Oak 78253
Ostrom Dr 78212
Oswego Dr 78250
Otono 78223
Ottawa Run 78231
Ottawa Way St 78260
Otter Dr 78227
Otter Pass 78254
Otter Trl 78232
Otto St
100-298 78211
400-498 78224
Outer Circle Rd 78235
Outlook Rdg 78233
Outrider 78247
Outwood Ct 78250
Oval Mdws 78244
Ovencenn St 78232
Overbrook Dr
300-398 78201
401-499 78228
Overglen 78231
Overhill Dr 78228
Overlake St 78230
Overland Crk 78245
Overland Dr 78218
Overland Run 78254
Overland Way 78254
Overlook Blf 78233
Overlook Crk 78260
Overlook Path 78249
Overlook Pkwy 78260
Overlook Rd 78233
Overpool St 78228
Overridge Dr 78221
Overton Rd 78217
Owasso St 78211
Owenwood Dr 78264
Owl Haven St 78250
Owl Ridge St 78250
Owl Tree St 78253
Owlwolf Crk 78245
Ox Bow 78228
Ox Bridge St 78232
Ox Eye Trl 78258
Ox-Eye Daisy 78261
Oxalis 78260
Oxford Bnd 78249
Oxford Dr 78213
Oxford Hall 78209
Oxford Trace St 78240
Oxhill Dr 78238
Oxted 78254
Oxydol St 78211
Ozalid St 78224
Ozark 78201
Ozark Ter 78266
Ozona Cv 78253
Ozona Ml 78253
Ozona Rnch 78245
Pace St 78207
Pacer Trl 78240
Pacific Grv 78259
Pacific Maple 78254
Pack Saddle Trl 78255
Packard St 78211
Packtrain Pass 78255
Paddington Way 78209
Paddle Crk 78245
Paddlebrook 78253
Paddlefish Crk 78245
Paddling Pass 78253
Paddock Dr 78238
Padgitt Dr 78228
Padie Smt 78251
Padiski Ct 78251
Padre Cir & Dr 78214
Paeglow St 78235
Paesanos Pkwy 78231
Pageland Dr 78219
Pagoda Oak 78230
Pagodia Vw 78245
Paige Trl 78249
Paint Ave 78227
Painted Daisy 78253
Painted Horse St 78242
Painted Oak 78255
Painted Post Ln 78231
Painted Ridge Dr 78239
Painted Rock 78255
Painted Sky St 78238
Painted Teepee St 78242
Painted Wagon 78254
Painter Grn & Way 78240
Paisano Pass 78255
Paisley St 78231
Palace Trl 78248
Palace Place Dr 78248
Palacio St 78233
Palacios Cv 78242
Palamon Farm 78228
Palatine Hl 78253
Palazzo Torre 78253
Paldeld St 78233
Paldenco Dr 78217
Pale Horse Ln 78254
Pale Valley St 78227
Palestine Blvd 78211
E & W Palfrey St 78223
Palisades Dr 78233
Palladio Pl 78253
Palm Cir 78213
Palm Dr 78228
Palm Grv 78227
Palm Pt 78259
Palm Bay Dr 78218
Palm Beach St 78211
Palm Bluff St 78211
Palm Crest St 78211
Palm Leaf St 78211
Palm Park Blvd 78223
Palm Springs Dr 78228
Palma Mesa 78259
Palma Noce 78253
Palma Nova St 78253
Palmdale St 78230
Palmer Vw 78260
N Palmetto Ave
200-498 78202
500-1199 78202
1418-1598 78208
1600-1815 78208
1817-1899 78208
S Palmetto Ave
201-799 78203
800-2600 78210
2602-2698 78210
Palmetto Pass 78245
Palmetto Pl 78254
Palmetto Way 78253
Palmilla Ct 78257
Palo Alto Rd 78211
Palo Blanco St 78210
Palo Corto 78211
Palo Duro Cyn 78258
Palo Duro St 78232
Palo Duro Peak 78255
Palo Grande St 78232
Palo Pinto St 78232
Palo Solo 78223
Paloma Crk 78249
Paloma Dr 78212
Paloma Pass 78259
Paloma Trl 78249
Paloma Wood 78259
Palomar 78250
Palomar Hls 78238
Palomino Blf 78245
Palomino Bnd 78254
Palomino Cv 78244
Palomino Dr 78227
Palomino Path 78254
Palomino Pl 78254
Palomino Oaks 78254
Pamela Dr 78223
N Panam Expy 78219
S Panam Expy 78225
Panama Ave 78210
Pancho Villa Dr 78238
Pandale 78261
Pandora Seco 78223
Pandorea 78253
Panola Cv 78253
Panola Dr 78216
Panola Way 78253
Panoramic Ct 78258
Pantheon Way 78232
Panther Pass 78254
Panther Bay 78245
Panther Peak 78247
Panuco St 78237
Panzano Pl 78258
Papoose Pass 78260
Par Five 78221
Par Four 78221
Par One 78221
Par Three 78221
Par Two 78221
Parade Dr 78213
Paradise Crk 78253
Paradise Pass 78266
Paradise Rd 78244
Paradise Vly 78227
Paradise Oak Dr 78227
Paradise Woods St 78249
Paradiso Loop 78260
Paramount Ave 78228
Parchman 78214
Pardo Cir 78228
Parham 78227
Parhaven Dr 78232
E Park Ave 78212
W Park Ave 78212
N Park Blvd 78204
S Park Blvd 78204
Park Bnd 78227
Park Cir 78259
Park Crk 78259
Park Ct
1-99 78226
100-199 78212
Park Dr 78212
N Park Dr 78216
Park Fls 78259
Park Holw 78259
Park Hvn 78244
Park Lk 78244
Park Mtn 78255
Park Plz 78237
Park Pt 78253
Park Rnch 78259
Park Ter 78237
Park Trl 78250
Park Xing 78217
Park Bluff St 78259
Park Canyon Dr 78247
Park Central 78216
Park Corner St 78230
Park Deville 78248
Park Farm 78259
Park Field Dr 78227
Park Forest St 78230
Park Gate St 78230
Park Grove Dr 78227
Park Hill Dr 78212
Park Lane Ct & Dr 78266
Park Manor St 78230
Park Meadow Dr 78227
Park Oak Dr 78232
Park Royal Ln 78229
Park Summit Cv 78258
Park Ten Blvd 78213
Park Valley St 78227
Park View Dr 78266
Park Village Dr 78227
Park Vista Dr 78250
Park West Dr 78250
Parkcrest Dr 78239
Parkdale Cv 78249
Parkdale St 78229
Parker Ave 78210
Parkett 78223
Parkford 78249
Parkhurst St 78232
Parkland Dr 78230
Parkland Green Dr 78240
Parkland Hills Dr 78254
Parkland Oaks Dr 78240
Parklane Dr 78212
Parkmont Ct 78258
Parkmoor Ct 78201
Parkridge Dr 78216
Parkrow 78204
Parkside Dr 78237
Parksite Woods 78249
Parkstone Blvd 78232
Parkview Dr 78210
Parkway Dr 78228
Parkwood Dr 78218
Parkwood Way 78249
Parland Pl 78209
Parliament St
11600-11698 78213
11700-11799 78213
11800-11899 78216
11901-11999 78216
Parman Pl 78230
Parmenter St 78217
Parmly Ave 78211
Parnell Ave 78224
Parnu Mesa 78251
Paro Pl 78227
Parr 78244
Parsley 78240
Parsley Hl 78238
Parter Pond 78260
Parton Ln 78233
Partridge Hl 78247
Partridge Trl 78232
Party Slippers Dr 78255
Parview Cir 78260
Pasadena 78201
Paschal St 78212
Paseo Arbol 78252
Paseo Bajo 78252
Paseo Canada St 78232
Paseo Corto Dr 78266
Paseo Derecho 78252
Paseo Encinal St 78212
Paseo Grande 78245
Paseo Oaks 78255
Paseo Pinosa 78252
Paseo Rioja 78257
Paseo Valencia 78257
Paseo Verde 78207
Paseo Yrigoyen 78252
Pasiano St 78253
Paso Ave 78237
Paso Chico Aly 78207
Paso Del Norte St 78232
Paso Del Sur St 78207
Paso Doble Dr 78237
Paso Hondo 78202
Paso Rocoso 78258
Paso Valley Dr 78242
S Pass Rd 78255
Passiflora 78261
Passion Elm 78254
Passion Flower 78253
Pat Pkwy 78257
Pat Booker Rd 78233
Paterid 78251
Path Finder Ln 78230
Path View Pt 78247
Patmore Dr 78217
Patricia
200-899 78216
Patricia
900-1499 78213
1501-1799 78213
Patrick Henry St 78233
Patron 78224
Patterson Ave 78209
Patton Blvd
100-499 78207
500-1299 78237
1301-1599 78237
Patton Pt 78254
Paul St 78203
Paul Revere St 78233
Paul Wagner 78226
Paul Wilkins St 78216
Paula Dr 78222
Paulsun St 78219
Pavilion Pl 78250
Pavillion Cir 78217
Pavo Viejo 78223
Pavona Rdg 78240
Pawnee Pride 78261
Pawtucket Dr 78230
Pax Hl 78256
Peabody Ave 78211
Peace Pipe Dr 78238
Peaceful Grv 78250
Peaceful Hls 78250
Peaceful Ln 78264
Peaceful Mdws 78250
Peacemaker 78258
Peach Blossom St 78247
Peach Tree St 78238
Peach Valley Dr 78227
Peacock Ave 78201
Peacock Hvn 78260
Peacock Rdg 78228
Peacock Way 78217
N Peak 78245
Peak Pt 78242
Peale 78239
Peanneri St 78243
Pear Blossom St 78247
Pear Tree 78218
Pearl Ct 78212
Pearl Fld 78245
Pearl Pass 78222
Pearl Pkwy 78215
Pearl Spg 78258
Pearl Harvest 78259
Pearl Lagoon 78249
Pearl Woods 78249
Pearlstone 78232
Pearson 78226
Pease Holw 78258
Pebble Bch 78248
Pebble Cir 78217
Pebble Cv 78232
Pebble Fls 78232
Pebble Frst 78232
Pebble Gln 78217
Pebble Hl 78217
Pebble Holw 78217
Pebble Park 78232
Pebble Path 78232
Pebble Rnch 78249
Pebble Row 78232
Pebble St 78230
Pebble Trl 78232
Pebble Vly 78232
Pebble Walk 78217
Pebble Way 78231
Pebble Bow 78232
Pebble Breeze 78232
Pebble Creek Dr 78238
Pebble Crest Cir 78231
Pebble Dawn 78232
Pebble Den 78232
Pebble Dew 78232
Pebble Gate 78232
Pebble Glade 78230
Pebble Height St 78232
Pebble Oak Dr 78231
Pebble Peak 78232
Pebble Point Dr 78231
Pebble Sound 78232
Pebble Spring Dr 78249
Pebblebrook Dr 78220
Pebblestone 78250
Pebblewood 78250
Pecan Cyn 78252
Pecan Est 78222
Pecan Hts 78244
Pecan Pass 78247
Pecan Spgs 78249
E Pecan St 78205
Pecan Sta 78258
Pecan Acres Dr 78240
Pecan Creek Ln 78255
Pecan Cross 78240
Pecan Gap 78247
Pecan Glade 78249
Pecan Grove Dr 78222
Pecan Hollow Dr 78232
Pecan Trail St 78249
Pecan Tree 78240
Pecan Valley Cir 78223
Pecan Valley Dr
401-497 78220
499-1199 78220
1201-1297 78210
1299-2799 78210
2801-2899 78210
4400-4698 78223
4700-6899 78223
Pecan Way Dr 78240
Peche St 78207
Peck Ave 78210
Pecos Vly 78254
N & S Pecos La
Trinidad 78207
Pecos Parke 78254
Pecos Sunset 78255
W Peden 78204
Pedernales Dr 78223
Pedregoso Ln 78258
Pedroncelli 78253
Peg Oak 78258
Peg Sue Ct 78213
Pegasus Run Rd 78254
Peggy Dr 78219
Pelham Dr 78219
Pelican Crk 78258
Pelican Cv 78221
Pelican Ln 78217
Pelican Pass 78221
Pelican Coral 78244
Pelican Edge 78258
Pelican Oak Dr 78254
Pelicans Way 78245
Pemberton St 78254
Pembranch 78240
Pembriar Cir 78240
Pembridge Dr 78247
Pembroke Ct, Ln, Pl &
Rd 78240
Pemcanyon 78240
Pemcliff 78240
Pemcrest 78240
Pemelm Dr 78240
Pemhaven 78240
Pemleaf Ct 78240
Pemmont 78240
Pemoak Dr 78240
Pemspice 78240
Pemview 78240
Pemwoods 78240
Penchean Dr 78239
Pendant Pass 78232
Pendant Oak 78232
Pendenwo Ave 78211
Pendleton Ave 78204
Pendragon St 78254
Penguin Trl 78238
Peninsula Dr 78239
Penns Way 78231
Penny Ln 78209
Penny Royale 78253
Pennystone Ave 78223
Penrose St 78228
Penstemon Trl 78256
Pentas Vw 78245
Pentridge 78250
Peoples Dr 78253
Pepita 78261
Pepper Trl 78244

Pepper Bush St 78231
Pepper Oak 78258
Pepper Tree St 78230
Pepperdine Bay 78249
Pepperidge Cv 78213
Peppermill Run St 78231
Peppermint Dr & Ln 78219
Peppervine Ln 78249
Pepperwood St 78238
Perch Mdw & Mnr 78253
Perch Horizon 78253
Perch Ledge 78253
Perchin St 78247
Peregrine 78233
Peregrine Rdg 78260
Pereida St 78210
Perennial Dr 78232
Perez St 78207
E & W Perimeter Dr 78227
Perini Rnch 78254
Periwinkle St 78232
Perkins Dr 78240
Perks Pl 78223
Perla Joy 78253
Perlita St 78224
Perma Ln 78224
Permian Bay 78245
Perpetual 78247
Perrin 78226
Perrin Crk 78217
Perrin Beitel Rd
3800-3998 78217
8200-8399 78218
8500-10409 78217
10410-10410 78284
10410-10410 78265
10411-12099 78217
10412-12098 78217
Perrin Central Blvd 78217
Perry Ct 78209
Perryton 78251
Perseus Sound 78252
Pershing Ave 78209
Persian Gdn, Holw & Pass 78260
Persimmon Dr 78213
Persimmon Fall 78249
Persimmon Path 78258
Persimmon Trl 78256
Persimmon Wl 78247
Persimmon Gap 78245
Persimmon Hill Dr 78247
Persimmon Pond 78231
Personality 78248
Persuasion Dr 78216
Persyn St 78207
Pertelote Farm 78228
Pertshire St 78254
Pesa Cv 78266
Pescala Rdg 78252
Peshawar St 78243
Petal Dr 78216
E & W Petaluma Blvd 78221
Peter Baque Rd 78209
Peters Ct 78204
Petersburg St 78245
Peterson Ave 78224
Petit Blossom 78247
Petite St 78230
Petroleum Dr 78218
Petry Dr 78219
Petseri Park 78251
Pettus 78228
Petwood Dr 78264
Peuplier 78254
Peyton Pl 78210
Pfeiffer Dr 78255
Phantom Valley Cir & St 78232
Pharis St 78237
Pheasant 78223
Pheasant Crk 78240
Pheasant Rdg 78248
Pheasant Run 78253
Phillips Pl 78260
Phillips St 78233

Phlox Ln 78213
Phlox Mdw 78259
Phoebe Vw 78252
Phoebe Lace 78253
Photon Walk 78252
Phyllis St 78225
Piano Pl 78228
Piazza Pl 78253
Piazza Italia 78207
Picardie Dr 78219
Piccadilly Cir 78251
Piccolo Crk 78245
Pickering Dr 78238
Pickford Ave 78228
Pickwell Dr 78223
Pickwick 78260
Pico De Aguila 78255
Picolo Pl 78260
Picoso Pt 78252
N Picoso St 78207
S Picoso St 78207
Piedmont Ave
101-197 78203
199-730 78203
732-798 78203
800-2400 78210
2402-2598 78210
3500-3699 78223
Piedmont Gln 78249
E Piedras Dr 78228
Piegan St 78207
Pierce Ave 78208
Pierce Massie 78226
Pierian Ave 78211
Pike Mdw 78249
Pike Rd 78209
Pike Ridge Dr 78221
Pike Valley Dr 78242
Pilar St 78222
Pilgrim Dr 78213
Pillar Oak St 78226
Pima St 78211
Pimpernel 78260
Pin Oak Dr 78229
Pin Oak Forest St 78232
Pinafore St 78253
Pinckney St 78209
Pindale Clf 78259
Pine Br 78250
Pine Frst 78239
Pine Hvn 78244
N Pine St
101-297 78202
299-1399 78202
1400-1899 78208
S Pine St
101-197 78203
199-799 78203
800-2599 78210
2601-3099 78210
3301-3999 78223
Pine Vlg 78250
Pine Arbor 78254
Pine Breeze Dr 78247
Pine Country St 78247
Pine Creek Dr 78250
Pine Eagle Ln 78260
Pine Glade 78245
Pine Hollow St 78211
Pine Lake Dr 78244
Pine Manor Dr 78240
Pine Mesa Dr 78245
Pine Needles Ln 78244
Pine Valley Dr 78242
Pine View Dr 78247
Pine Warbler 78253
Pinebluff Dr 78230
Pinebrook Dr 78230
Pinecomb Woods St 78249
Pinecrest Blvd 78209
Pinedale Dr 78230
Pinehill St 78230
Pinehurst Blvd 78221
Pinehurst Run 78239
Pinehurst Mesa 78247
Pineridge Rd 78217

Pinetree Blf 78247
Pinetree Ln 78232
Pinetum Dr 78213
Pineville Rd 78227
Pineway St 78247
Pinewood Ln 78216
Pinewood Park Ct 78230
Piney Wood Run 78255
Piney Woods 78248
Pinkerton Way 78254
Pinn Rd 78227
Pinnacle Dr 78261
Pinnacle Fls 78260
Pinoak Knls 78248
Pinon Blvd 78260
Pinon Cyn 78249
Pinon Rnch 78254
Pintail 78253
Pintail Pt 78239
Pinto Crk 78244
Pinto Pass 78247
N Pinto St 78207
S Pinto St 78207
Pinto Trl 78251
Pinto Pony Ln 78247
Pintoresco St 78233
Pinyon Hl 78260
Pinyon Pne 78261
Pinyon Jay 78253
Pioneer Crk 78245
Pioneer Est 78245
Pioneer Mdws 78245
Pioneer Path 78253
Pioneer Rd 78210
Pioneer Rdg 78245
Pioneer Vly 78245
Pioneer Way 78245
Pioneer Gold 78249
Pioneer Point Dr 78244
Pioneer Sky 78245
Pioneer Trail Dr 78244
Pious 78247
Pipe Spring St 78238
Pipecreek St 78251
Piper Dr 78228
Piper Sonoma 78253
Pipers Blf, Ct, Hl, Ln, Path, Rdg, Trl & Way 78251
Pipers Creek St 78251
Pipers Crest St 78251
Pipers Cross St 78251
Pipers Dale St 78251
Pipers Field St 78251
Pipers Glade St 78251
Pipers Haven St 78251
Pipers Meadow St 78251
Pipers Run St 78251
Pipers Stone St 78251
Pipers Swan St 78251
Pipers Valley St 78251
Pipers View St 78251
Pipestone Dr 78232
Pirate Cv 78242
Pisces Pass St 78260
Pistol Ln 78227
Pitcairn 78254
Pitluk Ave 78211
Pitted Rock 78260
Placid Dr 78228
Placid Bay 78245
Placid Valley Dr 78242
Plains Way 78253
Plainview Dr 78228
Plan St 78203
Plantation Dr 78230
Planter Dr 78224
Plarkenw Dr 78266
Plarlist Dr 78244
Plateau Dr 78227
Player St 78217
Player Oaks 78260
Playmoor St 78210
N Plaza 78227
Plaza De Armas 78205
Plaza De Cadiz 78257
Plaza Del Sol St 78207

Plaza Lake Dr 78245
Pleadi 78201
Pleasant Dr 78201
Pleasant Frst 78239
Pleasant Knl 78260
Pleasant Lk 78222
Pleasant Mdw 78222
Pleasant Vw 78217
Pleasant Bay 78244
Pleasant Oak Dr 78227
Pleasant Park Dr 78227
Pleasant Valley St 78227
Pleasant Well Dr 78247
Pleasanton Blf 78221
Pleasanton Cir 78221
Pleasanton Cv 78221
Pleasanton Hts 78221
Pleasanton Pl 78221
Pleasanton Rd
101-197 78214
199-1399 78214
1400-20699 78221
20700-25699 78264
22238-1-22238-10 78264
Pleasanton Spg 78221
Pleasanton Sq 78221
Pleasantville Rd 78233
Pleasure Hill Dr 78229
Pleasure Park St 78227
Pletz Dr 78226
Plum Holw 78258
Plum Ln 78218
Plum Blossom St 78247
Plum Creek Dr 78245
Plum Ranch Rd 78266
Plum Valley Dr 78255
Plumbago 78261
Plumbago Pl 78218
Plumbrook Dr 78258
Plumeria St 78232
Plumnear 78211
Plumnelley Ln 78216
Plumtree Dr 78242
Plumwood St 78233
Plymouth Rd 78216
Pocahontas 78264
Poco Pass 78260
Pocono Dr 78230
Poconos Run 78255
Poerner Trl 78261
Poesta 78218
Poets Corner St 78232
Poinciana St 78245
Poinsettia 78202
Point Crk 78253
Point Crst 78253
Point Cv 78253
Point Cyn 78253
N Point Dr 78266
Point Mdw 78253
Point Ml 78253
Point Pass 78253
Point Smt 78253
Point Spgs 78253
Point Vly 78253
Point Xing 78253
Point Bell 78253
Point Bluff Dr 78258
Point Breeze 78253
Point Comanche St 78257
Point Gap 78253
Point Mesa 78253
Point Oak 78232
Point Quail 78250
Point Range 78253
Point Rise 78253
Point Sound 78253
Point Sunset 78253
Point West St 78224
Pointer Ct 78260
Points Edge 78250
Polar Bnd 78238
Polar Bear 78238
N Polaris 78202
S Polaris St
101-197 78203
199-899 78203
1001-1099 78210
Polk 78212
Pollote St 78224
Pollydale Ave 78223
Polo Pass 78260
Polynesian 78248
Pomeroy Cir 78233
Pomona St 78249
Pomona Park Dr 78249
Ponca Bnd 78231
Ponce De Leon 78239
Pond Lk 78244
Pond Pass 78260
Pond Hill Rd 78231
Ponder Rnch 78245
Ponderosa Bnd 78261
Ponderosa Dr 78240
Ponderosa Way 78266
Ponernes St 78247
Poniente Ln 78209
Pontiac Ln 78232
Pony Ln 78227
Pony Spur 78254
Pony Express St 78255
Pony Gate 78254
Pony Mesa 78254
Ponyfoot 78261
Ponytail 78247
Pool Dr 78223
Pop Gunn St 78219
Popes Creek St 78233
Poplar Pass 78254
W Poplar St
201-697 78212
699-1099 78212
1201-1297 78207
1299-3199 78207
3200-3799 78228
Popping Dr 78229
Poppy Cir 78260
Poppy St 78203
Poppy Mallow 78260
Poppy Peak St 78232
Poppy Sands 78245
Poppy Seed 78253
Poppy Seed Run 78238
N Port Blf 78216
S Port Blf 78216
Port Pl 78253
Port Bay 78242
Port Entry 78222
Port Hudson St 78245
Port Kenton 78240
Port Lavaca 78242
Port Of Call Dr 78242
Port Royal St 78244
Port Shire Dr 78242
Port Townsend Dr 78242
Port Victoria St 78242
Portage Path 78232
Porter St 78210
Porterhouse 78248
Portland Rd 78216
Portofino Pl 78266
Portola Blvd 78251
Portola Vw 78261
Portrait Ct 78217
Portside St 78242
Portsmouth Dr 78223
Posada Cir 78237
Poss Rd
6601-6697 78238
6699-6800 78238
6802-6998 78238
7200-7299 78240
Possum Cir 78232
Possum Cv 78232
Possum Hl 78232
Possum Path 78232
Possum Run 78232
Possum Trl 78224
Possum Way 78232
Possum Oak 78230
Possum Rock 78232
Possum Tree Rd 78232

Possum Trot 78264
Possum Wolf 78245
Post Ave 78215
Post Ml 78244
Post Cedar 78253
Post Oak Cir 78264
Post Oak Ln 78217
Post Oak Park 78264
Post Oak Vw 78264
Post Oak Way 78230
Post Office Dr 78284
Posthouse Cir 78216
Postoak Ct 78248
Postwood Dr 78228
Poteet Jourdanton Fwy
1001-8697 78224
8699-9499 78224
9501-9599 78224
9701-9799 78211
Potlatch St 78242
Potomac 78202
Potosi St 78207
Potranco Rd
7301-7501 78251
7503-11099 78251
11200-13299 78253
Potter Cir 78253
Potter Vly 78245
Pottesgrove 78254
Pow Wow Dr 78238
Powder Horn Trl 78232
Powder Keg 78264
Powder River St 78232
Powderhorn Run 78255
Powderhouse Dr 78239
Powell 78204
Powhatan Dr 78230
Prado St
500-599 78204
600-1199 78225
Prague 78230
Prairie Bnd 78244
Prairie Crk 78255
Prairie Mdws 78258
Prairie Pass 78254
Prairie Dunes 78248
Prairie Falcon 78233
Prairie Flower St 78242
Prairie Grass 78245
Prairie Hill St 78211
Prairie Lace 78249
Prairie Mountain Dr 78255
Prairie Oak St 78233
Prairie Springs Dr 78249
Prairie Sun Dr 78244
Prato Brezza 78253
Prato Palma 78253
Preakness Ln 78248
Preakness Pass 78254
Precious Dr & St 78237
Prelude Pl 78220
Prentiss Dr 78240
N Presa St 78205
S Presa St
201-497 78205
499-599 78205
600-3999 78210
4000-9799 78223
Prescott Dm 78233
Prescott Dr 78245
Prescott Fls 78255
Prescott Oaks 78258
Preserve Crst 78261
Preserve Trl 78254
Preserve Oak 78258
Preserve Peak 78261
President Dr 78216
Presidio Path 78253
Presidio Pkwy 78249
Presley Dr 78240
Prestige Dr 78260
Preston Ave 78210
Preston Trl 78244
Preston Court Dr 78247
Preston Cove Dr 78247
Preston Hall Dr 78247

Preston Hollow Dr 78247
Preston Pass Dr 78247
Preston Point Dr 78247
Prestonshire 78258
Prestwick Blvd 78223
Prestwood 78233
Previn St 78251
Price Ave 78211
Prickle Pear Dr 78233
Prickly Oak 78223
Prides Xing 78232
Prima Vista Dr 78233
Prime Time 78233
Primera Dr 78212
Primrose 78266
Primrose Hl 78251
Primrose Pl 78209
Primrose Post 78218
Primwood St 78233
Prince Hts 78254
Prince Charles 78240
Prince Forest Ct 78230
Prince George Dr 78230
Prince Solms 78253
Prince Valiant 78218
Princes Knls 78231
Princess Ct 78209
Princess Pass 78212
Princess Diane St 78229
Princess Donna St 78229
Princeton Ave 78201
Princeton Oak 78230
Prinz Dr 78213
Priors Way 78257
Priscilla St 78211
Privada Yesa 78257
Private Road 3701 78253
Private Road 3702 78253
Private Road 3710 78253
Private Road 3730 78253
Private Road 3808 78253
Private Road 3810 78253
Privet Pl 78259
Pro Cv 78221
Probandt
100-198 78204
Probandt
200-1699 78204
1800-1898 78214
1900-2010 78214
2012-2198 78214
Proclamation Dr 78240
Proctor Blvd 78221
Produce Row 78207
Profit St 78219
Progress Rd 78264
Promeneade St 78217
Promontory Cir 78258
Pronghorn Oak 78253
Prospect Crk 78260
Prospect Hl 78258
Prospect Pt 78255
Prospect St 78211
Prosperity Dr 78237
Prosser Ln 78238
Proton Rd 78258
Proton Smt 78252
Providence Dr 78220
Providence Way 78240
Providence Oak 78249
Provision St 78233
Prude Rnch 78254
Prue Rd
5000-6600 78240
6602-6698 78240
7400-8599 78249
Pruitt Ave 78204
Pue Rd
2200-2298 78245
2300-2400 78245
2402-5998 78245
8900-10299 78252
Puebla Ave 78221
Pueblo Run 78232
Pueblo St 78233
Pueblo Vis 78258

Street	ZIP
Pueblo Crossing Dr	78232
Pueblo Springs Dr	78232
Puente	78223
Puesta De Sol	78261
Puma Pass St	78247
Purcell St	78237
Purdue St	78228
Purdue Vly	78249
Pure Silver	78254
Purlane	78247
Purple Rdg	78233
Purple Finch	78256
Purple Martin	78233
Purple Mint	78245
Purple Sage Rd	78255
Purple Tansy	78260
Putman Farm St	78230
Putter	78244
Putting Grn	78217
Pyle St	78223
Pyrite Loop	78222
E Pyron Ave	
100-1700	78214
1702-1798	78214
1800-1900	78223
1902-1998	78223
W Pyron Ave	
100-598	78214
600-1199	78221
1200-2099	78211
Quail Br	78250
Quail Cir	78247
Quail Crk	78218
Quail Cyn	78249
Quail Fld	78263
Quail Gdns	78250
Quail Hl	78239
Quail Hvn	78263
Quail Knls	78231
Quail Lk	78244
Quail Lndg	78250
Quail Mtn	78217
Quail Pass	78249
Quail Pnes	78250
Quail Rdg	78263
Quail St	78223
Quail Trce	78250
Quail Way	78263
Quail Breeze	78250
Quail Covey Ln	78263
Quail Crown	78249
Quail Feather Ln	78233
Quail Fern	78250
Quail Foot St	78253
Quail Hollow St	78232
Quail Meadow St	78230
Quail Oak St	78232
Quail Path St	78232
Quail Rise	78249
Quail Run Dr	78209
Quail Sky	78250
Quail Sun	78250
Quail Tree	78250
Quail Valley Ln	78233
Quail Whisper	78250
Quail Wilde	78250
Quail Wood	78250
Quailbrook	78253
Quakertown Dr	78230
Quarles St	78247
Quarter J	78254
Quartett Ln	78266
Quartz Bnd & Run	78253
Quayle Mist	78254
Quebec Dr	78239
Queen Cir	78255
Queen Hts	78254
Queen Anne Ct	78209
Queen Bess Ct	78228
Queens Ct & Hl	78257
Queens Castle	78218
Queens Crescent St	78212
E & W Queens Crown St	78233
Queens Forest St	78230
Queens Gate	78218
Queens Heath	78257
Queens Oak	78258
Queensland	78232
Queenspoint Dr	78251
Queenston Dr	78253
Queensway St	78217
Quentin Dr	78201
Quentin Roosevelt Rd	78226
Queretaro St	78237
Querida Ave	78226
Quicksilver Dr	78245
Quiet Cyn	78252
Quiet Dr	78260
Quiet Frst	78239
Quiet Lk	78254
Quiet Mtn	78258
Quiet Pt	78260
Quiet Rpds	78260
Quiet Strm	78222
Quiet Creek St	78242
Quiet Elk	78253
Quiet Eve	78260
Quiet Glen Dr	78240
Quiet Meadow St	78247
Quiet Moon Dr	78266
Quiet Oak St	78232
Quiet Plain Dr	78245
Quiet Ridge Walk	78250
Quiet Valley St	78242
Quig Dr	78223
Quihi St	78211
Quihi Way	78254
E & W Quill Dr	78228
Quince Flower	78253
E Quincy St	
200-999	78215
1100-1199	78212
W Quincy St	78212
Quinta St	78210
Quintana Rd	78211
Quintard	78214
Quintin Way	78230
Quirt St	78227
Quitman St	78208
Quitman Oak	78258
Quiver Dr	78238
Quixote Walk	78207
Raba Dr	78251
Rabbit Run	78260
Rabbit Spgs	78245
Rabbitbrush	78261
Rabel Rd	78221
Raceland Rd	78245
Rachels Br	78254
Rada	78214
Radcliff Ct	78253
Rader Pass	78247
Radford Trl	78244
Radiance Ave	78218
Radiant Star	78252
Radisson	78259
Radium St	78216
Rafanelli	78253
Ragtime Rd	78260
Rail Dr	78233
Railway	78244
Rain Frst	78239
Rain Shr	78249
Rain Cloud Dr	78238
Rain Dance	78242
Rain Preserve	78254
Rain Song	78260
Rain Valley St	78255
Rainbow Bnd	78250
Rainbow Crk	78245
Rainbow Crst	78245
Rainbow Dr	78209
Rainbow Falls St	78233
Raindrop Dr	78216
Rainey Meadow Ln	78233
Rainfall Park	78249
Rainfall Ridge Dr	78239
Rainlilly Cv	78249
Rainmaker St	78238
Rains Ct	78230
Raintree Bnd, Frst, Path, Pl & Run	78233
Rainwood Cv	78213
Rainy Ave	78240
Raleigh Pl	78201
Ralph	78204
Ramada Cir	78237
Ramble Rdg	78266
E Ramblewood St	78261
Ramblin River Rd	78251
Rambling Dr	78220
Rambling Oak	78232
Rambling Rose	78253
Rambling Trail Dr	78240
Rambowllette Dr	78247
Ramelle Cv	78250
Ramona	78201
E & W Rampart Dr	78216
E & W Ramsey Rd	78216
Ramsgate St	78230
Ranch Cor	78250
Ranch Ct	78250
Ranch Fls	78245
Ranch Mdws	78258
E Ranch Rd	78222
Ranch Smt	78245
Ranch Hill Dr	78250
Ranch House Rd	78264
Ranch Peak	78250
Ranch Trail Rd	78264
Ranch Valley Dr	78227
Ranchero St	78240
Ranchers Rdg	78251
Ranchland Dr	78213
Ranchland Plns	78245
Ranchland Fox	78245
Rancho Blanco Blvd	78201
Rancho Diana	78255
Rancho Mirage	78259
Ranchwell Cv	78249
Randall Ave	78237
Randolph Blvd	78233
Randolph Brooks Pkwy	78233
E Range	78255
Range Fld	78245
Range Boss	78245
Range Finder	78245
Range Water	78261
Rangeland St	78247
Ranger	78203
Ranger Cyn	78251
Ranger Path	78238
Ranger Pt	78251
Ranger Cavern	78254
Ranger Oak St	78233
Ranger Peak	78251
Rangerider	78247
Ranier Ln	78260
Rankin St	78211
Ranmar Ave	78214
Ransom Hl	78258
Raphael	78258
Rapids Pass	78253
Rapla Xing	78251
Raptor Peak	78233
Raritan St	78254
Rasa Dr	78227
Raton Fls	78245
Rattler Blf	78251
Rattler Cir	78266
Rattler Pass	78266
Rattler Gap	78251
Raven Dr	78223
Raven Rdg	78255
Raven Feather	78260
Raven Field Dr	78245
Raven Glenn	78248
Ravenhill Dr	78214
Ravens Rnch	78253
Ravenscroft Dr	78253
Ravenswood Dr	78227
Ravina St	78222
Ravine Pass	78255
Raw Silver	78254
Rawhide Ln	78227
Rawhide Trl	78264
Rawley Chambers	78219
Ray Ave	78204
Ray Bon Dr	78218
Ray Ellison Blvd	
5500-5698	78242
5700-5800	78242
5802-5898	78242
8501-8599	78227
Ray Lieck	78253
Rayburn Dr	
101-197	78221
199-1199	78221
1201-1297	78224
1299-1999	78224
Raymond Medina St	78226
Raytel St	78253
Raywood St	78211
Reading Ln	78257
Readwell Dr	78220
Reagan St	78224
Real Dr	78263
Real Rd	78263
Real Rdg	78256
Real Delight	78248
Realitos	78261
Realto Cir	78232
Reata Cv & Trl	78258
Reawick Dr	78253
Rebeccas Trl	78251
Rebel Queen	78255
Rebel Ridge St	78247
Rebel Run St	78230
Recanto	78260
Recia Oak	78223
Recio St	
500-599	78204
600-1199	78225
Recoleta Rd	78216
E & W Rector St	78216
Red Blf	78218
Red Cyn	78252
Red Grv	78230
Red Pass	78255
Red Alder Trl	78256
Red Ascot	78254
Red Cedar	78230
Red Cloud Dr	78260
Red Clover St	78231
Red Deer Pass	78249
Red Eagle	78258
Red Elm	78227
Red Feather Ln	78245
Red Fig Trl	78256
Red Fox St	78247
Red Gate Dr	78264
Red Hawk Rdg	78258
Red Hawk St	78242
Red Head	78245
Red Heron	78261
Red Hill Ln	78264
Red Hill Pl	78240
Red Jacket Dr	78238
Red Lake Dr	78223
Red Leaf Dr	78232
Red Leg Dr	78240
Red Lion Ct	78259
Red Maple St	78247
Red Maple Way	78253
Red Maple Wood	78249
Red Mulberry Woods St	78249
Red Musket Trl	78245
Red Oak Ln	78230
Red Oak Vis	78250
Red Quill Dr	78213
Red Quill Nest	78253
Red Ripple St	78233
Red River Dr	78238
Red Robin Rd	78255
Red Rock Rnch & Xing	78245
Red Sand Dr	78264
Red Sky St	78242
Red Stable Rd	78254
Red Tree St	78247
Red Willow	78260
Redbird Cir	78253
Redbird Ln	78240
Redbird Mnr	78253
Redbird Pass	78253
Redbird Vly	78229
Redbird Chase	78253
Redbird Farm	78253
Redbird Ledge	78253
Redbird Song	78253
Redbird Sun	78224
Redbridge	78248
Redbrook Dr	78242
Redbud Trce	78245
Redbud Leaf	78253
Redbud Woods	78250
Redbush Park	78249
Redcap Dr	78222
Redcliff Dr	78216
Redding Ln	78219
Redeemer	78247
Redfern Dr	78264
Redfish Cavern	78245
Redforest Ln	78264
Redhorse Pass	78247
Redland Crk	78259
Redland Pt	78259
Redland Rd	
19200A-19298A	78259
19200F-19298F	78259
19200I-19298I	78259
19201A-19297A	78259
19201F-19297F	78259
19201I-19297I	78259
16600-16698	78247
16700-17099	78247
17101-17499	78247
18101-18797	78259
18799-19000	78259
19002-19298	78259
Redland Rnch	78247
Redland Trl	78259
Redland Downs	78247
Redland Mesa	78259
Redlands Park Dr	78249
Redlawn Dr	78230
Redondo St	78237
Redriver Hl, Pass & Trl	78259
Redriver Creek Dr	78259
Redriver Dawn	78259
Redriver Sky	78259
Redriver Song	78259
Redrock Crk	78259
Redrock Dr	78213
Redrock Pass	78259
Redrock Trl	78259
Redrock Vis	78250
Redrock Oak	78249
Redrock Woods	78259
Redsky Hl, Pass & Trl	78259
Redspear Fls	78245
Redstart Dr	78224
Redstone Dr	78219
Redstone Hl	78261
Redstone Rise	78251
Redstone Woods	78259
Redwood Path	78259
Redwood St	78209
Redwoods Crst	78232
Redwoods Mnr	78247
Reece Dr	78216
Reed Rd	78251
Reeds Cv	78242
Reefridge Pl	78242
Reel Dr	78224
Reenie Way	78258
Reeves Gdn	78253
Reforma Dr	78211
Refugio St	78210
Regal Pt	78254
Regal St	78216
Regal Vw	78220
Regal Oaks Dr	78233
Regal Rose	78259
Regency Bnd	78249
Regency Crst	78249
Regency Ct	78249
Regency Cv	78249
Regency Frst	78249
Regency Ln	78249
Regency Mnr	78249
Regency Pt	78231
Regency Run	78266
Regency Trl	78249
Regency Way	78249
Regency Row Dr	78248
Regency Wood	78249
Regent	78204
Regent Cir	78231
Regent Clf	78249
Regent Arms	78257
Regents Park	78230
Regiment Dr	78240
Regina St	78223
Regis Hts	78254
Rehmann St	78204
Reichert St	78203
Reid Ranch Rd	78245
Reigh Count	78248
Reina Dr	78201
Reindeer Trl	78238
Reininger St	78217
Reiter Pass	78244
Rejillas	78228
Relampago	78223
Rembrandt Hl	78256
Remigio St	78211
Remington Cir, Run & Way	78258
Remington Oaks	78261
Remolino	78237
Remount	78218
Remsen St	78251
Remuda Cir	78254
Remuda Dr	78227
Remuda Path	78254
Remuda Rdg	78254
Remuda Ter	78254
Remuda Briar St	78254
Remuda Brush Dr	78254
Remuda Oak	78254
Remuda Ranch Dr	78254
Remuda View Dr	78254
Rena	78228
Renault Dr	78218
Rendezvous Dr	78216
Rene Ave	78233
Rene La Salle	78239
Rene Levy	78227
Renker Dr	78217
Renner Dr	78201
Reno St	78208
Renoir	78258
Renova St	78214
Renwick Ct	78218
Renwick Dr	78227
Repose Ln	78228
Reposo	78261
Republic Dr	78216
Republic Pkwy	78223
Research Dr	78240
Research Plz	78235
Resort Pkwy	78261
Resort Vw	78255
Rest Haven Dr	78232
Restless Wind St	78250
Reston Dr	78232
Resurrection	78227
Retama Holw	78233
Retama Pl	78209
Retama Way Dr	78240
Retreat Run	78253
Retta St	78222
Return Dr	78214
Reunion Pl	78216
Reuters Bldg	78205
Reve	78239
Reveille St	78233
Reverie Ln	78216
Revlon Dr	78227
Rex St	78212
Rexford Dr	78216
Rexton Ln	78258
Reyes Ln & Pt	78245
Reyglen Dr	78255
Reynosa	78261
E & W Rhapsody Dr	78216
Rheims Pl	78258
Rhett Rd	78251
Rhett Butler	78223
Rhineland	78239
Rhinestone Dr	78233
Rhoda Ave	78224
Rhodes Villa	78249
Rhyder Rdg	78254
Rialto Way	78230
Riata Ave	78227
Riata Cir	78261
Riata Cyn	78258
Riata Rdg	78261
Riata Ranch Dr	78261
Ribbon Crk	78238
Ricardo St	78237
Rice Crst	78249
Rice Rd	78220
Ricegrass	78258
Rich Way	78251
Rich Quail	78251
Rich Trace St	78251
Richard Frank Way	78240
Richey Otis Way	78223
Richfield Dr	78239
Richland Dr	78219
Richland Pl	78244
Richland Hills Dr	
100-700	78245
702-798	78245
1100-1799	78251
Richmond	78215
Richmond Hill St	78250
Richter Rd	78223
N Richter St	78207
S Richter St	78207
Richwood Dr	78230
Ricks Cir	78251
Riddle St	78210
Ridenden Dr	78209
Riders Pt & Walk	78227
Ridge Blf	78216
Ridge Dr	78228
Ridge Lk	78250
Ridge Ml	78250
Ridge Path	78250
Ridge Riv	78230
Ridge Rnch	78247
Ridge Spur	78247
Ridge Ter	78251
Ridge Trce	78258
Ridge Arbor St	78250
Ridge Ash	78247
Ridge Basin	78250
Ridge Bay St	78250
Ridge Branch St	78250
Ridge Breeze	78250
Ridge Cave St	78247
Ridge Chase	78230
Ridge Circle Dr	78233
Ridge Cliff St	78251
Ridge Climb	78250
Ridge Cloud	78260
Ridge Cluster St	78247
Ridge Corner St	78247
Ridge Country St	78247
Ridge Court St	78247
Ridge Creek Dr	78233
Ridge Cross	78250
Ridge Crown St	78247
Ridge Dale Dr	78233
Ridge Dawn St	78247
Ridge Dove	78230
Ridge Elm Dr	78239
Ridge Falls Dr	78233
Ridge Farm	78230
Ridge Fern	78250
Ridge Field St	78250
Ridge Flower	78239
Ridge Forest Dr	78233

Ridge Garden Dr 78239
Ridge Gate St 78250
Ridge Glade St 78250
Ridge Glen Dr 78233
Ridge Grove St 78250
Ridge Hill Dr 78233
Ridge Hollow St 78250
Ridge Knoll St 78247
Ridge Leaf 78251
Ridge Meadow Dr 78233
Ridge Mile Dr 78239
Ridge Mist Dr 78239
Ridge Moon Dr 78239
Ridge Mountain St 78250
Ridge North Dr 78266
Ridge Oak 78250
Ridge Oak Pkwy 78249
Ridge Park St 78232
Ridge Pass Dr 78233
Ridge Peak Dr 78233
Ridge Pilot 78239
Ridge Place St 78250
Ridge Point Dr 78233
Ridge Pond St 78250
Ridge Post 78250
Ridge Rise 78250
Ridge Rock Dr 78228
Ridge Run St 78250
Ridge Shadow 78250
Ridge Sky St 78250
Ridge Smoke 78247
Ridge Song 78247
Ridge Square St 78250
Ridge Stone St 78251
Ridge Summit St 78247
Ridge Sun St 78250
Ridge Town 78250
Ridge Trail St 78232
Ridge Tree Dr 78233
Ridge Vale 78250
Ridge Valley Ln 78253
Ridge View Dr 78253
Ridge Village Dr 78233
Ridge Walk St 78250
Ridge Wilde St 78250
Ridge Willow Dr 78233
Ridge Wind 78250
Ridge Wine 78247
Ridgeboro Dr 78232
Ridgebrook St 78250
Ridgecrest Dr 78209
Ridgefront 78250
Ridgehaven Pl 78209
Ridgehurst 78250
Ridgeland St 78250
Ridgeline Dr 78228
Ridgemont Ave 78209
Ridgeside 78217
Ridgetop Dr 78230
Ridgeway Dr 78259
E Ridgewood Ct 78212
W Ridgewood Ct
  100-899 78212
  900-2000 78201
  2002-2098 78201
Ridgewood Pkwy 78259
Ridingate Farm 78228
Riebe Aly 78207
Rife Ave 78211
Rifle Gap Dr 78245
Rifleman Rd 78254
Rigel Bay 78252
Rigsby Ave
  101-197 78210
  199-2199 78210
  2201-2597 78222
  2599-5199 78222
Riley Ln 78260
Rilla Vista Dr 78216
Rilling Rd 78214
S Rim 78245
Rim Dr 78257
Rim Pass 78257
Rim Oak 78232
Rim Rock Trl 78251
Rimcrest Dr 78217

Rimfire Dr 78227
Rimfire Run Ln 78245
Rimhurst 78250
Rimkus Dr 78238
Rimline St 78251
Rimrock St 78228
Rimwood St 78233
Rindle Rnch 78249
Ring Of Roses 78227
Rio Spgs 78258
Rio Bravo Ct 78259
Rio Bravo St 78232
Rio Brazos 78259
Rio Cactus Way 78260
Rio Colorado 78259
Rio Comal 78259
Rio D Oro 78233
Rio Frio 78251
N Rio Grande 78202
S Rio Grande St 78203
Rio Guadalupe 78259
Rio Hato St 78233
Rio Linda St 78245
Rio Mist Dr 78244
Rio Niebla 78249
Rio Paloma 78249
Rio Pecos 78251
Rio Rancho 78253
Rio Sabinal 78259
Rio Sabine 78259
Rio Seco St 78232
Rio Verde 78207
Ripford St
  100-399 78204
  600-1000 78225
  1002-1098 78225
Ripley Ave 78212
Ripon 78228
Ripple Way 78266
Ripple Creek St 78231
Ripplewind 78203
Ripplewood 78253
Rippling Rill St 78232
Rippling Spring Dr 78261
Riptide 78264
Risada St 78233
E & W Rische 78204
Risen Bay 78254
Rising Hl 78260
Rising Sun 78245
Rita Ave 78228
Rita Elena 78250
Rita Leon 78250
Rittiman Plz 78218
Rittiman Rd
  100-799 78209
  801-999 78209
  1001-3997 78218
  3999-6399 78218
Ritzel Cv 78250
Riva Ridge St 78248
Rivas St
  200-298 78207
  300-1999 78207
  2000-3699 78228
Riventri Dr 78223
River Blf 78255
River Bnd 78247
River Cyn 78222
River Fls 78259
River Frk 78222
River Gln N 78216
River Gln W 78216
River Hls 78239
River Ml 78216
River Park 78216
River Rd
  401-999 78212
  12700-12799 78223
River Rnch 78255
River Trce 78255
River Vis N 78216
River Vis S 78216
River Vis W 78216
River Vlg 78245
River Vly 78249

River Way 78230
River Birch Dr 78227
River Brook Dr 78244
River Elms 78240
River Hollow Dr 78232
River Kenton 78240
River North Dr 78230
River Oak Ln 78232
River Path St 78230
River Post 78222
River Rock 78251
River Run St 78230
River Stroll St 78230
E River Walk St 78205
River Wind 78233
Rivera Cv 78249
Rivercenter Mall 78205
Riverdale Dr 78228
Riverside Dr
  100-298 78210
  300-499 78210
  500-600 78223
  602-698 78223
Riverside Park Dr 78249
Riverstone Dr 78258
Riverton Rise 78261
Rivertree 78203
Riverview Dr 78204
Riverwood 78233
Riviera Dr 78213
Rivulet 78239
Roadman Rd 78235
Roadrunner Rdg 78245
Roadrunner Way 78249
Roadstead Way 78253
Roamer Park 78245
Roan Blf 78259
Roan Brk 78251
Roan Crk 78259
Roan Ct 78259
Roan Dr 78227
Roan Fld 78251
Roan Frst 78259
Roan Hts 78259
Roan Ldg 78251
Roan Park 78259
Roan Path 78258
Roan Spg 78258
Roan Trce 78258
Roan Vly 78259
Roan Way 78259
Roan Xing 78259
Roan Chase 78259
Roan Hunt 78258
Roan Leap 78259
Roanoke Run 78240
Roanoke St 78228
Roanwood 78244
Roaring Frk 78260
Roark Dr 78219
Rob Roy Ln 78251
Robards Row St 78233
Robert Gln 78252
Robert Dover St 78226
Robert E Lee 78214
Robert Galer 78260
Robert Jared 78264
Robert Mondavi 78253
Roberts St 78207
Robeson Ave 78220
Robillard Ln 78221
Robin Frst 78239
Robin Mdw 78222
Robin Rdg 78248
Robin Vw 78255
Robin Feather 78255
Robin Hill Dr 78230
Robin Rest Dr 78209
Robin Willow 78260
Robinair Dr 78245
Robinhood Pl 78209
Robinsnest 78249
Robinson Pl 78202
Robinwood Ln 78248
Roble Vis 78258
Roble Fino 78258

Roble Real 78258
Robledo Verde St 78232
Robles Nuevo 78232
Rocco St 78207
Rochambeau 78214
Rochelle Rd 78240
Rock Blf 78233
Rock Fls 78248
Rock Rd 78229
Rock Bend Ln 78260
Rock Cliff Rd 78230
Rock Creek Run 78230
Rock Dove Rd 78260
Rock Elm Woods 78249
Rock Hollow Ln 78250
Rock Knoll Dr 78227
Rock Nettle 78247
Rock River St 78247
Rock Shelter 78260
Rock Squirrel 78231
Rock Valley Dr 78227
Rock View St 78230
Rockaway Ln 78232
Rockbrook Cv 78261
Rockdale Dr 78219
Rockey Shls 78244
Rockford St 78249
Rockgate St 78227
Rockhampton St 78232
Rockhill Dr 78209
Rockhurst St 78249
Rocking D 78253
Rockingham Cir 78247
Rockland Dr 78230
Rockline St 78251
Rocklyn Dr 78239
Rockmoor 78230
Rockport Rd 78264
Rockridge Ln 78209
Rockrimmon 78240
Rockside Dr 78258
Rocksprings St 78251
Rockwall Ml 78253
Rockwell Blvd 78224
Rockwell Vis 78249
Rockwood Ct 78210
Rocky Crk 78247
Rocky Holw 78258
Rocky Plns 78260
Rocky Pt 78249
Rocky Rdg 78255
Rocky Trl 78249
Rocky Cedar 78249
Rocky Hill Rd 78257
Rocky Mine 78253
Rocky Oak St 78232
Rocky Overlook 78249
Rocky Path St 78254
Rocky Pine Woods St 78249
Rocky Rim 78266
Rod Schaffe 78219
Roddy Rd 78263
Rodena St 78201
Rodeo Rnch 78260
Rodrick Dr 78224
Rodriguez Rd 78227
Roesler Rd 78220
Roft Rd 78253
Rogans Hbr 78244
Rogers Ave
  1000-1199 78202
  1500-1818 78208
  1820-1898 78208
Rogers Blf 78258
Rogers Bnd 78258
Rogers Cir 78258
Rogers Cv 78258
Rogers Frk 78258
Rogers Gln 78258
Rogers Isle 78258
Rogers Ky 78258
Rogers Lk 78258
Rogers Loop 78258
Rogers Pass 78258
Rogers Pike 78258
Rogers Pl 78258

Rogers Rd 78251
Rogers Rst 78258
Rogers Run 78251
Rogers Ranch Pkwy 78258
Rogers Wood 78248
Rohrdanz 78233
Roland Rd
  300-3599 78210
  3601-3799 78210
  3801-4097 78222
  4099-4499 78222
Roleto Dr 78213
Rolling Brk 78253
Rolling Crk 78253
Rolling Frk 78232
Rolling Grv 78253
Rolling Hls 78227
Rolling Path 78253
Rolling Riv 78249
N Rolling Vw 78253
S Rolling Vw 78253
Rolling Circle St 78254
Rolling Dale Dr 78228
Rolling Forest Dr 78250
Rolling Green Dr 78228
N & S Rolling Oaks Ln 78253
E & W Rolling Ridge Dr 78228
Rolling Rock Dr 78245
Rolling Stone St 78254
Rolling Trail Dr 78250
Rolling Wood Dr 78228
Rollingfield Dr 78228
Rollins Ave 78228
Roman Pl 78230
Roman Shade 78260
Romance Point St 78260
Romero 78237
Romin Dr 78264
Romney 78254
Rompel Dr 78217
Rompel Pass 78232
Rompel Oak 78232
Rompel Trail Dr 78232
Ronald Ln 78201
Ronald Reagan 78258
Ronan 78233
Ronda De Cadiz 78257
Roosevelt Ave
  101-197 78210
  199-2400 78210
  2402-2498 78210
  2600-10499 78214
  10501-10599 78214
Roper St 78208
Roping Horse 78260
Roping Star 78260
Roquefort 78250
Rosa St 78221
Rosa Trl 78253
Rosa Verde 78207
Rosa Verde Towers 78205
Rosabell St 78228
N Rosary St 78202
S Rosary St 78203
Rose Crst 78248
Rose Ln 78212
Rose Rdg 78247
Rose Anna Dr 78237
Rose Blossom St 78247
Rose Dawn 78250
Rose Valley Dr 78242
Roseborough St 78210
Rosebud Ln 78221
Rosedale Ct 78201
Rosefield 78240
Roseheart 78259
Rosehill Dr 78213
Roselawn Rd 78226
Rosemary Ave 78209
Rosemarys Farm 78244
Rosemire Way 78254
Rosemont Dr
  1-99 78201
  100-599 78228

Rosemoss 78249
Rosestone Pl 78254
Rosethorn Dr 78249
Rosetti Dr 78247
Roseview 78253
Roseville St 78219
E Rosewood Ave 78212
W Rosewood Ave
  100-899 78212
  900-1699 78201
Rosewood Crk 78245
Rosewood Crst 78238
N & S Rosillo St 78207
Rosillos Peak 78245
Rosin Jaw Trl 78245
Rosita Pl 78207
Roslin Frst 78233
Roslyn Ave 78204
Ross Ave 78225
Ross Oak St 78247
Rossmore Dr 78230
Rossolis Dr 78219
Rossridge 78248
Roswell Cyn 78245
Rosy Cloud 78245
Rosy Finch 78233
Roszell St 78217
Rotary 78202
Rothberger Way 78244
Rothbury Ln 78232
Rough Oak St 78232
Roughrider Dr 78239
Round Mtn 78255
Round Oak Dr 78228
Round Pond Pl 78245
Round Table Dr 78218
Roundhill St 78250
Roundleaf Ct 78231
Rounds Aly & St 78207
Roundtree Ln 78233
Roundup Dr 78213
Roundup Pass 78245
Rouse Ave 78201
Rousseau St
  10700-10798 78245
  11400-11799 78251
  11801-11899 78251
Routt St 78209
Roveen Trl 78244
Rowe Dr 78247
Rowland Park Dr 78249
Rowley Rd 78240
Roxbury Dr 78238
Roxcove Dr 78247
Roxio Dr 78238
Roxton Ave 78247
Roy Ln 78250
Roy Smith St 78215
Royal Blf 78239
Royal Bnd 78239
Royal Cir 78239
Royal Clb 78239
Royal Crk 78239
Royal Ct 78228
Royal Cv 78248
Royal Cyn 78252
Royal Est 78245
Royal Fld 78255
Royal Hts 78257
Royal Hvn 78239
Royal Land 78255
Royal Mdws 78239
Royal Prt 78247
Royal Pt 78239
Royal Rdg 78239
Royal Wl 78249
Royal Breeze 78239
Royal Coach 78239
Royal Crescent St 78231
Royal Forest St 78230
Royal Gardens Dr 78248
Royal Hunt 78250
Royal Oaks Dr 78209
Royal Orbit 78248
Royal Stable 78238
Royal Sun St 78238

Royal Valley St 78242
Royal Vista Dr 78247
Royal Waters Dr 78248
Royal Wood 78239
Royalgate Dr 78242
Royalton Dr 78228
Royalty Pt 78238
Royce St 78235
Royston Ave 78225
Rua De Matta St 78232
Rubens 78239
Rubidoux Dr 78228
Ruby Mdw 78251
Ruby Run 78259
Ruby Oaks 78232
Ruby Palm Pass 78218
Ruby Sunset 78232
Rudolph 78202
Rue Bourbon 78240
Rue Burgundy 78240
N & S Rue Charles 78217
Rue De Bois 78254
Rue De Lis 78250
Rue Des Amis 78238
Rue Des Lac 78249
Rue Francois St 78238
Rue Liliane St 78238
Rue Marielyne St 78238
Rue Orleans 78240
Rue Royale 78240
Rue Sophie St 78238
Ruelle Ln 78209
Ruffled Grouse 78233
Rugby Hts 78254
Rugby Ln 78257
Ruger Rnch 78254
Rugged Oak Dr 78233
Rugged Ridge St 78254
Rugosa Hl 78256
Ruidosa 78214
Ruidosa Rdg 78259
Ruiz St
  500-2599 78207
  2600-3100 78228
  3102-3398 78228
Rullman Ave 78208
Runnels Ave 78208
Running Rnch & Spgs 78261
Running Creek Dr 78218
Running Fawn 78261
Running Horse St 78242
Running Quail 78250
Running Springs Loop 78261
Rush Wood 78232
Rushhill St 78228
Rushing Crk 78254
Rushing St 78230
Rushing Oaks 78254
Rushing Waters St 78260
Rushing Winds 78254
Ruslin 78248
Russell Park 78260
E Russell Pl 78212
W Russell Pl
  400-498 78212
  500-1099 78212
  1100-1399 78201
Russi St 78223
Rustic Bnd 78230
Rustic Brk 78261
Rustic Frst 78239
Rustic Lgt 78260
Rustic Ln 78230
Rustic Mdws 78249
Rustic Park 78240
Rustic Rdg 78228
Rustic Ter 78249
Rustic Trl 78244
Rustic Vlg 78245
Rustic Vly 78254
Rustic Way 78247
Rustic Cabin 78260
Rustic Cactus 78260
Rustic Cedar 78245
Rustic Glade 78247
Rustic Horse 78260

Rustic Oak 78261
Rustic Spoke 78245
Rustic Stable 78227
Rustic Star 78260
Rustic Wagon 78253
Rustleaf Dr 78242
Rustlers Trl 78245
Rustlers Butte 78231
Rustlers Creek Dr 78230
Rustling Brk 78249
Rustling Cv 78251
Rustling Gln 78249
Rustling Mdws 78254
Rustling Rdg 78259
Rustling Way 78249
Rustling Branches 78254
Rustling Breeze 78254
Rustling Leaf 78254
Rustling Oaks 78259
Rustling Winds 78254
Rusty Leaf Ln 78264
Rutgers Gdn 78249
Ruth Lee St 78263
Rutledge St 78219
Ryan Dr 78223
Ryans Point Dr 78248
Ryden Dr 78233
Ryder Rd 78254
Rye Dr 78260
Ryelle 78250
Ryoak St 78217
Sabal Rdg 78260
Sabinal Riv 78253
Sabinal Maple 78261
N Sabinas St
101-297 78207
299-1599 78207
1601-1997 78201
1999-2499 78201
S Sabinas St 78207
Sabine 78223
Sabine Pass 78242
Sabine Smt 78258
Sabine Way 78253
Sabine Parke 78254
Sable Bnd 78259
Sable Clf 78258
Sable Crk 78259
Sable Cyn 78258
Sable Fls 78258
Sable Frst 78259
Sable Grn 78251
Sable Hts 78258
Sable Ln 78217
Sable Lndg 78232
Sable Path 78259
Sable Vly 78258
Sable Xing 78232
Sable Arrow 78251
Sable Leap 78251
Sable Mist 78259
Sable Range 78245
Sabyan Dr 78218
Sacagawea 78239
Sachem Dr 78242
Sackville Dr 78247
Sacramento
500-600 78212
Sacramento
602-698 78212
900-2399 78201
Sacre Couer 78232
Sacred 78247
Saddle Cp 78259
Saddle Crk 78238
Saddle Rdg 78217
Saddle Rnch 78254
Saddle Trl 78255
N Saddle Trl 78255
Saddle Bend Dr 78238
Saddle Blanket 78258
Saddle Horse 78260
Saddle Point St 78259
Saddle Rock 78260
Saddlebow 78240
Saddlebrook Dr 78245
Saddlefoot Way 78260
Saddlehorn St 78227
Saddletree Ct & Rd 78231
Saddlewood St 78238
Sadie St 78210
Sadler Grv 78249
Safari St 78216
Safe Hbr 78244
Saffron Way 78238
Saffron Plum 78261
Saffron Rose 78253
Sagail Pl 78249
Sagamore Dr 78242
Sage Blf 78216
Sage Dr 78228
Sage Holw
2400-2799 78251
5700-5799 78249
Sage Mdw 78222
Sage Run 78253
Sage Ter 78251
Sage Trl 78231
Sage Bluff Cir 78216
Sage Heights Dr 78230
Sage Hill St 78230
Sage Kenton 78240
Sage Oak St 78233
Sage Ridge Dr 78247
Sagebrush Ln 78217
Sagecrest Dr 78232
Sageglen 78254
Sageline St 78251
Sagerock Park 78250
Sagerock Pass 78247
Sagewood 78248
Sagitarius Ln 78260
Sago Palm 78261
Sahara St 78216
Sail Loft Cir 78242
Sailing Away St 78233
Saint Andrews 78248
Saint Ann 78201
Saint Anthony Ave 78210
Saint Charles 78202
Saint Christopher Walk 78207
Saint Cloud Rd 78228
Saint Cyr 78232
Saint Dennis Ave 78209
Saint Francis Ave 78204
Saint George 78202
Saint Ives 78254
Saint James 78202
Saint John 78202
Saint Julien Ct 78240
Saint Lawrence St 78245
Saint Leger St 78233
Saint Leonard St 78228
Saint Louis Ave 78237
Saint Lukes Ln 78209
Saint Martin Ave 78202
N Saint Marys St
100-198 78205
200-899 78205
901-997 78215
999-1699 78215
1700-3899 78212
3901-3999 78212
S Saint Marys St
100-1099 78205
1100-1899 78210
1901-1999 78210
Saint Nicholas St 78228
Saint Xavier 78232
Saints Hvn, Psge &
Vw 78220
Saints Arc Dr 78220
Saints Cape Dr 78220
Saints Retreat 78220
Saintsbury 78253
Saipan Pl 78221
Salado Blf 78223
Salado Cyn 78258
Salado Rdg 78217
N Salado St 78207
S Salado St 78207
Salado Creek Dr 78217
Salado Draw 78258
Salado Mist 78258
Salano 78259
Salazar Trl 78216
Saldana St
500-599 78204
600-1099 78225
Salem Dr 78201
Salerno Way 78253
W Salinas St 78207
Salisbury Dr 78217
Sally Agee 78238
Sally Gay Dr 78223
Salt Lick Rd 78232
Saltgrass St 78247
Saltillo St
200-498 78207
500-1999 78207
2801-2899 78237
Saltillo Way 78253
Salto Del Agua 78255
Salty Marsh 78245
Salvador Dr 78221
Sam Houston Pl 78212
Sam Nail Rnch 78245
Sam Snead St 78240
Samar Dr 78217
Samba 78260
Sammy 78253
Samoth Dr 78223
Sample St 78210
Sampson Dr 78251
Sams Dr 78221
Samuel St 78227
Samuel Chase St 78233
Samuel Prescott St 78233
San Acacia 78214
San Andreas St 78228
San Angelo
100-599 78212
San Angelo
800-1899 78201
San Anita St 78207
San Antonio Ave 78201
San Anza 78260
San Arturo St 78210
N San Augustine Ave 78228
S San Augustine Ave 78237
San Benito Dr 78228
N San Bernardo Ave 78228
S San Bernardo Ave 78237
San Blas 78214
San Carlos St 78207
San Casimiro 78214
San Clemente 78260
San Cristobal 78251
N San Dario Ave 78228
S San Dario Ave 78237
San Diego 78232
San Dizier 78232
San Dominique 78232
N San Eduardo Ave 78228
S San Eduardo Ave 78237
N San Felipe Ave
100-399 78237
400-699 78228
S San Felipe Ave 78237
San Felipe Bay 78255
San Fernando St
300-3799 78207
3800-5699 78237
San Fidel Way 78255
San Fidel Rio 78245
San Francisco 78201
N San Gabriel Ave
100-399 78237
400-699 78228
S San Gabriel Ave 78237
N San Horacio Ave
100-399 78237
400-699 78228
S San Horacio Ave 78237
N San Ignacio Ave
100-399 78237
400-699 78228
S San Ignacio Ave 78237
San Isidro 78261
San Jacinto St 78207
N San Jacinto St 78207
S San Jacinto St
300-2099 78207
2100-2399 78204
N San Joaquin Ave
100-399 78237
400-699 78228
S San Joaquin Ave 78237
San Jose Dr 78214
San Juan Rd 78223
San Judas 78237
San Lino St 78207
San Lucas St 78245
San Luis St
900-998 78207
1000-3699 78207
4000-4399 78237
N San Manuel St 78228
S San Manuel St 78237
N San Marcos
101-1099 78207
N San Marcos
1601-1699 78201
S San Marcos 78207
San Marguerite 78260
San Marino 78250
San Martin St 78207
San Mateo Walk 78207
San Miguel St 78233
San Miniato 78260
San Nicolas 78207
San Pablo Pl 78237
San Patricio St 78207
San Pedro Ave
101-197 78205
199-299 78205
300-5999 78212
6100-13499 78216
13601-13697 78232
13699-18199 78232
15681-3-15681-7 78232
7103-2-7103-6 78216
San Pedro Pl 78221
San Portola 78260
San Rafael St 78214
San Roman Dr 78213
N San Saba 78207
S San Saba
201-299 78207
S San Saba
801-899 78204
San Saba Blf 78258
San Salvador Ave 78210
San Simeon Dr 78228
Sanco 78214
Sanctuary Cv 78257
Sanctuary Dr 78248
Sand Hbr 78245
Sand Ash Trl 78256
Sand Castle 78239
Sand Cliff Dr 78264
Sand Holly 78253
Sand Pebble 78250
Sand Rock St 78263
Sand Wedge 78258
Sandalwood Ln 78216
E Sandalwood Ln 78209
Sandau Rd 78216
Sandbar Hl 78230
Sandbar Pt 78254
Sandbrook Hl 78254
Sanderling 78245
Sanders St 78203
Sandflat Pass 78245
Sandhill Crane 78253
Sandhurst Ln 78257
Sandia Blf 78240
Sandia St 78232
Sandiland 78217
Sandledge Dr 78219
Sandlet Trl 78254
Sandman St 78216
Sandmeyer St 78208
Sandown St 78239
Sandpiper 78233
Sandpiper Park Dr 78249
Sandpiper Tree 78251
Sandra Dr 78223
Sandringham 78258
Sandspring Ct 78227
Sandstone St 78230
Sandtrap Ct 78260
Sandtrap St 78217
Sandview 78264
Sandwick Dr 78238
Sandy Bnd 78264
Sandy Cir 78264
Sandy Crk 78264
Sandy Crst 78217
Sandy Ct 78207
Sandy Cv 78245
Sandy Cyn 78252
Sandy Fld 78245
Sandy Mdws 78254
Sandy Park 78264
Sandy Pass 78264
Sandy Shls 78247
Sandy Cedar 78254
Sandy Dunes 78253
Sandy Elms 78251
Sandy Lake St 78222
Sandy Oaks St 78233
Sandy Point Dr 78244
Sandy Trail Dr 78240
Sandy Valley St 78242
Sandy White 78253
Sandyglen 78240
Sanez 78214
Sangria 78253
Sangria Dawn 78249
Sangria Mist 78249
Santa Anita 78261
Santa Anna 78201
Santa Barbara 78201
Santa Catalina 78250
Santa Catalina Cv 78218
Santa Cathrena 78232
Santa Clara Pl 78210
Santa Cruz St 78228
Santa Fe Rdg 78245
Santa Fe Trail Dr 78232
Santa Gertrudis St
14600-14799 78217
14801-14899 78217
14900-15098 78247
Santa Helena 78232
Santa Lucia 78259
Santa Monica
500-699 78212
Santa Monica
701-799 78212
900-2399 78201
Santa Rita 78214
S Santa Rosa Ave
101-397 78207
399-400 78207
402-498 78207
600-799 78204
N Santa Rosa St 78207
Santee 78240
Santiago St 78207
Santolina 78261
Santos St 78210
Sapphire Dr 78220
Sapphire Cave 78222
Sapphire Oak 78232
Sapphire Rim Dr 78232
Sarah Ln 78222
Sarasota Woods 78250
Saratoga Dr 78213
Saratoga Pass 78254
Saratoga Spgs 78245
Saratoga Coach 78254
Sarazen Ct 78257
Sarepto 78239
Sargent St 78210
Sarita St 78224
Sas Dr 78224
Sassafras 78261
Satellite Dr 78217
Saturn St 78226
Saunders Ave 78207
Sausalito Ct 78258
Sausalito Fern 78261
Sauvignon 78258
Sava St 78214
Savannah Dr 78213
Savannah Pass 78216
Savory Gln 78238
Savoy Dr 78209
Sawgrass 78244
Sawgrass Rdg 78260
Sawtooth Dr 78245
Sawyer Rd 78238
Saxby Gln 78257
Saxon Dr 78213
Saxonhill Dr 78253
Sayanora Ct 78216
Saybrook 78250
E & W Sayers Ave 78214
Saylers Crk 78245
Scarborough Ct 78249
Scarborough Sq 78218
Scarlet Mdw 78254
Scarlet Ibis 78245
Scarlet Oak Dr 78220
Scarlet Ohara 78223
Scarlet Sage 78253
Scarlett Pl 78221
Scarsdale St 78217
Scates Dr 78227
Scattered Oaks St 78232
Scaup Ct 78245
Scenic Cir 78251
Scenic Knl 78258
Scenic Knls 78258
Scenic Ln 78230
Scenic Pass 78260
Scenic Pt 78254
Scenic Spgs 78255
Scenic Glade 78249
Scenic Hills Dr 78255
Scenic Loop Rd 78255
Scenic Rock 78255
Scenic Stroll 78260
Scenic Sunset 78249
Scenic View Dr 78255
Scheh 78214
Schertz Rd 78233
Schley Ave 78210
Schmeltzer Ln 78213
Schneider Ln 78266
Schoenthal Rd 78266
Scholz Way 78207
School St 78210
Schoolhouse Rd 78255
Schreiner Pl 78212
Schumacher Rd 78220
Scordato Dr 78266
Scotland Dr 78213
Scots Gln 78240
Scotsdale Dr 78209
Scotsman Dr 78219
Scott Alan 78261
Scott Carpenter Dr 78219
Scottshill 78209
Scottswood 78239
Scotty Dr 78227
Scout Pt 78266
Scrub Jay 78240
S Sea Ln 78216
Sea Eagle 78253
Sea Holly 78245
Sea Island Dr 78264
Sea Mist 78250
Sea Spray 78264
Sea World Dr 78251
Seabreeze Dr 78220
Seabrook Dr 78219
Seacliff St 78242
Seacomber Pl 78242
Seacroft Dr 78238
Seafarer Dr 78242
Seahorse Dr 78242
Seal Cv 78255
Seale Rd 78219
Searcy Dr 78232
Searkers St 78226
Seascape 78251
Seashell Dr 78242
Seatide Vis 78249
Seaton Grn 78209
Seaton Hts 78254
Sebastian Pl 78249
Sebec Cir 78250
Secession Ln 78240
Secluded Grv 78253
Seco Creek St 78256
Seco Tierra 78223
Secret Cv 78266
Secret Shrs 78244
Secret Trl 78247
Sedberry Ct 78258
Sedgewick Ct 78257
Seekers St 78255
Seeling Blvd 78228
Seford Dr 78209
Segovia St 78251
Segovia Way 78253
Seguin Rd 78219
Seguin St 78208
Segura St 78237
Seidel Rd 78209
Seiler Ln 78263
Seine 78250
Sekula Dr 78250
Selbourne Ln 78251
Selby Hts 78254
Seldon Trl 78244
Selendine 78239
Selkirk St 78232
Selwyn Way 78251
Seminario 78250
Seminole Pass 78266
Seminole St 78207
Seminole Oaks 78261
Semlinger Rd 78220
Semora Oak 78259
Sendera Ct 78245
Sendera St 78260
Sendero Fls 78232
Sendero Spg 78251
Sendero Verde 78261
Seneca Dr 78238
Senisa Dr 78228
Senisa Spgs 78251
Senna Hls 78266
Senna Trl 78256
Senova Dr 78216
Sentinel St 78217
Sentry Hl 78260
Sentry Pt 78233
Sequoia Cv 78251
Sequoia Dr 78232
Sequoia Fall 78251
Sequoia Pass 78251
Sequoia Height St 78251
Sequoia Wood 78249
Seraphim Ct 78251
Serapio Ln 78260
Serena 78248
Serena Vis 78251
Serenade Dr
200-899 78216
900-999 78213
Serenata Cir 78216
Serene Grv 78247
Serene Hls 78255
Serene Mdw 78258
Serene Creek Dr 78230
Serene Ridge Dr 78239
Serene Valley St 78227
Serene Woods St 78253
Serenity Ln 78232
Serenity Rdg 78260
Serna Park 78218
Service Ctr 78218
Sesame St 78232
Setting Moon 78255
Setting Sun St 78238
Settlement Way 78258
Settler Ct 78258

Settlers Crk 78258
Settlers Rdg 78238
Settlers Trl 78245
Settlers Vly 78258
Seven Iron Way 78221
Seven Oaks Dr 78217
Seven Pines St 78245
Seven Seas Dr 78242
Seven States 78244
Seven Winds 78258
Severn Rd 78217
Sevilla Cir & Way 78257
Sewanee St 78210
Sexauer 78214
Shadbush St 78245
Shadden Oaks 78233
Shade Crk 78238
Shade Tree 78254
Shadewood St 78238
Shadow Frst 78239
Shadow Gln 78240
Shadow Pass 78260
Shadow Pt 78260
Shadow Rdg 78250
Shadow Run 78250
Shadow Trl 78244
Shadow Way 78218
Shadow Bend Dr 78230
Shadow Cliff St 78232
Shadow Elm Woods 78249
Shadow Hill Dr 78228
Shadow Lake Dr 78244
Shadow Mist 78238
Shadow Moss Ct 78244
Shadow Oak Woods 78249
Shadow Oaks Ln 78231
Shadow Park St 78232
Shadow Path St 78230
Shadow Smith Ln 78264
Shadow Tree 78233
Shadow Valley Dr 78227
Shadowbluff Dr 78216
Shadowbrook 78254
Shadowdance St 78253
Shadowlight Terrace
St 78233
Shadowrock 78260
Shadrach St 78203
Shadwell Dr 78228
Shady Blf 78218
Shady Brk 78239
Shady Crk 78239
Shady Cv 78213
Shady Grn 78250
Shady Hls 78254
Shady Knl 78258
Shady Ln 78257
Shady Mdws 78245
Shady Vly 78254
Shady Acres 78260
Shady Bend Dr 78256
Shady Breeze 78217
Shady Canyon Dr 78248
Shady Cliff St 78232
Shady Crest Cir 78231
Shady Elms 78240
Shady Grove Dr 78227
Shady Hollow Ln 78255
Shady Lake Dr 78244
Shady Leaf 78254
Shady Oak St 78229
Shady Rill 78213
Shady Rock Cir 78231
Shady Springs Dr 78230
Shady Trail St 78232
Shady Tree Ln 78247
Shady Walk Dr 78231
Shady Way St 78244
Shady Winds 78254
Shadydale Dr 78228
Shadyglen 78240
Shadylane Dr 78209
Shadystone Dr 78254
Shadyview Dr 78201
Shadywood Ln 78216
Shaencrest 78254
Shaencrossing 78254
Shaenfield Ct, Pl & Rd 78254
Shaenleaf 78254
Shaenmeadow 78254
Shaenpath 78254
N & S Shaenridge 78254
Shaenview 78254
Shaenwest 78254
Shagbark 78264
Shakertown 78238
Shalimar Dr 78213
Shallow Grv 78247
Shallow Brook St 78247
Shallow Creek Dr 78251
Shallow Ridge Dr 78239
Shallow Water St 78233
Shamrock St 78219
Shamrock Way 78253
Shane Rd 78223
Shanetag 78232
Shannon Cir 78260
Shannon Dr 78221
Shannon Lee St 78216
Shannon Rose 78260
Shara Mist 78251
Sharer St 78208
Sharmain Pl 78221
Sharon Dr 78216
Sharpsburg St 78230
Shasta Ave 78221
Shasta Daisy 78245
Shavano Ct 78230
Shavano Dr 78231
Shavano Hl 78249
Shavano Holw 78230
Shavano Pl 78249
Shavano Pt 78230
Shavano Rdg 78230
Shavano Rnch 78257
Shavano Spgs 78230
Shavano Walk 78230
Shavano Way 78249
Shavano Arrow 78230
Shavano Ash 78230
Shavano Bark 78230
Shavano Birch 78230
Shavano Breeze 78230
Shavano Cross 78230
Shavano Downs 78230
Shavano Glenn 78230
Shavano Mist 78230
Shavano Oak 78249
Shavano Peak 78230
Shavano Wind 78230
Shavano Woods St 78249
Shawanee Pass St 78260
Shawn Marie St 78210
Shawnee Way 78261
Shay Cir 78251
Shearer Blvd 78201
Shearer Hl 78216
Sheep Hair 78245
Sheffield 78213
Sheffield Park Dr 78209
Sheila Dr 78209
Shelbritt Rd 78249
Shelburn Dr 78220
Shelby Dr 78211
Shelbys Run 78251
Shelbyville Ct 78244
Shell Brk 78252
Shell Creek St 78232
Shellbark 78264
Shellnut 78264
Shelly St 78238
Shemya Ave 78221
Shenandale St 78230
Shenandoah St 78210
Shepherds Way 78252
Sheppard Knl 78227
Sheraton Dr 78209
Sherborne Ln 78257
Sherborne Wood 78218
Sherbrooke Oak 78249
E & W Sheridan 78204
Sheringham 78218
Sherman 78202
Sherman Oak St 78232
Sherri Ann Rd 78233
Sherri Oaks St 78250
Sherril Brook Rd 78228
Sherry 78264
Sherry St 78242
Sherry Wood 78264
Sherwood Dr 78201
Sherwood Way 78217
Sherwood Forest Dr 78260
Shetland Bnd 78254
Shetland Brk 78254
Shetland Ct 78254
Shetland Dr 78223
Shetland Hls 78254
Shetland Park 78254
Shetland Trce 78254
Shetland Vw 78254
Shetland Gate 78254
Shetland Wind 78254
Shieldhall 78245
Shields Dr 78245
Shiloh Dr 78220
Shiloh Frst 78258
Shimmering Dawn St 78253
Shin Oak Dr 78233
Shiner St 78207
Shingle Oak Dr 78247
Shining Arrow 78258
Shining Elk 78266
Shining Elm Dr 78254
Shining Glow 78244
Shining Star 78239
Shining Waters 78222
Shinnecock Trl 78260
Shipman Dr 78219
Shire Country 78254
Shire Oak St 78247
Shirley Hts 78260
Shirley St 78208
Shivalik Way 78228
Shoal Trl 78250
Shoal Creek Dr 78251
Shoal Run St 78232
Sholom Dr & Pl 78230
Shoo Fly Trl 78245
Shook Ave 78212
Shooting Quail 78250
Shooting Star 78255
Shop Ln 78226
Shore Dr 78207
Shorebird Ln 78245
Shorecliff St 78248
Shoreham 78260
Shoreline Dr 78254
Shoreview Pl 78242
Short Rdg 78231
Short Trl 78245
Short Branch St 78247
Short Horn Dr 78247
Shoshoni Trl 78255
Shoshoni Rise 78261
Shostakovich 78260
Shotgun Dr 78254
Showboat Dr 78223
Showboat Dock 78223
Shrader Rd 78220
Shrine Ave 78221
Shropshire Dr 78217
Shuman Crk 78255
Shumard Oak Dr 78223
Shumard Oak Woods
St 78249
Sicily 78253
Sid Katz Dr 78229
Sidbury Cir 78250
Sidecliff Pl 78253
Sidney St 78203
Sidney Brooks St 78235
Siena Vw 78253
Sienna Cir & Ct 78249
Sierra 78214
Sierra Crst 78259
Sierra Holw 78261
Sierra Trl 78254
Sierra Vis 78233
Sierra Birch 78261
Sierra Blanca 78259
Sierra Encino 78232
Sierra Glen Dr 78245
Sierra Hermosa 78255
Sierra Madre Dr 78233
Sierra Oaks 78256
Sierra Oscura 78259
Sierra Peak 78261
Sierra Ridge Dr 78245
Sierra Salinas 78259
Sierra Seco 78240
Sierra Sky 78254
Sierra Verde 78240
Siesta Ln 78201
Siesta Valley Dr 78242
Sight Scape 78255
Sigma Rd 78258
Signature St 78263
Silent Cir 78250
Silent Crk 78255
Silent Hls 78250
Silent Holw 78260
Silent Lk 78244
Silent Mdw 78250
Silent Path 78250
Silent Spg 78250
Silent Strm 78250
Silent Cloud 78250
Silent Cross 78250
Silent Elks 78250
Silent Forest Dr 78250
Silent Oaks 78250
Silent Rain 78250
Silent Sunrise 78250
Silent Sunset 78250
Silent Wind 78250
Silent Wings 78250
Silentbluff Dr 78216
Silhouette St 78216
Silicon Dr 78249
Silver Br 78254
Silver Cir 78264
Silver Crk 78260
Silver Cyn 78244
Silver Grv 78254
Silver Knls 78258
Silver Mtn 78264
Silver Park 78254
Silver Pass 78254
Silver Pr 78254
Silver Riv 78222
Silver Strm 78259
Silver Vis 78254
Silver Arrow St 78224
Silver Bit 78227
Silver Bow Dr 78242
Silver Brush 78254
Silver Charm 78248
Silver City 78254
Silver Cloud Dr 78260
Silver Coins 78254
Silver Crown 78254
Silver Dollar 78254
Silver Eagle 78264
Silver Elm Pl 78254
Silver Fox 78247
Silver Hampton 78254
Silver Hill St 78224
Silver Horse 78254
Silver Lake Dr 78219
Silver Leaf 78264
Silver Mine 78254
Silver Moon 78254
Silver Oaks 78213
Silver Pointe 78254
Silver Pond 78254
Silver Quail 78250
Silver Radiance St 78230
Silver Ridge St 78232
Silver Rock 78255
Silver Saddle Dr 78264
E & W Silver Sands
Dr 78216
Silver Shadow 78239
Silver Spot 78254
Silver Spring St 78224
Silver Spruce St 78232
Silver Spur St 78232
Silver Willow 78254
Silver Wings Dr 78264
Silverado Way 78260
Silverberry Cv 78213
Silverbrook Pl 78254
Silvercrest 78228
Silverfeather 78254
Silverhollow 78232
Silverhorn Dr 78216
Silversmith 78260
Silverstar Dr 78218
Silverstone 78258
Silvertip Dr 78228
Silverton 78251
Silverton Ct 78261
Silverton Wind 78261
Silverwagon 78254
Silverway 78251
Silverwood Dr 78232
Simi Valley Dr 78259
Simler St 78227
Simon 78204
Simplicity Dr 78245
Simpson Trl 78251
Sims Ave
2-98 78214
100-199 78214
200-1299 78225
Sinclair Rd 78222
Singing Frst 78256
Singing Vw 78255
Singing Brook Dr 78227
Singing Rain 78260
Singing Wind Dr 78227
Singinghill Dr 78242
Single Spur 78254
Single Peak 78261
Single Tree Dr 78264
Sinsonte St 78230
Sinsonte Haven St 78230
Sioux Spgs 78261
Sioux St 78211
Sir Arthur Ct 78213
Sir Barton St 78248
Sir Galahad 78240
Sir Gareth Dr 78218
Sir Huon St 78248
Sir Lancelot 78240
Sir Phillip Dr 78209
Sir Robert Dr 78219
Sir Winston St 78216
Sirius Mesa 78252
Sirretta Dr 78233
Sissinghurst 78209
Sistine 78258
Sitka Spruce 78245
Six Iron 78221
Six Mile Dr 78224
Sixpence 78253
Skaggs Pl 78235
Skelton Dr 78219
Skip Jack 78242
S Skipper Dr 78216
Skolout St 78227
Skull Valley Dr 78245
Sky Loop & Vis 78266
Sky Blue Bnd 78252
Sky Cliff St 78231
Sky Country St 78247
Sky Dale Dr 78231
Sky Oaks 78253
Sky Ridge Ct 78258
Skybound 78245
Skye Hts 78254
Skyforest Dr 78232
Skyhawk Dr 78249
Skylark Ave 78210
Skyline Blvd 78217
Skyline Vis 78253
Skyline Mesa 78253
Skyline Ridge Dr 78239
Skyplace Blvd 78216
Skyridge Ave 78210
Skyridge Cv 78261
E & W Skyview Dr 78228
Slash Pine Woods 78249
Slate Rock St 78232
Slate Valley Dr 78242
Slattery St 78240
Slayden Dr 78228
Slayton Way St 78207
Sleepy Frst 78239
Sleepy Cove St 78230
Sleepy Daisy 78245
Sleepy Elm 78209
Sleepy Glade St 78224
Sleepy Hollow St 78230
Sleepy Oaks Ln 78253
Sleepy Valley Dr 78242
Slicers Hole 78260
Slickrock Way 78258
Slickrock Draw 78245
Sligo St 78223
Slimp Way 78207
Slimwood Dr 78240
Slippery Elm St 78240
Slippery Rock 78251
Sloan Dr 78228
Slumber Pass 78260
Small Crk 78260
Small Valley Dr 78242
Smallwood Dr 78210
Smincons Trl 78255
Smith 78239
Smith Aly 78207
N Smith St 78207
S Smith St 78207
Smithson Ridge Rd 78261
Smithson Valley Rd 78261
Smoke Crk 78245
Smoke Rdg 78217
Smoke Signal St 78242
Smoke Tree Dr 78227
Smokey Way 78217
Smokey Bend Way 78217
Smokey Wood Ln 78249
Smoking Oaks St 78233
Smoky Fennel 78245
Smoky Quartz 78222
Snake Cyn 78252
Snead St 78217
Snell Dr 78219
Snell Mdws 78247
Snip 78248
Snorkel Cv 78255
Snow Hl 78245
Snow Fox St 78242
Snow Goose 78245
Snow Trail St 78250
Snow Valley St 78242
Snowbell Trl 78256
Snowden Crst & Rd 78240
Snowflake Dr 78238
Snowshoe 78245
Snuggle Clf 78255
Snuggle Vly 78260
Soapberry Cv 78249
Soaring Breeze 78253
Soaring Cloud 78253
Soaring Mesa 78253
Soaring Oak 78255
Socorro 78214
Sofia St 78207
Softrain 78259
Softwood St 78250
Solar Crst 78245
Solar Dr 78227
Solar Mist 78252
Soledad St 78205
Soledad Bldg 78205
Solitaire Hl 78247
Solitude Cv 78260
Solo St & Vw 78260
Soltol Cv 78249
Somerall 78248
Somerset Rd 78211
Somerset Arms 78257
Somerton Ln 78260
Somerville Ct 78257
Somerville Bay 78244
Sommerdale 78217
Sommers Dr 78217
Sonata Ct 78266
Sonata Dr 78216
Sonata Park 78230
Sonesta Ln 78260
Song St 78216
Song Heights Dr 78230
E Songbird Ln 78229
Sonia St 78224
Sonnet Dr 78216
Sonni Fld 78253
Sonny Rdg 78244
Sonoma 78259
Sonoma Rdg 78255
Sonoma Spgs 78232
Sonora 78204
Sonora Crk 78232
Sonora Cavern 78254
Sonora Mesa 78232
Sonora Sunset 78239
Sonterra Blvd 78258
E Sonterra Blvd
100-1500 78258
1502-1698 78258
1801-1899 78259
2100-2198 78259
Sonterra Pl 78258
Soogan Trl 78245
Sophora 78261
Sopris Ln 78260
Sorrell Ln 78266
Sorrell Place Dr 78248
Sorrento 78217
Sotol Ln 78261
Sound Willow 78254
Sousa St 78260
South Bnd 78250
Southampton Dr 78228
Southbridge St 78216
E Southcross Blvd
100-1199 78214
1201-1297 78223
1299-3499 78223
3800-4799 78222
W Southcross Blvd
101-197 78221
199-699 78221
700-2999 78211
Southcross Ranch Rd 78222
Southeast Dr 78222
Southerland 78250
Southern Blf 78222
Southern Fld 78222
Southern Grv 78222
Southern Hls 78244
Southern Knl 78261
Southern Oaks 78261
Southern Sky 78222
Southern Sun 78245
Southface 78233
Southill Rd
1-99 78228
100-299 78201
Southlawn Ave 78237
Southolme 78204
Southpoint St 78229
Southport Dr 78223
Southton Rd, Run &
Way 78223
Southtrail Dr 78216
Southwalk St 78232
Southway Dr 78225
Southwell Rd 78240
Southwick St 78228
Southwood St 78220
Sovereign St 78229
Spaatz St 78211
Space Center Dr 78218
Spaceway Dr 78239
Spacious Sky 78260
Spanish Br 78222
Spanish Cv 78242
Spanish Flt 78222

Spanish Trce 78222
Spanish Bay 78260
Spanish Dagger 78218
Spanish Dawn 78222
Spanish Earth 78233
Spanish Grant Rd 78264
Spanish King 78222
Spanish Moss 78239
Spanish Oaks
1300-1599 78213
Spanish Oaks
22600-22699 78266
Spanish Wood 78249
Sparrow Crk 78238
Sparrow Lk 78244
Sparrow Ln 78217
Sparrow Rdg 78261
Sparrow Song 78260
Sparrows Nest 78250
Spear St 78237
Spear Head Dr 78238
Spearwood 78233
Specht Rd 78260
Spectrum Dr 78249
Spectrum One 78230
Speedway Dr 78230
Spello Cir 78253
Spencer Ln 78201
Spent Wing Dr 78213
Spice Mdw 78222
Spice Spg 78260
Spicewood Bnd 78255
Spicewood Dr 78213
Spider Lily 78258
Spiller Rd 78254
Spindle Ave 78211
Spindle Top Dr 78245
Spindrift 78239
Spinnaker Path 78263
Spiral Ave 78227
Spiral Crk 78238
Spiral Cyn 78261
Spirea 78261
Splashing Rock 78260
Splendor View Dr 78249
Splintered Oak 78233
Split Crk 78238
Split Fairway 78260
Split Oak 78248
Spofford Ave 78208
Spokane Rd 78222
Spoon Lake St 78244
Spoonbill Ct 78245
Spoonwood Path 78245
Spotswood Trl 78230
Spotted Cedar 78249
Spotted Deer St 78242
Spotted Eagle 78248
Spotted Oak Woods 78249
Spotted Trail Dr 78240
Spotters Rdg 78233
Spriggsdale Ave 78220
Spring Blf 78247
Spring Brg 78247
Spring Cor 78247
Spring Crk 78247
Spring Cv 78247
Spring Cyn 78232
Spring Fls 78247
Spring Gln 78247
Spring Grn 78247
Spring Hbr 78247
Spring Hts 78247
Spring Knls 78258
Spring Land 78247
Spring Rnch 78247
Spring Smt 78247
Spring Spur 78247
Spring Sq 78247
N Spring St 78207
S Spring St 78207
Spring Vly 78247
Spring Walk 78247
Spring Xing 78247
Spring Arbor St 78249
Spring Arrow 78247

Spring Ash 78247
Spring Beauty 78254
Spring Bend St 78209
Spring Bird 78247
Spring Bow 78247
Spring Branch St 78249
Spring Briar St 78209
Spring Brook St 78249
Spring Buck 78247
Spring Cabin 78247
Spring Club Dr 78249
Spring Cluster 78247
Spring Coral 78247
Spring Country St 78247
Spring Crest St 78249
Spring Crown 78247
Spring Dale Dr 78249
Spring Dawn St 78217
Spring Day 78247
Spring Dew 78247
Spring Dove St 78247
Spring Drops St 78249
Spring Farm St 78247
Spring Fire 78247
Spring Flower St 78249
Spring Forest St 78249
Spring Front Dr 78249
Spring Garden St 78249
Spring Gate 78247
Spring Grove St 78249
Spring Harvest 78254
Spring Haven St 78249
Spring Hollow St 78249
Spring Hurst St 78249
Spring Lake Dr 78248
Spring Lark St 78249
Spring Leaf St 78249
Spring Life 78249
Spring Manor St 78249
Spring Meadow Dr 78227
Spring Mint Dr 78249
Spring Mist 78247
Spring Mont St 78249
Spring Moon St 78247
Spring Morning St 78249
Spring Night St 78247
Spring Oak Dr 78219
Spring Park St 78227
Spring Pebble 78247
Spring Pine St 78249
Spring Point St 78249
Spring Quail 78247
Spring Rain 78249
Spring Ridge Dr 78249
Spring Robin 78247
Spring Rock 78247
Spring Rose St 78249
Spring Scent 78258
Spring Shadow St 78249
Spring Shower 78247
Spring Sky St 78247
Spring Smoke 78247
Spring Song Dr 78249
Spring Star St 78247
Spring Stone 78247
Spring Sun 78244
Spring Sunshine 78247
Spring Terrace Dr 78249
Spring Time St 78249
Spring Trail St 78249
Spring Village St 78247
Spring Watch 78247
Spring Water Cir 78247
Spring Well St 78249
Springfield Rd 78219
Springhill Dr 78232
Springhouse St 78251
Springline St 78251
Springside 78260
Springvale Dr 78227
Springview Dr 78222
Springwood Ln 78216
Sprouted Rock 78260
Spruce Crst 78245
Spruce Fls 78245
Spruce Lk 78245

Spruce St 78203
Spruce Strm 78247
Spruce Breeze 78245
Spruce Cove St 78247
Spruce Leaf St 78247
Spruce Mist 78245
Spruce Tree Ln 78247
Sprucewood Ln 78216
Spur Dr 78227
Spur Rdg 78264
Spur Valley St 78242
Spurs Ln 78240
Spurs Rnch 78245
Spyglass Hls 78253
Spyglass Trl 78247
Spyglass Vw 78247
Squanto Dr 78230
Squaw Creek Dr 78230
Squires Row 78213
Squirrel Trl 78253
St Charles Bay 78229
St Johns Way 78212
Staack Ave 78240
Staacke Stevens Bldg 78205
Stable Dr 78240
Stable Holw 78244
Stable Pass 78249
Stable Vis 78227
Stable Vw 78244
Stable Briar 78249
Stable Brook Dr 78249
Stable Creek Dr 78249
Stable Downs 78249
Stable Farm 78249
Stable Forest Dr 78249
Stable Fork Dr 78249
Stable Glen Dr 78245
Stable Knoll Dr 78249
Stable Point Dr 78249
Stable Pond Dr 78249
Stable Ridge Dr 78249
Stable Road Dr 78249
Stable Square Dr 78249
Stable Trail Dr 78249
Stable Wood 78249
Stace 78204
Staffel St 78210
Stafford Ct 78217
Stafford St 78208
Staffordshire 78257
Stag Mdw & Pt 78248
Stagecoach Dr 78227
Stagecoach Run 78253
Stagecoach Bay 78254
Stagehand Rd 78245
Stager Hls 78238
Staggering Crk 78254
Staghorn Gate 78233
Stags Leap 78253
Stagwood Hl & Pass 78254
N Stahl Park 78217
Stahl Rd
3800-4999 78217
5001-5197 78247
5199-5700 78217
5702-7198 78247
Stairock St 78248
Stallion Crk 78247
Stallion Cv 78244
Stallion Hls 78238
Stallion Run 78259
Stallion Bay 78254
Stallion Cross 78247
Stampede 78227
Stampede Stead 78254
Stams Cir 78266
Standing Bear St 78242
Standing Creek Ln 78230
Standing Oaks St 78233
Standing Rock St 78242
Standish Rd 78258
Standwood 78254
Stanfield Ave 78210
Stanford Dr 78212
Stanley Ct 78214
Stanteen Dr 78263

Stanton Dr 78253
Stanton Oaks 78259
Stanwood St 78213
Staplehurst St 78228
Stapleton St 78227
Star Cir 78266
Star Grv 78259
Star Vis 78221
Star Vw 78260
Star Creek Dr 78251
Star Glade 78245
Star Heights Dr 78230
Starbend St 78217
Starbright 78258
Starburst Cir 78219
Starcrest Dr
8300-8499 78218
8501-8597 78217
8599-10599 78217
10601-10699 78217
11601-11797 78247
11799-12099 78247
12300-12398 78216
12400-12499 78216
Stardream Dr 78216
Stardust Dr 78228
Starfire St 78219
Stargazer Pass 78260
Starhaven Pl 78227
Starhill Dr 78218
Stark 78204
Starlight Ct 78261
Starlight Pass 78260
Starlight Ter 78233
Starling Dr 78255
Starling Hl 78260
Starlit Pond 78260
Starlite Way 78260
Starr 78202
Starry Mountain St 78260
State St 78223
State Highway 151
4700-5698 78227
State Highway 151
5700-5800 78227
5802-6498 78227
8201-8397 78245
8399-8799 78245
8801-9697 78251
9699-15199 78251
State Highway 16 S
9800-13899 78224
14000-19199 78264
State Highway 211 78254
Statehouse St 78233
Stately Oaks 78260
Stathmore Dr 78217
Statice Hunt 78253
Staton Dr 78224
Stattler St 78251
Stayman Dr 78222
Steam Boat Run 78250
Steamboat 78249
Stebbins St 78240
Stedwick Dr 78251
Steen St 78219
Steeple Blf, Brk, Crse,
Dr, Park & Vw 78256
Steeple Oak 78256
Steepleway 78248
Stefnianne St 78255
Stella St 78203
Stella Doro 78259
Stemmons 78238
Stephanie St 78237
Stephen Foster 78223
Stephens Rnch 78251
Stepstone Dr 78258
Sterling Dr 78220
Sterling Browning Rd 78232
Sterling Green Dr 78254
Sterlingford Pl 78217
Stetson Grn 78258
Stetson Park 78223
Stetson Run 78223
Stetson Trl 78223

Stetson Vw 78223
Steuben Dr 78230
Steubing Oaks 78258
Stevens Ct 78233
Stevenwood Ln 78230
Steves Ave
400-599 78204
600-2999 78210
Steves Run 78232
Stieren St 78210
Stiffkey Dr 78228
Still Crk 78238
Still Lk 78244
Still Mdw 78222
Still Brook St 78238
Still Hollow Dr 78244
Still Moon 78245
Still Pond 78245
Stillforest 78250
Stillwater Crk 78254
Stillwater Pkwy 78254
Stillwater St 78238
Stillwell St 78209
Stimmel St 78227
Stirman Way 78216
Stirrup Cir 78240
Stirrup Ln 78240
Stirrup St 78227
Stockade St 78233
Stockbridge Ln 78230
Stockdale St 78233
Stockholm 78230
Stockman Dr 78247
Stockport 78239
Stockton Dr 78216
Stoddard Dr 78232
Stokely Hl 78258
Stolnet St 78220
Stone Cyn 78260
Stone Gdn 78254
Stone Vlg 78250
Stone Cave 78247
Stone Chase 78254
Stone Creek Pl 78254
Stone Crest Dr 78209
Stone Crop Ln 78249
Stone Edge Pl 78254
Stone Edge St 78232
Stone Fence Rd 78227
Stone Hill Ct & Dr 78258
Stone Hollow Dr 78232
Stone Lake Dr 78244
Stone Oak Loop 78258
Stone Oak Pkwy
18700-20899 78258
21200-21299 78259
21500-21598 78258
21601-21699 78258
21701-21799 78260
Stone Saddle 78258
Stone Tree St 78247
Stone Valley Dr 78242
Stonebridge 78240
Stonecroft 78254
Stonefield Pl 78254
Stonefruit St 78240
Stonegate Dr 78228
Stonehaven Dr 78230
Stonehenge Dr 78230
Stonehouse Dr 78227
Stonehue 78258
Stoneland Dr 78230
Stoneleigh Dr 78220
Stoneleigh Way 78218
Stoneridge Dr 78232
Stones Ml 78233
Stones River Dr 78245
Stones Throw 78248
Stoneshire 78218
Stoneside 78237
Stonetower Dr 78248
Stonewall Bnd 78256
Stonewall Hl 78256
Stonewall St
100-699 78214
700-1500 78211

1502-1598 78211
Stoneway Dr 78258
Stonewind Pl 78254
Stonewood St 78216
Stoney Brg 78247
Stoney Cv 78247
Stoney Dr 78247
Stoney Frk 78247
Stoney Gln 78247
Stoney Grv 78247
Stoney Hl 78231
Stoney Orch 78247
Stoney Park 78247
Stoney Pass 78247
Stoney Smt 78247
Stoney Spur 78247
Stoney Sq 78247
Stoney Vis 78247
Stoney Xing 78247
Stoney Ash 78247
Stoney Bend St 78247
Stoney Bluff St 78247
Stoney Branch St 78247
Stoney Briar 78247
Stoney Burke 78247
Stoney Circle St 78247
Stoney Climb St 78217
Stoney Cluster 78247
Stoney Country 78247
Stoney Creek Dr 78242
Stoney Crown 78247
Stoney Dawn 78247
Stoney Falls St 78247
Stoney Glade 78247
Stoney Leaf 78247
Stoney Meadow St 78247
Stoney Mist 78247
Stoney Pond 78247
Stoney Star 78247
Stoney Trail Cir 78231
Stoney View St 78217
Stony Forest Dr 78231
Stonybrook Dr 78242
Stonykirk Rd 78240
Storeywood Dr 78213
Storm Vw 78266
Stormy Crk 78255
Stormy Hls 78247
Stormy Rdg 78255
Stormy Trl 78247
Stormy Autumn 78247
Stormy Breeze 78247
Stormy Dawn 78247
Stormy Rock 78255
Stormy Skies 78247
Stormy Sunset 78247
Stormy Winds 78247
Story Ln 78223
Stout Dr 78219
Stowers Blvd 78238
Strada Privata 78253
Stradford Pl 78217
Straight Arrow 78258
Strait Song 78253
Strand Sq 78218
Stratford Ct 78223
Strathaven St 78240
Stratton Ln 78257
Straus Medina 78252
Strauss 78256
Straw Flower St 78238
Strawberry Park 78238
Strawhouse Way 78245
Stream Cir 78250
Stream Run 78249
Stream Vly 78250
Stream Cross 78250
Stream Water 78249
Strech Ave 78224
Streeter St 78233
Stribling 78204
Stringfellow St 78223
Strings Dr 78216
Strolling Ln 78233
Strong Box 78247
Strong Box Way 78254

Strong Oak 78247
Stuart Rd
3000-13300 78263
13302-13698 78263
14000-15899 78223
Stumberg 78204
Sturbridge St 78254
Sturdy Oaks Trl 78233
Sturgis Dr 78245
Stutts Dr 78219
Su Vino Dawn 78255
Sublett Dr 78223
Suddith Dr 78233
Sue Ellen Cir 78247
Sueno Ln 78256
Sueno Pt 78245
Suffolk Pl 78201
Sugar Trl 78251
Sugar Creek St 78244
Sugar Crest Dr 78232
Sugar Pine St 78232
Sugar Wood 78248
Sugarberry Way 78253
Sugarberry Woods St 78249
Sugarfoot Dr 78227
Sugarhill Dr 78230
Sugarloaf Dr 78245
Sulfur Cyn 78247
Sulky Ln 78240
Sullivan Dr 78213
Sumac Cir 78266
Sumac Cv 78266
Sumac Ln 78266
Sumac Rdg 78250
Sumantra Clf 78261
Summer Fall 78259
Summer Mdw 78222
Summer Pl 78250
Summer Trl 78250
Summer Vw 78258
Summer Way 78240
Summer Bluff Dr 78254
Summer Breeze Ln 78253
Summer Creek Cir &
Dr 78248
Summer Dawn 78258
Summer Fest Dr 78244
Summer Forest St 78249
Summer Glen Dr 78247
Summer Gold Dr 78222
Summer Knoll Dr 78258
Summer Park Ln 78213
Summer Springs St 78259
Summer Squall 78248
Summer Sun Ln 78217
Summer Susie 78233
Summer Tanager 78253
Summer Vail 78251
Summer Wind St 78217
Summerbrook 78254
Summerfield 78258
Summerhill Dr 78226
Summers Pass 78247
Summers Dream 78258
Summerstone 78254
Summertime Dr 78216
Summerton Oak St 78232
Summerwood Dr 78232
E Summit Ave 78212
W Summit Ave
100-899 78212
900-2399 78201
2400-2699 78228
Summit Blf 78258
Summit Cir 78256
Summit Crk 78258
Summit Crst 78258
Summit Cv 78258
Summit Hl 78258
Summit Holw 78258
Summit Lk 78245
Summit Pass 78229
Summit Pkwy
5300-5399 78228
5500-5598 78229
Summit Rdg 78258

Summit Spgs 78258
Summit Vw 78261
Summit Oak 78229
Summit Wood 78229
Sumner Dr
300-799 78209
900-1100 78218
1102-1198 78218
Sun 78204
Sun Fls 78244
Sun Frst 78239
Sun Gdn 78245
Sun Holw 78238
Sun Is 78245
Sun Ml 78254
Sun Mtn 78258
Sun Park 78217
Sun Spg 78245
Sun Bay 78244
Sun Beam Ln 78220
Sun Candle 78245
Sun Canyon Dr 78244
Sun Chase 78245
Sun Country St 78247
Sun Creek St 78238
Sun Dial St 78238
Sun Farm 78244
Sun Gate St 78217
Sun Harbour Dr 78244
Sun Oak St 78232
Sun Ridge Dr 78247
Sun Sierra 78245
Sun Spur St 78232
Sun Trail St 78232
Sun Valley Dr 78227
Sun Vista Ln 78217
Sun Wood St 78232
E Sunbelt Dr 78218
Sunbend Fls 78224
Sunbird Lk 78245
Sunbird Pass 78224
Sunbird Bay 78245
Sunburst St 78230
Suncatcher 78253
Suncliff Crst 78238
Suncrest Ln 78217
Sundance Fall 78245
Sundance Ft 78245
Sundance Ln 78238
Sundance Hunt 78245
Sundance Scape 78245
Sunday Song 78245
Sunderidge 78260
Sundew Cir 78266
Sundew Mist 78244
Sundown Dr 78217
Sundown Pass 78261
Sundrop 78260
Sundrop Fls 78224
Sundrop Pass 78245
Sundrop Bay 78224
Sunfire 78247
Sunflower Ln 78213
Sunflower Run 78240
Sunflower Way 78240
Sungate Park 78245
Sungate Bay 78224
Sunglo Dr 78221
Sungold 78222
Sungrove Vw 78245
Sunhaven Dr 78239
Sunkist 78228
Sunlight Dr 78238
Sunlit Brk 78240
Sunlit Grv 78247
Sunlit Pt 78240
Sunlit Glade 78247
Sunlit Pass Dr 78239
Sunlit Trail Dr 78244
Sunlit Well Dr 78247
Sunny Gln 78217
Sunny Grv 78217
Sunny Hl 78263
Sunny Mdw 78260
Sunny Pass 78260
Sunny Pt 78266

Sunny Walk 78217
Sunny Brook Dr 78228
Sunny Day 78240
Sunny Oaks 78250
Sunny Wonder 78253
Sunnycrest Dr 78228
Sunnydell Dr 78253
Sunnyland Dr 78228
Sunnyside 78258
Sunnyvale Ln 78217
Sunnyview Trl 78253
Sunrise Bch 78253
Sunrise Dr 78228
Sunrise Fld 78245
Sunrise Hl 78260
Sunrise Lk 78244
Sunrise Pass 78244
Sunrise Vlg 78244
Sunrise Bend Dr 78244
Sunrise Bluff Dr 78244
Sunrise Cliff Dr 78244
Sunrise Cove Dr 78244
Sunrise Creek Dr 78244
Sunrise Crest Dr 78244
Sunrise Glade Dr 78244
Sunrise Laurel 78244
Sunrise Point Dr 78244
Sunrise Terrace Dr 78244
Sunrise View Dr 78244
Sunrise Wood 78245
Sunriver Dr 78244
Sunscape Way 78250
Sunset Blf 78244
Sunset Bnd 78244
Sunset Clf 78261
Sunset Crst 78249
Sunset Ct 78209
Sunset Fld 78245
Sunset Grv 78247
Sunset Hts 78261
Sunset Knl 78261
Sunset Lk 78245
Sunset Loop 78266
Sunset Mdws 78258
Sunset Pl 78245
Sunset Pt 78242
Sunset Rd 78264
E Sunset Rd 78209
W Sunset Rd
100-499 78209
501-597 78216
599-600 78216
602-698 78216
Sunset Rdg 78261
Sunset Ter 78244
Sunset Trl 78233
Sunset Vis 78242
Sunset Vw 78258
Sunset Walk 78237
Sunset Bay 78245
Sunset Farm 78245
Sunset Glade 78240
Sunset Haven St 78249
Sunset Peak 78258
Sunset Rainbow 78245
Sunset Stone 78254
Sunset Valley St 78242
Sunset Village Dr 78249
Sunshadow St 78217
E Sunshine Dr 78228
W Sunshine Dr 78228
Sunshine Park 78244
Sunshine Peak 78244
Sunshine Ranch Rd 78228
Sunshine Tower Dr 78244
Sunshine Trail Dr 78244
Sunshine Tree Dr 78249
Sunstream Way 78260
Suntanti Ave 78212
Sunup Dr 78233
Sunview Blf 78224
Sunview Lk 78245
Sunview Park 78224
Sunview Pass 78245
Sunview St 78238
Sunview Vly 78244

Sunview Oaks 78245
Sunview Post 78224
Sunway Dr 78232
Supreme Dr 78220
Surfrider St 78242
Surfside 78264
Surrells Ave 78228
Surrels Ave 78237
Surrey Ave 78225
Surreywood 78258
Surveyor St 78219
Susan Cir 78255
Susan Carol Dr 78216
Susan Elaine St 78240
Susan Marie St 78220
Susancrest Dr 78232
Susanwood Dr 78220
Susie Ct 78216
Sussex Ave 78221
Sutter Home 78253
Sutters Park 78230
Sutters Rim 78258
Sutton Dr 78228
Sutton Pl 78249
Suzanne Dr 78239
Suzette Ave 78227
Swale 78248
Swallow Dr 78217
Swan Frst, Gdn & Ter 78222
Swandale Dr 78230
Swann Ln 78219
Swans Lndg 78217
Swans Xing 78250
Sway Tree 78233
Swayback Rnch 78254
Swaying Oaks Dr 78227
Sweet 78204
Sweet Desiree 78253
Sweet Destiny 78253
Sweet Emily 78253
Sweet Forest St 78251
Sweet Maiden St 78242
Sweet Mary 78255
Sweet Oak 78258
Sweet Olive 78261
Sweet Pea Run 78245
Sweet Rock Dr 78227
Sweet Sand 78253
Sweet Valley St 78242
Sweetbriar Ave 78228
Sweetbrush 78258
Sweetgum 78253
Sweetwood 78254
Swift Creek Dr 78238
Swift Eagle Dr 78242
Swinburne Ct 78240
Swinford 78239
Swing Rider 78245
Swinging Bow 78261
N Swiss 78202
Swiss Oaks 78227
Switch Oak 78230
Sycamore Brk 78254
Sycamore Cv 78245
Sycamore Moon 78216
Sylvan Woods 78249
Sylvanoaks Dr 78229
Sylvia Ave 78237
Symphonic Hl 78260
Symphony Ln 78214
Synandra St 78232
Synergy Hl & Ln 78260
Syracuse St 78249
Syrinx 78260
Tabak Farm 78239
Tabard Dr 78213
Tabernas Ln 78253
Tabletop Ln 78245
Tabor 78221
Tacco Dr 78244
Tacoma Ave 78221
Taft Blvd
100-699 78225
800-899 78226
Taft Crk 78254
Tahoe Vis 78253

Tahoka St 78227
Tahoka Daisy 78245
Talavera Pkwy 78232
Talavera Rdg 78257
Talavera Trl 78251
Talba Ln 78230
Talbot Sq 78249
Talcott Dr 78232
Talisman Rd 78210
Tall Hts 78255
Tall Cedar 78249
Tall Elm Woods 78249
Tall Oak Dr 78232
Tall Tree St 78230
Tallahasse Dr 78227
Talley Rd 78253
Tallow Cir 78253
Tallow Trl 78256
Tallowood St 78245
Tallulah Dr 78218
Tally Gate 78240
Tally Ho Ln 78216
Talmadge Ln 78249
Talon Brk 78238
Talon Path 78247
Talon Pt 78254
Talon Rdg 78253
Talon Run 78254
Tamarak Dr 78220
Tamarind St 78240
Tamarisk St 78240
Tamaron Hl, Knl, Park, Pass, Rnch & Vly 78253
Tamarron St 78217
Tamber Ln 78255
Tamburo Trl 78266
Tammy Dr 78216
Tampa Ave 78211
Tampico St 78207
Tampke Fls 78245
Tampke Park 78247
Tampke Pl 78247
Tamworth Dr 78213
Tanager Ct 78260
Tanbark Dr 78240
Tandom Ct 78217
Tangerine St 78247
Tangle Tree St 78247
Tanglebriar Ln 78209
Tanglewood Dr 78216
Tango Dr 78216
Tanner Peak 78247
Tanner Woods 78248
Tanoan 78258
Tansyl Dr 78213
Tantara Ct 78249
Tantivity 78249
Tanzanite Rim 78222
Taos Crk 78255
Taos St 78207
Taos Vly 78245
Tapia 78261
Tara Dr 78216
Tara Oak St 78231
Tarasco St 78227
Tarifa Way 78253
Tarkio Way 78247
Tarlac Dr 78239
Tarleton 78223
Tarpley St 78251
Tarragon Cv 78213
Tarrant 78214
Tarrasa 78239
Tarrytown St 78233
Tarton Ln 78231
Tarywood St 78238
Tavern Pt 78254
Tavern Oaks St 78247
Tawny Oak Dr 78230
Taylor Crst 78249
Taylor St 78205
Taylor Kenton 78240
Taylore Run 78259
Taylors Bnd 78247
Tayman St 78226
Tea Rose Gln 78259

Teaberry Dr 78250
Teagarden Ln 78232
Teak Ln 78209
Teakwood Dr 78266
Teakwood Ln
100-399 78216
9300-9499 78266
Teal Ave 78224
Teal Lk 78244
Teal Way 78239
Tealeaf St 78238
Teall Fls 78251
Teasdale Dr 78217
Teatro Way 78253
Tech Com Rd 78233
Tecumseh Dr 78260
Ted St 78224
Tedder St 78211
Tee St 78222
Tee Time 78221
Teecee Ln 78217
Tehama Ln 78245
Tehama Gate 78223
E & W Tejas Crk, Spg & Trl 78257
Tejasco 78218
Tejeda Dr 78227
Tejeda Rd 78221
Telder Path 78228
Telegraph St 78219
Tellez Ave 78228
Telstar St 78219
Tempestuous 78251
Temple Hl 78217
Temple Sq 78245
Temptation St 78216
Tenaca Trl 78266
Tenbury 78253
Tendick St 78209
Tennyson Dr 78217
Tenore 78259
Tequila Rnch 78245
Teresa
100-357 78214
Teresa
359-399 78214
400-499 78225
Terlingua 78233
Terlingua Bnd 78261
N Terminal Dr 78216
Terra Brk, Clf, Cyn, Dl & Run 78255
E & W Terra Alta Dr 78209
Terra Cotta 78253
Terra Elm 78255
Terra Ferna 78251
Terra Gate 78255
Terra Loop Rd 78233
Terra Mont Way 78255
Terra Oak 78250
Terra Rock 78255
Terra Rye 78240
Terra Stone 78255
Terra Summit Rd 78233
Terrabianca 78258
Terrace Crst 78223
Terrace Gln 78223
Terrace Hl 78245
Terrace Holw 78259
Terrace Park 78250
Terrace Pass 78259
Terrace Pl 78230
Terrace Pln 78223
Terrace Rdg 78223
Terrace Walk 78223
Terrace Wind 78223
Terrace Wood 78223
Terranova 78240
Terrell Ave 78214
Terrell Bnd 78264
Terrell Rd 78209
Territory 78223
Territory Oak 78253
Terron Rd 78222
Terry Ct 78212
Tersk 78253

Tesla Dr 78228
Tesoro Dr 78217
Tesoro Hls 78242
Tetford 78253
Teton Ln 78230
Teton Rdg 78233
Tex Woods St 78249
Tex-Con Rd 78220
Texana Cv 78253
Texana Dr 78249
Texas Ave
600-1799 78201
1800-2599 78228
Texas Cyn 78252
Texas Pt 78260
Texas Riv 78222
Texas Ash 78261
Texas Bldg 78205
Texas Buckeye 78261
Texas Elm 78230
Texas Emmy Ln 78258
Texas Gold 78253
Texas Hawthorn 78261
Texas Jack 78223
Texas Laurel 78256
Texas Mulberry 78253
Texas Sotol 78261
Texas Thistle 78253
Texoma Dr 78222
Tezel Blf 78250
Tezel Bnd 78250
Tezel Ct 78250
Tezel Lndg 78250
Tezel Pt 78250
Tezel Rd
5500-8199 78250
8300-8398 78254
8400-10599 78254
Tezel Oaks 78250
Thames Dr 78216
Thatch Dr 78240
Theis Dr 78222
Thelka 78214
Thelma Dr 78212
E Theo Ave
100-399 78214
700-798 78210
W Theo Ave
101-197 78214
199-599 78214
600-1399 78225
1401-1599 78225
Theo Pkwy 78210
Theodor Dr 78219
Thicket Pass 78254
Thicket Palm 78247
Thicket Trail Dr 78248
Thistle Dr 78238
Thistle Down 78217
Thomas Rdg 78251
Thomas Spgs 78254
Thomas Broughton Ct 78240
Thomas Jefferson Dr 78228
Thomas Oaks 78261
Thomas Paine Dr 78219
Thomas Rusk 78253
Thomas Sumter St 78233
Thomas York Blvd 78251
Thompson Pl
100-699 78225
800-2000 78226
2002-2398 78226
Thorain Blvd
100-599 78212
900-1899 78201
Thoreaus Way 78239
Thorman Pl 78209
Thorn Apple 78253
Thornbury St 78250
Thorncliff Dr 78250
Thornedike Dr 78245
Thornell St 78235
Thornhill St 78209
Thornhurst 78218
Thornridge Ln 78232
Thornwood 78218

Thornwood Dr 78264
Thoroughbred Trl 78253
Thousand Oaks Dr
1500-2899 78232
2900-3799 78247
3801-4197 78217
4199-4399 78217
4401-4497 78233
4499-4699 78233
3650-1-3650-5 78247
Thrasher Dr 78245
Thrasher Oak 78232
Threadneedle Ln 78227
Threadway St 78219
Three Frks 78258
Three Iron 78221
Three Lakes Dr 78248
Three Springs Dr 78244
Three Wood Way 78221
Thrush Gdns 78209
Thrush Rdg 78248
Thrush Bend St 78209
Thrush Court Cir 78248
Thrush Gate Ln 78248
Thrush View Ln 78209
Thunder Dr 78238
Thunder Basin 78261
Thunder Gulch 78245
Thunder Oaks 78261
Thunderbird Dr 78240
Thymus Dr 78245
Tianna Lace 78253
Tibbits Dr 78245
Ticonderoga Dr 78230
Tidecrest Dr 78239
Tideland St 78245
Tidewind St 78221
Tierra Cv 78258
Tierra Bonita 78263
Tierra Chita 78263
Tierra Mesa 78263
Tierra Nueva 78263
Tierra Rancho 78263
Tiffany Dr 78230
Tiffnilee Ln 78255
Tifton Dr 78240
Tiger Fld, Grv, Hls, Path & Way 78251
Tiger Bay 78251
Tiger Chase 78251
Tiger Horse Cv & Dr 78254
Tiger Hunt 78251
Tiger Lily 78260
Tiger Paw 78251
Tiger Tail Rd 78232
Tiger Woods 78221
Tilbury Ln 78230
Tilden St 78208
Tillie Dr 78222
Tillman 78228
Tillman Park 78253
Tilson Dr 78224
Tiltwood Ln 78251
Timber Blf 78253
Timber Bnd 78238
Timber Ct 78250
Timber Frk 78250
Timber Grv 78250
Timber Hts 78250
Timber Hvn 78250
Timber Knls 78250
Timber Ldg 78250
Timber Ml 78250
Timber Pass 78260
Timber Path 78250
Timber Pl 78250
Timber Pln 78250
Timber Pne 78250
Timber Rnch 78250
Timber Row 78250
Timber Run 78250
Timber Spg 78250
Timber Strm 78250
Timber Trl 78228
Timber Ash St 78250
Timber Bark 78250

Timber Basin St 78250
Timber Bay St 78232
Timber Beach St 78250
Timber Belt 78250
Timber Bough St 78250
Timber Breeze St 78250
Timber Bridge St 78250
Timber Bush St 78250
Timber Cabin 78250
Timber Canyon St 78250
Timber Chase St 78250
Timber Circle St 78250
Timber Climb 78250
Timber Cloud St 78251
Timber Coach St 78250
Timber Country 78254
Timber Crest St 78250
Timber Cross St 78250
Timber Crown St 78250
Timber Cut 78250
Timber Draw St 78250
Timber Elm St 78250
Timber Fair 78250
Timber Fall St 78250
Timber Farm 78250
Timber Fern St 78250
Timber Flat St 78250
Timber Flower St 78250
Timber Forest St 78230
Timber Gale St 78250
Timber Gate St 78250
Timber Glade St 78250
Timber Glen St 78250
Timber Grand 78250
Timber Hawk 78250
Timber Hunt 78250
Timber Jack 78250
Timber Laurel 78250
Timber Ledge St 78250
Timber Loche 78250
Timber Lookout 78250
Timber Meadow St 78250
Timber Moss 78250
Timber Oak St 78232
Timber Park St 78250
Timber Peak 78250
Timber Point St 78250
Timber Pond St 78250
Timber Post St 78250
Timber Rail 78250
Timber Rain 78250
Timber Range 78250
Timber Ridge Dr 78227
Timber Rise 78250
Timber Rose 78266
Timber Shade 78250
Timber Slope 78250
Timber Star 78250
Timber Terrace St 78250
Timber Trace St 78250
Timber View Dr 78251
Timber Wagon 78250
Timber Walk St 78250
Timber West St 78250
Timber Whip 78250
Timber Whisper 78250
Timber Wind 78250
Timber Wolf St 78242
Timberbranch St 78250
Timberbriar St 78250
Timberbrook Dr 78238
Timbercliff St 78250
Timbercreek Dr 78227
Timberhill 78238
Timberhurst 78250
Timberlake Run 78244
Timberlane Dr
100-199 78209
300-599 78218
Timberleaf St 78238
Timberlight 78250
Timberline Dr 78260
Timbermont St 78250
Timberrock Dr 78242
Timbersteep 78250
Timberstone St 78250

Timbervale St 78250
Timberway St 78247
Timberwick St 78250
Timberwilde St 78250
Timberwood 78264
Timco E & W 78238
Timers Edge 78260
Timilo Dr 78219
Timken Dr 78260
Timmermann Cv 78266
Timpson Cir 78253
Tiner Ave 78201
Tinson 78251
Tintagel St 78254
Tiny Tune 78260
Tioga Cv 78251
Tioga Dr 78230
Tippecanoe 78245
Tipperary Ave 78223
Tippit Trl 78240
Tips Jewels Ln 78258
Tipton Ave 78204
Tiptop Rdg 78252
Tiptop St 78253
Tisbury Pkwy 78251
Titan Dr 78217
Titus Trl 78253
Tivoli Gdns 78233
Tivoli Hl 78260
Tivoli Mdw 78260
Tivoli Mesa 78260
Tivoli Woods 78260
Toad Pond 78260
Todd 78214
Todds Farm 78244
Toepperwein Rd 78233
Toftrees Dr 78209
Tokalon 78258
Tokay 78254
Tokyo 78230
Toledo St 78203
Toltec 78237
Tom Kite Ct 78244
Tom Slick 78229
Tom Stafford Dr 78219
Tom Tom St 78238
Tom Watson Ct 78244
Tomahawk Trl 78232
Tomar Dr 78227
Tomas Cir 78240
Tommins Ave 78214
Tommy Trl 78266
Tomrob Dr 78220
Tondre St 78209
Tonkawa Pass 78266
Tonkawa Trl 78255
Tool Yard 78233
Top Rail St 78232
Topala St 78264
Topaz St 78228
Topcroft Dr 78238
Topeka Blvd 78210
Tophill Rd 78209
Topper Cir, Pkwy, Rdg & Run 78233
Toppling Ln 78233
Topsey St 78221
Torch Lily 78260
Torcido Dr 78209
Torena Loop 78261
Torey Mesquite 78261
Torino St 78229
Tornillo Dr 78258
Torreon St 78207
Torreys Post 78240
Torrington 78251
Tortuga St 78224
Tortuga Verde 78245
Tory Hill St 78232
Toscana Isle 78249
Toscana Sands 78249
Tosha St 78260
Touch Gold 78248
Toudouze 78214
Toudouze Rd 78264
Toulouse 78240

Toumey Oak Dr 78223
Tourant Rd 78240
Tournament Grn 78257
Tourney St 78254
Toutant Beauregard Rd 78255
Tower Dr 78232
S Tower Dr 78232
Tower Rd 78223
Tower Ter 78259
Tower Life Bldg 78205
Tower Of The Americas Way 78205
Towering Elm 78247
Towering Oaks St 78217
Towers Park Ln 78209
Town Rdg & Way 78238
Town Briar St 78238
Town Center Dr 78251
Town Cliff St 78238
Town Creek St 78238
Town Crest St 78238
Town Field St 78238
Town Gate Dr 78238
Town Grove Dr 78238
Town Leaf St 78238
Town Oak Dr 78232
Town Ville St 78238
Town Wood St 78238
Townbreeze St 78238
Towne Vue Dr 78213
Townhill Dr 78238
Townsend Ave 78209
Townsend House Dr 78251
Toyah Brk 78258
Tpc Pkwy
2600-2698 78259
2901-3199 78259
3300-4398 78261
4401-5799 78261
Trace Buckle Dr 78240
Trace Oak 78232
Traciney Blvd 78255
Tracy Dr 78260
Tradesman 78249
Tradeway St 78217
Tradewind Dr 78239
Trading Post St 78242
Trafalgar Rd 78216
Trail Lk 78244
Trail St 78212
Trail Xing 78250
Trail Bluff St 78247
Trail Valley Dr 78242
Trail Village Dr 78244
Trailcrest St 78232
Traildrive Rd 78264
Trailend Dr 78209
Trailhead Pass 78251
Trailing Oaks St 78233
Trailing Winds 78254
Trailmeadow 78240
Trailside Ln 78233
Trailview 78258
Trailway Oak 78240
Trailway Park St 78247
Trailwood Dr 78228
Tramonto Hl 78253
Tramore 78260
Trannera St 78235
Tranquil Crk & Ter 78251
Tranquil Oak 78260
Tranquil Park Dr 78254
Tranquil Rim 78260
Tranquil Trail Dr 78232
Tranquillo Way 78266
Trappers Run St 78245
Travertine Ln 78213
Travis Park N 78205
Travis Path 78253
Travis Smt 78218
E Travis St 78205
W Travis St
101-399 78205
1300-4199 78207
Travis Bldg 78205

Travis Park Plz 78205
Travois St 78238
Trawood 78250
Treasure Way 78209
Treasure Trail Dr 78232
Treaty Crk 78255
Treaty Oak 78258
Treble Crk 78258
N Tree 78254
Tree Mdw 78258
Tree Run 78245
Tree Vlg 78250
Tree Bend St 78263
Tree Crossing St 78247
Tree Grove Dr 78247
Tree Haven St 78245
Tree Hill St 78230
Tree Swallow 78253
Tree Top Cv 78266
Tree Top St 78250
Tree View St 78220
Treefrog Trl 78253
Treegarden St 78222
Treehouse Dr 78222
Treeline Park 78209
Treemont Park 78261
Treeridge Pl 78247
Treewell Gln 78249
Trelart 78261
Tremlett Ave 78210
Tremonto 78261
Trendwood 78250
Trenerth Dr 78229
Trent Rnch 78249
Trent St 78232
Trenton 78214
Trentwood 78231
Tres Caminos 78245
Tres Ritos St 78247
Tressard 78248
Triangle 78264
Trickling Rock 78260
Trident St 78224
Trigger Corral 78254
Triggers Crk 78254
Trilby 78253
Trill Hl 78260
Trillium Ln 78213
Trinity Bnd 78261
Trinity Ct 78261
Trinity Cv 78261
Trinity Fls 78261
Trinity Hl 78261
Trinity Hts 78261
Trinity Mdw 78260
Trinity Pass 78261
Trinity Pl 78212
Trinity Pt 78261
Trinity Rdg 78261
N Trinity St
200-298 78207
300-1599 78207
1601-2099 78201
S Trinity St 78207
Trinity Vw 78261
Trinity Cross 78260
Trinity Glade 78261
Trinity Mesa 78261
Trinity Oak 78230
Trinity Star 78260
Trinity Villas 78261
Trinity Woods 78261
Triola Dr 78230
Triple Bnd 78263
Triple Crk 78247
Triple Mdws 78263
Triple Acres Dr 78263
Triple Branch Dr 78263
Triple Crown Ln 78248
N & S Triple Elm St 78263
Triple Leaf 78263
Triple Oaks Dr 78263
Triple Pines St 78263
Triple Tree Dr 78263
Triple Wood 78263
Triple X 78253
Triplett St 78216

Tristan Run 78259
Tristant Rdg 78260
Trondary Dr 78219
Trone Trl 78238
Trophy Cir 78258
Trophy Grn 78257
Trophy Rdg 78258
Trophy Way 78258
Trophy Oaks Dr 78266
Tropical Dr 78218
Tropical Storm 78233
Tropical Wind 78233
Tropicana Pl 78242
Trotter Ln 78240
Trotters Bay 78254
Trout Ln 78223
Troy Dr 78221
Truax 78204
Trudell Dr 78213
Truman St 78245
Trumbal 78233
Trumbo Rd & Trl 78264
Trumbo Sands 78264
Tucker Dr 78222
Tucker Pl 78221
Tudor Dr 78216
Tudor Gln 78257
Tufted Crst 78253
Tulane Dr 78228
Tuleta Dr 78212
Tulia Cir & Way 78253
Tulip Bnd 78253
Tulip Farm 78249
Tulip Rose 78253
Tulip Tree 78264
Tulipan Walk St 78207
Tumbleweed Ln 78264
Tumbleweed Way 78245
Tumblewood Trl 78247
Tumbling Oaks 78260
Tumbling Water 78238
Tuna St 78214
Tunstall St 78204
Tupelo Ln 78229
Tupper Ave 78221
E & W Turbo Dr 78216
Turin Ct 78257
Turin Rdg 78255
Turkey Cir 78264
Turkey Cv 78264
Turkey Hl 78261
Turkey Trl 78232
Turkey Chase 78264
Turkey Creek Rd 78231
Turkey Feather Dr 78233
Turkey Flat Dr 78245
Turkey Ledge St 78232
Turkey Oak St 78232
Turkey Point St 78232
Turkey Ridge St 78232
Turkey Run St 78238
Turnberry 78231
Turnberry Way 78230
Turner 78204
Turner Rdg 78266
Turnmill St 78248
Turnpost Ln 78247
Turnstone Ln 78247
Turquoise Crk 78254
Turquoise Pl 78254
Turquoise Way 78251
Turquoise Sky 78261
Turret Run 78248
Turtle Cv 78255
Turtle Hl 78260
Turtle Ln 78230
Turtle Creek St 78230
Turtle Cross 78253
Turtle Rock St 78232
Turtle Village St 78230
Tuscan Cv, Cyn, Mdw & Park 78261
Tuscan Hills Dr 78266
Tuscan Oaks 78261
Tuscan Winter 78260
Tuscan Woods 78261

Tuscany Ct 78257
Tuscany Dr 78219
Tuscany Way 78249
Tuscany Stone 78258
Tuscarora Trl 78231
Tuttle Rd 78209
Tuxedo Ave 78209
Tuxford 78239
Tweed Willow 78258
Twilight Blf 78260
Twilight Rdg 78258
Twilight Terrace St 78233
Twin Crk 78238
Twin Arrows 78258
Twin Elm Woods 78249
Twin Falls Dr 78238
Twin Fox 78247
Twin Lake Dr 78244
Twin Oaks Ct 78250
Twin Oaks Dr 78250
Twin Oaks Path 78254
Twin Peak St 78261
Twinbear Crk 78245
Twining Dr 78211
Twinleaf Ln 78213
Twinpod 78247
Twinpost 78254
Twinspur St 78238
Twisted Creek St 78230
Twisted Oaks 78266
Twisted Oaks Dr 78217
Twisted Wood Dr 78216
Two Fls 78255
Two Iron 78221
Two Rock Oak 78254
Two Wells Dr 78245
Two Winds 78255
Two Wood Way 78221
Twohig Ave
101-399 78210
500-599 78220
Twohill Pass 78247
Tworivers Dr 78259
Twynbridge 78259
Ty Terrace St 78229
Tyler Ave 78204
Tyne Dr 78222
Typhoon St 78248
Tyrol Pl 78209
Uecker Rd 78220
Uhr Ln 78217
Ullman Dr 78219
Umber Oak St 78232
Umbra Hts 78252
Umbria 78230
Unbridled 78245
Unicorn Rnch 78245
Unintra St 78207
Union Shls 78244
Union St 78215
Union Ter 78244
Union Cavern 78247
Unity Ct 78214
University Ave 78201
University Hts 78249
University Row 78249
University Way 78224
University Oak 78249
University View Dr 78249
Up Mountain Rd 78255
Upland Crk 78245
Upland Rd
201-1299 78220
1401-1497 78219
1499-1599 78219
Upland Vw 78244
Upper Oaks Ln 78266
Upson St 78212
Upton 78254
Upton Crk 78260
Upton Cv 78260
Upton Hts 78260
Upton Park 78253
Upton Vlg 78260
Upwood Dr 78238
Urban Hl 78250

Urban Loop
401-499 78207
501-597 78204
599-699 78204
701-799 78204
Urban Crest Dr 78209
Ursula St 78224
S Us Highway 181 N 78223
Us Highway 281 N
2800-2898 78212
Us Highway 281 N
18400-18598 78259
18401-19297 78258
19299-26499 78258
26400-27800 78260
27802-28398 78260
Us Highway 281 S
20300-28099 78264
N Us Highway 281
8201-10097 78216
S Us Highway 281
10600-20199 78221
S Us Highway 81 78211
Us Highway 87 E
5200-6199 78222
6201-6599 78222
6600-6698 78263
6700-9700 78263
9702-9998 78263
W Us Highway 90
4600-4699 78237
5300-5398 78227
5400-7899 78227
7901-8799 78227
9339-10297 78245
10299-14499 78245
14501-15199 78245
Usaa Blvd 78240
Utah St 78210
Ute 78211
Utex Blvd 78249
Utica Pl 78212
Utopia Hts & Ln 78223
Utsa Blvd, Cir & Dr 78249
Uvalde Cir 78264
Uvalde St 78210
Vadalia St 78228
E Vado Pl 78214
Vail Crst 78217
Valdez Ave 78212
Vale 78245
Vale Pass 78255
Valencia 78237
Valencia Ct 78259
Valencia Pt 78259
Valencia Vis 78259
Valencia Peak 78261
Valentino Pl 78212
Valero St 78212
Valero Way 78249
Valewood Vw 78240
Valga Hl 78251
Valle Dezavala 78249
Valle Vista Dr 78223
Vallecito Ct, Pass, Run & Way 78250
Vallecito Mesa 78250
Vallenas St 78233
Valley Bnd 78250
Valley Clfs 78250
Valley Crk 78261
Valley Crst 78250
Valley Gdn 78245
Valley Hl 78250
Valley Hvn 78250
Valley Rd 78221
Valley Rdg 78250
Valley Spg 78250
Valley Wl 78249
Valley Bay Dr 78250
Valley Branch St 78250
Valley Cabin 78250
Valley Castle 78250
Valley Center Dr 78227
Valley Cove St 78250
Valley Dale St 78250

E Valley Forge Ave & Cir 78233
Valley Gate 78250
Valley Glen St 78250
Valley Green Rd 78240
Valley Hedge 78250
Valley Hi Dr 78227
Valley King 78250
Valley Knight 78250
Valley Lawn 78250
Valley Moss 78250
Valley Oak St 78233
Valley Park Dr
500-599 78227
21600-21699 78266
Valley Pawn 78250
Valley Pike St 78230
Valley Point St 78233
Valley Queen 78250
Valley Rock 78250
Valley Star Dr 78224
Valley Stone 78250
Valley Trails St 78250
Valley Tree 78250
E & S Valley View Ln 78217
Valley Villa 78250
Valley Vine 78250
Valley Way Dr 78250
Valley Wood 78250
Valleybrook 78238
Valleyfield St 78222
Valliant St 78216
Valmont Dr 78240
Valparaiso Way 78249
Valtosca 78253
Valverde 78214
Van Buren Ln 78217
Van Dyke Dr 78218
Van Ness 78251
Van Nest Cir 78266
Vance St 78210
Vance Jackson 78257
Vance Jackson Rd
200-298 78201
300-1099 78201
1064-1064 78213
1064-1064 78228
1100-1398 78201
1101-1399 78201
1413-1897 78213
1899-4099 78213
4101-4297 78230
4299-12499 78230
12501-12699 78230
13200-14098 78249
14100-14899 78249
Vandale St 78216
Vandenberg Way 78245
Vanderbilt St 78210
Vanderheck St 78209
Vanderhoeven Dr 78209
Vanderpool St 78251
Vandewalle 78227
N & S Vandiver Rd 78209
Vanity Hl 78256
Vanley Dr 78228
Vantage Dr 78230
Vantage Hl 78231
Vantage Pt 78251
Vantage Way 78249
Vantage View Dr 78228
Vantrani Dr 78231
Vaquero Pass 78247
Vardon Way 78248
Vargas Aly 78203
Varrientos St 78233
Varsity Dr 78228
Vassar Ln 78212
Vaughan Pl 78201
Vaughns Vw 78260
Vaux Hall 78209
Vecchio 78260
Veda Mae Dr 78216
Vega Gap 78252
Vega Horizon 78252
Vegas Vw 78233
Veining Way 78261
Veleta 78250
Velez Park Dr 78249
Velvet Ln 78219
Velvet Spg 78254
Velvet Rose 78260
Venado Hls 78260
Venado Trce 78240
Venado Trl 78240
Venado Vista Dr 78216
Venando Pass 78260
Venezia 78253
Venice 78201
Venice Ct 78257
Ventana Pkwy 78256
Ventura Dr 78232
Venus St 78226
Vera Rd 78260
Vera Cruz 78207
Veradero St 78216
Veranda Ct 78250
Veranda Ln 78258
Verano Dr 78266
Verbena Hl 78258
Verbena St 78240
Verdant St 78209
Verde Blf 78258
Verde Bnd 78245
Verde Cyn 78224
N Verde Dr 78240
S Verde Dr 78240
Verde Knl 78258
Verde Path 78258
Verde Rdg 78258
Verde Riv 78255
Verde Trl 78259
Verde Azul 78245
Verde Bosque 78223
Verde Mountain Trl 78261
Verde Mtn Trl 78261
Verde Oak 78258
Verde Vista Dr 78216
Vereda 78201
Vermont St 78211
Verne St 78221
Vernlyn Dr 78230
Verona Cyn 78255
Verona Park 78261
Veronica St 78224
Verrado 78261
Versailles Dr 78219
Vespero 78233
E Vestal Pl 78221
W Vestal Pl
100-1499 78221
1501-1799 78224
Vfw Blvd 78223
Vhoories St 78203
Via Acuna St 78263
Via Aragon 78257
Via Belcanto 78260
Via Compagna 78258
Via Del Arbol 78257
Via Del Oro 78257
Via Espana 78245
Via Finita St 78229
Via Hermosa 78245
Via La Cantera 78256
Via La Circula 78223
Via Mantova 78260
Via Milano 78260
Via Mirada 78245
Via Perfecto St 78233
Via Pescados 78245
Via Posada Dr 78266
Via Positano 78260
Via Se Villa 78260
Via Shavano 78249
Via Torre 78258
Via Vineda 78258
Via Vizcaya 78260
Viaduct Post 78240
Viajes 78261
Viandart Ave 78225
Vibrant Oak 78232
Vicar 78218
Vickers Ave 78211
Vickery 78250
Vicksburg St 78220
Victor St 78209
Victoria Xing 78245
Victorian Oaks 78253
Victors Hl 78254
Victory Grn 78257
Victory Row 78254
Victory Cavern 78254
Victory Palm 78247
Victory Pass Dr 78240
Vidor Ave 78216
Vidorra Ct 78216
Vidorra Circle Dr 78216
Vidorra Vista Dr 78216
Viejita St 78224
Viendo 78201
Vienna 78258
Viento Pt 78260
Viento Oaks 78260
Viesca St 78209
View Dr 78228
View Mdw 78258
View Pt 78229
View Oak 78232
View Top 78258
Viewcrest Rd 78217
Viewridge Dr 78213
Viewsite Dr 78223
Vigil Vw 78233
Vigness St 78214
Viking Trl 78250
Viking Coral 78244
Viking Oak 78247
Viljandi Moon 78251
Villa Dr 78239
Villa Ann St 78213
Villa Aqua 78255
Villa Arboles 78228
Villa Barbaro 78259
Villa Basilica 78255
Villa Bonita 78230
Villa Borghese 78259
Villa Camino 78233
Villa Del Lago 78245
Villa Del Luna 78237
Villa Del Sol 78237
Villa Flores 78237
Villa Grande 78228
Villa Jardin 78230
Villa Linda 78237
Villa Madama 78259
Villa Madero St 78233
Villa Mar 78230
Villa Marco 78233
Villa Medici 78259
Villa Mercedes 78233
Villa Nava St 78233
Villa Norte 78228
Villa Nueva 78233
Villa Placer 78237
Villa Rey 78245
Villa Rosa 78237
Villa Rufina 78259
Villa Toscana 78260
Villa Valencia 78258
Villa Verde 78230
Village Br 78245
Village Cir 78232
Village Clb 78250
Village Clf 78250
Village Crk 78251
Village Crst 78218
Village Ct 78218
Village Dr 78217
S Village Dr 78249
Village Gln 78218
Village Grn 78218
Village Hvn 78218
Village Knls 78232
Village Park 78250
Village Path 78218
Village Pkwy 78251
Village Pt 78250
Village Row 78218
Village Vw 78218
Village Way 78218
Village Arbor 78250
Village Basin 78250
Village Blacksmith 78255
Village Briar 78250
Village Brown 78250
Village Gate 78250
Village Lance 78250
Village Lawn 78218
Village Oak Dr 78233
Village Spring Dr 78240
Village Trail Dr 78218
Village Wood 78216
Villamain Rd 78223
Villareal St 78210
E Villaret Blvd 78221
W Villaret Blvd
100-198 78221
200-699 78221
700-1499 78224
1501-1699 78224
Ville Serene 78253
Villers St Paul 78257
Villita St 78205
Vinca Mnr 78260
Vinca Pass 78251
Vinca Reef 78260
Vincent St 78211
Vine Clf 78227
Vine Rd 78264
Vine St 78210
Vinecrest Cir & Dr 78219
Vineland 78239
Vinewood Ct 78209
Vineyard Dr 78257
Vineyard Mist 78255
Vinsant Cir 78235
Vintage Pt 78253
Vintage Trce 78257
Vintage Oaks 78248
Vintint St 78203
Viola Park 78259
Violet Cv 78253
Violet St 78247
Violeta Pl 78207
Virencom 78258
Virgil Dr 78218
Virgin Oak 78258
Virginia Blvd
200-399 78210
500-2300 78203
2302-2398 78203
Virgo Ln 78260
Virtuoso Pass 78266
Visor Dr 78258
Vista Crk 78247
Vista Ct 78247
Vista Grv 78242
Vista Hvn 78216
Vista Mdw 78242
Vista Pt 78242
Vista Rd 78210
E Vista Rdg 78260
W Vista Rdg 78260
Vista Trl 78247
Vista Arroyo 78216
Vista Azul 78213
Vista Bella 78260
Vista Bluff Dr 78247
Vista Bonita 78216
Vista Briar Dr 78247
Vista Butte 78239
Vista Colina 78255
Vista Del Avion 78216
Vista Del Cedro 78216
Vista Del Juez 78216
Vista Del La Laguna 78216
Vista Del Mar 78216
Vista Del Monte 78216
Vista Del Mundo 78216
Vista Del Norte 78216
Vista Del Prado 78216
Vista Del Puente 78216
Vista Del Rey 78216
Vista Del Rio 78216
Vista Del Sur 78207
Vista Fairway 78244
Vista Forest Dr 78247
Vista Glen St 78247
Vista Hill St 78213
Vista Lake St 78222
Vista Loma 78216
Vista Montan 78256
Vista Nogal St 78213
Vista Norte 78213
Vista Oaks Dr 78247
Vista Park Dr 78247
Vista Real 78216
Vista Robles St 78232
Vista Run Dr 78247
Vista Valet 78216
Vista Valley Dr 78242
Vista Verde 78255
Vista View St 78231
Vista Village Dr 78247
Vistawood 78249
Vitex 78261
Vitra Pl 78210
Viva Max Dr 78238
Vivian Ln 78201
Viz Rey Dr 78224
Voelcker Ln 78248
Voelcker Ranch Dr 78231
Voigt Dr 78232
Vollmer Ln 78254
Vollum Ave 78201
Volterra 78258
Volunteer Pkwy 78253
Von Braun Dr 78219
Von Rosk 78238
Von Scheele Dr 78229
Vormis Vw 78251
Vortsa Ledge 78251
Vosler Loop 78227
Votaw St 78211
Vuewood St 78213
Vyra St 78237
Wabash St 78211
Wacker Way 78207
Wacos Dr 78238
Waddesdon Blf 78233
Waddesdon Wood 78233
Waddle Farm 78249
Wade St 78210
Wagner Ave 78211
Wagner Way 78256
Wagon Boss 78254
Wagon Spoke St 78238
Wagon Trail Rd 78231
Wagon Wheel St 78217
Wagons W 78255
Wahada Ave 78217
Wahl Ln 78266
Wahrmund Ct 78223
Waikiki Dr 78218
Wainwright St 78211
Wake Forrest Dr 78228
Wake Robin 78253
Wakefield Dr 78216
Wakeman Dr 78247
Waketon 78250
Wakewood St 78233
Walden Elms 78257
Walden Oak 78260
Waldenshire 78209
Walder Trl 78260
Waldo Dr 78209
Waldon Hts 78254
Waldon Walk 78261
Waldon Pond 78245
Waleetka St 78210
Wales St 78223
Wales Reserve 78255
Walford Ct 78257
Walhalla Ave & Rd 78221
Walker Hl 78233
Walker Ranch Rd 78216
Walkers Way 78216
Walking Crk 78254
Walking Gait Dr 78240
Walla Walla Dr 78250
Wallace St 78237
Wallingford St 78217
Wallstreet 78230
Walmer St 78247
Walnut Crst 78245
Walnut Pass 78255
Walnut Trce 78239
Walnut Bank 78254
Walnut Creek Dr 78247
Walnut Hill St 78232
Walnut Lake Dr 78244
Walnut Mill Dr 78244
Walnut Park St 78227
Walnut Trail Dr 78247
Walnut Valley Dr 78242
Walnut Vista Dr 78247
Walnut Woods St 78249
Walsbrook 78260
Walsh Rd 78224
Walsh St 78212
Walt Schirra St 78219
Walter Raleigh 78239
N Walters
201-397 78202
N Walters
399-599 78202
601-1599 78202
1700-1798 78208
1800-1900 78208
1902-2298 78208
S Walters
300-698 78203
700-899 78203
900-1398 78210
1400-1699 78210
1701-2899 78210
3800-3999 78223
Walthampton St 78216
Walton Ave 78225
Walzem Rd
4400-4700 78218
4702-4898 78218
4801-4897 78218
4899-5899 78218
5901-5999 78218
6100-6799 78239
7201-7299 78244
Wampum St 78238
Wandering Trl 78249
Wandesta Way 78245
Wapiti Trl 78228
War Admiral 78248
War Arrow 78238
War Bonnet St 78238
War Bow Dr 78238
War Cloud Dr 78242
War Dance St 78238
War Emblem 78245
War Feather 78238
War Horse Dr 78242
War Knife St 78238
War Lodge Ln 78238
War Pony St 78238
War Princess St 78238
Warbler Vw 78255
Warbler Way 78231
Ward Ave 78223
Ward Spg 78245
Warden St 78245
Ware Blvd
100-799 78221
800-1000 78214
1002-1098 78214
Warfield St 78216
Warhawk St 78238
Waring Dr 78216
Warley Hts 78254
Warm Winds 78253
Warner Ave 78201
Warpath St 78238
Warren St 78212
Warrior Trl 78244
Warriors Creek Dr 78230
Warwich St 78216
Washington 78204
Washita Way 78256
Watchers 78255
Watchtower St 78254
Water St 78255
Water Vly 78249
Water Lily 78260
Water Quail 78250
Water Wood Dr 78266
Waterbury 78251
Watercress Dr 78238
Waterfall 78239
Waterford Dr 78217
Waterford Gln 78257
Waterford Oaks 78250
Waterhole Ln 78261
Watering Point Dr 78247
Watering Trail Dr 78247
Waterleaf 78247
Waterlily Way 78254
Watermill 78217
Waters Edge Dr 78245
Waters Edge Way 78248
Waterside 78239
Watertown 78249
Watertrout Bay 78244
Waterway Rdg 78249
Waterwell Oaks 78261
Watkins Ln 78228
Watson Rd 78235
Watt Cir 78233
Waugh St 78223
Waukee Pass St 78260
Wave Dance 78251
Wave Digger 78251
Waverly Ave
600-698 78201
700-1899 78201
1900-2699 78228
Wavy Crk 78260
Waxachie Way 78256
Waxberry Trl 78256
Waxwing Cir 78239
Waxwood Ln 78216
Waycrest Dr 78239
Waycross Ln 78220
Waycross Rd 78264
Waydele Cir 78213
Wayfarer Pl 78242
Wayland Run 78247
Wayman Rdg 78233
Wayne Dr 78222
Wayne Path 78253
Waynesboro St 78233
Wayside Crk 78255
Wayside Dr 78213
Wayside Trl 78244
Wayside Oaks St 78232
Wayview St 78220
Wayward Dr 78217
Wayward Daisy 78245
Wayward Oaks 78248
Wayword Trl 78244
Weathercock Ln 78239
Weathered Post St 78238
Weatherford 78248
Weatherford Dr 78266
Weathering Crk 78238
Weathering Run 78254
Weatherly Dr 78239
Weaver St 78210
Webb 78223
Webbles Dr 78218
Webbwood Way 78250
Webster 78214
Wedge 78244
Wedgewood Dr 78230
Weeping Oak Trl 78233
Weeping Willow St 78232
Wega St 78245
N & S Weidner Rd 78233
Weigela 78261
Weimer Way 78233
Weinberg Ave 78214
Weir Ave 78226
Weizmann St
100-199 78212
201-297 78213

299-1099 78213
Welch Fls 78254
Welch St 78227
Welch Hallow 78254
Welcome Dr 78233
Welhausen St
201-299 78203
401-499 78210
Wellam Ct 78260
Wellcrest 78232
Welles Hbr, Park & Way 78240
Welles Arbor Cir 78240
Welles Brook Dr 78240
Welles Creek Cir & Dr 78240
Welles Dale Dr 78240
Welles Edge Cir & Dr 78240
Welles Fawn Cir 78240
Welles Glenn Cir 78240
Wellesley Blvd 78209
Wellesley Loop 78231
Wellesley Manor Dr 78240
Wellington 78214
Wellock Ct 78245
Wells Pt 78261
Wellsprings Cir & Dr 78230
Wellstone Run 78249
Wellwood St 78250
Welsch Vw 78249
Welsford 78233
Welsh Vly 78254
Wendover St 78254
Wendy St 78210
Wenrich 78233
Wensledale Cir 78251
Wentink Ave 78261
Wentworth Way 78260
Wenzel Rd 78233
Wesco Loop 78247
Wescott Ave 78237
Wesley Park 78261
Wesley Pl 78209
Wesleyan St 78249
West Ave
400-498 78201
500-3099 78201
3100-11699 78213
11700-13599 78216
Westbend Dr 78227
N Westberry Dr 78228
Westbluff Dr 78227
Westboro Pl 78229
Westbriar 78227
Westchase 78240
Westchester Dr 78217
Westcliff Ln 78227
Westcloud Ln 78227
Westcourt Ln 78257
Westcreek Plz 78253
Westcreek Oaks 78253
Westelm Cir, Gdns & Pt 78230
Westerleigh 78218
Western Mdw 78261
Western Park 78228
Western Way 78254
Western Cactus 78245
Western Pine Woods 78249
Western Skies 78240
Western Star 78260
Western Sun 78240
Western Tack
800-899 78260
Western Tack
19400-19499 78266
Western Trail Dr 78244
Westernhill Dr 78251
Westfall Ave 78210
Westfield Blvd 78227
Westfield Pl 78240
Westgard Pass 78245
Westgate Ln 78209
Westglade Dr 78227
Westgrove Dr 78240
Westhaven Pl 78227
Westhill Pl 78201
Westknoll Dr 78227
Westlake Dr 78227
Westlawn Dr 78227
Westleaf St 78227
Westlyn Dr 78227
Westmar St 78227
Westmark 78259
Westminster Ave 78228
Westminster Ct 78257
Westmont Dr 78227
Westmoor St 78227
Westmoreland Dr 78213
Westoak Rd 78227
Weston 78251
Weston Center Bldg 78205
Westover Blf 78251
Westover Cir 78251
Westover Park 78251
Westover Rd 78209
Westover Vw 78251
Westover Hills Blvd 78251
Westplain Dr 78227
Westport Way 78227
Westridge Dr 78237
Westrock Dr 78227
Westrun 78249
Westshire Dr 78227
Westspring Dr 78258
Westvale Dr 78227
Westvalley Dr 78227
Westville Dr 78227
Westward Dr 78227
Westway Dr 78225
Westwind Cir 78239
Westwood Dr 78212
Westwood Loop
6400-10899 78254
10900-11299 78253
Westwood Way 78218
Wethersfield St 78216
Wetmore Bnd 78247
Wetmore Knl 78247
Wetmore Rd
8901-11099 78216
11701-13397 78247
13399-13499 78247
13501-13599 78247
12983-1-12983-2 78247
Wetmore Rdg 78247
Wetmore Trl 78247
Wetmore Cross 78247
Wetz Dr 78217
Wever Xing 78250
Wexford Brk 78240
Wexford Crk 78240
Wexford Cv 78240
Wexford Gln 78240
Wexford Grv 78240
Wexford Holw 78240
Wexford Pl 78240
Wexford Rdg 78240
Wexford Sq 78240
Wexford St 78217
Weybridge 78250
Weyburn 78248
Weyfield 78248
Weymouth St 78212
Wharton St 78210
Whata Vw 78260
Wheatfield Dr 78228
Wheathill 78253
Wheatland St 78219
Wheatley Ave 78220
Wheelhouse St 78242
Whippoorwill 78263
Whirlwind Dr 78217
Whisper Cir 78230
Whisper Cyn 78258
Whisper Mtn 78258
Whisper Pt 78240
Whisper Bells St 78230
Whisper Bluff St 78230
Whisper Bow St 78230
Whisper Breeze St 78230
Whisper Brook St 78230
Whisper Dawn St 78230
Whisper Dew St 78230
Whisper Dove St 78230
Whisper Falls St 78230
Whisper Fawn St 78230
Whisper Fern St 78230
Whisper Forest St 78230
Whisper Glen St 78230
Whisper Green St 78230
Whisper Hill St 78230
Whisper Hollow St 78230
Whisper Lark St 78230
Whisper Leaves St 78230
Whisper Ledge St 78230
Whisper Meadow St 78230
Whisper Moss St 78230
Whisper Path St 78230
Whisper Quill St 78230
Whisper Ridge St 78230
Whisper Rock St 78230
Whisper Sloe St 78230
Whisper Sound St 78230
Whisper Spring Dr 78230
Whisper Trail St 78230
Whisper Valley St 78230
Whisper View St 78230
Whisper Willow St 78230
Whisper Wood Ln 78216
Whispering Crk 78220
Whispering Lake St 78222
Whispering Oaks 78266
Whispering Oaks St 78233
Whispering Wind St 78230
Whispering Winds Dr 78264
Whispine 78218
Whistler 78239
Whistling Acres 78261
Whistling Duck 78253
Whistling Wind 78257
Whitby Rd 78240
Whitby Tower 78258
E White 78214
W White 78214
White Crk 78255
White Cyn 78260
White Ash St 78245
White Birch St 78245
White Bonnet St 78240
White Cloud 78238
White Cross 78253
White Deer Ln 78245
White Dove Pass 78255
White Eagle Dr 78260
White Elm Woods St 78249
White Fawn Dr 78255
White Feather St 78242
White Magnolia 78227
White Mulberry 78254
White Oak Cv 78253
White Oak Dr 78230
White Pine St 78232
White Quail 78250
White River Dr 78254
White Rock St 78245
White Sands St 78233
White Star St 78242
White Tail Dr 78228
Whitechurch Ln 78257
Whitecliff Dr 78227
Whitefield Ave 78223
Whitegate 78253
Whitehall St 78216
Whitehaven 78232
Whiteoak Peak 78248
Whitestone St 78227
Whitewing Ln 78230
Whitewood St 78242
Whithers Ln 78240
Whiting Ave 78210
Whitland 78239
Whitley Dr 78224
Whitman Ave 78211
Whitney Ave 78223
Whitney Cir 78254
Whitney Grn 78244
Whitneys Ct 78260
Whitson Rd 78230
E & W Whittier St 78210
Whittlewood St 78250
Whittney Rdg 78239
Wichita Ct 78225
Wichita Pass 78258
Wickahoney 78250
Wickersham St 78254
Wickes St 78210
Wickfield St 78217
Wickford Way 78213
Wickham Wood 78218
Wickheather St 78254
Wicklow Dr 78250
Widefield Ln 78245
Widgeon Ct 78245
Wiggins Crk 78253
Wiggins Pl 78214
Wigwam Dr 78238
Wikieup St 78211
Wilborn Dr 78217
Wilby Ln 78253
Wilchester St 78220
Wilcox Ave 78211
Wild Crst, Holw & Trce 78266
Wild Basin 78258
Wild Bloom 78260
Wild Cat Lair 78253
Wild Deer Cir, Pass & Run 78248
Wild Eagle St 78255
Wild Fire 78251
Wild Flower Way 78244
Wild Grape Dr 78230
Wild Horse St 78238
Wild Oak Dr 78219
Wild Olive Trl 78256
Wild Onion 78258
Wild Peak 78258
Wild Pecan 78254
Wild Persimmon St 78245
Wild Pistachio 78254
Wild Plum 78222
Wild Root 78264
Wild Rose Bay 78254
Wild Springs Dr 78258
Wild Thicket 78254
Wild Trails St 78250
Wild Turkey E 78232
Wild Turkey W 78232
Wild Turkey Rd 78260
Wild Valley Dr 78242
Wild Wind Park 78266
Wildacres Dr 78249
Wildberry Ct 78258
Wildcat Cv 78254
Wildcat Cyn 78252
Wilde Gln 78240
Wilder St 78250
Wilder Pond 78260
Wilderness Blf 78261
Wilderness Cv 78261
Wilderness Hl 78231
Wilderness Pkwy 78232
Wilderness Pt 78231
Wilderness Rdg 78261
Wilderness Trl 78233
Wilderness Creek Dr 78231
Wilderness Elm 78261
Wilderness Gap 78254
Wilderness Oak
10700-10799 78261
Wilderness Oak
20701-21197 78258
21199-24299 78258
24301-24499 78258
25001-25099 78260
25700-25799 78261
Wilderness Paw 78261
Wilderness Rim 78261
Wilderness Sun 78254
Wilderness Wood St 78231
Wildfern St 78238
Wildflower Dr 78228
Wildflower Trl 78250
Wildgrass Spur 78244
Wildgrove Ln 78258
Wildhorse Pkwy 78254
Wildhorse Run 78251
Wildrose Ave 78209
Wildrose Hl 78230
Wildstone Cir 78232
Wildstone Pl 78254
Wildt Rd 78222
Wildwind Dr 78239
E Wildwood Dr 78212
W Wildwood Dr
100-599 78212
800-2499 78201
Wildwood Rdg 78250
Wilhelm 78266
Wilkins Ave 78210
Willacy Trl 78253
Willard Dr 78228
Willard Path 78261
Willee Dr 78228
Willet Way 78223
William Grv 78254
William Bonney 78254
William Carey 78253
William Classen Dr 78232
William Penn Dr 78230
William Rancher Rd 78238
William Travis Dr 78238
Williamsburg Pl 78201
Willim St 78209
Willis Rnch 78260
Willmon Way 78239
Willow
100-699 78202
Willow
900-1399 78208
Willow Bnd 78232
Willow Holw 78254
Willow Knl 78258
Willow Trl 78232
Willow Walk 78259
Willow Way 78214
Willow Country 78254
Willow Creek St 78251
Willow Crest St 78247
Willow Cross 78239
Willow Farm 78249
Willow Glen Dr 78250
Willow Green Dr 78217
Willow Grove Dr 78245
Willow Heights Dr 78254
Willow Hill St 78247
Willow Knoll Cv 78216
Willow Moss St 78232
Willow Oak St 78249
Willow Rain 78244
Willow Run St 78247
Willow Tree 78259
Willowbluff Dr 78216
Willowbrook Dr 78228
Willowick Ln 78217
Willowridge St 78249
Willowthorn Ln 78249
Willowwood Blvd 78219
Wilma Jean Dr 78224
Wilmington Ave
301-399 78215
500-699 78212
Wilmot St 78237
Wilson
200-298 78228
Wilson
300-2199 78228
2201-2699 78228
2700-2899 78201
2901-2999 78201
Wilson St 78226
Wilson Oaks 78249
Wilsons Creek St 78245
Wilted Oak 78264
Wiltshire Ave 78209
Wimberly Blvd 78221
Wimberly Oaks 78261
Wimbledon St 78254
Wincheap Farm 78228
Winchester Way 78254
Wind Spgs 78258
Wind Ter 78239
Wind Vly 78261
Wind Arbor 78239
Wind Cave St 78232
Wind Crown 78239
Wind Dancer 78251
Wind Gate Pkwy 78254
Wind Talker 78251
Windbluff Dr 78239
Windboro Dr 78239
Windbreak Ct 78258
Windbridge 78250
Windbrooke St 78249
Windchase 78232
Windcliffe 78259
Windcrest Dr 78239
Windemere 78230
Windfall 78260
Windgap Dr 78230
Windgarden 78239
Windhaven Dr 78239
Windhurst 78258
Winding Br 78230
Winding Crk 78231
Winding Hl 78217
Winding Ln 78231
Winding Vw 78260
Winding Elm Pl 78254
Winding Farm 78249
Winding Oak Dr 78247
Winding Ridge Dr 78239
Winding Way Dr 78232
Windlake St 78230
Windline St 78251
Windmill Rd 78231
Windmill Way 78232
Windmill Hill St 78229
Windmill Palm 78216
Windmore Ct 78258
Windover Dr 78218
Windrock Cir & Dr 78239
Windsor Dr 78228
Windsor Hl 78239
Windsor Holw 78239
Windsor Castle 78218
Windsor Cross 78239
Windsor Oaks 78239
Windsor Wood 78258
Windspirit 78260
Windstone Crk 78254
Windswept Cv 78266
Windswept St 78217
Windtree 78253
Windvale Dr 78239
Windview Dr 78239
Windview Way 78244
Windwalk 78253
Windward Trce 78254
Windward Way Dr 78227
Windway Dr 78239
Windy Cv 78239
Windy Frst 78239
Windy Holw 78239
Windy Knl 78239
Windy Trl 78232
Windy Cross 78239
Windy Mist 78254
Windy Oaks St 78230
Windy Pond 78260
Windy Ridge Ct 78259
Windyhill Dr 78242
Wine Cup 78228
Wine Rose Path 78255
Wineberry Dr 78240
Winecup Hl 78256
Winesap Dr 78222
Winewood Dr 78213
Winfield Blvd & Cir 78239
Wing Fls 78253
Wingate Ave 78204
Wingfoot 78260
Wingheart 78253
Wingstar 78253
Wink Cir 78224
Winkle Ct 78227
Winlock Dr 78228
Winnco Dr 78218
Winnetka Rd 78229
Winneway Dr 78222
Winning Colors 78248
W Winnipeg Ave 78225
Winridge Dr 78228
Winsford 78239
Winslow St 78208
Winsome 78224
Winsong Dr 78239
Winston Cv 78260
S Winston Ln 78213
Winston Oaks 78249
Winter Crk 78254
Winter Hl 78258
Winter Park 78250
Winter Cherry 78245
Winter Gorge 78259
Winter Lake St 78244
Winter Mist Dr 78247
Winter Oaks 78260
Winter Sky 78250
Winter Sunrise Dr 78244
Winter View Dr 78247
Winterhaven Dr 78239
Winterpath Dr 78233
Winters Edge 78253
Winterstone Dr 78254
Winterwood Pl 78229
Winthop St 78249
Winthrop Downs 78257
Winton Park Dr 78250
Wisdom Rdg 78252
Wiseman Blvd 78251
Wishing Wl 78260
Wishing Lake Dr 78222
Wishing Oaks St 78233
Wishing Star 78258
Wisteria Dr 78213
Wisteria Hl 78218
Wisteria Way 78259
Wisteria Woods 78251
Wistful Trl 78244
Witt St 78228
Wittenburg 78256
Wobaker Cir 78224
Woburn St 78254
Woley Dr 78228
Wolf Crst 78248
Wolf Pt 78251
Wolf Rd
101-397 78216
399-499 78216
10101-10799 78252
Wolf Creek St 78232
Wolf Ridge St 78247
Wolfe Xing 78239
Wolfeton Way 78218
Woller Crk, Path, Pl, Rd, Trl & Vly 78249
Woltwood 78248
Wonder Pkwy 78213
Wondering Oak 78247
Wonderview Dr 78230
Wood Blf 78240
Wood Byu 78249
Wood Cir 78251
Wood Fls 78251
Wood Frst 78251
Wood Grv 78232
Wood Hbr 78249
Wood Knls 78251
Wood Ln 78216
Wood Park 78264
Wood Pass 78249
Wood Pl 78251
Wood Pt 78231
Wood Rnch 78227
Wood Run 78251
Wood Ter 78233
Wood Wl 78261
Wood Arbor 78251
Wood Bench 78233
Wood Bow 78251
Wood Branch St 78232

Wood Canyon St 78248
Wood Cave 78251
Wood Chuck 78260
Wood Climb St 78233
Wood Dew 78251
Wood Fern St 78232
Wood Glen Dr 78244
Wood Meadow St 78232
Wood Moss St 78248
Wood Oak 78233
Wood Peak 78251
Wood Quail 78248
Wood Rush St 78232
Wood Shadow St 78216
Wood Sorrel 78247
Wood Walk St 78233
Wood Wind 78251
Woodbell 78233
Woodbine St 78209
Woodbrace St 78217
Woodbreeze St 78217
Woodbridge Way 78257
Woodbrook 78218
Woodburn Dr 78218
Woodbury Dr 78217
Woodby Ct 78212
Woodchase 78240
Woodchester St 78232
Woodcliffe St 78230
Woodcock Dr 78228
Woodcraft 78218
Woodcrest Dr 78209
Woodcutter Ct 78231
Wooded Crk 78259
Wooded Knl 78258
Wooded Acres 78260
Wooden Fox 78245
Woodfield 78244
Woodfin Dr 78264
Woodflame Ct 78227
Woodford 78239
Woodgate Dr 78227
Woodglow Cir 78244
Woodgreen 78218
Woodhaven St 78209
Woodheather St 78254
Woodhill 78218
Woodhollow 78218
Woodhuff Dr 78214
Woodlake Ctr 78244
E Woodlake Dr 78229
Woodlake Pkwy
5100-6899 78244
7101-7299 78218
Woodlake Pt 78244
Woodlake Trl 78244
Woodlake Vw 78244
Woodlake Club Dr 78244
Woodland 78264
Woodland Bnd 78255
Woodland Cv 78266
Woodland Hls 78250
Woodland Pnes 78254
Woodland Deer 78254
Woodlark 78231
E Woodlawn Ave 78212
W Woodlawn Ave
100-899 78212
900-2099 78201
2101-2399 78201
2400-3799 78228
Woodlawn Rdg 78259
Woodley St 78232
Woodlief St 78212
Woodline St 78251
Woodmanor Dr 78228
Woodmen Dr 78209
Woodmont 78260
Woodmoor St 78249
Woodpecker Way 78256
Woodridge Blf 78249
Woodridge Cv 78249
Woodridge Dr 78209
Woodridge Frst 78249
Woodridge Hl 78249
Woodridge Park 78249
Woodridge Path 78249
Woodridge Oaks 78249
Woodridge Rock 78249
Woodrock St 78251
Woodrose Cir 78247
Woodrose Park 78255
Woodrow 78204
Woods End St 78240
Woods Hole Dr 78233
Woodsage Dr 78224
Woodseer St 78248
Woodside Dr 78228
Woodsrim St 78233
Woodstock Dr 78223
Woodstone Dr 78230
Woodstone Way 78233
Woodstream 78231
Woodthorn Way 78249
Woodtrail 78250
Woodview Dr 78233
Woodville Dr 78223
Woodvine Cir 78232
Woodward Pl 78204
Woodwaters Way 78249
Woodway Ct 78249
Woodway Ln 78209
Woodway Pl 78249
Woodway Forest Dr 78216
Woodwick Dr 78239
Woody Ln 78233
Woollcott St 78251
Worbler Pass 78245
Worchester Knls 78233
Worchester Wood 78233
Wordsworth St 78217
World Trade Ctr 78205
Worldland Dr 78217
Wormack Way 78251
Worth Pkwy 78257
Worthington 78248
Worthsham Dr 78257
Wottlin Rd 78213
Wounded Knee 78261
Wr Larson Rd 78261
Wrangler Run 78223
Wrangler St 78227
Wrangler Vw 78223
Wrangler Way 78223
Wren Hvn 78248
Wren Lk 78244
Wren St 78223
Wrenwood St 78233
Wrexham Hts 78254
Wright Carpenter 78221
Wright Patterson St 78233
Wright Way St 78240
Wrought Iron 78260
Wroxton Rd 78217
Wt Montgomery 78252
Wurzbach Rd
3101-3197 78238
3199-6100 78238
6102-6198 78238
6300-7299 78240
7301-7797 78229
7799-8399 78229
8401-8499 78229
8500-9500 78240
9502-9598 78240
9900-10098 78230
10100-11200 78230
11202-11898 78230
Wuthering Heights St 78254
N Ww White Rd 78219
S Ww White Rd
100-499 78219
500-1899 78220
1900-7999 78222
9200-9999 78223
Wyanoke Dr 78209
Wyatts Run 78254
Wyckham Rise St 78209
Wycliff Dr 78220
Wycliff Rise 78231
Wycombe St 78216
Wye Dr 78217
Wynberry 78260
Wyndale St 78209
Wyoming Pass 78254
Wyoming St 78203
Yacht Hbr 78242
Yakima Dr 78250
Yale Ave 78201
Yanticaw Brook St 78260
Yantis St 78237
Yarrow Blvd 78224
Yateswood 78248
Yaupon Trl 78256
Yellow Knife St 78242
Yellow Oak Cir 78232
Yellow Rose St 78238
Yellow Sand Dr 78227
Yellow Sky 78264
Yellow Warbler 78233
Yellow Wood Dr 78219
Yellowstone St 78210
Yett Ave 78221
Yew Dr 78232
Yoakum Aly 78202
Yoakum Trl 78253
Yodel Hls 78260
Yolanda Dr 78228
York Bnd 78245
York Crst 78245
York Dr 78216
York Creek Cir 78230
York Woods 78249
Yorkhaven 78259
Yorkshire Ct 78249
Yorkshire Pl 78210
Yorktown Dr 78230
Yormis Nest 78251
Yosemite Cv 78251
Yosemite Dr 78232
Yosemite Oaks Cir 78213
E & W Young 78214
Young Bear St 78242
Yuba Trl 78245
Yucca St
100-399 78203
400-498 78220
500-899 78220
901-1099 78220
Yucca Vly 78242
Yukon Blvd 78221
Yukon Straight 78261
Yuma St 78211
Yvonne Ave 78211
Zabra St 78227
Zacatecas Ct 78253
Zachry Dr 78228
Zambrano Rd 78209
Zangs Dr 78238
Zapata St 78210
N Zarzamora St
101-197 78207
199-1599 78207
1600-2799 78201
2801-3199 78201
S Zarzamora St
100-2699 78207
2700-2798 78225
2800-3800 78225
3802-4298 78225
4500-6699 78211
6701-6797 78224
6799-12899 78224
E & W Zavalla 78204
Zebra Dl 78253
Zebulon Dr 78240
Zenia Cir 78237
Zenia Ln 78260
Zephyr Cv 78266
Zephyr Dr 78239
Zercher Rd 78209
Zerm Rd 78214
Zerrcliff Ln 78220
Zeta Cir & Vw 78258
Zeus Cir 78260
Zeuty St 78227
Zigmont Rd 78263
Zilla St 78212
Zinnia Flds 78245
Zornia Dr 78213
Zulema Ave 78237
Zupan St 78227
Zurich 78230

NUMBERED STREETS

1st Ave 78216
1st St 78266
2nd St
2000-2199 78221
18400-18499 78266
3rd St
201-397 78205
399-400 78205
402-498 78205
18400-18599 78266
4th St
201-299 78205
2100-2199 78221
18400-18499 78266
5th St
2100-2199 78221
18400-18499 78266
6th St
201-297 78215
299-500 78215
502-598 78215
2100-15399 78221
7th St 78221
7th Tee Cir & Vis 78221
8th St 78215
9th St
100-499 78215
8000-8099 78235
10th St 78215
NW 18th St 78207
1700-1799 78201
SW 18th St 78207
NW 19th St
401-697 78207
1600-1699 78201
SW 19th St 78207
NW & SW 20th 78207
NW 21st St 78207
SW 21st St
500-2298 78207
2500-2599 78226
NW 22nd St
101-597 78207
1600-1699 78201
NW 23rd St
301-397 78207
1600-1698 78201
NW & SW 24th 78207
NW 25th St
301-399 78207
1100-1198 78228
SW 25th St 78207
NW 26th St
200-698 78237
1001-1197 78228
1199-1699 78228
SW 26th St 78237
NW 27th St 78228
SW 27th St 78237
NW 28th St 78228
SW 28th St 78237
SW 29th St 78237
SW 30th St 78237
NW 34th St 78237
NW 34th St 78237
400-498 78228
500-1000 78228
1002-1098 78228
SW 34th St 78237
SW 35th St 78237
NW 36th St 78237
NW 36th St 78237
900-998 78228
1000-2499 78228
2501-2699 78228
SW 36th St 78237
SW 37th St 78237
NW 38th St 78237
1000-1298 78228
SW 38th St 78237
NW & SW 39th 78237
NW & SW 40th 78237
SW 41st St 78237
SW 42nd St 78237
91st St 78214
96th St 78214
99th St 78214

SAN MARCOS TX

General Delivery 78666

POST OFFICE BOXES MAIN OFFICE STATIONS AND BRANCHES

Box No.s
All PO Boxes 78667

NAMED STREETS

Abernathy Ave 78666
Academy St 78666
Acorn Ln, Path, Trl & Way 78666
Adrian St 78666
Advance St 78666
Airport Dr 78666
Alabama St 78666
Alamo St 78666
Algarita St 78666
Alhambra Dr 78666
Allegheny Ct 78666
Allen St 78666
Allison Ln 78666
Alpine Trl 78666
Alta Vista Dr 78666
Alto St 78666
Amelia 78666
Amherst St 78666
Amy Ln 78666
Anchor Hill Rd 78666
Anderson Acres Ln 78666
Andra Ln 78666
Annes Trl 78666
Appalachian Trl 78666
Aquarena Springs Dr 78666
Archers Way 78666
Arid 78666
Arizona St 78666
Armament Ln 78666
Armstead St 78666
Armstrong St 78666
Arrow Hl 78666
Arrowcrest Ln 78666
Arroyo Doble 78666
Ash St 78666
Ashley Ct 78666
Aspen St 78666
Autumn Cv 78666
Avalon Ave 78666
Avian Dr 78666
Azolar St 78666
Backbone Rdg 78666
Backhorn Ln 78666
Backus Rd 78666
Baker Ave 78666
Baker Creek Loop 78666
Bandera St 78666
Bar B Que Way 78666
Barbara Dr 78666
Barclay St 78666
Barnes Dr 78666
Barrientos Ln 78666
Barton Rd 78666
Baylor Ave 78666
Beback Inn Rd 78666
Belmont Dr 78666
Belvin St 78666
Benito Ln 78666
Benning 78666
Bert Brown St 78666
Bethke Rd 78666
Big Daddy 78666
Billy Bluff Trl 78666
Birmensdorf Dr 78666
N & S Bishop St 78666
Black Cv 78666
Blanco St 78666
Blanco River Ranch Rd 78666
Blanco Vista Blvd 78666
Blessing Ln 78666
Bliss St 78666
E & W Bluebonnet Dr & Pass 78666
Bob White Ct 78666
Bobcat Dr 78666
Bogie Dr 78666
Booth Dr 78666
Boulder Blf 78666
Bracewood Cir 78666
Braune Rd 78666
Brazoria Trl 78666
Breezewood Dr 78666
Briar Meadows Rd 78666
Briarwood Dr 78666
Bridlegate Cir 78666
Bridlewood Dr 78666
Bridlewood Ranches Dr 78666
Broadway St 78666
Brown St 78666
Browne Ter 78666
Buena Vista St 78666
Buffalo Run Dr 78666
Buffle Head Cv 78666
Bugg Ln 78666
Bunnyrun Ln 78666
Burleson St 78666
Burt St 78666
Buttercup St 78666
N & S C M Allen Pkwy 78666
Caliche Trl 78666
Calixto Ct 78666
Camaro Way 78666
Camino Alto 78666
Candlelight Ln 78666
Canvas Back Cv 78666
Canyon Frk & Rd 78666
Capistrano Dr 78666
Cardinal St 78666
Carlson Cir 78666
Casa Verde 78666
Cascade Trl 78666
Casida Ln 78666
Casita Cv 78666
Castle Bluff Dr 78666
Castle Creek Dr 78666
Castle Gate Cir 78666
Castle Guard Ln 78666
Catclaw Cv 78666
Cazador Dr 78666
Cedar Ln & Park 78666
Cedargrove 78666
Cedarside St 78666
Center Point Rd 78666
Centerview Dr 78666
Central Texas Dr 78666
Centre St 78666
Cerro Vista Dr 78666
Champion Blvd 78666
Chaparral St 78666
Char Crest Ct 78666
Charles Austin Dr 78666
Cheatham St 78666
Cherry Blossom Ct 78666
Chestnut St 78666
Chicago St 78666
Chico St 78666
Christopher St 78666
Chula Vista St 78666
Cielo Ranch Dr & Rd 78666
Cimarron Ct 78666
City Park St 78666
Civic Center Loop 78666
Claire Dr 78666
Clara St 78666
Claremont Dr 78666
Clarewood Dr 78666
Clark St 78666
Clear Path Ln 78666
Clearview Cir 78666
Cloverleaf St 78666
Clovis R Barker Rd 78666
Clyde Ct & St 78666
Clydesdale Dr 78666
Coers Dr 78666
Coffee Rd 78666
Colleen Ct 78666
Columbia Cir & St 78666
Comacho St 78666
Comal St 78666
N & S Comanche St 78666
Concho St 78666
Condor Dr 78666
Conway Dr 78666
Coral Ln 78666
Cordero Dr 78666
Corporate Dr 78666
Corrie Ct 78666
Country Estates Dr 78666
Covey Ct 78666
Cowan Rd 78666
Craber Ln 78666
Craddock Ave 78666
Crepe Myrtle St 78666
Crest Dr 78666
Crest Circle Dr 78666
Cross Rd 78666
Crossbow Ln 78666
Crossover Rd 78666
Crystal Cv 78666
Cypress Ct & St 78666
Dachshund Dr 78666
Dailey St 78666
Daisy St 78666
Dale St 78666
Dandelion Trl 78666
Dara Ln 78666
Dartmouth St 78666
Dashwood Dr 78666
Davis Ln 78666
Davis Ranch Rd 78666
Day Dr 78666
W De Zavala Dr 78666
Debbie Ct 78666
Dedeke Pl 78666
Deer Creek Dr 78666
Deer Stand Loop 78666
Deertrail Dr 78666
Deerwood Dr 78666
Dees St 78666
Delmar St 78666
Derby Ct 78666
Discovery Ln 78666
Dolly St 78666
Dreibrodt Rd 78666
Duncan Dr 78666
Durango St 78666
Dutton Dr 78666
Dylan Rd 78666
Earle St 78666
Easton Dr 78666
Eastwood Ln & St 78666
Easy St 78666
Ebony St 78666
Ed Jl Green Dr 78666
Edgemont Dr 78666
Edward Gary St 78666
Eisenhower St 78666
El Camino Way Dr 78666
El Paseo Dr 78666
Ellis St 78666
Elm Holw 78666
Elm Hill Ct 78666
Emerald Acres Dr 78666
Encina 78666
Encino St 78666
End Brook Ln 78666
N & S Endicott St 78666
Espada Dr 78666

Fairview Rd 78666
Falconwood Dr 78666
Faris St 78666
Farm House Rd 78666
Feltner St 78666
Fence Line Dr 78666
Fenway Loop 78666
Field St 78666
Field Corn Ln 78666
Fir St 78666
Fleming Pass 78666
Fm 1978 78666
Fm 1979 78666
Fm 32 78666
Fm 3353 78666
Fm 621 78666
Ford Rd 78666
Forssell Ln 78666
Foster Ln 78666
Fox Rd 78666
Fox Creek Cir 78666
Foxtail Run 78666
Frances Harris Ln 78666
Franklin Dr 78666
N & S Fredericksburg St 78666
Freeman Aquatic Building 78666
Freeman Ranch Rd 78666
Furman Ave 78666
Gadwall Cv 78666
Garden Ct & Way 78666
Gary Cir & Ct 78666
Geneva Grove Ct 78666
Georgia St 78666
Girard St 78666
Gladney Dr 78666
Gm Ln 78666
Golden Leaf Ln 78666
Goldeneye Cv 78666
Goldenrod 78666
Gomez St 78666
Gordon St 78666
Grace Ln 78666
Grandview Dr 78666
Grant Ct 78666
Grant Harris Rd 78666
Gravel St 78666
Great Oaks Dr 78666
Green Leaf 78666
Greenpointe 78666
Greenridge Cv 78666
E & W Grove St 78666
N Guadalupe St
101-197 78666
199-300 78666
301-301 78667
301-499 78666
302-698 78666
S Guadalupe St 78666
Gustav Ln 78666
Gypsy Cv 78666
Hackberry St 78666
Hamilton St 78666
Hamilton Hollow Rd 78666
Handlers Holw 78666
Hansen St 78666
Harmons Way 78666
Harper Dr 78666
Harris Hill Rd 78666
Harvard St 78666
Harvey St 78666
Harwood Dr 78666
Haven Crest Ln 78666
Hay Barn St 78666
Haynes St 78666
Hays St 78666
Hazelton St 78666
Hearthstone Dr 78666
Heartridge 78666
Henk Ln 78666
Hermann Rd 78666
Herndon St 78666
Hidden Brook Ln 78666
Hidden Farms Dr 78666
High Rd 78666
High Ridge Cir 78666
Highland Dr & Ter 78666
Highline Dr 78666
Highway 21 78666
Highway 80 78666
Hill Dr 78666
E & W Hillcrest Dr 78666
Hilliard Rd 78666
NW Hills Rd 78666
Hilltop Dr 78666
Hillyer St 78666
Hines St 78666
Hofheinz St 78666
E & W Holland St 78666
Hollys Way 78666
Holmes Ln 78666
Holt Dr 78666
E & W Hopkins St 78666
Horace Howard Dr 78666
Horseshoe Bend Rd 78666
House Wren Hl 78666
Howard Pl 78666
Hoya Ln 78666
Hughson Ct & Dr 78666
Hugo Rd 78666
Hull St 78666
Hunter Rd & Rdg 78666
Hunters Cir 78666
Hunters Glen Dr 78666
Hunters Run Trl 78666
E & W Hutchison St 78666
Indian Blanket St 78666
Indiana St 78666
N & S Interstate 35 78666
Invasion St 78666
Inwood Dr 78666
Iris St 78666
Irvin Dr 78666
Jackman St 78666
Jackson Ln 78666
Jacob Ln 78666
James St 78666
Jasmine Ln 78666
Johns St 78666
N & S Johnson Ave 78666
Joleen St 78666
Jones St 78666
Juarez St 78666
Juniper Ct 78666
Kaitlyn Ln 78666
Kasch St 78666
Kathryn Cv 78666
Kays Cv 78666
Kid Ranch Ln 78666
Kingswood St 78666
Knight St 78666
Knox St 78666
Kutscher Rd 78666
Lacey Ln 78666
Lady Bird Ln 78666
Lago Vista St 78666
Lamar Ave 78666
Lancaster St 78666
Lance Ln 78666
Laredo St 78666
Larue Dr 78666
E & W Laurel Hl, Ln & Rdg 78666
Lazy Ln 78666
N & S Lbj Cv & Dr 78666
Leah Ave 78666
Leather Oak Loop 78666
Lee St 78666
Lehmann Rd 78666
Leslie Ln 78666
Lewis St 78666
Ligustrum Ct 78666
Lily St 78666
Lime Kiln Rd 78666
Linda Dr 78666
Linden Ln 78666
Lindsey St 78666
Lisa Ln 78666
Little Backbone 78666
Live Oak Rd 78666
Live Oak Hills Ct 78666
Llano Dr 78666
Lockhart St 78666
Lockwood St 78666
Long St 78666
Longbranch Dr 78666
Longcope Loop 78666
Lookout Ridge Rd 78666
N & S Loop St 78666
Loquat St 78666
Losoya Dr 78666
Lost Prairie Ln 78666
Love St 78666
Lovejoy Ln 78666
Luciano Flores St 78666
Luck St 78666
Lupine Trl 78666
Magnolia St 78666
Mallard Loop 78666
Mandalay St 78666
Manor Park Rd 78666
Maple St 78666
Mariposa St 78666
Marita G Rd 78666
Marlow Ln 78666
Marlton St 78666
Marshall St 78666
E & W Martin Luther King Dr 78666
Martindale Rd 78666
Martins Crst 78666
Mary Ln & St 78666
Maury St 78666
Mcallister St 78666
Mcarthur St 78666
E & W Mccarty Ln 78666
Mcgehee St 78666
Mckie St 78666
Mckinley Place Dr 78666
Mead St 78666
Meadow Blf, Pass & Pkwy 78666
Meadow Brook Ln 78666
Meadow Rise 78666
Meadow View Dr 78666
Meadowridge Cv 78666
Medical Pkwy 78666
Meiners St 78666
Meredith St 78666
Merrywood Ln 78666
Mesquite Rd & St 78666
Midway St 78666
Military Dr 78666
Mill St 78666
Miller Trce 78666
E & W Mimosa Cir 78666
Mira Loma Ln 78666
Missum Pt 78666
Missy Ln 78666
N & S Mitchell St 78666
Mockingbird Dr 78666
Monica St 78666
Monterrey Oaks 78666
Moore St 78666
Morningmist Ct 78666
Morningwood Dr 78666
Mosscliff Cir 78666
Mostyn Ln 78666
Mountain Dr 78666
Mountain High Dr 78666
Mountain View Dr 78666
Mr Pete Rd 78666
Mulberry Ct 78666
Mustang Ln 78666
Nance St 78666
Nevada St 78666
Newberry Trl 78666
Nichols Dr 78666
Nicola Aly 78666
Nimitz St 78666
Norcrest Dr 78666
North St 78666
Northfork Rd 78666
Northpoint Dr N 78666
Northview Dr 78666
Oak Cv, Holw, Ldg, Mdws, Pkwy & St 78666
Oak Grove Rd 78666
Oak Haven Dr 78666
Oak Mesa 78666
Oak Shadow 78666
Oakdale Dr 78666
Oakridge Dr 78666
Oakwood Loop 78666
Offermann Hill Rd 78666
N & S Old Bastrop Hwy & Rd 78666
Old Gin Rd 78666
Old Martindale Rd 78666
Old Ranch Road 12 78666
Old Seguin Rd 78666
Old Settlers Dr 78666
S Old Stagecoach Rd 78666
Old Zorn Rd 78666
Olive St 78666
Orchard St 78666
Oregon St 78666
Oscar Smith St 78666
Overlook Way 78666
Owens St 78666
E Owl Hollow Rd 78666
Ozark Dr 78666
Paintbrush St 78666
Palermo Dr 78666
Palomino Ln 78666
Pampas Pass 78666
Panorama Dr 78666
Park Dr, Ln & Pl 78666
Parkdale Dr 78666
Parker Dr 78666
Parkview Ln 78666
Paso Del Robles 78666
Pat Garrison St 78666
Patricia Dr 78666
Patton St 78666
Pauls Dr 78666
Peach Blossom Ct 78666
Peach Tree St 78666
Pearce Ct 78666
Pecan St 78666
Pecan Park Dr 78666
Peques St 78666
Peregrine Dr 78666
Perkins St 78666
Perry St 78666
Peter Garza Dr 78666
Petmecky Ln 78666
Petunia St 78666
Philo St 78666
Picasso Dr 78666
Pico Ct 78666
Piedras Pass 78666
Pincea Pl 78666
Pine St 78666
Pintail Loop 78666
Pinto Ln 78666
Pioneer Trl 78666
Pisano Dr 78666
Pitt St 78666
Plarande St 78666
Plum St 78666
Pluma Ct 78666
Poplar St 78666
Porter St 78666
Posey Rd 78666
Post Rd 78666
Potomac Cir 78666
Powder Horn Trl 78666
Preston Trl 78666
Primrose Way 78666
Progress St 78666
Prospect St 78666
Purgatory Pass & Rd 78666
Purple Martin Dr 78666
Quail Run 78666
Quail Creek Dr 78666
Quarry St 78666
Quarry Crest Cir 78666
Quarry Springs Dr 78666
Rachel St 78666
Railroad St 78666
Rainwood Dr 78666
Ramona Cir 78666
Ramsay St 78666
Ranch Road 12 78666
Rancho Encino Dr 78666
Randi Ln 78666
Rattler Rd 78666
Raynaldo Way 78666
Red Head Cv 78666
Redbud Ct 78666
Redwood Rd 78666
S Reimer Ave 78666
Reyes St 78666
Ridge Dr 78666
Ridge View Dr 78666
Ridgecrest St 78666
Ridgeway Dr 78666
Ridgewood 78666
Rim Rock Ranch Rd 78666
Rimrock Ln 78666
Rivas Rd 78666
River Rd 78666
River Hills Dr 78666
River Ridge Pkwy 78666
Riverbend Blvd & Dr 78666
Riverside Dr 78666
Riviera St 78666
Roadrunner Rd 78666
Robbie Ln 78666
Robin Way 78666
Rock Bluff Ln 78666
Rodriquez St 78666
Rogers St 78666
Rogers Ridge St 78666
Rolling Oaks 78666
Roosevelt St 78666
Rose Trl 78666
Rosewood Cv 78666
Ruddy Cv 78666
Rush Hvn 78666
Russell Cir 78666
Ryleas Ct 78666
Saddlebow Ln 78666
Sadler Dr 78666
Sagewood Trl 78666
Sahalee Path 78666
Salas Dr 78666
Salerno Dr 78666
Salinas Rd 78666
Saltillo St 78666
Samantha 78666
E & W San Antonio St 78666
San Marcos Hwy & Pkwy 78666
Sarah Dr 78666
Schulle Dr 78666
Scott St 78666
Scull Rd 78666
Segovia Rd 78666
Seguin St 78666
Sendero Dr 78666
Senisa Ct 78666
E & W Sessom Dr 78666
Seth St 78666
Settlers Rd 78666
Shadowpoint 78666
Shadowwood Dr 78666
Shady Ln 78666
Shelley Ln 78666
Sherbarb Ave 78666
Sherwood St 78666
Shetland Ln 78666
Short St 78666
E & W Sierra Cir 78666
Sierra Ridge Dr 78666
Sierra Vista St 78666
Silo St 78666
Silvercrest Ln 78666
Silverpeak Dr 78666
Six Pines Cv & Rd 78666
Skyline Rdg 78666
Smith Ln 78666
Smoky Mountain Dr 78666
Snyder Hill Dr 78666
Soul Harvest Pass 78666
Southfork Rd 78666
Southpoint Dr 78666
Spanish Eyes 78666
Split Rail Dr 78666
Spring Rd 78666
Spring Hollow St 78666
Springtown Way 78666
Spruce St 78666
Squirrel Run 78666
Stacy St 78666
Stagecoach Trl 78666
S Stagecoach Trl
200-299 78666
210-210 78667
300-798 78666
301-699 78666
Staples Rd 78666
N State Highway 123 78666
Steeplebrook Dr 78666
Stillwell St 78666
Stokes Dr 78666
Stone Mountain Trl 78666
Stonehaven 78666
Straight Ln 78666
Student Center Dr 78666
Sturgeon St 78666
Summer Mountain Dr 78666
Summerwood Cv 78666
Summit Pass 78666
Summit Ridge Dr 78666
Sunderland Cv 78666
Sunflower Ln 78666
Sunnywood Ln 78666
Sunset Rdg 78666
Suttles Ave 78666
Sycamore St 78666
Talbot 78666
Tampico St 78666
Tanglewood St 78666
Tate Trl 78666
Teal Cv 78666
Technology Way 78666
Telegraph Trl 78666
Telluride St 78666
Teron Dr 78666
Teton Cir 78666
Texas Ave 78666
The Low Rd 78666
Thermon Dr 78666
Thorpe Ln 78666
Thousand Oaks Loop 78666
Thurman Rd 78666
Timber Ridge Dr 78666
Timbercrest St 78666
Tomas Rivera 78666
Trails End 78666
Travis St 78666
Trestle Tree 78666
Trinket Ln 78666
Triple Crown Run 78666
Turkey Hollow Cir 78666
Turkey Trail Dr 78666
Uhland Rd 78666
United Dr 78666
University Ave & Dr 78666
Valero Dr 78666
Valley Cir & St 78666
Valley View Dr 78666
Valley View West Rd 78666
Vanessa St 78666
Ventura Dr 78666
Veramendi St 78666
Village Rd 78666
Village West Dr 78666
Viola St 78666
Virginia St 78666
Vista St 78666
Vogel Ln 78666
Vogel Hill Ln 78666
Waco St 78666
Walker Rd 78666
Wall St 78666
Walnut St 78666
Warden Ln 78666
Water Tower Rd 78666
Wavell St 78666
Wayne Ridge Dr 78666
West Ave 78666
Wheatfield 78666
Whitetail Dr 78666
Widgeon Cv 78666
Wild Plum 78666
William Evans St 78666
Willis Way 78666
Willow Arbor 78666
Willow Creek Cir 78666
Willow Ridge Dr 78666
Willow Springs Dr 78666
S Wilson St 78666
Wind Song Ln 78666
Windemere Rd 78666
Windmill Dr 78666
Wisteria Way 78666
Wolf Creek Rd 78666
Wonder World Dr 78666
Woodland Trl 78666
Woodrose St 78666
W Woods St 78666
Wren Haven Dr 78666
Xavier Dr 78666
Yale St 78666
Yarrington Rd 78666
Yaupon Ct 78666
Yawkee St 78666
Younger St 78666
Zain Ln 78666
Zunker St 78666

NUMBERED STREETS

All Street Addresses 78666

SANTA FE TX

General Delivery 77510

POST OFFICE BOXES MAIN OFFICE STATIONS AND BRANCHES

Box No.s
1 - 1760 77510
1 - 1039 77517

RURAL ROUTES

01, 02, 03, 04, 07, 08, 10 77510
05, 06 77517

NAMED STREETS

A Bar Dr 77510
Allen Dr 77510
Alles House St 77510
Anders Ln 77510
Anna Ct 77517
Anne Ln 77510
Ash Rd & St 77517
Autry Dr 77510
Avenue E 77510
Avenue A 77510
Avenue B 77510
Avenue C 77510
Avenue C 1/2 77510
Avenue D 77510
Avenue D 1/2 77510
Avenue E 1/2 77510
Avenue F 77510
Avenue G 77510
Avenue G 1/2 77510
Avenue H 77510
Avenue I 77510
Avenue J 77510
Avenue J 1/2 77510
Avenue K 77510
Avenue K 1/2 77510
Avenue L 77510
Avenue L 1/2 77510
Avenue M 77510

Avenue M 1/2 77510
Avenue N 1/2 77510
Avenue O 77510
Avenue P 77510
Avenue Q 77510
Avenue Q 1/2 77510
Avenue R 77510
Avenue T 77510
Avenue U St 77517
Avenue V 77510
B Bar Dr 77510
Baker St 77510
E Bar Dr 77510
Bar O Ranch Rd 77517
E Baylan St 77517
Beaver Rd 77517
Becker Ln 77517
E Bellaire St 77510
Beriton St 77517
Bethel Ct 77510
Birch St 77517
Bluebird St 77517
Bob White Dr 77510
Bolin St 77510
Bolton Ave 77510
Briar Ln 77510
Bringham Ln 77517
Brittain Rd 77510
Broken Arrow Rd 77517
Bruce Hall Rd 77510
Bunde St 77510
Burditt St 77510
Burdock Dr 77510
C Bar Cir & Dr 77510
Canal Rd 77517
Cardin St 77510
Cark St
3600-3708 77510
3710-3722 77510
3733-3799 77517
3801-4999 77517
Carolyn St 77517
Casey Rd 77517
Castle Dr 77510
Cedar Rd & St 77517
Cemetery Rd 77517
Cherry Ln & St 77517
Chisholm Trl 77510
Christi Ln 77510
Cimarron Rd 77517
Cloud Dr 77510
Colston Pl & Rd 77510
Colton Ln 77510
Country Ln 77517
Country Meadow Ln 77517
Country Side St 77517
Courtney St 77517
Cowan Rd 77517
Crendelm Rd 77517
Crescent Dr 77517
Crescent Moon Dr 77517
Crews Rd 77517
D Bar Dr 77510
D Wagner Ln 77510
Davis Hall Rd 77510
Derrick Dr 77510
Dickey Ln 77517
Donna Ln 77510
Doris St 77517
Dover Ave 77510
Downey St 77517
Eaton Dr 77510
Edgemore St 77517
Eldridge 77517
Elizabeth Dr 77510
Elizabeth Ln 77517
N & S Elm Ave & Rd 77517
Everest Glen Dr 77510
F Bar Dr 77510
Faye St 77517
Fir Rd 77517
Fm 1764 Rd
10611-A-10611-D 77510
4100-4299 77517
10400-13599 77510
13600-13899 77517
10612-1-10612-4 77510
11622-1-11622-1 77510
Fm 2004 Rd 77510
Fm 646 Rd N & S 77510
Frost St 77517
Gamble Rd 77517
Garden St 77517
Garrett Ct 77510
Garris Rd 77510
Georgia St 77517
Gibbs St 77517
Gibson Ln 77510
Giles Rd 77510
Ginger St 77517
Gonsoulin St 77510
Greenbriar St 77510
Guisti Ln 77510
Halfmoon E & W 77517
Hammond Ln 77510
Harriett Ln 77510
Henkel Ln 77510
Henley St 77510
Highland Rd 77517
Highway 6
10400-13539 77510
Highway 6
13541-13599 77510
13542-13598 77517
13600-16999 77517
12995-1-12995-8 77510
15711-1-15711-1 77517
Hudson Rd 77517
Ike Frank Rd 77517
Jack Beaver Rd 77517
N Jackson St 77517
Jamie Ln 77510
Jan Ln 77510
Jana Ln 77510
Jeena Ln 77510
Jensen St 77517
Joe St 77510
Julia Ln 77510
Kaylee Ln 77510
Kids Ln 77517
Lago Cv 77517
Lago Circle Dr N 77517
Lamar St 77510
Landrum Rd 77510
Langford St 77510
Larou Ln 77517
Linda Ln 77517
Lone Pine Dr 77510
Longmire St 77510
Lynn Ln 77510
Madden Rd 77517
Main St 77510
Mandy Ln 77510
Manianco 77510
Maple St 77517
Martin St 77510
Mauldin St 77510
Mccarty St 77517
Mcclendon Dr 77510
Mcginnes Rd 77517
Mcgregor St 77517
Michael Ln 77510
Middleham Ln 77510
Milan Cir 77510
Montgomery Rd 77510
Moore Rd 77517
N Morning Glory Dr 77517
N & S Morningview 77517
Mount Vernon St 77510
Mulberry St 77510
Navagation St 77517
Oak Ln 77517
Old Spanish Trl 77510
Oleo St 77517
Orchard Ln 77517
Orcutt 77517
Oregon Trl 77510
Orem Rd 77517
Park St 77510
Parkman St 77510
Parkview 77517
Parrish St 77510
Pearson Rd 77517
Pecan Cir & Grv 77510
Peck St 77517
Penny Ln 77510
Pine St 77517
Polk St 77510
Poplar St 77510
Power Rd 77510
Prairie Knoll Dr 77510
Prairie Oaks Dr 77510
Primrose Ln 77517
Quartermoon Ct 77517
Raford Ln 77510
Rene Cir 77510
Robert Ln 77510
Rochester Ct 77510
Rush Rd 77510
Ryan Rd 77510
Sandy Ln 77510
Santa Fe Dr 77517
Santa Fe Trl 77510
Santa Gertrudus Rd 77517
S Sayko St 77510
Schattel Rd 77510
Scott St 77517
Self St 77517
Sesame St 77510
Shady Ln 77517
Shirley Ln 77510
Shouse Rd 77510
Sias St 77517
Speed Rd 77517
Stroud Ct 77510
Sunset Cir & St 77510
Susan Rd 77517
Suzanne St 77517
Tallow St 77517
Temple Cir 77510
Terry St 77517
Three Oaks Blvd & Dr 77517
Tibaldo Ln 77510
Tomahawk Dr 77510
S Tower Rd 77517
Tree Point Rd 77510
Trista Ct 77510
Troy St 77510
Twin Dr E & W 77510
Vacek Rd & St 77517
Veronica St 77517
Vista Real 77510
Wade St 77517
Walker St 77510
Walnut St 77517
Warpath Ave 77510
Washington St 77510
Webb Rd 77517
Weir St 77517
Williams St 77517
Winding Trail Rd & St 77517
Winding Trails Way 77517
Windsor Ct 77510
Windstalkers Way 77517
Winston Dr
13200-13399 77510
13400-13499 77517
Young Cir 77510
Zaro Rd 77510

NUMBERED STREETS

W 1st 77517
2nd St 77517
3rd St
12000-12299 77510
13800-14699 77517
4th St
12000-13600 77510
13601-13797 77517
13602-13698 77510
13799-14699 77517
4th 1/2 St 77510
5th St 77517
6th St 77517
W 6th St
11800-13599 77510
13701-13733 77517
7th St 77510
7th 1/2 St 77510
8th St
13200-13299 77510
14100-15099 77517
9th St 77510
10th St 77510
11th St 77510
12th St 77510
13th St 77510
14th St 77510
15th St 77510
16th St 77510
17th St 77510
18th St 77510
19th St 77510
20th St 77510
21st St 77510
22nd St 77510
23rd St 77510
24th St 77510
25th St 77510
26th 1/2 St 77510
27th St 77510
28th St
10600-13899 77510
13900-14699 77517
11825-1-11825-1 77510
13520-2-13520-2 77510
29th St 77510
30th St 77510
32nd St 77510
32nd 1/2 St 77510
33rd St 77510
33rd 1/2 St 77510
34th 1/2 St 77510
29 1/2 St 77510

SEGUIN TX

General Delivery 78155

POST OFFICE BOXES MAIN OFFICE STATIONS AND BRANCHES

Box No.s
All PO Boxes 78156

NAMED STREETS

A J Malone Dr 78155
Adams St 78155
Adobe Vis 78155
Adriana 78155
Agape Ln 78155
Agua Dulce 78155
Agua Verde 78155
Aguila St 78155
Aja Cir 78155
Albers Ln 78155
Albrecht Rd 78155
Aldama St 78155
Alexander Dr 78155
Allende St 78155
Allison Ranch Rd 78155
Alsup Ln 78155
Alternate 90 78155
Amanda Ln 78155
Ander St 78155
Anderson Hl & St 78155
Angel Ln 78155
Antelope Ln 78155
Apache Trl 78155
Arbolas Ct 78155
Arlington St 78155
Arminta Berry 78155
Arrowhead Blf 78155
Arroyo 78155
Arvin St 78155
Ashby St 78155
Ashley Ranch Rd 78155
Augusta Dr 78155
N & S Austin Pass & St 78155
Autumn Vis 78155
Auxiliary Airport Rd 78155
Avenue E 78155
Avenue A 78155
Avenue B 78155
Avenue C 78155
Avenue D 78155
Avenue G 78155
B And B Rd 78155
Baer Creek Trl 78155
Bailey St 78155
Baker 78155
Ball St 78155
Barbarossa Rd 78155
Barcus St 78155
Barnes Dr 78155
Bartels Rd 78155
Barth St 78155
Bartholomae St 78155
Barton Dr 78155
N & S Bauer St 78155
E & W Baxter St 78155
Beale St 78155
Becker Ln 78155
Beechcraft Ln 78155
Beicker Rd 78155
Bell Rd 78155
Belmarez Ave 78155
Benbo St 78155
Bennett St 78155
Berkeley St 78155
Bermuda Dunes Dr 78155
Bernie Ln 78155
Bert St 78155
Berthot Ln 78155
Best Dr 78155
Beutnagel Ln 78155
Big Oaks Rd 78155
Bismark St 78155
Blackjack Oak Rd 78155
Blanca St 78155
Blanks St 78155
Blue Stem Rd 78155
Bluebonnet Rdg & St 78155
Blumberg Park & St 78155
Bobwhite Trl 78155
Boenig Rd & St 78155
Boon St 78155
Bosque 78155
N Bowie St 78155
Boyd Rd 78155
Brackenridge Ln 78155
Braden St 78155
Branch Rd 78155
Brazos Ln 78155
Breezy Hill Ln 78155
Breustedt St 78155
Bridlewood Path 78155
Brietzke Rd 78155
Bronco Trl 78155
Brook St 78155
Bruns St 78155
Bryans Dr 78155
Buckeye 78155
Buerger Ln 78155
Buffalo Gap 78155
Bunny Trl 78155
Burges St 78155
Burkett Dr 78155
Burr Oak St 78155
Burroughs 78155
Butherne Rd 78155
Butler Rd 78155
C H Matthies Jr 78155
Caddell Ln 78155
Callaway Rd 78155
N & S Camp St 78155
Campbell St 78155
Canary Ln 78155
Capote Oaks Dr 78155
Castle Breeze Dr 78155
Castlewood Dr 78155
Caulkins Rd 78155
E & W Cedar Pkwy & St 78155
Cemetary Ave 78155
Cenizo Ln 78155
Champa Ln 78155
Champions Dr 78155
Chapman St 78155
Chapparral Dr 78155
Cherokee Bnd 78155
N & S Cherry St 78155
Cherry Hill Dr 78155
Cheshire Cir 78155
Chico St 78155
Chiero Ln 78155
Chisholm Trl 78155
Church Rd 78155
Ciela Vis 78155
Cimmarron Cir 78155
Clare Ln 78155
Clark St 78155
Clay St 78155
Clift Ln 78155
Clingingsmith Ln 78155
Club Vw E 78155
Colima St 78155
E & W College St 78155
Collins Ave 78155
Colorado Ln 78155
Comanche Hill Cir 78155
Conrad St 78155
Continental Dr 78155
E & W Convent St 78155
Copperhead Rd 78155
Cordova Loop & Rd 78155
Cottage St 78155
Cottonwood Ln 78155
Country Gdns & Ln 78155
Country Acres Dr 78155
Country Club Dr 78155
Country Place Dr 78155
E Court St 78155
W Court St
1-600 78155
531-531 78156
601-1799 78155
602-1798 78155
Coventry Ln 78155
Covey Ln 78155
Cowboy Cv 78155
Cowey Ranch Rd 78155
Coyote Bnd & Trl 78155
Creekside St 78155
Creekstone Trl 78155
Creekway Ln 78155
Crescent 78155
N & S Crockett St 78155
Cross Rd 78155
Crossroads Blvd 78155
Crosswind Dr 78155
Crystal Ln 78155
Curry Rd 78155
Cussie Ln 78155
Cypress Shadow Ln 78155
Danny Ln 78155
Dans Hl 78155
Darst Creek Ln 78155
Datt Ln 78155
David St 78155
Davila St 78155
Deep Woods Dr 78155
Deer Rdg 78155
Deer Slayer Dr 78155
Delany St 78155
Dennis Dr 78155
Dewey Ln 78155
Dibrell Ave 78155
Dietert Rd 78155
Dinks Ln 78155
Dittmar Ln 78155
Doctor S J F Rd 78155
Dolle Ave 78155
Dolle Farm Rd 78155
Domino Five 78155
E & W Donegan St 78155
Double M Ln 78155
Dove Ln 78155
Dowdy Rd 78155
Dresner Rd 78155
Driftwood Dr 78155
Duggan St 78155
Dugger Rd 78155
Dunn St 78155
Eagle Rdg 78155
Eastridge Pkwy 78155
Eastwind Rd 78155
Eastwood Dr 78155
Easy St 78155
Echo Ln 78155
Eden Rd 78155
Edgewater Ln 78155
El Dorado Ln 78155
El Rhea Dr 78155
Elizabeth 78155
Elley St 78155
Ellis St 78155
Elm St 78155
Elm Creek Rd 78155
Elm Grove Rd 78155
Elmwood Dr 78155
Elsik St 78155
Emily Ln 78155
Encantada 78155
Engbrock 78155
Engelmann Ln 78155
Engler Ave 78155
Engler Dairy Rd 78155
N & S Erkel Ave 78155
Ermel St 78155
N & S Erskine St 78155
Erskine Ferry Rd 78155
Erwin St 78155
Escondido 78155
Esther Ln 78155
Ethel 78155
Fair St & Walk 78155
Fairfax Cir 78155
Fermin Ln 78155
Fern Gully Ln 78155
Field Rd 78155
Fisherman Ln 78155
Fleming Dr 78155
Fletcher Ln 78155
Flint Rock Ln 78155
Flores St 78155
Floyd Ln 78155
Fm 1101 78155
Fm 1117 78155
Fm 1620 78155
Fm 20 78155
Fm 2438 78155
Fm 2538 78155
Fm 2623 78155
Fm 464 78155
Fm 465 78155
Fm 466 78155
Fm 467 78155
Fm 477 78155
Fm 539 78155
Fm 725 78155
Fm 758 78155
Fm 775 78155
Fm 78 78155
Forest Bnd & Dr 78155
Forshage Blvd 78155
Fox Run St 78155
Fox Trotter Rd 78155
Franch Rd 78155
Fred St 78155
Fred Byrd Dr 78155
Freeport Way 78155
Friedens Church Rd 78155
Friesenhahn Rd 78155
Fritz Zwicke Rd 78155
Frontier Way 78155
Frye Ln 78155
Galvin Dr 78155
Gamecock Rd 78155
Garcia St 78155
Gardenridge Dr 78155
Garnet St 78155
Gerdes St 78155
Geronimo Dr, St & Trl 78155

Gin Rd & Spur 78155
Gin View Ln 78155
Glag Ln 78155
Glen Cove Dr 78155
Glenewinkel Rd 78155
Gloria Dr 78155
Gold Dust Rd 78155
Goldensage Dr 78155
Gomez Ln 78155
E & W Gonzales St 78155
Good Luck Rd 78155
N & S Goodrich St 78155
Gordon St 78155
Governor Ireland Park 78155
Gracewind Ln 78155
Gravel St 78155
Gravel Pit Rd 78155
Gray Dove Ln 78155
Gray Stone Rd 78155
Greenway Dr 78155
Gregg Ln 78155
N & S Guadalupe St 78155
Guadalupe Hills Ln 78155
Guadalupe Ranch Ln 78155
Guadalupe River Dr 78155
Guenther Ln 78155
Gus Beicker Rd 78155
Haberle Rd 78155
Hackberry St 78155
Hallie Cir 78155
Halm Rd 78155
E Hampton Dr 78155
Harborth Hl & Rd 78155
Hargett Ln 78155
Harper St 78155
Hartfield Rd 78155
Hartmann Ln 78155
Harvest Holw 78155
Hays St 78155
Headwind Dr 78155
N & S Heideke St 78155
Heinemeyer 78155
Henri Ln 78155
Heritage Dr 78155
Hermitage St 78155
Hermosa 78155
Herreras Ln 78155
Hickory Dr 78155
Hickory Forrest Dr 78155
Hidalgo St 78155
Hidden Mdw 78155
Hidden Oak Ln 78155
High Country Dr 78155
High Point Dr & Rdg 78155
High Ridge Dr 78155
High Sierra Dr 78155
Highview Ln 78155
N & S Highway 123 Byp 78155
Hillside St 78155
Hilltop Dr 78155
Hoffman Rd 78155
Hollamon Dr 78155
Hollow Pass 78155
Hollub Ln 78155
Holt Way 78155
Horizon Hl 78155
Huber Rd 78155
Huckleberry Ln 78155
Hummingbird Ln 78155
E & W Humphreys St 78155
Hunters Ct, Pl & Way 78155
Hurst Ln 78155
Hysaw Rd 78155
Ilka Rd 78155
Ilka Switch 78155
Imperial Dr 78155
Indian Trl 78155
E & W Interstate 10 78155
E & W Ireland St 78155
Jackson Cir 78155
Jahns Rd 78155
Jakes Colony Rd 78155
Jas Ln 78155
Jay Rd 78155
Jefferson Ave 78155

Jenny Ln 78155
Joe Carrillo Blvd 78155
Johns Ave 78155
Johnson Ave 78155
Johnson Ranch Rd 78155
Jones Ave 78155
Journeys End 78155
Joye Ln 78155
Juarez St 78155
Kathy Dr 78155
Katie Ln 78155
Keller Ln 78155
Kenwood Cir 78155
Kickapoo Trl 78155
Kimbrough Rd 78155
N & S King St 78155
E & W Kingsbury St 78155
Kiowa Trl 78155
Kitty Ln 78155
E & W Klein St 78155
Koebig Rd 78155
Koepp St 78155
Koepsel St 78155
Kothmann Dr 78155
Krams Creek Rd 78155
E & W Krezdorn St 78155
Krueger Rd 78155
Kubena Rd 78155
Kunde Rd 78155
Kunkel St 78155
Lacy Ln 78155
Laguna Vis 78155
Laguna Rio 78155
Lake Dr 78155
Lake Forrest Dr 78155
Lake Placid Dr 78155
Lake Ridge Dr 78155
Lake Village Rd 78155
Lakeside Dr 78155
Lakeview Dr 78155
Lakewood Dr 78155
Lamar 78155
Land Ranch Rd 78155
Lange Rd 78155
Larkin Ave 78155
Las Brisas Blvd 78155
Las Hadas 78155
Laubach Rd 78155
Laurel Oaks 78155
Lay Ln 78155
Leaning Oaks Cir 78155
Lee St 78155
Legette St 78155
Leissner St 78155
Leissner School Rd 78155
Lennox Ave 78155
Lenz Dr 78155
N & S Leonard Ln 78155
E Lettau Ave 78155
Liberty Ave 78155
Lifegate Ln 78155
Lillian Ln 78155
Lina Ln 78155
Lincoln St 78155
Link Rd 78155
Linne Rd 78155
Little Oak Rd 78155
Little Quail Ln 78155
E & W Live Oak St 78155
Loch Ln 78155
Lone Oak St 78155
Longhorn Trl 78155
Lookout Hl 78155
Loop Dr 78155
S Loop 123 78155
Lopez St 78155
Lorine Ln 78155
Los Nietos Ln 78155
Los Nogales Ct 78155
Louise St 78155
Lucille St 78155
Lueb Ln 78155
Luensmann Rd 78155
Lullwood Ln 78155
Luther Rd 78155
Lyon Rd 78155

Maalish Ln 78155
Mackie Ln 78155
Maderas 78155
Madison Ln 78155
Magnolia 78155
Mahan Dr 78155
Maldonado Ave 78155
Malmsten Rd 78155
Mandel Rd 78155
Manor Dr 78155
Markgraf St 78155
Marrou Rd 78155
E & W Martindale Rd 78155
Mary Jane Ln 78155
Matador Dr 78155
Matamoros St 78155
Max Rd 78155
Mckay St 78155
Mckee St 78155
Mckinley Rd 78155
Mcknight Rd 78155
Meadow Run 78155
Meadow Lake Dr 78155
Meadow Park Ln 78155
Medical 78155
Medlin St 78155
Melina Ln 78155
Melrose St 78155
Memory Ln 78155
Merriweather Rd 78155
Mesa Trl 78155
Mesquite Pass, St & Vw 78155
Michna St 78155
Middle Rd 78155
Middletowne Rd 78155
Midway 78155
Milagros 78155
N & S Milam St 78155
Mill Creek Rd 78155
Mill Oak Ln 78155
Miller Ave & Walk 78155
Millford 78155
Mills Run & Way 78155
Miltex Rd 78155
Mitchell Ave 78155
Mockingbird Ln 78155
Mondin Rd 78155
Montclair St 78155
Monterrey Oak 78155
Monticello St 78155
Montwood 78155
Moody Rd 78155
Moore St 78155
Morelos St 78155
Morris Hl 78155
Mosheim St 78155
N & S Moss St 78155
E & W Mountain St 78155
Mountain Oaks Ln 78155
Mt Vernon 78155
Mud Track Ln 78155
Muehl Rd 78155
Mueller Ln 78155
Mulberry Ln 78155
Mustang Mdw 78155
Myers Farm Ln 78155
Nagel St 78155
Naumann Rd 78155
Navajo Trl 78155
Navarro Dr 78155
Navasota Ln 78155
Nelda St 78155
Nesbit Ln 78155
Neumann Rd 78155
E & W New Braunfels St 78155
New Salem Rd 78155
New World 78155
Newton Ave 78155
Nickerson Farms Rd 78155
Nockenut Rd 78155
Nogal 78155
Nogalitos Ln 78155
Nolan St 78155
E & W Nolte St 78155

Nordberg 78155
Nueces Ln 78155
Oak Crk, Hvn & Ter 78155
Oak Forrest Ln 78155
Oak Hill Dr 78155
Oak Mott Ct 78155
Oak Shadow 78155
Oak Springs Dr 78155
Oak Tree Rd 78155
Oakcreek Pkwy 78155
Odaniel Rd 78155
Odaniel School Rd 78155
Oestreich Dr 78155
Old St 78155
Old Campbell Rd 78155
Old Colony Rd 78155
Old Homestead 78155
Old Ilka Rd 78155
Old Lehmann Rd 78155
Old Luling Rd 78155
Old School Rd 78155
Old Seguin Luling Rd 78155
Old Spanish Trl 78155
Old Woehler Rd 78155
Oldtowne Rd 78155
N Olive St 78155
Olmos Loop & Rd 78155
Ostberg 78155
Otha Walk 78155
Paige St 78155
Palm St 78155
Palmer Rd 78155
Paloma St 78155
Palomino Pass & Run 78155
Pankau Rd 78155
Pape St 78155
Park Ln & St 78155
Park Village Ln 78155
Parkcreek Dr 78155
Parkridge Cir 78155
Partnership Rd 78155
Paseo Del Rio 78155
Patricia Park Ct 78155
Patterson Ln 78155
Patton Dr 78155
Peach St 78155
Peacock St 78155
Pecan Orch, Pt & St 78155
Peggy Ln 78155
Pet St 78155
Pfullman Rd 78155
Pin Oak Ln 78155
E & W Pine St 78155
Pine Meadow Rd 78155
Pine Ranch Rd 78155
Pioneer Pass & Rd 78155
Pioneer Home 78155
Pitts St 78155
Placid Hts 78155
Plantation Dr 78155
Pleasant Bnd 78155
Pleasant Acres Dr 78155
Ploetz Rd 78155
Pokey St 78155
Poloma Ln 78155
Pony Ln 78155
Post Oak Ln 78155
Pradera Walk 78155
Prairie Blf, Hl & Smt 78155
Prairie Pointe 78155
Prairie Rose 78155
Prarie Flower 78155
Pratt Rd 78155
Preston Dr 78155
Prexy Dr 78155
Proform Rd 78155
Prospect St 78155
Purple Sage Dr 78155
Quail Ln, Run & Xing 78155
Quintana Rd & Trl 78155
Raccoon Springs Rd 78155
Railroad 78155
Randow Rd 78155
Range Rd 78155
Rangel Ln 78155
Rangeland Rd 78155

Rawhide Rd 78155
Raymond St 78155
Reco Ln 78155
Red Rd 78155
Red Fox Run 78155
Red Oak St 78155
Redberry Rd 78155
Redwood St 78155
Reiland Rd 78155
Reiley Rd 78155
Renee St 78155
Resort Ln 78155
Reyna Ln 78155
Rhone St 78155
Ridge Crest Dr 78155
Ridge Run Dr 78155
Riley St 78155
Rill Rd 78155
Rio Azul 78155
Rio Grande Dr 78155
Rio Nogales Dr 78155
Rio Vista Dr 78155
N & S River Dr, Rd, St & Trl W 78155
River Oak Dr 78155
River Springs Dr 78155
Riverview Ter 78155
Rob Roy St 78155
Robert St 78155
Robin Ln 78155
Rock Bridge Trl 78155
Rodeo Dr 78155
Rogues Holw 78155
Rohlf Rd 78155
Romberg St 78155
Roosevelt Dr 78155
Roselawn St 78155
E Rosemary Dr 78155
Rosewood St 78155
Royal Crest Cir 78155
Royal Sage Dr 78155
Rudeloff Rd 78155
Runnel St 78155
Running Crk 78155
Sabrina St 78155
Saddlehorn Dr 78155
Sagebiel Rd 78155
Sagewood Pkwy 78155
Saint James 78155
Salinas St 78155
San Antonio Ave 78155
N & S San Marcos St 78155
Sandstone Ln 78155
Sandy Ln 78155
Sandy Oaks Dr 78155
Santa Anna Dr 78155
S Santa Clara Rd 78155
Sante Fe Rdg & Trl 78155
Sarah Ln 78155
N & S Saunders St 78155
Savage Ranch Rd 78155
Savannah Pr 78155
Saw Mill Rd 78155
Sawlog Creek Rd 78155
Schley Dr 78155
N & S Schmidt Rd 78155
Schneider Rd 78155
Schriewer 78155
Schroeder Ln 78155
Schuberts Pl 78155
Schuenemann Rd 78155
Schuessler St 78155
Schumann Rd 78155
Schwab Rd 78155
Seay St 78155
Seay World Ln 78155
E & W Seideman St 78155
Seitz Rd 78155
Seminole Cir 78155
Settlers Way 78155
Severn Dr 78155
Shady Ln 78155
Shannon Ave 78155
Shawn Ln 78155
Sheffield Rd 78155
E & W Shelby St 78155

Sherman St 78155
Short Ave 78155
Sierra Cir 78155
Signal Hl 78155
Silo Rdg 78155
Silva St 78155
Silver Wolf Ln 78155
Single Oak 78155
Ski Plex Dr 78155
Smith Ln 78155
Smith Falor Rd 78155
Sol Del Rio 78155
Sonka St 78155
Southsalem Rd 78155
Southwick Cir 78155
Southwind Loop 78155
Sowell St 78155
Spanish Oak St 78155
Split Rail Ln 78155
Springs Rnch & St 78155
Springs Hill Cir 78155
Spruce St 78155
Spur Trl 78155
Stagecoach Rd 78155
Stagecoach Hill Dr 78155
Stahl Rd 78155
Starburst Trl 78155
Starcke St 78155
N & S State Highway 123 78155
N & S State Highway 46 78155
Steel Mill Dr 78155
Steffens Rd 78155
Sterling Rd 78155
Stewart Ln 78155
Still Meadow Rd 78155
Stoneham Cir 78155
Stratton St 78155
Strempel St 78155
Strey Ln 78155
Sudberg 78155
Sunbelt Loop & Rd E, S & W 78155
Sunfire Trl 78155
Sunrise Dr 78155
Sunset Dr & St 78155
Sutherland Springs Rd 78155
Swallows Ln 78155
Swanson Rd 78155
Sweet Home Rd 78155
Sycamore St 78155
Tabernacle St 78155
Tabler Dr 78155
Taft St 78155
Tailwind Dr 78155
Tampico St 78155
Tanglewood Dr 78155
Tangram Rnch 78155
Tangram Mesquite 78155
Tannenbaum Ln 78155
Tausch Ln 78155
Taylor Ave 78155
Tejas Trl 78155
Terrell St 78155
Thormeyer Rd 78155
Three Oaks Rd 78155
Thunderbird Ln 78155
Tiemann Rd 78155
Timber Elm 78155
Timmermann Rd 78155
Tips Ct & St 78155
Tomahawk Trl 78155
Tonto Trl 78155
Tony Lee St 78155
Topaz Ave 78155
Tor Dr 78155
Tower Rd 78155
Townesend Rd 78155
Trails End 78155
N & S Travis St 78155
Trinity Ln 78155
Troell Holw & St 78155
Tschoepe Rd 78155
Tumbleweed 78155
Turkey Run 78155

Turkey Tree Trl 78155
Turnaround Rd 78155
Turtle Ln 78155
Twin Creeks 78155
Twin Oak Rd 78155
Twink Ln 78155
Ubry Ranch Ln 78155
Uncle Dicks Rd 78155
Unity Rd 78155
University Ln 78155
E & W Us Highway 90 78155
Val Walk 78155
Vanbooven 78155
N & S Vaughan Ave 78155
Vera Cruz St 78155
Veterans St 78155
Via Verde 78155
Vickers Ave 78155
Villa Vis 78155
Violet St 78155
Vivroux Ranch Rd 78155
Voges Ln 78155
Volunteer St 78155
Wagon Trl 78155
Wakefield 78155
Wallace St 78155
E & W Walnut Cir & St 78155
Waltons Way 78155
Wampum Way 78155
E & W Washington St 78155
Water Tower Rd 78155
Wayside Dr 78155
Weber Cir & Rd 78155
Wedgewood 78155
E & W Weinert St 78155
Wendy Ln 78155
Westbend Cir 78155
Westberg 78155
Westgate St 78155
Westview 78155
Westwind Ln 78155
Wetz 78155
Whitetail Holw 78155
Wieding Ln 78155
Wilcox Rd 78155
Wildflower Ln 78155
Williams Rd & St 78155
Williams Ranch Rd 78155
Willmann Rd 78155
Willow Ln 78155
Willow Creek Rd 78155
Wilson Rd 78155
Windmill Hl & Pr 78155
Windsong Cir 78155
Windwood Cir 78155
Windy Hl 78155
Windy Dawn 78155
Wingate Ct 78155
Wishing Star Ln 78155
Woehler Ln 78155
Woelke Rd 78155
Wood Ln 78155
Woodland Dr 78155
Woodstone St 78155
Wosnig Rd 78155
Wurzbach St 78155
Youth Haven Rd 78155
Zachary St 78155
Zaragoza St 78155
Zion Hill Rd 78155
Zorn St 78155
Zunker St 78155
Zwicke St 78155

NUMBERED STREETS

All Street Addresses 78155

SHERMAN TX

General Delivery 75090

POST OFFICE BOXES MAIN OFFICE STATIONS AND BRANCHES

Box No.s
All PO Boxes 75091

RURAL ROUTES

01, 04, 07, 08, 11 75090
02, 03, 05, 06, 10, 12 75092

NAMED STREETS

Aaron Ln 75092
Adams Rd 75090
Akers Rd 75090
Aletha Ln 75092
N Alexander St 75092
E Alma Ave 75090
Alpine Dr 75092
W Alta Vista St 75092
N & S Andrews Ave 75090
Andy Dr 75092
Angel Ridge Ln 75090
W Anita St 75092
E Ann Ave 75090
Anthony Dr 75092
Arapaho E & W 75092
Archer Cir & Dr 75092
Arizona St 75090
Arkansas Cir & St 75090
Arroyo Trl 75090
Atkinson Dr 75092
Auburn Ct 75092
Augusta Cir 75092
S Austin St 75090
Avendale Ct 75092
Ayers Dr 75090
Baker Rd 75090
Baker Park Dr 75092
Baker Ridge Rd 75090
Ballow Rd 75092
Bandera Dr 75092
Bar 7 Dr 75092
Barbara Ln 75090
Beaver Run Rd 75090
Beavers Dr 75092
W Belden St 75092
Bello Vista Cir, Ct & Dr 75090
Bennett Ave 75090
Bennett Ln 75092
Bentbrook Ln 75092
Bentcreek Ln 75090
Bethany Rd 75090
Biggerstaff Rd 75090
Bill Ln 75090
N & S Binkley St 75092
Binkley Park Dr 75092
W Birge St 75092
W Biscayne Dr 75092
Blanton Dr & Pl 75092
N Bledsoe St 75090
Blue Creek Cir 75090
Blue Flame Rd 75090
Blue Jay Ln 75092
Bluebonnet Ln 75092
Bluegrass Ln 75092
Bluffview Dr 75092
Boddie Rd 75090
Bois D Arc Cir 75090
Bois D Arc Dr 75092
Boone Dr 75090
Bordeaux St 75090
N & S Branch St 75090
Branchford Dr 75090
Breezy Meadow Ln 75092
N Brents Ave 75090
Breyonna Ln 75090
E Brockett St 75090
W Brockett St
100-299 75090
600-1899 75092
Brookhollow St 75092
Brookshire Ln 75092
N Broughton St 75090
Brown Rd 75090
Brushey Creek Dr 75090
N & S Bryant Ave 75090
Buffalo Ridge Trl 75092
N & S Burdette Ave 75090
Burgandy Ln 75090
Burkett Rd 75090
W Burton St 75092
Butterfield Trl 75092
Byler Dr 75092
Calais Dr & St 75090
Calf Creek Ln 75090
Calgary Dr 75092
Calle Cedro Dr 75090
Cambridge Dr 75092
Camino Dos Lagos Dr 75090
Camp Verde Cir 75092
Campground Rd 75090
Cannon Ln 75092
Canopy Dr 75090
Canterbury Cir & Dr 75092
Canyon Creek Dr 75092
Cardinal Dr 75092
N Carl St 75090
S Carolina Dr 75090
Carolyn Ct 75092
N & S Carr Ave 75090
Carriage Cir 75092
Carriage Estates Rd 75092
E Carter St 75090
W Cascade Dr 75092
Case Rd 75092
Cassidy Rd 75090
Catalina Cir 75092
Cathleen Ln S 75092
W Cedar Park & Rd 75090
E Centennial St 75090
W Center St
400-599 75090
701-1097 75092
1099-1400 75090
1402-1498 75092
E Chaffin St 75090
Chamberlain Rdg 75090
Chandler Ct 75092
Chapman Aly 75090
S Charles St 75090
Chateau Cir 75092
Chavarria Dr 75090
E Cherry St 75090
W Cherry St
100-599 75090
701-799 75092
Cherry Park Dr 75090
Chisholm Trl 75092
Choctaw Est Cir 75090
Churchill Way 75092
Cimmaron Trl 75092
Cinrose Ln 75092
Clay Ln 75092
N & S Cleveland Ave 75090
Cliff Hestand Rd 75090
Club House Dr 75092
Cobblestone Ln 75092
Cody Ln 75092
Coker Rd 75090
N & S Colbert Ave 75090
Cole Ave & Dr 75090
E College St 75090
W College St
100-299 75090
700-1899 75092
Collins Dr 75092
Colonial Cir 75092
Colorado St 75090
Comfort Way Dr 75092
Compress St 75090
Constitution Dr 75090
S Contemporary Dr 75092
Copley St 75090
Cormorant Dr 75092
N Cornerstone Dr 75092
E Cottage St 75090
Cottonwood Dr 75090
Country Ln 75092
Country Hill Cir 75090
Country Styx Ln 75090
Covington Ct 75092
Cox St 75090
N Craycroft St 75090
Creekbend Cir 75092
Creekside Ave 75092
Creekview Ln 75092
Crescent Dr 75092
Crestview Dr 75092
Crimsonwood Dr 75090
N Crockett St
101-109 75090
111-826 75090
1801-1897 75092
1899-2299 75092
S Crockett St 75090
Crow Rd 75092
Cundiff Dr 75092
Cypress Grove Rd W 75092
S Dakota Dr 75090
Dauphine Dr 75090
Davenport Rd 75090
Deaver Rd 75092
Deborah Dr 75090
Deer Run 75092
Denton Dr 75092
Devonshire Dr 75092
S Dewey Ave 75090
W Dexter St 75092
Df Edwards Rd 75090
Diana Dr 75092
Dickson Cir 75090
E Dorchester St 75090
N Doris St 75090
Dorset Dr 75092
Double D Ranch Rd 75092
Dove Ln 75090
Dover Dr 75092
Dripping Springs Rd 75090
N Duchess Dr 75090
E Dugan St 75090
N Duke Dr 75090
W Dulin St 75090
Dundale Cir 75092
W Dupree St 75092
Dusty Ln 75092
Eagle Ln 75090
Eagle Ridge Trl 75092
N & S East St 75090
W Easy St 75092
Ec Blythe Rd 75092
Elizabeth St 75090
Elk Rd 75090
N Ellington Ave 75090
Elliott Rd 75092
N Elliott St 75090
W Ellis St 75092
N & S Elm St 75090
Elm Hollow Ct 75092
Enterprise Rd 75092
E Epstein St 75090
Erma Ln 75090
Estate West Rd 75092
E Evergreen St 75090
Fair Oaks Cir 75092
W Fairview St 75092
Fairway Dr 75090
Falcon Dr 75092
Fallon Dr 75090
Farmington Rd 75092
Fellowship Ln 75092
E Fermapl St 75090
W Fern St 75092
S First St 75090
W Fischer St 75092
Flanary Rd 75092
Fm 1417 NE 75090
E Fm 1417 75090
N Fm 1417 75092
S Fm 1417 75092
W Fm 1417 75092
N Fm 1417 Ext 75090
Fm 691 75090
Fm 697 75090
Fm 902
601-1097 75090
Fm 902
1099-2999 75090
7701-7797 75092
7799-7800 75092
7802-8298 75092
Ford Rd 75092
E & W Forest Ave 75090
Forest Creek Dr 75092
Fossil Creek Cir 75092
Frank Ln 75092
Franklin Rd 75090
Frankwood Rd 75092
W Freeman St 75092
Friendship Rd 75092
N Frisco Rd 75090
Frog Pond Rd 75092
Gage Rd 75092
Gail Hill Ln 75092
Gallagher Dr 75090
Gant Rd 75092
Gibbons Rd 75092
S Glacier Dr 75092
Glasgow Dr 75092
Glenway Dr 75092
Golden Rd 75090
Goodnight Cir 75092
S Gordon St 75092
Graham Dr 75092
N & S Grand Ave 75090
N Grant Dr 75092
Gray Ln 75090
E Graystone Rd 75090
Green Rd 75092
Greenbrier Dr 75092
S Gribble St 75090
Grigg Rd 75090
Haliburton Ln 75092
Hall Rd 75090
Hara Ln 75092
Hardenberg Ln 75092
Harmony Loop 75092
Harriet Dr 75090
N & S Harrison Ave 75092
Haun Rd 75090
N Haven Dr 75092
Hawk Ln 75092
Hayes Rd & St 75090
Hazelwood Rd 75092
S Hazelwood St 75090
Heatherwood Ln 75092
W Hester St 75090
N Hickory St 75092
Hidden Valley Trl 75092
Higgins Rd 75092
High Country Rd 75092
High Point Rd 75090
Highgrove Dr 75090
N Highland Ave 75092
S Highland Ave 75092
Highland Mdws 75090
Hightower Rd 75092
E Hill St 75090
E Hillbrook St 75090
Hillcrest Dr 75092
Hillside Dr 75090
Hilltop Dr 75092
Hilre Dr 75092
E Hilton St 75090
N Hoard Ave 75090
Hog Skin Rd 75090
Holiday Dr 75090
N & S Holly Ave 75092
N Hopson St 75092
E Houston St 75090
W Houston St
100-330 75090
332-524 75090
701-703 75092
705-4700 75092
4702-5198 75092
Howe Dr 75092
S Hub St 75090
Hudgins Rd 75092
Hummingbird Dr 75092
W Hunt St 75092
N Hurt St 75090
E Ida Rd 75090
S Idlewild Dr 75090
Idlewood Dr 75092
Independence Dr & Spgs 75090
Indio Ln 75092
Industrial Dr 75092
S Inwood St 75090
Iowa St 75090
Iron Ore Creek Dr 75092
Jamaica Ln 75092
James St 75090
Jason Cir 75092
W Jay Ln 75090
N Jennings Dr 75090
Jeremy Cir 75092
Jim Lamb Rd 75090
Jody Ln 75092
John Fielder Dr 75092
E & W Jones Cir & St 75090
Joni Cir 75092
Joyce Ln 75092
Jp Cave Rd 75090
Judge Elliott Dr 75092
Judy Dr 75090
Junction Rd 75090
Juniper Dr 75090
Kansas St 75090
Kathleen Ct 75090
Katie Rose Ln 75092
Kay Ct 75090
Kelsoe Dr 75090
Ken Dr 75092
Kennedy Rd 75092
Kent Dr 75092
E Kentucky St 75090
Kerr Chapel Rd 75092
Kessler Blvd 75092
Kevin Ct 75090
Key Rd 75090
Keyes Rd 75092
E & W King St 75090
Klas Rd 75092
Knollwood Dr & Rd 75092
Kusch Rd 75092
La Cima Rd 75092
La Salle Dr 75090
Ladd Rd 75090
E & W Lake St 75090
Lakeside Dr 75092
Lakeview Cir 75092
Lakewood Dr 75092
E Lamar St 75090
W Lamar St
108-208 75090
210-599 75090
717-723 75092
725-1601 75092
Lamberth Cir 75092
E Lamberth Rd
115-197 75092
199-206 75090
208-298 75092
501-597 75090
599-799 75090
W Lamberth Rd 75092
W Lark Ln 75090
Laughlin Rd 75092
W Laurel St
100-399 75090
800-1400 75090
1402-1498 75092
Laurel Creek Dr 75092
Laurel Ridge Cir 75092
Lawrence Rd 75092
Leacrest Dr 75090
N & S Lee Ave 75090
Legend Ln 75092
N Leslie Ave 75092
E Leslie Ln 75090
E Lewis St 75090
Lexington Dr 75090
Liberty Hill Cir 75090
Liberty Hill Trl 75092
Linda Dr 75090
Lindley Dr 75090
Little Ln 75092
Live Oak Cir 75092
N Lockhart St 75090
Logston Rd 75092
Lone Grove Way 75092
Lonesome Dove Dr 75090
Longhorn Trl 75092
Lopez Dr 75090
Lotus Cir 75092
S Loving Ave 75090
E Lowell St 75090
Loy St 75090
Loy Lake Plz 75090
N Loy Lake Rd
1700-3999 75090
4000-4298 75092
4300-4900 75092
4902-5098 75092
Luby Dr 75090
N Luckett St 75090
S & W Luella Hts & Rd 75090
Lwsc Rd 75090
S Lyon St 75092
Madison Pl 75092
E Magnolia St 75090
Mahan Dr 75090
S Main St 75092
Mallard Dr 75092
N Maple St 75092
Marlborough St 75092
E & N Marseille Ln 75090
Marshall St 75090
E & W Martin Ln 75090
Mary Fitch Rd 75090
N Masters Dr 75090
Mathis Ln 75090
N & S Maxey St 75090
E May St 75090
Mayes Dr 75090
Mayfly Ct 75092
Mccall St 75090
E Mcgee St 75090
W Mcgee St 75092
Mcgraw Ln 75090
N & S Mckown Ave 75092
W Mclain Dr 75092
E Mcreynolds Ave 75090
Meadow Hill Ln 75090
Meadowlake Dr 75092
W Meadowridge Rd 75092
Meadows Cir & Ln 75092
Meandering Way 75092
Melody Cir 75090
Melrose Trl 75092
Melton Rd 75092
Mercer Dr 75090
Merrimac Rd 75090
Merriman Pkwy 75090
Mesquite Ridge Trl 75092
Meyers Dr 75092
Michelle Dr 75092
W Middleton St 75090
E Mildred St 75090
Miller Dr 75090
Mimosa Dr 75092
Mission Dr 75092
Mitchell Rd 75090
E & W Mockingbird Ln 75090
Mohican St 75092
Monett Dr 75092
Monfort Dr 75092
E Monroe St 75090
Montana St 75090
Montclair Dr & Rd 75092
Monte Cristo Cir, Dr & Way 75092
N & S Montgomery St 75090
W Moore St
100-599 75090
1300-1398 75092
1400-1899 75092
1901-2199 75092
Moreland Dr 75090
Morman Grove Rd 75092
Motors Dr 75092
Mountain Climb Rd 75092
Mountain View Cir 75090
E Mulberry St 75090
W Mulberry St
110-110 75090
112-221 75090
223-315 75090
1201-1397 75092
1399-1499 75092
N Music St 75090
E Nall St 75090
Nantucket Dr 75092
Nash Rd 75090
Navajo Rd 75092
Naylor Rd 75092
Nelson Rd 75090
Newman Rd 75090
Nichols Rd 75090
Norman Rd 75092
Normandy Dr 75090
E & W North Creek Dr 75092
Northaven Ln 75092
Northbrook Ln 75092
Northgate Dr 75092
Northpoint Rd 75090
Northridge Dr 75090
Norwood Rd 75092
Oak Creek Cir & Dr 75092
Oak Hollow Ln 75092
Oakbrook Cir 75092
Oakhill Dr 75092
Oakmont Ct 75092
Ob Groner Rd 75092
E Odneal St 75090
Old Dorchester Rd 75092
Old Gunter Hwy 75092
Old Ida Rd 75090
Old Perrin Rd 75092
Old Quail Run Rd 75092
Old Scoggins Rd 75092
Old Southmayd Rd 75092
E & W Olive St 75090
Opposum Trl 75092
E Orange St 75090
Ostrich Dr 75090
Outback Rd 75090
Overland Trl 75092
Oxford Dr 75092
E Pacific St 75090
W Pacific St 75092
Park Ave 75092
E Park Ave 75090
W Park Ave 75090
Park Pl 75092
Park Vista Blvd 75090
Patricia Dr 75090
Payne Dr 75092
Peachtree Pl 75090
Pebblebrook Ln 75092
Pebblecreek Ln 75092
E Pecan St 75090
W Pecan St
105-115 75090
117-499 75090
700-700 75092
702-1025 75092
1027-1913 75092
Pecan Grove Rd E 75090
Pecan Valley Ct 75090
Peggeys Cv 75092
W Pelton St 75092
Pennell Rd 75090
Perry St 75090
E Peyton St
300-1798 75090
701-1799 75090
701-701 75091
Pheasant Dr 75092
Pine Ridge Cir 75092
Pintail 75092
Pistachio Ln 75092
Plainview Rd 75092
Playa Ct & Dr 75090
Pleasant Home Rd 75092
W Plover Ln 75090
Poco Redondo Dr 75090
Ponderosa Rd 75092
N Porter St 75090
Portsmouth Pl 75092
Post Oak Dr 75092
Post Oak St 75090
Post Oak Xing 75092

Preston Dr 75092
Preston Club Dr 75092
Preston Meadows Rd 75092
Primrose Ln 75092
Princess Dr 75090
Progress St 75092
Pumping Jack Rd 75092
Quail Run Rd
1-800 75090
802-898 75090
4100-4698 75092
Raccoon Dr 75092
Railroad St 75090
W Rainey St 75090
Rams Ln 75092
S & W Raven Dr & Ln 75092
Red Rd 75090
Red Oak Ct 75092
Redbud Ln 75090
Redbud Trl 75092
Refuge Rd 75092
Regency Cir 75092
Remuda Dr 75092
Rex Cruse Dr 75092
Reynolds Ln 75092
Riata Dr 75092
E Richards St 75090
Richelieu St 75090
N & S Ricketts St 75092
Riddels Rd 75092
Ridgecrest Ln 75092
Ridgeview Dr 75090
Ridgeview Rd 75092
Ridgeway Dr 75092
Ridgewood Dr 75092
River Oak Cir 75092
Rivercrest Dr 75092
Roan Ln 75090
Roberts Dr 75090
Roberts Run 75092
Robin Dr 75092
W Robin Ln 75090
Rockport Rd 75092
Roelke Dr 75092
Rolling Hills Dr 75092
Rose Garden Dr 75092
E Rosedale St 75090
N Ross Ave 75090
N & S Rusk St 75090
Salvage Dr 75092
N & S Sam Rayburn Fwy 75090
Samuel 75090
San Juan Dr 75092
San Miguel St 75092
Sand Creek Cir 75092
Sandra Dr 75092
Sara Swamy Dr 75090
Savannah Dr 75092
Schneider Rd 75090
Scott Cir 75090
E Scott St 75090
W Scott St 75092
Seasons W 75092
Sedalia Cir & Trl 75092
Seminole Rd 75092
Shadow Trl 75092
Shady Oaks Cir & Ln 75092
Shannon Rd 75090
N Shannon St 75092
Sharp Rd 75090
Shenandoah Cir 75092
W Shepherd Dr 75092
Shepherd Rd 75090
Sherbrooke Ct & Pl 75092
E Sherman St 75090
Sherwood Dr 75092
W Shields Dr 75092
Shoreline Dr 75092
Short Ln 75092
Siebert Hill Ln 75092
Silver Mine Dr 75092
Silverado Trl 75092
Simpson Dr 75092
Sistrunk Dr & St 75090
Skaggs Rd 75090
Skyline Dr 75092
Smith Row 75090
Smith Oak Rd 75090
Snap Rd 75090
Snowbird 75092
Southfork Dr 75090
Southridge Ln 75092
Spalding Dr & Rd 75092
Sparrow Ln 75090
E & W Spring St 75090
Stanford Ct 75092
W Staples St 75090
Stark Ln 75090
Starlight Dr 75090
State Highway 11 75090
N State Highway 289 75092
State Highway 56
7000-7898 75090
State Highway 56
7900-11099 75090
11101-11399 75090
14800-17700 75092
17702-18398 75090
W State Highway 56 75092
W Steadman St
200-599 75090
1201-1299 75092
Steeplechase Dr 75092
Stephen Cir 75092
Stewart Ln & Rd 75092
Stonebrook Ln 75092
Strait Ln 75092
Stroud Dr 75092
E Summit St 75090
Sumner Ct 75090
Sunny Dr 75092
Sunset Blvd 75092
Swan Ridge Dr 75092
W Swanner Dr 75092
E Sycamore St 75090
W Sycamore St 75090
Taho Dr 75092
Talley Dr 75092
Tate Cir 75090
E Taylor St
100-198 75092
300-398 75090
400-899 75090
W Taylor St 75092
Teague Dr 75090
Teal 75092
Tee Taw Cir 75092
Tejas Dr 75092
W Tennessee St 75090
Terrace Oaks 75092
Terrell Rd 75092
Terry Ln 75092
W Texas St 75092
Texoma Dr & Pkwy 75090
Theresa Dr 75090
E Thomas St 75090
N & S Throckmorton St 75090
Timbercreek St 75092
Timberline Ct & Ln 75092
Timberview Dr 75090
Tolbert Ave 75092
Town Ctr 75092
Trailridge Rd 75092
Trails End Cir 75092
N Travis Ct 75092
N Travis St
100-1099 75090
1101-1199 75090
1201-1225 75092
1227-5399 75090
5141-5299 75092
5401-5599 75092
S Travis St 75090
Tribble Rd 75090
E Tuck St 75090
E Turley St 75090
Turtle Creek Cir & Dr 75092
N & S Us Highway 75 75090
Us Highway 82 E
700-3700 75090
E Us Highway 82
301-499 75092
W Us Highway 82 75092
Utah St 75090
N & S Vaden St 75090
S Valentine Dr 75090
Valerie Ln 75092
Valley Ranch Rd 75092
Valley Ridge Ln 75092
Van Deren Ln 75090
Vancouver Pl 75092
Verdi Ln 75090
Vernon Holland Memorial Dr 75090
Versaille Dr 75090
Victoria Dr 75090
Village Dr 75090
Vista Lagos Dr 75090
Vivaldi Xing 75090
Wagon Wheel Trl 75092
W Walcott St 75090
E & W Wall St 75090
N & S Walnut St 75090
Wanda Dr 75090
Warleang Dr 75092
W Washington St
100-399 75090
700-4099 75090
4101-7499 75092
E Water St 75090
Watkins Rd 75090
Wd Hill Rd 75092
Webb Smith Rd 75090
Wellington Dr 75092
E Wells Ave 75090
Western Hills Dr 75092
Westhaven Ct 75092
S Westridge Trl 75092
Westside Dr 75092
Westwood Dr 75092
N Wharton St 75092
White Mound Rd 75090
White Mound Cemetery Rd 75090
White Way Rd 75092
Whitney Rd 75090
Wible Rd 75092
Wilder Trl 75092
Wildflower Dr 75090
E Williams St 75090
N & S Willow St 75090
Willow Ridge Cir 75092
E & W Wilson Ave 75090
Wilsonwood Way S 75092
Windsor Dr 75092
Windy Ln 75092
Windy Hill Rd 75092
Wiship Dr 75092
Wolff Dr 75092
Woodard Ln 75090
Woodland Hills Dr 75092
Woodlawn Rd 75090
N & S Woods St 75092
Wright Rd 75092
Wyndham Ct 75092
Yarborough Dr 75092
Yorkshire Dr 75092

SNYDER TX

General Delivery 79550

POST OFFICE BOXES MAIN OFFICE STATIONS AND BRANCHES

Box No.s
All PO Boxes 79550

RURAL ROUTES

01, 02, 03 79549

HIGHWAY CONTRACTS

67, 69 79549

NAMED STREETS

All Street Addresses 79549

NUMBERED STREETS

All Street Addresses 79549

SPRING TX

General Delivery 77373

POST OFFICE BOXES MAIN OFFICE STATIONS AND BRANCHES

Box No.s
1 - 3352 77383
4070 - 9996 77387
11001 - 12359 77391
130001 - 135020 77393

NAMED STREETS

Abberton Hill Dr 77379
Abbey Ct 77389
Abbey Brook Pl 77381
Abbott Lakes Ln 77386
Abby Ln 77379
Abby Lane Cir 77379
Abelia Creek Dr 77379
Aberdeen Crossing Pl 77381
Aberton Ct & Ln 77379
N & S Abram Cir 77382
N & S Acacia Park Cir & Pl 77382
Academy Trace Dr 77386
Acadia Branch Pl 77382
Acorn Chase Dr 77389
Acorn Cluster Ct 77381
Acorn Grove Dr 77389
Acorn Oak St 77380
Acorn Springs Ln 77389
Acorn Tree Ct 77388
Acorn Valley Dr 77389
Acorn Way Ln 77389
Acornrun Ln 77389
Acrewoods Pl 77382
Adalyn Arbor Dr 77389
Adambury Ct 77373
Adamwood Ct 77388
Adarange Dr 77388
Addison Park Ln 77373
Adkins Forest Dr 77379
Admiralty Bend Ln 77380
Adobe Falls Dr
1800-1999 77388
29900-30099 77386
30101-30199 77386
Adonis Dr 77373
Adowa Spring Loop 77373
Adrian Hills Ln 77386
Adrienne Arbor Dr 77389
African Violets Pl 77382
Afton Oak Ln 77386
Agassi Ace Ct 77379
Agate St 77389
Agate Stream Pl 77381
Agusta Ct 77379
Alamosa Ln 77379
Alan Lake Ln 77388
Alana Ln 77386
Alba Rose Dr 77386
Albany Park Ct & Ln 77379
Alcea Ct 77379
Aldeburgh Ct 77379
Alden Bend Dr 77382
Alden Bridge Dr 77382
Alden Glen Ct & Dr 77382
Aldenham Pl 77379
Alder Pl 77380
Alder Bend Ln 77389
Aldergrove Dr 77388
Alderleaf Pl 77388
Alderly Dr 77389
Aldermoor Dr 77388
Alderon Woods Pl 77382
Alderwood Dr 77388
Aldine Westfield Rd
22500-26999 77373
29900-31299 77386
Aleah Ct 77388
Aleta Dr 77379
Alexandra Park Dr 77379
Alexandra Springs Ln 77386
Alexandria Ct 77379
Alfonso Ct 77388
Algernon Dr 77373
Algrave Ln 77379
Alhaven Dr 77388
Alina Ln 77386
Alivia Ct 77373
Alladdin Ln 77380
Allentown Dr 77389
Alley Ct 77388
Allie Ct 77386
Allis St 77373
Allison Ct 77389
Allison Meadows Ct 77386
Allyson Ct & Ln 77373
Almond Ct 77386
Almond Branch Pl 77382
Almond Dale Ct 77382
Almondwood Dr 77389
Alp Springs Ln 77373
Alshire Dr 77373
Altai Terrace Dr 77379
N & S Altwood Cir 77382
Alvin A Klein Dr 77379
Amandas Way 77386
Amara Ct 77381
E & W Ambassador Bnd 77382
Amber Fire Pl 77381
Amber Leaf Ct 77381
Amber Leigh Pl 77382
Amber Mills Dr 77389
Amber Sky Pl 77381
Ambercrest Ct & Dr 77389
E & W Amberglow Cir & Ct 77381
Amberlee Ct 77386
Ambler Dr 77379
Ambrosia Pl 77381
Amelia Ct 77381
Amelia Springs Dr 77379
American Elm Ln 77389
Amersham Ct 77389
Ames St 77373
Amesbury Meadow Ln 77379
Amidon Dr 77379
Ammick Ct 77389
Amorgas Isle Dr 77388
Ampton Dr 77379
Amulet Oaks Ct & Pl 77382
Amwell Rd 77389
Amy Willow Ln 77386
Anacacho Dr 77386
Anark Ct 77379
Anchor Point Pl 77381
Andante Trail Pl 77381
Anderson Point Ln 77388
Andover St 77373
Andree Forest Ct 77386
Andrew Chase Ln 77386
Andrew Springs Ln 77386
Andris Ln 77386
Angel Dove Pl 77382
Angel Leaf Rd 77380
Angela Ct 77379
Angela Way Dr 77386
Angelique Way 77382
Angels Rest Ct 77373
Angling Ln 77386
Anise Tree Pl 77382
Annawood Cir 77388
Annes Ct 77380
Annola Ln 77379
Anthony Trails Ln 77386
Antico Ct 77382
Antique Cedar Ln 77389
Antique Rose Ct 77382
Anzalone Dr 77373
Appin Falls Dr 77379
Apple Ct 77386
Apple Arbor Dr 77373
N & S Apple Springs Cir & Ct 77382
Applecrest Way 77388
Applegate Dr 77373
Appomattox Dr 77380
April Rain Ct 77382
Aquagate Dr 77373
Aquamarine Pl 77389
Aquiline Oaks Pl 77382
Arbor Bend Ct 77379
Arbor Breeze Ct 77379
E & W Arbor Camp Cir 77389
Arbor Rose Ln 77379
Arbor Spring Ct 77379
Arbor Terrace Ct & Dr 77388
Arborg Dr 77386
Arborgate Dr 77373
Arbroath Ct 77389
Arcade Dr 77379
Arcane Ct 77389
Archbriar Pl 77382
Archer Oak Pl 77382
Archgate Dr 77373
N Archwyck Cir 77382
Arden Forest Dr 77379
Ardmore Cove Dr 77386
Ardsley Square Pl 77382
Arendale Ln 77386
Argonne Pl 77382
Aria Ln 77382
Arica Ln 77373
Aristis Path 77382
Arkdale Ct 77379
Arlan Lake Dr 77388
Arnica Ct 77381
Arromanches Ln 77388
N & S Arrow Canyon Cir 77389
Arrow Creek Ln 77379
Arrowfeather Pl 77389
Artesia St 77373
Arthur Rd 77373
E & W Artist Grove Cir & Pl 77382
Asbury Glen Ct 77386
Ascot Way Ct 77382
Ash Branch Ct 77381
Ash Glen Ct & Dr 77388
Ash Valley Dr 77379
Ashbridge Ct 77379
Ashdown Forest Dr 77379
Ashgate Dr 77373
Ashland Park Ln 77386
Ashlane Way 77382
Ashlar Pt 77381
S Ashley Grn 77382
Ashley Manor Dr 77389
Ashley Pines Dr 77373
Ashlyn Grv 77382
Ashlyn Ridge Ln 77386
Ashmere Ln 77379
Ashridge Park Dr 77379
Ashton Pines Ln 77379
Ashton Village Ct & Dr 77386
Ashwell Ct 77389
Aspen Cir 77389
Aspen Brook Ln 77388
Aspen Dale Dr 77386
Aspen Fair Trl 77386
Aspen Glen Ln 77388
Aspen Oak Ct 77379
Asphodel Ct & Ln 77379
Asprey Ct 77379
Aster Crest Ct 77379
Astilbe Ct 77379
Astipalia Dr 77388
Astley Ln 77379
Astwood Ct 77379
Atherington Pl 77379
Atherstone St 77386
Atrium Woods Ct 77381
Auburn Bend Dr 77389
Auburn Forest Dr 77379
Auburn Jewel St 77389
Auburn Lakes Dr 77389
Auburn Mills Dr 77389
Auburn Park Ln 77379
N Auburn Path Dr 77382
Auburn Ridge Ln 77379
Auburn Sands Dr 77389
Auburn Terrace Ct & Dr 77389
Audra Ln 77386
Audubon Park Dr 77379
Auger Pl 77380
Aughton Ct & Dr 77389
August Meadows Ln 77379
Augusta Falls Ln 77389
W Augusta Pines Cv, Dr & Pkwy E 77389
Aulia Ln 77386
Austin Spgs 77373
Austin Manor Ct 77379
Autumn Cres 77381
Autumn Branch Cir & Dr 77382
Autumn Breeze Ct & Dr 77379
Autumn Canyon Ln 77386
Autumn Joy Dr 77379
Autumn Oak Ct & Way 77379
Autumn Point Ln 77373
Autumn Rain Ln 77379
Autumn Springs Ln 77373
Autumn Sunset Ln 77379
N Autumnwood Ct & Way 77380
Avalon Aqua Way 77379
Avalon Bend Cir 77379
Avalon Castle Dr 77386
Avalon Forest Ct 77386
Avalon Oaks Ct & Pl 77381
Avalon Queen Dr 77379
Avalon Spring Ln 77386
Avanak St 77389
Avenswood Pl 77382
Aventura Pl 77389
Avera Creek Dr 77386
Avery Hill Ln 77373
Avonglen Ln 77389
N & S Avonlea Cir, Ct & Dr 77382
Aylesbury Ln 77379
Azalea Way 77379
Azalea Park Dr 77389
Azalea Sands Dr 77386
Aztec Canyon Dr 77386
Azure Crystal Ct 77373
Azure Sky Dr 77373
Backland Ct 77373
N & S Bacopa Dr 77389
N & S Badger Lodge Cir 77389
Baffin Bay Ct 77379
Bainbridge Ln 77379
Bainbridge Estates Dr 77388
Baker Lake Dr 77386
Bakerswood Dr 77386
Bala Lake Ct 77379
Balch Spgs 77373
Ballard Ct 77388
Ballardwood Ct 77373
Ballin David Dr 77379
Balmoral Pl 77382
E & W Balsam Fir Cir, Ct & Ln 77386
Balson Forest Ln 77386

Balthasar St 77373
Baltzell Dr 77389
Baluchi Dr 77379
Bampton Dr 77379
Banchory Ave 77379
Baneberry Dr 77373
Bank Birch Pl 77381
Banquo Dr 77373
N & S Bantam Woods Cir & Dr 77382
Barcarole Dr 77388
Barclay Lake Ln 77388
Barco Ct 77386
N & S Bardsbrook Cir 77382
Barker Ridge Ct 77382
Barley Hall St 77382
Barlow Ct 77382
Barmby Ct & Dr 77389
Barn Lantern Pl 77382
Barnstable Ct 77379
Barnstable Pl 77381
Baron Gate Ct 77379
Baronet Woods Ct 77382
Barongate Ct 77382
Baronial Cir 77382
Barretts Crossing Dr 77379
Barronton Dr 77389
Barrow Glen Ct 77388
Barrygate Cir, Ct & Dr 77373
Barstow St 77389
Barwick Dr 77373
Barwood St 77380
Basal Briar Ct 77381
Bashaw Dr 77386
Basil Trace Dr 77386
Basket Flower Dr 77379
Bassbrook Dr 77388
Basswood Dr 77386
Batesbrooke Ct 77381
S Bauer Point Cir & Ct 77389
E & N Bay Blvd 77380
Bay Branch Dr 77382
Bay Cliff Ct 77389
Bay Mills Pl 77389
Bayer Rd 77373
Bayeux Ln 77388
Bayginger Pl 77381
Baylark Pl 77382
Bayleaf Dr 77373
Bayleaf Ln 77380
Bayonne Dr 77389
Bayou Bluff Ct & Dr 77379
N & S Bayou Club Ct 77389
Bayou Elm Dr 77373
Bayou Springs Ct 77382
Bayport Ct 77386
Baywick Dr 77389
Baywood Ct 77386
Beacon Chase Ct 77373
Beacon Creek Ct 77386
Beacon Green Ln 77386
Beacon Grove St 77389
Beacon Park Ct 77373
Bearborough Dr 77386
Beaubridge Ln 77379
Beaufort Dr 77379
Beauty Bower Pl 77382
Beaver Dam St 77389
Beaverhead Cir & Ct 77380
Beaverwood Dr 77373
Becker Line Dr 77379
Beckets Crossing Ln 77373
Beckett Hill Pl 77382
Beckham Springs Ct 77373
Beckins Cliff Dr 77379
E & W Beckonvale Cir & Ct 77382
Beebrush Pl 77389
Beech Bark Pl 77382
Beech Hill Dr 77388
N & S Beech Springs Cir 77389
Beeston Hall Ct 77388
Bekonscot Dr 77379
Bel Canto Grn 77382

Belcarra Pl 77382
N & S Belfair Pl 77382
Belham Ridge Ct 77379
Bella Vis 77381
Bella Cascata 77381
Bella Donna 77381
Bella Dulce Ct 77379
Bella Flora Ct 77379
Bella Jess Dr 77379
Bella Luce 77381
Bella Luna 77381
Bella Luna Ct 77379
Bella Mountain Dr 77379
Bella Noche Dr 77379
Bella Sera Dr 77379
Bella Sole 77381
Bellbird Ct 77380
Bellchase Cir 77373
Belle Vernon Dr 77389
Bellgate Ct 77373
E & W Bellmeade Pl 77382
Bellweather Ct 77381
Belted Kingfisher Trl 77389
Belton Lake Dr 77386
Bembridge Dr 77386
Benders Ln 77386
Benders Crossing Ct & Dr 77386
Benders Dock Ct 77386
E & W Benders Landing Blvd 77386
Benderwood Ct 77386
Bending Bough Dr & Ln 77388
Bending Branch Pl 77381
Bending Pines Ln 77379
Benedict Canyon Loop 77382
Bennet Trails Dr 77386
Benson Springs Ln 77386
Bent Cypress Dr 77388
Bent Elm Dr 77388
Bent Green Ln 77389
Bent Oak Ln 77379
Bentgate Dr 77373
Bentgrass Pl 77381
Bentgrass Run Ln 77386
Benton Brook Ct 77386
N & S Benton Woods Cir & Ct 77382
Bentwood Elm St 77379
Benwest Ct 77388
Benwick St 77379
Berkley Hall Ct 77379
Berners-Lee Ave Ct 77381
Bernshausen Dr 77389
Berry Ln 77389
Berry Blossom Ct & Dr 77380
Berry Cresent Dr 77389
Berry Grove Dr 77388
Berry Oaks Ln 77379
Berry Pine Dr 77373
Berryfrost Ln 77380
Berryhill Ln 77388
N & S Berryline Cir 77381
Berrypick Ln 77380
Berryview Ct 77380
Berwick Manor Ct 77379
Bessdale Ct 77382
Bessemer Ct 77381
N & S Bethany Bend Cir, Ct & Dr 77382
Betony Pl 77382
Bettina Ln 77382
Beufort Way 77389
Bickett Ln 77373
Big Creek Falls Ct 77379
Big Cypress Dr 77388
E & W Bigelow Oak Ct 77381
Billingham Ct 77379
Binefield St 77389
Binion Forest Ln 77389
Birch Forest Ln 77379
Birch Green Way 77386
Birchbrook Ct 77380

Birchcane Ct & Dr 77381
Birchgate Dr 77373
Birchline Dr 77379
Birchwood Dr 77386
Birchwood Park Pl 77382
Birdseye Maple Ln 77389
Birksbridge Ct 77379
Birnam Wood Blvd 77373
Birnamwood Dr 77373
Birnham Bend Cir 77386
Birnham Woods Dr 77386
Birsay St 77379
Biscay Ct & Pl 77381
Biscayne Hill Ct 77379
Bishops Place Dr 77379
Bitterwood Cir & Ct 77381
Bivens Bnd 77379
Black Cherry Ct 77381
Black Cormorant Pl 77380
Black Forest Dr
200-299 77388
8100-8399 77389
Black Hawk Trail Ct 77373
E & W Black Knight Dr 77382
Black Spruce Ct 77389
Blackberry Terrace Dr 77379
Blackbristle Ln 77379
N & S Blackjack Oak Cir & Pl 77380
Blackstar Pl 77382
Blaine Oaks Ln 77386
Blakeley Trails Ct 77386
Blanco Lake Ct 77388
Blanco River Loop 77386
Blanketflower Ct 77381
Blazing Star Ct 77380
Blenheim Dr 77379
Blooming Rock Ln 77379
Blossom Crest Ln 77373
Blossom Grove Ln 77379
Blue Bungalow Dr 77389
Blue Candle Dr 77388
Blue Cedar Ct & Ln 77386
Blue Creek Ct & Pl 77382
Blue Cruls Way 77379
Blue Cypress Dr 77388
Blue Fovant Ct 77388
Blue Fox Ct & Rd 77380
Blue Lake Dr 77388
Blue Mesa Ct 77389
Blue Ridge Dr 77381
Blue Ridge Park Ln 77386
Blue Sage Ter 77388
Blue Shadow Dr 77388
Blue Vervain Dr 77386
Bluebonnet Meadow Ln 77388
Bluebonnet Trace Dr 77386
Bluestone Springs Ln 77379
N & S Bluff Creek Cir, Ct & Pl 77382
Blundell Dr 77388
Blushwood Pl 77382
Boden Ln 77386
Bolinas Ct 77386
Bon Hill Ct 77379
Bonds Creek Ln 77388
Bonnaire Dr 77382
Bonnard Cir 77379
E Bonneymead Cir 77381
Bonnie Sean Dr 77379
E & W Bonny Branch St 77382
Bonnybrook Ct 77373
Bonwick Ct 77382
Booker Dr 77373
Bordace Ct 77379
Border St 77373
Borg Breakpoint Dr 77379
Borough Ln 77379
Borough Park Dr 77380
Bosque River Ct 77386
Boudreaux Rd 77379
Bough Leaf Pl 77381
Boulder Cliff Ln 77386

Bovington Dr 77389
Bow Wood Ct 77389
Bowden Chase Ct & Dr 77379
Bowles Ct 77388
Bowman Ct 77388
Box Oak Pl 77380
Box Turtle Ln 77380
Boxberry Ct 77380
Boxford Ct 77373
Boyton Ln 77379
E & W Bracebridge Cir & Dr 77382
Bracken Fern Ct 77380
Brackenfield Dr 77388
Brackenton Crest Ct & Dr 77379
Bradbury Path Ct 77373
Bradford Village Dr 77386
Braemar Forest St 77381
Brakendale Pl 77389
Brampton Ct 77379
Branch Ln & Rd 77373
W Branch Crossing Dr 77382
Branchberry Ln 77388
Branchdale Ln 77379
Brandenberry Ct 77381
Brandt Rd 77373
Brandy Bend Dr 77373
Brandygate Ct 77373
Brannon Park Ln 77373
Brantley Ln 77389
Braxton Grove Ln 77379
Braydon Ct 77386
Brea Ct 77386
Breckenridge Forest Ct & Dr 77373
Breen Vista Dr 77386
Breezin Ct 77380
Breezy Way 77380
Breezy Point Pl 77381
Breezy Retreat Ct 77386
Bremerton Ln 77388
Brendon Ct 77379
Brendon Trail Ct & Ln 77386
Brendon Trails Ct & Dr 77379
Brenton Oaks Dr 77379
Brentonridge Ln 77379
Brentwood Lakes Cir 77379
Brentwood Oaks Ct 77381
Breton Point Dr 77373
Brianwood Ct 77379
Briar Rock Rd 77380
Briarcreek Blvd 77373
Briarfield Dr 77379
Briarhorn Dr 77389
Briarstone Ct & Ln 77379
Briarvine Ct 77389
Brickhill Dr 77389
Brickstone Ct 77386
Bridal Oak Ct 77380
Briden Oak Ct 77379
Bridenwood Ct 77379
Bridge Way 77389
Bridge Creek Falls Ct 77379
Bridge End Ln 77388
Bridgeberry Ct & Pl 77381
Bridgebrook Dr 77373
Bridgecrossing Ct 77379
Bridgegate Dr 77373
Bridgeharbor Ct 77379
Bridgeland Ln 77388
Bridgemont Ln 77388
Bridgepoint Ln 77388
Bridgestone Ln 77388
Bridgestone Bend Dr 77388
Bridgestone Canyon Dr 77388
Bridgestone Cedar Dr 77388
Bridgestone Cliff Ct 77388
Bridgestone Crossing Dr 77388
Bridgestone Eagle Ct 77388
Bridgestone Glenridge Dr 77388

Bridgestone Hawk Ct 77388
Bridgestone Lakes Dr 77388
Bridgestone Maple Dr 77388
Bridgestone Oak Dr 77388
Bridgestone Palm Ct 77388
Bridgestone Park Ln 77386
Bridgestone Path Dr 77388
Bridgestone Pine Ct 77388
Bridgestone Point Ct & Dr 77388
Bridgestone Ridge Dr 77388
Bridgestone Shadow Ct 77388
Bridgestone Trails Dr 77388
Bridgestone Valley Dr 77388
Bridgestone Way Ct 77388
Bridgevalley Ct 77379
Bridgeview Cir & Ln 77388
Bridgevillage Dr 77373
Bridgeville Ln 77388
Bridgewater Cir & Dr 77373
Bridgewood Cove Ct 77381
Briervine Ct 77381
Bright Bloom Ln 77379
Bright Oak Ct 77373
Bright Sky Ct 77386
Bright Star Dr 77373
Bright Timber Landing Dr 77386
Brighton Brook Ln 77386
Brightonwood Ct & Ln 77379
Brightridge Ln 77379
Brightwork Way 77380
Brimstone Ct 77380
Bringewood Chase Dr 77379
Brinson Ct 77379
Brisk Spring Ct 77373
N & S Bristle Pine Dr 77379
Bristlecone Pl & Trl 77380
Bristlecone Pine Ln 77389
Bristol Bend Cir 77382
N & S Bristol Gate Pl 77380
Bristol Memorial Dr 77379
S & W Bristol Oak Cir & Ct 77382
Brittany Creek Dr 77388
Britton Key Ln 77386
Broad Branch Ct 77373
Broad Hollow Ct 77373
Broad Timbers Dr 77373
Broad Valley Ct 77373
Broadhead Manor Ct & Dr 77379
Broadwater Ct 77381
Broadweather Pl 77382
Brock Meadow Dr 77389
N & S Broken Bough 77380
Broken Brook Cir 77381
Broken Elm Dr 77388
E & W Broken Oak Ct 77381
N & S Brokenfern Dr 77380
N & S Brook Pebble Ct 77380
E & S Brookberry Ct 77381
Brookchase Dr 77386
Brookflower Rd 77380
Brookgate Dr 77373
Brookhaven St 77386
Brookline Ct 77381
N & S Brooksedge Cir & Ct 77382
Brooktree Ln 77380
Brookway Berch Ct 77379
Brookway Cedar Ct 77379
Brookway Cypress Ct 77379
Brookway Maple Ct 77379
Brookway Oak Ct 77379
Brookway Park Ct 77379
Brookway Pine Ct 77379
Brookway Willow Dr 77379
Brookway Wind Ct 77379
Broughton St 77373
Brown Hill Dr 77373
Brownlee Ln 77379
Brush Hl 77379
Brushwood Ct 77380

Bryanhurst Ln 77379
Bryberry Ct 77381
Bryce Branch Cir 77382
Bryce Canyon Ct 77379
Brywood Pl 77382
Buchans Dr 77386
N & S Buck Rdg 77381
Buck Trail Pl 77389
Buckminster Dr 77386
Buckthorne Pl 77380
Budde Rd 77380
Budde Cemetary Rd 77388
Buena Way 77386
Buffalo Canyon Dr 77386
Buffalo Springs Ct & Way 77373
Bull Pine Dr 77379
Bullinger Dr 77379
Bunnelle Way 77382
Bur Oak Ct & Dr 77379
N & S Burberry Park Cir 77382
Burcan Ct 77373
Burgess Bend Way 77389
Burgh Castle Dr 77389
Burkegate Dr 77373
E, N & W Burnaby Cir & St 77373
Burnt Candle Dr 77388
Burnt Leaf Ln 77379
Burrard St 77373
Burris Park Dr 77373
Burro Springs Ln 77386
Burton Ridge Dr 77386
Burwood Park Dr 77379
Bush Oak Ln 77380
Bushell Mill Pl 77382
Bushwood Dr 77388
Butler Oaks Ct 77389
Buttercup Cove Ln 77386
Butterfly Branch Pl 77382
Butteroak Dr 77379
Butterwick Dr 77389
Buttonbush Ct 77380
Byron Ct 77379
Cabaniss Cir 77379
Cabanna Rd 77389
Cabbage St 77379
Cactus Creek Dr 77386
Cade Hills Ln 77386
Cadena Ct 77379
Cadence Ct 77389
Cades Cove Dr 77373
Caelin Ct 77382
Cairn Meadows Dr 77379
Cairn Oaks Pl 77381
Calaveras Lake Dr 77386
Calico Corners Ln 77373
Calico Ridge Ln 77373
Calliope Knolls Dr 77379
Calmar Dr 77386
Calumet St 77389
Calvert Cove Ct 77386
Calwood Cir 77379
Camber Pine Pl 77382
Camberleigh Ln 77388
Camberwell Ct 77380
Cambria Pines Ct 77382
Camden Village Dr 77386
Camellia Bend Cir 77379
N & S Camellia Grove Cir 77382
Camelot Oaks Ct 77382
Cameron Park Ln 77386
Camino Ct 77382
Campden Ct & Dr 77379
Camplight Ct 77389
Camrose Ct 77373
Canadian River Ct 77386
Candle Bend Dr 77388
Candle Cabin Ln 77388
Candle Grove Dr 77388
Candle Hill Dr 77388
Candle Hollow Dr 77388
Candle Park Dr 77388
Candle Pine Pl 77381

Candle Place Dr 77388
Candle Pond Ln 77388
Candle River Ln 77388
Candlebrook Cir & Dr 77388
Candlechase Dr 77388
Candlecreek Dr 77388
Candleknoll Dr 77388
Candlelight Crescent Rd 77388
Candlelon Dr 77388
Candlenut Pl 77381
Candleoak Dr 77388
Candlepine Dr 77388
Candleridge Dr 77388
Candlespice Pl 77382
Candletrail Dr 77388
Candleview Dr 77388
Candleway Dr 77388
Candlewisp Cir & Dr 77388
Candlewood Oaks Ln 77379
Candy Ct 77379
Cane Mill Pl 77382
Canmore Springs Dr 77386
Cannaberry Way 77388
Cannon Ball Dr 77380
Cannongate Dr 77373
Canoe Bend Ct & Dr 77389
Canoe Birch Pl 77382
Canston Ct 77389
Cantwell Way 77382
Canvasback Glen Ct 77388
Canyon Back Ln 77373
Canyon Branch Ln 77386
Canyon Lake Dr 77373
Canyon Laurel Ct 77379
Canyon Oak Pl 77380
Canyon Pine Dr 77379
Canyon Ridge Ct & Dr 77379
Canyon Side Ct & Ln 77386
Canyon Square Dr 77386
Canyon Summer Ln 77386
E & W Canyon Wren Cir & Dr 77389
Cape Chestnut Dr 77381
Cape Cottage Ct & Ln 77373
Cape Harbour Pl 77380
Cape Jasmine Ct & Pl 77381
Cape May Ct 77386
Cape Vista Ct 77386
Capella Park Dr 77379
Capewood Ct 77381
E Capstone Cir & Pl 77381
Caradoc Springs Ct 77386
Caraquet Ct & Dr 77386
Carbrook Ct 77388
Cardigan Bay Cir 77379
Carelia Ln 77379
Caribou St 77389
Carl Road Ext 77373
Carleen Creek Trl 77379
Carley Cove Ct & Ln 77386
Carlton Woods Dr 77382
Carlton Woods Creekside Dr 77389
Carlyle Pl 77382
Carmeline Dr 77382
Carneys Point Ln 77379
Carolina Cherry Ct & Ln 77389
Caroline St 77373
Caroline Green Ct 77373
Caroline Park Ln 77386
Carolyn Ct 77379
Carriage Dale Ct 77379
Carriage Pines Ct 77381
Carrick Bend Dr 77389
Carrie Cove Ct 77386
Carroll Lake Dr 77379
Carrot St 77379
Carson Ridge Dr 77386
Carter Gate Dr 77373
Cartgate Ln 77381
E & W Cartouche Cir 77382
Cartwright Rdg 77380
Cascade Hollow Ln 77379
Cascade Springs Pl 77381

Casemont Dr 77388
Cash Oaks Dr 77373
Cashier Ct 77373
Casper Ct & Dr 77373
Cass Ct 77386
Cassandra Park St 77379
Cassina Dr & Ln 77388
Cassini Ct 77381
Cassowary Ct 77373
Cassowary Ln 77380
Casting Springs Way 77373
Castle Forest Dr 77386
Castle Hollow Dr 77389
Castle Manor Dr 77386
Castle Pine Ln 77379
Castle Terrace Ct 77379
Castlebrook St 77389
Castlegap Ct & Dr 77379
N Castlegreen Cir 77381
S Castlegreen Cir 77381
Castlegreen Dr 77388
Castlemist Dr 77386
Castlemont Ln 77388
Castleton Farms Rd 77379
Castletown Park Ct 77379
Castlewood Dr 77386
Cat Feet Ct 77381
Catalina Leaf Ln 77379
Catoosa Dr 77388
Cattail Pl 77381
Caulfield Ct 77382
Cayahoga Ct 77389
Caymus Dr 77373
Cayuga Pond Ct 77389
Cece Glen Ct 77386
Cedar Brush Cir 77379
Cedar Chase Pl 77381
Cedar Edge Dr 77379
Cedar Fern Ct 77386
Cedar Flats Ln 77386
Cedar Glen Ln 77388
Cedar Oaks Dr 77379
Cedar Run Cir 77379
Cedar Springs Pl 77373
Cedar Trace Dr 77379
Cedarshade Ln 77380
Cedarwing Ln 77380
Cedarwood Dr 77381
Cembra Walk 77379
Center Court Cir & Dr 77379
Center Park Dr 77373
Center Spring Ct 77373
Centerlake Ln 77379
Centre Court Pl 77379
Centre Place Cir 77379
Cezanne Woods Dr & Pl 77382
Chadington Ln 77388
Chagall Ln 77379
Challe Cir E & W 77373
Chalton Ct 77379
Chamberlain Ct 77382
Chamomile Ct 77382
Champagne Falls Ct 77379
Champion Dr 77379
Champion Forest Cir & Dr 77379
Champion Lake Ct & Dr 77380
Champion Pines Dr 77379
Champion Springs Cir 77379
Champions Cove Cir, Ct & Dr 77379
Chanas Ct 77388
Chancellor Dr 77379
Chancery Pl 77381
N & S Chandler Creek Cir & Ct 77381
Channelbrook Ln 77379
Channing Springs Dr 77386
N & S Chantsong Cir 77382
Chaparral Way 77380
Chapel Pine Ct & St 77379
Chapel Pines Dr 77379
Chapel Ridge Ln 77373
Chapel Rock Ln 77386
Chapel Square Dr 77388
Chapwood Ct 77373
Charis Pl 77388
Charmaine Way 77382
Charming River Dr 77373
Charrington Dr 77389
Chaseloch St 77379
Chasemore Dr 77379
Chateau Cv 77386
Chateau Creek Way 77386
Chateau Springs Ct 77386
Chatterbird Ln 77380
Cheddar Ridge Dr 77379
Chelmsford Ln 77379
Chelsea Bridge Ct 77382
Chelsea Creek Ln 77386
Chelsea Fair Ln 77379
Chelshurst Way 77379
Chelshurst Way Ct 77379
Cherry Blossom Pl 77381
Cherry Laurel Dr 77386
Cherry Springs Ln 77373
Cherryvale Ct 77382
Cherrywood Ln 77381
Cheshire Glen Ct 77382
Chessnut Glen Dr 77388
Chester Fort Dr 77373
Chestergate Dr 77373
Chesterpoint Dr 77386
Chestnut Creek Ct 77379
Chestnut Hill Ct 77380
Chestnut Oak Pl 77380
Cheswood Manor Ct & Dr 77382
Cheyne Cir 77379
Childers Ln 77373
Childres Pond Ct 77389
Chiltren Cir 77379
China Spgs 77373
China Rose Ct 77381
Chinkapin Oak Dr 77386
Chipped Sparrow Pl 77389
Chippewa Trl 77389
Chipstead Cir, Ct & Dr 77379
Chipwyck Way 77382
Chisos Trl 77388
Chivary Oaks Ct 77382
Chris Ridge Ct 77386
Churchdale Pl 77382
Churchhill Falls Ct 77379
Cias Trail Ln 77386
Cider Mill Ct 77382
Ciderwood Dr 77373
Cimarron Pass Dr 77373
Cimber Ln 77373
Cimmaron Creek Ct 77379
Cinnamon Run 77389
Cinnamon Teal Pl 77382
Circlegate Dr 77373
N & S Circlewood Gln 77381
Cirrus Ct 77380
Clachern Pl 77382
E & W Clady Ct & Dr 77386
Clarion Rdg 77382
Clarkgate Dr 77373
Clarkston Ln 77379
Clary Sage Ct 77382
Classic Oaks Pl 77382
Claytons Bend Ct 77386
Claytons Cove Ct 77386
Clear Springs Way 77373
Clear Wing St 77373
Clearlight Ln 77379
Clee Ln 77379
Cleerebrook Pl 77382
Clements Square Pl 77389
Cliff Swallow Ct 77373
Clingstone Pl 77382
Clipper Hill Ct & Ln 77373
Cloud Bank Pl 77382
Cloudleap Pl 77381
Clouds Hill Ct 77379
Clover Hills Cir 77380
Clover Trace Dr 77386
S Clovergate Cir 77382
Clovermeadow 77379
Cloverwick Ln 77379
Club Ridge Ct 77382
Clubview Ct 77382
Cluny Ct 77382
Cluster Ct 77379
Coachgate Dr 77373
Coachman Ridge Pl 77382
Cobble Ln 77379
Cobble Gate Pl 77381
E, S & W Cobble Hill Cir & Pl 77381
Cobble Manor Ln 77379
Cochet Spring Dr 77379
Cochrans Crossing Dr 77381
N & S Cochrans Green Cir 77381
Codero Creek Ct 77389
Cokeberry Ct & St 77380
E & W Coldbrook Cir & Ct 77381
Coldde Meadow Ln 77379
Coldsprings Ct 77380
Colechester Ct 77373
Colewick Ct 77373
Colewood Ct 77382
Colin Springs Ln 77386
Colleville Sur Mer Ln 77388
Collingtree Dr 77389
Collins Manor Dr 77389
Colonial Forest Cir & Ln 77379
Colonial Oaks Ln 77379
Colonial Pines Ct 77389
Colonial Row Dr 77380
Colonial Springs Ln 77386
Colonialgate Dr 77373
Colony Cove Dr 77379
Colony Creek Dr 77379
Colony Haven Cir 77379
Colony Hurst Trl 77373
Colony Oaks Ct 77379
Colony Stream Dr 77379
Colony Wood Pl 77380
Colonypond Dr 77380
Colonyway Ct 77379
Colorado Springs Ct 77373
Colter Stone Dr 77388
Coltwood Dr 77388
Columbia Crest Pl 77382
Columbia Glen Ct 77389
Columbine Dr 77386
Comal Karst Dr 77386
Comal River Ct & Loop 77386
Comoro Ln 77379
Compass Cove Cir 77379
Compton Manor Dr 77379
Concho River Ct 77386
N & S Concord Forest Cir 77381
E, N & S Concord Valley Cir & Pl 77382
Conefall Ct 77373
Congressional Cir 77389
Conica Ct 77389
Conners Ace Dr 77379
Connordale Ln 77386
Cooper Springs Dr 77373
E Copper Sage Cir 77381
Coppercrest Dr 77386
N & S Copperknoll Cir 77381
Copperleaf Dr
1-99 77381
31100-31399 77386
Copperwood Park Ln 77386
Coral Bridge Ln 77388
Coral Park Dr 77386
Coralberry Ct & Rd 77381
Coralvine Ct 77380
Corbin Gate Dr 77389
Cordella Pl 77382
Corinthian Park Dr 77379
Cornerbrook Pl 77381
Coronado Springs Dr 77379
Cory Crossing Ln 77386
Cory Terrace Ct 77386
Cotillion Ct 77382
E & W Cottage Green St 77382
Cottage Grove Pl 77381
Cottage Hill Ln 77373
Cottage Mill Pl 77382
Cottage Stream Ct & Ln 77379
Cotter Dr 77373
Cotton Forest Ct 77386
Cottonshire Dr 77373
Cottonwood Walk 77388
Cottonwood Cove Ln 77380
Cottonwood Walk Ct 77388
Cougar Falls Ct 77379
Coughton Ct 77382
Country Boy Ct 77373
Country Breeze Ct 77388
Country Canyon Dr 77388
Country Dell Dr 77388
Country Forest Ct 77380
Country Green Dr 77388
Country Land Ct 77388
Country Mill Way 77388
Country Mountain Ct 77388
Country Ranch Ct 77388
Country Village Dr 77388
Country Walk Dr 77379
Countrycloud Dr 77388
Countrycrossing Dr 77388
Countryheights Ct 77388
Countryhills Ct 77388
Countrymeadow Ln 77388
Countrymeadows Dr 77388
Countryoaks Ct 77388
Countrypark Dr 77388
Countrypines Dr 77388
Countryriver Ct 77388
Countryroad Dr 77388
Countryside View Ct 77388
Countrytrails Ct 77388
Course View Ln 77389
Courseview Ct 77389
Courtland Cir 77379
Courtland Green St 77382
Courtney Pine Cir 77379
E & W Cove View Trl 77389
Cove View Trail Ct 77389
Coventry Blvd 77389
Coverdell Park 77382
Coveredgate Ct 77373
Coverlea Ct 77388
Covington Bridge Dr 77388
Cow Oak Dr 77389
Coyote Springs Ct 77373
Crabtree Ct 77382
Craggy Bark Dr 77388
Craggy Rock St 77381
Craigchester Ln 77388
Craigshire Ct 77379
Craigway Rd 77389
Crail Dr 77379
Crampton Ln 77379
Cranberry Bnd 77381
Cranberry Cir 77373
Cranberry Trl 77373
Cranebrook Dr 77382
Cranwood Dr 77379
Creek Bend Dr 77388
Creek Forest Cir & Ln 77380
Creek Park Dr 77389
Creek Ridge Dr 77373
Creek Run Dr 77388
Creek Shade Dr 77388
Creek Water Dr 77379
Creek Wood Dr 77389
Creekbridge Ct 77379
Creekfield Ct & Dr 77379
Creekland Cir 77389
Creekmore Cir 77389
Creekside Forest Dr 77389
Creekside Green Dr 77389
Creekside Timbers Dr 77389
Creekview Dr 77389
Crescenda Ct 77373
N & S Crescendo Path Pl 77381
Crescent Arbor Ln 77379
Crescent Bend Rd 77388
Crescent Clover Dr 77379
Crescent Falls Ct 77381
Crescent Fountain Rd 77388
Crescent Heights St 77388
Crescent Hollow Ct 77388
Crescent Oaks Park Ln 77386
Crescent Star Rd 77388
Crescent View Ct 77381
Crescent Wood Ln 77379
Cresent Hollow Ct 77388
E & W Cresta Bend Pl 77389
Crestbridge Ln 77388
Crested Cloud Ct 77380
Crested Jay Ln 77380
Crested Pines Ct 77381
Crested Point Pl 77382
Crested Tern Ct 77380
Creston Dr 77386
Creston Springs Ct 77379
Crestone Pl 77381
Crestwood Dr 77381
E, N & S Cricket Cir & Dr 77388
Cricket Hollow Pl 77381
Cricklewood Ln 77379
N & S Crimson Clover Cir & Ct 77381
Crimson Grove Dr 77389
Crimson Ridge Ct 77381
Crinkleroot Ct 77380
N & S Crisp Morning Cir & Ct 77382
Crisp Spring Ln 77373
Cristiwood Ct 77379
Crocus Petal St 77382
Cromdale Manor Ct 77379
Crooked Oak Way 77379
Crooked Post Rd 77373
S Cross Ln 77379
Cross Fox Ln 77380
Cross Green Ln 77373
Cross Lake Dr 77382
Cross Saddle Ct 77373
Crossbow Dr 77386
Crossbridge Dr 77373
Crosscut Pass Dr 77373
N & S Crossed Birch Pl 77381
Crossfell Rd 77388
Crossglen Ct 77373
Crossing Links Ln 77389
Crossout Ct 77373
Crossvine Cir 77380
Crownberry Ct 77381
Crowned Oak Ct 77381
Crownridge Dr 77382
Crownsedge Dr 77379
E & W Crystal Canyon Cir, Ct & Pl 77389
Crystal Cascade Ln 77379
Crystal Creek Ct 77379
Crystal Dove Dr 77388
Crystal Lake Ln 77380
Crystola Park 77373
Culico Falls Ct 77386
Cullen Ter 77380
Culverdale Pl 77382
Cumbria Dr 77379
Cupids Bower Ct 77388
Currymead Pl 77382
Cypress Bank Dr 77388
Cypress Bayou Ct 77382
Cypress Breeze Ct 77379
Cypress Chateau Dr 77388
N & S Cypress Estates Cir, Ct & Dr 77388
Cypress Hill Ct & Dr 77388
Cypress Hurst 77373
Cypress Key Dr 77388
Cypress Lake Dr 77388
Cypress Lake Pl 77382
Cypress Loch Dr 77379
Cypress Mound Ct 77379
Cypress Mountain Dr 77388
Cypress Oaks Dr 77388
N & S Cypress Pine Dr 77381
Cypress Spring Dr 77388
Cypress Square Ct & Dr 77379
Cypress Tree Ln 77388
S & W Cypress Villas Dr 77379
Cypressdale Ct & Dr 77388
Cypressgate Dr 77373
Cypresstree Dr 77373
Cypresswell Ct 77379
Cypresswick Cir & Ln 77379
Cypresswood Bnd 77373
Cypresswood Brk 77373
Cypresswood Crk 77373
Cypresswood Ct 77388
Cypresswood Cv 77373
Cypresswood Dl 77373
Cypresswood Dr
100-4399 77388
4400-9599 77379
21600-27299 77373
E Cypresswood Dr 77373
Cypresswood Fls 77373
Cypresswood Gln 77373
Cypresswood Hl 77373
Cypresswood Hvn 77373
Cypresswood Knl 77373
Cypresswood Ml 77373
Cypresswood Rdg 77373
Cypresswood Shr 77373
Cypresswood Spgs 77373
Cypresswood Sq 77373
Cypresswood Trce 77373
Cypresswood Bough 77373
Cypresswood Chase 77373
Cypresswood Estates Ln & Run 77373
Cypresswood Forest Ct 77388
Cypresswood Glen Dr 77388
Cypresswood Green Ct & Dr 77373
Cypresswood Harbor Cir 77373
Cypresswood Lake Ct & Dr 77373
Cypresswood Manor St 77379
Cypresswood Meadows Ct & Dr 77388
Cypresswood Shadows 77373
Dahlia Trail Pl 77382
Dairy Gate Dr 77373
Dakota Ridge Pl 77381
Dalea Pl 77382
Dalmally St 77379
Dalton Park Ct 77373
Dalton Trace Ct 77373
Damask Rose Way 77382
Dancing Breeze Pl 77382
Dane Hill Dr 77389
Daneswood Ct 77388
Danette Ct 77379
E Daniel Oak Cir 77389
Dapple Gray St 77382
Dappled Sun Pl 77381
Dara Springs Ln 77386
Darbey Trace Dr 77379
Darby Way 77389
Darby Ridge Ct 77379
Dark Hollow Ln 77379
Darone Ct 77386
Dartford Ct 77379
Dashwood Forest St 77381
David Memorial Dr 77385
David Vetter Blvd 77385
Dawn Creek Ln 77388
Dawn Falls Ln 77379
Dawn Lily Dr 77388
Dawn Rose Ct 77379
Dawn Wind Ln 77386
Dawngate Dr 77373
Dawnglen Ct 77379
Dawnwood Dr 77380
Day Lily Pl 77381
Day Trail Ln 77379
Dayhill Dr 77379
Daylight Rdg 77382
Daylily Hills Dr 77388
Dayln Ct 77379
De Chirico Cir 77389
De Lagos Cir 77389
Deadwood Ln 77381
Dean St 77373
Deasa Dr 77373
Deauville Dr 77388
Debray Dr 77388
December Pine Ln 77379
Deep Brook Dr 77379
Deep Pines Dr 77379
Deer Creek Ct & Dr 77379
Deer Forest Dr 77373
Deer Lake Ct 77381
Deer Plain Dr 77389
Deer Point Dr 77389
E & W Deer River Cir 77389
Deer Trail Dr 77389
Deer Valley Dr 77373
Deerbend Ct 77386
Deerberry Ct 77380
Deerfern Pl 77381
N & S Deerfoot Cir & Ct 77380
Deerhaven Dr 77388
Deerwood Park Ln 77386
Degas Park Dr 77382
Dekadine Ct 77379
Delachase Cir 77379
Delaney Knl 77389
Deleon Fields Dr 77386
Deleon Trail Dr 77379
Dellforest Ct 77381
Dellhaven Ln 77379
Delmar Green Pl 77381
Delmar Terrace Dr 77386
Delores Ln 77373
Delphinium Pl 77382
Delridge Dr 77388
Democracy Ct 77379
N & S Denham Ridge Ln 77389
Denny Rd 77389
Desert Oak Ct & Way 77379
Desert Palms Dr 77379
Desert Rose Pl 77382
Destiny Cv 77381
Devon Mill Pl 77382
Dew Fall Ct 77380
Dew Wood Ln 77373
Dewdrift Pl 77382
Dewthread Ct 77380
Dewy Meadow Run Ct 77386
Diamond Falls Ln 77389
Diamond Oak Ct 77381
Diamond Park Cir 77373
Diane Ct & Dr 77373
Diane Oaks Dr 77373
Dianeshire Ct & Dr 77388
Dibello Forest Ln 77373
Dickson Park Dr 77373
Diehlwood Pl 77388
Dimmett Way 77388
Discovery Creek Blvd 77386
Divellec Ln 77388
Dodson Trace Dr 77386
S Doe Run Dr 77380
Doerre Rd 77379
Doeskin Pl 77382
Dogwood Bloom Ct 77379
Dogwood Branch Ln 77386
Dogwood Walk Ct 77388
Domer Dr 77379
Donalbain Dr 77373
Donald Rd 77373
Dornoch Dr 77379

Dorset Sq 77381
Dorthmund 77386
E & W Double Green Cir 77382
Double Jack Ct 77373
Douglas Creek Ln 77386
Douvaine Ct 77382
S Dove Trce 77382
Dove Call Ct 77382
Dove Manor Ct 77379
S Dove Trace Cir 77382
Dove Tree Ln 77379
Dovecote 77382
Doveplumb Pl 77382
Dover Ln 77373
Dover Way 77389
Dover House Way 77389
Dover Mills Dr 77379
Dover Oaks Ln 77386
Doversgreen Ln 77388
Dovershire 77389
Dovetail Pl 77381
Doveton Ln 77388
Dovewing Pl 77382
Dovewood Ln 77373
Dovewood Pl 77381
Dovie Dr 77380
Dovington Ct 77388
Dowcrest Dr 77389
Dowdell Rd 77389
Downington Ct 77379
N & S Downy Willow Cir 77382
Doyle Sands Ct 77389
Dragon Hill Pl 77381
Dragon Spruce Pl 77382
N & S Dragonwood Pl 77381
N & S Dreamweaver Cir 77380
Dresden Pl 77382
Dresher Dr 77373
Drew Haven Ln 77379
Drewdale Ct 77382
Driftdale Pl 77389
N & S Drifting Leaf Ct 77380
Driftoak Cir 77381
Driftstone Dr 77379
Driftwood Ln 77381
Druids Glen Pl 77382
Drybrook Rd 77389
Drywood Crossing Ct 77373
Duke Lake Dr 77388
Dukedale Dr 77382
N & S Dulcet Hollow Cir & Ct 77382
Dunbar Point Ct 77379
Dundalk St 77379
Dunleith Ln 77379
Dunlin Meadow Ct & Dr 77381
Dunloggin Ln 77380
Dunston Falls Dr 77379
Dunwell Ct 77386
Dunwood Springs Ct 77381
Durango Canyon Ln 77386
Durham Knoll Ln 77389
Durham Trace Dr 77373
Dusk Valley Ct 77379
N & S Duskwood Pl 77381
Dusky Meadow Pl 77381
Dusty Glen Ln 77379
Dutch Oak Cir 77379
Dyer Park Dr 77373
Dyersville Ct 77373
Eagle Ct 77380
Eagle Ln 77379
Eagle Ter 77381
Eagle Xing 77373
Eagle Brook Ln 77379
Eagle Chase Ln 77389
Eagle Grove Ln 77379
Eagle Mead Pl 77382
Eagle Pines Ln 77389
Eagle Rise Pl 77382
Eagle Rock Cir, Ct & Pl 77381

Eaglestone Ct 77388
Eaglewood Green Ln 77379
Earlington Manor Ct & Dr 77379
Earlmist Dr 77373
Early Dawn Ct 77381
Early Frost Pl 77381
Eastgate Village Dr 77373
Eastloch Dr 77379
Eastridge Dr 77386
Eastvale Dr 77386
Eastwood Dr 77386
Eastwood Pl 77382
Easybrook Ln 77379
Ebbets Fields Dr 77389
Ebony Oaks Pl 77382
Echo St 77380
Echo Canyon Ct 77386
Echobend Ln 77379
Ed English Dr 77385
Eday Dr 77379
Eden Ct & Pnes 77379
E & W Eden Elm Cir & Pl 77381
Eden Meadows Dr 77386
Eden Valley Dr 77379
Edenbridge Ct & St 77379
Edenwalk 77379
Edenway Dr 77379
Edenwood Dr 77389
Edgecliff Pl 77382
Edgegate Dr 77373
Edgeloch Dr 77373
Edgemire Pl 77381
Edgewood Forest Ct 77381
Edgewood Place Dr 77379
Edinston Pl 77388
Edsall Dr 77388
Egan Lake Pl 77382
Egret Ct 77386
El James Dr 77388
Elaine Rose Ct 77379
Elberry Rd 77389
Electra Cir 77382
Elephant Walk St 77389
Elfen Way 77382
Elijah Hills Ln 77386
Elk Bend Dr 77379
Elk Crossing Dr 77381
Ella Blvd 77388
Ellesborough Ln 77388
Ellscott Ct & Dr 77386
Ellwood St 77380
E Elm Cres 77382
W Elm Cres 77382
Elm Ln 77389
Elm St 77373
N & S Elm Branch Ct & Pl 77380
Elm Creek Dr 77380
Elm Crossing Trl 77386
Elm Green St 77373
Elm Ridge Dr 77386
Elm Willow Ct 77382
Elmbrook Dr 77388
Elmfield Dr 77389
Elmgrove Rd 77389
Elmley Pl 77389
Elmwood Ct
200-299 77386
23500-23599 77389
Elmwood Dr 77381
Eloquence Way 77382
Elwood Hills Ct 77381
Ember Trail Ln 77386
Emerald Manor Ln 77389
Emerald Pathway Dr 77388
Emerald Pool Ln 77379
Emerald Run Ln 77379
Emerald Terrace Way 77389
Emerson Creek Dr 77386
Emerson Ridge Dr 77388
Emery Cliff Pl 77381
Emilia Ct 77379
Emma Gardens Ln 77386
Emory Trl 77388

N & S Emory Bend Pl 77381
Emory Oak Ct 77381
Empire Forest Pl 77382
Empress Crossing Ct & Dr 77379
Enchanted Dr 77381
Enchanted Ln 77388
Enchanted Grove Dr 77388
Enchanted Hollow Dr & Ln 77388
Enchanted Oaks Ct & Dr 77388
Enchanted Park Dr 77386
Enchanted River Dr 77388
Enchanted Rock Ln 77388
Enchanted Spring Dr 77388
Enchanted Stream Dr 77388
Enchanted Trail Dr 77388
Enchantedgate Dr 77373
Enchantford Ct 77388
Enchantington Cir 77388
Endor Forest Pl 77382
Energy Dr 77389
English Glade Ct 77381
English Heather Pl 77382
English Ivy Ln 77379
English Lavender Pl 77382
English Oak Dr 77373
Enns Ln 77379
Enstone Cir 77379
Epic Dr 77386
Ericson Ct 77379
Erie Cove Ct 77386
Erinwood Ct & Dr 77379
Ernst Ct 77388
Estancia Pl 77389
Esteban Point Ln 77386
Estelle Ln 77373
Estonia Ct 77379
Etchstone Dr 77389
Ethan Trails Ln 77386
Etonshire Ct 77381
Etude Ct 77382
Evan Ridge Ct 77381
Evening Oaks Ct 77379
Evening Shadows Ln 77373
Evening Song Ct 77380
Evening Trail Dr 77388
Evergreen Cir 77380
Evergreen Bend Dr 77389
Evergreen Hills Dr 77386
Evergreen Springs Ct & Ln 77379
Everleaf Dr 77379
Evian Path Ct 77382
Fair Light Ct 77382
N & S Fair Manor Cir 77382
E & W Fairbranch Cir 77382
Fairbrook Ln 77373
Fairbrook Park Ct & Ln 77379
E Fairfax Village Cir 77373
Fairfax Village West Dr 77373
Fairidge Ct 77389
Fairmeade Ct 77381
Fairmeade Bend Dr 77381
Fairtide Ct 77381
Fairview Glen Dr 77389
Fairway Cove Ct 77389
Fairway Manor Ln 77373
Fairway Meadow Ln 77379
Fairway Oaks Ct 77379
Fairway Oaks Dr 77379
Fairway Oaks Pl 77380
Fairway Trails Ln 77379
Falcon Chase Ct 77379
Falcon Trail Ct & Dr 77373
Falconwing Dr 77381
Falconwood Ln 77373
Faldo Dr 77389
Falher Dr 77386
Fallengate Ct & Dr 77373
Fallenstone Dr 77381
Fallentimber Ct 77379
Falling Spg 77373

Falling Harbor Ln 77379
Falling Leaf Ln 77380
Falling Oak Dr 77389
Falling Oak Way 77379
Falling Star Ct & Rd 77381
Falling Waters Dr 77379
Fallsbury Ct & Way 77382
Fallshire Dr 77381
Falun Ct 77386
Falvel Dr 77389
Falvel Rd 77388
Falvel Cove Dr 77388
Falvel Lake Dr 77388
Falvel Misty Dr 77388
Falvel Shadow Creek Dr 77388
Falvel Sunrise Ct 77388
Falvelsunset Ct 77388
Far Pines Dr 77373
Faraday Ct 77381
Farington Way 77382
Farm Hill Rd 77373
Farnaby Ct 77379
Farnell Ct 77379
Fawn Point Ct 77389
Fawn Ridge Forest Dr 77373
N & W Fawn River Cir & Dr 77379
Fawn View Ln 77386
Fawnchase Ct 77381
Fawnlily St 77380
Fawnmist Pl 77381
Fawnwood Dr 77389
Fawnwood Ln 77386
N & S Fazio Ct & Way 77389
Feather Branch Ct 77381
Featherfall Pl 77381
Feliciana Ln 77379
Felicity Trace Pl 77382
Fellowship Ln 77379
Fellowship Pine Cir 77379
Felton Springs Dr 77386
Fenchurch Dr 77379
Fenny Bridge Ln 77379
Fenway Park Way 77389
Ferident Dr 77389
Fern Hill Dr 77373
Fern Lacy Ct & Dr 77388
Fern Rock Falls Ct 77379
Fern Trace Ct 77386
Fern Wing Ct 77381
Fernbluff Ct & Dr 77379
Ferncroft Ct 77382
Ferngate Dr 77373
Fernglen Dr 77380
Fernhollow Ln 77388
Fernoaks Dr 77388
Fernwillow Dr 77379
Ficus Ct 77388
Fiddleleaf Ct 77381
Fiddlers Cove Pl 77381
Field Flower Ct 77380
Fields Ln 77389
Filigree Pines Pl 77382
Fillgrove Pl 77382
Finland Ct 77379
Finn Corner Way 77389
Finney Knoll Ln 77386
Fir Creek Ln 77388
Fir Forest Dr 77388
Fire Flicker Pl 77381
Fire Wheel Dr & Ln 77386
Fire Wind Ct 77379
Firebrook Ct 77389
Firefall Ct 77380
Firegate Dr 77373
Fireside Dr 77379
Firethorn Pl 77382
Firethorne Creek Ct 77389
Firewillow Pl 77381
Firewood Ln 77373
Fish Hook Ct 77386
Fisher Trace Ct 77373
Fishermans Ct 77386
Fitzwater Dr 77373

Five Ashes Dr 77379
Five Forks Dr 77379
Five Oaks Dr 77389
Five Spot Ct 77379
Flagg Ranch Ct & Dr 77388
Flagstone Path 77381
N & S Flagstone Path Cir 77381
Flaming Candle Dr 77388
Flanners Ct 77373
Flashing Ridge Dr 77389
Flat Stone St 77381
Flatcreek Pl 77381
Flaxen Manor Ct 77379
Flecherwood Ct 77388
Fledgling Path St 77382
Fleeman Cir 77389
Fleming Mdw 77389
Fleming Downe Ln 77388
Fleury Way 77382
Flewellen Falls Ln 77379
Flickering Candle Dr 77388
N & S Flickering Sun Cir & Ct 77382
Flintshire Pl 77382
Flora View Ct 77379
Floragate Dr 77373
N & S Floral Leaf Cir 77381
Floral Ridge Dr 77388
Floret Ct 77382
Florette Ln 77388
Florham Park Dr 77379
Flower Gate Dr 77373
Flower Hill Ct 77379
Flower Valley Cir 77379
Flowertuft Ct 77380
Flycaster Dr 77388
Fm 2920 Rd
5032A-5032B 77388
1800-5999 77388
6000-8999 77379
Folklore Ct 77389
Fondness Park Dr 77379
Fonthill Dr 77379
Footbridge Way 77389
Forbes Field Trce 77389
Fordingbridge Ct & Dr 77379
Forest Dr 77388
Forest Xing 77381
Forest Bend Creek Way 77379
Forest Breeze Ln 77379
Forest Canyon Ct 77379
Forest Elms Dr 77388
Forest Floor Ln 77386
Forest Glen St 77380
Forest Hurst Dr & Gln 77373
Forest Mist Dr 77379
Forest Muse 77382
Forest Park Ln 77379
Forest Path Ct 77373
Forest Perch Pl 77382
Forest Ridge Rd 77379
Forest Springs Lk 77373
Forest Steppes Ct 77382
Forest Terrace Dr 77373
Forestbrook Dr 77373
Forestburg Ct & Dr 77386
Forestcrest Dr 77389
Forestgate Dr 77373
S Forestgate Dr 77382
Forestry Dr 77386
Forge Hill Pl 77381
Fort Augusta Ct & Dr 77389
Fort Path Dr 77373
Fort Settlement Dr & Trl 77373
Fort Timbers Ct & Dr 77373
Fortuneberry Pl 77382
Fossil Trails Dr 77388
Foster Ln 77386
Foster Rd 77388
Fountainbrook Park Ct & Ln 77386
Fountaingrove Ln 77379
Fox Cyn 77386

Fox Chapel Pl 77382
Fox Crossing Cir & Ln 77379
Fox Fountain Ln 77386
Fox Hollow Blvd & Ct 77389
Fox Hunt Dr 77389
Fox Lynn Dr 77386
Fox Mill Ln 77389
Fox Mountain Dr 77386
Fox Pitt Rd 77386
Fox Ravine Dr 77386
Fox River Dr & Ln 77386
Fox Run Blvd 77386
Fox Run St 77389
Fox View Cir 77386
Fox Water Dr 77386
Foxbriar Ln 77373
E & W Foxbriar Forest Cir 77382
Foxingham Cir 77386
Foxland Ct 77379
Foxtail Pl 77380
Foxview Dr 77386
Fraiser Fir Pl 77389
Frampton Ct 77379
Francisco Ct 77386
Franklin Park Ct 77379
Fraser Point Ct 77379
Frassati Way 77389
Freestone Pl 77382
Freestone Stream Pl 77389
Freida Ln 77379
N & S Fremont Ridge Loop 77389
E, N, S & W French Oaks Cir 77382
Fresh Pond Pl 77382
Freshwater Bay Ct 77379
Friar Cir 77379
Friar Lake Ln 77373
Friars Court Ln 77379
Friars Legends Dr 77386
Friesian Estates Dr 77379
Frio River Loop 77386
Fritz Ln 77389
Frontenac Way 77382
E, N & W Frontera Cir 77382
N & S Frosted Pond Dr & Pl 77381
Frostwood Ln 77386
Fuller Bluff Dr 77386
Fulshear Ct 77382
Fulton Point Dr 77379
Fury Ranch Pl 77389
Gable Meadows Ln 77379
Gabled Pines Pl 77382
Gaddis Oaks Dr 77389
Gage Spring Ct 77373
Gallant Oak Pl 77381
Gallery Cove Ct 77382
Galleta Ct 77389
Galley Mist Dr 77388
Galston Ln 77379
Galway Pl 77382
Gambrel Oak Pl 77380
Gamewood Ct & Dr 77386
Gannet Hollow Pl 77381
Garden Brook Ln 77379
Garden Creek Dr 77379
Garden Lodge Pl 77382
Garden Wind Ct 77379
Gardenia Trace Dr 77386
Gardenspring Brook Ln 77379
Garland Grove Pl 77381
N & S Garnet Bnd 77382
Garnet Bend Ct 77382
Garrison Run Dr 77386
Garrison Trail Ln 77386
Gary Ln 77380
N & S Gary Glen Cir 77382
E & W Gaslight Pl 77382
Gate Canyon Ct 77373
Gate Hill Dr 77381
Gateshead Pl 77382
Gateway Park Pl 77380
Gatlin Ln 77386

Gauntlet Dr 77382
Gavin Ct 77379
Gaylin Hills Ct 77386
Geffert Wright Rd 77386
Genesis Cove Ct 77379
Genesse Valley Dr 77389
Geneva Dr 77386
Geneva Hills Ln 77386
Geneva Springs Ln 77386
Gentle Haze Ct 77382
Gentlewind Pl 77381
Gentry St 77373
Gentry Oak Ct 77381
George Wayne Way 77379
Georgia Pine Dr 77373
Georgian Row 77380
Gilcrest Forest Ct 77381
Gilded Crest Ct 77382
Gilded Pond Pl 77381
Gilford Crest Dr 77379
Gillium Bluff Pl 77382
Gilmore Grove Pl 77382
Giltspur Way 77389
Ginger Dr 77389
Ginger Bay Pl 77382
Ginger Creek Ln 77386
Ginger Jar St 77382
Ginger Trace Dr 77386
Gingerwilde Pl 77381
Ginny Cove Ct 77386
Giverny Ct 77379
Glade Bank Pl 77382
Glade Canyon Dr 77388
Gleannloch Estates Dr 77379
Gleannloch Farm Rd 77379
Glen Canyon Pl 77381
Glen Erin Dr 77382
Glen Lake Dr 77388
Glen Lief Ct 77379
Glen Loch Dr
23800-26499 77380
26500-27799 77381
Glen May Park Ct & Dr 77379
Glenboro Dr 77386
Glenbranch Dr 77388
Glendower Dr 77373
Glenfair Ct 77379
Glenfinch Ln 77379
Glengate Dr 77373
Glenhill Dr 77389
Glenleigh Pl 77381
Glenmere Ln 77379
Glenmore Meadow Dr 77386
Glenn Elm Dr 77379
Glenn Haven Estates Cir & Dr 77379
Glenn Leigh Dr 77379
Glensheen Way 77382
Glentrace Cir 77382
N & S Glenwild Cir 77389
Glenwood Ridge Dr 77386
Glistening Pond Pl 77382
Glory Garden Way 77389
Glorybower Ct 77380
Glowing Star Pl 77382
Godstone Ln 77379
Goedecke Rd 77373
Gold Candle Dr 77388
Gold Crest Ct 77389
Golden Pl 77381
Golden Rd 77380
E, N, S & W Golden Arrow Cir 77381
Golden Bell Dr 77389
Golden Dove Dr 77388
Golden Grove Dr & Ln 77373
Golden Hollow Ct 77373
Golden Oak Chase Ct 77386
Golden Scroll Cir 77382
Golden Shadow Cir 77381
Golden Sunset Cir 77381
Golden Thrush Pl 77381
Golden Vines Ln 77386
Goldengrove Dr 77379
Goldensong Ct 77373

N & S Goldenvine Cir & Ct 77382
Goldking Cross Ct 77373
Goldspring Ln 77373
Goldthread Ct 77381
Goldwood Pl 77382
Good Dale Ln 77373
Goodfellow Dr 77373
Goodfield Ct 77379
Gore Grass Ct 77379
Gosling Rd
4700-4799 77381
7400-7599 77382
8600-9098 77381
9100-10599 77381
10601-10999 77381
10800-10998 77381
10800-10800 77393
22000-26199 77389
23626-1-23626-2 77389
23710-1-23710-2 77389
24309-1-24309-2 77389
24313-1-24313-2 77389
24331-1-24331-2 77389
24407-1-24407-7 77389
25011-2-25011-3 77389
25110-1-25110-1 77389
25126-1-25126-2 77389
Gosling Cedar Pl 77388
Goss Spring Ct 77373
Grable Cove Ln 77379
Graceful Elm Ct 77381
Graceful Path Way 77386
Graff Net Ct 77379
Gramond Hall Ct & Dr 77379
Granby Ter 77373
Grand Bayou Pl 77382
Grand Colonial Dr 77382
Grand Fairway 77381
Grand Garden Ct 77381
Grand Lakeview Dr 77388
Grand Rapids Ln 77373
W Grand Regency Cir 77382
Grand Vista Pl 77380
Grandview Park Dr 77379
Granite Gorge Dr 77379
Granite Path Pl 77389
Granum Dr 77386
Grape Arbor Ct 77382
Grassy Hill Ln 77388
Graven Hill Dr 77379
Gray Oak Pl 77380
Grayfeather Ct 77388
Graylin Woods Pl 77382
Graymont Hls 77379
Great Laurel Ct 77381
Great Owl Ct 77389
Green Blade Ln 77380
Green Bough Ct 77380
Green Bower Ln 77380
Green Candle Dr 77388
Green Elm Ln 77379
Green Estate Ct 77373
Green Fern Ct 77388
Green Field Pl 77380
Green Gable Mnr 77389
E Green Gables Cir & Ct 77382
Green Haven Dr
1-99 77381
25800-25999 77380
Green Hollow Ln
7800-7899 77389
8600-8899 77379
Green Jade Dr 77386
Green Jute Ledge Dr 77386
Green Lodge Cir 77373
Green Mill Ct 77386
E & W Green Pastures Cir 77382
Green Slope Pl 77381
Green Square Ct 77373
Green Thicket Ct 77388
N & S Greenbud Ct 77380
Greencreek Meadows Ln 77379
N Greenfield Dr 77379
Greenfield Rd 77373
Greenforest Dr 77388
Greengate Dr
21200-21999 77388
22100-22299 77389
Greenglade Ct 77381
Greenglade Ln 77386
Greenham Ct & Dr 77388
Greenheath Ct 77389
E & W Greenhill Terrace Pl 77382
Greeningdon St 77381
Greenlake Dr 77388
Greenland Oak Ct 77373
Greenleaf Dr 77389
Greenlet Ct 77373
Greenridge Forest Ct & Dr 77381
Greenridge Manor Ln 77389
Greenside Pl 77381
Greentwig Pl 77381
N & W Greenvine Cir & Ct 77382
Greenway Manor Ln 77373
Gresak St 77380
Grey Birch Pl 77381
Grey Finch Ct 77381
Greycrest Pl 77382
E, W & S Greywing Cir, Ct & Pl 77382
Griffin Hill Ct 77382
Grogans Mill Rd 77380
Grogans Park Dr 77380
Grogans Point Ct & Rd 77380
Ground Brier Ct 77381
Grove Creek Dr 77379
Grove Mesa Trl 77379
Groveleigh Park Ct 77386
Grovetrail Ln 77379
Guinstead Dr 77379
Gull Rock Pl 77389
Gumspring Ln 77373
Gun Oak Pl 77380
Gunters Ridge Dr 77379
Gunther Ct 77379
Gwenfair Dr 77373
Hackberry Ct 77388
Hackinson Dr 77386
Haderia Ct 77379
Hadley Springs Ln 77386
Hadlock Pl 77389
Hales Hunt Ct 77388
Haley Ln 77386
Halfmoon Ct 77380
Halkin Ct 77379
Halkirk St 77379
Hallbrook Way 77389
Hallimore Dr 77386
Hallmark Oak St 77386
Halstead Dr 77386
Hamilton Bend Ln 77386
Hamilton Falls Ln 77379
Hamlet Park Ct 77373
Hammock Dunes Pl 77389
Hampton Ct 77389
Hampton Ldg 77381
Hampton Park 77379
Hampton Pl 77381
Hampton Dale St 77379
Hampton Forest Ln 77389
Hampton Oak Ct & Dr 77379
Hampton Oaks Dr 77389
Hampton Pines Ln 77389
Hampton Way Ct 77389
Hanna Rd 77386
Hannock Glen Ln 77373
Hannover Frst & Way 77388
Hannover Estates Dr 77388
Hannover Pines Dr 77388
Hannover Ridge Dr 77388
Hannover Valley Ct 77388
Hannover Village Ct & Dr 77388
Hannover Way Ct 77388
Hanover Hollow Ln 77386
Hans Ct 77386
Hansom Trail St 77382
Hansons Ct 77386
Harbinger Ct 77382
Harbor Cove Dr 77381
Harbor Springs Ln 77379
Harburly Ct 77379
Hardsville Dr 77388
E & W Hardy Rd 77373
Hardy Elm St 77379
Hardy Toll Rd 77373
Harmon Crest Ct 77373
Harmony Arbor Ct 77382
Harmony Hill Ct & Dr 77379
Harmony Links Pl 77382
Harness Path Ct 77373
Harnwell Crossing Dr 77379
Harper Ln 77380
Harpergate Dr 77373
Harpost Mnr 77379
Harpstone Pl 77382
Harrison Lakes Cir 77379
Harrow Ln 77379
Harrowby Dr 77373
Hartfield Ln 77388
Harvest Green Pl 77382
Harvest Grove Ct 77388
Harvest Oak Landing Dr 77386
Harvest Terrace Ct & Ln 77379
Harvest Wind Pl 77382
Harwick Dr 77379
Hassler Rd 77389
Hasting Oak Ct 77381
Hatchmere Pl 77379
Hatchmere Place Ct 77379
Haude Rd 77388
Haughton Ct & Dr 77389
Hausworth Ct 77373
Havelock Dr 77386
Havenhouse Dr 77386
N & S Havenridge Dr 77381
Haverford Rd 77389
Havergate Dr 77389
Havering Ln 77379
Haverstrom Ln 77388
Hawk Haven Ln 77379
Hawksbill Pl 77382
Hawkseye Pl 77381
Hawkwood Dr 77373
Hawley Creek Dr 77386
Hawn Rd 77389
E & W Hawthorne Dr 77386
Hawthorne Blossom Dr 77389
Hawthorne Creek Dr 77379
Haydee Rd 77388
Hayden Ct 77386
Haylie Hollow Ct 77386
Hazelcrest Cir & Dr 77382
Hazy Forest Ln 77386
Hazy Landing Ct 77386
Hazy Mills Ln 77386
Hazy Stone Ct 77373
Hazycrest Dr 77379
N Head Dr 77386
Hearthstone Ct 77386
Hearthstone Hill Ln 77373
Heartleaf Ct 77381
Heartridge Ct 77382
Heath Hollow Dr 77379
Heath Meadow Ct 77373
Heathcote Ct 77380
Heather Bank Pl 77382
Heather Springs Dr 77379
Heather Wisp Ct & Pl 77381
Heatherknoll Dr 77373
Heatherland Dr 77379
Heatherwood Dr 77386
Heathrow Ln 77379
Heathstone Pl 77381
Heathwood Brook Ln 77379
Heaven Tree Pl 77382
Heddon Oaks Ct 77379
Heden Rd 77379
Hedgebell Ct 77380
Hedgedale Way 77389
Hedgerow Dr 77379
Hedgeton Ct 77389
Hedgewick Ct 77388
Heiden Cir 77379
Helen Dr 77386
Helenium Ln 77386
Hemingstone Ln 77388
Henderson Rd 77373
Hendricks Lakes Dr 77388
Hennessy Ln 77389
Hennington Dr 77388
Hepplewhite Way 77382
Herald Oak Ct 77381
N Heritage Hill Cir 77381
Heritage Maple Dr 77389
Hermit Thrush Pl 77382
Heron Hollow Ct 77382
Herons Flight Pl 77389
Hertfordshire Cir & Dr 77379
Herts Rd 77379
Hexham Ct & Dr 77379
Hickory Hill Rd 77380
Hickory Hollow Ln 77386
Hickory Hollow Pl 77381
Hickory Hollow Rd 77380
Hickory Oak Dr
1-99 77381
4200-4299 77389
Hickory Ridge Dr 77381
Hickory Terrace Dr 77386
Hickory Twig Way 77388
Hickory Valley Ln 77373
Hickorybark Dr 77381
Hickorycrest Dr 77389
Hickorygate Dr 77373
Hidden Deer Corner Ct 77381
Hidden Forest Cir & Dr 77379
Hidden Grove Landing Dr 77386
Hidden Maple Dr 77373
Hidden Meadow Dr 77382
Hidden Pond Pl 77381
Hidden Spring Falls Dr 77386
Hidden Spring Vale Dr 77386
Hidden Trail Ct & Ln 77379
N & S Hidden View Cir & Pl 77381
Hidden Winds Dr 77386
Hiddenbay Ct & Way 77379
Hideaway Ct E 77389
Hideaway Ct W 77389
Hideaway Ln 77388
Hideaway Lake Cir & Ct 77389
Hideaway Run Dr & Way 77389
High Creek Dr 77379
N High Oaks Cir 77380
High Park Cir 77373
High Point Pines Dr 77373
High Thicket Ct 77373
High Timbers Dr 77380
Highbush Ct 77381
Highclere Park Dr 77379
Highfield Ridge Ln 77373
N & S Highland Cir & Ct 77381
Highland Bluff Ln 77373
Highland Green Pl 77381
Highland Point Ct & Ln 77373
Highland Sage Ln 77373
Highlandgate Dr 77373
Highpointe Grn 77379
Highway 75 N 77389
Highworth Dr 77379
Hildebrandt Rd 77389
Hildene Way 77382
Hill Creek Rd 77373
Hill Haven Ct 77379
Hill View Ln 77379
Hilldale Park Ct & Ln 77386
Hillmeadow Dr 77388
Hillock Woods 77380
Hillside Ct & Dr 77386
Hillside Meadow Dr 77389
Hillside View Pl 77381
Hillswind Cir 77379
Hilltop Dr 77386
Hillway Dr 77373
Hirschfield Rd 77373
History Row 77380
Hithervale Ct 77382
Hoads Deuce Ct 77379
Hobart St 77389
Hogan Bridge Ct & Dr 77389
Holden Mills Dr 77389
Holleygate Ct 77373
Hollow Sage Ln 77386
Hollow Springs Ln 77386
Holly Walk 77388
Holly Creek Ct 77381
Holly Crest Dr 77386
Holly Hill Ct & Dr 77381
Holly Lake Ln 77373
Holly Shade Ct 77379
Holly Springs Pl 77373
Holly Tree Ln 77373
Holly Walk Ln 77388
Holly Walk Lane Ct 77388
Hollybush Ln 77373
N & S Hollylaurel Cir & Dr 77382
Hollyleaf Dr 77379
Hollymead Dr 77381
Holyoke Ln 77373
Holzwarth Rd
19601-19601 77388
19699-21599 77388
22800-23699 77389
Homed Lark Pl 77389
E & W Honey Grove Pl 77382
Honey Locust Hill Dr 77388
Honeybear Ln 77373
Honeycrest Ln 77389
Honeyfield Ln 77379
Honeysuckle Walk 77386
Honor Oaks Ct 77382
Hoover 77379
Hope Valley Pl 77382
Hopeton Dr 77386
Hopvine Ct 77381
Horierad Dr 77373
N, S, E & W Horizon Ridge Ct & Pl 77381
N & S Hornbeam Pl 77380
Hornbill Ct 77380
Hornerne Dr 77386
Hornsilver Pl 77381
Horse Cave Cir 77379
Horseshoe Run Dr 77373
Howell Creek Pl 77382
Howes Dr 77386
Hoyte Park Ln 77379
Huckelton Ln 77388
Huckinston Ct 77379
Huckleberry Branch Ct 77388
Huddersfield Ct 77379
Hughes Landing Blvd 77380
Huisache Branch Ct 77388
E & W Hullwood Cir & Ct 77389
Hunnewell Ct & Way 77382
Huntbrook Dr 77379
Hunter Creek Ct & Dr 77386
Hunter Spring Cir 77373
Hunters Crossing Cir, Ct & Dr 77381
Hunters Hollow Dr 77380
Hunting Path Pl 77381
Huntley Manor Dr 77386
Huntsmans Horn Cir 77380
Hurlock St 77380
Huron St 77389
Hurst Park Dr 77379
Hyland Greens Ln 77373
Iberian Ct 77379
Iceland Ct 77379
Ikes Pond Dr 77389
Ikes Tree Dr 77389
Imperial Bluff Ct 77386
Imperial Ivy Ct 77373
Imperial Leaf Ln 77379
Imperial Legends Dr 77386
Imperial Oaks Blvd 77386
N & S Imperial Path Ln 77386
Imperial Ridge Ln 77379
Imperial Walk Ct & Ln 77386
Indian Brook Ct 77373
Indian Cedar Ln 77380
Indian Clearing Trl 77386
Indian Clover Dr 77381
Indian Forest Dr 77373
Indian Hill Rd 77389
E Indian Sage Cir 77381
Indian Springs Way 77373
Indian Summer Pl 77381
N & S Indigo Cir 77381
Indigo Bunting Pl 77389
Indigo Park Dr 77386
Indigo Ruth Dr 77379
Ingleside Ct 77388
Innerwoods Pl 77382
Inspire Crest Ln 77386
Interfaith Way 77381
Interstate 45
18500-23998 77373
Interstate 45
18701-21999 77388
22001-23999 77389
24000-26998 77386
24001-28099 77380
28101-28599 77380
28601-29999 77381
17001-19677 77385
18200-18598 77384
Invermere Dr 77386
Inway Dr 77389
Inway Trail Dr 77389
Iris Bloom Ct 77386
Irish Ivy Ct 77386
Irish Moss Pl 77381
Ironcrest Ln 77388
Ironharp Dr 77379
Ironside Rd 77373
Island Spring Ct 77373
Islandbreeze Dr 77379
W Isle Pl 77381
Islewood Blvd 77380
Ivory St 77389
Ivory Forest Ln 77386
N & S Ivory Mall Cir 77382
Ivory Moon Pl 77381
Ivy Castle Ct 77382
Ivy Garden St 77382
Ivy Pond Pl 77381
Ivycroft Ln 77373
Ivygate Dr 77373
Jacobs Path Ln 77386
Jadecrest Ct, Dr & Rdg 77389
Jadestone Ct 77381
Jadestone Ln 77388
Jadewing Ct 77381
E & W Jagged Ridge Cir 77389
Jake Springs Ct 77386
James Rd 77373
James C Leo Dr 77373
Jan Glen Ln 77379
Jander Dr 77386
Jara Ct 77388
Jasmine Place St 77379
Jasmine Terrace Dr 77373
Jason Ct 77386
Jasper Stone Ct 77373
Jaspers Pl 77389
Jay Dr 77373
Jaya Loch Ct 77379
Jayden Ct 77386
Jean St 77373
Jenkins Rd 77373
Jennifer Heights Ct 77389
Jenny Lake Dr 77379
Jenny Wren Ct 77382
Jeremy Ct 77386
Jerson Rd 77379
Jessica Hills Ln 77386
Jessica Rose Ln 77379
Jester Oaks Pl 77381
Jetty Point Dr 77380
Jewel Point Dr 77386
Jewelsford Ct & Dr 77382
Jill Cir 77388
Jillian Oaks Ct & Ln 77386
Jillian Way Ct 77389
Jimbo Ln 77389
Joan Leigh Cir 77388
Joanleigh Dr 77388
Joey Cir 77373
John Bank Dr 77379
John Cooper Dr 77381
Johnathan Landing Ct 77389
Jonsport Ln 77389
Joshua Lee Ln 77386
Journal Leaf Pl 77382
Journeys End 77381
Jules Ct 77386
Julia Park Dr 77386
Julian Woods Pl 77382
Julienne Trce 77381
July Sky Ct 77386
June Breeze Pl 77382
Juniper Ln 77389
Juniper Grove Pl 77382
Juniper Meadows Dr 77388
Juniper Skies Ln 77379
Jupiter Landing Ct 77386
Kailees Ct 77386
Kalebs Pond Ct 77389
Kalithea Ct 77388
Kallie Hills Ln 77386
Kardy St 77388
Karpathos Ln 77388
Karsten Creek Ct & Way 77389
Karu Dr 77373
Kasey Springs Ln 77386
Kasos Isle Ct & Dr 77388
Kathy Cir 77389
Katie Grace Cir 77379
Katie Mill Trl 77379
Katlyn Ln 77386
Katner Ln 77386
Kayak Ridge Dr 77389
Kearny Brook Pl 77381
Keegan Hollow Ln 77386
Keelrock Pl 77382
Keith St 77373
Kelly St 77373
Kelly Kay Ct 77388
Kelly Spring Cir 77379
Kellydale Ct 77388
Kelona Dr 77386
Kelsey Springs Ct 77379
Kemp Crest Ct 77379
Kempton Park Dr 77379
Kendrick Pines Blvd 77389
Kenmare Ct 77382
Kenna Ct 77386
Kenna Cove Ln 77379
Kennedale Ln 77379
Kennerly Nanor Dr 77386
Kennet Valley Rd 77379
Kennington Way 77389
Kennoway Park Dr 77379
Kensington Park Cir & Dr 77386
Kent Hollow Ct 77386
Kent Springs Ct 77386
Kentwood Dr 77380
Kenwood Park Ln 77386
Kepler Mcvey Ct 77389
Kerloch Pt 77379
Kerouac Ct 77382
Kerri Leigh Ct 77388
Kerrigan Ct 77379

Kershope Forest Ct 77379
Ketan Loch Ct 77379
Ketelby Reach Dr 77386
Kettle Creek Dr 77379
Kevington Ct 77386
Key Hollow Way 77388
Keygate Dr 77388
Keystone Bend Ct 77386
Kielder Pointe Dr 77379
Kilborne Park Ln 77379
Kilbride Way Ct 77379
Kilrenny Ct & Dr 77379
Kim Dr 77373
Kimberly Glen Ln 77373
Kimberwicke Ct 77373
Kimstone Ln 77379
King Arthur Ct 77379
King Pine Ct 77382
King Point View Ln 77388
Kingbriar Cir, Ct & Dr 77373
Kingcup Ct 77382
Kingmont Knoll Ct 77373
Kings Cove Ln 77386
Kingsbury Park Ln 77386
Kingscote Way 77382
E & W Kingscrest Cir & Ln 77389
Kingsdown Dr 77389
Kingston Terrace Ln 77379
Kingston Village Dr 77386
Kingsway Park Ln 77386
Kinmont Ct 77379
Kino Ct 77380
Kirkchapel Ct & St 77379
Kirkleigh St 77379
Kirkstone Dr 77379
Kirkstone Manor Dr 77379
Kirkstone Terrace Ct & Dr 77379
Kirkwell Manor Ct 77379
Kirston Dr 77389
Kittatinny Pl 77389
Kittiwake Ct 77380
Klee Cir 77379
Klein Cemetary Rd 77379
Klein Church Rd 77379
Klein Oak Ln 77389
Kleingreen Ln 77379
Kleinwood Dr 77379
Knightrider Dr 77379
Knights Crossing Dr 77382
N & S Knightsgate Cir 77382
Knob Pines Ct 77389
Knoll Pines Ct 77381
Knollbridge Ln 77379
Knollbrook Ln 77373
Knollview Dr 77389
Knollwood Trl 77373
Knotty Post Ln 77373
Knotwood Ct 77389
Knotwood Pl 77382
Knurled Oak Ln 77379
Koback Corners St 77373
Kobi Park Ct 77373
Kodes Clay Ct 77379
Kodiac St 77389
Korbel Ct 77382
Kotar Ct 77388
Krahn Rd 77388
Krayola Ln 77379
Kreinhop Rd 77388
Kristen Ct 77373
Kudzu Dr 77386
Kuykendahl Rd
6700-10599 77382
10600-10898 77381
10601-10899 77389
17200-22399 77379
22400-22999 77389
19830-1-19830-2 77379
22912-1-22912-2 77389
Kyle Chase Ct 77373
Kylie Ct 77386
Kyren Ln 77389
La Arbre Ln 77388
La Cote Cir 77388
La Fleur Ln 77388
La Mer Ln 77388
La Seine Ln 77388
Lace Pt 77382
N & S Lace Arbor Dr 77382
Lacewing Pl 77380
E & W Lacey Oak Cir 77380
Lacoste Love Ct 77379
Lacreek Ln 77379
Lafone Dr 77379
Lagato Pl 77382
Lagos Azul Ct 77389
Lagos Lagoon Way 77389
Lain Rd 77379
Lajuana Ct & Ln 77388
Lake Cove Point Ln 77379
E, N & S Lake Falls Cir & Ln 77386
Lake Front Cir 77380
Lake Kent Ln 77389
Lake Lawn Dr 77380
Lake Leaf Pl 77381
Lake Oaks Dr 77388
Lake Paloma Trl 77389
Lake Ridge Bnd 77380
Lake Robbins Dr 77380
Lake Springs Way 77373
Lake Sterling Gate Dr 77379
Lake Terrace Ct 77380
Lake Voyageur Dr 77389
Lake Woodlands Dr
1100-2299 77380
6601-6697 77382
6699-6999 77382
E & W Lakemist Cir 77381
N & S Lakemist Harbour Pl 77381
E & N Lakeridge Cir, Ct & Dr 77381
Lakeside Blvd 77381
Lakeside Cv 77380
Lakeside Grn 77382
Lakeside View Dr 77388
Laketree Ln 77373
Lakeview Bend Ln 77386
Lakeway Dr 77373
Lakota Trl 77388
Lamaster Ln 77373
Lambourne Cir 77379
N & S Lamerie Way 77382
Lamps Glow Pl 77382
Lampwick Cir 77388
Lamson Ct 77373
Lancaster Pine Dr 77389
E & W Lance Leaf Rd 77381
Lancepine Pl 77382
Lancewood Dr 77373
Landau Park Ct & Ln 77379
Landing Way Ct & Dr 77373
Landon Springs Ln 77373
Landrum Point Ln 77388
Landry Blvd 77379
Landsdowne Pointe Ct & Dr 77379
Lane Ln 77386
Lanesend Pl 77382
Laneside Dr 77379
Langham Ct 77381
Langley Rd 77389
Langstone Pl 77389
E Lansdowne Cir 77382
Lantana Trl 77382
Lantern Hollow Pl 77381
Lapeer Ct 77379
Lapis River Dr 77379
Lapwing Ct 77381
Laremont Bend Dr 77386
Largo Woods Pl 77382
Largs Cir & Dr 77379
Larkmount Dr 77389
Larkridge Ln 77379
Larks Aire Pl 77381
Larksberry Pl 77382
Larksong Ln 77388
Larkspur Trl 77382
E & W Lasting Spring Cir 77389
Lattice Gate St 77382
Latticeleaf Pl 77382
Latvia Ct 77379
Laughing Brook Ct 77380
Laura Hills Ln 77386
Laurel Cherry Way 77380
Laurel Green St 77373
Laurel Hollow Dr 77388
Laurel Maple Ct 77379
Laurel Oak Pl 77380
Laureldale Park Ln 77386
W Laurelhurst Cir 77382
Lauren Cove Ln 77386
Lauren Creek Ln 77386
Laurens Lndg 77386
Lauri Lynn Dr 77386
Lavender Candle Dr 77388
Lavender Haze Ct & Pl 77381
Lavender Trace Dr 77386
Laver Love Dr 77379
Laverock Rd 77388
Lawson Knoll Dr 77389
Laxey Glen Dr 77379
Layton Meadows Ln 77379
Lazy Ln
1-99 77380
7600-8499 77389
29400-30198 77386
30200-30299 77386
Lazy Hill Ln 77379
N & S Lazy Meadow Way 77386
Lazy Morning Pl 77381
Lazy Moss Ln 77379
Lazy Springs Ln 77373
Lazy Trail Path Ct 77373
Lea Oak Ct 77381
Leaf Meadows Ct 77386
Leaf Spring Pl 77382
Leaf Trace Ct 77381
Leaf Vines Dr & Ln 77386
Leafbrook Ct & Ln 77379
Leaflet Ln 77388
Leafsage Ct 77381
Leafstalk Ct 77382
Leafstone Ln 77373
Leafygate Dr 77373
Leafywood Dr 77386
Leah Manor Ln 77386
Leanne Trail Ln 77386
Leathergate Dr 77373
Leblanc Landing Dr 77389
Ledbury Park Ln 77379
Ledgestone Pl 77382
Lee Rd 77379
Leedscastle Mnr 77379
Leedscastle Manor Ct 77379
Leemyers Ln 77388
Leestead Ct 77388
Leeward Cove Dr 77381
Legacy Pines Dr 77386
E & W Legacy Point Cir 77382
Legato Way 77382
Legend Hollow Ct 77382
Legend Mill Ct 77382
Legends Beam Dr 77386
E, N & S Legends Bend Dr & Ln 77386
Legends Bluff Dr 77386
Legends Branch Ln 77386
N & S Legends Chase Cir & Ct 77386
N & S Legends Creek Ct & Dr 77386
Legends Crest Dr 77386
Legends Garden Dr 77386
Legends Gate Dr 77386
Legends Glen Dr 77386
Legends Green Dr 77386
Legends Hill Ct & Dr 77386
Legends Knoll Dr 77386
Legends Landing Dr 77386
Legends Line Dr 77386
Legends Meade Dr 77386
Legends Mill Dr 77386
Legends Mist Dr 77386
Legends Pass Ct & Ln 77386
Legends Peak Dr 77386
Legends Pine Ln 77386
Legends Place Dr 77386
Legends Ranch Ct & Dr 77386
Legends Ridge Dr 77386
Legends Shadow Dr 77386
Legends Shore Dr 77386
Legends Smith Ln 77386
Legends Stone Dr 77386
Legends Trace Dr 77386
E & W Legends Trail Ct & Dr 77386
Legends Valley Dr & Ln 77386
N & S Legends Village Cir, Ct & Ln 77386
Legends Wick Dr 77386
Legends Wild Dr 77386
Legends Willow Dr 77386
Legends Worth Dr 77386
Legends York Dr 77386
Lehigh Springs Dr 77381
Leichester Dr 77386
Leigh Creek Dr 77388
Leisure Ln 77380
Leithcrest Way 77379
Lemm Ct 77373
Lemm Road 1 77373
Lemm Road 2 77373
Lemmingham Dr 77388
Lemmon Arbor Dr 77389
Lemon Grove Dr 77373
Lena Trail Dr 77388
Lenora Springs Dr 77386
Lenox Hill Ct & Dr 77382
Lenox Knoll Dr 77389
Lenze Rd 77389
Leon River Ct 77386
Lesa Ln 77373
Lestergate Dr 77373
Letchfield Hollow Dr 77379
Letham Way St 77373
Level Oak Pl 77380
Leverwood Ct 77381
Levi Rd 77389
Lewisham Ln 77379
Lexanne Ct 77388
Lexington Blvd & Rd 77373
Lexington Park Dr 77373
Lexington Woods Dr 77373
Liberty Branch Blvd 77389
Liberty Elm Ct 77379
Liberty Springs Way 77373
E & W Liberty Square Pl 77389
Libretto Ct 77382
Lichen Ln 77379
Lieren Ct & Ln 77373
Lietner Way Dr 77388
Light Bluff Ct 77373
Lightwood Trce 77382
Ligustrum Flower Dr 77388
Lilac Meadows Ln 77379
Lilacbrook Ct 77379
Lilium Ct 77380
Lillian Spgs 77373
Lillington Manor Ct 77379
Lily Hollow Ct 77379
Lily Trace Ct 77386
Lincolns Meadow Dr 77373
Lindale Manor Ct 77379
Lindell Rd 77373
Linden Ct 77379
Linden Manor Ct 77373
Linden Park Ln 77386
Linden Springs Ct 77386
Lindenberry Cir 77389
Linder Green Dr 77386
Lindonwood Ct 77379
Lindsey Terrace Ln 77386
Links Crossing Ln 77389
Linksgate Pl 77380
Linnet Chase Pl 77381
Linseed Dr 77388
Linshire Dr 77388
Linton Downs Pl 77382
N & S Linton Ridge Cir & Ct 77382
Litchfield Ln 77379
Little Forest Ct 77373
Little Fox Crst 77386
Little Mill Pl 77382
E & W Little Oak Ct 77386
Little River Ct 77386
Little Spring Cir 77373
Little Wind Ln 77373
Little Wing Dr 77388
Littlecroft Dr 77386
Live Oak Ln 77389
Live Oak Pl 77379
Lively Oaks Pl 77382
Liza Ct 77386
Llano River Ln & Loop 77386
Lobelia Manor Ct & Dr 77379
Loblolly Ln 77380
Loblolly Vista Dr 77389
Lobo Ln 77379
Loch Ln 77389
Loch Dane Dr 77379
Lochbury Ct & Dr 77379
Lochflora Dr 77379
Lochlea Ridge Dr 77379
Lockeridge Bend Dr 77386
Lockeridge Cove Dr 77386
Lockeridge Creek Dr 77386
Lockeridge Farms Dr 77386
Lockeridge Oaks Dr 77386
Lockeridge Pines Dr 77386
Lockeridge Place Dr 77386
Lockeridge Springs Dr 77386
Lockeridge View Dr 77386
Lockeridge Village Dr 77386
Lockgate Dr 77388
Lockridge Dr 77373
Lockshire Ridge Ct 77373
Loddington St 77386
Loetsch Ridge Way 77379
E & W Loftwood Cir 77382
Lofty Ln 77379
Lofty Falls Ct 77386
Log Tram Ct 77382
Logan Park Dr 77379
Loggers Chase Ct 77386
Loggers Luck Pl 77380
N & S Logrun Cir 77380
Logston Ln 77389
Loma Ct & Ln 77386
London Town Dr & Pl 77389
London Way Dr 77389
Lone Elm Dr 77373
Lone Fir Dr 77379
Lone Wolf Trl 77373
Lonesome Pine Rd 77389
Long Castle Dr 77388
Long Cypress Dr 77388
Long Hearth Pl 77382
Long Hill Ln 77373
Long Iron Ct 77389
Long Lake Pl 77381
Long Pine Dr 77389
Long Shadow Ln 77388
Long Shadows Cir 77388
Long Shadows St 77380
Long Ship Ct 77379
Long Springs Pl 77382
Long Trail Path Ct 77373
Longcroft Dr 77379
N & S Longsford Cir 77382
N & S Longspur Dr 77380
Longstone Rd 77389
Longstraw Pl 77380
Loone Ct 77386
Lora Meadows Ct 77386
Lorikeet St 77373
Loring Ln 77388
Losoya Ct 77388
Lost Brook Ln 77373
Lost Cove Ln 77373
Lost Hill Ct 77386
Lost Lake Ln 77388
Lost Mine Trl 77388
Lost Oak Dr 77388
W Lost Pond Cir & Ct 77381
Lotus Creek Ct 77379
Lou Ln 77388
Louetta Rd
300-899 77373
1400-4899 77388
4900-7800 77379
7717-7717 77391
7801-9999 77379
7802-9998 77379
E Louetta Rd 77373
Louetta Xing 77373
Louetta Brook Ct & Ln 77388
Louetta Crossing Dr 77388
Louetta Falls Ln 77388
Louetta Green Dr 77379
Louetta Lakes Dr 77388
Louetta Lee Dr 77388
Louetta Mist Dr 77388
Louetta Oak Ct & Dr 77388
Louetta Park Cir 77388
Louetta Point Ct 77388
Louetta Reach Dr 77388
Louetta Spring Dr 77388
Louetta Woods Dr 77388
Louise Oak Ct 77379
W Lovegrass Ln 77386
Lovenote Ct 77382
Lovett Ln 77379
Low Country Ln 77380
Low Ridge Rd 77379
Lowick St 77379
Loxanhachee Pl 77389
Loyanne Dr 77373
Lozar Dr 77379
Lucas Creek Dr 77389
Lucida Ln 77373
Lucky Leaf Ct 77381
Ludgate Dr 77373
Lullaby Ln 77380
Lullwater Pl 77381
Luna Lakes Dr 77386
Lush Meadow Pl 77381
Lynbriar Ln 77373
Lyndaleigh Ln 77388
Lyndhurst Village Ln 77379
Lynngate Dr 77373
Lynwood Rd 77373
Lynx Ln 77380
Lyon Springs Ct 77373
Lyons School Rd 77379
Lyrebird Dr 77380
Lyreleaf Pl 77382
E Lyric Arbor Cir & Ct 77381
Lysander Pl 77382
Lytton Spgs 77373
Macaw St 77380
Macbeth Dr 77373
Mackenzie Mesa Dr 77379
Macon St 77389
Macrantha Ct & Dr 77379
Macy Hills Ct 77386
Maddie Springs Ct 77386
Madelin Manor Ln 77386
Maggie Ridge Ct 77386
Magic Oaks Ct & Dr 77388
Magnolia St 77373
Magnolia Walk 77388
Magnolia Estates Dr 77386
Magnolia Fair Way 77386
N & S Magnolia Pond Pl 77381
Magnolia Shadows Pl 77382
Magnolia Warbler Crest Ln 77389
Mahogany Creek Ct 77379
Mahogany Forest Dr 77379
Maiden Way Dr 77379
Maidstone Manor Ct 77379
Main St 77373
Maize Meadow Pl 77381
Majestic Forest Dr 77379
Majestic Park Ln 77386
E & W Majestic Woods Pl 77382
Majesty Row 77380
Majolica Pl 77382
Malac Rd 77389
Mallard Glen Pl 77381
Mallards Pond Ct 77386
Malmaison Ridge Dr 77379
Mammoth Springs Ct 77382
Manchester Trail Dr 77373
Mandarin Glen Cir 77388
Mandeville Ct 77379
Manningtree Ln 77379
Manon Ln 77388
E & W Manor Cir 77389
Manor Brook Ln 77379
Manor Lake Estates Cir & Dr 77379
N & S Manorcliff Pl 77382
Mansfield Bluff Ln 77379
Mansfield Park Ln 77379
Mantana Ct & Dr 77388
Many Oak Dr 77380
Many Pines Rd 77380
Maple Allee Dr 77389
Maple Branch St 77380
N & S Maple Glade Cir 77382
Maple Loft Pl 77381
Maple Path Pl 77382
Maple Rapids Ct & Ln 77386
Maple Run Dr 77373
Maple View Dr 77373
Maple Vista Ln 77373
Maplegate Dr 77373
Maplehurst Dr 77379
Maplewood Dr 77386
Maplewood St 77381
Marabou Pl 77380
Marble Creek Falls Ct 77379
Marble Falls Dr 77379
Marble Oak Ct 77379
Marble Rock Pl 77382
Marble Wood Ct & Pl 77381
Marblecrest Ln 77386
Marchelle Ln 77379
Marcin Dr 77388
Margaux Way 77382
Margie Ct 77379
Margo St 77389
Marilyn Ln 77388
Marin Creek Pl 77389
Marion Meadow Dr & Ln 77386
Mariscal Pl 77389
Markham Grove Pl 77381
Markridge Dr 77379
Marksey Ct 77386
Markspring Ln 77388
Marlan Woods Ct 77386
Marle Point Ct 77388
Maroon Creek Ct 77389
Marquise Oaks Pl 77382
Marsh Millet Ct 77380
Marshall Fls 77379
Marshbrook Ln 77389
N & S Marshside Pl 77389
Marufo Vega Dr 77386
Marywood Dr 77388
Mason Pond Pl 77381
Masson Ct 77388
E & W Matisse Meadow Ct 77382
Matson Manor Ct 77379
Matthew Hills Ln 77386
Maurita Dr 77373
Max Conrad Dr 77379
Maxwood Dr 77379
May Valley Dr 77382
Mayborough Ct 77382
Mayday Run Ct 77373
Mayfair Grove Ct 77381
Mayfair Park Ln 77379

Mayglen Ln 77379
Maymont Way 77382
Maystar Ct 77380
Maywind Ct 77381
Mcbeth Way 77382
Mccleester Dr 77373
Mcdonald Ct & Rd 77380
Mcgoey Cir 77381
Mcgowen St 77373
Meadow Beauty Ct 77381
Meadow Brook Pl 77382
Meadow Cove Dr 77381
Meadow Edge Ln 77388
Meadow Owl Pl 77389
Meadow Rose Pl 77382
Meadow Rue St 77380
Meadow Star Ct 77381
Meadow Tree Ct & Ln 77388
Meadowfair Ct 77381
Meadowfield Creek Way 77379
Meadowfox Pl 77389
Meadowgate Dr 77373
Meadowhigh Ln 77373
Meadowhill Ct 77388
Meadowhill Dr
20800-21999 77388
22000-22200 77389
22202-22298 77389
Meadowlake Hills Ct 77389
Meadowlark Ln 77388
N & S Meadowmist Cir & Ct 77381
Meadowridge Pl 77381
Meadowrock Dr 77389
Meadowspring Cir & Ct 77381
Meadowtrace Dr 77389
Meandering Springs Dr 77389
Medical Plaza Dr 77380
Medina River Ct, Ln & Loop 77386
Mediterra Way 77386
Mediterra Way Ct 77389
Medley Ln 77382
Medway Dr 77386
Megan St 77373
Megan Springs Dr 77379
Meirwoods Dr 77379
Melanie Park Dr 77388
Melcrest Estates Dr 77386
Melda Rd 77380
Melham Ln 77373
Meline Fields Dr 77386
Melissa Dr 77386
Melita Dr 77386
Mellishaw Ct 77379
Mellow Leaf Ct 77381
Mellow Ridge Dr 77379
Mellow Wood Pl 77381
Mellowgrove Ct & Ln 77379
Melody Mist Dr 77389
Memorial Pass 77379
Memorial Blossom Dr 77379
Memorial Creek Dr 77379
Memorial Crest Dr 77379
Memorial Estates Dr 77379
Memorial Grove Dr 77379
Memorial Hills Dr 77379
Memorial Manor Dr 77379
Memorial Mills Dr 77379
Memorial Oaks Ln 77379
Memorial Pines Way 77379
Memorial Ridge Dr 77379
Memorial Trace Dr 77379
Memorial Trail Dr 77379
Memorial Valley Dr 77379
Memory Ln 77380
Menor Crest Dr 77388
Mentmore Dr 77379
Mercoal Dr 77386
Mercury Run Ct 77373
Mercutio Ct 77382
Meridian Hill Dr 77386
Meriglen Ln 77388

Merit Oaks Dr 77382
Merit Woods Pl 77382
Merlins Oaks Ct & Dr 77379
Merrick Meadow Dr 77386
Merrimac Ridge Ln 77373
Merry Oaks Dr 77373
Merry Pine Ct 77379
Merryglen Ct 77373
Merryvale Dr 77382
Mesa Valley Dr 77386
Meskil Oaks Dr 77386
Mesquite Branch Ct 77388
Mesquite Trail Ln 77373
Messara Dr 77379
Methil Dr 77379
Metzler Creek Dr 77389
N & S Mews Wood Ct 77381
Meyrick Ct 77379
Mia Ridge Ln 77386
Mickleham Dr 77379
Mid Oak Ct 77379
Midday Sun Pl 77382
Middle Gate Pl 77382
Midsummer Pl 77381
Midway St 77373
Midway Pass Ct 77373
Milani Ridge Ct 77386
Milano Ln 77379
Mileham Ln 77388
Milepost Ct 77382
Milholland Dr 77386
Mill Point Pl 77380
Mill Pond Ln 77373
Mill Springs Dr 77379
N & S Mill Trace Dr 77381
Millay Ct 77382
N & S Millbend Dr 77380
Millennium Forest Dr 77381
Millers Rock Ct 77389
Millgate Dr 77373
Millpark Dr 77380
N & S Millport Cir & Dr 77382
Millsap Cir 77382
Millstone Valley Ct 77373
Millwright Pl 77382
Mimosa Glen Dr 77388
Minden Oaks Dr 77388
Mineral Creek Ct 77379
Mineral Run Ln 77386
Minsmere Cir 77379
Mint Trace Ct 77386
Mintwood Ln 77379
Miro Ct 77388
Mirror Ct 77388
Mirror Lake Dr 77388
E & W Mirror Ridge Cir, Ct & Dr 77382
Mission Rd 77373
Mission Bend Pl 77382
Mist Green Ln 77373
Misted Lilac Pl 77381
Mistflower Pl 77381
Mistral Wind Pl 77382
Misty Pt 77380
Misty Brook Bend Ct & Ln 77379
Misty Cliff Ln 77386
Misty Cloud St 77381
Misty Creek Dr 77379
Misty Crossing Ln 77379
Misty Grove Cir 77380
N & W Misty Morning Trce 77381
Misty Mountain Trail Ln 77389
Misty Spring Ln 77379
Misty Village Ct 77373
E & W Mistybreeze Cir 77381
Mistygate Ct 77373
Mistyhaven Pl 77381
Moatwood Ct 77382
Moccasin Bend Dr 77379
Mockingbird Meadows Ct 77389

Modbury St 77379
Moggy Ct 77388
Mohawk Path Pl & Trl 77389
Molly Hills Ct 77386
Monarda Manor Ct 77379
Monet Bend Pl 77382
Monique Ridge Ln 77386
Montague Dr 77373
Montana Blue Dr 77373
Montay Bay Dr 77389
Montclair Oaks Ln 77386
Montclair Park Ln 77373
W Monteagle Cir 77382
Monteith Dr 77373
E & W Montfair Blvd 77382
Montfair Park Cir 77382
Moon Beam Ct 77381
Moonseed Pl 77381
Moonvine Ct 77380
Moor Lily Ct 77388
Moran Crest Dr 77388
Moreton Ct & Ln 77379
Morgan Spgs 77373
Morgan Hill Ct 77386
Morgan Park Dr 77388
Morgan Ridge Ln 77386
Morgans Pond Ct 77389
Moriah Ct 77386
Morley Park Ln 77373
Morning Arbor Pl 77381
E & N Morning Cloud Cir & Pl 77381
Morning Dove Bend Ln 77389
Morning Forest Ct 77381
Morning Glory Ln 77380
Morning Leaf Ct 77388
Morning Ridge Ln 77386
Morning Story Dr 77373
Morningbrook Ct & Dr 77379
Morningcrest Ct 77389
Morningsong Ct 77389
N & S Morningwood Ct 77380
Morris Park Ct 77389
Mosaic Point Pl 77389
Moss Agate Ct 77388
Moss Bluff Ct 77388
Moss Falls Ln 77373
Moss Point Ct & Dr 77379
Mossdale Cir 77379
Mossgrey Ln 77373
N & S Mossrock Rd 77380
Mossy Bluff Ct 77379
Mossy Branch Ln 77386
Mossy Bridge Dr 77379
Mossy Creek Pl 77381
Mossy Field Ln 77388
Mossy Oaks Rd 77389
Mossy Place Ln 77388
Mossy Spring Ln 77388
Mossygate Dr 77373
Moston Dr 77386
Mountain Bluebird Pl 77389
Mountain Crest Dr 77379
Mountain Grove Ct 77379
Mountain Mistral Pl 77382
Mountain Shade Dr 77388
Mountain Spring Dr 77379
Mountain View Creek Ct 77379
Mountbury Ct 77373
Mouring Ct 77389
Mourning Dove Dr 77388
Movado Ct 77386
Mrsny Ct & Dr 77386
Mt Hunt Dr 77388
Mueller Ln 77379
Muirfield Bend Ct 77389
Muirwood Place Ln 77379
Mulberry Glen Pl 77382
Musewood Ct 77382
Musgrove Pl 77382
Musk Rose Ct 77382
Muskmallow Ct 77380
Mustang Hill Ln 77389

Mustang Point Ct 77382
Myrtle Spgs 77373
Mystic Arbor Pl 77382
Mystic Canyon Dr 77386
Mystic Glade Ct 77382
Mystic Lake Cir 77381
Mystic Pines Ct 77382
Mystic Valley Ct 77381
Nagshead Pl 77389
Nagy Hill St 77379
Nannette Ln 77388
Nanton Dr 77386
Nantucket Point Ln 77389
Napfield Dr 77379
Naples Dr 77373
Naremore Ct & Dr 77379
Narrow Creek Pl 77381
Nashland Ct 77379
Nature Park Ln 77386
Natures Harp Ct 77381
Navajo Trail Dr 77388
Neches Ct 77386
Neches Trail Ln 77388
Needham Cross Dr 77379
Needlewalk Ln 77379
Nelson St 77373
Nelson Bridge Dr 77389
Nesting Crane Ct 77389
Nestlewood Pl 77382
Netherfield Way 77382
Nevelson Cir 77379
E & W New Avery Pl 77382
New Forest Rd 77379
W New Harmony Trl 77389
New Light Pl 77382
New Pines Dr 77373
New Trails Dr 77381
Newberry Trail Ct 77382
Newfoundland Ct 77379
Newgate Dr 77373
Newkay Ln 77379
Newland Ct 77382
Newmill Ct 77379
Newport Ct & Ln 77386
Nichilo Dr 77389
Nicholforest Ln 77389
Nickerton Ln 77388
Nickwill Way 77388
Night Beacon Point Dr 77379
Night Hawk Pl 77380
Night Heron Pl 77382
Night Rain Ct 77381
Night Song Ct 77380
Nightfall Pl 77381
Nightowl Trl 77373
Nightshade Ct 77388
Nightwind Pl 77381
Nikki Hills Ct 77386
Nina Ridge Ln 77386
Noah Ln 77379
Noah Ridge Ct 77386
Noahpines Ct 77386
E Noble St 77373
Noble Bend Dr & Pl 77382
Noble Pointe Ct & Dr 77379
Nobles Crossing Dr 77373
Nocturne Woods Pl 77382
Nodaway Ln 77379
Nodding Pines St 77380
Noontide Cir 77380
Norchester Way 77389
Norlund Way 77382
Normandy Forest Ct & Dr 77388
Norseman Ct 77379
E North Hill Dr 77373
W North Hill Dr 77388
Northampton Forest Dr 77389
Northampton Pines Dr 77389
Northampton Terrace Dr 77389
Northbridge Cir, Ct & Dr 77379
Northcastle Ln 77373
Northchapel St 77379
Northcrest Ct & Dr 77389

Northcrest Village Way 77388
Northgate Dr 77380
Northgate Crossing Blvd 77373
Northgate Ridge Dr 77373
Northgate Springs Dr 77373
Northoak Forest Ln 77389
Northpine Dr 77388
Northpointe Blvd & Dr 77379
Northridge Forest Dr 77386
Northridge Terrace Ct & Ln 77373
Northridge Trace Ln 77379
Northway Dr
6100-6599 77389
8200-8299 77382
Norvara Trl 77379
Norwood Oaks Dr 77379
Nottinghill Dr 77388
Nueces Dr 77389
Nueces River Ct & Loop 77386
Null Ct 77379
Nursery Rd 77380
Nursery Rd Rd 77380
Nutcracker Ln 77380
Nutmeg Ct 77381
Nutwood Ln 77389
Oak St 77373
Oak Bridge Ln 77388
Oak Castle Dr 77389
Oak Churn Pl 77373
Oak Creek Ln 77379
Oak Crest Ct 77379
Oak Dale Dr 77379
Oak Edge Ct 77379
Oak Forest Hollow Ln 77386
E Oak Hill Dr 77386
Oak Hollow Way 77379
Oak Knot Ct & Dr 77389
Oak Lace Dr 77389
Oak Masters Ct & Dr 77379
Oak Moss Dr 77379
Oak Plain Dr 77389
Oak Ridge Dr 77380
Oak Ridge Grove Cir & Dr 77386
Oak River Dr 77373
Oak Rock Cir 77373
Oak Star Dr 77389
Oak Trunnel Ct 77386
Oak Villa Ct & Dr 77389
Oakdale Mdws 77379
Oakdale Creek Ct 77379
Oakhill Gate Dr 77373
Oakhurst Dr 77386
Oakley Downs Pl 77382
Oaklynn Dr 77373
Oakmere Lake Ct 77379
Oakmont Creek Dr 77379
Oakmoss Ct & Trl 77379
Oakridge Forest Ct & Ln 77386
Oaksedge Ln 77388
Oaksham Ln 77373
Oakway Dr 77388
Oakwood Dr 77386
Oakwood Chase Dr 77379
Oakwood Glen Blvd & Cir 77379
Oarwood Pl 77389
Ocenda Dr 77380
October Shadow Ct 77379
Ofallon Mills Dr 77386
Ogdenburg Falls Dr 77379
Okra St 77379
Old Aldine Westfield Rd 77373
Old Carriage Ln 77373
Old Castle Ct 77382
N & S Old Cedar Cir 77382
Old Chapel Dr 77373
Old Field Pl 77380
Old Hannover Dr 77388
Old Holzwarth Rd 77388
Old Louetta Loop 77388

Old Louetta Rd 77379
Old Ox Rd 77386
Old River Pl 77382
Old Spring Cypress Rd 77379
W Old Sterling Cir 77382
Old Timber Ln 77379
Old Westfield Rd 77373
Olde Lantern Way 77380
Olde Rose Ct 77382
Oldsquaw Glen Ct 77388
Oldstream Ct 77381
Olivia Springs Ln 77386
Olivine Ln 77388
Olmstead Row 77380
Omaha Beach Ct & Ln 77388
Ontonagon Way 77386
Opaline Pl 77382
Orangevale Ct & Dr 77379
Orca Ct 77388
Orchard Dale Cir 77382
Orchard Dale Dr 77389
Orchard Hill Ln 77386
Orchard Pines Pl 77382
Orchard Valley Ln 77386
Orchid Trace Dr 77386
Oreana Ct 77386
Orie Ct 77373
S Oriel Oaks Cir & Ct 77382
Orion Star Ct 77382
Oscoda Ct 77386
N Ossineke Ct & Dr 77386
Otter Lodge Pl 77382
Otter Pond Pl 77381
Otto Rd 77373
Outervale Pl 77381
Overcup Dr 77389
Overlake Dr 77380
N Overlyn Ct & Pl 77381
Owens Creek Ln 77388
Owl Canyon Dr 77388
Owls Cove Pl 77382
Owosso Ct 77386
Oxalis Ct 77379
Oxbow Trl 77373
Oxfordshire Dr 77379
Oxhill Ct & Rd 77388
Oxted Ln 77379
Pacific Ocean Dr 77388
Paddle Wheel Dr 77379
Paddock Run 77389
Paddock Pines Pl 77382
Pagan Cir 77379
Pagehurst Ct 77382
Painted Canyon Pl 77381
Painted Post Pl 77389
Painted Sunset 77380
Paintedcup Ct 77380
Painton Ln 77389
Paladera Place Ct 77386
Pale Dawn Pl 77381
Pale Sage Ct 77382
Palisander Ct 77388
Palm Shores Ct & Dr 77379
E Palmer Bnd 77381
W Palmer Bnd 77381
Palmer Crst 77381
E Palmer Pt 77381
W Palmer Pt 77381
Palmer Way 77380
Palmer Bend Ct 77381
Palmer Cove Dr 77389
Palmer Crest Ct 77381
Palmer Green Pl 77381
Palmer Woods Dr 77381
N & S Palmiera Cir & Dr 77382
Paloma Dr 77389
Paloma Bend Pl 77389
Paloma Pines Pl 77389
Paloma Springs Dr 77389
Palomar Valley Dr 77386
Pamela Way 77379
Pampas St 77389
Panamint Ct 77389

Panterra Way 77382
Panther Pass 77388
E, N, S & W Panther Creek Dr & Pne 77381
Panther Peak 77388
Par Point Ct 77389
Paradise Gate Dr 77373
Parham Cir 77388
Parish Hall Dr 77379
S Park Dr 77380
Park Gable Dr 77373
Park Gwen Dr 77373
Park Lodge Dr 77379
Park Pine Ln 77386
Park Shadow Ct 77386
Park Spring Ln 77373
Parkerton Ln 77386
Parkeston Dr 77388
N & S Parkgate Cir 77381
Parliament Hills Dr 77386
Parsonfield Ct 77373
Parsonsgate Dr 77373
Parwood Ct 77382
Pascale Creek Pl 77382
Pastel Ln 77389
Pastoral Pond Cir 77380
Pateway Ct 77386
E Pathfinders Cir 77381
N Pathfinders Cir 77381
S Pathfinders Cir 77381
Pathfinders Pass 77373
Patina Pines Ct & Pl 77381
Patricia Oaks Ct 77386
Pawprint Pl 77382
Pea Ridge Dr 77373
Peace River Dr 77379
N & S Peaceful Canyon Cir & Ct 77381
Peaceful Valley Dr 77373
Peachglen Ln 77373
Peachridge Pl 77382
Peachstone Pl 77389
Pear Side Ct 77386
Pearl Crest Ln 77389
Pebble Cove Ct & Dr 77381
Pebble Hollow Ct 77381
Pebblegate Ct 77373
Pebworth Pl 77373
Pecan Cir 77381
Pecan Brook Ct 77379
Pecan Leaf Dr 77379
Pecan Valley Cir 77380
Pecangate Dr 77373
E & W Pecos River Ct & Dr 77386
Pedernales River Ln 77386
Peerless Dr 77373
Peerless Pass Ct 77373
Pelham Chase Dr 77389
Pembroke Spgs 77373
Pendelton Trace Dr 77386
Pendleton Park Pt 77382
Penguin Ct 77380
Pennsgrove Rd 77373
Pennwell Dr 77389
N & S Pentenwell Cir 77382
Peony Springs Ct 77382
Peper Hollow Ln 77386
Pepper Crest Ln 77379
Pepper Ridge Ln 77373
Pepperberry Trl 77388
Perlican Dr 77386
Perry Ln 77389
Perry Pass Ct 77379
Petal Park Pl 77382
Petalcup Pl 77381
Petaldrop Pl 77382
Pheasant Glen Dr 77379
Phibes Trl 77379
Philbrook Way 77382
Philip Springs Ln 77386
Picasso Path Pl 77382
Pico Meadow Ct 77386
Picture Rock Pl 77389
Piddler Dr 77373
Pikard Way Ct 77386

Pikecrest Dr 77389
Pilgrims Cir 77379
Pilgrims Gate Ln 77373
Pimberton Ln 77379
Pin Oak Dr 77389
Pin Oak Ln 77389
Pin Oak Pl 77379
Pinaster Pointe Ln 77379
Pincher Creek Dr 77386
Pine Ln 77389
Pine Acres Cir 77380
Pine Arrow Ct 77389
Pine Bay Dr 77386
Pine Branch Dr 77388
Pine Brook Ct 77381
Pine Canyon Dr 77380
Pine Crossing Ct & Dr 77373
Pine Dust Ln 77373
Pine Edge Dr 77380
Pine Grove Ct 77381
Pine Hill Dr 77381
Pine Island Pl 77382
Pine Lock Ln 77388
Pine Lodge Pl 77382
Pine Mist Ln 77373
Pine Needle Pl 77382
Pine Post Ln 77373
Pine Reserve Dr 77389
Pine Rest Dr 77389
Pine Rose Dr 77386
Pine Run Ct & Dr 77388
Pine Song Pl 77381
Pine Thicket Ct 77373
Pine Thistle Ct & Ln 77379
Pine Walk Trl 77388
Pine Wood Hills Ct 77386
Pine Wood Meadows Ln 77386
Pineash Ct 77381
Pinebridge Ln 77388
Pinebrook Bridge Ln 77379
Pinebrook Hollow Ln 77379
Pinecandle Dr 77388
Pinecreek Pt 77373
Pinecreek Point Ct 77373
Pinecreek Ridge Ct & Ln 77379
Pinecrest Dr 77389
Pinecroft Dr
9100-9299 77380
9300-9499 77380
9450-9450 77387
Pinefern Ln 77379
Pineglen Terrace Dr 77389
Pinehaven Ln 77379
Pinehearth Ct 77379
Pineholly Ct 77381
Pinelake Crossing Ct & Dr 77379
Pinelakes Blvd 77379
Pinellas Park 77379
Pinellas Park Ct 77379
Pinemill Hollow Dr 77386
Pinepath Pl 77381
N & S Pineplank Ct 77381
Pinery Ridge Pl 77382
Pinesplit Way 77389
Pinetop Glen Ln 77379
Pineville Ln 77388
Pinewalk Brook Ln 77379
Pinewood Forest Ct 77381
Pinewood Forest Dr 77379
Pinewood Glen Dr 77388
Pinewood Heights Dr 77389
Pinewood Ridge Dr 77386
Pinewoods Way 77386
Piney Ct 77373
Piney Bend Ct 77389
Piney Creek Ln 77388
Piney Heights Ln 77389
Piney Hill Ln 77388
Piney Lake Dr 77388
N & S Piney Plains Cir 77382
Pinnacle Point Pl 77386
Pinpoint Dr 77373
Pinsonfork Dr 77379
N & S Pinto Point Cir, Dr & Pl 77389
Pintuck Pl 77389
Pinyon Pl 77380
Pinyon Trail Dr 77389
S Piper Trce & Trl 77381
E & W Pipers Green St 77382
Pipers Meadow St 77382
Pirouette Pl 77382
Pitcataway Cir & Dr 77379
Pitkin Rd 77386
Pixie Springs Ln 77386
Place Vendome Ct 77379
E Placid Hill Cir 77381
N & S Planchard Cir & Ct 77382
Plato Point Ln 77386
Player Bend Dr 77382
N & S Player Crest Cir 77382
Player Green Pl 77382
Player Grove Ct 77382
N & S Player Manor Cir & Dr 77382
Player Oaks Pl 77382
Player Pines Ct 77382
Player Point Dr 77382
Player Pond Pl 77382
Player Ridge Ct 77382
Player Vista Pl 77382
Players Trl 77382
Pleasant Bend Dr & Pl 77382
Pleasant Meadow Dr 77379
Pleasant Point Ct & Pl 77389
Pleasant Shadows Dr 77389
Pleasantglen Ct 77379
Pleasantwood Dr 77379
Pleasure Cove Dr 77381
Plover Ln 77380
Plum Blossom Ct & Pl 77381
N & S Plum Creek Dr 77386
Plum Crest Cir 77382
Plumcove Ct 77381
Plymouth Ridge Ln 77379
Pocket Flower Ct 77382
Pomerelle Pl 77382
Poole Rd 77379
Poplar Hill Pl 77381
Portico Pt 77380
Portside Dr 77388
Post Bridge Rd 77389
Post Gate Dr 77373
Post Oak Ct & Holw 77379
Post Oak Hill Dr 77388
Post Shadow Estate Ct & Dr 77389
Postvine Ct 77381
Postwood Ct & Dr 77388
Postwood Glen Ln 77373
Postwood Green Ln 77373
Postwood Oaks Dr 77373
Postwood Park Ln 77373
Postwood Point Dr 77373
Powell Rd 77373
Powerline Pass Dr 77373
Powers Bend Way 77382
Prairie St 77373
Prairie Bird Dr & Ln 77373
Prairie Clover Ln 77379
Prairie Falcon Ct & Pl 77389
Prairie Forest Trl 77373
Prairie Spring Ln 77379
Prairie Trails Dr 77379
Precious Pl 77389
Prelude Springs Ln 77386
Preserve Bend Cir 77389
Preserve Glen Cir 77389
Preserve Park Dr 77389
Preserve View Cir 77389
Presswood Dr 77386
Preston Ave 77373
Preston Grove Dr 77389
Prides Crossing Dr 77381
Primm Valley Ct 77389
Primo Pl 77379
Primrose Trace Ln 77389
Prism Cove Pl 77381
Prism Point Pl 77389
Profit Pine Ln 77389
Pronghorn Pl 77389
Prose Ct 77389
Prosewood Ct & Dr 77381
N & S Provence Cir 77382
Pruitt Rd
100-1299 77380
27000-27199 77373
Puget Ln 77388
Purdue Park Ln 77386
Purple Martin Pl 77381
Purple Slate Pl 77381
Purpletop Ct 77381
Quail Haven Rd 77373
Quail Oak Park Ln 77386
Quail Rock Pl 77381
Quail Shute 77389
Quailgate Dr 77373
Queens Oak Ct 77379
N & S Queenscliff Cir & Ct 77382
Quick Stream Pl 77381
Quicktime Ct 77379
Quiet Oak Cir & Dr 77381
Quiet Peace Pl 77381
Quiet Pointe Dr 77389
Quiet Rose Ln 77379
Quiet Sky Pl 77386
Quiet Sky Place Dr 77386
Quintelle Ct 77382
Rabbit Run Pl 77382
Rabinow Ct 77381
Raccoon Ln 77380
Raccoon Run 77373
E & W Racing Cloud Ct 77381
Radley Ct & Dr 77379
Raes Creek Dr 77389
Raestone St 77386
Rafters Row 77380
Rain Fern Ct 77380
N & S Rain Forest Ct 77380
Rain Walk Ct 77380
Rainbird Pl 77381
E Rainbow Ridge Cir 77381
Raindream Pl 77381
Raintree Pl 77380
Raintree Crossing Dr 77381
Rainwood St 77388
Rainwood Park Ln 77386
Ralick Ct 77379
Rambling Brook Dr 77373
Rambling Springs Way 77382
Rambling Wood Ct 77380
Ramey Heights Ct 77381
Ramos Dr 77386
Rams Bottom Ct 77388
Ramsgate Dr 77388
Ranchers Trl 77389
Randal Way 77388
Randal Lake Ln 77388
Randal Point Ct 77388
Rannock Way 77379
Ransten Ln 77379
Rathlin Ct 77379
Raven Cliffs Ln 77379
Raven Ridge Ln 77380
Ravenno Ln 77379
Ravens Bluff Ln 77386
Ravens Manor Ct 77379
Rayford Rd
1-4000 77386
4002-4098 77386
23700-23899 77389
W Rayford Rd 77389
Rayford Crest Dr 77386
Razorback Dr 77389
Rebecca Field Ln 77386
Red Adler Pl 77382
Red Barn Way 77389
Red Candle Dr 77388
E Red Cedar Cir 77380
Red Corner Way 77389
Red Deer Ln 77380
Red Glade Ct 77373
Red Leo Ln 77389
Red Meadows Dr 77386
Red Oak Dr 77389
Red Oak Ln 77379
Red River Ct & Loop 77386
Red Rover Ct 77373
Red Sable Ct, Dr, Pl & Pt 77380
Red Sky Ct & Dr 77373
Red Wagon Dr 77389
Redberry Ct 77381
Redbud Hill Ct 77388
Redbud Ridge Pl 77380
Redchurch Dr 77379
Redcrested Glen Ct 77388
Reddingwood Ct 77373
Reddleston Ct 77389
Redhaven Pl 77381
Redland Pl 77382
Redstone Manor Dr 77379
Redwick Ct & Dr 77388
Redwood Terrace Ln 77389
Redwood Village Cir 77386
Reed Creek Ln 77388
Reedy Pond Ct & St 77381
Reflection Pt 77381
Regan Ct 77382
N & S Regan Mead Cir & Ct 77382
Regency Pl 77379
Regent Sq 77381
N & S Regent Oak Ct 77381
Remington Manor St 77379
Rendale Ct 77388
Rendezvous Ct 77373
Rene Creek Ct 77388
Rene Hills Ln 77386
Renee Springs Ct 77379
Reno Ranch Ln 77388
Renoir Trail Pl 77382
Research Forest Dr
1-99 77380
1100-1199 77380
1201-2099 77380
1400-1698 77381
1700-2098 77380
1700-1800 77381
1802-6198 77381
2101-2299 77380
2301-6599 77381
7500-8199 77382
Research Park Dr 77381
Reston Cliff Ct 77386
Rettendon Ct 77389
Rex Creek Ct 77379
Reynaldo Dr 77373
Reynolds Creek Dr 77388
Rhapsody Bend Dr 77382
Rhetta Ln 77389
Rhodes Rd
19700-19999 77379
20000-21999 77388
Riata Hills Ln 77379
Ribbon Creek Way 77389
Ribbon Hill Ln 77386
Ribbonwood Park Ln 77386
Ricegrass Pl 77389
Richards Rd 77386
Richardson St 77373
Richglen Ct 77389
Richland Falls Ln 77379
Richlawn Dr 77379
Ridge Beam Ln 77389
Ridge Path Ct & Rd 77388
Ridgebrook Cir 77380
Ridgecrest Dr 77389
Ridgecross Pl 77381
Ridgeline Ct 77381
Ridgewood Dr
200-299 77386
21700-21999 77388
Riley Fuzzell Rd
200-999 77373
1000-8899 77386
299-1-299-1 77373
319-1-319-2 77373
630-1-630-2 77373
Riley Woods Ct 77386
Rillwood Pl 77382
S Rim Trl 77388
Ringneck Glen Dr 77388
Ringwald Ct 77379
Ringwood St 77373
Rio Grande River Dr 77386
Ripple Ln 77389
Ripple Rush Ct 77381
Rippled Pond Cir 77382
Rippling Hollow Dr 77379
Rippon Dr 77373
Rittenhouse Park Ct 77379
Riva Row 77380
Rivendell Dr 77379
River Birch Ln 77380
River Lodge Dr 77379
River Mill Ct & Dr 77379
River Ridge Loop 77389
River Valley Dr 77373
River Willow Dr 77379
Riverbank Dr 77381
Riverbridge Ct 77379
Rivergate Dr 77373
Rivershadows Ln 77388
Riverstone Springs Dr 77386
Rivertree Ln
4600-4899 77388
5100-5699 77379
Riverwood Trl 77386
Riviere Ln 77388
Rivington Ct 77389
Roaming Woods Ln 77380
Roaring Creek St 77380
Robbs Xing 77379
Robin Caper Ct 77382
Robin Run Dr 77381
Robin Springs Pl 77381
Robin Walk Ln 77380
Robinhoods Well Dr 77379
Robins Forest Dr 77379
Robins Nest Ln 77389
Robinson Rd 77386
Robinwick Ct 77379
Robinwood Dr 77386
Rock Daisy Dr 77386
Rock Hollow Ln 77389
Rock Oak Pl 77380
Rock Pine Ct 77381
E & W Rock Wing Pl 77381
N Rockfern Ct & Rd 77380
Rockford Hall Dr 77379
Rockgate Dr 77373
Rocking Pine Pl 77381
Rockledge Ct & Dr 77382
Rockridge Ct & Dr 77381
Rockside Ln 77379
Rockwell Park Blvd & Dr 77389
Rockwell Square Pl 77389
Rocky Glen Ct & Ln 77373
N & S Rocky Point Cir, Ct & Dr 77389
Rockygate Dr 77373
Roger Dell Ct 77382
Rogue Creek St 77380
Roland Orchard Ct 77386
Rolling Forest Dr 77388
Rolling Glen Dr 77373
Rolling Links Ct 77380
Rolling Mill Ln 77380
Rolling Oaks Dr 77389
Rolling Stone Pl 77381
Rolling Terrace Dr 77388
Rollinson Park Dr 77379
Romulus Ct 77386
N & S Rondelet Dr 77386
Rookwood Ct 77382
Root Rd 77389
Rosalind Ln 77382
Rose Ln 77373
Rose Clover Ln 77386
Rose Crossing Ln 77379
Rose Dawn Ln 77379
Rose Petal Pl 77381
Rose Quartz Ln 77388
Rose Trace Dr 77386
Rose Vervain Dr 77386
Rose Willow Ln 77379
Roseberry Manor Dr 77379
Rosebrook Cir & Ln 77379
Rosebud Ridge Way 77379
Rosecastle Dr 77379
Rosedale Brook Ct 77381
Rosedown Pl 77382
Rosegate Dr 77373
Rosehill Park Ln 77386
Roseling Rd 77380
Rosemary Trace Dr 77386
Roserock Ln
4600-4899 77388
5100-5699 77379
Roserush Ct 77380
Rosespring Ln 77379
Rosestone Ln 77379
Rosethorn Pl 77381
Roseville Dr
21300-21999 77388
22300-22399 77389
Roseville Park Ct 77386
Rosewater Pl 77381
Rosewood Dr 77381
Rosewood Pl 77380
Rosholt Dr 77386
Rosillos Peak Dr 77386
Roslyn Bend Ct 77382
Roslyn Springs Dr 77388
Rossmore Hill Ct 77389
Rosswood Ln 77388
Rosy Finch Pl 77389
Roth Forest Ln 77389
Rotherham Dr 77388
Rothko Ln 77379
Rothshire Ct 77373
Rothwood Rd 77389
Rothwood Oaks Dr 77389
Round Rose Ct 77379
Roundtop Pl 77381
Routhland Dr 77379
Rowena Dale Dr 77379
Royal Crest Ct 77379
N & S Royal Fern Dr 77380
Royal Lagoon Ct 77388
Royal Oak Pl 77380
Royal Oaks Dr 77380
Royal Ridge Pl 77382
Royal Tern Ln 77380
Roydencrest Dr 77388
Rubylace Ct 77382
Rudgewick Ln 77379
Rudy Brook Way 77379
Rudy Glen Ct 77388
Ruffin Ln 77380
Rugby Ct 77379
Rui Cove Ct 77386
E & W Rumplecreek Pl 77381
Rundell Dr 77389
Running Brook Ln 77379
Running River Dr 77373
Running Vine Ln 77379
N & S Rush Haven Cir, Ct & Dr 77381
Rushstone Ln 77373
N & S Rushwing Cir & Pl 77381
Russell Creek Ct 77386
Russell Point Dr 77386
Russet Springs Ln 77389
Russet Wood Ct 77381
Russwood Ct 77379
Rustic Bend Pl 77382
Rustic Gardens Dr 77386
Rustic Oak Ct 77373
Rustic Pines Ct 77386
Rustic View Ct 77381
Rustington Dr 77379
Rustling Chestnut St 77389
Rustling Pines St 77380
Rustling Springs Dr 77389
Rustling Timbers Ct & Ln 77379
Rustling Trees Way 77373
Rusty Bridge Ct 77386
Rusty Ridge Pl 77381
Rustygate Dr 77373
Rutherford Way 77379
Rutley Cir 77379
Ryans Ridge Ln 77386
Ryansbrook Ln 77386
Rycroft Dr 77386
Rye St 77380
Rymwick Ct 77381
Sable Hill Ct 77386
Saddle Rdg 77380
Saddle Path Ct 77373
Saddlewood Cir 77381
Saffron Hills Dr 77379
Sagamore Bend Pl 77382
Sagamore Ridge Pl 77389
Sage Ct 77381
Sage Blue Ct 77382
E & W Sage Creek Pl 77382
Sage Grass Ln 77379
Sage Hollow Dr 77386
N & S Sage Sparrow Cir & Ct 77389
Sage Trace Ct 77386
Sagecombe Ct & Ln 77388
Sagegate Dr 77373
Sagehampton Ct 77379
Sagewalk Ct 77379
Sagewood Dr 77386
Sagging Oaks Dr 77388
Saginaw Bay Ct 77373
Saint Emilion Ct 77379
Saint Helen Ct 77379
Saint Peters Gate 77382
Sainte Mere Eglise Ln 77388
Salem Fields Dr 77386
Salmon Ln 77379
Sampras Ace Ct 77379
San Antonio River Dr 77386
San Bernard River Loop 77386
San Jacinto River Ct & Dr 77386
Sanctuary Cypress Ln 77388
Sanctuary Halls 77388
Sanctuary Hills Ct 77388
Sanctuary Hollow Ln 77388
Sanctuary Meadow Ct 77388
Sanctuary Oak Ct 77388
Sanctuary Pine Ct 77388
Sanctuary Place Dr 77388
Sanctuary Robin Ln 77388
Sanctuary Rose Bud Ln 77388
Sanctuary Trails Dr 77388
Sanctuary Valley Ln 77388
Sand Cove Ct 77381
Sand Piper Pl 77381
E & W Sandalbranch Cir & Dr 77382
Sandleigh Dr 77388
Sandlily Ct 77380
Sandown Park Dr 77379
Sandpebble Dr 77381
Sandpiper Trl 77373
Sandprint Ct 77381
Sands Terrace Ln 77389
Sandwedge Point Ct 77389
Sandwell Pl 77389
Sandy Briar Ct 77379
Sandy Fields Cir & Ln 77386
Sandy Isle Ln 77389
Sandy Knolls Dr 77379
Sandypine Cir, Ct, Dr & Ln 77379
Santa Elena Cyn 77388
Santa Elena Canyon Ct 77388
Sapling Pl 77382
Sapling Trail Ct 77388

Saragosa Pond Ln 77379
Sarah Springs Ct 77373
Savannah Dr 77381
Savannah Springs Way 77373
S Sawbridge Cir & Ct 77389
Sawdust Rd 77380
Sawmill Pass 77373
Sawmill Rd 77380
Sawmill Cross Ln 77373
Sawmill Grove Ct & Ln 77380
Sawmill Terrace Ln 77389
Sawyer Bend Ln
3600-3699 77386
5800-6099 77379
E & W Sawyer Ridge Dr 77389
N & S Scarlet Elm Ct 77382
Scarlet Plume Ct 77388
Scarlet Sage Pl 77381
Scarlet Woods Ct 77380
Scatterwood Ct 77381
Scenic Brook Ct 77382
Scenic Gardens Dr 77379
Scenic Mill Pl 77382
Scenic Park Dr 77386
Scenicside Ln 77379
Scented Candle Way 77388
Scented Path Ln 77381
Schaumburg Dr 77388
Schults Meadow Ln 77389
Schumann Oaks Dr 77386
Sciaaca Rd 77373
Scoresby Manor Ct & Dr 77379
Scotch Pine Ct 77382
E Scribewood Cir 77382
Scullers Cove Ct 77381
N & S Seasons Trce 77382
Seaton Valley Dr 77379
Secluded Trl 77380
Seders Walk 77381
Sedgefield St 77386
Sedgewick Pl 77382
Sedona Ranch Ln 77388
Sedona Springs Ln 77379
Sego Lily Ct 77389
Sekola Ln 77386
Seminole Lodge Ln 77379
Seminole Park Ln 77373
Seneca Pl 77382
Seneca Pt 77379
Senterra Bend Cir 77379
Senterra Lakes Blvd 77379
Sentinel Pl 77382
Sentinel Point Ct 77382
Sentry Maple Pl 77382
Sequin Dr 77388
Sequoia Trce 77379
Sequoia Trace Ct 77379
Serein Meadows Dr 77386
Serenade Pines Pl 77382
Serene Creek Pl 77382
Serene Spring Ln 77373
Serenity Loch Dr 77379
Serenity Woods Pl 77382
Serrano Hill Ln 77379
E & W Settlers Way 77380
Seven Pines Dr 77379
Seward St 77389
Sgt Taylor Memorial 77386
Shaddon Manor Ct 77379
Shadeberry Pl 77382
Shaded Arbor Dr 77389
Shaded Springs Ln 77389
Shadow Bend Pl 77381
Shadow Creek Ridge Ct & Dr 77389
E Shadow Creek Villas Loop 77389
Shadow Glen Ln 77386
Shadow Pond Dr 77389
Shadow River Ln 77379
Shadow Stone St 77381
Shadow Valley Ct, Dr & Ln 77379
Shadowbrook Dr 77380
Shadowcrest Ln 77380
E & W Shadowpoint Cir 77381
Shady Arbor Ln 77379
Shady Bayou Ln 77373
Shady Hills Landing Ln 77386
Shady Lodge Ln 77373
Shady Pine Dr 77388
Shady Pond Pl 77382
Shady Trace Dr 77386
W & E Shaker Ct & Ln 77380
E & W Shale Creek Cir & Ct 77382
Shale Run Pl 77382
Shalford Ct & Dr 77389
Shallow Pond Ct & Pl 77381
Shallow River Ct 77379
Shalom Creek Ln 77388
Shane Creek Ln 77388
Shanewood Ct 77382
Shannondale Ln 77388
Sharon Pkwy 77379
Sharptree Ct 77389
Shasta Bend Cir 77389
Shauna Ln 77386
Shavon Ct 77388
Shavon Springs Dr 77388
Shawna Lyn Dr 77373
N & S Shawnee Ridge Cir, Ct & Dr 77382
Shayna Ct 77388
Shearling Ct 77389
Shearwater Pl 77381
Sheep Meadow Pl 77381
Sheerborne Ct 77382
Shelburne Cir & Ln 77379
Shelby Ct 77373
Sheldon Pnes 77379
Shell Port Sq 77380
Shellbark Pl 77382
Shelter Rock Ct 77382
Sheltered Arbor Ct 77382
Shenandoah Dr 77381
Shenandoah Park Dr 77385
Sherilynn Dr 77373
Sherioaks Ln 77389
Sherrod Ln 77389
Sherrylee Ln 77373
Sherwick Rdg 77379
Sherwood Ct 77381
Sheryl Ct 77379
Shibe Park Ct 77389
Shiloh Bend Ct 77389
N & S Shimmering Aspen Cir & Dr 77389
Shimmering Pines Rd 77379
Shining Creek Ln 77386
Shining Lakes Pl 77381
Shiny Pebble Pl 77381
Shinyrock Pl 77381
Shipman Ln 77388
Shirefield Ct & Ln 77373
Shooting Star Pl 77381
E Shore Dr 77380
Shore Bend Ct 77379
N Shoreline Point Dr 77381
Shores Ct 77386
Short Path Ct 77373
Shrewsbury Cir 77379
Shumard Ct 77388
Siandra Creek Ct & Ln 77386
E & W Sienna Pl 77382
Sienna Pines Ct 77379
Sierra Springs Ln 77373
Sifton Dr 77386
Signature Crest Ct 77382
Silent Brook Ct & Pl 77381
Silent Timber Path Ln 77386
Silk Ct 77386
Silkbay Pl 77382
Silktassel Ln 77380
Silliso Pl 77381
Silver Arrow Ct 77389
Silver Bluff Ct 77382
Silver Canyon Pl 77381
Silver Cliff Ln 77373
N & S Silver Crescent Cir & Ct 77382
Silver Elm Pl 77381
Silver Iris Way 77382
Silver Jade Ct & Dr 77386
Silver Leaf Dr 77388
Silver Lute Pl 77381
Silver Maple Pl 77382
Silver Shadows Ln 77379
Silver Tip Dr 77379
Silver Village Dr 77386
Silvermont Dr 77382
N & S Silvershire Cir 77381
Silverstrand Pl 77381
Silverthorn Glen Dr 77379
Silverthorne Ln 77379
Silverton St 77373
Silverton Star Ct 77386
Silverwood Oaks Ct 77386
Silverwood Park Ln 77386
Simpson Springs Ln 77389
Singing Creek Ln 77373
Single Oak St 77373
Single Pine Ct 77373
Sir William Ct & Dr 77379
Siros Isle Ct & Dr 77388
Sitca St 77389
Six Pines Dr 77380
Skipwith Pl 77382
Sky Terrace Pl 77381
Skyflower Ct, Dr & Pl 77381
Skyhaven Ct & Ln 77373
Skyland Pl 77381
Skyoak Ct 77386
Skyridge Ct 77373
Skywing Ct 77373
N & S Slash Pine Park & Pl 77380
Slashwood Ln 77379
Slate Path Dr 77382
Slate Valley Ln 77373
Slatestone Cir 77382
E Slatestone Cir 77382
W Slatestone Cir 77382
Slatestone Ln 77386
Sleeping Colt Pl 77389
Sleepy Hollow Ln 77388
Sleepy Hollow St 77386
Sleepy Knoll Dr 77373
Sleepygate Dr 77373
Sliding Rock Cir 77379
Slippery Creek Ln 77388
Slippery Rock Ln 77388
Sloangate Dr 77373
Smith Spgs 77373
Smoke Rock Dr 77373
Smokerise Pl 77381
Smokestone Dr 77381
Smokey Forest Ln 77386
Smokey Oak Rd 77381
Smokeygate Ct 77373
Smooth Brome Ln 77386
Smooth Rock Falls Dr 77379
Snag Ln 77388
Snapdragon Ct 77381
Snappy Creek Ln 77388
Snow Goose Ct 77388
Snow Pond Pl 77382
Snowbell Pl 77381
Snowbird Pl 77381
Snowbird Meadow Dr 77373
Snowdance Ct 77382
Snowden Point Ln 77386
Snowwood Ct & Dr 77388
Soapstone Ln 77379
Soledad Ridge Dr 77373
Solo Ridge Dr 77373
Solvista High Ct 77386
Somerset Pond Pl 77381
Song Sparrow Pl 77381
Songful Woods Pl 77380
Songwind Ln 77379
Sonnet Grove Ct 77382
Sonora Creek Ln 77388
Sorrel Ridge Dr 77388
Sorrell Glen Ct 77388
Sorrell Ridge Dr 77388
Sotherloch Lake Dr 77379
Southampton Dr 77379
Southern Cres 77380
Southern Coast Dr 77380
Southern Cross Ct 77373
Southern Hunters Crossing Cir 77381
Southfork Pines Cir, Ct & Pl 77381
Southgate Dr 77380
Southleigh Dr 77379
Southpine Ct 77389
Spanish Acorn Ln 77389
Spanish Moss Ct 77379
Spanish Oak Way 77379
Spanish Oak Hill Ct 77388
Sparkleberry St 77380
Sparklewood Pl 77381
Sparkling Creek Dr 77386
Sparrow Hawk Ct 77380
Sparrows Glen Ln 77379
Speckled Egg Pl 77381
Spence Park Ct 77373
Spencers Gate Ct 77373
Spiceberry Pl 77382
Spicebush Ct 77381
Spicewood Springs Ln 77379
Spiller Dr 77379
N & S Spincaster Ct & Dr 77389
Spindle Ridge Dr 77386
E & W Spindle Tree Cir 77382
Spindrift Pl 77381
Spinks Creek Ln 77388
N & S Spinning Wheel Cir 77382
Spiral Leaf Ct 77381
N & S Spiral Vine Cir 77381
Split Creek Dr 77373
Split Rail Pl 77382
Split Rail Rdg 77373
Split Rock Ct, Cv & Rd 77381
Spoon Creek Ln 77373
Spooner Ridge Ct 77382
Spotted Deer Dr 77381
Spotted Fawn Ct 77381
Spreading Oaks Dr 77380
N Spring Dr 77373
Spring Acres Dr 77386
Spring Aspen Ln 77388
Spring Basket Trl 77389
Spring Bend Dr 77386
Spring Bluff Ln 77388
Spring Briar Ct & Ln 77373
N & S Spring Brook Ct 77382
Spring Brook Plaza Dr 77379
Spring Chase Dr 77386
Spring Cliff Ct 77373
Spring Colony Dr 77386
Spring Creek Dr
1100-1899 77386
2000-4199 77373
24800-25999 77380
Spring Creek Ln 77379
Spring Creek Trl 77373
Spring Creek Forest Dr 77379
Spring Creek Grove Ln 77379
Spring Creek Oaks Cir, Ct & Dr 77379
Spring Crossing Dr 77373
Spring Crystal Ct 77373
Spring Cypress Rd
6706A-6706B 77379
100-1499 77373
1500-4699 77388
4700-9699 77379
2914-1-2914-2 77388
6706-1-6706-2 77379
Spring Dane Dr 77373
Spring Day Ct & Ln 77373
Spring Dusk Ln 77373
Spring Elms Dr 77373
Spring Fair Ct 77388
Spring Falling Way 77373
Spring Flower Ln 77388
Spring Forest Dr 77386
Spring Forge Dr 77373
Spring Fork Dr 77373
Spring Grove Ln 77373
Spring Gum Dr 77373
Spring Harbor Dr 77373
Spring Heather Ct 77379
Spring Heights Dr 77373
Spring Hill Dr 77386
Spring Hill Pl 77373
Spring Hills Dr 77386
Spring Ivy Ln 77379
Spring Lake Park Ln 77386
Spring Lakes Hvn 77373
Spring Lakes Haven Ct & Dr 77373
Spring Leaf Dr 77379
Spring Lilac Ln 77388
Spring Lily Ct 77373
Spring Link Ct 77373
Spring Meadow Dr 77373
Spring Mill Ln 77373
Spring Mission Ln 77388
Spring Mist Dr 77386
Spring Mist Pl 77381
Spring Moss Dr 77373
Spring Oak Dr 77373
Spring Oak Holw 77379
Spring Oaks Dr 77389
Spring Orchard Ln 77388
Spring Park Center Blvd 77373
Spring Pines Dr 77386
Spring Plaza Dr 77388
Spring Rain Dr 77379
Spring Ranch Ln 77388
Spring Ridge Dr 77386
Spring River Cir 77379
Spring School Rd 77373
Spring Source Ct & Pl 77373
Spring Stuebner Loop 77389
Spring Stuebner Rd
100-1399 77373
1500-6799 77389
5807-1-5807-3 77389
Spring Sunset Dr 77373
Spring Terrace Dr 77386
Spring Town Dr 77388
Spring Towne Dr 77373
Spring Trails Bnd 77386
N & S Spring Trellis Cir 77382
Spring Village Dr 77389
Spring Way Dr 77373
Spring Woods Dr 77386
Springberry Ct 77379
Springbrook Garden Ln 77379
Springbrook Hollow Ct 77379
Springerton Cir 77373
Springfield Garden Ln 77379
Springgate Dr 77373
Springlight Ln 77379
Springstone Dr 77386
Springton Ln 77379
Springwoods Village Pkwy 77389
Sprite Woods Pl 77382
Spruce Cyn 77382
Spruce Run Dr 77379
Spurwood Ct 77381
Squash St 77379
Squirecrest Dr 77389
Squires Ct 77389
Squirrel Tree St 77389
Squyres Rd 77379
St Bernadette Dr 77379
St Domnina Dr 77379
St Hildegarde Ct 77379
St Joanna Ct 77379
St Marcella Dr 77379
St Placidia Dr 77379
St Rosalia Dr 77379
St Winfred Dr 77379
Stallion Brook Ln 77388
Standing Cypress Dr 77379
Standing Hill Ct 77386
Standing Oak Dr 77389
Standing Rock Dr 77386
Stanwick Pl 77382
Stapleford St 77386
Star Fern Pl 77380
Star Gazer Way 77386
Star Ledge Ct 77389
Star Light Ct 77386
Star Pine Ct 77381
N & S Star Ridge Cir 77382
Starcroft Ct 77379
Stardust Pl 77381
Stargazer Pl 77381
Stargazer Pt 77373
Stargrass Dr 77388
Starkstone Ct 77386
Starlight Pl 77380
Starlight Hill Ct 77386
Starling Stream Ct & Dr 77386
Starrush Ct 77380
Starviolet St 77380
Steam Springs Dr 77379
Steepbank Dr 77381
Stemwood Dr 77388
Stepinwolf Ln 77373
Steppinstone Ct & Way 77379
Sterling Dale Pl 77382
Sterling Gate Cir & Ct 77379
Sterling Manor Dr 77379
Sterling Pines Ct 77379
E & W Sterling Pond Cir & Ct 77382
Sterling Ridge Dr 77382
Sterling Village Dr 77386
Sternwood Manor Dr 77379
Stewarts Grove Dr 77379
Stickley Ct 77382
Still Corner Pl 77381
Still Glen Ct 77381
Still Meadow St 77389
Still Oaks Ln 77386
Stiller Ridge Way 77386
Stillgate Ct 77373
E & W Stockbridge Landing Cir, Ct & Dr 77382
Stockport Dr 77379
Stockton Springs Dr 77379
Stone Arrow Pl 77382
Stone Creek Pl 77382
Stone Fox Dr 77386
Stone Hill Rd 77389
Stone Ivory Ct 77388
Stone Mill Ln 77373
Stone Moss 77379
Stone Point St 77388
Stone Springs Cir 77381
Stone Trail Ln 77379
Stonebridge Church Dr 77382
Stonecroft Pl 77381
Stonegate Park Ct 77379
Stonehaven Dr 77389
Stonehaven Village Cir 77386
Stonesfield Pl 77389
Stoney Ct 77373
Stoney Bend Dr 77379
Stoney Plain Dr 77386
Stoney River Ct & Dr 77379
Stoneydale Ln 77388
E, S & W Stony Bridge Cir & Ct 77381
E & W Stony End Ct & Pl 77381
Stony Run Pl 77381
Storm Mist Pl 77381
Stormwood Pl 77381
Stormy Pine Ln 77379
Stornoway Dr 77379
Strack Dr 77379
Strack Farm Rd 77379
Strake Dr 77389
Stratmor Ct 77389
Stratton Park Dr 77379
Stratus Ct 77386
Strawberry Canyon Pl 77382
Streeter Ln 77388
Streeter Place Ct 77388
Stuebner Airline Rd 77379
Sue Ann Ln 77373
Sugar Bear Dr 77389
Sugar Grove Ct 77382
Sugar Leaf Trl 77389
Sugar Valley Ln 77373
Sugarloaf Dr 77379
Sullivan Oaks Dr 77386
Sulphur River Ct 77386
Sumac Ln 77389
Summer Ct & Prt 77381
Summer Bridge Ln 77379
Summer Chase Dr 77389
Summer Cloud Dr 77381
Summer Creek Dr 77379
Summer Crest Cir 77381
Summer Green Ln 77373
Summer Grove Cir 77379
E Summer Haze Cir & Ct 77382
Summer Lark Pl 77382
Summer Morning Ct 77381
Summer Oak Ct 77379
Summer Pine Dr & Ln 77373
Summer Sprig Rd 77380
Summer Spring Dr 77373
N & S Summer Star Ct 77380
E & W Summer Storm Cir & Pl 77381
Summer Trace Ct & Ln 77379
Summerfield Ln 77379
Summergate Dr 77373
Summersweet Pl 77380
Summerton Dr 77386
Summerwalk Pl 77381
Summit Grove Ln 77386
Summit Oaks Ln 77379
Summit Springs Ln 77386
Summithill Pl 77381
Sumner Isle Ct 77379
Sun Loft Ct 77382
Sun Shadow Ln 77386
Sun Shower Ct 77381
Sun Spring Ct 77373
Sunbeam Pl 77381
Sunbird Ct 77380
Sunbury Springs Dr 77379
E & W Sundance Cir 77382
Sundance Springs Ln 77379
Sundance Woods Ct 77386
Sunfall Trail Ln 77386
Sunflower Springs Ct 77373
Sungail Dr 77386
Sunlight Hill Ct 77379
Sunlight Hill Ln 77386
E Sunlit Forest Dr 77381
Sunlit Grove St 77382
Sunny Point Dr 77379
Sunny Sky Pl 77386
E & N Sunny Slope Cir 77381
Sunnygate Dr 77373
Sunrise Brook Ln 77379
Sunrise Glen Ct & Ln 77379
Sunrise Point Ct 77379
Sunset Bend Ln 77379
Sunset Falls Ct 77379
Sunset Falls Dr 77386
Sunset Glen Ln 77373
Sunset Loch Dr 77379

Street	ZIP
Sunset Oak	77379
Sunset Oaks Ln	77386
Sunset Pines Dr	77373
Sunshine Ln	77388
Sunspree Pl	77382
Sunwillow Creek Dr	77386
Surreygate Dr	77373
Surreywest Ln	77379
Susanna Ln	77389
Sussex Ct	77389
Sutter Springs Ln	77386
Sutton Mill Pl	77382
Suzanne Ct	77379
Swallow Tail Ct	77381
Swan Song Pl	77381
Swansea Bay Dr	77379
Sweden Ct	77379
Sweet Birch Pl	77382
W Sweet Gum St	77388
Sweet Louetta Ln	77388
Sweet William Ct	77379
Sweetbeth Ct	77380
Sweetdream Pl	77381
Sweetglen Ct	77373
Sweetgum Hill Ct	77388
Sweetjasmine Ln	77379
Sweetleaf Ct	77381
Sweetmeadow Dr	77379
Sweetspire Pl	77380
Sweetwind Ln	77373
Swift Brook Glen Way	77389
Swiftstream Pl	77381
Switchbud Pl	77380
Sylvan Forest Dr	77381
Sylvia Springs Ln	77386
Syndee Loch Ct	77379
T C Jester Blvd	77379
Taidswood Dr	77379
Tall Cypress Dr	77388
Tall Sky Pl	77381
Tall Tree Trl	77379
Tall Tree Ridge Way	77379
Tallgrass Ct & Way	77389
Tallow Chase Ln	77379
Tallow Hill Pl	77382
S & W Tallowberry Dr	77381
Tamarind Pl	77381
Tamerton Dr	77388
Tamina Rd	77385
Tammany Manor Ln	77379
Tanager Trl	77381
Tangle Brush Dr	77381
N Tangle Creek Ln	77388
Tanguey Ct	77388
Taper Glow Pl	77381
Tapestry Forest Pl	77381
E & W Tapestry Park Cir & Dr	77381
Tarawood Ct	77388
Tarra Firma Dr	77379
Tartan Manor St	77379
Tatton Crest Ct	77388
Tatum Ln	77389
Tatum Bend Ln	77386
Taylor Way	77389
Taylor Point Dr	77382
Taylor Ridge Dr	77373
Taymouth Dr	77386
Tea Olive Ct	77389
Teaberry Ln	77389
Teak Mill Pl	77382
Teakwood Forest Dr	77379
Teal Dr	77386
Teal Trl	77389
Teal Forest Ln	77379
Tealbriar Cir	77381
Tealcrest Estates Dr	77386
Tealgate Dr	77373
Technology Forest Blvd & Pl	77381
Teddy Rd	77389
Tee Tree Ct	77386
Telegraph Creek Ct & Dr	77379
Telkwa Dr	77386
Teller Blvd	77388
Temple Bell Dr	77388
Ten Curves Cir, Ct & Rd	77379
Tender Violet Pl	77381
Tenison Ct	77379
Teri Ct	77386
Terra Run Ct	77386
N & S Terrace Mill Cir	77382
Terrace Vine Ln	77379
Terraceglen Ct	77379
Terraglen Dr	77382
Terrain Park Dr	77373
Terramont Dr	77382
Terranova West Dr	77379
Terravale Ct	77381
Terravita Dr	77379
Terrawren Ln	77379
Tessie Cove Ln	77386
Tessie Hills Ln	77386
Tethered Vine Pl	77382
Texian Ct	77388
Thadds Trl	77373
N & S Thatcher Bend Cir	77389
Theiss Hill Dr	77379
Theiss Mail Route Rd	77379
Theiss Park Ln	77379
Theissetta Dr	77379
Theisswood Cir, Ct, Ln & Rd	77379
Thelfor Ct	77379
Thicket Run Dr	77388
Thimbleberry Ct	77380
Thistle Brook Pl	77382
Thistle Wind Ct	77381
Thistleberry Ln	77379
Thistlebury Ln	77373
Thistlegate Ct	77373
Thistlewaite Ln	77373
Thistlewood Pl	77381
Thora Ln	77381
Thorhill St	77379
Thorn Berry Pl	77381
Thornblade Cir	77389
Thornbush Pl	77381
Thorncreek Ct	77381
Thorngrove Ln	77389
Thornhedge Ct	77381
Thornmead Ln	77379
Thornwood Dr	77381
Thorsby Dr	77386
Thorton Knolls Dr	77389
Thrush Grove Pl	77381
Thrushwood Ln	77373
Thunder Hollow Pl	77381
Thundercove Pl	77381
Thundercreek Pl	77381
Thurber Ridge Dr	77379
E & W Thymewood Pl	77382
Tiburon Ct	77389
Tickleseed Ln	77379
Tidy Tips Ln	77379
Tillamook Ct	77379
Timber Dust Cir	77373
Timber Gardens Dr	77386
Timber Lakes Dr	77380
Timber Lane Dr	77386
Timber Line Dr	77380
Timber Mill St	77380
Timber Nook Ct	77389
Timber Pines Dr	77388
Timber Point Ct	77379
N & S Timber Top Dr	77380
Timber Trail St	77386
Timberbrook Dr	77373
Timbercrest Village Dr	77389
Timberjack Pl	77380
Timberland Path Dr	77373
Timberlea Pl	77382
Timberloch Pl	77380
E & W Timberspire Ct & Ln	77380
Timberstand Ln	77373
Timberstar St	77382
Timberstone Ln	77379
E & W Timberwagon Cir	77380
Timberwild St	77380
Timberwilde Dr	77389
Timberwork Rd	77379
Tinsley Trl	77388
E & W Titan Springs Dr	77389
Titleist Dr	77373
Tiverton Ct	77386
Tivoli Garden Ct	77382
Tizerton Ct	77379
Todd Ct	77386
Tomato St	77379
Tonydale Ln	77388
Tophill Dr	77388
Topside Row	77380
Topway Dr	77373
E & W Torch Pine Cir & Ct	77381
Torrington Ct	77379
Tortoise Creek Pl & Way	77389
Towergate Dr	77373
Towering Pines Dr	77381
Towermont Ln	77388
Towerstone Ct & Dr	77379
Town Moor Ct	77379
Towne Terrace Dr	77379
Townsend Pl	77382
Township Elm St	77373
E, N, S & W Trace Creek Dr	77381
Trace Forest Dr	77379
Tracy Ridge Ct	77386
Trailhead Pl	77381
Trailing Vine Rd	77373
Trailway Ln	77379
Trammel Dr	77388
S Tranquil Path	77380
Tranquil Glade Pl	77381
Tranquil Park Ct & Dr	77379
N & S Tranquil Path Dr	77380
Trapper Lake Dr	77388
Treadwell Ct	77381
Treaschwig Rd	77373
Treasure Cove Dr	77381
Treasure Mountain Dr	77388
Trebeck Ln	77379
Tree Bright Ln	77373
Tree Cove Ct	77381
Tree Crest Cir	77381
Tree House Cir, Ct & Ln	77373
Tree Shallow Bluff Path	77389
Tree Trunk Dr	77388
Treeloch Ln	77379
Treeridge Pl	77380
Treescape Cir	77381
Treestar Pl	77381
Treetop Ln	77388
Treevine Ct	77381
Trellis Gate St	77382
Trembling Creek Cir	77373
Tremont Woods Ct	77381
Trench Ln	77386
Tres Lagos Dr	77389
Treshire Ln	77388
Trestletree Pl	77380
Trickling Springs Ct	77373
E & W Trillium Cir & Ct	77381
S Trinity Oaks Cir & Ct	77381
Trinity Park Ln	77386
Trinity Pass Ct	77373
Trinity River Ct & Dr	77386
Trinket Dr	77386
Triple Spur Ln	77373
Tristan Bay Ct	77386
Tristandale Ln	77379
Tropper Ct	77386
Tropper Hill Ln	77386
Trummel Ct	77381
Truvine Pl	77382
Tuckahoe Ln	77373
Tudor Glen Pl	77382
Tulip Glen Ct	77379
Tulip Hill Ct	77380
Tulip Trace Dr	77386
Tulipa St	77380
Tunica Pass Ct	77389
E & W Tupelo Green Cir	77389
Turley St	77373
Turnberry Park Ln	77373
Turnbury Elm Ct	77386
Turnbury Village Dr	77386
Turner Slate Ln	77386
Turnip St	77379
Turnmill Ct	77379
N Turtle Rock Ct	77381
Tuscany Woods Dr	77381
Twain St	77373
Tweedbrook Dr	77379
Twelve Pines Ct	77381
Twilight Pl	77381
Twilight Glen Ct	77381
Twilight Plain Pl	77381
Twin Feather Pl	77381
Twin Leaf Dr	77379
Twin Mills Ln	77386
Twin Oaks Dr	77389
Twin Point Ln	77386
Twin Springs Pl	77381
Twin Woods Ln	77386
E & W Twinberry Pl	77381
Twining Oaks Ln	77379
Twisted Birch Ct	77373
Twisted Birch Place Ct	77381
Twisted Oak Ct & Dr	77381
Twister Trl	77373
Twisting Falls Dr	77373
Twisting Maple Ct	77373
Twisting Pine Ct & Dr	77373
Twisting Rose Cir & Dr	77373
Two Trail Dr	77373
Tylergate Dr	77373
Tynecreek Ln	77379
Tynham Springs Dr	77386
Tyrone St	77373
Umbria Ln	77382
Underwood Pl	77381
Unity Candle Trl	77388
Upland Brook Ln	77379
Upland Hill St	77373
Upper Falls Ct & Ln	77373
Urban Forest Ct	77386
Utah Beach Ct	77388
Uther Ct	77379
Valcourt Pl	77382
Vale Brook Dr	77373
Vale Haven Dr	77373
W Valera Ridge Dr & Pl	77389
Valerie Ln	77380
Valhalla Dr	77379
Valiant Woods Dr	77379
Valka Rd	77379
Valkyrie Dr	77379
Valley Center Dr	77386
Valley Cottage Pl	77389
N Valley Oaks Cir	77382
W Valley Palms Dr	77379
Valley Scene Way	77379
Valley Springs Pl	77373
Valley Wood Dr	77380
Valleybrook Pl	77382
Valleyview Creek Ct	77379
Van Allen Dr	77381
Vandyke Dr	77388
Vanessa Springs Ln	77389
Vanhorn Ct	77379
Vannevar Way	77381
Vanterne Dr	77379
Vashon Ln	77388
Vasser Ridge Dr	77388
Veilwood Cir	77382
Velvet Grass Ct	77382
Velvet Leaf Pl	77380
Velvet Sky Ct & Way	77386
Veranda Ln	77382
Veranda Ridge Dr	77382
Verbena Bend Pl	77382
Verdant Valley Pl	77382
Verdecove Ln	77388
Verdin Pl	77389
Vernal Glen Cir	77388
Verngate Ct & Dr	77373
Vernier Woods Ln	77379
N & S Vesper Bend Cir	77382
Viamonte Ln	77379
Vickridge Ln	77379
Victoria Estates Dr	77386
Victoria Falls Dr	77379
Victoria Lakes Cir	77379
N & S Victoriana Cir	77389
Victory Ln	77386
Viking Landing Ct	77388
Villa Canyon Pl	77382
Villa Mountain Ln	77379
N & S Villa Oaks Dr	77382
Villa Way Dr	77379
Village Creek Loop	77386
Village Crossing Trl	77373
Village Hills Dr	77379
E, N, S & W Village Knoll Cir & Pl	77381
Village Leaf Dr	77386
Villeroy Way	77382
Vinca Trl	77382
Vincent Ct	77382
Vincent Crossing Dr	77386
Vinebriar Dr	77386
Vinebrook Rd	77380
Vinland Shores Ct	77379
Vintage Creek Dr	77379
Vintage Path Pl	77381
Vintage Wood Cir & Ln	77379
Viola Bloom Ct	77382
Violetta Ct	77381
Vision Park Blvd	77384
Vista Cove Cir & Dr	77381
Vista De Tres Lagos Dr	77389
Vista Mill Pl	77382
Vista Springs Dr	77379
Vivian Ct	77379
N & S Vlg Of Bridgestone Ln	77379
Volunteer Ln	77380
Vorgen Ct	77379
Vuskou Ct	77386
Wakerobin Ct	77380
Walcott Mills Dr	77379
N & S Walden Elms Cir	77382
Wales Ct	77379
Walford Dr	77379
Wallingham Ct & Dr	77379
Wallstone Ct	77388
Walnut St	77373
Walnut Fair Ln	77373
Walnut Forest Ct & Ln	77388
Walnut Grove Cir	77380
Walnut Valley Dr	77389
Walnutgate Dr	77373
Walston Ridge Ct & Dr	77379
Waltham St	77386
E Wandering Oak Dr	77381
Wandflower Pl	77381
Wandsworth Dr	77379
Waning Moon Dr	77389
Waning Star Ct	77379
Warbler Pl	77381
N & S Warbler Bend Cir	77382
Ward Ln	77389
Warm Terrace Ln	77389
E & W Warwick Lake Ln	77389
Washington Park Ct	77379
Water Elm Pl	77382
Water Mark Way	77381
Water Oak Hill Dr	77388
Water Park Way	77386
Waterbend Ct, Cv & Way	77386
Waterbrook Pl	77381
Watercliff Ct	77388
Waterford Bnd, Cir & Lk	77381
Watermill Ct	77380
Watertree Ct & Dr	77380
Waterway Ave & Ct	77380
Waterway Square Pl	77380
Watt Point Ln	77388
Waverly Park Ln	77379
E, N, S & W Wavy Oak Cir	77381
N & S Waxberry Rd	77381
Waxcandle Dr	77388
Waymare Ln	77388
Waynegate Dr	77373
Weald Way Ct & St	77388
Wealden Forest Dr	77379
Webb Creek Pl	77382
Wedgehollow Ct & Ln	77389
E & W Wedgemere Cir & Ct	77381
Wedgewood Ct	77386
E Wedgewood Gln	77381
W Wedgewood Gln	77381
Wedgewood Pt	77381
Wedgewood Bluff Ct	77379
Wedgewood Forest Dr	77381
Weeping Oak Ct	77388
Weeping Oaks Ln	77388
Weller Oaks Dr	77389
Wellington Court Blvd	77389
Wellington Pass Dr	77373
Wells St	77373
E & W Welsford Dr	77386
Wenoah Loop & Pl	77389
Wensley Dr	77386
Westbridge Ln	77379
Westbrook Oaks Way	77379
Westgate Village Ln	77373
Weston Village Dr	77386
Westover Park Cir	77386
Westridge Rd	77380
N Westwinds Cir	77382
Westwood Ct & Dr	77386
Wheaton Crest Ln	77379
Whetstone Ridge Ct & Way	77382
Whidbey Ct	77388
Whisper Ln	77380
Whisper Wind Pl	77382
Whispering Maple Dr	77373
Whispering Maple Way	77386
Whispering Oaks Ln	77386
Whispering Rock Ln	77388
Whispering Springs Dr	77373
Whispering Willow Dr	77373
Whisperwillow Pl	77380
Whispy Fern Pl	77381
Whistlers Ct	77380
Whistlers Walk Pl	77381
Whistling Pines Ct & Dr	77389
N & S Whistling Swan Pl	77389
White Bark Pl	77381
White Birch Run	77386
White Candle Dr	77388
White Fawn Dr	77381
White Marsh Ct	77379
White Meadow Ct	77379
N & S White Pebble Ct	77380
White Sage Cove Ln	77386
White Shore Ln	77379
White Springs Ct	77373
White Tail Dr	77379
E & W White Willow Cir	77381
White Wing Ct	77382
Whitebrush Ln	77380
Whitelake Dr	77373
Whitelaw Dr	77386
Whitewood Dr	77373
Whittaker Way	77373
Wickburn Dr	77386
Wickerdale Pl	77382
Wickman Reach Dr	77386
Wickwilde St	77389
Wickwood Dr	77386
Widmore Ct & Pl	77379
Wied Rd	77388
Wilcox Point Ct & Dr	77388
Wild Aster Ct	77382
Wild Bird Dr	77373
Wild Colt Pl	77382
Wild Ginger Ct	77380
Wild Indigo Pl	77381
Wild Meadow Ct	77380
Wild Poppy Dr	77379
Wild Ridge Dr	77380
Wild Rose Dr	77386
Wild Wind Pl	77380
Wildcandle Dr	77388
Wilde Woods Way	77380
E, N, W & S Wilde Yaupon Ct	77381
Wilderness Rd	77380
Wildever Pl	77382
Wildfern Trl	77386
Wildflower Trace Pl	77382
Wilding Wimbledon Ct	77382
Wildsage Ct	77379
E Wildwind Cir	77380
Wildwood Creek Way	77379
Wildwood Dale Ln	77379
Wildwood Forest Dr	77380
Wildwood Green Way	77373
Willie Way	77380
Willow Ct	77379
Willow St	77373
Willow Loch Dr	77379
Willow Pine Dr	77379
N & S Willow Point Cir & Pl	77382
Willow Run Pl	77382
Willow School Dr	77389
Willow Springs Pl	77373
Willow Switch Rd	77379
Willow Wisp Cir & Ln	77388
Willowcreek Stables Rd	77389
Willowcrest Ct	77389
Willowcrest Pl	77381
Willowgate Dr	77373
Willowherb Ct	77380
Willowick Dr	77389
E & W Willowood Cir & Ct	77381
Wilsford Dr	77388
Wilson Reach Ln	77389
Wilting Oak Ln	77389
Wilton Park Ct & Dr	77379
Wimbledon Champions Dr	77379
Wimbledon Estates Dr	77379
Wimbledon Forest Ct & Dr	77379
Wimbledon Trail Rd	77379
Wimbledon Villas Dr	77379
Winchmore Hill Dr	77379
Wind Brush Dr	77388
Wind Field Ln	77379
Wind Harp Pl	77382
Wind Poppy Ct	77381
Wind Ridge Cir	77381
Wind Ridge Ln	77379
Wind Trace Ct	77381
Wind Trace Ln	77379
Wind Whisper Ct	77380
Windbluff Ct	77382
Windbury Ct	77379
Windcrest Park Ct & Ln	77386
Windfall Path Dr	77373

Windfellow Pl 77381
Windfern Pl 77382
Windflower Pl 77381
Windgap Ct 77380
Windhaven Dr 77381
Winding Creek Pl 77381
Winding Hill Ln 77379
Winding Oak Ln 77379
Winding Ridge Dr 77379
Winding Spring Dr 77379
Winding Willow Ln 77373
Windledge Pl 77381
Windmeadow Pl 77381
Windridge Pl 77381
Windrose Bend Dr 77379
Windrose Hollow Ln 77379
Windrow Dr 77379
Windrush Dr 77379
N & S Windsail Pl 77381
Windsong Ct 77381
Windsor Canyon Ct 77389
Windsor Castle Dr 77388
Windsor Chase Ln 77373
Windstar Ct & Dr 77381
Windtree Ln 77379
W Windward Ct & Cv 77381
Windy Briar Ln 77379
Windy Isle Ct 77389
Windy Pines Cir & Dr 77379
Windy Plain Ct 77388
Windy Point Dr 77379
Windy Run Ct 77379
Windygate Dr 77373
Windypine Dr 77379
Wine Cup Ct 77379
Wineberry Pl 77382
Winford Ct 77379
Wingfield Ln 77373
Wingspan Dr 77381
Winlock Trails Dr 77386
Winrock Pl 77382
Winslow Way 77382
Winsome Path Cir 77382
Winter Breeze Dr 77379
Winter Forest Dr 77379
Winter Mountain Ln 77379
Winter Pines Ct 77373
Winter Wheat Pl 77381
Winterberry Pl 77380
Wintercorn Pl 77382
Wintergate Dr 77373
Wintergrass Pl 77382
Wintergreen Trl 77382
N & S Winterport Cir 77382
Winton Wood Way 77386
Wintress Dr 77382
Wishbonebush Rd 77380
Wishing Oak Lndg 77386
Wisteria Walk 77388
Wisteria Brook Ln 77379
Wisteria Trace Dr 77386
Wisteria Walk Cir 77381
Wistful Vista Pl 77382
E & W Wolf Cabin Cir 77389
Wolf Rose Ln 77386
Wolfhound Ln 77380
Wolfs Crossing Ct 77373
Wollaston Ct 77389
Wolly Bucket Pl 77380
Wolverton Dr 77379
Wood Bark Cir & Rd 77379
Wood Cove Dr 77381
Wood Manor Pl 77381
Wood Place Ct 77379
Wood River Dr 77373
Wood Scent Ct 77380
Wood Tower Ct 77386
Woodbark Rd 77379
Woodberry Manor Dr 77379
Woodborough Way 77389
Woodbury Springs Ln 77379
Woodchuck Ln 77380
Woodcliff Lake Dr 77379
Wooded Brook Cir & Dr 77382
Wooded Park Pl 77380
Wooded Path Pl 77382
Wooded Way Dr 77389
Woodelves Pl 77381
Woodglen Dr 77386
Woodglen Point Ct 77379
Woodgum Dr 77388
Woodhaven Wood Ct & Dr 77380
Woodhouse Dr 77379
Woodhue Ct & Dr 77386
Woodland Heights Ln 77373
Woodlands Pkwy
1001-1997 77380
1999-2999 77380
4400-4699 77381
4701-6499 77381
6600-10199 77382
Woodlily Pl 77382
Woodline Dr 77386
Woodloch Forest Dr 77380
Woodlode Ln 77379
Woodlot Ct 77380
Woodmere Pl 77381
Woods Edge Dr 77388
Woodsboro Ct & Dr 77388
Woodson Trace Dr 77386
Woodsong Ln 77389
Woodsons Lake Dr 77386
Woodstead Ct 77380
N Woodstock Circle Dr 77381
E & W Woodtimber Ct 77381
Woodville Ln 77379
Woodway Ct 77386
Woolf Rd 77379
Worcester Dr 77379
Worgan Ct 77379
Wrangler Pass Dr 77389
Wrens Song Pl 77382
Wrest Point Ct 77388
Wrexham Springs Ct 77373
Wunder Hill Dr 77379
Wunsche Loop
800-1499 77373
1411-1411 77383
1219-1-1219-4 77373
Wyanngate Dr 77373
Wyckham Cir 77382
Wyeth Cir 77379
Wyndham Rose Ln 77379
N & S Wynnoak Cir & Dr 77382
Wyoma Trl 77379
Yarbrough Bend Ct 77389
Yarrow Ct 77382
Yarrowdale Ct 77382
Yaupon Green Ct 77379
Yellow Pine Cir & Ln 77380
Yellowood Ct 77380
Yewleaf Ct, Dr & Rd 77381
N & S York Gate Ct 77382
York Minster Dr 77379
Yorkgate Dr 77373
Yorkshire Manor Ct 77379
Young Oak St 77379
Youpon Ln 77389
Youpon Lake Ln 77373
Zephyr Bend Pl 77381

NUMBERED STREETS

All Street Addresses 77373

STAFFORD TX

General Delivery 77477

POST OFFICE BOXES MAIN OFFICE STATIONS AND BRANCHES

Box No.s
All PO Boxes 77497

NAMED STREETS

Aberdeen St 77477
Adams St 77477
Ainsworth Dr 77477
W Airport Blvd 77477
Akj St 77477
Alexandria St 77477
Allisa St 77477
Alpine Dr 77477
Alston Dr 77477
Amblewood Dr 77477
Angela Ln 77477
Annes Way 77477
Antonia St 77477
Applecreek Bend Dr 77477
Arcott Ln 77477
Ariel Ct 77477
Ashley Grove Ct 77477
Ashling Dr 77477
Aspen Ln 77477
Audubon Ct 77477
Avenue E 77477
Avenue B 77477
Avenue F 77477
Baptist St 77477
Barker St 77477
Bates Ln 77477
W Bellfort St 77477
W Bend Dr 77477
Betty Ln 77477
S Beverly Cir 77477
Blair Meadow Dr 77477
Bloomington Ln 77477
Bluebonnet Dr
3901-3921 77477
3923-4199 77477
4110-4110 77497
4200-4498 77477
4201-4499 77477
Boardwalk Pkwy 77477
Bold Ruler Dr 77477
Bolero Ct 77477
Bonnie Ln 77477
Bowen St 77477
Brand Ln 77477
Brandy St 77477
Breezy Meadow Dr 77477
Brighton Ln 77477
Brocket Pl 77477
Brook Meadows Ct & Ln 77477
Buckingham Pl 77477
Buena Vista St 77477
Caesar Dr 77477
Canonero St 77477
Capricorn St 77477
Carl Ct 77477
Carlie Way 77477
Carriage Ln 77477
Cash Rd 77477
Castle Pl 77477
Cedar Brook Ct 77477
Cedar Form Ln 77477
Center St 77477
Century Dr 77477
Chariot Dr 77477
Chesterfield Ln 77477
Childers Ct 77477
Christopher St 77477
Citation Dr 77477
Clay St 77477
Colony Lake Estates Dr 77477
Commerce Business Dr 77477
Corine St 77477
Corporate Dr 77477
Corridor Pl & Way 77477
Country Club Blvd 77477
Country Place Dr 77477
Cravens Rd 77477
Crescent Ln 77477
Crest Ct 77477
Crestmont Dr 77477
Cymbal Dr 77477
Dairy Ashford Rd 77477
Deborah St 77477
Demia Ct 77477
Directors Dr 77477
Doe Meadow Dr 77477
Dorrance Ln 77477
Dove Country Dr 77477
Dublin Ct 77477
Duchess Way 77477
Dukes Bnd 77477
Dulles Ave 77477
Easy Jet Dr 77477
Elana Ln 77477
Elk Meadow Dr 77477
Ellis St 77477
Elm View Ct 77477
Enclave Ct 77477
Eppolito St 77477
N & S Esplanade Ln, Pl & Way 77477
Essex Pl 77477
Ester St 77477
Exchange Dr 77477
Executive Dr 77477
Fair Oak Ct & Dr 77477
Farrah Ln 77477
Fern Meadow Dr 77477
Ferro St 77477
Fir Crest Ct 77477
Flaxseed Way 77477
Fm 2234 Rd 77477
Folkcrest Way 77477
Folklore Way 77477
Folknoll Dr 77477
Ford Rd 77477
Fountain Lake Cir & Dr 77477
Fountaingate Dr 77477
Fox Meadow Dr 77477
Frances St 77477
Frank Ln 77477
Gala Ct 77477
Gallant Fox Dr 77477
Gambit Dr 77477
Gina St 77477
Glenmeadow Dr 77477
Go Man Go Dr 77477
Golf Ct 77477
Gondola Dr 77477
Grapevine Ct 77477
Green Trails Dr 77477
Greenbough Dr 77477
Greenbriar Dr 77477
Greenland Ct & Dr 77477
Gregory Ct 77477
Grove Meadow Dr 77477
Grove Stone Ct 77477
Grove West Blvd 77477
Guadalupe St 77477
Guillen Ln 77477
Hackberry St 77477
Harvey Ln 77477
Hill Cris Rd 77477
Hoggard Dr 77477
Hollyhock Dr 77477
Horace St 77477
Illiad Ct 77477
Jaguar Dr 77477
James Ln 77477
Jays Ln 77477
Jebbia Ln 77477
Jersey Meadow Dr 77477
Jester Ln 77477
Jo Ann St 77477
Joan St 77477
Josephine St 77477
Juniper Ct 77477
Kangaroo Ct 77477
Katherine St 77477
Katy St 77477
Kelso Ct 77477
Kenzie Ct 77477
Kings Ct & Way 77477
S Kirkwood Dr & Rd 77477
Kitty St 77477
Knights Cir 77477
Lance Ln 77477
Laurel Ct 77477
Lawrence Ln 77477
Lebon Ln 77477
Leisure Dr 77477
Lelia St 77477
Level Run St 77477
Lilac Ct 77477
Linda St 77477
Lindsey Ln 77477
Live Oak Dr 77477
Llama Ln 77477
Louise St 77477
Ludwig Ln 77477
Lyrical Dr 77477
Mackworth Dr 77477
Magnolia Ct 77477
N & S Main St 77477
Maple Leaf Ln 77477
Maple Tree Ct 77477
N & S Marathon Pl & Way 77477
Mark St 77477
Maurice Way 77477
Mcintosh Bend Dr 77477
Meadow Ln 77477
Meadow Bend Ct 77477
Meadow Berry Dr 77477
Meadow Briar Dr 77477
Meadow Crest Ct & Dr 77477
Meadow Gate Dr 77477
Meadow Knoll Dr 77477
Meadow Lane Ct 77477
Meadow Park Ct 77477
Meadow Pines Ct & Dr 77477
Meadow Ridge Dr 77477
Meadow Valley Ln 77477
Meadowdale Dr 77477
Meadowglen Ct & Dr 77477
Meadowhollow Dr 77477
Meadowtrail Ln 77477
Monticeto Ct & Ln 77477
Moore Rd 77477
Mula Cir, Ct, Ln & Rd 77477
Mulholland Dr 77477
Murphy Rd 77477
Nadia Way 77477
Naples Cir & Ln 77477
Nashua Dr 77477
Nepau Dr 77477
Nikki Ln 77477
Nina Ln 77477
Nobility Dr 77477
Norenerr Dr 77477
Oak St 77477
Oak Meadow Dr 77477
Oakdale Ct & Dr 77477
Oldcrest Dr 77477
Orchard Ct 77477
Overland St 77477
Oyster Cove Ct 77477
Packer Ln 77477
Pagoda Dr 77477
Palace Dr 77477
Pamela Sue Ct 77477
Parc Crest Dr 77477
Pecan Ln 77477
Pender Ln 77477
Penwood Ct 77477
Perez St 77477
Picket Ln 77477
Pike Rd 77477
Pine Brook Dr 77477
Plantation Ln 77477
Present St 77477
N Promenade Blvd 77477
Queens Ct 77477
Quiet Meadow Ct 77477
Randall St 77477
Rastus Ave 77477
Redfish Ln 77477
Reva Ridge Dr 77477
Richard St 77477
Richton Rd 77477
River Meadow Ln 77477
Robin Meadow Cir 77477
Robins Way 77477
Robinwood Dr 77477
Rosas St 77477
Rose Ann St 77477
Rothwell St 77477
Royal Dr 77477
Ruffian Ln 77477
Ruth Ave 77477
Sandy Walk 77477
Saunter Dr 77477
Scarcella Ln 77477
Scarpinato Rd 77477
Scottsdale Ct & Dr 77477
Secretariet Dr 77477
Shady Brook Dr 77477
Shady Dale Dr 77477
Shirleen Dr 77477
Snowbird Ct 77477
Solano Ct 77477
Southmeadow Dr 77477
Southwest Fwy 77477
Squires Bnd 77477
Stafford Pkwy & Rd 77477
Stafford Centre Dr 77477
Stafford Colony Ln 77477
Stafford Point Dr 77477
Stafford Run Rd 77477
Stafford Springs Ave 77477
Staffordshire Rd 77477
Straus Ct 77477
Strolling Way 77477
Sturdivant St 77477
Success Ct 77477
Sugar Grove Blvd 77477
Sugar Ridge Blvd 77477
Sugardale Dr 77477
Summer Park Dr 77477
Sundance Ct 77477
E, N, S & W Sutton Sq 77477
Suzanne St 77477
Sweetwater Ct 77477
Swords Bnd 77477
Tambourine Dr 77477
Tanglewood Ct 77477
Taylor Ln 77477
Techniplex Dr 77477
Terrence Ct & Dr 77477
Thompson Cir 77477
Trinity Dr 77477
Troyan Dr 77477
Tyler Ct & Ln 77477
Valencia St 77477
Venice Cir & Ln 77477
Victory Dr 77477
Wallaby Ct 77477
War Admiral Dr 77477
Wesley Dr 77477
West St 77477
Westwood Dr 77477
Wheelhouse Ct & Dr 77477
Whirlaway Dr 77477
Whitehall Pl 77477
Whitney Oaks Ln 77477
Willards Way 77477
Willow Dr 77477
Winesap Bend Dr 77477
Wright Rd 77477
Youngcrest Dr 77477

NUMBERED STREETS

All Street Addresses 77477

SUGAR LAND TX

General Delivery 77478

POST OFFICE BOXES MAIN OFFICE STATIONS AND BRANCHES

Box No.s
1 - 5099 77487
16001 - 25006 77496

NAMED STREETS

Abbey Ln 77498
Abbott Cir 77498
Abellfield Ln 77478
Aberdeen Cir 77479
Abigal Dr 77498
Abingdon Ct 77479
Acacia Dr 77479
Adair St 77479
Adams Mill Ln 77498
Addison Ave & Pl 77479
Adelfina St 77498
Adlerspoint Ln 77479
Adobe Ct 77479
Adobe Meadows Ct 77479
Adobe Oaks Ct 77479
Adobe Trails Ct & Dr 77479
Adonia Pl 77479
Aegean Trl 77479
Agora Cir 77479
W Airport Blvd
12400-13499 77478
13500-16699 77498
Alamo Ave 77479
Alamosa Ct 77498
Alcorn St 77478
Alcorn Bayou Dr 77479
Alcorn Bend Dr 77479
Alcorn Crossing Dr 77479
Alcorn Glen Ln 77479
Alcorn Hill Dr 77479
Alcorn Oaks Dr 77479
Alden Ct 77479
Alderbrook Dr 77498
Alderwick Dr 77498
Alderwood Dr 77479
Alhambra Ct 77478
Alicant Dr 77479
Alice Dr 77478
Alice Foster St 77498
Aliso Ridge Ct 77479
W Alkire Lake Dr 77478
Alleyan Trl 77479
Alston Rd 77478
Althea Ct 77479
Amanda Ct 77478
Amber Ridge Dr 77498
Amber Trace Ct 77479
Amberstone Dr 77479
Ambleside Crescent Dr 77479
Ambrose Dr 77479
Amelia St 77478
Amelia Terrace Ct 77479
American Elm Ct 77479
Amersham Way 77479
Ames Xing 77479
Amesbury Ct & Ln 77478
Amherst Ave & Ct 77479
Amphora Cir 77479
Ancrum Hill Ln 77479
Andover Ct & St 77478
Angel Meadow Ct 77498
Angel Springs Dr 77479
Angleside Ln 77498
Ann Arbor Ct 77478
Annabella Pl 77479
Annies Way 77479
Anson Grove Ln 77498
Antrim Trl 77479
Apple Dr 77498
Apple Bluff Ct 77479
Apple Rock Ct 77479
Applebee Ct 77479
April Meadow Way 77479
April Run Ct 77479
Aprilmont Dr 77498
Arbor Pl 77479
Arbor Hill Ct 77479
Arbor View Ct & Dr 77479
Arborwood Ln 77479
Arcadia Dr 77498
Arctic Tern Ct 77478

Arden Oaks Dr 77479
Ardwell Dr 77498
Argonne Trl 77479
Ari Ct 77479
Armitage Ln 77498
Arrowhead Ct 77478
Arrowhead Dr 77479
Arundel Crossing Dr 77479
Arundel Gardens Ln 77498
Asbury Ct & Park 77479
Asbury Park Ct 77479
Ascot Ln 77479
Ascot Meadow Dr 77479
Ash St 77498
Ash Point Ln 77498
Ashbury Trails Ct 77479
Ashdale Dr 77498
Ashfield Place Ct 77479
Ashford Pne & Pt 77478
Ashford Falls Ln 77479
Ashford Glen Ct 77478
Ashford Green Ct 77478
Ashford Haven Dr 77478
Ashford Hills Dr 77478
Ashford Hollow Dr 77478
Ashford Lakes Dr 77478
Ashford Meadows Dr 77478
Ashford Park Dr 77478
Ashford Place Dr 77478
Ashford Pond Dr 77478
Ashford Valley Dr 77478
Ashford Willow 77478
Ashford Wind Dr 77478
Ashland Bridge Ln 77498
Ashland Grove Ln 77498
Ashley Garden Ct 77479
Ashley Ridge Ln 77498
Ashley Way Ct 77479
Ashmore Reef Ct 77498
Ashton Villa Ct 77479
Ashwood Dr 77498
Ashworth Dr 77479
Aspen Cove Ct 77479
Aspen Farms Ln 77479
Aspen Hollow Ln 77479
Astor Ct 77498
Atterbury Dr 77498
Auburn Path & Trl 77479
Auburn Brook Ln 77479
Auburn Key Ct 77479
Auckland Dr 77498
Audubon Ct 77478
Aurora St 77498
Austin Pkwy 77479
Austin Meadow Ct &
Dr 77479
Austins Pl 77478
Autumn Trl 77479
Autumn Bend Dr 77479
Autumn Fall Ct 77479
Autumn Glen Dr 77498
Autumn Ridge Dr 77479
Autumn Rose Ln 77479
E & W Autumn Run
Cir 77479
Avalon Pl 77479
Avana Glen Ln 77498
Avenue E 77498
Avenue A 77498
Avenue D 77498
Avenue F 77498
Avenue G 77498
Avenue H 77498
Avery Dr 77479
Avery Park Dr 77498
Avon Landing Ln 77479
Avon Rock Ct 77479
Avondale Dr 77479
Ayers Rock Rd 77498
Aylesbury Ct 77479
Azalea Bnd 77479
Azalea St 77478
Azalea Trail Ln 77479
Azucar Ct 77498
Babbling Brook Ct 77479
Bahama Cove Ct 77479
Baileys Place Ct 77479
Bainbridge Ct 77478
Bainbridge Dr 77479
Balboa Dr 77479
Baldwin Xing 77479
Balmorhea Ln 77498
Balsam Park Ct 77479
Bamberg Way 77479
Banbury Ct 77479
Bandicoot Dr 77498
Bannon Trl 77479
Barksdale Ave 77479
Barnett Rdg 77479
Barnhill Ln 77479
Baron Hill Ln 77479
Barons Gln 77478
Barons Point Ct 77479
Barrel Hoop Cir 77479
Barrett Ct 77479
Barrington Ct 77478
Barrington Place Dr 77478
Barronett Bnd 77479
Barrons Way 77479
Barrowgate Dr 77498
Barton Grove Ct 77479
Bartons Ct & Ln 77479
Bartrum Trl 77479
Basewood Ct 77498
Battle Ridge Ln 77479
Baumeadow Ln 77498
Baxley Ct 77479
Bay Bridge Dr 77478
Bay Gardens Dr 77498
Bay View Dr 77479
Bayberry Way 77479
Bayhill Dr 77479
Bayou Xing 77479
Bayou Bend Ct 77479
Bayou Green Ln 77479
Baytree Dr 77498
Beacon Hl & Pt 77479
Beacon Springs Ln 77479
Beacon View Ct 77479
Beamer Creek Ct 77479
Becket Woods Ln 77498
Bee Bayou Ln 77479
Beech Fork Ln 77498
Beecroft Dr 77498
Beewood Glen Ct &
Dr 77498
Bel Mar St 77478
Beldon Ln 77479
Belknap Ct 77479
Belknap Rd 77498
S Belknap St 77478
Bell Towne Dr 77498
Belle Grove Ln 77479
Belle Manor Ln 77479
Bellevue Falls Ln 77479
W Bellfort Ave
12401-13499 77478
13400-13498 77498
13500-13699 77498
W Bellfort St 77498
Bellingrath Ct 77479
Bellmont Park Ct 77479
Bend Ct 77478
Bending Key Ct 77479
Bendwood Dr 77478
Bennetts Mill Ln 77498
Bent Knoll Ct 77479
Bent River Ct & Dr 77479
Bent Trail Ct 77479
Benwick Dr 77498
Berenger Pl 77479
Berkoff Ct & Dr 77479
Berkshire Ct 77479
Berkshire Ridge Dr 77479
Bermuda Dr 77479
Berrytree Dr & Ln 77479
Berwick Ct 77479
Bettong Ct 77498
Big Bend Dr 77479
Big Horn Ct 77478
Birch Falls Ln 77479
Birch Hill Dr 77479
Birch Vale Ln 77479
Birdnest Trl 77498
Birnam Glen Dr 77479
Birnam Wood Dr 77479
Biscayne Ct 77478
Bishops Ct 77479
Black Canyon Ct 77479
Black Falls Ct & Ln 77498
Black Locust Dr 77479
Black Oak Dr 77479
Blacksmith Ln 77479
Blake Rd 77478
Blakely Ct 77479
Blakely Bend Dr 77479
Blancroft Ct 77478
Blanton Ln 77478
Blossomwood Ln 77498
Blue Falls Dr 77479
N & S Blue Meadow
Cir 77479
Blue Mist Cir, Ct & Dr 77498
Blue Mountain Ln 77479
Blue Vista Ct & Dr 77498
Bluebeard Ct 77479
Bluebonnet St 77478
Bluffstone Ct 77479
Bogard Ct 77479
Bonaventure Way
700-799 77479
800-999 77478
Bonneau Way 77479
Bonnetbriar Ln 77498
Borden St 77478
Boss Gaston Rd 77498
Boulder Oaks Ln 77479
Bountiful Crest Ln 77479
Bournewood Dr 77479
E Bournewood Dr 77478
Box Bluff Ct 77479
Boxwood Ct 77498
Bracebridge Ct 77498
Bradford Cir 77479
Bradham Way 77479
Braelinn Ln 77479
Braesmeadow Ln 77479
Bramblebury Dr 77498
Bramlett Ct 77479
Branchport Ct 77479
Branchwater Ln 77498
Brannon Hill Ct & Ln 77479
Bratton Ct & St 77479
Brazos Dr 77479
Brazos Ridge Dr 77479
Brazos Springs Dr 77479
Breaux Bridge Ln 77479
Breeland Park Ct 77498
Breezy Point Ln 77479
Brenner Ct 77478
Brentwood Ct 77479
Briar Ct 77478
Briar Bend Ct 77479
Briar Cliff Ct 77479
Briar Cottage Ct 77479
Briar Glen Ct 77479
Briar Hill Ct 77479
Briar Knoll Ct 77479
Briar Meadow Dr 77479
Briar Point Ct 77498
Briar Stone Ln 77479
Briarbank Dr 77498
Briarbend Dr 77479
Briarcross Ct 77479
N & S Briarpark Ln 77479
Briarwick Meadow Ln 77479
Bridge Hampton Way 77479
Bridge Oak Ln 77498
Bridgeton Ct 77479
Bridgeton Place Ln 77479
Brigade Ct 77479
Bright Trl 77479
Brightfield Dr 77498
Bristol Ct 77478
Bristol Path Ln 77479
Brittany Dr 77479
Broad Thicket Ct 77498
Broadknoll Ln 77498
Broadley Dr 77498
Broadmoor Dr 77479
Broadoak Grove Ln 77498
Brobeck Ct 77479
Broken Oak Ln 77479
Broken Pine Ct 77479
Broken Rock Ln 77479
Broken Trail Ct 77479
Brompton Ct 77479
E Brook Ct 77479
Brook Arbor Ln 77479
Brook Bend Dr 77478
Brook Forest Trl 77478
Brook Hollow Dr 77498
Brook River Ct 77479
Brook Shore Ct 77478
Brook View Ln 77498
Brookbend Ln 77479
Brookdale Ct 77479
Brooks St 77478
Brookside Dr 77478
Brookstone Ln 77479
Brookview Dr 77479
Brookwood Bridge Ln 77498
Brookwood Lake Pl 77498
Brown Bridge Ct 77498
Browning Ct 77479
Brunswick Cir & Dr 77479
Brush Field Ln 77479
Brush Meadow Ct 77498
Brushmeade Ln 77479
Brushy Creek Dr 77478
Brushy Knoll Ln 77498
Brynwood Ln 77498
Buckeye Furnace Ln 77498
Bucknell Ct 77478
Bucks Bridge Ln 77498
Buckskin Bridge Ct 77498
Buffalo Trl 77479
Buffalo Springs Ct 77479
Bumelia Ct 77479
Burbury St 77479
Burchton Dr 77479
Burclare Ct 77479
Burkdale Dr 77478
Burkwood Ct 77479
Burmese Ln 77478
Burney Rd 77498
Burnham Cir 77479
Burwick St 77479
Cabeza Dr 77478
Cabin Pl 77479
Cabin Run Ln 77498
Cabrera Dr 77479
Cadogan Ct 77479
Cairns Ct 77498
Caladium Dr 77479
Caledonia Trl 77479
Calera Ct & Dr 77479
Calico Creek Ct 77479
Calico Hill Ln 77478
Calisout Dr 77479
Callavance 77479
Calleston Ct 77479
Calley Path 77479
Calloway Dr 77479
Calumet Dr 77478
Calverton Dr 77498
Cambria Ln 77479
Cambrian Park Ct 77479
Cambridge Ct & St 77479
Cambry Landing Ln 77479
Camden Ct 77479
Camden Springs Ln 77479
Camellia St 77478
Camelot Pl 77479
Cameron Crest Ln 77498
Campwood Dr 77478
Canadian River Dr 77478
Canaveral Creek Ln 77479
Candle Cove Ct 77479
Candle Light Ct 77479
Cane Field Dr 77479
Cane Lake Ct 77498
Canebreak Xing 77478
Cannon Ln 77479
Cannon Pass Ct 77478
Cannons Point Ct &
Dr 77478
Canterbury Ct & Ln 77479
Canterbury Green Ct &
Ln 77498
Cantor Trails Ln 77479
Cantrell Ct 77479
Canyon Brook Ct 77479
Canyon Crest Dr 77479
Capri St 77478
Caprock Canyons Ln 77498
Capstan Way 77479
Cardinal Ave & Mdw 77478
Careywood Dr 77478
Carissa Ct 77479
Carnoustie Ct 77479
Caroline Ct 77479
Carriage Way 77478
Carriage Point Dr 77479
Carrington Ct 77479
Carya Cir 77479
Cascade Ct 77479
Casey Cir 77479
Castle Ln 77478
Castlebrook Ct 77478
Castlemaine Ct 77498
Castlewood St 77479
Catesby Pl 77479
Cedar Creek Pt 77478
Cedar Elm Ln 77479
Cedar Locust Ct 77479
Cedar Terrace Ct 77479
Cedaredge Ct 77479
Cedartowne Ln 77498
Cedarwood Ct 77498
Celeste Ct 77479
Centennial Bridge Ct &
Ln 77498
Century Square Blvd 77478
Chalford Dr 77498
Chalice Pl 77479
Chandler Ct 77479
Chandler Creek Ct 77479
Chaneybriar Ave 77479
Charlbrook Dr 77498
Charles Ln 77498
Charleston St N & S 77478
Charleston Heights Ln 77479
Charleton Mill Ln 77498
Charlton St 77479
Charterhouse Way 77498
Chatfield Ct 77479
Chatham Ave 77479
Chatham Green Dr 77479
Chatham Trails Ct 77479
Chatsworth Cir 77479
Chattaroy Pl 77478
Chelston Ct 77478
Cherry Brook Ct 77479
Cherrydown St 77498
Chesapeake Pl 77479
Cheshire Bend Dr 77479
Chessley Chase Dr 77479
Chesswood Cir 77479
Chestnut Glen Ct 77479
Chestnut Meadow Ct &
Dr 77479
Cheswick Cir 77479
Chevy Chase Cir 77478
Cheyenne River Cir 77478
Chianti Ct 77479
Chimneystone Cir 77479
Chippendale Ct 77478
Chipping Ct 77479
Chipping Rock Ct &
Dr 77479
Chipwood Hollow Ct 77498
Choke Canyon Dr 77498
Chritien Point Ct 77478
E & W Church Dr 77498
Circle Dr 77498
City Walk 77479
Claire Ct 77478
Clansmoor Ct 77479
Claremont Ct 77498
Clarenda Falls Dr 77479
Clark Towne Ln 77498
Clarktower Ct & Ln 77498
Clawson Fls 77479
Clawson Falls Ln 77479
Clear Forest Dr 77498
Clear Springs Ct 77479
Clearwater Ct 77478
Clearwater Creek Dr 77478
Clemson Ln 77479
Cleveland Dr 77498
Clover Lodge Ct 77498
Clover Point Dr 77498
Clover Ridge Ln 77479
Coachlight Ln 77479
Coatsworth Dr 77498
Cobalt Glen Dr 77498
Cobb Circle Dr 77479
Cobble Ridge Dr 77498
Cobble Springs Ct 77498
Cobbler Crossing Dr 77498
Cobblerstone Ct 77479
Cobblestone Point Ct &
Dr 77498
Coggins Point Way 77479
Coldstream Ct 77479
Coldwater Bridge Ct 77498
Coleridge St 77479
Coles Farm Dr 77478
Coley Park 77479
Collingsfield Ct & Dr 77478
Collingwood Ct 77479
Colonade Trl 77479
Colonial Dr 77479
Colonist Park Dr 77478
Colony Ct & Dr 77479
Colony Crossing Dr 77479
Colony Glen Ct 77479
Colony Hills Dr 77479
Colony Lakes Dr 77479
Colony Oaks Ct & Dr 77479
Colony Park Dr 77479
Colony Terrace Dr 77479
Colony Woods Dr 77479
Colson Way 77479
Colton Trails Dr 77479
Commerce Green Blvd 77478
Commonwealth Blvd 77479
Community Ct 77478
Concho River Ct 77478
Concord Falls Ln 77498
Constatine Ct 77479
Cook Ln 77479
Cool Springs Ln 77498
Cool Water Ct & Dr 77479
Coopers Creek Ct 77479
Coopers Post Ln 77478
Copano Bay Dr 77479
Copperas Creek Dr 77498
Coral Bean Dr 77498
Coral Wood Ln 77498
Corbin Bridge Ln 77498
Cordelia Pl 77479
Cordes Dr 77479
Corporate Dr 77478
Cotswold Ln 77479
Cottage Arbor Ct 77498
Cottage Lake Ct 77498
Cotton Stock Dr 77479
Cottonfield Way 77479
Cottonmist Ct 77479
Cottonwood Ct 77498
Country Brook Ct 77479
Country Club Blvd 77478
Country Manor Dr 77498
Court St 77478
Court Of St Jude 77479
Courtshire Ln 77478
Coventry Ct 77479
Coventry Place Dr 77479
Cozac Ln 77498
Cranbrook Canyon Ct 77479
Cranford Ct 77479
Cranston Ct 77479
Crawford Hill Ln 77479
E Creek Dr 77498
Creek Bend Dr 77478
Creek Glen Dr 77478
Creek Shadow Dr 77479
Creek Valley Ln 77478
Creek View Ct 77478
Creek Way Dr 77478
Creekford Cir & Ct 77478
Creekshire Dr 77478
Creekside Dr 77478
Creekstone Dr 77479
Creekview Dr 77479
Creighton Ln 77479
Crescent Lakes Cir 77479
Crestbrook Ct 77479
Crestridge Dr 77479
Crestwood Cir 77478
Crimson Ct 77479
Crisfield Dr 77479
Crocket Ct 77478
Cromwell Ct 77498
Crooked Arrow Dr 77498
Cross Spring Dr 77479
Cross Trail Dr 77479
Cross Valley Dr 77479
Crystal Creek Ct & Dr 77478
Crystal Run Dr 77498
Cumberland Bridge Ln 77498
Cunningham Creek
Blvd 77479
Cypress Hl 77479
Cypress Bend Ln 77478
Cypress Ridge Ln 77479
Cypress Run Ct & Dr 77478
Cypress Valley Ct 77479
Cypress Village Dr 77479
Dabney Hill Ct 77479
Dahlgren Trl 77479
Dairy Ashford Rd 77478
Dairybrook Cv 77479
Dallerton St 77479
Dalton Ln 77479
Dalton Ranch Ln 77479
Danbury Ln 77479
Darby Trails Dr 77479
Dargail St 77478
Darmascus Ct 77479
Dartmoor Ct & St 77479
David Searles Blvd 77479
Davids Bend Dr 77479
Davis Mountains Dr 77498
Dawn Marie Ln 77498
Dawn Mist Ct 77479
Dawncrest Way 77498
Dawnington Pl 77479
Deep Cove Ln 77498
Deepwater Ln 77479
Deer Creek Dr 77478
Deer Hollow Dr 77479
Deer Run Bnd 77479
Deerbourne Chase Dr 77479
Deerbrook Dr 77479
Delamotte Ln 77479
Delander Way 77479
Delford Way 77479
Delta Bridge Ct 77498
Demsey Mill Dr 77498
Denver Miller Rd 77498
Desert Vine Ct 77498
Deverell Dr 77498
Devonshire St 77479
Dew Bridge Ct & Dr 77479
Dew Point Ln 77479
Dexter Bluff Ct 77479
Dinosaur Valley Dr 77498
Dixie Ct 77478
Dockside Ct 77478
Dogwood St 77478
Dolan Lake Dr 77498
Dora Ln 77498
Dora Meadows Dr 77498
Dorchester Ct 77478
Dorothea Ln 77479
Dorsette Ct 77498
Doscher Ln 77479
Doughty Pl 77479
Dover Bluff Ln 77479

Drake Elm Ct & Dr 77479
Drakeview Ct 77479
Drakewood Dr 77498
Drayton Ct 77479
Dresden Ave 77479
Driftwood Ct 77478
Driver Ct & Ln 77498
Du Pont Cir 77479
Duke Trail Ln 77479
Dulles Ave 77478
Dumfries St 77479
Dunbar Grove Ct 77498
Dunbarton Dr 77479
Dunleigh Ct 77479
Dunmeyer Ct 77479
Dunrobin Way 77498
Dunston Ct 77479
Dunvegan Ln 77479
Durham Ln 77479
Dusty Grove Ln 77498
Dusty Meadow Ln 77479
Dusty Mill Dr E & W 77498
Dusty Rose Cir 77479
Dutch Ridge Dr 77498
Eagle Eye Ln 77498
Eagle Pointe Ct 77479
Eagle Run Ct 77479
Eagle Trace Ct 77479
Eaglewood Glen Trl 77498
Eaglewood Shadows Dr 77498
Easton Bend Ct 77479
Eastwood Ct 77478
Echo Rdg 77478
Eden Cove Ct 77479
Edenbrook Ct & Dr 77479
Edenfield Ln 77479
Edgemere Ct 77498
Edgewater Blvd 77479
Edgewick Ct 77478
Edgewood Ct & Dr 77479
Edinburgh Ct 77479
Ehrhardt Ln 77479
El Fleta Ln 77479
Elder Bridge Dr 77498
Elder Mill Ln 77498
Elderberry Trce 77479
Eldridge Rd 77478
Eldridge Park Way 77498
Eldridge Villa St 77498
Elkins Rd 77479
Ellcreek Ct 77479
Ellicott Way 77479
Elm Ct 77498
Elm Grove Dr 77479
Elm Trace Dr 77479
Elm Tree Ct 77479
Elmhurst Ct 77479
Elmscott Dr 77498
Elmwood Ct 77498
Elmwood Point Ln 77498
Ember Hollow Cir & Ln 77498
Emberwood Way 77479
Emerald Bay Ln 77498
Emerald Forest Ct 77498
Emerald Glen Ct & Dr 77479
Emerald Haven Dr 77479
Emerald Pointe Ct & Ln 77479
Emerald Trace Ct 77479
Emerson Ln 77479
Emery Hill Ct & Dr 77498
Emily Ct 77478
Emma Cove Ct 77479
Emmit Creek Ln 77479
Enchanted Cir E & W 77498
Enchanted Spring Ct 77479
Encino Ln 77478
Enclave Ter 77478
Endicott Ln 77478
Ennis Rd 77498
Entelman Ln 77479
Epperson Way 77479
Epperson Way Ct 77479
Epping Forest Way 77479

Erin Ct 77498
Erin Hills Ct 77498
Evandale Ln 77479
Evening Bend Ct 77479
Evening Light Dr 77479
Eves Landing Ct 77498
Executive Dr 77478
Explorer Cv 77479
Fagan Way 77479
Fairacres Dr 77498
Fairford Dr 77479
Fairmont Ct 77478
Fairpark Ln 77479
Fairview Dr 77479
Fairway Dr 77478
Fairway Glen Ct & Ln 77498
Fairway View Ct 77479
Fall Forest Ln 77479
Fall River Ct 77479
Fall Wood Dr 77479
Falling Briar Ln 77479
Falling Brook Ct 77479
Falling Water Ct 77478
Fallsbrook Ct 77479
E & W Farmington Ln 77479
Farrell Ridge Dr 77479
Fawn Hill Ct 77479
Fawn Nest Trl 77479
Fawnbrake Dr 77498
Featherbrook Ct 77479
Featherton Ct 77478
Feldman Ln 77479
Felicia Dr 77479
Fenian Ct 77498
Fenimore Ct 77478
Fenton Ln 77498
Fenwick Way Ct 77479
Ferainda Dr E 77498
Fern Vale Ct 77479
Ferncastle Ln 77479
Ferndale Ct 77479
Fernhill Dr 77498
N & S Ferrisburg Ct 77478
Ferry Lndg 77479
Field Briar Ln 77479
Field Crossing Ln 77498
Field Line Dr 77479
Fieldbloom Ln 77498
Fieldstone St 77479
Firefly Ln 77479
Fireside Ct 77479
First Colony Blvd 77479
First Crossing Blvd 77478
Fitzgerald Ct 77479
Flagstone Pass Ct 77479
Flanagan Rd 77479
Flanders Field Ln 77498
Fletcher Bridge Ct & Ln 77498
Flint Bridge Ct 77498
Flint Run Way 77498
Flintrock Ct & Ln 77479
Flintwood Dr 77479
Florence Rd 77498
Floret Hill Ln 77479
Floriencia St 77479
Flowermound Dr 77479
Fluor Daniel Dr
1-199 77478
200-299 77479
Fm 1464 Rd 77498
Fontana Dr 77479
Forest Brk & Ln 77479
Forest Bend Ct & Dr 77479
Forest Fern Ct 77479
Forest Gate Cir & Dr 77479
Forest Haven Dr 77479
Forest Knoll Ln 77479
Forest Leaf Dr 77498
Forest Rain Dr 77479
Forest Shadow Dr 77479
Forest Trace Dr 77479
Forester Canyon Ln 77498
Forestlake Dr 77479
Forsythe Ln 77479
Fosters Ct 77479

Fosters Green Dr 77479
Fountain Dr 77478
Fountainbrook Ln 77479
Fountainview Cir 77479
Four Leaf Dr 77479
Foursome Ln 77498
Fox Briar Ln 77478
Foxbrush Ln 77479
Foxhall Crescent Dr 77479
Foxland Chase St 77479
Foxworth Ct 77479
Frampton Ln 77479
Frank Rd 77498
Frontier Dr 77479
Furman Way 77479
Gable Meadows Dr 77479
Gable Wing Ln 77479
N & S Gabriel River Cir 77478
Gaines Rd 77498
Gallion Dr 77479
Gannoway Lake Ct 77498
Garden Bnd, Brk & Ln 77479
Garden Hills Dr 77479
Garden Home Dr 77479
Garden Place Dr 77498
Garden Row Dr 77498
Gardner Park Ln 77498
Garnet Fls 77479
Garrett Way 77479
Gates Farm Ln 77498
Gatesprings Ln 77479
Gatmere Ct 77498
Genesta Path 77479
Genova St 77478
Gentlewood Ln 77479
Georgetown Dr 77478
Gideon Ct 77479
Gillingham Blvd & Ln 77478
Ginger Run Way 77498
Gingerwood Crest Ct 77479
Gladden Way 77479
Glen Eagles Dr 77479
Glen Eden Ct 77479
Glen Heather Ct 77479
Glen Hollow St 77479
Glen Lake Dr 77498
Glen Loch Ct 77479
Glen Oak Ct 77479
Glendale Ct & Dr 77479
Glengary Ct 77479
Glenholly Park Dr 77498
Glenkirk Pl 77479
Glenmist Ct 77479
Glenwood Dr 77479
Gloria Ct 77478
Goanna Ct 77498
Golden Pond Ct 77479
Goldenmere Ct 77498
Goldenview Park Ln 77498
Goldfinch Ave 77478
Gondola St 77478
Goodlowe Park 77479
Goodnight Ct 77479
Gossamer Ln 77479
Grace Meadow Ln 77498
W Grand Mnr, Pkwy & Ter S 77479
Grand Cayman Ct & Dr 77479
Grand Haven Ln 77479
Grand Manor Ct 77479
Grand Pines Dr 77498
Grants Lake Blvd
2500-3000 77479
3002-3198 77479
3130-3130 77496
Grants Lake Cir 77479
Grants River Cir 77479
Grassland Ct 77478
Grassy Knls 77479
Grassy Knoll Ct 77478
Gray Birch Dr 77478
Gray Hills Ct 77478
Gray Moss Ct 77478
Great Lakes Ave 77479

Great Oak Ln 77479
Great Pecan Ln 77479
Greatwood Pkwy 77479
Greatwood Glen Ct & Dr 77479
Greatwood Grove Dr 77479
Greatwood Lake Dr 77479
Greatwood Trails Ct & Dr 77479
Green Ash Dr 77479
Green Belt Dr 77498
Green Fields Dr 77479
Green Hills Cir 77479
Green Knoll Dr 77479
Green Leaf Oaks Dr 77479
Green Path Ct 77479
Green Valley Dr 77479
Greenbriar Dr 77498
Greencove Ln 77479
Greenhaven Dr 77479
Greenlaw Ct & St 77479
Greenridge Dr 77498
Greensward Ln 77479
Greentree Dr 77479
Greenway Dr 77498
Greenwood Dr 77478
Greystone Ct & Way 77479
Greywood Dr 77498
Griggs Point Ln 77498
Grind Stone Ln 77498
Groveshire Ct 77478
Guenther St 77479
Guinevere Dr 77479
Gulfstream Ct & Ln 77498
Gunston Ct 77478
Guyer St 77498
Habersham Ave 77479
Hadfield Ct 77479
Hadley Cir 77478
Hagans Ct 77498
Hagerson Rd 77479
Half Penny Ct 77479
N & S Hall Dr 77478
Halstead St 77479
Halston Dr 77498
Hampden Ct 77479
Hampton Ct 77498
S Hampton St 77479
Hampton Park Ln 77479
Hanbury Ct 77498
Hannahs Way Ct 77479
Hansford Ln 77479
Harbor View Dr 77479
Harbortown Dr 77498
Harbour Pl 77478
Harmony Ave 77479
Harpeth Oak Ln 77479
Hartford Ct 77498
Hartman Dr 77478
Hartwood Ct 77478
Harvest Bend Ct 77479
Harwood Dr 77479
Hathaway Ln 77479
Hatteras Ct 77479
Haven Falls Ln 77478
Haven Glen Dr 77479
Haven Manor Ct 77479
Hawkesbury Ct 77498
Hawksbury Ct 77479
Hawsley Way 77479
Hayden Creek Dr 77479
Haywood Ct 77478
Hearth Hollow Ln 77479
Hearthglen Ln 77479
Hearthside Dr 77479
Heath River Ln 77479
Heatheglen Ln 77479
Heather Dale Ct 77479
Heather Park Ct 77479
E & W Heatherock Cir 77479
Heatherwilde St 77479
Heathrow Ln 77479
Heddon Falls Dr 77479
Heflin Colony Dr 77498
Hemlock Bridge Ct 77498
Henley Ct 77479

Heritage Pl 77479
Herndon Pl 77479
Heron Ct & Way 77478
Hessenford St 77479
Hickory Hill Ct 77478
E & W Hickory Park Cir 77479
Hickory Run Dr 77479
Hidden Creek Dr 77479
Hidden Crest Way 77479
Hidden Gate Ct 77498
Hidden Hollow Ln 77498
Hidden Knoll Ct 77478
Hidden Lake Ln 77498
Hidden Meadow Dr 77498
Hidden Terrace Dr 77479
Hidden Trails Ct 77479
High Gate Ct 77478
High Knoll Dr 77479
High Meadows Ct & Dr 77479
High Plains Dr 77498
High Terrace Dr 77479
Highcroft Frst 77479
Highland Ct 77478
Highland Bluff Dr 77479
Highland Forest Dr 77479
Highland Green Dr 77479
Highland Hills Dr 77478
Highland Ridge Ct 77479
Highland Way Ln 77498
Highland Woods Dr 77498
Highway 6
300-4699 77478
Highway 6
4700-4710 77479
S Highway 6 77498
Highway 90a
4800-6599 77498
6600-6699 77478
6700-7299 77498
7300-7398 77478
7301-7399 77498
7400-10499 77478
Hill Canyon Ct 77479
Hill Spring Dr 77479
Hillary Cir 77498
Hillbrook Ct 77498
Hills Bridge Ct & Ln 77498
Hillsboro Pl 77479
Hillsdale Bridge Ln 77498
Hillside Ct 77479
Hillside Forest Dr 77479
Hillsman Ln 77498
Hillstone Dr 77479
Hillswick Ct & Dr 77479
Hitherfield Dr 77498
Hobart Dr 77479
Hodge Lake Ln 77478
Hodges Bend Cir 77479
Hogan Ct 77479
Holles Dr 77498
Hollinfare Ct 77479
Hollington Way 77479
Hollow Bank Ln 77478
Hollow Canyon Ct & Dr 77498
Hollow Oak Ct 77479
Hollsbrook Ct 77478
Holly Glade Ln 77479
Holly Hill Dr 77498
Hollyberry Ln 77479
Hollybush Dr 77498
Hollys Way 77479
N & S Home Pl 77479
Homeward Way 77479
Honey Brook Ct 77479
Honey Creek Dr 77478
Honeylocust Dr 77479
Honeymoon Bridge Ln 77498
Honeysuckle Ln 77479
Hope Ranch Ln 77479
Horizon View Cir 77479
Horse Creek Ln 77498
N Horseshoe Dr 77478
Houghton Ct 77479

Howell Ln 77479
Hudson Ct 77498
Hudson Grove Ln 77479
Hueco Tanks Dr 77498
Huggins Fry 77479
Hundred Bridge Ln 77498
Hunters Gate Ct 77479
Hunters Locke St 77479
Hunters Point Dr 77479
Huntleigh Way 77478
Huntley Dr 77479
Hyde Park Dr 77479
Imperial Blvd & Ct 77498
Imperial Canyon Ct & Ln 77498
Indian Hills Ln 77479
Indian Plains Ln 77479
Indian Springs Ct 77479
Indian Summer Ct & Dr 77479
Indian Trail Dr 77479
Indigo Dr 77479
Indigo River Ln 77479
Industrial Blvd 77478
Ingham Ct 77498
Inks Lake Dr 77498
Innsbrook Pl 77479
Inverrary Ln 77479
Inwood Ct 77478
Iron Rdg 77478
Issacks Way 77479
Ivory Meadow Ln 77479
Ivy Bend Ln 77479
Ivy Cross Ln 77498
Ivycrest Ct 77479
Ivymist Ct 77479
Ivymount Dr 77498
Ivystone Ct 77479
Ivyvine Ct 77479
Jackson Sawmill Ln 77498
Jade Cove Ct & Ln 77479
Jade Glen Ct 77498
Jamaica Dr 77479
Jasons Bend Dr 77479
Jaubert Ct 77498
Jaymar Dr 77479
Jenny Dr 77479
Jess Pirtle Blvd
12800-13399 77478
13700-13799 77498
Jessica Ct 77479
Jessie Parker Rd 77498
Jim Davidson Dr 77498
Jo Ann Ln 77498
Johnson Ln 77479
Jourdan Way 77479
Jowett Pl 77498
Julie Rivers Dr 77478
Jurgensen Ln 77479
Justina Ct 77478
Kathi Lynn Ln 77498
Katie Leigh Ln 77479
Kayleigh Ct 77479
Keating Ct 77479
Keelson Way 77479
Keeran Point Ct & Ln 77498
Kelly Dr 77478
Kelsey Place Ct 77479
Keltwood Ct 77479
Kempner St 77498
Kempwood Dr 77479
Ken Pl 77478
Kendall Creek Dr 77479
Kendall Hill Ct & Ln 77479
Keneshaw Ct & St 77479
Kenilworth Dr 77479
Kennewick Ct 77479
Kensington Dr 77479
Kent Towne Ln 77498
Kentshire Ave 77479
Kentwood Ridge Ct 77479
Kerri Ct 77478
N & S Keswick Ct 77479
Kettle Run 77479
Kindall Tate Ln 77479
King Arthurs Ct 77478

King Ranch Ln 77498
Kingfisher Dr 77478
Kingsland Ct 77479
Kingsmill Dr 77478
Kipling Glen Ct 77479
Kirkwall Ct & Dr 77479
Kirkwood Ct 77479
Kitchen Hill Ln 77479
Kittiwake Ct 77478
Knights Branch Dr 77479
Knightsbridge Blvd 77479
Knoll Crest Ct 77479
Knoll Forest Ct & Dr 77479
Knoll Park Dr 77479
Knottinghill Dr 77498
Krisford Ct 77479
Kyle St 77478
Kyle Hill Ln 77479
Laconia Ct 77498
Ladson Trl 77479
W Lake Dr 77478
Lake Bend Dr 77479
Lake Canyon Ct 77498
Lake Estates Ct & Dr 77498
Lake Haven Ct 77479
Lake Knoll Ct 77479
Lake Mist Ct & Dr 77479
Lake Pointe Pkwy 77479
Lake Trail Dr 77498
Lake Woodbridge Ct & Dr 77498
Lakebend Dr 77478
Lakefield Blvd & Way 77479
Lakefront Ct 77478
Lakeglen Ct 77478
Lakehill Park Ct & Ln 77498
Lakemeade Ct 77498
Lakeridge Canyon Dr 77498
Lakeshore Dr 77478
Lakeside Blvd 77478
Lakeside Plaza Dr 77479
Lakespur Dr 77479
Lakeview Dr
100-899 77498
1200-1299 77478
Lakewood Oaks Dr 77498
Lamonte Ct 77479
Lancer Xing 77479
Landcircle Ct 77478
Landers Dr 77479
Laney Way 77498
Lantana Ct & Dr 77479
Larimer Point Ct 77479
Lark Creek Ct 77479
Lark Glen Way 77479
Larkhill Gardens Ln 77498
Larkway Dr 77498
Larkwood Ln 77479
Larocke Trl 77479
Lathrop Ct 77479
Laurel Dr 77479
Laurel Bush Ln 77479
Laurel Creek Ln 77498
Laurel Hill Ct 77479
Laurel Springs Ct 77478
Laurel Terrace Ln 77498
Laurelstone Ct 77498
Lauren Way 77479
Laurette Ct 77479
Lavender Field Ct & Dr 77479
Lavington Way 77479
Lawick Cir 77478
Lawton Cir 77478
Laytham Ln 77498
Lazy Brook Dr 77479
Lazy Trail Ct 77479
Leaf Springs Ct 77479
Leamington St 77479
Lee Ln 77479
Lee Duggan Dr 77498
Legacy Ridge Ln 77479
Legend Park Dr 77479
Legend Woods Ct 77479
Leigh Ct 77479
Leigh Gardens Dr 77479

erin Ln 77498
exington Blvd
13800-15799 77478
15900-17099 77479
exington Meadows Ct 77479
iberty Point Ln 77478
iberty Woods Ln 77479
imeshade Ln 77498
imestone Hill Ln 77479
imewood Ln 77498
incoln Crest Way 77498
inden St 77498
inden Grove Ct 77479
inden Rose Ln 77479
indencrest Ct 77479
inenhall Dr 77498
inmont Falls Ln 77479
inney Blvd 77479
issa Ln 77479
ittle Gap Ct 77498
ive Oak St 77498
ively Ln 77479
ocke Ln 77478
ocksley Ln 77479
ockwood Bend Ln 77479
odge Vine Ct 77479
ogan Bridge Ln 77498
ogan Creek Ln 77479
oggers Depot Dr 77478
ombardy Dr 77478
one Rock Ln 77479
one Star Dr 77479
onesome Ridge Ct 77498
ong Briar Ln 77498
ong Hollow Ct 77479
ong Leaf Dr 77478
ong Reach Dr 77478
ong River Cir, Ct &
' 77498
ong Shadows Dr 77479
onghorn Cavern Dr 77478
ongview Dr 77478
oralie Ln 77479
orena Ridge Ln 77479
orfing Ln 77479
ost Falls Ct 77479
st Maples Dr 77498
ouan Ct 77498
ouisa Ct 77478
w Bridge Ln 77498
owerby Ln 77479
owther Landing Ct 77479
ssier Dr 77479
nbrook Ct 77478
ndhurst Pl 77479
nnwood Ln 77498
nx Ln 77478
tham Ct 77479
acoma Ct 77479
adeleine Ct 77478
agnolia Ln 77478
agnolia Crest Ln 77479
agnolia Forest Dr 77479
agnolia Run Dr 77478
agnolia Woods Ct 77479
aidenhair Ln 77479
aily Meadowlane 77478
ain St 77498
aleewan Ln 77498
allard Fields Ct 77479
anchester Ct 77479
andenco Dr 77478
angrove Falls Ct 77479
anor Dr 77479
anor Lake Ln 77498
anorbier Ln 77498
anorfield Ct 77479
anorwood St 77478
anzanilla View Ln 77479
aple Bough Ct 77479
aple Downs Ln 77498
aple Hollow Dr 77498
aple Run Dr 77479
aranatha Dr 77479
arburg Ct 77479
arden Ct & Ln 77478

Margate Dr 77479
Marigold Dr 77479
Marilee Chris Ct 77479
Marina Bay Ln 77498
Mariner Cv 77498
Marlowe Grove Dr 77498
Marshall Bridge Ln 77498
Martinez St 77498
Martinique Pass 77479
Martins Way 77479
Mary Sue Ct 77498
Mason Ct 77479
Mason Dr 77498
Masonglen Ct 77479
Massey Row 77479
Mast Ct 77479
Matagorda Ln 77498
Matisse 77479
Matlage Way
200-300 77478
225-225 77487
301-599 77478
302-398 77478
Mayberry Cir 77479
Mayfair Ct 77478
Mayfair Ln 77479
Maygrove Dr 77498
Maykirk St 77478
Mcallister Ave 77479
Mcclellan Ln 77479
Mcdonald Ct 77479
Mckaskle Rd 77498
Mckinney Falls Ct &
Ln 77498
Mcvey Ln 77479
Meadow Rd 77479
Meadow Bay Ct 77479
Meadow Branch Dr 77479
Meadow Briar Dr 77479
Meadow Canyon Dr 77479
Meadow Edge Dr 77479
Meadow Glade Ct 77479
Meadow Green Dr 77479
Meadow Hill Dr 77479
Meadow Lakes Dr 77479
Meadow Landing Ct &
Ln 77479
Meadow Rue Ct 77479
Meadow Spring Dr 77479
Meadow Valley Ln 77498
Meadowcrest Ln 77479
Meadowcroft Blvd 77479
Meadowfair Ct 77479
Meadowlark Ln 77478
Meadowleigh Ct 77479
Meadowlocke Ln 77479
S, E & W Meadows Ct &
Dr 77479
Meadowside Dr 77479
Meadowstar Dr 77479
Meadowsweet Dr 77479
Medford Ct 77478
Medinah Ct 77479
N & S Medio River Cir 77478
Melissa Ct 77479
Mellow Oaks Ln 77498
Mendenhall Way 77479
Menlo Park Dr 77479
Merganser Ln 77479
Merrick Dr 77478
Merriweather St 77478
Merry Meadow Ct 77479
Mesa Crossing Ln 77479
Mesquite Dr 77479
Mesquite Hollow Ln 77478
Metzger Ct 77479
Michele Dr 77498
Midway Dr 77498
Milas Way 77478
Mill Branch Ln 77498
Mill Bridge Ct 77498
Mill Creek Dr 77478
Mill Dale Ct 77479
Mill Place Ct 77479
Mill Rock Cir 77479
Mill Run Dr 77498

Mill Shadow Ct & Dr 77498
Mill Song Ct 77498
Mill Stream Ct 77479
Mill Trail Ct & Dr 77479
Mill Valley Dr 77498
Millcroft Pl 77479
Miller Ridge Ln 77479
Miller Shadow Ln 77479
Millers Oak Ln 77498
Millers Run Ln 77498
Millglen Ct 77498
Millpond Dr 77498
Millstone Ct 77498
Millstone Canyon Ln 77479
Millwright St 77479
Mimosa Way 77479
Miramar Heights Cir 77479
Misty Ml 77479
Misty Briar Ct 77479
Misty Lake Ct & Dr 77498
Misty Morn Ln 77479
Misty Oaks Ln 77479
Misty Orchard Ln 77498
Misty Park Ln 77479
Misty Ridge Ct 77479
Misty Rose Ct 77479
Mistyleaf Ct & Ln 77479
Mockingbird Way 77478
Monarch Dr 77479
Monarch Bluff Ct 77479
Monet Dr 77479
Monrovia Ln 77479
Montclair Blvd 77478
Montcliff Bend Ct & Ln 77479
Montford Ct 77479
Monticello Dr 77479
Monvale Ln 77479
Moon Shadow Ct 77479
Moorcroft Ct 77498
Moorland Ct 77479
Morgan St 77478
Morgan Mist Ct 77479
Morgan Park Ln 77479
Morgans Chase Ln 77479
Morning Cloud Ln 77479
Morning Mist Ct 77498
Morning Shadows Dr 77479
Morningside Dr 77479
Morningstar Dr 77479
Mornington Dr 77479
Morrow Ct 77479
Mosaic Ln 77498
Mosby Dr 77479
Moss Bridge Ln 77498
Moss Cove Ct 77479
Moss Dale Dr 77479
Moss Hammock Way 77479
Moss Meadow Ct 77479
Moss Stone Dr 77479
Moss Wood Dr 77479
Mound Airy Ct 77479
Mount Vernon Ave 77479
Mountain Laurel Ln 77479
Muirfield Way 77479
Muirwood Ln 77498
Mulberry Run Ct 77479
Mulligan Ct 77498
Mulrain Dr 77479
Museum Square Dr 77479
Mustang Island Dr 77498
Myrtle Dr 77498
Mystic Bay Ct 77498
Nails Creek Dr 77478
Nanak Dr 77498
E Nantucket Dr & Rd 77478
Naples Bridge Rd 77498
Nashmor Dr 77479
Nassau Dr 77479
Natural Bridges Ct &
Ln 77498
Neal Dr 77479
Needle Ridge Ct 77498
Needleleaf Ln 77479
Nelson Bay Ct 77498
New Forest Ln 77479
New Kent Ct & Dr 77498

N & W New Meadows Ct
& Dr 77479
New Territory Blvd 77479
New Village Ln 77498
Newberry St 77478
Newbury Trl 77479
Newfield Bridge Ln 77498
Newington Ln 77479
Newport Bridge Cir, Ct &
Ln 77498
Newton Falls Ln 77498
Nighthawk Ct 77478
Nightingale Ct 77479
Noble Hollow Dr 77498
Noblewood Ct 77498
Normandy Ct 77498
Norsworthy Dr 77479
Northcliff Pl 77478
Northumbria Park 77479
Northwoods Dr 77479
Nottaway Ct 77478
S Oak Cir 77479
Oak Branch Ln 77479
Oak Glen Ln 77479
Oak Green Ct 77479
Oak Grove Ct 77479
Oak Knoll Ct & Dr 77498
Oak Lake Glen Cir, Ct &
Dr 77498
Oak Lake Park Dr 77498
Oak Lake Point Dr 77498
Oak Lake Ridge Ct 77498
Oak Lake Vista Ct 77498
Oak Place Dr 77479
Oak Shade Dr 77479
Oak Shadow Ct 77479
Oak Shadows Ct 77479
Oak Trail Ct 77479
Oak Tree Ct 77479
Oak View Trl 77479
Oakburl Ct & Ln 77479
Oakhurst Pkwy 77479
Oakland Ct 77498
Oakland Dr 77479
Oaklawn St 77498
Oakman Ln 77479
Oakmead Dr 77498
Oakmere Pl 77479
Oakmont Ct & Dr 77479
Oakview St 77498
Oakville Ct 77479
Oakwood Ln 77498
Oakwood Run Dr 77498
Oakworth Ct 77498
Odessa Dr 77479
Ogden Trl 77479
Oglesby Ct 77479
Oilfield Rd 77479
Old Bridge Ct 77479
Old Elm Trl 77479
Old English Ct 77479
Old Fort Rd 77479
Old Legend Ct & Dr 77478
Old Manse Ct 77478
Old Masters Dr 77479
Old Mill Ct 77498
Old Mill Rd 77498
Old Oak Cir 77479
Old Oyster Trl 77478
Old Quarry Dr 77479
Old Richmond Rd 77498
Old Stone Ct 77479
Old Towne Ln 77498
Old Trail Ct 77479
Old Tree Ct 77479
Old Village Ln 77498
Old Windsor Way 77479
Oldtown Bridge Ct 77498
Oleta Ln 77479
Olive Hill Blvd 77479
Olmstead Park Dr 77479
Onion Crk 77479
Open Sands Ct 77479
Orchard Ln 77498
Orchard Arbor Ln 77498
Orchard Bend Dr 77498

Orchard Blossom Dr 77479
Orchard Falls Dr 77479
Orchard Garden Ct 77479
Orchard Gate St 77479
Orchard Hills Ln 77479
Orchard Mews Dr 77498
Orchard Springs Ct 77479
Orchard Summit Dr 77498
Orchid Breeze Ln 77498
Orkney Isle Ct 77479
Overdell Dr 77479
Overland Pass Dr 77478
Overlook Hill Ln 77479
Overview Dr 77498
Oxford Mills Ln 77479
Oyster Bank Cir 77478
Oyster Bay Dr 77478
Oyster Cove Dr 77478
Oyster Creek Dr & Ln 77478
Oyster Loop Ct & Dr 77478
Oyster Point Dr 77478
Pablo Picasso Dr 77479
Paddington Way 77479
Pademelon Dr 77498
Padgett Ct & Dr 77498
Paige Ct 77498
Paintbrush Ln 77498
Palace Spgs 77479
Paleo Ct 77478
Palm Grove Cir 77498
Palm Meadow Ct 77479
Palm Royale Blvd 77479
Palmer Ct 77479
Panhandle Dr 77498
Paradise Point Dr 77478
Park Holw 77479
E Park St 77498
W Park St 77498
Park Bend Ln 77478
Park Field Ct 77479
Park Glen Dr 77498
W Park One Dr 77478
Park Springs Ln 77479
Park Two Dr 77478
Park West Dr 77478
Parkbrook Way Ln 77498
Parkdale Ct 77479
Parkhaven Dr 77478
Parkland Woods Dr 77498
Parklane Blvd 77478
Parklane Colony Ct 77479
Parkriver Xing 77479
Parkstone Ct 77479
Parkview Ct 77498
Parkwater Cove Ct 77479
Parkway Blvd 77479
Parkwood Ln & Pl 77478
Pasture Ct & Ln 77479
Paul Rd 77498
Pawlett Ct 77479
Paxton Ct 77479
Peachwood Ln 77479
Peachwood Hollow Ln 77498
Peachwood Lake Dr 77498
Pearl Pass Ct & Ln 77498
Peatwood Way 77479
Pebble Bluff Ln 77479
Pebble Heights Ln 77479
Pebble Hill Ct 77479
Pebble Lake Dr 77479
Pebblebrook Ct 77478
Pebbledowne Cir 77479
Pebblestone Walk 77479
Pecan Dr 77498
Pecan Grv 77479
Pecan Acres Dr 77498
Pecan Bay Ct 77498
Pecan Crest Ct 77479
Pecan Draw Ct 77479
Pecan Gorge Ct 77479
Pecan Mill Dr 77498
Pecan Point Cir & Dr 77478
Pecan Ridge Dr 77498
Pecan Trace Ct 77479
Pecan Tree Ct 77478
Pecan Walk Ln 77498

Pedernales Falls Ln 77498
Pelham Pl 77479
Pembroke St 77479
Pendelton Place Cir &
Dr 77479
Pendergrass Trl 77479
Penny Green St 77479
Penny Worth Dr 77479
Penrose Ct 77479
Pensacola Oaks Ln 77479
Penton Dr 77498
Pepper Hill Ln 77479
Pepper Tree Ct 77479
Pepper Wood Dr 77479
Peppervine Way 77479
Percy St 77479
Periwinkle Ct 77479
Permian Dr 77498
Perry Knoll Ct 77479
Petitt Rd 77498
Pettigrew Dr 77479
Pheasant Creek Ct &
Dr 77498
Pheasant Ridge Dr 77498
Pheasant Trail Dr 77498
Pickney Ave 77479
Pickwell Ct 77498
Piedmont Ave 77479
Piedmont St 77478
Pin Oak Ct 77479
Pine St 77498
Pine Shadows Dr 77479
Pinecroft Dr 77498
Pineleaf Dr 77479
Pineridge Dr 77479
Pinetown Bridge Ln 77498
Pinewood Ct 77498
Pioneer Pass & Trl 77479
Pioneer Ridge Ct 77479
Piper Pass Ln 77479
Pipers Walk 77479
Pittsford Ct & St 77479
Placid Woods Ct 77498
Planetree Ct 77479
Plantation Ln & Trl 77478
Plantation Bend Dr 77478
Plantation Colony Ct &
Dr 77478
Plantation Run Dr 77478
Planters Row 77479
Planters St 77479
Planters Point Ct 77479
Plato Park Dr 77479
Plaza Dr 77479
Plum Point Ct 77479
Plumbridge Ln 77479
Pointe Loma Dr 77479
Pompano Lake Ln 77479
Pool Forge Ct 77498
Poplar Pl 77479
Possum Kingdom Ln 77498
Poundstone Ct 77479
Power Ct 77478
Poydras St 77498
Prairie Pl 77479
Prairie Dog Run 77498
Presley Way 77479
Preston Ct 77479
Prestwick Ave 77479
Priber Dr 77479
Primrose Glen Ct 77498
Pristine Way 77479
Prudential Cir 77478
Pulp Mill Ct 77498
Quail Ridge Ln 77498
Quarry Hill Rd 77478
Queen Mary Ct 77479
Queensbridge Dr 77498
Queensbury Ct 77479
Quiet Trl 77479
Quiet Creek Ct 77498
Quiet Glen Ct & Dr 77479
Quiet Park Dr 77498
Quiet Path Dr 77498
Quiet Pond Dr 77479
Quiet Town Ln 77498

Quiet Vista Dr 77498
Quiet Water Ct 77479
Quiet Way Ln 77498
Rabbs Xing 77479
Radcliff Pl 77479
Radcliffe Dr 77498
Radley Dr 77498
Rads Pt 77498
Ragus Lake Dr 77498
Rain Fall St 77479
Rainbow Run 77479
Rainford Ct 77479
Raintree Cir 77479
Raintree Dr 77478
Ralston Branch Way 77479
Ramblebrook Ln 77479
Ramp Creek Ln 77498
Rancho Bernardo Ln 77498
Randall Oak Dr 77478
Randons Bell Dr 77479
Randons Point Dr 77478
E & W Rangecrest Pl 77479
Ranger Run 77479
Ranna Ct 77498
Ravenel Ln 77479
Ravens Crest Dr 77478
Ravens Mill Ct 77479
Ravenscourt Dr 77498
Ravensthorpe Ct 77479
Raynor Way 77479
Rebel Ridge Dr 77478
Red Bud Ln 77479
Red Gully Dr 77498
Red Hawk Ct 77479
Red Oak Ct 77479
Redbush Dr 77498
Redcliff Dr 77479
Reddington Rd 77478
Redmond Ct 77479
Redwood Ct 77498
Redwood Forest Ct 77498
Reed Rd 77478
Regal Oak Way 77479
Regal Shadow Ln 77479
Regal Stone Ln 77479
Regency Dr 77479
Regent Ct 77478
Regents Park 77479
Reinhart Ave 77479
Remington Ct 77479
Rene Ct 77479
Renoir 77479
Reseda St 77479
Reynor Creek Ct 77479
Ribbonridge Dr 77498
Rich Valley Ln 77498
Richland Ct & Dr 77478
Richland Spring Ln 77479
Richtown Ln 77498
Ridge Wood Ln 77479
Ridgepoint Cir 77479
Rifle Gap Ln 77478
Riley Way Ln 77479
Ripplemoor Ct 77479
Ripplewave Dr 77498
Rippling Creek Dr 77479
Rippling Mill Dr 77498
Rippling Water Ct &
Dr 77479
River Trl & Xing 77479
River Birch Dr 77479
River Creek Way 77478
River Gable Ct 77479
River Glen Dr 77498
River Grove Rd 77478
River Lodge Ln 77479
E & W River Park Dr 77479
River Wind Dr 77478
Riverbend Xing 77478
Riverbrook Dr 77479
Rivercoach Ln 77479
Rivercrest Dr 77478
Riverglade Ct 77479
Riverhollow Ct & Ln 77479
Riverstone Crossing
Dr 77479

Riviera Ct & Dr 77479
Robins Way 77479
Robinsons Fry 77479
Rock Bridge Ln 77498
Rock Mill Ln 77498
Rock Spring Ct 77479
Rockdale Bridge Ct & Ln 77498
Rockmoor Ct 77478
Rockport Ct 77498
Rockton Hills Ln 77479
Rockwall Ct 77479
Rocky Bend Dr 77479
Rocky Ponds Ct 77479
Roller Mill Ln 77498
Rolling Brook Ct 77479
Rolling Mill Dr 77498
Rolling Plains Dr 77479
Rosalyn Ct 77479
Rose Arbor Ct 77478
Rosebank Ct 77478
Rosebay Ct 77479
Rosecrest Ct 77478
Rosedale Path Ct 77479
Rosehaven Ct 77479
Rosehill Ct 77479
Rosewood Ln 77479
Rosewood Hill Ct 77498
Rosstown Ct & Dr 77478
Round Rock Ct 77479
Royal Bend Ln 77479
Royal Hampton Ct 77479
Royal Lytham Ct 77479
Rozelle Ave 77498
Runney Meade Dr 77479
Rushwood Ln 77479
Russett Ln 77479
Rustic Arbour Ln 77498
Rustic Colony Dr 77479
Rustic Hills Ct 77479
Ruston Ln 77479
Rutherford Ct 77479
Ryans Run Ct 77478
Saber Riv 77479
Sadler Ct 77479
Sage Brush Ln 77479
Sage Hollow Ct 77479
Sage River Ct 77479
Sage Walk Ln 77479
Sailfish Pt 77479
Saint Albans Ct 77479
Saint Annes Dr 77479
Saint Christopher Ct 77479
Saint George Ct 77479
Saint Ives St 77479
Saint Marks St 77478
Saint Michaels Ct 77479
Saint Peters Walk 77479
Saint Simons Ct 77479
Salem Ct 77479
Salerno St 77478
Salisbury Dr 77498
Sam Rd 77498
Sam Brookins St 77498
Sam Houston Dr 77479
Samantha Ct 77479
Samual Bluff Ct 77479
San Lorenzo Ruiz Dr 77498
San Marino St 77478
Sand Dollar Ct 77479
Sand River Ct 77479
Sandcroft Ln 77479
Sanderling Ln 77478
Sanders Ridge Ct 77479
Sandflower Ln 77498
Sandhill Dr 77479
Sandpiper Dr 77478
Sandy Ripple Ct 77498
Sandy River Dr 77479
Sandy Springs Ln 77498
Santa Chase Ln 77479
Santa Maria St 77478
Santa Rosa Ln 77478
Sapling Ridge Dr 77498
Sapphire Bay Ct 77479
Saradon Dr 77478
Sarahs Cv 77479
Saratoga Dr 77479
Sarento Vlg 77498
Sartartia Rd 77479
Savoy St 77478
Sawmill Bend Ln 77479
Sawyer Bend Ln 77479
Sawyers Crossing Ln 77498
Saxony Dr 77498
Scarlet Maple Ct & Dr 77479
Scarlet Ridge Ct 77479
Scarlet Sunset Ct 77478
Scenic Rivers Dr 77479
Scenic Shore Ct 77478
Scenic Valley Ln 77479
Schaley Ct 77479
Schiller Park Ln 77479
Schlumberger Dr 77478
Schubach Dr 77479
Schumann Trl 77498
Scot Ct 77479
Scotsmoor Ct 77479
Scramble Ct 77498
Sea Myrtle Ln 77498
Seahorse Cv 77498
Seaton Ct 77479
Secluded Dr 77498
Selkirk Dr 77479
Seminole Ct 77479
Seminole Canyon Dr 77498
Senna Pl 77479
Sentinal Oaks St 77478
Sentry Oak Way 77479
Serene Pl 77498
Serene Oak Dr 77478
Settlers Way Blvd
2200-2399 77478
2400-3100 77479
3102-3298 77479
Severo Rd 77498
Shadow Bend Dr 77479
Shadow Lake Dr 77479
N & S Shadow Mist Ln 77479
Shadow Wood Dr 77498
S Shadowmist Ln 77479
Shady Ln 77479
Shady Bay Ct 77498
Shady Bend Dr 77479
Shady Ridge Trl 77498
Shady Valley Dr 77479
Shady Way Dr 77479
Shadywood St 77479
Shallow Pond Ct 77479
Shamrock Park Ln 77498
Shannondale Dr 77479
Shawnee Dr 77479
Sheffield Ct 77479
Shelby Row 77479
Sheldrake Ct 77478
Shepherds Pl 77479
Sherwood St 77498
Shetland Isle Ct 77479
Shirebrook Dr 77498
Shoal Haven Ct 77479
Shorewood Ln 77479
Siamese Ln 77479
Sierra Oaks Dr 77479
Silas Creek Ct 77479
Silent Dr 77498
Silent Circle Dr 77498
Silent Forest Dr 77479
Silent Lake Ct 77498
Silent Manor Dr 77498
Silent Spring Dr 77479
Silent Way Dr 77498
Silent Willow Ln 77479
Silver Bay Ct 77479
Silver Glade Ln 77498
Silver Lining Ln 77498
Silver Pond Ct & Dr 77479
Silverlake Dr 77479
Silverloch Ct 77479
Silverthorne Dr 77479
Sitella Ct 77498
Skimmer Ct 77478
Skipping Stone Ln 77479
Skycrest Dr 77479
Skyview Dr 77498
Sleepy Hollow Dr 77479
Sleepycove Ct 77479
Slippery Rock Ct & Dr 77498
Sloan Falls Ct 77479
Smada Ct 77478
Smith Bridge Ln 77498
Smithville St 77498
Smoke Tree Ct & Ln 77479
Smooth Pine Ln 77498
Snead Ct 77479
Snow Hill Ct 77498
Soaring Eagle Dr 77498
Solana Springs Dr 77479
Solano Pointe Ct 77479
Solara Ledge Ln 77479
Soldiers Field Dr 77479
Somerset Dr 77479
Sophie Ct 77479
Sophora Pl 77479
Sorrelwood Ln 77479
Sorrento St 77478
Sotoria Ln 77479
Southline Rd 77498
Southwest Fwy
13100-15900 77478
15902-15998 77479
16000-16098 77479
16100-20199 77479
20201-20899 77479
Southwestern Blvd 77478
Spanish Grant Dr 77498
Sparrow Branch Ct 77479
Spartan Trl 77479
Spencers Glen Dr & Way 77479
Spindle Pine Way 77479
Spinnaker Way 77479
Sporting Hill Ln 77498
Spring Arbor Ln 77479
Spring Bloom Ct 77479
Spring Bluebonnet Dr 77479
Spring Mist Ct 77479
Spring Trail Ct & Dr 77479
Spring Valley Ct 77479
Springbrook Ct 77479
Springcrest Ct & Dr 77479
Springdale Ct & Dr 77479
Springfield Ct & Dr 77498
Springfield Lakes St 77479
Springhill Ln 77479
Springwood Dr 77479
Spruce River Ct 77479
Squire Dobbins Dr 77478
St Theresa Blvd 77498
Stadium Dr 77498
Stalybridge Ct & St 77479
Stancliff Oaks St 77479
Stanwick St 77479
Star Creek Ct 77479
Starlite Field Dr 77479
Steamboat Run 77478
E & W Steepbank Cir 77479
Stephens Creek Ct & Ln 77478
Stephens Grant Dr 77479
Sterling Ct & St 77479
Sterling Green Ct 77479
Stiles Ln 77478
Stillmeadow Ct 77479
Stillwater Ln 77479
Stilwell Ln 77479
Stockbridge Dr 77479
Stocklin Ct 77498
Stockman Ln 77498
Stone Ter 77479
Stone Arbor Dr 77479
Stone Canyon Dr 77479
Stone Edge Ct 77479
Stone River Ln 77479
Stone Trail Dr 77479
Stoneburg Ct 77479
Stonebury Ct & Ln 77479
Stonecliff Cir 77479
Stonehenge Dr 77498
Stoneleigh Ct & Dr 77479
Stonelick Bridge Ln 77498
Stonepass Ct 77479
Stoney Mist Dr 77479
Stoney Point Ct 77479
Stoney Ridge Ct 77479
Stovepipe Ln 77479
Stratford Ln 77479
Stratford Arms Ln 77498
Stratford Bend Dr 77498
Stratford Cottage Dr 77479
Stratford Gardens Dr 77479
Stratford Green Dr 77498
Stratford Heights Dr 77498
Stratford Manor Dr 77498
Stratford Mill Ln 77498
Stratford Plaza Ln 77498
E Stratford Pointe Dr 77498
Stratford Town Ln 77498
Strawfield Dr 77478
Stream Meadows Ln 77479
Streamcrest Ln 77479
Streamhurst Ln 77479
Streamside Ln 77479
Stretford Ct 77479
Strutton Dr 77498
Sturbridge Ln 77479
Sugar Creek Blvd & Ln 77478
Sugar Creek Center Blvd 77478
Sugar Crossing Ct & Dr 77478
Sugar Crystal Ct 77498
Sugar Cup Ct 77498
Sugar Falls Ct 77498
Sugar Lakes Dr 77478
Sugar Land Howell Rd 77498
Sugar Line Ct & Dr 77479
Sugar Mill Dr 77498
Sugar Mist Ln 77498
Sugar Mountain Ct 77498
Sugar Park Ln 77478
Sugar Peak Dr 77498
Sugar Place Ct & Dr 77498
Sugar Sands Ct & Dr 77498
Sugar Stone Dr 77498
Sugar Sweet Dr 77498
Sugar Trace Dr 77498
Sugarblossom Ln 77498
Sugarbridge Trl 77498
Sugardale Ct 77498
Sugarfield Ct 77498
Sugarhollow Ct & Dr 77498
Sugarplum Cir 77498
Sugarwood Dr 77478
Summer Brk & Lks 77479
Summer Ash Ln 77479
Summer Bay Cir, Ct & Dr 77478
Summer Brook Ct 77479
Summer Forest Dr 77479
Summer Hill Dr 77479
Summer Hollow Dr 77498
Summer Rain Dr 77479
Summer Terrace Dr 77479
Summer Trail Dr 77479
Summer Wind Ct & Dr 77479
Summerfield Pl 77478
Summerfield Ridge Ct & Dr 77498
Summit Springs Ln 77498
Sun Canyon Ct 77498
Sunclair Park Ln 77479
Sundance Hill Ln 77479
Sunderland Dr 77479
Sunny Trail Ct & Ln 77479
Sunrise Ct 77479
Sunrise Creek Ln 77498
Sunset Trl 77478
Sunset Cliff Ct 77478
Sunset Lake Dr 77478
Sunset Park Ln 77479
Sunshine Cir & Dr 77479
Sunswept Ct 77478
Supplejack Ct 77479
Susan Ct 77498
Sutters Chase Ct & Dr 77479
Swallow Cir 77478
Sweet Hollow Ct 77498
Sweet Rose Ct 77479
Sweetglen Ct 77479
Sweetwater Blvd & Ct 77479
Swift Creek Ct 77479
Swift River Ln 77498
Swiftwater Bridge Ln 77498
Sydney Park Ln 77479
Synott Rd 77498
Taco Ct 77498
Tahoe Valley Ln 77479
Tahoka Ln 77498
Taimer Ct 77479
Talbot Ct 77479
Talcott Ln 77479
Talshire Ln 77498
Tamara Heights Ln 77479
N & S Tamarino Park Ln 77479
Tarlton Way 77478
Tarpon Bay Ct 77479
Tarver Ct 77479
Tasmania Ct 77498
Taylor Medford Ln 77479
Teague Cir 77478
Teakwood Pl 77478
Teal Ln 77478
Teal Brook Ln 77479
Telfair Central Blvd 77479
Templar Ln 77498
Terminal Ln 77498
Terrace Hollow Ln 77498
Terrace View Dr 77479
Terralyn Way 77478
Terry St 77478
Terscott Ct & Ln 77479
Tessa Lakes Ct 77479
Tessie Ct 77479
Texas Dr & Trl 77479
The Highlands Dr 77478
The Oval St 77479
Thetford St 77479
Thistle Hill Ct 77479
Thistlegrove Ln 77498
Thistlerock Ln 77498
Thomas Mill Ln 77479
Thompson Chapel Rd 77479
Thompson Ferry Rd 77479
Thorncrest Ct 77498
Three Rivers Dr 77479
Thunder Lake Ln 77479
Tiburon Trl 77479
Tiedmann Park Way 77479
Tiffany Sq 77478
Timber Glen Ln 77479
Timber Hill Ct & Dr 77479
Timber Ridge Trl 77479
Timber View Ct & Dr 77479
Timberlake Dr 77479
Timbertrail Dr 77479
Tolken Way 77498
Tomasa St 77498
Topaz Trail Dr 77479
Torrington Ct 77479
Tory Hill Ln 77478
Toulouse Ln 77498
Tower Point Dr 77498
Town Center Blvd N 77479
Town Center Blvd S 77479
Town Center Dr 77478
Town Square Pl 77479
Towne Brook Ln 77498
Towne Mist Ct & Dr 77498
Towne Oak Ln 77498
Towne Square Rd 77498
Towne Tower Ln 77498
Towne Way Dr 77498
Towne West Blvd 77498
Towneview Dr 77498
Townhall Ln 77498
Trail Creek Dr 77479
Trail West St 77478
Trailbrook Dr 77479
Trailside Ct 77479
Trailwood Ct & Dr 77479
Tranquil Dr 77498
Travis Park Dr 77479
Traynor Ln 77479
Treasure Trl 77479
Tredington St 77479
Treeline Dr 77479
Tremont Ct 77479
Trent St 77479
Treverstone Ct 77479
Trexler St 77479
Trillium Dr 77479
Trinity Sta 77478
Trudeau Ln 77498
Truslow Point Ln 77478
Turnabout Ct 77478
Turnberry Dr 77479
Turner Shadow Ln 77479
Turning Leaf Ct & Ln 77479
Turning Manor Ln 77479
Turphin Way 77498
Turtle Creek Mnr 77479
Turtle Trails Ln 77479
Tuscany St 77478
Tuscany Place Dr 77479
Twin Lakes Dr 77498
Twin Rivers Ct & Ln 77479
Twin Valley Dr 77479
Twining Trail Ln 77479
Tyler Run 77479
Ulrich St 77498
Union Spgs 77479
Union Chapel St 77479
University Blvd
11500-11799 77478
11900-18799 77479
20400-20499 77478
Upland Park Ct & Dr 77479
Upland Shadows Dr 77479
Utopia Dr 77498
Valentine Bridge Ln 77498
Valleria Ct 77479
Valley Bend Ct 77498
Valley Country Ln 77479
Valley Field Dr 77479
Valley Pike Ct 77498
Valleyview Ct 77479
Vaughn Creek Ct 77479
Veera Ln 77498
Venice St 77478
Venice Villa Ln 77498
Veramonte Ct 77479
Verdant Vly 77479
Vickery Dr 77498
Victoria Ct 77478
Victors Chase Dr 77479
Villa Del St 77498
Village Dr 77498
Village Forest Dr 77479
Village Point Ln 77498
Village View Trl 77498
Vinces Brg 77478
Vinehill Dr 77498
Vineyard Ct 77498
Vineyard Trail Ln 77479
Vintage Oak Ln 77498
Virgin Island Dr 77479
Virginia Grace Dr 77498
Vista Blue Ln 77479
Vista Creek Ct & Dr 77479
Vista Lake Ct & Dr 77478
Voss Rd 77498
Wagner Way 77479
Wagon Run 77479
Wagon Trail Dr 77479
Walbrook Dr 77498
Walden Cir 77498
Walker School Rd 77479
Walkers Park N & S 77479
Walkers Park Dr 77479
Wallberry Way 77479
Walnut Creek Ct 77479
Walston Bend Dr 77479
Warner Hollow Ct 77498
Warwick Ct & Dr 7747
Water Locust Dr 7747
Water Rest Dr 7747
Water View Bnd 7747
Waterfall Way 7747
Waterford Pointe Cir 7747
Watermill Pl 7747
Waters View Dr 7747
Waters Way Dr 7747
Watersedge Dr 7747
Waterwood Dr 7747
Watson Mill Ct 7749
Waumsley Way 7749
Waverdale Ct 7747
Waverly Canyon Ct 7747
Waverton Ct 7749
Waybridge St 7747
Wayson Dr 7749
Weatherfield Ct 7747
Weatherstone Cir 7747
Webb Ln 7749
Wedgefield Pl 7747
Wedgewood Ct & Dr 7747
Weldon Park Dr 7747
Weldridge Dr 7749
Wellford Trl 7747
Wellington Ct, Dr & Ln 7747
Wellshire Village Ct 7749
Wellsley Ct 7749
Welshwood Ln 7747
Wentworth Ave 7747
Westbrook Forest Dr 7747
Westedge Dr 7749
Westmoreland Dr 7747
Westport Bridge Ln 7749
Westside Ct 7747
Westwind Ct 7747
Wexford Trl 7747
Whetrock Ln 7747
Whimbrel Dr 7747
Whisper Ridge Dr & Pl 7747
Whisper Trace Ln 7747
Whispering Ct 7749
Whispering Willow Ct 7747
Whistle Ct 7747
Whitby Cir & Ct 7747
White Barrow Crk 7747
White Bridge Ln 7749
White Forge Ct & Ln 7749
White Oak Ct 7747
White River Pass Ln 7747
Whitfield St 7747
Whitman Ln 7747
Whittier Bridge Ln 7749
Whitworth Way 7747
Wickford Cir 7747
Wickham Ct 7747
Wicklowe St 7747
Wild Rye Trl 7747
Wild Violet Ct 7747
Wildacre Dr 7747
Wildcat Bridge Ln 7749
Wilde Forest Ct 7749
Wildewood Ct 7747
Wildgrass Ct 7749
Wilkins Ln & Xing 7747
Williams Bridge Ln 7749
Williams Glen Dr 7747
Williams Grant St 7747
Williams Landing Dr 7747
Williams Trace Blvd
1700-2399 7747
2500-2599 7747
Willingham Ct 7747
Willow Bank Dr 7747
Willow Bend Ct 7747
Willow Brook Ct 7747
Willow Cliff Ln 7747
Willow Lakes Dr 7747
Willow Pond Ct 7747
Willow Springs Ln 7747
Willowfield Ct 7747
Willowick Ct 7747
Willowview Ct 7747
Wilmington Ct 7747

Wimbledon Dr ... 77498
Winchester Way ... 77479
Wind Fall Ln ... 77479
Wind Trace Cv ... 77479
Windbreak Ln ... 77479
Windcroft Ln ... 77479
Windermere Park Ln ... 77479
Winding River Dr ... 77478
Windmill St ... 77479
Windover Ct ... 77479
Windrift Ct ... 77479
Windshore Way ... 77479
Windsor Pl ... 77479
Windwood Ct ... 77479
Windy Meadow Dr ... 77478
Winnsboro Ct ... 77478
Winnstream Ln ... 77498
Winston Ln ... 77479
Winter Crest Ct ... 77479
E & W Wisteria Cir ... 77479
Wittenberg Ave ... 77479
Wolf Springs Ct ... 77479
Woma Ct ... 77498
Wood Park ... 77479
Wood St ... 77498
Wood Bridge Cir ... 77498
Wood Cove Ln ... 77479
Wood Fern Dr ... 77479
Wood Haven Ct ... 77479
Wood Song Dr ... 77479
Woodbriar Ct ... 77479
Woodbrook Ln ... 77478
Woodchester Dr ... 77498
Woodcrest Ct ... 77479
Wooddale Bridge Ct ... 77498
Woodglen Ct ... 77479
Woodhollow Ct ... 77479
Woodlake Cir ... 77498
Woodlawn Terrace Ct ... 77479
Woodley Bnd ... 77479
Woodmere Ln ... 77478
Woodsage Dr ... 77479
Woodside Ct & Dr ... 77479
Woodstream Blvd & Pl ... 77479
Woodwick Dr ... 77479
Woody Bend Pl ... 77479
Worfield Ct ... 77498
Worthington St ... 77478
Wyndham Way ... 77479
Yabbie Dr ... 77498
N & S Yegua River Cir ... 77478
Yorkshire St ... 77479
Zachary Ln ... 77479
Zachary Stuart Cir ... 77479
Zimmerly Ct ... 77479

NUMBERED STREETS

1st St ... 77498
2nd St ... 77498
4th St ... 77498
5th St ... 77498
6th St ... 77498
7th St ... 77498
1200-1299 ... 77478

SULPHUR SPRINGS TX

General Delivery ... 75482

POST OFFICE BOXES MAIN OFFICE STATIONS AND BRANCHES

Box No.s
All PO Boxes ... 75483

RURAL ROUTES

01, 01, 01 ... 75482

HIGHWAY CONTRACTS

01, 01, 01 ... 75482
01, 01, 01 ... 75482
01, 01, 01 ... 75482

NAMED STREETS

All Street Addresses ... 75482

NUMBERED STREETS

All Street Addresses ... 75482

TEMPLE TX

General Delivery ... 76501

POST OFFICE BOXES MAIN OFFICE STATIONS AND BRANCHES

Box No.s
A - D ... 76503
1 - 3260 ... 76503
3001 - 5498 ... 76505
6100 - 6138 ... 76503

RURAL ROUTES

01, 03, 04 ... 76501
05, 09 ... 76502

NAMED STREETS

Abbey Rdg ... 76504
Aberdeen Ct ... 76502
Acres Rd ... 76502
N Acres Rd ... 76501
Acres Spur ... 76502
E Adams Ave ... 76501
W Adams Ave
2-198 ... 76501
200-699 ... 76501
1000-1098 ... 76504
1100-4399 ... 76504
5101-5197 ... 76502
5199-9599 ... 76502
9601-10799 ... 76502
Adams Ln ... 76502
Airport Rd
1701-1997 ... 76504
1999-3399 ... 76504
5000-5698 ... 76502
5700-8576 ... 76502
8578-8898 ... 76502
Airport Trl ... 76504
Airville Loop & Rd ... 76501
Alabama Ave ... 76502
Alamo Ct ... 76501
Alamo Trl ... 76502
Alaska Ave ... 76502
Alderwood Ln ... 76502
Alexandria Dr ... 76502
Allegiance ... 76504
Allena Ln ... 76502
Alta Vista Loop ... 76502
Amber Dawn Dr ... 76502
Amber Meadow Loop ... 76502
Anacacho Dr ... 76502
Anchor Ln ... 76502
Andy Ln ... 76502
Angelina ... 76502
Anna Cir ... 76502
Antelope Trl ... 76504
N Apache Dr ... 76504
Apple Cider Rd ... 76501
April Dawn ... 76502
Arapaho Dr ... 76504
Armadillo Ln ... 76502
Arrangement Way ... 76504
Arrowhead Cir & Dr ... 76502
Arthur Rd ... 76502
Asa Rd ... 76504
Ascot Pkwy ... 76502
Ash Ln ... 76502
Aspen Trl ... 76502
Aster Dr ... 76502
Austin Cir ... 76502
Autumn Wood ... 76502
Avalon Rd ... 76502
Ave B Heidenheimer ... 76501
Ave C Heidenheimer ... 76501
E Avenue E ... 76501
E Avenue N ... 76504
W Avenue E ... 76504
W Avenue N ... 76504
W Avenue S ... 76504
E Avenue A ... 76501
W Avenue A
2-298 ... 76501
W Avenue A
300-399 ... 76501
401-499 ... 76501
1001-1197 ... 76504
1199-1500 ... 76504
1502-1798 ... 76504
E Avenue B ... 76501
W Avenue B
2-298 ... 76501
300-399 ... 76501
1500-1598 ... 76504
2101-2199 ... 76504
E Avenue C ... 76501
W Avenue C ... 76504
E Avenue D ... 76501
W Avenue D ... 76504
E Avenue F
2-98 ... 76504
301-399 ... 76504
400-698 ... 76501
700-800 ... 76501
802-1398 ... 76501
W Avenue F ... 76504
E Avenue G
1-97 ... 76504
99-100 ... 76504
102-498 ... 76504
1900-2298 ... 76501
W Avenue G ... 76504
E Avenue H
2-98 ... 76504
100-499 ... 76504
501-599 ... 76504
900-1698 ... 76501
1700-3100 ... 76501
3102-3598 ... 76501
W Avenue H ... 76504
E Avenue I
2-98 ... 76504
100-500 ... 76504
502-598 ... 76504
801-2299 ... 76501
W Avenue I ... 76504
E Avenue J
101-197 ... 76504
199-200 ... 76504
202-598 ... 76504
1000-1598 ... 76501
1600-1799 ... 76501
W Avenue J ... 76504
E Avenue K
100-498 ... 76504
500-599 ... 76504
601-799 ... 76504
1801-2199 ... 76501
W Avenue K ... 76504
W Avenue L ... 76504
E & W Avenue M ... 76504
W Avenue O ... 76504
W Avenue P ... 76504
W Avenue Q ... 76504
W Avenue R ... 76504
W Avenue T ... 76504
W Avenue U ... 76504
W Avenue V ... 76504
W Avenue Z ... 76504
Avrshire Ln ... 76502
Aycock Rd ... 76502
Azalea Dr ... 76502
Babu Ct ... 76502
Baker Blvd ... 76501
Banbury ... 76502
Barnhardt Rd
1800-1998 ... 76502
2101-2199 ... 76502
2300-2699 ... 76501
Barrington Ct ... 76502
E Barton Ave ... 76501
W Barton Ave
2-698 ... 76501
801-899 ... 76501
1100-1798 ... 76504
Basalt Ct ... 76502
Bashaw Loop ... 76502
Bay Dr ... 76502
Beagle Rd ... 76501
Bearing Ln ... 76504
Beaver Loop ... 76502
Bedrock Way ... 76502
Bell Dr ... 76502
Bellmont ... 76504
S Belmont ... 76504
Benbrook ... 76502
Bent Oak Dr ... 76502
Bentwood Ct & Ln ... 76502
Berger Rd ... 76501
Berkley Dr ... 76502
Betsy Ross Dr ... 76504
Big Timber ... 76502
Birch Blvd & Cir ... 76502
Birch Tree Dr ... 76502
Birdcreek Dr & Ter ... 76502
Blackfoot Dr ... 76504
E Blackland Rd ... 76502
Blue Gill Ln ... 76501
Blue Jay Dr ... 76502
Blue Leaf Dr ... 76502
Blue Meadow Dr ... 76502
Blue Star Blvd ... 76502
Bluebird Ln ... 76502
Bluebonnet Cir & Ln ... 76502
Bluegrass Ct ... 76502
Bluestem Ct ... 76502
Bob White Rd ... 76501
Bobcat Trl ... 76502
Bois D Arc Rd ... 76502
S Bongerne St ... 76504
Bonham Ave ... 76502
Bordeaux Pl ... 76502
Bottoms Rd ... 76501
Bottoms East Rd ... 76501
Boutwell Dr & Ln E ... 76502
Bowie Ct ... 76501
Bowie Trl ... 76502
Bowsprit Ln ... 76502
Box Canyon Dr ... 76502
Branchwood Way ... 76502
Brandon Dr ... 76502
Brandywine Dr ... 76504
Brazos Ct ... 76502
Brazos Dr
500-598 ... 76504
600-799 ... 76504
15900-16099 ... 76502
Breaker Cir ... 76502
Breezeway Ln ... 76502
Brewster Rd
5801-5997 ... 76504
5999-6099 ... 76504
6101-6199 ... 76504
6600-8799 ... 76501
Briar Cliff Rd ... 76502
Briarcrest Cir ... 76502
Briarwood Dr ... 76502
Bridgepointe Dr ... 76502
Bridgeport Dr ... 76502
Bright Ln ... 76502
Brighton Pl ... 76502
Broken Spoke Dr ... 76502
Brookhaven Dr ... 76504
Brooklawn Dr ... 76502
Brooks Dr ... 76502
Brunswick ... 76502
Brutus Ln ... 76502
Brykerwood Rd ... 76502
Buchanan Ct ... 76502
Buckeye Ln ... 76502
Buckingham Ct ... 76502
Buckskin Trl ... 76502
Buffalo Trl ... 76504
Buggy Ride Rd ... 76502
Bulleyes Ln ... 76501
Bunker Hill Dr ... 76504
Buoy Dr ... 76502
Burgandy Ln ... 76504
Burgess Rd ... 76501
Burlington ... 76504
Burnham Dr ... 76502
Burton Ln ... 76502
Butterfly Ct & Dr ... 76502
Cactus Trl ... 76502
Caddo ... 76504
E Calhoun Ave ... 76501
W Calhoun Ave
2-298 ... 76501
300-800 ... 76501
802-898 ... 76501
1100-1198 ... 76504
Callahan Loop ... 76501
Calle Nogal St ... 76502
Calle Olmo ... 76502
Calle Roble ... 76502
Calle Secoya St ... 76502
Calvin Dr ... 76501
Cambridge Ct ... 76502
Camellia Cir, Dr & Ln ... 76502
Camelot Ln ... 76502
Camp Creek Rd ... 76501
W Campus Dr ... 76502
Canterbury Cir ... 76502
Canyon Ct & Rdg ... 76502
Canyon Cliff Cir & Dr ... 76502
Canyon Creek Ct & Dr ... 76502
Canyon Oaks Ct ... 76502
Capstan Dr ... 76502
Capstone Cv ... 76502
N Cardinal Rd ... 76502
Cardinal Feather Ln ... 76502
Carnation Ln ... 76502
Carriage Rd & Spur ... 76502
Carriage House Dr ... 76502
Cart Rd & Spur ... 76502
Case Rd ... 76504
Casler Cir ... 76502
Cearley Rd ... 76504
N Cedallan St ... 76501
N & S Cedar Ln & Rd ... 76502
Cedar Creek Rd ... 76504
Cedar Oaks Cir ... 76502
Cedar Ridge Park Rd ... 76502
Celeste Trl ... 76504
Cemetery Rd ... 76501
Cen Tex Loop ... 76501
Center St ... 76504
E Central Ave ... 76501
W Central Ave
1-97 ... 76501
99-599 ... 76501
1001-1097 ... 76504
1099-1499 ... 76504
Central Pointe Pkwy ... 76504
Chadwick Dr ... 76502
Chamberlain Ln ... 76502
Chaparral Dr ... 76502
Charlya Ct & Dr ... 76502
Charter Oak Dr & Loop ... 76502
Chelsea Pl ... 76502
Cherokee Dr ... 76504
Cherry Ln ... 76502
Chestnut Rd ... 76502
Chevy Cir ... 76504
Cheyenne Dr ... 76504
Chief The Land ... 76501
Chimney Cir ... 76502
Chimney Hill Dr ... 76502
Chisholm Trl ... 76504
Choctaw Dr ... 76504
Cindy Ln ... 76501
Clarence Rd ... 76501
Claridge Ct ... 76502
Cleghorn Ln ... 76504
Cliff Ln ... 76502
Cliff Estates Rd ... 76502
Clover Ln ... 76502
Coach Stop Dr ... 76502
Coastal Dr ... 76502
Cole Ave ... 76501
Cole Porter Dr ... 76502
Colonel Travis St ... 76502
Comanche Ct & Rd ... 76502
Commanche Dr ... 76504
Commerce Dr ... 76504
Concord Dr ... 76504
Connecticut Ave ... 76502
Content School Rd ... 76501
Copper Ridge Loop ... 76502
Cordova Dr ... 76502
Cottingham Dr ... 76504
Cottontail Trl ... 76501
Cottonwood Ln ... 76502
Cottonwood Creek Rd ... 76501
Country Lane Dr ... 76504
Cove Point Rd ... 76502
Coventry Dr ... 76502
Covington Ln ... 76502
Cow Page Ct ... 76502
Cozy Creek Dr ... 76502
Creasey Dr ... 76501
N Creek Ln ... 76504
Creek Rd ... 76501
Creek Side Dr ... 76502
Creekview Trl ... 76504
Crestwood Ct ... 76502
Cricket Ln ... 76501
Cripple Creek Dr ... 76502
Crocker Dr ... 76502
Crockett Ct ... 76501
Crockett Dr ... 76502
Cryer Ln ... 76502
Crystal Dr ... 76502
Curtis B Elliott Dr ... 76501
Daffodil Dr ... 76502
Dairy Rd ... 76501
Daisey Ln ... 76502
Dakota Dr ... 76504
Dalgoner Ln ... 76502
Danbury Dr ... 76502
Dandridge Dr ... 76502
Daniel Boone Trl ... 76502
Daniels Dr ... 76502
Daugherty Ln ... 76502
Davis Ln ... 76504
Davy Crockett St ... 76502
Deck Dr ... 76502
Deep Dr ... 76502
Deer Trl ... 76504
Deerfield Dr ... 76502
Del Norte Blvd ... 76502
Delaware Ave ... 76502
Delaware Dr ... 76504
Devin Dr ... 76502
Dewberry Ln ... 76502
Dodge Dr ... 76504
Dogwood Ln ... 76502
Dons Trl ... 76502
Dove Cir & Ln ... 76502
E Downs Ave ... 76501
W Downs Ave
101-297 ... 76501
299-799 ... 76501
1100-1199 ... 76504
Draper Dr ... 76504
Driftwood Cir ... 76502
Dubose Rd ... 76502
Duck Hollow Ln ... 76502
Dudley Rd ... 76501
Dudleys Draw Dr ... 76502
Duke Dr ... 76502
Dunbar Rd ... 76504
Durango Dr ... 76504
Durant Dr ... 76502
Dusty Ln ... 76502
Duval Ct ... 76501
Eagle Rd ... 76502
Eagles Nest Cv ... 76502
East Dr ... 76502
Eberhardt Rd ... 76504
Echo Village Dr ... 76502
Edge Hill Dr ... 76502
Edgewood Ln ... 76502
El Camino Dr ... 76502
El Capitan Dr ... 76502
Elk Trl ... 76504
Ellen Ct ... 76501
Ellington Ct ... 76502
E Elm Ave ... 76501
W Elm Ave
100-298 ... 76501
300-400 ... 76501
402-698 ... 76501
1101-1199 ... 76504
Elm Dr ... 76502
N Elm Loop ... 76501
Emerald Gate Dr ... 76502
Emerald Ridge Dr ... 76502
Enterprise Rd ... 76504
Epperson Rd ... 76504
Erath Dr ... 76501
Erie Dr ... 76504
Ermine Trl ... 76504
Estes Pkwy ... 76501
Evanwood Dr ... 76502
Evergreen Farm Dr ... 76502
Everton Dr ... 76504
Exchange Plz ... 76504
Executive Dr ... 76504
Fair Hill Dr ... 76502
Fairfield ... 76502
Fairway Dr ... 76502
Falcon Dr ... 76502
Fall Creek Ln ... 76504
Fallen Leaf Ln ... 76502
Fannin Loop ... 76501
Fantail Ln ... 76502
Fawn Trl ... 76504
Fawn Lily Dr ... 76502
Fawn Meadows Dr ... 76502
Field Rd ... 76501
Fieldstone Dr ... 76502
Filly Ln ... 76504
Flint Rock Ln ... 76502
Fm 1237
300-398 ... 76501
Fm 1237
400-2999 ... 76501
3400-3998 ... 76504
4000-9199 ... 76504
Fm 2086 ... 76501
Fm 2409 ... 76504
Fm 2904 ... 76501
Fm 3117 ... 76501
Fm 3369 ... 76501
E Fm 436 ... 76501
Fm 437 ... 76501
Fm 438 Loop ... 76501
E Fm 93
100-1900 ... 76502
1902-2998 ... 76502
3200-4998 ... 76501
W Fm 93 ... 76502
W Fm 93 Hwy ... 76502
Fm 93 Spur ... 76502
Forest Trl ... 76502
Forrester Rd ... 76502
Fowler Dr & Rd ... 76501
Fox Trl ... 76504
Fox Glen Ln ... 76502
Foxhill Rd ... 76502
Foxtail ... 76502
Fredrick Ln ... 76502
Freedom Ct & Dr ... 76502
E French Ave ... 76501
W French Ave
2-98 ... 76501
100-900 ... 76501
902-998 ... 76501
1101-1199 ... 76504
Friars Grove Dr ... 76502
Friendship Ln ... 76501
Frontier Dr ... 76504

Fryers Creek Cir & Dr .. 76504
Galleta Ct ... 76502
Garden Green Dr ... 76502
E & W Garfield Ave ... 76501
Gazelle Trl ... 76504
N General Bruce Dr
2-98 ... 76504
100-2000 ... 76504
2002-2298 ... 76504
2500-7799 ... 76501
S General Bruce Dr
100-3799 ... 76504
3800-7499 ... 76502
7501-7799 ... 76502
George Dr ... 76504
Georgia Ave ... 76502
Geronimo Dr ... 76504
Gianotti Ct ... 76502
Gila Trl ... 76504
Gillmeister Ln ... 76502
Glenwood Dr ... 76502
Goliad Cir ... 76502
Goliad Dr ... 76502
Goliad Loop ... 76502
Goliad St ... 76501
Gorden Rd ... 76501
Granbury Cv ... 76502
Green Pasture Dr ... 76502
Greenbriar Ct ... 76502
Greenview Dr ... 76502
Greenway Rd ... 76501
Grizzly Bear Trl ... 76502
Gun Club Rd ... 76501
Gunbarrel Dr ... 76502
Guy Dr ... 76504
W H Ave ... 76504
H K Allen Pkwy ... 76502
NE H K Dodgen Loop .. 76501
NW H K Dodgen Loop
6201-6299 ... 76502
9601-10599 ... 76504
10900-10998 ... 76504
12300-12398 ... 76501
SE H K Dodgen Loop
14501-18499 ... 76501
21800-23398 ... 76504
21901-22699 ... 76502
SW H K Dodgen Loop
100-5798 ... 76504
201-6299 ... 76502
Hampton Dr ... 76502
Hancock Dr ... 76504
Hansom Cab Cir & Dr .. 76502
Harbor Dr ... 76502
Harrington ... 76504
Hart Rd ... 76501
Hartrick Cir ... 76502
Hartrick Bluff Rd ... 76502
Hartrick Canyon Dr ... 76502
Harvest Mdw ... 76502
Hawthorn ... 76502
Heather Marie Ct ... 76502
Heidenheimer Rd ... 76501
Helm Ln ... 76502
Hemlock Blvd, Cir &
Ct ... 76502
Henderson St ... 76501
E Heritage Ave ... 76501
Hernandez Dr ... 76504
Hickory Rd ... 76502
Hidden Valley Dr ... 76502
High Bluff Cir ... 76502
High Meadow Dr ... 76502
High Pointe Dr ... 76502
Highland Trl ... 76502
E Highway 36 ... 76501
Highway 95 ... 76502
Hillcrest Rd ... 76501
Hilliard Rd ... 76502
Hogan Rd ... 76502
Holly Ln ... 76502
Honeysuckle ... 76502
Hope St ... 76501
Hopi Cir & Trl ... 76504
Hopkins Dr ... 76502
Horseshoe Bnd ... 76502

E & W Houston Ave ... 76501
Hruskaville Rd ... 76501
Hummingbird Ln ... 76502
Huntington Dr ... 76502
Hyacinth Dr ... 76502
Idaho Ave ... 76502
Iglesia Ln ... 76504
Independence Ct ... 76502
Indian Trl ... 76502
Indian Bluff Rd ... 76502
Indian Grove Dr ... 76502
Indian Mallow Dr ... 76502
Indian Springs Rd ... 76502
Industrial Blvd
500-798 ... 76501
1100-1198 ... 76504
1200-2899 ... 76504
2901-4099 ... 76504
Inks Cv ... 76502
N Interstate Hwy 35 ... 76501
Inwood Rd ... 76502
Iowa Ave ... 76502
Ira Young Dr ... 76504
Iris Cir ... 76502
Irish Ln ... 76502
Iroquois Trl ... 76504
E & W Irvin Ave ... 76501
Ivanhoe Dr ... 76502
J I Bruce Dr ... 76502
Jack Rabbit Rd ... 76502
E Jackson Ave ... 76501
Jaguar Trl ... 76504
Jayline Dr ... 76501
Jeanine Dr ... 76502
Jib Ln ... 76502
John Paul Jones Dr ... 76504
Jubilee Springs Rd ... 76502
Juniper Dr ... 76502
Jupiter ... 76502
Kacie Dr ... 76502
Kahlig Rd ... 76501
Kansas Ave ... 76502
Karey Dr ... 76502
Karla Way ... 76502
Kasberg Dr ... 76502
Kathy Dr ... 76502
N Katy St ... 76501
N & S Kegley Ln &
Rd ... 76502
Kegley Place Ct & Ln .. 76502
Keller Rd ... 76504
Kelly Dr ... 76502
Ken Cir ... 76502
Kendra Dr ... 76502
Kensington Ct ... 76502
Kevin Dr ... 76502
Key Stone ... 76502
Kiddieland Rd ... 76502
E & W Killen Ln ... 76501
Kimi Ln ... 76502
E & W King Ave & Cir .. 76501
King Arthur Blvd ... 76502
King George Dr ... 76504
Kingsbury Dr ... 76502
Kinne Rd ... 76502
Klein Dr ... 76502
S Knob St ... 76501
Knob Creek Rd &
Spur ... 76501
Kton Loop ... 76502
Kuykendall Mountain
Rd ... 76502
Kuykendall Springs Rd . 76502
Kyle Dr ... 76502
Lake Pointe Dr ... 76502
Lake Whitney Dr ... 76502
Lakeaire Blvd & Cir ... 76502
Lakeview St ... 76502
E & W Lamar Ave ... 76501
Lamplight Ct ... 76502
Lancelot Ln ... 76502
Landfill Rd ... 76501
Lark Trl ... 76502
Larkspur Ln ... 76502
Las Cienega Blvd ... 76502
Las Colinas Dr ... 76502

Las Cruces Blvd ... 76502
Las Lomas Ct ... 76502
Las Moras Dr ... 76502
Las Palmas Ln ... 76502
Laurel Rd & Rdg ... 76502
Lavendusky Dr ... 76501
Lavon Ln ... 76502
Lawnwood Cir & Dr ... 76502
Lawsons Point Rd ... 76502
Ledge Rd ... 76502
Ledgestone Trl ... 76502
Legacy Oaks Dr ... 76502
Legend Oaks Dr ... 76502
Lemonwood Ln ... 76501
Leona Park Ln ... 76504
Level Acres Dr ... 76502
Lexington Dr ... 76504
Liberty Dr & Hl ... 76504
Liberty Bell Ct ... 76502
Lightner Ln ... 76502
Lilac Ln ... 76502
Limewood Ln ... 76501
Lindo Vista Dr ... 76501
Linwood Rd ... 76502
Little Elm Loop ... 76501
Little Flock Rd ... 76501
Little Mexico Rd ... 76504
Little River Rd ... 76502
Live Oak Dr ... 76504
Livingston Ct ... 76502
Lobo Trl ... 76502
Lone Star Trl ... 76502
Lonesome Oak Dr ... 76502
Longhorn Trl ... 76502
W Loop ... 76504
Loop Dr ... 76502
Lorraine Ave ... 76501
Lost Creek Ct ... 76502
Lost Prairie Ln ... 76501
Lovetta Ln ... 76502
Lower Troy Rd ... 76501
Lowes Dr ... 76502
Lucius Mccelvey Dr ... 76504
Luna Ln ... 76501
Lynx Trl ... 76504
Madden Rd ... 76502
Madison ... 76504
Magnolia Blvd ... 76502
N Main St
1-500 ... 76501
401-499 ... 76503
501-2999 ... 76501
502-2898 ... 76501
S Main St
1-210 ... 76501
300-398 ... 76504
400-1399 ... 76504
Mama Dog Cir ... 76504
Mama Dog Ln ... 76501
Maplewood Ct ... 76502
Mardean Ln ... 76501
Margie Lou Ln ... 76501
Mariam Rd ... 76502
Market Loop ... 76502
Marlandwood Cir & Rd . 76502
Mars Cir ... 76502
S Martin Luther King
Blvd ... 76504
Martin Luther King Jr Dr
& Ln ... 76504
E Marvin R Felder Dr .. 76504
Mayborn Dr ... 76501
Mccullough Loop ... 76502
Mcfaddan Ln ... 76502
Mcgregor Park Rd ... 76502
Mcgugan Ln ... 76502
Mclane Pkwy ... 76504
Mclaughlin Ln ... 76502
Meadow Creek Ln ... 76504
Meadow Lark Ln ... 76501
Meadow Oaks Dr ... 76502
Meadow Wood Ct &
Dr ... 76502
Meadowbrook Dr ... 76502
Melany Ln ... 76501
Melrose Ln ... 76502

Mendoza Cir ... 76501
Mesquite Dr ... 76502
Michaels Dr ... 76502
Middle Rd ... 76501
Midway Dr ... 76502
Mikey Ln ... 76502
Milan Ct ... 76502
Misty Creek Ln ... 76502
Misty Gail ... 76502
Misty Morning Ln ... 76502
Misty Pine Dr ... 76502
Mitchell Dr ... 76501
Mockingbird Ln ... 76502
N Mockingbird Rd ... 76501
S Mockingbird Rd ... 76501
Mockingbird Hill Ln ... 76501
Moffat Loop, Rd &
Spgs ... 76502
Montana Dr ... 76502
Monticello Rd ... 76501
N Montpark Rd ... 76502
Montscotia Ln ... 76502
Moody Ln ... 76504
Moon Shadow ... 76502
Moores Mill Rd
901-1097 ... 76501
1099-1700 ... 76501
1701-1821 ... 76504
1702-1798 ... 76501
1823-2600 ... 76504
2602-3598 ... 76504
Morgan Dr ... 76502
Morning Dove Cv ... 76502
Morning Glory Dr ... 76502
Motl Ln ... 76501
Mountain Laurel Loop .. 76502
Mouser Rd ... 76504
Mt Calvary Dr ... 76504
E & W Munroe Ave ... 76501
Nairm Ln ... 76502
Naples Dr ... 76502
Navajo ... 76504
Neches Cir ... 76504
Neuberry Cliffe ... 76502
Nibling Ln ... 76502
Night View Dr ... 76502
Nighthawk Cir ... 76502
Northwood Rd ... 76502
E Nugent Ave ... 76501
W Nugent Ave
2-598 ... 76501
600-799 ... 76501
1600-1998 ... 76504
2000-3799 ... 76504
Oak Xing ... 76502
Oak Bluff Cir ... 76502
Oak Chase Trl ... 76502
Oak Hills Dr ... 76502
Oak Villa Dr ... 76502
Oakbend Cv ... 76502
Oakcreek Dr ... 76504
Oakdale Dr ... 76502
E & W Oakland Ave ... 76501
Oaklawn Dr ... 76502
Oakridge Dr & Rd ... 76502
Oakview Dr ... 76502
Oakwood Ct ... 76504
Oakwood St ... 76502
Ocker Rd ... 76501
Oenaville Loop ... 76501
Oil Loop ... 76501
Olaf Dr ... 76504
Old Glory ... 76502
Old Highway 95 ... 76502
Old Howard Rd ... 76504
Old Hwy 81 ... 76501
Old Waco Ln & Rd ... 76502
Olde Oaks Dr ... 76502
Olympia Dr ... 76502
Open Prairie Dr ... 76502
Orion Dr ... 76502
Osage ... 76504
Osage Ln ... 76501
Oscar Ln & Spur ... 76501
Oscar School Rd ... 76501
Ottoway Dr ... 76501

Owen Ln ... 76502
Oxford Dr ... 76502
Paint Brush Ln ... 76502
Painted Vly ... 76502
Palermo Pkwy ... 76502
Palmetto Dr ... 76502
Palomino Dr ... 76502
Pamela Rd ... 76502
Panda Dr ... 76501
Pappus Ct ... 76502
W Park Ave ... 76501
Park Place Ln ... 76504
Parkdale ... 76502
Parkfield ... 76502
Parkside Dr ... 76502
Parkway Dr ... 76504
Parnell Dr ... 76504
Paseo Del Cobre ... 76502
Paseo Del Oro ... 76502
Paseo Del Plata ... 76502
Pat Cole Rd ... 76502
Patrick Henry St ... 76504
Patriot Ct ... 76502
Paul Revere St ... 76504
N & S Pea Ridge Rd ... 76502
Peach Orchard Ln &
Rd ... 76501
Peanut Dr ... 76502
Pecan Blf ... 76504
Pecan Dr ... 76502
Pecan Rd ... 76501
Pecan Valley Dr ... 76502
Pecos Dr ... 76504
Pegasus Dr ... 76501
Pendleton St ... 76504
Penrose Ln ... 76502
Pepper Creek Rd ... 76504
Pepper Spring Ct ... 76502
Pheasant Run Ln ... 76502
Phoenix Dr ... 76504
Pima ... 76504
Pin Oak Dr ... 76502
Pino Circulo ... 76502
Pleasant View Rd ... 76501
Poison Oak Rd ... 76502
Ponderosa Ln ... 76502
Poplar Rd ... 76502
Possum Creek Rd ... 76501
Post Oak Cir ... 76502
Prairie Lark Dr ... 76502
Prairie View Rd ... 76502
Prcin Ln ... 76502
Preston Oaks Dr ... 76504
Prewitt Dr ... 76501
Primrose Trl ... 76501
Pritchard Rd ... 76501
Profesional Dr ... 76504
Profit Pl ... 76502
Providence Park ... 76504
Pullman Place Blvd ... 76502
Pumpkin Dr ... 76502
Quail Trl ... 76502
Quail Hollow Dr ... 76502
Quartz Ct ... 76502
Rabbit Rd ... 76501
Raindance Dr ... 76502
Raleigh Dr ... 76502
Ramcon Dr ... 76504
Ranch Rd ... 76502
Range Rd ... 76504
Ravenwood ... 76502
Rawhide Trl ... 76502
Red Barn Ln ... 76501
Red Bud Rd ... 76502
Red Cliff Cir ... 76502
Red Coat Dr ... 76504
Red Oak Cir ... 76502
Red Ranger Rd ... 76501
Red River Cir ... 76504
Red Valley Way ... 76502
Redbird Ln ... 76502
Redbrush ... 76502
Redstone Dr ... 76502
Redwing Dr ... 76502
Reeds Lake Loop &
Rd ... 76501

Reef Ln ... 76502
Revis Dr ... 76502
Rickey Dr ... 76502
E & W Ridge Blvd ... 76502
Ridge Way Dr ... 76502
Ridge Wood ... 76502
Ridgeview Dr ... 76502
Riggs Rd ... 76502
River Hills Ct ... 76504
River Land Ct ... 76502
River Oaks Cir ... 76504
River Ranch Rd ... 76502
Riverside Trl ... 76502
Robin Rd ... 76502
Robinhood Dr ... 76502
Rock Ct ... 76502
Rock Hill Loop ... 76502
Rogers St ... 76504
Rollingwood Dr ... 76502
Rosehall Ln ... 76504
Rosemary Ln ... 76502
Rosewood Dr ... 76502
Ross Cole Ln ... 76502
Roxbury Ave ... 76502
W Royal Ave ... 76501
Ruggles Loop ... 76501
Runway Ln ... 76504
Rusty Nail Dr ... 76502
Sabine Cir ... 76504
Saddle Brook Dr ... 76502
Sage Loop Ct ... 76502
Sage Meadow Dr ... 76502
Sage Valley Dr ... 76502
Salac Ln ... 76501
Salado Dr ... 76502
Salado St ... 76504
Salt Creek Rd ... 76501
Sam Houston ... 76502
San Jacinto Rd ... 76502
Sandstone Dr & Loop .. 76502
Sanincom Dr ... 76502
Sarahs Way ... 76502
Saratoga Dr ... 76504
Saturn Cir ... 76502
Saulsbury Dr ... 76504
Sawyer Ln ... 76502
Scarlet Oak Dr ... 76501
Scott Blvd ... 76504
Sean Patrick Gln ... 76502
Seaton Rd ... 76501
Seven Coves Rd ... 76502
Shadow Canyon Dr ... 76502
Shadow Creek Cv ... 76502
Shady Hill Cir & Dr ... 76502
Shady Oaks Ct & Ln ... 76504
Shale Rock Run ... 76502
Shallow Ford Rd ... 76502
Shallow Ford West Rd . 76502
Shaw Rd ... 76501
E & W Shell Ave ... 76501
Shelton Dr ... 76502
Sherwood Ln ... 76502
Shine Branch Rd ... 76504
Shoal Dr ... 76502
Short Cut Rd ... 76501
Sienna Cv ... 76502
Sierra Blanca Blvd ... 76502
Silver Leaf Ct ... 76502
Silver Springs Ct ... 76502
Silver Stone Dr ... 76502
Silver Wood Ct ... 76502
Single Bend Trl ... 76502
Sioux ... 76504
Skyline Dr ... 76504
Skyview ... 76502
Sleepy Hollow Ln ... 76502
Slough Dr ... 76502
Smock Mill Ln ... 76502
Somerville ... 76502
Sorento Cir ... 76502
Southern Crossing Dr .. 76502
Southern Draw Dr ... 76502
Spanish Oak Rd ... 76502
Spar Cir ... 76502
Spray Ln ... 76502
Springwood Ct ... 76502

Stagecoach Trl ... 76502
Stallion Rd ... 76501
Stan Cir ... 76502
Stanford Dr ... 76502
Starlight Dr ... 76502
Starview St ... 76502
State Highway 317 ... 76504
W State Highway 36 ... 76502
State Highway 53 ... 76501
State Highway 95 ... 76502
Station Rd ... 76502
Stecher Ct ... 76502
Steeplechase Ct ... 76502
Sterling Dr ... 76502
Sterling Manor Ct &
Dr ... 76502
Stone Rd ... 76501
Stone Pointe Dr ... 76502
Stone Ridge Dr ... 76502
Stonebrook Dr ... 76502
Stoneham ... 76504
Stonehaven Dr ... 76502
Stonehill Ct ... 76502
Stonehollow Dr ... 76502
Stratford Ct & Dr ... 76502
Stringtown Rd ... 76501
Sturbridge Dr ... 76502
Sugar Brook Dr ... 76502
Sugar Cane Ln ... 76501
Sumac Dr ... 76502
Summerhill Ln ... 76502
Summerwood Dr ... 76502
Sundance Dr ... 76502
Sundrop Ln ... 76502
Sunflower Ln ... 76502
Sunny Side Ln ... 76502
Sunrise Blf ... 76502
Sunset Ln & Trl ... 76502
Sunset Canyon Dr ... 76502
Surrey Ct & Dr ... 76502
Sutton Loop & Pt ... 76504
Swanflower Ln ... 76502
Sycamore St ... 76502
Tanglehead Dr ... 76502
Tanglewood Rd ... 76502
Tarver Dr ... 76502
Taylor Ridge Rd ... 76502
Taylors Dr ... 76502
Taylors Valley Rd ... 76502
Taylors Valley Creek
Dr ... 76502
Teesh Dr ... 76502
Telephone Loop ... 76502
Tem Bel Ln ... 76502
Terra Cotta ... 76502
S Terrace St ... 76501
Terrell Ln ... 76502
W Thompson Ave ... 76501
Thornton Ln ... 76502
Ticonderoga Dr ... 76504
Tiger Cir ... 76502
Tiller Ln ... 76502
Timber Ridge Dr ... 76502
Timberline St ... 76502
Tobosa Dr ... 76502
Tower Rd ... 76501
Trade Pl ... 76504
Trader Rd ... 76501
Trail Dr ... 76502
Trailridge Dr ... 76502
Trailview Dr ... 76502
Trailwood Dr ... 76502
Travis Ct ... 76502
Trenton Dr ... 76504
Trinity Dr ... 76504
Triple Heart Ln ... 76504
Troy St ... 76504
Truelove Ln ... 76502
Tucson Dr ... 76504
Tully Weary Ln ... 76502
Tumbleweed Trl ... 76502
Turley Dr ... 76502
Turtle Creek Trl ... 76502
Twelve Oaks Ct & Dr ... 76504
Twin City Blvd ... 76502
Twin Oaks Dr ... 76504

Twisted Oak Dr 76502
Tyler Trl 76504
E Union 76501
Upland Bend Dr 76502
E & W Upshaw Ave 76501
Upson Ave 76501
E Us Highway 190 76501
Valerie Ln 76502
Valley Park 76502
Valley Forge Ave 76504
Valley Mist Ct & Dr 76502
Valley View Dr 76502
Van Dyke Dr 76504
Van Pelt Ave 76501
Venice Pkwy 76502
Venus 76502
Verbena Dr 76502
Victorian Dr 76502
E & W Victory Ave 76501
W Virginia Ave 76501
Vista Ct 76502
Vista Valley Dr 76502
Wagon Rd & Trl 76502
Wahle Ln 76501
E & W Walker Ave 76501
Walnut Rd 76502
Warren Lawson Loop 76502
Warwicke Ct & Dr 76502
Water Ridge Rd 76502
Water Supply Rd 76502
Waterbury Ct & Dr 76502
Waterford Ct & Dr 76502
Waters Dairy Rd 76502
Wedel Cemetery Rd 76501
Wedgwood Dr 76502
Weeping Willow Dr 76502
Wellington Ct 76502
W Welton Ave 76501
Wendland Rd 76504
Wendy Oaks Dr 76502
Westbury 76504
Westchester Ct 76502
Westend Dr 76502
Westfield Blvd 76502
Westoak Cv 76502
Westpoint Dr 76504
Westway Cv & Dr 76502
Westwood Rd 76502
Westwood Hills Blvd 76502
Whispering Oaks 76504
Whistle Stop Dr 76502
White Chapel Rd 76502
White Oak Dr 76502
White Owl Ln 76501
S Whitehall Rd 76504
Whiterock Dr 76502
Whitesail Ln 76502
Wickersham Dr 76502
Wild Buck Run 76502
Wild Wood 76504
Wildcat Dr 76502
Wildflower Ln 76502
Williams Dr 76502
Williamson Cir 76504
Willow Rd
800-2299 76501
3200-3299 76502
Willow Grove Rd 76504
Willowood Ln 76502
Wilshire Dr 76502
Wilson Pl 76504
Winchester Dr 76502
Windchime Way 76502
Windcliff Dr 76502
Windsong Ln 76502
Windy Cir 76502
Winrock Cir 76502
Witter Ln 76502
Wolverine Trl 76502
Wood Creek Dr 76502
Woodbridge Blvd 76504
Woodbury Dr 76502
Woodcrest Rd 76502
Wooded Creek Cv 76502
Woodford Rd 76501
Woodhollow Dr 76502
Woodolee Dr 76502
Woodstone Cir 76502
Wren Cir & Rd 76502
Wyndcrest 76502
Wyndham Hill Pkwy 76502
E & W Xavier Ave 76501
Yaupon Rd 76502
Yorktown Dr 76504
E & W Young Ave 76501
Yuma 76504
E & W Zenith Ave 76501

NUMBERED STREETS

N 1st St 76501
S 1st St
1-199 76501
201-299 76501
300-2400 76504
2402-2698 76504
N 2nd St 76501
S 2nd St
1-299 76501
301-399 76501
401-497 76504
499-1499 76504
N 3rd St 76501
S 3rd St
1-99 76501
400-498 76504
N 4th St 76501
S 4th St
2-298 76501
300-399 76501
401-597 76504
599-1400 76504
1402-1498 76504
N 5th St 76501
S 5th St
2-98 76501
100-199 76501
201-297 76504
299-2599 76504
2601-2699 76504
3200-4898 76502
4900-4999 76502
5001-6199 76502
N 6th St 76501
N 6th St W 76501
S 6th St
100-200 76501
202-498 76501
500-598 76504
600-1499 76504
N 7th St 76501
2-198 76501
300-2199 76504
N & S 8th 76501
N 9th St 76501
1-99 76501
400-2199 76504
N 10th St 76501
S 10th St
1-599 76501
700-1400 76504
N 11th St 76501
1-99 76501
400-2199 76504
N 12th St 76501
S 12th St
2-198 76501
200-399 76501
800-998 76504
1000-1399 76504
1401-1499 76504
N 13th St 76501
400-2499 76504
2901-2999 76502
N & S 14th 76501
N 15th St 76501
S 15th St 76504
N & S 16th 76501
N 17th St 76501
S 17th St 76504
N & S 18th 76501
N & S 19th 76504
N & S 20th 76501
N & S 21st 76504
N & S 22nd 76501
N & S 23rd 76504
S 24th St 76501
N & S 25th 76504
S 26th St 76501
N & S 27th 76504
S 28th St 76501
N & S 29th 76504
S 30th St
700-900 76501
902-1498 76501
2101-2197 76504
2199-2200 76504
2202-2298 76504
N 31st St 76504
S 31st St
1-2699 76504
2900-3098 76502
3100-5599 76502
5601-6399 76502
S 32nd St 76501
N & S 33rd 76504
N & S 34th 76501
S 35th St 76504
N & S 36th 76501
S 37th St 76504
S 38th St 76501
S 39th St 76504
S 40th St 76501
N & S 41st 76504
N 42nd St 76501
N & S 43rd 76504
S 45th St 76504
S 47th St 76504
S 49th St 76504
N & S 50th 76501
51st St & Ter 76504
S 53rd St 76504
55th St & Ter 76504
S 57th St 76504
S 61st St
1700-2199 76504
2400-2499 76502
205 Loop 76502

TERRELL TX

General Delivery 75160

POST OFFICE BOXES MAIN OFFICE STATIONS AND BRANCHES

Box No.s
All PO Boxes 75160

RURAL ROUTES

03, 04, 06, 07 75160
01, 02, 05 75161

NAMED STREETS

Abner Rd 75161
Adams St 75160
N & S Adelaide St 75160
Airport Rd 75160
Airport East Dr 75160
E & W Alamo St 75160
E & W Alamosa Dr 75160
Allen Ln 75161
Allen St 75160
Amy Ln 75161
Anglin Way 75161
N & S Ann St 75160
Apache Trl 75160
Armstrong 75160
Artesia St 75160
Athens St 75160
Baker St 75160
Banks St 75160
Barnes Ln 75161
Bedrick Ln 75160
Beesley Ct 75160
Belmont Ln 75160
Bennett St 75160
Bethlehem St 75160
Betty Dr 75160
Beverly Dr 75160
Bill Ln 75161
Birdsong Ct & Ln 75160
N & S Blanche St 75160
Boathouse Dr 75160
Bob White Ln 75161
Boone St 75160
Bowling Ln 75161
Bowser St 75160
Bradeen Dr 75161
Bradshaw St 75160
Brent Ave 75160
E & W Brin St 75160
W British Flying School Blvd 75160
E Broad St 75160
Brookhollow Dr 75160
Brooks St 75160
Brookwood Dr 75160
Brushy Creek Ln 75160
N & S Burch St 75160
Burnett St 75160
Business Cir 75160
Butler Ln 75160
Campbell St 75160
Canton St 75160
Carl Lee Cir 75160
Carroll St 75160
Cartwright St 75160
N & S Catherine St 75160
Champion Rd 75160
Chandler Ln 75161
Chapman Ln 75160
Chappell St 75160
Charles Ln 75160
Cherokee St 75160
Cherrend 75161
Chestnut Cir 75160
Cheyenne Ln & Trl 75160
Christie Ln 75161
Churchill Downs Cir 75160
Circle Dr 75160
Cleaver Ln 75160
E & W College St 75160
College Mound Rd 75160
College Mound Acres 75161
Collins Dr 75160
Colquitt Rd 75160
Corrall Ln 75160
E & W Cottage St 75160
Cottonwood Ln 75160
Country Corner Ln 75161
Country Meadows Dr 75160
County Road 125 75161
County Road 126 75161
County Road 129 75161
County Road 130 75161
County Road 131 75161
County Road 131a 75161
County Road 131b 75161
County Road 132 75161
County Road 133 75161
County Road 133a 75161
County Road 136 75161
County Road 136a 75161
County Road 136b 75161
County Road 136c 75161
County Road 137 75161
County Road 138 75161
County Road 139 75161
County Road 164 75161
County Road 215 75160
County Road 216 75160
County Road 2312 75160
County Road 2316 75160
County Road 2320 75160
County Road 2322 75160
County Road 2323 75160
County Road 2324 75160
County Road 2326 75160
County Road 2328 75160
County Road 2329 75160
County Road 2332 75160
County Road 234 75160
County Road 236 75160
County Road 237 75160
County Road 237a 75160
County Road 237b 75160
County Road 238 75160
County Road 239 75160
County Road 239a 75160
County Road 2400 75160
County Road 2426 75160
County Road 2428 75160
County Road 243 75160
County Road 2430 75160
County Road 2431 75160
County Road 2432 75160
County Road 2433 75160
County Road 2434 75160
County Road 245 75160
County Road 2450 75160
County Road 2451 75160
County Road 2452 75160
County Road 2454 75160
County Road 2456 75160
County Road 2458 75160
County Road 246 75160
County Road 2460 75160
County Road 2462 75160
County Road 2464 75160
County Road 2466 75160
County Road 2468 75160
County Road 247 75160
County Road 248 75160
County Road 249 75160
County Road 250 75160
County Road 251 75160
County Road 253 75160
County Road 255 75160
County Road 271 75160
County Road 272 75160
County Road 273 75160
County Road 274 75160
County Road 275 75160
County Road 276 75160
County Road 283 75160
County Road 286 75160
County Road 301 75160
County Road 302 75160
County Road 303 75160
County Road 304 75160
County Road 305 75160
County Road 307 75161
County Road 308 75161
County Road 309 75161
County Road 310 75161
County Road 311 75161
County Road 312 75161
County Road 313 75161
County Road 314 75161
County Road 314a 75161
County Road 315 75161
County Road 316 75161
County Road 316a 75161
County Road 316b 75161
County Road 316c 75161
County Road 318 75160
County Road 319 75161
County Road 319b 75161
County Road 321 75160
County Road 322
15201-15297 75161
15299-16099 75161
16101-16299 75160
17000-18999 75160
County Road 322a 75160
County Road 323 75160
County Road 324 75160
County Road 329 75161
County Road 330 75161
County Road 331 75161
County Road 331a 75161
County Road 332a 75161
County Road 333a 75161
County Road 336 75161
County Road 338 75161
County Road 339 75161
County Road 340 75161
County Road 341 75161
County Road 342 75161
County Road 343 75161
County Road 343a 75161
County Road 344 75161
County Road 345 75161
County Road 346 75161
County Road 346a 75161
County Road 347 75161
County Road 348 75161
County Road 349 75161
County Road 350 75161
County Road 351 75161
County Road 351a 75161
County Road 352 75161
County Road 353 75161
County Road 354 75161
County Road 355 75161
County Road 356 75161
County Road 357 75161
County Road 358 75161
County Road 358a 75161
County Road 359 75161
County Road 360 75161
County Road 364 75160
County Road 369 75161
County Road 370 75161
County Road 371 75161
County Road 374 75161
County Road 375 75161
County Road 376 75161
County Road 377 75161
County Road 378 75161
County Road 379 75161
County Road 381 75161
County Road 390 75161
Creekside Dr 75160
Crenshaw St 75160
E Cresent St 75160
Crockett St 75160
Crosby Ln 75160
Crow Ln 75161
Curtis Ln 75160
Dallas St 75160
W Damon St 75160
Daniels St 75160
Davidson Dr 75160
Davis Ln 75160
Dee Dr 75160
Dellis St 75160
Delphine St S 75160
Denali Ct 75160
Denim St 75160
Dixon St 75160
Dogpatch Dr 75161
Douglas Cir 75160
Dove Ln 75161
Dower Ct, Dr & Rd 75160
Dry Creek Run 75160
Duck Ln 75161
Duck Creek Rd 75161
Eason St 75160
Eastgate Dr 75160
Ed Hardin Ln 75161
Edwards St 75160
Elizabeth St 75160
Elm Dr 75160
Emerald Ln 75161
Emily St 75160
W End St 75160
Estate Ln 75161
Eulalia Dr 75160
Evelyn Dr 75160
Everett Dr 75160
Ewing Ln 75161
Fall Creek Rd 75160
Feather Ln 75161
Flash Ln 75161
Fm 1392 75160
N Fm 148 75160
Fm 1565 75160
Fm 1641 75160
Fm 2578 75160
Fm 2727 75161
Fm 2728 75161
Fm 2932 75160
Fm 429 75161
S Fm 548 75160
Fm 986 75160
Fm 987 75160
Foolish Pleasure Dr 75160
Forest Creek Ln 75160
Forest Trail Cir 75160
Four Post Ln 75160
N Fox St 75160
N & S Frances St 75160
Frank St 75160
Frazier St 75160
Freeman St 75160
Gantt St 75160
Gate Ln 75160
George Trl 75160
Gilbert St 75160
Giles Ln 75160
Glenda St 75160
Gold Meadow Dr 75161
Gordon Dr 75160
W Goss Ln & St 75160
Grabbs Ln 75161
Grace Ln 75160
Green St 75160
Green Meadow Ln 75160
Greenwood St 75160
Griffith Ave, Ct & Rd 75160
E & W Grove St 75160
Hackberry St 75160
Hamilton Dr 75160
Hammond St 75160
Hanging Tree Rd 75161
Hardin St 75160
Harrisee St 75160
N & S Hattie St 75160
Hawkins St 75160
Haynes Cir 75160
Heath St 75160
Heather Way 75160
Heather Lane Cir 75160
Helen St 75160
Henderson St 75160
Heritage Ln 75160
E & W High St 75160
High Meadow Ct & Dr 75160
High Point Rd 75160
Hill St 75160
Hilltop Dr 75161
Hiram Rd 75161
Hollow Ct 75161
Holly Ct 75160
Holly Creek Rd 75160
Homer Cir 75160
Hood St 75160
Houston St 75160
Howard St 75160
Ida St 75160
Industrial Blvd 75160
Interstate 20 75161
E Interstate 20
301-399 75160
8401-8499 75161
10900-11798 75161
Iron Horse Dr 75160
Ivan Ct 75161
Jacks Dr 75161
Jackson Dr
100-199 75160
6600-6899 75161
W Jackson St 75160
James St 75160
Jamison Ct 75160
Jaycee St 75160
Jerry Dr 75160
John Wayne Trl 75160
Johnson St 75160
W Jones St 75160
Jordan Ln 75161
June St 75160
Karen Ln 75160

Kennedy Dr 75160
Kings Creek Dr 75161
Lamar St 75160
Lane St 75160
Laroe St 75160
Laurel Trl N 75160
Laurel Trail Dr 75160
Lawrence Ave & Cir 75160
Lazy Cir 75161
Lee St 75160
Leighton Dr 75160
Lexington Dr 75160
Lincoln Ln 75160
Linda Dr 75160
Live Oak Ln 75160
Lone Star Blvd & Trl 75160
Longspur Ln 75160
Louisiana Downs Cir 75160
Lovers Ln 75160
Lydia St 75160
Main St 75160
Maple Dr & St 75160
Maplewood Dr 75160
Maryell St 75160
E & W Mccoulskey St 75160
Mccurdy Ln 75161
Meadow Way 75160
Meadowcrest Dr 75160
Meadowview Ct 75160
S Medora St 75160
Mellon St 75160
Melody Ln 75160
Meridith Dr 75160
Metro Dr 75160
Metrocrest Way 75160
Michael Talty Ave 75160
Mineral Wells St 75160
Mira Pl 75160
Mitchell Dr & St 75160
E & W Moore Ave 75160
Morris St 75160
Mount Olive St 75160
Music Row 75160
Myers St 75160
E & W Nash Ct & St 75160
New Hope St 75160
E & W Newton St 75160
Nike Dr 75160
North Ln 75161
Northgate Dr 75160
Northridge Dr 75160
Northview Dr 75160
Norton Ct & Dr 75160
Oak Dr 75160
Oak Ln 75161
Oak St 75160
Oak Post Dr 75160
Oak Ridge Dr 75160
Oakcrest Cir 75160
E & W Oaklawn Dr 75160
Old Bridge Rd 75160
Old George Dr 75160
Out Crop 75160
Overrado 75160
Pacific Ave 75160
Paloma Cir 75160
Pam Ln 75161
N & S Park Ave & St 75160
Pebble Creek Ln 75160
Pecan St 75160
Pecos St 75160
Pin Oak Dr 75161
Pinkston St 75160
Plant Rd 75161
Poetry Ln & Rd 75160
Poinsetta Cir 75160
Point Dr 75160
Polk St 75160
Preakness Cir 75160
Princeton Cir 75160
Private Road 2321 75160
Private Road 2325 75160
Private Road 2327 75160
Private Road 2329 75160
Private Road 2330 75160
Private Road 2331 75160
Private Road 2425 75160
Private Road 2427 75160
Private Road 2428 75160
Private Road 2429 75160
Quail Ct & Ln 75160
Ragsdale St 75160
Ranchette Rd 75161
Rash Ln 75160
Redwood 75160
Rellia Dr 75160
E & W Remington Park Dr 75160
Retama Park Dr 75160
Rexall Ct 75160
Ridge Ct & Rd 75160
Ridgecrest Dr 75160
Roadsend Cir 75160
Roberts Ave & St 75160
Robin Rd 75161
W Rochester St 75160
N & S Rockwall Ave & Ct 75160
Rocky Rd 75160
Rodeo Dr 75160
Roosevelt Ave & Ct 75160
Rose St 75160
Rose Hill Dr & Rd 75160
Rosewood Dr 75160
Ross St 75160
Ruby St 75160
Ruidoso Downs Dr 75160
Runnells St 75160
Saddle Ridge Cir 75160
Sage St 75160
Saint James St 75160
Saint Luke St 75160
Sam Walton Way 75160
Samples Ln 75160
Samuels Rd 75160
San Jacinto St 75160
Sandlewood Dr 75160
Sarah Ln 75161
Scott St 75160
E & W Secretariat Dr 75160
Shadow Brook Ct 75160
Shadow Ridge Ln 75161
Shady Creek Ln 75160
Shady Oaks Cir 75160
Silent Wings Blvd 75160
Skinner Rd 75161
Skyline Dr 75160
Sleepy Ln 75161
Sleepy Hollow Dr & Rd 75161
Sparks St 75160
Stallings St 75160
E & W State St 75160
State Highway 205 75160
State Highway 34 S 75160
N State Highway 34
7201-7697 75161
N State Highway 34
7699-8699 75161
8701-8799 75161
14300-14599 75160
14601-14899 75160
15301-15497 75161
15499-22000 75161
22002-22198 75161
Stonebriar Way 75160
Stonegate St 75160
Stoney Creek Ln 75160
Sue Ln 75160
Sue Ann Ln 75161
Talty Rd 75160
Tanger Dr 75160
Tejas Dr 75160
Tem Tex Blvd 75160
E Temple St 75160
Texas Trl 75160
Therrell Ln 75160
Thomas St 75160
Thunder Rd 75161
Tiffany Cir 75160
Timber Ct 75160
Timber Wood Cir 75160
Timberside 75161
Tom Ln 75161
Tower Cir 75160
Town North Dr 75160
Trails End 75160
Trailview Dr 75160
Trinity Meadows Dr 75160
Truman Ct 75160
Tyler St 75160
E Us Highway 80 75161
W Us Highway 80 75160
Valverde Loop 75161
Vine St 75160
N & S Virginia St 75160
Volney Dr 75160
Wade St 75160
Wall St 75160
Walnut St 75160
War Admiral Dr 75160
Warren St 75160
Washington St 75160
Westgate Dr 75160
Westvue St 75160
Westway Dr 75160
E Wheeler St 75160
Whirlaway Dr 75160
Williams St 75160
Willie Dennis 75160
Willow Cir & Ln 75160
Willow Brook Cir 75160
Willow Creek Ln 75160
Willowbrook Dr 75160
Wilson Rd 75161
Windsor Ave 75160
Wisteria Ct 75160
Wood Ln & St 75160
Woodland Estates Rd 75160
Wright St 75160
Yellow Rock Rdg 75161
Yosemite Ln 75160
Zagota Crossing Rd 75161
Zajic Dr 75160

NUMBERED STREETS

1st St 75160
3rd St 75160
4th St 75160
5th St 75160
6th St 75160
7th St 75160
S 7th St 75161
8th St 75160
9th St 75160
10th St 75160
11th St 75160

TEXARKANA TX

General Delivery 75501

POST OFFICE BOXES MAIN OFFICE STATIONS AND BRANCHES

Box No.s
1 - 3640 75504
3761 - 3993 75501
4941 - 9700 75505

RURAL ROUTES

02, 06, 09, 11, 13, 15, 17, 22, 23 75501
03, 05, 14, 16, 20, 24 75503

NAMED STREETS

Aaron Ln 75503
Adams St 75501
Airline Dr 75503
Akin Rd 75503
N Akin St 75501
S Akin St 75501
Akins Rd 75501
Alamo St 75501
Alan St 75501
Alexander Ave 75501
Alford St 75501
Allen Ln 75501
Alpine Dr 75501
Alpine Mhp 75501
Alumax Dr & Rd 75501
Amesdale Dr 75503
Amis Rd 75501
Amy Dr 75503
Ann St 75501
Anthony Dr 75503
Apache Trl 75501
Apple St 75501
Arbor Dr 75503
Arista Blvd 75503
Arizona Ave 75501
Arlington St 75501
Arnold Cir & Ln 75503
Arrington Rd 75503
Arroyo Dr 75503
Ashleigh Cir 75501
Ashley 75501
Aspen 75501
Atlanta St 75501
Austin St 75501
Autumn Cir & Ln 75501
Avenue A 75501
Azalea Dr 75503
B K Pickering Dr 75501
Babb Ln 75501
Bamboo St 75503
Bandera St 75503
Barber Ln 75503
Barentine Ln 75501
Barkwood St 75503
Baxter Dr 75501
Baylor St 75501
Beacon Hill Dr 75503
Beaumont St 75501
Beaver Creek Run 75501
Beaver Lake Cir & Dr 75501
Beechwood Ln 75501
Bel Air Dr 75503
Bell St
2100-2499 75501
2501-2599 75503
Bella Ln 75501
Bella Vista Cir 75503
Belt Rd 75501
Ben Burrough Rd 75503
S Bend Rd 75501
Bender Rd 75501
Benson 75501
Bent Tree Ct & Rd 75503
Bergt Rd 75501
Berry Dr 75501
Bertha St 75501
Bethany 75501
Bethany Ln 75503
Beuville Cir 75503
Bevil Pl 75503
Big Oak Ln
1-99 75503
200-299 75501
301-399 75501
Bill Rogers Dr 75503
Birchwood Cir 75503
N & S Bishop St 75501
Bivins Ln 75503
Blackfriar Rd 75503
Blake St 75501
Blankenship Rd 75501
Blanton Ave 75501
Bluebird Ln 75501
Bluebonnet Dr 75501
Boardwalk Ave 75501
Bobcat Trl 75503
Boondock Ln 75501
Border St 75501
Bottoms Rd 75501
Bowie St 75501
Boyce Ln 75501
Bradley Ln 75503
Branson 75503
Brazos St 75503
Breckenridge St 75501
Brenda St 75503
Briarwood Cir 75503
Briarwood St 75501
Bridlewood Dr 75503
Bright St 75501
Bringle Rdg 75503
Bringle Lake Rd 75503
Brinley Rd 75501
Brittan Pl 75503
Brittney Ln 75503
Britton St 75501
W Broad St 75501
Broadleaf 75503
Broken Post Rd 75503
Brooke Rd 75501
Brookfield St 75501
Brookhollow Cir & Dr 75503
Brookwood Dr 75501
Broussard Ln 75501
Brower Ln 75501
Brown Cir, Dr & St 75501
Bryant St 75501
Buchanan Rd 75501
Buchanan Loop Rd 75501
Burger Ln 75501
Burma Rd 75501
Butler Ave & St 75501
Caldwell St 75501
Camelia Ln 75503
Camelia Rd 75501
Cameron 75503
Canadian Cir, Pl & St 75503
Cancun 75501
Candlewood St 75503
Capp St 75501
Cardinal Ln 75501
Carol Ln 75501
Carrie Ln 75503
Carrie Smith Rd 75501
Carroll Ave 75501
Carter Cir 75503
Carver Cir 75501
Cascades Blvd 75503
Casteel St 75501
Castleberry 75501
Cavite Pl 75501
Cayman 75501
Cedar St 75501
Cedar Creek Cir & Dr 75501
Cedar Hill Rd 75503
Cedar Ridge Cir 75501
Central Ave 75501
Central Mall 75503
Central St 75501
Century Ln 75503
Cerrato Ln 75503
Champion Pl & St 75501
Chaparral St 75503
Charlestine St 75503
Charlotte St 75501
Charmwood Ct 75503
Chartwell 75503
Chatman Ln 75501
Chelf Rd 75501
Cherokee Trl 75501
Cherry Hill Rd 75503
Cheyenne Pl 75501
Christus Dr 75503
Cindy Ave 75503
Cindywood Cir & Dr 75503
N & S Circle Dr 75503
Circle Y Ranch Rd 75503
Citation St 75501
Citizens Trl 75501
Claiborne Ln 75501
Claire Ave 75503
Clara Ln 75501
Clara Sorsby Ln 75501
Clay Ave 75503
Clayborn St 75503
Clear Creek Cir & Dr 75503
Clear Springs Rd 75501
S Clearview Dr 75501
Clem Ranch Rd 75503
Clover Ln 75501
Cody Cir & St 75501
Coke Dr 75501
College Dr
101-797 75503
799-2399 75503
2400-3099 75501
Collier St 75501
Collins Ln 75503
Collins Rd 75501
Collom St 75501
Colonial Cir 75503
Colorado St 75503
Columbia Ave 75503
Columbine Ln 75503
Columbus St 75501
Comanche Ln 75501
Concord Pl 75503
Congress St 75501
Connella St 75501
Connie Ln 75503
Constitution Dr 75503
Conway Dr & Rd 75501
Cooks Ln 75503
Cooper Ln 75503
Copper Ridge Rd 75503
Coppercreek Cir 75503
Cork Ln 75503
Corley Cir 75501
Corporate Dr 75503
Cottonwood St 75501
Country Ln 75501
Country Lane Park 75501
Country Paradise Cir & Ln 75501
County Road 1213 75501
County Road 1214 75501
County Road 1215 E & W 75501
County Road 1223 75501
County Road 1224 75501
County Road 1227 75501
County Road 1230 75501
County Road 1231 75501
County Road 1232 75501
County Road 1242 75501
County Road 1251 75501
County Road 1302 75501
County Road 1303 75501
County Road 1304 75501
County Road 1313 75501
County Road 1317 75501
County Road 1329 75501
County Road 1337 75501
County Road 1376 75501
County Road 1404 75501
County Road 2203 75503
County Road 2204 75503
County Road 2206 75501
County Road 2213 75503
County Road 2216 75501
County Road 2220 75503
County Road 2301 75503
County Road 2302 75503
County Road 2304 75503
County Road 2305 75503
County Road 2306 75503
County Road 2307 75503
County Road 2308 75503
County Road 2309 75503
County Road 2310 75503
County Road 2311 75503
County Road 2312 75503
County Road 2313 75503
County Road 2320 75503
County Road 2342 75503
Court St 75501
Courtney Way 75501
S Cowhorn Creek Loop & Rd 75503
Coyote Trl 75503
Cozumel 75501
Crestridge Dr 75503
Crestview St 75501
Crockett St 75501
Cross St 75501
Crudip Ln 75501
Crumpton Dr 75503
Cruthers Creek Rd 75501
Culebra St 75503
Cummings Ln 75501
Cypress St 75503
Daffodil Ln 75503
Dallas St 75501
Dan Haskins Way 75501
Dan Michael Dr 75501
Dana Ln 75503
Daniels St 75501
Danube Ave 75503
David Dr 75503
Davis St 75501
Dawn St 75501
Deer Creek Cir 75503
Deer Creek Dr 75503
Deer Creek Ln 75501
Deer Ridge Dr 75501
Deerfield Dr 75503
Deerwood St 75503
Defee St 75501
Dekalb St 75503
Della St 75501
Deloach St 75501
Demarce Ln 75501
Dennis Ln 75501
Denver Pl 75501
Desoto Cir 75503
Destin St 75501
Devon Ln 75503
Dewey St 75501
Diamond Cir 75503
Diane Dr 75501
Dill Ln 75501
Dillon St 75501
Dodd St 75503
Dogwood Ln & Pl 75503
Dogwood Lake Dr 75503
Double L Rd 75501
Douglas Rd 75501
Dove Holw 75501
Dreyer Pl 75503
Dunbar Ave 75501
Dunham Dr 75503
Dyer Ln 75501
Dyke Thomas Rd 75501
Earnest Rd 75503
Eastline Rd 75501
Eastloop Dr 75501
Easy St 75503
Eddings Ave 75503
Edgewood Cir & Ln 75501
Elaine Dr 75501
Ele St 75501
Eli St 75503
Elinor Dr 75501
Elizabeth Ln 75503
Elizabeth St
2001-2199 75501
3600-5099 75503
Elizabeth Ann St 75503
Ellen Ave 75501
Ellen Cir 75503
Elliott Rd & St 75501
Elm St 75501
N Elmwood Dr 75501
S Elmwood Dr 75501
Elmwood Ln 75501
Elmwood Pl 75503
Elton St 75501
Emily Rd 75501
English Ln 75503
Esther St 75501
Evans Rd 75501
Evergreen Dr 75503
Eylau Hills Rd 75501
Eylau Loop Rd 75501
F M Dr 75503
Factory St 75501
Fagan Ln 75501

air Oaks Dr ... 75503
airground Ave ... 75503
airway St ... 75501
alvey Ave ... 75501
annin St ... 75501
armers Ln ... 75503
arren Rd ... 75503
ernwood Dr ... 75503
ielden St ... 75501
indley St ... 75501
leming Ln ... 75501
lower Acre Rd ... 75501
m 1397 ... 75503
Fm 2148
901-997 ... 75501
Fm 2148
999-2400 ... 75501
2402-2898 ... 75501
3000-5000 ... 75503
5002-5098 ... 75503
Fm 2148 ... 75501
m 2253 ... 75503
m 3244 ... 75501
m 3287 ... 75501
m 559 ... 75503
m 989 S ... 75501
m 991 E ... 75501
oraill St ... 75501
orest Cir ... 75501
orest Grove Rd ... 75503
orest Lake Dr ... 75503
orrest Brook Ln ... 75503
orrest Villa Ln ... 75501
orrestburg Dr ... 75501
orsyth Cir ... 75501
ortune Ave ... 75503
oster St ... 75501
ountain View St ... 75501
rame Ln ... 75501
ranklin Dr & St ... 75501
ricks Ln ... 75501
Front St ... 75501
alleria Oaks Dr ... 75503
alloping Way ... 75503
arber St ... 75501
arden Dr ... 75503
arrett Dr ... 75501
arrett Ln ... 75503
atling St ... 75501
azola St ... 75501
eneva Dr & Rd ... 75501
eorge Thomas Rd ... 75501
hio Fish Blvd ... 75503
ibson Ln ... 75503
Gibson Ln ... 75501
Gibson Ln ... 75501
iles Ln ... 75501
illiam Ave ... 75501
in Rd ... 75503
lass St ... 75501
off Ln ... 75501
olden Rule Dr ... 75503
oldfinch Rd ... 75501
oree St ... 75503
ould Ln & Pl ... 75503
race Ln ... 75501
reen St ... 75501
reen Forest Ln ... 75501
reenbriar St ... 75501
reenbriar Forest Cir ... 75503
& W Greenfield Dr ... 75501
reenview Dr ... 75501
reenwood Rd ... 75501
regory Ln ... 75503
riffin St ... 75501
uam St ... 75501
uitar Rd ... 75501
un Club Rd ... 75501
unstock ... 75501
us Orr Dr ... 75503
agler Ln ... 75501
amilton Ln ... 75501
ampton Rd ... 75503
andley St ... 75501
aney St ... 75501
annah Cir ... 75501

Harlen St ... 75501
Harrisburg Ln ... 75503
Harrison Ln ... 75501
Haskell Way ... 75501
Hatton St ... 75501
Hawk Ln ... 75503
Hawkins Ave & Cir ... 75501
Hazel St
1100-2399 ... 75501
2400-4299 ... 75503
Heather Dr ... 75501
Heatherwood Dr ... 75503
Henry Ln ... 75501
Heritage Blvd ... 75501
Heritage Ln ... 75503
Heritage Oaks Rd ... 75503
Hermitage Dr ... 75501
Hickam Dr ... 75501
Hickerson Ave ... 75501
Hickory Bridge Rd ... 75501
Hickory Hills Dr ... 75503
Hickory Oak Ln ... 75501
Hickory Ridge Cir &
Dr ... 75503
Hickory Wood Dr ... 75501
Hidalgo Cir ... 75501
Hidden Acres ... 75503
Hidden Valley Cv &
Rd ... 75501
Hideaway Ln ... 75503
High Dr ... 75503
High Point Dr ... 75503
Highcrest Pl ... 75503
Highland Villa St ... 75503
Hill St ... 75501
Hillcrest Dr ... 75503
N Hills Dr ... 75503
Hillside Dr ... 75503
Hilltop Ln ... 75501
Hillview St ... 75501
Hilton Ln ... 75503
Hines Ln ... 75501
Holiday Ln ... 75503
Holloway Dr & Pl ... 75503
Holly Dr ... 75501
Holly Ln ... 75503
Holly Creek Rd ... 75503
Holly Ridge Dr ... 75503
Hollywood St ... 75501
Holmes Ln ... 75503
Honeysuckle Ln ... 75503
Hoot Plant Rd ... 75501
Hoover St ... 75501
Horseshoe Dr & Loop ... 75501
Houff Ln ... 75501
Houston St ... 75501
Howard St ... 75501
Howard Teel Cir ... 75501
Howell Ln ... 75503
Hubbard St ... 75501
Huckabee St ... 75501
Hudson Ln & St ... 75503
Hughes Ln ... 75501
Hughes Rd ... 75503
S Hunt Cir & St ... 75501
Hunters Cv ... 75501
Hunters Rdg ... 75503
Idaho St ... 75501
Idalou Dr ... 75503
Independence Cir ... 75503
Indiana St ... 75501
Industrial St ... 75503
W Interstate 30 ... 75503
Inwood Rd ... 75501
Iowa St ... 75501
Iris Ln ... 75501
Irongate Dr ... 75503
Ironwood Dr ... 75503
Ivy Ln ... 75503
Jack St ... 75503
James St
2001-2297 ... 75501
2299-2400 ... 75501
2402-2498 ... 75501
2500-2599 ... 75503
Jamison St ... 75501

Jamiston St ... 75501
Jan Cir ... 75503
Japonica Dr ... 75501
Jasmine Ln ... 75503
Jason Ln ... 75503
Jeff Dr ... 75501
Jeffrey Cir & Ln ... 75501
Jenkins St ... 75501
Jennings St ... 75501
Jerome St ... 75501
Jesse Hughes Rd ... 75501
Joe Davis Ln ... 75501
Joe Thomas Rd ... 75501
Joe Tyl Rd ... 75501
Johnson Ave & Ln ... 75501
Jonathan St ... 75503
Jones Dr ... 75501
Jones Ln ... 75503
Jones St ... 75501
Jonquill Rd ... 75501
Jordan Ln ... 75503
Joyce St ... 75503
Judson St ... 75503
Juniper Ln ... 75503
Kansas St ... 75503
Katherine Cir ... 75503
Keel St ... 75501
Keller Ave ... 75503
Kelli Ct ... 75501
Kelly Rd ... 75501
Kennedy Ln ... 75503
N & S Kenwood Rd ... 75501
Kevin Ave ... 75503
Key West St ... 75501
Kidd Ln ... 75501
N & S Kilgore St ... 75501
Kimball Cir & Dr ... 75501
King Rd & St ... 75501
N Kings Hwy
400-1000 ... 75501
500-822 ... 75501
824-898 ... 75501
1002-1098 ... 75501
4100-9199 ... 75503
S Kings Hwy ... 75501
Kings Way ... 75501
Kings Row Cv ... 75501
Knightsbridge Pl & Rd ... 75503
Knottingham St ... 75501
Knotty Pine Pl & St ... 75503
Kramer Ln ... 75501
Krobot Cir, Ln & Pl ... 75501
W Kyle Rd ... 75503
La Grange Dr ... 75501
Ladera Dr ... 75503
Ladybird Dr ... 75501
Lafayette St ... 75501
N Lake Dr ... 75501
S Lake Dr ... 75501
Lake Vis ... 75503
Lake Breeze Dr ... 75501
Lakeridge Cir, Dr, Ln &
Pl ... 75503
Lakeshore Dr ... 75501
Lakeview Dr & Pl ... 75503
Lambeth Cir, Pl & Rd ... 75503
Lampasas Way ... 75501
Landon Ln ... 75501
Landrum Ln ... 75501
Lanshire Dr ... 75503
Larkspur Ln ... 75501
Larry Dr ... 75503
Lauren Ln ... 75503
Lavaca St ... 75503
Lawson Cir ... 75503
Lazy Ln ... 75503
Leana St ... 75501
Leary Rd
1-499 ... 75501
500-1199 ... 75503
Lee St ... 75501
Leeway St ... 75501
Leggett Dr ... 75503
Lela Cir ... 75501
Lelia Ave & St ... 75501
Lemon St ... 75501

Lemon Acres Ln ... 75501
Lemontree Cir ... 75501
Leo Ln ... 75503
Leopard Dr ... 75501
Lesley Ln ... 75503
Lester St ... 75501
Letter Carrier Dr ... 75501
Letterman Ln ... 75501
Levi Jackson Rd ... 75501
Lewis Ln & Rd ... 75501
Lewis Akin Rd ... 75503
Lexington Pl ... 75503
Liberty Ln ... 75501
Liddell St ... 75501
Liggett St ... 75501
Lilac St ... 75501
Lincoln Ave ... 75503
Linda Ln ... 75501
Lionel Ave ... 75503
Loma Linda St ... 75501
Lone Star Pkwy ... 75503
Longhorn Rd ... 75501
Longview St ... 75501
Lonnie Ln ... 75501
Lost Antlers ... 75503
Lost Creek Cir & Dr ... 75503
Lott Ln ... 75503
Lotus St ... 75503
Louise Ln ... 75501
Loving St ... 75501
Lubbock St ... 75501
Lucas St ... 75501
Lumpkin St ... 75501
Lynch St ... 75501
Lynda Ave ... 75503
Lynn Dr ... 75503
Lynwood Dr ... 75501
Lyons St ... 75501
Macarthur Ave & Dr ... 75501
Macedonia Rd ... 75501
Madison Dr ... 75501
Magnolia St
1201-1897 ... 75501
1899-2399 ... 75501
2400-4399 ... 75503
Mahafey St ... 75501
Main St
101-197 ... 75501
199-2399 ... 75501
2900-4200 ... 75503
4202-4298 ... 75503
Mall Dr ... 75503
Mall Ln ... 75501
Mallard Dr ... 75501
Mamie Dr ... 75501
Manila Dr ... 75501
Maple St
1-99 ... 75501
101-2399 ... 75501
2400-2899 ... 75503
Maplecrest St ... 75503
Marcell Cir ... 75503
Mariana Dr ... 75501
Marion St ... 75501
Marissa Ct ... 75501
Market St ... 75501
Markham Rd ... 75501
Marshall Ridge Dr ... 75501
W Martin Luther King Jr
Blvd ... 75501
Martine St ... 75501
Maryland Dr ... 75501
Mason St ... 75501
Matlock St ... 75501
Matthews Ln ... 75501
May Den Dr ... 75503
Mcbride St ... 75501
Mccartney Blvd ... 75503
Mccormick St ... 75501
Mcgary St ... 75501
Mcintyre St ... 75501
Mckinney Pl ... 75503
Mcknight Rd ... 75503
Mcshane St ... 75501
Meadow Ln ... 75503
Meadow Lake Dr ... 75503

Meadow Vista Cir ... 75503
Meadowbrook Ln ... 75501
Meadowland Dr ... 75503
Meadows Dr ... 75501
Meandering Pl ... 75503
Medical Parkway Dr ... 75503
Medina Dr ... 75503
Melody Ln ... 75503
Melrose Dr ... 75501
Melton St ... 75501
Memorial Dr ... 75501
Mercer St ... 75501
Mercury St ... 75501
Meredith Way ... 75501
Merritt Dr ... 75501
Meyer St ... 75501
W Midway Dr ... 75501
Milam St ... 75501
Miller Rd ... 75501
Millrose St ... 75501
Mimosa Dr ... 75501
Misty Ln ... 75501
Mitchell Ryan ... 75501
Mockingbird Ln ... 75501
Monroe Dr ... 75503
Montgomery St ... 75501
Moore Dr ... 75503
Moores Ln ... 75503
Morgan Ln ... 75501
Morris Ln ... 75503
Morton Ln ... 75503
Moser St ... 75501
Mulberry St ... 75501
Myrtle Springs Rd ... 75503
Neff St ... 75501
Nettie St ... 75503
W New Boston Rd ... 75501
New Castle St ... 75503
Newport Ave ... 75503
Newton St ... 75501
Nicholas Dr ... 75503
Nichols Dr ... 75503
Nicole Ln ... 75501
Nile Ave ... 75503
Noah Ave ... 75503
Nolthenius St ... 75501
Norris Cooley Dr ... 75501
North St ... 75501
Northcrest Dr ... 75501
Northridge Cir ... 75503
Northview St ... 75503
Northwest Dr ... 75501
Norton Ln & St ... 75503
Oak St ... 75501
S Oak St ... 75501
Oak Trl ... 75503
Oak Creek Rd ... 75503
Oak Flat Ave ... 75503
Oak Forest Ln ... 75501
Oak Haven Dr ... 75501
Oak Hill Pl ... 75503
Oak Hill Rd ... 75501
Oak Meadow Ln ... 75503
Oakhollow Dr ... 75503
Oaklawn Dr & Vlg ... 75501
Oakridge Cir & Dr ... 75503
Oakview Dr ... 75501
Ohio St ... 75501
Old Boston Rd ... 75501
Old Red Lick Rd
2500-2799 ... 75501
3101-3299 ... 75503
Old Redwater Rd ... 75501
Old Spanish Dr ... 75503
Olive St
401-597 ... 75501
599-2399 ... 75501
2400-4899 ... 75503
Orange St ... 75503
Orangewood Rd ... 75501
Oregon St ... 75501
Orr Dr ... 75501
Overcup St ... 75503
Overlock Ln ... 75503
Owens Dr ... 75503
Pacific Ave ... 75501

Page St ... 75501
Palisades Dr ... 75503
Palm Dr ... 75503
Pansy St ... 75501
Paradise Cv ... 75501
Parish St ... 75503
W, N & S Park Blvd, Cir,
Ln & Rd ... 75503
Parker St ... 75503
Parkview Ln ... 75501
Parkway Dr ... 75501
Parkwood St ... 75501
Patrick Dr ... 75501
Patriot Way ... 75501
Paul Dr ... 75503
Pavilion ... 75503
Payton Rd ... 75501
Peach St ... 75501
Pearson Ln ... 75503
Pebble Creek Cir ... 75501
Pebblebrook Dr ... 75503
Pecan Cv ... 75503
Pecan Creek Cir ... 75503
Pecos Pl ... 75501
Pecos St ... 75503
Penneran Dr ... 75503
Perry Suggs Ln ... 75503
Peter Alan ... 75501
Phenie St ... 75501
Phillips Cir & Ln ... 75501
Pickering Ln ... 75501
Picoma Dr ... 75501
Pierce Rd ... 75501
Pierre St ... 75501
Pine St
201-397 ... 75501
399-2399 ... 75501
2400-4299 ... 75503
Pine Creek Pl ... 75503
Pine Forest St ... 75501
Pine Knoll Rd ... 75503
Pine Meadow Cir & Dr ... 75503
Pine Ridge Cir ... 75503
Pine Valley Rd ... 75501
Pinecrest Dr ... 75501
N & S Pineview Dr ... 75501
N & S Pinewood Dr ... 75501
Piney Rd & St ... 75501
Piney Grove Cir ... 75501
Pinoak St ... 75503
Pintail Ave ... 75501
Pinto Cir ... 75503
E & W Pioneer St ... 75501
Pipes Cir ... 75501
Pittman Ln ... 75503
Plant St ... 75503
Plantation Rd ... 75501
Plantivigne Dr ... 75501
Plaza W ... 75501
Plaza Cir ... 75503
Plaza Dr ... 75503
Pleasant Ln ... 75503
Pleasant Grove Rd ... 75503
Plum Ln & St ... 75501
Poinsetta Dr ... 75503
Polly Cir & Dr ... 75503
Ponderosa Dr ... 75503
Poplar St ... 75501
Porter Dr ... 75503
Post St ... 75501
Potomac Ave, Cir & Pl ... 75503
Presidio Pl ... 75501
Presley Rd ... 75501
Prestige Ln ... 75503
Private Road 12161 ... 75501
Private Road 12162 ... 75501
Private Road 12175 ... 75501
Private Road 12301 ... 75501
Private Road 13091 ... 75501
Private Road 13121 ... 75501
Private Road 13141 ... 75501
Private Road 13142 ... 75501
Private Road 13251 ... 75501
Private Road 13261 ... 75501
Private Road 13301 ... 75501
Private Road 13461 ... 75501

Private Road 13481 ... 75501
Private Road 13501 ... 75501
Private Road 13561 ... 75501
Private Road 21481 ... 75501
Private Road 22111 ... 75503
Private Road 23110 ... 75503
Private Road 25161 ... 75501
Private Road 25162 ... 75501
Private Road 25163 ... 75501
Private Road 25164 ... 75501
Private Road 25165 ... 75501
Private Road 32441 ... 75501
Private Road 55901 ... 75503
Private Road 59001 ... 75501
Private Road 59002 ... 75501
Private Road 59003 ... 75501
Private Road 59004 ... 75501
Private Road 59006 ... 75501
Private Road 67003 ... 75501
Private Road 67007 ... 75501
Private Road 98905 ... 75503
Proctor St ... 75501
Proetz Ln ... 75501
Prof David Brown Ave ... 75501
Quail Cir, Ln & Trl ... 75501
Quail Brook Dr ... 75501
Quail Hollow Dr ... 75503
Quail Ridge Rd ... 75501
Ralph Dr ... 75501
Randall Rd ... 75501
Randolph Cir ... 75501
Randy Dr ... 75501
Reading Ave ... 75501
Red Dot Rd ... 75503
Red Oak Ln ... 75501
Red River Rd N ... 75501
Red Springs Rd ... 75501
Redbird Cir ... 75501
Redbridge Rd ... 75501
Redbud St ... 75501
Redhill Rd ... 75501
Redwater Blvd & Rd ... 75501
Redwood Dr ... 75501
Rhine Ave ... 75503
Rhozine Ln ... 75503
Richill Dr ... 75503
N Richland Dr ... 75503
Richmond Mdws, Pl, Rd
& Sq ... 75503
Richmond Ranch Rd ... 75503
Richwood Dr & Pl ... 75503
Ridge Row Cir ... 75503
Ridgecrest Pl ... 75503
Rio Grande Ave ... 75503
River Bnd ... 75501
River Oaks Dr ... 75503
River Plantation ... 75503
River Ridge Dr ... 75503
Riverside Pl ... 75503
Robbins St ... 75501
Roberta Ln ... 75503
Roberts St ... 75501
Robin Cir & Ln ... 75503
Robinhood Ln ... 75501
Robison Pl ... 75501
N Robison Rd
800-2212 ... 75501
2211-2211 ... 75505
2214-3698 ... 75501
2301-3699 ... 75501
3700-3798 ... 75503
S Robison Rd ... 75501
Robison Ter ... 75501
Rochelle Ln ... 75503
Rock School Rd ... 75501
Rogers Ln ... 75503
Rolling Hls ... 75503
Rollins Ln ... 75501
Ronny St ... 75501
Roosevelt Rd ... 75501
Rose Acres Rd ... 75501
Rose Hill Dr ... 75501
Rose Of Sharon ... 75501
Roseboro St ... 75503
Rosedale St ... 75501
Rosewood St ... 75501

Rosey St 75501
Rothwell Dr 75501
Royale Dr 75503
Rozzell Ave 75501
Ruston Rd 75503
Ryan Loop Rd 75501
Sabine Ave 75503
Saddlebrook Dr 75501
Sagebrush Ave 75503
Saint Michael Dr 75503
Sam Thomas Rd 75501
San Saba Ln 75503
Sanderson Loop 75501
Sandlin Ave 75503
Sara Rd 75501
Sarah Cir & Ln 75503
Sayers St 75501
Scott Lynn Dr 75501
Scott Wright Rd 75503
Serenity Ln 75503
Shadow Brk 75503
Shadow Dr 75501
Shady Ln 75503
Shady Acres Ln 75501
Shady Grove Ln 75501
Shady Pines Rd 75501
Shady Tree Ln 75501
Shadyside Ln 75503
Shavers Ln 75501
Shellwood Dr 75501
Shepherd Day Dr 75503
Sheri Ln 75503
Sherman St 75501
Sherry Rdg 75501
Sherwood Acres Ln 75501
Sherwood Forest Dr 75501
Shields Ct 75503
Shields St 75501
Shilling Cir, Pl & Rd 75503
Shiloh Rd 75503
Shirley Ln 75501
Short Capp St 75501
Short Pierre St 75501
Sidney Dr 75503
Sierra Madre Ln 75503
Silverhill Dr 75503
Silverleaf Ln 75503
Singapore Dr 75501
Skaggs Cir 75501
Skylark Dr 75503
Skyline Blvd 75503
Sleepy Hollow Ave 75503
Smelser St 75501
Smith Rd & St 75501
Sneed 75501
Southridge St 75501
Sowell Ln 75501
Space Dr 75503
Spicer Ln 75503
Spotswood Pl 75503
Spring Cv 75503
Spring Creek Pl 75501
Spring Holmes Dr 75501
Springcreek Rd 75503
Springridge Dr & Ln 75501
Springwood Cir & Dr 75503
Spruce St
101-197 75501
199-2399 75501
2401-2499 75503
2600-2698 75503
S Spruce St 75501
Stanford Dr 75503
Stanley Ln 75501
W Starlite Dr 75501
N State Line Ave
100-198 75501
201-2399 75501
2401-7897 75503
7899-8499 75503
8501-9099 75503
S State Line Ave 75501
Steeplechase Dr 75503
Sterling Rd 75503
Stevens Rd 75501
Stevenson St 75501
Stewart St 75501
Stillwell Dr 75501
Stipp Ln 75501
Stone Rd 75501
Stone Creek Dr 75503
Stonegate Cir & Dr 75503
Stoneledge Dr 75503
Stoneridge Cir & Dr 75503
Stonewall Cir, Dr &
Trce 75503
Straight St 75501
Strange Rd 75501
Stroupe 75501
Stuart Ln 75501
Stuckey St 75501
Sugden St 75501
Sulpher Point Rd 75501
Sulphur St 75501
Summer Ln & Xing 75503
Summer Glenn Pl 75503
Summerfield Dr 75503
Summerhill Pl 75503
Summerhill Rd
901-2097 75501
2099-2499 75501
2501-2599 75501
2600-6999 75503
7001-7399 75503
Summerhill Sq 75503
Sundance Rdg 75503
Sunny Ln 75501
Sunny St 75501
Sunray Rd 75501
Sunset Cir, Pl & Rd 75501
Suzanne Ave 75503
Sweetbrush Ave 75503
Sylvia Dr 75503
T P Lake Rd 75501
T V Ave 75503
Taft St 75501
Talbert St 75501
Talisman Cir 75501
Tamar Dr 75503
Tanglewood Dr 75501
Taylor St 75501
Tealwood Dr 75503
Teepee St 75501
Tejas Trl 75503
Telka Pl 75501
Terrace Ln 75503
Terrace Plaza Dr 75501
Terry St 75501
Texarkana Ave 75501
Texas Blvd
100-198 75501
200-2399 75501
2400-4899 75503
4901-4999 75503
Thames Ave & Cir 75503
Thomas Ln
100-198 75503
3700-4200 75501
4202-4298 75501
Thompson Ln & St 75501
Tiffany Dr 75501
Tigres Ave 75503
Timber Bark Ln 75501
Timber Oaks Cir & Ln 75501
Timberlake Dr 75501
Timberlane St 75501
Timberwilde St 75503
Timberwood Dr 75501
Tomahawk Rd 75503
Tommy Hines Rd 75501
Tony Ln 75501
Tracey Ave 75501
Tracola St 75501
Trailwood Ln 75501
Trammels Trce 75503
Travis St 75501
Treasure Hill Dr 75503
Trexler Rd 75501
Tri State Rd 75501
Trinity St 75503
Tropicana Ln 75501
Trotter Ln 75503
Truman Ln 75501
Trumbles Ln 75501
Tucker St 75501
Tulip Dr 75503
Turner St 75501
Turtle Creek Dr 75503
Tv Rd 75503
Twilight Cir 75501
Twin Oak Dr 75503
Tyler St 75501
Underwood Dr 75501
Unity Dr 75501
Univeristy Ave 75501
University Ave & Park 75503
Urban Dr 75501
Us Highway 59 S 75501
Utah St 75501
Val Verde Trl 75501
Valley Rd 75503
Valley Hill Rd 75503
Valley Run Dr 75501
Valleyview Cir 75503
Vaughn St 75501
Verbena St 75503
Vernon St 75501
Veronica Ln 75503
Veterans Memorial Dr 75501
Victory Pl 75501
Village Cir, Ln & Pl 75501
Village Terrace Plz 75501
Virginia St 75501
Volga Ave & Cir 75503
Waco St 75501
Wade Ln 75501
Wain Wright St 75501
Wainwright St 75501
Wake Ave 75501
Wake Forest Dr 75501
S Wake Village Rd 75501
Walker Ln 75501
Wall Cir 75501
Waller Ln 75501
Walnut St
801-1197 75501
1199-2399 75501
2500-4799 75503
Walnut Hill Rd 75503
Walton Dr 75501
Ward St 75501
Warren Thomas Rd 75501
Waterall St 75501
Waterman St 75501
Waters Rd 75503
Waterworks Rd 75501
N & S Watlington Cir &
Dr 75501
Watts St 75501
Waverly Dr 75501
Weaver Pl 75501
Webb St 75501
Wesley Aaron Dr 75503
West St 75501
Westfork Dr 75503
Westlawn Dr 75501
Westline Ct & Rd 75501
Westpoint St 75501
Westridge Ave 75503
Westwood Dr 75501
Wg Sorsby Rd 75501
Wheeler St
100-398 75501
400-1099 75501
1100-1199 75503
1201-1299 75503
Whippoorwill Ln 75501
Whispering Pnes 75501
Whispering Pines Cir 75501
Whitaker St 75501
White Rd E & W 75501
White Oak Cir 75501
White Oak Ln
1-99 75501
9100-9199 75503
White Oak Pl 75501
Whitmarsh Pl 75501
Whitney Cir & Ln 75503
Wild Oak Cir 75503
Wild Rose St 75501
Wildcat Dr 75501
Wilderness Cv 75501
Wildwood Dr 75501
Will Smith Rd 75501
Williams Cir 75501
Williams Ln 75503
Williamsburg Cir & Ln 75501
Willis St 75501
Willow Bend St 75503
Willow Glen Ln 75503
Willowcreek Cir 75503
Wilshire Dr 75503
Wilson St 75501
Winchester Dr 75503
Windham Ln 75501
Windmere Dr 75503
Windsor Dr 75501
Wisteria Dr 75503
Witt Ln 75501
Wood St
800-2399 75501
2401-2497 75503
2499-4299 75503
Wood Bridge Dr 75503
Wood Duck Ln 75501
Woodberry Dr 75501
Woodbriar Way 75501
Woodcliff Dr 75503
Woodgate Dr 75503
Woodland Cir 75501
Woodland Pl 75503
Woodmere Ct 75503
Woodmont St 75501
Woodmont Crossing
St 75503
Woodridge Dr 75503
Woodstock Ln 75503
Wormington 75503
Wren Rowe Dr 75503
Ww Rd 75501
Wyatt Ln 75503
Yarborough Ct 75503
Yorktown Pl 75503
Yucca St 75503
Yukon Ave 75503

NUMBERED STREETS

W 3rd St 75501
W 4th St 75501
W 5th St 75501
W 6th St 75501
W 7th St 75501
S 8th St 75501
S & W 9th 75501
W 10th St 75501
W 11th St 75501
W 12th St 75501
W 13th St 75501
W 14th St 75501
W 15th St 75501
W 16th St 75501
W 17th St 75501
W 18th St 75501
W 19th St 75501
W 20th St 75501
W 21st St 75501
W 22nd St 75501
W 23rd St 75501
W 24th St 75503
W 24th St 75503
W 24th St 75503
1700-1799 75501
1801-1899 75501
W 25th St 75503
W 26th St 75503
W 27th St 75503
W 28th St 75503
W 29th St 75503
W 30th St 75503
W 31st St 75503
W 32nd St 75503
W 34th St 75503
W 35th St 75503
W 36th St 75503
W 37th St 75503
W 38th St 75503
W 39th St 75503
W 40th St 75503
W 41st St 75503
W 42nd St 75503
W 48th St 75503
W 52nd St 75503
W 53rd St 75503

TEXAS CITY TX

General Delivery 77590

POST OFFICE BOXES MAIN OFFICE STATIONS AND BRANCHES

Box No.s
All PO Boxes 77592

NAMED STREETS

Abbott Dr 77590
Acorn Cir 77591
S Albert St 77591
S Algeria St 77591
Allen Ave 77591
Allen Cay Dr 77590
Amberjack Dr 77591
N & S Amburn Rd 77591
Anderson St 77591
Andrews St 77591
Appomattox Dr 77591
Armstrong Dr 77591
Ash Rd 77591
Aspen St 77591
Babin Dr 77590
Barracuda Dr 77591
Bates St 77591
Bay St N & S 77590
Bay Street Ext 77590
Beach Dr 77590
N & S Bell Dr 77591
Big Oak Dr 77591
Birch St 77591
S Black Oak St 77591
Blackhawk Dr 77590
Blanchard St 77591
Blue Bonnet Dr 77591
Blue Crab Dr 77591
Bluejay Dr 77591
Bonito Dr 77591
Brigantine Cay Ct 77590
Britton Dr 77591
Brown Dr 77591
Bryce Ave 77591
Burr Oak Ln 77591
Buttonwood Dr 77591
Camino Ct 77590
Campbell St 77591
N Canal St 77591
Canary Cir 77591
Cardinal Cir 77591
Carver Ave 77591
Catalpa St 77591
Cedar Oaks Ct & Dr 77591
Century Blvd 77591
Cherry Ave 77590
Clara Ln 77590
Clemons Ln 77591
Clover Hill Ln 77591
S Cobb St 77591
Cobia Ct 77591
College Ave 77591
Crestwood Ct & Dr 77591
Crockett St 77591
Crown Ct 77591
Curlew Ln 77590
Danforth Dr 77590
Diamond Ct 77591
Diamond Oak Dr 77591
Dickson Ave 77591
Dogwood St 77591
Dolphin Cir 77591
Downey Cv 77591
S East Rd 77591
Edgebrook Dr 77591
Edward St 77591
Emerald Ln 77591
Emerald Oak Dr 77591
Emmett F Lowry Expy
3600-3798 77590
4100-10799 77591
Estelle Cir 77591
Ethel St 77591
Eugenia Ave 77591
Eunice St 77591
Evelyn St 77591
Fairfield Ave 77590
Fairhill Cir 77591
S Fallen Oak Ln 77591
Fawnwood Dr 77591
Fm 1760 77591
Fm 1765
2900-3599 77590
Fm 1765
3600-8598 77591
Fm 2004 Rd 77591
N & S Foster Rd 77591
N & S Fulton St 77591
Garenern St 77591
Garnet Ct 77591
Gary Ave 77591
Gettysburg Ave 77591
Glacier Ave 77591
N & S Golden Oak Dr 77591
Grant Ave S 77590
Groveshire Dr 77591
Gulf Fwy 77591
Hemphill St 77591
Herbert Ln 77591
N & S Heritage Oaks
Dr 77591
Heron Ln 77591
Highborne Cay Ct 77590
Highland St 77591
Highway 146 N & S 77590
Highway 1764 77591
Highway 3 N 77591
Hobgood Ave 77591
Hollow Mist Dr 77591
Hummingbird Ln 77591
Hunter Dr 77590
Indigo Sky Ln 77591
Jackson Ln 77591
Jennings St 77590
Jones Rd 77591
Jonquil Dr 77591
S Justice St 77591
Kingfish Rd 77591
Kingston Dr 77590
Lake Point Dr 77590
Lane Rd 77591
Lantana Dr 77591
Larkspur Dr 77591
Laughing Gull Ln 77590
Leaning Oak Dr 77591
S Leroy St 77591
N Lincoln St 77591
N Linden Dr 77591
Ling Cir 77591
Linton Ln 77591
Live Oak Dr 77591
Loch Haven Dr 77591
N & S Logan St 77590
Lone Trail Dr 77591
Longfellow Dr 77591
Louisiana St 77591
Luttrell St 77591
Lynn Cir 77590
Mackerel Dr 77591
Magnolia St 77590
Mainland Dr 77590
Mainland Center Dr 77591
Mallard Dr 77591
Marlin Dr 77591
Martin Luther King
Blvd 7759
Mayflower Dr 7759
Meadow Ln 7759
Meadowlark Ln 7759
Medical Center Dr 7759
Memorial Dr 7759
Mentor Dr 7759
Mockingbird Ln 7759
Monarch Oak Ln 7759
Monticello Dr 7759
Moonstone Ct 7759
Morningstar Cir 7759
N Natchez Dr 7759
Nightingale Cir 7759
N & S Noble Rd 7759
Norton St 7759
N & S Oak Ln & St 7759
Oleander Ave 7759
Oliver St 7759
Onyx Ct 7759
Opal St 7759
Orange Ave 7759
N & S Orchid Dr 7759
Oriole St 7759
Palm Ave 7759
Palmer Hwy 7759
Park Ave 7759
Park Ln 7759
Parkwest St 7759
Paseo Lobo 7759
Peachtree Ct 7759
N & S Pecan Dr 7759
Pelican Harbour Dr 7759
Phillips St 7759
Pilgrim Estates Dr 7759
S Pin Oak Dr 7759
N & S Pine Rd 7759
Pineapple St 7759
Plantation Dr 7759
Plover Cir 7759
Pompano Rd 7759
Post Oak Ln 7759
Preston St 7759
Princeton Pl 7759
Quaker Dr 7759
Quetzal St 7759
Ramada Ct 7759
Raymond Ct 7759
W Red Oak Ln 7759
Redfish Dr 7759
Rice St 7759
Roberts St 7759
Robertson St 7759
Robin St 7759
Robinson Blvd 7759
S Rose St 7759
Royal Oak Dr 7759
Ruckett St 7759
Ruisenor St 7759
Rust Ave 7759
Ruth Cir 7759
San Jacinto Ave 7759
San Jose Ave 7759
Sapphire Ct 7759
Schamera Ave N 7759
Seaside Ln 7759
Shady Oak Ln 7759
Shark Cir 7759
Shiloh St 7759
Siers St 7759
Silver Oak Dr 7759
Silvercrest Dr 7759
Skyline Dr 7759
Somerset Ave 7759
Sparks Ln 7759
N & S Sparrow Way 7759
Stingray Ct 7759
Sunnycrest Dr 7759
Sunset Ln 7759
Swallow Ln 7759
Tara Cir 7759
Tarpey Ave 7759
Tarpey Rd 7759
Tarpon Dr 7759
Teel St 7759

Terrace Dr 77591
Texas Ave 77590
N Texas St 77591
S Texas St 77591
Thelma Ln 77591
Timothy St 77591
Topaz Way 77591
Truman St 77591
Tuna Cir 77591
Turpail St 77591
Twelve Oaks Dr 77591
Vance Ave 77590
S Vauthier Rd 77591
Verde Meadow Dr 77591
Vicksburg Ave 77591
N Vionett Ln 77591
Wahoo Cir 77591
N & S Washington Ave & St 77591
Wayside Dr 77590
S West Rd 77591
Westbury Ln 77590
N & S Westward St 77591
Whippoorwill Ln 77591
White Ibis Ave 77590
White Oak St 77591
Widgeon Cv 77590
Williams Dr 77591
Willis Cir 77591
N & S Willow St 77591
Woodrow St 77591
Wren Cir 77591
Yellowfin Cir 77591
Yucca Dr 77591

NUMBERED STREETS

1st Ave & St N & S 77590
1st 1/2 Ave N 77590
2nd Ave & St N & S 77590
3rd Ave & St N & S 77590
3rd 1/2 Ave N 77590
4th Ave & St N & S 77590
5th Ave N
1-3799 77590
4000-4599 77591
5th Ave S 77590
5th St N 77590
5th St S 77590
6th Ave & St N & S 77590
7th Ave & St N & S 77590
8th Ave & St N & S 77590
9th Ave & St 77590
10th Ave & St N & S 77590
11th Ave & St 77590
11th 1/2 St N 77590
12th Ave & St 77590
12th 1/2 St N 77590
13th Ave & St 77590
14th Ave & St 77590
15th Ave & St 77590
16th Ave & St 77590
17th Ave & St 77590
18th Ave & St 77590
19th Ave & St 77590
20th Ave & St 77590
21st Ave & St 77590
22nd Ave & St 77590
23rd Ave & St 77590
24th Ave & St 77590
25th Ave N
101-297 77590
8200-8299 77591
25th 1/2 St N 77590
26th Ave & St 77590
27th Ave & St 77590
28th Ave & St 77590
28th 1/2 St S 77590
29th Ave & St 77590
30th Ave N
2300-3099 77590
10600-11999 77591
30th St N 77590
30th St S 77590
31st Ave N
2300-3099 77590
10900-11499 77591
31st St N 77590
31st St S 77590
31st 1/2 St N 77590
32nd Ave N
2300-2899 77590
10000-11999 77591
32nd St N 77590
33rd Ave & St 77590
34th Ave & St 77590
35th Ave & St 77590
36th Ave & St 77590
37th Ave N 77590
38th Ave N 77590
39th Ave N 77590
40th Ave N 77590
41st Ave N 77590
42nd Ave N 77590
110th St N 77591
111th St N 77591
112th St N 77591

TOMBALL TX

NAMED STREETS

Aberdeen Hollow Ln 77377
Adam Ct 77375
Adobe Canyon Ln 77377
Adrienne Dr 77375
Aerie Dr 77377
Afton Ct 77375
Agg Rd 77375
Ajuga Ct 77377
Albury Park Ln 77375
Alcina Dr 77375
Alcove Glen Ln 77375
Alice Ln 77375
Alice Rd 77377
Alicia Dr 77375
Alma St 77375
Almonte Ln 77377
Altair Dr 77375
Amber Bay Dr 77377
Ambler Springs Dr 77377
Ambrosia Falls Dr 77375
Amistad Ct & Dr 77375
Amurwood Dr 77375
Ancient Lore Dr 77375
Ancient Willow Dr 77375
Angeli Dr 77377
Anna St 77375
Antonia Ln 77375
Apache Hills Dr 77377
Arabian Trl 77375
Arbor Pne 77375
Arbor Hollow Ln 77377
Arbor Lake Dr 77377
Arcadian Springs Ln 77375
Arcott Bend Dr 77377
Ardwick Ct 77375
Arlington Meadows Ln 77377
Arneway Dr 77375
Arnold St 77375
Arrow Mill Ln 77377
Arroyo Creek Ln 77375
Arthurian Dream Ct 77375
Artoys Dr 77377
Ash St 77375
Ashford Square St 77375
Ashley Ct 77375
Ashmond Ln 77375
Ashvale Dr 77377
Auburn Dr 77375
Auburn Hills Dr 77377
Auburn Mane Dr 77375
August Leaf Dr 77375
Austin Bluff Ln 77375
Austrian Pine Pl 77375
Autumn Strm 77375
Autumn Briar Ln 77377
Autumn Willow Dr 77375
Avalon Springs Dr 77375
Avenfield Rd 77377
Avenplace Rd 77377
Avery Ridge Ln 77377
Ayston Dr 77375
Babbling Spring Ct 77375
Bailey Dr 77375
Baker Dr 77375
Baldswelle Dr 77377
Baldwin Springs Ct 77377
Baldwin Spruce Trl 77377
Balthamwood Ln 77377
Banestone Blvd 77375
Banewood Dr 77375
Bank Shade Ct 77375
Barbara St 77375
Barmby Dr 77375
Barnsford Ln 77375
Barnwood Ct 77375
Barrell Springs Ln 77375
Barrister Creek Dr 77377
Bauer Hockley Rd 77377
Bay Laurel Ct 77375
Bayberry Ct 77377
Bayberry Park Ln 77375
Bayonne Cir 77377
Beacons Light Pl 77375
Bearden Lake Dr 77377
Bearing Star Ln 77375
Beauline Abbey St 77377
Beaverdell Dr 77375
Beckendorf Bend Ln 77377
Beckerdell Ln 77377
Beckton Cypress Dr 77377
Begonia Meadows Dr 77375
Bella Ava Dr 77377
W Bellefontaine Way 77377
Belmont St 77375
Belmont Farms Dr 77375
Benevolent Way 77375
Bennie St 77375
Benton Park Ln 77375
Bermondsey Ct & Dr 77377
Berry Hill Ln 77375
Berry Hill Rd 77377
Berry Orchard Ln 77375
Berry Ridge Ln 77375
Berry Shoals Ln 77375
Berry Vine St 77375
Berrybriar Ln 77375
Berrypatch Ln 77375
Berrystone Ln 77375
Berrywood Bend Dr 77375
Bettywood Ct & Ln 77375
Big Pnes 77375
Big Rock Ln 77375
Birchview Dr 77377
Bitternut Hickory Ln 77375
Black Birch Ln 77375
Black Willow Dr 77375
Blackshear St 77375
Blanefield Ct & Ln 77375
Blasdell Ct 77377
Blissfull Valley Ln 77375
W Bluebird Ln 77377
Bluestone Hollow Ln 77377
Bobby St 77375
Bobolink Cir 77375
Bogs Ct & Rd 77375
Bold River Rd 77375
Bolte Timbers Ln 77377
Bolton Ct 77375
Boquillas Canyon Dr 77377
Boudreaux Cir 77377
Boudreaux Rd
9000-12999 77375
13000-15400 77377
15402-15998 77377
Boudreaux Estates Dr 77377
Boulder Springs Ln 77375
Bounty Ln 77377
Bourgain Dr 77375
Bowsman Dr 77377
Brady Ln 77375
Brandy Ln 77375
Brandywood Cir 77375
Brannok Ln 77375
Brantfield Park Ln 77377
Brantley Haven Dr 77375
Breezy Cove Ct 77375
Brentcross Dr 77377
Brenthaven Springs Ln 77375
N & S Brenton Knoll Ct & Dr 77375
Bressingham Dr 77375
Briar Canyon Ct 77377
Briar Harbor Dr 77377
Briar Meadow Rd 77377
Bridle Grove Ct 77377
Bridle Meadow Ln 77377
Bright Point Ct 77375
Brighton Trail Ct & Ln 77377
Brill Ln 77375
Bristol Point Ln 77377
Brittany Rose Pl 77375
Broad Oak Ct 77377
Brogan Ct 77375
Brown Ln 77375
Brown Rd 77377
Brown Trl 77377
Brownwood Ln 77377
Bruns Glen Ln 77377
Brush Canyon Dr 77377
Buck Springs Trl 77375
Buckhead Ct 77377
Buckingham Dr & Ln 77375
Bucks Run 77377
Buckskin Dr 77377
Buescher Rd 77377
Burkhardt Rd 77377
Buster Cir 77375
Butternut Grove Pl 77375
Buvinghausen St 77375
Cabbot Cove Ct 77375
Cactus Wren Dr 77377
Calico Canyon Dr 77375
Callepine Ln 77377
Calvert Rd 77377
Camden Meadow Dr 77375
Camden Woods Ct 77377
S Camellia Park Cir 77375
Cameron Reach Ct & Dr 77377
Camille Dr 77377
Camillia Trl 77375
Campbellford Dr 77377
Cannion Falls Dr 77377
Cannon Creek Trl 77375
Canterborough Pl 77375
Canterbury Forest Dr 77377
Canyon Bay Ct & Dr 77377
Canyon Bend Dr 77377
Canyon Breeze Dr 77377
Canyon Drop Dr 77377
Canyon Falls Dr 77375
Canyon Frost Dr 77377
Canyon Gate Dr 77377
Canyon Lake Dr 77377
Canyon Mill Ln 77377
Canyon Mist Ln 77377
Canyon Rock Ln 77377
Canyon Rose Dr 77377
Canyon Royal Dr 77377
Canyon Star Ct & Ln 77377
Canyon Sun Ln 77377
Canyon Timbers Dr 77377
Canyon Valley Ct & Dr 77377
Canyon Vista Ct & Ln 77377
Canyon Woods Dr 77377
Capella Cir 77375
Caprice Bend Pl 77375
Carbon Canyon Ln 77377
Cardinal Ln 77377
Cardston Ct 77377
Caribou Ridge Dr 77377
Carlton Oaks St 77377
Carlton Vale Ct 77377
Carneswood Dr 77375
Carrell St 77375
Carriage Glen Dr 77377
Carriage Vale Ln 77377
Cascade Basin Fls 77375
Cascade Timbers Ln 77377
Castlegrove Ct 77377
Castlehead Dr 77375
Castlerock Springs Ln 77375
Castor St 77375
Catskill Crest Dr 77375
Cavern Springs Dr 77375
Cedar Ln 77377
Cedar Post Ct 77377
Cedar Run Fls 77375
Cedar Walk Dr 77375
Cedarberry Ln 77375
Cedarvale Ln 77377
Celeste Ct 77375
Chaddington Ct 77375
E, S & W Champagne Cir, Ct & Dr 77377
Champion Wood Dr 77377
Champions Lakes Trl 77375
Champions Lakeway 77375
Chase Mills Pl 77375
Chateau Dr & Trl 77377
Chateau Ridge Ct 77375
Chatfield Manor Ln 77377
Checkerberry Park Ln 77375
Cheddar Ct 77375
Cherokee Bluff Dr 77375
N & S Cherry St 77375
Cherry Canyon Ln 77377
Cherry Laurel Dr 77375
Cheslyn Ct 77375
N Chestnut St 77375
S Chestnut St 77375
Chestnut Trl 77375
Chestnut Path Way 77375
Chewton Ct 77377
Chewton Glen St 77377
Chickadee Ln 77377
Chinaberry Park Ln 77375
Chris Ln 77377
Chuck Wagon Ride Ln 77375
Cidercreek Ln 77377
Cimarron Fls 77375
Cinder Creek Ct 77375
Cinnaberry Ln 77375
Clairhill Dr 77375
Clarence St 77375
Claresholm Dr 77377
Clayton St 77375
Clepper Dr 77375
Cloud Peak Dr 77377
Cloudberry Ln 77375
Cloverview Dr 77377
Cobble Shores Dr 77375
Cobbler Ln 77375
Coconino Ln 77377
Cohasset Pl 77375
Colbert Ct 77375
Colby Ln 77375
Collinsville Dr 77377
Columba Ct 77375
Commerce St 77375
Commercial Ln 77375
Commercial Park Rd 77375
Concho Valley Dr 77375
Condrey Ct 77375
Cook Rd 77375
Coons Rd 77375
Cooper Canyon Dr 77377
Copper Bean Dr 77375
Coral Cyn 77377
Corbel Point Way 77375
Corral Ct 77375
Cottage Ivy Cir 77377
Cotton Brook Ct 77375
Cotton Creek Dr 77375
Cougar Peak Dr 77377
Coulter Pine Ct 77375
Country Cir 77375
Country Hls 77377
Country Ln 77377
Country Trl 77377
N & S Country Club Green Cir, Dr & Way 77375
Country Gate Dr 77375
Country Hill Ct 77375
Country Meadow Ln 77375
Country Meadows Dr 77375
Country Pine Ct 77375
Country Time Cir 77375
N Cove Ln 77377
Cove Timbers Ct & Ln 77375
Cowboy Ct & Way 77375
Coxwold Ln 77375
Cranes Park St 77377
Creek Willow Dr 77375
Creekpine Ln 77375
Creekside Gate Ct 77375
Creekside Timbers Dr 77375
Creekside Willow Ct & Dr 77375
Crescent Dr 77375
Crescent Pass Dr 77375
Crestbrook Park Ln 77375
Crossfence Dr 77375
Curry Ridge Ln 77377
N Cypress Ln 77377
Cypress Garden Dr 77375
Cypress Rosehill Rd 77375
Cypress Shores Dr 77375
Dahlia Dale Dr 77375
Dakota Springs Dr 77377
Dana Dr 77377
Danbridge Ct 77375
Danby Pl 77375
Dandyline Way 77375
Danphe Landing Ct 77375
Dappled Filly Dr 77375
Darrell Springs Ln 77375
Date Meadow Ln 77375
Datewood Ln 77375
Days Dawn Dr 77375
De Luca Ln 77377
Decker Prairie Rosehi Rd 77377
Deep Meadow Dr 77375
Deerpath Ct 77375
Deerwick Ct 77375
Del Norte Canyon Dr 77377
Dement Ln 77375
Denise Ln 77375
Devon Dale Dr 77375
Di Jon Dr 77377
Di Mambro Ln 77377
Diablo Canyon Ln 77377
Diego Springs Dr 77375
Dillingham Dr 77375
Diversion Dr 77375
Dogwood Dr 77375
Dogwood Trl 77377
Dolan Springs Dr 77375
Dorado Cir 77375
Dove Trl 77375
Doverton Ln 77375
Doverwick Dr 77375
Doves Landing Ave 77375
Dovewood Springs Ln 77375
Dowdell Rd 77375
Downford Dr 77377
Dragon Fly Dr 77377
Draper Rd 77377
Drum Heller Ln 77377
Dusty Rose Ln 77377
Dylan Hills Ln 77377
Eagle Ledge Dr & Ln 77377
Echo Canyon Dr 77377
Edengrove Dr 77377
Edens Dawn Dr 77377
Edgecroft Ct 77377
Edgewood Manor Ct 77375
Edison Trace Ln 77377
Edmond Thorpe Ln 77375
Edward Ln 77377
Eganville Cir 77377
Elderberry Park Ln 77375
N Eldridge Pkwy 77377
Elgar Ln 77375
Eli Cove Ln 77377
Elizabeths Glen Ln 77375
Elkwood Glen Ct & Ln 77375
Ella St 77375
N & S Elm St 77375
Elm Bark St 77375
Elmira St 77375
Elverson Oaks Dr 77377
Ember Village Ln 77377
Emerald Point Ln 77375
Emerald Pool Falls Dr 77375
Emery Meadows Ln 77377
Empress Cove Ln 77377
Encinitas Cove Ct & Dr 77375
English Pine Ct 77375
Epps St 77375
Evening Glen Cir, Ct & Dr 77375
Evening Primrose Ln 77375
Evergreen Dr 77375
Everhart Pointe Dr 77377
Exbury Ct 77377
Ezekiel Dr & Rd 77375
Fairwyck Ct 77375
Falling Stream Dr 77375
Fannin St 77375
Fanwick Ct & Dr 77375
Fawnmist Cv 77377
Fawns Crossing Dr 77375
Faye St 77377
Feathers Landing Dr 77377
Finborough Dr 77377
Finnery Dr 77375
Fisher Dr 77377
Fisher Ridge Ln 77377
Flaghorne Ct 77375
Flattop Ln 77377
Flax Ct 77377
Florence St 77375
Florence Run Ln 77377
Flower Mist Ct 77377
Flying Geese Ln 77375
Fm 2920 Rd
8701-8997 77375
8999-11399 77375
14000-20599 77377
Fm 2978 Rd 77375
Fones Rd 77377
Fontana St 77377
Forest Creek Dr 77375
Forest Haven Trl 77375
Forest Hills Estates Dr 77375
Forest Vine Ct 77377
Fortrose Garden Ct 77377
Foster St 77375
Fountain Bend Dr 77375
Fountaine Bleau Dr 77377
Foxbluff Dr 77375
Fred J Petrich Rd 77375
Frederick Dr 77377
Freesia Ct 77375
Frey Ln 77375
Friar Village Dr 77375
Friardale Ct 77375
Fritz Falls Ct 77377
Frost River Ct 77377
Gable Woods Dr 77377
Gables Bend Dr 77377
Galena Falls Dr 77375
Galium Mdws 77377
Gallant Flag Dr 77375
Gallatin Ln 77377
Garden Path Pl 77375
Garden Pool Ln 77375
Garland Falls Dr 77375
Gatesden Dr 77377
Gehan Woods Dr 77375
Gettysburg Ct & Dr 77377
Gila Bend Ln 77375
Gilbertyn Dr 77377
Gilbough Dr 77375
Gildwood Pl 77375
Ginger Fields Ln 77377
Ginger Ridge Ln 77377
Glacier Falls Dr 77375
Glade River Ln 77377
Gladebeck Ln 77377
Gladesmore Ln 77377
Gladewater Ct & Dr 77375
Glen Willow St 77375

Glezman Ln 77377
Gold Rush Springs Dr 77375
Golden Mane Rd 77375
Goldfinch Ln 77377
Goldstream Ct 77377
Graham Dr 77375
Granberry Gate Dr 77377
Grand Ashford Dr 77375
Grand Creek Ln 77375
Granite Rock Ln 77375
Granite Springs Dr 77375
Grassnook Dr 77375
Gravenhurst Ln 77377
Gray Forest Trl 77377
Gray Trail Ct 77377
Green Bark St 77375
Green Meadow Rd 77377
Green Tree Dr 77375
Green Willow Falls Dr 77375
N & S Greenprint Cir 77375
Gregson Rd 77377
Grosbeak Ln 77377
Guernsey Dr 77377
Haigshire Dr 77375
Haleys Comet Cir 77375
Halston Ridge Ct 77375
Hamish Rd 77377
Hamlin Lake Dr 77375
Hammersmith Dr 77377
Hammerwood Ct 77375
Hampton Wood Dr 77377
Hamptonmere Ln 77377
Hamsfield Ct 77377
Handbridge Pl 77375
Hardy Trace Dr 77377
Harlow Dr 77375
Harston Dr 77375
Hart Hollow Ln 77377
Hatfield Hollow Dr 77375
Haven Trl & Way 77375
Haven Lake Dr 77375
Haven Woods Way 77375
Havenmist Dr 77377
Hawkin Ln 77377
Hawthorne Ct 77375
Hayden Cove Dr 77375
Hayden Wood Dr 77375
Hazyl Shadow Dr 77375
Headstall Dr 77375
Hearthwick Pl & Rd 77375
Hebburn Ct 77375
Heidi Ln 77375
Helen Ln 77375
Hemington Cir & Dr 77375
Hemlock St 77375
Hereford Dr 77377
Heritage Dr 77377
E Heritage Mill Cir 77375
Hermit Thrush Dr 77377
Hermitage Oaks Ct & Dr 77377
Heron Ln & Trl 77377
N Hickory St 77375
Hickory Post Ct 77375
Hickory Trace Ct 77375
Hicks St 77375
Hidden Grove Ct & Trl 77375
Hiddenbriar Loop 77375
High St 77375
High Canyon Ln 77377
High Meadow Ln & Rd 77377
High Sea Dr 77377
Highet Pl 77375
Hill Creek Fls 77375
Hillegeist Ln 77377
Hillingdon Ln 77377
Hillington Ct 77375
Hillsgate Ct 77377
Hilltop Ln 77377
Hinterwood Way 77375
Hirschfield Rd 77377
Hobbs Terrace Dr 77377
Hodges Grove Ln 77377
Hoffman Estates Blvd 77377
Holderrieth Blvd 77375
N Holderrieth Blvd
104-198 77375
122-122 77377
Holderrieth Rd 77375
Holiday St 77375
Hollington Dr 77375
Hollis Garden Dr 77375
Hollow Bend Ln 77377
Hollow Glen Ln 77375
Holly Branch Dr 77375
Holly Creek Trl 77375
Holly Hills Dr 77375
Holly Hollow St 77377
Holly Lakes Dr 77377
Holly Thorn 77375
Hollybranch Dr 77375
Hollywick Dr 77375
Holsberry Ct 77377
Horden Creek Dr 77377
Horsetail Falls Dr 77375
Hospital St 77375
Hostler Dr 77375
E Houston St 77375
N & S Howard St 77375
Hufsmith Rd 77375
Hufsmith Cemetery Rd 77375
Hufsmith Kohrville Rd 77375
Hufsmith Kuykendahl Rd 77375
Humble Rd 77375
N Humble Lake Rd 77377
Hummingbird Ln 77377
Hunters Bend Dr 77377
Huntington Woods Estates Dr 77377
Iberis Meadows Dr 77375
Imperial Creek Dr 77375
Imperial Crossing Dr 77375
Imperial Hills Dr 77375
Indian Creek Fls 77375
Indian Hills Cir 77377
Indian Trails Dr 77377
Indigo Creek Ln 77375
Industry Ln 77375
Inland Prairie Dr 77375
Innisfall Cir 77377
Invergyel Ln 77375
Inverness Park Blvd 77375
Inwood Dr & St 77375
Iris Canyon Dr 77375
Isbell Dr 77375
Island Dr 77375
Island Spring Ln 77375
Ivy Wick Ct 77375
Jack Pine Cir & Pl 77375
Jacobs Ladder Ct 77375
Jade Canyon Ln 77375
James St 77375
Jane Ln 77375
E Jane Ln 77375
W Jane Ln 77375
Jane Rd 77375
Jasmine Springs Dr 77377
Jeanie Dr 77377
Jeckell Isles Ct & Dr 77375
Jenner Dr 77377
Johnson Rd 77375
Jordi Dr 77375
Jordyn Lake Dr 77375
Joseph Ct 77375
Joshua Ln 77375
Juergen Rd 77375
Julia Ln 77375
Julie Ln 77375
Juniper Ct 77375
Juniper Ridge Ln 77375
Justin Ct 77375
Justinwood Pt 77375
Kane St 77375
Kathywood Dr 77377
Keefer Rd 77375
Keen Rd 77375
W Kelly Ln 77377
Kendahlwood Ln 77377
Kenny Dr 77377
Kensal Bay Ln 77377
Kenswick Cove Ct & Dr 77375
Kent Park Dr 77375
Kerr Dr 77377
Kimbrough Dr 77375
King Rd 77375
Kingbird Dr 77377
Kingsbarn Ct 77377
Kingsnorth Dr 77375
Kinnel Ln 77375
Kleppel Rd 77375
Knight Quest Dr 77375
Kobs Rd 77377
Kobs Hill Ln 77377
Krug Rd 77377
Krug Glen Ct 77377
Kuykendahl Rd 77375
La Fouche Ct & Dr 77377
Lacey Rd 77375
Lacy Willow Ct 77375
Lago Villa Dr 77377
Laguna Woods Dr 77375
Lake Breeze Dr 77375
Lake Front Dr 77377
Lake Grove Bnd, Ct & Frst 77377
Lake Reverie Ct & Pl 77375
Lake Stone Ct 77377
Lake Vista Dr 77377
Lakecrest Ln 77377
Lakestone Dr 77377
Lakeway Park 77375
Lakewodd Springs Dr 77377
Lakewood Gln 77375
Lakewood Trl 77375
Lakewood Crossing Dr 77377
Lakewood Field Ct & Dr 77377
E & W Lakewood Forest North Ct 77377
Lakewood Grove Dr 77377
Lakewood Hills Dr 77377
Lakewood Villa Dr 77377
Lantern Cove Ln 77375
Larchfield Ct 77377
Larkmist Ln 77375
Laurel Cv 77377
Laurel Meadow Dr 77377
Laurelwood Ln 77375
Lavon Dr 77375
Lawrence St 77375
Lawson Cypress Dr 77377
Lazy Tee Ln 77375
Le Berge Dr 77377
Leeside Ct & Dr 77377
Leyton Ct 77377
Leytonstone St 77377
Liberty Ln 77377
Ligustrum Trl 77377
Ligustrum Trail Ct 77377
Lillian Ln 77377
Lily Creek Dr 77377
Limerick Ln 77375
Limestone Lake Dr 77375
Linda Ln 77375
Linda Leigh Ln 77375
Lindsey Rd 77375
Little Falls Pl 77375
Little Green St 77375
Little Orchard Ct 77377
Littlefield Ct 77377
N Live Oak St 77375
S Live Oak St 77375
Live Oak Trl 77375
Lizzie Ln 77375
Loblolly Dr 77375
Lochberry Ct 77377
Lodgepole Pl 77375
Log Cabin Ln 77375
Logan Briar Dr 77377
Logan Timbers Ln 77375
London Way Dr 77375
Longs Peek Ct 77375
Lost Creek Ct & Rd 77375
Louden Dr 77377
Lovett Ct & St 77375
Lowell Ave 77377
Lucas Hollow Ln 77377
Lucien Ln 77377
Lucky Meadow Dr 77375
Lufberry Pl 77375
Luna Falls Ct & Dr 77377
Lundar Ln 77377
Lutheran Cemetery Rd 77377
Lutheran Church Rd 77377
Lutheran School Rd 77377
Lynnrose Springs Dr 77375
Lyric Way Dr 77377
Madera Canyon Ln 77377
Madisons Crossing Ln 77375
Magic Falls Dr 77377
Magic Spell Dr 77377
E & W Maglitto Cir 77375
N & S Magnolia St 77375
Magnolia Arbor Ct & Ln 77377
Mahaffey Rd 77375
Maidenfair Dr 77375
Main Blvd 77377
E Main St 77375
W Main St 77375
Mainer Ln 77375
Malone St 77375
Mammoth Falls Dr 77375
Manleigh Ct 77377
Manor Spring Ct 77377
Maple Falls Ct & Dr 77377
Maple Glen Dr 77377
Maplewick Dr 77377
Marfield Ct 77377
Mariposa Canyon Dr 77377
Market St 77375
Marmite Dr 77377
Marrat Ct 77375
Martens Rd 77375
Martin Creek Ln 77377
Mary Jane Ln 77377
Mason St 77375
Mathews Rd 77375
May Basket Dr 77375
Maycrest Ct 77377
Mckinney Dr 77375
Mcmahon Cir 77377
Mcphail St 77375
Meadow Fls & Ln 77377
Meadow Lark Ln 77375
Meadowhurst Cir 77377
Meadowview Ln 77377
Mechanic St 77375
Medical Complex Dr
13400-13799 77375
14000-14799 77377
Medina Lake Dr 77377
Melina Ln 77375
Melissa Springs Dr 77375
Memorial Crossing Ct & Dr 77375
Memorial Falls Dr 77375
Memorial Mist Ln 77375
Memorial Springs Ct, Dr & Pass 77375
Memorial Trail Dr 77375
Memorial Way Dr 77375
Mercer Dr 77375
Mesa Wells Dr 77375
Metzler Hills Ln 77377
Michel Rd 77375
Middleburgh Dr 77377
Middlecrest Ln 77375
Midland Creek Dr 77375
Millstream Bend Ln 77377
Milo Pass Ln 77375
Mimosa Spring Dr 77377
Miramar Crest Ct & Dr 77375
S Miramar Lake Blvd 77375
Misty Ln 77375
Misty Blue Ln 77375
Misty Meadow Ct 77375
Misty Moores Dr 77375
Misty Willow Ln 77375
Moccasin Ct 77377
Mockingbird Ln 77377
Molasses Meadow Ln 77375
Montebello Manor Ln 77377
Monterrey Pine Pl 77375
Moonlit Ridge Ct 77375
Moore St 77375
Moose Cove Ct 77375
Morgan Dr 77375
Morning Rain Dr 77377
Mossey Forest Ct 77375
Mosshall Ct 77375
Mosswillow Ln 77375
Mossy Ledge Dr 77377
Mossy Pointe Ln 77375
Mossy Woods Dr 77375
Mueschke Rd 77377
Mulberry St 77375
Mulberry Park Ln 77375
Muller Sky Ct 77377
Mutineer Ln 77377
Mutiny Ln 77377
Myrtle Creek Fls 77375
Mystic Stone Dr 77375
Nancy Ln 77375
Napper Dr 77377
Nara Vista Dr 77377
Nasworthy Dr 77375
Navajo Place Dr 77375
Navarro Mills Dr 77375
Neal Dr 77375
New Hampton Dr 77377
Newcourt Place St 77375
Newcroft Ct 77375
Newlands Ct 77377
Newpark Dr 77377
Niagra Falls Dr 77375
Noble Crusade Ct 77375
Noco Dr 77375
Norhill Fair Ln 77375
Northam Dr 77375
Northcanyon Dr 77377
Northfork Bend Ct & Ln 77377
Northpointe Blvd 77377
Northpointe Bend Dr 77377
Northpointe Meadows Dr 77377
Northpointe Ridge Ln 77377
Northpointe Terrace Dr 77377
Northwood Glen Ln 77377
Norway Maple Ln 77377
Norway Spruce Ln 77375
N & S Oak St 77375
Oak Hollow Ln 77377
Oak Island Dr 77377
Oak Landing Dr 77377
Oakner Dr 77377
Oconee Ct & Dr 77375
Oden Trace Dr 77377
Okehampton Dr 77377
Old Court Dr 77377
Olde Mint House Ln 77375
Oldwick Brook Dr 77375
Olin Rd 77377
Opal Valley Dr 77377
Orange Hill Ln 77375
Orchard Grove Dr 77375
Orion Dr 77377
Orleans Ave 77377
Owens Falls Dr 77375
Oxenberg Manor Ln 77377
Oxenford Dr 77377
Oxford St 77375
Oxford Trails Dr 77375
Oxley Ct 77377
Pacer Cir 77375
Painted Canyon Dr 77377
Painted Pony Ln 77375
Palmetta Spring Dr 77375
Palomino Creek Ct 77375
Papago Ct & Dr 77377
Paradise Summit Dr 77377
Park Dr, Ln & Rd 77377
Park Cedar Ct 77377
Park Island Ct 77377
Park Place Dr 77377
Parker Ct 77375
Parker Rd 77377
Pauls Trl 77377
Pavilion Ct 77377
Peach St 77375
Peachvine Ln 77375
Pebble Falls Ln 77375
Pebble Sands Dr 77375
E Pecan Dr 77375
Pecan Canyon Ct 77377
Pecks Park Ct 77377
Pedder Way Dr 77377
Pedlars Ct 77377
Pelican Isle Ct 77377
Pemford Dr 77377
Pennridge Ln 77377
Peralta Hill Ln 77377
Perch Brook Ct 77377
Percival St 77375
Perdenales Falls Ct 77375
S Persimmon St 77375
Petrich Ln 77377
Petuma Meadows Dr 77375
Pheasant Ln 77377
Pikes Peek Ct 77375
Pilot Rock Pl 77375
Pin Cherry Dr 77377
N & S Pine Brk, St & Trl 77375
Pine Bark Ln 77377
Pine Bluff Dr 77377
Pine Canyon Fls 77375
Pine Canyon Falls Cir 77375
Pine Cone Ln 77377
Pine Country Blvd 77377
E, N, S & W Pine Ivy Ln 77375
Pine Meadow Ln 77377
Pine Meadows St 77375
Pine Plains Dr 77377
Pine Trace Bend Dr 77375
Pine Trace Crossing Dr 77375
Pine Tree Dr 77377
Pine Warbler Dr 77377
Pine Water Ln 77375
Pine Woods St 77375
Pineleigh Ct 77375
Pinemeade Ln 77375
Pinewille Park Ln 77377
Pinewood Pl 77375
Pinewood Point Ln 77377
Piney Bend Ct & Dr 77375
Piney Way Ct, Dr & Ln 77375
Pinos Altos Dr 77377
Pinto Ct 77375
Piper Pointe Ln 77375
Pirate Cove Dr 77377
Pitcairn Dr 77377
Pitchford Rd 77375
Pitchstone Ct & Dr 77377
Placid Trails Dr 77377
Plantation Pines Ln 77375
Platinum Springs Dr 77375
Plaza 290 Blvd 77377
Pleasant Green Cir 77377
Pocatello Dr 77375
Point Arbor Ct 77375
Point Pendleton Dr 77375
Polaris Blvd 77375
Pollux Ct 77375
Pondera Point Dr 77375
Ponderosa Pine Pl 77375
Pony Trl 77375
N & S Poplar St 77375
Poplar Trails Ln 77375
Porinert Blvd 77377
Portales Pointe Ln 77377
Powder Mill Dr 77375
Prancer Dr 77375
Princeton Place Dr 77375
Quail Ln 77377
Quaking Aspen Dr 77377
Quiet Yearling Pl 77375
Quinn Rd 77375
Rachels Way 77375
Rain Creek Ct & Dr 77375
Raindark Rd 77375
Rampy Green Dr 77377
Ranch Hand Rd 77375
Randon Ln 77377
Randy Riley Way 77377
Raven Cliff Falls Dr 77375
Ray Falls Dr 77375
W Rayford Rd 77375
Raymond St 77375
Red Canyon Ln 77377
Red Fox Rd 77377
Red Moon Pl 77375
Red Oak Trl 77377
Red Pine Dr 77375
Red Wing Trl 77375
Redrock Fls 77375
Reflecting Point Pl 77375
Rhinefield St 77377
Ribbon Falls Ct & Dr 77375
Ribbonwood Point Ct 77375
Ridgewick Ct 77377
N Riding Dr 77375
Rigel Ct 77375
Rippling Brook Ln 77375
River Birch Dr 77375
River Breeze Dr 77375
River Vine Ct 77377
Rivergrove Ct 77377
Rivermist Ct 77377
Roaring River Fls 77375
Robeck St 77377
Robin Ln 77377
Robins Crest Dr 77377
Rock Elm Dr 77375
Rocky Bank Dr 77375
Rocky Briar Ct & Ln 77377
Rocky Brook Fls 77375
Rocky Shores Dr 77375
Rollick Dr 77375
Rolling Glen Ln 77375
Rolling Meadow Dr 77375
Rolling Oaks Dr 77375
Rolling Stream Dr 77375
Rose Hurst Dr 77375
Rosebud Ln 77377
Rosehill Rd 77377
Rosehill Church Rd 77377
Rosehill Manor Ct 77377
Rosehollow Trl 77375
Rosehurst Blvd & Dr 77377
Rosel Oaks Ln 77377
E Roselake Dr 77377
Rosevale Ct 77377
Roseway Rd 77377
Rosewood Trl 77377
Roseworth Ct 77377
Roundtable Dr 77377
Rouselle Ln 77377
Roxanne St 77377
Royal Bend Ln 77377
Royal Isle Ct & Dr 77375
Royal Mist Ln 77377
Royalwick Dr 77375
Rudel Dr 77375
Rudolph Rd 77377
Rue Beaujon Ct 77377
Rue La Fontaine Dr 77377
Rue Montebello Ct & Dr 77377
Rue Saint Honore Ct & Dr 77377
Rue Saint Lazare Ct 77377
Rumbling Creek Ln 77375
Rumfolo Dr 77377
Running Deer Dr 77375
Running Eagle Fls 77375
Rushing Springs Ct & Dr 77375
Rushing Stream Ct 77375
Russett Green Dr 77377
Rustic Springs Dr 77375
Rustica Dr 77375
Rustling Ridge Ln 77375
Rusty Pine Ln 77375
Rye St 77375

Saddlebrook Ct & Ln ... 77375
Saddlebrook Champion Way ... 77375
Saddlebrook Ranch Dr ... 77375
Saddlebrook Village Dr ... 77375
Sage Thrasher Dr ... 77377
Saint Florent Ct & Dr ... 77377
Saint Johns Wood Dr ... 77377
Salt Grass Ln & Trl ... 77375
Sandpiper Ln ... 77377
Sandstone Fls ... 77375
Sandusky Ct & Dr ... 77375
Sandy Bank Dr ... 77375
Sandy Stream Ct & Dr ... 77375
Sandy Woods Dr ... 77375
Sarah Rd ... 77377
Saratoga Ln ... 77375
Saratoga Ranch Dr ... 77375
Sardis Lake Dr ... 77375
Sasquatch Dr ... 77377
Satinleaf Pl ... 77375
Sawston Dr ... 77375
E, N, S & W Sawtooth Canyon Dr ... 77377
Saybrook Point Ln ... 77375
Scarlet Cove Dr ... 77377
Scarlet Forest Dr ... 77377
Scarlet Oak Dr ... 77377
Scenic Trl ... 77375
Scherer Woods Ct ... 77377
School St ... 77375
Scotch Pine Pl & St ... 77375
Scott St ... 77375
Scotts Point Dr ... 77375
Scrub Jay Dr ... 77377
Seabiscuit Dr ... 77375
Seber Dr & Ln ... 77375
Sedgemoor Dr ... 77375
Seidel Rd ... 77377
Seidel Cemetary Rd ... 77377
Seidelstone Ct ... 77377
Self Rd ... 77377
Serene Trl ... 77375
Serrano Lake Ct ... 77375
Seven Sisters Dr ... 77375
Shadow Pass Trl ... 77377
Shady Bank Dr ... 77375
Shady Canyon Ln ... 77377
Shady Fort Ln ... 77377
Shady Willow St ... 77375
Shale Creek Dr ... 77375
Shallow Oak Ct ... 77377
Shallowford Pl ... 77375
Sherlock Acres Dr ... 77377
Shieldhall Ln ... 77375
Shingle Oak Dr ... 77377
Shoreland Ct ... 77377
Shores Edge Dr ... 77375
Short Trail Ln ... 77377
Side Way ... 77375
Sienna Trails Dr ... 77377
Sierra Dawn Dr ... 77375
Sierra Falls Ct ... 77377
Silent Meadow Ct ... 77375
Silverleaf Ln ... 77375
Singleleaf Ln ... 77375
Sir Alex Dr ... 77375
Sky Haven Dr ... 77375
Skydale Dr ... 77375
Slash Pine Pl ... 77375
Sleepy Ln ... 77375
Smoke Lk ... 77375
Snook Ln ... 77375
Snowblossom Ln ... 77375
Snowbridge Ct ... 77377
Snowcrest Ct ... 77377
Socorro Ln ... 77377
Solebrook Path ... 77375
Solomon Rd ... 77375
Solomon Road Ext ... 77375
Solon Springs Ct & Dr ... 77375
Songhollow Dr ... 77377
Sonora Springs Dr ... 77375
Sorrel Meadows Dr ... 77375
Southmore St ... 77375
Spell Rd ... 77375
Spellbrook Point Ln ... 77377
Spica St ... 77375
Spicewood ... 77375
Split Rd ... 77377
Split Rock Fls ... 77375
Spring Ct ... 77375
Spring Alp Ct ... 77375
Spring Cypress Rd
10700-10898 ... 77375
11000-12999 ... 77377
Spring Forest Way ... 77377
Spring Hollow Dr ... 77375
Spring Knoll Dr ... 77375
Spring Mountain Dr ... 77377
Spring Path Ct ... 77377
Spring Pines Dr ... 77377
Spring Rapid Way ... 77375
Spring Willow Dr ... 77375
Springcroft Ct ... 77375
Spruce Cir ... 77375
Spur Ln ... 77377
Spurlin Meadow Dr Dr ... 77377
Stamford Dr ... 77375
Stamford Oaks Dr ... 77375
Stanbury Park Ln ... 77377
Standing Pine Ln ... 77375
Stanolind Rd ... 77375
Star Iris Pl ... 77375
State Highway 249 ... 77375
Stella Ln ... 77375
Stetson St ... 77375
Still Pond Dr ... 77375
Stillhouse Dr ... 77375
Stone Cannon Ct ... 77377
Stone Creek Ct ... 77377
Stone Gate Ct ... 77375
Stone Lake Cir & Dr ... 77375
Stone Mountain Fls ... 77375
Stonebridge Pl ... 77375
Stonebridge Crossing Ln ... 77375
Stonebridge Lake Ct & Dr ... 77375
Stonegrove Ct ... 77375
Stoneleigh Ct ... 77375
Stonepine Creek Dr ... 77377
Stonepine Meadow Ct ... 77377
Storybrook Forest Dr ... 77377
Strackfield Ln ... 77377
Stratford Pl ... 77375
Stuebner Dr ... 77375
Stuebner Airline Rd ... 77375
Sugar Bowl Dr ... 77375
Sugar Orchard Ln ... 77375
Sugar Pine Pl ... 77375
Sugarberry Way ... 77375
Sugarbloom Ln ... 77377
Sugarbridge Ln ... 77375
Sugarglen Ln ... 77375
Sugarmeade Ln ... 77375
Sugarvine Ln ... 77375
Summer Breeze Ln ... 77375
Summerberry Ln ... 77375
Summercliff Ct & Ln ... 77375
Summerstone Ct ... 77377
Summerville Lake Dr ... 77377
Summit Dr ... 77375
Sun Canyon Ct ... 77375
Sun Pass Dr ... 77377
Sun River Ct & Ln ... 77377
Suncross Ln ... 77377
Sundance Creek Ln ... 77375
Sundown Ridge Pl ... 77375
Sunny Gallop Dr ... 77375
Sunny Stream Dr ... 77377
Sunrise Canter Dr ... 77375
Sunset Arbor Dr ... 77377
Sunset Canyon Dr ... 77377
Sunset Pond Dr ... 77377
Sunset Trail Ln ... 77377
Surrey Ct ... 77375
Sutton Ln ... 77375
N & S Swanwick Pl ... 77375
Sweet Grv ... 77375
Sweet Blossom Ln ... 77375
Sweet Grass Ln ... 77375
Sweet Olive Way ... 77375
Sweet Pasture Dr ... 77375
Sweet Rain Dr ... 77377
Sweet River Ln ... 77375
Sweet Song Dr ... 77377
Sweetberry Ln ... 77375
Sweetbloom Ln ... 77375
Sweetnectar Ln ... 77375
Sweetrock Ln ... 77375
Sweetvine Ln ... 77375
Sweetwater Fields Ln ... 77377
Swift Water Bnd ... 77375
N & S Sycamore St ... 77375
Sydney Park Ln ... 77377
T K C Rd ... 77375
Tacoma Ridge Dr ... 77377
Talcott Way Dr ... 77375
Tall Pine Vista Ln ... 77375
Tallcrest Ln ... 77375
Tan Oak Cir ... 77375
Tanager Ln ... 77377
Tangler Ct & Ln ... 77375
Tannery Hill Rd ... 77375
Taper Reach Dr ... 77377
Tara Ct ... 77375
Tawakom Dr ... 77375
Taylor Springs Ln ... 77375
Taylors Crossing Dr ... 77375
Tea Leaf Dr ... 77375
Teal Hollow Ln ... 77375
Tealight Pl ... 77375
Teasly Ln ... 77375
Telford Way ... 77375
Telge Rd & Ter ... 77377
Ten Oaks Dr ... 77375
Terra Valley Ln ... 77375
Terrero Ct ... 77377
Texas St ... 77375
Theis Ln ... 77375
Theis Trail Ln ... 77375
Thistleberry Ln ... 77375
Thorn Valley Ct ... 77375
Thornecrest Dr ... 77375
Thornridge Ln ... 77377
Three Lakes Blvd ... 77375
Three Stone Ln ... 77375
Tidwillow Pl ... 77375
Timber Dove Ln ... 77375
Timber Grove Ct ... 77375
Timber Tech Ave ... 77375
Timbercrest Dr ... 77375
Timberlake Creek Rd ... 77377
Timberlake Forest Ln ... 77377
Timberlake Grove Ln ... 77377
Timberlake Oaks Dr ... 77377
Timberlake View Ln ... 77377
Timberlake Village Rd ... 77377
Timberlake Woods Ln ... 77377
Timberwild Ct ... 77375
Timkin Rd ... 77375
Timpnogos Dr ... 77377
Tioga Pl ... 77375
Tisha Ln ... 77377
Todd St ... 77375
Tomball Cemetery Rd ... 77377
Tomball Waller Rd ... 77377
Torrance Ct ... 77377
Torrens Ct ... 77375
Torrey Pine Pl ... 77375
Torrisdale Ln ... 77375
Towne Bridge Dr ... 77377
Trail Point Dr ... 77377
Trailwood Ln ... 77377
Treichel Rd ... 77375
Troy St ... 77375
Tularosa Ln ... 77377
Tumbleweed Trl ... 77375
Tupper Creek Ct ... 77377
Turnervine Dr ... 77375
Turtles Corner Ln ... 77375
Tuwa Rd ... 77375
Twin Buttes Dr ... 77375
Twin Flower Dr ... 77377
Twin Rivers Dr ... 77375
Twisted Creek Dr ... 77375
Two Lakes Dr ... 77375
Tyler St ... 77375
Ulrich Rd ... 77375
Union St ... 77377
Ute Mountain Ln ... 77377
Valley Cliff Ct ... 77377
Velvet Shadow Ct ... 77375
S Vernon St ... 77375
Village Breeze Dr ... 77377
Village Commons Dr ... 77377
Village Crest Ct ... 77377
Village Meadow Ct ... 77375
Village Ridge Dr ... 77375
Village Square Dr ... 77375
Virginia Pine Ct & Dr ... 77375
E & W Wading Pond Cir ... 77375
Wading River Dr ... 77375
Wagner Point Ct ... 77377
Walden Way ... 77375
Waldwick Dr ... 77377
N & S Walnut St ... 77375
Wandering Streams Dr ... 77377
Ward Rd ... 77375
Warm Winds Dr ... 77377
Warwickshire Dr ... 77377
Wasatch Dr ... 77377
Water Oak Trl ... 77377
Waterfall Way ... 77375
Waterflower Dr ... 77375
Waterford Estates Ct ... 77375
Waterstone Estates Cir & Ct E, N, S & W ... 77375
Wealdstone Dr ... 77377
Weirich Rd ... 77375
Wellock Ln ... 77375
Wenbury Dr ... 77375
Wendy Glinn Way ... 77375
Westlock Ct, Dr & St ... 77377
Westwold Dr ... 77377
Whispering Grv E & W ... 77377
Whispering Thicket Pl ... 77375
White Elks Blvd ... 77375
White Horse Dr ... 77377
White Pine Pl ... 77375
White River Dr ... 77375
Whitland Ln ... 77377
Whitney Meadows Dr ... 77377
Wickford Dr ... 77375
Wilbur Ln ... 77375
Wild Goose Dr ... 77375
Wild Grove Ct ... 77377
Wild Moss St ... 77375
Wildrose Ln ... 77377
Wildvine Ct ... 77377
Wildwood Dr ... 77375
Will Rogers Taxiway ... 77377
William Juergens Dr ... 77375
N Willow Gln, Path, Run, St & Way ... 77375
Willow Bough St ... 77375
Willow Branch Ln & St ... 77375
Willow Breeze Dr ... 77377
Willow Creek Dr ... 77375
Willow Creek Bridge Ln ... 77375
Willow Downs Dr ... 77375
Willow End St ... 77375
Willow Forest Dr ... 77375
Willow Grove Dr ... 77375
Willow Leaf St ... 77375
Willow Shade Ln ... 77375
Willow Shadows Dr ... 77375
Willow Spur Ct & Dr ... 77375
Willow Wilde Dr ... 77375
Willow Wood St ... 77375
Willowbank Dr ... 77377
Willowcrest ... 77375
Willowick St ... 77375
Willowpark Dr ... 77377
Wilson Ln & St ... 77375
Wind Pine Ln ... 77375
Windbourne Dr ... 77375
Winding Hollow Ln ... 77375
Winding Wood Ln ... 77375
Windsinger Ct ... 77375
Windsor Bay Ct ... 77375
Windsor Pointe Ct & Dr ... 77375
Windy Brook Ln ... 77375
Windy Meadow Rd ... 77377
Winfrey Ln ... 77375
Winfro Dr ... 77375
Winkler Willow Ct ... 77377
Winspring Ct & Dr ... 77377
Winter Canyon Ln ... 77377
Winterhaven Dr ... 77377
Witherbee Pl ... 77375
Wixford Ln ... 77375
Woburn Dr ... 77377
Wondering Forest Dr ... 77377
Wondering Stream Dr ... 77377
Wood Drake Ct & Pl ... 77375
Wooded Overlook Dr ... 77375
Woodglade Way ... 77375
Woodland Shore Dr ... 77375
Woody Hollow Dr ... 77375
Wrangler Ln ... 77375
Wren Ln ... 77377
E, N, S & W Yaupon Cir ... 77377
Yellow Canyon Falls Dr ... 77375
Yorkmonte Dr ... 77375
Yosemite Falls Dr ... 77375
Yuma Crest Ln ... 77377
Zion Rd ... 77375
Zion Luther Cmtery Rd ... 77375
Zula Dr ... 77375

TYLER TX

General Delivery ... 75702

POST OFFICE BOXES MAIN OFFICE STATIONS AND BRANCHES

Box No.s
1 - 2525 ... 75710
4001 - 5800 ... 75712
6001 - 10140 ... 75711
120001 - 120418 ... 75712
130001 - 133246 ... 75713

RURAL ROUTES

16, 31 ... 75701
04, 08, 13, 18, 23, 24, 27, 30, 43 ... 75703
02, 17, 22, 37 ... 75704
03 ... 75705
05, 09, 38 ... 75706
10, 15, 25 ... 75707
12, 42 ... 75708
11, 21 ... 75709

NAMED STREETS

Abbey Ct ... 75703
Abbeywood Ct ... 75703
Aberdeen Dr ... 75703
Acacia Dr ... 75707
S Academy St ... 75701
Acadia Dr ... 75703
Ada Ave ... 75702
S Adams Ave ... 75702
Airline Dr ... 75701
Airport Dr ... 75704
Airway Ave & Dr ... 75704
Airways Dr ... 75704
Aj Blvd ... 75705
Alamo Dr ... 75701
N Albertson Ave ... 75702
Alexandria Pl ... 75701
N Alfred Ave ... 75702
Alice Ln ... 75703
Alice St ... 75702
Allen Ave ... 75701
Allendale Dr ... 75701
Alma St ... 75704
Alpine Dr ... 75701
Alta Mira Dr ... 75701
Amber Cir ... 75707
Amber Leaf Ct ... 75707
Amberwood Cir ... 75701
Ambrose Ave ... 75704
American Legion Rd ... 75708
Amesbury Cir ... 75701
Amesbury Pl ... 75703
E & W Amherst Dr ... 75701
Amy Dr ... 75709
Amy Ln ... 75701
N Anderson Ave ... 75702
Andover Dr ... 75707
Andy Ln ... 75701
N Angeline Ave ... 75702
Angy Dr ... 75703
Anita Ln ... 75701
Ann Ave ... 75706
Anne Pl ... 75703
Anthony Dr ... 75701
Antlers Dr ... 75703
Apache Rd ... 75705
Apache Trl ... 75707
Appletree Ln ... 75701
Arapaho St ... 75705
Arbor Oak Dr ... 75707
N Ardmore Ave ... 75702
Arizona Dr ... 75707
Arlington Ave ... 75701
Arnette Way ... 75707
E Arnold St ... 75701
Ash Ln ... 75703
Ashbury Ct ... 75703
Ashford Cir & Ct ... 75703
Ashmore Ln ... 75703
Ashton Ct ... 75703
Ashwood Dr ... 75703
Aspen Cir ... 75703
Athens Dr ... 75703
Atlanta Ave ... 75703
Auburn Dr ... 75703
Augusta Ave ... 75701
S Augusta Ave ... 75702
Aurora St ... 75701
Austin Dr ... 75701
Autumn Dr ... 75703
Autumn Leaves Dr ... 75702
Avenham Ct ... 75703
Avoyelles ... 75703
N Azalea Dr ... 75701
Bailey Dr ... 75702
Bain Pl ... 75701
Baker Dr ... 75702
Baldwin Dr ... 75702
Balmoral Dr ... 75703
Balsam Gap ... 75703
Bama Ln ... 75701
Bandera Dr ... 75702
Banks St ... 75701
E Barbara St ... 75701
Barbee Dr ... 75703
Barclay Dr ... 75703
E Barger St ... 75702
Barkwood Cir ... 75707
Barnes St ... 75701
Barney Ln ... 75705
E & W Barrett St ... 75702
N Baron Ave ... 75702
Baruth Dr ... 75702
Bateman Ave ... 75701
S Baxter Ave
101-197 ... 75702
199-504 ... 75702
506-598 ... 75701
601-817 ... 75701
819-1099 ... 75701
1101-1799 ... 75701
Baylor Dr ... 75703
Beall Cir ... 75701
Bearwood Ln ... 75703
Beauregard Dr ... 75703
N Beckham Ave ... 75702
S Beckham Ave
100-599 ... 75702
601-697 ... 75701
699-1799 ... 75701
1801-2099 ... 75701
Becky Dr ... 75703
Bedford Dr ... 75703
Bedshire Ct ... 75703
Beechwood Dr ... 75701
N Belcher Ave ... 75702
Bellaire Dr ... 75702
Belle Chase ... 75703
Belle Mere St ... 75701
Bellehaven Ct ... 75703
Bellwood Rd
1501-1897 ... 75701
1899-3200 ... 75701
3202-3498 ... 75701
3800-4499 ... 75709
Bellwood Golf Club Rd ... 75709
Belmead Ln ... 75701
Belmont Dr ... 75701
Belvedere Blvd ... 75702
Ben St ... 75701
Benbrook Dr ... 75702
S Bennett Ave ... 75701
Bent Trl ... 75707
Bent Oak Ln ... 75708
Bent Tree ... 75706
Bent Tree Ln ... 75703
Bentley Ct ... 75703
Bentridge Ct ... 75707
N Bergfield Ave ... 75702
Berkeley Dr ... 75707
Bernice Ave ... 75701
Berrinco ... 75708
Berry Dr ... 75701
Berry Ln ... 75707
Berryhill Dr ... 75702
E Berta St ... 75702
Beth Dr ... 75703
Betts St ... 75701
N & S Beverly Ave ... 75702
Bienville Dr ... 75701
Big Oak Dr ... 75707
Big Oak Bay Rd ... 75707
Big Timber Rd ... 75703
Big Tree ... 75703
Bighorn Dr ... 75707
Bill Allen Dr ... 75706
Biltmore Cir ... 75703
Birch Cir ... 75701
Birch Dr ... 75701
Birch Pl ... 75705
Bird Point Trl ... 75703
Birdwell Dr
2800-3799 ... 75701
3801-3899 ... 75701
3900-4299 ... 75703
Black Jack Rd ... 75706
S Blackwell Ave ... 75701
Blackwood Dr ... 75703
Blancas Dr ... 75709
Blanche St ... 75708
Blanco Dr ... 75707
Blarney Stone St ... 75703
Blenheim Pl ... 75703
Blossom Ln ... 75701
Blue Bird Ln ... 75703
Blue Mountain Blvd ... 75703
Bluebonnet Dr ... 75701
Boca Raton Ct ... 75703
N Bois D Arc Ave ... 75702
S Bois D Arc Ave
100-308 ... 75702
310-525 ... 75702
527-527 ... 75702
600-999 ... 75701
1001-1099 ... 75701
S Boldt Ave ... 75701
Boliver Dr ... 75702
Bonita Ln ... 75702
N & S Bonner Ave ... 75702
Bonnie Brae Cir ... 75703
S Boon Ave ... 75702

N Border Ave … 75702
Bostick Dr … 75707
Boswell St … 75701
Bourn Dr … 75708
E & W Bow St … 75702
Bowie Cir & Dr … 75701
Boyd Ave … 75701
Boyd Ln … 75703
Bracken Dr … 75701
Bradbury Ct … 75703
Bradley Ave … 75702
Bradley Ct … 75703
Bradshaw Dr … 75702
Bradshaw Rd … 75707
Brandon Ct & Dr … 75703
Brandywine Dr … 75703
Brazos Blvd … 75702
Breckenridge St … 75702
Brentwood Dr … 75701
Briar Cove Dr … 75703
Briar Creek Dr … 75703
Briaridge Dr … 75703
Briarose Ln … 75702
Briarwood Dr … 75701
Briarwood Rd … 75709
Bridgewood Trl … 75707
Brigadoon St … 75703
Bright Star Ct … 75703
Brighton Ct … 75701
Brighton Creek Cir … 75707
Britton Ave … 75701
Brixworth Dr … 75703
Broadmoore Ct … 75707
N Broadway Ave … 75702
S Broadway Ave
100-599 … 75702
600-2628 … 75701
2627-2627 … 75711
2630-4298 … 75701
2701-4299 … 75701
4300-8400 … 75703
8402-9198 … 75703
Broken Bow … 75706
Brookdale Dr … 75701
Brookhaven Dr … 75701
Brookhollow Dr
2701-2899 … 75702
7100-8199 … 75707
Brooks Ln … 75701
Brookshire Dr … 75701
Brookside Dr … 75701
Brookview Ct … 75707
Brookwood Dr
300-3999 … 75701
10100-10199 … 75707
Broussard St … 75701
Brown St … 75708
S Bruck Ave … 75702
Brunton Ct … 75703
W Bryan St … 75702
Brynmar Cir & Ct … 75703
Buck Dr … 75701
Buckboard Cir … 75703
Buckingham Pl … 75701
S Buckley Ave … 75701
Bucknell Dr … 75703
Buddie St … 75701
Buena Vista Dr … 75701
Buffalo Trl … 75703
Bullock Dr … 75704
Bunche St … 75701
Bunker Dr … 75703
Burns Dr … 75708
Burro Dr … 75707
S Butler St … 75701
Buttercup Ln … 75703
Butterfield Cir … 75703
Butterfly Crk … 75703
Byrd Ln … 75707
Cabernet Pl … 75703
Cain St … 75701
Calais Dr … 75704
Calcasieu Dr … 75703
Caldwell Blvd … 75702
E Callahan St … 75701
Calloway Rd … 75707
Calumet Dr … 75703
Cambridge Bnd, Dr & Rd … 75703
Camden Psge … 75703
W Camellia St … 75701
S Cameron Ave … 75701
E Camp St … 75702
Campus Cir … 75701
Canal … 75703
Canary Cir … 75701
Canberra Ct … 75703
Candace Pl … 75703
Candleridge Dr … 75709
Candy Ln … 75701
Canopy Oaks Dr … 75707
Canterbury Ct … 75703
Cantina Dr … 75708
Canton St … 75702
Canyon Cir … 75706
Canyon Rd … 75703
Canyon Creek Cir … 75707
Caperton Blvd … 75701
Capital Dr … 75701
Carden Ln … 75701
Cardinal St … 75701
Cardwell Ln … 75701
Carli Cir … 75703
N Carlyle Ave … 75702
Carmel Ct … 75703
Carnegie Cir … 75701
Carol Ln … 75701
Caroline Dr … 75703
Carpenter Dr … 75709
Carriage Dr … 75703
Carson Dr … 75704
Carter Blvd E & W … 75702
Cartwright St … 75701
Carver St … 75701
Cascade Rd … 75709
Cascades Blvd & Ct … 75709
Cascades Shoreline Dr … 75709
Castle Pines Ct … 75703
Castleton Way … 75703
Catherine Ct … 75703
Cecil Ave … 75702
Cedar Holw … 75708
Cedar Pl … 75705
E Cedar St … 75702
W Cedar St … 75702
Cedar Creek Dr … 75703
Cedar Hill Cir … 75703
Cedar Ridge Dr … 75708
Cedar Spur St … 75703
Cedarvale Dr … 75708
Cedarwood Cir … 75703
Centennial Pkwy … 75703
N & S Center Ave … 75702
N Central Ave … 75702
Chad Dr … 75703
Chadbourne St … 75703
Chadwick Pl … 75703
Chancery Ln … 75703
Chandler Hwy & St … 75702
Chaparrel Run … 75703
Chapel Ct & Rdg … 75707
Chapel Quarters … 75707
Chapel Woods Blvd … 75707
Chapman Rd … 75708
Charity Dr … 75709
W Charles St … 75702
Charleston Dr … 75703
Charleston Park … 75701
Charlotte Dr … 75702
Charlotte Ann Ln … 75707
E & W Charnwood St … 75701
Chase Dr … 75701
Chasewood Dr … 75703
Chelsea Dr … 75701
Cherokee Dr … 75709
Cherokee St … 75705
Cherokee Trl … 75703
Cherry St … 75704
Cherryhill Dr … 75703
Cherrylaurel Cv … 75703
Cheryl Dr
11700-12899 … 75707
13600-13799 … 75709
Chester Dr … 75701
Chestnut Dr … 75704
Cheyenne St … 75705
Chickasha Dr … 75703
S Chilton Ave
400-599 … 75702
600-2799 … 75701
Chimney Rock Dr … 75703
Chipco Dr … 75703
Chisholm Trl … 75703
Chisum Trl … 75703
Choctaw Dr … 75709
Choctaw St … 75705
Chris Ln … 75703
N Church Ave … 75702
Churchill Dr … 75703
Cimmarron Dr … 75709
Cimmarron Trl … 75703
Circle Dr … 75703
Cityview Dr … 75708
Clarion Ln … 75707
Clark St … 75701
W Claude St … 75702
N Clayton Ave … 75702
S Clayton Ave
100-110 … 75702
112-521 … 75702
523-599 … 75702
600-626 … 75701
628-700 … 75701
702-1598 … 75701
Clear Cove Dr … 75703
Clemson Cir & Dr … 75703
Clemera … 75704
Clinic Dr … 75701
Cloverdale Dr
3400-4099 … 75701
4900-5299 … 75703
Club Cir … 75702
Club Lake Dr … 75702
Clubview Dr … 75701
Clyde Dr … 75701
W Cochran St … 75702
Colby Cir … 75707
Cold Water Cv & Dr … 75703
Coleman St … 75704
Colgate Ave … 75701
Colina Trl … 75707
N College Ave … 75702
S College Ave
100-509 … 75702
511-599 … 75702
600-2099 … 75701
Colonial Cir & Dr … 75701
Colony Park Dr … 75701
Colston Dr … 75703
Colt Ln … 75703
Columbia Dr … 75703
Commanche Trl … 75707
E Commerce St
800-898 … 75702
900-2599 … 75702
2601-2699 … 75702
2700-2799 … 75708
Commons Dr … 75701
Commonwealth Dr … 75702
Community Ln … 75706
Concord Pl … 75701
N Confederate Ave … 75702
S Confederate Ave
101-199 … 75702
432-598 … 75702
600-632 … 75701
634-999 … 75701
W Connally St … 75701
Constantine Ave … 75708
Contenders Way … 75703
Conway Ln … 75709
Cooks Xing … 75703
Cope St … 75702
Copeland Dr … 75703
Copper Cir & Ct … 75706
Copper Ridge Blvd … 75706
Copperoaks Dr … 75703
Cordoba Dr … 75707
Cornell Pl … 75701
Cornerstone Trl … 75701
Cottage Dr … 75701
Cotten Rd … 75704
Cottonwood Cir … 75701
Cottonwood Dr … 75706
Country Gln & Vw … 75706
Country Estates Dr … 75708
Country Hills Blvd … 75708
Country Oaks Dr … 75706
County Road 1100 … 75703
County Road 1101 … 75703
County Road 1111 … 75704
County Road 1113
11100-14000 … 75709
County Road 1113
14001-14097 … 75703
14002-14098 … 75709
14099-15799 … 75703
16300-16399 … 75708
County Road 1114 … 75709
County Road 1115 … 75709
County Road 1117 … 75709
County Road 1118 … 75709
County Road 112 … 75703
County Road 1120 … 75704
County Road 1121 … 75709
County Road 1124 … 75709
County Road 1125
500-7999 … 75704
8700-8798 … 75709
8800-14099 … 75709
14301-14397 … 75703
14399-15799 … 75703
County Road 1126 … 75709
County Road 1128 … 75704
County Road 113 … 75703
County Road 1130 … 75703
County Road 1131 … 75703
County Road 1134 … 75709
County Road 1138 … 75709
County Road 1139 … 75709
County Road 1140 … 75709
County Road 1141
8900-13499 … 75709
13500-14399 … 75703
County Road 1143 … 75704
County Road 1145 … 75704
County Road 1146 … 75704
County Road 1147 N & S … 75704
County Road 1148 … 75704
County Road 1149 … 75704
County Road 115 … 75703
County Road 1150 … 75704
County Road 1151 … 75704
County Road 1155 N … 75704
County Road 116 … 75703
County Road 1161 … 75703
County Road 1168 … 75703
County Road 1169 … 75703
County Road 1184 … 75704
County Road 1185 … 75704
County Road 1188 … 75709
County Road 119 … 75703
County Road 1192 … 75709
County Road 1204 … 75703
County Road 1205 … 75703
County Road 1206 … 75703
County Road 1207 … 75703
County Road 1208 … 75703
County Road 1209 … 75703
County Road 1211 … 75703
County Road 1216 … 75703
County Road 1217 … 75703
County Road 1218 … 75703
County Road 122 … 75703
County Road 1222 … 75709
County Road 1223 … 75709
County Road 1227 … 75709
County Road 1235 … 75709
County Road 1237 … 75703
County Road 1238 … 75709
County Road 1248 … 75709
County Road 1250 … 75709
County Road 1252 … 75709
County Road 1267 … 75704
County Road 1275 … 75703
County Road 1283 … 75709
County Road 1289 … 75709
County Road 129 … 75703
County Road 1293 … 75703
County Road 1295 … 75704
County Road 1297 … 75704
County Road 130 … 75703
County Road 1303 … 75704
County Road 131 … 75703
County Road 1319 … 75703
County Road 1346 … 75709
County Road 136 … 75703
County Road 145 … 75703
County Road 146 … 75703
County Road 147 … 75703
County Road 15 … 75703
County Road 152 E & W … 75703
County Road 154 … 75703
County Road 159 … 75703
County Road 164 … 75703
County Road 165 … 75703
County Road 166 … 75703
County Road 167 … 75703
County Road 168 … 75703
County Road 178 … 75703
County Road 180 … 75703
County Road 192 … 75703
County Road 193 … 75703
County Road 194 … 75703
County Road 195 … 75703
County Road 196 … 75703
County Road 198 … 75703
County Road 21
200-2999 … 75705
4000-10399 … 75707
County Road 210 … 75707
County Road 211 N … 75708
County Road 211 S … 75707
County Road 212 … 75707
County Road 2120 … 75707
County Road 2121 … 75707
County Road 2122 … 75707
County Road 2123 … 75707
County Road 213 … 75707
County Road 214 … 75707
County Road 215 … 75707
County Road 219 … 75707
County Road 2190 … 75707
County Road 220 … 75707
County Road 2202 … 75707
County Road 2205 … 75707
County Road 2206 … 75707
County Road 2208 … 75705
County Road 2209 … 75707
County Road 221 … 75707
County Road 2210 … 75707
County Road 2213 … 75707
County Road 2215 … 75707
County Road 2216 … 75707
County Road 2219 … 75707
County Road 2223 … 75707
County Road 2225 … 75707
County Road 223 … 75707
County Road 2241 … 75707
County Road 2243 … 75707
County Road 2245 … 75707
County Road 2246 … 75707
County Road 2247 … 75707
County Road 2248 … 75707
County Road 2249 … 75707
County Road 225 … 75707
County Road 2250 … 75707
County Road 2253 … 75707
County Road 2254 … 75707
County Road 2255 … 75708
County Road 2256 … 75705
County Road 2258 … 75707
County Road 2259 … 75707
County Road 226 … 75707
County Road 2262 … 75707
County Road 2265 … 75707
County Road 2273 … 75707
County Road 2278 … 75707
County Road 2279 … 75705
County Road 228 E … 75707
County Road 2285 … 75707
County Road 2286 … 75707
County Road 2292 … 75707
County Road 2293 … 75707
County Road 2298 … 75707
County Road 23 … 75705
County Road 2301 … 75707
County Road 2305 … 75707
County Road 2306 … 75707
County Road 2315 … 75707
County Road 2320 … 75707
County Road 2326 … 75707
County Road 233
500-3899 … 75705
4001-5797 … 75707
5799-10599 … 75707
County Road 2331 … 75707
County Road 2335 … 75707
County Road 2337 … 75707
County Road 234 … 75707
County Road 2344 … 75707
County Road 2347 … 75708
County Road 235 … 75707
County Road 236 … 75705
County Road 237 … 75705
County Road 238 … 75705
County Road 24 … 75705
County Road 240 … 75705
County Road 246 N & S … 75705
County Road 25 … 75705
County Road 26
13400-19899 … 75707
20100-21399 … 75705
County Road 262 … 75707
County Road 27 … 75707
County Road 272 … 75707
County Road 273 … 75707
County Road 274 … 75707
County Road 278 … 75707
County Road 279 … 75705
County Road 28 … 75707
County Road 280 … 75707
County Road 284 … 75707
County Road 285 … 75707
County Road 287 … 75707
County Road 288 … 75707
County Road 289 … 75707
County Road 290 … 75707
County Road 291 … 75707
County Road 293 … 75707
County Road 310 E & W … 75706
County Road 311 … 75706
County Road 312 … 75706
County Road 3126 … 75708
County Road 313 E
100-10699 … 75706
11200-13799 … 75708
County Road 313 W … 75706
County Road 3133 … 75708
County Road 314 … 75706
County Road 3140 … 75706
County Road 3146 … 75706
County Road 3147 … 75706
County Road 3150 … 75708
County Road 3151 … 75708
County Road 3152 … 75708
County Road 3156 … 75708
County Road 3157 … 75708
County Road 3158 … 75708
County Road 3159 … 75708
County Road 317 … 75706
County Road 3173 … 75706
County Road 3174 … 75708
County Road 318 … 75706
County Road 3180 … 75706
County Road 3183 … 75708
County Road 319 E & W … 75706
County Road 3190 … 75706
County Road 3193 … 75706
County Road 32 … 75706
County Road 320 … 75706
County Road 3201 … 75706
County Road 3205 … 75708
County Road 3216 … 75705
County Road 322 … 75706
County Road 326 E & W … 75706
County Road 328 E
300-3099 … 75706
3300-4599 … 75708
County Road 328 W … 75706
County Road 329 … 75706
County Road 330 … 75708
County Road 331 … 75708
County Road 333 … 75708
County Road 334
100-1799 … 75706
2100-12599 … 75708
County Road 335 … 75708
County Road 336 … 75708
County Road 337 … 75708
County Road 339 … 75706
County Road 34 … 75706
County Road 340 … 75706
County Road 341 … 75706
County Road 342 … 75706
County Road 343 … 75708
County Road 347 … 75706
County Road 35 … 75706
County Road 353 … 75708
County Road 37 … 75706
County Road 376 … 75708
County Road 379 … 75708
County Road 38 … 75706
County Road 380 … 75708
County Road 381 … 75708
County Road 382 … 75708
County Road 383 … 75708
County Road 384 … 75708
County Road 385 … 75708
County Road 386 … 75708
County Road 388 … 75708
County Road 389 … 75705
County Road 39 … 75706
County Road 390 … 75705
County Road 391 … 75708
County Road 392 … 75708
County Road 393 … 75708
County Road 395 … 75708
County Road 396 … 75708
County Road 397 … 75708
County Road 398 … 75705
County Road 41 … 75706
County Road 410 … 75704
County Road 411
10600-12299 … 75704
12500-15099 … 75706
County Road 412
11900-12999 … 75704
13000-13099 … 75706
13101-13299 … 75706
County Road 413 … 75704
County Road 4134 … 75704
County Road 4135 … 75704
County Road 4136 … 75706
County Road 4138 … 75706
County Road 414 … 75704
County Road 4149 … 75704
County Road 415 … 75704
County Road 4150 … 75704
County Road 4153 … 75704
County Road 4155 … 75704
County Road 4156 … 75706
County Road 4159 … 75706
County Road 416 … 75704
County Road 4160 … 75706
County Road 4162 … 75704
County Road 4163 … 75704
County Road 4165 … 75704
County Road 4167 … 75704
County Road 4168 … 75706
County Road 417 … 75704
County Road 4170 … 75704
County Road 4172 … 75704
County Road 4173 … 75704

County Road 4175 ... 75706
County Road 4176 ... 75704
County Road 418 ... 75704
County Road 4180 E &
W ... 75704
County Road 419 ... 75704
County Road 42 ... 75704
County Road 420 ... 75704
County Road 4201 ... 75704
County Road 4202 ... 75704
County Road 4203 ... 75706
County Road 421 ... 75704
County Road 4215 ... 75706
County Road 4218 ... 75704
County Road 4220 ... 75706
County Road 427
3200-5899 ... 75704
7801-7897 ... 75706
7899-9399 ... 75706
County Road 428 ... 75704
County Road 429
7900-10899 ... 75704
11000-11199 ... 75706
County Road 43 ... 75704
County Road 431 ... 75706
County Road 433
11300-12099 ... 75704
12500-15699 ... 75706
15701-15799 ... 75706
County Road 45 ... 75704
County Road 46 ... 75704
County Road 461 ... 75706
County Road 463 ... 75706
County Road 468
12200-13026 ... 75706
13027-13029 ... 75704
13028-13030 ... 75706
13031-14099 ... 75706
County Road 469 ... 75706
County Road 47 ... 75704
County Road 470 ... 75704
County Road 471
12500-15799 ... 75706
15900-16099 ... 75704
County Road 472 ... 75706
County Road 475 ... 75706
County Road 48 ... 75704
County Road 485 ... 75706
County Road 486 ... 75706
County Road 487 ... 75706
County Road 488 ... 75706
County Road 489 ... 75706
County Road 49 ... 75704
County Road 490 ... 75706
County Road 492 ... 75706
County Road 493 ... 75706
County Road 494 ... 75706
County Road 495 ... 75706
County Road 496 ... 75706
Couples Ct ... 75709
Court Crst & Rdg ... 75703
Courtney Dr ... 75701
Courtview ... 75703
Coventry Rd ... 75703
Covewood Dr ... 75703
Covey Ln ... 75703
Craftdale St ... 75701
Craig Ct ... 75702
Creek Bend Dr ... 75707
Creekside Cir & Dr ... 75703
Creekview Cir & Trl ... 75707
Crescent Cir ... 75703
Crescent Ct ... 75703
Crescent Dr ... 75702
Crestridge ... 75707
Crestview Dr ... 75707
Crestview St ... 75701
Crestway Dr
400-599 ... 75702
700-799 ... 75701
Crestwood Dr ... 75701
Cripple Creek Dr
3200-3499 ... 75707
15200-15598 ... 75703
15600-15899 ... 75703
Criss St ... 75701

Crockett Dr ... 75701
Crooked Trl ... 75703
Crosby St ... 75701
Cross Rd ... 75703
Cross Creek Cir ... 75703
Cross Fence Trl ... 75706
Cross Timbers Rd ... 75705
Crow Rd ... 75703
Crumpler ... 75707
W Cumberland Rd ... 75703
Curtis Dr ... 75701
Cushing Dr ... 75702
Cypress Cir ... 75703
Danica Dr ... 75701
Danley Ave ... 75701
N Dargan Ave ... 75702
Darrell Ln ... 75701
Dartmouth Dr ... 75701
Dave St ... 75701
David Dr ... 75703
Davis St ... 75701
Dawn Ln ... 75709
E Dawson St ... 75701
Dayton St ... 75702
Dc Dr ... 75701
Deauville St ... 75704
Debby Ln ... 75701
Decharles St ... 75701
Deepwood Dr ... 75703
Deer Creek Dr ... 75707
Deer Ridge Ln ... 75703
Deerbrook Dr ... 75703
Deerfield Dr ... 75703
Deerwood Dr ... 75703
Del Norte Dr ... 75703
Delano Rd ... 75701
Delaware St ... 75708
N Della Ave ... 75702
Delmar Dr ... 75701
Dennis Dr ... 75701
Dennis Ln ... 75703
Depriest Ave ... 75701
Derrick Ct ... 75703
E Devine St ... 75701
Devonshire Dr ... 75703
Diane St ... 75708
Dietz Ln ... 75701
Dinah Ln ... 75701
Division Ave ... 75702
E & W Dixie Ln ... 75706
Dixson Rd ... 75703
E Dobbs St ... 75701
W Dobbs St ... 75701
Dobbs Ter ... 75706
Dockside Ct ... 75703
Doctors Dr ... 75701
E Dodge St ... 75701
Dogwood St ... 75701
Dolores St ... 75703
Dominion Plz ... 75703
E Don St ... 75701
Donna Dr ... 75702
Donnybrook Ave ... 75703
S Donnybrook Ave ... 75701
Doral Pl ... 75703
Dorchester Dr ... 75703
Douglas Blvd ... 75702
Dover Ln ... 75703
Downing St ... 75703
W Drake Pl ... 75702
Dreamcatcher ... 75703
Dressage Ln ... 75703
Drexel Pl ... 75701
Driftwood Dr ... 75707
Driftwood Ln ... 75701
Dry Creek Rd ... 75705
Dublin Ave ... 75703
Duchess Dr ... 75701
Duckenfield Ave ... 75701
Dudley Dr ... 75709
Dueling Oaks Dr ... 75703
E Dulse St ... 75701
E Duncan St ... 75702
Dundee Dr ... 75703
Dunmore Dr ... 75703
Duran Ln ... 75706

Eagle St ... 75701
Eagles Nest Blvd ... 75703
Eaglewood Cir & Dr ... 75703
Earl Campbell Pkwy ... 75701
E Earle St ... 75702
Earlene St ... 75708
Eastgate Dr ... 75703
Eastside Rd ... 75707
Easy St
1400-1599 ... 75701
1700-4499 ... 75703
Echo Ln ... 75708
Echo Glen Dr ... 75703
Edgar Ln ... 75708
Edgewood Dr ... 75701
Edinburgh Dr ... 75703
N Edwards Ave ... 75702
Eileen St ... 75701
Eisenhower Dr ... 75704
El Cerrito Pl ... 75703
Elaine Dr ... 75703
Elderwood Dr ... 75703
Eldorado Dr ... 75705
Eleanor St ... 75708
Elgem St ... 75701
Elizabeth Dr ... 75701
Elk River Rd ... 75703
Elkton Trl ... 75703
N Ellis Ave ... 75702
W Ellis Dr ... 75701
E & W Elm St ... 75702
Elm Tree Cir ... 75703
Elmridge Dr ... 75703
Elmwood St ... 75706
N Emerson Ave ... 75702
Emily Ln ... 75701
Emma St ... 75701
N Emmett Ave ... 75702
Emory Ct ... 75703
N Englewood Ave ... 75702
S Englewood Ave
101-197 ... 75702
199-299 ... 75702
600-1999 ... 75701
Epps Ave ... 75708
Equestrian Ln ... 75703
Erin Dr ... 75701
Erma St ... 75701
Erwin St W
12190-12198 ... 75704
E Erwin St
101-207 ... 75702
209-2699 ... 75702
2700-2999 ... 75708
W Erwin St
100-198 ... 75702
Esperanza Pl ... 75703
Estates Dr ... 75703
Estrella Del Mar Dr ... 75703
Evansburg Ln ... 75703
Everett Dr ... 75706
Everglades Dr ... 75703
Fair Ln ... 75701
Faircroft Dr ... 75703
Fairfax Dr ... 75701
Fairlawn Dr ... 75702
Fairmead Cir ... 75703
S Fairmont Ave ... 75702
Fairmont Dr ... 75701
Fairway Ave ... 75702
Faith Ln ... 75701
Fallcrest ... 75703
Fallmeadow Dr ... 75703
Fannie St ... 75701
N Fannin Ave ... 75702
S Fannin Ave
100-198 ... 75702
200-599 ... 75702
600-1299 ... 75701
Fannin Pkwy ... 75708
E Faulkner St ... 75701
N & S Fenton Ave ... 75702
E Ferdell St ... 75701
E & W Ferguson St ... 75702
Fernwood Dr ... 75701
Ferrell Pl ... 75702

Festoon Ct ... 75703
W Fields St ... 75702
Fillbrook Ln ... 75707
Firestone Cir ... 75703
Fisher Dr ... 75701
Flagstaff Dr ... 75707
Flagstone Dr ... 75707
Flat Rock Ln ... 75703
Fleetwood Dr ... 75701
N Fleishel Ave ... 75702
S Fleishel Ave
101-197 ... 75702
199-599 ... 75702
600-2599 ... 75701
Fleta Ct ... 75703
Flint St ... 75701
Fm 14 ... 75706
Fm 16 E ... 75706
Fm 16 W
100-5099 ... 75706
Fm 16 W
22100-22199 ... 75708
Fm 1995 ... 75704
Fm 2015
9300-14299 ... 75708
14300-18699 ... 75706
Fm 2016
10600-11699 ... 75706
11700-12299 ... 75704
Fm 206 ... 75709
Fm 2261 ... 75704
Fm 2493 ... 75703
Fm 2661
200-11199 ... 75704
11200-11799 ... 75709
Fm 2767
2900-14299 ... 75708
14300-17699 ... 75705
Fm 279 ... 75704
Fm 2908
400-498 ... 75705
500-2299 ... 75705
3300-11599 ... 75708
Fm 2964 ... 75707
Fm 3226 ... 75707
Fm 3270 ... 75708
Fm 3271
11800-11999 ... 75706
12100-13799 ... 75704
Fm 3311 ... 75708
Fm 344 E ... 75703
Fm 346 E ... 75703
Fm 724 ... 75704
Fm 756 ... 75703
Fm 757
100-3399 ... 75705
12300-12599 ... 75708
Fm 848 ... 75707
Fm 850
4100-4199 ... 75708
4200-11499 ... 75705
11500-15399 ... 75707
Forbes Rd ... 75703
E Ford St ... 75701
N Forest Ave ... 75702
Forestwood Blvd ... 75703
Foster St ... 75701
Fox Rdg ... 75709
Fox Cove St ... 75703
Fox Hollow Dr ... 75703
Foxcroft Rd ... 75703
Foxglove Cir & Ln ... 75703
Foxwood Cir ... 75703
Franchel St ... 75701
S Francis St ... 75701
N Frank Ave ... 75702
E & W Franklin St ... 75702
Frankston Hwy ... 75701
Frazier St ... 75701
Freliste ... 75705
E & W Front St ... 75702
Frostwood Dr ... 75703
Fry Ave ... 75701
N Fuller Ave ... 75702
Furman Ct ... 75703
G E Dr ... 75701

Gabriel Dr ... 75701
Gaelic Hills Dr ... 75703
Gail Ln ... 75701
Gallion Ave & Cir ... 75708
Garden Lake Rd ... 75703
Garden Park Cir ... 75703
Garden Valley Rd ... 75702
Gardner Ave ... 75701
Garland St ... 75704
Garrett Dr ... 75703
N Gaston Ave ... 75702
S Gaston Ave ... 75701
Gateridge Dr ... 75703
Gatewood Dr ... 75703
Gaut Ave ... 75708
Gena Dr ... 75709
E Gentry Pkwy
500-2023 ... 75702
2400-2799 ... 75708
W Gentry Pkwy ... 75702
Gentry St ... 75704
N George Ave ... 75702
George Dr ... 75703
Gilmore Rd ... 75704
Gish Ln
1400-1499 ... 75707
1500-3699 ... 75701
3701-3799 ... 75701
Glascow Rd ... 75707
N Glass Ave ... 75702
Glen Abbey Ln ... 75703
Glen Arbor St ... 75703
Glen Cove Cir ... 75701
Glenbrook Dr ... 75701
Glenda Ave ... 75704
Glendale Dr ... 75701
Gleneagles Dr ... 75703
Glenhaven Dr ... 75701
Glenrose St ... 75701
Glenview Ave ... 75701
N Glenwood Blvd ... 75702
S Glenwood Blvd
105-197 ... 75702
199-599 ... 75702
601-619 ... 75701
621-1499 ... 75701
1501-1599 ... 75701
W Glenwood Blvd ... 75701
Gloucester Dr ... 75707
E & W Gold St ... 75702
Gold Leaf Ct ... 75707
Golden Rd ... 75701
Golden Oaks Dr ... 75703
Golf Ave ... 75702
Goliad St ... 75701
W Goodman St ... 75702
Goss St ... 75701
Grace Ave ... 75707
Graemont Blvd ... 75703
Graham Dr ... 75701
Granbury Ct ... 75707
N Grand Ave ... 75702
Grand Coteau ... 75703
Grand Oaks Cir ... 75703
E & W Grande Blvd ... 75703
Grandview St ... 75704
E Granville St ... 75702
Grassy Ridge Ln ... 75703
Gray St ... 75702
Great Oaks Cir ... 75703
Green Ln & St ... 75701
Green Berry Dr ... 75707
Green Ridge Cv ... 75703
Green Valley Ln ... 75703
Greenbriar Lake Rd ... 75709
Greenhill Dr ... 75703
Greenland Blvd ... 75704
Greenland Hl ... 75702
Greenoak Pl ... 75701
Greenock Ct ... 75703
Greenway Cir ... 75701
Greenwood Ln ... 75701
Greer Dr ... 75703
Greg Ln ... 75701
Gretna Green Ln ... 75703
W Grove St ... 75701

Grubbs St ... 75706
Guinn Dr ... 75701
Guinn Farms Rd ... 75707
Habitat Cir ... 75701
Haden St ... 75701
Hall St ... 75701
Hallmark Pl ... 75701
Hallye Ln ... 75703
Hampton Ln ... 75701
Hampton Rd ... 75708
Hampton Hill Dr ... 75703
Hamvasy Ln ... 75701
Hancock Dr ... 75707
Handley Dr ... 75708
E Hankerson St ... 75701
Hanover Pl ... 75701
Hansford Pl ... 75701
Happy Acres ... 75706
W Harmony St ... 75702
Harpole St ... 75702
N Harris Ave ... 75702
Harvard Dr ... 75703
Harvestwood Dr ... 75703
Harwood Dr ... 75701
Havens Trl ... 75707
Haverhill Dr ... 75707
N Hawthorne Ave ... 75702
Hayes Ave ... 75707
N Haynie Ave ... 75702
Heather Ln ... 75703
Hebron Rd ... 75708
Heines Dr ... 75701
Hemingway ... 75701
Henderson Dr ... 75701
Henson Ave ... 75701
E & W Heritage Cir &
Dr ... 75703
Hermitage Ct ... 75703
S Herndon Ave ... 75702
Hichilla ... 75706
W Hickory St ... 75702
Hidden Lake Dr ... 75703
S High Ave ... 75702
High Point Cir ... 75703
S Highland Ave ... 75701
Highland Park Cir &
Ct ... 75701
Highlands Ct & Ln ... 75703
Highmeadow Dr ... 75703
Highmont Ct ... 75703
Highridge St ... 75709
Hightech Dr ... 75703
N Hill Ave ... 75702
S Hill Ave ... 75702
N Hill Rd ... 75706
Hill N Dale Rd ... 75709
Hillcrest Ave ... 75702
Hillcrest Rd ... 75708
E & W Hillsboro St ... 75702
Hillside Dr
2700-2899 ... 75707
9900-10098 ... 75709
10100-10300 ... 75709
10302-10398 ... 75709
12100-18998 ... 75703
19000-19299 ... 75703
Hilltop Dr ... 75701
Hillview Rd ... 75703
Hinson St ... 75708
Hitts Lake Rd ... 75706
Hobbs Rd ... 75708
Hogan Ct & Dr ... 75709
Holcomb Cir ... 75703
Holiday Ln ... 75703
Holiday Pkwy ... 75704
Holiday Hills Cir & Rd ... 75708
Holley St ... 75701
Hollow Oak Cir ... 75707
Hollowbrook Dr ... 75707
Holly Creek Dr ... 75703
Holly Hill Dr ... 75703
Holly Leaf Dr ... 75703
Holly Square Ct ... 75703
Holly Star Dr ... 75703
Hollybranch Dr ... 75703
Hollybrook Dr ... 75703

Hollyglen Dr ... 75703
Hollylake Cir ... 75703
Hollyoak Dr ... 75703
Hollyridge Dr ... 75703
Hollystone Dr ... 75703
Hollytree Cir, Dr & Pl ... 75703
Hollywest Dr ... 75703
N Holmes Ave ... 75702
Holtz Claw Dr ... 75706
Homestead Ln ... 75701
Honor Ln ... 75708
N & S Horace Ave ... 75702
N Horn Ave ... 75702
Horseshoe Ln ... 75708
Horseshoe Trl ... 75702
Hospital Dr ... 75701
N House Ave ... 75702
E & W Houston St ... 75702
Howard Dr ... 75701
Hoyt Rd ... 75706
Hubbard Dr ... 75703
Huckabee St ... 75709
Huckleberry Hl ... 75703
Hudnall Dr ... 75701
E Hudson St ... 75701
Hughey Dr ... 75701
Hunt St ... 75701
Hunter St ... 75701
Hunters Ct ... 75702
Huntington Dr ... 75703
Huntwick Ln ... 75703
Hurst Dr ... 75703
S Hurt Ave ... 75701
Hyde Park Dr ... 75701
Iberia Dr ... 75703
Iberville Dr ... 75701
E Idel St ... 75701
Idlewood Dr ... 75701
Independence Pl ... 75703
Indian Dr ... 75709
Indian Trce ... 75708
Indian Springs Dr ... 75703
N Industrial Ave
2200-2699 ... 75702
2701-2799 ... 75702
2900-3099 ... 75708
Inner Cir ... 75703
Interstate 20 E
401-597 ... 75706
Interstate 20 E
599-699 ... 75706
11100-16999 ... 75708
Interstate 20 W ... 75706
Inverness Dr ... 75703
Inwood Cir ... 75701
Irish Moss Dr ... 75703
Itten Dr ... 75701
Ivy Trl ... 75703
J Cupit Ct ... 75709
Jackie Ave ... 75701
Jackson Ave ... 75705
W Jackson St ... 75701
Jade Forest Trl ... 75707
James Ave ... 75706
Jamestown Dr ... 75701
Jan Ave ... 75701
Janan Dr ... 75707
S Jarrel Ave ... 75701
Jaysid St ... 75706
S Jean Ave ... 75702
Jeb Stuart Dr ... 75703
Jeff Davis Dr ... 75703
Jefferson Ave ... 75706
Jeffery Dr ... 75703
Jennifer Dr ... 75703
Jersey St ... 75701
Jessie Hale Rd ... 75707
Jewell Ln ... 75703
Jill Cir ... 75701
Jimmie St ... 75708
Jimmy Frank St ... 75706
Jo Bar Dr ... 75703
Joe St ... 75702
Joel Dr ... 75703
N John Ave ... 75702
John Carney Dr ... 75701

E Jones St ... 75702
Joni Dr ... 75709
Jordan St ... 75702
Jordan Plaza Blvd ... 75704
Joseph Dr ... 75702
Joseph Rd ... 75707
Joy Dr ... 75703
Julia Dr ... 75708
Juniper Ln ... 75701
Juniper Pl ... 75705
Kallan Ave ... 75703
Kara Lynn Pl ... 75704
Karen Dr ... 75703
Karren Ave ... 75708
Kathy Cir ... 75702
Katie Dr ... 75703
S Keaton Ave ... 75701
Keenan Dr ... 75701
Kelli Dr ... 75703
Kelly Green St ... 75703
Kellywood Ln ... 75706
Kenilworth Ave ... 75702
Kennebunk Ln ... 75703
S Kennedy Ave ... 75701
Kennedy Rd ... 75702
Kenshire Dr ... 75706
Kensington Dr ... 75703
Kent Dr ... 75707
Kevin Dr ... 75703
Keystone Dr ... 75704
Kiamichi Dr ... 75703
Kidd Dr ... 75703
Kilrush Dr ... 75703
Kimwood Ln ... 75703
King St ... 75701
Kingsbury Dr ... 75701
Kingsmill Cir ... 75703
Kingspark Dr ... 75703
Kingston Ct ... 75703
Kingswood Dr & Pl ... 75703
Kinsey Dr ... 75703
Kirkcaldey Dr ... 75703
Knob Hill Dr ... 75701
Knollwood Dr ... 75703
Knowles Trce ... 75708
Knoxville Dr ... 75703
Koberlin St ... 75703
Kyle Dr ... 75706
La Mobile Ave ... 75707
La Vista Dr ... 75703
Lacebark Cir ... 75703
Lacosta Dr ... 75703
Lafayette Dr ... 75703
Lafourche ... 75703
Lake Rd E ... 75709
Lake Rd W ... 75709
E Lake St ... 75701
Lake Forest Dr ... 75707
Lake Pines Dr ... 75707
Lake Placid Rd ... 75701
Lake Pointe Cv ... 75703
Lake Vista Cir ... 75707
Lakeland Dr ... 75708
Lakemont Dr ... 75707
Lakepine Cir ... 75707
Lakeshore Dr
7600-10799 ... 75707
18900-19599 ... 75703
E Lakeshore Dr ... 75709
W Lakeshore Dr ... 75709
Lakeside Ct ... 75707
Lakeside Dr ... 75707
Lakeside Ln ... 75703
Lakeview Ave ... 75701
Lakeview Rd ... 75704
Lakeway Dr
8000-8500 ... 75703
8502-8598 ... 75703
11800-11999 ... 75704
Lakewood Dr ... 75702
Lamar St ... 75701
Lamb Dr ... 75709
Lamern Dr ... 75707
Lamont Dr ... 75708
Lamont St ... 75701
Lamp Post Cv ... 75703

Lamplight Ln ... 75701
Lancashire Dr ... 75703
Laney Rd ... 75708
Lansdowne Ter ... 75703
Lariate Cir ... 75704
Larkridge St ... 75709
Larkspur Ln ... 75703
Larry Ln ... 75709
Las Palmas Dr ... 75707
Las Vegas Dr ... 75704
Latosha Ln ... 75706
Laurel Pl ... 75701
E Laurel St ... 75702
Laurel Springs Ln ... 75703
Laurelwood Dr ... 75703
Lawler Pl ... 75702
Lawndale Dr ... 75701
E Lawrence St ... 75702
Lazy Ln ... 75703
Lazy Acres Ln ... 75707
Lazy Creek Dr ... 75707
Le Harve Dr ... 75704
Leard Ln ... 75701
Lee St ... 75702
Lehigh Pl ... 75701
Leisure Ln ... 75703
Lemay Dr ... 75704
Lemmert Dr ... 75709
Lenora Ave ... 75702
S Lenox St ... 75701
Leo Lynn St ... 75703
Leon Dr ... 75702
Letha Ct ... 75702
Levine Aly ... 75702
Lex Ave ... 75702
Lexington Dr ... 75701
Libbie St ... 75707
N Liberty Ave ... 75702
Light Horse Ct ... 75703
Lila Ln ... 75707
Limerick St ... 75703
Linda Ave ... 75708
Lindale Industrial Pkwy ... 75706
Lindbergh St ... 75703
Lindsey Ln ... 75701
E & W Line St ... 75702
Lingner Dr ... 75701
Linwood Dr ... 75707
Linwood St ... 75708
Lisa Ln ... 75701
Littlefield Dr ... 75708
Live Oak St
2400-2499 ... 75702
16200-16499 ... 75707
Lively Ln ... 75702
Loblolly Ln ... 75701
E & W Locust St ... 75702
Loftin St ... 75701
W Lollar St ... 75702
Londonderry Dr ... 75703
Lonetree Cir ... 75706
Long Leaf Dr ... 75707
Lookout Ct ... 75708
W Lorance St ... 75702
Lori Ln ... 75709
Louise Ct ... 75709
Low Ave ... 75708
Luann Ln ... 75703
N Luberta St ... 75702
Lucky Ave ... 75708
Luther St ... 75701
N Lyndon Ave ... 75702
Lynn Dr ... 75702
Lynwood Dr ... 75701
S Lyons Ave
200-799 ... 75702
800-1399 ... 75701
1401-1599 ... 75701
Macallan Cv ... 75703
Macarthur St ... 75704
Macbeth Ct ... 75703
N Machalls Ave ... 75702
Macon St ... 75701
Madera Dr ... 75707
Madison St ... 75701
Magnolia Dr ... 75701

S Mahon Ave
100-599 ... 75702
700-1799 ... 75701
S Main St ... 75706
Malabar Dr ... 75701
Malisa Cir ... 75707
Mallory Ct ... 75703
Manassas Ln ... 75703
Manchester Ct ... 75703
Mandy Ln ... 75703
Manhatton Dr ... 75701
Manilee Ln ... 75702
Manorway St ... 75702
Mansion Creek Cir ... 75707
Maple Dr ... 75709
Maple Rdg ... 75708
W Maple St ... 75702
Maple Leaf Ct ... 75707
Maplewood Pl ... 75702
Marcella Cir ... 75709
Marian St ... 75701
Marilyn Dr ... 75701
Mark Dr ... 75709
Mark Hayes Ct ... 75709
Market Dr ... 75701
Market Square Blvd ... 75703
Marlee Ct ... 75706
Marquette Ln ... 75703
Martha St ... 75702
Martha Carol Ln ... 75707
Martin Ln ... 75701
E Martin Luther King Jr Blvd ... 75702
W Martin Luther King Jr Blvd
100-2101 ... 75702
2100-2100 ... 75710
2100-2100 ... 75712
2103-2299 ... 75702
Mary Ln ... 75701
Mary Ann St ... 75708
Massey Ave
1501-1599 ... 75702
11900-12599 ... 75708
Masters Cir ... 75701
Matise St ... 75706
Matney Ln ... 75707
Matt Ln ... 75701
Mattie St ... 75706
Maxine Dr ... 75709
Maxwell Dr ... 75702
May St ... 75702
Mccain Dr ... 75702
Mcclain St ... 75701
Mcclenny Dr ... 75703
Mccormick Ln ... 75701
Mccullar Dr ... 75702
Mccurley Dr ... 75702
Mcdonald Rd ... 75701
Mcgowan Dr ... 75707
Mckellar Rd ... 75702
Mckenzie Dr ... 75701
Mcmillan Dr ... 75701
Mcmurrey Dr ... 75702
Mcnew St ... 75702
Meadow Ln ... 75702
Meadow Creek Dr ... 75703
Meadowglen Ct ... 75707
Meadowland Ct ... 75707
Meadowlark Ln ... 75701
Meadowood Ln ... 75703
Medical Dr ... 75701
Medina Dr ... 75701
Melanie Ct ... 75707
Melba Dr & Pl ... 75701
Melinda Ln ... 75702
Melody Ln ... 75701
Melrose Ave ... 75701
Melwood Pl ... 75706
Memory Ln ... 75701
Merlot Ln ... 75703
Merrill Dr ... 75701
Merrimac St ... 75701
Merry Ln ... 75701
Mesa Dr ... 75704
Mesquite Dr ... 75707

Meyer Ave ... 75701
Michael St ... 75706
S Mike Ave ... 75702
Milam Dr ... 75701
Mill Ct ... 75703
Mill Creek Dr ... 75703
Miller Dr ... 75701
Millpond Ln ... 75706
Mills Dr ... 75703
Milwood Pl ... 75703
Mimosa Dr ... 75701
E & W Mims St ... 75702
Mineola Hwy ... 75702
Mirabeau Dr ... 75703
Mistletoe Cir ... 75701
Mitchell Ave ... 75701
Mobile Dr ... 75703
Mobley Ln ... 75707
Mockingbird Ln ... 75701
Mohave Dr ... 75704
Monarch Rd ... 75707
Mondalli Dr ... 75701
Monroe St ... 75701
Montgomery Gdns ... 75708
Montrose Dr ... 75701
N Moore Ave ... 75702
Moorehill Dr ... 75701
Moorhead St ... 75701
Morgan Ave ... 75702
Morgan Dr ... 75701
Morning Mist Dr ... 75707
Morning Star ... 75703
Morning Tide Cv ... 75703
Morningside Dr
2100-2200 ... 75708
2202-2698 ... 75708
12600-12999 ... 75704
W Morris St ... 75702
Mosely St ... 75701
Moses Ct ... 75704
Moss Gln ... 75707
Mosswood Dr ... 75703
Mount Vernon St ... 75708
Mugsy Dr ... 75707
Mulberry Grv ... 75703
E Mulberry St ... 75702
Muller Garden Rd ... 75703
Mustang Trl ... 75707
Myers St ... 75707
Myracle St ... 75704
Nancy Dr ... 75702
Nature Trl ... 75709
Navaho St ... 75705
Navaho Trl ... 75707
Navasota Dr ... 75702
Neches Dr ... 75702
Neches Pkwy ... 75704
Neeley St ... 75701
Negem Dr ... 75702
Neighbors Rd ... 75703
Nell St ... 75701
Nell Lynn Ln ... 75707
Nellis Dr ... 75704
Nelray Ave ... 75708
Nettles Dr ... 75702
New Copeland Rd
2200-4102 ... 75701
4104-4198 ... 75701
4300-6399 ... 75703
New Sunnybrook Ave ... 75701
Newberry St ... 75701
Newbury Ct ... 75703
Newcastle Dr ... 75703
Niblack Pl ... 75701
Nichols Ct ... 75704
Nicholson Dr ... 75707
Nicklaus Ct ... 75709
Night Hawk ... 75706
Nimitz St ... 75704
E Noble St ... 75702
Nolan Dr ... 75709
Norma Ln ... 75701
Normandy Ave ... 75702
North Dr ... 75703
Northcrest Dr ... 75702

E Northeast Loop 323
200-699 ... 75706
E Northeast Loop 323
700-1999 ... 75708
N Northeast Loop 323 ... 75708
Northridge Dr ... 75702
Northstar Blvd ... 75703
Northview Dr ... 75702
Northwest Rd ... 75707
N Northwest Loop 323 ... 75702
W Northwest Loop 323
900-1298 ... 75706
1300-1399 ... 75706
1401-1499 ... 75706
1500-2498 ... 75702
2500-3299 ... 75702
Northwood Dr ... 75703
Nottaway Dr ... 75703
E & W Nutbush St ... 75702
Oacacia Dr ... 75707
Oak Aly ... 75703
Oak Bnd ... 75707
Oak Ln ... 75701
Oak Pl ... 75705
Oak Creek Cir ... 75703
Oak Crest Dr ... 75701
Oak Garden Cir ... 75703
Oak Haven Cir ... 75706
Oak Hill Blvd ... 75703
Oak Hill Dr ... 75707
Oak Hurst Pl ... 75703
Oak Knob St ... 75701
Oak Knoll Dr ... 75707
Oak Leaf Cir ... 75707
Oak Spring Rd ... 75709
Oak Village Dr ... 75707
Oakbrook Rd ... 75703
Oakdale Dr ... 75707
Oakhurst Cir ... 75701
S Oakland Ave
200-500 ... 75702
502-598 ... 75702
600-799 ... 75701
Oakleigh Dr ... 75707
Oakmeadow Cir ... 75703
Oakridge St ... 75706
Oaks West Dr ... 75704
Oakvale Dr ... 75704
E & W Oakwood St ... 75702
Oberlin Ct ... 75703
Old Bullard Rd
2001-2097 ... 75701
2099-4299 ... 75701
4301-5025 ... 75703
5027-6100 ... 75703
6102-6198 ... 75703
Old Chandler Rd ... 75702
Old Creek Dr ... 75703
Old Farm Rd ... 75703
Old Gladewater Hwy ... 75702
Old Grande Blvd ... 75703
Old Henderson Hwy ... 75702
Old Hickory Rd ... 75703
Old Jacksonville Hwy ... 75703
Old Jacksonville Rd ... 75701
Old Noonday Rd ... 75701
Old Oak Cir & Dr ... 75703
Old Omen Rd
900-1598 ... 75701
1600-3099 ... 75701
3101-3399 ... 75701
3400-3600 ... 75707
3602-4398 ... 75707
Old Troup Hwy
1900-2099 ... 75701
2101-3399 ... 75701
3700-4999 ... 75707
Oleander Dr ... 75707
E Olive St ... 75702
Olive Branch Cir & Dr ... 75709
Oliver St ... 75701
Olympia Ln ... 75709
Olympic Plaza Cir ... 75701
Omega Dr ... 75701
Oneall St ... 75704
Orchard Dr ... 75704

Orr Dr ... 75702
Osler Dr ... 75701
Outer Dr ... 75701
Outwood Dr ... 75701
Overbrook Dr ... 75703
Overhill Dr ... 75701
Overland Trl ... 75703
Overland Stage Dr ... 75703
N Owens Ave ... 75702
Oxford Cir & Dr ... 75703
N Pabst Ave ... 75702
Pac Rd ... 75707
Pachins ... 75709
Pacific Ave ... 75701
N Palace Ave ... 75702
S Palace Ave
100-599 ... 75702
600-999 ... 75701
N Palace Cts ... 75702
Palendow ... 75707
Palestine St ... 75701
S Palmer Ave
100-599 ... 75702
600-1099 ... 75701
1101-1199 ... 75701
Palo Pinto Dr ... 75707
Paloma St ... 75703
Paluxy Cir ... 75701
Paluxy Dr
3100-3299 ... 75701
3301-3699 ... 75701
3700-4298 ... 75703
4300-9299 ... 75703
9301-9399 ... 75703
Pam Dr ... 75703
Pamela Dr ... 75702
N Parish Ave ... 75702
Park Hl ... 75709
Park Ln ... 75708
Park Pl ... 75703
W Park St ... 75702
Park Center Dr ... 75701
Park Heights Cir ... 75701
Park Ridge Dr ... 75703
Park Road 16 ... 75706
Park Slope ... 75703
N & S Parkdale Dr ... 75702
N Parker Ave ... 75702
Parklen St ... 75701
Parkview Dr ... 75703
Parkway Pl ... 75701
Parkwood Dr ... 75707
Parliament Dr ... 75701
Pat Ln ... 75701
Patricia Ct ... 75702
Patrick Dr ... 75701
Patridge St ... 75701
Patriot Dr ... 75701
Patton Cir ... 75704
Patton Ln
100-699 ... 75704
700-800 ... 75709
802-5498 ... 75709
W Paul St ... 75702
Paula Dr ... 75709
Pawnee Dr ... 75703
Pawnee St ... 75705
Peaceful Acres ... 75706
S Peach Ave
100-599 ... 75702
700-898 ... 75701
900-1599 ... 75701
Pearl St
2800-2899 ... 75701
2901-2999 ... 75701
6400-8299 ... 75708
Pebblebrook Cir & Dr ... 75707
Pecan Dr ... 75701
Pecan Hill Cv ... 75703
Pecanridge Dr ... 75703
Peggys Pl ... 75701
Pegues Ave ... 75702
Peninsula Dr ... 75707
Perry St ... 75707
Persimmon Dr ... 75707
Peterson Rd ... 75708

Pettit Dr ... 75701
W Phillips St ... 75701
Phoenix Dr ... 75707
Picadilly Pl ... 75703
W Pickney St ... 75702
Pickwick Ln ... 75701
Pilot Dr ... 75707
Pin Oak Rdg ... 75707
Pin Oak St ... 75702
W Pine St ... 75702
Pine Bend Cir ... 75703
Pine Bluff Cir ... 75707
Pine Cone Dr ... 75704
Pine Cone Ln ... 75707
Pine Haven Rd ... 75702
Pine Knoll St ... 75703
Pine Lake Blvd ... 75709
Pine Manor Dr ... 75701
Pine Springs Dr ... 75708
Pine Terrace Dr ... 75709
Pine Tree Cir ... 75703
Pine Tree Rd ... 75707
Pinebrook Dr ... 75703
Pineburr Rd ... 75702
Pinecreek Dr ... 75707
Pinecrest Dr ... 75701
Pinedale Pl ... 75701
Pinehaven ... 75703
Pinehurst St ... 75703
Pineridge Dr ... 75704
Pinetree Pl ... 75703
Pineview Dr ... 75704
Pinewood Dr ... 75703
Pinkerton Dr ... 75701
Pinnacle Cir ... 75703
Pioneer Dr ... 75704
E Plainview St ... 75701
Plantation Dr ... 75703
Plaquemine ... 75703
Plaza Ave ... 75702
Pleasant Dr ... 75701
Pleasant Hill Cir ... 75707
Pleasant Hollow Rd ... 75709
Plume Dr ... 75703
Plumridge Cir ... 75703
Plymouth Cir ... 75707
Pointe North Dr ... 75702
Pollan St ... 75704
Pollard Dr ... 75701
Polo Ct ... 75703
Ponderosa Trl ... 75707
N Poplar Ave ... 75702
S Porter Ave ... 75701
Post Oak Rd ... 75701
Potomac Dr ... 75703
Pounds Ave ... 75701
Pounds Dr ... 75709
Powell Dr ... 75703
Powers Dr ... 75701
Poydras ... 75703
Preston Ave ... 75701
Prestonwood Cir ... 75703
Prestwick Ln ... 75703
Price St ... 75702
Primera Rd ... 75705
Princedale ... 75703
Princess Pl ... 75704
Princeton Dr ... 75703
Private Road 2244 ... 75707
Professional Dr ... 75701
Profit Dr ... 75707
Pruitt Pl ... 75703
Public Rd ... 75702
Pueblo St ... 75705
Purdue Dr ... 75703
Putting Ln ... 75709
Quail Creek Dr ... 75703
Quail Run Rd ... 75709
E & W Queen St ... 75702
Queenspark St ... 75703
Quiet Bay Dr ... 75707
Quiet Water ... 75703
Quinby Ln ... 75701
Rachel Ave ... 75701
Radcliffe Dr ... 75703
Rainbow Pt ... 75707

Rainbow Ridge Cir 75707
Raine Rd 75708
Rainmaker 75703
Raintree Dr 75703
Raleigh Dr 75703
N Ramey Ave 75702
Ranch Rd 75703
Rasberry Ln 75703
Raveneaux Ln 75703
Reagan St 75707
Red Bird Ln 75706
Red Fern Rd 75703
Red Oak Dr 75708
Red Oak Rd 75707
Red Rock Dr 75706
Redbud Ave 75701
Redcoat Ln 75703
Reed Aly 75702
Reed Rd 75707
E Reeves St 75702
Regency Ln 75703
Regents Row 75703
Renee Ave 75701
Reno Rd 75704
Republic Dr 75701
Reserve Ct 75707
Reynolds Rd 75708
Rhinehart St 75701
Rhodes Dr 75701
Rhones Quarter Rd 75707
Rhudy Dr 75703
Rice Rd 75703
E Richards St 75702
Richardson Dr 75702
Richfield Dr 75703
Richmond Rd 75703
Rickety Ln 75703
Ridge Ln 75701
Ridge Bluff Cir 75707
Ridge Creek Dr 75703
Ridge Place Cir 75703
Ridgecrest Dr 75701
Ridgeline Rd 75703
Ridgetop Rd 75703
Ridgeview Cir 75703
Ridgeview Dr 75701
Ridgeview St 75709
Ridgewood Dr 75701
Ridgewood St 75709
Riding Rd 75703
E & W Rieck Rd 75703
River Bend Dr 75703
River Oaks Ct 75707
Riviera Dr 75707
E Rix St 75701
Roanoke Ln 75701
W Robbins St 75701
Robert E Lee Dr 75703
Roberts Ave 75701
Roberts Rd 75707
Robertson Ave & Rd 75701
Robinson Dr 75703
Rochester Way 75703
Rock Rd 75707
Rock Creek Dr 75707
Rockbridge Rd 75701
Rockpoint Cir & Ln 75703
Rockway Dr 75702
Rockwood Dr 75703
Rocky Ln 75703
Rocky Mountain Ln 75703
Rodessa Dr 75701
Rodge Dr 75701
E Rogers St 75702
Rolling Green Cv 75703
Rolling Hill Dr 75702
Rolling Pines Dr 75707
Rollingwood Dr 75701
Rollins Dr 75703
Ronald Cir 75709
Ronnette Dr 75703
Roosevelt Dr 75705
W Rose Rd & St 75701
Rose Circle Dr 75701
Rose Park Dr 75702
Rosebud Ln 75709
Rosecrest Ln 75704
E Rosedale St 75702
Roseland Blvd 75701
Rosemary Ln 75701
Rosemont Pl 75701
W Rosemont St 75702
Rosewood Dr 75701
N Ross Ave 75702
S Ross Ave
100-599 75702
600-899 75701
Rowland Pl 75701
Roy Rd 75707
Roy St 75701
Royal Oak Dr 75703
Rudman Rd 75701
W Rusk St 75701
Ruth Dr 75709
Ryan Cir 75703
Sabine Dr 75702
Saddle Creek Dr 75703
Sagemont Ln 75707
Saint Anthony Dr 75703
Saint James Ct 75701
Saint Patrick Pl 75703
S Saleh Ave 75702
Salisbury Ln 75703
Sampson Dr & Pl 75701
Samuel Dr 75701
San Antonio St 75701
San Augustine Dr 75704
San Jacinto Dr 75701
Sandalwood Ln 75701
Sande Ln 75706
Sandy Oaks Ln 75706
Sandy Point Dr 75707
Santa Elena Dr 75701
Santa Fe Trl 75703
Santa Rosa Dr 75701
Sara St 75701
Sarasota Dr 75701
S Saunders Ave
100-699 75702
700-799 75701
1000-1099 75702
Savannah St 75703
Sawgrass Cir & Dr 75703
Scenic Dr 75709
Scenic Hollow Ct 75707
Scotland Cir 75707
S Scott Ave
100-399 75702
1000-1098 75701
1100-1499 75701
Seagle St 75701
Seaton St 75701
W Selman St 75702
Sequoia Dr 75703
Seven Hills Rd 75708
Seville Ln 75704
Shaddock Rdg 75703
Shadow Gln 75707
Shady Blf 75707
Shady Ln
2700-2798 75702
2800-2899 75702
2901-2999 75702
16700-17799 75707
Shady Bend Ct 75703
Shady Cove St 75707
Shady Creek Rd 75705
Shady Oaks Dr 75703
Shady Trail Dr 75702
Shadyridge Dr 75703
Shadywood Dr 75703
Shaffer Ln 75702
Shane Cir 75703
Shannon Dr 75701
Shaquille Dr 75709
W Shaw St 75701
Shawnee Blvd 75702
Shawntae Ln 75703
Sheffield Dr 75703
Sheila Dr 75709
Shelby Ln 75707
Sheldon Ln 75703
Shelley Dr 75701
Shelley Park Plz 75701
Shenandoah Dr 75701
Shepherd Ln 75701
Sherbrooke Dr 75703
E Sheridan St 75701
Sherra St 75706
Sherry Ln 75701
W Sherwood St 75702
Sherwood Forest Dr 75703
Sheryl Ln 75701
Shiloh Rd
300-3099 75703
3100-3899 75707
Shiloh Ridge Dr & St 75703
Shiloh Village Dr 75703
Shirley Dr 75708
Shofner Dr 75706
Shoreline Dr 75703
W Short St 75702
Shoshone Dr 75703
Sierra Ln 75709
Silkwood Dr 75707
Silver Creek Dr 75702
Silvermaple Cv 75703
Silverwood Dr 75701
Skidmore Ln 75703
Skipping Stone Ln 75703
Skyline St 75701
Skyway Blvd 75704
Smith St 75702
Smuts Dr 75701
S Sneed Ave 75701
E Social St 75702
W South St 75706
E & W South Town Dr 75703
E Southeast Loop 323 75701
S Southeast Loop 323
100-999 75702
S Southeast Loop 323
1010-1198 75701
1200-2799 75701
2801-3099 75701
Southgate Ave 75702
Southland Dr 75703
Southpark Dr 75703
Southplace Dr 75703
Southpoint Cir 75707
Southpoint Dr 75701
Southport Dr 75703
Southridge Dr 75702
S Southwest Loop 323
100-599 75702
700-898 75701
900-3999 75701
W Southwest Loop
323 75701
Southwind St 75709
Southwood Dr 75707
Sparks Dr 75704
Sparrow Cir 75701
Spartanburg 75701
Speciality Dr 75707
Speedway Ct 75703
Spencer Ln 75704
N & S Spring Ave 75702
Spring Branch Dr 75703
Spring Club Lk 75706
Spring Creek Dr 75703
Springbrook Dr 75707
Spruce Pl 75707
Spruce Pine Ln 75703
Spur 124 75707
Spur 164 75709
Spur 248 75707
Spur 323 75708
Spur 364 75709
Spyglass Ct 75703
Stagecoach St 75703
Staley Dr 75702
Standing Rock Ln 75703
Stanford Ct & St 75701
State Highway 110 N 75704
State Highway 110 S 75707
State Highway 155 N 75708
State Highway 155 S 75703
State Highway 31 E
2901-3199 75702
8000-23199 75705
State Highway 31 W 75709
State Highway 64 E 75707
State Highway 64 W 75704
Steel Rd 75703
Steeple Ct 75703
Sterling Dr 75701
Stewart Way 75709
Stockman Cir 75703
Stone Creek Dr
9000-9112 75703
14400-14599 75709
Stonebank Xing 75703
Stonebridge Way 75703
Stonebrook Ln 75707
Stonecreek Dr 75703
Stonecrest Blvd 75703
Stonegate Blvd, Cir, Pl &
Trl 75703
Stonegate Valley Dr 75703
Stonehaven Ct 75703
Stonehill Dr 75703
Stoneking Ln 75708
Stoneleaf Dr 75703
Stoneleigh Dr 75703
Stonewall Ct 75701
Stoney Glen Cir 75703
Storey Lake Dr 75707
Storey Place Dr 75708
Story Dr 75702
Stratford Dr 75703
Suanne Dr 75701
Suel Dr 75702
Sugar Maple Ct 75703
W Summerkamp St 75702
N Summit Ave 75702
Sundown St 75709
Sunny Ln 75702
Sunnybrook Dr 75701
Sunnyhill Dr 75702
Sunnyside Dr 75702
Sunrise Lake Ct 75707
Sunset Dr
1200-1499 75701
12600-12999 75704
Sunset Trl 75706
Sunshine Dr 75703
Surrey Cir 75701
Surrey Ln 75705
Surrey Trl 75705
Susan Dr 75703
Susie Cir 75703
Sutherland Dr 75703
Swan Ln 75706
Swann St 75702
Sweetbriar Ln 75703
Sybil Ln 75703
Sycamore Ave & St 75704
Syrah Ln 75703
N Taft Ave 75702
Talihina Cir 75703
Tall Pines Dr 75703
Tall Timber Dr 75703
S Talley Ave 75701
Tallow Oaks Cir 75707
Tallyho Cir 75703
Tammi Trl 75709
Tandem Dr 75708
Tanglewood Dr 75701
Tanya Dr 75709
Tartan Ct 75703
Teague Dr 75701
Teakwood Dr 75701
Teal Flight Way 75703
Tech Pl 75701
Telephone Rd 75701
N Tenneha Ave 75702
Tepee Trl 75709
Terilinga Dr 75701
Terre Haute Dr 75701
Terrebonne Dr 75703
Teton Rd 75709
Texas College Rd 75702
Thibodaux Dr 75703
Thigpen Dr 75703
Thistle Dr 75703
Thomas St 75702
Thomas Nelson Dr 75707
S Thompson Ave 75702
Thompson Ln 75704
Thompson Pl 75707
Thornton St 75702
Thornwood 75703
Three Lakes Pkwy 75703
Tidwell Dr 75708
Timber Cir 75708
Timber Creek Cir 75707
Timber Creek Dr
1500-1598 75703
1600-5199 75703
5201-6099 75703
10900-11299 75707
Timber View Dr 75703
Timbercrest Dr 75703
Timberidge Dr 75703
Timberlake Cir 75703
Timberlane Dr 75701
Timberline Dr 75703
Timberwilde Dr 75703
Timms St 75701
Timothy Ct 75703
Tina Dr 75703
Tinsley St 75709
Tipperary Dr 75703
S Tipton Ave 75701
Tol Ave 75701
Toledo Ln 75704
Top Hill Dr 75703
N Topeka Ave 75702
Tournament Rd 75702
Tower Dr 75701
Towne Oaks Dr 75701
Towne Park Dr 75701
Towne Way Dr 75701
Townhouse Dr 75701
N Townsend Ave 75702
Tracer Ln 75701
Tracy Ln 75709
Tradewind St 75709
Trafalgar Sq 75701
Trail Rdg 75703
Trailwood Ct 75707
E Travis St 75701
Tremont St 75701
Trenton Dr 75701
W Trezevant St 75702
Triggs Trce 75709
Trinity Dr 75702
Troup Hwy
100-398 75701
400-3399 75701
3320-3320 75713
3401-3599 75701
3500-3598 75701
3600-4899 75703
5000-6599 75707
Tryon Ct 75703
Tubbs St 75701
Tucson Oaks Dr 75707
Tulsa St 75702
Turnberry Ct & Dr N 75703
S Turner Ave 75701
Turner Cir 75704
W Turney St 75702
Turtle Cove Ct 75703
Turtle Creek Dr 75701
Tweed Ct 75703
E & W Twin Lakes Dr 75704
Twin Oaks Dr 75707
Tyler Ave 75702
Ulster Dr 75703
University Blvd 75701
University Dr 75707
University Pl 75702
Us Highway 271 75708
Us Highway 69 N 75706
Us Highway 69 S 75703
Us Jones Dr 75705
Utah Ave 75704
E & W Valentine St 75702
Valley View Dr 75709
Valley View Ln 75703
Valley View Rdg 75709
Valley View St 75701
Van Hwy
2700-3499 75702
3600-4898 75704
W Van St 75702
Van Buren St 75703
E & W Vance St 75702
Vanderbilt 75703
Vantage View Dr 75707
Varsity Dr 75701
S Vaughn Ave 75702
Vermillion 75703
Vernon Ave 75708
N Vernon Ave 75702
Vickery Dr 75704
Vicksburg St 75703
Victoria Ct & Park 75703
Victory Dr 75701
Victory Ln 75703
Vieux Carre 75703
Villa Ct & Dr 75703
Vincent Way 75705
S Vine Ave
100-599 75702
600-3599 75701
Vine Hts 75701
Vineyard 75701
N & S Virginia Ave 75702
Vivian Ct 75703
Wade St 75701
Wakefield Dr 75701
Walden Dr 75703
Waljim St 75703
Walker St 75701
S Wall Ave 75701
Walling Dr 75704
Walnut Dr 75702
Walton Rd 75701
N Ward Ave 75702
Washington Ave & Ct 75702
Washita Dr 75703
Waterford Ct 75703
Waters Edge Way 75703
Waterwood Dr 75703
E Watkins St 75701
Watson St 75701
Waunell Dr 75701
Waverly St 75701
Waydak Cir 75701
Wayne Dr 75708
Wayside Dr 75701
Wedgewood Pl 75701
Welch Dr 75709
Wellington Pl 75704
Wellington St 75703
Wellington Trce 75709
E Wells St 75701
Wendell Dr 75706
Wendover Pl 75703
Wesson Way 75708
Westbluff Ct 75707
Westbrook Dr 75704
Westchester Dr 75703
Westfield St 75701
Westminster Dr 75701
Weston Ct 75703
Westridge St 75709
Westway St 75703
Wexford Dr 75709
Wheaton Ct 75703
Whetstone Ln 75703
Whippoorwill Ct & Dr 75703
Whispering Ln 75707
White Deer Trl 75703
White Oak Cir 75707
White Tail Dr 75707
Whiteforest Cv 75703
Whiteoak Ln 75703
Whiteside Rd
300-699 75702
700-1099 75709
N Whitten Ave 75702
Whittle St 75701
Wichita Ave 75702
Wicket Ct 75703
Wilana Dr 75703
Wild Horse 75706
Wilder Pl & Way 75703
Wilder Woods 75703
Wilderness Rd 75703
Wildfern Rd 75707
Wildflower 75706
Wildwood Dr
100-299 75705
400-500 75702
502-610 75702
10500-10599 75707
S Wiley Ave 75701
Wilken Plz 75703
Wilkinson Dr 75707
Willard Dr 75707
William Spear Dr 75704
Williams Ct & St 75702
Williamsburg Cir & Dr 75701
Willingham Dr 75704
Willow Bnd 75703
Willow Cove Ter 75703
Willow Oak Ln 75703
Willowbrook Ave 75702
Willowbrook Ln 75701
Willowwood Dr 75703
Willscott Dr 75703
Wilma St 75701
Wilmington Pl 75701
Wilshire Dr 75703
Wilson 75704
Wilson Rd 75707
W Wilson St 75702
Wimbledon Dr 75703
Winchester Dr 75701
Wind Dancer 75706
Winding Way 75707
Winding Brook Ln 75703
Windmill Xing 75706
Windomere Cir 75701
Windsor Pl 75701
Winner Cir 75703
N Winona Ave 75702
Winterberry Cv 75703
Winthrop 75703
Wisteria Dr 75702
W Woldert St 75702
N Wolford Ave 75702
Wood Ln 75707
Wood Springs Rd 75706
Woodbine Blvd 75701
Woodbridge Dr & Pl 75703
Woodcrest St 75704
Woodglen Dr 75703
Woodhall Ct 75703
Woodhaven Dr 75701
Woodhue Dr 75702
Woodlake Dr 75701
Woodland Hills Dr 75701
Woodlands Dr 75703
Woodlark Dr 75701
Woodlark St 75704
Woodlawn St 75702
Woodley St 75701
Woods Blvd 75707
Wynnwood Dr 75701
Yale Dr 75703
Yancy Ln 75707
York Pl 75702
Yorktown Dr 75704
Yorktown St 75701
Yosemite Dr 75703
Young Pl 75708
Yucca Ln W 75704
Zelwood Dr 75701

NUMBERED STREETS

W 1st Ave 75706
1st Pl 75702
1st St 75704
E 1st St 75701
W 1st St 75701
1st Xing 75703

E & W 2nd 75701
3 Lakes Rd 75703
E & W 3rd 75701
4th St 75708
E 4th St 75701
W 4th St 75701
E & W 5th 75701
E & W 6th 75701
7 League Rd 75703
E & W 7th 75701
8th St 75708
E 8th St 75701
W 8th St 75701
E & W 9th 75701
W 10th St 75701
18th Ave 75708
19th Ave 75708
E & W 24th 75702
E & W 25th 75702
W 26th St 75702
W 27th St 75702
W 28th St 75702
W 29th St 75702
W 30th St 75702
W 31st St 75702
W 32nd St 75702
W 33rd St 75702
W 34th St 75702

UVALDE TX

General Delivery 78801

POST OFFICE BOXES MAIN OFFICE STATIONS AND BRANCHES

Box No.s
All PO Boxes 78802

HIGHWAY CONTRACTS

32, 33, 34, 77 78801

NAMED STREETS

Acacia Dr 78801
Adela St 78801
Airfield 78801
Airline Dr 78801
W Alley 78801
Alvarez Ln 78801
E & W Anglin St 78801
E & W Antonio St 78801
Apolino St 78801
Arrow Head Ln 78801
N & S Ashby Dr 78801
Augustin St 78801
B P Ln 78801
Bar S Rd 78801
Barnes Rd 78801
Barry St 78801
Barton St 78801
Bates Aly & St 78801
Beavers Knl, Ln & Trl 78801
Behland Cir 78801
N & W Benson Rd & St 78801
Bent Oak Trl 78801
Birch Cir 78801
Black St 78801
E Bluebonnet Dr 78801
Bob White Trl 78801
Bobwhite Loop 78801
Bohme St 78801
Boone St 78801
Booth St 78801
Bowie St 78801
E & W Brazos St 78801
Briar Ct 78801
Briar Crown 78801
Brice Ln 78801
Brook St 78801
Buena Vista Cir 78801
Bunting Ln 78801
E & W Calera St 78801
N & S Camp St 78801
E & W Campbell St 78801
E & W Canales St 78801
Cap Rock Ranch Rd 78801
Capitan St 78801
E Cardwell St 78801
E & W Cargile St 78801
Castro St 78801
Cenisa Dr 78801
Cenizo Blvd 78801
Chalk Bluff Rd 78801
Chaparral St 78801
Charles Pl 78801
Cherry St 78801
N & S Claudia St 78801
Cobb St 78801
College Ln 78801
E & W Commerce St 78801
Como St 78801
Cottonwood 78801
Country Ln 78801
Country Club Ln 78801
County Road 101 78801
County Road 103 78801
County Road 105 78801
County Road 106 78801
County Road 107 78801
County Road 108 78801
County Road 109 78801
County Road 110 78801
County Road 111 78801
County Road 112 78801
County Road 201 78801
County Road 202 78801
County Road 203 78801
County Road 205 78801
County Road 365 78801
County Road 367 78801
County Road 368 78801
County Road 368a 78801
County Road 369 78801
County Road 370 78801
County Road 372 78801
County Road 373 78801
County Road 375 78801
County Road 400 78801
County Road 402 78801
County Road 403 78801
County Road 404 78801
County Road 405 78801
County Road 406 78801
County Road 407 78801
County Road 408 78801
County Road 411 78801
County Road 412 78801
County Road 413 78801
County Road 414 78801
County Road 415 78801
County Road 416 78801
County Road 417 78801
County Road 421 78801
County Road 423 78801
County Road 425 78801
County Road 428 78801
County Road 429 78801
County Road 429a 78801
County Road 429b 78801
County Road 429c 78801
County Road 429d 78801
County Road 429e 78801
County Road 429f 78801
Coyote Trl 78801
N & S Crisp St 78801
Crockett St 78801
Crystal City Hwy 78801
Cummings St 78801
Cypress Cir 78801
Dalrymple 78801
E & W Daniel St 78801
De Leon Aly 78801
Dean St 78801
Deer Ln 78801
Deer Valley Ranch Rd 78801
Diaz St 78801
Donna Dr 78801
Doolie St 78801
Dorothy Jo Cir 78801
E & W Doughty St 78801
Dove Cir 78801
Eagle Pass Trl 78801
N & S East Ln & St 78801
El Norte Cir 78801
Elizabeth St 78801
Encino St 78801
Evans St 78801
E & W Evergreen St 78801
Fair Oaks Dr 78801
E & W Fannin St 78801
Farel Cir 78801
N & S Farrar St 78801
Fenley St 78801
Florence St 78801
Flores St 78801
Fm 1023 78801
Fm 1052 78801
N Fm 117 78801
Fm 140 78801
Fm 1403 78801
Fm 1574 78801
Fm 187 78801
Fm 2369 78801
Fm 2690 78801
Fm 3447 78801
Fm 481 78801
Fort Clark Rd 78801
Forty Ln 78801
Fox Run Rd 78801
Friends Trl 78801
E & W Frio St 78801
E & W Front St 78801
E & W Garden St 78801
Garner Field Rd 78801
Garza Ct 78801
Geraldine St 78801
N Getty St 78801
S Getty St
100-200 78801
103-103 78802
201-1199 78801
202-1198 78801
Gibson Ln 78801
Glennwood Dr 78801
Goldbeck St 78801
Gonzales St 78801
Greenbriar Ln 78801
N & S Grove St 78801
E & W Hacienda Ln & Rd 78801
Hackberry Dr 78801
Ham Ln 78801
Hardin St 78801
Hernandez St 78801
Heyne Ranch Rd 78801
N & S High Ln & St 78801
Hightower 78801
Homestead Rd 78801
Hood St 78801
Hornby Pl 78801
Houston St 78801
Howard Langford Dr 78801
Indian Trl 78801
Industrial Park 78801
James Bros Ranch Rd 78801
Javelina Pass 78801
Joe Carper Dr 78801
Jolley St 78801
Juarez St 78801
Kaylyn St 78801
Kennedy St 78801
King Fisher Ln 78801
Kings Ct 78801
E & W Knippa St 78801
Knox St 78801
La Hacienda Dr 78801
Lane Hill Rd 78801
Laredo St 78801
Larkspur Dr 78801
Laurel St 78801
E & W Leona Hts, Rd & St 78801
Live Oak Rd 78801
Lou Stroup Dr 78801
Louise Dr 78801
Mackenzie St 78801
Magnolia St 78801
E & W Mahaffey St 78801
E & W Main St 78801
Maple St 78801
Margarita St 78801
Marlinville Dr 78801
Marsh Ln & St 78801
Martin St 78801
Martinez St 78801
Mary Ann St 78801
Matamoros St 78801
Mayhew St 78801
Mcglasson St 78801
Melody Ln 78801
Mendoza Aly 78801
E & W Mesquite St 78801
Milam St 78801
Military Ln 78801
E & W Mill St 78801
Mills Ln 78801
Minter St 78801
E & W Modesta St 78801
Monterrey St 78801
Moonwind Dr 78801
Mueller St 78801
Mulberry St 78801
Myrtle St 78801
Nava St 78801
Nicholas St 78801
E & W Nopal St 78801
W & E North Ln & St 78801
W Nueces St 78801
Nueces River Rd 78801
Nunn Pl 78801
E & W Oak St 78801
Old Carrizo Rd 78801
E & W Oppenheimer St 78801
E & W Pacific St 78801
N & S Park St 78801
Pashanso St 78801
Patricia Pl 78801
Pecan St 78801
E & W Pecos St 78801
Perez St 78801
N & S Piper Ln 78801
Prairie St 78801
Private Road 1035 78801
Private Road 1040 78801
Private Road 2000 78801
Private Road 2040 78801
Private Road 2080 78801
Private Road 2085 78801
Private Road 2165 78801
Private Road 2200 78801
Private Road 2205 78801
Private Road 2235 78801
Private Road 2310 78801
Private Road 2315 78801
Private Road 2320 78801
Private Road 2325 78801
Private Road 2330 78801
Private Road 2340 78801
Private Road 2345 78801
Private Road 2350 78801
Private Road 2370 78801
Private Road 2400 78801
Private Road 2405 78801
Private Road 2410 78801
Private Road 2415 78801
Private Road 2430 78801
Private Road 2431 78801
Private Road 2485 78801
Private Road 2560 78801
Private Road 2575 78801
Private Road 2715 78801
N Private Road 2735 78801
Private Road 2750 78801
Private Road 2760 78801
Private Road 2765 78801
Private Road 2779 78801
Private Road 2780 78801
Private Road 2840 78801
Private Road 3226 78801
Private Road 4235 78801
Private Road 428 78801
Private Road 4330 78801
Private Road 4450 78801
Private Road 4650 78801
Private Road 4990 78801
Private Road 5000 78801
Private Road 5002 78801
Puccinni Ln 78801
Pulliam Ave 78801
Quail Cir, Trl & Way 78801
Ranch Road 1022 78801
Ranch Road 1051 78801
Ranch Road 334 78801
Rene St 78801
Reyes Aly & St 78801
Reynosa St 78801
Rio St 78801
Rio Grande St 78801
Rio Seco 78801
Riverside Dr 78801
Roach St 78801
Robbin St 78801
W Roberts Ln 78801
Rocking N Ranch Rd 78801
Rocky Ridge Rd 78801
Rose St 78801
Rosebud Cir 78801
Royal Ln 78801
Ruth St 78801
E & W Sabinal St 78801
Sage Ln 78801
Sage Brush Ln 78801
Salinas St 78801
San Diego St 78801
San Jacinto St 78801
Saunders Ln 78801
E & W School Ln 78801
Schwartz St 78801
Seleste Cir 78801
Sgt Joey Alvarez Ln 78801
Shook St 78801
Silvestre St 78801
Sky Way 78801
Skylane Dr N & S 78801
W & E South Ln & St 78801
Spanish Oaks Dr 78801
Sparks Ln 78801
Squirrel Bnd 78801
State Highway 55 78801
Stewart St 78801
Studer Cir, Ct, Park & St 78801
Sul Ross Dr 78801
Summit Vw 78801
Sunday Ct 78801
Sunnyvale Pl 78801
Sunrise Ave 78801
Sunshine Ln 78801
N Sutton Pl 78801
Sycamore St 78801
Tanglewood St 78801
Tellez Ln 78801
Timber Wood 78801
Tinsley Ln 78801
Travis St 78801
Tucker St 78801
Turkey Trot Rd 78801
Twins Ln 78801
N & S Us Highway 83 78801
W Us Highway 90 78801
Uvalde Estates Dr 78801
Uvalde Oaks Dr 78801
Valley Vw 78801
Valley View Dr 78801
Vanessa St 78801
Vanham St 78801
Veterans Ln 78801
Victoria Pl 78801
Villa St 78801
Walnut Cir 78801
Weeping Willow 78801
Wesley Aly 78801
N & S West St 78801
Westward Trl 78801
White Ln 78801
White Tail Dr & Run 78801
White Wing Cv 78801
William St 78801
Wilson St 78801
Wimberly St 78801
Windmill Rd 78801
Windsong Dr 78801
N & S Wood St 78801
E & W Zaragosa St 78801

NUMBERED STREETS

All Street Addresses 78801

VERNON TX

General Delivery 76384

POST OFFICE BOXES MAIN OFFICE STATIONS AND BRANCHES

Box No.s
All PO Boxes 76385

RURAL ROUTES

01, 02, 03 76384

NAMED STREETS

All Street Addresses 76384

NUMBERED STREETS

All Street Addresses 76384

VICTORIA TX

General Delivery 77901

POST OFFICE BOXES MAIN OFFICE STATIONS AND BRANCHES

Box No.s
A - F 77902
1 - 2984 77902
3001 - 103000 77903

RURAL ROUTES

05 77905

NAMED STREETS

Abby Dr 77904
Aberdeen St 77904
Abrameit Rd 77905
W Acorn Dr 77905
Adcock Rd 77905
Adcock Dairy Rd 77905
Adcock Ranch Rd 77904
E Airline Rd
100-198 77901
200-2999 77901
3001-3499 77901
5101-5199 77904
Al Beamon Dr 77905
Alabama Ave 77905
Alameda Cir 77904
Alamo Dr 77901
Alamogordo Dr 77904
Albany St 77904
Albert Ave 77905
Albrecht Rd W 77905
Alcoa St 77901
Algie St 77901
Allen St 77901
Allendale St 77901
Allie St 77901
Alma St 77901
Alnita 77905
Aloe Rd N 77905
Alpine Pl 77905
Alvin St 77901
Amber 77905
Amberglow Ct 77904
Amhurst St 77904
E Anaqua Ave 77901
Andover St 77904
Andrew Dr 77904
Angus St 77904
Ann St 77901
Antelope Cir 77904
Anthony Rd 77901
Antietam Dr 77904
Antlers Ln 77905
Appalachian Dr 77904
Appaloosa Ct & Dr 77904
Apple St 77905
Arabian Dr 77904
Arbor Lake St 77904
Arizona Ave 77905
Arkansas Ave 77905
Armadillo Dr 77905
Arnold Rd 77905
Arrington Ln 77905
Arroyo Dr 77901
Ash St 77901
Ashford Dr 77904
Ashland Crk 77901
Ashton Gln 77904
Aster Ln 77904
Auburn Hl 77904
Austin Ave 77901
Avalon Dr 77901
Avant Garde Dr 77901
Avenue E 77901
Avenue A 77901
Avenue C 77901
Avenue D 77901
Avon 77901
Avondale St 77901
N Azalea St 77901
Baass Ln 77905
Bachelor Dr 77904
Bahia St 77904
Bailey Dr 77904
Baker St 77901
Balboa Ct 77901
Ball Airport Rd 77904
Bambi Dr 77904
Banbury Ln 77904
Banyan Ct 77901
Barbara Dr 77905
Barbara St 77901
Bartlett Rd 77905
Basin St 77901
Basswood St 77904
E Bates St 77901
Bayer Rd E 77905
Beauvoir Ln 77901
Beck Rd W 77905
Bedgood Ln 77905
Bedivere Dr 77904
Beechwood Dr 77901
Begonia St 77904
Bella Vista St 77905
Bellevue St 77904
Belmoor Ln 77904
N Ben Jordan St 77901
N & S Ben Wilson St 77901
Bennett St 77901
Berger Rd 77905
Berkman Dr 77904
Berkshire Ln 77904
Berwick St 77904

Street	ZIP
Beverly Dr	77905
Bexar Ave	77901
Bianchi Dr	77904
Big Bend Dr	77904
Big State Rd	77905
Billy Dr	77901
Biltmore Dr	77904
Bingham Rd	77904
Birchwood Dr	77901
Bishop St	77901
Bivouac Ln	77905
Black St	77901
Blake St	77905
Blanco Ln	77905
Block Rd	77905
Bloomingdale Cir	77904
Blue Quail Ct	77905
Blue Rock Ct	77904
Bluebird Rd	77905
Bluebonnet St	77901
Bluestem St	77904
N Bluff St	77901
Blyth Rd	77904
Bob White Rd	77905
Bobbie Circle Dr	77905
Bobolink St	77901
Boehm Rd	77905
Bois Darc Ln	77905
Bon Aire Ave	77901
Bonham Dr	77901
Booker St	77901
Bottom Rd	77905
Bottom St	77901
Bowie Dr	77901
Bowling Green Dr	77904
Bradley St	77901
Bramble Bush Ln	77904
Branch Creek Rd	77904
Brandywine Ln	77901
E & W Brazos St	77901
Brenna Cir	77901
Briarmeadow Ln	77904
Briarwood St	77904
N & S Bridge St	77901
Bridle Ln	77904
Briggs Blvd	77904
Brinkley Ln	77905
Bristol Ct	77904
Broadmoor St	77904
Brocton St	77904
Brook Vw	77904
Brooks Rd	77904
Brookwood	77901
Brown St	77901
Brownson Rd	77905
N Brownson St	77901
S Brownson St	77901
Brunhild St	77901
Brushy Crk	77904
Bubenik Ln	77905
Buck Square St	77905
Buckey Ln	77905
Buckingham St	77904
Bucksin Trl	77904
Buena Vista Ave	77901
Buentello Rd	77905
Bugle Ln	77905
Bunny Ln	77905
Bures Rd	77905
Burkhart Rd	77905
Burning Tree St	77904
Burroughsville Rd	77905
Byron Ln	77901
Cabana Dr	77901
Calle Corta	77905
Calle Del Sol	77905
Calle Ricardo	77904
Callis St	77901
Calypso Ct	77901
Cambridge St	77905
Camellia St	77904
Camelot Dr	77901
N & S Cameron St	77901
Camino Dr	77905
Camino Del Oro	77905
Camino Real	77905
Camp Colet Rd	77905
Canadian	77905
Canal Rd	77905
Cannon Rd	77904
Canterbury Ln	77904
Canyon Crk	77901
Cardinal St	77901
Carefree Dr	77905
Carlsbad Dr	77904
Caroline St	77901
Carsner St	77901
Carter St	77905
Castleway St	77904
Catalpa St	77901
Catherine Cir	77901
Cavalry Rd	77905
Cedar St	77901
Center St	77901
Cercis Dr	77901
Cervantes St	77901
Chama Dr	77904
Champions Ct & Row	77904
Champlain St	77905
Chamrad Ln	77905
Chantilly St	77904
Chaparral Dr & Rd	77905
Charles St	77901
Charleston Dr	77904
Cherokee Ln	77901
Cherry St	77901
Cherrystone Cir	77904
Chesapeake Ave	77904
Chimney Rock Dr	77904
Chippendale Ln	77904
Chris Thompson Rd	77905
Chukar Dr	77905
Church Ln	77905
Church St	77905
E Church St	77901
W Church St	77901
Cimarron Dr	77904
Cinco Oaks	77905
Circle Ln	77904
Circle St	77901
E Circle St	77901
Citizens Plz	77901
Clark School Rd	77904
Clay Dr	77904
Clayton St	77905
N & S Cleveland St	77901
Cloverbloom Dr	77904
Club Dr	77905
Clydesdale Ln	77904
Cobble Stone Ct	77904
Cody Dr	77904
Coffey St	77901
Colake Dr	77905
Coleto Dr	77905
Coleto Bluff Rd	77905
Coleto Oaks Dr	77905
Coleto Park Rd	77905
Coletoville Rd E, S & W	77905
College Dr	77901
Collins St	
1700-1799	77901
12901-12999	77905
Cologne Rd S	77905
Colony Dr	77905
Colony Creek Dr	77904
E & W Colorado St	77901
Commerce Ave	77905
Commerce St	77901
E & W Commercial St	77901
Concord Ln	77901
E & W Constitution St	77901
Contento St	77905
Conti Ln	77904
E & W Convent St	77901
Cook Ln	77905
Copper Rock Cv	77904
Copper Spur Ln	77905
Copperhead Ln	77905
Cornwall Dr	77904
Corpus Christi Dr	77904
Costa Del Oro St	77904
Cotswold Ln	77904
Cottonwood St	77904
Country Ln	77904
Country Club Dr	77904
County Rd	77905
Cowboy Rd	77905
Cozzi Cir	77901
N Craig St	77901
Crane St	77904
Crawford Dr	77904
Creek Ln	77905
Creekridge Dr	77904
Creekside Dr	77904
Crescent Dr	77905
N Crescent Dr	77901
S Crescent Dr	77901
Crestview Dr	77905
E & W Crestwood Dr	77901
Crockett Ave	77901
Crockett Dr	77905
Cromwell Dr	77901
Crosswind Dr	77904
Crouch Rd	77905
Culver Rd	77905
Cumberland Gap	77904
Curlew St	77905
Cynthia St	77904
Cypress St	77901
Dahlia Ln	77904
Dairy Rd	77904
Dale St	77905
Davidson Rd	77905
Davis Ln	77905
Dawn Dr	77905
De La Garza Rd	77905
N & S De Leon St	77901
Debbie St	77905
Deer Chase	77901
Deer Circle Ln	77904
Deer Trot Dr	77905
Deerwood St	77904
Del Papa St	77901
Delmar Dr	77901
Delores Dr	77905
N & S Depot St	77901
Dernal Dr	77905
Derrick Rd	77905
Dewberry Ln	77904
Dianna Dr	77905
Dick St	77901
Diebel Dr & Rd	77905
Dike 2 Service Rd	77905
Dillon Dr	77905
Dina St	77901
Dixie Ln	77904
Dogwood St	77901
Don St	77901
Donna Dr	77905
Dove	77905
Dover St	77905
Dover Dell	77904
Dreyer Ln	77905
Dry Creek Rd	77905
Duck Dr	77905
Dudley St	77901
Dunbar Dr	77904
Duncan St	77901
Dundee St	77904
Dupont Dr	77904
Dupont St	77901
Durango St	77904
Easley Rd	77904
N & S East St	77901
Eddie St	77905
Eden Roc St	77904
Edgewater	77904
Edgewood Dr	77905
Edinburgh St	77904
Eisenhower St	77901
Ekstrum St	77905
El Corral St	77901
Elaine St	77904
Elder St	77901
Eleanor St	77904
N Elizabeth St	77901
Elk St	77904
Ellis St	77901
Elm Hollow Rd	77904
Encino Dr	77905
Enterprise Dr	77905
Entrada Dr	77905
Erie St	77905
Ernst St	77901
Erwin Ave	77901
Esquire Pl	77901
Estelle Ln	77905
Eton Grn	77904
Evan Cir	77901
Evergreen St	77904
Fagan Cir	77901
Fairview St	77904
Fairway St	77904
Falcon Ln	77905
Faltysek Rd	77905
Fannin Dr	77901
Fannin Rd	77905
Fannin Oaks	77905
Faupel Dr	77905
Fawn Dr	77905
Felder Dr	77904
Fenway St	77904
Fern Ln	77904
Fernwood Cir	77901
Fieldstone	77901
Fig Ln	77905
Fillmore Ave	77901
Fisher Rd	77905
Flamingo Dr	77901
Fleetwood Dr	77901
Fleming Prairie Rd	77905
Flint Rock Ct	77904
Fm 1432	77905
Fm 1685	77905
Fm 1686	77905
Fm 236	77905
Fm 237	77905
Fm 2615	77905
Fm 2987	77905
Fm 3085	77905
Fm 446	77905
Fm 447	77905
Fm 616	77905
Fm 622	77905
Fordyce Rd	77905
Forest View Dr	77905
E & W Forrest St	77901
Foster Field Dr	77904
Francis St	77901
Fricka St	77901
E Frontage Rd	77905
Gail Ln	77905
Galahad St	77904
Garden Pl	77904
Garden Gate Ln	77904
Gardenia Ln	77904
Garfield St	77901
Garrett	77901
Gayle St	77901
Geistman Ln	77904
Gemini Ct	77901
Gene St	77905
Gentle Breeze St	77905
N & S George St	77901
Georgia Ln	77901
Gettysburg Dr	77904
Girdy Rd	77905
Givens Rd	77905
Glacier Ct	77904
Glascow St	77904
N & S Glass St	77901
Glendale St	77901
Glenmore St	77904
Golden Eye Loop	77905
Golden Glow St	77905
Goldenrod Ave	77904
Goldman Hl	77905
N Goldman St	77901
E & W Goodwin Ave	77901
Gotfried St	77905
Grand Ave	77905
Grand Canyon Ct	77904
Grant St	77901
Grapevine Dr	77905
Green Way	77904
Green Gable Dr	77904
Greenwood St	77901
Griffith Dr	77901
Groll Ln	77905
E Grouse Rd	77905
Guadalupe Rd	77905
E Guadalupe St	77901
W Guadalupe St	77901
Guinevere St	77904
Gunther St	77901
Gussie Schmidt Rd	77905
Guy Grant Rd	77904
Hackamore Ln	77904
Hackberry St	77901
Halsey St	77901
Hamlet Ct	77901
Hampshire St	77904
Hampton Ct	77904
Hand Rd	
1301-2399	77901
2700-2999	77905
Handley Rd	77905
Hangar Dr N & S	77904
Hanselka St	77901
Hanselman Rd	
3700-4400	77901
4402-4498	77901
4600-5098	77905
5100-7700	77905
7702-7798	77905
Harpers Ferry St	77904
Harrison St	77904
Harry St	77901
Hartman Rd	77905
Harvey Ln	77901
Haschke Rd	77905
Hathaway St	77904
Havana St	77904
W Haven	77904
Havenwood Dr	77901
Haynes Rd	77904
Heather St	77904
Henderson Rd	77905
Henderson St	77901
Herbert Ln	77905
Heritage Oak Ct	77901
Hester Rd	77905
Hickory Dr	77904
Hickory Knoll St	77901
Hilex Dr	77901
Hill Rd	77905
Hill Creek Ln	77905
E Hiller St	77901
Hillside Rd	77905
Hilltop Dr	77905
Hkr Ranch Rd	77904
Holly Dr	77905
Holly Ln	77905
Holly St	77901
Holly Oak Ct	77901
Hollywood Blvd	77904
Holt Rd	77905
Honey Dr	77904
Hopkins St	77901
Horseshoe Dr	77904
Hosek Rd	77905
Hospital Dr	77901
Houston Hwy	
1500-1698	77901
1700-8099	77901
8201-8299	77904
Houston St	77905
Huisache St	77901
N & S Hummel St	77901
Hummingbird St	77901
Hunding St	77901
Hunters Cir	77905
Hunters Way	77904
Huntington Dr	77904
Huron St	77905
Huvar St	77904
Hyak Ln	77905
Hyak St	77901
Hybiscus Ln	77904
Idylwood Pl	77901
Imperial Dr	77901
Independence Dr	77901
E Industrial Dr	77901
Industrial Park Dr	77905
E Industry Way	77901
Inverness Dr	77901
Iola St	77904
Ira Ln	77905
Iris Ln	77904
Irma Dr	77905
Iron Gate	77904
Isabell Ivy Rd	77905
Isolda St	77901
Ivanhoe Dr	77901
Jackson Rd	77901
Jacobs Rd	77905
Jade Dr	77904
James Coleman Dr	77904
Jared Rd	77905
Jason St	77901
N Jecker St	77901
Jeffery St	77905
Jessica Dr	77904
Jewett St	77905
Jim Ln	77905
Jj Fishbeck Rd	77904
Jocelyn Cir	77901
Joe Beaver Ln	77905
John St	77901
John Stockbauer Dr	
100-3500	77901
3502-3598	77901
3600-5699	77904
5701-5899	77904
John Wayne Trl	77905
Johnson Rd	77905
Joplin St	77904
Josephine Ln & Rd	77905
Joyce Ln	77901
Juan Antonio Rd	77904
E & W Juan Linn St	77901
Juglan Dr	77901
Julius St	77901
Kainer Rd	77905
Kathy St	77905
Kay Dr	77901
Keith St	77905
Kelly Dr	77904
Kelly Crick Rd	77904
Kemble St	77904
Kemper City Rd E	77905
Kendal Dr	77904
Kenilworth Glen St	77904
Kensington Dr	77901
Kerh Blvd	77904
Kern Dr	77901
Key Rd	77905
Kilt St	77904
Kim	77905
King Dr	77904
King Arthur St	77904
Kingwood Dr	77901
Kingwood Forest Dr	77904
Kinney Dr	77904
Kipling St	77901
Kirkwall St	77904
Klimitchek Rd	77905
Knowland Ave	77901
Kobitz Rd	77905
Kohl Rd	77905
Kohutek Rd	77904
Kolodzey Rd	77905
Kramer St	77901
Krause St	77901
Kreekview Dr	77904
La Luz Dr	77905
La Valliere St	77901
Laguna Dr	77904
Lake Dr	77905
Lake Forest Dr	77904
Lakefront Dr	77905
Lakeoak	77905
Lakeplace	77905
Lakeshore Dr	77905
Lakeside Rd	77905
Lakeview Dr	77905
Lakeway Ct	77905
Lala Ln	77905
Lala St	77901
Lamar Dr	77901
Lamorak St	77904
Lancaster St	77904
Lance Ln	77904
Lancelot St	77904
Lansdown St	77904
Lantana Ave	77901
Laramie Dr	77904
Largo Ct	77901
Lariat Ln	77901
Larimore St	77904
Lark Ln	77901
E Larkspur St	77904
Lasalle Xing	77904
S Lastro St	77901
Laurel Ave	77901
Laurel Ln	77905
N Laurent St	
100-298	77901
300-4400	77901
4402-4598	77901
4700-4798	77904
S Laurent St	77901
Lawndale Ave	77901
Lazy Ln	77905
Leaning Oak Rd	77904
Leary Ln	77901
Lee St	77905
Lee Marshall Dr	77905
Leeper Ln	77904
Legend Dr	77904
Leisure Ln	77904
Lenora Dr	77901
Leuschner Rd	77905
Levi Rd	77905
N Levi St	77901
Levi Sloan Rd	77904
Levis Rd	77901
Lexie Ln	77905
Lexington Ln	77901
N & S Liberty St	77901
Lilac Ln	
4400-4599	77901
4600-5099	77904
5101-5399	77904
Lillian St	77901
Linam Ln	77905
Lincoln St	77901
Linda Dr	77901
Line Drive Rd	77905
Lingo Ln	77904
Linwood Dr	77901
Live Oak Ln	77905
E Locust Ave	77901
E Loma Vista Ave	77901
Londonderry Dr	77901
Lone Oak	77905
Lone Tree Rd	
1600-1798	77901
1800-5899	77901
5901-5999	77901
6501-7297	77905
7299-8400	77905
8402-8498	77905
Lonestar Rd	77905
Longfellow Ln	77904
Longview Dr	77904
Lookout Ln	77905
Lott Rd	77905
N Louis St	77901
Louisiana Ave	77905
Lova Dr	77901
Love Rd	77904
Love St	77901
Lower Mission Valley Rd	77905
Lucero	77905
Lynmore St	77901
Macarthur St	77901
Macon Crk	77901
Madera St	77905
Magdalena Dr	77904

Magnolia Ave 77901
E & W Magruder Dr 77904
Maguey Dr 77905
N Main St
100-298 77901
300-4299 77901
4401-4897 77904
4899-4999 77904
5001-6999 77904
S Main St
100-399 77901
312-312 77902
400-1098 77901
401-1099 77901
Majestic Ln 77904
Mallard Rd 77905
Mallette Dr & St 77904
Manassas Loop 77904
Mandarin Dr 77901
Manor Dr 77901
N & S Mantz St 77901
Maplewood Dr 77901
Marigold St 77904
Marilyn Dr 77901
Marimba Ct 77901
Mariner Dr 77901
Marr Rd 77905
Marshall St 77901
Marvelle St 77901
Mason Cir 77904
Massena Rd 77905
Massouh St 77901
Masters Ct & Dr 77904
Matchett Dr & Rd 77905
Matthews Rd 77905
Mayfair Dr 77901
Mcclanahan Rd 77905
Mccormick Dr 77904
Mccoy Rd 77905
Mccright Dr 77901
Mcdow St 77901
Mclane St 77904
Mcqueens Ln 77904
Mead Rd 77904
Meadow Vw 77904
Meadow Creek St 77905
Meadowlane St 77901
Meadowlark St 77901
Medical Dr 77904
Mejia St 77901
Melrose Ave 77901
Memorial Dr 77901
Menke Rd 77905
Mercury Dr 77904
Mercy River Ln 77905
Merlin St 77904
Mernerth Rd 77905
N Mesquite Dr 77905
S Mesquite Dr 77905
E Mesquite Ln 77901
Mexico Rd 77905
Meyer St 77901
Michigan St 77905
Milam Dr 77901
Milann St 77901
Milton St 77901
E Mimosa Ave 77901
Mincent Dr 77904
Miori Ln 77901
Mission Dr 77901
Mission Bell Rd 77905
Mission Valley Acres Rd 77905
Missy Ln 77901
E Mistletoe Ave 77901
Mitchell St 77901
Mockingbird Cir 77901
E Mockingbird Ln 77904
W Mockingbird Ln 77904
Monte Vista St 77905
Montego Ct 77901
Monterrey Dr 77904
Montezuma Dr 77904
N Moody St 77901
S Moody St 77901
SW Moody St
1100-2299 77901
2301-2599 77901
3400-3598 77905
3600-5700 77905
5702-6298 77905
Morales St 77905
Morgan Dr 77901
Moritz Ln 77905
Morninglory Ln 77904
Morningside St 77901
Morris St 77901
Morris Town Rd 77905
Mossy Oaks Ln 77904
Mueller Rd 77905
Mulberry St 77901
Mumphord Rd 77905
Mumphord St 77901
Murphy Rd 77905
E & W Murray St 77901
Musket Dr 77905
Nagel Rd 77905
Nantucket Ave 77904
Navajo Dr 77904
N Navarro St
8306-A-8306-B 77904
100-198 77901
200-4399 77901
4400-13699 77904
S Navarro St 77901
Navidad St 77901
Neal St 77905
Neil Fox Dr 77901
Nelson Ave 77901
Neu Rd 77904
Newcastle St 77905
Newhaven St 77904
Newport Dr 77904
Nightingale St 77901
N Nimitz St 77901
E & W North St 77901
Northampton Cir 77904
Northcross St 77904
Northfork Rd 77904
Northgate Rd 77904
Northpark Dr 77901
Northshire St 77904
Northside Rd 77904
Norwich Glen St 77904
Nottingham Dr 77904
Nova St 77901
E & W Nueces St 77901
Nursery Dr & Rd 77904
E Oak St 77901
Oak Colony Dr 77905
Oak Ridge St 77905
Oak Village Ln 77905
Oaklawn St 77901
Oakmont Dr 77904
W Oaks 77905
Oakside 77905
Oakway St 77905
Oakwood St 77904
Oconnor Plz 77901
Odem St 77901
Ohrt Rd 77905
Old Bloomington Rd N 77905
Old Goliad Rd 77905
Old Port Lavaca Rd 77905
Old Refugio Rd 77905
Old River Rd 77905
Oleander Dr 77901
Oliver Rd 77904
Oliver St 77901
Ontario St 77905
Opravil Rd 77905
Orangewood St 77904
Oriole St 77901
Osage Rd 77905
Otilia St 77901
Owens St 77901
Owl Rd 77905
Oxford St 77904
Ozark St 77901
Paco Rd 77904
Padre Ln 77905
Paisano Dr 77904
Palm Dr 77901
Palmetto Ave 77901
Palmwood Dr 77901
Paloma Rd 77905
Palomino Ln 77904
Paradise Ranch Rd 77905
E Park Ave 77901
Park Ln 77904
Park Vw 77904
Parkstone Dr 77904
Parsifal St 77901
Parsons Rd 77904
E & W Partridge Rd 77905
Pasadena Dr 77904
Patricia Ln 77905
Patterson Dr 77901
Patterson Ln 77905
Peach St 77905
Pear St 77905
Pebble Brk 77904
Pebble Dr 77905
Pecan Bnd 77901
Pecan Dr 77905
Pecan St 77901
Pecos Dr 77904
Pembrook St 77905
Penn Ave 77904
Pennsylvania Ave 77904
Perdido Ct 77905
Perdido Oaks Dr 77905
Perdido Pointe Cir 77905
Perth St 77904
Pheasant Dr 77905
Pickering Rd W 77905
Pin Oak Ct 77901
Pine St 77901
Pineoak St 77905
Pintail Dr 77905
Plainview St 77901
Plantation Rd 77904
Planters Dr 77901
Pleasant Green Dr
300-1398 77905
1400-1899 77905
1901-1997 77901
1999-3600 77901
3602-3898 77901
Plover St 77901
Plum St 77905
W Point St 77905
E Polk Ave 77901
Polly St 77904
E Poplar Ave 77901
Port St 77901
Port Lavaca Dr
1101-1897 77901
1899-3899 77901
3901-4199 77901
4507-4599 77905
Portsmouth Cir 77904
Post Oak Dr 77905
E & W Power Ave 77901
Pozzi Rd 77905
Prairie View Rd 77904
Price Rd 77905
S Price Rd 77905
Price St 77901
Primrose St 77904
Prince St 77901
Proctor St 77901
Professional Park Dr 77904
Profit Dr 77901
Progress Dr 77905
Providence Ct 77904
Putney St 77901
Quail Creek Dr 77905
Queenswood Trl 77901
Raab Rd 77905
Raab St 77901
Rabbit Run Rd 77905
Rabel Rd 77905
Rae St 77901
Raisin Rd 77905
Ramona Ln 77904
Ramos Rd 77905
Rattan Dr 77901
Raven Rd 77905
Raven St 77901
Raymond Ln 77905
Reaser Dr 77905
Rebecca Ln 77901
Rebel St 77904
Red Oak Ct 77901
E & W Red River St 77901
Redbird Ct 77905
Redding Ln 77905
Redwood Dr 77901
Reeves Oaks 77905
Reeves Ranch Rd 77905
Reeves Ranch Park Rd 77905
Refugio Hwy 77905
Regency Ave 77904
Reid Dr 77904
Reimann Rd 77905
Reinecke Rd 77905
Reissig Rd 77905
Rendon St 77901
Reoh Rd 77905
Reserve Strip St 77901
Retama Cir & Dr 77901
Rhinegold St 77901
Rhodes Rd 77904
Riata 77901
Richmond Dr 77904
Rico Dr 77905
Ridge Dr & Vw 77904
Ridgewood Dr 77901
E & W Rio Grande St 77901
Rio Vista Dr 77904
Ripple Rd 77905
River Rd 77905
E River St 77901
W River St 77901
River Ranch Rd 77905
Riverwood 77904
Roanoke Dr 77904
Robert E Lee St 77905
Robin St 77901
Robles St 77905
Rochelle St 77905
Rockwood Dr 77905
Rocky Creek Dr 77905
Rogers Rd 77905
Rose Dr 77901
Rose Way N 77905
E Rosebud Ave 77901
Roseland Ave 77901
Rosemary Ave 77901
Rosewood Dr 77901
Rotary Rd 77905
Royal Dr 77905
Royal Oak St 77905
Rubin Ln 77905
Ruidoso Dr 77904
Rupley Lk 77905
Russell Rd 77904
Ryan Rd 77904
Rye St 77904
E & W Sabine St 77901
Sagemont Ave 77904
Salem Rd 77904
Salisbury Ln 77904
Salziger St 77901
Sam Houston Dr
100-198 77901
200-2599 77901
2700-2899 77904
2804-2804 77903
2901-3899 77904
3000-3598 77904
E & W San Antonio St 77901
San Antonio River Rd 77905
San Jacinto Ave 77901
San Polo Ct 77904
Sanchez St 77901
Sandpiper Dr 77905
Sandra Ln 77905
Sandstone Ct 77904
Sandy Ln 77905
Santa Barbara St 77904
Santa Fe 77904
E & W Santa Rosa St 77901
Savannah Dr 77904
Scarborough Dr 77901
Schaar Rd 77905
Schaefer Rd 77905
Schell Rd 77904
Schmidt Dr 77905
Schrade Ln 77905
Schubert Rd 77905
E Scott St 77901
Seagull St 77901
Seguin Ave 77901
Seibert Ln 77905
Selma Ln 77905
Senecio St 77901
Sentry Rd 77905
Sequoia Dr 77904
Serene Dr E & W 77905
Sertuche St 77901
Shade Ln 77905
Shadow Ln 77905
Shady Hollow Rd 77904
Shannon Dr 77904
Shannon Valley Dr 77904
Sherwood Dr 77901
Sheryl Dr 77905
Shiloh Dr 77904
Shin Oak Rd 77904
Sidneyville Ln 77905
Siegfried St 77901
Siegmond St 77901
Sierra Ct 77904
Silverado Trl 77901
Simpson Rd 77904
Sirocco Dr 77904
Sky Ct 77904
Skyline 77905
Skytop Rd 77905
N Smith St 77901
Solar Dr 77904
Somerset Pl 77904
E Sonoco Dr 77901
E South St 77901
Sparrow Ln 77905
Spiegelhauer Ln 77901
Spokane St 77904
Spring Rdg 77904
Spring St 77901
Spring Creek Rd 77904
Springwood 77905
Spur Dr 77904
Stanford Ln 77905
Stange Ln 77905
Stanly St 77904
N Star Dr 77904
State Highway 185 S 77905
E & W Stayton Ave 77901
Stehle Rd 77905
Stephenson St 77904
Sterling Ct 77904
Stevenson Rd 77905
Stevie St 77901
Stirrup Rd 77905
Stockade Dr 77905
Stolz St 77901
Stone Mdw & St 77905
Stone Gate Dr 77904
Stoner Rd 77901
Stonewood Pl 77901
Stoney Ln 77905
Storehouse Dr 77904
Stratford St 77905
Strobel Rd 77905
Stubbs School Rd 77905
Sulphur Creek Ests Rd 77905
Summer Ln 77905
Summerwind Dr 77904
Summit Vw 77904
Sun Ct 77904
Sun Valley Dr 77904
Suncrest Ln 77905
Sundance Dr 77901
Sunrise Ct 77901
Sunrise Ln 77905
Sunset Dr
101-107 77901
173-197 77905
199-200 77905
201-213 77901
202-214 77905
215-221 77901
400-410 77905
412-800 77905
802-898 77905
Superior St 77905
Susie St 77905
Sussex Dell Dr 77904
Sutton Mott Rd 77905
Suzanne Ln 77901
Swan Dr 77901
Swanson Rd 77905
Swift Ct 77901
Sycamore St 77901
Sylvan Cir 77905
Sylvia St 77904
Tagliabue Rd 77905
Tampa Dr 77904
Tampico Ct 77904
Tanglewood Dr 77901
Taos Dr 77904
Tate Rd 77904
Tater Ln 77905
Taylor Ave 77901
Taylorcrest St 77905
Teakwood Dr 77901
Teal 77905
Tern Ct 77901
Terrace Ave 77901
Terravista Trl 77904
Texas Ave 77905
Thompson St 77901
Thurmond St 77901
Tibiletti Dr 77901
Tibiletti Rd 77905
Tiffany Dr 77904
Tiki Ct 77904
Tilley Ln 77905
Timber Dr 77904
Timber Rd 77905
Timberlane Dr 77901
Timberline Dr 77905
Tipton Rd W 77905
Tonto Cir 77904
Topaz Dr 77904
Tournament Dr 77904
Tracy Ln 77904
Tradewind Dr 77904
Tranquillo Dr 77905
Travis Ave 77901
Travis Dr 77905
Trent St 77905
Trentwood Cir 77901
E & W Trinity St 77901
Tristan St 77901
Troon Rd 77904
Tropical Dr 77904
N & S Troy St 77901
Turtle Rock Dr 77904
Tuscany Dr 77904
Tweed St 77904
Twin Fountains Dr 77904
Twin Lakes Cir & Dr 77905
Twin Oak Dr 77905
Tyne Rd 77904
Uresti Ln 77905
Us Highway 59 N & S 77905
Us Highway 77 N 77904
Us Highway 77 S 77905
Us Highway 87 N 77904
Us Highway 87 S 77905
Valkyrie St 77901
Valley View St 77905
Valley Vista Rd 77905
Vanchelm St 77901
Vanessa Ln 77901
Vernon St 77905
Versailles St 77904
Victor Dr 77904
N & S Victoria St 77901
Victoria Station Dr 77901
Viking St 77905
Villafranca Rd 77904
Villafranca Rh Rd 77904
Village Dr 77901
Village Grn 77904
Village Ln 77905
N Vine St
101-397 77901
399-4099 77901
4101-4399 77901
4700-4898 77904
4900-4999 77904
S Vine St 77901
Virada 77905
E Virginia Ave 77901
Vista Cv 77904
Vista Alta St 77904
Vogt Dr 77901
Vogt Rd 77905
Volsung St 77901
Vrana Ln 77904
Waco Cir 77904
Wade Dr 77904
Wade Way 77905
Wagner Way St 77904
Wagon Trl 77905
Waida Rd 77905
Wallace Ln 77904
Wally Ln 77905
E Walnut Ave 77901
Walter St 77901
Warburton Rd 77905
Warehouse Rd 77905
E Warren Ave 77901
Warwick Glen St 77904
N Washington St 77901
E Water St 77901
Water Oak Ct 77901
Waterford Dr 77901
Watermark 77904
Waters Edge Dr 77905
Waterstone 77901
Watts St 77901
Wayside Dr 77901
Wearden Dr 77904
Weber Ln & Rd 77905
Wellspring Blvd 77904
N West St 77901
Westbrook Dr 77904
Westchester Dr 77904
Westlake Trl 77905
Westpark Ave 77905
Westwood St 77901
Wharf St 77901
N & S Wheeler St 77901
Whispering Creek St 77904
Whispering Oaks St 77905
White Oak Ct 77901
Whitechurch Ln 77904
Whitewing St 77905
Wickerwood Dr 77901
Wilden St 77901
Wildrose Dr 77904
Wildwood St 77901
Will Heard Rd 77904
Willard St 77901
Willemin Ln 77905
N & S William St 77901
Williamsburg Ave 77904
Willie St 77901
Willow St 77901
Willow Way 77904
Willow Creek Rd 77904
Willow Creek Ranch Rd 77904
Willowick Dr 77901
Wilshire Dr 77904
Windcrest Dr 77904
Winding Way Dr 77905
Windrock Dr 77904
Windsor St 77901
Windward Ct 77901
Windwood Ln 77904
Windy Hollow St 77904
Windy Way Dr 77904
Winnipeg St 77905

Winston Ct 77904
Winter Ln 77905
Wischkaemper Rd 77905
Wischkaemper School Rd 77905
Wisteria Ave 77901
Wolfram St 77901
Wood Duck Ct 77905
Wood Hi Rd 77905
Woodchase Dr 77904
Woodcreek Cir 77904
Woodglenn Dr 77904
Woodhall Dr 77904
Woodhaven Dr 77904
Woodland Way 77905
Woodlands Ln 77904
Woodlawn St 77901
Woodmere Dr 77904
Woodridge Dr 77904
Woodsprite Rd 77905
Woodway Dr 77904
Woodwind Dr 77904
Wren St 77904
Ybarra Rd 77905
Yellowstone Dr 77904
York Rd 77905
Yorkshire Ln 77904
Yosemite Dr 77904
Young Dr 77901
Yucca Dr 77904
Yuma Dr 77904
Yupon Ave 77901
NE Zac Lentz Pkwy 77904
NW Zac Lentz Pkwy 77905
Zephyr Dr 77904

NUMBERED STREETS

All Street Addresses 77901

VIDOR TX

General Delivery 77662

POST OFFICE BOXES MAIN OFFICE STATIONS AND BRANCHES

Box No.s
All PO Boxes 77670

RURAL ROUTES

07, 08, 09 77662

NAMED STREETS

All Street Addresses 77662

NUMBERED STREETS

All Street Addresses 77662

WACO TX

General Delivery 76702

POST OFFICE BOXES MAIN OFFICE STATIONS AND BRANCHES

Box No.s
1 - 2494 76703
2500 - 2900 76702
3001 - 3615 76707
4001 - 5999 76708
6011 - 6443 76706
7000 - 9148 76714
9997 - 9997 76702
11003 - 11882 76716
20001 - 24302 76702
32501 - 32746 76703
154001 - 156100 76715

RURAL ROUTES

04, 05, 07, 08, 09, 17, 19, 22 76705
10, 16 76708

NAMED STREETS

Abbott St 76704
Abby Ln 76708
Acree St 76711
Acree Acres 76711
Adams St 76704
Addie Ln 76705
Adeline Dr 76708
Adobe Ct 76712
Adrian Dr 76706
Air Base Rd 76705
Airline Dr 76705
Airport Rd 76708
Alaska St 76705
Alex Gill Ln 76705
Alexander Ave 76708
Alford Dr 76710
Algonquin St 76707
Alice Ave 76708
Allen St 76705
Alma Rohn Dr 76705
Alston Dr 76705
Alta Vista Cir & Dr 76706
Alto Ln 76705
Alvin Dr 76708
Ambassador Dr 76712
Amber Cir 76712
Amberway 76705
American Plz 76712
S And T Dr 76706
Andalusian Ln 76706
N & S Andrews Dr 76706
Angle Ln 76705
Anlo Ave 76710
Ann St 76711
Anthony Dr 76705
Apache Dr 76712
Apple Ln 76704
Apple Cross Ct 76706
Applegrove Cir 76704
Apron Rd 76705
Aquilla Trl 76708
Aragon Dr 76708
Arapaho 76706
Armstrong Dr 76704
Arra St 76704
Arroyo Rd 76710
Ashburn St 76704
Ashleman St 76705
Athens Ave 76710
E Athens St 76704
W Aubrey Dr 76706
Audrey Ave 76705
Aurora Dr 76708
Austin Ave
300-2499 76701
2500-4199 76710
Autumn Wood Dr 76711
Avenue E 76705
Avenue A 76705
Avenue B 76705
Avenue C 76705
Avenue D 76705
Avenue F 76705
Avenue G 76705
Avenue H 76705
Avenue I 76705
Aviation Pkwy 76705
Avon Dr 76708
Avondale Ave 76707
Aztec Cir & Dr 76706
B B Burt 76708
Babcock Dr 76705
Badger Trl 76705
Bagby Ave
100-798 76706
800-2399 76706
2600-5699 76711
Baker Ln
100-198 76706
200-400 76706
400-699 76708
402-498 76706
701-1399 76708
Bank Dr 76705
Bar W Ranch Rd 76705
N & S Barbara St 76705
Barcelona Dr 76708
Barker Ln 76705
Barksdale St 76705
Barlow St 76705
Barnard St 76701
Barron Ave
400-499 76701
501-599 76701
1300-1699 76707
Barry Hand Ln 76705
Barton Creek Dr 76708
Bavarian Rd 76705
Baxter Loop 76705
Baylor Ave
901-1197 76706
1199-2499 76706
2600-2899 76711
Beachwood 76705
Beale St 76705
Bear Pl 76798
Bear Run 76711
Beard Ave 76706
Beauford St 76706
Beauregard St 76705
Beaver Ln & St 76705
Beaver Lake Rd 76705
Bedrock Trl 76708
Behrens Cir 76705
Belfast Cir 76712
E Bell Rd 76705
W Bell Rd 76705
Bell St 76711
Bellcrest St 76705
Bellmead Dr 76705
Belmont Dr 76711
Bennett St 76704
Benson Rd 76706
Bent Tree Cir 76708
Benton Dr 76706
Bentwood 76706
Berkshire St 76705
Berlinger Dr 76710
N & S Bermuda St 76705
Berry Dr 76706
Berry St 76710
Berwick Ct 76706
Berwyn Dr 76708
Bestyett Ln 76708
Bethard St 76705
N Betsy Dr 76706
Betting Way 76705
Beverly Dr 76711
Beverly Cox Dr 76705
Big Mailbox Rd 76706
W Billington Dr 76706
Birch St 76705
Birdie Cir 76708
Bishop Dr 76710
Bismark Ct 76708
Blackjack Cir 76705
Blackmon St 76708
Blackwell St 76705
Blair St 76707
Blanco Dr 76708
Blanton Pl 76705
Bluebird St 76705
Bobcat Dr 76705
E Bode Rd 76705
Bogey Ln 76708
Bolling Dr 76705
Bongard Cir 76705
Booker St 76705
Boone Tucker Ln 76705
Borman Ln 76705
Bosque Blvd
201-397 76707
399-3399 76707
3400-7399 76710
Boston St 76705
Bowden St 76710
Bowen Ln 76705
Bowers St 76704
Bowie St 76705
Boyd St 76706
Boys Ranch Rd 76705
Bradford St 76711
Braemar St 76710
Brame St 76705
Brandon Ln 76705
Brandy Ln 76705
Brandywine 76705
Brannon Dr 76710
Brazos Loop 76705
Brazos Oaks Dr 76705
Brazos Point Dr 76705
Brazos Ridge Trl 76705
Breckenridge Dr 76706
Breezy Dr 76712
Brenda St 76705
Breton St 76706
Brewster St 76706
Briar Dr 76710
Briarcliff Dr 76710
Briarwood Ln 76705
E Bridge St 76704
Brint Ln 76706
Broad Ave 76712
Broadway St 76704
E Broadway St 76705
Broken Arrow Dr 76705
Bronco 76705
Brook Ave 76708
Brook Cir
3300-3399 76707
3400-3499 76710
Brookcrest Cir 76710
Brooklyn Cir & St 76704
Brooks Dr 76710
Brooks Ln 76705
E Brookview Dr
3300-3399 76707
3401-3699 76710
W Brookview Dr 76710
Brown Ave 76706
Browning Dr 76710
Bryan Ave 76708
Buckboard Xing 76706
Buckskin Ln 76706
Bud Dr 76705
Buffalo Loop 76705
Buffalo Rdg 76712
Bulldog Run 76708
Bumpy Rd 76705
N Bunker Dr 76706
Bunting Dr 76708
Burberry 76712
Burgan St 76704
Burleson St 76707
Burnell Cir 76712
Burnett Ave
1000-1498 76706
1500-2599 76706
2600-2899 76711
Burnham Dr 76708
Busch Ln 76705
Buster Chatham Rd 76705
Buttercup 76705
Buttercup Cir 76708
Butterfly Way 76705
C C Carpenter Ln 76705
Cadet Way 76705
Calaveras 76708
Caldwell St 76710
E Calhoun Ave 76704
Calumet St 76704
Calvery St 76705
Cambridge Cir 76712
Cameron Ct 76708
Camp Dr 76710
Camp Ground Rd 76705
Campbelton St 76705
Campus Dr 76705
Caney Creek Dr 76708
Cannon Ln 76708
Cannon St 76704
Canterbury Dr 76712
Cantrell St 76704
Canyon Dr 76708
Canyon Ridge Dr 76705
Carl Dr 76705
Carla St 76705
W Carlos St 76706
Carlton Ln 76705
Carlyle Dr 76710
Carolinda Dr 76710
Caron St 76706
Carondolet Blvd 76710
Carriage Sq 76708
Carroll Dr 76708
Carswell St 76705
Carter Dr 76706
Carter Rd 76705
Carver St 76704
Casa Linda Dr 76708
Cashearb Ave 76707
Cassie Trl 76708
Castillo Village Rd 76708
Castle Ave 76710
Catalina Dr 76712
Catherine St 76705
Cathy Dr 76706
Catto Ave 76710
Caudill Ln 76705
Cedar St 76705
Cedar Creek Cir & Dr 76705
Cedar Crest Dr 76708
Cedar Mountain Dr 76708
Cedar Point Dr 76710
N Cedar Ridge Cir 76706
S Cedar Ridge Cir 76706
Cedar Ridge Rd 76708
Celeste Dr 76706
Central St 76705
Chado Ln 76706
Chamber Ln 76706
Chandler St 76705
Chantilly St 76706
Chanute St 76705
Chaparral Dr 76710
Chapel Rd 76712
Chapel Creek Rd 76712
Chapel Downs Rd 76712
Chapel Hill Dr 76712
Chapel Ridge Rd 76712
Chapel Trail Cir 76712
Chapel View Rd 76712
Chapelwood Dr 76712
Chappel Hill Rd 76705
Charboneau Dr 76710
Charleston 76705
Charlotte Dr 76708
Charlton Ave 76711
Charping St 76705
Chartwell Dr 76712
Chateau Ave 76710
Chattanooga St 76704
Cherokee Ln 76712
Cherokee St 76705
Cherry St 76704
Cherry Hill Sq 76708
Cheshire Dr 76712
Chesser Dr 76706
Chestnut St 76704
Chimney Corner Dr 76708
Chimney Hill Dr 76708
Chimney Place Dr 76708
Chimney Ridge Dr 76708
China Creek Dr 76708
China Spring Rd 76708
Choctaw Ct 76704
Christina Dr 76706
Christopher Ln 76708
Church Ave 76706
S Church Ave 76706
E Church St 76704
Church Camp Ln 76706
Churchill Cir 76712
Cimmarron Dr 76712
Cindy Cir 76710
Cindy St 76706
Circle Rd 76706
Circle C Dr 76705
Claire Newell Ln 76705
Clark Ave 76708
Clater Powell Rd 76705
Clay Ave
100-198 76706
200-499 76706
424-424 76703
424-424 76706
424-424 76716
501-2599 76706
600-2598 76706
2600-3400 76711
3402-3498 76711
E Clay St 76704
Clear Creek Ln 76706
Cleveland Ave
701-797 76706
799-2599 76706
2600-2899 76711
Cliffdale Dr 76708
Cliffview Rd 76710
Clifton St 76704
Cline Rd 76706
Clover Ln 76710
Clover St 76705
Cloverland 76708
Cloverleaf Dr 76706
Cloverleaf Rd 76705
Club Estates Ct 76710
Clydesdale Way 76706
Coahuila Dr 76706
Coastal Ln 76705
Cobbs Dr
3800-4099 76708
4101-4197 76710
4199-6499 76710
Cobbs Ln 76708
Colcord Ave 76707
Cold Water Dr 76712
Cole Ave
2201-2297 76707
2299-3299 76707
4600-4799 76710
Cole Rd 76705
Coleman St 76705
Colina Ln 76705
College Dr 76708
Collins Dr 76710
Colonial Ave
1800-3199 76707
4600-4799 76710
Colonial St 76705
Colonnade Pkwy 76712
Colony Dr 76708
Columbia St 76711
Columbus Ave
400-2499 76701
2500-2900 76710
2902-2998 76710
Comal St 76708
Comanche Cir 76706
Comanche Dr 76706
Comanche Trl 76712
Commerce Dr 76710
Compton Ln 76705
Concho Bend Dr 76712
Concord Rd 76705
Concorn Way 76705
Condor Loop 76708
Conestoga 76706
Congress St
300-699 76705
1100-1299 76704
Conine Dr 76706
Connally St 76711
Connor Ave
1100-1398 76706
1400-2499 76706
2600-2999 76711
Cooksey Ln 76706
Coral Reef 76705
Cordoba Ct 76708
Cornell St 76711
Cortivo Rd 76705
Costa Dr 76712
Cotter Ln 76705
Cotton Dr 76712
Cottonbelt St 76704
Cottonwood St 76706
Cougar Ridge Pkwy 76708
Country Dr 76705
Country Aire Dr 76708
Country Club Rd 76710
Country Lake Dr 76708
County Road 421 76706
County Road 422 76706
Cove Dr 76705
Cowpoke Cir 76705
Coxs Oak Valley Rd 76705
Coyote Run 76705
Cozie Cir 76708
E & W Craven Ave 76705
Creek Rdg 76708
Creekwood Cir 76710
Crescent Rd 76710
Crescent St 76705
E Crest Dr 76705
Cresthill Cir 76710
Cresthill Dr 76705
Crestline St 76705
Crestview St 76710
Crestwood Dr 76710
Cricket Dr 76705
Crockett St 76705
Crosby Dr 76706
Cross Cir 76708
Crosslake Pkwy 76712
Crow Dr 76705
Crozier Cir 76705
Crunk Rd 76706
Cumberland Ave 76707
Curtis Dr 76710
Dahlia St 76708
Dal Paso Dr 76706
Dale St 76706
Dallas Cir & St 76704
Dan Rowe St 76704
Dana St 76706
Darby Ln 76712
Darden Dr 76706
Darryl Ln 76708
Dartmouth St 76711
Darwin St 76705
Daughtrey Ave
66-398 76706
400-2399 76706
3000-3398 76711
3400-3599 76711
Daughtrey Cir 76711
David Dr 76707
Davis St 76704
E Dawn Dr 76706
Dawson St 76704
Daybreak St 76705
Dayton Dr 76706
Dean Dr 76706
Deanna St 76706
Dearborn St 76704
Deer Crk 76705
Deer Creek Dr 76708
Deerwood Dr 76710
Del Mar Ct 76706
Delakerm Ave 76708
Delano St 76704
Delila Dr 76706
Delview Dr 76705
Denise Dr 76706
W Denison Dr 76706
Denton Cir 76710
Denver Ave 76708
Depot Dr 76712
Deshong Smith St 76704
Desperado 76708

Development Blvd 76705
Dever Dr 76708
Dewberry Ln 76708
Dewey Pickney 76705
Dickens Dr 76710
N Dison Dr 76706
Docs Run 76705
Dogwood Ln 76705
Dogwood St 76706
Donald St 76705
Donaldson Ln 76706
Donlo St 76706
N Donna Dr 76706
Dossett St 76705
Double Ee Ranch Rd 76705
Dove St 76706
Downsville Rd 76706
Drake Ct 76710
Dreyer Ln 76705
Driftwood St 76706
Dry Creek Rd 76705
Dublin Dr 76712
Dugger St 76705
Dunbar St 76704
Dunn St 76710
Durand Ct 76705
Durango Trl 76712
Durie 76706
Dustin Dr 76705
Dutton Ave
501-997 76706
999-2599 76706
2600-3300 76711
3302-3398 76711
Duty Ave 76706
Dyer Ave 76708
Eagle Ct 76708
Eagle Point Ct 76705
Eagles Mtn 76712
Earle Ave 76704
Eastgate Plz 76705
Eastland Lake Dr 76706
Eastwood Way 76705
Easy St 76704
Easy Acres Rd 76705
Edgeway St 76704
Edgewood Ave 76708
Edinburgh Dr 76710
Edmond Ave
2800-3299 76707
4600-7199 76710
Edna Ave 76708
Edward Dr 76708
Egan Ln 76705
El Blanco Ln 76705
Elden Cir 76705
Eldon Ln 76710
Eldridge Ln 76710
Elizabeth Cir 76711
W Elizabeth Dr 76706
Elk Rd 76705
Elk Road Spur 76705
Elling Dr 76705
Ellington St 76705
Elliott Dr 76711
Elm St 76704
W Elm Mott Dr 76705
N Emberwood Dr 76706
Emerald Dr 76708
Emerson Dr 76710
Emily Ln 76708
Enchanted Rock 76712
Enclave Ct 76708
Ender Rd 76706
Erath St 76710
Erskine Ln 76706
Estella Ln 76706
Esther St 76710
Ethel Ave 76707
Evans Dr
1400-1498 76704
1500-1699 76704
1800-1899 76705
Evergreen Cir 76710
Ewing Ave 76706
E Ewing St 76704

Factory Dr 76710
Fadal Ave 76708
Fairview Dr 76710
Falcon 76706
Fall St 76708
Fallbrook Rd 76708
Fannie Lee Dr 76708
Fannin St 76705
Far Paddock Rd 76705
Faulkner Ln
100-1899 76704
2200-2299 76705
Faye St 76705
Fenton St 76705
Fern Hill Cir 76708
Fern Valley Rd 76708
Ferndale Dr 76706
Fieldstone Cir 76708
Fincher Dr 76706
Fish Pond Rd 76710
Fisher St 76705
Fisseler St 76704
Fitzpatrick Ave 76708
Flat Creek Dr 76706
Flat Rock Rd 76708
Flint Ave
1500-1598 76706
1600-2599 76706
2600-2899 76711
Florida St 76705
Flyer St 76705
Flying Heart Rd 76706
Fm 2491 76705
Fm 2839 76706
Fm 434 76706
W Fork Trl 76705
Forrest St 76704
Forrester Ln 76708
Fort Ave
1800-3399 76707
3400-3598 76710
3600-5199 76710
Fort Gates 76708
Fort Graham Cir & Rd 76705
Fort Hill Rd 76705
Fossil Rdg 76712
W Foster Dr 76706
Foundation Dr 76712
Fountain Pkwy 76705
Four Winds Rd 76705
Fox Glenn Rd 76705
Fox Hill Dr 76705
Fox Hollow Cir 76708
Foxview Dr 76708
Fran Ln 76705
Frances Rd 76706
Franklin Ave
2-98 76701
100-2499 76701
2500-5200 76710
5202-6098 76710
Frederick Ave 76707
Freedom Ct 76708
French Ave 76706
Frost Ave 76708
E Frost St 76705
Frow St 76704
Gail Dr 76708
Galleywinter Ln 76708
Garden Dr 76706
E Garden Dr 76706
Garden Ln 76705
Gardendale Dr 76710
Garland Ave 76707
Garnet Dr 76708
Garrett Ave 76706
Garrison St 76704
Gary Ln 76708
Georges Cir 76705
Georgia Ln 76706
Germania Rd 76705
Gholson Rd
1100-2999 76704
3001-3097 76705
3099-3200 76705
3202-3298 76705

3300-3399 76704
3401-3597 76705
3599-18399 76705
Gill Ln 76705
Gilliam St 76705
Glasgow Dr 76710
Glen Lake St 76710
Glendale Dr 76710
Glenwood Cir 76708
Glenwood Dr 76705
Gloryland Rd 76705
Goebel Ln 76705
Gold Camp Cir 76712
Goldman Ln 76708
Gorham Cir & Dr 76708
Gorman Ave
1800-2999 76707
3600-4299 76710
Gram Ln 76705
Granada Dr 76708
E Grant St 76704
Gravel Rd 76708
Great Oak Trl 76705
Green Acres Trl 76705
Green Oak Dr 76710
Green Point Dr 76710
Green Valley Dr 76710
Greenbriar Dr 76705
W Greenbriar St 76706
Greenfield Dr 76705
Greenleaf Dr
400-499 76705
3200-3498 76710
3500-3999 76710
4001-4199 76710
Greenway Dr 76705
Greenwood Dr 76708
Greenwood Ln 76705
Greer St 76710
Gregory Ln 76708
Greig Dr 76706
Grice St 76710
Grim Ave
2400-2999 76707
3001-3099 76707
3600-4299 76710
Grove Crk 76708
Groveland St 76705
Guittard Ave 76706
Gunsmoke Dr 76705
Gurley Ave
1300-2499 76706
2501-2599 76706
2600-2899 76711
2901-3099 76711
Gurley Ln 76706
Guthrie Cir & Dr 76705
Hacienda Wesley 76706
Hackberry Ave & Cir 76706
Haden Dr 76710
Haferkamp Ln 76705
Hahn Dr 76706
Halbert Ln 76705
Half Pint Rd 76705
Hall Dr 76705
Hallsburg Rd 76705
Hamilton Dr 76705
Hamilton Ln 76706
Hamilton St 76705
Hand Dr 76705
Hannah Ln 76706
Hannah St 76705
Hanover Dr 76710
Happy Ln 76708
Harlan Ave 76710
Harlem Ave 76704
Harrington Ave 76706
Harris St 76705
Harrison Ave 76704
Harrison Rd 76705
Harrison St 76705
Harry James Dr 76705
Harvard St 76711
Harvey Dr 76710
Haskell Rd 76708
Hassie Ln 76705

Hatcher St 76705
Hatton St 76704
Hawk Rdg 76705
Hawkins Ct 76706
Hawthorne Dr 76710
Hay Ave 76711
Hayes Ln 76705
Hazelwood Ave 76705
Headrick Dr 76706
Hearthwood Cir 76708
Heatherstone Cir 76708
Heese Ln 76705
Helen Dr 76708
Helmsdale 76706
Hermanson Dr 76710
Hermosa St 76705
Herrera Rd 76705
Herring Ave 76708
E Herring Ave 76704
Herwol Ave 76710
Hesston Cir 76706
Hiawatha Dr 76712
Hickory Vly 76705
Hicks Dr 76704
Hicks Ln 76706
Hidden Oaks Dr 76705
Hidden Valley Dr 76710
Hideaway Loop 76706
High Ln 76705
High Point Dr
200-299 76705
12300-12499 76708
E Highway 6 76704
E Highway 84 76705
Hiland Dr 76711
Hillandale Rd 76710
Hillcrest Dr
3201-3297 76708
3299-3700 76708
3702-3998 76708
4100-5399 76710
Hillcrest Medical Blvd 76712
Hillsboro Dr 76704
Hillside Dr 76706
Hillside St 76710
Hilltop Dr 76710
N Hillview St 76706
Hines Ave 76706
Hirsch Dairy Rd 76706
Hobbs Ln 76706
Hodde Dr 76710
Hoffman St 76705
Hoffmeyer Ln 76706
Hogan Ln 76705
Holly Vista St 76711
Hollywood Dr 76704
Holmes St 76705
Holt Ave 76706
Holtkamphill 76706
Holze Cir 76710
Homan Ave 76707
Honey Ln 76706
Hood St 76704
Hooks St 76705
Hoosier Park 76706
Horne Cir 76705
Horseshoe Dr 76711
Horseshoe Bend Rd 76708
Horton Dr 76705
Hour Glass Cir 76708
Houston St 76704
Howard St 76711
Howe Hill Rd 76706
Huaco Ln 76710
Hubby Ave
2900-2999 76707
3600-4299 76710
Hubert St 76704
Hunter Ridge Cir 76708
Huntington Dr 76710
Hunton Ln 76706
Hyacinth Ln 76708
Ida St 76705
Idaho St 76705
Idlewood Dr 76705
Idylwood Ln 76705

Ike St 76704
Imperial Dr 76712
Independence Trl 76708
Indian Wls 76705
Indian Springs Dr 76708
Indiana Ave 76707
E Industrial Blvd 76705
W Industrial Blvd 76711
Industrial Dr 76710
N Industrial Dr 76710
S Industrial Dr 76710
Inez Dr 76706
Ingred St 76705
Inmon St 76705
Interstate 35 N
100-106 76704
Interstate 35 N
108-598 76704
800-1498 76705
1500-6400 76705
6402-6698 76705
Interstate 35 S 76706
N Interstate 35
701-999 76705
Inverness Dr 76710
Inwood Dr 76711
Ione Dr 76708
Iowa St 76705
Iris Ln 76708
Iron Horse Trl 76708
Irving Lee St 76711
Ivan 76706
Ivy Ave 76706
J J Flewellen Rd 76704
J L Brazzil Loop 76705
N Jack Kultgen Expy 76704
S Jack Kultgen Expy 76706
Jackson Ave 76701
Jake Sparks Dr 76705
James Ave
600-798 76706
800-2399 76706
3000-4199 76711
E James St 76704
James Wesley Dr 76706
Jami Ln 76708
Jancy St 76706
Jane St 76711
Janice Dr 76706
January St 76705
Jasmine Ln 76706
Jason St 76705
Jefferson Ave
300-1499 76701
2100-2199 76707
Jeffrey St 76710
Jennifer Dr 76706
Jeran Dr 76711
Jerico Rd 76706
Jewel Ln 76705
Jewell Dr 76712
Jim Tom Dr 76706
Jimenez Dr 76706
Jo Dr 76706
Joanne Dr 76705
Joey Dr 76711
John Spur 76705
E Johnson St
100-199 76704
200-999 76705
Jonquil 76708
Josephine Dr 76705
Journeys End 76705
Joy Dr 76708
N & S Joyce St 76705
Judy Dr 76705
Juniper Ln 76706
Kane St 76705
Kansas St 76705
E & W Karels Dr 76706
Karem Rd 76710
Karen Dr 76706
Karl May Dr 76708
W Karnes Dr 76706
Kate St 76705
Kathryn Ln 76708

Katy Ln & St 76705
Kay Dr 76706
Keesler Ln 76705
Kellum St 76704
Kelly St 76710
Kempner Park 76706
Kendall Ln 76705
Kendrick Ln 76711
Kenna Ln 76708
Kennedy Cir 76706
Kenny Ln 76710
Kenwood St 76706
Kestrel Ct 76708
Kettler Dr 76706
Keys Creek Dr 76708
Kilgore Ln 76705
Kim Ln 76706
Kimberly Dr 76708
King Cole Dr 76705
Kingman St 76710
Kings Hwy 76704
Kingston Dr 76712
Kiowa Cir & Ln 76706
Kipling Dr 76710
Kirkland Ln 76708
Knight Ln 76705
Knoll Dr 76708
Knust Cir 76705
Kristi St 76706
La Clede St 76705
La Porte Dr 76710
La Salle Ave 76706
La Vega St 76705
La Village Ave 76712
Lacey Cir 76708
N & S Lacy Dr 76705
Lady Bug Cir 76705
Lafayette Cir 76705
Laguna Vista Dr 76708
Lajuana Dr 76705
Lake Air Dr 76710
Lake Arrowhead Dr 76710
Lake Charles Dr 76710
W Lake Creek Rd 76705
Lake Crest Dr 76710
Lake Englewood Dr 76710
Lake Felton Pkwy 76705
Lake Forest Dr 76708
Lake Haven Dr 76710
Lake Heights Dr 76708
Lake Highlands Dr 76710
Lake Hurst Dr 76710
Lake Jackson Dr 76710
Lake James Dr 76710
Lake Killarney Dr 76710
Lake Lindenwood Dr 76710
Lake Oaks Rd 76710
Lake Placid Pl 76710
Lake Ridge Cir 76710
Lake Ridge Dr 76706
Lake Shore Dr
900-2899 76708
2901-4099 76708
4100-4198 76710
4200-5299 76710
E Lake Shore Dr
900-998 76705
1100-1199 76708
1201-1899 76708
2200-2298 76705
2300-2599 76705
Lake Shore Villa Dr 76710
Lake Success Dr 76710
Lakeland Cir 76710
Lakemont Cir 76710
Lakemoor Dr 76710
N & S Lakeview Dr 76705
Lakewood Dr 76710
Landmark Dr 76710
Landon Branch Rd 76708
Landsdown Dr 76708
Langley Dr 76705
Lankart Cir 76706
Lapis Cir & Dr 76708
Lapsley St 76704
Larry Ln 76705

Larry Don Ln 76708
Lasker Ave 76707
Lassetter Ln 76705
Latimer St 76705
Laurel Park 76706
Laurel Lake Dr 76710
Lawhon Ln 76708
Lawndale St 76706
Lawrence Dr 76710
Lazy Oaks Dr 76705
E League St 76704
N & S League Ranch Rd 76705
Lee St 76711
E Lee St 76704
Legend Ln 76706
Legend Lake Pkwy 76712
Leggott Dr 76706
Leland Ave 76708
Lemley Ln 76705
Lenamon St 76710
Lenox St 76704
Leon Dr
100-499 76705
6200-6599 76708
E Leona Pkwy 76706
Lewis St 76705
Lexington St
1100-1799 76711
4600-4799 76705
Liberty St 76705
Lilac 76708
Lillian St 76704
Lilry Rd 76708
Limestone Trl 76712
Limited St 76705
Lincoln St 76705
Linda Ln 76705
Linda St 76708
Linda Vista Ln 76706
Lindsey Ln 76708
Lindsey Hollow Rd 76708
Links Cir & Dr 76708
Linn St 76704
Linnett Dr 76706
Lippizan St 76706
Lisa St 76705
Lisbon Dr 76706
Live Oak Ave
1500-3799 76708
4400-5299 76710
E Live Oak St 76704
Live Oak Valley Cir 76710
Loch Lomond Dr 76710
Lochinvar Ct 76710
Locklar Loop 76705
Lockwood Dr 76710
Lockwood Ln 76706
Loftin Rd 76710
Logue Ln 76708
Lola Ln 76705
Loma Vista Dr 76708
Londonderry Dr 76712
Lone Star Dr 76708
Lonely Pine Rd 76708
Longfellow St 76710
S Lontonge St 76706
N Loop Dr
301-1399 76705
500-1398 76704
S Loop Dr 76704
E Loop 340 76705
N Loop 340 76705
S Loop 340 76706
W Loop 340 76711
Lopez St 76705
Lorraine Dr 76707
Los Alamitos 76706
Los Arboles Ln 76711
Losak Rd 76706
Lost Gold Rd 76708
Lost Oaks Dr 76705
Lost Trails Dr 76712
Lottie St 76704
Louis St 76705
Loyee Ln 76708

Luanne 76705
Lux Dr 76706
Lyle Ave
1400-3499 76708
4100-4199 76710
E & W Lyndale Ave 76706
Lyndon Cir 76706
M J R Rd 76706
Mabry St 76711
Macarthur Dr 76708
Machintosh Ct 76706
Madera Dr 76705
Madison Dr 76706
Madrid Ct 76708
Maehr Rd 76705
Mahalia Dr 76705
Mahan Holw 76704
Main St 76704
Majestic Oaks Ln 76705
Majors St 76704
Mall Dr 76712
Mamie Ballew Ln 76705
Mammoth Springs Dr 76708
Mammy Ln 76705
Manchaca Pl 76705
N Mann St 76704
Manor Dr 76706
Maple Ave 76707
Maple Hill Cir 76708
Marble Dr 76705
W Margaret St 76706
Marie Dr
900-1099 76712
2000-2099 76706
Marigold Rd 76708
Market St 76704
Market Place Dr 76711
Marlin Hwy 76705
Marquita St 76711
Mars Dr 76712
Marsha Cir 76707
Marsha St 76705
Marshall Ave 76708
Martin Ave 76706
N Martin Luther King Jr Blvd
300-398 76704
400-2599 76704
3801-3899 76708
S Martin Luther King Jr Blvd 76704
Mary Ave
100-2499 76701
2901-3399 76710
Mary Ware Dr 76705
Maryland Ave 76707
Massey Ln 76706
Mather St 76705
Mathews St 76705
Matthys Dr 76705
Matus Ln 76705
Maxfield St 76705
Maxwell Ln 76705
May Dr 76710
May St 76705
Mazanec Rd 76705
Mccloney St 76704
Mcdonald Ln 76705
Mcferrin Ave 76708
Mcgary Rd 76708
Mckeen St 76704
Mckenzie Aly 76708
Mckenzie Ave
1501-1525 76708
1527-3199 76708
4200-4298 76710
N & S Mclendon Dr 76706
Mcnamara Ln 76708
Meadow Rd 76710
Meadow Brook Rd 76710
Meadow Mountain Dr 76712
Meadow Park Cir 76705
Meadow Wood Dr 76710
Meadowbrook St 76706
Mecca Rd 76710
Medallion Cir 76706

Medical Pkwy 76712
Meinzer St 76711
Meixner Rd 76705
Melissa Dr 76708
Melrose Dr 76710
Memorial Dr 76711
Merganser Way 76706
Meridian Ave 76708
Merrimac Cir 76710
Merriwood Ln 76708
Mesa 76708
Mesa Verde Dr 76712
Mesquite Bend Rd 76708
Mesquite Tree Ct 76708
Mesquite Tree Rd 76705
Methodist Ranch Rd 76705
Meyers Ln 76705
Micah Dr 76708
Michigan St 76705
Mickler Ln 76708
Mike St 76705
Mikel Ln 76708
Mildred St 76706
Mill St 76704
Mill Creek Rd 76712
Miller St 76704
Mira St 76711
Mistletoe St 76706
Misty Dr 76712
Mitchell Ave 76708
Mitchell Rd
3300-3599 76708
4200-4299 76710
E Mitchell St 76704
Mockingbird Cir & Ln 76708
Modoc Ave 76705
Monkey Run Rd 76708
Montana Gap 76712
Montclair Dr 76710
Monte Vista St 76711
Monthie Rd 76705
Montrose St 76705
E & W Moonlight Dr 76706
Morning Vw 76708
Morningview Cir 76708
Morris St 76706
Morrow Ave
900-3399 76707
3400-4299 76710
W Morse Dr 76706
Mosley Dr 76705
Mount Carmel Dr 76710
Mount Lookout Rd 76708
Mount Rockwood Cir 76710
Mount Selma Dr 76710
Mount Terminal Dr 76710
Mountainview Dr 76710
Mt Pleasant Dr 76706
Muhl Circle Dr 76705
Mule Barn Ln 76705
Mundo Dr 76712
Myrtle Way 76705
Nathaniel Mccoy 76704
Nealton St 76705
Neil Dr 76710
Nellis Dr 76705
Nelson St 76706
Nelva St 76711
N New Rd
100-198 76710
200-1499 76710
1700-1800 76707
1802-2198 76707
S New Rd
100-199 76710
900-2499 76711
3100-3198 76706
3200-3299 76706
S New Dallas Hwy 76705
New Wood Ln 76710
E Newland Dr 76706
Nicky Ln 76705
Nicole Ln 76705
Nogal Ln 76706
Nolan Harris Ln 76705
N & S Norma Dr 76705

Northcrest Dr 76710
Northwood Ave 76705
Novelty St 76707
Novice Rd 76710
Oak Dr 76705
E Oak St 76704
N Oak St 76705
S Oak St 76705
Oak Cliff Dr 76710
Oak Lake Rd 76705
Oakland Dr 76705
Oaklawn St 76705
Oakridge Ln 76708
Oakview Cir 76705
Oakview St 76710
Oakwood Ave 76706
Obrien Cir 76708
Ocampo Ct 76708
Ocampo Ln 76706
W Old Axtell Rd 76705
Old Briarstown Rd 76710
Old Central Rd 76705
Old China Spring Rd 76708
S Old Dallas Rd 76705
Old Fort Graham Rd 76705
Old Hewitt Rd 76712
Old House Loop & Rd 76705
Old Marlin Rd 76705
Old Mexia Rd 76705
Old Mill Rd 76710
Old Mill Creek Dr 76712
Old Oaks Dr 76710
Old Robinson Rd 76706
Old Sawmill Rd 76705
Old Springfield Rd 76705
Old Steinbeck Rd 76708
Oldelley 76798
Oleander St 76708
Olive St 76704
Operations Rd 76705
Orchard Ln
700-900 76704
902-1098 76704
1701-2097 76705
2099-5699 76705
Orchid Ln 76708
Oregon St 76705
Oriental Rd 76710
Ouida Dr 76705
Our Way Rd 76705
Overlook Dr 76708
Overture Ct 76706
Owen Ln 76710
Oxford Dr 76712
Paddock Ln 76706
Paintbrush 76705
Palomino 76712
Palomino Trl 76706
Pamela Ave 76705
Pamela Rd 76708
Pandi Loop 76705
Pantherway 76712
Paradise Island Rd 76705
Park Ave
1300-1398 76706
1400-2499 76706
2700-2999 76711
N Park Ave 76708
E Park St 76705
Park Lake Dr 76708
Parkdale Dr 76710
Parker Ln 76705
Parker Springs Dr 76708
Parkside Dr 76710
Parkwood St 76710
Parrish St 76705
Parrott Ave 76707
Pascal Ct 76706
Paso Fino St 76706
Paterali Dr 76710
N & S Patricia St 76705
Patrick Rd & Xing 76708
Patton Br 76705
Paul Quinn St 76704
Pavelka Dr 76705
Pawnee St 76705

Payne St 76704
Peaceful Ln 76705
Peach St 76704
Peachtree St 76705
E Pearl St 76705
Pebble Bch 76705
Pebbles Ln 76708
E Pecan Ave 76704
Pecan Dr 76705
Pecan Ln 76705
Pecan Ter 76710
Pecan Village Cir 76710
Pecos Dr 76708
Pedernales Dr 76708
Peevey Ln 76706
N Peggy Dr 76706
Pembrook Dr 76710
Penton Ln 76705
Peony Ln 76708
Peplow Dr 76706
Perrin St 76705
Petit Rd 76708
Petty Pl 76705
Pewitt Dr 76706
Phillips St 76704
Pine Ave
1500-3899 76708
4101-4397 76710
4399-5299 76710
Pinto Loop 76706
Pioneer Pkwy 76708
Pipkin Ln 76705
Placid Cir 76706
Plantation Dr 76708
Pleasant St 76704
Pleasant Grove Ln 76712
Pleasant Grove Rd 76705
Pleasantview Dr 76705
Plum Cir 76706
Plum St 76706
E Plum St 76704
Point Vw 76710
Pointwood Cir 76710
Polk St 76705
Polo Park Cir 76712
Pompano Park 76706
Pool Side 76705
N & S Possum Creek Rd 76708
Post Oak Dr 76705
Powell Dr 76705
Powers St 76705
Praise Ln 76708
Precision Dr 76710
Preston St 76704
S Price St 76704
Primrose Dr 76706
Princelett Pl 76710
Princeton St 76711
Private Rd 76708
Proctor Ave 76708
Prose St 76706
Providence Dr 76707
Pryor St 76704
Pueblo Dr 76712
Purdue St 76711
Purvis St 76705
Quail Crk 76705
Quail Run St 76706
Quarter Horse Trl 76706
Queens Ct 76705
Quillian Trce 76705
Raceway Rd 76705
Radio Tower Rd 76705
Radle Rd 76706
Rambler Dr 76710
Rance Ln 76708
Ranchito Rd 76705
Randolph Cir 76705
Rantrans St 76704
Rayburn Way 76708
Real Dr 76712
Red Bud Cir 76710
Red Sage Dr 76708
Redbird St 76705
Redding Ln 76706

Redfish Ln 76705
Reese St 76705
Regency Dr 76710
Rejcek Way 76705
Remington Park 76706
Renick St 76704
Renner Rd 76706
Reno Dr 76712
Republic Dr 76708
Research Pkwy
100-198 76704
600-698 76705
Retoma Park 76706
Reuter Ave 76708
Revere Dr 76705
Rey Dr 76712
Reynolds St 76707
Riata Dr 76712
Rice Ave 76708
Richards Dr 76710
Richfield Ave 76707
Richland Dr 76710
Richland West Cir 76712
Richter Ave 76711
Rickert Dr 76710
Rico Dr 76710
Riddle St 76704
Riders Way 76712
N Ridge Dr 76710
Ridgecrest Cir 76710
Ridgeview Dr 76710
Ridgewood Dr 76710
Riggins St 76706
Rio Bonito Dr 76706
N & S Rita St 76705
Ritchie Rd 76712
River Ln 76708
River Rd 76705
River St 76706
River Bend Ln 76705
River Ridge Dr 76705
Riverview Rd 76706
Roanoak Ave 76705
Roberts Dr 76710
Robin Loop 76705
Robin Rd 76708
Robin May Cir 76706
Robinson Dr 76706
Robinson Industrial Park 76706
Robinwood Dr 76708
N & S Rock Creek Loop & Rd 76708
Rocking K Dr 76705
Rocking R Ranch Rd 76705
Rockview Dr 76710
Rocky Ledge Cir 76708
Rodeo Dr 76712
Rogene Dr 76705
Rogers Hill Rd & Spur 76705
Rolando Ave 76711
Rolling Oaks Trl 76705
Rosalie Dr 76708
Rose St 76704
Roselawn Dr 76710
Rosemary St 76705
Rosemere St 76705
Rosenfeld Rd 76706
Rosewood Dr 76710
Ross Ave
701-897 76706
899-2599 76706
2600-2899 76711
Ross Rd 76705
E Ross St 76704
Ross Road Spur 76705
Rough Creek Ct 76708
Roxanne Dr 76710
W Roy Dr 76706
Roy Beatty Ln 76705
Royal Oaks Dr 76710
Rozell Pass 76705
Ruby Ave 76710
Ruby Dell Ln 76705
Ruidoso St 76712
S Ruidoso Downs Dr 76706

Rusk St 76704
Rustler Dr 76705
Ruth Dr 76706
Ryff Ln 76705
Sabine Dr 76708
Saddle Creek Rd 76708
Saddlebrook 76712
Saddlewood 76705
Saffle Rd 76706
Salem Ct & Way 76708
Sam Dr 76706
Sam Houston St 76705
Samaritan Way 76705
Sames St 76705
E San Benito St 76706
San Jacinto St 76705
San Jose St 76705
San Pedro St 76705
Sand Field Ln 76705
Sandera Dr 76710
Sandy Ln 76708
Sanger Ave
1701-1797 76707
1799-3099 76707
3600-7029 76710
7031-7039 76710
7101-7197 76712
7199-7399 76712
7401-7499 76712
E Santa Anna St 76706
Sarah St 76706
Saratoga
600-899 76706
Saratoga
1300-1499 76705
Savannah Ct 76710
Saxet Rd 76706
N Scarlett Dr 76705
Schaeper Rd 76706
Schroeder Dr 76710
Scott Cir 76705
Scott Ln 76708
Scottwood Dr 76708
Scroggins Dr 76705
Sean St 76706
Sedwick Ave 76708
Segovia Dr 76708
Selby Ln 76705
Seley Ave 76704
Selman St 76704
Seneca Ave 76707
Seville Ct 76708
Sgt Rich Rd 76705
Shady Ln 76705
Shady Glen Dr 76708
Shady Oaks Dr 76710
Shady Place Dr 76712
Shadywood Dr 76710
Shallow Creek Dr 76708
E & W Shamrock St 76706
Shawnee Trl 76712
Shelburne St 76711
Shelby Ave 76711
Shelton St 76705
Sheppard St 76711
Shepperd Rd 76705
Sherman St 76704
Sherry Ln 76711
Sherwood Cir 76710
Sherwood Forest St 76710
Sherwood Oaks Dr 76705
Shetland Ct 76706
Shirley Dr 76705
Shoofly Ln 76708
N Shore Cir 76708
Short St 76704
Sierra West Dr 76712
Silver Vly 76705
Silver Fox 76705
Silver Lake Cir 76710
Silver Maple Dr 76706
Silver River Rd 76705
Silver Rose Ranch Rd 76705
Silver Saddle Dr 76706
Silverthorn Dr 76708
Simons Ave 76706

Skeet Eason Rd 76708
Skyline Dr 76710
Skyview 76705
Sleeper Ave 76707
Smith St 76705
Snow Pea Dr 76708
Soaring Eagle 76705
Somerset St 76705
Sommerfeld Dr 76705
Southerland Dr 76706
Southern Dr 76710
Southey St 76704
Spanish Oak 76710
Speight Ave
201-2599 76706
500-500 76798
800-2598 76706
2600-4799 76711
Spencer St 76705
Spring St 76704
Spring Branch Rd 76705
Spring Branch St 76711
Spring Creek St 76705
Spring Flower Ct & Ln 76705
Spring Lake Dr & Rd 76705
Spring Oak St 76705
Spring Willow St 76705
Springdale St 76710
Springhill St 76705
Springwood Dr 76706
Spruce Terrace Ave 76710
Stallion Dr 76706
Stanfield Dr 76705
Starlight Dr 76705
Starr Dr 76710
State St 76704
E State Highway 6 76705
W State Highway 6
301-1299 76710
W State Highway 6
430-430 76702
Station Creek Dr 76708
Staton St 76710
Stead Dr 76705
N Stefka Dr 76706
E & W Stegall Rd 76706
Steinbeck Bend Dr 76708
Steinke Rd 76705
Stephanie 76705
Stewart Cir & Dr 76708
Stillhouse Holw 76708
Stillwater Rd 76708
Stone Ln 76705
Stoneleigh Rd 76710
Stoney Creek Cir 76708
N Stovall Dr 76706
Stratford Dr 76710
N & S Strauss Dr 76706
Strickland St 76705
Student Union St 76798
Sturgis Ln 76708
Sturgis Rd 76708
Sturgis St 76706
Sublett Aly 76704
Sugg Dr 76710
Summer Ave 76708
Summit Ridge Dr 76710
Sun Valley Rd 76706
Sunbird Dr 76706
Sunflower Dr 76708
Sunland Park 76706
Sunnycrest Dr 76705
Sunnydell Ave 76711
Sunset Rd 76706
Sunset St 76710
E Sunset St 76704
Surratt St 76705
Surrey Ridge Ln 76706
Susan St 76706
Susanna St 76705
Swan Lk 76708
Swan Lake Dr 76710
Swiss Cir 76706
Sydney Dr 76708
Sylvia St 76708
Szanto Ln 76705

T Boy Loop ... 76706
T Bury ... 76708
Tabor St ... 76704
Tailspin ... 76705
Tanglewood Ave ... 76708
Tarton Ct ... 76706
E & W Tate St ... 76706
Taylor Ln ... 76705
Taylor St
  100-1499 ... 76704
  1501-1899 ... 76704
  2101-2297 ... 76705
  2299-2399 ... 76705
Taylor Oaks Dr ... 76705
Taylorville Ln ... 76705
Telluride Dr ... 76712
Tennessee Ave ... 76707
Tennie Dr ... 76705
Tennyson Dr ... 76710
Terrell Rd ... 76705
Texas St
  1000-1099 ... 76705
  1100-1299 ... 76704
Texas Central Pkwy ... 76712
Texas Ranger Trl ... 76706
The Land ... 76708
Theresa St ... 76705
Thistle Park ... 76706
Thomas Dr ... 76706
Thompson Cattle Rd ... 76705
Timber Creek Rd ... 76705
Timber View Dr ... 76705
Timbercrest Ln ... 76705
Timberleaf Cir ... 76708
Timberline St ... 76705
Timbermill Rd ... 76710
Tiner Ln ... 76705
W & E Tinsley Dr & Rd ... 76706
Tipton Dr ... 76710
Tokio Rd ... 76705
Tom Mccartney Ln ... 76705
Tomahawk Dr ... 76705
Tony Dr ... 76706
Torrance St ... 76705
Torres Ln ... 76708
Towne Oaks Dr ... 76710
Tracey Dr ... 76708
Trading Post Rd ... 76705
Tradinghouse Ln ... 76705
Trail Ridge Dr ... 76705
Tranquil Ct ... 76708
Travis St
  1500-1699 ... 76705
  1700-2099 ... 76711
  1622-1-1622-4 ... 76705
Treasure Island Rd ... 76705
Tree Grove Cir ... 76712
Tree Lake Dr ... 76708
Triangle Pl ... 76710
Trice Ave ... 76707
Trinity Dr ... 76710
Trinity Meadows Ln ... 76706
Triple Oaks ... 76705
Tulane St ... 76711
Turfway Park Dr ... 76706
Turner St ... 76704
Turtle Cv ... 76711
Turtle Creek Rd ... 76710
Twilight Dr ... 76705
Twin Ln ... 76705
Twin Lake Dr ... 76705
Twin Oaks Dr ... 76705
Twin Rivers Cir ... 76712
Tyler St ... 76704
Tyndall Cir ... 76705
Tynes Rd ... 76706
Union St ... 76705
University St ... 76706
N University Parks Dr
  100-599 ... 76701
  601-699 ... 76701
  1000-1098 ... 76707
S University Parks Dr
  100-399 ... 76701
  500-9700 ... 76706
  9702-9898 ... 76706
Utah St ... 76705
Val Halla Park ... 76706
Valencia Dr ... 76708
Valentine Ave ... 76706
Valeska Dr ... 76710
N Valley Mills Dr ... 76710
S Valley Mills Dr
  200-298 ... 76710
  300-399 ... 76710
  500-1899 ... 76711
  1901-1999 ... 76711
  2100-2199 ... 76706
Valley View Dr
  200-299 ... 76706
  5400-5499 ... 76710
Valview Dr ... 76708
Van American Dr ... 76712
Van Matre Rd ... 76706
Vance Ave ... 76705
Velma Dr ... 76706
Vernon Ln ... 76706
Victor St ... 76705
Victoria St ... 76705
Victory Dr ... 76711
Viking Dr ... 76710
Villa Dr ... 76710
Village Cir ... 76710
Village Green Dr ... 76710
Village Lake Cir ... 76708
Village Oak Dr ... 76710
Village Park Dr ... 76708
Vine St ... 76704
Virginia Dr & Rd ... 76705
Vista Cove Dr ... 76706
Vivian Ave ... 76708
E Waco Dr
  101-297 ... 76704
  299-1799 ... 76704
  1900-2500 ... 76705
  2502-2598 ... 76705
W Waco Dr
  201-3399 ... 76707
  400-2498 ... 76701
  2500-3498 ... 76710
  3500-5299 ... 76710
  5301-6003 ... 76710
Waco Sand Rd ... 76708
Wagon Wheel Cir ... 76706
Wagoner Rd ... 76705
Walker St ... 76704
Walkers Xing ... 76705
Walley Way ... 76708
E Walnut St ... 76704
N Walnut St ... 76705
S Walnut St ... 76705
Walton Dr ... 76705
E & W Ward Dr ... 76706
Washington Ave
  100-2499 ... 76701
  2500-2999 ... 76710
Washington Ln ... 76708
Waters St ... 76704
Watkinville Trl ... 76706
Watt Ave ... 76710
Waverly St ... 76706
Wayside ... 76705
Webb Dr & St ... 76705
Webster Ave
  201-297 ... 76706
  299-2100 ... 76706
  2102-2298 ... 76706
  2600-2698 ... 76711
  2700-2799 ... 76711
E Webster St ... 76704
Welborn St ... 76705
Wendy Ln ... 76710
Wenz Ave ... 76708
Wesley Chapel Rd ... 76705
Wesley Robinson Rd ... 76705
West Ave ... 76707
Westbury Cir ... 76710
Westchester Dr ... 76710
Western Ridge Dr ... 76712
Western Star ... 76706
Westlawn Dr ... 76710
Westover Rd ... 76710
Westview Dr & Vlg ... 76710
Westwood St ... 76710
Wheeler St ... 76705
Whispering Ave ... 76705
Whistler Dr ... 76712
White Rock Ln ... 76705
Whitney Ln ... 76705
Whitney Trce ... 76708
Whittier Cir ... 76710
Wiethorn Dr ... 76710
Wigley St ... 76706
Wilbanks Dr ... 76705
Wildcat Cir & Dr ... 76705
Wildwood Cir ... 76708
Wildwood Dr ... 76705
N Willard Dr ... 76706
Williams Rd ... 76705
Williams Landing Rd ... 76711
Willis Ln ... 76704
Willow Vly ... 76705
Willow Bend Cir ... 76708
Willowbrook St ... 76711
N & S Willowwood ... 76705
Wilshire Dr ... 76710
Wilson Ave ... 76708
Wilson Rd ... 76705
Winchell Dr ... 76712
Winding Oaks Dr ... 76705
Windmill Ln ... 76705
Windmill Hill St ... 76710
Windsor Ave ... 76708
Wingate Dr ... 76706
Winter Ln ... 76708
Winter St ... 76711
Wisconsin St ... 76705
Wisdom Ct ... 76708
Wisdom Ln ... 76705
Wisteria St
  1-39 ... 76708
  41-99 ... 76708
  400-4099 ... 76705
Witt St ... 76704
Wolf Ln ... 76705
Wolverine Dr ... 76705
Wood Ave
  700-2199 ... 76706
  3400-4699 ... 76711
Wood Lake Dr ... 76710
Woodall St ... 76705
Woodbine St ... 76705
Woodcastle Dr ... 76710
Woodcock Dr ... 76706
Woodcrest Dr ... 76710
Wooddale Cir ... 76710
Wooded Acres Dr
  800-800 ... 76710
  800-800 ... 76714
  801-897 ... 76710
  899-3299 ... 76710
Woodhill Cir ... 76710
Woodland Blvd ... 76705
Woodland Dr ... 76710
Woodmont Cir ... 76710
Woodrow Ave ... 76708
Woodruff Rd ... 76705
Wortham Bend Rd ... 76708
Wrangler ... 76705
Wren Dr ... 76706
Wynmore Dr ... 76706
Yale St ... 76711
Yancy Cir ... 76704
Yorelank Ave ... 76711
Yorestra St ... 76705
Yorktown ... 76705
Youngblood Rd ... 76706
Zavalla Dr ... 76708
Zettie Ln ... 76705
Ziegler Ln ... 76708
Zoo Park Rd ... 76708

NUMBERED STREETS

S 1st St ... 76706
S 2nd St
  200-399 ... 76701
  500-3000 ... 76706
N 3rd St
  101-597 ... 76701
  599-699 ... 76701
  800-898 ... 76707
S 3rd St
  100-399 ... 76701
  401-597 ... 76706
  599-4099 ... 76706
S 3rd A St ... 76706
S 3rd St Rd ... 76706
E 4th St ... 76704
N 4th St
  100-799 ... 76701
  800-1699 ... 76707
  1701-1799 ... 76707
  2000-2298 ... 76708
S 4th St
  100-399 ... 76701
  400-4099 ... 76706
  4101-4199 ... 76706
E 5th St ... 76704
N 5th St
  100-799 ... 76701
  800-998 ... 76707
  1900-2199 ... 76708
S 5th St
  100-399 ... 76701
  400-598 ... 76706
  1311-1312 ... 76798
  1500-1598 ... 76706
E 6th St ... 76704
N 6th St
  100-799 ... 76701
  901-1097 ... 76707
  1099-1899 ... 76707
  1900-2199 ... 76708
  2201-2299 ... 76708
S 6th St
  100-399 ... 76701
  701-797 ... 76706
  799-999 ... 76706
E 7th St ... 76704
N 7th St
  100-699 ... 76701
  1401-1497 ... 76707
  1900-2099 ... 76708
S 7th St
  100-399 ... 76701
  600-999 ... 76706
  1111-1111 ... 76798
  1113-2699 ... 76706
  1300-1398 ... 76798
  1800-2298 ... 76706
N 8th St ... 76701
S 8th St
  100-399 ... 76701
  400-1400 ... 76706
  1402-2898 ... 76706
  1425-1425 ... 76798
  1701-2899 ... 76706
9th St ... 76705
E 9th St ... 76704
N 9th St
  100-699 ... 76701
  700-898 ... 76707
  900-1699 ... 76707
S 9th St ... 76706
S 9th A St ... 76706
N 10th St
  200-699 ... 76701
  700-1899 ... 76707
S 10th St ... 76706
E 11th St ... 76704
N 11th St
  200-298 ... 76701
  300-599 ... 76701
  700-1800 ... 76707
  1802-1898 ... 76707
S 11th St
  200-299 ... 76701
  301-399 ... 76701
  500-598 ... 76706
  600-2199 ... 76706
N 12th St
  301-497 ... 76701
  499-699 ... 76701
  700-1999 ... 76707
  2000-2099 ... 76708
  2101-2199 ... 76708
S 12th St
  100-399 ... 76701
  500-598 ... 76706
  600-2999 ... 76706
  3001-3399 ... 76706
S 12th A St ... 76706
S 12th St Rd ... 76706
N 13th St
  101-197 ... 76701
  199-599 ... 76701
  700-1999 ... 76707
S 13th St
  200-399 ... 76701
  401-497 ... 76706
  499-500 ... 76706
  502-2098 ... 76706
N 14th St
  101-197 ... 76701
  199-399 ... 76701
  401-521 ... 76701
  523-1200 ... 76707
  1202-1298 ... 76707
S 14th St
  100-399 ... 76701
  1100-1898 ... 76706
  1900-2799 ... 76706
N 15th St
  300-499 ... 76701
  500-1999 ... 76707
  2001-2297 ... 76708
  2299-3399 ... 76708
S 15th St
  200-399 ... 76701
  400-2699 ... 76706
N 15th A St
  1501-1597 ... 76707
  1599-1899 ... 76707
  1901-1999 ... 76707
  2001-2497 ... 76708
  2499-3400 ... 76708
  3402-3498 ... 76708
N 16th St
  300-399 ... 76701
  401-499 ... 76701
  500-1700 ... 76707
  1702-1898 ... 76707
  2000-3399 ... 76708
S 16th St
  100-399 ... 76701
  400-598 ... 76706
  600-2600 ... 76706
  2602-2698 ... 76706
N 17th St
  100-300 ... 76701
  302-398 ... 76701
  501-797 ... 76707
  799-1999 ... 76707
  2000-3100 ... 76708
  3102-3298 ... 76708
S 17th St
  100-399 ... 76701
  400-2000 ... 76706
  2002-2098 ... 76706
N 18th St
  200-400 ... 76701
  501-513 ... 76707
  2000-2198 ... 76708
S 18th St
  100-199 ... 76701
  401-597 ... 76706
N 18th A St ... 76707
N 19th St ... 76708
  600-1999 ... 76707
  2000-2298 ... 76708
  4428-4428 ... 76707
  4428-6598 ... 76708
S 19th St
  200-399 ... 76701
  501-897 ... 76706
E 20th St ... 76705
N 20th St
  500-1899 ... 76707
  2201-2297 ... 76708
S 20th St
  101-197 ... 76701
  400-498 ... 76706
N 20th A St ... 76708
S 20th A St ... 76706
E 21st St ... 76705
N 21st St
  300-398 ... 76701
  500-798 ... 76707
  2000-2098 ... 76708
S 21st St
  200-299 ... 76701
  401-1297 ... 76706
N 21st A St ... 76708
E 22nd St ... 76705
N 22nd St
  500-1999 ... 76707
  2000-2298 ... 76708
  2300-4399 ... 76708
S 22nd St
  200-298 ... 76701
  501-597 ... 76706
  599-2099 ... 76706
  2101-2199 ... 76706
E 23rd St ... 76705
N 23rd St
  400-1999 ... 76707
  2100-2298 ... 76708
  2300-4399 ... 76708
S 23rd St ... 76706
N 24th St
  100-198 ... 76701
  200-300 ... 76701
  302-398 ... 76701
  401-697 ... 76707
  699-1899 ... 76707
  2300-4199 ... 76708
S 24th St
  100-298 ... 76701
  700-2699 ... 76706
E 25th St ... 76705
N 25th St
  100-199 ... 76710
  201-399 ... 76710
  400-498 ... 76707
  500-1999 ... 76707
  2000-4199 ... 76708
  4201-4299 ... 76708
S 25th St
  101-299 ... 76710
  1600-2799 ... 76706
E 26th St ... 76705
N 26th St
  500-1899 ... 76707
  2801-2997 ... 76708
  2999-4100 ... 76708
  4102-4198 ... 76708
S 26th St
  100-198 ... 76710
  201-399 ... 76710
  500-598 ... 76706
  600-2799 ... 76706
S 26th A St ... 76706
E 27th St ... 76705
N 27th St
  200-399 ... 76710
  400-1899 ... 76707
  2100-3098 ... 76708
  3100-4299 ... 76708
S 27th St
  200-398 ... 76710
  1100-1400 ... 76711
  1402-1598 ... 76711
  2400-2799 ... 76706
N 28th St
  300-398 ... 76710
  600-898 ... 76707
  2500-2698 ... 76708
S 28th St
  101-399 ... 76710
  600-698 ... 76711
N 29th St
  301-399 ... 76710
  501-697 ... 76707
  699-1900 ... 76707
  1902-1998 ... 76707
  2500-3799 ... 76708
S 29th St ... 76711
N 29th A St ... 76708
N 30th St
  100-198 ... 76710
  500-1799 ... 76707
  2200-4199 ... 76708
S 30th St ... 76711
N 31st St
  500-1899 ... 76707
  2217-3197 ... 76708
S 31st St ... 76711
N 32nd St
  500-1899 ... 76707
  2300-2398 ... 76708
S 32nd St ... 76710
N 33rd St
  500-2099 ... 76707
  2100-2198 ... 76708
N 34th St
  500-1499 ... 76710
  2101-2997 ... 76708
N 35th St
  500-799 ... 76710
  2000-2099 ... 76707
S 35th St ... 76710
N 36th St
  501-597 ... 76710
  1600-1699 ... 76707
  2200-2298 ... 76708
N 37th St
  501-697 ... 76710
  699-800 ... 76710
  802-898 ... 76710
  1500-1699 ... 76707
N 38th St
  201-497 ... 76710
  499-699 ... 76710
  701-799 ... 76710
  1700-1999 ... 76707
  2212-2298 ... 76708
N 39th St
  200-398 ... 76710
  400-499 ... 76710
  1700-2099 ... 76707
  2300-2399 ... 76708
N 39th A St ... 76707
N 40th St ... 76710
  2000-2099 ... 76707
N 40th A St ... 76707
N 41st St ... 76710
N 41st St ... 76710
  1700-1799 ... 76707
  2200-2500 ... 76708
  2502-2598 ... 76708
N 42nd St ... 76710
N 43rd St ... 76710
N 44th St ... 76710
N 45th St ... 76710
N 46th St ... 76710
N 49th St ... 76710
N 50th St ... 76710
N 51st St ... 76710
N 52nd St ... 76710
N 57th St ... 76710
N 58th St ... 76710
N 59th St ... 76710
N 60th St ... 76710
N 61st St ... 76710
N 62nd St ... 76710
N 63rd St ... 76710
N 64th St ... 76710
N 65th St ... 76710
N 66th St ... 76710

WAXAHACHIE TX

General Delivery ... 75165

POST OFFICE BOXES MAIN OFFICE STATIONS AND BRANCHES

Box No.s
All PO Boxes ... 75168

RURAL ROUTES

01, 02, 04, 06, 07, 08, 10, 14, 16 ... 75165
03, 05, 09, 12 ... 75167

NAMED STREETS

Abbey Rd ... 75165
Abela Dr ... 75165
Adams St ... 75165
Adays Rd ... 75165
Adobe Ct ... 75165
Affirmed Rd ... 75165
N & S Aiken St ... 75165
Alamo St ... 75165
Aldridge St ... 75165
Alexander Dr ... 75165
Alliance Blvd ... 75165
Almond St ... 75165
Althea Dr ... 75165
Alto Rd ... 75167
Alvis Ln ... 75165
Alysa Ln ... 75167
Amanda Ln ... 75165
Amherst Dr ... 75165
Anderson Rd ... 75167
Anderson St ... 75165
Angus Dr ... 75165
Angus Rd ... 75167
Anita Ln ... 75165
Annette Ave ... 75165
Antonio Ln ... 75165
Apache Ct ... 75165
April Ln ... 75165
Arabian Rd ... 75165
Arena Rd ... 75165
Armstrong Way ... 75167
Arrowhead Rd ... 75167
Ash Dr ... 75165
Atlantic Ave ... 75165
Auburn St ... 75165
Aucuba Ln ... 75165
Audra Ave ... 75165
E & W Avenue C ... 75165
Azalea Ln & Trl ... 75165
Aztec Ct ... 75165
Bakers Branch Rd ... 75167
Barbara Way ... 75165
Bardwell Cir ... 75165
Barger Dr ... 75165
Bateman St ... 75165
Bates Dr ... 75167
Baucum Rd ... 75167
Bauder St ... 75165
Bear Trl ... 75165
Bearden Rd ... 75167
Beaver Creek Dr ... 75165
Becky Ln ... 75165
Belgian St ... 75165
Bells Chapel Cir & Rd ... 75165
Bent Creek Ct & Dr ... 75165
Berkshire Ln ... 75165
Bethel Rd ... 75167
Bethel St ... 75165
Big Bend Blvd ... 75165
Big Sky Dr ... 75167
Bigham Rd ... 75167
Bird Ln ... 75165
Birdie Ln ... 75165
Bison Meadow Dr ... 75165
Black Champ Rd ... 75167
Blair Rd ... 75165
Blue Moon Dr ... 75165
Blue Ribbon Rd ... 75165
Blue Roan Dr ... 75165
Bluebonnet Ln ... 75165
Boardwalk Ave ... 75165
Bob White Rd ... 75167
Bogey Ct ... 75165
Boren Dr ... 75165
Boyce Rd ... 75165
Boyce First St ... 75165
Boyce Second St ... 75165
Boyce Third St ... 75165
Boz Rd ... 75167
Boze St ... 75165
Brackens St ... 75165
Bradburry Ln ... 75167
Bradshaw Ct & St ... 75165
Brady St ... 75165
Brandie Mac Ln ... 75165
Branding Iron Dr ... 75165
Brandy Ln ... 75165
Breanna Way ... 75165
Breezeway St ... 75165
Brenna Rd ... 75165
Brian Pl ... 75165
Briar Ln ... 75165
Briggs St ... 75165
Broadhead Rd ... 75165
Broken Arrow St ... 75165
Brookbend Ct & Dr ... 75165
Brookcrest Ct ... 75165
Brooke Ln ... 75165
Brookglen Ct ... 75165
Brookhaven Ct ... 75165
Brookside Dr ... 75165
Brookside Rd ... 75167
Brookstone Ct & Dr ... 75165
Brookvista Ct E & W ... 75165
Brown St ... 75165
Brown Industrial Rd ... 75167
Bryn Mawr Ln ... 75165
Bryson St ... 75165
Buchanan Dr ... 75165
Buckhorn ... 75165
Buckingham Dr ... 75165
Buckskin Dr ... 75167
Bud Run Rd ... 75165
Buena Vista Rd ... 75167
Buffalo Creek Cir & Dr ... 75165
Bunker Ct ... 75165
Burnett St ... 75165
Butcher Rd ... 75165
Butler Ln ... 75165
Cactus Ct & Rd ... 75165
Calvert St ... 75165
Cambridge Ct ... 75167
Cambridge St ... 75165
Campbell Rd ... 75167
Cantrell St ... 75165
Canyon Ct ... 75167
Cardinal Rd ... 75165
Cardinal Ridge Ct ... 75165
Carlton Pkwy ... 75165
Carnation Ct ... 75165
Carriage Dr ... 75165
Carter Ct ... 75165
Catawba Rd ... 75165
Cathy Dr ... 75165
Cattail Ct ... 75165
Cedar St ... 75165
Cedar Park Ct ... 75167
Center St ... 75165
N & S Central Ave ... 75165
Chambers Cir ... 75165
Chapel Ct ... 75165
Chapel Hill Ln ... 75165
Chapman Cir ... 75165
Charlotte Ave ... 75165
Chautauqua Dr ... 75165
Chazlynn Ct ... 75165
Cherokee Ct ... 75165
Chesterfield Cir ... 75165
Chestnut Dr ... 75165
Chevy Chase Ln ... 75165
Cheyenne Dr ... 75165
Chieftain Dr ... 75165
Childress Rd ... 75165
Childs ... 75165
Chiles Dr ... 75165
Chimney Rock Dr ... 75167
Chisholm Trl ... 75165
Choctaw Ln & Trl ... 75165
Cholla Way ... 75165
Christie Ln ... 75165
Church St ... 75165
Cimarron Meadows Dr ... 75167
Circle St ... 75165
Citation Ln ... 75165
Civic Center Ln ... 75165
Clark Ln ... 75165
Cleaver Rd ... 75165
Clemson Ct ... 75165
Clift St ... 75165
Clopton Lake Rd ... 75165
Clover Ln ... 75165
Clydesdale St ... 75165
Coats St ... 75165
Coleman St ... 75165
N College St
100-399 ... 75165
316-316 ... 75168
400-598 ... 75165
401-599 ... 75165
S College St ... 75165
Colorado Dr ... 75167
Colt Dr ... 75165
Columbia Ave ... 75165
Comanche Ct ... 75165
Comfort Ct ... 75165
Commonwealth Cir ... 75165
Compton Dr & Ln ... 75167
Conner St ... 75165
Cook St ... 75165
Cornell Ln ... 75165
Corral Rd ... 75167
Country Dr & Hls ... 75165
Country Club Pl ... 75165
Country Crest Dr ... 75165
Country Meadows Blvd & Dr ... 75165
Courtney Cir ... 75165
Coventry Ln ... 75165
Covey Run Cir ... 75165
Cox Rd ... 75167
Coyote Run ... 75165
N & S Creek Cir ... 75165
Creekside Way ... 75165
Creekview Dr ... 75165
E & W Criddle St ... 75165
Cross Creek Ct ... 75167
Crownover Rd ... 75167
Crystal Cv ... 75165
Culberson Rd ... 75165
Cumberland Rd ... 75165
Cunningham Meadows Rd ... 75167
Curry Rd ... 75167
Cynisca St ... 75165
N D Ranch Rd ... 75167
Dahl ... 75165
Daniel Rd ... 75167
Darierai Rd ... 75167
Dartmouth Dr ... 75165
Davenport Dr ... 75167
Davenport Ln ... 75165
Dawn Dr ... 75165
Dawson Rd ... 75167
Dean Box Dr ... 75165
Deercreek Dr ... 75165
Deerwood Ln ... 75165
Desert ... 75165
Devonshire Dr ... 75167
Dewberry St ... 75165
Dixie Ln ... 75165
Dogwood Ln ... 75165
Dollar Ct ... 75165
Dover Dr ... 75165
Dr Martin Luther King Jr Blvd ... 75165
Drexel Dr ... 75165
Driftwood Ln ... 75165
Dublin Cir ... 75165
Dubose Way ... 75167
Dunaway Rd ... 75167
Dunaway St ... 75165
Dunlap St ... 75165
Dunn St ... 75165
Eagle Feather Dr ... 75165
Eagle Point Dr ... 75165
Eagle Ridge Dr ... 75165
N Edgefield Rd ... 75165
Edmondson Rd ... 75167
Edna Rd ... 75165
Eggar St ... 75165
El Camino ... 75167
Elder St ... 75165
Ellis St ... 75165
N & S Elm St ... 75165
Elmwood Trl ... 75165
Emanuel St ... 75165
Ennis St ... 75165
Equestrian Dr ... 75165
Etta Ave ... 75165
Executive Ct ... 75165
Fair Weather Farm Rd ... 75165
Fairview St ... 75165
Fairway Dr ... 75165
Faith Ln ... 75167
Falcon Ridge Dr ... 75165
Fallen Rock Dr ... 75165
N & S Falling Leaves Dr ... 75167
Farley St ... 75165
Farrar Rd ... 75165
Fawn Ridge Dr ... 75165
Feaster Rd ... 75165
Ferris Ave ... 75165
Finley St ... 75165
Flat Ct ... 75167
N Flat St ... 75165
S Flat St ... 75165
Flower Meadows Dr ... 75165
Flowers St ... 75165
Floyd St ... 75165
Fm 1387 ... 75167
Fm 1446 ... 75167
Fm 1493 ... 75167
Fm 387 ... 75165
Fm 55 ... 75165
Fm 66 ... 75167
Fm 664 ... 75167
Fm 813 ... 75165
E Fm 875 ... 75167
Fm 876 ... 75167
Fm 877 ... 75165
Fm 878 ... 75165
Fm 879 ... 75165
Fordyce Cir ... 75165
Forreston Rd ... 75165
Fox Grove Dr ... 75165
E & W Franklin St ... 75165
Frierson St ... 75165
Frost Creek Rd ... 75167
Garden Valley Pkwy ... 75165
Gardenia Ln ... 75165
Gardner St ... 75165
Gayleh Ln ... 75165
N & S Getzendaner St ... 75165
Ghost Rider Rd ... 75165
Gibb Rd ... 75167
N & S Gibson Rd & St ... 75165
Gingerbread Ln ... 75165
Givens St ... 75165
Glen Brook Dr ... 75165
Glenwick Dr ... 75167
Glory Dr ... 75165
Goodnight Ln ... 75165
Grace St ... 75165
Graham St ... 75165
Grainery Rd
100-199 ... 75165
300-798 ... 75167
800-899 ... 75167
N & S Grand Ave ... 75165
Grande Casa Rd ... 75167
Grassy Ct ... 75167
Gravel St ... 75165
Greathouse Cir & Rd ... 75167
Green Meadows Dr ... 75167
Greenbark Ct ... 75167
Greenbrier St ... 75165
Greenoaks Cir ... 75165
Griffin St ... 75165
Grove Creek Rd ... 75165
Hacienda Dr ... 75165
Hampshire Dr ... 75165
S Hampton Pl ... 75165
Hanover Dr ... 75165
Harbin Ave ... 75165
Harding St ... 75165
Hardwood Ln ... 75165
Harrington Rd ... 75165
Hart Cir ... 75165
Hartfield Dr ... 75165
S & E Haven Pl & Rd ... 75165
N & S Hawkins St ... 75165
Hawthorn ... 75165
Heartland Dr ... 75165
Heather Ln ... 75165
Hedgewood Dr ... 75165
Henderson St ... 75165
Henrietta St ... 75165
Henry St ... 75165
Hibiscus Trl ... 75165
Hidalgo Rd ... 75167
Hideaway Rd ... 75165
Higgins Rd ... 75167
High Line Dr ... 75167
High Meadow Dr ... 75165
High School Dr ... 75165
Highland Ave ... 75165
E Highland Rd ... 75167
Hight Rd ... 75167
Highview Dr ... 75165
S Highway 287 ... 75165
W Highway 287 Byp
1-1617 ... 75165
1619-1799 ... 75165
1800-3199 ... 75167
E Highway 287 Business ... 75165
W Highway 287 Business
1500-2042 ... 75165
W Highway 287 Business
2044-2098 ... 75165
2200-2599 ... 75167
Highway 342 ... 75165
N & S Highway 77 ... 75165
S Hill Ln & St ... 75165
Hillside Dr ... 75165
Hilltop Dr ... 75165
Hillview Dr ... 75165
Hiwasee Rd ... 75165
Holder Rd ... 75165
Hollis Rd ... 75167
Holly St ... 75165
Honeysuckle Ln ... 75165
Honeytree Cir ... 75165
Horseshoe Bnd & Dr ... 75165
Houston St ... 75165
Howard Rd ... 75165
Howland Ln ... 75167
Hoyt Rd ... 75167
Hunter Pass ... 75165
Hunter Pass Cv ... 75165
Hunters Glen Dr ... 75167
Huntington Ct ... 75165
Ike Rd ... 75165
Indian Ct & Dr ... 75165
Indian Hills Dr ... 75165
Indian Trace Ln ... 75165
Indigo Way ... 75165
Industrial Dr ... 75165
N Interstate Highway 35 E
100-498 ... 75165
500-2000 ... 75165
2002-9998 ... 75165
2401-2499 ... 75167
2801-9999 ... 75165
S Interstate Highway 35 E ... 75165
Iroquois Ln ... 75165
N & S Jackson St ... 75165
James Ct ... 75165
Janis Ln ... 75165
Jarrett St ... 75165
Jasmine Ln ... 75165
E & W Jefferson St ... 75165
Jennings Dr ... 75165
Jim St ... 75165
John Arden Dr ... 75165
Johnston Blvd ... 75165
Johnston Rd
100-199 ... 75165
500-1099 ... 75167
Jolly Way ... 75165
Jordan Ln ... 75165
Joseph St ... 75165
Katy Lake Dr ... 75165
Kaufman St ... 75165
Kelley Bnd ... 75167
Kelly Dr ... 75167
Keowee Cir ... 75165
Kinchum St ... 75165
Kingdom Cir ... 75167
Kings Ct ... 75165
Kings Court Dr ... 75165
Kiowa Ln ... 75165
Kirksey St ... 75165
Kirven Ave ... 75165
Lacy Oak Ln ... 75165
Laguna Vista Dr ... 75165
Lake Park Ave ... 75165
Lakecrest Cir, Ct, Dr & Pl ... 75165
Lakefront Dr ... 75165
Lakeshore Dr ... 75165
Lakeside Dr ... 75165
Lakeview Cir & Dr ... 75165
Lakeway Dr ... 75165
Lakewood Dr ... 75165
Lancaster St ... 75165
Lance Dr ... 75165
Lantana Ter ... 75165
Lariat Trl ... 75165
Laurie Ln ... 75165
Lavista St ... 75165
Lawndale Dr ... 75165
Leatherwood St ... 75165
Legion St ... 75165
Leisure Ln ... 75165
Leisure Rd ... 75167
Lewis St ... 75165
Lexie Ln ... 75167
Lexington Dr ... 75165
Liberty Way ... 75167
E & W Light St ... 75165
Lilly Ln ... 75165
Linda Ln ... 75165
Link Crest Dr ... 75167
Lions Park Rd ... 75165
Liriope Ln ... 75165
Little Branch Rd ... 75167
Little Creek Dr ... 75165
Lofland Dr ... 75165
Logan Ln ... 75165
Lois St ... 75165
Lone Elm Rd ... 75167
Long Branch Rd ... 75167
Longhorn Dr ... 75165
Lonzo St ... 75165
Loycie Cir ... 75165
Lucas St ... 75165
Lynn St & Way ... 75165
Lyon Ln ... 75165
Maddox Rd ... 75165
E & W Madison St ... 75165
Magnolia Dr ... 75165
E & W Main St ... 75165
Maledon St ... 75165
Mallory Ct & Dr ... 75167
Maloney Rd ... 75165
Manchester Dr ... 75165
Mangrum Dr ... 75167
Manor Ln ... 75165
Maree Ct & Dr ... 75165
Margaret Dr ... 75167
Mariam Ave ... 75165
Mark Trl ... 75165
Marshall Rd ... 75167
Martha St ... 75165
E & W Marvin Ave & Gdns ... 75165
Mary Ave ... 75165
Mary Ct ... 75167
Mary Dr ... 75167
Mason Ln ... 75167
Mathew St ... 75165
Mattie Ln ... 75167
Maumee Rd ... 75165
Mavis Ave ... 75167
Mcclain St ... 75165
Mccuen St ... 75165
Mcdonnell Ct ... 75167
Mcfarland Dr ... 75167
Mckenzie St ... 75165
Mcmillan St ... 75165
Mcmurry ... 75165
Mcnaughton St ... 75165
Meadow Crest Dr ... 75167
Meadow Glen Dr ... 75165
N Meadowview Dr ... 75165
Meagan St ... 75165
Meghann Ln ... 75167
Melissa Ct & Dr ... 75167
Memory Ln ... 75167
Mesa Rd ... 75167
Misty Ct ... 75165
Modene Ave ... 75165
Mohawk St ... 75165
Monarch Ct ... 75165
N & S Monroe St ... 75165
Montgomery St ... 75165
Monticello Dr ... 75165
Moonlight Trl ... 75165
Morene Ave ... 75165
Morgan Ct ... 75167
Morning Star Ln ... 75165
Mulkey Rd ... 75167
Mulligan Ct ... 75165
Munchus St ... 75165
Murdock St ... 75165
Mushroom Rd ... 75165
Muskingum Rd ... 75165
Mustang Rd ... 75165
Mustang Creek Dr ... 75165
Myers St ... 75165
Myrtle Ave ... 75165
Nandina Way ... 75165
Nash Howard Rd ... 75165
Neal St ... 75165
Newcastle St ... 75165
Newt Ln ... 75167
Nocona Dr ... 75165
Noel St ... 75165
Norman Rd ... 75165
Northgate Dr ... 75165
Northstar Ln ... 75165
Northview Dr ... 75165
Nottingham Dr ... 75165
Oak Ln ... 75167
N & S Oak Branch Cir, Ct, Rd & Trl ... 75167
Oak Creek Ct & Dr ... 75165
Oak Hill Ct ... 75167
Oak Ridge Dr ... 75165
Oak Tree Dr ... 75165
Oak Vista Rd ... 75167
Oaklawn ... 75165
Ocotillo Dr ... 75165
Odom St ... 75165
Odonna Dr ... 75165
Old Boyce Rd ... 75165
Old Bridge Rd ... 75165
Old Buena Vista Rd ... 75167
Old Church Rd ... 75165
Old Highway 287 ... 75165
Old Howard Rd ... 75165
Old Italy Rd ... 75165
Old Maypearl Rd ... 75167
Old Reagor Springs Rd ... 75165
Old Settlers Trl ... 75167
Old Spanish Trl ... 75167
Old Waxahachie Rd ... 75165
Oldham St ... 75165
Oleander Pl ... 75165
Olive St ... 75165
Oliver Ln ... 75165
Olvido Rd ... 75167
Omaha Ct ... 75165
Oneida St ... 75165
Opal St ... 75165
Oregon Trl ... 75167
Osage Dr ... 75165
Oscar St ... 75165
Otter ... 75165

Overhill Dr 75165
Ovilla Rd 75167
Owen Way 75165
Oxford Ranch Ct & Rd 75167
Pacific Ave 75165
Paddock Rdg 75167
Palomino Dr 75165
Paluxy Ct 75167
Panorama 75165
Park Dr 75165
Park Hills Dr 75165
Park Meadows Dr 75165
Park Place Blvd 75165
E & W Parks Ave 75165
Parks School House Rd 75165
Pasley St 75165
Patrick Rd 75167
Patrick St 75165
Patsy Ln 75167
Patterson St 75165
Peaceful Trl 75165
Pecan Mdws & St 75165
E Pecan Tree Rd 75165
W Pecan Tree Rd
201-299 75165
300-799 75167
Pecan Valley Ln 75165
Penn Cv & St 75165
Pensacola Ave 75165
Perry Ave 75165
Peters St 75165
Pickett St 75165
Pigg Rd 75165
Pine St 75165
Pinkston St 75165
Pinto Dr 75165
Pioneer Ct 75167
Pleiade Cir 75165
Plentris Rd 75165
Pommel Ct 75167
Poplar St 75165
Post Oak Dr & Ln 75165
Professional Pl 75165
Pueblo Cir & Dr 75165
Pulaski St 75165
Purdue Dr 75165
Quarterhorse Rd 75165
Queens Dr 75165
Railroad St 75165
Rain Cloud Dr 75165
Rainbow Ln 75167
Randal Cir 75165
Randy Rd 75165
Range Rd 75165
Rawhide St 75165
Red River Ct & Dr 75167
Redbud St 75165
Redman Ln 75165
Reese Ct & Rd 75167
Remington Dr 75165
Richard Rd 75167
Richh St 75165
Richmond Dr & Ln 75165
Ridge Creek Rd 75167
Ridgecrest Dr 75165
S Ring Rd 75165
River Oaks Blvd 75165
Robin Ridge Dr 75165
Robinett Rd 75165
Rock Springs Ct 75165
Rocky Dr 75167
Rodeo Rd 75165
N & S Rogers St 75165
Rolling Hills Rd 75167
Rosa St 75165
E & W Ross St 75165
Rough Creek Rd 75167
Roundup Rd 75165
Rousseau St 75165
Royal St 75165
Royal Park Ln 75165
Running Deer Ln 75165
Rusty Ln 75165
Rutherford Rd 75165
Rvg Pkwy 75165

Ryburn St 75165
Sabine Ct 75167
Saddle Rdg 75167
Saddle Horn Ln 75167
Saddlebrook Ln 75165
Sadler St 75165
Sagebrush Ln 75165
Saguaro Rd 75165
Sam St 75165
San Jacinto St 75165
Sandhurst Dr 75165
Sandy Ln 75165
Sanger Creek Way 75165
Santa Fe Cir & Trl 75165
Sargent Pl 75165
Savannah St 75165
Saxon St 75165
Secretariat St 75165
Sendero Dr 75165
Seneca Dr 75165
Serenity Cir 75165
E, N, S & W Sharpshire Ct & Dr 75165
Shawnee Rd 75165
Shea St 75165
Shenendoah Dr 75165
Shetland St 75165
Shields Pkwy 75165
Shoreway Cir 75165
Short Branch Rd 75167
Short Putt Dr 75165
Sierra Dr 75167
Silver Spur Dr 75165
Sims Rd 75167
Singleton Rd 75165
Sioux Ct, Dr & Pl 75165
Smith Cemetery Rd 75165
Smokey Ln 75165
Smooth Creek Rd 75167
Solon Rd
1-1199 75165
1200-2799 75167
Solon Place Way 75165
Southview Dr 75165
Spencer St 75165
Spider Rd 75167
Sports Row 75165
Spring Branch Rd 75167
Spring Creek Dr 75165
Spring Grove Dr 75165
Spring Lake Cir 75167
Springfield Cir & Ln 75165
St Johns Dr 75167
Stable Dr 75165
Stadium Dr 75165
Stallion Rd 75165
Stampede St 75165
Stanford Dr 75165
Stardust Trl 75165
Stephens St 75165
E Sterrett Rd 75165
W Sterrett Rd
100-199 75165
300-1199 75167
Stone 75165
Stone Field Ct 75167
Stone Haven Pl 75165
Stones Ct 75165
Stroud St 75165
Sullivan Way 75167
Sumac Dr 75165
Sumner Ln 75165
Sunburst Dr 75165
Sunny Ln 75165
Sunnyside Dr 75165
Sunrise Dr 75165
Sycamore St 75165
Tamarron Dr 75167
Tanglewood Ln 75165
Tanner Dr 75165
Taos Cir 75165
Taylor Rd 75165
Tecumseh Pkwy 75165
Tee Side Dr 75165
Textile St 75165
Thames Cir 75165

Thompson St 75165
Thoroughbred Rd & St 75165
Tierra Ln 75167
Timber Dr 75165
Timberline Dr 75167
Tishomingo Rd 75165
Toccoa Rd 75165
Todd St 75165
Tracy Dr 75165
Tranquil Pl 75167
Tranquillity Ln 75165
Traveller St 75165
Trey Ct 75165
Trinity Ln 75165
Triple Crown Rd 75165
Tugaloo Cir 75165
Tuggle St 75165
Tulane Dr 75165
Tumbleweed Dr 75167
Turner St 75165
Twin Lakes Dr 75165
University Ave 75165
Vaca 75167
Valley Rd 75165
Valley Ranch Ct & Dr 75165
Valley View Dr 75167
Vanderbilt Ln 75165
Vassar Ct 75165
Vermont St 75165
Victorian Dr 75165
Village Dr 75165
Village Gate Dr 75165
Village Green Ct 75165
Villanova Ct 75165
Vine St 75165
Vineyard View Ln 75165
Vintage Dr 75165
Vinyard Dr 75167
Virginia Ave 75165
Vivian Dr 75165
Waco Rd 75165
Wagon Mound 75167
Wagon Wheel Dr 75167
Wakeland Rd 75165
Walker Ct N & S 75167
Watauga Dr 75165
Water St 75165
Water Garden Dr 75165
Waterford Dr & Xing 75167
Waterfront Dr 75165
Wellington Ct 75165
West Ave & Rd 75165
Westgate Dr 75165
Westminister Dr 75165
S Westmoreland Rd 75167
Wildflower Dr 75165
Will St 75165
Williams St 75165
Willow Ln & Run 75165
Willow Bend Dr 75167
Willowcrest 75165
Wilmington Ave 75165
Wilshire Cir 75165
Wilson Rd 75165
Windermere St 75165
Windmill Ct 75167
Windsor Cir 75165
Woodridge Rd 75165
Wright Rd 75167
Wyatt St 75165
Y O Rd 75167
Yinger St 75165
Ymca Dr 75165
Yorkshire Ct 75165
Young St 75165
Youngblood Rd 75165

NUMBERED STREETS

All Street Addresses 75165

WEATHERFORD TX

General Delivery 76086

POST OFFICE BOXES MAIN OFFICE STATIONS AND BRANCHES

Box No.s
All PO Boxes 76086

RURAL ROUTES

01, 03, 10, 17, 23, 27 76085

HIGHWAY CONTRACTS

51, 54 76085
53 76086
02, 06, 07, 08, 09, 12, 13, 14, 15, 19, 20, 21, 24, 26, 28, 29, 32, 33, 34 76087
04, 05, 11, 16, 18, 22, 25, 30, 31 76088
52 76088

NAMED STREETS

Abby Ln 76086
Adair Ln 76088
Adams Dr 76086
Addison Ct & Dr 76087
Adell Cir & Rd 76088
Adobe Ct 76087
Advance Rd 76088
E & W Akard St 76086
Alameda St 76086
Alamo Rd 76088
N Alamo St 76086
S Alamo St 76086
Aleman St 76087
Alexander Dr 76086
Alford Dr 76087
Alice Springs Ln 76085
Allen St 76086
Allie Ct 76087
Alma Ct & Dr 76086
Alpine Dr 76086
Alyssa Ct 76085
Amantes Ln 76088
Amber Ct 76087
Ames Cir 76087
Ancient Bnd 76087
E & W Anderson St 76086
Andi Way 76086
Andrews Ct 76087
Andy Dr 76088
Angie Ln 76087
Angus Dr 76088
Ann St 76086
Ann Brown Dr 76085
Annie Mae Ct 76085
Anns Ln 76085
Anvil Ct 76088
Apache Rdg & Trl 76087
Applebee Ct 76088
Appleton Dr 76088
Arapahoe Rdg 76087
Archers Way 76088
Arena Run 76087
Arrowhead Dr 76087
Arrowpoint Dr 76087
Arroyo Ct & Dr 76087
Arunda Ct 76085
Ashley Ln 76086
Ashlyn Ln 76085
Athens Dr 76087
Atkins Dr 76086
Atlee Dr 76087
Atwood Ct 76086
Austen Dr 76087
Austin Ave & Ct 76086

Autumn Springs Ct 76087
Autumn Wood Ct 76087
Avendale Dr 76086
E & W Aycock Ct 76088
Azle Hwy 76085
Azle St 76087
Aztec Trl 76087
E B B Fielder Dr & Rd 76087
Baggett Rd 76085
Baker Rd 76087
Baker Cut Off Rd 76087
W Ball St 76086
Ballard Rd 76088
Ballew Springs Rd 76088
Bankhead Ct 76087
E Bankhead Dr 76086
E Bankhead Hwy 76087
W Bankhead Hwy 76086
Banks Dr 76087
Barber St 76088
Barnett Dr 76087
Bartallen Ln 76088
Barton Ln 76085
Basswood Ct 76087
Bay Ct 76088
Bay Laurel Dr 76086
E & W Baylor St 76086
Bear Creek Rd 76087
Beaudelaire Dr 76087
Beaumont Dr 76086
Bedford Ct 76087
Bedinger Ln 76087
Beech Ct 76087
Beech St 76088
Bella Ct 76088
Bellenger Ln 76088
N Bend Rd 76085
Bennett Hills Dr 76088
Bent Oak Rd 76086
Berry Ln 76087
Bethel Rd
1700-2099 76086
2100-7999 76087
Bielss Ln 76087
Big Jake Ct 76088
Big Oak Ln 76085
Billabong Ct 76085
Billie Dr 76085
Billo Ct 76087
Bishop Dr 76088
W Bishop St 76086
Black Forest Dr 76086
Blackfoot Trl 76087
Blair Dr 76086
Blue Bell Ct 76088
Blue Bird Rd 76085
Blue Castle Ct 76088
N & S Blue Jay Ct 76088
N & S Blue Meadow Ct 76088
Blue Quail Dr 76087
Blue Ribbon Trl 76087
Blue Ridge Dr 76088
Blue Ridge Rd 76087
Blue Sage Ct 76088
N & S Blue Stem Ct 76087
Bluebonnet Cir 76087
Bluebonnet Dr 76087
Bluebonnet Ln 76086
Bluff Creek Ct & Rd 76087
Bluff Heights Dr 76085
Bluff Ridge Rd 76087
Bob White Ave 76086
Boeing Trl 76087
Bois D Arc Ln & St 76086
Bolivar Dr 76085
Boone Ct 76087
Boot Hill Dr 76087
N Boundary St 76086
N Bowie Dr 76086
S Bowie Dr 76086
Bowie Rd 76088
Boyd Ln 76088
Brandon Dr 76087
Brandy Dr 76087

Brazos Cir 76087
Brazos Ln 76086
N Brazos St 76086
S Brazos St 76086
Brazos Trl 76087
Brazos Hills Dr 76087
Brazos Mountain Dr 76087
Brazos Ridge Dr 76087
Brazos Valley Ln 76087
Brazos Vista Ct 76087
Brewster Trl 76087
Briarhaven Blvd 76086
Briarwood St 76087
W Bridge St 76086
Brim St 76087
Brock Hill Ln 76088
Brock Springs Trl 76087
Broken Rd 76088
Broken Bow Rd 76087
Bronco Ln 76087
Brook Hollow Ln 76088
Brooke Arbor Ct 76087
Brookview Ct 76087
Browder Ln 76087
Brown Creek Rd 76085
Brush Creek Dr 76087
Bryan St 76086
Brynns Ct 76087
Bryon Dr 76085
Buck Ct 76088
Buckboard Trl 76087
Buckingham Ct 76088
Bullard St 76086
Burette Dr 76086
Burkburnett Dr 76087
Burning Tree Ct 76087
Burton Dr 76087
Burton Hill Rd 76087
Butternut Ct 76088
Cabaniss Ln 76088
Cactus Rio Dr & Ln 76087
Cahill Ct 76088
Cain Ln 76088
Camelia St 76086
Camelot Ct & Dr 76086
Candle Ln 76088
Candleridge Ct 76087
Canull Ln 76087
Canyon Rd 76085
E & W Canyon Creek Cir, Ct, Dr & Ln 76087
Canyon Trail Ct & Rd 76087
Canyon Valley Ct & Ln 76085
Canyon View Ct 76087
Canyon West Dr 76087
Caraway Dr 76087
Cardinal Ct 76086
Carlisle Dr 76085
Carlton Ct 76085
Caroline Dr 76087
Carriage Hill Ct 76087
Carson Dr 76087
Carter Dr 76086
Carter Ln 76087
Carter Hall Ln 76088
Carter Hills Ct & Ln 76085
Carter Ranch Trl 76087
Carter View Ct 76085
Cartwright Rd 76087
Cartwright Park Rd 76088
Case St 76086
Cat Track Rd 76085
Causbie Rd 76087
Cedar Rd 76087
Cedar St
200-299 76086
3500-3699 76088
Cedar Trl 76087
Cedar Crest Ct 76087
Cedar Hill Dr 76087
Cedar Ranch Dr 76087
Cedar Ridge Dr 76087
Cedar Springs Ct & Ln 76087
Center Point Rd 76087

Central Rd 76088
Champion Ct 76087
Chappel Hill Ct 76088
Charles St 76086
Charlie Way 76087
Chavez Trl 76087
Chelsey Ct 76087
Cherokee St 76086
Cherokee Trl 76087
Cherry St 76086
Cheyenne Trl 76087
Chilton St 76086
Chimney Rock Ct & Dr 76086
Chippewa Trl 76087
Chisholm Trl 76087
Chisholm Hills Rd 76087
Choctaw Rdg 76085
Chris Ct
100-199 76087
3500-3599 76088
Christine St 76085
Christopher Ct 76088
Christopher Dr 76085
E & W Church St 76086
Churchill Cir & Ct 76085
Cimmaron Loop & Trl 76087
Cimmarron Rd 76087
Cindy Ct & Ln 76085
Cinema Dr 76087
Cinnamon Ct 76088
Circle Ct 76087
Circleview Dr 76087
Clark Ave 76085
Clark Lake Rd 76088
Clear Creek Ct & Dr 76087
Clear Lake Ct 76087
Clear Lake Ln 76087
Clear Lake Rd
1200-2099 76086
2100-2899 76087
Clearview Ct 76087
Cleburne Ave 76086
Cleburne Hwy 76087
Cleveland Ave 76086
Cliff View Ct & Loop 76087
Clinton Dr 76086
Club House Dr 76087
Coates Trl 76087
Cochran Rd 76085
Cody Ct 76088
Cohiba Ct 76085
Cold Springs Rd 76088
Coldwater Creek Ln 76088
Coleman Ln 76087
College Ave 76086
College Dr 76088
College Park Dr 76086
Collett Ct 76088
Colonial Creek Ln 76088
Colton Dr 76087
E & W Columbia St 76086
Comanche Crk & Trl 76087
Comer Ln 76085
Common St 76086
Condor Vw 76087
Cool Ln 76088
Coolibar Ct 76085
Cooparoo Ct 76085
Copper Field Ct 76087
Cornstubble Ln 76088
Coronado Ct & Trl 76087
Cortez Trl 76087
Corto Trl 76087
Cottontail Ln 76088
Cottonwood Ct 76087
Cottonwood Ln 76086
Cottonwood St 76086
Country Rd 76088
Country Brook Ct & Dr 76087
Country Green Ct 76087
Country Oaks Ln 76088
Country Place Rd 76087
Countryside Ct 76087
Courthouse Sq 76086
W Couts St 76086

Cox Dr 76088
Coy Rd 76087
Coyote Run 76086
Creek Crossing Dr 76087
Creek Side Dr 76087
Creek View Ct 76088
E & S Creighton Dr 76087
Crest Rd 76087
Crest Ridge Ct 76087
Crestview Dr 76087
Crockett Rd 76088
Cross Timbers Ct 76085
Crossbow Ct 76088
Crossfire Ct 76088
Crossing Point Dr 76088
Crossland Dr 76087
Crow Ave 76085
Crown Pointe Blvd 76087
Crown Valley Cir, Ct &
Dr 76087
Crystal Ln 76088
Curtis Dr 76086
Cutters Trl 76087
Cutting Horse Ct 76087
Cynthia Ln 76087
Cynthia Ann Parker Ln 76087
Cypress St 76086
D J Ln 76088
Daffodil Ct 76088
Dakota Trl 76087
Dalering Rd 76088
Dalhart Ct & Dr 76086
Dallas Ave 76086
Dalton St 76086
Dana Ct 76085
Daniel Rd 76087
Danielle Dr 76087
Daniels Rd 76087
Davis Ln 76088
Davis St 76086
Dawn Cir 76086
De La Cruz St 76085
De Leon Dr 76088
Dean Rd & St 76087
Deanna Ln 76087
Debbie Ct 76087
Deep Wood Ln 76088
Deer Butte St 76088
Deer Path Ln 76085
Deer Track Rd 76085
Deer Valley Rd 76085
Deerfield Blvd 76088
Deerwood Ct 76087
Del Rio Ct 76086
Delaware Trl 76087
Dennis Rd 76087
Dennis Junction Rd 76088
N & S Denton St 76086
Denton Heights Ln 76085
Derek Ct & Dr 76087
Devon Ct 76087
Diamond Oaks Dr 76087
Diamond Ridge Ln 76087
Dicey Rd 76085
Dill Rd 76085
Dillingham Ln 76085
Dirkson St 76086
Dixie Rd 76087
Docs Rd 76088
Dominique Dr 76087
Donna Ct 76087
Dornerle Rd 76087
Dorris Ct & Dr 76087
Dove Dr 76088
Dove Haven Ln 76085
Dove Hill Ln 76085
Driftwood Ranch Trl 76087
N & S Dubellette St 76086
Dugan Ct & Ln 76088
Duke St 76086
Duke Trl 76088
N & S Duncan Creek
Ct 76087
Dunn Ln 76088
Dusk Dr 76088
Dustin Cir 76087

Eagle Pass Ln 76087
Eagle Spirit Ln 76087
Eagle View Ct 76087
Eagles Crest Ln 76087
Eastmeadow Ln 76087
Eastview Dr 76086
Eaton Ct 76085
Echo Valley Rd 76087
Eden Rd 76085
Edge Hill Ter 76086
Edna St 76086
Edward Farris Rd 76085
Effie Ln 76088
E & W El Camino
Real 76087
El Colina Rd 76085
Elaine St 76086
Elbow Ct 76087
Elizabeth Pl 76086
Elk Hollow Ln 76085
Ellis Dr 76088
Ellis Creek Ct, Dr &
Ln 76085
Ellis Pond Ct 76085
Ellis Ridge Dr 76085
Ellis Spring Dr 76085
Elm St
100-199 76087
400-3699 76088
N Elm St 76086
S Elm St 76086
Elm Crest Ct 76087
Elmira St 76086
Elmwood Trl 76087
Embers Ln 76085
Emerald Dr 76087
Emerald Way 76085
Emilie Ct 76087
Enchanted Oaks Ct 76087
Encino Springs Ln 76088
Endive 76088
English Lake Ct 76088
Equine Rd 76087
Erica Ct 76085
Estate Dr 76086
Estel St 76086
Ethan Ct 76088
Ethan Dr 76087
Euless Ct 76087
Eureka St 76086
Evergreen Ct & Trl 76087
Fain Ln 76087
Falcon Dr 76088
Falcons Eye Ct 76087
Falling Star Ct 76088
Farmer Rd 76087
Fawn Ct 76088
Fegan St 76086
Fiddlers Trl 76087
Field Creek Ct 76085
Fingerbanks Ln 76088
Finney Dr 76085
Finneyoaks Ln 76085
Fir St 76088
Flamingo Ct 76087
Fletcher Rd 76087
Florine Ct 76087
Floyd Ct & Rd 76087
N Fm 113 76088
Fm 1189 76087
Fm 1708 76087
W Fm 1885 76088
N Fm 51 76085
N Fm 52 76088
Fm 920 76088
Fondren Ln 76088
Foot Hills Dr 76087
Forest Ln 76088
Forest Trl 76085
Forest Bend Ln 76087
Forest Creek Cir 76088
Forest Glen Ct & Ln 76087
Forest Hill Dr 76087
Forest Park Dr 76087
Forest Trail Ct 76085
Fork Ct & Dr 76087

Forrest View Ct 76087
Fort Worth Hwy
100-2299 76086
2300-4399 76087
2600-3599 76088
S Forty Dr 76085
Fossil Hill Rd 76087
Foster Ln 76086
Four Trees Dr 76087
Fox Ln & Rd 76088
Fox Chase Dr 76088
Foxpointe Cir 76087
Frank Plumlee Ln 76088
Franklin St 76086
Franko Switch Rd 76088
Fredricksburg Ct 76087
Friendship Rd 76085
N & S Frio Ct 76087
Front St 76086
Futurity Ln 76087
Gail Dr 76085
Gammill Dr 76085
Garden Ln 76085
Gardner Rd 76087
Garner Rd 76086
Garner Adell Rd 76088
Garner School Rd 76088
Garnet Dr 76087
Georgetown Ct 76087
Gibson Ln 76088
Gilbert Dr 76087
Gilley Ln 76085
Glenn Dr 76086
Golden Arrow Dr 76087
Goldfinch Ln 76088
Golf View Cir 76086
Gopher Rd 76088
Grace St 76086
Granada Ct & Dr 76088
Granbury Hwy 76087
Grant Dr 76086
Grapevine Ct 76087
Gray Wolf Trl 76087
Green Acres Rd 76088
Green Branch Rd 76085
Green Canyon Ct 76087
Green Gables Ln 76088
Green Oaks Ct & Trl 76087
Green Pointe Dr 76087
Green Tree Dr 76087
Greenbriar St 76087
Greenfield Ln 76088
Greenlee Park 76088
Greenridge Dr 76087
Greenwood Rd 76088
Greenwood Cut Off
Rd 76088
Greenwood Oaks Dr 76087
Gregory St 76087
Grimes Rd 76088
Grindstone Rd 76087
Grover Dallas Rd 76088
Grumman Trl 76087
Guadalupe Trl 76087
Guinevere Ct & Dr 76086
E & W Gumm Ct 76085
Gumtree Ct 76087
Gun Barrel Ct 76085
Gun Barrel Dr 76087
Gun Barrel Rd 76085
Gustine Ct 76087
Haciendas Ct & Dr 76087
Hall Rd & St 76088
Hamilton Ct 76087
Hancock Dr 76087
Hannah Ct 76085
Hanover St 76086
Harcourt St 76086
Harlan Dr 76085
Harmon St 76086
Harmony Cir, Rd &
Spur 76087
Harold Ln 76085
Harris Dr 76087
Harwell Ln 76088
Harwell Lake Rd 76088

Hawkins Lilly Rd 76085
Hawthorne Ct 76087
Hayley Dr 76085
Haynes Rd 76087
Hearndale Dr 76085
Hearthstone Ct 76087
Heather Ct 76086
Heather Ridge Ct 76085
Heathington Rd 76088
Hedges Cir 76085
Henigan Ct 76088
Henry Ln 76086
Henson Ct 76086
Heritage Hts 76085
Heritage Ln 76087
Hickory Ln 76086
Hico Ct 76087
Hidden Acres Ln 76087
Hidden Creek Loop 76085
Hidden Oaks Dr 76087
Hide Away Ln 76088
High Meadows Dr 76088
High Point Ct & Rd 76088
High View Ct
100-199 76086
500-599 76085
High View Dr 76085
High View Rd 76085
Highlake Dr & Ln 76087
Highland Cir 76085
Highway 171 76087
S Hill Dr 76086
Hill Top Cir 76085
Hillcroft Dr 76087
Hilltop Dr 76086
Hilltop Ter 76088
Hillview Ct 76087
Hiner Rd 76088
Hines Ln 76088
Hitching Post Dr 76087
Hobson St 76086
Hobson Bend Rd 76088
Hogle St 76086
Holders Chapel Rd 76088
Holland Lake Dr 76086
Holly Oak Dr 76087
Holly Oaks Ln 76087
Holmes Ln 76085
Hopi Trl 76087
Horseshoe Ct 76087
Horseshoe Dr 76087
Horseshoe Trl 76085
Horseshoe Bend Rd &
Trl 76087
Hott Ln 76088
Houston Ave 76086
Houston Rd 76088
Howard Rd 76088
Howell Garner Rd 76087
Hubbard Dr 76087
Hummingbird Dr & Ln 76088
Hunters Cir 76088
Huron Trl 76087
Hurst Ct 76087
Hutcheson Ln 76087
Hyde Away Ln 76085
Ice House Cir & Rd 76085
Ikard Ln 76086
Imperial Mammoth Valley
Ln 76085
Indian Camp Rd 76088
Indian Gap St 76087
Industrial St 76086
Inspiration Dr 76087
E Interstate 20
100-2898 76087
E Interstate 20
101-2499 76086
2501-2899 76087
2900-4099 76087
W Interstate 20
100-998 76086
101-7699 76087
1500-7698 76088
Inverness Dr 76086
Iroquois Trl 76087

Irving Ct 76087
Ivie Ln 76087
Izella Ln 76085
J B Ln 76085
Jabez Ct 76087
Jack Borden Way 76086
Jackson St 76086
Jade Ct 76087
Jade Ln 76086
Jamar Dr 76088
James Dr 76087
James C Rd 76085
Jameson St 76086
Jane Ln 76085
Jefferson St 76086
Jennifer Ct 76086
Jenny Ln 76085
Jeremy Ln 76088
Joalene Dr 76087
Jodie Dr 76087
John Chisholm Rd 76087
Johnson St 76086
Johnson Bend Rd 76088
Jolin Ln 76088
Jonathan Ct 76086
Jones Rd 76088
E & W Josephine St 76086
Joshua Rd 76087
Joyce Ct 76087
Joyce St 76085
Juan Ct 76087
Julia Ct 76085
Julie St 76086
Juniper Ct 76087
Jupiter Trl 76088
Kachnovich Ln 76085
Kailyn Ln 76085
Kaitlyn Dr 76087
Kalinga Dr 76085
Karbo Ln 76085
Karen St 76088
Kari Linda Ct 76085
Kate Ct 76087
Kathey St 76088
Kay Dr 76086
Keechi St 76086
Kelley Dr 76085
Kelly Ct 76087
Kelly Brook Cir & Ln 76087
Kemp Rd 76087
Kenshire Ct 76086
Keri Ct 76085
Kevin Dr 76087
Key Ln 76088
Kickapoo Trl 76087
Kinbrook Ln 76087
King St
100-199 76087
900-1499 76086
King Arthur Ct & Dr 76086
Kirby Rd 76088
Kirkland Ln 76085
Kortney Dr 76087
Kourtney Ct 76086
Kristi Way 76087
Kuranda Ct 76085
La Arroya Dr 76088
N La Colina Rd 76085
La Costa Cir 76088
La Estada Dr 76088
La Mesa Dr 76085
La Vega Trl 76088
La Vista Ct 76088
Lake Dr 76085
E Lake Dr 76087
N Lake Dr 76085
W Lake Dr 76087
Lake Circle Ct 76087
Lake Country Dr 76087
Lake Hollow Dr 76087
Lake Shore Trl 76087
Lakeforest Ct & Dr 76087
Lakeridge Ct & Dr 76087
Lakeshore Dr 76087
Lakeview Ct
100-199 76087

200-299 76088
Lakeview Ter 76087
Lakeview Trl 76087
Lakeway Dr 76087
Lakewood Dr 76087
N & S Lamar St 76086
N & W Lambert Rd 76088
Lancelot Dr 76086
Lands Way Rd 76087
Laser Ln 76087
Laura St 76086
Laurel Valley Ct 76087
Lauren Ct 76087
Lazy Bend Rd 76087
Leatherman Ln 76088
E Lee Ave 76086
W Lee Ave 76086
Lee Ln 76087
Leea Ln 76087
Legacy Blvd 76085
Lemmuel Dr 76085
Lexington St 76086
Liberty St 76086
Linda Ln 76087
Lindas Creek Ln 76088
Lindentree Dr 76086
N & S Line St 76086
Link St 76086
Linville Ln 76086
Lipan Trl 76087
Lisa Leigh Ct 76087
Little Cat Track Rd 76085
Little Reba Ranch Rd 76088
Live Oak Dr 76087
Live Oak Ln 76086
Live Oak Trl 76087
Livingston Ct & Rd 76087
Llano Ct 76087
Llano Dr 76087
Llano Rd 76088
Lochness Cir 76086
Lockheed Trl 76087
Lockwood Ln 76087
Lois Ln 76088
Loma Vista Dr 76085
Lone Oak Rd 76087
Lone Star Rd 76085
Longhorn Dr
1-99 76085
1100-1198 76086
N Longhorn Dr 76085
S Longhorn Dr 76085
Longhorn Trl 76087
Longley Ln 76085
Looney Ln 76087
Lora Ln 76088
Lorrie Ln 76087
Louis Trl 76087
Louis Scherer Ln &
Rd 76088
Love St 76086
Lucas Rd 76085
Lution Dr 76087
Lynn St 76086
Lytle Ln 76085
Macanudo Ln 76085
Mad Canyon Rd 76087
Maddux Rd 76088
Madison St 76086
Magnolia Dr 76086
N Main St
100-1699 76086
1700-1899 76085
S Main St
100-2399 76086
2401-2499 76086
2500-2799 76087
Manley Ln 76088
Maple St 76088
Maplewood Dr 76087
Mariah Dr 76087
Marian Dr 76085
Marilyn St 76085
Marina View Ct 76087
Mark Layne Rd 76088
Marlboro Country Trl 76087

Martin Dr 76086
Mary Dr 76085
Marys Ln 76086
Marys Shady Ln 76088
Mason Pond Dr 76085
Mastadon Way 76085
Matthew Dr 76086
May Ct 76088
Mc Kay Ln 76088
Mccarthy Dr 76088
Mccarty St 76086
Mcclendon Rd 76088
Mcclintock Ct 76088
Mcclure Ct 76087
Mcfarland Ln 76088
Mckinzie Ln 76087
Meadow Ct 76086
Meadow Dr 76086
Meadow Ln 76087
Meadow Arbor Dr 76085
Meadow Bridge Dr 76085
Meadow Creek Dr 76085
Meadow Lark Ln 76087
Meadow Ridge Dr 76087
Meadow Vista Cir 76087
Meadowglenn Dr 76087
Meadowview Ct & Rd 76087
Meadowwood Ln 76087
Meandering Way 76086
Mearl Ct 76087
Measures Rd 76088
Megan Ct 76087
Melody Ln 76087
Merlin Dr 76086
N & S Merrimac St 76086
Merritt Ln 76086
Mesa Ct 76087
Mesa St 76086
Mesa Trl 76087
Mesa Springs St 76086
Mesquite Dr 76086
Mesquite St 76086
Mesquite Trl 76087
Michael Ln
100-399 76088
1700-1799 76085
Michele Ct 76088
Middleton Ct 76087
Middleton Rd 76088
Midway Ln 76087
Midway Rd 76085
Mikus Rd 76087
N & S Mill St 76086
Mill Branch Ln 76085
Mill Creek Dr 76085
S Mill Creek Dr 76085
Mill Creek Ln 76087
Mimosa St 76086
Mineola St 76086
Mineral Wells Hwy
1200-1699 76086
1700-12300 76088
12302-12798 76088
Mini Ranch Dr 76088
Miramar Cir 76085
Mission Rd 76088
Misty Ridge Ln 76085
Mitchell Blvd 76087
Mockingbird Ln 76086
Mohawk Trl 76087
Molly Ln 76085
Montclair Dr 76087
Montecristo Dr 76085
Monterrey Dr 76087
Monterrey Rd 76088
Montgomery Ln 76087
Morris Ct 76088
Mosley Ct 76086
Moss Ln 76088
Mount Zion Rd 76088
Mountain View Dr 76087
Moyer Ct & Ln 76087
Murls Lake Cir, Dr &
Rd 76085
Mylea Ln 76087
Naibara Trl 76088

Narrow St 76087
Narry Ln 76087
Navajo Trl 76087
Neal Ln 76088
New Authon Rd 76088
New Tin Top Rd 76087
Newcastle Dr 76086
Newell Dr 76087
Newman Ln 76088
Newport Rd 76086
Newsom Mound Rd 76085
Nicole Ln 76087
Nighthawk Ln & St 76088
Nikki Trill Ln 76088
Noahs Ct 76085
Nocona Trl 76087
Noelle Ln 76087
Norman Dr 76087
Norris Cir 76087
North St 76086
Northwood Rd 76088
Norton St 76086
Oak Cir 76088
Oak Dr 76088
Oak Ln 76088
E Oak St 76086
W Oak St 76086
Oak Country Est 76085
Oak Crest Dr 76087
Oak Glen Dr 76087
Oak Hill Dr 76087
Oak Hollow Dr 76087
Oak Leaf Dr 76087
Oak Park Dr 76087
Oak Ridge Est 76085
Oak Ridge Ter 76086
Oak Tree Cir & Ln 76086
Oakbend Ct 76088
Oakley Cir 76085
Oakmont Dr 76088
Oakridge Dr 76086
N Oakridge Dr 76087
S Oakridge Dr 76087
Oakview Dr 76087
Oakwood Dr 76086
Oakwood Creek Ct & Ln 76088
Obrien Ct 76086
Odel Dr 76085
Old Agnes Rd 76088
Old Airport Rd 76087
Old Authon Ln & Rd 76088
Old Brock Rd
100-1899 76088
1900-8099 76087
8100-8999 76087
Old Dennis Rd 76087
Old Foundry Rd 76087
Old Garner Rd 76088
Old Millsap Rd 76088
Old Mineral Wells Hwy 76088
Old Ranch Ct 76087
Old Springtown Rd 76085
Old Tin Top Rd 76087
Olive Branch Rd 76087
Oliver St 76086
Onyx Ct 76087
Opal Dr 76087
Oralings Rd 76085
Orcheade St 76086
Oriole St 76086
Otto Dr 76087
Our Ln 76088
Overton Dr 76086
Overton Ridge Cir 76088
Owen Cir 76087
E & W Owens St 76086
Ox Mill Creek Rd 76087
Oxen Ln 76088
Oxford School Ln 76087
Oykey Trl 76087
Oyster Hill St 76086
Pack Saddle Ct & Trl 76088
Paige St 76088
Paintbrush Ct 76087
Palo Pinto St 76086
Pamela Dr 76086
Pamela Kay Ln 76088
E & W Park Ave & Ct 76086
Park Meadow Dr 76087
Park Ridge Dr 76087
Parker Oaks Ct & Ln 76087
Partagas Dr 76085
Patrick Dr 76087
Patrick Creek Rd 76087
Patriot Dr 76087
Pats Ct 76087
Patsy Lee Ct 76087
Patti Ct 76085
Patti Pl 76086
Paul St 76088
Pawnee Trl 76087
Payne St 76086
Peaceful Ln 76088
Peacock Dr 76085
Pearl Ct 76087
Pearson Ranch Rd 76087
Peaster Hwy
600-699 76086
700-1899 76088
Pebblebrook Dr 76087
Pecan Dr 76086
Pecan Grove Dr 76087
Pecan Park Dr 76087
Pecos Dr
300-399 76086
4900-4999 76087
Pepper Ln 76088
Perdue Ln 76085
Pheasant Dr 76088
Pickard Ln 76087
Pin Oak Trl 76087
Pine St 76086
Ping Ct 76087
Pinnacle Peak Ln 76087
Pintail Ln 76088
Pioneer Rd & Trl 76087
Piper Trl 76087
Pittman Rd 76087
Pleasant Valley Ln 76087
Pleasant View Dr 76086
Pleasant Wood Cir 76086
Pogue Branch Ct 76086
Point Ct 76087
Ponderosa Ln 76085
Possum Pass 76085
Post Oak Trl 76087
Powell Rd 76088
Prachyl Rd 76087
Prairie Ln 76087
Precinct Rd 76088
Price Ln 76085
Primrose Dr 76086
Pritchard Ln 76085
Pueblo Trl 76087
Quail Ridge Dr 76087
Quail Run Ct 76086
Quail Run Rd 76088
Quail Springs Dr 76088
Quanah Trl 76087
Quanah Hill Rd 76087
Quincy Ln 76087
Quinn Ct 76085
R T Ln 76085
Rachel Rd 76086
Rafter J Rd 76086
Ragle Rd 76087
Rains St 76086
Raintree Ct 76087
Raley Ct & Rd 76085
Ramble Oak Dr 76087
SE Rambling Loop & Trl 76087
N Rambling Fork St 76087
Ranch Ct & Ln 76088
Ranch Oak Dr 76087
Ranchoma Ct 76087
Ranchview Trl 76087
Randall Rd 76087
Randy Dr 76086
Ranger Hwy
1200-1599 76086
1600-3299 76088
Raven Bnd 76087
Rawhide Trl 76088
Rayna Dr 76086
Reata Dr 76087
Rebecca Ln 76085
Red Bird Ln 76088
Red Bud Dr 76087
Red Eagle Trl 76087
Red Fox Ct 76088
Red Oak Ln 76086
Red Oak St S 76087
Red Oak Trl 76087
Redbud Ln 76086
Redtail Ct 76088
Remington Cir 76086
Remington Ct 76085
Remington Ln 76085
Renee Dr 76087
E & W Rentz St 76086
Rentz Place Cir 76086
Rey Del Mar Cir 76085
N Ric Williamson Memorial Hwy 76088
Rider Ln 76085
W Ridge Rd 76086
Ridge Crest Dr 76088
Ridge Hollow Trl 76087
Ridgecrest Dr 76087
N & S Ridgeoak Ct 76087
N & S Ridgeview Dr 76087
Ridgeway Blvd 76086
Ridgmar Dr 76088
Rifle Rd 76087
Rifleman Rd 76087
Rio Bravo Ct 76088
Rippy Rd 76088
Rising View Ct 76085
Rivendell Ln 76088
River Trl 76087
N & S River Buck Ct 76087
River Oak Ct 76087
River View Ct 76087
Riverwood Dr 76087
Roadrunner Dr 76088
Roark Ln 76088
Rob Ln 76087
Roberts Bnd 76086
Robin Ave 76086
Robinson Rd 76087
Roble Ct 76088
Rock Church Rd 76088
Rockridge Ct 76087
Rocky Ridge Ln 76085
Rona St 76086
Rooster Cogburn Ct 76088
Roselawn Dr 76086
Royal Ct & Dr 76085
Royal View Ct 76087
Running Creek Ct 76087
Rupert Ct 76087
N & S Rusk St 76086
Russell Ct 76087
Russell Ln 76087
Russell Rd 76087
W Russell St 76086
Russell Bend Rd 76088
Rustic Harbour Ct 76087
Sabathney Dr & Rd 76085
Saddle Brook Dr 76087
Saddle Club Rd 76088
Saddle Ridge Trl 76087
Sage Brush Dr 76087
Sagewood Dr 76087
Salado Trl 76087
Samuel Dr 76085
Sanchez Ct 76088
Sanchez Creek Ct & Dr 76088
Sandalwood Ct 76085
Sanders Rd 76085
Sandhill Ct 76085
Sandpiper Dr 76088
Sandpoint Ct 76085
Sandridge Dr 76085
Sandstone Ln 76085
Sandwood Ct 76085
Sandy Ln 76088
Sandy Creek Ct & Trl 76085
W Sandy Lee Ln 76085
Santa Clara Dr 76085
Santa Fe Dr 76086
Santa Fe Trl 76087
Sarahs Ct 76088
N & S Savage Creek Ln 76087
Savannah Dr 76087
Scarlett Rd 76087
W Scenic Trl 76088
Scenic Ridge Ct & Dr 76087
Scherer Ln 76088
Scott Ct 76085
Scott Ln 76085
Scott Rd 76088
Scotts Meadow Ct 76087
Seminole Trl 76087
Serenity Ln 76087
Serrano Ct 76087
Shadow Run 76086
Shadowglenn Dr 76087
Shady Ln 76085
Shady Creek Ct 76087
Shady Grove Ln & Rd 76088
Shady Oak Ct, Dr & Ln 76087
Shady Oaks Dr 76085
Shady Valley Cir 76086
Shady Wood Ct 76087
Shanes Ln 76087
Shannon Dr 76087
Shannon St 76086
Sharla Smelley Rd 76087
Shawnee Trl 76087
Shelbi Ct 76088
Sherri Ln 76085
Sherry Ct & Trl 76086
Shiloh Ct 76085
Shirley Cir 76087
Shoreline Cir 76088
Shoreline Ct 76087
Shotgun Dr 76087
Signature Ct 76087
Silent Springs Ct 76085
Silver Saddle Cir 76087
Silver Sage Ct 76087
Silver Spur Dr 76087
Silverado Dr 76087
Silverstone Dr 76087
E & W Simmons St 76086
Sioux Trl 76087
Slay Ln 76087
Sleepy Hollow Ln 76085
Sloan St 76086
Smith Trl 76088
Smokey Br 76085
Smokey Terrace Ln 76085
Soapberry Dr 76086
Songwood Dr 76087
Sonora Canyon Rd 76087
Sophies Pl 76087
Sorrel Ct 76087
Sosebee Bend Rd 76088
Southerland Ln 76088
Southland Dr 76086
Southridge Dr 76087
Southview Dr 76087
Southwinds Dr 76087
Soward Ave 76086
Spalding Ct 76087
Spanish Trl 76087
Spirit Ct 76087
Spring Ct 76087
E Spring St 76086
W Spring St 76086
Spring Creek Pkwy & Rd 76087
Spring Lake Dr 76087
Springwood Ln 76087
Spur Rd 76087
Stacy Ln 76087
Stafford Rd 76088
Stage Coach Trl 76087
N Star Crossing Ln 76088
Star Designs Way 76088
Star Point Ln 76088
Starr Dr 76085
Starwood Dr 76086
State St 76086
Stetson Dr 76087
Stonebridge Ct, Dr, Ln & Trl 76085
Stoneridge Cir, Ct & Trl 76087
Story Book Ln 76086
Sugar Sand Ct 76085
Sumac Trl 76087
Summer Ct 76087
Summer Brook Dr 76087
Summer Stone Ct 76087
Sun Valley Ln 76087
Sunburst Ct 76087
Sundance Ct 76087
Sunflower Dr 76087
Sunny Oaks Ct 76087
Sunray Ct 76087
Sunrise Trl 76088
Sunset Ct 76088
Sunset Hill Ct 76087
Sunshine Meadows Ct 76088
Suzanne Trl 76087
Swancy Ln 76088
Sweet Springs Rd 76088
Sweetwater Dr
100-399 76086
400-599 76085
Sycamore St 76086
Sylvan Creek Dr 76087
Sylvan Valley Dr 76087
Sylvia St 76086
T D Studio Ln 76087
Tabernacle St 76088
Tackett Ln 76087
Tahoe Ln 76087
Tahoka Trl 76087
Tail Spin Cir 76087
Tanglewood Dr 76087
Tanglewood Ln 76087
Tanglewood St 76085
Tango Rd 76087
Tankersley Ln 76087
Tay Ct 76088
Taylor Dr & Rd 76087
Tejas Rd 76085
Teresa Ct 76086
Terrace Dr 76086
Terry Trl 76086
Texas Dr 76086
The Farm Rd 76085
Thistle Hill Trl 76087
Thomas Ln 76088
Thompson Rd 76087
Thorp Ln 76088
Thorpe Springs Rd 76087
Thousand Oaks Cir 76086
Threatt Ln 76088
Throckmorton St 76086
Thrush St 76086
Tidwell Rd 76087
Tiffany Trl 76086
Tigers Eye Ct 76087
Timaaron Ct 76085
Timber Trl 76087
Timber Cove Ct & Dr 76087
Timber Creek Dr 76086
Timber Ridge Rd 76088
Timber Wild Dr 76087
Tin Top Hwy 76087
Tin Top Rd
1800-2199 76086
2200-6199 76087
Tin Top Estates Rd 76087
Titelist Dr 76087
Toowoomba Ln 76085
Top Flight Dr 76087
Tory St 76086
Toto Rd 76088
N & S Tower St 76086
Trace Dr 76087
Trace Ridge Dr 76087
Trail Rdg 76087
Trails End St 76087
Trailview Ln 76088
Trailwood Dr 76085
Travis Rd 76088
Tremble Rd 76085
Tremont St 76086
Trenton St 76086
Trevor Dr 76087
Trey Dr 76087
Trinity St 76086
Trinity Ranch Rd 76087
Trinity River Dr 76087
Trinity View Rd 76087
Triple K Ct 76087
True Grit Ct 76088
Truitt Dr 76087
Tucker Dr 76085
Tula Trl 76087
Tumbleweed Dr 76087
Tusk Ct 76085
Twin Hill Ct 76087
Twin Springs Ranch Ln 76087
Tyler Ct 76086
Ultra Ct 76087
Upper Denton Ct 76085
Upper Denton Rd
300-399 76086
400-5899 76085
Utopia Trl 76087
Valley Cir 76086
Valley Dr 76087
Valley Ln 76085
Valley Rd 76087
Valley Oak Rd 76087
Valley Ranch Rd 76087
Valley Trail Dr 76087
Valley View Cir & Ln 76087
Van Winkle St 76086
Vance Ln 76088
Vaughn Ln 76088
Vaughna Dr 76087
Veal Station Rd 76085
Vigortone Blvd 76086
Vine St 76086
Vineyard St 76087
Vivienne St 76086
N & S Waco St 76086
Wagon Wheel Trl 76087
Walden Rd 76087
Walker Bend Rd 76088
Walkers Pl 76087
Wall St 76086
Walnut Ct 76087
N Walnut St 76086
S Walnut St 76086
Walters Ln 76087
Waltzing Brook Ct 76085
Wandering Ct & Ln 76086
Ward St 76086
Washington Dr 76086
E & W Water St 76086
Water Oak Ln 76086
Water View Ct & Ln 76085
Watkins Trl 76088
Waverly Ct 76085
E & W Weatherford St 76086
Weaver Ln 76087
Weiland Rd 76088
N Weilland St 76086
Wellington Trl 76085
Wells Ln 76085
Wendy Ln 76086
Westbriar Dr 76086
Westend Ln 76088
Western Lake Dr 76087
Westmeadow Ln 76087
Westridge Dr & Trl 76087
Westwind Ct 76087
Westwood Dr 76086
Wheeler St 76086
Whippoorwill Trl 76085
Whispering Dell Ln 76085
White Oak Ct 76087
White Settlement Rd 76087
White Wing Ct 76088
Whiterock Ct & Dr 76086
Whitestone Way 76085
Whitetail Run 76088
Whitney Dr 76087
Whitt Cir 76088
Wiggins Ct 76087
Wiggs Ln 76086
Wild Plum Ct 76087
Wild Rose Ct 76087
Wild Turkey Trl 76087
Wilderness Way 76085
Wildflower Ln 76088
Wildflower Trl 76087
Wildwood Trl 76085
Williams Rd
2-98 76087
100-299 76087
801-899 76085
Willow Cir 76087
Willow St 76088
Willow Creek Dr 76085
Willow Glen Dr 76087
Willow Wood Dr 76087
Willowglenn Dr 76087
Wilson Ln 76087
Winbrook St 76087
Winchester Ln 76085
Windcrest Ct 76087
Windhaven Ct 76087
Winding Creek Dr 76087
E Windmill Rd 76088
Windowmere Trl 76085
Windriver Ct 76088
Windsong Ct 76087
Windsor Ct 76086
Windview Ct 76087
E & W Windwalker Ct 76088
Winfield St 76087
Winona St 76086
Wintergreen Ct 76085
Wonder Oak Ct 76085
Wood Ave 76086
Wood Bend Ct 76087
Wood Creek Ct 76087
Wood Hollow Dr 76087
Wood Oak Trl 76088
Woodcrest St 76087
Woodhaven Ct 76087
Woodland Trl 76085
Woodland Hills Ln 76087
Woodmont Dr 76087
Woodrun Ct 76087
Woods Edge Ct 76087
Woodside Ct 76087
Wooley Ct 76085
Wright Ln 76085
Wyche Rd 76085
York Ave 76086
Yorkshire Ct & Dr 76086
Young Bend Rd 76087
Yucca Dr 76087
E Yucca Vw 76085
W Yucca Vw 76085
Yukon Ct 76087
Zachary Dr 76087
Zion Hill Loop & Rd 76088

NUMBERED STREETS

All Street Addresses 76086

WESLACO TX

General Delivery 78596

POST OFFICE BOXES MAIN OFFICE STATIONS AND BRANCHES

Box No.s
All PO Boxes 78599

RURAL ROUTES

03, 05, 07 78596
01, 03, 06, 09, 10 78599

NAMED STREETS

W Abilene Dr 78599
Abraham Dr 78599
Abraham Lincoln St 78599
Ac St 78596
Academy Dr 78596
Acapulco St 78596
Adams St 78599
W Adelita St 78599
Agate Dr 78596
Aggassi Dr 78599
E & W Agostadero St .. 78596
Aguila 78596
N Airport Dr
400-598 78596
600-799 78596
801-899 78596
901-999 78599
1600-1698 78599
S Airport Dr 78596
Alabama St 78599
Alamo St 78599
Alexandra Dr 78596
Alicia Dr 78596
Alma Ave 78599
Aloha Dr 78596
Alondra Dr 78599
Alpine Rd 78599
Alvarez St 78599
Alyssum St 78599
S Amanda St 78596
Amaryllis 78599
Amber Dr 78596
Ambrosia 78596
America St 78596
Amethyst Dr 78596
Amistad Dr 78596
Amistad Ln 78599
Anacua Cir 78599
Anaqua St 78599
Angel St 78599
Angelita Dr 78599
Annie St 78599
Anthony St 78596
Arboledas Dr 78599
Armadillo Run 78596
Arthur Cir 78596
S & W Ash Dr & St 78596
Ashley Dr 78596
Aster Dr 78596
Audrey Dr 78596
Augusta St 78596
Aurora Dr 78596
E Austin St 78599
B Shea 78596
Babb Dr 78596
Bahamas 78596
E & W Baker Dr 78596
Bald Cypress 78596
Ballard St 78599
Barclay St 78596
W Beaumont Dr 78599
Belen St 78599
Belinda Dr 78599
Bella Vis 78596
Bently Dr 78599
N & S Bermuda St 78596
Beryl Cir 78596
E Bethany Dr 78599
Beto Ave 78596
N Beto Garcia Dr 78599
Big Pine Ky 78596
Big Valley Dr 78599
Bill Clinton St 78599
Bill Summers
International Blvd 78596
E Birdnest Ln 78599
Birdwing St 78599
Black St 78599
Blue Sky 78599

Bluebonnet St 78599
Bluejay St 78596
N Border Ave
101-199 78596
109-109 78599
400-498 78596
500-1099 78596
1500-1698 78599
1700-2100 78599
2102-3498 78599
S Border Ave 78596
Borg 78599
Bougainvillea Ave 78596
Bowie St 78599
Bowl Dr 78599
Braeside 78596
Brenda Ln 78596
N Bridge Ave
101-297 78596
299-699 78596
701-899 78596
1001-1397 78599
1399-3399 78599
3401-4399 78599
S Bridge Ave 78596
Bridget St 78596
Brightwood Ave 78596
S Broadway St 78599
Bronco Dr 78596
Brush Dr 78599
Buena Suerte 78596
Buena Ventura 78596
Buena Vista Dr 78596
Burns St 78596
E & W Business 83 78596
N Business Fm 1015 78596
Bustamante St 78596
Cabos Dr 78599
Cactus Dr 78599
California St 78599
W Calle Santiago
Galvan 78596
Camelot Dr 78596
Camino De Verdad Rd . 78596
Camino Real Viejo Rd .. 78596
Cancun St 78599
N & S Cantu St 78596
Canyon Dr 78599
Cardenas St 78599
Cardinal 78599
Carnelian Dr 78596
Carol Ave 78599
Cary St
1700-1999 78599
2000-2098 78596
2001-2099 78599
Casandra St 78596
Cascade Dr 78599
Castaneda St 78599
Catarina Rd & St 78596
Cedar Cv 78599
Cedar St 78596
N & S Cedro St 78596
Celeste
1701-1797 78599
Celeste
1799-1800 78599
1801-1899 78596
1802-2098 78599
1901-2099 78596
Ceniza Dr 78599
Chalcedony 78596
Chapa Dr 78599
W Chaparral St 78596
Charlene Ave 78599
Charlotte Ave 78599
E Cherry Blossom Cir .. 78596
Chilton St 78596
China St 78596
Chloe Rae Cir 78599
Christian Ct 78596
Chrysolite Dr 78596
Chula Vis 78596
Cielo Blanco 78596
Citrine Dr 78596
Citrus Ct & Dr 78596

Citrus Hills Cir & Dr 78599
Claudio Gomez St 78599
S Clavel Ave 78599
Clear Creek Cir 78596
Clifford Dr
500-600 78596
602-798 78596
2900-3099 78599
Clifton St 78596
Club De Amistad 78596
W Coast Dr 78599
Coco Dr 78599
Colorado St 78596
Colosio Ct & St 78599
E Commercial Dr 78599
Conch Ky 78596
Connors 78599
Coral Ave 78599
Corporate Dr 78599
W Corpus Christi Dr 78599
Corral Cir 78596
Cortez St 78599
Corto St 78596
Costa Rico 78596
Country Ln 78599
Country Way Dr 78599
Countryside Dr 78599
Cowboy Dr 78599
Coyote Trl 78596
Crockett St 78599
Cronicas Ct & St 78599
Crosswinds Circle Dr ... 78596
Cruz Rocha Sr Dr 78596
Cypress Dr 78599
Daily Ave E 78596
Daisy Dr 78599
W Dallas Dr 78599
Danita Jo St 78596
Dario St 78599
Darlene Ave 78599
Date Dr 78599
Davenport St 78596
Dawson St 78596
De La Madrid 78599
De Leon St 78599
De Los Santos Ave 78599
Del Oro 78599
Delaware St 78596
Delma St 78596
Desiga Way 78596
Dewberry 78596
Diamond Blvd 78599
Diaz St 78599
Don Bruno St 78596
Dover Dr 78599
Drain St 78596
Dunn St 78599
Durango St 78596
Edgewood Dr 78596
Edna St 78599
Eisenhower Dr 78599
El Camino Dr 78599
El Jardin 78596
El Nido St 78596
El Paseo Dr 78596
El Salvador St 78596
El Sol Dr
700-2598 78599
2600-2799 78599
2800-2998 78596
2801-2999 78599
El Triunfo Rd 78599
Elena St 78599
Elma St 78596
Emerald Dr 78599
Encantado Dr 78599
Encanto Sr 78596
Encino Dr & St 78596
Esperanza St N & S 78599
E & W Esplanada St 78596
Estrella St 78596
Eucalyptus St 78596
Eve Ave 78596
Evelyn Ave 78599
Everglade Dr 78599
Express Ave 78596

E Expressway 83
201-4099 78599
E Expressway 83
500-1998 78596
2000-2098 78599
2300-3698 78596
3700-4098 78599
W Expressway 83
100-3298 78599
301-2199 78596
2201-2299 78599
2301-2399 78596
2401-2499 78599
2901-2999 78596
3001-3201 78599
3203-3299 78596
Fairfield Blvd 78596
Falcon Dr 78599
Felix Garcia St 78599
Fern Dr 78599
Fernando St 78599
Fica Dr 78599
Filbert St 78599
Flagtstone Ter 78596
Flores St 78599
Florida Ave 78596
Flushing Mdws 78596
N Fm 1015
101-397 78596
399-700 78596
702-798 78596
4401-4999 78599
5001-5099 78596
5701-5799 78599
S Fm 1015 78596
N Fm 88
13701A-13799A 78599
4001-4197 78599
4199-10400 78599
10402-11798 78599
10601-10699 78596
10901-13299 78599
11900-11998 78596
13500-17298 78599
13701-13799 78596
14201-17499 78599
17501-17599 78596
17801-17999 78599
Ford St 78596
Forest Ln 78596
Forest Hills Dr 78596
Fox St 78599
Fresno Dr 78596
Fresno Ln 78599
Frost Proof Dr 78599
Gabriela 78599
Gallahad Cir 78596
Garcia St 78599
Gardenia St 78599
Garnet Dr 78596
Gary Ln 78596
Garza Ave 78596
Garza Cir 78599
Garza St 78596
Gateway Dr 78599
Gemstone 78596
George Bush St 78599
George Washington St . 78599
N Georgia Ave 78599
S Georgia Ave 78596
Geronimo 78599
Ginger Ave 78596
E Gonzales Rd 78596
N & S Gonzalez Rd 78596
Grace Ave 78596
Granada 78599
Gray Lane Ave 78596
Grove Cir 78599
N Gte Ave 78599
Guadalupe St 78599
N Guadalupe St 78596
Guava Dr 78596
S Guerra Ave 78599
Guinivere Ln 78596
Gutierrez St 78599
Hacienda Del Sol 78599
W Hackberry Dr & St ... 78596

Haggar St 78599
W Harrison St 78599
Hawaii 78596
Hermosillo St 78599
Hibiscus Ave 78596
W Hidalgo St 78596
Hidden Trce 78599
Hidden Valley Dr 78596
Highland Dr 78599
E & W Highway 281 ... 78596
Hollow Rd 78599
Homer Ave 78596
Honey Tree St 78596
Honolulu Dr 78596
Hospital Dr 78596
Huatulco St 78599
Huerta St 78596
E & W Huisache St 78596
Huron Dr 78599
Hydrangea St 78599
N & S Illinois Ave 78596
S Indiana Ave 78596
Industrial Dr
1000-1199 78596
1201-1299 78596
1401-1497 78599
1499-1599 78596
2000-2098 78596
S Industrial Dr 78596
N International Blvd
300-998 78599
1000-1014 78599
1015-1015 78596
1016-4898 78599
1201-5299 78599
S International Blvd 78596
N & S Iowa Ave 78596
Iris Ave & St 78596
Isaac St 78599
Isabel Dr 78599
Island St 78596
Iturbide St 78599
J St 78596
J P Garza St 78599
J R Becerra Ave 78596
Jacinth St 78596
Jade Dr 78599
Jade St 78596
Jade Lynn St 78599
Jaime St 78599
Jalapa St 78599
Jamaica St 78596
James St 78596
Janie St 78599
Jasmine St 78596
Jasper Dr 78596
E & W Jefferson St 78599
Jesse St 78596
Jimmy Carter St 78599
Joe Stephens Ave 78599
Johann Ave 78596
John F Kennedy St 78599
John T Eberly Dr 78599
Johnson Cir 78596
Jose St N & W 78596
Joyce St
1100-1199 78599
1200-1298 78596
1201-1699 78599
1600-1698 78596
Juarez St 78599
Judi St 78599
K St 78596
Kalanchoe Dr 78596
Kalhua St 78599
N & S Kansas Ave 78596
Katie St 78596
Kennedy Dr & St 78599
Kerps St 78599
Kerria St 78596
Key Biscayne 78596
Key Largo 78596
Key West Dr 78596
Kotol 78599
L St 78596
La Ciniega Dr 78596

La Estrella Dr 78599
La Hacienda 78596
La Paz St 78596
La Perla St 78596
La Quinta Dr 78596
La Quinta Ln 78599
Lagos Verdes 78596
Lake Way Dr 78596
Lakeview Dr 78596
Lancelot Dr 78596
Lantana Dr 78596
Lantana Ln 78599
Largo St 78596
Las Brisas Dr 78599
Las Cruces St 78596
Las Nubes 78599
Laurel Dr 78596
Lazaro St 78599
Lazy River Rd 78596
Lee Garza St 78596
Leisure Ln 78596
E Levee Rd 78596
Leyenda St 78599
N & S Liberty St 78596
Lilia Dr 78599
Lime Blvd 78596
Linares 78596
Lincoln St 78599
Lindsey St 78596
Linsay 78596
Lion Lake Dr N & S 78596
W Live Oak Ave & Dr .. 78596
E & W Llano Grande
St 78596
Llave St 78596
Lobelia St 78599
Lobo Ln 78596
Longhorn Dr 78596
E & W Loop 19th St ... 78596
Lopez Dr 78599
Los Arcos Cir 78599
Los Palomos St 78596
E & W Los Torritos St .. 78596
N Louisiana Ave
600-899 78596
2500-2899 78596
S Louisiana Ave 78596
Lucille St 78599
E Lulac St 78596
Lulus Dr 78599
M Flores St 78596
Mac 78599
Mackenzie Dr 78599
Madison Dr 78599
Magdalena St 78599
Magnolia Pt 78599
Maingate Dr 78596
W Malone Dr & St 78596
Mango Ct 78596
E & W Manzanillo 78599
Maria St 78596
Maria Isabel Dr 78599
Marin St 78599
Mariposa 78599
Maritza St 78596
Mark Ave 78596
Marlen St 78599
Martha St 78596
Martin Morales Rd 78599
Martinez Ave & St 78596
Matamoros St 78596
Meadow Dr 78599
Meadow Lark Cir & Dr . 78596
Meadow Wood 78596
Medrano Rd 78599
Mel C Gray 78599
Melissa St 78599
Mercedes St 78596
W Merida St 78599
Mesquite Cir
11700-11799 78596
11800-11999 78599
Mesquite Dr 78596
E Mesquite St 78596
Mexico Ave 78596
Mi Cielo 78599

Mi Tierra Dr 78599
Mi Vida St 78596
Michigan Ave 78596
Midvalley Dr 78599
Midway Rd 78596
N Midway Rd 78599
S Midway Rd 78596
N & S Milanos Rd 78596
E & W Mile 10 78599
E Mile 11 N
101-697 78599
E Mile 11 N
699-2200 78599
2201-2299 78596
2202-3298 78599
2401-3199 78599
W Mile 11 N 78599
E & W Mile 12 78599
E & W Mile 12 1/2 78599
E & W Mile 13 78599
E & W Mile 13 1/2 78599
E & W Mile 14 78599
E & W Mile 14 1/2 78599
E & W Mile 15 78599
Mile 15 1/2 N 78599
W Mile 16 N 78599
Mile 2 1/2 W 78599
S Mile 2 1/2 W
700-798 78599
1100-1298 78596
N Mile 3 1/2 W
2901-4097 78599
4099-4799 78599
4800-4898 78596
4801-6599 78599
5000-7098 78599
E Mile 4 W 78599
N Mile 4 W 78599
S Mile 4 W 78596
N Mile 4 1/2 W 78599
E & W Mile 5 78596
N Mile 5 1/2 W 78599
W Mile 5 1/2 N 78596
N Mile 6 W
7111-8900 78599
8901-8999 78596
8902-10598 78599
9001-18299 78599
10600-10698 78596
10700-11898 78599
11900-11998 78596
12600-18598 78599
S Mile 6 W 78599
Mile 6 1/2 N 78596
Mile 6 1/2 W 78596
N Mile 6 1/2 N 78599
N Mile 6 1/2 W
7200A-7298A 78599
7200D-7298D 78599
1401-1697 78599
1699-6000 78599
6002-7098 78599
7200-7298 78596
S Mile 6 1/2 W 78596
W Mile 6 1/2 N 78596
W Mile 7 78596
E Mile 8 N 78599
W Mile 8 1/2 N 78599
E Mile 9 78599
W Mile 9 1/4 N 78599
Mills Ave 78596
Mimosa Dr 78599
Mina 78596
Miracle Dr 78596
Mireles St 78599
Mis Padres 78599
N Missouri Ave
100-699 78596
1700-2200 78599
2202-2698 78599
S Missouri Ave 78596
Misty Ln 78596
E Molby St 78596
Monarch St 78599
Monica 78599
Monterey Dr 78599
Moon Lake Dr N & S ... 78596

E Moreland 78599
Moreland Dr 78596
N Morgan Ave 78596
Mourning Dove 78599
Mulberry 78596
Nadia St 78596
Narcissus St 78596
Natalie St 78596
N Nebraska Ave 78599
S Nebraska Ave 78596
Nellie St 78596
N & S Nevada Ave 78596
Nicolas Cir & Ln 78599
Nicole Ave 78599
Nieves Rodriguez St 78599
Nogales St 78599
Nora St 78596
North Ln 78599
Northcross Ln 78599
Northgate Cir & Dr 78599
Oak Ln 78599
Oak St 78596
Oak Preserve 78599
N Ohio Ave
900-999 78596
1001-1099 78596
2600-2899 78599
S Ohio Ave 78596
N Oklahoma Ave 78599
S Oklahoma Ave 78596
Old Military Rd 78596
Olivarez Dr 78599
Onyx Dr 78599
Opal Dr 78599
Orange Ave & Dr 78596
Orange Blossom 78596
Orchard Ct 78596
Orchard Dr 78596
Orchard Ln 78599
S Oregon Ave 78596
Orizaba 78599
Orlando Tijerina Rd 78599
N Outlet Ave 78596
Ovalles St 78599
N Padre Ave 78596
Page 78596
W Paisano Ln 78599
Palestina 78596
S Palm Dr 78596
Palm Parkway Dr & St 78596
N & S Palmas St 78596
Palmetto Dr 78599
N & S Palo Blanco Ln 78596
Palos Altos Dr 78599
Palos Azulez Dr 78599
Palos Grandes Dr 78599
Palos Nuevos Dr 78599
Palos Ricos Dr 78599
Palos Rojos Dr 78599
Palos Verdes Dr 78599
Panama 78596
Panchita St 78596
Panther Dr 78596
Papaya Dr 78599
Paraiso Dr 78599
N Park Place Dr 78599
N & S Pat Cannon St 78596
Pecan Grove Dr 78599
Pena Ave & St 78599
N Perez Ave 78596
S Petunia Ave 78596
Phoebie Dr 78599
E Pike Blvd
101-197 78596
199-1499 78596
1501-1599 78596
1700-3699 78599
W Pike Blvd 78596
Pine St 78596
Pineda St 78599
Pinehurst St 78596
N & S Pino Dr & St 78596
Plata Dr 78596
E & W Plaza St 78596
Plaza Los Encinos 78596

N Pleasantview Dr
100-199 78596
201-299 78596
4200-4299 78599
S Pleasantview Dr 78596
Polanco Ave 78599
Portillo Ct 78599
Primrose 78596
Professional Dr 78596
Prolongacion Gonzalez Rd 78596
Pueblo St 78596
Pueblo Del Sol W 78599
Puerto Rico St 78596
Puerto Vallarta Dr 78599
Puesta Del Sol Dr 78599
Quail Hollow Dr 78596
Quinta Ave 78596
Quintero St 78599
R St 78596
R J Johns Ave 78599
Rachel Ave 78599
E & W Railroad St 78596
Ramos Dr 78596
Ranchito St 78596
Rancho Toluca 78599
Rancho Viejo St 78599
Rebecca St 78596
Red Ant Dr 78599
Regency Ln 78596
Reginald Dr 78596
Remuda Dr 78596
Renee Way 78599
N & S Republic St 78596
N & S Retama Ln 78596
Ricardo St 78599
Ricardo Andrea St 78599
Rico St 78596
Rimrock Dr 78599
Rio St 78599
Rio Bravo St 78596
Rodeo Dr 78599
Rone Dr 78596
E & W Roosevelt St 78599
Roper Dr 78599
Rosalinda St 78599
Rose Ave 78599
Roselawn Dr 78596
Rosewood Dr 78596
Ruben Navarro St 78599
Ruby Ave 78599
Ruiz St 78599
Sabatini Dr 78599
Sable Dr 78599
Saddle St 78599
Sage 78596
Sago Dr 78599
Sahara Dr 78599
Salazar St 78599
Salinas St 78599
E, N, S & W Saltillo Cir 78599
Samoa Dr 78599
San Angelo St 78599
San Benito St 78596
San Carlos St 78599
San Felipe St 78599
San Ignacio 78599
San Joaquin St 78596
San Jose St 78599
San Juana St 78599
San Maria St 78599
San Miguel 78596
San Pedro 78599
San Vicente Norte 78599
San Vicente Sur 78599
Sanoma Dr 78599
Santa Anna St 78596
Santa Elena St 78599
Santa Fe St 78596
Santa Maria Ave & St 78599
Santo Cielo St 78596
Sapphire Dr 78599
Sara Ave 78599
Sarab St 78599
Sasha Cir 78599

E Sathire Cir 78599
N Sathire Cir 78599
S Sathire Cir 78599
W Sathire Cir
10501-10599 78596
10601-10699 78599
Sawgrass St 78596
Seles 78599
Serengeti Way 78596
Servando Barrera St
15700-15799 78599
15801-16299 78599
16400-16498 78596
E Sgt M C Garcia St 78596
Sgt Rosas St 78599
Shady Grove Trl 78599
Shane St 78596
Shilo Dr 78599
Shirel St 78596
E Short Morgan St 78596
Silva Dr 78596
N & S Sinclair Ave 78596
N & S Sky Soldier Rd 78596
South Ln 78599
Southgate Blvd & Cir 78596
Southland Dr 78596
Spanish Oak Dr 78599
Spear Dr 78596
Spicewood Dr 78596
Spur St 78599
Steer Dr 78596
Steffy Dr 78596
W Steve Dr 78599
Stewart Dr 78599
Stone St 78599
Stone Cliff Ct 78596
Stoneridge 78599
Stuart Rd 78599
Suarez Dr 78599
E & W Sugar Cane Dr 78596
Sugar Sweet 78599
Summerfield St 78599
Summerview Dr 78599
Sundance Cir 78599
Sunny Dr 78596
Superior Dr 78596
Swallow St 78599
Sylvia Handy St 78599
Taft St 78599
Tahiti Dr 78599
Tahoe Dr 78599
Tamaulipas St 78596
Tampico St 78599
Tangerine Dr 78596
Tanglewood Ln N 78596
Tasha Lee Dr 78599
Taylor 78599
Tejas St 78599
Tennessee Ave 78596
Teran 78596
Terrace Ln 78599
Tesoro Dr 78596
N Texas Blvd
100-1100 78596
1102-1198 78599
1300-1498 78599
1500-4000 78599
4002-4098 78599
S Texas Blvd 78596
Thicket Dr 78599
Tierra Bella 78596
Tierra Bonnita St 78596
Tierra De Oro 78596
Tierra Encantada 78596
Tierra Escondida 78596
Tierra Prometida 78596
Tierra Rica Cir 78596
Tierra Santa Dr 78596
Timothy Dr 78599
N & S Tio Ave 78596
Tio Juan 78596
Tolu St 78599
Tomatillo 78596
Topaz Cir 78599
Toro Ave 78599
Tower St 78599

Town Center Blvd 78596
Travis St 78599
Trinidad St 78596
Troy Ave 78599
Truman St 78599
Tula Ave 78599
S Tulipana Ave 78596
Turquoise Ave 78599
N & S Utah Ave 78596
Valencia 78596
Valentino St 78596
Valley Trace Dr 78599
Valley View Dr 78596
Venezuela 78596
Venture Dr 78599
Vera Cruz St 78596
Viceroy Dr 78599
Victor Garcia Dr 78599
Victory Dr 78596
Vida Dulce 78596
Vida Grande 78596
Vida Santa 78596
Villas Del Norte 78599
Virginian Dr 78599
Vo Tech Dr 78599
Walter Wagers St 78599
Wardlow Ave 78596
E & W Washington St 78599
Water St 78599
Water Plant Rd 78599
Water Willow 78596
Western Dr 78599
N Westgate Dr
201-297 78596
299-1099 78596
1400-5399 78599
5401-6599 78596
6100-6198 78596
6300-6698 78599
6601-6697 78596
6699-6799 78596
6800-6900 78596
6902-7298 78599
7201-7299 78596
7601-7699 78599
S Westgate Dr 78596
Westhaven Dr 78599
Westmont Dr 78596
Whitetail Dr 78596
Wildturkey Dr 78596
Wildwood Dr 78596
N Wilson Dr 78599
Wimbledon Dr 78596
Windcrest Dr 78596
Witmer St 78596
Woodland Dr 78596
W Woodlawn St 78596
Yarbrough St 78596
Yasmin St 78596
Yolanda St 78596
Yucatan St 78596
W Zacatecas St 78599
Zamora Ave 78596
Zapata St 78599
Zelma St 78596
Zinnia Dr 78599

NUMBERED STREETS

E 1st St
200-300 78596
301-399 78599
302-2098 78596
601-2099 78596
W 1st St 78596
E 2nd St 78599
200-2099 78596
W 2nd St 78596
E & W 3rd 78596
E & W 4th 78596
E & W 5th 78596
E & W 6th 78596
E & W 7th 78596
E & W 8th 78596
E & W 9th 78596
E & W 10th 78596
E & W 11th 78596
E & W 12th 78596
E & W 13th 78596
W 14th St 78596
E & W 15th 78596
E & W 16th 78596
W 17th St 78596
E & W 18th 78596
E & W 19th 78596
E & W 20th 78596
E 22nd St 78596
E 23rd St 78596
E & W 24th 78596
E 25th St 78596
E 26th St 78596
E 27th St 78596
E 28th St 78596
E 29th St 78596
E & W 34th 78596

WICHITA FALLS TX

General Delivery 76307

POST OFFICE BOXES MAIN OFFICE STATIONS AND BRANCHES

Box No.s
1 - 2611 76307
3001 - 3897 76301
4001 - 4894 76308
5001 - 8672 76307
9001 - 94905 76308
97000 - 97998 76307

RURAL ROUTES

01, 04, 05, 07, 10 76305
02, 03, 06, 08 76310

NAMED STREETS

Abbott Ave 76308
Abby Ln 76308
Aberdeen Dr 76302
Adrian Ave 76306
Air Force Dr 76306
Airport Dr
900-999 76305
1900-2399 76306
3100-4499 76305
Alabama Ave 76309
Alamo Dr 76302
Aldrich Ave 76302
Alexandria St 76310
Alice Ave 76301
Allegheny Dr 76310
Allen Rd 76309
Allendale Rd 76310
Allison Dr 76308
Alma St 76301
Alpine Dr 76302
Amber Ave 76306
Amber Joy 76310
Amherst Dr 76308
Amy Cir 76310
Anchor Rd 76310
Andrews Dr 76301
Andria Dr 76302
Angelina Ave 76308
Anita Ln 76306
Antigua 76308
Apache Trl 76310
Approach Ave 76308
April St 76310
Arapaho Trce 76310
Arborgate Ter 76308
Archer City Hwy 76302
Archway Ct 76310
Ardath Ave 76301
Arena Rd 76310

Arlington St 76302
Armada Ln 76308
Armory Rd 76302
Armstrong Dr 76305
Arnold Dr 76302
Arnold Rd 76305
Arrowhead Dr 76309
W Arrowhead Dr 76310
W Arrowhead Ln 76310
Arthur St
1900-2999 76309
3100-3699 76308
Ash Ln 76310
Asharanc St 76301
Ashgrove Dr 76309
Ashley Ct 76310
Ashleyanne Cir 76310
Aspen St 76306
Astin Ave 76301
Atoka Cir 76302
Atoka Dr 76310
Atoka Trl 76310
August Ln 76310
Augusta Ln 76302
Austin St 76301
N Austin St 76306
Avalon Pl 76306
Avenue E 76309
Avenue N 76309
Avenue S 76309
Avenue W 76308
Avenue A 76309
Avenue B 76309
Avenue C 76309
Avenue D 76309
Avenue F 76309
Avenue G 76309
Avenue H 76309
Avenue I 76309
Avenue J 76309
Avenue K 76309
Avenue L 76309
Avenue M 76309
Avenue N S 76309
Avenue O 76309
Avenue Q 76309
Avenue R 76309
Avenue T 76309
Avenue U 76308
Avenue V 76308
Avenue Y 76308
Avery Row Ct 76309
Avondale St 76308
B W Stone Ranch Rd 76310
Bachman Rd 76305
Bacon St 76301
Bacon Switch Rd 76305
Bahama Dr 76310
Bailey Ave 76301
Bailey Rd 76305
Baker Rd 76305
Balboa Dr 76310
Baltimore Rd 76309
Bandera Blvd 76301
Bandera Cir 76302
S Bandera Dr 76302
Barbados 76308
Barcelona Ct 76308
Barker Dr 76306
Barna Rd 76302
Barnett Dr 76308
Barnett Rd 76310
Barrett Pl 76308
Barry Ln 76301
Barrywood Dr 76309
Bartley Dr
1-99 76310
5000-5099 76302
Bartosh Ln 76310
Barwise St 76301
Basin St 76309
Basswood Dr 76310
Bayberry Ct & Dr 76310
Baylor St 76301
Bazely Cir 76306
Beard Ave 76308

Bebe Ln 76301
Becky Dr 76306
Beech St 76309
Beefeater Dr 76308
Bekendam Ct 76309
Bel Air Blvd 76310
Belgrave Ct 76309
Belinda Dr 76310
Bell St 76309
Belmede Dr 76302
Belmount Dr 76308
Belue Rd 76306
Bent Rd 76305
Berkley Dr 76308
Bermuda Ln 76308
Berner St 76310
Bernhardt Pl 76302
Berryman Rd 76310
Bert Dr 76302
Berwick Dr 76309
Best Blvd 76301
Beth Dr 76302
E & N Bevering Ln & Rd 76305
Beverly Dr 76309
N Beverly Dr 76306
Big Bend Dr 76310
Billie Cir & Dr 76306
Billie Joyce St 76308
N Billye Ln 76310
Birch St 76309
Blackfeet Trl 76310
Blair House Ln 76306
Blake Dr 76305
Blanco St 76308
Bland St 76302
Blankenship St 76308
Blanton St 76308
Blazing Star Ct & Ln 76310
Blonde St 76301
Blue Bird Dr & Trl 76310
Blue Heron Trl 76310
Blue Herron Dr 76310
Blue Ridge Dr 76310
Blue Sage Ct 76309
Blue Star Ct 76310
Blue Stem Dr 76310
Bluebonnet Dr 76301
Bluff St
200-2199 76301
3000-3799 76302
Bluff View Cir 76309
Boanza Ln 76306
Bob Ave 76308
Bobby Point Rd 76305
Bonds St 76301
Bonita Dr 76308
Bonner St 76301
Bonny Cir & Dr 76302
Boren Ave 76308
Borland Ln 76305
Borton St 76306
Bosque Cir 76309
Boulder Dr 76306
Bowman Est 76310
Bowman Rd 76308
Bradford Ct 76310
Brandy Ln 76306
Brass Lantern Ct 76308
Brazos St 76309
Breezewood Ct 76308
Brenda Hursh Dr 76302
Brenna Dr 76302
Brentwood Dr 76308
Bretton Rd 76308
Brewster St 76302
Briandale Ct 76310
Briar Cliff Dr 76309
Briargrove Dr 76310
Briarwood Dr 76310
Brick St 76301
Bridge St
1-99 76301
400-1099 76306
Bridge Creek Dr 76308
Bridwell Rd 76310

Bridwell St
1500-2599 76301
3000-3199 76302
Bristol Ln 76301
Britain St 76309
Broad St 76301
Broadmoor Pl 76306
N Broadway St 76306
Broday Rd 76305
Brook Ave 76301
N Brook Ave 76306
Brook Hollow Dr 76308
Brookdale Dr 76310
Brookwood Dr 76302
Brown St 76309
Brownlee St 76306
Bryan Rd 76301
Bryan Glen St 76308
Buchanan St
800-999 76301
1200-2699 76309
2900-3599 76308
Buckingham Dr 76310
Buena Vista Way 76308
Bullington St 76301
Bunny Run Dr 76310
Burkburnett Rd
400-5699 76306
7400-8499 76305
Burks Ln 76305
Burlington St 76302
Burnett St 76301
N Burnett St 76306
Burroughs St 76309
Business Highway 287j
E 76305
N Butler Rd 76305
Buttercup Cir 76310
Byrne Pl 76306
Caddo Trl 76310
Caden Ln 76310
Calhoun St 76306
California St
200-2599 76301
2900-2999 76302
Call Field Rd 76308
Callahan Dr 76305
Callie Ct 76310
Cambridge Ave 76308
Cameron Ln 76305
Canberra Dr 76308
Candlewood Cir & Ct 76308
Cannan Dr 76308
Canyon Crk 76308
Canyon Bluff Ct 76309
Canyon Cliff Ct 76309
Canyon Crest Ct 76309
Canyon Ridge Dr 76309
Canyon Trails Dr 76309
Canyon View Ct 76309
Cap Rock Cv 76308
Cape Cod Dr 76310
Capri St 76306
Carlene Dr 76310
Carlson St 76302
Carlyle Ct 76309
Carol Ln 76302
Carol Ann St 76309
E Carolina St 76306
Carriage Ln 76305
Carrigan St 76301
Carswell Cir 76306
Carter Ave 76308
Carter Rd 76310
Cartwright Rd 76305
Casa Grande Ct 76310
Cascades Dr 76310
Cashion Rd 76305
Castle Dr 76306
Caston Ln 76302
Catalina Dr 76310
Catskills Dr 76310
Caushatta Ln & Trl 76310
Cedar Ave 76309
Cedar Elm Ln 76308
Cedar Spring Ct 76310
Celia Dr 76302
Centennial Ct 76306
Centime Dr 76305
W Central Dr 76301
Central Fwy
1-5599 76306
5600-6299 76305
Central Fwy E
100-320 76301
322-3198 76301
401-2999 76302
3001-3199 76310
Central Fwy N 76305
Central St 76305
Chadwick Ct 76310
Champions Ct 76302
Chance St 76301
Chandler Rd 76301
Chanute Cir 76306
Chaparral Dr 76308
Chaparral Ln 76310
Charing Ct 76309
Charlie Cir 76305
Chase Dr 76308
Chateau Ct 76302
Chelsea Dr 76309
Cherokee St 76301
Cherokee Trl 76310
Cherry Ave 76309
Cheryl St 76309
Chester Ave 76301
Chestnut Cir 76301
Cheyenne Trl 76310
Chickasaw Cir 76310
Chimney Rock 76310
Chinaberry Dr 76310
Chip N Dale Cir 76301
Chippewa Trl 76310
Choctaw St 76301
Chris Dr 76308
Christine Rd 76302
Chuck Dr 76310
N Church St 76308
Cimarron Trl 76306
Cindy Ln 76305
Circle Dr 76309
Circles Edge 76302
City View Dr
1000-2999 76306
3000-5299 76305
Clantres Rd 76305
Clarinda Ave 76308
Clark St 76301
Clay Rd 76305
Clay St 76306
Clayton Ln 76308
Clements St 76306
Cleveland Ave 76301
Cliffside Dr 76302
Clift St 76301
Clipper Ln 76308
Clothesline Rd 76305
Clover Ct 76310
Clover Ln 76305
Clovis Dr 76306
Clower Rd 76305
Club View St 76302
Clyde Morgan Rd 76310
Coastal St 76305
Cochese Cir 76310
Cochise Trl 76310
Cole St 76301
Colina Cir 76309
Colleen Dr 76302
Collins Ave 76301
Colonial Ct & Dr 76306
Colquit Rd 76309
Columbia Rd 76310
Commerce St 76301
Compton Rd 76309
Concho Ln 76309
Concord Rd 76310
Conkling Dr 76301
Conner Cir 76301
Cooke Ave 76308
Cooper Rd 76305
Copper Kettle Ct 76308
Copperas Cv 76310
Coronado Ave 76310
E Cortez Ct & Dr 76306
Corwin St 76306
Cotton St 76305
N Cottonwood Rd 76301
Country Holw & Rd 76310
Court Capistrano 76310
Court De Casita 76310
Coushatta Ln 76302
Cove Rd 76310
Coventry Cir 76310
Covey Cv 76302
Covington St 76306
Cox Ln 76305
Coyote Blvd 76309
Craigmont Dr 76309
Cranbrook Ln 76308
Crescent Ln 76306
Crest St 76302
Crest Trl 76310
Crestview 76306
Crestview Memorial
Rd 76310
Crestway 76301
Cromwell Ave 76309
Crown Ln 76310
Crown Ridge Dr 76310
Crumpler Dr 76305
Cuba Ct 76309
Culley Rd 76310
Cumberland Ave 76309
Cunningham Dr 76308
Curly Rd 76305
Cutter Cv 76308
Cy Young Dr 76306
Cynthia Ln 76302
Cypress Ave 76310
Daisy Cir 76310
Dallas St 76301
Danberry Pl 76308
Dartmouth St 76308
Darwin Dr 76308
David St 76310
Davis Dr 76306
N Davis Rd 76305
Dawn Cir 76301
Dayton Ave 76301
Dean School Rd 76305
Deanna Cir 76302
Decker Rd 76310
Dee Dr 76301
Deer Creek Rd 76302
Deer Park Way 76306
Deerwood St 76301
Deggs St 76301
Dehaven Dr 76302
Del Rio Trl 76310
Delia Ct 76302
Della Dr 76302
Delta Dr 76308
Dencendi Dr 76302
Denison Ave 76301
Dennis Blvd 76310
Denver St 76301
Denzil St 76301
Desert Willow Ct 76309
Detroiter St 76306
Deville St 76306
Devon Rd 76308
Devonshire Dr 76302
Dewey St 76306
Diane Dr 76302
Dickens St 76308
Dirks Dr 76302
Ditto Ln 76302
Dockman Dr 76305
Dodge St 76301
Dog Rd 76305
Donna St 76308
Donnie Cir 76310
Doris St 76306
Dorothy St 76306
Dove Ln 76305
Dowdy Dr 76310
Dowdy Rd 76305
Downhill Dr 76302
Downing St 76308
Driftwood Dr 76309
Dubonnet Ct 76310
Dunbar Dr 76302
Dunbarton Dr 76302
Duncan St 76301
Dundee Dr 76302
Dunn St 76310
Durango Trl 76310
Duty Ln 76306
Duval St 76301
Eagle Ridge Cir 76309
Eagles Lndg 76310
Earl St 76302
East Rd 76305
Eastland Ln 76305
Eastridge Dr 76302
Easy St 76302
Echo Ln 76302
Ecleto Blvd 76308
Eddie Ln 76301
Eden Ln 76306
N & S Eden Hills Cir 76306
Edgecliff Dr 76302
Edgefield Ct 76302
Edgehill 76306
Edgerins Dr 76306
Edgewater Dr 76308
Edgewood St 76308
Edwards Way 76308
El Capitan Dr 76310
Eldorado Dr 76310
Eldridge Ln 76306
Elizabeth Ave 76301
Ellingham 76308
Elliott Rd 76310
Elliott St 76308
E Elliott St 76308
Elm St 76301
Elmwood Ave 76308
Elmwood North Ave &
Cir 76308
Elwood St 76301
Emerson St 76309
Emilie Ln 76301
Emmert Rd 76305
Enterprise St 76306
Ernest Cir 76308
Essex Dr 76308
Euel St 76306
Eureka Cir 76308
Evans Rd 76305
Evergreen Dr 76306
Evington Ct 76302
Fain St 76308
Fairfax Ave 76306
Fairway Blvd
2700-3999 76310
4200-4699 76308
4700-5299 76310
Fairway Dr 76301
Faith Rd 76308
Falcon Crest Blvd 76310
Falls Dr 76306
Farington Rd 76308
Farris St 76301
Fawn Dr & Trl 76310
Fawnwood Ct 76310
Featherston Ave 76308
Felena Trl 76305
Fell Ln 76305
Fenoglio Ave 76308
Fillmore St
100-999 76301
1100-2699 76309
First Circle Dr 76306
Fisher Rd
1500-1699 76305
2100-2899 76302
Flagstone St 76310
Flat Top Cir 76308
Fleming Rd 76308
Flo Dr 76302
Flood St 76301
Florance Dr 76310
Florist St 76302
Fm 1177 76305
W Fm 171 76305
Fm 1740 76305
Fm 1954 76310
Fm 2393
100-14199 76305
Fm 2393
14444-22599 76310
Fm 2650 76310
Fm 3393 76305
Fm 367 76305
Fm 368 S 76310
Fm 440 76310
Fm 810 76305
Forcher Rd 76310
Ford Cir 76306
Forest Cove Dr 76310
E Fort Worth St 76301
Foster Ave 76308
Four Sixes Cir 76308
Fourth Circle Dr 76306
Foxy Ln 76302
Foyce Rd 76305
Fran Ln 76301
Franklin St 76301
Frauline St 76306
Fre Mar Vly 76301
Freedom Cir 76306
Friberg Ln 76306
Friberg Church Rd 76305
Front St 76301
Fry St 76308
Fuchs Dr 76305
Fuller Cir 76301
Fuller Rd 76310
Fulmer Way 76310
Fulton St 76309
Galleon Dr 76308
Galloway Rd 76306
Galveston St 76301
Garden St 76301
Garden Grove Ln 76308
Gardiner Rd 76308
Garfield St
800-999 76301
1400-2999 76309
3100-3699 76308
Garnett Ave 76308
Gateway Ct 76306
Gay St 76306
Gayle Ave 76308
Gayle St 76310
Gee Ln 76305
General Custer Dr 76310
George St 76302
Gerald St 76301
Geronimo Dr 76310
Giddings St 76309
Gilbert Ave 76301
Gladiolus St 76301
Gladney Ln 76308
Glasgow Dr 76302
N & S Glencoe Cir 76302
Glendale Dr 76302
Glendora Dr 76302
Glenhaven Dr 76306
Glenn Dr 76306
Glenwood Ave 76308
Glidewell Ave 76301
Gloria Cir & Ln 76309
Goldenrod Ct 76308
Goodman Rd 76305
Gorman Rd 76302
Gossett Dr 76308
Grace St
800-2299 76301
2900-3699 76302
Granada Dr 76308
Grandview E 76306
Grant St
800-999 76301
1300-2899 76309
2900-3699 76308
Grant Gill Ln 76301
Grants Gln 76309
Gray Moss Ct 76309
Graydon Cir 76308
Grayfox Pl 76306
Greenbriar Rd 76302
Greenhollow 76308
Greenleaf Dr 76309
Greenridge 76306
Greentree Ave 76306
Greenwood Dr 76301
Gregory St 76308
Gunnison Dr 76306
Hairpin Curv 76301
Half House Rd 76310
Hamilton Blvd
1700-1799 76308
2600-2699 76301
2700-3299 76308
Hamlin Ave 76301
Hammon Rd 76310
Hampstead Ln 76308
Hampton Rd
1500-1999 76301
2000-2399 76305
Hanover Rd 76302
Happy Hill Dr 76306
Happy Hollow Dr 76308
Harbor Rd 76310
Harding St
400-1699 76301
1700-3099 76305
Harlan Ave 76306
Harrell Ln 76301
Harrell St 76308
Harriet St 76309
Harris Ln 76306
Harris Rd 76305
Harrison St
600-999 76301
1000-2099 76309
2200-3599 76308
Harvard Ave 76301
Harvey Dr 76302
Hatton Rd 76302
E Hatton Rd
100-1300 76302
1302-1398 76302
1400-3199 76310
Hawes Ave 76301
Hawthorne St 76301
Hay Rd 76305
Hayes St
800-999 76301
1300-2699 76309
Hazel Ct 76308
Heather Ln 76308
Heaven Ln 76308
Heisman Dr 76310
Helmcamp Dr 76310
Helwig Dr 76305
Henrietta St 76301
Henry S Grace Fwy 76302
Hensley St 76306
Herring Ln 76302
Hiawatha Blvd 76309
Hickory Ln 76301
Hickory Downs 76308
High Rd 76310
Highland Dr 76308
Highway 79 S 76310
Hill St 76302
Hillsboro 76306
Hillside Dr & Trce 76310
Hilltop Ave 76301
Hines Blvd 76301
Hirschi Ln 76306
Hld Rd 76310
Hollandale Ave 76302
Holliday Rd
1800-2899 76301
2900-3300 76302
3302-3398 76302
Holliday St 76301
Hollow Ridge Ct & Dr 76309
Holly Dr 76301
Hollywood Ave 76309
Homes Ave 76301
Homestead Ln 76305
Homestead Access Rd 76305
Homeward Way 76302
Hooper Dr 76306
Horseshoe Bnd 76301
Horton Ln 76305
Hudson St 76309
Huff Rd 76310
Huff St 76301
Hughes Dr 76308
Humphreys St 76301
Hunt St 76302
Hunter St 76308
E Hunters Gln 76306
Huntington Ln 76305
Hursh Ave 76302
Hurson Ln 76302
Huskie Dr 76306
Hy Bridges Pr 76310
Hyde Park Ct 76309
Idlewood Dr 76308
Indian Heights Blvd 76309
Indiana Ave 76301
Indigo Cir 76310
Industrial Blvd & Dr 76306
Ingleside Dr 76308
Inglewood Dr 76301
Inlet Dr 76310
E & W Inwood Dr 76301
Ireland St 76301
Irene Ln 76301
Irving Pl 76308
Itasca Trl 76310
Itaska Ln 76310
Ivanhoe Ter 76306
Ivy Ln 76306
Jack St 76308
Jacksboro Hwy 76310
Jackson Cir 76301
Jacob Ct 76310
Jacqueline Rd 76306
Jalich Dr 76301
Jalonick St 76301
Jamaica Cir & Dr 76310
James St 76308
Jarmon St 76302
Jasmine Ct 76310
Jasper St
2200-2600 76301
2601-2605 76302
2602-2606 76301
2607-2999 76302
Jay Rd 76305
Jayden Ct 76302
Jeannie Ct 76308
E Jefferson St 76306
Jeffrey Cir 76306
Jeffus Ct 76308
Jenney Lee Dr 76302
Jennifer Ct 76310
Jennings Ave 76310
E & W Jentsch Rd 76310
Jerry Ln 76305
Jessica Ct 76310
Jo Ann Cir & Dr 76306
John Lee St 76306
Johnathan Pl 76310
Johnny Ct 76302
Johnson Rd 76310
Joline St 76309
Jones St 76309
Joy Ct 76308
Joyce Ln 76302
Juarez St 76301
Judson Cir 76308
Judy Cir 76309
Juniper Ln 76308
K Mart Dr 76308
Kalee Ct 76302
Karen Ct 76310
Karen St 76306
Karla St 76310
Katherine Dr 76306
Keeler Ave 76301
Keith St 76308

Street	ZIP
Kell Blvd	
900-2099	76301
2100-4598	76309
2101-3923	76308
4600-6899	76310
Kelly St	76302
Kellygreen Ct	76310
Kemp Blvd	
500-999	76301
1200-2699	76309
2900-6599	76308
Kenesaw Ave	76309
Kenley Ave	76306
Kennedy Rd	76305
Kent Ln	76308
Kentucky Ave	76301
Kenwood St	76310
Kessler Ave & Blvd	76309
Kevin Cir & Dr	76306
Kiel Ln	76305
Kimbell Dr	76302
Kimberly Ln	76301
Kincall Rd	76305
King Dr	76309
Kings Hwy	76301
Kingsbury Dr	76309
Kingston Dr	76310
Kinsale Ct	76306
Kinta Trl	76310
Kiowa Ct	76310
Kirk Dr	76308
N & S Kirkwell Cir	76302
Kit Carson Trl	76310
Kitchings St	76301
Kitty St	76310
Knight Cir	76301
Knoll St	76302
Knowles Dr	76305
Kovarik Rd	76310
Krajca Rd	76305
Kristy Ln	76310
Kyle Cv	76308
La Juana Cir	76306
Laci Ln	76310
Lackland Cir	76306
Ladera Cv	76309
Lafayette St	76309
Lake St	76301
Lake Bend Dr	76310
Lake Creek Rd	76310
S Lake Park Dr	76302
Lake Shore Dr	76310
Lake View Dr	76308
Lake Wellington Pkwy	76310
Lakefront Dr	76310
Lakewood Dr	76301
Lamar St	
200-999	76301
1000-1598	76301
1000-1000	76307
1001-1599	76301
N Lamar St	76306
Lambeth Way	76309
Lancaster Ln	76310
Lancer Cir	76306
Landon Ln	76306
Lands End	76308
Lanfair Rd	76305
Langford Ln	76310
Lansing Blvd	76309
Lansing Place Dr	76309
Lantana Dr	76310
Larchmont Pl	76302
Lark St	76306
Las Cruces Ln	76306
Las Vegas Trl	76306
Latricia Ln	76302
Laura Ln	76301
Lavell Ave	76308
Lawrence Rd	
2600-3099	76309
3100-3999	76308
Lb Dr	76310
Leath Rd	76305
Lebanon Rd	76309
Lee St	76301
Leffall Cir	76301
Legacy Dr	76310
N & S Leighton Cir	76309
Lela Ln	76306
Lennox Ct	76309
Lenore Dr	76306
Leon Cir	76309
Lerma Ln	76306
Leroy Dr	76305
Lesley Hts	76310
Lexington Ave	76309
Libby Ct & Dr	76310
Liberty Ct	76306
Likins Cir	76308
Lilac Ln	76306
E Lincoln St	76306
Linda Ln	76301
Lindale Dr	
4500-4599	76308
4600-5099	76310
Linden Pl	76301
Lindsey Dr	76301
Lingle Dr	76305
Linville Rd	76305
Linwood Ave	76306
Lisa Ln	76309
Little Beaver Ln & Trl	76310
Liveoak St	76301
Lobban Ln	76306
Loch Lomond Dr	76302
Locke Ln	76306
Lockwood Dr	76308
Lois Ln	76306
Loma Linda Ln	76308
Lombard Dr	76309
Lone Wolf Trl	76310
Long Leaf Dr	76310
Longview St	76306
Loop 11	76306
Loop 47	76310
Loretta St	76306
Lori Ln	76306
Lou Ln	76308
Louis Esquibel Ave	76306
Louis J Rodriguez Dr	76308
Louise Ln	76306
Lournere St	76309
Lovers Ln	76310
Lucas Ave	76301
Lucile Ave	76301
Lucky Ln	76306
Lucy Cir	76301
Luecke Ln	76305
Lura Maie Rd	76305
Lydia Dr	76308
Lynda Sue Ln	76301
Maag Rd	76310
Madiliz Way	76302
Madison St	76306
Magnolia St	76302
Mahler Rd	76310
Malcolm Ln	76302
Mallard Dr	76308
Mallory Ln	76309
Malone Rd	76305
Manchester Rd	76306
Manor Ln	76302
Maple St	76301
Maplewood Ave & Ct	76308
March Dr	76306
Marconi St	76301
Marella Ter	76309
Margaret Dr	76306
Margie St	76308
Marian Ln	76306
Marie St	76301
Marigold Ln	76308
Marika Cir	76308
Market St	76301
Marlette Cir	76306
Marlow St	76306
Marsha Ln	76302
Marshal St	76301
Martha Ln	76306
Martin Blvd & St	76308
Martinique	76308
Mary Ln	76302
Masterson Cir	76308
Mastrad Rd	76310
Mathews Rd	76305
Matterhorn Dr	76310
Mattie Cir	76310
Maurine St	76306
Maverick Trl	76310
Mayfair Ter	76308
Mccauley Dr	76305
Mccleod Dr	76302
Mccrory Ave	76308
Mccullough Ln	76310
Mccutchen Ave	76308
Mcgaha Ave	76308
Mcgrath Ln	76309
Mcgregor Ave	76301
Mckinley Rd	76305
Mckinney Rd	
1500-2499	76301
3000-4199	76310
Mclaughlin St	76301
Mcnabb Cir	76306
Mcniel Ave	
2400-3199	76309
3400-4599	76308
Meadow Green Ct	76308
Meadow Lake Dr	76310
Meadowbrook Dr	76308
Meadowcliff Dr	76302
W Medical Ct	76310
Melissa Lea Ln	76308
Melody Ln	76302
Melrose Dr	76310
Memorial Dr	76302
Merle Cir	76310
Merrimac Dr	76308
Merryhill Cir	76309
Mesa Rd	76305
Mesquite St	76302
Miami Ave	76309
Michigan Ave	76301
Michna Ln	76302
Midway St	76306
Midwestern Pkwy	
900-900	76302
902-1999	76302
2000-3299	76308
4900-4998	76302
Midwestern Pkwy E	76302
Milby Ave	76308
N Mill St	76301
Mill Valley Dr	76308
Miller Ct	76308
Miller Dr	76305
Miller Rd	76308
Milliron Ave	76301
Milo St	76305
Milton St	76310
Mimosa Ln	76310
Minnetaska Ave	76309
Minnetonga Trl	76310
Miramar St	76308
Miriam Ln	76305
Missile Rd	76306
Mission Ln	76302
Mississippi Ave	76301
Mistletoe Dr	76310
Misty Vly E & W	76310
Mitchell St	76301
Mitzi Cv	76302
Mlk Jr Blvd	76301
N Mlk Jr Blvd	76306
Mobley Dr	76305
Mockingbird Ln	76308
Moffett Ave	76308
Mohawk Ln & Trl	76310
Mojave Trl	76310
Monroe St	76309
Montague Dr	76306
Montego Dr	76308
Monterrey Dr	76310
Montgomery Pl	76308
Montgomery St	76302
Montgomery East Pl	76308
Montreal Dr	76310
Moralins Dr	76308
Morgan Ln	76301
Morningside Dr	76301
Morrow St	76301
Mount Everest Dr	76310
Mount Scott Dr	76310
Mourning Dove Ln	76305
Mowery St	76310
Murphy Rd	76310
Musgrave Rd	76305
Mustang St	76306
Nakomis Rd & Trl	76310
Napier Rd	76305
Nashua Dr	76306
Nassau Dr	76308
Natchez Trce	76310
Navajo Trl	76310
Navasota Cir	76309
Neff Ave	76301
Neta Ln	76302
New Haven Rd	76306
New Moon Ln	76306
Newcomb Ter	76308
Newsom Cir	76308
Newsome Rd	76310
Nitana Ln	76309
Norman St	76302
Normandy Dr	76301
Norriss Rd	76302
Northeast Dr	76306
Northview Dr	76306
Northwest Dr	76306
Northwest Fwy	
2000-4599	76306
5500-7399	76305
Nottinghill Ln	76308
Nunn St	76306
Nunneley Pl	76306
Nursery St	76302
Oak St	76301
Oak Grove Cir	76310
Oakhurst Dr	76302
Oakmont Dr	76310
Oakwood Ct	76308
Oceola Ave	76301
Odin St	76301
Offutt St	76301
Ohio Ave	76301
Old Bacon Rd	76305
Old Burk Hwy	76306
Old Friberg Rd	76305
Old Iowa Park Hwy	76306
Old Iowa Park Rd	
1400-3799	76306
3800-4799	76305
Old Jacksboro Hwy	
700-2299	76301
2300-6199	76302
Old State Rd S	76310
Old T Bone Rd	76305
Old Windthorst Rd	
1700-2499	76301
2500-6899	76310
Olen St	76301
E Olive St	76310
Olive Branch Ct	76308
Olivia Ln	76310
Olympic Dr	76310
Onaway Trl	76309
Opal St	76310
Opportunity Dr	76302
Orchard Ave	76301
N Oriole St	76301
Osage Ave	76301
Outlet Ave	76308
Oxford Ln	76310
Oxley Dr	76310
Ozmun St	76306
P B Ln	76302
Page Dr	76306
Palmetto Dr	76306
Palomino St	76306
Paluxy Cir	76309
Pamela Ln	76302
Paradise St	76301
Parish St	76308
N Park Dr	76306
Park St	76301
Park Place Ct	76302
Park Road 63	76310
Park View Dr	76306
Parkdale Dr	76306
Parker Blvd	76302
Parker Rd	76310
Parker Ranch Rd	76310
Parkhill Rd	76310
Parklane Dr	76310
Parsons St	76309
Pasadena Ave	76310
Patterson St	76301
Pawhuska Dr	76309
Pawnee Pathway	76310
Peach St	76301
Peachtree Ct & Ln	76308
Pearl Ave	76301
Pearlie Cir & Dr	76306
Pebblestone Dr	76306
Pecan St	76301
Pecanway Dr	76305
Peckham St	76308
Pecos St	76306
Peggy Dr	76306
Pembroke Ln	76301
Pendleton Dr	76310
Pennsylvania Rd	76309
Pepperbush	76310
Perigo St	76301
Periwinkle Dr	76310
Perkins Rd	76305
Perrin Dr	76306
Pershing Dr	76309
Peterson Rd	76305
Peyton Ct	76310
Phila St	76310
Phillips Dr	76308
Phoenix Dr	76306
Picadilly Ln	76309
Picasso Dr	76308
Piedmont Pl	76308
Piegan Trl	76310
Pillars Ct	76302
Pilot Point Dr	76306
Pine St	76301
Pinehurst Dr	76310
Pitchfork Ln	76308
Pitts Rd	76305
Piute Dr & Trl	76310
Plateau Ct	76310
Plaza Pkwy	76308
Pleasant View Dr	76306
Pocahontas Dr & Trl	76310
Polk St	
200-999	76301
1000-2599	76309
Ponderosa Dr & Ln	76310
Pool St	76308
Post Oak Dr	76310
Powell Ln	76306
Powell Rd	76305
Prairie Way	76310
Prairie Lace Ct & Ln	76310
Pratt Ct	76302
Preece Rd	76308
Preston Dr	76308
Primrose Dr	76302
Prince Edward Dr	76308
Princeton Ave	76301
Priscilla Ln	76306
Production Blvd	76302
Professional Dr	76302
Prothro Ave	76308
Puckett Rd	76306
Pullin Dr	76305
Pyrenees Dr	76310
Quail Rdg & Run	76310
Quail Creek Dr	76308
Quail Springs Dr	76302
Queen Anne Ter	76309
Quincy Rd	76310
Radio Ln	76306
Radney Ln	76309
Rain Lily Ct	76310
Rainbow Dr	76310
Rama Dr	76306
Ramona Ct	76310
Ranch Dr	76305
Randel Dr	76308
Randolph Dr	76306
Randy Dr	76306
W Rathgeber Rd	76310
Ratt Rd	76305
Ravens Ct	76309
Ray Rd	76305
Raylett Dr	76306
Raymond Cir	76308
Red Blf	76308
Red Cloud Cir & Trl	76310
Red Fox Rd	76306
Red Oak Dr	76308
Red Robin Ln	76310
Red Rock Rd	76305
Redbud Ln	76306
Reddy Dr	76302
Redford Ter	76308
Redlands Ct	76308
Redwood Ave	76301
Regan St	76310
Regent Dr	76308
Regina Cir	76308
Reginald Dr	76308
Reilly Ave	76301
Reilly Rd	
2300-2699	76306
4000-7399	76305
Rembrandt Cir	76306
Rene Cir	76306
Residence Rd	76310
Retta Ter	76309
Reyes St	76306
Reynolds Ln	76301
Rhea Rd	76308
Rhone Dr	76306
Ricci St	76302
Richard Rd	76308
Richmond Dr	76309
Ridge St	76308
Ridgecrest Dr	76310
Ridgemont Dr	76309
Ridgeview Ln	76310
Ridgeway Dr	76306
Rigsby Ln	76305
River Ln & Rd	76305
River Creek Dr & Est	76305
Rivercrest Dr	76309
Riviera Dr	76310
Roanoke Dr	76306
Rob Roy Ln	76302
Roberts Ave	76301
Robertson St	76301
Robin Ln	76308
Robinson Rd	76305
Rock Island Cir	76308
Rock Point St	76310
Rockcliff Cir	76309
Rockhill Rd	76306
Rockridge Dr	76310
Rockwood Dr	76301
E Rogers Dr	76309
W Rogers Dr	76309
Rogers Ln	76305
Roosevelt St	76301
Rose St	76301
Rosedale St	76310
Roselawn Ave	76308
Rosemary Dr	76306
Rosemont Rd	76310
N & S Rosewood Ave	76301
Ross Ave	76306
Ross Creek Ln	76310
Roundrock Ct	76310
Rowland Rd	76301
Royal Rd	76308
Royal Oak St	76308
Royalwood Dr	76302
Rubsam St	76308
Rugby Ln	76310
Rugeley St	76308
Ruidosa Dr	76306
Running Bear Ln & Trl	76310
Rushing St	76308
Ruskin Rd	76309
Russell Dr	76306
Ryan Collins Dr	76306
Rye St	76305
Sabota Ave	76310
Sagebrush Ct	76310
Saint Andrews Ct	76309
Saint Helena Dr	76310
Saint James Ter	76309
Saint John St	76302
Saint Stephens Ct	76310
Sally Cir	76301
Salt Flat Ln	76310
San Antonio St	76301
San Simeon Dr	76308
Sand Beach Rd	76310
Sand Piper	76308
Sandcastle Rd	76306
Sandra Lee Ct	76308
Sandy Rd	76305
Sandy Hill Blvd	76310
Santa Barbara Cir & Dr	76302
Santa Fe St	76309
Saramy St	76306
Sarasue Ln	76302
Saratoga Trl	76310
Saxet St	76306
Schooner Dr	76308
Scotland Dr	76306
Scott Ave	76301
E Scott Ave	76301
N Scott Ave	76306
Scottsdale Ln	76302
Scurry St	76301
Seabea Dr	76308
Seabury Dr	76308
Second Circle Dr	76306
Seel Rd	76310
Sellers St	76301
Selma Dr	76306
Seymour Hwy	
1501-1697	76301
1699-3199	76301
3200-4599	76309
4600-9899	76310
Seymour Rd	76309
Shadow Ridge Ct	76308
Shady Ln	76309
Shady Brook Ct	76310
Shady Grove Ln	76308
Sharon Ln	76301
Shasta Dr	76306
Shawnee Trl	76305
Sheffield Dr	76306
Shelly Cir	76302
Shenandoah Dr	76310
Shepherd St	76309
S Shepherds Ct & Gln	76308
Sheppard Access Rd	76306
Sheridan Rd	76302
Sherman Rd	76309
Sherry Ln	76310
Sherwood Ln	76308
Shiver Cir	76301
Shoal Creek Dr	76310
Shore Cir & Dr	76310
Shore Line Dr	76308
Sibley St	76301
Sierra Dr	76306
Sierra Blanca	76310
Sierra Madre Dr	76310
Silver Crest Dr	76310
Silver Sage Dr	76310
Silverwood Ter	76308
Simmons Ln	76301
Singleton Ave	76302
Sisk Rd	76310
Sitting Bull Cir & Trl	76310
Skelly Dr	76306
Ski Shore St	76308
Skyline Dr	76306
Skyline Rd	76308
Sleepy Holw	76308

Sligar Rd 76310
Smith St 76301
Smoke Rise Cir 76306
Soaring Ct 76310
Soaring Eagle Trl 76310
Sondra Dr 76308
Sonora Dr 76310
South Dr 76306
Southeast Dr 76306
Southern Ave 76301
Southfork Dr 76310
Southmoor Ln 76302
Southridge Dr 76302
Southwest Dr 76306
Southwest Pkwy
1400-2099 76302
2200-4599 76308
4600-6799 76310
Spanish Trce 76310
Sparks St 76302
Spearman Dr 76306
Speedway Ave
1500-2099 76301
2100-3299 76308
Spencer Dr 76308
Spindletree Dr 76310
Spiser Ln 76302
Sports St 76308
Sprague Dr 76302
Spring Hill Dr 76310
Spring Park Ln 76308
Spring Shadow Dr 76310
Springlake Dr 76301
Springlake Rd 76305
Springwood Ln 76310
Spur 325 76306
Stanford Ave 76308
Stansbury Ln 76310
Star Ave 76301
Star Vista Dr 76301
Starwood Ave 76310
State Highway 258 E 76310
State Highway 79
200-499 76301
State Highway 79
2901-2997 76310
2999-3900 76310
3902-3998 76310
800-10699 76305
2501-2797 76310
Stearns Ave 76308
Stephens Dr 76310
Stephens Ranch Rd 76310
Sternadel Ln 76305
Stesco Ave 76301
Stillwood Dr 76302
Stirling St 76310
Stone Lake Dr 76310
Stone Ridge Dr 76310
Stonegate Dr 76310
Stratford Ave 76306
Sturdevandt Pl 76301
Suburban Ave 76301
Sudan St 76305
Sue Ln 76305
Sue Ann Ave 76309
Sullivan St 76301
Summer Tree Ct 76308
Summit Cir & Dr 76310
Sumner Ter 76306
Sun Stone Ct & Dr 76310
Sun Valley Dr 76302
Sundial Ct 76308
Sunflower Trl 76310
Sunnybrook Ln 76310
Sunnyside Ln 76301
Sunset Dr 76301
Sunset Ln 76306
Surrey Cir 76309
Sutton Cir 76309
Swallow St 76301
Swartz Ave 76301
Sweetbriar Dr 76302
Swenson Cir 76308
T Bone Rd 76310
Taft Blvd 76308
Taft St 76309
Talley Ln 76305
Talon Trl 76310
Talunar Ln 76301
Tamarron Ct & Dr 76308
Tammen Rd 76305
Tammy Dr 76306
Tampico Dr 76306
Tanbark Rd 76306
Tanglewood Blvd & Dr 76309
Tanner Dr 76310
Tarry St 76308
Taylor Rd 76305
Taylor St
300-999 76301
1100-2599 76309
Telephone Dr 76306
Terrace Ave 76301
Texas Ave
100-999 76301
2700-2799 76308
Texas Star Ct & Ln 76310
Thaten Dr 76306
Thelma Cir & Dr 76306
Third Circle Dr 76306
Thomas Ave 76308
Thompson Rd 76301
Three Way Rd 76310
Tica Rd 76305
Tilden St
800-999 76301
1300-2399 76309
Tillie Dr 76310
Tinker Trl 76306
Tippecanoe Trl 76310
Tobago 76308
Tomahawk Trl 76310
Tortuga Trl 76309
Towanda Trl 76310
Tower Dr 76310
Town And Country Dr 76306
Tradewinds Rd 76310
Trails Crest Cir 76310
Trailwood Dr 76310
Travis St
200-1699 76301
2700-3799 76302
N Travis St 76306
Trenton Ter 76308
Triangle Cir 76308
Trigg Ln 76306
Trinidad Ct & Dr 76310
Tripple D Ranch Ln 76310
Tripple T Ln 76310
Trout Rd 76305
Trout St 76301
Trueheart St 76301
Tucker Rd 76305
Tucson Dr 76306
Tulip St 76301
Tulsa St 76301
Tumbleweed Ct 76310
Turkey Ranch Rd 76310
Turtle Creek Rd 76309
Twelve Oaks Ct 76310
Twin Oaks St 76302
Tyler St
700-999 76301
1000-1299 76309
Ulen Ln 76310
Underwood St 76301
University Ave 76308
Untalan St 76306
Upper Garner Rd 76305
Us Business Highway
287 N 76305
Us Business Highway
287 S 76310
Us Highway 277 S 76310
Us Highway 281 76310
Us Highway 287 N
4500-4600 76305
Us Highway 287 N
4602-12998 76305
10227-14399 76310
Us Highway 287 North
Access Rd 76305
Us Highway 287 South
Access Rd 76310
Valencia Ct 76306
Valley Ridge Rd 76309
Valley View Rd 76306
Van Buren St 76301
Van Dorn Dr 76310
Vera Ct 76310
Vermont St 76306
Vernon Ave 76301
Vicars Dr 76305
Vickers Dr 76310
Vickie Dr 76306
Victoria St 76308
Victory Ave 76301
Viewpark 76306
Villa Ct 76308
Village Gln 76302
Vinson P R 76310
Virginia Ave 76301
Virginia Dr 76309
Vista St 76302
Waco St 76301
Waggoner Cir 76309
Wagon Wheel 76310
Wakefield Ln 76310
Wallace Rd 76305
Walnut St 76301
Wampum Trl 76310
Wanami Ln & Trl 76310
War Path St & Trl 76310
Ward St 76310
Warford St 76301
Warren St 76306
Warwick Ct 76309
E Washington St 76306
Waterford Dr 76310
Watkins Rd 76305
Waurika Fwy 76305
Waverly Pl 76301
Wayne Ave 76308
Wb Stone Rd 76310
Webb Ave 76310
Webster St 76306
Wedgewood Ave 76301
Weeks St 76302
Weeks Park Ln 76308
Welch St 76301
Wellington Ln 76305
Wells Rd 76310
Wendover Ct & St 76309
Wendy Rdg 76302
E & W Wenonah Ave &
Blvd 76309
Weruk Rd 76305
Wesley Dr 76306
Westcliff Dr 76306
Westerly Pl 76309
Western Hills Dr 76310
Westgate St 76308
Westlake Dr 76309
Westminister St 76309
Westridge Dr 76302
Westside Dr 76301
Westward Dr 76308
Wheat St 76305
Whirlwind Dr 76310
Whisper Wind Dr 76310
Whispering Creek Ln 76310
White Rd 76305
White St 76301
White Oak Ct 76308
White Rock Ct 76310
Whitehall Ln 76309
Whitfield Ln 76301
Whitney St 76301
E Wichita St 76306
Wichita Wood Rd 76305
Widows Ln 76301
Wigwam Dr & Trl 76310
Wildflower Ln 76310
Wildwood Dr 76302
Williams Ave 76301
S Williams Rd 76310
Willis Rd 76305
Willow Dr 76306
Willow Bend Dr 76310
Willow Run St 76310
Willowick Dr 76309
Wilson Ave 76301
Wimberly Ter 76308
Wimbledon Ln 76310
Windjammer Way 76308
Windmill Lake Ave 76309
S Winds Dr 76302
Windsong Dr 76310
Windsor Ln 76308
Wisconsin Ave 76310
Wolcott Ln 76306
Wolf Rd 76305
Wolfe St 76308
Woodcrest Cir 76309
Wooddale Ave 76301
Woodhaven East Dr 76302
Woodland Creek Cir 76302
Woodlawn 76308
Woodridge Dr 76310
Woodrow Ave 76301
Woods St 76301
Worthington Ct 76306
Wrangler Dr 76306
Wranglers Retreat 76310
Wyneth Dr 76306
Wynn Cir 76308
Wynnwood Dr 76308
Wyoming Ave 76310
Yale Ave 76301
York St 76309
Yucca Dr 76305
Yuma Trl 76306

NUMBERED STREETS

N 1st St 76306
2nd St 76301
E 2nd St 76301
N 2nd St 76306
3rd St 76301
E 3rd St 76301
N 3rd St 76306
4th St 76301
E 4th St 76301
N 4th St 76306
5th St 76301
E 5th St 76301
N 5th St 76306
6th St 76301
N 6th St 76306
7th St 76301
N 7th St 76306
8th St 76301
N 8th St 76306
9th St
500-3199 76301
3200-3499 76309
N 9th St 76306
10th St
500-2199 76301
2200-3399 76309
N 10th St 76306
11th St 76301
12th St 76301
13th St 76301
14th St 76301
15th St 76301
16th St 76301
17th St 76301
20th St 76301
21st St 76301
22nd St 76301
23rd St 76301
24th St 76301
25th St 76301
26th St 76301
28th St 76302
29th St 76302
30th St 76302
31st St 76302
32nd St 76302
33rd St 76302
34th St 76302
35th St 76302
36th St 76302
37th St 76302
38th St 76302
N 77 Ranch 76305

WILLIS TX

General Delivery 77378

POST OFFICE BOXES MAIN OFFICE STATIONS AND BRANCHES

Box No.s
All PO Boxes 77378

RURAL ROUTES

03, 12 77378

NAMED STREETS

N Acres Rd 77378
African Hill Rd 77378
Afton Park Rd 77378
Altair Ct 77318
Amber Cv 77378
Amblewood St 77318
Anchor Ct 77318
Anchorage Marina Rd 77318
Anderson Ln & Rd 77318
Andromeda Ct 77318
Andwood St 77318
Antares Dr 77318
Apache Bnd, St & Trl 77378
Apple Tree St 77318
Applewood Dr 77378
Aquila Ct E & W 77318
Arbor Oak 77318
Arcturus Dr 77318
Arden Ct 77318
Aries Loop S 77318
Arrowhead Bnd & Loop
E
& W 77378
Ashba Ln 77378
Aspen Way 77318
Aspen Way Ct & Dr 77318
Austin Rd 77378
S Avenue A 77378
Bagwell Rd 77378
Balboa Dr 77318
Balsam St 77318
Bandera Bnd 77378
Barberry St 77318
Bazell Ln 77318
Bee Creek Dr 77378
S Bell St 77378
Ben Milam Rd 77378
S Bend Ct 77378
Big Bow Bnd 77378
Big Spring Cir 77378
Bighorn Trl 77378
Bill Cody Trl 77378
Bill Hales Rd 77378
Bilnoski Rd 77378
Binnacle Ct 77318
Birchwood Dr 77378
Black Gum 77318
Blackland Rd 77378
Blue Bell Dr 77318
Blue Haven Dr 77318
Blueberry Hl 77318
Bluff View Dr 77318
Boggy Creek Ln 77378
Bonham Ln 77378
Bourbon St 77318
Bowie Ln 77378
Bowsprit Pt 77318
Brandi Ct & Ln 77378
Brandon Ln 77378
Brazos Dr 77378
Breeland Rd 77378
Breezy Pt 77318
Briarwood Dr 77378
Bridgepoint Ct 77318
Bridges Rd 77378
Brigadier Dr 77318
Broken Arrow Dr & St 77378
Bronte Courts Dr 77378
Brook Oaks Ct 77378
Brookhaven Farm Rd 77378
Browder Traylor Rd 77378
Brown Rd 77378
Bruce Rd 77318
Brushwood Dr 77318
Bryan Ln 77378
Buckskin Dr 77318
E, N, S & W Buffalo
Cir 77378
Bunker Hill Dr 77318
Burleson Ln 77378
Burnett Ln 77378
Burnt Mls 77318
Business Park Dr 77378
Bybee St 77378
C Goffney Rd 77378
Calendar St 77318
Calhoun St 77378
Calvary Rd
1-99 77378
9800-15799 77318
Camp Creek Way 77318
Camp Robinwood 77318
N & S Campbell St 77378
Canal St 77318
Canyon Ct 77318
Canyon Falls Blvd 77318
Canyon Hill Dr 77318
Canyon Park Ln 77318
Capricornus Dr 77318
Captain Cir 77318
Cargill St 77378
Carmel Dr 77318
Carrol Ct, Ln & Rd 77318
Catalina Rd 77318
Cedar Ct, Grv & Ln 77378
Cedar Lane Loop 77318
Cedar Ridge Ct 77318
Cedarwood Dr 77318
Cemetary Ln 77378
Centaurus Ct 77318
Cetus Ct 77318
Challenger Dr 77318
Champions Loop 77378
Chapa Rd 77378
Charred Oaks Dr 77318
Chevelle Ln 77378
China Grove Ln 77378
Church St 77378
Circle Dr 77378
Citron Ct 77378
Clearwater Dr 77318
Clipper Ct 77318
Clipper Circle Dr 77318
Club House Dr 77378
Coaltown Rd 77378
Coastal Dr 77318
S Cochran Rd & St 77378
Collier Rd 77378
Colt Ln 77378
S Comanche Cir 77378
Commander Cir 77318
Commodore Cir 77318
Conroe Bay Blvd 77318
Conroe Heights Ln 77318
Constellation Cir E &
W 77318
Cook Rd 77318
Corinthian Way 77318
Corona Ct 77318
Corvus Dr 77318
Country Oak Dr 77318
Country Run Dr 77378
County Line Rd 77378
Coushatta Trl 77318
Cox Rd 77378
Coyote Run 77378
Cozy Cove Ln 77318
Crater Dr 77318
Creek St 77318
Creek Edge Ct 77378
Creek Meadow Dr 77378
Creek Park Way 77378
Creek Vista Ln 77378
Creekside Dr 77378
Creekway Ct 77378
Crest Dr 77318
Crestwood Dr 77378
Crockett Rd 77378
Cross St 77378
Crown Royal Dr 77378
Crystal Park Cir 77378
Cude Cemetery Rd 77318
Cunningham Trl 77318
Cygnus Ct 77318
Cypress Dr 77318
Dairyland Dr 77378
Daniel St 77378
Daniel Boone Trl 77378
W Danville Rd 77318
N Danville St 77378
S Danville St 77378
Darkwood St 77318
Dauphine St 77318
Dave Moore Rd 77378
Decatur St 77318
Deer Haven Cir & Run 77378
Delagarza Rd 77378
Diamond Shrs 77378
Dobraski Rd 77378
Dogwood Dr 77378
Dolphin Dr 77318
E & W Double Crk 77378
Double Creek Ct & Dr 77378
Dream Point Ln 77318
Dry Creek Ln 77318
Easy St 77378
Eden Ln 77378
Edgewater Ct & Dr 77318
Edmonds Rd 77378
Edwards Ln 77378
Elder St 77378
Elkwood St 77318
Ell Dr 77318
Elm Mnr & St 77318
Elmore Dr 77318
Emerald Lakes Dr 77378
Emerson Ct 77318
Enchanted Ct, Cv &
Vis 77318
Enchanted View Ct 77318
Enchanted Waters Dr 77318
Escondido Dr 77318
Esperanza Rd 77378
Estates Way 77318
Everitt Rd 77378
Everwood St 77318
Falling Oak Dr 77318
Falls Ct 77318
Family Ln 77318
Fannin Rd 77318
Farrell Rd 77378
Felder St 77378
Ferguson Rd 77378
Ferris Rd 77378
Fieldstone Ln 77378
First View Ct 77318
Fisher Ln 77318
Fm 1097 Rd W 77318
E Fm 1097 Rd 77318
Fm 1725 Rd 77378
Fm 2432 Rd 77378
Fm 3081 Rd 77378
Fm 830 Rd
1000-1200 77378
1201-1299 77378
1202-14098 77378
2001-14099 77318
N Forest Dr 77378
Forest Cove Dr 77318
Forest Creek Dr 77318

Forest Glen Dr 77318
Forest Trace Ln 77378
Forest Trails Dr 77318
Fox Fire Ln 77378
Foxhall St 77318
Frank Novark Rd 77318
Frontier Rd 77378
Gable Dr 77318
Gale Haven Rd 77378
Garrett Ln 77378
Gemini Blvd 77318
Gentle Breeze Dr 77318
George Goosby Dr 77378
Gerald St 77378
Gibbs Pipeline Rd 77378
Gladewood St 77318
Glenmar 77318
Golden Ln & St 77378
Goliad Ln 77378
Goosby Rd 77378
Grand Lake Dr 77318
Grand Oaks Dr 77378
Green Meadow Ln & Loop 77318
Green Pine Blvd 77378
Greenbriar 77318
Greenridge Dr 77318
Greenwater Ct & Dr 77318
Grove E & W 77378
Gulf Coast Dr 77378
Gunwale Cir 77318
Hackberry Dr 77318
Hackberry Manor Dr 77378
Hairston Cir & Dr 77318
Hamlet 77378
Hasara Ln 77378
Hawthorne Dr 77378
Heavenly Acres Dr 77318
Helm Ct 77318
Henry Calfee Dr 77378
Hibbard Hicks Ln 77378
Hickock Ln 77378
Hickory Knl 77318
Hickory Ln 77378
Hidden Springs Ranch Dr 77378
Hidden Trail Ct 77318
High Creek Ln 77378
W Highway 150 77378
N Highway 75 N 77378
Hill Dr 77318
Hill Rd 77378
Hill St 77378
Hillcrest Cir 77318
Hillcrest Manor Dr 77318
Hillshire Dr 77318
Hillside Dr & Ln 77318
Hilltop Cir, Ct & Dr 77318
Hines Ave 77378
N Holland St 77378
Holly St 77378
Hollywood Dr 77378
Honey Hill Ln 77378
Hooper Ranch Rd 77378
Hostetter Creek Rd 77378
Huck Finn St 77318
Hughes Loop 77378
Hulon Dr 77318
Hydra Ct 77318
I O Ct 77318
Indian Creek Cir 77378
Indian Hill Trl 77378
Industrial Park Ln 77378
Inkjet Way 77378
Interstate 45 77318
Interstate 45 N
  1000-2099 77378
Interstate 45 N
  12100-12399 77318
  12400-12798 77378
  12401-12899 77318
  12800-12898 77378
  12900-12999 77378
  13000-18599 77318
Invermark Way 77318
Inwood 77318

Jack Gibbs Rd 77378
Jamaica Cir & Dr 77378
Janet St 77378
Jayton Wood Way 77318
Jbk Memorial Dr 77378
Jennifer Dr 77318
Jennings Rd 77378
Jerapi 77378
Joann St 77318
John St 77378
Jones Rd
  1-999 77378
  13400-13999 77318
Joos Rd 77378
Keel Ct 77318
Kelli Ln 77378
Kelly Rd 77378
N & S Kennedy St 77378
Ketch Ct 77318
Kickapoo Trl 77378
Kingston Cv 77318
Kingston Cove Cir, Ct & Ln 77318
Kristen Ln 77378
Kuo Dr 77318
Laguna Way 77318
Lake Dr 77318
Lake Dr E 77378
Lake Dr W 77378
N Lake Dr 77318
Lake Breeze Ln 77318
Lake Conroe Bay Rd 77318
Lake Conroe Hills Dr 77318
Lake Haven Dr 77318
S Lake Mist Ln 77318
Lake Paula Dr 77318
Lake Shore Dr 77318
Lake Sunset Dr 77318
Lake Villa Ln & St 77318
Lake Vista Ct & Dr 77318
Lakepoint Dr 77318
Lakeshore Cir, Ct, Dr & Ln 77318
Lakeside Place Dr 77318
Lakeview Dr 77318
Lakeview Manor Dr 77318
Lakeway Dr 77318
Lakewood Ct 77318
Lakewood Dr 77318
Lakewood Oaks Dr 77318
Lamar Rd & St 77378
Laurie Ln 77378
Lazy Ct & Ln 77318
Lazy Cove Dr 77318
N Lee Shore Dr 77318
Leisure Ln 77378
Lemay Ln 77378
Lepus Dr 77318
Levi Rd 77318
Lewis Creek Cir 77318
Libby Cir 77378
Libra Ct 77318
Lindley Dr & St 77378
Little Bill Ln 77378
Live Oak Trl 77318
Lochness Dr 77318
Longstreet Rd
  100-499 77378
  9600-14699 77318
  13336-40-13336-42 77318
Longwood Cir & Dr 77318
Lookout Cir & Ct 77318
Louise Dr 77378
Lucher Rd 77378
Lukes Rd 77378
Lyra Dr 77318
Maggie Ln 77318
Main Dr 77318
Main Sail Loop 77318
Malibu E & W 77318
Mandy Ln 77378
Maple Ridge Dr 77318
Maplewood Dr 77318
Marigold St 77318
Marina Loop 77318
Mariner Dr 77318

Mariners Ct 77318
Mark Dr 77318
E & W Marlin St 77378
E & W Martin Luther King Blvd 77378
Mary Wagner Rd 77318
Maverick Dr 77378
Maxwell St 77378
Maywood St 77318
Mccrory Rd 77378
Mcdonald Rd 77378
Mcgehee Rd 77378
Mcgoffney Rd 77378
Mckay Rd 77378
Meadow Ln 77378
Meadow Wood Ln 77378
Mendez Rd 77378
Midway Dr 77378
N Mill St 77378
Mill Creek Dr 77378
Miller Ln 77318
E & W Mink St 77378
Misty Glen Ln 77318
Mohawk Bnd 77378
Molk Rd 77378
Monroe St 77378
Montego Cove Dr 77318
Monterrey Cir 77318
E Montgomery St 77378
W Montgomery St
  100-999 77378
  1000-1099 77318
Moon Rd 77378
Moonlight Dr 77378
Mopac 77378
Mosley Rd 77378
Munchkin Ln 77378
Mustang Ave & Rd 77318
Navajo Trl 77378
Needham Pl 77378
Nelwood St 77378
Newport Dr 77318
North Dr 77378
Northline Rd 77378
Nursery Ln 77378
Oak Ln 77378
Oak Apple Ct 77318
Oak Branch Dr 77378
Oak Falls Dr 77318
Oak Glen Dr 77318
Oak Hill Dr 77318
Oak Lynn Dr 77318
Oak Manor Ct 77318
Oak Meadow Dr 77318
Oak Meadows Dr 77318
Oak Moss Ln 77318
Oak Ridge Rd 77378
Oak Shores Dr 77318
Oak Springs Dr 77318
Oak Terrace Dr 77318
Oak Trace Ln 77318
Oak Tree Ln 77318
Oak Woods Ct & Dr 77318
Oaken Timber Ln 77318
Oakridge Manor Dr 77318
Oaks Dr 77318
Oakwood Dr 77318
Old County Rd 77378
Old Creek St 77318
Old Danville Rd 77318
Old Montgomery Rd 77318
E & W Old Oak Trl 77318
Old Salem Church Rd 77318
Old Waverly Rd 77318
Olde Oaks Ln 77318
Opal Trl 77318
Ophiuchus Ct 77318
Orion Ct E 77318
Orleans Dr 77318
Osage Trl 77378
Osprey Ct 77318
Outpost Cove Dr 77318
Outrigger Dr 77318
Overstreet Dr 77378
Paddock St 77378
Pagewood St 77378

Palms Marina Rd 77318
Papoose Trl 77378
Paradise Ct 77318
Paradise Cove Dr 77318
Paradise Point Dr 77318
Paradise View Ct & Dr 77318
Park Dr 77378
Park Ln 77318
Park Slope Dr 77318
Park View Dr 77318
Parker Dr 77318
Parker Hill Dr 77378
Parkside Cir & Dr 77318
Parkway Manor Dr 77318
Parret Ln 77318
Pearl Cv 77378
Pearwood St 77318
E Pecan Mnr & St 77378
Pecan Tree Ct & Dr 77318
Pecos Pl 77318
Pegasus Dr 77318
Peggy Ln 77378
Pelican Blvd 77318
Pelican Island Dr 77318
Perkins St 77378
Persimmon St 77378
Pettigrew Ln 77318
Philpot St 77378
Pin Oak 77378
Pine Cir 77378
Pine St 77378
Pine Circle Dr 77378
Pine Trail Ct 77318
Pineloch Dr & St 77378
Pinemont Dr & Rd 77378
Pineway Dr 77318
Pleasure Lake Dr & Ln 77318
Pocahantis Bnd 77378
Point Dr 77318
Point Aquarius Blvd 77318
Pollard Rd 77378
Pollux Dr 77318
Poplar 77378
Port Cir 77318
Post Mill Rd 77378
Post Oak Rd 77378
E & W Powell St 77378
N & S Puffin Ln 77318
R Hales Rd 77378
R Robinson Ln 77378
Ranch Road One 77378
Rancho Dr 77378
E & W Ravine Run 77318
Rayford 77378
Rebecca Ln 77378
Red Bird 77378
Redbud Vw 77318
Reese St 77378
Regulus St 77318
Ridgecrest Dr 77378
Ridgepoint Cir 77378
N & S Ridgeway Dr 77318
Robin Ln 77378
Rock Creek Dr 77378
E & W Rogers Rd & St 77378
Rose Rd 77378
Roy Bean Rd 77378
Ruby Dr 77378
Runnels St 77378
Running Bear Dr 77378
Runnymeade 77378
Rusty Ln 77378
Sagittarius Dr E & W 77318
Salem Church Rd 77318
Sam Houston Rd & St 77378
San Saba Way 77378
Sanchart Dr 77378
Sandy Cv 77318
Sandy Ln
  10500-10599 77318
  12500-12699 77378
Sandy Creek Ln & Rd 77318
Sapphire Shrs 77318
Sarah Circle Dr 77378

Sassafras St 77318
Scarlet Oak 77378
Schooner Pt 77318
Scott Ln 77378
Seminole St 77378
Serenity Ct 77318
Serenity North Dr 77318
Serenity Woods Dr 77318
Seven Coves Rd 77378
Shadow Bay Dr 77318
Shadow Brook Dr 77318
Shadow Lake Dr 77318
Shadowbrook Ln 77318
Shady Cove Dr 77318
Shady Knoll Ln 77318
Shark Aly 77318
Sharon Ln 77378
Shatterway Ln 77318
Shelter Bay Cv 77318
Shepard Hill Rd 77318
Shirley Ln 77378
E & W Shore Dr 77318
Shoreline Dr 77318
Shorewood Dr 77318
Short Rd 77378
Sirius Ct 77318
Skyline Dr 77318
Sleepy Pt 77318
E & W Small Oak Ln 77378
Snoe Hl & Rd 77318
Snow Ln 77318
Snow Grein 77378
Souni Rd 77378
South Ct & Dr 77378
Southway Rd 77378
Spica Ct 77318
Spinnaker Cv 77318
Squirrel Tree Rd 77318
St Ann Ct 77318
St Louis Ct 77318
St Peter Ct 77318
Standing Oak Dr 77318
Starboard Dr 77318
Stark St 77378
Starks Rd 77378
Starr Way 77318
State Highway 150 Loop W 77378
E & W Stewart St 77378
Stillwater Dr 77318
Stone Creek Dr 77318
Straughter St 77378
Summer Chase Blvd 77318
E, N & S Summerchase Cir & Dr 77318
Summit Dr 77378
Sunfish Rd 77378
Sunflower Dr 77318
Sunset Mnr 77318
Sunshine Pt 77318
Sutton Dr & Pl 77318
Sutton Place St 77318
Syphrett Rd 77378
Tanglewood Dr 77378
Tanning Ln 77378
Tanyard Rd 77378
Taurus Dr 77318
Taylor Ct 77378
Teal Way 77318
Texas National Blvd 77378
N & S Thomason St 77378
Thompson Rd 77318
Thousand Trl 77318
Tierwood Ct 77378
Timberline Estates Dr 77378
Timothy Dr 77318
Tom Sawyer St 77318
Topaz Ct, Cv & Trl 77318
Torrey Pines Dr 77318
Travis Ln 77378
Treadwell Rd 77378
Trero Ln 77378
N & S Trice St 77378
Troy Cir & Ln 77318
Turner Dr 77378
Turquoise Trl 77378

Twelve Oak St 77378
Twelve Oaks 77378
Twin Forks Dr 77378
Twin Shores Dr 77318
Tyra Dr 77378
Underwood St 77378
Upland St 77318
Val Verde Way 77378
Valley Dr N & S 77318
Valleywood Cir 77318
Vanwood St 77318
Vega Ct 77318
Ventura Rd 77318
Vernwood St 77318
View Cir 77318
Viniarski Rd 77318
Virginia Ln 77318
Virgo Dr 77318
Vistawood St 77318
Walco Hills Dr 77318
Walker Rd 77378
Walker Hill Ln 77318
Walkwood St 77318
Warm Spg 77318
Warm Spring St 77318
Water Oak 77318
Waterline Way 77318
Waterview Dr 77318
Waterway Dr 77318
E & W Watson St 77378
Waywood 77318
Weeping Bow 77378
Weir Creek Rd 77318
Whispering Wind Dr 77318
White Rd 77378
White Cedar St 77318
White Oak Dr 77318
White Oak Hills Blvd 77378
Whitehorse Ln 77378
Wickdome Dr 77318
Wildercroft 77318
Will St 77378
Williamson Ln 77378
Willow Dr 77378
Willwood Dr 77378
Wilson Ln 77378
Windlass Ln 77318
Windswept Way 77318
Windwood Way 77318
N & S Wood St 77378
Wood Acres Dr 77318
Wood Hollow Dr 77318
Woodcreek Cir & Dr 77318
Woodcrest Dr 77318
Wooded Oak Ct 77378
Woodland Lks 77378
Woodland Lakes Dr & Loop 77378
Woodland Manor Dr 77318
Woods Ct 77378
N & S Woodson St 77378
W Worsham St 77378
Wren Cv 77318
Wright Wood Ln 77378
Wyatt Earp Ln 77378
Young St 77378
Zachary Taylor Rd 77378
Zapata Way 77378
Zephyr Ln 77318

NUMBERED STREETS

All Street Addresses 77378

Utah

People QuickFacts	Utah	USA
Population, 2013 estimate	2,900,872	316,128,839
Population, 2010 (April 1) estimates base	2,763,885	308,747,716
Population, percent change, April 1, 2010 to July 1, 2013	5.0%	2.4%
Population, 2010	2,763,885	308,745,538
Persons under 5 years, percent, 2013	8.8%	6.3%
Persons under 18 years, percent, 2013	30.9%	23.3%
Persons 65 years and over, percent, 2013	9.8%	14.1%
Female persons, percent, 2013	49.7%	50.8%
White alone, percent, 2013 (a)	91.6%	77.7%
Black or African American alone, percent, 2013 (a)	1.3%	13.2%
American Indian and Alaska Native alone, percent, 2013 (a)	1.5%	1.2%
Asian alone, percent, 2013 (a)	2.3%	5.3%
Native Hawaiian and Other Pacific Islander alone, percent, 2013 (a)	1.0%	0.2%
Two or More Races, percent, 2013	2.3%	2.4%
Hispanic or Latino, percent, 2013 (b)	13.4%	17.1%
White alone, not Hispanic or Latino, percent, 2013	79.7%	62.6%
Living in same house 1 year & over, percent, 2008-2012	82.6%	84.8%
Foreign born persons, percent, 2008-2012	8.3%	12.9%
Language other than English spoken at home, pct age 5+, 2008-2012	14.4%	20.5%
High school graduate or higher, percent of persons age 25+, 2008-2012	90.6%	85.7%
Bachelor's degree or higher, percent of persons age 25+, 2008-2012	29.9%	28.5%
Veterans, 2008-2012	146,524	21,853,912
Mean travel time to work (minutes), workers age 16+, 2008-2012	21.5	25.4
Housing units, 2013	1,006,106	132,802,859
Homeownership rate, 2008-2012	70.4%	65.5%
Housing units in multi-unit structures, percent, 2008-2012	21.3%	25.9%
Median value of owner-occupied housing units, 2008-2012	$217,800	$181,400
Households, 2008-2012	880,873	115,226,802
Persons per household, 2008-2012	3.09	2.61
Per capita money income in past 12 months (2012 dollars), 2008-2012	$23,794	$28,051
Median household income, 2008-2012	$58,164	$53,046
Persons below poverty level, percent, 2008-2012	12.1%	14.9%

Business QuickFacts	Utah	USA
Private nonfarm establishments, 2012	70,454	7,431,808
Private nonfarm employment, 2012	1,070,986	115,938,468
Private nonfarm employment, percent change, 2011-2012	4.1%	2.2%
Nonemployer establishments, 2012	199,393	22,735,915
Total number of firms, 2007	246,393	27,092,908
Black-owned firms, percent, 2007	0.5%	7.1%
American Indian- and Alaska Native-owned firms, percent, 2007	0.6%	0.9%
Asian-owned firms, percent, 2007	1.9%	5.7%
Native Hawaiian and Other Pacific Islander-owned firms, percent, 2007	0.3%	0.1%
Hispanic-owned firms, percent, 2007	3.7%	8.3%
Women-owned firms, percent, 2007	24.9%	28.8%
Manufacturers shipments, 2007 ($1000)	42,431,657	5,319,456,312
Merchant wholesaler sales, 2007 ($1000)	25,417,368	4,174,286,516
Retail sales, 2007 ($1000)	36,574,240	3,917,663,456
Retail sales per capita, 2007	$13,730	$12,990
Accommodation and food services sales, 2007 ($1000)	3,980,570	613,795,732
Building permits, 2012	13,007	829,658

Geography QuickFacts	Utah	USA
Land area in square miles, 2010	82,169.62	3,531,905.43
Persons per square mile, 2010	33.6	87.4
FIPS Code	49	

(a) Includes persons reporting only one race.
(b) Hispanics may be of any race, so also are included in applicable race categories.
FN: Footnote on this item for this area in place of data
NA: Not available
D: Suppressed to avoid disclosure of confidential information
X: Not applicable
S: Suppressed; does not meet publication standards
Z: Value greater than zero but less than half unit of measure shown
F: Fewer than 100 firms
Source: US Census Bureau State & County QuickFacts

3 DIGIT ZIP CODE MAP

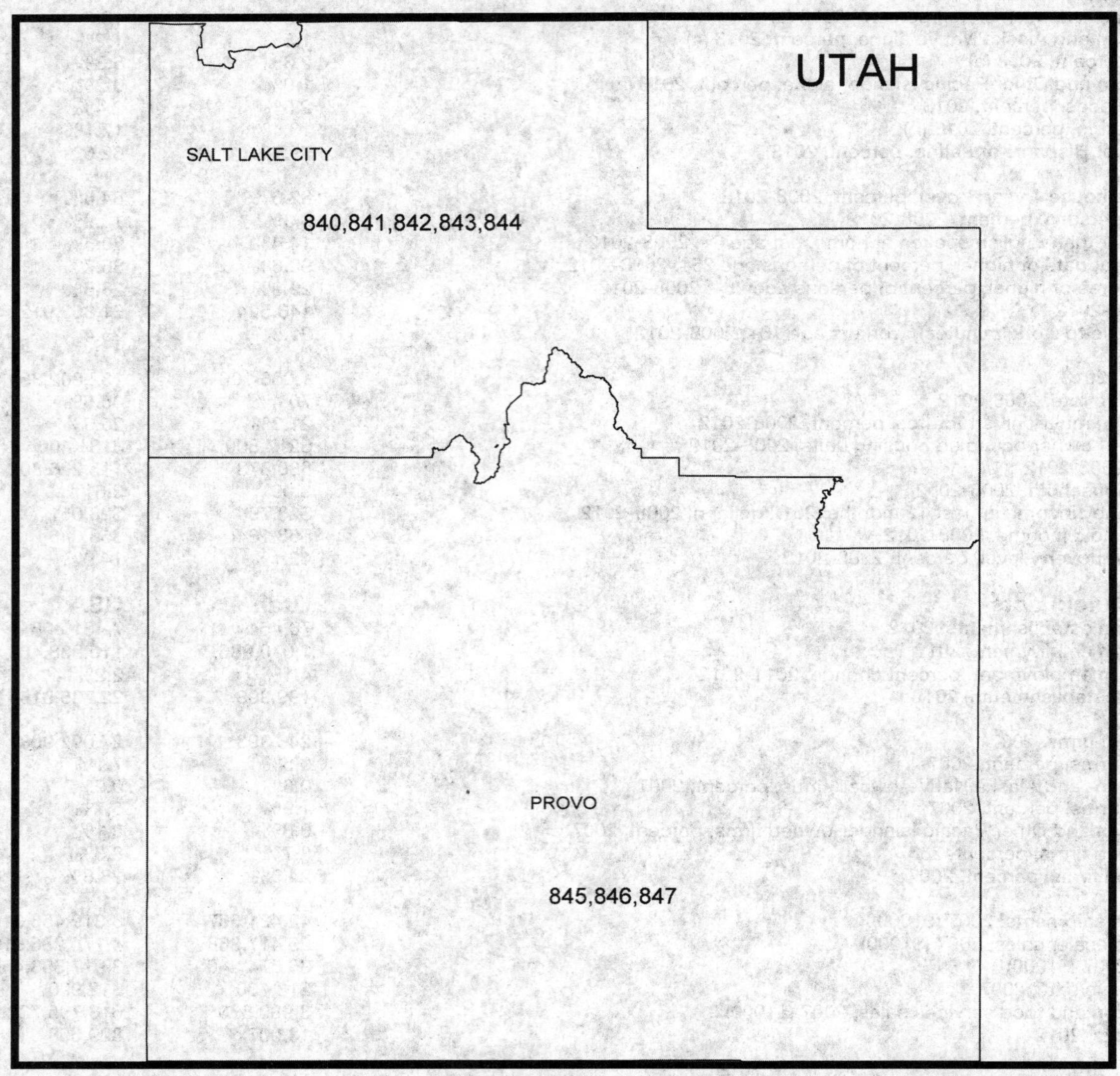

Utah

(Abbreviation: UT)

Post Office, County — ZIP Code

Places with more than one ZIP code are listed in capital letters, See pages indicated.

Abraham, Millard 84635
Adamsville, Beaver 84731
Alpine, Utah 84004
Alta, Salt Lake 84092
Altamont, Duchesne 84001
Alton, Kane 84710
Altonah, Duchesne 84002
Amalga, Cache 84335
American Fork, Utah 84003
Aneth, San Juan 84510
Annabella, Sevier 84711
Antimony, Garfield 84712
Apple Valley, Washington 84737
Aurora, Sevier 84620
Austin, Sevier 84754
Axtell, Sanpete 84621
Ballard, Duchesne 84066
Bear River City, Box Elder 84301
Beaver, Beaver 84713
Beaverdam, Box Elder 84306
Benjamin, Utah 84660
Benson, Cache 84335
Beryl, Iron 84714
Bicknell, Wayne 84715
Big Water, Kane 84741
Bingham Canyon, Salt Lake 84006
Blanding, San Juan 84511
Bluebell, Duchesne 84007
Bluff, San Juan 84512
Bluffdale, Salt Lake 84065
Bonanza, Uintah 84008
Boulder, Garfield 84716
BOUNTIFUL, Davis
(See Page 4014)
Brian Head, Iron 84719
Bridgeland, Duchesne 84021
Brigham City, Box Elder 84302
Brighton, Salt Lake 84121
Brookside, Washington 84782
Bryce, Garfield 84764
Bryce Canyon, Garfield 84764
Bryce Canyon City, Garfield 84764
Bullfrog, San Juan 84533
Burrville, Sevier 84744
Cache Junction, Cache 84304
Callao, Tooele 84034
Cannonville, Garfield 84718
Canyon Point, Kane 84741
Castle Dale, Emery 84513
Castle Valley, Grand 84532
CEDAR CITY, Iron
(See Page 4014)
Cedar Fort, Utah 84013
Cedar Hills, Utah 84062
Cedar Valley, Utah 84013
Centerfield, Sanpete 84622
Centerville, Davis 84014
Central, Washington 84722
Central Valley, Sevier 84754
Chester, Sanpete 84623
Circleville, Piute 84723
Cisco, Grand 84515
Clarkston, Cache 84305
Clawson, Emery 84516
CLEARFIELD, Davis
(See Page 4016)
Cleveland, Emery 84518
Clinton, Davis 84015
Coalville, Summit 84017
Collinston, Box Elder 84306
Copperton, Salt Lake 84006
Corinne, Box Elder 84307
Cornish, Cache 84308
Cottonwood
(See Salt Lake City)
Cottonwood Heights, Salt Lake 84047
Cottonwood Heights City
(See Salt Lake City)
Cove, Cache 84320
Croydon, Morgan 84018
Dammeron Valley, Washington 84783
Daniel, Wasatch 84032
Deer Valley, Summit 84060
Delta, Millard 84624
Deseret, Millard 84624
Deweyville, Box Elder 84309
Draper, Salt Lake 84020
Duchesne, Duchesne 84021
Duck Creek Village, Kane 84762
Dugway, Tooele 84022
Dutch John, Daggett 84023
Eagle Mountain, Utah 84043
East Carbon, Carbon 84520
Echo, Summit 84024
Eden, Weber 84310
Elberta, Utah 84626
Elk Ridge, Utah 84651
Elmo, Emery 84521
Elsinore, Sevier 84724
Elwood, Box Elder 84337
Emery, Emery 84522
Emigration Canyon, Salt Lake 84108
Enoch
(See Cedar City)
Enterprise, Washington 84725
Ephraim, Sanpete 84627
Erda, Tooele 84074
Escalante, Garfield 84726
Eureka, Juab 84628
Fairfield, Utah 84013
Fairview, Sanpete 84629
Farmington, Davis 84025
Farr West, Weber 84404
Fayette, Sanpete 84630
Ferron, Emery 84523
Fielding, Box Elder 84311
Fillmore, Millard 84631
Fort Duchesne, Uintah 84026
Fountain Green, Sanpete 84632
Francis, Summit 84036
Fremont, Wayne 84747
Fruit Heights, Davis 84037
Fruitland, Duchesne 84027
Garden City, Rich 84028
Garland, Box Elder 84312
Garrison, Millard 84728
Genola, Utah 84655
Glendale, Kane 84729
Glenwood, Sevier 84730
Goshen, Utah 84633
Grantsville, Tooele 84029
Green River, Emery 84525
Green River, Grand 84540
Greenhaven, Tooele 84083
Greenville, Beaver 84731
Greenwich, Piute 84732
Grouse Creek, Box Elder 84313
Gunlock, Washington 84733
Gunnison, Sanpete 84634
Gusher, Uintah 84026
Halls Crossing, San Juan 84533
Hanksville, Wayne 84734
Hanna, Duchesne 84031
Harrisville
(See Ogden)
Hatch, Garfield 84735
Heber City, Wasatch 84032
Helper, Carbon 84526
Henefer, Summit 84033
Henrieville, Garfield 84736
Herriman, Salt Lake 84065
Herriman, Salt Lake 84096
Hideout, Summit 84036
Highland, Utah 84003
Hildale, Washington 84784
Hill Afb, Davis 84056
Hill Air Force Base, Davis 84056
Hinckley, Millard 84635
Hite, San Juan 84533
Holden, Millard 84636
Holladay
(See Salt Lake City)
Holladay Cottonwood
(See Salt Lake City)
Honeyville, Box Elder 84314
Hooper, Weber 84315
Hooper, Weber 84401
Howell, Box Elder 84316
Huntington, Emery 84528
Huntsville, Weber 84317
Hurricane, Washington 84737
Hyde Park, Cache 84318
Hyrum, Cache 84319
Ibapah, Tooele 84034
Ivins, Washington 84738
Jensen, Uintah 84035
Joseph, Sevier 84739
Junction, Piute 84740
Kamas, Summit 84036
Kanab, Kane 84741
Kanarraville, Iron 84742
Kanesville, Weber 84315
Kanosh, Millard 84637
Kaysville, Davis 84037
Kearns, Salt Lake 84118
Kenilworth, Carbon 84529
Kingston, Piute 84743
Koosharem, Sevier 84744
La Sal, San Juan 84530
La Verkin, Washington 84745
Lake Point, Tooele 84074
Lake Powell, San Juan 84533
Lakeside, Tooele 84029
Laketown, Rich 84038
Lapoint, Uintah 84039
LAYTON, Davis
(See Page 4016)
Leamington, Millard 84638
Leeds, Washington 84746
Lehi, Utah 84005
Levan, Juab 84639
Lewiston, Cache 84320
Liberty, Weber 84310
Lindon, Utah 84042
Loa, Wayne 84747
LOGAN, Cache
(See Page 4018)
Lyman, Wayne 84749
Lynndyl, Millard 84640
Magna, Salt Lake 84044
Mammoth, Juab 84628
Manila, Daggett 84046
Manti, Sanpete 84642
Mantua, Box Elder 84324
Mapleton, Utah 84664
Marriott Slaterville
(See Ogden)
Marriott-Slaterville City
(See Ogden)
Marysvale, Piute 84750
Mayfield, Sanpete 84643
Meadow, Millard 84644
Mendon, Cache 84325
Mexican Hat, San Juan 84531
Midvale, Salt Lake 84047
Midway, Wasatch 84049
Milford, Beaver 84751
Millcreek
(See Salt Lake City)
Millville, Cache 84326
Minersville, Beaver 84752
Moab, Grand 84532
Modena, Iron 84753
Mona, Juab 84645
Monroe, Sevier 84754
Montezuma Creek, San Juan 84534
Monticello, San Juan 84535
Monument Valley, San Juan 84536
Morgan, Morgan 84050
Moroni, Sanpete 84646
Mount Carmel, Kane 84755
Mount Pleasant, Sanpete 84647
Mountain Green, Morgan 84050
Mountain Home, Duchesne 84051
Ms City
(See Ogden)
Murray
(See Salt Lake City)
Myton, Duchesne 84052
Naples, Uintah 84078
Neola, Duchesne 84053
Nephi, Juab 84648
New Harmony, Washington 84757
Newcastle, Iron 84756
Newton, Cache 84327
Nibley, Cache 84321
North Logan, Cache 84341
North Ogden
(See Ogden)
North Salt Lake, Davis 84054
Oak City, Millard 84649
Oakley, Summit 84055
Oasis, Millard 84624
OGDEN, Weber
(See Page 4019)
Ophir, Tooele 84071
Orangeville, Emery 84537
Orderville, Kane 84758
OREM, Utah
(See Page 4024)
Ouray, Uintah 84026
Panguitch, Garfield 84759
Paradise, Cache 84328
Paragonah, Iron 84760
PARK CITY, Summit
(See Page 4026)
Park Valley, Box Elder 84329
Parowan, Iron 84761
Partoun, Tooele 84083
Payson, Utah 84651
Penrose, Box Elder 84337
Peoa, Summit 84061
Perry, Box Elder 84302
Pine Valley, Washington 84781
Pintura, Iron 84720
Plain City, Weber 84404
Pleasant Grove, Utah 84062
Pleasant View
(See Ogden)
Plymouth, Box Elder 84330
Portage, Box Elder 84331
Price, Carbon 84501
Providence, Cache 84332
PROVO, Utah
(See Page 4027)
Provo Canyon, Utah 84604
Randlett, Uintah 84063
Randolph, Rich 84064
Red Canyon, Daggett 84023
Redmond, Sevier 84652
Richfield, Sevier 84701
Richmond, Cache 84333
River Heights, Cache 84321
Riverdale, Weber 84405
Riverside, Box Elder 84334
Riverton, Salt Lake 84065
Riverton, Salt Lake 84095
Rockville, Washington 84763
Rocky Ridge Town, Juab 84645
Roosevelt, Duchesne 84066
Roy, Weber 84067
Roy, Weber 84401
Rush Valley, Tooele 84069
SAINT GEORGE, Washington
(See Page 4029)
Salem, Utah 84653
Salina, Sevier 84654
SALT LAKE CITY, Salt Lake
(See Page 4031)
SANDY, Salt Lake
(See Page 4042)
Santa Clara, Washington 84765
Santaquin, Utah 84655
Saratoga Springs, Utah 84043
Saratoga Springs, Utah 84045
Scipio, Millard 84656
Scofield, Carbon 84526
Sevier, Sevier 84766
Sigurd, Sevier 84657
Skull Valley, Tooele 84029
Slc
(See Salt Lake City)
Smithfield, Cache 84335
Snowbird, Salt Lake 84092
Snowville, Box Elder 84336
Snyderville, Summit 84098
Solitude, Salt Lake 84121
South Jordan, Salt Lake 84095
South Ogden
(See Ogden)
South Rim, Tooele 84071
South Salt Lake
(See Salt Lake City)
South Weber
(See Ogden)
Spanish Fork, Utah 84660
Spring City, Sanpete 84662
Springdale, Washington 84767
Springdale, Washington 84779
Springville, Utah 84663
Springville, Utah 84664
Ssl, Salt Lake 84165
St George
(See Saint George)
Stansbury Park, Tooele 84074
Sterling, Sanpete 84665
Stockton, Tooele 84071
Sugarville, Millard 84624
Summit, Iron 84772
Sundance, Utah 84604
Sunnyside, Carbon 84539
Sunset, Davis 84015
Sutherland, Millard 84624
Syracuse, Davis 84075
Tabiona, Duchesne 84072
Talmage, Duchesne 84073
Taylor, Weber 84401
Taylorsville, Salt Lake 84119
Teasdale, Wayne 84773
Terra, Tooele 84022
Thatcher, Box Elder 84337
Thistle, Sanpete 84629
Thompson, Grand 84540
Ticaboo, San Juan 84533
Tooele, Tooele 84074
Toquerville, Washington 84774
Torrey, Wayne 84775
Tremonton, Box Elder 84337
Trenton, Cache 84338
Tridell, Uintah 84076
Tropic, Garfield 84776
Trout Creek, Tooele 84083
Uintah
(See Ogden)
Venice, Sevier 84701
VERNAL, Uintah
(See Page 4045)
Vernon, Tooele 84080
Veyo, Washington 84782
Vineyard
(See Orem)
Virgin, Washington 84779
Wales, Sanpete 84667
Wallsburg, Wasatch 84082
Wanship, Summit 84017
Washington, Washington 84780
Washington Terrace, Weber 84405
Wellington, Carbon 84542
Wellsville, Cache 84339
Wendover, Tooele 84083
West Bountiful, Davis 84010
West Bountiful, Davis 84087
West Haven, Weber 84401
WEST JORDAN, Salt Lake
(See Page 4045)
West Point, Davis 84015
West Valley, Salt Lake 84081
West Valley City
(See West Jordan)
White Mesa, San Juan 84511
Whiterocks, Uintah 84085
Willard, Box Elder 84340
Woodland Hills, Utah 84653
Woodruff, Rich 84086
Woods Cross, Davis 84010
Woods Cross, Davis 84087
Zion National Park, Washington 84767

BOUNTIFUL UT

General Delivery 84010

POST OFFICE BOXES MAIN OFFICE STATIONS AND BRANCHES

Box No.s
All PO Boxes 84011

NAMED STREETS

Aliwood Way 84010
Amby Cir 84010
Applewood Dr 84010
Arlington Way 84010
Artistic Cir 84010
Ashley Cir 84010
Barton Ct 84010
Barton Creek Cir & Ln 84010
Beverly Way 84010
Bluebell Cir & Dr 84010
Bona Vista Cir & Dr 84010
Bonneview Dr 84010
E & W Bonneville Dr 84010
Boulton Way 84010
Bountiful Blvd 84010
Bountiful Hills Dr 84010
Bountiful Ridge Dr 84010
Brentwood Cir & Ln 84010
Bridlewood Dr 84010
Briggs Dr 84010
Browns Park Dr 84010
Cambridge Ct 84010
Canyon Creek Dr 84010
Canyon Crest Dr 84010
Canyon Estates Cir & Dr 84010
Canyon Oaks Cir 84010
Canyon Park Rd 84010
Canyon View Cir 84010
Cardiff Way 84010
Carolyn Way 84010
Carriage Ln 84010
Cassidy Cir 84010
Cave Hollow Way 84010
Cedar Cir 84010
S Censone W 84087
E & W Center St 84010
Chapel Dr 84010
Charlene Dr 84010
Chelsea Dr 84010
Chokecherry Cir & Dr 84010
Claremont Dr 84010
Clark St 84010
Concord Way 84010
Coronation Cir & Way 84010
Cottonwood Cir 84010
Councilman Cir 84087
Country Springs Cir, Dr & Ln 84010
Cove Ln 84010
Crestview Cir 84010
Crestwood Cir 84010
Dadola Dr 84010
N Davis Blvd 84010
Deborah Cir & Dr 84010
Deer Run Cir 84010
Devon Dr & Ln 84010
Devonshire Dr 84010
Eagle Glen Cir 84087
Eagleridge Dr 84010
Easthills Cir & Dr 84010
Edgehill Dr 84010
Elaine Dr 84010
Emerald Hills Dr 84010
Evergreen Cir 84010
Fair Oaks Dr 84010
Fairway Cir & Dr 84010
Fairwind Cir 84087
Fawn Ln 84010
Foothill Cir & Dr 84010
Foss Cir 84010
Franklin Cir 84010
Fremont Rd 84010
Glade Hollow Way 84010
Golf Course Dr 84010
Governors Cir & Way 84087
Granada Cir & Dr 84010
Grand Oak Cir 84010
Green Oaks Dr 84010
Heritage Dr 84010
Heritage Point Cir & Ln 84087
Hidden Hollow Ct & Dr 84010
Hidden Lake Cir & Dr 84010
Hidden Ridge Dr 84010
High Pointe Dr 84010
Highland Ct 84010
Highland Oaks Dr 84010
S Highway 89 84010
Hilltop Cir 84010
Holbrook Rd 84010
Horsley Cir 84010
Huntington Cir & Dr 84010
Indian Springs Rd 84010
Indian Trail Cir & Rd 84010
Irene Dr 84010
Jenkins Ln 84010
Jeri Dr 84010
Jessis Meadow Cir, Dr & Way 84087
Lago Vista Cir 84010
Lakecrest Rd 84010
Lakeview Dr 84010
Larsen Dr 84010
Leah Cir 84010
Lewis Park Cir, Cv & Dr 84010
Lexington Dr 84010
Lillian Cir 84010
Linden Cir, Ln & St 84010
Lorien Ct & Dr 84010
Lyman Ln 84010
Madera Hills Dr 84010
N Main St 84010
S Main St
20-20 84010
20-20 84011
50-98 84010
100-2299 84010
2300-2398 84010
2301-2849 84010
2400-2599 84010
2601-2699 84010
Maple Ln 84010
Maple Cove Dr 84010
Maple Grove Way 84010
Maple Hills Dr 84010
Maple Hollow Way 84010
Maple Ridge Dr 84010
Mapleview Dr 84010
Maxine Cir 84010
Mayors Cir 84087
Mckean Ln 84087
Meadowland Cir 84087
Meadowlark Ln
500-699 84010
900-999 84087
Medford Dr 84010
Medical Dr 84010
Mill St 84010
Millbridge Ln 84087
E & S Millbrook Way 84010
Millcreek Way 84010
Millcrest Cir 84010
Millstream Way 84010
Monarch Dr 84010
Monterey Cir 84010
E Moss Hill Dr 84010
S Mountain Crest Dr 84087
Mountain Oaks Dr 84010
S Mountain View Blvd & Ct 84087
Mueller Park Rd 84010
Newport Cir 84010
E North Canyon Rd 84010
Northcanyon Cir 84010
Northern Hills Cir & Dr 84010
Northridge Dr 84010
Oakhollow Ct 84010
Oakmont Dr 84010
Oakridge Cir, Ct, Dr & Ln 84010
Oakview Ln 84010
Oakwood Cir & Dr 84010
Ocenew Dr 84010
Olsen Way 84087
Orchard Dr & Pl 84010
Orchard Pines Loop 84010
Oxford Way 84010
W Pages Cir 84087
E Pages Ln 84010
W Pages Ln
101-197 84010
199-499 84010
500-1099 84087
Pages Pl 84010
Park Shadows Cir, Ct & Ln 84010
Park View Cir 84010
Peach Ln 84010
Penman Ln 84010
Peregrine Ln 84010
Pheasant Cir & Way 84010
Pheasant Ridge Cir 84010
Pinetree Cir 84087
Plum Tree Ln 84010
Porter Ln 84087
Presidential Dr 84087
Raintree Cir 84087
Renaissance Towne Dr 84010
Ridge Crest Cir 84010
Ridge Point Dr 84010
Ridgehill Dr 84010
Ridgehollow Dr 84010
Ridgeview Dr 84010
Ridgewood Ln & Way 84010
San Simeon Way 84010
Scenic Cir 84010
Senator Cir 84087
Sereno Cir 84010
Seville Way 84010
Shari Cir 84010
Skyline Dr 84010
Sorrento Dr 84087
Southview Cir 84010
Spring Creek Dr 84010
Spring Meadow Cir & Dr 84010
Stellaria Cir 84010
Sterling Dr 84010
N Stone Creek Cir 84010
Stone Hollow Ct & Dr 84010
Stone Ridge Cir & Dr 84010
Summer Tree Dr 84087
Summermeadow Cir & Dr 84010
Summerview Cir & Rd 84010
Summerwood Cir & Dr 84010
Sundance Cir 84010
Sunrise Pl 84010
Sunset Cir, Dr & Way 84010
Sunset Hollow Dr 84010
Sunset Loop Rd 84010
Tartarian Cir 84010
Temple Ct 84010
Temple Hill Cir 84010
Templeview Dr 84010
Terrace Dr 84010
Thunderbird Dr 84087
Tierra Vista Ct 84010
Timothy Way 84010
S & W View Point Ct & Dr 84087
Viewcrest Cir & Dr 84010
Vineyard Cir & Dr 84010
N Vintage Cir 84010
Vista Cir 84010
Westwood Rd 84010
E & W Wicker Ln 84010
Willowbrook Dr 84087
Windsor Ct & Ln 84010
Windsor Park Cir 84010
Wood Hollow Way 84010
Woodland Cir & Ln 84010
Woodland Hills Cir & Dr 84010
Woodmoor Cir & Dr 84010
Woods Dr 84010
Yarrow Cir 84010

NUMBERED STREETS

All Street Addresses 84010

CEDAR CITY UT

General Delivery 84720

POST OFFICE BOXES MAIN OFFICE STATIONS AND BRANCHES

Box No.s
1 - 3474 84721
7000 - 9963 84720

NAMED STREETS

W Aaron Tippets Rd 84721
N Abby Way 84721
N Aime Ave 84720
W Ainsworth Dr 84721
N Airport Rd 84721
N Albert Dr 84721
E Altamira Dr 84720
N Amberwood Ln 84721
Appaloosa Loop 84721
E & N Apple Blossom Ln 84721
N Arabian Way 84721
S Artifact 84720
E & N Ashdown Forest Rd 84721
N Ashlee Ct 84721
W Ashton Ct 84721
Aviation Way 84721
S Azalea Cir 84720
W Azalea Ct 84721
N Azalea Ln 84721
N Bald Eagle Dr 84721
N Bandtail Cir 84721
S Bareback Rd 84720
W, N & S Beacon Cir & Dr 84720
S Bentley Blvd 84720
E Blue Sky Dr N 84721
Bramblewood Dr 84721
Bridgewater Rd 84721
W Bristlecone Dr 84720
Brook St 84721
W Browse Rd 84720
N Buckboard Dr 84721
N Bulldog Rd 84721
N Bulloch Cir & Pl 84721
W Bumble Bee Springs Rd 84720
S Bumble Bee View Dr 84720
California Trl 84721
S Campus Dr 84720
S Canyon Dr 84720
W Canyon Rd 84721
E Canyon Commercial Ave 84721
N Canyon Ranch Dr 84721
Canyon Ridge Dr 84721
E Canyon View Dr 84721
Caplanto 84720
S & W Carmel Canyon Cir & Dr 84720
Carmel Estates Cir & Dr 84720
S Carmel Ridge Cir 84720
W Carousel Cir 84720
S Casa Loma Ln 84720
N Cedar Blvd 84721
Cedar Knls 84720
Cedar Knls N 84720
Cedar Knls S 84720
Cedar Knls W 84720
E Cedar Berry Ln 84721
S Cedar Bluffs Dr 84720
S & W Cedar Hills Cir & Dr 84720
Cedar View Dr 84721
Cedarwood Cir, Ln & Ter 84720
E Cellowood Ln 84721
E & W Center St 84720
N Chandler Dr 84721
S Chaparral Dr 84720
W Church St 84720
Churchfield Ln 84721
N Cimarron Cir 84720
Circleway Dr 84720
N & W Clark Pkwy N 84721
N & W Cliffrose Cir, Dr & Ln 84721
W Clubhouse Loop 84720
Coal Creek Rd 84721
E & N Cobblecreek Dr 84721
W Cody Cir & Dr 84720
E, W & N College Ave & Way 84720
W Columbia Dr 84721
Columbia Way 84720
N Commerce Center Dr 84721
Comstock Rd 84720
W Cookie Jar Cir 84720
E & N Cottontail Cir & Dr 84721
W, N & E Cottonwood Cir, Dr & Ln 84721
N & S Cove Dr 84720
W, N & S Cove Canyon Cir & Dr 84720
W Cove Heights Cir 84720
W Cove View Dr 84720
N Covered Wagon Dr 84721
W Crescent Heights Dr 84720
W Crestview Cir 84720
S & W Cross Hollow Dr & Rd 84720
N Cypress Ln 84721
E & N Dana Dr 84721
Desert Pines Dr 84720
S Dewey Ave 84720
Dl Sargent Dr 84721
N Double Tree Way 84721
N Driftwood Ln 84721
S & W Eagle Ridge Loop 84720
S East Canyon Dr 84720
S Eastgate Dr 84720
N Elderwood Ln 84721
N Enoch Rd 84721
Escalante Trl 84721
N Fairview Dr 84721
N Fairway Dr 84721
E Fenwick Way 84721
E Fiddlers Canyon Rd 84721
E Fiddlers Ranch Rd 84721
Fir St 84720
N Foothill Dr 84721
N Forest Cir 84721
S Fountain Dr 84720
Frontier Cir 84721
N & W Gemini Meadows Ln 84721
S George Perry Rd 84720
W Ginny Way 84721
S Glen Canyon Dr 84720
Gold Dust Trl 84721
Golden Leaf Cir 84721
S Graff Farm Frontage Rd 84720
Green Acre Cir 84721
W Greenslake Dr 84720
N Guidelight Dr 84720
Half Mile Rd 84721
N Halterman Rd 84721
S Hamilton Dr 84720
W & N Hampshire Cir & Dr 84721
N Harbor Cir 84720
W Harding Ave 84720
Harmony Ln 84720
S Hawk Dr 84720
N Hawthorne Ln 84721
W Heather Ln 84720
N Heather Hue Rd 84721
S Heavenly View Cir 84720
E Heritage Dr 84721
Hidden Hills Dr & Loop 84720
E Hide A Way Rd 84721
E & N Highland Cir & Dr 84721
E Highland Trails Rd 84721
W Highway 56 84720
E Highway 91 84721
N Highway 91 84721
S Highway 91 84720
N Hillcrest Cir 84721
S Hillcrest Dr 84720
W Hillcrest Dr 84720
Hillside Pl 84721
E Hillview Dr 84721
W Holly Cir 84720
E Homestead Blvd 84721
W Hoover Ave 84720
W Horse Aly 84721
N Horseshoe Dr 84721
House Rock Cir & Dr 84720
E & N Hovi Hills Dr 84721
W Industrial Rd 84721
W Industry Way 84721
S Interstate Dr 84720
N Iron Springs Rd 84721
Irontown Lodc Mt Rd 84720
Ironwood Cir 84720
Josie Cir 84720
S & W Juniper Dr 84720
N Juniper Ridge Rd 84721
Kanarra Mountain Rd 84720
E Katie Ct 84721
Kayenta Cir 84720
W Kendall Ct 84721
S Kimberly Ct 84720
S & W Kingsbury Dr 84720
Kittyhawk Dr 84721
Knoll St 84721
Knoll Ridge Dr 84721
E La Croix Cir 84721
S Laurie Ln 84720
Legacy Park Ave 84720
N Lerae Ln 84721
N Liberty Cir 84720
S Little Pinto Creek Rd 84720
S Lobo Ln 84720
W Lone Rock Cir 84720
W Longhorn 84721
N Lovell Ln 84721
N Lumberjack 84721
N Lund Hwy 84721
Lunt Cir 84721
N Magnolia Dr 84721
N Mahogany Cir 84721
N Main St
1-7 84720
9-199 84720
200-300 84721
302-2698 84721
333-333 84720
333-2699 84721
S Main St 84720
Maple Cir & Ln 84721
N Maplewood Ln 84721
Marble Canyon Cir & Dr 84720
N Marshal Trl 84721
E & N Matchstick Way 84721
N Matheson Way 84721
S Maverick Way 84720
Maxwell Rd 84721
E Mcarthur Ave 84720
Meadow Dr & St 84720
Meadowbrook Dr 84721
N Meadowlark Ln 84721
Melling Dr 84721
S & W Mesa Hills Dr 84720
E & W Midvalley Rd 84721
E & N Mill Hollow Way 84721
N Millard Ln 84721
Millstone Cir 84721
N Minersville Hwy 84721
N Monarch Cir & Dr 84721
Monterey Dr 84720
Moonlight Dr 84720
N Morgan Dr 84721
E Moriah 84721
Morningside Cir 84720
N Mountain Valley Trl 84721
Mountain View Cir 84721
S Mountain View Dr 84720
W Mountain View Dr 84720
N Mule Train Dr 84721
Mustang 84721
N Native Dancer Dr 84721
N Nature View Dr 84720
E Nichols Canyon Cir & Rd 84721
W North Cedar Blvd 84721
Northern View Dr 84720
Northfield Rd 84721
W Old Beaty Ranch Rd 84720
W Old Irontown Rd 84720
E Old Mill Rd 84721
N Old Scout Trl 84721
N & W Pachea Cir & Trl 84720
Padre Cir & Dr 84720
N Paiute Dr 84721
Palomino Dr 84721
S Panorama Dr 84720
E Paradise Canyon Rd 84720
N & W Park Ave 84721
N Parkside Dr 84721
E Parkway Dr 84721
S Peaceful Ct 84720
N Pearly Ln 84721
Pinecone Dr 84720
Pinewood Dr W 84720
S Pinto Cir 84720
W Pinto Cir 84721
E Pinto Rd 84720
W Pinto Rd 84720
Pintura Water 84720
N Pioneer Dr 84721
N Plandark W 84721
Port Orr Ln 84721
E Primrose Ln 84721
N Production Rd 84721
N Prospector 84721
S Providence Center Dr 84720
N Quarterhorse Ln 84721
E Rachel Ln 84721
E Rainbow Canyon Dr 84721
E Ravine Rd 84721
N Red Cedar Cir 84721
N Redwood Ln 84721
S & W Regency Rd 84720
S Ridge Rd 84720
Ridgeview Cir 84721
S Ridgeview Loop 84720
N Ridgeway Dr 84721
N Riverwood Ln 84721
Robbers Roost Ln 84720
E & N Rose Cir & Ln 84721
S Rose Hill Rd 84720
W & N Rosewood Cir & Ln 84721
N Roundabout Way 84720
Rountree Dr 84720

/ Royal Hunte Dr 84720
/ Saddleback Rd 84720
. Saddleback View Dr . 84721
age Cir & Dr 84720
/ Sage Hills Dr 84721
Sage View Ct 84721
agebrush Dr 84721
& N Sagewood Ln ... 84721
Saint James Pl 84720
anta Fe Trl 84721
Sawmill St 84721
cenic Dr 84721
/ Secretariat Way 84721
Serviceberry Cir 84721
Shady Place Ln 84721
hanna Ln 84720
heltie Ln 84721
/ Shetland Cir 84721
Shirley Ln 84721
hurtz Canyon Dr 84720
/ Signal Cir 84720
/ Silvercrest Cir 84720
Silverspur Dr 84720
Skyline Dr 84721
/ Skyview Dr 84720
Smokey Trail Way ... 84721
nowfield Rnch 84720
South Pointe Cir 84721
outhern Homestead
lvd 84721
outhern Utah
niversity 84720
outhern View Dr 84720
Southview Dr 84720
panish Trails Dr 84721
Splinter Wood Ln 84721
Spring Ave 84721
pring Canyon Rd 84720
pruce St 84720
Staci Ct 84720
tagecoach Ln 84721
Sugar Plum Cir 84721
Sumack Cir 84721
Summer Rain Cir 84721
ummer Tree Dr 84721
ummit Frontage Rd ... 84721
Sunbow St 84721
undown Ave 84720
Sunny Brook Row 84721
& W Sunnyside Dr ... 84720
Sunnyvale Cir 84720
unnyview Rd 84720
unrise Ave & Dr 84721
Sunset Dr 84720
Sunset Dr 84720
Sunset Dr 84720
Sunset Rd 84721
& W Sunset Pointe
r 84720
& N Sunshine Cir &
n 84721
ju 84720
Sycamore Ln 84721
Taba Dr 84720
Tahquitz Dr 84720
alon Cir & Dr 84720
amarisk Cir 84721
& W Thoroughbred
ay 84721
hree Fountains Dr 84720
pple Rd 84720
omahawk Dr 84721
Torrey Pines Cir 84720
iple Deuce Cir 84721
Tumbleweed Dr 84721
niversity Ave & Blvd .. 84720
tah Trl 84721
Vaquero Way 84720
eterans Memorial Dr .. 84721
Village Green Rd 84721
& N Wagon Trail Dr .. 84721
Wagon Wheel Dr 84721
Wecco Rd 84721
edgewood Cir & Ln ... 84721
Welch Cir 84721
West Canyon Dr 84720
N Western View Dr 84721
N & S Westview Dr 84720
Westward Ave 84721
Wildflower Ln 84720
N Wildrose 84720
N Wonser 84721
N Wood Cir 84721
N Woodland Pointe
Cir 84721

NUMBERED STREETS

E 4-D Bar Cir 84721
N 100 E
2-98 84720
100-199 84720
200-4799 84721
2300-4999 84721
4200-4900 84720
4902-5198 84720
N 100 W
1-199 84720
100-199 84721
200-499 84721
300-399 84721
5001-5199 84720
S 100 E 84720
S 100 W
1-67 84720
300-399 84720
W 1000 N
200-6699 84721
4100-4299 84720
W 100 S
3900-5299 84720
4300-6099 84720
S 1020 W 84720
S 1025 W 84720
W 1020 South Cir 84720
W 1045 N 84721
N 1050 W
1-199 84720
3500-3599 84721
W 1050 N 84721
N 1070 W 84721
W 1070 S 84720
E 11000 N 84721
N 1100 W 84721
S 110 W 84720
S 1100 W
300-799 84720
W 1100 N 84721
N 1120 E 84721
W 1125 N 84721
W 1120 S
1200-1399 84720
W 1125 S
4700-5299 84720
N 1150 W 84720
W 1150 N 84721
W 1150 S 84720
S 11600 W 84720
E & N 1170 N & E 84721
S 1175 W 84720
W 1175 N 84721
S 11900 W 84720
W 1200 S 84720
N 1225 W 84720
W 1225 N 84721
W 1225 S 84720
E 1225 Cir N 84721
W 125 N 84720
W 1250 N 84721
S 1265 W 84720
S 12675 W 84720
S 12700 W 84720
400-599 84720
W 1275 N 84721
W 1275 S 84720
E 1275 Cir N 84721
W 1300 N 84721
W 1325 N 84721
W 1325 S 84720
W 1350 N 84721
W 1350 S 84720
S 13600 W 84720
W 1375 N 84721
W 1380 S 84720
N 1400 E 84721
N 1400 W 84721
S 14000 W 84720
1-299 84720
W 1400 N 84721
W 1400 S 84720
W 1425 N 84721
W 1420 S 84720
N & W 1450 W & N 84721
W 1475 N 84721
N & W 1500 W & N 84721
600-4599 84721
S 150 E 84720
S 150 W 84720
W 150 N 84720
W 150 S 84720
W 1525 N 84721
W 1525 S 84720
N 1550 W 84720
W 1550 N 84721
N 1575 E 84721
W 1575 S 84720
E 1600 N 84721
N 1600 E 84721
N 1600 W 84721
W 1600 N 84721
W 1600 S 84720
N 1600 North Access
Rd 84721
N 1630 E 84721
S 1650 W 84720
W 1650 N 84721
W 165 S 84720
W 1650 S
1200-1499 84720
W 1675 N 84721
N 170 E 84721
N 1700 W 84721
S 170 W 84720
W 1700 S 84720
W 1725 N 84721
S 17300 W 84720
S 17475 W 84720
N 175 W
1500-2999 84721
N 1750 W
4600-4799 84721
S 1750 W 84720
1200-1499 84720
W 175 S
3900-4199 84720
N 1765 E 84721
S 17675 W 84720
S 17725 W 84720
W 1775 N 84721
W 1775 S 84720
S 17800 W 84720
S 17825 W 84720
S 17900 W 84720
N 1800 E 84721
W 1800 N 84721
W 1800 S 84720
S 18100 W 84720
S 1840 W 84720
N 1850 W 84720
S 1850 W 84720
W 1850 N 84721
S 18700 W 84720
N 1900 E 84721
W 1900 S 84720
W 1925 N 84721
E 1935 N 84721
S 1950 W 84720
W 1950 N 84721
W 1950 S 84720
S 1950 West Cir 84720
E 200 N 84720
E 200 S 84720
N 200 E
1-199 84720
4900-4999 84721
N 200 W
1-199 84720
251-4999 84721
S 200 E 84720
S 200 W 84720
W 200 N
1-5499 84720
W 2000 N
400-599 84721
W 200 S
1-91 84720
W 2000 S
7600-11899 84720
E 2015 N 84721
N 2050 W 84720
S 2050 W 84720
W 2050 N 84721
S 2075 W 84720
W 2075 N 84721
N 2100 E 84721
E 2100 North Cir 84721
N 2125 W 84720
N 2150 W 84721
W 2150 N 84721
W 2150 S 84720
E 2150 North Cir 84721
N 2175 W 84721
W 2175 S 84720
E 2200 N 84721
N 2200 W 84721
W 2200 N 84721
W 2200 S 84720
W 2210 S 84720
N & W 2225 W & N 84721
N 2225 West Cir 84721
E 2250 N 84721
N 225 W 84721
S 225 E 84720
S 225 W 84720
W 225 N 84720
W 2250 S 84720
N 2275 W 84721
W 2280 S 84720
N 230 W 84721
N 2300 W 84721
N 2325 W 84721
E 2350 N 84721
N 2375 W 84721
N & S 2380 84720
N 2400 W 84721
W 2400 N 84721
W 2400 S 84720
E 2400 North Pkwy 84721
N 2425 W 84721
W 2450 N 84721
N 2475 W
100-299 84720
4200-4999 84721
S 2475 W 84720
N 25 E 84721
S 25 E 84720
W 25 N 84720
W 25 S 84720
N 250 E 84721
N & W 2500 W & N 84721
W 250 N
1600-1799 84721
3900-4299 84720
W 250 S 84720
N 2525 W 84721
E & W 2530 84721
W 2575 N 84721
N 2600 W 84721
W 2600 S 84720
W 2650 N 84721
W 265 S 84720
W 2675 N 84721
N 2700 W 84721
W 2700 S 84720
E 275 N 84721
W 275 N 84721
E & W 2775 84721
N 2774 W 84721
N 280 W 84721
N 2800 W
3400-5399 84721
W 2800 N 84721
W 2800 S 84720
W 2825 North Cir 84721
S 2875 W 84720
W 2875 N 84721
W 2875 North Cir 84721
N 2900 W 84721
W 2925 North Cir 84721
N 2950 W 84721
W 30 N 84720
N 300 E 84720
N 300 W
1-199 84720
200-699 84721
N 3000 W
5100-5399 84721
S 300 E 84720
S 300 W 84720
W 3000 N
100-2099 84721
300-399 84721
4000-4399 84720
W 300 S
2700-5599 84720
W 3000 S
13100-18899 84720
E 3025 N 84721
N 3100 W 84721
N 3175 W 84721
W 3200 N 84721
W 320 S 84720
W 3200 S
5100-6049 84720
E 325 S 84720
N 3250 W 84721
W 325 South Cir 84720
W 3275 N 84721
N 330 W 84721
N 3300 W 84721
N 3325 W 84721
W 3345 N 84721
W 3350 N 84721
W 3380 N 84721
N 3400 W 84721
W 3400 S 84720
W 3415 S 84720
N & W 3425 W & N 84721
N 3450 W 84721
S 3450 W 84720
W 3450 N 84721
W 3450 S 84720
E & N 3475 N & W 84721
N 350 E 84721
N & W 3500 W & N 84721
W 350 S 84720
S 3525 W 84720
N 3525 West Cir 84721
N & W 3550 W & N 84721
N 3575 W 84721
E 3600 N 84721
N 3600 W 84721
W 3600 N 84721
W 3600 S 84720
N 3625 W 84721
N 3650 W 84721
W 3695 N 84721
N 3700 W 84721
W 3700 N 84721
W 370 S 84720
W 3700 S
5200-5299 84720
W 3750 N 84721
375 N & S 84720
N 3775 W 84721
W 3770 N 84721
N 3800 W 84721
W 3800 S 84720
E 3810 N 84721
N 3900 W 84721
S 3900 W 84720
E 400 N 84721
E 400 S 84720
N 4000 W
1-199 84720
100-199 84720
200-2699 84721
5500-5599 84721
S 400 E 84720
S 400 W
1100-1299 84720
2500-3099 84720
W 400 N
100-1699 84721
2100-5099 84720
2300-4299 84721
5700-6099 84721
W 400 S
2-72 84720
5301-5897 84720
E 4025 N 84721
N 4050 W
1-399 84720
400-498 84721
S 4050 W 84720
N 4100 W
1-399 84720
2801-2997 84721
2999-5699 84721
S 4100 W 84720
W 4100 N 84721
N 4125 W 84720
N 4150 W 84720
S 4175 W 84720
E 4200 N 84721
N 4200 W
1-399 84720
500-5999 84721
S 4200 W 84720
W 4200 N 84721
W 420 S 84720
17500-17599 84720
N 4225 W 84721
S 4225 W 84720
E 4250 N 84721
N 4250 W 84720
S 4250 W 84720
W 425 N 84721
W 425 S 84720
N 4275 W
1-199 84720
500-5999 84721
N 4300 W
100-299 84720
5000-5599 84721
S 4300 W 84720
W 4300 N 84721
N 4325 W 84721
E 4350 N 84721
N 4350 W 84721
W 4350 S 84720
N 4375 W 84721
S 4375 W 84720
W 4375 N 84721
W 4390 N 84721
E 440 S 84720
N & W 4400 W & N 84721
S 4425 W 84720
S 4450 W 84720
N 4475 W 84721
S 4475 W 84720
W 45 N 84720
N 4500 W 84721
N 450 W
1400-1499 84721
S 450 W 84720
S 4575 W 84720
N & W 4600 W & N 84721
W 460 S 84720
N 4650 W 84721
N & W 4675 W & N 84721
E 4700 N 84720
S 4700 W 84720
W 4700 N 84721
W 4725 N 84721
N 475 E 84721
N 475 W 84721
S 475 W 84720
W 4750 N 84721
4000-4187 84721
W 475 S 84720
W 4800 N 84721
S 4850 W 84720
W 4850 N 84721
W 4875 N 84721
W 4875 S 84720
S 4900 W 84720
W 4900 N 84721
E 4930 N 84721
E & W 4950 84721
E 4960 N 84721
50 N & S 84720
E & W 5000 84721
N 500 E 84721
N 500 W
100-199 84720
200-396 84721
398-398 84721
S 500 E 84720
S 500 W 84720
W 500 N 84721
W 500 S 84720
E 5020 N 84721
W 5025 N 84721
E 5030 N 84721
S 5050 W 84720
W 5050 N 84721
W 5075 N 84721
E 5080 N 84721
E 5100 N 84721
S 5100 W 84720
W 5100 S 84720
W 5125 N 84721
E 5140 N 84721
N 515 E 84721
S 515 W 84720
W 5150 N 84721
S 5175 W 84720
E 5200 N 84721
N 5200 W 84721
S 5200 W 84720
W 5200 N 84721
S 5225 W 84720
E 5250 N 84721
N 525 E 84721
W 525 N 84721
W 525 S 84720
W 5275 N 84721
N 5300 W
1-399 84720
800-4699 84721
S 5300 W 84720
W 5300 N 84721
W 5325 N 84721
W 535 S 84720
S 540 E 84720
W 5400 N 84721
S 5425 W 84720
W 546 S 84720
W 55 S 84720
N 5500 W
2-399 84720
700-799 84721
N 550 W
1800-2699 84721
S 550 W 84720
W 5500 N 84721
S 555 W 84720
W 5550 N 84721
N 5575 W 84721
N & W 5600 W & N 84721
W 560 N 84721
N 5675 W 84721
N 5700 W 84720
S 5700 W 84720
W 5700 N 84721
E 575 N 84721
W 577 N 84721
S 580 E 84720
S 580 W 84720
W 580 N 84721
W 5875 N 84721
N & W 5900 W & N 84721
N 600 E 84721
N 600 W
100-199 84720
200-1399 84721
S 600 W 84720
W 6000 N 84721
3300-3399 84721
5300-5399 84720

5500-6099 84721
W 600 S 84720
E 600 South Cir 84720
N 6100 W 84721
S 6100 W 84720
W 6100 N 84721
S 6125 W 84720
W 6200 N 84721
E 625 N 84721
N 625 W 84721
S 625 W 84720
W 625 N 84721
W 625 S 84720
N 6300 W 84721
S 6300 W 84720
W 6300 N 84721
E 6400 N 84721
S 640 W 84720
N 6425 W 84721
N 6450 W 84721
N 6500 W
1000-1099 84721
N 650 W
1200-1399 84721
S 6500 W 84720
W 650 S 84720
E 650 South Cir 84720
N 6525 W 84721
N 6550 W 84721
E & W 6600 84721
N 6625 W 84721
N 6650 W 84721
E 670 S 84720
N 6700 W 84721
S 6700 W 84720
N 6725 W 84721
N 6724 W 84721
N 6775 W 84721
E 680 S 84720
N 6900 W 84721
N 700 W
1-97 84720
99-199 84720
200-399 84721
S 700 W 84720
W 7000 N 84721
3700-3899 84721
W 700 S 84720
N 725 W 84721
S 7300 W 84720
W 7400 N 84721
S 75 E 84720
W 750 N 84721
S 7700 W 84720
E 775 N 84721
N 775 W 84721
W 775 S 84720
S 780 W 84720
E 800 N 84721
N 800 W
1-199 84720
200-699 84721
S 800 W 84720
W 800 N 84721
W 800 S 84720
S 8100 W 84720
E & W 820 84720
S 8300 W 84720
W 850 N 84721
S 860 W 84720
S 8900 W 84720
W 895 S 84720
W 90 S 84720
N 900 W
2-98 84720
100-199 84720
200-399 84721
S 900 W 84720
W 900 N 84721
S 9100 W 84720
S 9300 W 84720
N 935 W 84721
N 940 E 84721
S 940 W 84720
W 940 N 84721
N 950 E 84721
S 9500 W 84720
W 970 N 84721
W 970 South Cir 84720
W 975 S 84720
W 995 S 84720

CLEARFIELD UT

General Delivery 84015

POST OFFICE BOXES MAIN OFFICE STATIONS AND BRANCHES

Box No.s
1 - 9998 84089
160001 - 169998 84016

NAMED STREETS

Airlane Dr 84015
Ann St 84015
Aspen Cv 84015
Barlow St 84015
Birch Cir & St 84015
Bruce St 84015
Canyon Cv 84015
Center St 84015
E Charrans 84016
Chelemes Way 84015
E & S Chris Cir 84015
Cranefield Rd 84015
S Demetro Dr 84015
Depot St 84015
Eurasian Crane Rd 84015
Fern Dr 84015
S Freeport Industrial Pkwy 84015
Grey Crown Crane Dr & Ln W 84015
Hilltop Dr 84015
Hooded Crane Cir, Ct, Dr & Ln 84015
E & S James Cir & St 84015
Jenny Ln 84015
Katies Way 84015
E Lakeview Dr 84015
Legend Hills Dr 84015
Lindon St 84015
Locust St 84015
Lynnwood Dr 84015
N Main St
1-99 84015
98-98 84089
100-998 84015
101-2699 84015
N Main St N 84015
S Main St 84015
Maple St 84015
Marilyn Dr 84015
Pacific Ave 84015
Parc Cir 84015
Parkway Dr 84015
Patrol Rd 84016
Pine Creek Rd 84015
Ridge Point Dr 84015
Ross Dr 84015
E & S Sam Cir 84015
Sarus Crane Dr 84015
Stanley Crane Dr 84015
S State St 84015
Sycamore Cir 84015
N & S Terrace Dr 84015
University Park Blvd 84015
Valhalla Dr 84015
Vickie Ln 84015
Villa Dr 84015
Vine Cir & St 84015

NUMBERED STREETS

13th St 84016
E, N, S & W 100 N, W, E & S 84015
E, N, S & W 1000 S, W, E & N 84015
W 1010 N 84015
S & W 1025 W & N 84015
W 1020 N 84015
W 1045 S 84015
E, N, S & W 1050 S, W, E & N 84015
W 1055 N 84015
N & W 1060 W & N 84015
N, S & W 1075 W, E & N 84015
W 1080 N 84015
W 1090 N 84015
E, N, S & W 1100 S, W & N 84015
N 1110 W 84015
W 1115 N 84015
N 1120 W 84015
N 1125 W 84015
W 1130 N 84015
W 1145 N 84015
E, N, S & W 1150 S, W & N 84015
N 1155 W 84015
N 1160 W 84015
N 1170 W 84015
N 1175 W 84015
N & W 1185 W & N 84015
N, S & W 1200 W, E, N & S 84015
N 1205 W 84015
E 1225 S 84015
N & W 1220 W & N 84015
N & W 1235 W & N 84015
N & W 1230 W & N 84015
W 1240 N 84015
E, N, S & W 1250 S, W, E & N 84015
N & S 125 E & W 84015
N & W 1260 W & N 84015
N 1275 W 84015
N 1285 W 84015
S 1280 W 84015
E, N, S & W 1300 S, W & N 84015
N 1320 W 84015
N & S 1325 84015
N 1335 W 84015
W 1340 N 84015
E, N, S & W 1350 S, W, E & N 84015
N & W 1360 W & N 84015
N & S 1375 84015
W 1370 N 84015
N & W 1385 W & N 84015
N 1390 W 84015
W 1395 N 84015
E 1400 S 84015
N 140 W 84015
N 1410 W 84015
N 1415 W 84015
N & W 1420 W & N 84015
S & W 1425 W & N 84015
N 1435 W 84015
N & W 1445 W & N 84015
E, N, S & W 1450 S, W & N 84015
W 1460 N 84015
W 1470 N 84015
W 1475 N 84015
S 1480 W 84015
N, S & W 150 W, E, N & S 84015
N 1500 W 84015
E 1525 S 84015
W 1520 N 84015
N 1535 W 84015
S & W 1550 W & N 84015
N 1575 W 84015
W 1570 N 84015
W 1580 N 84015
N & W 1590 W & N 84015
W 1595 N 84015
N, S & W 1600 W, E, N & S 84015
N 160 W 84015
N 1615 W 84015
S & W 1625 E & N 84015
W 1620 N 84015
W 1635 N 84015
W 1630 N 84015
W 1640 N 84015
S & W 1650 E & N 84015
N & S 1660 84015
W 1675 N 84015
W 1680 N 84015
E 1700 S
2-1098 84015
391-699 84015
391-391 84016
N 1700 W 84015
S 1700 W 84015
W 170 N 84015
1100-2900 84015
W 1700 S
20-22 84016
50-999 84015
N 1720 W 84015
N & W 1725 W & N 84015
N 1735 W 84015
W 1730 N 84015
W 1740 N 84015
E 1750 S 84015
N 175 W 84015
N 1775 W 84015
E, N & W 1800 S, W & N 84015
W 180 N 84015
N 1825 W 84015
W 1835 N 84015
W 1850 N 84015
W 1860 N 84015
N 1875 W 84015
W 1870 N 84015
W 1890 N 84015
E, N & W 1900 S, W & N 84015
W 1915 N 84015
E & W 1925 N & S 84015
N & W 1930 W & N 84015
N 1940 W 84015
E & W 1950 N & S 84015
N & W 1960 W & N 84015
E 1975 S 84015
W 1985 N 84015
W 1980 S 84015
E, N, S & W 200 S, W, E & N 84015
E, N, S & W 2000 S, W, E & N 84015
W 2005 N 84015
E & W 2025 N & S 84015
N 2030 W 84015
E, N & W 2050 S, W & N 84015
W 2060 N 84015
N 2070 W 84015
W 2075 N 84015
W 2080 N 84015
W 2085 N 84015
N 2095 W 84015
N 2090 W 84015
E, N & W 2100 S, W & N 84015
N & W 2125 W & N 84015
W 2120 N 84015
N & W 2140 W & N 84015
E, N & W 2150 S, W & N 84015
N 2155 W 84015
N 2165 W 84015
W 2175 N 84015
N 2195 W 84015
E, N & W 2200 S, W & N 84015
E, N & W 2225 S, W & N 84015
N & W 2220 W & N 84015
W 2240 N 84015
E 225 S 84015
W 2250 N 84015
W 2265 N 84015
E & N 2275 S & W 84015
N 2290 W 84015
N 2300 W 84015
E 2325 S 84015
N & W 2340 W & N 84015
N & W 2350 W & N 84015
N 2360 W 84015
W 2375 N 84015
E, N & W 2400 S, W & N 84015
N 2405 W 84015
W 2415 N 84015
N 2430 W 84015
E 2450 S 84015
N & W 2475 W & N 84015
25 N & S 84015
E, N, S & W 250 S, W & N 84015
E, N & W 2500 S, W & N 84015
E 2525 S 84015
N 2530 W 84015
E 2550 S 84015
N & W 2575 W & N 84015
N 2585 W 84015
N & W 2580 W & N 84015
N 2595 W 84015
E 2600 S 84015
N 2615 W 84015
N 2625 W 84015
N 2645 W 84015
N & W 2650 W & N 84015
W 265 N 84015
N 2660 W 84015
E 2675 S 84015
N 2700 W 84015
N 2710 W 84015
N 2740 W 84015
N 2750 W 84015
N 275 W 84015
N & S 2775 84015
S 2770 W 84015
N 2800 W 84015
N 2825 W 84015
N 2835 W 84015
S 2830 W 84015
N 2845 W 84015
N 2850 W 84015
N 2865 W 84015
N 2870 W 84015
N & S 2875 84015
N 2890 W 84015
N 2895 W 84015
N & S 2900 84015
N 2925 W 84015
N 2930 W 84015
N 2950 W 84015
N 2975 W 84015
E, N, S & W 300 E, N, S & W 84015
N & S 3000 84015
N 3025 W 84015
N 3050 W 84015
N 3060 W 84015
N 3100 W 84015
N 3125 W 84015
N 3150 W 84015
N 3200 W 84015
N 3225 W 84015
N 325 W 84015
N 3275 W 84015
N 3335 W 84015
N 3330 W 84015
N 3425 W 84015
N 3420 W 84015
N 3455 W 84015
E, N, S & W 350 S, W, E & N 84015
N 3500 W 84015
N 360 W 84015
N 3600 W 84015
N 3650 W 84015
N 3675 W 84015
N 375 W 84015
N 3775 W 84015
N 3830 W 84015
N 3850 W 84015
N 390 W 84015
N 40 W 84015
E, N, S & W 400 S, W, E & N 84015
N 4000 W 84015
N 4050 W 84015
N 4100 W 84015
N 4150 W 84015
N 425 W 84015
N 4300 W 84015
N 4325 W 84015
N 4350 W 84015
E, N, S & W 450 S, W, E & N 84015
N & S 4500 84015
N 4550 W 84015
N 4600 W 84015
N 4625 W 84015
N 4700 W 84015
W 470 N 84015
N 4750 W 84015
N & W 475 W & N 84015
N 4850 W 84015
N 4875 W 84015
N 4920 W 84015
N 4950 W 84015
N, S & W 50 W, E, N & S 84015
E, N, S & W 500 E, N, S & W 84015
N 5000 W 84015
W 520 N 84015
E, N, S & W 525 S, W & N 84015
E 550 S 84015
W 570 N 84015
N & S 575 E & W 84015
N 600 W 84015
N 625 W 84015
N 630 W 84015
E, N, S & W 650 N, W & E 84015
N 660 W 84015
N & W 670 W & N 84015
N & W 675 W & N 84015
N 690 W 84015
E, N, S & W 700 S, W, E & N 84015
N 720 W 84015
N 725 W 84015
N 730 W 84015
W 735 N 84015
N 75 W 84015
E, N, S & W 750 S, W, E & N 84015
N 770 W 84015
N 775 W 84015
N 780 W 84015
E 800 S 84015
N 810 W 84015
N 820 W 84015
N 825 W 84015
N 840 W 84015
N & W 850 W & S 84015
N 865 W 84015
N & W 870 W & N 84015
N & S 875 E & W 84015
N 890 W 84015
W 90 N 84015
E 900 S 84015
W 910 N 84015
E & W 925 N & S 84015
W 930 N 84015
E, N & W 950 S, W & N 84015
W 955 N 84015
W 960 N 84015
N 970 W 84015
N & W 975 W & S 84015
W 985 N 84015

LAYTON UT

General Delivery 8404

POST OFFICE BOXES MAIN OFFICE STATIONS AND BRANCHES

Box No.s
All PO Boxes 8404

NAMED STREETS

Adams St 8404
N Adamswood Rd 8404
N & W Afton Cir 8404
Aircraft Ave 8404
Alder St 8404
Alex Dr 8404
Alfred Dr 8404
E & N Allanwood Pl & Rd 8404
Amethyst St 8404
N & S Angel St 8404
Ann St 8404
E Antelope Dr
1-849 8404
850-2600 8404
2602-2698 8404
W Antelope Dr 8404
S Arbor Way 8404
Arnold Dr 8404
N Artists Way 8404
Ash Dr 8404
Aspen St 8404
Aspen Way 8404
Aspen East Dr 8404
Atherton Way 8404
E Avian Way 8404
Balsam Dr 8404
Barbara St 8404
Barrington Way 8404
Beacon Ave 8404
E & N Beechwood Dr 8404
N & W Belvedere Way 8404
Bennett St 8404
Bing Cherry Way 8404
Birch Cir 8404
Blue Sage Ln 8404
Blue Spruce Dr 8404
Bonne Way 8404
Boulder Dr 8404
Boulder Creek Ln 8404
Boyce Cir 8404
Boynton Rd 8404
Brady Way 8404
Brent Ave 8404
N Bridge Ct 8404
Bridge Park Way 8404
Bridgecreek Ln 8404
Bridgeview Dr 8404
Brinton Cir & Way 8404
N Broadwing Dr 8404
N Brom Cir 8404
Bruce Cir 8404
Cambridge Cir 8404
E & N Canyon Creek Cir 8404
E Canyon Rim Dr 8404
Canyon View Dr 8404
Carol Dr 8404
N & W Celia Cir & Way 8404
Chapel St 8404
E & N Cherry Cir & Ln 8404
Cherry Meadows Ln 8404
N Cherry Stem Cir 8404
Cherrywood Dr 8404
Cheryle Way 8404
Child Dr 8404
Church St 8404
N Church St 8404
Cistena Cir 8404

lara St 84041
Clark St 84041
& S Clearwater Ct &
r 84041
Clearwater Falls Dr 84041
liff Pl 84041
lyde St 84041
oates Ave 84041
olchester Ct & Rd 84040
old Creek Way 84041
olonial Ave & St 84041
ook Dr 84041
orral Dr 84040
Cottage Way 84041
ountry Creek Dr 84041
ountry Hills Dr 84040
ountry Oaks Dr 84041
ountry View Way 84041
ove Cir & Ln 84040
owley St 84041
raftsman Ct 84041
reekside Dr 84041
& S Creekview Dr 84041
Crescent Cir 84040
restwood Rd 84040
ross St 84041
ushing Way 84041
aley Ave 84041
an Dr 84040
arlington Way 84041
avis Dr 84041
awson St 84041
eer Run Ln 84040
eere Valley Dr 84040
eere View Dr 84040
elayne Cir 84041
Diamond St 84041
ixie Ave & St 84041
East Lisa St 84040
Eastcrest Dr 84040
astside Dr 84040
dgehill Cir 84040
gan St 84041
llison St 84041
lm St 84041
merald Dr
1-299 84041
1000-1098 84040
1100-1599 84040
1601-1699 84040
ngstrom Way 84041
vans Cove Loop 84041
verette St 84041
vergreen Ln 84040
& S Fairfield Rd 84041
airmont Ln 84041
& N Falcon Way 84040
ernwood Cir & Dr 84040
Fiddlers Creek St 84040
ield Stone Way 84041
lint St 84041
oothill Way 84040
orbes St 84041
Forest Creek Ln 84041
orest Ridge Dr 84040
& S Fort Ln 84041
ox Run 84041
rancis Ave 84041
Franklin Rd 84040
eemont Way 84041
arden Ln 84041
arnet St 84041
Gentile St
1-1099 84041
1100-2899 84040
Gentile St 84041
ilman Dr 84040
len Ave & Pl 84041
oddard Cir 84041
& W Golden Ave 84041
& N Golden Eagle Dr
Way 84040
Gordon Ave
1-849 84041
851-897 84040
899-1374 84040
1376-1798 84040
W Gordon Ave 84041
N Goshawk Way 84040
S & W Granite Dr 84041
E Greatblack Cir 84040
Green Dr 84041
N & W Gregory Dr 84041
Grover St 84041
S Harmony Dr 84041
Harriger Way 84041
Harris Blvd 84041
Hawthorne Dr 84041
Hayes Dr 84040
Heather Cir & Dr 84040
Heritage Park Blvd 84041
Hidden Dr 84041
E Highway 193
600-738 84041
E Highway 193
740-849 84041
850-2399 84040
2401-2899 84040
W Highway 193 84041
N Highway 89 84040
Hill Blvd 84041
N & W Hill Field Rd 84041
Hill Villa Dr 84041
Hillgate Way 84041
N Hills Dr 84040
Hillsboro Dr 84040
E Hillsden Rd 84040
Hobbs Creek Dr 84040
Hobbs View Cir 84040
Holly Cir 84040
Holmes Creek Ln 84041
N Hope Cir 84040
N Horseman 84040
Hunters Gln 84041
N Icabod Ln 84040
Indian Hills Ln 84040
E & S Indian Springs Cir
& Dr 84040
N Isabella Dr 84040
W Jack D Dr 84041
E Jacobs Cir 84040
Jeff St 84040
Jensen St 84041
John St 84041
Joni Dr 84041
Julie Dr 84041
E Juniper St 84040
Katie Cir 84041
N Katrina Ct 84040
E Kay Ct 84040
Kays Creek Cir, Dr &
Pl 84040
Kent Cir 84041
Kimball Dr 84041
Kimberly Dr 84040
King St 84041
Kingston Ave 84041
Kirk St 84041
Knowlton St 84041
La Verde St 84041
Lakeview Cir 84040
Lakeview Dr 84040
Larchmont Way 84041
Larsen Ln 84041
Layton Cir 84041
Layton Hills Mall &
Pkwy 84041
E & N Layton Ridge
Dr 84040
Laytona Dr 84041
Liberty St 84041
W Lindi St 84041
Lindsay St 84041
Loch Lomond Dr 84040
Luke St 84041
N & S Main St 84041
Mala Dr 84041
E Maple Way 84040
Maplewood Cir 84041
Marilyn Dr 84041
N & W Mark St 84041
Marshall Way 84041
Marva Ave 84041
Matthew Dr 84041
Maxine Dr 84040
Mccormick Way 84041
Meadow Brook Ct 84041
Meadow Way Dr 84041
Melody Ave 84041
Mica Ln 84041
Mill Cir & Rd 84041
Miller Ave 84041
Mindella Way 84041
Morgan St 84041
Mountain Shadow Dr 84040
S Muddy Ln 84040
Mutton Hollow Rd 84040
Nalder Cir & St 84040
Nayon Dr 84040
E North Lisa St 84040
W North Star Cir 84041
N Northern Harrier
Way 84040
Oak Ln 84040
Oak Forest Dr 84040
Oak Hills Cir & Dr 84040
Oak Hollow Dr 84040
Oakridge Cir & Dr 84040
Oakwood Dr 84040
Onyx St 84041
Orson F Dr 84040
E & N Osprey Way 84040
Overlook Dr 84041
Owens St 84041
Page Cir 84041
Park St 84041
Parkdale Cir 84041
Parkside Ln 84041
Paul Ave 84041
Payne Cir 84041
N Peacefield Dr 84040
S Peach Tree Cv 84040
Pebble Brook Ln 84041
S & W Pebblecreek
Dr 84041
Peregrine Cv & Way 84040
E & S Pheasant View
Dr 84041
Phillips St 84041
Pine Cone Cir 84041
Pinewood Cir & Ln 84040
N Pinion St 84040
Plum Tree Dr 84040
E Poets Rst 84040
E Ponderosa St 84040
Poplar Cir 84041
Prows Cir 84041
Raelyn Way 84040
Rainbow Cir 84041
Rainbow Dr 84041
Ralph St 84041
E & N Redshoulder Dr 84040
E & N Redtail Way 84040
Reid Dr 84041
E & N Ridge Rd 84040
Ridgeview Cir 84040
Ring Rd 84041
S & W Rock Creek
Cor 84041
Rockbridge Dr 84041
Roger Ave 84041
Roger Cir 84040
E & N Rolling Oaks
Ln 84040
Ronald Ave 84041
Rose Blossom Dr 84041
Rosewood Ln 84041
E Rosewood Ln 84040
N Rosewood Ln 84040
Rosewood Way 84041
Sandi St 84041
Sapphire Dr 84041
Scott Cir 84041
W & N Seraphim Ct &
Ln 84041
Sherma Ave 84041
Sherwood Dr 84041
N Shoreline Cir 84040
Sierra Way 84041
Sill St 84041
W Silvercreek Dr 84041
Sky View Dr 84040
Sleepy Hollow Rd 84040
Snoqualmie Dr 84040
E & N Snowcreek Cir &
Dr 84040
E South Lisa St 84040
Spring Creek Dr 84041
Springtree Dr 84040
Spurlock St 84041
E St Josephs St 84040
N Stallion Cir 84041
Stanford St 84041
N Stein Way 84040
W Stone Brook Ln 84041
Stone Creek Cor & Ln 84041
S & W Stonebridge Dr 84041
Sugar St 84041
Summerview Ct 84041
Summerwood Dr 84040
Sundance Cir 84040
Sunflower Cir 84040
Sunrise Dr 84041
Sunset Dr 84041
E Sunset Dr 84040
N Sunset Dr 84040
S Sweet Apricot Cv 84040
N Swift Creek Dr 84041
N & S Talbot Dr 84041
Tanglewood Dr 84040
Tartan Way 84040
W Timbercreek Ln 84041
S Trailside Dr 84041
W Treners N 84041
Twin Peaks Cir & Dr 84040
Twin Trees Ln 84041
University Park Blvd 84041
Valeria Dr 84041
Valley View Dr 84040
N Vangtont E 84040
N View Dr 84040
Walburk Ave 84040
Wasatch Dr
101-423 84041
425-849 84041
901-999 84040
Weaver Ln 84041
Westminister Cir 84040
Westside Dr 84041
Whitesides St 84041
E & N Whitetail Dr &
Way 84040
N Wilcox Way 84040
Willow St 84041
N Willow Creek Dr 84040
Wind River Dr 84040
Wintergreen Cir 84040
Woodland Park Dr 84041
Woodridge Dr 84040
E & N Wyndom Way 84040
Zircon Cir 84041

NUMBERED STREETS

N 10 W 84041
E, N, S & W 100 S, E,
W & N 84041
N 1000 E 84040
N 1000 W 84041
S 1000 E 84040
S 1000 W 84041
W 1000 S 84041
E 1025 N 84040
N 1025 E 84040
W 1025 N 84041
W 1025 S 84041
N 1050 E 84040
N 1050 W 84041
S 1050 E 84040
W 1050 N 84041
W 1060 N 84041
N 1075 E 84040
N 1075 W 84041
W 1070 N 84041
1300-3299 84041
W 1075 S 84041
N 1085 W 84041
E 1100 N 84041
1100-1199 84040
N 1100 E 84040
N 1100 W 84041
W 1100 N 84041
W 1100 S 84041
N 1125 E 84040
N 1125 W 84041
S 1125 W 84041
W 1120 N 84041
2400-3699 84041
E 1150 N
1-399 84041
901-1697 84040
1699-1899 84040
N 1150 E 84040
N 1150 W 84041
S 1150 W 84041
W 1150 N 84041
N 1175 E 84040
N 1175 W 84041
W 1175 N 84041
W 1175 S 84041
E 1200 N
400-499 84041
1000-3050 84040
3052-3198 84040
N 1200 E 84040
N 1200 W 84041
W 1200 N 84041
E 1225 N 84040
N 1225 E 84040
W 1225 N 84041
W 1245 N 84041
W 1240 N 84041
E 1250 N
1-399 84041
1100-3199 84040
E 125 S 84040
N 125 E
1000-1599 84041
1900-1999 84040
N 1250 W
1000-1199 84041
1500-2499 84041
S 1250 E
400-499 84041
784-812 84041
S 125 W 84041
W 1250 N 84041
E 1275 N 84040
N 1275 E 84040
W 1275 N 84041
N 1285 E 84040
E 1300 N 84041
1100-3300 84040
3302-3398 84040
N 1300 E 84040
N 1300 W 84041
S 1300 E 84041
W 1300 N 84041
E 1325 N
1-399 84041
1400-2099 84040
N 1325 E 84040
S 1325 E 84040
W 1325 N 84041
W 1345 N 84041
E 1350 N 84040
N 1350 W 84041
W 1350 N 84041
E 1375 N 84041
N 1375 E 84040
S 1375 E 84040
S 1375 W 84041
W 1375 N 84041
E 1400 N 84040
N 1400 E 84040
N 1400 W 84041
W 1400 N 84041
E 1425 N 84040
N 1425 E 84040
S 1425 W 84041
W 1425 N 84041
E 1450 N
100-348 84041
1400-1499 84040
N 1450 E 84040
N 1450 W 84041
W 1450 N 84041
N 1470 E 84040
N & W 1475 W & N 84041
N 1480 E 84040
W 1480 N 84041
E 1500 N
100-399 84041
1000-1199 84040
E 150 S
900-999 84041
2500-2599 84040
N 1500 E
100-999 84040
700-1699 84041
N 150 W
700-1999 84041
1100-1799 84041
S 1500 W 84041
W 150 N 84041
W 150 S 84041
E 1525 N
1-399 84041
1000-2799 84040
N 1525 E 84040
N 1525 W 84041
W 1525 N 84041
N 1540 W 84041
N 1550 E 84040
W 1550 N 84041
N 1575 E 84040
N 1575 W 84041
S 1575 W 84041
E 1600 N 84040
N 1600 E 84040
N 160 W 84041
1100-1799 84041
W 1600 N 84041
E 1625 N 84041
N 1625 E 84040
N 1625 W 84041
S 1625 W 84041
W 1620 N 84041
N 1640 W 84041
E 1650 N 84040
N 1650 E 84040
W 1650 N 84041
N 1675 E 84040
N 1675 W 84041
S 1675 E 84040
W 1675 N 84041
N 1690 W 84041
E 1700 N 84040
N 1700 E 84040
N 1700 W 84041
S 1700 W 84041
W 1700 N 84041
E 1720 N 84041
N 1725 E 84040
N 1725 W 84041
E 1750 N 84040
E, N, S & W 175 S, E,
W & N 84041
N 1750 E 84040
W 1750 N 84041
E 1770 N 84041
W 1775 N 84041
E 1800 N 84041
N 1800 E 84040
W 1800 N 84041
E & N 1825 N & E 84040
N 1845 E 84040
E 1850 N 84040
N 1850 E 84040
N 1850 W 84041
W 1850 N 84041
E 1875 N
1-99 84041
3200-3299 84040
W 1875 N 84041
E 1900 N 84040
W 1900 N 84041
N 1925 E 84040
W 1920 N 84041
W 1925 N
200-499 84041
E 1930 N
1-99 84041
2500-2599 84040
E 1950 N 84040
N 1965 E 84040
W 1960 N 84041
E & N 1975 N & E 84040
E 1980 N 84040
E 200 N 84040
E 200 S
700-899 84041
1900-1998 84040
2000-2199 84040
N 200 E
1100-1699 84041
N & S 2000 84040
N 200 W 84041
S 200 E 84041
W 200 N 84041
W 200 S 84041
N 2025 W 84041
E 2050 N 84040
N 2075 E 84040
E 2100 N 84040
N 2100 E 84040
N 2100 W 84041
E 2125 N 84041
N 2125 E 84040
W 2125 N 84041
E 2150 N
1-299 84041
2200-2399 84040
N 2150 E 84040
N 2150 W 84041
W 2150 N 84041
N 2175 E 84040
W 2175 N 84041
E 2200 N
1-99 84041
1000-2599 84040
N 2200 E 84040
N 2200 W 84041
S 2200 W 84041
W 2200 N 84041
N 2225 E 84040
N 2225 W 84041
W 2225 N 84041
N 2240 E 84040
E, N, S & W 225 N, E,
W & S 84041
E 2250 N 84041
1420-2799 84040
N 2250 E 84040
W 2250 N 84041
N 2260 E 84040
N 2275 E 84040
N 2275 W 84041
W 2275 N 84041
N 2295 E 84040
E 2300 N 84041
1100-1299 84040
N 2300 E 84040
W 230 N 84041
1-199 84041
N 2325 E 84040
N 2325 W 84041
W 2325 N 84041
E 2350 N
1-99 84041
1100-2399 84040
N 2350 E 84040
N 2350 W 84041
W 2350 N 84041
E 2375 N 84040
N 2375 E 84040
N 2375 W 84041
E 2400 N 84041
N 2400 E 84040
W 2400 N 84041
E 2425 N 84040

N 2425 W ... 84041
E 2450 N
1-99 ... 84041
1000-1399 ... 84040
N 2450 E ... 84040
W 2450 N ... 84041
E 2475 N ... 84040
N 2475 E ... 84040
N 2475 W ... 84041
W 2475 N ... 84041
E 25 S ... 84040
N 25 E ... 84041
S 25 E ... 84041
W 25 N ... 84041
W 25 S ... 84041
E & S 2500 N & E ... 84040
1200-2299 ... 84040
E 250 S ... 84041
N 250 E ... 84041
N 250 W ... 84041
S 250 E ... 84041
S 250 W ... 84041
W 250 N ... 84041
E 2525 N ... 84040
N 2525 E ... 84040
N 2525 W ... 84041
W 2525 N ... 84041
E 2550 N ... 84040
E 255 S ... 84041
N 2550 E ... 84040
N 2550 W ... 84041
S 2550 E ... 84040
N 2575 E ... 84040
N 2570 W ... 84041
N 2575 W
1000-1499 ... 84041
E 2600 N ... 84040
E 260 S ... 84041
N 2600 E ... 84040
W 2600 N ... 84041
E 2625 N
300-799 ... 84041
1100-1199 ... 84040
N 2625 E ... 84040
N 2625 W ... 84041
S 2625 E ... 84040
N 2650 E ... 84040
E 2675 N ... 84040
N 2675 E ... 84040
N 2675 W ... 84041
W 2675 N ... 84041
E 2700 N ... 84040
N 2700 E ... 84040
N 2700 W ... 84041
S 2700 E ... 84040
N 2725 W ... 84041
E & N 2750 N & E ... 84040
1300-1599 ... 84040
E 275 S ... 84040
N 275 E ... 84041
N 275 W ... 84041
S 275 W ... 84041
W 275 N ... 84041
W 275 S ... 84041
N 2775 E ... 84040
N 2775 W ... 84041
S 2775 E ... 84040
E & N 2800 N & E ... 84040
E 2825 N ... 84040
N 2825 E ... 84040
N 2825 W ... 84041
S 2825 E ... 84040
W 2825 N ... 84041
285 E & W ... 84041
N 2850 E
1500-1699 ... 84040
N 2850 W ... 84041
N & W 2875 W & N ... 84041
E & N 2900 N & E ... 84040
N 2925 W ... 84041
N 2975 E ... 84040
N 2975 W ... 84041
E 300 N
800-926 ... 84041
928-998 ... 84041
1100-1499 ... 84040

E & N 3000 N & E ... 84040
N 300 E ... 84041
N 300 W ... 84041
S 300 E ... 84041
W 300 S ... 84041
E 3025 N ... 84040
E 3050 N ... 84040
N 3050 E ... 84040
N 3050 W ... 84041
E 3075 N ... 84040
E 3100 N ... 84040
N 3100 E ... 84040
N 3100 W ... 84041
E 3125 N ... 84040
N 3125 E ... 84040
N 3125 W ... 84041
E & N 3150 N & E ... 84040
E 315 S ... 84041
N 3175 E ... 84040
E 320 S ... 84041
N 3200 E ... 84040
N 3200 W ... 84041
S 3200 W ... 84041
E 3225 N ... 84040
N 3225 W ... 84041
S 3225 E ... 84040
E & N 3250 N & E ... 84040
E 325 S
900-999 ... 84041
1548-1599 ... 84040
N 325 E ... 84041
W 325 N ... 84041
W 325 S ... 84041
E 3300 N ... 84040
N 3300 E ... 84040
N 3300 W ... 84041
E 3325 N ... 84040
E 3350 N ... 84040
N 3350 W ... 84041
N 3375 W ... 84041
E 3400 N ... 84040
N 3425 W ... 84041
E 3450 N ... 84040
N 3450 W ... 84041
W 345 S ... 84041
N & S 3475 ... 84041
E 350 N ... 84041
E 3500 N
2200-2399 ... 84040
2200-2399 ... 84040
E 350 S ... 84040
N 350 E ... 84041
N 3500 W
900-1099 ... 84041
1000-2999 ... 84041
S 350 W ... 84041
W 350 N ... 84041
W 350 S ... 84041
E 3525 N ... 84040
S 3525 W ... 84041
N 3550 W ... 84041
E 3575 N ... 84040
N 3575 W ... 84041
E 3600 N ... 84040
N 3600 W ... 84041
S 3600 W ... 84041
N 3625 W ... 84041
E 3650 N ... 84040
N 3675 W ... 84041
E 3700 N ... 84040
E 370 S ... 84041
N 3700 W ... 84041
E 3725 N ... 84040
E 3750 N ... 84040
E 375 S ... 84041
E, N & W 400 S, W &
N ... 84041
E 405 S ... 84041
E 425 N ... 84040
E 425 S ... 84041
W 425 N ... 84041
W 425 S ... 84041
N 440 W ... 84041
N, S & W 450 W, N &
S ... 84041
E 475 N ... 84040

W 475 N ... 84041
N 490 W ... 84041
N 5 E ... 84041
E 50 S ... 84040
N 50 W ... 84041
S 50 E ... 84041
S 50 W ... 84041
W 50 N ... 84041
E 500 N ... 84040
N 500 W ... 84041
S 500 W ... 84041
W 500 S ... 84041
E 525 N
1-199 ... 84041
1400-1574 ... 84040
1576-1588 ... 84040
W 525 N ... 84041
W 525 S ... 84041
E 530 N ... 84040
N 550 W ... 84041
E 575 N ... 84041
1000-1048 ... 84040
1050-1699 ... 84040
N 575 W ... 84041
W 575 S ... 84041
N & W 590 W & N ... 84041
N 60 E ... 84041
E, N, S & W 600 N, W,
E & S ... 84041
E 625 N ... 84040
E 625 S ... 84041
N 630 W ... 84041
E, N, S & W 650 S, E,
W & N ... 84041
675 E & W ... 84041
E, N, S & W 700 N, S &
W ... 84041
N 725 W ... 84041
E 75 S ... 84041
1800-2199 ... 84040
N 75 E ... 84041
N 75 W ... 84041
S 75 W ... 84041
W 75 N ... 84041
W 75 S ... 84041
E, N, S & W 750 N, E,
W & S ... 84041
S 755 E ... 84041
E 775 N ... 84040
E 775 S ... 84041
S 775 E ... 84041
W 775 N ... 84041
W 775 S ... 84041
E 780 N ... 84040
N 80 E ... 84041
E 800 N ... 84040
E 800 S ... 84041
N 800 W ... 84041
S 800 E ... 84041
S 800 W ... 84041
W 800 S ... 84041
E 825 N
17-24 ... 84041
900-1099 ... 84040
S 825 E ... 84041
W 825 N ... 84041
W 840 N ... 84041
E 850 N ... 84040
E 850 S ... 84041
N 850 E ... 84041
S 850 E ... 84041
S 850 W ... 84041
W 850 N ... 84041
W 850 S ... 84041
E 875 N ... 84041
E 900 N ... 84041
E 900 S ... 84041
N 900 E ... 84040
N 900 W ... 84041
S 900 E ... 84041
W 900 N ... 84041
W 900 S ... 84041
E 925 S ... 84041
N 925 E ... 84040
S 925 E ... 84041
S 925 W ... 84041

W 925 N ... 84041
E 935 S ... 84041
N 935 E ... 84040
N 935 W ... 84041
E, N, S & W 950 S, W,
E & N ... 84041
E 975 N ... 84040
E 975 S ... 84041
N 975 E ... 84040
N 975 W ... 84041
S 975 E ... 84041
W 975 N ... 84041
W 975 S ... 84041

LOGAN UT

General Delivery ... 84321

POST OFFICE BOXES MAIN OFFICE STATIONS AND BRANCHES

Box No.s
1 - 4986 ... 84323
6001 - 6838 ... 84341
23001 - 23001 ... 84323

NAMED STREETS

Aggie Vlg ... 84341
Apple Dr ... 84321
Aspen Dr ... 84341
Aspen Meadow Dr ... 84341
W Aspen Park Cir ... 84321
Aspen Park Ln ... 84341
Beech Ct ... 84321
Birch Cir ... 84341
Black Walnut Dr ... 84341
Blacksmith Ct ... 84321
Blake Ct ... 84321
N Bonestat E ... 84341
Bonneville Ave ... 84341
Boulevard ... 84321
Box Elder Cir ... 84341
Boxwood Cir ... 84341
Braxton Pl ... 84321
Bridger Dr ... 84321
Bristol Rd ... 84341
Brookside Pl ... 84321
Bullen Hall ... 84321
W Cache Valley Blvd ... 84341
Camelot Dr ... 84341
Canterbury Cir, Dr &
Ln ... 84321
Canyon Cv & Rd ... 84321
Canyon Ridge Dr ... 84341
Cedar Heights Dr ... 84341
Cedarwood Ln ... 84341
E & W Center Ave &
St ... 84321
Chestnut Ln ... 84321
Church St ... 84321
Circle View Dr ... 84341
Clear Creek Cir & Rd ... 84321
Cliffside Dr ... 84321
Clover Cir ... 84321
Conifer Pl ... 84321
Cottonwood Cir & Ln ... 84341
Country Club Dr ... 84321
Country Manor Dr ... 84321
Coventry Pl ... 84341
Crayon Ct ... 84321
Crescent Dr ... 84341
Crockett Ave ... 84321
Crystal Ave ... 84321
Daines Way ... 84341
W Darielaw S ... 84321
Darwin Ave ... 84321
Davis Ave ... 84321
Dee Ave ... 84321
Deerhaven Dr ... 84341
Douglas Dr ... 84341

Eastridge Cir, Dr & Ln ... 84321
Elderberry Cir ... 84341
W Elkhorn Dr ... 84321
Ellendale Ave ... 84321
Emme Way ... 84321
Evergreen Dr ... 84321
Fairway Ln ... 84321
Federal Ave ... 84321
Fonnesbeck Ave ... 84321
Foothill Dr ... 84341
Fox Farm Rd ... 84321
Garden Cir ... 84321
Ginger Cir ... 84321
E Golf Course Rd ... 84321
Greaves Hall ... 84321
Green Field Cir ... 84321
Hampton Pl ... 84341
W Haven Dr ... 84321
Hawthorne Dr ... 84321
Hayden Ct ... 84321
W Henrys Pt Dr ... 84321
S Heritage Cv & Dr ... 84321
Highland Dr ... 84341
E Highway 101 ... 84321
E Highway 89 ... 84321
Hillcrest Ave ... 84321
Hillside Cir & Dr ... 84321
Hollow Rd ... 84321
Hollyhock Ln ... 84321
Hyclone Dr & Rd ... 84321
Island Dr ... 84321
Johnson Rd ... 84321
Juniper Cir ... 84341
Juniper Dr ... 84321
Kc Ln ... 84321
Kensington Pl ... 84341
Kings Ct ... 84321
Knowles Ln ... 84321
Lamplighter Dr ... 84321
Larkspur Dr ... 84321
Lauralin Dr ... 84321
Law Ct ... 84321
Legend Dr ... 84321
Legrand ... 84321
Leruisseau Dr ... 84321
Lexington Loop ... 84321
Linden Ct ... 84321
Lone Brook Ct ... 84321
Lynnwood Ave ... 84341
N Main St
1-999 ... 84321
1000-3600 ... 84341
3602-3798 ... 84341
S Main St ... 84321
Majestic Dr ... 84321
Mallard Loop ... 84321
Maple Cir ... 84341
Maple Dr ... 84321
Maple Valley Rd ... 84321
Marindale Ave ... 84321
Meadow Cir ... 84321
Meadow Ln ... 84341
Meadow View Ln ... 84321
Meadowbrook Dr ... 84321
Merrill Hall ... 84321
Moen Hall ... 84321
Mount Logan Dr &
Loop ... 84321
Mountain Rd ... 84321
Mountain View Dr ... 84321
Mountain View Towers ... 84321
Naomi Cir & Dr ... 84341
Oak Pl ... 84321
Oakbrook Cir ... 84321
Oakcreek Pl ... 84321
Oakview Dr ... 84321
Oakwood Ct & Dr ... 84321
Orchard Dr & Hts ... 84321
Paintbrush Cir ... 84321
Palisade Cir ... 84321
Palomino Cir ... 84341
Park Ave & Cir ... 84321
Parkview Cir ... 84321
Pebble Creek Ct ... 84341
Penhurst Pl ... 84341
Penny Ln ... 84341

Pheasant Creek Dr ... 84321
Pinewood Dr ... 84321
Pioneer Ave ... 84321
Poplar Ave ... 84321
Preston Ave ... 84321
Ptarmigan Loop ... 84321
Quail Way ... 84321
Quail Canyon Dr ... 84321
Quail Hollow Rd ... 84321
Quarter Cir ... 84321
Rainbow Dr ... 84321
Raymond Ct ... 84321
Red Fox Trce ... 84321
Red Oak Dr ... 84341
Reeder Hall ... 84321
Research Park Way ... 84341
Richards Hall ... 84321
River Circle Dr ... 84321
River Heights Blvd ... 84321
River Park Dr ... 84321
River Pointe Dr ... 84321
Riverbend Rd ... 84321
Riverdale Ave ... 84321
Riverside Dr ... 84321
Riverview Ave ... 84321
Riverwalk Cir & Pkwy ... 84321
Riverwood Ct & Dr ... 84321
Rose St ... 84341
Rosewood Cir ... 84321
Rsi Dr ... 84321
Saddle Hill Dr ... 84321
Sage Cir ... 84321
Sagewood Ln ... 84341
Schiess Ct ... 84321
Shadow Mountain Dr ... 84321
Sheridan Cir ... 84321
Sheridan Ridge Ln ... 84321
Skyridge Cir ... 84341
Sleepy Hollow Ln ... 84321
Somerset Pl ... 84321
Southgate Ct ... 84321
W Southview Cir ... 84321
Southwest St ... 84321
Spring Cir ... 84321
Spring Ln ... 84341
E Stadium Dr ... 84341
S State Highway 89 ... 84321
Stewart Hill Ct & Dr ... 84321
Stirling Pl ... 84341
Stone Creek Dr ... 84321
Stonebridge Dr ... 84321
Stonecrest Ln ... 84341
Stuart Ct ... 84321
Sumac Dr ... 84321
Summerwild Ave ... 84321
Sundown Way ... 84321
Sunset Cir, Dr & Rdg ... 84321
Sunstone Cir & Ct ... 84321
Talon Dr ... 84321
Teal Loop ... 84321
Temple Ave ... 84321
Temple View Dr ... 84321
Terrace Pl ... 84321
Thomas Ct ... 84321
Three Point Ave ... 84321
N Thrushwood Dr ... 84321
Trail Cir & Dr ... 84321
University Hillway ... 84321
Usu Trailer Ct ... 84341
Valley View Dr ... 84321
Valley View Towers ... 84321
Viewcrest Cir ... 84341
Wasatch Dr ... 84341
Water St ... 84321
Weston Dr ... 84321
White Pine Pl ... 84341
Willow Cir ... 84341
Willow Dr ... 84321
Willow Way ... 84341
Winding Way ... 84341
Windsor Dr ... 84321
Woodside Dr ... 84321

NUMBERED STREETS

E 1000 N
1-1399 ... 84321

53-97 ... 8432
E 100 S ... 8432
N 100 E
30-98 ... 8432
1600-2999 ... 8434
1800-2398 ... 8434
N 100 W
1-999 ... 8432
75-1699 ... 8432
1600-1698 ... 8434
S 1000 E
1-400 ... 8432
1-699 ... 8432
S 100 W
1-97 ... 8432
400-3199 ... 8432
W 100 N
1-599 ... 8432
1-47 ... 8432
W 100 S
1-699 ... 8432
500-1899 ... 8432
W 1010 S ... 8432
S 1020 W ... 8432
E 1030 N ... 8434
W 1030 S ... 8432
W 1040 S ... 8432
W 1050 N ... 8434
N 1060 E ... 8434
S 1060 W ... 8432
W 1060 N ... 8434
W 1060 S ... 8432
S 1070 W ... 8432
E 1080 N ... 8434
S 1080 W ... 8432
E 1100 N ... 8434
N 1100 E ... 8434
S 1100 W ... 8432
W 1100 N ... 8434
W 1100 S ... 8432
W 1110 N ... 8434
E 1120 N ... 8434
N 1120 E ... 8432
S 1120 W ... 8432
W 1124 N ... 8434
E 1140 N ... 8434
N 1140 W ... 8432
W 1140 N ... 8434
E 1150 N ... 8434
N 1150 E ... 8434
S 1150 W
1600-1799 ... 8432
S 1155 W
2300-2399 ... 8432
W 1150 N
2-50 ... 8434
W 1155 N
400-499 ... 8434
N 1170 E ... 8432
N 1175 W ... 8432
E 1185 N ... 8434
W 1190 N ... 8434
E 1200 N ... 8434
E 1200 S ... 8432
N 1200 E
800-948 ... 8432
1400-3300 ... 8434
3302-3498 ... 8434
N 120 W ... 8434
S 1200 W ... 8432
W 1200 N ... 8434
W 1200 S ... 8432
E 1225 N
301-399 ... 8434
1400-1799 ... 8434
N 1220 E ... 8432
S 1220 E ... 8432
S 1225 W
401-499 ... 8432
1600-1699 ... 8432
E 1240 N ... 8434
S 1240 W ... 8432
E 1250 N ... 8434
N 1250 E
1-199 ... 8432
1900-2699 ... 8434
2701-2799 ... 8434

S 1250 E 84321
S 1250 W 84321
W 1250 S 84321
E 1260 N 84341
W 1260 S 84321
E 1270 N 84341
S & W 1275 W & S 84321
E 1280 N 84341
S 1280 W 84321
W 1285 S 84321
S & W 1290 W & S 84321
E 1300 N 84341
N 1300 E
  1-99 84321
  2000-2098 84341
N 130 W 84341
S 1300 E 84321
W 1309 S 84321
W 1305 S 84321
W 130 S
  1000-1099 84321
W 1310 S 84321
W 1315 S 84321
E 1325 N 84341
N 1325 E 84341
S 1325 W 84321
W 1320 S 84321
  1-99 84321
S 1330 W 84321
W 1330 N 84341
E & N 1340 N & E 84341
E 1350 N 84341
N 1350 E 84341
S 1350 E 84321
S 1350 W 84321
W 1350 N 84341
S 1360 W 84321
S 1365 W 84321
E 1370 N 84341
N 1375 W 84321
E 1370 South Pl 84321
E 1385 N 84341
N 1380 E 84341
S 1380 W 84321
W 1380 N 84341
W 1395 S 84321
E 1400 N 84341
N 1400 E
  700-999 84321
  1101-1197 84341
N 1400 W 84321
S 1400 E 84321
S 1400 W 84321
W 1400 N
  175-400 84341
  800-999 84321
W 1400 S 84321
E 1400 South Pl 84321
N 1410 E 84341
S 1416 W 84321
E 1425 N 84341
N 1420 E 84321
N 1430 E 84321
E 1455 N 84341
N 1450 E
  800-899 84321
  2000-3299 84341
W 1458 S 84321
E 1460 N 84341
S 1460 W 84321
W 1465 N 84341
N 1475 E 84341
S 1470 W 84321
W 1470 N 84341
N 1480 E 84321
W 1490 N 84341
E 1490 South Pl 84321
E 150 N 84321
  1201-1447 84341
N 1500 E
  700-850 84321
  852-998 84321
  1200-1399 84341
S 1500 W 84321
E 1500 South Pl 84321
N 1515 E 84341
N 1520 E 84341
N 1525 E
  1400-1599 84341
S 1525 W 84321
E & W 1530 84341
E 1540 N 84341
S 1540 W 84321
E 1550 N 84341
N 1550 E 84341
W 1550 S 84321
N 1560 E 84341
S 1565 W 84321
N 1570 E 84321
W 1570 N 84341
E 1580 N 84341
S 1580 W 84321
W 1595 N 84341
E 1600 N 84341
N 1600 E
  901-999 84321
  1000-3499 84341
S 1600 W 84321
W 1600 N 84321
W 1610 S 84321
W 1615 S 84321
E 1625 N 84341
W 1625 S 84321
E 1630 N 84341
N 1640 E 84341
E & N 1650 N & E 84341
S & W 1690 W & S 84321
E 1700 N 84341
E & S 170 S & W 84321
N 1700 E 84341
W 1700 N 84321
W 1700 S 84321
N 1720 E 84341
W 1725 N 84321
E & N 1730 N & E 84341
W 1740 N 84341
N 175 E 84321
N 1750 E
  1100-1899 84341
W 1750 S 84321
E & N 1770 N & E 84341
N 1775 E 84341
E 1780 N 84341
N 1780 E 84341
W 1780 N 84321
W 1780 S 84321
E 1800 N 84341
N 1800 E 84341
N 180 W 84341
S 180 W 84321
W 1800 N
  95-397 84341
  399-500 84341
  502-598 84341
  600-799 84341
  801-815 84321
W 1800 S 84321
E 1815 N 84341
W 1825 S 84321
W 1845 S 84321
E & N 1850 N & E 84341
N 1875 E 84341
E 1890 N 84341
E 1900 N 84341
N 1900 E 84341
S 1900 W 84321
W 1900 S 84321
W 1925 S 84321
E & N 1950 N & E 84341
W 1960 S 84321
E 1980 N 84341
E 200 N
  1-49 84321
  1-1599 84341
E 200 S 84321
N 200 E
  1-900 84321
  1000-2799 84341
  1700-1899 84341
N 200 W
  1-999 84321
  1000-3099 84341
S 200 E 84321
S 200 W
  1-3799 84321
  600-1172 84321
W 200 N
  73-99 84321
  75-75 84323
  100-3199 84321
W 200 S
  1-2399 84321
  1100-1200 84321
E & N 2050 N & E 84341
E 2060 N 84341
E & N 2100 N & E 84341
E 2120 N 84341
N 2150 E 84341
E 2160 N 84341
E 2175 N 84341
E 2170 N 84341
E 2180 N 84341
E 2200 N 84341
N 220 W 84341
S 220 W 84321
W 2200 S 84321
E 2230 N 84341
E 2250 N 84341
N 225 E 84341
E 2280 N 84341
W 2280 S 84321
E 2290 N 84341
E 2300 N 84341
230 E & W 84341
W 2320 S 84321
E 2330 N 84341
W 2350 S 84321
W 2395 S 84321
E 2400 N 84341
N 240 W 84341
S 2400 W 84321
W 2400 N
  2-98 84341
W 240 N
  400-499 84321
W 2401 S 84321
  1100-1199 84321
W 2415 S 84321
W 2420 S 84321
W 2432 S 84321
E 2440 N 84341
W 2445 S 84321
E 2450 N 84341
W 2450 N 84341
W 2450 S 84321
E 2475 N 84341
W 2470 S 84321
W 2475 S
  600-799 84321
N 25 W 84321
E 2500 N 84341
N 250 E
  700-799 84321
  1100-1299 84341
N 250 W
  801-869 84321
  871-899 84321
  1000-1099 84341
S 250 E 84321
S 250 W 84321
W 2500 N
  1-27 84341
  1035-1035 84321
W 2500 S 84321
E 2520 N 84341
W 2550 S 84321
W 2575 S 84321
E 2600 N
  1-1699 84341
  1300-1499 84321
N 260 E 84341
N 260 W 84341
S 260 W 84321
W 2600 S 84321
W 2625 S 84321
W 2640 S 84321
E 2650 N 84341
E 2650 S 84321
W 2650 S 84321
E 2660 N 84341
W 2675 S 84321
W 2680 S 84321
E 2700 N 84341
N 270 E 84341
S 270 W 84321
W 2700 S 84321
E 2720 N 84341
W 2730 S 84321
W 2740 S 84321
E 2750 N 84341
E 275 N 84321
W 2775 S 84321
W 2770 S 84321
E 2780 N 84341
S 2800 W 84321
S & W 280 W & S 84321
E 2820 N 84341
W 2840 S 84321
E 2850 N 84341
W 2850 S 84321
W 2880 S 84321
E 2900 N
  700-1000 84341
E 290 N
  1300-1499 84321
E 2900 S 84321
N 290 W 84341
W 2930 S 84321
E 2950 N 84341
W 2965 S 84321
W 2960 S 84321
W 2980 S 84321
E 3000 N 84341
  1-1299 84321
E 300 S 84321
N 300 E
  100-999 84321
  1500-2799 84341
N 300 W
  1-999 84321
  1400-3099 84341
S 300 E 84321
S 300 W 84321
W 300 N 84321
W 300 S 84321
E 3025 N 84341
W 3020 S 84321
W 3045 S 84321
E 3075 N 84341
E 3100 N 84341
N 310 W 84341
N 315 W 84321
W 3170 S 84321
E 320 N
  801-897 84321
  1800-1999 84341
N 320 W 84341
S 3200 W 84321
W 3200 N 84341
W 3200 S 84321
W 3220 S 84321
E 3250 N 84341
N 325 W 84341
N 330 E 84341
W 3300 S 84321
W 330 S
  800-999 84321
W 3310 S 84321
W 3335 S 84321
E 3375 N 84341
W 3390 S 84321
N 340 W 84341
S & W 3400 W & S 84321
W 3430 S 84321
E 3450 N 84341
W 3450 S 84321
W 3480 S 84321
E, N, S & W 350 S, E & W 84321
W 3515 S 84321
E 3550 N 84341
W 3550 S 84321
W 3575 S 84321
360 E & W 84341
S 3600 W 84321
W 3650 S 84321
W 365 S 84321
E 3700 S 84321
N 370 E 84341
S 370 W 84321
W 370 S 84321
N 375 W
  900-999 84321
  1000-1099 84341
W 3800 S 84321
E 3850 S 84321
S 385 W 84321
E 400 N 84341
E 400 S 84321
N 400 E
  1-999 84321
  1000-2599 84341
N 400 W
  1-900 84321
  1000-1800 84341
S 400 E 84321
S 400 W 84321
W 400 N 84321
W 4000 S 84321
  1-1199 84321
N 420 W 84341
N 425 W 84341
E 4300 S 84321
W 430 S 84321
N 440 W 84341
E 442 N 84321
N 450 W
  600-699 84321
  1500-1599 84341
S 450 W 84321
N 460 E 84341
N 460 W 84341
S 460 E 84321
S & W 470 E & N 84321
N 480 W
  800-999 84321
  1100-1199 84341
E, N & S 50 N, S & W 84321
E 500 N 84341
E 500 S 84321
N 500 E
  1-999 84321
  1000-2899 84341
N 500 W
  1-679 84321
  1700-2499 84341
S 500 E 84321
S 500 W 84321
W 500 N 84321
W 500 S 84321
W 505 S 84321
N 510 W 84341
S 515 W 84321
N 520 W 84341
N & S 525 84321
S & W 530 W & S 84321
S & W 535 W & S 84321
N 540 W
  900-999 84321
  1500-1599 84341
S 540 E 84321
N 550 E
  600-899 84321
  1400-1998 84341
  2000-2099 84341
N 550 W 84341
S 550 E 84321
W 550 N 84321
W 550 S 84321
N 560 W 84341
S 560 E 84321
S 560 W 84321
N 565 W 84341
N 570 E 84341
S 575 W 84321
N 580 E 84341
N 590 W 84341
E 60 S 84321
E 600 N 84321
E 600 S 84321
N 600 E
  200-999 84321
  1000-1018 84341
N 600 W 84321
S 600 E 84321
S 600 W 84321
W 600 N 84321
W 600 S 84321
W 620 S 84321
N 630 E 84341
N 630 W 84321
W 630 S 84321
N 640 E 84341
S 640 W 84321
W 640 N 84321
W 640 S 84321
E, N, S & W 650 S, E, W & N 84321
S 660 W 84321
N & S 670 84321
W 675 S 84321
N 680 E 84341
W 680 N 84321
W 690 S 84321
E 700 N 84321
E 700 S 84321
N 700 E
  301-697 84321
  1200-2098 84341
S 700 E 84321
S 700 W 84321
W 700 N 84321
W 700 S 84321
N & W 710 W & S 84321
E 716 S 84321
S & W 720 W & S 84321
W 725 N 84321
N 728 E 84341
N 730 E 84341
N 730 W 84321
W 730 N 84321
N 740 E 84341
E 750 S 84321
N 750 E
  1-799 84321
  2100-2199 84341
N 750 W 84321
S 750 E 84321
W 750 N 84321
W 750 S 84321
W 760 S 84321
E & S 770 N & W 84321
W 775 N 84321
N 780 W 84321
W 790 S 84321
N & S 80 E & W 84321
E 800 N 84321
E 800 S 84321
N 800 E
  601-627 84321
  1001-1397 84341
N 800 W 84321
S 800 E 84321
S 800 W 84321
W 800 N 84321
W 800 S 84321
810 N & S 84321
W 815 S 84321
E & S 820 N & W 84321
S & W 830 W & S 84321
S 845 W 84321
N 850 W 84321
E & S 860 N & W 84321
E 870 N 84321
N 870 E 84341
N 870 W 84321
W 870 N 84321
N 875 E 84321
880 N & S 84321
W 890 S 84321
E, N, S & W 900 N, W & S 84321
W 910 N 84321
N 920 E 84341
W 925 N 84321
W 930 N 84321
W 940 S 84321
N 950 E 84341
N 950 W 84321
W 950 N 84321
S 960 W 84321
E & N 970 N & E 84321
S & W 980 W & N 84321

OGDEN UT

General Delivery 84401

POST OFFICE BOXES MAIN OFFICE STATIONS AND BRANCHES

Box No.s
1 - 2419 84402
3001 - 3999 84409
6001 - 6350 84402
9001 - 10518 84409
12001 - 14216 84412
29998 - 29998 84402
129998 - 129998 84412
150001 - 159998 84415
409101 - 409107 84409

NAMED STREETS

A Ave 84401
Acorn Cir 84403
Adams Ave
  100-1700 84404
  1702-1798 84404
  2000-2680 84401
  2682-2698 84401
  2700-5099 84403
  5100-5199 84405
N Adams Ave 84404
W Addison Way 84401
Adobe Mill Ct & Ln 84404
Airport Rd 84405
Alder Creek Dr 84414
Allen Rd 84401
Allen Peak Cir 84404
Alta Vista Cir 84404
American Way 84401
W Amidan Dr 84404
Anasazi Dr 84403
S Andover St 84401
Angel Heights Cir 84414
Apache Way 84403
Arapaho Cir & Dr 84403
Arlington Dr 84403
Arlington Way 84414
Arrowhead Ln 84403
Aspen Ct & Dr 84403
Avalon Hills Dr 84404
Avc Ln 84404
Aztec Dr 84403
B Ave 84401
Baker Dr 84403
Banbury Ln 84403
Barker Pkwy 84414
E Bateman Way 84405
Bee Ct 84401
Bel Mar Dr 84403
Belnap Cir 84403
Ben Lomond Ave 84403
E Benchview Dr 84404
E Berkley St 84404
Beus Dr 84403
Beverly Dr 84403
Bill Bailey Blvd 84404
W Binford St 84401
W Bingham Way 84404
Birch Ave 84403
Birch Creek Rd 84401
Black Mountain Cir & Dr 84404
Blossom Ln 84404

Street	ZIP
Bobwhite Ct	84403
Bona Villa Dr	84403
Bonneville Ter	84403
Borg Cir	84403
Boston Ave	84401
Boughton St	84403
Boulder Canyon Dr	84404
Bowman Way	84405
Bramwell Ct	84401
Breeze Cir	84403
N Brickyard Rd	84404
Bridlewood Ct	84404
Brinker Ave	
500-1599	84404
1800-2699	84401
2700-4899	84403
N Brinker Ave	84404
Brittany Rd	84403
Broadmoor Ave	84404
Brookdale Cir	84404
Brookmeadow Dr	84404
Brookshire Dr	84405
Brookside Cir	84404
Browning Cir	84403
Brynn Ave	84401
Buchanan Ave	
1900-2599	84401
2601-2649	84401
2700-2899	84403
Budge Ln	84414
Buena Vista Dr	84405
S Burbidge Ave	84404
E Burch Creek Dr & Holw	84403
Burnham Dr	84414
N Burns St	84404
Burton Ct	84403
Bybee Dr	84403
C Ave	84401
Cahoon St	84401
Calvert Ct	84404
Cambridge Ave	84414
Cameron Ct	84404
S Cameron Dr	84401
Canfield Dr	84404
Canterbury Rd	84403
Canyon Cv	84401
Canyon Dr	84405
E Canyon Dr	84405
Canyon Rd	84404
E Canyon Vw	84404
Canyonwoods Dr	84404
W Capitol St	84401
Carney St	84403
Carriage Ct & Ln	84403
Carson Ave	84401
Carter Dr	84405
Casey Ln	84414
Cassie Dr	84405
Cattail Dr	84404
Cedar Cir	84405
Cedar Ct	84405
Cedar Ln	84403
Cedar Bench Dr	84405
Cedar Glen Cir	84405
Cedar Loop Dr	84405
N Centennial Way	84404
Center Ave	84404
Century Dr	84404
Chambers St	84403
Charenton Cove Cir	84403
Charleen Cir	84403
Charleston Ave	84414
Chatelain Rd	84403
Chelsea Ln	84403
Cherokee Cir	84403
Cherry Ct	84403
Cherry Dr	
300-499	84405
2800-2999	84414
Cherry Wood Way	84403
Chester St	84404
Chestnut St	84404
Cheyenne Cir	84403
Childs Ave	
100-1799	84404
2601-2639	84401
2641-3399	84401
3800-3898	84405
N Childs Ave	84404
Chilly Peak Cir	84404
Chimes Cir	84405
Chimes View Dr	84405
Choctaw Rdg	84403
Chokecherry Ct	84403
Christensen Ave	84403
Christmas Box Ln	84404
Christoffersen Cir	84403
Chugg Ln	84404
Chukar Ln	84403
Circle Way	84403
N Clark Ave	84404
Clover Cir	84404
Club View Ln	84405
Clydesdale Ct	84404
Coachman Way	84405
Cobblestone Ln	84404
E & N Cold Water Way	84404
College Dr	84403
Collins Blvd	84404
Colonial Dr	84414
Comanche Cir	84403
Combe Rd	84403
Commerce Way	84401
N & W Concord Cir & Dr	84404
Connecticut Ave	84404
Constitution Way	84403
Cook St	84404
E Copper Cir	84404
E Cornia Dr	84405
Cottonwood Dr	
100-199	84414
600-899	84405
4400-4500	84414
4502-4598	84414
W Country Boy Dr	84404
Country Club Dr	84405
Country Cove Way	84401
Country Hills Dr	84403
Country View Dr	84403
E Countryside Way	84404
S Cozy Dale Dr	84405
N Cragun Way	84404
Craig Dr	84403
Creekside Dr	84404
Crestwood Dr	84405
Critchlow Dr	84404
Cross St	84404
Cross Creek Rd	84401
Custer Ave	
400-598	84404
600-1599	84404
1900-2499	84401
3600-3738	84403
D Ave	84401
Dan St	84404
Darling Cir & St	84403
Davis Ct & Ln	84401
Daybreak Dr	84403
Deer Meadows Dr	84414
Deer Run Dr & Way	84405
Deerwalk Ln	84404
Degiorgio St	84401
N & S Depot Dr	84404
W Diamond Cv	84404
Diana St	84403
Dillon Dr	84404
Dixie Cir	84403
Dixie Dr	84405
Dominion Ct	84403
Donna Ave	84404
N & W Dorchester Ave	84414
Doren Dr	84403
Douglas St	84404
Downs Cir & Dr	84404
Doxey St	
100-199	84401
400-1800	84403
1802-1898	84403
W Doxey St	84401
Dunsinane Cir	84401
E Ave	84401
W Eagle Pl	84404
Earl Dr	84404
Eastwood Blvd	84403
Easy St	84403
Eccles Ave	
500-699	84404
1800-2699	84401
2800-4099	84403
N Eccles Ave	84404
S Eccles Ave	84404
Edgehill Dr	84403
Edgewood Dr	84403
Edvalson St	84403
E & W Elberta Dr	84414
Elderberry Ct	84403
W Ellis St	84401
N Erastus Dr	84404
E & S Erica Way	84405
Evelyn Rd	84403
Evergreen Dr	84414
Evergreen Way	84404
Exchange Rd	84401
Eyrie Dr	84404
F Ave	84401
Fairgrounds Dr	84404
W Fallow Way	84414
Farr Ct	84401
Farr Dr	84404
Farr West Dr	84404
Fashion Point Dr	84403
Fawn Dr	84414
Fern Dr	84403
W Fernside St	84401
Fillmore Ave	
900-1350	84404
1352-1398	84404
1901-1997	84401
1999-2699	84401
2700-5399	84403
Firth Farm Rd	84405
Foothill Dr	84403
Forest Green Dr	84403
Fort Ln	84404
Fowler Ave	
100-1699	84404
2100-2599	84401
2700-4399	84403
N Fowler Ave	84404
Fox Chase Dr	84403
W Foxwood St	84401
Franklin Cir	84404
Franklin St	
101-197	84401
199-399	84401
800-1399	84403
Freedom Ln	84401
Freeway Park Dr	84405
Fruitland Dr	
1601-1699	84404
1700-2599	84414
G Ave	84401
Garden Ct	84403
Gavin St	84404
N & S Genetti Ave	84404
Georgia Ave	84404
Gettysburg Way	84401
Gibbs Cir	84405
Gibson Ave	84404
Gilmour St	84401
Glasmann Way	84403
Goddard St	
300-399	84401
800-950	84403
952-998	84403
Golden Spike Ct	84404
W Goodale Dr	84404
Grace Ave	84404
Gramercy Ave	
200-298	84404
300-1699	84404
2000-2699	84401
2700-4599	84403
N Gramercy Ave	84404
Grandview Dr	84403
Grant Ave	
300-1749	84404
1751-1799	84404
1801-1897	84401
1899-3599	84401
3700-3799	84405
3801-3899	84405
Grenwood Cir	84405
Gwen St	84404
H Ave	84401
Hampton Cir & Rdg	84403
Hampton Green Way	84403
W Hancock Cir	84404
Haredara St	84404
W Harleran S	84405
Harper Way	84405
E & W Harris St	84401
Harrison Blvd	
100-1499	84404
1801-1997	84401
1999-2699	84401
2700-5899	84403
N Harrison Blvd	84404
S Harrison Blvd	84405
N & W Harrisville Rd	84404
Harrop St	84404
W Haven Rd	84401
Haven Creek Rd	84401
Hawthorne Ave	84403
Healy St	
300-399	84401
600-1099	84403
1101-1149	84403
Heather Cir	84404
S Heights Cir	84403
Henderson Dr	84404
Heritage Dr	84404
Heritage Ranch Dr	84404
Herman St	84404
N Hidden Cv	84404
Highland Dr	84405
Highland Springs Cir & Rd	84403
N Highway 126	84404
E Highway 39	84401
Highway 89	84405
N Highway 89	84404
N Higley Rd	84404
Hiland Rd	84404
Hill Dr	84403
Hillcrest Cir	84405
Hillsborough Dr	84414
Hillside Cir	84403
Hinckley Dr	84401
Hinkley Dr	84401
Hislop Dr	84404
Holiday Dr	84414
Holly Ct	84403
Holroyd Dr	84403
Hudson St	84404
Hunter Ct	84401
Independence Blvd	84404
Indian Camp Rd	84404
Industrial Dr	84401
Iowa Ave	
121-597	84404
599-999	84404
2300-2699	84401
3000-3699	84403
N Iowa Ave	84404
Iroquoi Way	84403
S Issac Newton Ct	84404
Jace Ln	84405
Jackson Ave	
200-1099	84404
1800-1898	84401
1900-2699	84401
2700-3999	84403
N Jackson Ave	
100-1299	84404
3600-4199	84414
Jacqueline Dr	84403
Jared Way	84403
Jefferson Ave	
100-1699	84404
2000-2699	84401
2700-4899	84403
N Jefferson Ave	84404
Jennifer Dr	84403
Jenny Ln	84414
Jessie Creek Dr	84414
Joe Dean Cir	84403
N Jorgensen Ave	84404
Junction Way	84401
Juniper Ct	84405
Kanesville Meadows Ln	84401
Karen Dr	84403
Kay Ln	84405
Kenna Ln	84401
Kershaw St	
300-399	84401
600-1799	84403
W Kershaw St	84401
Kiesel Ave	
301-397	84404
399-1699	84404
2201-2297	84401
2299-3199	84401
3201-3299	84401
3700-3800	84405
3802-3898	84405
King Hill Dr	84414
Kingston Cir & Dr	84403
Kiwana Dr	84403
S Knights Way	84401
Knollwood Dr	84403
Kylee Ln	84404
Laine Ave	84401
W Lake St	84401
Lakerview Dr	84403
Lakeview Cir	84403
Lakeview Dr	
3301-3397	84414
3399-3749	84414
3751-3799	84414
4001-4097	84403
4099-4300	84403
4302-4398	84403
Lakeview Way	84403
Lamplighter Way	84405
W Lancelot Ln	84401
Lankshire Dr	84414
Lark Cir	84403
Larkspur Ln	
3400-3499	84404
4900-4999	84403
Larsen Ln	84404
Laurel Dr	84403
S Laurel St	84401
Laurel Hurst Ct	84401
Lavina Dr	84403
Leona Dr	84403
E Lester Dr	84405
Lewis Dr	84404
N Lewis Peak Dr	84404
Lexi Ln	84401
Liberty Ave	
100-1699	84404
2000-2699	84401
2700-4299	84403
N Liberty Ave	84404
Lincoln Ave	
500-598	84404
600-1799	84404
1800-1898	84401
1900-3599	84401
3600-3698	84405
Lockwood Dr	84404
Loffredo St	84404
Logan Ave	84401
E & W Lomond View Dr	84414
W Lone Pine Dr	84404
Lorin Cir	84401
Lorl Ln	84404
N & S Lynne School Ln	84404
Macintosh Way	84414
Madie Ln	84401
Madison Ave	
112-112	84404
114-1699	84404
2000-2699	84401
2700-4799	84403
N Madison Ave	84404
Main Point Blvd	84405
Majestic Cir	84414
Malan Ave & Ct	84403
Manderley Ln	84403
Maple St	84403
Maple Grove Way	84401
Maplewood Dr	84405
Marco Ln	84404
Marilyn Dr	84403
Marlette Dr	84404
N Marshal Ln	84404
Martinet Ln	84403
Massachusetts Cir	84404
Matrixx Plz	84405
Maule Dr	84403
Maxfield Dr	84404
Mcfarland St	84403
N Meadow Ct	84404
W Meadow Ct	84404
Meadow Dr	84403
Meadow Ln	84403
Meadow Creek Ln	84403
Meadow View Dr	84404
Meadow Wood Dr	84405
Meadowbrook Dr	84404
Megan Cir	84403
Melanie Ln	84403
Melling Way	84404
Melody Ln	84404
N Meteor Pl	84404
Midland Dr	84401
Mile High Cir	84403
Millcreek Dr	84404
Mitchell Dr	84403
Mohawk Cir & Ln	84403
Mond St	84404
Monroe Blvd	
101-397	84404
399-1699	84404
1700-1798	84401
1800-2699	84401
2700-4699	84403
4701-4799	84403
N Monroe Blvd	84404
Morning Mist Ct & Ln	84404
Mound Fort Dr	84404
Mount Lomond Dr	84414
Mount Ogden Cir & Dr	84403
Mount Orchard Dr	84414
Mountain Rd	
900-1600	84404
1602-1698	84404
1700-1798	84414
1800-3499	84414
E Mountain Rd	84414
N Mountain Rd	84404
Mountain Pines Ln	84403
Mountain View Dr	84414
Nancy Dr	84403
Navajo Dr	84403
Nebo Ave	84414
New Jersey Ave	84404
New York Ave	84404
W Newbury Ln	84414
Newgate Mall	84405
Nordin Ave	84403
W North St	84404
W North Plain City Rd	84404
Oak Dr	84403
Oak St	84401
W Oak St	84401
Oakcrest Cir & Dr	84403
Oakridge Dr	84403
Oaks Cir & Dr	84404
Oakwood Ct	84403
Oakwood Dr	84405
Ogden Ave	
300-1699	84404
1701-1799	84404
2000-2599	84401
2601-3499	84401
2900-2998	84403
3000-3498	84401
3500-3999	84403
N Ogden Ave	84404
Ogden Cyn	84401
Ogden Peak Cir	84404
E Old Fort Rd	84405
Old Post Rd	84403
Old Springs Rd	84404
S Olivia St	84401
Olympic Ln	84404
Oram Cir	84403
Orchard Ave	
100-1399	84404
2000-2599	84401
2900-4599	84403
N Orchard Ave	84404
Orchard Cir	84403
Orchard Park Dr	84404
Osmond Dr	84403
Oxford Dr	84403
Oxford Ln	84414
Pacific Ave	
1700-1798	84404
2100-3500	84401
3502-3680	84401
3680-3680	84409
3690-3690	84401
3700-4099	84405
Painter Ln	84401
Palmer Dr	84405
Panorama Dr	84403
Park Blvd	84401
W Park Cir	84404
Park Ln	84403
Park Vista Dr	84405
Parker Dr	84405
Parkland Blvd	84404
Parkview Dr	84403
Parry St	84404
Partridge Way	84403
Patterson St	
100-399	84401
600-1199	84403
W Patterson St	84401
Peach Dr	84404
Peachwood Dr & Way	84405
Pebblebrook Rd	84404
N Pelican Dr	84404
Pennsylvania Ave	84401
Pennsylvania Dr	84404
Peterson Pkwy	84405
Pierce Ave	
1900-2699	84401
2700-5200	84403
5202-5298	84403
Pine Cir	84414
Pine Ct	84404
S Pine Cone Way	84404
Pinecrest Dr	84403
Pingree Ave	
1700-1798	84404
2100-3299	84401
N Pingree Ave	84404
S Pingree Ave	84404
N & W Pioneer Rd	84404
Pleasant Valley Dr	84405
E & W Pleasant View Dr	84414
Plum Creek Ln	84404
Pole Patch Dr	84414
Polk Ave	
100-899	84404
2000-2699	84401
2700-3599	84403
N Polk Ave	84404
Porter Ave	
201-297	84404
299-1299	84404
2500-2599	84401
2800-4699	84403
N Porter Ave	84404
Prairie Cir	84404
Price Ln	84414
Pringle Cir	84403
Quail Ln	84403
Quail Run Dr	84403

uincy Ave
100-199 84404
2000-2699 84401
2700-3899 84403
Quincy Ave 84404
uinn Ct 84404
ancho Blvd 84404
ancho Vista Dr 84404
ay St 84404
aymond Ave 84403
aymond Dr 84405
Red River Way 84404
ed Rock Dr 84404
& W Red Sand Rd 84401
edwood Ln 84403
eeves Ave
1201-1299 84404
2100-3199 84401
egency Dr 84403
emuda Dr 84404
hode Island Cir 84404
idge Canyon Rd 84414
idge Place Dr 84404
dgecrest Dr 84403
idgedale Cir & Dr 84403
Ridgeline Dr 84405
idgeview Dr 84403
itter Dr 84405
iver Dr 84404
iver Valley Dr 84405
iverbend Ln 84404
Riverdale Rd 84405
iverwalk Dr 84405
obins Ave
300-799 84404
2000-2199 84401
obins Cir 84404
ond Cir 84403
ose Anne Cir 84414
oss Dr 84403
oyal Oaks Dr 84404
ue Ann Ct 84401
ulon White Blvd 84404
Rushton St 84401
utherford Ridge Rd 84403
yan Cir 84403
& S Sam Gates Rd 84404
am Williams Dr 84401
& S Sandalwood Dr 84405
ara Ln 84404
avannah Ln 84414
axonbrook 84404
Scott Ln 84401
ecluded Cir 84403
Sego St 84401
ellwood Ct 84401
even Oaks Ln 84403
hadow Mountain Cir &
84403
adow Ridge Cir 84403
hadow Valley Dr 84403
hamrock Dr 84403
haron Cir 84403
harp Mountain Cir &
84404
harron Ct 84404
hawnee Ln 84403
hay Ln 84405
heridan Dr 84404
herwood Dr 84404
hoshone Cir & Dr 84403
hupe Ln 84401
igne Ln 84405
Silverton Rd 84404
imoron Dr 84404
ioux Cir 84403
kate St 84401
kyhaven Cv 84405
kyline Dr 84403
Skyline Dr 84405
South Point Ter 84405
& W South Weber
84405
outhwell St 84404
pring Rd & St 84403
pring Canyon Rd 84403

W Spring Valley Ln 84404
Spruce Ct 84403
Staci Ct 84404
Standard Way 84404
Stayley Ave 84401
Stephens Ave 84401
Stephens Cir 84403
Stephens Ct 84403
Stewart St 84404
W Stock Rd 84401
Stone Ct 84404
Stone Creek Rd 84401
Stone Mountain Cir 84403
Stone Pond Rd 84404
Stonefield Way 84404
Stowe Dr 84404
Stringer Ave 84404
Sullivan Rd 84403
Sun Valley Ln 84404
Suncrest Dr 84404
Sunflower Dr 84404
Sunset Dr 84403
N Sunset Dr 84404
Sunset Ln 84403
Sunview Cir & Dr 84404
Swan St 84401
Swanner Pl 84401
Sylvia Dr 84405
Symphony Cir 84404
Taylor Ave
100-1399 84404
2000-2699 84401
2700-5199 84403
Taylor Cir 84404
Tomahawk Ln 84403
E Trennerm N 84414
Tyler Ave
100-1599 84404
2001-2047 84401
2049-2699 84401
2700-3699 84403
N Tyler Ave 84404
Tyler Cir 84404
Tyler View Way 84401
Union Ave 84401
Valley Dr 84401
Valley View Cir 84403
Van Buren Ave
200-1099 84404
1800-2699 84401
2700-4899 84403
N Van Buren Ave 84404
E Verona Creek Way 84405
Victoria Ct 84403
Victory Ln 84404
View Dr 84405
Viking Dr 84403
Village Cir 84403
E Village Rd 84404
N Village Rd 84404
Village Way 84403
N Virginia Ave 84404
W Virginia Ave 84404
Virginia Way 84403
Vista Dr 84403
Vitt Dr 84404
Waco Dr 84403
Wade Ct 84401
Wadman Dr 84401
Wagonwheel Ln 84403
Wahlen Way 84404
Walcott St 84403
Wall Ave
100-298 84404
300-1700 84404
1702-1798 84404
1800-3599 84401
3600-3999 84405
N Wall Ave 84404
Wallace Cir 84403
Warren Row 84401
Wasatch Ct & Dr 84403
Washakie Cir 84403
Washington Blvd
100-198 84404
200-1799 84404

1801-1897 84401
1899-2731 84401
2730-2730 84402
2732-3498 84401
2733-3499 84401
3500-4200 84403
4202-4598 84403
N Washington Blvd
100-222 84404
221-221 84412
224-1698 84404
225-1699 84404
2003-2597 84414
2599-2699 84414
Water Tower Way 84401
Waterfall Dr 84414
Waterfall Ln 84403
Wayment Way 84401
S Weber Dr 84405
Weber River Dr 84405
Wellington Ave 84414
West Ct 84401
Westgate Ln 84404
Westwind Ct 84405
Westwood Dr 84414
Wheelock Ave 84403
Whispering Meadow
Ln 84404
Whispering Oaks Dr 84403
Whisperwood Ct 84401
Whiston St 84401
White St 84404
White Barn Dr 84414
White Rail Ln 84401
Wild Rose Way 84404
Wildcat Ln 84403
Wildflower Cir 84404
Willard Ct 84403
Willard Peak Cir & Dr 84404
N Williamsburg Ave 84414
Willow Crk 84404
W Willow St 84401
Willow Way 84414
Willow Wood Ct & Ln 84403
Willowbrook Ln 84404
Wilson Ln 84401
Winchester Ln 84403
Windemere Ln 84403
Wood St 84404
W Woodbury Dr 84404
Woodland Cir & Dr 84403
Woodshire Ct & Pl 84403
W Woodstone Dr 84401
Yale Dr 84405
Yorkshire 84403

NUMBERED STREETS

W 1st 84404
W 2nd 84404
3rd St 84404
W 4th 84404
5th St 84404
6th St 84404
W 7th 84404
8th St 84404
W 9th 84404
10th St 84404
11th St 84404
W 12th 84404
W 13th 84404
W 14th 84404
15th St 84404
16th St 84404
W 17th 84404
18th St 84401
W 18th St 84404
19th St 84401
20th St 84401
21st St 84401
E & W 22nd 84401
23rd St 84401
W 24th 84401
W 25th 84401
W 26th 84401

27th St
100-499 84401
500-1899 84403
W 27th St 84401
28th St
100-499 84401
500-1899 84403
W 28th St 84401
29th St
100-499 84401
500-1799 84403
W 29th St 84401
30th St
100-499 84401
500-1399 84403
W 30th St 84401
31st St
100-499 84401
500-1399 84403
W 31st St 84401
32nd St
101-197 84401
500-1499 84403
W 32nd St 84401
33rd St
100-299 84401
500-1552 84403
W 33rd St 84401
34th St
200-499 84401
500-1699 84403
35th St
101-197 84401
400-1399 84403
36th St
100-198 84405
400-448 84403
450-1699 84403
W 36th St 84405
37th St
201-347 84405
349-399 84405
400-1300 84403
1302-1398 84403
38th St 84403
39th St
200-298 84405
400-999 84403
40th St
100-326 84405
328-348 84405
401-447 84403
449-1099 84403
41st St 84403
42nd St 84403
E 1000 N 84404
N 100 E
1100-1499 84404
2001-2097 84414
2099-4099 84414
2700-3098 84414
N 1000 W
2601-2697 84414
3000-3299 84414
S 100 E
4100-5599 84405
4500-4899 84403
5432-5472 84405
S 1000 W
100-199 84404
4000-4399 84405
4300-5599 84405
W 1000 N
2100-2299 84404
4400-4599 84404
W 1000 S 84404
E 1015 S 84404
E 1025 S 84404
N 1025 E
900-1099 84404
2800-3099 84414
N 1020 W 84414
S 1025 E
4600-4999 84403
5400-5492 84405
5494-7499 84405
S 1025 W 84405

W 1025 N 84404
N 1030 W 84414
S 1035 E 84403
S 1040 E 84404
E 1050 N 84404
N 1050 E 84414
N 10500 W 84404
1600-1699 84404
3000-3999 84414
S 1055 E
1400-1699 84404
4600-5099 84403
5500-5798 84405
5800-5999 84405
S 1055 E
5900-5999 84405
S 1050 W 84405
W 1050 S 84404
S 1060 E 84405
S 1065 E 84404
N 1075 E
1100-1199 84404
3100-3199 84414
N 1070 W 84404
1400-1599 84404
3000-3399 84414
S 1075 E
4600-5099 84403
5600-7499 84405
S 1085 E 84404
E 1100 N 84404
N 1100 E 84414
N 1100 W 84414
S 1100 E
4600-5099 84403
5500-7199 84405
S 1100 W
1500-1699 84404
1800-1898 84401
4000-5599 84405
W 1100 N 84404
W 1100 S
600-699 84404
1800-1898 84401
E 1120 S 84404
N 1125 E 84414
E 1140 S 84404
E 1150 N 84404
E 1150 S 84404
N 1150 E 84414
S 1150 E
4800-5199 84403
5600-6099 84405
S 1150 W 84405
W 1150 S 84404
S 1165 E 84404
S 1160 E 84405
E 1175 N 84404
S 1175 E
1400-1499 84404
4000-4100 84403
4102-4198 84403
S 1175 W 84405
S 1185 E 84404
S 1195 E 84404
E 1200 N 84404
N 1200 E 84414
N 1200 W 84404
S 1200 E
1400-1499 84404
5000-5299 84403
6000-7399 84405
S 120 W 84404
101-197 84404
2100-2299 84401
5100-5699 84405
W 1200 N 84404
W 1200 S 84404
E 1225 N 84404
E 1225 S 84404
N 1225 E 84414
S 1225 E 84403
S 1225 W 84405
E 125 N 84404
E 125 S
900-1099 84404
900-1799 84404

N 125 E
1100-1199 84404
2400-3175 84414
N 125 W
2501-4399 84414
3000-3399 84414
S 1250 E
4201-4299 84403
5200-5499 84405
6000-7399 84405
S 1250 W
700-899 84404
1900-2899 84401
4300-4699 84405
4500-5174 84405
W 1250 N
100-299 84404
100-299 84404
W 1250 S 84404
E 1275 N 84404
N 1275 E 84414
S 1275 E
1900-1999 84401
6000-6099 84405
6101-6299 84405
S 1275 W 84405
W 1275 N 84404
E 1300 N 84404
N 1300 E 84414
S 1300 E
1945-1999 84401
5101-5197 84403
7200-7300 84405
S 1300 W
700-999 84404
4700-4798 84405
W 1300 N 84404
E 1325 N 84404
N 1325 E 84414
N 1325 W 84414
S 1325 E
4200-4299 84403
5750-5798 84405
5800-6099 84405
S 1325 W 84401
S 1345 W 84405
E 1350 N 84404
E 1350 S 84404
N 1350 E 84414
N 135 W 84404
1200-1899 84404
3100-3399 84414
S 1350 E
5200-5599 84403
6000-6299 84405
S 1350 W 84401
W 1350 S 84401
E 1375 N 84404
E 1375 S 84404
N 1375 E 84414
N 1375 W 84414
S 1375 E
5500-5599 84403
5800-7699 84405
W 1375 N 84404
N 1385 E 84414
E 1390 S 84404
S 1390 E 84405
E 1400 N 84404
N 1400 E 84414
S 140 E
2500-2599 84401
5300-5399 84403
5800-7599 84405
S 1400 W 84401
W 140 N
100-199 84404
900-5999 84404
W 1400 S 84401
S 1410 E 84403
E 1425 N 84404
E 1420 S 84404
N 1425 E 84414
5500-5600 84403
S 1420 E
5801-5899 84405
E 1450 N 84404

E 1450 S 84404
S 1450 E
5000-5099 84403
6100-7499 84405
E 1475 N 84404
E 1470 S 84404
1000-1699 84404
S 1475 E
5600-5799 84403
7400-7499 84405
S 1475 W 84401
W 1480 N 84404
E 1500 N 84404
N 150 E 84414
N 1500 W
100-2424 84404
1200-1699 84404
1800-2999 84414
3700-3799 84414
S 150 E
4300-5599 84405
4700-4999 84403
6500-7499 84405
S 1500 W
100-299 84404
300-499 84404
3300-3400 84401
3501-4497 84405
4499-5599 84405
4600-5199 84405
W 1500 N 84404
W 150 S
200-2099 84404
1000-1099 84404
E 1510 N 84404
E 1525 N 84404
4700-4899 84403
6100-6299 84405
W 1520 N 84404
S 1540 E 84405
E 1550 N 84404
E 1550 S 84404
N 1550 E 84414
S 1550 E
1100-1298 84404
4700-4799 84403
6000-7599 84405
S 1550 W 84401
W 1550 N 84404
S 1575 E
4600-4899 84403
6200-6399 84405
S 1575 W 84401
W 1575 N 84404
S 1590 E 84405
N 160 E
200-299 84404
2500-2575 84414
N 1600 W 84404
S 1600 E
1401-1499 84404
S 160 E
2500-2599 84401
4900-4999 84403
6700-6798 84405
6800-7399 84405
S 1600 W 84405
W 1600 N 84404
W 1600 S 84401
S 1615 E 84404
E & W 1625 84404
S 1620 W 84401
S 1635 E 84404
E 1640 S 84404
N 1650 W 84404
S 1650 E
1400-1499 84404
6600-7799 84405
S 1650 W 84405
W 1650 N 84404
W 1650 S 84401
1675 N & S 84404
1675 N & S 84401
E 1700 N 84414
E 1700 S 84404
N 1700 W 84404
S 1700 E 84405

S 1700 W
1100-1199 84404
2600-3198 84401
4800-4999 84405
W 1700 N
200-399 84414
2800-3400 84404
W 1700 S 84401
N 1710 W 84414
E 1725 N 84414
N 1725 W
1200-1899 84404
3800-3899 84414
S 1725 E 84405
W 1725 S 84401
S 1740 E 84405
E 1750 N 84414
N 175 E 84414
N 1750 W
1200-1299 84404
3000-4499 84414
S 175 E
4300-5599 84405
5500-5598 84403
6700-7899 84405
S 175 W 84405
W 175 N
100-299 84404
100-199 84414
1300-2899 84404
S 1760 W 84401
E 1775 N 84414
N 1775 W 84404
S 1775 E 84405
S 1775 W 84401
W 1775 N
200-399 84414
3300-3499 84404
W 1775 S 84401
E 1800 N 84414
N 180 E 84404
N 1800 W 84404
S 1800 E
5600-5699 84403
6600-6698 84405
6700-7899 84405
W 1800 N 84404
W 1800 S 84401
S 1825 E 84401
W 1825 N 84414
E 1850 N 84414
N 1850 W 84404
S 1850 E
1900-2099 84401
6400-7899 84405
S 1850 W 84401
W 1850 N 84404
W 1850 S 84401
E 1875 N 84414
N 1875 W 84404
W 1875 N
100-399 84414
3800-3999 84404
E 1908 N 84414
201-397 84414
N 1900 W 84404
S 1900 E
4700-4800 84403
7400-7498 84405
S 1900 W
500-999 84404
1300-3299 84401
W 1900 N 84404
W 1900 S 84401
E 1925 N 84414
S 1925 E 84405
W 1925 N 84414
W 1940 N 84414
E 1950 N 84414
E 1950 S 84401
S 1950 E 84405
W 1950 N
200-399 84414
6200-6599 84404
W 1950 S 84401
E 1960 S 84401
S 1960 E 84405
E 1975 N 84414
200-399 84414
2700-4699 84404
N 1980 W 84404
S 1980 E 84405
S 1980 W 84404
E 1990 S 84401
E 2000 N 84414
N 200 E
1100-1199 84404
2000-3699 84414
N 200 W
128-1599 84404
300-3500 84404
1700-2899 84414
S 200 E
4600-5599 84405
6000-6099 84403
6400-7899 84405
S 200 W
300-999 84404
700-1199 84404
1500-1599 84401
4300-5599 84405
W 2000 N
116-498 84414
700-6699 84404
2400-6299 84404
W 200 S
1200-2799 84404
3400-3499 84401
E 2025 N 84414
E 2025 S 84401
N 2025 E 84404
N 2020 W 84404
S 2025 E
6100-6199 84403
S 2020 E
7500-7999 84405
100-199 84404
200-499 84404
2800-2805 84401
W 2025 N
100-199 84414
2800-2899 84404
W 2025 S 84401
E 2050 N 84414
S 2050 E
6200-6299 84403
7200-7999 84405
S 2050 W
500-699 84404
1600-3299 84401
W 2050 N
100-599 84414
4400-6199 84404
W 2050 S 84401
N 2075 W 84404
S 2075 W 84404
W 2075 N
400-499 84414
2600-2899 84404
E 2100 N 84414
S 2100 E 84405
S 2100 W 84404
W 2100 N
500-599 84414
3400-4399 84404
W 2100 S 84401
N 2125 W 84404
S 2125 E
5900-6299 84403
6600-8133 84405
W 2125 N
400-499 84414
2600-4699 84404
E 2143 N 84414
E 2150 N 84414
N 2150 W 84404
S 2150 E 84405
S 2150 W 84404
W 2150 N
89-89 84414
91-700 84414
702-798 84414
800-5899 84404
W 2150 S 84401
E 2175 N 84414
N 2175 W 84404
S 2175 E
6100-6299 84403
6400-8128 84405
W 2175 N 84404
W 2175 S 84401
E 2200 N 84414
N 2200 W 84404
S 2200 E 84405
S 2200 W
300-399 84404
2200-2399 84401
W 2200 N
500-599 84414
2900-4999 84404
W 2200 S 84401
E 2225 N 84414
S 2225 E
6163-6165 84403
7700-8199 84405
E 2250 N 84414
E 2250 S 84401
N 225 E 84414
N 2250 W
900-2699 84404
1200-1650 84404
1652-1698 84404
1700-3400 84414
3402-3498 84414
S 225 E
4300-5599 84405
6101-6147 84403
6149-6156 84403
6158-6164 84403
6300-8099 84405
S 2250 W 84404
W 2250 N 84414
S 2260 E 84405
E 2275 N 84414
S 2275 E
6200-6299 84403
6550-8199 84405
W 2275 N
200-299 84414
4200-4599 84404
E 2300 N 84414
N 2300 W 84404
S 2300 E
6100-6199 84403
7700-8099 84405
S 2300 W 84401
W 2300 N 84414
S 2310 E 84405
E 2325 N 84414
S 2325 E 84405
W 2325 N 84404
W 2325 S 84401
E 2350 N 84414
S 2350 E 84405
S 2350 W 84401
W 2350 N
300-399 84414
1200-4500 84404
4502-4598 84404
W 2350 S 84401
S 2375 E 84403
S 2380 W 84401
E 2400 N 84414
N 240 E 84404
N 2400 W 84404
S 240 E
5000-5099 84405
5900-6299 84403
6300-6398 84405
W 2400 N 84404
W 2400 S 84401
W 2410 N 84404
S 2420 E 84405
S 2425 E
8100-8199 84405
S 2425 W 84401
300-699 84414
3400-4499 84404
E 2450 N 84414
N 2450 W 84404
S 2450 E
5900-5999 84403
7800-7999 84405
W 2450 N
300-399 84414
2500-2699 84404
W 2450 S 84401
E 2475 N 84414
N 2475 W 84404
S 2475 E 84405
W 2475 N 84404
W 2475 S 84401
E 2500 N 84414
N 250 E
900-998 84404
2000-3299 84414
N 250 W
1500-1549 84404
1800-2598 84404
2200-4399 84414
4401-4499 84414
S 250 E
4300-5599 84405
8000-8099 84405
S 2500 W
2200-2399 84401
3600-3698 84405
W 2500 N
500-599 84414
1400-1598 84404
2000-4499 84404
E 2525 N 84414
N 2525 W 84404
S 2525 E 84405
W 2525 N
100-199 84414
2500-3399 84404
S 2530 E 84405
W 2530 N 84404
E 2550 N 84414
N 2550 W 84404
S 2550 E
5800-5899 84403
8000-8099 84405
S 2550 W
100-199 84404
1200-3099 84401
W 2550 N
100-800 84414
802-998 84414
1600-4199 84404
W 2550 S 84401
S 2560 E 84405
W 2565 N 84404
N 2575 W 84404
S 2570 E 84405
S 2575 E
8000-8099 84405
W 2575 N 84404
E 2600 N 84414
N 2600 W 84404
S 2600 E 84405
W 2600 N 84404
W 2600 S 84401
E 2625 N 84414
N 2625 W 84404
S 2625 E 84405
S 2625 W 84401
W 2625 N 84404
E 2650 N 84414
N 2650 W 84404
S 2650 E 84405
S 2650 W 84401
W 2650 N 84404
W 2650 S 84401
E 2675 N 84414
N 2675 W 84404
W 2675 N 84404
E 2700 N 84414
N 2700 W 84404
S 2700 E 84405
S 2700 W
200-999 84404
1801-2197 84401
2199-2399 84401
2500-3899 84401
W 2700 N
200-999 84414
1100-5199 84404
W 2700 S 84401
S 2725 E 84405
S 2725 W 84401
W 2725 N 84404
E 2735 S 84403
W 2740 N 84404
E 2750 N 84414
N 275 E
1000-1100 84404
1102-1198 84404
2000-3099 84414
3101-3799 84414
N 2750 W
1500-3999 84404
1700-1999 84414
S 275 E
4700-4799 84405
8000-8099 84405
S 275 W 84405
W 2750 N 84404
W 2750 S 84401
S 2775 W 84401
W 2775 N 84404
E 2800 N 84414
N 2800 W 84404
S 2800 E
6200-6500 84403
6502-6598 84403
7600-7999 84405
S 2800 W 84404
W 2800 N 84404
W 2800 S 84401
E 2825 N 84414
N 2825 W 84404
S 2825 W 84401
W 2825 N
600-799 84414
2400-2699 84404
E 2850 N 84414
N 285 W 84414
1600-2399 84404
S 2855 E 84403
6000-6098 84403
S 2850 W 84401
W 2875 N 84404
E 2900 N 84414
S 2900 E 84403
S 2900 W 84401
W 2900 S 84401
E 2925 N 84414
S 2925 E 84403
E 2950 N 84414
N 2950 W 84404
W 2950 N 84404
N & W 2975 W & N 84404
N & W 2975 W & N 84401
S 2985 W 84401
E 3000 N 84414
N 300 E 84414
N 3000 W
1000-3599 84404
1700-4299 84414
S 300 E 84405
S 3005 W 84401
900-999 84404
2700-2899 84401
4100-5699 84405
W 3000 N
500-1099 84414
5500-5699 84404
W 3000 S 84401
E 3025 N 84414
W 3025 S 84401
E 3050 N 84414
N 3050 W 84404
S 3050 W 84401
W 3050 N 84414
W 3050 S 84401
E 3075 N 84414
S 3075 W 84401
E 3090 N 84414
E 3100 N 84414
1-1399 84414
2000-2799 84404
W 3100 S 84401
E & W 3125 84414
E & W 3150 84414
E & W 3150 84401
E 3175 N 84414
N 3175 W 84404
W 3175 N 84414
W 3175 S 84401
E & W 3200 84414
E & W 3225 84414
E 3250 N 84414
N 325 E 84404
N 325 W
900-998 84404
1000-1099 84404
1900-3299 84414
S 325 E 84405
S 3250 W 84401
W 3250 N
1000-1099 84414
2800-2899 84404
E 3275 N 84414
N 3275 W 84404
W 3275 N 84414
E 3300 N 84414
N 3300 W 84404
S 3300 W 84401
W 3300 N
1000-1399 84414
2100-2575 84404
W 3300 S 84401
E & W 3325 84414
E & W 3325 84401
E 3350 N 84414
N 3350 W 84404
S 3350 W 84401
W 3350 N 84414
W 3350 S 84401
E 3375 N 84414
N 3375 W 84404
S 3375 W 84401
W 3375 S 84401
W 3380 S 84401
E 3400 N 84414
N 3400 W 84404
S 3400 W 84404
W 3400 N 84414
E 3425 N 84414
N 3425 W 84404
S 3425 W 84401
W 3425 N 84404
W 3425 S 84401
E 3450 N 84414
N 3450 W 84404
S 3450 W 84401
W 3450 N
200-499 84414
2600-3099 84404
W 3450 S 84401
E 3460 N 84414
E 3475 N 84414
N 3475 W 84404
S 3475 W 84401
E 3500 N 84414
N 350 E 84414
N 3500 W
1000-2999 84404
N 350 W
1700-4699 84414
S 350 E 84405
S 3500 W
800-1249 84404
1250-3402 84401
3529-4699 84401
W 3500 N
400-799 84414
2500-2999 84404
W 3500 S 84405
E 3525 N 84414
N 3525 W 84404
S 3525 W 84401
W 3520 S 84401
E 3550 N 84414
N 3550 W 84404
S 3550 W 84401
W 3550 N 8441
W 3550 S
500-699 8440
3400-3498 8440
E 3560 N 8441
E 3575 N 8441
W 3575 S 8440
E 3600 N 8441
N 360 W 8440
100-2599 8440
S 3600 W
100-899 8440
3600-4599 8440
W 3600 N
700-799 8441
2500-4299 8440
W 3600 S
500-799 8440
2500-4899 8440
E 3625 N 8441
W 3625 S 8440
E 3650 N 8441
N 3650 W 8440
S 3650 W 8440
W 3650 N 8441
W 3650 S
500-699 8440
3600-3799 8440
E 3675 N 8441
S 3675 W 8440
W 3675 N 8440
W 3675 S
601-697 8440
2800-2899 8440
E 3700 N 8441
N 3700 W 8440
S 3700 W 8440
500-699 8440
3500-3899 8440
E 3725 N 8441
N 375 E
900-1099 8440
3300-3699 8441
N 375 W 8441
S 375 E 8440
S 375 W
500-699 8440
S 3750 W
2100-2199 8440
4600-4799 8440
W 3750 N 8441
W 375 S
201-299 8440
W 3750 S
600-649 8440
W 3765 N 8441
S 3775 W 8440
W 3775 N 8441
W 3775 S 8440
E 3800 N 8441
S 3800 W 8440
W 380 N 8440
W 3800 N
900-1399 8441
W 3800 S 8440
N 3825 W 8440
W 3825 S 8440
E 3850 S 8440
S 3850 W 8440
W 3850 N 8441
W 3850 S
600-699 8440
4200-4699 8440
E 3875 N 8441
S 3875 W 8440
W 3875 N 8441
W 3875 S 8440
S 3885 W 8440
E 3900 N 8441
N 3900 W 8440
S 3900 W 8440
W 3900 N
500-1399 8441
2600-2699 8440
W 3900 S 8440
S 3925 W 8440
W 3925 N 8441

3925 S 84401
3950 W 84401
3950 N
200-899 84414
2650-2699 84404
3950 S
500-999 84405
3600-3799 84401
3965 S 84401
3975 W 84404
300-499 84414
2700-2799 84404
3975 S 84401
400 N 84404
400 E 84414
400 W
1501-1547 84404
1549-1699 84404
1700-4499 84414
400 E 84405
4000 W
3900-4124 84401
4500-5599 84405
400 N
600-1799 84404
4000 N
800-1399 84414
3200-4299 84404
500-899 84405
2900-2998 84401
3700-4699 84404
4025 W 84401
4050 N 84414
4050 S 84403
4050 W 84401
4050 N 84414
4050 S
600-1199 84405
4500-4799 84401
4075 N 84414
700-799 84405
3300-5099 84401
4100 S 84403
4100 W 84404
410 W 84404
400-1299 84404
4100-4599 84401
4100 N
100-999 84414
2200-2298 84404
4100 S
700-1199 84405
3900-4999 84401
4125 N 84414
4125 S 84401
4150 S 84405
800-899 84403
4150 W 84404
4150 W 84401
4150 S
600-1099 84405
3300-3899 84401
4175 W 84404
4175 N 84414
1000-1199 84405
4900-5099 84401
4200 W 84404
4200 W 84401
4200 N 84414
4200 S
600-1199 84405
3900-4498 84401
4225 S 84403
4225 N 84414
621-699 84405
3200-3899 84401
425 N 84404
4250 S
600-699 84403
600-799 84404
425 E
900-1098 84404
1700-3599 84414
4255 W 84404
4250 W
1400-1499 84404
1900-4299 84414

S 425 W 84405
W 4255 S 84401
100-299 84404
W 4250 S
700-1199 84405
3200-5099 84401
E 4275 S 84403
N 4275 W 84404
600-699 84405
3200-4699 84401
E 4300 S 84405
E 4300 S 84405
500-899 84403
N & S 430 E & W 84404
N 4300 W 84404
S 4300 W
900-1299 84404
1300-3300 84401
3925-4578 84401
4580-4698 84401
W 4300 N 84414
W 4300 S
1-1199 84405
3500-4899 84401
N 4325 W 84404
E 4350 S 84405
900-999 84403
N 4350 W 84404
W 4350 N 84414
W 4350 S
700-999 84405
3300-4699 84401
S 4375 W 84401
700-999 84405
3200-3699 84401
E 4400 S 84405
E 4400 S 84405
E 4400 S 84405
400-999 84403
N & S 440 84404
700-1699 84404
W 4400 N 84414
W 4400 S
1-97 84405
99-1200 84405
1202-1498 84405
4200-5099 84401
E 4425 S 84405
N 4425 W 84404
W 4425 S 84401
E 4450 S 84405
S 4450 W
400-599 84404
2700-2799 84401
W 4450 S
860-898 84405
3300-4699 84401
E & W 4475 84405
E & W 4475 84401
E 450 N 84404
E 4500 S 84403
N 450 E
900-1699 84404
1700-3299 84414
N 4500 W
1900-2499 84404
2300-2599 84414
S 4500 W
2300-2388 84401
4500-5299 84405
W 4500 N 84414
W 4500 S
100-1299 84405
4500-4899 84401
E 4525 S
200-399 84405
900-1099 84403
300-499 84405
3300-3899 84401
N 4550 W 84404
S 4550 W 84401
900-1299 84405
3900-4299 84401
E 4575 S 84405
N 4575 W 84404
S 4575 W 84401
W 4575 N 84414

W 4575 S 84405
W 4585 S 84401
E 4600 S 84405
500-1200 84403
1145-1145 84415
1202-1898 84403
1301-1899 84403
N 4600 W 84404
S 4600 W
100-399 84404
1300-1399 84401
4400-4499 84401
W 4600 S
100-1299 84405
3400-4899 84401
E 4625 S 84403
S 4625 W 84401
W 4625 S 84405
E 4650 S 84405
N 4650 W 84404
S 4650 W 84401
100-1199 84405
4500-4599 84401
E & W 4675 84405
W 4695 S 84405
E 4700 S 84405
E 4700 S 84405
1500-1599 84403
N 4700 W 84404
S 4700 W
100-1199 84404
1200-3299 84401
3300-3800 84401
3802-4274 84405
W 4700 S 84405
E 4725 S 84403
N 4725 W 84404
300-499 84405
4700-4899 84401
E 475 N 84404
E 4750 S 84403
N 475 E
1000-1699 84404
1700-3799 84414
S 475 E 84405
S 475 W 84405
W 4750 S 84401
100-199 84404
E 4775 S 84405
S 4775 W 84401
W 4775 S 84405
E 4800 S
100-198 84405
800-1299 84403
N 4800 W 84404
S 4800 W 84401
W 4800 S
100-1799 84405
4300-4698 84401
E 4825 S 84403
N 4825 W 84404
W 4825 S 84405
E 4850 S 84405
N 4850 W 84404
W 4850 S 84405
E 4875 S 84403
S 4875 W 84401
E 490 N 84404
E 4900 S 84405
1100-1199 84405
N 4900 W 84404
S 4900 W 84401
W 4900 S 84405
E 4925 S 84403
S 4925 W 84401
W 4925 S 84405
S 4950 W 84401
W 4950 S 84405
E 4975 S 84403
S 4975 W 84401
E 4980 S 84403
S 50 E 84405
E 500 N 84404
E 5000 S
100-399 84405
700-1074 84403
1076-1298 84403

N 500 E
900-1099 84404
1800-3699 84414
N 500 W 84414
S 500 E 84405
S 5000 W
400-499 84404
3800-4399 84401
4200-4299 84405
W 5000 S
100-699 84405
2000-4799 84404
E 5015 S 84403
S 5025 W 84401
W 5025 S 84405
E 5050 S 84405
1000-1399 84403
S 5050 W 84401
W 5050 S 84405
E 5100 S
100-299 84405
900-1399 84403
N 5100 W 84404
S 5100 E 84401
S 5100 W
1100-1299 84404
1300-2199 84401
2201-2899 84401
3300-4698 84401
W 5100 S 84405
W 5125 S 84405
E 5150 S 84405
1000-1399 84403
N 515 E 84414
N 5150 W 84404
W 5150 S 84405
W 5175 S 84405
E 5200 S 84405
1300-1399 84403
N 5200 W 84404
S 5200 W 84404
W 5200 S 84405
W 5225 S 84405
E 525 N 84404
E 5250 S
100-299 84405
1000-1399 84403
N 525 E
1000-1299 84404
2200-3999 84414
N 5250 W 84404
S 5250 W
1100-1299 84404
4800-4822 84405
W 5250 S 84405
E 5275 S 84403
W 5275 S 84405
E 5285 S 84403
E & W 5300 84405
N 530 W 84404
E & W 5350 84405
S 535 W 84405
E 5375 S 84403
W 5375 S 84405
E 5400 S 84405
E 5400 S 84405
E 5400 S 84405
1200-1298 84403
S 540 W 84405
W 5400 S 84405
E 5425 S 84403
W 5425 S 84405
E & W 5450 84405
E & W 5475 84405
E 550 N 84404
E 5500 S
500-598 84405
600-800 84405
700-849 84404
802-898 84405
1100-1198 84403
1200-1499 84403
N 550 E
900-1099 84404
1900-3099 84414
N 5500 W
200-999 84404

2000-4099 84414
S 550 E 84405
S 550 W 84405
W 550 S
300-399 84404
400-1199 84405
W 5525 S 84405
E 5530 S 84405
E 5540 S 84405
E 5550 S 84405
1100-1298 84403
W 5550 S 84405
E & W 5575 84405
E 5600 S 84405
E 5600 S 84405
1200-1899 84403
W 5600 S 84405
E 5625 S
900-1099 84405
1750-1898 84403
E 5630 S 84403
E 5640 S 84403
E 5650 S 84405
1701-1947 84403
W 5650 S 84405
E 5665 S 84403
E 5675 S 84405
E 5675 S 84405
1900-2099 84403
E 5700 S
700-1199 84405
1600-2498 84403
W 5700 S 84405
E 5725 S 84403
E 575 N 84404
E 5750 S
700-1074 84405
1076-1198 84405
1700-1899 84403
N 575 E
800-899 84404
2000-3699 84414
N 575 W 84414
S 575 W 84405
E 5775 S
900-1099 84405
1800-1900 84403
E 5800 S
1000-1399 84405
1900-1999 84403
E 5825 S
1000-1099 84405
1101-1299 84405
1700-1799 84403
E 5850 S
1000-1399 84405
1900-1992 84403
E 5875 S
800-1499 84405
1900-2099 84403
E 5900 S
900-1074 84405
1900-2499 84403
N 5900 W 84404
S 5900 W 84404
E 5950 S
1000-1099 84405
2000-2599 84403
N 60 W 84404
E 6000 S
1100-1599 84405
2700-2799 84403
N 600 E 84414
N 600 W
100-299 84404
2000-3751 84414
3753-3899 84414
S 600 E 84405
S 600 W
100-199 84404
3700-5599 84405
W 600 S 84404
E 6025 S 84403
E 6075 S 84403
E 6100 S 84405
E 6125 S 84405

E 6150 S 84405
2100-2198 84403
2200-2374 84403
2376-2498 84403
S 6150 W 84404
E 6175 S
1200-1399 84405
2000-2499 84403
E 6200 S
1500-1700 84405
1702-1798 84405
1800-1898 84403
1900-2000 84403
2002-2398 84403
N 6200 W 84404
E 6225 S
1200-1599 84405
1900-2125 84403
E 625 N 84404
E 6250 S 84405
600-699 84404
N 625 E 84414
S 625 W 84405
E 6275 S 84403
N 630 E 84404
S 635 E 84403
S 635 W 84405
E 6400 S 84405
E 6425 S 84403
E 6450 S 84405
E 650 N 84404
E 6500 S 84403
700-899 84404
N 650 E 84414
N 650 W 84414
S 650 E 84404
S 650 W 84405
W 650 S 84404
E 6525 S 84403
E 6550 S 84405
E 6575 S 84405
E 6600 S 84405
E 6600 S 84405
2800-2898 84403
N & S 660 84404
E 6625 S 84405
E 6650 S 84405
670 N & S 84404
E 6700 S 84405
N 6700 W 84404
S 6700 W 84404
E 675 N 84404
E 6750 S 84405
N 675 E 84414
S 675 E
4200-4299 84403
6800-7099 84405
E 6775 S 84405
E 6800 S 84405
E 6850 S 84405
E 6900 S 84405
E 6980 S 84405
E 700 N 84404
N 700 E 84414
N 700 W
100-299 84404
2100-3399 84414
S 700 E 84405
S 700 W 84405
W 700 N 84404
W 700 S 84404
S 7100 W 84404
E 7150 S 84405
E 7240 S 84405
E 725 N 84404
N 725 E
1500-1675 84404
1677-1699 84404
1801-2397 84414
2399-2599 84414
S 725 E 84405
E 7325 S 84405
E 7375 S 84405
E 7400 S 84405
E 7425 S 84405
E 7450 S 84405

E 7470 S 84405
E 750 N 84404
E 7500 S 84405
N 750 E 84414
N 750 W
1301-1697 84404
1699-1999 84404
2001-2199 84404
2150-2298 84414
2300-3399 84414
S 750 E 84405
S 7500 W
600-2399 84404
3900-4399 84405
E 7510 S 84405
E 7550 S 84405
E 760 N 84404
E 7600 S 84405
E 7640 S 84405
E 7650 S 84405
E 7700 S 84405
E 775 S 84404
N 775 E
1500-1599 84404
1700-2499 84414
N 775 W 84414
S 775 E 84404
S 775 W 84405
W 775 S 84404
E 7775 S 84405
E 7800 S 84405
E 7825 S 84405
E 7840 S 84405
S 785 E 84403
E 7875 S 84405
E 7870 S 84405
E 7880 S 84405
S 7900 W 84404
E 7925 S 84405
E 7950 S 84405
E 7975 S 84405
E 800 N 84404
N 800 E 84414
N 800 W
100-1699 84404
3400-4199 84414
S 800 E
4800-4822 84403
4824-4999 84403
5300-5699 84405
S 800 W 84405
E 8100 S 84405
E 8125 S 84405
E 8150 S 84405
E 8200 S 84405
E 8225 S 84405
E 8240 S 84405
E 825 N 84404
N 825 E 84414
N 825 W 84414
S 825 E 84405
S 825 W 84405
E 8300 S 84405
E 850 N 84404
N 850 E 84414
N 850 W 84414
S 850 E
4100-4999 84403
5301-5397 84405
5399-7499 84405
S 850 W 84405
S 865 E 84404
E 875 N 84404
N 875 E
1500-1599 84404
1700-3599 84414
N 875 W 84414
S 875 E
3900-5199 84403
5400-5548 84405
5551-5573 84405
S 885 E 84404
S 895 E 84403
E 900 N 84404
N 900 E 84414
N 900 W
1375-1397 84404

3500-3528 84414
S 900 E
4000-4399 84403
5700-7399 84405
S 900 W 84405
W 900 N 84404
W 900 S 84404
N 910 E 84404
S 920 E 84404
E 925 N 84404
N 925 E
100-1399 84404
1700-1799 84414
N 925 W 84404
S 925 E 84405
S 925 W
2900-2999 84401
4100-4199 84405
S 9300 W 84404
E 940 N 84404
E 950 N 84404
N 950 E
700-1199 84404
2600-3599 84414
N 950 W
1500-2199 84404
3500-4199 84414
S 950 E
1200-1298 84404
4100-5199 84403
5700-5899 84405
S 950 W 84405
W 950 N 84404
W 950 S 84404
E 960 N 84404
S 960 E 84405
N 975 E
700-798 84404
800-1599 84404
2800-3099 84414
N 975 W 84404
S 975 E 84405
E 980 N 84404
E 990 N 84404

OREM UT

General Delivery 84057

POST OFFICE BOXES MAIN OFFICE STATIONS AND BRANCHES

Box No.s
1 - 599998 84059
970001 - 972998 84097

NAMED STREETS

A St 84057
S & W Alta Vista Dr 84058
Alturas Cir 84058
N & W Amiron Way 84057
S Anne Cir 84058
Artesian Rd 84058
Atlantis Dr 84057
Austin Ave 84097
N Bella Vista Dr 84097
Beverly Ave 84057
Birchwood Dr 84057
Bluebird Rd 84097
Bowl Dr 84097
E Bretonwoods Ln 84097
W Business Park Dr 84058
Campus Dr 84097
N Canyon Hills Dr 84097
W Carriage Cir 84058
S Carterville Rd 84097
Cascade Dr 84097
Cedarwood Dr 84057
E Center St
2-92 84057
94-100 84057
102-398 84057
400-1099 84097
W Center St
1-223 84057
222-222 84059
224-1598 84057
225-1599 84057
Chapel Cir 84058
Cherapple Cir & Dr 84097
S Cherry Dr 84058
Chokecherry Cir 84058
W Clachall N 84057
College Dr 84058
S Columbia Ln 84097
Commerce Loop & Rd 84058
S Commercial St 84058
S & W Countryside Cir, Dr & Ln 84058
Coventry Cir 84058
Crest Dr 84057
Daniel Dr 84057
Del Def 84097
Eastwood Dr 84097
S Ellen Cir 84058
Ellis Dr 84097
Elmwood Dr 84057
Emery Ave 84057
Fairway Ct & Ln 84058
Farm Lane Cir 84057
S & W Fox Trail Ln 84058
Foxmoor Dr 84057
E Gammon Rd 84058
N & W Garden Dr & Park 84057
N Geneva Rd 84057
S Geneva Rd 84058
Gilbert Cir 84057
Gillman Cir 84097
Glendell Dr 84058
Gold River Cir & Dr 84057
Gold Tip Dr 84058
W Golden Pond Way 84058
S Graff Cir 84058
Hanover Dr 84058
Heather Cir 84057
Heather Dr 84097
Heather Rd
100-399 84057
400-1999 84097
W Hidden Ct 84058
Hidden Hollow Cir & Dr 84058
High Country Dr 84097
E & S Holdaway Rd 84058
S Honey Ln 84058
W Industrial Dr 84058
Industrial Park Rd 84057
Inglewood Dr 84097
Keyridge Cir 84058
Kwanzan Cir 84058
Laguna Vista Cir & Dr 84058
E Lake View Dr 84058
W Lakeview Ct 84058
Lakewood Dr 84058
Lambert Dr 84097
N Lecheminant Dr 84058
Lupe Cir 84057
Lynnwood Dr 84097
N Main St 84057
S Main St 84058
Meadowlark Rd 84097
Memo Dr 84057
Monterey Dr 84057
Moor Ln 84057
Mountain Oaks Dr 84097
Mountain View Ct 84057
Mountain Way Dr 84058
Mountainlands Dr 84058
Ninetta Cir 84057
Nu Vue Cir 84057
Oak View Cir 84097
Oakcrest Dr 84097
Oakwood Cir 84057
Orchard Dr 84057
N Orem Blvd 84057
S Orem Blvd 84058
Orlean Dr 84097
N Pachariv E 84097
N & S Palisades Dr 84097
Palos Verdes Dr 84058
E & N Paradise Dr 84097
Park Ln E 84058
Pembroke Cir 84097
Penni Ln 84097
S & W Pheasant Run 84058
Pleasant Cir 84097
Quail Rd 84097
Regent Ct 84057
Research Way 84097
Ribbonwood Dr 84057
Ridge Rd 84057
S Ridgecrest Dr 84058
S Ridgeview Dr 84058
S River Breeze Dr 84097
River Ridge Ln 84097
E Riverhaven Cir 84097
Riverside Ln 84097
Robin Rd 84097
Royal Ann Cir 84058
N Rue Borda 84058
E Rue Cournot 84058
E Rue De Borda 84058
E & N Rue De Matth 84058
E & N Rue Hugo 84058
Sage Cir & Dr 84097
Sage Hen Rd 84097
Sandhill Rd 84058
Sarah Cir 84058
W Scorinti S 84058
W Serenity Ct 84058
W Shoreline Ct 84058
Skyline Dr 84097
S Sleepy Ridge Dr 84058
Springwater Dr 84058
Starcrest Dr 84058
N State St 84057
S State St
1-799 84058
800-2099 84097
N & W Sun Village Dr 84057
Sunny Ln 84058
Sunrise Dr 84097
N & S Sunset Dr 84058
Sunshine Ct 84097
N Technology Ave & Way 84097
Terrace Dr 84097
Timpanogos Cir & Pkwy 84097
W Twilight Ct 84058
E University Pkwy
40-399 84058
400-498 84097
500-899 84097
W University Pkwy 84058
Village Dr & Ln 84058
N & S Vineyard Rd 84058
S Virginia Cir 84058
Westlake Dr 84058
Westview Cir & Dr 84058
Westwood Dr 84097
Wildwood Holw 84058
S Willowspring 84097
Woodland Dr 84097
Woodmore Dr 84058
Xactware Plz 84097
Zobell Dr 84097

NUMBERED STREETS

W 10 N 84057
E 100 N
1-399 84057
200-399 84057
600-1199 84097
E 1000 S
1-399 84058
400-599 84097
500-899 84097
N 1000 E
1-1299 84097
200-1960 84057
N 1005 W 84057
500-598 84057
700-799 84057
S 1000 E
1-1399 84097
900-1780 84058
S 1000 W
40-98 84058
201-297 84058
W 100 N
300-698 84057
400-899 84057
W 1000 S
100-1799 84058
200-999 84058
E 1010 N 84097
E 1010 S 84097
N 1015 W 84057
S 1015 W 84058
101-199 84057
W 1010 N
400-499 84057
E 1020 N 84057
1-97 84057
N & W 1025 W & N 84057
S 1020 W 84058
E 1030 N 84097
N 1035 W 84057
100-1769 84057
S 1030 E 84097
S 1030 W 84058
W 1030 N 84057
E 1040 N
300-399 84057
E 1045 N
1000-1199 84097
1100-1199 84097
1201-1299 84097
N 1040 E 84097
N 1040 W 84057
S 1040 E 84097
S 1045 W
400-599 84058
600-699 84058
W 1040 N 84057
W 1040 S 84058
E 1050 N 84097
N 1050 E 84097
N 1050 W 84057
S 1050 W 84058
W 1055 N 84057
W 105 N 84057
800-899 84057
E 1060 N
100-199 84057
1300-1599 84097
E 1060 S 84097
N 1060 W 84057
S 1065 W 84058
W 1060 S 84058
E 1070 S 84097
W 1075 N 84057
W 1070 N
1-99 84057
E & W 1085 84057
800-999 84097
N 1080 E 84097
N 1080 W 84057
S 1080 E 84097
E 1090 N
200-399 84057
400-1299 84097
N 1090 W 84057
W 1090 N 84057
E 1100 N
1-99 84057
900-1199 84097
E 1100 S
1-299 84058
501-797 84097
N 1100 E 84097
N 1100 W
700-1498 84057
N 110 W
1300-1699 84057
S 1100 E
100-1399 84097
S 110 E
801-1599 84058
S 1100 W
400-550 84058
S 110 W
1000-1099 84058
W 1100 N 84057
W 1100 S 84058
E 1110 N 84097
N 1110 E 84097
N 1110 W 84057
S 1115 W 84058
1301-1399 84058
E 1120 S 84097
N 1120 E
200-599 84097
N 1125 E
700-799 84097
N 1120 W
400-499 84057
N 1125 W
1101-1129 84057
S 1120 W
201-299 84058
S 1125 W
1201-1299 84058
W 1120 N 84057
E 1130 N
100-199 84057
600-1299 84097
N 1130 W 84057
W 1130 N 84057
W 1130 S 84058
E 1140 N
200-399 84057
E 1145 N
400-1199 84097
700-799 84097
N 1140 W 84057
S 1140 E 84097
S 1145 W 84058
W 1140 N 84057
E 1150 N 84097
E 1150 S 84097
N 1150 W 84057
S 1150 W 84058
W 1150 N 84057
E 1165 N
200-399 84057
400-1399 84097
N 1160 E 84097
N 1160 W
500-1499 84057
N 1165 W
1100-1199 84057
S 1160 W
1-699 84058
S 1165 W
300-399 84058
W 1160 N 84057
E 1170 N 84097
N 1170 E 84097
S 1170 W 84058
W 1170 N 84057
N 1180 E 84097
N 1180 W 84057
S 1180 W 84058
W 1185 N 84057
S 1190 W 84058
W 1190 N 84057
E 1200 N
1-399 84057
400-1299 84097
1000-1099 84097
E 1200 S
1-399 84058
700-748 84097
900-1199 84097
N 1200 E
1-599 84097
600-1799 84057
N 1200 W
2-98 84057
1700-1798 84057
S 1200 W
2-98 84058
1900-1999 84058
W 1200 N
1-1150 84057
400-799 84057
W 1200 S 84058
E 1220 N 84097
S 1220 W 84058
N 1230 E 84097
N 1235 W 84057
1300-1399 84057
S 1230 W 84058
W 1230 N 84057
W 1230 S 84058
N 1240 E 84097
W 1240 N 84057
E 1250 N
200-399 84057
900-999 84097
N 1250 E 84097
N 1250 W 84057
S 125 E 84058
S 1250 W 84058
W 1250 N 84057
W 1250 S 84058
S 1260 W 84058
W 1260 N 84057
W 1260 S 84058
W 1275 S 84058
E & N 1280 N & E 84097
N & W 1285 W & N 84057
E 1290 S 84097
W 1295 S 84058
W 1290 S
1000-1199 84058
E 1300 N 84057
200-298 84057
400-498 84097
N 130 E 84057
S 130 W 84058
W 130 N 84057
W 130 S 84058
W 1310 N 84057
W 1315 S 84058
E 1320 N 84097
E 1325 N
400-498 84097
S 1325 W 84058
W 1325 N 84057
N 1330 W
1-200 84057
N 1335 W
1400-1599 84057
W 1330 N 84057
1000-1098 84058
W 1335 S
1101-1199 84058
E 1340 N 84057
E 135 N 84057
E 1350 S 84097
N 135 W 84057
S 1350 W
1100-1108 84058
S 135 W
1400-1599 84058
W 1350 N 84057
W 1350 S 84058
N 1360 E 84097
W 1360 N 84057
W 1360 S 84058
N 1370 W 84057
S 1370 W 84058
W 1375 N 84057
N 1380 W 84057
S 1380 W 84058
W 1380 N 84057
W 1390 N 84057
W 1390 S 84058
E 140 N 84097
E 1400 S
300-398 84058
400-499 84058
501-547 84097
549-999 84097
N 140 E 84057
S 140 E 8405
S 140 W 8405
W 1400 N 8405
W 1400 S
1-97 8405
1700-1999 8405
W 1415 N 8405
W 1410 S 8405
E 1420 S 8405
N 1420 E 8409
S 1420 W 8405
W 1420 N 8405
W 1428 S 8405
E 1430 N 8405
N 1430 W 8405
W 1435 S 8405
W 1430 S
400-499 8405
N 1445 W 8405
W 1440 N 8405
E 1450 N
1-99 8405
E 145 N
1-99 8405
400-499 8409
E 1450 S
2-298 8405
300-399 8405
800-1099 8409
N 1450 E 8409
S 145 E 8405
W 1450 N
500-799 8405
W 1455 N
901-997 8405
200-299 8405
300-399 8405
E 1460 N 8405
E 1460 S 8405
W 1465 N 8405
S 1470 W 8405
W 1475 N 8405
S 1480 W 8405
W 1485 N 8405
W 1480 N
1-1399 8405
W 1480 S 8405
S 1490 W 8405
W 1490 N 8405
E 1500 N
1-99 8405
300-399 8405
400-499 8409
600-1199 8409
E 1500 S
1-400 8405
501-627 8409
N 150 E 8405
N 1500 W
400-1099 8405
1000-1899 8405
S 150 E 8409
S 1500 W
1-599 8405
300-1599 8405
W 1500 N
200-1199 8405
401-447 8405
N 1510 E 8409
N 1515 W 8405
W 1510 N 8405
E 1520 N 8405
E 1525 S 8405
N 1520 E 8409
S 1525 W
600-799 8405
900-998 8405
W 1525 N
1-199 8405
300-399 8405
E 1535 N 8405
N 1530 E 8409
W 1530 N 8405
W 1530 S 8405
N 1540 W 8405
S 1545 W 8405

S 1540 W
500-699 84058
W 1540 N 84057
E 1550 N 84097
E 1550 S
300-356 84058
358-399 84058
800-899 84097
N 1550 E 84097
S 1555 W 84058
W 1550 N 84057
N 1560 E 84097
N & W 1565 W & N 84057
W 1560 N 84057
W 1560 S 84058
E 1570 N 84057
E 1575 N
1-99 84057
E 1575 S 84058
N 1580 W 84057
S 1580 W 84058
W 1580 N 84057
S 1590 W 84058
E 1600 N
1-205 84057
201-299 84057
401-417 84097
425-426 84057
441-699 84097
E 1600 S
1-499 84058
500-598 84097
N 160 W 84057
S 160 E 84058
S 1600 W 84058
W 1600 N
1-1299 84057
1200-1299 84057
W 1600 S 84058
E 1610 N 84097
N 1610 W 84057
E 1620 N 84057
E 1636 N 84097
E 1630 S 84097
N 1630 E 84097
S 1635 W 84058
W 1630 N 84057
E 1640 N 84097
S 1640 W 84058
W 1645 N 84057
1-199 84057
W 1640 S 84058
E 1650 N
300-399 84057
600-698 84097
E 1655 S 84058
250-252 84058
600-799 84097
N 165 E 84057
N 1650 W 84057
S 165 W 84058
W 1650 N 84057
W 165 S 84058
E 1660 N 84057
W 1665 N 84057
S 1675 W 84058
W 1670 N 84057
W 1670 S 84058
S & W 1680 W & S 84058
E 1700 N 84057
E 1700 S
1-199 84058
500-799 84097
N & W 170 E & N 84057
W 1700 N 84057
W 1700 S
1-400 84058
N & W 170 E & N 84058
E 1725 N 84097
E 1720 S 84097
100-999 84057
W 1725 N
600-699 84057
E 1730 N 84097
E 1730 S 84058
S 1730 W 84058
E 1740 S 84097
W 1740 N 84057
E 1750 N 84057
E 1750 S 84058
S 175 E 84058
W 1750 N
300-859 84057
W 175 N
400-499 84057
E 1775 N 84057
E 1775 S 84097
S 1770 W 84058
W 1770 N 84057
W 1770 S 84058
E 1780 S 84058
S 1780 W 84058
W 1780 N 84057
E 1800 N
1-99 84057
1-99 84057
1100-1199 84097
E 1800 S 84058
N 180 W 84057
S 180 E 84058
S 180 W 84058
W 1800 N
400-799 84057
900-1199 84057
W 1800 S
1-499 84058
800-1999 84058
E 1810 N 84097
S 1810 W 84058
W 1810 N 84057
E 1825 S 84058
E 1820 S
1-99 84058
W 1820 N 84057
E 1834 S 84058
E 1838 S 84058
E 1830 S
300-399 84058
W 1830 N 84057
E 1840 N 84097
S 1840 W 84058
W 1840 S 84058
E 1850 N 84057
N 185 W 84057
S 1850 W
100-199 84058
S 185 W
1400-1499 84058
W 1850 N 84057
W 185 S 84058
E 1864 S 84058
W 1860 N 84057
E 1870 N 84097
S 1875 W 84058
S 1870 W
600-699 84058
W 1870 N 84057
W 1880 N 84057
W 1885 N 84057
E & W 1890 84057
N 190 E 84057
S 190 W 84058
W 190 N 84057
E 1910 S 84058
S 1920 W
500-699 84058
S 1925 W
900-999 84058
200-299 84057
W 1920 N
800-899 84057
E 1930 N 84097
W 1930 N 84057
W 1945 N 84057
E 1950 N
300-399 84057
500-799 84097
E 1950 S 84058
S 195 E 84058
W 1950 N 84057
E 1960 N 84057
E 1960 S 84058
W 1960 N 84057
S 1990 W 84058
S 20 E 84058
W 20 N 84057
E 200 N
1-197 84057
2-398 84057
400-1135 84097
540-598 84097
600-699 84097
E 2000 S
1-399 84058
101-197 84058
800-1099 84097
N 200 E 84057
N 200 W 84057
S 200 E 84058
S 200 W 84058
W 2000 N
47-999 84057
800-900 84057
W 2000 S 84058
S 202 E 84058
S 2020 W 84058
W 2030 S 84058
S & W 2040 W & S 84058
E 2050 S 84058
N & W 205 W & N 84057
S 2060 W 84058
E 2075 S 84058
W 2070 S 84058
E & S 2100 S & W 84058
N 210 E 84057
N 210 W 84057
S 210 W 84058
W 210 N 84057
W 210 S 84058
W 2170 S 84058
N 220 W 84057
S 220 E 84058
S 220 W 84058
W 220 S 84058
W 225 S 84058
E 230 S
200-399 84058
1000-1099 84097
N 230 E 84057
N 230 W 84057
S 230 E 84058
S 230 W 84058
W 230 N 84057
W 230 S 84058
N 235 E 84057
N 235 W 84057
S 235 W 84058
E 240 N 84057
E 240 S 84097
N 240 E 84057
N 240 W 84057
S 240 E 84058
S 240 W 84058
W 240 N 84057
W 240 S 84058
N 25 W 84057
E 250 N 84097
E 250 S 84097
N 250 E 84057
S 250 E 84058
S 250 W 84058
W 255 N 84057
W 255 S 84058
E 260 N 84097
E 260 S
200-399 84058
1000-1099 84097
N 260 W 84057
S 260 E 84058
S 260 W 84058
W 260 N 84057
W 260 S 84058
E 265 N 84058
W 265 S 84058
N 270 E 84057
S 270 W 84058
W 270 N 84057
W 270 S 84058
E 275 N 84097
N 275 E 84057
N 275 W 84057
E 280 N 84097
E 280 S 84097
N 280 W 84057
S 280 E 84058
S 280 W 84058
W 280 N 84057
N 285 E 84057
W 285 S 84058
E 290 N 84057
S 290 E 84058
W 290 N 84057
W 290 S 84058
E 30 N 84097
E 30 S 84058
S 30 E 84058
S 30 W 84058
W 30 S 84058
E 300 N
1-299 84057
700-1199 84097
E 300 S 84097
N 300 E 84057
N 300 W 84057
S 300 E 84058
S 300 W 84058
W 300 N 84057
W 300 S 84058
E 310 S 84097
W 310 N 84057
E 315 S 84097
W 315 S 84058
E 320 N
301-399 84057
500-599 84097
N 320 W 84057
S 320 E 84058
S 320 W 84058
W 320 S 84058
N 325 E 84057
N 325 W 84057
S 325 W 84058
E 330 N 84097
N 330 E 84057
S 330 W 84058
W 330 S 84058
S 335 W 84058
E 34 S 84097
E 340 S 84058
N 340 E 84057
N 340 W 84057
S 340 E 84058
E 350 N
1-199 84057
1100-1199 84097
E 350 S 84097
N 350 E 84057
N 350 W 84057
S 350 E 84058
S 350 W 84058
W 350 N 84057
W 350 S 84058
N 355 W 84057
W 355 S 84058
E 360 S 84097
N 360 E 84057
N 360 W 84057
S 360 W 84058
W 360 S 84058
E 370 S 84097
W 370 N 84057
E 375 N 84097
N 375 E 84057
N 375 W 84057
S 375 E 84058
N 380 W 84057
E 40 N 84097
N 40 E 84057
N 40 W 84057
S 40 W 84058
W 40 N 84057
W 40 S 84058
E 400 N
1-399 84057
400-1199 84097
E 400 S
1-97 84058
400-999 84097
N 400 E
1-1999 84097
1600-1699 84057
N 400 W 84057
S 400 E
2-32 84097
1400-1498 84058
S 400 W 84058
W 400 N 84057
W 400 S 84058
N 420 E 84097
W 420 N 84057
S 424 E 84058
N 425 W 84057
E 430 N 84097
E 430 S 84058
N 430 E 84097
N 430 W 84057
S 430 E 84097
S 430 W 84058
W 430 S 84058
E & N 435 N & E 84097
E 440 N 84097
N 440 W 84057
S 440 W 84058
W 440 N 84057
W 440 S 84058
E 445 S 84097
W 445 S 84058
N 45 W 84057
S 45 E 84058
S 45 W 84058
E 450 N 84057
E 450 S 84097
N 450 E 84097
N 450 W 84057
S 450 E
1-1099 84097
1500-1799 84058
S 450 W 84058
W 450 N 84057
W 450 S 84058
E 460 S 84097
N 460 W 84057
S 460 W 84058
W 460 N 84057
W 460 S 84058
S 465 W 84058
W 465 N 84057
W 465 S 84058
E 470 N 84097
N 470 E 84097
N 470 W 84057
S 470 E 84097
E 475 N 84097
N 475 E 84097
S 475 E 84097
W 475 S 84058
N 480 W 84057
E 485 S 84097
N 490 W 84057
S 490 E 84058
S 490 W 84058
W 490 N 84057
W 490 S 84058
S 5 E 84058
E 50 S 84097
N 50 E 84057
N 50 W 84057
S 50 E 84058
S 50 W 84058
E 500 N
1-299 84057
500-1160 84097
E 500 S 84097
N 500 E 84097
N 500 W 84057
S 500 E
500-1199 84097
1700-1750 84058
S 500 W 84058
W 500 N 84057
W 500 S 84058
N 510 E 84097
N 520 E 84097
N 520 W 84057
S 520 E
400-499 84097
1900-1999 84058
S 520 W 84058
W 520 N 84057
W 520 S 84058
W 525 S 84058
E 530 N 84097
E 530 S 84058
N 530 E 84097
S 530 E 84097
W 530 N 84057
W 530 S 84058
N 540 E 84097
N 540 W 84057
S 540 W 84058
W 540 N 84057
W 540 S 84058
S 543 E 84058
S 545 E 84097
E 550 N
200-299 84057
1300-1399 84097
E 550 S 84097
N 550 E 84097
N 550 W 84057
S 550 E 84097
W 550 N 84057
W 550 S 84058
N 555 W 84057
E 560 N 84097
N 560 E 84097
N 560 W 84057
S 560 E 84097
S 560 W 84058
W 560 N 84057
W 560 S 84058
E 570 N 84097
W 570 N 84057
E 575 S 84097
W 575 S 84058
N 580 E 84097
N 580 W 84057
S 580 W 84058
W 580 N 84057
W 580 S 84058
E & S 590 S & E 84097
E 60 N 84097
N 60 E 84057
S 60 W 84058
W 60 S 84058
E 600 N
1-97 84057
400-1399 84097
E 600 S
1-199 84058
400-448 84097
N 600 E 84097
N 600 W 84057
S 600 W 84058
W 600 N 84057
W 600 S 84058
S 605 E 84097
S 605 W 84058
S 610 E 84097
W 610 S 84058
E 620 N 84097
E 620 S 84097
S 620 E 84097
S 620 W 84058
W 620 N 84057
W 620 S 84058
N 625 W 84057
E 630 N 84057
N 630 E 84097
S 630 E 84097
S 630 W 84058
W 630 N 84057
W 630 S 84058
S & W 635 W & S 84058
E 640 N 84097
N 640 W 84057
S 640 E 84097
W 640 N 84057
N 645 W 84057
W 645 S 84058
S 65 W 84058
E 650 N
300-399 84057
1000-1099 84097
E 650 S 84097
N 650 E 84097
N 650 W 84057
S 650 E 84097
W 650 N 84057
W 650 S 84058
E 660 N 84097
E 660 S 84058
N 660 E 84097
N 660 W 84057
S 660 W 84058
W 665 N 84057
S 670 E 84097
W 675 N 84057
E 680 N 84097
E 680 S 84058
N 680 W 84057
S 680 E 84097
W 680 N 84057
W 680 S 84058
N 685 W 84057
E 690 S 84097
N 690 E 84097
W 690 S 84058
N 70 W 84057
S 70 E 84058
S 70 W 84058
E 700 N
1-299 84057
400-899 84097
E 700 S
1-99 84058
400-999 84097
N 700 E 84097
N 700 W 84057
S 700 E 84097
S 700 W 84058
W 700 N 84057
W 700 S 84058
N 705 W 84057
S 705 E 84097
N 710 E 84097
N 710 W 84057
W 710 N 84057
E 720 N
300-399 84057
500-898 84097
900-1199 84097
E 720 S 84058
N 720 W 84057
S 720 E 84097
W 720 N 84057
W 720 S 84058
N 725 W 84057
S 725 W 84058
N 730 E 84097
S 730 E 84097
W 730 S 84058
E 740 N 84057
E 740 S 84058
N 740 E 84097
N 740 W 84057
S 740 E 84097
W 740 N 84057
W 740 S 84058
N 75 E 84057
S 75 E 84058
W 75 N 84057
E 750 N
100-199 84057
700-1400 84097
E 750 S 84097
N 750 E 84097
N 750 W 84057
S 750 E 84097
S 750 W 84058
W 750 N 84057
W 750 S 84058

Street	ZIP
S 754 W	84058
E 760 N	
201-297	84057
299-399	84057
1000-1099	84097
E 760 S	
1-199	84058
1000-1099	84097
N 760 W	84057
S 760 E	84097
S 760 W	84058
W 760 N	84057
W 761 S	84058
W 765 S	84058
E 770 N	84097
N 770 W	84057
E 780 N	84097
N 780 E	84097
W 780 N	84057
W 795 S	84058
E 80 N	84097
E 80 S	84097
N 80 E	84057
N 80 W	84057
S 80 E	84058
S 80 W	84058
W 80 N	84057
E 800 N	
2-98	84057
400-498	84097
E 800 S	
1-200	84058
300-1000	84097
N 800 E	84097
N 800 W	84057
S 800 E	84097
S 800 W	84058
W 800 N	84057
W 800 S	84058
W 815 S	84058
E 820 N	84097
N 820 W	84057
E 825 S	84058
N 830 W	84057
S 830 E	84097
W 830 N	84057
E 835 N	84097
N 835 W	84057
E 840 N	84097
E 840 S	84058
N 840 E	84097
N 840 W	84057
S 840 W	84058
W 840 S	84058
N 85 E	84057
N 85 W	84057
W 85 S	84058
E 850 N	84097
E 850 S	
1-199	84058
400-499	84097
N 850 E	84097
N 850 W	84057
S 850 E	84097
S 850 W	84058
W 850 S	84058
E 860 S	84058
N 860 W	84057
S 860 E	84097
W 860 S	84058
E 865 N	84057
E 870 S	84097
N 870 E	84097
S 870 E	84097
W 870 N	84057
W 870 S	84058
E 875 N	84097
N 875 E	84097
S 875 W	84058
E 880 N	84097
S 880 W	84058
W 880 N	84057
W 880 S	84058
N 885 E	84097
N 890 E	84097
N 890 W	84057
S 890 E	84097
E 90 N	84097
N 90 E	84057
N 90 W	84057
E 900 N	
300-399	84057
400-1099	84097
E 900 S	
1-199	84058
300-899	84097
N 900 E	84097
N 900 W	84057
S 900 E	84097
S 900 W	84058
W 900 N	84057
W 900 S	84058
E & W 905	84057
E 910 N	
100-199	84057
500-799	84097
N 910 E	84097
N 910 W	84057
E 920 N	84097
N 920 E	84097
N 920 W	84057
S 920 E	84097
W 920 N	84057
E 925 N	84057
S 925 E	84097
S 925 W	84058
W 925 S	84058
E 930 N	84097
E 930 S	84058
N 930 W	84057
S 930 W	84058
W 930 N	84057
N 940 W	84057
S 940 E	84097
S 940 W	84058
W 940 N	84057
N 945 W	84057
E 950 N	84097
E 950 S	
200-300	84058
302-398	84058
800-899	84097
N 950 E	84097
N 950 W	84057
S 950 E	84097
S 950 W	84058
W 950 N	84057
N 960 E	84097
N 960 W	84057
S 960 E	84097
W 960 N	84057
E 965 N	84097
W 965 N	84057
E 970 N	84097
N 970 W	84057
W 970 N	84057
W 975 N	84057
E 980 N	84057
N 980 W	84057
S 980 W	84058
W 980 S	84058
N 985 W	84057
S 990 W	84058
W 990 N	84057
W 990 S	84058
N 995 W	84057

PARK CITY UT

General Delivery 84068

POST OFFICE BOXES MAIN OFFICE STATIONS AND BRANCHES

Box No.s	ZIP
1 - 28020	84060
680001 - 689998	84068
980001 - 983056	84098

NAMED STREETS

Street	ZIP
Abilene Way	84098
Ability Way	84060
Aerie Dr	84060
Aiden Ct	84098
Alice Ct	84098
American Saddler Dr	84060
Angus Ct	84098
Annie Oakley Dr	84060
Antler Ct	84098
Apache Trl	84098
Appaloosa Ln	84098
April Mountain Dr	84060
Arabian Dr	84060
Arrowhead Trl	84098
Ashley Ct	84060
Aspen Cir, Dr, Ln, Pl, Pt & Ter	84098
Aspen Camp Loop	84098
Aspen Springs Dr	84060
Aspenleaf Dr	84098
Atkinson Ave	84098
Augusta Ct	84060
Back Nine Cir	84098
Bald Eagle Dr	84060
Balsam Dr	84098
Basin Canyon Rd	84098
Bear Hollow Dr	84098
Bear Ridge Dr	84098
Bear View Dr	84098
Beehive Dr	84098
Belle Star Ct	84060
Biathlon Loop	84098
Big Spruce Way	84098
Bitner Rd	84098
Bitner Ranch Rd	84098
E Bitter Brush Dr	84098
Blacksmith Rd	84098
Blue Sage Cir & Trl	84098
Bluebird Ln	84098
Bobsled Blvd	84098
Bonanza Ct & Dr	84060
Boothill Dr	84098
Broken Hill Dr	84098
Broken Spoke Way	84060
Brook Hollow Loop Rd	84098
Brookside Dr	84060
Brookwood Dr	84098
Browning Ct	84098
Buckboard Cir & Dr	84098
Buffalo Bill Dr	84060
Bufflehead Dr	84098
Business Park Loop Rd	84098
Butch Cassidy Ct	84060
Calumet Cir	84060
Canyon Ct	
1-99	84060
6800-6899	84098
Canyon Dr	84098
Canyon Basin Rd	84098
E Canyon Gate Rd	84098
Canyon Link Dr	84098
Canyon View Dr	84098
Canyons Resort Dr	84098
Cedar Ct, Dr & Way	84098
Centennial Cir	84060
Center Dr	84098
Central Pacific Trl	84098
Chancey Dr	84098
Charlais Ln	84098
Cheyenne Way	84098
Chuck Wagon Ct	84098
Claim Jumper Ct	84060
E Cliff Rose Ct	84098
Club Ct	84098
Coalition View Ct	84060
Cochise Ct	84098
Cody Cir & Trl	84098
Columbine Ct	84060
Commanche Trl	84098
Comstock Dr	84060
Cooke Dr	84060
Cooper Ln	84098
Cottage Ct & Loop	84098
Cottonwood Ln & Trl	84098
Countryside Cir	84098
Courtyard Loop	84098
Cove Ct	84060
Cove Canyon Dr	84098
Cove Hollow Ln	84098
Creek Ct	84060
Creek Dr	84060
Creek Rd	84098
Creek Side Ln	84098
Creek Stone Ct	84098
Creekside Dr	84098
Crescent Dr N	84098
Crescent Dr S	84098
Crescent Rd	84060
Crest Ct	84060
Crestline Dr	84060
Crestview Cir, Dr, Ln & Ter	84098
Crestwood Ct	84060
Cross Country Way	84098
Crosstie Ct	84098
Cutter Ln	84098
Cynthia Cir	84098
Dakota Trl	84098
Daly Ave	84060
Daybreaker Dr	84098
Daystar Cir	84060
Deer Crest Estates Dr	84060
Deer Hollow Ct, Dr & Rd	84060
Deer Pointe Dr	84060
Deer Valley Dr & Loop	84060
Division Rd	84098
Doc Holiday Dr	84060
Double Jack Ct	84060
Douglas Dr	84098
Duck Hook Dr	84060
Dye Cabins Dr	84098
Eagle Ct, Cv & Way	84060
Eagle Landing Ct	84060
Eagle Point Ct	84098
Eagle View Ct	84060
Echo Ln	84098
Ecker Hill Dr	84098
Eladar Pl	84060
Elk Run Dr	84098
Empire Ave	84060
Enclave Ln & Way	84098
Engen Loop	84098
Equestrian Way	84060
Escala Ct	84098
Estates Cir, Dr & Pl	84060
Euston Dr	84060
Evening Star Dr	84060
Evergreen Cir	84098
Fairview Dr	84098
Fairway Hills Ct	84060
Fairway Village Dr	84060
Fawn Dr	84098
Fenchurch Dr	84060
Fiddlers Holw	84098
Fire Ring Glade	84098
Flanders Way	84098
Fletcher Ct	84098
Flint Way	84098
Forestdale Dr	84098
E & W Fort Rd	84098
Four Lakes Dr	84060
Fox Glen Cir	84098
Fox Hollow Ln	84098
Fox Pointe Cir	84098
Fox Tail Trl	84060
Foxcrest Ct & Dr	84098
Foxglove Ct	84098
Foxwood Ct	84060
Fradongt Dr	84098
Freestyle Way	84098
Frostwood Blvd	84098
Gallivan Ct & Loop	84060
Galts Gulch	84098
Gambel Dr	84098
Geronimo Ct	84060
Gilmore Way	84060
Glenwild Dr	84098
Gold Dust Ln	84060
Golden Way	84060
Golden Eagle Dr	84060
Golden Spike Ct	84060
Good Trump Ct	84060
Gorgoza Dr	84098
Gorgoza Pines Rd	84098
Goshawk Ranch Rd	84098
Goshawk Ridge Rd	84098
Greenfield Dr	84098
Hackney Ct	84060
Haystack Ct	84098
Heather Ln	84098
Heber Ave	84060
Heuga Ct	84098
Hidden Ct	84060
Hidden Cove Rd	84098
N Hidden Hill Loop	84098
Hidden Oaks Ln	84060
Hidden Splendor Ct	84098
High St	84060
W High Mountain Rd	84098
Highfield Rd	84098
Highland Dr	84098
Highway 224	
3601-3697	84060
Highway 224	
3699-3700	84060
3702-3798	84060
4000-6599	84098
Hilltop Ct & Dr	84098
Hitching Post Dr	84098
Holiday Curve Dr	84098
Holiday Ranch Loop Rd	84060
Hollyhock St	84098
Home Run Ct	84060
Homestake Rd	84060
Homestead Rd	84098
Ina Ave	84060
Innsbruck Way	84098
Innsbruck Strasse	84098
Iron Canyon Ct & Dr	84060
Iron Horse Dr	84060
Iron Mountain Dr	84060
Jeremy Cir & Rd	84098
Jeremy Point Ct	84098
Jeremy Ranch Rd	84098
W Jeremy Woods Dr	84098
Jordanelle Way	84060
Jordanelle View Dr	84060
Julia Ct	84098
Julies Dr	84098
Juniper Dr	84098
Juniper Draw	84098
Jupiter View Dr & Way	84060
Justice Center Rd	84098
Katies Xing	84098
Kearns Blvd	84060
Keystone Ct	84060
Kidd Cir	84098
Kilby Rd	84098
Kimball Canyon Rd	84098
King Dr	84060
Kings Ct	84060
Kingsford Ave	84098
Knob Hl	84098
Kodiak Way	84098
Lake Front Ct	84098
Lake View Ct & Ln	84060
Lakeview Dr	84060
N Landmark Dr	84098
Lariat Cir & Rd	84098
Larkspur Dr	84060
Last Run Dr	84098
Last Spike Ln	84098
Last Stand Dr	84098
Liberty Peak Ln	84098
Lillehammer Ln	84098
Lily Langtree Ct	84060
Lincoln Ln	84098
Linger Ln	84098
Little Bessie Ave	84060
Little Kate Rd	84060
Little Lake Dr	84098
Lone Pine Ct	84098
Long Rifle Rd	84098
Longspur Ln	84098
Lookout Dr	84060
Lookout Ln	84098
Lowell Ave	84060
Lower Evergreen Dr	84098
Lower Iron Horse Loop	84060
Lower Lando Ln	84098
Lower Saddleback Rd	84098
Lucky John Dr	84060
Luge Ln	84098
Lupine Dr	84098
Lupine Ln	84060
Mahre Dr	84098
Main St	84060
Mallard Cir	84098
Maple Cir & Dr	84098
Marilyn Ct	84060
Market St	84098
Marmot Cir	84098
Marsac Ave	84060
Martingale Ln	84098
Matterhorn Cir, Dr & Ter	84098
Mckinney Ct	84098
Meadow Creek Ct & Dr	84060
Meadow Loop Rd	84098
Meadows Dr	84060
E Meadows Dr	84098
Meadows Connection	84098
Meadowview Ct, Dr & Rd	84098
Mellow Mountain Rd	84060
Monarch Dr	84060
Monitor Dr	84060
Moon Dog Ct	84098
Moosehollow Rd	84098
Moray Ct	84060
Moridens Dr	84060
Morning Sky Ct	84060
Morning Star Ct & Dr	84060
Mountain Ln	84060
Mountain Crest Rd	84098
Mountain Holly Rd	84098
Mountain Meadow Ln	84098
Mountain Oak Ct	84060
Mountain Ranch Dr	84098
Mountain Ridge Ct	84098
Mountain Top Ln & Rd	84060
Mountain View Dr	84098
Mountain Willow Ln	84098
Mourning Dove Way	84098
Munchkin Rd	84060
Murnin Way	84098
Mustang Loop Rd	84098
Nail Driver Ct	84060
Nanson Ct	84060
Narrow Leaf Ct	84098
Navajo Trl	84098
Nelson Ct	84098
Newpark Blvd	84098
Niblick Dr	84098
Nicklaus Club Dr	84098
Nicklaus Valley Rd	84098
Nighthawk Cir	84098
Norfolk Ave	84060
Normans Way	84060
Northchurch Rd	84098
Northcove Dr	84098
Northshore Ct	84098
Oak Leaf Ct	84060
Oak Rim Ln	84060
Oakbrush Dr N	84098
Oakridge Rd N & S	84098
Oakwood Ct & Dr	84060
Old Highway 40	84098
Old Meadow Ln	84098
Old Rail Ln	84098
Old Ranch Rd	84098
Old Stone House Way	84098
Olympic Pkwy	84098
Ontario Ave	84060
Oslo Ln	84098
Outcrop Rd	84098
Outpost Way	84098
Overhill Rd	84098
Pace Dr, Pl & Rd	84098
Pace Frontage Rd	84098
Packsaddle Cir	84098
Paddington Dr	84060
Palomino Trl	84098
Panorama Dr	84098
Par Ct	84098
Paradise Rd	84098
Park Ave	
100-2101	84060
2100-2100	84068
2103-2299	84060
2200-2298	84060
Park Pl	84098
Parkridge Dr	84098
Parkview Cir, Dr, Pl & Ter	84098
Parkway Dr	84098
Parleys Ln & Rd	84098
Payday Dr	84060
Pete Dye Draw	84098
Pheasant Way	84098
Picabo St	84098
Pine Ridge Dr	84098
Pinebrook Blvd & Rd	84098
Pinebrush Dr	84098
Pinecrest	84098
Pinehurst Ct	84060
Pintail Cir	84098
Pioche Ct	84060
Pointe Dr & Rd	84098
Polar Way	84098
Ponderosa Ct & Dr	84098
Powderhorn Ct	84098
Powderwood Rd	84098
Prairie Schooner Trl	84098
Primrose Pl	84098
N Promontory Ranch Rd	84098
N Promontory Ridge Dr	84098
N Promontory Rock Rd	84098
N Promontory Summit Dr	84098
Prospector Ave & Dr	84060
Ptarmigan Ct & Loop	84098
Purple Sage	84098
Quail Meadow Rd	84098
Quaking Aspen Ct	84060
Quarry Rd	84098
Quarry Mountain Ln, Rd & Way	84098
Queen Esther Dr	84060
Quick Draw	84098
N Rabbit Brush Ct	84098
Ranch Pl	84098
N Ranch Club Ct, Dr & Trl	84098
N Ranch Creek Ln	84098
N Ranch Garden Rd	84098
Rasmussen Rd	84098
Red Fox Ct & Rd	84098
Red Hawk Ln & Trl	84098
Red Hawk Ridge Rd	84098
Red Maple Ct	84060
Red Pine Ct	84060
Red Pine Rd	84098
W Red Pine Rd	84098
Redden Rd	84098
Redstone Ave	84098
Redstone Center Dr	84098
Remington Ln	84098
Richmond Dr	84098
Ridge Way	84098
Ridgecrest Dr	84098
Ridgeview Dr	84060
Rio Grande Rd	84098
Rising Star Ln	84060
River Birch Ct	84060
N Rockport Ridge Rd	84098
Roffe Rd	84098
Rossie Hill Dr	84060

Round Valley Dr & Way 84060
Royal Ct & St 84060
Ruminant Rd 84060
Sackett Dr 84098
Saddle Ct 84098
Saddle View Way 84060
Saddleback Cir & Rd 84098
Saddleback Ridge Dr 84098
Saddlehorn Dr 84098
Sage Meadow Ct & Rd 84098
Sagebrook Dr 84098
Sagebrush Pl & Rd 84098
Sagewood Dr 84098
Saint Andrews Ct 84060
Saint Moritz Cir, Ter & Way 84098
Saint Moritz Strasse 84098
Samuel Colt Ct 84060
Sand Trap Ct 84098
Sandhill Ct 84098
Sandridge Ave 84060
Sandstone Cv 84060
Santa Fe Rd 84098
E & W Sawmill Rd 84098
Scenic Grade 84098
Seasons Dr 84060
Settlement Dr 84098
Shepherd Way 84098
Shortline Rd 84060
Sidewinder Dr 84060
Signal Hill Ct 84098
Silver Berry Ct 84098
Silver Cloud Ct & Dr 84060
Silver Creek Dr & Rd 84098
Silver King Dr 84060
Silver Lake Dr 84060
Silver Meadows Dr 84098
Silver Queen Ct 84060
Silver Sage Dr 84098
Silver Springs Dr & Rd 84098
Silver Spur Cir & Rd 84098
Silver Star Ct 84060
Silver Summit Pkwy 84098
Single Jack Ct 84060
Snow Berry St 84098
Snow Cloud Cir 84060
Snow Creek Dr 84060
Snow Top Ct & Rd 84060
Snows Ln 84060
Snowview Dr 84098
Snyders Way 84098
Solamere Dr 84060
Southridge Ct & Dr 84098
Southshore Dr 84098
Spotted Owl 84098
Springshire Dr 84098
Spur Ln 84098
Spyglass Ct 84060
Stagecoach Dr 84098
Stanford Ct 84060
Starview Dr 84098
Station Loop Rd 84098
Stein Way 84060
Stonebridge Dr 84060
Stryker Ave 84060
Summer Hill Dr 84098
Summit Dr 84098
Summit View Dr 84060
Sun Peak Dr 84098
Sun Ridge Ct, Cv & Dr 84060
Sundial Ct 84098
Sunny Knoll Ct 84060
Sunny Slopes Ct & Dr 84060
Sunnyside Dr 84060
Sunridge Dr 84098
Sunrise Cir 84060
Sunrise Dr 84098
Sunrise Loop 84098
Sunset Cir 84098
Sunset Ct 84060
Susans Cir 84098
Swede Alley Dr 84060
Tall Oaks Cir & Dr 84098
Talon Way 84060
Tatanka Trl 84098
Teal Dr 84098
Telemark Dr 84060
Thaynes Canyon Dr & Way 84060
Thistle St 84060
Three Kings Ct & Dr 84060
Three Mile Cyn 84098
Tollcreek Vlg 84098
Tollgate Rd 84098
Tommy Moe Ct & Pl 84098
Trading Post 84098
Trails Dr 84098
Trailside Ct 84060
Trailside Dr 84098
Trailside Loop 84098
Trelawney Ln 84098
Trout Creek Ct 84098
Twilight Ct 84060
W & N Two Creeks Cir & Ln 84098
Uinta Way 84098
Uintah Ct 84060
Union Pacific Trl 84098
Upland Cir 84060
Upper Evergreen Dr 84098
Upper Lando Ln 84098
Ute Blvd 84098
Valley Dr 84098
Venus Ct 84060
Victoria Cir 84060
Victory Ln 84060
View Dr 84098
View Pointe Dr 84098
Village Rd 84098
Village Rim Rd 84098
Village Round Dr 84098
Vista Cir 84098
Voelker Ct 84098
Wagon Wheel Cir & Way 84098
Walker Ct
1-99 84060
1700-1799 84098
E Wapiti Canyon Rd 84098
Wasatch Ln & Way 84098
Waterloo Cir 84060
Webster Ct & Dr 84060
Wedge Cir 84098
Western Sky 84098
N Westhills Trl 84098
Westsilver Springs Rd 84098
Westview Ct & Trl 84098
Westview Draw 84098
Westwood Rd 84098
Whileaway Rd E & W 84098
White Pine Ct & Ln 84060
White Pine Canyon Ln & Rd 84060
Wild Rose 84060
W & N Wildflower Ct & Dr 84098
Williamstown Ct 84098
Willow Ln & Loop 84098
Willow Creek Dr 84098
Willow Draw Dr 84098
Winchester Ct 84098
Windrift Ln 84060
Wolfe Cir 84098
Woodbine Way 84060
Woodland Dr & Pl 84098
Woodside Ave 84060
Worthington Dr 84098
Wrangler Way 84098
Wyatt Earp Way 84060
Yorkton Ln 84098
Zermat Strasse 84098

NUMBERED STREETS

All Street Addresses 84098

PROVO UT

General Delivery 84601

POST OFFICE BOXES MAIN OFFICE STATIONS AND BRANCHES

Box No.s
A - U 84603
1 - 5152 84603
5900 - 5900 84605
6000 - 6000 84603
7001 - 7536 84602
19000 - 19684 84605
20000 - 20000 84603
20101 - 29998 84602
39998 - 39998 84603
50001 - 59998 84605

RURAL ROUTES

03 84604

NAMED STREETS

A Richards Hall 84604
Alabama St 84606
Alaska Ave 84606
Alpine Loop & Way 84606
Alpine Air Way 84601
N Alpine Loop Rd 84604
Alumni House 84602
Andrus Ln 84604
Apache Ln & Way 84604
Apple Ave 84604
Arapahoe Ln 84604
Arizona Ave 84606
Arlington Dr 84606
Arthur Dr 84601
Asb 84602
Ash Ave 84604
Aspen Ave 84604
Aspen Ridge Ln 84604
Aviation Dr 84601
Bannock Dr 84604
E Bay Blvd 84606
W Beashil N 84601
Bedford Dr 84604
Belmont Pl 84606
E Big Canyon Rd 84604
Birch Ln 84604
Bnsn 84602
Bowen Hall 84604
Brentwood Cir 84604
Brereton Dr 84604
Briar Ave 84604
Bristol Cir 84604
Brittlebush Dr 84604
Brmb 84602
Broadbent Hall 84604
Brook Ln 84604
Brookshire Cir & Dr 84604
Brookside Dr 84604
Brwb 84602
Buckley Ln 84606
Budge Hall 84604
Byu 84602
California Ave & Cir 84606
Cambridge Cir & Ct 84604
Camelot Dr 84601
E Campus Dr 84602
Candlewood Pl 84604
N Canyon Rd 84604
Canyon Meadow Dr 84606
Canyon Vista Rd 84606
Carroll Hall 84604
Cascade Dr 84604
Cb 84602
Cedar Ave & Cir 84604
E Center St 84606
W Center St 84601
Chapel View Cir 84604
Cherokee Ln 84604
Cherry Cir & Ln 84604
Chipman Hall 84604
Chippewa Way 84604
Chokecherry Ln 84604
Churchill Dr 84604
Cinnamon Hills Dr 84606
Cinnamon Ridge Cir, Dr, Ln & Way 84606
Cobblestone Dr 84604
Colorado Ave 84606
Columbia Cir 84601
Columbia Ln 84604
Comanche Ln 84604
Conf 84602
Conference Ctr 84602
N Cottonwood Ln 84604
Country Club Dr 84604
N Cove Dr 84604
Cove Point Ln 84604
Coventry Ln 84604
Crestview Ave 84604
Ctb 84602
Dakota Ave & Ln 84606
Devonshire Cir & Dr 84604
Dover Dr & Ln 84604
Draper Ln 84601
Driftwood Dr 84604
S East Bay Blvd 84606
Eastcliff Ave 84604
Eastgate Dr 84606
Edgewood Dr 84604
Elderberry Ln 84604
Elm Ave & Cir 84604
Elwc 84602
Esc 84602
F Smith Hall 84604
Fairfax Dr 84604
Fb 84602
Felt Hall 84604
Fir Ave & Cir 84604
Flight Line Dr 84601
Fob 84602
E Foothill Dr 84604
Fox Hall 84604
N Freedom Blvd
2-98 84601
100-600 84601
602-798 84601
801-1227 84604
1229-1699 84604
1701-2299 84604
S Freedom Blvd 84601
S Frontage Rd 84601
Fugal Hall 84604
W Galinch N 84604
Gates Hall 84604
N Geneva Rd 84601
Glenwood Cir 84604
N Goodridge Ln 84601
Grand Ave & Cir 84604
Grandview Ln 84604
Green Dr 84604
Green Canyon Rd 84606
H Tracy Hall Pkwy 84606
Harbor Pkwy 84601
Harris Hall 84604
Hbll 84602
Hceb 84602
W Heather Ln 84601
Helaman Halls 84604
Heritage Dr 84604
Heritage Halls 84604
Heritage School Dr 84604
Hfac 84602
Hgb 84602
Hickory Ln 84604
Hillsdale Cir & Ln 84606
Hillside Cir & Dr 84604
Hinckley Hall 84604
Holly Cir 84604
Horne Hall 84604
Hrcb 84602
Huron Way 84604
Hyde Park Ct 84604
Idaho Ave 84606
Imperial Way 84604
Independence Ave
600-698 84601
800-1198 84604
Indian Hills Cir & Dr 84604
S Industrial Pkwy 84606
Ironton Blvd 84606
Iroquois Cir & Dr 84604
Itb 84602
Ivy Ln 84604
Jfsb 84602
Jkb 84602
John Hall 84604
Jordan Ave 84604
Jrcb 84602
Jsb 84602
Juniper Dr 84604
Kimball Hall 84604
N Lakeshore Dr 84601
Lakeview Dr 84604
Lakewood Dr 84601
Lambert Ln 84604
Lancelot Dr 84601
E Lawn Dr 84604
W Le Bon Cir 84601
Little Rock Ct, Dr, Ln & Ter 84604
E & N Locust Cir & Ln 84604
Lupine Dr 84604
M Smith Hall 84604
Maeser Hall 84604
Maple Ln 84604
Marrcrest E 84604
Marrcrest North Cir 84604
May Hall 84604
Mc 84602
W Mcclellan Ct 84601
Mckb 84602
Meadow Dr 84604
Meadow Fork Rd 84606
E Mearente S 84606
Merlin Dr 84601
Merrill Hall 84604
Mike Jense Cir & Pkwy 84601
Mile High Dr 84604
Moa 84602
Mohawk Cir & Ln 84604
Mohican Ln & Way 84604
Mojave Ln 84604
Montana Ave 84606
Moon River Dr 84604
Morris Ctr 84602
Mountain Ridge Rd 84604
Mountain View Pkwy 84606
S Mountain Vista Ln & Pkwy 84606
Msrb 84602
Navajo Cir & Ln 84604
Nevada Ave & Cir 84606
Nicb 84602
Norfolk Cir 84604
E Normandy Dr 84604
Northgate Dr 84604
W Northwood Ln 84604
Novell Pl 84606
Nuskin Plz 84601
Oak Ln 84604
Oak Cliff Dr 84604
Oak Hill Cir 84604
Oak Ridge Cir 84604
Oakcrest Cir, Ln & Ter 84604
Oakmont Ln 84604
Oakview Cir 84604
Old Willow Ln 84604
Oneida Cir & Ln 84604
Oquirrh Dr 84604
E & S Oregon Ave 84606
Osmond Ln 84604
Park Ave & St 84606
S & W Parkside Ct, Dr & Pl 84601
E Parkview Dr 84604
Parkway 84604
Pebble Ln 84604
Penrose Hall 84604
Pine Ln 84604
W Pinnacle Peak 84604
Pioneer Cir 84601
Piute Dr 84604
Prichead 84602
E Provo Canyon Rd 84604
Quail Run 84604
Quail Ridge Dr 84604
Quail Summit Dr 84604
Quail Valley Dr 84604
Rb 84602
Red Oak Cir 84604
Redford Dr 84604
Reese Dr 84601
E Richards Hall 84604
Riderwood Way 84601
N Ridge Dr 84606
River Bend Ln 84604
River Park Dr 84604
Riverpark Way 84604
Riverside Ave 84604
Riverwood Cir & Dr 84604
Robison Hall 84604
Rock Canyon Cir 84604
Rogers Hall 84604
Rolling Knolls Dr 84604
Royalwood Cir 84604
Sagewood Ave 84604
Sasb 84602
E & N Scenic Dr 84604
Sego Ln 84604
N Seven Peaks Blvd 84606
Sfh 84602
Shadowbrook Cir & Dr 84604
N Shadyside Dr 84604
Sheffield Dr 84604
Sherwood Dr 84604
Shipp Hall 84604
Sioux Cir 84604
S Slate Canyon Dr 84606
Snlb 84602
Snow Hall 84604
Southfork Rd 84604
Springdell Cir & Dr 84604
Stadium Ave, Cir & Ln 84604
Stafford Ct 84604
N State St 84604
S State St 84606
Stone Brook Ln 84604
Stone Creek Ln 84604
Stone Gate Ln 84604
Stonecrossing 84604
Stover Hall 84604
S Stubbs Ave 84601
Sumac Ln 84604
N Summit Dr 84606
Sundance Resort 84604
Swkt 84602
Taylor Hall 84604
N Temple Dr 84604
Temple Hill Dr 84604
Temple View Dr 84604
Tennessee Ave 84606
Terrace Dr 84604
Teton Dr 84604
Texas Ave 84606
Three Fountains Dr 84604
Timpanogos Dr 84604
Timpview Dr 84604
Tingey Hall 84604
Tmcb 84602
Tnrb 84602
Towne Centre Blvd 84601
Uinta Dr 84604
N University Ave
2-2 84601
4-799 84601
800-5600 84604
5602-5698 84604
S University Ave 84601
N University Hl 84602
E University Pkwy 84602
N University Pkwy 84604
Upb 84602
Utah Ave 84606
E Valley Vista Way 84606
Victoria Cir 84604
Village Ln 84604
Vintage Cir & Dr 84604
Vivia Cir 84604
Walnut Ave 84604
Wasatch Dr 84604
Washington Ave & Cir 84606
Waterford Ct & Ln 84604
Wells Hall 84604
West Ln 84601
Westbridge Cir & Dr 84601
Westlane Ct 84601
Whitney Hall 84604
Widb 84602
Willow Ln 84604
Willowbrook Dr 84604
Wimbledon Dr 84604
Windsor Dr 84604
Woodland Dr 84604
Woodside Dr 84604
Wsc 84602
Wymount Ter 84604
N Wymount Terrace Dr 84604
Young Hall 84604

NUMBERED STREETS

E 100 N 84606
E 100 S
45-97 84606
901-1397 84606
N 100 E
1-699 84606
100-799 84606
2300-2599 84604
3300-3398 84604
N 1000 W
1-499 84601
1-97 84601
800-4599 84604
800-898 84604
900-2399 84604
S 100 E
100-899 84606
100-1299 84606
S 1000 W
1-37 84601
2-198 84601
W 100 N
2-98 84601
1400-1699 84604
W 100 S 84601
W 1010 N
1700-1899 84604
2800-3099 84601
W 1010 S 84601
N 1020 E
300-399 84606
3700-3799 84604
N 1025 W 84601
401-447 84601
W 1020 N 84604
W 1020 S 84601
E 1040 S 84606
S 1040 W 84601
E 1050 S 84606
N 1050 E 84606
N 1050 W
500-598 84601
600-799 84601
900-1799 84604
S 1050 W 84601
W 1050 N 84604
E 1060 S 84606
N 1060 E 84604
N 1060 W
300-451 84601
453-499 84601
2001-2097 84604
2099-2299 84604
S 1060 E 84606
W 1060 N
1000-1799 84604
2600-3099 84601
E 1080 S 84606

N 1080 E 84606
N 1080 W 84601
S 1080 E 84606
W 1080 N 84604
E 1090 S 84606
N 1100 E
400-799 84606
800-898 84604
N 1100 W
1-699 84601
1000-1199 84604
N 110 W
1900-1999 84604
S 1100 W 84601
W 1100 N
1000-1799 84604
W 110 N
2700-2799 84601
2800-2950 84601
2952-2998 84601
W 1110 N 84604
E 1120 S 84606
N 1120 W
300-399 84601
1800-1999 84604
W 1120 N
800-898 84604
2700-2799 84601
E 1130 S 84606
N 1130 E 84606
N 1130 W
200-299 84601
800-899 84604
W 1130 N 84601
E 1140 S 84606
N 1140 W 84604
W 1140 N 84604
N 1150 E
700-799 84606
2500-2598 84604
N 1150 W 84601
S 1150 E 84606
W 1150 N 84604
W 1150 S 84601
E 1160 S 84606
N 1160 W 84604
W 1160 N 84604
N 1170 W 84601
1500-1699 84604
2800-2999 84601
E 1180 S 84606
W 1180 N 84601
E 1190 S 84606
W 1190 N 84601
E 1200 S 84606
N 1200 E
501-597 84606
800-900 84604
N 1200 W
256-399 84601
N 120 W
2000-2199 84604
S 1200 E 84606
S 1200 W 84601
W 1200 N
700-1399 84604
2300-2499 84601
W 120 N
3000-3099 84601
W 1200 S
2-998 84601
W 120 S
1600-1899 84601
W 1210 N 84601
N 1220 E 84604
N 1220 W
300-899 84601
1001-1097 84604
1099-1499 84604
S 1220 E 84606
S 1220 W 84601
W 1225 N 84604
W 1220 S 84601
E 1230 N 84604
E 1230 S 84606
S 1230 E 84606
W 1230 N 84604

N 1240 W 84601
E 1250 S 84606
N 1250 E 84606
N 125 W 84604
800-1699 84604
W 1250 N 84604
N 1260 E 84604
N 1260 W 84601
E 1270 S 84606
N 1270 W 84604
E 1280 S 84606
N 1280 W 84601
S 1280 E 84606
W 1280 N 84604
W 1280 S 84601
N 1290 W 84604
E 1300 S 84606
N 1300 W 84601
S 1300 E 84606
S 1300 W 84601
W 1300 N
300-1299 84604
3000-3099 84601
W 130 S 84601
400-499 84601
W 1310 N 84601
E 1325 S
200-299 84606
E 1320 S
1400-1699 84606
W 1325 N
1200-1298 84604
W 1320 N
1350-1799 84604
S 1330 E 84606
S 1330 W 84601
N 1340 E 84606
W 1340 N 84604
W 1340 S 84601
E 1350 S 84606
N 1350 W
500-699 84601
800-1999 84604
S 1350 E 84606
W 1350 N 84601
E 1370 S 84606
N 1375 W 84604
S 1370 E 84606
W 1370 N 84604
W 1380 N 84604
S & W 1390 W & N 84601
E 1400 S 84606
N 1400 E
1701-1797 84604
140 E & W 84604
N 1400 W 84604
S 1400 E 84606
S 1400 W 84601
W 1400 N 84604
W 1400 S 84601
N 1410 E 84606
N 1410 W 84604
S 1410 E 84606
N 1420 E 84606
N 1420 W 84604
S 1420 E 84606
N 1430 E 84604
S 1430 E 84606
W 1430 S 84601
E 1440 S 84606
N 1440 E 84606
S 1440 E 84606
S 1440 W 84601
W 1440 N 84601
W 1440 S 84601
N 1450 E 84604
N 1450 W 84604
S 1450 E 84606
W 1450 N 84604
W 1450 S 84601
S 1460 E 84606
W 1460 N 84604
S 1470 E 84606
S 1470 W 84601
N & S 1480 84606

E 150 N
700-1099 84606
1401-1497 84604
E 150 S 84606
N 150 E
801-999 84604
1277-1597 84604
N 1500 W
1001-1097 84604
3100-4599 84604
S 1500 E 84606
S 1500 W 84601
W 1500 N
300-1499 84604
1600-1810 84601
W 1500 S 84601
S 1510 E 84606
W 1520 N 84601
S 1530 W 84601
S 1540 E 84606
N 1550 E 84604
N 1550 W 84604
S 1550 E 84606
W 1550 N 84604
W 1560 S 84601
E & N 1575 N & W 84604
1570 N & S 84601
N 1590 W 84604
S 1590 E 84606
E 1600 S 84606
N 1600 W
1-99 84601
N 160 W
801-1897 84604
S 1600 W 84601
W 1600 N
1201-1267 84604
W 160 N
2800-2999 84601
W 1610 S 84601
W 1625 N 84604
N 1640 W 84604
E 1650 N 84604
N 1650 W 84604
S 1650 E 84606
S 1660 W 84601
N 1670 W 84604
W 1670 S 84601
S & W 1680 W & N 84601
E 1700 N 84604
E 1700 S 84606
N 170 W 84604
S 170 E 84606
W 1700 N
900-2399 84604
2700-2799 84601
W 170 S 84601
S 1710 E 84606
W 1720 N 84604
W 1720 S 84601
W 1730 N 84604
N 1740 W 84604
S 1740 W 84601
N 175 E 84604
N 1750 W 84604
N 1760 W 84604
W 1770 S 84601
N 180 E 84604
S 180 E 84606
S 1800 W 84601
W 1800 N 84604
W 180 S 84601
N & S 1810 84601
N 1820 W 84604
W 1825 N 84604
W 1820 S 84601
N 1830 W 84604
E 1850 N 84604
N 1850 W 84604
S 1850 W 84601
W 1850 N 84604
E 1860 S 84606
S 1860 W 84601
W 1870 N 84604
N 1880 W 84604
N 1890 W 84601

E & N 1900 N & W 84604
N 190 W 84604
E 1910 S 84606
S 1920 W 84601
W 1925 N 84604
N 1930 W 84604
W 1930 N 84601
W 1940 N 84604
E 1950 N 84604
W 1975 N 84604
W 1970 N 84604
E 1980 N 84604
N 1980 W 84604
S 1980 W 84601
W 1980 N 84604
E & W 1990 84604
E 200 N
1-1099 84606
1200-1299 84604
E 200 S
2-98 84606
1400-1499 84606
N 200 E
1-799 84606
2100-4899 84604
N 200 W
391-399 84601
1600-1899 84604
S 200 E 84606
W 200 N
1-2999 84601
700-1099 84604
2600-2699 84601
W 200 S 84601
E 2020 N 84604
N 2025 W 84601
N 2040 W 84604
E 2050 N 84604
N 2050 W 84604
S 2050 W 84601
W 2050 N 84604
W 2060 N 84604
E 2080 N 84604
E 2090 N 84604
E 2100 N 84604
N 210 W 84604
W 210 N 84601
E 2120 N 84604
S 2120 W 84601
S 2130 W 84601
N 2150 W 84601
W 2150 N 84604
W 2170 N 84604
E 2190 N 84604
E 2200 N 84604
N 220 E 84604
N 2200 W
100-198 84601
1500-1598 84604
W 220 N 84601
W 220 S 84601
N & S 2210 84601
N 2220 W 84601
E & W 2230 84604
N 2250 W 84601
E 2260 N 84604
E 2260 S 84606
N 2260 W 84601
E 2270 N 84604
N 2270 W 84601
S 2280 W 84601
W 2280 N 84604
E 2300 N 84604
E 230 S 84606
N 230 E 84604
N 2300 W
200-299 84601
1500-1599 84604
1601-1699 84604
W 2300 N
701-797 84604
2800-2999 84601
W 230 S 84601
N 2310 W 84601
E 2320 N 84604
N & S 2330 84601

N 2350 W 84601
N 2370 W 84601
S 2370 W 84601
W 2370 N 84604
N 2380 W 84601
E 2390 N 84604
S 2390 W 84601
N 2400 W 84601
W 240 N 84601
N 2410 W 84601
N 2420 W 84601
N & S 2430 84601
N 2460 W 84601
N 2475 W 84601
N & S 2470 84601
N 2480 W 84601
N 25 W 84604
E 2500 N 84604
N 250 E 84604
N 250 W 84604
S 250 E
900-998 84606
936-936 84605
1000-1099 84606
S 250 W 84601
N 2520 W 84601
N & S 2530 84601
E 2540 N 84604
N 2540 W 84601
E 2550 N 84604
N 2550 W 84601
N 2560 W 84601
E 2570 N 84604
N 2580 W 84601
E 2600 N 84604
N 2600 W 84601
E 2620 N 84604
N 2620 W 84601
N 2630 W 84601
N 265 E 84604
N 2650 W 84601
E 2660 N 84604
N 2660 W 84601
N 2670 W 84601
E 2680 N 84604
N 2690 W 84601
N 270 E 84604
N 2700 W 84601
W 270 S 84601
N 2710 W 84601
N 2720 W 84601
E 2730 N 84604
N 2740 W 84601
N 2750 W 84601
N 2760 W 84601
N 2770 W 84601
E 2780 N 84604
N 2780 W 84601
E 2800 N 84604
N 2800 W 84601
W 280 S 84601
N 2810 W 84601
E 2825 N 84604
N 2820 W 84601
N 2830 W 84601
N 2850 W 84601
E 2875 N 84604
N 2870 W 84601
N 290 E 84604
S 290 W 84601
N 2920 W 84601
S 2945 W 84601
E 2950 N 84604
N 2950 W 84601
W 2950 N 84604
N 2960 W 84601
N 2970 W 84601
E 300 N 84606
E 300 S 84606
N 300 E
1-799 84606
2201-2237 84604
N 3000 W 84601
2-2 84601
800-5199 84604
S 300 E 84606

S 300 W 84601
W 300 N 84601
W 300 S 84601
N 3020 W 84601
E 3030 N 84604
E 3050 N 84604
N 3050 W 84601
E 3060 N 84604
N 3080 W 84601
E 3100 N 84604
N 3100 W 84601
S 310 W 84601
W 3100 N 84604
N & S 3110 84601
E 3125 N 84604
E & W 3140 84604
E 3180 N 84604
E & W 3200 84604
E 320 N
1300-1399 84606
N 320 E 84604
S 320 W 84601
E 3230 N 84604
E & W 3250 84604
330 N & S 84606
W 3300 N 84604
E 3400 N 84604
E 3450 N 84604
E 3460 N 84604
E 350 N 84606
N 350 E 84604
S 350 E 84606
W 350 N 84601
W 350 S 84601
E 3530 N 84604
E & W 3540 84604
E 3550 N 84604
E 360 S 84606
N 360 E 84604
W 360 N 84601
W 360 S 84601
W 3610 N 84604
E 3620 N 84604
E 3630 N 84604
E 3650 N 84604
E & W 3700 84604
N 370 E 84604
N 370 W 84604
W 370 N 84601
E 3750 N 84604
E & W 3800 84604
N 380 W
700-799 84601
800-4100 84604
W 380 S 84601
E 3850 N 84604
E 3860 N 84604
E & W 3900 84604
N 390 E 84604
W 390 N 84601
E & W 3950 84604
W 3960 N 84604
N 40 W 84604
S 40 E 84606
E 4000 N 84604
1-1499 84606
E 400 S 84606
N 400 E
1-699 84606
2500-2599 84604
N 400 W
1-499 84601
3600-3699 84604
S 400 E 84606
S 400 W 84601
W 400 N 84601
W 400 S 84601
E & W 4020 84604
E 4075 N 84604
W 4100 N 84604
W 410 S 84601
W 4130 N 84604
W 4150 N 84604
E 4190 N 84604
E & W 4200 84604
600-699 84606

E 420 S 84606
N 420 E 84604
N 420 W 84604
W 420 S 84601
E 4220 N 84604
N 425 E 84604
E 4300 N 84604
N 430 E 84604
W 430 N 84601
W 430 S 84601
E 4320 N 84604
E 4380 N 84604
E 440 N 84606
N 440 E 84604
N 440 W
700-799 84601
800-3699 84604
W 440 S 84601
W 4420 N 84604
E 4450 N 84604
E 450 N 84606
N 450 W 84604
S 450 E 84606
S 450 W 84601
W 4500 N 84604
1000-2199 84601
E 460 S 84606
N 460 E 84604
W 4600 N 84604
2300-2398 84601
W 460 S 84601
E & W 4620 84604
E 4635 N 84604
W 4630 N 84604
E 4640 N 84604
W 4650 N 84604
E 4680 N 84604
E 4695 N 84604
E 4700 N 84604
N 470 E 84604
W 470 N 84601
W 470 S 84601
E 4735 N 84604
E & W 4750 84604
N 475 E 84604
W 4770 N 84604
N 480 E 84604
W 4800 N 84604
W 480 N
2100-2300 84601
E 4840 N 84604
N 490 E 84604
W 490 N 84601
W 490 S 84601
E 4960 N 84604
N 4967 E 84604
E 50 S 84606
N 50 E 84604
N 50 W 84604
W 50 N 84601
E 500 N 84606
E 500 S 84606
N 500 E
1-799 84606
1702-1712 84604
N 500 W
1-799 84601
800-1149 84604
S 500 E 84606
S 500 W 84601
W 500 N 84601
W 500 S 84601
W 5050 N 84604
510 N & S 84601
E 520 S 84606
W 520 N 84601
W 520 S 84601
N 530 E 84604
W 530 N 84601
540 N & S 84601
N 550 E 84604
N 550 W 84604
S 550 E 84606
W 550 S 84601
E 560 N 84606
N 560 E 84604

560 W 84601
560 S 84601
& W 570 W & N 84601
580 N 84606
580 S 84606
580 E 84606
580 N 84601
590 N 84601
600 N 84606
600 S 84606
600 E
1-97 84606
2700-3799 84604
600 W
1-97 84601
800-939 84604
600 E 84606
600 W 84601
600 N 84601
600 S 84601
610 N 84606
610 N 84601
620 N 84606
620 N 84601
640 S 84606
650 E 84604
650 W 84604
650 W 84601
650 N 84601
660 N 84606
670 N 84606
680 S 84606
680 W 84601
680 N 84601
690 S 84601
70 W 84604
70 S 84601
700 N 84606
700 S 84606
700 E
1-899 84606
2200-3899 84604
700 W
1-799 84601
800-1999 84604
700 E 84606
700 W 84601
700 N 84601
700 S 84601
710 N 84601
720 N 84606
720 E 84606
720 W 84601
0 N & S 84601
750 N 84606
750 E
300-499 84606
2300-2398 84604
750 W
500-799 84601
800-2100 84604
750 E 84606
750 N 84601
750 S 84601
760 E 84604
760 W 84601
770 W 84601
780 S 84606
790 E 84606
80 E 84604
80 W 84604
80 S 84601
800 N 84606
800 S 84606
800 E
150-799 84606
2200-2299 84604
800 W
1-799 84601
800-2399 84604
800 W 84601
800 N 84601
810 E 84606
810 W 84601
820 N 84606
820 E 84604

S 820 W 84601
W 820 N 84601
W 830 N 84604
840 E & W 84604
E 850 S 84606
N 850 E 84604
N 850 W
500-799 84601
900-2699 84604
S 850 E 84606
W 850 N 84601
W 850 S 84601
N 860 E 84604
S 860 W 84601
W 860 N 84604
E 870 N 84606
N 870 E 84604
S 870 W 84601
N 880 E 84604
W 880 N
1-299 84604
301-499 84604
2200-3099 84601
W 880 S 84601
S 890 W 84601
W 890 N 84604
W 890 S 84601
W 90 S 84601
E 900 N
1-99 84604
700-798 84606
800-898 84604
E 900 S 84606
N 900 E
1-799 84606
821-897 84604
2001-2029 84602
N 900 W
1-499 84601
800-1999 84604
S 900 E 84606
S 900 W 84601
W 900 N 84604
W 900 S 84601
S & W 910 W & S 84601
E 920 S 84606
N 920 E 84604
N 920 W 84604
W 920 S 84601
E 930 N 84604
E 930 S 84606
N 930 E 84604
N 940 W 84604
S 940 W 84601
W 940 N 84604
E 950 S 84606
N 950 E 84604
N 950 W 84604
S 950 E 84606
S 950 W 84601
W 950 N
1300-1699 84604
2600-2999 84601
E 960 S 84606
S 960 E 84606
S 960 W 84601
W 960 N
1-1999 84604
2201-2297 84601
2299-2500 84601
2502-2598 84601
W 960 S 84601
N 970 E 84604
N 970 W 84601
W 970 S 84601
S 980 W 84601
W 980 N 84604
S 990 W 84601
W 990 N 84604

SAINT GEORGE UT

General Delivery 84790

POST OFFICE BOXES MAIN OFFICE STATIONS AND BRANCHES

Box No.s
1 - 719998 84771
910001 - 919998 84791

RURAL ROUTES

01 84790

NAMED STREETS

Abronia Cir 84790
Acacia Pl 84790
N & S Acantilado Cir & Dr 84790
Accolade Cir 84790
W Acowa Cir 84770
Adonis Cir 84790
S Agate Cir 84790
Agate Ct 84770
Agate Rd 84770
S Airport Pkwy 84790
S Airport Rd 84770
S Airy Hill Dr 84790
Alba Dr 84770
Alder Cir 84790
Alienta Dr 84770
Allison Row 84790
Almond Cir 84790
Altamira Way 84790
Amanda Cir 84790
E Amaranth Dr 84790
S & W Ambassador Dr 84790
Amber Cir 84790
N & W Amethyst 84770
Amethyst Garden Cir 84790
Anasazi Trl 84770
W Ancestor Point Cir 84790
S Ancient Shore Dr 84790
Apache Cir 84790
Apparation Ct 84790
Aquarius Cir 84790
W Aquifer Cir 84770
Arnica Cir 84790
S Arrowhead Canyon Dr 84790
Arroyo Dr 84790
N Artesia Dr 84770
Ash Cir 84790
Ash Springs Ln 84790
E Ashby Dr 84790
S Aspen Glow Dr 84790
W Aspiration Point Cir 84790
Auburn Cir & Dr 84790
Augusta Dr & Ln 84790
N & S Avallon Cir & Dr 84770
Azalea Cir 84790
Aztec Rd 84790
Azzurro Dr 84770
W Balanced Rock Dr 84770
Balboa Way 84770
S Banded Hills Dr 84790
Baneberry Dr 84790
E & S Barcelona Dr 84790
Basswood Cir 84790
Bayberry Cir 84790
Bear Claw Dr 84790
Beech St 84790
Belford Pl 84790
Bella Rosa Cir & Dr 84790
Bella Viaggio Cv 84770
Belmont Dr 84790
Bentley Rd 84790
S Big River Dr 84790
Birch Cir 84790
S Black Ridge Dr 84770
W Blackberry Cir 84790
S Bloomington Dr E 84790
Bloomington Hills Dr 84790
W Blue Duck Ln 84770
Blueberry Cir 84790
Bluegrass Way 84790
N & S Bluff St 84770
W Bonita Bay Cir & Dr 84790
Boulder Cove Cir 84790
Boulder Mountain Rd 84790
Boulder Springs Cir & Rd 84790
N Box Canyon Rd 84770
Box Elder Cir 84790
S & W Bridge Pointe Way 84770
E & W Brigham Rd 84790
S Broadmoor Dr 84790
W Brook View Ln 84770
Bunker Cir 84770
W Burgundy Way 84770
Butternut Cir 84790
Buttonbush Cir 84790
Cactus Cir 84790
Caddy Cir 84770
Calanus Cir 84790
E Calgary Dr 84790
Calla Cir 84790
Calle Del Sol 84790
Calle Las Casitas 84790
Calliandra Cir 84790
Cambridge Dr 84770
Cameron Pl 84790
S Cantamar Dr 84790
S Canterbury Rd 84770
Canyon Cove Cir 84790
Canyon Ridge Dr 84770
S & W Canyon View Dr 84770
Canyon Voices Dr 84790
Capri Dr 84770
Caribbean Cir 84790
Carisa Dr 84790
S & W Carmel Bluffs Cir & Dr 84790
Carmine Dr & St 84790
Carolina Cir 84790
Cascade Canyon Cir & Dr 84770
Casper Cir 84790
Cassidy Cir 84790
Castle Rock Rd 84770
Catalpa Cir 84790
Cathedral Dr 84790
N & W Cedar Dr 84770
Centennial Dr 84790
Chaco Trl 84770
W Chandler Dr 84770
Chaparral Dr 84790
W Chapel View Ln 84770
N Charbonne Dr 84770
Chasing Light Dr 84790
W Chateau Cir 84770
Cherry Cir 84790
Chestnut Cir 84790
Chettro Trl 84790
N Chinle Cir 84770
Chippenham Ct 84770
Chokeberry Dr 84790
Churchill Dr 84790
Cinder Cone 84770
Cinnamon Field Cir 84790
E & S Circle Ridge Dr 84790
Citation Cir 84790
E & N City Center St 84770
Clear Creek Ln 84790
S & E Cliff Point Cir & Dr 84790
Cliff Rose Dr 84790
Clinton Cir & Way 84790
Cloudcrest Cir 84790
Clubhouse Way 84770
E & S Cobalt Dr 84790
Cobble Cove Cir 84790
Cobblestone Ln 84770
Cohonina Cir & Trl 84770
Cold River Dr 84790
Colorado Dr 84770
Columbia Cir 84790
Columbine Cir 84790
Comanche Rd 84790
E Commerce Dr 84790
Concord Way 84770
S Convention Center Dr 84790
Copper River Dr 84790
Corkwood Cir 84790
Cottam Ct 84790
Cottonwood Cir 84790
Cottonwood Springs Dr 84770
W Cougar Rock Cir 84770
Count Fleet Rd 84790
N Country Ln 84770
Country Club Dr 84790
Covington Dr 84770
Coyote Springs Cir & Dr 84790
Crescent Cir 84770
Cresole Dr 84770
N & S Crestline Cir & Dr 84790
E & S Crimson Cir 84790
E Crimson Ridge Dr 84790
Crockett Cir 84790
Crystal Dr 84770
S Crystal Lakes Dr 84770
W Curly Hallow Dr 84770
Cypress Cir 84790
Damascus Dr 84790
S Datura Hill Dr 84790
N Daybreak Dr 84770
S Deer Poppy Cir 84790
Del Mar Dr 84790
Del Rio Cir 84790
E Deseret Dr 84790
Desert Hills Dr 84790
Desert Rose Dr 84790
N Desert Springs Rd 84770
E Desmo Way 84790
W Destiny Point Cir 84790
Diagonal St 84770
N Diamond Rdg 84770
S & W Diamond River Dr 84790
N & W Diamond Valley Ct & Dr 84770
N & S Dixie Dr 84770
N Dixie Downs Rd 84770
Dogwood Cir 84790
W Dolce Cv 84770
N & S Donlee Dr 84770
N Dove Ln 84770
S & W Dover Way 84770
Dreamcrest Cir 84790
E Ducati Way 84790
N & W Dusk Dr 84770
Eagle Cir 84770
Eastlake Dr 84790
N & S Eastridge Dr 84790
Ebony Cir 84790
Echo Springs Cir 84790
Eclipse Dr 84770
W Edge Hill Ln 84770
Elder Cir 84790
Elm Cir & St 84790
Elrose 84790
N & W Emerald Dr 84770
Emeraud Dr 84770
Empress Cir 84790
Englemann Pl 84790
E & S Enterprise Dr 84790
W Entrada Trl 84770
Erin Dawn Cir 84790
Escalante Dr 84790
W Estela Cir 84770
Eucalyptus Cir 84790
N Evening Star Dr 84770
Everest Dr 84790
Evergreen Dr 84790
E Factory Dr 84790
Fairway Cir 84770
Fairway Rd 84790
Fairway Hills Dr 84790
Falcon Cir & Dr 84770
W Fandango Dr 84770
S Festival Park Cir 84790
Fig Cir 84790
Fir Cir 84790
S First Light Dr 84790
S Five Sisters Dr 84790
Flagstone Dr 84790
S Flaming Arch Dr 84790
Flatrock Rd 84790
S Flowering Hills Dr 84790
Foothill Cir 84790
E Foremaster Dr 84790
W Forest Hill Dr 84790
Fort Pierce Dr 84790
W Fountain Cir 84770
Franklin Cir & Dr 84790
Fuente Cir 84790
Gardenia Cir 84790
Garnet 84770
Garnet Ridge Cir & Dr 84790
Geronimo Rd 84790
W Glen Canyon Cir 84770
E & S Golda Dr 84790
W Golden Eagle Cir 84770
Goldenrod Cir 84790
Golf Cart Ln 84770
W Grand View Dr 84770
Granite Way 84790
S Grapevine Dr 84790
S Grass Valley Dr 84790
Grayson Dr 84790
N Great Basin Dr 84770
S & W Green Valley Ln 84770
Greystone Dr 84790
Guardian Cir 84790
Gunlock Cir & Ct 84790
N & W Gunsight Dr 84770
Hagen Cir 84790
Hamlet Hill Dr 84790
Hammock Dunes Cir 84790
S & W Hampton Rd 84770
Harmony Cir & Pl 84790
Harrison Dr 84770
Harvest Heights Dr 84790
Hawkins Cir 84790
Hawthorne Cir 84790
W Heather Glen Dr 84790
Hedera Pl 84790
Hemlock Cir 84790
W Heritage Dr 84770
Hibiscus Cir 84790
Hickory Way 84790
S Hidden Valley Dr 84790
High Park Dr 84790
E Highland Dr 84770
Hiko Springs Dr 84790
Hill Rd 84790
Hillrise Ave & Cir 84790
S & W Hilton Dr 84770
Hogan Cir 84790
Holly Grape Ln 84790
Homestead Cir 84770
Honey Locust Cir 84790
E & W Hope St 84770
Hopi Cir 84790
Horizon View Dr 84790
E Horsemans Park Dr 84790
E Howard Ln 84790
Hubbard Pl 84790
Hummingbird Dr 84770
Idlewood Ln 84770
Inca Cir 84790
S & W Indian Hills Dr 84770
Industrial Rd 84770
S Iris Cir 84790
Ironwood Dr 84790
Jacob Hamblin Dr 84790
N Jade 84770
W Jade 84770
E Jade Dr 84770
Jarvis Cir 84790
Jasmine Pl 84790
S Jaycee Dr 84770
N Jefferson St 84770
Jeter St 84790
E & S Joe Cir 84790
Jolley Cir 84790
Jones Cir 84790
Joshua Cir 84790
Juniper Cir 84790
Junipero Serra Dr 84790
Kaibab Cir 84790
Kanab Cir 84790
Kennedy Pl 84790
N Kimette 84790
S Kiva Hill Dr 84790
S Knob Oak Dr 84790
E Knolls Dr 84790
W Kolob Dr 84790
La Grasse Cir & Dr 84790
Labyrinth Cir & Dr 84770
S Lake Cir 84790
S Lake Placid 84790
N & W Lakota Dr 84770
N & W Laquinta Dr 84770
Larkspur Rd 84790
W Las Colinas 84790
W Las Hurdes Dr 84770
Lasal Cir 84790
Latonia Cir 84790
S Laurel Green Dr 84790
Lava Flow Dr 84770
Lava Point Dr 84790
Laverkin Cir 84790
Lazy River Dr 84790
Ledgerock Cir & Dr 84790
Ledges Pkwy 84770
N Lee Ln 84790
S Legacy Dr 84770
Lepido Way 84790
Lexington Dr 84770
Limestone Dr 84790
Little Valley Rd 84790
Lizzie Ln 84790
Lloyd Dr 84770
Loblolly Cir 84790
Locust Cir 84790
W Lomaki Cir 84770
Lone Coyote 84790
Lone Rock Dr 84770
N & W Long Sky Cir & Dr 84770
Los Alamitos Dr 84790
Los Padres Dr 84790
Lost Crk 84770
S Luce Del Sol 84770
W Luna Cir 84770
Lupin Way 84790
Madera Pl 84790
W Magatsu Cir 84770
Magellan Dr 84790
Magenta Mist Cir 84790
Mahogany Cir 84790
N Main St
1-179 84770
180-180 84771
181-499 84770
182-498 84770
S Main St 84770
N & S Mall Dr 84790
Man O War Rd 84790
W Mantua Dr 84770
Manzanita Rd 84790
Maplewood Way 84790
Marigold Way 84790
Mariposa Cir 84790
Mathis Park Pl 84770
Maya Cir 84790
Mckinley Way 84790
S & E Meadow Mist Cir & Way 84790
Meadow View Ln 84770
S & W Medallion Dr 84790
E & S Medical Center Dr 84790
Mesa Palms Dr 84770
N Mesquite Dr 84770
E Middleton Dr 84770
Moab Cir 84790
Modena Cir 84790
N Moenavi Cir 84770
Mojave Hts 84770
N & W Monroe St 84770
N & W Monterey Dr 84770
Montezuma Cir 84790
Monticello Cir 84790
Moody Cir 84790

N & W Moonglow Pl ... 84770
Moqui Dr ... 84790
Morane Manor Dr ... 84790
E & S Morningside Dr ... 84790
S Mosaic Dr ... 84790
Mountain Ledge Dr ... 84790
Mountain View Cir ... 84790
Mulberry Dr ... 84790
E & S Munich Dr ... 84790
E Nagano Dr ... 84790
Nannyberry Dr ... 84790
Nashua Rd ... 84790
Navajo Dr ... 84790
Nelson Cir ... 84790
Nicklaus Cir ... 84790
Nightfall Cir ... 84790
Ninebark Cir ... 84790
Normandy Ct ... 84770
Northridge Ave ... 84770
Northstar Dr ... 84770
Oak Cir ... 84790
Oakley Cir ... 84790
Oakmont Ln ... 84790
Oasis Dr ... 84770
Observation Cir ... 84790
Obsidian Dr ... 84770
W Old Marsh Dr ... 84790
Oleander Cir ... 84790
Onyx ... 84770
Onyx Way ... 84790
Opal Ct ... 84770
Opal Way ... 84790
Osage Cir ... 84790
E Overlook Dr ... 84790
Oxford Pl ... 84790
Paintbrush Way ... 84790
N Painted Sky Dr ... 84770
S Paiute Rd ... 84790
Palm Cir ... 84790
Palmer Cir ... 84790
Palmetto Cir ... 84790
N & W Palo Verde Dr ... 84770
Panorama Pkwy ... 84790
Par Three Cir ... 84770
E & N Paradise Way ... 84790
S Paragon Dr ... 84790
Paria Cir ... 84790
E Paris Dr ... 84790
E & N Park St ... 84770
S Parkside Cir ... 84770
Pavant Cir ... 84790
Peaceful River Dr ... 84790
Pear Cir ... 84790
Pebblecreek Dr ... 84770
Pecan Cir ... 84790
W Phoenix Dr ... 84770
Picturesque Dr ... 84770
Pikes Dr ... 84770
Pimlico Dr ... 84790
S & W Pinebrook Ln ... 84770
E & S Pinnacle Cir &
Dr ... 84790
Pintura Dr ... 84790
S Pioneer Rd ... 84790
Plantation Dr ... 84770
W Plateau Ln ... 84770
Player Cir ... 84790
Plum Cir ... 84790
Point Dr ... 84790
Pomegranate Way ... 84790
W Poppy Hills Cir ... 84790
E Portofino Cir ... 84790
E Price Hills Dr ... 84790
N & W Primrose Cir, Ct
& Dr ... 84770
Princeton Cir ... 84790
Province Way ... 84770
Provost Rd ... 84790
Purple Lupine Dr ... 84790
Putters Cir ... 84790
Quail Cir ... 84790
Quartz Dr ... 84790
Rain Lily Cir ... 84790
Rainier Dr ... 84770
Rancho Cir ... 84790
E Rasmussen Dr ... 84790

N Raven Ln ... 84770
Red Bud Cir ... 84790
Red Cliffs Dr ... 84790
Red Cloud Cir & Dr ... 84770
E Red Hills Pkwy ... 84770
Red River Dr ... 84790
Red Rock Rd ... 84770
Redstone Way ... 84790
Redwood Tree Cir &
St ... 84790
N & S Reflection Way ... 84770
Ridge Rim Way ... 84770
Ridgecrest Cir ... 84790
Ridgeview Dr ... 84770
E & S Rimcrest Cir &
Dr ... 84790
Rio Lobo Dr ... 84770
Rio Virgin Dr ... 84790
Rio Vista Dr ... 84790
N & W Rising Sun Cir &
Dr ... 84770
E River Rd ... 84790
River Of Fortune Dr ... 84790
W Rivers Edge Ln ... 84770
E Riverside Dr
100-1151 ... 84790
1150-1150 ... 84791
1153-2999 ... 84790
1200-2998 ... 84790
N & W Roadrunner Dr ... 84770
S Rockcress Cir ... 84790
Rocket Bar Rd ... 84790
Rocky Rd ... 84790
S Roja Vista Dr ... 84770
Rolling Hills Dr ... 84770
Rolling Stone Cir ... 84790
E Rome Dr ... 84790
W Rose Garden Ln ... 84770
Rosewood Cir ... 84790
Round Hill Cir & Dr ... 84790
N & W Royal Cir ... 84790
Ruby River Ln ... 84790
Russell Cir ... 84770
Rustic Dr ... 84770
Saddle Dr ... 84770
Sage Cir & Dr ... 84770
E Saint George Blvd
1-999 ... 84770
1400-1499 ... 84790
W Saint George Blvd ... 84770
Saint James Ln ... 84790
San Carlos Ct ... 84790
San Juan Cir ... 84790
San Marcus Cir ... 84770
San Rafael Pl ... 84790
Sand Feather Cir ... 84790
Sandalwood Cir ... 84790
S Sandscape Dr ... 84790
Sandstone Cir ... 84770
Sanford Pl ... 84790
Santa Anita Dr ... 84790
Santa Clara Cir ... 84790
Santa Maria Ct ... 84790
N & W Sapphire Ct &
Trl ... 84770
Saratoga Dr ... 84790
Scenic Mountain Ln ... 84790
S Seabrook Dr ... 84790
Secret Springs Cir &
Dr ... 84790
Seegmiller Rd ... 84790
W Sego Lily Ln ... 84770
Segovia Cir & Dr ... 84790
N Serenity Dr ... 84770
Sevier Rd ... 84770
Shadow Point Dr ... 84770
Shady Spgs ... 84770
Shasta Dr ... 84770
Shavano Pl ... 84790
S Shellee Dr ... 84790
Sherman Cir & Rd ... 84790
S Sherwood Dr ... 84790
Shiloh Cir ... 84790
W Shinnecock ... 84770
Shivwits Dr ... 84790
Sierra Vista Cir ... 84790

S Siesta Dr ... 84790
S & W Silicon Cir &
Way ... 84770
Silk Tree Cir ... 84790
N & W Silver Cloud
Dr ... 84770
Sinagua Trl ... 84770
Single Track Ln ... 84790
S & W Sir Monte Dr ... 84770
Skyline Dr ... 84770
S & E Slate Ridge Cir &
Dr ... 84790
Smoke Tree St ... 84790
Snead Cir ... 84790
Snow Cir ... 84790
N & W Snow Canyon
Pkwy ... 84770
Snow Hill Ln ... 84770
Solano Way ... 84790
Solar Cir ... 84770
S Sonata Cir ... 84790
W Songbird Dr ... 84790
Sonoma Ln ... 84770
N Sonoran Dr ... 84770
Southgate Hills Dr ... 84770
Southwind Dr ... 84770
Spirit Walker Dr ... 84790
Springs Cir & Dr ... 84790
Spruce Cir ... 84790
W Stardust Dr ... 84770
Starling Cir ... 84770
Stone Canyon Cir &
Dr ... 84790
Stone Cliff Dr ... 84790
Stone Crest Cir &
Way ... 84790
N & S Stone Mountain
Dr ... 84770
Stonebridge Dr ... 84770
Sugar Leo Cir & Rd ... 84790
W Summer Poppy Dr ... 84790
Summit Ridge Dr ... 84790
W Sun Kissed Dr ... 84790
W Sunbrook Dr ... 84770
Sundance Cir ... 84790
N Sunflower Dr ... 84790
Sunland Dr ... 84790
Sunrise Ct ... 84770
Sunriver Pkwy ... 84790
Sunsation Cir ... 84790
W Sunset Blvd ... 84770
Sunstar Cir & Dr ... 84790
Swaps Dr ... 84790
Sweetgum Cir ... 84790
Sweetwater Cir ... 84790
E & W Tabernacle St ... 84770
N & W Tacheene Dr ... 84770
Tamarisk Dr ... 84790
Taviawk Cir ... 84770
Tavimaus Cir ... 84770
Tee Cir ... 84770
S Terra Ridge Dr ... 84790
Three Bars Rd ... 84790
Three Marys Pl ... 84790
W Ticaboo ... 84770
Tobin Cir ... 84790
Toltec Cir ... 84790
Tonaquint Dr ... 84790
S Tonaquint Dr ... 84770
W Tonaquint Dr ... 84770
N Topaz ... 84770
W Topaz ... 84770
E Topaz Way ... 84790
S Torino Dr ... 84790
N Tower Butte Dr ... 84770
Tranquility Bay Dr ... 84790
Travellers Ter ... 84770
S Trebruk Cir ... 84770
Tusher Cir ... 84790
N Tuweap Dr ... 84770
Twin Cir ... 84790
Twin Lakes Dr ... 84770
Ute Rd ... 84790
Uxbridge Cir ... 84770
E Valley Springs Dr ... 84790
Valley View Dr ... 84770

E Venture Dr ... 84790
Verbena Cir ... 84790
S & W Verde Ridge
Rd ... 84770
Vermillion Ave ... 84790
Versailles Ct ... 84770
Via Linda Way ... 84790
S & W Victoria Ln ... 84790
View Point Dr ... 84790
S Village Rd ... 84770
S Ville Franche Cir ... 84770
Vision Point Cir ... 84790
Vista Ct ... 84790
Wagon Rd ... 84770
Walnut Cir ... 84790
Walton Cir ... 84790
N Wapatki Trl ... 84770
Warm River Dr ... 84790
S Washington Fields
Rd ... 84790
S Waterfront Dr ... 84790
Waterworks Dr ... 84770
Webb Cir ... 84790
Wedgewood Cir & Dr ... 84770
Wesley Powell Dr ... 84790
Westcliff Dr ... 84790
Westridge Dr ... 84770
Whipple Ct ... 84790
Whisper Point Cir &
Dr ... 84790
E White Ridge Dr ... 84790
Whitestone Dr ... 84790
Whitney Dr ... 84770
Wide River Dr ... 84790
Willow Dr ... 84790
N & W Winchester Dr ... 84770
N Winchester Hills Dr ... 84770
Windom Pl ... 84790
Windsong Way ... 84790
Windsor Dr ... 84770
Windswept Dr ... 84790
Witch Hazel Cir ... 84790
Wonderstone Dr ... 84790
Woodbury Cir ... 84790
Woodlen Cir ... 84790
S & W Woods View Cir
& Ln ... 84770
Yarrow Way ... 84790
Young St ... 84790
Yucca Cir ... 84790

NUMBERED STREETS

E 10 S ... 84790
W 10 N ... 84770
W 10 S ... 84770
E 10 North Cir ... 84790
E 100 S
1-1099 ... 84770
1100-2199 ... 84790
N 100 E
1-399 ... 84770
1-299 ... 84770
N 100 W
1-499 ... 84770
500-799 ... 84770
S 1000 E
1-99 ... 84770
1-999 ... 84770
101-399 ... 84770
600-1700 ... 84790
1702-1798 ... 84790
S 100 W ... 84770
W 100 N ... 84770
W 100 S ... 84770
E 1000 South Cir ... 84790
E 1000 North Cir ... 84770
E 1010 S ... 84790
W 1010 N ... 84770
E 1010 South Cir ... 84790
N & W 1020 W & N ... 84770
E 1030 N ... 84770
E 1030 S ... 84790
S 1030 E ... 84790
W 1030 N ... 84770
W 1040 N ... 84770

E 1050 S ... 84790
N 1050 W ... 84770
W 1050 N ... 84770
E 1050 South Cir ... 84790
E 1060 N ... 84770
E 1070 S ... 84790
N 1070 W ... 84770
W 1070 S ... 84770
N & S 1080 E & W ... 84770
S 1090 West Cir ... 84770
110 N & S ... 84790
E 1100 S ... 84790
N 1100 E ... 84770
N 1100 W ... 84770
S 1100 E ... 84790
S 1100 W ... 84770
W 1100 N ... 84770
E 110 North Cir ... 84790
E 1100 South Cir ... 84790
W 110 South Cir ... 84770
N 1110 West Cir ... 84770
W 1130 N ... 84770
W 1130 North Cir ... 84770
W 1140 N ... 84770
E 1150 N ... 84770
E & N 1160 S & W ... 84770
S 1160 East Cir ... 84790
S 1160 West Cir ... 84770
N 1175 W ... 84770
W 1170 N ... 84770
N 1180 W ... 84770
E 1190 S ... 84790
W 1190 N ... 84770
W 1190 North Cir ... 84770
E 1200 N ... 84770
E 1200 S ... 84790
S 1200 E
100-298 ... 84790
S 120 E
2600-2699 ... 84790
S 1200 W ... 84770
W 120 N
1100-1199 ... 84770
1217-1259 ... 84770
E 1200 North Cir ... 84770
W 120 South Cir ... 84770
N & S 1210 ... 84770
S 1220 East Cir ... 84790
W 1230 N ... 84770
E 1240 S ... 84790
N 1240 W ... 84770
S 1240 W ... 84770
E 1250 S ... 84790
N 1250 W ... 84770
S 1250 W ... 84770
W 1250 N ... 84770
S 1260 W ... 84770
N 1275 W ... 84770
W 1270 N ... 84770
N 1280 W ... 84770
S 1280 E ... 84790
W 1280 N ... 84770
S 1280 East Cir ... 84790
E 1290 S ... 84790
E 130 N ... 84790
E 1300 S ... 84790
N 1300 E ... 84770
N 1300 W ... 84770
S 1300 E ... 84790
S 1300 W ... 84770
W 1300 N ... 84770
W 1300 S ... 84770
E 1300 South Cir ... 84790
W 1300 North Cir ... 84770
W 1310 N ... 84770
N 1320 W ... 84770
S 1340 W ... 84770
N 1340 West Cir ... 84770
S 1340 East Cir ... 84790
S 1350 E ... 84790
W 1350 N ... 84770
S & W 1360 W & N ... 84770
W 1375 N ... 84770
W 1370 N ... 84770
N & W 1390 W & N ... 84770

E 140 S ... 84790
200-2799 ... 84790
N 1400 E ... 84770
N 1400 W ... 84770
S 1400 E ... 84790
W 1400 N ... 84770
W 1400 S ... 84770
E 1400 South Cir ... 84790
E 140 South Cir ... 84790
S 1420 E ... 84790
W 1425 N ... 84770
W 1420 N
2100-2199 ... 84770
S 1430 East Cir ... 84790
N & W 1440 W & N ... 84770
S 1440 East Cir ... 84790
E & S 1450 S & E ... 84790
W 145 N ... 84770
N 1460 W ... 84770
W 1465 N ... 84770
S 1470 E ... 84790
S 1470 W ... 84790
W 1470 N ... 84770
W 1470 S ... 84770
E 1480 S ... 84790
N 1480 West Cir ... 84770
S 1480 East Cir ... 84790
N 1490 W ... 84770
S 1490 West Cir ... 84770
S 1490 East Cir ... 84790
W 15 North Cir ... 84770
E 150 N
1-99 ... 84770
2700-2798 ... 84790
2800-2999 ... 84790
E 150 S
500-599 ... 84770
E 1500 S
2600-2699 ... 84790
N 1500 W ... 84770
S 150 E ... 84770
W 150 S ... 84770
S 1500 East Cir ... 84790
W 150 North Cir ... 84770
N & W 1510 W & N ... 84770
W 1525 N ... 84770
N 1530 W ... 84770
E 1530 South Cir ... 84790
E 1540 S ... 84790
N 1540 W ... 84770
S 1540 E ... 84790
E 1540 South Cir ... 84790
N 1550 W ... 84770
S 1550 W ... 84790
W 1550 N ... 84770
N 1560 West Cir ... 84770
N 1570 W ... 84770
S 1570 E ... 84790
W 1575 N ... 84770
S 1570 East Cir ... 84790
E 1580 S ... 84790
W 1580 N ... 84770
N 1590 W ... 84770
E 160 S
600-699 ... 84770
2200-2599 ... 84790
N 1600 W ... 84770
S 1600 E ... 84790
W 1600 N ... 84770
W 1600 S ... 84770
N 160 West Cir ... 84770
N 1600 West Cir ... 84770
N 1610 W ... 84770
S 1610 W ... 84790
W 1610 N ... 84770
N 1610 West Cir ... 84770
N 1620 W ... 84770
S 1620 W ... 84790
N 1620 West Cir ... 84770
W 1620 North Cir ... 84770
S 1630 E ... 84790
N 1640 W ... 84770
N 1650 W ... 84770
S 1650 E ... 84790
S 1660 W ... 84790
W 1660 N ... 84770

N 1660 West Cir ... 8477
N 1680 E ... 8479
E 170 N ... 8479
E 170 S ... 8479
N 1700 E ... 8477
S 1700 E ... 8479
S 1700 W ... 8479
W 170 N
1200-1299 ... 8477
1800-2099 ... 8477
W 1700 S ... 8477
E 170 South Cir ... 8479
E 1710 S ... 8479
W 1710 N ... 8477
W 1710 North Cir ... 8477
E 1720 S ... 8479
N 1725 W ... 8477
W 1720 N ... 8477
S 1730 W ... 8479
N 1740 W ... 8477
S 1740 E ... 8479
S 1740 W ... 8479
W 1740 N ... 8477
E 175 N ... 8479
S 1750 E ... 8479
W 1750 N ... 8477
E 1750 South Cir ... 8479
N & W 1760 W & N ... 8477
S & W 1770 W & N ... 8477
W 1780 N ... 8477
N 1790 East Cir ... 8477
S 1790 West Cir ... 8477
E 180 S ... 8479
1400-1599 ... 8479
N 1800 E ... 8477
S 1800 E ... 8479
W 1800 N ... 8477
E 180 South Cir ... 8479
N 1800 West Cir ... 8477
W 180 South Cir ... 8477
W 1820 N ... 8477
S 1820 West Cir ... 8477
N 1830 East Cir ... 8477
S 1840 W ... 8477
E 1850 S ... 8479
N 1850 W ... 8477
W 1860 N ... 8477
N & S 1870 ... 8477
S 1880 E ... 8479
S 1890 East Cir ... 8479
N 1900 E ... 8477
N 1910 W ... 8477
W 1920 N ... 8477
W 1920 North Cir ... 8477
S 1930 E ... 8479
W 1940 N ... 8477
N 1950 E ... 8479
900-1099 ... 8477
N 1955 W ... 8477
1800-1999 ... 8477
S 1950 E ... 8479
S 1950 W ... 8477
S 1960 E ... 8479
S 1960 East Cir ... 8479
N 1975 W ... 8477
S 1970 E ... 8479
E 1975 South Cir ... 8479
W 1970 North Cir ... 8477
W 1980 N ... 8477
S 1990 E ... 8479
E 200 N ... 8477
E 200 S
1-700 ... 8477
1100-2499 ... 8479
2500-3399 ... 8479
N 2000 E
1-699 ... 8479
1-1 ... 8477
800-1099 ... 8477
N 200 W
1-299 ... 8477
900-998 ... 8477
S 200 E
1-670 ... 8477
1-2799 ... 8479
S 200 W ... 8477

W 200 N
1-97 84770
2000-2399 84770
W 200 S 84770
N 2010 E 84770
S 2010 E 84790
N 2020 W 84770
N & W 2025 W & S 84770
S 2020 East Cir 84790
N 2040 E 84790
N & S 2040 East 84790
W 2040 South Cir 84770
N 2050 East Cir 84770
N 2065 W 84770
S 2060 E 84790
E 2070 S 84790
N 2070 E 84790
N 2070 W 84770
S 2070 E 84790
N 2075 East Cir 84770
S 2070 East Cir 84790
N 2080 East Cir 84770
W 2080 South Cir 84770
E 2090 South Cir 84790
N 2100 E 84790
N 2100 W 84770
S 2100 E 84790
S 2110 E 84790
N & S 2110 East 84790
N 2120 East Cir 84790
N & W 2130 W & S 84770
N 2140 East Cir 84790
W 2140 South Cir 84770
E 2150 South Cir 84790
S 2160 E 84790
E & S 2170 S & E 84790
N 2170 East Cir 84790
S 2180 E 84790
E 2190 S 84790
N 2190 W 84770
E 2190 South Cir 84790
W 2190 South Cir 84770
N 2200 E 84790
N 2200 W 84770
S 2200 E 84790
E 220 South Cir 84790
W 220 North Cir 84770
E & S 2220 S & E 84790
S 2220 East Cir 84790
N 2230 E 84790
W 2230 S 84770
N 2240 E 84790
S 2240 E 84790
W 2240 S 84770
N & S 2250 84790
E 2250 South Cir 84790
S 2260 E 84790
S 2260 East Cir 84790
E 2270 S 84790
N 2270 E 84790
W 2270 S 84770
N 2270 East Cir 84790
W 2270 South Cir 84770
N 2280 E 84790
E 2290 S 84790
E 2300 S 84790
E 2300 South Cir 84790
E 230 Cir S 84790
N 2300 West Cir 84770
N & S 2310 84790
S 2310 East Cir 84790
N & W 2320 W & S 84770
S 2320 East Cir 84790
E 2330 S 84790
N 2330 E 84790
N 2330 W 84770
N 2330 West Cir 84770
S 2340 E 84790
S 2350 E 84790
N 2350 East Cir 84790
N 2360 E 84790
E 2370 S 84790
N 2370 E 84790
S 2370 E 84790
W 2370 S 84770
N 2380 East Cir 84790
S 2390 E 84790
E 2390 South Cir 84790
E 240 S 84790
W 2400 S 84770
E 2410 S 84790
W 2410 South Cir 84770
E 2420 Cir S 84790
S 2420 East Cir 84790
S 2430 E 84790
N 2430 East Cir 84790
S 2440 E 84790
S 2440 East Cir 84790
E 2450 S 84790
S 2460 E 84790
E & N 2480 S & E 84790
S 2490 E 84790
E 250 N 84770
N 2500 W 84770
S 2510 E 84790
S 2520 E 84790
S 2530 E 84790
E 2540 S 84790
E 2550 S 84790
S 2565 E 84790
E & S 2580 S & E 84790
E 2580 South Cir 84790
E & N 2590 S & E 84790
E 2590 South Cir 84790
N 260 West Cir 84770
E & S 2610 S & E 84790
E & S 2620 S & E 84790
S 2620 East Cir 84790
E 2630 South Cir 84790
S 2640 E 84790
N 2650 E 84790
W 265 S 84770
N & S 2660 84790
S 2670 E 84790
E & S 2680 S & E 84790
S 2690 E 84790
E & S 270 S & E 84790
N & S 2700 84790
S 2700 East Cir 84790
N & S 2710 84790
E & W 2710 South 84790
E & N 2720 S & E 84790
S 2740 E 84790
S 2740 W 84770
N & S 2750 84790
S 2760 East Cir 84790
S 2780 E 84790
N & S 2790 84790
S 2790 East Cir 84790
E 280 N 84790
E & S 2800 S & E 84790
S 2810 E 84790
N & S 2820 84790
E 2830 S 84790
E 2860 S 84790
E 2860 South Cir 84790
N 2860 East Cir 84790
S 2870 E 84790
S 2880 E 84790
N 2890 E 84790
E 290 S 84790
N 2900 E 84790
S 2910 E 84790
N & S 2940 84790
S 2950 E 84790
S 2970 E 84790
E 30 N 84790
E 300 N 84770
E 300 S
1-699 84770
1100-1198 84770
N 300 E 84770
N 300 W 84770
S 3000 E 84790
1-669 84770
S 300 W 84770
W 300 N 84770
W 300 S 84770
S 3030 E 84790
N 3050 E 84790
S 3070 E 84790
E 3090 South Cir 84790
S 3120 E 84790
E 3150 S 84790
E 3160 E 84790
E 3190 S 84790
E 3200 S 84790
S 320 E 84790
W 320 N 84770
S 3210 E 84790
S 3220 E 84790
E 3240 S 84790
E 330 S 84790
W 330 N 84770
E 3330 S 84790
E 3350 S 84790
E 3380 S 84790
E 3390 S 84790
E 3400 S 84790
E 340 South Cir 84790
E & S 3430 S & E 84790
E 3460 S 84790
E 3470 S 84790
E 350 N
1100-1399 84770
2001-2597 84790
W 350 N 84770
E 3510 S 84790
E & W 3530 84790
E 3540 South Cir 84790
W 3550 S 84790
E 3580 S 84790
W 3590 South Cir 84790
W 360 N 84770
W 3600 S 84790
E 3610 South Cir 84790
E 3630 S 84790
W 3640 S 84790
W 3650 South Cir 84790
E 3670 S 84790
E 370 N 84790
W 3700 N 84770
3710 Cir 84790
W 3750 S 84790
E 3770 S 84790
W 3780 S 84790
E 380 N 84790
E 380 South Cir 84790
E & S 3850 S & E 84790
E 3860 S 84790
E 390 N 84790
W 390 N 84770
E 390 North Cir 84790
W 390 North Cir 84770
E 3910 S 84790
E 3950 S 84790
E 40 N 84790
W 40 S 84770
E 40 South Cir 84790
E 400 N 84790
E 400 S
1-999 84770
1101-1199 84790
N 400 E 84770
N 400 W 84770
S 400 E
1-999 84770
1300-1398 84790
S 400 W 84770
W 400 N 84770
W 400 S 84770
E 410 N 84790
W 410 N 84770
W 4100 S 84790
E 4130 S 84790
E 4150 S 84790
W 4200 N 84770
W 4230 N 84770
W 425 N 84770
E & S 430 N & E 84790
E 430 North Cir 84790
W 430 North Cir 84770
E 4340 South Cir 84790
W 4400 N 84770
E 440 North Cir 84790
S 440 East Cir 84770
E 450 N 84790
W 450 N 84770
W 450 S 84770
S 460 E 84790
S 460 East Cir 84790
W 470 N 84770
W 475 North Cir 84770
E 480 North Cir 84790
S & W 490 W & N 84770
E 490 South Cir 84790
E 50 N 84790
E 50 S 84790
N 50 E 84770
W 50 N 84770
E 50 North Cir 84790
E 50 South Cir 84790
S 50 West Cir 84770
E 500 S
1-600 84770
602-698 84770
1000-1099 84790
N 500 E 84770
N 500 W 84770
S 500 E 84770
W 500 N 84770
W 500 S 84770
S 500 East Cir 84790
W 500 South Cir 84770
W 510 N 84770
S 510 West Cir 84770
W 510 North Cir 84770
S 5160 E 84790
W 5300 N 84770
W 530 S 84770
E 540 N 84790
S 540 E 84790
W 5400 N 84770
W 540 N
1000-1899 84770
E 540 South Cir 84790
W 5484 N 84770
N 55 West Cir 84770
E 550 N 84790
S 550 E 84790
W 550 N 84770
E 550 South Cir 84790
W 5530 N 84770
W 5540 N 84770
W 5550 N 84770
W 5560 N 84770
560 N & S 84770
W 5630 N 84770
W 5650 N 84770
W 570 North Cir 84770
W 5745 N 84770
E 575 N 84790
W 580 N 84770
E 580 South Cir 84790
W 5830 N 84770
W 5870 N 84770
W 590 S 84770
E & S 60 S & E 84790
E 600 N 84790
E 600 S
1-97 84770
1000-1100 84790
N 600 E 84770
N 600 W 84770
S 600 E 84770
W 600 N 84770
W 600 S 84770
S 600 East Cir 84770
E 610 N 84790
W 610 North Cir 84770
E & S 620 N & E 84790
W 620 North Cir 84770
W 625 N 84770
E 630 N 84790
N 630 W 84770
W 630 S 84770
W 65 S 84770
E 650 N 84790
E 650 S 84790
S 650 E 84790
W 650 N 84770
W 650 S 84770
E 650 North Cir 84790
W 650 North Cir 84770
N 660 W 84770
S 660 E 84790
S 660 W 84770
E 660 North Cir 84790
S 660 East Cir 84770
E & W 670 N & S 84770
S 670 East Cir 84790
W 670 North Cir 84770
680 N & S 84770
E 680 South Cir 84790
S 690 W 84770
W 690 North Cir 84770
W 70 North Cir 84770
E 70 South Cir 84790
W 70 South Cir 84770
E 700 N
1200-1298 84770
2200-2699 84790
E 700 S
1-799 84770
900-1199 84790
N 700 E 84770
N 700 W 84770
S 700 E 84770
W 700 N 84770
W 700 S 84770
W 710 N 84770
730 N & S 84770
W 730 North Cir 84770
E & W 740 N & S 84770
E 740 South Cir 84790
E 750 N 84790
E 750 S 84770
W 750 N 84770
E 750 North Cir 84790
E 760 South Cir 84790
E 770 N 84770
S 770 E 84790
E 775 S 84770
W 790 N 84770
E 790 South Cir 84790
E 80 North Cir 84790
E 80 South Cir 84790
E 800 N 84770
E 800 S 84790
N 800 E 84770
S 800 E 84770
S 800 East Cir 84790
S 810 E 84790
S 840 E 84790
E 840 South Cir 84770
W 8450 N 84770
E 850 N 84790
N 850 W 84770
S 850 E 84790
W 8500 N 84770
E 850 South Cir 84790
W 870 South Cir 84770
890 E & W 84790
W 8900 N 84770
E 90 S 84790
W 90 S 84770
E 90 South Cir 84790
E 900 S
200-299 84770
400-698 84790
N 900 E 84770
S 900 E
2-98 84770
700-1099 84790
W 900 N 84770
W 900 S 84770
N 920 W 84770
S 930 E 84790
E 930 South Cir 84790
E & S 940 S & E 84790
E 950 S 84790
N 950 W 84770
S 950 E 84790
W 950 N 84770
W 950 S 84770
S 960 E 84790
S 960 East Cir 84790
W 960 South Cir 84770
W 970 N 84770
E 970 South Cir 84790
W 975 N 84770
W 980 N 84770
S 980 East Cir 84790
E 990 South Cir 84790

SALT LAKE CITY UT

General Delivery 84101

POST OFFICE BOXES MAIN OFFICE STATIONS AND BRANCHES

Box No.s
1 - 4940 84110
9001 - 9996 84109
9998 - 9998 84110
11001 - 11999 84147
16001 - 16998 84116
17001 - 17992 84117
18001 - 18999 84118
22001 - 22996 84122
25001 - 25957 84125
26001 - 26977 84126
27001 - 27997 84127
30000 - 30997 84130
31001 - 31990 84131
45000 - 45925 84145
57001 - 57999 84157
58001 - 58994 84158
65000 - 65999 84165
70001 - 70994 84170
71001 - 71980 84171
91001 - 91318 84109
112012 - 119998 84147
140100 - 148941 84114
161001 - 168888 84116
171001 - 171439 84117
221001 - 229998 84122
259998 - 259998 84125
269998 - 269998 84126
271001 - 279998 84127
457000 - 457000 84145
510002 - 511624 84151
520001 - 526459 84152
571001 - 579998 84157
581001 - 589998 84158
651000 - 652001 84165
701001 - 704008 84170
711001 - 713800 84171

HIGHWAY CONTRACTS

30 84121

NAMED STREETS

A St 84103
N A St 84111
S Aaron Way 84118
W Aaron Park Cir 84123
S Abbey Ct 84123
S Abinadi Rd 84124
S Achilles Dr 84124
S Acorn Ct 84111
E & S Adaley Ave 84107
Adams Cir & St 84115
S Adams Garden Cv 84106
N Admiral Byrd Rd 84116
E & S Adonis Cir & Dr 84124
W Advantage Cir 84104
E Aerie Cv 84121
E & S Afton Ave 84107
E Ailee Ln 84107
E Alameda Ave 84102
S Alberly Way 84124
S Albertville Pl 84121
S Albright Dr 84124
S Alden St 84106
W Alder Rd 84123
E Aldo Cir 84108
S Alex St 84118
S & W Alfred Cir & Way 84123
S Alicia Park Way 84107
W Alida Pl 84103
E Alison Cir 84124
S & W Allegheny Dr 84123
E Allen Park Dr 84105
S Allendale Dr 84123
E Almira Ct 84121
N Almond St 84103
E Aloha Rd 84103
S & E Alpen Cir & Way 84121
S Alpine Dr 84107
E Alpine Pl 84105
W Alpine Brook Cir 84118
S Alpine Crest Cir 84118
W Alpine Flower Cir 84118
W Alpine Point Cir 84118
W Alps Way 84116
E & N Alta Cir & St 84103
S Alta Loma Dr 84106
S Alta Vista Dr 84106
W Altair Cir 84116
S & W Altamira Dr 84118
S Alton Way 84108
E & S Alva Cir 84109
S & E Alvera Cir & Dr 84117
S Amanda Ave 84105
S Ambassador Way 84108
E Amblewood Ln 84124
W Amelia Earhart Dr 84116
W American Ave
1-199 84107
300-399 84101
1100-1499 84104
N American Beauty Dr 84116
E Amesbury Cir 84121
W Amiga Dr 84104
S Ancestor Pl 84123
W Anderson Ave
300-398 84107
400-799 84123
S Andlor St 84117
N Andrea Cir 84116
W Andrew Ave
1-47 84115
49-99 84115
101-399 84115
1201-1225 84104
1227-2999 84104
E Angelina Ave 84106
E & S Angelita Ct 84106
E & W Angelo Ave 84115
S Angelus St 84107
E Anita Ave 84106
E Ann Dell Ln 84121
S Anna Raquel Cir 84123
S Annabow Cir 84117
E & S Anne Marie Dr 84121
W Anthony Cir 84104
N & W Antilles Cir & Dr 84116
E Antler Way 84121
E Apache Cir 84108
E Apollo Dr 84124
N Apollo Rd 84116
S Aposhian Cir 84124
E Apple Blossom Ln 84117
S Apple Creek Ct 84118
S & W Apple Cross Way 84107
E Apple Mill Cv 84109
Apple Park Pl & Way 84106
E Apple View Ct 84109
S Applevale Dr 84123
E Applewood Ave 84121
S & W Appomattox Way 84123
W Apricot Ave 84103
S Aqua Vista Cv 84121
S & W Aquarius Cir, Ct & Dr 84118
W Arapahoe Ave 84104
S Arapeen Dr 84108

S & E Arbor Cir & Ln 84117
S & W Arbroath Ln 84115
E Arcadia Ln 84124
S Arcadia Ln
4400-4499 84124
4500-4599 84117
E & S Arcadia Green Way 84107
E Arcadia Heights Cir 84109
E & S Arcata Rd 84124
W Archard Ave 84115
S Archer Garden Ct 84117
S Arco Cir 84124
N Arctic Ct 84103
S Arden Ct 84123
W Ardmore Pl 84103
N Argyle Ct 84116
W Aries Cir 84116
S Aries Dr 84118
E Arlington Ave 84107
N Arlington Cir 84103
E Arlington Dr 84103
S Arminta St 84117
E Arnecia Ct 84106
S & E Arnette Cir & Dr 84109
W Arnica Ridge Cir 84118
S & E Arrowhead Cir & Ln 84107
S Arroyo Rd 84106
E & S Artesian Way 84121
E & S Ash Cir 84109
E Ash Tree Cv 84106
S Ashbury Ln 84121
E & S Ashford Dr 84124
S & E Ashland Dr & Way 84109
E Ashton Ave 84106
E Ashton Cir 84109
E & S Ashwood Cir & Dr 84121
E Aspen Cir 84109
S Aspen Ln 84123
E & S Aspen Bend Ln 84121
S Aspen Haven Ln 84121
W Aspen Heights Dr 84123
S Aspen Hollow Ln 84117
E Aspen Meadows Ct 84107
S Astoria Ln 84123
S & E Astro Cir & Way 84109
S & W Atherton Ct & Dr 84123
E Atkin Ave
900-1999 84106
2000-2299 84109
S Atwood Blvd 84107
W Auburn Dr 84123
S Augusta Way 84108
E & S Aura Cir & Dr 84124
E Aurora Cir 84124
E Austin Ave 84106
E & S Austrian Way 84121
E & S Auto Blvd 84107
W Autumn Ave 84116
W Autumn Bluff Dr 84123
W Autumn Leaf Ln 84123
S Autumn Spice Ln 84123
S Avalon Dr 84107
E Aveline Ave 84109
E Aviary Pl 84117
E & S Avon Pl 84115
E & S Avondale Dr 84121
S Awl Cir 84104
S Ayrshire Dr 84107
B St 84103
E Badger Hollow Ln 84108
E Bagend St 84106
W Bailiff Dr 84118
S Bainbridge Cir 84121
Baird Ave & Cir 84115
S Baker St 84107
S Baldwin Park 84123
S Balfour Ln 84123
S Balmossie Ln 84115
S & W Balsam Ave & Cir 84123
E Balsam Forest Ln 84121
N Baltic Ct 84103
S Balveine Pl 84107
S Bambrough Pl 84108
W Bampton Ln 84118
S & E Banbury Cir & Rd 84121
E Bank Ave 84115
S Banks Ct 84102
E Barbara Pl 84102
E Barbara Way 84124
W Barberry Dr 84123
E Barbey Dr 84109
E Barcon Rd 84117
S Barke Cir 84123
E Barnhill Bay 84121
E Barnwood Bay 84121
N & W Baroness Pl & St 84116
E Barrows Ave 84106
W Barry Links Way 84115
S Battle Creek Ct 84118
S Bay Bridge Rd 84123
S & W Bayport Way 84123
S & E Baywood Cir & Dr 84117
E & S Beacon Dr 84108
S & W Beacon Hill Cir & Dr 84123
W Bearcat Dr 84115
E Beartrap Fork Rd 84121
W Beau Cir 84118
E Beaumont Cir 84121
N Beaumont Ct 84116
S Beaumont Dr 84121
S Beaverbrook Ln 84117
N Beck St
800-824 84103
826-1199 84103
1200-1900 84116
1902-1998 84116
S Becky Cir 84109
W Beebe Ln 84107
S & W Beechwood Cir & Rd 84123
S Bekkemellom Way 84121
S Belaire Dr 84109
E Beldon Pl 84111
W Bell Ave 84104
E Bell Plz 84111
E Bell Tower Ln 84109
S Bella Verde Ct 84107
E Bella Vie Ct 84121
S Bella Vista Dr 84121
S Belle Grove Way 84115
E Belle Meadows Way 84121
S & W Bellwood Ln 84123
E Belmont Ave
141-147 84111
149-299 84111
739-1099 84105
S Belmour Way 84117
E & S Belview Ave 84107
S Ben Davis Park 84123
E Benbow St 84107
S & E Benchmark Cir & Dr 84109
E Bendamere Cir 84109
S Bending River Rd 84104
S Benecia Dr 84121
E Bengal Blvd 84121
E Bengal Bend Cv 84121
S Bengal Heights Ct 84121
E Bengal Hills Cv 84121
S Bennett Rd 84104
W Berger Ln 84107
S Berkeley Cir 84109
S Berkeley St
1800-1898 84108
1900-1999 84108
2100-2499 84109
S & E Bernada Cir & Dr 84124
E Bernadine Dr 84109
E Beryl Ave 84115
E Best Ave 84106
S Betty Gene Dr 84107
S Beverly St 84106
S Bevwood Cir 84124
E & S Big Cottonwood Canyon Rd 84121
W Big Mountain Dr 84123
W Billinis Rd 84115
N Billy Mitchell Rd 84116
E Biltmore Ave 84107
E Birch Cir 84124
S Birch Dr
3700-3899 84109
3900-3999 84124
S Birch Point Rd 84117
E & S Birchfield Ln 84107
E & S Birchwood Dr 84121
S Birkhill Blvd 84107
S Biscayne Dr 84121
W Bishop Pl 84103
E Bishop Federal Ln 84115
W Black Angus Dr 84116
S & W Black Mica Ave & Cir 84118
S Black Swan Dr 84117
E Blackburn Cir 84117
S Blackhawk Way 84108
E & S Blackstone Rd 84121
E Blaine Ave
301-397 84115
399-499 84115
900-1699 84105
1700-2699 84108
E Blaine Cir 84108
S Blaine Dr 84107
S Blair Cir 84115
S Blair St
800-1199 84111
1300-2999 84115
3001-3099 84115
N Bliss Ct 84116
N Bloomfield Pl 84116
W Bloomsbury Cv 84123
S Blossom Valley Ln 84118
S Blue Flax Ln 84121
E Blue Grass Cir 84121
S Blue Iron Way 84118
S & E Blue Jay Cir & Ln 84121
S & E Blue Spruce Cir & Dr 84117
S Blue Stone Cir 84123
E Bluebell Dr 84124
W Bluebird St 84123
S & W Bluemont Cir & Dr 84123
E Bo Mar Dr 84121
S & E Boabab Cir, Ct & Dr 84117
E Bobcat Haven Ln 84121
S & W Bobolink St 84123
E & S Bonair St 84117
S Bonham Ln 84123
E Bonita Dr 84106
S & E Bonner Cir & Way 84117
S Bonneville Dr 84108
E Bonnie Ln 84115
E Bonnie Brae Ave 84124
S & W Bonnyview Ave 84107
E Bonview Dr 84109
Borax Ave & Cir 84118
W Borthwick Way 84123
E Bosham Ln 84106
S Boston Cir 84121
S Bothwell St 84104
Bouchelle Cv & Ln 84121
S Boulder Dr 84121
W Boulevard Gdns 84115
S Bourne Cir 84121
E Bowden Cir 84117
W Bowers Way 84115
S Bowers Vista Cir 84107
S Box Elder St 84107
S Boxwood Rd 84121
E & S Boyes St 84117
E Bradshaw Cir 84109
E Braewick Rd 84103
S & E Brahma Cir & Dr 84107
E Braintree Ct 84124
E Bramble Way 84117
S Bramblewood Ln 84118
S & W Brampton Way 84104
W Branbury Ct 84118
E Branch Dr 84117
W Brandermill Cv 84123
N Branding Cir 84116
S & W Brandonwood Dr 84123
E Brandt Ct 84107
S & W Brass Cir, Dr & Pl 84118
S Brava St 84104
S Braxton Ct 84121
S & W Breakwater Dr 84123
E & S Brekenridge Dr 84117
E Brenda Ave 84121
E & S Brent Ln 84121
S Brentwood Cir 84109
E Brentwood Dr 84121
S Brentwood Dr 84121
E Brewer Ave 84121
W Briar Rose Pl 84104
W Briarcliff Ave 84116
E & S Briarcreek Cir & Dr 84117
E Briarmeadow Ave 84107
S & E Briarwood Cir & Dr 84124
S Brick Oven Way 84107
E Brickyard Rd 84106
W Bridgecrest Cir 84116
E Bridgeport Ave 84121
W Bridger Rd 84104
E & S Bridges Ct & Ln 84121
S Bridgeside Way 84123
N & W Bridgestone Cir & Ln 84116
S & E Bridgewater Cir, Ct & Dr 84121
E Bridlebrook Cir 84117
E & S Bridlechase Ln 84107
E Bridlewalk Ln 84107
E Bridlewood Dr 84107
N Brigadier Cir 84116
E Brigadoon Ct 84117
E Brigham Fork Cir 84108
N Bright Ct 84116
S Bright Morning Cir 84123
E & S Brighton Cir, Ct, Loop, Pl & Way 84121
S Brighton Cove Cir 84121
E Brighton Lake Ln 84121
S Brighton Loop Rd 84121
E & S Brighton Point Dr 84121
S & W Brister Cir & Dr 84123
E Bristle Pine Pl 84106
E Bristlecone Cir 84121
E Brittany Dr 84107
S Brixen Ct 84102
S Broadmoor St
1900-1999 84108
2001-2099 84108
2101-2129 84109
2131-2245 84109
2247-2299 84109
E Broadway 84111
W Broadway 84101
E & S Brockbank Dr & Way 84124
E & S Brockway Cir & Dr 84117
S Bron Breck St 84117
W Brook Ridge Ln 84123
S Brook View Ln 84106
E Brookburn Rd 84109
W Brookbury Way 84123
E & S Brookhill Dr 84121
E & S Brooklane Cir & Dr 84124
W Brooklyn Ave
200-224 84101
226-300 84101
302-398 84101
1100-1199 84104
S Brookridge Dr 84107
S Brooks Way 84117
E Brookshire Dr 84106
S Brookwillow Cv 84117
Brookwood Cir & Dr 84117
S Broughtyferry Cv 84115
S Brown St 84107
S Brown Villa Cv 84123
E Browning Ave
200-299 84115
500-1699 84105
1700-2199 84108
E & S Bruce St 84124
S Brunswick Ct 84123
E Bryan Ave
1-499 84115
600-1599 84105
1700-2399 84108
E Bryan Cir 84108
W Bryanston Cv 84123
N Buccaneer Dr 84116
E Buchanan St 84115
E Buck Cir 84121
E Bueno Ave 84102
W Bugatti Dr 84115
W Bulldog Cir 84123
S & W Bullion St 84123
E Bulrush Way 84106
S & W Bunbury Cv & Ln 84104
E Bunkerhill Rd 84117
W Burbank Ave 84104
E Burnside Cir 84109
E Burnt Flat Rd 84121
N Burnt Fork Rd 84108
E & W Burton Ave 84115
Buster Cir & St 84118
E Butler Ave 84102
S Butler Cir 84107
S Butler Hills Dr 84121
Butterfield Cir & St 84123
E Butternut Cir 84124
S Butternut Rd
4300-4430 84124
4432-4450 84124
4500-4540 84117
S Buxton Ln 84108
S Byrum Cir 84118
C St 84103
E Cabrito St 84117
S Cadens Cv 84121
W Caesar Cir 84123
E Caitland Ct 84121
W Cajun Bay 84123
E & S Calann Dr 84121
W Caleb Pl 84107
S Calgary Ct 84121
W California Ave 84104
E Calinas Creek Cir 84107
S & W Callaway Ct 84123
S Camarilla Cir 84104
S Cambria Cir 84121
Cambridge Cir & Way 84103
W Cambridgetown Cv 84123
S & E Camelback Cir & Rd 84121
E Camila Ave 84107
E & S Camille Cir & St 84124
S & E Camino Cir, Ct, Pl & Way 84121
S Camino Bay 84121
S Camino Real Dr 84117
S Campbell Dr 84118
S Campus Cir 84121
E Campus Dr
1705-1825 84112
2310-2572 84121
2574-2576 84121
S Campus Dr
1-99 84112
7029-7037 84121
7039-7061 84121
7063-7071 84121
E & S Campus Center Dr 84112
W Canary St 84123
Cancento Dr 84109
S Canchina W 84101
S Candle Cv 84121
E Candytuft St 84121
S & W Canley Vale Ct & Ln 84115
E Cannes Way 84121
W Cannon Ave 84104
S & W Cannon Oaks Pl & St 84104
S & W Cannonwood Dr & Pl 84123
S Canterbury Dr 84108
E Canterbury Ln 84121
S Canterbury Ln 84121
N Canyon Rd 84103
S Canyon Way 84106
S & E Canyon Cove Cir, Ct, Dr & Pl 84121
S & E Canyon Creek Cir & Dr 84121
E & S Canyon Crest Dr 84121
E & N Canyon Oaks Way 84103
S Canyon Pines Cir 84121
E & S Canyon Ranch Rd 84121
E Canyon Rim Ln 84109
N Canyon Side St 84103
S & E Canyon View Cir & Dr 84109
E Canyon Winds Ln 84121
S Capehart St 84118
N Capistrano Dr 84116
E Capitol St 84103
E Capitol Oaks Ln 84103
E & N Capitol Park Ave 84103
W Caplan St 84118
S & W Capri Dr 84123
E Caprice Ct 84124
E Capricorn Way 84124
E Capstone Ave 84121
N Captain Cir 84116
S Captiva Cv 84121
S Caracol Cv 84121
S & E Cardiff Cir, Frk & Rd 84121
E Cardinal Way 84121
W Cardington Cir 84118
W Cargo Cir 84118
S Caribbean Way 84107
N Caring Cv 84103
S Carling Cir 84121
W Carlton Ct 84123
E Carmelita Dr 84106
S & W Carmellia Dr 84123
S Carnaby Ct 84123
E Carnahan Cir 84121
S Carol Jane Dr 84124
E Carole Cir 84115
E Carole Dr 84121
S Caroleen Way 84124
S Carolyn St 84106
N Carousel St 84116
E Carriage Ln 84117
E & S Carriage Park Cir 84121
S & W Carrick Dr 84115
S Carrigan Cir 84109
E Carrigan Canyon Dr 84109
E Carson Garden Ln 84124
S Carter Cir 84124
E & S Cascade Cir & Way 84109
E Casino Way 84121
W Cassatt Cir 84118
E & S Castle Hill Ave & Cir 84121
S & W Castle Park Ct & Ln 84118
S Castle Ridge Dr 84117
E & S Castlecreek Cir & Dr 84117
S Castlefield Ln 84107
S Castlegate Dr 84117
S & E Casto Cir & Ln 84117
S Casto Pines Cv 84117
E & S Catalina Dr 84121
S Cathay Cir 84123
Catherine Cir & St 84116
E & S Caton Way 84106
S & E Cavalier Cir & Dr 84121
N & W Cavallo Dr 84116
E Cecelia Cir 84121
E & S Cecil Dr 84124
S Cedar St 84107
S Cedar Creek Cir 84118
E Cedar Pine Ct 84106
S Cederlof Ln 84108
E & S Celeste Cir & Way 84109
S Celia Cv 84121
W Centennial Cir 84116
N Center St 84103
S Center St 84107
E & W Central Ave 84107
Central Campus Dr 84112
S Central Fork Ln 84121
S & W Century Dr 84123
W Century Park Way 84115
E Ceres Dr 84124
S Cezanne Cir 84118
E & S Chadbourne Dr 84121
S Chadwick St 84106
E Chalis Ln 84121
N Challenger Rd 84116
S & W Chama Way 84118
W Chambre Dr 84118
S & E Chancellor Cir, Pl & Way 84108
Chandler Cir & Dr 84103
E Channel Dr 84107
W Chantilly Cir 84118
S & W Chaparral Dr 84123
E Chaparral Oak Cir 84121
S Chapel Dr 84117
E Chapman Pl 84111
E Charity Cv 84103
N Charles Lindbergh Dr 84116
E Charleston Ln 84121
S Charlotte Ave 84118
Charlton Ave & Cir 84106
N Chartwell Ct 84103
E Chase Ave 84102
Chase St 84113
E & S Chase Brook Ln 84107
E Chase Creek Ct 84107
E Chateau Parc Cv 84121
E Chaucer Pl 84108
E Chaundra Ave 84124
N Chaz Ct 84116
S Cheerful Dr 84123
S Chegwidden Ln 84123
S Cherise Cir 84106
S Cherokee Cir 84108
S Cherry St 84123
E Cherry Blossom Ln 84117
S & W Cherry Oak Cir 84123
W Cherry Springs Ct 84118
S Cherry Tree Ln 84121
S Cherry Valley Pl 84118
E & S Cherrywood Cir 84106
S & W Chesapeake Cir 84123
W Chesterbrook Cv 84123
S Chestnut Cir 84121
S Chestnut St 84104
S Chestnut Glen Dr 84107

E & S Chevy Chase Cir & Dr 84117
S Cheyenne St 84104
N Chicago St 84116
S & W Chickadee St 84123
S Chickasha St 84107
S & W China Clay Cir & Dr 84118
Chinook Cir & Way 84107
S Chipeta Way 84108
S Choke Cherry Dr 84109
S Chris Ln 84121
E Christensen Ct 84106
E & S Christine Cir & St 84106
S Christos Cir 84123
E Chula Vista Cir 84121
E & S Church Rd 84121
E & N Churchill Dr 84103
E Cinnabar Ln 84121
E Circle Way 84103
Circle Of Hope Dr 84112
S Cirrus Cir 84118
S Citrus Cir 84106
S Claim Jumper Cir 84121
E Claremont Way 84108
S Clarenden Pl 84117
Claret Cir & St 84121
E Claridge Dr 84124
W Clark Ave 84116
E Clark St 84107
E Clawson Pl 84102
S Clay St 84107
S & W Clay Park Dr 84107
E Claybourne Ave
1-199 84115
201-299 84115
700-1999 84106
2100-2266 84109
2268-2398 84109
S Claybourne Ave 84109
S Claybourne Cir 84109
S Clayton St 84104
S Clear St 84107
E & S Clear Spring Ln 84117
S & W Clear Vista Cir & Dr 84118
S Clearview St 84117
S & W Clemates Dr 84118
E Cleveland Ave
1-499 84115
500-599 84105
S Cleveland Cir 84109
S Cliff Dr 84109
W & E Clinton Ave & St 84103
S Clover Ln 84124
W Clover Blossom Cir 84123
S & W Clover Creek Ln 84118
S & W Clover Crest Dr 84123
S & W Clover Meadow Cir & Dr 84123
S Clover Spring Ln 84121
S & W Clover View Dr 84123
E Cloverdale Rd 84121
S & W Clubhouse Dr 84123
S Coachman Cir 84121
S & W Coastal Ct 84123
E Coatsville Ave
1-499 84115
600-899 84105
S Coba Ct 84121
S Cobb Cir 84118
E & S Cobble Creek Rd 84117
E & S Cobblecrest Rd 84121
S Cobblerock Ln 84121
W Cole Ln 84123
S Colemere Way 84109
E Colfax Ave 84111
S College Dr 84123
E College St 84117
S Colleton Cir 84121
W Colmar Ave 84104

N & W Colonel Rd 84116
S Colonial Cir 84108
S Colonial Dr 84108
E Colonial Pl 84102
E Colony N 84106
E Colony S 84106
S Colony Cir 84117
E Colony Dr 84117
S Colony Dr 84117
N Colorado St 84116
S Colorow Dr 84108
S Colt Haven Cir 84124
S & W Colter Cir & Dr 84118
E Columbia Ave 84107
E Columbian Ct 84106
E & N Columbus Ct & St 84103
Comanche Cir & Dr 84108
S Comet Cir 84124
S Commerce Dr 84107
W Commercial Way 84104
W Commons Ln 84104
E Commonwealth Ave
100-250 84115
252-298 84115
500-599 84106
2400-2899 84109
W Commonwealth Ave 84115
E Compton Ct 84107
Comstock Cir & Dr 84121
S Concord St 84104
S Conestoga Cir 84118
W Confluence Ave 84123
S Congress Dr 84123
W Conifer Way 84123
E & N Connecticut Dr & Ln 84103
W Connie Way 84123
Connor Rd 84113
S Connor Rd 84112
S Connor St
800-1899 84108
2700-3199 84109
E Connor Park Cv 84109
S Conrad St 84124
S & W Contoy Cir 84123
S Conway Ct 84111
S Conway Rd 84121
S Coopers Hawk Bay 84117
W Copan Way 84118
S & W Copper City Cir & Dr 84118
E Coquina Ct 84121
S Coral Dr 84123
S Coral St 84124
W Coral Hill Cir 84118
W Coral Mount Ln 84118
Coral Pine Ct & St 84118
W Coral Ridge Ct 84118
S & W Coral View Cir & Ln 84118
E & S Corbin Creek Cv 84121
E Cordelia Ave 84115
W Corentine Cir 84118
S & W Coriander Ct, Dr & St 84118
S Cormorant Cir 84121
E Cornell Cir 84108
N Cornell St 84116
W Cornwall Pl 84116
S & W Coronado Way 84123
E Coronet Dr 84124
N Corral Ln 84116
N Cortez St 84103
S Cory Hill Cir 84121
S Costa Cv 84121
S Cotswold Ct 84121
E Cottage Ave 84111
S Cottage Creek Ln 84107
E Cottage Glen Ln 84107
S Cottage Grove Ln 84107
E & S Cottage Pines Cv 84121
E Cottage Wood Ln 84107
E Cotton Blossom Ln 84117

S Cotton Ridge Cir 84107
S Cotton Tree Ln 84117
S Cotton View Ct 84121
E Cotton Willow Ln 84117
E Cottonwood Cir 84117
E Cottonwood Ln 84117
S Cottonwood Ln 84117
E Cottonwood Pkwy 84121
S Cottonwood St 84107
E & S Cottonwood Club Cir & Dr 84117
E Cottonwood Cove Ln 84121
E Cottonwood Glen Ct 84117
S Cougar Ln 84118
E Country Ave 84121
S & E Country Club Cir & Dr 84109
E Country Hollow Dr 84121
E & S Country Manor Rd 84121
E Country Pine Cv 84117
E Country View Ln 84121
W Country Villa Ln 84123
E & S Countrylane Rd 84117
E Countryside Dr 84106
E County Rd 84121
S Courchevel Pl 84121
E Court Ave 84107
S Courtland Ave 84121
E Cove Rd 84108
S Cove Creek Ln 84107
W Cove Park Cir 84123
E & S Cove Point Dr 84109
S Covecrest Dr 84124
E & S Coventry Ln 84121
W Coventry View Dr 84116
E Covey View Ct 84106
E Coyote Run Ln 84121
Cradelak Dr 84123
E Craftsman Way 84124
W Crags Ct 84103
S & E Craig Cir & Dr 84109
Crandall Ave & Cir 84106
E Crawford Ave 84107
E Creek Dr 84107
W Creek Dr 84107
S Creek Ln 84107
E Creek Rd 84121
E Creek Crossing Ln 84121
E Creek Ledge Ln 84121
S Creek Park Ct 84106
E Creekside Cir 84107
S Creekview Cir 84107
E Creekview Cv 84121
S Creekview Cv 84121
E Creekview Dr 84107
S Creekview Dr 84107
E & S Creekwood Ln 84107
E & S Creighton Way 84121
Crellani Ave 84115
S Crescent Dr 84106
S & W Crest Flower Way 84118
W Crest Gate Cir 84123
E & S Crest Mount Cir & Dr 84121
Crest Oak Cir & Dr 84124
E & S Crestbrook Ln 84109
S & E Cresthill Cir & Dr 84117
N Crestline Cir 84103
E Crestone Ave 84115
S Crestview Cir 84108
S Crestview Ct 84121
E Crestview Dr 84108
S Crestview Dr 84124
S Crestwood Dr 84109
E Crimson Cir 84115
S Cristobal St 84121
S & W Crockett Dr 84118
S Croft Cv 84106
S Cromwell Ct 84123
S Cross Ct 84123
W Cross St 84118

S & E Cross Creek Cir & Ln 84107
S Crossbow Cir 84123
S & W Crosspark Dr 84123
Crosspointe Cir & Ct 84123
W Crossroad Sq 84115
E & S Crown Pointe Dr 84107
Crown Ridge Cir & Rd 84107
S & E Cruise Dr & Way 84109
E Cruise Bay Ct 84121
E & S Crusader Dr 84107
E Crystal Ave
600-1299 84106
2000-2199 84109
W Crystal Ave 84115
W Crystal Bluffs Dr 84123
E Crystal Hill Cir 84108
S & W Crystal River Dr 84123
W Crystal Rock Ave 84116
W Culloden Ct 84123
W Culpepper Cir 84123
E & S Cumberland Dr & Rd 84124
E & S Cummings Rd 84109
E Cumorah Dr 84124
S Cumulus Cir 84118
E & S Cupecoy Dr 84121
E & S Curtis Dr 84121
W Custer Rd 84104
E Cutler Rd 84106
E & S Cypress Way 84121
D St 84103
E & S Da Vinci Dr 84121
S & W Daisy Ln 84123
W Dale Ave 84104
S & W Dale Amour Dr 84118
W Dale Ridge Ave 84116
S Dallin St 84109
W Dalton Ave 84104
S & E Damon Cir & Way 84117
E & S Damsel Dr 84107
Dancedg Dr 84107
W Dancenes S 84129
E & S Daneborg Cir & Dr 84121
E Danforth Dr 84121
S & W Daniel Ct & Way 84123
E & S Danish Cir, Ct, Ln, Rd & Way 84121
E Danish Brook Cir 84121
S Danish Downes Ct 84121
E Danish Hills Cir 84121
S Danish Point Pl 84121
E & S Danish Ridge Way 84121
E Darby Cir 84117
W Darby Castle Way 84123
E Dard Pl 84109
S Dard Hills Ct 84109
E & N Dartmoor Ln, Pl & Way 84103
N Darwin St 84103
W Dauntless Ave 84116
S Davis Grove Ln 84115
E Dawn Dr 84121
E Dayspring Ln 84124
S Dazzling View Cir 84121
E De Lann Ln 84121
N De Soto St 84103
S De Ville Dr 84121
S Dearborn St 84106
E Deauville Ave 84121
W Debonair Dr 84116
E Debs Pl 84111
S Decathlon St 84124
E & S Deer Creek Cir, Cv & Rd 84121
S & W Deer Springs Ln 84118
S Deercreek Rd 84124
E Deerfield Rd 84107

E Del Mar Dr 84109
S Del Prado St 84117
E & S Del Rio St 84117
E Del Verde Ave 84109
E Delaware Ln 84117
S & E Delia Cir & Dr 84109
S Dell Rd 84121
S Dellron Dr 84123
S Delmar Ct 84101
E Delmont Dr 84117
Delno Cir & Dr 84107
S Delong St 84104
E Delsa Dr 84124
S Demerest Rd 84121
S Dempsey Ln 84104
E & S Denarles Cir 84121
E Denise Dr 84106
E Denmark Dr 84121
S Denver St
300-1199 84111
1300-1499 84115
1501-1699 84115
S Derbyshire Ct 84123
S Desert Ridge Cv 84121
W Desert Vista Cir 84118
Detrobriand St 84113
E & S Detroiter Cir 84107
S Devereaux Way 84109
E & S Devonshire Cir & Dr 84108
W Dewar Grove Ln 84115
S Dewcrest Cir 84124
S Dewdrops Dr 84118
W Dewflower Cir 84118
N Dexter St 84116
E & S Diamond Hills Ln 84121
W Diamond Rose Cir 84116
S Diana Way 84124
S & W Diane Cir & Dr 84123
S Diane Hollow Way 84108
E Dickens Pl 84108
S Diestel Rd 84105
E & S Dipo Pl 84117
W Directors Row 84104
S Distribution Dr 84104
S & W District Edge Way 84107
E Division Ln 84106
S Dokos Ln 84104
W Dokos View Ct 84104
E Dolce Vita Ct 84121
S & E Dolphin Cir & Way 84121
E Donegal Cir 84109
E Donelson Ln 84117
Donner Cir & Way 84108
N Donner Hill Cir 84108
E Donner Trail Cir 84108
S Dooley Ct 84102
N Doralma St 84116
E Dorchester Dr 84103
S & E Doreen Cir & St 84107
S Dorie St 84106
E & S Doris Way 84124
N Dorothea Way 84116
S Dorset Cir 84121
Double Eagle Cir & Dr 84118
S Douglas St
100-799 84102
900-998 84105
1000-2099 84105
2400-2599 84106
W Douglas Corrigan Way 84116
W Dove St 84123
S Dover Rd 84108
E & S Doverhill Dr 84121
E Downington Ave
100-499 84115
500-1699 84105
1700-2599 84108
W Dowry Ct 84123
S Drage Cir 84109
S & W Draper St 84118

S Driftwood Dr 84123
E Driggs Ave 84106
W Dry Bone Cir 84118
S Dubei Ct 84111
E Duck Creek Cir 84107
S & W Duck Pond Ln 84123
W Duck Tail Cir 84123
W Duehl Cir 84123
S Duftown Pl 84107
W Duluth Ave 84116
W Dun Robin Ct 84123
E & S Dunbarton Dr 84117
S Dunmore Ct 84123
E & S Dunyon Dr 84121
W Dupont Ave 84116
S Durango Ct 84123
S Dyce Cv 84115
S Dynasty Way 84121
E St 84103
E Eagle Way 84108
Eagle Gate Tower 84111
S & W Eagle Nest Dr 84123
E Eagle Ray Ct 84121
S Eaglepoint Dr 84109
E Eaglesland Cv 84121
S Earl Dr 84104
N & W Earnshaw Ln 84116
East Pl 84102
Eastbourne Cir & Dr 84121
Eastcapitol Blvd & St 84103
Eastcliff Cir & Dr 84124
Eastgate Rd 84117
S Eastlake Dr 84107
S Eastmoor Rd 84117
Eastoaks Dr 84124
S Eastridge Ln 84117
S Eastview Dr 84118
S Eastwood Cir 84107
Eastwood Dr 84109
S Eastwood Dr 84109
S Eastwood Ln 84109
S & W Easy Putt Dr 84123
W Eaton Way 84118
S Ebony Ave 84123
S & W Echo Dr 84123
W Eclipse Way 84116
W Eddington Ct 84118
S & W Edgeberry Dr 84123
E Edgecombe Dr 84103
E Edgehill Rd 84103
E Edgemoor Dr 84117
E Edgerock Cir 84117
Edgewood Cir & Dr 84117
E Edindrew Cir 84107
E Edison Ave 84107
S Edison St
200-999 84111
1300-3399 84115
E Edith Ave 84111
N Edmonds Pl 84116
E Edward Ave 84106
E Edward Cir 84124
S Edward Dr 84124
E Edward Way 84124
S Edwin Cir 84117
S Egli Ct 84102
S & W Eisenhower Way 84104
E & S El Amador St 84117
W El Cimarron Dr 84123
E & S El Monte Dr 84117
S El Rancho Rd 84109
S El Rey St 84108
E & S El Sendero Cir 84117
El Serrito Cir & Dr 84109
S Elderberry Ln 84123
E & S Eldorado Dr 84124
S Eldredge St 84115
E Elgin Ave 84106
E Elgin Dr 84109
E Elgin Heights Ln 84106
S Elida St 84107
S Elizabeth St
1-799 84102
1801-1899 84105
2000-2098 84105
2400-2570 84106
2572-2699 84107

E & S Ellerby Ave & Ct 84117
E Ellisonwoods Ave 84121
E Elm Ave
500-1099 84106
2400-2699 84109
E Elm St 84107
W Elm Hill Cir 84123
E Elm Leaf Cv 84117
W Elm Tree Pl 84116
E & S Elmcrest Dr 84107
S Elmwood St 84106
S & W Elsie Cir, Ct & Dr 84123
E Elwood Pl 84102
E Ely Pl 84102
S Embarcadero St 84123
Embassy Cir & Way 84108
E & S Emberly Ln 84107
E Emelita St 84117
E Emerald Hills Ct 84121
S & W Emerald Isle Ln 84107
S Emerald Ridge Cv 84121
S Emerald Spring Ln 84117
W Emeril Ave 84116
E Emerson Ave
301-397 84115
399-499 84115
500-1699 84105
2000-2499 84108
S & W Emery Cir & St 84104
Emigration Cir & St 84108
E & N Emigration Canyon Rd 84108
N Emigration Estates Rd 84108
W Emilion Cir 84118
N Emily Cir 84116
S Emma Cir 84124
S & W Emperor Dr & Pl 84123
E Empire Ave 84106
E Empire Cir 84106
S Empire Cir 84106
S Empire Rd 84104
E & S Enchanted Hills Dr 84121
E Enchanted View Dr 84121
S Encino St 84117
W Englishman Way 84118
Ensign Cir, Ct & Pl 84121
E Ensign Bay 84121
E & N Ensign Vista Dr 84103
E & S Erekson Ct & Ln 84107
E Erekson View Cir 84107
E Erickson Ln 84107
N Erie Pl 84116
S & W Erin Cir & Ln 84123
S Erv Cir 84118
E & S Escalade Ave & Cir 84121
S Escondido St 84117
S Esprit Dr 84118
S Esther Cir 84117
W Euclid Ave 84104
E & S Europa Dr 84106
E & S Evelyn Dr 84124
E Evening Star Dr 84124
W Everett Ave 84116
E Evergreen Ave
1900-1999 84106
2000-2098 84109
2100-3176 84109
3178-3198 84109
E Evergreen Ln 84106
S Evergreen Pl 84106
E Evergreen View Ct 84109
E Evesham Dr 84107
E Evry Ct 84117
S Ewell Dr 84107
S Excelsius Cir 84121

E Exchange Pl 84111
E Executive Park Dr 84117
F St 84103
S Faber Ln 84123
S Fairbourne Ave 84107
S Fairbrook Ln 84117
E Fairclough Dr 84106
E & N Fairfax Cir & Rd 84103
S & E Fairfield Cir & Rd 84124
S & W Fairhaven Cir 84123
E Fairmont Cir 84106
S Fairoaks Dr 84117
S Fairview Ave 84105
S Fairview Dr 84117
S Falkirk Dr 84107
N Fall St 84116
S & W Fallen Oak Rd 84118
E & S Fallon Rd 84109
W Falstaff Dr 84118
S Family Tree Pl 84123
S & W Far Vista Ct & Dr 84118
S & W Farah Cir & Dr 84118
E & S Fardown Ave & Ct 84121
S Farm Bridge Cir 84117
E & S Farm Hill Dr 84117
E & S Farm Meadow Cir & Ln 84117
S Fashion Blvd 84107
Fashion Square Dr 84107
E Fawn Cir 84121
W Fayelle Ave 84107
W Fayette Ave
  2-398 84101
  400-499 84101
  800-899 84104
W & N Featherstone Cir & Dr 84116
E Federal Way 84102
E & N Federal Heights Cir & Dr 84103
E Federal Pointe Dr 84103
E & S Fenton Ave & Cv 84115
S Fenton View Ct 84115
E Fenway Ave 84102
S Feramorz Dr 84124
W Fern Ave 84103
N Fernleaf St 84116
S & W Fernwood Dr 84123
S Field Cir 84118
E & S Field Rose Dr 84121
E & S Fieldcrest Ln 84117
E & S Fieldstone Cir & Ln 84121
S Fiesta Way 84121
W Fife Ct 84123
W Fig Tree Pl 84116
S Filbert Way 84118
W Filbert Park Cir 84118
S Filmore St
  1300-1399 84105
  2400-2999 84106
S Finch Ln 84102
W Fine Dr 84115
S & W Finlay Dr 84115
E & W Fireclay Ave 84107
S & W Fireweed Dr 84123
S & E Fisher Cir & Ln 84109
S Fitzpatrick Cir 84118
E Flamingo Dr 84117
S Fleetwood Dr 84109
S Fletcher Ct 84102
W Floisand Cir 84116
Flonderm Dr 84117
S Floral St 84111
S Florence Cir 84109
E Floribunda Dr 84117
N Flyer Way 84116
S Flynn Cir 84109
S Folker Cir 84109
S Folklore Pl 84123
W Folsom Ave 84104
Fontaine Bleu Cir & Dr 84121
Foothill Blvd 84113
E Foothill Cir 84108
Foothill Dr 84112
S Foothill Dr
  800-2000 84108
  2002-2098 84108
  2100-2399 84109
  2401-2499 84109
N Forbes Park Way 84116
E Ford Ave 84115
S Forefather Pl 84123
E & S Forest Bend Dr 84121
E Forest Brook Cir 84107
E & S Forest Creek Ln 84121
S Forest Dale Cir 84106
E Forest Farm Cir 84106
E Forest Glen Rd 84121
E & S Forest Hills Dr 84106
S Forest Oaks Ct 84121
E Forest Park Ct 84106
E & S Forest Side Cir & Ln 84107
S Forest Spring Way 84106
E Forest View Ave 84106
Fort Douglas Blvd 84113
E Fort Douglas Cir 84103
E Fort Union Blvd 84121
E & S Fortuna Cir, Dr & Way 84124
W Fortune Rd 84104
S Foss St 84104
E Foubert Ave 84124
S Foulger St 84111
W Fountain Cir 84123
E Four Woods Cir 84109
E Fox Point Ln 84107
W Fox River Ln 84118
W Foxberry Ct 84118
E Foxboro Dr 84106
S & W Foxglove Dr 84123
E Foxmont Ln 84117
W Framewood Ln 84123
W Frankie Cir 84104
N Freeze Creek Cir 84108
W Fremont Ave
  1-599 84101
  700-1199 84104
S Fremont Dr 84104
E Freshman Cir 84117
S Friesian Way 84107
E Front Ave 84115
E Frontier Rd 84121
E Fuller Ave 84102
E Fuller Dr 84124
S Fulton St 84104
S Furnace Creek Ct 84118
G St 84103
S Gainey Ranch Ct 84121
S Gale St 84101
E Gallagher Pl 84102
S Gallantry Way 84121
S Galleria Dr 84123
E Gallivan Ave 84111
W Gander Ln 84116
E Garden Ave
  100-118 84115
  120-299 84115
  500-799 84106
E Garden Cir 84115
S Garden Cir 84115
E Garden Dr 84124
S Garden Dr 84124
E & S Garden Farm Ln 84106
S Garden Meadows Cv 84106
E & S Garden Park Cir 84115
S & W Garden Ridge Rd 84118
S Garden Spring Ln 84117
E Gardena Ave 84115
E Garfield Ave
  142-238 84115
  240-499 84115
  600-1699 84105
  1700-2399 84108
Garkenc Ave 84108
S & W Garn Way 84104
S Garner Ct 84118
Garnette Cir & St 84116
S Gary Rd 84124
E Gateway Rd 84109
E Gaylar Cir 84109
W Gaylawood Cir 84123
E Gazebo Pl 84124
S Geary St 84123
N Gelding Ln 84116
W Gem Cir 84116
N Gemini Dr 84116
N & W General Dr 84116
W Genesee Ave 84104
E & S Georgetown Sq 84109
E Georgia Cir 84115
S & W Germania Ave & Pl 84123
E & W Gilbride Ave 84107
S Gilead Way 84124
E Giles Flat Ln 84121
S Gillen Ln 84107
W Gillespie Ave 84104
E Gilmer Dr 84105
E & S Gilroy Cir & Rd 84109
S Gingerwood Ct 84118
E Girard Ave 84103
W Girard Ave
  1-159 84103
  161-199 84103
  500-1199 84116
W Girard Pl 84103
S Gladiola St 84104
E Glen Arbor St 84105
E Glen Haven Ln 84117
E Glen Heather Ave 84121
E Glen Oaks Dr 84109
S Glen Oaks St 84107
E & S Glenbrook Cir & Dr 84121
S & W Glencoe Ct & Dr 84123
S Glencrest Ln 84107
Glendale Cir, Dr & St 84104
S Glendon St 84123
W Glengyle Ct 84123
S Glenmare St
  1300-1399 84105
  2400-2999 84106
W Glenmeadow Cir 84123
S Glenn St 84107
E & S Glenna Dr 84124
S Glenridge Way 84107
W Glenrose Dr 84104
E Gloria Ct 84115
S Gloria St 84109
E Glorieta Dr 84106
S Gloucester Ct 84123
W Gold Pl 84104
S Gold Valley Ct 84118
S Golden Cir 84124
S Golden Dr 84123
S Golden Chain Dr 84107
E Golden Hills Ave 84121
E Golden Oaks Dr 84121
S & W Goldfinch St 84123
W Goltz Ave 84101
S & W Goodway Dr 84123
W & N Goodwin Ave & Cir 84116
E, W & S Gordon Ave, Cir & Ln 84107
S Goshen St 84104
S Got Teeth Ln 84108
S Gowan Ln 84115
S Grace Ct 84111
S Grace St 84109
S Gramercy Rd 84104
S Granada Dr 84121
S Grand St 84102
E Grand Cayman Dr 84107
S Grand Oak Dr 84121
W Grand Pine Cir 84118
E & S Grand Vista Way 84121
E & S Grandeur Cir & Dr 84121
S & W Grandeur Peak Cir 84123
Grandridge Ct & Dr 84103
S Grandview Cir 84106
E Granite Ave 84115
E Granite Mill Ct 84106
S Granite Oaks Cv 84106
E & S Granite Park Cv 84106
N Grant St 84116
E Grape Ivy Way 84106
N Gravelly Ln 84108
S Gravenstein Park 84123
E Gray Ave 84103
E Graystone Way 84106
S Green St
  600-899 84102
  1300-1599 84105
  2100-2198 84106
  2200-3299 84106
  5101-5297 84123
  5299-5400 84123
  5402-5798 84123
E Green Blossom Ct 84107
E Green Flower Ct 84107
E Green Orchard Ln 84124
E & S Green Valley Dr 84107
E & S Green Vista Ct 84107
E & S Greenbriar Cir & Way 84109
S Greenbrook Ct 84123
S Greendale Rd 84121
E & S Greenfield Ave, Cir & Way 84121
S & W Greenleaf Dr 84123
E & S Greenmeadow Way 84107
S & W Greenoaks Dr 84123
S Greenpine Dr 84123
E & S Greens Basin Rd 84121
S Greenside Pl 84107
S Greenwood Dr 84123
S Greenwood Ter 84105
E Gregson Ave
  1-399 84115
  800-1699 84106
  1701-1759 84106
  2100-3399 84109
W Gregson Ave 84115
N Grenoble St 84116
E Grey Oak Cir 84121
W Griffin Ct 84118
S Griffiths Pl 84121
W Grove Ave 84115
E Grove Hollow Ct 84121
E Grover Ln 84124
Guardsman Way 84112
S Guardsman Way 84108
E & S Guardsman Pass Rd 84121
S Gudgell Ct 84111
E & W Guest Ave 84115
W Gumwood Ave 84123
E Gun Club Rd 84121
E Gunderson Ln 84124
E Gunn Ave 84106
W Gunnell Pl 84116
E Gunther Dr 84121
S Gurene Dr 84117
S Gustin Rd 84104
H St 84103
S Hagoth Cir 84124
W Halcyon Dr 84123
E Hale Ave 84121
S Hale Dr 84124
W Halford Cir 84118
W Halstead Ct 84118
E Hamilton Ln 84115
S Hamlet Cir 84118
S Hamlin St 84123
E Hampton Ave 84111
E Hampton Ct 84124
E & S Hampton Crest Cv 84124
E & S Hanauer Pl & St 84107
S Hancock Cir 84121
S Hannibal St 84106
E Hanover Dr 84103
W Hansen Ave 84115
S Hansen Cir 84107
E & S Hansen Hollow Pl 84124
W Harbor Pointe Dr 84123
S Harmony Cir 84109
S Harmony Ct 84102
N Harold St 84116
W Harold Gatty Dr 84116
S Harper St 84117
W Harris Ave
  1-197 84115
  199-250 84115
  252-298 84115
  1200-1499 84104
E Harrison Ave
  40-298 84115
  300-499 84115
  600-1699 84105
  1700-1899 84108
S Hartford St 84106
W Hartwell Ave 84115
E Harvard Ave
  2-98 84111
  100-499 84111
  900-1012 84105
  1014-1699 84105
  1700-1899 84108
E Harvard Oaks Cir 84108
W Harvest St 84116
E Harvest Park Ct 84121
E Harwood Ln 84107
W Haslam Cir 84116
S Hatchery Rd 84104
S Hathaway St 84123
S Hatton Cir 84107
E Haun Ave 84121
E Haven Ave 84115
W Haven Ave 84115
E Haven Dr 84109
E Haven Ln 84117
S Haven Ln 84117
S Haven Way 84109
E & S Haven Brook Cir 84121
E & S Haven Chase Ln 84121
E Haven Dale Ct 84121
E Haven Glen Ln 84121
S Haven Moor Cir 84121
S Haven Oaks Pl 84121
N Havenstone Ln 84116
S Havenwood Ln 84117
S Haverford Ct 84123
S Hawkes Ct 84102
S & W Hawksbill Cir & Dr 84123
E Hawthorne Ave 84102
S Haxton Pl 84102
W Hayes Ave 84104
S Haystack Way 84123
S Hazel Arlene Cir 84106
E Hazelwood Way 84121
S & W Heath Ave, Cir & Ct 84118
E Heather Cir 84117
S Heather St 84102
E Heather Lynn Ln 84117
Heatherton Cir & Way 84121
W Heathrow Cir 84118
W Heavens Gate Ave 84123
E Hedgewood Ct 84121
S Heirloom Pl 84123
S Helaman Cir 84124
E Helm Ave 84115
S Hemingford Ct 84123
E Hemingway Dr 84121
S & W Hemlock Dr 84123
Hempstead Rd 84113
W Henley Dr 84118
E Herbert Ave
  1-37 84111
  39-499 84111
  900-1199 84105
  1700-2099 84108
S Heredity Pl 84123
Heritage Ctr 84112
E Heritage Way 84109
E Hermansen Cir 84115
Hermes Cir & Dr 84124
E Hermitage Cir 84121
E & S Hermosa Way 84124
E Heughs Cir 84121
E & S Heughs Canyon Cir, Ct, Dr & Way 84121
E Hiawatha Cir 84108
E & S Hickory Ln 84121
S Hickory Hill Cir 84121
S Hidden Pl 84123
E Hidden Acres Cir 84109
S & W Hidden Cove Cir & Dr 84123
E Hidden Creek Ct 84117
E Hidden Garden Ln 84115
E Hidden Meadows Dr 84117
S Hidden Mill Cv 84121
E & S Hidden Oak Dr 84121
S Hidden Oaks Cir 84121
S Hidden Quail Cir 84124
W Hidden Villa Rd 84115
S Hidden Woods Ln 84107
W High Ave
  201-299 84115
  1500-1599 84104
S High Bluff Dr 84118
S Highland Cir 84117
S Highland Dr
  2100-3899 84106
  3900-4499 84124
  4500-5599 84117
  5600-8099 84121
  8101-8149 84121
E & S Highland Cove Ln 84106
E & S Highland Down Ln 84117
S Highland Park Ct 84121
E Highland Rose Ln 84117
E Highland View Cir 84109
E Highland Woods Ct 84106
S Highway 111 84118
S & W Highwood Dr 84118
E Hill Ave 84107
E Hill Park Cir 84107
E Hillcrest Ave 84106
W Hillcrest Cir 84107
S Hillcrest Dr 84107
E Hillrise Cir 84121
E & S Hillsden Dr 84117
E Hillside Ave 84103
E Hillside Cir 84109
E Hillside Dr 84107
S Hillside Dr 84107
S Hillside Ln 84109
E Hillside Pines Cir 84109
S & E Hillside Village Cir & Ct 84121
N Hilltop Rd 84103
E & S Hillview Dr 84124
S Himrod Ct 84123
E Hintze Dr 84124
W Hobbson Dr 84118
N & W Hodges Ln 84116
W Hoffman St 84118
E Holladay Blvd 84124
S Holladay Blvd
  4101-4197 84124
  4199-4499 84124
  4506-4540 84117
  4542-5599 84117
  5600-6299 84121
S Holladay Cir 84117
E & S Holladay Farm Ln 84117
E Holladay Oaks Ln 84117
S Holladay Pines Ct 84117
E Holladay View Pl 84117
S Holladay Wood Ln 84117
Holliday Village Plz 84117
S & E Hollow Dale Cir & Dr 84121
E & S Hollow Mill Dr 84121
S Hollow Oaks Cir 84121
S Hollow Ridge Rd 84121
Hollow Springs Cir & Dr 84123
S Holloway Dr 84124
E Holly Ave 84107
E Holly Cir 84107
S Holly Dr 84109
S Holly Ln 84117
E Holly Haven Cir 84107
S Hollyberry Cir 84123
E Hollyhock Hl 84121
E Hollywood Ave
  200-298 84115
  300-499 84115
  500-1599 84105
  1700-2299 84108
E & S Holstein Way 84107
S Homestead Ct 84107
S Honey Clover Ct 84123
E Honeybrook Pl 84106
S & E Honeycomb Cir & Rd 84121
E & S Honeycut Cir & Rd 84106
S Honeysuckle Way 84118
S Honeywood Cove Dr 84121
S Honeywood Hill Ln 84121
S & W Hoopes Cir & St 84118
E Hoover Pl 84111
W Hope Ave 84115
S Horizon Cir 84121
W Horn Silver Cir 84118
E Horne Ave 84106
E & S Howey Dr 84121
S Howick St 84107
W Hoyt Pl 84116
E Hubbard Ave
  200-399 84111
  1500-1599 84105
  1700-2299 84108
E & S Hudson Ave & Cir 84106
E & S Hugo Ave 84117
S Hulse Ave 84121
S & W Hummel Cir & Dr 84118
S Hummelstrasse 84117
S & W Hummingbird St 84123
E Hundley Haven Cir 84106
E & S Hunt Rd 84117
S Hunters Ridge Cir 84124
S Huntly Dr 84107
S Huntsman Way 84108
N Hyde Park Way 84116
S Hyland Cv 84121
E Hyland Hills Rd 84109
E Hyland Lake Dr 84121
I St 84103
S Ichabod St 84117
S Ida Cir 84106
E Ideal Ln 84115
Idlewild Cir & Rd 84124
W Illinois Ave 84104
S Imperial St
  1801-1897 84105
  1899-2099 84105
  2400-3242 84106
  3244-3244 84106
E & S Imperial Park Ln & Sq 84106
S & W Impressions Dr & Way 84118

Independence Blvd ... 84116
dian Hills Cir & Dr ... 84108
Indian Rock Rd ... 84117
Indian Summer Dr ... 84116
diana Ave & Cir ... 84104
& W Industrial Cir &
d ... 84104
Ingleby Cir ... 84104
Inglewood Ct ... 84105
Inheritance Ct ... 84123
Innsbruck Way ... 84121
Integra Ct ... 84106
Intermountain Dr ... 84107
Inverary Dr ... 84124
Inverkeithing Dr ... 84115
Iola Ave ... 84104
Iowa St ... 84102
& W Irie Ln ... 84116
Iris Ln ... 84106
Iron Blossom Cir ... 84121
& W Iron Rose Pl ... 84104
Ironwood Ave ... 84121
Ironwood Dr ... 84115
Irving St ... 84116
Isabella Ct ... 84102
Isom Pl ... 84103
Ivan Ct ... 84102
Iverson St ... 84111
Iverson Woods Pl ... 84117
Ivy Cir ... 84116
Ivy Ln ... 84115
Ivy Ln ... 84115
Ivy Gate Cir ... 84121
Ivybrook Cir ... 84123
Izapa Cv ... 84118
St ... 84103
& S Jackie Way ... 84107
Jackson Ave ... 84116
Jackson Park Pl ... 84116
Jacksonwood Ln ... 84124
Jacobs Cir ... 84121
Jake Garn Blvd ... 84104
amaica Cir & St ... 84123
James Ct ... 84111
& S James Pointe
r ... 84107
& E Jamestown Cir, Ct
Dr ... 84121
Jamiah Dr ... 84123
Jaren Cir ... 84108
argon Cir & Way ... 84118
Jarrad Rd ... 84118
Jarrah St ... 84123
Jasmine Dr ... 84123
& S Jasper Cir & St ... 84106
Jazz Ln ... 84117
Jeanne Ave ... 84121
Jeannine Dr ... 84107
Jedediah Dr ... 84118
Jefferson Cir ... 84115
Jefferson St
800-1099 ... 84101
1300-1799 ... 84115
6400-6899 ... 84107
Jennie Ln ... 84117
Jennifer Way ... 84116
& W Jenny Sue Ct ... 84123
Jensen Ln ... 84123
Jensen Meadow Ln ... 84116
Jepson Ave ... 84106
& W Jeremiah Cir &
r ... 84118
Jeremy Cir ... 84121
Jeremy Cir ... 84121
Jeremy Ct ... 84121
Jeremy Dr ... 84121
Jeremy St ... 84104
& S Jerrie Lee Ln ... 84117
& W Jerusalem Dr ... 84123
Jessieo Way ... 84123
Jester Dr ... 84123
Jewell Ave ... 84104
Jimmy Doolittle Rd ... 84116
& W Joaquin St ... 84118
John David Ln ... 84107
John Glenn Rd ... 84116

S Johnson Cir ... 84121
S & W Jolly Cir & St ... 84123
S Joma St ... 84107
S & E Jonathan Cir &
Dr ... 84121
S Jones Ct ... 84107
S Jonetta Dr ... 84109
W Jordan Bluff Cir ... 84123
W Josh Cir ... 84123
W Joust Ct ... 84116
E Joyce Dr ... 84109
E Joye St ... 84107
S Judith St ... 84106
E & S Julep Cir & Dr ... 84107
E & S Juliet Way ... 84121
E Juniper Way ... 84117
Juniperpoint Ct & Dr ... 84103
E Juno Cir ... 84124
E & S Jupiter Dr ... 84124
W Justin Dr ... 84123
S & W Justin Kay Ct ... 84104
K St ... 84103
N Kaia View Ct ... 84116
E & S Kaibab Cir &
Way ... 84109
S Kaitlyn Ann Cir ... 84123
S Kalani Ln ... 84117
W Kalia Cv ... 84123
E Kane Cir ... 84121
E Kara Ct ... 84121
E Karin Ct ... 84121
S Karos Cir ... 84123
E Karren St ... 84124
W Karsten Ct ... 84118
S Katherine Cir ... 84109
S Kathrine Ann Ct ... 84118
E Katie Lynn Ln ... 84117
S Kay Cir ... 84106
S & E Kayland Cir &
Way ... 84117
S Kaywood Cir ... 84109
E Keddington Ln ... 84117
E Keepler Ln ... 84109
E Keller Ln ... 84109
S & E Kelly Cir & Ln ... 84117
E & S Kelmscott Ct &
Ln ... 84124
E Kelsey Ave ... 84111
E Kelsey View Ln ... 84115
S Kemp Dr ... 84118
E & S Kempner Rd ... 84109
S Ken Rey St ... 84108
E Kenbridge Ct ... 84108
E Kennedy Dr ... 84108
E Kensington Ave
1-499 ... 84115
500-1699 ... 84105
1701-1725 ... 84108
1727-2599 ... 84108
S Kent Cir ... 84117
E Kenton Dr ... 84109
E Kentucky Ave ... 84117
E Kenwood Cir ... 84106
S Kenwood Dr ... 84107
S Kenwood St ... 84106
S Kerry Cir ... 84107
E Kessler View Ln ... 84121
E Keysview Ct ... 84117
E Kiera Ct ... 84124
E Kierstin Pl ... 84108
E Kikkert Cir ... 84124
S Kilbourne Ct ... 84102
S Kilby Ct ... 84101
N Killyons Ln ... 84108
E Killyons Canyon Ln ... 84108
S Kim Way ... 84121
S Kim Wood Ln ... 84106
S & E Kimbary Cir &
Way ... 84109
W Kimberly Cir ... 84116
S & W Kimman Cv &
Ln ... 84123
S King St ... 84109
E Kings Ln ... 84106
E & S Kings Cove Cir,
Dr & Way ... 84121

E & S Kings Hill Cir, Dr
& Pl ... 84121
S & E Kings Row Cir &
Dr ... 84117
S Kingston Cir ... 84121
S Kingston Way ... 84107
S Kinnell Dr ... 84115
S Kinsmen Cir ... 84118
S Kipling Cir ... 84121
S Kirk Cir ... 84106
E Kirstys Ln ... 84107
S Kiska Ln ... 84117
E Kline Ave ... 84117
E Knightsbridge Ln ... 84103
E & S Knollcrest St ... 84107
S Knudsen St ... 84109
S Knudsen Mill Cir ... 84121
S Knudsen Ridge Cir ... 84121
E Kohala Dr ... 84117
S Komas Dr ... 84108
S Koneta Ct ... 84102
N Kress Cir ... 84116
W Krista Ct ... 84123
W Kristeldell Ct ... 84123
S Kristian Pine Ln ... 84123
E Kristianna Cir ... 84103
S Kristie Ln ... 84108
S & W Kyle Dr ... 84118
S Kylie Cv ... 84123
L St ... 84103
S La Barranca Ct ... 84121
S La Brea St ... 84118
E & S La Contessa Dr ... 84117
E La Cresta Dr ... 84121
E La Dore Dr ... 84107
E La Joya Dr ... 84124
S La Mesa Rd ... 84109
S La Rosa Ct ... 84121
S La Rue Ln ... 84106
S & W La Salle Dr ... 84123
E & S La Tour Cir &
St ... 84121
E Labrum Ave ... 84107
S Laconia Ct ... 84111
W Lady Bank Way ... 84115
N & W Lafayette Dr ... 84116
E Lahar Dr ... 84106
S Laily Ct ... 84117
E Laird Ave
900-1699 ... 84105
1700-1899 ... 84108
E Laird Cir ... 84105
E Laird Dr ... 84108
E Laird Way ... 84108
E Lake Cir ... 84106
S Lake Cir ... 84106
S Lake St
600-837 ... 84102
838-2099 ... 84105
2100-2899 ... 84106
E & S Lake Mary Dr ... 84121
S Lake Pines Dr ... 84107
S Lake Placid Pl ... 84121
E & S Lake Springs
Ln ... 84117
Lakeline Cir & Dr ... 84109
E & S Lakepoint Dr ... 84107
S Laker Ct ... 84102
S Lakeside Dr ... 84121
E & S Lakeview Dr ... 84109
Lakewood Cir & Dr ... 84117
N Lamarne St ... 84116
E Lambourne Ave
300-499 ... 84115
1800-1999 ... 84106
2000-2699 ... 84109
S Lambourne Cir ... 84109
S Lanark Rd ... 84124
E Lancaster Dr ... 84108
W Lander Way ... 84118
E & S Lanebrook Cir &
Ln ... 84124
E Laneview Ct ... 84108
E Laney Ave ... 84117
S Larch Way ... 84123
E Larchmont Dr ... 84109

S & E Lares Cir &
Way ... 84124
S Larkwood St ... 84107
S Larson Way ... 84124
S Lasalle Cir ... 84123
W Lassen View Ct ... 84118
E Last Camp Cir ... 84108
E Last Monument Cir ... 84108
E Latimer View Ct ... 84106
S Laura Dr ... 84107
S Laurel Cir ... 84109
N Laurel St ... 84103
S & W Laurel Canyon
Dr ... 84118
S Laurelcrest Dr ... 84109
S Laurelhurst Dr ... 84108
E & S Laurelwood Cir &
St ... 84121
E Lauri Kay Dr ... 84124
S Lavar Dr ... 84109
S Lavell Ln ... 84106
Lavon Cir & Dr ... 84106
W Law Cir ... 84118
W Lawndale Dr ... 84115
N Laxon Ct ... 84116
W Layton Ave
1-199 ... 84115
700-798 ... 84104
800-899 ... 84104
S Lazy Bar Cir ... 84121
S & W Lazy River Dr ... 84123
E Le Banke Ave ... 84115
S Le Chateau Way ... 84118
S Le Corbusier Cir ... 84106
S Le Grand St ... 84108
E Le Jardin Pl ... 84117
W Leadville Ave ... 84116
W Learned Ave ... 84116
S Ledgemont Dr ... 84124
E Lee Way Cir ... 84109
E Lefthand Fork Ln ... 84108
S Legacy View St ... 84104
E Lehua Ln ... 84117
E & S Leland Ave &
Cv ... 84106
S Lemans Dr ... 84124
S Lemel Cir ... 84115
S Lemmon Ln ... 84124
S Lenora Cir ... 84121
S Lenora Joe Cv ... 84107
S Leo Way ... 84117
E Leona Ln ... 84107
S Leprechaun Ln ... 84118
W Lerwill Ave ... 84123
E Leslie Ave ... 84115
E & W Lester Ave ... 84107
W Levoy Dr ... 84123
S & W Lewis Clark Cir &
Dr ... 84118
W Lexington Ave ... 84104
E Lexington Cir ... 84124
N Libby Way ... 84116
S Liberty Oaks Cv ... 84107
S Liberty Wells Pl ... 84111
W Lieutenant Rd ... 84116
S Lighthouse Rd ... 84123
W Liljay Cir ... 84104
E Lillie Cir ... 84121
S Lily Meadows Ln ... 84124
E Lincoln Cir ... 84124
S Lincoln Cir ... 84106
E Lincoln Ct ... 84124
E Lincoln Ln ... 84124
E Lincoln Pl ... 84107
S Lincoln St
100-899 ... 84102
900-1969 ... 84105
1971-2099 ... 84105
2101-2159 ... 84106
2161-3175 ... 84106
4801-4897 ... 84107
4899-5099 ... 84107
E Lincoln Oak Ct ... 84106
E & S Lincoln Park Dr ... 84115
S Lincoln Pines Ct ... 84124
S Linda Cir ... 84109

E Linda Rosa Ave ... 84106
E Linden Ave ... 84102
E Linden Cir ... 84121
S Linden Way ... 84121
S Lindie Ct ... 84121
S & E Lindon St &
Way ... 84107
Lintrent Ctr ... 84112
E & S Lion Ln ... 84121
S Lisa Dr ... 84124
W Lisa Hills Cv ... 84123
W Lisa Rae Cir ... 84107
E Lisonbee Ave ... 84106
E Litson Cir ... 84107
S Little Farm Ln ... 84109
W Little Matterhorn Dr ... 84123
S & W Little Mountain
Dr ... 84123
E & N Little Tree Cir &
Rd ... 84108
N Little Valley Rd ... 84103
S Little Willow Cir ... 84121
E Live Oak Cir ... 84117
W Livingston Ave ... 84116
E Loch Lomond Way ... 84117
W Lochlevan Ln ... 84123
S Lochnivar Ct ... 84107
E Lockhart Rd ... 84117
S Locust Ln ... 84117
S Loder Dr ... 84118
S & W Lodestone Ave &
Cir ... 84118
E Logan Ave
300-499 ... 84115
700-1599 ... 84105
1700-2299 ... 84108
E Logan Cir ... 84108
E Logan Way ... 84108
E Lois Ln ... 84124
S Lola Cir ... 84109
N Loma Ln ... 84103
E & S Lombardy Cir, Ct,
Dr & Pl ... 84121
E London Plane Rd ... 84124
E Lone Brook Ln ... 84121
E Lone Peak Dr ... 84117
S Longfellow Ln ... 84107
S & W Longmore Dr ... 84118
E Longview Dr ... 84124
S Longview Dr ... 84107
E & S Lonsdale Dr ... 84121
W Loomis Ln ... 84118
E Lora Lee Cir ... 84121
E Loran Heights Dr ... 84109
E & S Loredell Dr &
St ... 84117
E & S Loren Von Cir &
Dr ... 84124
S Loretta Dr ... 84106
E & S Lori Way ... 84117
E & S Lori Leigh Ln ... 84117
S Lorien Ct ... 84109
S Lornadale Cir ... 84121
E & S Lorraine Ave, Cir
& Dr ... 84106
E & S Lorreen Cir, Ct, Dr
& Pl ... 84121
S Los Altos St ... 84109
N Los Angeles St ... 84116
S Lost Canyon Cir ... 84121
Lost Creek Ln ... 84107
E Lost River Rd ... 84109
E Lost Spring Ln ... 84121
E Louise Ave
1-299 ... 84115
2700-3399 ... 84109
W Louise Ave ... 84115
E Loveland Ave ... 84106
W Lovely Rd ... 84123
S Lovendahle Ct ... 84107
E Lowell Ave ... 84102
W Loxwood Ave ... 84104
W Loyal Dr ... 84123
S Luchars Ln ... 84115
E Luck Ln ... 84106
E Luck Spring Dr ... 84106

S & W Lucky Clover Cir
& Ln ... 84123
W Lucy Ave
100-399 ... 84101
800-899 ... 84104
E & S Luetta Dr ... 84124
E & S Luna Cir &
Way ... 84121
S Lupine Way ... 84121
E Lupine Ridge Rd ... 84121
S Lyman Ct ... 84105
E Lyndzie Ln ... 84121
S Lynne Ln ... 84124
E Lynwood Dr ... 84109
M St ... 84103
E Mabey Dr ... 84109
W Macarthur Ave ... 84115
W Macfarland Dr ... 84116
E & S Macintosh Cir &
Ln ... 84121
S Mackay St ... 84123
W Mackinac Dr ... 84123
S Macondray Cir ... 84123
S Madrid St ... 84121
E Magda Ln ... 84124
S & W Magic Dr ... 84107
E & S Magic Hills Cir &
Dr ... 84121
S & W Magic Isle Ln ... 84107
S Magic Morning Ln ... 84123
S & E Magic View Cir &
Dr ... 84121
N Main St ... 84103
S Main St
1-9 ... 84133
4-1298 ... 84101
21-1299 ... 84111
1301-1347 ... 84115
1349-3800 ... 84115
3802-3898 ... 84115
3900-6099 ... 84107
S Majerus Ct ... 84123
E Majestic Dr ... 84124
E & S Majestic Pine
Dr ... 84107
E & S Majestic Ridge Cir
& Dr ... 84121
S Majestic Village Cir ... 84123
S Major St
1031-1097 ... 84111
1099-1299 ... 84111
1301-1361 ... 84115
1363-1799 ... 84115
6700-6798 ... 84107
6800-6830 ... 84107
6832-6898 ... 84107
E Makenna Ct ... 84117
E Malibu Dr ... 84107
S Mallontr E ... 84105
W Mallow Ridge Cir ... 84118
S & W Malstrom Ct &
Ln ... 84107
E Malvern Ave
1-99 ... 84115
900-1299 ... 84106
W Malvern Ave ... 84115
N Mandalay Rd ... 84116
S & W Mango Cir &
Rd ... 84123
E Manor Cir ... 84124
E Manor Dr ... 84121
S Manor Dr ... 84121
S Manor Ridge Pl ... 84124
E Manorcrest Ct ... 84121
S Manorly Cir ... 84121
E Manorview Ct ... 84121
E Mansfield Ave
300-399 ... 84115
500-1099 ... 84106
S Mantyla St ... 84123
W Manzanita Dr ... 84123
E Maple Ave ... 84106
S Maple Cv ... 84106
E Maple St ... 84107
E Maple Crest Ct ... 84106
N Maple Tree Ct ... 84116
E & S Maple View Dr ... 84106

E & S Maplewood Cir &
Dr ... 84121
E Mar Jane Ave ... 84107
E Mar Vian Dr ... 84124
S Marabow Cir ... 84117
E & N Marathon Cir &
Ln ... 84108
S March St ... 84104
S Marco Rd ... 84121
E Mardonna Way ... 84109
W Margaret Ave ... 84104
N Margarethe Ln ... 84108
E Margie Ave ... 84109
E & S Marie Ave &
Cir ... 84109
S Marilyn Dr ... 84117
E & S Marinda Way ... 84121
S & W Marinwood Ave &
Cir ... 84123
Mario Capecchi Dr ... 84113
Mario Capechi Dr ... 84112
N Marion St ... 84116
E Mariposa Ave ... 84106
E Mark Ave ... 84106
E Markea Ave ... 84102
W Market St ... 84101
S Markinch Way ... 84115
E Marley Pl ... 84109
S Marquis Way ... 84124
Marriott Honors ... 84112
Marrwood Cir & Dr ... 84124
S Mars Way ... 84124
W Marshall Ave ... 84104
E & S Marshwood Ln ... 84107
W Martin Ln ... 84107
Marvelle Cir & Ct ... 84118
E Marvin Gardens St ... 84121
E Mary Cir ... 84121
E Mary Dott Way ... 84106
W Mary Etta Ave ... 84115
S Mary Lake Ln ... 84121
E Mary Rose Dr ... 84107
S Maryfield Dr ... 84108
E Maryland Cir ... 84124
S Masonic Cir ... 84115
E Mateo Way ... 84117
E & S Mathews Way ... 84124
S Matson Cir ... 84124
E Matthew Ave ... 84121
E Maurice Dr ... 84124
S Maverick Cir ... 84121
S Maxfield Dr ... 84121
E Maxwell Ln ... 84115
S Maybeck Pl ... 84124
E Mayfair Cir ... 84105
S & E Maywood Cir &
Dr ... 84109
S Mc Callan Way ... 84107
S Mcbeth Ct ... 84123
S Mccall St ... 84115
S Mcclelland St
100-899 ... 84102
900-2099 ... 84105
2100-3000 ... 84106
3002-3198 ... 84106
E & S Mccormick Cir &
Way ... 84121
E Mcdonald Pl ... 84102
E Mckell Ct ... 84121
E & S Mclain Mountain
Cir ... 84121
S & E Mcmillan Cir &
Ln ... 84107
W Mead Ave
100-199 ... 84101
1100-1108 ... 84104
1110-1399 ... 84104
S Mead Cir ... 84104
E Meadow Dr ... 84121
S Meadow Dr ... 84121
E Meadow Ln ... 84106
E Meadow Rd ... 84107
S Meadow Rd ... 84107
S & W Meadow Acres
Cir ... 84123
E & S Meadow Downs
Way ... 84121

W Meadow Hollow Cv 84123
E Meadow Pine Ct 84106
S Meadow View Cir 84107
S Meadow View Dr 84123
S Meadow View Rd 84107
S Meadoway St 84107
W Meadowbrook Expy 84123
S Meadowcrest Dr 84107
S Meadowcrest Rd 84121
Meadowmoor Cir & Rd 84117
Medical Dr 84112
N Medical Dr 84113
Medical Plz 84112
S Megan Cir 84107
S Melbourne St 84106
E & S Melinda Ln 84109
E Melodie Ann Way 84124
E Melony Dr 84124
S Melvina St 84106
S Memory Ln 84117
S Mendon Ct 84105
E Menlo Ave 84102
W Menzel Ct 84118
S Mercedes Way 84108
W Mercer Way 84115
S Mercury Dr 84124
S & W Meridian Cir 84123
S Meridian Park Rd 84104
E & S Merlyn Cir & Dr 84117
E Merribee Way 84121
W Merrimac Ave 84115
E Merritt Cir 84117
E Metro Way 84109
S Metropolitan Way 84109
S Meyers Ln 84107
N & W Miami Cir & Rd 84116
E Michael Mills Pl 84106
E Michigan Ave
1100-1600 84105
1602-1698 84105
1700-2499 84108
S Middle Fork Ln 84117
N Middle Oak Ln 84108
W Middlesex Rd 84123
E Middleton Way 84124
S & W Middlewood Ave & Cir 84118
S Midhurst Way 84117
W Milan Dr 84116
W Mildred St 84118
E & S Mile High Dr 84124
S Milestone Dr 84104
S Milhan Ct 84123
S Military Dr
900-999 84108
1000-1099 84105
E Military Way 84103
S Milky Way 84124
S Mill Cir 84109
E Mill Ln 84106
E Mill Corner Cir 84106
E Mill Garden Ln 84107
S Mill Stone Ln 84121
S & W Mill Valley Ct & Ln 84118
E & S Millbert Ave & Dr 84106
S & E Millbrook Cir, Dr, Rd & Ter 84106
E Millcreek Cir 84106
S Millcreek Cir 84106
E Millcreek Rd 84109
S Millcreek Rd 84109
E Millcreek Way 84106
S Millcreek Way 84106
E Millcreek Canyon Rd 84109
E Millcreek Dell Ln 84109
E Millcreek Park Cir 84106
S Millcrest Rd 84109
E Miller Ave
1-99 84115
1201-1297 84106
1299-1399 84106
E Miller St 84107
W Miller St 84107
S Millhaven Cir 84109
S Millhollow Cir 84106
E Millicent Dr 84108
S Millicentview Ln 84121
E & S Millpoint Pl 84115
S Millrace Ln 84107
S & W Millrace Park Ct & Ln 84123
E & S Millrock Dr 84121
E Millstream Dr 84109
E Millstream Ln
1300-1499 84106
2000-3599 84109
E Milo Way 84117
S & W Milstead Ln 84118
E Milton Ave
300-499 84115
600-1199 84105
E & S Minden Dr 84121
E Mint Green Cir 84107
S Mirador Ct 84118
S Miramar Way 84109
S Mission Rd 84104
S Misty Way 84118
S Misty Morning Cir 84123
S & W Misty View Cir & Way 84123
E & S Mitchell Cv 84115
S Mitt Ln 84121
E & S Mobina Ct 84117
S & W Modesto Ave & Cir 84104
S Moffat Ct 84111
S Moffat Farm Ln 84121
Mohawk Cir & Way 84108
S Mohican Cir 84123
W Mojave Dr 84116
E & S Monaco Ave & Cir 84121
S Monarch Way 84124
S Monet Ct 84118
S Monica Cv 84121
W Monifieth Pl 84115
W Montague Ave
440-498 84101
800-999 84104
E Montana Vista Ln 84124
E & S Montclair Dr 84106
W Monte Azul 84123
W Monte Bella Dr 84123
W Monte Blanco 84123
E Monte C Ct 84115
E & S Monte Carlo Dr 84121
W Monte Del Oro 84123
S Monte Grande Dr 84123
W Monte Hermosa St 84123
S Monte Verde Dr 84109
S Monte Vista Cir 84108
S Monte Vista Dr 84123
S Montecito St 84106
E & S Montego Pl 84117
E Monterey Dr 84121
N Montgomery St 84116
S Montgomery St 84104
W Monticello Ln 84123
W Montrose Ave 84101
S Montrose St 84107
S Monument Park Cir 84108
E Monza Dr 84109
W Moon Flower Cir 84118
W Moon Ridge Dr 84107
S & E Moor Dale Cir & Ln 84117
S & E Moor Mont Cir & Dr 84117
E & S Moore Crest Ct 84121
E Moose Ln 84121
E Moose Creek Ln 84121
E & S Moose Haven Ln 84121
E Moose Loop Rd 84121
S Moose Meadow Ln 84121
E & S Moose Run Ln 84121
E Moose Track Ln 84121
E Moraine Cir 84109
E Morgan Dr 84124
S & W Morgan Wood Bay 84118
S Morning Breeze Dr 84118
S & W Morning Crest Dr 84123
S & W Morning Dew Cir & Dr 84123
S Morning Mesa Cir 84123
S & W Morning Oaks Dr 84123
S Morning Sky Cir 84123
E & S Morning Star Dr 84124
S & W Morning Sun Dr 84123
S & W Morning Vista Ct & Dr 84123
E & S Morning Wood Ct 84106
Morningside Cir & Dr 84124
Morris Ave 84115
S Morro St 84121
N & W Morton Dr 84116
N Morton Hills Cir 84116
S & E Moss Creek Cir & Dr 84107
E & S Mossy Springs Ln 84117
W Motor Ave 84116
E Mott Dr 84109
S & W Mount Adams Dr 84118
S & W Mount Baldy Dr 84123
S Mount Cedar Ct 84118
E Mount Crest Dr 84109
S & W Mount Flora Cir 84118
E Mount Haven Ln 84121
E Mount Manor Cir 84121
W Mount Montana Dr 84118
W Mount Nebo Dr 84123
S Mount Olympus Way 84124
W Mount Shasta Ct 84118
S & E Mount Springs Ct & Rd 84117
S & W Mount Tuscarora Dr 84123
E & S Mount Vernon Cir & Dr 84107
S & W Mount Whitney Ln 84118
E & S Mountain Cv, Ln & Pl 84124
S Mountain Estates Dr 84121
S Mountain Glen Ln 84121
Mountain Men Cir & Dr 84118
S & E Mountain Oaks Cir, Cv & Dr 84121
E Mountain Sun Ln 84121
E Mountain View Dr
100-299 84107
1700-1899 84106
2800-2999 84109
S Mountair Dr 84106
S Muirfield Dr 84124
E Mule Hollow Ln 84121
S Mulholland St 84124
S Murdoch Woods Pl 84121
E Murphys Ln 84106
S & W Murray Blvd 84123
S & W Murray Bluffs Ct & Dr 84123
E Murray Holladay Rd 84117
S Murray Links Dr 84107
S Murray Oaks Cir 84123
E & S Murray Park Ave & Ln 84107
S Murray Parkway Ave 84123
S Musser Ct 84102
E Myrtle Ave 84107
N St 84103
Namba Cir & Way 84107
E & S Naniloa Cir & Dr 84117
E & S Nantucket Dr 84121
E Nashua St 84107
S Nathan Cir 84117
S Nations Way 84121
S Natura St 84104
S & W Nautilus Dr 84118
S Navajo St 84104
S Naylor Ct 84105
S Naylor Ln 84107
W Nebula Way 84116
E & S Neffs Cir & Ln 84109
S Neighbor Ln 84117
N Neil Armstrong Rd 84116
W Nelson Farm Ct 84123
S Nena Way 84107
S Neptune Dr 84124
S Nerual Cir 84108
E & S Netties Pl 84124
S Nevada St 84108
E New Baldwin Cir 84117
E New Bedford Dr 84103
N New Bonneville Pl 84103
E New Century Ln 84115
W New Hampshire Ave 84116
S & W New Hampton Dr 84123
S New Haven Dr 84121
N New Star Dr 84116
New Terminal Dr 84122
S New Vintage Ct 84124
W New York Dr 84116
S Newberry Rd 84108
E Newmans Ln 84121
E & S Newport Cir & Way 84121
E Newsome Park Ln 84115
S Newton Ct 84123
N Newton Park St 84116
E Newtopia Cir 84121
S Nez Perce Dr 84118
Niagara Cir & Way 84118
E Nibley Cir 84106
S Nibley Garden Pl 84106
S Nibley Park Pl 84106
E Nibley View Ct 84106
E Nichols Cv 84106
S & W Nickle Way 84118
E Nila Way 84124
W Niles Ave 84116
S Nimbus Way 84118
S Nina Marie Cir 84123
W Ninigret Dr 84104
W Noah Cir 84107
E & S Noal Dr 84124
W Nobility Cir 84116
E Noble Pl 84102
S Noble Oaks Cir 84123
N Nocturne Dr 84116
E & S Nod Hill Rd 84121
S Noma Linda Cir 84109
S & E Nora Cir & Dr 84124
E Norma Cir 84121
E Normandie Cir 84105
S Normandie Ln 84107
S Normandy Oaks Cir 84123
E Normandywoods Ct 84117
S Normawood Dr 84123
E Norris Pl 84102
E North Hills Dr 84103
W North Temple
144-298 84103
W North Temple
500-2399 84116
2401-2499 84116
E North White Cir 84109
E Northbonneville Dr 84103
E Northcliffe Cir & Dr 84103
E Northcrest Dr 84103
E Northlake Dr 84107
Northland Dr 84103
Northmont Way 84103
Northpoint Ct & Dr 84103
Northshore Dr 84103
W Northstar Dr 84116
E Northvale Way 84103
Northview Cir & Dr 84103
S Northwest Ave 84118
W Northwood Ave 84116
E Northwood Rd 84117
S Northwood Rd 84117
E Northwoodside Dr 84124
W Norwalk Rd 84123
E & S Norwood Rd 84121
E Nottingham Way 84108
S Nova Dr 84107
S Nowell Cir 84115
E Nunley Cir 84121
E Nutmeg St 84121
E & S Nutree Dr 84121
E & S Nye Cir & Dr 84121
O St 84103
S Oak Ter 84124
S Oak Canyon Dr 84121
E & N Oak Forest Rd 84103
S Oak Hills Cir 84121
S Oak Hills Way 84108
E & S Oak Knoll Dr 84121
S Oak Meadows Dr 84123
E Oak Mountain Cir 84108
E Oak Park Ln 84117
E Oak Side Cir 84121
S Oak Springs Dr 84108
N Oak Tree Ct 84116
E Oakbrook Cir 84108
E Oakcliff Dr 84124
S & E Oakcrest Cir & Ln 84121
E & S Oakdale Dr 84121
E & S Oakhill Dr 84121
E Oakhurst Dr 84108
E & W Oakland Ave 84115
E & S Oakledge Rd 84121
N Oakley St 84116
E Oakmont Ave 84107
E Oakridge Dr
1700-1899 84106
2800-2999 84109
E Oakrim Way 84109
S Oakshadow Cir 84121
E Oakview Cir 84121
E Oakview Dr 84124
E & S Oakwood Cir & St 84109
S & W Obsidian Way 84118
S & W Ocean Ct 84123
Officers Cir 84113
E Okeson Cir 84117
E Old Colony Cir 84117
E Old Farm Rd 84107
S Old Fashion Pl 84123
E Old Granite Cv 84115
S Old Honeycomb Rd 84121
E Old Maple Ct 84117
E & S Old Mill Cir 84121
S Old Millbrook Cir 84115
W Old Miller Ct 84118
S & W Old Millrace Ln 84123
N Old Oak Rd 84108
E & S Old Orchard Cir & Ln 84121
S Old Oxford Rd 84118
S Old Prospect Ave 84121
E & S Old Ridge Cir 84121
S Old Stage Rd 84121
S Old Trenton Way 84123
E Old Williams Ct 84106
S Oles Ln 84121
S Olive Cir 84123
E Olive Dr 84124
S Olive Dr 84124
W Olive St 84123
E & S Oliver Cir & Dr 84124
S Olivet Dr 84121
E & S Olivia Ct 84107
E & S Olivia View Ln 84107
S Olympic Way 84124
E Olympus Dr 84124
E Olympus Oaks Ln 84124
E Olympus Park Dr 84117
E Olympus Ridge Cv 84117
E & S Olympus View Dr 84124
E Olympus Vista Ct 84124
W & N Omni Ave, Cir & Dr 84116
S Oneida St
1700-1799 84108
2100-2399 84109
S & W Ontario Dr 84104
E Oquirrh Dr 84108
N Orange St 84116
S Orange St
46-99 84116
200-400 84104
402-498 84104
E Orchard Cir 84106
E Orchard Dr
1500-1999 84106
2900-2999 84109
W Orchard Pl 84101
S Orchard St 84106
S Orchard Park Ct 84124
S Oregon St 84106
S Origin Pl 84123
E Oros Ave 84124
W Ortons Bend Way 84123
E Osage Orange Ave 84124
S Oslo Bay 84121
W Ouray Ave
300-399 84103
800-1399 84116
S Overhill Cir 84121
W Overlook Point Pl 84123
S Overlook Rim Rd 84123
S & W Oxbow Cir 84123
E & S Oxford Hollow Ct 84107
S Ozone Cir 84118
P St 84103
W Pacific Ave 84104
W Packlan Pl 84123
S Padley St 84108
E Pagos Ave 84124
S Paige Cir 84109
E & S Painter Way 84106
W Palace Way 84123
W Palenque Dr 84118
E Palisade Dr 84109
Palleado Dr 84116
W Palm Dr 84123
E Palma Way 84121
E & S Palo Verde Way 84121
S & W Palomar Pl 84118
E Pamela Dr 84121
N Pamela Way 84116
E & S Pan American Dr 84107
S Panama St 84115
E & S Panorama Cir, Dr & Way 84124
E & S Pantera Ln 84106
E & S Par Three Ln 84107
W Paradise Ln 84123
W Paramount Ave 84115
E Paris Ln 84124
E Park Cir 84109
S Park Ct 84106
W Park Ln 84118
E Park Pl N 84121
S Park Pl 84106
S Park Pl E 84121
S Park Pl W 84121
S Park St
600-899 84102
1300-1999 84105
2300-2699 84106
4200-4399 84107
E & S Park Centre Dr 84121
E Park Creeke Ln 84115
S Park Hill Dr 84124
E Park Hill Way 84107
S Park Manor Dr 84117
S Park Meadows St 84106
E Park Oak Pl 8410
S Park Row St 8410
S Park Terrace Dr 8412
S Park Wood Dr 8411
E Parkcrest Cir 8412
S Parkcrest Ct 8412
E Parker Ln 8410
S Parkfield Pl 8411
W Parkham Way 8411
S & E Parkridge Cir & Dr 8412
S Parkside Dr 8410
S & E Parkview Cir & Dr 8412
E Parkway Ave
700-798 8410
800-1699 8410
2066-2098 8410
2100-2299 8410
S & E Parleys Cir, Ter & Way 8410
E Parleys Canyon Blvd
1700-1851 8410
1853-1999 8410
2000-2099 8410
W Parliament Ave 8412
W Parramatta Ln 8411
S Parrish Dr 8411
S & W Parrott St 8412
S Pasadena St 8410
S Paschal Cir 8410
S & W Pasque Dr 8412
Pathesta 8411
W Patricia Way 8411
E Pax Cir 8412
W Paxton Ave
42-98 8410
100-399 8410
700-799 8410
S Peach St
3600-3749 8410
4400-4599 8411
E Peaks Cir 8411
S Pearblossom Cir 8410
N Pearl Harbor St 8411
E Pebble Glen Cir 8410
S Pebble Ridge Ln 8411
S Pecan Cir 8412
S Penguin Cir 8411
S Penn St 8410
E & S Penney Ave & Cv 8411
E Pennsylvania Pl 8410
E Penny Parade Dr 8410
E Penrose Dr 8410
Pentreli Dr 8412
Perandi Dr 8411
E Perry Ave 8410
E & N Perrys Hollow Dr & Rd 8410
E Perrywill Ave 8412
S & W Persimmon Pl 8412
W Perth Pl 8411
W Peten Way 8411
E Peterborough Rd 8412
E Peyton Ct 8411
S & W Pharaoh Cir & Rd 8412
E & S Pheasant Cir, Ln & Way 8412
S Pheasantridge Rd 8410
E Phebe Ln 8410
S & W Phillips Ln 8412
E Phylden Dr 8411
W Pickett Cir 8411
N & W Picture Dr 8411
S Pieper Blvd 8411
W Pierpont Ave
100-399 8410
901-997 8410
999-1099 8410
E Pika Peak Ln 8412
S Pike Cir 8411
S Pin Oak St 8412
S Pin Tail Ct 8411
E Pine St 8412

S Pine Cone St ... 84121
S Pine Knot Dr ... 84121
S Pine Mountain Dr ... 84121
Pine Rock Cir & Dr ... 84121
W Pine Shade Pl ... 84118
S & W Pine Valley Ln ... 84118
N Pinecrest Canyon Rd ... 84108
S Pinehill Dr ... 84107
S Pinemont Dr ... 84123
S Pinetree Dr ... 84124
Pinetree Vlg ... 84121
S & E Pineview Cir & Dr ... 84121
E Pineway Dr ... 84107
S & W Pinewood Dr ... 84123
S Piney Park Cir ... 84118
S & W Piney Ridge Dr ... 84118
W Piney View Ct ... 84118
E Pink Coral Cir ... 84121
S Pinnacle Pl ... 84124
E Pinnacle Terrace Way ... 84121
W Pinnocchio Dr ... 84116
E Pinon Pl ... 84121
E Pioneer Cir ... 84109
W Pioneer Cir ... 84104
S Pioneer Rd ... 84104
S Pioneer St ... 84109
E & N Pioneer Fork Rd ... 84108
N Pioneer Oak Rd ... 84108
E & N Pioneer Ridge Cir & Rd ... 84108
S Pippin Dr ... 84121
W Pitchfork Rd ... 84123
W Planada Way ... 84118
S Plateau Dr ... 84109
S Plaza Way ... 84109
W Pleadinc ... 84180
S Pleasant Ct ... 84101
W Pleasant Ridge Dr ... 84118
S Plum St ... 84123
W Plumbago Ave ... 84118
S Pluto Way ... 84124
W Plymouth Ave ... 84115
S Plymouth View Dr ... 84123
W Poacher Cir ... 84118
N Poinsettia Dr ... 84116
S Polaris Ct ... 84118
W Polaris Way ... 84116
Pollock Rd ... 84113
E Pond View Way ... 84106
S Ponderosa Dr ... 84121
E Pondoray Cir ... 84117
S & E Pontiac Cir & Dr ... 84107
S Poplar Ct ... 84101
S Poplar St ... 84107
W Port Mann Row ... 84123
S & W Portside Way ... 84123
E & S Portsmouth Ave ... 84121
S Post St ... 84104
S & W Potomac Cir & Dr ... 84123
Potter St ... 84113
S Poulos Ln ... 84117
S Powers Cir ... 84124
S Prairiewood Dr ... 84115
S Pralern E ... 84111
Presidents Cir ... 84112
S Preston St
1400-1599 ... 84108
2100-2951 ... 84106
2953-2999 ... 84106
W Price Ave ... 84115
E Princeton Ave
701-739 ... 84105
741-1699 ... 84105
1700-2099 ... 84108
E Privet Dr ... 84121
W Professional Cir ... 84104
E & S Promenade Cir & Dr ... 84121
S Promontory Dr ... 84109
S & W Prospect Cir & St ... 84104
E & S Prospector Cir & Dr ... 84121
W Prosperity Ave ... 84116
E & S Providence Ct ... 84121
S Pueblo St ... 84104
N Pugsley St ... 84103
E & S Purcell Ct ... 84107
W Putters Cir ... 84123
Q St ... 84103
E Quad Rd ... 84108
E & S Quail Estates Way ... 84106
E Quail Grove Cir ... 84121
S Quail Haven Cir ... 84106
S Quail Hollow Dr ... 84109
S Quail Meadow Cir ... 84121
E & S Quail Park Dr ... 84117
S Quail Point Rd ... 84124
E Quail Trail Ln ... 84107
W Quail Trax Pl ... 84107
E & S Quail Vista Ct, Cv & Ln ... 84117
E Quakie Ln ... 84121
S & W Quaking Aspen Dr ... 84123
W Quarry Hill Cir ... 84118
W Quarter Horse Ave ... 84116
E Quarter Mile Rd ... 84108
W Quayle Ave
2-98 ... 84115
900-999 ... 84104
S Quercus Cv ... 84123
S Quicksilver Dr ... 84121
S Quiet Cir ... 84107
S Quiet Spring Cv ... 84117
N Quince St ... 84103
S Quinette Ln ... 84124
R St ... 84103
E Rachelwood Ln ... 84124
E & S Racquet Club Cir & Dr ... 84121
S Ragsdale Dr ... 84121
S Rain Crest Ct ... 84121
Rainbow Cir & Dr ... 84107
E Rainbow Point Dr ... 84124
E Rainforest Dr ... 84107
S Rainier Ave ... 84109
S & E Rainsborough Cir & Rd ... 84121
S Rainy Ln ... 84107
S Ralph St ... 84124
N & W Rambler Dr ... 84116
E Ramona Ave
200-399 ... 84115
500-1599 ... 84105
1700-2299 ... 84108
W Ranch Hollow Ln ... 84123
E Ranch View Dr ... 84124
S Ranchfield Rd ... 84117
S & E Range Cir & Rd ... 84117
S Rappahannock Cir ... 84123
S & W Raton Ln ... 84123
W Rayco Cir ... 84123
S Rayford Cir ... 84118
E & S Rebecca Cir ... 84117
W Red Angus Dr ... 84116
E Red Brick Ct ... 84103
S Red Cliff Dr ... 84123
E Red Hill Ln ... 84108
Red Lodge Cir & Dr ... 84118
S & W Red Oaks Dr ... 84123
W Red Ridge Ln ... 84118
W Red Rose Ln ... 84123
S & E Red Sage Ct & Ln ... 84107
S & W Red Zinc Dr ... 84118
W Redclover Dr ... 84116
W Redfield Ave ... 84115
E & S Redmaple Cir & Rd ... 84106
E Redondo Ave
1-297 ... 84115
299-499 ... 84115
500-1699 ... 84105
1700-2599 ... 84108
E Redondo Pl ... 84108
S Redtail Hawk Bay ... 84117
S Redwood Dr ... 84104
N Redwood Rd ... 84116
S Redwood Rd
50-52 ... 84116
54-99 ... 84116
200-398 ... 84104
400-1899 ... 84104
1901-2099 ... 84104
3900-6599 ... 84123
W Reed Ave ... 84103
S Reeves Ter ... 84102
Regal St ... 84107
E Regal Stream Cv ... 84121
E & S Regalia Rd ... 84121
E Regan Ct ... 84121
S Regency St ... 84117
S Regent St ... 84111
S Reindeer Dr ... 84121
S & W Remington Way ... 84104
N Rendon Ct ... 84116
E Renoir Cir ... 84121
Research Rd ... 84112
S Reva Cir ... 84123
N Reveille Cir ... 84116
E Revelle Way ... 84106
E & S Revere Cir & Dr ... 84117
E Rexford Pl ... 84121
S Reynolds Ct ... 84117
E & S Ribbon Ln ... 84117
E & S Rich Way ... 84121
S Richards St
800-1179 ... 84101
1181-1199 ... 84101
1300-3299 ... 84115
E Riches Ave ... 84106
N Richland Dr ... 84103
S Richmond St ... 84106
Rickenw Rd ... 84113
W Ridge Brook Way ... 84118
Ridge Creek Cir & Rd ... 84107
S & W Ridge Flower Way ... 84118
S & W Ridge Hollow Cir & Way ... 84118
W Ridge Stone Dr ... 84118
S Ridge Village Dr ... 84118
Ridgedale Cir & Ln ... 84106
E Rigdon Ave ... 84115
W Riley Cir ... 84104
S Riley Ln ... 84107
S Riley Commons Ln ... 84107
W Rimrock Ln ... 84123
N & S Rio Grande St ... 84101
E Ripple Way ... 84121
S & W River Bluffs Rd ... 84123
W River Cross Ct ... 84123
S & W River Edge Ln ... 84123
S & W River Glen Cir & Dr ... 84123
S & W River Hollow Rd ... 84123
W River House Cir ... 84123
S & W River Meadow Way ... 84123
S River Park Dr ... 84123
S & W River Point Cir ... 84123
S & W River Rock Pl ... 84118
S & W River Trail Ter ... 84123
S & W Riverbend Dr ... 84123
S Riverboat Rd ... 84123
W Riverdell Rd ... 84123
S Rivers End Rd ... 84121
W Riverside Cir ... 84116
N Riverside Dr ... 84116
S Riverside Dr
1400-1499 ... 84104
1501-1699 ... 84104
4500-4598 ... 84123
4600-5099 ... 84123
5101-5599 ... 84123
W Riverside Dr ... 84123
E & S Riviera Cir & Dr ... 84106
S & W Roanoke Cir & Dr ... 84123
E & W Robert Ave ... 84115
S Roberta St
700-1099 ... 84111
1300-2199 ... 84115
E & S Robie Hill Ln ... 84109
E & S Robie View Pl ... 84109
W Rock Rose Cir ... 84118
W Rock Springs Ln ... 84118
S Rockford St ... 84118
S & W Rockhill Cir, Ln & Pl ... 84123
W Rockhill Point Cv ... 84123
E Rockingham Ct ... 84115
W Rocky Meadows Pl ... 84118
S & W Rocky Ridge Ct, Dr & Rd ... 84118
S Rodeo Ln ... 84121
W Roenewood Cir ... 84123
S Roeoaks Ct ... 84121
E & S Roger Dr ... 84124
S Rogers Dr ... 84118
S & W Rogue River Ct & Ln ... 84118
E Rolling Knolls Way ... 84121
S Rome Beauty Park ... 84123
W Ron Hollow St ... 84123
E Roosevelt Ave
300-399 ... 84115
600-1699 ... 84105
2100-2299 ... 84108
W Ropcke Dr ... 84123
S Rosalind Cir ... 84121
W Rose Cir
1-99 ... 84107
4200-4299 ... 84118
S Rose Garden Ln ... 84124
W & N Rose Park Cir & Ln ... 84116
E Rosecrest Dr ... 84108
S Roseleaf Dr ... 84123
E & S Rosemore Ct ... 84107
E Rosewood Ave ... 84115
S Rossbern Cv ... 84121
E & S Rothmoor Cir & Dr ... 84121
E Rouen Cir ... 84117
E Roundtoft Dr ... 84103
W Roundup Cir ... 84116
E & S Rowland Dr ... 84124
E Rowley Dr ... 84107
E & S Roxbury Cir & Rd ... 84108
E Royal Cir ... 84108
E Royal Coventry Ct ... 84121
E Royal Farm Dr ... 84121
E Royal Garden Ter ... 84115
E & S Royal Harvest Way ... 84121
S Royal River Rd ... 84123
E Royal Troon Dr ... 84124
S Royalton Dr ... 84107
E Roycroft Pl ... 84124
S Ruby Ridge Cv ... 84121
S Rugby Ct ... 84123
E & S Russell Cir & St ... 84117
S Russell Park Rd ... 84121
W Russett Ave ... 84115
S Rustic Dr ... 84123
E Rustic Spring Ln ... 84121
E Ruth Dr ... 84124
W Ruth Dr ... 84118
S Ruth Meadows Cv ... 84117
E Rutland Pl ... 84121
S & W Ryker Vista Ln ... 84123
S St ... 84103
E & S Sabal Ave ... 84121
S & W Saddle Bluff Dr ... 84123
N Saddle Hill Rd ... 84103
S Saddleback Dr ... 84117
S Sadie Ln ... 84121
S Sage Cir ... 84124
S Sage St ... 84124
E Sage Way ... 84109
E Sage Park Ln ... 84117
E & S Sagebrush Cir & Way ... 84121
E Sagehill Dr ... 84124
S Sagewood Dr ... 84107
E Sahara Dr ... 84124
E & S Saint Charles Pl ... 84121
S Saint Francis Cir ... 84124
E & S Saint James Pl ... 84121
E Saint Marks Ct ... 84124
Saint Marys Cir, Dr & Way ... 84108
S & W Salem Ave, Cir & Ct ... 84118
E Sallie Ave ... 84103
S Salt Creek Cir ... 84118
S Sam Oliver Dr ... 84107
W Sams Blvd ... 84118
S San Bartolo Ct ... 84118
W San Fernando Dr ... 84116
S San Lucas Ct ... 84117
E San Rafael Ave ... 84109
N Sandhurst Dr ... 84103
E & S Sandpiper Cir, Dr & Way ... 84117
E Sandra Cir ... 84121
N & S Sandrun Rd ... 84103
E Sands Dr ... 84124
S Sandusky Cir ... 84123
S Sandwedge Cir ... 84123
S Sanford Dr ... 84123
E Sanibel Cv ... 84121
E & S Santa Cruz Dr ... 84121
E & S Santa Rosa Ave & Dr ... 84109
S Santa Ynez Cir ... 84104
W Santee Cir ... 84123
E Santiago Ln ... 84121
S & W Sarah Jane Cir & Dr ... 84118
E Saratoga Rd ... 84117
S & W Sarbo St ... 84118
E & S Sarto Ave ... 84121
N Satori Cir ... 84116
S Saturn Ave ... 84124
E Saunders St ... 84107
S Saunter Ln ... 84123
S & E Saxony Cir & Pl ... 84117
W Saxton Pl ... 84123
S Scenic Cir ... 84109
S Scenic Dr
1901-1997 ... 84108
1999-2099 ... 84108
2100-2599 ... 84109
W Scenic Park Cir ... 84118
W Scenic Ridge Cir ... 84118
S & W Scorpio Dr ... 84118
W Scots Field Ct ... 84123
E Scott Ave
300-499 ... 84115
500-899 ... 84106
S Scott Cir ... 84115
S Scott Ct ... 84106
S Scott Park Ln ... 84106
E & S Searle Ave & Cir ... 84117
S Secluded Oak Cir ... 84121
S Secord St ... 84115
W Secret Garden Pl ... 84104
E Sego Ave
400-499 ... 84111
600-798 ... 84102
800-899 ... 84102
S Senate Cir ... 84104
W Senior Way ... 84115
S Senoma Dr ... 84121
S & W September Morn Cir & Ln ... 84123
S Sequoia Ave ... 84109
W Sequoia Vista Cir ... 84104
E Seraphine Cv ... 84121
E Serenity Oak Ln ... 84107
W Sergeant Dr ... 84116
S & W Settlers Way ... 84123
E & S Severn Cir & Dr ... 84124
S Seville Rd ... 84121
E Seychelles Ct ... 84121
E & S Shadow Cv ... 84121
E Shadow Wood Cir ... 84117
W Shadow Wood Dr ... 84123
S Shadowwood Dr ... 84123
S Shady Ct ... 84106
E & S Shady Creek Pl ... 84106
S Shady Farm Ln ... 84107
S Shady Grove Cir ... 84121
E Shady Lake Dr ... 84106
E & S Shady Maple Cv ... 84117
W Shady Pine Ln ... 84118
S & W Shady River Way ... 84123
E Shady Tree Ct ... 84106
E Shadybrook Ln ... 84121
E Shakespeare Pl ... 84108
S Shalee St ... 84118
S Shamrock Cir ... 84118
E Shamrock Dr ... 84107
S Shamrock Dr ... 84107
S Shangri Ln ... 84121
S Shanna St ... 84124
W Shannon Cir ... 84116
S Shannon St ... 84105
E Shays Grove Ln ... 84121
W Shea Dr ... 84104
S & W Shelbourne Ln ... 84123
E Shelby Ct ... 84121
W Shelley Ave ... 84115
S Shelmerdine Ct ... 84115
W Shenandoah Cir ... 84123
S Shenandoah Park Ave ... 84121
E Sheridan Rd ... 84108
E Sherleen Cir ... 84124
E Sherman Ave
300-499 ... 84115
501-537 ... 84105
539-1699 ... 84105
2100-2199 ... 84108
Sherwood Cir & Dr ... 84108
E Shiloh Way ... 84107
S Shiloh Park Ln ... 84117
S Shirecliff Rd ... 84108
S Shirl St ... 84123
S Shirley Ln ... 84124
S Short Iron Cir ... 84123
S Shorthills Dr ... 84121
W Shortline Ave ... 84116
W Siena Cir ... 84116
W Sienna Way ... 84123
E Sierra Way ... 84106
S Sierra Park Cir ... 84106
S Sierra Point Pl ... 84109
E Sierra Ridge Ct ... 84109
E Sierra View Cir ... 84109
E Siggard Dr ... 84106
S Signal Point Cir ... 84109
W Signora Dr ... 84116
E Sigsbee Ave ... 84103
N Silent Glen Ln ... 84116
S Sillored E ... 84106
W Silver Ave ... 84115
Silver Frk ... 84121
S Silver Bell Dr ... 84107
S & E Silver Fork Dr & Rd ... 84121
S & W Silver Fox Dr ... 84118
E Silver Hawk Dr ... 84121
S Silver King Cir ... 84121
E & S Silver Lake Dr ... 84121
E & N Silver Oak Rd ... 84108
E Silver Shadows Dr ... 84107
E Silver Snow Ln ... 84121
N Silver Star Dr ... 84116
S Silver Valley Dr ... 84118
S & W Silvertip Dr ... 84118
S Simmental Dr ... 84123
W Simondi Ave ... 84116
E Simpson Ave
601-697 ... 84106
699-999 ... 84106
1001-1099 ... 84106
2400-2699 ... 84109
W Sir Andrew Way ... 84116
Sir Anthony Cir & Dr ... 84116
W Sir Charles Dr ... 84116
Sir James Cir, Dr & Way ... 84116
Sir Jeffrey Cir, Dr & Way ... 84116
N & W Sir Joseph Way ... 84116
N Sir Michael Dr ... 84116
N Sir Patrick Dr ... 84116
N Sir Philip Dr ... 84116
W Sir Robert Dr ... 84116
W Sir Timothy Ave ... 84116
Skiview Rd ... 84121
E Sky Pines Ct ... 84117
E & S Skycrest Cir & Ln ... 84108
E Skycrest Park Cv ... 84108
Skyline Cir & Dr ... 84108
E Skyline View Ln ... 84121
E Skyridge Cir ... 84109
S & E Skyview Cir & Dr ... 84124
E Slade Pl ... 84102
E Sleepy Hollow Dr ... 84117
E Slopeside Ln ... 84121
S & W Smiley Dr ... 84123
S Smokey Ln ... 84108
S Snake Creek Rd ... 84121
W Snow Queen Pl ... 84104
S Snowmass Ct ... 84124
E Snowy River Ct ... 84115
E Social Hall Ave ... 84111
S & E Solar Cir & Dr ... 84124
S Solaris Way ... 84115
Soldiers Cir ... 84113
S Soleil Cv ... 84108
E & S Solitaire Dr ... 84106
S Solitude Dr ... 84121
E Somerset Dr ... 84121
E Somerset Way ... 84117
S Somerset Way ... 84117
E & S Sommet Dr ... 84117
N Sonata St ... 84116
S Sonia Rose Ct ... 84124
S Sonnet Dr ... 84106
E Sonoma Ct ... 84106
W Sophia Cir ... 84123
E Sophomore Cir ... 84117
S Sorenson Way ... 84109
E South Temple
10-10 ... 84133
E South Temple
20-98 ... 84111
100-499 ... 84111
500-1449 ... 84102
W South Temple
15-97 ... 84101
99-163 ... 84101
165-399 ... 84101
600-698 ... 84104
700-999 ... 84104
W Southampton Rd ... 84123
E Southcampus Dr ... 84112
E Southgate Ave ... 84115
E Southlake Dr ... 84107
S & E Southmoor Cir & Dr ... 84117
E Southwood Dr ... 84107
E Southwoodside Dr ... 84124
S Sovereign Way ... 84124
S & W Spacerama Dr ... 84123
S & W Spanish Oak Way ... 84123
S Specialty Cir ... 84115
E Spencer Ave ... 84115
N Spencer Ct ... 84103
W Speyside Way ... 84107
S & W Spinnaker Row ... 84123
E & S Splendor Cir & Way ... 84124
N Split Rail Ln ... 84116

Street	ZIP
E Spriande	84133
E Spring Ln	84117
W Spring St	84116
S & W Spring Clover Dr	84123
E & S Spring Creek Rd	84117
E & S Spring Gate Dr	84117
E Spring Haven Dr	84109
E Spring Hill Dr	84107
E & S Spring Hollow Dr	84109
E & S Spring House Ln	84107
E & S Spring Leaf Dr	84117
E Spring Meadow Rd	84107
E & S Spring Run Dr	84117
E & S Spring Valley Ct	84117
E Spring View Dr	84106
S Springbrook Way	84121
W Springfield Rd	84116
W Springshire Ln	84123
E & S Springtree Ln	84107
S & E Spruce Cir & Dr	84124
S & E Spruce Glen Cir & Rd	84107
S Spruce Hill Rd	84121
E & S Spruce View Ct & Ln	84109
S Spurrier Rd	84107
S Squire Ct	84124
E Stablewood Cir	84117
E Staker Cir	84121
N Stallion Ln	84116
S Standel Dr	84108
E & S Stanford Ln	84117
S Stanida Cir	84121
E Stanley Ave	84115
W Stanley Glen Ln	84123
S Stansbury Way	84108
E Stanton Ave	84111
E & S Stanwick Rd	84121
S Starboard Ln	84123
N Starcrest Dr	84116
E Starling Dr	84121
S Starlite Dr	84107
W State Cir	84104
N State St	
2-98	84103
100-299	84103
300-499	84114
S State St	
2-12	84111
14-100	84111
101-125	84138
102-1298	84111
127-1299	84111
1300-3899	84115
3900-5000	84107
4989-4989	84157
5001-6799	84107
5002-6798	84107
State Capitol Building	84114
State Office Building	84114
E & W Stauffer Ln	84107
E & S Stauning Cv	84121
S Steele St	84118
S Steeple Chase Ln	84121
S Steffensen Dr	84121
S Steller Jay Way	84121
E Stephie Marie Ln	84115
W Sterling Dr	84116
W Stern Dr	84123
Stetson Cir & Way	84104
S & W Stewart Cir & St	84104
E Stillman Ln	84109
S & E Stillwood Cir & Dr	84117
E & S Stockbridge Ln	84117
W Stockton St	84118
E & S Stone Rd	84121
S & W Stone Bluff Way	84118
S Stone Crest Dr	84107
S & W Stone Flower Way	84118
S Stone Mill Dr	84121
S Stone Pine Ln	84117
E Stonehedge Dr	84107
E & S Stonehill Ln	84121
E Stonemoor Cir	84121
S & W Stony Brook Cir & Way	84118
W Stony Park Dr	84118
W Stony Ridge Cir	84118
W Stony Vista Dr	84118
S & W Storm Mountain Dr	84123
S Strata Cir	84107
E Stratford Ave	84106
W Stratford Ave	84115
E Stratford Dr	84109
S Stratler St	84107
E & S Stratton Dr	84117
W Stratus St	84118
S Stream Side Ct	84109
Strielia St	84103
S Stringfellow Ct	84111
E Stringham Ave	
500-599	84106
2300-2699	84109
S Strongs Ct	84102
S & E Suada Cir & Dr	84124
S Sue St	84115
S Sugar Hill Cir	84123
E Sugar Leaf Ln	84109
S Sugarhouse Ln	84108
E Sugarmont Dr	84106
S Sultan Cir	84107
E & S Sumac Way	84121
N Summer St	84116
E Summer Estates Cir	84121
E Summer Oaks Cir	84121
E Summer Pine Ln	84115
S Summer View Way	84123
S & E Summerhill Cir, Ct & Dr	84121
S & E Summerspring Ct & Ln	84124
S Summerwood St	84123
S Summit Cir	84109
W Summit Brook Cir	84118
W Summit Flower Cir	84118
W Summit Point Cir	84118
S & W Sun Dr	84118
N Sun Arbor Ter	84116
W Sun Cliff Ct	84118
E Sun Meadow Cir	84106
W Sun Ridge Ct	84118
W Sunberry Dr	84123
Sunbow Ct & Dr	84118
S Sunburst Cir	84121
Sunbury Pl & Way	84118
S Suncrest Dr	84117
W Suncrest View Pl	84118
Sundown Ave & Cir	84121
E Sundrift Cir	84121
W Sundrop Cir	84118
W Sunfalls Ct	84118
W Sunglow Cir	84118
Sunhill Cir & Rd	84121
E & S Suniland Cir & Dr	84109
S & W Sunkist Dr	84118
S Sunlight Dr	84118
E Sunny Pl	84115
S Sunny End Way	84121
E Sunny Flowers Ln	84107
W Sunny Peak Cir	84118
S & W Sunny River Rd	84123
E Sunnybrook Way	84124
S Sunnydale Dr	
3601-3697	84109
3699-3899	84109
3900-3999	84124
E Sunnydale Ln	84108
S Sunnyoak Cir	84121
E Sunnyside Ave	
1100-1199	84102
1400-1698	84105
1700-1898	84108
1900-2300	84108
2255-2255	84158
2302-2698	84108
2601-2699	84108
N Sunrise Ave	84103
S Sunrise Hills Cir	84121
S Sunrise Vista Cir	84118
E Sunset Ave	84115
W Sunset Ave	84115
W Sunset Dr	84116
S & W Sunset Links Dr	84123
S Sunset Oaks Dr	84108
S & W Sunset Peak Ln	84123
S Sunset View Dr	84124
S Sunset Vista Dr	84118
S Sunstone Rd	84123
Sunview Ct & Dr	84118
W Superior Peak Dr	84123
E & S Supernal Cir & Way	84121
S & E Surrey Ct & Ln	84121
E & S Surreyrun Rd	84107
E & S Susan Way	84121
S & W Susan Grove Ln	84115
S & W Susquehanna	84123
S Sutter St	84123
E & S Sutton Cir & Way	84121
E Sutton Commons Cir	84121
S Suwannee Cir	84123
E Suzette Cir	84106
S Swallow St	84123
W Swanbridge Dr	84118
S Swaner Rd	84104
E Swasont Way	84117
S Sweetwood Cir	84123
S & E Sycamore Dr & Ln	84117
E Sylvan Ave	84108
T St	84103
N Taffeta Dr	84116
S Tahnia Bay	84121
E Tahnia Park Cir	84121
E Taitlynn Cir	84106
W & N Talisman Cir & Dr	84116
S Tall Oak Ln	84121
E Tall Pine Ln	84121
W Tally Ho St	84116
S & W Talon Cir	84118
W Tamarack Rd	84123
S Tanglewood Dr	84117
Tanner Ln & Way	84121
S Tanner Gardens Ct	84109
E Tara Ln	84117
S Taroona Dr	84117
S Tarragon Ct	84118
E & S Tartan Ave	84108
S Taryton Ct	84123
N Taurus Cir	84116
E Taylor Ln	84107
S & W Taylors Hill Cv & Dr	84123
S & W Taylors Meadow Ct	84123
S & W Taylors Park Cir & Dr	84123
W Teakwood Dr	84123
W Telegraph Hill Dr	84123
Terianch Dr	84121
N Terminal Dr	84122
E Terra Linda Dr	84124
W Terra Nova Cir	84118
E & S Terra Sol Dr	84115
Terrace Heights Cir & Rd	84109
N Terrace Hills Dr	84103
E & S Terrace View Cir & Dr	84109
S Teton Dr	84109
S Texas St	
1700-2099	84108
2100-2299	84109
E Thackeray Pl	84108
W Thackie Cir	84104
W Thames Ct	84123
E Thistle Ave	84102
S & W Thorncrest Way	84118
S & W Thornhill Dr	84123
E Thornton Ave	84105
S Thornwood Ave	84123
E & S Thousand Oaks Cir & Dr	84124
E & S Three Fountains Cir & Dr	84107
W Thrush Rd	84123
E Thunderbird Dr	84109
E Tiara St	84117
W Tidwell St	84118
S Tierra Dr	84118
S Tikal Way	84118
S Timber Way	84117
E & S Timberline Dr	84121
W Tin Stone Cir	84118
E & S Tina Way	84107
S Titian St	84121
E & S Tolcate Ln	84121
E Tolcate Hills Dr	84121
S Tolcate Woods Ln	84121
E Tomahawk Dr	84103
N Tommy Thompson Rd	84116
E Tompkins Dr	84121
E & S Tonalea Dr	84107
E & S Toni Cir	84121
S & E Top Of The World Cir & Dr	84121
N Topaz Dr	84116
S & W Topowa Dr	84107
E Topps Ln	84106
W Torrington Ct	84118
E Tortuga Cv	84121
W Torwood Ct	84123
S Towncrest Dr	84121
S & E Towne Cir & Dr	84121
E Townhouse Ct	84115
E Townhouse Villa	84115
S & W Townsend Cir & Way	84118
W Trafalga Way	84116
E Trailorama Ave	84107
E Trails End Way	84108
S & W Travis James Ln	84107
S Treasure Farm Cir	84123
S Treasure Ridge Cir	84121
S Treasure View Cv	84123
E Tree Farm Ln	84121
E Tree View Dr	84124
S Treetop Cir	84107
S Tressler Rd	84118
Triad Ctr	84180
S & W Trident Cir & Dr	84118
W Triderli S	84104
W Tripp Ln	84123
S & W Tripp View Ln	84123
S Tripp Vista Ct	84123
E & S Triton Ct & Dr	84107
Trolley Sq	84102
E Troon Cir	84121
S Trout Ln	84108
S Trowbridge Way	84118
E Troy Way	84107
E & W Truman Ave	84115
E & S Trunk Bay Cir	84107
W Tuckington Cir	84118
S Tumerick Ct	84118
N & W Turin Dr	84116
E & S Turnagain Cv	84121
S & W Turnberry Pl & Way	84123
S Turner Dr	84121
S Turpin St	84107
W Turtle Creek Ct	84118
S Tuscan St	84118
N Tuttle Ct	84116
N Twickenham Dr	84103
S & W Twilight Cir & Dr	84118
S Twin Aspen Cv	84121
E & N Twin Creek Cir & Rd	84108
S Twin Lake Cir	84121
S & W Twin River Way	84123
E Twin View Dr	84109
S Twin Willows Cir	84123
S Twinbrook St	84109
S Tyler St	84105
S & W Tytus Dr	84107
U St	84103
E Uintah Cir	84105
E Unintana S	84102
S University St	84102
University Vlg	84108
University Of Utah	84112
E Upland Dr	84109
S Urban Way	84107
S Urban Corner Cv	84107
E Urbandale Ln	84106
S Utah St	84104
S Utahna Cir	84104
S Utahna Dr	
1300-1499	84104
5600-5899	84107
E Ute Cir	84107
S Ute Cir	84107
S Ute Dr	84108
E & W Utopia Ave	84115
E & S Vagabond Dr	84107
Valdez Dr	84113
E Valencia Park Ln	84106
S Valene St	84117
N Valentine St	84116
S & W Valewood Dr	84123
S Valiant Dr	84121
S Vallejo Dr	84124
S Valley Dr	84107
W Valley Dr	84107
S Valley St	84109
E Valley View Ave	84117
S Valley Vista Dr	84124
W Van Buren Ave	
1-399	84115
1300-1499	84104
W Van Buren Cir	84104
S Van Cott Rd	84121
Van Gogh Cir	84118
E Van Ness Pl	84111
S Van Winkle Expy	
5500-5598	84117
6100-6198	84121
W Varden Way	84123
S Vegas Way	84124
S Venar Cir	84109
E & S Ventnor Ave	84121
W Venture Way	84115
E & S Venus Cir	84124
E Vera Cir	84121
S Verdant Cir	84109
Verde St	84118
Verdugo Dr	84118
S Verness Cv	84121
S Vernon Cir	84124
E Verona Cir	84117
E Verona Meadows Ct	84107
S Via Terra St	84115
E Victoria Pl	84103
N Victoria Way	84116
N Victory Rd	84103
E Vidas Ave	84115
S View St	84105
Viewcrest Cir & Dr	84124
Viewmont Cir & St	84117
S Viking Rd	84109
S Villa Dr	84109
E Villa Park Ln	84121
E Village Cir	84108
E Village Rd	84121
S Village Rd	84121
E & S Village 3 Rd	84121
E & S Village Green Rd	84121
W & N Village Hill Ave & Cir	84116
W Village Park Ave	84116
N Village View St	84116
E Villaire Ave	84121
S Villandrie Ln	84121
E Vimont Ave	84109
S Vincent Ct	84102
E Vine St	
1-899	84107
900-1911	84121
1913-1999	84121
N Vine St	84103
S Vine St	84107
W Vine St	
2-98	84107
100-349	84107
350-750	84123
752-798	84123
S Vine Way	84121
S Vine Bend Ln	84121
E Vine Creek Cir	84107
S Vine Field Ln	84121
E Vine Gate Dr	84121
S Vine Hill Ln	84121
E Vine Meadow Cir	84121
S Vine Park Dr	84121
E Vine Ridge Way	84121
E & S Vinecrest Cir & Dr	84121
S Vineway Cir	84121
E & S Vineyard Ct	84106
E Vintage Ln	84124
E & S Vintage Oak Ln	84121
E Vintage Woods Ct	84117
E & S Vintry Cir & Ln	84121
E Virginia St	84107
N Virginia St	84103
S Virginia Way	84109
S Virginia Hills Dr	84121
S Viscayne Dr	84121
E Vista Bonita Cir	84121
E & S Vista Grande Cir & Dr	84121
W Vista Point Dr	84118
S & W Vista Ridge Cir & Way	84118
S Vista View Dr	84108
S Von Baron Pl	84104
S Voyager Pl	84107
S Wabash Cir	84123
E Wagstaff Dr	84117
S Wahlquist Ln	84123
E Wailua Way	84117
S Waimea Way	84117
S Wainwright Rd	84109
S Wakara Way	84108
S Wakefield Way	84118
S Walden Glen Dr	84123
S & W Walden Hills Dr	84123
S & W Walden Meadows Cir, Ct, Dr & Pl	84123
W Walden Park Dr	84123
S & W Walden Ridge Dr	84123
S & W Walden Wood Cir & Dr	84123
E Waldo Dr	84117
N Walersid W	84122
E Walker Ln	84117
S Walker Estates Cir	84117
S Walker Haven Cir	84124
E Walker Meadows Cir	84117
E & S Walker Mill Ct & Dr	84121
E Walker Oaks Ct	84121
S Walker Woods Ln	84117
N Wall St	84103
S Wallace Ln	
4400-4458	84124
4460-4486	84124
4500-5099	84117
S Wallace Rd	84104
W Wallin St	84107
N Walnut Cir	84116
W Walnut Dr	84116
E Walnut Way	84121
S Walnut Way	84121
E Walnut Brook Dr	84107
W Walnut Creek Ct	84118
E Walnut Mill Cv	84106
S & W Walnut Ridge Cir & Dr	84118
S & W Walnut View Cir & Dr	84118
S & W Walnut Wood Dr	84118
S Walpole Way	84121
W Walton Ave	84115
E Wanda Way	84117
E Wandamere Ave	84106
E Wander Cir	84117
S Wander Ln	
4200-4419	84124
4421-4499	84124
4500-5299	84117
E Wanderbrook Ln	84124
S & W Warbler St	84123
E Wardway Dr	84124
S Warehouse Rd	84118
N Warm Springs Rd	84116
E Warnock Ave	
400-499	84115
600-1299	84106
E & S Warr Rd	84109
W Wasatch Ave	84104
S Wasatch Blvd	
2901-3899	84109
3901-4999	84124
5700-8412	84121
8414-8598	84121
E Wasatch Cir	84105
Wasatch Dr	
100-151	84112
153-199	84112
500-599	84113
E Wasatch Dr	84108
S Wasatch Dr	
36-36	84112
900-1198	84108
1200-2099	84108
2101-2103	84109
2105-2176	84109
2178-2298	84109
S Wasatch St	84107
S Wasatch Cove Cir	84109
E & S Wasatch Grove Ln	84121
E & S Wasatch Haven Ct	84121
E Wasatch Hills Ln	84121
E Wasatch Oaks Cir	84124
E Washington Ave	84107
W Washington Ave	84107
S Washington St	
600-1000	84101
1002-1098	84101
3100-3200	84115
3202-3298	84115
E & S Water Lily Dr	84106
S & E Waterbury Cir, Dr & Way	84121
S Waterfront Dr	84123
Watermill Cir & Way	84121
W Waters Edge Cir	84123
S Waterton Cir	84121
S Watson Creek Ln	84109
S Waverly Ct	84123
S & W Waxwing St	84123
S Way Mar Cir	84121
S Wayman Ln	84117
E Wayman View Ct	84117
E & S Waymark Cir	84109
S Wayne Cir	84121
S Wayne Ct	84101
S Weathervane Dr	84117
S Wedgewood Rd	84106

E Welby Ave
200-499 84115
1000-1099 84106
S Welch Cir 84118
E Wellington Cir 84117
S Wellington St
2100-3699 84106
4500-4699 84117
S Wells Fargo Plz 84101
Wenco Cir & Dr 84104
S & E Wendell Cir, Dr & Way 84115
E & W Wentworth Ave 84115
E & S Wesley Rd 84117
S West Ct 84102
N West Temple 84103
S West Temple
2-52 84101
S West Temple
54-1200 84101
1202-1298 84101
1300-1398 84115
1400-3170 84115
3161-3161 84165
3171-3899 84115
3172-3898 84115
3900-4100 84107
4102-4114 84107
S Westbench Cir & Dr 84118
N Westcapitol St 84103
E & S Westerling Way 84121
E Westminster Ave
101-197 84115
199-499 84115
800-1699 84105
1800-2599 84108
S Westmoor Rd 84117
E Westmoreland Dr 84105
W Weston Ave 84107
N Westpointe Cir 84116
S Westridge Blvd 84118
S Westridge St 84107
Westside Cir & Dr 84118
Westslope Cir & Dr 84118
E & S Westview Cir & Dr 84124
S Westwind Way 84118
W Westwood Ave 84115
S Westwood Dr 84109
E Wheeler Farm Cv 84121
S & E Whispering Pine Cir & Dr 84107
W Whistler Cir 84118
S Whitby Ct 84123
E White Ave 84106
E White Cir 84109
S White Cir 84109
E White Pl 84115
E White Way 84124
S White Aspen Cv 84121
E White Oaks Cir 84121
W White Pine Dr 84123
S White Springs Dr 84123
E Whitemaple Way 84106
S & E Whitewater Cir & Dr 84121
E Whitlock Ave
100-299 84115
1100-1299 84106
W Whitlock Ave 84115
E & S Whitmore Way 84121
Whitney Ave 84115
S Wicklow Pl 84109
E & S Wild Duck Ln 84117
W Wildberry Cir 84118
E Wilderness Rd 84121
W Wildflower Dr 84116
S Wildflower Ln 84123
S Wildrose Ln 84109
S & E Wildwood Cir & Dr 84121
W Wiley Post Way 84116
E Wilford Ave 84107
E Williams Ave
100-499 84111
1000-1099 84105
E Williams Ct 84107

E Williams Way 84107
W Willingcott Way 84118
E Willow Ave 84107
S Willow Ln 84107
S Willow Rd 84117
E Willow Way 84121
S Willow Way 84121
E Willow Canyon Dr 84121
E Willow Fork Ln 84121
S Willow Grove Ln 84123
E Willow Loop Rd 84121
E Willow Oak Cir 84121
E & S Willow Ridge Rd 84121
W Willow Run Dr 84123
S & E Willowcrest Cir & Rd 84121
E Willowood Ave 84107
E Wilmington Ave
500-1899 84106
2000-2008 84109
2010-2699 84109
S Wilmington Cir 84109
E Wilmott Dr 84109
S Wilshire Cir 84109
E Wilshire Dr 84109
S Wilshire Dr 84109
E Wilshire Pl 84102
E Wilson Ave
1-99 84107
100-399 84115
401-499 84115
500-1699 84105
1700-2499 84108
W Wilson Ave 84107
S Wilton Way 84108
E Winchester St 84107
W Winchester St
1-19 84107
21-449 84107
451-497 84123
499-1299 84123
S Windell Cir 84124
E Winder Ln 84124
S Winder Farm Pl 84124
S Winder Meadow Cir 84124
E Winder Park Pl 84124
S & E Winderbrook Ct & Way 84124
E Windflower Ln 84121
E Windham Cir 84109
S Windsor Cir 84106
S Windsor St
101-497 84102
499-799 84102
900-2099 84105
2200-2399 84106
E Windsor Park Dr 84117
S Windwood Cir 84121
E & S Windy Garden Ln 84107
S & E Winesap Cir, Ct & Rd 84121
S Winfield Rd 84123
E Winslow Ave 84115
N Winter St 84116
S Winter Ridge Ln 84118
S Winterdale Cir 84121
S Wintergreen Cir 84123
E Winward Dr 84117
W Wirthlin Dr 84123
N Wolcott St 84103
S Wolcott St 84102
W Wolf Creek Ct 84118
E Wolf Hollow Ln 84117
E Wood Ave
2-98 84115
500-1100 84105
1102-1298 84105
S Wood Cir 84107
E & S Woodbridge Dr 84117
E & S Woodcrest Dr 84117
S Woodduck Ln 84117
S Wooded Cv 84117
N Wooden Ln 84116
S & W Woodhaven Cir & Dr 84123

Woodlake Cv, Dr & Ln 84107
E Woodland Ave
400-499 84115
1300-1699 84106
S Woodline Dr 84124
S Woodmont Dr 84117
E Woodoak Ln
600-700 84107
702-898 84107
900-958 84117
960-999 84117
E Woodridge Cir 84121
S & W Woodrow St 84107
S Woodruff Way 84108
S & W Woodsborough Cir & Way 84118
Woodshire Ave & Cir 84107
E & S Woodside Dr 84124
E Woodstock Ave 84121
S & W Woodview Cir & Dr 84118
E & S Woodwillow Cir 84109
E Worchester Dr 84121
S & E Wren Cir & Rd 84117
S Wren Hollow Cir 84117
E & S Wrenhaven Ln & Rd 84121
W Wright Cir 84104
S Wright Ct 84105
N Wright Brothers Dr 84116
E Wyndom Ct 84108
E & S Wynford Cir & St 84121
S Wyoming St
1800-2099 84108
2100-2399 84109
S Xanadu Cir 84123
E Yale Ave
100-199 84111
700-1699 84105
1700-2099 84108
E Yalecrest Ave
1501-1597 84105
1599-1699 84105
1700-1999 84108
S & W Yarrow Ln 84123
W Yeager Rd 84116
S Yellow Fin Way 84107
E Yermo Ave 84109
S York St 84117
E & S Yorktown Cir & Dr 84117
E & S Yosemite Dr 84109
S Young Haven Cir 84109
N Young Oak Rd 84108
S & W Yucca Dr 84123
S Yuma Cir 84109
S Yuma St
1300-1899 84108
2100-2799 84109
E Yuma View Dr 84109
W Zachary Dr 84116
W Zane Ave 84103
S Zarahemla Dr 84124
E Zenda Way 84121
E & S Zenia Meadows Ct 84107
E & S Zenith Ave & Cir 84106
E Zeuthen Ln 84124
S Zevex Park Ln 84123
S & W Zodiac Dr 84118

NUMBERED STREETS

E 1st Ave 84103
E 2nd Ave 84103
E 3rd Ave 84103
E 4th Ave 84107
100-1399 84103
W 4th Ave 84107
E 5th Ave 84107
E 5th Ave 84107
E 5th Ave 84107
200-1299 84103
W 5th Ave 84107
E 6th Ave 84103
E 7th Ave 84103
E 8th Ave 84103
E 9th Ave 84103
9th South Cir 84108
E 10th Ave 84103
E 11th Ave 84103
E 12th Ave 84103
E 13th Ave 84103
E 14th Ave 84103
E 16th Ave 84103
E 17th Ave 84103
E 18th Ave 84103
E 100 S 84111
E 100 S 84111
E 100 S 84111
500-1341 84102
1343-1453 84102
1455-1499 84112
N 1000 W 84116
S 1000 E
2-98 84102
900-2099 84105
2100-3452 84106
3900-4099 84124
5000-5199 84117
S 1000 W
1-1699 84104
5200-5248 84107
W 1000 N 84116
W 100 S
1-599 84101
600-999 84104
S 1021 E 84117
S 1025 E 84124
4501-4599 84117
W 1020 N 84116
S 1030 E 84106
S 1034 E 84117
S 1035 E 84121
S 1040 E
3900-3969 84124
S 1045 E
4000-4199 84124
4900-4998 84117
5000-5190 84117
5192-5234 84117
S 1045 W
1700-1899 84104
S 1040 W
6400-6599 84123
W 1040 S 84104
S 1050 E 84121
S 1055 W 84123
S 1065 E 84117
S 1065 W 84123
S 1070 E 84117
S 1085 E 84121
S 1080 E 84121
S 1090 W 84123
N 1100 W 84116
S 1100 E
1-899 84102
900-1918 84105
1930-1954 84106
1953-1953 84152
1955-3799 84106
3900-3998 84124
5000-5098 84117
S 1100 W
100-198 84104
4300-4398 84123
W 1100 N 84116
S 1110 E 84117
S 1115 E 84117
S 1135 E 84124
S 1130 W 84123
S 1140 E 84124
4800-4899 84117
S 1145 E
5700-5899 84121
4300-4399 84123
S 1140 W
6400-6599 84123
S 115 W 84107
N 1160 W 84116
S 1160 E 84124

S 1175 E 84124
S 1175 W 84123
S 1180 E 84121
S 1185 E 84121
S 1195 W 84123
S 1190 W 84123
N 1200 W 84116
S 1200 E
1-800 84102
900-1999 84105
2800-3699 84106
3900-3999 84124
4500-4600 84117
6200-6228 84121
S 120 W 84107
200-234 84104
4301-4399 84123
W 1200 N 84116
S 1215 E 84106
S 1210 W 84123
S 1225 E 84117
S 1220 E 84124
5800-5899 84121
S 1230 W 84123
S 1250 E
3800-3899 84106
5600-6299 84121
S 1250 W 84123
S 1260 E
3600-3699 84106
4401-4499 84124
S 1260 W 84119
N 1280 W 84116
S 1280 E 84121
S 1280 W 84123
S 129 W 84107
S 1290 W 84123
E 1300 S
2-44 84115
46-499 84115
500-1699 84105
1700-2699 84108
N 1300 W 84116
S 1300 E
2-98 84102
900-2099 84105
2100-3799 84106
3931-3997 84124
4500-5399 84117
5600-5698 84121
S 1300 W
200-1699 84104
4000-4098 84123
S 130 W
6500-6599 84107
W 1300 N 84116
W 1300 S
1-200 84115
700-1599 84104
W 130 S
1175-1175 84104
N 1320 W 84116
4750-4750 84117
5900-5999 84121
N 1330 W 84116
S 1335 E 84106
S 1330 E
4750-4750 84117
7200-7299 84121
N 1340 W 84116
S 1340 E 84117
E 135 S 84112
S 1350 E 84124
4750-4750 84117
S 1355 W 84123
W 1355 S 84104
S 1380 E 84124
W 1385 S 84104
S 1395 E 84117
W 1390 S 84104
N 1400 W 84116
S 1405 E 84121
115-267 84112
800-2099 84105
2800-2999 84106
3956-4399 84124
S 1400 W 84104

W 140 N 84116
W 1400 S
100-199 84115
900-1399 84104
S 1410 E 84117
S 1420 E 84121
S 1425 W 84123
S 1420 W
4093-4199 84123
S 1430 E 84121
S 1440 E 84121
S 1450 E 84124
S 1452 E 84112
N 1465 W 84116
200-298 84116
S 1460 E
100-299 84112
4100-4199 84124
S 1460 W 84123
S 1475 W 84123
S 1470 W 84123
S 1480 E 84121
S 1480 W 84123
S 1490 E 84121
S 1495 E 84121
N 1500 W 84116
S 1500 E
240-292 84112
900-1999 84105
2400-2999 84106
3900-3928 84124
S 1500 W
200-1099 84104
3900-5799 84123
S 150 W
4682-4798 84107
W 1500 N 84116
W 1500 S
300-499 84115
1700-2799 84104
W 150 S
5100-5199 84104
S 151 W 84107
S 1515 W 84123
S 1525 E 84121
W 1520 S 84104
W 1525 S
4600-4698 84104
S 1530 E
300-398 84112
3100-3299 84106
5600-6899 84121
S 1535 W 84123
S 1540 E 84121
S 1540 W 84123
S 1550 E 84121
S 1555 W 84123
S 1560 E 84121
S 1575 E
3101-3197 84106
S 1570 E
3300-3399 84106
4000-4099 84124
6500-6599 84121
S 157 W 84107
S 1575 W
4800-4898 84123
S 1585 E 84121
S 1580 E
5700-6599 84121
W 1580 N 84116
S 1590 E 84117
S 1600 E
1429-2099 84105
7100-7198 84121
7200-7399 84121
S 1600 W
3901-4099 84123
S 160 W
4501-4597 84107
W 1600 N
800-898 84116
W 160 N
2200-2298 84116
W 1600 S 84115
S 1610 E
4000-4161 84124

S 1615 E
4110-4117 84124
4163-4199 84124
5600-6498 84121
S 1610 E
6401-6499 84121
S 1620 E
3301-3399 84106
S 1625 E
4100-4198 84124
4900-4999 84117
S 1620 E
5600-6598 84121
W 1625 S 84104
S 1640 E 84106
S 1645 E
4900-5099 84117
6500-6599 84121
S 1655 E 84121
S 1650 E
4100-4271 84124
4273-4299 84124
6400-6499 84121
S 1650 W 84123
S 1660 E 84121
S 1670 E
4800-4899 84117
6500-6599 84121
S 1670 W 84123
S 1680 E 84121
S 1690 E 84117
E 1700 S 84115
500-1600 84105
1700-2599 84108
S 1700 E
900-2040 84108
2100-2699 84106
6900-6998 84121
S 170 W 84115
W 1700 N 84116
W 1700 S
1-499 84115
600-698 84104
S 1715 E 84106
S 1710 E
4800-4899 84117
6500-7238 84121
S 1720 E 84117
S 1730 E 84106
W 1730 S 84104
S 1740 E 84117
W 1740 S 84104
S 1768 E 84112
W 1760 S 84104
N 1775 W 84116
N 1800 W 84116
S 1800 E
1101-1197 84108
1199-1999 84108
2001-2099 84108
2100-3099 84106
W 180 N 84116
S 1810 E 84106
W 1820 S 84104
S 1835 E 84121
S 1830 E
6000-6098 84121
W 1830 S 84115
S 1840 E 84121
S 1850 E
250-300 84112
7000-7099 84121
S 1860 E 84106
S 1865 E 84124
S 1865 E 84124
6400-6499 84121
S 1870 E 84117
S 1885 E 84106
N 1900 E 84112
S 1905 E 84106
800-2000 84108
2002-2098 84108
2100-3799 84106
5800-5999 84121
S 190 W 84107
W 1900 N 84116
W 1900 S 84104

S 1915 E 84106
S 1925 E 84124
S 1935 E
3000-3099 84106
7000-7099 84121
S 1945 E 84121
S 1940 E
3100-3375 84106
6400-6499 84121
N 1950 W 84116
3700-3899 84106
7200-7399 84121
W 1980 S 84104
W 1987 S 84104
S 20 E 84107
E 200 N 84103
E 200 S
1-23 84111
501-537 84102
N 200 W 84103
S 200 E
1-47 84111
10-72 84112
800-1955 84108
1300-3899 84115
2100-2399 84106
2600-2698 84109
2700-3899 84109
3900-6099 84107
3900-4180 84124
4182-4188 84124
S 200 W
100-272 84101
4500-4698 84107
W 200 N
2-98 84103
500-1000 84116
W 200 S
1-99 84101
230-230 84110
700-1449 84104
N & S 2030 84112
S 2035 E 84109
S 2045 E 84109
S 2040 E 84121
S 2050 E 84117
S 2060 E 84109
S 2065 E 84121
S 2070 E 84109
S 2075 E
3000-3099 84109
6000-6198 84121
S 2090 E 84121
E 2100 S 84106
E 2100 S 84115
E 2100 S 84115
1301-1699 84105
1302-1998 84106
2000-2899 84109
N 2100 W 84116
S 2100 E
800-1132 84108
2100-3299 84109
5000-5299 84117
5800-5820 84121
W 2100 S
2-18 84115
700-1258 84119
1760-1760 84125
1760-1760 84126
1760-1760 84127
1800-3598 84119
3600-4498 84120
S 2110 E
3501-3597 84109
5201-5399 84117
S 2124 E 84117
S 2125 E 84109
S 2120 E 84117
S 2135 E 84121
S 2130 E 84109
S 2140 E 84109
S 2145 E 84109
S 2155 E 84121
S 2160 E 84121
S 2175 E
3500-3699 84109

3900-3999 84124
S 2180 E 84121
W 2180 N 84116
E 2200 S 84115
N 2200 W 84116
S 220 E 84107
800-2099 84108
2100-2400 84109
2402-3598 84109
4500-4500 84117
6300-7399 84121
7401-7499 84121
S 2210 E 84109
N 2220 W 84116
S 2225 E
3000-3099 84109
S 2220 E
4500-4800 84117
S 2225 E
4601-4799 84117
S 2220 E
7100-7299 84121
S 2235 E 84109
S 2230 E 84121
S 2245 E 84109
S 2240 E 84121
E 2250 S 84115
3901-3999 84124
7100-7199 84121
N 2265 W 84116
S 2260 E 84121
W 2260 S 84115
N 2270 W 84116
S 2275 E 84121
S 2270 E
4500-4500 84117
7200-7299 84121
S 2280 E 84124
S 2290 E 84117
N 2300 W 84116
S 2300 E
800-2099 84108
2100-3899 84109
3900-4499 84124
4525-4561 84117
5900-5998 84121
6890-6890 84171
6892-7598 84121
W 2300 N 84116
N 2325 W 84116
S 2325 E 84121
N 2330 W 84116
S 2340 E 84121
S 2345 E 84121
S 235 E 84107
N 2360 W 84116
S 2365 E 84121
N 2370 W 84116
S 2375 E 84121
S 2380 E 84121
E 2400 S 84115
N 2400 W 84116
S 2400 E
1400-1599 84108
3500-3699 84109
S 2400 W 84116
W 240 N 84116
W 2400 S 84115
S 2410 E 84109
S 2425 E 84121
S 2430 E 84121
S 2440 E 84109
S 2445 E
3500-3699 84109
6600-6799 84121
S 2455 E 84109
S 2475 E
2700-2899 84109
6401-6497 84121
S 2475 W 84104
S 2485 E 84121
S 2490 E 84124
S 2500 E
1700-2099 84108
2300-3600 84109
250 E & W 84107
S 2510 E 84121

S 2520 E
2700-3099 84109
6400-6599 84121
S 2540 E 84109
S 2555 E 84117
S 2600 E
1700-2099 84108
3001-3047 84109
6400-6599 84121
W 260 N 84116
S 2650 W 84104
W 2670 N 84116
S 2680 E 84121
E 2700 S 84115
E 2700 S 84115
501-697 84106
2001-2049 84109
S 270 E 84107
2701-2757 84109
3900-4499 84124
7000-7699 84121
W 2700 S 84115
S 2710 E 84121
W 2720 S 84115
S 2740 E
3700-3899 84109
7000-7299 84121
S 2750 E 84109
S 275 E
3300-3399 84115
S 275 W 84107
S 2760 E 84117
S 2760 W 84104
S 2770 E
3300-3350 84109
4551-4600 84117
S 2780 E
3701-3797 84109
7000-7399 84121
S 2790 E 84109
S 2800 E 84109
W 280 N 84116
E 2815 S 84109
E 2825 S 84106
S 2820 E 84124
S 2825 E
7000-7320 84121
S 2835 E 84124
E & S 2850 S & E 84109
W 2855 S 84115
E 2860 S 84109
S 2870 E
2801-2899 84109
4800-5199 84117
7000-7399 84121
E 2880 S 84109
S 2880 E 84109
W 2880 S 84115
S 2890 E 84109
W 2890 S 84115
E 2900 S 84109
S 2900 E
2962-2998 84109
3000-3899 84109
3900-4499 84124
5400-5499 84117
S 2910 E 84109
S 2930 E 84121
E & S 2940 S & E 84109
S 2955 E 84121
S 2950 E
4300-4344 84124
W 2950 S 84115
E 2965 S 84109
E 2960 S 84109
E 2980 S 84109
S 2985 E 84121
S 2980 E
7200-7321 84121
E 2990 S 84106
S 2995 E 84117
S 2990 E
4300-4499 84124
E 300 N 84103
E 300 S
400-499 84111
500-1300 84102

1301-1897 84106
1899-1999 84106
2000-2799 84109
N 300 W
53-95 84101
100-799 84103
S 300 E
1-1299 84111
1300-3899 84115
3900-6301 84107
4100-4198 84124
6300-6398 84121
6400-7099 84121
S 300 W
100-1299 84101
1321-1367 84115
3900-6200 84107
W 300 N
2-28 84103
500-1399 84116
W 3000 S
300-399 84115
700-6099 84104
E 3015 S 84106
E 3010 S
1300-1699 84106
S 3010 E 84109
E 3020 S 84109
E 3035 S 84109
S 3030 E 84124
S 3035 E
4300-4499 84124
S 3030 E
7300-7399 84121
W 3030 S 84115
E 3045 S 84115
1400-1699 84106
S 3040 E 84109
S 3050 E 84121
W 3050 S 84115
E 3060 S 84106
E 3065 S
500-699 84106
2001-2099 84109
S 3065 E 84124
E 3070 S 84109
S 3075 E
3100-3299 84109
3900-4099 84124
E 3085 S
500-599 84106
1800-1999 84106
S 3080 E
4212-4248 84124
7100-7299 84121
S 3085 E
7300-7399 84121
E 3100 S 84109
S 3100 E
3631-3697 84109
3699-3841 84109
3843-3899 84109
4141-4299 84124
E 3115 S 84106
E 3110 S 84109
E 3120 S 84109
S 3125 E 84109
S 3120 E
3900-3999 84124
E 3135 S 84109
S 3130 E 84109
W 3130 N 84116
S 3145 E 84109
E 3150 S 84106
E 3155 S 84106
S 3165 E 84124
E 3170 S
1700-1899 84106
E & S 3175 S & E 84109
S 3170 E 84109
E 3185 S 84115
2000-2800 84109
E 3195 S 84106
E 3205 S
1300-1399 84106
2000-2299 84109
N 3200 W 84116

S 320 E 84107
S 3200 E
3900-3900 84124
S 3200 W 84104
E 3215 S 84109
1700-1798 84106
1800-1899 84106
2545-2551 84109
2553-2699 84109
S 3210 E 84124
E 3220 S 84109
E 3225 S 84109
S 3230 W 84104
S 3275 E 84109
E 3300 S 84115
600-1999 84106
2000-3241 84109
3243-3299 84109
S 3305 E 84124
3300-3399 84109
W 3300 N 84116
W 3300 S 84115
S 3320 E 84124
E 3335 S 84115
E 3335 S 84115
2000-2099 84109
E 3345 S
1300-1370 84106
3000-3098 84109
S 3340 E
3000-3199 84109
4001-4097 84124
E 3350 S 84115
E 3355 S 84106
E 3350 S
1400-1799 84106
S 335 E 84115
W 3350 S 84115
E 3365 S 84109
E 3360 S
300-499 84115
S 3360 E 84109
E 3375 S
800-824 84106
E 3370 S
901-999 84106
2201-2891 84109
S 3375 E 84121
E 3385 S 84106
E 3380 S
1901-1999 84106
2100-2299 84109
S 3380 E 84109
E 3390 S 84106
E 3395 S
2300-2399 84109
S 3395 E 84121
E 3400 S 84115
2700-2899 84109
S 340 E 84107
W 3400 S 84115
S 3435 E 84109
W 3440 S 84115
S 345 E 84107
W 3450 S 84115
S 3480 W 84104
S 3500 E 84121
S 350 W 84123
5900-6199 84107
E 3510 S 84109
S 3530 E 84109
E 3545 S 84106
S 3545 E 84121
W 3560 S 84115
S 3570 E 84109
E 3585 S 84106
E 3580 S 84106
E 3600 S
1800-1899 84106
1901-1999 84106
2700-2899 84109
S 360 E 84115
S 3600 W
800-2000 84104
S 360 W
4500-4598 84123
W 3600 S 84115

E 3610 S 84106
S 3610 E 84109
W 3615 S 84115
E 3625 S 84106
W 3620 S 84115
E 3635 S 84106
E & S 3650 S & E 84109
E 3665 S 84106
E 3670 S 84106
E 3685 S 84106
E 3680 S
700-799 84106
W 3680 S 84115
E 3690 S 84106
E 3700 S 84115
700-799 84106
2300-2399 84109
N 3700 W
300-399 84122
400-499 84116
S 370 E 84107
E 3715 S 84109
E 3710 S 84106
E 3720 S
700-799 84106
2400-2499 84109
E 3735 S 84109
E 3730 S
701-1297 84106
S 3730 W 84104
E 3745 S 84106
E 3740 S
1000-1099 84106
W 3740 S 84115
E 3750 S 84115
2300-2499 84109
S 3760 W 84104
W 3765 S 84115
E 3770 S 84106
E 3780 S
1800-1999 84106
2000-2199 84109
E 3790 S 84106
E 3805 S 84106
1200-1299 84106
3580-3698 84109
N 3800 W 84116
380 E & W 84107
S 3800 W 84104
W 3815 S 84123
E 3825 S 84106
E 3820 S
3600-3699 84109
W 3820 S 84115
E 3835 S 84109
S 3850 W 84104
E 3900 S
1-97 84107
99-899 84107
900-3399 84124
S 390 E 84107
W 3900 S
1-200 84107
202-298 84107
400-498 84123
500-699 84123
701-1141 84123
E 3925 S 84124
E 3935 S 84124
E 3930 S
1300-1399 84124
N 3930 W 84116
E 3945 S 84107
W 3940 S 84123
E 3955 S 84107
600-700 84107
1000-1099 84124
N 3950 W 84116
E 3960 S 84124
E 3975 S 84107
E 3970 S
501-597 84107
1500-2199 84124
E 3980 S 84124
E 3982 S 84107
E 3990 S
500-899 84107

1401-1449 84124
E 400 S 84111
E 400 S 84111
E 400 S 84111
500-1340 84102
E 4000 S
1300-2299 84124
N 400 W
1-55 84101
101-297 84103
N 4000 W
1200-1299 84116
S 400 E
2-38 84111
1300-3899 84115
3900-6399 84107
S 400 W
2-204 84101
1300-1498 84115
4601-4699 84123
6500-6699 84107
W 400 N
1-27 84103
500-1999 84116
W 400 S
50-114 84101
701-845 84104
W 4000 S
800-899 84123
E 4010 S 84107
S 4015 W
4722-4722 84118
5495-5499 84129
E 4020 S
300-399 84107
E 4025 S
600-699 84107
1000-1099 84124
E 4020 S
1100-1199 84124
W 4020 S 84123
E 4030 S 84107
N 4030 W 84116
E 4045 S 84124
S 404 E 84107
S 4040 W 84118
E 4055 S
500-699 84107
E 4050 S
510-598 84107
600-699 84104
S 4055 W
4776-5899 84118
E 4065 S
600-699 84107
1300-1399 84124
S 4060 W 84118
W 4060 S 84123
E 4075 S 84107
700-800 84107
1500-1599 84124
W 4070 S 84123
E 4085 S 84124
501-599 84107
1400-1461 84124
W 4080 S 84123
E 4090 S
300-400 84107
E 4095 S
1500-1599 84124
3300-3399 84124
S 4095 W
4800-4999 84118
5800-5999 84118
E 4100 S 84107
W 4100 S 84123
E 4110 S 84107
E 4115 S 84107
E 4116 S 84107
E 4119 S 84107
E 4125 S 84107
E 4129 S 84107
E 4128 S 84107
E 4120 S
476-488 84107
S 4120 W 84118

4130 S
1200-1299 84124
4135 S
2700-2899 84124
4130 W
1700-1999 84104
4135 W
4800-4999 84118
4149 S 84107
4145 S 84124
4140 S
301-377 84107
4140 W 84118
4150 S 84124
4150 W 84104
4165 S 84124
4160 S 84124
4170 S
800-862 84107
864-899 84107
1300-1399 84124
4170 W 84118
4170 S 84123
4181 S 84107
4180 W 84118
4180 S 84123
4190 S 84124
4190 W 84104
4200 S
400-698 84107
1300-1499 84124
420 W 84123
4200 S 84123
4215 S 84124
4220 W 84118
4230 S 84124
4240 W 84118
4255 S 84107
4250 S
3315-3350 84124
4250 W 84104
4250 S 84107
4260 W 84118
4270 S 84124
4270 W 84118
4270 S 84123
4280 S 84107
4285 S 84107
4302 S 84107
430 E 84107
4300 W 84118
4300 S 84123
4315 S 84107
4310 W 84118
4325 S 84124
4325 W 84116
4320 W 84118
4330 S 84123
4345 S 84124
4340 S
2400-2500 84124
4340 W 84118
4340 S 84107
& W 4350 84107
4365 S 84123
4370 S 84107
4370 W 84104
4370 S 84123
4380 S 84124
4385 W 84118
4380 W
4700-4999 84118
4390 S 84124
4390 W 84118
440 E
2200-3399 84115
6200-6399 84107
4400 W
801-1097 84104
3490-3490 84170
4400 S 84107
4425 S 84124
4420 S
1100-1199 84124
4420 W 84118
4430 S 84124

S 4430 W 84118
S 4450 W 84104
W 4450 S 84107
E 4460 S 84107
S 4460 W 84118
S 4475 W 84118
W 4470 S 84123
S 4480 W 84118
S 4490 W 84104
W 4490 S 84107
E 4500 S
2-8 84107
900-2411 84117
E 4505 S
2900-3099 84117
S 450 E 84107
1700-1798 84115
5600-5698 84118
W 4500 S
1-197 84107
400-448 84123
W 4505 S
1100-1699 84123
E 4510 S 84117
S 4520 W 84118
E 4530 S 84117
S 4540 W 84118
E 4550 S 84117
E 4555 S
430-499 84107
900-1099 84117
S 455 E 84115
E 4565 S 84107
E 4580 S 84117
S 4580 W 84118
S 4590 W 84118
E 4600 S 84107
460 E & W 84115
E 4620 S
1600-1799 84117
E 4625 S
1800-1893 84117
S 4620 W
4700-5415 84118
S 4625 W
6000-6199 84118
E 4630 S 84107
W 4640 S 84107
E 4650 S 84117
S 465 E 84107
S 4650 W 84104
W 4650 S 84107
E 4660 S 84107
S 4660 W 84118
E 4675 S 84117
E 4680 S 84107
S 4680 W 84118
E 4705 S 84117
S 4700 W 84104
W 4700 S
1201-1299 84123
4800-4998 84118
5000-5999 84118
6001-6399 84118
W 4715 S 84118
S 4720 W 84118
W 4745 S 84118
E 4750 S 84117
W 4775 S 84118
S & W 4780 W & S 84118
E 4800 S 84107
S 480 E 84115
S 4800 W
1000-1999 84104
4700-4798 84118
W 4805 S 84118
3-97 84107
99-299 84107
301-349 84107
351-379 84123
381-1699 84123
S & W 4820 W & S 84118
W 4835 S 84118
S 4840 W 84118
E 4850 S 84117
300-398 84123
4900-4998 84118

S 4860 W 84118
W 4865 S 84118
W 4860 S
100-299 84107
S 4880 W 84118
E 4895 S 84117
W 4890 S 84123
W 4895 S
4400-4899 84118
E 4900 S 84107
S 490 E 84107
S 4900 W 84118
W 4900 S 84118
W 4915 S 84123
W 4925 S 84118
W 4920 S 84123
W 4935 S 84118
S 4940 W 84118
S 4950 W 84118
W 4955 S 84118
W 4950 S
1400-1599 84123
W 4960 S 84118
S 4980 W 84118
W 4985 S 84118
W 4980 S
1400-1699 84123
W 4990 S 84118
S 50 W 84107
W 50 N 84101
E 500 N 84103
E 500 S
150-499 84111
500-548 84102
E 5000 S
1000-1099 84117
N 500 W 84116
S 500 E
2-98 84102
900-1298 84105
2101-2197 84106
3900-4400 84107
S 500 W
1-1100 84101
1300-3821 84115
3900-4499 84123
W 500 N
2-98 84103
500-1899 84116
W 500 S
100-499 84101
800-3700 84104
W 5000 S
1101-1247 84123
E 5014 S 84117
W 5010 S 84118
W 5015 S 84118
S 5020 W 84118
S 5030 W 84118
W 5035 S 84118
W 5055 S 84118
W 5050 S 84123
4000-4199 84118
E 5065 S 84107
S 5075 W 84118
S 5070 W 84104
W 5085 S 84118
S 510 E 84107
S 5100 W
1-100 84104
5900-6099 84118
W 510 N 84116
W 5100 S 84118
W 5115 S 84118
S 5120 W 84118
W 5135 S 84118
E 5140 S 84117
E 5150 S 84117
W 5150 S 84118
S 5160 W 84118
W 5175 S 84118
S 5180 W 84118
S 5185 W 84118
E 5190 S 84117
W 5195 S 84118
E 5205 S 84117

S 520 E 84107
S 5200 W
200-2099 84104
4850-5098 84118
S 520 W
6400-6599 84123
W 5200 S 84118
W 5215 S 84118
S 5220 W 84118
E 5235 S 84117
E 5245 S 84117
S & W 5240 W & S 84118
S 525 E 84107
W 5255 S 84118
E 5290 S 84117
W 5295 S 84118
E 5300 S 84107
S 530 E 84107
S 5300 W
700-799 84104
S 530 W
3700-3899 84115
4800-4899 84118
W 5300 S
1-199 84107
350-398 84123
400-700 84123
702-798 84123
E 5315 S 84117
S 5325 W 84118
W 5320 S 84123
W 5325 S
100-151 84107
W 5320 S
4900-5199 84118
W 5335 S 84118
E 5340 S 84117
W 5345 S 84118
S 5350 W 84104
E 5360 S 84117
W 5360 S 84118
W 5375 S 84118
E 5400 S 84107
N 540 W 84116
S 540 E 84106
S 540 W 84115
W 5400 S
200-399 84107
1500-1599 84123
4800-4958 84118
4960-8299 84118
S & W 5415 W & S 84118
S 5420 W 84118
S 5425 W 84118
E 5440 S 84117
W 5440 S 84118
S 545 E 84106
S 5450 W 84118
E 5460 S 84107
W 5465 S 84123
W 5460 S
4300-4580 84118
S 5475 W 84118
W 5485 S 84118
E 5495 S 84117
S 5495 W 84118
S 550 E 84107
S 5500 W 84104
W 5505 S 84118
W 5500 S
4000-4581 84118
W 5510 S 84123
W 5540 S 84118
E 5550 S 84117
S 555 W 84123
W 5550 S 84123
E 5560 S 84107
W 5566 S 84123
S 5575 W 84118
W 5570 S 84118
W 5580 S 84118
E 5600 S
100-574 84107
576-898 84107
900-1999 84121
N 5600 W 84116

S 560 E 84107
S 5600 W
700-799 84104
4700-5898 84118
W 5615 S 84118
S 5625 W 84118
E 5640 S 84107
E 5645 S 84121
E 5650 S 84121
S 565 E 84107
S 565 W 84115
W 5655 S 84118
E 5660 S 84121
S 5665 W 84118
E 5685 S 84121
E 5690 S 84121
E 5700 S 84121
S 570 E 84107
S 5700 W 84104
W 5700 S 84118
E 5720 S 84107
E 5730 S 84121
W 5735 S 84123
E 5740 S 84121
W 5740 S 84118
E 5750 S 84121
S 575 E 84107
S 575 W 84115
W 5750 S
1-199 84107
501-597 84123
E 5770 S 84107
W 5770 S
1400-1448 84123
1450-1460 84123
1462-1498 84123
5700-5799 84118
W 5785 S 84107
W 5780 S 84118
S 580 E
3600-3799 84106
5301-5399 84107
W 5818 S 84107
W 5820 S 84118
E 5840 S 84121
W 5845 S 84123
W 5855 S 84118
W 5850 S 84123
W 5865 S 84118
E & W 5878 84107
W 5885 S 84107
E 5900 S 84107
S 590 E 84107
S 590 W 84123
W 5905 S 84118
1-7 84107
9-399 84107
419-481 84123
483-699 84123
4000-4199 84118
W 5910 S 84123
W 5925 S 84123
E 5935 S 84121
E 5930 S
1512-1512 84121
W 5930 S 84118
W 5965 S 84107
W 5960 S
301-399 84107
5601-5663 84118
E 5975 S 84121
E 5980 S 84107
E 5985 S 84121
W 5987 S 84123
E 600 S
2-144 84111
146-499 84111
500-1399 84102
N 600 W 84116
S 600 E
1-872 84102
1300-2099 84105
2100-3299 84106
4200-5199 84107
S 600 W
1-325 84101
2200-2398 84115

6000-6099 84123
W 600 N
100-122 84103
501-797 84116
W 6000 S 84107
100-550 84101
600-1600 84104
E 6015 S 84121
W 6015 S 84118
W 6025 S 84107
W 6020 S
1-199 84107
1300-1475 84123
E 6030 S 84121
E 6045 S 84121
E 6050 S 84121
S & W 6055 W & S 84118
E 6060 S 84121
W 6060 S 84118
E 6070 S 84121
S 6070 W 84118
W 6090 S 84118
W 6095 S 84118
E & W 6100 84107
S 610 E 84106
S 6105 W 84118
S 610 W
5900-5999 84123
W 6110 S
300-498 84107
4800-4898 84118
W 6120 S 84118
E 6135 S 84121
W 6130 S 84118
W 6140 S 84123
E 6150 S 84107
S 615 E 84107
E 6165 S
1000-1099 84121
E 6160 S
1001-1099 84121
300-399 84107
1600-1699 84123
W 6165 S
4300-4599 84118
E 6170 S 84107
E 6185 S 84121
W 6190 S 84123
E 6200 S 84121
S 620 E 84107
W 6200 S 84118
E 6210 S 84121
E 6215 S
300-319 84107
1000-1099 84121
E 6220 S 84107
E 6230 S 84107
W 6235 S 84123
E 6240 S 84107
S 625 E 84107
E 6270 S 84107
E 6280 S 84107
E 6295 S 84107
E 6290 S 84121
S 630 W 84123
W 6300 S 84123
E 6310 S 84107
E 6325 S 84107
E 6320 S 84121
E 6340 S 84107
S 635 E 84107
E 6360 S 84107
E 6380 S 84121
E 6385 S 84121
E 6400 S 84121
S 640 W 84123
E 6410 S 84107
W 6415 S 84123
E 6425 S 84121
E 6430 S 84121
E 6450 S 84121
S 645 E
3600-3799 84106
4301-4399 84107
E 6470 S 84121
E 6485 S 84121

E 6480 S
1600-1698 84121
W 6480 S 84107
E 6505 S 84121
S 650 E 84107
S 650 W 84123
W 650 N 84116
W 6500 S 84107
E 6520 S 84121
E 6525 S 84121
E 6535 S 84121
E 6550 S 84121
W 6570 S
1-99 84107
500-699 84123
E 6595 S 84121
E 6600 S 84121
S 660 E 84107
W 6600 S 84123
E 6630 S 84121
W 6645 S 84123
W 6640 S 84123
S 665 W 84123
E 6660 S 84121
E 6670 S 84121
E 6675 S
2100-2299 84121
W 6675 S 84123
W 6690 S 84123
S 670 E 84107
S 670 W 84123
E 6710 S 84121
E 6720 S 84121
S 675 E 84107
E 6765 S 84121
E 6780 S 84121
W 6830 S 84107
E 6850 S 84121
S 685 E 84107
E 6895 S 84121
S 70 W 84107
E 700 N 84103
E 7000 S 84121
1-499 84111
500-1399 84102
N 700 W 84116
S 700 E
1-899 84102
901-1397 84105
2100-3899 84106
3900-4600 84107
S 700 W
100-398 84104
3500-3599 84115
3900-6699 84123
W 700 N
200-399 84103
701-1597 84116
W 700 S
1-599 84101
600-6199 84104
E 7020 S 84121
E 7050 S 84121
E 7070 S 84121
E 7075 S 84121
E 7080 S 84121
E 7090 S 84121
E 7105 S 84121
E 7115 S 84121
E 7110 S 84121
E 7120 S 84121
E 7130 S 84121
E 7145 S 84121
E 7150 S 84121
S 715 E 84106
E 7160 S 84121
E 7180 S 84121
E 7200 S 84121
E 7205 S 84121
E 7230 S 84121
E 7240 S 84121
S 725 E 84107
E 7260 S 84121
S 730 E 84107
E 7325 S 84121
E 7320 S 84121

E 7335 S 84121
E 7350 S 84121
E 7375 S 84121
E 7380 S 84121
S 740 E 84106
E 7480 S 84121
E 7495 S 84121
S 75 W 84107
S 750 E 84106
S 750 W 84123
W 750 N 84116
E 7590 S 84121
S 760 E 84107
E 7635 S 84121
E 7645 S 84121
E 7650 S 84121
S 765 S 84102
S 765 W 84104
E 7745 S 84121
S 775 E 84106
E 7800 S 84121
S 780 W 84123
S 785 E 84107
S 790 W 84123
E 800 S 84111
E 800 S 84111
500-1199 84102
N 800 W 84116
S 800 E
1-899 84102
900-2099 84105
2100-2130 84106
4001-4097 84107
S 800 W
1-1300 84104
5201-5597 84123
W 800 N
300-375 84103
900-1999 84116
W 800 S
1-599 84101
600-3799 84104
S 805 E
3500-3599 84106
3900-3999 84107
S 810 E 84106
S 820 E 84107
S 825 E 84106
E 8350 S 84121
S 840 E 84107
S 8400 W 84118
S 840 W
4601-6397 84123
S 845 E 84107
E 8505 S 84121
S 850 E 84107
W 850 S 84104
S 855 E 84107
S 860 E
3500-3699 84106
5100-5299 84107
S 870 W 84104
E 8740 S 84121
S 875 E 84107
S 890 W 84123
E 900 S 84111
501-697 84105
699-1699 84105
1700-2440 84108
2442-2450 84108
N 900 W 84116
1-880 84102
882-898 84102
900-2000 84105
2002-2098 84105
2100-3899 84106
3900-4499 84124
4500-5599 84117
5600-6600 84121
6602-6698 84121
S 900 W 84104
300-499 84103
900-1999 84116
1-440 84101
442-598 84101
600-1098 84104
1100-3699 84104
S 920 E 84121
W 920 N 84116
S 925 E 84117
S 935 E 84117
S 938 E 84117
S 940 W 84123
S 945 E 84106
S 95 W 84107
S 950 E 84117
S 960 E 84117
S 975 E 84117
S 980 E 84106
S 990 W 84123

SANDY UT

General Delivery 84070

POST OFFICE BOXES MAIN OFFICE STATIONS AND BRANCHES

Box No.s
1 - 7811 84091
8000 - 8000 84092
9998 - 9998 84091
708001 - 709796 84070
900001 - 909998 84090
929000 - 929998 84092

HIGHWAY CONTRACTS

62 84092

NAMED STREETS

E Abbedale Ln 84092
S Abbey Ridge Ln 84092
E & S Abbotts Ford Ct & Ln 84070
E & S Acorn Ln 84093
E Addington Cir 84094
E Aerie Heights Cv 84092
E Afton Cir 84070
E & S Akers Way 84094
E Alan Cir 84070
S & E Albion Cir & Dr 84092
Albion Village Way 84070
E & S Albury Rd 84092
E Alexander Ct 84094
E Alla Panna Way 84093
S Allen St 84070
S Allison Cir 84070
E Aloha Ln 84070
S Alondra Way 84094
S Alpine Fir Cv 84070
E & S Alpine Valley Cir 84092
E Alta Approach 84092
E & S Alta Canyon Cir & Dr 84093
E & S Alta Cove Cir & Dr 84093
E & S Alta Heights Dr 84094
S & E Alta Hills Cir & Dr 84093
S Alta Mesa Cir 84094
E & S Alta Ridge Cir 84092
S & W Alta View Cir, Ct & Way 84070
Alta Wood Ln 84092
E & S Altair Cir & Dr 84093
E & S Altamont Cir & Dr 84092
E Altamont Lake Ln 84094
E Altara Cir 84094
E Altara Hills Dr 84094
S Altavilla Dr 84092
E Altura Cir 84070
S Alvey Ln 84093
E Amalfi Way 84093
S Amaryllis Dr 84094
S Amber Ln 84094
S Amberley Ln 84094
E Amberwick Ln 84093
E Andermatt Cir 84093
S Andorra Ln 84093
E Andover Ct 84094
E & S Angel Ct & St 84070
E Annabelle Ln 84094
E & S Annalyn Cir & Dr 84070
Antimony Cir & Ln 84094
Aplomado Cir & Dr 84092
E Apollo Way 84070
S Apple Ct 84070
Apple Hill Cir 84092
E Apple Hollow Cv 84092
E Apple Tree Dr 84070
E Arborfield Cir 84092
S Ardonna Way 84070
E Arlen Way 84093
E Arlo Ave 84070
E Arosa Cir 84093
S Arrington Pl 84092
E & S Ascot Cir & Pkwy 84092
Ashley Ave & Cir 84093
S Ashley Downs Ct 84093
S Ashley Hills Cir 84092
S Ashley Meadows Cir 84092
E & S Ashley Mesa Ln 84092
S Ashley Park Dr 84092
E & S Ashley Ridge Rd 84092
E Ashley Valley Ln 84092
E Ashridge Cir 84093
E & S Aspen Way 84093
S & E Aspen Hills Cir, Dr & Pl 84092
S Aspen Ridge Rd 84094
E Aspen View Ct 84092
E Aspenwood Way 84092
S Aster Ln 84094
S & W Auto Mall Dr 84070
E Autumn Field Dr 84094
E & S Autumn Hill Cir & Dr 84094
S & E Autumn Ridge Cv & Dr 84092
E & S Avila Ct & Dr 84094
S Azul Way 84093
E & S Bainbridge Rd 84092
Bannor Hill Cir & Rd 84092
E Barcelona Dr 84093
Barium Ln & St 84094
E & S Barnwood Way 84094
S Baronay Cir 84093
S & E Barrett Park Cir & Dr 84092
S Basin St 84070
E & S Bavarian Ct 84093
S Bay Meadow Cir 84092
S Bay Meadows Dr 84092
E & S Beagle Dr 84092
E Bear Canyon Rd 84094
S Beaumont Dr 84093
S Bedrock Ln 84092
E Beetdigger Blvd 84070
S Bell Canyon Cir 84092
E Bell Canyon Dr 84094
E Bell Canyon Rd 84092
S Bell Canyon Rd 84092
E Bell Castle Cir 84094
E & S Bell Oaks Cir & Dr 84092
S Bell Ridge Dr 84094
E Bell View Cir 84094
E Belle Glenn Cir 84070
S Bellingham Dr 84070
Belmont Canal Rd 84070
E Belsaw Cir 84094
E & S Belton Cir & Ln 84093
E & S Benson Way 84070
Bentbrook Ln 84092
S Bentham Ave 84093
S Bently Cir 84093
Bentwood Ln 84092
E Bernay Cir 84094
S Berrywood Ct 84070
S Bettina Ln 84093
E & S Big Pine Cir & Dr 84094
E Big Rock Ln 84093
E & S Big Sky Dr 84070
S Big Willow Ct 84092
Birchtree Ln 84092
S Birchwood Way 84092
E & S Black Forest Dr 84094
E Black Horn Pl 84092
E Blithfield Cir 84092
E & S Blossom Dr 84092
S Blossom Tree Ln 84070
E Blossomwood Cir 84093
S Blue Roan Ln 84092
E Blueberry Hl 84093
S Bluff View Dr 84092
E & S Bluffside Cir & Dr 84092
E & S Bob Ln 84092
E & S Bohm Cir & Pl 84094
S & E Boise Cir & St 84070
S Bonnet Dr 84093
S Bordeaux Way 84093
E & S Borg Ct & Dr 84092
E & S Bowden St 84070
E & S Boysenberry Cir & Dr 84093
E Bradley Way 84070
Brady Creek Cir, Ct & Dr 84093
S & E Brandon Park Dr, Pl, Ter & Way 84092
S Brandy Creek Dr 84070
S Brandy Spring Ln 84070
E Brent Cir 84070
S Brentmar Cir 84070
S Brian Head Cir 84093
E & S Briar Glen Dr & Ln 84092
E Bridger Blvd 84093
S Brighton View Dr 84070
E & S Brisbane Dr 84094
E & S Broadview Ct & Way 84092
E & S Broken Ridge Ct & Dr 84094
E Bronze Ln 84094
E Brook Ln 84092
S Brookbend Ln 84093
E & S Brookglen Dr 84092
E & S Brookmill Ln 84092
S Bryce Dr 84070
E Buchnell Dr 84094
S & E Buckingham Ct & Way 84093
Budding Cir & Dr 84092
E & S Buddlea Dr 84094
S Buena Vista Dr 84094
S Bur Oak Ln 84092
S Burgundy St 84070
E & S Buttercup Dr 84092
S & E Buttonwood Cir & Dr 84092
E Bypass Rd 84092
S Caballero Dr 84093
E Calbourne Ln 84070
E & S Calla Lily Way 84092
E Calnette Dr 84070
S Camberley Cir 84092
S Cambridge Cir 84070
E Cameley Cir 84093
E & S Cameo Way 84093
E & S Cameron Pl 84092
E Cana Cir 84094
E & S Canberra Dr 84094
E & S Candle Spruce Cv 84092
E & S Candle Tree Cv & Ln 84092
E & S Candlewood Cir, Ct & Dr 84092
E & S Canterwood Cir & Ln 84093
S & E Canton Ct & Ln 84092
Canyon Gate Cir & Rd 84093
E & S Canyon Oak Cir 84092
E Canyon View Pl 84092
E & S Capella Way 84093
E & S Carmel Pt 84093
S Carmen Ct 84070
E & S Carnation Dr 84094
E & S Carriage Chase Ln 84092
S Carriagehouse Ln 84092
S Carrington Ct 84092
S Carrington St 84094
Cascade Pl & St 84070
E & S Cascade Park Dr 84070
S & E Casper Pl & Rd 84092
E & S Cassowary Cir & Dr 84092
E Castle Dale Cir 84094
S Castle Ridge Dr 84092
E Castle Rock Rd 84094
E Catamount Ridge Way 84092
E Cavendish Cir 84093
E & S Cedar Crest Dr 84092
S & E Cedar Ridge Cir & Rd 84094
Cedar Terrace Cir & Dr 84094
S & E Cedar View Cir & Dr 84094
E Cedro Cir 84093
S Centennial Pkwy 84070
S Center St 84070
E Center Fork Cir 84094
S Cervantes Cir 84092
S Cessna Cir 84093
S Chablis Cir 84093
Chalet Cir & Rd 84093
E & S Chapada Cir & Way 84094
E Chapel Oaks Cir 84093
E & S Chariot Cir & Dr 84094
Charleston Cir & St 84094
E Charros Rd 84092
E Charter Oaks Cir 84093
S & W Chartres Ave 84070
E & S Chateau Ridge Way 84092
S Chatsworth Ct 84093
S Chelsea Cir 84070
S Cherbourg Pl 84093
S Cherry Creek Dr 84094
S Cherry Hill Dr 84094
S & E Cherry Knoll Cir & Dr 84094
E Cherry Plum Ct 84070
Cherrywoods Ln 84092
S & E Cheshire Cir & Dr 84093
E Chestnut Ridge Dr 84070
S Chickadee Cir 84093
S Chickasaw Ln 84070
S Chinaberry Cir 84092
S Christopher Cir 84092
E Churchill Downs Dr 84092
S Chylene Dr 84092
E & S Cima Dr 84093
S Cindy Cir 84092
S Cinnamon Ridge Rd 84094
Circle Oaks 84092
S Citori Dr 84070
W Civic Center Dr 84070
S Clairmont Cir 84070
E & S Clear Creek Dr 84070
S Clearview Dr 84070
S Cliff Lodge Dr 84092
E & S Cliff Side Ct & Dr 84094
E Cliff Swallow Dr 84093
S Clifford Cir 84092
E Clover Ridge Dr 84070
S & W Club Oaks Dr 84070
E Coal Creek Cir 84094
S & E Cobalt Cir & Ln 84094
S & E Cobble Canyon Cir & Ln 84093
E Cobble Stream Cir 84093
S Cobblecrest Ln 84093
E & S Cobblemoor Ln 84093
E & S Cobblestone Way 84093
E Cobblestone Village Cir 84092
Cobblewood Cv 84092
E & S Colchester Ct & Dr 84092
S Cold Water Dr 84094
E & S Colemere St 84092
S Colene Dr 84094
S & E Colima Cir & Dr 84094
Columbine Cir & Way 84094
E Commotion Dr 84093
S Copper Creek Cir 84093
E Coppercreek Rd 84093
S Copplestone Cir 84092
E Corby Cir 84092
E & S Cordova Cir & Way 84093
S Corinth Rd 84070
S Cornell Dr 84094
E Cornwall Ct 84092
E Corrie Cir 84070
E Corrie Ann Cir 84093
S Cortina Pl 84092
E Cotswold Cir 84093
W Cottage Ave 84070
S & E Cottonwood Hills Cir, Ct & Dr 84094
S Country Glen Cir 84093
E Country Terrace Cir 84092
E & S Countrywood Ct & Dr 84092
S Courage Dr 84070
Courtside Ln 84092
E Covington Ct 84094
S Cranberry Cir 84093
S Cravalan Cir 84093
W Crawford Pl 84070
S Creative Pl 84093
S & E Creek Cir, Rd & Way 84093
W Creek Bluff Cv 84070
S Creek Hollow Cv 84093
E & S Creek Villas Ln 84093
S Creponette Dr 84093
E & S Crescent Bend Dr 84070
S Crescent Elm Cv 84070
S Crescent Glen Cir 84070
S Crescent Oak Way 84070
S & E Crescent Park Cir & Way 84070
E Crescent Pine Ln 84070
Crescent View Cir & Dr 84092
E & S Crescent Vista Ln 84070
E & S Crescentwood Dr 84070
E Crest Cir 84093
S Crest Point Cir 84093
S Crestridge Cir 84094
S Crestridge Dr 84070
E Crestridge Rd 84094
E & S Crocus Cir & St 84094
Crosshill Ln 84092
S & E Crosswood Cir & Ln 84092
S Cypress Pine Cv 84070
E Daisy St 84094
S Daisy Ridge Dr 84070
S Dana Cir 84070
E Dancehall Ln 84092
E & S Danish Rd 84093
E & S Danish Oaks Ct & Dr 84093
E Danish Springs Cv 84093
S Dante Rd 84092
E Danville Dr 84092
E & S Darin Cir & Dr 84070
E & S David Cir, Ct & St 84070
E Dawn Dr 84070
Dawn Hill Dr 84092
Daybreak Cir & Dr 84093
E & S Debbie Cir 84070
E Debeers Dr 84093
S Deborah Ann Ct 84070
S Dedication Dr 84070
S Deer Brook Cir 84092
E & S Deer Hollow Cir & Dr 84092
E Deer Ridge Pl 84092
S Deer Run Pl 84092
E Delphinium Way 84094
S Despain Way 84093
E Diamond Way 84094
E Diana Hills Way 84094
E & S Dimple Dell Cir, Dr, Ln & Rd 84092
S Dimple View Ln 84092
Dolomite Ln & Way 84094
E Donna Cir 84070
E Dorothy Cir 84070
S Double Down Ct 84093
S Douglas Fir Cv 84094
E & S Dry Creek Rd 84094
E & S Dry Gulch Cir & Rd 84094
E & S Drystone Ave, Cir & Rd 84094
S Dunston Ave 84093
E Dupler Rd 84094
Durant Ave 84070
E & S Durban Rd 84093
W Durdham Ln 84070
E Durham St 84070
E Dusty Creek Ave 84094
Dusty Rock Cir & Pl 84094
S & E Eagle Bend Cir & Rd 84094
E & S Eagle Cliff Ct & Way 84092
E Eagle Crest Cir 84092
E & S Eagle Ridge Cir & Dr 84094
E & S Eagle View Cir, Cv & Dr 84092
E Eaglebrook Dr 84070
Eaglewood Ln 84092
E Earl Way 84094
S Eastdell Dr 84092
W Eastgate Dr 84070
E & S Easthills Cir & Dr 84093
S Eastpoint Cir & Dr 84092
Eastridge Cir & Rd 84094
Eastwood Pl 84092
E Edelweiss Cir 84092
S Eden Dr 84094
E & S Edenbrook Dr 84094
E & S Edgecliff Cir & Dr 84092
E Edgefield Rd 84094
S El Manicero Way 84093
E & S Elderberry Way 84092
E & S Eldon Way 84093
E & S Electra Ln & St 84094
E Elise St 84070
S & E Elk Horn Cir & Ln 84093
E Ellen Way 84092
S Elm Ridge Rd 84094
E Elswood Ave 84094
E Emerald Dr 84094
E Emilee Kaye Cir 84070
S Enchanted Oak Ln 84094
E English Way 84093
S English Oaks Cv 84093
S Equestrian Park Cir 84092
S Erique Way 84093
S Escalante Dr 84093

E Estrellita Dr 84093
E & S Etienne Way 84093
S Eton Cir 84070
S Evening Moon Way 84070
W Evening Star Way 84070
E & S Evergreen Pine Ln 84070
E Everleigh Cir 84093
E Exeter Cir 84093
S & E Fairoaks Cir & Way 84070
S Fairway Cir 84092
S & W Fairway View Dr 84070
S & E Falcon Cir & Way 84093
E & S Falcon Heights Ln 84093
E & S Falcon Hill Cir & Dr 84092
S Falcon Park Cir 84093
E & S Falconhurst Cir, Ct & Dr 84092
E & S Falconview Dr 84092
Falconwood Ln 84092
E Fall View Dr 84093
S & E Fallbrook Cir & Way 84094
E Fallentine Rd 84093
E Family Cir 84070
E Farley Cir 84092
E Farm Cir 84093
E & S Farm Brook Way 84093
S Farm Creek Cir 84093
S Farnsworth Ln 84070
E & S Faunsdale Cir & Dr 84092
Fawn Grove Ln 84092
E Fawnwood Cv 84092
E & S Faye Cir 84070
S Fayeway Dr 84094
E Field Point Cir 84092
S & E Finlandia Cir, Ct & Way 84093
E Fireice Rose Ln 84070
E Firelight Way 84092
E Fireside Cir 84093
S Flanders Rd 84092
E & S Flatiron Dr 84093
E Flicker Dr 84070
S Flint Dr 84094
E Floyd Dr 84070
E Forbush Dr 84093
S Forest Pointe Cir 84092
E Forest Ridge Rd 84094
E Forget Me Not Ave 84094
S Four Sox Cv 84092
S Fox Cir 84092
E & S Fox Hunt Dr 84092
E & S Foxmoor Cir, Dr & Pl 84092
E & S Foxwood Cir & Ln 84092
W Freedom Ave 84070
S & E Fruitwood Ct & Ln 84070
S & E Fur Hollow Cir & Dr 84092
E & S Gad Way 84093
S Gad Valley Cir 84094
E Gad Valley Dr 84092
E & S Gadzooks Dr 84094
E Galaxie Dr 84093
E Galena Dr 84094
S Gambel Cv 84092
S & E Gambel Oak Cir & Dr 84092
E Garden Bend Pl 84094
S Gardners Pl 84092
E Garmish Cv 84092
S Garnet Dr 84094
E Gary Ave 84070
Gatehouse Ln 84092
E Gatewood Dr 84094
E Gaylene Cir 84094
S & E Geode Cir & Way 84094
E & S Georgia Way 84092
E Geranium St 84094
E Germania Cir 84093
S Gerona Cir 84093
E Geta Way 84092
E & S Glacier Ln 84092
S Glacier Park Ln 84092
E & S Glacier Ridge Dr 84092
E Glacier View Dr 84092
E & S Gladiator Way 84094
S Glass Slipper Rd 84092
S Glen Croft Ln 84070
E & S Glendover Way 84092
E & S Glenn Abbey Cir & Way 84093
E & S Glider Ln 84093
S & E Godatia Cir & Ln 84094
E Golden Eye Dr 84093
E & S Golden Field Way 84094
S Golden Rain Cir 84070
E & S Golden Willow Cir & Dr 84070
E & S Gracey Ln 84092
E & S Grambling Way 84094
Granada Cir & Dr 84093
E Grand Point Cir 84092
S & E Grandview Cir, Dr & Way 84092
S Granite Dr 84094
E Granite Pl 84092
E Granite Bench Ln 84092
S Granite Canyon Dr 84092
E Granite Cliffs Rd 84092
E & S Granite Crest Cir & Ln 84092
S Granite Farm Rd 84092
E & S Granite Hills Cir & Dr 84092
E Granite Hollow St 84092
E Granite Knob Ln 84092
E Granite Meadow Ln 84092
S Granite Mesa Cir 84092
E Granite Pass Ct 84092
E Granite Peak Dr 84094
E Granite Point Cir 84092
E Granite Quarry Ln 84092
S & E Granite Slope Dr & Ln 84092
S Granite View Dr 84092
S Granite Vista Dr 84092
S & E Granite Woods Cir & Ln 84092
S Granville Cir 84093
S Grape Arbor Pl 84070
S Grapevine Cv 84070
E & S Gravel Hills Dr 84094
S Graybouldor Ct 84092
S Grayrock Ct 84092
E Grayson Ct 84094
S Green Way 84094
S Green Bend Ct 84094
S Green Ridge Dr 84070
E & S Greenhills Dr 84093
E & S Greenwich Cir & Ln 84093
S Greenwood Dr 84070
S Greer Ln 84093
S Grouse Cir 84093
E & S Grouse Creek Cir 84092
S & E Gyrfalcon Ct, Dr & Ln 84092
E & S Hagan Cir & Rd 84092
S Haley Cir 84094
S & E Handcart Cir & Way 84070
E Harmony Grove Way 84092
S Harrison St 84070
S Harvard Park Dr 84094
S Harvel Dr 84070
S Havre Cir 84093
E Hawk Cir 84092
S Hawkins Ct 84092
S Hawkwood Dr 84094
S Heartwood Cv 84070
E Heather Cir 84094
E & S Heather Ridge Cir & Dr 84070
E Heatherwood Cir 84092
S Hedgelawn Way 84092
S Heights Dr 84094
S Heytesbury Ln 84092
E Hibiscus Ave 84094
E & S Hickory Point Cir & Dr 84092
E & S Hickory Valley Cir & Dr 84092
S Hidden Cir 84092
S & W Hidden Bluff Cv & Way 84070
S Hidden Brook Blvd 84092
E & S Hidden Canyon Ln 84092
S Hidden Park Ln 84093
S Hidden Pine Ln 84092
S Hidden Point Dr 84070
S Hidden Ridge Ln 84092
S Hidden Springs Cv 84094
S Hidden Vale Ln 84070
S Hidden Valley Blvd 84092
E Hidden Valley Cir 84092
E Hidden Valley Dr
- 1000-1299 84094
- 1300-1328 84092
- 1330-1599 84092

S Hidden Valley Dr 84094
E Hidden Valley Rd 84092
S Hidden Valley Rd 84092
E & S Hidden Valley Club Cir & Dr 84092
E & S Hidden View Dr 84070
E & S Hidden Village Cir & Dr 84092
E Hidden Wood Dr 84092
E & S Hiddenwood Dr 84092
E High Danish Rd 84093
E & S High Mesa Dr 84092
S & E High Mountain Cir & Dr 84092
E & S High Point Ln 84092
E & S High Ridge Ln 84092
S Highland Dr
- 8150-8298 84093
- 8300-8699 84093
- 8701-9299 84093
- 9265-9265 84090
- 9301-9399 84093
- 9400-9600 84092
- 9602-11898 84092

S Highland Oaks Cir 84092
S Hilden Ct 84093
E Hill Climb Cir 84092
S Hill Haven Ln 84093
E & S Hillsboroughheights Rd 84092
E Hilo St 84070
S Holiday Park Dr 84070
S Hollow Cv 84070
E & S Hollow Bend Dr 84070
E & S Holly Cir 84070
E Holly Ridge Rd 84094
E Hollyhock Ave 84094
S Hosta Ln 84094
E Howard Dr 84070
E & S Huckleberry Cir & Ct 84093
Hummingbird Cir & Ln 84094
E & S Hunters Meadow Cir 84093
E & S Hunts End Dr 84092
S Hyacinth Cir 84094
S Hyrum Pl 84070
E & S Ida Cir & Ln 84093
E & S Indian Ridge Cir & Dr 84092
S Inspiration Cir 84092
E Interlaken Cir 84093
W Iron Way 84070
S Irwin Rd 84092
S Ivy Hills Cir 84093
Ivy Oaks Ln 84092
S Jackson Cir 84092
S Jackson Hole Dr 84093
E Jacob Rd 84092
E & S Jade Cir & Dr 84094
E James Cir 84070
S Jameson Point Cv 84092
E Jane Cir 84092
Janella Cir & Way 84093
E & S Jardim Cir & Way 84093
E Jasmine Ave 84092
S Jason Dr 84094
S Jason K Cir 84070
S Jean Dr 84070
S & W Jefferson Cv, Ln & Pl 84070
E & S Jene Dr 84070
E Jerand Way 84070
S Jesse Valley Cir 84092
E & S Jessica Ln 84092
S Joanna Cir 84070
E Joey Cir 84092
E Johns Way 84070
S & E Johnson Way Cir & Dr 84094
Johnstone Cir & Dr 84093
S Jolley Acres Cir 84092
S Jordan Gtwy 84070
S Jordan Meadow Ln 84070
S & W Jordan Oaks Ct & Dr 84070
E & S Jordan Point Cir & Dr 84092
E & S Jordan View Cir & Dr 84070
E Julho St 84093
E Julie Ann Cir 84094
S & E Julie Anna Ct & Dr 84070
E & S Justin Park Dr 84092
E & S Kalinda Dr 84092
E Karalee Way 84092
E Karon Cir 84094
S Katey Ct 84092
E Kathryn Cir 84070
E Kathy Dr 84092
E & S Keith Dr 84094
S Kelly Brook Dr 84092
E & S Kelsch Dr 84093
E Kennelly Ave 84094
E & S Keswick Rd 84093
S & E Kimsbrough Ct & Rd 84092
S & E Kirkwood Cir, Pl & Way 84094
E Klosters Cir 84093
S & E Knollwood Cir & Dr 84092
S & E Kramer Cir & Dr 84092
E & S Kristin Dr 84070
E & S Ksel Cir & Dr 84092
La Casa Cir & Dr 84094
S La Croix Dr 84070
S La Grange Way 84093
La Montagne Ln 84092
E La Vera Ln 84070
S Lafayette Ct 84092
E Lafayette St 84094
S Lamasa Cir 84092
E Lancaster Cir 84092
S Landover Cir 84093
E Lane Cir 84070
E Langdale Cir 84093
E & S Lannae Dr 84094
E & S Lantern Hill Ct 84093
S & E Larkspur Cir & Dr 84094
S Laura Anne Way 84094
S Laura Lane Dr 84092
E Lauralane Dr 84092
E & S Laurel Dr 84070
Laver Ct & St 84092
S & E Lazon Cir & Dr 84094
W Lazy Oak Way 84070
E & S Leafwood Ln 84094
E Lee Ln 84070
E Legacy Park Ln 84093
Legend Ln 84092
E & S Leilani Cir & Dr 84070
E Leonard Cir 84093
S Lexann Cir 84093
S & E Lexington Cir & Dr 84092
S & E Lexington Hills Cir & Dr 84092
S & E Liberty Bend Dr & Ln 84094
E Lindell Ave 84070
S Lindfield Cir 84093
S Lindon Rd 84092
E & S Lindsay Wood Ln 84092
S & E Lipman Cir & Dr 84092
E & S Little Cloud Cir & Rd 84093
E & S Little Cottonwood Ln, Pl & Rd 84092
E Little Kay Cir 84070
E & S Littler Cir & Rd 84092
S Littlewood Cir 84094
E & S Locksley Cir & Rd 84092
E Locust St 84070
E Lodge Dr 84092
E & S Lodgepole Dr 84094
S Logan Meadow Ln 84070
W Lola Cir 84070
E Loma Way 84092
S Londonderry Dr 84092
E Lone Eagle Ln 84092
Lone Hollow Cv & Dr 84092
E Lone Springs Cv 84092
E & S Longdale Cir & Dr 84092
Longwood Ln 84092
E & S Loredo Dr 84094
E Lori Cir 84094
S Loridan Ln 84092
S Lorimer Ln 84070
S Lorinder Dr 84092
E Lorita Way 84093
E Lost Eden Dr 84094
S Lost Trail Dr 84092
E & S Lostwood Dr 84092
W Loyal Ave 84070
S Lyndbrook Way 84092
S Lynford Dr 84092
E Lynn Cir 84070
S Lynwood St 84070
E & S Mach Schnell Dr 84094
E Madrid Way 84093
S & E Madsen Ct & Ln 84093
E Main St 84070
S & E Maio Ct & Dr 84093
S Maison Dr 84093
S Majestic Canyon Rd 84092
E Majesty Cir 84094
S Mallard Cir 84093
S Manchester Ln 84093
E Manshire Cir 84094
S Manzano Dr 84093
E Maple Creek Ln 84092
S Maple Hill Cir 84092
Maple Ridge Cir & Rd 84094
S & E Marbella Cir & St 84093
S Marble St 84094
S Margie Dr 84070
S Marion Cir 84094
S Marion View Cir 84094
E Marion Village Rd 84094
S Mariposa Way 84094
S Marksbury Cir 84092
E Mars Way 84070
S Marsha Kaye Cir 84070
E Marthas Cv 84093
S Mary Dr 84092
S Mary Esther Cir 84093
E Marymore Cir 84092
E Matlock Ct 84093
E & S Mayfly Way 84070
E Mcneill Cir 84093
S Meadow Ct 84093
S & E Meadow Hill Cir & Dr 84070
E Meadow Lark Way 84093
E Meadow Ridge Rd 84094
S Meadow River Dr 84070
S Meadowlark Cir 84093
S Meckailee Cv 84094
S Melbury Cir 84093
S Melissa Cir 84092
S Melissa Kaye Dr 84070
E Merewood Ct 84094
E Mesa Cir 84092
S Mesa Dr 84093
S Meyer Vista Cv 84093
E & S Michael Way 84093
S Michaels View St 84070
S Michelle Way 84093
E Milky Way 84094
S Mill Canyon Dr 84094
Mill Ridge Cir & Rd 84094
E & S Millbury Way 84092
S Millerberg Dr 84070
S Millwood Dr 84092
E & S Mingo Park Dr 84070
E Mingo View Ave 84070
E & S Miranda Ln 84093
E Misty Meadows Cir 84093
Mistywood Ln 84092
S Mivu Cir 84093
S & E Mockingbird Cir & Ln 84094
E & S Mombo Dr 84092
S Monitor Dr 84093
S Monroe St 84070
S Monroe Plaza Way 84070
E Montana Dr 84070
E Monte Luca Way 84093
E Montebello Dr 84092
S Monterey Cir 84093
E Montgomery Dr 84070
S Montreaux Ln 84093
S Moonglow Way 84070
S Moonlight Dr 84070
S Morgan Grove Way 84092
S Morning Mist Ct 84093
S Morning Star Way 84070
S Morning View Cir 84094
S Morningview Dr 84094
W Motor Park Ave 84070
E & S Mount Jordan Rd 84092
S Mount Majestic Rd 84093
E & S Mount View Cir & Dr 84070
S Mountain Ridge Cir 84092
S Mountain Shadow Rd 84092
E & S Mountain Valley Way 84092
E Mountain View Dr 84070
Mountain Wood Ln 84092
E & S Mulberry Way 84093
S & E Mumford Cir & Dr 84094
E Mums Cir 84092
E Mystic Grove Cv 84093
S & E Mystic Hills Cv & Ln 84093
E & S Mystic Meadow Cv & Ln 84093
E Naomi Dr 84070
E New England Dr 84094
E & S New Horizon Dr 84093
S Newbury Dr 84092
S & E Newcastle Cir, Ct & Dr 84093
E & S Nichole Cir & Dr 84093
E & S Nicklaus Cir & Rd 84092
E & S Nighthawk Dr 84094
E & S Noelle Rd 84092
S & E Nordic Cir & Dr 84093
S Norfolk Pine Way 84094
E North Eden Cir 84094
E North Fork Cir 84094
S Northforty Rd 84093
Northridge Cv, Ln & Way 84092
E Nottingham Cir 84093
S Nutwood Cir 84094
S Oak Cir 84093
S Oak Brush Dr 84070
E & S Oak Creek Cir & Dr 84093
W Oak Green Dr 84070
E Oak Grove Dr 84092
E Oak Haven Pl 84093
E & S Oak Hollow Cir 84093
S & E Oak Leaf Pl & Way 84092
E & S Oak Manor Dr 84092
E & S Oak Valley Cir & Dr 84093
E & S Oakridge Cir & Rd 84094
E & S Oakshire Cir & Ln 84092
S Oakwood Ln 84092
E & S Oakwood Park Cir 84094
E Oakwood Vista Cv 84093
E & S Oberland Rd 84092
S October Cv 84092
S Ohenry Rd 84070
S Old Barn Dr 84094
S Old Coventry Cir 84093
E & S Old Dairy Rd 84094
S Old England Rd 84092
E & S Old Mission Rd 84093
Old Oak Ln 84092
S Old Ranch Pl 84092
E Old Sandy Ct 84094
E Onyx Ln 84094
S Opal Cir 84094
E Opequon Rd 84070
E & S Orangewood Ln 84070
E Owenwood Cir 84092
S & W Oxford Cir & Rd 84070
E Pali St 84070
S Paloma Way 84094
S Pampas Dr 84094
S Parakeet Dr 84093
S Paralers Dr 84094
S & E Park Hurst Cir & Ln 84094
E Park Knoll Cir 84070
E Park Mesa Way 84094
E & S Park Rise Way 84070
W Parkland Dr 84070
Parkside Ln 84092
S & E Partridge Cir & Way 84093
E Paty Cir 84070
S & W Paula Cir & Dr 84070
E Paulista Way 84093
E & S Peach Blossom Cir & Dr 84094
S Peacock Dr 84093
S & E Pear Tree Cir & Dr 84094
E Pebble Beach Cir 84092
S Pebble Creek Cir 84093
S Pebble Glen Cir 84094
E & S Pebble Hills Cir & Dr 84094
S Pebble Springs Ct 84093
E Pebblewood Cir 84092

E Pecos Dr 84094
S Peony Way 84094
S Pepper Cir 84092
E Pepperell Cir 84094
E Pepperwood Dr 84092
Pepperwood Pointe 84092
E & S Peregrine Ln & Pl 84094
E & S Peruvian Cir & Dr 84093
E Petal Cir 84092
E & S Petunia Way 84092
E Pheasant Brook Rd 84092
S Pheasant Wood Dr 84093
S Phlox St 84094
E Pico St 84070
E Pimlico Pl 84092
S Pine Springs Cv 84093
E & S Pinecreek Cir & Ln 84093
E Pinecrest Ln 84092
S Pinedale Cir 84092
S Pinehurst Dr 84092
E & S Pineridge Rd 84094
E & S Pinewood Cir & Dr 84094
E Pioneer Ave 84070
Piper Cir & Ln 84093
E Plantation Dr 84094
E Plata Way 84093
E Platinum Way 84094
Player Cir & Rd 84092
Pleasant Hill Cir & Dr 84092
E Pleasant Valley Ct 84092
S Pleasant View Dr 84092
S Plum Creek Ln 84093
S & E Ponderosa Cir, Dr & Way 84094
S Poppy Ln 84094
E & S Portal Way 84093
E & S Porto Fino Ct 84093
Powder Horn Ct & Dr 84093
E Powderkeg Dr 84093
S Power Plant Rd 84092
E & S Prescott Dr 84092
S Prescott Park Cir 84092
S Prestbury Pl 84094
S Primrose Dr 84094
S Proctor Farm Cir 84093
E & S Promontory Way 84094
E & S Purple Lilac Ln 84070
S & E Quail Creek Cir & Dr 84094
E Quail Crossing Ln 84092
S & E Quail Hollow Cir & Dr 84093
S Quail Ridge Rd 84092
E & S Quail Run Cir & Dr 84093
E Quail Stream Ln 84093
E Quailwood Cir 84092
E Quarry Dr 84092
S Quarry Bend Dr 84094
E Quarry Park Dr 84094
E Quarry Sands Ln 84094
E & S Quarry Stone Way 84094
E Quarry View Way 84094
E Quarry Vista Cir 84094
E & S Quartzridge Dr 84092
E Quiet Ridge Cir 84092
Quietwood Ln 84092
S Quindaro Rd 84070
E Raddon Dr 84092
E Rainbow Oaks Cir 84092
E Raintree Ave 84094
E Raintree Cir 84092
S Raintree Dr 84092
S Raintree Pl 84092
S Raptor Cv 84094
Ravenwood Ln 84092
S Ray Cir 84094
S Red River Rd 84093
S Red Willow Cir 84093
E Redbirch Cv 84093
E Redding Ct 84094
E & S Redhaven Dr 84094
S Reliance Dr 84070
E & S Rembrandt Cir & Ln 84070
E & S Renegade Rd 84093
E & S Resaca Dr 84070
E Richard Rd 84093
S Ridge Bend Ct 84094
S Ridge Gate Cir 84092
S Ridge Point Rd 84093
E Ridgemark Dr 84092
S & E Riggs Cir & Dr 84092
Rio Cir, Ct & Way 84093
S & E River Oaks Cir & Dr 84093
S Riverside Dr 84070
S Riverwood Dr 84093
E & S Robidoux Rd 84093
E & S Robins Way 84094
S Robinson Cir 84092
S Roble Cir 84093
E & S Rockhampton Dr 84092
S & E Rocklin Cir & Dr 84092
S & E Rockview Cir & Dr 84092
E & S Rockwell Dr 84093
S Rodnia Cir 84092
Rollingwood Ln 84092
E & S Romaine Cir & Dr 84070
E Rondelle Cir 84093
E Rosa Cir 84092
E Rose Bowl Ct 84070
E & S Roseboro Cir & Rd 84092
S Rossett Green Ln 84093
E & S Royal Ln 84093
E & S Royal Birch Cv 84093
S Royal Creek Cv 84093
E Royal Oak Cir 84092
E Royal Pine Cv 84093
E & S Rua Branco Cir & Dr 84093
S & E Ruskin Cir & Ct 84092
S Rustler Rd 84093
E & S Ryan Park Ave 84092
S Saddle Brook Cir 84093
Saddlewood Ln 84092
S Sady Ln 84070
S Sage Mesa Dr 84094
S & E Sage Ridge Cir & Rd 84094
S Sagecrest Cir 84093
E Saint Moritz Cir 84093
S Saint Tropez Cv 84093
S Sako Way 84070
S Salisbury Ct 84094
E & S Sample Cv 84093
E & S Sand Dollar Dr 84094
S & E Sandcrest Cir & Dr 84094
S Sanders Cir 84092
E Sanders Rd
1100-1299 84094
1301-1327 84092
1329-1359 84094
1361-1499 84092
S Sanders Rd 84094
E Sanders Hill Cir 84094
E & S Sandia Hills Dr 84094
S Sandridge Cir 84093
S Sandridge Dr 84092
E Sandstone Cir 84094
E, S & W Sandy Cir & Pkwy 84070
S Sandy Creek Dr 84094
E & S Sandy Dunes Cir & Dr 84094
E & S Sandy Gulch Cir, Pl & Rd 84094
E & S Sandy Hills Dr 84093
E & S Sandy Oaks Dr 84070
E & S Sandy Point Dr 84094
S & E Sandy Ridge Cir & Dr 84094
S Sandy Willows Cv 84070
E Sandys Grove Ln 84092
S & E Saphire Cir & Dr 84094
E Sarah Ln 84070
E & S Savannah Ct & Dr 84094
S & E Scandia Cir, Ct & Way 84093
E Scenic Oaks Cv 84092
E Scenic Valley Ln 84092
S Schofield Cir 84093
E & S Scirlein Dr 84094
S Scobey Cir 84070
S Scotia Ln 84093
S Scottish Dr 84093
E & S Secret View Dr 84092
E Sego Lily Dr
120-699 84070
800-1280 84094
1282-1298 84094
1520-1558 84092
1560-2599 84092
S Sego Lily Dr
9800-9999 84094
10200-10369 84092
10371-10399 84092
W Sego Lily Dr 84070
S Segovia Cir 84094
S Senda Cir 84093
S September Cv 84092
S Sequoia Tree Ln 84094
S & E Serpentine Cir & Way 84094
S Set Point Cir 84093
S & E Seven Springs Cir & Dr 84092
Shad Cir & Ln 84093
E Shadow Gate Cir 84094
E Shadow Oak Ln 84092
Shadow Wood Ln 84092
S Shady Dell Dr 84094
S Shady Meadow Dr 84093
S Shady Oak Ln 84092
S Shady Willow Cir 84093
E Shalisan Cir 84092
E Shane Cir 84092
S Shangrila Cir 84094
S Sharons Ln 84070
S Sheffield Way 84093
S Shelba Ct 84070
S Shellond Dr 84093
E Shelly Louise Dr 84070
E Sheraton Cir 84094
E Sherwood Cir 84093
E & S Shoshone Ave, Cir & Ct 84092
S Showcase Ln 84094
E Sienna Oak Ct 84092
E & S Siesta Dr 84093
S Siesta Hills Ct 84093
E & S Silica Dr 84094
S Silver Buckle Way 84092
S Silver Charm Ln 84092
S Silver Hills Cir 84094
E Silver Mesa Cir 84094
S Silver Mountain Dr 84094
S Silver Queen Cir 84094
S Silver Ridge Dr 84094
E Silver Sage Dr 84094
S & E Silver Willow Cir & Dr 84070
E & S Silvercrest Dr 84093
S & E Silversmith Cir & Dr 84094
E & S Silverstone Cir & Way 84093
E & S Sitka Dr 84093
E & S Sitzmark Dr 84092
S Six Shooter Cir 84093
E Ski View Dr 84092
S & E Sleepy Hollow Cir & Ln 84094
E & S Smart Ln 84094
S Smoketree Cir 84092
S Sneddon Dr 84070
E Snow Cir 84092
E & S Snow Basin Cir & Dr 84093
Snow Forest Cv & Ln 84092
E & S Snow Iris Cir & Way 84092
S & E Snow Mountain Cir & Dr 84093
E Snowball Cir 84092
Snowbird Cir & Dr 84093
E Snowbird Center Dr 84092
Snowstar Ln 84092
S Snowville Dr 84093
S Solar Way 84070
S Solena Way 84093
S Solomon Cir 84092
S Somerton Cir 84093
E Somerville Dr 84093
S Sophie Ln 84070
E South Eden Cir 84094
E South Fork Cir 84094
E Southbridge Way 84093
S Southwood Dr 84070
E & S Spartan Dr 84094
S Spectrum Cv 84093
S & E Spring Ridge Cir & Dr 84094
S Springwood Ln 84093
E Spruce Mesa Way 84094
E & S Spruce Tree Ln 84094
E Spyglass Cir 84092
E & S St Germain Way 84070
S Stacey Cir 84070
E Stalbridge Cir 84093
E & S Stanley Dr 84093
S Star Cir 84092
S Starburst Cir 84094
S Stargazer Cir 84093
E & S Starpine Dr 84094
Starwood Ct & Dr 84094
S State St 84070
E State Highway 210 84092
E & S Statice Ave & Cir 84094
E Station St 84070
E & S Station Landing Way 84070
E Stephanie Cir 84070
S Sterling Dr 84093
W Still Blossom Ln 84070
S Stillwater Cir 84093
S Stone Cliff Dr 84092
S Stone Gate Cir 84092
S Stone Mesa Ct 84092
S & E Stone Mountain Cv & Ln 84092
S Stone Point Pl 84093
S Stone Ridge Cir 84093
E & S Stone Valley Way 84094
S Stone View Cv 84093
E Stonebrook Cir 84092
E & S Stonefield Cir & Rd 84094
E Stonefly Dr 84070
S Stonewall Ct 84092
E & S Stonewood Cir, Ct & Dr 84093
S Stony Bend Ct 84094
Stormy Creek Cir & Rd 84094
S Strasbourg Cir 84093
S Stratford Cir 84070
E & S Strato Dr 84093
E & S Stream View Dr 84093
S Streatham Rd 84070
S & E Sublette Cir & Pl 84093
E Success Ln 84092
E Sudbury Ave 84093
S Sugarloaf Cir 84093
E Sugarloaf Dr 84092
S Sugarloaf Dr 84093
E Sugarloaf Ln 84093
S Sugarloaf Ln 84093
E & S Summer Crest Cv & Dr 84093
E & S Summer Meadow Cir & Dr 84093
S Summer Mesa Cir 84093
E Summer Oak Cir 84092
E Summer Park Cir 84093
E Summer Stone Ct 84092
Summer Willow Dr & Pl 84093
E Summerborne Cir 84093
S & E Summerfield Cir & Ln 84092
S Summit View Dr 84092
S Sun Valley Dr 84093
S & E Sunburn Cir & Ln 84094
S Sunburst Ct 84093
E & S Sundance Dr 84093
S Sunderland Cir 84092
S Sunfire Rose Ln 84070
S Sunflower Ln 84094
S Sunny Brea Cir 84093
E Sunny Glen Cir 84093
E & S Sunridge Cir & Dr 84093
S Sunrise Cir 84093
E Sunrise Meadow Dr 84093
E & S Sunrise Park Cir & Dr 84093
S & E Sunset Ridge Cir & Dr 84092
E Sunspot Cir 84093
Sunwood Ln 84092
Superior Cir & Dr 84094
E Susan Cir 84070
E Susan Dr 84092
S Susan Dr 84092
E & S Sutton Ct & Way 84093
Swallow Wood Ln 84092
S & W Sweet Meadow Ln 84070
E Sweetbriar Ln 84092
E Swiss Oaks Dr 84093
S Sycamore Tree Cv 84094
E Syrena Cir 84094
Taft Hill Ct & Dr 84093
S & E Tall Pines Cv & Way 84092
E Tallowood Cir 84093
E & S Tamara St 84094
S Tamarack Dr 84094
S & E Tameron Cir & Dr 84092
S Taos Dr 84093
S Tapp Ln 84070
S & E Teakwood Cir & Dr 84092
S & E Teal Cir & Way 84093
S Telford Way 84093
E & S Tennyson Ave & Cir 84070
S Terendale Ln 84092
E Terra Vista Way 84093
E & S Terrace Ct & Dr 84093
S Terrace Creek Cir 84093
S Terri Lynn Dr 84094
E Thistle Down Dr 84092
E Thistlewood Way 84092
E Tierney Cir 84094
S Tifftan Cir 84094
E & S Tiger Eye Dr 84094
S Tiger Tail Cir 84094
E Timber Crest Cv 84093
E Timpie Dr 84094
Tiny Wood Dr 84070
E & S Tj Cir & Dr 84070
S Tolman Farms Cir 84070
S Tolman Field Way 84070
E & S Tonya Dr 84070
E Torry Cir 84070
S Tortellini Dr 84093
W Towne Ridge Pkwy 84070
S & E Tracy Cir & Dr 84093
S Trailridge Cir 84092
S Trailwood Cv 84092
S & E Tramway Cir & Dr 84092
E Transwest Dr 84092
S Treasure Way 84093
E & S Treasure Mountain Cir & Dr 84093
Trendland Cv 84092
E Trevino Rd 84092
E Tritoma Ave 84094
E Tulane Cir 84094
E & S Tulip Dr 84094
S Turnpike Ln 84070
S & E Turquoise Cir & Way 84094
E Tuscan Oak Way 84092
E Tuscan Ridge Cv 84092
Tuxedo Cir & Way 84093
E & S Twelve Pines Cir & Dr 84094
S Tynedale Ct 84093
E & S Union Sq 84070
W Universal Cir 84070
S Urry Cir 84093
E Vail Cir 84093
E Valde Neige Cir 84093
Valencia Cir & Pl 84093
E Valley Cir 84070
S Valley Bend Ct 84094
E Valley Ridge Dr 84093
S Vaquero Dr 84094
S Vauna Lee St 84093
E Verbenia Ave 84094
E Verde Cir 84093
S Vermer Way 84070
S Veronica St 84094
S Via Riviera Way 84093
E & S View Point Dr 84094
S Vilas Dr 84092
Villa Bluff Dr & Way 84070
W Villa Ridge Way 84070
S Villa Springs Cv 84070
E & S Village Cir & Way 84094
E & S Village Oak Ln 84092
E & S Village Point Way 84093
S Village Shop Dr 84094
E & S Violet Cir & Dr 84094
S & E Viscounti Cir, Cv & Dr 84093
S Vista Way 84070
S Vista Glen Ct 84092
S Wagner Cir 84093
E Wagonwheel Cir 84093
Wanderwood Way 84092
E Wasatch Blvd 84092
S Wasatch Blvd
8900-9068 84093
9070-9299 84093
9500-11197 84092
11199-11499 84092
E Wasatch Pines Ln 84092
E Wasatch Resort Rd 84092
E Wassail Rd 84070
E Water Vista Way 84093
S & E Waters Cir & Ln 84093
E & S Watson Rd 84092
S & E Wayside Cir & Dr 84094
E Webster Dr 84094
S Wedgefield Dr 84093
S Weeping Willow Dr 84070
S & E Weybridge Cir & Ln 84092
S Whirlaway Ln 84092
E & S Whisper Cove Rd 84094
E Whisperwood Cir 84092
E & S White Pine Way 84094
E & S White River Dr 84070
S White Sands Dr 84070
E White Spruce Cv 84070
S & E Wild Willow Cir & Ln 84093
Wildcreek Cir & Rd 84092
E Wilde Cherry Way 84070
E & S Wildfire Rose Ln 84070
E & S Wildflower Rd 84092
E & S Williamsburg Park Cir 84070
E Williamson Cir 84092
S Willow Cir 84093
S Willow Bank Cir 84070
E & S Willow Bend Dr 84093
S & E Willow Brook Cir & Way 84092
E & S Willow Creek Dr 84093
E Willow Glen Cir 84093
Willow Green Cir, Ct & Dr 84093
S Willow Hill Dr 84092
S & E Willow Hills Ct & Dr 84093
E Willow Park Ln 84093
S Willow Stream Dr 84093
E & S Willow View Cir & Way 84092
Willow Vista Cir & Dr 84093
Willow Wick Ct & Dr 84093
S Wimbleton Dr 84092
S & W Windflower Ln 84070
Windsong 84092
E Windsor Oak Cv 84092
Windy Peak Cir & Way 84094
S Windy Peak Ridge Dr 84094
E Winter Canyon Way 84094
S Winter Wren Dr 84093
E & S Winterwood Cir & Dr 84092
S Wolf Point Cir 84070
E Wood Glen Rd 84092
S Woodbine Cir 84092
Woodchuck Cir & Way 84093
S Woodglen Cir 84092
E & S Woodhampton Cir & Dr 84092
E & S Woodhill Cir & Dr 84092
E Woodleaf Way 84094
S Woodridge Rd 84094
S & E Woodthrush Cir & Dr 84093
S Worthington Ct 84092
E Wright Way 84094
E Wyandotte Ave 84070
E & S Wyndcastle Dr 84092
E & S Wyngate Cir & Ln 84092
S Yorielak E 84070
S Yorkridge Rd 84094
E Zermatt Cir 84093
E & S Zinnia Way 84094
W Zona Cir 84070

NUMBERED STREETS

E 10065 S 84070
E 10095 S 84092
E 10000 S 84092
S 1000 E 84094
100 E & W 84070
E 10105 S 84070
E 10120 S 84070
E 10145 S 84070
E 10185 S 84070
E 10195 S 84070
E 10180 S 84092
E 10140 S 84092
E 10230 S 84070
E 10260 S 84092
E 10265 S 84092
E 10285 S 84092

E 10225 S 84092
E & W 10200 84070
S 1025 E 84094
E 10305 S 84092
E 10315 S 84070
E 10375 S 84070
300-499 84070
2101-2197 84092
E 10450 S 84070
E 10425 S 84070
E 10430 S 84070
S 1040 E 84094
E 10560 S 84070
E 10500 S 84070
S 1050 E 84094
E 10655 S 84094
E 10695 S 84070
1-630 84070
632-698 84070
700-1299 84094
1301-1597 84092
1599-1900 84092
1902-1998 84092
S 1060 E 84094
W 10600 S 84070
E 10735 S 84070
E 10715 S 84094
E 10760 S 84094
E 10765 S 84092
S 1070 E 84094
E 10980 S 84092
E 10900 S 84092
E 10930 S 84070
S 1090 E 84094
E 11000 S
1-699 84070
700-1299 84094
S 1100 E 84094
W 11000 S 84070
E 11150 S 84094
E 11190 S 84094
E 11170 S 84092
E 11100 S 84070
E 11125 S 84070
E 11245 S 84092
E 11265 S 84092
E 11270 S 84092
E 11200 S 84070
E 11205 S 84092
S 1120 E 84094
E 11370 S 84092
E 11340 S 84092
E 11460 S 84092
1-199 84070
901-997 84094
999-1099 84094
1300-1899 84092
W 11400 S 84070
E 11500 S 84092
E 11570 S 84092
S 115 E 84070
E 11660 S 84092
E 11620 S 84092
E 11780 S 84094
S 1185 E 84094
S 1195 E 84094
S 1205 E 84094
S 120 E 84070
S 1210 E 84094
S 1225 E 84094
S 1240 E 84094
S 1260 E 84094
S 1270 E 84094
S 1275 E 84094
S 1280 E 84094
S 1300 E 84094
S 1320 E 84092
S 1325 E 84093
S 1330 E 84093
S 1335 E 84092
S 1330 E
11100-11299 84092
S 1350 E 84093
9401-9499 84092
S 1370 E
8300-8399 84093
11200-11299 84092
S 1380 E
8400-9299 84093
9301-9455 84093
9500-11699 84092
S 1390 E 84093
S 1395 E 84093
S 1400 E 84093
9400-9465 84093
9466-9468 84093
9467-9599 84092
9470-9598 84092
S 1425 E 84093
S 1430 E 84093
S 1475 E 84093
S 1480 E 84093
S 150 E 84070
S 1520 E 84093
S 1540 E 84093
S 1555 E 84093
S 1575 E 84093
S 1595 E 84093
S 160 E 84070
S 1620 E 84093
S 1645 E 84093
S 1660 E 84093
S 1700 E 84093
S 1700 E 84093
S 170 E 84070
9500-11770 84092
S 1715 E 84093
S 1730 E 84092
S 1740 E 84092
S 1800 E 84092
S 180 E 84070
S 1835 E 84092
S 1900 E 84092
S 1925 E 84093
S 1980 E 84092
S 198 E 84070
S 2000 E 84092
S 2020 E 84093
10000-10199 84092
S 2050 E 84092
S 210 E 84070
S 2100 E 84093
S 2125 E 84092
S 2130 E 84092
S 2165 E 84092
S 220 E 84070
S 2220 E 84092
S 2230 E 84092
S 2240 E 84092
S 2260 E 84092
S 2270 E 84092
S 2280 E 84092
S 230 E 84070
S 2375 E 84092
240 E & W 84070
S 2415 E 84092
S 2420 E 84092
S 2460 E 84092
S 2465 E 84092
S 250 E 84070
S 2505 E 84092
S 2550 E 84092
S 255 W 84070
S 260 E 84070
S 2600 E 84092
S 2660 E 84093
S 2680 E 84093
S 270 E 84070
S 2700 E 84093
9800-9848 84092
S 2720 E 84092
S 2760 E 84092
S 280 E 84070
S 285 E 84070
S 2875 E 84092
S 2900 E 84092
S 2980 E 84092
300 E & W 84070
S 3030 E 84092
S 3100 E 84092
S 3200 E 84092
S 325 E 84070
S 3350 E 84092
S 360 E 84070
S 3605 E 84093
S 370 W 84070
S 3775 E 84092
S 385 E 84070
S 390 E 84070
S 40 E 84070
S 400 E 84070
S 415 E 84070
S 420 E 84070
S 440 E 84070
S 450 E 84070
455 E & W 84070
S 460 E 84070
S 465 E 84070
S 475 E 84070
S 480 W 84070
500 E & W 84070
S 510 E 84070
S 520 E 84070
S 530 E 84070
S 535 E 84070
S 540 E 84070
S 550 E 84070
560 E & W 84070
S 570 E 84070
S 575 E 84070
S 580 E 84070
S 60 E 84070
S 600 W 84070
S 610 E 84070
S 615 E 84070
S 620 E 84070
S 630 E 84070
S 650 E 84070
S 660 E 84070
S 670 W 84070
S 700 E
7800-8849 84070
8850-11298 84070
8850-8850 84091
8851-11399 84070
S 700 W 84070
S 730 E 84070
S 740 E 84094
E 7450 S 84093
S 745 E 84094
S 760 E 84094
E 7800 S 84070
E 7845 S 84070
E 7850 S 84094
E 7865 S 84094
E 7890 S 84070
E 7905 S 84094
E 7945 S 84094
E 7985 S 84094
E 8000 S 84070
S 800 E 84094
E 8020 S 84093
E 8045 S 84070
S 805 E 84094
E 8085 S 84093
E 8080 S 84094
E 8080 S 84094
1700-1799 84093
E 8100 S 84070
E 8120 S 84070
E 8125 S 84094
E 8125 S 84094
1300-1499 84093
E 8135 S 84070
E 8175 S 84070
E 8175 S 84094
1300-1499 84093
E 8180 S
400-599 84070
1700-1799 84093
E 8200 S 84070
E 8220 S
300-599 84070
1100-1299 84094
E 8230 S 84094
E 8245 S 84094
E 8240 S 84070
E 8255 S 84070
E 8260 S 84070
E 8265 S 84070
E 8270 S 84094
E 8285 S
500-511 84070
1100-1299 84094
E 8300 S 84070
S 830 E 84094
E 8320 S 84094
E 8325 S 84094
1800-1999 84093
E 8330 S 84070
E 8355 S 84070
S 835 E 84094
W 8360 S 84070
E 8375 S
100-198 84070
700-899 84094
E 8380 S 84094
E 8400 S 84070
E 8425 S 84094
E 8420 S 84093
E 8425 S
1300-1599 84093
E 8475 S 84094
E 8490 S 84070
S 85 E 84070
E 8545 S 84093
E 8555 S 84093
S 855 E 84094
E 8560 S 84094
1500-1599 84093
E 8575 S 84070
E 8600 S
500-599 84070
601-699 84070
701-773 84094
775-1299 84094
1300-1700 84093
1702-1794 84093
S 860 E 84094
E 8620 S 84070
E 8640 S
1-299 84070
1500-1699 84093
S 865 E 84094
E 8680 S 84070
E 8685 S 84093
W 8710 S 84070
E 8725 S 84094
E 8730 S 84093
E 8760 S 84070
E 8800 S
1-37 84070
901-999 84094
S 880 E 84094
W 8835 S 84070
E 8840 S 84070
E 8850 S 84093
W 8850 S 84070
W 8865 S 84070
E 8880 S 84070
E 8920 S 84093
S 895 E 84094
E 8960 S 84070
S 90 E 84070
E 9000 S
2-598 84070
700-799 84094
W 9000 S 84070
E 9045 S 84094
E 9055 S 84093
E 9050 S
500-599 84070
3500-3698 84093
E 9060 S 84093
E 9085 S 84094
E 9090 S 84093
E 9100 S
100-299 84070
2000-2100 84093
S 910 E 84094
E 9120 S 84070
E 9125 S 84070
E 9140 S 84070
E 9150 S 84070
E 9165 S 84070
E 9180 S 84070
E 9200 S
100-200 84070
1300-1499 84093
S 920 E 84094
W 9210 S 84070
E 9230 S 84070
W 9240 S 84070
W 9260 S 84070
E 9275 S 84094
E 9270 S 84070
S 930 E 84094
W 9320 S 84070
E 9355 S 84092
S 935 E 84094
W 9365 S 84070
E 9400 S
1-699 84070
701-767 84094
769-1100 84094
1102-1298 84094
1300-2199 84093
2201-2399 84093
3200-3298 84092
W 9400 S 84070
E 9425 S 84092
E 9430 S
200-299 84070
1000-1199 84094
E 9460 S 84092
W 9460 S 84070
E 9510 S 84092
E 9520 S 84094
E 9530 S 84092
W 9535 S 84070
E 9545 S 84070
W 9560 S 84070
E 9585 S 84070
E 9590 S 84094
S 96 W 84070
S 960 E 84094
E 9620 S 84092
E 9630 S 84094
E 9655 S 84092
S 965 E 84094
E 9670 S 84070
E 9690 S 84092
E 9725 S 84092
E 9765 S 84070
E 9800 S 84092
W 9800 S 84070
E 9845 S 84092
E 9840 S 84092
E 9850 S
600-699 84070
2500-2598 84092
S 985 E 84094
E 9880 S 84092
E 9900 S
400-699 84070
2500-2599 84092
E 9940 S 84070
E 9950 S 84070
E 9990 S 84094

VERNAL UT

General Delivery 84078

POST OFFICE BOXES
MAIN OFFICE STATIONS
AND BRANCHES

Box No.s
1 - 1954 84078
790001 - 791260 84079

HIGHWAY CONTRACTS

73 84078

NAMED STREETS

All Street Addresses 84078

NUMBERED STREETS

All Street Addresses 84078

WEST JORDAN UT

General Delivery 84088

POST OFFICE BOXES
MAIN OFFICE STATIONS
AND BRANCHES

Box No.s
All PO Boxes 84084

NAMED STREETS

S & W Abbey Glen Way 84128
W Abbey Springs Cir 84084
S & W Abbey View Rd 84088
W Abbotsbury Ln 84081
S Abercrombie Ln 84088
W Aberford Dr 84081
S & W Acoma St 84120
S & W Acord Cir & Way 84120
S Acord Meadows Pl 84119
W Adamson Cir 84081
W Addison Ct 84128
S Adventure Way 84081
S & W Aerie Hill Cir & Dr 84081
W Aire Dr 84088
S Airport Rd
6400-7600 84084
7602-7698 84084
7901-7999 84088
W Alabama Ave 84084
S Alamo St 84120
W Alan Ave 84119
S Alane St 84120
Alane Hollow Rd 84081
S Alba Lucia Dr 84088
S Albany Bay 84128
W Alberta Pl 84084
W Albion View Cir 84088
S Alby Way 84119
S Alderstone Bay 84128
S Alderwood Ct 84120
W Alesa St 84119
W Alexander St 84119
S Alfalfa Cir 84084
W Ali Cir 84120
W Alice Dr 84088
S Alice Way 84119
W Alice Way 84119
S & W Alice Susanna Ln & Pl 84084
S & W Alida Cir & Dr 84084
W Almina Rd 84120
W Almond Ln 84088
W Almont Cir 84128
S & W Alpine Meadows Cir & Dr 84120
W Alpine Ridge Cir 84088
S & W Alsace Way 84119
S Altonia Cir 84120
W Amber Ridge Ln 84120
S Amber Sky Ct 84081
W Amberview Cv 84120
S American Dr 84119
S & W American Park Cir & Dr 84119
W Amethyst Dr 84081
W Amherst Ave 84119
W Ancora Ct 84128
W Anders Ridge Way 84128
S Anderson Way 84084
S Andra Dr 84120
S Angelico Ct 84119
S Angelsea Dr 84084
S Ann Dr 84119
Anna Caroline Dr 84128
W Annapolis Dr 84120
S Annas Cir 84084
Annie Lee Way 84081
W Antelope Rd 84128
W Apaloosa Dr 84128
S & W Apple Farms Cir & Rd 84119
S & W Appleseed Rd 84119
W Appleton Dr 84119
S April Meadows Dr 84084
S & W Arabian Cir & Way 84128
S Arbor Meadows Ln 84088
W Arbutus Cir 84081
W Archer Ln 84120
S Archmore Ct 84128
W Argaus Cir 84128
S Argenta Dr 84088
S Argonaut Dr 84120
W Aristada Ave 84081
S Arlington Ct 84088
S & W Arlington Park Dr 84120
S Armor Ct 84120
Arno Ct & Way 84084
S Arnold Way 84119
S Arrow Wood Ct 84081
W Arthur Dr 84084
S Arthurs Ct 84120
S Asbury Ln 84120
S & W Ash Briar Ln 84084
S Ashburton Ln 84120
S & W Ashby Cv & Way 84128
S Ashby View Cv 84128
W Ashland Cir 84084
S Aspen Fork Dr 84081
W Aspen Park Dr 84081
S & W Aspen Shadow Ct 84081
S & W Aspen View Dr 84081
S Asplund Cir 84119
S Assembly Ct 84120
W Athens Dr 84088
W Athleen Dr 84084
W Atlanta Cir 84084
S Atlas Way 84120
W Atmore Rd 84084
S Aubrey Ln 84128
S & W Audrey Ct & St 84128
S & W August Ln 84081
S & W August Farms Cir & Dr 84119
W August Field Dr 84119
W August View Cir 84081
S Autumn Dr 84084
S & W Autumn Ash Ct 84084
S Autumn Blaze Cv 84128
S Autumn Gold Cir 84081
S Autumn Meadow Cir 84084
W Autumn Oak Cir 84088
S & W Autumn Vistas Dr 84128
W Aviator Dr 84084
S Avignon Pl 84088
W Avion St 84120
W Axel Park Rd 84081
S Azimuth Ct 84081
S & W Bagley Park Rd 84081
S Baldwin Ave 84084
S & W Baldy Dr 84088
S & W Balm Willow Pl 84128
S Balmoral Way 84119
S & W Balsa Ave & Cir 84081
W Balsam Pine Dr 84088

S & W Bamburgh Way 84128
W Barnell Dr 84128
S & W Bannock Cir, Dr & St 84120
W Banquet Ave 84081
W Bar M Cir 84119
W Barbara Cir 84084
S Bard Ln 84088
S & W Barker Rd 84119
W Barletta Ct 84084
W Barley Cir 84084
S Barney St 84119
W Barnfield Way 84119
S Barnstable Dr 84081
S & W Barrington Cir & Dr 84088
W Bartels Cir 84084
S Barton Crest Ct 84120
S & W Barton Hollow Dr 84084
S & W Barton Park Dr 84081
W Basalt Cv 84081
W Basils Way 84120
S & W Basin Ridge Ct & Dr 84128
S Bass Bay 84120
S Basswood Cv 84120
W Bateman Pl 84084
S Bateman Dell Way 84084
S Bateman Field Dr 84084
S & W Bateman Point Dr 84084
S & W Bateman Ponds Cir & Way 84084
S Battlefield Cv 84084
W Baty Dr 84119
W Bawden Ave 84120
W Bayard Ln 84081
S & W Beagley Cir 84128
S Bear Lake Ct 84081
W Bear Valley Cv 84081
S Beargrass Rd 84081
W Beau View Ct 84120
S Beaven Cir 84128
Beaver Cir & St 84119
W Beckford Cir 84088
W Beckton Ct 84120
W Bedford Rd 84119
S & W Bedrock Flats Ln 84081
Beehive Cir & St 84119
S & W Begonia Cir, Dr, Pl & Way 84081
W Belfort Dr 84120
W Bellaviti Cir 84084
W Bello Ave 84128
S & W Belmont Downs Ct & Ln 84128
S Belnap Cir 84088
S & W Bendixon Cir, Dr & Way 84128
S Bent Willow Pl 84119
W Bentoak Dr 84120
Benview Ave & Dr 84120
S Berault Ct 84081
S Berry Glen Cir 84081
S Berula Cir 84081
W Berwick Pl 84119
S & W Beth Park Cir & Dr 84120
S Betty Dr 84088
W Beverly Glen Ave 84084
S Bexley Ct 84120
S Big Bar Ct 84081
S & W Big Oak Ct & Dr 84119
S & W Big Spring Dr 84081
S & W Big Sycamore Dr 84081
S Big Village Ct 84119
W Bighorn Cir 84081
S Bilbo Ave 84084
S & W Bills Dr 84128
W Bingham Creek Dr 84088
S Bingham Hills Ct 84088
S & W Bingham Park Dr 84088
S & W Bingham View Cir & Dr 84088
W Birch Canyon Dr 84081
S Birch Fork Dr 84081
S Birch River Rd 84119
S & W Birch View Ct 84120
S & W Birch Water Ln 84081
W Bird Ct 84088
S Bird Haven Rd 84119
W Birdsong Rd 84119
S Bishop St 84119
S Black Diamond Cv 84081
W Black Elk Way 84088
W Black Goose Cir 84081
S & W Black Granite Way 84120
W Black Oak Dr 84081
S Black Pine St 84088
S Black Village Ct 84119
S Blackfriar Cir 84084
S Blackhawk Dr 84120
S Blue Flower Ct 84081
W Blue Grouse Way 84119
W Blue Haven Dr 84119
W Blue Holly Ct 84081
W Blue Iris Dr 84081
S Blue Jay St 84120
W Blue Kestrel Cv 84119
W Blue Lake Ln 84120
S & W Bluebird Cir & Dr 84120
W Bluebonnet Cir 84081
W Bluecrest Dr 84119
W Bluevail Ct 84081
S & W Bluff Ridge Dr 84128
S Bobwhite Way 84120
W Bona Dea Blvd 84128
W Bonnie Arlene Dr 84128
S Bonniewood St 84119
S & W Boothill Cir & Dr 84120
W Bora Bora Dr 84084
S Bornite Rd 84081
S Botticelli Ct 84119
W Bottlebrush Ln 84081
S & W Bouck Cir 84120
S & W Boulder Creek Rd 84081
W Boulder Glen Cir 84081
S & W Boulder Wash Ln 84081
S Bourdeaux Way 84120
S Box Canyon Rd 84081
W Boys Ranch Ln 84081
W Bradford Cir 84119
W Bradford Park Dr 84119
S Brae Lin Way 84084
W Braemar Ct 84128
S Braewood Pl 84120
S Branden Dr 84120
S Branding Iron Way 84081
S Brandon Ct 84128
W Brandy Cir 84084
S Brandy Wood Dr 84120
W Braveheart Ct 84119
S Bravery Ct 84119
S Breeze Hill Rd 84081
W Brentford Ct 84120
W Brett Ave 84119
W Brewski Bay 84084
S Brians Way 84119
S & W Briar Dr 84084
W Bridge Maple Ln 84081
W Bridge Point Cir 84128
W Bridgeport Way 84084
S & W Bridle Creek Dr 84081
W Bridle Farms Rd 84128
W Bridle Hollow Pl 84081
S Bridle Mark Way 84081
S Bridle Ridge Cir 84081
W Bridle Vista Cir 84081
W Brigadoon Park Dr 84088
S & W Bristol Way 84119
W Bristol Ridge Rd 84088
W Brittany Ct 84120
S Brittany Park Ave 84084
S Brittany Town Dr 84084
W Brittney Downs Dr 84120
S & W Brixham Way 84120
S Broad Creek Dr 84128
S Brock St 84119
S Bromley Rd 84084
S & W Brook Hollow Ct & Dr 84128
S & W Brook Maple Way 84081
Brookfield Cir & Way 84120
S Brookhurst Cir 84120
S & W Brookpoint Dr 84128
S Brookside Dr 84120
W Brookview Cir 84128
S & W Brookway Dr 84119
W Brower Cir 84084
S Brown Ave 84088
S Brown Park Dr 84081
W Brud Dr 84128
W Brush Creek Bay 84120
W Brush Fork Dr 84081
S Brushwood Bay 84120
W Brynn Cir 84088
W Brynwood Pine Bay 84088
W Buckskin Ln 84088
S Buckthorn Cir 84081
S & W Bueno Vista Dr 84088
W Bull Creek Ct 84081
W Bull Moose Ct 84088
S Burdock Dr 84128
S & W Burkman Way 84120
S & W Burlingame Dr 84120
W Burning Sky Ct 84081
S & W Burningham Cir & Dr 84119
S Burnt Oak Dr 84081
W Burrey Ct 84119
S Bury Rd 84081
S Busman Pl 84128
S Byde A Wyle Rd 84119
W Byron Cir 84119
W Cable Ct 84084
W Cache Creek Cir 84088
S & W Cadenza Dr 84081
S & W Cajean Cir & Way 84088
W Calais Ct 84119
S Calendula Ln 84081
S Calico Way 84120
S & W Caliente Dr 84081
S Calkary Cir 84120
S Callao Dr 84128
W Callery Ln 84081
S Callie Dr 84084
S Calvin Dr 84120
W Calvo Dr 84119
S Calvo View Cir 84119
S Calypso St 84120
W Calyx Cir 84081
S Camas Meadows Cir 84081
S & W Cambridge Dr 84119
S & W Camelot Way 84084
S Campfire Cir 84119
S Campo St 84119
S & W Campus View Dr 84084
W Camstone Dr 84120
W Canal Rd 84084
W Candice Wood Cir 84120
Caney Rd 84081
S Canmore Dr 84081
W Cannon Creek Cir 84119
S Cantwell St 84119
W Cape Cod Dr 84128
S & W Cape Ridge Ln 84128
S & W Cape Vista Way 84128
S & W Capernaum Rd 84088
S Caprine Ct 84084
W Caraway Bay 84088
S Carbon Cir 84120
S Cardoness Way 84088
S Carla St 84120
W Carlos Dr 84119
S Carnegie Tech St 84120
W Carolee Hill Cir 84081
W Caroleen Park Cir 84128
W Carolina Dr 84084
W Carpell Ave 84081
S Carrie Dr 84120
S & W Carson Cir & Ln 84084
S Carter Cir 84084
S Casa Bonita Pl 84119
S Cascade Springs Ln 84088
S & W Case Mountain Cv & Rd 84081
S Casino Camino St 84119
S Cassell St 84119
S & W Cassidy Cir & Ln 84084
S Castle Rd 84128
W Castle Pines Way 84084
S & W Castle View Dr 84128
S Castleford Dr 84084
S Cave Bay 84128
Cedar Cir & St 84088
W Cedar Fork Dr 84081
S & W Cedar Hill Ct & Rd 84081
S Celebration Dr 84128
W Center Hollow Ct 84119
S & W Center Park Dr 84084
S & W Center View Ct, Dr & Way 84084
S & W Centerbrook Dr 84119
W Cerro Ln 84128
S Chalice Way 84120
W Chantay Dr 84128
S & W Chantry Rd 84120
S Chari Cir 84084
W Charing Cross Rd 84084
S Charisse Cir 84084
W Charlene Ln 84120
S & W Charles Dr & Way 84120
W Charlesworth Cir 84088
S Charter Way 84081
S Chatham St 84119
S & W Chatterleigh Ave & Rd 84128
S Cheerful Vista Rd 84120
W Cheltonham Way 84084
S Cherry Blossom Cir 84120
S Cherry Hollow Cir 84120
W Cherry Laurel Ln 84081
S Cherry Leaf Dr 84084
S & W Cherry View Dr 84120
W Cherrywood Ln 84120
S Cheryl St 84119
W Chester Rd 84120
W Chester Park Dr 84119
S Chesterfield St 84119
W Chets Ct 84120
S Chilwell Cv 84081
S & W Chippewa Pl & Rd 84120
S & W Chiswick Ct 84081
W Choctaw Ave 84120
S Christalee Ct 84084
S & W Christopherson Cir & Dr 84120
W Christy Ave 84119
S Chromalloy Cir 84088
S & W Chula Cir & Dr 84128
S & W Cilma Cir, Dr & Pl 84128
S & W Cimmarron Dr 84128
W Cinnamon Tree Cir 84120
W Cisco Ct 84081
S Citadel St 84120
W City Center Ct 84119
S & W City Vistas Way 84128
W Cj Way 84119
S Clare Dr 84119
W Clark View Cv 84120
S Claudia St 84120
S & W Claudia Hill Ln 84081
W Clavinet Cir 84088
W Clay Hollow Ave 84081
W Claybourne Ave 84119
S Clayton Ridge Way 84084
S & W Clearbrook Cir & Dr 84119
S & W Clematis Way 84081
W Clermont Dr 84120
Clemates Cir & Dr 84081
W Cliff Rose Ct 84081
S & W Cliffhaven Ln 84128
S Clover Cir 84084
W Club Ln 84088
S Clubside Cv 84119
S Clydesdale Dr 84128
S Coachman Way 84088
S & W Cobble Cir 84081
S & W Cobble Creek Dr 84081
S Cobble Hollow Ln 84081
W Cobble Ridge Dr 84084
S & W Cochise Dr 84120
S Cody Ln 84084
W Colander Dr 84088
S & W Colby Ave 84128
S & W Cold Stone Ln 84081
S Colebrook Cv 84128
S Coleus Ct 84081
W Coley Cir 84120
S Colgate St 84120
S Collie Dr 84128
S Collins Camp Ct 84128
S Colt Ct 84120
S Colt Plaza Dr 84128
S Colter Bay Cir 84088
W Colton Mill Ct 84120
S & W Columbia Dr 84084
S Comet Hill Cir 84081
S & W Como Ln 84081
W Compass Point Ln 84084
W Concord Cir 84084
W Condie Park Cir 84120
W Condie View Dr 84120
S Coneflower Ct 84081
W Conewood St 84120
S Congregation Ct 84120
Constitution Blvd & Dr 84119
S & W Contadora Cir, Ct, Dr & Ln 84128
W Continental Dr 84120
S Cool Creek Way 84081
S & W Cool Water Way 84081
S Copper Ln 84088
W Copper Brook Cir 84088
S & W Copper Canyon Way 84081
W Copper Cloud Ln 84081
W Copper Dale Pl 84088
S & W Copper Dust Ln 84081
W Copper Glen Ct 84088
W Copper Meadow Ln 84081
S & W Copper Pot Ln 84088
W Copper Valley Ln 84088
S Copper Vista Cir 84081
W Coppergate Cir 84084
W Copperhill Dr 84128
S Coppering Ave 84081
S & W Copperwood Dr 84081
W Coquille Ave 84120
W Coral Rose Pl 84120
S Coralroot Cir 84081
S Corbin Dr 84081
W Corbin Bay 84120
W Cordelle Cir 84084
W Corilyn Cir 84120
S Cork Oak Dr 84081
S Corliss Ave 84088
W Cornflower Cir 84081
W Corona Cir 84084
S Corporate Park Dr 84120
W Corral Cir 84088
S Corridor Ln 84119
S & W Cortney Dr & Pl 84120
S & W Cosmo Cir, Dr & Pl 84081
W Cottage Brook Cir 84120
W Cottage Point Dr 84081
W Cottontail Dr 84128
S Cougar Ln
6300-6698 84081
6951-6999 84084
S & W Country Home Ln 84084
W Country Meadow Ln 84120
S Country Mill Ct 84084
S & W Country Squire Dr 84088
W Countryside Ln 84084
W Countrywood Ln 84088
W Courtney Ct 84088
S & W Cousin Cv 84120
W Coventry Park Dr 84119
S Covered Wagon Cir 84088
S & W Covewood Pl 84088
S Cowan Way 84120
S Coyote Cv 84088
S Cozy River Pl 84119
W Cranston Cv 84128
S & W Cree Dr 84120
Creekwood Cir & Dr 84088
S Crescent Mine Ln 84081
S Crespi Ct 84119
W Crest St 84128
S & W Crestfield Dr 84119
W Crestmoor Ct 84088
S Crews Hill Ct 84120
S Crichton Cv 84128
S Cricket Ln 84081
S Crimson King Cv 84128
S Crimson Sky Ct 84081
S Cripple Creek Cir 84088
W Croftwood Cv 84128
W Crow Cir 84128
W Crowder Cir 84120
S & W Crown Ave & Dr 84120
W Crownpointe Dr 84120
S & W Crowsnest Dr 84081
S & W Crus Corvi Rd 84081
W Crystal Ave 84119
S Crystal Creek Dr 84081
S Crystal Downs Ln 84084
S Crystal Lake Way 84120
W Crystal Ridge Dr 84084
S Crystal Vista Ln 84088
S Cumbria Cir 84119
S & W Cyclamen Cir, Ct, Cv, Dr, Pl, Sq & Way 84081
W Cygnus Hill Cv 84081
S & W Daffodil Ave & Way 84081
S Dairy Hill Ct 84084
S Dale Park Cir 84084
S & W Dalmatian St 84128
S Damascus Way 84088
S Dan Dr 84084
S Dana Shelby Ct 84119
W Dannon Way 84081
W Dansere Cir 84088
W Darle Ave 84128
S Darlington Dr 84081
S & W Dartmouth Cir & Dr 84120
S David Pl 84119
W Davis View Ln 84128
S & W Dawn Vista Rd 84081
W Day Park Dr 84120
S Days End Ct 84081
W De Loss Ct 84081
S De Mass Dr 84128
S & W Dean Cir & Dr 84120
S Deann Dr 84128
W Debenham Pl 84119
W Deborah Dr 84088
W Decatur Cir 84084
Decker Lake Blvd, Dr & Ln 84119
S & W Decora Way 84081
S & W Deep Creek Cir & Dr 84081
W Deer Wood Dr 84120
W Deerbrush Cir 84081
W Deercrest Dr 84120
S & W Deermeadow Cir & Dr 84120
S Deitrick Cir 84081
W Del Cir 84120
S Delaney Ct 84128
W Delfina Ct 84120
S Delicate Arch Dr 84081
W Dell Wood Ct 84081
W Delta Park Cir 84120
S Denby Dale Rd 84084
S & W Denman Ave 84081
S & W Dennis Cir & Dr 84120
S & W Deno Ct & Dr 84120
W Denton Cir 84084
S Derby Cir 84088
W Derby Cir 84088
S Derby St 84119
S Derby Way 84088
W Derby Way 84088
S Derbyshire 84120
S & W Desert Willow Dr 84119
S & W Designer Ct 84119
W Detevis Cir 84120
S & W Devonna Rd 84081
S Dewdrops Dr 84081
S Diamond Dove Dr 84088
S Diamond Point Cir 84128
S Diamond Ridge Cir 84128
S & W Diamondleaf Way 84081
W Dimond Dr 84084
S & W Discovery Ct & Dr 84081
W Dixie Cir 84084
S Dixie Dr 84084
W Dixie Dr 84128
S Dixieann Dr 84119
S Dolley Ct 84128
S Domian Ct 84128
S Donatello Ct 84119
S Doodle Bug Pl 84128
S & W Dorilee Dr 84088
S Double Arch Cir 84081
S & W Dove Creek Ln 84081
S & W Dove Meadows Ln 84088
W Dove Point Rd 84119
S Dovetail Dr 84128
S Downs Way 84119
W Drake Ln 84084
S Drawbridge Way 84120
W Dry Sycamore Ln 84081
S Duane Cv 84088
S & W Dublin Cir & Dr 84119
S & W Duchess St 84081
S Duck Ridge Way 84081
S & W Duffys Ln 84084
S Dukewater Cir 84120
W Dunford Ct 84128
S Dunham Ln 84119
S & W Dunlop Ct & Dr 84088
S & W Dunraven Dr 84119
S & W Dunsmoore Way 84120
W Duquesne St 84120
S Durrans Ln 84120
S & W Dusky Dr 84081
W Eagle Ct 84088
W Eagle Glen Way 84120
W Eagle Heights Dr 84120
W Eagle Hill Cir 84081
W Eagle Park Ln 84120

S & W Eagle Rock
Way 84120
W Eagle Wood Dr 84120
W Eaglemann Ct 84084
W Eagles Peak Cv 84128
S & W Early Dawn Dr 84081
S & W Early Duke Dr &
St 84120
S Eastcrest Rd 84120
S Eastern Park Ln 84119
Echo Ridge Dr 84081
S Echo View Dr 84081
W Eclipse Hill Dr 84081
S Edenbrook Way 84088
W Edgewater Cir 84120
W Edinburgh Ln 84081
S Edith Grove Ln 84120
S Education Cir 84128
W El Cabrio Dr 84119
S & W El Cajon Cir &
Dr 84119
W El Centro 84119
S El Dorado Pl 84088
W El Glen Ave 84120
S & W Elaine Ave &
Dr 84120
W Elba Ave 84119
S & W Elbow River
Cir 84081
W Elizabeth Cir 84084
S & W Elk Meadows
Dr 84088
S & W Elk Ridge Cir &
Dr 84084
W Elk Run Ln 84088
S Elkwood Cir 84081
W Ella St 84088
W Ellis Dr 84128
S & W Elma Cir & St 84120
S Elmhearst Dr 84088
S Eloni Cir 84084
W Elwood Way 84088
W Emerald Green St 84120
W Emma Sue Cir 84081
S & W Emmons Dr 84088
S & W Empress Ct &
Ln 84081
S & W Enterado Ave &
Cir 84119
S Equator Ln 84084
W Erica Cir 84084
W Erickson Park Dr 84084
S & W Eskesen Cir &
Dr 84120
Etruscan Ct & Way 84084
S Etude Dr 84088
S & W Eucalyptus
Way 84119
S Eugenia Pl 84119
S Evan Hill Rd 84081
W Evening Dove Cir 84119
S Evening Glow Ct 84081
S & W Eveningshade
Dr 84084
S Excaliber Way 84088
S & W Executive Cir &
Dr 84084
W Facet Way 84081
W Fahnian Cir 84088
S Fair Isle Ln 84128
S & W Fairgrove Ln 84120
S Fairlane Cir 84120
W Fairmount Cir 84084
S Fairwind Dr 84084
S Falcon St 84120
Fanfare Ct & Dr 84128
Faraninc Dr 84128
S Fargo Rd 84084
S Fargo St 84119
W Farm Rd 84088
S Farm Oak Ct 84081
W Farm Station Way 84120
W Farmer Cir 84120
S & W Farrell Ln 84088
W Farrington Ct 84084
W Farthington Cir 84088

W Fassio Cir 84120
W Feldspar Way 84081
W Fenchurch Rd 84084
W Fern Cir 84084
W Fescue Cir 84128
S & W Festival Dr 84120
S Festive Way 84088
S & W Feulner Ct &
Dr 84128
S & W Feulner Park Cir
& Rd 84081
W Field Creek Way 84081
W Fieldbury Cir 84120
S Fieldmint Ln 84128
W Fieldview Dr 84128
W Figure Skate Cir 84084
Finair Dr & St 84120
S Finsbury Ln 84120
W Fiona Cir 84120
S Fire Lily Ln 84081
S Fire Sky Ct 84081
S Firefox Cir 84081
S & W Firenze Pl 84081
W Fish Lake Dr 84081
S Fisher Way 84119
Flacharr Dr 84084
W Flag Ave 84119
S & W Flagstone Dr 84128
S Flair St 84120
W Flaming Sky Ct 84081
S Flamingo Way 84084
W Flat Creek Cir 84088
W Flats Cir 84119
S & W Flaxton Ln 84081
S Florentine Way 84084
S & W Florlita Ave &
Cir 84119
W Fly Catcher Ln 84119
W Foggia Ct 84084
S Forest Wood Dr 84120
S Forsythia Dr 84119
W Founders Ln 84128
S & W Fox Den Dr 84084
W Fox Park Dr 84088
S & W Fox Pointe Ct &
Dr 84088
S Fox Ridge Way 84081
W Fox Shadow Dr 84120
S Fox Tail Bay 84084
W Fox Trot Cir 84084
S Foxflower Ct 84081
S Foxtail Pine Way 84088
W Foxton Cir 84084
S Franklin Cir 84084
S & W Frederick Pl 84119
W Freedom Ln 84084
W Friar Way 84084
W Friardale St 84120
S Frodo Ave 84084
S & W Fuchsia Cir, Dr &
Pl 84081
S Gaelic Cir 84088
W Gala Way 84128
S Galaxy Hill Rd 84081
W Galaxy Park Pl 84088
S & W Galilee Cir, Ct &
Way 84088
W Garden Breeze Ct 84128
W Garden Creek Way 84088
W Garden Crest Cir 84088
S & W Garden Gate
Dr 84128
W Garden Green Cir 84120
W Garden Vista Cv 84120
W Gardner Ln 84088
S & W Garonne Ave &
Ct 84084
W Gaskill Way 84081
W Gates Ave 84128
S & W Gateshead Dr 84120
S Gazelle Rd 84128
S Geitz St 84120
W Gemstone Dr 84084
W Gentry Ln 84088
W Georges Rd 84084
S Georgia Dr 84084

S Geralee Ln 84084
W Geronimo Way 84081
W Ghost Hill Dr 84081
S & W Ginny Cir & Dr 84128
S & W Glen Eagle Dr 84128
S & W Glen Hill Cir &
Dr 84120
W Glen Livet Ct 84128
W Glen Park Ct 84120
W Glen Springs Way 84088
S Globe Willow Ct 84119
S & W Goblin Valley Cv
& Dr 84081
S Goddard Cir 84088
S Gold Cir 84084
W Gold Bullion Ct 84081
S Gold Finch Cir 84081
S Gold Medal Dr 84084
W Gold Rush Cir 84084
S Golden Arrow Cv 84128
S & W Golden Gate
Cir 84081
S Golden Grain Cir 84120
S & W Goldenpointe
Way 84088
W Goldrush Pl 84128
W Good Springs Cv 84081
S Goslin Ct 84088
W Graceland Way 84081
S & W Granada Hills Ct
& Dr 84088
S & W Grand Teton
Dr 84088
S Grand Valley Pl 84081
S Granger Dr 84119
W Grantham Ln 84120
S Grasmere Ln 84119
S Grayline Ct 84081
W Great Lakes Dr 84120
W Great Pasture Rd 84088
W Grecian Dr 84128
W Green Acre Dr 84088
W Green Ash Cir 84081
W Green Grove Ln 84120
W Green Hedge Way 84084
W Green Mesa Way 84088
S Green Spire Cir 84128
Greenmont Cir & Dr 84120
S & W Greensand Dr 84084
W Grevillea Ln 84081
S & W Greystock Cir 84120
S Grizzly Way 84081
W Grouse Cir 84120
W Grovewood Cir 84120
W Guard Ct 84088
W Hacienda Dr 84119
Hadley Ave & Ct 84128
S Hadwen Dr 84128
W Half Penny Cir 84088
S Halifax Park Dr 84119
W Hall Cir 84119
S Hall Dr 84084
W Hall Dr 84084
S & W Hallmark Cir &
Dr 84119
W Halter Creek Way 84128
W Halton Ln 84120
S Hamden Ct 84120
S Hamilton Cir 84084
S Hammonton Cir 84119
S Hampshire Cir 84119
W Hampstead Ln 84120
S Hampton Park Dr 84119
W Hanover Park Dr 84119
S Harbonne Ln 84084
W Harbor St 84120
W Harker Cir 84120
S & W Harkness Dr 84088
W Harlech Ln 84128
S Harley Cv 84081
S Harlingen Cir 84119
W Harman Dr 84120
S & W Harrisonwood Cir
& Dr 84119
S Harrow Ct 84120
S Hartford Park Ave 84081

S & W Hartley Ct &
Ln 84081
S & W Harvest Cir &
Ln 84084
S Harvest Ridge Dr 84084
W Harvest Skies Ct 84081
S & W Harvest View
Way 84084
W Harvestmill Dr 84081
W Haun Dr 84088
S & W Havasu Way 84120
W Haven Maple Dr 84081
S & W Haven Ridge
Way 84128
Hawarden Cir & Dr 84119
S Hawk Nest Cir 84120
S & W Hawker Ln 84128
S & W Hawkeye Cir, Dr
& St 84120
S Hawley Park Rd 84081
S Hawthorne Glen Cir 84081
W Hayden Peak Dr
4600-4798 84088
5000-5198 84081
W Hayloft Cv 84120
S Heather Way 84084
S Heather Downs Dr 84088
S Heathercrest Cir 84120
S Heatherview Ct 84120
W Hector Dr 84119
S Hedron Pl 84119
W Heidelberg Ln 84084
S & W Helenic Ct &
Ln 84088
W Hellas Dr 84120
S Hempstead St 84119
W Henry Alice Ct 84084
S & W Henrys Fork
Way 84081
W Hercules Dr 84120
W Herdan Cir 84128
W Herdon Way 84128
S Heritage Dr 84119
W Heritage Oaks Cv 84084
S & W Herman Cir &
Dr 84119
W Heron Way 84119
S Hertford Dr 84119
S & W Heywood Dr 84081
S & W Hialeah Rd 84119
S & W Hidden Peak
Dr 84088
W Higate Ave 84128
S Higbee Cir 84119
S High Bluff Dr 84081
S High Commons
Way 84120
W High Market Dr 84120
S High Summit Cir 84088
W Highbury Pkwy 84120
S & W Highland Hollow
Cv & Dr 84084
S Highlander St 84128
S Highway 111 84081
S Hilgard Dr 84088
W Hill Vista Ct 84081
S Hillers Dr 84088
W Hillsboro Cir 84084
S Hillsdale Dr 84119
S Hilltop Oak Dr 84081
S Hinton Ct 84128
W Hockey Ln 84084
S Hogan St 84119
S & W Holder Dr 84120
S Holder Knoll Dr 84120
W Hollandia Ln 84084
S Hollow Moor Cv 84084
S & W Hollow View
Way 84084
S & W Holly Lily Ln 84081
S Holly Oak Dr 84081
S Holmberg St 84119
S Homecrest Dr 84119
W Homestead Farms
Ln 84119
W Honda Ave 84119

S Honeywood Ln 84120
Hopalong Cir 84088
S Hopi Cir 84081
S Hopi Dr
4100-4261 84119
4263-4299 84119
6200-6249 84081
6251-6299 84081
W Horizon Peak Way 84128
S Horse Rd 84128
S Hoyle Cir 84081
S Huckleberry Cir 84088
S Humboldt Ct 84081
W Hummingbird Way 84120
S & W Hunter Ct & Dr 84120
W Hunter Ash Cir 84128
W Hunter Birch Cir 84128
S Hunter Canyon Dr 84128
S & W Hunter Crest Cir
& Dr 84128
S & W Hunter Dawn
Way 84128
S & W Hunter Dell Pl 84128
S & W Hunter Farm Cir
& Way 84128
Hunter Hollow Cir &
Dr 84128
W Hunter Maple Cir 84128
S & W Hunter Mesa
Dr 84128
S & W Hunter Oak
Way 84128
W Hunter Park Cir 84128
W Hunter Peak Cir 84128
W Hunter Pine Cir 84128
S Hunter Point Cir 84128
S Hunter Spring Dr 84128
W Hunter Valley Dr 84128
S Hunter View Dr 84128
S & W Hunter Villa Ln 84128
S Hunter Village Dr 84128
W Hunter Vista Cir 84128
W Hunter Wood Cir 84128
W Hyannis Ave 84119
W Ice Skate Cir 84084
W Icehouse Way 84081
S Impala Cir 84128
S & W Imperial Oak
Dr 84081
S Inca Cir 84120
S Independence Dr 84119
W Indian Ln 84120
S Indian Gulch Cv 84081
S & W Indian Oak Dr 84081
S Industry Cir 84088
S Ingram Dr 84088
S Interlochin Ln 84084
Inverness Cir & Dr 84084
Island Cir & Way 84120
S & W Island Creek
Dr 84081
S & W Island Park Dr 84081
Islington Ln 84120
Italian Ct & St 84084
S Ivana St 84120
S Ivanhoe Ct 84120
S & W Ivy Gable Dr 84081
S Ivy Leaf Pl 84088
S & W Ivy Park Ct &
Dr 84119
S Ivy Springs Ln 84081
W Ivy Terrace Ct 84081
W Jack Cir 84120
S & W Jackling Way 84081
S Jackson Lake Dr 84081
W Jacob Hill Cir 84081
W Jacquelyn St 84088
S Jade Hill Cv 84081
S Jamboree St 84120
S & W Jana Lee Dr 84088
S Jane Cir 84120
S Janet Way 84088
W Janette Ave 84120
W Jasmine St 84120
S Jason Pl 84119
S Jasper Hill Dr 84081

S Jayden Cv 84120
W Jean Way 84084
S Jefferson Cir 84084
S & W Jeffs Cir 84128
S Jenelles Bay 84119
S Jenkins Ln 84088
S & W Jenny Lake Dr 84088
S Jensen Cir 84120
S Jerry Way 84088
W Jersey Cir 84120
W Jewkes Cir 84088
S Jills Pl 84120
S & W Jocelyn Way 84128
Jodie Cir & Ln 84128
W Jody St 84088
S John Way 84120
S John Henry Dr 84119
S John Robert Cir 84120
S & W Johnson Ridge
Cir & Ln 84084
W Jonestead Way 84084
S Jordan Close Cir 84084
S Jordan Dale Rd 84084
S & W Jordan Landing
Blvd 84084
Jordan Meadows Cv &
Ln 84084
W Jordan River Blvd 84088
S Jordan Valley Way 84088
S & W Jordan Villa Dr 84088
S Jordan Village Rd 84084
S Jordanelle Ct 84081
W Joshua Cir 84081
S Joycelyn Cir 84120
W Joyes Ln 84088
W Joyli Cir 84088
Jubilee Ct & Way 84128
S & W Judd Cir & Ln 84088
S & W Julie Ann Way 84088
W Juniper Fork Dr 84081
S Justice St 84119
S Kallie Cir 84120
S & W Kapford Dr 84128
W Karma Ave 84120
W Kate Cv 84088
S & W Kathleen Ave &
Cir 84120
S & W Kathy Ave &
Cir 84119
S Keelcrest Dr 84084
S Keltic Ct 84128
S Kendrick Dr 84119
S & W Kensington Park
Dr 84088
S & W Kentucky Cir &
Dr 84084
S Kenyon Cir 84088
S Kenyon Park Dr 84120
W Kenyons Claim Cir 84081
W Kestrel Dr 84120
W Ketchum Dr 84128
S & W Kewanee Cir &
Dr 84120
S Keys St 84119
S Kiesta Ct 84081
W Kiku Ct 84120
S Kildare Cir 84119
S Kilee Ct 84128
S Killarney Cir 84119
S Kilt Rock Ct 84128
S Kimberly Way 84128
S King Arthur Dr 84119
S & W King Valley Cir,
Dr, Ln, Rd, St & Way 84128
S Kingdom Ct 84119
S Kings Ct 84128
S Kings Bridge Dr 84084
S & W Kings Estate Cir,
Ct & Dr 84128
W Kingsbarn Way 84119
S & W Kingsbury Ln 84119
W Kingsley Ct 84084
S & W Kingspointe Cir &
Ln 84119
W Kingstonvale Dr 84081
W Kinloch Way 84119

W Kintail Ct 84128
Kiowa Ct & Way 84120
S Kit Cir 84084
S & W Klondyke Dr 84081
W Knights Way 84084
S & W Knowley Rd 84081
S Knowsley Dr 84120
S Kokopelli Ct 84081
S Kristilyn Ln 84084
W La Questa Ct 84120
S La Suesue St 84119
W La Vista Dr 84088
W Labrador Cir 84128
S & W Lago Grande
Dr 84128
S & W Laguna Cir &
Dr 84088
W Lake Breeze Ln 84120
S Lake Erie Dr 84120
S Lake Meadow Dr 84120
S Lake Park Blvd 84120
W Lake Park Blvd 84120
S Lake Park Cir 84119
W Lake Park Dr 84119
S & W Lake Powell Cir &
Rd 84081
S Lakecrest Dr 84119
W Lamus Cir 84128
S Lancashire Cir 84119
S Lance St 84119
W Lanceleaf Ln 84084
W Lancelot Dr 84119
W Land Dr 84119
W Landen Cir 84120
S Lantana Dr 84088
S Larabrook Way 84084
S & W Laredo Cir &
Way 84120
S Laree St 84120
W Lariat Dr 84120
W Lark Way 84120
S & W Larkin Way 84120
W Larry Cir 84120
S Las Flores St 84119
S Latigo Cir 84128
S Latimer Dr 84120
W Latitude Ln 84084
S Laurel Green Dr 84120
W Laurel Hill Cir 84081
S Laurel Oak Dr 84081
S & W Laurel Ridge Cir
& Dr 84088
W Laytham Way 84088
S Lazy J Cir 84120
S & W Le Rosier Ct 84088
S & W Leafy Hollow
Ln 84119
S Lee Ann St 84119
S Lee Maur St 84119
S Leeds Cv 84128
W Legacy Hill Dr 84081
S & W Lehi Dr 84119
W Lehman Ave 84119
S & W Leichen Ave &
Ct 84081
W Leisure Cir 84084
W Leisure Villas Ct 84084
W Leland Dr 84084
W Lemar Way 84120
W Lemay Ave 84119
S & W Lemonwood Cir &
St 84120
S Lena Dr 84088
W Leo Park Rd 84081
W Leon Ave 84119
W Leonardo Ln 84119
S Leslie Dr 84088
S Lester St 84119
W Leticia Ct 84081
W Lewis Acres Ct 84120
S & W Lewisport Dr 84084
S & W Lexington Dr 84081
S & W Lexington Park
Dr 84119
W Lexington View Dr 84088
W Liberty Dr 84119

Street	ZIP
S Liesel St	84084
W Lilac Ave	84081
S Lilloet St	84120
W Lillyvale Pl	84081
S Lime Ln	84081
W Linda Vista Dr	84119
W Links Dr	84120
S & W Linton Cir & Dr	84088
W Lionel St	84081
S Lionheart Way	84119
S Lisa Ave	84088
S Lismore Ln	84088
S Little Cir	84084
W Little Cir	84084
W Little Ln	84119
S & W Little Creek Dr	84088
S & W Little Oak Ct & Dr	84119
S & W Liza Ln	84081
S Lobelia Dr	84081
W Loch Raven Ct	84128
W Lochness Ave	84128
S & W Lockwood Dr	84120
S Lona Cir	84084
W Lone View Ct	84088
Lonebellow Dr	84081
W Lonesome Cir	84088
S & W Long Ct & Dr	84088
W Long Leaf Dr	84088
S & W Long Valley Ct & Dr	84128
S Longitude Ln	84084
S Loon Ct	84119
W Lopalena Cir	84081
W Loren Way	84120
W Lorient Ave	84084
S & W Lorna Cir & Dr	84120
W Losee Dr	84120
S & W Losser Dr	84119
S Lotus Way	84081
S & W Lotus Blossom Dr	84120
W Louisville Cir	84084
W Lower Huntly Way	84088
W Lower Newark Way	84088
S Loyola St	84120
S Lucerne Ln	84084
W Lucia Cir	84088
W Lucky Cv	84084
W Luella Cir	84084
W Lugano Dr	84081
W Luge Ln	84084
S & W Lusterpointe Ct & Ln	84088
S & W Luxor Park	84120
S Lynaria Ct	84081
S Lynn Ln	84088
S Lynn Ridge Ln	84128
S Lyoni Ct	84081
W Maasai Dr	84081
S Mac Duff Ln	84088
S & W Mackay Meadows Pl	84119
S Macks Inn Cir	84081
S Madill Cir	84119
S Madison Cir	84084
S Madison Nan Dr	84081
W Magnolia Tree Cir	84084
S & W Magnum Vista Dr & Pl	84128
S & W Mahogany Pl	84081
S Maiden Ct	84120
S & W Maidie Ln	84119
S Mainstay Pl	84128
S & W Majestic Loop Rd	84081
W Majestic Meadows Pl	84128
S Mallard Ln	84088
W Malvern Ave	84119
W Mandan Ave	84120
W Mandy Cir	84084
S Manhattan Ct	84120
S & W Manhatten Dr	84120
S & W Mann Way	84120
W Mansfield Cir	84084
S Mantova Way	84081
S Maple Way	84119
W Maple Canyon Rd	84081
S Maple Fork Dr	84081
S & W Maple Grove Dr	84088
S & W Maple Meadows Dr	84120
S Maple Water Dr	84081
S & W Mapleleaf Way	84088
S & W Marcrest Cir & Dr	84128
S & W Marcus Rd	84119
S & W Mardi Gras Ln	84088
S & W Maren Pl	84081
S Maricopa Cir	84120
S Marin Cv	84128
W Marion Dr	84084
W Marjorie Ct	84088
W Mark Ave	84119
S Mark Iv Ct	84119
S Market St	84119
S Markread St	84119
W Markwood Ct	84120
S & W Marseilles Way	84119
S Marsha Dr	84128
S Marshrock Rd	84081
W Martin Way	84128
W Marty Cir	84084
S Marylebone Rd	84084
S Mascaro Way	84081
W Mask Dr	84119
S & W Masters Cir, Ct & Dr	84128
S Matisse Ln	84119
W Maudine Ave	84120
S Maul Oak Dr	84081
S Maxine St	84120
S May Cir	84120
W Mayapple Way	84119
S & W Mayflower St	84081
S Mcclanahan Ln	84081
S Mccune Ct	84081
S Mcdowell Ct	84081
S & W Mcginnis Ln	84081
S Mcgregor Ln	84088
S & W Mcintyre Ct & Way	84081
S Mckenzie Ln	84081
S Mcnae Way	84084
S & W Meadow Breeze Way	84128
S & W Meadow Clover Ct & Ln	84128
S Meadow Estates Dr	84081
W Meadow Farm Dr	84128
S & W Meadow Gate Cir & Dr	84120
S & W Meadow Glen Way	84088
W Meadow Green Dr	84120
S Meadow Green Way	84088
W Meadow Green Way	84088
S & W Meadow Leaf Ct	84119
S Meadow Lily Ln	84081
S Meadow Loop Bay	84128
S Meadow Point Ct	84128
W Meadow Ridge Dr	84088
S & W Meadow Stream Rd	84119
Meadowbrook Cir & Dr	84119
W Meadowland Ave	84084
S Meadowlark Dr	84119
S Meadowlark Ln	84088
W Meander Ave	84128
Meashang St	84088
S Mel Helen Way	84084
W Melanie Place Ln	84088
S Melbrook Ln	84081
W Melville Cir	84088
W Merlot Way	84081
S Merrick Ct	84081
W Merril Cir	84120
W Merrilie Cir	84128
S Merry Ln	84120
S & W Mesa Arch Dr	84081
S Mesa Maple Dr	84081
S Messina Ct	84119
W Meteor Hill Cv	84081
S Michaelangelo Ct	84119
S & W Michaelsen Way	84088
S Midas Cir	84128
S Middlepark Ln	84119
S & W Midvalley Cir, Ct & Dr	84088
S & W Midway Dr	84120
W Miera Ln	84120
S Mignon Dr	84120
Milden Cir & Ln	84128
S Milfoil Cir	84081
S & W Milky Hollow Ln	84084
W Millen Cir	84128
W Millerama Ave	84119
W Millerberg Way	84084
S Millet Cir	84120
S Millrace Bend Rd	84088
S Millrace View Cir	84088
S & W Millsden Ln	84084
W Milos Dr	84120
S Mindy Cir	84120
S Mineral Mount Dr	84081
W Miners Mesa Dr	84081
S & W Minuet Ave, Cir & Ct	84119
S Mira Loma St	84119
W Mirror Lake Dr	84081
W Misty Dr	84084
W Misty Fen Way	84088
S & W Misty Hollow Way	84084
S Moat Cir	84120
S & W Mock Orange Dr	84119
S & W Mockingbird Cir & Way	84119
S & W Mohave Way	84120
S Moki Cir	84081
W Mona Ln	84084
W Monroe Cir	84084
S Montaia Dr	84119
W Monterey Pine Ln	84088
S & W Montrone Dr	84119
W Moody Skies Ct	84081
W Moon Crest Ct	84081
W Moonshine Cir	84088
W Moor Ln	84084
S & W Moorgate Ave & Cir	84120
W Moose Horn Ct	84088
W Moreland Cir	84084
W Morning Dove Cir	84119
W Morning Laurel Ln	84081
S & W Morning Lily Ct & Ln	84081
S & W Moshier Ln	84120
W Moshier View Cir	84120
S Mount Spencer Cir	84088
S & W Mountain Aura Dr	84081
W Mountain Brook Dr	84081
S Mountain Goat Way	84128
S & W Mountain Hill Dr	84081
S & W Mountain Iris Way	84081
S & W Mountain Laurel Ln	84081
S Mountain Meadow Dr	84088
W Mountain Park Cir	84081
S Mountain Pass Cir	84088
W Mountain Pine Dr	84088
W Mountain View Ct	84084
S & W Mountain Vista Dr	84081
Muirkirk Cir & Rd	84081
S Mullien Dr	84081
W Muriel Way	84119
W Mustang Cir	84088
W Mya Nichol Cir	84084
W Nancy Dr	84120
W Natalie Ct	84120
W Nathanael Way	84088
S Navigator Dr	84084
S Naylor Farm Dr	84088
S & W Nebo Dr	84088
W Nellies St	84081
W Neville Ct	84119
W New Bingham Hwy	
4300-4599	84088
5401-5897	84081
5899-7399	84081
W New Flaxton Ct	84081
S & W New Heritage Cir & Dr	84088
W New London Rd	84084
S New Snowbell Ln	84081
W New Sycamore Dr	84081
W New Village Rd	84084
W New World Dr	84084
S Newcastle Rd	84088
S & W Newell Dr	84088
W Newellwood Cir	84088
S Newmark Dr	84128
W Nicole Cir	84084
S & W Nielsen Way	84119
W Nigel Way	84119
W Nightjars Ln	84119
W Nike Dr	84088
S Nina Cir	84084
S Nob Hill St	84120
W Norman Dr	84119
S & W Norris View Ln	84088
W Northlilac Ave	84081
W Norwich Dr	84088
Nottingham Cir & Dr	84084
S Novice Cir	84128
S & W Nugget Dr	84128
S Oak Ln	84088
S Oak Acorn Ct	84081
W Oak Bridge Dr	84081
S & W Oak Farms Dr	84081
W Oak Fork Dr	84081
S & W Oak Gate Dr	84081
S & W Oak Lawn Ct & Way	84119
S Oak Mill Dr	84081
S Oak Run Dr	84081
S & W Oak Vista Dr	84081
S Oakland Hills Dr	84084
S & W Oakshade Ln	84081
S Oakvale Ct	84120
S Oakwood Pl	84088
S Oberlin Rd	84120
S & W October Way	84120
W Odell Dr	84120
W Odin Ln	84088
S & W Ogallala Dr	84119
W Olani Way	84120
S Old Arbor Ln	84120
S Old Bingham Hwy	84088
W Old Bingham Hwy	
3500-3598	84088
3600-3999	84088
4001-4199	84088
5200-5598	84081
W Old Church Ct	84084
W Old Creek Rd	84081
S Old Factory Dr	84088
S Old Flaxton Ct	84081
S & W Old Hollow Way	84084
S Old Homestead Ln	84088
S Old Silo Way	84119
S Olden Ln	84081
Oldham Cir & St	84120
S Olene Cir	84120
S Olive Dunn Dr	84120
S & W Olive Grove Way	84088
S & W Olive Leaf Ct & Ln	84088
W Olive Tree Cir	84088
W Omega Way	84120
S & W Opal Hill Dr	84081
S Oquirrh Meadows Dr	84088
W Oquirrh Point Rd	84081
S & W Oquirrh Ridge Ct & Rd	84081
S Oquirrh Vistas Ln	84128
Oranchen Sq	84081
S Orange Sky Ct	84081
S & W Orchard Hills Way	84128
S Orchid Cir	84120
S & W Oriole Cir & Way	84119
S Oriole Grove Way	84119
S & W Orion Cir & Way	84119
S Orion Hill Rd	84081
W Orion Hills Cv	84081
S Orleans Way	84120
W Orton Cir	84119
W Oskaloosa Dr	84084
W Osprey Ave	84120
S Othello Way	84128
S & W Ottawa Dr	84119
S & W Otter Creek Dr	84081
S & W Ovation Ct & Dr	84128
S Overton Dr	84081
S & W Overview Way	84084
S & W Owensboro Dr	84084
S Oxford Way	84119
W Oxford Park Dr	84119
W Oxford Row Dr	84081
S Oxley Cir	84120
Paddington Cir & Rd	84084
S Pagentry Pl	84120
S Pagoda Tree Ln	84088
S Paintbrush Dr	84081
S Paisley Way	84084
W Paiute Dr	84119
S Palladium Dr	84088
S & W Palm Frond Ct	84081
Palmer Ct & Dr	84120
W Palomino Dr	84128
W Panamint Rd	84120
S Pando Way	84084
W Par Cir	84088
S & W Parachute Cv & Dr	84120
S Park Brook Ct	84120
S & W Park Commons Way	84120
S Park Dale Ct	84120
S Park Glen Ct	84081
S Park Green Dr	84120
S Park Maple Dr	84081
S & W Park Point Dr	84081
S & W Park Springs Dr	84120
W Park Vale Dr	84081
S & W Park Village Dr	84081
S & W Park Vista Ct & Dr	84120
W Park Wood Ct	84081
S Parkcrest Dr	84119
W Parkway Ave	84119
W Parkway Blvd	
1701-1797	84119
1799-3400	84119
3402-3598	84119
3600-4099	84120
5600-5998	84128
6000-6800	84128
6802-7198	84128
S Parkway Ln	84119
W Parkway Ln	84119
S & W Parr Ct & Dr	84081
S Partridge Run Way	84088
S Partridge View Ln	84088
W Paskay Dr	84120
W Passenger Ln	84081
S & W Patti Cir & Dr	84128
W Paulette Ave	84120
W Pauline Way	84088
S & W Pavant Ave, Cir & Dr	84120
W Pawnee Cir	84081
S Pawnee Dr	84081
W Pawnee Dr	84081
W Pawnee St	84119
W Paynter Cv	84120
W Peach Creek Ct	84088
S Peach Flower Ln	84128
S & W Peach Ridge Way	84128
S Peachwood Dr	84119
S & W Peak Dr	84088
S Pear Apple Cir	84119
Pearce Dr & St	84119
S Pearson Cir	84128
S Pebble Crest Way	84081
S Pebblecreek Rd	84081
W Pebblerock Cir	84081
W Pebblestone Cir	84081
S Pecan Cir	84088
S & W Peggy Cir, Ct, Dr, Ln & Way	84120
S Pelican Cv	84119
S Pembroke Ln	84120
W Pence Dr	84088
W Penny Cir	84088
W Pensacola Cir	84084
S Penstemmon Ln	84081
W Pepper Pond Ln	84128
W Pepper Tree Ct	84120
S & W Perigrine Way	84120
W Peron Ln	84128
W Pescara Ct	84084
W Petersen Ln	84120
S & W Pheasant Glen Dr	84120
S Pheasant Hill Cir	84120
S Pheasant Park Dr	84120
S & W Pheasant Run Cir & Dr	84088
S & W Philadelphian Ct	84081
W Piagentini Way	84084
W Piccadilly Cir	84088
W Piera Cir	84084
S Pika Dr	84128
S & W Pilgrim Dr	84081
S & W Pin Oak Dr	84081
S Pine Cir	84088
S & W Pine Crossing Cir & Dr	84088
S Pine Lake Cir	84081
S & W Pine Landing Way	84084
S & W Pine Laurel Ln	84081
S Pine Vistas Cir	84128
S & W Pinecastle Dr	84081
W Pinehurst Cir	84120
S Pinenut Cir	84088
S & W Pines Point Way	84084
S Pinevale Ct	84120
S Piney Ct	84088
S Pinion Ln	84088
S Pinta Cir	84084
W Pinyon Cir	84128
S & W Pioneer Pkwy	84120
W Placer Claim Way	84081
W Placer Mine Ln	84081
S Placerville Cv	84081
S & W Platinum Cir & Dr	84084
S Plaza Center Dr	84084
S Plover Ct	84119
S Plum Blossom Cir	84088
S & W Plum Creek Cir & Dr	84088
S Point Ridge Ct	84084
S Point Vista Cir	84128
S & W Pointer Ln	84120
S & W Poison Oak Dr	84081
W Polo Ln	84088
W Ponderosa Ln	84088
S Ponds Lodge Dr	84081
W Porter Cir	84084
S Poseidon Dr	84120
W Postwood Cir	84120
W Potenza Ct	84084
S Powder Ridge Dr	84128
S Powder View Cir	84128
S & W Powderwood Dr	84128
S & W Prairie Dunes Dr	84084
W Prairie Lake St	84081
S Presidents Dr	84120
W Prichard St	84119
W Primavera Way	84084
Prince Cir & Dr	84120
W Prodo Vista Dr	84119
S Progress Dr	84119
S & W Prosperity Rd	84119
W Puma Ct	84120
S Pumpkin Patch Cir	84120
S Purple Sage Dr	84081
S Purple Sky Ct	84081
Putnam Ct & Dr	84128
S Quartz Hill Dr	84081
Queenspointe Cir & Ln	84119
S Quest Cir	84120
S Quick Water Way	84081
W Rachelle Dr	84084
S Radcliffe St	84120
W Radley Cir	84128
S & W Rae St	84120
W Rain Tree Way	84120
W Ramford Way	84081
S Rams Horn Dr	84088
S Ramsey Cir	84120
S Ranch House Rd	84081
W Ranch Park Dr	84088
W Ranches Loop Rd	84081
W Ranches Park Ln	84081
S Ranchhand Rd	84081
W Rancho Martin Cir	84128
S & W Rancho Vista Ln	84120
S Ranchwood Ct	84081
S Raphael Ct	84119
S Rappel Ct	84081
S Raquel Cir	84120
W Rawhide Dr	84120
W Reaper Cir	84084
S Red Acorn Ct	84119
S Red Blossom Cir	84120
S Red Bur Ct	84119
S Red Castle Way	84120
S Red Cherry Cir	84120
S Red Cloud Way	84081
S Red Elm Cir	84081
S & W Red Heather Ln	84084
W Red Narrows Dr	84081
W Red Oakleaf Ct	84119
W Red Orchard Way	84084
S Red Pine Cir	84088
W Red Robin Rd	84119
S Red Springs Way	84081
W Red Spruce Dr	84088
W Redflower Cir	84120
S Redhawk Rd	84119
S Redwing St	84119
W Redwood Pl	84119
S Redwood Rd	
2100-3899	84119
6600-6648	84084
6650-7799	84084
7800-9400	84088
9402-9404	84088
S Regal Hill Dr	84081
W Regency Park Dr	84119
W Regene Way	84119
W Relative Pl	84120
S & W Renae St	84084
S Renardo Pl	84119
S Renault Cir	84119
S Rendezvous Way	84120
W Research Way	84119
W Reuben Cir	84128
W Reunion Woods Ct	84120

W Revere Cir 84084
W Rhinehurst Cir 84084
S & W Rhonda Ave 84084
S & W Rialto Way 84081
S & W Richardson Cir & Ln 84128
S & W Richfield Ave, Cir & Ct 84120
W Richland Cir 84084
S & W Rickys Dr 84119
W Ridge Dr 84119
W Ridge Mesa Cir 84128
S Ridge Vistas Dr 84128
S & W Ridgeland Cir & Dr 84119
S & W Ridgeland Park Dr & Ln 84119
S Ridgewood Pl 84088
S Rio Bravo Pl 84088
S Rio Camino St 84119
W Rio Grande Pl 84088
W Rio Vista St 84119
S & W Ripple Dr 84088
W Ripple Creek Cir 84088
W Rishel Cir 84128
W Rivendell Dr 84081
S River Ln 84119
W River Bank Rd 84119
W River Bed Dr 84119
S River Bottom Way 84119
S River Dock Ct 84119
W River Fringe Pl 84119
W River Harvest Ct 84119
S & W River Horse Rd 84119
S & W River Ridge Dr 84088
S River Village Ln 84119
S Robert Cir 84084
W Robin Rd 84119
S Robin Way 84084
W Robin Way 84084
W Robin Hill Rd 84081
S Rochelle Cir 84120
S Rock Brook Cir 84128
W Rock Ridge Ln 84081
W Rock River Rd 84119
W Rockport Dr 84081
W Rockwood Way 84120
S & W Rocky Creek Dr 84081
W Rocky Vista Cir 84081
S & W Rodonda Linda Pl 84128
W Rolling River Rd 84119
S Rome Cv 84119
S & W Romney Park Dr 84084
S Ron Cir 84120
W Rooster Tail Rd 84128
S & W Rosa Arbor Cir 84128
S Rose Blossom St 84120
S & W Rose Hollow Ln 84119
S Rose Petal Way 84120
S & W Roseberry Ct & St 84081
W Rosedale Row Dr 84081
S Rosehaven Ct 84120
Rosemary Cir & St 84120
S & W Rothchild Cir & Dr 84119
S & W Roundstem Rd 84081
S & W Roundtable Cir & Rd 84120
S & W Roxborough Ct 84119
S & W Roxborough Park St 84119
W Roxey Ct 84128
S Roy Del Cir 84088
S & W Royal Ann Cir & Dr 84120
S Royal Crest Dr 84088
S Royal Scott Dr 84128
S Royal Wulff Ln 84120
W Ruddy Way 84119
S & W Rundlestone Dr 84081
W Rundquist Dr 84084
S & W Running Springs Dr 84084
S & W Rural Rd 84084
S & W Rushford Ct 84128
S & W Rushton Acres Ct & Ln 84120
S Rushton Park Dr 84120
W Russett Ave 84119
S Rustic Oak Ct 84081
W Rutgers Ave 84120
W Ryan Bennett Ln 84119
S Rye Cir 84084
W Saddle Creek Cir 84081
W Saddle Hollow Pl 84081
W Saddle Mount Cir 84081
S Saddle Oaks Ct 84081
S & W Saddle Park Dr 84081
W Saddlecrest Cir 84081
S & W Saddler Cir & Dr 84088
S Safari Dr 84081
W Sage Fork Rd 84081
S Sagers Way 84128
W Saguaro Dr 84081
S Saint Ives Ln 84088
W Sakura Ct 84081
S Salix Cir 84081
W Sallybrooke Way 84081
S Salt Grass Rd 84119
S & W Salto Sierra Way 84128
W Salvia Pl 84119
W San Andreas Ct 84088
S & W San Carlos Dr & Pl 84119
W San Juan Ct 84088
W San Marcos Cir 84119
S San Miguel St 84088
W San Rafael Ct 84088
S Sandlily Cir 84081
S & W Sandwell Dr 84120
S & W Sandy Creek Cir 84088
S Santa Maria Cir 84084
S Santa Rita Pl 84088
S Santa Rosa Pl 84088
W Sarah Cir 84128
S Saralee Dr 84088
S Saris Cir 84120
W Savannah Cir 84084
S Savoie Ct 84084
S & W Saw Timber Way 84081
S Sawston Rd 84081
S & W Sawtell Cir & Way 84081
S Sawtooth Oak Dr 84081
S Saxby Pl 84088
S & W Saybrook Ln 84128
S & W Scarlet Oak Dr 84081
S & W Scarsborough Ln 84084
S Schmidt Cir 84088
Schorr Cir & Dr 84084
W Schuler Ave 84128
Scomeriv Dr 84120
W Scotch Pine Ln 84088
S Scottsdale Dr 84120
S & W Scranton Dr 84084
W Scrub Oak Dr 84081
W Seagull Dr 84120
S Sean Heights Cir 84081
S Seaton Pl 84088
S Sedgemoor Ln 84088
S Sedonia Ct 84081
S & W Sefton Dr 84120
W Segal Cir 84120
W Seneca Rd 84120
S Senegal Dove Dr 84088
S Sentinel Hill Ct 84128
W Serena Cir 84120
S & W Serenera Way 84081
W Serenity View Dr 84084
W Settlers Point Dr 84128
S Sextant Ln 84084
W Shadberry Cir 84081
W Shadow Park Dr 84119
S Shady Red Ct 84119
S & W Shadyvale Ln 84120
S Shadywood Way 84119
S Shafer Ln 84119
S Shalimar St 84128
S Shalise Cir 84120
S Shallow Creek Rd 84081
S & W Sharal Park Cir & Dr 84128
W Sharlyn Hill Cir 84081
S Shatton Ln 84088
S & W Shayla Dr 84088
W Shayn Hill Dr 84081
W Shelley Ave 84119
S Shepard Ln 84120
S Sheri Way 84120
S Sherington Dr 84120
W Sherlene Cir 84120
S Sherm Cir 84120
S & W Sherwood Cir 84084
S Shetland Dr 84128
W Shingle Oak Ct 84081
S & W Shooting Star Ave 84081
S Shoreline Dr 84120
S & W Short Leaf Dr 84088
S & W Shoshone Lake Dr 84088
S Shulsen Ln 84088
W Shumard Oak Dr 84081
W Sierra Vis 84119
W Sierra Dawn St 84119
S & W Sierra Oaks Dr 84081
S & W Silo Dr 84081
S Silver Cir 84084
S Silver Glen Dr 84128
W Silver Meadow Way 84088
W Silver Park Dr 84081
S Silver Pine Ct 84088
S Silverleaf Cir 84081
W Silverton Cir 84084
S Silverwood Cir 84128
S Simba Way 84081
W Singing Wood Ct 84084
S Sky Meadow Dr 84081
W Skyhawk Dr 84084
S Skyhawk View Cir 84128
S & W Skyline Arch Dr 84081
S & W Skyvue Cir 84088
S Slalom Way 84084
S & W Slate Canyon Dr 84081
W Snapdragon Cv 84081
W Snow Bell Dr 84081
S Snow Canyon Dr 84081
W Snow Hollow Dr 84128
S & W Snow Vistas Ln 84128
W Snowbush Ln 84128
S Snowdon Park Dr 84119
W Snowdrop Pl 84081
S Snowshoe Dr 84128
S Soft Breeze Cir 84128
S Sol Rise Dr 84081
S Solace Ct 84081
S Solano Cir 84120
Soliai Cir 84081
S Solstice Ct 84081
S Somerset Dr 84084
W Songbird Dr 84120
S & W Sorrento Way 84081
S Sortive Sky Ct 84081
W Soulero Cir 84088
S & W Southbourne Cir & Way 84119
W Southgate Ave 84119
S Sparrowtail Rd 84081
S & W Spaulding Ct, Ln & Rd 84088
W Speed Skate Cir 84084
W Spencer Crest Ln 84084
W Spike Ave 84120
S Spinner Ln 84120
S Spiral Jetty Cir 84081
S & W Spratling Dr 84081
W Spray Lake Dr 84081
S & W Spring Dr 84084
S & W Spring Glen Cir & St 84119
W Spring Oak Dr 84081
S & W Spring Vista Cir & Dr 84120
S & W Spring Water Dr 84120
S & W Springbrook Dr 84084
S & W Springside Ct 84119
W Sprucewood Cir 84120
W Spur Cir 84128
Squirewood Cir & Dr 84120
S & W Stafford Cir, Pl & Way 84119
W Stane Ave 84120
S Stanton Dr 84120
S Star Brook Cir 84128
S Star Lily Cir 84081
S Star View Cir 84128
W Stardust Cir 84088
S & W Starflower Way 84081
Starling Ave & Cir 84119
W Starlite Dr 84088
S & W Starwood Cir & St 84120
S Steadman Cir 84084
S & W Stillridge Dr 84128
S & W Stillwater Pl & Way 84120
S Stirrup Dr 84128
S & W Stone Butte Ln 84120
S & W Stone Creek Dr 84119
W Stone Meadow Dr 84088
W Stone Quarry Cir 84081
S Stone Slab Way 84128
S Stone Spring Cir 84081
S & W Stone Vista Ln 84081
S Stonecam Ave 84120
S Stonecutter Cir 84081
S Stonewood Dr 84119
S Stoney Creek Cir 84128
W Stork Cv 84119
W Stratford Ave 84119
S Stratford Ln 84088
W Straw Cir 84084
S & W Strawberry Cv, Dr & Loop 84084
W Strickland Pl 84128
S Suffolk Cir 84119
W Sugar Pl 84088
W Sugar Beet Dr 84120
S & W Sugar Bowl Ln 84128
S & W Sugar Creek Way 84088
W Sugar Factory Rd 84088
W Sugar Maple Cir 84120
W Summer St 84084
S Summer Trail Dr 84120
W Summer Tree Ln 84088
W Summerstar Cv 84088
S Summertime Pl 84120
S & W Summit Valley Dr 84088
W Sumter Dr 84084
W Sun Blossom Cir 84088
W Sun Hollow Cir 84088
S Sun Leaf Dr 84088
S Sunbrook Pl 84119
W Sunburst Dr 84084
S & W Sundew Ct & Ln 84081
S & W Sunlit Way 84081
S & W Sunny Vista Ln 84081
W Sunnybrook Dr 84119
S Sunnypark Ln 84119
S & W Sunnyvale Dr 84120
S Sunoak Cir 84128
W Sunrise Cir 84084
S Sunrise Pl E 84084
S Sunrise Pl W 84084
W Sunrise Pl 84084
W Sunrise Pl N 84084
W Sunrise Pl S 84084
S Sunrise Rd 84119
S & W Sunrise Oak Dr 84081
W Sunrose Pl 84119
W Sunset Ave 84119
S Sunset Cir 84084
S Sunset Way 84084
S & W Sunset Maple Dr 84081
Sunset Park Cir & Ln 84081
S & W Sunshade Cv & Dr 84120
W Sunshine Dr 84120
S Sunspring Dr 84088
W Suntree Ave 84120
W Surf Ct 84084
Susan Cir & Way 84088
S Susie Cir 84120
S & W Sussex Ct & Pl 84119
S & W Swan Hill Cv & Dr 84081
S & W Swan Ridge Way 84081
W Sweetwater Cir 84120
W Swift Creek Rd 84081
W Swift Water Way 84081
S Swordsman Cv 84084
W Sycamore Farm Rd 84081
S Sycamore Glen Cir 84081
S Symphony Cir 84119
W Tafoya Cir 84081
S Tafton Rd 84120
W Tangiers Cir 84120
S & W Tanya Ave 84088
S Targhee Dr 84088
S Tarlton Cir 84120
W Taryns Ln 84088
S Taunton Ln 84081
S & W Teal Vista Cir 84120
W Teasel Ave 84128
S & W Technology Dr 84119
S Technology Park Way 84119
S Tecumseh St 84120
W Ted Way 84120
W Telluride Cv 84081
W Tenway Dr 84128
S Terra Pointe Way 84088
S & W Terrace Ridge Dr 84128
W Tess Ave 84119
S & W Teton Estates Dr 84088
Thayn Cir & Dr 84120
W Theresa Cv 84119
S Thimbleleaf Cir 84081
S Thomas Cir 84084
W Thor Way 84120
S & W Thorndale Way 84084
S Thorpe Creek Rd 84128
S Thorpe View Cir 84128
S Thorup Cir 84119
W Thresher Ct 84081
S & W Thrush Hill Dr 84081
S & W Ticklegrass Rd 84081
S Tico Dr 84081
S Tiger Ct 84081
W Tiger Lily Ct 84081
S & W Tilbury Ln 84081
S Timber Oaks Ln 84128
S Timeron Dr 84128
W Timmerman Pl 84128
S Timothy Cir 84084
S & W Tintic Ln 84081
S & W Tolin Cir & St 84120
W Tolkin Ave 84084
S Tolman Crest Way 84119
W Toni Dr 84119
S & W Toni Lee Cir & St 84088
W Tonopah Cv 84081
W Torbay Ct 84120
S & W Toulouse Cir & St 84120
S Tourist Ln 84081
S Tower Hill Way 84120
S Tower View Way 84119
S & W Towerbell Ln 84120
S Town View Cir 84081
S & W Townley St 84081
S Township Ct 84128
W Trail Ave 84120
S Trailblazer Cv 84128
S Tralee Cir 84119
S & W Traveler Ln 84081
Travis Cir & Ln 84088
S Treeline Dr 84088
S Treena Cir 84084
W Treille Ct 84119
S Trento Cir 84081
W Trimble Ln 84088
S & W Trimble Creek Dr 84088
W Trinity Ave 84120
S Triumph Ln 84084
S Trojan Dr 84120
W Trophy Cir 84120
W Tudor Ct 84120
S Tuft Ct 84081
S Tukford Cir 84081
S Tundra Ln 84119
W Tungsten Ct 84081
W Tupelo Ln 84081
S Turnstone Ct 84081
W Turtle Dove Ln 84088
W Tuscaloosa Way 84084
S Tuscany Downs Way 84128
W Twin Oaks Dr 84088
W Twin Tree Dr 84081
W Udine Ct 84084
S Ufizzi Ct 84084
S & W Uinta Hills Ct & Dr 84088
S Upland Lake Dr 84119
W Upper Huntly Way 84088
W Upper Newark Way 84088
S Uranium Dr 84084
S Uyeda Ct 84081
S & W Valcrest Cir, Ct & Dr 84119
W Valdown Ave 84120
S Valence Ln 84084
W Valerian Cir 84081
S Valle Verde Dr 84128
W Valley Breeze Ct 84128
S & W Valley Haven Ct 84120
S Valley High Rd 84128
W Valley Home Ave 84119
S & W Valley Maple Dr 84081
W Valley Oak Dr 84081
S & W Valley Pointe Ct & Dr 84128
W Valley View Dr 84120
W Valley Villa Dr 84120
W Valley West Dr 84088
W Van St 84088
W Van Cherry Way 84120
S Van Dyck Ct 84119
S & W Vassar Cir & St 84120
W Vendee Ave 84084
S Verano Cir 84081
S Vermont Ct 84128
S Verna Cir 84120
S & W Vespa Dr 84119
S Viburnum Ave 84081
W Vickie Cir 84084
S Victoria Park Dr 84119
S View Vista Rd 84119
S & W Villa View Dr 84120
S & W Village Dell Dr 84081
W Village Ford Rd 84084
S & W Village Glen Cir & Dr 84081
W Village Main Dr 84119
S & W Village Meadow Ct & Dr 84128
S Village Pine Cv 84128
S & W Village Wood Ct & Dr 84120
S Villosa Cir 84081
S Vinson Cir 84120
S Virden Cir 84120
W Virginia Pine Ln 84088
S & W Vironcia Way 84119
S & W Vista Mesa Dr 84128
S Vista Montana Way 84128
W Vista Peak Dr 84081
S Vista Villa Ln 84120
S & W Vistas Haven Way 84128
S & W Vistawest Dr 84088
W Vivante Way 84119
S & W Volta Ave 84120
S Wade Way 84119
W Wake Cir 84084
W Wake Robin Dr 84081
S Wakefield Way 84081
W Wakepoint Dr 84120
S Wakeport Bay 84128
S Waller Ln 84081
S & W Walter Cir, Ct & Way 84120
W Warley Bay 84081
W Warnock Ave 84119
W Warr Barton Cir 84120
W Wasa St 84088
S & W Wasatch Meadows Dr 84088
S Wasatch Peak Cir 84088
W Washoe Cv 84081
S Water Oak Dr 84081
S & W Water Pointe Dr 84088
S Water View Rd 84119
S Water Wood Dr 84120
S Waterleaf Way 84128
S Waterloo Cir 84084
W Watkins Way 84084
W Watt Ln 84128
W Wave Ct 84084
S Wayward Cir 84128
W Webwood Ct 84119
W Wedgecliffe Dr 84120
S Welby Farm Rd 84088
S & W Welby Hills Dr 84088
S Welby Park Dr 84088
S Wells Cir 84081
W Wells Park Rd 84081
W Wending Ln 84128
S & W Wendy Ave & Cir 84120
S West Heather Dr 84084
S Westborough Way 84084
Westcove Dr 84119
S Westcrest Rd 84120
Westfield Cir 84084
S Westgene Cir 84119
Westhaven Dr 84120
Westlake Ave 84120
Westlake Cir 84119
Westlake Dr 84119
S Westlake Dr 84119
Westlake Rd 84119
Westland Dr 84088
S Westlilac Dr 84081
S Westmoor Way 84084
S Westpoint Cir, Dr & Way 84120
S Westshire Cir & Dr 84119
S & W Weymouth Cir, Pl & Rd 84119
W Wheatcrest Cir 84081
S & W Wheatridge Ct & Ln 84081
W Wheatwood Cir 84084
S Whipoorwhil St 84120
S Whisper St 84120
S Whistling Ln 84119
S & W White Blossom Way 84120
S & W White Cherry Way 84120

S & W White Cony Cir 84128
S & W White Diamond Way 84120
S & W White Flower Cir & Way 84120
S White Village Ct 84119
W Whitebird Cir 84120
W Whitehall Dr 84119
W Whitlock Ave 84119
S Wickford Way 84081
S & W Wights Fort Rd 84088
S & W Wild Acres Dr 84081
S Wild Cherry Cir 84120
S Wild Clover Ln 84081
S & W Wild Oak Dr 84081
S & W Wildrose Dr 84120
W Willette Cir 84084
S William Cir 84084
W Williamsburg Cir
  2200-2399 84088
  6300-6399 84128
S Williamsburg Ct 84088
S Williamsburg Dr 84128
S Willow Hollow Rd 84119
S Willow River Rd 84119
S Willow Wood Way 84088
S Willowpond Way 84081
S & W Wilshire Park Ave 84081
S & W Wiltshire Way 84119
S Wimbledon Ct 84084
S & W Wimbledon Ridge Ln 84084
S Wimbleton Pl 84088
S & W Winchester Cir & Dr 84119
S Wind Caves Ln 84081
S & W Wind River Cir & Dr 84088
W Windcrest Cir 84120
W Windfield Ct 84088
S & W Windmill Dr 84081
S Window Ranch Way 84081
W Windrift Bay 84088
S Windsor Pl 84088
S & W Winners Cir 84084
S Winsted Way 84120
S Winston Dr 84128
S Winter Berry Dr 84081
S & W Winter Hill Cv & Ln 84081
S & W Winthrope Cir & Dr 84088
S Winton St 84119
S & W Wisteria Way 84081
S Witfield Ct 84088
S Wollemi Pine Way 84088
W Wood Meadow Ct 84120
S Wood Mesa Dr 84081
S & W Wood Shade Ct 84081
W Wood Spring Dr 84081
W Wood Village Ct 84120
W Woodacre Rd 84081
W Woodash Cir 84120
S & W Woodbend Rd 84081
W Woodburne Rd 84081
S Woodcreek St 84119
W Woodcutter Ln 84120
S & W Wooded Park Ct 84120
W Woodgate Cir 84120
S Woodgreen Rd 84084
S & W Woodgrove Cir & Dr 84120
S Woodhue Ct 84081
W Woodledge Ave 84120
S Woodman Ct 84088
W Woodstep Ave 84120
W Woodtree Cir 84120
W Woodward Pl 84088
W Woodworth Rd 84081
S & W Wormwood Dr 84120
W Wright Ln 84119
S Wynridge Ln 84128
S Yarrow Cir 84120
S Yellow Pine St 84088
S & W Yellow Poppy Dr 84081
W Yellow Rose Cir 84119
S Yellow Sky Ct 84081
S Yellowwood Ln 84081
S Yorkshire Rd 84119
W Zadok Ln 84088
S Zeus Dr 84128
W Zina Cir 84128
S Zinnia Ct 84081

NUMBERED STREETS

S 1000 W 84088
W 10120 S 84081
S 1030 W 84088
S 1030 W 84119
S 1050 W 84088
S 1075 W 84088
S 1070 W 84088
S 1070 W 84119
S 1095 W 84088
S 1100 W 84088
S 1100 W 84119
S 1115 W 84084
S 1130 W 84084
S 1150 W 84088
S 1155 W 84084
S 1160 W 84084
S 1170 W 84084
S 1185 W 84119
S 1190 W 84084
S 1205 W 84084
S 1220 W 84088
S 1245 W 84084
S 1240 W
  7700-7798 84084
  8800-8999 84088
S 1250 W 84088
S 1275 W 84088
S 1300 W
  2200-2300 84119
  6700-7799 84084
  7800-7898 84088
S 1320 W 84084
S 1320 W 84119
S 1335 W 84084
S 1330 W 84088
S 1365 W 84088
S 1360 W 84088
S 1360 W 84119
S 1365 W 84119
S 1370 W 84084
S 1380 W
  7100-7200 84084
  8400-8599 84088
S 1405 W 84088
S 1400 W 84119
S 1410 W 84088
S 1425 W 84084
S 1440 W 84088
S 1440 W 84119
S 1460 W
  6700-6780 84084
  8000-8198 84088
S 1470 W 84084
S 1480 W
  2300-2399 84119
  6800-6959 84084
  8200-8598 84088
S 1500 W 84088
S 1505 W 84119
S 1510 W 84088
S 1510 W 84119
S 1525 W 84084
S 1520 W
  6700-6999 84084
  8200-8499 84088
S 1530 W
  7600-7799 84084
  7800-7900 84088
S 1540 W 84119
S 1550 W 84084
S 1560 W 84088
S 1565 W 84119
S 1570 W 84084
S 1575 W 84119
S 1580 W 84119
S 1590 W 84088
S 1600 W
  6700-6799 84084
  8200-8300 84088
S 1640 W 84088
S 1645 W 84084
S 1655 W 84084
S 1670 W 84088
S 1725 W 84119
S 1750 W 84088
S 1755 W 84119
S 1800 W 84119
S 1825 W 84088
S 1845 W 84119
S 1850 W 84088
S 1850 W 84119
S 1855 W 84119
S 1870 W 84088
S 1890 W 84088
S 1900 W 84088
S 1900 W 84119
S 1920 W
  7700-7799 84084
  8700-8798 84088
S 1940 W 84119
S 1950 W 84088
S 1950 W 84119
S 1960 W 84084
S 1975 W 84084
S 1980 W 84088
S 2000 W 84119
S 2010 W 84088
S 2040 W 84088
S 2040 W 84119
S 2045 W 84119
S 2050 W 84119
S 2070 W 84088
S 2075 W 84084
S 2100 W 84119
S 2110 W 84088
W 2150 S 84120
S 2160 W 84084
S 2172 W 84084
S 2180 W 84084
W 2180 S 84119
S 2200 W
  3441-3497 84119
  6600-7799 84084
  7800-7998 84088
W 2200 S
  1201-1597 84119
  4000-4199 84120
W 2210 S 84119
S 2230 W 84084
S 2245 W 84088
S 2240 W 84088
W 2240 S 84119
S 2250 W 84084
W 2250 S 84119
W 2270 S 84120
S 2280 W 84088
S 2290 W 84084
W 2300 S 84119
W 2305 S 84120
S 2310 W 84084
S 2315 W 84088
S 2320 W 84084
W 2320 S 84119
S 2345 W 84084
S 2340 W 84088
W 2340 S 84120
S 2350 W 84084
S 2360 W 84088
W 2365 S 84119
S 2370 W
  7100-7299 84084
  8200-8299 84088
S 2385 W 84088
S 2390 W 84088
S 2400 W 84084
S 2405 W 84084
S 2400 W 84119
W 2410 S 84119
S 2420 W
  7000-7098 84084
  8100-8199 84088
S 2440 W 84088
S 2450 W 84084
W 2455 S 84120
S 2475 W 84119
S 2470 W
  7000-7199 84084
  8100-8148 84088
S 2480 W
  7300-7599 84084
  7872-7903 84088
S 2490 W 84088
S 2500 W 84084
S 2500 W 84119
S 2520 W 84119
S 2530 W 84084
S 2540 W 84084
S 2540 W 84119
S 2550 W 84084
W 2555 S 84119
S 2570 W 84084
S 2570 W 84119
S 2580 W 84119
S 2595 W 84084
W 2590 S 84119
W 2600 S 84119
S 2625 W 84084
S 2620 W 84088
S 2620 W 84119
S 2645 W 84084
W 2640 S 84119
S 2665 W 84119
S 2670 W 84119
W 2680 S 84119
S 2700 W
  6600-7700 84084
  7702-7798 84084
  7801-7897 84088
  7899-9300 84088
  9302-9398 84088
W 2700 S
  1586-1598 84119
  1600-1699 84119
  3801-3999 84120
W 2720 S 84119
S 2730 W 84084
S 2735 W 84119
W 2730 S 84119
W 2745 S 84119
S 2760 W 84088
S 2770 W 84084
W 2770 S 84119
S 2785 W 84119
W 2780 S 84119
S 2795 W 84084
W 2795 S 84119
S 2805 W 84119
S 2800 W
  7000-7599 84084
  7800-8299 84088
  2501-3299 84119
S 2820 W 84119
S 2835 W 84119
S 2840 W
  7500-7599 84084
  7900-7999 84088
S 2850 W 84084
S 2850 W 84119
S 2855 W 84119
W 2865 S 84119
S 2870 W
  3500-3598 84119
  6800-7199 84084
  7800-7999 84088
S 2880 W
  7600-7699 84084
  8400-8598 84088
S 2890 W 84119
S 2895 W 84119
S 2900 W 84088
W 2900 S 84128
S 2910 W 84119
S 2920 W
  7400-7677 84084
  8300-8399 84088
W 2925 S 84120
W 2920 S
  2900-3099 84119
  3900-4999 84120
  6000-6599 84128
S 2930 W 84119
W 2935 S 84119
S 2940 W 84088
S 2950 W 84084
S 2955 W 84119
S 2956 W 84119
S 2960 W
  6600-6699 84084
  8300-8399 84088
  2800-3099 84119
S 2970 W 84119
S 2975 W 84119
S 2980 W
  7000-7180 84084
  7900-8099 84088
W 2995 S 84119
S 3000 W
  2700-2798 84119
  2800-3899 84119
  6601-6699 84084
  8000-8099 84088
  4933-4997 84120
W 3015 S 84120
S 3020 W 84088
S 3025 W 84119
W 3020 S 84120
W 3035 S 84120
S 3040 W
  6600-6699 84084
  9200-9399 84088
  2900-3099 84119
  4400-4499 84120
S 3050 W 84119
S 3060 W 84119
S 3075 W 84084
S 3080 W 84119
S 3085 W 84119
S 3090 W 84088
S 3095 W 84119
S 3100 W 84084
W 3100 S 84119
S 3110 W 84088
S 3115 W 84119
W 3125 S 84120
S 3140 W 84088
S 3140 W 84119
S 3145 W 84119
S 3150 W 84088
S 3155 W 84088
S 3150 W 84119
W 3160 S 84120
W 3170 S 84119
W 3175 S 84120
W 3180 S 84119
W 3185 S 84120
S 3190 W 84084
W 3190 S 84119
S 3200 W
  2100-4699 84119
  6601-7197 84084
  7199-7799 84084
  7800-7900 84088
  7901-7901 84084
  7901-8999 84088
  7902-8998 84088
W 3205 S 84120
  3700-4299 84120
W 3210 S 84128
S 3220 W 84088
W 3225 S 84120
S 3235 W 84084
W 3235 S 84120
S 3245 W 84119
W 3240 S 84120
S 3250 W 84084
S 3250 W 84119
W 3255 S 84119
S 3260 W 84088
W 3260 S 84119
W 3265 S 84119
S 3270 W 84084
S 3270 W 84119
W 3275 S 84120
S 3280 W 84088
W 3280 S 84119
W 3285 S 84120
S 3290 W 84119
S 3300 W 84084
W 3300 S 84119
S 3310 W 84088
S 3310 W 84119
W 3315 S 84128
S 3320 W 84088
S 3320 W 84119
S 3325 W 84119
S 3335 W 84084
W 3335 S 84120
S 3341 W 84084
S 3340 W 84119
W 3350 S 84119
W 3360 S 84119
S 3370 W 84084
W 3375 S 84120
S 3380 W
  4500-4699 84119
  6600-6699 84084
  8400-8598 84088
  6200-6399 84128
W 3395 S 84119
S 3400 W 84088
S 3400 W 84119
S 3410 W 84088
S 3420 W 84088
S 3420 W 84119
S 3425 W 84119
S 3430 W 84084
W 3435 S 84128
S 3440 W 84119
S 3450 W 84088
S 3452 W 84084
S 3450 W 84119
S 3455 W 84119
S 3460 W 84119
W 3470 S 84119
W 3475 S 84120
S 3485 W 84119
S 3490 W 84088
S 3500 W 84088
W 3500 S 84119
S 3515 W 84119
S 3520 W 84088
S 3520 W 84119
S 3535 W 84084
S 3530 W
  7500-7799 84084
  7900-8099 84088
  6400-6599 84128
S 3540 W 84088
W 3540 S 84119
S 3550 W 84119
S 3560 W 84119
W 3570 S 84119
W 3575 S 84128
S 3580 W 84088
W 3590 S 84119
W 3595 S 84119
S 3600 W 84119
W 3605 S 84119
W 3615 S 84119
S 3620 W 84088
W 3620 S 84128
S 3630 W 84120
W 3635 S 84128
S 3640 W 84088
S 3645 W 84088
W 3640 S 84128
W 3650 S 84119
S 3660 W 84120
S 3670 W 84120
W 3675 S 84120
S 3685 W 84088
S 3680 W 84088
S 3680 W 84120
S 3690 W 84120
S 3700 W 84120
W 3705 S 84128
S 3715 W 84088
S 3710 W 84120
S 3715 W 84120
S 3720 W 84088
S 3725 W 84088
S 3720 W 84120
W 3725 S 84128
S 3740 W 84120
W 3750 S 84120
S 3760 W 84088
S 3760 W 84120
W 3765 S 84119
S 3780 W 84088
S 3780 W 84120
W 3785 S 84119
S 3795 W 84084
S 3800 W
  7571-7671 84084
  7800-8199 84088
  1960-2068 84119
  2070-3599 84119
  3600-4200 84120
  4202-4298 84120
  6700-7199 84128
W 3815 S 84128
S 3820 W 84088
S 3825 W 84088
S 3820 W 84120
S 3825 W 84120
S 3830 W 84088
W 3835 S 84119
W 3830 S 84120
W 3840 S 84119
S 3850 W 84088
S 3850 W 84120
W 3855 S 84120
S 3860 W 84088
S 3860 W 84120
W 3870 S 84119
W 3875 S 84119
W 3880 S 84128
W 3890 S 84119
W 3895 S 84120
S 3900 W 84088
S 3900 W 84120
W 3910 S 84128
S 3920 W 84088
S 3920 W 84120
S 3930 W 84088
W 3935 S 84119
W 3930 S 84120
W 3940 S 84128
W 3950 S 84119
S 3960 W 84088
S 3965 W 84088
S 3960 W 84120
W 3965 S 84119
W 3970 S 84119
W 3980 S 84120
W 3995 S 84119
W 3990 S 84120
S 4000 W 84088
S 4000 W 84120
W 4015 S 84128
W 4020 S 84119
W 4025 S 84120
W 4030 S 84119
W 4035 S 84128
S 4045 W 84120
W 4040 S 84119
S 4050 W 84120
W 4055 S 84119
S 4060 W 84120
W 4065 S 84120
S 4075 W 84120
W 4070 S 84119
S 4080 W 84120
W 4085 S 84128
S 4100 W 84120
S 4110 W 84120
W 4120 S 84120
W 4135 S 84119
S 4140 W 84120
W 4145 S 84128
S 4150 W 84120
S 4155 W 84120

S 4167 W 84088
S 4165 W 84120
S 4170 W 84120
W 4175 S 84120
S 4180 W 84120
W 4190 S 84120
S 4200 W 84120
S 4205 W 84120
S 4210 W 84120
W 4215 S 84128
S 4220 W 84120
W 4235 S 84120
S 4240 W 84120
W 4250 S 84120
S 4265 W 84120
W 4260 S 84120
S 4275 W 84120
S 4280 W 84120
S 4290 W 84088
W 4290 S 84120
S 4300 W 84088
S 4300 W 84120
S 4305 W 84120
S 4310 W 84120
S 4320 W 84120
W 4330 S 84120
S 4340 W 84120
S 4355 W 84120
W 4360 S 84120
W 4365 S 84120
S 4387 W 84088
S 4385 W 84120
W 4390 S 84120
S 4400 W 84120
W 4410 S 84120
W 4415 S 84120
S 4420 W 84088
S 4425 W 84120
W 4420 S 84128
W 4430 S 84128
S 4440 W 84120
S 4445 W 84120
S 4450 W 84084
S 4455 W 84088
S 4460 W 84088
W 4460 S 84119
S 4470 W 84084
S 4475 W 84120
W 4480 S 84128
S 4490 W 84120
W 4495 S 84120
S 4500 W 84120
S 4515 W 84120
W 4510 S 84128
S 4520 W 84120
S 4525 W 84120
S 4560 W 84120
S 4565 W 84120
W 4570 S 84119
S 4580 W 84120
S 4590 W 84088
W 4595 S 84120
W 4600 S 84119
W 4605 S 84120
S 4610 W 84088
W 4610 S 84119
S 4620 W 84120
S 4625 W 84120
W 4630 S 84119
W 4645 S 84120
S 4650 W 84120
S 4665 W 84120
W 4660 S 84119
S 4670 W 84088
S 4675 W 84120
S 4680 W 84088
S 4690 W 84084
W 4695 S 84120
S 4710 W 84120
S 4730 W 84084
S 4745 W 84120
S 4755 W 84120
S 4760 W 84120
S 4770 W
  7500-7799 84084
  8400-8799 84088
S 4780 W 84084
S 4780 W 84120
S 4800 W
  3100-4699 84120
  6901-7697 84084
  7699-7799 84084
  8201-8337 84088
  8339-8400 84088
  8402-8998 84088
S 4830 W 84081
S 4840 W 84120
S 4850 W 84120
S 4870 W 84081
S 4880 W 84081
S 4880 W 84120
S 4900 W 84081
S 4900 W 84120
S 4910 W 84081
S 4920 W 84120
S 4940 W 84081
S 4950 W 84081
S 4960 W 84120
S 4980 W 84081
S 4985 W 84120
S 4990 W 84081
S 5000 W 84120
S 5020 W 84120
S 5030 W 84081
S 5040 W 84081
S 5040 W 84120
S 5055 W 84081
S 5060 W 84081
S 5070 W 84081
S 5080 W 84081
S 5090 W 84081
S 5095 W 84081
S 5130 W 84081
S 5135 W 84081
S 5140 W 84081
S 5150 W 84081
S 5170 W 84081
S 5180 W 84081
S 5200 W 84081
S 5200 W 84120
S 5220 W 84081
S 5230 W 84081
S 5240 W 84081
S 5260 W 84081
S 5260 W 84120
S 5280 W 84081
S 5310 W 84081
S 5320 W 84081
S 5320 W 84120
S 5345 W 84120
S 5360 W 84081
S 5370 W 84081
S 5370 W 84120
S 5375 W 84120
S 5385 W 84120
S 5390 W 84081
S 5400 W 84120
S 5410 W 84120
S 5420 W 84081
S 5440 W 84120
S 5445 W 84120
S 5450 W 84120
S 5475 W 84120
S 5490 W 84081
S 5500 W 84081
S 5505 W 84120
S 5510 W 84120
S 5525 W 84120
S 5530 W 84120
S 5565 W 84120
S 5570 W 84120
S 5600 W 84081
S 5600 W 84120
S 5620 W 84128
S 5630 W 84128
S 5655 W 84081
S 5650 W 84128
S 5665 W 84128
S 5700 W 84128
S 5710 W 84128
S 5720 W 84128
S 5725 W 84128
S 5740 W 84128
S 5750 W 84128
S 5785 W 84081
S 5780 W 84128
S 5800 W 84128
S 5820 W 84081
S 5990 W 84128
S 6000 W 84128
S 6035 W 84128
S 6045 W 84081
S 6060 W 84128
S 6070 W 84128
S 6100 W 84128
S 6115 W 84128
S 6115 W 84081
S 6150 W 84081
S 6160 W 84081
S 6165 W 84128
S 6180 W 84128
S 6220 W 84081
S 6220 W 84128
S 6225 W 84128
W 6225 S 84081
S 6250 W 84081
S 6250 W 84128
S 6260 W 84081
S 6265 W 84128
W 6275 S 84081
S 6285 W 84128
S 6290 W 84081
S 6290 W 84128
S 6300 W 84128
W 6300 S 84084
S 6310 W 84128
S 6320 W 84128
S 6325 W 84128
S 6335 W 84081
S 6340 W 84128
S 6350 W 84128
S 6355 W 84128
S 6360 W 84128
S 6400 W 84128
W 6400 S 84081
S 6430 W 84081
S & W 6435 W & S 84081
S 6440 W 84128
W 6440 S 84081
S 6465 W 84081
S 6460 W 84128
S 6470 W 84128
S 6485 W 84128
S 6500 W 84128
S 6505 W 84128
S 6515 W 84128
W 6515 S 84081
S 6520 W 84081
S 6530 W 84128
S 6535 W 84128
S 6540 W 84081
S 6545 W 84128
S 6555 W 84081
S 6555 W 84128
W 6560 S 84081
S 6580 W 84128
W 6600 S 84081
W 6610 S 84084
S 6620 W 84128
W 6620 S 84084
W 6635 S 84081
S 6640 W 84128
W 6655 S 84081
S 6660 W 84128
S 6670 W 84081
S 6670 W 84128
W 6685 S 84084
W 6680 S 84084
W 6695 S 84084
W 6700 S 84081
S 6715 W 84081
W 6720 S 84084
W 6735 S 84084
S 6740 W 84128
S 6750 W 84128
W 6750 S 84081
S 6775 W 84128
W 6775 S 84084
S 6780 W 84128
W 6785 S 84084
S 6800 W 84128
S 6820 W 84128
W 6825 S 84084
S 6830 W 84128
W 6830 S 84084
S 6840 W 84128
W 6850 S 84084
S 6865 W
  3900-4099 84128
  7900-7999 84081
W 6865 S 84084
W 6870 S 84084
W 6875 S 84084
S 6880 W 84128
W 6880 S 84084
S 6900 W 84128
W 6900 S 84084
W 6915 S 84084
W 6925 S 84084
W 6920 S 84084
S 6935 W 84128
S 6955 W 84128
W 6960 S 84084
  4800-5045 84081
W 6975 S 84084
S 6990 W 84128
S 700 W 84119
  3800-3899 84128
W 7000 S
  1200-3600 84084
  4800-5198 84081
S 7025 W 84081
S 7025 W 84128
S 7030 W 84128
S 7040 W 84128
W 7050 S 84084
W 7055 S 84084
S 7060 W 84081
S 7080 W 84128
W 7085 S 84084
W 7095 S 84084
S 7105 W 84128
W 7105 S 84084
S 7110 W 84081
S 7120 W 84128
W 7125 S 84084
W 7130 S 84084
W 7140 S 84084
S 7160 W 84128
S 7175 W 84081
W 7180 S 84084
W 7200 S 84084
W 7225 S 84084
S 7260 W 84081
W 7265 S 84084
W 7268 S 84084
W 7260 S
  3400-3440 84084
W 7290 S 84084
W 7305 S 84084
S 7320 W 84081
W 7325 S 84084
W 7340 S 84084
S 7365 W 84081
W 7370 S 84084
W 7380 S 84084
W 7410 S 84084
W 7420 S 84084
  5189-5229 84081
W 7455 S 84084
W 7460 S 84084
W 7470 S 84084
W 7500 S 84084
W 7510 S 84084
W 7525 S 84084
W 7520 S 84084
W 7530 S 84084
  5290-5399 84081
W 7545 S 84084
W 7550 S 84084
  4900-4999 84081
W 7560 S 84084
W 7575 S 84084
W 7580 S 84084
W 7590 S 84084
W 7600 S 84084
W 7625 S 84084
W 7640 S 84081
W 7655 S 84084
W 7660 S 84084
W 7660 S 84084
  5000-5198 84081
W 7675 S 84084
  3001-3097 84084
  4900-4999 84081
W 7680 S 84084
  5100-5199 84081
W 7700 S 84084
W 7705 S 84084
W 7720 S 84084
W 7730 S 84084
W 7735 S 84084
W 7730 S
  4900-5199 84081
W 7740 S 84084
W 7770 S 84081
W 7800 S 84088
W 7800 S 84088
  5210-5388 84081
W 7825 S 84088
W 7820 S 84081
W 7865 S 84088
W 7875 S 84088
W 7870 S 84081
W 7888 S 84088
W 7895 S 84081
W 7900 S 84088
W 7910 S 84088
  5000-5099 84081
W 7925 S 84088
W 7950 S 84088
W 7965 S 84088
W 7970 S 84088
W 7980 S 84088
  5000-5099 84081
W 7990 S
  3600-3699 84088
  6400-6499 84081
W 8010 S 84088
W 8025 S 84088
W 8020 S 84088
W 8030 S 84088
W 8040 S 84088
W 8050 S 84088
  7013-7199 84081
W 8070 S 84088
W 8090 S 84081
W 8110 S 84088
W 8120 S 84088
W 8130 S 84081
W 8140 S 84088
  4900-4999 84081
W 8170 S 84081
W 8180 S 84088
  4900-5399 84081
W 8200 S
  2700-4499 84088
  4501-4599 84088
  6000-6881 84081
W 8220 S 84088
W 8235 S 84081
W 8230 S 84088
  5200-5300 84081
W 8245 S 84088
W 8250 S 84088
W 8260 S 84081
W 8270 S 84088
  5100-5199 84081
W 8280 S 84088
W 8295 S 84088
W 8300 S 84088
W 8305 S 84081
W 8315 S 84088
W 8310 S 84081
W 8320 S 84081
W 8340 S 84088
W 8350 S 84088
W 8370 S 84088
W 8375 S 84081
W 8380 S 84088
W 8390 S 84088
W 8395 S 84088
W 8400 S 84088
W 8410 S 84088
W 8420 S 84088
W 8430 S 84088
W 8450 S 84088
W 8475 S 84088
W 8470 S 84088
W 8480 S 84088
W 8490 S 84088
W 8500 S 84088
W 8510 S 84088
W 8525 S 84088
W 8540 S 84088
W 8550 S 84088
W 8565 S 84088
W 8575 S 84081
W 8580 S 84088
W 8605 S 84088
W 8600 S 84088
W 8620 S 84088
W 8620 S 84088
  4800-5199 84081
W 8660 S
  1301-1397 84088
  4800-4999 84081
W 8680 S 84088
W 8690 S 84088
W 8700 S 84088
  4800-4999 84081
W 8730 S
  3976-3999 84088
  4800-4899 84081
W 8745 S 84088
W 8740 S
  1500-1999 84088
  4800-4999 84081
W 8750 S 84088
W 8760 S 84088
W 8770 S 84088
W 8780 S 84088
  4800-4959 84081
W 8790 S 84088
W 8800 S 84088
W 8820 S 84088
  4800-5199 84081
W 8830 S 84088
W 8850 S 84088
W 8860 S 84081
W 8870 S 84088
W 8890 S 84088
W 8900 S 84088
W 8910 S 84088
W 8920 S 84088
W 8925 S 84088
W 8940 S 84088
W 8970 S 84088
W 9000 S 84088
W 9000 S 84088
  4800-5498 84081
W 9050 S 84088
W 9070 S 84088
W 9100 S 84088
W 9110 S 84088
W 9140 S 84088
W 9150 S 84088
W 9170 S 84088
W 9190 S 84088
W 9230 S 84088
W 9240 S 84088
W 9260 S 84088
W 9270 S 84088
W 9300 S 84088
W 9305 S 84088
W 9330 S 84088
W 9335 S 84088
W 9340 S 84088
W 9380 S 84088
W 9390 S 84088
W 9470 S 84081
W 9790 S 84081
W 9860 S 84081
W 9930 S 84081

Vermont

People QuickFacts	Vermont	USA
Population, 2013 estimate	626,630	316,128,839
Population, 2010 (April 1) estimates base	625,745	308,747,716
Population, percent change, April 1, 2010 to July 1, 2013	0.1%	2.4%
Population, 2010	625,741	308,745,538
Persons under 5 years, percent, 2013	4.9%	6.3%
Persons under 18 years, percent, 2013	19.6%	23.3%
Persons 65 years and over, percent, 2013	16.4%	14.1%
Female persons, percent, 2013	50.7%	50.8%
White alone, percent, 2013 (a)	95.2%	77.7%
Black or African American alone, percent, 2013 (a)	1.2%	13.2%
American Indian and Alaska Native alone, percent, 2013 (a)	0.4%	1.2%
Asian alone, percent, 2013 (a)	1.4%	5.3%
Native Hawaiian and Other Pacific Islander alone, percent, 2013 (a)	Z	0.2%
Two or More Races, percent, 2013	1.8%	2.4%
Hispanic or Latino, percent, 2013 (b)	1.7%	17.1%
White alone, not Hispanic or Latino, percent, 2013	93.8%	62.6%
Living in same house 1 year & over, percent, 2008-2012	86.3%	84.8%
Foreign born persons, percent, 2008-2012	4.0%	12.9%
Language other than English spoken at home, pct age 5+, 2008-2012	5.3%	20.5%
High school graduate or higher, percent of persons age 25+, 2008-2012	91.3%	85.7%
Bachelor's degree or higher, percent of persons age 25+, 2008-2012	34.2%	28.5%
Veterans, 2008-2012	50,705	21,853,912
Mean travel time to work (minutes), workers age 16+, 2008-2012	22.1	25.4
Housing units, 2013	323,920	132,802,859
Homeownership rate, 2008-2012	71.2%	65.5%
Housing units in multi-unit structures, percent, 2008-2012	23.1%	25.9%
Median value of owner-occupied housing units, 2008-2012	$215,800	$181,400
Households, 2008-2012	256,830	115,226,802
Persons per household, 2008-2012	2.34	2.61
Per capita money income in past 12 months (2012 dollars), 2008-2012	$28,846	$28,051
Median household income, 2008-2012	$54,168	$53,046
Persons below poverty level, percent, 2008-2012	11.6%	14.9%

Business QuickFacts	Vermont	USA
Private nonfarm establishments, 2012	21,161	7,431,808
Private nonfarm employment, 2012	265,460	115,938,468
Private nonfarm employment, percent change, 2011-2012	0.5%	2.2%
Nonemployer establishments, 2012	59,836	22,735,915
Total number of firms, 2007	78,729	27,092,908
Black-owned firms, percent, 2007	S	7.1%
American Indian- and Alaska Native-owned firms, percent, 2007	0.5%	0.9%
Asian-owned firms, percent, 2007	0.8%	5.7%
Native Hawaiian and Other Pacific Islander-owned firms, percent, 2007	S	0.1%
Hispanic-owned firms, percent, 2007	0.6%	8.3%
Women-owned firms, percent, 2007	26.0%	28.8%
Manufacturers shipments, 2007 ($1000)	10,751,461	5,319,456,312
Merchant wholesaler sales, 2007 ($1000)	5,121,694	4,174,286,516
Retail sales, 2007 ($1000)	9,310,119	3,917,663,456
Retail sales per capita, 2007	$15,005	$12,990
Accommodation and food services sales, 2007 ($1000)	1,367,630	613,795,732
Building permits, 2012	1,301	829,658

Geography QuickFacts	Vermont	USA
Land area in square miles, 2010	9,216.66	3,531,905.43
Persons per square mile, 2010	67.9	87.4
FIPS Code	50	

(a) Includes persons reporting only one race.
(b) Hispanics may be of any race, so also are included in applicable race categories.
FN: Footnote on this item for this area in place of data
NA: Not available
D: Suppressed to avoid disclosure of confidential information
X: Not applicable
S: Suppressed; does not meet publication standards
Z: Value greater than zero but less than half unit of measure shown
F: Fewer than 100 firms
Source: US Census Bureau State & County QuickFacts

Vermont

3 DIGIT ZIP CODE MAP

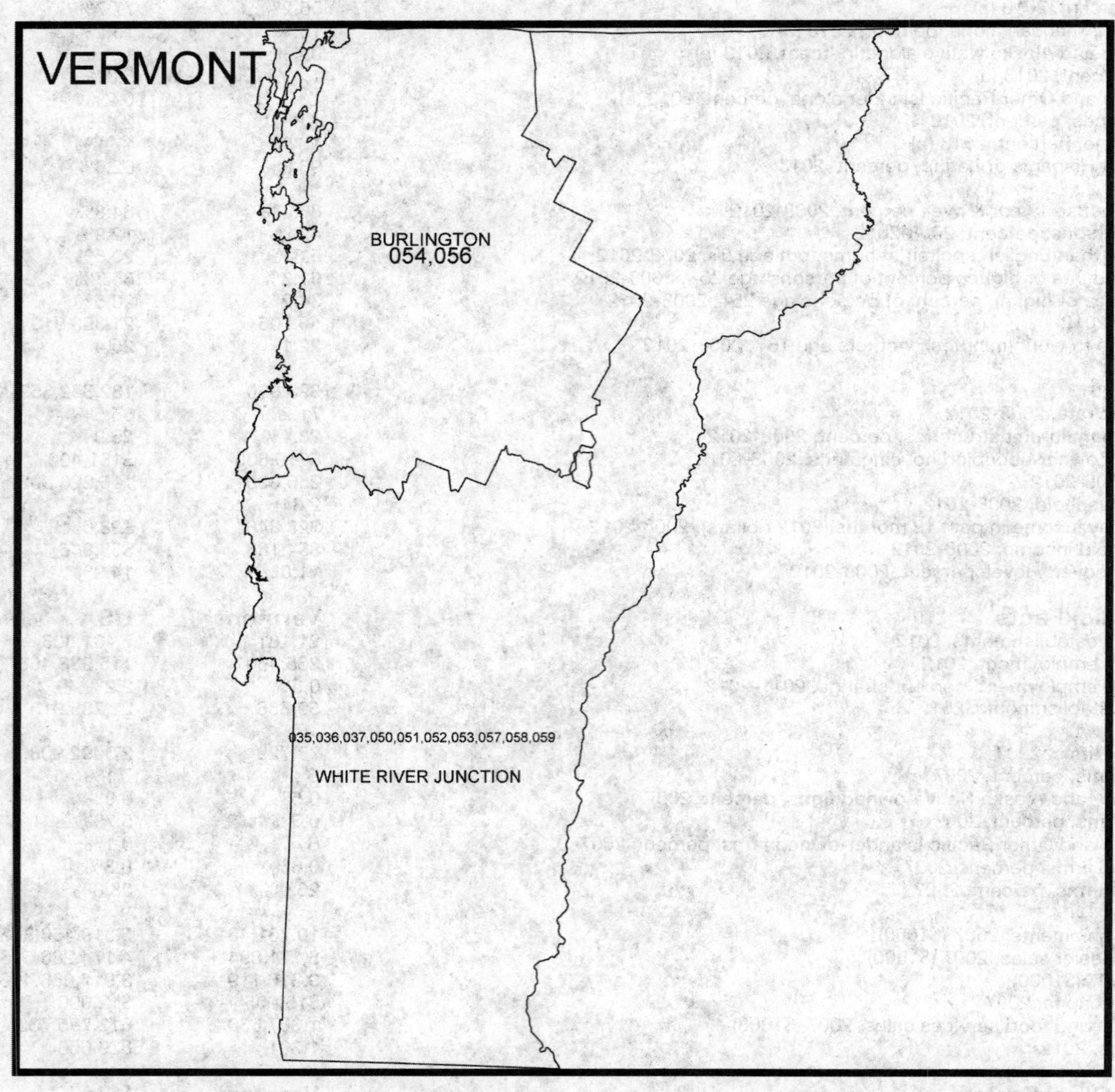

Vermont

(Abbreviation: VT)

Post Office, County — ZIP Code

Places with more than one ZIP code are listed in capital letters, See pages indicated.

Adamant, Washington 05640
Addison, Addison 05491
Albany, Orleans 05820
Alburg, Grand Isle 05440
Alburgh, Grand Isle 05440
Andover, Windsor 05143
Arlington, Bennington 05250
Ascutney, Windsor 05030
Athens, Windsor 05143
Averill, Essex 05901
Bakersfield, Franklin 05441
Baltimore, Windsor 05143
Barnard, Windsor 05031
Barnet, Caledonia 05821
Barre, Washington 05641
Barton, Orleans 05822
Beebe Plain, Orleans 05823
Beecher Falls, Essex 05902
Bellows Falls, Windham 05101
Belmont, Rutland 05730
Belvidere Center, Lamoille 05442
Bennington, Bennington 05201
Benson, Rutland 05731
Benson, Rutland 05743
Berlin, Washington 05602
Bethel, Windsor 05032
Bloomfield, Essex 05905
Bolton Valley, Chittenden 05477
Bomoseen, Rutland 05732
Bondville, Bennington 05340
Bradford, Orange 05033
Braintree, Orange 05060
Brandon, Rutland 05733
BRATTLEBORO, Windham
(See Page 4056)
Brdgewtr Cors, Windsor 05035
Bridgewater, Windsor 05034
Bridgewater Corners, Windsor 05035
Bridport, Addison 05734
Bristol, Addison 05443
Brookfield, Orange 05036
Brookline, Windham 05345
Brownington, Orleans 05860
Brownsville, Windsor 05037
Brunswick, Essex 05905
BURLINGTON, Chittenden
(See Page 4056)
Cabot, Washington 05647
Calais, Washington 05648
Cambridge, Chittenden 05444
Cambridgeport, Windham 05141
Canaan, Essex 05901
Canaan, Essex 05903
Castleton, Rutland 05735
Cavendish, Windsor 05142
Center Rutland, Rutland 05736
Charlotte, Chittenden 05445
Chelsea, Orange 05038
Chester, Windsor 05143
Chittenden, Rutland 05737
Clarendon Springs, Rutland 05777
COLCHESTER, Chittenden
(See Page 4056)
Concord, Essex 05824
Corinth, Orange 05039
Cornwall, Addison 05753
Coventry, Orleans 05825
Craftsbry Cmn, Orleans 05827
Craftsbury, Orleans 05826
Craftsbury Common, Orleans 05827
Cuttingsville, Rutland 05738
Danby, Rutland 05739
Danville, Caledonia 05828
Derby, Orleans 05829
Derby Line, Orleans 05830
Dorset, Bennington 05251
Dummerston, Windham 05301
East Arlington, Bennington 05252
East Barre, Washington 05649
East Berkshire, Franklin 05447
East Burke, Caledonia 05832
East Calais, Washington 05650
East Charleston, Orleans 05833
East Concord, Essex 05906
East Corinth, Orange 05040
East Corinth, Orange 05076
East Dorset, Bennington 05253
East Dover, Windham 05341
East Dummerston, Windham 05346
East Fairfield, Franklin 05448
East Hardwick, Caledonia 05836
East Haven, Essex 05837
East Middlebury, Addison 05740
East Montpelier, Washington 05651
East Orange, Orange 05086
East Poultney, Rutland 05741
East Randolph, Orange 05041
East Ryegate, Caledonia 05042
East Saint Johnsbury, Caledonia 05838
East Thetford, Orange 05043
East Wallingford, Rutland 05742
Eden, Lamoille 05652
Eden, Lamoille 05653
Eden Mills, Lamoille 05653
Elmore, Lamoille 05661
Enosburg Falls, Franklin 05450
Essex, Chittenden 05451
ESSEX JUNCTION, Chittenden
(See Page 4057)
Fair Haven, Rutland 05743
Fairfax, Chittenden 05454
Fairfield, Franklin 05455
Fairlee, Orange 05045
Ferrisburgh, Addison 05456
Florence, Rutland 05744
Forest Dale, Rutland 05745
Franklin, Franklin 05457
Gaysville, Windsor 05746
Gilman, Essex 05904
Glover, Orleans 05839
Goshen, Rutland 05733
Grafton, Windham 05146
Granby, Essex 05840
Grand Isle, Grand Isle 05458
Graniteville, Washington 05654
Granville, Addison 05747
Greensboro, Orleans 05841
Greensboro Bend, Orleans 05842
Grnsboro Bend, Orleans 05842
Groton, Caledonia 05046
Guildhall, Essex 05905
Guilford, Windham 05301
Hancock, Addison 05748
Hardwick, Caledonia 05843
Hartford, Windsor 05047
Hartland, Windsor 05048
Hartland Four Corners, Windsor 05049
Highgate Center, Franklin 05459
Highgate Springs, Franklin 05460
Hinesburg, Chittenden 05461
Huntington, Chittenden 05462
Hyde Park, Lamoille 05655
Hydeville, Rutland 05750
Irasburg, Orleans 05845
Island Pond, Essex 05846
Isle La Motte, Grand Isle 05463
Jacksonville, Windham 05342
Jamaica, Windham 05343
Jay, Orleans 05859
Jay Peak, Orleans 05859
Jeffersonville, Lamoille 05464
Jericho, Chittenden 05465
Jericho Center, Chittenden 05465
Johnson, Lamoille 05656
Jonesville, Chittenden 05466
Killington, Rutland 05751
Lake Elmore, Lamoille 05657
Landgrove, Windham 05148
Leicester, Rutland 05733
Lemington, Essex 05903
Lincoln, Addison 05443
Londonderry, Windham 05148
Lowell, Orleans 05847
Lower Waterford, Caledonia 05848
Ludlow, Windsor 05149
Lunenburg, Essex 05906
Lyndon, Caledonia 05849
Lyndon Center, Caledonia 05850
Lyndonville, Caledonia 05851
Maidstone, Essex 05905
Manchester, Bennington 05254
Manchester Center, Bennington 05255
Marlboro, Windham 05344
Marshfield, Washington 05658
Mc Indoe Falls, Caledonia 05050
Mendon, Rutland 05701
Middlebury, Addison 05753
Middlesex, Washington 05602
Middlesex Center, Washington 05602
Middletown Springs, Rutland 05757
Milton, Chittenden 05468
Monkton, Addison 05469
Montgomery, Franklin 05470
Montgomery Center, Franklin 05471
MONTPELIER, Washington
(See Page 4057)
Moretown, Washington 05660
Morgan, Orleans 05853
Morgan Ctr, Orleans 05853
Morristown, Lamoille 05661
Morrisville, Lamoille 05661
Moscow, Lamoille 05662
Mount Holly, Rutland 05758
Mount Snow, Windham 05356
Mount Tabor, Rutland 05739
New Haven, Addison 05472
Newbury, Orange 05051
Newfane, Windham 05345
Newport, Orleans 05855
Newport Center, Orleans 05857
North Bennington, Bennington 05257
North Chittenden, Rutland 05763
North Clarendon, Rutland 05759
North Concord, Essex 05858
North Ferrisburgh, Addison 05473
North Hartland, Windsor 05052
North Hero, Grand Isle 05474
North Hyde Park, Lamoille 05665
North Middlesex, Washington 05682
North Montpelier, Washington 05666
North Pomfret, Windsor 05053
North Pownal, Bennington 05260
North Springfield, Windsor 05150
North Thetford, Orange 05054
North Troy, Orleans 05859
Northfield, Washington 05663
Northfield Falls, Washington 05664
Northfld Fls, Washington 05664
Norton, Essex 05907
Norwich, Windsor 05055
Orange, Washington 05641
Orleans, Orleans 05860
Orwell, Addison 05760
Panton, Addison 05491
Passumpsic, Caledonia 05861
Pawlet, Rutland 05761
Peacham, Caledonia 05862
Perkinsville, Windsor 05151
Peru, Bennington 05152
Pittsfield, Rutland 05762
Pittsford, Rutland 05763
Plainfield, Washington 05667
Plymouth, Windsor 05056
Post Mills, Orange 05058
Poultney, Rutland 05741
Poultney, Rutland 05764
Pownal, Bennington 05261
Proctor, Rutland 05765
Proctorsville, Windsor 05153
Putney, Windham 05346
Quechee, Windsor 05059
Randolph, Orange 05060
Randolph Center, Orange 05061
Reading, Windsor 05062
Readsboro, Bennington 05350
Readsboro, Bennington 05352
Richford, Franklin 05476
Richmond, Chittenden 05477
Ripton, Addison 05766
Riverton, Washington 05663
Rochester, Windsor 05767
Roxbury, Addison 05669
Rupert, Bennington 05768
RUTLAND, Rutland
(See Page 4057)
Ryegate, Caledonia 05042
Saint Albans, Franklin 05478
Saint Albans Bay, Franklin 05481
Saint George, Chittenden 05495
Saint Johnsbury, Caledonia 05819
Saint Johnsbury Center, Caledonia 05863
Salisbury, Addison 05769
Sandgate, Bennington 05250
Saxtons River, Windham 05154
Searsburg, Windham 05363
Shaftsbury, Bennington 05262
Sharon, Windsor 05065
Sheffield, Caledonia 05866
Shelburne, Chittenden 05482
Sheldon, Franklin 05455
Sheldon, Franklin 05483
Sheldon Springs, Franklin 05485
Shoreham, Addison 05770
Shrewsbury, Rutland 05738
South Barre, Washington 05670
SOUTH BURLINGTON, Chittenden
(See Page 4057)
South Chittenden, Rutland 05701
South Duxbury, Washington 05660
South Hero, Grand Isle 05486
South Londonderry, Windham 05155
South Newfane, Windham 05351
South Pomfret, Windsor 05067
South Reading, Windsor 05153
South Royalton, Windsor 05068
South Ryegate, Caledonia 05069
South Strafford, Orange 05070
South Woodstock, Windsor 05071
Springfield, Windsor 05156
St George, Chittenden 05495
Stamford, Bennington 05352
Starksboro, Addison 05487
Stockbridge, Windsor 05772
Stowe, Lamoille 05672
Strafford, Orange 05072
Stratton, Windham 05360
Stratton Mnt, Windham 05155
Stratton Mountain, Windham 05155
Sudbury, Rutland 05733
Sunderland, Bennington 05250
Sutton, Caledonia 05867
Swanton, Franklin 05488
Taftsville, Windsor 05073
Thetford, Orange 05074
Thetford Center, Orange 05075
Tinmouth, Rutland 05773
Topsham, Orange 05076
Townshend, Windham 05353
Troy, Orleans 05868
Tunbridge, Orange 05077
Underhill, Chittenden 05489
Underhill Center, Chittenden 05490
Vergennes, Addison 05491
Vernon, Windham 05354
Vershire, Orange 05079
Victory, Essex 05858
Waitsfield, Washington 05673
Wallingford, Rutland 05773
Wardsboro, Windham 05355
Warren, Washington 05674
Washington, Orange 05675
Waterbury, Washington 05671
Waterbury Center, Washington 05677
Waterford, Caledonia 05819
Waterville, Lamoille 05492
Websterville, Washington 05678
Wells, Rutland 05774
Wells River, Orange 05081
West Arlington, Bennington 05250
West Berlin, Washington 05663
West Braintree, Addison 05669
West Brattleboro, Windham 05301
West Brookfield, Orange 05060
West Burke, Caledonia 05871
West Charleston, Orleans 05872
West Cornwall, Addison 05778
West Danville, Caledonia 05873
West Dover, Windham 05356
West Dummerston, Windham 05357
West Fairlee, Orange 05083
West Glover, Orleans 05875
West Halifax, Windham 05358
West Hartford, Windsor 05084
West Haven, Rutland 05743
West Marlboro, Windham 05363
West Newbury, Orange 05085
West Pawlet, Rutland 05775
West Rupert, Bennington 05776
West Rutland, Rutland 05777
West Topsham, Orange 05086
West Townshend, Windham 05359
West Wardsboro, Windham 05360
West Windsor, Windsor 05089
Westfield, Orleans 05874
Westford, Chittenden 05494
Westminster, Windham 05158
Westminster Station, Windham 05159
Westminster West, Windham 05346
Weston, Windsor 05161
Weybridge, Addison 05753
White River Junction, Windsor 05001
Whiting, Addison 05778
Whitingham, Windham 05361
Wilder, Windsor 05088
Williamstown, Orange 05679
Williamsville, Windham 05362
Williston, Chittenden 05495
Wilmington, Windham 05363
Windham, Windham 05359
Windsor, Windsor 05089
Winhall, Bennington 05340
Winooski, Chittenden 05404
Wolcott, Lamoille 05680
Woodbury, Washington 05681
Woodford, Bennington 05201
Woodstock, Windsor 05091
Worcester, Washington 05682

BRATTLEBORO VT

General Delivery 05301

POST OFFICE BOXES MAIN OFFICE STATIONS AND BRANCHES

Box No.s
1 - 1998 05302
2001 - 2740 05303
6001 - 6480 05302
8001 - 8480 05304

NAMED STREETS

All Street Addresses 05301

NUMBERED STREETS

All Street Addresses 05301

BURLINGTON VT

General Delivery 05402

POST OFFICE BOXES MAIN OFFICE STATIONS AND BRANCHES

Box No.s
1 - 1916 05402
3001 - 3420 05408
4001 - 4638 05406
5001 - 8898 05402
64641 - 65379 05406

NAMED STREETS

Adams Ct & St 05401
Adsit Ct 05401
Alder Ln 05401
Alexis Dr 05408
Alfred St & Ter 05401
Algird St 05408
Allen St 05401
Ambrose Pl 05401
Appletree Point Ln & Rd 05408
Archibald St 05401
Arlington Ct 05408
Austin Dr 05401
Avenue A 05408
Avenue B 05408
S Avenue C 05408
Bacon St 05401
Baird St 05401
Balsam St 05408
Bank St 05401
Barley Rd 05408
Barrett St 05401
Batchelder St 05401
Battery St 05401
Bayview St 05401
Beachcrest Dr 05408
Beech St 05401
Bennington Ct 05408
Berry St 05401
Billings Ct 05408
Bilodeau Ct & Pkwy 05401
Birch Ct 05408
Birchcliff Pkwy 05401
Birchwood Ln 05408
Bittersweet Ln 05401
Blodgett St 05401
Blondin Cir 05408
Booth St 05401
Borestone Ln 05408
Bradley St 05401
Brandywine St 05408
Brierwood Ln 05408
Briggs St 05401
Bright St 05401
Brook Dr 05408
Brookes Ave 05401
Browe Ct 05408
Browns Ct 05401
Buell St 05401
Burlington Sq 05401
Calarco Ct 05401
Canfield St 05401
Caroline St 05401
Case Pkwy 05401
Cathedral Sq 05401
Catherine St 05401
Cayuga Ct 05408
Cedar Ln & St 05401
Centennial Ct 05401
Center St 05401
Central Ave 05401
N & S Champlain St 05401
Charity St 05408
Charles St 05401
Charlotte St 05401
Chase Ln & St 05401
Cherry Ln & St 05401
Chestnut Ter 05401
Chittenden Dr 05401
Church St 05401
Claire Point Rd 05408
Clarke St 05401
Cliff St 05401
Clistine Sq 05408
Cloarec Ct 05401
Clover Ln 05408
Clymer St 05401
Colchester Ave & Ct 05401
College St 05401
Colonial Sq 05401
Conger Ave 05401
Convent Sq 05401
Converse Ct 05401
Cottage Grv 05408
N Cove Rd 05408
S Cove Rd 05401
Crescent Rd & Ter 05401
Crescent Beach Dr 05408
Crombie St 05401
Cross Pkwy 05408
Crowley St 05401
Cumberland Rd 05408
Curtis Ave 05408
Dale Rd 05408
Dans Ct 05401
Davis Rd 05401
Decatur St 05401
Deforest Hts & Rd 05401
Depot St 05401
Derway Dr 05408
Dewey Dr 05408
Dodds Ct 05408
Dorset Ln 05408
Drew St 05401
Driftwood Ln 05408
Dunder Rd 05401
East Ave 05401
Eastman Farm Rd 05408
Eastman Way Dr 05401
Edgemoor Dr 05408
Edgewood Ln 05401
Edinborough Dr 05408
Edson St 05401
Elm Ter 05401
Elmwood Ave
1-19 05401
11-11 05402
20-299 05401
Ethan Allen Pkwy 05408
Ethan Allen Homestead 05408
Fairholt 05401
Fairmont Pl 05408
Fairmount St 05401
Faith St 05408
Farrell St 05401
Farrington Pkwy 05408
Ferguson Ave 05401
Fern St 05408
Fletcher Pl 05401
Flynn Ave 05401
Forest St 05408
Foster St 05401
Franklin Sq 05408
Front St 05401
Gazo Ave 05408
George St 05401
Germain St 05401
Glen Rd 05401
Glenwood Ln 05408
Golden Pl 05401
Gosse Ct 05408
Gove Ct 05401
Grant St 05401
Green St 05401
Green Acres Dr 05408
Grey Meadow Dr 05408
Grove St 05401
Hale Ct 05408
Handy Ct 05401
Harbor Watch Rd 05401
Hardy Ave 05408
Harrington Ter 05401
Harrison Ave 05401
Haswell St 05401
Hayward St 05401
Heineberg Rd 05408
Henderson Ter 05401
Henry St 05401
Hickok Pl 05401
High Grove Ct 05401
Hildred Dr 05401
Hillcrest Rd 05401
Hillside Ter 05401
Holly Ln 05408
Holt St 05401
Home Ave 05401
Hoover St 05401
Hope St 05408
Howard St 05401
Hungerford Ter 05401
Hyde St 05401
Industrial Pkwy 05401
Institute Rd 05408
Intervale Ave & Rd 05401
Ira Ln 05408
Iranistan Rd 05401
Isham St 05401
Ivy Ln 05408
Jackson Ct 05401
James Ave 05408
Janet Cir 05408
Johnson St 05401
Juniper Ter 05401
Kilburn St 05401
Killarney Dr 05408
King St 05401
King Street Dock 05401
Kingsland Ter 05401
Lafayette Pl 05401
Lafountain St 05401
Lake St 05401
Lake Forest Dr 05401
Lakeside Ave 05401
Lakeview Ter 05401
Lakewood Pkwy 05408
Latham Ct 05401
Laurel Ct 05408
Lavalley Ln 05401
Lawson Ln 05401
Leddy Park Rd 05408
Ledge Rd 05401
Ledgemere St 05401
Leonard St 05408
Linden Ter 05401
Little Eagle Bay 05408
Loaldo Dr 05401
Locust St & Ter 05401
Loomis St 05401
Lopes Ave 05408
Lori Ln 05408
Luck St 05401
Ludwig Ct 05401
Lyman Ave 05401
Main St 05401
Manhattan Dr 05401
Mansfield Ave 05401
Maple St 05401
Marble Ave 05401
Margaret St 05401
Marion St 05401
Market Sq 05401
Marshall Dr 05408
Matthew Ave 05408
Mcauley Sq 05401
S Meadow Dr 05401
Mechanics Ln 05401
Meridian St 05408
Mill St 05401
Monroe St 05401
Moore Ct & Dr 05408
Morgan St 05408
Morrill Dr 05408
Morse Pl 05401
Mountview Ct 05401
Muirfield Rd 05408
Murray St 05401
Myrtle St 05401
Nash Pl 05401
North Ave
1-499 05401
600-3199 05408
3201-3299 05408
North St 05401
Northgate Rd 05408
Northshore Dr 05408
Northview Dr 05408
Nottingham Ln 05408
Oak St 05401
Oakbeach Dr 05408
Oakcrest Dr 05408
Oakland Ter 05408
Oakledge Dr 05401
Orchard Ter 05401
Overlake Park 05401
Parielis St 05401
Park St 05401
Pearl St 05401
Pennington Dr 05408
Penny Ln 05401
Perrotta Pl 05401
Peru St 05401
Pine Pl & St 05401
Pitkin St 05401
Plattsburg Ave 05408
Pleasant Ave 05408
Poirier Pl 05408
Pomeroy St 05401
Poplar St 05401
Proctor Pl 05401
N & S Prospect Hl, Pkwy & St 05401
Railway Ln 05401
Randy Ln 05408
Raymond Pl 05401
Red Maple Ln 05408
Redstone Ter 05401
Revere Ct 05408
Richardson St 05401
Ridgewood Dr 05408
Rivermount Ter 05408
Rivers Edge Dr 05408
Riverside Ave 05401
Riverview Dr 05408
Robinson Pkwy 05401
Rock Point Rd 05408
Rockland St 05408
Rose St 05401
Roseade Pkwy 05408
Rumsey Ln 05401
Russell St 05401
Saint Louis St 05401
Saint Mary St 05401
Saint Paul St 05401
Sandra Cir 05408
Sandy Ln 05408
Saratoga Ave 05408
Scarff Ave 05401
School St 05401
Sears Ln 05401
Shelburne Rd
1-371 05401
370-370 05406
372-690 05401
373-699 05401
Sherman St 05401
Shore Rd 05408
Simms St 05408
Sky Dr 05408
South St 05401
Southcrest Dr 05401
Southwind Dr 05401
Spring St 05401
Spruce Ct & St 05401
Stanbury Rd 05408
Staniford Rd 05408
Starr Farm Bch & Rd 05408
Steele St 05401
Stirling Pl 05408
Strong St 05401
Summer St 05401
Summit Rdg & St 05401
Sunset Clfs 05408
Sunset Ct 05401
Sunset Dr 05408
Surf Rd 05408
Tallwood Ln 05408
Temple St 05408
Thibault Pkwy 05401
Tower Ter 05401
Tracy Dr 05408
Turf Rd 05408
N & S Union St 05401
University Rd & Ter 05401
University Of Vermont 05401
Valade Rd 05408
Van Patten Pkwy 05408
Venus Ave 05408
Vermont Park 05401
Vest Haven Dr 05408
E Village Dr 05401
Village Grn 05401
Vine St 05408
Volz St 05401
Walnut St 05401
Ward St 05401
Washington St 05401
Wells St 05401
West Rd 05408
Western Ave 05408
Westminster Dr 05408
Weston St 05401
Westward Dr 05408
White Pl 05401
Wildwood Dr 05408
N & S Willard St 05401
N & S Williams St 05401
Willow St 05401
Wilson St 05401
Wing St 05408
N & S Winooski Ave 05401
Woodbury Rd 05408
Woodcrest Ln 05401
Woodlawn Rd 05408
Woodridge Dr 05408
Woods St 05408
Wright Ave 05401
York Dr 05408

COLCHESTER VT

General Delivery 05446

POST OFFICE BOXES MAIN OFFICE STATIONS AND BRANCHES

Box No.s
1 - 1068 05446
2001 - 2212 05449

NAMED STREETS

Abigail Dr 05446
Acorn Ln 05446
Aikey Ln 05446
Al Shir Rd 05446
Andrea Ln 05446
Annas Ct 05446
Arbor Ln 05446
Ashford Ln 05446
Aurielle Dr 05446
Austin House Rd 05446
Autumn Woods 05446
Barbara Ter 05446
Barnes Ave 05446
Bartletts Way 05446
Basswood Rdg 05446
Bay Cir & Rd 05446
Bay Meadow Ests 05446
Bayview Rd 05446
N Beach Rd 05446
Bean Rd 05446
Belair Dr 05446
Belwood Ave 05446
Billado Ct 05446
Birch Dr 05446
Birchwood Dr 05446
Biscayne Hts 05446
Bissette Dr 05446
Blackberry Cir 05446
Blakely Rd 05446
Bloomfield Dr 05446
Bluebird Dr 05446
Bluff Rd 05446
Bonanza Park 05446
Braeloch Rd E 05446
Brennan St 05446
Brentwood Dr 05446
Briar Ln 05446
Brickyard Rd 05446
Brighton Ln 05446
Broadacres Dr 05446
Broadlake Rd 05446
Brookside Way 05446
Brown Ledge Rd 05446
Buckingham Dr 05446
Buff Ledge Rd 05446
Burnham Ln 05446
Cable Ln 05446
Caleb Ct 05446
Calm Cove Cir 05446
Camels Hump Ave 05446
Camp Holy Cross Rd 05446
Camp Kiniya Rd 05446
Canyon Rd 05446
Canyon Estate Dr 05446
Carriage Way 05446
Casey Ln 05446
Catamount Ln 05446
Causeway Rd 05446
Cedar Creek Rd 05446
Cedar Ridge Dr 05446
Champlain Dr 05446
Chase Ln 05446
Chestnut Ln 05446
Chimney Hill Dr 05446
Chipmunk Ln 05446
Church Rd 05446
Clay Point Rd 05446
Cliff Rd 05446
Coates Island Rd 05446
Cobbleview Dr 05446
Colchester Point Rd 05446
Colchester Pond Rd 05446
Colden Rd 05446
College Pkwy 05446
Colonial Dr 05446
Commerce Dr 05446
Commonwealth Dr 05446
Conquest Cir 05446
Coolidge Ct 05446
Coon Hill Rd 05446
Cortland Ln 05446
Cottonwood Xing 05446
Country Mdws 05446
Coventry Rd 05446
Creek Gln 05446
Creek Farm Plz & Rd 05446
Crooked Creek Rd 05446
Crossfield Dr 05446
Curve Hill Rd 05446
Dalton Dr 05446
Deer Ln 05446
Depot Rd 05446
Diane Ln 05446
Don Mar Ter 05446
Donnas Way 05446
Douglas Dr 05446
Dunlop Way 05446
Eagle Park Dr 05446
East Ave & Rd 05446
Edgewater Dr 05446
Edgewood Dr 05446
Eighth St 05446
Elderberry Ln 05446
Elm Ct 05446
Emmas Way 05446
Entrance Rd 05446
Ethan Allen Ave 05446
Evening Sun Dr 05446
Everbreeze Dr 05446
Evergreen Cir 05446
Farnsworth Rd 05446
Fastnet Cir 05446
Fern Ct 05446
Ferndell Ln 05446
Field Green Dr 05446
Fifth St 05446
First St 05446
Foley Rd 05446
Ford Ln 05446
Forest Trl 05446
Forman Dr 05446
Fourth St 05446
Fox Run 05446
Galvin Hill Rd 05446
Garden Ln 05446
Giffin Ct 05446
Gilman Cir 05446
Goodsell Pt 05446
Gorge Rd 05446
Grand View Rd 05446
Granite Creek Rd 05446
Greenbrier Ln 05446
Greenwood Dr 05446
Gregg Ln 05446
Grey Birch Dr 05446
Haileys Way 05446
Half Moon Ter 05446
Hannahs Pl 05446
N Harbor Ln & Rd 05446
Harvest Ln 05446
Hawkes Way 05446
Hawthorne Ln 05446
Hazelwood Pl 05446
Hazen Lyon 05446
Heartwood Ln 05446
Heather Cir 05446
Hedman Rd 05446
Hegeman Ave 05446
Heineberg Dr 05446
Hercules Dr 05446
Heritage Ln 05446
Heros View Rd 05446
Hickory Ln 05446
Hidden Oaks Dr 05446
High Point Ctr 05446
Hill Spring Ln 05446
Hillcrest Ln 05446
Hilltop Ct 05446
Holbrook Ct 05446
Hollow Crk 05446
Holy Cross Rd 05446
Horizon Vw 05446
Horseshoe Ln 05446
Hummingbird Dr 05446
Indian Cir 05446
Ira Allen Ct 05446
E Island Rd 05446
Jakes Pl 05446
James Way 05446
Jason Dr 05446

Jasper Mine Rd 05446
Jefferson Dr 05446
Jeffrey Dr 05446
Jen Barry Ln 05446
Jimmo Dr 05446
Jocelyn Ct 05446
Joey Dr 05446
Johnson Ave 05446
Julie Dr 05446
Juniper Dr 05446
Justin Morgan Dr 05446
Kathleen Ln 05446
Kensington Rd 05446
King St 05446
Kylies Way 05446
E & W Lakeshore Dr 05446
Lakewood Ct 05446
Lamoille Blf 05446
Landing Ave 05446
Laura Ln 05446
Lavigne Rd 05446
Lawrence J Dr 05446
Leclair Dr 05446
Ledge Rd 05446
Lee Ct 05446
Leorey Ct 05446
Lesage Ln 05446
Lexington Rd 05446
Liberty Ln 05446
Lilac St 05446
Lily Ln 05446
Lincoln Dr 05446
Lindale Dr 05446
Logan Dr 05446
Lois Ln 05446
Lone Birch St 05446
Longmeadow Village Rd 05446
Longwood Cir 05446
Lost Cove Rd 05446
Lower Mountain View Dr 05446
Lupine Dr 05446
Macrae Rd 05446
Main St 05446
Mainieri Ln 05446
Mallard Dr 05446
Malletts Bay Ave
29-103 05446
105-219 05446
218-218 05449
221-2899 05446
268-2898 05446
Malletts Bay Campground 05446
Malletts Bay Club Rd 05446
Malletts Head Rd 05446
Maple Ridge Dr 05446
Marble Island Rd 05446
Marcou Ln 05446
Mariner Hts 05446
Mariners Ln 05446
Marsh Ln 05446
Mayo Rd 05446
Mazza Ct 05446
Mcharrington Ln 05446
Mchawk Dr 05446
Mcneil Way 05446
Meadow Dr 05446
Mercier Dr 05446
Merganser Way 05446
Middle Rd 05446
Midnight Pass 05446
Midship Way 05446
Mill Pond Rd 05446
Mills Point Rd 05446
Moonlight Rdg 05446
Morehouse Dr 05446
Morellen Ln 05446
Mount Mansfield Ave 05446
Mount Sterling Ave 05446
Mountain View Ave, Dr & Rd 05446
Munson Rd 05446
Murdock Gln 05446
Naomis Way 05446
National Guard Rd 05446
New England Ave 05446
Nice Way 05446
Niquette Bay Rd 05446
North St 05446
Northland Ct 05446
Norway Dr 05446
Nottingham Ct 05446
S Oak Cir & Ter 05446
Oakridge Dr 05446
Old Sawmill Rd 05446
Old Well Rd 05446
Orchard Cir & Dr 05446
Orchard Shore Rd 05446
Orion Dr 05446
Outer Bay Ln 05446
Overlake Dr 05446
S Park Dr 05446
Parkwood Dr 05446
Parsons Rd 05446
Partridge Hl 05446
Peach Tree Ln 05446
Pebble Beach Rd 05446
Perimeter Ln 05446
Pheasant Woods 05446
Pierre Ct 05446
Pine Ln 05446
Pine Haven Rd 05446
Pine Island Rd 05446
Pine Meadow Dr 05446
Place Saint Michel 05446
Platt Rd 05446
Point Red Rock 05446
Pond Brook Rd 05446
Ponderosa Dr 05446
Poor Farm Rd 05446
W Porters Point Ct & Rd 05446
Potter Rd 05446
Pretty Rd 05446
Prim Rd 05446
Princess Ann Dr 05446
Radford Ln 05446
Rail Rd 05446
Rathe Rd 05446
Raymond Rd 05446
Rea Janet Dr 05446
Red Can Dr 05446
Red Oak Dr 05446
Red Pines Ln 05446
W Red Rock Rd 05446
Renkin Dr 05446
Reynolds Dr 05446
Richfield Ln 05446
Ridge Top Way 05446
River Rd 05446
Riverbend Ln 05446
Robert Frost Cir 05446
Robin Rd 05446
Roosevelt Hwy 05446
Rudgate Rd 05446
Ryan Pl 05446
Saint Michaels College 05446
Sand Rd 05446
Sand Dunes Rd 05446
Sandy Shore Ter 05446
Second St 05446
Seventh St 05446
Severance Grn & Rd 05446
Shady Ln 05446
Shannon Rd 05446
Sharrow Cir 05446
Shetland Ln 05446
Shore Acres Dr 05446
Sixth St 05446
Smith Rd 05446
South St 05446
Spaulding East Shr 05446
Spauldings Bay Ct 05446
Spinnaker Way 05446
Starboard Way 05446
Stone Dr 05446
Student Ln 05446
Sugarbush Farm Rd 05446
Summit Rdg 05446
Suncrest Ter 05446
Sunderland Woods Rd 05446
Sunset Dr 05446
Sunset View Rd 05446
Tamorac Pl 05446
Tanglewood Dr 05446
Terry Ln 05446
Thayer Bay Cir & Rd 05446
Thayer Beach Rd 05446
Thibault Dr 05446
Third St 05446
Thomas Dr 05446
Three Islands Rd 05446
Timberlake Dr 05446
Tower Ridge Cir 05446
Transom Way 05446
Troy Ave 05446
Truman Dr 05446
Tuckaway Pond Ln 05446
Turquoise Dr 05446
University Ln 05446
Us Route 7 05446
Valiquette Ct 05446
Valleyfield Dr 05446
Vermont Ave 05446
Vermont National Guard Rd 05446
Village Dr 05446
Village Commons 05446
Walden Rd & St 05446
Wall St 05446
Walnut Grv 05446
Walnut Ledge Ln 05446
Watertower Cir 05446
Waterview Rd 05446
Watkins Rd 05446
Waverly Cir 05446
Waybury Rd 05446
Webley St 05446
Wedgewood Rd 05446
Wellington St 05446
Wells Ave 05446
Wentworth Rd 05446
Westbrook Condos 05446
Westview Rd 05446
Westward Dr 05446
Wexford Ln 05446
Wheatly Ct 05446
Whispering Pnes 05446
White Cap Rd 05446
White Lilac Way 05446
Wilderness Rise Rd 05446
Wildflower Ln 05446
Wiley Rd 05446
Williams Rd 05446
Willow Cir 05446
Wilmington Rd 05446
Windemere Way 05446
Windswept Dr 05446
Windy Ln 05446
Wintergreen Dr 05446
Wolcott St 05446
Woodbine By The Lk 05446
Woodland Shores Dr 05446
Woodlins Cir 05446
Woodridge 05446
Woodrose Ln 05446
Woodside Dr E 05446
Wright Farm Rd 05446
Wyndham Rd 05446
Yardley Ln 05446
Young St 05446

ESSEX JUNCTION VT

General Delivery 05452

POST OFFICE BOXES MAIN OFFICE STATIONS AND BRANCHES

Box No.s
All PO Boxes 05453

NAMED STREETS

All Street Addresses 05452

MONTPELIER VT

General Delivery 05602

POST OFFICE BOXES MAIN OFFICE STATIONS AND BRANCHES

Box No.s
All PO Boxes 05601

NAMED STREETS

All Street Addresses 05602

NUMBERED STREETS

All Street Addresses 05602

RUTLAND VT

General Delivery 05701

POST OFFICE BOXES MAIN OFFICE STATIONS AND BRANCHES

Box No.s
1 - 999 05702
1001 - 1858 05701
6001 - 9505 05702

NAMED STREETS

All Street Addresses 05701

NUMBERED STREETS

All Street Addresses 05701

SOUTH BURLINGTON VT

POST OFFICE BOXES MAIN OFFICE STATIONS AND BRANCHES

Box No.s
All PO Boxes 05407

NAMED STREETS

Adams Ct 05403
Adirondack St 05403
Aiken St 05403
Air Guard Rd 05403
Airport Dr, Pkwy & Rd 05403
Allen Rd E 05403
Anderson Pkwy 05403
Andrews Ave 05403
Appletree Ct 05403
Arbor Rd 05403
Arlington Grn 05403
Arthur Ct 05403
Aspen Dr 05403
Austin Rd 05403
Autumn Hill Rd 05403
Aviation Ave 05403
Bacon St 05403
Baldwin Ave 05403
Barber Ter 05403
Barnsley St 05403
Barrett St 05403
Bartlett Bay Rd 05403
Bay Ct 05403
Bayberry Ln 05403
Baycrest Dr 05403
S Beach Rd 05403
Beacon St 05403
Bedford Grn 05403
Beechwood Ln 05403
Berard Dr 05403
Berkley St 05403
E Birch Ln & St 05403
Birchwood Ct 05403
Black Lantern Ln 05403
Blackberry Ln 05403
Bluestar Ln 05403
Bluff Ct 05403
Bouyea Ln 05403
Bowdoin St 05403
Bower St 05403
Braeburn St 05403
Brand Farm Dr 05403
Brewer Pkwy 05403
Brigham Rd 05403
Brookwood Dr 05403
Brownell Way 05403
Butler Dr 05403
Cabot Ct 05403
Calkins Ct 05403
Catkin Dr 05403
Cedar Ct & Gln N 05403
Central Ave 05403
Charles St 05403
Charleston Grn 05403
Cheese Factory Ln 05403
Cheesefactory Rd 05403
Chelmsford Grn 05403
Chelsea Cir 05403
Chickadee Cir 05403
Chipman St 05403
Cinda St 05403
Circle Dr 05403
Clinton St 05403
Clover St 05403
Cobblestone Cir 05403
Comcast Way 05403
Commerce Ave 05403
Community Dr 05403
Concord Grn 05403
Cortland Ave 05403
Cottage Grove Ave 05403
Country Club Dr E 05403
Cranwell Ave 05403
Crispin Dr 05403
Customs Dr 05403
Dairy Ln 05403
Davis Pkwy 05403
Deane St 05403
Deborah Dr 05403
Deerfield Rd 05403
Delaware St 05403
Derby Cir 05403
Dewey Pl 05403
Dorey Rd 05403
Dorset Hts & St 05403
Dover St 05403
Dubois Dr 05403
Duchess Ave 05403
Dumont Ave 05403
Duval St 05403
Eagle Dr 05403
East Ter 05403
Eastwood Dr 05403
Economou Farm Rd 05403
Eldredge St 05403
Elizabeth St 05403
Elsom Pkwy 05403
Ethan Allen Dr 05403
Executive Dr 05403
Fairway Dr 05403
Falcon St 05403
Farrell St 05403
Fayette Dr 05403
Fielding Ln 05403
Fieldstone Dr 05403
Finch Ct 05403
E & W Fisher Ln 05403
Flanders Ln 05403
Floral St 05403
Folsham Hollow Rd 05403
Forest St 05403
Four Sisters Rd 05403
Fox Run Ln 05403
Frost St 05403
Gilbert St 05403
Goldenrod St 05403
Golf Course Rd 05403
Grandview Dr 05403
Green Dolphin Dr 05403
Green Mountain Dr 05403
Green Tree Dr 05403
Greening Ave 05403
Gregory Dr 05403
Hadley Rd 05403
Hanneford Dr 05403
Hanover St 05403
Harbor Ridge Rd 05403
Harbor View Rd 05403
Hawthorne Cir 05403
Hayden Pkwy 05403
Hayes Ave 05403
Haymaker Ln 05403
Heath St 05403
Helen Ave 05403
Hemlock Ln 05403
Henry Ct 05403
Hermit Thrush Ln 05403
Hickory Ln 05403
Hidden Meadow Ln 05403
Highland Ter 05403
Hinesburg Rd 05403
Holbrook Rd 05403
Holmes Rd 05403
Hopkins St 05403
Howland Farm Rd 05403
Hummingbird Ln 05403
Iby St 05403
Idx Dr 05403
Imperial Dr 05403
Industrial Pkwy 05403
Iris Ln 05403
Irish Cove Rd 05403
Irish Farm Rd 05403
N & S Jefferson Rd 05403
John Fay Rd 05403
Jonathan Ave 05403
Joy Dr 05403
Juniper Dr 05403
Karen Dr 05403
Kaylyns Way 05403
Keari Ln 05403
Kendrick Dr 05403
Kennedy Dr 05403
Kimball Ave 05403
Kindness Ct 05403
Kingfisher Ct 05403
Kinsington St 05403
Kirby Rd 05403
Kitty St 05403
Knoll Cir 05403
Koda Way 05403
Lakeview Ln 05403
Landfill Rd 05403
Larch Rd 05403
Laurel Hill Dr 05403
Ledoux Ter 05403
Lexington Grn 05403
Lilac Ln 05403
Lily Ln 05403
Lime Kiln Rd 05403
Lime Rock Rd 05403
Lincoln Grn 05403
Lindenwood Dr 05403
Link Rd 05403
Logwood St 05403
Lupine Ln 05403
Lynn Ave 05403
Lyons Ave 05403
Lyons Avenue Ext 05403
Madison Ln 05403
Mansfield View Ln 05403
Maple Ave 05403
Maple Wood Dr 05403
Market St 05403
Mary St 05403
Maryland St 05403
Mayfair St 05403
Mcintosh Ave 05403
Meadow Rd 05403
Meadowland Dr 05403
Meadowood Dr 05403
Midas Dr 05403
Middlesex Grn 05403
Mill Pond Ln 05403
Millham Ct 05403
Mills Ave 05403
Mockingbird Ln 05403
Moss Glen Ln 05403
Mountain View Blvd 05403
Myers Ct 05403
National Guard Park 05403
Nco Dr 05403
Nesti Dr 05403
Newton Ave 05403
Nicklaus Cir 05403
Nowland Farm Rd 05403
Oak Creek Dr 05403
Oak Hill Dr 05403
Oakwood Dr 05403
Obrien Dr 05403
Old Cross Rd 05403
Old Farm Rd 05403
Old Schoolhouse Rd 05403
Olde Orchard Park 05403
Orchard Rd 05403
Overlook Dr 05403
Park Rd 05403
Patchen Rd 05403
Patrick St 05403
Pavilion Ave 05403
Peterson Ter 05403
Pheasant Way 05403
Picard Cir 05403
Pine Pl & St 05403
Pine Tree Ter 05403
Pinnacle Dr 05403
Pleasant Ave 05403
S Pointe Dr 05403
Proctor Ave 05403
Prouty Pkwy 05403
Pump Ln 05403
Quail Run 05403
Quarry Hill Rd 05403
Queen City Park Rd 05403
Queensbury Rd 05403
Richard Ter 05403
Royal Dr 05403
Ruth St 05403
San Remo Dr 05403
Sandalwood Dr 05403
Scotsdale Rd 05403
Sebring Rd 05403
Shamrock Rd 05403
Shaw Ave 05403
Shea Dr 05403
Shelburne Rd 05403
Shepard Ln 05403
Sherry Rd 05403
Shunpike Rd 05403
Simpson Ct 05403
Slocum St 05403
Songbird Rd 05403
South Rd 05403
Southview Dr 05403
Spear St 05403
Springhouse Rd 05403
Stanhope Rd 05403
Sterinti Rd 05403
Stonehedge Dr 05403
Stonehouse Cmn 05403
Stonington Cir 05403
Suburban Sq 05403
Sugar Tree Ln 05403
Sunset Ave 05403
Swift St 05403

Street	ZIP
Tabor Pl	05403
Tanglewood Dr	05403
Technology Park Way	05403
Thompson St	05403
Tilley Dr	05403
Timber Ln	05403
Tumblebrook Dr	05403
Twin Brook Ct	05403
Twin Oaks Ter	05403
Upswept Ln	05403
Vale Dr	05403
Valley Rd	05403
Valley Ridge Rd	05403
Van Sicklen Rd	05403
Victoria Dr	05403
Victory Dr	05403
Village Green Dr	05403
Wealthy Ave	05403
Weeping Willow Ln	05403
Westview Dr	05403
Whately Rd	05403
White St	
2-28	05403
30-61	05403
60-60	05407
62-460	05403
63-499	05403
Whiteface St	05403
Wildflower Dr	05403
Williston Rd	05403
Winding Brook Dr	05403
Windsor Ct	05403
Winesap Ln	05403
Woodbine St	05403
Woodcrest Dr	05403
Woodland Pl	05403
Woodside Dr	05403
Woodthrush Cir	05403
Worcester St	05403
Worth St	05403
Wright Ct	05403
Yandow Dr	05403

Virgin Islands

Virgin Islands

3 DIGIT ZIP CODE MAP

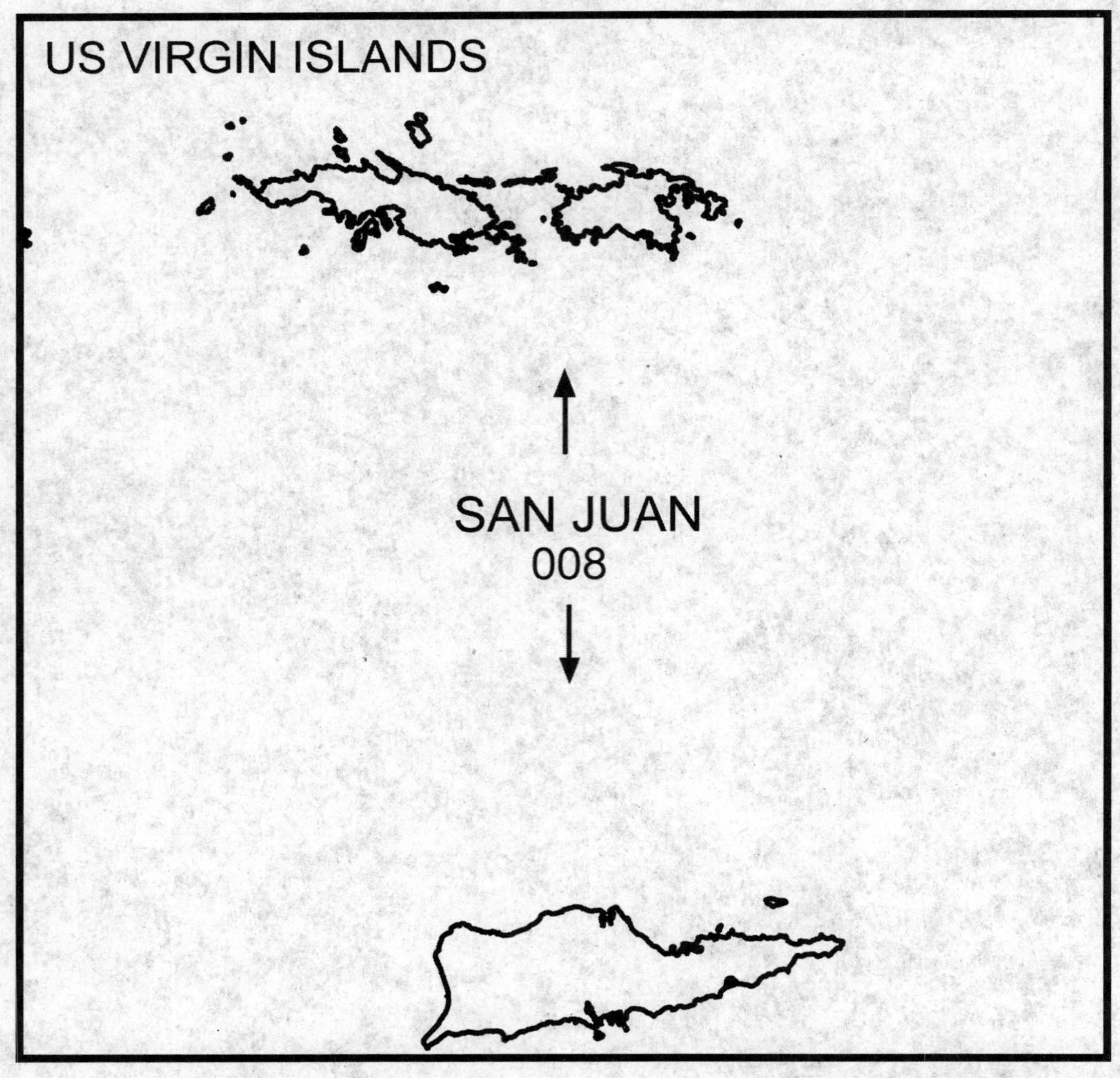

Virgin Islands

(Abbreviation: VI)

Post Office, County — ZIP Code

Places with more than one ZIP code are listed in capital letters, See pages indicated.

Charlotte Amalie
(See St Thomas)
CHRISTIANSTED, Saint Croix
(See Page 4062)
Cruz Bay
(See St John)
FREDERIKSTED, Saint Croix
(See Page 4062)
KINGSHILL, Saint Croix
(See Page 4062)
St Croix
(See Christiansted)
ST JOHN, Saint John
(See Page 4062)
ST THOMAS, Saint Thomas
(See Page 4062)

CHRISTIANSTED VI

General Delivery 00820

POST OFFICE BOXES MAIN OFFICE STATIONS AND BRANCHES

Box No.s
1 - 1800 00821
2255 - 4622 00822
4951 - 9998 00823
24001 - 26580 00824
222501 - 224670 00822

RURAL ROUTES

09 00820

NAMED STREETS

All Street Addresses 00820

FREDERIKSTED VI

General Delivery 00841

POST OFFICE BOXES MAIN OFFICE STATIONS AND BRANCHES

Box No.s
All PO Boxes 00841

HIGHWAY CONTRACTS

63 00840

NAMED STREETS

All Street Addresses 00840

KINGSHILL VI

General Delivery 00851

POST OFFICE BOXES MAIN OFFICE STATIONS AND BRANCHES

Box No.s
All PO Boxes 00851

RURAL ROUTES

01, 02 00850

NAMED STREETS

All Street Addresses 00850

ST JOHN VI

General Delivery 00830

POST OFFICE BOXES MAIN OFFICE STATIONS AND BRANCHES

Box No.s
All PO Boxes 00831

HIGHWAY CONTRACTS

61, 62 00830

NAMED STREETS

All Street Addresses 00830

ST THOMAS VI

General Delivery 00801

POST OFFICE BOXES MAIN OFFICE STATIONS AND BRANCHES

Box No.s
1 - 6880 00804
7001 - 12440 00801
301701 - 309900 00803
502001 - 503374 00805
600101 - 600216 00801

HIGHWAY CONTRACTS

58, 60 00802

NAMED STREETS

All Street Addresses 00802

Virginia

People QuickFacts	Virginia	USA
Population, 2013 estimate	8,260,405	316,128,839
Population, 2010 (April 1) estimates base	8,001,031	308,747,716
Population, percent change, April 1, 2010 to July 1, 2013	3.2%	2.4%
Population, 2010	8,001,024	308,745,538
Persons under 5 years, percent, 2013	6.2%	6.3%
Persons under 18 years, percent, 2013	22.6%	23.3%
Persons 65 years and over, percent, 2013	13.4%	14.1%
Female persons, percent, 2013	50.8%	50.8%
White alone, percent, 2013 (a)	70.8%	77.7%
Black or African American alone, percent, 2013 (a)	19.7%	13.2%
American Indian and Alaska Native alone, percent, 2013 (a)	0.5%	1.2%
Asian alone, percent, 2013 (a)	6.1%	5.3%
Native Hawaiian and Other Pacific Islander alone, percent, 2013 (a)	0.1%	0.2%
Two or More Races, percent, 2013	2.7%	2.4%
Hispanic or Latino, percent, 2013 (b)	8.6%	17.1%
White alone, not Hispanic or Latino, percent, 2013	63.6%	62.6%
Living in same house 1 year & over, percent, 2008-2012	84.7%	84.8%
Foreign born persons, percent, 2008-2012	11.1%	12.9%
Language other than English spoken at home, pct age 5+, 2008-2012	14.7%	20.5%
High school graduate or higher, percent of persons age 25+, 2008-2012	86.9%	85.7%
Bachelor's degree or higher, percent of persons age 25+, 2008-2012	34.7%	28.5%
Veterans, 2008-2012	734,151	21,853,912
Mean travel time to work (minutes), workers age 16+, 2008-2012	27.5	25.4
Housing units, 2013	3,412,460	132,802,859
Homeownership rate, 2008-2012	67.8%	65.5%
Housing units in multi-unit structures, percent, 2008-2012	21.5%	25.9%
Median value of owner-occupied housing units, 2008-2012	$249,700	$181,400
Households, 2008-2012	3,006,219	115,226,802
Persons per household, 2008-2012	2.59	2.61
Per capita money income in past 12 months (2012 dollars), 2008-2012	$33,326	$28,051
Median household income, 2008-2012	$63,636	$53,046
Persons below poverty level, percent, 2008-2012	11.1%	14.9%

Business QuickFacts	Virginia	USA
Private nonfarm establishments, 2012	192,730	7,431,808
Private nonfarm employment, 2012	3,089,241	115,938,468
Private nonfarm employment, percent change, 2011-2012	2.0%	2.2%
Nonemployer establishments, 2012	529,636	22,735,915
Total number of firms, 2007	638,643	27,092,908
Black-owned firms, percent, 2007	9.9%	7.1%
American Indian- and Alaska Native-owned firms, percent, 2007	0.5%	0.9%
Asian-owned firms, percent, 2007	7.0%	5.7%
Native Hawaiian and Other Pacific Islander-owned firms, percent, 2007	0.1%	0.1%
Hispanic-owned firms, percent, 2007	4.5%	8.3%
Women-owned firms, percent, 2007	30.1%	28.8%
Manufacturers shipments, 2007 ($1000)	92,417,797	5,319,456,312
Merchant wholesaler sales, 2007 ($1000)	60,513,396	4,174,286,516
Retail sales, 2007 ($1000)	105,663,299	3,917,663,456
Retail sales per capita, 2007	$13,687	$12,990
Accommodation and food services sales, 2007 ($1000)	15,340,483	613,795,732
Building permits, 2012	27,278	829,658

Geography QuickFacts	Virginia	USA
Land area in square miles, 2010	39,490.09	3,531,905.43
Persons per square mile, 2010	202.6	87.4
FIPS Code	51	

(a) Includes persons reporting only one race.
(b) Hispanics may be of any race, so also are included in applicable race categories.
FN: Footnote on this item for this area in place of data
NA: Not available
D: Suppressed to avoid disclosure of confidential information
X: Not applicable
S: Suppressed; does not meet publication standards
Z: Value greater than zero but less than half unit of measure shown
F: Fewer than 100 firms
Source: US Census Bureau State & County QuickFacts

Virginia

3 DIGIT ZIP CODE MAP

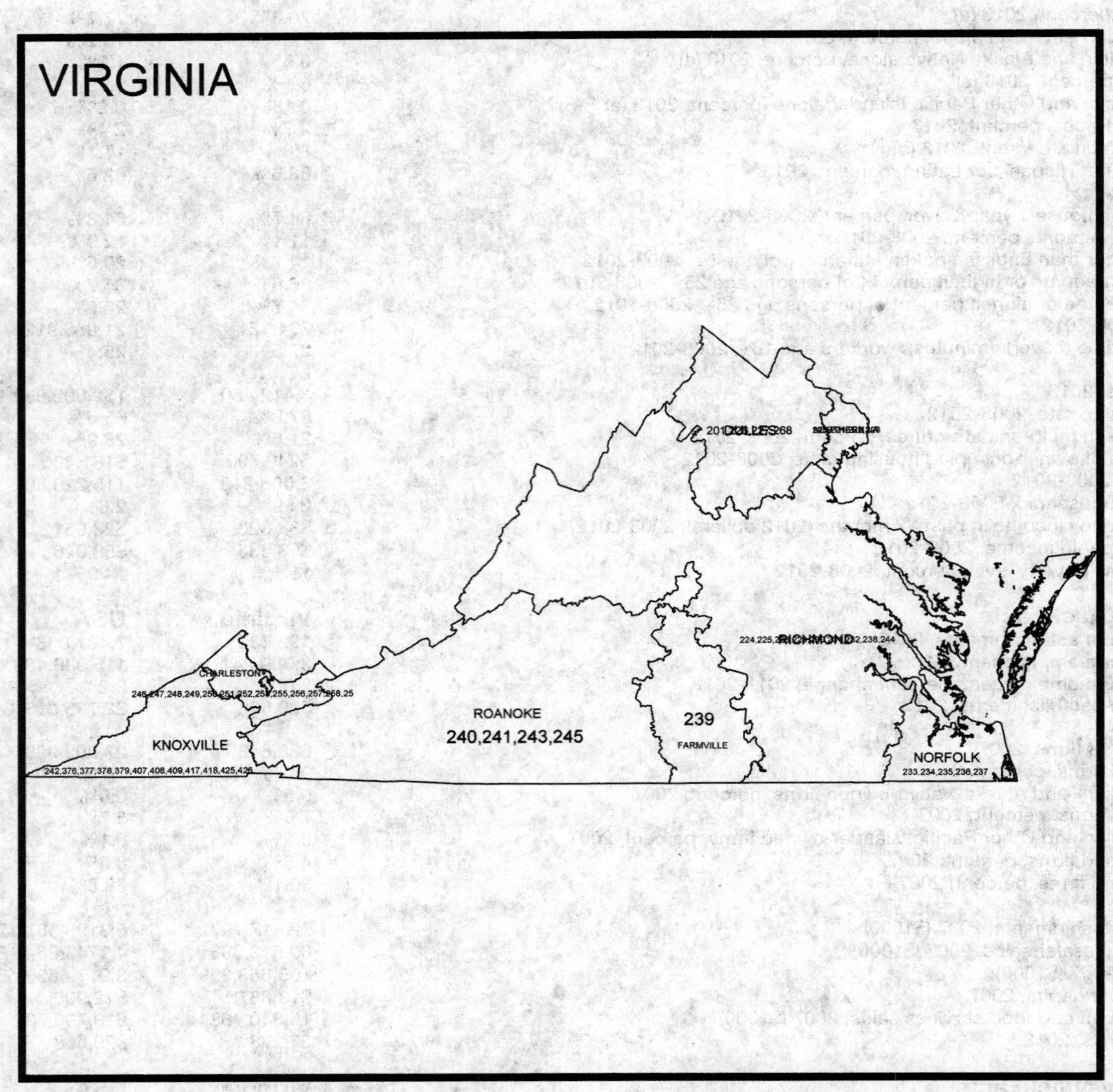

Virginia

(Abbreviation: VA)

Places with more than one ZIP code are listed in capital letters, See pages indicated.

Post Office, County	ZIP Code
ABINGDON, Washington (See Page 4068)	
Accomac, Accomack	23301
Achilles, Gloucester	23001
Advance Mills, Greene	22968
Afton, Nelson	22920
Alberta, Brunswick	23821
Aldie, Loudoun	20105
ALEXANDRIA, Alexandria City (See Page 4069)	
Alfonso, Lancaster	22503
Alleghany, Covington City	24426
Allisonia, Pulaski	24347
Altavista, Campbell	24517
Alton, Halifax	24520
Alum Ridge, Floyd	24091
Amelia Court House, Amelia	23002
Amherst, Amherst	24521
Amissville, Culpeper	20106
Ammon, Dinwiddie	23822
Amonate, Tazewell	24601
Ampthill, Chesterfield	23234
Andover, Wise	24215
Annandale, Fairfax	22003
Appalachia, Wise	24216
Appomattox, Appomattox	24522
Ararat, Patrick	24053
Arcola, Loudoun	20166
Ark, Gloucester	23003
ARLINGTON, Arlington (See Page 4074)	
Aroda, Madison	22709
Arrington, Nelson	22922
Arvonia, Buckingham	23004
ASHBURN, Loudoun (See Page 4076)	
Ashland, Hanover	23005
Assawoman, Accomack	23302
Atkins, Smyth	24311
Atlantic, Accomack	23303
Augusta Springs, Augusta	24411
Austinville, Wythe	24312
Axton, Henry	24054
Aylett, King William	23009
Bacova, Bath	24412
Baileys Crossroads, Fairfax	22041
Banco, Madison	22711
Banco, Madison	22727
Bandy, Tazewell	24602
Barboursville, Orange	22923
Barhamsville, New Kent	23011
Barren Springs, Wythe	24313
Baskerville, Mecklenburg	23915
Bassett, Henry	24055
Bastian, Bland	24314
Basye, Shenandoah	22810
Batesville, Albemarle	22924
Battery Park, Isle Of Wight	23304
Bavon, Mathews	23138
Bealeton, Fauquier	22712
Beaumont, Goochland	23014
Beaverdam, Hanover	23015
Beaverlett, Mathews	23109
Bedford, Bedford	24523
Bee, Dickenson	24217
Bellamy, Gloucester	23061
Belle Haven, Accomack	23306
Belleview, Fairfax	22307
Belspring, Pulaski	24058
Ben Hur, Lee	24218
Bena, Gloucester	23018
Bent Mountain, Roanoke	24059
Bentonville, Warren	22610
Bergton, Rockingham	22811
Berryville, Clarke	22611
Big Island, Bedford	24526
Big Rock, Buchanan	24603
Big Stone Gap, Wise	24219
Birchleaf, Dickenson	24220
Birdsnest, Northampton	23307
Bishop, Tazewell	24604
Blackridge, Mecklenburg	23950
BLACKSBURG, Montgomery (See Page 4079)	
Blackstone, Nottoway	23824
Blackwater, Lee	24221
Blairs, Pittsylvania	24527
Blakes, Mathews	23035
Bland, Bland	24315
Bloxom, Accomack	23308
Blue Grass, Highland	24413
Blue Ridge, Botetourt	24064
Bluefield, Tazewell	24605
Bluemont, Clarke	20135
Bohannon, Mathews	23021
Boissevain, Tazewell	24606
Bolar, Bath	24484
Bon Air, Chesterfield	23235
Boones Mill, Franklin	24065
Boonesville, Greene	22935
Boston, Culpeper	22713
Bowling Green, Caroline	22427
Boyce, Clarke	22620
Boyd Tavern, Albemarle	22947
Boydton, Mecklenburg	23917
Boykins, Southampton	23827
Bracey, Mecklenburg	23919
Brambleton, Loudoun	20148
Branchville, Southampton	23828
Brandy Station, Culpeper	22714
Breaks, Dickenson	24607
Bremo Bluff, Fluvanna	23022
Bridgewater, Rockingham	22812
Brightwood, Madison	22715
BRISTOL, Bristol City (See Page 4080)	
Bristow, Prince William	20136
Broad Run, Fauquier	20137
Broadford, Tazewell	24316
Broadlands, Loudoun	20148
Broadway, Rockingham	22815
Brodnax, Brunswick	23920
Brooke, Stafford	22430
Brookneal, Campbell	24528
Brownsburg, Rockbridge	24415
Browntown, Warren	22610
Brucetown, Frederick	22622
Bruington, King And Queen	23023
Buchanan, Botetourt	24066
Buckingham, Buckingham	23921
Buena Vista, Buena Vista City	24416
Buffalo Junction, Mecklenburg	24529
Bumpass, Louisa	23024
Burgess, Northumberland	22432
BURKE, Fairfax (See Page 4082)	
Burkes Garden, Tazewell	24608
Burkeville, Nottoway	23922
Burnleys, Orange	22923
Burnsville, Bath	24487
Burnt Chimney, Franklin	24184
Burr Hill, Orange	22433
Bybee, Fluvanna	22963
Callands, Pittsylvania	24530
Callao, Northumberland	22435
Callaway, Franklin	24067
Calverton, Fauquier	20138
Campbell, Albemarle	22947
Cana, Carroll	24317
Cape Charles, Northampton	23310
Capeville, Northampton	23313
Capron, Southampton	23829
Cardinal, Mathews	23025
Caret, Essex	22436
Carrollton, Isle Of Wight	23314
Carrsville, Isle Of Wight	23315
Carson, Dinwiddie	23830
Cartersville, Cumberland	23027
Casanova, Fauquier	20139
Cascade, Pittsylvania	24069
Castleton, Rappahannock	22716
Castlewood, Russell	24224
Catawba, Roanoke	24070
Catharpin, Prince William	20143
Catlett, Fauquier	20119
Cauthornville, King And Queen	23148
Cave Spring, Roanoke	24018
Cedar Bluff, Tazewell	24609
Center Cross, Essex	22437
CENTREVILLE, Fairfax (See Page 4083)	
Ceres, Bland	24318
Champlain, Essex	22438
Chance, Essex	22438
CHANTILLY, Fairfax (See Page 4084)	
Charity, Franklin	24088
Charles City, Charles City	23030
Charlotte Court House, Charlotte	23923
CHARLOTTESVILLE, Albemarle (See Page 4085)	
Chase City, Mecklenburg	23924
Chatham, Pittsylvania	24531
Check, Floyd	24072
Cheriton, Northampton	23316
CHESAPEAKE, Chesapeake City (See Page 4089)	
CHESTER, Chesterfield (See Page 4095)	
Chester Gap, Rappahannock	22623
CHESTERFIELD, Chesterfield (See Page 4097)	
Chilhowie, Smyth	24319
Chincoteague Island, Accomack	23336
Christchurch, Middlesex	23031
CHRISTIANSBURG, Montgomery (See Page 4098)	
Church Road, Dinwiddie	23833
Church View, Middlesex	23032
Churchville, Augusta	24421
Cismont, Albemarle	22947
Claremont, Surry	23899
Clarksville, Mecklenburg	23927
Claudville, Patrick	24076
Clear Brook, Frederick	22624
Cleveland, Russell	24225
Clifford, Amherst	24533
Clifton, Fairfax	20124
Clifton Forge, Alleghany	24422
Clinchburg, Washington	24361
Clinchco, Dickenson	24226
Clinchport, Scott	24244
Clintwood, Dickenson	24228
Clover, Halifax	24534
Cloverdale, Botetourt	24077
Cluster Springs, Halifax	24535
Cobbs Creek, Mathews	23035
Cobham, Albemarle	22947
Coeburn, Wise	24230
Coleman Falls, Bedford	24536
Coles Point, Westmoreland	22442
Collinsville, Henry	24078
Cologne, King William	23181
Colonial Beach, Westmoreland	22443
Colonial Heights, Colonial Heights City	23834
Columbia, Goochland	23038
Community, Fairfax	22306
Conaway, Buchanan	24603
Concord, Campbell	24538
Copper Hill, Floyd	24079
Corbin, Caroline	22446
Council, Russell	24260
Courtland, Southampton	23837
Covesville, Albemarle	22931
Covington, Covington City	24426
Craddockville, Accomack	23341
Craigsville, Augusta	24430
Crewe, Nottoway	23930
Criders, Rockingham	22820
Crimora, Augusta	24431
Cripple Creek, Wythe	24322
Critz, Patrick	24082
Crockett, Wythe	24323
Cross Junction, Frederick	22625
Crozet, Albemarle	22932
Crozier, Goochland	23039
Crystal Hill, Halifax	24539
Cullen, Charlotte	23934
Culpeper, Culpeper	22701
Cumberland, Cumberland	23040
Cunningham, Fluvanna	22963
Dabneys, Goochland	23102
Dahlgren, King George	22448
Dale City, Prince William	22193
Daleville, Botetourt	24083
Damascus, Washington	24236
Dante, Russell	24237
DANVILLE, Danville City (See Page 4099)	
Darlington Heights, Appomattox	23958
Davenport, Buchanan	24239
Davis Wharf, Accomack	23345
Dayton, Rockingham	22821
Deerfield, Augusta	24432
Delaplane, Fauquier	20144
Deltaville, Middlesex	23043
Dendron, Surry	23839
Dewitt, Dinwiddie	23840
Dhs, Loudoun	20598
Diggs, Mathews	23045
Dillwyn, Buckingham	23936
Dinwiddie, Dinwiddie	23841
Disputanta, Prince George	23842
Doe Hill, Highland	24433
Dogue, King George	22451
Dolphin, Brunswick	23843
Doran, Tazewell	24612
Doswell, Hanover	23047
Drakes Branch, Charlotte	23937
Draper, Pulaski	24324
Drewryville, Southampton	23844
Dry Fork, Pittsylvania	24549
Dryden, Lee	24243
Dublin, Pulaski	24084
Duffield, Scott	24244
Dugspur, Carroll	24325
Dulles, Loudoun	20189
DUMFRIES, Prince William (See Page 4102)	
Dundas, Lunenburg	23938
Dungannon, Scott	24245
Dunn Loring, Fairfax	22027
Dunnsville, Essex	22454
Dutton, Gloucester	23050
Dyke, Greene	22935
Eagle Rock, Botetourt	24085
Earlysville, Albemarle	22936
East Stone Gap, Wise	24246
Eastville, Northampton	23347
Ebony, Brunswick	23845
Edinburg, Shenandoah	22824
Edwardsville, Northumberland	22456
Eggleston, Giles	24086
Eheart, Orange	22923
Elberon, Surry	23846
Elk Creek, Grayson	24326
Elk Garden, Russell	24260
Elkton, Rockingham	22827
Elkwood, Culpeper	22718
Elliston, Montgomery	24087
Emory, Washington	24327
Emporia, Greensville	23847
Engleside, Fairfax	22309
Esmont, Albemarle	22937
Etlan, Madison	22719
Etlan, Madison	22727
Evergreen, Appomattox	23939
Evington, Campbell	24550
Ewing, Lee	24248
Exeter, Wise	24216
Exmore, Northampton	23350
Faber, Nelson	22938
FAIRFAX, Fairfax City (See Page 4102)	
Fairfax Station, Fairfax	22039
Fairfield, Rockbridge	24435
Fairlawn, Radford	24141
FALLS CHURCH, Falls Church City (See Page 4106)	
Falls Mills, Tazewell	24613
Falmouth (See Fredericksburg)	
Fancy Gap, Carroll	24328
Farmville, Prince Edward	23901
Farnham, Richmond	22460
Ferrum, Franklin	24088
Fieldale, Henry	24089
Fife, Goochland	23063
Fincastle, Botetourt	24090
Fishers Hill, Shenandoah	22626
Fishersville, Augusta	22939
Fleet, Norfolk City	23511
Flint Hill, Rappahannock	22627
Floyd, Floyd	24091
Foneswood, Richmond	22572
Ford, Dinwiddie	23850
Forest, Bedford	24551
Fork Union, Fluvanna	23055
Forksville, Mecklenburg	23950
Fort A P Hill, Caroline	22427
Fort Belvoir, Fairfax	22060
Fort Blackmore, Scott	24250
Fort Chiswell, Wythe	24360
Fort Defiance, Augusta	24437
Fort Eustis, Newport News City	23604
Fort Hunt, Fairfax	22308
Fort Lee, Prince George	23801
Fort Mitchell, Lunenburg	23941
Fort Monroe, Hampton City	23651
Fort Myer, Arlington	22211
Fort Story, Virginia Beach City	23459
Fort Valley, Shenandoah	22652
Foster, Mathews	23056
Foster Falls, Wythe	24360
Franconia, Fairfax	22310
Franklin, Franklin City	23851
Franktown, Northampton	23354
Fredericksburg, Fredericksburg City	22401
Free Union, Albemarle	22940
Freeman, Brunswick	23856
Fries, Grayson	24330
Front Royal, Warren	22630
Ft Belvoir, Fairfax	22060
Ft Myer, Arlington	22211
Fulks Run, Rockingham	22830
Fx Station, Fairfax	22039
GAINESVILLE, Prince William (See Page 4107)	
Galax, Galax City	24333
Garrisonville, Stafford	22463
Gasburg, Brunswick	23857
Gate City, Scott	24251
Glade Hill, Franklin	24092
Glade Spring, Washington	24340
Gladstone, Nelson	24553
Gladys, Campbell	24554
Glasgow, Rockbridge	24555
GLEN ALLEN, Henrico (See Page 4108)	
Glen Lyn, Giles	24093
Glen Wilton, Botetourt	24438
Glou Point, Gloucester	23062
Gloucester, Gloucester	23061
Gloucester Point, Gloucester	23062
Goldbond, Giles	24150
Goldvein, Fauquier	22720
Goochland, Goochland	23063
Goode, Bedford	24556
Goodview, Bedford	24095
Gordonsville, Orange	22942
Gore, Frederick	22637
Goshen, Rockbridge	24439
Grafton, York	23692
Graves Mill, Madison	22727
Great Falls, Fairfax	22066
Green Bay, Prince Edward	23942
Greenbackville, Accomack	23356
Greenbush, Accomack	23357
Greenville, Augusta	24440
Greenway, Fairfax	22067
Greenwood, Albemarle	22943
Gretna, Pittsylvania	24557
Grimstead, Mathews	23064
Grottoes, Rockingham	24441
Grundy, Buchanan	24614
Gum Spring, Goochland	23065
Gwynn, Mathews	23066
Hacks Neck, Accomack	23358
Hacksneck, Accomack	23358
Hadensville, Goochland	23067
Hague, Westmoreland	22469
Halifax, Halifax	24558
Hallieford, Mathews	23068
Hallwood, Accomack	23359
HAMILTON, Loudoun (See Page 4110)	
Hampden Sydney, Prince Edward	23943
HAMPTON, Hampton City (See Page 4110)	
Hanover, Hanover	23069
Harborton, Accomack	23389
Hardy, Franklin	24101
Hardyville, Middlesex	23070
Harman, Buchanan	24628
HARRISONBURG, Harrisonburg City (See Page 4114)	
Hartfield, Middlesex	23071
Hartwood, Stafford	22471
Hayes, Gloucester	23072
Hayfield, Frederick	22603
HAYMARKET, Prince William (See Page 4116)	
Haynesville, Richmond	22472
Haysi, Dickenson	24256
Haywood, Madison	22722
Head Waters, Highland	24442
Heathsville, Northumberland	22473
HENRICO, Henrico (See Page 4117)	
Henry, Franklin	24102
HERNDON, Fairfax (See Page 4121)	
Highland Springs, Henrico	23075
Hightown, Highland	24465
Hillsboro (See Purcellville)	
Hillsville, Carroll	24343
Hiltons, Scott	24258
Hinton, Rockingham	22831
Hiwassee, Pulaski	24347
Hollins, Roanoke	24019
Hollins College, Roanoke	24019
Honaker, Russell	24260
Hood, Madison	22723
Hopewell, Hopewell City	23860
Horntown, Accomack	23395
Horsepen, Tazewell	24619
Hot Springs, Bath	24445
Howardsville, Buckingham	24562
Howertons, Essex	22454
Huddleston, Bedford	24104
Hudgins, Mathews	23076
Hume, Fauquier	22639
Huntly, Rappahannock	22627
Huntly, Rappahannock	22640
Hurley, Buchanan	24620
Hurt, Pittsylvania	24563
Hustle, Essex	22476
Independence, Grayson	24348
Indian Neck, King And Queen	23148
Indian Valley, Floyd	24105
Ingram, Halifax	24597
Iron Gate, Alleghany	24448
Ironto, Montgomery	24087
Irvington, Lancaster	22480
Isle Of Wight, Isle Of Wight	23397

Ivanhoe, Wythe 24350
Ivor, Southampton 23866
Ivy, Albemarle 22945
Jamaica, Middlesex 23079
James Store, Mathews 23128
Jamestown, James City 23081
Jamesville, Northampton 23398
Jarratt, Greensville 23867
Java, Pittsylvania 24565
Jefferson Manor, Fairfax 22303
Jeffersonton, Culpeper 22724
Jenkins Bridge, Accomack 23399
Jersey, King George 22481
Jetersville, Amelia 23083
Jewell Ridge, Tazewell 24622
Jewell Valley, Tazewell 24622
Jonesville, Lee 24263
Jordan Mines, Covington City 24426
Keeling, Pittsylvania 24566
Keen Mountain, Buchanan 24624
Keene, Albemarle 22946
Keezletown, Rockingham 22832
Keller, Accomack 23401
Kenbridge, Lunenburg 23944
Kents Store, Fluvanna 23084
Keokee, Lee 24265
Keswick, Albemarle 22947
Keysville, Charlotte 23947
Kilmarnock, Lancaster 22482
King And Queen Court House, King And Queen 23085
King George, King George 22485
King William, King William 23086
Kingstowne, Fairfax 22315
Kinsale, Westmoreland 22488
La Crosse, Mecklenburg 23950
Lacey Spring, Rockingham 22833
Lackey, York 23694
Ladysmith, Caroline 22501
Lafayette, Montgomery 24087
Lake Frederick, Warren 22630
Lake Of The Woods, Orange 22508
Lake Ridge, Prince William 22192
Lambsburg, Carroll 24351
Lancaster, Lancaster 22503
Laneview, Essex 22504
Lanexa, New Kent 23089
Langley Afb, York 23665
Lansdowne, Loudoun 20176
Laurel Fork, Carroll 24352
Lawrenceville, Brunswick 23868
Lebanon, Russell 24266
Lebanon Church, Shenandoah 22641
Lee Mont, Accomack 23421
LEESBURG, Loudoun (See Page 4123)
Lennig, Halifax 24577
Leon, Madison 22725
Lewisetta, Northumberland 22511
Lexington, Lexington City 24450
Lightfoot, York 23090
Lignum, Culpeper 22726
Lincoln, Loudoun 20160
Lincolnia, Fairfax 22312
Linden, Warren 22642
Linville, Rockingham 22834
Lithia, Botetourt 24066
Little Plymouth, King And Queen 23091
Lively, Lancaster 22507
Locust Dale, Madison 22948
Locust Grove, Orange 22508
Locust Hill, Middlesex 23092
Locustville, Accomack 23404
Long Island, Pittsylvania 24569
Loretto, Essex 22509
LORTON, Fairfax (See Page 4125)
Lottsburg, Northumberland 22511
Louisa, Louisa 23093
Lovettsville, Loudoun 20180
Lovingston, Nelson 22949
Low Moor, Alleghany 24457

Lowesville, Nelson 22967
Lowry, Bedford 24570
Lunenburg, Lunenburg 23952
Luray, Page 22835
Lynch Station, Campbell 24571
LYNCHBURG, Lynchburg City (See Page 4126)
Lyndhurst, Augusta 22952
Machipongo, Northampton 23405
Macon, Powhatan 23139
Madison, Madison 22719
Madison, Madison 22727
Madison Heights, Amherst 24572
Madison Mills, Orange 22960
Maidens, Goochland 23102
Manakin Sabot, Goochland 23103
MANASSAS, Manassas City (See Page 4129)
Manassas Park (See Manassas)
Mangohick, Hanover 23069
Mannboro, Amelia 23105
Manquin, King William 23106
Mappsville, Accomack 23407
Marion, Smyth 24354
Marionville, Northampton 23408
Markham, Fauquier 22643
MARSHALL, Fauquier (See Page 4132)
MARTINSVILLE, Martinsville City (See Page 4132)
Maryus, Gloucester 23107
Mascot, King And Queen 23108
Mason Neck, Fairfax 22079
Massanutten, Rockingham 22840
Massies Mill, Nelson 22967
Mathews, Mathews 23109
Mattaponi, King And Queen 23110
Maurertown, Shenandoah 22644
Mavisdale, Buchanan 24627
Max Meadows, Wythe 24360
Maxie, Buchanan 24628
Mc Clure, Dickenson 24269
Mc Coy, Montgomery 24111
Mc Dowell, Highland 24458
Mc Gaheysville, Rockingham 22840
Mc Kenney, Dinwiddie 23872
MC LEAN, Fairfax (See Page 4132)
Meadows Of Dan, Patrick 24120
Meadowview, Washington 24361
Mears, Accomack 23409
MECHANICSVILLE, Hanover (See Page 4134)
Meherrin, Prince Edward 23954
Melfa, Accomack 23410
Mendota, Washington 24270
Meredithville, Brunswick 23873
MERRIFIELD, Fairfax (See Page 4136)
Merry Point, Lancaster 22513
Middlebrook, Augusta 24459
MIDDLEBURG, Loudoun (See Page 4136)
MIDDLETOWN, Frederick (See Page 4136)
Midland, Fauquier 22728
MIDLOTHIAN, Chesterfield (See Page 4137)
Miles, Mathews 23025
Milford, Caroline 22514
Millboro, Bath 24460
Millers Tavern, Essex 23115
Millwood, Clarke 22646
Mine Run, Orange 22508
Mineral, Louisa 23117
Mint Spring, Augusta 24463
Mission Home, Albemarle 22940
Mitchells, Culpeper 22729
Mobjack, Mathews 23056
Modest Town, Accomack 23412
Mollusk, Lancaster 22517
Moneta, Bedford 24121
Monroe, Amherst 24574

Montclair, Prince William 22025
Montebello, Nelson 24464
Monterey, Highland 24465
Montezuma, Rockingham 22821
Montford, Orange 22960
Monticello, Charlottesville City 22902
Montpelier, Hanover 23192
Montpelier Station, Orange 22957
Montross, Westmoreland 22520
Montvale, Bedford 24122
Moon, Mathews 23119
Morattico, Lancaster 22523
Morrisville, Fauquier 22712
Mosby, Fairfax 22042
Moseley, Chesterfield 23120
Mount Crawford, Rockingham 22841
Mount Holly, Westmoreland 22524
Mount Jackson, Shenandoah 22842
Mount Sidney, Augusta 24467
Mount Solon, Augusta 22843
Mount Vernon, Fairfax 22121
Mount Weather, Clarke 20135
Mouth Of Wilson, Grayson 24363
Mustoe, Highland 24468
Narrows, Giles 24124
Naruna, Campbell 24576
Nasons, Orange 22960
Nassawadox, Northampton 23413
Nathalie, Halifax 24577
Natural Bridge, Rockbridge 24578
Natural Bridge Station, Rockbridge 24579
Naval Base, Norfolk City 23511
Naval Weapons Station, York 23691
Naxera, Gloucester 23061
Nellysford, Nelson 22958
Nelson, Mecklenburg 24580
Nelsonia, Accomack 23414
New Baltimore, Fauquier 20187
New Canton, Buckingham 23123
New Castle, Craig 24127
New Church, Accomack 23415
New Hope, Augusta 24469
New Kent, New Kent 23124
New Market, Shenandoah 22844
New Point, Mathews 23125
New River, Pulaski 24129
Newbern, Pulaski 24126
Newington, Fairfax 22122
Newport, Giles 24128
NEWPORT NEWS, Newport News City (See Page 4139)
Newsoms, Southampton 23874
Newtown, King And Queen 23126
Nickelsville, Scott 24271
Ninde, King George 22526
NOKESVILLE, Prince William (See Page 4143)
Nora, Dickenson 24272
NORFOLK, Norfolk City (See Page 4143)
Norge, James City 23127
North, Mathews 23128
North Chesterfield (See Richmond)
North Dinwiddie (See Petersburg)
North Garden, Albemarle 22959
North Prince George, Hopewell City 23860
North Springfield, Fairfax 22151
North Tazewell, Tazewell 24630
Norton, Norton City 24273
Nortonsville, Greene 22935
Norwood, Nelson 24581
Nottoway, Nottoway 23955
Nuttsville, Lancaster 22528
Oak Grove, Westmoreland 22443
Oak Hall, Accomack 23396
Oak Hill, Fairfax 20171
Oakpark, Madison 22730

Oakton, Fairfax 22124
Oakton, Fairfax 22185
Oakwood, Buchanan 24631
Occoquan, Prince William 22125
Oilville, Goochland 23129
Oldhams, Westmoreland 22529
Onancock, Accomack 23417
Onemo, Mathews 23130
Onley, Accomack 23418
Ophelia, Northumberland 22530
Orange, Orange 22960
Ordinary, Gloucester 23131
Oriskany, Botetourt 24130
Orkney Springs, Shenandoah 22845
Orlean, Fauquier 20128
Oyster, Northampton 23419
Paeonian Springs, Loudoun 20129
Paint Bank, Craig 24131
Painter, Accomack 23420
Palmyra, Fluvanna 22963
Pamplin, Appomattox 23958
Paris, Clarke 20130
Parksley, Accomack 23421
Parrott, Pulaski 24132
Partlow, Spotsylvania 22534
Patrick Springs, Patrick 24133
Patterson, Buchanan 24631
Pearisburg, Giles 24134
Peary, Mathews 23138
Pembroke, Giles 24136
Penhook, Franklin 24137
Penn Laird, Rockingham 22846
Pennington Gap, Lee 24277
PETERSBURG, Prince George (See Page 4147)
Phenix, Charlotte 23959
Philomont, Loudoun 20131
Pilgrims Knob, Buchanan 24634
Pilot, Montgomery 24138
Pimmit, Fairfax 22043
Pinero, Gloucester 23061
Piney River, Nelson 22964
Pittsville, Pittsylvania 24139
Plain View, King And Queen 23156
Pleasant Valley, Rockingham 22848
Pocahontas, Tazewell 24635
Poquoson, Poquoson City 23662
Port Haywood, Mathews 23138
Port Republic, Rockingham 24471
Port Royal, Caroline 22535
PORTSMOUTH, Portsmouth City (See Page 4148)
Potomac, Alexandria City 22301
Potomac Falls, Loudoun 20165
Pound, Wise 24279
Pounding Mill, Tazewell 24637
Powhatan, Powhatan 23139
Pratts, Madison 22731
Prince George, Prince George 23875
Prince William, Prince William 22192
Princess Anne, Virginia Beach City 23456
Prospect, Prince Edward 23960
Providence Forge, New Kent 23140
Pulaski, Pulaski 24301
Pungoteague, Accomack 23422
PURCELLVILLE, Loudoun (See Page 4151)
Quantico, Prince William 22134
Quicksburg, Shenandoah 22847
Quinby, Accomack 23423
Quinque, Greene 22965
Quinton, New Kent 23141
Raccoon Ford, Culpeper 22701
RADFORD, Radford (See Page 4151)
Radiant, Madison 22732
Randolph, Charlotte 23962
Raphine, Rockbridge 24472
Rapidan, Culpeper 22733

Rappahannock Academy, Caroline 22538
Raven, Buchanan 24639
Rawlings, Brunswick 23876
Rectortown, Fauquier 20140
Red Ash, Tazewell 24640
Red House, Charlotte 23963
Red Oak, Charlotte 23964
Redart, Mathews 23076
Redwood, Franklin 24146
Reedville, Northumberland 22539
Regency, Henrico 23229
Regina, Lancaster 22503
Reliance, Warren 22649
Remington, Fauquier 22734
Republican Grove, Halifax 24577
Rescue, Isle Of Wight 23424
RESTON, Fairfax (See Page 4151)
Reva, Madison 22735
Rhoadesville, Orange 22542
Rice, Prince Edward 23966
Rich Creek, Giles 24147
Richardsville, Culpeper 22736
Richlands, Tazewell 24641
RICHMOND, Richmond City (See Page 4153)
Richmond Int Airport, Henrico 23250
Ridge, Henrico 23233
Ridgeway, Henry 24148
Rileyville, Page 22650
Riner, Montgomery 24149
Ringgold, Pittsylvania 24586
Ripplemead, Giles 24150
Riverton, Warren 22630
Rixeyville, Culpeper 22737
ROANOKE, Roanoke City (See Page 4161)
Rochelle, Madison 22738
Rockbridge Baths, Rockbridge 24473
Rockfish, Nelson 22971
Rockville, Hanover 23146
Rocky Gap, Bland 24366
Rocky Mount, Franklin 24151
Rollins Fork, King George 22544
Rose Hill, Lee 24281
Rosedale, Russell 24280
Roseland, Nelson 22967
Roseland, Nelson 22976
Rosslyn, Arlington 22209
ROUND HILL, Loudoun (See Page 4166)
Rowe, Buchanan 24646
Ruby, Stafford 22545
Ruckersville, Greene 22968
Rural Retreat, Wythe 24368
Rustburg, Campbell 24588
Ruther Glen, Caroline 22546
Ruthville, Charles City 23147
Saint Charles, Lee 24282
Saint Davids Church, Shenandoah 22652
Saint Paul, Wise 24283
Saint Stephens Church, King And Queen 23148
Salem, Salem 24153
Saltville, Smyth 24370
Saluda, Middlesex 23149
Sandston, Henrico 23150
Sandy Hook, Goochland 23153
Sandy Level, Pittsylvania 24161
Sandy Point, Westmoreland 22577
Sanford, Accomack 23426
Saxe, Charlotte 23967
Saxis, Accomack 23427
Schley, Gloucester 23154
Schuyler, Nelson 22969
Scottsburg, Halifax 24589
Scottsville, Buckingham 24562
Scottsville, Albemarle 24590
Seaford, York 23696
Sealston, King George 22547
Seaview, Northampton 23429
Sedley, Southampton 23878

Selma, Alleghany 24474
Seven Corners, Fairfax 22044
Seven Fountains, Shenandoah 22652
Seven Mile Ford, Smyth 24354
Severn, Gloucester 23155
Shacklefords, King And Queen 23156
Shadow, Mathews 23163
Shadwell, Albemarle 22947
Sharps, Richmond 22548
Shawsville, Montgomery 24162
Shenandoah, Page 22849
Shenandoah Caverns, Shenandoah 22847
Sherando, Augusta 22952
Shiloh, King George 22485
Shipman, Nelson 22971
Shortt Gap, Buchanan 24647
Simpsons, Floyd 24072
Singers Glen, Rockingham 22850
Skippers, Greensville 23879
Skipwith, Mecklenburg 23968
SMITHFIELD, Isle Of Wight (See Page 4166)
Snell, Spotsylvania 22553
Somerset, Orange 22972
Somerville, Fauquier 22739
South Boston, Halifax 24592
South Chesterfield, Petersburg City 23803
South Chesterfield, Colonial Heights City 23834
South Hill, Mecklenburg 23970
South Norfolk, Chesapeake City 23324
South Prince George, Petersburg City 23805
South Riding, Loudoun 20152
Southbridge, Prince William 22026
Sparta, Caroline 22552
Speedwell, Wythe 24374
Spencer, Henry 24165
Sperryville, Rappahannock 22740
SPOTSYLVANIA, Spotsylvania (See Page 4167)
Spottswood, Augusta 24476
Spout Spring, Appomattox 24593
Spring Grove, Surry 23881
SPRINGFIELD, Fairfax (See Page 4168)
Sprouses Corner, Buckingham 23936
St George, Greene 22935
St Stephens Church, King And Queen 23148
STAFFORD, Stafford (See Page 4171)
Staffordsville, Giles 24167
Stanardsville, Greene 22973
Stanley, Page 22851
Stanleytown, Henry 24168
Star Tannery, Frederick 22654
State Farm, Goochland 23160
STAUNTON, Staunton City (See Page 4173)
Steeles Tavern, Augusta 24476
Stephens City, Frederick 22655
Stephenson, Frederick 22656
STERLING, Loudoun (See Page 4174)
Stevensburg, Culpeper 22741
Stevensville, King And Queen 23161
Stone Ridge, Loudoun 20105
Stonega, Wise 24216
Stony Creek, Sussex 23882
STRASBURG, Shenandoah (See Page 4176)
Stratford, Westmoreland 22558
Stuart, Patrick 24171
Stuarts Draft, Augusta 24477
Studley, Hanover 23162
Sudley Springs, Prince William 20109
SUFFOLK, Suffolk City (See Page 4177)

Sugar Grove, Smyth 24375
Sully Station, Fairfax 20120
Sumerduck, Fauquier 22742
Supply, Essex 22436
Surry, Surry 23883
Susan, Mathews 23163
Sussex, Sussex 23884
Sutherland, Dinwiddie 23885
Sutherlin, Pittsylvania 24594
Sweet Briar, Amherst 24595
Swoope, Augusta 24479
Swords Creek, Russell 24649
Syria, Madison 22743
Syringa, Middlesex 23169
Tabb, York 23693
Tamworth, Cumberland 23027
Tangier, Accomack 23440
Tannersville, Tazewell 24377
Tappahannock, Essex 22560
Tasley, Accomack 23441
Tazewell, Tazewell 24608
Tazewell, Tazewell 24651
Temperanceville, Accomack .. 23442
Thaxton, Bedford 24174
The Plains, Fauquier 20198
Thornburg, Spotsylvania 22565
Thornhill, Orange 22960
Timberlake, Lynchburg City ... 24502
Timberville, Rockingham 22853
Tiptop, Tazewell 24630
Toano, James City 23168
Toms Brook, Shenandoah 22660
Topping, Middlesex 23169
Townsend, Northampton 23443
Trammel, Russell 24237
Trevilians, Louisa 23170
Triangle, Prince William 22172
Triplet, Brunswick 23868
Troutdale, Grayson 24378
Troutville, Botetourt 24175
Troy, Fluvanna 22974
Turbeville, Halifax 24592
Tye River, Nelson 22922
Tyro, Nelson 22976
Tysons, Fairfax 22102
Tysons Corner, Fairfax 22102
Union Hall, Franklin 24176
Unionville, Orange 22567
University, Charlottesville City 22903
Uno, Madison 22738
UPPERVILLE, Fauquier (See Page 4180)
Urbanna, Middlesex 23175
Va Bch (See Virginia Beach)
Va Beach (See Virginia Beach)
Vab (See Virginia Beach)
Valentines, Brunswick 23887
Vansant, Buchanan 24656
Venia, Russell 24260
Vernon Hill, Halifax 24597
Verona, Augusta 24482
Vesta, Patrick 24177
Vesuvius, Rockbridge 24483
Victoria, Lunenburg 23974
VIENNA, Fairfax (See Page 4180)
Viewtown, Culpeper 20106
Viewtown, Culpeper 22746
Village, Richmond 22570
Villamont, Bedford 24178
Vint Hill Farms (See Warrenton)
Vinton, Roanoke 24179
Virgilina, Halifax 24598
VIRGINIA BEACH, Virginia Beach City (See Page 4182)
Virginia State University, Petersburg City 23806
Volney, Grayson 24363
Wachapreague, Accomack 23480
Wake, Middlesex 23176
Wakefield, Sussex 23888
Walkerton, King And Queen .. 23177
Wallops Island, Accomack 23337
Walters, Isle Of Wight 23315
Wardtown, Northampton 23482
Ware Neck, Gloucester 23178
Warfield, Brunswick 23889
Warm Springs, Bath 24484
Warner, Middlesex 23175
WARRENTON, Fauquier (See Page 4193)
Warsaw, Richmond 22572
Washington, Rappahannock .. 22747
Washingtons Birthplace, Westmoreland 22443
Water View, Middlesex 23180
Waterford, Loudoun 20197
Wattsville, Accomack 23483
Waverly, Sussex 23890
Waynesboro, Waynesboro City 22980
Weber City, Scott 24290
Weems, Lancaster 22576
Weirwood, Northampton 23413
West Augusta, Augusta 24485
West Mclean, Fairfax 22102
West Mclean, Fairfax 22103
West Point, King William 23181
West Springfield, Fairfax 22152
Weyers Cave, Augusta 24486
Whitacre, Frederick 22625
White Hall, Albemarle 22987
White Marsh, Gloucester 23183
White Plains, Brunswick 23893
White Post, Clarke 22663
White Stone, Lancaster 22578
Whitetop, Grayson 24292
Whitewood, Buchanan 24657
Wicomico, Gloucester 23184
Wicomico Church, Northumberland 22579
Wildwood, Fluvanna 22963
WILLIAMSBURG, James City (See Page 4194)
Williamsville, Bath 24487
Willis, Floyd 24380
Willis Wharf, Northampton 23486
Wilmington, Fluvanna 22963
Wilsons, Dinwiddie 23894
WINCHESTER, Winchester City (See Page 4198)
Windsor, Isle Of Wight 23487
Wingina, Buckingham 24599
Winston, Culpeper 22701
Wintergreen Resort, Nelson .. 22967
Wirtz, Franklin 24184
Wise, Wise 24293
Withams, Accomack 23488
Wolford, Buchanan 24658
Wolftown, Madison 22748
Woodberry Forest, Madison .. 22989
WOODBRIDGE, Prince William (See Page 4200)
Woodford, Caroline 22580
Woodlawn, Carroll 24381
Woods Cross Roads, Gloucester 23190
Woodstock, Shenandoah 22664
Woodville, Rappahannock 22749
Woolwine, Patrick 24185
Wylliesburg, Charlotte 23976
Wytheville, Wythe 24382
Yale, Sussex 23897
Yancey Mills, Albemarle 22932
Yards, Tazewell 24605
YORKTOWN, York (See Page 4204)
Zacata, Westmoreland 22581
Zanoni, Gloucester 23061
Zion Crossroads, Orange 22942
Zuni, Isle Of Wight 23898

ABINGDON VA

General Delivery 24210

POST OFFICE BOXES MAIN OFFICE STATIONS AND BRANCHES

Box No.s
All PO Boxes 24212

NAMED STREETS

A St SE 24210
Abbey Ln NW 24210
Abingdon Pl 24211
Academy Dr NW 24210
Adare Ln 24210
Ahoy Ln 24211
Aliff Dr 24210
Allegheny Dr 24211
Alma Ct 24211
Alpine Dr 24211
Altamont Dr SE 24210
Alvarado Rd 24211
Amanda Ln 24211
Ambler Way 24210
Amelia Dr 24211
Amish Dr 24211
Anchor Ln 24211
Annie Ln 24211
April Ln 24211
Arden Ct 24210
Argyle Ln 24210
Arnold St 24210
Arrowhead Ln 24211
Ash St NW 24210
Ashley Hills Cir 24211
Astor Rd 24210
Athens Dr 24211
Atlantis Ln 24211
Augusta Dr 24211
Augustine Ln 24211
Avanta Dr 24211
Aven Ln 24211
Avondale Rd 24211
Azure Ln 24211
B St SE 24210
Badger Dr 24211
Bailey Dr 24210
Baltimore St NW 24210
Banjo Dr 24211
Barclay Dr 24210
Barn Hill Rd 24211
Barter Dr 24210
Baugh Ln NE 24210
Beech Cir 24211
Beech Hideaway 24211
Beechwood Dr 24210
Bellevue Rd 24210
Bermuda Dr 24211
Berry Creek Dr 24211
Besclaren Rd 24211
Bethany Ln 24210
Bethel Rd 24211
Beverly Dr 24210
Big Bass Camp Rd 24211
Big Horn Dr 24211
Big Horse Cove Rd 24210
Big Jack Dr 24211
Birdie Dr 24211
Biscay Dr 24211
Black Hollow Rd 24210
Black Wolf Dr 24211
Blacks Fort Ln 24210
Blake Dr 24210
Blue Sky Dr 24211
Bluegrass Dr 24211
Bobby Ln 24211
Bogey Dr 24211
Bonnie Ln 24211
Bonnycastle Dr 24211
Boone St SW 24210
Bow Hunter Dr 24210
Bowers Dr 24210
Bowman Rd 24211
Bradley St SW 24210
Branch St 24210
Braudy Ln 24210
Braxton Ln 24210
Breckenridge Ct 24211
Breezy Point Rd 24211
Brewers Aly SE 24210
Briarwood Ln 24210
Bridgeview Dr 24211
Bridle Dr 24210
Briel Rd 24211
Bright Star Rd 24211
Brinkley Rd 24210
Brookhill Dr 24210
Browning Rd 24211
Brumley Gap Rd 24210
Bryce Ln 24211
Bryson Cove Rd 24210
Buckingham Ct NE 24210
Burkes Ln 24210
Butler Dr 24210
Butt St SW 24210
Cabin Creek Rd 24210
Calima Dr 24210
Calla Rd 24210
Cambridge St NE 24210
Camp Comfort Hts 24211
Camp Sequoya Dr 24211
Campbell St SW 24210
Campbell Hollow Rd 24211
Campus Dr 24210
Canebrake Rd 24210
Canjle Dr 24210
Canterbury Ln 24210
Canyon Dr 24211
Capella Ln 24210
Capri Ave 24211
Carol Jane Ln 24211
Carousel Rd 24210
Carterton Ln 24210
Cary Dr 24210
Case Cove Dr 24211
Cash Ln 24210
Cashmere Ct 24210
Castlegate Dr 24210
Cave Creek Rd 24211
Cavendish Dr 24210
Cedar Tree Ln 24210
Cedarwood Dr 24211
Celebrity Ln 24211
Center St NE 24210
Chandler Dr 24211
Chantilly Way 24210
Chaparral Dr 24211
Charwood Dr 24210
Chase Ln 24210
Chatham Ct 24210
Cherry St 24210
Cherry Hill Dr 24210
Chestnut St 24210
Cheyenne Trl 24211
Childress Hollow Rd 24210
Chip Ridge Rd 24210
Christy Ln 24210
Church St 24210
Circle Dr 24210
Clapp Ln 24210
Clark St 24210
Clay Dr 24210
Clearview Dr 24211
Clemson Dr 24210
Cleveland Rd 24211
Cleveland Church Rd 24211
Cliffhanger Rd 24210
Clinchside Dr 24210
Clipper Ln 24211
Cloudview Rd 24210
Clubhouse Dr 24211
Clydes Ln 24210
Coal Yard Rd 24210
Coffee Ln 24210
College St NW 24210
Colonade Dr 24210
Colonial Rd SW 24210
Comet Rd 24211
Commerce Dr 24211
Concord Ln 24211
Condor Ln 24210
Conklin Dr 24210
Connie Sue Ct 24211
Conway Dr 24211
Cook St E 24210
Cool Breeze Dr 24211
Copperfield Rd 24211
Cornelius Dr 24211
Cosby Ln 24210
Countiss Rd 24210
Country Dr 24211
Country Club Dr 24211
Country Lake Dr 24211
Country Side
Apartment 24210
Counts Ln 24210
County Park Rd 24211
Court St 24210
Cox Mill Rd 24211
Creamery Dr 24211
Crestview Dr NW 24210
Cricket Ln 24210
Crigger St SW 24210
Cross Ln 24210
Crosscreek Dr 24211
Crosswinds Dr 24211
Cruise Dr 24211
Cullop Ln 24210
Cummings St
100-699 24210
700-1199 24211
Daisy Ln 24210
Dale St NW 24210
Dallas Dr 24211
Dandelion Dr 24211
Dauphin Dr 24211
Davids Xing 24210
Deadmore St NE &
SE 24210
Deep Woods Rd 24211
Deer Run Dr 24211
Delano Dr 24211
Delray Dr 24210
Denham Dr 24210
Denmark Dr 24211
Dennison Dr 24211
Denton Valley Rd 24211
Depot Sq SW 24210
Derby Dr 24210
Destiny Ln 24210
Dogwood Dr 24210
Dollar Ln 24211
Donegal Dr 24210
Dons Pl 24211
Doral Pl 24211
Doris Kay Ct 24211
Douglas Ln 24210
Drake Rd 24211
Driftwood Ln 24211
Drugan Ln 24211
Druid Dr 24210
Dublin Ln 24210
Duchess Dr 24211
Duff Ln 24211
Duncan Pl 24211
Dylan Dr 24210
Dysart Dr 24210
Eagle Site Dr 24211
Eastwood Dr 24210
Ebony Ln 24210
Eden Ln 24211
Edgemont Ter 24210
Edgemont North St
NE 24210
Edmond Dr 24211
Eggers Pl 24210
Elderspirit Ct 24210
Elementary Dr 24210
Elliott St 24210
Elm St SW 24210
Empire Dr SW 24210
Enterprise Rd
14300-14499 24210
14500-15400 24211
15402-27298 24211
Erie Ln 24210
Erin Dr 24210
Essex Dr 24211
Everett Hagy Rd 24210
Ewing Dr 24210
Fairground Dr 24210
Fairhaven Rd 24211
Fairoaks Ln 24211
Fairway Dr 24211
Falcon Dr 24211
Falcon Place Blvd 24211
Fall Hill Rd 24210
Falls Dr NW 24210
Farnsworth Rd 24211
Fathom Ln 24211
Feathernest Dr 24211
Fenton Dr 24210
Fern Cir 24210
Fernbank Dr 24211
Fields Ln 24210
Fiesta Dr 24211
Filigree Rd 24211
Filly Run Rd 24211
Finley Ln 24210
Fire Department Rd 24210
Firebird Ln 24210
Fisherman Dr 24210
Flamingo Dr 24211
Flax Rd 24211
Florence Dr 24210
Florist Dr 24210
Floyd St SW 24210
Food City Cir E 24210
Foran Dr 24210
N Fork River Rd 24210
Fortunes Way 24210
Fox Hall Dr 24210
Foxchase Ln 24210
Fredia Ln 24210
Fremont Ln 24211
French Moore Jr Blvd 24210
Front St SW 24210
Fudge Rd 24210
Fugate St SW 24210
Fulkerson St SW 24210
Fuller St SW 24210
Galen Dr 24211
Garden Path Ln 24211
Gardenia Ln 24211
Garrett Creek Rd 24210
Genesis Ln 24210
Gentry Pl 24211
Gibson St SE 24210
Gilbert Dr 24210
Gillespie Dr 24210
Gilliam St SW 24210
Glen Dr 24210
Glenrochie Dr 24211
Glenview Dr 24211
Glenwood Dr 24211
Glory Ln 24210
Golden View Dr 24211
Goldenrod Dr 24210
Good Hope Rd 24211
Government Center
Way 24210
Grahams Dr 24211
Granada Pl 24210
Grandview Rd 24210
Grant St 24210
Gravel Lake Rd 24211
Gray Dr 24210
Green Vlg 24210
Green Spring Rd
300-599 24210
18200-24699 24211
Green Springs Church
Rd 24211
Greenevers Ct 24210
Greenhill Dr NE 24210
Grey Heron Ct 24211
Griffey Ln 24210
Grove Terrace Dr SW 24210
Guilford Dr 24210
Gunsmith Ln 24211
Gunthers Rdg 24210
Hagy St SW 24210
Halifax Rd 24211
Hall St 24210
Hallock Cir, Dr & Pl 24210
Halls Apartments 24210
Halter Trl 24210
Hampton Dr 24210
Harbor Light Cir 24211
Harmony Way 24210
Harmony Hills Ln 24211
Harrison Rd 24210
Hart Run Dr 24211
Hassinger St SW 24210
Havens Rest Rd 24210
Hawks Mdws 24210
Hayter St SW 24210
Hayters Gap Rd 24210
Hearl Dr 24210
Heart Of The Woods
Ln 24210
Heartwood Cir 24210
Heath Dr 24210
Hemingway Dr 24210
Henderson Ct 24210
Hendricks Dr NE 24210
Henry St NW 24210
Hereford Ln 24210
Heritage Dr 24211
Heron Cir 24211
Hickman St SE 24210
Hickory Ridge Rd 24210
Hidden Hills Ln 24211
Hidden Valley Rd 24210
High St NW 24210
Highfall Rd 24211
Highland St SE 24210
Highlands Log Dr 24210
Hill Dr & St 24210
Hill Top Ct 24211
Hillandale Rd 24210
Hillman Hwy NE 24210
Hillside Dr NE 24210
Hilltop Dr SW 24210
Hillview Dr 24210
Hite Ln 24210
Holston St NW 24210
Homeview Dr 24211
Honey Locust Rd 24211
Hooters Vill Dr 24210
Hopkins St 24210
Horizon Dr 24211
Horse Run Ln 24210
Horsemans Ln 24210
Horseshoe Trl 24210
Hortenstine Pl 24211
Hospital Dr 24210
Hubbard Ln 24211
Hughes St SW 24210
Humes St 24211
Hummingbird Ln 24210
Hunt Club Rd 24211
Hunter Brown Ln 24211
Huron Ln 24210
Hurt St SW 24210
Hutton St 24210
Huxley Rd 24210
Ian Ln 24210
Ibex Dr 24211
Idaho Dr 24211
Imogene Ct 24211
Ingle Dr 24210
Ingram Pl NW 24210
Inlet Cir 24211
Inspiration Dr 24210
Inwood Dr 24210
Ironwood Loop 24211
Ivy St NW 24210
Jackson St NE 24210
Jacobs Way 24210
Jamison St SW 24210
Jeb Stuart Hwy 24211
Jefferson Cir 24210
Jeffrey Dr 24211
Jennifer Dr 24211
Jerry Ln 24210
Jessica Ln 24211
Joe Derting Dr 24210
Joe Pesto Dr 24210
John Ashley Dr 24211
Johnson Dr 24211
Johnson St 24210
Johnson Hill Dr 24211
Johnston Memorial Dr 24211
Jomean Dr 24211
Jones Ln 24210
Jones Rd 24211
Jonquil Dr 24210
Josh Dr 24211
Josh Allen Dr 24211
Jubilee Dr 24211
Judith Way 24211
Kara B Dr 24210
Keeneland Ln 24211
Keller Rd 24211
Kendricks Dr NE 24210
Kennedy Dr 24211
Kenwarn Ln 24210
Kesner Ln 24210
Keswick Ln 24210
Ketron Ln 24211
Keys Dr 24210
Keystone Dr 24210
Kildee Dr 24210
Kimberlin Rd 24210
King St NW 24210
Kings Mountain Dr 24210
Kipling Dr 24210
Knights Bridge Rd 24210
Lacy Dr 24211
Lagoon Dr 24211
Lake Rd 24211
Lake Crest Dr 24211
Laken Ln 24211
Lakeshore Dr 24211
Lakeside Dr 24210
Lakeview Dr 24211
Lakewood Dr 24211
Lancaster Dr 24211
Landfall Ct 24210
Landridge Way 24211
Large Hollow Rd 24210
Lariat Loop 24211
Lateen Dr 24211
Laura Ln 24211
Laura Lee Ct 24211
Lauren Dr 24210
Leaf Ln 24211
Leatherwood Rd 24210
Leaward Ln 24211
Lee Hwy
25267A-25267Z 24211
17000-19499 24210
24400-28099 24211
Leisure Ln 24211
Leonard St NW 24210
Lexi Dr 24210
Lilly Ln 24210
Limestone Dr 24210
Lindell Rd 24210
Lindy Dr 24211
Litchfield Rd 24210
Little Duck Rd 24211
Little Mountain Rd 24210
Litton Rd 24210
Lizmarye Ln 24211
Locust St NW 24210
Lombardy Ln 24211
Long Shadow Dr 24211
Longview Dr 24211
Lorimer Branch Ln 24211
Lost Valley Dr & Rd 24211
Lowland St SE 24210
Lowry Dr SW 24210
Lucky Ln 24210
Lundy Ln 24210
Lycoming Dr 24211
Macedonia Rd 24211
Madge Hl 24211
Madison St SE 24210
Mahogany Dr 24210
Maiden St 24210
Maiden Creek Rd 24210
E Main St 24210
W Main St
966A3-966A3 24210
100-301 24210
300-300 24212
302-1298 24210
303-1299 24210
Major Dr 24211
Mallard Ln 24210
Mallicote Dr 24210
Mandalay Ln 24211
Marcus Way 24210
Marianne Dr 24211
Maringo Rd 24211
Marshall Dr 24210
Mary St 24210
Mary Lee Dr 24210
Mason Pl NW 24210
Matney Dr 24211
Matthew Dr 24211
Mcbroom St NW 24210
Mcconnell Ln 24211
Mccray Dr 24211
Mcculloch Dr 24210
Mcguffie Rd 24210
Meade Dr 24211
Meadowbrook Dr 24211
Meadows Dr 24211
Melrose St 24210
Mendota Rd 24210
Mercedes Dr 24210
Merion Cir 24211
Merman St 24211
Middle Dr 24211
Middle Pointe Ct 24210
Middlewood Dr 24210
Midland Dr 24211
Midwest Cir 24211
Millbrook Dr 24211
Miller Ln SW 24210
Millsap Ln 24211
Millstone Ln 24210
Milton Dr 24211
Mimis Ln 24210
Mink Pl 24210
Minton Ln 24211
Miracle Valley Dr 24210
Misty Rd 24210
Moccasin Cir 24210
Mock Knob Rd 24211
Mohawk Ln 24211
Molly Ln 24211
Mongle Dr 24210
Mont Calm St 24210
Montego Bay Rd 24211
Montgomery Rd 24211
Montview Dr 24210
Moonlight Bay Rd 24211
Moonshine Dr 24211
Moonstone Rd 24210
Morningside Dr & Ln 24210
Morris Ln 24210
Mosby St SW 24210
Mossy Oak Ln 24211
Moulin St 24210
Mountain Pass Rd 24211
Mountain Spring Rd 24210
Mountain View Dr SW 24211
Muirfield Cir 24211
Muster Pl 24210
Nassau Dr 24211
Neal Rd 24211
Nestlewood Rd 24211
New Hope Rd 24210
Newbanks Rd 24210
Newton Ln 24211
Nicholas St SE 24210
Noel Rd 24211
Norfolk St 24210
Northridge Rd 24210
Northwoods Trl 24210
Nugget Dr 24211
Oak Hill St NE 24210
Oak Park Dr 24210

Oakland St SW 24210
Oakmont Dr 24211
Oakwood Dr 24211
Oates Dr 24211
Old 11 Ct & Dr 24210
Old Homestead Ln 24211
Old Jonesboro Rd
100-199 24210
17700-17798 24211
17800-19699 24211
Old Saltworks Rd 24210
Old South Way 24211
Old Timber Rd 24210
Old Trail Rd 24210
Ole Berry Rd 24210
Olson Dr 24210
Onalee Dr 24211
Ontario Ln 24210
Orleans Dr 24210
Osceola Rd 24211
Otter Ln 24210
Out Of Bounds Dr 24211
Overlook Dr 24210
Oxford St NE 24210
Oyhee Ln 24210
Paddock Pl 24211
Page St NW 24210
Painter Creek Rd 24211
Palmer St NW 24210
Palmwood Dr 24211
Panacella Dr 24210
Panorama Dr 24210
Par Pl 24211
Paradise Ln 24210
Park St SE 24210
Park Ridge Dr 24211
Parks Rd 24211
Parks Creek Ln 24210
Parks Mill Rd 24211
Partnership Cir
1-1 24210
1200-1300 24211
1302-2198 24211
Pats Ln 24210
Patton St NW 24210
Pauls Way 24210
Pawnee Dr 24211
Peaceful Valley Rd 24210
Pecan St NE & SE 24210
Pecota Dr 24210
Petals Ln
18100-18199 24211
18200-18299 24210
Pewter Ln 24211
Phillips St NW 24210
Phipps Farm Rd 24210
Phoenix Dr 24210
Picardy Dr 24210
Pickett Ln 24211
Piggly Wiggly Aly 24210
Pilgrim Ln 24211
Pilot Ln 24211
Pincour Rd 24210
Pine St 24210
Pine Hedge Dr 24210
Pine Hedge
Townhouses 24210
Pinehurst Ct 24211
Piper Springs Ave 24210
Pippin St NW 24210
Pleasant View Dr 24211
Plumb Aly 24210
Plummer St 24210
Pond Dr 24211
Ponderosa Dr 24211
Poplar St NW 24210
Porter Ln 24211
Porterfield Hwy SW 24210
Powderhorn Dr 24210
Pratt Ln 24210
Prehaps Ln 24211
Preston St SW 24210
Preston Place Dr 24211
Primrose Ln 24210
Providence Rd 24210
Puckett Knob Rd 24211
Quail Rd 24210
Quail Ridge Way 24210
Rabbit Hill Rd 24210
Racking Horse Rd 24210
Radio Dr 24210
Railroad St SE 24210
Raintree Dr 24210
Randolph Dr 24211
Ratcliffe St 24210
Ratite Way 24210
Rattle Creek Rd 24210
Red Wolf Dr 24211
Redbird Ln 24211
Reedy Creek Rd 24210
Reflection Ln 24211
Regal Dr 24211
Regency Dr 24211
Remington Dr 24211
Repass St 24210
Reservoir St NW 24210
Rich Valley Rd 24210
Richardson Ave 24210
Rickard St NW 24210
Ridgecrest Dr 24210
Ridgeview Dr 24211
Ridgewood Rd 24210
Riffe Way 24211
Rim Rd 24210
River Forest Dr 24210
Rivermont Dr 24211
Riverwalk Trl 24210
Roark Mountain Dr 24211
Roberta St SW 24210
Robinson Rd 24211
Rockledge Ln 24210
Rockwall Dr 24210
Rodefer St SW 24210
Roebuck Rd 24211
Roger St 24210
Rooster Ln 24211
Rose St NW 24210
Rose Down Ln 24210
Roxbury Ln 24210
Rugby Ter NE 24210
Russell Rd NW 24210
Rust Hollow Rd 24210
Rustic Ln 24210
Ruth St SW 24210
Saddletree Ln 24210
Samantha Dr 24211
Sams Way 24210
Sand Hill Ln 24211
Sandcastle Rd 24210
Sappo Rd 24211
Saras Way 24211
Saturn Dr 24211
Sawgrass Cir 24211
Saybrook Dr 24211
Scott Ridge Rd 24210
Sedona Dr 24211
Self Hill Dr 24210
Senior Dr NE 24210
Serenade Pl 24210
Shady St 24210
Shallow Ford Dr 24211
Shannon Hill Dr 24210
Sheffield Ct 24210
Shell Rd 24210
Shelton Dr 24210
Shepard Ln 24211
Shetlane Dr 24210
Shiloh Dr 24211
Shirley Dr 24210
Shoreline Dr 24211
Short St 24210
Shortsville Rd 24210
Show Horse Ln 24210
Shutters Cv 24210
Silver Lake Rd 24211
Sims Rd 24211
Sky King Dr 24210
Skyward Dr 24211
Sleepy Hollow Ln 24211
Smartview Ln 24210
Smoke Tree Dr 24211
Snowbird Ln 24210
Sophie Dr 24211
Southwood Dr 24210
Sparrow Rd 24210
Spearmint Dr 24211
Spice Ln 24210
Spoon Gap Rd 24211
Sportsman Dr 24211
Spring St 24210
Spring Creek Rd
18400-18499 24210
18500-19299 24211
Spring Lake Rd 24210
Spring Valley Rd 24210
Spur Ln 24210
Stagfield Rd 24210
Stanley St 24210
Starboard Ln 24211
Starlight Dr 24211
Steeple Chase Dr 24211
Steinman Rd 24210
Stella Dr 24211
Sterling Dr 24211
Sterling Manor Dr 24211
Stillwater Ln 24211
Stirrup Dr 24211
Stone St 24210
Stone Mill Rd 24211
Stone Mill Rd SW 24210
Stone Mountain Rd 24211
Stonewall Hts NE 24210
Stoneybrook Dr 24210
Storybook Ln 24211
Stover Ln 24211
Strawberry Fields Rd 24211
Stuart Dr 24211
Suffolk Dr 24210
Sugar Cove Rd 24210
Sugarbush Ln 24211
Summers St NE 24210
Summerwood Dr NE 24210
Sun Valley Dr 24210
Sunbrite Dr 24211
Suncatcher Rd 24211
Sunset Dr 24210
Surrey Ln 24210
Sutton St SW 24210
Swan Dr 24210
Sweet Hollow Rd 24211
Sweetland Ct 24211
Swiss Ln 24210
Sydney Dr 24211
Tall Oaks Dr 24211
Tandy Rd 24210
Tanner St NE & SE 24210
Tartan Dr 24210
Tate Dr 24210
Taylor Pl 24210
Taylor St NW 24210
Teal Dr 24211
Thistledown Rd 24211
Thomas Ct 24211
Thompson Dr 24210
Tigger Dr 24210
Tiki Way 24211
Timberland Ct NE 24210
Tioga Dr 24211
Tipperary Ln 24210
Tobyhanna Rd 24210
Toole Creek Rd 24210
Towne Center Dr 24210
Trailview Dr 24210
Treeline Dr 24210
Trigg St 24210
Trinity Dr 24211
Triple Crown Dr 24211
Troopers Aly 24210
Trotters Ln 24211
Troublesome Holw 24211
Trout Rd 24210
Tuckaway Dr 24210
Turfway Ln 24211
Turtle Creek Rd 24211
Twain Dr 24210
Twin Ash Ln 24211
Twin Oaks Rd 24211
Twin Rivers Trl 24211
Tycho Dr 24211
Tyco Dr 24211
Underwood Ln 24211
Upland Dr 24211
Valley St NE & NW 24210
Valley Street Ext NE 24210
Valley View Dr NE 24210
Vances Mill Rd 24211
Viandent Rd 24211
Viceroy Dr 24211
Village Blvd, Ct &
Loop 24210
Vintage Vw 24210
Vols Dr 24210
Voyager Way 24211
Wake Pl SW 24210
Walden Rd NE 24210
Waldon Ridge Condos 24210
Wall St NW 24210
Wallace Pike 24210
Watauga Rd 24211
Waters Way 24210
Waylon Dr 24211
Wayne Ave NE 24210
Webb Dr 24211
Weeping Willow Dr 24210
Welcome Ln 24211
Welsh Ln 24210
Wes Gentry Dr 24211
Westchester Cir 24211
Westinghouse Rd 24210
Westminster Ave 24211
Westwood Dr 24211
Wexmouth Dr 24211
Wheeler St NW 24210
Whitaker Hollow Rd 24211
White St NE 24210
White Top Vw 24210
Whiteridge Dr 24211
Whites Mill Rd 24210
Whites Point Dr 24211
Whitney Ln 24211
Wichita Ln 24211
Wild Cherry Ln 24211
Wildflower Ln NW 24211
Wiley St NW 24210
Wilkinson Dr 24211
Williams St SW 24210
Willow Run Dr 24210
Windbreak Ln 24210
Windmere Cir 24211
Windsor Ln 24211
Windy Ridge Ln 24211
Winfield Rd 24210
Wingedfoot Ct 24211
Winter Hvn 24210
Winterham Dr 24211
Wise Ln 24210
Witts End 24210
Wolf Creek Trl 24210
Wonderland Dr 24211
Woodby Ln 24211
Woodcliffe Dr 24210
Woodland Hills Rd 24210
Woodlawn Ter NE 24210
Woolwine Pl SW 24210
Worthing Way 24210
Wycoff Dr 24211
Wyldwood Rd 24211
Wyndale Rd 24210
Wynscape Dr 24210
York Dr 24211
Zikan Dr 24211

NUMBERED STREETS

All Street Addresses 24210

ALEXANDRIA VA

General Delivery 22313

POST OFFICE BOXES MAIN OFFICE STATIONS AND BRANCHES

Box No.s
9504A - 9505A 22304
9137A - 9160A 22304
178A - 178A 22313
268B - 268B 22313
323A - 323B 22313
456B - 456B 22313
1 - 880 22313
5 - 5 22302
901 - 1180 22313
1200 - 1200 22302
1201 - 1992 22313
2185 - 2959 22301
3001 - 3650 22302
4001 - 4950 22303
6001 - 6980 22306
7001 - 7900 22307
8001 - 8738 22306
9001 - 9998 22304
9998 - 9998 22313
10001 - 10899 22310
10001 - 10001 22302
11001 - 11999 22312
12001 - 12116 22304
13000 - 13170 22312
15001 - 15640 22309
16001 - 17358 22302
20834 - 20834 22320
22001 - 24000 22304
25001 - 26477 22313
28000 - 28000 22304
30000 - 31638 22310
90001 - 90834 22309
150001 - 151974 22315
230403 - 230499 22304
230500 - 230599 22305
230700 - 230700 22307
231200 - 231299 22312
320001 - 321074 22320
2230100 - 2230100 22301

NAMED STREETS

Abbottsbury Row 22315
W & E Abingdon Ct &
Dr 22314
Accotink Pl 22308
Achilles Ct 22315
Ackley St 22309
Adams Ave 22301
Admetus Ct 22315
Admiral Dr
7300-7499 22307
7600-7699 22308
Admiral Vernon Ter 22309
Admiralty Ct 22315
Adonis Ct 22315
Adrienne Ct & Dr 22309
Agnew Ave 22309
Alabama Ave 22305
Alameda Ct 22309
Albany Ave 22302
Albee Ln 22309
Albemarle Dr 22303
Albro Ln 22312
Alcott St 22309
Alden Rd 22308
Alderman Dr 22315
Alexander Ave 22310
Alexander St 22314
Alexandria Ave 22308
E Alexandria Ave 22301
W Alexandria Ave
1-199 22301
200-499 22302
Alforth Ave 22315
N & S Alfred St 22314
Algona Ct 22310
Alicia Ct 22310
Allborough Dr 22315
Allison St 22302
Allwood Ct & Dr 22309
Alyce Pl 22308
Ambassador Way 22310
Ambler St 22310
Amblewood Rd 22309
Amesbury Ct 22315
Amlong Ave & Pl 22306
Ampthill Dr 22312
Ancell St 22305
Ancilla Ct 22307
Andalusia Dr 22308
Anderson Ct & St 22312
Andover Dr 22307
Andrus Ct & Rd 22306
Anesbury Ct & Ln 22308
Anker St 22306
Annandale St 22312
Anne Ly Ln 22310
Anne Tucker Ln 22309
Annie Rose Ave 22301
Anthony St 22306
Appian Ct 22306
Apple Hill Rd 22308
Apple Tree Dr 22310
Appleford Dr 22315
Applegarth Ct 22312
Applemint Ln 22310
Apsley House Ct 22310
Aragon Pl 22309
Arapaho Ln 22312
Arcadia Rd 22312
Arch Hall Ln 22314
Archer Ct 22312
Archstone Ct & Way 22310
Arco St 22310
Arcross Ct 22310
Arcturus Ln 22308
Arcturus On The
Potomac 22308
Arell Ct 22304
Arendale Sq 22309
Argall Pl 22314
Argyle Dr 22305
Arkendale Rd 22307
Arlington Dr 22306
Arlington Ter 22303
N Armistead St 22312
Arrow Park Dr 22306
Arundel Ave 22306
Asbury Ct 22312
Ascot Ct 22311
Ashboro Dr 22309
Ashby Ln 22315
Ashby St 22305
Ashby Heights Cir 22315
Ashby Manor Pl 22310
Ashfield Rd 22315
Ashford Ln 22304
Ashleigh Manor Ct 22315
Ashton St 22309
N Ashton St 22312
Ashwood Dr 22308
Aspen Dr 22309
Aspen Pl 22305
Aspen St 22305
Aspen Glen Ct 22309
Aspinwall Ln 22304
Auburn Ct 22305
Auburn Leaf Ln 22312
Audubon Ave 22306
Audubon Meadow
Way 22306
Augustine St 22309
Austin Ave & Ct 22310
Autumn Cove Ct 22312
Autumn Glen Ct 22312
Avalon Ct 22314
Avalon Pl 22315
Avermara 22331
Avery Park Ct 22306
Avon Pl 22314
Ayers Dr 22309
Azalea Cove Ter 22315
Badger Dr 22309
Baggett Pl 22314
Bainbridge Rd 22308
Ballenger Ave 22314
Ballycastle Cir 22315
Baltimore Rd 22308
Banchory Ct 22315
Bangor Dr 22303
Banks Pl 22312
Barbara Rd 22315
Barbmor Ct 22310
Barbour Dr 22304
Barclay Dr 22315
Barcroft Ln 22312
Barnum Ln 22312
Barrett Pl 22304
Barrister Pl
5400-5499 22304
6300-6399 22307
Barry Rd 22315
Bartley Way 22315
Basha Ct 22310
Bashford Ln 22314
Bass Ct 22306
Basset St 22308
Battersea Ln 22309
Battery Pl 22314
Battery Rd 22308
Battlement Way 22312
Bayberry Dr 22306
Baychester Ct 22315
Bayliss Dr 22302
Bayliss Pl 22310
Bayliss Knoll Ct 22310
Baylor Dr 22307
Beacon Hill Rd 22306
Beatty Dr 22308
Beauchamp Dr 22309
Beauregard St 22312
N Beauregard St
300-499 22312
501-1199 22312
1400-3002 22311
3004-3198 22311
3400-3499 22302
Becherer Rd 22309
Beckner Ct 22309
Beddoo St 22306
Bedford Ln 22307
Bedford Ter 22309
Bedlington Ter 22304
Bedrock Ct & Rd 22306
Bee St 22310
Beech Tree Dr 22310
Beechcliff Dr 22306
Beechcraft Dr 22306
Beechwood Rd 22307
Beekman Pl 22309
Belfield Rd 22307
Belford Dr 22306
Bellaire Rd 22301
Belle Haven Rd 22307
Belle Haven Meadows
Ct 22306
Belle Pre Way 22314
Belle Rive Ter 22309
Belle View Blvd 22307
Belle Vista Dr 22307
Belleau Woods Ln 22315
E & W Bellefonte Ave 22301
Bellemeade Ln 22311
Belleview Ave 22303
Bellvue Pl 22314
Belvedere Dr 22306
Belvoir Dr 22306
Belwood Ct 22309
Benecia Ct 22309
Benfield Dr 22310
Benning Ct 22312
S Benson Dr 22306
Bent Willow Dr 22310
Bentley Mill Pl 22315
Berielia Dr 22306
Berkeley Rd 22307
Berkshire Ct 22303
Berkshire Dr 22310
Berlee Dr 22312
Bermuda Green Ct 22312
Bernard Ave 22310
Bernard St 22314
Bertram Ln 22306
Berwick Ct 22315
Beryl Rd 22312
Bessley Pl 22304
Bethel Rd 22310

Street	ZIP
Beulah St	
6300-6999	22310
7000-7899	22315
Beverley Dr	22302
Beverly Dr	22305
Bianca Pl	22309
Bibbings Way	22315
Bing Ct	22315
Bingley Rd	22315
Birch Ln	22312
Birch St	22305
Birch Branch Ter	22315
Birchlake Ct	22309
Birchleigh Cir & Way	22315
Birds View Ln	22312
Birkenhead Pl	22315
Biscayne Dr	22303
Bishop Ln	22302
Bishop Walker Cir	22304
Bismach Dr	22312
Bitternut Dr	22310
Black Alder Dr	22309
Blaine Dr	22303
Blakiston Ln	22308
Blanford Ct	22315
Blankenship St	22309
Bloomfield Dr	22312
Blossom Ln	22310
Blowing Rock Rd	22309
Blue Grass Dr	22310
Blue Jay Ct	22306
Blue Mallard Lndg	22306
Blue Slate Ct & Dr	22306
Blue Wing Dr	22307
Bluebill Ln	22307
Bluebird Ln	22306
Bluedale St	22308
Bluemont Ave	22301
Bluestone Rd	22304
Blunt Ln	22303
Blyth Pl	22309
Bob White Ct	22306
Boland Pl	22309
Bold Lion Ln	22315
Bolling Dr	22308
Bond Ct	22315
Boothe St	22309
Bordeaux St	22309
Boswell Ave	22306
Bouffant Blvd	22311
E Boulevard Dr	22308
W Boulevard Dr	22308
Boulevard Vw	22307
Bound Brook Ln	22309
Boyce Dr	22311
Boyle St	22314
Bracey Ln	22314
Braddock Ave	22309
Braddock Ct	22304
Braddock Pl	
1200-1399	22314
1715-1739	22302
Braddock Rd	22312
E Braddock Rd	
1-499	22301
500-599	22314
W Braddock Rd	
1-199	22301
200-3899	22302
4000-4499	22304
4501-4599	22304
4600-4698	22311
4700-4899	22311
Bradford Ct	22311
Bradgate Ct & Rd	22308
Bradley Blvd	22311
Bradmore St	22315
Brady St	22309
Braeleigh Ln	22315
S Bragg St	22312
Brambly Ln	22309
Brampton Ct	22304
Branch Ave	22302
Brawner Pl	22304
Braxton Pl	22301
N Breckinridge Pl	22312
Breezy Ter	22303
Bren Mar Dr	22312
Brenman Park Dr	22304
Brent St	22303
Brentwood Pl	22306
Brevard Ct	22309
Brewster Dr	22308
Briarleigh Way	22315
Briarmoor Ln	22310
Briarview Ct	22310
Brick Hearth Ct	22306
Bricker Ln	22315
Brickleigh Ct	22315
Bridgehaven Ct	22308
Bridgewater Ct	22315
Bridle Ln	22308
Brighouse Ct	22315
Brighton Ct	22305
Brindle Heath Way	22315
Bristol Ct	22312
Bristol Way	22310
Broadmoor St	22315
Broadwing Pl	22312
Brocketts Aly	22314
Brocketts Xing	22315
Brockham Dr	22309
Brookington Ct	22306
Brookland Ct & Rd	22310
Brookleigh Way	22315
Brookmay Ct	22309
Brookside Dr	22312
Brookview Ct & Dr	22310
Brosar Ct	22306
Brown Ct	22306
Browns Mill Dr	22304
Bruce St	22305
Bryan Pl & St	22302
Bryant Towne Ct	22306
Bryce Rd	22312
Buchanan St	22314
Buckboard Dr	22308
Buckhaven Ct	22315
Buckingham Palace Ct	22315
Buckman Ct & Rd	22309
Buckner Rd	22309
Budd Way	22310
Bulfinch Ct	22315
Bunker Hill Rd	22308
Burdon Ct	22315
Burgess Ave	22305
Burgundy Pl & Rd	22303
Burgundy Leaf Ln	22312
Burke Ave	22301
Burke Dr	22309
Burlingame Pl	22309
Burnett St	22310
Burnside Pl	22304
Burnt Pine Ct	22312
Burr St	22303
Burtonwood Ct & Dr	22307
Bush Hill Dr	22310
Bushie Ct	22312
Bushrod Rd	22308
Business Center Dr	22314
Buttercup Ct	22310
Butterfly Ln	22304
Butterworth Ct	22315
Buxton Ct	22315
Byers Dr	22309
Byrd Ln	22303
Byron St	22303
Cabin Creek Rd	22314
Cadbury Row	22315
Cahill Dr	22304
Calabria Ct	22315
Calderon Ct	22306
Caleb Ct	22315
Caledonia St	22309
Calhoun Ave	22311
California Ln	22304
Callahan Dr	22301
Callcott Way	22312
Calvert Ave	22301
Cambridge Rd	22314
Camden St	22308
Camellia Dr	22306
Cameron Mews	22314
Cameron Rd	22308
Cameron St	22314
Cameron Farms Pl	22310
Cameron Mills Rd	
2300-3399	22302
3400-3999	22305
Cameron Parke Ct & Pl	22304
Cameron Run Ter	22303
Cameron Station Blvd	22304
Camfield Ct & Dr	22308
Campbell Dr	22303
Canal Center Plz	22314
Canard St	22312
Candlelight Ct	22310
Candlewood Dr	
2200-2499	22308
7800-8099	22306
Cane Hill Way	22315
Cannes Ct	22315
Cannon Ln	22303
Canterbury Ln	
500-599	22314
7000-7099	22307
Canterbury Sq	22304
Canyon Dr	22305
Capistrano Pl	22309
Caprice Ct	22310
Captains Row	22308
Captains Cove Ct	22315
Care Dr	22310
Carlby Ln	22309
Carlisle Dr	22301
Carlos Ct	22309
Carlwood Rd	22309
Carlyle Pl	22308
Carolina Pl	22305
Carpenter Rd	22314
Carriage Dr	22310
Carriage House Cir	22304
Carriage House Ct	22309
Carson Pl	22304
Carter Farm Ct	22306
Caryn Ct	22312
Casa Grande Pl	22309
Casdin Dr	22310
Casey Ct	22306
Cashland Ct	22315
Casperson Rd	22315
Cassel Glen Ct	22310
Castle Bar Ct & Ln	22315
Castle Riding Ct	22315
Castleberg Ct	22315
Castlefin Way	22315
Castletown Way	22310
Castlewellan Dr	22315
Cathedral Dr	22314
Catlin Ln	22311
W Caton Ave	22301
Catts Tavern Dr	22314
Cauba Ct	22310
Cavalier Dr	22307
Cavendish Dr	22308
Cedar Ct	22309
Cedar Rd	22309
W Cedar St	22301
Cedar Dale Ln	22308
Cedar Landing Ct	22306
Cedardale Dr	22308
Cedarlake Ct	22309
Celtic Dr	22310
Cencolli Ct	22315
Centennial Ct	22311
Centerbrook Pl	22308
Central Ave	
2400-2899	22302
8200-8499	22309
Central Park Cir & Dr	22309
Centre Plz	22302
Century Ct	22312
Century Dr	22304
Century Pl	22304
Chaco Rd	22312
Chadwick Ave	22308
Chahotkin Dr	22308
Chalfonte Dr	22305
N Chambliss St	
800-1599	22312
1800-2699	22311
4600-4799	22312
Chancel Pl	22314
Chancery Ct	22308
Chapel Cove Ct	22315
Chapel Gate Ct	22315
Chapel Hill Dr	22304
Chapin Ave	22303
E & W Chapman St	22301
Charles Ave	22305
Charles Alexander Ct	22301
Charles Arrington Dr	22310
Charles Augustine Dr	22308
Charles Green Sq	22315
Charlton Ct	22315
Chase Ct	22312
Chaucer Ln	22304
Chaucer View Cir	22304
Chauncey Ct	22314
Cheatham Ct	22310
Chelsea Ct	22304
Cherokee Ave & Ct	22312
Cherry Valley Ln	22309
Cherrytree Dr	22309
Cherwell Ln	22315
Cheshire Ct & Ln	22307
Chesley Search Way	22315
Chestnut Pl	22311
Chetworth Ct & Pl	22314
Chevell Ct	22310
Cheyenne Dr	22312
Cheyenne Knoll Pl	22312
Chickawane Ct	22309
Chicory Pl	22310
Chieftain Cir	22312
Childs Ln	22308
Chili St	22303
Chimney Wood Ct	22306
China Grove Ct	22310
Chippewa Pl	22312
Chiswick Ln	22310
Chollman Ct	22308
Chowan Ave	22312
Christine Pl	22311
Chrysanthemum Dr	22310
Church St	22314
Churchman Ct	22310
Cilantro Dr	22310
Cinnamon Ct	22310
Circle Ter	22302
Circle Hill Rd	22305
Clames Dr	22310
Clapham Rd	22315
Clara Edward Ter	22310
Claremont Woods Dr	22309
Clarence Ave	22311
N Clarens St	22304
Clark Pl	22308
Clay St	22302
Clayborne Ave	22306
Claymont Dr	22309
Clayton Ln	22304
Clayton Pl	22308
Clemson Dr	22307
Clermont Ave	22304
Clermont Dr	22310
Cleveland St	22302
Cliff Dr	22315
E Cliff St	22301
N Cliff St	22301
Clifford Ave	22305
Clifton Dr	22308
Clifton St	22312
Clifton Farm Ct	22306
Clifton Knoll Ct	22315
Climbhill Rd	22310
Clinton Rd	22312
Clonmel Ct	22315
Cloudes Mill Ct, Dr & Way	22304
Clouds Mill Dr	22310
Clovercrest Dr	22314
Clovergrass Dr	22310
Cloverway Dr	22314
Clyde Ave	22301
Coachleigh Way	22315
Cobblestone Ct	22306
Cobbs Rd	22310
Cobbs Creek Ct	22310
Cockrell St	22304
Cockspur Dr	22310
Cold Spring Ct, Ln & Pl	22306
Coldbrooke Ct	22306
Colebrook Pl	22312
Colecroft Ct	22314
Colette Dr	22315
Colfax Ave	22311
Colgate Dr	22307
Collard St	22306
Colliers Ln	22312
Colling Ridge Ct	22308
Collingwood Ct & Rd	22308
Collins Meade Way	22315
Colonel Ellis Ave	22304
Colonel Johnson Ln	22304
Colonial Ave	
1000-1299	22314
3700-4299	22309
Colonial Springs Blvd & Ct	22306
Colonial Woods Dr	22308
Colony Ct	22309
Columbia Dr	22307
Columbia Rd	22302
N & S Columbus St	22314
Colville Dr	22304
Colvin St	22314
Comay Ter	22304
Commerce St	22314
Commonwealth Ave	
2-2599	22301
2600-3600	22305
3602-3898	22305
Concord Pl	22308
Condit Ct	22302
Condor Ct	22306
Congressional Ct	22309
Conover Pl	22308
Conoy St	22301
Conrad Rd	22312
Continental Dr	22309
Convair Dr	22306
Cook St	
432B-432C	22314
400-499	22314
3900-3999	22311
Cool Brooke Way	22306
Cool Spring Dr	22308
Cool Valley Ct	22310
Cooper Rd & St	22309
Coral Ln	22309
Corcoran St	22309
Cornell Dr	22307
Cornish Way	22315
Cornith Dr	22306
Cornwallis Ct	22309
Coryell Ln	22302
Cotswold Ct	22308
Cottingham Pl	22304
Cottonwood Dr & Pl	22310
Courthouse Sq	22314
Courtland Cir	22305
Courtland Rd	22306
Courtney Ave	22304
Coventry Ln	22304
Coventry Rd	22306
Coverdale Way	22310
Cowling Ct	22304
Coxton Ct	22306
Cozy Glen Ct & Ln	22312
Craft Rd	22310
Craig Ave	22309
Crane Pl	22306
Crater Pl	22312
Crawford Ct	22315
Credos Ct	22309
Creek Dr	22308
Creek Point Way	22315
Crescent Dr	22302
Crest St	22302
Crestleigh Cir & Way	22315
Crestwood Dr	
500-1799	22302
6200-6399	22312
Crocus Ct	22310
Cromarty Dr	22315
Cromley Aly	22314
Cromwell Pl	22315
Cross Dr	22302
Cross Gate Ln	22315
Crossley Pl	22308
Croton Dr	22308
Crow Ct	22306
Crowley Pl	22308
Crown Pl	22308
Crown Court Rd	22308
Crown Royal Cir & Dr	22310
Crown View Dr	22314
Culpeper Rd	22308
Culver Pl	22308
Cunningham Dr	22309
Curtier Dr	22310
Curtis Ave	22309
Cushman Pl	22308
E Custis Ave	22301
W Custis Ave	22301
Custis St	22308
Cygnet Dr	22307
Cypress Point Rd	22312
Cyrus Pl	22308
Dade Ln	22308
Dadson Ct	22310
Dahill Pl	22312
Daingerfield Rd	22314
Daisy St	22306
Dakota Ct	22312
Dale St	22305
Dalebrook Dr	22308
Dandridge Ter	22309
Danewood Dr	22308
Dannys Ln & Pl	22311
Danton Ln	22308
Daphne Ln	22306
Darby Towne Ct	22315
Darden Row	22315
Dare Ct	22308
Darleon Pl	22310
Dartmoor Ln	22310
Dartmouth Ct	22314
Dartmouth Dr	22307
Dartmouth Rd	22314
Darton Dr	22308
Davenport St	22306
David Ln	22311
Davis Ave	22302
Davis St	22306
Dawes Ave	22311
Dawn Dr	22306
Day Ln	22314
Daybreak Ct	22306
Deane Ct	22312
Deanery Dr	22304
Dearborn Pl	22304
N Dearing St	22302
Declaration Sq	22312
Deer Gap Ct	22310
Deer Run Ct & Dr	22306
Del Norte Ct	22309
E & W Del Ray Ave	22301
Delafield Pl	22306
Delia Dr	22310
Deming Ave	22312
Denfield Dr	22309
Densmore Ct	22309
Derby Ct	22311
Derek Rd	22306
Derrell Ct	22307
Derth Ct	22315
Derwood Ln	22309
Desiree Ct & St	22315
Devereux Ct	22315
Devereux Circle Dr	22315
Devon Pl	22314
Devonshire Rd	22307
Dew Grass Dr	22310
Dewey Dr	22310
Dewitt Ave	22301
Dewolfe Dr	22308
Diablo Ct	22309
Diagonal Rd	22314
Diamond Ave	22301
Diana Ln	22310
Digby Grn	22315
Dijohn Court Dr	22315
Doctor Craik Ct	22306
Doeg Indian Ct	22309
Dogue Ct & Dr	22309
Dogue Forest Ct	22315
Dogwood Dr	22302
Dolphin Ln	22309
Domain Pl	22311
Dominion Mill Dr	22304
Dona Ave	22303
Donegan Ct	22315
Donelson St	22309
N Donelson St	22304
Donival Sq	22315
Donora Dr	22306
Donovan Dr	22304
Doris Dr & Pl	22311
Dorothy Bolton Ct	22310
Dorothy Giles Ct	22315
Dorset Dr	
5500-5599	22311
6300-6699	22310
Doter Dr	22308
Douglas St	22306
Dove Dr	
5900-5999	22310
7700-7899	22306
S Dove St	22314
Dover Ct	22312
Dover Pl	22311
Doyle Dr	22308
Drake Ct	22311
Dreams Way Ct	22315
Dresden Ct	22308
Drews Ct	22309
Driftwood Dr	22310
Drury Ln	22307
Dubin Dr	22310
Dubois St	22310
Duddington Dr	22315
Duffield Ln	22307
Duke Dr	22307
Duke St	
1300A-1300D	22314
4241A-4241D	22304
4251A-4251D	22304
4311A-4311D	22304
4321A-4321D	22304
1-3399	22314
3400-6099	22304
6200-6299	22312
Dulany St	22314
Dumas St	22306
Dunbar St	22306
E Duncan Ave	22301
Dungeness Ln	22315
Dunman Way	22315
Dunnington Pl	22315
Dunsmore Rd	22315
Dunstable Ln	22315
Dunster Ct	22311
Dunwich Way	22315
Dupree Ct	22303
Duvall Parish Ln	22315
Duvawn St	22310
Duxbury Pl	22308
Eagle Ave	22306
Eagle Ridge Ln	22312
Eaglebrook Ct	22308
Earl St	22314
Earldale Ct	22306
Earlston Ct & Dr	22315
N Early St	
2-16	22304
18-199	22304
2100-2399	22302
S Early St	22304

East Dr 22303
Eastchester Cir 22310
Eastgate Ln 22315
Eaton Pl 22310
Echols Ave 22311
Eddington Ter 22302
Eden Ct 22308
Edge Cliff Dr 22315
Edgehill Ct 22303
Edgehill Dr
1800-1899 22307
2900-3199 22302
5800-5941 22303
Edgemont Dr 22310
Edgemoor Ln 22312
Edgeware Ln 22315
Edgewood Dr 22310
Edgewood Ln 22310
Edgewood Ter 22307
Edison Dr 22310
Edison St 22305
Edsall Rd
5600-6199 22304
6200-6500 22312
6502-6598 22312
Edsall Ridge Pl 22312
Edward Gibbs Pl 22309
Edwards St 22312
Effingham Sq 22315
Eighth Cir & St 22312
Eisenhower Ave
5380LL-5380LL 22304
1500-1698 22314
1700-2460 22314
2461-2461 22331
2462-3498 22314
2463-3499 22314
3600-5700 22304
5702-5798 22304
El Camino Pl 22309
El Cerrito Pl 22309
El Soneta Pl 22309
Elaine Ct 22308
Elati Ct 22310
Elba Ct & Rd 22306
Elbert Ave 22305
Elbetee Ln 22312
Eldon Dr 22302
Eleanor Ct 22303
Eliot Ct 22311
Elizabeth Ln 22314
Elk Park Ct 22310
Elkin St 22308
Ellerali Ave 22305
Ellesmere Ct 22315
Ellicott St 22304
Ellingham Cir 22315
Ellsworth St 22314
Elm Dr 22306
Elm St 22301
Elmdale Rd 22312
Elmore Dr 22302
Elmwood Dr
3000-4099 22303
4200-4599 22310
Elmwood Towne Way 22303
Elton Way 22315
Em St 22310
Embry Spring Ln 22315
Emerald Dr 22308
Emerson Aly & Ave 22314
Emmett Dr 22307
Emory St 22312
Empress Ct 22308
Enderby Dr 22302
Enfield Dr 22310
Engleside St 22309
Engleside Office Park 22309
English Ter 22304
Enid Pl 22312
Ericka Ave 22310
Essex Ct 22311
Essex House Sq 22310
Essex Manor Ct & Pl 22308
Estates Dr 22310
Eton Ct 22312

Eubank St 22309
Eugene Pl 22308
Euille St 22314
Eureka Ct 22309
Evangeline Ln 22312
Evans Ln 22305
Evening Ln 22306
Everglades Dr 22312
Evergreen Farm Pl 22306
Evergreen Knoll Ct 22303
Ewing Pl 22310
Executive Ave 22305
Exeter Ct 22311
Eyler Dr 22315
Fairbanks Ave 22311
Fairchild Dr 22306
Fairfax Pkwy 22312
Fairfax Rd 22308
Fairfax St 22309
N Fairfax St 22314
S Fairfax St 22314
Fairfax Ter 22303
Fairfield Ct 22306
Fairfield Pl 22310
Fairglen Dr 22309
Fairhaven Ave 22303
Fairland St 22312
Fairview Ct 22311
Fairview Dr 22306
Fairview Ter 22303
Fairway Downs Ct 22312
Faith Ct 22311
Falkstone Ln 22309
Fallen Tree Ct 22310
Falster Ct & Rd 22308
Fannon St 22301
Farland Ct 22315
Farm Rd 22302
Farmington Dr 22303
Farmwood Ct 22315
Farnsworth Dr 22303
Farrington Ave
2100-2399 22303
5800-6299 22304
N & S Fayette St 22314
Featherstone Pl 22304
Felton Ln 22308
Fendall Ave 22304
Fenimore Pl 22309
Fenton Ct 22312
Fenwick Dr 22303
Ferdinand Day Dr 22304
Fern St 22302
Fernlake Ct 22309
Ferry Hall Ct 22309
Ferry Harbour Ct 22309
Ferry Landing Ct & Rd 22309
Fieldhurst Ct 22315
Fielding St 22309
Fifer Dr 22303
Fifth St 22312
Fillmore Ave 22311
Finch Ct 22306
Finley Ln 22304
Fircrest Pl 22308
First St
200-1299 22314
6400-6499 22312
First Statesman Ln 22312
Fiske Pl 22312
Fitzgerald Ln 22302
Fitzhugh Way 22314
Fitzroy St 22309
Flagstone Ter 22306
Flamingo Dr 22306
Flat Rock Rd 22310
Flaxton Pl 22303
Fleet Dr 22310
Fleetside Ct 22310
Fleetwood Ct 22308
Fleming St 22306
Flintstone Rd 22306
Florence Dr 22305
Florence Ln 22310
Flower Ln 22310
N & S Floyd St 22304

Fogle St 22310
Foldi St 22310
Foley St 22303
Fontaine St 22302
Forbush Ct 22310
Ford Ave 22302
Fordham Dr 22307
Fordham Rd 22302
Fords Landing Way 22314
Fordson Ct & Rd 22306
Forest Ave 22310
Forest Dr 22302
Forest Haven Dr 22309
Foresthill Rd 22307
Forrest St 22305
Forrestal Ave 22311
Fort Dr
2000-2099 22307
2300-2899 22303
Fort Ellsworth Ct 22310
Fort Farnsworth Rd 22303
Fort Hill Dr 22310
Fort Hunt Ct 22307
Fort Hunt Rd
6000-7599 22307
7600-8999 22308
Fort Ward Pl 22304
Fort Willard Cir 22307
Fort Williams Pkwy 22304
Fort Worth Ave & Pl 22304
Foster Ave 22311
Founders Crossing Ct 22310
Founders Hill Ct & Dr 22310
Foundry Way 22314
Four Mile Rd 22305
Four Seasons Ct 22309
Fourth St 22312
Fox Haven Ln 22304
Foxboro Ct 22315
Foxcroft Rd 22307
Foxleigh Way 22315
Fran Pl 22312
Frances Dr 22306
Francis Ct 22314
Francis Hammond
Pkwy 22302
Franconia Rd 22310
Franconia Commons Ct
& Dr 22310
Franconia Forest Ct &
Ln 22310
Franconia Station Ct &
Ln 22310
Franklin Ct 22302
Franklin St
1-1299 22314
2800-3199 22306
Frazier St 22304
Freeport Ave 22315
N & S French St 22304
Frenchmens Dr 22312
Freshwood Ct 22315
Fresno Ln 22309
Friars Ct 22306
N Frost St 22304
Frost Lake Ln 22315
Frye Rd 22309
Fucci Ct 22304
Fuerte Ct 22309
Fuller Ct 22310
Fulton St 22305
Furman Ln 22306
N Furman St 22304
Gadsby Pl 22311
Gadsby Sq 22315
Gage Rd 22309
Gahant Rd 22308
N Gaillard St 22304
Galen St 22309
Gallahan Ct 22309
Garden Dr 22304
Gardenia Ct 22310
Gardner Dr 22304
N Garland St 22304
Garnett Dr 22311
Gary Ave & Pl 22311

Gates St 22303
Gateshead Rd 22309
Gatewood Ct & Dr 22307
Gatton Sq 22315
Gayfields Rd 22315
Gene St 22315
General Green Way 22312
General Washington
Dr 22312
Gentele Ct 22310
Gentle Ct & Ln 22310
Gentry Ave 22305
S George Mason Dr 22302
George Mason Pl 22305
Gibbon St 22314
Gibbs St 22309
Gifford Ct 22315
Gila Ct 22309
Gildar St 22310
Gilden Dr 22305
Gillingham Row 22315
Ginger Dr 22312
Gingham Ct 22310
Gladden Ct 22303
N Gladden St 22304
Gladstone Pl 22308
Gladys May Ln 22310
Glamis Dr 22315
Glasgow Rd 22307
Glassell Ct 22310
Gleaves Ct 22309
E & W Glebe Rd 22305
Glen Dr 22307
Glen Cove Ct 22308
Glen Green Ct 22315
E Glendale Ave 22301
W Glendale Ave 22301
Glendale Ter 22303
Glenmullen Pl 22303
Glenshire Row 22315
Glenview Ct 22312
Glenwood Ct & Dr 22310
Glenwood Mews Ct &
Dr 22315
Gloucester Rd 22312
Glyn St 22309
Goddard Way 22304
Godfrey Ave 22309
Goldenrod Ct & Dr 22310
Golf Course Sq 22307
Good Lion Ct 22315
Gooden Way 22308
Gopost
105-105 22301
Gopost
214-214 22302
304-304 22303
307-307 22303
405-405 22304
616-622 22306
1403-1403 22314
1406-1406 22314
1417-1417 22304
1419-1419 22314
1507-1507 22315
N & S Gordon St 22304
Gorgas Pl 22311
Gourock Ct 22315
Governors Ct 22308
Governors Crest Ct 22310
Governors Hill Dr 22310
Governors Pond Cir 22310
Governors View Ln 22310
Grackle Ct 22306
Grafton St 22312
Gramercy Cir 22309
Granada St 22309
Grand Pavilion Way 22303
Grand View Dr 22305
Grange Ln 22315
Grassymeade Ln 22308
Gravel Ave 22310
Graves St 22309
Gray Heights Ct 22315
N Grayson St 22304
Great Lakes St 22306

Great Neck Ct 22309
Great Swan Ct 22306
Green St 22314
Green Glade Ct 22315
Green Glen Ct & Ln 22315
Green Meadow Ct 22310
Green Spring Ln 22306
Green Spring Rd 22312
Greendale Rd 22310
Greenhaven Pl 22310
Greenleaf St 22309
Greenleigh Ln 22315
N & S Greenmount Dr 22311
Greenway Pl 22302
Greenway Rd 22308
Greenwood Pl 22304
Gregory Dr 22309
Greshem Pl 22305
Greta Ct 22309
Gretna Green Ct 22304
Gretna Green Way 22312
Gretter Pl 22311
Grey Goose Way 22306
Greyledge Ct 22310
Greylock St 22308
Greystone Pl 22309
Griffin Dr 22307
Griffith Pl 22304
Grigsby St 22311
Grimm Dr 22304
Grimsley St 22309
Grist Mill Rd 22309
Grist Mill Woods Ct &
Way 22309
Groombridge Way 22309
Grove Dr 22307
Grove Rd 22306
Grovedale Ct & Dr 22310
Grovehurst Pl 22310
Grovenor Ct 22315
Groves Ave 22305
Groveton St 22306
Groveton Gardens Rd 22306
Grumman Pl 22306
Guest Ln 22312
Guilford Dr 22310
Gulf Hill Ct 22315
Gum St 22310
Gum Springs Village
Dr 22306
Gunston Rd 22302
Guthrie Ave 22305
Gwyn Pl 22312
Gypsy Ct 22310
H St 22307
Habersham Way 22310
Hackamore Ln 22308
Hadrian Ct 22310
Halcyon Dr 22305
Halfe St 22309
Hall Pl 22302
Halley Farm Ct 22309
Hallie Rose Pl & St 22309
Haltwhistle Ln 22315
Halwis St 22303
Hamilton Ln 22308
Hammond St 22309
Hammonds Ct 22314
Hampton Ct 22306
N Hampton Dr
2400-3099 22311
3100-3101 22302
Hampton Rd 22306
Hancock Ave 22301
Hanrahan Pl 22309
Hanson Ln 22302
Harbin Dr 22310
Harbor Ter 22308
Harbor Court Dr 22315
Hard Rock Ct 22306
Hardbower Way 22303
Hardee Pl 22304
Harding Ave 22311
Hare Ct 22304
Harold Secord St 22304
Harrington Falls Ln 22312

Harris Pl 22304
Harrison Cir 22304
Harrison Ln 22306
Hartshorne Sq 22315
Harvard Dr 22307
Harvard St 22314
Harvey Ln 22312
Harvey Pl 22303
Harwich Ct 22311
Hatcher St 22303
Hatherleigh Ct 22315
Hatton Ct 22311
Havenwood Pl 22309
Hawaii Ct 22312
Hawk View Ct & Ln 22312
Hawkins Way 22314
Hawthorne Ave 22311
Hayes St 22302
Hayfield Pl 22310
Hayfield Rd 22315
Haynes Point Way 22315
Haystack Rd 22310
Hazeltine Ct 22312
Hearthstone Mews 22314
Heather Ct 22310
Heather Glen Dr 22309
Heatherfield Ln 22315
Heatherington Pl 22315
Heatherway Ct 22315
Heatherwood Ct & Dr 22310
Helen St 22305
Helen Winter Ter 22312
Helmsdale Ln 22315
Helmuth Ln 22304
Hemlock Ave 22305
N & S Henry St 22314
Henshaw Pl 22311
Hensley Ct 22308
Herbert St 22305
Herbert Springs Rd 22308
Hereford Ct 22315
Heritage Ln 22311
Heritage Hill Ct & Dr 22310
Heritage Springs Ct 22306
Hermitage Ct 22302
Hershey Ln 22312
Hickman Ter 22315
Hickory St 22305
Hiddenite Ct 22310
High St 22302
High Meadow Rd 22310
High Valley Ln 22315
Higham Dr 22310
Highdale Cir 22310
Highgate Rd 22308
Highland Dr 22310
Highland Ln 22309
Highland Pl 22301
Highland Green Ct 22312
Highland Meadows Ct 22315
N & S Highview Ln 22311
Hill Ct 22303
Hillary Ct & St 22315
Hillcrest Pl 22312
Hilldale Dr 22310
Hillside Ct 22306
Hillside Ln 22306
Hillside Ter 22302
Hilltop Ter 22301
Hillvale Pl 22307
Hillview Ave & Ct 22310
Hilton St 22314
Hinson Farm Rd 22306
Hitching Post Ln 22308
Hocking Pl 22309
Hoffman I 22331
Hoffman Ii 22332
Holiday Dr 22308
Holland Ct 22306
Holland Ln 22314
Holland Rd 22306
Hollindale Ct & Dr 22306
Hollinwood Dr 22307
Hollis Aly 22314
Holly St 22305
Holly Hill Rd 22306

Holly Tree Dr 22310
Hollyford Ln 22315
Holmes Ln 22302
Holmes Run Pkwy
4500-5599 22304
6200-6299 22311
Hooffs Run Dr 22314
Hoover Ln 22308
Hopa Ct 22306
Hopark Dr 22310
Hopkins Ct 22314
Houndsbury Ct 22315
Houston Ct 22310
N Howard St 22304
E & W Howell Ave 22301
Howells Rd 22310
S Hudson St 22304
Huerta Ct 22309
Huffman Pl 22306
Hulvey Ter 22306
Hume Ave 22301
Hunter Creek Ln 22315
Hunter Murphy Cir 22309
Hunting Cove Pl 22307
Hunting Creek Ct 22303
Hunting Creek Dr 22314
Hunting Creek Ln 22303
Hunting Creek Rd 22303
Huntington Ave 22303
Huntington Grove Sq 22306
Huntington Park Dr 22303
Huntington Station Ct 22303
Huntley Creek Pl 22306
Huntley Manor Ln 22306
Huntley Meadows Ln 22306
Huntley Run Pl 22306
Huntly Pl 22307
Hunton Pl 22311
Huron Pl 22310
Hyacinth Dr 22310
Hydrangea Dr 22310
Hyman Way 22309
I St 22307
Ians Way 22315
Ice House Rd 22314
N Imboden St 22304
Imperial St 22309
Independence Cir &
Way 22312
Indian Ct & Dr 22303
Indian Run Pkwy 22312
Indian Trail Ct 22310
Ingalls Ave 22302
Ingemar Ct 22308
Ingersol Rd 22309
Ingle Pl 22304
Ingram Pl 22308
S Ingram St 22304
Inter Parcel Rd 22315
Interlachen Ct 22312
Inyo Ct 22309
Iona Way 22312
Ireland St 22306
S Iris St 22304
Iron Willow Ct 22310
Irvin Ct, Pl & Sq 22312
Irving Ct 22314
Irwell Ln 22315
Island Creek Ct 22315
Ivanhoe Ct 22304
Ivanhoe Ln 22310
Ivanhoe Pl 22304
N Ivanhoe St 22304
N Iverson St 22304
Ivor Ln 22304
Ivy Cir 22302
Jackies Ln 22306
Jackson Pl
400-499 22302
4200-4499 22309
Jackson Rd 22308
Jacobsen Pl 22303
Jake Pl 22309
Jamaica Dr 22303
James Dr 22303
James Franklin Ct 22309

James Gunnell Ln 22310
Jamestown Ln 22314
Jamestown Rd 22308
Jamieson Ave 22314
Jane Way 22310
Janelle St 22303
Janna Lee Ave
7900-7999 22306
8000-8199 22309
Janneys Ln 22302
Jason Ave 22302
Jasper Pl 22304
Javins Dr 22310
Jay Ave 22302
Jean Louise Way 22310
Jefferson Ct 22314
Jefferson Dr 22303
Jefferson St 22314
Jefferson Davis Hwy
1800-2899 22301
2900-3999 22305
S Jenkins St 22304
Jepson Pl 22309
Jesmond St 22315
Jewel St 22312
Jewell Ct 22312
Jinetes Ct 22309
Joanne Dr 22312
John Carlyle St 22314
John Roccato Ct 22310
John Thomas Dr 22315
John Ticer Dr 22304
Johnston Pl 22301
Joliette Ct 22307
Jon Paul Dr 22306
Jones Pt 22314
N & S Jordan Ct & St 22304
Joseph Edgar Ct 22310
Joseph Makell Ct 22306
Joshua Pl 22309
Joust Ln 22315
Jowett Ct 22315
Joyce Rd 22310
Jube Ct 22307
Judith Ave 22315
Julep Dr 22306
Juliana Pl 22304
Juneberry Ct 22310
Junior St 22301
Juniper Pl 22304
Jupiter Hills Cir 22312
Justin Rd 22309
Justis Pl 22310
Kahn Pl 22314
Kane Ct 22308
Karl Rd 22308
Katelyn Ct 22310
Katelyn Mary Pl 22310
Kathmoor Dr 22310
Kathryn St 22303
Kearney Ct 22311
Keates St 22303
Keble Dr 22315
Keeler Ct & St 22309
Keiths Ln 22314
Kell Ln 22311
Keller Ave 22302
Kelley Ct 22312
Kelsey Point Cir 22315
Kemp Ct 22311
Kemper St 22309
N Kemper St 22304
Kemper Lakes Ct 22312
Kendall Pl 22303
Kenley Ct 22308
Kenmore Ave 22304
Kennedy St 22305
Kent Pl 22305
Kent Rd 22308
Kentucky Ave 22305
Kenwood Ave 22302
Kenyon Dr 22307
Keota St 22303
Kerrybrooke Dr 22310
Kestner Cir 22315
Kestrel Crossing Dr 22312

Keswick Rd 22309
Key Dr 22302
Keyser Way 22310
Kidd St 22309
Kiernan Ct 22315
Kilburn St 22304
Kilt Ct 22308
Kimberly Anne Way 22310
Kimbrelee Ct 22309
Kimbro St 22307
Kincardine Ct 22315
King St
4656B1-4656B10 22302
1-1899 22314
1900-2699 22301
2700-4800 22302
4802-4898 22302
King Centre Dr 22315
King Duncan Rd 22312
King Henry Ct 22314
King James Dr 22310
King James Pl 22304
King Louis Dr 22312
Kingfisher Ln 22312
Kingham Ct 22310
Kingland Rd 22306
Kings Ct 22302
N Kings Hwy 22303
S Kings Hwy
6300-6899 22306
6901-6937 22310
6939-6949 22310
6951-6999 22310
Kings Arm Dr 22308
Kings Cloister Cir 22302
Kings Cross Rd 22303
Kings Hill Ct 22309
Kings Landing Rd 22310
Kings Manor Dr 22315
Kings Station Ct 22306
Kings Village Rd 22306
Kingsbury Rd 22315
Kingsgate Ct 22302
Kingston Ave & Pl 22302
Kingstowne Blvd & Ctr 22315
Kingstowne Commons
Dr 22315
Kingstowne Towne Ctr 22315
Kingstowne Village
Pkwy 22315
Kinsey Ln 22311
Kirchner Ct 22304
Kirk Pl 22312
Kirkcaldy Ln 22315
Kirke Ct 22304
Kirkland Pl 22311
Kirkpatrick Ln 22311
Kirkside Dr 22306
Kling Dr 22312
Knapp Pl 22304
Knickerbocker Dr 22310
Knight Pl 22311
Knights Ridge Way 22310
Knole Ct 22311
Knox Pl 22304
Komes Ct 22306
La Faye Ct 22306
La Grande Ave 22301
La Ronde Ct 22307
La Salle Ave 22304
La Vista Dr 22310
Lachine Ln 22312
Ladson Ln 22306
Lady Anne Ct 22310
Lafayette Dr 22308
Lafitte Ct 22312
Laguna Ct 22309
Lake Cook Dr 22304
Lake Cove Ct & Dr 22315
Lake Village Dr 22315
Lakepark Dr 22309
Laker Ln 22310
Lakeshire Dr 22308
Lakota Rd 22303
Lambert Dr & Pl 22311
Lamberts Ln 22309

Lamond Pl 22314
Lamoyne Ct 22315
Lamp Post Ln 22306
Landess St 22312
Landover St 22305
Lands End Ln 22315
Landsdowne Ctr 22315
Lane Dr
5800-5899 22310
6000-6099 22304
Langleigh Way 22315
N Langley St 22304
Langton Dr 22310
Lannon Ct 22304
Lantern Pl 22306
Laramie Pl 22309
Larchmont Ave 22302
Lark Ln 22310
Larkspur Dr 22310
Larno Dr 22310
Larochelle Ct & Dr 22315
Larpin Ln 22310
Larrup Ct 22315
Larstan Dr 22312
Lassen Ct 22312
N Latham St 22304
Latour Ct 22315
Latrobe Pl 22311
Laura Mews Pl 22303
Laurel Rd 22309
Lauriefrost Ct 22309
Lavenham Lndg 22315
Laverne Ave 22305
Lavinus Ln 22315
Lawrence Ave 22304
Lawrence St 22309
Lawsons Hill Ct & Pl 22310
Lawton Way 22311
Layne Estates Ct 22310
Lea Ln 22309
Leadbeater St 22305
Leaf Rd 22309
Lebanon Rd 22310
Lee Ave 22308
E Lee Ave 22306
Lee Cir 22305
Lee Ct
200-299 22314
3500-3599 22302
N Lee St 22314
S Lee St 22314
Leesburg Ct & Pike 22302
Leeward Ln 22315
Leewood Dr 22310
Leisure Ct 22310
Leith Pl 22307
Lemon Thyme Dr 22310
Lenclair St 22306
Lenore Ln 22303
Lensfield Ct 22315
Leo Ln 22308
Leric Ln 22306
Lerwick Ct 22315
Les Dorson Ln 22315
Leslie Ave 22301
Lester Ct 22311
Leverett Ct 22311
Levtov Lndg 22312
Lewin Dr 22310
Liberty Dr 22303
Liberty Springs Cir 22306
Lichen Ct 22306
Lida Ct 22306
Lilac Ln 22308
Lillian Dr 22310
Lincoln Ave 22312
Lincolnia Rd 22312
Lindberg Dr 22306
E & W Linden St 22301
Lindsay Pl 22304
Linleigh Way 22315
Linmar Ct 22312
Linnean St 22303
Linton Ln 22308
Lisbon Ln 22306
Little St 22301

Little Creek Ln 22309
Little Hunting Creek
Dr 22309
Little Potters Ln 22310
Little River Tpke 22312
Little Valley Way 22310
Littlethorpe Ln 22315
Livermore Ln 22304
Liverpool Ct & Ln 22315
Lloyds Ln 22302
Lochleigh Ct 22315
Lockheed Blvd 22306
Locust Ln
200-299 22302
3800-3999 22310
Locust Leaf Ln 22315
Locust Tree Ln 22312
Lodestone Ct 22306
Lofthill Ct 22303
Lofty Oak Pl 22309
Logan Ct 22310
Lomack Ct 22312
Lombardy Ln 22308
Londonderry Rd 22308
Longfields Ln 22309
Longstreet Ln 22311
Longview Dr 22314
Longworthe Sq 22309
Lookout Ct 22306
Loraine Ave 22308
Lory Ct 22306
Louis Pl 22304
Lowell Ave 22312
Loyola Ave 22304
Lucia Ln 22308
Ludgate Dr 22309
Ludwood Ct 22306
Lukens Ln 22309
Luna Park Dr 22305
Lund Ct 22315
E & W Luray Ave 22301
Luton Pl 22315
Lyles Ln 22314
Lyndale Dr 22308
Lynhaven Dr 22305
Lynley Ter 22310
Lynn Ct 22302
Lynnfield Dr 22306
Lynnhall Pl 22309
Lyons Ln 22302
Macadams Pl 22308
Macarthur Rd 22305
Mack St 22308
Macklin Ct 22309
Madge Ln 22309
Madison Pl & St 22314
Madison Hill Ct 22310
Magnolia Ln 22311
Magnolia Manor Way 22312
Maid Marian Ct 22306
Main St 22309
Main Line Blvd 22301
Major Ct & St 22312
Malcolm Pl 22302
Mallaral Dr 22307
Mallinson Way 22308
Mallory Cir & Ln 22315
Malone Ridge St 22312
Malvern Ct 22304
Manchester Blvd 22310
Manchester Lakes Dr 22310
Manchester Park Cir 22310
Mangum Pl 22308
Manhasset Ln 22312
Manigold Ct 22315
Manitoba Dr 22312
Manning St 22305
Manor Dr 22309
Manor Rd 22305
Manorhaven Ct 22306
Manorview Way 22315
N Mansfield St 22304
Mansion Dr 22302
Mansion Farm Pl 22309
Manzanita Pl 22309

E Maple St
1-199 22301
2600-2699 22306
W Maple St 22301
Maple Hill Pl 22302
Maple Tree Ct 22304
Maplefield Pl 22310
Maplewood Pl 22302
Marble Arch Way 22315
Marble Dale Ct 22308
E & W Marcia Ct 22309
Marcy Ct 22310
Margay Ct 22309
Marilyn Dr 22310
Marina Dr 22314
Marine Dr 22307
Mariners Mill Ct 22315
Marionet St 22312
Mariposa Pl 22309
Maris Ave 22304
Marjoram Ct 22310
Mark Dr 22305
Mark Center Dr 22311
Markham Grant Ln 22315
Marl Pat Dr 22310
Marlan Dr 22307
Marlboro Dr 22304
Marshall Ln 22302
Marsham Ct 22315
Martha St 22309
Martha Custis Dr 22302
Martha Washington St 22309
Marthas Rd 22307
Martin Ln 22304
Martin St 22312
Martin Allen Ct 22315
Martinique Ln 22315
Mary Baldwin Dr 22307
Mary Beth Way 22315
Mary Caroline Cir 22310
Mary Evelyn Way 22309
Mary Meindl Ct 22312
Maryland St 22309
Maryview St 22310
Masefield Ct 22304
Maskell St 22301
E & W Mason Ave 22301
Mason Grove Ct 22306
Mason Hill Dr
1600-2099 22307
2100-2199 22306
Masondale Rd 22315
E & W Masonic View
Ave 22301
Massey Ct 22303
Massey Ln 22314
Masters Ct 22308
Maury Ln 22304
Maury Pl 22309
Mavis Ct 22309
Maxine Ct 22310
May Blvd 22310
Mayapple Pl 22312
Maybrook Ct & Pl 22309
Mayer Pl 22302
Mayfair Ct & Ln 22310
Mayflower Ct 22312
Mayhunt Ct 22312
Mayor Pl 22310
Mcclelland Pl 22309
Mcgeorge Ter 22309
Mcguin Dr 22310
Mckenna Way 22315
Mckenzie Ave 22301
Mclendon Ct 22310
Mcnair Ct & Dr 22309
Meadow Rose Ct 22310
Meadowleigh Way 22315
Meadows Ln 22304
Medallion Ct 22303
Medinah Ln 22312
Medlock Ln 22304
Meeting House Way 22312
Melon St 22309
Melrose St 22302
Melvern Pl 22312

Memorial St
2600-3499 22306
3500-3599 22310
Memorial Heights Dr 22306
Memphis St 22303
Menard Ct 22309
Menniefield Ct 22306
Menokin Dr 22302
Mercedes Ct 22308
Merle Pl 22312
Merritt Ct & Rd 22312
Mersey Oaks Way 22315
Merton Ct 22311
Mesa Way 22312
Metro Rd 22304
Metro Park Dr 22310
Metroview Pkwy 22303
Michigan Ave & Ct 22314
Midday Ln 22306
Middlebury Dr 22307
Midered Dr 22302
Midtown Ave 22303
Midwood St 22308
Milan Dr 22305
Mill Rd 22314
Mill Towns Ct 22309
Millbrook Pl 22309
Millburn Ct 22309
Miller Dr 22315
Miller Ln 22314
Milton St 22303
Milway Dr 22306
Mina Loma Ct 22309
Minda Ct 22304
Minor Cir 22312
Minor Pl 22312
Minor St 22302
Mint Pl 22306
Miramonte Pl 22309
Mission Ct 22310
Mission Ln 22304
Mitchell St 22312
Mittendorff Ln 22315
Mohawk Ln 22309
Monacan St 22314
Moncure Dr 22314
E & W Monroe Ave 22301
Monte Vista Pl 22309
Montell Dr 22310
Montgomery Pl & St 22314
Monticello Ave 22308
Monticello Blvd 22305
Monticello Rd 22303
Montrose Ave 22305
Montrose St 22312
Moody Ct 22312
Moon St 22306
Moon Rock Ct 22306
Moore Pl 22305
Morey Ln 22308
N Morgan Ct & St 22312
Morin St 22312
Morning Brook Ter 22315
Morning Glen Ct & Ln 22315
Morning Glory Rd 22310
Morning Meadow Ct &
Dr 22315
Morning Mist Ln 22312
Morning Ride Cir & Ct 22315
Morning View Ct & Ln 22315
Morningside Ln 22308
Mosby St 22305
Moss Pl 22304
Mount Pl 22305
Mount Eagle Dr 22303
Mount Eagle Pl 22302
E Mount Ida Ave 22301
W Mount Ida Ave 22305
Mount Vernon Ave
708A-708B 22301
3108A-3108B 22305
Mount Vernon Memorial
Hwy 22309
Mount Vernon Square
Ctr 22306
Mount Woodley Pl 22306

Mount Zephyr Dr & St 22309
Muir Pl 22312
Muirs Ct 22314
Mulberry Ct 22310
Mums Dr 22306
Munhall Ln 22310
Munstead Dr 22311
Murrys Ave 22301
Murtha St 22304
E & W Myrtle St 22301
Nagy Pl 22312
Nalls Rd 22309
Namassin Rd 22308
Nancy Hanks Ct 22312
Napper Rd 22306
Navaho Dr 22312
N Naylor Pl & St 22304
Neal Dr 22308
Nealon Pl 22312
Nedra Ave 22310
Needles Pl 22309
Neely Ann Ct 22310
Neitzey Pl 22309
Nellie Custis Ct 22309
E & W Nelson Ave 22301
Nemeth Ct 22306
Neptune Dr 22309
Netties Ln 22315
Neville Ct 22310
Nevitt Way 22315
New Market Rd 22308
New Orleans Dr 22308
New Valley Way 22310
Newcomb Pl 22304
Newton St 22301
Nice Pl 22310
Nicholson Ln 22302
Nicky Ln 22311
Nightwind Ct 22312
Ninian Ave & Ct 22310
Nob Hill Ct 22314
Noel St 22309
Nogales Ct 22309
Nomini Ln 22309
Noradenw Ct 22311
Noral Pl 22308
Nordok Pl 22306
Norfolk Ln 22314
Norham Dr 22315
Normandy Hill Dr 22304
Norris Pl 22305
Northdown Rd 22308
Northern Spruce Ln 22309
Northrop Rd 22306
Norton Ct 22314
Norton Rd 22303
Norwich Ter 22309
Norwood Dr 22309
Norwood Pl 22305
Notabene Dr 22305
Oak Dr 22306
E Oak St 22301
W Oak St 22301
Oak Hill Pl 22310
Oak Leaf Dr 22309
Oak Ridge Dr 22312
Oakbrooke Ave 22308
Oakcrest Dr 22302
Oaklake Ct 22309
Oakland Dr 22310
Oakland Ter 22302
Oaklawn Dr 22306
Oakley Pl 22302
Oakville St 22301
Oakwood Ln & Rd 22310
Oberlin Dr 22307
Observation Way 22312
Odessa Dr 22309
Old Brentford Ct & Rd 22310
Old Carriage Dr, Ln, Trl
& Way 22315
Old Coach Ct 22315
Old Colony Way 22309
Old Dominion Blvd 22305
Old Franconia Rd 22310
Old Mansion Rd 22309

Old Marsh Ln 22315
Old Mill Rd 22309
Old Mount Vernon Rd 22309
Old Parsonage Ct 22315
Old Quarry Ter 22306
Old Richmond Hwy 22303
Old Rolling Rd 22310
Old Stage Rd 22308
Old Stratford Ct 22315
Old Telegraph Rd
6000-6399 22310
7300-7800 22315
7802-7898 22315
Old Town Ct 22314
Old Valley Ct 22310
Old Vernon Ct 22309
Olde Mill Ct 22309
Olde Towne Ct & Rd 22307
Oldham Way 22315
Olmi Landrith Dr 22307
Olympic Way 22312
Oneill Ln 22304
Orange Ct 22309
Orchard St 22302
Ordsall St 22315
Oregano Ln 22310
Orinda Ct 22309
Oriole Ln 22306
Orlando Pl 22305
Orleans Pl 22304
Ormond Ave 22304
Oronoco St 22314
Orville St 22309
Osage St 22302
Osman Dr 22309
Osprey Point Ln 22315
Otley Dr 22310
Ousley Pl 22315
Oval Dr 22305
Overleigh Ln 22315
Overlook Dr 22312
N Overlook Dr 22305
S Overlook Dr 22305
Overly Dr 22310
N Owen St 22304
Oxbow Ct 22308
E Oxford Ave 22301
Oxpen Ct 22315
Pace Ln 22306
Page Ter 22302
Paldel Ave 22301
Palin Pl 22303
Palladium Ct 22315
Palmer Pl 22304
Pantano Pl 22309
Parenham Way 22310
Parish Glebe Ln 22315
Park Pl 22303
Park Rd
200-399 22301
4400-4699 22312
Park Ter 22310
Park Center Dr 22302
Park Terrace Dr 22307
Parker Gray School Way 22314
Parkers Ln 22306
Parkhill Dr 22312
Parkleigh Way 22315
Parkridge Ln 22310
Parkway Ter 22302
Parramore Dr 22312
Parrot Pl 22306
Parry Ln 22308
Parsley Dr 22310
Parsons Ct 22306
Pastando Dr 22303
Patent Parish Ln 22315
Patience Ct 22315
N & S Patrick St 22314
Patton Blvd 22309
Patuxent Knoll Pl 22312
Patuxent Vista Dr 22312
Paul St 22311
Paul Spring Pkwy 22308
Paul Spring Rd 22307
Paulonia Rd 22310
N Paxton St 22304
N & S Payne St 22314
Peaceful Ter 22303
Peach St 22302
Peachtree Pl 22304
Peacock Ave 22304
Peacock Pl 22306
Pear Tree Village Ct 22309
Pearson Ln 22304
Peartree Lndg 22309
Peele Pl 22304
N Pegram St 22304
N Pelham St 22304
Pelican Pl 22306
Pembrook Village Dr 22309
Pender Ct 22304
Pendleton St 22314
Penn Pl 22308
Pennsylvania Blvd 22308
Penwood Dr 22310
Percethony Ct 22315
Perch Pl 22309
Pete Jones Way 22314
Peverill Dr 22310
N & S Peyton St 22314
Pheasant Ct 22306
Phillips Dr 22306
Phlox Ct 22310
Phoenix Mill Pl 22304
Phyllis Ln 22312
Phylliss St 22309
Picardy Ct 22309
Pickering Pl 22309
Pickett St 22306
N Pickett St 22304
S Pickett St 22304
Picketts Ridge Way 22304
Pickwick Ln 22307
Picot Rd 22310
Pieco Ct 22315
Piedmont Dr 22310
Pierpont St 22302
Pike Ct & Rd 22310
Pike Branch Dr 22310
Pilgrim Ct 22308
Pima St 22312
Pine Ln 22312
Pine Rd 22312
Pine St 22305
Pine Brook Rd 22310
Pine Grove Cir 22303
Pine Stand Ln 22312
Pinecrest Office Park Dr 22312
Pinelake Ct 22309
Piney Run Dr 22315
Piney Woods Ct 22315
Pintail Ct 22306
Piper Ct & Ln 22306
Pipit Dr 22306
N & S Pitt Mews & St 22314
Plarint Dr 22312
Pleasant Point Ct 22315
Pleasure Cove Ct 22315
Plerri Rd 22308
Plymouth Rd 22308
Poag St 22303
Pocosin Ln 22304
Poinsettia Dr 22306
Pole Rd 22309
Polins Ct 22306
Polk Ave 22304
Pomegranate Ct 22309
Pommander Walk 22314
Pondside Ter 22309
Popkins Ln
2100-2299 22307
2300-3099 22306
Popkins Farm Rd 22306
Poplar Dr 22310
Porter Ln 22308
Portner Pl & Rd 22314
Potomac Ave
2000-2498 22301
6300-6699 22307
Potomac Ct 22314
Potomac Ln 22308
Potomac St 22314
Potomac Greens Dr 22314
Potters Ln 22310
Powatan Knoll Ct 22312
Powhatan St 22314
Poyntz Pl 22310
Pram Way 22309
Pratt Ct & St 22310
Preldenc Dr 22309
President Ford Ln 22302
Presidential Dr 22309
Preston Ave 22306
Preston Rd 22302
Price St 22301
Prices Ln 22308
Prince St 22314
Princess St 22314
Princeton Blvd 22314
Princeton Dr 22307
Priscilla Ln 22308
Prospect Pl 22304
Prospect Ter 22310
N Pryor St 22304
Pullman Pl 22305
Purks Ct 22309
Putnam Pl 22302
N Quaker Ln
1-599 22304
601-797 22302
799-1999 22302
S Quaker Ln
1-199 22314
5500-5699 22303
Quaker Hill Ct & Dr 22314
Quander Rd 22307
Quantrell Ave 22312
Quay St 22314
Queen St 22314
Queens Rd 22306
Queens Gate Ct 22303
Quincy St 22302
Quisenberry Dr 22309
Racepoint Way 22315
Rachael Whitney Ln 22315
Radcliff Rd 22307
Radcliffe Dr 22307
Radford Ave 22309
Radford St 22302
Raleigh Ave 22304
Ralston Way 22310
Rampart Ct & Dr 22308
Ramsey Aly 22314
Ramsey St 22301
Ramsgate Ct & Ter 22309
Randall Ct 22307
E Randolph Ave 22301
Randolph Macon Dr 22307
Range Rd 22306
Ransom Pl 22306
Rantred St 22314
Rapidan Ct 22304
Ravensworth Pl 22302
Rayburn Ave 22311
E Raymond Ave 22301
Reading Ave 22311
Rebecca Dr 22307
Rebecca Jane Way 22310
Rebel Ln 22312
Recard Ln 22307
Redcoat Dr 22303
Reddick Ave 22309
Redins Dr 22310
Redondo Pl 22309
Redwing Dr 22312
Redwood Ln 22310
E & W Reed Ave 22305
Reef Ct 22309
Regan St 22306
Regency Pl 22304
Regent Dr 22307
Reinekers Ln 22314
Remington Dr 22309
Renault Pl 22309
Renee St 22315
Republic Ct 22306
Reservoir Heights Ave 22311
Revere Dr 22308
S Reynolds St 22304
Rhoades Pl 22304
Richard Casey Ct 22307
Richards Ln 22302
Richenbacher Ave 22304
Richmarr Pl 22304
Richmond Ave 22309
Richmond Hwy
7706B1-7706B2 22306
7609B-1-7609B-4 22306
7611C-1-7611C-2 22306
6700-B-6700-B 22306
7849E-2-7849E-2 22306
7698A-7698B 22306
9000A-9000D 22309
5800-6299 22303
6300-8099 22306
8100-8899 22309
8901-9023 22309
6700-1-6700-10 22306
Richmond Ln 22305
Ricketts Walk 22312
Riddle Walk 22312
Ridge Dr 22306
Ridge Road Dr 22302
Ridge View Dr 22310
Ridgecrest Dr 22308
Ridgewood Rd 22312
Ridley Ct 22315
Riefton Ct 22310
N Ripley St 22304
Ripon Pl 22302
Rippon Rd 22307
Rita Ct 22306
Rita Gray Loop 22315
Rive Dr 22309
River Downs Rd 22312
River Farm Dr 22308
River Tweed Ln 22312
Rivergate Pl 22314
Riverside Rd 22308
Riverton Ln 22308
Riverview Ter 22303
Riverwood Ct & Rd 22309
Rixey Dr 22303
Roan Ln 22302
Roanoke Ave 22311
Roanoke Dr 22307
Robert E Lee Pl 22306
Robert Todd Ct 22312
Roberts Ct & Ln 22314
Robertson Blvd 22309
Robinhood Ct 22306
Robinson Ct 22302
Rock A By Rd 22310
Rock Cliff Ln 22315
Rock Creek Ct & Rd 22306
Rock Ridge Ln 22315
Rockleigh Way 22315
Rockshire Ct & St 22315
Rolfe Pl 22314
Rolling Creek Way 22315
Rolling Hills Ave 22309
Rolling Stone Way 22306
Rollingbrooke Ct 22306
Rollins Dr 22307
Ronson Ct & Dr 22310
Roosevelt St 22302
Rose Sq 22314
Rose Hill Ct & Dr 22310
Rose Hill Falls Way 22310
Rosecrest Ave 22301
Rosemary Lena Way 22309
Rosemont Ave 22309
E Rosemont Ave 22301
W Rosemont Ave 22301
Rosemont Cir 22309
Ross Aly 22314
Ross St 22306
N Rosser St 22311
Rossiter Pl 22308
Roth St 22314
Roudsby Ct & Ln 22315
Rouge Ct 22312
Roundhill Rd 22310
Roundhouse Ln 22314
Roxann Rd 22315
Roxbury Ct, Dr & Ln 22309
N & S Royal St 22314
Royal Crest Ln 22310
Royal Patents Ln 22315
Royal Thomas Way 22315
Ruby Virginia Ct 22310
Rucker Pl 22301
Ruffner Rd 22302
Rundale Ct 22315
Russell Rd
1-2699 22301
2700-3899 22305
7900-8299 22309
Rutland Pl 22304
Rye Ct 22310
Ryegate Ln 22308
Rynex Dr 22312
Sabine St 22309
Sable Dr 22303
Sacramento Dr 22309
Sacramento Mews Pl 22309
Saddle Tree Dr 22310
Sage Dr 22310
Sahalee Ct 22312
Saint Annes Ct 22309
N & S Saint Asaph St 22314
Saint Elliott Ct 22306
Saint Genevieve Pl 22315
Saint Giles Way 22315
Saint Gregorys Ln 22309
Saint John Dr 22310
Saint John Pl 22311
Saint Mark Ct 22306
Saint Stephens Rd 22304
Salford Ct 22315
San Leandro Pl 22309
Sanborn Pl 22305
Sand Wedge Ct 22312
Sandbrook Ct 22307
Sandlin Ct 22310
Sandpiper Ct 22306
Sandra Marie Cir 22310
Sandringham Ct 22315
Sandyford St 22315
Sanford St 22301
Sanger Ave 22311
Sano St 22312
Sapphire Ct 22310
Saratoga St 22310
Saucon Valley Ct 22312
Saul Rd 22306
Sausalito Pl 22309
Saville Ct 22306
Sawgrass Ct 22312
Saylor Pl 22304
Scarborough Sq 22309
Scarburgh Way 22314
Schebish Ln 22310
Schelhorn Rd 22306
School St 22303
Schooley Dr 22306
Schoonmaker Ct 22310
Schopan St 22306
Schurtz Dr & St 22310
Scotch Dr 22310
Scotland Rd 22309
Scott Pl 22308
N Scott St 22311
Scottswood Ct & St 22315
Scoville St 22311
Scroggins Rd 22302
Seaport Ln 22314
Seaton St 22306
Seay St 22314
Second St
300-999 22314
6400-6499 22312
Segundo Pl 22309
Seminary Rd
3600-3734 22304
3736-4799 22304
4900-5500 22311
5502-5698 22311
Seminole Ave & Ct 22312
Sequoia Ct 22312
Seth Hampton Dr 22315
Seven Woods Dr 22309
Seventh St 22312
Sevor Ln 22309
Sexton St 22309
Shackelford Ter 22312
Shade Tree Ln 22310
Shadow Walk 22310
Shadwell Ct & Dr 22309
Shaffer Dr 22310
Shalott Ct 22310
Shannon Ct 22306
Shannon Hill Rd 22310
Shannons Green Way 22309
Sharon Chapel Rd 22310
Sharon Kay Ct 22310
Sharp Pl 22304
Shaw Park Ct 22306
Shawnee Rd 22312
Sheffield Ct 22311
Sheldon Dr 22312
N Shelley St 22311
Shenandoah Rd 22308
Sheridans Point Ct 22309
Sheridonna Ln 22310
Sherwood Hall Ln 22306
Shetland Green Rd 22312
Shields Ave 22303
Shirley St 22309
Shirley Hunter Way 22315
Shiver Dr 22307
Shoal Creek Ct 22312
Shooters Ct 22314
Shorter Ln 22305
Shropshire Ct 22315
Shuttington Dr 22315
Sibel Pl 22310
Sibley St 22311
E Side Dr 22306
Signature Cir 22310
Silo Rd 22310
Silver Lake Blvd 22315
Silver Ridge Cir 22315
Silverada Pl 22309
Simms Rd 22315
Simsbury Pl 22308
Sir Cambridge Way 22315
Sir Viceroy Dr 22315
Sixth St 22312
Sky Blue Ct & Dr 22315
Sky View Dr 22309
Skyhill Rd 22314
Skyline Ct 22307
Skyline Heights Ct 22311
Skyline Village Ct 22302
Slaters Ln 22314
Small St 22302
Smithway Dr 22307
Snowden Hallowell Way 22314
Snowpea Ct 22306
Snug Harbor Ct 22315
Somervelle St 22304
Sonia Ct 22309
Sonora Pl 22309
South Pl 22309
Southdown Rd 22308
Southgate Dr 22306
Southland Ave 22312
Southlawn Ct 22309
Southward Way 22315
Southwood Dr 22309
Sparrow Dr 22306
Spect Ct 22310
Split Creek Ct & Ln 22312
Split Rock Rd 22310
Spotswood Dr 22308
Sprayer Ct & St 22309
Spring Dr 22306
E Spring St 22301
W Spring St 22301
Spring Faire Ct 22315
Spring Valley Dr 22312
Springirth Ter 22315
Springleigh Way 22315
Springman St 22309
Squire Ln 22310
Squiredale Sq 22309
Stable Dr 22308
Stacey Rd 22308
Stafford Rd 22307
Staghorn Ct 22315
Stanby Ct 22312
Standish Rd 22308
Stanford Dr 22307
Stanton Pl 22304
Steadman Pl & St 22309
Stegen Dr 22310
Steinway St 22315
Stephenson Way 22312
Stephies Ct 22309
Sterling Ave 22304
N Stevens St 22311
Stevenson Ave & Sq 22304
Stewart Ave 22301
Still Spring Pl 22315
Stillwell Ave 22309
Stinson Rd 22306
Stirrup Ln 22308
Stockade Dr 22308
Stockton Pkwy 22308
Stoddard Ct 22315
Stokes Ln 22307
Stone Hedge Dr 22306
Stone Mansion Ct 22306
Stone Mill Pl 22306
Stone Terrace Rd 22308
Stone Valley Ct 22310
Stone Wheat Ct 22315
Stonebridge Ct 22306
Stonebridge Rd
1600-1799 22304
3800-3999 22306
Stonewall Rd 22302
Stoneybrooke Ct, Dr & Ln 22306
Stonnell Pl 22302
Stork Rd 22306
Stovall St 22332
Stovepoint Ct 22306
Stover Ct & Dr 22306
Stratford Dr & Ln 22308
Strathblane Pl 22304
Strathdon Ct 22315
Strawbridge Square Dr 22312
Strawn Ct 22306
Stream Bed Way 22306
Strutfield Ln 22311
Stultz Rd 22304
Sturbridge Pl 22310
Sudbury Pl 22309
Suffolk Ct 22315
Sulgrave Dr 22309
Sulky Ct 22308
Sullivan Cir & Way 22315
Summer Leaf Ln 22312
Summer Moon Ln 22312
Summer Park Ln 22315
Summers Ct & Dr 22301
Summers Grove Rd 22304
Summerset Ln 22308
Summit Ave 22302
Summit Pl 22312
Summit Ter 22307
Summit Point Ct 22310
Sumner Rd 22310
Sun Up Way 22309
Sunburst Ct 22303
Sunburst Way 22315
Sunbury Dr 22303
Sunderland Ct 22315
Sunny View Dr 22309
Sunset Dr 22301
Surrey Ct & Dr 22309
Surry Pl 22304
Susan Barkley Ct 22315
Sussex Pl 22307
Sutcliffe Dr 22315
Suter St 22314

Sutton Pl 22304
Swain Dr 22306
Swallow Ct 22306
Swamp Fox Rd 22314
Swan Ter 22307
Swann Ave 22301
Swarthmore Dr 22307
Sweeley St 22314
Sweet Pea Ct 22310
Sweetbriar Dr 22307
Swift Aly 22314
Sword Ln 22308
Sycamore St 22305
Sylvan Ct 22304
Taft Ave 22304
Tahalla Dr 22306
Tahoe Ct 22312
Talavera Ct 22310
Talbois Pl 22310
Talbot Pl 22304
Talbott Farm Dr 22309
Taliaferro Way 22315
Tally Ho Ln 22307
Tammy Dr 22310
Tancil Ct 22314
Tancreti Ln 22304
Taney Ave 22304
Tarpon Ln 22309
Tartan Vista Dr 22312
Tassia Dr 22315
Tatum Dr 22307
Tauxemont Rd 22308
Tavenner Ln 22306
Tayack Pl 22312
Taylor Ave 22302
E Taylor Run Pkwy
1-699 22314
901-1199 22302
W Taylor Run Pkwy
1-699 22314
800-1198 22302
Teak Ct 22309
Telegraph Rd
100-399 22314
5600-5799 22303
5800-6999 22310
7001-7097 22315
7099-8099 22315
Telegraph Corner Ln 22310
Temple Ct 22307
Templeton Pl 22304
Tenley St 22308
Tennessee Ave 22305
Tennessee Dr 22303
Teresa Ann Ct 22308
Terrace Ct & Dr 22302
Terrapin Pl 22310
Terrett Ave 22301
Terrett Ct 22311
N Terrill St 22304
Terry Pl 22304
Tessie Ter 22309
Teton Pl 22312
Thackwell Way 22315
Thayer Ave 22304
The Pkwy 22310
The Strand 22314
Thetford Pl 22310
Third St
300-399 22314
6400-6499 22312
Thomas St 22302
Thomas Edison Ct 22310
Thomas Grant Ct & Dr 22315
Thompsons Aly 22314
Thornwood Dr 22310
Thorpe Ter 22315
Thrush Ct 22306
Thurlton Dr 22315
Tiburon Pl 22309
Tidewater Ct 22309
Tilbury Rd 22310
E & W Timber Branch Dr & Pkwy 22302
Timothy Pl 22303
Tipton Ln 22310
Tis Well Dr 22306
Tivoli Psge 22314
Tobacco Quay 22314
Toll Ct 22306
Toll Bridge Ct 22308
Tolliver St 22306
Tonto Ct 22312
Topper Ct 22315
Toron Ct 22306
Torrey Pl 22302
Towanda Rd 22303
Towchester Ct 22315
Tower Ct 22304
Tower Dr 22306
Tower Hill Cir 22315
Tower House Pl 22308
Towne Manor Ct 22309
Tracey Ct 22310
Traci Joyce Ln 22310
N Tracy St *22311
Traies Ct 22306
Tranquil Ct 22310
Trask Ter 22315
Treebrooke Ln 22308
Treetop Ln 22310
Tremont Ct & Dr 22303
Trent Ct 22311
Trenton Dr 22308
Triadelphia Way 22312
Trigger Ct 22310
Trin St 22310
Trinity Dr
1100-1499 22314
3500-3699 22304
Triumph Ct 22308
Trotter Rd 22304
Truman Ave 22304
Trumpington Ct 22315
Tuckahoe Ln 22302
Tudor Pl 22307
Tulane Dr 22307
Tull Pl 22304
Tulsa Ct 22307
Tulsa Pl 22304
Tunlaw Ct & St 22312
Tupelo Pl 22304
Turbridge Ln 22308
Turtle Dove Nook 22306
Twin Knolls Ct 22312
Tyler Pl 22302
Tyne Pl 22310
E & W Uhler Ave & Ter 22301
Uline Ave 22304
Underhill Pl 22305
Underwood Pl 22304
N & S Union St 22314
Union Farm Rd 22309
University Dr 22307
Upland Dr 22310
Upland Pl
400-699 22301
700-799 22314
Upland Woods Dr 22310
Usher Ave & Ct 22304
Utica Ave 22304
N Vail St 22304
Vale Ct & St 22312
Valley Cir 22302
Valley Dr 22302
Valley St 22302
Valley Forge Dr
5200-5399 22304
8900-8999 22309
Valley View Dr 22310
Valon Ct 22307
Van Ct 22309
N Van Dorn St
416-598 22304
600-1799 22304
1801-2299 22304
2500-2699 22302
S Van Dorn St
1-1099 22304
5600-6100 22310
6102-6398 22310
6400-6598 22315
6600-6999 22315
Van Dyke St 22306
Van Port St 22303
Vanderbilt Dr 22307
Vantage Ct & Dr 22306
Vassar Pl & Rd 22314
Venable Ave 22304
Vengo Ct 22312
Venoy Ct 22309
Venture Dr 22315
Verde Ct 22312
Vermont Ave & Ct 22304
Vernon Ave 22309
Vernon St 22314
Vernon Ter 22307
Vernon Square Dr 22306
Vernon View Dr 22308
Vianiank 22320
Vicar Ln 22302
Vicharan 22332
Vicki Ct 22312
Victor Gray Ct 22315
Victoria Dr 22310
Victoria Ln 22304
Victory Dr 22303
N View Ter 22301
S View Ter 22314
W View Ter 22301
Viewpoint Rd 22314
Villa St 22310
Village Way 22309
Village Green Ct & Dr 22309
Village Square Dr 22309
Villamay Blvd 22307
Vincent Gate Ter 22312
Vinchale Dr 22310
Vine St 22310
Virginia Ave 22302
Virginia St 22312
Virginia Hills Ave 22310
Volley Ct 22308
Volunteer Dr 22309
Vos Ln 22304
Wagon Dr 22303
Wagon Wheel Rd 22309
Wake Forest Dr 22307
Wakefield Ct 22307
Wakefield Dr 22307
E Wakefield Dr 22307
W Wakefield Dr 22307
Wakefield St 22308
Waldo Ct & Dr 22315
Wales Aly 22314
Walhaven Dr 22310
Walker Ln 22310
Walkers Croft Way 22315
Walking Ln 22312
Walleston Ct 22302
E & W Walnut St 22301
Walter Dr 22315
Waltonway Rd 22307
Walutes Cir 22309
Waple Ln 22304
Warburton Ct 22309
Warren Point Ct 22315
Warrington Pl 22307
Warwick Cir & Sq 22315
Washington Ave
7900-8099 22308
8300-8699 22309
Washington Cir 22305
Washington Ct 22302
Washington Rd 22308
N Washington St
100-199 22314
200-200 22320
201-1101 22314
202-998 22314
S Washington St
100-125 22314
126-126 22320
127-1299 22314
128-1298 22314
Washington Woods Dr 22309
Water Pl 22314
Waterfield Rd 22315
Waterford Pl 22314
Waterford Rd 22308
Waterlily Ct 22310
Waterside Ln 22309
Watkins Mill Dr 22304
Waverley St 22312
Waycross Dr 22310
Wayne St 22301
Waynewood Blvd 22308
Wayside Pl 22310
Welch Ct 22315
Welford St 22309
Wellesley Dr 22307
Wellington Rd
3100-3299 22302
7701-7797 22306
7799-7899 22306
7900-8199 22308
Wellington Commons Dr 22310
Wendell Dr 22308
Wendron Way 22315
Wescott Hills Way 22315
Wesmond Dr 22305
Wessex Ct & Ln 22310
Wessynton Way 22309
N & S West St 22314
Westchester St 22310
Westfield Ct 22306
Westfield St 22308
Westford View Ct 22306
Westgate Dr 22309
Westgrove Blvd 22307
Westhampton Dr 22307
Westman Ct 22306
Westminister Pl 22305
Westmoreland Rd 22308
Westridge Ct 22310
Wexford Pl 22315
Weyanoke Ct 22312
Wharf St 22314
Wheat Ct 22311
Wheeler Ave 22304
Whetstone Rd 22306
N Whinerie St 22304
Whiskey Ln 22314
White Heron Trl 22306
White Post Ct 22304
Whiteoaks Dr 22306
S Whiting St 22304
Wickford Dr 22315
Wigmore Ln 22315
Wilby Ct 22310
Wilcox Ct 22310
Wild Turkey Ln 22314
Wild Valley Ct 22310
Wiley Creek Way 22315
Wilkes St 22314
Wilkinson Pl 22306
William And Mary Dr 22308
William Edgar Dr 22310
Williams Dr 22307
Williamsburg Rd 22303
Williamsburg St 22314
Willowood Ln 22310
Wills St 22310
Wilmer Ln 22304
Wilson Ave 22305
Wilton Rd 22310
Wilton Crest Ct 22310
Wilton Hall Ct 22310
Wilton Hill Ter 22310
Wilton Knoll Ct 22310
Wilton Woods Ln 22310
Windbreak Dr 22306
Windham Ave 22315
Windham Hill Run 22315
Windmill Ct & Ln 22307
Windsor Ave 22315
E Windsor Ave 22301
W Windsor Ave
1-299 22301
400-699 22302
Windsor Rd 22307
Wingate St 22312
Wingfield Pl 22308
Winston Ct 22311
Winston Pl 22310
Winter View Dr 22312
Winthrop Dr 22308
Wittington Blvd 22308
Wivenhoe Ct 22315
Wolfe St 22314
Wood Dr 22309
Wood Haven Rd 22307
Wood Pile Ct 22310
Woodacre St 22308
Woodbine St 22302
Woodcliff Ct & Dr 22308
Wooden Valley Ct 22310
Woodfield Estates Dr 22310
Woodhue Pl 22309
Woodlake Ln 22315
Woodland Ln 22309
Woodland Ter 22302
Woodland Heights Ct 22309
Woodland Lake Dr 22310
Woodland Stream Dr 22310
Woodlawn Ct
3800-3899 22304
8500-8699 22309
Woodlawn Ln 22306
Woodlawn St 22309
Woodlawn Trl 22306
Woodlawn Gable Dr 22309
Woodlawn Green Cir & Ct 22309
Woodlawn Manor Ct 22309
Woodley Dr 22309
Woodmire Ln 22311
Woodmont Rd 22307
Woodpecker Way 22306
Woodridge Cir 22308
Woodridge Rd 22312
Woods Ave & Pl 22302
Woodside Rd 22310
Woodstone Pl 22306
Woodwalk Ct 22306
Woodward Ave 22309
Woodway Dr 22310
Woodway St 22312
Worsley Way 22315
Worthing Ct 22315
Wrenleigh Row 22315
W Wyatt Ave 22301
Wycklow Ct 22304
Wyndham Cir 22302
Wynema Ct 22315
Wyngate Manor Ct 22309
Wyomissing Ct 22303
Wyres St 22309
Wythe St
300-1099 22314
1100-1100 22313
1101-1399 22314
1102-1398 22314
Yadkin Ct 22310
Yale Dr
1-499 22314
2100-2299 22307
Yardley Ct & Dr 22308
Yeaton Aly 22314
Yellowstone Dr 22312
Yoakum Pkwy 22304
York Rd 22310
Yorktown Dr 22308
Yosemite Dr 22312
Yuma Ct 22312
Zabriskie Dr 22304
Zion Ct 22312
Zircon Dr 22312
Zohra Ct 22310
Zoysia Ct 22312

NUMBERED STREETS

10th St 22307
11th St 22307
13th St 22307
14th St 22307
S 14th St 22302
15th St 22307
16th St 22307
S 28th St 22302

ARLINGTON VA

General Delivery 22210

POST OFFICE BOXES MAIN OFFICE STATIONS AND BRANCHES

Box No.s
1 - 5 22205
501 - 994 22216
2001 - 2986 22202
3011 - 3907 22203
3300 - 3300 22206
4001 - 4760 22204
5101 - 5980 22205
6000 - 6946 22206
7001 - 7768 22207
9101 - 13998 22219
15000 - 16754 22215
17001 - 17886 22216
20001 - 20120 22219
25001 - 25360 22202
26000 - 26304 22215
40001 - 42218 22204
50001 - 51072 22205
90002 - 90020 22210
91010 - 91010 22202
100001 - 101974 22210
220200 - 220299 22202
220300 - 220399 22203
220400 - 220499 22204
220500 - 220599 22205
220601 - 220699 22206
220700 - 220799 22207
221001 - 221099 22210
221600 - 221699 22216
221800 - 222399 22219

NAMED STREETS

N Aberdeen St
1100-1198 22205
4000-4099 22207
S Aberdeen St 22204
N Abingdon St
100-899 22203
1200-4099 22207
S Abingdon St
1-599 22204
2800-3199 22206
N Adallewo St 22205
N Adams Ct 22201
N Adams St 22201
S Adams St
200-999 22204
2500-2799 22206
Air Force Memorial Dr 22204
N Albemarle St
700-799 22203
2000-3899 22207
N Arizona St 22213
Arlington Blvd
1001-1497 22209
1499-1799 22209
2101-3499 22201
2400-5998 22204
4203-5999 22203
N Arlington Mill Dr 22205
S Arlington Mill Dr
2564A-2564E 22206
2586A-2586H 22206
2592A-2592H 22206
2596A-2596H 22206
2606A-2606J 22206
700-898 22204
2500-2799 22206
S Arlington Ridge Rd 22202
Army Navy Dr
200-2099 22202
2301-2397 22206
2399-2499 22206
N Avenerid St 22201
S Ball St 22202
S Barton Ct 22206
N Barton St 22201
S Barton St 22204
N Bedford St 22201
Beechwood Cir & Pl 22207
S Bell St 22202
N Bluemont Dr 22203
Boundary Channel Dr 22202
N Brandywine St 22207
N Brookside Dr 22201
N Bryan St 22201
N Buchanan Ct 22207
N Buchanan St
600-899 22203
1100-1599 22205
1600-3499 22207
S Buchanan St
100-1499 22204
2100-3099 22206
N Burlington St
800-899 22203
2200-2399 22207
N Calvert St 22201
N Cameron St 22207
Campbell Ave 22206
N Carlin Springs Rd 22203
S Carlin Springs Rd 22204
Carpenter Rd
1-28 22204
29-29 22214
30-98 22204
31-99 22204
Cathedral Ln 22203
N Chesterbrook Rd 22207
S Chesterfield Rd 22206
Clarendon Blvd
1500-1799 22209
1800-3100 22201
3102-3198 22201
Clark Pl & St 22202
N Cleveland St 22201
S Cleveland St
100-1899 22204
2700-2799 22206
N Cloriew St 22213
N Coliando St 22203
Colonial Ct & Ter 22209
Columbia Pike 22204
N Columbus St
1-299 22203
1100-1299 22205
1800-3399 22207
S Columbus St
1-1599 22204
2100-3099 22206
N Courthouse Rd 22201
S Courthouse Rd 22204
Crystal Dr 22202
Crystal Mall Arc 22202
Crystal Plaza Arc 22202
Crystal Square Arc
1600-1631 22202
1632-1632 22215
1633-1699 22202
1634-1698 22202
N Culpeper St 22207
S Culpeper St 22206
Custis Rd 22201
N Daniel St 22201
N Danville St
700-1999 22201
2300-2399 22207
N Delaware St 22207
N Dickerson St 22207
S Dickerson St 22204
N Dinwiddie St
1200-1299 22205
1700-3599 22207
S Dinwiddie St
700-1099 22204
1300-2999 22206

Dittmar Rd ... 22207
orelist ... 22214
Dumbarton St ... 22207
Eads St ... 22202
Edgewood St
100-2364 ... 22201
2365-2499 ... 22207
Edgewood St ... 22204
Edison St
1-799 ... 22203
800-1599 ... 22205
1600-3899 ... 22207
Edison St ... 22204
Emerson St
200-799 ... 22203
800-999 ... 22205
1900-3499 ... 22207
Emerson St ... 22204
Evergreen St
200-299 ... 22203
1100-1299 ... 22205
1301-1399 ... 22205
2300-2399 ... 22207
Fair St ... 22202
airfax Dr
2504A-2504B ... 22201
Fenwick St ... 22201
Fenwick St ... 22204
Fern St ... 22202
Fillmore St
1-2305 ... 22201
2306-2799 ... 22207
Fillmore St
1-2199 ... 22204
2200-2299 ... 22206
Florida St
400-641 ... 22203
642-698 ... 22205
700-899 ... 22205
2300-3099 ... 22207
Florida St ... 22204
Forest Dr ... 22204
ort Myer Dr ... 22209
ort Scott Dr ... 22202
Four Mile Run Dr
5401-5499 ... 22205
5900-6098 ... 22205
6900-6999 ... 22213
Four Mile Run Dr
2600-4060 ... 22206
4061-4297 ... 22204
4062-4298 ... 22206
4299-4699 ... 22204
Fox St ... 22202
Fralliso St ... 22207
ranklin Rd ... 22201
Frederick St
300-721 ... 22203
722-1400 ... 22205
1402-1498 ... 22205
3200-3399 ... 22207
Frederick St ... 22204
Galveston St ... 22203
Garfield St ... 22201
Garfield St
1-1799 ... 22204
2200-2298 ... 22206
George Mason Dr
100-799 ... 22203
800-998 ... 22205
1000-1800 ... 22205
1801-2197 ... 22207
1802-2198 ... 22205
2199-3499 ... 22207
George Mason Dr ... 22204
eorge Washington Mem
kwy ... 22202
Glebe Rd
1-999 ... 22203
1000-1199 ... 22201
1201-1299 ... 22201
1300-4799 ... 22207
Glebe Rd
1-2199 ... 22204
2200-2202 ... 22206
2201-2203 ... 22204
2204-3099 ... 22206

3100-3699 ... 22202
Gopost
112-113 ... 22201
Gopost
115-125 ... 22201
210-210 ... 22202
212-214 ... 22202
216-224 ... 22202
308-308 ... 22203
405-405 ... 22204
606-614 ... 22206
718-718 ... 22207
N Granada St
1-499 ... 22203
2500-2599 ... 22207
S Granada St ... 22204
S Grant St ... 22202
N Greenbrier Ct ... 22207
N Greenbrier St
1-629 ... 22203
630-2099 ... 22205
2101-2299 ... 22205
2400-2999 ... 22207
S Greenbrier St
600-899 ... 22204
1300-4999 ... 22206
N Greencastle St ... 22207
S Grove St ... 22202
S Hamilton Dr ... 22204
N Hancock St ... 22201
N Harrison St
400-615 ... 22203
616-2399 ... 22205
2400-3899 ... 22207
S Harrison St ... 22204
N Hartford St ... 22201
N Harvard St ... 22201
S Hayes St ... 22202
N Henderson Rd ... 22203
Henderson Hall ... 22214
N Herndon St ... 22201
S High St ... 22202
N Highland St ... 22201
S Highland St ... 22204
S Hill St ... 22202
N Hollister St ... 22205
N Hudson St ... 22201
S Hudson St ... 22204
N Huntington St ... 22205
N Illinois St
500-599 ... 22203
600-2499 ... 22205
S Illinois St ... 22204
S Inge St ... 22202
N Inglewood St
1100-2199 ... 22205
3100-3199 ... 22207
N Irving St ... 22201
S Irving St ... 22204
N Ivanhoe St ... 22205
S Ives St ... 22202
N Ivy St ... 22201
S Ivy St ... 22204
N Jackson St ... 22201
S Jackson St ... 22204
N Jacksonville St ... 22205
N Jefferson St
300-399 ... 22203
500-2110 ... 22205
2112-2198 ... 22205
2400-3699 ... 22207
S Jefferson St ... 22204
Jefferson Davis Hwy ... 22202
John Marshall Dr
2200-2398 ... 22205
2400-3799 ... 22207
N Johnson St
1100-1699 ... 22201
1800-1999 ... 22207
S Joyce St
801-899 ... 22204
1100-2899 ... 22202
S June St ... 22202
N Kansas St ... 22201
Kemper Rd ... 22206
N Kenilworth St
1100-2199 ... 22205

2500-3699 ... 22207
S Kenmore Cir ... 22204
S Kenmore Ct ... 22206
N Kenmore St
300-1499 ... 22201
1800-2099 ... 22207
2100-2350 ... 22201
2351-3299 ... 22207
S Kenmore St
2036A-2036B ... 22204
1900-2199 ... 22204
2200-2499 ... 22206
N Kennebec St ... 22205
N Kennesaw St ... 22205
N Kensington St
200-398 ... 22205
400-2412 ... 22205
2413-3799 ... 22207
S Kensington St ... 22204
N Kent St ... 22209
S Kent St ... 22202
N Kentucky St ... 22205
S Kenwood St ... 22206
Key Blvd
1400-1699 ... 22209
1800-3199 ... 22201
King St ... 22206
Kirkwood Pl & Rd ... 22201
S Knoll St ... 22202
N Lancaster St
1400-1599 ... 22205
3600-3699 ... 22207
S Lancaster St ... 22204
S Lang St ... 22206
S Langley St ... 22204
S Larallet St ... 22206
N Larrimore St ... 22205
S Larrimore St ... 22204
N Lebanon St ... 22205
Lee Hwy
1300-1799 ... 22209
1800-2144 ... 22201
2146-3199 ... 22201
3200-5999 ... 22207
6000-6799 ... 22205
6800-6999 ... 22213
N Lexington St
800-2399 ... 22205
2400-2999 ... 22207
S Lexington St ... 22204
N Liberty St
2-299 ... 22203
800-1049 ... 22205
1051-1099 ... 22205
N Lincoln St
300-1599 ... 22201
1600-3699 ... 22207
S Lincoln St
700-2199 ... 22204
2400-2499 ... 22206
Little Falls Rd
4700-6299 ... 22207
6400-6999 ... 22213
N Littleton St ... 22203
N Livingston St
400-699 ... 22203
800-1299 ... 22205
N Lombardy St ... 22203
Long Bridge Dr ... 22202
N Longfellow St
500-599 ... 22203
800-1699 ... 22205
Lorcom Ln ... 22207
S Lorton St ... 22204
S Lowell St
1700-2199 ... 22204
2200-2499 ... 22206
N Lynn St ... 22209
S Lynn St ... 22202
N Lynnbrook Dr ... 22201
N Madison St
1-699 ... 22203
801-897 ... 22205
899-2499 ... 22205
N Manchester St
1-599 ... 22203
601-699 ... 22203

1000-1099 ... 22205
S Manchester St ... 22204
Marcey Rd ... 22207
N Mckinley Rd ... 22205
N Mckinley St ... 22207
N Meade St ... 22209
S Meade St
2300-2499 ... 22202
2800-2899 ... 22206
Meridian St ... 22213
Military Rd ... 22207
N Monroe St
300-1499 ... 22201
1600-3699 ... 22207
S Monroe St
600-2199 ... 22204
2200-2599 ... 22206
N Montague St ... 22203
S Montague St ... 22204
N Montana St
500-599 ... 22203
900-1099 ... 22205
S Montana St ... 22204
N Moore St ... 22209
N Nash St ... 22209
S Nash St ... 22202
Nellie Custis Dr ... 22207
N Nelson St
200-399 ... 22201
400-999 ... 22203
1000-1499 ... 22201
1600-3899 ... 22207
S Nelson St
1300-2199 ... 22204
2200-2799 ... 22206
N Nicholas St ... 22205
N Norwood St
400-599 ... 22203
2700-2799 ... 22207
S Norwood St ... 22204
N Nottingham St
100-499 ... 22203
800-2399 ... 22205
2400-3599 ... 22207
N Oak Ct ... 22209
N Oak St ... 22209
S Oak St ... 22204
S Oakcrest Rd ... 22202
N Oakland St
1-999 ... 22203
1800-3899 ... 22207
S Oakland St
600-2199 ... 22204
2200-2799 ... 22206
N Ode St ... 22209
S Ode St
700-999 ... 22204
2300-2399 ... 22202
N Ohio St
800-2000 ... 22205
2002-2198 ... 22205
2400-3599 ... 22207
Old Dominion Dr
4870-A-4870-G ... 22207
3200-3299 ... 22201
4000-5299 ... 22207
N Old Glebe Rd ... 22207
S Old Glebe Rd ... 22204
S Oldelans St ... 22202
S Orme St ... 22204
N Ottawa St
2400-2499 ... 22205
3500-3599 ... 22213
N Oxford St
300-699 ... 22203
2900-3199 ... 22207
S Oxford St
2100-2199 ... 22204
2400-2799 ... 22206
N Park Dr ... 22203
S Park Dr ... 22204
S Paterani St ... 22204
Patrick Henry Dr ... 22205
N Peary St ... 22207
S Pershing Ct ... 22204
N Pershing Dr
2100-3699 ... 22201

3700-4599 ... 22203
S Pershing Dr ... 22204
N Piedmont St
200-799 ... 22203
3100-3699 ... 22207
N Pierce Ct ... 22209
N Pierce St ... 22209
S Pierce St
1200-1399 ... 22204
2100-2399 ... 22202
N Pocomoke St
1401-1697 ... 22205
1699-2399 ... 22205
2400-3399 ... 22207
3500-3699 ... 22213
S Poe St ... 22204
N Pollard St
500-999 ... 22203
1700-3199 ... 22207
S Pollard St ... 22204
S Potomac Ave ... 22202
N Potomac St
900-2199 ... 22205
2400-2699 ... 22207
3400-3699 ... 22213
N Powhatan St
900-2399 ... 22205
2400-2899 ... 22207
3400-3699 ... 22213
N Quantico St
900-2399 ... 22205
2400-2799 ... 22207
N Quebec St
300-398 ... 22203
1600-3599 ... 22207
S Quebec St ... 22204
N Queen St ... 22209
S Queen St
1000-1499 ... 22204
2300-2499 ... 22202
N Queens Ln ... 22201
N Quesada St ... 22205
N Quincy St
1104A-1104F ... 22201
500-999 ... 22203
1000-1012 ... 22201
1014-1399 ... 22201
1400-3199 ... 22207
S Quincy St
600-2399 ... 22204
2700-2999 ... 22206
N Quinn St ... 22209
S Quinn St ... 22204
N Quintana St
900-2299 ... 22205
2400-2499 ... 22207
N Radford St ... 22207
N Randolph Ct ... 22207
N Randolph St
500-999 ... 22203
1000-1199 ... 22201
1500-4199 ... 22207
S Randolph St
800-2299 ... 22204
2700-3099 ... 22206
N Rhodes St
1300-1699 ... 22209
1700-1999 ... 22201
N Richmond St ... 22207
N Ridgeview Rd ... 22207
N River St ... 22207
N Rixey St ... 22207
Robert Walker Pl ... 22207
Roberts Ln ... 22207
N Rochester St
900-1200 ... 22205
1202-1298 ... 22205
2800-3299 ... 22213
Rock Spring Rd ... 22207
N Rockingham St
1100-1199 ... 22205
2400-2699 ... 22207
3500-3699 ... 22213
N Rolfe St ... 22209
S Rolfe St
900-1499 ... 22204
2300-2399 ... 22202

N Roosevelt St
1000-2399 ... 22205
2400-3099 ... 22207
Round Hill Rd ... 22207
N Scott St ... 22209
S Scott St ... 22204
S Shirlington Rd
2000-2199 ... 22204
2200-2899 ... 22206
N Smythe St ... 22201
N Somerset St
2200-2299 ... 22205
2701-2797 ... 22213
2799-3599 ... 22213
Southgate Rd ... 22214
Spout Run Pkwy ... 22201
N Stafford St
800-999 ... 22203
1000-1399 ... 22201
1500-4099 ... 22207
S Stafford St
600-1899 ... 22204
2701-3599 ... 22206
N Stuart St ... 22201
N Sycamore St
1100-2199 ... 22205
2201-2299 ... 22205
2400-2999 ... 22207
N Tacoma St ... 22213
N Taft St ... 22201
N Taylor St
2135A-2135I ... 22207
1111A-1111C ... 22201
801-999 ... 22203
1000-1499 ... 22201
1500-4099 ... 22207
S Taylor St
300-1799 ... 22204
2700-3699 ... 22206
N Tazewell Ct ... 22207
N Tazewell St
600-799 ... 22203
3700-4099 ... 22207
N Thomas St
1-599 ... 22203
2100-3499 ... 22207
S Thomas St ... 22204
N Toronto St ... 22213
N Trenton St
1-299 ... 22203
2200-2399 ... 22207
N Trinidad St ... 22213
N Troy St ... 22201
S Troy St ... 22206
N Tuckahoe St
1300-2499 ... 22205
2800-3099 ... 22213
N Uhle St ... 22201
S Uhle St ... 22206
N Underwood St
1800-2499 ... 22205
2500-3199 ... 22213
N Upland St ... 22207
N Upshur St ... 22207
N Upton St ... 22207
N Utah St
1000-1499 ... 22201
1500-3599 ... 22207
S Utah St
100-999 ... 22204
3200-3599 ... 22206
Vacation Ln ... 22207
N Valley St ... 22207
N Van Buren Ct ... 22205
N Van Buren St
1800-1999 ... 22205
2800-2899 ... 22213
S Vance Ct ... 22206
N Vance St ... 22201
N Vanderpool St ... 22213
N Veitch St ... 22201
S Veitch St
200-999 ... 22204
2600-2799 ... 22206
N Venable St ... 22213
N Venice St ... 22207

N Vermont St
600-799 ... 22203
1001-1097 ... 22201
1099-1499 ... 22201
1900-3799 ... 22207
N Vernon St
1100-1499 ... 22201
2000-3899 ... 22207
N Wakefield Ct ... 22207
N Wakefield St
100-899 ... 22203
1300-3999 ... 22207
S Wakefield St
2821A-2821F ... 22206
300-1199 ... 22204
2800-3699 ... 22206
S Walter Reed Dr
2402A-2402C ... 22206
500-2199 ... 22204
2300-2799 ... 22206
Washington Blvd
6835A-6835G ... 22213
2100-2198 ... 22204
2300-3119 ... 22201
3118-3118 ... 22210
3120-4698 ... 22201
3121-4699 ... 22201
4700-6499 ... 22205
6501-6699 ... 22205
6700-7099 ... 22213
S Washington Ct ... 22204
S Wayne Ct ... 22206
N Wayne St ... 22201
S Wayne St
200-1099 ... 22204
2700-2799 ... 22206
N Welianin St ... 22209
N Westmoreland St ... 22213
Williamsburg Blvd
4700-6499 ... 22207
6500-7099 ... 22213
Wilson Blvd
1000-1100 ... 22209
1101-1799 ... 22209
1101-1101 ... 22219
1102-1798 ... 22209
1800-2044 ... 22201
2043-2043 ... 22216
2045-3699 ... 22201
2046-3698 ... 22201
3700-5099 ... 22203
5100-6199 ... 22205
6201-6407 ... 22205
N Winchester St ... 22213
S Wise St ... 22204
N Woodley St ... 22207
S Woodley St ... 22206
N Woodrow St
800-899 ... 22203
1900-3899 ... 22207
S Woodrow St
100-199 ... 22204
2800-3099 ... 22206
N Woodstock St ... 22207
S Woodstock St
2927A-2927E ... 22206
2929A-2929D ... 22206
600-699 ... 22204
2900-2999 ... 22206
N Wyoming St ... 22213
Yorktown Blvd ... 22207
N Yucatan St ... 22213

NUMBERED STREETS

1st Pl N
3111-3299 ... 22201
5300-5399 ... 22203
1st Pl S ... 22204
1st Rd N ... 22201
1st Rd S ... 22204
1st St N
2900-3399 ... 22201
4700-6099 ... 22203
1st St S ... 22204
2nd Rd N
2500-3399 ... 22201

4200-4899 ... 22203
2nd St N
2200-3199 ... 22201
3800-6099 ... 22203
2nd St S ... 22204
3rd Rd N ... 22203
3rd St N
2400-3699 ... 22201
4600-5999 ... 22203
3rd St S ... 22204
4th Ct N ... 22203
4th Rd N ... 22203
4th St N
2500-3299 ... 22201
3600-5099 ... 22203
5600-5698 ... 22205
5700-5799 ... 22205
5900-6099 ... 22203
4th St S ... 22204
5th Pl N ... 22203
5th Rd N ... 22203
5th Rd S ... 22204
5th St N
3000-3399 ... 22201
3600-5399 ... 22203
5600-5799 ... 22205
5801-5899 ... 22205
5900-5999 ... 22203
5th St S ... 22204
6th Pl S ... 22204
6th Rd N ... 22203
6th Rd S ... 22204
6th St N
3100-3599 ... 22201
3820-3824 ... 22203
5600-5799 ... 22205
6000-6099 ... 22203
6th St S
300-399 ... 22202
1900-5699 ... 22204
7th Pl S ... 22204
7th Rd N ... 22203
7th Rd S ... 22204
7th St N
2800-3599 ... 22201
3700-4999 ... 22203
5600-5799 ... 22205
7th St S ... 22204
8th Pl N ... 22205
8th Pl S ... 22204
8th Rd N
4700-4899 ... 22203
5100-5999 ... 22205
8th Rd S ... 22204
8th St N
3100-3599 ... 22201
5100-5799 ... 22205
8th St S ... 22204
9th Pl N ... 22205
9th Rd N
3100-3199 ... 22201
5400-5498 ... 22205
5500-6199 ... 22205
9th Rd S ... 22204
9th St N
2300-3699 ... 22201
3700-4899 ... 22203
5100-6099 ... 22205
9th St S ... 22204
10th Pl S ... 22204
10th Rd N ... 22205
10th St N
2300-3699 ... 22201
5000-5999 ... 22205
10th St S
300-399 ... 22202
1600-5099 ... 22204
5101-5107 ... 22204
11th Pl N ... 22201
11th Rd N ... 22205
11th Rd S ... 22204
11th St N
2300-4599 ... 22201
4700-6199 ... 22205
6201-6499 ... 22205
11th St S
400-499 ... 22202

1500-5299 ... 22204
12th Ct N ... 22201
12th Pl N ... 22205
12th Rd N
3400-3499 ... 22201
6100-6399 ... 22205
12th Rd S ... 22204
12th St N
1424A-1424E ... 22209
2500-2699 ... 22201
5200-6399 ... 22205
12th St S
200-299 ... 22202
1500-5138 ... 22204
5200-5499 ... 22204
13th Ct N ... 22201
13th Rd S ... 22204
13th St N
1800-1899 ... 22209
1900-1998 ... 22201
2000-3999 ... 22201
4001-4499 ... 22201
4600-4699 ... 22207
4700-5099 ... 22205
13th St S ... 22204
14th Rd N ... 22205
14th Rd S
500-598 ... 22202
1701-1707 ... 22204
14th St N
1300-1899 ... 22209
2000-3999 ... 22201
4600-4699 ... 22207
4700-6199 ... 22205
14th St S
1600-4999 ... 22204
5000-5099 ... 22206
15th Pl N ... 22205
15th Rd N ... 22205
15th St N
1900-3599 ... 22201
4001-4197 ... 22207
4199-4699 ... 22207
4700-5999 ... 22205
15th St S
100-1199 ... 22202
1700-3599 ... 22204
16th Pl N ... 22207
16th Rd N
1500-1535 ... 22209
4700-5099 ... 22207
5300-5399 ... 22205
16th Rd S ... 22204
16th St N
1536-1598 ... 22209
1900-3399 ... 22201
4300-4699 ... 22207
4700-6699 ... 22205
16th St S
900-1199 ... 22202
2600-4399 ... 22204
17th Rd N ... 22207
17th Rd S ... 22204
17th St N
1300-1398 ... 22209
3100-3399 ... 22201
3400-5099 ... 22207
5200-5600 ... 22205
5602-6398 ... 22205
17th St S
900-1199 ... 22202
2800-3599 ... 22204
18th Rd N
4000-4199 ... 22207
5500-6299 ... 22205
18th St N
1501-1597 ... 22209
2100-3199 ... 22201
3300-4999 ... 22207
5300-6300 ... 22205
18th St S
201-597 ... 22202
2401-4199 ... 22204
19th Ct ... 22201
19th Rd N
3200-3299 ... 22201
4400-5299 ... 22207

6000-6899 ... 22205
19th Rd S ... 22202
19th St N
1000-1699 ... 22209
2100-3299 ... 22201
3600-5299 ... 22207
5400-6700 ... 22205
19th St S
600-1200 ... 22202
2600-4099 ... 22204
20th Ct S ... 22204
20th Pl N ... 22207
20th Rd N
1901-2497 ... 22201
3200-4799 ... 22207
5800-5899 ... 22205
20th St N
2100-2198 ... 22201
3300-5199 ... 22207
5200-5298 ... 22205
20th St S
200-598 ... 22202
2800-3099 ... 22204
21st Ave N ... 22207
21st Ct N
1500-1599 ... 22209
2164-2180 ... 22201
21st Rd N
1637-1645 ... 22209
2100-2135 ... 22201
4000-4799 ... 22207
21st Rd S ... 22204
21st St N
1600-1899 ... 22209
2000-2010 ... 22201
4000-5199 ... 22207
5400-6299 ... 22205
21st St S
600-1499 ... 22202
3501-3599 ... 22204
22nd Ct N ... 22209
22nd Rd N
4800-4999 ... 22207
5400-6499 ... 22205
22nd St N
1500-1721 ... 22209
2900-3399 ... 22201
3500-5199 ... 22207
5200-6500 ... 22205
22nd St S
500-1699 ... 22202
2900-3899 ... 22204
5000-5099 ... 22206
23rd Rd N
2500-2699 ... 22207
2700-3323 ... 22201
4300-5199 ... 22207
23rd Rd S
1100-1513 ... 22202
4800-4899 ... 22206
23rd St N
2817-3322 ... 22201
3700-4899 ... 22207
5400-6399 ... 22205
23rd St S
201-297 ... 22202
2900-5099 ... 22206
24th Rd N
2900-4899 ... 22207
6600-6699 ... 22205
24th Rd S ... 22206
24th St N
2100-5199 ... 22207
5400-5699 ... 22205
6300-6499 ... 22207
6500-6699 ... 22205
24th St S
500-1899 ... 22202
3000-5099 ... 22206
25th Ct S ... 22206
25th Pl N ... 22207
25th Rd N ... 22207
25th St N
2500-6499 ... 22207
6600-6799 ... 22213
25th St S
500-1299 ... 22202

2300-5099 ... 22206
26th Ct S ... 22206
26th Pl S ... 22202
26th Rd N
4100-6299 ... 22207
6500-6599 ... 22213
26th Rd S
500-1299 ... 22202
2400-2435 ... 22206
26th St N
2900-6499 ... 22207
6500-6999 ... 22213
26th St S
500-1299 ... 22202
1600-2399 ... 22206
27th Ct S ... 22206
27th Pl N ... 22207
27th Rd N
3900-6099 ... 22207
6900-7199 ... 22213
27th Rd S ... 22206
27th St N
2800-6499 ... 22207
6500-6899 ... 22213
27th St S
1000-1099 ... 22202
2000-3699 ... 22206
28th Rd S ... 22206
28th St N
4800-6499 ... 22207
6500-6999 ... 22213
28th St S
900-999 ... 22202
1100-1499 ... 22206
1501-1699 ... 22206
1800-1899 ... 22202
4000-4999 ... 22206
29th Rd S
600-612 ... 22202
4900-4999 ... 22206
29th St N
4800-6499 ... 22207
6500-6999 ... 22213
29th St S
601-613 ... 22202
4000-4899 ... 22206
30th Pl N ... 22207
30th Rd N
3700-3899 ... 22207
6800-6899 ... 22213
30th Rd S ... 22206
30th St N
3700-6499 ... 22207
6900-6999 ... 22213
30th St S ... 22206
31st Rd N ... 22207
31st Rd S ... 22206
31st St N
3900-6399 ... 22207
6600-6899 ... 22213
31st St S
500-899 ... 22202
4000-4999 ... 22206
32nd Rd N ... 22207
32nd Rd S ... 22206
32nd St N
4500-5699 ... 22207
6600-6699 ... 22213
32nd St S ... 22206
33rd Rd N ... 22207
33rd St N ... 22207
33rd St S ... 22206
34th Rd N ... 22207
34th St N ... 22207
34th St S ... 22206
35th Rd N
4500-5699 ... 22207
6500-6599 ... 22213
35th St N
4000-6099 ... 22207
6100-6399 ... 22213
35th St S ... 22206
36th Rd N ... 22207
36th St N
3500-5899 ... 22207
6100-6599 ... 22213
36th St S ... 22206

37th Pl, Rd & St ... 22207
38th Pl, Rd & St ... 22207
39th St N ... 22207
40th Pl & St ... 22207
41st St N ... 22207

ASHBURN VA

General Delivery ... 20147

POST OFFICE BOXES MAIN OFFICE STATIONS AND BRANCHES

Box No.s
1 - 4000 ... 20146
4001 - 4894 ... 20148
9998 - 18090 ... 20146

NAMED STREETS

Abbeyfields Dr ... 20147
Abbott Pl ... 20147
Aberdeen Ter ... 20147
Academic Way ... 20147
Acushnet Ter ... 20147
Adagio Ter ... 20148
Adams Mill Pl ... 20147
Adams Point Ter ... 20148
Adare Manor Sq ... 20147
Addlestone Pl ... 20148
Adena Ter ... 20147
Adirondack Ter ... 20147
Advantage Ct ... 20147
Afton Ter ... 20147
Agawam Ter ... 20147
Ainsley Ct ... 20148
Airmont Hunt Dr ... 20148
Airmont Woods Ter ... 20148
Albion Ln ... 20147
Alderleaf Ter ... 20147
Alexandras Grove Dr ... 20147
Alford Rd ... 20148
Alicent Ter ... 20147
Allderwood Ter ... 20147
Allison Way ... 20148
Allisons Ridge Ter ... 20148
Allspice Ct ... 20148
Altavista Way ... 20147
Alum Creek Ct ... 20147
Amanda Kay Ct ... 20147
Amber Grove Ter ... 20147
Amber Meadows Ln ... 20148
Amberjack Sq ... 20148
Amberleigh Farm Dr ... 20148
Amberly Ter ... 20147
Amberview Ct ... 20147
Ambleside Ct ... 20147
Amendola Ter ... 20148
Amity Pl ... 20147
Andreas Ct ... 20147
Angel Wing Way ... 20148
Angela Faye Sq ... 20148
Angelique Dr ... 20148
Annenberg Dr ... 20147
Antiquity Ct ... 20147
Apache Cir ... 20147
Apollo Ter ... 20147
Appalachian Vista Ter ... 20147
Applegrove Ct ... 20147
Appleyard Pl ... 20148
April Mist Pl ... 20148
Arapaho Ter ... 20147
Arbor Glen Ct ... 20148
Arbor Greene Way ... 20148
Arbor View Dr ... 20148
Arborvitae Dr ... 20147
Arcadia Ct ... 20147
Arcola Grove Dr ... 20148
Arcola Manor Ct ... 20148
Ardmore St ... 20147
Armstrong Ter ... 20148

Arora Heights Dr ... 20148
Arrowhead Ct ... 20147
Arthur Amos Ct ... 20148
Artsmith Ter ... 20147
Arundell Ct ... 20148
Ascot Ct ... 20147
Ash Tree Dr ... 20148
Ashbrook Pl ... 20147
Ashbrook Commons Plz ... 20147
Ashburn Rd ... 20147
Ashburn Farm Pkwy ... 20147
Ashburn Heights Dr ... 20148
Ashburn Run Pl ... 20147
Ashburn Shopping Plz ... 20147
Ashburn Station Pl ... 20147
Ashburn Tillett Dr ... 20148
Ashburn Valley Ct ... 20147
Ashburn Village Blvd ... 20147
Ashby Oak Ct ... 20148
Ashby Ponds Blvd ... 20147
Ashlar Ter ... 20147
Ashlawn Ct ... 20147
Ashley Green Dr ... 20148
Ashley Heights Cir ... 20148
Ashley Inn Ter ... 20148
Ashmeadow Ct ... 20148
Ashton Woods Dr ... 20148
Ashwood Moss Ter ... 20148
Aspendale Sq ... 20147
Athens St ... 20148
Atherton St ... 20147
Atwater Dr ... 20147
Auction Barn Dr ... 20148
Audobon Sq ... 20147
Augusta Village Pl ... 20147
Augustine Pl ... 20147
Autumn Harvest Ct ... 20148
Autumn Rain Cir ... 20148
Autumn Sky Ct ... 20148
Autumnwood Sq ... 20148
Avens Ct ... 20148
Avonworth Sq ... 20148
Awbrey Pl ... 20148
Ayr Hill Ct ... 20148
Aztec Ct ... 20147
Babbling Brook Ter ... 20147
Babcock Ter ... 20148
Backcountry Ct ... 20148
Backhand Ter ... 20147
Backlot Aly ... 20147
Balduck Ter ... 20148
Ballantine Pl ... 20147
Balmoral Ter ... 20147
Baltray Cir ... 20147
Baltusrol Ter ... 20147
Bancroft Ct ... 20147
Bandon Dunes Ct ... 20147
Bankbarn Ter ... 20148
Banshee Heights Ter ... 20148
Bar Harbor Ter ... 20147
Barborsville Mansion Sq ... 20148
Barley Ct ... 20147
Barley Hall Ter ... 20147
Barnsdale View Ct ... 20148
Barnstead Dr ... 20148
Barretts Sq ... 20147
Baseline Ter ... 20147
Basil Ct ... 20148
Bass Rocks Ter ... 20147
Bayard Ter ... 20148
Baymeadow Ct ... 20147
Beacon Crest Ter ... 20148
Beaumeade Cir ... 20147
Beaverdam Dr ... 20148
Beckett Ter ... 20148
Becontree Ter ... 20148
Beechdrop Dr ... 20147
Beechwood Ter ... 20147
Belgreen Dr ... 20147
Bellair Ct ... 20147
Belle Terra Dr ... 20148
Belmont Executive Plz ... 20147
Belmont Glen Pl ... 20148
Belmont Manor Ln ... 20147

Belmont Park Ter ... 2014
Belmont Ridge Rd
19800-20799 ... 2014
20900-23899 ... 2014
Belmont Station Dr & Pl ... 2014
Belmont View Ter ... 2014
Belvedere Ct ... 2014
Belvoir Woods Ter ... 2014
Benefold Sq ... 2014
Bent Twig Ter ... 2014
Bentley Grove Pl ... 2014
Benwood Ter ... 2014
Berkeley Meadows Dr ... 2014
Bethpage Ct ... 2014
Bidwell Ct ... 2014
Big Trail Ter ... 2014
Biggers Farm Ter ... 2014
Birch Manor Ter ... 2014
Birchmere Ter ... 2014
Birdsnest Pl ... 2014
Bishop Meade Pl ... 2014
Bissell Ter ... 2014
Bitterroot Ter ... 2014
Bittner Sq ... 2014
Black Diamond Pl ... 2014
Black Horse Sq ... 2014
Blackheath Way ... 2014
Blackmar Ter ... 2014
Blacksmith Sq ... 2014
Blackwolf Run Pl ... 2014
Blair Park Sq ... 2014
Blanco Ter ... 2014
Blantyre Ct ... 2014
Bliss Ter ... 2014
Bloomfield Path St ... 2014
Blossom Hill Ter ... 2014
Blue Bill Ct ... 2014
Blue Copper Way ... 2014
Blue Elder Ter ... 2014
Blue Water Ct ... 2014
Bluengrey Ct ... 2014
Blueridge Meadows Dr ... 2014
Bluestone Ct ... 2014
Blythwood Ct ... 2014
Boca Field Ter ... 2014
Bold Forbes Ct ... 2014
Bollinger Ter ... 2014
Bonlee Sq ... 2014
Bonnieblue Ct ... 2014
Bourne Ter ... 2014
Bowditch Sq ... 2014
Bowfonds St ... 2014
Bowmantown Bridge Ct ... 2014
Boxford Ter ... 2014
Boxwood Pl ... 2014
Bozman Ct ... 2014
Brae Ter ... 2014
Braemount Cir ... 2014
Braeton Bay Ter ... 2014
Bramblebush Ter ... 2014
Brambleton Plz ... 2014
Branderburgh Dr ... 2014
Branower St ... 2014
Breadalbane Cir ... 2014
Breeders Run Ct ... 2014
Breezy Hollow Dr ... 2014
Breezyhill Dr ... 2014
Breitling Ter ... 2014
Briar Creek Ter ... 2014
Brickshire Cir ... 2014
Bright Star Ct ... 2014
Brightcrest Ter ... 2014
Brimfield Dr ... 2014
Bristow Cir ... 2014
Bristow Manor Dr ... 2014
Broad Vista Ter ... 2014
Broadlands Blvd ... 2014
Broadlands Center Plz ... 2014
Broadnax Pl ... 2014
Broadrun Meadow Cir ... 2014
Broadwell Ct ... 2014
Bronstein Ln ... 2014
Bronte Pl ... 2014
Brookford Sq ... 2014

Street	ZIP
Brookline Ter	20147
Brookshade Dr	20148
Brookton Way	20147
Brookview Sq	20147
Brookwash Ter	20148
N Brown Sq	20148
Brownstone Ct	20147
Broxton Ter	20148
Bruceton Mills Cir	20147
Buckland Farm Ter	20148
Buckley Ter	20147
Builders Ln	20147
Bulwark Ter	20148
Bunker Hill Way	20147
Bunker Woods Pl	20148
Burnt Hickory Ct	20148
Burnthill Ct	20147
Burrell Sq	20147
Butterfield Ct	20147
Buttermere Ter	20147
Cadbury Ter	20147
Calais Ter	20147
Calderwood Ln	20148
Calhoun Corners Ter	20147
Calistoga Sq	20147
Callalily Way	20148
Callaway Sq	20147
Cambridgeport Sq	20148
Camellia St	20147
Cameron Hunt Pl	20147
Cameron Parish Dr	20148
Camptown Ct	20147
Candice Dr	20148
Cape Ct	20147
Capilano Ct	20147
Capitol View Ter	20148
Capri Pl	20148
Cardiff Ct	20147
Cardinal Pond Ter	20147
Cardinal Trace Ter	20148
Carnegie Pl	20148
Carrleigh Ct	20147
Carson Ct	20147
Carters Station Ct	20148
Carthagena Ct	20147
Cartier Ter	20148
Carys Brook Ct	20147
Casablanca Dr	20147
Castle Pines Ter	20147
Castle Ridge Sq	20148
Castlehill Ct	20147
Caterham Dr	20148
Cather Ct	20147
Catlett Pl	20147
Cattail Meadows Pl	20148
Catton Pl	20147
Cavalier Ct	20147
Cayuga Ct	20147
Cedar Forest Ter	20148
Cedar Glen Ter	20147
Cedar Heights Dr	20147
Cedar Springs Ct	20148
Cedarpost Sq	20147
Center Point Cir	20147
Center Post Ter	20148
Centergate Dr	20148
Central Station Dr	20147
Century Corner Dr	20147
Cessna Ln	20147
Chadds Ford Ct	20147
Chadwick Ter	20148
Chamberlain Ter	20147
Championship Pl	20147
Champney Ct	20148
Chancery Ter	20148
Channing Ct	20147
Charity Ter	20147
Charmay Pond Pl	20148
Charter Oak Dr	20147
Chatelain Cir	20148
Chatham Way	20147
Chelsy Paige Sq	20148
Cheltenham Cir	20147
Cherrystone Pl	20147
Chertsey St	20148
Chervil Ln	20148
Chestermill Ter	20147
Chesterton St	20147
Chestwood Acres Ter	20148
Chetwood Ter	20147
Chickacoan Trail Dr	20148
Chilum Pl	20147
Chisholm Dr	20148
Chloe Ter	20147
Choctaw Sq	20147
Chokeberry Sq	20147
Choptank Ter	20147
Christina Ridge Sq	20148
Christopher Thomas Ln	20148
Christophers View Ter	20147
Churchill Downs Dr	20147
Citation Dr	20147
Claiborne Pkwy 20301-21099	20147
Claiborne Pkwy 21901-21999	20148
Clancy Ter	20147
Clappertown Dr	20147
Clarks Mill Ter	20148
Clary Ct	20147
Claxton Ter	20148
Claybrooke Cir	20147
Clear Lake Sq	20147
Clearfork Ct	20147
Clearnight Ter	20147
Clearwater Ct	20147
Cleland Dr	20148
Clemens Ter	20147
Clifton Ter	20147
Clivedon Ct	20147
Clover Meadow Ct	20148
Clover Valley Ct	20148
Cloverknoll Ct	20147
Cloverleaf Ct	20148
Coach House Sq	20147
Coal Bed Ct	20147
Cobb Run Ter	20147
Cobble Pond Ter	20147
Cobham Ct	20147
Cobham Station Ct	20147
Coburn Ter	20147
Cochrans Lock Dr	20148
Codman Dr	20147
Cog Hill Ter	20147
Cohasset Ter	20147
Coldstream Ter	20147
Colecroft Sq	20147
Collingdale Ter	20147
Colonial Hills Dr	20148
Colonial Village Way	20147
Colter Ct	20147
Coltsfoot Ter	20147
Columbus St	20147
Comfort Ct	20147
Comus Ct	20147
Concord Station Ter	20148
Conesus Sq	20147
Confidence Ct	20147
Conklin Ridge Ct	20148
Connie Marie Ter	20148
Conquest Cir	20148
Conservancy Dr	20148
Cool Fern Sq	20147
Coolspring Ln	20147
Coppersmith Dr	20147
Corder Pl	20147
Cornerpost Sq	20147
Cornerstone Sq	20147
Corning Way	20147
Cornish Ln	20147
Cornstalk Ter	20147
Coronado Ter	20148
Corro Pl	20148
Cortez Ter	20148
Cotton Grass Way	20148
Coulwood Ter	20148
Countrywalk Ct	20147
Courier Ridge Pl	20147
Courtland Dr	20147
Courtland Park Dr	20148
Covent Garden Dr	20147
Cowgill Ct	20147
Cox Mills Ct	20147
Crab Orchard Ct	20147
Crandall Sq	20148
Crane Ct	20147
Crape Myrtle Ter	20147
Creek View Plz	20147
Creighton Rd	20148
Crescent Park Sq	20148
Crescent Pointe Pl	20148
Crested Quail Dr	20148
Crew Sq	20147
Cricket Hill Ct	20148
Cripple Creek Sq	20147
Crocus Ter	20147
Crofton Ct	20147
Crooked Stick Ter	20147
Croson Ln	20148
Cross Breeze Pl	20147
Cross Timber Dr	20148
Crossbeam Sq	20148
Crossbow Ct	20147
Crossroads Dr	20147
Crosswind Ter	20148
Crow Ct	20147
Crowfoot Ct	20147
Crucible Ct	20147
Cruden Bay Dr	20147
Cuba Mills Ct	20147
Cypress Village Dr	20147
Daisy Meadow Dr	20148
Dana Ct	20148
Darby Ter	20147
Day Lily Ter	20147
Deep Furrow Ct	20147
Deepspring Ct	20147
Deepwood Ter	20147
Deer Chase Pl	20147
Deer Run Way	20147
Deerview Dr	20147
Deerwatch Pl	20147
Deirdre Sq	20148
Deleon Dr	20147
Delightful Pl	20148
Demott Dr	20148
Depascale Sq	20148
Desert Forest Dr	20147
Desoto Ter	20148
Devin Shafron Dr	20147
Devonwood Way	20148
Dewberry Ct	20147
Dexter House Ter	20148
Difrank Ct	20147
Digital Loudoun Plz	20147
Dillonvale Ter	20147
Dilworth Sq	20148
Dobson Ct	20147
Dodge Ter	20147
Dolomite Hills Dr	20147
Donnington Pl	20147
Dorothy Ann Ter	20147
Doswell Pl	20147
Dove Wing Ct	20147
Dovetail Pl	20147
Downing Ct	20147
Downington Ct	20147
Dragons Green Sq	20147
Dray Ter	20147
Dreamweaver Dr	20148
Dry Ridge Ter	20148
Dryden Ct	20147
Dublane Pl	20148
Dubois Ct	20147
Ducato Ct	20148
Duck Creek Sq	20148
Dulles Gap Ct	20148
Dunhill Cup Sq	20148
Dunlop Heights Ter	20147
Duryea Ter	20147
Duxbury Ter	20147
Eagle Harbor Ter	20147
Eagle Watch Ct	20148
Earls Ct	20147
Early Light Pl	20148
Eastcreek Dr	20148
Eastern Kingbird Plz	20147
Easthampton Plz	20147
Edgebrook Ct	20147
Edgecliff Ter	20147
Edgemere Ter	20148
Edgemont Sq	20147
Edison Club Ct	20147
Edisto Sq	20147
Edson Ter	20148
Education Ct	20148
Eildon Ter	20147
Elise Pl	20148
Elk View Ter	20147
Ellzey Dr	20148
Elm Grove Ter	20147
Elm Valley Ln	20148
Elmhurst Ct	20147
Emerald Chase Pl	20148
Emperor Dr	20148
Engleside Pl	20148
Epperson Sq	20148
Erskine Ter	20147
Estancia Ter	20148
Estate Pl	20147
Evening Breeze Ct	20148
Evening Primrose Sq	20147
Evergold Ter	20147
Evergreen Mills Rd	20148
Evergreen Ridge Dr	20148
Eversole Ter	20148
Exchange St	20147
Expedition Dr	20148
Explorer Dr	20148
Fairhunt Dr	20148
Fairlawn Dr	20148
Fairweather Ct	20148
Faith Ter	20148
Falcon Ridge Ct	20148
Fallen Hills Dr	20148
Fallen Timber Ln	20148
Falling Ter	20148
Falling Leaf Ct	20148
Falling Rock Ter	20148
Falmouth Ct	20147
Fanshaw Sq	20148
Far Hills Ct	20147
Farmgate Ter	20148
Farmingdale Dr	20147
Farmwell Rd	20147
Farmwell Hunt Plz	20147
Fawn Ridge Ct	20148
Fawngrove Ct	20147
Felicity Pl	20148
Fellowship Sq	20147
Fenway Cir	20148
Fenwick Dr	20147
Fernbrook Ct	20148
Ferncliff Ter	20147
Ferncrest Ter	20148
Fernridge Way	20147
Field Station Ter	20148
Fieldgrass Sq	20147
Fieldthorn Ter	20148
Filigree Ct	20147
Fincastle Dr	20147
Findon Ct	20147
Firedrake Ter	20148
Fishers Island Ct	20147
Fitzgerald Dr	20147
Flagstaff Plz	20148
Flanders Ct	20147
Flattop Ct	20147
Fling Ct	20147
Flora Mure Dr	20148
Flora Springs Ter	20147
Florence Ter	20147
Flowing Spring Sq	20148
Flushing Meadows Ct	20147
Foche Ter	20148
Fontenoy Way	20148
Foothill Ter	20147
Footstep Ter	20147
Fordham Ter	20147
Forest Crest Ct	20148
Forest Edge Sq	20148
Forest Farm Ln	20147
Forest Highlands Ct	20147
Forest Manor Dr	20148
Forest Run Dr	20148
Forest View Ct	20148
Founders Dr	20148
Fountain Grass Ter	20148
Fountain Grove Sq	20148
Fowlers Mill Cir	20147
Fox Fire Ter	20148
Fox Tracks Ter	20148
Foxgrove Ct	20147
Foxthorn Ter	20147
Foyt Ter	20147
Frame Sq	20148
Franklin Benjamin Ter	20148
Free Stone Ter	20147
Freedom Station Plz	20148
French Open Ct	20147
Frenchmans Creek Ter	20147
Frogs Leap Ter	20147
Frogtown Way	20148
Frontier Dr	20148
Frost Ct	20147
Frugality Ct	20147
Fullerton St	20147
Fultonham Cir	20147
Gala Cir	20148
Galbraith Sq	20148
Gardengate Cir	20147
Gardenpost Sq	20147
Gardenwalk Dr	20148
Gardenwall Ter	20148
Gatehouse Way	20148
Gatwick Sq	20147
Gayton Ter	20147
Geddes Ter	20147
Generation Dr	20147
Gentle Falls Dr	20148
Gentle Heights Ct	20148
Genuine Reward Ct	20147
George Washington Blvd	20147
Ginghamsburg Pl	20147
Girdland Ct	20147
Gladwyne Ct	20147
Glebe View Dr	20148
Gleedsville Manor Dr	20148
Glen Castle Ct	20147
Glenburn Ter	20147
Glendower Ct	20147
Glenelder Ter	20147
Glenhazel Dr	20147
Glenorchy Ct	20148
Glenrobin Ter	20147
Glenside Dr	20148
Globe Mills Ct	20147
Gloucester Pkwy	20147
Glyndebourne Ct	20147
Golden Autumn Pl	20148
Golden Bear Ct	20147
Golden Meadow Cir	20147
Golden Plover Pl	20148
Golden Ridge Dr	20147
Goldenrod Dr	20148
Goldenseal Sq	20148
Goldsborough Ter	20148
Good Hope Ln	20148
Goodwin Ct	20148
Goodwood Ter	20147
Goose Cross Ter	20148
Goose Glen Ln	20147
Goose Preserve Dr	20148
Goosefoot Sq	20148
Gordon Park Sq	20147
Gotham Way	20147
Grace Bridge Dr	20147
Graceford Ter	20148
Grahams Stable Sq	20148
Grainery Ct	20147
Granite Mountain Ter	20147
Grantner Pl	20147
Graves Ln	20147
Gray Falcon Sq	20148
Grayling Ter	20148
Great Harvest Ct	20147
Great Heron Sq	20148
Great Sky Pl	20148
Green Stable Sq	20147
Green Teal Ct	20148
Greenbrier Ct	20147
Greenlook Ln	20148
Greenside Dr	20148
Greenspring Ct	20147
Greenway Corporate Dr	20147
Greenwich Sq	20147
Gresham Dr	20147
Grey Slate Ct	20147
Greymont Ter	20147
Greyswallow Ter	20147
Gristmill Ct	20147
Grottoes Dr	20147
Grove Ter	20147
Grovemont Ter	20147
Guildhall Dr	20148
Guilford Dr	20147
Gulicks Landing Ct	20148
Gullane Way	20148
Halburton Ter	20148
Hales Trace Dr	20148
Haley Ct	20147
Hamilton Chapel Ter	20148
Hammersmith Pl	20148
Hampton Woods Ter	20148
Hansberry Ter	20147
Hanworth St	20148
Haraden Ter	20148
Hardage Ter	20148
Hardwood Ter	20147
Harmony Ct	20147
Harper Manor Ct	20148
Harroun Ter	20147
Harry Byrd Hwy	20147
Harte Ct	20147
Hartley Pl	20147
Hartsville Ter	20147
Hartwell St	20147
Harvest Green Ter	20148
Harwich Sq	20147
Hastings Dr	20147
Hatten Cross Ct	20147
Haven Crest Way	20147
Hawkbill Sq	20148
Hawksbury Ter	20148
Hay Rd	20147
Hayshire Ct	20147
Haystack Ct	20147
Hazeltine Pl	20147
Hazleton Way	20147
Hearford Ln	20147
Heart Pine Sq	20148
Hearthstone Ct	20147
Heathbrook Way	20148
Heather Leigh Ct	20147
Heather Meadow Dr	20148
Heather Mews Dr	20148
Heatherton Ct	20147
Hedgeapple Ct	20147
Hedgerow Ter	20147
Helen Marie Ct	20147
Helix Dr	20147
Hemingway Dr	20147
Hempland Dr	20147
Hensley Hunt Ct	20148
Hepatica Ct	20148
Heritage Oak Ct	20148
Hermitage Ct	20148
Hibiscus Dr	20147
Hickory Corner Ter	20147
Hickory Hill Sq	20148
Hickox Dr	20148
Hidden Creek Ct	20147
Hidden Pond Pl	20148
Hiddengrove Ct	20147
Higbee Ln	20148
High Haven Ter	20148
High Rock Ter	20147
Highcrest Cir	20148
Highcroft Ter	20148
Highgate Ter	20148
Highgrove Ter	20148
Highland Vista Dr	20147
Highview Trail Pl	20148
Hillary Way	20147
Hillgate Ter	20148
Hillmont Ter	20148
Hillsboro Hunt Dr	20148
Hollister Pl	20148
Hollowind Ct	20148
Holly Knoll Ct	20148
Hollyberry Ct	20147
Hollyhock Ter	20148
Hollywood Park Pl	20147
Holyoke Dr	20147
Homecrest Ct	20147
Homeland Ter	20147
Homestead Landing Ct	20148
Hope Spring Ter	20147
Hopewell Manor Ter	20148
Hopi Dr	20147
Hornbeam Pl	20147
Houseman Ter	20148
Howardsville Woods Ct	20148
Howe Dr	20147
Hoysville Manor Dr	20148
Hughesville Manor Ct	20148
Humbolt Sq	20147
Hunt Manor Ct	20148
Hunters Green Sq	20148
Huntford Ter	20147
Huntland Ct	20147
Huntsman Sq	20148
Huron Ter	20147
Huxley Ter	20147
Hyde Park Dr	20147
Hyrst Grove Ter	20147
Iannis Spring Dr	20148
Ice Pond Dr	20147
Ice Rink Plz	20147
Incas Ter	20147
Ingersoll Way	20148
Inglewood Ct	20148
Inman Park Pl	20147
Interlachen Cir	20147
Inverness Sq	20147
Iredell Ter	20148
Irongate Way	20147
Isherwood Ter	20147
Island Ave	20147
Island West Sq	20147
Ivy Glen Ct	20148
Ivy Walk Ter	20148
Ivymount Ter	20147
Ivywood Ter	20148
Jackpit Ln	20147
Janelia Ln	20147
Janelia Farm Blvd	20147
Janneys Corner Ct	20148
Jarvis Sq	20147
Jenkins Ln	20147
Jennifer Ann Dr	20147
Jersey Mills Pl	20147
Jessica Farm Ter	20148
John Danforth Ct	20147
Judith Ln	20147
Julia St	20148
Julie Martin Ct	20147
Junction Plz	20147
Kathleen Elizabeth Dr	20147
Katie Leigh Ct	20147
Keane Ct	20147
Keiller Ter	20147
Keller Sq	20147
Kelsey Sq	20147
Kenilworth Ter	20147
Kennerly Ter	20148
Kentmere Ct	20147
Kentucky Oaks Ct	20147
Keverne Ct	20148
Kiawah Island Dr	20147
Killarney Way	20147
Killawog Ter	20147
Kimberly Anne Ct	20147
Kindred Ter	20148
Kings Arms Sq	20147
Kings Crossing Ter	20147
Kingsdale Ter	20148
Kingston Station Ter	20148

Street	ZIP
Kirkland St	20147
Kisko Way	20147
Kitchen Prim Ct	20148
Kittanning Ln	20147
Kitts Hill Ter	20147
Kleinsmith Way	20148
Klondike Ct	20148
Knob Hill Pl	20148
Knoll Sq	20147
Knolls Hill Sq	20147
Knotty Oak Ter	20148
Kouros Ct	20147
Kristin Marie Ct	20147
La Belle Pl	20147
La Bete Ct	20147
La Riva Dr	20148
Laburnum Sq	20147
Laceyville Ter	20147
Ladiesburg Pl	20147
Lady Fern Pl	20148
Ladyslipper Sq	20147
Lago Gallerie Ct	20148
Lago Stella Pl	20148
Lakeview Center Plz	20147
Lakeview Overlook Plz	20147
Lamoreaux Landing Sq	20148
Lansing Ter	20147
Lantana Dr	20148
Laplume Pl	20147
Laporte Ter	20147
Larchmont Way	20148
Larue Ct	20148
Lauder Ter	20147
Laughing Quail Ct	20148
Laurel Creek Way	20147
Laurel Leaf Ct	20147
Laurel Ridge Dr	20148
Laurier Dr	20148
Lavender Meadow Pl	20148
Lawnsberry Sq	20147
Lazy River Ter	20147
Lcsa Campus Ln	20147
Leah May Ct	20147
Leanne Ter	20148
Leesylvania Ct	20148
Lefevre Inn Dr	20148
Legacy Park Dr	20148
Leier Pl	20147
Leithtown Mill Ct	20148
Lemon Springs Ter	20147
Lenox Park Ter	20148
Lentils Ln	20148
Lexington Dr	20147
Lightsey Ridge Ter	20147
Lincoln Woods Ct	20148
Linden Oaks Ln	20148
Lindsay Marie Dr	20147
Lindsey Heights Pl	20148
Lister Ter	20147
Litchfield Ter	20147
Liverpool St	20147
Livery Sq	20147
Livingston Ter	20148
Livonia Ter	20147
Locust Dale Ter	20147
Lofthill Dr	20148
Loganberry Ter	20148
Logans Ridge Ter	20148
Loganwood Ct	20147
Logmill Ct	20147
Lohengrin Ct	20147
Lois Ln	20148
London Way	20148
London Bridge Ter	20147
Longfeather Way	20148
Longview Dr	20147
Lonsdale Dr	20148
Lord Fairfax Pl	20147
Lord Nelson Ter	20147
Lords Valley Ter	20147
Lost Branch Cir	20148
Lost Creek Ter	20148
Lost Moccasin Ter	20147
Loudoun St	20147
Loudoun County Pkwy	20147
Loudoun Reserve Dr	20148
Loudoun Water Way	20147
Louisa Dr	20147
Lovettsville Knoll Ct	20148
Lowry Park Ter	20148
Lucinda Ct	20147
Luck Ln	20147
Lucketts Bridge Cir	20148
Ludlum Ct	20147
Macauley Pl	20148
Macdougall Ter	20148
Macedonia Ct	20147
Macglashan Ter	20147
Madison Renee Ter	20147
Magellan Sq	20148
Maiden Creek Ct	20147
Maidsville Ct	20147
Maison Blanc Sq	20148
Maison Carree Sq	20148
Maitland Ter	20147
Majestic Knolls Dr	20148
Malachite Ter	20148
Malden Pl	20147
Malin Ct	20147
Maltese Falcon Sq	20147
Mandalay Ct	20147
Manitoba Ct	20148
Mantua Sq	20148
Maple Branch Ter	20147
Maplegrove Ct	20147
Mapleton Ct	20148
Marble Chip Ct	20147
Marble Summit Ter	20147
Marblehead Dr	20147
Marburg Ter	20148
Marchand Ln	20147
Mare Ter	20147
Marigold Mill Pl	20148
Markham Pl	20147
Marquette Ct	20148
Marsh Creek Dr	20148
Mary Rita Ter	20147
Marymount Ter	20147
Mason Ridge Ct	20148
Matchlock Ct	20147
Mayburgh Ter	20148
Mayflower Ter	20148
Maynard Sq	20147
Mccollough Ct	20147
Mccroskey Ct	20148
Mchenry Sq	20147
Meadfoot Ter	20148
Meadow Field Ct	20148
Meadow Grove Dr	20147
Meadow Overlook Pl	20147
Meadow Sage Dr	20147
Meadowsweet Ct	20147
Meadowthrash Ct	20147
Meander Crossing Ct	20148
Meandering Ter	20147
Mears Ter	20147
Mechanicsville Glen St	20148
Medalist Dr	20147
Medinah Ct	20147
Medix Run Pl	20147
Medley Ter	20147
Melanie Ct	20147
Mellon Cir	20147
Melville Ter	20148
Memorial Heights Ct	20148
Menges Mill Ct	20147
Meridian Hill Dr	20148
Merion St	20147
Meriweather Ct	20148
Merryoak Way	20147
Merrywood Ct	20147
Michener Dr	20147
Middle Ridge Pl	20148
Middlebrook Ter	20147
Middleburg Chapel Ct	20148
Middlebury St	20147
Middleham Ct	20148
Midsummer Way	20148
Midvale Ct	20147
Milestone Sq	20147
Milford Dr	20148
Mill Quarter Pl	20148
Millay Ct	20147
Millstead Dr	20147
Milltown Farm Ct	20148
Millwick Ter	20148
Minerva Dr	20148
Mingo Ter	20147
Minthill Ter	20147
Mintwood Ct	20147
Mirror Pond Pl	20148
Mistflower Cir	20148
Mistletoe Ter	20147
Misty Creek Pl	20147
Misty Meadow Ct	20147
Mitcham Sq	20148
Mitchell Ct	20147
Mizner Ter	20147
Moccasin Ter	20147
Mohave Dr	20147
Mohegan Dr	20147
Monmouth Ter	20147
Monti Cimini Ct	20147
Moonglow Ct	20148
Mooreview Pkwy	20148
Moreland Point Ct	20148
Morning Walk Dr	20148
Morrisonville Corner Ct	20148
Morven Sq	20147
Morven Woods Ct	20148
Moss Landing Ct	20148
Mossy Brook Sq	20147
Mossy Glen Ter	20147
Mount Auburn Pl	20148
Mount Hope Rd	20148
Mount Middleton Sq	20148
Mount Pleasant Ter	20147
Mountville Woods Dr	20148
Muirfield Village Ct	20148
Muirwood Ct	20148
Munday Hill Pl	20148
Mustoe Pl	20147
Myan Gold Dr	20148
Myerstown Manor Dr	20148
Naismith Ter	20147
Napier Ter	20148
Naples Lakes Ter	20147
Narragansett Ter	20148
Nashua St	20147
Natalie Ter	20147
Navajo Dr	20147
Ned Dr	20148
Needham Way	20147
Needleleaf Way	20147
Needlepine Ct	20147
Needmore Ct	20147
Neponset St	20147
New Dawn Ter	20148
Newbridge Sq	20148
Nichols Farm Way	20148
Nickens Pl	20148
Nightshade Pl	20147
Nightwatch St	20147
Nokes Corner Ter	20148
Nootka Ter	20147
Northville Hills Ter	20147
Norwalk Sq	20148
Norwich Pl	20147
Nottingham Sq	20147
Novi Ter	20147
Oak Post Ct	20148
Oakencroft Ct	20147
Oakhill Heights Ct	20148
Oakmont Manor Sq	20147
Oakville Ter	20147
Oatlands Grove Pl	20148
Oatyer Ct	20148
Ocean Forest Ct	20147
Ogilvie Sq	20148
Oglethorpe Ct	20148
Ohara Ct	20147
Old Gallivan Ter	20148
Old Grey Pl	20147
Old Kinderhook Dr	20147
Old Ryan Rd	20148
Oldetowne Pl	20147
Olive Green Ct	20147
Olmsted Dr	20148
Olympia Dr	20148
Olympic Club Ct	20147
Omeara Ter	20147
Orchard Grass Ter	20148
Orchard Oriole Dr	20147
Ordinary Pl	20147
Orefield Ter	20148
Osage Ct	20147
Overland Park Dr	20147
Owings Ter	20147
Owls Nest Sq	20147
Oyster Reef Pl	20147
Pablo Creek Ct	20147
Paget Ter	20147
Pagoda Ter	20147
Pale Iris Ter	20148
Palladian Ct	20147
Palladian Blue Ter	20148
Pallan Ter	20148
Palmer Classic Pkwy	20147
Pandora Ct	20147
Panmure Ct	20148
Panther Ridge Dr	20147
Paradise Spring Ct	20148
Park Brooke Ct	20148
Park Creek Dr	20148
Park Glenn Dr	20148
Park Grove Ter	20147
Parkhurst Plz	20147
Parkland Farms Ter	20148
Parkview Dr	20148
Parliamentary Sq	20147
Parlor Sq	20147
Parsells Ridge Ct	20148
Partlow Rd	20148
Pascale Ter	20147
Pasture Rose Pl	20148
Patching Pond Sq	20148
Patrick Wayne Sq	20148
Pattyjean Ter	20147
Paw Paw Ct	20147
Pawnee Ter	20147
Peckham St	20147
Pecos Ln	20148
Pelican Hill Ct	20148
Pennesto Ter	20147
Pennyroyal Sq	20148
Peregrine Ter	20148
Perennial Ln	20147
Petersham Dr	20148
Petworth Ct	20147
Phelps Ter	20147
Philomont Ridge Ct	20148
Piccadilly Plz	20147
Piccadilly Circus Ct	20147
Pickens Way	20148
Pickerelweed Ter	20147
Pickett Corner Ter	20148
Piedmont Hunt Ter	20148
Pilate Sq	20147
Pimlico Way	20147
Pine Ridge Ct	20148
Pine Top Ct	20148
Pinkhorn Way	20148
Pioneer Ridge Ter	20147
Pipeline Plz	20147
Plainfield St	20147
Plantation Ter	20147
Player Ct	20147
Pleasant Forest Ct	20148
Plum Ridge Ter	20147
Plymouth Pl	20147
Plympton Sq	20148
Pocosin Ct	20148
Point Bay Ter	20147
Pomeroy Ct	20148
Poole Ct	20148
Port Royal Cir	20147
Portico Pl	20148
Portsmouth Blvd	20147
Postrail Sq	20147
Potomac Dr	20148
Potomac Trail Cir	20148
Potter Ter	20147
Powderhorn Ct	20147
Prairie Aster Ct	20148
Prairie Dunes Ter	20147
Preakness Ct	20147
Preddy Ct	20147
Premier Plz	20147
Prentice Dr	20146
Presidents Cup Ter	20147
Preston Ct	20147
Princeville Ct	20147
Professional Plz	20147
Prosperity Ridge Pl	20148
Providence Forge Dr	20148
Pueblos Sq	20147
Puller Ter	20148
Pumpkin Ridge Ct	20147
Pushmore Ct	20148
Pyrocantha Way	20147
Quail Hollow Dr	20147
Quail Pond Pl	20148
Quante Sq	20148
Queensbridge Dr	20148
Quiet Walk Ter	20147
Quillback Ct	20148
Rachelle Ann Ct	20147
Rachels Row Ter	20148
Radcliff Ter	20148
Railstop Ter	20147
Rainsboro Dr	20148
Raintree Ct	20147
Raleigh Pl	20147
Ramblin Ct	20148
Rampsbeck Ter	20148
Ravenglass Dr	20148
Rawnsley Dr	20148
Raymond Way	20147
Reamy Way	20148
Rectors Chase Way	20148
Red Admiral Pl	20148
Red Rum Dr	20147
Red Shale Ct	20148
Red Tartan Way	20148
Redeemer Ter	20147
Redfield St	20147
Redgate Way	20148
Redpath Ter	20147
Redskin Park Dr	20147
Redstone Ter	20148
Regal Wood Dr	20148
Reigate Way	20148
Reliance Ct	20147
Renova Ter	20147
Research Pl	20147
Reservoir Ridge Pl	20148
Revival Dr	20148
Reynwood Pl	20148
Rhett Dr	20148
Ribboncrest Ter	20147
Richfield Way	20147
Richland Grove Dr	20148
Rickenbacker Sq	20147
Ridenour Ridge Ln	20148
Riders Sq	20147
Ridgecrest Sq	20147
Ridgeview Pl	20147
Ridgeway Dr	20148
Riding Mill Pl	20148
Riggins Ridge Ter	20148
Ringneck Pl	20148
Ringold Dr	20147
Ringtail Ct	20148
Rising Moon Pl	20148
Rising Sun Ter	20147
River Ridge Ter	20147
Rivermont Ter	20147
Riverside Pkwy	20147
Riverstone Ct	20148
Roaming Shores Ter	20147
Robindale Ct	20147
Rochelle Ct	20147
Rock Bar Ter	20147
Rock Cove Ter	20147
Rock Harbor Cir	20147
Rockfield Ct	20147
Rockrose Sq	20148
Rockslide Ter	20148
Rocky Knoll Sq	20147
Romans Dr	20147
Rootstown Ter	20147
Rosalind St	20148
Rose Leigh Ter	20148
Rose Quartz Sq	20148
Rosedale Ct	20147
Rosetta Pl	20147
Rosewood Manor Sq	20147
Roslindale Dr	20147
Rosses Point Ct	20147
Rostormel Ct	20147
Rothschild Ct	20147
Rowley Ter	20147
Royal Crest Sq	20147
Royal Fern Ter	20148
Rubble Ter	20147
Rubles Mill Ct	20147
Ruby Dusk Way	20148
Ruffsdale Ct	20147
Runnymeade Ter	20148
Rush Run Ter	20147
Rushmore Ct	20148
Russell Branch Pkwy	20147
Ryan Rd	20148
Ryan Center Way	20147
Ryan Corner Pl	20147
Ryan Park Ter	20147
Ryder Cup Sq	20147
Ryder Mills Ct	20147
Safe Habor Ter	20148
Safflower Ct	20148
Sagamore Sq	20148
Sailfish Sq	20148
Saint Germain Ct	20147
Saint Helena Ter	20147
San Joaquin Ter	20147
Sandburg Sq	20147
Sandhurst Ct	20148
Sandi Louise Ct	20147
Sandwort Ter	20148
Saranac St	20147
Saratoga Ct	20147
Saratoga Springs Pl	20147
Savin Hill Dr	20147
Sawyer Sq	20147
Saxony Ter	20147
Scara Pl	20148
Scarlet Rush Ct	20147
Scattersville Gap Ter	20148
Schenley Ter	20147
Schoolhouse Ct	20148
Scientific Way	20147
Scioto Ter	20147
Scotchbridge Pl	20148
Sebago Ln	20147
Secretariat Ct	20147
Seneca Sq	20147
Settlers Trail Ter	20148
Shadow Creek Ct	20147
Shadow Walk Sq	20147
Shady Glen Ter	20147
Shady Wood Ter	20148
Shadyside Ter	20147
Shandali Rd	20148
Sharpie Sq	20148
Shawbury Cir	20148
Sheffield Ct	20147
Shehawken Ter	20147
Shellhorn Rd	20147
Shockey Farms Ln	20148
Shy Beaver Ct	20148
Sibbald Sq	20147
Sidney Pl	20148
Silken Moss Ct	20148
Silkworth Ter	20147
Silo Creek Ter	20147
Silver Bluff Ln	20148
Silver Creek Ter	20147
Silver Queen Ter	20147
Silverdale Dr	20148
Silverthistle Ct	20147
Silverthorne Ct	20148
Simonet Blanc Ter	20147
Slate Range Ter	20147
Small Branch Pl	20148
Smith Cir	20147
Smith Switch Rd	20147
Smokehouse Ct	20147
Smollet Ter	20147
Snickersville Kiln Ct	20148
Snow Powder Ter	20148
Snowpine Pl	20148
Snowpoint Pl	20147
Snowshoe Sq	20147
Soave Dr	20148
Soft Breeze Ter	20148
Solheim Cup Ter	20148
Somerset Crossing Pl	20148
Somerset Hills Ter	20147
Sonara Ln	20147
Song Sparrow Ln	20148
Songbird Ct	20148
Sorrel Grove Ct	20147
Southern Walk Plz	20148
Southolme Way	20147
Southview Manor Dr	20148
Southwind Ter	20147
Southwoods Ter	20148
Sperrin Ct	20147
Spice Bush Ter	20148
Spiceberry Ct	20147
Splitrock Way	20148
Spring Dew Dr	20148
Spring Morning Ct	20148
Spring Splendor Dr	20148
Springwater Ct	20147
Springwell Dr	20148
Sprucegrove Sq	20147
Spyglass Hill Ct	20147
St Theresa Ln	20147
Stableford Sq	20147
Stanford Hall Pl	20147
Stardust Way	20148
Starflower Way	20147
Statesboro Pl	20148
Steamside Pl	20147
Steatite Ct	20147
Steinbeck Sq	20147
Stepney Dr	20147
Still Creek Dr	20148
Stillbrook Farm Dr	20148
Stillforest Ter	20148
Stillpond Ct	20147
Stillwater Ter	20148
Stockham Way	20148
Stoke Chapel Ter	20148
Stone Hollow Dr	20148
Stone Roses Cir	20147
Stonebridge Dr	20147
Stonecottage Pl	20147
Stonecrop Pl	20147
Stonegarden Ter	20148
Stonehill Ct	20147
Stonestile Pl	20148
Stonewheel Way	20148
Stoneyglen Ct	20147
Stoneyrun Pl	20147
Straloch Ter	20147
Stratford Landing Dr	20148
Strawrick Ter	20147
Stronghold Ct	20147
Stubble Rd	20147
Sturman Pl	20148
Sugarview Dr	20148
Summer Rain Ct	20148
Summerhouse Pl	20148
Summersweet Pl	20148
Summerwood Cir	20147
Summithill Ct	20147
Sunbury St	20148
Sundance Sq	20148
Sunderland Ter	20148
Sunderleigh Sq	20148
Sundial Ct	20148
Sungrove Ter	20148
Sunset Ter	20147
Sunset Maple Dr	20147
Sunset Ridge Sq	20148
Sunstone Ct	20148
Susan Leslie Dr	20147
Suscon Sq	20147
Suzanne Hope Way	20147

Swallowtail Way 20148
Swampfox Ct 20147
Sweet Andrea Dr 20148
Sweet Bay Ter 20148
Sweet Clover Pl 20147
Sweet Grass Way 20147
Sweet Jen Ter 20148
Sweetair Ct 20147
Sweetbells Ct 20148
Sweetpine Ln 20148
Sycolin Rd
20700-20798 20148
20900-20998 20147
21000-21012 20147
21014-21098 20147
Tall Pines Ct 20147
Tally Ho Ct 20147
Tandridge Way 20148
Tannahill Ter 20147
Tara Ct 20148
Tattinger Ter 20148
Tavern Dr 20147
Tavernsprings Ct 20147
Taylorstown Hunt Ct 20148
Tealbriar Pl 20148
Telford Ter 20147
Terra Rosa Pl 20148
Thatcher Ter 20147
Thimbleberry Sq 20148
Thimbleweed Ct 20147
Thistledown Ter 20148
Thistlewood Ct 20147
Tholen St 20147
Thornblade Cir 20148
Thorncroft Ter 20148
Thorndike St 20147
Thornhill Pl 20148
Thoroughfare Gap Ter 20148
Thurgood Ter 20147
Tiger Lily Pl 20147
Tilberg St 20147
Tillman Ter 20147
Tiltonsville Ter 20147
Timber Ridge Ter 20147
Timberbrooke Pl 20147
Tioga Ter 20147
Tippecanoe Ter 20147
Tithables Cir 20148
Tivoli Ln 20148
Tobacco Sq 20147
Tolamac Dr 20147
Toulouse Ter 20147
Tourmaline Ln 20148
Tournament Pkwy 20147
Tradewind Dr 20148
Trails End Ter 20147
Trajans Column Ter 20148
Trappe Rock Ct 20148
Trask Pl 20147
Treeside Pl 20148
Trellis Sq 20148
Triple Crown Ct 20147
Trout Ter 20147
Trowbridge Sq 20147
Truro Parish Dr 20148
Tucker Ln 20148
Tumbletree Ter 20148
Tunstall Ter 20148
Twain Ter 20147
Twelve Oaks Way 20147
Twin Falls Ter 20148
Twinleaf Dr 20148
Twitter Sq 20148
Tyler Too Ter 20148
Tyrone Ter 20147
Unison Knoll Cir 20148
University Dr 20147
Upland Ter 20147
Upperville Heights Sq 20148
Urbancrest Ct 20147
Uunet Dr 20147
Val Aosta Dr 20148
Val Varaita Dr 20148
Valhalla Sq 20147
Valle Ducale Dr 20148
Valley Falls Sq 20147
Valley Preserve Ct 20147
Vanguard Way 20148
Vantage Pointe Pl 20148
Velvet Grass Ln 20148
Vendome Ct 20147
Verde Gate Ter 20148
Verlaine Ct 20147
Vermeer St 20147
Vernon Ridge Ter 20148
Vestals Gap Dr 20148
Vestry Ct 20148
Via Veneto Way 20148
Vickery Park Dr 20148
Victorias Cross Ter 20147
Vienna Green Ter 20148
Vineland Sq 20147
Vineyard Ter 20147
Vino Rosso Ct 20148
Violet Mist Ter 20148
Virginia Manor Ter 20148
Virginia Oak Ct 20148
Virginia Rae Ct 20148
Virginia Rose Pl 20148
Volley Ter 20148
Vosburg Ter 20147
Waccamaw Sq 20147
Walkley Hill Pl 20148
Walsheid Ter 20147
Walter Ter 20148
Wardlaw Ter 20148
Washburn Ter 20148
Watch Hill Ter 20147
Water Run Ct 20148
Waterberry Ter 20148
Waterleaf Dr 20148
Waterpointe Ter 20148
Watershed Ct 20147
Watertown Ter 20147
Watson Heights Cir 20148
Waverly Ct 20147
Waxpool Rd
42500-42799 20148
42800-43200 20148
43202-43298 20148
43300-44699 20147
Wayside Cir 20147
Weatherwood Dr 20147
Webster Ct 20148
Wedgeford Way 20147
Welborne Manor Sq 20148
Welbourne Walk Ct 20148
Welbourne Woods Dr 20148
Welby Ter 20148
Wellfleet Dr 20147
Wellhouse Ct 20147
Wellsboro Dr 20147
Welty Ct 20147
Westdale Ct 20148
Westmont Ter 20147
Weybridge Sq 20148
Wheatlands Chase Ct 20148
Whelplehill Ter 20148
Whetstone Ct 20147
Whisperhill Ct 20148
Whisperwood Ter 20147
Whistling Straits Pl 20147
White Birch Way 20147
White Ibis Dr 20148
White Post Way 20148
White Yarrow Ct 20148
Whitford Sq 20147
Wild Iris Ter 20148
Wild Meadow Ct 20147
Wild River Sq 20148
Wild Timber Ct 20147
Wildbrook Ct 20147
Wildflower Sq 20147
Wildly Ter 20148
Wildrose Ct 20147
Willington Sq 20148
Willow Bend Dr 20148
Willow Creek Way 20148
Willowbrook Dr 20147
Willowdale Pl 20147
Wilmar Sq 20148
Windflower Dr 20148
Winding Brook Sq 20147
Windmill Dr 20147
Windover Dr 20148
Windrow Ct 20147
Windsor Locks Sq 20148
Windy Oaks Sq 20148
Windy Pine Ct 20148
Wingfoot Ct 20148
Winkle Dr 20147
Winola Ter 20147
Winter Haven Dr 20148
Winter Lake Ct 20148
Winter Wind Ter 20148
Winterbourne Sq 20148
Wintergrove Dr 20147
Wintersrun Ct 20148
Winthrop Ct 20147
Wispy Green Ter 20148
Witham Sq 20148
Withers Grove Ct 20148
Withorne Way 20148
Woodspice Ct 20148
Woodworth Ct 20147
Woolsey Dr 20148
World Woods Ct 20147
Wrathall Dr 20148
Wythridge Ct 20148
Yancey Ter 20148
Yarmouth Dr 20147
Yeats Sq 20148
Yellow Star Ter 20148
Yellowbloom Ct 20147
York Crest Ter 20148
Yorkshire Ct 20147
Yorkville Ter 20147
Yukon Dr 20147
Zander Ter 20147
Zion Chapel Dr 20148
Zuknick Ter 20147
Zulla Chase Pl 20148
Zulla Manor Pl 20148

BLACKSBURG VA

General Delivery 24060

POST OFFICE BOXES MAIN OFFICE STATIONS AND BRANCHES

Box No.s
A - U 24063
1 - 1014 24063
10001 - 90005 24062

NAMED STREETS

Adams Marke Dr 24060
Aden Ln 24060
Airport Rd 24060
Albemarle Ln 24060
Albert Ln 24060
Aleph Ln 24060
Algonquin Ct 24060
Alice Dr 24060
Alleghany St 24060
Allendale Ct 24060
E & W Ambler Johnston 24060
Anchor Rd 24060
Anne Dr 24060
Anthracite Ln 24060
Apartment Heights Dr 24060
Appalachian Dr 24060
Apperson Dr 24060
Arden Ln 24060
Ardmore St 24060
Arrington Rd 24060
Artis Ct 24060
Ascot Ln 24060
Asher Ln 24060
Ashford Ct 24060
Ashlawn Dr 24060
Auburn Dr 24060
Augusta National Dr 24060
Autumn Ln 24060
Autumn Splendor Way 24060
Azalea Dr 24060
Backwoods Ln 24060
Ballard Ct 24060
Bannister Ln 24060
Barger St 24060
Barringer Dr 24060
Batavia Ln 24060
Batts Rd 24060
Bay Tree Pl 24060
Bee Ln 24060
Belaire Dr 24060
Bennett St 24060
E & W Benoit Dr 24060
Berkeley Ct 24060
Berryfield Ln 24060
Bet Dr 24060
Big Falls Rd 24060
Big Run Rd 24060
Big Sky Trl 24060
Big Vein Rd 24060
Birchleaf Ln 24060
Bishop Rd 24060
Bixby Ct 24060
Blacksburg Ln 24060
Blossom Trl E & W 24060
Blue Jay Ln 24060
Blue Ridge Dr 24060
Bobcat Ln 24060
Bobwhite Dr 24060
Boxwood Dr 24060
Bradley Ln 24060
Branch St 24060
Brattle Ln 24060
Breckenridge Dr 24060
Brevard Ln 24060
Briarwood Dr 24060
Brighton Ct 24060
Brightwood Manor Dr 24060
Broce Dr 24060
Brockton St 24060
Brodie 24060
Broken Oak Dr 24060
Brook Cir 24060
Brooksfield Rd 24060
Bruin Ln 24060
Brumfield Rd 24060
Brunswick Dr 24060
Brush Mountain Cir & Rd 24060
Brush Mountain Creek Rd 24060
Bryant Ln 24060
Buchanan Dr 24060
Buck Mountain Rdg 24060
Buckingham Pl 24060
Buckshot Ln 24060
Buckskin Rd 24060
Bunny Trail Dr 24060
Burley Ln 24060
Burruss Dr 24060
Butternut Rd 24060
Caldwell Dr 24060
Calico Ln 24060
Cambridge Rd 24060
Camelot Ct 24060
Cameo Ln 24060
E Campbell 24060
Campus Edge Ct 24060
Canterbury Ct 24060
Capistrano St 24060
Cara Ct 24060
Cardinal Ct 24060
Carlson Dr 24060
Carroll Dr 24060
Cascade Ct 24060
Cascades Rd 24060
Catawba Rd 24060
Catnip Ln 24060
Cedar Walk 24060
Cedar Hill Dr 24060
Cedar Orchard Dr E & W 24060
Cedar Run Rd 24060
Cedarview Dr 24060
Centennial Rd 24060
Center St 24060
Charles St 24060
Charlotte Dr 24060
Chateau Ct 24060
Chelsea Ct 24060
Cherokee Dr & Trl 24060
Cherry Ln 24060
Chestnut Dr 24060
Chickadee Cir 24060
Chickahominy Dr 24060
Chowning Pl & Trl 24060
Christine Ct 24060
Christopher Dr 24060
Church St NE & SE 24060
Circle Dr 24060
Clairmont Dr 24060
Clay Cir & St 24060
Claytor Sq 24060
Cleo Ln 24060
Clover Valley Cir 24060
Clubhouse Rd 24060
Coal Bank Hollow Rd 24060
Coalwood Way 24060
Cochrane 24060
Cohee Rd 24060
College Ave 24060
College View Dr 24060
Collegiate Ct 24060
Colonial Dr 24060
Commerce St 24060
Conner Ln 24060
Copper Croft Run 24060
Cork Dr 24060
Cottonwood Dr 24060
Council Ln 24060
Country Acres Rd 24060
Country Club Dr SE & SW 24060
Countryside Ct 24060
Court Ln N 24060
Courtney Cir 24060
Craig Dr 24060
E Craig Creek Rd 24060
Cranberry Ln 24060
Cranwell Cir 24060
Creasy Reynolds Ln 24060
Crestview Dr 24060
Crestwood Dr 24060
Crimson Dr 24060
Cupp St 24060
Cypress Ln 24060
Dairy Rd 24060
Daisy Rd 24060
Dalet Dr 24060
Davis St 24060
Deer Run Rd 24060
Deercroft Dr 24060
Deerfield Dr 24060
Dehart St 24060
Dickerson Ln 24060
Doe Run 24060
Dogwood Cir 24060
Donaldson Brown 24060
Donlee Dr 24060
Dori Del Hls 24060
Dove Ln 24060
Draper Rd NW & SW 24060
Dry Run Rd 24060
Duluth Rd 24060
Dunton Dr 24060
Eakin St SE & SW 24060
Eastview Ter 24060
Echols St 24060
Edge Way 24060
Edgewood Ln 24060
Edison Ln 24060
Edwards Ln 24060
W Eggleston 24060
Eheart St 24060
Elizabeth Dr 24060
Ella Ln 24060
Ellett Rd 24060
Elliott Dr 24060
Emerald St 24060
Emerson Ln 24060
Emil Ct 24060
Energy Dr 24060
Englewood Ct 24060
Essex Ct 24060
Estates Dr 24060
Evergreen Trl & Way 24060
Faculty St 24060
Fairfax Rd 24060
Fairview Ave 24060
Falcon Ridge Rd 24060
Falcun Dr 24060
Fallam Rd 24060
Fallen Acorn Trl 24060
Fallen Acre Trl 24060
Farmingdale Ln 24060
Farmview Dr 24060
Faulkner Rd 24060
Faystone Dr 24060
Ferguson Dr 24060
Field Dr 24060
Fincastle Dr 24060
Fleets Way 24060
Flippin Cir 24060
Floyd St 24060
Forecast Dr 24060
Forest Ln 24060
Forest Hill Dr 24060
Forest Service Rd 24060
Forest View Ln 24060
N Fork Farms Rd 24060
Fortress Dr 24060
Four Wheel Dr 24060
Foxhunt Ln 24060
Foxridge Ln 24060
Foxtrail Ln 24060
Frame Ln 24060
Francis Ln 24060
Franklin Dr 24060
Gallion Ridge Rd 24060
Gardenspring Dr 24060
Gedney Park Dr 24060
Georgia St 24060
Gigi Dr 24060
Gilbert St 24060
Giles Rd 24060
Gimmel Cir 24060
Ginger Ln 24060
Givens Ln 24060
Glade Rd 24060
Gladewood Dr 24060
Glen Cove Ln 24060
Gloucester Dr 24060
Gobblers Knob 24060
Golden Harvest Cir 24060
Golfview Dr 24060
Gooseberry Ln 24060
Gordon Dr 24060
Gracelyn Ct 24060
Grandview Dr 24060
Graves Ave 24060
Grayland St 24060
Great Valley Dr 24060
Green St 24060
Green Meadow Dr 24060
Greenbrier Cir 24060
Greendale Cir & Dr 24060
Greenwood Dr 24060
Grissom Ln 24060
Grove Ave 24060
Halfpenny Ln 24060
Hamilton Ct 24060
Hampton Ct 24060
Hanna St 24060
Happy Hollow Rd 24060
Harding Ave & Rd 24060
Hardwick St 24060
Hardwood Dr 24060
Harper Hall 24060
Harrell St 24060
Harvest Ridge Ln 24060
Hawthorne Rdg 24060
Haywood Ln 24060
Hearthstone Dr 24060
Heartwood Xing 24060
Heather Dr 24060
Heights Ln 24060
Hemlock Dr SE & SW 24060
Henry Ln 24060
Henry Eaves Dr 24060
Heritage Ln 24060
Hethwood Blvd 24060
Hibiscus Ln 24060
Hickory Hill Cir 24060
Hidden Nest Dr 24060
Hidden Valley Rd 24060
High Meadow Dr 24060
High Ridge Dr 24060
Highland Cir 24060
Hightop Rd 24060
Highview Dr 24060
S Hill St 24060
Hillcrest Dr 24060
Hillman Ln 24060
Holiday Ln 24060
Hollow Oak Ct 24060
Hollyhill Pl 24060
Homeplace Dr 24060
Honeysuckle Dr & Ln 24060
Hoogendam Ln 24060
Horse Farm Rd 24060
Horse Shoe Ln 24060
Hospital Dr 24060
Houndschase Ln 24060
Houston St 24060
Hoyt St 24060
Hubbard St 24060
Huckleberry Ln 24060
Huff Ln 24060
Hunt Club Rd 24060
Hunters Mill Rd 24060
Huntington Ln 24060
Hutcheson Dr 24060
Indian Meadow Dr 24060
Industrial Park Rd SE & SW 24060
Ingles Ct 24060
Innovation Dr 24060
Isabel Ct 24060
Ivan Dr 24060
J E Jones Ln 24060
Jackson St 24060
Janie Ln 24060
Jefferson St 24060
S Jefferson Forest Ln 24060
Jennelle Rd 24060
Jennifer Dr 24060
Jim Meadows Dr 24060
Johnson 24060
Kabrich St 24060
Kam Dr 24060
Karr Ln 24060
Keisters Branch Rd 24060
Kelly Ln 24060
Kelsey Ln 24060
Kennedy Ave 24060
Kent St 24060
Kentwood Dr 24060
King St 24060
Kings Arms Ln 24060
Kipps Ln 24060
Knob Hill Dr 24060
Knollwood Dr 24060
Knox Ln 24060
Kraft Dr 24060
Lacy Ln 24060
Ladyslipper Ln 24060
Lakewood Dr 24060
Lancaster Dr 24060
Landsdowne Dr & St 24060
Lark Ln 24060
Laurel Dr 24060
Laurence Ln 24060
Layman Ct 24060
Lew Ln 24060
Lee St 24060
Leisure Ln 24060
Liberty Ln 24060
Lick Run Rd 24060

Lightfoot Ln 24060
Lilly Rd 24060
Lincoln Ln 24060
Lindale Dr 24060
Linden Ct 24060
Linkous Dr 24060
Linwood Ln 24060
Little Cir 24060
Litton Ln 24060
Locust Ave 24060
Lombardi Dr 24060
Long Shop Rd 24060
Lookout Dr 24060
Lora Ln 24060
Loudon Rd 24060
Lucas Dr 24060
Lusters Gate Rd 24060
Lynn Dr 24060
Mabry Ln 24060
Maddy Dr 24060
Madison Ln 24060
N Main St
100-119 24060
118-118 24063
120-2698 24060
121-2699 24060
S Main St 24060
Main Campbell 24060
Main Eggleston 24060
Manchester St 24060
Maple Ln 24060
Maplewood Ln 24060
Marla Dr 24060
Marlington St 24060
Marsh Rd 24060
Martin Dr 24060
Mary Jane Cir 24060
Masada Way 24060
Mash Run Rd 24060
Mason Dr 24060
Matamoros Ln 24060
Mateer Cir 24060
Mathews Ln 24060
Maxine St 24060
Maywood St 24060
Mcbryde Dr & Ln 24060
Mcconkey St 24060
Mccoy Rd 24060
Mcdonald St 24060
Mcdowell Ct 24060
Mcever Rd 24060
Mclean Ct 24060
Mcpherson Rd 24060
Meadow Dr 24060
Meadowbrook Dr 24060
Meadowview Cir 24060
Melissa Ln 24060
Merrimac Rd 24060
Mid Pines Rd 24060
Miles 24060
Milhurst St 24060
Mill Creek Rd 24060
Mill Pointe Rd 24060
Mill Wood Ln 24060
Miller St 24060
Millstone Ridge Rd 24060
Minor Cir 24060
Misty Hills Cir 24060
Mockingbird Ln 24060
Mockorange Dr 24060
Monarch Ct 24060
Monte Vista Dr 24060
Monteith 24060
Monterey Ct 24060
Montgomery St 24060
Monticello Ln 24060
Mossy Spring Rd 24060
Mount Mission Church Rd 24060
Mount Tabor Rd 24060
Mount Vernon Ln 24060
Mount Zion Rd 24060
Mountain Breeze Dr 24060
Mountain Laurel Rdg 24060
Mountain View Dr 24060
Mountainside Dr 24060
Mourning Dove Dr 24060
Mulberry Dr 24060
Murphy St 24060
Murril Ln 24060
Mustang Ln 24060
Myers Pl 24060
Nathan Dr 24060
Natures Waye Rd 24060
Neil St 24060
Nellies Cave Rd 24060
Nelson St 24060
New Hall W 24060
New Kent Rd 24060
New London Ct 24060
New Residence Hall E 24060
New River House 24060
Newman Ln 24060
Newport Ter 24060
Newton Ct 24060
Nicholas Way 24060
Nik Ryan Dr 24060
Nikkel Ln 24060
Norris Run Rd 24060
North Dr 24060
Northside Dr 24060
Northview Dr 24060
Nottingham Ct 24060
Nuthatch Way 24060
Oak Dr 24060
Oak Pointe Ct 24060
Oakland Sq 24060
October Glory Ct 24060
Oilwell Rd 24060
Old Cedarfield Dr 24060
Old Creek Rd 24060
Old Farm Rd 24060
Old Fort Rd 24060
Old Harding Ave 24060
Old Mill Rd 24060
Olinger Rd 24060
Opal Ln 24060
Orange Ln 24060
Orchard St 24060
Orchard View Ln 24060
Oriole Dr 24060
Oshaughnessy 24060
Otey St 24060
Overlook Dr 24060
Owens St 24060
Owl Xing 24060
Oxford Ct 24060
Palmer Dr 24060
Pamela Way 24060
Pandapas Pond Rd 24060
Panorama Dr 24060
Park Dr 24060
Partnership Dr 24060
Patrick Henry Dr 24060
Patton Ct 24060
Payne Dr 24060
Pearl Ln 24060
Pearman Rd 24060
Pebble Beach Rd 24060
Peddrew Yates 24060
Penn St NE & SE 24060
Pepper Run Rd 24060
Petra Pass 24060
Pheasant Run Ct & Dr 24060
Piedmont St 24060
Pine Dr 24060
Pineridge Dr 24060
Pippen Ln 24060
Plank Dr 24060
Plantation Rd 24060
Pleasant View Cir 24060
Plymouth St 24060
Poplar Ridge Cir 24060
Porter St 24060
Poverty Creek Rd 24060
Pratt Dr 24060
Preston Ave 24060
Preston Forest Dr 24060
Price St 24060
Prices Fork Rd 24060
Prices Mountain Rd 24060
Prices Station Rd 24060
Primrose Dr 24060
Pritchard Hall 24060
Proadin Rd 24060
Professional Park Dr SE 24060
Progress St NE & NW 24060
Prospect St 24060
Prosperity Rd 24060
Puller Ln 24060
Pumpkin Dr 24060
Quail Dr 24060
Quailwood Dr 24060
Quartz Ln 24060
Quez Dr 24060
Quincy Ct 24060
Rainbow Ridge Dr 24060
Ramble Rd 24060
Rasche 24060
Raspberry Rd 24060
Reagan Rd 24060
Red Maple Dr 24060
Redbud Rd 24060
Remington Rd 24060
Research Center Dr 24060
Reynolds St 24060
Rhea Ridge Dr 24060
Rich Cir 24060
Richmond Ln 24060
E & W Ridge Dr & Rd 24060
Ridgeview Dr 24060
Rim Rock Rd 24060
River Rise Rd 24060
Riverside Dr 24060
Roanoke St E & W 24060
Robin Rd 24060
Robinson St 24060
Rocky Acres Ln 24060
Rose Ave 24060
Roundhouse Rd 24060
Roy Ln 24060
Royal Ln 24060
Rucker Rd 24060
Rutherford Dr 24060
Rutledge St 24060
Sage Ln 24060
Saint Andrews Cir 24060
San Marcos St 24060
Sanders St 24060
Sandy Cir 24060
Scott Dr 24060
Scott Alan Cir 24060
Seminole Dr 24060
Seneca Dr 24060
Seymour Dr 24060
Shadow Lake Rd 24060
Shady Grove Ln 24060
Shale St 24060
Shawnee Trl 24060
Sheffield Dr 24060
Sheliah Ct 24060
Shelor Ln 24060
Shenandoah Cir 24060
Sheppard Dr 24060
Sherwood Ct 24060
Shiela Ct 24060
Shilo Way 24060
Showalter Dr 24060
Silverleaf Ln 24060
Skyview Dr 24060
Slusher 24060
Smith Wood Ln 24060
Smithfield Dr 24060
Smithfield Plantation Rd 24060
Snyder Ln 24060
Somerset Pl 24060
Southgate Dr 24060
Southhampton Ct 24060
Southpark Dr 24060
Southwoods Dr 24060
Special Purpose Home E & N 24060
Special Purpose Home A 24060
Special Purpose Home B 24060
Special Purpose Home C 24060
Special Purpose Home D 24060
Special Purpose Home F 24060
Special Purpose Home G 24060
Special Purpose Home H 24060
Special Purpose Home I 24060
Special Purpose Home J 24060
Special Purpose Home K 24060
Special Purpose Home L 24060
Special Purpose Home M 24060
Special Purpose Home O 24060
Special Purpose Home P 24060
Special Purpose Home Q 24060
Special Purpose Home R 24060
Spickard St 24060
Spotswood Rd 24060
Springhollow Ln 24060
Spur St 24060
State St 24060
Stayman Ct 24060
Steinbeck Rd 24060
Sterling Dr 24060
Sterling Heights Ln 24060
Still Hollow Rd 24060
Stonegate Dr 24060
Stradford Ln 24060
Straley Vly 24060
Stratford View Dr 24060
Strider Rd 24060
Stroubles Creek Rd 24060
Summer Ln 24060
Summit Dr 24060
Sunridge Dr 24060
Sunrise Dr 24060
Sunset Blvd 24060
Sunshine Farm Ln 24060
Surface View Cir 24060
Susannah Dr 24060
Sussex Rd 24060
Sutton Pl 24060
Sweeny Rd 24060
Sycamore Trl 24060
Sylvan Ln 24060
Tabor Village Dr 24060
Talheim Cir 24060
Tall Oaks Dr 24060
Tarby Ln 24060
Taylor Hollow Rd 24060
Tech Center Dr 24060
Tech Village Dr 24060
Tee St 24060
Terra Bella St 24060
Thomas Ln 24060
Tipple Rd 24060
Toggle Ln 24060
Toms Creek Rd 24060
Tory Springs Rd 24060
Totem Ln 24060
Towhee Aly 24060
Trade St 24060
Transportation Research Plz 24060
Treetop Ridge Rd 24060
Triangle St 24060
Tribble Rd 24060
Trillium Dr & Ln 24060
Tucker Rd 24060
Turner St NE & NW 24060
Turning Leaf Ln 24060
University Ter 24060
University City Blvd
600-698 24060
700-910 24060
909-909 24062
911-1399 24060
912-1498 24060
Upland Rd 24060
Valleyview Dr 24060
Vawter 24060
Vest Cir 24060
Village Way N & S 24060
Vinyard Ave 24060
Virginia St 24060
Virtue Ln 24060
Vista Ter 24060
Vpi 24060
Wake Forest Rd 24060
Wakefield Dr 24060
Wall St 24060
Walls Branch Rd 24060
Walnut Dr 24060
Walnut Spring Rd 24060
Walters Ct 24060
Warm Hearth Dr 24060
Warren St 24060
Washington St SE & SW 24060
Watson Ave & Ln 24060
Weatherly Ct 24060
Webb St 24060
Welcome Rd 24060
Wellesley Ct 24060
Westminister Ct 24060
Westover Dr 24060
Wharton St NE & SE 24060
Whipple Dr 24060
Whitethorne Rd 24060
Whitney Ct 24060
Whittaker Hollow Rd 24060
Whittier Ln 24060
Wildflower Ln 24060
Willard Dr 24060
Wilson Ave 24060
Windy Ridge Ln 24060
Winslow Dr 24060
Winston Ave 24060
Wise Ln 24060
Wood Haven Ct 24060
Woodbine Dr 24060
Woodland Dr 24060
Woodland Hills Dr 24060
Woods Edge Ct 24060
Woodside Ter 24060
Woolwine St 24060
Wren Ct 24060
Wrights Way 24060
Yarrow Rd 24060
Yellow Sulphur Rd SW 24060
Yod Ln 24060
York Dr 24060
Yorkshire Ct 24060

BRISTOL VA

General Delivery 24203

POST OFFICE BOXES MAIN OFFICE STATIONS AND BRANCHES

Box No.s
1 - 8930 24203
16001 - 17754 24209

RURAL ROUTES

03 24202

NAMED STREETS

Abbie Ln 24202
Abrams Falls Rd 24202
Acorn Ln 24202
Adaline Dr 24202
Agate Ln 24202
Akard Ln 24202
Albert Ln 24201
Alexis Dr 24202
Alisa Ln 24202
Alley Oop Hl 24202
Amy St 24201
Anaconda Ln 24202
Andover Dr 24201
Angus Dr 24202
Antelope Dr 24202
Apache Ln 24202
Appaloosa Dr & Rd 24202
Apple Aly 24201
Applejack Rd 24202
Appleton Dr 24202
Arapahoe Trl 24202
Arbutus Ln 24202
Arcadia Ln 24202
Archery Range Rd 24202
Argonne Dr 24202
Arlington Ave 24201
Arrington Private Dr 24202
Ashley Cir 24202
Ashley Dr 24201
Aspen Cir 24201
Atoka Rd 24202
Auction Dr 24202
Augusta Ct 24202
Autumn Dr 24201
Autumn Rd 24202
Avery Ln 24202
Avondale Ln 24201
Ayres Ln 24202
Babbling Brook Ln 24202
Bailey St 24201
Baker Ln 24202
Bandit Dr 24201
Barger Dr 24202
Barker Ln 24201
Barytes Dr 24201
Battle Hill Dr 24202
Baytree Rd 24202
Beacon Rd 24201
Beaver St 24201
Beaver Creek Ln 24202
Beaverview Dr 24201
Bee Dr 24202
Beech St 24201
Belleair Ln 24201
Bellehaven Dr 24201
Bellemeade Cir 24201
Benhams Rd 24202
Bethesda Rd 24202
Bethlehem Rd 24202
Bexley Dr 24202
Big Knob Rd 24202
Birch St 24201
Black Smith Trl 24202
Blevins Blvd 24202
Blue Grass St 24201
Blue Spruce Rd 24202
Bluejay Dr 24202
Bluff St 24201
Bob Morrison Blvd 24201
Bobs Rd 24201
Bohner Rd 24202
Bond Dr 24202
Bonham Rd
1-299 24202
300-899 24201
Booher Ln & Rd 24201
Boohers Chapel Ln 24202
Boone St 24201
Boozie Creek Rd 24202
Boozy Creek Rd 24202
Bordwine Rd 24202
Bradley St 24201
Braemar St 24202
Bramble Ln 24201
Brandon Ln 24201
Brandywine Rd 24202
Briscoe Dr 24202
Bristol Hwy 24202
Bristol East Rd 24202
Bristol View Dr 24201
Britts Ln 24202
Brook Ln 24201
Brookdale Cir 24201
Brooks Way 24202
Brookwood Cir 24201
Browns Aly 24201
Brunswick Ln 24202
Bryant Dr 24201
Brynwood Dr 24202
Buchanan St 24201
Buckner St 24201
Buffalo Pond Rd 24202
Buffner Rd 24202
Buford St 24201
Burning Bush Ln 24202
Burson Ln 24202
Cadle Ln 24202
Cain Rd 24202
Campground Rd 24202
Canary Ln 24202
Candlelight Ln 24202
Caney Valley Rd 24202
Canter Ln 24202
Cardinal Dr 24201
Carmack Dr 24201
Carroll St 24202
Carson Ln 24202
Carter St 24201
Cartwright Ln 24202
Castle Yonder Ln 24202
Catalina Ln 24202
Cathedral Hill St 24202
Catherine St 24201
Cavalier Cir 24202
Cedar Ln 24201
Celebrity Ct 24202
Center St 24201
Central Ave 24202
Central Ct 24201
Chateau Mountain Dr 24202
Chelshea Ln 24202
Cherokee Rd 24201
Cherry Ln 24201
Cherry Hill Ln 24201
Chester St 24201
Chester Hill Rd 24201
Chesterfield Ln 24202
Cheyenne Rd 24201
Chippewa Dr 24201
Christopher Dr 24202
Church St 24201
Circle Dr 24201
E Circle Dr 24202
W Circle Dr 24202
Claremont Cir 24201
Clark St 24201
Clayman Valley Rd 24202
Claymore Dr 24202
Clear Creek Rd 24202
Clinton Ave 24201
Cloud Nine Dr 24202
Clover Ln 24201
Club Ct 24202
Clubhouse Rdg 24202
Coachman Rd 24202
Cocke Dr 24202
Cody St 24201
Colchester Dr 24202
Cole Ln 24202
Colleton Ct 24202
Collie Ct 24202
Collins St 24201
Colony Cir 24201
Colony Ln 24202
Columbia Ave 24201
Combs Valley Dr 24202
Comer Rd 24201
Commerce Ct 24202
Commonwealth Ave 24201
Commonwealth Avenue Ext 24201
Concord Cir 24201
Condalt St 24201
Conner Ln 24202
Constitution Row 24202

Coral Aly 24201
Corona St 24202
Coronet Dr 24201
Corporation Rd 24202
Corporation St 24201
Cougar Pl 24202
Country Folk Rd 24202
County Cork Ln 24202
Court Dr 24201
Courtland Cir 24202
Courtney Ln 24201
Cove Creek Rd 24202
Coventry Ct 24201
Cowan Dr 24202
Cox Rd 24202
Cozy Ln 24202
Crabtree Ct 24202
Crawford Rd 24202
Crescent Dr 24201
Crimson Dr 24202
Crockett St 24201
Cross St 24201
Crossway Rd 24201
Crusenberry Dr 24202
Cumberland St 24201
Cunningham Rd 24202
Czoka Rd 24201
Dakin Dr 24201
Dakota Dr 24202
Dakota Rd 24201
Dalhia Dr 24202
Dameron Dr 24202
Dane Dr 24202
Danville Ave 24201
Darlington Dr 24202
Dartmore Dr 24202
Dawn Pl 24201
Dean Allen Dr 24202
Decatur Ln 24202
Deepwater Dr 24202
Deertrack Ln 24201
Dennis Dr 24202
Denton Ln 24201
Derrik Dr 24202
Dettor Rd 24202
Dewberry Dr 24202
Dewdrop Pl 24201
Dewey Ct 24202
Dianes Way 24201
Dickey St 24201
Dishner Valley Rd 24202
Dixie St 24201
Dogwood Ln 24201
Dorsett Dr 24202
Douglas St 24201
Dover Cir 24202
Downy Pl 24201
Duff Ln 24201
Duke St 24201
Dunlap St 24201
Dunmore Rd 24202
Eads Ave 24201
Eagle Ridge Ln 24202
Earley Ln 24202
Edgewood Dr 24202
Edmond St 24201
Elbert Way 24202
Elk Dr 24202
Elkton Ln 24201
Elm St 24201
Elmo St 24201
Enchanted Ln 24202
Equistrian Rd 24202
Euclid Ave 24201
Euclid Avenue Ext 24201
Evans Dr 24202
Everett St 24201
Fairfield Dr 24202
Fairfield St 24201
Fairmount Ave 24201
Fairview Rd 24202
Fairview St 24201
Fantasy Ct 24202
Fayette Dr 24202
Federal Rd 24202
Fentriss Rd 24202
Fido Dr 24202
Fieldcrest Ln 24202
Flame Leaf Dr 24202
Flannagan Dr 24202
Fledgling Cir 24202
Fleenors Memorial Rd 24202
Flintlock Cir 24201
Floyd St 24201
Foothills Trl 24202
Forest Ln 24201
Forest Meadow Rd 24202
Forsythe Rd 24202
Four Seasons Dr 24202
Four Winds Dr 24202
Fox Meadow Ln 24201
Foxcroft Rd 24201
Frances Dr 24201
Freedom Rd
100-199 24201
6300-6399 24202
Freedom Hollow Rd 24202
Fuller St 24201
Gale Ave 24202
Garden Ln 24201
Gas Well Rd 24202
Gate City Hwy
1-97 24201
99-899 24201
2200-7199 24202
Gateway Dr 24202
Gazelle Dr 24202
Genchela Rd 24202
Georgia St 24201
Glenway Ave 24201
Gloucester Ln 24202
Golden View Dr 24202
Goldspier Dr 24202
Goode St 24201
Goodson St 24201
Goose Creek Rd 24202
Gordon Ave 24201
Gouge St 24201
Grable Rd 24201
Grand St 24201
Grandview Cir & Rd 24201
Green Acres Rd 24201
Green Hill Rd 24201
Green Valley Rd 24202
Greenbriar Dr 24202
Greentree Circle Rd 24201
Grindstone Branch Rd 24202
Grove St 24201
Grove Park Dr 24201
Guernsey Dr 24202
Gum Hill Rd 24202
Haddon St 24201
Halls Bottom Rd 24202
Hamlet Ln 24202
Hampshire Dr 24202
Harleywood Rd 24202
Harlow Pl 24201
Harmeling St 24201
Harmony Dr 24201
Harvest Rd 24201
Haskell Station Rd 24202
Hassen Heights Rd 24201
Haverhill Rd 24201
Hazel Dr 24201
Hazelwood Dr 24202
Hearst Rd 24202
Heather Dr 24202
Heather Rd 24201
Hedgerow Hl 24202
Helen Ln 24202
Helms Dr 24202
Henrys Ln 24202
Heritage Dr 24201
Hickory Dr 24201
High St 24201
High Meadow Trl 24202
Highland Ave 24201
Highland Dr 24201
Highland Rd 24202
Highlands Trl 24202
Highlands Center Blvd 24202
Highpoint Rd 24202
Hill Dr 24201
Hill Park Dr 24201
Hillbilly Ln 24202
Hilliard Ln 24202
Hillside Ave 24201
Hilltop Dr 24202
Hite Dr 24202
Hobbs Rd 24202
Holbrook St 24202
Hollis Ln 24202
Holly Ln 24201
Holly Mountain Ln 24201
Holt Dr 24202
Homestead Dr 24201
Hoot Owl Rd 24202
Hudson Ln 24201
Hughes St 24201
Hughes Mountain Rd 24202
Huron Rd 24201
Impala Dr 24202
Independence Dr 24201
Indian Creek Ln 24202
Indiana St 24201
Indigo Cir 24202
Industrial Park Rd 24202
Inez Ave 24201
Intermont Dr 24201
Inverness Way 24202
Iris Ln 24201
Iroquois Rd 24202
Island Rd
2-198 24201
200-1951 24201
1953-1999 24201
9201-10097 24202
10099-10199 24202
10201-11199 24202
Ivanhoe Rd 24202
Ivory Ln 24202
Ivy Rd 24202
Jackson Ln 24201
Jade Ln 24202
Jade Woods Dr 24202
James St 24201
Jane Ln 24201
Jani Hammit Dr 24201
Jasper Creek Rd 24202
Jeff Gordon Dr 24202
Jefferson Dr 24201
Jericho Rd 24202
Jewell Dr 24202
Johnson St 24201
Johnson Chapel Rd 24202
Jolly St 24201
Jordan Ln 24202
Joshua Dr 24202
Joy Dr 24202
Judson Dr 24202
Junction Dr 24202
Justice Dr 24202
Kami Cir 24201
Keeler Ln 24201
Kels Pl 24202
Kerin Dr 24202
Kestrel Dr 24202
Kettlefoot Ln 24202
Keys St 24201
Keywest 24202
Kilgore Dr 24201
Kim Dr 24202
King St 24201
King Mill Pike
1401-1497 24201
1499-2799 24201
12400-15499 24202
15501-24099 24202
King Mountain Aly 24201
King Terry Dr 24202
Kingsbridge St 24202
Kingsolver St 24201
Kingston Ln 24202
Knob Hill Dr 24202
Knoll Dr 24202
Krimmel Creek Dr 24202
Kriswood Dr 24201
Ladd Dr 24202
Ladybug Ln 24202
Lamont Rd 24201
Lancaster St 24201
Large Hollow Rd 24202
Larwood Ln 24202
Latham Dr 24202
Latture Ln 24202
Lauren Dr 24202
Lavender Ln 24202
Lavinia St 24201
Lawndale Dr 24201
Lawrence Ave 24201
Lawson Rd 24202
Leabs Hillside Dr 24202
Lee Ct 24201
Lee Hwy
1200-2003 24201
2002-2002 24209
2004-2146 24201
2005-2145 24201
2200-17200 24202
17202-17298 24202
Lee Ln 24202
Lee St 24201
Lena St 24201
Leonard St 24201
Lester St 24201
Lewis St 24201
Lexington Ave 24201
Liberty Pl 24201
Lime Hill Rd 24202
Limerick Ln 24202
Lincoln Dr 24202
Linden Dr 24202
Linden Square Dr 24202
Lindsey St 24201
Little Creek Rd 24202
Little Wolf Run Rd 24202
Livingston Creek Rd 24202
Log Cabin Way 24202
Lola Ln 24201
Lone Eagle Dr 24202
Lone Star Rd 24202
Lone Willow Dr 24202
Long Crescent Dr 24201
Long Hole Rdg 24202
Longdale Rd 24201
Look Out Rdg 24202
Lookout Rdg 24202
Loretta Ln 24202
Lori Ln 24202
Lottie St 24201
Loudon Dr 24202
Love Hollow Rd 24202
Lovers Ln 24202
Lovins Dr 24202
Lowry Hills Rd 24202
Luttrell St 24201
Lyle Ln 24202
Lynn St 24202
Lynnwood Dr 24201
Mabe Hill Rd 24202
Madison St 24201
Magnolia Dr 24201
Main Ct 24202
Majestic Dr 24202
Manchester Dr 24202
Maple St 24201
Margay Dr 24202
Marietta Dr 24202
Marshall Rd 24201
Martin Rd 24201
Martin Luther King Jr
Blvd 24201
Mary St 24201
Marys Chapel Rd 24202
Massachusetts Ave 24201
Masters Ct 24202
Mathis Dr 24202
Maya Rd 24202
Mayfield Ln 24201
Maywood Loop 24202
Mcarthur Cir 24201
Mccall Gap Rd 24202
Mcchesney Dr 24201
Mckinley Ave 24201
Mcnamara Cir 24202
Mcneil St 24201
Meadow Dr & St 24201
Meadowcrest Dr 24201
Meadowood Dr 24202
Melina Ln 24202
Mellow Ln 24201
Memphis Ln 24202
Merrimac Dr 24202
Midway St 24201
Milburn Dr 24201
Millard Dr 24202
Millard St 24201
Miller St 24201
Miller Hill Rd 24202
Milsap St 24201
Ming Ct 24202
Mock Knob Rd 24202
Monarch Dr 24201
Moneta Cir 24201
Monticello Dr 24202
Montpelier Ave 24201
Montrose Dr 24201
Montvale St 24201
Montvue St 24201
Moore St 24201
Mosby Ave 24202
Mosswood Ln 24201
Mount Vernon Cir &
Rd 24202
Mumpower Dr 24201
Music Dr 24202
Musick Dr 24202
Navaho Trl 24201
Nelson St 24201
Nevada St 24201
New Castle Dr 24202
New Hampshire Ave 24201
New York St 24201
Newton St 24201
Neyland Dr 24202
Nightingale Way 24202
Nininger Rd 24202
Noble Dr 24202
Noonkester Rd 24202
Nordyke Rd 24202
Norfolk Ave 24201
North St 24201
Norway St 24201
Norwood Dr 24201
Nunley Ct 24202
Oak St 24201
Oak Grove Rd 24202
Oakcrest Cir 24201
Oakview Ave, Cir & Dr 24201
Oakwinds Cir 24202
Ohio Dr 24202
Ohio St 24201
Old Abingdon Hwy 24201
Old Airport Rd
1-1099 24201
1100-1199 24202
Old Dominion Rd 24202
Old Home Pl 24202
Old Jonesboro Rd 24202
Olde Timber Mill Rd 24202
Olen St 24201
Omaha Rd 24201
Orchid Rd 24201
Orion Ave 24202
Osborne St 24201
Osprey Ridge Rd 24202
Overhill Rd 24201
Overlake Dr 24202
Overland Rd 24202
Pace Dr 24201
Page St 24201
Pairgin Rd 24202
Paladin Rd 24202
Park St 24201
Patrick Ln 24202
Patriot Cir 24201
Patsy Rd 24202
Paulena Dr 24202
Paw Prints Ln 24202
Peaceful Ln 24202
Peachtree Cir 24201
Peacock Valley Dr 24202
Pearl St 24201
Pebble Dr 24201
Pebble Beach Dr 24202
Pebble Creek Condos 24201
Peltier Ln 24202
Pembroke Cir 24202
Pendergrass Rd 24201
Penn Rd 24202
Penny Ln 24202
Perchion Rd 24202
Peregrine Dr 24202
Peters St 24201
Peyton Dr 24202
Phillips Rd 24202
Piedmont Ave 24201
Piedmont Cir 24202
Pin Oak Cir 24202
Pine St 24201
Pine Circle Dr 24201
Pine Hill Rd 24202
Pinebrook Dr 24202
N Pinecrest Ln 24201
Pineview Dr 24201
Pinzgauer Ln 24202
Pioneer Dr 24202
Pippin Ln 24202
Pittstown Rd 24201
Plantation Rd 24202
Poplar St 24201
Portsmouth Ave 24201
Potter Rd 24202
Powers Ln 24202
Preston Aly & St 24201
Prestonwood Dr 24202
Prince St 24201
Prospect Ave 24201
Pullontown Ln 24202
Quarry St 24201
Queens Lace Dr 24202
Quillen Dr 24201
Quintana St 24202
Ragsdale Dr 24202
Rainbow Cir 24201
Rainbow Rd 24202
Raintree Cir 24201
Ranchero Rd 24202
Randall Street Expy 24201
Randolph St 24201
Rankin Rd 24202
Raven Dr 24202
Rebecca St 24201
Red Ct 24202
Red Robin Ln 24202
Redbud Ln 24201
Redstone Dr 24202
Redwood Cir 24202
Reece School Rd 24202
Reedy St 24201
Reedy Creek Rd 24202
Regal Ridge Dr 24202
Reserve Blvd 24202
Reservoir St 24201
Resting Tree Dr 24202
Rhode Island Ave 24201
Rich Valley Rd 24202
Richard Rd 24202
Ridge Crest Ct 24202
Ridgewood Ct 24201
Risto Rd 24201
Rivelet Dr 24202
Riverside Dr 24201
Roark Ln 24202
Roark Farm Ln 24202
Robin Cir 24202
Rocky Hill Rd 24202
Rocky Top Rdg 24202
Rollins Dr 24202
Roo Pl 24201
Rory Ln 24202
Running Brook Ln 24202
Russell St 24201
Rutherford Rd 24202
Rutter Rd 24201
Rye Rd 24202
Safari Dr 24202
Saffron Ln 24202
Saint Andrews Dr 24202
Salem Rd 24202
Santa Monica Rd 24201
Saranac Ln 24202
Saratoga St 24201
Satinwood Rd 24202
Saul Dr 24201
Saxon Dr 24202
Scott St 24201
Second Taylor St 24201
Seminole Rd 24201
Serenity Ln 24202
Seward Ave 24201
Shadow Grove Cir 24201
Shadowhill Ln 24201
Shady Oak Dr 24202
Shaffertown Rd 24202
Shakesville Rd 24201
Shankle Mill Rd 24201
Sharrett Rd 24202
Shawnee Rd 24201
Sheffey Ct 24202
Shell Aly 24201
Shelley Rd 24202
Shelleys Rd 24202
Sherwood Rd 24201
Shipley Dr 24201
Short St 24201
Sierra Dr 24202
Siesta Ave 24202
Silk Rd 24202
Simcox Dr 24202
Singing Wood Ln 24202
Sinking Creek Rd 24202
Sioux Rd 24201
Skye Knob Trl 24202
Skyland Ave 24202
Slaughter Rd 24202
Smallmouth Dr 24202
Smith Creek Rd 24202
Snaffle Bit Ln 24202
Snapp Ln 24202
Solar St 24201
Solar Street Ext 24201
Sorah St 24202
South St 24201
Southampton Cir 24202
Southern View Rd 24202
Spencer St 24201
Spencer Street Ext 24201
Spring Cir & St 24201
Spring Branch Rd 24201
Spring Hill Ter 24201
Spring Valley Rd 24201
Springlake Rd 24201
Springview Rdg 24202
Spur Strap Rd 24202
Spurgeon Ln 24201
Spyglass Ct 24202
Stables Rd 24202
Stage Ln 24202
Stagecoach Rd 24201
Stanfield Dr 24202
Starburst Way 24202
Stardust Pl 24201
State St 24201
Steele Creek Rd 24201
Stevens Dr 24202
Stone Dr 24202
Stonewall Rdg 24202
Strada Cir 24202
Straight St 24201
Sue Ave 24201
Suffolk Ave 24201
Sugar Hollow Rd 24202
Sullins St 24201
Sullins Academy Dr 24202
Summer Pl 24201
Summit St 24201
Sunbird Dr 24202
Suncrest Dr 24201
Sundale Cir 24201
Sundance Rd 24202
Sunny Acres 24202

Sunrise Ave 24201
Sunrise St
200-299 24201
10000-10199 24202
Sunshine Pl 24202
Superior Cir 24201
Superior Ln 24202
Sutherlin St 24201
Sycamore St 24201
Tad Ct 24202
Tadlock Dr 24202
Talent Ln 24202
Tall Timbers Est 24201
Talon Crest Cir 24202
Tanase Hls 24202
Taryn Ct 24201
Teakwood Ct 24202
Temple Ln 24202
Terra Caro Cir 24202
Terrace Dr 24202
Terrance Cir 24201
Terry Dr 24201
Texas Ave 24201
Thistle Hill Dr 24202
Thomas Rd 24201
Thor Dr 24202
Tiffany Sq 24201
Tilley Dr 24201
Timber Bend Rd 24202
Timber Oak Dr 24201
Timber Ridge Rd 24201
Timberbrook Dr 24201
Timbertree Branch Rd 24202
Timothy Ln 24201
Titan Dr 24202
Toncray Dr 24202
Topeka Dr 24202
Townsend Dr 24202
Tracy St 24201
Trading Post Ln 24202
Trail Rd 24201
Tranbarger Rd 24202
Travalite Dr 24202
Tri State Lime Rd 24202
Trojan Dr 24202
Tuffy Dr 24202
Tulsa Dr 24202
Turkey Ln 24202
Turkey Hollow Ln 24202
Turnberry Ct 24202
Tyler Cir 24202
Tyree Ln 24202
Underpass Rd 24202
Unicorn Dr 24202
Upshur Ln 24202
Utah St 24201
Vale Dr 24201
E & W Valley Dr 24201
Valley View Rd 24202
Van St 24201
Vance St 24201
Vanguard Dr 24202
Veda Dr 24201
Venable Aly 24201
Ventura Cir 24201
Vermont Ave 24201
Vernon St 24201
Victory Ln 24202
Village Cir 24201
Virginia Dr 24201
Virginia St 24201
Virginia Trl 24202
Vista Cir 24201
Wagner Rd
600-1099 24201
8100-9299 24202
Wagner St 24201
Wagners Aly 24201
Walker Mountain Rd 24202
Wallace Pike 24202
Wallace Meadows Way 24202
Walling Rd 24201
Walton Ridge Rd 24202
Warrior Trl 24202
Warwick Ln 24202
Washington St 24201
Washington Way 24202
Washington Lee Dr 24201
Weatherly Aly 24201
Wellmore Dr 24201
Wendover Rd 24201
Wesley Way 24201
West St 24201
Westfield St 24201
Westlawn St 24201
Westmoreland Dr 24202
White Oak Rd 24202
White Pine Cir 24202
Whitt St 24201
Wilby Ln 24202
Wilderness Rd 24202
Williams St 24201
Williamsburg Cir & Rd 24202
Willow Cir 24201
Willow Ln 24202
Willow Branch Rd 24202
Willow Creek Cir 24202
Willow Oak Ct 24201
Willowcrest Dr 24202
Wills Dr 24202
Wilson Cir 24202
Wilson Haus Rd 24202
Winchester Ln 24202
Winding Way Rd 24201
Windmere Hts 24201
Windmill Cir 24201
Windon Acres Ln 24202
Winston St 24201
Wolf Run Rd 24202
Wood St 24201
Wood Howell Rd 24202
Woodland Cir & Dr 24201
Woodridge Cir 24202
Woodstock Ln 24201
Woodstone Cir 24202
Woodway Rd 24202
Wyandotte Rd 24201
Yamaha Cir 24202
Yancy Ln 24202
Yokum Dr 24202
Young Dr 24202
Yukon Dr 24202

NUMBERED STREETS

2nd St 24201
3rd St 24201
6th St
111-111 24203
112-112 24209
18th St 24201
19th St 24201
20th St 24201
21st St 24201

BURKE VA

POST OFFICE BOXES MAIN OFFICE STATIONS AND BRANCHES

Box No.s
All PO Boxes 22009

NAMED STREETS

Acorn Knoll Ct 22015
Advantage Ct 22015
Alison Dr 22015
Amber Ct 22015
Andromeda Dr 22015
Annaberg Ct & Pl 22015
Aplomado Dr 22015
Apple Wood Ct & Ln 22015
Arbutus Ct 22015
Arrit Ct 22015
Ashbourn Dr 22015
Ashbridge Ct 22015
Atherstone Ct 22015
Backstay Ct 22015
Bakersville Ln 22015
Bald Hill Pl 22015
Ballast Ct 22015
Banning Pl 22015
Barnacle Pl 22015
Barnstable Ct 22015
Basket Oak Ct 22015
Battalion Landing Ct 22015
Beacon Pond Ln 22015
Beaconsfield Ct 22015
Bear Oak Ct 22015
Belleair Rd 22015
Bestwicke Ct & Rd 22015
Biggers Rd 22015
Birch Leaf Ct 22015
Blackburn Dr 22015
Blake House Ct 22015
Blincoe Ct 22015
Bloom Ct 22015
Blue Jug Lndg 22015
Bluffwood Ct 22015
Bonnie Bern Ct 22015
Boothe Dr 22015
Braddock Rd 22015
Bradfield Dr 22015
Bridgetown Ct & Pl 22015
Britford Dr 22015
Brixham Ct 22015
Broadwick Ct 22015
Broken Oak Pl 22015
Bromyard Ct 22015
Bronte Dr 22015
Brook Ford Rd 22015
Buffie Ct 22015
Bunker Woods Ct & Ln 22015
Burdett Rd 22015
Burke Rd
8800-9500 22015
9501-9501 22009
9501-9699 22015
9502-9600 22015
Burke Centre Pkwy 22015
Burke Commons Rd 22015
Burke Lake Rd 22015
Burke Manor Ct 22015
Burke Pond Ct & Ln 22015
Burke Towne Ct 22015
Burke View Ave & Ct 22015
Burke Woods Dr 22015
Burkewood Way 22015
Burley Ct 22015
Burning Branch Rd 22015
Burnside Landing Ct & Dr 22015
Burr Oak Way 22015
Byron Ter 22015
Calico Pool Ln 22015
Calstock Ct 22015
Candleberry Ct 22015
Canvasback Rd 22015
Capella Ave 22015
Capon Hill Pl 22015
Capricorn Ct 22015
Cardington Ct 22015
Carrindale Ct 22015
Carters Oak Ct & Way 22015
Carthage Ln 22015
Castlebury Ct 22015
Caulking Pl 22015
Centaurus Ct 22015
Chapel Hill Dr 22015
Chase Commons Ct & Dr 22015
Chelmsford Ct 22015
Cherry Oak Ct 22015
Chestnut Wood Ln 22015
Church Way 22015
Claychin Ct 22015
Cleat Ct 22015
Clerkenwell Ct 22015
Clermont Landing Ct 22015
Cloverdale Ct 22015
Coffer Woods Ct, Pl & Rd 22015
Colston Ct 22015
Compass Ct 22015
Conistone Ct 22015
Coopers Landing Ct 22015
Cordwood Ct 22015
Cork Pl 22015
Cotswold Dr 22015
Counter Pl 22015
Courageous Cir 22015
Cove Landing Rd 22015
Covered Bridge Rd 22015
Crayford Ct & St 22015
Crevenna Oak Dr 22015
Crossin Ct 22015
Crossrail Ct & Dr 22015
Crowfoot Dr 22015
Crown Point Rd 22015
Crownleigh Ct 22015
Crownwood Ct 22015
Dahlgreen Pl 22015
Dalby Ln 22015
Dam View Ct 22015
Daventry Ct 22015
De Soto Ct & St 22015
Debra Spradlin Ct 22015
Deckhand Dr 22015
Deep Lake Way 22015
Degen Dr 22015
Dellford Ct 22015
Devon Ln 22015
Digory Ct 22015
Dobbin Ct 22015
Doolittle St 22015
Dory Landing Ct 22015
Dove Nest Ct 22015
Downeys Wood Ct 22015
Downhaul Ln 22015
Draco St 22015
Draycott Ct 22015
Drifter Ct 22015
Dundas Oak Ct 22015
Dunleer Ln 22015
Dunleigh Ct & Dr 22015
Dunleigh Glen Ln 22015
Duxford Pl 22015
Eagle Landing Ct & Rd 22015
Ebbtide Ln 22015
Edgewater Oak Ct 22015
Erik Charles Ct 22015
Erman Ct & St 22015
Faire Commons Ct 22015
Fairleigh Ct 22015
Fairweather Ct 22015
Falcon Landing Ct 22015
Falling Brook Dr 22015
Fathom Ct 22015
Fenestra Ct 22015
Fern Park Dr 22015
Fern Pool Ct 22015
First Landing Way 22015
Fitzhugh St 22015
Flint Tavern Pl 22015
Fort Corloran Dr 22015
Fort Craig Dr 22015
Fort Fisher Ct 22015
Four Oaks Ln 22015
Fox Lair Dr 22015
Freds Oak Ct & Rd 22015
Fultons Landing Ct 22015
Fushsimi Ct 22015
Gabon Ct 22015
Gaines St 22015
Garretson St 22015
Gatecross Pl 22015
Gemini Ct 22015
General Banks Ct 22015
Georgian Woods Ct 22015
Gladeview Ct 22015
Glenarm Ct 22015
Glenbard Ct & Rd 22015
Glenway Ct 22015
Goldfield Ln 22015
Gooding Pond Ct 22015
Gopost 22015
Goshen Ln 22015
Greenough Pl 22015
Grovers Theater Ct 22015
Guildhall Ct 22015
Guinea Rd 22015
Hall St 22015
Halyard Pl 22015
Harford Ln 22015
Harr Ct 22015
Harrowhill Ln 22015
Harvester Ct 22015
Haskin Ct 22015
Hatches Ct 22015
Heathwick Ct 22015
Heathwood Ct 22015
Hemlock Woods Ln 22015
Herbert St 22015
Herberts Crossing Dr 22015
Heritage Landing Ct & Rd 22015
Heritage Square Dr 22015
Heron Pond Ct & Ter 22015
Hersand Dr 22015
Hickory Tree Ct 22015
High Ln 22015
High Bluff Ct 22015
High Water Ct 22015
Hillock Ct 22015
Hollins Ln 22015
Hollow Oak Ct 22015
Holly Prospect Ct 22015
Home Guard Dr 22015
Honey Creeper Ct 22015
Honey Tree Ct 22015
Huber Ct 22015
Humphries Dr 22015
Ironmaster Dr 22015
Jackson St 22015
Jacksons Oak Ct 22015
Jerell Ct 22015
Judson Ct 22015
Kara Pl 22015
Katharines Dr 22015
Kemp Ln 22015
Kendrick Ln 22015
Kenilworth Dr 22015
Kerrwood St 22015
Kersey Ct 22015
Kestrell Ct 22015
Kings Grove Ct 22015
Kinnerly Ct 22015
Kirkfield Rd 22015
Kite St 22015
Klimt Ct 22015
Koziara Dr 22015
Lake Braddock Dr 22015
Lake Meadow Ct & Dr 22015
Lakehaven Ct 22015
Lakepointe Ct & Dr 22015
Lakeside Oak Ct & Ln 22015
Lapstrake Ln 22015
Leathersmith Ct 22015
Lee St 22015
Lee Chapel Rd 22015
Lee Prescott Dr 22015
Legendgate Pl 22015
Leslie Ct 22015
Liberty Bell Ct 22015
Light Infantry Dr 22015
Lighthorne Rd 22015
Lighthouse Ln 22015
Lightship Ct 22015
Lincolnwood Ct & Dr 22015
Little Cobbler Ct 22015
Longmead Ct 22015
Lucas Pond Ct 22015
Lundy Ct & Pl 22015
Luria Commons Ct 22015
Lyngate Ct 22015
Lyon Park Ct 22015
Lyra Ct 22015
Macmahon Dr 22015
Mainsail Ct & Dr 22015
Manet Rd 22015
Manteo Ct 22015
Mantle Rd 22015
Mantlepiece Ct 22015
Mardale Ln 22015
Marianna Ct 22015
Marquand Dr 22015
Marshall House Ct 22015
Marshall Pond Rd 22015
Martins Landing Ct & Ln 22015
Mason Bluff Ct & Dr 22015
Mccarthy Woods Ct 22015
Meadow Brook Dr 22015
Meadow Grove Ct 22015
Meadowpond Ct 22015
Meadowrill Ln 22015
Mellett Ct 22015
Meridian Hill Pl 22015
Merridith Cir 22015
Mersea Ct 22015
Meyers Landing Ct 22015
Midship Ct 22015
Mill Cove Ct 22015
Millgate Pl 22015
Minstead Ct 22015
Mizzen Pl 22015
Mockingbird Pond Ct & Ter 22015
Mount Burnside Way 22015
Mount Corcoran Pl 22015
Mount Greenwich Ct 22015
Mount Lookout Ct 22015
Myrtle Oak Ct 22015
Narnia Ct 22015
Natick Ct & Rd 22015
Nativity Ln 22015
Neaptide Ln 22015
New England Woods Ct & Dr 22015
Newchandler Ct 22015
Nordeen Oak Ct 22015
Novak Woods Ct 22015
Oak Apple Ct 22015
Oak Bluff Ct 22015
Oak Bucket Ct 22015
Oak Fern Ct 22015
Oak Green Ct & Way 22015
Oak Ladder Ct 22015
Oak Leather Dr 22015
Oak Moss Ter 22015
Oak Ridge Ct 22015
Oak Stake Ct 22015
Oak Tanager Ct 22015
Oak Thrush Ct 22015
Oak Wilds Ct 22015
Oakenshaw Ct 22015
Oakland Park Dr 22015
Oakshore Ct 22015
Oatley Ln 22015
Odyssey Ct 22015
Ohara Landing Ct 22015
Old Blacksmith Dr 22015
Old Burke Lake Rd 22015
Old Keene Mill Rd 22015
Old Landing Way 22015
Olivia Pl 22015
Olley Ln 22015
Onion Patch Dr 22015
Orion Ct 22015
Ormandy Dr 22015
Outhaul Ln 22015
Packard Way 22015
Parakeet Dr 22015
Park Woods Ln & Ter 22015
Parliament Dr 22015
Passageway Pl 22015
Pebble Weigh Ct 22015
Peppercorn Dr 22015
Peregrine Dr 22015
Peter Roy Ct 22015
Pierrpont St 22015
Pilothouse Rd 22015
Pin Oak Commons Ct 22015
Pine Crossing Ln 22015
Pine Meadows Ln 22015
Pine View Ct 22015
Poburn Landing Ct 22015
Pohick Rd 22015
Poindexter Ct 22015
Point Longstreet Way 22015
Point Roundtop Ct 22015
Pond Lily Ct 22015
Pond Spice Ln & Ter 22015
Poplar Spring Ct 22015
Portside Dr 22015
Powells Landing Rd 22015
Premier Ct 22015
Prince Caspian Ct & Ln 22015
Protest Ct 22015
Pueblo Ct 22015
Pulham Rd 22015
Queen Victoria Ct 22015
Queens Wood Dr 22015
Quiet Oak Ct 22015
Quiet Pond Ct & Ter 22015
Quintana Ct 22015
Raftelis Rd 22015
Raillear Ct 22015
Raintree Rd 22015
Rand Dr 22015
Rapid Run Ct 22015
Reeds Landing Cir 22015
Rehanek Ct 22015
Rein Commons Ct 22015
Renaissance Ct 22015
Renoir Port Ln 22015
Renton Dr 22015
Renwick Ct 22015
Retriever Rd 22015
Rich Ct 22015
Ridge Ford Dr 22015
Rilian Ct 22015
Roberts Pkwy 22015
Roberts Common Ct & Ln 22015
Robins Nest Ct & Ln 22015
Rockwell Ct & Rd 22015
Rolling Rd 22015
Rossetti Ct 22015
Round Top Ln 22015
Ruffner Woods Ct 22015
Rumsford Ln 22015
Rymney Ln 22015
Saddlebrook Ct 22015
Saddlehorn Ct 22015
Sailcloth Pl 22015
Sanctuary Woods Ct 22015
Sand Creek Ct 22015
Sara Alyce Ct 22015
Sassafras Woods Ct 22015
Scarborough Commons Ct & Ln 22015
Schmidt Dr 22015
Schoolcraft Ln 22015
Schoolhouse Woods Ct & Rd 22015
Scorpio Ct & Ln 22015
Shackle Pl 22015
Shana Pl 22015
Shingle Oak Ct 22015
Shiplett Blvd 22015
Shipwright Dr 22015
Signal Hill Dr 22015
Signal House Ct 22015
Signal Point Ct 22015
Silas Burke St 22015
Silchester Ct & St 22015
Simpson Ln 22015
Skinner Dr 22015
Sloop Ct 22015
Southern Cross Ln 22015
Spalding Ct 22015
Spanker Dr 22015
Spillway Ct 22015
Split Oak Ln 22015
Spring Lake Dr 22015
Spring Oak Ct 22015
Sprucewood Rd 22015
Stanchion Ln 22015
Stavendish St 22015
Staysail Ct 22015

Steamboat Landing Ct & Ln 22015
Stewart St 22015
Stillwater Ct 22015
Stipp St 22015
Stone Wood Ct 22015
Stonecutter Dr 22015
Stoneway Ct 22015
Strattondale Ct 22015
Summer Oak Ct & Way 22015
Summerday Ct & Dr 22015
Summit Oak Way 22015
Sunset Woods Ct 22015
Sutherland Ct 22015
Swan Landing Ct 22015
Swift Current Ct 22015
Sydenstricker Rd 22015
Tara Ct 22015
Teakwood Ct 22015
Tibbitt Ln 22015
Ticonderoga Ct 22015
Tilia Ct 22015
Tillary Ct 22015
Timarron Cove Ln 22015
Tinker Ct 22015
Tinsmith Ln 22015
Tiny Ct 22015
Tisbury Dr 22015
Todman Landing Ct 22015
Torrence St 22015
Tregaron Pl 22015
Tripolis Ct 22015
Truxion Ct 22015
Tucker Woods Ct 22015
Turnbuckle Dr 22015
Twinbrook Rd 22015
Ulysses Ct 22015
Vandola Ct 22015
Veering Ln 22015
Velilla Rd 22015
Vernons Oak Ct 22015
View Park Dr 22015
Villagesmith Way 22015
Virgo Ct 22015
Walden Commons Ct 22015
Wallingford Dr 22015
Walnut Wood Ct & Ln 22015
Walthorne Ct 22015
Wards Grove Cir 22015
Waterline Dr 22015
Waters Edge Landing Ct & Ln 22015
Waterside Dr 22015
Wax Myrtle Ct 22015
Weetman St 22015
Wenlock Way 22015
Wesley Pond Ct 22015
Westcliff Ct 22015
Westport Ln 22015
Westwood Manor Ct 22015
Wheaton Dr 22015
Whidbey Ln 22015
Whippany Way 22015
Whitewater Dr 22015
Wicklow Dr 22015
Wigfield Way 22015
William Kirk Ln 22015
Willow Pond Ln 22015
Wilmette Dr 22015
Wilmington Dr 22015
Winbourne Rd 22015
Windsor Way 22015
Windward Dr 22015
Winnepeg Ct & Dr 22015
Winter Park Dr 22015
Wolcott Dr 22015
Wood Astor Ct 22015
Wood Duck Ct 22015
Wood Flower Ct 22015
Wood Green Way 22015
Wood Grouse Ct 22015
Wood Laurel Ct 22015
Wood Mouse Ct 22015
Wood Poppy Ct 22015
Wood Sorrels Ct & Ln 22015
Woodcarver Ct 22015
Wooded Glen Ave 22015
Woodedge Ct & Dr 22015
Wooden Dove Ct 22015
Wooden Hawk Ct & Ln 22015
Wooden Spoke Ct & Rd 22015
Wooden Spoon Ct 22015
Woodfahl Ct 22015
Woodhenge Ct 22015
Wye Oak Commons Cir & Ct 22015
Wyeth Ln 22015
Wynyard Pl 22015
Wythal Ln 22015
Yachthaven Dr 22015
Yardarm Ln 22015
Yawl Ct 22015

CENTREVILLE VA

General Delivery 20120

POST OFFICE BOXES MAIN OFFICE STATIONS AND BRANCHES

Box No.s
1 - 2380 20122
230001 - 238391 20120

RURAL ROUTES

02, 23 20120

NAMED STREETS

Adolphus Dr 20121
Affinity Ct 20120
Ajuga Ct 20120
Alcove Path 20120
Algretus Dr 20120
Ampstead Ct 20120
Ann Grigsby Cir 20120
Anne Marie Ter 20121
Antonia Ford Ct 20121
Arrowhead Park Dr 20120
Artillery Ct 20121
Ashcomb Ct 20120
Asher Ct & Vw 20121
Ashington Ct 20120
Ashmere Ln 20120
Astilbe Ct 20120
Astrid Cv 20120
Audrey Dr 20120
Ausable Ct & Way 20121
Autumn Cir 20121
Avocado Ct 20121
Awbrey Patent Dr 20120
Barnesdale Path 20120
Barnsley Pl 20120
Baron Kent Ln 20120
Barren Springs Ct 20121
N & S Barros Ct & Dr 20120
Barrymore Rd 20120
Basingstoke Ct & Loop 20120
Batavia Dr 20120
Baton Rouge Ct 20121
Battalion St 20121
Battery Ridge Ct & Ln 20120
Baugher Dr 20120
Bay Valley Ln 20121
Bayberry Ln 20121
Baywood Ct 20120
Beaumeadow Ct & Dr 20120
Bebe Ct 20121
Beckford Way 20120
Beddingfield Ct & Way 20121
Belcher Farm Ct & Dr 20120
Bella Dr 20121
Belle Plains Dr 20120
Belle Pond Dr 20120
Belt Buckle Ct 20121
Bent Maple Ln 20120
Bent Tree Cir & Ln 20121
Bentley Sq 20120
Betsy Ross Ct & Ln 20121
Big Yankee Ln 20121
Billingsgate Ln 20120
Birchleaf Park Ct 20120
Black Horse Ct 20120
Blue Aster Cir 20120
Blue Post Rd 20121
Blueridge View Dr 20120
Bobann Dr 20120
Bodley Sq 20120
Bolton Rd 20121
Bonham Pl 20121
Bonnet Ter 20121
Boydell Dr 20120
Braddock Rd
13800-13899 20121
13900-43599 20120
Braddock Ridge Dr 20120
Braddock Springs Rd 20121
Branham Ct 20120
Brass Button Ct 20121
Braywood Dr 20120
Brenham Dr 20121
Bridlington Ct 20120
Brim Ln 20121
British Manor Ct 20120
Brittney Elyse Cir 20120
Broad Brook Ct 20120
Bromfield Trce 20120
Bronze Post Ct & Rd 20121
Brookmere Dr 20120
Brookmoor Ln 20121
Brown Post Ln 20121
Brushwood Way 20121
Buffalo Run Ln 20120
Buggy Whip Dr 20120
Bull Run Dr 20121
Bull Run Post Office Rd
6000-6899 20120
6900-7399 20121
26300-26899 20120
Bungleweed Ln 20120
Cabells Mill Ct & Dr 20120
Caddington Rd 20121
Calamint Ct 20120
Caliper Ct 20120
Callaway Ct 20121
Calvary Pl 20121
Canteen Ct 20121
Cardigan Sq 20120
Carlbern Dr 20120
Carriage Way Ct 20120
Castle Harbor Way 20120
Castleford Ct 20121
Cat Tail Ct 20120
Cedar Walk 20121
Cedar Break Dr 20120
Cedar Key Lndg 20121
Cedar Knoll Dr 20120
Cedar Loch Ct 20121
Cedar Post Ct 20120
Cedar Spring Rd 20121
Cedarhurst Ct 20120
Centre Square Dr 20120
Centreville Rd & Sq 20121
Centreville Crest Ln 20121
Centreville Farms Rd 20120
Chandley Farm Cir & Ct 20120
Chapel Run Ct 20120
Chasewood Cir 20121
Chelsey Pl 20121
Chestnut Hollow Ct 20121
Cheverly Ct 20120
Choptank Ct 20120
Cider Barrel Cir 20121
Cider House Ln 20121
Clarendon Springs Ct & Pl 20121
Claret Pl 20120
Clay Pipe Ct 20121
Clay Spur Ct 20121
Claybank Ln 20120
Climbing Rose Way 20121
Clubside Ln 20120
Coachway Dr 20120
Coble Laskey Ct 20121
Cochran Pl 20120
Coleman Ct 20120
Colonel Taylor Ln 20121
Compton Ln & Rd 20121
Compton Valley Ct, Pl & Way 20121
Compton Village Dr 20121
Coneflower Ct 20120
Confederate Ridge Ln 20121
Connor Dr 20120
Cool Fountain Ln 20120
Cool Oak Ln 20121
Coreopsis Ct 20120
Cottingham Ln 20121
Cranoke St 20120
Creek Bed Ct 20121
Creek Branch Ct 20120
Creek Run Dr 20121
Creek Valley Ct 20120
Creekstone Ln 20120
Crenshaw Dr 20120
Crim Station Rd 20121
Crimson Sky Ct 20120
Cristo Ct 20120
Croatan Ct & Dr 20120
Crystalford Ct & Ln 20120
Cub Run Ct 20121
Cub Run Park Dr 20120
Cub Stream Dr 20120
Cupids Dart Dr 20120
Darkwood Cir & Dr 20121
Darrington Way 20120
Day Valley Ct 20120
Deer Hill Ct 20121
Deer Lake Ct & Ln 20120
Deer Pond Ct & Rd 20120
Derring St 20120
Destin Ct 20121
Devereaux Ct 20120
Deviar Dr 20120
Dianthus Ct 20120
Doyle Ln 20120
Drifton Ct 20121
Drill Field Ct 20121
Dumas Ct 20120
Eagle Button Ct 20121
Eagle Tavern Ln & Way 20120
Ealing Ct 20120
Eames Ave 20120
Early Autumn Dr 20120
Eastcliff Cir 20120
Eddy Ct 20120
Edgecomb Ct 20120
Edman Cir & Rd 20121
Elkheart Ct 20120
Ellicott Ct & Dr 20120
Elliston Ct 20120
Emerald Green Ct 20121
Emerald Pool Dr 20120
Emeric Ct 20120
English Saddle Ct 20121
Euphrates Ct 20120
Faircloth Ct 20120
Fairfax National Way 20120
Fallscliff Ln 20120
Farm Pond Ct 20120
Farming Way 20120
Farnam Cluster 20120
Farrahs Cavalry Rd 20121
Fawn Hollow Pl 20120
Federation Dr 20121
Fence Post Ct 20121
Fernbrook Ct & Dr 20120
Field Flower Trl 20121
Fiery Dawn Ct & Dr 20120
Filly Ct 20120
Fire Fox Run 20120
Flag Staff Ct 20121
Flagler Ct & Dr 20120
Flomation Ct 20121
Flourcastle Ct 20120
Flower Hill Ct & Dr 20120
Flowerdew Hundred Ct 20120
Folkers Lndg 20121
Forest Pond Ct 20121
Fort Dr 20121
Fount Beattie Ct 20121
Four Chimney Dr 20120
Fox Meadow Ct 20120
Frankford Cir 20120
Franklin Fox Dr 20121
Frosty Winter Ct 20120
Gabrielle Way 20121
Gatwick Sq 20120
General Johnston Pl 20120
General Lee Dr 20121
Generals Ct 20121
George Baylor Dr 20121
Giant Oak Ct 20121
Gill Brook Ln 20121
Glade Spring Dr 20121
Gladewright Dr 20120
Glassford Pl 20120
Glen Meadow Ct, Dr, Pl & Rd 20120
Glencrest Cir 20120
Glory Creek Trl 20120
Gold Post Ct 20121
Golden Oak Ct & Rd 20121
Goldmoore Ct 20120
Gopost 20122
Gordon Dr 20120
Gothic Dr 20121
Gothwaite Dr 20120
Grainery Rd 20121
Grande Forest Ct 20120
Granite Step Trl 20120
Granville Ln 20120
Grape Holly Grv 20121
Gray Post Ct 20121
Gray Valley Ct 20120
Great Rocky Run 20120
Green Park Way 20120
Green Post Ct 20121
Green Trails Blvd & Ct 20121
Greenhouse Ter 20120
Gresham Ln 20120
Greymont Dr 20120
Gringsby Ct 20120
Grisby House Ct 20120
Gristmill Square Ln & Trce 20120
Grobie Pond Ln 20120
Grogans Ct 20121
Grumble Jones Ct 20121
Guard Mount Ct 20121
Gulliver Rd 20120
Gun Cap Ct 20121
Gun Mount Ct 20121
Gunners Pl 20121
Gunther Ct 20120
Hallissey Ct 20120
Hancock Ct 20120
Hanna Ct 20121
Hardee Chambliss Ct 20120
Harmony Hill Ct 20120
Harness Hill Ct 20121
Harrison House Ct 20120
Hart Forest Dr 20121
Hartlaub Ct 20120
Hartwood Ct & Ln 20121
Harvest Ct 20120
Harvest Mill Ct 20121
Hatfield Sq 20120
Havener House Ct & Way 20120
Haversack Rd 20121
Haymarket Ln 20120
Haysickle Ct 20121
Haystack Ct 20120
Heathrow Ln 20120
Hedgerow Ct 20120
Helmsly Ct 20120
Heritage Crossing Ct & Ln 20120
Heron Dr 20120
Hibner St 20120
Hickory Post Ct 20121
Hidden Canyon Rd 20120
High Grove Hills Ln 20120
Highbourne Ln 20120
S Hills Ct 20120
Hirst Valley Way 20120
Hollow Oak Ln 20121
Hollyspring Ln 20120
Honey Hill Ct 20121
Honeysuckle Ct 20120
Honnicut Dr 20121
Honsena Dr 20120
Hoskins Hollow Cir 20121
Hovingham Ct 20121
Hoxton Sq 20120
Hunt Chase Ct 20120
Hunting Path Pl 20120
Illuminati Way 20120
Indian Rock Rd 20120
Indian Summer Ct 20120
Insignia Ct 20121
Iron Stone Ct 20120
Jackson Fields Ct 20121
Jacob Ln 20120
Jade Post Ln 20121
James Harris Way 20121
Jameson Ct 20120
Jarnigan St 20120
Jarrett Ct 20120
Jarski Ct 20120
Jaslow St 20120
Jeb Stuart Sq 20120
Jenlar Dr 20121
Jenn Ct 20120
Jennifer Ct 20121
Jenny Leigh Ct 20121
Jillians Forest Way 20120
Joel Beach Ln 20120
John Charles Lndg 20121
John Ewell Ct 20121
Johnny Moore Ct 20120
Johnson Ave 20120
Jordans Journey Dr 20120
Joseph Johnston Ln 20120
Jovet Ct & Way 20120
Juglan Ct 20120
Jule Star Dr 20120
Kamputa Dr 20120
Kearns Ct 20120
Keepers Park 20121
Kendra Way 20121
Kentwell Cir 20120
Kerrywood Cir 20121
Kertscher Ter 20120
Kettle Mountain Dr 20120
Kimanna Dr 20120
Knapsack Ln 20121
Knoll View Pl 20120
Knoughton Way 20120
Kyle Dr 20120
La Petite Pl 20121
Lady Madonna Ct 20120
Lalos St 20120
Lambeth Sq 20120
Lamium Ln 20120
Lampec St 20120
Latshaw Rd 20120
Laura Ratcliff Ct 20121
Lavatera Ct 20120
Lavender Mist Ct & Ln 20120
Lawnes Creek Ct 20120
Lee Hwy
14098A-14098D 20120
14120A-14120A 20122
13300-14198 20120
13301-16099 20121
14400-16098 20120
13830-1-13830-18 20120
Lee Forest Path 20120
Leicester Ct 20120
Leland Rd 20120
Level Green Ln 20121
Lierman Cir 20120
Lightburn Ct & Ln 20121
Lilva Dr 20120
Linden Creek Ct 20120
Little Rocky Mountain Ct 20120
Little Rocky Run Cir 20121
Littlefield Ct 20121
Lock Dr 20120
Locust Branch Ct 20120
Locust Grove Ct 20120
London Towne Sq 20120
Lotus Ln 20120
Ludington Pl 20121
Lynhodge Ct 20120
Machen Rd 20121
Mackenzie St 20120
Maidstone Ct 20120
Malabar Ct 20121
Malcolm Jameson Way 20120
Malton Ct 20121
Manassas Gap Ct 20120
Manorwood Dr 20120
Mansonti Ct 20121
Maple Creek Ln 20120
Maple Mountain Dr 20120
Maple Rock Ct 20121
Maple Valley Ct 20120
Marshall Crown Rd 20120
Marston Cluster 20120
Martins Brandon Way 20120
Martins Hundred Dr 20120
Mary Todd Ct & Ln 20121
Massaponax Pl 20121
Matthews Vista Dr 20120
Mcalester Way 20121
Mccambell Cluster 20120
Mcconnell Ct 20120
Mccoy Rd 20121
Meadow Crest Ct 20121
Meadow Glade Ln 20121
Meeting Camp Rd 20121
Meherrin Ct & Dr 20120
Melton Pl 20120
Middle Creek Pl 20121
Middlebourne Ln 20120
Midnight Blue Pl 20120
Millicent Ct 20120
Mist Flower Dr 20120
Misty Meadow Way 20120
Montjoy Ct 20121
Montverd Ct 20121
Moore Rd 20121
Morning Dove Ln 20121
Mossy Bank Ln 20121
Mount Gilead Rd 20120
Mount Olive Ct & Rd 20121
Muddy Creek Ct 20120
Multiplex Dr 20120
Munsey Pl 20120
Musket Ball Dr 20121
Muskett Way 20121
Muster Ct 20121
Nandina Ct 20120
Nanticoke Ct 20120
Naylor Rd 20121
Netherton St 20120
New Braddock Rd 20121
Newgate Blvd 20120
Newgate Tavern Ct 20120
Newhall Ct 20120
Newton Patent Ct 20120
Nicholas Schar Way 20121
Northbourne Dr 20120
Oak Cluster Dr 20120
Oak Rock Ct 20121
Oakengate Way 20120
Oakham Pl 20120
Oakmere Dr & Pl 20120
Oday Dr 20120
Old Centreville Rd 20121
Old Mill Rd 20121
Olddale Rd 20120
Olde Kent Rd 20120
Olinerai Dr 20120

Street	ZIP
Ordway Rd	20121
Ormond Stone Cir	20120
Oshay Ct	20120
Ottawa Rd	20120
Outpost Ct	20121
Overcoat Ln	20121
Overland Ct	20120
Owens Wood Ct	20120
Pachysandra Ln	20120
Paddington Ct	20121
Paddington Ln	20120
Pale Moon Way	20120
Palisades Dr	20121
Palmerston Sq	20120
Palmetto Pl	20121
Palmetto Bay Ct	20120
Pamela Dr	20120
Papilion Way	20121
Paradise Mill Rd	20121
Patriarch Ct	20120
Patrick Ct	20120
Peaceful Meadow Ln	20120
Pearson Valley Ln	20120
Pebblebrook Dr & Trce	20120
Pelhams Trce	20120
Pendleton Pl	20121
Picket Oaks Rd	20121
Pickets Post Rd	20121
Pickwick Rd	
5500-5699	20120
5700-5798	20121
5701-5799	20120
Pittman Ct	20121
Pleasant Forest Dr	20120
Pleasant Valley Rd	20120
Plumbago Dr	20120
Point Cir & Ct	20120
Pond Field Dr	20120
Ponderlay Dr	20120
Pony Hill Ct	20121
Poplar Valley Ct	20120
Portage Pl	20120
Post Corners Trl	20120
Powder Flask Ct	20121
Powers Ln	20120
Prairie Mallow Ln	20120
Prairie Willow Ln & Way	20120
Preacher Chapman Pl	20121
Prince Way	20120
Purple Dusk Ct	20120
Quail Pond Ct	20120
Quiet Cedar Ln	20120
Rabbit Hill Ct	20121
Rabbit Run Ct	20120
Rachael Alice Ln	20120
Raina Dr	20120
Rainy Spring Ln	20120
Rampant Lion Ct	20120
Ravenscar Ct	20121
Red Barn Ct	20120
Red House Dr	20120
Red Post Ct	20121
Red River Dr	20121
Redwood Square Ctr	20121
Regents Park Rd	20120
Regimental Ct	20120
Richard Simpson Ln	20121
Ridge Haven Ct	20120
Ridge Pond Rd	20121
Ridge Water Ct	20121
Ridgemont Dr	20120
Ridings Manor Pl	20120
Rinard Dr	20120
Ritchie Rd	20120
Riverland Run	20120
Riverwind Ter	20120
Roamer Ct	20121
Rock Ter	20120
Rock Canyon Dr	20121
Rock Forest Ct	20121
Rock Landing Ct	20121
Rockbridge Pl	20120
Rockdale Ct	20121
Rockledge Pl	20121
Rockton Ct	20121
Rocky Branch Ct	20120
Rocky Run Dr	20120
Rocky Valley Dr	20121
Rocky Way Ct	20120
Rockymount Ct	20120
Rosalie Ridge Dr	20120
Rosebud Ln	20121
Rosemallow Cir	20120
Rosy Ln	20121
Round Lick Ln	20120
Round Post Ct	20121
Rowena Dr	20120
Royal Oak Ln	20120
Running Post Ct	20120
Rushbrook Dr	20120
Rustling Leaves Ln	20121
Rydell Rd	20121
Sacred Ln	20121
Saddle Downs Pl	20120
Saguaro Pl	20121
Saint Germain Dr	20121
Saint Hubert Ln	20121
Saint Timothys Ln	20121
Salisbury Plain Ct	20120
Sammie Kay Ln	20120
Sapphire Sky Ln	20120
Sara Marie Ter	20121
Sawteeth Way	20121
Schoolfield Ct	20120
Scotch Run Ct	20120
Scott Ter	20121
Seasons Dr	20120
Secret Hollow Ln	20120
Selby Ct	20121
Sequoia Farms Dr	20120
Serviceberry St	20120
Sharps Dr	20121
Sharpsburg Dr	20121
Sheals Ln	20120
Shelburne Ct & St	20120
Sherborne Knls	20120
Shetler Way	20120
Shipley Ct	20120
Shirey Ln	20121
Shreve St	20120
Silo Valley Vw	20121
Singletons Way	20121
Skipton Ct	20121
Skylemar Trl	20121
N Slope St	20120
Smethwick Pl	20120
Smithaven Pl	20120
Smithfield Ct & Pl	20120
Smiths Trce	20120
Smithwood Dr	20120
Snellings Ct	20120
Snowhill Ct & Ln	20120
Sorrel Chase Ct	20121
Soucy Pl	20120
Sour Gum Dr	20120
Southwarke Pl	20120
Spence Pl	20121
Spindle Ct	20120
Spruce Run Ct	20120
Starbird Ct	20120
Stargazer Ter	20120
Starry Night Ln	20120
Stillfield Ct & Pl	20120
Stilsby Ct	20121
Stone Rd	
5500-6299	20120
6300-6399	20121
Stone Chase Way	20121
Stone Creek Ct & Dr	20120
Stone Crossing Ct	20120
Stone Maple Ter	20121
Stone Range Dr	20120
Stone Ridge Dr	20120
Stonepath Cir	20120
Stonewater Ct	20121
Stoney Branch Ct	20120
Store House Ct & Dr	20121
Strasburg Dr	20121
Stratton Major Ct	20120
Stream Pond Ct & Dr	20120
Stringfellow Rd	20120
Stroud Ct	20120
Sudley Rd	20120
Sudley Forest Ct	20120
Sully Rd	20120
Sully Lake Ct & Dr	20120
Sully Park Dr	20120
Sully Station Dr	20120
Summer Garden Walk	20120
Summer Pond Dr	20121
Summer Tree Rd	20121
Summerlake Way	20120
Summit St	20120
Sun Meadow Ct	20120
Suncatcher Ct	20121
Sunset Ridge Ct	20121
Surrey House Way	20120
Sutler Store Ct	20121
Sweet Woodruff Ln	20120
Sweetwater Ln	20121
Sydell Ln	20120
Tanners House Way	20121
Tarleton Dr	20120
Terrycloth Ln	20120
Thera Way	20120
Thorndyke Ct	20120
Top Sergeant Ln	20121
Tracy Schar Ln	20121
Travis Edward Way	20120
Tre Towers Ct	20120
Tree Line Dr	20120
Trevilian Pl	20121
Trillium House Ln	20120
Trinity Pkwy	20120
Trinity Post Way	20120
Triplett Dr	20120
Truitt Farm Ct & Dr	20120
Truro Parish Ct	20120
Tulip Leaf Ct	20120
Turin Ln	20121
Twilight Glow Dr	20120
Twin Creeks Ct	20120
Twin Pine Ct	20120
Ulderic Dr	20120
Uniform Dr	20121
Upperridge Ct & Dr	20121
Verona Ln	20121
Veronica Rd	20120
W View Dr	20121
Village Center Dr	20120
Village Fountain Pl	20120
Village Square Dr	20120
Vine Cottage Dr	20120
Vinson Pl	20120
Virgin Rock Rd	20120
Virginia Chase Ct & Dr	20120
Virginia Infantry Rd	20121
Virginia Pine Ct	20121
Wakley Ct	20121
Walney Rd	20120
Walter Bowie Ln	20121
Water Pond Ct	20121
Water Springs Ct	20121
Waterdale Ct	20121
Waterflow Ct & Pl	20121
Watermark Cir	20120
Waters Creek Dr	20120
Watery Mountain Ct	20120
Wealdstone Ct	20120
Weinstein Ct	20120
Welton Ct & Dr	20120
Westbourne Pl	20120
Westfields Blvd	20120
Westwater Ct	20121
Wetherburn Ct & Dr	20120
Wharton Ln	20120
Wharton Park Ct	20120
Wheat Mill Way	20121
Whispering Glen Ct	20120
White Post Ct & Rd	20121
Whitechapel Ct	20120
Wicker Ln	20121
Wild Brook Ct	20121
Wildflower Ct	20120
William Carr Ln	20120
William Colin Ct	20120
William Mosby Dr	20121
Willoughby Newton Dr	20120
Willow Creek Dr	20120
Winding Oak Cir	20121
Winding Ridge Ln	20121
Winding Woods Ct & Dr	20120
Windrift Ct	20120
Winterfield Ct & Dr	20120
Wisteria Arbor Ln	20120
Wood Creek Ln	20120
Wood Home Rd	20120
Wood Lilly Ln	20120
Wood Meadow Way	20120
Wood Rock Way	20121
Woodfield Dr	20120
Woodford Dr	20120
Woodgate Manor Cir & Pl	20120
Woodland Ridge Ct & Dr	20121
Woodleaf Ct	20120
Woodmere Ct, Dr & Pl	20120
Woods Run Ct	20121
Woodspring Ct	20120
Worth Ct	20120
Worthington Woods Way	20120
Woven Willow Ln	20121
Wycoff Sq	20120
Wycombe St	20120
Wyndham Rose Cv	20120
Yellow Poplar Dr	20120

CHANTILLY VA

General Delivery 20151

POST OFFICE BOXES MAIN OFFICE STATIONS AND BRANCHES

Box No.s

All PO Boxes 20153

NAMED STREETS

Street	ZIP
Adamstown Ct	20152
Adelphi Ct	20151
Ahlea Ln	20152
Ahmadiyya Dr	20151
Air And Space Museum Pkwy	20151
Airline Pkwy	20151
Albemarle Point Pl	20151
Aldie Mill Ct	20152
Alumni Ter	20152
Amber Gate Ter	20152
Amberwood Plz	20152
America Sq	20152
Amethyst Ln	20152
Anabell Ln	20152
Anderby Ln	20152
Angelica Ct	20151
Anthem Ter	20152
Appaloosa Trail Ct	20152
Armfield Farm Dr	20151
Arthur Pl	20152
Ashbury Dr	20152
Ashgarten Dr	20152
Astell St	20152
Astors Beachwood Ct	20152
Atchison Ter	20152
Atrium Village Ct	20152
Auto Park Cir	20151
Autumn Ln	20152
Autumn Glory Ct & Way	20151
Autumn Vale Ct	20151
Avenza Ter	20152
Avion Pkwy	20151
Avion Park Ct	20151
Avonlea Dr	20152
Aythorne Ln	20152
Balcombe Ter	20152
Bald Eagle Ter	20152
Baltzer Glenn Ct	20152
Banff Springs Pl	20152
Bannockburn Ter	20152
Bannon Hill Ct	20151
Bare Island Dr	20151
Barford Ct	20151
Barons St	20152
Beach Pl	20152
Beachall St	20152
Beaujolais Ct	20151
Becerra Ter	20152
Beech Down Dr	20151
Beeker Mill Pl	20151
Belcourt Castle Dr	20152
Bell Ridge Ct	20151
Bellerose Dr	20151
Benjamin Cross Ct	20151
Bennet Pond Ct	20151
Bennett St	20152
Bentree Ct	20151
Beresford Dr	20152
Bernadette Ct	20151
Bessemer Ln	20152
Bicentennial Ct	20151
Biddle Ln	20152
Birch Dr	20151
Bixby Ct	20151
Black Gum Ct	20151
Black Spruce Way	20151
Blackstone Ct	20152
Blue Sky Ln	20152
Blue Springs Dr & Ln	20152
Boac Cir	20151
Bogle Dr	20151
Bokel Dr	20151
Bordolino Dr	20151
Braddock Rd	20152
Bradfords Telegraph Ct	20152
Bradshaw Dr	20152
Braniff Cir	20151
Braxton Rd	20151
Brentwall Ct & Dr	20151
Brewerton Ct	20151
Briarton Dr	20151
Brickell Dr	20152
Bridgehampton Sq	20152
Bridgewater Pl	20152
Bridle Pl	20152
Brockmeyer Ct	20151
Brodie Ter	20152
Broken Branch Ct	20151
Bromall Ct	20151
Brookbark Ter	20152
Brookfield Ct & Dr	20151
Brookfield Corporate Dr	
4449A-4449C	20151
4200-4411	20151
4410-4410	20153
4412-4698	20151
4413-4699	20151
Brookfield Tower Dr	20151
Brownburg Pl	20152
Bryson Dr	20152
Burke Dale St	20152
Buser Ct	20152
Cabernet Ct	20151
Cabin Point Ct	20152
Cadmor Plz	20152
Camden Ln	20152
Cancello Ter	20152
Capital Ter	20152
Carberry Dr	20152
Carbury Ct	20151
Carls Ct	20151
Carmel Ln & Ter	20151
Carrier Ct	20151
Carrington Dr	20152
Carroll Ct	20151
Casale Ter	20152
Castle Ct	20151
Castlebar St	20152
Castleton Dr	20152
Caversham Ter	20152
Cedar Hedge St	20152
Cedar Hollow Dr	20152
Cedar Pond Pl	20152
Cedar Ridge Blvd	20152
Celbridge Way	20152
Celest Ter	20152
Center St	20152
Centerview Dr	20151
Centreville Rd	20151
Chambers Dr	20152
Chantilly Rd	20151
Chantilly Crossing Ln	20151
Chantilly Lace Ct	20151
Chantilly Shopping Center Dr	20151
Chase St	20152
Chevy Chase Ct & Ln	20151
Chianti Ct	20151
Chicama Dr	20152
Chilmark Dr	20152
Chiswick Ter	20152
Chorley Wood St	20152
Churchill Glen Dr	20152
Clarecastle Dr	20152
Claremorris Way	20152
Claret Ct	20151
Clary Sage Dr	20151
Clifton Forge Way	20152
Coatesly Dr	20151
Colonists Ter	20152
Commons Sq	20152
Concorde Pkwy	20151
Conference Center Dr	20151
Conrad Ter	20152
Constitution Ct	20151
Corcoran Ln	20152
Corsair Ct	20151
Country Crossing Ct & St	20151
Creek Run Ter	20152
Creekmore Ter	20152
Cross Meadow Pl	20151
Crossfield Dr	20152
Crusher Dr	20152
Crystal Rock Ct	20151
Cub Run Rd	20151
Cunard Aly	20152
Currey Ln	20151
Cutleaf Ct	20151
Dabner Dr	20152
Dallas St	20151
Dallas Hutchison St	20151
Daly Dr	20151
Dapper Ct	20152
Darkwoods St	20152
Daventry Sq	20152
Dawn Valley Ct	20151
De Haven Dr	20151
Dean Chapel Sq	20152
Deerhurst Ter	20152
Deerwatch Dr	20151
Defender Dr	20152
Demarco Ter	20152
Demerrit St	20152
Demilton Ter	20152
Dempsey Ln	20152
Dittany Ct	20151
Dominion Glen Way	20152
Donegal Dr	20152
Donegal Church Ct	20151
Donerails Chase Dr	20152
Donovan Dr	20152
Doolittle Ln	20152
Downfield St	20152
Downs Dr	20151
Dressmaker Ln	20152
Drillfield Ter	20152
Dulles South Ct	20151
Dunvegan Sq	20152
Eagle Chase Cir	20151
Earlsdon Ter	20152
Earlsford Dr	20152
Eastern Marketplace Plz	20152
Easterwood Ln	20152
Eastgate View Dr	20152
Eden Way	20151
Edenfield Ln	20152
Edgartown St	20152
Edge Rock Ct & Dr	20151
Edgewater St	20152
Eggleston Ter	20152
Eisenhower Dr	20152
Eldridge Ter	20152
Elk Pl	20152
Elk Lick Rd	20152
Elk Run Rd	20151
Ellendale Dr	20151
Elmwood St	20151
Elwen Ter	20152
Emerald Ln	20152
Enterprise Ct	20151
Entre Ct	20151
Equality St	20152
Equine Ct	20152
Equine Trail Ct	20152
Esther Ct	20152
Etna Ter	20152
Eustis St	20152
Evans Sq	20152
Evian Ln	20152
Exart Ter	20152
Fair Hope Way	20152
Fair Ponds Ln	20152
Fairbanks Pl	20152
Fairdoun Farm Ln	20152
Fallen Oak Ct & Dr	20151
Falling Cedars Ct	20152
Falling Spring Way	20152
Farmneck Ct	20152
Fawn Meadow Pl	20152
Feltre Ter	20152
Femoyer Ter	20152
Fenian Ct	20152
Ferrara Ct	20151
Field Post Sq	20152
Fieldsman Ln	20152
Fillingame Dr	20151
Finders Ln	20152
Firefly Ln	20152
First Frost Way	20152
Fishers Hill Ct	20152
Flagg Ct	20151
Flannigan Ter	20152
Flatlick Branch Dr	20151
Flemming Dr	20152
Flight Line Rd	20151
Flint Lee Rd	20151
Flint Rock Ct	20151
Flintonbridge Dr	20152
Flowing Brook Ct	20151
Flushing Ct	20151
Flyaway Ct	20152
Flynn Ln	20152
Fortitude Ter	20152
Fox Creek Ct	20151
Foxwarren Way	20152
Francis Sq	20152
Francisco Ter	20152
Freda Ln	20152
Freedom St	20152
Fretton Sq	20152
Friendship St	20152
Frontier Spring Dr	20152
Fulmer Dr	20151
Gabriel Sq	20152
Galesbury Ln	20151
Gallitzin Ln	20152
Gaston St	20151
Gateway Village Pl	20152
Gayfeather Dr	20152
Gazelle Ct	20152
Gelding Sq	20152
General Kearny Ct	20151
General Stevens Ct	20151
George Carter Way	20151
Gertrudes View Way	20152
Gideon Ln	20152

Gilead Ct 20151
Gimbel Dr 20152
Gladehill Ct 20152
Gladwyn Ct 20151
Glasgow Dr 20152
Glen Aspen Way 20152
Golf View Dr 20152
Gopost 20151
Gothic Sq 20152
Gover Dr 20152
Granite Rock Ct & Dr 20151
Green Fern Ct 20152
Gregory Ct 20152
Gum Spring Rd 20152
Gumwood Ct 20151
Gunnery Sq 20152
Gwynneth Sq 20152
Hagen Ct 20152
Hallmark St 20152
Hamlin Ave & Ct 20151
Hampstead Ct 20151
Harris St 20152
Hartwood Dr 20152
Harvest Hills Dr 20152
Harvest Horn Way 20152
Haughton Sq 20152
Haverford Ct 20151
Hazel Park Ct 20151
Hazelnut Ct 20151
Heathfield Cir 20152
Heathman Pl 20152
Henninger Ct 20151
Henry Pond Ct 20151
Heritage Gap Ter 20152
Herndon Ave 20151
Herring Creek Dr 20152
Hetrick Ln 20152
Heyer Sq 20152
Hillpark St 20152
Historic Sully Way 20151
Hollingsworth Ter 20152
Hollowstone Ct 20151
Holly Tree Ln 20152
Hollybank Pl 20152
Holtby Sq 20152
Holton Pl 20151
Homefront Ter 20152
Hopefield Pl 20152
Hopestone Ter 20152
Hopton House Ter 20152
Howerton Dr 20152
Hubbard Sq 20152
Huddleston Ln 20152
Hundonmoore Dr 20152
Hussar Ter 20152
Hyland Hills St 20152
Iberia Cir 20151
Icelandic Pl 20151
Impala Ct 20152
Indian Hill Cir 20152
Interval St 20152
Intrepid St 20152
Iron Bit Pl 20152
Iverson Dr 20152
Ivory Ln 20152
Ivory Coast Ct 20151
James Cross St 20151
Janes Ct 20152
Jenny Ln 20152
Jerpoint Ct 20152
John Mosby Hwy 20152
Jolly Ln 20152
Jonquil Ln 20152
Jubilee St 20152
Juniper Glen Dr 20152
Justice Dr 20152
Kaiser Pl 20152
Katama Sq 20152
Katebini Ln 20152
Katling Sq 20152
Kearney Ter 20152
Kellamugh Ter 20152
Kelly Ter 20152
Kenai Ct 20152
Kenmore Ln 20152
Kenna Ct 20151
Kennebec Dr 20152
Kennywood Sq 20152
Kettle Ln 20152
Kew Garden Ct 20151
Keys Run Ct 20152
Khalid Ln 20151
Kimberley Glen Ct 20151
Kimberly Rose Dr 20152
Kincaid Ct & Pl 20151
King Charles Dr 20151
Kingscote Ct 20152
Kiplington Sq 20152
Kirby Ln 20152
Kirkwood Sq 20152
Knotty Log Ct 20151
Krebs Ln 20152
Lafayette Center Dr 20151
Laidlow St 20152
Lake Central Dr 20151
Lake Mist Sq 20152
Lake Shore Sq 20152
Lambert Ln 20152
Lands End Dr 20152
Langdon Ter 20152
Lanica Cir 20151
Larks Ter 20152
Latrobe St 20152
Lavin Ln 20152
Lawrence Park Ct 20151
Leaflet Ln 20152
Lee Rd 20151
Lee Jackson Memorial
Hwy 20151
Lees Corner Rd 20151
Leeton Cir 20151
Leighfield St 20151
Leighfield Valley Dr 20151
Leith Ct 20151
Lemon Tree Pl 20152
Lennox Ct 20152
Leonard Dr 20152
Lewis Leigh Ct 20151
Lewis Mill Way 20151
Lewis Woods Ct 20151
Lewiston Dr 20152
Leyland Ln 20152
Lightfoot St 20151
Lighthouse Pl 20152
Lilypad Ln 20152
Lindendale Ln 20151
Little Cedar Ct 20152
Lochdon Ln 20152
Locket Ln 20152
Locklear Ter 20152
Loganshire Ter 20152
Logquarter Ln 20152
Logwood Ln 20151
Lomax Ter 20152
Londontown Ter 20152
Longacre Dr 20152
Longforest Dr 20152
Longleaf St 20152
Longworth Ter 20152
Loudoun Barn Way 20152
Loudoun County Pkwy 20152
Louis Mill Dr 20151
Louise Ave 20151
Lowe St 20151
Lowry Dr 20151
Lufthansa Cir 20151
Lynncroft Dr 20151
Lyon Ter 20152
Maderiv Dr 20152
Madturkey Run Pl 20152
Magistrate Ct 20152
Majestic Prince Pl 20152
Malin Ct 20151
Malmsbury Ter 20152
Mandeville Dr 20152
Mandolin St 20152
Maple Cross St 20152
Mapleton Dr 20151
Marble Rock Ct & Dr 20151
Marble Wood Ln 20151
Marcy Way 20152
Mariah Ct 20151
Marsden Ct 20151
Mason Dale Ter 20152
Mason Dixon Dr 20151
Matties Ter 20152
Maverick Ln 20152
Mayhew Ln 20152
Mayville Ct 20152
Mcbryde Ter 20152
Mccloskey Ct 20151
Mccomas Ter 20152
Mccoy Ct 20152
Mcdeeds Ln 20152
Mcgill Dr 20151
Mcintyre Sq 20152
Mckay Ter 20152
Mckinzie Ln 20152
Meadow Wood Ln 20151
Meadowhouse Ct 20152
Meadowland Ct 20151
Melville Ln 20151
Menemsha Ln 20152
Metrotech Dr 20151
Mews Ter 20152
Middlecoff Ln 20152
Middlesex Dr 20152
Miltec Ter 20152
Mimosa Tree Ct 20152
Mink Meadows St 20152
Mixed Willow Pl 20151
Monet Ct 20151
Monteith Ter 20152
Morningdale Dr 20151
Morse Dr 20151
Moselle Dr 20151
Moshupe Way 20152
Mountain View Dr 20152
Mountcastle Dr 20152
Murdock St 20151
Murrey Dr 20151
Myers Glen Pl 20151
National Dr 20151
Nations St 20152
Natures Ln 20152
Necklace Ct 20151
Neighborly Ln 20152
Nellie Ct 20152
Neptune Ter 20152
Nesbit Ln 20152
Nesting Sq 20152
Newbrook Dr 20151
Newcastle Dr 20152
Newcomer Ter 20152
Newport Dr & Ln 20151
Nicklaus Ln 20152
Nimbleton Sq 20152
Norrington Sq 20152
Norris Ct 20151
Northeast Pl 20151
Northern Dancer Ct 20151
Northridge Dr 20151
Northwest Pl 20151
Novar Dr 20151
Oasis Ct 20152
Oberon Ln 20152
Obrien Sq 20152
Ocala Cir 20152
Offenham Ter 20152
Olander Sq 20152
Old Chatwood Pl 20151
Old Lee Rd 20151
Old Nursery Ct 20151
Oleary Ln 20152
Olive Tree Ln 20152
Omaha Ter 20152
Orr Dr 20151
Orson St 20152
Otis Ln 20152
Over Ridge Ct 20151
Overlord Ter 20152
Overly Sq 20152
Owen Park Way 20152
Ox Riding Ln 20152
Oxen Ln 20152
Oyster Point Ct 20151
Paddock Trail Pl 20152
Palm Cove Ct 20152
Pamplin Ter 20152
Pan Am Ave 20151
Panagra Pl 20151
Paoli Ct 20151
Paradise Pl 20152
Paramount Pl 20152
Parish St 20152
Park Meadow Dr 20151
Parke Long Ct 20151
Parkeast Cir 20151
Parkside Manor Ct 20151
Parkstone Dr 20151
Peacock Market Plz 20152
Peirosa Ter 20152
Pelican Dr 20152
Pemberton Sq 20152
Pembrooke Cir 20152
Pennsboro Ct, Dr & Pl 20151
Penny Tree Pl 20151
Penrose Pl 20151
Penwith Ct 20151
Pepsi Pl 20151
Phar Lap Ct 20152
Philip Lee Rd 20151
Picasso Pl 20151
Pilgrim Sq 20152
Pine Forest Dr 20152
Pinebluff Dr 20152
Pinebrook Rd 20152
Piney Stream Ct 20152
Pitch Pine Ct 20151
Pitkin Ct 20151
Placid Lake Ct 20151
Planting Field Dr 20152
Pleasant Meadow Ct 20151
Pleasant Valley Rd
4100-5099 20151
25200-25799 20152
Pleasant Woods Ct 20152
Plum St 20152
Point Pleasant Dr 20151
Poland Rd 20152
Pond View Sq 20152
Ponderosa Dr 20152
Poplar Branch Dr 20151
Poplar Forest Ct 20151
Poplar Tree Ct & Rd 20151
Poplar Woods Ct 20151
Post Oak Ct 20151
Post Time Ct 20152
Potomac Twain Ter 20152
Presgraves Ct 20151
Priesters Pond Dr 20152
Primanti St 20152
Providence Ridge Dr 20152
Puma Sq 20152
Quartz Rock Ct 20151
Quentin St 20152
Quiet Brook Ct 20151
Quiet Stream Ct 20151
Quietway Ct 20151
Quigley Ln 20152
Quilting Ln 20152
Quinlan St 20152
Quits Pond Ct 20152
Rachel Hill Dr 20152
Radke Ter 20152
Raflo Ln 20152
Rainbow Ranch Ln 20152
Randfield Ln 20152
Rawley Springs Dr 20152
Rembrandt Way 20151
Renoir Ter 20151
Rickmansworth Ln 20152
Ridge Rock Dr 20151
Riding Blvd & Plz 20152
Riding Center Dr 20152
Riffleford Sq 20152
Ripleys Field Dr 20152
Ritter Ln 20152
Roan Ct 20152
Robert Paris Ct 20151
Rockland Village Dr 20151
Rocky Gap Ct 20152
Roger Mack Ct 20151
Rolling Rock Sq 20152
Roper Ln 20152
Rose Ln 20152
Rose Lodge Pl 20151
Rosetree Ct 20151
Rowdelbury Sq 20152
Royal Burkedale St 20152
Royal Red Ter 20151
Sackwheat Sq 20152
Saddle Trail Ct 20152
Samuels Pine Rd 20151
San Sebastian Ter 20152
Sand Pine Pl 20152
Sand Rock Ct & Ln 20151
Sandman Ter 20152
Sangiovese St 20151
Sarazen Dr 20152
Sauterne Ct & Way 20151
Savoy Woods Ct 20152
Scarlet Sq 20152
Schooley Mill Ter 20152
Sealock Ln 20152
Seawolve Sq 20152
Selby Bay Ct 20151
Sellman Ln 20152
Shady Grove Ln 20152
Shady Point Pl 20151
Shaler St 20152
Shelanti Dr 20151
Shelbourne Sq 20152
Sherando Ct 20152
Ship Sq 20152
Shipley Ter 20152
Shoover Sq 20152
Shultz Ter 20152
Silas Hutchinson Dr 20151
Silversmith Ct 20151
Singer Ct 20151
Singleton Ln 20152
Skiff Ln 20152
Skyhawk Dr 20151
Smallwood Ct 20151
Smallwood Ln 20151
Smallwood Ter 20152
Snead Ln 20152
Somerby Dr 20152
Sonora Seed Ter 20152
Sorbonne Ln 20152
Southernwood Ct 20151
Southgate Pl 20151
Southpoint Dr 20152
Sovereign Pl 20151
Spectacular Run Pl 20152
Spring Farm Cir 20152
Spring Run Ct 20151
Springdale Dr 20152
Springhaven Dr 20151
Spurling Ln 20152
Spyder Pl 20152
St Andrews St 20152
St Huberts Pl 20152
Stable Ct 20152
Stadler Ln 20152
Stallion Branch Ter 20152
Star Flower Ct & Dr 20151
Stepney Ln 20151
Stinger Dr 20152
Stires Dr 20152
Stone Pine Ct 20151
Stonecroft Blvd 20151
Stonecroft Center Ct 20151
Stonewall Pond St 20152
Strathaven Ct 20152
Stream Valley Dr 20151
Stringfellow Rd 20151
Sully Rd 20151
Sullyfield Cir 20151
Sulser Pl 20151
Summer Hollow Ct 20151
Summerbank Ct 20152
Sun Devil Sq 20152
Sun Orchard Dr 20151
Suny Bay Ct 20152
Sutton Oaks Dr 20151
Sweet Ct 20152
Sweetwater Ln 20152
Swissair Pl 20151
Sykes Ter 20152
Sylvia Ln 20152
Tabor House Ln 20152
Tabscott Dr 20151
Tadman Ln 20152
Talamore Dr 20152
Talent St 20152
Tall Cedars Pkwy 20152
Talmont Dr 20152
Tanner Ln 20152
Tashmoo Ln 20152
Taylor Crescent Dr 20152
Taylor Tree Ter 20152
Technology Ct 20151
Thomas Bridges Ct 20152
Thompson Rd 20151
Thorley Pl 20152
Thornburg Ct 20152
Thoroughgood Dr 20152
Thunderbolt Pl 20151
Ticonderoga Rd 20152
Tippman Pl 20152
Tisbury Ct 20152
Tonys Pl 20151
Town Hall Plz 20152
Trans World Ave 20151
Travers Ct 20151
Tremaine Ter 20152
Tulip Tree Ct 20151
Tullow Pl 20152
Turf Field Sq 20152
Turkey Foot Ct 20151
Turlough Ter 20152
Tuthill Ln 20152
Twelve Cedars Ct 20152
Ulster Ln 20152
Ulysses St 20152
Unbridleds Song Pl 20152
Unicorn Dr 20152
United Dr 20151
Upper Clubhouse Dr 20152
Upper Cub Run Dr 20151
Vaira Ter 20152
Valiant Dr 20152
Valley Country Dr 20151
Valleyvista Ln 20152
Vance Rd 20152
Vernacchia Dr 20151
Vernon St 20151
S Village Dr 20152
Virginia Dare Ct 20151
Virginia Mallory Dr 20151
Virginia Pine Ct 20152
Voormeade Ter 20152
Wade Dr 20152
Wakestone Park Ter 20152
Walbern Ct & Dr 20151
Waldo Cir 20152
Walney Rd & Way 20151
Walney Knoll Ct 20151
Walney Park Dr 20151
Walney Village Ct 20151
Walnutgrove Ln 20152
Warner Ln 20151
Watercrest Sq 20152
Waverly Creek Ct 20151
Waverly Crossing Ln 20151
Wayfarer Sq 20152
Week Pl 20151
Weeping Willow Ct 20152
Wembley Ln 20152
Wendell St 20152
Westbrook Pl 20151
Westfax Dr 20151
Westfields Blvd 20151
Westone Plz 20151
Wheadon Ter 20152
Wheat Berry Ter 20152
Whippoorwill Ter 20152
White Cap Ter 20152
White Fir Ct 20152
White Sands Dr 20152
Whitlow Pl 20151
Willard Rd
14150A-14150J 20151
13800-14999 20151
25100-25299 20152
Willoughby Ct 20151
Windmoore Ct 20151
Winter Ln 20152
Winter Harbor Ct 20151
Woods Edge Ct 20151
Woodside Pl 20151
Woodville Ct 20152
Woodward Ct 20151

CHARLOTTESVILLE VA

General Delivery 22906

POST OFFICE BOXES MAIN OFFICE STATIONS AND BRANCHES

Box No.s
A - B 22905
1 - 2998 22902
4201 - 5858 22905
6001 - 9077 22906
9998 - 9998 22901
400000 - 400999 22904

RURAL ROUTES

02, 12, 14, 15, 17, 24, 28 22901
10, 20 22903

NAMED STREETS

Abbey Rd 22911
Abbot Ct 22902
Abelia Way 22911
Abington Dr 22911
Ackley Ln 22903
Acorn Ct 22902
Acorn Ln 22903
Acorn Hill Ct 22911
Adams Ct 22911
Agnese St 22901
Airport Rd 22911
Airport Acres Pl & Rd 22911
Albemarle Sq 22901
Albemarle St 22903
Albert Ct 22901
Albie Ln 22903
Alder Rd 22911
Alderman Rd 22903
Alderman Library 22903
Aldersgate Way 22911
Allen Dr 22903
Allendale Dr 22901
Allens Way 22911
Allied Ln & St 22903
Allister Grn 22901
Alpine Ct 22902
Altamont Cir & St 22902
Altavista Ave 22902
Althea Dr 22903
Alwood Ln 22901
Amber Ridge Ct & Rd 22901
Amberfield Ct, Dr & Trl 22911
Ambrose Way 22901
Ambrose Commons Dr 22903
Amherst Cmn & St 22903
Anchorage Farm 22903
Anderson Ct 22911
Anderson Ln 22911
Anderson St 22903
Andrew Ln 22901
Angler Ct 22902
Angus Ct & Rd 22901
Antoinette Ave & Ct 22903
Appian Way 22911
Apple Ln 22903

Apple Tree Ln 22901
Apple Tree Rd 22903
Arbor Cir 22902
Arbor Ct 22911
Arbor Ter 22911
Arbor Trce 22911
Arbor Crest Dr 22901
Arbor Lake Dr 22911
Arden Dr 22902
Arden Creek Ct, Ln, Pl & Way 22901
Arlanda Ln 22911
Arlington Blvd 22903
Arrow Wood Dr 22902
Arrowhead Farm Ln 22903
Arrowhead Valley Rd 22903
Ashby Pl 22901
Ashcroft Mtn Rd 22911
Asheville Dr 22911
Ashland Dr 22911
Ashlawn Highland Dr 22902
Ashley Ct 22901
Ashley Dr 22902
Ashmere Dr 22902
Ashton Church Rd 22911
Ashwood Blvd 22911
Aspen Dr 22911
Aspenwood Rd 22911
Auburn Dr 22902
Auburn Hill Farm 22902
Augusta St 22903
Austin Dr 22911
Autumn Grove Ct 22902
Autumn Winds Ln 22903
Autumn Woods Dr 22911
Avemore Ln 22911
Avemore Pond Rd 22911
Avemore Square Pl 22911
Aviano Way 22911
Aviation Dr 22911
Avinity Ct, Dr & Loop 22902
Avon Ct & St 22902
Avon Street Ext 22902
Azalea Dr 22903
Bache Ln 22911
Bailey Rd 22903
Baileys Ct 22901
Baileys Retreat 22901
Bainbridge St 22902
N Baker St 22903
Ballard Ridge Dr 22901
Ballard Woods Ct 22901
Balz Dobie 22904
Banbury St 22901
Banyan Ct 22911
Barbour Dr 22903
Barclay Hl 22901
Barclay Place Ct 22901
Barefoot Ct 22901
Barn Rd 22911
Barnsdale Rd 22911
Barracks Ct 22901
Barracks Hl 22901
Barracks Pl 22901
Barracks Rd
1800-2299 22903
2300-3399 22901
Barracks Farm Rd 22901
Barracksdale Ln 22901
Barrackside Farm 22901
Barron Ct 22911
Barrsden Farm 22911
Battles Aly 22901
Bayberry Way 22911
Baylor Ln & Pl 22902
Beam Rd 22911
Bear Run 22901
Bear Den Ct 22903
Beau Mont Farm Rd 22901
Beau Pre Ln 22901
Beaver Creek Park 22901
Beaver Hill Dr & Ln 22901
Beaver Hill Lake Dr 22901
Becker Ln 22911
Beckoning Ridge Rd 22901
Bedford Pl 22903
Bedford Park Rd 22903
Bee Ct 22902
Beech Grv 22911
Beechcrest Ct 22903
Beechwood Dr 22901
Bellafield Rd 22911
Bellair Farm 22902
Belleview Ave 22901
Belmont Ave & Park 22902
Belmont Cottage Ln 22902
Belvedere Blvd, Dr, Pl & Way 22901
Bending Branch Rd 22901
Bennington Ct & Rd 22901
Bent Tree Ct 22902
Bentivar Dr 22911
Bentivar Farm Ct & Rd 22911
Berkmar Cir, Ct & Dr 22901
N Berkshire Pl & Rd 22901
Berring St 22902
Berwick Cir 22901
Berwick Ct 22901
Berwick Rd 22903
Bethel Station Rd 22911
Beverley Dr 22911
Big Oak Rd 22903
Biltmore Dr 22901
Bing Ln 22903
Birch Ln 22911
Birchcrest Ln 22911
Birdwood Ct, Dr & Rd 22903
Birnam Dr 22901
Bishop Ln 22902
Bishop Hill Rd 22902
Bishops Ridge Dr 22911
Bitternut Ct & Ln 22902
Bixham Ln 22901
Black Oak Rd 22903
Blackburn Blf & Way 22901
Blackthorn Ln 22902
Blackwood Rd 22901
Bland Cir 22901
Blandemar Dr & Ln 22903
Blandemar Farm Dr 22903
Blenheim Ave, Ln & Rd 22902
Blenheim Cove Ln 22902
Blenheim Farm 22902
Blincoe Ln 22902
Blithe Ct 22901
Bloomfield Rd 22903
Blue Ridge Ln 22901
Blue Ridge Rd 22903
Blue Rock Rdg 22903
Blue Springs Ln 22903
Blueberry Rd 22911
Bluejay Way 22911
Boars Head Ln & Pl 22903
Boars Head Pointe 22903
Bobwhite Ct 22901
Bolling Ave 22902
Bollingbrook Dr 22911
Bollingwood Rd 22903
Bond St 22901
Bonnycastle 22904
Booker St 22903
Boone Trl 22903
Boston Creek Dr 22902
Boulder Spring Ct 22902
Boulders Rd 22911
Bowen Loop 22911
Bowles Aly 22901
Box Holly Ln 22903
Boxley Dr 22901
Boxwood Ct 22902
Boxwood Estate Rd 22903
Branch Hill Rd 22911
Branchlands Blvd & Dr 22901
Brandermill Pl 22911
Brandlin Dr 22902
Brandon Ave 22903
Brandywine Ct & Dr 22901
Branham Pl 22903
Bravo Hall 22903
Breckenridge Ct 22901
Breezemont Dr 22911
Brenda Ct 22901
Brentwood Rd 22901
Briarcliff Ave 22903
Briarwood Dr 22911
Brightfield Pl 22901
Brinnington Rd 22901
Bristlecone Ln 22911
Britts Mountain Holw 22903
Broad Ave 22903
Broad Axe Rd 22903
Broad Crossing Rd 22911
Broadleaf Way 22911
Broadway St 22902
Brook Rd 22901
Brook Hill Ln 22901
Brook Mill Ln 22911
Brookhill Ave 22902
Brookmere Rd 22901
Brookside Dr 22901
Brookway Dr 22901
Brookwood Dr 22902
Broomley Rd 22901
Brown St 22903
Browns Gap Tpke 22901
Brownstone Ln 22901
Brownsville Rd 22903
Bruce Ave 22903
Brunswick Rd 22903
Bryan Ct 22902
Bryan Hall 22903
Buck Island Rd 22902
Buck Island Woods 22902
Buckeye Ct 22903
Buckeyeland Ln 22902
Buckingham Cir & Rd 22903
Bunker Hill Dr 22901
Burchs Creek Rd 22903
Burgess Ln 22902
Burgundy Ln 22911
Burnet St & Way 22902
Burnley Ave 22903
Burnt Mill Rd 22911
Burton Ct 22901
Butler St 22901
Buttercup Ln 22902
Cabell Ave 22903
Cabell Hall 22903
Cairn Heights Ct 22903
Calhoun St 22901
Calvary Cir 22911
Camargo Dr 22901
Cambridge Cir 22903
Camellia Dr 22903
Camelot Dr 22911
Cameron Ln 22903
Cami Ln 22902
Camp Rd 22902
Campbell Farm Ln 22902
Campbell Hall 22903
Candlewood Ct 22903
Candlewyck Dr 22901
Canfield Ln 22903
Cannon Pl 22901
Cannon Brook Way 22901
Canterbury Rd 22903
Canvas Back Dr 22903
Capri Way 22911
Caravan Ct 22902
Cardinal Ridge Rd 22901
Cargil Ln 22902
Caribbean Ln 22902
Carlins Way 22903
Carlton Ave & Rd 22902
Carlyle Pl 22903
Caroline Ave 22902
Carriage Ln 22901
Carrington Pl 22901
Carrollton Ter 22903
Carrs Hill Rd 22903
Carrsbrook Ct & Dr 22901
Carter Ln 22901
Carters Mountain Rd & Trl 22902
Carya Ct 22902
Cason Farm Rd 22911
Castalia St 22902
Castle Ct 22901
Catalpa Ct & Ter 22903
Catlett Rd 22901
Catlin Rd 22901
Caty Ln 22901
Cauthen Hall 22904
Cavalier Dr 22901
Cedar Bluff Rd 22901
Cedar Grove Ln 22902
Cedar Hill Rd 22901
Cedar Hill Farm 22902
Cedar Knoll Ln 22901
Cedar Ridge Ln 22901
Cedarbrook Ct 22901
Cedars Ct 22903
Cedarwood Ct 22903
Center Ave 22903
Chancellor St 22903
Chandler Ct 22902
Chapel Hill Rd 22901
Charles Ct 22911
Charlotte Cir 22901
Charlton Ave 22903
Charter Oaks Dr 22901
Chatham Ct & Rdg 22901
Chaucer Rd 22901
Chelsea Dr 22903
Cherokee Ct 22901
Cherry Ave 22903
Cherry St 22902
Cherry Bark Ln 22911
Cherry Hill Farm 22903
Chesapeake St 22902
Chesapeake Bay Pl 22903
Cheshire Ct 22901
Chesi Cir 22901
N & S Chesterfield Ct 22911
Chestnut St 22902
Chestnut Oak Ln 22903
Chestnut Ridge Rd 22911
Chestnut Ridge Farm 22901
Chimney Rdg & Spgs 22911
Chippendale Ct 22901
Chisholm Pl 22902
Chopin Dr 22903
Chris Greene Lake Rd 22911
Christa Ct 22903
Church St 22902
Church Plains Dr 22901
Churchill Ln 22903
Cindy Ln 22911
Cinnamon Ridge Rd 22901
City Walk Way 22902
Clark Ln 22901
Clark Hall 22903
Clarke Ct 22903
Clay Hill Rd 22901
Clear Springs Ct 22911
Clearbrook Ln 22911
Clements Hollow Ln 22903
Cleveland Ave 22903
Clifden Grn 22901
Clifton Inn Dr 22911
Clover Lawn Ln 22903
Clover Ridge Ct & Pl 22901
Clubhouse Way 22901
Cobblestone Ln 22901
Cocke Hall 22903
Coffey Dr 22911
Cola Woods Ln 22901
Cold Spring Rd 22903
Colderic Rd 22903
Cole St 22901
Coleman Ct, Dr & St 22901
Colle Ln 22902
College Dr 22902
Collina Farm 22911
Colonial Dr 22911
Colonnade Aly & Dr 22903
Colonnades Hill Dr 22901
Colony Dr 22903
Colridge Dr 22903
Colston Dr 22903
Colthurst Dr 22901
Colvin Aly 22901
Commerce St 22903
Commonwealth Cir, Ct & Dr 22901
Community St 22911
Concord Ave 22903
Concord Dr 22901
Connor Dr 22911
Cool Spring Rd 22901
Coopers Ln 22902
Copeley 22904
Copeley Rd 22903
Copper Hill Dr 22902
Copper Knoll Rd 22911
Copperstone Dr 22902
Coralberry Pl 22911
Corktree Ln 22901
Corner Vlg 22911
Cornwall Rd 22901
Cory Ct 22903
Cottage Ln
900-999 22903
1900-1999 22902
Cottage Green Way 22903
Cottage View Ln 22901
Cottonwood Rd 22901
Country Ln 22903
Country Club Cir 22901
Country Green Ln 22902
Country Green Rd
653-679 22902
681-799 22903
Country Woods Ln 22903
Court Pl 22901
Court Sq 22902
Court Square Anx 22902
Courtenay Glen Way 22902
Courtenay Hall 22904
Courtyard Ct & Dr 22903
Cove Ln & Trce 22911
Cove Pointe Rd 22911
Covey Hill Rd 22901
Cow Path Ln 22901
Crackerbox 22903
Craigland Rd 22902
Craven Aly 22901
Cream St 22903
Creekside Cir & Dr 22902
Creekview Ln 22911
Crenshaw Ct 22901
Crenshaws Trailer Park 22901
Cresap Rd 22903
Crestfield Ct 22911
Crestmont Ave 22903
Crestview Ln 22902
Crestwood Dr 22903
Crickenberger Ln 22911
Cricket Ln 22901
Cricklewood Ct 22911
Crispell Dr 22903
Critta Ln 22901
Cross Timbers Rd 22911
Crossfield Ln 22911
Croydon Rd 22901
Crumpet Ct 22901
Crutchfield Park 22911
Culbreth Rd 22903
Cumberland Rd 22901
Cutler Ln 22901
Cynthianna Ave 22903
Cypress Dr 22911
Cypress Pointe Dr 22901
Dabney 22904
Dairy Rd 22903
Daisy Ln 22901
Dale Ave 22903
Danbury Ct 22902
Daniel Morris Ln 22902
Darden Blvd 22903
Darden Towe Park 22911
Darien Ter 22902
Daventry Ln 22911
David Rd 22902
David Ter 22903
Davis 22904
Davis Ave 22901
Dawn St 22902
Dawsons Row 22903
Debenham Ct 22902
Decca Ln 22901
Deer Path 22903
Deer Crest Hts 22903
Deer Ridge Farm 22902
Deer Run Rd 22903
Deer Valley Ct 22902
Deerfield Ln 22903
Deerwood Bnd, Dr & Rd 22911
Defense Hwy 22911
Del Mar Dr 22903
Delevan St 22903
Delila Dr 22901
Dell Ln 22901
Dellmead Ln 22901
Dellwood Rd 22901
Delphi Dr 22911
Denali Way 22903
Denice Ln 22901
Derby Ln 22911
Dettor Rd 22903
Devon Rd 22903
Devon Spring Ct 22903
Devonshire Rd 22901
Dew Maw Ln 22911
Diamond Ct 22902
Dice St
200-299 22902
300-699 22903
Dick Woods Rd 22903
Dickerson Rd 22911
Dillard 22904
Discovery Dr 22911
District Ave 22901
Dobleann Dr 22911
Doctors Xing 22911
N Dogwood Ln 22901
Dollens Hollow 22903
Dominion Dr 22901
Doncaster Ln 22903
Dorchester Pl 22911
Doringh Pl 22901
Dorrier Dr 22911
Dorset Ct 22911
Dots Dr 22903
Douglas Ave 22902
Dover Ct & Rd 22901
Druid Ave 22902
Dry Bridge Rd 22903
Dryden Ln & Pl 22903
Dublin Rd 22903
Dudley Mountain Rd 22903
Dunglison 22904
Dunlora Dr 22901
Dunlora Farm Rd 22901
Dunmore Rd 22901
Dunnington 22904
Dunova Ct 22903
Dunromin Rd 22901
Dutchman Rd 22911
Eagle Hill Farm 22901
Earhart St 22903
Early St 22902
Earlysville Rd 22901
Eastbrook Ct & Dr 22901
Eastham Hl & Rd 22911
Easy Ln 22911
Echo Hill Dr 22902
Echo Hill Farm 22901
Echo Ridge Rd 22911
Echols 22904
Eclipse Ct 22902
Ed Jones Rd 22902
Eden Ln 22901
Edge Hill Rd 22903
Edgehill Dr 22911
Edgemont Rd 22903
Edgewater Dr 22911
Edgewood Ln 22903
Edlich Dr 22911
Ednam Cir, Ctr, Dr & Pl 22903
Ednam Village St 22903
Eglinton Ln 22903
Eight Woods Ln 22903
Elizabeth Ave 22901
Elizabeth Ln 22903
Elk Dr 22911
Elkhorn Rd 22903
Ellerslie Dr 22902
Elliewood Ave 22903
Ellington Bnd 22903
Elliott Ave 22902
Elm St 22903
Elm Tree Ct & Knl 22911
Elmwood Ct 22903
Elsom St 22903
Emerald Ln 22903
Emerson Dr 22901
Emmet 22904
Emmet St N
100-1499 22903
1501-1597 22901
1599-2000 22901
2002-2098 22901
Emmet St S 22903
Empress Pl 22911
English Oaks Cir N 22911
Eric Pl 22903
Essex Rd 22901
Estes St 22903
Eton Rd 22903
Evergreen Ave 22902
Exeter Ct 22901
Explorers Rd 22911
Exton Ct 22901
Fair Hill Ln 22903
Fairview Dr 22901
Fairway Ave 22902
Fairway Ln 22901
Falcon Dr 22901
Fall Fields Dr 22911
Fallen Leaf Ln 22901
Far Hills Rd 22903
Farish St 22902
Farm Ln 22902
Farm Brook Pl 22901
Farm Vista Rd 22903
N Farmington Dr & Hts 22901
Farriers Ct 22903
Farrish Cir 22903
Farrow Dr 22901
Faulconer Dr 22903
Faulkner 22904
Faulkner Way 22903
Fayerweather Hall 22903
Fendall Ave & Ter 22903
Fern Ct 22901
Fernleaf Rd 22911
Fiddlestick Ln 22903
Field Rd 22903
Field Creek Ln 22903
Fieldhaven Dr 22903
Fielding Dr 22902
Fields Of Boaz Dr 22903
Fieldstone Rd 22903
Filly Run 22903
Fin Ct 22902
Finch Ct 22911
Finders Way 22901
Fiske Kimball Hall 22903
Fitzgerald Rd 22903
Fitzhugh Hall 22904
Five Springs Rd 22902
Flagstone Ter 22902
Flannigan Branch Ln 22911
Flicker Dr 22911
Flordon Dr 22901
Florence Rd 22902
Fly Ct 22902
Foal Ln 22901
Folly Rd 22901
Fontaine Ave 22903
Fontaine Avenue Extended 22903
Fontana Ct & Dr 22911
Foothill Ct 22903
Forest St 22903

Street	ZIP
Forest Hills Ave	22903
Forest Lodge Ln	22903
Forest Ridge Rd	22903
Forest View Rd	22902
Forloines Dr	22911
Forrest Rd	22902
Forsythia Ln	22911
Fortune Park Rd	22911
Foster Rdg	22903
Fosters Branch Rd	22911
Fountain Ct	22901
Four Leaf Ln	22903
Four Seasons Dr	22901
Four Winds Ln	22901
Fox Crest Way	22902
Fox Hill Rd	22903
Fox Horn Ct & Ln	22902
Fox Run Ln	22901
Foxbrook Ln	22901
Foxchase Rdg	22902
Foxdale Ln	22903
Foxhaven Farm	22903
Foxpath Ct	22901
Foxtail Pnes	22911
Foxvale Ln	22902
Fralist Rd	22911
Francis Fife Way	22903
Frank Tate Rd	22903
Franklin Ct	22901
Franklin Dr	22911
Franklin St	22902
Frays Mill Rd	22911
Frederick Cir	22901
Free Bridge Ln	22911
Free State Rd	22901
Free Union Rd	22901
Frog Rock Ln	22901
Frontier Ln	22903
Frys Path	22902
Gables Run Rd	22902
Galaxie Farm Ln	22902
Galloway Dr	22901
Gander Dr	22901
Garden Ct	22901
Garden Dr	22903
Garden St	22902
Garden Trail Path	22901
Gardens Blvd	22901
Garland Ln	22902
Garnet Center Dr	22911
Garrett St	22902
Garrett Hall	22903
Garth Ln & Rd	22901
Garth Gate Ln	22901
Garth House Ln	22901
Garth Oaks Pt	22901
Garthfield Ln	22901
Gasoline Aly	22901
Gate Post Ln	22901
Gateway Cir	22911
Gatewood Cir	22911
Gazebo Ct	22901
Gelletly Rd	22902
Gencoun St	22902
Gentry Ln	22903
George Dean Dr	22903
George Rogers Rd	22911
Georgetown Grn, Rd & Way	22901
Georgianna Aly	22901
Gersandy Pl	22901
Gibbons Aly	22901
Gibson Mountain Ln	22903
Gibsons Hill Dr	22903
Gibsons Hollow Ln	22903
Gildersleeve	22904
Gildersleeve Wood	22903
Gillespie Ave	22902
Gilliams Mountain Ct & Rd	22903
Gillums Mountain Ln	22903
Gillums Ridge Ln & Rd	22903
Gilmer Hall	22903
Gimbert Ln	22902
Girtha Ln	22911
Glade Ln	22901
Gleco Mills Ln	22903
Glen Echo Farm	22911
Glenaire Dr	22901
Glendale Rd	22901
Glenn Ct	22901
Glenside Grn	22901
Glenview Ct	22903
Glenwood Rd	22901
Glenwood Station Ln	22901
Gloucester Ct & Rd	22901
Go Ct	22902
Gobblers Rdg	22902
Gold Eagle Dr	22903
Golden Chain Ln	22901
Goldenrod Ct	22902
Goldentree Pl	22911
Gooch	22904
Goodman St	22902
Goodwin Farm Ln	22903
Gooseneck Ln	22903
Gordon Ave	22903
Gordon Hill Ln	22911
Grace St	22902
Grady Ave	22903
Grand Cru Dr	22902
Grand Forks Blvd	22911
Grand View Dr	22901
Grande Vista Dr	22911
Grassmere Rd	22903
Grassmere Farm Rd	22903
Grassy Knl	22901
Graves St	22902
Gray Fox Spur & Trl	22901
Gray Stone Ct	22902
Grayson Ln	22903
Green Hts & St	22902
Green Acre Ln	22901
Green Beech Dr	22901
Green Meadows Ln	22901
Green Turtle Ln	22901
Greenbrier Dr, Pl & Ter	22901
Greene Edge Ln	22911
Greenfield Ct, Ln & Ter	22901
Greenleaf Ln	22903
Greenmont Farm	22902
Greenmurray Hl	22903
Greentree Park	22901
Greenway Rd	22903
Greenwich Ct	22902
Grenville Dr	22903
Grey Dove Ln	22903
Grimes Pl	22902
Gristmill Dr	22902
Grove Ave	22902
Grove Rd	22901
Grove St	22903
Grove Street Ext	22903
Grover Ct	22901
Guilford Ln	22901
Halsey Hall	22903
Hammocks Gap Rd	22911
Hammond St	22903
Hamner Rd	22903
Hampshire Ct	22901
Hampton St	22902
Hancock	22904
Hanover St	22903
Hansen Rd	22911
Hansens Mountain Rd	22911
Hardware River Rd	22903
Hardwood Ave	22903
Hardy Dr	22903
Harmon St	22903
Harmony Dr	22901
Harris Rd	
100-599	22903
600-899	22902
Harris St	22903
Harris Creek Rd & Way	22902
Harrison	22904
Harrow Rd	22903
Hartford Ct	22902
Hartland Ct	22911
Hartmans Mill Rd	22902
Harvest Dr	22903
Hatcher Ct	22903
Hathaway St	22902
Haunted Hollow Rd	22911
E Haven Ct	22911
S Haven Acres Ln	22903
Hawkshill Ln	22911
Hawkwood Ct	22901
Hawthorne Ln	22911
Hayrake Ln	22903
Hazel St	22902
Heartbreak Rdg	22903
Hearthglow Ct & Ln	22901
Heather Ct	22911
Heather Crest Pl	22903
Heather Glen Rd	22911
Hedge St	22902
Hedgerow Ln	22903
Heiskell Ln	22901
Hemlock Ln	22903
Hench	22904
Henry Ave	22903
Heritage Ct	22903
Herndon Rd	22903
Herold Cir	22901
Heron Ln	22903
Hessian Rd	22903
Hessian Hills Cir, Rdg & Way	22901
Hickman Rd	22911
Hickory Ln	22911
Hickory St	22902
Hickory Hill Ln	22903
Hickory Nut Ln	22902
Hidden Knoll Dr	22903
Hidden Ridge Rd	22902
Hidden Valley Trl	22903
E & W High St	22902
High View Dr	22901
Highland Ave	22903
Highland Ridge Rd	22911
Highlands Dr & Pl	22901
Highview Ln	22901
Hildridge Dr	22902
Hill St	22903
Hill Top View Ln	22911
Hillcrest Rd	22903
Hillsdale Dr	22901
Hillsdale Farm Ln	22902
Hilltop Rd	22903
Hillview Ct	22902
Hillwood Pl	22901
Hilton Dr	22903
Hilton Heights Rd	22901
Hinton Ave	22902
Hobbit Hl	22903
Holiday Dr	22901
Holiday Trails Ln	22903
Holkham Dr & Ln	22901
Holly Ct	22901
Holly Dr	22903
Holly Rd	22901
Holly Knoll Ln	22901
Hollymead Dr	22911
Holmes	22904
Holmes Ave	22901
Home Port Ln	22903
Homestead Ln	22902
Honeysuckle Ln	22902
Hopkins Ct	22901
Horseshoe Bend Rd	22901
Howard Dr	22903
Hoxton	22904
Hubbard Ct	22903
Hummingbird Ln	22911
Humphreys	22904
Hunt Ln	22903
Hunt Country Ln	22901
Hunters Pl & Way	22911
Hunterstand Ct	22911
Huntington Rd	22901
Huntley Ave	22903
Huntwood Ln	22901
Hydraulic Cir & Rd	22901
Hydraulic Ridge Rd	22901
Hyland Creek Cir	22911
Idlewood Dr	22901
Ilex Ct	22911
Incarnation Dr	22901
Independence Way	22902
India Rd	22901
Indian Laurel Rd	22911
N & S Indian Spring Rd	22901
Ingle Ct	22901
Inglecress Dr	22901
Ingleridge Farm	22901
Ingleside Dr & Ln	22901
Ingleside Farm Ln	22901
Inglewood Ct & Dr	22901
Inn Dr	22911
Innovation Dr	22911
Insurance Ln	22911
Ipswich Pl	22901
Iris Ct	22902
Ironwood Ln	22901
Isolina Ln	22902
Ivy Dr	22903
Ivy Hl	22903
Ivy Ln	22901
Ivy Rd	22903
Ivy Commons	22903
Ivy Creek Dr	22901
Ivy Creek Farm Rd	22903
Ivy Depot Rd	22903
Ivy Farm Dr	22901
Ivy Ridge Rd	22901
Ivy Rose Ln	22903
Ivy Springs Ln	22901
Ivy Vista Dr	22903
Ivywest Ln	22901
Ivywood Ln	22903
Jackson Dr	22902
James Ln	22903
James Monroe Pkwy	22902
Jamestown Dr	22901
Jasmine Ter	22911
Java Ct	22902
Jeanette Lancaster Way	22903
Jeffers Dr	22911
Jefferson Ct	22911
E Jefferson St	22902
W Jefferson St	22902
Jefferson Lake Dr	22902
Jefferson Park Ave & Cir	22903
Jersey Pine Rdg	22911
Jessies Ln	22911
Jester Ln	22911
John St	22903
Johnson	22904
Jones St	22903
Jones Mill Rd	22901
Jordan Ln	22903
Jordan Run Ln	22902
Journeys End Ln	22902
Joy Ct	22902
Judge Ln	22911
Jumpers Run	22911
Juniper Ln	22911
Jurlando Ln	22911
Kearney Ln	22903
Kearsarge Cir	22903
Keelona Farm	22902
Keenwood Pl	22911
Keiser Ridge Rd	22911
Keith Valley Rd	
1600-1604	22903
1605-1699	22901
Kellogg	22904
Kellogg Dr	22903
Kelly Ave	22902
Kelsey Ct & Dr	22903
Kemper Ln	22901
Kempton Pl	22911
Kendalwood Ln	22911
Kenridge Ct	22901
Kensington Ave	22903
Kent	22904
Kent Rd	22903
Kent Ter	22903
Kenwood Cir & Ln	22901
Kerchof Hall	22903
Kernwood Pl	22911
Kerry Ln	22901
Key West Dr	22911
Keyhole Ct	22902
Keystone Pl	22902
Kimbrough Cir & Ct	22901
King St	22903
King George Cir	22901
King Mountain Rd	22901
King William Dr	22901
Kingston Rd	22901
Kirtley Ln	22903
Knight Ct	22901
Knightsbridge Ct	22911
Knoll St	22902
Knoll Ridge Dr	22903
Labrador Ln	22903
Lacebark Ter	22903
Lafayette Ln & St	22902
Lake Rd	22901
Lake Albemarle Rd	22901
Lake Club Ct	22902
Lake Forest Dr & Ln	22901
Lakeside Dr	22901
Lakeview Dr	22901
Lambeth	22904
Lambeth Ln	22903
Lambs Ln & Rd	22901
Lamkin Way	22911
Lanark Farm	22902
Lancaster Ct	22901
Landin Cir	22902
Landmark Dr	22903
Landonia Cir	22901
Lane Rd	22903
Lanford Hills Dr	22911
Langford Dr & Pl	22903
Lankford Ave	22902
Larkspur Ct & Way	22902
Latrobe Ct	22903
Laurel Cir & Gln	22903
Laurel Cove Rd	22911
Laurelwood Ln	22903
E & W Lawn	22903
Lawrence Rd	22901
Layla Ln	22903
Layton Dr	22903
Le Parc Ter	22901
Leaf Ct	22902
Leake Ln	22902
Leake Sq	22911
Leaping Fox Ct & Ln	22902
Leeds Ln	22901
Lefevre	22904
S Lego Dr & Rd	22911
S Lego Farm	22911
Lehigh Cir	22901
W Leigh Dr	22901
Leigh Pl	22902
Leigh Way	22901
Lenora Rd	22902
Lenox Hill Rd	22903
Leonard St	22902
Lester Dr	22901
Levering Hall	22903
Levy Ave	22902
Lewis	22904
Lewis St	22903
Lewis And Clark Dr	22911
Lewis Mountain Cir & Rd	22903
Lexington Ave	22902
Leyland Dr	22911
Liberty Hall Ln	22901
Liberty Oaks Ct	22901
Lide Pl	22902
Lilac Ct	22901
Lile-Maupin	22904
Lili Ln	22901
Linda Ct	22901
Linden Ave & St	22902
Line Dr	22901
Linlier Ct	22911
Lions Watch Farm	22902
Little Fox Ln	22903
Little Graves St	22902
Little High St	22902
Little Ivy Ln	22903
Little Mountain Farm	22911
Little Mtn Farm	22911
Llama Farm Ln	22902
Lobban Pl	22903
Loblolly Ln	22903
Loch Brae Ln	22901
Locke Ln	22911
Lockesley Ter	22903
Lockwood Dr	22911
Locust Ave	
400-899	22902
900-1199	22901
Locust Ln	22901
Locust Grove Ln	22901
Locust Hill Dr	22901
Locust Hollow Rd	22903
Locust Lane Ct	22901
Locust Shade Ct & Ln	22911
Lodge Creek Cir	22903
Loma Ln	22902
London Rd	22901
Lonesome Mountain Holw & Rd	22911
Lonesome Pine Ln	22911
Long	22904
Long St	22901
Long Branch Ivy Ln	22903
Longacre Farm Ln	22901
Longbranch Farm	22902
Longwood Dr	22903
Lonicera Way	22911
Lords Ct	22901
Loring Cir, Pl & Run	22901
Lost Hollow Path	22911
Louisa Rd	22911
Lowelina Rd	22901
Lower Holly	22904
Lupine Ln	22911
Luxor Terrace Dr	22901
Lyman St	22902
Lyman Hills Dr	22902
Lyman Mansion Rd	22902
Lynchburg Dr	22903
Lynnwood Ln	22901
Lynx Farm Ln	22903
Lyons Ave & Ct	22902
Lyons Court Ln	22902
Madison Ave	22903
Madison Ct	22911
Madison Ln	22903
Magnolia Bnd	22911
Magnolia Dr	22901
Mahogany Pl	22911
Mahonia Dr	22911
Maiden Ln	22911
E Main St	22902
W Main St	
100-299	22902
300-1400	22903
1402-1498	22903
Malbon Dr	22911
Malcolm Cres	22902
Mall Dr	22901
Mallet	22904
Mallside Forest Ct	22901
Malone	22904
Malvern Farm Dr	22903
Manchester Ct	22901
Manilla St	22903
Mansfield Ct	22903
Maple St	22902
Maple Ridge Dr	22911
Maple View Ct & Dr	22902
Maranatha Ln	22903
Marchant St	22902
Marchia Ln	22902
Marie Pl	22901
Marion Ct & Dr	22903
E & W Market St	22902
Marlboro Ct	22901
Marsh Ln	22903
Marshall Ct	22902
Marshall St	22901
Martha Jefferson Dr	22911
Martin St	22901
Martin Farm Ln	22901
Martin Kings Rd	22902
Mary Munford	22904
Mason Ln	22903
Mason St	22902
Masseys Woods Rd	22903
Massie Rd	22903
Massie Branch Ln	22902
Math Building	22903
Mattox Ct	22903
Maupin Dr	22901
Maury Ave	22903
Maury Hall	22903
Mawyer Farm Ln	22901
Maxwelton Rd	22903
Maymont Ct & Dr	22902
Maywood Ln	22903
Mccauley Ct	22911
Mccauley Mountain Ln	22903
Mcclary Ct	22911
Mccormick Rd	
---	22904
100-199	22904
200-298	22903
201-999	22904
300-998	22904
Mcelroy Dr	22903
Mcguffey	22904
Mcintire Rd	22902
Mclane Rd	22911
Mcleod Hall	22903
Meade Ave	22902
Meadow St	22903
Meadow Vista Dr	22901
Meadowbrook Ct	22901
Meadowbrook Rd	22903
Meadowbrook Heights Rd	22901
Meadowfield Ln & Way	22911
Meadowlark Ct	22911
Mechum Pl	22901
Mechum Banks Dr	22901
Mechum Heights Rd	22901
Mechum View Dr	22903
Mechums Dr W	22903
Mechums Depot Ln	22903
Mechums River Rd	22901
Mechums School Hl	22903
Mechums West Dr	22903
Megan Ct	22901
Melbourne Rd	22901
Melbourne Park Cir	22901
Melissa Pl	22901
Merano Ln	22911
Meridian St	22902
Merion Greene	22901
Meriwether Dr	22901
Meriwether St	22902
Meriwether Hill Ln	22901
Merlin Ct	22911
Metcalf	22904
Metchums River Rd	22903
Mews Aly	22903
Michael Pl	22901
Michelangelo Ct	22911
Michie Dr	22901
Michie Tavern Ln	22902
Middlesex Dr	22901
Middleton Ln	22903
Midland St	22902
Midmont Ln	22903
Midway Rd	22903
Midway Farm Rd	22901
Milford Ter	22902
Mill Creek Ct & Dr	22902
Mill Park Dr	22901
Mill Park Drive Ext	22901
Mill Ridge Rd	22901
Miller School Rd	22903
Millers Manor Ln	22911

Millie Ln 22911
Millington Rd 22901
Millmont St 22903
Millpond Rd 22902
Mills Ln 22902
Millstone Ct 22901
Milton Rd 22902
N Milton Rd
900-999 22911
1100-1199 22902
Milton Farm 22902
Milton Hills Dr 22902
Milton Village Ln 22902
Mimosa Ct & Dr 22903
Mine Creek Trl 22911
Minor Dr 22902
Minor Rd 22903
Minor Court Ln 22903
Minor Mill Rd 22911
Minor Ridge Ct & Rd 22901
Mint Meadow Ln 22911
Mist Ct 22902
Mitchell 22904
Mobile Ln 22903
Mockingbird Way 22901
Mollifield Ln 22911
Molly Ln 22902
E & W Monacan Dr 22901
Monacan Trail Rd 22903
Monet Hl 22911
Monroe Ct 22911
Monroe Ln 22903
Monroe Hall 22903
Montalcino Way 22911
Montalto Loop Rd 22902
Monte Vista Ave 22903
Montebello Cir 22903
Monterey Dr 22901
Montessori Ter 22911
Montgomery Ln 22903
Montgomery Ridge Rd 22911
Monticello Ave, Loop & Rd 22902
Montpelier St 22903
Montrose Ave 22902
Montvue Dr 22901
Moore Ave 22902
Mooreland Ln 22903
Moores St 22902
N Moores Creek Ln 22902
Morewood Ln 22901
Morgan Ct 22903
Morgantown Rd 22903
Morning Glory Hl 22902
Morningside Ln 22903
Morris Hl 22902
Morris Rd 22903
Morris Knoll Ln 22902
Morris Paul Ct 22903
Morrowdale Farm 22901
Morton Dr & Ln 22903
Morven Dr 22902
Mosby Rch 22901
Moseley Dr 22903
Mossing Ford Rd 22911
Moubry Ln 22911
Mountain Rd 22901
Mountain Brook Dr 22902
Mountain Laurel Rdg 22903
Mountain View Dr 22903
Mountain View St 22902
Mountainside Ct & Pl 22903
Mountainwood Rd 22903
Mountford Ct 22901
Mowbray Pl 22902
Mt Aire Rock Ln 22901
Mulberry Ave 22903
Murray Ln 22903
Myers Dr 22901
Myrtle St 22902
Nahor Rd 22902
Nalle St 22903
Nandina Ct 22911
Napier Hl 22902
Nash Dr 22903
Nassau St 22902

Natali Ln 22911
Natl Radio Ast Obs 22903
Natural Resources Dr 22903
Naylor St 22903
Neidin Farm 22903
Nelson Dr 22902
Nettle Ct 22903
New House Dr 22911
Newburg Hts 22903
Newcastle Ct 22911
Newcomb Hall 22904
Newcomb Mountain Ln 22903
Nicholas Page Ln 22903
Nix Way 22902
Nob Hill Cir 22903
Noble Hts 22902
Nomad Dr 22902
Norford Ln 22911
Normandy Dr 22903
Norris 22904
North Ave 22901
North Hl 22911
Northfield Ct & Rd 22901
Northridge Rd 22903
Northside Dr 22911
Northwest Dr 22901
Northwest Ln 22911
Northwood Ave & Cir 22902
Northwoods Grove Rd 22901
Northwoods Park Rd 22911
Northwoods Pointe Dr 22901
Nottingham Rd 22901
Nunley St 22903
Nutmeg Farm 22902
Oak Cir 22901
Oak St
100-299 22902
300-499 22903
Oak Forest Cir 22901
Oak Hill Ct, Dr & Pl 22902
Oak Tree Ln 22901
Oakencroft Cir & Ln 22901
Oakhurst Cir 22903
Oakleaf Ln 22903
Oakmont St 22902
Oakridge Ct 22911
Observatory Ave 22903
October Ln 22903
Old Ballard Rd 22901
Old Ballard Farm Ln & Rd 22901
Old Banks Farm 22902
Old Brook Rd 22901
Old Cabell Hall 22903
Old Farm Rd 22903
Old Fifth Cir 22903
Old Forge Rd 22901
Old Free Union Rd 22901
Old Garth Hts & Rd 22901
Old Ivy Rd & Way 22903
Old Lynchburg Rd
100-500 22903
501-599 22902
502-598 22903
601-699 22902
700-2499 22903
Old Mill Rd 22901
Old Oaks Dr & Spur 22901
Old Preston Ave 22902
Old Reservoir Rd 22903
Old Scottsville Rd 22902
Old Three Notch D Rd 22901
Old Turner Mountain Ln 22901
Old Via Rd 22901
Olinda Dr 22903
Olton Pl 22902
Olympia Dr 22911
Orange St 22902
Orangedale Ave 22903
Orchard 22904
Orchard Rd 22903
Orchard Hill Ln 22911
Orchard House Rd 22903
Oriole Ct 22911
Otter St 22901

Out Of Bounds Rd 22901
Overangt 22904
Overlook Dr 22903
Owen Ct 22911
Owensfield Ct & Dr 22901
Owensville Rd 22901
Oxford Pl & Rd 22903
Pace Ln 22902
Page 22904
Page St 22903
Pagebrook Farm 22903
Painted Sky Ter 22901
Palatine Ave 22902
Pallas Hill Ln 22901
N & S Pantops Ctr & Dr 22911
Pantops Cottage Ct 22911
Pantops Mountain Pl & Rd 22911
Paoli St 22903
Parham Cir 22902
W Park Dr 22901
Park Hl 22902
Park Ln E 22902
Park Ln W 22903
Park Pl 22903
Park Plz 22902
Park Rd 22903
Park St
300-899 22902
900-1399 22901
Park Forest Ct 22901
Parker Pl 22903
Parkway St 22902
Parkwood Pl 22901
Parsons Dr 22901
Parsons Green Ln 22903
Partridge Ln 22901
Paton St 22903
Patriot Way 22903
Pavilion Cir 22911
Payne Jackson Dr 22911
Paynes Ln 22902
Pea Ridge Rd 22901
Peacock Dr 22903
Peartree Ln 22901
Pebble Dr 22902
Pebble Hill Ct 22903
Pebblebrooke Ln 22902
Pebblecreek Ct 22901
Pen Park Ln & Rd 22901
Pendleton Ct 22901
Penfield Ln 22901
Penick Ct 22902
Pennbrook Farm 22902
Pennwood Farm 22902
Penny Ln 22903
Penwood Farm 22902
People Pl 22911
Pepper Pl 22902
Pepperidge Ln 22911
Peppervine Ct 22911
Pepsi Pl 22901
Peregory Ln 22902
Perry Dr 22902
Petal Ln 22903
Peter Jefferson Pkwy 22911
Peters 22904
Peterson Pl 22901
Pewter Ct 22911
Peyton Ct 22903
Peyton Dr 22901
Peyton Ridge Rd 22901
Pheasant Ln & Xing 22901
Physics Department 22903
Pickett Ln 22901
Piedmont Ave N & S 22903
Pike Pl 22901
Pin Oak Ct 22901
Pinch Em Slyly Pl 22911
Pinch Hill Ln 22903
Pine Ln 22901
Pine St 22903
Pine Cone Cir 22901
Pine Garth Run 22901
Pine Haven Ct 22901

Pine Hill Ln 22903
Pine Top Rd 22903
Pinedale Rd 22901
Pinehurst Ct 22902
Pineridge Ln 22911
W Pines Dr 22901
Piney Knoll Ln 22911
Piney Mountain Rd 22911
Pinnacle Pl 22911
Pintail Ln 22903
Pioneer Ln 22903
Pippin Ln 22903
Pireus Row 22902
Plains Dr 22901
Plank Rd 22903
Plantation Ct 22903
Plateau Rd 22903
Pleasant Pl 22911
Pleasant Ridge Ct & Rd 22911
Pleasant View Ln 22901
Pliney Rd 22902
Pliny Rd 22902
Plymouth Rd 22903
Poe Aly 22903
Poes Ln 22911
Polo Grounds Rd 22911
Ponderosa Trl 22903
Poorhouse Rd 22903
Poplar Dr 22903
Poplar St 22902
Poplar Glen Ct & Rd 22903
Poplar Ridge Rd 22911
Porter Ave 22903
Portico Way 22911
Post Ct 22902
Pounding Creek Rd 22903
Powell Rdg 22911
Powell Creek Ct & Dr 22911
Powhatan Cir 22901
Preddy Creek Rd 22911
Premier Cir 22901
Prescelly Pl 22901
Preston Ave
300-399 22902
400-1399 22903
1401-1799 22903
Preston Pl 22903
Price Ave 22903
Primrose Ln 22902
Pritchett Ln 22911
Pritchett Ridge Ln 22911
Proffit Rd 22911
Proffit Crossing Ln 22911
Proffit Station Rd 22911
Promised Land Ln 22903
Prospect Ave 22903
Providence Rd 22901
Pryors Mountain Ln 22903
Purple Sage Ct 22911
Putt Putt Pl 22901
Quail Run 22911
Quail Xing 22902
Quail Hollow Ln 22901
Quandary Dr 22902
Quandary Farm 22902
Quarles Rd 22911
Quarry Rd 22902
Queens Ct 22901
Quest Ct 22902
Quiet Acres Ln 22911
Quince Ln 22902
Quintas Das Torres Farm 22903
Radford Ln 22903
Ragged Mountain Dr, Ln & Rd 22903
Ragged Ridge Ln 22903
Ragged View Ct 22903
Rainier Rd 22903
Raintree Dr 22901
Raleigh Rd 22903
Raleigh Mountain Trl 22903
Ramblewood Pl 22901
Randall Hall 22903
Randolph Ct 22911

E & W Range 22903
Ranson Ct 22911
Ravens Pl 22911
Ravenscroft Way 22911
Ravenswood Ct 22911
Ray C Hunt Dr 22903
Raymond Ave 22903
Raymond Rd 22902
Rayon St 22902
Reas Ford Rd 22901
Red Hill Rd 22903
Redbud Ln 22911
Redfields Rd 22903
Redhawk Trl 22903
Redington Ln 22901
Redlands Farm 22902
Redwing Ln 22911
Regency Ct 22901
Regent St 22911
Reivers Run 22901
Remington Pl 22903
Remson Ct 22901
Research Park Blvd 22911
Reserve Blvd 22901
Reservoir Rd 22903
Reservoir Ridge Rd 22901
Retriever Run 22903
Reynard Dr 22901
Reynard Woods Rd 22901
Reynovia Dr 22902
Rhett Ct 22903
Rialto St 22902
Richland Dr 22903
Richmond Rd 22911
Ricky Rd 22901
Ridge Rd 22901
Ridge St 22902
Ridge Lee Dr 22903
Ridge Mcintire Rd 22903
Ridgefield Rd 22911
Ridgeley Ct 22901
Ridgetop Dr 22903
Ridgeview Cir 22902
Ridgeway Ln 22911
Ridgeway Farm 22911
Ridgewood Cir & Dr 22911
Ridgewood Trailer Park 22911
Riggory Ridge Rd 22911
Rio Rd E & W 22901
Rio East Ct 22901
Rio Hill Ctr & Dr 22901
Rivancrest Dr 22901
Rivanna Ave 22903
Rivanna Farm 22911
Rivanna Plaza Dr 22901
Rivanwood Dr & Pl 22901
River Ct & Rd 22901
River Brook Ct 22901
River Chase Ln & Rdg 22901
River Inn Ln 22901
River Oaks Ln & Rdg 22901
River Ridge Rd 22901
River Vista Ave 22901
Riverbend Dr 22911
Riverbluff Cir 22902
Riverdale Dr 22902
Riverrun Dr 22901
Rivers Edge Rd 22911
Riverside Ave 22902
Riverview Ln 22911
Riverview St 22902
Riverview Farm 22911
Rives St 22902
Roades Ct 22902
Roberta Gwathmey 22904
Robertson Ave 22903
Robertson Ln 22902
Robin Ln 22911
Robin Hill Ct 22901
Robinson Pl 22902
Robinson Woods 22903
Rock Chimney Ln 22903
Rock Creek Rd 22903
Rockbrook Dr 22901
Rockfish Gap Tpke 22903

Rockland Ave 22902
Rockledge Dr 22903
Rocks Farm Ct & Dr 22903
Rocks Mill Ct & Ln 22903
Rocky Run 22901
Rocky Hollow Rd 22911
Rocky Top Rd 22911
Rodes Dr 22903
Rodgers 22904
Rodman Dr 22901
Rolkin Ct & Rd 22911
Rolling Hill Rd 22901
Rolling Valley Ct 22902
Rookwood Dr & Pl 22903
Roosevelt Blvd 22903
Roosevelt Brown Blvd 22903
Rosa Ter 22902
Rose Arbor Ct 22901
Rose Hill Dr 22903
Rose Hill Church Ln 22902
Rosebud Ln 22903
Rosedell Ln 22903
Rosemont Dr 22903
Rosemont Farm Way 22903
Rosenwall Hl 22911
Rosewood Ln 22903
Roslyn Forest Ln 22901
Roslyn Heights Rd 22901
Roslyn Ridge Ct & Rd 22901
Ross Ct 22902
Rosser Ave & Ln 22903
Rothery Rd 22903
Rotunda 22903
Rougemont Ave 22902
Round Hill Dr 22901
Roundtop Farm 22902
Rouss Hall 22903
Rowledge Pl & Rd 22903
Royal Ct 22901
Royal Oak Ct 22902
Royer Dr 22902
Roys Pl 22902
Rubin Ln 22911
Ruffin Hall 22903
Ruffner Hall 22903
Rugby Ave, Cir, Pl & Rd 22903
Running Cedar Ct 22911
Running Fox Ct & Ln 22902
Ruppel Dr 22903
Ruskin Dr 22901
Rustic Willow Ln 22911
Rustling Oaks Dr 22901
Rutherford Rd 22901
Rutledge Ave 22903
Rye Hollow Ln 22903
Sachem Pl 22901
Sacre Meadow Ln 22911
Saddlebrook Ln 22911
Saddlewood Dr, Pl & Trl 22902
Sadler St 22903
Sagebrush Ct 22911
Sagewood Dr 22902
Saint Annes Rd 22901
Saint Charles Ave
600-899 22902
900-1099 22901
1101-1199 22901
Saint Charles Ct 22901
Saint Clair Ave
700-899 22902
900-1199 22901
Saint George Ave 22901
Saint Ives Rd 22911
Saint James Cir 22902
Salisbury Sq 22901
Samara Ct 22903
Samuel Miller Loop 22903
Samuels Rd 22903
Sandridge Ct & Ln 22902
Sandstone Rd 22911
Saranac Ct 22911
Sassafras Cir & Hl 22911
Sawgrass Ct 22901
Saxon Ct 22901

Scarborough Pl 22903
Scarlet Oak Ln & Rdg 22911
Schelford Farm 22901
Schoolhouse Hl 22903
Scott Ct & Rd 22902
Scottsville Rd 22902
Secretarys Rd 22902
Secretarys Sand Rd 22903
Seminole Ct 22901
Seminole Ln 22901
Seminole Trl
900-1154 22901
1155-1155 22906
1156-2350 22901
1157-2199 22901
2400-2499 22911
2500-2598 22901
2501-5099 22911
2600-5098 22911
Sequoia St 22911
Serpentine Ln 22911
Seven Hills Ln 22901
Seymour Rd 22903
Shadow Oaks Pl 22901
Shadwell Station Ln 22911
Shady Ln 22903
Shady Forest Way 22901
Shady Grove Ct 22902
Shady Spring Dr 22901
Shadybrook Trl 22911
Shale Pl 22902
Shamrock Rd 22903
Shannon 22904
Shasta Ct 22903
Shawnee Ct 22901
Sheffield Rd 22901
Shelby Dr 22901
Shelton Mill Rd 22903
Shepards Hill Pl & Rd 22903
Shepherd Run 22903
Shepherds Ridge Cir & Rd 22901
Sheridan Ave 22901
Sherwood Rd 22903
Sherwood Farm 22902
Shiloh Rd 22903
Shoppers World Ct 22901
Short 18th St 22902
Silas Jackson Ct 22901
Silk Wood Ct 22911
Silverbell Ct & Ter 22903
Simeon Ct & Ln 22902
Singleton Ln 22903
Skylark Ct 22901
Skyline Crest Dr 22903
Skyline View Ln 22903
Slate Pl 22902
Slate Mill Branch Rd 22903
Sleepy Hollow Ln 22911
Smith 22904
Smith St 22901
Smithfield Ct & Rd 22901
Sneads Hill Ln & Rd 22911
Snl Plz 22902
Snow Point Ln 22902
Snowden Dr 22901
Solitude Wayside Ln 22902
Solomon Rd 22901
Somer Chase Ct 22911
Somerset Ct 22901
Somerset Farm Dr 22902
Somesso Ct 22902
Sonoma St 22902
Sourwood Pl 22911
E & W South St 22902
Southampton Dr 22901
Southern Ridge Dr 22903
Southwood Ct 22902
Sowell Branch Ln 22902
Sparrow Ln 22911
Spotnap Rd 22911
Spottswood Rd 22903
Sprigg Ln 22903
Spring Ct 22901
Spring Ln 22903
Spring St 22903

Spring Brook Dr 22901
Spring Creek Ln 22901
Spring Hill Farm 22903
Spring Mountain Rd 22902
Springfield Rd 22911
Spruce St 22902
Squire Hill Ct 22901
Squirrel Path 22901
Stable Ln 22901
Stadium Rd 22903
Stagecoach Rd 22902
Starcrest Rd 22902
Stargate Ln 22911
State Farm Blvd 22911
Station Ln 22901
Station 1 22904
Station 2 22904
Steephill St 22902
Steeplechase Run 22911
Steubin Ln 22911
Stevenson Pl 22903
Stewart Cir 22903
Stewart St 22902
Still Meadow Ave, Cv & Xing 22901
Stillfried Ln 22903
Stillhouse Rd 22901
Stillhouse Ridge Ln 22903
Stirling Ct 22901
Stockton Rd 22903
Stone Creek Ln & Pt 22902
Stone Mill Ct 22902
Stonecrop Ct 22902
Stonefield Ln 22903
Stonehenge Ave 22902
Stonehenge Rd 22901
Stonewood Dr 22911
Stoney Creek Dr 22902
Stoney Ridge Rd 22902
Stony Point Rd 22911
Stowe Ct 22901
Stratford Ct 22903
Stratford Glen Way 22911
Stribling Ave 22903
Stribling Avenue Ext 22903
Stuart Pl 22903
Sturbridge Rd 22901
Suffolk Rd 22901
Sugar Maple Ct & Ter 22903
Sulphur Mine Rd 22911
Summerfield Ct 22911
Summerfield Farm Ln 22903
Summit Rd 22901
Summit St 22903
Summit Ridge Pt & Trl 22911
Summit View Ln 22903
Sumter Ct 22901
Sun Ridge Rd 22901
Sundown Pl 22911
Sundrops Ct 22902
Sunny Meadows Dr 22903
Sunrise Park Ln 22902
Sunset Ave 22903
Sunset Cir 22901
Sunset Rd 22903
Sunset Avenue Ext 22903
Sunset Lodge Ct 22903
Surrey Rd 22901
Surry Hill Ct 22901
Sutlers Rd 22902
Sutton Ct 22901
Swan Lake Dr 22902
Swan Ridge Rd 22903
Swanson Dr 22901
Sweet Hollow Ln 22903
Swift Ln 22901
Sycamore Ct 22901
Sycamore St 22902
Sylvan Ln 22911
Tall Tree Ct 22901
Tally Ho Dr 22901
Tandem Ln 22902
Tanglewood Rd 22901
Tarleton Dr 22901
Tattersall Farm Ln 22903
Tavernor Ln 22911
Taylors Gap Rd 22903
Taylors Gate Dr 22903
Taylors Mountain Farm Ln 22903
Teakwood Cv & Dr 22911
Tearose Ln 22903
Teel Ln 22903
Tennis Dr & Rd 22901
Terrell Ct & Rd 22901
Terrell Forest Ln 22903
Terrybrook Dr 22911
Thomas Dr 22903
Thomas Jefferson Pkwy 22902
Thomas Ridge Ln 22902
Thompson Farm Rd 22901
Thomson Rd 22903
Thorn Rose Ln 22902
Thornridge Way 22911
Thornton Hall 22903
Three Notch D Rd 22901
Three Notched Trce 22903
Thrush Rd 22901
Thuja St 22911
Thurmans Tract 22911
Tilman Rd
600-699 22903
700-1399 22901
Timber Ln 22911
Timber Mdws 22911
Timber Pt 22901
Timber Pointe Rd 22911
Timber Trail Dr 22901
Timberbranch Ct 22902
Timbercreek Farm 22901
Timberlake Rd 22901
Timberwood Blvd & Pkwy 22911
Tinkers Cove Rd 22911
Tintern Ct 22901
Todd Ave 22903
Tompkins Dr 22911
Towler Pl 22902
Town And Country Ln 22911
Townbrook Ct & Xing 22901
Towncenter Blvd & Ln 22911
Towne Ln 22901
Townsend Ct & Ln 22902
Townwood Ct & Dr 22901
Trailridge Rd 22903
Treesdale Way 22901
Treesdale Park Ct & Ln 22901
Treetop Dr 22903
Trellis Ln 22903
Tremont Rd 22911
Treviso Ln 22911
Triangle Ct 22901
Tripper Ct 22903
Troost Ct 22903
Tuckahoe Farm Ln 22901
Tucker 22904
Tudor Ct 22902
Tufton Ave 22902
Tufton Farm 22902
Tulip Tree Ct 22903
Tunlaw Pl 22903
Tupelo Ct & Ter 22903
Turkey Run 22911
Turkey Ridge Ln & Rd 22903
Turnberry Cir 22911
Turner Mountain Rd 22903
Turner Mtn Wood Rd 22903
Turnstone Dr 22903
Turtle Creek Rd 22901
Tuttle-Dunnington 22904
Twentyninth Place Ct 22901
Twin Creeks Rd 22901
Twin Sycamores Ln 22903
Twyman Rd 22903
Tyler Pl 22901
Tyree Ln 22901
Underhill Ln 22911
Unicorn Ln 22901
University Ave, Cir, Ct, Gdns, Mnr & Way 22903
Upper Holly 22904
Valley Cir & Rd 22903
Valley Road Ext 22903
Valley View Cir 22902
Varsity Hall 22903
Vdot Way 22911
Vegas Ct 22901
Venable 22904
Verdant Lawn Ln 22903
Verde Pl 22901
Vermira Pl 22901
Verona Ct & Dr 22911
Via Creek Dr 22903
Via Florence Rd 22911
Viburnum Ct 22911
Vicar Ct 22901
Victorian Ct 22901
E View St 22902
Viewmont Ct 22911
Viewmont Farm 22902
Viewmont West Dr 22902
Villa Ln, Ter & Way 22903
Villa Deste Ct & Dr 22903
Village Ct & Rd 22903
Village Green Cir 22903
Villaverde Ln 22902
Vincennes Ct & Rd 22911
Vine St 22902
Vinton Ct 22901
Viola Way 22902
Virginia Ave & Mnr 22903
Vivarium Ln 22902
Wahoo Way 22903
Wakefield Ct & Rd 22901
Walbert Cir 22902
Waldemar Dr 22903
Walden Ct 22901
Waldorf School Rd 22901
Walker Ln 22902
Walker Sq 22903
Walnut Ln 22911
Walnut St 22902
Walnut Hill Farm 22911
Walnut Ridge Ct & Ln 22911
Walnutside Ln & Pl 22901
Ward Ave 22902
Ware St 22902
Warren Ln 22901
Warwick Ct 22901
Washington Ave 22903
Washington Ct 22911
Washington Hall 22903
E & W Water St 22902
Water Oak Ct 22903
Waterbury Ct 22902
Watercrest Dr 22911
Waterwheel Ct & Dr 22902
Watson Ave 22901
Watson-Webb 22904
Watts Psge 22911
Watts Farm Rd 22911
Watts Station Dr & Rd 22911
Waverly Dr 22901
Wayles Ln 22911
Wayne Ave 22901
Wayside Pl 22903
Weatherwood Dr 22911
Webland Dr, Park, Ter & Vw 22901
Weedon 22904
Welk Pl 22903
Wellford St 22903
Wellington Dr & Pl 22903
Wells Ct 22902
Wendover Dr 22901
Wendover Ln 22911
Wentworth Farm 22902
Wertland St 22903
West Dr 22901
West St 22903
Westbrook Pl 22903
Westerly Ave 22903
Westfield Ct & Rd 22901
Westminster Rd 22901
Westmoreland Ct & Rd 22901
Westover Cir & Dr 22901
Westvaco Blvd 22902
Westview Rd 22903
Westwood Cir & Rd 22903
Weybridge Ct 22911
Wharton Dr 22902
Wheeler Rd 22903
Whetstone Pl 22901
Whippoorwill Rd 22901
Whispering Hollow Ln 22911
Whispering Oaks Dr 22902
Whispering Pines Ln 22901
Whispering Woods Dr 22911
Whitcover Cir 22901
White Cedar Ln 22911
White Eagle Ln 22903
White Gables Ln 22903
White Oak Ln 22911
White Pine Way 22911
White Rock Rd 22902
Whitehead Rd 22903
Whites Farm Ln 22911
Whitewood Rd 22901
Whitney Ct 22911
Whittington Dr 22911
Whyburn 22904
Wickham Pl & Way 22901
Wickham Pond Dr 22901
Wild Berry Ln 22903
Wild Flower Dr 22911
Wild Orchid Rdg 22903
Wild Turkey Ln 22903
Wilder Dr 22901
Wildmere Pl 22901
Wildwood Ct 22901
Wiley Dr 22903
Willard Dr 22903
William Ct 22903
Williamsburg Rd 22901
Williston Ct & Dr 22901
Willow Dr 22902
Willow Dale Ln 22911
Willow Lake Dr 22902
Willow Oak Cir 22901
Wilson Ct 22901
Wilson Hall 22903
Wilton Country Ln 22911
Wilton Farm Rd 22911
Wilton Pasture Ln 22911
Wimbledon Way 22901
Wind River Rd 22901
Windfield Cir 22902
Winding River Ln 22911
Windsor Rd 22901
Windy Knl 22903
Windy Ridge Rd 22903
Wine St 22902
Winecellar Cir 22902
Winery Hill Dr 22902
Wingfield Rd 22901
Winston Rd & Ter 22903
Winstons Run 22911
Winter Creek Farm 22901
Winterberry Ct 22911
Winterfield Cir 22911
Wintergreen Ln 22903
Winthrop Dr 22911
Wise Ct 22903
Wise St 22905
Wisteria Dr 22911
Wolf Trap Rd 22911
Wood Ln 22901
Wood St 22903
Wood Duck Pl 22902
Woodberry Rd 22901
Woodberry Hill Ln 22901
Woodbrook Ct & Dr 22901
Woodburn Ct & Rd 22901
Woodchuck Ln 22902
Woodcreek Dr 22911
Wooded Acres Ln 22911
Woodfolk Dr 22902
Woodgate Ct 22901
Woodhaven Ct 22902
Woodhurst Ct & Rd 22901
Woodlake Dr 22901
Woodland Dr 22903
Woodlands Rd 22901
Woodmont Dr 22901
Woodrow St 22903
Woodson Mountain Ln 22903
Woodstock Dr 22901
Woody 22904
Worrell Dr 22911
Worth Park & Xing 22911
Worthington Dr 22903
Wren Ct 22911
Wright Ln 22911
Wyant Ln 22903
Wyngate Rd 22901
Wynridge Dr & Ln 22901
Yellow Brick Rd 22903
Yellow Mountain Farm Dr 22903
Yellow Springs Pl 22902
Yellow Wood Dr 22901
Yellowstone Dr 22903
Yorktown Dr 22901
Younger 22904
Yule Farm 22901
Zack Ln 22901
Zan Rd 22901

NUMBERED STREETS

1st N & S 22902
2nd St NE 22902
3rd NE & SE 22902
4 H Way 22901
4th St NE 22902
4th St NW 22903
4th St SE 22902
4th St SW 22903
5th St NE 22902
5th St NW 22903
5th St SE 22902
5th St SW
100-699 22903
700-1399 22902
1401-1511 22902
5th Street Ext 22902
6 1/2 St SW 22903
6th St NE 22902
6th St NW 22903
6th St SE 22902
6th St SW 22903
7 1/2 St SW 22903
7th St NE 22902
7th St NW 22903
7th St SW 22903
8th St NE 22902
8th St NW 22903
9 1/2 St NE 22902
9th St NE 22902
9th St NW 22903
9th St SW 22903
10th St NE 22902
10th St NW 22903
11th St NE 22902
11th St NW 22903
11th St SW 22903
12th St NE 22902
12th St NW 22903
13th St NE 22902
13th St NW 22903
14th St NW 22903
15th NW & SW 22903
16th St NE 22902
16th St NW 22903
17th St NW 22903
18th St NE 22902
10 1/2 St NW 22903
12 1/2 St NW 22903
250 Byp 22901

CHESAPEAKE VA

General Delivery 23320

POST OFFICE BOXES MAIN OFFICE STATIONS AND BRANCHES

Box No.s
500 - 919 23322
1000 - 4940 23327
5001 - 5832 23324
6001 - 7039 23323
7171 - 7784 23324
9001 - 9916 23321
13001 - 14100 23325
15001 - 17130 23328

RURAL ROUTES

27 23321

NAMED STREETS

A St 23324
Aaron Ct & Dr 23323
Aaron Culbreth Ct 23322
Abbey Cir 23324
Abelia Way 23322
Aberdeen Ln 23322
Abilene Ct 23322
Abingdon St 23324
Able St 23324
Acentala Quay 23321
Acorn St 23324
Acorn Grove Ln 23320
Adair Ln 23323
Adams Ct 23320
Admiralty Ct 23323
Aguila Ct & Dr 23322
Ahoy Ct & Dr 23321
Airline Blvd 23321
Airport Dr 23323
Akron Ave 23322
Alackend Ave 23325
Alamoot Ct & Dr 23322
Albemarle Ct & Dr 23322
Albert Ave 23323
Albertine Ct 23320
Albury Ct 23321
Alder Ct 23320
Aldershot Ln 23320
Aldrich Ct 23323
Aldwell St 23323
Aleck Way 23323
Alexander Ln 23322
Alexandria Ln 23320
Alfred Loop 23320
Algona Rd 23324
Alice St 23323
Alixis Way 23320
Allegheny Way 23320
Allen Dr 23322
Allison Ct & Dr 23325
Almond Ct 23323
Alpine Ct & Dr 23322
Althea Ct 23322
Alton Cir 23320
Altoona St 23320
Amanda Ct 23322
Amber Cv 23321
Amberdale Dr 23322
Amberline Ct & Dr 23322
Amberwood Cmn 23320
Ambrose St 23322
Amelia Ct 23320
American Legion Rd 23321
Ames Cir & Ct E, N, S & W 23321
Amherst Ct 23320
Amick Rd
600-799 23325
800-999 23324
Amie Dr 23322
Ampo Ct 23322
Amster Ln 23323
Amy Marie Ln 23322
Anchor Ave 23321
Anchor Bend Ct 23321
Anderson Rd 23324
Andiron Arch 23323
Andover Ct 23322
Andrea Ln 23320
Andrea Lynne Ct 23321
Andrews Dr 23323
Angel Ct 23320
Angeli Arch 23322
Angelica Lndg 23322
Angler Ct & Ln 23323
Angora Ct & Dr 23325
Angus Rd 23322
Anita Cir 23321
Anjal Ln 23323
Anna Joy Ct 23320
Anna Maria Way 23323
Annabranch Trce 23323
Annaka Loop 23323
Annandale Dr 23321
Anne Ave 23324
Annette St 23324
Annias Way 23320
Annie Cir 23323
Ansell Rd 23322
Anthony Ct 23320
Appalachian Ct 23320
Appaloosa Trl 23323
Apple Tree Ln 23325
Applewood Ln 23324
April Ct 23323
Arabian Arch 23322
Arbor Ct 23325
Arbor Glen Dr 23324
Arbutus Cir 23323
Arcadia Rd 23320
Arce Ct 23322
Arch Rd 23322
Archer Ct, Dr & Pl 23322
Archery Ct & Dr 23323
Ardmore Ave & Cir 23324
Arena Ct 23322
Argyll St 23320
Arlean Dr 23321
Arlington Ave 23325
Arlo Ct 23323
Armada Ct & Dr 23321
Armentrout Ct 23324
Armor Ln 23325
Arnold Ct 23322
Arondale Cres & Ct 23320
Arrowhead Ct 23321
Arthurs Ct 23322
Artis Ave 23323
Artisan Ave 23323
Arundel Ln 23321
Asbury Ct 23322
Ash Hill Ct & Lndg 23322
Ash Pine Cv 23323
Ashburn Ct 23322
Ashforth Way 23322
Ashland Dr 23321
Ashley Rd 23322
Ashley Caroline Ct 23323
Ashton St 23321
Ashwell Way 23322
Ashwood Dr 23321
Askew Rd 23321
Aspen Arch 23320
Aspen Forest Ct 23322
Aspinock St 23322
Aston Pl 23322
Astor Way 23323
Athens Ct 23323
Atkinson Mews 23320
Atlantic Ave 23324
Attwick Ct 23320
Audubon Cir 23320
Aundre Ct 23321
Austenwood Ct 23322
Austin Dr 23320
Autumn Green Ln 23320
Autumn Oaks Dr 23322
Avalon Ave 23324
Avebury Way 23322
Averill Dr 23323
Avery Ct & Trce 23322
Avon Rd 23322
Avondale Ct 23321
Avonlea Ct & Dr 23322
Avonlea Pointe 23322
Aylesbury Dr 23322
Ayrshire Ct 23322

Azalea Ct 23322
B St 23324
Back Rd 23322
Backwoods Rd 23322
Baffy Loop 23320
Bahama Way 23322
Bailey Ln 23321
Bainbridge Blvd
700-4399 23324
4400-5599 23320
Bakerloo Ct 23322
Balboa Cres 23321
Bald Cypress Ct 23320
Baldwin Ln 23320
Balford Ln 23320
Ball St 23323
Balladeer Ct 23322
Ballahack Rd 23322
Ballance Ct 23321
Ballast Ct & Ln 23323
Ballentine Rd 23322
Balmoral Ln 23322
Bandock St 23323
Banff Ct 23320
Bangor Cres, Ct & Dr 23321
Bankbury Way 23322
Banks St 23324
Bannister St 23324
Bar Harbor Ct 23323
Barbara Ct 23322
Barbury Arch 23323
Barcelona Cir, Ct & Dr 23322
Barco Ct & Ln 23323
Bard Cir 23324
Barger St 23320
Barksdale Rd 23321
Barlingame Pl 23320
Barn Way 23323
Barn Owl Ln 23321
Barn Swallow Ct & Dr 23321
Barnes Rd 23324
Barnwell Ln 23322
Baron Ct 23323
Barred Owl Ln 23323
Barrington Ct 23322
Bartell Ct & Dr 23322
Bartlett Dr 23322
Barwick Ct 23320
Basin Rd 23322
Basing Ct 23322
Basnight Ct 23322
Bassett St 23324
Basswood Ct 23320
Bastian Ct 23322
Bateau Lndg 23321
Battery Cir 23323
Battery Park Rd 23323
Battlefield Blvd N
100-1426 23320
1425-1425 23327
1427-1899 23320
1428-1798 23320
1900-2099 23324
Battlefield Blvd S
100-1101 23322
1100-1100 23328
1102-4798 23322
1103-4799 23322
Battlefield Woods Ct 23322
Batton Door Pl 23323
Baugher Ave 23323
Baum Rd 23322
Bay Cres 23321
Bay Laurel Ct 23322
Bay Oak Ct & Dr 23323
Bayberry Ct & Pl 23320
Baydon Ln 23322
Bayford Ct 23321
Bayhaven Ct 23323
Baylor Ct 23320
W Baylor Ct 23324
Baywater Ct 23322
Baywood Trl 23323
Beacon Hill Pl & Rd 23322
Beacon Key Ct 23322
Beagle Gap Ct 23320

Bear Creek Ln 23323
Beardsly Ct 23322
Bearsden Ct 23322
Beatrice Ln 23323
Beau Lndg 23322
Beaujue St 23321
Beauregard Dr 23322
Beaver Creek Ct 23322
Beaver Dam Ct & Rd 23322
Becca Anne Ct 23322
Beckley Ln 23322
Becks Ct 23320
Beckwood Cmn 23320
Bedford St 23322
Bedstone Cir 23323
Beech St 23324
Beech Forest Ct 23322
Beecher Stowe St 23323
Beechwood Rd 23323
Begonia Ln 23325
Belem Dr 23322
Belfry Ct 23325
Bell Tower Arch 23324
Belle Haven St 23322
Belle Ridge Ct 23322
Bellechase Ct 23321
Bellingham Ct & Dr 23322
Bellpage Ave 23322
Bells Lndg 23323
Bells Creek Ct 23322
Bells Hollow Ct 23322
Bells Mill Rd 23322
Belmont St 23320
Belton Rd 23325
Belvedere Dr 23321
Belvin Ct 23322
Benefit Rd 23322
Bennett Way 23322
Benson Ln 23322
Bent Branch Ct 23323
Bentham Ln 23321
Bently Pl 23320
Beretta Ct 23321
Berkely Ct 23322
Berkley Ave
800-1198 23324
1200-1300 23324
1302-2398 23324
2400-3099 23325
Berkshire Dr 23321
Bernard St 23324
Berndale Dr 23322
Bernies Ct N & S 23321
Berrick Ct 23322
Bersoury St 23324
Bertram St 23323
Bertwick Ln 23325
Bethel Rd
500-799 23325
800-1199 23324
1201-1299 23324
Bettes Way 23320
Bexhill St 23323
Bickford Ct 23321
Biddle Ln 23321
Biernot Ave 23321
Big Bend Ct & Dr 23321
Big Game Way 23321
Big Pond Ln 23323
Bill Ct 23322
Bill Reid Ct 23324
Birch Forest Ct 23322
Birch Leaf Rd 23320
Birch Trail Cir 23320
Birchwater Ave 23320
Birchwater Arch 23320
Birchwood Ave 23321
Birsay Ct 23321
Biscayne Dr 23321
Bisco St 23321
Bisham Ct 23322
Bishop St 23323
Bishops Ct 23323
Black Bear Ct 23323
Black Walnut Ct 23322
Blackberne Ct 23322

Blackboard Dr 23322
Blackgum Ct 23323
Blackhawk Ct 23323
Blackhawk Pl 23321
Blacksmith Trl 23322
Blackstone Walk 23322
Blackthorne Ct & Dr 23322
Blackwater Rd 23322
Blade Ct 23320
Blair Ct 23320
Blairwood Ln 23320
Blake St 23320
Blanche Ct & Dr E, S & W 23323
Blaywicke Ct 23322
Bloom Ave 23325
Blossom Arch 23320
Blue Beech Way 23320
Blue Bill Ct 23320
Blue Goose Ct 23321
Blue Heron Ct 23321
Blue Jay Ct 23321
Blue Moon Cres 23320
Blue Ridge Rd 23322
Blue Spruce Cir 23322
Blueberry Bank 23325
Bluebird Dr 23322
Bluebonnet St 23324
Bluecastle Way 23323
Bluestem Ct 23323
Bluewater Ct 23320
Bluewing Ln 23323
Bobby Ryan Way 23322
Bobolink Cir 23321
Bobwhite Ct 23322
Bodine Ct 23322
Bogus Ln 23322
Bolton Cir 23323
Bomar Dr 23321
Bond Ave 23323
Bonnie View Arc 23320
Bonsack Ct 23320
Booker St 23320
Booth Ct 23322
Bordeaux St 23321
Border Ct & Rd 23324
Boston Ave 23322
Bostwyck Pl 23320
Bosun Dr 23321
Boswell Dr 23320
Botetourt Ct 23320
Bottom Quay 23320
Boundary St 23324
Bounds Ave 23323
Bourbon Ct 23322
Bow Ct & St 23325
Bowden Ave 23323
Bowling Green Ct & Trl 23320
Boxelder Ln 23320
Boxer Dr 23320
Boxwood Dr 23323
Boyette Ct 23322
Boyle Ct 23320
Bracey Way 23320
Bracknell Arch 23320
Braddock Landing Rd 23321
Bradford Ct 23322
Bradwell Reach 23322
Bragg St 23323
Braishfield Ct 23320
Bramblewood Ct 23323
Bramley Rd 23323
Branch Dr 23321
Branchview Way 23321
Brandermill Ct & Dr 23322
Brandon Ct & Way 23320
Brandon Quay 23320
Brandy Ct 23322
Brandywine Dr 23321
Brant Ct 23320
Brassie Ct 23320
Braves Trl 23325
Breckenridge Ct 23320
Breeze Ave 23323
Breeze Hill Cres 23322

Breeze Port Arch 23321
Breezy Pt 23322
Breezy Pines Ct 23321
Brennhaven Trl 23323
Brentwood Ct 23320
Brentwood Arch 23320
Brians Way 23321
Briarcliff Pl 23323
Briarfield Dr 23322
Briars Lndg 23320
Briarwood Ct & Dr 23322
Brice Ct 23322
Brickhouse Ln 23323
Bridge Dr 23322
Bridgefield Blvd 23322
Bridgeview Cir 23322
Bridgewood Way 23320
Bridle Ct 23323
Brier Cliff Cres 23320
Brigade Dr 23322
Brigantine Ct 23320
Brightleaf Pl 23320
Brighton Ln 23321
Brinn Quay 23322
Brinsmayd Arch 23322
Brisa Ct & Dr 23322
Bristlewood Ct 23320
Bristol Cir 23320
British Oak Ct 23323
Brittany Way 23321
Britwell Dr 23322
Broad St 23324
Broad Bend Cir 23322
Broad Reach Rd 23320
Broadleaf Xing 23320
Broadmoor Ave & Way 23323
Broadnax Cir & Dr 23323
Broadwater Ct & Dr 23323
Broadwinsor Cres 23322
Brockenbraugh Rd 23322
Bromay St 23321
Brook Stone Dr 23321
Brookcrest Arch 23320
Brookedale Ct 23322
Brookfield Ln 23321
Brookhaven Ct 23320
Brookland Dr 23324
Brookmont Ln 23320
Brookrun Chase 23322
Brookshire Dr 23323
Brookside Ct 23322
Brookside Lndg 23320
Brookside Arch 23322
Brougham Ct 23322
Broward Way 23322
Brown Rd 23323
Browning Cir 23321
Bruce Rd & Sta 23321
Bruce Station Ct 23321
Bruin Dr & Pl 23321
Bruno Dr 23323
Brunswick Ct 23320
Bruton Ct 23322
Bryan Ct 23320
Bryant Dr 23320
Bryson Arch 23323
Buchanan St 23324
Buck St 23323
Buckingham Dr 23320
Buckland St 23324
Buckthorn Ct 23323
Bud Dr 23322
Buddy Ct 23321
Buell St 23324
Buff St 23324
Bufflehead Dr 23320
Buford Ct 23322
Bugle Dr E 23321
Bulldog Dr 23320
Bulrush Ct 23320
Bunch Walnuts Rd 23322
Bunker Ridge Arch 23320
Burdett St 23322
Burfoot St 23324
Burford Ln 23325

Burkett Ct 23321
Burks Mill Ln 23323
Burns Ct & St 23320
Burnside Pl 23325
Burr Ct 23320
Burrow Ave 23324
Burrowin Dr 23321
Burson Dr 23323
Burton Ct & Pl 23322
Business Center Dr 23323
Business Park Dr 23320
Buskey Rd 23322
Bute St 23321
Butler St 23323
Butrico Rd 23325
Butt St 23324
Butterfly Dr 23322
Butternut St 23324
Butterwick Ct 23320
Buttonwood St 23324
Butts Station Rd 23320
Buxton Dr 23322
Byrd Ave 23324
Byrd Ct 23320
Byron St 23320
Bywood Ave 23323
Caboose Ct 23322
Cahoon Pkwy 23322
Calabria Dr 23323
Caleb Dr 23322
Calico Ct 23322
Calisha Ct 23321
Calista Dr 23320
Callery Ct 23323
Callison Dr 23322
Callorin Rd 23322
Calloway Ave 23324
Calm Wood Way 23320
Calonia Arch 23323
Calumet St 23322
Calvert Ct 23320
Calverton Ct & Way 23321
Camberley Way 23320
Camberly Ct 23320
Cambridge Ct & Way 23320
Camden Pl 23320
Camellia Ct 23322
Camelot Blvd & Ct 23323
Cameo Ter 23323
Campbell Rd 23322
Campostella Rd
1000-1098 23320
1100-1599 23320
1600-3099 23324
Canal Dr 23323
Canary Ct 23321
Candlelight Dr 23325
Candlewood Cir & Ct 23324
Candy Ln 23321
Cannon Point Dr 23321
Canoe St 23323
Canterbury Rd 23320
Canton Ave 23325
Cantor St 23320
Canvasback Ct 23320
Cap Stone Arc 23323
Capital Ave 23324
Capri Cir 23321
Captain Carter Cir 23321
Captain Cooke Way 23322
Captains Ct 23320
Caravelle Ct & Dr 23322
Carawan Ln 23322
Cardiff Ln 23321
Cardigan St 23324
Cardinal St 23322
Cardover Ave 23325
Carey Ct 23322
Carissa Way 23322
Carlisle Rd 23321
Carlton Dr 23320
Carmichael Way 23322
Carnation Ln 23325
Caroga Ct 23322
Carol Dr 23322
Carolina Rd 23322

Carolyn Dr 23320
Carriage Ct 23322
Carrick Ct 23321
Carrington Ave 23325
Carrollwood Cmn 23320
Carrolton Way 23320
Carter Rd 23322
Carver St 23320
Cascade Blvd 23324
Casey Martin Ct 23321
Cassway Arch 23323
Castaway Ct 23321
Castle Ct 23323
Castle Forbes Way 23322
Castleberry Dr 23322
Catalina Ct 23322
Catamount Ct 23322
Catrina Ln 23322
Causeway Dr 23322
Cavalier Blvd 23323
Cawdor Xing 23322
Cayce Cir, Ct & Dr 23324
Cayland Ct 23322
Caymon Ct 23321
Caymus Rd 23320
Cecilia Ct & Ter 23323
Cedar Ln 23322
Cedar Rd
100-1699 23322
1700-2999 23323
Cedar Commons 23322
Cedar Cove Ln 23323
Cedar Craft Ln 23323
Cedar Creek Ter 23322
Cedar Grove Cres 23321
Cedar Lakes Dr 23322
Cedar Mill Sq 23320
Cedar Pointe Ct & Ln 23323
Cedarlane Ct 23322
Cedarville Rd 23322
Cedarwood Ct, Ln & Trce 23322
Center Mast Crst 23322
Centerville Tpke N 23320
Centerville Tpke S 23322
Chablis St 23321
Chadswyck Rd 23321
Chalbourne Ct & Dr 23322
Challis Ct & Dr 23321
Champion Ct 23322
Chancery Ln 23321
Chandler Dr 23322
Channel Pl 23320
Channing Way 23322
Channing Arch 23322
Chantilly Ln 23322
Chapel Ave 23323
Charca Ct 23322
Charing Cross 23322
Charisse Ct 23322
Charles St 23320
Charlotte St 23321
Charlotte Ann Ct 23321
Charlton Ct & Dr 23321
Chasebury Pl 23320
Chasewyck Pl 23320
Chateau Cir 23322
Chattanooga St 23322
Chaz Ct 23321
Chelbrook Rd 23322
Chelsea Ln 23322
Cheltingham Ct 23322
Cherie Ct 23322
Cherry Ln 23323
Cherry Forest Ct 23322
Cherryhill Ln 23325
Cherrytree Ln 23320
Cherrywood Ct 23321
Chesapeake Ave, Cir, Ct & Dr 23324
Chesapeake Square Blvd 23321
Chesapeake Square Ring Rd 23321
Cheshire Forest Dr 23322
Cheslie Ct 23323

Cheslie Arch 23323
Chessie Ct 23322
Chessire Ct 23322
Chesslawn Cir E & W 23320
Chesterfield Loop 23323
Chesterfield Ter 23320
Chestnut Ave 23325
Chickadee St 23322
Chipada Ct 23321
Chowan Ave 23325
Chris Ct 23322
Christa Dr 23322
Christian Ave 23324
Christopher Dr 23321
Church Court Ln 23320
Churchill Dr 23322
Churchland Blvd 23321
Cicero Ct 23322
Cinnamon Ct 23321
Circlewood Dr 23323
Cistern Cir 23323
Citizen Cir 23325
Clara Dr 23320
Clarendon Cir 23323
Clark Ct 23320
Clarks Cir 23321
Clay Ave 23323
Clayton Ct 23323
Claytor Ct 23320
Clear Springs Ct 23320
Clearfield Ave 23320
Clearwater Ln 23322
Clemson Ave 23324
Cleona Dr 23324
Clifton St 23321
Clipperton St 23320
Cloud Nine Ct 23323
Clove Ct 23321
Clover Dr
100-199 23322
3400-3499 23321
Clover Rd 23321
Clover Rd E 23321
Clover Hill Ct 23322
Clover Meadows Dr 23321
Club House Dr 23322
Club Pines Ct 23320
Club Point Rd 23322
Clydes Way 23320
Coachman Dr 23325
Coastal Ln & Way 23320
Cobb Ave 23325
Cobb Island Ct 23322
Cobble Scott Way 23322
Cobblestone Ct 23325
Cobblewood Bnd 23320
Cobblewood Arch 23320
Codorus St 23323
Coffman Blvd 23321
Cogliandro Ct & Dr 23320
Coinbrook Ln 23322
Coker Pl 23320
Cole Dr 23320
Coleshill Ln 23321
Colgin Way 23320
Colindale Rd 23321
Collington Dr 23322
Collingwood Ave 23324
Collins Blvd & Ct 23321
Colonel Byrd St 23323
Colonial Vw 23322
Colonial Way 23325
Colony Dr 23322
Colony Manor Rd 23321
Colony Pointe Dr 23321
Colt Arch 23321
Colton Ct 23322
Columbo Ave 23321
Columbus Ave 23321
Commerce Ave & St 23324
Commish Ln 23320
Common Ln 23324
Commonwealth Ave 23325
Compaz Rd 23321
Concord Dr 23324
Concorde Pl 23321

Condor Ct, Dr & Lndg 23321
Conference Center Dr 23320
Connie Ln 23322
Conrad Ave 23323
Conservancy Dr & Way 23323
Conservation Ct & Xing 23320
Constance Dr 23322
Contrell Ct 23320
Conway Rd 23322
Cook Blvd 23323
Cookes Mill Rd 23323
Cookham Arch 23322
Cool Brook Trl 23320
Copeland Ct & Dr 23322
Copley Ct 23320
Copper Way 23320
Copper Knoll Ln 23320
Copper Stone Cir & Ct 23320
Copperfield Dr 23321
Cora St 23324
Coral Ave 23324
Coral Ivy Ct & Ln 23323
Coral Maple Ct 23321
Coral Water Ct 23322
Corapeake Dr 23322
Corbin Dr 23320
Corby Cir 23320
Corby Glen Ave 23322
Corden Ave 23324
Cordgrass Ct 23320
Cordova Ct 23323
Corkwood Cir 23320
Corlew Ct 23320
Cornet St 23321
Cornick Ave 23325
Cornland Rd 23322
Corporate Ln 23320
Corsini Way 23322
Corwood Ct 23323
Cory Ln 23321
Costa Ave 23320
Cottage Pl 23322
Cotton Mill Ct 23323
Cottonwood Ln 23320
Country Cir & Rd 23324
Country Club Blvd & Ct 23322
Country Mill Ct & Run 23322
Country Trail Ct & Rd 23322
Cove Cir 23325
Coventry Close 23320
Coveside Ln 23320
Covey Ct 23323
Cox Ave 23323
Cozy Cor 23320
Crabtree Ct 23321
Cranberry Dr 23320
Cranham Rd 23322
Cranston Dr 23320
Creef Ln 23320
S Creek Ct 23325
N Creek Dr 23323
Creek Ln 23320
Creeks Edge Ct 23323
Creekside Cres & Ct 23320
Creekview Ct & Dr 23321
Creekwood Dr 23323
Crepe Myrtle Ln 23325
Crescent Trce 23320
Crescentwood Arch 23320
Crestmont Pl 23320
Crestwood Ln 23324
Crestwynd Cir & Dr 23322
Cricket Ct 23320
Cricket Ln 23321
Cricket Hollow Ln 23321
Crimson Ivy Ln 23320
Crittenden Ct 23321
Croatan Ct 23322
Croft Xing 23320
Cromwell Ave & Ct 23325
Cronin Ct 23322
Crooked Stick Xing 23320
Cross St 23323
Cross Creek Quay 23320
Cross Quay 23320
Crossbow Ct 23321
Crossings Ct & Dr 23321
Crossland Dr 23320
Crosstie Ct & Ln 23323
Crossways Blvd 23320
Crossways Shopping Ctr 23320
Crosswinds Dr 23320
Crosswood Ct & Ln 23322
Crowell Ave 23324
Crowley Cir 23320
Crown Cres & Ct 23325
Crystal Ave 23324
Crystalwood Cir 23320
Cuddy Ct 23323
Cuervo Ct 23322
Cuffee Rd 23322
Cullen Ave 23324
Cully St 23321
Culpepper Ave 23323
Cumberland Ct 23322
Curlew Ct 23321
Curling Ct 23322
Currie Ave 23323
Currituck Dr 23322
Custis Ave 23323
Cuthrell Ln 23320
Cutspring Rd & Trce 23322
Cutter Ct 23321
Cypress Pl 23320
Cypress Mill Ct & Rd 23322
Cypress Wood Cv 23323
Cyprine Cv 23321
D St 23324
Daffodil Ln 23325
Daggerboard Dr 23321
Dahlia St 23324
Dahoon Ct 23322
Dale St 23323
Dalmore Ct 23321
Dalton Ct 23322
Damsel Ct 23322
Damyien Arch 23320
Dana Dr 23321
Danali Ct 23323
Dandridge Way 23323
Dane St 23323
Danielle Ct 23322
Dapple Grey Ct 23322
Darby Run Dr 23322
Darden St 23322
Darius Ct 23323
Darley Ln 23323
Dartmoor Ct 23321
Daverlin Way 23323
David Ct 23320
Davids Mill Dr 23321
Davis Ave 23325
Dawnee Brook Trl N & S 23320
Dawson Cir 23322
Daylily Dr 23320
Daystone Ct 23323
Daystone Arch 23323
Daytona Dr 23323
Deal Dr 23323
Deal Island Ct 23322
Deans Ct 23321
Deaton Ct & Dr 23323
Debaun Ave & Loop 23320
Debbs Ln 23320
Deborah Ct 23321
Debreck Way 23320
Decatur St 23324
Deep Branch Way 23323
Deep Creek Blvd, Cmn & Run 23323
Deep Run Dr 23321
Deepspring Dr 23321
Deepwater Dr 23322
Deer Path 23320
Deer Trl 23321
Deer Xing 23323
Deer Neck Dr 23323
Deer Neck Arch 23323
Deer Ridge Ct 23322
Deerbrook Ct 23323
Deerfield Cres & Ct 23321
Deerview Ct & Dr 23321
Deerwood Ct & Dr 23320
Deland Ct 23322
Delaura Ct 23320
Delegate Ln 23323
Delia Dr 23322
Delta Ct 23325
Delwood Rd 23323
Dena St 23324
Denham Arch 23322
Denise Ct 23320
Denning Ln 23321
Dent Pl 23325
Denver Ave 23322
Derby Ct 23322
Dermott St 23320
Derry Dr 23323
Desertmartin Way 23323
Destiny Way 23320
Devon Dr 23321
Devonshire Ct & Dr 23323
Devonwood Cmn 23320
Dewald Rd 23322
Dewberry Dr 23320
Dexter St E & W 23324
Diamond Ave 23323
Diamond Hill Rd 23324
Diana Lynn Ct 23322
Dickens Pl 23322
Dietz Dr 23323
Dillwyn Dr 23322
Dinwiddie Ct 23322
Discovery Dr 23320
Dismal Swamp Canal Trl 23322
Dissdale Ct & Ln 23320
Dobbs Ferry Ct 23320
Dock Harbour Dr 23321
Dock Landing Rd 23321
Dock Point Arch 23321
Docking Post Dr 23323
Dockside Ct 23323
Dockwood Trl 23321
Dockyard Lndg 23321
Dodd Dr 23323
Doe Run Ct & Dr 23322
Dogwood Ter 23321
Dogwood Forest Ct 23322
Dolph Cir 23322
Dolphin Ct 23321
Dominion Blvd N 23320
Dominion Blvd S
100-399 23322
400-1309 23323
Dominion Commons Way 23322
Dominion Lakes Blvd & Ct 23320
Donnington Ct & Dr 23322
Doolittle Ave 23322
Dorcas Rd 23320
Dorchester Ct 23322
Dordon St 23321
Doria Trl 23320
Doris Ave 23324
Dorothy Ct 23323
Dorset Ct 23322
Douglas Ave 23323
Douglas Rd 23322
Douglas A Munro Rd 23322
Dove Dr 23322
Downing Dr 23322
Dragon Ln 23323
Drake Cir 23320
Draughon Rd 23322
Drawbridge Ct & Dr 23323
Drayton Ct & Rd 23324
Driftwood Ct & Dr 23320
Drum Creek Rd 23321
Drum Point Cir, Cres & Ln 23321
Drumcastle Ln 23323
Drummond Ln 23322
Drury Ln 23322
Duchess Of York Quay 23320
Duck Blind Trl 23321
Duffield Pl 23320
Duke Of Gloucester Ct & Dr 23321
Duke Of Suffolk 23320
Duke Of York Ct & Dr 23321
Dunbar Ct 23322
Dunbarton Ct & Dr 23325
Dundas Ct 23322
Dundee Ln 23322
Dunedin Ct & Dr 23321
Dunleavy St 23322
Dunmore Dr 23323
Dunn St 23320
Dunning Ln 23322
Dunstan Ct 23322
Dunwich Rd 23325
Dunwood Ct 23322
Dunworken Dr 23321
Dupont St 23320
Duquesne Dr 23321
Durham Ave 23320
Dustin Ct 23320
Dusty Rd 23322
Dutch Ln 23323
Dyanax St 23324
Eady Dr 23323
Eagle Dr 23323
Eagle Glen Dr 23322
Eagle Hill Dr 23321
Eagle Pointe Way 23322
Eagles Nest 23322
Eagles Trace Path 23320
Eaglestone Arch 23322
Earhart St 23322
Earle Ave 23324
Earley St 23324
Eason Rd 23322
East Rd 23321
Eastern Way 23320
Easton Ct 23322
Eastwood Ave 23324
Eaton Way 23320
Eddington Ct 23322
Eddystone Dr 23323
Eden Sq & Way 23320
Edenbridge Dr 23322
Edgerton Rd 23320
Edgeware Ct 23322
Edgewood Ave & Ct 23324
Edgewood Arch 23322
Edinburg Ave 23324
Edna St 23322
Edwards Ct 23321
Egret Ct 23320
Eider Ct 23320
Eight Star Ct & Way 23323
Elberon Ct 23322
Elbow Rd 23320
Elbyrne Ct & Dr 23325
Elco St 23324
Elder Ave 23325
Elderberry Ct 23320
Elderwood Cmn 23320
Eley St 23321
Elgin Ct 23320
Elias Ct 23322
Elijah St 23323
Elindra Ct 23323
Elizabeth Ave 23324
N Elizabeth Harbor Dr 23321
Elkhart St 23323
Elkton Ct & Dr 23321
Ellen Ln 23321
Ellena St 23320
Elliston Way 23323
Elm Ave 23325
Elm Forest Ct 23322
Elmhurst Ave 23322
Elmsford Pl 23321
Elon Ct 23322
Elverton Ct 23321
Elysian Pl 23320
Emberhill Ct & Ln 23321
Emerald Ct 23320
Emerald Sea Dr 23323
Emerald Woods Dr 23321
Emmbrook Ct 23323
Emmett Dr 23325
Emmham Ct 23322
Emporia Ave & Ct 23325
Emsworth Dr 23320
Enfield Ct 23323
Engle Ave 23320
Englewood Dr 23320
English Ave 23320
Enoch Rdg 23322
Enterprise Cir & Ct 23321
Epping Ct 23321
Equinox Lndg 23322
Eric Ct 23323
Erie St 23322
Erik Paul Dr 23322
Erin Ln 23323
Ervin Ct 23322
Esmont Ct 23322
Esplanade Pl 23320
Essex Dr 23320
Estates Way 23320
Estella Dr 23325
Ethel James Dr 23323
Etheridge Ct & Rd 23322
Eugenia Ave 23324
Eunice Way 23320
Eustis Ave 23325
E & S Eva Blvd & Ct 23320
Evans Ln 23322
Everett St 23324
Evergreen Ct 23321
Evers Ct 23324
Ewell Ln 23322
Excalibur Ct & St 23323
Executive Blvd & Ct 23320
Executive Center Dr 23321
Exeter Cir 23320
Fair Oak Dr 23322
Faire Chase 23322
Fairfax Ter 23320
Fairfield Dr 23322
Fairhaven Rd 23322
Fairview St 23325
Fairway Ct & Dr 23320
Fairways Lookout 23320
Fairwind Dr 23320
Falcon Ave 23324
Fall Ridge Ct & Ln 23322
Fallcreek Run 23322
Fallen Leaf Ln 23320
Fallhaven Ct 23320
Falls Brook Run 23322
Falls Creek Ct & Dr 23322
Falmouth Ct & Dr 23321
False Creek Way 23322
Farange Dr 23323
Fargo Ct 23322
Farington Cir 23320
Farman Ct 23322
Farmer Ln 23324
Farmhouse Rd 23322
Farnsworth Dr 23321
Farringdon Way 23321
Faulk St 23321
Fawn Lake Ct 23323
Fawnwood Cmn 23320
Faye St 23324
Featherbed Ct & Dr 23325
Feldspar Quay 23321
Fenton Quay 23320
Fentress Rd 23322
Fentress Airfield Rd 23322
Fenway Ave 23323
Ferebee Ave 23324
Ferguson Cv 23323
Fern Dr 23320
Fern Mill Ct & Ln 23323
Fern Quay 23320
Fernbridge Pl 23320
Ferncliff Ct 23323
Ferndale Rd 23323
Fernham Ln 23322
Fernwood Farms Ct & Rd 23320
Ferrum Ln 23322
Ferryman Quay 23323
Field Crest Ct 23322
Fieldstone Ln 23323
Fife St 23321
Fillmore Pl 23325
Filly Run 23323
Finch St 23322
Fincham Ct 23324
Finck Ln 23320
Fire Box Ct 23323
Firebird Ct 23323
Fireside Rd 23324
Firethorn Rd 23320
Fireweed Ct 23320
Firman St 23323
Fisher Ave 23320
Fitchett St 23324
Flag Rd 23323
Flatrock Ln 23320
Flax Mill Dr & Way 23322
Flaxton Trce 23322
Fleetway Dr 23323
Fleetwood Rd 23325
Fleming Cir 23323
Fletcher Ct 23321
Flint St 23322
Flint Chip Dr 23320
Flintfield Cres 23321
Flintlock Ct & Rd 23322
Flintshire Dr 23323
Flower Ln 23324
Flume Ct 23323
Fluridy Rd 23322
Flyfisher Trl 23321
Flying Star Ct 23323
Fontana Ave & Ct 23325
Ford St 23323
Fordham Ln 23320
Fordsmere Ct & Rd 23322
Fordson Way 23320
Fordyce Ct & Dr 23322
Forehand Dr 23323
Foreman Lndg 23323
Forest Rd 23322
Forest Cove Dr 23322
Forest Glade Ct & Dr 23322
Forest Haven Ln 23321
Forest Lake Blvd 23322
Forest Lakes Cir & Dr 23322
Forest Mills Rd 23322
Forest Point Dr 23320
Forestview Ct 23321
Forsythe Ct 23321
Foster Ct 23325
Fox Ridge Ct & Trl 23322
Foxcroft Ct 23322
Foxfield Dr 23323
Foxgate Quarter 23322
Foxglove Ct 23321
Foxgrove Ln 23321
Foxton St 23323
Foxwood Dr 23323
Foxxglen Run 23321
Foxxglen Quay 23321
Fragrant Cv 23320
Frances Ct 23322
Franconia Dr 23322
Frank Dr 23322
Franklin St 23324
Frederick Ct 23321
Freeman Ave 23324
Freers Ct 23322
Fresno Dr 23322
Friar Tuck Ct 23322
Friesian Ct 23322
Frost Flower Ct 23323
Frosty Rd 23325
Fryar Pl 23322
Fulcrum Ct 23323
Furnace Rd 23325
Gable Way 23320
Gadwall Ct 23320
Gaff Rd 23321
Gainsborough Cir, Ct & Sq E 23320
Galberry Rd 23323
Gale Ave 23323
Galeasha Dr 23320
Galies Pointe Ln 23322
Gallbush Rd 23322
Gallenway Ter 23322
Galleon Dr 23321
Gallop Ave 23324
Galston Ct 23321
Gammon Trl 23322
Gannet Ct 23320
Garden Ct 23322
Garden Tree Rd 23322
Gardenia Cir 23325
Garland Dr 23322
Garnes Ave 23323
Garrett St 23324
Garrison St 23323
Garth Way 23323
Garwood Ln 23323
Gaskin Ct 23323
Gaston Ct & Dr 23323
Gatefield Ln 23322
Gates Lndg 23323
Gateway Ct 23320
Gatewood Ct 23320
Gauntlet Ct & Dr 23323
Gavin Rd 23323
Gene Cres 23320
Geneva Ave 23323
Genoa Cres 23321
Genovese Reach 23322
George Dr 23323
George Washington Hwy N & S 23323
Georgetown Blvd 23325
Georgia Rd 23321
Georgie Ct 23323
Geranium Ln 23325
Gerrey Dr 23323
Gibson Dr 23320
Gideon Cres 23324
Gilbert Ct 23323
Gilbys Ct 23323
Gilchrist Ct 23320
Giles Dr 23322
Gillette Ct 23322
Gilmerton Rd 23323
Ginger Ct 23320
Girard Ave 23323
Glades Ct 23322
Gladesdale Dr 23322
Glasgow St 23322
Glemmings Ct 23321
Glen Ct 23325
Glen Oak Cv & Xing 23322
Glencoe St 23322
Glenda Cres 23322
Glendale Ave 23323
Gleneagle Ct 23322
Glenmar St 23323
Glenrose Ct 23322
Glenview Rd 23321
Glenwood Dr 23322
Global Cir 23322
Gloria Ct 23321
Gloria Dr 23322
Gloss St 23322
Glouchester Cir 23320
Glovers Ct 23322
Godwin Ave 23324
Goldcrest Dr 23325
Golden Ct 23323
Golden Cypress Ct 23320
Golden Hind Ct & Rd 23321
Golden Leaf Dr 23324
Golden Maple Dr 23322
Golden Oaks Ln 23321
Goldeneye Dr 23320
Golfview Dr & Way 23323
Goodman St 23321
Goose Creek Ct 23321

Street	ZIP
Goose Creek Flyway	23321
Goshawk Dr	23321
Gould Ave	23320
Grace St	23323
Gracie Rd	23325
Grady Cres & St	23324
Graham St	23323
Grain Way	23323
Granada Dr	23322
Grand Isle Dr	23323
Grandy Ct, Dr & Rd	23322
Grant Ct	23321
Grant St	23320
Grantham Ln	23322
Granton Ter	23322
Grassfield Pkwy	23322
Grassfield Rd	23323
Gratton St	23320
Graver Ln	23322
Gray Rock Rd	23322
Grayson Way	23320
Great Bridge Blvd	23320
Great Heron Ct	23322
Great Marsh Ave & Cir	23320
Great Oak Ct	23320
Grebe Ct	23320
Green Meadow Dr	23320
Green Oaks Ct	23322
Green Point Dr	23321
Green Tree Cir & Rd	23320
Greenbrier Cir, Pkwy & Rd	23320
Greendell Rd	23321
Greenfield Ln	23322
Greengable Way	23322
Greenleaf Dr	23321
Greenmoor Ct	23322
Greens Edge Ct & Dr	23322
Greenspring Ct	23322
Greenview Rd	23321
Greenway Dr	23322
Greenwell Ln	23320
Greenwing Ct & Dr	23323
Greenwood Rd	23321
Greer St	23324
Gregg St	23320
Gregory St	23320
Grenadier Ct & Dr	23322
Gresham Way	23323
Gretna Ct	23321
Grey Fox Ct	23323
Greystone Ln	23320
Grizzly Trl	23323
Grover Ct	23320
Gruen St	23323
Guadal Ct	23320
Guenevere Ct & Dr	23323
Guerriere St	23324
Guildford Mews	23320
Guisborne Ct	23322
Gulfwind Rd	23320
Gum Ct & Rd	23321
Gum Tree Ct	23321
Gunston Ct	23322
Gunston Bridge Ct	23323
Gust Ln	23323
Guynn Ave	23323
Gwaltney Ct	23321
Habitat Xing	23323
Hadley Ct	23323
Hadleybrook Dr	23320
Hagenspring Rd	23320
Hailey Ct	23321
Hails Ln	23323
Haledon Rd	23320
Half Hitch St	23321
Halifax Ln	23324
Hall Dr	23322
Hallbridge Dr	23322
Hallmark Way	23323
Halsey St	23324
Halter Arch	23320
Halton Ln	23320
Halyard Ln	23323
Hambledon Loop	23320
Hamill Ln	23320
Hamilton St	23324
Hanbury Ct & Rd	23322
Hancock Dr	23323
Hanes St	23324
Hanna Rose Ct	23320
Hanover Ln	23321
Happy Acres Rd	23323
Harbor Lndg	23323
Harbor Quay	23320
Harbor Watch Dr	23320
Harbour Pl	23320
Harbour North Dr	23320
Harding Dr	23321
Hardwick Cir	23320
Hardwick Ct	23321
Hardwick Ter	23321
Hardwood Ct & Dr	23320
Harlequin Ct & Way	23321
Harling Dr	23325
Harper Ct	23323
Harrell Rd	23323
Hartford Ct	23320
Harton Cir & Ln	23323
Hartswood Ter	23322
Hartwell Ct	23320
Harvard Dr	23324
Harvest Trl	23320
Harvest Green Ln	23320
Harvesttime Cres	23321
Harway Ave	23325
Harwich Ct & Dr	23322
Hassell Dr	23322
Hastings Ct	23320
Hathaway Ct	23322
Hatteras Cres	23322
N Haven Cir	23322
Havenwood Ct	23321
Haverford Dr	23320
Haverhill Ct	23322
Haviland Ct & Rd	23320
Hawick Ter	23322
Hawk Blvd	23322
Hawkhurst Dr	23322
Hawks Ave	23323
Hawksley Dr	23321
Hawley Ct	23322
Hawthorne Dr	23325
Haysi Way	23322
Hayward Ave	23320
Haywood Ave	23324
Hazel Ave & Ct	23325
Hazel Grove Way	23322
Hazelwood Rd	23323
Head Of River Rd	23322
Head Water Way	23323
Hearndon Ct	23322
Hearring Way	23323
Hearthside Ct E	23325
Hearthstone Lndg	23320
Heathway Trl	23323
Hedgerow Ct	23322
Heidi Dr	23323
Helen Ave	23322
Helensburgh Dr	23321
Helmsdale Ct & Way	23320
Hemlock Dr	23321
Hemple St	23324
Hempstead Ct	23322
Henley Ct	23320
Henphil Farms Ct	23320
Henry Ave	23323
Henwick Ct	23320
Herberts Ln	23322
Heritage Cir, Dr & Pt	23322
Heritage Oak Dr	23320
Hermit Thrush Way	23323
Herring Ditch Rd	23323
Herrington Ln	23325
Herron Dr	23320
Hertz Rd	23321
Heydon Ct	23322
Hibben Rd	23320
Hickory Rd E & W	23322
Hickory Forest Dr	23322
Hickory Hinge Way	23323
Hickory Hollow Ct	23320
Hickory Ridge Ct & Rd	23322
Hickory Station Dr	23322
Hickory Woods Ct	23322
Hidden Falls Ct & Ln	23320
Hidden Harbor Ct	23322
Higgins Ave, Ct & St	23324
High Point Cir, Ln & Pl	23322
High Ridge Ct	23322
High Rock Ct	23322
High Tide Way	23321
Highgate Ct	23322
Highlands Ct	23320
Hilda Pine Dr	23322
E Hill Ln	23322
N Hill Ln	23322
S Hill Ln	23322
Hill St	23324
Hill Point Ct	23322
Hillard St	23323
Hillbrook Dr	23323
Hillburn Dr	23323
Hillcrest Pkwy	23322
Hillingdon Bnd	23321
N Hills Dr	23320
Hillside Ave, Ct & Trce	23322
Hillston Ct	23322
Hillston Arch	23322
Hilltop Ct & Dr	23322
Hillwell Ct & Rd	23322
Hilton Ave & Ct	23324
Hines St	23324
Hinksley Ct	23322
Hinton Ave	23323
Hodges Rd	23322
Hoffman Ave	23325
Holbrook Trce	23322
Holland Blvd	23323
Hollins Ct	23322
Hollow Ct	23320
Hollowell Ln	23320
Holly Ave	23324
Holly Berry Ln	23325
Holly Cove Dr	23321
Holly Glen Dr	23325
Holly Point Blvd & Ln	23325
Holly Ridge Ct & Dr	23323
Hollygate Ln	23322
Hollywood Dr	23320
Holmes Trl	23322
Holston River Ct	23320
Holt Dr	23322
Holyoke Ln	23320
Homecrest Blvd	23324
Homestead Rd	23321
Honey Flower Ct	23323
Honey Locust Way	23320
Hook St	23324
Hoover Ave	23324
Hopewell Dr	23323
Hornsea Ct & Rd	23325
Hornswood Ct	23322
Horse Run Dr	23322
Horseback Run	23323
Horseshoe Dr	23322
Hot Mill Ct	23323
Howard Rd	23320
Hoyt Dr	23323
Hubard Dr	23325
Hudson St	23324
Hugh Ln	23322
Hughes Ave	23324
Hulen Dr	23323
Hull St	23324
Hummingbird St	23322
Humphries Ln	23322
Hungarian Rd	23322
Hunningdon Lakes Blvd	23320
Hunningdon Woods Blvd	23320
Hunt Trl	23321
Hunt Club Ln	23323
Hunter Green Ct	23320
Hunters Bridge Dr	23320
Hunters Glen Ct	23323
Hunters Quay	23320
Huntersbow Ct	23321
Hunthaven Ct	23320
Hunting Wood Rd	23321
Huntly Ct & Dr	23320
Hurdle Dr	23322
Hydenwood Cres	23321
Hywood Ct	23322
Ians Way	23320
Ida St	23324
Ike St	23324
Ilex St	23320
Ilkly Cir	23320
Independence Pkwy	23320
Indian Cedar Dr	23320
Indian Creek Rd	23322
Indian River Rd	23325
Indiana Ave	23321
Indianola Ct	23323
Indigo Rd	23325
Industrial Ave	23324
Inez Ln	23321
Inkwell Ct	23322
Inland Rd	23322
Inlet Quay	23320
Innovation Dr	23320
International Plz	23323
Iowa St	23323
Iris St	23324
Iron Bridge Ln	23323
Iron Clad Ct	23321
Isabel Ct	23320
Isabella Dr	23321
Ivanhoe Ct	23322
Iverness Ct	23320
Ivy Brg	23320
Ivy Cres	23325
Ivy Ct	23325
Ivy Trl	23320
Ivystone Sq & Way	23320
Jackie Dr	23324
Jackson Ave	23324
Jacob Ct	23324
Jake Ln	23320
Jamaica Ave	23322
James Lndg & St	23321
James Earl Dr	23322
Jana Ct	23322
Janell Ct	23320
Janes Way	23320
Janice Lynn Ct	23323
Janson Dr	23321
Jardin Cv	23321
Jarman Rd	23320
Jarvis Rd	23323
Jaye Cir	23321
Jean Ct	23323
Jean Shackelford Dr	23321
Jefferson St	23324
Jenna Ct	23320
Jennell Ct	23321
Jennifer Cres	23321
Jeremy Way	23322
Jerome St	23324
Jerry Locker St	23322
Jerryville St	23322
Jersey Cir	23320
Jester Ct	23321
Jill Cres	23321
Jo Anne Cir	23322
Joan Ct	23322
Jockey Ct	23322
Jodi Lynn Trl	23322
John St	23321
John Anthony Ct	23320
John Etheridge Rd	23322
Johnson Ave	23320
Johnson Ln	23322
Johnstown Cres & Rd	23322
Jolliff Rd	23321
Jolliff Woods Dr	23321
Jones Ln & St	23320
Jonquil Ct	23321
Joplin Ln	23323
Jordan Trce	23323
Jordan Crossing Rd	23322
Joseph Ave	23324
Jousting Ct	23323
Joyce Ct	23321
Joyner Rd	23320
Judah Way	23320
Jule Dr	23322
June Berry Ct	23325
Juniper Cres	23320
Jury Rd	23322
Justin Lee Way	23322
Justin Quay	23322
Justis St	23325
Kaitlyn Ct	23321
Kalmar Dr	23320
Kate Dr	23320
Kathleen Ln	23322
Kay Ave	23324
Keaton Ct & Way	23321
Keats Lndg, St & Sta	23320
Keel St	23324
Keelee Tree Ct	23322
Keeling Ct & Dr	23322
Keeter Run	23320
Kegman Rd	23322
Keith Ct	23325
Kelland Dr	23320
Kelly Run	23320
Kelsey Bay Ct	23323
Keltic Cir	23323
Kemet Rd	23325
Kemp Ln	23325
Kemp Ln E	23325
Kemp Xing	23320
Kemp Bridge Ct, Dr & Ln	23320
Kemp Meadow Dr & Way	23320
Kempsville Rd	23320
Kendale Cir	23322
Kendra Ct	23322
Kenelm Ct & Dr	23323
Kenley Ct	23321
Kennedy St	23324
Kennedy Trl	23322
Kenny Ln	23321
Kensington Ct & Way	23322
Kent Pl	23320
Kentucky Trl	23323
Kenyon Way	23320
Keri Ct	23320
Kerwyck Pl	23320
Keswick Cir	23320
Ketch Ct	23320
Kettle Creek Ter	23322
Kids Ct	23323
Kilbride Ct & Dr	23325
Kilby Dr	23320
Kildeer Ct	23322
Killington Sq	23320
Killington Arch	23322
Kimberly Ct	23320
Kincaid Ter	23320
Kinderly Ln	23320
Kindlewood Cres & Ct	23321
King Ct	23324
King Arthur Cir, Ct & Dr	23323
King George Quay	23325
King Maple Ct	23320
King Richard Way	23321
Kingfisher Ct	23321
Kinglet Ave	23324
Kings Bishop Ct	23320
Kings Cross Quay	23320
Kings Gate	23320
Kings Mill Ct	23320
Kingsborough Sq	23320
N & S Kingsbridge Pl & Way S	23322
Kingsbury Ct & Dr	23322
Kingsley Ln	23323
Kingston Way	23320
Kingsway Dr	23320
Kinser Ct	23324
Kinsington Dr	23321
Kinston Waters Ct	23323
Kirkwall Ct	23320
Knells Ridge Blvd & Dr	23320
Knight Rd	23323
Knollwood Ct	23320
Knox Ct	23321
Koppens Way	23323
Kramer Pl	23320
Kresler Pl	23324
Kristina Way	23320
Kyle Ct	23322
Lacy Oak Dr	23320
Lady Ashley Dr	23320
Lafayette Ave	23324
Lago Rd	23322
Lagoon Ln	23322
E Lake Cir	23322
S Lake Cir	23322
W Lake Cir	23322
Lake St	23323
Lake Crest Dr	23323
Lake Drummond Cswy	23322
Lake Point Ct & Dr	23320
Lake Ridge Ct & Xing	23322
Lake Shore Ct & Dr	23321
Lake Thrasher Pkwy	23320
Lake Village Dr	23323
Lakeford Pl	23322
Lakeside Ct	23322
Lakeview Ct & Dr	23323
Lakewood Cir & Ln	23321
Lambardi Ct	23322
Lambert Ct	23320
Lambert Trl	23323
Lambourne Ct	23322
Lamont St	23324
Lamp Post Ct & Dr	23325
Lanae Ct	23321
Lance Ct	23325
Lancing Way	23323
Lancing Crest Cir & Ln	23323
Land Of Promise Rd	23322
Landers Dr	23322
W Landing Ct & Dr	23322
Landing Creek Dr	23323
Landmark Ct	23322
Lands End Dr	23322
Landsworth St	23324
Langshire Cres	23322
Lanier St	23324
Lanphier Cir	23323
Larkspur Ct & Ln	23322
Larkwood Ct	23321
Las Gaviotas Blvd & Lndg	23322
Las Olas Ct	23322
Latham St	23324
Lathbury Ct	23322
Lauderdale Dr	23322
Launton Ct	23322
Laura St	23320
Laurel Ave	23325
Laurel Ridge Ln	23322
Lauren Ashleigh Dr	23321
Lavery Ct	23322
Laxey Ct	23321
Lear Close	23321
Leary Ct	23323
Leckford Dr	23320
Ledgebrook Ct	23322
Lee Cres	23323
Lee Ct	23322
Lee Shore Ct	23320
Leeds Ct	23321
Leeward Ct & Dr	23321
Lehman Rd	23322
Lehman Pines Rd	23322
Leicester Ct	23322
Lela Ln	23322
Leleon Ct	23322
Lemonwood Rd	23323
Lenore Trl	23320
Lenox Ct & Trce	23322
Lenwil Dr	23325
Leonard Ave	23324
Leshea Ct	23322
Lester St	23324
Letcher Ct	23323
Levee Ct & Ln	23323
Leyte Ave	23324
Leytonstone Dr	23321
Liam Close	23321
Liberton Ct	23321
Liberty St	23324
Libertyville Rd	23320
Lido Ct	23323
Lil Walnut Ln	23320
Lilac Ave	23325
Lilley Cove Dr	23321
Lilly St	23324
Lima Ct	23322
Limestone Ct	23320
Linbay Ct	23323
Lincoln Ct & Rd	23320
Lincolnshire Ct	23322
Lindale Dr	23320
Lindbergh Ave	23325
Linden Ave	23325
Lindenbrook Ln	23322
Lindenwood Dr	23321
Lindsey Ave	23320
Lingale Ct	23322
Lingale Arch	23322
Linkenborough Dr	23322
Links Ct	23320
Linster St	23324
Linton Cir	23322
Lisas Cove Way	23321
Lisbon Rd	23321
Little Beaver Rd	23325
Little John Trl	23322
Little Marsh Ln	23320
Live Oak Dr	23320
Liverpool Ct	23322
Livesay Rd	23323
Livingston Ave	23324
Lloyd Dr	23325
Lobdell Ct	23322
Loblolly Ct	23322
Loch Island Dr	23320
Lockard Ave	23320
Lockhaven St	23320
Lockheed Ave	23322
Locks Ln	23320
Locks Lndg	23323
Locks Rd	23320
Locks Landing Cres	23323
Locksdale Ct	23322
Lockspar Ct	23321
Lodge Cv	23322
Lofurno Rd	23322
Logans Mill Trl	23323
Lola B Ct	23321
Lolly Pine Ct	23323
Lombard St	23321
London Plane Crst	23323
Long Ave & Pt	23322
Long Beeches Ave	23322
Long Brooke Ct	23320
Long Meadow Ln	23322
Long Parish Way	23320
Long Ridge Rd	23322
Longdale Cres & Ct	23325
Loose Strife Pl	23320
Lord Bradford Ct	23321
Lord Byron Ct	23320
Lord Nelson Ct	23320
Lords Landing Ct	23322
Loretta Ln	23322
Lorton Ct	23323
Louis Dr	23320
Louise James Ct	23323
Lovegrove Ave	23323
Loxdell Ct	23322
Loxley Ct	23322
Lucas Ave	23324
Ludgate Ct & Dr	23321
Luid Dr	23322

Luray St 23323
Luray Ter 23322
Lusk St 23325
Luther St 23322
Luxenbay Ln 23323
Luxford Ct 23321
Luxor Ave 23325
Lydney Cir 23320
Lynchs Ln 23323
Lynnfield Ct & Rd 23323
Lynnhurst Blvd 23321
Lynnwood Gold Ct 23320
Lyons Ave 23324
Mabry Mill Pl 23320
Macdonald Rd 23325
Mactaggert Ave 23325
Madera Ct & Rd 23322
Madison Plz 23320
Madison Garden Ct 23322
Madri Dr 23321
Madrid Pl 23321
Magnum Rd 23322
Maid Marion Cir 23322
Maiden Ln 23325
Main St 23320
Mains Creek Rd 23320
Mainsail Ln 23321
Majestic Ct 23323
Malbon Dr 23320
Malcolm Ct 23324
Malibu St 23323
Mallard Ct 23320
Mallet Way 23323
Mallow Ct 23321
Manchester Ln 23321
Mandarin Ln 23323
Mangrove Dr 23323
Mann Dr 23322
Manning Ct 23321
Manor View Ct 23321
Manorwyck Pl 23320
Manteo Ct 23322
Maori Ct & Dr 23321
Maple Dr 23321
Maple St 23324
Maple Bridge Ct 23320
Maple Forest Ct 23322
Maplefield Dr 23321
Mapleshore Dr 23320
Mapleton Cres 23321
Maplewood Ln 23323
Marble Arch 23322
Marcia Ct 23323
Marco Dr 23323
Marcus Ct & St 23320
Mardean Dr 23321
Margaret Ct 23321
Margaret Dr 23322
Margaret Ann Ct 23321
Margaret Booker Dr 23323
Marge Dr 23320
Marigold Ct 23324
Marilla Ln 23322
Marina Ct 23320
Marina Reach 23320
Mariner Dr 23321
Marion Dr 23322
Marjorie Ln 23320
Mark St 23324
Market Pl 23321
Markland Dr 23325
Marla Ct 23323
Marlbank Ct 23322
Marlboro St 23323
Marlin Ct 23323
Marlow Ct 23322
Marquis Ct 23322
Marsh Island Dr 23320
Marsh Quay 23320
Marsh Wren Ct 23322
Marshwood Ct 23322
Marston Dr 23322
Marta Ln 23321
Martha Dr 23323
Martin Ave 23324
Martin Johnson Rd 23323

Mary Ann Ct 23323
Mary Ellen Ave 23324
Maryview Ave 23324
Mason Ct 23320
Mast Head Way 23321
Masters Ct & Row 23320
Mathews Ct & Dr 23320
Matt Chase 23323
Mattox Dr 23325
Matty Trce 23322
Maude St 23323
Maulden St 23324
Maxim Ct 23323
Maxwell St 23322
Mayapple Ct 23323
Mayfair Ct 23322
Mayfield Ave 23324
Mayon Dr 23325
Maysiett St 23324
Maywood St 23323
Mccaan Quay 23321
Mccloud Rd 23320
Mccosh Ct & Dr 23320
Mcdaniels Ave 23323
Mcdonough St 23324
Mckenna Close 23321
Mckinley Ave 23324
Mckinzie Ct 23320
Mclain St 23324
Mcneal Ave 23325
Mcrae Close 23321
Mcrowland Ln & Way 23320
Mcsherry Ct 23322
Meadow Ct & Dr E & W 23321
Meadow Creek Ct & Dr 23323
Meadow Forest Ct & Rd 23321
Meadow Trail Rd 23322
Meadow Wood Ct & Dr E & W 23321
Meadowbrook Ln 23321
Meadowgate Ct 23321
Meadowgreen Ct 23321
Meadowhill Ct 23320
Meadowlark St 23322
Meadowridge Dr 23321
Meadows Lndg & Way 23321
Meadowview Rd 23321
Meads Ct 23323
Meaford St 23324
Meanley Dr 23323
Meannew Dr 23321
Medical Pkwy E 23320
Meggett Dr 23322
Meherrin River Ct 23320
Meiggs Rd 23323
Melonie Ct & Dr 23322
Melton St 23324
Menands Dr 23325
Mendel Ct 23324
Mercantile St 23323
Mercer Ct 23323
Merchants Ct & Way 23320
Meredith Dr 23322
Merganser Ct 23320
Meridian Dr 23322
Merle Ct 23322
Merlin Ct 23323
Merrimac Ct 23321
Merry Cat Ct 23320
Meta St 23323
Meta Pointe Ct & Dr 23323
Miami Dr 23323
Miarfield Arc 23321
Miars Grn 23321
Miars Farm Cir 23321
Miars Quay 23321
Michael Dr 23323
Michael Thomas Ct 23321
Michelle Ct 23321
Mid Estates Way 23322
Middle St 23324
Middle Oaks Dr 23322
Middle Ridge Dr 23322

Middleburg Ln 23321
Midhurst Ln 23321
Midlands Ln 23320
Midship Ct 23323
Midway Ave 23324
Midway Dr 23322
Milano Ct 23322
Milbrook Arch 23322
Milby Dr 23325
Mildenhall Dr 23322
Mile Creek Ln 23322
Miles St 23324
S Military Hwy
1000-2599 23320
2600-2699 23324
2700-3799 23323
3800-4599 23321
W Military Hwy 23321
Mill Run 23322
Mill Bridge Way 23323
Mill Creek Pkwy 23323
Mill Lake Quarter 23320
Mill Landing Rd 23322
Mill Pond Dr 23320
Mill Pond Arch 23320
Mill Stone Rd 23322
Mill Stream Way 23320
Millborough Pl 23321
Miller Ave 23320
Millgate Ct 23322
Millgrove Ct 23321
Millhouse Ct & Ln 23323
Millpike Ct 23322
Millville Ct & Rd 23323
Millwood Ave 23322
Millwright Way 23323
Mimosa Ct 23321
Mineola Dr 23325
Mingo Trl 23325
Mintwood Dr 23321
Minuteman Dr 23323
Mishannock Way 23323
Mistletoe Ct & Way 23323
Mistral Pl 23322
Misty Ct 23323
Misty Vw 23320
Misty Hollow Ct 23323
Misty Point Rd 23323
Mitchum Way 23320
Moat Ln 23323
Mobile Dr 23323
Mockingbird Ct 23322
Monaco Ct 23321
Monarch Ct 23320
Monarch Reach 23320
Moneta Dr 23321
Monitor Ct 23321
Monroe Ct 23320
Montauk Ln 23320
Montclair Ave 23325
Montebello Cir 23322
Monterey Ct 23321
S Monterey Dr 23320
Montevale Dr 23322
Monticello St 23324
Montrose Ct 23320
Montross Ct 23322
Mooney Rd 23325
Moonraker Dr 23320
Moor Dale Ct 23322
Moore Cir 23321
Mooregate Ct 23322
Moorehouse Cres 23322
Moores Lndg 23322
Mooring Ct 23321
Moors Lndg 23323
Morningside Dr 23321
Mornington Dr 23321
Morris Ct 23323
Morrison Pl 23324
Morven Ct 23322
Mosby Ct 23324
Mosely Cir 23320
Moses Grandy Trl 23323
Moss Lndg 23323
Moss Quay 23320

Mossgate Ct 23323
Mossvale Way 23322
Mostiler Ct & Pl 23323
Motley Ct 23322
Mount Pleasant Rd 23322
Mountain Stone Way 23320
Mowbry Ct 23322
Mulberry Cres 23320
Mullen Rd 23320
Mulligan Ct 23322
Munden St 23324
Munford Ln 23321
Murphy Ln 23324
Murray Dr 23322
Muscovy Ct 23320
Musket Ct 23322
Muskrat Ct 23323
Mustang Dr 23322
Mustoe Ct 23322
Myers Rd 23324
Myrtle Ave 23325
Mystic Cv 23321
Naples Ct 23322
Napoli Ct 23322
Narrow St 23324
Natchez Trce 23322
Nathaniel Ct 23322
Nautilus Ave 23325
Neal St 23320
Neck Rd 23322
Needlerush Ct 23320
Nelson St 23324
Neptune Ave & Ct 23325
Nesbit Dr 23323
Nesting Pl 23320
Network Sta 23320
New Born Ct 23322
New Land Rd 23322
New Mill Dr & Lndg 23322
New River Ct 23320
New Zealand Reach 23322
Newberry Dr 23322
Newport Dr 23321
Newstead Cir 23320
Niblick Ct 23320
Nicholas Ct 23320
Nicholson Ct 23320
Nicked Pin Pl 23323
Nicks Pl 23323
Nightingale Ln 23321
Nightshade Ct 23323
Niles Ct 23322
Nina Dr 23321
Nixon Ct 23321
Noble Ct 23323
Noelle Ct 23322
Noggin Cir 23323
Nollie Ct 23323
Norcova Ct & Dr 23320
Norfolk St 23321
Norlina Dr 23322
Norman Way 23322
Normandy Ct 23321
Norris Ln 23321
North Rd 23321
Northfield St 23320
Northmoor Ct 23322
Northview Dr 23322
Northwest Blvd 23322
Northwood Dr 23322
Norwood Arch 23320
Nottaway Ct & Dr 23320
Nottingham Dr 23322
Nottoway River Ct 23320
Nugent Dr 23322
Number Ten Ln 23323
Oak Dr E 23321
Oak Bark Ln 23323
Oak Forest Ct 23322
Oak Gate Dr 23320
Oak Grove Rd & Run 23320
Oak Hill Way 23320
Oak Knoll Ln 23320
Oak Lake Dr, Run, Sq, Ter & Way 23320
Oak Lake Run Cres 23320

Oak Lake Way Ct & Sq 23320
Oak Leaf Ct 23320
Oak Manor Dr 23323
Oak Mears Cv 23323
Oak Moss Ct 23321
Oak Ridge Dr 23322
Oak Ridge Ln 23320
Oakdale Ln & Way 23324
Oakford Crst 23322
Oaklette Ave & Dr 23325
Oakstone Trl 23320
Oakwell Ct 23322
Oakwood Rd 23323
Odman Dr 23321
Ohio St 23324
Oil Bird Ln 23321
Oklahoma Dr 23323
Old Dr 23322
Old Atlantic Ave 23324
Old Barnes Rd 23324
Old Battlefield Blvd S 23322
Old Bridge Ln 23320
Old Butts Station Rd 23320
Old Centerville Tpke 23322
Old Coach Rd 23322
Old Dock Landing Rd 23321
Old Farm Ave 23320
Old Fields Arch 23320
Old Fox Trl 23321
Old Galberry Rd 23323
Old George Washington Hwy N 23323
Old Grandad Ln 23323
Old Greenbrier Rd
1900-2199 23320
2200-2599 23325
Old Gum Rd 23321
Old Jolliff Rd 23321
Old Manor Rd 23323
Old Mill Rd 23323
Old Oak Grove Rd 23320
Old Oaks Cir & Ter 23322
Old Pughsville Rd 23321
Old Spice Ct 23321
Old State Rd 23321
Old Taylor Rd 23321
Old Vintage Rd 23322
Old Virginia Rd 23323
Old Woodland Dr 23321
Old Woodmont Dr 23322
Olde Stone Way 23321
Oldwood St 23324
Oleander Ave 23325
Oliver Ave 23324
Olympic Ave 23322
Omar St 23324
Onawa Ln 23325
Oneford Pl 23321
Ontario Ave 23325
Opoho Cres & Ct 23321
Orangewood Rd 23323
Orchard Way 23320
Orchard Grove Dr 23320
Orchard Trail Rd 23322
Oregon Xing 23322
Orford Cir 23320
Oriole Dr 23321
Orkney Ct 23322
Ormer Rd 23325
Orville Ave 23324
Osborn Ave 23325
Osprey Ct 23322
Otterbourne Cir & Ct 23320
Otterbourne Quay 23320
Outlaw St 23320
Overbrook Ave 23323
Overshot Arch 23323
Owens Ter 23323
Oxbow Ct 23322
Oxford Rd 23324
Pacels Way 23322
Paddington Ct 23322
Page Ct 23323
Page St 23324
Palomino Ct 23322

Pamela Ct 23321
Pamlico Blvd 23322
Pampus Ln 23321
Pamunkey River Ct 23320
Pantigo Ln 23320
Paperbark Trl 23323
Paradisio Way 23322
Paramont Ave
2000-2298 23320
2300-2399 23325
Parapet Ct & Rd 23323
Park Ave 23324
S Park Ct 23320
Park Row 23324
Parker Rd 23322
Parkerson Ln 23323
Parkside Dr 23324
Parkview Dr 23320
Parkway Rd 23321
Parr Ln 23323
Parrish St 23324
Partridge Ave 23324
Patrick St 23324
Patrick Henry Dr 23323
Patriot Ln 23325
Pattie Ln 23321
Patton Pl 23320
Paul Eason Dr 23322
Paula Dr 23322
Pawnee St 23321
Paxson Ave 23324
Payne Rd 23323
Peaceful Rd 23322
Peach Rd 23321
Peachtree Dr 23322
Pearl St 23321
Peartree St 23324
Pebble Quay 23320
Pebble Rock Ct 23320
Pecan Forest Ct 23322
Pecan Point Ct 23320
Peek Trl 23321
Pelham St 23324
Pelican Cir 23322
Pendragon Ct 23323
Penhook Ct 23322
Penny Ln 23322
Penrose Ln 23320
Penryth Ct 23323
Penton Mews 23320
Penzance Cir 23320
Peoples Rd 23322
Pepper Cir 23322
Pepper Ridge Ct 23321
Pepper Tree Ln 23322
Peppercorn Dr & Way 23321
Pepperwood Dr 23320
Percheron Ct 23322
Perdue Ln 23325
Peren Ave 23322
Perry St 23324
Pershing Ct 23320
Persimmon St 23324
Personnel Support Det NW 23322
Pescado Ct 23322
Petre Rd 23325
Petunia Path 23325
Peyton Ln 23320
Pheasant Way 23321
Philadelphia St 23320
Phillips St 23324
Philmont Ave 23325
Phoenix Dr 23321
Phyllis Dr 23325
Picadilly Ct 23322
Piedmont Arch 23320
Pierce Ln 23321
Piers Lndg 23323
Pierside Lndg 23321
Pile Ave 23320
Pin Oak Pl 23322
Pine Bnd 23320
Pine Bark Dr 23322
Pine Bluff Ct 23320
Pine Forest Ln 23322

Pine Grove Cir 23321
Pine Grove Ln 23321
Pine Grove Lndg 23322
Pine Harbor Ct 23320
Pine Hill Cres 23321
Pine Island Quay 23322
Pine Level Ln 23322
Pine Valley Run 23320
Pine View Ct & Ln 23320
Pine Wood Ct 23320
Pinecliffe Ct & Dr 23322
Pinecroft Ln 23323
Pinedale Ln 23322
Pinehurst Dr 23323
Pineridge Ct & Dr 23321
Pines Of Warrick Dr 23322
Pinmaul Arch 23323
Pino Ct 23322
Pinta Dr 23321
Pintail Ln 23323
Pioneer Ln 23323
Piping Rock Dr 23322
Pitchback Ln 23323
Pitt Saw Ln 23323
Pittway Ct 23321
Placid Ct & Way 23320
Plainfield Ave 23320
Plane Tree Mews 23320
Plantation Dr 23323
Plantation Xing 23320
Plantation Lakes Cir 23320
Plantation Woods Way 23320
Pleasant Way 23322
Pleasant Ridge Ct & Dr 23322
Pleasure St 23324
Plover Ct 23321
Plow Ln 23324
Plum Ln 23321
Plumlee Dr 23323
Plummer Dr 23323
Pocahontas Ave 23324
Pocaty Rd 23322
Pocaty Creek Ln 23322
Pods Way 23320
Poindexter St 23324
Poinsettia Ln 23325
E Point Cres, Ct & Dr 23321
Point Elizabeth Ct & Dr 23321
Point Harbor Ct 23321
Point Reel Rd 23325
Pointers Trl 23321
Pompano Arch 23322
Ponce Ct 23322
Pond Ln
600-799 23325
2000-2099 23324
Pontiac St 23322
Pontonge Dr 23322
Poplar Ave 23323
Poplar Forest Ct 23322
Poplar Hill Ct & Rd 23321
Poplar Ridge Ct & Dr 23322
Poquoson Cir & Xing 23320
Port Rd 23321
Port Chambers Ct 23321
Portal Rd 23324
Porter St 23324
Portland St 23324
Portlock Rd 23324
Portobello Ct 23321
Ports Lndg 23323
Portsmouth Blvd 23321
Post Ave 23324
Potter Rd 23320
Powell Cir 23323
Powhatan Sq 23320
Pratt St 23324
Precon Dr 23320
Prentiss Dr 23322
Prescott Cir 23323
Preservation Loop 23320
Preservation Reach 23320
Preston Arch 23321
Prestwick Ct 23320

Price Ct 23320
Primrose Ln 23320
Prince Andrew Ct 23320
Prince Charles Dr 23322
Prince Edward Dr 23322
Prince George Ct 23320
Prince John Ct 23320
Prince Michael Ct 23320
Prince Of Wales Ct & Dr 23321
Prince Phillip Ct 23320
Princess Anne Cres & Ct 23321
Princeton Ave 23325
Principal Ct & Ln 23320
Prindle Ct 23321
Pringle Dr 23325
Printers Pl 23325
Priority Ln 23324
Priscilla Ln 23322
Professional Pl W 23320
Profit Way 23323
Progress Ct & Dr 23322
Progressive Dr 23320
Prospect Ct, Dr & Trce 23322
Prosperity Way 23320
Providence Rd
1-199 23324
200-4399 23325
4401-4599 23325
Prudden Trce 23323
Pryor Ct 23323
Pucknall Dr 23320
Pughsville Rd 23321
Pummis Ln 23320
Quail Ave 23324
Quail Creek Holw 23320
Quail Meadow Dr 23323
Quail Ridge Ct 23321
Quailshire Ct & Ln 23321
Quailshire Arch 23321
Quaker Pl 23325
Quarter Path Trl 23320
Queen St 23321
Queen City Rd 23325
Queens Ct 23320
Queens Grv 23322
Queens Gate 23320
Queensbury Dr 23322
Queenswood Ter 23322
Quinby Ct 23323
Quivers Keep 23321
Rabbit Run 23320
N Radcliffe Ln 23321
Radford Cir 23321
Raeside Ave 23321
Raewick Ct 23321
Railroad Ave 23324
Railway Ct 23320
Rainbow Ln & Run 23320
Raintree Ct & Rd 23321
Raleigh Ct & Rd 23321
Ramblewood Ct 23320
Rams Horn Ln S 23323
Ramsgate Ln 23322
Randy Ct 23322
Ransom Ct 23321
Rapidan River Ct 23320
Rathwell Ct N & S 23322
Raton Ct 23323
Raven Rd 23322
Ravenna Crse 23322
Ravenna Arch 23322
Ravenstone Ct & Dr 23322
Ravenwoods Dr 23322
Ray Ave 23320
Raytee Ct & Dr 23323
Reardon Ct 23322
Rebecca Dr 23322
Rebel Rd 23322
Red Bay Cir & Ln 23322
Red Cedar Ct 23320
Red Head Ct 23320
Red Maple Rd 23323
Red Oak Trl 23320
Red Rider Ln 23323
Redbrick Ct & Dr 23325
Redbud Cir 23325
Redcoat Chase 23323
Redding Ct 23322
Redfern Ln 23321
Redleafe Cir 23320
Redmere Ct 23322
Redstart Ave 23324
Redwing St 23322
Redwood Dr 23320
Reef Knot Ct 23321
Reefwood Rd 23323
Refuge Xing 23320
Regal Ct 23321
Regina Way 23321
Reid St 23324
Relay Rd 23322
Rellen Ct & St 23320
Remington Ct & Dr 23322
Renaissance Ct 23320
Renan Arch 23322
Republic Rd 23324
Research Dr 23320
Reservation Rd 23322
Resh Ct 23322
Resource Row 23320
Revella Arch 23322
Rex Cir 23321
Rhodes St 23324
Rhonda Cres 23321
Ricardo Ct 23322
Rice St 23324
Richmond Ave 23324
Richmond Cedar Wks Rd 23322
Richwood Ave 23322
Rick Fletcher Ct 23321
Ricka Ct 23322
Ricks Ct 23322
Riddick St 23321
Riddlehurst Ave 23320
Ridge Cir 23320
Ridgeboard Pl 23323
Ridgecrest Pl 23320
Ridgeline Pt 23321
Ridgeway Ave 23321
Ridgewood Ct & Rd 23325
Riley Dr 23322
Ring Rd 23320
Rio Dr 23322
Rio Mar Ct 23323
Ripley St 23323
Riston Ct 23322
Rivanna River Reach 23320
River Dr 23321
N River Dr 23323
S River Dr 23323
River Arch Ct & Dr 23320
River Birch Ct & Run 23320
River Breeze Cir 23321
River Creek Rd 23320
River Gate Ct & Rd 23322
River Oaks Dr 23321
River Pearl Way 23321
River Rock Reach 23321
River Strand 23320
River Walk Pkwy 23320
Rivercrest Pl & Way 23325
Rivers Edge Cv & Trce 23323
Riverstone Way 23325
Riverton Ct & Way 23322
Riverwood Cres 23322
Riviara Pl 23322
Rixtown Ct 23322
Roadside Ln 23325
Roanoke Ct 23322
Roanoke Arch 23322
Robert Ct & St 23322
Robert Frost Rd 23323
Robert Hall Blvd & Ct 23324
Robert Welch Ct & Ln 23320
Robertson Blvd 23324
Robin Ct 23322
Robinhood Rd 23322
Robinold Ct 23322
Roble Ct 23322
Rochelle Ct 23321
Rock Dr 23323
Rock Bridge Mews 23320
Rock Cliff Reach 23320
Rock Creek Ct & Dr 23325
Rockbridge Ct 23320
Rockglen Cir & Ct 23320
Rockland Ct & Ter 23322
Rockwood Dr 23323
Rocky Point Run 23320
Rodgers St 23324
Rokeby Ave
1500-1699 23325
1700-1900 23320
1902-2198 23320
3300-4099 23325
Rollesby Way 23320
Rollingswood Ct & Rd 23325
Rollis Rd 23321
Romaron St 23323
Romsey Cir 23320
Romulus Pl 23322
Ronlynn Rd 23322
Rosana Ct 23322
Rose Ash Way 23320
Rose Garden Ln 23320
Rose Leigh Dr 23322
Rose Wind Ct 23320
Rosebud Ln 23322
Rosehill Dr 23320
Rosemary Ln 23321
Rosemont Ave 23324
Rosewell Ave 23325
Rosewind Arch 23320
Rosewood Ter 23320
Rotan Ct 23325
Rotunda Ave
1401-1499 23323
4200-4299 23321
Roundtable Ct & Dr 23323
Roundtree Cir 23323
Rountree Ct & Dr 23322
Rowland Ave 23324
Rowlock Ct & Rd 23321
Roxbury Ct 23320
Royal Ct 23321
Royal Grant Dr 23322
Royal Grove Ct & Way 23320
Royal Oak Dr 23320
Royal Tern Ct 23321
E & W Royce Dr 23322
Ruby Ct 23320
Ruddy Ct 23320
Rue Marseille 23320
Rue Saint La Rogue 23320
Ruffin Way 23322
Rumford Ct 23322
Running Stone Way 23323
Ruritan Blvd 23324
Russell Ln 23320
Rutgers Ave 23324
Ruth St 23324
Rutherford Cir, Ct & Dr 23322
Rutledge Rd 23320
Ruxton Ct 23322
Rystrom Run 23320
Sabal Palm Ln 23322
Sabbath Ln 23320
Saber Dr 23322
Saddle Ct 23320
Saddleback Lndg 23320
Saddleback Trail Ct & Rd 23322
Saddlehorn Dr 23322
Sage Ct 23320
Sagebrook Run 23322
Sagen Arch 23323
Sail Ct 23321
Sail Fish Quay 23320
Saint Andrews Way 23320
Saint Andrews Reach 23320
Saint Brides Rd E & W 23322
Saint Clair Ct & Dr 23321
Saint James Pl 23320
Saint Julian Dr 23323
Saint Kitts Way 23322
Saint Lawrence Dr 23325
Saint Lukes Church Rd 23320
Saint Michaels Ct 23322
Salton Dr 23325
Saltwood Ct 23320
Samantha Ln 23322
Sams Cir & Dr 23320
San Juan Dr 23322
San Pedro Dr 23322
San Roman Ct & Dr 23322
San Salvador Dr 23321
Sand Bunker Arch 23320
Sand Drift Ct 23322
Sand Pebble Ct 23320
Sand Trap Ct 23320
Sand Wedge Ct 23320
Sand Willow Ct & Dr 23320
Sandcastle Ct & Way 23320
Sandchip Ter 23320
Sanderson Rd 23322
Sandhurst Ct 23323
Sandlewood Ln 23322
Sandown Crst 23323
Sandpiper Ln 23325
Sandy Rd 23322
Sandy Hill Way 23322
Sandy Pines Ct & Way 23321
Sandy Point Ln 23320
Sanjo Farms Dr 23320
Santa Maria Dr 23321
Santeetlah Ave 23325
Santiago Ct 23323
Sara Dr 23320
Sarasota Arch 23322
Sarvin Ct 23320
Sasparilla Ct 23320
Satinwood Ct 23322
Saul Ct & Dr 23320
Saunders Ln 23321
Savannah Dr 23322
Savory Cres 23320
Saw Mill Ct 23321
Sawblade Cir 23323
Sawgrass Ln 23321
Sawmark Ct 23323
Sawmill Arch 23323
Sawtooth Cir 23323
Sawyers Arch 23323
Sawyers Mill Xing 23323
Saxe Ct 23322
Saxon Ct 23323
Scaleboard Cir 23323
Scarborough Dr 23322
Scarlet Oak Ct N & S 23320
Scarlett Dr 23322
Scaup Ct 23320
Scenic Blvd 23322
Scenic Pkwy 23323
Schaefer Ave 23321
Schiemann Ct 23321
Scholastic Way 23323
School House Rd 23322
Schooner Trl 23321
Scone Castle Loop 23322
Scoonie Pointe Dr 23322
Scotchwood Ct 23320
Scoter Ct 23320
Scotfield Dr 23321
Scotia Dr 23325
Scotland Ln 23320
Scotsman Run 23321
Scott Ave 23320
Scotties Ln 23324
Screech Ct 23321
Sea Cliff Rd 23321
Sea Palling Ln 23323
Sea Pines Run 23320
Seaboard Ave 23324
Seaborn Way 23322
Seabreeze Ct 23320
Seabrooke Ln & Pt 23322
Seaforth Rd 23321
Seagrass Reach 23320
Seagull Ct 23322
Seahorse Run 23320
Sean Dr 23323
Seastone Trce 23321
Seaton Cir 23320
Sebriell Way 23323
Secretariat Way 23322
Seddon Ct 23322
Sedgefield Ct 23322
Sedgewood Ct 23320
Seldon Rd 23321
Seldorn Pl 23320
Sendero Ct 23322
Seneca Ave 23325
Sentinel Dr 23320
Sentry Dr 23323
Septaria Quay 23321
September Ln 23322
Sequoia Pl 23320
Serf Ct 23323
Sero Ct 23325
Settlement Ct 23321
Seven Eleven Rd 23322
Seville Dr 23322
Sextant St 23321
Shadow Brooke Dr 23320
Shadowberry Crst 23320
Shadowfield Ct 23322
Shadowlake Ct & Dr 23320
Shadowood Ln 23322
Shadwell Ter 23322
Shady Ln 23324
Shady Cove Ct 23320
Shady Tree Way 23323
Shadyside Ln 23321
Shamrock Garden Rd 23323
Shannon St 23324
Sharon Dr 23320
Shawnee Rd 23325
Shea Dr 23322
Shearwater Ct 23320
Sheffield Ct 23322
Shelia Cres 23321
Shell Rd 23323
Shell Drake Ct 23320
Shelley St 23320
Shelter Rock Ln 23322
Shelview Cir 23323
Shenandoah Pkwy 23320
Shenandoah River Dr & Rd 23320
Shepherds Ct 23320
Shepherds Gate 23320
Sherando Ct 23320
Sherborn Trce 23322
Sherbrooke Rd 23323
Sheriff Ct 23322
Sherman Dr 23320
Sherrard Ct 23322
Sherringfield Ter 23322
Sherrington Dr 23320
Sherwood Dr 23322
Sherwood Forest Rd 23322
Shetland Dr 23322
Shield Ln 23325
Shifford Ln 23322
Shillelagh Rd 23323
Ships Lndg & Xing 23323
Shipton Ct 23320
Shipyard Rd 23323
Shire Ln 23325
Shoal Creek Trl 23320
Shoal Quay 23320
Shoemaker Dr 23325
Shore Rd 23323
Shore Side Rd 23320
Shorebird Ct & Ln 23323
Shorewood Dr 23321
Short Spoon Ct 23320
Shortleaf Ln 23320
Shotgun Rd 23322
Shoveller Ct 23320
Sidley Ct & Rd 23321
Sierra Dr 23322
Sign Pine Rd 23322
Signal Quay 23320
Silk Tree Ln 23320
Silver Leaf Dr 23324
Silver Maple Dr 23322
Silver Rail Ln 23323
Silverthorne Ct 23321
Silvertown Ave 23322
Silverwood Blvd 23321
Simms Arch 23322
Simon Dr 23320
Sinclair Ln 23322
Sippel Dr 23320
Sir Francis Drake Dr 23321
Sir Galahad Dr 23323
Sir Gawaine Dr 23323
Sir Kay Ct & Dr 23323
Sir Knight Ct 23322
Sir Lance Dr 23325
Sir Lancelot Ct & Dr 23323
Sir Meliot Ct & Dr 23323
Sir Raleigh Dr 23322
Sir Thomas Ct & Dr 23321
Sir Tristram Ct 23323
Sir Walter Cres & Ct 23321
Sitka Spruce Rd 23320
Sivills Lndg 23322
Sivills Farm Dr 23322
Skipjack Ln 23323
Skylark Ct 23321
Skyline Cir 23320
Slate St 23322
Sloop Trl 23321
Sluice Ct 23323
Smith Ave
2100-2199 23320
2201-2299 23320
2300-2499 23325
Smith Douglas Rd 23320
Smithson Dr 23322
Smokestack Ln 23323
Smokey Mountain Ct & Trl 23320
Snow Goose Dr 23320
Snowberry Ln 23320
Snowden St 23321
Sol Thorpe Ln 23325
Solomon St 23320
Somerton Ln 23322
Sommerton Way 23320
Sommerville Cres 23320
Sondej Ave 23321
Sorrento Dr 23321
Sound Ct 23322
South Rd 23321
Southall Ct E & W 23323
Southampton Ct 23320
Southern Oak Dr 23322
Southern Pines Dr 23323
Southfield Dr 23322
Southport Ave 23324
Southway St 23323
Southwind Dr 23320
Southwood Ct & Dr 23322
Spadina Ave 23324
Spanish Moss Dr 23320
Spar Ct & St 23321
Sparks Trce 23322
Sparrow Ct 23325
Sparrow Ln 23325
Sparrow Rd
100-1699 23325
1700-2299 23320
E Sparrow Rd 23325
Speedy Ave 23320
Speight Lyons Loop 23322
Spencer Ln 23323
Spice Bush Ct 23320
Spice Quay 23320
Spincaster Ln 23321
Spinnaker Ct 23320
Spinners Way 23323
Spoonbill Ct 23320
Spring Rd 23321
Spring Maple Ct 23320
Spring Meadow Cres 23321
Springbrook Ln 23320
Springdale Rd 23323
Springer Ln 23320
Springfield Ave 23325
Springwood Ct 23321
Spruce Ln 23320
Spruce Forest Ct 23322
Spurlane Cir 23322
Spurlock Ct & Way 23322
Squire Ct 23323
Squirrel Run 23321
Stadium Dr 23322
Stafford Dr 23321
Staffordshire Ct 23322
Staley Crest Way 23323
Stalham Rd
100-398 23325
400-799 23325
2000-2999 23324
Stanhope Gdns 23320
Stanhope Close 23320
Stanley Dr 23323
Stanmore Ct 23322
Star Ct 23322
Starboard Rd 23321
Stardale Cir & Dr 23322
Starina Ct 23320
Starling St 23322
Starmount Pkwy 23321
State St 23323
Station Rd 23322
Station House Rd 23321
Station Square Ct & Ln 23320
Steed Ct 23323
Steel St 23323
Steeleman Ln 23320
Steeton Ct 23321
Stefanie Ct 23323
Stephanie Way 23320
Stephanie Boyd Dr 23321
Steppingstone Sq 23320
Sterling Ct 23322
Stewart St 23324
Still Harbor Cir 23320
Stillmeadows Ct 23320
Stillwater Dr 23320
Stillwood St 23320
Stilton Arch 23320
Stilworken Dr 23321
Stockleybridge Dr 23322
Stone Moss Reach 23320
Stonebridge Ct & Lndg 23321
Stonegate Pkwy & Way 23322
Stonehurst St 23324
Stoneleigh Ct & Rd 23322
Stones Throw Ct 23320
Stonewood Ct 23320
Stoney Brook Lndg 23320
Stoney Creek Arch 23320
Stout Ct 23323
Stowaway Ct 23321
Stowe St 23324
Stratford Ct & Dr 23321
Strathmore Ln 23322
Strawberry Ln 23324
Strawman Ct 23323
Strayhan Way 23322
Stream Arch 23322
Streamside Ct 23322
Stubbs Ct & Dr 23323
Stuben St 23324
Sue Cres 23321
Suffolk Ave 23324
Sugar Run 23321
Sugar Maple Ln 23322
Sugar Tree Ct 23320
Sullivan Ln 23322
Summerall Ln 23322
Summerest Dr 23321
Summerfield Cres 23322

Summerset Ct 23320
Summit Ridge Dr 23322
Sun Ave 23325
Sun Jack Ct 23321
Sun Valley Cres 23321
Sundance Arch 23322
Sunderland Ct & Ter 23322
Sundon Ct 23322
Sunkist Rd 23321
Sunlight Dr 23322
Sunnybrook Ter 23321
Sunnyside Arch 23320
Sunray Ave 23321
Sunrise Ave & Ct 23324
Sunset Dr 23323
Sunset Maple Ct & Ln 23323
Sunsprite Loop 23323
Supplejack Ct 23320
Surf Ave 23325
Surrey Rd 23321
Susan Dr 23320
Sussex Ct 23320
Sutherland Ct & Dr 23320
Sutherland Arch 23320
Sutherlyn Ct 23322
Suzette Ln 23322
Swain Ave 23324
Swan Lake Cres 23321
Sweet Autumn Arch 23320
Sweet Gum Ct 23322
Sweet Leaf Pl 23320
Sweetbay Ct & Dr 23322
Swindell St 23324
Swinson Lndg 23323
Sword Dr 23323
Sybilla St 23323
Sycamore Ln 23322
Sydenham Blvd 23322
Sydney Ct 23320
Sylvia Ct 23322
Taft Rd 23322
Tafton Way 23322
Talbert Ave 23323
Tall Oak Ct 23320
Tallahassee Dr 23322
Tallwood Cir 23320
Tamer Ave 23325
Tampa Dr 23323
Tanager Xing 23321
Tangerine Trl 23325
Tanglewood Trl 23325
Tannahill Ct 23322
Tanners Green Ct 23320
Tapestry Park Dr & Loop 23320
Tapgallant Quay 23321
Tapscott Ave 23324
Tara Cir 23322
Taralynn Ln 23320
Tarkington Ct N & S 23322
Tarneywood Ct & Dr 23320
Tartan Arch 23321
Tasley Cir 23323
Tasman Ct 23321
Tatemstown Rd 23325
Tattenhall Ln 23323
Tattinger Trl 23321
Taughtline Loop 23321
Tawnyberry Ln 23325
Taxus St 23320
Taylor Ct & Rd 23321
Taylor Acres Ct 23321
Taylor Point Dr 23321
Taylorwood Blvd & Ct 23321
Teakwood Ct 23322
Teal Ct 23320
Tealwood Ln 23320
Technology Dr 23320
Tejo Ln 23321
Tekoa Rd 23325
Telfon Cir 23320
Telfyan Dr 23320
Temple St 23323
Tennessee Dr 23323
Tennis Dr 23320
Tennyson St 23320
Teresa Dr 23322
Tern Ct 23321
Terry Dr 23321
Terwillinger Rd 23323
Tether Wood Ct 23321
Teton Ct 23320
Texas St 23323
Thaddeus Ct 23322
Thames Cir 23320
Thatcher Way 23320
Theodora Ct 23322
Thistle Ct 23322
Thistlewood Ct & Ln 23320
Thistley Ln 23322
Thomas Ln 23321
Thomas St 23323
Thomason Trl 23320
Thorn Rose Ct 23322
Thorngate Ct 23320
Thornloe Ln 23320
Thornton Cir 23322
Thornwood Ln 23320
Thoroughbred Ln 23320
Thrasher Rd 23320
Three Oaks Dr 23320
Thrower St 23323
Thrush Ct 23322
Thyme Trl 23320
Tidal Island Way 23320
Tidewater Chemical Rd 23322
Tiffany Green Ct 23320
Tiger Dr 23320
Tigertail Dr 23320
Tiki Way 23322
Tilden Ave 23320
Tiller Ln 23321
Tillman Arch 23322
Timber Ln 23324
Timber Neck Mall 23320
Timber Neck Close 23320
Timber Quay 23320
Timber Ridge Ct & Rd 23322
Timberlake Ct 23320
Timberline Ct 23322
Timmons Ct 23322
Tintern Ct & St 23320
Tisbury Dr 23322
Tiswood Ct 23323
Titchfield Dr 23320
Tiverton Pl 23320
Toll Plaza Rd 23322
Topsail Lndg 23321
Torre Pine Ct 23322
Tournament Dr 23323
Towanda Ct & Rd 23325
Towering Oak Ct 23320
Towhee Ln 23323
Towne Point Rd 23321
Townhouse Ln 23323
Traciene Dr 23322
Track Xing 23320
Tracker Ln 23321
Trade St 23323
Trade Wind Pl 23323
Trademark Crst 23322
Trafalgar Ct 23322
Trail Bend Dr 23321
Trailwood Ct 23321
Trajan Reach 23322
Tranquility Trce 23320
Transylvania Ave 23324
Trappers Run 23321
Trapshoot Ct 23321
Travelers Way 23321
Travis Ct 23322
Treasure Way 23322
Tree Duck Ct 23320
Tree Fern Dr 23322
Treeland Ter 23322
Treemont Ct 23323
Treetop Ln 23320
Trellis Trl 23320
Trent Ave 23323
Trescott Way 23323
Trestle Way 23324
Trevor Ct 23322
Trey Ln 23322
Trilby Ct 23325
Triple Crown Cir 23320
Triton Trce 23323
Trolley Xing 23320
Trotman Way 23320
Trotters Ln 23322
Troy Ln 23323
Truitt Rd 23321
Trumpet Ct 23323
Trumpet Rd 23321
Truxton St 23324
Tuck St 23322
Tuckaway Reach 23320
Tudor Pl 23325
Tulip Dr 23322
Tundrah Ct 23323
Tunnel Ct 23320
Tupelo Xing 23320
Turin Ct 23321
Turnberry Ct 23320
Turnbuckle Ct 23322
Turning Leaf Ln 23320
Turtle Rock Trce 23320
Tuskegee Ave 23320
Tuttle St 23323
Twelve Oaks Ct 23322
Twilight Arch 23323
Twin Cedar Trl 23323
Twin Oaks Ct 23320
Twin Peak Ct 23320
Two Gates Cir 23322
Tybourne Ct 23322
Tyler Way 23322
Tyre Neck Rd 23321
Uffington Ct 23321
Undershot Ct 23323
Unicorn Trl 23322
Union Forge Ln 23322
Unser Ct & Dr 23322
Upperville Ct 23321
Upton Cir 23320
Urquhart St 23324
Us Navy Radio Sta 23322
Vail Ct 23320
Valencia Rd 23321
Valera Ct 23322
Valley Point Cres 23321
Valley Stream Rd 23325
Valleyjo Pl 23321
Valmire Dr 23320
Valor Ct 23322
Van Buren Ct 23322
Van Luik Ct 23325
Vance Cir & Ln 23320
Vanderploeg Dr 23320
Vanette Dr 23322
Varsity Ct & Dr 23324
Vaughn St 23320
Veery St 23323
Vellen St 23320
Vellines Ave 23324
Velva Dr 23325
Venetian Way 23320
Ventosa Dr 23322
Ventures Way 23320
Vepco St 23323
Veranda Way 23320
Vernon Ct 23324
Vernon Mills Ct 23323
Vero St 23323
Vespasian Cir 23322
Vicker Ave 23324
Vicksdell Cres 23322
Vico Dr 23321
Victoria Dr 23322
Victory Blvd 23323
Vikingfield Ter 23322
Villa Ct & Dr 23322
Village Ave 23323
Villanova Ave 23324
Vincek Way 23323
Vincent St 23324
Vineyard Ct & Dr 23322
Vinsa Ct 23320
Vinton Cir 23323
Virginia Ave 23324
Volunteer Trl 23322
Volvo Pkwy 23320
Volvo Penta Dr 23320
Voyager Ct 23321
Waddell Woods Dr 23322
Wade St 23324
Wadena Rd 23320
Wake Ave 23324
Wakedale Arch 23322
Walbury Ct 23322
Walden St 23324
Walkers Bend Dr 23321
Wallace Ln 23323
Wallboard Dr 23323
Walnut Ave 23325
Walnut Forest Ct 23322
Walnut Neck Ave & Cir 23320
Waltham Way 23320
Walton Rd 23322
Wampler Pl 23321
Wanchese Ct 23322
Warbler Ct 23322
Warfield St 23324
Warhawks Rd 23322
Warren Ave 23322
Warrick Rd 23322
Warrington Blvd & Sq 23320
Warwick Cir 23320
Washington Dr 23322
Watch Island Reach 23320
Water Birch Ct 23323
Water Elm Ct 23320
Water Hickory Ct S 23320
Water Oak Ct 23322
Watercrest Pl 23324
Waterfall Way 23322
Waterfern Cv 23321
Waterfield Ave 23320
Waterford Ct & Dr 23322
Waterfront Dr 23322
Waterlawn Ave 23323
Watermill Grv 23321
Waters Rd 23322
Waterside Dr N & S 23320
Waterstock Ct 23322
Waterstone Ct 23320
Waterstone Cv 23321
Waterstone Way 23321
Watertown Way 23320
Waterview Cir 23322
Waterway Cir & Ct 23322
Waterwheel Rd 23322
Watson Rd 23320
Watson Way 23321
Watsons Glen Ct & Rd 23322
Waverton Ct & Pkwy 23324
Waxwing Ct 23321
W Way Ct 23321
Waycroft Reach 23320
Waylen Loop 23320
Wayne Ave 23320
Weatherby Ct 23322
Weaver Ln 23320
Weaver St 23324
Weber Ave
1600-1699 23325
1700-2299 23320
Webster Ave 23325
Wecht Ct 23320
Wedgewood Cir & Dr 23321
Weeping Cedar Ct & Trl 23323
Weeping Willow Dr 23322
Weiss Ln 23323
Welch Ln 23320
Welcome Rd 23324
Welles Ct 23320
Wellington Ave 23324
Wendover Ct 23323
Wenger Rd 23322
Wentworth Dr 23322
Wesley Rd 23323
Wessex Dr 23322
West Rd
800-2299 23323
2300-2599 23322
Westborough Dr 23321
Westbrook Ln 23320
Westcove Ln 23320
Westerly Ct 23322
Western Branch Blvd 23321
Westfield Ct 23322
Westgate Ct & St 23324
Westmoreland Ct 23320
Weston Arch 23325
Westonia Rd 23323
Westwood Ave 23324
Wexford Ct 23322
Wharfs Lndg 23323
Wheatfield Way 23320
Wheeling Ave 23325
Whimbrel Ave 23322
Whippoorwill Trce 23322
Whisper Walk 23322
Whisper Hollow Dr 23322
Whispering Oak Cir 23320
Whistle Town Ct & Rd 23322
Whitburn Ter 23322
White Cap Cres & Crst 23321
White Cedar Dr 23323
White Dogwood Dr 23322
White Egret Cv 23322
White Head Ct 23320
White Heron Run 23325
White Manor Ln 23321
White Oak Ct N & S 23320
White Owl Cres 23321
White Pine Dr 23323
White Rock Bnd 23320
White Swallow Way 23321
White Tail Ct 23323
Whitebark Rd 23320
Whitechapel Arch 23321
Whitehall Ct 23322
Whitehaven Cres & Ct 23325
Whitehurst Lndg 23320
Whitehurst Rd 23322
Whites Lndg 23321
Whitestone Ave 23323
Whitlock Ct 23324
Whitney Ct 23322
Whittamore Rd 23322
Wickford Ct & Dr 23320
Wickwood Ct & Dr 23322
Widgeon Ct 23320
Wilbur Ave 23324
Wilcox St 23324
Wild Cherry Ct 23322
Wild Duck Cir & Xing 23321
Wild Horse Rdg 23322
Wilderness Rd 23322
Wildlife Trce 23320
Wildwood Rd 23323
Wilkins Ln 23324
Will Scarlet Way 23322
Willard Dr 23322
William Crst 23323
William Clarke Ct 23324
William Hall Way 23322
Williams Ave 23323
Williamsburg Dr & Sq 23322
Williamson St 23324
Willis St 23323
Willow Ave 23325
Willow Arch 23323
Willow Bend Ct & Dr 23323
Willow Bridge Ct 23320
Willow Brook Ct, Rd & Way 23320
Willow Creek Ct 23321
Willow Green Ct 23320
Willow Lake Rd 23321
Willow Oak Dr 23322
Willow Point Arch 23320
Willow Spire Arch 23320
Willows Arch 23323
Willowstone Ct 23320
Willowstone Arch 23320
Willowwood Ct & Dr 23323
Wilrose Trce 23322
Wilson Dr 23322
Wilson Rd 23324
Wilson Spruce Ct 23323
Wilton St 23324
Wimbledon Sq 23320
Wimbledon Chase 23320
Wimbley Ln 23322
Winchester Way 23320
Windlesham Dr 23322
Windmill Pt 23322
Windom Blvd 23320
Windsong Ct 23321
Windsor Pt 23320
Windsor Rd 23322
Windswept Cir 23320
Windward Dr & Pl 23320
Windy Rd
700-799 23325
2000-2099 23324
Windy Oak Run 23320
Windy Pine Ln 23320
Winery Dr 23321
Winfall Dr 23322
Winged Foot Ct 23320
Wingfield Ave
100-1699 23325
1700-2999 23324
Winnie Dr 23321
Winscott Ct 23322
Winslow Ave 23323
Winston Ter 23323
Winter Jasmine Ct 23323
Winter King Ct 23323
Winter Stone Ct 23320
Winter Wren Ln 23322
Winterberry Ct 23322
Wintercress Way 23320
Wintergreen Dr 23323
Winterhawk Ct 23323
Winterside Loop 23320
Winterwater Ct 23320
Winterwood Ct 23320
Winwood Dr 23323
Wise St 23321
Wisecamp Ct 23323
Wisteria Ct 23321
Witt Ct 23320
Wittington Dr 23322
Wood Ave 23325
Wood Bird Ct 23323
Wood Duck Ct & Ln 23323
Wood Stork Dr 23321
Woodards Ford Rd 23322
Woodbaugh Dr 23321
Woodberry Dr 23322
Woodbriar Ln 23323
Woodbridge Ct & Dr 23322
Woodcliff Arch 23320
Woodcott Dr 23322
Woodcroft Ln 23321
Wooddale Ct 23323
Woodford Dr 23322
Woodgate Arch 23320
Woodglen Dr 23322
Woodgrove St 23320
Woodhurst Ln 23322
Woodlake Cir & Dr 23320
Woodland Dr 23321
Woodland Terrace Dr 23323
Woodmark Trl 23321
Woodmill St 23320
Woodmont Dr 23322
Woodmoor Ct 23321
Woodrow Ct 23322
Woods Way 23323
Woods Edge Ct 23323
Woodshire Cir & Ct 23323
Woodside Ct N & S 23320
Woodsmans Ct 23320
Woodsmans Reach 23320
Woodsmere Rd 23322
Woodspring Arch 23320
Woodstock Ct 23320
Woodstream Ct & Way 23322
Woodview Lair 23322
Woodwind Way 23320
Woodworkers Ct 23322
Woody Ridge Ct 23322
Wooten Ln 23323
Wormington Dr 23322
Wortham Ct E & W 23323
Worthing Ln 23321
Wren St 23322
Wright Ave 23324
Wyant Ct 23321
Wye Oak Way 23323
Wyfold Ct 23320
Wymers Ct 23322
Wynngate Ct & Dr 23320
Yacht Dr 23320
Yadkin Rd 23323
Yager Ct 23324
Yakima Rd 23325
Yale Ct 23324
Yancy Ct 23322
Yateley Ct 23322
Yates Cir 23323
Yeadon Rd 23324
Yellow Pine Cres 23321
York Dr 23320
York St 23321
Yorkshire Ct, Dr & Trl 23322
Youngman Rd 23323
Youngstown Ct 23322
Yucca St 23324
Yupo Ct 23320
Zari Run 23322

NUMBERED STREETS

All Street Addresses 23324

CHESTER VA

General Delivery 23831

POST OFFICE BOXES MAIN OFFICE STATIONS AND BRANCHES

Box No.s
All PO Boxes 23831

NAMED STREETS

Abbeydale Ct & Dr 23831
Advantage Storage Dr 23831
Alberta Ct 23836
Alderwood Ct, Loop, Ter & Way 23831
Alderwood Turn 23831
Algroup Way 23836
Alliance Cir 23831
Allied Rd 23836
Anchor Landing Ct, Dr & Pl 23836
Angarde Dr 23831
Anglewood Ct & Dr 23831
Appleford Ct & Dr 23831
Appomattox St 23836
Arbor Banks Ct & Ter 23831
Arbor Croft Way 23831
Arbor Green Ct & Dr 23831
Arbor Highlands Ter 23831
Arbor Lake Dr 23831
Arbor Landing Ct & Dr 23831
Arbor Meadows Dr & Ter 23831
Arbor Park Dr 23831
Arbor Point Ter 23831
Arbor Ridge Dr & Ter 23831
Arbor View Ter 23831
Arcadia Ave & Ct 23831
Ashley Forest Dr 23831

Ashley Landing Ct 23831
Ashley Oak Ter 23831
Ashton Creek Rd 23831
Ashton Dell Rd 23831
Aspen Ave 23831
Astwood Cove Dr 23836
Austin Ct & Rd 23836
Autumn Landing Ct 23831
Back Stretch Ct 23836
Baldwin Rd 23831
Baltustrol Ave 23831
Banbury Rd 23831
Baptist Dr 23836
Barberry Ct & Ln 23836
Barkwood Ct 23831
Basilia Ct 23836
Battery Dantzler Ct & Rd 23836
Battista Ct 23836
Bay Hill Dr 23836
Beachmere Ct, Dr & Ter 23831
Beau Springs Dr 23831
Beckinham Dr 23831
Beginners Trail Loop 23836
Bel Arbor Dr 23831
Bel Jour Pl 23831
Bel Lac Dr 23831
Belspring Ct & Rd 23831
Belvoir Rd 23831
Ben Fry Dr 23831
Benhill Dr 23831
Bent Tree Pl 23831
Bermuda Ave & Ct 23836
Bermuda Crossroad Ln 23831
Bermuda Hundred Rd 23836
Bermuda Orchard Ln 23836
Bermuda Place Dr 23836
Bermuda Point Ct 23836
Bermuda Triangle Rd 23836
Berrystone Rd 23831
Bethesda Ct & Dr 23831
Birchleaf Ct & Rd 23831
Birdie Ln 23831
Birds Eye Pl & Ter 23831
Black Gum Ter 23831
Blithe Dr 23831
Blossom Point Rd 23831
Blossom Pointe Rd 23836
Blue Rock Dr 23836
Bluemont Rd 23831
Bluewater Dr & Ter 23836
Bolling Ave 23836
Bonjour Ln 23836
E & W Booker Blvd 23831
Boyd Rd 23831
Bradley Bridge Rd 23831
Branders Bridge Rd 23831
Branders Creek Rd 23831
Branner Pl & Way 23836
Brentwood Arbor Ct 23831
Bridgetown Cir & Ct 23831
Briggs Rd 23831
Broadwater Cir, Ct, Ln, Rd & Way 23831
Brook Ln 23831
Brooks Point Ter 23831
Bruce Rd 23831
Buccaneer Dr 23836
Buckhurst St 23831
Buckingham Ct & St 23831
Buckland Pl & Rd 23831
Buena Vista Blvd 23831
Burgess Rd 23836
Burkwood Ct 23831
Burley Ridge Ln & Ter 23831
Burnettedale Ct & Dr 23831
Buxton Ct & Dr 23831
Cadbury Ct 23831
Calvingate Ter 23831
Cameron Ave 23836
Canterbury Rd 23831
Captain Dr 23836
Cara Hill Ct & Ln 23831
Carmel Dr 23831
Caronado Dr 23831
Carty Bay Dr 23836
Carver Heights Dr 23831
Castlebury Dr 23831
Castlewellan Ct, Dr & Ter 23836
Cedar Ln 23831
Cedar Cliff Ct, Rd & Ter 23831
Cedar Landing Ter 23831
Celanco Ct 23831
Celebration Ave 23831
Central Ave 23836
Centralia Rd 23831
Centre St 23831
E Chagford Dr & Ter 23831
S Chalkley Rd 23831
Champion Ct 23831
Channel View Dr & Ter 23836
Chaplin Bay Dr 23836
Charlotte Ct 23836
Cherry St 23831
S Chester Rd 23831
Chester Garden Cir, Loop & Trl 23831
Chester Grove Ct & Dr 23831
Chester Square Rd 23831
Chester Station Dr 23831
Chester Village Cir, Dr & Ln 23831
Chestertowne Rd 23831
Chestnut Hill Rd 23836
China Cat Ter 23831
Chip Ct 23831
Chippoke Ct, Pl & Rd 23831
Chipstead Ct, Pl & Rd 23831
Chrisfield Dr 23831
Churchill Ct 23831
Cicero Pkwy 23831
Circleview Ct & Dr 23831
Claimont Mill Dr 23831
Clarence Cove Dr 23836
Claybon Ln & Ter 23831
Cliff Lawn Dr 23831
Cliffside Dr 23836
Clipper Bay Dr 23831
Club Crest Blvd 23836
Club Ridge Ct, Dr & Ter 23836
Coastline Cir 23831
Cobble Glen Ct 23831
Cobbs Ave 23836
Cobbs Point Dr, Ln & Way 23836
Colby Cove Ct 23831
Cole St 23836
Cool Spring Dr 23831
Cooperton Cir 23836
Cornwall Ln 23836
Corvus Ct 23836
Cougar Trl 23831
Courtland Dr 23831
Courtyard Rd 23831
Cove Dr 23836
Coxendale Rd
500-1298 23836
1300-1799 23831
1801-1999 23836
2001-2097 23831
2099-2499 23831
Coyote Dr 23836
Creek Way 23831
N & S Cresthill Ct & Rd 23831
Crestway Dr 23831
Crofton Cir, Ct & Rd 23831
Crossgate Rd 23831
Crystal Downs Ct & Ln 23836
Currier Ct 23831
Curtis Cir & St 23831
Dale Ln 23831
Dalhart Ct 23831
Dampier Ct & Dr 23831
Daniels St 23831
Dawson Dr 23836
Declaration Ave 23836
Deford Ct 23831
Delamere Dr 23831
Delavial St 23831
Dell Hill Ct 23831
Demaret Dr 23836
Derbycreek Ln 23836
Dewberry Ln 23831
Discovery Dr & Rd 23836
Dockside Ct & Dr 23831
Dodomeade St 23831
W Dogwood Ave 23831
Dogwood Ridge Ct 23831
Donnaford Dr 23831
Dottie Dr 23831
Drayton Rd 23831
Drayton Landing Ct & Dr 23831
Driscoll Rd 23831
Drumvale Dr 23831
Dudley Dr 23831
Dunkirk Dr 23831
Dunlop Crescent Dr 23836
Duxton Ct & Dr 23831
Dylans Walk Rd 23831
Eagle Point Rd 23831
Eagle Rock Ave & Ct 23831
Easy St 23831
Eatonberg Ln 23836
Ecoff Ave 23831
Edenshire Rd 23831
Edenton Pl 23831
Edgewood Dr 23831
Elfinwood Rd 23831
Elkington Ct & Dr 23836
Ellenbrook Dr & Pl 23831
Elm St 23831
Elmwood Ln 23831
Elokomin Ave 23831
Empire Pkwy 23831
English Wells Way 23831
Enon Ave 23836
N Enon Church Rd 23836
Enon Oaks Ln 23836
Erin Rd 23831
Erin Green Ct 23831
Erlene Ct & Dr 23831
N & S Esther Ct & Ln 23836
Ethens Castle Dr 23831
Ethens Mill Rd 23831
Ethens Point Ct & Ln 23831
Euphoria Rd 23831
Evelyn Dr 23831
Evergreen Arbor Pl 23831
Eves Ln 23831
Executive Dr 23831
Exhall Ct & Dr 23831
Exton Ln 23831
Fairway Woods Ct & Dr 23836
Fall Harvest Dr 23831
Fantail Ct 23831
Faraday Ct, Dr, Pl & Ter 23831
Farm Field Ct & Dr 23831
Farmstead Way 23836
Feddo Ct 23831
Festival Park Plz 23831
Fieldwood Rd 23831
Finney Ct & Pl 23831
Florence Ave 23836
Forest Glenn Cir 23836
Forest Lake Rd 23831
Forrestal Rd 23831
Fortview Dr 23831
Fox Chappel Rd 23831
Foxwood Rd 23831
Fulcher Ln 23831
Furlong Ter 23831
Gadwell Landing Ct 23831
Gala Ct 23831
Galsworthy Dr 23831
Gamblers Cove Ln 23836
Ganesh Ln 23836
Garden Springs Ln 23831
Gary Ave 23831
Gayle Rd 23831
George Ct 23831
Gill St 23831
Gimbel Dr 23836
Gladehill Rd 23831
Glen Oaks Ct & Dr 23831
Glendale St 23831
Glenmorgan Ct & Dr 23831
Gloria Ct 23831
Golden Garden Cir & Pkwy 23836
Golf Course Rd 23836
Goyne Loop & Ter 23831
Grand Oaks Forest Cir & Ct 23831
Grantshire Rd 23831
Gravel Neck Dr 23831
Great Branch Dr 23831
Great Coastal Dr 23836
Green Apple Pl 23836
Green Garden Cir, Ct, Pl, Ter & Way 23836
Green Orchard Ct & Dr 23836
Green Spire Cir, Ct & Dr 23836
Green Vista Ct & Dr 23836
Greenbriar Ct & Dr 23831
Greenham Ct & Dr 23831
Greenside Ct, Dr & Ter 23836
Greenyard Rd & Way 23831
Greyfield Dr & Pl 23831
Greyledge Blvd, Ct, Mews, Pl & Ter 23836
Greyledge Turn 23836
Greymont Ln 23836
Greyshire Dr 23836
Greywater Ct & Dr 23831
W Grove Ave & Pl 23831
Grover Ct 23836
S Hackberry Rd 23836
Hamilton Dr 23831
Hamlin Cir, Ct, Dr, Pl, Ter & Way 23831
Hamlin Creek Ct, Pkwy & Pl 23831
Hanbury Dr 23831
Hanover St 23836
Happy Hill Rd 23831
W Harbour Dr 23836
Harmeadow Ln 23831
Harrow Dr 23831
Harrowgate Rd 23831
Heather Landing Pl 23831
Heather Stone Dr 23836
Heathstead Ct & Rd 23831
Hemlock Rd 23831
Hemway Rd 23831
Henrico St 23836
Henricus Park Rd 23836
Henry Ln 23836
Heritage Dr 23831
Hickory Glen Rd 23831
Hickory Landing Pl 23831
Hidden Arbor Pl 23831
Hidden Valley Rd 23831
Hiddenwell Ct & Ln 23831
Highpaige Way 23831
Hill Spring Dr & Ter 23831
Hiller Dr 23831
Hillside Rd 23831
Hilltop Farms Dr & Ter 23831
Hilltop Field Dr 23831
Hogans Aly, Ct, Dr & Pl 23836
Hollingsford Dr 23836
Hollis Rd 23831
Holly Rd 23831
Holly Arbor Ct & Dr 23831
Holly Hill Ct & Rd 23831
Hopkins Rd 23831
Horseshoe Bend Dr 23831
Hp Way 23836
Hubert Ln 23836
E Hundred Rd 23836
W Hundred Rd
1-2100 23836
2102-2198 23836
2201-2297 23831
2299-5599 23831
Hyde Park Dr 23831
Ida Ave 23831
Inge Rd 23836
Inverness Dr, Pl & Way 23836
Iron Bridge Plz & Rd 23831
Iron Creek Rd 23831
Ironbridge Pkwy 23831
Irvenway Ln 23836
Ivy Ln 23831
Ivyridge Ct, Dr & Ter 23831
Ivyridge Turn 23831
Ivytree Ter 23831
Ivywood Ct & Rd 23831
Janeburn Dr 23831
Jefferson Ave 23836
Jefferson Davis Hwy 23831
Johnson Creek Dr 23836
Jolly Ln & Pl 23831
Karlyn Ct 23836
Karma Rd 23831
Kaybridge Rd 23831
Keel Dr 23836
Kelsey Pointe Ct 23831
Ken Dr 23831
Kentshire Ln 23831
Kentwood Forest Ct, Dr & Pl 23831
Kiefer Rd 23831
Kilt Dr 23836
Kings Ct 23831
Kings Gate Rd 23831
N Kingston Ave 23836
Kingstream Layne 23831
Knobbly Ct 23831
Koyoto Ct & Dr 23836
Krag Cir, Ct & Rd 23831
Kralan Ct & Dr 23831
Krenmore Ct & Ln 23831
Kriserin Cir 23831
Kristen Ln 23836
Lafon St 23831
Lake Dale Rd 23831
Lake Falls Dr 23831
Laketree Dr 23831
Lakeview Dr 23831
Lalonde Dr & Pl 23831
Landfill Dr 23831
Lanter Ln 23836
Lanyard Ct 23831
Laprade St 23831
Larryvale Dr 23831
Laughlin Way 23831
Laughter Ct & Ln 23831
Laurel Hill Dr 23836
Laurel Spring Ct & Rd 23831
Lawn Dr 23836
Lazy Stream Ct 23831
Lee St 23831
Leeward Dr 23836
Leighworth Blvd 23831
Leslie Ln 23836
Lewis Rd 23831
Liberty Way 23836
N Light Dr 23831
Lilking Ct & Rd 23831
Lippingham Cir, Dr, Ln & Ter 23831
Littlebury Ct & Dr 23831
Littlefield Rd 23836
Litwack Cove Dr & Ter 23836
Lively St 23831
Liverpool Cir & Ln 23836
Long Creek Ln 23831
Long Feather Ct 23831
Lora Lynn Rd 23831
Loren Ct & Dr 23836
Louise Dr 23831
Lucia Dr 23831
Ludgate Ct, Pl & Rd 23831
Lunswood Rd 23831
Lyndhurst Ct, Dr & Pl 23831
Magnolia Bluff Ct 23831
Magnolia Cove Cir 23831
Magnolia Shore Ln 23831
Malcolm Dr 23831
Malerren Rd 23836
Malibu St 23831
Mangrove Bay Ct, Dr & Ter 23836
Maple Landing Pl 23831
Maplevale Pl & Rd 23831
Maranatha Ave 23836
Maria Dr 23831
Maritime Ct 23831
Marsden Rd 23831
Martineau Dr 23836
Mason Ave 23831
Mathenay Dr 23831
Maughan House Ter 23831
Mayfair Dr 23836
Maynooth Ct 23836
Mcallister Dr 23831
Mccabe Ct & Dr 23831
Meadowville Ln & Rd 23836
Meadowville Technology Pkwy 23836
Medinah Ct & Pl 23831
Medora Pl 23831
Mercer Ct 23836
Meridian Ave 23831
Merry Dr 23831
Michmar Dr 23831
Mid City Rd 23831
N & S Middlebrook Ct & Rd 23831
Middlecoff Dr 23836
Midhurst Dr 23831
Millwood Rd 23831
Milsmith Rd 23831
Mimi Ave 23831
Mineola Dr 23831
Mistora Rd 23831
Mistwood Forest Ct & Dr 23831
Misty Arbor Pl 23831
Mooring Way 23831
Morehead Dr 23831
Mount Blanco Ct & Rd 23836
Mount Clair Rd 23831
Mountshire Ln, Pl & Ter 23836
Nairn Ct, Ln, Pl & Rd 23831
Naylors Blue Ct & Dr 23836
Nena Grove Ln 23831
Nesting Way 23831
New Found Ln 23831
Nightingale Ct & Dr 23836
Nile Rd 23831
Nomini Ct 23836
Norlanya Dr 23836
North St 23831
Nottington Ct 23831
Oak Rd 23831
Oak Arbor Ct, Dr & Ter 23831
Oak Bluff Dr, Ter & Trl 23831
Oak Hollow Rd 23831
Oak Landing Dr 23831
Oakbrook Ln 23831
Oakhaven Ct 23831
Oakland St 23831
Okuma Dr 23836
Old Ln 23831
Old Beaver Ln 23831
Old Bermuda Hundred Rd
100-2499 23836
2500-2598 23831
Old Centralia Rd 23831
Old Cheshire Ct, Dr & Ln 23831
Old Hampstead Ct & Ln 23831
Old Happy Hill Rd 23831
Old Hundred Rd 23831
Old St Andrews Pl 23836
Old Stage Rd 23836
Olivers Way 23831
Orchard Harvest Dr 23836
Orchard Leaf Ct & Pl 23836
Orchard Wood Ct 23836
Osborne Rd
1800-1899 23836
2000-3499 23831
Overridge Dr 23831
Owendale Rd 23831
Owls Hollow Ln 23836
Oxley Ct & Dr 23831
Paces Ferry Rd 23831
Par Dr 23831
Parker Ln 23831
Parkers Battery Rd 23836
Parkgate Dr 23831
Parsons Bay Dr 23836
Passage Way Dr 23831
Passaic Ave 23831
Pauline Ave 23831
Perch Point Dr 23836
Percival St 23831
Perdue Ave, Ct, St & Ter 23831
Perdue Springs Ct, Dr, Ln & Loop 23831
Perkinson Dr 23836
Permilla Springs Dr 23836
Petersburg St 23831
Pheasant Run Dr 23831
Pine St 23831
Pine Knoll Ct & Way 23831
Pine Meadows Cir 23831
Pine Vista Ln 23831
Piney Ridge Ct 23831
Pintail Landing Pl 23831
Placid Ave 23831
Player Ct & Ln 23836
Plum Harvest Way 23836
Poinsetta Ct & Dr 23831
Point Of Rocks Rd 23836
Pompton Ln 23831
Poplar View Pl 23831
Prince George Ave 23836
Prindell Ct 23831
Quay St 23831
Quiet Pine Cir & Dr 23831
Quixton Ln 23831
Railgate Ter 23831
Railroad St 23831
Ramblewood Dr 23836
Ramsey Ct & Dr 23831
Randall Dr 23831
Random Rd 23836
Redbird Dr 23836
Redwater Dr 23836
Redwater Creek Rd 23831
Redwater Ridge Rd 23831
Reflections Pt 23831
Richmond St
12100-12899 23831
15400-15599 23836
Riderwood Way 23831
Rieves Pond Dr 23831
Ringle Way 23831
Rio Vista St 23831
River Fork Pl & Way 23836
River Haven Ave 23836
River Rock Dr & Rd 23836
River Shore Pl 23836
River Tree Ct & Dr 23836
River Walk Ave, Pl & Ter 23836
Rivermont Rd 23836
Rivers Bend Blvd, Cir, Ct & Rd 23836
Riverview Ct & Dr 23836
Riviera Ct 23831
Rivington Dr 23831
Robertson St 23831

Rochelle Rd 23831
Rock Hill Rd 23831
Rock Orchard Ln 23836
Rockbasket Ct, Ln, Pl & Ter 23836
Rockbasket Turn 23836
Rockharvest Ct 23836
Rockhaven Ct & Dr 23836
Rockridge Ct, Pl & Rd 23831
Roland Dr 23831
Roland View Ct, Dr & Ter 23831
Rolling Brook Rd 23831
Rose Arbor Ct 23831
Rossington Blvd & Pl 23831
Rothschild Dr 23836
Rotunda Ct & Ln 23836
Royal Mews Ct 23831
Ruffin Mill Rd 23836
Rufford Ct, Pl & Rd 23831
Rystock Ct 23836
Saffron Ln 23836
Sand Hills Dr 23831
Sandwave Rd 23831
Sandy Oak Ct, Rd & Ter 23831
Santana St 23831
Santell Dr 23836
Sarazen Ln 23836
Saromont Ave 23831
School St 23831
Schooner Dr 23836
Scrimshaw Cir, Ct & Dr 23836
Sculley Rd 23836
Seahorse Dr 23836
Seamist Rd 23831
Searchlight Ct 23831
Seasigh Ct 23831
Seminole Ave 23831
Sentinel Ln 23836
Shady Ln 23831
Shale Ct & Pl 23836
Shallow Cove Dr 23836
Shallow Creek Ln 23831
Sherbet Ln 23831
Sherri Dr 23831
Shields Rd 23831
Shop St 23831
Shumark Dr 23836
Silver Crest Rd 23831
Silverdust Ct, Ln & Pl 23836
Sinker Creek Dr 23836
Sir Peyton Dr 23836
Sir Scott Dr & Ter 23831
Sloan Dr 23836
Snead St 23831
Somerlane Cir & Rd 23831
Sonnenburg Ct & Dr 23831
South St 23831
Southland Dr 23831
Split Creek Ct & Dr 23831
Spring Arbor Ct 23831
Spruce Ave 23836
Starboard Dr 23836
Stardown Ct 23831
Starpine Ln 23836
State Ave 23836
Staten Rd 23831
Stebbins St 23831
Stephens Point Ct & Dr 23831
Stepney Rd 23831
Stevenhurst Dr 23831
Stilton Ct & Dr 23831
Stockleigh Dr & Ln 23831
Stone Manor Cir 23831
Stonebridge Ln 23836
E Stonepath Garden Dr 23831
Stoneway Dr 23831
Stoney Creek Ct, Ln, Pkwy & Ter 23831
Sula Dr 23831
Sulphur Springs Ter 23836
Summer Arbor Ln 23831
Sunset Ave 23831
Sunset Blvd 23836
Surry Cir, Ct, Pl & Rd 23831
Swallow Rd 23831
Sweetbay Arbor Pl 23831
Sweetberry Ct 23831
Swiftrun Rd 23831
Switchback Ln 23831
Sycamore Springs Ct & Dr 23836
Sylvania Ct, Pl & Rd 23831
Talleywood Ct & Ln 23831
Tanner Slip Cir 23831
Tarris Ln 23831
Tazewell Ave 23836
Terjo Ln 23831
Terminal Ave 23836
Teterling Ct & Rd 23831
Thornhill Ct, Dr, Pl & Ter 23836
Thornsett Dr & Ln 23831
Thrushwood Ct & Way 23831
Thrushwood Turn 23831
Timonium Dr 23831
Timsberry Cir & Ter 23831
Timsbury Pointe Ct & Dr 23831
Tobacco Bay Ct & Pl 23836
Tolbert Ter 23836
Tooley Ct, Dr, Pl & Ter 23831
Tosh Ln 23831
Trailview Cir 23831
Tralee Ct, Dr & Pl 23836
Tranor Ave 23836
Traywick Ct & Dr 23836
Treebeard Ter 23831
Treely Rd 23831
Tri Gate Rd 23831
Tributary Ct 23831
Trollingwood Ln 23831
Tuscola Dr 23831
Twin Cedars Ct, Rd & Ter 23831
Twin Cliffs Ln 23831
Valley Rd 23836
Vance Dr 23836
Vanhorn Ct 23831
Vicki Ct 23831
Victoria Arbor Ct 23831
Village Creek Dr 23831
Village Garden Cir, Ct & Dr 23831
Village Park Ave 23831
Village Woods Ln 23831
Villas Ct & Dr 23836
Vogt Ave 23836
Vonda Ct 23831
Walnut Dr 23836
Walnut Cove Ct 23831
Walnut Landing Way 23831
Walters Dr 23831
Ware Bottom Spring Rd 23836
Warfield Estates Ct, Dr, Pl & Ter 23831
Warfield Ridge Dr & Ter 23831
Warwick Longbay Dr 23836
Waterview Dr 23831
Weatherby Dr 23831
Webb Tree Ter 23831
Wedge Dr 23831
Weir Pl & Rd 23831
Wellington Cross Way 23831
Wellington Farms Dr & Pl 23831
Wellshire Pl 23836
Wellspring Dr 23831
Wensley Ln 23831
Werth St 23831
West St 23831
Weybridge Rd 23831
N White Mountain Dr 23836
Whitebirch Dr 23831
Whitley Ct & St 23836
Williams Mill Rd 23831
Willow Landing Way 23831
Willowynde Ct & Rd 23836
Wilton Ct & Dr 23831
Wind Seeker Ct 23831
Windcry Dr 23831
Windsor Rd 23831
Windward Dr 23831
Windy Marsh Ct 23831
Winfree Cir & St 23831
Winners Cir 23836
Womack Rd 23831
Wood Dale Rd 23831
Woodbridge Ct 23831
Wooded Glen Ct 23831
Woodland Rd 23831
Woodleigh Dr 23831
Woodside Rd 23831
Wooten Ct 23836
Wraywood Ave 23831
Yantis Ct 23831
Yard Arm Dr 23831
Yoko Ct 23831
Zack Rd 23831

CHESTERFIELD VA

General Delivery 23832

POST OFFICE BOXES MAIN OFFICE STATIONS AND BRANCHES

Box No.s
All PO Boxes 23832

NAMED STREETS

Able Ct, Pl, Rd & Ter 23832
Adventure Hill Ln 23838
Ainsdale Ln 23832
W & E Alberta Cir, Ct, Mews, Rd & Ter 23832
Alcove Grove Rd & Way 23832
Aldera Ln 23838
Allerdice Ter 23838
Allworthy Ln 23832
Ambridge Rd 23832
Amsden Dr 23832
Amstel Bluff Ter & Way 23838
Amstel Ridge Ct 23838
Amstel View Pl 23838
Andradell Ln 23832
Apamatica Ln 23838
Appleway Ct 23838
Applewhite Ln 23838
Aquia Ct 23838
Arabella Dr 23832
Ashbourne Hollow Cir 23832
Ashbrook Pkwy 23832
Ashby Ln 23832
Ashdale Ct & Way 23832
Ashenberry Ct 23838
Ashmeade Pl 23832
Asia Way 23838
August Ct & Rd 23832
Autumn Mist Ct, Dr & Way 23832
Avent Ln 23832
Aviemore Ct 23838
Avocet Ct & Dr 23838
Badestowe Ct & Dr 23832
Bakers Hill Ln, Pl & Rd 23838
Baldwin Creek Rd 23832
Ball Cypress Rd 23832
Ballater Pl 23838
Balta Ct, Rd & Ter 23838
Balta Turn 23838
E & W Banes Ct 23832
Banff Ct & Ter 23838
Baniff Dr 23838
Barefoot Trl 23832
Barkbridge Cir, Ct & Rd 23832
Baron Dr 23832
Barretta Ln 23838
Barrister Rd 23832
Barrows Hill Ct & Ter 23838
Barrows Ridge Ct & Ln 23838
Bay Colony Ct 23838
Beach Rd
7200-9299 23838
9301-17999 23838
10300-10300 23832
11300-17798 23838
Beachcrest Ct, Pl, Rd & Ter 23832
Beaver Bridge Rd 23838
Beaverwood Dr 23832
Becket Dr 23832
Beechgrove Dr 23832
Beechwood Forest Dr 23838
Belcherwood Rd 23832
Beldon Dr 23838
Belmont Rd 23832
Belmont Downs Mews 23832
Benefice Rdg 23838
Berkley Davis Ct, Dr & Ter 23838
Berry Patch Dr 23832
Berryridge Ter 23832
Bethia Rd 23832
Bexwood Ct & Dr 23832
Birchlake Cir 23832
Bixby Ln 23838
Black Rd 23838
Black Isle Ct & Way 23838
Blackrail Pl & Rd 23832
Blind Trap Ln 23838
Blossomwood Cir, Ct & Rd 23832
Blue Cedar Dr & Pl 23832
Blue Heron Cir & Loop 23838
Blue Stack Ct 23832
Bluff Ridge Ct & Dr 23838
Boones Bluff Mews & Way 23832
Boones Trail Cir, Ct, Pl, Rd & Ter 23832
Bradley Bridge Rd 23838
Braidstone Ln & Ter 23838
Brambleton Rd 23832
Branding Iron Rd 23838
Brandy Oaks Blvd, Dr, Pl, Rd, Ter & Way 23832
Brandy Wood Pl, Rd & Ter 23832
Brandycrest Dr 23832
Brandyfield Pl 23832
Brandygrove Ct 23832
Brant Hollow Ct 23832
Brattice Mill Ct, Pl & Rd 23838
Braystone Ct, Dr & Ln 23838
Breaker Point Ct 23832
Brechin Ln 23838
Brenspark Rd 23832
Breslin Dr 23832
Brickell Ln 23832
Brickhaven Dr 23832
Bridlewood Ct 23838
Bright Hope Rd 23832
Brightridge Ct, Ln, Rd & Way 23832
Brixton Rd 23832
Broadreach Dr 23832
Bronholly Rd 23832
Bronze Penny Ct 23838
Brook Point Pl 23838
Brookridge Pl, Rd & Way 23832
Buckhorn Rd 23832
Bundle Rd 23838
Burnage Ct 23832
Burnett Dr 23832
Burray Ct & Rd 23838
Buttermere Ct 23838
Buttevant Dr 23838
Candlelamp Ln 23832
Cannock Rd 23832
Canvasback Cir 23838
Caribbean Ln 23832
Carlow Rd 23838
Carlton Forest Ct 23832
Carol Anne Rd 23832
Carteret Rd 23832
Carters Creek Ct, Dr, Pl & Ter 23838
Carters Crossing Ct, Rd & Way 23838
Carters Garden Ct, Dr & Ter 23838
Carters Hill Ct, Dr & Pl 23838
Carters Valley Ct, Pl, Rd & Ter 23838
Carters Valley Turn 23838
Carters Way Blvd, Ct, Pl & Rd 23838
Cascade Creek Ct, Ln & Pl 23832
Cattail Rd 23838
Cedar Creek Rd 23838
Cedar Mill Ct 23838
Cedar Springs Rd 23832
Celestial Ln 23832
Celtic Rd 23838
Centerbrook Ct, Ln & Pl 23832
Centralia Rd 23832
Chandon Ct & Pl 23838
Chanelka Ln 23832
Chantry Dr 23838
Charter Oak Dr 23838
Chesdin Crossing Dr & Ter 23838
Chesdin Green Way 23838
Chesdin Landing Ct, Dr, Pl & Ter 23838
Chesdin Manor Ct & Dr 23838
Chesdin Point Ct & Dr 23838
Chesdin Shores Dr, Pl & Ter 23838
Chesmount Dr 23832
Chesterfield Meadows Dr 23832
Chiasso Ter & Way 23838
Chickamauga Ct & Dr 23832
Christina Ct, Rd & Way 23832
Church Point Rd 23832
Claridge Dr 23832
Clay Ridge Dr & Ter 23832
Claypoint Rd 23832
Clearbrook Ct & Pl 23832
Clearpoint Dr 23832
Clearwater Trl 23832
Clearwood Ct & Rd 23832
Clover Hill Rd 23838
Clover Ridge Ln & Pl 23832
Cloverfield Cir & Ct 23838
Coalboro Rd 23838
Cogbill Rd 23832
Coldwater Cir & Run 23832
Collingswood Dr 23832
Colorstone Pl 23832
Commons Plz 23832
Conerald Rd 23838
Conestoga Pl 23832
Copperpenny Ct, Rd & Ter 23832
Corapeake Pl & Ter 23838
Corcoran Ct, Dr & Pl 23832
Cordova Ln 23832
Cornus Ave 23832
Corte Castle Ct, Pl, Rd & Ter 23838
Cosby Rd 23832
Courthouse Rd 23832
Courtview Ln 23832
Covina Ct & Ln 23838
Creek Bluff Ridge Dr 23838
Creek Stone Ct & Dr 23838
Creekbed Rd 23838
Creekbend Ct 23832
Crimson Crest Ln 23838
Cromarty Ct 23838
Crooked Creek Ct & Dr 23832
Crumpland Rd 23832
Culloden Ln 23838
Danforth Rd 23838
Darcy Ct, Dr & Ln 23832
Decoy Ln 23832
Deeley Ln 23832
Deer Dr 23838
Deerbrook Rd 23832
Deerfield Dr 23832
E & W Denny Ct 23832
Derryvech Dr 23832
Devette Ct, Dr, Pl & Ter 23838
Devlin Dr 23838
Dogwood Villas Dr 23832
N Donegal Ct, Dr, Pl, Rd & Ter 23832
Dortonway Ct, Dr & Pl 23832
Double Creek Ct 23832
Drexelbrook Rd 23832
Dry Creek Rd 23832
Duchess Way 23832
Dunnottar Ct, Dr & Ter 23838
Dunrobin Ct 23838
Dunroming Ct & Rd 23832
Duntrune Ct & Dr 23838
Dunvegan Ct 23838
Eades Ct 23832
Eagle Pass Ct & Dr 23838
Eaglenest Dr 23832
Eagles Crest Dr & Ln 23832
Eastfair Ct & Way 23838
Easton Ridge Pl 23838
Edgecliff Ln 23832
Egan Pl & Rd 23832
Egret Ct & Ln 23838
Eider Lndg 23838
Elementary Way Loop 23832
Elvas Ln 23838
Emerald Dunes Cir 23832
Emerald Valley Cir 23832
Enderly Ct 23832
Eppes Falls Rd 23838
Erinton Ct, Dr & Ter 23838
Escada Ct & Dr 23832
Europa Dr 23838
Exter Mill Rd 23838
Fair Isle Ct, Dr & Ter 23838
Fairpines Ct & Rd 23832
Falling Hill Ter 23832
Fallow Dr 23832
Family Ln 23832
Farmhill Ln 23832
Fawndale Dr 23832
Featherchase Ct, Dr, Pl & Ter 23832
Fermanagh Dr 23832
Fern Hollow Ct & Dr 23832
Fernway Dr & Pl 23832
Finstown Ln 23838
First Branch Ct & Ln 23838
Five Forks Ln 23832
Flagstone Ct 23838
Folkstone Dr 23838
Fore Cir 23832
Fox Grn E & W 23832
Foyle Dr 23832
Gadwell Ct & Ter 23832
Gamewell Rd 23832
Ganton Ct 23832
Garden Grove Ct & Rd 23832
Garden Ridge Ct, Pl, Rd & Trce 23832
Gates Bluff Ct, Dr, Pl & Ter 23832
Gatesgreen Dr 23832
Generation Ln 23838
Genito Ln & Rd 23832
Genlou Cir, Ct & Rd 23832
Gention Ct, Pl & Rd 23832
Ghent Cir, Ct & Dr 23832
Gills Gate Ct, Dr, Pl & Ter 23832
Glamis Ct 23838
Glebe Point Rd 23838
Glen Kilchurn Dr 23838
Glendevon Cir, Ct, Dr, Rd & Ter 23838
Golden Nugget Ct 23832
Goldenbrook Ct & Dr 23832
Government Center Pkwy 23832
Grampian Ct & Ln 23838
Granite Point Ct 23838
Grizzard Ct & Dr 23832
Ground Fern Dr & Pl 23832
Hadden Hall Ct & Dr 23838
Hadley Ln 23832
Hagerty Ln 23838
Haggis Dr & Ter 23838
Hagood Ln 23832
Halls Run Rd 23832
Halyard Ct & Ter 23832
Hampton Arbor Cir, Ct & Ter 23832
Hampton Bluff Ter & Trl 23832
Hampton Chase Way 23832
Hampton Colony Ct & Way 23832
Hampton Crest Cir, Ct, Mews, Pl, Ter & Way 23832
Hampton Crest Turn 23832
Hampton Crossing Ct, Dr, Mews & Pl 23832
Hampton Forest Dr & Ln 23832
Hampton Glen Ct, Dr, Ln, Mews, Pl & Ter 23832
Hampton Green Cir, Dr & Mews 23832
Hampton Manor Ct & Ter 23832
Hampton Meadows Cir, Ct, Cv, Ln, Pl & Ter 23832
Hampton Park Blvd, Cir & Dr 23832
Hampton Springs Rd 23832
Hampton Station Ct 23832
Hampton Summit Cir, Ct, Dr, Ln, Pl & Ter 23832
Hampton Valley Cir, Ct, Dr, Mews, Pl & Ter 23832
Hampton Valley Turn 23832
Hancock Farm Ln & Pl 23832
Hancock Ridge Ct 23832
Hancock Village Dr & St 23832
Harley Dr 23832
Hartsdale Ct & Rd 23832
Heartside Pl 23832
Heathbluff Ct 23832
Heathermist Ct 23838
Heathside Dr 23832
Helmsman Ct 23832
Hembrick Rd 23838
Hereld Green Dr 23832
Herton Cross Rd 23832
Hickory Hollow Rd 23838
Highcrest Ridge Dr 23838
Highgate Hill Ct & Dr 23838
Highland Glen Dr 23838
Hollow Branch Ct 23832
Hollow Ridge Ct 23832
Hollow Wood Ct 23832
Holly Pines Dr 23832
Holly Trace Ct, Dr & Ter 23832

Hollytree Ct & Ter 23832
Holridge Ct & St 23832
Homeland Ct 23832
Hotchkiss Ct 23832
Houghton Ct, Pl & St 23832
Hourglass Ct 23832
Hull Street Rd 23832
Hulsey Dr 23838
Hunters Hawk Ct & Dr 23838
Hunters Lake Ln & Pl 23832
Hunters Lake Turn 23832
Hunters Landing Ct & Dr 23832
Huntsville Ct & Rd 23832
Husting Ct, Rd & Ter 23832
Inlet Ct 23832
Iron Bridge Rd 23832
Isadora Dr & Pl 23838
Isle Pines Dr 23838
N Ivey Mill Rd 23838
Ivory Bill Ct & Ln 23838
Jacobs Rd 23832
Janeka Ct & Dr 23838
Jean Machenberg Dr 23838
Jessup Loop & Rd 23832
Jones Neck Pl 23832
Junilla Ln 23832
Kalliope Ct, Dr & Pl 23838
Katy Reid Ct 23832
Kempwood Ct, Dr & Pl 23832
Kennemer Pl 23832
Ketcham Dr 23832
Killarney Ct 23832
Kimlynn Trl 23838
Kings Crest Ct, Dr & Pl 23832
Kings Grove Ct, Dr & Ter 23832
Kingsland Creek Ct, Dr & Ln 23832
Kintail Dr 23838
Kitchawam Ct 23832
Knightwood Ct, Ln & Pl 23832
Kousa Rd 23832
W Krause Rd 23832
Ladderback Ct 23838
Lady Anne Ln 23832
Lake Caroline Ct & Dr 23832
Lake Chesdin Pkwy 23838
Lamberts Creek Ln 23832
Lammermoor Ct, Dr & Ln 23838
Lantern Ridge Ct 23832
Larosa Rd 23832
Latane Wood Ct & Rd 23838
Laughton Ct & Dr 23832
Laurel Cove Ln & Pl 23838
Leamington Dr 23832
Leeds Ln 23832
Lenadoon Dr 23832
Lerwick Pl 23838
Lesser Scaup Lndg 23838
Licking Creek Dr 23832
Lifford Ln 23832
Lifsey Ln 23832
Lightwood Ct 23832
Linegar Dr 23832
Litchfield Dr 23832
Little Ridge Ct & Ln 23832
Llewellyn Ln 23832
Loamy Cir & Ct 23838
Logswood Rd 23832
Lollys Run 23832
Long Branch Ct & Dr 23832
Long Tom Ct & Ln 23832
Longhouse Ln 23838
Longlands Ct, Pl & Rd 23832
Lori Rd 23832
Lowwin Ter 23832
Lucy Corr Cir, Ct & Dr 23832
Lylwood Ct & Ln 23838
Lyndenwood Ct & Dr 23838
Macandrew Ct, Dr, Ln, Pl & Ter 23838
Maclachlan Ct & Dr 23838
Madison Pointe Way 23832
Madras Cir & Ct 23832
Mahogany Ct, Dr & Pl 23832
Malbon Way 23832
Manassas Ct, Dr & Ter 23832
Manitoba Rd 23832
Manning Rd 23832
Manordale Rd 23832
Mapleridge Ct 23838
Marek Dr 23838
Marsh Elder Ct 23838
Marshall Pointe Trl 23832
Masada Ct & Dr 23838
Melville Dr 23832
Memory Ln 23832
Mendota Rd 23838
Meredith Pointe Way 23832
Merganser Ter 23838
Mermainc Rd 23832
Merseyside Ln 23832
Meterie Ct 23832
Middlefield Ct, Ln, Mews & Pl 23832
Midship Woods Ct 23832
Mill River Ct, Ln & Trce 23832
Millay Dr 23838
Millhouse Ct & Dr 23832
Millvale Ct & Rd 23832
Mimms Loop 23832
Mission Hills Cir, Ln & Loop 23832
Molena Dr 23838
Monks Pl 23832
Morehouse Ter 23832
Morgan Trail Dr 23832
Morrisett Rd 23838
Mount Holly Ln 23832
Mountcastle Pl & Rd 23832
Nabor Way 23838
Nash Rd 23838
Natural Bark Dr 23832
Nestor Rd 23838
Newbys Ct 23832
Newbys Bridge Rd 23832
Newbys Mill Ct, Dr & Ter 23832
Newbys Wood Trl 23832
Nithdale Ct & Pl 23838
Noltland Ct 23838
Northbrook Cir 23838
Northford Ct, Ln, Mews & Pl 23832
Northwood Dr 23838
Nott Ln 23832
Nuttall Ct 23838
Oakforest Ct & Dr 23832
Oakhill Ln 23832
Oakton Rd 23838
Obisque Dr 23832
Offshore Dr 23832
Old Beach Rd 23838
Old Bond Ct & St 23832
Old Brompton Rd 23832
Old Creek Ct, Rd & Ter 23832
Old Glory Rd 23832
Old Squaws Ln 23838
Old Wrexham Cir, Pl & Rd 23832
Oldbern Ct & Rd 23832
Onnies Dr 23832
Orangeburg Way 23838
Orchid Ct, Dr, Pl & Ter 23832
Outpost Cir 23832
Owl Trace Ct & Dr 23838
Paddock Grove Ct 23832
Pampas Dr 23832
Park Bluff Ct & Ter 23838
Park Branch Ct & Ln 23838
Parrish Creek Cir, Ct, Ln, Pl & Ter 23832
Partridge Run 23832
Pebble Beach Ct 23832
Pennbrook Ct & Dr 23832
Physic Hill Rd 23838
Pierson Dr 23832
Pine Orchard Ct 23832
Pine Reach Ct & Dr 23832
Pintail Pl 23838
Plantation Trace Dr & Pl 23838
Pleasant Pond Ct, Ln & Pl 23832
Poachers Ct & Run 23832
Poplardell Ct 23832
Post Land Ct & Dr 23832
Precedent Rd 23832
Prince James Ct, Dr, Mews, Pl & Ter 23832
Prince James Turn 23832
Prince Philip Ct, Ln & Pl 23838
Princess Mary Pl, Rd & Ter 23838
Public Safety Rd 23832
Pullman Ln 23832
Pungo Ct & Ter 23838
Puritan Rd 23838
Pursuit Ct 23832
Putford Ct 23832
Pypers Pointe Dr 23838
Quail Ridge Rd & Ter 23832
Qualla Rd 23832
Qualla Farms Ct, Dr, Pl & Ter 23832
Rabbit Ridge Rd 23838
Ranger Rd 23838
Raven Wing Cir, Ct & Dr 23832
Ravenna Dr & Ter 23832
Reedy Branch Rd 23838
Regal Crest Ct, Dr & Ter 23832
Regal Grove Dr & Ln 23832
Regalia Ct, Dr & Pl 23838
Reinhold Dr 23838
Rhodes Ln 23838
Richland Rd 23832
Riddle Ct & Rd 23832
Ridgegreen Dr 23832
Ridgerun Ct, Pl, Rd & Ter 23832
River Rd 23838
River Otter Ct & Rd 23838
Riverpark Dr, Ter & Way 23838
Riverway Rd 23838
Robbie Rd 23832
Robinwood Ct & Dr 23832
Rock Run Rd 23838
Rock Valley Ln 23838
Rockyrun Ct & Rd 23838
Rolling Fields Ln & Pl 23832
Rollingmist Ln 23838
Rollingridge Ln 23832
Rollingway Ct, Rd & Ter 23832
Rosebud Rd 23832
Rosemead Ct & Ln 23838
Rossville Ct & Dr 23832
Round Hill Ct & Dr 23832
Round Ridge Pl 23838
Round Rock Ct, Pl & Rd 23838
Roundabout Bnd & Way 23832
Rowlett Rd 23838
Royal Birkdale Dr 23838
Saddlebrook Rd 23838
Sailors Creek Ct & Dr 23832
Saint Annas Ct 23832
Salix Grove Ln & Ter 23832
Salk Rd 23838
Salles Branch Rd 23838
Sambar Rd 23832
Sanchez Rd 23832
Sandrock Ridge Dr 23838
Sandy Ford Rd 23838
Sandy Shore Mews 23838
Sarata Ct & Ln 23838
Sawdust Trl 23838
Sawgrass Pl 23832
Scotts Bluff Ct, Ln, Ter & Way 23832
Scouters Cir & Pl 23832
Seabrook Cir 23832
Seaview Ct & Dr 23838
Second Branch Rd 23838
Sexton Dr 23832
Shady Banks Ct, Dr, Rd & Ter 23832
Shagreen Ct & Ln 23838
Shannon County Dr 23832
Shawonodasee Rd 23832
Shell Harbor Ct 23838
Shelton Ct 23832
Shepherds Mill Dr 23832
Shepherds Watch Dr 23832
Shore Lake Turn 23838
Shorecrest Ct & Ln 23838
Sidlaw Hills Ln & Ter 23838
Silliman Ct, Dr & Ter 23832
Simmons Branch Ct & Ter 23838
Simplicity Ct & St 23832
Sir Britton Ct, Dr & Mews 23832
Skybird Ct & Rd 23838
Slate Ct & Rd 23838
Snare Ct 23832
Snowbird Ct & Rd 23832
Solaris Cir, Ct & Dr 23832
Soundview Ln 23832
Southern Points Ct & Dr 23838
Southern Ridge Dr 23838
Southford Ct, Ln, Mews, Pl & Ter 23832
Southwind Dr 23832
Sparkleberry Ln 23832
Spelman Rd 23832
Spikehorn Ln 23838
Spring Glen Ct & Dr 23832
Spring Run Rd 23832
Springbok Rd 23832
Springhouse Ct, Dr & Way 23832
Springmount Rd & Ter 23832
Spyglass Hill Cir, Cres, Crk, Ct, Loop, Mews, Pl, Ter & Trl 23832
Spyglass Hill Turn 23832
Squirrel Tree Ct 23838
St Audries Dr 23838
Stagpenn Rd 23832
State Park Rd 23832
Statute Ct & St 23832
Sterling Cove Dr, Pl & Ter 23838
Sterling Tide Ct 23838
N & S Stevens Hollow Dr & Rd 23832
Stevens Wood Ct 23832
Stillwood Ct 23832
Stirrup Cir 23832
Stockport Ct, Dr, Pl & Ter 23832
Stockport Turn 23832
Stone Creek Dr & Ter 23832
Stonecreek Club Ct & Pl 23832
Stonewheel Ct 23832
Stonington Ct 23832
Summer Gate Ct 23832
Summercliff Ct, Ter & Trl 23832
Summercreek Ct, Dr, Pl & Way 23832
Summerford Ct & Dr 23832
Summerlook Ct, Ln & Pl 23832
Summers Trace Ct, Dr & Ter 23832
Summersedge Ter 23832
Summit Rd 23838
Sunne Ct 23832
Sunningdale Ter 23832
Sunny Creek Dr 23832
Sunnygrove Rd 23832
Sunswyck Ct 23832
Sussex Ct, Dr & Pl 23832
Swift Water Rd 23838
Swiftrock Ridge Ct, Dr, Pl & Ter 23838
Sylvan Ridge Ct, Pl & Rd 23838
Tamworth Rd 23832
Tavern Hill Ct 23832
Taylor Rd 23838
Taylor Landing Pl & Way 23838
Teelin Ct 23832
Third Branch Ct & Dr 23832
Thirsk Ln 23832
Thoreau Ct & Dr 23832
Thornton Heath Dr 23832
Timber Point Dr 23838
Timber Run Ct & Rd 23832
Tokay Ct & Rd 23832
Torrey Pines Cir & Dr 23832
Towchester Dr 23832
Townsbury Ct, Rd & Ter 23832
Tracker Ct & Dr 23832
Trailbrook Dr 23838
Trailwood Dr 23832
Trappers Creek Trl 23832
Tree Line Ter 23832
Trents Bridge Rd 23838
Trumpington Ct 23838
Tulip Oak Rd 23832
Turner Rd 23832
Turning Ln 23832
Tuskwillow Dr 23832
Twickenham Pl 23832
Twin Poplar Cir 23838
Twisted Cedar Ct, Dr, Pl & Ter 23832
Valencia Ct, Pl & Rd 23832
Ventura Rd 23832
Verdict Ct 23832
Vest Rd 23838
Wagners Way 23832
Walden Rd 23832
Walke Pointe Way 23832
Walkes Quarter Rd 23838
Walkmill Reach Trl 23832
Water Vista Dr 23838
Waterfall Cove Ct & Dr 23832
Waterfall Crest Way 23832
Waterfowl Ct & Pl 23838
Waterfowl Flyway 23838
Waterman Ln & Pl 23832
Wedgemere Rd 23832
Welch Ct & Dr 23832
Wellesley Dr 23838
West Cir, Ct, Rd & Ter 23832
Whistling Swan Pl & Rd 23838
Whitley Manor Dr 23838
Widgeon Way 23838
Wilconna Rd 23832
Wild Turkey Run 23838
Willow Grove Ct, Pl & Rd 23832
Willow Hill Ct, Dr, Ln & Loop 23832
Willow Walk Dr 23832
Willowcrest Ct & Ln 23832
Wilton Rd 23832
Winding Ash Ct, Dr, Pl & Ter 23832
Winding Creek Ln 23832
Windy Creek Cir, Ct, Dr, Pl & Way 23832
Winpic Pl 23832
Winterpock Rd
7000-10700 23832
10702-10798 23832
11000-12199 23838
14100-14199 23832
Wintic Pl 23832
Woodbluff Ct 23838
Woodgate Rd 23832
Woodland Pond Pkwy 23838
Woodpecker Rd 23838
Wryneck Ct 23838
Wynnstay Ct & Ln 23838
Yatesdale Dr 23832

CHRISTIANSBURG VA

General Delivery 24073

POST OFFICE BOXES MAIN OFFICE STATIONS AND BRANCHES

Box No.s
All PO Boxes 24068

NAMED STREETS

Agee St 24073
Akers St 24073
Akers Farm Rd 24073
Alder Ln 24073
Aldwych Ave 24073
Alexa Ln 24073
Alexander Ct 24073
Alleghany St SE 24073
Alma St 24073
Almetta Ave 24073
Alpine Dr 24073
Alta Ct 24073
Amethyst Dr 24073
Angle Dr 24073
Applewood Dr 24073
Arbolito Trl 24073
Arbor Dr
1-349 24073
350-350 24068
350-398 24073
351-399 24073
Arrowhead Trl 24073
Arry Spring Rd 24073
Arthur Ln 24073
Ash Dr 24073
Ashby St 24073
Ashton Ct 24073
Aspen St 24073
Aster Ln 24073
Atkinson Rd 24073
Auburn Dr 24073
Aurora Ln 24073
Austin Rd 24073
Authority Dr 24073
Avery Ln 24073
Aysha Ln 24073
Badger St 24073
Baldwin Ln 24073
Banjo Rd 24073
Bank St 24073
Barkwood St 24073
Barn Rd 24073
Barringer Mountain Rd 24073
Beaver Dr 24073
Beech Spring Ln 24073
Bell Rd 24073
Belmont Dr 24073
Belmont Trailer Park 24073
Berkshire Dr 24073
Bethel Park 24073
Betty Dr 24073
Beulah Ln 24073
Billy St 24073
Birch Ln 24073
Bishops Gate Rd 24073
Black Bear Run Rd 24073
Blair St 24073
Blake Dr 24073
Block Ln 24073
Blossom Rd 24073
Blue Heron Dr 24073
Blue Leaf Dr 24073
Blue Spruce Ct & Dr 24073
Bluegrass Rd 24073
Bow Hill Rd 24073
Bower St 24073
Boxwood Dr 24073
Brackens St 24073
Bradley Dr 24073
Brammer Ln 24073
Brandywine Dr 24073
Briarwood Dr 24073
Brilliant Dr 24073
Bristol Dr 24073
Bronze Leaf Dr 24073
Brooklyn Ave 24073
Brookside Dr 24073
Brown St 24073
Buckingham Ln 24073
Buffalo Dr 24073
Burbank St 24073
Business Center Rd 24073
Butterfly Ln 24073
Caboose Rd 24073
Cambria St NE & NW 24073
Camellia Ln NW 24073
Cameo Ct 24073
Canaan Rd SE 24073
Canterbury Ct SW 24073
Capital Via 24073
Carden St 24073
Cardinal Dr 24073
Carenchi Rd 24073
Carson Dr 24073
Carter Dr 24073
Cassatt Ln 24073
Castle Rd 24073
Cedar St 24073
Cedar Bluff Dr 24073
Cedarwood Dr 24073
Cemetery Rd 24073
Center St 24073
S Central Ave & Dr 24073
Chapel St 24073
Charles St 24073
Charleston Ln 24073
Chaucer Ln 24073
Chelsea Loop 24073
Cherokee Dr 24073
Cherry Ln 24073
Chestnut Dr 24073
Cheverly Rd 24073
Chickory St 24073
Childress Rd 24073
Chinquapin Trl 24073
Chrisman St 24073
Chrisman Mill Rd 24073
Christiana Ct 24073
Christie Ln 24073
Church St 24073
Cinnabar Rd 24073
Circle Dr SE 24073
Circle Brook Ln 24073
Citrine Ct 24073
Clark St 24073
Clearview Dr 24073
Coal Hollow Rd 24073
Colhoun St NE 24073
College St NW 24073
Collins St 24073
Colonial Dr 24073
Conners Trailer Park 24073
Constitution Via 24073
Conston Ave 24073
Cooper Ln 24073
Copper Beach Ct 24073
Corning Dr 24073
Corrells Trailer Ct 24073
Countrie Dr 24073
Country Dr 24073
Country Meadow Dr 24073
County Dr & Rd NE 24073
Crab Creek Rd 24073

Craig St 24073
Craigs Mountain Rd 24073
Crescent Dr 24073
Crestview St 24073
Cross St 24073
Crosscreek Dr 24073
Cullen Ct 24073
Cumberland Dr 24073
Currin Ln 24073
Curtis Dr 24073
Dabney Rd 24073
Dairy Rd 24073
Darci Dr SE 24073
Davey St 24073
Declaration Ln 24073
Dee Dee Dr 24073
Degas Ln 24073
Delta Ln 24073
Den Hill Rd 24073
Depot St NE & W 24073
Derby Rd 24073
Dezzie Ln 24073
Diamond Ave 24073
Diamond Crest Ct 24073
Diana Dr 24073
Divine Dr 24073
Dogwood Ln 24073
Dominion Dr 24073
Doubletree Ln 24073
Dow St 24073
Dry Valley Rd 24073
S Dudley Dr 24073
Dunkley St 24073
Dunlap Dr 24073
Dunnington Ct 24073
Eaglebrook Rd 24073
Eanes Cir 24073
East St 24073
Easy St 24073
Economy St 24073
Edgemont Rd 24073
Edgewood Dr 24073
Electric Way 24073
Elk Dr 24073
Elk Creek Dr 24073
Ellett Dr & Rd 24073
Elliott Creek Rd 24073
Elm St 24073
Emerald Blvd 24073
Epperly Dr SE 24073
Eskeridge Rd 24073
Evans St 24073
Evergreen Dr 24073
Fairview Dr & St 24073
Fairview Church Rd 24073
Fairview Trailer Park 24073
Falcon Run 24073
Falling Branch Rd 24073
Falls Ridge Rd 24073
Falor Ln 24073
Farmview Rd & St 24073
Fir Rd 24073
Fire Tower Rd 24073
Fisher St 24073
Flagg Ct 24073
Flanagan Dr 24073
Flint Dr 24073
Florence Dr 24073
Floyd St 24073
Food Lion Plz 24073
Forelmont St 24073
Forest St 24073
Fork Rd & St 24073
Fox St 24073
Fralin Aly 24073
N & S Franklin St 24073
Franklin Parke Ct 24073
Freedom Via 24073
Freeman Ln 24073
Freestone Dr NE 24073
Front St 24073
Gallimore St 24073
Gantt Dr 24073
Garnett Dr 24073
Gate Rd 24073
Geneva St 24073
George Edward Via 24073
Gibson Dr 24073
Giles Rd 24073
Gingerbread Rd 24073
Glade Dr 24073
Glasgow Rd 24073
Glen Ct 24073
Glouster St 24073
Gobblers Spur 24073
Gold Leaf Dr 24073
Gooseneck Dr 24073
Grand View Dr 24073
N & S Grant St 24073
Graves St 24073
Green Ridge Rd 24073
Greenway Dr 24073
Griggs St 24073
Grim St 24073
Groundhog Rd 24073
Grove Ave 24073
Gum Dr 24073
Gunston Rd 24073
Hagan St 24073
Halee Dr 24073
Hall St 24073
Hammes St 24073
Hampton Blvd 24073
Hanover St 24073
Hans Meadow Rd 24073
Harkrader St 24073
Harless St 24073
Harman Dr 24073
Harmon Cir SE 24073
Hawley Rd 24073
Haymaker St 24073
Haynes Trailer Park 24073
Hazelnut Rd 24073
Heather Dr 24073
Height St 24073
Hemlock St 24073
Henley Dr 24073
Hickok St 24073
Hickory Dr 24073
N High St 24073
Highview St 24073
Hill Dr & St NE 24073
Hillcrest Dr 24073
Hillside Dr 24073
Hitching Post Dr 24073
Holly Dr 24073
Holmes St 24073
Hornsby Rd 24073
Houchins Rd 24073
Howery St 24073
Hubble Dr 24073
Huckleberry St 24073
Huff Heritage Ln 24073
Hummingbird Dr 24073
Hungate Rd 24073
Hunters Path & Rdg 24073
Hyde St 24073
Ijaz Dr & Rd 24073
Imperial St 24073
Independence Blvd 24073
Indigo Rd 24073
Industrial Dr 24073
Interstate Trailer Park 24073
Ivy Ln 24073
Ivywoods Ln 24073
Izaak Walton Ln 24073
Jackson St 24073
James St 24073
Janna Rd 24073
Jarrett Dr 24073
Jennelle Rd 24073
Jennifer St SE 24073
Jessie Cir 24073
Jimmy Ln 24073
John Lemley Ln 24073
Johns Ct 24073
Johnson St 24073
Joi St 24073
Jones St SE & SW 24073
Juniper Dr & Ln 24073
Junkin St 24073
Justin Ln 24073
Kamran St 24073
Katie Ln 24073
Kays Dr 24073
Keith Ln 24073
Kensington Way 24073
Keystone Dr 24073
Kimball Ln 24073
King St 24073
King Charles Ct 24073
Kings Ct 24073
Kingston Branch Rd 24073
Kinser Ct 24073
Kirby Dr 24073
Kitty Ln 24073
Knoll Crest Dr 24073
Ladybug Rd 24073
Lagoon Dr 24073
Lake Vista Dr 24073
Lamb Cir 24073
Laurel St 24073
Lawn Dr 24073
Leather Rd 24073
Lee St 24073
Lee Hy Ct 24073
Lester Pl & St 24073
Lewis St 24073
Liberty St & Via 24073
Life Dr 24073
Light St 24073
Linden Ct 24073
Lions Dr 24073
Lithia Springs Rd 24073
Little John Ct 24073
Locust St 24073
Logenberry Ln 24073
Lomoor St 24073
Lonesome Pnes 24073
Lonesome Dove Dr 24073
Long St 24073
Longs Trailer Ct 24073
Longview Dr 24073
Loret Ln 24073
Lovely Mount Dr 24073
Lubna Dr 24073
Lucas St 24073
Lucky Ln 24073
Lupine Ln 24073
Lusters Gate Rd 24073
Lyle Ln 24073
Lynn Dr 24073
Lynnwood Ln 24073
Mac Ln 24073
Madison Ave 24073
Magna Carta Via 24073
Magnolia Ln 24073
Mahone St 24073
E Main St
1-899 24073
2-2 24068
2-898 24073
S Main St 24073
W Main St 24073
Majestic Dr 24073
Maple Dr 24073
Market St 24073
Marquise Dr 24073
Marshall Dr 24073
Marty Cir 24073
Mass Cir 24073
Massie Dr 24073
Maury Ln 24073
Maxwell Ln 24073
Mc Peak Dr 24073
Mcdaniel Dr 24073
Mchenry Ave 24073
Meadow Dr 24073
Meadow Creek Rd 24073
Meerkat Rd 24073
Melody Dr 24073
Meredith Rd 24073
Merrimac Rd 24073
Midway Rd 24073
Midway Plaza Dr NW 24073
Mill Ln 24073
Miller Ct & St 24073
Milton Ave 24073
Mink St 24073
Mitchell St SW 24073
Moccassin Rd 24073
Montague St 24073
Montgomery St 24073
Moore St 24073
Moose Dr 24073
Morning Mist Dr 24073
Morning Star Ln 24073
Morningside Trailer Park 24073
Motor Ln 24073
Mount Pleasant Rd 24073
Mountain Top Dr 24073
Mountain View Dr 24073
Mountain View Mobile Est 24073
Mud Pike 24073
Mudpike Rd 24073
Mulberry Dr 24073
Murray St 24073
Nancy Ct 24073
Nash Rd 24073
National Dr 24073
Nell Dr 24073
New St 24073
New River Rd 24073
New Village Dr NW 24073
Newcomb St 24073
Night Hawk Dr 24073
Nolen Rd 24073
North Dr 24073
Norwood St 24073
Nugget Ridge Rd 24073
Nursery Ln 24073
Oak Dr 24073
Oakland Dr 24073
Oaktree Blvd 24073
Old Farm Village Rd 24073
Orange Leaf Dr 24073
Orchard St 24073
Orchid Rd 24073
Overhill Rd 24073
Overland Dr 24073
Overlook Dr 24073
Palmer St 24073
Park St 24073
Parkway Dr 24073
Parsley Rd 24073
Patricia Ln NE 24073
E Patriot Way 24073
Patton Dr 24073
Peach St NE 24073
Peachtree Hl 24073
Peakland Way 24073
Pear St NE 24073
Peggy Dr 24073
Pelham Ln 24073
Pepper St N 24073
Peppers Ferry Rd NE & NW 24073
Perry St 24073
Phlegar St 24073
Phoenix Blvd NW 24073
Pickett St 24073
Pike Ln 24073
Pilot Rd 24073
Pin Oak Dr 24073
Pine St 24073
Pine Hollow Rd 24073
Piney Woods Rd 24073
Pioneer Apartments 24073
Plateau Dr 24073
Plum St 24073
Plum Creek Rd 24073
Poff Ct 24073
Pollard Rd 24073
Ponderosa Dr 24073
Poplar Ln 24073
Poppy Ln 24073
Pops Ln 24073
Powhatan St 24073
Prices Fork Rd 24073
Proclamation Ln 24073
Progress St 24073
Prominence Ln NW 24073
Prospect Dr 24073
Providence Blvd 24073
Pugh Rd 24073
Putter Ln 24073
Quality Rd 24073
Quesenberry St 24073
Radford Rd & St 24073
Ragan Dr 24073
Railroad St 24073
Rainbow St 24073
Reading Rd 24073
Red Hawk Run 24073
Red Leaf Dr 24073
Red Oak Dr NE 24073
Redwood Dr 24073
Republic Rd 24073
Revolution Cir 24073
Riddle Rd 24073
Ridge Rd SE 24073
Ridgeway Dr 24073
Ridinger St NW 24073
Rigby St 24073
Riner Rd 24073
Roanoke St 24073
Robert St 24073
Robin Rd 24073
Robin Hood Dr 24073
Rock Rd 24073
Rogers St 24073
Rolling Hills Dr 24073
Roman Dr 24073
Rosehill Dr 24073
Roseland Dr 24073
Rosemary Rd 24073
Roudabush Dr NW 24073
Round Meadow Dr 24073
Roundhill Dr 24073
Ruby Ct 24073
Ruffin Rd 24073
Running Buck Rd 24073
Runnymeade Ln 24073
Rusty Dr 24073
Sage Ln 24073
Salem Ln 24073
Sally Ann Dr 24073
Sapphire Ave 24073
Sara St 24073
Sassafrass Rd 24073
Scalehouse Dr 24073
Scattergood Dr NE & NW 24073
Scenic Dr 24073
School Ln 24073
Scott St 24073
Sequoia Cir NW 24073
Shaffer Dr & St 24073
Shelburne Dr 24073
Sheltman St 24073
Shepherds Trailer Ct 24073
Sheppy Hollow Rd 24073
Sherwood Dr 24073
Shooting Star Ln 24073
Shoppers Way 24073
Short St 24073
Siena Dr 24073
Silver Lake Rd 24073
Silver Leaf Dr 24073
Simmons Rd NE & SE 24073
Simpson Rd 24073
Skyline St 24073
Slate Creek Dr 24073
Sleepy Hollow Rd 24073
Smith Creek Rd 24073
Snapdragon Ln 24073
Somerset St 24073
Sophia Ln 24073
Southview Ter 24073
Sowers Trailer Ct 24073
Spaulding Rd 24073
Spradlin Farm Dr 24073
Spring House Rd 24073
Springbuck Dr 24073
Springview Dr 24073
Spruce St 24073
St Clair Ln 24073
Stafford Dr 24073
Stanley Rd 24073
Starlight Ct & Dr 24073
Stone St 24073
Stroubles Creek Rd 24073
Stuart St 24073
Sugar Grove Rd 24073
Sullivan St 24073
Sumac Rd 24073
Summit Ridge Rd 24073
Sunnyside Ln 24073
Sunrise St 24073
Sunset Dr 24073
Surry Cir N & S 24073
Swallow Ln 24073
Sweetbrier Dr 24073
Switchback Rd 24073
Sycamore St 24073
Tall Oak Blvd 24073
Talon Ln 24073
Talus Ln NW 24073
Tanglewood Dr 24073
Tarrytown Rd 24073
Taylor St 24073
Teaberry Rd 24073
Technology Dr 24073
Teel St 24073
Testerman Dr 24073
Texas Rd 24073
Thaddeus Ln 24073
Thelma Ln 24073
Thistle Ln 24073
Thomas Cir 24073
Thorn Cir 24073
Thrush Rd 24073
Tiffany Ln 24073
Tomahawk Dr 24073
Tower Rd 24073
Townhouse St 24073
Tranquility Via 24073
Trent Dr 24073
Triangle Trailer Ct 24073
Truman Ave 24073
Tula Cir 24073
Tunnel Cir 24073
Turpin Walk 24073
Turtle Xing 24073
Tyler Rd & St 24073
Underwood St 24073
Unicorn Ln 24073
Varsity Ln 24073
Vaughn Cir 24073
Vernon St 24073
Vickers Switch Rd 24073
Victory Hts 24073
W View Dr 24073
Viewland Cir 24073
Village Ln 24073
Vinnie Ave 24073
Violet Ln 24073
Virginian Dr 24073
Vj Dr 24073
Wades Ln 24073
Wakeman Ct 24073
Wall St 24073
Walnut Dr 24073
Walters Dr 24073
Walton Rd 24073
Warren Ct & St 24073
Warrior Dr 24073
Washington Ave 24073
Water St 24073
Wayside Dr 24073
Weddle Way 24073
Welch Cir NW 24073
Wenn St 24073
West St 24073
Wetherburn Rd 24073
Wheatland Ct & Dr 24073
Whiffletree Ln 24073
Whispering Pine Cir 24073
Whistler Rd 24073
White Oak Ln 24073
White Pine Dr 24073
Whitman Ln 24073
Wild Turkey Run 24073
Wildflower Rd 24073
Williams St 24073
Willow Dr 24073
Willow Oak Dr 24073
Wimmer St 24073
Windmill Ridge Rd E & W 24073
Windsong Ln 24073
Windsor Dr 24073
Windy Hill Ln 24073
Winesap Rd 24073
Wing St 24073
Wistaria Dr 24073
Wolf St 24073
Wooden Shoe Ct N 24073
Woodland Dr 24073
Woodridge Dr 24073
Woodrow Rd 24073
Woods Vista Dr 24073
Worrell Dr 24073
Yellow Sulphur Rd 24073
York Dr 24073
Ziegler St 24073
Zimmerman Ln 24073

NUMBERED STREETS

All Street Addresses 24073

DANVILLE VA

General Delivery 24541

POST OFFICE BOXES MAIN OFFICE STATIONS AND BRANCHES

Box No.s
1 - 1732 24543
2001 - 2778 24541
3100 - 4000 24543
4001 - 5482 24540
6170 - 6400 24543
7001 - 7206 24541
8000 - 12875 24543

NAMED STREETS

A And W Dr 24540
Abbott St 24540
Abercrombie Pl 24541
Aby Way 24541
Acorn Ln 24541
Adams Cir 24541
Adams St 24540
Adobe Pl 24540
Afton Rd 24540
Agnor Cir 24541
Aiken St 24541
Airport Dr 24540
Airside Dr 24540
Airview Dr 24540
Albert St 24541
Allen Pl 24540
Allison Dr 24541
Allwood Ct 24541
Almond Rd 24540
Alpine Dr & Ln 24540
Altice Dr 24540
American Legion Blvd 24540
Andes Dr 24540
Andover Pl 24541
Angie Rd 24540
Annhurst Dr 24540
Apollo Ave 24540
Apple Ln 24540
Applewood Dr 24541
April Ln 24540
Arbor Pl 24540
Arey Ct 24541
Arlington Pl & Rd 24541
Arnett Blvd 24540
Arnett Boulevard Ext 24540

Street	ZIP
Arnn Ln	24540
Arrowhead Ln	24540
Ash St	24540
Ashlawn Dr	24541
Ashlyn Dr	24541
Ashwood Pl	24541
Ashworth Ln	24540
Aspen St	24540
Astin Ln	24540
Astor Ct	24540
Astor St	24541
Audubon Dr	24540
Augusta Ave	24541
Austin Cir	24540
Autumn Ln	24541
Avalon Dr	24541
Averett Pl	24541
Avondale Dr	24541
Aye St	24541
Ayers St	24541
Azalea Ln	24540
B Jones Rd	24540
Bachelor Hall Ln	24541
Bachelor Hall Farm Rd	24541
Bailey Pl	24540
Baldwin St	24541
Baltimore Ave	24541
Banner St	24541
Bannister Ct	24540
Bansbury Ct	24541
Barrett St	24541
Barringer Dr	24540
Barter St	24541
Baskerville Ct	24541
Baugh St	24540
Baxter St	24540
Beach Hollow Rd	24541
Beacon Cir	24541
Beaufort St	24541
Beaumont St	24541
Beauregard St	24541
Beaver Dr	24540
Beaverbrook Ct	24541
Beavers Mill Rd	24540
Beccan Ct & Dr	24541
Beckham Ct & Ln	24541
Bee St	24541
Beech Ave	24541
Beechtree Ct	24541
Beechwood Ln	24541
Belaire Dr	24541
Bell Ct & Dr	24541
Bellevue St	24540
Bellmeade Ct & St	24540
Benefield St	24540
Benjamin Ct	24540
Bennett St	24541
Bent Creek Ct & Rd	24540
Berkley St	24540
Berkshire Dr	24541
Berman Dr	24540
Bermuda Rd	24540
Bernard Ct	24540
Berry Hill Ln & Rd	24541
Berryman Ave	24541
Bethel Ct	24540
Bethel Rd	24540
Bethel St	24541
Betts St	24541
Beverly Rd	24541
Big Rock Rd	24541
Big Sky Rd	24540
Birchwood Rd	24540
Bishop Ave	24541
Blackwell Dr	24541
Blaine St	24541
Blair Pl	24540
Blair Loop Rd	24541
Blairmont Dr	24540
Blue Jay St	24541
Blue Ridge View Dr	24541
Boatwright Ave & St	24541
Bonner Ave	24541
Booth Rd	24541
S Boston Rd	24540
Boswell St	24541
Bowe St	24541
Boxwood Ct	24540
Brackenhouse Rd	24540
Bradford St	24540
Bradley Rd	24540
Branch Ct	24540
Branch St	24541
Brandon Ct	
100-299	24541
1000-1199	24540
Brantley Pl	24540
Breezewood Dr	24541
Brentwood Dr	24540
Briarcliff Ln & Pl	24541
Briarwood Dr	24540
Bridge St	24541
Bridgewater Ct	24541
Bridgewood Dr	24540
Bridle Path Trl	24540
Bright Leaf Rd	24540
Brightwell Ct & Dr	24540
Bristol Ct	24541
W Broad St	24541
Broad Street Aly	24541
Broadnax St	24541
Brockton Pl	24541
Bromley Dr	24541
Brook Cir	24541
Brooke Dr	24540
Brookside Ave	24541
Brookview Rd	24540
Brosville Industrial Rd	24541
Brown Ln	24541
Brush Arbor Ct	24540
Bryant Ave	24540
Buckhorn Dr	24540
Buford Rd & St	24541
Bulldog Ln	24540
Burton Rd & St	24541
Burwood Pl	24540
Butt St	24541
Cabell St	24541
Cahill Ct	24541
Cain St	24540
Callahan Hill Rd	24541
Calvary St	24541
Cambridge Cir & Dr	24541
Camburides Dr	24540
Camden St	24541
Camp St	24540
Camp Grove Pl	24540
Campbell St	24540
Campview Rd	24540
Canary Dr	24540
Candlewood Rd	24541
Cane Creek Blvd	24540
Canterbury Rd	24541
Capri Ct	24541
Cardinal Pl	24541
Cardwell St	24540
Carlson Ave	24541
Carolina Ave	24541
Carolyn Ct	24540
Carriage Hill Cir, Ct & Dr	24540
Carrollton Rd	24540
Carson Jones Rd	24540
Carson Lester Ln	24540
Carter Dr	24540
W Carter Dr	24541
Carter St	24540
Carter Farms Ln	24540
Carver Dr	24540
Castle Ct	24540
Cathy Dr & Pl	24540
Cedar Pl	24541
Cedar Trl	24540
Cedar Crest Ln	24540
Cedar Spring Rd	24541
Cedarbrook Dr	24541
Cedarwood Ln	24540
Central Blvd	
300-399	24540
500-599	24541
Central St	24540
Chadwyck Dr	24541
Chambers St	24541
Charles St	24541
Charles Towne Dr	24541
Charlotte Ave	24541
Charming Rd	24541
Chatelaine Ave	24541
Chatham Ave	24541
Chatham Ct	24540
Chatham Dr	24540
Cheltenham Pl	24541
Cherokee Ct	24540
Cherry Ln	24541
Cherry St	24540
Cheryl Dr	24540
Chester Dr	24541
Chestnut Pl	24541
Chestnut Rd	24540
Chestnut St	24540
Cheyenne Dr	24540
Chickadee Rd	24540
Chilton Ct	24540
Christopher Ln	24541
Church Ave	24541
Church St	24540
Churchview Dr	24540
Claiborne St	24540
Clarendon Cir	24541
Clark St	24540
Clarks Mill Rd	24540
Clarkson Dr & St	24540
Clarksville Rd	24540
Clay St	24540
Clearview Dr	
100-199	24541
400-698	24540
700-1399	24540
1401-1699	24540
Clement Ave	24540
Cleveland St	24541
Cliff St	24540
Clifton St	24541
Cline St	24541
Clover Ln	24540
Cobblestone Ct & Dr	24540
Cole Ln	24540
Cole St	24541
Coleman St	24540
Coleman Estates Ct & Rd	24540
College Ave	24541
College Park Dr & Ext	24541
Collie Ter	24541
Collins Dr	24540
Colonial Ct & Pl	24540
Colquohoun St	24541
Commerce St	24541
Concord St	24541
Confederate Ave	24541
Conifer Dr	24541
Conrad Ct	24540
Conway Ct, Dr & Rd	24540
Cooper St	24540
Copper Ct	24540
Copperhead Rd	24540
Corcoran St	24541
Corn Tassel Rd	24540
Corning Dr	24541
Cornwallis Dr	24540
Cottage Grove Ct	24541
Cottonwood Ln & St	24540
Country Ln	24540
Country Club Dr	24541
Court St	24541
Courtland St	24541
Courtney St	24540
Craghead St	24541
Crandon Rd	24541
Crane Rd	24540
Creekside Dr	24540
Crescent St	24540
Crestview Dr & St	24540
Crestwood Dr	24541
Crews Aly	24541
Crosland Ave	24540
Cross Creek Ln	24540
Crown Dr	24540
Crystal Ln	24540
Cumberland Dr	24541
Cunningham St	24540
Custer St	24540
Dakota Dr & Rd	24540
Dallas Ave	24541
Dalton St	24540
Dame St	24541
Dan Ln	24540
Dan St	24541
Dan River Rd	24541
Dan View Dr	24541
Darby Rd	24541
Davenport St	24540
Davis Dr	24540
N Davis Dr	24540
Davis St	24541
Davis Farm Rd	24541
Dean St	24540
Deaton St	24541
Debbie Ln	24540
Dee St	24541
Deer Run Rd	24540
Deercrest Ln	24541
Deerfield Ct & Ln	24541
Delta Rd	24541
Devonshire Ct	24540
Dewey Pl	24541
Dibrell Aly	24541
Dodd St	24541
Dodson Dr	24540
Doe St	24541
Dogwood Dr	24541
Dogwood Ln	24540
Doolittle St	24541
Doubletree Ct	24540
Douglas Ct	24540
Douglas Pl	24540
Dover Cir	24540
Dover Pl	24541
Dovie Ct	24541
Downey Ln	24540
Downing Dr	24540
Druid Ct & Ln	24541
Drury Ln	24540
Dublin Ct	24540
Dudley St	24540
Dula St	24541
Duncan Dr	24541
Dunmore Ave & St	24540
Dyerwood Pl	24541
Eagle Ln	24540
Eagle Springs Rd	24540
East Ave	24540
Easter Dr	24540
Eastlawn Ave	24540
Eastwood Dr	24540
Easy Run Rd	24541
Echols Farm Rd	24541
Ecomnet Way	24540
Ed Hardy Rd	24541
Eden Pl	24540
Edgewood Dr	24540
Edmonds St	24541
Eds Way	24540
Edwards Ct	24541
Edwin Ct	24541
Elizabeth St	24541
Elizabeth Street Ext	24541
Ellarken St	24541
Elliott St	24540
Elon Pl	24540
Elwood Ave	24540
Elwood Ln	24541
Embry St	24541
W End Ave	24541
Englewood Ln	24541
Enterprise Dr	24540
Epps St	24541
Essex St	24541
Ethel Ct	24541
Evans Ln	24540
Evergreen Pl	24540
Exchange St	24541
Executive Ct & Dr	24541
Fagan St	24540
Fairfield Ave	24541
Fairhaven Cir	24540
Fairlawn Dr	24540
Fairmont Cir	24541
Fairview Ave	24541
Fairway Dr	24541
Faith Ct	24540
Falcon Ct	24540
Fall Creek Dr	24540
Falls Rd	24540
Falwell Ct	24540
Farrar St	24540
Fenton Pl	24541
Ferguson Ct	24541
Ferry Rd	24541
Ficklen Ave	24540
Finch Dr	24540
Fitzgerald St	24541
Flint St	24541
Floral Ave	24541
N & S Floyd St	24541
Forest Cir	24541
Forest Ct	24540
Forest St	24541
Forestdale Dr & Pl	24540
Forestlawn Dr	24540
Forestroad Dr	24540
Foster Rd & St	24541
Fox St	24541
Fox Trl	24540
Fox Berry Ln	24541
Fox Hollow Dr	24541
Foxwood Pl	24541
Franklin Ct	24540
Franklin Pl	24541
Franklin St	24541
Franklin Tpke	24540
Frazier Rd	24540
Freeze Rd	24540
Fritz Way	24540
Front St	24540
Fuller St	24540
Fulton Hts	24541
Gaither Rd	24541
Garden Grove Ave	24541
Gardner St	24540
Garfield St	24541
Garland St	24541
Gatewood Ave	24541
W Gay St	24541
Gemstone Ln	24541
Gerald Ln	24540
Gery St	24540
Gilbert Ct, Dr & St	24540
Gilliland Dr	24541
Ginger Dr	24540
Girard St	24540
Glen Oak Dr	24541
Glendale Ave	24540
Glenlyn St	24540
Glenn St	24540
Gloucester St	24540
Godfrey St	24541
Golf Club Rd	24540
Goode St	24541
Goodyear Blvd	24541
Gordon Ave	24540
Gough St	24540
Grace St	24541
Grand Ave	24541
Grandimere Dr	24541
Grandin Ct	24541
Granite Dr	24540
Grant St	24541
Grant Street Ext	24541
Granville Dr	24540
Gray St	24541
Graymont Pl	24541
Grays Park Rd	24541
E Green St	24541
Green Acre Dr	24540
Green Farm Rd	24541
Green Oak Ln	24540
Greencroft Pl	24541
Greenhill Dr	24540
Greentree Rd	24541
Greenwich Cir	24540
Greenwood Ave	24541
Greenwood Dr	24540
Greenwood Ln	24540
Grenadier Cir	24541
Gretna St	24540
Grove St	24541
Grove Park Cir	24541
Guerrant St	24540
Guilford St	24540
Gunns Aly	24540
Gypsum Rd	24541
Hairston Ln & St	24540
Haley St	24540
Halifax Rd & St	24540
Hamilton Ct & St	24541
Hamlin Ave	24540
Hampton Dr	24540
Hanks Ave & Ln	24541
Hanley Cir	24541
Haraway Rd	24540
Hardy Creek Ln	24541
Harley Ln	24540
Harris Pl	24541
Harrison St	24540
Hartford St	24540
Hawks Ridge Rd	24540
Hawthorne Ct & Dr	24541
Hayes Ave	24540
Hayes Ct	24541
Haymore St	24540
Haynesworth Dr	24541
Hazelwood Ct	24541
Hearp Ln	24540
Heather St	24541
Hedrick Ct	24540
Hemlock Dr	24540
Hemlock Ln	24541
Henry Rd & St	24541
Hereford Ln	24541
Hermitage Dr	24541
Herndon Pl	24541
Hickory Ct	24540
Hickory Forest Rd	24540
High St	24541
Highland Ct	24540
Hillcrest Ave	24540
N Hills Ct	24541
Hinesville Rd	24541
Holbrook Ave & St	24541
Holcomb St	24541
Holland Rd	24541
Holt Garrison Pkwy	24540
Homeport Ln	24540
Honey Rd	24540
Hopkins St	24541
Horseshoe Rd	24541
Howeland Cir	24541
Howerton Ln	24540
Howertons Bottom Rd	24540
Hughes St	24541
N & S Hunter St	24541
Hunters Rdg & Run	24540
Hunters Chase	24540
Hunting Hills Rd	24540
Huntington Pl	24541
Hurt St	24540
Hyler Cir	24540
Hyler Farm Ln	24541
Hylton Ave	24541
Ida St	24540
Idlewood Ter	24540
Indian Trail Rd	24540
Indian Valley Rd	24541
Industrial Ave	24541
Inge St	24540
Ingram Rd	24541
Ingram St	24540
Inman Rd	24541
Ireson St	24541
Iris Ct & Ln	24540
Isom Ct	24540
Ivy St	24540
Jackson Hts	24540
Jacob Pl	24540
Jamerson Rd N & S	24540
James Ct	24540
James Rd	24541
W James St	24540
Janice Ct	24541
Jay St	24541
Jeanette Dr	24540
Jefferson Ave	24541
Jefferson Rd	24540
Jefferson St	24541
Jenny Ln	24541
Jerry Dr	24541
Joanis Dr	24540
Joe Carter Rd	24541
John Dr	24540
John St	24541
Johnson St	24540
Johnson Oakes Rd	24540
Jones Xing	24541
Joplin St	24540
Jordon St	24540
Joy Cir	24541
Juless St	24541
Juniper Dr	24540
Justin Ln	24540
Kayewood Ln	24541
Keatts Ln	24541
Keen St	24540
Keister St	24540
Kemper Ct & Rd	24541
Kemper Road Ext	24541
Kendall Pl	24540
Kenilworth Ave	24541
Kenmore Dr	24541
Kennon Dr	24540
Kenridge Cir	24540
Kensington Ct	24541
Kent Ln & St	24541
Kentuck Rd	24540
Kerr Ln	24540
Keswick Dr	24540
Kimberly Ave	24541
King St	24540
Kingoff Dr	24540
Kings Ct	24540
Kingston Rd	24541
Kinsley Ct	24541
Kinzer Ave & St	24540
Kirk Dr	24540
Kirkwood Dr	24541
Kittyhawk Dr	24540
Knight Celotex Way	24541
Knollwood St	24541
Knollwood Ter	24540
Knottingham Way	24540
Kohler Rd	24540
Koyeton Way	24540
Kristen Ln	24540
Kristy Ln	24540
Kyle Rd	24541
Lady Astor Pl & St	24541
Lafayette Dr	24540
Lake Heron Dr	24541
Lakeside Dr	24540
Lakeview Ter	24540
Lakewood Dr	24540
Lamar St	24541
Lamberth Dr	24541
Lancaster St	24540
Lands End Rd	24541
Lanier Ave	24541
Laniers Mill Rd	24540
Lansbury Dr	24540
Lansdale Dr	24540
Laramie Cir	24541
Larchmont Way	24541
Laurel Ave	24541
Laurel Woods Dr	24541
Lawless Creek Rd	24540
Lawson St	24541
Layton Ave	24541
Leah Ct	24540
Lee St	24541
Leemont Ct	24540
Lemon Ln	24541
Lennox Ct	24540

Street	ZIP
Leslie Ln	24541
Lester Ln	24540
Levelton St	24541
Lewis Ln	24540
Lewis St	24541
Lexington Ave	24540
Liberty Bell Ct	24541
Lincoln St	24541
Linden Dr, Ln & Pl	24541
Lindhurst Dr	24540
Lion Ln	24540
Lipton Ln	24541
Lithia Springs Ave	24541
Little St	24540
Little Creek Ct & Rd	24540
Little River Rd	24541
Livestock Rd	24540
Lloyd St	24540
Lockerman Ln	24541
Lockett Cir, Dr & St	24541
Locust Ln & St	24540
Log Cabin Rd	24540
Lombardy Ct	24541
London Dr	24541
London Bridge Dr	24541
Long Cir	24541
Longview Ave & Ct	24541
Loomfixer Lake Rd	24541
Loretta Ln	24541
Lorillard Cir	24540
Lovelace Dr	24540
Lovell Dr	24541
Lowell St	24540
Lowery Ct	24540
Lowes Dr	24540
Loyal St	24541
Lucky Ln	24541
Luna Lake Rd	24541
Lynch Dr & St	24540
Lynn St	24541
Lynndale Dr	24540
Lynrock Ct	24540
Lynskey Farm Rd	24541
Mabin St	24541
Macon St	24540
Madison Ave & St	24540
Magnolia Dr	24541
Main St	24541
N Main St	24540
S Main St	24541
W Main St	24541
Major Ave & Ct	24540
Mall Dr	24540
Mallard Lake Dr	24541
Manchester Ave	24541
Mangrums Rd	24541
Manor Ln & Pl	24541
Maple Dr	24540
Maple Ln	24541
Maple Grove Ave	24541
Maplewood St	24540
N & S Market St	24541
Marshall Ter	24541
Martha St	24541
Martin Ave & Rd	24541
Martindale Dr	24541
Martinsville Hwy	24541
Mary Cir & Ln	24540
Mary Miles Dr	24540
Mason Ave	24541
Masonite Dr	24541
Matthew Cir	24540
Maury St	24541
Maxey Ln	24540
Maxine Rd	24541
Maybrook Ave	24540
Mayo St	24540
Mclaughlin Dr & St	24540
Meades Aly	24540
Meadowbrook Cir	24541
Meadowbrook Dr	24540
Meadowood Ln	24540
Meadowview Ct & Dr	24541
Meadowwood Ct	24540
Medical Center Rd	
100-800	24540
802-1498	24540
1701-1797	24541
1799-3599	24541
Melbourne Cir	24541
Melrose Ave & Dr	24540
Melville Ave	24541
Memorial Dr	24541
Merricks Branch Cir	24540
Middle St	24540
Midland St	24540
Milford Pl	24540
Mill Creek Rd	24540
Millerton Rd	24540
Millsville Ln	24540
Milton Ave	24541
Mimosa St	24541
Mitchell Ct & St	24541
Moanna Pl	24540
Mockingbird Ln	24540
Moffett St	24540
Monroe St	24541
Montague St	24541
Monument St	24540
Moorefield Ln	24541
Moorefield Bridge Rd	
200-1100	24540
1102-1598	24540
1901-1997	24541
1999-3200	24541
3202-3498	24541
Morris Ave	24541
Motley Ave	24540
Mount Cross Rd	24540
Mount Hermon Cir & Ln	24540
Mount Hermon School Rd	24540
Mount Olivet Ln	24540
Mount Vernon Ave	24541
Mount View Ct	24540
Mount View Dr	24541
Mount View Rd	24540
Mountain Hill Rd	24540
Mountain View Ave	24541
Mowbray Arch	24541
Mulberry Rd	24540
Murphy Cir	24540
Myrtle Ave	24540
Nannie G Edwards Dr	24540
Naples St	24541
Nathalie Ln	24540
Navajo Ct	24540
Neal Ct	24540
Nelson Ave	24540
New St	24540
New Hope Way	24541
New Ingram Rd	24541
Newbury Way	24541
Newgass St	24541
Newton St	24541
Niagara Ct	24540
Noble Ave	24540
Noel Ave	24541
Nor Dan Dr	24540
Norfolk Pl	24541
Normandale St	24540
North Ave	24540
Northern Dr	24540
Northmont Blvd & Ct	24540
Northpointe Ln	24540
Northridge Dr	24540
Northside Dr	24540
Northwest Blvd	24540
Norwood Dr	24540
O Briant Ave	24540
Oak Dr	24541
Oak Ln	24541
Oak St	24540
Oak Creek Dr	24541
Oak Crest Rd	24540
Oak Forest Cir	24540
Oak Hill Rd	24540
Oak Ridge Ave & Ln	24541
Oak Ridge Farms Rd	24541
Oak Tree Ln	24541
Oakhaven Dr	24541
Oakland Ave, Dr & Ln	24540
Oakmont Trl	24541
Oakvale Cir	24540
Oakwood Cir, Dr & Pl	24541
Old Farm Rd	24541
Old Greensboro Rd	24541
Old Halifax Rd	24540
Old Highway 360	24541
Old Mayfield Rd	24541
Old Mount Cross Rd	24540
Old Piney Forest Rd	24540
Old Quarry Rd	24540
Old Richmond Rd	24540
Old Riverside Dr	24541
Old South Main St	24541
Old Spring Ct & Rd	24540
Olde Hunting Trl	24540
E Orchard Dr & Rd	24541
Orphanage Rd	24540
Ottawa Ct, Dr & Ln	24540
Overby St	24540
Oxford Pl	24541
Oxford St	24540
Page Rd & St	24541
Palm St	24541
Park Ave, Cir & St	24541
Park Avenue Ext	24541
Parker Pl & Rd	24540
Parker Forest Trl	24540
Parkland Dr	24540
Parkmoor Ct	24541
Parkview Pl	24541
Parkway Dr	24540
Parrish Rd	24540
Parrott St	24540
Parsons St	24541
Patton St	24541
Paul St	24541
Paxton Ave & St	24541
Peach St	24541
Peachtree St	24540
Peacock Acres Trl	24541
Pearl St	24541
Peastank Rd	24540
Pecan Ct	24541
Pendleton Rd	24541
Pepper Ln	24541
Peters Ct	24541
Phillips Ct	24540
Piedmont Dr	24540
Piedmont Pl	24541
Pin Oak Ln	24541
Pine St	24541
Pine Hill Cir	24540
Pine Lake Rd	24541
Pine Tree Ln	24541
Pinecrest Dr	24540
Pinecroft Cir & Rd	24540
Pineview Dr	24540
Pineview Rd	24541
Piney Rd	24541
Piney Forest Rd	24540
Pittwood Dr	24540
Plantation Rd	24541
Pleasant View Ave	24541
Plum St	24540
Pocahontas Rd	24540
Poplar Rd	24540
Poplar St	24541
Poplar Trce	24540
Poplar Falls Dr	24540
Powell Ave	24540
Powhatan Dr	24540
Prather Dr	24540
Presley Ln	24540
Preston Pl	24541
Primrose Ct & Pl	24541
Princess Dr	24540
Princeton Dr	24540
Princeton Rd	24540
W Prospect St	24541
Pruitt Rd	24540
Pumpkin Creek Ln	24541
Purdum Rd	24540
Quail Dr	24540
Quarry St	24540
Quarry Access Rd	24541
R And L Smith Dr	24540
Radio Ln	24541
Ragsdale Rd	24540
Rainbow Cir	24540
Raintree Ct & Rd	24541
N & S Raleigh Ct	24540
Rambler Dr	24541
Ranch Dr	24541
Randolph St	24541
Red Bird Ln	24540
Red Bud Ln	
200-299	24540
301-399	24540
900-999	24541
Redwood Dr	24541
Reese Dr	24540
Reid Ct	24540
Reid St	24541
Reina Ct	24540
Reuben Ct	24541
Rhodenizer St	24540
Rice St	24540
Riceland St	24540
Richardson Ct	24541
Richardson St	24540
Richmond Ave & Blvd	24540
Ricketts St	24540
Ridge Rd	24540
N Ridge St	24541
S Ridge St	24541
Ridgecrest Ct & Dr	24541
Ridgeway Dr	24541
Ridgewood Dr	24541
Ringgold Rd	24540
Ringgold Industrial Pkwy	24540
Ripley Ct, Dr, Ln & Pl	24540
Ripple Meade St	24540
Rison St	24541
River St & Ter	24540
River Oak Dr	24541
River Park Dr	24540
River Ridge Rd	24541
River Run Rd	24541
Riverbend Rd	24541
Riverpoint Dr	24540
Riverside Dr	
100-2899	24540
2900-2922	24541
2901-2923	24540
2924-6799	24541
Rivertree Rd	24541
Riverview Ave, Dr & St	24541
Riviera Dr	24540
W Roberts St	24541
Robertson Ave	24541
Robertson Ln	24540
Robin Dr	24541
Robin Hood Ct & Dr	24540
Robindell Ct	24541
Robinwood Pl	24540
Rockford Pl	24541
Rocking Chair Rd	24540
Rocklawn Ave & Pl	24540
Rockwood Dr	24541
Rocky Ln	24540
Rocky Knoll Ln	24541
Rosedale Ct	24541
Roselane Dr	24540
Rosemary Ln	24541
Rosewood Ct	24540
Rosewood Ln	24541
Rosewood St	24540
Ross St	24541
Rover Ridge Dr	24540
Royham Dr	24541
Rugby Rd	24541
Ruskin St	24540
Rutledge St	24541
Saddle Rd	24541
Saint Paul Cir	24541
Salisburg Cir	24541
Salisbury Cir	24541
Sam Haley Rd	24541
Samuel Bnd, Ct & Rd	24540
Samuel Road Ext	24540
Sandy Ct	24541
Sandy Creek Rd	24540
Sandy River Dr	24541
Sanford Rd	24541
Sanitary Rd	24541
Saunders Dr	24541
Scales St	24540
Schoolfield Dr	24541
Scott St	24540
Searcy St	24541
Seay St	24541
Sedgefield Ct & Ln	24541
Seeland Rd	24541
Sellers Rd	24540
Selma Ave	24541
Seminole Dr & Trl	24541
Setliff St	24541
Shadowwood Ct	24540
Shady Ln	24541
Shamrock Dr	24541
Shannon Dr	24540
Sharon Ln & Way	24540
Shavers Johnson St	24540
Sheffield Dr	24541
Sheldon Ct	24540
Shelton St	24541
Shepherd Ave	24540
Sheridan Pl	24541
Sherman St	24541
Sherwood Dr	24540
Shields Rd	24541
Shoreham Dr	24541
Short St	24540
Shumate St	24541
Signet Rd	24540
Silas Cole Farm Rd	24540
Silver Creek Ct, Ln & Rd	24540
Sky Hawk Ct	24540
Skylark Ct & Dr	24541
Skyline Ave	24540
Slade St	24541
Slaughter Ave	24540
Slayton Ave	24540
Smith St	24541
Song Bird Ln	24540
South St	24541
Southampton Ave	24541
Southern St	24541
Southland Ct & Dr	24541
Spencer St	24540
Spring Ave & St	24541
Springfield Rd	24540
Springview Ct	24541
Spruce St	24541
St Clair Dr	24541
Stanley Ct & Dr	24541
Starling Ave	24540
Starmont Blvd & Dr	24540
Station Dr	24540
Steam Way	24540
Steel Soring Pl	24541
W Stephens St	24541
Still St	24541
Still Spring Dr	24541
Stinson Dr	24540
Stokes St	24541
Stokesland Ave	24541
Stokesland Avenue Ext	24541
Stone Creek Rd	24540
Stonegate Way	24541
Stoneridge Dr	24540
Stonewall Ct	24540
Stony Mill Rd	
100-1499	24540
1501-1699	24540
1900-4299	24541
4301-4399	24541
Stony Mill Elementary Cir	24541
Stony Mill School Rd	24541
Stratford Pl	24541
Stuart St	24541
Subletts Aly	24540
Suburban Dr	24540
Sugar Creek Ct	24541
Sugar Lake Dr	24541
Sugartree Church Rd	
200-1399	24540
1401-1499	24540
1600-1798	24541
1800-3799	24541
3801-4199	24541
Sugartree Manor Dr	24541
Summer Ln	24541
Summit Dr & Rd	24540
Sunny Knoll Ln	24540
Sunnyside St	24540
Sunset Dr	24540
Sunset Pl	24540
Sunset St	24541
Sunset Way	24541
Surry Ln	24541
Sussex Pl	24541
Sutherlin Ave & Pl	24541
Swain Dr	24540
Swanson Ave & St	24540
Sweet William Ct	24540
Sweetbriar Dr	24540
Sweetgum Ln	24540
Sycamore Cir	24540
Sycamore St	24541
Sydenham St	24541
Sylvan Rd	24540
Talbott Dr	24540
Tamworth Dr & Pl	24540
Target Dr	24541
Tarpley Pl	24540
Tate St	24540
Taylor Dr & St	24541
Teal Ct	24541
Temple Ave	24541
Terry Ave	24540
Thistle Trl	24540
E & W Thomas Ct & St	24540
Thompson Rd	24541
Thrush St	24540
Thunderbird Cir	24540
Timberlake Dr	24540
Tinsley Ct	24540
Tolliver Pl	24541
Tower Dr	24540
Townes St	24541
Trade St	24541
Treadway Dr	24541
Tree Ct	24541
Tree Lake Dr	24541
Truman Dr	24541
Tuckaway Lake Rd	24541
Tuggle Ct	24541
Tunstall Rd	24541
Tunstall High Rd	24540
Turpin St	24541
Tuscarora Dr	24540
Twin Arch Dr	24541
Twin Brook Rd	24541
Twin Oaks Ln	24541
Twin Springs Elementary Cir	24540
Tyler Ave	24541
Tyler Dr	24541
U S Highway 29	24540
N & S Union St	24541
Updike Pl	24541
Upper St	24541
V F W Dr	24541
Valley St	24541
Van Buren St	24540
Vance St	24540
Vance Hill Rd	24540
Vandola Rd	24541
Vandola Church Rd	24541
Vann St	24541
Vassar St	24541
Verne Blvd	24540
Vicar Pl & Rd	24540
Victoria St	24540
Vine Cir	24540
Vinton Pl	24540
Virginia Ave	24541
Virginia Ln	24540
Vista Ct	24541
Wade St	24541
Wagner St	24540
Walden Ct	24541
Walker Cir	24541
Walker Ct	24540
Walker Dr	24540
Walker Pl	24540
Walker St	24540
Wall St	24541
Walnut Rd	24541
Walnut St	24540
Walnut Creek Ln & Rd	24540
Walnut Hill Rd	24541
Walter Beavers Pl	24540
Walters St	24541
Walters Mill Rd	24541
Ward Ct	24540
Warren St	24541
Washburn Dr	24541
Washington St	24540
Water St	24540
Waterford Ct	24541
Watlington Ct	24540
Watson St	24541
Wayles St	24540
Wellington Pl	24541
Wendell Ct	24540
Wendell Scott Dr	24540
Wendin Ln	24540
Wentz Cir	24541
Wesley Dr	24540
West Ct	24541
Westhampton Ave	24541
Westhaven Dr	24541
Westminister Ct	24541
Westmore Dr	24541
Westmoreland Ct	24541
Westover Dr, Ln & Pl	24541
Westridge Dr	24541
Westview Dr & Pl	24540
Westwood Ct & Dr	24541
Wheatley Rd	24540
Whispering Pines Rd	24541
White St	24540
White Rock Rd	24540
Whitfield St	24541
Whitmell St	24541
Whitmell School Rd	24540
Whitmore Dr	24540
Whittington Dr	24541
Wigwam Dr	24540
Wilbourne Ave	24540
Wilderness Ln	24540
Wildflower Rd	24540
Wildhurst Ln	24540
Wildwood Ct & Ter	24540
Wilkerson Rd	24540
William Dr	24540
Williams Ct & St	24540
Williamson Rd	24540
Willoughby Pl	24541
Willow St	24540
Willow Briar Ln	24541
Wills St	24541
Wilson Rd & St	24541
Wilton Ave	24541
Wimbish Dr & Pl	24541
Windridge Ct	24540
Windsor Ct, Pl & Trl	24541
Winfield Pl	24541
Winslow St	24541
Winstead Dr	24541
Winston Cir	24540
Winston Ct	24541
Winston Dr	24541
Winston Rd	24541
Winterberry Rd	24540
Winthrop Ct & Dr	24540
W Withers Cir & Rd	24541
W Witt Rd	24540
Womack Dr	24540
Wood Ave	24541

Wood Avenue Ext 24541
N & S Woodberry Ave & Dr 24540
Woodcrest Hts 24541
Woodcroft Dr & Pl 24540
Woodfinch Cir 24541
Woodhaven Dr 24540
Wooding Ave 24541
Woodlake Dr 24540
Woodland Dr 24541
W Woodlawn Ct & Dr 24541
Woodrow Ln 24540
Woodside Dr & Rd 24540
Woodstock Way 24541
Woodview Dr 24540
Worsham Ct & St 24540
Wrenn Dr 24540
Wyatt Dr 24540
Wyllie Ave 24540
Wyndover Dr 24541
Yates St 24540
York Pl 24541

NUMBERED STREETS

1st Ct 24541
1st St 24540
2nd St 24540
3rd Ave & St 24540
4th St 24540
5th St 24540
6th St 24540
7th St 24540

DUMFRIES VA

General Delivery 22026

POST OFFICE BOXES MAIN OFFICE STATIONS AND BRANCHES

Box No.s
All PO Boxes 22026

RURAL ROUTES

50, 51, 52, 54, 55, 56, 57, 58, 59 22025
01, 02, 10, 13 22026

NAMED STREETS

Accolon Ct 22025
Acts Ln 22026
Afton Ct 22025
Alexander Pl 22025
Allen Dent Rd 22026
Allerton Ct 22026
Allstadt Farm Loop 22025
American Elm Ct 22026
Amsley Ct 22026
Andrews Pl 22025
Anglia Loop 22025
Antrim Cir 22026
Apple Ln 22026
Apple Cider Ct 22026
Ashgrove Dr 22025
Ashmere Cir 22025
Atterbury Ct 22025
Atwater Ln 22025
Autumn Ln 22025
Avenel Ln 22026
Avon Dr 22025
Azalea Sands Ln 22026
Backwater Ct 22025
Badger Ct 22026
Banks Ct 22026
Barger Pl 22025
Barnacle Pl 22025
Barrington Pl 22025
Barrley Ct & Dr 22026
Barron Heights Rd 22025
Bassett Ct 22026
Battersea Rd 22026
Bayou Bend Cir 22025
Beachland Way 22025
Beachview Dr 22025
Beachwater Ct 22025
Beacon Ct 22025
Beacon Hill Pl 22025
Beaver Dam Rd 22025
Belle Isle Dr 22026
Belleplain Ct 22026
Benecia Ln 22025
Benson Ct 22025
Birch Creek Ct 22026
Bishop Pl 22026
Blowing Leaf Pl 22025
Boxwood Dr 22025
Brandywine Rd 22025
Brawner Dr 22025
Breeze Way 22025
Brent Ridge Ct 22026
Briarwood Dr 22026
Bridgeport Dr 22025
Brockenbrough Dr 22026
Buck Ln 22025
Buckingham Ct 22025
Buell Ct 22026
Buena Vista Dr 22025
Buffel Duck Ct 22026
Bunker Ct 22025
Butler Pl 22025
Butterfly Way 22026
Cahill Ln 22026
Cajun Ct 22025
Camellia Ln 22025
Camelot Ct 22025
Cameron St 22026
Canal Rd 22026
Candlestick Ct 22025
Canton Ct 22026
Cape May Ct 22026
Capri Ln 22026
Catamaran Ct 22025
Caxton Pl 22025
Cedar Knoll Ct 22025
Celebration Way 22025
Chalice Ct 22025
Champion Oak Dr 22025
Chapman Pl 22025
Chapman Mill Trl 22025
Cherry Hill Rd 22026
Chesapeake Dr 22026
China Grove Mews 22025
Chisholm Ln 22026
Chogburn Ln 22026
Cindy Ln 22025
Clancy Dr 22026
Clearwater Ct 22025
Cliffbrook Ct 22025
Cliffview Dr 22025
Cockpit Point Rd 22026
Cogenbury Ct 22025
Colonial St 22026
Colonial Port Rd 22026
Confederate Ct 22026
Conqueror Ct 22026
Continental Dr 22025
Corwin Pl 22025
Cosgrove Way 22026
Country Club Dr 22025
Cove Ln 22025
Cranberry Ct 22026
Crestleigh Ct 22025
Crocus Ln 22025
Crosscut Ln 22026
Crystal Downs Ter 22026
Curtis Dr 22026
Cusack Ln 22026
Cypress Ct 22025
Dahlgren Pl 22026
Dalebrook Dr 22025
Dancing Leaf Pl 22025
Dartmoor Dr 22025
Deer Park Dr 22025
Denali Pl 22025
Desert Palm Ct 22026
Detrick Trl 22025
Devonald Pl 22025
Deweys Run Ln 22026
Diamond Point Mews 22026
Dickerson Pl 22025
Dolphin Dr 22026
Dominican Dr 22026
Dominion Dr 22025
Dovetail Ct 22026
Downy Flake Mews 22025
Dr David Cline Ln 22026
Dry Powder Cir 22026
Dryden Way 22025
Duke St 22026
Dumfries Dr 22026
Dumfries Pl 22026
Dumfries Rd
15900-17199 22025
17200-17399 22026
Dumfries Shopping Plz 22026
Duncan Pl 22025
Dunes Ct 22026
Dunnington Pl 22026
Ebb Tide Ct 22025
Eby Dr 22026
Edgehill Dr 22025
Edgewood Dr 22025
Equinox Way 22025
Eugene Pl 22026
Exeter Dr 22026
N Fairfax St 22026
Fairway Dr 22025
Fallstone Pl 22025
Fawn Pl 22025
Festival Spirit Way 22025
Fettler Park Dr 22025
Fishermans Cv 22025
Flatstick Ct 22026
Fort Donelson Ct 22026
Fort Fisher Ct 22026
Fort Henry Ct 22026
Fort Monroe Ct 22026
Fort Pemberton Ct 22026
Fort Pickens Ct 22026
Fort Pulaski Ct 22026
Fort Sumter Ct 22026
Fortuna Center Plz 22025
Four Seasons Dr 22025
N Fraley Blvd 22026
Francis West Ln 22026
Fresh Meadow Trl 22026
Friar Loop 22025
Garcia Way 22026
Garden Gate Ct 22025
Gentle Wood Ln 22026
Gibson Mill Rd 22026
Gilder Way 22026
Glastonbury Ct 22025
Glennville Dr 22026
Glouster Pointe Dr 22026
Golden Gate Way 22025
Golf Club Dr 22025
Graham St 22026
Graham Park Rd 22026
Grant Cottage Dr 22025
Great Harvest Ct 22025
Greenfield Pl 22025
Greentree Ln 22026
Grey Ghost Ct 22025
Groveside Ct 22025
Gullwing Dr 22026
Hampstead Ridge Ct 22026
Harbor Station Pkwy 22026
Harmony Pl 22025
Harmsworth Dr 22026
Harpers Ferry Dr 22025
Harwood Oaks Ct 22026
Hedgeman St 22026
Henderson Ln 22025
Heth Ct 22025
Hickory Creek Ct 22026
Hickory Nut Pl 22026
Hidden Valley Ct 22025
Hide A Way Dr 22025
Higgins Dr 22025
Historic Virginia Ct 22025
Holleyside Ct & Dr 22025
Holly St 22026
Holly Creek Ct 22026
Holly Hill Dr 22025
Hopkins Dr 22025
Horton Ct 22025
Hoskins Way 22026
Hot Springs Way 22025
Hour Glass Dr 22026
Howard St 22026
Hudson River Ct 22025
Hunley Mill Pl 22025
Huntgate Ln 22025
Hyacinth Pl 22025
Ibsen Pl 22025
Inlet Pl 22025
Interstate Dr 22026
Iris Ln 22025
Isle Royale Ter 22025
Islip Loop 22026
Jasper Loop 22025
Jasper Hill Ct 22026
Jefferson Davis Hwy 22026
Jester Ct 22025
John Pary Way 22026
John Robinson Ln 22026
John Rolfe Ct 22026
Jonathan Ct 22025
Kagera Dr 22025
Kensington Pl 22025
Kenton Cir 22025
Kersey Cir 22025
Keswick Ct 22025
Kevin Walker Dr 22025
Keys Ridge Rd 22025
Kildare Ln 22026
Kilkenny Way 22025
Kilpatrick Pl 22026
Kings Row Pl 22025
Kings Valley Dr 22025
Kirby Dr 22026
La Mauricie Loop 22025
Lands End Ct 22025
Lansdale Pl 22025
Lansing Ct 22026
Larchmont Ct 22026
Larkin Dr 22026
Larkspur Ln 22025
Laurel St 22026
Laurel Ridge Rd 22025
Lazy Day Ln 22025
Leonard St 22026
Lindenberry Ln 22026
Linton Ct 22026
Live Oaks Ct 22025
Locust Creek Dr 22026
Loganberry Ln 22026
London Pl 22025
Lounsbery Dr 22026
Lunar Eclipse Dr 22025
Lyda Ln 22026
Macrae Ct 22026
Madden Way 22026
Main St 22026
Malory Ct 22025
Mammoth Cave Loop 22025
Maple St 22026
Maple Glen Ct 22025
Marbury Heights Way 22025
Marhalt Pl 22025
Marjon Ct 22025
Marlington Dr 22025
Marsh Harbor Ln 22026
Marshlake Ln 22025
Maybury Pl 22025
Maywood Dr 22026
Mcclellan Ct 22026
Mcdowell Ct 22026
Medford Dr 22026
Melody Ln 22025
Melting Snow Pl 22025
Metheny Pl 22025
Middleton Loop 22025
Mill Spring Dr 22025
Milroy Dr 22026
Mimosa Trl 22025
Mina Ln 22025
Mine Rd
17000-17799 22025
17800-17899 22026
Miss Packard Ct 22026
Moncure Ct & Dr 22025
Monmouth Ct 22026
Montezuma Way 22025
Montview Dr 22025
Moot Dr 22025
Morgan Ct 22026
Mountain Laurel Loop 22025
Mulberry Point Ct 22025
Mulcaster Ter 22025
Myrtle Pl 22025
Myrtlewood Dr 22026
Mystic Ct 22025
Naples Ln 22026
Nelm Way 22025
Nicely Ct 22026
Nichols Ct 22026
Nightingale Pl 22025
Northgate Dr 22025
Nugent Ln 22026
Oak Crest Ct 22025
October Glory Loop 22025
Old Stage Rd 22025
Old Stage Coach Rd 22026
Olivia Way 22025
Oriole Ct 22025
Ostenbury Ct 22025
Outlook Pl 22025
Overlook Rd 22026
Oyster Bay Ct 22026
Pacific Rim Ter 22025
Paige Point Way 22025
Palton Dr 22025
Panther Pride Dr 22026
Peach Ct 22025
Pebblewood St 22025
Peppermill Ct 22025
Periscope Pl 22026
Philena St 22025
Pike Trl 22025
Pine Ct & St 22026
Pine Bluff Dr 22025
Pinecrest Ct 22025
Piper Glenn Ct 22026
Pleasant Rd 22025
Pleasant Hill Pl 22025
Point Pleasant Ln 22026
Pointe Center Ct 22025
Pony Ridge Turn 22026
Port Washington Ct 22025
Porters Inn Dr 22025
Possum Point Rd 22026
Potomac River Blvd 22026
Prendend Dr 22026
Presidential Hill Loop 22025
Prestwick Ct 22025
Prince Charles Ln 22026
Prince William Cir 22026
Purcival Ct 22025
Queens Ln 22026
Renton Ct 22025
Reservoir Loop 22026
Rhame Dr 22025
Riderli St 22025
Ridgecrest Dr 22025
Ridgewood Ct 22025
Rincon Pl 22025
Ring Necked Ct 22026
Rising Fawn Ter 22025
River Heritage Blvd 22026
River Ridge Blvd 22026
Rocky Mount Ln 22026
Rose Hill Cir 22026
Rotunda Way 22025
Royal Crescent Ct 22025
Russett Maple Ct 22026
Saltwater Dr 22026
Sanibel Ct 22025
Sassafras Tree Ct 22026
Sea Skiff Way 22026
Seal Pl 22025
Secret Grove Ct 22025
Sedgewick Pl 22026
Shadow Oak Ct 22025
Shadow Woods Ct 22025
Shady Knoll Ct 22025
Shaker Ct 22025
Sheffield Dr 22025
Shell Cast Loop 22026
Shorehaven Way 22025
Sigel Ct 22026
Silvan Glen Dr 22025
Silver Arrow Dr 22026
Silver Leaf Ct 22025
Singletree Ln 22025
Skiff Ct 22025
Skyline Dr 22025
Sligo Loop 22026
Solstice Ln 22025
Southwood Pl 22025
Spalding Dr 22025
Sparkling Brook Loop 22025
Spillway Ln 22025
Spriggs Lane Fire Rd 22025
Spring Branch Blvd 22025
Stedham Cir 22025
Steele Ct 22026
Stewart Ln 22026
Stockbridge Dr 22025
Stone Mountain Ct 22025
Streamside Ct 22025
Sugar Maple Ln 22025
Sugarbush Ln 22025
Summer Duck Dr 22026
Sunny Knoll Dr 22025
Sutersmill Way 22026
Swans Creek Ln 22026
Sycamore Valley Way 22026
Taconic Cir & Ct 22025
Takeaway Ln 22026
Tallowwood Dr 22025
Talon Dr 22025
Tangariro Sq 22025
Tebbs Ln 22026
Telegraph Station Loop 22026
Telescope Ln 22026
Terri Ct 22026
Thistle Ct 22025
Timber Ridge Dr 22025
Timid Creek Ct 22025
Tintagel Ct 22025
Tompkins Ct 22026
Toms River Loop 22025
Tony Ct 22026
Tranio Ct 22025
Triangle Shopping Plz 22026
Tripoli Blvd & Ct 22026
Trisail Ct 22025
Tuckahoe Ct 22026
Tulip Tree Pl 22026
Tweezer Ct 22026
Twin Six Ln 22026
Twist Ct 22026
Vals Way 22025
Van Buren Rd 22025
Vaughn Ln 22026
Vault Ln 22026
Victoria Falls Dr 22025
Vidalia Ct 22026
Viewpoint Cir 22025
Village Pkwy 22026
Vineland Pl 22026
Virginia Dr 22026
Vista Dr 22026
Washington St 22026
Waters Ln 22026
Waters Edge Ct 22025
Waterway Dr 22025
Wayside Dr 22026
Weeping Cherry Ct 22026
Wendy Ct 22025
Wexford Loop 22026
Whisperwood Ct 22025
White Haven Dr 22026
Whitings Brigade Dr 22026
Widewater Dr 22025
William Johnston Ln 22026
Williams Ct 22026
Williamstown Dr 22026
Willow Ln 22026
Willow Oak Pl 22025
Wilmer Porter Ct 22026
Wilson Ct & St 22026
Wiltshire Pl 22025
Winding Creek Dr 22025
Windsong Ln 22025
Windward Ct 22025
Wintercress Ct 22025
Woodglen Ct 22025
Yellow Stone Loop 22025
Yew Grove Pl 22026
Yorktown Dr 22026
Yost Ln 22026

FAIRFAX VA

General Delivery 22030

POST OFFICE BOXES MAIN OFFICE STATIONS AND BRANCHES

Box No.s
A - H 22031
1 - 1600 22038
2001 - 2999 22031
3001 - 10165 22038
10200 - 10230 22035
10222 - 10398 22038
10400 - 10500 22031

NAMED STREETS

Abernathy Ct 22032
Abington Ct 22032
Abner Ave 22030
Acacia Ln 22032
Acorn Ridge Ct 22033
Acosta Rd 22031
Adams Ct 22030
Adare Dr 22032
Addison Ct & Rd 22030
Adenlee Ave 22031
Akridge Ct 22032
Alba Pl 22031
Albany Ct 22031
Albion Ct 22031
Alcoa Dr 22033
Alder Woods Ct & Dr 22033
Alex Ct 22030
Alexander Cornell Dr 22033
Alice Ct 22032
Allenby Rd 22032
Allerton Rd 22032
Alliance Ct & Dr 22030
Allison Cir 22030
Almond St 22032
Alta Vista Ct & Dr 22030
Altura Ct 22030
Alwaes Dr 22031
Amber Hills Ct 22033
Amberleigh Way 22031
Amberley Ln 22031
Ames St 22032
Amnesty Pl 22030
Anchor Ct 22032
Anderson Ave 22030
Anderson Dr 22031
Andes Ct & Dr 22030
Andover Dr 22030
Andrew Ln 22030
Andrews Chapel Ct 22032
Ann St 22030
Ann Peake Dr 22032
Annamohr Dr 22030
Annapolis Ct 22032
Anne Pl 22031

Annhurst St ... 22031
Antietam Ave ... 22030
Antler Ct ... 22030
Antler Point Trl ... 22030
Anvil Ct ... 22030
Apple Orchard Ct ... 22033
Appleby Way ... 22030
Appling Valley Rd ... 22030
Ardath Pl ... 22032
Ardmore Pl ... 22030
Ardwick Ct ... 22031
Argonne Dr ... 22032
Aristotle Ct & Dr ... 22030
Arlington Blvd ... 22031
Armory Ct ... 22030
Armstrong St ... 22030
Arniel Pl ... 22030
Arrowhead Cir & Dr ... 22030
Arrowood St ... 22032
Artery Dr ... 22030
Ashby Pl ... 22030
Ashby Rd ... 22031
Ashcroft Ct & Way ... 22032
Ashford Ln ... 22032
Ashford Green Dr ... 22030
Ashleigh Ct & Rd ... 22030
Ashley Manor Ct ... 22032
Ashmeade Dr ... 22032
Ashton Oaks Ct & Dr ... 22030
Ashvale Dr ... 22033
Aspen Hollow Way ... 22032
Aspen Willow Dr ... 22032
Asquith Ct ... 22032
Assembly Dr ... 22030
Athens Rd ... 22032
Atlanta St ... 22030
Austrian Pine Ct ... 22030
Autumn Ct ... 22030
Autumn Leaf Ct ... 22031
Autumn Willow Dr ... 22030
Autumn Woods Way ... 22033
Avenel Ct ... 22033
Avery Rd ... 22033
Avondale Dr ... 22030
Aylor Rd ... 22032
Babashaw Ct ... 22031
Babson Ct ... 22032
Baccarat Dr ... 22032
Bacon Ct ... 22032
Bailey Ln ... 22031
Ballynahown Cir & Pl ... 22030
Banbridge Ct ... 22030
Bannockburn Ct ... 22030
Banting Ct & Dr ... 22032
Bantry Ter ... 22030
Barbara Ln ... 22031
Barbara Ann Ln ... 22032
Barbour Dr ... 22030
Barcellona Ct ... 22031
Barker Ct ... 22032
Barkley Dr ... 22031
Barkley Gate Ln ... 22031
Barkwood Ct ... 22032
Barley Rd ... 22031
Barlow Rd ... 22031
Barn Swallow Ct ... 22032
Barnard Ct ... 22031
Barnsbury Ct ... 22031
Barrick St ... 22031
Barrindo Ln ... 22033
Barringer Pl ... 22030
Barristers Keepe Cir ... 22031
Battenburg Ln ... 22030
Bay Hill Ct ... 22033
Bayard Pl ... 22032
Bayswater Ct ... 22031
Bea Mar Ct ... 22030
Beacon Grove Cir ... 22033
Beau Ln ... 22031
Beaumont Ct & St ... 22030
Becket Ct ... 22032
Beech Haven Ct ... 22032
Beech Ridge Ct & Dr ... 22030
Beech Tree Ct ... 22030
Beechstone Ln ... 22033
Beechwood Dr ... 22031

Bel Glade St ... 22031
Bellavia Ln ... 22030
Belle Cote Ln ... 22033
Bellmont Dr ... 22030
Benjamin Hill Ln ... 22033
Bentnail Ct ... 22032
Bentonbrook Dr ... 22030
Bentwood Ct ... 22031
Berkshire Woods Dr ... 22030
Berritt St ... 22030
Berry St ... 22030
Berrywood Ct ... 22032
Berwynd Ct & Rd ... 22030
Bessmer Ln ... 22032
Bevan Dr ... 22030
Bexley Ln ... 22032
Bideford Sq ... 22030
Billberry Dr ... 22033
Billingham St ... 22030
Birch Bark Ct ... 22033
Birch Pond Ln ... 22033
Birdsboro Dr ... 22033
Birkdale Way ... 22030
Birney Ln ... 22033
Black Ct ... 22032
Black Forest Cir ... 22031
Black Ironwood Dr ... 22030
Black Maple Dr ... 22031
Black Oak Dr ... 22032
Black Rock Ct ... 22032
Blackbird Pl ... 22033
Blackthorn Ct ... 22030
Blair Ridge Rd ... 22033
Blake Ln ... 22031
Blake Park Ct ... 22031
Blissful Valley Dr ... 22033
Blue Barn Way ... 22031
Blue Coat Dr ... 22030
Blue Fox Ln ... 22033
Blue Royale Ln ... 22031
Blue Topaz Ln ... 22030
Blueberry Ln ... 22033
Bluegate Dr ... 22031
Bluetill Ct ... 22033
Blythewood Dr ... 22030
Bob Ct ... 22030
Bobs Ford Rd ... 22030
Bohicket Ct ... 22031
Bolton Village Ct ... 22032
Bosworth Ct ... 22031
Bowler Dr ... 22031
Boxford Ct ... 22030
Boyett Ct ... 22032
Braddock Rd
9400-9498 ... 22032
9500-10299 ... 22032
10300-10698 ... 22030
10301-10699 ... 22032
10700-12799 ... 22030
Braddock Green Ct ... 22032
Braddock Knoll Way ... 22030
Bradshaw Ln ... 22030
Bradwater St ... 22031
Braeburn Dr ... 22032
Branch Brigade Ln ... 22033
Branch Side Ln ... 22031
Branchview Way ... 22032
Brandermill Ct ... 22030
Brandon Ridge Way ... 22032
Brandy Station Ct ... 22033
Braxton Wood Ct ... 22031
Breckinridge Ln ... 22030
Brecknock St ... 22033
Bredon Hill Ln ... 22030
Brentwood Farm Dr ... 22030
Briar St ... 22032
Briar Patch Ct & Ln ... 22032
Briarbush Way ... 22031
Briargate Ct ... 22033
Briarwood Pl ... 22032
Briarwood Farms Ct ... 22031
Briary Ln & Way ... 22031
Brices Ford Ct ... 22033
Brickell Dr ... 22033
Bridgend Run ... 22030
Bridgewood Dr ... 22032

Brigade Dr ... 22030
Briggs Ct & Rd ... 22030
Britwell Pl ... 22033
Broadrun Dr ... 22033
Broadview Dr ... 22030
Broadwater Dr ... 22032
Broadwire Dr ... 22032
Bronte Dr ... 22032
Brook Mist Ln ... 22033
Brookgreen Dr ... 22033
Brookings Ct ... 22031
Brookline Dr ... 22030
Brookridge Pl ... 22030
Brookwood Dr ... 22030
Broomsedge Ct ... 22033
Bruning Ct ... 22032
Buccaneer Ct ... 22031
Buckeye Ct & Ln ... 22033
Buckhorn Rdg ... 22030
Buckingham Rd ... 22032
Buckleys Gate Dr ... 22030
Bulova Ln ... 22030
Bumbry Ter ... 22030
Bunche Rd ... 22030
Burke Chase Ct ... 22032
Burke Station Ct & Rd ... 22032
Burkitts Rd ... 22033
Burnetta Dr ... 22032
Burning Bush Ct ... 22033
Burrows Ave ... 22030
Byrd Ct & Dr ... 22030
Cabat Lake Ct ... 22032
Cabot Ridge Ct ... 22032
Cabriolet Ct ... 22030
Cahoon Ct ... 22030
Caisson Rd ... 22030
Caithness Ct ... 22032
Calais Point Ct ... 22033
Caldicot Ln ... 22030
Calie Ct ... 22033
Calumet Grove Dr ... 22032
Camborne Ter ... 22030
Cambridge Ct ... 22030
Cambryar St ... 22030
Cameron Glen Dr ... 22030
Campbell Dr ... 22031
Canfield St ... 22030
Cannon Ridge Ct ... 22033
Cannonball Rd ... 22030
Cannongate Rd ... 22031
Canoe Birch Ct ... 22033
Canonbury Sq ... 22031
Cantrell Ln ... 22031
Capeway Ct ... 22030
Captain John Smith Ct ... 22030
Cardoness Ln ... 22030
Caribbean Ct ... 22031
Carisbrooke Ln ... 22030
Carol St ... 22030
Carolyn Ave ... 22031
Caronia Way ... 22030
Carriage Gate Ct ... 22030
Carriagepark Ct & Rd ... 22032
Carterwood Dr ... 22032
Casbeer Dr ... 22033
Cascade Ln ... 22032
Castle Branch Rd ... 22030
Castlecary Ln ... 22030
Castner Ct ... 22030
Casto Dr ... 22031
Catesby Row ... 22030
Catterick Ct ... 22032
Cavalier Ct ... 22030
Cavalier Landing Ct ... 22030
Cavalry Dr ... 22030
Cedar Ave ... 22030
Cedar Ln ... 22031
Cedar Crest Ln ... 22033
Cedar Farm Cir ... 22031
Cedar Forest Dr ... 22030
Cedar Grove Dr ... 22031
Cedar Lakes Dr ... 22033
Cedarest Rd ... 22031
Center St ... 22030
Center Way ... 22033
Centurion Ln ... 22033

Ceralene Ct & Dr ... 22032
Cerromar Pl ... 22030
Chain Bridge Rd ... 22030
Chalkstone Ct & Way ... 22030
Chancery Ct ... 22030
Chancery Park Dr ... 22030
Chandler St ... 22031
Chantal Ln ... 22031
Chantery Ct ... 22032
Chapel Hill Ter ... 22031
Chariot Ct ... 22030
Charles Dr ... 22030
Charles Stewart Ct & Dr ... 22033
Charleston Woods Dr ... 22032
Chartres Way ... 22030
Chatsworth Ct ... 22032
Cherry Dr ... 22031
Chesapeake Ln ... 22030
Chesham St ... 22031
Cheshire Meadows Way ... 22032
Chestermill Ct & Dr ... 22030
Chestnut St ... 22030
Chestnut Knolls Dr ... 22032
Chichester Ln ... 22031
Chipper Ln ... 22032
Christie Jane Ln ... 22030
Christopher St ... 22031
Chronical Dr ... 22030
Church St ... 22030
Circle Woods Dr ... 22031
Clanbrook Ct ... 22031
Clara Barton Ct ... 22032
Clares Ct ... 22033
Claridge Ct ... 22032
Cleveland St ... 22030
Clifford Dr ... 22031
Clocktower Pl ... 22031
Clovet Dr ... 22030
Cobb Dr ... 22030
Colbert Ct ... 22032
Colchester Rd ... 22030
Colchester Brook Ln ... 22031
Colchester Hunt Dr ... 22030
Colchester Meadow Ln ... 22030
Coleridge Dr ... 22032
Colesbury Pl ... 22031
Collier Rd ... 22030
Collin Chase Pl ... 22030
Collingham Dr ... 22032
Collis Oak Ct ... 22033
Colonel Mendez Way ... 22032
Colonial Ave ... 22031
Colony Rd ... 22030
Colony Park Ct & Dr ... 22032
Colony View Dr ... 22032
Colton St ... 22032
Commonwealth Blvd & Ct ... 22032
Concordia St ... 22032
Confederate Ln ... 22030
E & W Constable Ct ... 22032
Convento Ter ... 22031
Copeland Pond Ct ... 22031
Copper Ln ... 22030
Coralberry Dr ... 22033
Cordova Pl ... 22031
Corkwood Pl ... 22033
Cornell Rd ... 22030
Cornerstone Ct ... 22030
Cornwall Ct & Rd ... 22030
Coronado Ter ... 22031
Corot Ct ... 22032
Cortez Ct & Dr ... 22030
Cotswolds Hill Ln ... 22030
Cotton Farm Rd ... 22032
Cotton Top Ct ... 22033
Country Hill Dr ... 22030
Country Ridge Ln ... 22033
Country Squire Ln ... 22032
Courthouse Dr ... 22030
Courtley Ct ... 22031
Courtney Dr ... 22030
Cove Rd ... 22032
Covent Ct ... 22032

Cover Pl ... 22030
Covington St ... 22031
Covington Square Way ... 22031
Crable St ... 22030
Cranleigh Ct ... 22031
Crescent Dr ... 22030
Cresence Way ... 22032
Crest St ... 22030
Crestar Ct ... 22032
Crestview Dr ... 22031
Crewshore Dr ... 22030
Cristfield Ct ... 22032
Crofton Green Dr ... 22030
Cross Keys Ct ... 22033
Crouch Dr ... 22030
Crows Nest Ct ... 22032
Crupper Pl ... 22030
Cupp Dr ... 22030
Curtice Farm Dr ... 22033
Custom House Ct ... 22033
Cyrandall Valley Rd ... 22031
Dadmun Ct ... 22031
Dale Dr ... 22030
Dalroy Ct ... 22032
Danas Crossing Dr ... 22032
Daniels Run Ct & Way ... 22030
Dansk Ct ... 22032
Darby St ... 22030
Day Lilly Ct ... 22031
Decatur Ct & Dr ... 22030
Decour Ct ... 22030
Deer Glen Ct ... 22031
Deer Hollow Way ... 22031
Deerberry Ct ... 22033
Del Mar Ct ... 22033
Del Rio Dr ... 22030
Delburne Ct ... 22031
Delegate Ct ... 22030
Delfield Ln ... 22031
Deljo Dr ... 22030
Delsignore Dr ... 22030
Demby Dr ... 22032
Deming Dr ... 22030
Democracy Ln ... 22030
Deneale Pl ... 22032
Denise Ln ... 22031
Dequincey Dr ... 22032
Derring Ln ... 22030
Devilwood Ct ... 22030
Devin Green Ln ... 22030
Dickens Way ... 22033
Dillard Ct ... 22032
District Ave ... 22031
Dixie Hill Rd ... 22030
Dogberry Ln ... 22033
Dogwood Ln ... 22031
Dogwood Hills Ln ... 22033
Donaldson Ct ... 22033
Dorado Ct ... 22031
Dorforth Dr ... 22033
Dorr Ave ... 22031
Doulton Ct ... 22032
Doveville Ln ... 22032
Dowell Pl ... 22032
Dranes Tavern Dr ... 22030
Draper Dr ... 22031
Dudley Ct ... 22030
Dudley Heights Ct ... 22030
Duncan St ... 22031
Dundalk St ... 22032
Dungannon Rd ... 22030
Dunhill Dr ... 22030
Dunster Ct ... 22030
Duston Pl ... 22031
Dusty Wheel Ln ... 22033
Duvall St ... 22031
Dwight Ave ... 22032
Eagle Nest Ct ... 22032
Eakin Park Ct ... 22031
Earlham St ... 22032
Early Woodland Pl ... 22031
Earps Corner Pl ... 22032
East St ... 22030
Easter Ln ... 22030
Eastlake Dr ... 22032

Eastwick Ct ... 22033
Eastwood Ct ... 22032
Eaton Pl ... 22030
Edenderry Dr ... 22030
Edenvale Rd ... 22031
Egan Dr ... 22030
Eggleston Ter ... 22030
Eland Ct ... 22032
Elderberry Pl ... 22033
Elizabeth Ln ... 22032
Eljames Dr ... 22032
Ellenwood Dr ... 22031
Ellenwood Ln ... 22032
Ellington Ct ... 22032
Ellzey Dr ... 22032
Elm Forest Way ... 22030
Elmira Ct ... 22032
Elmont Ct ... 22030
Elsa Ct ... 22030
Elsmore St ... 22031
Embassy Ln ... 22030
Enford Ct ... 22032
Engelmann Oak Ln ... 22030
Englemeade Dr ... 22030
English Holly Dr ... 22030
English Maple Ln ... 22030
Englishwood Ln ... 22033
Erica Hill Ln ... 22033
Esabella Ct ... 22032
Eskridge Rd ... 22031
Espana Ct ... 22031
Estate Ct ... 22030
Estel Rd ... 22031
Ethels Pond Ct ... 22030
Evergreen Dr ... 22032
Everleigh Way ... 22031
Evesham Ln ... 22030
Excelsior Pl ... 22030
Executive Park Ave ... 22031
Fair Briar Ln ... 22033
Fair Crest Ct ... 22033
Fair Heights Dr ... 22033
Fair Knoll Dr ... 22033
Fair Lakes Cir, Ct & Pkwy ... 22033
Fair Lakes Promenade Dr ... 22033
Fair Lakes Shopping Ctr ... 22033
Fair Oaks Mall ... 22033
Fair Ridge Dr ... 22033
Fair Stone Dr ... 22033
Fair Valley Ct & Dr ... 22033
Fair Village Way ... 22033
Fairbury Ln ... 22031
Fairchester Dr ... 22030
Fairfax Blvd
9400-9799 ... 22031
9800-11299 ... 22030
Fairfax Sq ... 22031
Fairfax St ... 22030
Fairfax Center Creek Dr ... 22030
Fairfax Center Hunt Trl ... 22030
Fairfax Center Woods Trl ... 22030
Fairfax Commons Dr ... 22030
Fairfax Corner Ave ... 22030
Fairfax Estates Dr ... 22030
Fairfax Farms Rd ... 22033
Fairfax Green Dr ... 22030
Fairfax Hills Way ... 22030
Fairfax Hunt Rd ... 22030
Fairfax Meadows Cir ... 22030
Fairfax Ridge Rd ... 22030
Fairfax Towne Ctr ... 22033
Fairfax Village Dr ... 22030
Fairfax Woods Way ... 22030
Fairfield House Dr ... 22033
Fairhaven Ct ... 22030
Fairhill Rd ... 22031
Fairlee Dr ... 22031
Fairview Dr ... 22031
Falcon Wood Pl ... 22033
Falkirk Dr ... 22033

Falmead Rd ... 22032
Fanleaf Ct ... 22033
Faraday Ct ... 22032
Farm House Ln ... 22032
Farmington Dr ... 22030
Farmland Dr ... 22033
Farmview Ct ... 22032
Farndon Ct ... 22032
Farr Ave & Dr ... 22030
Farr Oak Cir & Pl ... 22030
Farrcroft Dr & Grn ... 22030
Fawn Wood Ln ... 22033
Featherfield Ct ... 22030
Feature Oak Way ... 22032
Federal Systems Park Dr ... 22033
Federalist Way ... 22030
Fern St ... 22030
Field Lark Ct & Ln ... 22033
Fieldbrook Pl ... 22033
Fieldwood Ct & Dr ... 22030
Fiesta Rd ... 22032
Finchem Ct ... 22030
Finchley Ct ... 22032
Finsbury Pl ... 22031
Fireside Ct ... 22032
Firestone Ct ... 22033
Firethorne Ct ... 22030
Fishers Hill Ct ... 22033
Five Oaks Rd ... 22031
Flatwood Cir ... 22033
Flintlock Rd ... 22030
Flintridge Ct ... 22032
Flower Box Ct ... 22030
Fogarty Ct ... 22030
Ford Rd ... 22030
Forest Ave
10100-10199 ... 22032
10200-10599 ... 22030
Forest Ct ... 22032
Forest Dr ... 22030
Forest Hill Ct & Dr ... 22030
Forest Mist Ln ... 22033
Forestdale Dr ... 22032
Forsgate Pl ... 22030
Fort Buffalo Cir ... 22033
Fountainside Ln ... 22030
Fox Run ... 22030
Fox Chapel Rd ... 22030
Fox Hunter Pl ... 22030
Fox Keep Run ... 22033
Fox Lake Ct, Dr & Pl ... 22033
Fox Sparrow Ct ... 22032
Foxfield Ln ... 22033
Foxhole Dr ... 22033
Franciscan Ln ... 22031
Francy Adams Ct ... 22032
Franklin Manor Ct ... 22033
Franklin View Ct ... 22033
Freehill Ln & Rd ... 22033
Freeland Ct ... 22030
Friendship Ct ... 22032
Frostleaf Ct ... 22033
Fyfe Ct ... 22032
Gadsen Dr ... 22032
Gagne Ct & Dr ... 22030
Gainsborough Ct ... 22030
Gainsborough Dr ... 22032
Galley Ct ... 22032
Galliec St ... 22030
Gallows Rd ... 22031
Galsworth Ct ... 22032
Garden Gate Dr ... 22031
Garden Grove Cir ... 22030
Garden Path Ln ... 22030
Garden Ridge Ln ... 22030
Garden Stone Ln ... 22031
Garland Tree Ct ... 22033
Gary Hill Dr ... 22030
George Mason Blvd ... 22030
George Mckay Ct & Ln ... 22030
Gilbertson Rd ... 22032
Ginger Tree Ct ... 22030
Glade Hill Rd ... 22031
Glade Meadow Dr ... 22030

Glanmore Ct 22032
Glasgow Woods Ct 22032
Glass Aly 22031
Glen Ct 22031
Glen Alden Rd 22030
Glen Chase Ct 22032
Glen Mist Ln 22030
Glenbrook Ct, Pl & Rd 22031
Glendale Way 22030
Glenmere Rd 22032
Glenn Rose St 22032
Glenvale Dr 22031
Glenville St 22032
Glostonbury Way 22030
Golden Meadow Ct 22033
Goldeneye Ln 22032
Golf Ridge Ct 22033
Golf Tee Ct 22033
Golf Trail Ln 22033
Goodview Ct 22031
Goodwood Dr 22030
Goolsby Way 22030
Goose Pond Ln 22033
Gopost
3102-3102 22031
Gopost
3121-3121 22031
3326-3328 22033
Goss Rd 22032
Gossamer Way 22033
Goth St 22030
Government Center Pkwy
11301-11499 22030
12000-12001 22035
12003-12099 22035
Governor Yeardley Dr 22032
Governor Yeardley Ln 22030
Graceland Pl 22031
Gramlee Cir 22032
Grand Commons Ave 22030
Grand Junction Ct & Dr 22033
Grassy Hill Ct 22033
Grays Pointe Ct & Rd 22033
Great Heron Cir & Ter 22033
Great Laurel Ln 22033
Great Oaks Way 22030
Great Pine Dr 22032
Great Tree Ct 22032
Green Cap Pl 22030
Green Duck Ln 22033
Green Leaf Ct 22033
Green Ledge Ct 22033
Green Look Ct & Pl 22033
Green Ridge Ct 22033
Greenshank Ct 22032
Greenway Ct 22033
Greenwood Ct 22033
Greer Ct 22031
Gregg Ct 22033
Grenshaw Dr 22030
Grinnell St 22032
Grosvenor Ct 22031
Grover Glen Ct 22033
Groves Ln 22030
Grovewood Way 22032
Guinea Rd 22032
Gunpowder Rd 22030
Guysborough Dr 22031
Hackney Coach Ln 22030
Hadley Ln 22032
Hall Dr 22032
Hallman St 22030
Halsted St 22033
Hamaker Ct 22031
Hamilton Dr 22031
Hamlet Hill Ct & Way 22030
Hampshire Green Ave 22032
Hampton Ln 22030
Hampton Forest Ct & Way 22030
Hanger Rd 22033
Harbor Town Cir & Ct 22033
Hargrove Ct 22031
Harper Dr 22030
Harrow Ct & Ln 22030

Harrowby Ct 22032
Hartwick Ln 22031
Harvest Pl 22030
Harvest Woods Ct 22033
Harvester Farm Ln 22032
Harvey Dr 22030
Haviland Ct 22032
Hayes Ct 22033
Haynsworth Pl 22031
Hazel Ferguson Dr 22030
Hazelwood Ct 22030
Head Ct 22032
Headly Ct 22032
Heart Leaf Ct 22030
Hearthside Ln 22033
Heatherford Ct & Pl 22030
Heatherstone Ct 22030
Hecate Ct 22032
Helenwood Dr 22032
Helm Ct 22032
Helmsford Ln 22033
Hemlock Way 22030
Henley Pl 22030
Henrico St 22032
Herend Pl 22032
Heritage Ln 22030
Hermitage Dr 22032
Hermosa Dr 22031
Heron Neck Ln 22033
Heron Ridge Dr 22030
Hershour Ct 22032
Herzell Woods Ct 22032
Heversham Ct 22032
Hexagon Pl 22030
Hickory Grove Ct 22031
Hickory Knoll Pl 22033
Hidden Meadow Dr 22033
Hideaway Rd 22031
Highland Ln 22031
Highland Pl 22033
Highland Ter 22030
Highland Oaks Ct & Dr 22033
Hightower Pl 22031
Hill Dr & St 22030
Hill Cumorah Dr 22033
Hillside Pl 22031
Hilltop Rd 22031
Hillyer St 22032
Hobart Ct 22032
Holbrook Ave 22030
Holden St 22032
Holiday Ln 22030
Hollinger Ave 22033
Hollow Tree Ln 22030
Hollowview Ct 22032
Holly Ave & St 22030
Holly Grove Ct 22033
Hollybrook Ln 22032
Hollyoak Pl 22032
Homewood Way 22030
Honey Brook Ct 22030
Honey Locust Ct 22033
Hope Park Rd 22030
Horner Ct 22031
Hound Run Dr 22033
Howerton Ave 22030
Howsen Ave 22030
Hoylake Ln 22030
Hummingbird Ln & Way 22033
Hunt Rd 22032
Hunt Club Cir 22030
Hunt Manor Ct & Dr 22033
Hunter Rd & St 22031
Hunters Branch Rd 22031
Hunters Glen Way 22031
Hunting Pines Ct & Pl 22032
Huntwood Manor Dr 22030
Hurst Ct 22030
Indale Ct 22033
Indigo Ln 22032
Inglenook Dr 22030
Inverness Ct & Rd 22033
Inverness Woods Ct 22032
Irish Moss Ct 22033

Iva Ln 22032
James St 22031
James Bergen Way 22033
James Halley Dr 22032
James Swart Cir 22030
James Wren Way 22030
Jancie Rd 22030
Jasper Ct & Rd 22033
Javier Rd 22031
Jean St 22030
Jefferson Oaks Cir 22033
Jennichelle Ct 22033
Jennifer Dr 22032
Jenny Ln 22032
Jenny Lynne Ln 22030
Jensen Pl 22032
Jeremy Grv 22030
Jermantown Rd 22030
Jersey Dr 22031
Jessie Ct 22030
John Ayres Dr 22032
John Barnes Ln 22033
John Mason Pl 22030
John Robert Way 22032
John Trammell Ct 22030
John Turley Pl 22033
Johns Pl 22033
Jomar Dr 22032
Jones St 22030
Joseph Siewick Dr 22033
Joshua Davis Ct 22032
Joyce Dr 22030
Joyce St 22030
Judicial Dr 22030
Juniper St 22031
Kahle St 22032
Kalmia Ct & Ln 22033
Karen Dr 22031
Katherine Hanley Ct 22030
Kathryn Jean Ct 22033
Kaywood Ct 22032
Kearny Ln 22033
Keefer Ct 22033
Keith Ave 22030
Kelley Dr 22030
Kenerson Ct & Dr 22032
Kenmore Dr 22030
Kennington Pl 22030
Kentmere Sq 22030
Kentshire Way 22030
Kentstone Way 22030
Kenwood Ter 22033
Kernstown Ct 22033
Kerrigan Ln 22030
Keys Ct 22032
Kieland Ridge Rd 22030
Kilbourne Dr 22032
Kildare Ln 22031
Kilmarnock Dr 22031
Kings Way 22033
Kings Color Dr 22030
Kings Crown Ct 22031
Kingsbridge Dr 22031
Kipp Ct 22033
Kirktree Ct 22032
Kirkwood Dr 22031
Kittery Ct 22031
Kitty Pozer Dr 22030
Knight Arch Ct & Rd 22030
Koke Way 22033
Kristin Ln 22032
Kristina Ct 22030
La Cross Ct 22032
La Messa Dr 22030
Laar Ct 22030
Ladbrook Way 22032
Ladue Ln 22030
Ladues End Ct & Ln 22030
Lady Somerset Ln 22033
Lafferty Ln 22030
Lake Ct & Dr 22033
Lake Glen Rd 22033
Lake Normandy Ct & Ln 22030
Lakewhite Ct 22032
Lamarre Dr 22030

Lamplight Dr 22033
Landau Ln 22030
Landmark Pl 22032
Landon Ct 22031
Langdon Gate Dr 22031
Laro Ct 22031
Larry Rd 22030
Latimer Ct 22032
Latney Rd 22032
Latona Ct 22033
Latrobe Ct 22031
Laura Belle Ln 22032
Laurel St 22032
Laurel Grove Way 22033
Laurel Lake Sq 22030
Laurel Leaf Ln 22031
Laurie Pl 22031
Lauries Way 22033
Lauriston Pl 22031
Lavender Keep Cir 22033
Lavery Ct 22032
Lawn Ct 22032
Layton Hall Dr 22030
Leafcrest Ln 22033
Leamington Ct 22031
Leclair Ct 22033
Lee Hwy
9526A-9526C 22031
11218A-11218C 22030
8200-9799 22031
11000-13299 22030
Lee St 22030
Lee Jackson Memorial Hwy
11200-11300 22030
11302-11498 22033
11700-13400 22033
13402-13598 22033
Lee Side Ct 22033
Leehigh Ct & Dr 22030
Lees Corner Rd 22033
Leeway Ct 22032
Legacy Ln 22030
Legato Rd
4000-4299 22033
4300-4799 22030
Leghorn Pl 22031
Lenox Dr 22032
Leonard Dr 22030
Leroy Pl 22031
Levau Ct 22033
Lewisham Rd 22030
Lewiston Pl 22030
Lexington Ct 22030
Libbey Dr 22032
Liberty Bridge Rd 22033
Lido Pl 22031
Lieutenant Nichols Ct & Rd 22033
Lillard Ct 22033
Lime Ct 22032
Limoges Dr 22032
Limpkin Ct 22032
Lincoln Dr 22030
Lincoln Lake Way 22030
Linda Maria Ct 22031
Linden St 22030
Linden Leaf Ct 22031
Lindenbrook St 22031
Lindenwood Ln 22031
Lindsay St 22032
Lindsey Meadow Ct 22032
Linfield St 22032
Lisa Marie Ct 22033
Lismore Ln 22031
Lister Ct 22032
Little River Tpke 22031
Littlebrook Ln 22030
Littleton St 22032
Llewellyn Ct 22030
Loch Linden Ct 22032
Lochleven Trl 22030
Locust Ln & St 22030
Log Ridge Dr 22030
Lone Oak Pl 22032
Long Pl 22032

Long Boat Ct 22032
Lord Ct 22032
Lord Culpeper Ln 22030
Loreleigh Way 22031
Loston Cir & Ct 22033
Lothbury Ct 22031
Lothian Rd 22031
Lower Park Dr 22030
Loyola Ln 22033
Lucas Dr 22033
Luxberry Dr 22033
Lynchburg Ct 22032
Lyndhurst Dr 22031
Lynford Ln 22030
Lynn Regis Ct 22031
Lynnhurst Dr 22031
Macduff Ct 22031
Maclura Ct 22032
Mactavish Hts 22030
Madeley Ct 22033
Madison Mews 22030
Madonna Ln 22033
Maepine Ct 22033
Main St
9671A-9671D 22031
Mainstone Dr 22031
Maintree Ct 22033
Majestic Ln 22033
Majestic Pine Ln 22033
Mallard Creek Trl 22033
Mallory Hill Ln 22033
Malone Ct 22032
Maltese Ln 22033
Manor Pl 22032
Manor Hall Ln 22033
Mantua Dr 22031
Maple Ave 22032
Maple Ln 22031
Maple St 22030
Maple Forest Ct 22030
Maple Hill Rd 22033
Maple Trace Cir 22032
Maple View Ln 22033
Marble Ln 22033
Marboro Ln 22033
Marcum Ct 22033
Marcus Ct 22032
Marengo Ct 22030
Margin Way 22033
Marietta Ct 22033
Marilta Ct 22030
Mariner Ln 22033
Market Commons Dr 22033
Markwood Ln 22033
Marlborough Rd 22032
Marley Rd 22032
Marlstone Ln 22033
Marly Garden Ln 22033
Marquis Ct 22030
Marsala Glen Way 22033
Marshal Farm Ct 22030
Marshall Hall Ln 22033
Marvell Ln 22033
Marycrest St 22031
Marymead Dr 22030
Mason St 22030
Mason Oaks Ct 22030
Mason Park Ct 22030
Mason Pond Dr 22030
Masser Ln 22032
Mathy Dr 22031
Matthews Ct 22033
Mattie Moore Ct 22030
Mauck Ct 22032
Maureen Ln 22033
Maury Ct & Rd 22032
Mavis Ct 22030
Maximilian Ct 22033
May Hill Ct 22033
Mayde Ct 22030
Maylock Ln 22033
Mayport Ln 22033
Maywood Ln 22031
Mazarin Pl 22033
Mazewood Ln 22033
Mccarty Crest Ct 22030

Mcclain Hill Ct 22033
Mcduffie Ln 22030
Mcfarland Ct & Dr 22032
Mckenzie Ave 22030
Mclean Ave 22030
Mclearen Ct 22030
Meadow Bridge Ln 22033
Meadow Estates Dr 22030
Meadow Field Ct & Dr 22033
Meadow Hill Ln 22033
Meadow Hunt Dr 22033
Meadowsweet Dr 22033
Mears St 22031
Measharr Dr 22030
Meath Ct & Dr 22033
Megan Dr 22030
Melissa Ct 22030
Mellwood Ln 22033
Melrae Ct 22033
Melville Ln 22033
Melvue Ct 22033
Members Way 22030
Memory Ln 22033
Mendell St 22030
Mercury Ln 22033
Meredith Dr 22030
Merion Ln 22030
Merrifield Ave 22031
Merrilee Dr 22031
Metcalf Cir 22030
Meyer Woods Ln 22033
Middle Ridge Dr 22033
Middlebrook St 22032
Middlegate Dr 22032
Middleton Ln 22033
Midfield Way 22033
Midland Rd 22031
Midstone Ln 22033
Milan Ln 22033
Milburn St 22033
Mill Ct 22033
Mill Meadow Ct 22033
Mill Point Ct 22033
Mill Rock Dr 22030
Mill Springs Dr 22031
Millard Way 22033
Millbank Ct 22031
Millbranch Pl 22031
Millpond Ct 22033
Millstone Way 22033
Milroy Way 22030
Milroy Crest St 22030
Miniature Ln 22033
Minoso Dr 22030
Minstrell Ln 22033
Minton Dr 22032
Miranda Ct 22031
Mirror Pond Dr 22032
Mission Square Dr 22031
Misty Ct 22033
Misty Creek Ln 22033
Misty Glen Ln 22033
Mitchell Ct 22033
Mobile Ct & Dr 22030
Modano Ct & Pl 22031
Mode St 22031
Mohr Oak Ct 22033
Monica Ct 22030
Monmouth St 22030
Monroe Ct 22030
Monteith Ln 22030
Monument Ct 22033
Monument Dr
11600-11698 22030
12100-12198 22033
Monument Corner Dr 22030
Monument Hill Way 22030
Monument Wall Way 22030
Moonstone Dr 22031
Moore St 22030
Morley Ct 22032
Morning Spring Ln 22033
Morningside Ct 22030
Morningside Dr 22031
Morningside Woods Pl 22031
Mornington Ct 22032

Morrisons Way 22030
Mosby Rd 22032
Mosby Woods Dr 22030
Moss Brooke Ct 22031
Moss Ranch Ln 22033
Mount Carriage Ln 22033
Mount Echo Ln 22033
Mount Royal Ln 22033
Mount Vineyard Ct 22032
Moylan Ln 22033
Mozart Brigade Ln 22033
Muddler Way 22030
Muirfield Ln 22033
Murdock Rd 22032
Murdstone Ct 22033
Musket Ct 22030
Myrtle Leaf Dr 22030
Mystic Way 22033
Nan Mill Ln 22032
Nancy Dr 22030
Nancyann Way 22030
Nantucket Ct 22032
Naoma Ct 22030
Nash Dr 22032
Nellie White Ln 22032
Nester Rd 22032
New Church Ct 22032
New Guinea Rd 22032
New London Park Dr 22032
Newbury Rd 22030
Newman Rd 22030
Nicholas Ct 22033
Nipper Way 22031
Nodding Pine Ct 22033
Nomes Ct 22030
Nomis Dr 22032
Nonquitt Dr 22031
Norman Ave 22030
North St 22030
Northwood Rd 22031
Nottinghill Ln 22032
Novak Ln 22030
Noyes Ct 22032
Nutley St 22031
Nuttall Rd 22032
Nutwood Way 22032
Oak Pl & St 22030
Oak Creek Ct & Ln 22033
Oak Hill Way 22030
Oak Ivy Ln 22033
Oak Mill Ln 22030
Oak Park Ct 22032
Oak Place Ct 22032
Oak Pond Ct 22031
Oak Rail Ln 22033
Oak Village Ldg 22033
Oakcrest Ct & Dr 22032
Oakdale Crescent Ct 22030
Oakshade Ct 22033
Oakwood Dr 22030
Octagon Ct 22030
Odie Ct 22030
Ofaly Rd 22030
Okla Dr 22031
Old Creek Dr 22032
Old Hickory Rd 22032
Old Lee Hwy
2800-2899 22031
3100-3999 22030
Old Pickett Rd 22031
Old Plains Rd 22033
Old Post Rd 22030
Old Reserve Way 22031
Old Sawmill Rd 22030
Olde Forge Ct 22032
Olive Mae Cir 22031
Oliver St 22030
Olivia Dr 22030
Olley Ln 22032
Omar Ct 22031
Omega Office Park 22031
Orchard Dr 22032
Orchard St 22030
Orchardson Ct 22032
Orkney Ct 22032
Overbridge Ln 22030

Overbrook Rd 22031
Overcup Ct 22032
Owens Ct 22031
Owens Glen Dr 22030
Ox Rd 22030
W Ox Rd
3418-3498 22033
3500-4499 22033
4500-4598 22030
4600-4799 22030
Ox Trl 22033
Ox Hill Rd 22033
Ox Ridge Ct & Rd 22033
Oxford Ln 22030
Page Ave
10500-10661 22030
10660-10660 22038
10662-10798 22030
10663-10799 22030
Pageant Ln 22033
Palace Way 22030
Paramount Rd 22033
Park Dr & Rd 22030
Park Chase Dr 22030
Park Green Ct & Dr 22030
Park Hill Pl 22030
Park Preserve Dr 22032
Park Vista Blvd 22030
Parkland Ct & Dr 22033
Parklane Rd 22030
Parkside Dr 22033
Parkside Ter 22031
Parson Ln 22033
Patriot Cir 22030
Patriot Park Ct 22030
Pavilion Ln 22033
Paxford Ct 22032
Paynes Church Dr 22032
Peaceful Creek Dr 22033
Peach Leaf Pl 22030
Peachwood Ct 22033
Peakview Ct 22033
Pearl St 22032
Pearsall Ln 22033
Pebble Ln 22033
Pebble Hill Ln 22031
Pecan Pl 22033
Peekskill Ln 22033
Peep Toad Ct 22030
Pelfrey Ln 22033
Pelham Ln 22030
Pembridge Ct 22031
Pender Dr 22030
Pender Creek Cir 22033
Pender Ridge Ter 22033
Pender Spring Dr 22033
Penderview Dr, Ln & Ter 22033
Penderwood Dr 22033
Penndale Ln 22033
Pennell St 22031
Penner Ln 22033
Pennerview Ln 22033
Penny Ln 22031
Pennypacker Ln 22033
Pentland Pl 22031
Peony Way 22033
Pergate Ln 22033
Perrott Ct 22031
Perry St 22030
Persimmon Cir & Dr 22031
Petal Ct 22033
Peterson St 22031
Petros Ct 22031
Pheasant Brook Ln 22033
Pheasant Ridge Rd 22030
Phoenix Dr 22030
Pickett Rd
3400-3999 22031
4000-4799 22032
Pickstone Ct & Dr 22032
Pimlico Ct 22032
Pine St 22030
Pine Forest Cir 22030
Pine Park Ct 22030
Pine Tree Dr 22033

Pineapple Henry Way 22033
Pinefield Ct 22033
Pinehurst Ave 22030
Pinehurst Greens Ct & Dr 22033
Pineland St 22031
Piney Branch Rd 22030
Piney Grove Ct & Dr 22031
Pixie Ct 22031
Plantation Pkwy 22030
Platte Pl 22032
Platten Dr 22031
Plaza Dr 22030
Plaza Ln 22033
Pleasantview Ln 22033
Plow Ct 22030
Plum Dale Dr 22033
Plum Run Ct 22033
Plymouth Meadows Ct 22032
Poet Ct 22033
Pohick Ln 22030
Point Hollow Ln 22033
Point Pleasant Dr 22033
Polaris Way 22033
Polo Dr 22033
Pommeroy Dr 22032
Ponce Pl 22031
Pond Way 22033
Popes Head Rd 22030
Popes Head View Ln 22030
Poplar St 22030
Poplar Creek Ct & Dr 22033
Poplar Leaf Ct 22031
Poplar Tree Rd 22033
Port Rae Ln 22033
Portloe Ter 22033
Portsmouth Rd 22032
Potomac Crossing Way 22030
Powell Rd 22032
Prado Pl 22031
Preservation Dr 22031
Preserve Oaks Ct 22030
Pressmont Ln 22033
Prestwick Dr 22030
Price Club Plz 22030
Prince William Dr 22031
Princess Anne Ct 22032
Professional Hill Dr 22031
Prosperity Ave 22031
Prosperity Ridge Ct 22031
Providence Pl 22031
Providence Way 22030
Provincetown Ct 22032
Pullman Pl 22031
Pumphrey Ct & Dr 22032
Pumpkin Pl 22030
Pylers Mill Ct 22032
Quail Creek Ln 22033
Queen Anne Dr 22030
Queens Brigade Ct & Dr 22030
Quiet Brook Rd 22030
Quiet Creek Dr 22033
Quiet Crossing Ct 22033
Quiet Hollow Ct 22033
Quiet Woods Ln 22033
Quincy Marr Dr 22032
Rachael Manor Dr 22032
Raeburn Ct 22032
Ragan Oaks Ct 22033
Raider Ln 22030
Railroad Ave & Ct 22030
Railroad Vine Ct 22031
Ramona Dr 22030
Ramrod Ct 22030
Randolph St 22030
Random Hills Rd 22030
Ranger Rd
3100-3199 22031
9700-10399 22030
Ratcliffe Manor Dr 22030
Readsborough Ct 22031
Rebel Run 22030
Red Admiral Pl & Way 22033
Red Patch Ln 22033

Red Spruce Rd 22032
Redford Ct 22030
Redwood Ct 22030
Regent Park Ct 22030
Regents Tower St 22031
Ren Rd 22030
Renfrew St 22030
Revercomb Ct 22030
Rhett Ln 22030
Richard Ave 22031
Richardson Dr 22032
Richardson Pl 22030
Ridge Ave 22030
Ridge Ct 22032
Ridge Knoll Ct & Dr 22033
Ridge Top Rd 22030
W Ridge View Dr 22030
Ridgelea Dr 22031
Ridgemist Ln 22033
Ridgeton Hill Ct 22032
Ridgewell Ct 22033
Rippling Pond Dr 22033
Rippon Lodge Dr 22032
Rittenhouse Cir 22031
Rivanna River Way 22030
River Forth Dr 22030
Riverboat Way 22032
Roanoke St 22031
Robert Evans Dr 22031
Roberts Rd 22032
Robertson Farm Cir 22030
Robeys Meadow Ln 22030
Robin Ridge Ct & Rd 22031
Rochester Dr 22030
Rock Garden Dr 22030
Rockaway Ln 22030
Rockcrest Dr 22032
Rocky Meadow Ct 22033
Rocky Mount Rd 22031
Rodgers Rd 22030
Rodney Ct 22032
Roger Stover Dr 22033
Roma St 22030
Rona Pl 22030
Rose Arbor Ct 22031
Rose Crest Ct & Ln 22033
Rose Path Cir 22033
Rose Thickett Ln 22030
Rosebay Ct 22033
Rosehaven St 22030
Roseline Rd 22030
Rosemeade Dr 22033
Rosemoor Ln 22031
Rothbury Sq 22030
Roundtop Ct 22032
Rowan Tree Dr 22030
Royal Mews 22030
Royal Astor Way 22031
Royal Commons Ct 22030
Royal Doulton Ln 22031
Royal Hannah Ln 22031
Royal Lytham Dr 22033
Royal Wolf Pl 22030
Royal Worcester Ln 22031
Ruben Simpson Ct 22033
Ruby Dr 22030
Ruffin Ct & Dr 22030
Rugby Rd 22033
Rumsey Pl 22032
Runabout Ln 22030
Rush St 22033
Rushton Rd 22033
Rust Rd 22030
Rust Hill Pl 22030
Rustburg Pl 22032
Ryers Pl 22032
Sabastian Dr 22030
Saber Cir 22030
Sablewood Ct 22030
Saddle Horn Dr 22030
Saddle Horse Pl 22030
Safe Harbor Ct 22032
Sager Ave 22030
Saint Andrews Dr 22030
Saint Charles Pl 22032
Saint Cloud Ct 22031

Saint Edwards Pl 22030
Saint Johns Pl 22030
Saint Marks Pl 22031
Saint Pauls Pl 22031
Saint Regents Ct & Dr 22031
Saintsbury Dr & Plz 22031
Salina Ct 22030
Sammy Joe Dr 22030
San Carlos Dr 22030
San Juan Dr 22030
San Marcos Ct & Dr 22030
Sandalwood Ct 22031
Sandra Ln 22030
Sandy Lewis Dr 22032
Sandy Ridge Ct 22031
Santa Clara Ct & Dr 22030
Santayana Dr 22031
Saranac Ct 22032
Sasher Ln 22030
Savoy Dr 22031
Saxon Flowers Dr 22031
Sayre Rd 22031
Scarlet Cir 22030
Scenic Ridge Trl 22033
School St 22030
Schuerman House Dr 22031
Scibilia Ct & Rd 22033
Scooter Ln 22030
Scott Dr 22030
Scout Dr 22030
Second St 22030
Sedgefield Rd 22030
Sedgehurst Dr 22033
Selkirk Dr 22032
Senatorial Ln 22030
Sessions Ct 22030
Settle Ct 22033
Sewickley Pl 22030
Shadow Oak Ln 22033
Shadow Valley Dr 22030
Shadowbrook Ln 22033
Shady Ridge Ln 22033
Shandwick Pl 22031
Shari Dr 22032
Sharon Ct 22032
Sharpes Meadow Ln 22030
Shasta Ct 22031
Shaughnessy Ct 22030
Shearman St 22032
Shellans Dr 22031
Shelly Krasnow Ln 22031
Sherford Dr 22033
Sherman St 22030
Sherman Oaks Ct 22032
Sherwood St 22030
Sherwood Forest Way 22030
Shiloh Cir & St 22030
Shirley Gate Ct & Rd 22030
Shooters Hill Ln 22032
Shoppes Ln 22033
Sideburn Ct 22032
Sideburn Rd
4100-4499 22030
4800-5599 22032
Silent Valley Dr 22031
Silver Cypress Ter 22030
Silver King Ct 22031
Silver Mill Pl 22031
Simpson Mews Ln 22030
Singleton Cir 22030
Skyview Ln 22031
Slatestone Ct 22030
Sleepy Lake Ct & Dr 22033
Smokewood Pl 22032
Snowy Owl Dr 22033
Snughaven Ln 22030
Sonata Ct 22032
Sonjo Ct 22032
Southern Elm Ct 22031
Southlea Ct 22031
Southport Ln 22030
Southwick St 22031
Sparrow Tail Ln 22033
Spartan Rd 22031
Sperrin Cir 22030
Spinning Wheel Ct 22032

Spode Ct 22032
Spring St 22031
Spring Lake Ct & Ter 22030
Spring Pond Pl 22033
Spring Rock Ct 22032
Springhaven Dr 22033
Springmann Dr 22030
Spruce Ave & St 22030
Spurlock Ct 22032
Stackler Dr 22030
Stafford Dr 22030
Staffordshire Ln 22030
Stallion Chase Ct 22030
Stallworth Ct 22032
Stanhope Pl 22032
Stanrich Ct 22030
Stanton Dr 22031
Star Opal Dr 22031
Starboard Ct 22032
Starling Ct 22033
Starlit Ponds Dr 22032
Starters Ct & Ln 22033
Stella Blue Ln 22031
Sterne Ct 22032
Steuben Pike 22030
Stevebrook Rd 22032
Steven Lee Ct 22032
Steven Martin Dr 22031
Stevens Battle Ln 22033
Stevenson St 22030
Stewarts Bridge Ct 22033
Stewarts Ford Ct 22033
Still Meadow Rd 22032
Stockton Tees Ln 22030
Stockwell Ln 22031
Stolen Moments Ter 22031
Stonehenge Way 22030
Stonehurst Dr 22031
Stoneleigh Ct 22031
Stonewall Ave 22032
Stonington Dr 22032
Stoughton Rd 22032
Stratford Ave 22030
Stringfellow Ct 22033
Stringfellow Rd 22030
Strong Ct 22033
Subtle Ln 22031
Sudley Ford Ct 22033
Suede Ct 22031
Summer Rain Ter 22033
Summit Dr 22030
Summit Corner Dr 22030
Summit Heights Way 22030
Summit Manor Ct & Dr 22033
Sumter Ct 22033
Sunflower Ln 22030
Sunrise Grn 22030
Superior Sq 22033
Surfbird Ct 22032
Susan Rosemary Ln 22031
Suteki Dr 22031
Sutherland Pl 22030
Sutherland Hill Ct 22031
Sutler Hill Sq 22033
Swallowtail Pl 22033
Swanee Ln 22031
Swarts Dr 22030
Swedes St 22030
Sweet Leaf Ter 22033
Sweethorn Ct 22033
Swift Ct 22032
Swinburne Ct 22031
Swinton Dr 22032
Sycamore Crest Dr 22031
Sydenham St 22031
Taba Cove Ct 22030
Talking Rock Dr 22031
Tall Pines Ct 22030
Tall Shadows Ln 22033
Tallow Tree Ct & Pl 22033
Talon Ct 22032
Tamar Woods Ct 22032
Tannery Ct 22033
Tanzanite Pl 22031
Tapestry Ct & Dr 22032

Tara Dr 22032
Tartan Oak Ct 22032
Tartan View Dr 22032
Taylor Dr 22032
Teaberry Ct 22032
Tecumseh Ln 22030
Tedrich Blvd 22031
Tenbury Ter 22030
Terry St 22031
Thackery Ct & Sq 22032
Tharper Way 22033
Thayer Ct 22030
Thomas Brigade Ln 22033
Thompson Rd 22033
Thompson Farm Ct 22031
Thompson Park Ln 22031
Thornaby Way 22030
Thornbury Dr 22030
Tiffin Pl 22032
Tiger Lily Ln 22030
Tilton Valley Dr 22033
Timber Log Way 22030
Timber Meadow Dr 22030
Timber Oak Trl 22033
Tobego Ct 22032
Tolman Rd 22033
Toms Ct 22032
Tooley Ct 22032
Topaz St 22031
Topsham Sq 22033
Tortoise Pl 22033
Tourmaline Way 22031
Tovito Dr 22031
Tower Side Dr 22031
Towlston Rd 22030
Townsend St 22031
Tracie Ann Ct 22032
Tractor Ln 22030
Tramore Ct 22032
Trapp Rd 22032
Traveler St 22033
Treasure Ct 22032
Treaty Oak Ct 22033
Tribune St 22033
Troon Ct 22033
Trowbridge Ct & St 22030
Trumbo Ct 22033
Trumpet Vine Dr 22030
Truro Ln 22030
Tuckaway Dr 22033
Tumbleweed Ct 22033
Tumbrel Ct 22033
Tusico Pl 22030
Twinbrook Rd 22032
Twinbrook Run Dr 22032
Tydfil Ct 22030
University Dr & Plz 22030
Upper Park Dr 22030
Vail Ridge Ln 22033
Valerank Dr 22032
Valley Rd 22033
Valley Oaks Ct & Dr 22033
Valley Ridge Cir & Dr 22033
Vanda Ln 22031
Vanderbilt Ct 22030
Varny Pl 22033
Vawter Trl 22030
Vennard Pl 22032
Verde Vista Dr 22030
Vernoy Hills Cmn, Ct & Rd 22033
Verret Dr 22030
Vertain Ct 22032
Via Dr 22030
Victoria Station Ct 22033
Viera Ln 22030
Village Dr 22030
Vineyard Ln 22030
Virginia St 22032
Virginia Willow Dr 22033
Vosger Ct 22031
Walcott Ave 22030
Walker St 22032
Waller Rd 22032
Walnut St 22030
Walnut Cove Cir 22033

Walport Ln 22032
Walters Ct 22030
Waples Mill Rd 22030
Ward Ct 22032
Warm Hearth Cir 22033
Warren Ln 22030
Warwick Ave & Cir 22030
Washington St 22030
Washington Brice Rd 22033
Watchwood Ln 22033
Water Birch Ct 22033
Water Crest Ct 22032
Water Elm Ln 22030
Water Oak Dr 22031
Waterloo Ln 22031
Waveland St 22033
Wavell Rd 22032
Waythorn Pl 22032
Weatherington Ln 22030
Wedgeway Ct & Pl 22033
Weirich Ct & Rd 22032
Welby Ct 22031
Wenzel St 22032
Werthers Ct 22030
West Dr 22030
Westbrook Dr 22030
Westbrook Mill Ln 22030
Western St 22030
Westfield Dr 22032
Westmore Dr 22030
Wheatfield Ct 22032
Wheatgrain Ln 22033
Wheatland Rd 22033
Wheatstone Dr 22032
Wheeled Caisson Sq 22033
Whisper Willow Dr 22030
Whitacre Rd 22032
White Dr 22030
White Birch Ct 22031
White Clover Ct 22031
White Daisy Pl 22031
White Oak Ct 22030
White Peach Pl 22031
White Rose Ln 22031
Whitefield St 22032
Whitehead St 22030
Whitfield Ct 22032
Whittemore Pl 22030
Wilburn Dr 22030
Wilcoxson Dr 22031
Wild Horse Dr 22033
Wildwood St 22032
Willa Mae Ct 22032
Willard Way 22030
Willcoxon Tavern Ct 22032
William Pl 22030
Williams Dr 22031
Williamsburg Ct 22032
Willoughby Point Dr & Ln 22033
Willow Crescent Dr 22030
Willow Oaks Corporate Dr 22031
Willow Springs School Rd 22030
Willow Stream Ln 22033
Willowmeade Dr 22030
Wilson St 22033
Wilson Valley Dr 22033
Wilson Woods Ct 22032
Windsor Gate Ln 22030
Windsor Hills Dr 22030
Winfield Rd 22030
Winford Ct 22032
Winscombe Ter 22030
Winston Pl 22030
Winter Pine Ct 22031
Winter Willow Cir & Dr 22030
Winterberry Ln 22032
Wisteria Way 22032
Wisteria Way Ct 22033
Wood Rd 22030
Wood Thrush Ct 22032
Wood Wren Ct 22032
Woodberry Meadow Dr 22033

Woodbury Knoll Ct 22032
Woodbury Woods Ct & Pl 22032
Woodfield St 22032
Woodhaven Ct & Dr 22030
Woodhill Pl 22031
Woodland Dr 22030
Worcester Dr 22032
Wren Hollow Ln 22033
Wrens Ct 22032
Wrought Iron Ct 22032
Wycliff Ln 22032
Wyndham Creek Ct 22030
Wynford Dr 22031
Yellow Brick Rd 22030
Yellow Rail Ct 22032
Yorktown Ct & Dr 22030
Zelkova Ct 22033
Zimpel Dr 22031
Zinnia Ln 22030
Zion Dr 22032
Zouave Ln 22033

NUMBERED STREETS

All Street Addresses 22030

FALLS CHURCH VA

General Delivery 22046

POST OFFICE BOXES MAIN OFFICE STATIONS AND BRANCHES

Box No.s
1 - 998 22040
1001 - 1976 22041
2001 - 2659 22042
4001 - 5152 22044
6001 - 7814 22040
8001 - 9000 22041
12003 - 12012 22042
16025 - 16070 22040

NAMED STREETS

Abbott Ln 22046
Adams Ln & Pl 22042
Add Dr 22042
Addey Ct 22043
Adrian Pl 22044
Afton Ct 22044
Aiken Hill Ct 22043
Alger Rd 22042
Alice Ct 22042
Allan Ave 22046
Allen St 22042
Anchorway Ct 22042
Anderson Rd 22043
Anna Ct 22042
Annandale Rd 22042
E Annandale Rd 22046
W Annandale Rd 22046
Anne St 22046
Anneliese Dr 22044
Apex Cir 22044
Appledore Ct 22043
Aqua Ter 22041
Arch Dr 22043
Ardley Ct 22041
Argyle Dr 22041
Arlington Blvd
6000-6399 22044
6400-8199 22042
Armand Ct 22043
Arnet St 22041
Arnold Ln 22042
Aronow Dr 22042
Arthur Dr 22046
Ashwood Pl 22041
Aspen Ln 22042
Aura Ct 22041
Autumn Chase Ct 22043
Avignon Blvd 22043
Avon Ln 22043
Barbour Ct & Rd 22043
Barcroft Mews Ct & Dr 22041
Barcroft View Ter 22041
Barger Dr 22044
Barley Walk 22042
Barrett Rd 22042
Bay Tree Ct & Ln 22041
Beachway Dr
6100-6299 22041
6300-6399 22044
Beacon Ln 22043
Beard Ct 22043
Beechtree Ln 22042
Beechview Dr 22042
Beechwood Ln 22042
Bell Manor Ct 22041
Bellview Dr 22041
Bent Branch Ct & Rd 22041
Bent Oak Ct 22043
Berkeley St 22043
Berry St 22042
Bethune St 22043
Birch St 22046
Birchwood Rd 22041
Bishops Ct 22046
Bisvey Dr 22042
Black Hickory Dr 22042
Blair Rd 22041
Blocker Pl 22043
Blue Heron Dr 22042
Blundell Cir & Rd 22042
Boat Dock Dr 22041
Bolling Rd 22042
Boston Dr 22041
Boxwood Dr 22043
Brad St 22042
Brandy Ct 22042
Brayden Ct 22043
Brice St 22042
Bridgehampton Ct 22042
Brill Ct 22041
Brilyn Pl 22046
Brittany Parc Ct & Dr 22043
E Broad St
100-899 22046
1000-1049 22042
1050-1099 22044
W Broad St
100-799 22046
800-800 22040
800-1298 22046
801-1299 22046
Broadmont Ter 22046
Broadway Dr 22043
Brook Dr
200-2999 22042
6000-6199 22044
Brook Run Dr 22043
Brooks Pl 22044
Brooks Square Pl 22043
Brush Dr 22042
Buckelew Dr 22046
Buffalo Ridge Rd 22044
Burfoot St 22043
Burke Farm Ln 22043
Burnside Ct 22043
Burroughs Ln 22043
Burton Cir 22041
Buxton Rd 22046
Cameron Rd 22042
W Cameron Rd 22046
Camp Alger Ave 22042
Cape Ct 22043
Capri Ct 22043
Carlin Springs Rd 22041
Carlton Ave 22042
Carlyn Ct 22041
Carlyn Hill Dr 22041
Carol Ln 22042
Carol Pl 22046
Carolyn Dr 22044
Caron Ln 22043
Carroll Pl 22042
Cartbridge Rd 22043
Carver Pl 22041
Casemont Dr 22046
Casilear Rd 22042
Castle Pl & Rd 22044
Cavalier Trl 22042
Cavalier Corridor 22044
Cedar Ln 22042
Cedar Hill Rd 22042
Cedarbrooke Ct 22042
Cedarwood Ct 22041
Cedarwood Ln 22042
Celadon Ln 22044
Center Ln 22041
Center St 22043
Centerside Ct 22043
Chambray Way 22042
Chanel Ter 22046
Chanute Pl 22042
Charing Cross Rd 22042
Charles St 22041
Chepstow Ln 22042
Cherri Dr 22043
Cherry St 22042
N Cherry St 22046
S Cherry St
100-199 22046
200-299 22042
Cheryl Dr 22044
Chestnut Ave 22042
Chestnut St
300-399 22046
2300-2499 22043
Chestnut Hill Ave 22043
Chicamuxen Ct 22041
Chrisland Cv 22042
Chummley Ct 22043
Church Pl 22046
Church St 22041
Church Walk 22042
Claremont Dr 22043
Clearview Dr 22042
Clearwood Ct 22042
Cleave Dr 22042
Cofer Rd 22042
Colby Crossing Way 22046
Collie Ln 22044
Colmac Dr 22044
Colonel Lindsay Ct & Dr 22043
Columbia Pike 22041
E Columbia St 22046
W Columbia St 22046
Conifer Ln 22046
Coors Park Ct 22043
Copa Ct 22044
Costner Dr 22042
Courtland Dr 22041
Covewood Ct 22042
Crane Dr 22042
Crane St 22046
Creek Wood Ct 22042
Crest Pl 22046
Crest Haven Ct 22042
Creswell Dr 22044
Crimmins Ln 22043
Crofton Pl 22043
Crooked Oak Ln 22042
Crossroads Ctr 22041
Crosswoods Cir & Dr 22044
Crutchfield St 22043
Culmore Ct 22041
Custis Pkwy 22042
Cypress Dr 22042
Dale Dr 22043
Darrells Grant Pl 22043
Darwin Ct & Dr 22042
Dashiell Rd 22042
Dauphine Dr 22042
Dearborn Dr 22044
Deborah Dr 22046
Deer Spring Ct 22043
Deerfield Ct 22043
Defense Dr 22042
Devon Dr 22042
Devonshire Garden Ct 22042
Dewey Jones Rd 22041
Dexter Dr 22043
Diamond Dr 22044
Diehl Ct 22041
Dinsmore St 22042
Diplomat Ct 22043
Division Ave 22043
Dockser Ter 22041
Dogwood Pl 22041
Dominion Dr & Way 22043
Dominion Heights Ct 22043
Donahue Ct 22042
Dorchester Rd 22046
Douglass Ave
200-299 22046
300-2899 22042
Dover Ln 22042
Driver Cir 22042
Duff Dr 22041
Dulany Pl 22046
Dunbar Ln 22046
Dunford Dr 22043
Durbin Pl 22041
Dye Dr 22042
Eastman Dr 22043
Echo Pl 22043
Edgar Ct 22043
Edgewater Dr 22041
Ellen Ave 22042
Ellery Cir 22041
Ellis Ct 22042
Ellison Sq & St 22046
Elm Ter 22042
Elmhirst Dr 22043
Elmwood Dr 22042
Elvira Ct 22042
Emilys Ln 22043
Emma Lee St 22042
Eppard St
6300-6438 22044
6439-6499 22042
Evans Ct 22043
Executive Ave 22042
Faber Ct 22046
Faber Dr 22044
E & N Fairfax St 22046
Fairmont St 22042
Fairview Pl 22041
Fairview Park Dr 22042
Fairwood Ln 22046
Fallfax Dr 22042
Fallowfield Dr 22042
W Falls Ave & Way 22046
Falls Gate Ct 22041
Falls Place Ct 22043
Falls Reach Dr 22043
Fallsmere Ct 22043
Fallswood Glen Ct 22044
Faragut Ct 22044
Farm Hill Dr 22044
Farragut Ave 22042
Fay Pl 22043
Federal Hill Dr 22044
Fellows Ct 22046
Fenwick Rd 22042
Fiddlers Grn 22044
Fieldcrest Ct 22042
Firehouse Ln 22041
Fisher Ave 22046
Fisher Ct 22043
Fisher Dr 22043
Flagmaker Ct & Dr 22042
Forest Dr 22046
Fowler St 22046
Foxwood Nook 22041
Franklin Walk 22042
Franklin Cluster Ct 22042
Frase Dr 22043
Frazier Pl 22042
Fredsen Pl 22042
Freedom Ln 22043
Freedom Pl 22041
Freehollow Dr 22042
Frenora Ct 22042
Frey Ct 22046
Friar Tuck Ct 22042
Friden Dr 22043
Friendship Ln & Pl 22043
Fulton Ave 22046
Gaddy Ct 22042
Gallows Rd 22042
Galway Pl 22043
Garden Ct 22046
Garland Dr 22041
Gary Ct 22042
Gate House Plz 22042
Gatehouse Rd 22042
Genea Way 22042
George C Marshall Dr 22043
S George Mason Dr 22041
W George Mason Rd
100-299 22046
2700-2899 22042
Georges Ln 22044
Gerard Ct 22043
Gervais Dr 22043
Gibson Pl & St 22046
Gillen Ln 22043
Gilson St 22043
Glavis Rd 22044
W Glen Dr 22046
Glen Carlyn Dr & Rd 22041
Glen Eagles Ct 22044
Glen Forest Dr 22041
Glenheather Dr 22043
Glenmont St 22042
Glenmore Dr 22041
Glenn Spring Ct 22043
Glenroy Cir 22042
Glenwood Pl 22041
Goldsboro Ct, Pl & Rd 22042
Goodwin Ct 22046
Gopost
4109-4109 22041
Gopost
4114-4114 22041
4220-4220 22042
4306-4312 22043
4314-4316 22043
4318-4318 22043
4420-4420 22044
4619-4619 22046
Gordon Ave 22046
Gordon Rd 22046
Gordon St 22041
Gordons Rd 22043
Gouthier Rd 22043
Governors Ct 22046
Grace Ln 22046
Graham Ct & Rd 22042
Grande Ln 22043
Grass Hill Ter 22044
Graydon St 22042
Grayson Pl 22043
Great Falls St
100-599 22046
2013-2209 22043
2210-2399 22046
Great Oak Ct 22042
Greentree Dr 22041
Greenway Blvd 22042
W Greenway Blvd 22046
Greenwich St
500-699 22046
2000-2299 22043
2300-2399 22046
Greenwood Dr 22044
Grenstead St 22042
Gresham Pl 22046
Griffith Rd 22043
Grove Ave 22046
Gundry Dr 22046
Half Moon Cir 22044
Hall Ct 22042
Hallran Rd 22041
Hallwood Ave 22046
Hampton Ct 22046
Hardwick Pl 22041
Harper Valley Ln 22042
Harriett St 22042
Harrison Rd 22042
Hartland Rd 22043
Hartwell Ct 22042
Haven Pl 22041
Hawthorne Ln 22042
Haycock Rd
100-199 22046
2000-7099 22043
Hazelton St 22044
Headrow Cir & Ln 22042
Heather Ln 22044
Helena Dr 22043
Hemlock Dr 22042
Herrell Ct 22043
Hessney Dr 22042
Hewitt St 22042
Hickory Ct 22042
Hickory St 22043
Hickory Hill Rd 22042
High St 22046
Highboro Way 22043
Highland Ave & Ter 22046
Highland Estates Pl 22043
Highview Pl 22044
Hileman Rd 22043
Hill Pl 22043
Hillier St 22046
Hillsborough Dr 22044
Hillside Dr 22043
Hillsman St 22043
Hilltop Pl 22043
Hillwood Ave
100A-100B 22046
1-399 22046
400-400 22042
401-499 22046
402-498 22046
500-1199 22042
Hockett St 22042
Hodge Pl 22042
Hoffmans Ln 22041
Hogan Ct 22043
Holloman Rd 22042
Holloway Rd 22042
Holly Ct 22042
Holly St 22044
Holly Berry Ct 22042
Holly Bush Way 22043
Holly Hill Dr 22042
Holly Manor Dr 22042
Hollywood Rd 22043
Holmes Run Dr & Rd 22042
Homespun Ln 22044
Hopewood Dr 22043
Horseman Ln 22042
Howard Ct 22043
Hughes Ct 22046
Hunton Ave 22046
Hurst St 22043
Hutchison St 22043
Hutchison Grove Ct 22043
Hyde Rd 22043
Hyson Ln 22043
Hyson Park Ct 22043
Ichabod Pl 22042
Idylbrook Ct 22043
Idylwood Ct & Rd 22043
Idylwood Station Ln 22043
Inglewood Ct 22043
Inversham Dr 22042
Iroquois Ct & Ln 22043
Irving St 22046
Irvington Rd 22042
Jaala Ln 22042
Jacks Ln 22042
Jackson Ave 22042
Jackson Ct 22046
Jackson Dr 22043
Jackson St 22046
Jaguar Trl 22042
James Ct & St 22046
James Lee St 22042
James Thurber Ct 22046
Jan Mar Dr 22041
Janet Pl 22046
January Ct 22043
Jay Miller Dr 22041
Jeanne St 22046
Jefferson Ave 22042
E Jefferson St 22046
S Jefferson St 22041
W Jefferson St 22046
Jefferson Hill Ct 22041
Jenkins Ln 22043
Jennifer Ln 22046
Joan Ct 22042
John Marshall Dr 22044
Johns Rd 22043
Johnson Rd 22042
Jonothan Pl 22042
Juniper Ln & Way 22044
Kadala Pl 22042
Kaiser Pl 22042
Kalmia Lee Ct 22042
Katie Ct 22046
Kaywood Dr & Pl 22041
Kelsey Ct 22044
S Kenfig Dr & Pl 22042
Kennedy Ln 22042
Kennedy St 22046
Kenney Dr 22042
Kent St 22046
Kerns Ct 22044
Kerns Rd
6504-6599 22044
6600-6799 22042
Kilgore Rd 22043
Kilmer Ct 22044
Kimberly Dr 22042
Kimble Ct 22041
Kincaid Ave 22042
Kings Chapel Rd 22042
Kings Garden Way 22043
Kings Lynn Rd 22043
Kings Mill Ct 22043
Kingwood Dr 22042
Kirby Ct 22043
Kirklyn St 22043
Knapp Ct 22043
Knoll Dr 22042
Knollwood Dr
600-699 22046
6000-6199 22041
Korte Ct 22042
Kristina Ursula Ct 22044
Labella Walk 22042
Lacy Blvd 22041
Lake St 22041
Lakeside View Dr 22041
Lakeside Village Dr 22042
Lakeview Dr & Ter 22041
Lakewood Dr 22041
Lancaster Ct 22043
Landing Ln 22043
Langston Ln 22046
Lanham Rd 22043
Lanier Pl 22046
Larchwood Rd 22041
Laura Dr 22046
Laurel Ct 22042
Lawndale Dr 22042
Lawrence Dr 22042
Lawton St 22046
Le Havre Pl 22042
Lea Ct 22046
Lebanon Dr 22041
Ledford St 22043
Lee Hwy
7101-7275 22046
7277-8199 22042
7300-7398 22046
7400-8198 22042
N Lee St 22046
S Lee St 22046
Lee Landing Ct & Dr 22043
Lee Oaks Ct & Pl 22046
Lee Park Ct 22042
Leeland Dr 22043
Leesburg Pike
5101-5197 22041
5199-6150 22041
6151-6399 22044
7049-7099 22046

7100-7899 22043
Leighton Dr 22043
Leonard Dr & Rd 22043
Lester Lee Ct 22042
Lewis Ln 22041
Lewis Pl 22042
Lexington Rd 22043
Liberty Ave 22042
Lily Dhu Ln 22044
Lily Pond Dr 22043
Linced Rd 22042
Lincoln Ave 22046
Linda Ln 22042
Linden Ln 22042
Lisle Ave 22043
Little Falls Pl 22042
Little Falls St 22046
Little John Ct 22042
Locker St 22042
Lockport Dr 22042
Locust St 22046
Locust Ridge Ct 22046
Longbranch Dr 22041
Longwood Dr 22041
Los Pueblos Ln 22043
Lounsbury Pl 22046
Luckey Ct 22041
Lunceford Ln 22043
Lusby Pl 22043
Lynn Pl 22046
Lyric Ln 22044
Machodoc Ct 22043
Madison Ln 22041
Madison Crest Ct 22041
Madison Overlook Ct 22041
Madison Park Dr 22041
Madison Pointe Ct 22041
Madison View Ln 22041
Madison Watch Way 22041
Magarity Ct & Rd 22043
Magnolia Ave & Ln 22041
Malbrook Dr 22044
Malibu Cir 22041
Mallory Ct 22043
S Manchester St 22044
Mankin Walk 22042
Mann Ct 22046
Manor Rd 22042
Mansfield Rd 22041
N Maple Ave 22046
S Maple Ave 22046
Maple Ct 22041
Mapledale Ct 22041
Maplewood Dr 22041
Marbo Ct 22046
Marbury Ct 22046
Marc Dr 22042
Marcer St 22044
Marian Ct 22042
Maries Dr 22041
Marlo Dr 22042
Marshall Dr 22041
Marshall St 22042
W Marshall St 22046
Marshall Heights Ct 22043
Marthas Ln 22043
Mary St 22042
Maryalice Pl 22041
Mason Ln 22042
Masonville Dr 22042
Matera St 22043
Mayberry St 22042
Maydan Ln 22043
Mayfair Dr 22042
Mayfair Mclean Ct 22043
Maynard Dr 22043
Mcconvey Pl 22043
Mccrea Pl 22042
Mckay St 22043
Mclean Greens Ct 22043
Mclean Park Rd 22043
Mclean Province Cir 22043
Mcsherry Dr 22042
Meadow Ln 22042
Meadow View Rd 22042
Meeting St 22044

Melarran Rd 22043
Mendota Ave 22042
Meridian St 22046
Merritt Pl 22041
Metropolitan Pl 22043
Michael Pl 22046
Middleboro Dr 22042
Middlecoff Pl 22043
Midhill Pl 22043
Midvale St 22046
Midway St 22046
Mildred Dr 22042
Military Dr 22044
Miracle Ln 22043
Mohegan Dr 22043
Moly Dr 22046
Moncure Ave 22041
Monroe Pl & St 22042
Montauk Ct 22042
Monticello Dr 22042
Montivideo Square Ct 22043
Montour Dr 22043
Montview Ct 22043
Moon Dr 22043
Moray Ln 22041
Morris St 22042
Morthene Dr 22041
Mount Daniel Dr 22046
Munson Ct, Pl & Rd 22041
Munson Hill Rd
6000-6049 22041
6050-6199 22044
Nanjemoy Ct 22046
Natahoa Ct 22043
Nealon Dr 22042
Nevius St 22041
New Providence Ct & Dr 22042
Nicholson Rd 22042
Nicholson St 22044
Nicosh Cir 22042
Nicosh Circle Ln 22042
Nigh Rd 22043
Noland Rd 22042
Noland St 22046
Nordlie Pl 22043
Norfolk Ln 22043
Normandy Ln 22042
Norsham Ln 22043
North St W 22046
Norwalk St 22043
Nottage Ln 22042
Nottingham Dr 22043
Oak St 22043
N Oak St 22046
S Oak St 22046
Oak Glen Ct 22042
Oak Haven Dr 22046
Oak Knoll Dr 22042
Oak Ridge Rd 22042
Oak Run Ct 22042
Oakland Ave 22042
Oakview Gardens Dr 22041
Oakwood Ct & Dr 22041
Offutt Dr 22046
Ogden Ct & St 22043
Old Farm Rd 22044
Oldewood Dr 22043
Olds Dr 22041
Olin Dr 22044
Olmstead Dr 22043
Olney Rd 22043
Orchid Dr 22046
Orland St 22043
Osborn St 22046
Oswald Pl 22043
Overbrook St 22043
Overhill Rd 22042
Packeran St 22046
Paldende Dr 22044
Parish Ln 22042
Park Ave & Pl 22046
Park Washington Ct 22046
Parker Ave & St 22046
Parkview Ave 22042
Parkwood Ct & Ter 22042

Pathway Ct 22042
Patricia Ct 22043
Patrick Henry Dr 22044
Patterson Rd 22043
Patterson St 22046
Paul Edwin Ter 22043
Paxton Rd 22043
Payne St 22041
Peabody Dr 22043
Peace Valley Ln 22044
Peach Orchard Dr 22043
Penguin Pl 22043
Pennsylvania Ave 22046
Pensa Dr 22041
Peyton Randolph Dr 22044
Pice Pl 22043
Pimmit Ct & Dr 22043
Pimmit Run Ln 22043
Pine St 22046
Pine Spring Rd 22042
Pinecastle Rd 22043
Pinedale Ct 22041
Pinetree Ter 22041
Pinewood St 22046
Pinewood Ter 22041
Pioneer Ln 22043
Placid St 22043
Plainfield St 22043
Poplar Ct 22042
Poplar Dr 22046
Poplar Ln 22041
Poplar St 22042
Poplar Tree Ln 22043
Porter Rd 22042
Potterton Dr 22044
Powell Ln 22041
Powhatan St 22043
Preston Square Ct 22043
Primrose Dr 22046
Prince Albert Ct 22042
Prince Charles Ct 22044
Princess Anne Ln 22042
Prout Pl 22043
Providence St 22043
Putnam St 22042
Quaint Acre Cir 22041
Quaker Ct 22042
Queen Anne Ter 22044
Quincy Ave & Pl 22042
Quinten St 22043
Radnor Pl 22042
Railroad Ave 22046
Randall Pl 22044
Randolph St 22046
Random Rd 22042
Random Run Ln 22042
Ransell Rd 22042
Ravenwood Dr 22044
Raymond Ct 22042
Recreation Ln 22041
Red Pine St 22041
Redd Rd 22043
Reddfield Ct & Dr 22043
Rees Pl 22046
Regent Ln 22042
Relda Ct 22043
Remington St 22046
Reservoir Heights Ave 22041
Reynolds St 22043
Rice St 22042
Ridge Pl 22046
Ridgeway Ter 22044
Riley St 22046
Rio Dr 22041
Robert Ln 22043
Robinson Pl 22046
Robinwood Ln 22041
N Rochester St 22043
Rock Spring Ave 22041
Rockford Dr 22043
Rockmont Ct 22043
Rogers Dr 22042
Rolfs Rd 22042
Rollin Rd 22042
Rolling Trce 22046
Rollins St 22046

Romney St 22043
Ronald St 22046
Roosevelt Ave 22042
Roosevelt Blvd 22044
Roosevelt St 22043
N Roosevelt St 22046
S Roosevelt St 22042
Rose Ln & Pl 22042
Rose Glen Ct 22042
Rosecroft Pl 22043
Rosemary Ln 22042
W Rosemary Ln 22046
Roswell Ct & Dr 22043
Roundtree Rd 22042
Roundtree Estates Ct 22042
Row Pl & St 22044
Rowell Ct 22046
Royal Lodge Dr 22043
Rudyard St 22043
Rustic Way Ln 22044
Rutland Pl 22044
Saint James Pl 22042
Saint Philips Ct 22042
Salem Rd 22043
Sampson St 22042
Sargent Dr 22044
Savannah St 22043
School Ln 22042
Scipio Ln 22042
Scoville St 22041
Seaton Cir & Ln 22046
Seminary Rd 22041
Senseney Ln 22043
Seoane Ct 22042
Seven Corners Ctr & Pl 22044
Seven Oaks Ct, Dr & Pl 22042
Sewell Ave 22046
Shadeland Dr 22044
Shadow Walk 22046
Shadwell Park Ln 22042
Shady Ln 22042
Sheffield Ct 22042
Shelby Ct & Ln 22043
Sheperds Ct 22041
Sherrow Ave 22046
Sherry Ct 22042
Sherwood Ct 22042
Shipyard Pl 22043
Shirley St 22046
Shreve Rd 22043
Sienna Ct 22043
Siesta Dr 22042
Sigmona St 22046
Sikes Ct 22043
Silver Maple Ln & Pl 22042
Siron St 22042
Skelton Cir 22042
Skyview Ter 22042
Slade Ct 22042
Slade Run Dr 22042
Sleepy Ln 22044
Sleepy Hollow Rd
2900-2999 22044
3000-3299 22042
3300-3520 22044
3521-3999 22041
Sleepy Ridge Rd 22042
Smallwood Way 22046
Snead Ln 22043
Snowbell Ln 22042
Sonnet Ct 22043
South St 22042
Sportsman Dr 22043
Spring Ct 22046
Spring Ln 22041
N Spring St 22046
S Spring St 22046
Spring Ter 22042
Spruce St 22046
Squires Hill Dr 22044
Stanford Cir 22041
Stanley Pl 22043
Steeples Ct 22046
Stephanie Marie Dr 22043

Steppes Ct 22041
Stillwood Cir 22042
Stockwell Manor Dr 22043
Stoneybrae Dr 22044
Storm Ct & Dr 22043
Strathmeade St 22042
Strathmore St 22042
Stratton Pl 22043
Strawberry Ln 22042
Stuart Dr 22042
Stuart Pl 22046
Summerfield Rd 22042
Summers Ln 22041
Surrey Ln 22042
Susans Ln 22043
Sycamore Dr 22042
Sycamore St 22046
N Sycamore St 22046
Sylvan Dr 22042
Tallwood Ter 22041
Taney Ln 22042
Tansey Dr 22042
Taylor Rd 22043
Taynton Rd 22042
Ted Dr 22042
Telestar Ct 22042
Tennis Ct 22041
Terry Ln 22042
Thomas Ct 22042
Tillman Dr 22043
Timber Ln 22046
Timberock Rd 22043
Tinner Hill Rd 22046
Tod St 22046
Tollgate Ter 22041
Tollgate Way 22046
Toronto St 22043
Tower St 22046
Tracy Pl 22046
Trail Run Rd 22042
Trevino Ln 22043
N Trinidad St 22043
E Tripps Run Rd 22042
Truman Ln 22043
N Tuckahoe St
900-1499 22046
2200-2299 22043
Tulip Dr 22046
Turner Ave 22043
Twin Oak Pl 22042
Tyler Ave 22042
Tyler St 22041
Tyson Dr 22046
N Underwood St
200-399 22046
2200-2299 22043
Upside Ct 22042
Vagabond Dr 22042
Valley Ct 22042
Valley Ln 22044
Valley Brook Dr
6600-6699 22044
6700-6999 22042
Van Buren Ct 22043
N Van Buren St 22046
Van Tuyl Pl 22043
Van Winkle Dr 22044
Venice Ct & St 22043
Veranda Ct 22043
Villa Ln 22044
Villa Ridge Rd 22046
Village Crossing Rd 22043
Vine Forest Ct 22044
Vinewood Pl 22044
Virginia Ave 22043
N Virginia Ave 22046
S Virginia Ave 22046
Virginia Ln 22043
Vista Dr 22041
Wade Pl 22042
Walden Ct 22042
Waldorf Ln 22046
Wallace Dr 22042
Walled Oak Ct 22043
Walnut St 22046
Walnut Hill Ct & Ln 22042

Walnut Manor Way 22042
Walters Woods Dr 22044
Ware Rd 22043
Washington Dr 22041
N Washington St 22046
S Washington St 22046
Waterway Dr & Pl 22044
Watters Glen Ct 22043
Wayne Rd 22042
Welcome Dr 22046
Wellfleet Ct 22043
Wentworth Dr 22044
West St 22046
Westcott Rd & St 22042
Westfall Pl 22042
Westford Ct 22043
Westlawn Dr & Pl 22042
Westley Rd 22042
Westminster Ct 22042
Westmoreland Rd 22042
W Westmoreland Rd 22046
Westmoreland St
2000-2228 22043
2229-2317 22046
2319-2319 22046
Weston Rd 22042
Westover St 22042
Westwood Pl 22043
Westwood Park Ln 22046
Wheatley Ct 22042
Whispering Ln 22041
Whitcomb Pl 22046
White St 22044
Whitestone Hill Ct 22043
Whittier Cir 22046
Wickersham Way 22042
Wicomico St 22043
Wieland Pl 22043
Wilkins Dr 22041
Williams Ln 22041
Williams Walk 22042
Williamsburg Pond Ct 22043
Willow Ln 22042
Willow St 22046
Willow Point Dr 22042
Willow Tree Ln 22044
Willston Dr & Pl 22044
Wilson Blvd 22044
Wincanton Ct 22043
Winchester Way 22042
Windsor Dr 22042
Wood Mist Ln 22043
Woodberry Ln 22042
Woodland Cir 22041
Woodland Dr 22046
Woodlawn Ave 22042
Woodley Ln 22042
Woodley Pl 22046
Woodville Dr 22044
Wooten Dr 22044
Worden Ln 22043
Worthington Cir 22044
Wraywood Pl 22042
Wrens Way 22046
Yancey Dr 22042
Yarling Ct 22042
Yarmouth Ct 22043
Yarn Ct 22042
N Yucatan St 22046
Zenith Ct 22042

NUMBERED STREETS

6th Rd & St 22041
11th St 22046
16th St 22046
26th St 22046
32nd St 22046
33rd St
6400-6599 22043
6600-6699 22046

GAINESVILLE VA

General Delivery 20155

POST OFFICE BOXES MAIN OFFICE STATIONS AND BRANCHES

Box No.s
All PO Boxes 20156

RURAL ROUTES

02, 04, 05 20155

NAMED STREETS

Abberley Loop 20155
Abbey Manor Ln 20155
Abernethy Ln 20155
Accord Ct 20155
Adirondack Ct 20155
Affirmed Pl 20155
Ainsworth St 20155
Akker Ct 20155
Albert Way 20155
Alderwood Way 20155
Alexander Sophia Ct 20155
Allaire Dr 20155
Alpine Bay Loop 20155
Alta Vista Ct 20155
Altenbury Loop 20155
Amal Ln 20155
Amsterdam Ct 20155
Anacortes Trl 20155
Ancestry Ct 20155
Anchor Mill Pl 20155
Angus Dr 20155
Anoka Way 20155
Arcadian Shore Ct 20155
Arrowleaf Turn 20155
Artemus Rd 20155
Arthur St 20155
Arthur Hills Dr 20155
Ashler Ln 20155
Atkins Way 20155
Atlas Walk Way 20155
Avalon Isle Way 20155
Avington Pl 20155
Baltusrol Blvd 20155
Banbury Dr 20155
Barley Field Pl 20155
Barn Owl Ct 20155
Barrymore Ct 20155
Basket Ring Ct 20155
Bearhurst Dr 20155
Belgrove Gardens Ln 20155
Bellingham Dr 20155
Berry Rd 20155
Beton Ct 20155
Bexhill Ct 20155
Bigleaf Maple Ct 20155
Birkenhead Pl 20155
Birnham Wood Ct 20155
Bitterroot Ct 20155
Bladen Pl 20155
Blue Heron Way 20155
Bluff Point Ct 20155
Bobedge Dr 20155
Bold Venture Way 20155
Bonnie Briar Loop 20155
Box Elder Loop 20155
Breeders Cup Dr 20155
Breezewood Ct 20155
Bridlewood Dr 20155
Brightview Way 20155
Broadleaf Ter 20155
Broadwinged Dr 20155
Brogue Ct 20155
Broughton Pl 20155
Brown Thrasher Ct 20155
Brunson Cir 20155
Buckland Mill Rd 20155
Buglecall Pl 20155

Bullen Bluff Ter 20155
Buschwood Mews 20155
Busick Ct 20155
Calbera Ct 20155
Calthorpe Pl 20155
Calumet Ct 20155
Calverts Mill Way 20155
Camdenhurst Dr 20155
Cancun Ct 20155
Cannondale Way 20155
Canterbury Ln 20155
Cantwell St 20155
Cartagena Dr 20155
Carver Rd 20155
Catbird Dr 20155
Catharpin Rd & Way ... 20155
Catharpin Valley Dr 20155
Cavaletti Ct 20155
Caybury Pl 20155
Cedar Branch Dr 20155
Cerro Gordo Rd 20155
Cerromar Way 20155
Charismatic Way 20155
Charlene Dr 20155
Chelmsford Dr 20155
Cheney Way 20155
Chimbote Ct 20155
Chipper Ct 20155
Chucks Pl 20155
Churchside Dr 20155
Cinch Ln 20155
Circuit Ct 20155
Clarkton Ct 20155
Clatterbuck Loop 20155
Clay Hill Ct 20155
Clearview Ave 20155
Cleveland Bay Ct 20155
Clubhouse Rd 20155
Cluster House Way 20155
Cobblers Green Ct 20155
Collier Ln 20155
Collingham Pl 20155
Colonel Wood Rd 20155
Conley Pl 20155
Cotswald Ct 20155
County Down Ct 20155
Covantry Ln 20155
Covewood Ct 20155
Crabtree Way 20155
Crackling Cedar Ln 20155
Crackling Fire Dr 20155
Creekbranch Way 20155
Crescent Park Dr 20155
Crimson Crossing Way . 20155
Crimson Leaf Ct 20155
Crooked Oaks Ct 20155
Crown Hollow Ct 20155
Culverhouse Ct 20155
Cumberstone Pl 20155
Currant Loop 20155
Dallas Ct 20155
Dancer Ct 20155
Dancing Twig Dr 20155
Danehurst Cir 20155
Darbey Knoll Dr 20155
Dartmouth Ln 20155
Daves Store Ln 20155
Deacons Way 20155
Debhill Ln 20155
Deming Dr 20155
Densworth Mews 20155
Derby Run Way 20155
Dewars Way 20155
Double Eagle St 20155
Douglas Fir Loop 20155
Dover Downs Ct 20155
Ducktan Loop 20155
Dunwoody Ct 20155
Eagle Island Ct 20155
Early Marker Ct 20155
Edgartown Way 20155
Edisto Ct 20155
Eldermill Ln 20155
Ellis Ford Pl 20155
Ellis Mill Dr 20155
Emmanuel Ct 20155
Enochs Ct 20155
Equinox Landing Ct 20155
Erie Ct 20155
Estate Manor Dr 20155
Everbreeze Ln 20155
Executive Dr 20155
Fairland Ct 20155
Falkland Dr 20155
Fallen Oaks Pl 20155
Fallsmere Cir 20155
Farebrook Pl 20155
Fenestra Pl 20155
Ferrier Ct 20155
Fieldstone Way 20155
Filly Ct 20155
Finish Line Dr 20155
Flamingo Dr 20155
Flicker Ct 20155
Flying Feather Ct 20155
Foal Ct 20155
Forbes Pl 20155
Forkland Way 20155
Fowlers Mill Dr 20155
Fox Hunt Way 20155
Framingham Ct 20155
Gaffney Cir 20155
Gainesville Village Sq .. 20155
Galena Ct 20155
Gallant Fox Ct 20155
Gallerher Rd 20155
Gallery Way 20155
Gap Way 20155
Gardner Manor Pl 20155
Gardner Park Dr 20155
Gary Fisher Trl 20155
Gateway Center Dr 20155
Gateway Promenade
Pl 20155
Gayleburg Pl 20155
Gelding Pl 20155
General Lafayette Way . 20155
Gillis Way 20155
Gingerwood Ct 20155
Glass Ridge Pl 20155
Glenkirk Rd 20155
Godfrey St 20155
Grace View St 20155
Grackle Ct 20155
Great Dover St 20155
Gumbo Ct 20155
Hackamore Trl 20155
Haddonfield Ln 20155
Halverton Pl 20155
Hamelin Ln 20155
Hamill Run Dr 20155
Hampton Bay Ln 20155
Hancock Ct 20155
Handel Pl 20155
Harefield Ln 20155
Harlingen Way 20155
Harness Shop Ct &
Rd 20155
Haro Trl 20155
Harrowhill Way 20155
Hastenbeck Dr 20155
Heathcote Blvd 20155
Henry Lee Way 20155
Heredity Ln 20155
Heritage Farms Dr 20155
Heritage Hunt Dr 20155
Heritage Valley Way 20155
Heritage Village Plz 20155
Heythorpe Ct 20155
Hillwood Dr 20155
Hollow Glen Ct 20155
Hollow Trunk Ct 20155
Holly Knoll Ln 20155
Holly Ridge Ln 20155
Holstein Pony Ct 20155
Hopewells Landing Dr .. 20155
Horse Shoe Bay Ct 20155
Hulfish Way 20155
Humbolt Bay Ct 20155
Hunters Run Way 20155
Huron Dr 20155
Hyde Park Pl 20155
Indigo Bunting Ct 20155
Innesfree Way 20155
Iron Bar Ln 20155
Jackpin Pl 20155
Jade Dr 20155
James Madison Hwy ... 20155
Jangle Ct 20155
Jansbury St 20155
Jennifer Ann Ln 20155
John Marshall Hwy 20155
Junco Ct 20155
Jutland Pony Ct 20155
Kamehameha Pl 20155
Kanawha Way 20155
Katie Lynn Ct 20155
Keenan Ct 20155
Kensington Palace Ct .. 20155
Kentish Fire St 20155
Kentucky Derby Ct 20155
Kerfoot Dr 20155
Kimberwick Ct 20155
King Hill Way 20155
Kingbird Ct 20155
Kinsley Mill Pl 20155
Kite Way 20155
Knight Ct 20155
Kona Dr 20155
Kylewood Way 20155
Ladderbacked Dr 20155
Lake Manassas Dr 20155
Lakeview Dr 20155
Landfall Ct 20155
Landseer Dr 20155
Latonia Ct 20155
Lattany Ct 20155
Laurianne Ter 20155
Lawnvale Dr 20155
Lee Hwy
12600-14688 20155
14689-16399 20155
14689-14689 20156
14690-16398 20155
Lee Carter Rd 20155
Legend Glen Ct 20155
Liber Ct 20155
Lick River Ln 20155
Limestone Dr 20155
Link Hills Loop 20155
Links Pond Cir 20155
Linton Hall Rd 20155
Lippizan Pl 20155
Little Thames Dr 20155
Loftridge Ln 20155
Logmill Rd 20155
Logos Way 20155
Lolan St 20155
Longmeade Ct 20155
Lords View Loop 20155
Lucas Ct 20155
Lucas Point Loop 20155
Lucknow St 20155
Lynn Forest Dr 20155
Macon Grove Ln 20155
Maidenhair Dr 20155
Majestic Prince Loop ... 20155
Malevich Ct 20155
Manahoac Pl 20155
Mandalay Ct 20155
Manns Harbor Ct 20155
Mantriel Rd 20155
Maracaibo Ct 20155
Marlow St 20155
Maurine Ct 20155
Mcgraws Corner Dr 20155
Meagan Loop 20155
Medalist Ct 20155
Melton Ct 20155
Metrica Ct 20155
Midy Ln 20155
Milestone Ct 20155
Milton Cir 20155
Misty Acres Ln 20155
Mongoose Trl 20155
Montour Heights Dr 20155
Morgan Island Way 20155
Morris Ct 20155
Morven Park Ln 20155
Moss Ledge Ct 20155
Mossy Pines Way 20155
Murphy Ter 20155
Narrow Branch Ct 20155
Neale Sound Ct 20155
Netherstone Ct 20155
New Caledonia Ct 20155
Newbern Loop 20155
Newfoundland Way 20155
Nicarter Ln 20155
Northbrook Ln 20155
Northington Ct 20155
Norwick Pl 20155
Old Carolina Rd 20155
Old Field Dr 20155
Old Linton Hall Rd 20155
Onan Ct 20155
Ontario Rd 20155
Open Valley Way 20155
Otter Creek Dr 20155
Paddock Ct 20155
Pageland Ln 20155
Paper Birch Ln 20155
Parula Way 20155
Parville Loop 20155
Pasture View Pl 20155
Pedigrue Ct 20155
Peggs Ln 20155
Peggys Ct 20155
Pelham Crossover Ln .. 20155
Penderlea Ct 20155
Pensacola Pl 20155
Percheron Trl 20155
Piedmont Center Plz ... 20155
Pine Knott Ct 20155
Piney Grove Way 20155
Plantation Mill Ct 20155
Post Point Way 20155
Preakness Pl 20155
Presidents Landing
Way 20155
Preswell Ct 20155
Prices Cove Pl 20155
Prickly Ash Way 20155
Progress Ct 20155
Promenade Commons
St 20155
Quaking Aspen Rd 20155
Rail Line Ct 20155
Rainy Day Way 20155
Raleigh Mews 20155
Ransom Oaks Ct 20155
Rathbone Pl 20155
Real Quite Ct 20155
Red House Rd 20155
Red Rock Ct 20155
Redstart Ct 20155
Redtailed Ct 20155
Reidhall Pl 20155
Rembert Ct 20155
Respite Ct 20155
Retriever Ln 20155
Rio Grande Way 20155
Robin Marie Pl 20155
Robledo Rd 20155
Rockingham Ln 20155
Rocky Run Rd 20155
Roderick Loop 20155
Rogue Forest Ln 20155
Roland Park Pl 20155
Rooster Ct 20155
Rosney Ct 20155
Roxborough Loop 20155
Royal Sydney Dr 20155
Ruffed Grouse Ct 20155
Ryton Ridge Ln 20155
Sabbarton Pl 20155
Saddle Run Way 20155
Saint Annes Ct 20155
Saint Clair Dr 20155
San Diego Ct 20155
Santander Dr 20155
Sapphire Lakes Ct 20155
Sauvage Ln 20155
Scarlet Maple Dr 20155
Screech Owl Ct 20155
Sedge Wren Dr 20155
Sedgefield Oaks Ct 20155
Sedgmoor St 20155
Sedona Dr 20155
Selbourne Ln 20155
Settlers Trail Pl 20155
Shadow Fox Ct 20155
Shady Hollow Ln 20155
Sharpshinned Dr 20155
Shelford Way 20155
Sheringham Way 20155
Shimmering Rock Rd ... 20155
Shire Pl 20155
Side Bay Ct 20155
Sierra Sunset Ln 20155
Silver Moon Ln 20155
Smallpath Ct 20155
Snead Loop 20155
Snickersville Dr 20155
Snow Hill Dr 20155
Soapstone Dr 20155
Somerset Crossing Dr .. 20155
Song Sparrow Dr 20155
Sour Gum Ct 20155
Sovereign Way 20155
Sparkling Water Ct 20155
Specialized Trl 20155
Springfield Ct 20155
Spyglass Hill Loop 20155
Stanwick Sq 20155
Stapleton Pl 20155
Starting Post Ct 20155
Stepney Dr 20155
Sterling Point Dr 20155
Stonewall Shops Sq 20155
Strawberry Dr 20155
Street Cry Ct 20155
Sudley Rd 20155
Suffolk Pl & Way 20155
Sunapple Pl 20155
Sunday Silence Ct 20155
Susquehanna Rd 20155
Sutton Oaks Way 20155
Swainley St 20155
Swift Way 20155
Tackhouse Ct & Loop .. 20155
Tall Timber Ct & Dr 20155
Tallyrand Way 20155
Tarleton Ct 20155
Tenbrook Dr 20155
Thornton Dr 20155
Thoroughfare Rd 20155
Thorpe Farm Ln 20155
Tillinghast Ln 20155
Timothy Dr 20155
Toccoa Ct 20155
Town Commons Way ... 20155
Traditions Trl 20155
Traphill Way 20155
Trappers Ridge Ct 20155
Tred Avon Pl 20155
Trek Way 20155
Triple Crown Loop 20155
Tryon Way 20155
Tullamore Estates Rd .. 20155
Turning Grass Way 20155
Turtle Ct 20155
Turtle Point Dr 20155
Tuscarora Ct 20155
Tuxedo Ln 20155
Tysons Oaks Ct 20155
Upland Meadow Ct 20155
Valderrama Ct 20155
Victory Gallop Way 20155
Village High St 20155
Village Stream Pl 20155
Vinewood Ct 20155
Vint Hill Rd 20155
Virginia Cedar Ct 20155
Virginia Oaks Dr 20155
Wales Ct 20155
Walnut Hill Dr 20155
Waverley Mill Ct 20155
Wavyleaf Ct 20155
Webb Dr 20155
Wellington Rd 20155
Wellington Branch Dr ... 20155
Wellington Center Cir ... 20155
Welsh Pony Ct 20155
Wharfdale Pl 20155
Wheeling Way 20155
Whirlaway Ct 20155
Whitney Rd 20155
Wild Raspberry Ct 20155
Willet Way 20155
Willingboro Ct 20155
Windy Hollow Cir 20155
Winnipeg Ct 20155
Witton Cir 20155
Woodpecker Ct 20155
Woodridge Dr 20155
Woodwill Ln 20155
Wulford Ct 20155
Wyngate Dr 20155
Yalta Way 20155
Yearling Ct 20155
Yellow Hammer Dr 20155
Yellowleg Ct 20155
Yellowthroat Ct 20155
Yesterlinks Ct 20155
Yewing Way 20155
Yountville Dr 20155
Zeeland Pl 20155

GLEN ALLEN VA

General Delivery 23060

POST OFFICE BOXES MAIN OFFICE STATIONS AND BRANCHES

Box No.s
761 - 1839 23060
2001 - 9999 23058

NAMED STREETS

W Abbey Ct 23059
Abbots Cross Ln 23059
Abbott Cir 23059
Abington Park Dr 23059
Abner Church Rd 23059
Abruzzo Pl 23059
Acworth Ct & Dr 23060
Agnes Dr 23060
Aldenbrook Way 23059
Alder Glen Way 23059
Alder Ridge Ct, Pl &
Ter 23059
Alf Ct 23060
Allen Ln 23059
Allenbend Cir & Rd 23060
Allens Xing 23060
Alor Ct 23059
Amberwell Pl 23059
Amberwood Cir, Dr &
Ln 23059
Amburg Ln 23060
Amershire Ct, Ln, Pl &
Way 23059
Anable Ln 23059
Anderson Rd 23060
Ann Michelle Ln 23060
Anna Marie Ct, Dr &
Way 23060
Anne Gate Ct 23059
Appling Rd 23059
Arapaho Ln 23059
Arapaho Trl 23060
Arbill Trce 23059
Archduke Ct & Rd 23060
Ardington Blvd 23059
Argonne Ct & Dr 23060
Armedon Dr 23059
Armentrout Ct 23060
Arrowleaf Ct 23060
Arthur Ct 23060
Ascot Glen Ct & Dr 23059
Ashborne Ct & Rd 23060
Ashburg Dr 23060
Ashdown Oaks Ct 23059
Ashford Park Dr 23059
Ashland Rd 23059
Ashleys Boreen Ln 23059
Ashmont Cir, Ct & Ln .. 23059
Ashton Mill Ter 23059
Ashton Park Ct, Dr &
Way 23059
Aspen Grove Dr 23059
Atkins Grove Ct 23059
Attems Ct & Way 23060
Atterbury Dr 23060
Aubs Ln 23060
Auburn Mill Ln & Rd ... 23059
Austin Healey Ct, Dr &
Pl 23059
Autumnwood Ct, Dr &
Way 23059
Avery Green Ct & Dr ... 23059
Averys Ct 23059
Axe Handle Ct, Ln &
Ter 23059
Ayers Way 23060
Back St 23060
Bacova Dr 23059
Baffy Ct 23059
Ballentine Ln 23059
Barda Cir 23060
Baria Dr 23060
Barn Owl Ln 23060
Barnsley Ct, Pl & Ter ... 23059
Barnstable Ct 23059
Barnyard Trl 23060
Barwood Rd 23060
Bastione Ct 23060
Battenfield Dr 23059
Battlefield Rd
9400-9499 23059
10100-10199 23060
Baxter Rd 23060
Bayon Way 23060
Bayswater Ct, Pl &
Ter 23059
Bazile Rd 23059
Becton Rd 23060
Bekah Ln 23059
Belair Pl 23059
Belfast Rd 23060
Bellamy Pl 23059
Belmont Park Ct, Ln &
Rd 23059
Belstead Ct, Dr & Ln ... 23059
Belva Ct, Ln & Rd 23059
Benjamin Hill Ct 23060
Bennett Ct & Ln 23059
Benning Oaks Ct & Dr . 23059
Bent Needle 23060
Bent Pine Rd 23059
Berrymeade Ave, Ct &
Pl 23060
Berrymeade Hills Ct &
Ter 23060
Big Apple Rd 23059
Birchill Ct & Ln 23059
Bishops Gate Ct & Dr .. 23059
Black Haw Ln 23059
Blackburn Rd E 23060
Blackstone Ave 23060
Blairmont Ct, Dr & Pl ... 23059
Bluebell Ct & Dr 23060
Bogey Pl 23059
Bohannon Dr 23060
Boscastle Ct & Rd 23060
Bosworth Ct, Dr & Pl ... 23059
Bottomley Pl 23059
Boulware Ct 23059
Bourne Rd 23059
Bowles Ln 23060
Bowman Ct 23059
Bradford Landing Dr &
Way 23059

Bradington Ct, Dr & Ter 23059
Bragdon Way 23059
Branch Rd 23059
Brandons Ct 23059
Brant Ln 23060
Brassie Ln 23059
Braxton Ave 23059
Brays Fork Dr 23060
Breithorne Ct 23060
Brennen Robert Ct & Pl 23060
Brentmoor Ct & Dr 23059
Bretton Ct & Ln 23060
Briar Wood Ln 23059
Bridgehead Pl 23059
Brighter Tower Ct 23060
Brilland Ct 23060
Brilland Meadows Ter 23060
Brilland Springs Pl 23060
Bristol Ln 23059
Britlyn Ct 23060
W Broad St 23060
Broad Meadows Ct & Rd 23060
Brockton Ct & Pl 23059
Brook Rd
8400-9499 23060
9601-9697 23059
9699-10299 23059
Brookemere Dr 23060
Brookemoor Ct, Ln & Pl 23060
Brookhollow Ct & Dr 23059
Brookley Rd 23060
Brookmeade Ct, Ln & Ter 23059
Brookriver Dr 23060
Brookwood Glen Dr, Ln & Ter 23060
Broward Pl 23059
Brownstone Blvd 23060
Brunson Way 23060
Brushwood Ave 23059
Brydes Ln 23059
Buchmill Dr 23060
Bud Ln 23059
Bundle Of Joy Ln 23059
Burberry Ct, Dr & Ln 23059
Burning Oak Ct 23060
Bush Dr & Ln 23060
Bush Lake Ct, Dr, Ln, Pl & Way 23060
Cadmus Ct 23059
Calabria Ct 23059
Caledon Dr 23060
Callao Way 23060
Callison Dr 23060
Calvin Ct 23059
Cameron Creek Ct & Rd 23059
Canaan Valley Ct 23060
Candace Ct & Ter 23060
Candlelight Ct, Ln & Pl 23060
Cannon Rd 23060
Capitol One Way 23060
Cardigan Cir 23060
Carriage Point Ln 23059
Carrington Green Ct, Dr & Pl 23060
Carrington Hills Ct & Dr 23060
Carrington Woods Dr 23060
Carrolls Way 23059
Caruthers Way 23059
Cason Rd 23060
Castle Point Ct, Dr, Ln & Rd 23060
Castle York Ct 23060
Cattle Pond Ln 23060
Cauthorne Rd 23059
Cavalry Farms Ln 23059
Cedar Ln 23059
Cedar Branch Ct 23060
Cedar Forest Ct, Pl & Rd 23060
Cedar Pines Ln 23059
Cedar Post Ct & Pl 23060
Cedarlea Pkwy 23059
Cemetery Rd 23060
Centerway Dr 23059
Chadsworth Ct, Dr, Pl & Ter 23059
Champion Pointe 23060
Chapel Lawn Ct & Ter 23059
Chappell Rd 23059
Chappell Ridge Ct, Pl & Ter 23059
Charing Cir & Ln 23059
Chariot Ct & St 23060
Chelsea Brook Ln 23059
Cherry Hill Ct & Dr 23059
Chestnut Hill Ct & Dr 23059
Chewning Rd 23059
Chickahominy Branch Dr 23059
Chickahominy River Ln 23059
Chicopee Rd 23060
Chiles Rd 23059
Chiltern Hills Ct 23059
Chislehurst Dr 23059
Christiano Dr 23060
Chriswood Rd 23059
Circus Farm Rd 23059
Classic Rd 23060
Claytonshire Ct 23060
Claytor Country Ln 23060
Claywood Rd 23060
Cleannew Rd 23060
Clerke Dr 23059
Cliffmore Dr 23060
Club Car Ln 23060
Club Commons Ct & Dr 23059
Coachmans Carriage Pl & Ter 23059
Coachmans Landing Ct 23059
Coal Spring Ct & Ln 23060
Cobblers Stone Ct & Pl 23059
Cobblestone Landing Ct, Pl & Ter 23059
Cobbs Rd 23059
Cody Pl 23060
Cole Blvd 23060
Coles Point Way 23060
Coleson Rd 23060
Colfax Rd 23059
Collier Ct 23060
Collinstone Ct, Dr & Pl 23059
Colonial Estates Cir, Ct & Ln 23059
Comanche Ln 23059
Concourse Blvd 23059
Connecticut Ave 23060
Contessa Ct & Dr 23060
Cord Ct 23060
Cordell Cir 23059
Correnty Dr 23059
Corrotoman Rd 23060
Corwin Dr 23059
Country Creek Ct, Ter & Way 23059
Country Hills Ct, Ln, Ter & Way 23059
Country Lake Dr & Pl 23059
Country Oaks Cir, Ct & Way 23059
Country Way Ct, Pl & Rd 23060
Countryview Dr 23059
Courtney Rd 23060
Covewood Ct & Rd 23060
Covington Hills Ln 23059
Cox Rd 23060
Craigs Mill Ct & Dr 23060
Cranston Ct 23059
Creek Mill Ct, Pl & Way 23059
Creekwalk Ct & Pl 23060
Creery Rd 23059
Creston Rd 23060
Croft Cir & Ct 23060
Crossridge Glen Way 23060
Crutchfields Ct 23059
Crystal Brook Ter 23060
Crystal Lake Ave 23059
Crystal Pointe Pl 23060
Cussons Rd 23060
Daffodil Cir 23060
Dalat Ct 23060
Dalecross Ct & Way 23059
Dalton Ln 23059
Daly Ct 23059
Damsel Stone Ct 23059
Darrel Lake Ct 23060
Darrowby Ct & Rd 23060
Davis Ave 23060
Dawson Mill Ct 23060
Dellwood Rd 23059
Delray Ct & Rd 23060
Denali Dr 23060
Denford Ct & Way 23059
Deputy Ct 23059
Diggs Ct 23060
Dillard Ct, Dr & Pl 23060
Dink Ln 23060
Doe Crossing Ln 23059
Dolmen Ct & Rd 23059
Dominion Blvd 23060
Dominion Club Dr 23059
Dominion Fairways Ct, Dr, Ln & Pl 23059
Dorin Hill Ct 23059
Dorrington Cir 23059
Dorton Ct & Ln 23060
Dove Hollow Ct, Ln & Pl 23060
Dovetail Ct 23060
Dravo Pl 23059
Drayton Cir & Dr 23060
Drumore Ct & Way 23059
Drystack Ct & Ln 23059
Dublin Rd 23060
Duckling Dr & Walk 23060
Dude Ranch Rd 23059
Duncan Park Ct & Ln 23060
Duncannon Ct & Pl 23059
Dunncroft Ct & Dr 23060
Dyers Ln 23059
Eagle Lake Dr 23060
Eastbranch Dr 23059
Eastshore Dr 23059
Echo Lake Dr 23060
Eddings Ct & Dr 23060
Edel Ct 23059
Edgelake Ct 23059
Edgeware Ln 23059
Edinburgh Rd 23060
Edmund Ct 23059
Edwardsville Dr 23060
Eggleston Circle Ln 23059
Eli Pl 23060
Elks Pass Ln 23060
Ellaberry Ln 23059
Ellington Woods Dr, Pl & Ter 23059
Elliot Ridge Way 23059
Ellis Meadows Ln 23059
Elmont Rd 23059
Elmont Glen Dr 23059
Elmont Woods Dr 23059
Elmwood Forest Ct 23059
Emmett Ct & Rd 23060
Englewood Rd 23060
English Cedar Ct 23060
English Ivy Ln 23059
Estelle Ct 23059
Ethelwood Rd 23059
Evelyton Ct 23060
Evergreen Mill Dr 23059
Everson Ter 23060
Faddenstone Dr 23060
Fair Port Cir 23060
Fairlake Ln 23060
Fairway Homes Way 23059
Fairways Pl 23059
Farm Meadow Dr 23060
Farmount Ter 23059
Farrington Rd 23059
Fauver Ave 23060
Fireside Dr 23060
Fish Pond Ln 23060
Fitchetts Ln 23060
Fleeton Ct 23060
Fontaine Ln 23060
Fords Country Ln 23059
Forest Way 23060
Forest Heights Ln 23059
Forest Lodge Ct & Dr 23060
Forest Trace Ct, Ln, Ter & Way 23059
W Fork Dr 23059
Fort Mchenry Pkwy 23060
Four Seasons Ter 23060
Foxford Ln 23059
Francis Rd
601-697 23059
699-1999 23059
2000-2199 23060
10000-10099 23059
Francis Marion Ct 23060
Francis Run Ct 23060
Francistown Rd 23060
Fremont Ct, Dr & Pl 23059
Friars Walk Ct, Ln & Ter 23059
Fuller Dr 23059
Gabriel Ct 23059
Gadsby Forest Pl 23059
Gadsby Park Ter 23059
Gadsby Trace Ct 23059
Gaelic Ln 23060
Garden Club Cir 23059
Garden Pond Dr 23059
Garden Spring Ln 23059
Garth Ln 23059
Gaskins Rd 23060
Gate House Ct, Dr & Pl 23059
Gathering Pl 23060
Gatwick Ter 23060
Geese Lndg 23060
Georgia Ave 23060
Gibson Hollow Ln 23060
Gilmans Cross Ct 23059
Ginda Ter 23059
Gladfelter Rd 23060
Glasgow Rd 23060
Glen Ct 23059
Glen Abbey Ct, Dr, Pl & Ter 23059
Glen Cove Ct 23060
Glen Lake Dr 23060
Glencoe Rd 23060
Glenmar Ct 23060
Glenshaw Ct & Dr 23059
Golf Villa Ln 23059
Good Oak Ln 23060
Goose Pond Ln 23059
Gordons Ln 23059
Grace Hill Ln 23059
Grayley Ct 23059
Greenbrooke Ct & Dr 23060
Greenmeadow Cir 23060
Greenstone Ct, Pl & Ter 23060
Greenwich Dr 23059
Greenwick Ct & Dr 23059
Greenwood Ct 23059
Greenwood Rd
9900-10399 23060
10400-14999 23059
Greenwood Glen Dr 23059
Gregory Ave 23059
Grey Oaks Estates Ct 23059
Grey Oaks Park Ln, Rd & Ter 23059
Grey Oaks Villas Dr 23059
Grinding Stone Cir 23060
Gwynns Pl 23060
Hackett St 23059
Hagan Rd 23060
Haleys Hollow Ct & Rd 23060
Halleys Cir 23060
Haltonshire Way 23059
Hames Ln 23059
Hamilton Rd 23060
Hanover Ln 23059
Harben Ct & Pl 23059
Harding Ave 23059
Hardwick Ct & Dr 23059
Hargrave Ct 23060
Harlow Farm Way 23059
Harmony Rd 23059
Harris Farm Ln 23059
Hart Mill Dr 23060
Hartley Hill Ct 23060
Harvest Glen Ct, Dr, Ln & Way 23059
Harwin Cir & Pl 23060
Hasting Mill Ln 23060
Hastings Mill Dr 23060
Haven Mews Cir 23059
Hawks Beak Ct 23060
Haybrook Ln 23059
Haylors Beach Way 23060
Hearthstone Ct, Dr & Rd 23059
Heather Brook Ln 23059
Heather Grove Rd 23059
Heatherford Ct & Pl 23059
Heathsville Ct 23060
Henrico Landfill Rd 23059
Heritage Ln 23060
Hermitage Way 23059
Herrick Ln & Pl 23059
Heverley Ct, Dr & Pl 23059
Hickory Ann Dr 23059
Hickory Downs Ct & Dr 23059
Hickory Lake Ct & Ter 23059
Hickory Meadows Ct 23059
Hickory Park Dr 23059
Hickory Place Way 23059
Hickson Dr 23059
High Bush Cir 23060
High Mountain Ct 23060
Highview Ave 23059
Highwoods Pkwy 23060
Hill Trace Ct 23060
Hillshire Cir, Ct & Way 23059
Hinsdale Pl 23059
Hinton Ct 23060
Hoehns Rd 23060
Holliman Dr 23059
Hollow Ct 23060
Holly Hill Rd 23059
Hollybriar Ct 23060
Holman Dr & Ln 23059
Holman Ridge Rd 23059
Honey Ln & Ter 23060
Hookers Ln 23059
Hope Rd 23059
Horizon Rd 23060
Horse Castle Ct 23060
Hoskins Dr 23060
Houze Ter 23060
Howards Mill Rd 23059
Howze Rd 23060
Hungary Rd 23060
Hungary Branch Ct 23060
Hungary Ridge Ct, Dr & Ter 23060
Hungary Spring Rd 23060
Hungary Woods Dr, Pl & Ter 23060
Hunter Hill Ter 23059
Hunters Glen Ct, Dr & Ter 23059
Hunting Hollow Ct & Rd 23060
Hunton Commons Ln 23059
Hunton Cottage Ct & Ln 23059
Hunton Crossing Ct, Dr & Pl 23059
Hunton Ridge Dr & Ln 23059
Hunton Station Ct 23059
Hurley Ct 23060
Hylas Blvd 23059
Indale Ct & Rd 23060
Inkberry Pl 23059
Innesbrook Rd 23060
Innslake Dr 23060
Ireland Ln 23060
Ironwoods Walk Dr & Pl 23059
Isleworth Ct & Dr 23059
Ismet Ct 23060
Ivy Hollow Ct 23059
Jacobs Creek Dr 23060
Jalbert Dr 23060
Jamerson Ct & Ln 23059
Jamieson Pl 23059
Jeb Stuart Pkwy 23059
Jebstone Ct 23059
John Cussons Dr 23060
Johnnetta Ln 23060
Jon Page Ct 23060
Jones Rd 23060
Jones Mill Ct & Dr 23060
Jordan Ct & Dr 23060
Joseph Ct, Dr & Way 23060
Journey Ln 23059
Joycelyn Ct 23060
Kain Rd 23059
Katy Brooke Ct & Pl 23060
Kay Frye Ln 23060
Kayhoe Rd 23060
Keats Grove Ct & Pl 23059
Keelwood Ct 23060
Keesee Meadow Ln 23059
Kelbrook Ln 23060
Kelleys Ford Ln 23059
Kellipe Rd 23059
Kelly Cv 23060
Kellywood Cir, Ct & Dr 23060
Kelston Green Ct & Dr 23060
Kempton Manor Ct 23060
Kenilworth Pl 23059
Kenley Tye Ln 23059
Kennedy Station Ln, Pl & Ter 23060
Kershaw Ct, Dr & Pl 23059
Ketterley Row 23059
Kevo Ct 23060
Kiefer Field Ct 23059
Killiam Ct 23060
Killington Rd 23060
Kilpatrick Ln 23059
Kimberly Lynn Cir 23060
Kimbermere Ct 23060
Kimberwick Dr 23060
Kimbolton Pl 23059
Kincaid Rd 23060
Kinglet Ct 23059
Kings Rd 23059
Kingscote Ln 23059
Kingscroft Dr 23060
Kingshurst Ct 23060
Kingsrow Cir, Ct & Dr 23060
Kittery Pl 23060
Klaus Cir & Ct 23060
Knotty Dr 23060
Knotty Pine Ln 23059
Knotty Way Dr 23060
Lake Dr 23059
Lake Brook Dr 23060
Lake Sharon Dr 23060
Lake Shore Ct 23059
Lake West Ter 23059
N Lakefront Dr 23060
Lakewood Rd 23060
Lambeth Rd 23060
Lanceor Dr 23060
Langley Dr 23060
Lansdowne Rd 23060
Larabrook Pl 23060
Laurel Lakes Ct & Dr 23060
Laurel Ridge Ct & Ter 23060
Lavecchia Way 23059
Lawford Hills Ct 23060
Layton Dr 23059
Leabrook Dr & Way 23059
Leander Ct & Dr 23060
Ledge Cir 23059
Lee Ave 23060
Lee Ann Ln 23060
Lees Crossing Ct 23059
Leighwood Ct 23060
Lemoore Ct & Dr 23059
Lerade Ct 23059
Lewisetta Dr 23060
Lexington Farm Dr 23059
Liesfeld Pkwy & Pl 23060
Lillian Ct 23059
Lincoln Ridge Ln 23060
Lincolnshire Ct & Pl 23059
Links Ln & Way 23059
Linsey Lakes Dr 23060
Lissie Ct 23060
Lito Rd 23060
Little Brighton Ct 23059
Lizfield Way 23059
Lizzie Anne Ln 23060
Locklies Dr 23060
Lofton Dr 23060
London Ct & Dr 23060
London Tower Ct 23060
Long Meadow Cir, Dr & Xing 23059
Longdale Ave 23060
Longest Rd 23059
Lottsburg Ct 23060
Lower Wyndham Ct 23059
Loxton Ct & Way 23059
Lumberjack Ct & Ln 23060
Luxford Ct, Pl & Way 23059
Lynwood Dr 23059
Macalpine Cir & Ct 23060
Magnolia Pointe Blvd, Cir, Ct & Pl 23059
Magnolia Ridge Dr 23059
Maher Mnr 23060
Main Blvd 23059
Malham Way 23059
Manaford Cir 23059
Manor Grove Cir 23059
Manor Park Ct, Dr, Ter & Way 23059
Manowar Ct 23060
Mantle Ct 23060
Maple Hill Ct & Pl 23059
Marbury Dr & Ter 23060
Marcross Ct 23059
Marlee Farm 23059
Marshall Run Cir 23060
Mary Beth Ln 23060
Maryland Ave 23060
Mason Park Way 23059
Masters Row 23059
Maurice Walk Ct 23060
Maybrook Ct, Dr, Ln & Way 23059
Mayo Ct 23060
Mcfall Ct 23059
Meadow Pond Ct 23059
Meadow Ridge Ct, Ter & Way 23059
Meadow Run Ct 23060
Meadowbrook Ct & Rd 23060
Meadowfield Ct & Ln 23060
Megan Ct, Dr & Way 23060
Melcroft Ct & Pl 23059
Melitta Ct 23060
Meltonberry Ct 23060
Mercil Ter 23060
Meredith Creek Dr & Ln 23060
Meredith Woods Ct & Rd 23060
Merediths Branch Dr 23060
Merkner Dr 23060
Merlin Ct & Ln 23060
Merritt Ct & Pl 23060
Mesquite Rd 23060
Mica Ct 23060
Middletown Way 23060

Mill Rd
11000-11399 23060
11400-11999 23059
Mill Cross Ter 23059
Mill Park Cir, Ct & Dr 23060
Mill Pine Ct 23060
Mill Place Ct, Dr & Ter 23060
Miller Ave 23060
Millstone Landing Dr 23059
Mineral Springs Ln 23060
Minor Rd 23059
Mistyview Ct & Pl 23060
Mobjack Ave 23060
Molly Ln 23060
Montfort Cir 23059
Moraticco Ct 23060
Morattico Cir 23060
Morestead Ct & Dr 23059
Morgans Glen Cir, Dr & Pl 23059
Moriano Ter 23060
Morning Creek Rd & Ter 23059
Morse Ln 23060
Moultrie Rd 23060
Mount Olive Ave 23060
Mountain Pl 23060
Mountain Rd
1200-4199 23060
13000-14999 23059
Mountain Ash Cir & Dr 23060
Mountain Cove Ct 23060
Mountain Gate Ln, Pl & Way 23060
Mountain Glen Pkwy 23060
Mountain Grove Rd 23060
Mountain Run Dr 23060
Mountain Spring Dr & Ter 23060
Mountainberry Ct 23060
Mulholland Dr 23059
Murano Way 23059
Nash Ln 23059
Nashly Way 23060
Nature Trail Rd 23060
Nectar Ct 23060
Needles Way 23060
Needles Eye Ter 23060
New Farrington Ct 23059
New Harvard Ct, Ln & Pl 23059
New Haven Ct, Dr & Pl 23059
New Town Ct 23059
New Trail Ct 23060
New Wade Ln 23059
New York Ave 23060
Newtonwood Ct 23060
Nicewood Rd 23060
Nightmuse Ct & Way 23059
Norfolk St 23060
Norwich Ct, Pkwy & Pl 23059
Nuckols Rd
10800-10999 23060
11000-12399 23059
Nuthatch Ct 23059
Oak Lawn Ln 23059
Oak Mill Ct 23059
Oakstone Dr 23060
Old Brick Rd 23060
Old Courtney Rd 23060
Old Farmhouse Ln 23059
Old Forester Ln 23060
Old Francis Rd 23059
Old Greenway Ct, Dr & Pl 23059
Old Greenwood Rd 23059
Old Keeton Rd 23059
Old Millrace Ct, Pl & Ter 23059
Old Mountain Rd
8700-11499 23060
11500-11699 23059
Old Nuckols Rd 23059
Old Route 33 23060
Old School Rd 23059
Old Scotland Rd 23059
Old Springfield Rd 23060
Old Springfield Farm Rd & Way 23060
Old Washington Hwy
10400-10599 23059
10700-10999 23060
11001-11007 23060
11008-11009 23059
11010-11018 23060
11011-11027 23059
11014-11098 23059
11031-11035 23060
11037-11099 23059
11100-11199 23060
11200-11999 23059
Old Woodman Rd 23059
Old Wyndham Dr 23059
Olde Belo Ct 23060
Olde Covington Ct, Pl & Way 23059
Olde Hartley Ct, Dr, Pl & Way 23060
Olde Milbrooke Dr & Way 23060
Olde Mill Pond Dr, Ln & Pl 23060
Olde Sage Ct 23059
Onslow Ct 23059
Opaca Ln 23059
Operator Ct 23060
Orchard Park Ct, Dr & Ln 23059
Oscar Pl 23060
Overhill Dr 23059
Overhill Lake Ln 23059
Oxbury Ct 23059
Packard Ct & Rd 23060
Pale Moon Ct, Dr & Pl 23059
Palmers Way 23059
Palomine Ct 23060
Par Farm Ct 23060
Park Commons Ct & Loop 23059
Park Creste Dr 23059
Park Forest Ct, Ln & Way 23059
Park Green Way 23060
Park Meadows Ct, Ln & Way 23059
Park Place Ct 23060
Park Tree Pl 23060
Parkcrest Ct 23059
Parkland Pl 23059
Parksburg Ct 23059
Parrish Ln 23059
Parsons Chapel Rd 23059
Parsons Walk Cir, Ct & Pl 23059
Parview Pl & Way 23059
Patch Ct, Rd & Ter 23059
Patjay Ln 23059
Patriot Cir 23059
Peace Ln 23060
Peace Mill Pl 23060
Peavey Ct & St 23059
Pennsylvania Ave 23060
Pepperbush Ct 23060
Perch Ln 23060
Perrywinkle Rd 23059
Persimmon Tree Ln 23060
Peterfield Ln 23059
Phelps St 23060
Pin Oak Estates Dr 23060
Pine Lodge Ct 23060
Pinedale Dr 23059
Pinenoble Ct 23060
Pinepoint Dr 23059
Pinkerton Pl 23060
Pond Mill Ct & Way 23059
Poquoson Ct 23060
Pornello Ln 23060
Porsche Dr 23059
Portsmouth St 23060
Pouncey Pl 23059
Pouncey Tract Rd
4100-4440 23060
4441-15499 23059
Powhatans Trl 23060
Prenderi Rd 23059
Presbytery Ct 23059
Prescott Pl 23059
Preston Square Loop 23059
Pruett Ct & Ln 23059
Pumpkin Seed Ln 23060
Purcell Pl & Rd 23060
Puttinham Ct 23059
Quail Challenge Ct 23059
Quail Roost Ct & Dr 23059
Quail Walk Dr 23059
Quail Whistle Ct & Dr 23059
Quarry Hill Ln 23059
Rachel Lake Ln 23060
Racquet Club Ln 23060
Radcliffe Ct 23060
Reba Ct 23060
Rebel Rd 23059
Red Cedar Ter 23060
Redbud Rd 23060
Redfield Ln 23059
Redmond Ct & Pl 23060
Reed Forest Ct 23059
Reedville Ave 23060
Regal Oaks Rd 23059
Reids Pointe Ky & Rd 23060
Renay Ct 23060
Renwick Ct, Dr & Pl 23059
Rhode Island Ave 23060
Richmond Rd 23060
Rickey Ct 23060
Ridgedale Ct & Dr 23059
Ridgegate Dr, Ln & Pl 23059
Ridgewood Park Ct 23060
Rigney Ct, Pl & Ter 23060
Rimbey Ct 23060
River Mill Ct 23060
River Run Dr & Ln 23059
Riverdale Ave 23060
Riverplace Ct & Ter 23059
Rivers Edge Pl 23059
Rivertop Ct 23059
Robin Lee Ln 23060
Robin Spring Ln 23060
Rocket Dr 23060
Rocky Ridge Rd 23059
Rolling Creek Pl 23059
Rollingwood Ct, Ln & Ter 23060
Rose Bowl Dr 23059
Rosebud Ln 23060
Rosebud Bend Ln 23059
Rosier Creek Way 23060
Round Top Rd 23060
Rudwick Rd 23060
N Run Rd 23060
Running Creek Rd 23060
Running Stone Ct 23059
Runnymeade Dr 23060
Runyon Dr 23060
Ruxton Rd 23060
Ryall Rd 23060
Saddleridge Ct & Rd 23059
Sadler Pl
4900-4999 23060
4990-4990 23058
5001-5099 23060
5020-5098 23060
Sadler Rd 23060
Sadler Glen Ct, Ln & Pl 23060
Sadler Green Ln & Pl 23060
Sadler Grove Ct, Rd & Way 23060
Sadler Oaks Ct & Dr 23060
Sadler Place Ct & Ter 23060
Sadler Walk Ln 23060
Salford Ct 23060
Saluda Ave 23060
Sampson Ln 23059
San Marco Dr 23060
Sanbet Ct 23060
Sand Castle Dr 23059
Sands Ct 23060
Sara Beth Cir 23060
Sara Jean Ct & Ter 23060
Savage Ct 23059
Sawdust Dr 23059
Scattered Flock Ct 23059
Scenic Pl 23060
Schaum Ct 23060
Scotland Ln 23060
Scots Hill Ter 23059
Scots Quarter Rd 23059
Scotsglen Ct, Dr & Ter 23059
Scotts Ridge Ct 23060
Serenity Ct 23059
Servo Dr 23060
Sethwarner Ct, Dr & Pl 23059
Shadow Run Dr & Ln 23059
Shadrach Ct 23059
Shady Grove Rd 23059
Shady Hills Ct & Way 23059
Shady Mill Ct & Way 23059
Shady Willow Ct, Pl & Ter 23059
Shadyford Ln 23060
Shae Pl 23059
Shamrock Farms Ct 23059
Sharbel Cir 23059
Sharonway Ct & Dr 23060
Shellbark Ct & Pl 23059
Sheppards Way Dr 23059
Sherwin Pl 23059
Sherwood Farms Ln 23059
Shifflett Ct 23059
Shirebrook Dr 23059
Short Spoon Ct 23059
Sideview Ln 23059
Sidney Ct 23059
Siena Ln 23059
Simsbury Ct & Pl 23059
Singletree Ct & Ln 23060
Sioux Ln 23060
Slenderleaf Dr 23060
Smith Point Way 23059
Smith Woods Pl 23059
Snow Goose Ln 23060
Snowberry Ct 23060
Snowmass Ct, Rd & Ter 23060
Snowshoe Ct 23060
Southerly Ct 23059
Southmill Ct & Dr 23060
Southwinds Ct, Dr & Pl 23059
Spray Ct 23060
Spring Lake Pl 23060
Spring Moss Cir, Ln & Ter 23060
Springfield Ct & Rd 23060
Springfield Church Ln 23060
Springfield Woods Cir & Ct 23060
Spurloch Ct 23059
Squaw Valley Ct & Pl 23060
St Anton Cir 23060
Stable Hill Pl & Ter 23059
Stable Ridge Ct 23059
Stanwood Ct & Way 23059
Staples Mill Rd
9600-11199 23060
11400-11499 23059
Staples Trace Ct & Rd 23059
Starling Ridge Ln 23059
Steamboat Dr 23060
Stepping Stone Ln 23059
Steuben Ct & Dr 23060
Stillman Pkwy 23060
Stone Arbor Ln 23059
Stone Bluff Dr 23060
Stone Horse Ct & Rd 23059
Stone Horse Creek Rd 23059
Stone Lake Dr 23059
Stone Valley Ct 23060
Stoneacre Ct, Dr & Pl 23059
Stonebrook Ct & Dr 23060
Stonehurst Estates Ter 23059
Stonemeadow Ct & Dr 23060
Stonewell Cir 23060
Stonewick Ct, Dr & Pl 23059
Strolling Ln 23060
Stuart Oaks Dr 23059
Sugar Ct 23060
Summer Breeze Dr 23059
Summer Creek Ct & Way 23059
Summerhaven Ct 23060
Summerhook Ct 23060
Sumner Ct & Pl 23059
Susan Sheppard Ct 23060
Sutton Park Ct 23060
Swanson Mill Ct & Way 23059
Swift Flight Ln 23059
Tabb Rd 23060
Tag Pl 23060
Tahoe Ct 23060
Taker Ct 23060
Tameo Ct & Rd 23060
Taos Ln 23060
Tates Way 23060
Tavern Way 23060
Tavern Green Rd 23060
Taylors Crossing Ct 23059
Technology Park Dr
800-1199 23059
1400-1499 23060
Telegraph Rd
8600-9799 23060
10100-10599 23059
10601-10699 23059
Telegraph Run Ln 23060
Telegraph Station Ln 23059
Telegraph Wire Ct 23060
Telegraph Woods Ct, Dr & Ln 23060
The Gardens Dr 23059
Thistle Hills Ln 23059
Thomas Kenney Dr 23060
Thomas Mill Dr 23059
Thomasville Ln 23060
Thornberry St 23060
Thorncroft Dr 23060
Tiller Rd 23060
Timber Pass & Pl 23060
Timber Hollow Ct & Pl 23060
Timbers Edge Ct 23060
Timberton Ct 23060
Tiverton Ln 23059
Tolson Ln 23060
Tom Leonard Dr 23060
Topping Ln 23060
Torno Dr 23060
Toston Ln 23060
Towering Rd 23059
Townsend Park Dr & Row 23060
Tracey Lynne Cir 23060
Tractor Barn Pl 23060
Trail Wynd Ct 23059
Tray Way 23060
Treasure Ct 23059
Trexler Rd 23060
Treyburn Dr, Pl & Way 23059
Trillium Ct & Pl 23060
Triple Lee Ln 23059
Triple Oak Estates Dr 23059
Trolley Ln 23060
Tudor Rose Ct 23060
Turnberry Park Ct, Dr & Ln 23059
Turner Mountain Pl 23060
Turning Branch Cir, Rd & Way 23059
Tutelo Ct & Pl 23059
Tweed Pl 23060
Twin Hickory Ln & Rd 23059
Twin Hickory Lake Dr 23059
Two Pond Ln 23059
Urbanna Ct 23060
Valleymeade Pl 23060
Velyton Pl 23059
Vesely Ln 23059
Vicars Ridge Ln 23059
Victory Ln 23059
Vienna Woods Pl 23060
Villa Pl 23059
Village Commons Walk 23060
Village Run Ct & Dr 23060
Village Townes Walk 23060
Village Views Dr & Pl 23059
Virginia Ave & Rd 23059
Virginia Center Pkwy 23059
Virginia Centerway Dr & Pl 23059
Virginia Forest Ct 23060
Virginia Village Dr 23059
Walborough Ct & Ln 23059
Walnut Trails Ct 23059
Walsinghamtown Ct 23059
Warbler Way 23059
Ward Rd 23059
Wares Wharf Cir 23060
Warnerwood Ct 23060
Warren Ct, Pl, Rd & Ter 23060
Warsaw Ter 23060
Washington Blvd 23059
Washington Hwy 23059
Washington Rd 23060
Waterfront Dr 23060
Watford Ct & Ter 23060
Wellston Ct & Pl 23059
Welshland Ct 23059
Wendhurst Dr 23060
Westcott Landing Cir, Ct & Pl 23059
Westcott Ridge Ct, Dr & Ter 23059
Western Riders Ln 23059
Westin Estates Ct, Dr & Ter 23059
Westward Pl & Ter 23059
Wheat Ridge Ct & Pl 23059
Whelford Way 23060
Whispering Breeze Ct 23059
Whispering Creek Cir 23059
White Chimneys Ct 23060
White Marsh Rd 23060
Whitford Cir, Ct & Ter 23060
Whittall Way 23060
Wiinterhawk Dr 23059
Wilary Rd 23059
Wild Goose Ln & Walk 23060
Wildtree Dr 23060
Wilf Ct 23060
Willane Rd 23059
Willow Gate Dr & Pl 23060
Willow Ridge Dr, Pl & Ter 23060
Willow Run Ct & Ter 23060
Willows Green Ln, Rd & Way 23059
Willscott Pl 23059
Wilshire Dr & Pl 23060
Wilson Ave 23060
Wind Haven Ct 23060
Windam Hill Rd 23059
Windwhistle Pass 23060
Windy Hollow Cir, Ct & Way 23059
Winfrey Rd 23059
Wingstem Ct 23060
Winns Church Rd 23059
Winona Blvd & Ct 23060
Winsted Ct 23060
Winston Blvd & Ct 23060
Winston Trace Cir 23060
Wintercreek Dr 23060
Wintergreen Rd 23060
Winterhawk Dr & Pl 23059
Winterset Pl 23060
Winterwood Dr 23060
Wolfe Manor Ct 23060
Wonder Ln 23060
Wood Brook Ct, Ln, Rd & Way 23059
Woodacres Ct 23060
Woodchuck Ct & Pl 23060
Woodford Ct & Pl 23059
Woodland Rd 23060
Woodman Ct & Rd 23060
Woodman Hills Ct & Ter 23060
Woodman Trace Ct, Dr & Ln 23060
Woodshire Pl & Way 23060
Woodstock Dr & Rd 23059
Woodstock Heights Dr 23059
Woody Ridge Pl 23059
Woolshire Ct, Dr & Pl 23059
Wylie Ln 23059
Wyndham Lake Dr 23059
Wyndham Park Dr 23059
Wyndham West Dr 23059
Yorkminster Dr 23060
Zermatt Ct 23060

HAMILTON VA

General Delivery 20158

POST OFFICE BOXES MAIN OFFICE STATIONS AND BRANCHES

Box No.s
All PO Boxes 20159

NAMED STREETS

All Street Addresses 20158

HAMPTON VA

General Delivery 23670

POST OFFICE BOXES MAIN OFFICE STATIONS AND BRANCHES

Box No.s
A - N 23666
A - I 23669
1 - 656 23669
1201 - 1560 23661
1701 - 1940 23669
3001 - 3808 23663
7001 - 8242 23666
9001 - 9819 23670
65001 - 66540 23665
69001 - 69232 23669

NAMED STREETS

Abba Way 23669
Abbey Ct 23661
Abbott Dr 23666
Aberdeen Rd
1-808 23661
809-809 23670
810-898 23661
811-899 23661
900-1699 23666
Abigail Ln 23669
Abingdon Cir 23669
Academy Ln 23669
Acorn St 23669
Adams Cir 23663
Addison Rd 23663
Admiral Ct 23669
Adrian Cir 23669

Adriatic Dr 23664
Agecroft Ct 23669
Agnes Ct 23669
Aidan Ct 23666
Airacobra Ct 23665
Al St 23664
Alamo Ct 23669
Alaric Dr 23664
Albany Dr 23666
Albert E Simpson St 23669
Alcove Dr 23669
Alder Wood Dr 23666
Alert Dr 23665
Alexander Dr 23664
Algernourne St 23664
Algonquin Rd 23661
Allainby Way 23666
Alleghany Rd 23661
Allen St 23669
Allendale Dr 23669
Allison Sutton Dr 23669
Alma Ct 23669
Almond Ct 23669
Altair Ln 23665
Alton Ct 23669
Aluminum Ave & Dr 23661
Alvin Dr 23664
Ambassador Dr 23666
Ambler Ct 23669
Ambrose Ln 23663
Ames Ct 23669
Amherst Rd 23663
Amy Ct 23663
Ancel Ct 23666
Anchorage Ct 23666
Andalusia Ct 23666
Anderson Ln 23661
Andrews Blvd
1300-1399 23669
1800-2499 23663
Andrews St 23665
Andros Isle 23666
Angela Ct 23669
Angelia Way 23663
Angus Ln 23669
Anita Ct 23663
Anne St 23664
Anne Burras Ave 23665
Anthony Dr 23663
Antietam Ct 23669
Antiqua Bay 23666
Antoinette Cir 23663
Apache Trl 23669
Apollo Dr 23669
Apollo Way 23665
Appaloosa Ct 23666
Apple Ave 23661
Applewood Dr 23666
Aqua Ct 23666
Arch St 23669
Ardmoor Dr 23666
Ares St 23665
Arlington Ter 23666
N Armistead Ave
1-1100 23669
1102-1198 23669
1400-3799 23666
S Armistead Ave 23669
Armistead Pointe Pkwy 23666
Armor Arch 23669
Armstrong Dr 23669
Arrollton Dr 23666
Arrowwood Ct 23666
Artillery Rd 23669
Ascot Ct 23666
Ash Ave 23665
Ashe Meadows Dr 23664
Ashleigh Dr 23666
Ashmont Cir 23666
Ashwood Dr 23666
Aspenwood Dr 23666
Aster Way 23663
Athens Ave 23669
Atlantic Ave 23664
Atlantis Ln 23665
Atwell Ln 23669
Auburn Ln 23666
Augusta St 23669
Autozone Way 23669
Autumn Ln 23669
Avon Rd 23666
Azalea Dr 23669
Baccus Ct 23664
N & S Back River Rd 23669
Bacon St 23669
Bailey Park Dr 23669
Bainbridge Ave 23663
Baines Rd 23666
Baker Farm Dr 23666
Baldwin Ter 23666
Balmoral Dr 23669
Bancroft Dr 23663
Banister Dr 23666
Banks Ln 23666
Bannon Ct 23666
Barba Dr 23669
Barfoot Cir 23664
Barksdale Rd 23669
Barnes Ct 23664
Barrack St 23666
Barrington Pl 23666
Barron Dr 23669
Barry Ct 23666
Barrymore Ct 23666
Basil Sawyer Dr 23666
Bassette St 23669
Bates St 23661
Battle Rd 23666
Baxter St 23669
Bay Ave 23661
Bay Front Pl 23664
E & W Bayberry Ct 23669
Bayhaven Dr 23666
Bayview Ct 23664
Beach Rd 23664
Beacon Cir 23664
Beacons Way 23669
Beall Dr 23663
Bear Creek Xing 23669
Beatrice Dr 23666
Beaumont St 23669
Beauregard Hts 23669
Beaver Castle Ct 23666
Becouvarakis Ct 23669
Bedford Ct 23664
Beechmount Dr 23669
Beechwood Rd 23666
Belfast Ave 23661
Bell St 23661
Bellgrade Dr 23666
Bells Island Dr 23664
Bellview Ter 23669
Bellwood Rd 23666
Belmont Ct & Pl 23666
Bending Oak Dr 23666
Benedict Ave 23665
Benevita Pl 23666
Benjamin Ter 23666
Bennett Ln 23666
Benson Dr 23664
Benthall Rd 23664
Bentley Dr 23666
Berkley Dr 23663
Berkshire Ter 23666
Bernard Ave 23669
Bethel Ave 23669
Betty Ct 23666
Betz Ln 23666
Beverly St 23669
Bexley Ln 23666
Bickfield Dr 23666
Bickford St 23663
Big Bethel Pl & Rd 23666
E & W Big Sky Dr 23666
Bimini Xing 23666
Birch Ave 23661
Birch St 23665
Black Oak Ct 23666
Black Widow Dr 23665
Blackberry Ln 23669
Blackburn Ln 23666
Blackmore Pl 23666
Blackwater Ln 23669
Blair Ave 23661
Blake Cir 23669
Bland St 23669
Blazer Ct 23666
Bleak Point Ln 23669
Blount Ct 23663
Bloxoms Ln 23664
Blue Ridge Hunt Rd 23666
Blue Run Cir 23666
Blueberry Hl 23669
Bluesage Path 23663
Boathouse Ln 23669
Bob Gray Cir 23666
Bobcat Dr 23665
Bobs Ct 23666
Boeing Ave 23669
Boger Cir 23664
Bogie Cir 23669
Bohnert Dr 23666
Bonaire Dr 23669
Bond St 23666
Bonifay Dr 23666
Bonita Dr 23664
Bonneville Dr 23664
Bonney Ln 23669
Bonwood Rd 23666
Booker St 23663
Boswell Dr 23669
Bounty Cir 23666
Bowen Dr 23666
Bowen St 23665
Box St 23661
Boxelder Ct 23666
N & S Boxwood St 23669
Boxwood Point Rd 23669
Boykin Ln 23663
Brackin Ct 23663
Braddock Rd 23661
Bradley Pl 23663
Braemar Dr 23669
Brafferton Cir 23663
Bragg Ct 23666
Bramston Dr 23666
Brandon Ct 23669
Brantleys Trce 23666
Braxton Ct 23665
Breaker Ct 23666
Breakwater St 23669
Breckinridge Ct 23666
Brentwood Dr 23669
Brians Ct 23664
Briar Dr 23661
Briarfield Rd
1500-1599 23666
1600-1643 23661
1644-1699 23669
1701-1725 23669
Briarwood Dr 23666
Bridge St 23669
Bridgeport Cove Dr 23663
Bridgewater Dr 23666
Brigham St 23663
Brightwood Ave 23661
Brimer Ct 23666
Brinkman Dr 23666
Bristol Ct 23666
Brittain Ln 23669
Broadstreet Rd 23666
Brockridge Hunt Dr 23666
Brogden Ln 23666
Bromsgrove Dr 23666
Bronco Dr & Ln 23665
Brooke Dr 23669
Brookfield Dr 23666
Brough Ln 23669
Broughton Ln 23669
Brout Dr 23666
Brown Cir 23663
Bruins Way 23666
Brunell Dr 23666
Bryant Ave 23665
Bryant Dr 23663
Bryson Cir 23666
Buchanan Dr 23669
Buck Cir 23666
Buckroe Ave 23664
Budweiser St 23661
Buffalo Dr 23664
Bufflehead Cv 23669
Build America Dr 23666
Bullock Pl 23666
Burgess Ave 23664
Burgh Westra Dr 23669
Burman Wood Dr 23666
Burnette Dr 23663
Burns St 23669
Burrell St 23665
Burrell Loop Rd 23665
Burton St 23666
Burwick Ct 23669
Bush St 23666
Butler Dr 23666
Butler Farm Rd 23666
Butternut Dr 23666
Buttonwood Dr 23666
Byrd St 23661
C And F Dr 23666
C C Spaulding Dr 23666
Cabell Ln 23664
Cabot Dr 23669
Caisson Xing 23669
Caldwell Dr 23666
Calhoun St 23669
Calvary Ter 23666
Calvert St 23669
Cambridge Pl 23669
Camden St 23669
Camellia Ln 23663
Cameo Dr 23666
Cameron St 23663
N Campus Pkwy 23666
Canal Rd 23664
Canavan Dr 23663
Canberra Ct 23665
Candlewood Dr 23666
Canford Dr 23669
Cannister Ct 23669
Cannonball Cir 23669
Cantamar Ct 23664
Canterbury Rd 23669
Canton Dr 23669
Cape Dorey Dr 23666
Capps Quarters 23669
Captains Ct 23669
Cardiff St 23666
Cardinal Dr 23664
Carlisle Ct 23666
Carlton Dr 23666
Carmel Ter 23666
Carmen Dr 23664
Carmine Pl 23666
Carolina St 23669
Carriage Dr 23664
Carrington Ct 23666
Carroll St 23663
Carters Grove Ct 23663
Carver St 23669
Cary St 23666
Cascade View Ct 23666
Cashinge Ave 23661
Castle Haven Rd 23666
Castlewood Ct 23669
Catalina Dr 23664
Catalpa Ave 23661
Catesby Jones Dr 23669
Cavalier Rd 23669
Cedar Dr 23669
Cedar St 23665
Cedar Point Dr 23669
Celey St 23661
Cellardoor Ct 23666
Cemetary Rd 23669
Center St 23669
Central St 23663
Challenger Ave 23665
Challenger Way 23666
Chalmers Ct 23666
Chamberlin Ave E & W 23663
Chancellor Rd 23661
Channel Ln 23664
Chantilly Ct 23669
Chapel St 23669
Charlene Loop 23666
Charles St 23669
Charlton Dr 23666
Charolais Run 23669
Charthouse Cir 23664
Chatham Ter 23666
Chattanooga Ct 23669
Cherokee Rd 23661
Cherry Ave 23661
Cherry St 23665
Cherry Acres Dr 23669
Chesapeake Ave
701-797 23661
799-2999 23661
3001-3743 23661
3745-4499 23669
Chesapeake Inlet Blvd 23665
Chesterfield Rd 23661
Chichester Ave 23669
Chickamauga Pike 23669
Childs Ave 23661
Chinaberry Pl 23666
Chipanbeth Ct 23669
Chippendale Ct 23666
Chipper Ln 23664
Chowning Dr 23664
Christin Way 23666
Christine Ct 23666
Christophers Ln 23666
Church Ln 23664
Churchill Ter 23666
Cindy Ct 23666
Cinnamon Ct 23666
Cisco Ct 23669
City Line Rd
2100-2121 23661
2123-2199 23661
5000-5000 23670
5002-5698 23661
Claiborne Sq E & W 23666
Claremont Ave 23661
Clark Rd 23664
Clarke Ave 23665
Classic Cv 23669
Claxton Ter 23664
Clay St 23663
Clay Pipe Ln 23666
Claymore Dr 23669
Clayton Dr 23669
Clear Stream Ln 23666
Clemwood Pkwy 23669
Cleopatra Ct 23669
Clifton St 23661
Cline Dr 23666
Clinton Cir 23666
Clipper Dr 23669
Clovelly Ln 23669
Clover St 23669
Clyde St 23669
Clydesdale Ct 23666
Coach St 23664
Cofer Ct 23666
Coffman Cir 23669
Colbert Ave 23669
Colebrook Dr 23669
Colgate Cir 23664
Coliseum Dr, Mall & Xing 23666
College Pl 23669
Collier Dr 23666
Collinwood Cir 23666
Colonial Ave 23661
Colonial Acres Dr 23664
Colonies Lndg 23669
Colonnade Ct 23666
Coltraine Cir 23669
Columbia Ave 23669
Columns Ln 23666
Comeangt Dr 23664
Commander Dr 23666
Commander Shepard Blvd 23666
Commerce Dr 23666
Commodore Dr 23669
Compass Cir 23669
Compton Ct 23666
Concord Dr 23666
Condor St 23669
Cone Dr 23666
Congress Ave 23669
Conner Rd 23663
Connie St 23664
Constant Rd 23664
Constellation Ln 23665
Continental Dr 23669
Cooks Cir 23669
Cooper St 23669
Copeland Dr 23661
Copley Ln 23669
Copper Kersey Dr 23666
Copperfield Rd 23666
Coral Pl 23669
Corbin Dr 23666
Cordova Dr 23666
Corey Cir 23663
Cornelius Dr 23666
Cornell Dr 23669
Cornwall Ter 23666
Corsair Dr 23665
Cortez Ct 23666
Corwin Cir 23666
Cottonwood Ave 23661
Counselor Ln 23669
Countess Ct 23669
E & W County St 23663
Courtland Ave 23661
Courtney Dr 23669
Covenant Ct 23666
Cranes Cv 23669
Craven St 23661
Creek Ave 23669
W Creek Ct 23666
Creek Landing Ln 23664
Creek Point Ln 23664
Creekside Pl 23669
Creekview Ln 23669
Crenshaw Ct 23666
Crescent Dr 23661
Crestwood Cir 23669
Crew House Rising 23669
Crispell Ct 23666
Critzos Ct 23669
Crockett Dr 23669
Cromer Ct 23661
Cronin Dr 23663
Crown Ct 23669
Crystal Cv 23666
Culotta Dr 23666
Cumberland Ave 23669
E & W Cummings Ave 23663
Cunniff Ct 23666
Cunningham Dr 23666
Cure Cir 23666
Curle Rd 23669
N & S Curry St 23663
Curtin Ct 23666
Curtis Ln 23669
Curtis Brooke Ln 23664
Cushing Post 23669
Custer Ct 23666
Cynthia Dr 23666
N & S Cypress St 23669
Dafia Dr 23666
Dahlia Ln 23663
Dale St 23661
Dale Lemonds Dr 23666
Dallas Ct 23669
Dan Leigh Ct 23666
Dandy Haven Rd 23664
Dandy Point Rd 23664
Dane Ct 23666
Danfield Cir 23666
Danforth Ave 23665
Daniel Ln 23664
Darby Ave 23663
Dare Ave 23661
Darnaby Ave 23661
Darville Dr 23663
Davenport Ct 23666
David Dr 23666
E Davis Rd 23666
Dawn Ln 23666
Day St 23661
Deaton Dr 23669
Debbie Dr 23666
Decesare Dr 23666
Deep Run Rd 23666
Deer Run Ln 23669
Deerfield Blvd 23666
Deerview Ln 23664
Deford St 23665
Delaware Ave 23661
Delbrook Way 23666
Delmont Ct 23666
Delta Pl 23666
Demetro Dr 23663
Denton Dr
1-99 23663
1501-1505 23664
1507-1599 23664
Denver Cir 23666
Derby Dr 23666
Derosa Dr 23666
Derry Rd 23663
Devils Den Rd 23669
Devonshire Ter 23666
Devore Ave 23666
Dewey Ave 23661
Diamond Hill Rd 23666
Diggs Dr 23666
Dillingham Ct 23669
Discovery Rd 23664
Dockside Dr 23669
Dodd Blvd 23665
Dogwood Ave 23665
Dogwood St 23669
Dolphin Ct 23669
Donald St 23669
Dooley St 23669
Doolittle Rd 23669
Dorene Ct 23663
Dornock Ct 23666
Dorris Carlson Dr 23666
Dorsetshire Ter 23666
Dotson Dr 23669
Douglas St
1-99 23663
101-111 23665
113-131 23665
133-199 23665
Dover Rd 23666
Downer Ln 23666
Downes St 23663
Downey Farm Rd 23666
Downey Green St 23666
Downing St 23661
Dragon Dr 23665
Drake Ct 23666
Draper Cir 23666
E & W Dressage Ct 23666
Driftwood Dr 23666
Drummonds Way 23669
Ducette Dr 23666
Duchess Ct 23669
Duke St 23669
Dulcy Ct 23666
Duluth Ct 23666
Dumont Cir 23669
Duncan Dr 23663
Dundee Rd 23669
Dunham Massie Dr 23669
Dunn Cir 23666
Dunnshire Ter 23666
Dunwoody Cir 23666
Durand Rd 23665
Durham St 23669
Dusk Ct 23666
Duval Ct 23669
E St 23661
Eagan Ave 23665
Eagle Ave & Loop 23665
Eagle Point Rd 23669
Eagles Lndg 23669
Earl St 23669
East Ave 23661

Street	ZIP
Eastbriar Ct	23666
Easterly Ave	23669
Eastfield Ct	23666
Easthill Ct	23664
Eastlawn Dr	23664
Eastmoreland Dr	23669
Easy St	23666
Easy Style Dr	23670
Eaton St	23669
Ebb Tide Ln	23666
Ebbing Quay	23666
Eberly Ter	23669
Echols Ct	23666
Edenbrook Dr	23666
Edgemont Dr	23666
Edgewater Rd	23664
Edgewood Dr	23666
Edinburgh Ln	23669
Edith Ct	23669
Edith Key St	23666
Edmonds Cove Rd	23664
Edson Ter	23663
Edward Dr	23666
Egger Cir	23663
Eggleston Ave	23669
Egret Cir	23666
Eisele Ct	23666
El Dorado Ct	23669
El Paso Ct	23669
Elite Ct	23666
Elizabeth Rd	23669
Elizabeth Lake Dr	23669
Ellington Ave	23661
Elliott Pl	23664
Elm Ave	23669
Elm St	23665
Elmwood Ln	23666
Eltham Ct	23669
Emeraude Plage	23666
Emma Dr	23664
Emmett Ln	23666
Emmonds Rd	23665
Emory Way	23666
Endeavor Ln	23665
Enfield Dr	23666
England Ave	23669
Enscore Ct	23666
Ensign Dr	23669
Enterprise Pkwy	23666
Eppington Cir	23669
Ericcson Dr	23669
Erskine St	23666
Ervin St	23661
Essex Park Dr	23669
Estate Dr	23666
Esterdale Ln	23669
Ethel Dr	23666
Eubank Dr	23666
Evans St	23669
Evergreen Pl	23666
Ewell Ct	23669
Executive Dr	23666
Exeter Ct	23666
Expedition St	23665
Exploration Way	23666
Explorer Trce	23665
Fairchild Ct	23666
Fairfax Dr	23661
Fairfield Blvd	23669
Fairland Ave	23661
Fairmont Dr	23666
Falcon Ct & Dr	23665
Falcon Creek Way	23666
Falcon Nest Pl	23666
Fallmeadow Ct	23666
N & S Fallon Ct	23661
Falmouth Turning	23669
Family Fun Pl	23666
S Farm House Ln	23669
Farmington Blvd	23666
Farrington Pl	23663
Fast Cir	23663
Faulk Cir	23663
Fawn Cir	23666
Felton Pl	23666
Fern St	23661
Ferncliff Dr	23669
Fernwood Cir	23666
Ferry Rd	23669
Ferry Landing Ln	23663
Fiddlers Grn	23669
Fields Dr	23664
N & S Fifth St	23664
Findley Sq & St	23666
Finland St	23661
Finns Point Ln	23669
Fir Ct	23666
N & S First St	23664
First Colony Trce	23665
Fiscella Ct	23669
Five Forks Ln	23669
Fleetwood Ave	23669
Fleming Dr	23669
E & W Flight Line Rd	23665
Flinton Dr	23666
Florence Dr	23666
Florida St	23669
Floyd Thompson Blvd	23666
Flyer Dr	23665
Flying D Ln	23666
Foley St	23669
Ford Rd	23663
Forrest St	23669
Forsyth Way	23666
Fort Worth St	23669
Founders Point Ave	23665
Fountain Way	23666
N & S Fourth St	23664
Fowler Ave	23661
Fox Run	23666
Fox Gate Way	23664
Fox Grove Dr	23664
Fox Hill Rd	23669
Fox Pond Ln	23664
Fox Wood Ln	23664
Foxtrot Rd	23665
Fran Cir	23661
Frankie P Engel St	23666
Franklin Ct	23665
Franklin St	23669
Franktown Rd	23663
Frazier Ct	23666
Freda Ct	23666
Freedom Cir	23666
Freeman Dr	23666
Frissell St	23663
Frost Ct	23666
Fruitwood Dr	23666
Fulcher Ct	23666
Fulton St	23663
Fulton Farm Rd	23669
G St	23661
Gabriel Pl	23661
Gabriel Archer Ln	23665
Gaines Mill Ln	23669
Galax St	23661
Gallaer Ct	23666
Galveston Ct	23669
Garland St	23669
Garrett Dr	23669
Garris Dr	23666
Garrow Cir	23663
Gary Ln	23661
Gateway Blvd & Dr	23666
Gatewood St	23666
Gatling Dr	23666
N & S Gawain Way	23669
Gayle St	23669
Geddy Dr	23669
Gemini Ln	23665
Gemini Way	23666
Gency Ln	23666
Genoa Dr	23664
George Ct	23663
Georgeanna Ct	23663
Georgia St	23661
Geyser Sq	23666
Gibbs Ct	23664
Gibson Rd	23669
E & W Gilbert St	23669
Gildner Rd	23666
Ginger Ct	23666
Gladstone Ct	23666
Glascock Ct	23666
Glascow Way	23669
Glen Forest Dr	23669
Glendale Rd	23661
Glenhaven Dr	23664
Glenrock Dr	23661
N Glenwood Rd	23669
Glica Ct	23666
Gloria Ct	23666
Gloucester St	23661
Glover Ave	23665
Godspeed Way	23663
Gold Cup Rd	23666
Gold Leaf Pl	23666
Golden Gate Dr	23663
Golden Willow Cir	23666
Goldmont Ct	23666
Gordon Ct	23666
Gosnold Ln	23665
Grace St	23669
Graham Heights Rd	23669
Grand View Dr	23664
Granella St	23669
Granger Dr	23666
Grant Cir	23669
Grant Allen Ct	23666
Gray Ave	23665
Grays Lndg	23666
Great Lakes Dr	23669
Green St	23669
Green Spring Ct	23669
Greenbriar Ave	23661
N & S Greenfield Ave	23666
Greenhill Ln	23666
Greenhouse Ln	23663
Greenlawn Ave	23661
Greenville Ct	23669
Greenwell Dr	23666
Greenwood Dr	23666
Gregg Rd	23665
Gregory Ct	23669
Gregson Ct	23666
Gretna Ct	23669
Griffin St	23669
Grimes Rd	23663
Grist Mill Dr	23669
Grouper Loop	23666
Grove St	23664
Grundland Dr	23664
Gumwood Dr	23666
Gunn Way	23669
Gunston Hall Ct	23669
Gunter Ct	23666
Gurley Ct	23663
Guthrie Rd	23666
Guy St	23669
Hackberry Pl	23666
Hale Dr	23663
Haley Dr	23661
Halifax Ave	23663
Hall Rd	23664
Hallmark Pl	23669
Hamilton Ct	23665
Hamilton St	23661
Hamlet Ln	23669
Hampshire Dr	23669
Hampshire Glen Pkwy	23669
Hampstead Ct	23669
Hampstead Heath Way	23666
Hampton Dr	23661
Hampton Ln	23669
Hampton Club Dr	23666
Hampton Harbor Ave	23669
Hampton Roads Ave	23661
Hamrick Dr	23666
Hankins Dr	23669
Hannah St	23661
Hanover Ave	23661
Happy Acres Rd	23669
Harbor Dr	23661
Hard Wood Dr	23666
Hardee Ct	23666
Hardy Ln	23669
Hardy Cash Dr	23666
Hare Rd	23666
Harland Ct	23666
Harlequin Dr	23669
Harlow Ct	23669
Harmony Ct	23666
Harper Ln	23666
Harriett St	23669
Harris Ave	23665
Harris Creek Rd	23669
Harris Landing Rd	23669
Harrison Ct	23665
Harrison St	23669
Harrogate Ln	23666
Hart Cir	23663
Hartford Rd	23666
Hartless Ct	23669
Harvest Ln	23664
Harwin Dr	23666
Harwood Ave	23664
Hastings Dr	23663
Hatteras Lndg	23669
Hatton Cir	23666
Haverford Ct	23666
Havoc Dr	23665
Hawk Ct	23665
Hawk Nest Ct	23666
Hawkins Ct	23666
Hawkstone Cv	23669
Hawthorn Pl	23666
Haywagon Trl	23669
Hazelwood Rd	23666
Headrow Ter	23666
Heather Cir	23669
Hedgelawn Ct	23669
Heffelfinger St	23669
Helms Ave & Rd	23665
Hemlock Ave	23661
Henderson Ln	23663
Henry Ct	23665
Henry St	23669
Henry Fork Dr	23666
Herbert Ave	23664
Hercules Dr	23669
Hermitage Pl	23664
Herring Pl	23666
Hickory St	
1-99	23665
200-299	23669
Hickory Hill Rd	23666
Hidalgo Dr	23669
Higgins Ln	23664
High Court Ln	23669
High Dunes Quay	23664
Highland Ave	23661
Hilda Cir	23666
Hilke Dr	23666
Hill St	23661
Hillcrest Cir	23666
Hillside Dr	23666
Hiram Crockett Ct	23669
Historic Trl	23665
Hobson Ave	23661
Hodges Dr	23666
Holiday Dr	23669
Hollis Wood Dr	23666
Hollomon Dr	23666
Hollow Creek Ct	23669
Holloway Dr	23666
Holly St	23669
Hollyberry St	23661
Hollywood Ave	23661
Holston Ln	23664
Holt Ave	23666
Home Pl	23663
Homeland St	23661
Homestead Ave	23661
Hondo Ct	23669
Honeysuckle Hl	23669
N & S Hope St	23663
Hopemont Cir	23669
Hopkins St	23663
Horseshoe Lndg	23669
Horsley Dr	23666
Horton Rd	23664
Houston Ave	23669
E Howard St	23663
Howe Rd	23669
Howmet Dr	23661
Huffman Dr	23669
Hughes Ln	23663
Hull Dr	23661
Hunlac Ave	23664
Hunt Club Blvd	23666
Hunter Trce	23669
Hunting Ave	23665
Hurst Dr	23663
Huskie Dr	23665
Hyde Park Ct	23669
E & W Hygeia Ave	23663
Ian Ct	23666
Ida St	23669
Ilex Ct	23666
Incubator Rd	23661
N & S Independence Dr	23669
Indian Rd	23669
Industry Dr	23661
Inglewood Dr	23666
Inlandview Dr	23669
Institute Dr	23663
Invader Ct & Dr	23665
Ira Ct	23666
Ireland St	23663
Iris Pl	23663
Iron Bridge Ct	23663
Ironwood Way	23666
Isaac Ln	23666
Island Cove Ct	23669
Ivory Gull Cres	23664
Ivy Home Rd	23669
Jacklyn Cir	23666
Jackson Ct	23665
Jakes Ln	23664
James Ter	23666
James River Trce	23665
Jameson Ave	23666
Jamestown Ave	23661
Janet Dr	23666
Janice Ct	23666
Jasmine St	23663
Jay Sykes Ct	23663
Jayhawk Dr	23665
Jaymoore Ln	23669
Jayne Lee Dr	23664
Jefferson Ct	23665
Jeffrey Ln	23666
Jenkins Ln	23664
Jennifer Ln	23666
Jennisons Fall	23669
Jerome Cir	23663
Jesse Ln	23664
Jib Ct	23664
Jimmy Cir	23666
Joan Dr	23666
Jodys Way	23666
John Smith Trce	23665
Johnson Ct	23669
Johnson Rd	23664
Jonquil Ln	23669
Jordan Dr	23666
Josephs Xing	23669
Joy Dr	23666
Joyce Lee Cir	23666
Joynes Rd	23666
Juanita Dr	23666
Judy Ct	23661
Julian Pl	23666
N & S Juniper St	23669
Kaitlyn Cir	23666
Kaleigh Ct	23666
Kanawha Ct	23669
Kansas Ct	23669
Katherine St	23661
Kecoughtan Rd	
700-3699	23661
3700-4799	23669
Keel Ct	23666
Keeton Ct	23666
N Keith Rd	23669
Keller Ct	23666
E & W Kelly Ave	23663
Kempers Charge	23669
Kempton St	23669
Kenan Ct	23666
Kenilworth Dr	23666
Kenmore Dr	23661
Kenneth St	23669
Kensington Dr	23663
Kent St	23661
Kentucky Ave	23661
Kenwood Dr	23666
Keswick Ln	23669
Kettering Ln	23666
Keystone Dr	23665
Kilgore Ave	23666
Killdeer Ln	23666
Kilverstone Way	23669
Kimberly Ave	23663
Kincaid Ln	23666
N & S King St	23669
King Cobra Ct	23665
King Kove Ln	23669
Kings Way	23669
Kings Landing Ln	23669
Kings Point Dr	23669
Kings View Ct	23669
Kingsbury Way	23666
Kingslee Ln	23669
Kingston Hall Ct	23663
Kingsway Ct	23669
Kinsmen Way	23666
Kirkwood Cir	23666
Kiwanis St	23661
Klich Dr	23666
Knickerbocker Cir	23666
Knight St	23669
Knodishall Way	23664
Knox Pl	23669
Kopek Ct	23666
Kostel Ct	23669
Kove Dr	23669
Kramer Ct	23664
Krause Ct	23664
Kyle St	23666
Kylee Ln	23664
Lacrosse St	23663
Ladd St	23669
Lafayette Dr	23664
Laguard Dr	23661
Lair Cir	23669
N & S Lake Cir & Loop	23666
Lake Cove Ln	23666
Lake Erie Ct	23669
Lake Ferguson Ct	23669
Lake Field Xing	23666
Lake Huron Ct	23669
Lake One Dr	23666
Lake Ontario Ct	23669
Lake Ovide Ct	23669
Lake Phillips Dr	23669
Lake Superior Ct	23669
Lake Tower Dr	23666
Lake View Dr	23666
Lake Walk Xing	23666
Lakeland Dr	23669
Lakeridge Rd	23666
E Lakeshore Dr	23666
Lakeside Cres	23669
Lakewood Dr	23666
E & W Lamington Rd	23669
Lampros Ct	23666
Lancaster Ter	23666
Lancer Ln	23665
Landmark Ct	23666
Lands End Cir	23669
Langholm Ct	23669
Langille Ct	23663
Langley Ave	23669
Langley Research Ctr	23665
Langston Blvd	23666
Lansdown Cir	23666
Lansing Dr	23663
Lantana Ln	23669
Larabee Ln	23663
Laralenc Dr	23670
Laredo Ct	23669
Lasalle Ave	
1-599	23661
600-1399	23669
Lassiter Dr	23666
Lauderdale Ave	23661
Laurel Dr	23669
Lavender Trce	23663
Lawndale Dr	23661
Lawrence Ave	23663
Leahs Trce	23666
Lee Ct	23665
Lee St	23669
Leeds Ter	23666
Leeland Ave	23661
Leencene St	23669
Leftwich Ct	23664
Lehman Ct	23666
Leicester Ter	23666
Lemaster Ave	23669
Lena Cir	23666
Leon Ln	23666
Leta Ct	23666
Level Green Ct	23669
Levingston Dr	23663
Lewis Ln	23664
E Lewis Rd	23666
W Lewis Rd	23666
Lexington St	23669
Libbey St	23663
Liberty Ln	23666
Lighthouse Dr	23664
Lightning Dr & Loop	23665
Lillian Ct	23669
Lincoln St	23669
Linda Cir	23666
Lindale St	23661
Lindbergh Way	23665
Linden Ave	23669
Litchfield Close	23669
E & W Little Back River Rd	23669
Little Farms Ave	23661
Little Neck Ln	23666
Little Oak Ln	23669
Little Rockwell Way	23669
Little Round Top	23669
Live Oak Ct	23669
Loch Cir	23669
Locksley Dr	23666
Lockwood Dr	23661
Locust Ave	23661
Lodi Ct	23666
Log Cabin Ln	23669
Logan Ct	23669
Lomax St	23666
Lombard St	23661
Londonshire Ter	23666
Lonerley Ave	23665
Long Ct	23666
Long Bridge Rd	23669
Long Creek Ln	23664
Long Green Ln	23663
Longleaf Ct	23666
Longstreet Ct	23666
Longwood Dr	23669
Lookout Pass	23669
Loon Ln	23669
Loquat Pl	23666
Lorigan Ln	23664
Loring Ct	23666
Lotus St	23663
Loura Ct	23666
Lowden Hunt Dr	23666
Lowrey St	23663
Lucas Dr	23666
Lucas Way	23666
Lucinda Ct	23666
Lucy Ct	23669
Lundy Ln	23666
Lyford Ky	23666
Lynnhaven Dr	23666
Lynnwood Dr	23666
M O Herb St	23664
Mabry Ave	23665
Macalva Dr	23669
Macon Rd	23666

Madison Ct 23665
Madison Chase 23666
Madrid Dr 23669
Madrone Pl 23666
Magnolia Pl 23669
Magnolia St 23665
Magruder Blvd 23666
Mainsail Dr 23664
Majestys Way 23669
Mallard Ct 23666
Mallard Run 23669
N Mallory St
 1-1508 23663
 1509-1515 23664
 1510-1516 23663
 1517-2299 23664
S Mallory St 23663
Malvern Hill Cir 23663
Manack Rd 23669
Manassas Ct 23669
Manchester Dr 23666
Manhattan Sq 23666
Manilla Ln 23669
Manning Ln 23666
Manor Hill Ct 23666
Mansford Dr 23664
Manteo Ave 23661
Maple Ave 23661
Maplewood St 23669
Marade Ln 23664
Marauder Ct 23665
Marcella Rd 23666
Margaret Dr 23669
Margereteaville Ln 23669
Marie Cir 23666
Marigold Ln 23663
Marina Rd 23669
Mariners Cove Rd 23669
Marion Rd 23663
Mark Dr 23661
Market Place Dr 23666
Markham Dr 23669
Markos Ct 23666
Marlborough Ct 23666
Marldale Dr 23666
Marlfield Cir 23669
Marlin Cir 23664
Marple Ln 23666
Marrow St 23669
Marsh Loop 23666
Marsh Point Ln 23666
Marshall Ave & St 23669
Martha Lee Dr 23666
Marval Cir 23666
Marvin Dr 23666
Mary St 23664
Mary Ann Dr 23666
N Mary Peake Blvd 23666
Maryfield Ct 23666
Maryland Ave 23661
Maser Ct 23666
Mason St 23669
Matoaka Rd 23661
Maume Cir 23666
Maverick Ct 23669
Maxwell Dr 23661
May St 23661
Mayer Ct 23664
Maynard St 23661
Maywood Dr 23666
Mccall Ct 23666
Mcculloch Rd 23663
Mcdonald Rd 23669
Mcelheney Ln 23669
Mcgivney Ln 23664
Mckenzie Pl 23666
Mcmenamin St 23666
Mcsweeney Cir 23663
Meadow Ln 23666
Meadowbrook Dr 23666
Medical Dr 23666
Mehrens Ct 23663
Melborne Pl 23669
Melissa Ct 23669
E & W Mellen St 23663
Melson Ln 23664
Melville Rd 23661
Memory Ln 23664
Merchant Ln 23666
E Mercury Blvd
 1-299 23669
 300-1099 23663
W Mercury Blvd
 1-299 23669
 400-4900 23666
 4902-4988 23666
Meredith St 23669
Merrick Rd 23666
Merrimac Ave 23661
Mesquite Pl 23666
Micale Ave 23666
Michael St 23666
Michaels Woods Dr 23666
Michele Dr 23669
Michigan Dr 23669
Micklebring Ln 23666
Micott Dr 23666
Middleboro Ter 23661
Middleburg Hunt Rd 23666
Middleton Ct 23661
Midlothian Sq 23669
Miles Cary Mews 23669
Milford Ave 23661
Mill Creek Ter 23663
Mill Point Dr 23669
Miller Dr 23666
Millicent Ct 23666
Millwood Ct 23666
Milton Dr 23666
Mimosa Cres 23661
Minetti Ct 23666
Mingee Dr 23661
Miranda Ct 23663
Missionary Rdg 23669
Misty Cv 23666
Misty Creek Ln 23669
Mitchell Rd 23669
Mizzen Cir 23664
Mockingbird Ln 23669
Moger Dr 23663
Mohawk Rd 23669
Monitor Dr 23669
Monroe Ct 23665
Monroe Dr 23669
Monte Volpe Ln 23664
Monterey Ave 23661
Monticello Mews 23666
Montpelier Pl 23666
Montrose Dr 23666
Moore St 23661
Morgan Dr 23663
Morningview Ct 23664
Morris St 23663
Morton Cir 23666
Mosby Ct 23666
Moss Ave 23669
Mount Stirling Cir 23663
Mountain Ashe Pl 23666
Muir Ct 23666
Mulberry Turn 23669
Mullins Ct 23666
Murray Ave 23666
Murray Ct 23665
Musket Ln 23666
Mustang Ct 23665
My Ln 23664
N Myra Dr 23661
Myrtle St 23669
Nancy Dr 23669
Nasa Dr 23666
Nassau Pl 23666
Natalie Dr 23666
Nathan St 23669
National Ave 23663
Naturewood Cir 23666
Neal St 23661
Nealy Ave & Blvd 23665
Ned Dr 23666
Neff Dr 23669
Nelson Ct 23665
Nelson Pkwy 23669
Nelson House Ln 23669
Neptune Dr 23669
Nettles Ln 23666
Neville Cir 23663
New St
 800-899 23669
 900-998 23661
 1000-1099 23661
New Bern Ave 23669
New Frontier Way 23665
New World Ln 23665
New York Ave 23661
Newby Dr 23666
Newcastle Ct 23666
Newcombe Ave 23669
Newgate Village Rd 23666
Newport News Ave
 200-799 23669
 800-999 23661
Newsome Pl 23661
Newton Rd 23663
Nickerson Blvd
 1700-2099 23663
 2300-2399 23669
Nicole Ct 23669
Nighthawk Way 23665
Noble Rd 23666
Norris Ct 23666
North St 23663
Northampton Dr 23666
Northcutt Dr 23664
Northwood Dr 23661
Norwood Cir 23661
Nottingham Dr 23669
Nurmi Ln 23666
Oak St 23665
Oakcrest Dr 23663
Oakland Ave 23663
Oakville Rd 23669
Ocanoe Pl 23661
Okeefe Ln 23669
Old Aberdeen Rd 23661
Old Armistead Ave 23666
Old Big Bethel Rd 23666
Old Buckroe Rd
 100-1499 23663
 1500-1899 23664
Old Celey Rd 23666
Old Fox Hill Rd 23669
Old Hampton Ln 23669
Old Meribeth Rd 23669
Old Oak Ct 23666
Old Point Ave
 300-499 23669
 500-899 23663
Old Pond Ct 23666
Old Town Ln 23669
Olde Buckingham Rd 23669
Oldenburg Ln 23664
Oldfield St 23663
Olga Ct 23669
Olson Ct 23666
Omera Pl 23666
Oneda Dr 23663
Orange Plank Rd 23669
Orchard Ave 23661
Orchard Rd 23669
Orcutt Ave 23666
Osage Ln 23669
Oser Ln 23669
Osprey Ave 23661
Otley Rd 23669
Overbrooke Pl 23669
Overlook Ct 23669
Overton Dr 23666
Owens St 23669
Owl Creek Ct 23669
Oxford Ter 23661
Oyster Shell Ln 23664
Pacers Pt 23669
Pacific Dr 23666
Paddington Pl 23669
Paddock Ln 23669
Page Dr 23669
Palace Ct 23666
Palisade Pt 23666
Palmerston Dr 23669
Pamela Dr 23666
Pansy St 23663
Paquette Ct 23666
Paradise Cv 23669
N Park Ln 23666
W Park Ln 23666
Park Pl 23669
Parkdale Ave 23669
Parkinson Rd 23661
Parkside Ave 23669
Parkview Pl 23664
Parkway Dr 23669
Parliment Ct 23669
E Parris Pl 23669
Parsonage Ln 23669
Pasadena Ct 23666
Pasture Ln 23669
Patrician Dr 23666
Patrick Ct & St 23669
Patriot Cres 23666
Patterson Ave 23669
Paul Jack Dr 23666
Pauline Dr 23663
Paulson Ln 23664
Pavilion Pl 23664
Peabody Dr 23666
Peacemaker Ave 23665
Peachtree Ln 23669
Pear Ave 23661
Pearcewood Ln 23664
Pebble Beach Ct 23666
Pecan Rd 23666
Peek St 23669
Pelchat Dr 23666
Pelham Dr 23669
Pelican Shores Dr 23666
E Pembroke Ave
 1-1399 23669
 1400-1999 23663
 2000-2799 23664
W Pembroke Ave
 1-1099 23669
 1100-2699 23661
Pendleton Ct 23669
Pennington Ter 23666
Pennsylvania Ave 23661
Pennwood Dr 23666
Peppermint Way 23666
Percy Ln 23669
Perkins Ln 23669
Perry St 23663
Pershing Ct 23666
Persimmon Ct 23666
Perth Ct & Pl 23669
Peterborough Dr 23666
Phantom Trce 23665
Phelps Cir 23663
Phenix Ct 23661
Phillips Ln 23669
Philmont Dr 23666
Phyllis Ln 23666
Piazza Pl 23666
Pickett St 23669
Piedmont Ave 23661
Pilgrim Ct 23666
Pilot Ave 23664
Pin Oak Ct 23666
Pine Ln 23664
Pine St 23665
Pine Chapel Rd 23666
Pine Cone Dr 23669
Pine Creek Dr 23669
Pine Grove Ave 23669
Pine Lake Ct 23669
Piney Branch Cir 23666
E & W Pinto Ct 23666
Pioneer Way 23666
Pirates Cv 23669
Plachalt Rd 23663
Plantation Dr 23669
Plaza Dr 23669
Pleasant Way 23666
Plum Ave 23661
Plumb St 23665
Pocahontas Pl 23661
Pochin Pl 23661
Point Comfort Ave 23664
Point Comfort Loop 23665
Polaris St 23669
Polly Ct 23666
Ponderosa Dr 23666
Pooles Ln 23669
Pop Lamkin Cir 23666
Poplar Ave 23669
Poplar Rd 23665
Poppy Ct 23666
Portally Ln 23663
Porte Harbour Arch 23664
Porter Ave 23669
Poseidon Pl 23666
Post Oak Ct 23666
Potter Ln 23666
Poulas Ct 23669
Powells Cv 23669
Power Plant Pkwy
 1500-1599 23669
 1600-1699 23666
 1700-1799 23669
 1900-2199 23666
Powhatan Pkwy
 1-97 23661
 99-899 23661
 1700-1799 23669
 2000-2099 23666
Pratt St 23669
Preakness Ln 23666
Predator Ln 23665
Prentiss Ln 23669
Pressy Ln 23669
E & W Preston St 23669
Prestwick Way 23669
Price St 23663
Pridgen Rd 23663
Priest Ct 23669
Primrose Ave 23663
Prince George Dr 23669
Prince James Dr 23669
Princess St 23669
Probasco Ln 23669
Providence St 23669
Provider Ct & Dr 23665
Purdue Ct 23666
Puryear Cir 23661
Pyron Hunt Cir 23666
Quaker Rd 23669
Quarry Cir 23669
Quarter Path Ln 23666
Quarterhorse Turn 23669
Quash St 23669
E Queen St 23669
W Queen St
 190-1599 23669
 1600-2199 23666
E & W Queens Way 23669
Queens View Ct 23669
Queensbury Way 23666
Quincy St 23661
Quinn St 23669
Radford Dr 23666
Rainbow Ct 23666
Raintree Dr 23666
Raleigh Ave 23661
Ramsey Ct 23666
Ranalet Dr 23664
Randall Ct 23666
Ranger Way 23666
Ranhorne Ct 23661
Ransone St 23669
Rapidan Rd 23669
Raptor Blvd 23665
Rattray Dr 23666
Raven Ln 23665
Ravenscroft Ln 23669
Rawhunt Loop 23665
Rawood Dr 23663
Ray Cir 23669
Raymond Dr 23666
Reaper Ln 23665
Reba Dr 23669
Rebecca Ct 23666
Rebel St 23669
Red Leaf Pl 23666
Red Oak Pl 23666
Red Robin Turn 23669
Redford Rd 23663
Redheart Dr 23666
Redman Ct 23669
Redwood St 23669
Reed St 23669
Reef Ln 23666
Reese Dr 23666
Reflection Ln 23666
Regal Way 23669
Regent St 23669
Regina Ct 23669
Regional Dr 23661
Rendon Dr 23666
Renee Ct 23664
Renn Rd 23663
Research Dr 23666
Reservoir Ln 23666
S Resort Blvd 23664
Revere Dr 23664
Reynolds Dr 23664
Rhoda Ct 23664
Rhonda Cir 23669
Richard Ave 23664
Richmond Dr 23664
Rick Ct 23663
Rickenbacker Rd 23665
Ridge Lake Dr 23666
Ridge Wood Dr 23666
Ridgecrest Dr 23666
Ridgemont Cir 23666
Ridgeway Ave 23661
Riding Path 23669
Rigsby Ct 23666
Riley Dr 23666
Rileys Way 23664
Rip Rap Rd 23669
River St 23669
River Run Ct 23669
River Shore Ln 23669
River Walk Ct 23669
Riverchase Dr 23669
Riverdale Dr 23666
W Riverpoint Dr 23669
Riversedge Dr 23669
Riverside Dr 23669
Riverview Dr 23669
Roads View Ave 23669
Roane Dr 23669
Roaring Springs Cir 23663
Robert Connor Dr 23669
Roberta Dr 23666
Roberts Rd & Trce 23666
Robins Way 23669
Robinson Rd 23661
Rockingham Dr 23669
Rockwell Rd 23669
E & N Roger Peed Dr 23663
Rogers Ave 23664
Roland Dr 23669
Rolfe St 23661
Rollins Cir 23663
Roma Rd 23665
Roosevelt St 23669
Rosalee Dr 23661
Rose Ln 23664
Rose Briar Pl 23666
Rosewood Dr 23669
Ross Ct 23669
Rosser Dr 23669
Rotary St 23661
Rotherham Ln 23666
Roundtree Cir 23661
Routten Rd 23664
Rowe St 23669
Roxbury Ter 23666
Roy Ct 23666
Royal Oak Ct 23666
Royston Dr 23669
Rozzelle Rd 23663
Ruby Ct 23666
Rudd Ln 23669
Rudisill Rd 23669
E Russell Rd 23666
Rust St 23664
Ruth Cir 23666
Rutherford St 23661
Rutland Dr 23666
Ryan Ave 23665
Ryland Rd 23661
Saber Dr 23665
Sabre Ct 23665
Sacramento Dr 23666
Saddle Ln 23666
Sage Ct 23669
Saint Albans Dr 23669
Saint Ashley Pl 23669
Saint George Way 23669
Saint Paul Ct 23666
Salem St 23669
Salina St 23669
Salisbury Way 23669
Salt Marsh Quay 23666
Salt Pond Rd 23664
Salt Water Ln 23664
Salters Creek Rd 23661
Samantha Ct 23663
Sampson Ave 23661
Sandpiper Ct 23669
Sandra Ct 23669
Sandy Lake Dr 23666
Sanford Dr 23661
Sanlun Lakes Dr 23666
Santa Barbara Dr 23666
Santa Clara Dr 23666
Sarfan Dr 23664
Sargeant St 23663
Saunders Rd 23666
Saville Row 23666
Saxony Pl 23669
Saxton Dr 23669
Scarborough Dr 23666
Schaffer Ln 23669
Scher Ct 23666
Schley Ave 23661
Schooner Dr 23669
Scollin Cir 23663
Scones Dr 23666
Scotland Rd 23663
Scott Dr 23661
Scotts Pt 23663
Sea Breeze Ct 23669
Sea Cove Ct 23669
Sea Ventures Ln 23665
Seabee Pt 23669
Seaboard Ave 23664
Seabreeze Farm 23664
Seafarer Ct 23669
Seagull Ct 23669
Sealey Farm Ln 23666
Searcy Dr 23666
Seaview Dr 23664
N & S Second St 23664
Secota Dr 23661
Secretariat Ln 23666
Segar St 23663
S Seldendale Dr 23669
Seminary Rdg 23669
Seminole Rd 23661
Semple St 23663
Semple Farm Rd 23666
Sesco Dr 23664
Settlers Landing Rd 23669
Severn St 23669
Seward Dr 23663
W Sewell Ave 23663
Shady Grove Pl 23666
Sharon Ct 23666
Sharon Bass Dr 23664
Sharpley Ave 23666
Shatto Dr 23661
Shaughanassee Ct 23666
Shawen Dr 23669
Sheffield St 23666
Sheila Dr 23664
Shell Rd
 500-3799 23661
 3800-3999 23669
Shelley Ct 23669
Shelton Rd 23663
Shenandoah Rd 23661

Sheralyn Pl 23663
Sherazi Dr 23663
Sherman Ct 23665
Sherry Dell Dr 23666
E & W Sherwood Ave 23663
Shetland Ct 23666
Shields St 23669
Shifting Log Dr 23669
Shiloh Park 23669
Shirley Dr 23666
Shooting Star Dr 23665
Shore Rd 23669
Shorecrest Ln 23669
Shoreline Dr 23669
Shoveler Ct 23669
Shrike Ct 23665
Shuttle Ct 23666
Signature Way 23666
Sijan Rd 23665
Silk Tree Pl 23666
Silver Isles Blvd 23664
Sinclair Rd 23669
Singleton Dr 23666
Sir Walter Ln 23661
Sitka Ct 23666
N & S Sixth St 23664
Skipper Ct 23669
Skyland Dr 23663
Skyraider Ct 23665
Skytrain Ct 23665
Slater Ave 23664
Sloop Ct 23666
Smiley Rd 23663
Smith St 23661
Smithman Cir 23663
Smythe Rd 23665
Snow St 23663
Snug Harbor Dr 23661
Soho St 23666
Somerset Ln 23669
Somerville Dr 23663
Sonora Dr 23669
Sourwood Dr 23666
South St 23669
Southall Lndg 23664
E & W Southampton Ave 23669
Southerland Dr 23669
Southwind Dr 23669
Spaatz Dr 23665
Spanish Trl 23669
Sperry Ct 23669
Spitfire Dr 23665
Spottswood Pl 23661
Spring St 23669
Springdale Way 23666
Springfield Ave 23669
Springmeadow Ct 23666
Springwood Pl 23666
Spruce St
2-98 23665
49-49 23665
700-799 23661
E & W Spur Ct 23666
St Johns Dr 23666
Stacey Cir 23663
Staghorn Ct 23666
Stanford Ct 23666
Stanton Ct 23669
Stapleford Way 23669
Starfighter Ct 23665
N & S Starfish Ct 23669
State Park Dr 23664
Staton Dr 23666
Stedlyn Cir 23664
Steeler Cir 23666
Steeplechase Loop 23666
Stella June Ln 23666
Stephanies Rd 23666
Stephen Conway Ct 23666
Sterling Ct 23669
Stevens Ct 23666
Stewart St 23669
Stickle Ln 23669
Still Harbor Ct 23669
Sting Ray Point Ln 23665
Stirrup Ct 23664
Stockton St 23669
Stonehurst Rd 23669
Stonewall Ter 23666
Stratford Rd 23669
Stratofortress Ln 23665
Stratum Way 23661
Strawberry Banks Blvd 23663
Strother Dr 23666
Stroup Ct 23663
Suburban Pkwy 23661
Sugarberry Run 23669
Summit Ct 23666
N Summit Ridge Cir & Dr 23666
Sunbriar Way 23666
Sunny Meade Cv 23666
Sunnyside Dr 23666
Sunrise Cv 23666
E & W Sunset Rd 23669
Surry Ct 23669
Susan Ct 23661
Susquehanna Ct 23669
Sutton Pl 23666
Swanns Point Cir 23669
Swartmore Dr 23666
Sweeney Blvd 23665
Sweeney Ln 23663
Sweet Gum Pl 23666
Sycamore Dr 23666
Sydney Jay Ln 23669
Syms St 23669
Szetela Ct 23666
Tabatha Cir 23666
Tabb St 23661
Tall Pine Dr 23666
Tall Tree Pl 23666
Talley Farm Retreat 23669
Tallwood Dr 23666
Tallyho Turn 23666
Talon Dr 23665
Tamarisk Quay 23666
Tanglewood Dr 23666
Tappan Ave 23664
Tarrant Rd 23666
Tartan Ln 23663
Taylor Ave E 23663
Taylor Ave W 23663
E Taylor Rd 23665
Teach St 23661
Teakwood Ct 23666
Tecumseh Dr 23661
Temple St 23664
Templewood Dr 23666
Tender Foot Ct 23669
Tennis Ln 23663
Teresa Dr 23666
Terrace Rd 23661
Terrell Ln 23666
Terri Sue Ct 23666
Terry Ct 23666
Tetra Ct 23669
Texan Ct 23665
Thames Dr 23666
Theodore St 23669
Thimble Shoals Ct 23664
Thollinc Dr 23666
Thom Hall Dr 23663
Thomas St 23669
Thomas Athey Ct 23666
Thomas Nelson Dr 23666
Thompson St 23665
Thornbriar Ct 23661
Thornell Ave 23665
Thornette St 23669
Thornhill Dr 23661
Thornrose Ave 23669
Thoroughbred Dr 23666
Threechopt Rd 23666
Thunderchief Ct 23665
Thurgood Ct 23663
Tidal Ln 23666
Tide Mill Ln 23666
Tidewater Dr 23666
Tiffany Ln 23664
Tiller Cir 23669
Tilstone Rd 23669
Timberline Dr 23666
Timberneck Ct 23663
Timothy Dell 23669
Tindalls Way 23666
Tiona Ct 23669
Todds Ln 23666
Toddsbury Ct 23663
Toledo Ct 23666
Tom Jones Ct 23666
Tomahawk Rd 23669
Topping Ln 23666
Topsail Ct 23666
Tower Pl 23666
Towler Dr 23666
Town Center Way 23666
Town Park Dr 23669
Townsend Dr 23666
Tradewinds Quay 23666
Trail St 23669
Tratman Ct 23666
Travis Cir 23669
Treasure Ky 23666
Treebark Pl 23666
Treeclad Pl 23666
Treefern Pl 23666
Treslyn Trce 23666
Trincard Rd 23669
Trinity Ln 23669
Triple Crown Ct 23666
Tripp Ter 23666
Triton Way 23666
Troy Cir 23666
Tucker Ln 23669
Tudor Ct 23669
Tulip St 23663
Tupelo Cir 23666
Turner Ter 23666
Turret Ln 23669
Twin Lakes Cir 23666
Twin Oaks Dr 23666
Tyburn Ct 23669
Tyler St 23669
Tyndall Cir 23663
Tyndall Pl 23665
Tysinger Dr 23669
Union St 23669
Upland Dr 23666
Valentine Ct 23666
Valirey Dr 23669
Valor Pl 23669
Van Patten Dr 23669
Vanasse Ct 23666
Vaughan Ave 23661
Veneris Ct 23669
Venture Ln 23664
Verde Quay 23666
Verell St 23661
Vernon Cir 23666
Victor St 23669
Victoria Blvd
401-597 23661
599-3699 23661
3700-4799 23669
Vienna Ct 23666
Viking Way 23666
Village Dr 23666
Violet St 23663
Viper Ct 23666
E & W Virginia Ave 23663
Vista Point Dr 23666
Von Schilling Dr 23666
Voodoo Ct 23665
Voyager Dr 23666
Waco Ct 23669
Wade Rd 23664
Wakefield Ave 23661
Wales Cir 23666
E Walker Rd 23666
Wallace Rd 23664
Walnut Ave 23665
Walnut St 23669
Walters Ln 23666
Waltham St 23666
Ward Dr 23669
Ward Rd 23665
Warhawk Dr 23665
Warner Rd 23666
Warren Ln 23666
Warren St 23663
Warrington Cir 23669
Washington Ct 23665
Washington St 23669
Water St 23663
Water Way 23666
Waterford Cir 23666
Waters Edge Cir 23669
Waterside Dr 23666
Waterview Pt 23666
Watkins Dr 23669
Watson Ln 23669
Watts Ave 23665
Watts Dr 23666
Waverly St 23669
E & W Weaver Rd 23666
Weber Ln 23663
Webster St 23663
Wedgewood Dr 23669
Welcome Way 23666
Wellington Dr 23666
Wells Ct 23666
Wendell Dr 23666
Wentworth Pl 23666
West Ave 23669
Westbriar Dr 23666
Westbrook Dr 23666
Westfield Pl 23661
Westlawn Dr 23664
Westley Ct 23669
Westminister Dr 23666
Westmont Dr 23666
Westmoreland Dr 23669
Westover St 23669
Westphal Dr 23669
Westview Dr 23666
Westwood Ave 23661
Wexford Hill Ct & Rd 23666
Weyanoke Ct 23666
Weyland Rd 23665
Weymouth Ter 23666
Whartons Way 23669
Whealton Rd 23666
Wheatland Dr 23666
Wheeler Ave 23661
Whetstone Dr 23666
Whipple Dr 23663
Whitaker Ave 23664
White Hall Cir 23669
White Marsh Ct 23669
White Oak Trl 23669
Whitecedar Ct 23666
Whiting St 23669
Whitman Pl 23663
Whitney Ct 23669
Wigner Ct 23663
Wild Duck Ct 23666
Wild Flower Cir 23669
Wilderness Rd 23669
Wildwood Dr 23666
N & S Willard Ave 23663
Williams St 23663
Williamsburg Dr 23666
Willis Church Yard 23669
Willnew Dr 23669
Willoughby Pl 23661
Willow Rd 23664
Willow St 23665
Willow Oaks Blvd 23669
Willowtree Rd 23666
Wills Way 23666
Wilson Ln 23669
Wilton Ave 23663
Wiltshire Pl 23664
Wimbledon Ter 23666
Winchester Dr 23666
Wind Mill Point Rd 23664
Winder Ct 23666
Winder Farm Ln 23666
Windjammer Dr 23669
Windsor Dr 23666
Windy Cv 23666
Wine St 23669
Winfree Rd 23663
Wingfield Dr
1500-1604 23666
1605-1699 23661
Winnard Rd 23669
Winona Dr E & N 23661
Winthrop Ter 23666
Wise Rd 23663
Wisteria Ln 23669
Woltz Ct 23669
Womack Dr 23663
Womble Ct 23663
Wood Ave 23664
Woodall Dr 23666
Woodbridge Dr 23666
Woodburn Dr 23664
Woodbury Forrest Dr 23666
Woodcreek Ct 23666
Woodcrest Dr
1300-1399 23669
1400-1499 23663
Wooded Hill Dr 23669
Woodlake Ln 23666
Woodland Rd
1-199 23663
200-599 23669
Woodlawn Dr 23666
Woodmansee Dr 23663
Woodpath Ln 23666
Woodrose Pl 23666
Woods Ln 23666
Woodside Dr 23669
Woodsman Rd 23666
Woodview Ln 23666
Woody Cir 23669
Worden Ave 23669
Worley Rd 23665
Worster Ave 23669
Wrexham Ct 23669
Wright Ave 23665
Wyndham Dr 23666
Wyse Ct 23666
Wythe Ct 23665
Wythe Pkwy 23661
Wythe Creek Rd 23666
Wythe Crescent Dr 23661
Yale Dr 23666
Yellow Wood Rd 23666
Ymca Way 23669
York St 23661
Yorkshire Ter 23666
Yukon St 23663
Yulee Ct 23669
Zelkova Reach 23666
Zilber Ct 23669
Zinzer Rd 23663

NUMBERED STREETS

1st St 23665
2nd St 23665
3rd St
1200-1299 23661
1500-1599 23665
4th St 23665
5th St 23665
6th St 23665
7th Ave 23665
8th St 23665
9th St 23665
10th St 23665
11th St 23665
48th St 23661
50th St 23661
52nd St 23661
56th St 23661
58th St 23661
60th St 23661

HARRISONBURG VA

General Delivery 22801

POST OFFICE BOXES MAIN OFFICE STATIONS AND BRANCHES

Box No.s
1 - 1620 22803
193 - 1007 22801
1701 - 1820 22803
1821 - 20040 22801
20003 - 20005 22803

RURAL ROUTES

01, 05, 06, 07, 08, 11, 12, 14, 16, 17, 18, 21 22801

NAMED STREETS

Abbott Cir & Ln 22801
Aberdeen Loop 22801
Academy St 22801
Ace Ct 22802
Acorn Dr 22802
Adair Way 22802
Ajax Ct 22801
Albert Long Dr 22801
Alexander Hamilton Ln 22802
Alleghany Dr 22802
Allen Rd 22801
Alnwick Ct 22801
Aloha Ln 22802
Alpine Dr 22802
Alston Cir 22802
Amberly Rd 22802
Amherst Ct 22801
Andergren Dr 22801
Angle Dr 22801
Annandale Ct 22801
Antioch Rd 22802
Apple B Ln 22802
Apple Ridge Ct 22801
Apple Tree Dr 22802
Arbor Ln 22801
Archers Ln 22801
Argyle Ct 22801
Armstrong Ln 22802
Arrowhead Rd 22801
Arrowwood Dr 22801
Ash Tree Ln 22801
Ashburn Dr 22802
Ashby Ave 22802
Ashford Ct 22801
Ashwood St 22802
Aspen Heights Ln 22801
Auburn Hill Ln 22801
Augusta Cir 22801
Autumn Ln 22801
Avalon Woods Dr 22801
Avonlea Ln 22801
Aynsley Ln 22801
Azure Vista Dr 22802
Bald Eagle Cir 22801
Ballantrae Ln 22801
Barracuda Dr 22801
Barrington Dr 22801
Bartlett Ct 22801
Battery Park Pl 22801
Battlefield Rd 22801
Baxter Dr 22801
Bay St 22801
Bayberry Ln 22801
Baybrook Dr 22801
Beacon Hill Rd 22802
Beagle Ln 22802
Bear Wallow Ln 22802
Beard Woods Ln 22802
Beauford Rd 22801
Bedford Pl 22801
Beery Rd 22801
Bel Ayr View Dr 22801
Belle Cir 22801
Bellview Rd 22802
Belmont Dr 22801
Bending Tree Ln 22802
Bennington Pl 22801
Berryfield Dr 22801
Berwick Dr 22801
Bethany Ct 22801
Betsy Ross Ct 22802
Betts Ct 22801
Betts Rd 22802
Big Spring Dr 22802
Birch Dr 22802
Birdie Cir 22802
Birkdale Ct 22801
Black Walnut Ln 22802
Blackberry Ln 22802
Blakely Ct 22802
Blaze Ct 22801
Blue Mountain Ct 22801
Blue Ridge Dr 22802
Blue Stone Hills Dr 22801
Bluebird Ct 22802
Bluestone St 22801
Bluewater Rd 22801
Bobwhite Pl 22802
Boxwood Ct 22801
Boyd Ln 22801
Boyers Rd 22801
Bradley Dr 22801
Brady Ln 22802
Breckenridge Ct 22801
Brenneman Church Rd 22802
Brentwood Dr 22801
Briarcrest Dr 22801
Briarwood Ct 22801
Bridle Ct 22801
Broad St 22802
Broad Acres Ln 22802
Broadridge Dr 22801
Broadview Dr 22802
Brompton Ct 22801
N Brook Ave 22802
S Brook Ave 22801
Brookhaven Dr 22801
Brookshire Dr 22801
Brookside Pl 22802
Brookstone Dr 22801
Brown Roan Ln 22801
E & W Bruce St 22801
Buck Run Ct 22802
Buckingham Dr 22801
Buckland Dr 22801
Buckskin Ln 22801
Buffalo Dr 22802
Burgess Rd 22801
N & S Burkwood Ct 22802
Burt St 22802
Butler St 22801
Buttermilk Creek Rd 22802
Buttonwood Ct 22802
Cable Dr 22802
Cadogan Ct 22801
Calina Ct 22801
Callaway Cir 22801
Cambridge Cir 22801
Camden Pl 22801
Camelot Ln 22801
Campbell St 22801
Campus View Cir 22801
Canterbury Ct 22801
Cantrell Ave 22801
Cantubury Ct 22801
Cardinal Dr 22801
N Carlton St 22802
S Carlton St 22801
Caroline Ct 22801
Carpenter Ln 22801
Carriage Dr 22801
Carter Ln 22801
Cecil Wampler Rd 22801
Cedar Dr & St 22801
Cedar Hill Dr 22802
Cedar Point Ln 22802
Cedar Rock Dr 22802
Central Ave
900-999 22802
1300-1799 22801
Central Park Blvd 22801
Cf Pours Dr 22802
Charles St 22802
Charleston Blvd 22801
Chase Ct 22801
Chelsea Cir 22801
Cherry Tree Ln 22801
Cherrybrook Dr 22802
Chesapeake Ave 22801

Street	ZIP
Chestnut Dr	22801
Chestnut Ridge Dr	22801
Chicago Ave	22802
Chicory Ln	22802
Chinkapin Dr	22802
Chris St	22802
Chrisman Rd	22802
Christy Ln	22801
Circle Dr	22801
Clara Ct	22802
Claremont Ave	22801
Claudes Ln	22801
Clay St	22802
Clayborn Rd	22802
Clear Mountain Cir	22802
Clear View Dr	22802
Clement Dr	22801
Clinton St	22802
Clubhouse Hill Rd	22801
Cobblestone Dr	22801
College Ave	22802
Collicello St	22802
Colonial Dr	22801
Comfort Ct	22802
Commerce Dr	22802
Commercial Ct	22802
Community St	22802
Congress St	22801
Constitution Ct	22802
Cooks Creek Rd	22802
Copper Beech Cir	22801
Coral St	22801
Cornerstone Dr	22802
Cory Ln	22802
Cottage Ln	22801
Council St	22801
Country Boy Ln	22802
Country Club Ct & Rd	22802
Court Sq	
1-1	22802
2-79	22801
80-80	22802
81-99	22801
82-98	22801
Covenant Dr	22801
Craigmore Dr	22801
Craun Ridge Ln	22802
Crawford Ave	22801
Crepe Myrtle Dr	22801
S Crescent Dr & Rd	22801
Crestridge Ct	22802
Crestview Ln	22801
Crist Mill Rd	22802
Cromer Rd	22802
Cross Keys Rd	22801
Crystal Ln	22801
Crystal Spring Ln	22801
Cullison Ct	22801
Cumberland Dr	22801
Custers Rd	22802
Dahlia Ct	22801
Dakota Ln	22802
Dale Cir	22801
Dale Enterprise Rd	22801
Dalt Dr	22801
Danbury Ct	22801
Daniel Smith Ln	22802
Davis Corner Ln	22802
Davis Mills Dr	22801
Dawn Dr	22801
Daylilly Dr	22802
Dealton Ave	22801
Deavers Ln	22802
Debbie Ct	22801
Decca Dr	22801
Denim Dr	22802
Derrer Ln	22802
Devon Ln	22801
Dexter Dr	22801
Deyerle Ave	22801
Diamond Ct	22801
Diamond Spring Ln	22801
Diana Ct	22801
Divot Dr	22802
Dixie Ave	22801
Dogtown Rd	22802
N Dogwood Dr	22802
S Dogwood Dr	22801
W Dogwood Dr	22802
Dorval Rd	22801
Double Dean Ln	22802
Drake St	22802
Driver Dr	22801
Dromedary Dr	22801
Drumheller Ln	22801
Dutch Mill Ct	22801
Eagle Ln	22802
Early Rd	22801
Earmans Loop	22802
East Ct	22801
Easthampton Ct	22801
Eastover Dr	22801
Echo Mountain Rd	22801
Eckert Cir	22801
Eden Valley Rd	22802
Edgelawn Dr	22801
Edgerton Ct	22801
Edgewood Rd	22801
Edom Rd	22802
Effinger St	
300-400	22802
401-499	22801
402-498	22802
Elgin Ct	22801
E & W Elizabeth St	22802
Elmwood Dr	22801
Emerald Dr	22801
Emerson Ln	22802
Emery St	22801
Emmaus Rd	22801
Endless View Dr	22802
Erickson Ave	22801
Etna Rd	22802
Evelyn Byrd Ave	22801
Evergreen Dr	22801
Eversole Rd	22802
Fairdell St	22801
E & W Fairview Ave	22801
Fairway Dr	22802
Falcon Ct	22802
Family Tree Ln	22802
Fancy Hill Ct	22802
N Federal St	22801
S Federal St	22801
Fellowship Rd	22802
Ferguson Dr	22802
Ferguson Trailer Park	22802
Fieldale Pl	22801
Fieldcrest Ln	22802
Fir St	22801
Flint Ave	22801
Flook Ln	22802
Flowing Spring Ln	22802
Flyntshire Pl	22801
Foken Ln	22802
Foley Rd	22801
Forest Hill Rd	22801
Forest Oaks Ln	22801
Fort Lynne Rd	22802
Fort View Dr	22802
Fortune Dr	22802
Founders Way	22802
Fox Ln	22801
Foxcroft Dr	22801
Franklin St	22801
Frederick Rd	22801
Freedom Ct	22801
Fridleys Gap Rd	22802
Friendship Dr	22802
Frost Pl	22802
Fry Ave	22801
Gailcrist Dr	22802
Garber Dr	22802
Garbers Rd	22801
Garbers Church Rd	22801
Garnet Cir	22801
Gary Ln	22802
Gaslamp Ln	22801
E & W Gay St	22802
Gen Jackson Ln	22801
Gilmer Cir	22801
Gladwell Ln	22802
Glanzer Ct	22801
Glen Lea Ln	22801
Glen Loch Ct	22801
Glendale Dr	22802
Glenfield Ct	22802
Glenmoor Dr	22801
Glenside Dr	22801
Golda St	22802
Goldenrod Ln	22802
Goldfinch Dr	22802
Goode Dr	22802
Goods Mill Rd	22801
Gospel Mountain Ln	22802
Governors Ln	22801
E & W Grace St	22801
Grace Chapel Rd	22801
Graham St	22801
Grandview Dr	22802
Grant St	22802
Grassland Ln	22802
Grassy Creek Rd	22801
E & W Grattan St	22801
Grattan Price Dr	22801
Gravels Rd	22802
Green St	22802
Greenbriar Dr	22801
Greendale Rd	22801
Greenmount Rd	22802
Greenport Dr	22801
Greenway Ct	22802
Greenwood Pass & St	22801
Greystone St	22802
Grist Mill Rd	22802
Grove St	22801
Guinea Ln	22802
Hamlet Dr	
900-1098	22801
901-1097	22802
1099-1199	22802
Hamshire Ests	22801
Harman Rd	22802
Harmony Dr	22802
Harness Ln	22801
Harolds Ln	22802
Harpine Hwy	22802
Harris St	22802
Harrison St	22801
Harrisonburg Mobile Hm Park	22801
Hartman Dr	22802
Hastings Ct	22801
Hawkins St	22801
Hawthorne Cir	22802
Health Campus Dr	22801
Hearthstone Ln	22801
Heatwole Rd	22802
Hebron Ct	22801
Hemlock St	22801
Henry Grant Hl	22801
Henton Mill Ln	22802
Heritage Dr	22801
Heritage Center Way	22801
Heritage Estates Cir	22801
Hermitage Dr	22801
Hickory Cv	22801
Hickory Grove Cir	22801
Hickory Hill Dr	22801
Hidden Creek Ln	22801
Hidden Hollow Ln	22801
Hidden Oaks Ln	22802
N High St	22802
S High St	22801
Highland Ave & Ct	22801
Highlands Pl	22801
Hightown Ln	22802
Hill St	22802
Hillandale Ave	22801
Hillcrest Dr	
1000-1299	22801
1300-1699	22801
Hillmeadow Dr	22802
Hillmont Cir	22801
Hillside Ave	
800-1299	22802
1300-1599	22801
Hilltop Rd	22801
Hilton Ln	22802
Hobart Ct	22801
Holly Ct	22801
Hollybrook Ln	22801
Honeysuckle Ln	22802
Hope St	22801
Hopkins Gap Rd	22802
Horizons Way	22802
Horseshoe Ln	22801
Hounds Chase Ln	22801
Hudson Cir	22801
Huffman St	22801
Hughes Ln	22802
Hunters Rd	22801
Huntington Springs Dr	22801
Huron Ct	22801
Impression Ct	22801
Indian Ridge Ln	22802
Indian Trail Rd	22802
Industry Ct	22802
Inglewood Dr	22801
Interstate View Dr	22801
Irish Path	22802
Iroquois Path	22802
Isaac Ln	22801
Ivy Ln	22802
Izaak Walton Dr	22801
Jackson St	22802
James Pl	22801
James Branch Rd	22802
James Evelyn Ln	22802
Janie Ln	22801
Jefferson St	22802
Jericho Rd	22801
Jewell St	22802
John Hancock Pl	22802
John Paul Jones Ln	22802
John Tyler Cir	22801
John Wayland Hwy	22801
E & W Johnson St	22802
Joppa Ct	22801
Juniper Ct	22801
Karawood Ln	22801
Katie Grove Way	22801
Kaylor Ln	22801
W Kaylor Park Dr	22801
Keezletown Rd	
600-899	22802
900-999	22801
1800-2799	22802
Kelley St	22801
Kelsey Ln	22801
Kendall Ln	22801
Kenmore St	22801
Kentshire Dr	22801
Kenworth Ln	22802
Kiln Dr	22801
Kimberly Ct	22801
King Arthurs Ct	22801
King Edwards Way	22801
Kingston Ct	22801
Koehn Dr	22802
Koffee Ln	22801
Koontz Corner Rd	22802
Kramer Ct	22801
Kratzer Ave & Rd	22802
Kyle St	22801
Lacey Ln	22802
Lacey Heights Ave	22802
Lacey Spring Rd	22802
Lady Slipper Ct	22801
Lake Pointe Dr	22801
Lake Terrace Dr	22802
Lakeview Cir & Dr	22801
Lakewood Dr	22801
Lamplighter Ln	22802
Lancelot Ln	22801
Landon Dr	22801
Lanny St	22802
Laurel St	22801
Layman Ave	22801
Layman Trestle Rd	22802
Leaky Pond Ln	22802
Lee Ave	22802
Lendale Ln	22801
Leonard Ct	22801
Leray Cir	22801
Lewis St	22801
Lewis Byrd Rd	22801
N Liberty St	22802
S Liberty St	22801
Lilac Ln	22802
Lime Kiln Dr	22802
Lincoln Cir	22802
Lincolnshire Dr	22802
Linda Ln	22802
Linstead Farm Ln	22802
Linville Edom Rd	22802
Liskey Rd	22801
Little Ln	22802
Little Sorrell Dr	22801
Locust Cir	22801
Locust Hill Dr	22801
Log Homes Dr	22801
Logan Ln	22801
Lois Ln	22801
Londonderry Ct	22801
Long Ave	22801
Longs Pump Rd	22802
Longview Dr	22802
Louderback St	22802
Lucy Dr	22801
Lucy Long Dr	22801
Lupine Dr	22801
Lynden Pl	22801
Lynne Pl	22801
Lynwood Ln	22801
Macallister Way	22801
Madison St	22802
Maggie Ln	22801
Magnolia Ridge Dr	22801
Maid Marian Ln	22801
N Main St	22802
S Main St	
1-4199	22801
2-4	22802
6-4198	22801
Mannheim Ct	22801
Manor Dr	22801
Maple Dr	22802
Maplehurst Ave	22801
Maplewood Ct	22802
Marble Ridge Dr	22801
Mariette Way	22802
Marigold Cir	22801
E & W Market St	22801
Markham Pl	22801
Martin Luther King Jr Way	22801
Martys Ln	22802
Martz Rd	22802
Maryland Ave	22801
N Mason St	
1-300	22802
281-281	22803
301-499	22802
302-498	22802
S Mason St	22801
Massanetta Springs Rd	22801
Massanutten St	22802
Mattie Dr	22801
Mcdorman Hill Dr	22802
Mckeever Ln	22802
Meadow Ct	22801
Meadowlark Dr	22802
Media Ln	22801
Medical Ave	22801
Melrose Rd	22802
Memorial Ln	22801
Memory Ln	22802
Meridian Cir	22802
Merlins Way	22801
Mesinetto Creek Dr	22801
Middlebrook St	22801
Mill Race Ct	22801
Miller Cir	22801
Miller Spring Ct	22801
Millwood Loop	22801
Mineral Springs Rd	22801
Mint Springs Rd	22801
Misty Ct	22801
Mockingbird Dr	22802
Moffett Ter	22801
Molly Pitcher Pl	22802
Mollys Way Ln	22801
Monroe St	22802
Monte Vista Dr	22802
Monticello Ave	22801
Monument Ave	22801
Moon View Ct	22801
Moore St	22802
Morgan Rd	22801
Morningglory Ct	22802
E, S & W Mosby Ct & Rd	22801
Mossy Rock Ln	22802
Mount Clinton Pike	22802
Mountain Spring Ln	22801
Mountain Valley Rd	22802
Mountain View Dr	22801
Muddy Creek Rd	22802
Mulberry Ln	22801
Munchkin Ln	22801
Myers Ave	22801
Myrtle St	22802
Mystic Woods Ln	22801
Natasha Ct	22802
Nathan Hale Ct	22802
National Coach Est	22801
Natural Spring Ln	22801
Needmore Ln	22802
Neff Ave	22801
Nehi Ln	22802
Nelson Dr	22801
New Beginnings Ln	22802
New York Ave	22801
Newcomer Ln	22801
Newman Ave	22801
Newton Mill Rd	22802
Neyland Dr	22801
Niswander Ln	22802
Noland Dr	22802
Noll Dr	22802
Northampton Ct	22801
Northfield Ct	22802
Northglen Ln	22802
Northwood Ln	22802
Northwood Trailer Park	22802
Norwood St	22801
Nutmeg Ct	22801
Oak Dr	22801
Oak Grove Ln	22801
Oak Hill Dr	22801
Oak Ridge Rd	22801
Oak Shade Rd	22801
Oak Tree Ln	22801
Oak View Ct	22802
Oak Villa Ln	22801
Oakdale Ct	22801
Oakland St	22802
Oakwood Dr	22801
Offspring Dr	22802
Ohio Ave	22801
Old 33 St W	22801
Old Depot Ln	22801
Old Furnace Rd	22802
Old Orchard Ln	22802
Old Richmond Cir	22802
Old Sawmill Rd	22802
Old South High St	22801
Old Thirty Three Rd	22801
Old Trail Way	22802
Old Windmill Cir	22802
Onyx Cir	22801
Opal Dr	22801
Orchard Ln	22801
Oriole Ln	22802
Osage Ln	22802
Osceola Springs Rd	22801
Ott St	22801
Par Ln	22802
Paradise Ln	22802
Park Ave, Cir, Ln, Pl & Rd	22802
Park Lawn Dr	22801
Parkway Dr	22802
Parkwood Dr	22802
Party Ln	22802
Patrick Henry Pl	22802
Patterson St	22801
Paul St	22801
Paul Revere Ct	22802
Peaceful Ln	22802
Peach Grove Ave	22801
W Peake Ln	22802
Peake Mountain Rd	22802
Pear St	22801
Pearl Ln	22801
Pelham Pl	22801
Penshurst Pl	22801
Peoples Dr	22801
Periwinkle Ln	22801
Perry St	22801
Petes Ln	22802
Pheasant Ct	22802
Pheasant Run Cir	22801
Pike Church Rd	22801
Pin Oak Dr	22801
Pindelin Rd	22802
Pine Ct	22802
Pine Harbor Ln	22801
Pine Tree Ln	22802
Pinto Pl	22801
Pirkey Ln	22801
Pleasant Hill Rd	22801
Pleasant Run Dr	22801
Pleasant Valley Rd	22801
Pleasants Dr	22801
Poets Ct	22802
Pointe Dr	22801
Polecat Hollow Rd	22802
Pond View Ln	22802
Poplar Cir	22802
Port Republic Rd	22801
Portland Dr	22801
Powderhorn Pl	22801
Prairie Ln	22801
Preston Dr	22801
Preston Lake Blvd	22801
Preston Shore Dr	22801
Pro Pointe Ln	22801
Pulses Hill Ln	22802
Purple And Gold Way	22801
Putter Ct	22801
Quail Oaks Ln	22801
Quarles Ct	22801
Queen Anne Ct	22801
Quince Dr	22801
Radnor Ct	22801
Raggedy Ann Ln	22802
Ragtown Rd	22802
Ralston Rd	22802
Ramblewood Rd	22801
Rawley Pike	22801
Rebecca Ridge Ct	22801
Red Oak St	22802
Red Wing Ct	22802
Redbud Ln	22801
Redcliff Ln	22801
Reedy Cir	22801
Research Dr	22802
Reservoir St	22801
Retreat Ln	22801
Rex Rd	22801
Rhianon Ln	22801
Rhodes Ln	22802
Richmond Rd	22801
Ridge Rd	22801
Ridgecrest Ct	22801
Ridgedale Rd	22801
Ridgeline Dr	22802
Ridgeville Ln	22801
Ridgewood Rd	22801
Riga Dr	22802
Rising Rock Ct	22802
Roberts Ct	22802
Robin Ct	22802
Robinhood Ct	22801
Rocco Ave	22801
E & W Rock St	22802
Rock Fence Ln	22802
Rock Spring Ln	22802

Rockbridge Cir 22801
Rockingham Dr 22802
Rockinham Sq 22801
Rocky Ln 22802
Rodeo Dr 22802
Roosevelt St 22801
Rorrer Cir 22801
Rosedale Ct & Dr 22801
Royal Ct 22802
Ruby Dr 22801
Ruffs Ridge Rd 22802
Running Bear Dr 22802
Russell Dr 22801
Rutledge Ct 22801
Sagefield Dr 22801
Sandtrap Ln 22802
Sawdust Ln 22802
Scarlet Oak Ct 22801
Secrist Ln 22801
Seneca Rd 22801
Serenity Dr 22802
Settlers Ln 22802
Shands Trl 22802
Shank Dr 22802
Sharon Ln 22802
Sharon St 22801
Sharpes Dr 22801
Shen Lake Dr 22801
Shenandoah Ave & St 22802
Shenstone Dr 22802
Sherry Ln 22801
Sherwood Ct 22801
Shetland Ln 22801
Shiloh Dr 22802
Shipp Ln 22802
Shire Cir 22801
Shirley St 22802
Shirttail Aly 22802
Shrum Ct 22801
Silver Lake Rd 22801
Silver Oaks Dr 22801
Silverbell Dr 22801
Simmers Valley Rd 22802
Simms Ave 22802
Singers Glen Rd 22802
Sipe Ln 22802
Skidmore Rd 22802
Sky Rd 22802
Skylark Ln 22801
Skyview Ln 22802
Sloan Ct 22801
Smith Ave 22802
Smithland Rd
600-699 22802
700-899 22801
900-2699 22802
Snapps Creek Rd 22802
Snowberry Ln 22801
Snowmass Dr 22801
Sour Cherry Ct 22801
South Ave 22801
Southampton Ct & Dr 22801
Southgate Ct 22801
Southview Dr 22802
Spaders Church Rd 22801
Sparrow Ct 22802
Spotswood Dr 22802
Spotswood Ter 22802
Spotswood Trl 22801
Spring Oaks Dr 22801
Springfield Dr 22801
Springhouse Cir 22802
Springside Dr 22801
Spruce Ct 22802
Star Cir 22801
N Star Ter 22802
Star Crest Dr 22802
Starlight Ct 22801
Statton St 22802
Steam Engine Dr 22801
Steel Rd 22801
Sterling St 22802
Stingray Dr 22802
Stockings Cir 22801
Stone Hill Ln 22802
Stone Spring Rd 22801
Stonechris Dr 22802
Stonefield Ct 22802
Stoneleigh Dr 22801
Stonewall Dr 22801
Stony Point Rd 22802
Straite Way 22801
Stratford Dr 22801
Stuart St 22802
Sugar Maple Ln 22801
Sully Dr 22801
Summers Ln 22802
Summit Ave & St 22802
Sumter Ct 22802
Sunchase Dr 22801
Suncrest Cir 22801
Sunlit Way 22802
Sunny Acres Ln 22801
Sunny Slope Ln 22801
Sunnyside Dr 22801
Sunrise Ave 22801
Sunshine Ct 22802
Suter St 22802
Sweet Corn Ln 22801
Sweet Magnolia Ln 22802
Swiftwater Ct 22801
Switchboard Rd
1-99 22802
100-299 22801
300-1499 22802
Sylvan Dr 22801
Tabb Ct 22801
Tahoe Ct 22801
Taliaferro Dr 22802
Tamela Ct 22801
Tan Bark Dr 22801
Tanners Ct 22802
Tasha Cir 22801
Taylor Grove Ln 22801
Taylor Spring Ln 22801
Teaberry Ln 22801
Teak Cir 22801
Technology Dr 22802
Teddy Bear Trl 22802
Terri Dr 22802
The Grn 22802
The Tee 22802
Thistle Ln 22802
Thomas Paine Dr 22802
Thompson Rd 22802
Tilbury Ct 22801
Toll Gate Ln 22802
Toni St 22802
Topaz Cir 22801
Toppin Blvd 22801
Tower St 22802
Towman Ln 22802
Traveler Rd 22801
Tredarth Rd 22801
Trinity Church Rd 22802
Triple H Ln 22802
Triple Ridge Ln 22802
Tulip Ter 22801
Tumbleweed Ln 22801
Tupelo Dr 22801
Turkey Run Rd 22801
Turner Ashby Ln 22801
Turners Mill Ln 22802
Turquoise Dr 22801
Turtle Ln 22802
Twin Gables Ct 22801
Twin Oaks Dr 22802
Two Penny Dr 22802
Ty Way Xing 22802
University Blvd 22801
Upland Dr 22802
Usman Cir 22801
Vale Cir 22801
N Valley Pike 22802
S Valley Pike 22801
Valley St 22801
Valley View Mob Home
Park 22802
Vera Vista Path 22801
Verdant Spring Ln 22801
Vernon St 22802
Victorian Village Dr 22802
W View St 22801
Viewmont Ct 22802
Villa Dr 22802
Village Ln 22801
Village Sq 22802
Vine St 22802
Virginia Ave 22802
Vista Ln 22801
Vista Glen Dr 22801
Wakefield Pl 22801
Walk Up Ln 22801
Walker St 22801
Walnut Ln 22801
Walnut Creek Dr 22801
Walnut Springs Ln 22801
Wandering Ln 22802
Wapiti Ln 22802
War Branch Rd 22802
War Spring Ln 22802
Warehouse Rd 22801
Warner Ln 22802
Warren St 22801
Warsaw Ave 22801
E & W Washington St 22802
E & W Water St 22801
Waterman Dr 22802
E & W Weaver Ave 22801
Weavers Rd 22802
Welch Ln 22801
Well Hollow Rd 22802
Wellington Dr 22802
Welstone Dr 22801
Wesley Chapel Rd 22802
West Ave & Ct 22801
Westbrier Dr 22802
Westfield Ct 22802
Westhampton Ct 22801
Westmoreland Dr 22801
Westwind Dr 22801
Whippoorwill Ln 22802
Whispering Oak Ln 22802
Whispering Springs Rd 22801
Whissen Ln 22802
Whistling Wind Ln 22802
White Oak Cir & Dr 22801
Whitmore Shop Rd 22802
Wild Cherry Ln 22801
N Willow St 22802
S Willow St 22801
Willow Hill Dr 22801
Willow Run Rd 22802
Willow Spring Rd 22801
Wilson Ave 22802
Wilton Pl 22801
Wiltshire St 22802
Windsor Rd 22801
Windy Heights Ln 22802
Windy Knoll Dr 22802
Wine Dr 22801
Winona Ln 22801
Winter Park Ln 22801
Wishing Well Ct 22801
Wits End Way 22802
E & W Wolfe St 22802
Woodbury Cir 22802
Woodcrest Cir 22801
Woodland Dr
700-799 22801
1300-1399 22802
4000-4299 22801
Woodland Hills Dr 22802
Woodland Park Cir 22802
Woodleigh Ct 22802
Woods Rd 22801
Woodside Dr 22801
Wordsworth Ct 22802
Wren Way 22802
Wyndam Wood Ln 22801
Wyndham Dr 22801
Wyndham Woods Cir 22801
Wynnwood Ln 22802
York Pl 22801

NUMBERED STREETS

All Street Addresses 22802

HAYMARKET VA

General Delivery 20169

POST OFFICE BOXES MAIN OFFICE STATIONS AND BRANCHES

Box No.s
All PO Boxes 20168

NAMED STREETS

Acerville Pl 20169
Addlerfield Way 20169
Admiral Baker Cir 20169
Adriatic Ct 20169
Alderbrook Dr 20169
Alderdale Pl 20169
Alexanders Mill Ct 20169
Alexandras Keep Ln 20169
Allens Mill Blvd 20169
Almansor Pl 20169
Alvey Dr 20169
Amber Ridge Rd 20169
Amberfield Ln 20169
Amelia Springs Cir 20169
Annenberg Ct 20169
Antioch Rd 20169
Antioch Ridge Dr 20169
Armour Ct 20169
Arnold Palmer Dr 20169
Arrowfield Ter 20169
Ashby Grove Loop 20169
Ashby Oak Ct 20169
Aster Haven Cir 20169
Avens Creek Dr 20169
Averadon Rd 20169
Aviara View Ct 20169
Babbling Brook Ct 20169
Bakerwood Pl 20169
Bear Hollow Trl 20169
Bencrest Way 20169
Benford Dr 20169
Bengal Pl 20169
Bent Grass Dr 20169
Benvenue Rd 20169
Berkeley Dr 20169
Berry Pond Pl 20169
Berryville Ct 20169
Besselink Way 20169
Bethpage Ln 20169
Blair Brook Ct 20169
Bleight Dr 20169
Blossom Hill Dr 20169
Bonnie Brae Farm Dr 20169
Boothe Ln 20169
Bos Cir 20169
Bowers Hill Dr 20169
Boydton Plank Ct 20169
Brandon Hill Loop 20169
Brave Ct 20169
Brier Creek Dr 20169
Brinestone Pl 20169
Brown Deer Ct 20169
Bull Run Estates Dr 20169
Burnley Glen Ct 20169
Burnside Farm Pl 20169
Caboose Trl 20169
Camptown Ct 20169
Canyon Creek Way 20169
Caribbean Ct 20169
Carlsmore Ct 20169
Carlton Oaks Pl 20169
Carnoustie Ln 20169
Cedarville Ct 20169
Celeste Ct 20169
Chaffins Farm Ct 20169
Chalfont Dr 20169
Chamberry Cir 20169
Championship Dr 20169
Charles St 20169
Cheal Ct 20169
Cherokee Run Ct 20169
Chestnut Ridge Ct 20169
Cheyenne Way 20169
Chimneys West Dr 20169
China Ct 20169
Clementine Way 20169
Clifton Manor Pl 20169
Coach Way 20169
Coachview Ct 20169
Cody Spring Pl 20169
Colby Hunt Ct 20169
Collins Ct 20169
Comanche Ct 20169
Comptown Ct 20169
Conklin Way 20169
Contest Ln 20169
Cool Spring Dr 20169
Corbin Woods Ct 20169
Corner Post Pl 20169
Costello Way 20169
Courtyard Way 20169
Cousteau Pl 20169
Cove Mountain Ct 20169
Cox Creek Ct 20169
Cranswick Ct 20169
Crescent Hills Dr 20169
Crestview Ln 20169
Crusade Ct 20169
Cullen Pl 20169
Curran Creek Dr 20169
Cypress Park Ln 20169
Dabneys Mill Ct 20169
Dan Ct 20169
Dane Valley Ct 20169
Danube Way 20169
Dean Chapel Ct 20169
Delashmutt Dr 20169
Desert Forest Ct 20169
Doe Ridge Ct & Rd 20169
Dogwood Park Ln 20169
Dogwood Tree Ct 20169
Dominion Valley Dr 20169
Donna Marie Ct 20169
Doral Pl 20169
Dowden Downs Dr 20169
Drake Ln 20169
Duck Ln 20169
Duffey Dr 20169
Dunbars Sawmill Dr 20169
Dunnbrook Ter 20169
Dustin Ct 20169
East Dr 20169
Emily Ct 20169
Emmys Mill Ct 20169
Empire Lakes Ct 20169
Enfield Chase Ct 20169
Erin Dr 20169
Erinblair Loop 20169
Faldo Dr 20169
Fassels Ct 20169
Fayette St 20169
Fells Bridge Pl 20169
Fishers Hill Way 20169
Flynnsbrooke Ter 20169
Fog Mountain Cir 20169
Foleys Mill Pl 20169
Forest Lake Ln 20169
Fourmile Creek Ct 20169
Freedmen Ln 20169
Gaines Mill Cir 20169
Gap Way
14658-14798 20169
14658-14658 20168
14800-14899 20169
Garnetts Farm Dr 20169
George Lansdowne Dr 20169
Gilesburg Dr 20169
Glass Mountain Way 20169
Golf View Dr 20169
Gore Dr 20169
Gossom Manor Pl 20169
Gossoms Store Ct 20169
Gossum Ct 20169
Graduation Dr 20169
Grand Beech Ct 20169
Green Bay St 20169
Greenhill Crossing Dr 20169
Greenville Dr 20169
Greymill Manor Dr 20169
Grigsby Pl 20169
Guard Hill Ct 20169
Guilford Ridge Rd 20169
Gypsum Hill Rd 20169
Hagen Way 20169
Haig Point Pl 20169
Hall Manor Ln 20169
Harclief Ct 20169
Hardwood Hill Way 20169
Hartzell Hill Ln 20169
Haymarket Dr 20169
Heathcote Blvd 20169
Heather Mill Ln 20169
Hickory Ln 20169
High Ridge Rd 20169
Hillsman Farm Ln 20169
Hinman Pl 20169
Holcrest Ct 20169
Holshire Way 20169
Hopewell Ct 20169
Hortons Mill Ct 20169
Hull Dr 20169
Hunting Path Rd 20169
Hunton Ln 20169
Hurd Ln 20169
Hylamore Ct 20169
Ingram Dr 20169
Interlachen Ct 20169
Iris Meadow Ln 20169
Jackson Dr 20169
Jackson Hollow Rd 20169
Jackson Mill Rd 20169
Jacobs Creek Pl 20169
James Madison Hwy 20169
Janneys Mill Cir 20169
Jefferson St 20169
Jennifer Ln 20169
Jockey Club Ln 20169
John Marshall Hwy 20169
Jordan Ln 20169
Jordan Crest Ct 20169
Judy Ter 20169
Jupiter Hills Ln 20169
Kapp Valley Way 20169
Keavy Pl 20169
Keavy Ridge Ct 20169
Kedzie St 20169
Kernstown Ct 20169
Kilgore St 20169
Kroll Ln 20169
La Jolla Ct 20169
Lansdowne Ln 20169
Largo Vista Dr 20169
Latham Dr 20169
Lawson Dr 20169
Lea Berry Way 20169
Learning Ln 20169
Legacy Way 20169
Lightner Rd 20169
Lightning Dr 20169
Lilywood Ln 20169
Little John Ct 20169
Little River Rd 20169
Lloyd Ct 20169
Log Cabin Dr 20169
Logmill Rd 20169
Londons Bridge Rd 20169
Lone Eagle Ct 20169
Lookout Rd 20169
Loudoun Dr 20169
Lupine Haven Dr 20169
Macintosh Loop 20169
Mackenzie Manor Dr 20169
Macklin St 20169
Madison Ct & St 20169
Malvern Hill Ct 20169
Market Ridge Blvd 20169
Marlbank Pl 20169
Martin Ter 20169
Martinwood Dr 20169
Masters Ct 20169
Mcleod Way 20169
Meander Creek Ln 20169
Medinah Ct 20169
Mellon Ct 20169
Mendelmore Way 20169
Mercer Rd 20169
Merchants View Sq 20169
Mercury Ave 20169
Michener Dr 20169
Mill Creek Rd 20169
Misty Ridge Dr 20169
Mortons Ford Way 20169
Mount Atlas Ln 20169
Mountain Rd 20169
Mountain Crest Ct 20169
Mountain View Dr 20169
Mozambique Ct 20169
Muirfield Dr 20169
Myradale Way 20169
Nelson Dr 20169
Neptune Ct 20169
Newhope Dr 20169
Northwood Estates Dr 20169
Noyes Ave 20169
Oak Ln 20169
Oakland Ridge Rd 20169
Oakton Ave 20169
October Way 20169
Old Carolina Rd 20169
Old Waterfall Rd 20169
Olga Ct 20169
Olympia Fields Pl 20169
Omland Pl 20169
Orrington Ln 20169
Otis Ct 20169
Padgett Dr 20169
Painter Ct 20169
Painters Cove Way 20169
Palmer Ln 20169
Palmers Ridge Ct 20169
Paloma Ct 20169
Parchment Ct 20169
Parkers Ford Ct 20169
Parnell Ct 20169
Patent Cir 20169
Pattie Ct 20169
Paynes Farm Dr 20169
Pennshire Dr 20169
Peyton Chapel Dr 20169
Picketts Store Pl 20169
Piedmont Vista Dr 20169
Pitner St 20169
Plain Tree Way 20169
Plantation Grove Ln 20169
Players Cir 20169
Popes Creek Pl 20169
Poplar Hill Rd 20169
Presgrave Pl 20169
Prosperity Dr 20169
Quaker Rd 20169
Quarters Ln 20169
Quintessence Ct 20169
Rail Post Pl 20169
Rainer Heights Ct 20169
Raymond Pl 20169
Red Fox Ct 20169
Ridge Rd 20169
Riding Club Dr 20169
Ripple Stone Ct 20169
Rising Sun Ln 20169
Roan Chapel Dr 20169
Rock Hill Ln 20169
Rodgers Ter 20169
Rodriquez Ln 20169
Rolling Ridge Rd 20169
Rosemont Manor Dr 20169
Rothschild Ct 20169
Royal Crest Dr 20169
Ruddy Ct 20169
Ryder Ct 20169
Ryder Cup Dr 20169
Sage Run Rd 20169
Saint Paul Dr 20169
Saltville Ter 20169
Sawgrass Pl 20169
Scotts Valley Dr 20169
Seneca Knoll Way 20169
September Way 20169
Serengeti Ct 20169

Seven Pines Ct 20169
Shady Oak Ln 20169
Shawbrook Ct 20169
Shelter Ln 20169
Shelter Manor Dr 20169
Sherman Oaks Ct 20169
Shoal Creek Dr 20169
Shortgrass Ln 20169
Signature Ct 20169
Silica St 20169
Silver Lake Rd 20169
Simmons Grove Dr 20169
Simon Kenton Rd 20169
Slatemore Ct 20169
Slippery Rock Rd 20169
Smithey Dr 20169
Smooth Stone Pl 20169
Solheim Cup Dr 20169
Sorrell Hunt Rd 20169
Southern Crossing St 20169
Spout Spring Ct 20169
Spring Lake Dr 20169
Spruce Grove Ct 20169
Stepping Stone Dr 20169
Stonewall Farms Dr 20169
Stoney Creek Ct 20169
Stormy Dr 20169
Stourcliffe Ln 20169
Strayer Ln 20169
Stream Valley Ct 20169
Sudley Rd 20169
Summit Dr 20169
Sumney Dr 20169
Swift Creek Ct 20169
Sycamore Hills Pl 20169
Sycamore Park Dr 20169
Tanning House Pl 20169
Tansill Dr 20169
Tanyard Ln 20169
Taylors Mill Pl 20169
Thoroughfare Rd 20169
Thousand Oaks Dr 20169
Thunder Rd 20169
Tiffany Ln 20169
Timor Ct 20169
Tinley Mill Dr 20169
Toledo Pl 20169
Tory Gate Ct 20169
Tournament Dr 20169
Track Ct 20169
Trading Sq 20169
Trevino Dr 20169
Troon Ct 20169
Tucson Ct 20169
Tulloch Spring Ct 20169
Tumble Creek Ct 20169
Turara Ct 20169
Turnberry Dr 20169
Turning Leaf Pl 20169
Twin Branch Ct 20169
Tyler Mill Ct 20169
Utterback Ln 20169
Vailmont Ct 20169
Valhalla Ct 20169
Venus Ct 20169
Verde Pl 20169
Victorias Crest Pl 20169
Village Cove Pl 20169
Wake Crest Ct 20169
Wakefield Ct 20169
Walkerton Ct 20169
Walking Stick Way 20169
Wallasey Ct 20169
Walnut Park Ln 20169
Walter Robinson Ln 20169
Wandering Run Ct 20169
Warburton Dr 20169
Warwick Hills Ct 20169
Washington St 20169
Waterfall Rd 20169
Waterloo Bridge Cir 20169
Waverly Farm Dr 20169
Weiskopf Ct 20169
Wheelwright Way 20169
Whiskers Ridge Way 20169
Whitworth Ct 20169
Wiley Ter 20169
Wishing Rock Way 20169
Woodley Hills Rd 20169
Woodruff Springs Way 20169
Woolen Mill Ct 20169
Woolman Dr 20169
Wythridge Way 20169
Yellow Tavern Ct 20169
Yorktown Run Ct 20169
Youngs Dr 20169
Zacharys Mill Ter 20169
Zoysia Ct 20169

HENRICO VA

General Delivery 23075
General Delivery 23228
General Delivery 23229
General Delivery 23233
General Delivery 23294

POST OFFICE BOXES MAIN OFFICE STATIONS AND BRANCHES

Box No.s
31004C - 31004C 23231
90508C - 90523C 23242
90002C - 90002C 23231
1 - 490 23075
2901 - 3400 23228
7501 - 7899 23231
9401 - 28992 23228
29001 - 29981 23242
31335 - 32706 23294
38001 - 38980 23231
42301 - 42412 23242
70001 - 72140 23255
90522 - 90522 23242
90775 - 90799 23228
90905 - 90909 23242
734400 - 734413 23255
905020 - 905020 23242

NAMED STREETS

A P Hill Ave 23075
Abbey Ln 23233
Abelia Rd 23228
Abundance Ct 23231
Academy Rd 23229
Accomac St 23231
Ackley Ave 23228
Acreview Dr 23075
Acton St 23231
Adair Ave 23228
Adamo Ct 23233
Adamson St 23075
Adelphi Rd 23229
Adingham Ct 23229
Adrian Dr 23294
Aeronca Ave 23228
Agra Dr 23228
Aiken Dr 23294
N & S Airport Ct, Dr & Pl 23075
Airy Cir 23238
Airycrest Dr 23075
Aisquith Rd 23229
Ajay Ct 23231
Alameda Ave 23294
Alamosa Dr 23075
Aldeburgh Dr 23294
Alder Grove Dr & Ln 23228
Aldershot Dr 23294
Alendale Rd 23229
Alexander Rd 23231
Alexis Dr 23231
Allegro Dr 23231
Allen Woods Ln 23231
Allenshaw Dr 23231
Allistair Ct 23228
Almond Creek Ct, Ln & Pl 23231
Almond Creek North Ln, Pl & Ter 23231
Almond Tree Dr & Ter 23231
Almondberry Pl 23231
Almora Ave 23228
Aloe Ct 23228
Alsatia Dr 23238
Alston Ln 23294
Altair Rd 23231
Altman Rd 23228
Alvarado Dr & Rd 23229
Alvis Ct & Pl 23231
Alycia Ave 23228
Alyssalaine Dr & Pl 23231
Amber Ter 23233
Americana Dr 23228
Amherst St 23231
Anaconda Dr 23228
Anderson Rd 23228
Andover Rd 23229
Andover Hills Pl 23294
Angelsea Dr 23294
Anglican Ct, Pl & Way 23233
Anna Way 23233
Anneslie Ct 23229
Anoka Rd 23229
Ansley Rd 23231
Antietam Dr 23231
Apple Ridge Ct 23229
Aprilbud Ct, Dr & Pl 23233
Aqua Vista Ln 23231
Ara Rd 23228
Arbor Creek Dr & Way 23233
Arborhill Rd 23238
Arcadia Ln 23233
Archie Ln 23231
Ardmore Rd 23294
Argyll Cir 23075
Arlington Cir 23229
Armstrong Rd 23228
Arrahatteck Trl 23231
Arrington Rd 23294
Arrowdel Ct & Rd 23229
Arrowview Ct 23229
Art Ave 23231
Asbury Ct & Rd 23229
N Ash Ave 23075
Ashbridge Pl 23238
Ashburton Ct 23233
Ashcliff Ct & Way 23228
Ashcreek Dr 23238
Ashcrest Ct & Pl 23238
Asheville Ct 23231
Ashford Rd 23229
Ashford Lake Pl 23233
Ashinghurst Rd 23238
Ashley Glen Dr 23233
Ashton Glen Ct 23238
Asker Ct 23233
Aspen Ave 23228
Aspen Pl 23233
Aspen Way 23233
Aspen Shades Pkwy 23231
Aspen View Ct, Dr & Pl 23228
Aspinwald Dr 23233
Aston Ln 23238
Aubery Rd 23229
Audubon Dr 23231
Autumn Chase Ct, Dr & Pl 23233
Autumn Honey Ct 23229
Avalon Dr 23229
Avenham Way 23238
Axel Ct 23233
Azrock Ct 23231
Azure Ct 23233
Babcock Rd 23075
Bailey Dr 23231
Baird St 23228
Bald Eagle Ct 23231
Baldwin Rd 23229
Balineen Ct 23228
Balla Ct 23228
Ballantrae Ct 23229
Ballyshannon Ct 23228
Balmoral Ave 23228
Balster Ln 23233
Bambacus Rd 23229
Banbridge Ct 23228
Bandera Dr 23228
Bandock Rd 23229
Bandy Rd 23229
Bangor Ct 23228
N Bank Rd 23238
Banks St 23075
Bankside Mews 23231
Banstead Rd 23231
Barbara Ct, Ln & Pl 23233
Barbour Rd 23228
Barclay Rd 23228
Barksdale Rd 23231
Barnard Dr 23229
Barnesway Ln 23231
Barnett Cir 23233
Barnside Cir 23233
Barony Cres 23233
Barrett Pl 23231
Barribee Ln 23229
Barringer Ln 23233
Barrington Branch Ct 23233
Barrington Bridge Ct, Pl & Ter 23233
Barrington Hill Ct & Dr 23233
Bartlett Rd 23231
Bartley Pond Ct, Dr & Pl 23233
Baseline Ct 23294
Basie Rd 23228
Basildon Ct 23229
Basswood Rd 23229
Bateleur Ct 23231
Battery Ave 23228
Battery St 23231
N Battery St 23075
Battery Gregg Ct, Dr & Pl 23231
Battery Hill Dr 23231
Battlefield Park Rd 23231
Battlefield Run Ct 23231
Bayapple Ct & Dr 23294
Bayleaf Ct 23238
Bayly Ct 23229
Baymeadows Way 23233
Baypines Ln 23238
Baysdale Ln 23229
Beacontree Ln 23294
Beagle Dr 23228
E & W Beal St 23075
Beauregard Ave 23075
Beaver Ln 23229
Beaver Rd 23075
Beaver Creek Dr 23233
Bedell Rd 23229
Bedford St 23231
Bedfordshire Sq 23238
N & S Beech Ave 23075
Beechwood Dr 23229
Beechwood Park Ln 23075
Belcrest Ct 23294
Belfort Rd 23229
Belgrave Rd 23229
Belhaven Ct 23233
Bell Tower Ct & Pl 23233
Belle Air Ln 23229
Belle Grove Ln 23229
Bellefonte Rd 23229
Bellona Ct 23233
Benham Ct 23228
Benjamin Pl 23233
Bentbrook Dr 23231
Bentridge Ln 23229
Beowulf Ct & Dr 23231
Berkeley Pointe Dr 23233
Berkshire Dr 23229
Berman Ct 23238
Bernal Cir 23231
Bernice Ln 23238
Bernie Ct 23075
Berryhill Rd 23231
Berrywine Ct 23294
Berwickshire Dr 23229
Beryl Ct 23233
Beth Rd 23228
Bethania Ct 23228
Bethlehem Rd 23228
Bethnalgreen Dr 23229
Beulah Rd 23231
Beverly Dr 23229
Beverstone Rd 23075
Bevlynn Way 23229
Bexhill Rd 23229
Bexley Ct 23233
Bickerstaff Pl & Rd 23231
Biddeford Pl 23233
Billingsgate Cir 23238
Birch Point Ct, Dr & Ln 23228
Birchbrook Rd 23228
Birchcrest Rd 23238
Birchview Ct 23228
Birchwood Rd 23294
Biscayne Ct & Rd 23294
Bisley Ct 23238
Black Duck Ct 23231
Blackberry Patch Ct & Rd 23231
Blackthorn Ln & Way 23233
Blairs Bluff Ct 23238
Blandfield St 23233
Blankenship Cir & Rd 23294
Blendon Ln 23238
Bloomingdale Ave 23228
Blossom View Ln 23231
Blue Jay Ln 23229
Blue Lake Dr 23233
Blueberry Hill Ct 23229
Bluefield Swamp Dr 23231
Boardman Ln 23238
Bobbiedell Ln 23229
Bogan Rd 23294
Bogle Ct 23231
Boissevain Rd 23233
Bolelyn Dr & Way 23231
Bonanza St 23228
Bonnie Dale Rd 23229
Bonruth Pl 23238
Boothbay Ct 23233
Bootsie Blvd 23231
Borden Rd 23229
Borris Ct 23228
Bothwell Ct & St 23233
Boulder Run Ct, Dr & Pl 23238
Bowden Rd 23229
Bowerton Rd 23233
Bowler St 23228
Boxwood Ct, Pl & Rd 23228
Bradbury Rd 23231
Bradbury Knoll Dr 23231
Bradway Ct & Ln 23233
Braeburn Dr 23238
Bramall Rd 23229
Bramblewood Ln 23228
Bramsford Ct 23238
Branberry Ct & Ln 23233
Branchview Cir & Ct 23229
Brandon Creek Pl 23233
Brandon Forest Ct 23228
Brandonview Ave 23231
Brandy Ln 23231
Brandyview Ln 23233
Bransford Dr 23228
Branway Ct & Dr 23229
Brass Hill Way 23294
Brawner Dr 23229
Breezy Bay Cir 23233
Bremerton Dr 23233
Bremner Blvd 23228
Brendonridge Ct & Ln 23238
Brennan Rd 23229
Brewer Ct & Rd 23233
Brewington Rd 23238
Brewster Ct & Dr 23233
Briar Ln 23228
Briardale Ln 23229
Briargrove Ct 23238
Briarview Ct 23233
Brick Dr 23075
Bridge St 23075
Bridgehampton Pl 23229
Bridgehaven Ter 23233
Bridgetender Dr 23233
Bridgeview Ln 23233
Bridgewater Dr 23228
Bridle Ln 23229
Brieryle Rd 23229
Brigadoon Ct 23228
Brightmoor Ct 23238
Brighton Rd 23231
Brightwater Ln 23233
E & W Brightway Cir, Ct & Dr 23294
Brinley Meadows Dr 23231
Britain Way 23238
Brittles Ln 23231
Britton Rd 23231
W Broad St
7000-9599 23294
11401-11497 23233
11499-12499 23233
Broadford Ln & Ter 23233
Broadmoor Dr 23229
Broadview Ln 23233
Broadway Ave 23228
Brockwood Ct 23294
Bromby St 23231
Bronwood Rd 23229
Bronwyn Rd 23238
Brookmont Ct & Dr 23233
Brooks Hall Pl 23238
Brookschase Ln 23229
Brookside Rd 23229
Brookstone Ln 23233
Brooktree Ct 23238
Brookwater Dr 23233
Browning Ct & Pl 23233
Bryan Park Ave 23228
Bryans View Ct 23233
Bryn Mawr Rd 23229
Bryson Dr 23233
Buchanan Ct 23233
Buckeye Dr 23228
Buckingham Ave 23228
Buckner St 23231
Buffapple Ct & Dr 23233
Buffin Rd 23231
Bufflehead Ct 23231
Bull Run Ct & Dr 23231
Bunche St 23228
Bunclody Ct 23228
Burgoyne Rd 23229
Burkhart Dr 23229
Burley Ave 23228
Burma Ct 23231
Burning Tree Rd 23231
Burnlake Ct 23233
Burnley Ave 23228
Burnside Ln 23233
Burrard Ct & St 23233
Burtfield Ct & Dr 23231
Butler St 23231
Butterfield Ave 23229
Buttonwood Dr 23238
Byfield Ct & Pl 23233
Byrd Industrial Dr 23231
Byrdhill Rd 23228
Bywater Dr 23233
Cabot Pl 23233
Caithness Pl 23075
Caitlin Cir & Ct 23233
Caliber Dr 23231
California Dr 23233
Calloway Rd 23228
Calm Harbor Dr 23233
Camberwell Ct 23233
Cambie Pl 23233
Cambrai Ave 23231
Cambridge Cir, Ct & Dr 23238
Camden Dr 23229
Camelot Cir & Dr 23229
Camero Ct 23075
Cameron Rd 23229
Camille Ave 23228
Camolin Ct 23228
Camp Hill Rd 23231
Camp Holly Dr 23231
Camrose Rd 23229
Candle Ct 23238
Candlebrook Ct 23233
Canesville Ln 23231
Capehart Rd 23294
Capilano Pl 23233
Capri Rd 23229
E & W Cardinal Ct & Rd 23228
Cardinal Woods Ln 23231
Careybrook Dr 23238
Carisbrook Dr 23238
Carlisle Ave & Ct 23231
Carlstone Ct, Dr & Pl 23075
Carlway Ct 23228
Carmel Rd 23228
Carmon Ct & St 23233
Caroline Vines Ct & Way 23231
Carousel Ln 23294
Carriage Ln 23229
Carriage Pond Ct & Dr 23233
Carrick St 23228
Carrington Pl 23238
Carrollwood Ct 23238
Carterham Ct & Rd 23229
Carters Mill Rd 23231
Carters Pond Ct 23231
Carterswood Ct 23233
Carterwood Ct, Pl & Rd 23229
Cartwright Ct & Ln 23233
Casco Bay Ct 23233
Cassell Ct 23238
Castile Ct, Pl & Rd 23238
Castle Dr 23231
Castlebar Ct 23228
Catesby Ln 23238
Catriona Ct 23233
Cattle Dr 23231
Causeway Dr 23233
Cavalry Dr 23229
Cavan Green Ct 23228
Cavedo Ln 23231
Cavedo Farm Rd 23231
N & S Cedar Ave 23075
Cedar Bay Ct 23233
Cedar Cone Dr 23233
Cedar Crest Ln 23231
Cedar Croft St 23228
Cedar Grove Ter & Way 23228
Cedar Hill Ct 23233
Cedar Hollow Ct 23238
Cedar Knoll Ct & Ln 23233
Cedar Lawn Ave 23231
Cedar Mountain Ct 23228
Cedar Station Ct 23233
Cedar Valley Ln 23231
Cedar Works Row 23231
Cedarbluff Dr 23238
Cedarbrooke Ln 23229
Cedarfield Ct, Ln & Pkwy 23233
Cedarglen Rd 23238
Cedaridge Rd 23229
Cedarpine Rd 23231
Cedarwood Rd 23075
N Cendisti Ave 23075
Center Ridge Dr 23233
Century Dr 23229
Ceres Rd 23294
Chadwick Dr 23229
E & W Chaffin Rd 23231
Chaffins Bluff Ln 23231
Champagne Way 23231
Chancer Dr 23233
Chancery Ct & Pl 23233
Chandler Cir & Dr 23229

Street	ZIP
Chapaqua Ct & Dr	23229
Chaparral Ct	23228
Chapelwood Ln	23233
Chapin Dr	23238
Chardon Rd	23231
Charles City Cir, Pl & Rd	23231
Charlesfield Ct	23238
Charnwood Rd	23229
Chase Gayton Cir, Dr & Ter	23238
Chase Wellesley Ct, Dr & Pl	23233
Chatham Woods Dr	23233
Chatsworth Rd	23231
Chatterleigh Ct & Dr	23238
Chauncey Ln	23238
Checkerberry Dr	23231
Chellbrook Pl	23229
Chelton Rd	23228
Cherry View Ct	23228
Cherrydale Dr	23238
Cherrystone Ave	23228
Cherrywood Dr	23238
Chesham St	23231
Cheshire Rd	23229
Chesley Rd	23231
Chesterbrook Ct & Way	23233
Chestnut Grove Ct	23233
Chestnut Springs Pl	23233
Cheswick Ln	23229
Chichester Ct	23228
Chimney Stone Ct	23233
Chipewyan Dr	23238
Chipoax Ave	23231
Chipper Ct & Way	23075
Chiswick Park Rd	23229
Choate Pl	23238
Chowan Rd	23229
Chowning Cir, Ct, Pl & Rd	23294
Chris Travis Dr	23231
Christi Ct	23238
Chumley Ln	23294
Church Ct & Rd	23233
Church Creek Pl	23233
Church Grove Ct	23233
Church Run Pkwy	23233
Churchwood Ct & Pl	23229
Citadel Dr	23229
Clarinbridge Ct	23228
Clarke St	23228
Clary Preston Dr	23233
Claxton Rd	23238
Claymont Dr	23229
Clayton Rd	23231
Clearwood Rd	23238
Cleveland St	23228
Clinard Ct	23228
Cloister Ct & Dr	23238
Cloisters E & W	23229
Clover Ln	23228
Cloverdale St	23228
Club Rd	23228
Club House Ct	23294
Club View Ct	23229
Club Vista Ln	23229
Cluck Ln	23231
Coachford Ct	23228
Coachlite Dr	23238
Coachman Ln	23228
Coachouse Ln	23233
Coalport Rd	23229
Coalville Dr	23294
Coat Bridge Ln	23238
Cobbler Ct	23228
Cokesburg Ln	23229
Colemant Ct & Ter	23231
Coleridge Ln	23229
College Rd	23229
College Valley Ct, Ln & Way	23233
Collinwood Dr	23238
Colonel Dr	23075
Colonist Dr	23238
Colony Bluff Dr & Pl	23238
Colony Lake Dr	23238
Colthurst Pl	23233
Colwyn Rd	23229
Comet Rd	23294
Compton Rd	23228
Concord Ave	23228
Condover Rd	23229
Confederate Run Ct	23075
Congressional Ct	23238
Constitution Dr	23238
Convair Ln	23228
Cookes Farm Ct & Dr	23231
Cool Brook Dr	23229
Cool Stream Dr	23233
Coolwind Ln	23233
Copley Dr	23229
Copper Cove Ln	23294
Copper Pond Ct	23294
Copperas Ln	23233
Coppermill Trce	23294
Coralberry Pl	23229
Cornelia Rd	23228
Cornett St	23075
Cornwall Rd	23229
Coronet Dr	23229
Corum Dr	23294
Cosby St	23075
Costin Ct & Dr	23229
Cotley Ct & Ln	23233
Cottage St	23228
Cottage Cove Ct & Dr	23233
Cottage Creek Ct	23233
Cottesmore Ct, Ln & Ter	23228
Cotton Patch Ct	23233
Cottrell Rd	23233
Count St	23228
Country Squire Ln	23229
Countryside Ct & Ln	23229
Countryside Crossing Ct	23231
Court St	23228
Courtyard Ln	23233
Courtyard Glen Pl	23233
Covemeadow Dr	23238
Covent Rd	23238
Covey Run Dr	23233
Cox Rd	23233
Coxley Ct	23231
Coxson Rd	23231
Craddock Ave	23231
Cragmont Cir	23238
Cragmont Dr	
9200-9699	23229
9700-9799	23238
Craighill Rd	23238
Cranbrook Rd	23229
Cranbury Ct & Dr	23238
Crandall Ct	23233
Cranemore Rd	23231
Craven Ln	23228
Creek Cross Way	23233
Creekridge Rd	23231
Creekside Ct & Dr	23238
Crested Eagle Ln	23231
Cresthaven Ct	23238
Crickett Ct	23229
Crickhollow Ct	23233
Crimson Ct	23233
Crockett St	23228
Crofton Ln	23238
Cross Country Ct	23294
Cross Keys Ct	23233
Crossfield Rd	23233
Crown Ct	23294
Crown Grant Ct & Rd	23233
Crown Prince Cir	23238
Crown Squire Rd	23231
Crowncrest Ct, Dr, Pl & Way	23233
Crystal Ridge Rd	23233
Crystal Springs Ln	23231
Crystalwood Ln	23294
Culpeper Rd	23229
Curles Neck Rd	23231
Curtisdale Rd	23231
Cutler Ridge Dr	
12400-12499	23238
12500-12699	23233
Cynthia Ct & Dr	23231
Cypress Spring Ct	23294
Cyril Ln	23229
Dacono Dr	23228
Daffodil Meadow Ln	23231
Dairy Farm Ct	23231
N & S Daisy Ave	23075
Dale St	23075
Dalewood Dr	23238
Dalkeith Dr & Ln	23233
Dalmain Dr	23228
Dan St	23231
Dancer Rd	23294
Danewood Dr	23233
Daniels Rd	23238
Danielsdale Dr	23294
Danley Ln	23228
Danrett Ct & Ln	23231
Danville St	23231
Darbytown Ct, Pl & Rd	23231
Darjoy Dr & Ln	23231
Darnell Rd	23294
Darracott Rd	23228
Dartford Rd	23229
Dartmoor Rd	23229
Dasher Rd	23294
Davenport Ave	23228
David Dr	23229
E & W Davista Ave	23228
Dawndeer Ln	23238
Dawnfield Ln	23231
Deborah Ridge Pl	23238
Dee Kay Dr	23228
Deep Bottom Rd	23231
Deep Ridge Ct	23233
Deep Rock Rd	23233
Deephaven Ct	23233
Deepwood Cir	23238
Dehaven Dr	23238
Delafayette Pl	23238
Delaney St	23229
Delbert Dr	23075
Delham Dr	23294
Della Dr	23238
Dellbrooks Pl	23238
Dellrose Ave	23228
Dellwood St	23228
Delma Dr	23228
Delta Cir	23228
Demaree Ct	23231
Dena Dr	23229
Denham Ct & Rd	23229
Denison Rd	23231
Densmore Ct & Pl	23233
Dentana Ct	23228
Denver St	23231
Derby Dr	23229
Derbyshire Rd	23229
Derek Ln	23229
Derryclare Dr	23228
Desota Dr	23229
Devon Rd	23229
Diamond Ridge Ct	23231
Diamond Springs Dr	23231
Digby Ct	23233
Dilton Ct & Dr	23238
Dinwiddie Ave	23229
Discovery Dr	23229
Distribution Dr	23231
Dixon Powers Dr	23228
Dobbin Rd	23229
Dodds Creek Dr	23229
Dogwood Rd	23229
Dogwood Oaks	23231
Dolphin Rd	23231
Donaldwood Dr	23294
Donder Rd	23294
Donegal Trace Ct	23228
Donora Ct & Dr	23229
Donovan Ct	23228
Doran Pl & Rd	23231
Dorey Park Dr	23231
Dornoch Rd	23294
Dotson Rd	23231
Dover Hunt Ct & Pl	23233
N & S Dover Pointe Ct & Rd	23238
Doverland Ct & Rd	23229
Doverton Rd	23233
Dowdy Dr	23231
Downing Ct & St	23238
N & S Downs Dr & Sq	23238
Downy Ln	23228
Dragana Dr	23233
Drammen Ct & Pl	23233
Dresden Rd	23229
Drexel Ln	23228
W Drive Cir	23229
S Drouin Dr	23238
Dryden Ln	23229
Duck Blind Ct	23231
Duffy Ct	23233
Dulaney Ct	23233
Dumbarton Rd	23228
Dunham Rd	23233
Dunnington Ct	23294
Dunsmore Rd	23229
Durango Rd	23228
Durley Ct	23231
Durvin Dr	23229
Durwood Cres	23229
Dwyer St	23231
Eagle Ridge Rd	23233
Eagles Landing Ave	23231
Eagles Nest Ct	23231
Eagles View Ct, Pl & Ter	23233
Eanes Ln	23231
Easley Ct	23228
Eastborough Ct	23238
Eastkent Sq	23238
Eastover Ave	23231
Eastport Blvd	23231
Eastridge Rd	23229
Eden Ave	23231
Eden St	23228
Edenbridge Ct	23233
Edenbrook Dr	23228
Edenburry Dr	23238
Edgelawn Cir & St	23231
Edgemore St	23228
Edgewood Farm Ct	23233
Edinborough Sq	23238
Edith Hill Ct	23231
Ednam Forest Dr	23238
Edson Rd	23229
Eglantine Cir	23238
Eildonway Pl	23238
El Dorado Dr	23229
Electra Ct & Ln	23228
Ella Rd	23231
Ellerbee Rd	23228
Ellis Ave	23228
Ellis Ln	23294
N & S Elm Ave	23075
Elmbrook Ct & Rd	23228
Elmhurst Dr	23229
Elmington Dr	23238
Elmshadow Ct & Dr	23231
Elon Rd	23229
Elsing Green Ct, Pl & Way	23075
Elswick Ln	23294
Elwell Ln	23229
Emerald Brook Ln	23233
Emerald Forest Ln	23231
Emerald Lakes Dr	23233
Emerywood Pkwy	23294
Emily Ln	23229
Emporia St	23231
Empress Ct	23233
W End Dr	23294
England Dr	23229
Englehart Way	23231
English Holly Cir	23294
English Horn Ct	23233
Ensley Ct & Pl	23233
Enterprise Pkwy	23294
Environmental Pkwy	23231
Epson Downs Ct & Dr	23229
Erin Crescent St	23231
N & S Erlwood Ct & Rd	23229
Erma Ln	23229
Erskine St	23228
Esmont Rd	23228
Essex Ave	23229
Essex Rd	23228
Etna Cir	23231
Eubank Rd	23231
Eugene Dr	23231
Eunice Ct & Dr	23228
Evansdale Rd	23233
N & S Eversham Ct & Rd	23294
Everville Dr	23294
Fairbury Rd	23075
Fairfield Green Ct, Pl & Rd	23238
Fairhaven Ln	23228
Fairlake Ct, Ln & Pl	23294
Fairway Ave	23228
Fairwind Cir	23238
Fairystone Ct & Rd	23075
Falcon Creek Ct & Dr	23231
N & S Falconbridge Ct & Dr	23238
Fallon Ln	23231
Falstaff Ct	23238
Fanwood Ct & Pl	23233
Fargo Rd	23229
Farmer Ct	23233
Farmington Ct & Dr	23229
Farnwood Dr	23229
Farrand Dr & St	23231
Farrell Ct	23228
Favero Ct & Rd	23233
Fawcett Ln	23231
Fawn Ln	23229
Fawnwick Dr	23231
Felspar Dr	23231
Fenrother Ct	23228
Fenton St	23231
Fergus Blvd	23231
N & S Fern Ave	23075
Fern Church Ct	23294
Fernhill Ave	23228
Fernwood Ct & St	23228
Fife Ct	23075
Finborough Ct	23228
Finlay St	23231
Finnegan Ct	23228
Finsbury Rd	23228
First Colonial Ct & Pkwy	23231
First Landing Ct	23231
Fishduck Ct & Pl	23231
Fisher Crest Ln	23231
Fisherton Dr	23233
Fisk Rd	23229
Fitzgerald Ct	23228
Flagstaff Ln	23228
Flanders Rd	23229
Flannagan Ct	23228
Flat Branch Ct & Dr	23233
Fleet Ave	23228
Flintwood Dr	23238
Flippen Ct	23228
Fon Du Lac Rd	23229
Fordson Rd	23229
Fordson Farm Ln	23231
Forest Ave	23229
Forest Cove Dr	23228
Forest Edge Ct	23294
Forest Glen Rd	23228
Forest Light Ct	23233
Forest Park Ct	23294
Forest Ridge Ct	23229
Forest Run Dr	23228
Forestford Rd	23294
Forestway Dr	23238
Forge Rd	23228
Fort Alvis Ct, Ln & Way	23231
Fort Gilmer Ct, Dr & Way	23231
Fort King Rd	23229
Fortress Ct & Pl	23231
Fortune Rd	23294
Fountain Ave	23228
Fountain Ln	23229
Four Mile Run Dr & Pkwy	23231
Fourdale Ln	23231
Fox Downs Ct, Dr & Pl	23231
Fox Meadow Dr	23233
Fox Rest Dr	23228
Foxborough Dr	23238
Foxbush Ct	23233
Foxcreek Cir	23238
Foxcroft Rd	23229
Foxfield Cir, Ct, Pl & Ter	23233
Foxfire Cir	23238
Foxhall Ln	23228
Foxlawn Ct	23233
Foxmere Dr	23238
Foxmoore Ave & Ct	23233
Francis Drake Ct & Dr	23233
Francisco Rd	23229
Francistown Rd	23294
Frankham Rd	23294
Franklin Farms Dr	23229
Fraser Ct	23233
Freeless St	23231
Freeport Pl	23233
Freestone Ave	23229
French Horn Ct	23233
Freshet Ct	23231
Frisco Dr	23233
Front Royal Dr	23228
Fruehauf Rd	23228
Fundy Bay Ct	23233
Fussells Ridge Dr	23231
Futura Ave	23231
Galax Rd	23228
Galaxie Cir & Rd	23228
Gallant Dr	23229
Galway Ln	23228
Gardenia Dr	23228
Gardiner Rd	23229
Garinger Ct	23233
Garland Estates Ct	23229
Garron Point Ct	23228
Garvey Ct	23228
Garyson Ln	23231
Gaskins Rd	
1100-2600	23238
2602-2698	23238
3800-3999	23233
N Gaskins Rd	23238
S Gaskins Rd	23238
Gaslight Ct, Dr, Pl & Ter	23229
Gately Dr	23238
Gateway E	23229
Gatewood Ave	23075
Gay Ave	23231
Gaylin Ridge Ln	23233
Gaylord Rd	23229
Gaymont Rd	23229
Gayton Rd	
8701-8797	23229
8799-9599	23229
9600-12499	23238
13000-13099	23233
N Gayton Rd	23233
Gayton Bluffs Ct & Ln	23233
Gayton Centre Dr	23238
Gayton Downs Ct	23233
Gayton Grove Ct & Rd	23233
Gayton Hills Ln	23233
Gayton Manor Pl	23233
Gayton Meadows Pl & Ter	23233
Gayton Oaks Ct	23229
Gayton Station Blvd	23233
Geffert Dr	23231
Georges Bluff Rd	23229
Gibbs Ln	23231
Gibraltar Dr	23228
Gibsons Landing Dr	23233
Gilchrist Ave, Ct & Pl	23231
Gildenfield Ct	23294
Gill Dale Rd	23231
Gillespie Ave	23228
Gillis Ct & St	23228
Giltspur Rd	23238
Ginger Way Ct & Dr	23229
Ginter St	23228
Girard Ave	23229
Glades End Ln	23233
Gladewater Ct & Rd	23294
Glastonbury Dr, Pl & Trce	23233
Glazebrook Ave	23228
Glebe Rd	23229
Glen Pkwy	23229
Glen Alden Dr	23231
Glen Eagles Dr	23233
Glen Gary Cir, Ct, Dr & Pl	23233
Glen Hollow Ct	23233
Glen Point Cir	23233
Glen Willow Cir	23238
E & W Glenbrooke Cir	23229
Glendale Dr	23229
Glendale Acres Pl	23231
Glendale Estates Ct & Dr	23231
Glendale Woods Dr, Pkwy & Xing	23231
Glenfinnian Dr	23231
E & W Glenkirk Ct & Rd	23233
Glenmore Rd	23229
Glenside Dr	23228
Glenstone Pl	23233
Glenwood St	23228
Gobbler Ct	23231
Golden Way Ct	23294
Goldeneye Ct & Ln	23231
Goldenrod Ct	23231
Goldthread Ct & Ln	23228
Golf Ln	23228
Golfview Ave	23228
Goneway Dr	23238
Goodwick Sq	23238
Gorman Rd	23231
Graham Meadows Ct, Dr & Pl	23233
Grainmill Ct	23233
Grand Ledge Ct	23231
Grand Oaks Dr, Pl & Ter	23233
Grande Ct & Dr	23229
Granger Rd	23229
Grants Cir	23238
Granville Ave	23231
Grassmount Ct & Ln	23228
Grattan Rd	23229
Grayson Hill Way	23229
Greatwood Dr	23231
Green St	23075
Green Mount Rd	23238
Green Run Ct & Dr	23228
Greenaire Pl	23233
Greencourt Rd	23228
Greendale Rd	23228
Greene Ridge Rd	23229
Greenfield Ct	23233
Greenford Dr	23294
Greengate Dr	23229
Greenhill Ct	23294
Greenhurst Dr	23229
Greentree Dr	23229
Greenview Dr	23231
Greenway Ave	23228
Greenwing Ln & Pl	23231
Gregg Rd	23231
Grelangs Rd	23294
Grenadier Ct	23238

Grenoble Rd 23294
Gresham Ave 23228
Grey Forge Pl 23233
Grey Rock Ln 23231
Greybattery Pl 23231
Greycliff Rd 23294
Greystone East Cir 23229
Greystone West Cir 23229
Grigg St 23231
Grinn Ct 23231
N & S Grove Ave 23075
Grove Gate Ct & Ln 23233
Grumman Dr 23229
Gunby Dr 23229
Gunston Rd 23294
Gurley Rd 23294
Guyana Ct & Dr 23233
Gwendolyn Ave 23231
Gwinnett Rd 23229
Habersham Dr 23231
Habwood Ln 23238
Hackamore Ln 23233
Hagen Dr 23233
Halbrooke Ct & Pl 23233
Hampshire Rd 23229
Hampton Ridge Ct 23229
Hampton Woods Dr 23233
Hanford Dr 23229
Harborough Ct, Pl, Rd &
Way 23238
Harbour Ct 23233
Harcourt Ln, Pl & Ter 23233
Hardings Trace Ct, Ln, Pl
& Way 23233
Hare Rd 23231
Harewood Ln 23231
Harmony Ave 23231
Harmony Woods Way 23229
Harness Pl 23231
Harpers Ferry Ct 23228
Harpoon Ct 23294
Harrison Ave 23228
Hart St 23075
Hatcher St 23231
Haupts Ln 23231
Havenwood Dr 23238
Haviland Dr 23229
Hawkesbury Ct 23233
Hawkins Rd 23228
Hawkshead Rd 23231
Hazel Tree Ct & Dr 23233
Hearthglow Ct & Ln 23238
Hearthrock Ct 23233
Heather Cir 23075
Heather Ridge Ct &
Dr 23231
Heather Spring Dr 23238
Heathfield Rd 23229
Heavenly Valley Dr 23231
Heiber Ct 23233
Heisler Ave 23228
Helmsdale Dr 23238
Henrico Ave 23229
Henrico Arms Pl & St 23231
Hepler Rd 23229
Heritage Hill Cir & Dr 23238
Herman St 23231
Hermitage Rd 23228
Hermitage Trace Cir &
Ct 23228
Herndon Rd 23229
Herringbone Ct & Pl 23233
Hibiscus Ct & Dr 23075
Hickory Ave 23231
Hickory Creek Cir, Ct,
Dr, Pl & Ter 23294
Hickory Ridge Way 23228
Hickoryridge Rd 23238
Hidden Oaks Ct, Ln &
Pl 23233
Hideaway Ln 23231
Higginbotham Pl 23229
Highfield Rd 23229
Highland Dr 23075
Highland Rd 23229
E Highland Rd 23229

Hilbingdon Rd 23238
Hill Cir 23229
Hill Dr 23228
N Hill Dr 23228
Hillaire Ln 23229
Hillbrook Ave 23231
Hillcrest Ave 23075
Hillcrest Rd 23231
Hillcroft Dr 23238
Hillery Ct 23228
Hillgate Ct & Ln 23233
Hilliard Rd 23228
Hillsboro Dr 23238
Hillsdale Dr 23229
Hillside Ave 23229
Hillview Ave 23229
Hines Pl & Rd 23231
Hitchcock Ave 23075
Hitchin Dr 23238
Hob Nob Hl 23231
Hobart Rd 23228
Hodder Ln 23075
Hoke Brady Rd 23231
Holbrook Dr 23229
Holland St 23231
Hollandale Rd 23238
Hollins Rd 23229
Hollins Glen Ct 23228
N & S Holly Ave 23075
Holly Hill Rd 23229
Hollybrook Ave 23294
Hollyhock Ct & Pl 23233
Hollyport Rd 23229
Holmbank Ct & Ln 23233
Holmes Ave 23229
Holt Dr 23228
Homestead Ln 23238
Homeview Dr 23294
Honey Grove Dr 23229
Honeysuckle Ct 23075
Honor Dr 23228
Hooper Rd 23228
Horncastle Pl 23233
Horrigan Ct 23294
Horselydown Ct & Ln 23233
Horsepen Rd 23229
Horseshoe Curv 23228
Horsley Dr 23233
Hounds Way 23231
Houndstooth Ct &
Way 23233
Hudgins Rd 23228
Hudson Dr 23229
Huneycutt Dr 23238
Hungary Rd
400-2999 23228
8901-8997 23294
8999-9199 23294
Hungary Creek Ln 23228
Hungary Glen Ter 23294
Hungary Spring Ct 23294
Hungary Spring Rd
2201-2397 23294
2399-2799 23294
2800-9699 23228
Hunt Club Ln 23228
Huntcliff Ct 23294
Hunter Green Ct 23294
Hunters Knoll Dr 23231
Hunters Meadow Dr &
Pl 23231
Huntmaster Ct & Ln 23233
Huntsmoor Dr 23233
Huntsteed Ct & Way 23233
Huntwick Ct 23233
Huron Ave 23294
Hyde Ln 23229
Hyner Cir & Ct 23231
Idlebrook Ct & Dr 23238
Impala Dr & Pl 23228
Imperial Dr 23229
Indarado Rd 23229
Independence Ct 23238
Independence Park Dr 23233
Indian Trl 23231
Indianola Dr 23228

Indigo Run Dr 23233
Inez Rd 23229
Ingallston Rd 23233
Ingleside Ave 23228
Inglewood St 23228
Inman Ave 23231
International Trade Ct &
Dr 23231
Ireton Rd 23228
Irisdale Ave 23228
Irving Ln 23229
Islandview Ct & Dr 23233
Ivory Ct & Ter 23233
N & S Ivy Ave 23075
Ivy Cliffs Ct 23075
Ivy Heights Ln 23075
Ivy Home Ct, Pl & Ter 23233
Ivyglen Ct & Dr 23233
Ivystone Ct & Dr 23238
Jack Burd Ln 23294
Jahodi Ct, Ln & Pl 23231
James St 23231
James And Cheryl Ln 23231
N James Estates Dr 23231
James River Golfcourse
Rd 23238
Jan Rd 23231
January Ct, Dr & Way 23238
Janway Rd 23228
Jarwin Ln 23231
Jennell Crescent Ct 23231
Jennings Rd 23075
E & W Jerald St 23075
Jerome Rd 23228
Jesse Senior Dr 23229
Jewel Park Ln 23233
Jewett Dr 23228
Jockey Ct & Trce 23231
John Rolfe Pkwy
1500-2098 23238
2100-2200 23233
2202-2398 23233
Joi Cir & Dr 23228
Jones Oak Grove Ln 23231
Jonquill Dr 23238
Joppa Ct & Pl 23233
Julian Rd 23229
Junior Dr 23075
N Juniper Ave 23075
Kalark Ct 23231
Kalb Rd 23229
N & S Kalmia Ave &
Pl 23075
Kamankeag Rd 23229
Kambis Dr 23231
Kanawha Dr 23229
Kara Dr 23231
Karem St 23294
Kavanagh Ct 23228
Keats Rd 23229
Keeney Ct 23238
Keller Rd 23229
Kelly Ridge Rd 23233
Kemp Ave & St 23231
Kenbridge St 23231
Kendyl Knoll Ln 23231
Kenmore Rd 23228
Kennebrook Ct 23294
Kennedy Rd 23233
Kenneth Dr 23228
Kent St 23228
Kenwood Ave 23228
Kerry Ln 23231
Ketelby Rd 23294
Kevin Dr 23229
Kexby Rd 23228
Kidwelly Ln 23231
Kiftsgate Ct 23229
Kilburn Cir 23233
Kilchurn Ct 23231
Kilcolman Dr 23228
Kilgore St 23231
Kilmarnock Dr 23229
Kilpeck Ct & Dr 23294
Kilrush Ct 23228
Kimbershell Pl 23229

Kimway Dr 23228
King Eider Dr 23231
Kings Dr 23231
Kings Bishop Rd 23231
Kings Grant Ct & Dr 23233
Kings Hill Rd 23231
Kings Passage Dr 23238
Kingsbridge Rd 23238
Kingsbrook Dr 23238
Kingsbury Ct 23233
Kingsdown Ct 23229
Kingsland Rd 23231
Kingsland Pointe Dr 23231
Kingsthorpe Ter 23229
Kingston Rd 23229
Kinloch Ct & Ln 23231
Kinsale Cir & Ct 23228
Kinvan Rd 23231
Kira Ct 23233
Kirkwood St 23228
Klarey Ct 23228
Kleindale Dr & Pl 23233
Klockner Dr 23231
Knights Gate Ct 23238
Knockadoon Ct 23228
Knowland Cir 23229
Kraft Ct 23228
Kramer Dr 23075
Kukymuth Rd 23231
Lab Ct 23233
Labonte Ct 23231
Labrador Ct 23233
S Laburnum Ave 23231
Laclede Ave 23233
Lady Vixen Ct 23233
Lafayette Ave 23228
Laflin Pl 23228
Lake Ln 23229
Lake Loreine Ln 23233
Lake Meadow Pl 23238
Lakecrest Ct 23238
Lakefield Dr 23231
Lakefield Mews Ct, Dr &
Pl 23231
N Lakefront Dr 23294
Lakeland Cir, Ct, Dr, Pl
& Ter 23229
Lakeside Ave 23228
Lakewater Ct & Dr 23229
Lakeway Ct & Dr 23229
Lakewood Dr 23229
Lambay Ct 23228
Lammrich Rd 23231
Lampworth Cir, Ct, Pl,
Rd & Ter 23231
Lancaster Ln 23229
Landmark Rd 23228
Landon Rd 23294
Landsworth Ave 23228
E & W Langham Ct 23233
Langtree Dr 23233
Lanier Ave 23231
Lansdowne Rd 23229
Lanver Ln 23294
Larcom Ln 23229
Laredo Ct 23228
Largo Rd 23238
Larkwood Rd 23294
Lashley Ln 23238
Lateefa Ct 23233
Lauderdale Dr
1200-2499 23238
2500-4099 23233
Laurandrew Cir & Ct 23228
Laurel Hill Ln 23231
Laurel Pine Dr 23228
Laurel Village Dr 23228
Laurel Woods Ln 23233
Laurelton Ct & Pl 23228
Lawland Dr 23294
Lawndell Rd 23229
Lawnmeadow Ct & Dr 23233
Lawrence Ave 23228
Layne Ct 23233
Le Suer Rd 23229
Ledbury Rd 23229

Lee Ave & Ct 23075
Leeland Ct, Dr & Pl 23231
Leewal Ct 23238
Leffingwell Ct & Pl 23233
Leighton Ct 23238
Lemonwood Ct 23228
Lennox Rd 23228
Leonard Ave 23231
Leslie Ct & Ln 23228
Lester Ln 23229
Lexy Ct 23228
E & W Leyburn Ct 23228
Liberty Bell Ct 23238
Library Rd 23231
Lighthouse Ct 23294
Lilly Meadow Ct 23229
Lily Valley Farm Ln 23231
Linbrook Dr 23228
Lincoln Ave 23228
N Linden Ave 23075
Lindenshire Ln 23238
Lindsay Ct 23229
Lindsey Gabriel Dr 23231
Lisa Ln 23294
Little Acre Ln 23231
Little Brook Ln 23228
Little Buck Trl 23231
Little League Dr 23233
Little Margaret Ln 23075
Littlefox Dr 23233
Littleton Blvd 23228
Local St 23231
Locarno Ct 23231
Locbury Ln 23228
Lochaven Ave 23231
Lochwood Ct & Dr 23238
Lockport Ct, Pl, Ter &
Way 23233
Lockton Dr 23233
Lockwood Rd 23294
Locust St 23228
Locust Hill Rd 23238
Locustdale Dr 23228
Locustgrove Ct & Rd 23238
Logan Estates Run 23233
Logwood Cir 23238
Lomas Ct 23229
Loncroft Rd 23238
London Rd 23233
Lonepine Rd 23294
Long St 23231
Long Bridge Rd 23231
Longboat Ct 23294
Longford Dr 23228
Longleaf Dr 23294
Longstreet Ave 23075
Longview Landing Ct &
Dr 23233
Longwood Rd 23229
Loreines Landing Ct, Ln
& Ter 23233
Lorenas Pl 23231
Lorraine Station Rd 23238
Lost Country Ln 23231
Lothbury Ln 23238
Loudon St 23231
Louisa St 23231
Lourdes Rd 23228
Lous Lore Ln 23231
Loveridge Ct 23294
Lovey Ct & Ln 23231
Lower Ralston Ct 23229
Lucas Rd 23228
Lucerne Ln 23229
Lucie Ln 23238
Lucy Long Ln 23231
Ludlow Rd 23231
Ludton Ct 23294
Lullington Dr 23238
Lundie Ln 23231
Lupine Rd 23228
Lurgan Pl 23228
Luscombe Ln 23228
Luther Rd 23075
Lycoming Rd 23229
Lydell Dr 23228

Lynchell Pl 23238
Lyndonway Dr 23229
Lynn Ave 23294
Macallan Pkwy 23231
Macie Dr 23228
Macilroy Ct 23228
Macon Dr 23228
Madeline Ct 23231
Madison Ln 23228
Mae St 23075
Maelee Mews 23228
Maida Ct 23233
Main Sail Ct 23233
Mainmast Ct 23294
Maintenance Way 23231
Majestic Way 23231
Maji Dr 23228
Mallards Ct & Xing 23233
Mallicotte Ct, Ln & Pl 23231
Malvern Hill Ln 23231
Manlyn Rd 23229
Mansfield Woods Dr 23231
Maple Creek Ct 23294
Maple Run Dr & Ln 23228
Maple Tree Ct 23228
N Mapleleaf Ave 23075
Mapleton Cir, Ct & Rd 23229
Mapleview Ave 23294
Mapleway Rd 23229
Maplewood Rd 23228
Mara Dr 23238
Marble Hill Dr 23238
Marcliff Ct 23228
Marcuse Ave 23228
Maremont Cir, Ct, Dr &
Pl 23238
Margaret Ave 23228
Marianna Rd 23231
Mark Lawn Dr 23229
Markham Ct 23233
Marlborough Ter 23229
Marleigh Ct 23231
Marnelan Dr & Pl 23233
Marney Ct 23229
Marquis Ter 23238
Marroit Rd 23229
Martin St 23228
Mary Washington St 23075
Marywood Ln 23229
Masonic Ln 23231
Matilda Cv 23294
Matterhorn Dr 23228
Maybeury Dr 23229
Mayfair Ave 23228
Mayland Ct 23233
Mayland Dr
7500-9799 23294
9800-9999 23233
Mays Dr 23231
Maywood Rd 23229
Mccabes Grant Ct &
Ter 23233
Mcclary Dr 23231
Mccoul St 23231
Mcgill St 23231
Mcintyre Ct, St & Way 23233
Mclean Ct & St 23231
Meadbrook Ct & Pl 23238
Meadowcrest Rd 23238
Meadowgreen Ct &
Rd 23294
Meadowlark Ct 23231
Meadowlark Ln 23228
Meadowview Rd 23294
Media Park Rd 23231
Meghans Bay Ct 23233
Meherrin Rd 23229
Melaway Dr 23228
Melissie Ct 23238
Melwood Ln 23229
Mendota Dr 23229
Merle St 23231
Merrick Rd 23294
Messer Rd 23231
Michael Ave 23228
Michael Rd 23229

Michaels Rd 23229
Michaux Ln 23229
Michelle Pl 23229
Middle Quarter Ct &
Ln 23238
Middle Ridge Way 23233
Middleberry Ct & Dr 23231
Middleham Ct 23231
Midvale Rd 23229
N Midview Rd 23231
Midway Rd 23229
Migration Ct & Dr 23231
Milbank Rd 23229
Milbranch Ct & Pl 23233
Milbrier Pl 23233
Milbury Run St 23233
Milford Rd 23229
Milhaven Ct, Dr & Sq 23238
Milhouse Ln 23231
Mill Rd 23231
Milledge Ct 23233
Miller Rd 23231
Millers Ct & Ln 23231
Millers Crossing Trl 23231
Millers Glen Ln 23231
Millington Ct, Dr & Ln 23238
Millrun Pl 23238
Millstone Rd 23228
Millstream Dr & Ln 23228
Millwheel Ln & Way 23228
Milshire Ct & Pl 23233
Milwright Dr 23231
Minna Dr 23229
Minter Ave 23228
Misty Cove Ct 23233
Misty Dawn Ct 23238
Mizar Rd 23231
Monahan Rd 23231
Monarch Cres 23228
Monarda Rd 23229
Moncure Ave 23231
Monida Rd 23294
Monimia Ct 23238
W Monmouth Ct, Dr &
Pl 23238
Montfort Loop 23294
Montpelier St 23231
Moonwind Pl 23238
Moorefield Rd 23229
N & S Mooreland Ct, Pt
& Rd 23229
Moorgate Rd 23238
Morgan Ln 23231
Morgan Run Rd 23233
Mormac Rd 23233
Mornell St 23075
Morrison Ave 23228
Morshedi Ct 23238
Moss Ct 23231
Mosswood Rd 23231
Mountainbrook Ct &
Dr 23233
Muldoon Ct 23228
Mulford Rd 23231
N Mullens Ln 23075
Mundy Ct & Dr 23228
Murdoch Rd 23229
Myradare Dr 23229
Myrtle Grove St 23228
Nalla Rd 23229
Naman Rd 23229
Nanassas Ct 23231
Nandina Dr 23228
Nandun Rd 23231
Narrowridge Ct & Rd 23231
Narvik Ct 23233
Naselle Ln 23228
Nassington Ct 23229
Natalie Ct 23294
National St 23231
Navarre Ct 23238
Navion St 23228
Needham Ct 23231
Nelson St 23228
Nesslewood Dr & Rd 23229
Nettleham Ct 23233

Nettlestone Ct 23233
Neuson Ct 23229
N New Ave 23075
New Berne Rd 23228
New Harvest Dr & Rd 23231
New Market Rd 23231
New Market Heights Ln 23231
New Market Village Blvd & Pkwy 23231
New Orleans St 23231
New Osborne Tpke 23231
New Point Dr 23233
New Scott Ln 23231
New Settlement Dr 23231
Newhall Rd 23229
Newlands Ave & Ct 23233
Newman Rd 23231
Newross Ct 23228
N & S Newton Cir 23231
E & W Nine Mile Rd 23075
Nolte Dr 23238
Nomas Ln 23238
Norman Ave 23228
Normandy Dr 23229
Northbourne Ct 23228
Northbury Ave & Ct 23231
Northglen Ln 23238
Northlake Ct, Dr & Pl 23233
Northside Ave 23228
Northwind Ct, Dr & Pl 23233
Nortonia Rd 23229
Norwick Cir & Rd 23229
Notre Dame Dr 23228
November Ave 23231
Nutfield Ct 23231
Nuthall Pl 23231
Nutley Ct 23233
N & S Oak Ave 23075
Oak Back Ct 23231
Oak Bay Ct & Ln 23233
Oak Front Ct 23231
S Oak Grove Dr 23228
Oak Middle Ct 23231
Oak Place Blvd 23231
Oak Point Ct & Ln 23233
Oak Ridge St 23294
Oak Run Ln 23228
Oak Springs Ct 23229
Oakano Dr 23231
Oakcroft Dr 23229
Oaken Walk Pl 23233
Oakham Ct 23231
Oakhampton Ct, Pl & Ter 23233
Oakington Dr 23231
Oakland Ave 23228
Oakland Rd 23231
Oakland Chase Pkwy & Pl 23231
Oakland Trace Ct 23231
Oakleigh Ct 23233
Oakley Pointe Dr, Ter & Way 23233
Oakleys Ln
4391-4399 23075
4401-4497 23231
4499-4999 23231
Oakmere Ct 23231
Oakmont Dr 23228
Oakridge Ave 23075
Oakvale St 23231
Oakview Ave 23228
Oakway Ct, Dr & Pl 23233
Oakwood Ln 23228
Obannon Ct 23228
Ocala Rd 23229
Oceana Ct 23238
Oconnor Ct 23228
Odendron Ct 23233
Odonnell Ct 23228
Ogden Ave 23294
Ohl St 23231
Okeith Ct 23228
Old Bridge Ln 23229
Old Britton Rd 23231

Old Bronze Rd 23231
Old Brookewood Ct & Way 23233
Old Charles City Rd 23231
Old Club Trce 23238
Old Coach Ct & Ln 23238
Old Coleman Rd 23231
Old Compton Rd 23238
Old Country Trce 23238
Old Cox Rd 23233
Old Dell Trce 23238
Old Gaskins Rd 23238
Old Hearth Ct 23233
Old Hilliard Rd 23228
Old Kingsland Rd 23231
Old Main St 23231
Old Mayland Ct, Pl, Rd & Way 23294
Old Nelson Hill Ave 23229
Old Oak Rd 23229
Old Oakland Rd 23231
Old Oakleys Ln 23231
Old Osborne Tpke 23231
Old Parham Rd 23294
Old Point Dr 23233
Old Prescott Ct, Pl & Rd 23238
Old Pump Rd 23233
Old Rebel Trl 23231
Old Staples Mill Rd 23228
Old Three Chopt Rd 23233
Old Wick Ln 23231
Olde West Ct 23228
Oldhouse Dr 23238
Omega Rd 23228
Opal Ave 23228
Oregon Ave 23231
Orion Ct & Rd 23231
Orkney Rd 23238
Ormond Dr 23233
Osborne Lndg & Tpke 23231
Otlyn Pl 23238
Overhill Rd 23229
Overland Dr 23231
Overlook Rd 23229
Overton Rd 23228
Pachight 23238
Pachight Dr 23233
Paigefield Ct 23229
Paigley Pl 23229
Palace Ct & Way 23238
Palm Grove Ter 23228
Palmer Dr 23228
Palmer Place Ct 23238
Pamela Dr 23229
Panorama Dr 23229
Paragon Dr 23228
Parchment Cir, Ct & Ln 23233
E Parham Rd
900-4399 23228
7500-7598 23294
7600-7899 23294
N Parham Rd
400-2499 23229
2600-2606 23294
2608-3499 23294
Paris Dr 23229
Paris Ridge Ln 23229
Park Ave 23231
Parkline Dr 23229
Parkshire Ln 23233
Parkside Ave 23228
Parma Rd 23229
Parrish St 23231
Pathfinder Cir, Ct & Pl 23294
Patricia Rd 23231
Patterson Ave
7100-9699 23229
10000-10600 23238
10509-10509 23242
10601-11399 23238
10602-11398 23238
Pavilion Dr 23229
Pavlovich Ln 23231
Peadwal Rd 23228

Pearces Creek Ln 23231
Pebblebrook Pl 23238
Pegasi Rd 23231
Pell St 23233
Pellington Pl 23294
Pemberton Rd
1400-2199 23238
2200-3599 23233
Pemberton Creek Ct & Dr 23233
Pemberton Crossing Ct & Dr 23294
Pendragon Trl 23231
Penick Rd 23228
Penniman Ct, Pl & Ter 23228
Pennington Rd 23294
Pennmardel Ct & Ln 23233
Pennsbury Pl 23294
Penola Dr 23229
Penquin Rd 23229
Pepperhill Ct & Ln 23238
Peppertree Dr 23238
Pepperwood Ct 23228
Pershing Ave 23228
Persimmon Ct 23233
Persimmon Trek 23233
Peyton St 23228
Pheasant Chase Dr & Pl 23231
Pheasant Hollow Dr 23231
Phillips Woods Dr 23231
Philmont Dr 23294
Piccadilly Rd 23231
Pickett River Dr 23231
Pickwick Ln 23231
Pillary Ct 23238
N Pine Ave 23075
Pine Cliff Ter 23228
Pine Dell Ave 23294
Pine Edge Ln 23229
Pine Grove Dr 23294
Pine Shadow Ct & Dr 23238
Pine Top Ct & Dr 23294
Pine Trails Ct 23294
Pineberry Ct 23229
Pinebluff Dr 23229
Pinefields Ct, Dr & Pl 23231
Pinefrost Ct & Rd 23231
Pinehill Dr 23228
Pinehurst Rd 23228
Pinetree Rd 23229
Pinewood Ct & Dr 23238
Pinyon Rd 23229
Plain View Rd 23238
Pleanina Rd 23231
Pleasant St 23075
Pleasant Lake Ct, Dr, Pl & Ter 23233
Pleasant Run Ct 23233
Pleasant Run Dr
1-2599 23238
2600-2799 23233
Pleasant Run Ter 23233
Plum Shade Ct 23233
Poates Dr 23228
Pocahontas Pkwy 23231
Point Grey Rd 23233
Point Pleasant Rd 23228
Pomeroy Ct 23228
Pond View Ln 23231
Poole Ct 23228
Poplar Grn 23238
Poplar Forest Ct 23238
Poplar Forest Dr
12200-12399 23238
12400-12498 23233
12401-12499 23238
12500-12899 23233
Poplar Hill Ct 23229
Poplar Spring Rd 23231
Poplar Stand Ct 23228
Poppy Ct 23294
Pops Ln 23231
Port View Ct 23233
Portadown Ct 23228
Portwest Ct & Ter 23238

Potomac Hunt Ln 23233
Powderhorn Dr 23231
Prairieview Ct 23228
Premier Dr 23229
Presidential Dr 23228
Presquile Rd 23231
Prestondale Ave 23294
Prestwick Cir, Ct & Rd 23294
Prince Rd 23228
Prince Regent Pl 23238
Princess Rd 23228
Priscilla Ct 23233
Probst St 23231
Produce Rd 23231
Professor Ct 23228
Prospect Ave 23228
Prosperity Ter 23231
Province Dr 23229
Pump Rd
900-2199 23238
2200-3599 23233
Purcell Rd 23228
Putney Rd 23228
Quail Covey Rd 23238
Quarry Lake Dr 23233
Quarter Creek Cir, Ct & Ln 23294
Quarter Mill Rd 23294
Quarterdeck Ct 23294
Quarterpath Pl 23233
Queens Ct 23231
Queens Crosse Ct 23238
Queens Point Dr 23238
Queensland Dr 23294
Queensmere Pl 23294
Quietwood Ct 23238
Quinby Ct 23075
N Quince Ave 23075
Quincy Maie Dr 23231
Quioccasin Ct 23229
Quioccasin Rd
1-9399 23229
9400-9699 23238
Rainbow Dr 23229
Rainbow Spring Ct 23294
Rainbrook Dr 23238
Raintree Dr 23238
Raintree Commons Ct, Dr & Ln 23238
Raleigh Rd 23231
Raleigh Manor Ct, Pl & Rd 23229
Ralston Rd 23229
Rambler Dr 23228
Ramsbury Ct & Way 23238
Ramsey Ct 23228
Ranch Dr 23229
Ranco Rd 23228
Randall Ave 23231
Random Winds Ct 23238
Raspberry Patch Ln 23231
Raven Rock Ct, Ln & Rd 23229
Ravenscraig Cres 23231
Ravenstone Ct 23238
Rawlings Ct & St 23231
Raymond Ave & Ct 23228
E & W Read St 23075
Reagan Rd 23228
Reaping Ct 23231
Rearden Rd 23229
Recreation Rd 23231
Red Fox Ln 23228
Red Hawk Rd 23229
Red Hill Club Ct 23231
Red Maple Ln 23238
Red Wing Ln 23231
Redstone Dr 23294
Regal Dr 23075
Regency Woods Rd 23238
Regents Crosse Ln 23238
Regirer Pl 23229
Reilly St 23231
Reinland Dr 23294
Remington Ct & Rd 23231
Renard Ter 23231

Renee Ct & Ln 23075
Renmark Rd 23229
Repp Cir, Ct & St 23075
Retrievers Ridge Rd 23233
Rexford Rd 23229
Reynard Ct & Ln 23233
Rhonda Dr 23229
Richie Ave 23229
Richneil Rd 23231
Rickde Ct 23294
Ridge Rd 23229
Ridge Meadow Pl 23238
Ridge Stone Ct 23238
Ridge Top Rd 23229
Ridgecrest Dr 23229
Ridgefield Pkwy 23233
Ridgefield Rd 23229
Ridgefield Green Pl & Way 23233
Ridgehaven Rd 23229
Ridgeley Ln 23229
Ridgemere Ct & Dr 23233
Ridgeview Dr 23229
Rio Grande Rd 23229
Rio Hondo Cir 23229
Rivendell Ct 23231
Rivenmore Cir 23231
River Rd
6200-9699 23229
9700-10099 23238
River Bend Rd 23231
River Bend Estates Ct & Dr 23231
River Court Ln 23238
River Trace Ct 23229
Riverchase Ct, Dr & Pl 23233
Rivermont Dr 23229
Riverwood Dr 23229
Roaringbrook Ct & Dr 23233
Roberts Creek Ct 23228
Robin Grey Ln 23231
Robins Rd 23231
Robins Nest Ct 23238
Robson Ct, Pl & St 23233
Rochampton Sq 23238
Rock Creek Rd 23229
Rock Garden Ln 23228
Rocketts Way 23231
Rockingham St 23231
Rockstone Ct & Pl 23238
Rockview Curv 23228
Rockwater Ter 23238
Rockwell Rd 23229
Rocky Branch Ln 23228
Rocky Creek Ln 23238
Rocky Hill Farm Dr 23231
Rocky Point Ct, Pkwy & Pl 23238
Rocliffe Rd 23238
Rolando Dr 23229
Rolfe Way 23238
Rolfield Way 23238
Rolling Hills Dr 23229
Rollingrock Ct 23238
Rolridge Rd 23233
Roost Hill Ct 23231
Roscommon Ct 23228
N Rose Ave 23075
Rose Hill Rd 23229
Rosecroft Rd 23229
Roslyn Hills Dr 23229
Ross Rd 23229
Roswell Rd 23229
Rothland Dr 23294
Roundabout Rd 23231
Rounding Run 23238
Roundtree Rd 23294
Roxana Rd 23075
Royerton Ct & Dr 23228
Rudd Pl 23231
Ruddy Duck Ct & Dr 23231
Rudolph Ct, Rd & Ter 23294
Ruggles Pl & Rd 23229
Rumford Rd 23228

Running Cedar Cir & Ln 23229
W Runswick Dr 23238
Rupert Ct & Ln 23233
Rustling Cedar Ln 23231
Rutgers Ct, Dr & Ln 23233
Ruthland Rd 23228
Ryan Rd 23228
Ryandale Rd 23238
Ryerson Rd 23294
Sable Ct & Rd 23233
Saddlehorse Pl 23231
Saddleseat Ct & Pl 23233
Sage Ct & Dr 23233
Sagebrush Trl 23228
Salua Dr 23228
Salvo Dr 23231
Samara Dr 23231
San Juan Rd 23229
San Ramon 23231
Sancrest Rd 23238
Sanctuary Dr 23228
Sandalwood Dr 23229
Sanderling Ave 23075
Sandown Cir 23229
Sandy Bluff Ct, Dr & Pl 23233
Sandy Spring Cir, Ct & Way 23294
Sanford Dr 23228
Santa Anna Rd 23229
Santa Clara Dr 23229
Santa Rosa Rd 23229
Sarellen Rd 23231
Sargeant Ct 23228
Sawmill Rd 23229
Saxby Rd 23231
Schaaf Dr 23229
School Ave 23228
School House Rd 23231
Schooner Ct 23233
Seagull Ct 23294
Seahaven Ct & Dr 23233
Sebring Dr 23233
Second Ave 23228
Sedgemoor Dr 23228
Seldondale Ln 23229
Selkirk Ln 23228
Sentury Meadow Ct & Dr 23233
September Dr 23229
Settler Rd 23231
Settlers Ridge Ct 23231
Seven Hills Blvd 23231
Severn Rd 23229
Seymour Ter 23233
Shadow Ln 23229
Shadowbrook Ct & Dr 23231
Shadowood Ct 23228
Shady Branch Ct & Trl 23238
Shady Knoll Ct 23233
Shady Lake Ct & Pl 23233
Shady Tree Ct 23238
Shady Wood Ct 23233
Shaleigh Ln 23231
Shane Rd 23229
Shannon Green Ct 23228
Shannon Hill Rd 23229
Shari Dr 23228
Sharon Ln 23229
Sharon Shade Way 23231
Sharpsburg Ct 23228
Sharron Rd 23075
Shawn Ct 23075
Shecardee Ln 23228
Shelbourne Ct & Dr 23233
Sheldrake Ct 23238
Shelley Rd 23229
Shellfish Ct 23294
Shepton Cir & Dr 23294
Sherilyn Dr 23075
Sherry Ln 23231
Sheryl Rd 23229
Shewalt Cir & Dr 23228
Shirleydale Ave & Ct 23231
Sholey Rd 23231

Shore View Dr 23233
Shoveler Dr 23231
Shrader Ct 23228
Shrader Rd
7700-7799 23228
7800-8099 23294
8700-8799 23228
Shrewsbury Rd 23229
Sierra Rd 23229
Silent Wood Ct & Pl 23233
Silver Stream Ln 23294
Silverbrook Dr 23233
Silverbush Ct & Dr 23228
Silverlace Ct 23228
Silverspring Dr 23229
Silvertail Ct 23231
Singingwoods Ln 23233
Sinton Rd 23229
Sir Barry Ct & Dr 23229
Sir James Ct 23233
Sir Thomas Pl 23075
Sir Walter Dr 23229
Sir William Ct 23075
Sithean Way 23233
Skeet St 23294
Skipwith Rd
1100-1999 23229
2000-3299 23294
N Skipwith Rd 23294
Skipwith Green Cir 23294
Skirmish Run Ct & Dr 23228
Skylark Dr 23229
Skyview Ct & Dr 23229
Slaughter Rd 23228
Sleepy Duck Pl 23229
Sleepy Hollow Rd 23229
Sloman Pl 23238
Small Glen Ct 23229
Smith Ave 23228
Smithers Ct 23238
Snowcrest Ct 23233
Snughaven Rd 23229
Somerbrook Ct 23233
Sommersworth Ln 23233
Sommie Ln 23229
Somoa Dr 23228
Sorrento Pl 23238
South St 23075
Southall Ct 23233
Southbay Dr 23233
Southbury Ave & Ct 23231
Southern Ct 23075
Southside Ave 23228
Southwark Ln 23229
Sovereign Ct & Ln 23233
Spalding Dr 23229
Sparrow Dr 23229
Spencely Pl 23229
Spendthrift Cir, Ct & Dr 23294
Spider Dr 23228
Spilsby Ct 23229
Spinnaker Ct 23233
Spinning Wheel Way 23233
Split Oak Ln 23229
Splitwood Cir 23229
Spottswood Rd 23229
Spratley Rd 23228
Sprenkle Ct & Ln 23228
Spring Brook Ct & Ln 23229
Spring Oak Dr 23233
Spring Park Pl 23233
Spring Ridge Way 23229
Spring Tree Ct 23228
Springcrest Ln 23231
Springfield Rd 23294
Springrock Ct & Dr 23233
Springsberry Pl 23233
Springwater Dr & Ln 23228
Sprouse Dr 23231
N Spruce Ave 23075
Spruce View Ter 23228
Squire Ct 23228
St Albans Way 23229
St James Rd 23231
St Julians Ln 23238

St Marc Ln 23233
St Martins Ln & Trl 23294
St Michaels Ln 23229
St Pages Ln 23233
Stanberry Dr 23238
Stancraft Way 23231
Standish Ln 23229
Stansfield Ct 23231
Stanton Way 23238
Staples Mill Rd 23228
Starling Cir 23229
Starling Ct 23229
Starling Dr
800-2000 23229
2000-2000 23255
2000-2000 23294
Starwood Dr 23229
Statler Rd 23231
Steam Brewery Ct 23231
Stembridge Ct 23238
Sterlingwood Ct & Trce 23233
Stevens St 23231
Stillman Pkwy 23233
Stillwater Ln 23228
Stingray Ct 23233
Stockbridge Dr 23228
Stokesley Ct 23233
Stone Meadow Ct & Dr 23228
Stone Post Ter 23233
Stonebriar Ct, Ln & Pl 23233
Stoneheather Rd 23238
Stonehollow Rd 23238
Stoneleigh Rd 23228
Stoneman Ct & Rd 23228
Stonemark Ct 23238
Stonemeade Dr 23231
Stonemill Ct, Pl & Rd 23233
Stonequarter Ct & Rd 23238
Stoneridge Ln 23229
Stoney Ct 23233
Stoneycreek Ct & Dr 23238
Stony Force Dr 23228
Storrow Rd 23233
Strangford Ct & Pl 23233
Stratford Glen Dr 23233
Strath Rd 23231
Straw Bridge Chase E & W 23233
Strawhill Ct & Rd 23231
Strum Ct 23294
Stuart Hall Rd 23229
Suecla Ct & Dr 23231
Sulky Dr 23228
Sumac Ln 23229
Summer Ct & St 23075
Summer Stream Dr 23233
Summerest Ave 23231
Summerview Dr 23233
Summerwood Dr 23233
Summit Ct 23228
Summit Dr 23229
Summit Gayton Cir & Ct 23233
Summit Oak Ct 23228
Sunburst Rd 23294
Sundance Way 23294
Sunday Dr 23231
Sunderland Rd 23229
Sundial Ct 23294
Sunny Bank Dr 23228
Sunnybrook Rd 23294
Sunrise Ct & Rd 23233
Sunset Dr 23229
Surfscoter Ct 23231
Sussex Square Dr 23238
Sutton Pl 23233
Swanhollow Cir, Ct, Dr & Way 23233
Swansbury Dr 23238
Swartwout Ave 23228
Sweeney Cir 23231
Sweeney Landing Rd 23231
Sweet Creek Ct & Way 23233

Sweetbriar Rd 23229
Sweetwater Ln 23229
Swinging Bridge Dr 23233
Swinton Ln 23238
Swissvale Pl 23229
Switchgrass Ct 23294
Sycamore Ln 23228
Sycamore Crest Dr 23231
Sydclay Dr 23231
Sydnor Rd 23231
Taft Pl 23238
Talley Rd 23228
Tamarack Rd 23229
Tanager Rd 23228
Tanelorn Dr 23294
Tanfield Dr 23228
Tangle Dr 23228
Tanya Ave 23228
Tarheel Ter 23228
Tarrytown Dr 23229
Tartuffe Dr 23238
Tatton Park Cir 23229
Taymat Ct 23238
Teasdale Ct 23233
Tech Dr 23075
Templemore Ct 23238
Terrace Ave 23228
Terrapin Ct 23228
Terrell Dr 23229
Terrence Bay Ct 23233
Terry Ct & Dr 23228
Thacker Ln 23228
Thaddeus Dr 23233
Thalia Cres 23231
Thames Dr 23238
Thamesford Ct & Way 23233
Thicket Greene 23233
Thistle Rd 23238
Thistlebrook Ln & Pl 23294
Thistledown Dr 23233
Thom Rd 23229
Thomashire Ct 23229
Thor Dr 23229
Thornbury Ct, Dr & Pl 23233
Thornrose Ave 23228
Thorpe Ave 23228
Thousand Oaks Dr 23294
Three Chopt Ln 23233
Three Chopt Rd
7500-9999 23229
10000-12499 23233
Three Foxes Dr 23231
Three Sisters Ln 23228
Three Willows Ct 23294
Tide Ter 23231
Tilbury Ln 23229
Timber Ct & Rd 23228
Timber Mill Ln 23228
Timber Run Ln 23228
Timbercrest Ct & Ln 23238
Timbercross Cir, Ct & Pl 23233
Timberlake Ave 23228
Timberly Ct 23238
Timberly Waye 23238
Timbermead Ct & Rd 23238
Timberwood Pl 23294
Timken Dr 23229
Tina Dr 23075
Tingewood Ter 23233
Tobak Ct 23238
Tolliver Rd 23229
Tolman Rd 23229
Topaz Rd 23228
Topsham Rd 23229
Torno Dr 23228
Tottenham Ct & Pl 23233
Tournament Ln 23233
Towhee Ln 23231
Town Hall Ct & Dr 23231
Towne Center West Blvd 23233
Towngate Ct 23233
Townhouse Rd 23228
Townley Rd 23229
Township Blvd 23231

Tracewood Cir 23233
Tracy Ct 23238
Traditional Ct & Dr 23294
Trafalgar Park 23228
Trail Dr 23228
Trailing Ridge Ct & Rd 23231
Tree Ridge Ct, Pl & Rd 23231
Treetop Ln 23229
Trellis Ln 23075
Trellis Crossing Ln 23238
Trellis Green Cir 23233
Tresco Rd 23229
Trevvett Dr 23228
Tricia Pl 23233
Trickling Brook Ct & Dr 23228
Trimble Ct 23228
Trimmer Dr 23294
Trinity Ct 23233
Trinity Dr 23229
Trinity Pl 23233
Triple Notch Ct, Ter & Way 23233
Triple Oak Ct 23231
Trojan Ct 23294
Trowbridge Rd 23238
Tuckahoe Club Ct 23229
Tuckaway Ln 23229
Tuckernuck Dr 23294
Tudor Springs Ln 23231
Tumbleweed Cir 23228
Tunbridge Dr 23238
Tupelo Rd 23294
Turf Club Ct & Ln 23294
Turkey Island Rd 23231
Turnbull Ave 23229
Turner Rd 23231
Turner Forest Ct, Pl & Rd 23231
Turner Woods Ct & Rd 23231
Turret Ct 23231
Turtle Creek Dr 23233
Turtle Run Dr 23233
Tweed Ct & Rd 23228
Twin Lake Ct & Ln 23229
Twin Oak Dr 23228
Tyburn Ln 23238
Tyler Ln 23231
Tyverton Ct 23233
Union Grove Rd 23231
Union Jack Pl 23233
United Ct 23238
University Blvd, Ct, Dr & Pl 23229
University Park Blvd 23229
Upper Western Run Ln 23231
Urban Dr 23229
Uxbridge Ct 23294
Vale St 23228
Valentine Rd 23228
E & W Valley Dr 23229
Valley Wood Rd 23229
Valleybrook Dr 23233
Valleyfield Rd 23228
Van Ness Pl 23231
Vandover Rd 23229
Vanna Ln 23233
Vanta Rd 23294
Varann Rd 23231
Varina Rd 23231
Varina Chase Dr 23231
Varina On The James 23231
Varina Point Ln 23231
Varina Station Ct & Dr 23231
Varney Rd 23231
Vassar Rd 23229
Venetian Way 23229
Verna Ct & Dr 23228
Vernelle Ln 23229
Vernon Rd 23228
Verona Rd 23229
Viking Ln 23228
Villa Park Dr 23228

Village Field Dr & Pl 23231
Village Grove Rd 23238
Villageway Dr 23229
Vincennes Rd 23229
W Vine St 23075
Vintage Dr 23229
Virden Ct 23231
Virgil Ct, Dr & Ter 23231
Virginia Pine Ct 23228
Virginia Way Ct 23238
Vollmer Rd 23229
Voyager Dr 23294
Waco St 23294
Waddill Dr 23228
Wade Ct 23229
Wadeward Rd 23229
Wakefield Rd 23228
Walbrook Dr 23238
Waldo Ln 23228
Wales Dr 23075
Walkenhut Dr 23228
Walker Ave 23228
Wall Ave 23231
Wallaby Trce 23294
Wallo Rd 23231
Walnut Forest Ct 23231
Walnut Knoll Ln 23229
Walsh Dr 23231
Walsham Ct 23238
Walsing Dr 23229
Waltham Ct & Dr 23238
Walton Farms Ct & Dr 23294
Wanstead Ct 23238
Wanymala Rd 23229
Ware Rd 23229
Warfield Rd 23229
Warren View Rd 23233
Warrenton Cir & Dr 23229
Warriner Rd 23231
Warrington Ct 23233
Warwick Park Rd 23231
E, N & W Washington Ct & St 23075
Wasp Ln 23228
Water Birch Ct 23228
Waterbury Dr 23229
Waterfall Rd 23228
Waterford Dr 23229
Waterford Way E 23233
Waterford Way W 23233
Waterford Rhye Cir & Dr 23229
Waterford Way Pl 23233
Waterford Way East Ct 23233
Waterloo Ct 23229
Waterside Ct 23294
Waterville Ct 23233
Watlington Rd 23229
Waveny Rd 23229
Waycross Dr 23233
E & W Wayfare Ct 23238
Weather Vane Ct & Rd 23238
Webb Rd 23228
Webfoot Ct 23231
Wedgewood Ave 23228
Welborne Dr 23229
Weldon Dr 23229
Wellesley Terrace Cir, Ct & Ln 23233
Wellington Ridge Rd 23231
Wellington Woods Rd 23231
Welwyn Ct, Pl & Rd 23229
Wembly Rd 23229
Wendell Dr 23231
Wentworth Ave 23228
Westbluff Ct 23228
Westbriar Dr 23238
Westbury Dr 23229
Westcastle Dr 23238
Westdale Ln 23229
Westek Dr 23233
Western Run Rd 23231
Westerre Pkwy 23233
Westfield Rd 23229

Westgate Pkwy 23233
S Westham Grn & Pkwy 23229
Westham Station Rd 23229
Westham Woods Dr 23229
Westhampton Glen Ct, Dr & Pl 23238
Westmoor Cir & Dr 23229
Westney Rd 23231
Westoe Rd 23229
Weston Ct, Ln & Way 23238
Westover Ave 23231
Westridge Rd 23229
Westriver Dr 23229
Westshire Ct & Ln 23238
Westwick Rd 23238
Westwind Ct 23228
Wetherburn Ct 23233
Wetherly Dr 23229
Wexleigh Dr 23229
Wharfside Rd 23228
Wheat Ct & Ter 23233
Wheeler Rd 23229
Whispering Wood Ct & Dr 23233
Whistling Arrow Ct & Dr 23231
Whitaker Woods Rd 23238
Whiteclift Dr 23233
Whitegate Dr 23231
Whitehaven Ct & Pl 23231
Whitelake Dr 23231
Whitemont Dr 23294
Whitfield Ave 23231
Whitmore Ct & Dr 23229
Whitney Cir 23233
Wicker Dr 23231
Wicker Meadows Cir 23231
Wilber Cir 23228
Wildbriar Ln 23229
Wilde Lake Ct, Dr & Pl 23233
Wilderness Ct & Dr 23231
Wildflower Ter 23238
Wildwood St 23231
Wilkins St 23228
Willard Rd 23294
Willbrook Ct & Dr 23233
Williams St 23228
Williamsburg Rd 23231
Williamson Ct 23229
Willingham Rd 23238
Willis Ln 23228
Willis Church Rd 23231
E & W Willow St 23075
Willow Bend Pl 23233
Willow Cove Cir 23228
Willow Crossing Ter 23228
Willow Glen Ct & Ln 23228
Willow Leaf Ct & Pl 23228
Willow Pine Ct & Pl 23228
Willow Wind Cir 23238
Willowbrook Dr 23228
Willowick Ct, Ln & Pl 23238
Willowtree Dr 23229
Willpage Pl 23233
Willson Ct & Rd 23231
Willson Cove Ct 23231
Wilmecote Ave 23228
Wilson Ave 23228
Wilton Rd 23231
Wilton Farm Rd 23231
Wiltonshire Dr 23233
Wimberly Dr 23238
Wimgrow Rd 23233
Winchester St 23231
Winchester Green Ct & Dr 23233
Winchmere Ct 23294
Windbluff Ct & Dr 23238
Windingdale Dr 23233
Windingridge Cir, Ct, Dr, Pl & Way 23238
Windover Ct 23229
Windsong Ter 23238
Windsor Castle Way 23231

Windsordale Dr 23229
Windy Cove Cir & Ct 23294
Winesap Dr 23231
Winespring Pl 23233
Wingate St 23231
Winkler Rd 23294
Winnwood Rd 23228
Winthrop St 23231
Wishart Cir, Ct & Rd 23229
Wistar Ct 23294
Wistar Pl 23294
Wistar Rd 23228
Wistar St 23294
Wistar Village Dr 23228
Wolverine Dr 23228
Wolverton Dr 23294
Wood Rd 23229
Wood Creek Ct 23228
Wood Grove Cir 23238
E & W Wood Harbor Ct 23231
Wood Mill Ct & Dr 23231
Wood Run Blvd 23228
Wood Sorrel Ct & Dr 23229
Wood Thrush Cir 23231
Woodbaron Ct & Way 23233
Woodberry Rd 23229
Woodcrest Rd 23229
Woodcut Pl 23233
Woodhall Dr 23229
Woodhurst Rd 23238
Woodlake Dr 23294
Woodley Rd 23229
Woodlynne Pl 23233
Woodman Rd 23228
Woodmark Ct 23233
Woodpost Dr 23075
Woodrow Ter 23228
Woodside Ct, Mews & St 23231
Woodstream Dr 23238
Woodthorne Ct 23238
Wrva Rd 23231
Wykehurst Dr 23238
Wymerman Pl 23231
Wyndhurst Dr 23229
Wytheland Rd 23229
Yahley Mill Holw & Rd 23231
E & W Yardley Ct & Rd 23294
Yarnell Ct & Rd 23231
Yellow Tavern Ct 23228
Yellow Warbler Ln 23231
Yellow Wing Ct 23231
Yeomans Dr 23238
Yester Oaks Ln 23231
Yolanda Rd 23229
York Ave 23075
Zell Ln 23229
Ziontown Rd 23229

NUMBERED STREETS

All Street Addresses 23231

HERNDON VA

General Delivery 20170

POST OFFICE BOXES MAIN OFFICE STATIONS AND BRANCHES

Box No.s
1 - 1958 20172
2000 - 5000 20171
5001 - 5534 20172
5500 - 9000 20171
10810 - 10900 20172
77777 - 711620 20171

NAMED STREETS

Acorn Hollow Ln 20171

Acorn Hunt Pl 20171
Adams St 20170
Adele Garden Way 20170
Admiral Zumwalt Ln 20170
Aiken Pl 20170
Alabama Dr 20170
Alfred Mill Ct 20171
Allness Ln 20171
Alton Sq 20170
Amber Oaks Ct 20171
Amy Way 20171
Angeline Dr 20171
Anthem Ave 20170
Anvil Pl 20171
Apgar Pl 20170
Apple Barrel Ct 20171
Applegrove Ct & Ln 20171
April Way 20170
Arboroak Pl 20170
Archer Ct 20170
Arkansas Ave 20170
Armada St 20171
Arnsley Ct & Dr 20171
Artic Quill Rd 20170
Ashburn St 20170
Ashburton Ave 20171
Ashburton Manor Dr 20171
Ashdown Forest Dr 20171
Ashleigh Oaks Ct 20171
Ashnut Ln 20171
Aspen Dr 20170
Astoria Cir 20170
Asturian Ct 20171
Attorney Ct 20170
Austin Ln 20170
Autumn Pl 20170
Autumn Breeze Ct 20170
Autumn Crest Ct & Dr 20171
Autumn Hill Ct & Ln 20171
Autumnhaze Ct 20170
Avalon Bay Ln 20171
Avonmore Dr 20171
Awbrey Ct 20171
Azalea Woods Way 20171
Bakers Creek Ct 20170
Bal Harbor Ct 20170
Ballou St 20170
Bandy Run Rd 20170
Bankfoot Ct 20171
Bannacker Pl 20171
Banshire Dr 20171
Barbaralynn Pl 20170
Barker Hill Rd 20170
Barksdale Dr 20171
Barnsfield Rd 20171
Barnside Ct 20171
Barton Way 20171
Barton Oaks Pl 20170
Bastian Ln 20171
Bathgate Dr 20171
Baxley Hollow Ct 20171
Bayflower Ct 20170
Bayou Ct & Dr 20170
Bayshire Ct, Ln & Pl 20170
Beauford Ct 20170
Beckingham Dr 20171
Belcroft Pl 20171
Ben Nevis Ct 20171
Benicia Ln 20170
Bennett Rd 20171
Bennett St 20170
Bennett Farms Ct 20171
Bennett Oaks Pl 20171
Berger Pl 20170
Berry Farm Ct 20171
Betsy Ln 20171
Bexhill Ct 20171
Bicksler Ct & Dr 20170
Big Boulder Rd 20171
Bill Waugh Dr 20170
Birch Ct 20170
Birch Cove Rd 20171
Birch Run Cir 20171
Bitter Sweet Ct 20171
Blacksmith Ln 20170
Blakesley Hall Ct 20171

Blue Holly Ln 20171
Blue Ridge Ct 20170
Blue Robin Ct 20171
Blueberry Farm Ln 20171
Bluemont Ct 20170
Bond St 20170
Boros Ct 20170
Boulder Crest Ct 20170
Bowers Ln 20170
Bradley Acres Ct 20171
Bradley Farm Dr 20171
Bradley Woods Ct 20171
Bradwell Rd 20171
Brafferton Ct 20171
Bramblewood Ln 20171
Branch Dr 20170
Branding Iron Ct 20171
Brass Harness Ct 20171
Breezy Knoll Ct 20171
Briargrove Ct 20171
Briery River Ter 20170
Brightfield Ct & Ln 20171
Broad Creek Pl 20170
Broad Oaks Dr 20170
Brofferton Ct 20171
Bronze Stone Pl 20171
Bronzegate Ct 20171
Brook Mill Ct 20171
Brook Overlook Ct 20171
Browns Ferry Rd 20170
Browns Mill Ct & Dr 20170
Brownsville Dr 20170
Bruce Ct 20170
Bryce Ct 20170
Brynwood Ct & Pl 20171
Builders Ct & Rd 20170
Burchlawn St 20171
Burrough Farm Dr 20171
Burwick Dr 20170
Butter Churn Ct & Dr 20170
Bywater Ct 20171
Cabin Creek Rd 20171
Calhoun Ct 20170
Calkins Rd 20171
Camberley Forest Dr 20171
Camberwell Ct 20171
Cameo Ct 20170
Campbell Way 20170
Capstone Cir 20170
Caris Glenne Dr 20170
Carlisle Dr 20170
Carlsbad Ct 20171
Caroline Ct 20171
Carson Overlook Ct 20170
Casper Dr 20170
Cassia St 20170
Castlevine Ct 20171
Catoctin Ct 20170
Cavendish St 20170
Cedar Chase Ct & Rd 20170
Cedar Glen Ln 20171
Cedar Run Ln 20171
Cellar Creek Way 20170
Center St 20170
Centre Park Cir 20171
Centreville Rd
2100-2279 20170
2280-3399 20171
Chamblee Pl 20170
Champion Lake Ct 20170
Charles St 20170
Charlton Pl 20170
Chasbarb Ct & Ter 20171
Chase Wellesley Dr 20171
Cherry Ct 20170
Cherry Branch Ln 20171
Chestnut Ct 20170
Cheviot Dr 20170
Chiswell Pl 20171
Christy Pl 20170
Chriswell Pl 20171
Cinnamon Oaks Ct 20171
Clareth Dr 20171
Clarke St 20170
Classic Ct 20171
Claxton Dr 20171
Clear Lake Ct 20171
Clearwater Ct 20170
Cleeve Hill Ct 20171
Cliff Edge Dr 20170
Clinch Rd 20170
Cliveden St 20170
Clover Field Cir 20171
Coat Ridge Rd 20170
Coates Ln 20171
Cobra Ct & Dr 20171
Cockerill Ct 20171
Cockerill Farm Ln 20171
Cold Harbor Ct & Dr 20170
Colewood St 20171
Colvin Ct 20170
Commodore Ct 20171
Congreve Ct 20171
Conquest Pl 20171
Coomber Ct 20170
Cooper Station Rd 20170
Cooperative Way 20171
Coopers Branch Ct 20171
Copper Bed Rd 20171
Copper Brook Way 20171
Copper Cove Way 20171
Copper Creek Ct & Rd 20171
Copper Hill Rd 20171
Copper Kettle Pl 20171
Copper Ridge Dr 20171
Copperfield Ln 20170
Coppermill Dr 20171
Coppermine Rd 20171
Cordell Way 20170
Corn Crib Ct 20171
Cornelia Rd 20171
Coronation Rd 20171
Corporate Park Dr 20171
Courtney Ct 20170
Covered Wagon Ct & Ln 20171
Crayton Ct & Rd 20171
Crest Dr 20170
Crestview Dr 20170
Criton St 20170
Crosen Ct 20171
Cross Creek Ct & Ln 20171
Cross Hollow Ct 20170
Crossfields Way 20171
Crosstitch Dr 20170
Crystal Wood Ct 20171
Curie Ct 20171
Curved Iron Rd 20171
Cuttermill Ct 20170
Cuzco Ct 20170
Cypress Cove Cir 20171
Cypress Green Ln 20171
Cypress Tree Pl 20170
Dairy Lou Ct & Dr 20171
Dakota Dr 20170
Dakota Lakes Dr 20171
Dan Patch Ct 20171
Daniel Webster Dr 20171
Danlea Ct 20170
Dardanelle Ct 20170
Dashco Way 20171
Davinci Ln 20171
Deer Wood Ct & Way 20171
Delevan Dr 20171
Denmark Dr 20171
Devon St 20170
Dew Meadow Ct 20171
Diamond Mill Dr 20171
Dick Wright St 20170
Doe Run Ct 20171
Dogwood Ct 20170
Dominion Ridge Ln & Ter 20170
Dornock Ct 20171
Doug Brooks Rd 20170
Dower House Dr 20171
Dranesville Rd 20170
Dranesville Manor Dr 20170
Dublin Pl 20170
Duck Pond Ct 20171
Dulles Ct & Pl 20170
Dulles Corner Blvd, Ln & Park 20171
Dulles Park Ct 20170
Dulles Station Blvd 20171
Dulles Technology Dr 20171
Dulles View Dr 20171
Dunbarton Ct 20170
Dwight St 20171
Dylan Schar Ct 20171
Early Fall Ct 20170
Eddyspark Dr 20170
Eds Dr 20171
Einstein St 20171
Elden St 20170
Elder Ct 20170
Eldridge Ln 20170
Elevation Ln 20171
Elliott An Ct 20171
Elm Tree Ct & Dr 20171
Emerald Chase Dr 20171
Endeavour Dr 20171
English Garden Ct 20171
Enright Pl 20170
Equus Ct 20171
Eric Ct 20170
Etruscan Dr 20171
Exbury St 20170
Exchange Pl 20170
Fairbrook Dr 20170
Fairfax Ln 20170
Fall Pl 20170
Fall Oaks Pl 20171
Fallon Dr 20171
Fanieul Hall Ct 20171
Fantasia Cir & Dr 20171
Farm Buggy Ct 20171
Farmbell Ct 20171
Farmcrest Ct & Dr 20171
Farmsted Ct 20171
Farougi Ct 20170
Farthingale Dr 20171
Feldman Pl 20170
Ferdinand Porsche Dr 20171
Ferguson Pl 20170
Fern Hollow Ct & Pl 20171
Ferndale Ave 20170
Fieldcreek Dr 20171
Fillmore St 20171
Firenze Ct 20171
Firewood Ct 20171
Fishers Mill Ct 20170
Flagship Ave & Ct 20170
Flat Meadow Ct & Ln 20171
Flintwood Ct & Pl 20171
Florence Pl 20171
Florida Ave 20170
Floris Ln & St 20171
Floyd Pl 20171
Flying Squirrel Dr 20171
Flynn Ct 20170
Folkstone Dr 20171
Folley Lick Ct 20170
Fones Pl 20171
Forbes Glen Dr 20170
Forest Heights Ct 20171
Fort Lee St 20171
Fortnightly Blvd 20171
Forty Oaks Ct & Dr 20170
Founders Way 20171
Fox Hound Ct 20171
Fox Hunt Ln 20171
Fox Mill Rd 20171
Fox Mine Ln 20171
Fox Ripple Ln 20171
Fox Stream Ln 20171
Fox Woods Dr 20171
Foxlease Ct 20171
Framingham Ct 20171
Franklin Corner Ln 20171
Franklin Farm Rd 20171
Franklin Oaks Dr 20171
Franklins Way 20171
Fraternal Ct 20171
Frear Pl 20171
Fred Morin Rd 20171
Freshrain Ct 20170
Frinks Ct 20170
Frog Hollow Ct 20171
Frying Pan Rd 20171
Garberry Ct 20170
Gatepost Ct & Ln 20171
Gentle Breeze Ct 20170
George Wythe Ct 20171
Gibson Oaks Dr 20171
Gilman Ct & Ln 20170
Gingell Pl 20170
Glen Echo Cir & Rd 20171
Glen Taylor Ln 20171
Glenbrooke Woods Dr 20171
Glendundee Dr 20171
Glenlawn Pl 20171
Golden Harvest Ct 20171
Goldenchain Ct 20171
Gordon Ct 20171
Grace St 20170
Gracie Park Dr 20170
Grand Hamptons Dr 20170
Granite Wood Ct 20171
Grant St 20170
Grassmere Ct 20171
Graypine Pl 20171
Greear Pl 20170
Green Grass Ct 20171
Greenhorn St 20171
Greenstone Ct & Way 20171
Greg Roy Ln 20171
Grey Friars Pl 20171
Grove St
300-591 20170
590-590 20172
593-599 20170
N & S Gunnell Ct 20170
Halterbreak Ct 20171
Hamer Ct 20170
Hanna Overlook Ct 20170
Hannahs Pond Ln 20171
Harrington Ct 20171
Harrison Hollow Ln 20171
Harvest Glen Ct 20171
Havencrest St 20171
Hawks Nest Ct 20170
Hay Meadow Pl 20171
Hay Rake Ct 20171
Heather Way 20170
Heather Down Dr 20170
Hedgetop Dr 20171
Hemlock Ct 20170
Henson Ct 20171
Heritage Farm Ct & Ln 20171
Herman Ct 20170
Herndon Pkwy 20170
Herndon Mill Cir 20170
Herndon Station Sq 20170
Herndon Woods Ct 20170
Hertford St 20170
Hickory Ct 20170
Hickory Meadows Ct 20171
Hickory Nut Ln 20171
Hidden Meadow Ct & Dr 20171
Hidden Park Pl 20170
Hiddenbrook Dr 20170
Higgs Ct 20171
Highcourt Ln 20170
Highland Crossing Dr 20171
Highland Mews Ct & Pl 20171
Hill Haven Ct 20171
Hillwood Ct 20170
Holkein Dr 20171
Hollingsworth Ter 20170
Holly Ct 20170
Holly Meadow Ln 20171
Horizon Ct 20170
Horsepen Woods Ct & Ln 20171
Horton Hill Rd 20171
Hughsmith Ct & Way 20171
Hungerford Pl 20170
Hunt Way Ct & Ln 20170
Huntington Dr 20171
Huntmar Park Dr 20170
Huntsfield Ct 20171
Huntsman Pl 20170
Hurdle Ct 20171
Huston Pl 20170
Hutumn Ct 20171
Icy Brook Dr 20170
Iron Forge Rd 20171
Iron Ridge Ct 20170
Isham Randolph Dr 20171
Jackson St 20170
James Cirone Way 20170
James Madison Cir 20171
James Maury Dr 20171
James Monroe Cir 20171
Jeannie Anna Ct 20171
Jeff Ryan Dr 20170
Jefferson St 20170
Jefferson Way 20171
Jefferson Commons Ct 20171
Jefferson Park Dr 20171
Jenny Ann Ct 20170
Jensen Pl 20170
Jocelyne Ct 20171
John Donnelly St 20170
John Eppes Rd 20171
John Milton Ct & Dr 20171
Jonathons Glen Way 20170
Jonquil Ln 20170
Jonquilla Ct 20171
Jorss Pl 20170
Jubilation Ct 20170
Judd Ct 20170
Juniper Ct 20170
Keach Pl 20170
Keele Dr 20171
Keisler Ct 20171
Kelly Ct 20170
Kensal Green Ct 20171
Kensington Pl 20170
Kettering Dr 20171
Kidwell Field Rd 20171
Kilbrennan Ct 20171
Kinbrace Rd 20171
Kinfolk Ct 20171
Kings Ct 20170
Kings Valley Ct 20170
Kingstream Cir & Dr 20170
Kingsvale Cir 20170
Kinross Cir & Ct 20171
Kinship Dr 20171
Kirkwell Pl 20171
Knight Ln 20170
Kristin Pl 20171
Kyler Ln 20171
Lady Fairfax Cir 20170
Ladybank Ln 20171
Lake James Dr 20171
Lake Shore Dr 20171
Landerset Dr 20170
Laneview Ct & Pl 20171
Laura Mark Ln 20171
Laurel Way 20170
Laurel Tree Ln 20171
Lauren Oaks Ct 20171
Lawyers Rd 20171
Lazy Glen Ct & Ln 20171
Leefield Dr 20171
Leesburg Pike 20170
Lefrak Ct 20170
Legacy Cir 20171
Legacy Pride Dr 20170
Leona Ln 20170
Lexus Way 20170
Leyland Ridge Rd 20171
Liberty Meeting Ct 20171
Lillian Chase Ln 20170
Lincoln Park Dr 20171
Linden Ct 20170
Lions Pride Dr 20170
Lisa Ct 20170
Litchfield Dr 20171
Little Current Dr 20171
Little Stones Ln 20170
Liz Ct 20171
Lockgate Ct & Pl 20171
Locksley Ct 20171
Locust St 20170
Logan Wood Dr 20171
Longfellow Ct 20170
Longleaf Ln 20170
Longview Ct & Pl 20170
Lopez Ln 20170
Lopp Ct 20170
Lou Alice Way 20171
Loughrie Way 20171
Loveless Ln 20170
Lyme Bay Dr 20171
Lynn St 20170
Macao Ct & Dr 20171
Madden Ct 20171
Madison St 20170
Madison Forest Dr 20170
Madison Manor Ct 20170
Madison Ridge Ln 20170
Mager Dr 20170
Magna Carta Rd 20171
Magnolia Ct & Ln 20170
Mahogany Tree Ln 20171
Main Dr 20170
Maleady Dr 20170
Malvern Hill Pl 20170
Manderley Way 20171
Mansarde Ave 20171
Mansway Dr 20171
Maple Ct 20170
Maple Sugar Ln 20171
Marcey Creek Rd 20171
Mares Neck Ln 20171
Marionwood Ct 20171
Marjorie Ln 20170
Marstan Moor Ln 20171
Martha Jefferson Pl 20171
Mary Etta Ln 20171
Mary Powell Ln 20171
Mason Mill Ct 20170
Masons Ferry Dr 20171
Maverick Ln 20171
Mcdaniel Ct 20170
Mcgrane Ct 20171
Mclearen Rd 20171
Mcmaster Ct 20171
Mcnair Farms Dr 20171
Meadow Chase Dr 20170
Meadow Hall Ct & Dr 20171
Meadow Willow Cir 20171
Meadowstream Ct 20170
Meadowville Ct 20170
Meeting House Station Sq 20170
Melchester Dr 20171
Merlins Ct & Ln 20170
Merricourt Ln 20171
Merrybrook Ct & Dr 20171
Methven Ct 20170
Micheal Lawrence Pl 20171
Middleton Farm Ct & Ln 20171
Mill Heights Ct & Dr 20171
Millbank Way 20170
Millikens Bend Rd 20170
Millstream Ct 20171
Millwood Pond Ct & Dr 20170
Mississippi Dr 20170
Missouri Ave 20170
Misty Dawn Ct & Dr 20171
Misty Water Dr 20170
Mistyvale St 20170
Mockernut Ct 20171
Moffett Forge Rd 20170
Monaghan Dr 20170
Monroe St
600-1499 20170
2200-2599 20171
Monroe Chase Ct 20171
Monroe Hill Ct 20170
Monroe Manor Dr 20171
Monroe Mills Ln 20170
Monsouni St 20170
Montalto Dr 20170
Monterey Estates Dr 20171
Morningside Ct 20170
Morton Mills Ln 20170
Mosby Ct 20170
Mosby Hollow Dr 20170
Mother Well Ct 20171
Mount Aubern Ct 20171
Mountain Mill Pl 20171
Mountain View Ct 20171
Muirkirk Ln 20171
Mustang Dr 20171
Myra Virginia Ct 20171
Myterra Way 20171
Nash St 20170
Nathan Ct & Ln 20170
Nathaniel Chase Ln 20170
Nathaniel Oaks Ct & Dr 20171
Navy Dr 20171
Neil Armstrong Ave 20171
Nestlewood Ct & Dr 20171
Netherleigh Pl 20171
Network Pl 20171
New Ambler Ct 20171
New Arden Ct 20171
New Aspen Ct 20171
New Austin Ct 20171
New Banner Ln 20171
New Belmont Ct 20171
New Carson Dr 20171
New Concorde Ct 20171
New Parkland Dr 20171
Newnan Ridge Ct 20171
Nicklaus Ct 20170
Nickleback Ct 20171
Northern Valley Ct 20171
Northpoint Glen Ct 20170
Nubian Ct 20171
Nureyev Ln 20170
Oak St 20170
Oak Farms Dr 20171
Oak Lawn Pl 20171
Oak Shadow Dr 20171
Oak Trail Ct 20170
Oakhampton Pl 20171
Oakshire Ct 20170
Oakton Chase Ct 20171
Old Dairy Ct & Rd 20171
Old Dominion Ave 20170
Old Dorm Pl 20170
Old Farmhouse Ct 20171
Old Heights Rd 20170
Old Hunt Way 20170
Old Pine Way 20171
Old Silo Ct 20171
Oliver Cromwell Dr 20171
Oram Pl 20170
Orchard Glen Ct 20171
Otsego Dr 20171
Overcup Oak Ct 20171
Owlsley Way 20171
W Ox Rd 20171
Ox Hunt Rd 20171
Ox Meadow Ct & Dr 20171
Oxford Forest Dr 20171
Oxon Rd 20171
Paddock Gate Ct 20171
Page Ct 20170
Palmer Dr 20170
Paradise Ln 20170
Parapet Way 20171
Parcher Ave 20170
Park Ave 20170
Park Center Rd 20171
Park Crescent Cir 20171
Parklawn Ct 20171
Parkstream Ter 20170
Parkvale Ct 20170
Pascal Pl 20171
Patrick Ln 20170
Peachtree St 20170
Pearl St 20170
Pellow Circle Ct & Trl 20170
Pelmira Ridge Ct 20171
Pemberton Ct 20170
Pembrook Ct & St 20170
Pennymoor Ct 20171

Percheron Ln 20171
Permit Ct 20170
Peter Jefferson Ln 20171
Petersborough St 20171
Philmont Dr 20170
Pickett Ln 20170
Pinafore Ct 20171
Pine St 20170
Pine Oaks Way 20171
Pinecrest Rd 20171
Pinecrest View Ct 20171
Piney Glade Rd 20171
Piney Point Pl 20171
Piney Ridge Ct 20171
Plato Ln 20170
Player Way 20170
Pleasant Glen Ct & Dr 20171
Pleasantree Ct 20171
Plotner Farm Rd 20171
Plowman Ct 20170
Pocono Ct & Pl 20170
Poener Pl 20170
Point Rider Ln 20171
Polly Jefferson Way 20171
Pond Crest Ln 20171
Pond Mist Way 20171
Post Dr 20170
Powells Tavern Pl 20170
Preference Way 20170
Preuit Pl 20170
Pride Ave 20170
Prince Harold Ct 20171
Proffitt Estates Ct 20171
Promenade Pl 20171
Pumpkin Ash Ct 20171
Puritan Ct 20171
Purple Martin Pl 20171
Queens Ct 20171
Queens Row St 20170
Quick St 20171
Quietwalk Ln 20170
Quimpers Pl 20170
Quincy St 20170
Quincy Adams Ct & Dr 20171
Rainbow Ct 20170
Ramesses Ct 20171
Raven Tower Ct 20170
Ravenscraig Ct 20171
Rayjohn Ln 20171
Reams Station Pl 20170
Red Squirrel Way 20171
Redskin Dr 20171
Redwood Ct & Pl 20170
Reign Ct & St 20171
Reneau Way 20170
Reston Ave 20170
Reston Pkwy 20171
Richland Ln 20171
Ridgegate Dr 20170
Ripplemeade Ct 20171
River Birch Rd 20171
Robaleed Way 20171
Robin Glen Ct 20171
Rock Chapel Ct & Rd 20170
Rock Hill Rd 20170
Rock Manor Ct 20171
Rock Ridge Ct & Rd 20171
Rock Spray Ct 20171
Rogers Ln 20171
Rolling Fork Cir 20171
Rolling Plains Ct & Dr 20171
Rose Grove Dr & Ter 20171
Rose Petal Cir 20171
Rosemere Ct 20171
Rosiers Branch Dr 20170
Rounding Run Cir & Ct 20171
Rover Glen Ct 20171
Rowland Dr 20170
Rowles Pl 20170
Royal Elm Ct 20170
Ruby Lace Ct 20171
Rudds Store Pl 20170
Running Pump Ct & Ln 20171
Rushing Brook Ln 20171
Saber Ln 20170
Sadlers Wells Ct & Dr 20170
Safa Ct & St 20170
Saffron Dr 20171
Saint Johns Wood Pl 20171
Salk St 20171
San Moritz Cir 20170
Sandbourne Ln 20171
Sandy Ct 20170
Sasscers Hill Ct 20171
Saunders Dr 20170
Saylers Creek Ln 20170
Sayward Dr 20171
School St 20170
Schwenger Pl 20170
Scotsmore Way 20171
Scranton Ct 20170
Seaman Ct 20170
Searsmont Pl 20171
Senate Ct 20170
Seskey Glen Ct 20171
Seven Pines Ct 20170
Shady Mill Ln 20171
Shaker Dr 20170
Shaker Knolls Ct 20170
Shaker Meadows Ct 20170
Shaker Woods Rd 20170
Shallow Ford Ct & Rd 20170
Shannon Pl 20170
Shea Pl 20170
Shellbark Pl 20170
Sheridan Run Ct 20170
Sheringham Dr 20171
Shrewsbury Ct 20171
Silk Ct 20171
Silver Beech Rd 20170
Silver Spur Ct 20171
Simpkins Farm Dr 20171
Sir Ramsay Way 20171
Skyhaven Ct 20170
Smith Farm Way 20171
Snead Pl 20171
Snow Shoe Ct 20170
Snowflake Ct 20170
Society Ct & Dr 20170
Soft Breeze Ct 20171
Southfield Ct & Dr 20171
Southington Ln 20170
Spofford Rd 20171
Spring St 20170
Spring Chapel Ct 20171
Spring Knoll Dr 20170
Spring Mill Ln 20171
Spring Rain Ct 20171
Springer Dr 20170
Springpark Pl 20170
Springtide Pl 20170
Spruce Ct 20170
Squirrel Hill Rd 20171
Stable Brook Way 20171
Stalwart Ct 20170
Stanton Pl 20171
Stanton Park Ct 20170
Star Ct 20171
Station St 20170
Sterling Ct & Rd 20170
Stevenson Ct 20170
Still Pond Ct & Ln 20171
Stoa Ct 20170
Stone Church Ct 20170
Stone Fence Ln 20171
Stone Heather Ct & Dr 20171
Stone Mountain Ct 20170
Stourhead Ct 20170
Stratford Glen Pl 20171
Streamvale Cir 20170
Striped Maple Cir 20171
Stuart Ct & Rd 20170
Stuart Hills Way 20170
Stuart Pointe Ln 20170
Stuart Ridge Dr 20170
Sugar Creek Ct 20170
Sugar Maple Dr & Ln 20170
Sugar Mill Way 20171
Sugarland Rd 20170
Sugarland Meadow Dr 20170
Sugarland Valley Dr 20170
Sugarloaf Ct 20170
Summer Pl 20171
Summerfield Dr 20170
Summerset Pl 20170
Summershade Ct 20171
Sundale Ct 20170
Sunny Fields Ln 20171
Sunnyvale Ct 20171
Sunrise Ct 20170
Sunrise Valley Dr 20171
Sunset Ct 20170
Sunset Park Dr 20170
Sutters Mill Dr 20171
Sycamore Ct 20170
Sycamore Lakes Cv 20171
Sycamore View Ln 20171
Syrup Mill Rd 20170
Taji Ct 20170
Tallyrand Ct 20171
Tamani Dr 20170
Tamarack Way 20170
Tarleton Corner Dr 20171
Tarragon Ct 20171
Tatnuck Ct 20171
Taustin Ln 20170
Tayloe Ct 20171
Taylor Makenzye Ct 20171
Terra Cotta Cir 20171
Terrylynn Ct 20170
Terrymill Dr 20170
Tewksbury Dr 20171
Thacker Hill Ct 20171
Thistleberry Ct 20171
Thistlethorn Dr 20171
Thomas Jefferson Dr 20171
Thomas Young Ct & Ln 20171
Thornapple Pl 20171
Thornburg Ln 20170
Thorncroft Pl 20171
Thorngate Ct & Dr 20171
Thoroughbred Rd 20171
Thurber St 20170
Timber Knoll Ct 20170
Timber Wood Way 20171
Tingewood Ct 20171
Topsfield Ct 20171
Tori Glen Ct 20170
Towerview Rd 20171
Tranquility Ct & Ln 20171
Trapper Crest Ct 20170
Travelers Pl 20170
Treadwell Ln 20171
Tredgerr Dr 20171
Treeside Ln 20170
Trevino Ln 20170
Trinity Gate St 20170
Trossack Rd 20170
Tuckaway Ct & Dr 20171
Turberville Ct & Ln 20171
Turquoise Ln 20170
Tway Ln 20170
Tyburn Tree Ct 20171
Tyler St 20170
Tyler Swetman Dr 20170
Tympani Ct 20170
Unicorn Ct 20171
Upper Wynnewood Ct & Pl 20171
Valebrook Ln 20170
Valley High Rd 20170
Valley Mill Ct 20170
Van Buren St 20170
Veenendaal Ct 20170
Venturi Ln 20171
Verisign Way 20171
Victory Dr 20170
Viking Ct & Dr 20170
Vine St 20170
Virginia Ave 20170
Virginia Randolph Ave 20171
Wall Rd 20171
Walnut Leaf Ln 20171
Walnut Rocker Ln 20171
Wasser Ter 20171
Waterford Pl 20170
Weather Vane Way 20171
Weathered Oak Ct 20171
Weeping Cherry Walk 20171
Wellhouse Ct 20171
Wendell Holmes Rd 20171
Westcourt Ln 20170
Westlodge Ct 20170
Westwood Hills Dr 20171
Wexford Ct 20170
Weyers Cave Ct 20170
Whaley Ct 20171
Wheat Meadow Cir & Ct 20171
Wheeler Way 20171
Whirlaway Cir 20171
Whisonant Ct 20170
White Barn Ct & Ln 20171
White Oak Ct 20170
Whitefur Ln 20170
Whitewater Pl 20170
Whitewood Ln 20171
Whitworth Ct 20170
Wilbury Rd 20171
Wildmere Pl 20171
Wilkes Ct & Way 20170
William Short Cir 20171
William Taft Ct 20171
Williams Meadow Ct 20171
Willow Falls Dr 20170
Willow Glen Ct & Dr 20171
Willow Spring Ct 20170
Wilshire Dr 20170
Windcroft Glen Ct 20170
Winding Way Dr 20170
Windsor Hall Way 20170
Windy Oak Way 20171
Winter Oaks Way 20171
Winter Sun Ter 20171
Winter Wren Ct 20171
Winterberry Ct 20170
Winterborne Ct 20170
Winterhaven Pl 20170
Winterland Ct 20170
Winterwood Ct & Pl 20170
Wintrol Ct 20170
Wood St 20170
Wood Crescent Cir 20171
Wood Oak Dr 20171
Woodcock Ct & Ln 20171
Woodgrove Ct 20170
Woodland Crossing Dr 20171
Woodland Park Rd 20171
Woodland Pond Ln 20171
Woodrow Wilson Dr 20171
Woodshire Ln 20170
Woodvale Ct 20170
Worchester St 20170
Wordsworth Ct 20170
Worldgate Dr 20170
Wrenn House Ct & Ln 20171
Wrexham Ct & Rd 20171
Yellow Tavern Ct & Rd 20170
Young Ave 20170
Young Dairy Ct 20170
Youngs Point Pl 20170
Yukon Rd 20171
Zachary Taylor Cir 20171
Zosimo Pl 20170

NUMBERED STREETS

All Street Addresses 20170

LEESBURG VA

General Delivery 20175

POST OFFICE BOXES MAIN OFFICE STATIONS AND BRANCHES

Box No.s
1 - 978 20178
347 - 6000 20177
6001 - 6480 20178
7000 - 9100 20177

RURAL ROUTES

01, 02, 05 20175
04, 06 20176

NAMED STREETS

Aberlour Ln 20175
Accokeek Ter 20176
Adams Dr NE 20176
Adarenew Rd 20176
Agape Ln 20176
Aging Oak Dr 20175
Aldie Burn Ln 20175
Alex St 20176
Allenby Way 20176
Allman Way SW 20175
Alpine Dr SE 20175
Alshami Ct 20176
Alysheba Dr 20176
Amanda Ct 20175
Amber Ct NE 20176
Amori Ln 20175
Amur Ct 20176
Andover Ct NE 20176
Andromeda Ter NE 20176
Anne St SW 20175
Anthony Ct SE 20175
Apache Wells Ter 20176
Appletree Dr NE 20176
Arcadian Dr 20176
Ariel Dr NE 20176
Arrow Creek Dr 20175
Arroyo Ter 20176
Artillery Ter NE 20176
Ash Mill Ter 20176
Ashford Ct NE 20176
Ashton Dr SW 20175
Augusta National Ter 20176
Aurora Ct NE 20176
Avebury Manor Pl 20176
Ayr St NW 20176
Ayr St SW 20175
Ayrlee Ave NW 20176
Babson Cir SW 20175
Baish Dr SE 20175
Balch Dr S 20175
Balch Springs Cir SE 20175
Bald Hill Rd 20176
Balderstone Ct NE 20176
Balls Bluff Rd NE 20176
Ballybunion Ter 20176
Banshee Dr 20175
Barbara Ct NE 20176
Barclay Ct 20175
Barksdale Dr NE 20176
Barnfield Sq NE 20176
Barnhouse Pl 20176
Barnwick Ct NE 20176
Barnwood Ct 20175
Barton Creek Pl 20176
Baskerville Ct 20176
Basque Ct 20176
Batey Ct 20175
Battery Ter NE 20176
Battery Point Pl 20176
Battlefield Pkwy NE 20176
Beacon Hill Dr 20176
Bear Creek Ter 20176
Beauregard Dr SE 20175
Beaver Creek Ter 20176
Beechnut Rd 20175
Belforest Ct 20175
Belleville Dr NE 20176
Bellingham Ln 20175
Bellview Ct NE 20176
Belmont Dr & Pl 20175
Beningbrough Pl 20176
Bent Creek Ter 20176
Bent Tree Ter 20176
Berkhamstead Pl 20176
Bermuda Dunes Ter 20176
Berwyn Ct 20176
Bethal Ct SW 20175
Bethany Dr 20175
Big Pines Ln 20175
Big Spring Ln 20176
Big Springs Ct 20176
Big Spruce Sq 20176
Binkley Cir 20176
Binns Ct SW 20175
Birch St NE 20176
Birdwood Ct 20176
Black Branch Pkwy 20175
Black Gold Pl 20176
Black Walnut Ln 20176
Blacksburg Ter NE 20176
Blaise Hamlet Ln 20176
Blessed Ln 20175
Blincoe Ct 20175
Blue Ridge Ave NE 20176
Blue Seal Dr SE 20175
Blue View Ct 20176
Bluefield Sq NE 20176
Bluff Ct NE 20176
Bold Venture Dr 20176
Bonnie Ridge Dr NE 20176
Bournville Ct SE 20175
Bow Lake Pl NE 20176
Boyer Fields Pl 20176
Bradfield Dr SW 20175
Braemar Pl 20175
Breckinridge Sq SE 20175
Brian Thomas Ct SE 20175
Briarberry Pl 20176
Bridges Farm Ln 20175
Bridgette Pl NE 20176
Bridle Crest Sq NE 20176
Brigadier Ct SE 20175
Brightwood Ln 20176
Brindley Pl SW 20175
Brookridge Ct 20176
Browns Creek Pl 20175
Browns Farm Ln 20175
Browns Meadow Ct NE 20176
Brumsey Ct SW 20175
Bryn Bach Ln 20175
Buccaneer Ter 20176
Buchanan Ct SE 20175
Buena Vista Sq 20176
Bugle Ct NE 20176
Buna Mae Ln 20176
Burberry Ter SE 20175
Burnell Pl SE 20175
Burning Sands Ter 20176
Burning Tree Pl 20176
Burnside Ter SE 20175
Burnt Bridge Dr 20176
Burrows Ct NE 20176
Burstall Ct 20176
Burt Ct NE 20176
Bushnell Way 20175
Bushveld Aly 20176
Butler Pl 20175
Butterfly Way 20175
Buttonwood Ter NE 20176
Caddy Ct 20176
Cagney Ter SE 20175
Calamus Creek Ct 20176
Caldwell Ter SE 20175
Caledonia Ct 20176
Callaway Gardens Sq 20176
Calphams Mill Ct 20176
Calvary Ct SE 20175
Cambria Ter NE 20176
Camelback Ter 20176
Camelot Pl 20175
Campbell Ct NE 20176
Canal Creek Pl 20176
Canal Ford Ter 20176
Canby Rd 20175
Candlewick Sq 20176
Candlewood Pl NE 20176
Cannon Ct NE 20176
Cannonade Dr 20176
Canoe Landing Ct 20176
Canongate Dr 20175
Canova Ct 20175
Cardinal Park Dr SE 20175
Cardston Pl 20176
Carlton St SW 20175
Carnaby Way NE 20176
Carradoc Farm Ter 20176
Carry Back Ln 20176
Carter Ridge Ln 20176
Casla Ct SE 20175
Castle Harbour Ter 20176
Castleguard Ct 20176
Catchfly Ter 20176
Catesby Ct SW 20175
Catoctin Cir NE 20176
Catoctin Cir SE
1-26 20175
25-25 20177
28-222 20175
37-219 20175
Catoctin Cir SW 20175
Catoctin Springs Ct 20176
Catskill Ct NE 20176
Cattail Ln NE 20176
Cattail Branch Ct 20176
Cattail Spring Dr 20176
Cavell Ct 20176
Cedar Walk Cir NE 20176
Cedargrove Pl SW 20175
Chadfield Way NE 20176
Chancellor St SW 20175
Channel Ridge Ct 20176
Chapel Ln 20176
Chapel View Ln 20176
Charandy Dr 20175
Charles Ln 20176
Chartered Creek Pl 20176
Chartier Dr 20176
Chatfield Ct NE 20176
Chathill Ter 20176
Chaucer Pl NE 20176
Chauncey Ln 20175
Chelsea Ct NE 20176
Cherry Ln NE 20176
Cherry Spring Ln 20176
Chesterfield Pl SW 20175
Chestnut Hill Ln 20175
Chestnut Orchard Ln 20176
Chevington Ln 20175
Chicacoan Creek Sq 20176
Chickasaw Pl NE 20176
Childrens Center Rd SW 20175
Chimney Ct NE 20176
Church St NE 20176
Church St SE 20175
Cisco Ln 20175
Citrine Dr 20176
Clagett St SW 20175
Clairmont Ct NE 20176
Clark Ct NE 20176
Clarksridge Rd 20176
Classic Path Way SE 20175
Claude Ct SE 20175
Claudia Dr 20175
Claymont Dr 20175
Cliff Cir 20175
Cloister Pl 20176
Clove Ter NE 20176
Clubhouse Dr SW 20175
Clymer Ct NE 20176
Cobbler Ter SE 20175
Cochran Mill Rd 20175
Colleen Ct NE 20176
Collett Mill Ct 20176
E Colonial Hwy 20175
Colston Ct 20176
Coltrane Sq 20175
Coltsridge Ter NE 20176
Commonwealth Ter 20176
Compressor Ln 20175
Conklin Dr 20176
Connery Ter SW 20175
Consolidated Ln 20175
Constellation Sq SE 20175
Cool Breeze Sq 20176

Cool Hollow Ln 20176
Cope Dr 20175
Coppermine Sq 20176
Coralbells Pl 20176
Coreopsis Ter 20176
Cornwall St NE & NW 20176
Cory Ct 20176
Coton Commons Dr 20176
Coton Farm Ct 20176
Coton Hall St 20176
Coton Holdings Ct 20176
Coton Manor Dr 20176
Coton Reserve Dr 20176
Count Turf Pl 20176
Country Club Dr SW 20175
Courage Ct 20175
Courier Ct NE 20176
Courtland Village Dr 20175
Cove Point Ln 20175
Covington Ter NE 20176
Cranberry Ln 20176
Cranbrook Dr NE 20176
Cranwell Pl SW 20175
Creek Bend Pl 20175
Creek Field Cir 20176
Creekbank Ct 20176
Creighton Farms Dr 20175
Crestwood St SW 20175
Crimson Pl 20175
Crimson Clover Ter 20175
Cristabel Ln 20176
Crooked Bridge Ln 20175
Crosstrail Blvd SE 20175
Crystal Lake St 20176
Culps Hill Ln 20176
Currant Ter NE 20176
Curtin Pl SE 20175
Cypress Point Ter 20176
Cypress Ridge Ter 20176
Dahlia Ct 20175
Dailey Pl SW 20175
Daleview Ln 20176
Dalhart Dr SE 20175
Dalton Points Pl 20176
Dandelion Ter SE 20175
Daniels St NW 20176
Darden Ct 20176
Davis Ave & Ct SW & SE 20175
Dawson Mill Pl 20175
Dearmont Ter 20176
Deerfield Ave 20176
Deermeadow Pl SW 20175
Deerpath Ave SW 20175
Delphinium Cir 20176
Demory Ter 20176
Depot Ct SE 20175
Desert Inn Ct 20176
Determine Ct 20176
Dettington Ct 20176
Diamond Ct 20175
Diamond Lake Dr 20176
Diggins Ct 20175
Dinah Pl 20175
Diskin Pl SW 20175
Dodd Ct & Dr 20175
Dodona Ter 20175
Dogwood Run Ln 20175
Donaldson Ln SW 20175
Dorati Sq 20175
Dorneywood Dr 20176
Dove Ln 20176
Doyle Ter NE 20176
Dressage Ct 20176
Drummond Pl 20176
Dry Hollow Rd 20176
Dry Mill Rd SW 20175
Duff Rd NE 20176
Duncan Pl SE 20175
Dunlop Mill Rd 20175
Durham Ct 20175
Duvall Ct SE 20175
Eagle Bend Sq 20176
Eagle Mine Ter 20176
Eagle Point Sq 20176
Eagle Springs Dr 20175

Eagles Rest Dr 20176
Eaglesham Ct 20175
Ebaugh Dr SE 20175
Eckbo Dr 20175
Edmonton Ter NE 20176
Edwards Ferry Rd NE 20176
Eldorado Way 20176
Eleni St 20176
Elia Ct SE 20175
Elk Run Ct 20176
Elkridge Way NE 20176
Ellerslie Ct SE 20175
Elysian Dr 20176
Emerald Dunes Pl 20176
Emerald Hill Dr NE 20176
Emerald Park Dr 20176
Emmet Ct SW 20175
English Ct SW 20175
English Yew Pl 20176
Evans Pond Rd 20176
Evans Ridge Ter NE 20176
Evard Ct SW 20175
Evergreen Mill Rd SE 20175
Evergreen Mills Rd 20175
Ewing Cir 20176
Exmoor Ct NW 20176
Fairfax St SE 20175
Fairfield Way SW 20175
Fairleigh Ct NE 20176
Fairview St NW 20176
Fairway Oaks Sq 20176
Falls Overlook Ct 20176
Falls View Sq 20176
Farewell Dance Dr 20176
Farm Ln 20176
Farm Market Rd 20175
Farmstead Dr 20175
Farnborough Pl 20176
Farnham Ct 20176
Featherbed Ln 20176
Featherstone Ln NE 20176
Fern Valley Ln 20176
Ferndale Ter NE 20176
Ferriers Ct 20176
Ferry Field Ter 20176
Field Ct NE 20176
Fieldmaster Cir 20176
Fieldstone Dr NE 20176
Fieldsview Ct 20175
Firefly Hill Ln 20175
Firehill Ln 20175
Firestone Pl 20176
First St SW 20175
Flag Ct NE 20176
Flameflower Ter SE 20175
Fleur Dr 20176
Flowering Dogwood Ter SE 20175
Forbes Ct NE 20176
Fording Branch Ct 20175
Forest Glen Dr 20175
Forest Mills Rd 20175
Forest Oaks Ct 20175
Forest Spring Dr 20175
Forestgrove Rd 20175
Forsyth Ln 20175
Fort Evans Rd 20176
Fort Evans Rd NE 20176
Fort Evans Rd SE 20176
Fort Johnston Rd 20176
Fort Macleod Ter NE 20176
Fortress Cir SE 20175
Foster Pl SW 20175
Fountain Hall Ct NE 20176
Fox Chase Ct 20176
Fox Creek Ln 20176
Fox Hollow Ln 20175
Fox Manor Dr 20175
Fox Run Ln 20175
Fox Trot Way NW 20176
Foxborough Dr SW 20175
Foxden Ln 20175
Foxfield Ln 20175
Foxgreen Cir 20175
Foxhill Rd 20175
Foxhunt Ter NE 20176

Foxridge Dr SW 20175
Foxtail Cir NE 20176
Franklin Ct SW 20175
Freedom Center Ln 20175
Front St 20176
Frost Leaf Ln 20176
Gaines Ct SW 20175
Gallorette Pl 20175
Galloway Dr SE 20175
Gap Rd 20175
Gardner View Sq 20176
Garriland Dr 20176
Garrison Ct NE 20176
Gateshead Way 20175
Gateway Dr SE 20175
Gawthorpe Ln 20176
Gemstone Ct 20175
Generals Ct SE 20175
Georgetown Ct NE 20176
Gibbon Ct 20176
Gibson St NW 20176
Giddings Ln 20175
Ginger Sq NE 20176
Ginkgo Ter NE 20176
Glade Fern Ter SE 20175
Glastonbury Ln 20176
Glaydin Ln 20176
Glaydin Woods Ln 20176
Gleedsville Rd 20175
Glen Abbey Ct 20176
Glen Oak Way 20176
Glenrose Ter 20176
Glynn Tarra Pl 20175
Godfrey Ct SE 20175
Gold Hill Sq 20176
Golden Larch Ter NE 20176
Goldfinch Ln 20175
Goldsworth Ter SW 20175
Golf Club Rd 20175
Golf Vista Plz 20176
Goodhart Ln 20176
Goose Bluff Ct 20176
Goose Creek Ln 20176
Gooseberry Ln 20176
Gooseview Ct 20176
E Gopost 20176
Gore Ln 20175
Goshen Farm Ct 20176
Gospond Ln 20175
Governors Dr SW 20175
Grafton Way NE 20176
Granite Falls Ln 20176
Grant Ln 20176
Graywood Way NE 20176
Great Laurel Sq SE 20175
Great Woods Dr 20176
Green Island Ter 20176
Green Meadow Ln 20176
Greenfield Farm Ln 20176
Greenham Dr 20175
Greenhow Ct SE 20175
Greenmont Way NE 20176
Greenway Dr SW 20175
Grenata Preserve Pl 20175
Grey Fox Ln 20176
Grey Oak Way 20176
Greyhouse Pl 20175
Greystone Sq 20176
Griffin Farm Ln 20175
Grindstone Ct 20176
Grogan Ct 20175
Grouse Ter 20176
Grove Church Ct 20175
Guinness Way 20175
Gulick Mill Rd 20175
Gunpowder Ct SE 20175
Gusty Knoll Ln 20176
Habitat Cir 20176
Hagley Pl 20175
Hague Dr SW 20175
Halifax Pl SE 20175
Hallbrook Ct 20176
Hallyard Ct SE 20175
Halprin Ct 20176
Hambrick Manor Ln 20176
Hampshire Sq SW 20175

Hampshire Crossing Sq 20176
Hampstead Ct NE 20176
Hanberry Ct NE 20176
Hancock Pl NE 20176
Hanrahan Ct SE 20175
Harbor Hills Ter 20176
Harbour Town Ter 20176
Hardy Ct NE 20176
Harle Pl SW 20175
Harlow Sq 20176
Harmony Church Rd 20175
Harrier Ln 20175
Harrison St NE 20176
Harrison St SE 20175
Harrison Hill Ln 20176
Hartford Ct NE 20176
Hartshire Ter 20176
Hasbrouck Ln 20176
Haversack Ct NE 20176
Hawks Run Ct SE 20175
Hawks View Sq SE 20175
Hawling Pl SW 20175
Heartleaf Ter SE 20175
Heaters Island Ct 20176
Heatherstone Ter 20176
Heavenly Cir 20176
Hebron Ln 20176
Hedgestone Ter NE 20176
Heritage Way NE 20176
Herndon Ct 20176
Hertz Rd 20175
Hetzel Ter SE 20175
Hibler Rd 20175
Hidcote Manor Ln 20176
Hiddenhollow Ln 20175
Higham Ct NE 20176
Highland Creek Dr 20175
Hill Head Pl 20175
Hillside Cir 20176
Hillview Pl SW 20175
Hogback Mountain Rd 20175
Hogeland Mill Rd 20175
Honeycreeper Pl 20175
Hooded Crow Dr 20175
Hopkins Mill Ter 20176
Howitzer Ter NE 20176
Hughesville Rd 20175
Hume Ct SW 20175
Hundred Acres Ln 20175
Hunter Pl 20175
Hunters Crossing Ln 20176
Huntfield Ct NE 20176
Huntmaster Ter NE 20176
Hunton Pl NE 20176
Hunts End Pl 20175
Hutton Cir 20175
Icehouse Ter 20175
Ida Lee Dr NW 20176
Ilam Park Ln 20176
Indian Fields Ct 20176
Indigo Pl 20175
Industrial Ct SE 20175
Ingalls Ct 20176
Inula Sq 20176
Invermere Dr NE 20176
Inverrary Cir 20175
Iron Liege Ct 20176
Ivybridge Ln 20175
Jackson Hole Cir 20175
Jacob Ct SW 20175
Jade Ct 20175
James Monroe Hwy
12400-12448 20176
12450-17399 20176
19200-20599 20175
James Rifle Ct NE 20176
Janney St SW 20175
Jared Sq NE 20176
Jennifer Ct NE 20176
Jennings Ct SE 20175
Jernigan Ter 20176
Jodhpur Dr 20175
Jupiter Hills Ter 20176
Kalmia Sq NE 20176
Kapalua Ter 20176

Kates Ct 20176
Kemper Lakes Ct 20176
Kendra Ter NE 20176
Kenneth Pl SE 20175
Kenslee Hill Ln 20176
Keokuk Ter NE 20176
Kepharts Mill Ter 20176
Kimberley Ct 20176
Kincaid Blvd SE 20175
N King St 20176
S King St 20175
Kingsmill St 20176
Kingsport Dr 20176
Kinloch Ridge Ct 20175
Kinnaird Ter NE 20176
Kintyre Ct 20176
Kipheart Dr 20176
Kittiwake Dr 20176
Kitty Ln 20176
Koslowski Sq 20176
Kristin Ct SE 20175
Lacey Ct SW 20175
Lackawanna Way NE 20176
Lafayette Pl & Ter 20175
Lake Ridge Pl 20176
Lake View Way NW 20176
Lamz Pl 20176
Lanier Island Sq 20176
Lansdowne Blvd 20176
Larch Valley Ct NE 20176
Lark Song Ct SE 20175
Lasswell Ct SW 20175
Laurel Hill Ct 20176
Laurel Springs Dr 20175
Laurel Wood Ct 20175
Lawford Dr SW 20175
Lawnhill Ct SW 20175
Lawson Rd SE 20175
Le Notre Pl 20175
Lecroy Cir 20175
Lee Ave SW 20175
Lee Patent Dr 20175
Leeland Orchard Rd 20175
Leelynn Farm Ln 20176
Lees Crossing Ln 20176
Lees Mill Sq 20176
Leesburg Mobile Park 20175
Legrace Ter NE 20176
Leighfield Ln 20175
Leisure World Blvd 20176
Lennon Ct SE 20175
Lester Ct NE 20176
Levade Dr 20175
Lewis Ct 20175
Liberty St NW 20176
Liberty St SW 20175
Liebchen Ln 20175
Lilac Ter NE 20176
Lime Kiln Rd 20175
Limestone Ct 20175
Limestone Branch Pl 20176
Limestone School Rd 20175
Linden Hill Way SW 20175
Linfield Ter NE 20176
Lismore Ter NE 20176
Little Angel Ct 20175
Little Oatlands Ln 20175
Little Sorrel Ln 20175
Little Spring Rd 20176
Llewellyn Ct 20175
Lochiel Ln 20176
Locust Hill Ln 20176
Locust Knoll Dr NW 20176
Logans Creek Ln 20175
London Council Ln 20175
Longfellow Dr NE 20176
Longhouse Pl 20175
Lost Corner Rd 20176
Loudoun St SE & SW 20175
Loudoun Center Pl 20175
Loudoun Orchard Rd 20175
Lounsbury Ct NE 20176
Loyalty Rd 20176
Lucarno Ln 20175
Lucketts Rd 20176
Lynchburg Ter NE 20176

Macalister Dr SE 20175
Madison Ct SE 20175
Madison Hill Pl 20175
Magnolia Grove Sq 20176
Magruder Pl SE 20175
Mahala St 20176
Mahogany Run Ct 20176
Malloch Pl 20176
Malvosin Pl 20176
Manbar Ln 20175
Manor House Rd 20175
Maple Spring Ct 20176
Maple View Ln 20176
Maplewood Ln 20175
E Market St 20176
Marlow St SW 20175
Marshall Dr NE 20176
Maruca Ct 20176
Marvins Mill Ter 20176
Maryanne Ave SW 20175
Masons Ln SE 20175
Max Ct SE 20175
Maximillian Ct SW 20175
Mayfair Dr NE 20176
Mcarthur Ter NE 20176
Mcconnell Way 20176
Mcdowell Sq 20176
Mcintosh Pl 20175
Mcleary Sq SE 20175
Meade Dr SW 20175
Meadow Brook Ct SW 20175
Meadowood Ct 20176
Meadows Ln NE 20176
Meadowview Ct 20175
Mechling Farm Ln 20175
Meherrin Ter SW 20175
Melody Ct SE 20175
Melrose Spring Ln 20176
Memorial Dr NW 20176
Menlow Dr NE 20176
Merchant Mill Ter 20176
Merlon Ct 20176
Merritt Farm Ln 20176
Michael Patrick Ct SE 20175
Mid Ocean Pl 20176
Mill Branch Dr 20175
Mill Dam Pl 20175
Mill House Sq 20176
Mill Park Ct 20176
Mill Race Ter 20176
Mill Ridge Ter 20176
Mill Run Ct 20176
Mill Site Pl 20176
Mill Spring Ct 20176
Millbrook Ter NE 20176
Miller Dr SE 20175
Millwright Ter 20176
Mindy Ct SE 20175
Miramonte Ter 20176
Mission Hills Way 20176
Monarch Beach Sq 20176
Monroe St SE 20175
Monroe Glen Ln 20175
Montacute Ln 20176
Montauk Ct NE 20176
Montevista Sq 20176
Montjoy Ct 20175
Montresor Rd 20176
Montview Sq 20176
Moore Pl SW 20175
Moorland Ct 20176
Morrisett Ct SE 20175
Morrisworth Ln 20175
Morven Park Ct NW 20176
Morven Park Rd NW 20176
Morven Park Rd SW 20175
Mosby Dr SW 20175
Moselle Way 20176
Moss Valley Ln 20175
Moultrie Ter NE 20176
Mount Gilead Rd 20175
Mount Holly Pl NE 20176
Mountain Meadow Ln 20176
Mountain Spring Ln 20175
Moxley Dr NE 20176
Muffin Ct SE 20175

Mullfield Village Ter 20176
Musket Ct NE 20176
Myers Pl 20175
Myersville Ln 20176
Nansemond St SE 20175
Natalma Ct 20176
Nathan Pl NE 20176
Nautical Jive Dr 20176
Needles Ct 20176
Nelson Ct NE 20176
Nestlewood Rd 20176
Neville Ct SE 20175
Newberry Ter 20176
Newhall Pl SW 20175
Newington Pl NE 20176
Newton Pl 20175
Newton Pass Sq 20176
Newvalley Church Rd 20176
Nickels Dr & Pl 20175
Nickman Way 20175
Nikki Ter SE 20175
Nikos St 20176
Niven Ct SW 20175
Nolands Ferry Rd 20176
Nolen Ct 20175
Norborne Ct 20176
Norman Pl 20175
Normandy Dr NW 20176
Norris Ct SW 20175
North St NE & NW 20176
Northampton Ln 20175
Northlake Blvd 20176
Northlake Overlook Ter 20176
Northridge Pl 20175
Nottoway St SE 20175
Oak Bucket Ln 20175
Oak Lake Ct 20176
Oak View Dr SE 20175
Oakcrest Manor Dr NE 20176
Oakland Green Rd 20175
Oatlands Chase Pl 20175
Oatlands Mill Rd 20175
Oatlands Plantation Ln 20175
Occoquan Ter SW 20175
Oconnors Cir 20175
Octorora Pl NE 20176
Old Dory Ln 20176
Old English Ct SW 20175
Old Hickory Ln 20175
Old Reilly Ln 20175
Old Waterford Rd NW 20176
Olympic Blvd 20176
Oneills Way 20175
Opal Ct 20175
Orchard Manor Ln 20175
Orchid Dr 20176
Orr Cir SW 20175
Osterly Ln 20176
Over Reach Ct 20176
Overview Pl 20175
Paddington Way NE 20176
Paddock Ct NW 20176
Palliser Ct 20176
Palmetto Dunes Ter 20176
Panorama Pl 20176
Panther Ct 20176
Parallel Bluffs Ct 20176
Park Gate Dr SE 20175
Park Hunt Ct 20176
Park Meadow Ct 20175
Parker Ct SE 20175
Parkers Ridge Dr 20176
Partridge Pl 20175
Pathway Ct & Pl 20175
Patrice Dr SE 20175
Patterson Ct NW 20176
Paw Print Ln 20176
Peaceful Stream Dr 20176
Peale Ln 20175
Pearce Cir 20176
Pearlbush Sq NE 20176
Peers Sq 20176
Pelicans Nest Way 20176
Pencader Way 20176

Peppermill Ter NE 20176
Perdido Bay Ter 20176
Periwinkle Way SW 20175
Pershing Ave NW 20176
Perthshire Ct 20175
Peters Ct 20176
Petunia Ter SE 20175
Pheasant Pl SW 20175
Phillips Ct & Dr 20176
Pickett Ridge Pl 20176
Piedmont Ridge Sq 20176
Pierpoint Ter 20176
Pileated Ter 20176
Pineview Sq 20176
Pink Azalea Ter SE 20175
Pinnacle Ln 20176
Planters Ter NE 20176
Plaza St NE 20176
Plaza St SE 20175
Pon Farr Ct 20175
Popes Creek Sq 20176
Potomac Overlook Ln 20176
Potomac Station Dr NE 20176
Potomac Woods Ln 20176
Powhatan Ct NE 20176
Primrose Ct SW 20175
Prince St NE 20176
Princeton Ct NE 20176
Principal Drummond Way SE 20175
Promenade Dr 20176
Prospect Dr & Pl 20175
Prosperity Ave SE 20175
Purple Aster Ter 20176
Putters Green Ct 20176
Quail Hill Ln 20175
Quarter Horse Ln 20176
Queen St NE 20176
Quinton Oaks Ln 20175
Quiver Ridge Dr 20176
Radford Ter NE 20176
Randi Dr SE 20175
Rangers Way SE 20175
Ranleigh Ter 20176
Raspberry Dr 20176
Raspberry Plain Ln 20176
Red Cedar Dr 20176
Red Hill Rd 20175
Red House Dr 20176
Red Raspberry Ter 20175
Red Rock Way 20176
Redbud Ln NE 20176
Redhill Manor Ct 20175
Renee Ct 20176
Reservoir Rd 20175
Revelstore Ter NE 20176
Revere Ct NE 20176
Rhonda Pl SE 20175
Richard Dr SE 20175
Richmond Sq NE 20176
Riders Success Ln 20175
Ridgeback Ct 20176
Riding Trail Ct NW 20176
Rim Rock Cir 20176
Ripken Way 20176
Rivanna Ter SW 20175
River Farm Ln 20176
River Frays Dr SW 20175
Rivercreek Pkwy 20176
Riverlook Ct 20176
Riverpoint Dr 20176
Riverside Pkwy 20176
Riviera Way 20176
Roanoke Dr SE 20175
Robin Cir 20175
Rock Spring Dr SW 20175
Rockbridge Dr SE 20175
Rockford Sq NE 20176
Rockland Ln 20176
Rocks Way 20176
Rocky Creek Dr 20176
Rocky Crest Ter 20176
Rocky Meadow Ln 20176
Rocky Ridge Ct 20176
Rodney Ln 20175
Roland Ct 20176
Rollins Dr & Pl 20175
Rosebrook Ct NW 20176
Rosefinch Cir 20176
Rosehaven Pl 20176
Rosemeade Pl SW 20175
Rossback Ter 20176
Rothbury Ln 20175
Rouges Sq 20176
Roxbury Hall Rd 20175
Roy Ct SE 20175
Royal St SE & SW 20175
Royal Autumn Ln 20175
Rozier Ct SW 20175
Rubicon Farm Ln 20176
Ruby Dr 20176
Rudy Ter 20176
Rundle Ter 20176
Running Colt Pl 20175
Running Ridge Way 20176
Rusert Dr SE 20175
Rust Dr NE 20176
Rustling Woods Ct 20175
Saber Ct SE 20175
Saddle Tree Pl 20176
Saddleback Pl NE 20176
Saddlebrook Pl 20176
Salem Ct SE 20175
Salyor Way SW 20175
Samuels Mill Ct 20175
Sandpiper Pl 20176
Sandpoint Ct NE 20176
Sandridge Way 20176
Sandy Landing Dr SE 20175
Santmyer Dr SE 20175
Saxon Shore Dr 20176
Scenic Creek Way 20176
Scherazade Pl 20176
Scholar Plz 20176
Sea Island Pl 20176
Seaton Ct SE 20175
Selkirk Greene Ct 20175
Selma Ln 20176
Seminole Ct 20176
Sentinel Dr NE 20176
Shadetree Way SW 20175
Shadow Ter 20176
Shadwell Ter SE 20175
Shady Creek Ct 20175
Shady Oak Ln SW 20175
Shalimar Pointe Ter 20176
Shana Dr SE 20175
Shanks Evans Rd NE 20176
Shelburne Glebe Rd 20175
Shenandoah St SE 20175
Shenstone Run Ct 20175
Sherbrooke Ter 20176
Sheridan Way SW 20175
Sherry Ann Ct SE 20175
Shields Ter NE 20176
Shiloh Pl SE 20175
Shinniecock Hills Pl 20176
Shirley Sq SE 20175
Shiso Ct 20176
Shoal Creek Dr 20176
Showers Ln 20175
Shreve Mill Rd 20175
Shropshire Ct 20176
Shumate Ct 20175
Sidesaddle Ct 20176
Sierra Springs Sq 20176
Silver Charm Pl 20176
Silver Hill Ln 20175
Silverado Ter 20176
Silverbell Ter NE 20176
Silverside Dr 20176
Silverwood Ter 20176
Skillsusa Way 20176
Skinner Sq 20176
Skip Away Ct 20176
Slack Ln NE 20176
Slatestone Ct 20176
Small Island Ln 20176
Smarts Mill Ln 20176
Smartts Ln NE 20176
Smith Ferry Sq 20176
Smythe Way 20175
Snider House Ct 20175
Snowberry Ct 20176
Snowden Ct SW 20175
Solti Way 20175
Somercote Ln 20175
Somerset Park Dr SE 20175
South St SE & SW 20175
Southern Planter Ln 20176
Southpaw Pl 20175
Southview Pl NE 20176
Spanish Bay Ct 20176
Sparkleberry Ter NE 20176
Spectacular Bid Pl 20176
Spencer Ter SE 20175
Spinks Ferry Rd 20176
Spirit Ct NE 20176
Spotted Owl Dr 20175
Spring Cellar Ct 20176
Spring Creek Ln 20176
Springfield Ln 20175
Springhollow Ln 20175
Springhouse Sq SE 20175
Springrun Ln 20176
Springvalley Ln 20175
Springview Ct 20176
Squirrel Ridge Pl 20176
St Clair Ln 20176
St Georges Ct 20176
Stable View Ter NE 20176
Stagecoach Ln 20175
Stallion Sq NE 20176
Stanford Farm Ln 20175
Star Violet Ter 20175
Stargell Ter 20176
Steed Hill Ln 20176
Steger Pl 20176
Stone Ct NE 20176
Stone Fence Ter 20176
Stone Fox Ct 20175
Stone Haven Dr 20176
Stone School Ln 20175
Stonefield Sq NE 20176
Stoneledge Pl NE 20176
Stoney Brook Sq 20176
Stowers Ln SE 20175
Stratford Pl SW 20175
Stream Crossing Ct 20176
Stream Farm Ln 20176
Stribling Ct SW 20175
Stumptown Rd 20176
Sugarbush Ct 20176
Sugarloaf View Ln 20176
Summit Ash Ct 20176
Sundrum Pl NE 20176
Sunrise View Ct 20176
Sunset Course Ter NE 20176
Sunset View Ter SE 20175
Surreyfield Way 20175
Susquehanna Sq 20176
Sweet Spring Ln 20176
Sweet William Ct SE 20175
Sweetberry Ct 20176
Sweig Ter 20176
Swiftwater Dr 20176
Sycolin Rd SE 20175
Sydney Ter NE 20176
Sydnor Hill Ct 20175
Sylvan Bluff Dr 20176
Tall Oaks Sq SE 20175
Talmadge Ct SE 20175
Tammy Ter SE 20175
Tanager Pl 20175
Tantara Ter 20176
Tarara Ln 20176
Tavistock Dr SE 20175
Taylor Springs Ct 20175
Taylorstown Rd 20176
Taymount Ter NE 20176
Teaberry Dr 20176
Tearose Pl SW 20175
Tecumseh Ter NE 20176
Temple Hall Ln 20176
Tenaya Way NE 20176
Tennessee Dr NE 20176
Tess Dr 20175
Thaddeus Ln 20176
The Woods Rd 20176
Thistle Way NE 20176
Thomas Lee Way 20176
Thomas Mill Rd 20175
Thornberry Sq 20176
Tides Inn Way 20176
Tim Tam Ct 20176
Timber Sq 20176
Timoney Ct 20176
Tina Dr SE 20175
Tinsman Dr NE 20176
Tobermory Pl 20175
Tolbert Ln SE 20175
Tomkal Ln 20176
Tomworth Ct NE 20176
Tonquin Pl NE 20176
Toucan Way 20175
Tow Path Ter 20176
Town Branch Ter SW 20175
Tracy Ct NE 20176
Trailview Blvd SE 20175
Travelers Run Ln 20176
Treehouse Ct 20176
Trengwinton Pl 20176
Trenton Cir 20175
Trident Sq 20176
Trimble Plz SE 20175
Trongate Ct 20176
Trottingpath Ct 20176
Tuckaway Pl 20176
Tudor Ct NE 20176
Tuliptree Sq NE 20176
Tupelo Ridge Ter 20176
Turnberry Isle Ct 20176
Turner Farm Ln 20175
Turning Leaf Ln 20176
Tuscarora Dr SW 20175
Tutt Ln 20176
Twin Maple Ln 20176
Twintree Ter NE 20176
Twynholme Ln 20175
Tyrrell Ct 20176
Union St NW 20176
Upper Belmont Pl 20176
Upper Meadow Dr 20176
Valemount Ter NE 20176
Valley View Ave SW 20175
Valleybrook Ln 20176
Vanderbilt Ter SE 20175
Verleard Rd 20175
Vermillion Dr NE 20176
Vestals Pl 20176
Victory Ln 20176
Village Green Dr 20176
Village Market Blvd SE 20175
Viola Ct 20176
Virginia Wildflower Ter 20175
Vista Grande Ct SW 20175
Vista Ridge Dr NE 20176
Wage Dr SW 20175
Wakehurst Pl 20176
Walker Run Dr 20175
Wallace Dr SE 20175
Warbler Sq 20176
Ward Cir SW 20175
Ward Hill Rd 20175
Warner Ct SW 20175
Warren Glen Ln 20175
Warrenton Ter NE 20176
Warwick Hills Ct 20176
Washington St NE 20176
Water Bay Ter 20176
Waterfield Ter NE 20176
Waterford Woods Ct 20176
Waters Overlook Ct 20176
Watson Rd 20175
Waxwing Dr 20175
Weaver Ct 20175
Westchester Sq 20176
Westerville Way 20175
Whipp Dr SE 20175
Whirlaway Ct 20176
Whisper Ct 20176
Whispering Brook Pl 20175
White Pl SW 20175
White Clay Pl 20175
White Gate Pl 20175
Whitegate Rd 20175
Whitehorse Ct SW 20175
Whites Ferry Rd 20176
Whitney Pl NE 20176
Wide Meadow Sq 20176
Wiggum Sq 20176
Wild Dunes Sq 20176
Wild Ginger Ter 20176
Wild Goose Ln 20175
Wild Indigo Ter 20176
Wild Onion Ter 20175
Wild Turkey Way SW 20175
Wilderness Acres Cir 20175
Wildman St NE 20176
Wilkinson Dr NE 20176
William St NW 20176
Wilson Ave NW 20176
Wilt Store Rd 20176
Wilton Dr 20175
Windowsills Way 20175
Windy Creek Ln 20176
Windybush Cir & Dr 20175
Wing Tip Ct SW 20175
Wingate Pl SW 20175
Winmeade Dr 20176
Winning Colors Pl 20176
Winterberry Dr SE 20175
Wirt St NW 20176
Wirt St SW 20175
Wolfe Ct SW 20175
Woodberry Rd NE 20176
Woodbridge Ct NE 20176
Woodburn Rd 20175
Woodchester Ct 20176
Woodcock Ct 20175
Woodcrest Ln 20176
Woodfield Ter NE 20176
Woodlea Dr SW 20175
Woodridge Pkwy 20176
Woods Edge Dr NE 20176
Woodside Pl 20175
Woodstar Ct 20176
Woodwinds Dr 20175
Woolsthorpe Dr 20176
Wrenbury Ln 20175
Wythe Ct NE 20176
Xerox Dr 20176
York Ln SE 20175
Young Ln 20176
Zachary Ln 20176

NUMBERED STREETS

All Street Addresses 20175

LORTON VA

General Delivery 22079

POST OFFICE BOXES MAIN OFFICE STATIONS AND BRANCHES

Box No.s
All PO Boxes 22199

NAMED STREETS

Accotink Rd 22079
Acheson Ct 22079
Adams Chase Cir 22079
Ainsley Ct 22079
Albert Ln 22079
Alexandra Nicole Dr 22079
Allen Park Rd 22079
Allerdale Ct 22079
Almeda Ct 22079
Alverton St 22079
American Holly Rd 22079
Amity St 22079
Amsterdam St 22079
Angleton Ct 22079
Anita Dr 22079
Annette Dr 22079
Anzio Ln 22079
Apollo St 22079
Arcade St 22079
Arch Hall Rd 22079
Ardglass Ct & Dr 22079
Armistead Rd 22079
Ashland Woods Ln 22079
Ashmeadow Ct 22079
Aspenpark Ct & Rd 22079
Ataturk Way 22079
Athey Rd 22079
Aurora Ct 22079
Aventon Ct 22079
Ayden Ln 22079
Backlick Rd 22079
Baird Ct 22079
Bakers Dr 22079
Ballendine Ct 22079
Bard St 22079
Barrow Furnace Ln 22079
Bates Rd 22079
Bellwether Ct 22079
Belmont Blvd 22079
Belmont Landing Rd 22079
Belvoir View Pl 22079
Benham St 22079
Bennington Blvd 22079
Bertsky Ln 22079
Billsam Ct 22079
Birch Bay Cir 22079
Birch Crest Way 22079
Birchfield Way 22079
Bitterroot Ct 22079
Blackfoot Ct 22079
Blanche Dr 22079
Blu Steel Way 22079
Blue Bird Woods Ct 22079
Blue Rock Ln 22079
Bluebird Way 22079
Bluebonnet Dr 22079
Boot Ct 22079
Braleant Rd 22079
Brook Estates Ct 22079
Broughton Craggs Ln 22079
Buckland Pl 22079
Bulkley Rd 22079
Cacapon Ct 22079
California Poppy Ln 22079
Calla Lily Ct 22079
Calvert Cliff Ct 22079
Canaan Ct 22079
Capron Ct 22079
Cardiff St 22079
Cardinal Forest Ln 22079
Cardinal Woods Ct 22079
Carpenters Hall Dr 22079
Carsley Ct 22079
Carson Rd 22079
Catbird Cir 22079
Catskill Rd 22079
Chapman Rd 22079
Charlesborough Ct 22079
Chaucer House Ct 22079
Chauncey Ln 22079
Cherokee Rose Way 22079
Cherwek Dr 22079
Chippewa Ct 22079
Cinder Bed Rd 22079
Clematis Trl 22079
Clementine Ct 22079
Cockburn Ct 22079
Colgrove Ct 22079
Conell Ct 22079
Corder Ln 22079
Cranford St 22079
Cranford Farm Cir 22079
Crepe Myrtle Ct 22079
Cresswell Lndg 22079
Crosby St 22079
Cross Chase Cir 22079
Crossbrook Ct 22079
Crosspointe Glen Ct & Way 22079
Cullum Dr & St 22079
Cumbria Valley Dr 22079
Daniel French St 22079
Davis Dr 22079
Day St 22079
Dayton St 22079
Deer Xing 22079
Delphinium Trl 22079
Denali Way 22079
Derwent Valley Ct 22079
Devries Ct & Dr 22079
Dixon St 22079
Dockray Ct 22079
Dogue Hollow Ln 22079
Dogue Indian Cir 22079
Dolly Dr 22079
Dolsie Grove Dr 22079
Dorcey Pl 22079
Douglas Fir Dr 22079
Dove Cottage Ct 22079
Duck Hawk Way 22079
Dudley Dr 22079
Dutchman Dr 22079
Eaton Woods Pl 22079
Edgemar Woods Ct 22079
Edwardene Ln 22079
Elk Horn Rd 22079
Elkhorne Run Ct 22079
Enochs Dr 22079
Evergreen Trl 22079
Fairfield Woods Ct 22079
Fallswood Way 22079
Fascination Ct 22079
Finnegan St 22079
Fisher Woods Dr 22079
Fitt Ct 22079
Flowering Dogwood Ln 22079
Forest Greens Dr 22079
Fox Glove Trl 22079
Fran Ct 22079
Franklin Dr 22079
Franklin Woods Pl 22079
French Rd 22079
Frosty Ct 22079
Furey Rd 22079
Furnace Rd 22079
Galvin Ln 22079
George Fox Pl 22079
Giles Run Rd 22079
Gilmore Dr 22079
Gilroy Dr 22079
Gingerspice Pl 22079
Golden Ridge Ct 22079
Grace Church Ln 22079
Graceway Dr 22079
Grady Ct 22079
Grandwind Dr 22079
Graysons Mill Ln 22079
Green Heron Way 22079
Greencastle Ln 22079
Greene Dr 22079
Guadalcanal Dr 22079
Gunston Dr 22079
Gunston Plz
7700-7726 22079
7726-7726 22199
7728-7798 22079
Gunston Rd 22079
Gunston Commons Way 22079
Gunston Corner Ln 22079
Gunston Cove Rd 22079
Gunston Hill Ln 22079
Gunston Road Way 22079
Gunston Woods Pl 22079
Hagel Cir 22079
Haines Dr 22079
Haislip Ln 22079
Halley Ct 22079
Hallowing Dr 22079
Hamilton Ct & Rd 22079
Hampton Station Ct 22079
Hanson Ln 22079
Harley Rd 22079

Harrogate Ct 22079
Harrover Pl 22079
Hassett St 22079
Hawkshead Dr 22079
Haywood Ave 22079
Heather Ridge Ct 22079
Heller Rd 22079
Henry Pl 22079
Henry Knox Dr 22079
Hibiscus Ct 22079
High Point Rd 22079
Higham Rd 22079
Highgrove Ct 22079
Highland Woods Ct 22079
Hill Ct, Dr & Way 22079
Hill Park Ct & Dr 22079
Hollister Ct 22079
Holly Pl 22079
Hollymeade Dr 22079
Hooes Rd 22079
Horseshoe Cottage Cir 22079
Hucks Bridge Cir 22079
Hundith Hill Ct 22079
Igoe St 22079
Indian Paintbrush Way 22079
Inverary Ct 22079
Jameson St 22079
Jandell Rd 22079
Jasmine Trl 22079
Jenerio Ct 22079
John Sutherland Ln 22079
Kanawha Ct 22079
Kelford Ct 22079
Kenosha Ct 22079
Kentia Trl 22079
Kernon Ct 22079
Khalsa Ct 22079
Kiger St 22079
Kincannon Pl 22079
Kirby Lionsdale Dr 22079
Koluder Ct 22079
Koopman Ct 22079
Lagrange St 22079
Lake Hill Dr 22079
Lakeland Fells Ln 22079
Lambkin Ct 22079
Lancer Ridge Ct 22079
Landerfield Ct 22079
Lantana Trl 22079
Larne Ct & Ln 22079
Laurel Crest Dr 22079
Laurel Crossing Ln 22079
Laurel Heights Loop 22079
Laurel Overlook Dr 22079
Laurel Ridge Crossing Rd 22079
Lazy Point Ln 22079
Lee Masey Dr 22079
Legion Dr 22079
Lewis Chapel Cir & Rd 22079
Linden Oaks Ct 22079
Linnett Hill Dr 22079
Lockport Pl 22079
Lone Star Ct & Rd 22079
Lorfax Dr 22079
Lorraine Carol Way 22079
Lorton Rd 22079
Lorton Market St 22079
Lorton Station Blvd 22079
Lorton Valley Rd 22079
Lyndam Hill Cir 22079
Macsvega Ct 22079
Madison Dr 22079
Mahoney Dr 22079
Mallard Rd 22079
Mallow Trl 22079
Mariah Jefferson Ct 22079
Marie Ct 22079
Marin Woods Ct 22079
Marion Pl 22079
Marovelli Forest Dr 22079
Masey Mcquire Ct 22079
Mayhew Ct 22079
Mccandlish Trl 22079
Mccarty Rd 22079
Mccauley Way 22079
Mccloud Ct 22079
Meadowcreek Ln 22079
Middle Ruddings Dr 22079
Midway Ln & Pl 22079
Milford Haven Ct & Dr 22079
Millom Ct 22079
Mims St 22079
Mistletoe Ln 22079
Mockingbird Woods Ct 22079
Monacan Ct & Rd 22079
Mooregate Ct 22079
Mordor Dr 22079
Mount Vernon Blvd 22079
Mountain Larkspur Dr 22079
Native Violet Dr 22079
Newby Bridge Dr 22079
Newington Rd 22079
Newington Commons Rd 22079
Newtowne Ct 22079
Nicotine Trl 22079
Nirvana Ct 22079
Oak Grove St 22079
Oakridge Woods Ct 22079
Occoquan Overlook Dr 22079
Old Beech Ct 22079
Old Colchester Rd 22079
Old Pohick Ct & Way 22079
Old Spring Dr 22079
Old Vicarage St 22079
Ona Dr 22079
Orange Blossom Trl 22079
Osprey Ridge Ln 22079
Owens View Ct 22079
Ox Rd 22079
Palmer Dr 22079
Paper Birch Dr 22079
Paris St 22079
Park Rd 22079
Parson Massey Pl 22079
Parsonage Ln 22079
Pasquel Flower Pl 22079
Pasture Rose Ct 22079
Peace Lily Ct 22079
Peach Blossom Trl 22079
Penfield Ct 22079
Peniwill Dr 22079
Periwinkle Blue Ct 22079
Phelps Lake Ct 22079
Pinion Pl 22079
Pink Carnation Ct 22079
Pinnacle Rock Ct 22079
Plaskett Ln 22079
Plaskett Forest Ln 22079
Pohick Rd 22079
Pohick Bay Dr 22079
Pohick River Dr 22079
S Pointe Ln 22079
Pollen St 22079
Porters Hill Ln 22079
Potomac Rd 22079
Potomac View Blvd 22079
Pott Ct 22079
Potters Hill Cir 22079
Purple Lilac Cir & Ct 22079
Purvis Dr 22079
Rainwater Pl 22079
Ravenglass Ct 22079
Red Bird Woods Ct 22079
Red Carnation Ct 22079
Red Eagle Ct 22079
Reiser Ln 22079
Rhododendron Cir & Ct 22079
Rhondda Dr 22079
Richmond Hwy 22079
Ridgely Dr 22079
River Dr & Rd 22079
Robert Lundy Pl 22079
Rocky Gap Ct 22079
Rocky Knob Ct 22079
Rommel Dr 22079
Royal Robin Ln 22079
Royal Tern Way 22079
Saint Catherines Ln 22079
Salisbury Hollow Ln 22079
Saluda Ct 22079
Samuel Wallis St 22079
Sanderling Way 22079
Sanger St 22079
Saunas Ct 22079
Seafarer Way 22079
Sebrell St 22079
Sego Lily Ct 22079
Shannons Landing Way 22079
Sheffield Green Way 22079
Sheffield Hunt Ct & Rd 22079
Sheffield Village Ln 22079
Shepherd Hills Ct & Dr 22079
Shirley Woods Ct 22079
Silassie Ct 22079
Silver Ann Dr 22079
Silverbrook Rd 22079
Silverdale Ct & Rd 22079
Silvershadow Ct 22079
Silverview Ct & Dr 22079
Singleleaf Cir & Ln 22079
Skiddaw Dr 22079
Sloway Coast Dr 22079
Snapdragon Pl 22079
Snowy Egrit Way 22079
Southern Oaks Ct 22079
Springfield Dr 22079
Springwood Meadow Ln 22079
Stana Ct 22079
Stargazer Lily Ct 22079
Stationhouse Ct 22079
Stonegarden Dr 22079
Stovall Ct 22079
Sullenberger Ct 22079
Summerhill Ct 22079
Surry Grove Ct 22079
Susquehanna St 22079
Swans Creek Way 22079
Sweet Pecan Dr 22079
Sylvania St 22079
Talbert Rd 22079
Tangerine Pl 22079
Tanyard Ln 22079
Tea Table Dr 22079
Telegraph Rd 22079
Telegraph Crossing Ct 22079
Telegraph Square Dr 22079
Terminal Rd 22079
Thomas Baxter Pl 22079
Thomas Nevitt St 22079
Thwaite Howe Dr 22079
Tiddle Way 22079
Timarand Ct 22079
Titleist Trl 22079
Treasure Oak Ct 22079
Trestle Ct 22079
Two Bays Rd 22079
Unity Ln 22079
Usher Dr 22079
Virginia Ter 22079
Waites Way 22079
Waldren Dr & Way 22079
Wasdale Head Dr 22079
Weatherly Way 22079
Wells Rd 22079
Western Hemlock Way 22079
Whernside Ct & St 22079
White Feather Ct 22079
White Orchid Pl 22079
Whitehaven Ct 22079
Whitly Way 22079
Whitsell Way 22079
Wild Prairie Rose Way 22079
Wildwood Ct & St 22079
Wiley Dr 22079
William Augustus Ct 22079
Wilma Ln 22079
Windermere Hill Rd 22079
Windrush Dr 22079
Windstead Manor Dr 22079
Winstead Manor Ct & Ln 22079
Wolford Way 22079
Wood Spice Ln 22079
Woodside Ln 22079
Workhouse Rd & Way 22079
Wounded Knee Rd 22079
Wrights Hollow Ln 22079
Wynnefield Ct 22079
Yellow Daisy Pl 22079
Yorkshire View Ct 22079

NUMBERED STREETS

All Street Addresses 22079

LYNCHBURG VA

General Delivery 24506

POST OFFICE BOXES MAIN OFFICE STATIONS AND BRANCHES

Box No.s
1 - 1660 24505
1 - 2 24502
2000 - 2000 24506
2001 - 2960 24505
3001 - 3620 24503
4001 - 4816 24502
6001 - 9000 24505
10001 - 12300 24506
15001 - 15240 24502
20000 - 41000 24506

RURAL ROUTES

06, 10 24502
04, 07, 12 24503
03, 08 24504

NAMED STREETS

Aaron Pl 24502
Abbey Ct 24503
Abert Rd 24503
Acorn St 24501
Acres Ct 24502
Adam Hill Ct 24503
Adammay Ln 24501
Adams Dr 24502
Adams St 24504
Adams Ridge Trl 24503
Adams View Ln 24503
Addie Way 24501
Adele St 24503
Airpark Dr 24502
Airport Cir & Rd 24502
Alabama Ave 24502
Albemarle Dr 24503
Albert Lankford Dr 24501
Alclif Dr 24503
Alleghany Ave 24501
Alpine Dr 24502
Alta Ln 24502
Alum Springs Rd 24502
Alydar Pl 24503
Amaya Dr 24503
Amelia St 24501
Amherst St
200-299 24503
400-599 24504
Ann St 24504
Anniebelle Ln 24501
Anslem Dr 24504
Anthony Pl 24501
Apache Ln 24502
Aragon St 24501
Archway Ct 24502
Ardmore Cir & Dr 24501
Arkansas Ave 24501
Arlington Pl & St 24503
Arlington Heights Dr 24501
Arrow St 24503
Arrowhead Dr 24502
Arthur Dr 24502
Arts Aly 24502
Ash St 24503
Ash Grove Dr 24502
Ashbourne Dr 24501
Ashland Pl 24503
Ashley Dr 24501
Ashmont Ct 24503
Atherholt Rd 24501
Atlanta Ave 24502
Audubon Dr & Pl 24503
Augusta Pl 24503
Augusta St 24501
Aultice Ln 24504
Autumn Dr 24502
Avalon Rd & St 24501
Averill Ct 24501
Avondale Dr 24502
Ayers Rd 24504
Azalea Pl 24503
B St 24504
Bailey St 24504
Baker Rd 24502
Baldwin Cir 24502
Ballard Ct 24501
Banbury Ln 24503
Bard Ln 24502
Barkley Ct 24503
Barrington Way 24502
Bass St 24501
Bateau Dr 24503
Battery St 24503
Bay St 24501
Bcc Dr 24503
Beacon Ct 24502
Beacon Hill Pl 24503
Bear Den Trak 24502
Beasley Rd 24501
Beaver Creek Xing 24501
Beck Ln 24504
Bedford Ave
900-1899 24504
1900-2399 24503
Bedford Springs Rd 24502
Bee Dr 24502
Beech St 24504
Beechnut Dr 24504
Beechwood Dr 24502
Beemer Trl 24503
Belfield Pl 24503
Bell Rd & St 24501
Bell Tavern Rd 24503
Bella Ct 24502
Belle Terre Dr 24501
Bellwood Dr 24501
Belmont Pl 24502
Belmont St 24504
Belvedere St 24503
Bennett Dr 24501
Bennie Ln 24501
Bennington Dr 24503
Bent Oak Ct 24502
Bentridge Ct & Way 24501
Berger St 24501
Berkley Pl 24501
Berkshire Dr 24504
Berkshire Pl 24502
Bethel Park Dr 24502
Beverly St 24501
Beverly Hills Cir 24502
Bexley Dr 24502
Biltmore Ave 24502
Birch St 24503
Birch Haven Dr 24502
Birchwood Dr 24501
Bishops Ln 24503
Blackberry Ct 24502
Blackburn St 24501
Blackford St 24504
Blackhawke Dr 24502
Blackstone Pl 24503
Blane Dr 24502
Blenheim Dr 24502
Blue Dr 24502
Blue Buckle Aly 24501
Blue Gap Cir & Rd 24503
Blue Ridge St 24501
Bluff St 24504
Blumont Dr 24503
Bocock Rd 24501
Bon Ton Cir & Rd 24503
Bonair Cir 24503
Bonneville Pl 24501
Bonsack St 24501
Boone Hill Dr 24503
Boonsboro Dr, Pl & Rd 24503
Border St 24502
Boston Ave
200-399 24503
1600-1699 24504
1700-1999 24503
Botetourt St 24504
Box Ln 24501
Bradford Ln 24502
Bradley Ct 24502
Bradley Dr 24501
Bramble Pl 24502
Brambleridge Ct 24502
Brandi Ct 24504
Brandon Rd 24502
Bransford St 24504
Breckenbridge St 24501
Breeze Hill Ln 24504
Breezewood Dr 24502
Brenleigh Ct 24501
Brenna Ln 24501
Brentwood Ave 24502
Brevard St 24501
Briar Cliff Cir 24502
Briarwood Ln 24501
Briarwood St 24503
Bridge St 24504
Bridgeton Ct 24502
Bridle Rock Ct 24503
Bright Star Ct 24501
Brightside Dr 24501
Bristol St 24501
Broadway St 24501
Brook St 24501
Brookfield Rd 24503
Brooklawn Cir & Dr 24502
Brookside Ln 24501
Brookville Cir & Ln 24502
Brookwood Dr 24501
Brown Haven Ln 24501
Browns Dr 24502
Brunswick Dr 24502
Brunswick Rd 24503
Brush Tavern Dr 24502
Bryant Rd 24502
Buchanan St 24501
Buckhead Rd 24502
Buckingham Dr 24502
Buena Vista St 24504
Burnham Ln 24502
Burnt Bridge Rd 24503
Burr Oak Rd 24502
Burton Creek Pl 24502
Buxton Dr 24502
Byrd St 24504
C St 24504
Cabell St 24504
Cabin Field Rd 24504
E & W Cadbury Dr 24501
Callaham St 24501
Callaway Ct 24502
Calloway Cottage Trl 24503
Calumet Ct 24503
Cambria St 24502
Cambridge Dr 24502
Cambridge Pl
1-1299 24502
2200-2299 24503
Camp Ave 24501
Camp Hydaway Rd 24501
Campbell Ave 24501
Campbell Dr 24502
Campbell Hwy 24501
Campbell Hwy N 24501
Campbell 1 Ave 24501
Candlers Mountain Rd 24502
Candlewood Ct 24502
Canterbury Ct 24503
Cape Charles Sq 24502
Cape Fear Ct 24502
Cape Henry Ct 24502
Cape Lookout Ct 24502
Cape Point Ct 24502
Capital St 24502
Capstone Dr 24502
Cardinal Pl 24503
Cardwell Ln 24504
Carnell Ln 24504
Caroline St 24501
Carra St 24502
Carriage Way 24503
Carrington Ln 24503
Carrington Rd 24501
Carroll Ave 24501
Carter St 24501
Carters Grove Ln 24503
Carver St 24502
Cary St 24501
Cascade Ct 24502
Casey Dr 24502
Castle Pl 24503
Catalina Pl 24502
Catalpa Rd 24502
Catherine Ct 24501
Cavalier Ct 24502
Cavalry Ln 24502
Cedar Dr 24503
Cedar St 24504
Cedar Branch Rd 24502
Cedar Creek Ln 24503
Cedar Hill Dr 24502
Cedar Hills Dr 24503
Cedar Lane Ct 24503
Cedar Ridge Dr 24503
Center St 24501
Centerdale St 24501
Chadwick Dr 24502
Chambers St 24501
Chambersville St 24503
Channie Ln 24504
Chapel Ln 24501
Charldon Rd 24501
Charlotte St 24503
Chateau Pl 24502
Cheese Creek Rd 24503
Chelsey Ct 24502
Cherokee Ave 24502
Cherokee Dr 24501
Cherry St 24504
Chesney Dr 24502
Chesterfield Pl & Rd 24502
Chestnut Hill Dr 24502
Chestnut Hill Rd 24503
Chestnut Mountain Rd 24504
Chevy Ln 24501
Cheyenne Dr 24502
Chikasaw Rd 24502
Chilarna Ln 24503
Chinook Dr 24501
Chinook Pl 24502
Chowan Ave 24502
Chris Ln 24502
Church St 24504
Churchill Dr 24502
Circle Ct 24504
Circle Dr 24504
Circle Rd 24501
Citation Ln 24503
Clair Ct 24503
Clair Ln 24501
Clarke St 24502
Clay St 24504
Claymont Dr 24502
Clayton Ave 24503
Clearview Dr 24503
Clennest St 24504
Cleveland Ave 24503

liff St 24501
lifton St 24501
linton St 24503
lipton Ct 24503
loseburn Manor Dr 24502
lover Ln & Pl 24501
lub Dr & Ter 24503
lubhouse Dr 24502
lubridge Rd 24503
lydesdale Dr 24501
oal St 24504
obblestone Dr 24502
obbs St 24501
offee Rd 24503
og Ln 24501
ohen Pl 24501
olby Rd 24501
ollege Dr & St 24501
ollege Park Dr 24502
ollington Dr 24502
olonial Ct 24503
olonnade St 24502
olumbia Ave 24503
omanche Pl 24502
ommerce St 24504
oncord Tpke 24504
oncrete Dr 24501
one Dr 24501
onfederate Ave 24501
onnecticut Ave 24502
onnie Dr 24503
onstitution Ln 24502
ooks Branch Rd 24501
ool Springs Dr 24501
oolidge Dr 24503
opley Pl 24502
ora Lee Rd 24502
ork St 24503
orner Ln 24501
ornerstone St 24502
ornwallis Dr 24502
oronado Ln 24502
osby St 24504
ottontown Rd 24503
ottonwood Rd 24502
ountry Rd 24504
ountry Club Dr 24503
ountry Woods Rd 24504
ountryplace Ln 24501
ourt St 24504
ozy Home Dr 24501
raddock St 24501
raig St 24501
raighill St
3500-3599 24501
3600-3900 24502
3902-3998 24502
raigmont Dr 24501
ranehill Dr 24503
reek Side Dr 24502
reekside Ln 24502
reekview Ct 24502
reekview Ln 24501
renshaw Ct 24503
rescent Rd 24502
rest Hill Rd 24504
restwood Cir 24502
rews Shop Rd 24504
rocetti Ln 24501
rossway Rd 24502
rowell Ln 24502
rozier Dr 24502
upola St 24502
uster Dr 24502
ynthia Ct 24503
St 24501
abney St 24504
ale Ave 24502
ale St 24504
anbury Dr 24502
andridge Dr 24501
aniel Ave 24502
avis Cup Rd 24502
awnridge Dr 24502
ean St 24502
earing St 24503

Deaton St 24503
Deborah Dr 24501
Deer Creek Dr 24502
Deer Haven Dr 24501
Deer Haven Trl 24503
Deerfield Ln 24502
Deerwood Dr 24502
Del Ray Cir 24502
Delaney Dr 24501
Dellwood Cir 24503
Delta St 24502
Demott St 24501
Denson Dr 24502
E Denver Ave 24503
Devonshire Rd 24501
Dewitt St 24501
Dianne Dr 24504
Dinwiddie St 24504
Dodd St 24502
Dodson Dr 24501
Dogwood Ln 24503
Dogwood Pl 24502
Donington Ct 24501
Dorchester Ct 24503
Doulton Cir 24503
Dove Ct 24501
Dover Pl 24502
Downing Dr 24503
Doyle Ter 24503
Dragon Fire Ln 24501
Dreaming Creek Dr 24502
Driftwood Ln 24501
Drinkard Rd 24504
Drury Rd 24504
Dublin St 24502
Ducks Ln 24503
Dudley St 24504
Duiguid Dr 24502
Duke Ln 24502
Duke St 24501
Dulaney St 24503
Dumas St 24502
Dunbar Dr 24504
Duncraig Dr 24502
N Durham St 24501
Duval Pl 24503
E St 24504
Eagle Cir 24503
Eagle Eyrie Dr 24503
Earls Ct 24503
Early St 24503
Easley Ave 24501
Eastbrook Rd 24501
Easton Ave 24503
Eastwood Ln 24503
Edenboro Ct 24503
Edgar St 24501
Edgeway Dr 24502
Edgewood Ave, Ct & Dr
E 24502
Edinboro Ave 24502
Edley Pl 24502
Edmunds St 24501
Eisenhower Dr 24502
Eldon St 24501
Elk St 24503
Elm St 24504
Elmhurst St 24501
Elmwood Ave 24503
Emeline Dr 24502
Emily Ln 24501
Englewood St 24501
English Tavern Rd 24501
Enterprise Dr 24502
Equestrian Ct 24503
Erskine Ave 24501
Essex St 24503
Etowah 24501
Euclid Ave 24501
Eutis Ln 24501
Evenc St 24501
Evergreen Ln 24501
Evergreen Rd 24503
Evergreen Ridge Dr 24503
Evergreen Trailer Park 24501
Eyrie View Dr 24503

F St 24504
Faculty Dr 24501
Fair Oaks Ln 24503
Fairfax Ct 24503
Fairlea Ct 24503
Fairmont Ave 24502
Fairview Ave 24501
Fairway Pl 24503
Fairwood Ct 24503
Falcon Hill Pl 24503
Fallen Oaks Ln 24503
Farfields Dr 24502
Farley Branch Dr 24502
Farmington Pl 24503
Farmington Rd 24502
Fastener Dr 24502
Fauquier St
300-499 24503
500-599 24504
Federal St 24504
Fenwick Dr 24502
Ferguson Dr 24502
Ferncliff Dr 24502
Fieldale Rd 24503
Fieldstone Ct 24502
Fieldview Rd 24502
Filbert St 24504
Fillmore St 24501
Firefly Ln 24504
Flat Creek Ln & Rd 24501
Flattop Ln 24504
Fleetwood Dr 24501
Fleming Way 24503
Fleming Mountain Dr 24503
Flint St 24504
Florida Ave
200-1099 24504
1300-2299 24501
Floyd St 24501
Fnb Dr 24502
Fonda Dr 24502
Ford St & Ter 24501
Forest Ave 24502
Forest Dr 24502
Forest Rd
18101-18197 24502
18199-19299 24502
19301-19431 24502
19400-19430 24501
19432-19499 24501
Forest Brook Rd 24501
Forest Hills Cir 24501
Fort Ave
1800-3799 24501
3800-6299 24502
Fort Manor Dr 24502
Foster Ln 24501
Fountain Dr 24501
Fowler St 24502
Fox Dr 24502
Fox Hall Ln 24502
Fox Hill Rd 24503
Fox Hollow Rd 24503
Fox Hunt Way 24503
Fox Meadows Rd 24503
Fox Runn Dr 24503
Foxcrest Dr 24502
Frances Horner Ln 24503
Franklin Dr 24502
Franklin Pl 24502
Franklin St 24504
Franklin Farm Rd 24502
Frederick Dr 24502
Fredonia Ave 24503
Freeman Dr 24502
Front St 24504
Fulks St 24501
Fulton St 24501
G St 24504
Gable Dr 24502
Gaddy Rd 24502
Gaertner Pl 24503
Gala Dr 24503
Garbee Pl 24501
Garbo Dr 24502
Gardenpark Ave 24502

Garfield Ave 24501
Garland Dr & St 24504
Garnett St 24504
Gates St 24502
Gatlin St 24502
Gaymoor Ter 24503
Gentry Dr 24502
George St 24502
Georgetown Dr 24501
Georgia Ave 24501
Geppetto Way 24502
Giles St 24504
Gills St 24501
Gilmore Cir 24501
Gladwood Pl 24503
Glasgow Ct 24503
Glenbrooke Dr 24503
Glencove Pl 24503
Glenfield Dr 24502
Glenn St 24504
Glenoak Ln 24503
Globe St 24504
Gloucester Dr 24501
Goldenrod Pl 24502
Goldfinch Dr 24502
Golf Park Dr 24502
Goodview St 24502
Gordon Dr 24502
Gordon St 24501
Gorman Dr 24503
Grace St 24504
Grady St 24501
Graham St 24504
E Grand Ave 24501
Grand Summit Dr 24502
Grand View Cir 24502
Granite Ln 24501
Granville St 24502
Grapewood Ln 24501
Graves Mill Rd 24502
Grayson St 24503
Greenbriar Dr 24502
Greene St 24501
Greenfield Dr 24501
Greenhill Ln 24503
Greenview Cir & Dr 24502
Greenway Ct & Pl 24503
Greenwell Ct 24502
Greenwood Dr 24502
Gregory Ln 24503
Greystone Dr 24502
Griffin St 24501
Grist Mill Rd 24501
Grove Ave 24502
Grove Rd 24502
Grove St 24501
Guffey Ter 24502
Gum St 24504
H St 24504
Haden St 24501
Halifax Ave 24501
Halsey Rd 24501
Hamilton Dr 24503
Hampden Dr 24502
Hampton St 24504
Hancock St 24504
Handy St 24501
Hanger Rd 24502
Hanover St 24501
Hansouni Rd 24503
Harbor Dr 24504
Harbor St 24503
Harding St 24502
Haredald Dr 24503
Harris Ln 24501
Harrison St 24504
Harrods Ct 24503
Hartford St 24502
Hartless Ln 24502
Harvest Ct 24502
Harvest Basket Rd 24503
Harvey St 24504
Harveys Ln 24504
Hastings Ct 24503
Haven Ct 24504
Havenwood Dr 24502

Hawes St 24503
Hawkins Farm Rd 24503
Hawkins Mill Rd 24503
Hawthorne Rd 24503
Hayes Dr 24502
Hayfield Dr 24503
Hazel St 24504
Heath Ave 24502
Heather Dr 24501
Hefferman St 24501
Hemlock St 24504
Hendricks Ave 24501
Herbert St 24501
Heritage Cir 24502
Heritage Dr 24503
Hermitage Rd 24502
Heronhill Pl 24503
Hexam Dr 24502
Hexham Dr 24502
Hickok Rd 24502
Hickory Dr 24504
Hickory Hill Dr 24503
Hicks Rd 24502
High St 24504
High View Pl 24502
Highland Dr 24502
Highland Oaks Rd 24503
Hightrail Ln 24501
Hilda Dr 24501
Hiley Ter 24504
Hill St 24501
Hill N Dale Dr 24504
Hill Top Dr 24504
Hillsdale Rd 24501
Hillside Ct 24501
Hillsman Ln 24501
Hilltop Dr 24502
Hillview Dr 24502
Hillview St 24501
Hillwood Dr 24502
Hilton Pl 24503
Hines Cir 24502
Hobbs Ln 24502
Holcomb Path Rd 24501
Holcomb Rock Rd 24503
Holcombe Rd 24502
Holiday Ln 24504
Holiday Bob Ct 24503
Holliday St 24501
Hollins St 24504
Hollins Mill Rd
500-598 24504
1601-1697 24503
1699-2299 24503
Hollow Hill Rd 24503
Holly St 24503
Holly Haven Dr 24502
Holly Hill Rd 24502
Hollywood Dr 24501
Holmes Cir 24501
Homewood Dr 24502
Honey Tree Ln 24502
Honeysuckle Ct 24502
Hood St 24501
Hook Dr 24502
Hopkins Rd 24502
Horner Dr 24503
Horseford Rd 24504
Horseman Dr 24502
Howard Dr 24503
Huckleberry Ln 24503
Hudson St 24504
Hughes Ave 24501
Hunt St 24501
Hunterdale Dr 24502
Hunterland Rd 24503
Huntingwood Blvd 24503
Hurdle Hill Rd 24503
Huron Ave 24503
Hut Pl 24504
Hydro St 24503
I St 24504
Idaho Ave 24501
Igloe Dr 24502
Indered Farm Rd 24503
Indian Ln 24501

Indian Hill Rd 24503
Indian Ridge Dr 24502
Industrial Cir & Dr 24501
Inge Ln 24504
Inglewood Rd 24503
Interlink Rd 24503
Irish Ct 24503
Irma Dr 24502
Irvington St 24503
Irvington Springs Rd 24503
Ivanhoe Trl 24504
Ivy Dr 24503
Ivy St 24504
Ivy Creek Ln 24502
Ivy Ridge Ln 24503
Ivy Ridge Rd 24504
Ivylink Pl 24503
Jackson St 24504
James St 24501
James River Pl 24503
James View Dr 24503
Jameson Ct 24503
Jasper Cir 24501
Jean Pl 24502
Jefferson Dr 24502
Jefferson St 24504
Jefferson Ridge Pkwy 24501
Jennings Dr 24503
Jesup Way 24502
Jeter Ct 24501
Joe Watson Dr 24503
Joel St 24501
John Ada Dr 24504
John Capron Rd 24501
John Lynch Pl 24502
John Scott Dr 24503
Johnson Rd 24502
Johnson St 24504
Jonathan Pl 24502
Jonathans Lndg 24502
Jones St 24504
Jordan Dr 24502
Journey Ln 24502
Jubilee Dr 24501
Judd Ct 24501
Judith St 24501
Judith Creek Rd 24503
Juniper Dr 24502
Kanawha Ln 24503
Kanawha Rd 24502
Kavanaugh Rd 24504
Keeneland Ct 24503
Kemper St 24501
Kenbridge Pl & Rd 24502
Kendrick Pl 24502
Kenmore Dr 24503
Kensington Ave 24503
Kentucky Ave 24501
Kenwood Dr & Pl 24502
Kenyon St 24501
Kerry Ln 24502
Kesterson Dr 24502
Keswick Dr 24503
Kettering Ln 24501
Kettle Ln 24501
Keystone Rd 24503
Keywood Dr 24501
Killarney Ct & Pl 24502
Kimball Ave 24501
King St 24501
Kings Dr 24501
Kings Rd
1-199 24501
201-299 24501
600-799 24502
Kings Way 24502
Kingston Ave 24501
Kingswood Ln 24504
Kiowa Rd 24504
Kirby St 24501
Kitty Hawk Sq 24502
Knight St 24504
Knott St 24502
Knotty Pine Rd 24501
Krise Cir 24503
Kulman Pl 24501

L St 24503
La Salle Ct 24502
Lady Slipper Ln 24502
Lafayette St 24501
E Lake Dr 24502
N Lake Dr 24502
S Lake Dr 24502
W Lake Dr 24502
Lake Pl 24504
Lake Court Ave 24502
Lake Crest Ln 24502
Lake Forest Dr & Pl 24502
Lake Shore Ln 24502
Lakehaven Dr & Pl 24502
Lakeside Dr
1-299 24504
800-2699 24501
2700-2899 24502
Lakeview Dr 24502
Lakewood St 24501
Lambeth Ct 24503
Lancaster St 24501
Landon Ct & St 24503
Landover Pl 24501
Langhorne Ln 24501
Langhorne Rd
900-1800 24503
1802-1898 24503
1900-2999 24501
Langhorne Sq 24501
Lanier St 24504
Lankford Ln 24504
Lansdown Pl 24501
Lansing Ave 24503
Lark Pl 24503
Latham St 24502
Laurel Ln 24502
Laurel St 24504
Laverne Loop 24502
Lawton Cir & Ln 24501
Lawyers Rd 24501
Laxton Rd 24502
Ledger Ln 24502
Lee Cir 24503
Lee Pl 24502
Lee Jackson Hwy 24503
Leesville Rd
500-999 24502
1001-17299 24502
18201-18397 24501
18399-18800 24501
18802-18998 24501
19100-20399 24502
20401-20499 24502
Leewood Dr 24503
Legacy Oaks Cir, Ct &
Pl 24501
Lemon Dr 24501
Lemontvue Dr 24503
Lennox St 24501
Leroy Bowen Dr 24502
Leslie St 24501
Lewis Way 24502
Lexington Dr 24503
Ley St 24504
Leyburn St 24501
Liberty St 24504
Liberty Mountain Dr 24502
Liberty View Ln 24502
Liberty Village Blvd 24502
Library St 24504
Lichford Ln 24502
Liggates Rd 24502
Light St 24501
Lighthouse Dr 24502
Lilac Ln 24502
Lillian Ln 24502
Lime Rock Rd 24501
Lindberg St 24501
Linden Ave 24503
Lindsay St 24502
Link Rd 24503
Linkhorne Dr 24503
Lisa Ln & Pl 24502
Little Creek Rd 24502
Lively Ln 24501

Loch Ter ... 24503
Lockewood Dr ... 24502
Locksview Rd ... 24503
Locust Ln ... 24502
Locust St ... 24504
Lodge St ... 24501
Lofty View Ln ... 24501
Logan Ln ... 24502
Logans Ln ... 24502
Lone Jack Rd ... 24501
Lonesome Oak Trl ... 24504
Long Meadows Dr ... 24502
Long Mountain Dr ... 24504
Longfellow St ... 24503
Longview Rd ... 24501
Longwood Cir ... 24504
Longwood Rd ... 24503
Lookout Dr ... 24502
Lookout Rdg ... 24501
Loraine St ... 24504
Lotus Rd ... 24501
Loudon St ... 24503
Lovell St ... 24501
Low Cir ... 24502
Lower Basin ... 24504
Lucado Pl ... 24504
Luck St ... 24504
Lyn Dan Dr ... 24502
Lynbrook Rd ... 24501
E Lynch St ... 24504
Lynchburg Hwy ... 24502
Lynchpin Ln ... 24501
Lynette Dr ... 24502
Lynndale Pl ... 24502
Lynview Dr ... 24502
Lynx Dr ... 24502
Macarthur Dr ... 24502
Macel Dr ... 24502
Mackel St ... 24501
Macleod St ... 24503
Macon Loop ... 24503
Macon St ... 24501
Madewood Rd ... 24503
Madison St ... 24504
Magnolia St ... 24503
Maher St ... 24501
Main St ... 24504
Majestic Cir & Rd ... 24502
Mal Ln ... 24502
Mallard Dr ... 24503
Manassas St ... 24501
Manor View Ct ... 24503
Mansfield Ave ... 24501
Mantle Dr ... 24501
Manton Dr & Ln ... 24503
Maple Ln & St ... 24504
Maple Hills Dr ... 24502
Margate Dr ... 24502
Marguerite Dr ... 24502
Marsh St ... 24501
Marshall St ... 24503
Martin Rd ... 24503
Martin St ... 24501
Marvin Pl ... 24503
Mary Ann Dr ... 24502
Maryland Ave ... 24501
Mason Brooks Ln ... 24503
Massies Rd ... 24501
Mathews St ... 24503
Maybrook Dr ... 24502
Mayfield Dr ... 24502
Mayflower Dr ... 24501
Mccausland St ... 24501
Mcconville Rd ... 24502
Mccorkle St ... 24504
Mcdonald St ... 24504
Mcguffey Ln ... 24503
Mcintosh Dr ... 24503
Mcivor St ... 24504
Mckenna Cir ... 24503
Mckinley St ... 24504
Mckinney Ave ... 24502
Mcveigh Rd ... 24502
Mcwane Cir ... 24501
Meadhill Ln ... 24504
Meadow Ct ... 24501

Meadowbrook Rd ... 24502
Meadowridge Dr ... 24503
Meadowview Dr ... 24502
Mechel Pl ... 24502
Medina Ln ... 24503
Meem St ... 24501
Megginson Ln ... 24504
Melinda Dr ... 24502
Melody Ln ... 24504
Memorial Ave ... 24501
Memphis Ave ... 24503
Mercury St ... 24502
Meredith Pl ... 24503
Meridian St ... 24502
Meriwether Cir & Rd ... 24503
Mesena Dr ... 24502
Middle St ... 24502
Middleboro Pl ... 24502
Middleview St ... 24502
Midland Ave ... 24501
Midvale St ... 24502
Miles Pl ... 24502
Milford Ln ... 24501
Milkweed Ln ... 24501
Mill Acres Dr ... 24503
Mill Lane Rd ... 24503
Mill Ridge Rd ... 24502
Mill Stream Ln ... 24502
Mill View Ln ... 24502
Miller Dr ... 24501
Miller St ... 24504
Miller Park Sq ... 24501
Millners Dr ... 24502
Millrace Dr ... 24502
Millstone Rd ... 24502
Millwheel Ct ... 24503
Millwoods North Rd ... 24503
Millwoods West Rd ... 24503
Milton St ... 24501
Mimosa Dr ... 24503
Mirror Lake Ln ... 24503
Missionary Mnr ... 24501
Missouri Ave ... 24501
Mist Ln ... 24504
Misty Mountain Rd ... 24502
Mobile Rd ... 24503
Modac Pl ... 24502
Mohawk Dr ... 24502
Molly Stark Trl ... 24503
Monica Blvd ... 24502
Monkey Wrench Dr ... 24504
Monroe Ct ... 24502
Monroe Pl ... 24503
Monroe St ... 24504
Monsview Pl ... 24504
Monte Carlo Dr ... 24502
Montgomery Rd ... 24503
Monticello Ave ... 24501
Montridge Pl ... 24501
Montview Rd ... 24502
Montview Forest Dr ... 24502
Moonlight Dr ... 24501
Moonlit Cove Ln ... 24503
Moorman Dr ... 24501
Moormans Rd ... 24501
Moreview Dr ... 24502
Morey Pl ... 24502
Morgan St ... 24501
Morningside Dr ... 24503
Morris Ln ... 24502
Morrison Dr ... 24503
Morson St ... 24501
Morton Dr ... 24502
Morton Creek Rd ... 24504
Mosby Ave ... 24501
Moseley Dr ... 24502
Moultire Pl ... 24502
Mount Athos Rd ... 24504
Mount Olivet Church Rd ... 24504
Mount Sterling Dr ... 24502
Mount Vista Dr ... 24504
Mountain Dr ... 24504
Mountain Lake Ct & Rd ... 24502
Mountain Laurel Dr ... 24503

Mountain Peak Dr ... 24502
Mountain Ridge Ln ... 24503
Mountain View Dr & Rd ... 24502
Mowry Ln ... 24502
Moyer Ln ... 24501
Mulberry Cir ... 24502
Mullbury Pl ... 24502
Munford St ... 24501
Murger St ... 24501
Murray Pl
3900-4299 ... 24501
4300-4699 ... 24502
Murrell Rd ... 24501
Myrtle Ln & St ... 24502
Nags Head Ct ... 24502
Narragansett Dr ... 24502
Narrows Ln ... 24503
Nationwide Dr ... 24502
Navaho Dr ... 24501
Navajo Cir ... 24502
Naval Reserve Rd ... 24501
Neal St ... 24503
Neighbors Ln & Pl ... 24501
Nelson Dr ... 24502
Nelson St ... 24501
Nest Ln ... 24501
Nester Ln ... 24501
Nettie Ct ... 24502
New Britain Dr ... 24503
New Hampshire Ave ... 24502
New London Dr & Pl ... 24502
New Park Cir ... 24502
New Towne Rd ... 24502
Newberne St ... 24501
Newport Dr ... 24502
Nicholas St ... 24502
Nichols Tavern Dr ... 24503
Nickerson Rd ... 24504
Nickolas Berten Way ... 24502
Nicoles Way ... 24502
Night Hawk Rd ... 24504
Nippon Loop ... 24501
Norcross Rd ... 24502
Norfolk Ave ... 24503
Norma St ... 24501
North St ... 24502
Northwood Cir ... 24503
Northwynd Cir ... 24502
Norvell St ... 24502
Norvell House Ct ... 24503
Norwood St ... 24504
Nottingham Cir ... 24502
Nowlins Ct ... 24501
Oak Ln ... 24503
Oak Trl ... 24502
Oak Haven Dr ... 24502
Oak Hill Ave ... 24501
Oak Hill Dr ... 24502
Oak Park Pl ... 24503
Oak Spring Rd ... 24503
Oak Tree St ... 24501
Oakdale Cir & Dr ... 24502
Oakland Ave ... 24501
Oakland Cir ... 24502
Oakley Ave ... 24501
Oakmont Cir ... 24502
Oakmont Ct ... 24503
Oakridge Blvd
1-99 ... 24501
100-699 ... 24502
Oakwood Ct & Pl ... 24503
Odd Fellows Rd
3000-3299 ... 24501
3300-3300 ... 24506
3301-3499 ... 24501
3400-3498 ... 24501
Old Abert Rd ... 24503
Old Boonsboro Rd ... 24503
Old Courthouse Tpke ... 24501
Old Dominion Dr ... 24503
Old Farm Rd ... 24503
Old Forest Rd ... 24501
Old Graves Mill Rd ... 24502
Old Mill Rd ... 24502
Old Plantation Dr ... 24502

Old Post Rd ... 24502
Old Rustburg Rd ... 24501
Old Spring Way ... 24503
Old Stable Rd ... 24503
Old Tavern Cir ... 24501
Old Timberlake Rd ... 24502
Old Trents Ferry Rd ... 24503
Old Wiggington Rd ... 24502
Olive St ... 24504
Omega Ct & Dr ... 24502
Opal St ... 24504
Opossum Creek Ln ... 24501
Orchard St ... 24501
Oriole Pl ... 24503
Otey St ... 24501
Otter Pl ... 24503
Otterview Pl ... 24503
Overbrook Rd ... 24501
E Overbrook Rd ... 24502
Overlink Ct ... 24503
Overstreet Ln ... 24503
Overton Dr ... 24501
Oxford St ... 24502
Oxford Furnace Rd ... 24504
Oxford Point Rd ... 24502
Ozone Ct ... 24503
Pacos St ... 24502
Paddington Ct ... 24503
Page St ... 24501
Palm St ... 24501
Palmer Dr ... 24502
Panorama Pt ... 24502
Pansy St
900-999 ... 24503
1000-1199 ... 24504
1900-2099 ... 24503
Park Ave
1100-1199 ... 24504
1200-2499 ... 24501
Park Ln ... 24501
Park Pl ... 24501
Parkland Dr ... 24503
Parkview Dr ... 24502
Parkwood Ave & Dr ... 24501
Pastime Ln ... 24501
Patricia Dr ... 24501
Patrick St ... 24501
Patriot Dr ... 24502
Patton Dr ... 24502
Paulette Cir ... 24502
Pawnee Dr ... 24502
Pawtucket Dr ... 24502
Payne St ... 24501
Peabody Rd ... 24502
Peace St ... 24501
Peach Tree Ln ... 24504
Peachtree Rd ... 24502
Peakland Pl ... 24503
Peaks View Dr ... 24501
Pearl St ... 24504
Pearson Dr ... 24502
Pebbleton Ln ... 24503
Pecan Dr ... 24504
Peck Ln ... 24501
Peg Ln ... 24502
Peninsular St ... 24501
Pennsylvania Ave ... 24502
Perch Rd ... 24503
Perrymont Ave ... 24502
Pershing Ave ... 24503
Pershing Dr ... 24502
Peters Ln ... 24501
Petite Ct ... 24503
Peyton St ... 24504
Pheasant Ridge Rd ... 24502
Phillips Cir ... 24502
Piedmont Pl ... 24502
Pierce St ... 24501
Pilgrim Rd ... 24502
Pimlico Pl ... 24503
Pine Dr
1-499 ... 24502
500-699 ... 24503
Pine St ... 24504
Pine Acres Dr & Est ... 24504
Pine Bluff Dr ... 24503

Pine Haven Dr ... 24502
Pine Woods Ln ... 24504
Pinecrest Ln ... 24504
Pinehurst St ... 24501
Pines Village Dr ... 24502
Pinoak Ln ... 24504
Pioneer Ct ... 24503
Plantation Dr ... 24501
Pleasant St ... 24501
Pleasant Hill Rd ... 24501
Pleasant Ridge St ... 24503
Pleasant Valley Rd ... 24504
Pleasant View Dr ... 24501
Plum Branch Rd ... 24504
Plymouth Pl ... 24503
Pocahontas St ... 24501
Poe Ln ... 24501
Poindexter St ... 24501
Point Dr ... 24502
Pokeys Creek Rd ... 24503
Polk St ... 24504
Pollard St ... 24501
Poor House Rd ... 24504
Poplar St ... 24504
Poplar Terrace Dr ... 24502
Portico St ... 24502
Poston St ... 24504
Powhatan St ... 24501
Powtan Dr ... 24502
Preserve Dr ... 24503
Preston Pl ... 24502
Preston St ... 24504
Prestwood Rd ... 24502
Price St ... 24501
Primrose Ln ... 24501
Prince St ... 24501
N Princeton Cir ... 24503
Principal Ct ... 24502
Pritchett Dr ... 24501
Progress Dr ... 24502
Pryor Ridge Trl ... 24503
Pughs Dr ... 24501
Pulaski St ... 24501
Putnam St ... 24501
Quail Ln ... 24502
Quail Rd ... 24504
Quaker Pkwy ... 24502
Quarry Rd ... 24503
Quartz Rd ... 24502
Quiet Hills Dr ... 24501
Quinlan St ... 24503
Race St ... 24504
Radcliff Ave ... 24502
Raiford Cir ... 24503
Rainbow Cir ... 24501
Rainbow Forest Dr ... 24502
Raleigh St ... 24501
Rambling Creek Dr ... 24504
Ramsey Pl ... 24501
Ramsgate Ln ... 24501
Randall Ln ... 24502
Randolph Ln ... 24502
Randolph Pl E ... 24503
Randolph St ... 24504
Range St ... 24501
S Rangoon Rd ... 24502
Raven Stone Ct ... 24503
Ravenwood Dr ... 24503
Red Hawk Rd ... 24503
Red Maple Ct ... 24501
Reed St ... 24501
Reese St ... 24501
Regal Ct ... 24504
Regency Woods Pl ... 24503
Regent Pl ... 24502
Reno Dr ... 24502
Reusens Rd ... 24503
Rhode Island Ave ... 24502
Rhodes Cir ... 24502
Rhonda Rd ... 24502
Richeson Dr ... 24501
Richland Dr ... 24502
Richmond Ave ... 24502
Richmond Hwy
4100-4798 ... 24501
4101-4797 ... 24504

4799-11200 ... 24504
11202-13498 ... 24504
Richmond St ... 24501
Ridge Ave ... 24501
N Ridge Ln ... 24502
Ridgecroft Dr ... 24503
Ridgelawn Pl ... 24503
Ridgeline Dr ... 24502
Ridgeview Dr ... 24503
Ridgewood Dr ... 24503
Rise Ln ... 24504
Rittenhouse St ... 24502
Riverbirch Trce ... 24502
Rivermont Ave
300-1399 ... 24504
1400-3599 ... 24503
Rivermont Ter ... 24503
Riverside Dr ... 24503
Riverview Ln & Pl ... 24503
Roberts Ave ... 24501
Roberts Trailer Ct ... 24501
Robin Dr ... 24502
Robin Hood Pl ... 24503
Robins Rd ... 24504
Robinson Dr ... 24502
Rockbridge Ave ... 24501
Rockview Ln ... 24503
Rockwell Rd ... 24504
Rolfe Ave ... 24503
Rome Dr ... 24503
Rose Ln ... 24501
Rose St ... 24504
Roslyn Pl ... 24504
Rothowood Rd ... 24503
Rotunda St ... 24502
Round Hill Rd ... 24503
Roundelay Cir & Rd ... 24502
Rowland Dr ... 24503
Rowse Dr ... 24502
Roxbury St ... 24501
Royal Blvd ... 24503
Royal Oak Cir, Dr & Way ... 24503
Ruffled Grouse Ln ... 24503
Ruffner Pl
1300-1399 ... 24504
1600-1699 ... 24503
Rugby Cir ... 24501
Rugby Ln ... 24501
Rugby Rd ... 24503
Running Cedar Way ... 24503
Russell St ... 24501
Russell Springs Dr ... 24501
Russell Woods Dr ... 24502
Rustic Ct ... 24503
Rustic Ln ... 24504
Rutherford St ... 24501
Sabine Ave ... 24501
Sackett St ... 24501
Saddle Rock Rd ... 24503
Saddleback Way ... 24503
Sagamore Ct ... 24503
Sage Dr ... 24501
Saint Augustine St ... 24501
Saint Cloud Ave ... 24502
Saint David Dr ... 24502
Saint James Pl ... 24503
Salisbury Cir ... 24502
San Jose ... 24502
Sandbridge Ct ... 24502
Sanders Ln ... 24503
Sandown Cir ... 24503
Sandusky Dr ... 24502
Sandy Dr ... 24502
Sangloe Pl ... 24502
Sanhill Dr ... 24502
Sarah Lynch Pl ... 24503
Saratoga Dr
1-99 ... 24502
100-105 ... 24503
106-106 ... 24502
106-106 ... 24503
107-159 ... 24502
161-200 ... 24502
201-211 ... 24503
212-212 ... 24502

213-213 ... 24503
214-499 ... 24502
Saturn Ln ... 24501
Saturn St ... 24502
Savannah Ave ... 24502
Savoy Pl ... 24503
School Ln ... 24501
Schothum St ... 24502
Scott St ... 24504
Scotts Farm Rd ... 24504
Seabury Ave ... 24501
Sedgebrook Ct ... 24502
Sedgewick Dr ... 24503
Selene St ... 24503
Seminole Ave ... 24502
Senoia Pl ... 24502
Settlement Dr ... 24502
Settlers Row ... 24504
Seven Oaks Dr ... 24502
Shadowwood Ln ... 24501
Shadwell Dr ... 24503
Shady Grove Ln ... 24502
Shady Tree Ln ... 24504
Shaffer St ... 24501
Sheffield Dr ... 24502
Shelby Ct ... 24501
Shelly Ct ... 24501
Shelor Dr ... 24502
Sherbrook Apartments ... 24504
Sherbrooke Dr ... 24502
Sheringham Pl ... 24503
Sherman Dr ... 24502
Sherwood Pl ... 24503
Shirley Rd ... 24502
Shore Line Dr ... 24501
Short St ... 24502
Shrader Ln ... 24502
Sierra Way ... 24501
Silver Creek Dr ... 24503
Silver Springs Dr ... 24502
Simons Run ... 24502
Sky Pl ... 24502
Sky View Pl ... 24503
Skylark Ln ... 24502
Skylark Pl ... 24503
Sleepy Hollow Rd ... 24502
Smitty Cir ... 24501
Smoketree Ln ... 24502
Smoky Hollow Rd ... 24504
Smyth St ... 24501
Soapstone Dr ... 24502
Somerset Dr ... 24503
Somerset Shire Pl ... 24503
Sommers St ... 24501
Sound Ridge Ln ... 24502
Sparrow Dr ... 24502
Spencer Pl ... 24504
Spicer Rd ... 24504
Spinoza Cir ... 24504
Spottswood Pl ... 24503
Spring St ... 24504
Spring Mountain Rd ... 24503
Spring Oaks Dr ... 24501
Springfield Rd ... 24501
Springlake Rd ... 24504
Springvale Dr ... 24502
Sprouse Ln ... 24502
Spruce Ln ... 24501
St Andrews Cir ... 24503
St Paul Dr ... 24503
St Johns Dr ... 24503
Stadium Rd ... 24501
Stafford St ... 24501
Stage Rd ... 24504
Standish Cir ... 24501
Statham Rd ... 24504
Staunton St ... 24501
Stayman Rd ... 24503
Steeple Run ... 24501
Stephenson Ave ... 24501
Stepping Stone Rd ... 24504
Stevens Rd ... 24501
Stillhouse Run ... 24503
Stonehouse Dr ... 24502
Stonemill Dr ... 24502
Stoneridge St ... 24501

Stonewall St 24504
Stormy Hill Rd 24504
Stratford Rd 24502
Stuart St 24501
Sublett Ct 24502
Suburban Rd 24501
Summerville St 24503
Summit St 24503
Sumpter St 24503
Sumter Ln 24504
Sun Dance Dr 24504
Sunburst Rd 24501
Sunbury Pl 24502
Suncrest Dr 24502
Sunderland Pl 24502
Sunflower Ln 24503
Sunnybank Dr 24502
Sunnymead Rd 24501
Sunnymeade Rd 24501
Sunset Dr 24503
Surrey Ln & Pl 24503
Susannah Pl 24502
Sussex St
300-4399 24501
4400-4499 24502
Swan Pl 24501
Sweetwater Rd 24501
Sycamore Pl 24502
Takoma St 24502
Talbot St 24501
Tamer Ln 24503
Tanglewood Dr 24502
Tanglewood Ln 24503
Tanzalon Dr 24502
Tate Springs Rd 24501
Taylor Rd 24502
Taylor St
1-99 24504
400-599 24501
600-1999 24504
Taylor Farm Rd 24503
Tazewell Ave 24501
Teal Ct 24503
Temple Cir 24502
Templeton Ln 24503
Templeton Mill Rd 24503
Tenbury Dr 24501
Tennessee Ave 24501
Terminal Dr 24502
Terminal St 24501
Terra Way 24501
Terrace Hill Dr 24502
Terrell Pl 24503
Terry Ct 24501
Texas Ave 24501
Thomas Rd
100-599 24501
600-799 24502
Thomson Dr 24501
Thornfield Dr 24502
Three Creeks Ct 24502
Thurman Ave 24501
Tilden Ave 24501
Tiller Ln 24501
Timber Ct 24501
S Timberlake Dr & Rd 24502
Timberoak Ct 24502
Timbrook Pl 24502
Toddsbury Rd 24502
Toledo Ave 24502
Tolleys Ln 24502
Tomahawk Dr 24502
Tomahawk Industrial Park 24502
Tommie Wood Ln 24501
Top Ridge Dr 24501
Tottenham Ct 24503
Town Fork Rd 24502
Towne Crier Rd 24502
Townson Ct 24502
Tradewynd Dr 24502
Training Center Rd 24502
Traylor Ln 24502
Treadway Cir 24501
Tremont St 24502
Trents Dr 24504
Trents Ferry Ct & Rd 24503
Trents Meadow Ln 24503
Trents Trailer Ct 24504
Trey Ct 24502
Triangle Pl 24501
Trinity Ct 24502
Trolley Ct 24503
Tudor Dr 24501
Tulane St 24502
Tule Rd 24502
Tulip St 24504
Tumblewood Trl 24501
Tunbridge Rd 24501
Turf Rd 24501
Turkey Foot Rd 24502
Turner Ln 24504
Turner Rd 24503
Turnpike Dr 24502
Turtle Creek Rd 24501
Twin Court Ter 24502
Twin Oak Dr 24502
Two Creek Dr 24502
Tyree St 24504
Tyreeanna Rd 24504
Union Dr 24502
Union St 24504
University Blvd 24502
V E S Rd 24503
Valley St 24501
Valleydale Dr 24502
Valorie Ct 24502
Ventura Dr 24502
Vermont Ave 24502
Vernon Cir 24502
Vernon St 24501
Victor Dr 24501
Victoria Ave 24504
View Pl 24502
Viking Dr 24502
Villa Rd 24503
Villa View Pl 24502
Village Hwy 24504
Village Rd 24502
Village Park Ct 24501
Villas Way Dr 24502
Vine St 24504
Virginia St 24504
Vista Ave 24503
Vista Ln 24502
Wade Ln 24502
Wadsworth St 24501
Wagon Cir 24501
Wakefield Rd 24503
Wall St 24504
Wallace St 24503
Walnut Ln 24504
Walnut Pl 24502
Walnut St 24504
Walnut Hollow Rd 24503
Walton Dr 24502
Walton Rd 24501
Wampum Ln 24502
Wards Rd
2000-4799 24502
13000-13298 24501
13300-13999 24501
14000-14030 24502
14001-14031 24501
14032-15299 24502
Wards Ferry Rd 24502
Warfield Rd 24503
Warner Rd 24504
Warner Rose Pl 24502
Warren Ave 24501
Warwick Ln 24503
Washington St 24504
Water Gate Dr 24502
Waterlick Rd
1-2099 24501
2101-2299 24501
2300-3332 24502
3334-3498 24502
Waterton Dr 24503
Waterview Pl 24502
Watkins Pl 24502
Watson Dr 24501
Watts St 24501
Waverly Pl 24503
Wayne Dr 24502
Webber Ln 24503
Wedgewood Rd 24503
Weeping Willow Dr 24501
Wellington Dr 24502
Wendover Sq 24503
Wesley Pl 24502
Wessex Rd 24501
West St 24501
Westbrook Cir 24501
Westburg Dr 24502
Westchester Dr 24502
Westdale Dr 24501
Westerly Dr 24501
Westfield Dr 24502
Westhaven Pl 24501
Westminster Way 24503
Westmoreland Pl & St 24503
Westover Blvd 24501
Westridge Cir 24502
Westview Cir 24504
Westview Dr 24502
Westwood Ave 24501
Wetbanks Dr 24501
Wexford Ct 24503
Wexford Pl 24502
Wexview Ln 24502
Wheatland Ct 24503
Wheeler Rd 24504
Whispering Pines Ct 24502
Whispering Stream Ln 24501
Whistlewood Ct 24502
White St 24502
White Oak Dr 24502
White Pine Dr 24501
Whitehall Rd 24501
Whitestone Dr 24502
Whitley Way 24503
Widgeon Ct 24503
Wiggington Rd 24502
Wild Turkey Rd 24502
Wildwind Pl 24503
Wildwood Dr 24502
Willard Way 24502
William Craighead Pl 24503
Williams Rd 24503
Williamsburg Pl 24503
Willis Dr 24502
Willow St
1-299 24503
300-399 24504
Willow Bend Dr 24502
Willow Lawn Dr 24503
Wilson Ave & Dr 24501
Wilton Ave 24501
Wimbledon Way 24503
Winchester St 24501
Windcrest Dr 24502
Windemere Pl 24501
Windham Ct 24503
Winding Cedar Way 24502
Winding Creek Ln 24503
Windingway Rd 24502
Windsor Ave, Ln & Rd 24502
Windy Ridge Dr 24503
Winebarger Cir 24501
Winesap Dr 24503
Winfree Pl 24502
Winston Ridge Rd 24501
Wise St
300-999 24501
1000-1599 24504
Wood Ln 24501
Wood Rd 24501
Wood St 24504
Woodall Rd 24502
Woodberry Ln 24502
Woodberry Square Pl 24502
Woodbine Dr 24502
Woodbourne Dr 24502
Woodcock Rd 24503
Woodcrest Dr 24503
Woodhaven Dr 24502
Woodland Ave 24503
Woodland Cir 24502
Woodland Dr 24503
Woodlawn Cir 24502
Woodlawn Dr 24503
Woodridge Pl 24503
Woodrow St 24501
Woodruff Cir 24503
E Woodside Ave 24503
Woodson Ln 24503
Woodway Dr 24501
Wooldridge Cir 24502
Wren Ln 24503
Wyndale Dr 24501
Wyndhurst Dr 24502
Wyndpark Cir 24502
Wyndsong Pl 24502
Wyndview Dr 24502
Wythe Rd 24501
Yale St 24502
Yancey St 24503
Yeardley Ave 24501
Yeatts Ct 24502
Yellowstone Dr 24502
York Dr 24502
N York Ln 24503
S York Ln 24503
York St 24501
Yorkshire Cir 24502
Yorktown Ave 24501
Young Pl 24501

NUMBERED STREETS

1st St
600-999 24504
1001-1099 24504
1400-1799 24501
2nd St
700-1099 24504
1500-1999 24501
3rd St
800-1099 24504
1600-2099 24501
4th St
800-1099 24504
1200-1499 24501
5th St
100-298 24504
300-1199 24504
1200-1599 24501
6th St
301-497 24504
1500-1599 24501
7th St
1-1299 24504
1300-1699 24501
8th St
100-1299 24504
1500-2199 24501
9th St
1-1199 24504
1300-1400 24501
10th St 24504
1300-1699 24501
11th St
100-1199 24504
1400-1699 24501
12th St
100-1399 24504
1400-2499 24501
13th St
100-1399 24504
1400-2499 24501
14th St
700-1399 24504
1400-2399 24501
15th St
800-1399 24504
1400-2100 24501
16th St
900-1399 24504
1400-1799 24501
17th St
900-1299 24504
1300-1799 24501
18th St 24504
19th St 24504
1400-1499 24501

MANASSAS VA

General Delivery 20110

POST OFFICE BOXES MAIN OFFICE STATIONS AND BRANCHES

Box No.s
1 - 598 20108
601 - 978 20113
1001 - 5034 20108
7510 - 7510 20113
9000 - 10259 20108
11001 - 11320 20113

RURAL ROUTES

50, 51, 60 20109
13, 61, 62 20110
07, 09, 12, 16, 18, 30, 31, 32 20111

NAMED STREETS

Abbey Oaks Ct 20112
Abbie Ln 20112
Abbott Ct & Rd 20110
Abingdon Ct 20109
Abington Way 20110
Acer Ct 20112
Acer Ln 20110
Adams St 20111
Adamson St 20110
Adel Dr 20112
Aden Rd 20112
Adrienne Pl 20110
Afton Ct 20110
Alan Ct 20109
Albemarle Dr 20111
Albert Myer Ct 20111
Albrite Ct 20112
Alendale Ct 20112
Alessi Dr 20112
Alexa Ct 20111
Alexander Way 20111
Alistair Dr 20112
Alleghany Rd 20111
Allegro Dr 20112
Allen St 20110
Allwood Ct 20110
Almond St 20110
Almond Tree Ct 20110
Alpaugh St 20112
Alpha Ct 20110
Alpine St 20111
Amaryllis Ave 20110
Ambassador Dr 20109
Amberleigh Ct 20110
Amberview Ct 20112
Amblewood Dr 20112
Ambrose Ct 20109
Amelia Ct 20111
American Legion Dr 20112
Amherst Ct & Dr 20111
Ancient Oak Ct 20111
Anderson Ct 20109
Andrew Dr 20111
Anita Ct 20110
Anjou Ct 20110
Anna Ct 20111
Annagreen Ct 20112
Anne Marie Ln 20112
Ansley Ct 20112
Antique Way 20110
Antonia Ave 20110
Apache Ridge Ct 20109
Apple Tree Ct 20112
Appomattox Ave 20111
Aragon Ct 20110
Ariel Ct 20110
Arlington Ave 20111
Arnie Ct 20111
Arrington Ct 20112
Arrington Farm Ct 20111
Arrowood Dr 20111
Artillery Rd 20110
Aruba Ct 20109
Ash Lawn Ct 20111
Asheville St 20109
Ashland Ave 20109
Ashland Community Sq 20112
Ashley Ct 20112
Ashton Ave
7600-8299 20109
8900-9198 20110
Aspen Pl 20110
Aspen Wood Ct 20110
Assateague Pl 20112
Assett Loop 20109
Associates Ct 20109
Atlas Pl 20112
Attingham Ct 20111
Aubrey Dr 20111
Augusta Rd 20111
Austin Way 20110
Automotive Dr 20109
Autumn Pl 20110
Autumn Brook Ln 20112
Aviation Ln 20110
Avondale Dr 20111
Azalea Grove Dr 20110
Azure Ct 20110
Baber Dr 20112
Backus Ln 20111
Bainbridge Ct 20110
Baker St 20111
Ballantrae St 20110
Balls Ford Rd 20109
Baneberry Cir 20112
Bank St 20111
Bank Beaver Ct 20112
Bankhead Dr 20110
Bannerwood Dr 20109
Barbados Ln 20109
Barnett St 20110
Barnwood Rd 20111
Barrett Dr 20109
Barrington Park Cir 20110
Barron St 20112
Bartow Pl 20110
Basil Ct 20112
Basilwood Dr 20110
Bass Pond Ct 20112
Basswood Dr 20112
Battery Heights Blvd 20110
Battle Ct & St 20110
Battlefield Dr 20110
Battleview Pkwy 20109
Bayberry Ave & Ct 20110
Bayonet Way 20109
Beadfield Ct 20112
Beamer Way 20109
Bear Creek Dr 20111
Bears Den Ct 20111
Beauregard Ave 20110
Beaver Mill Ln 20112
Beck Ln 20110
Beckham Ct 20111
Becky Ct 20111
Bedford Rd 20109
Beech Pl 20110
Belle Grae Dr 20109
Belo Gate Dr 20111
Ben Lomond Park Dr 20109
Bennett Dr 20110
Bens Way 20110
Bent Tree Ln 20111
Bentfield Dr 20110
Berkshire St 20110
Bermuda Ln 20109
Bernard Ct 20110
Berry Orchard Ct 20112
Bertalice Ct 20110
Bertha Ct 20110
Bessie Watson Ln 20112
Bethany Ct 20110
Bethany Springs Mews 20109
Bethel Rd 20112
Bethlehem Rd 20109
Big Oak Cir 20112
Birch St 20111
Birchwood Ct 20110
Birmingham Dr 20111
Black Hawk Ct 20111
Black Horse Ct 20109
Blackstone Rd 20110
Bland Dr 20109
Blandsford Dr 20111
Blendia Ln 20109
Blooms Rd 20111
Blooms Quarry Ln 20111
Blossom Ln 20112
Blue Bell Ct 20111
Blue Gray Cir 20109
Blue Ridge Ct 20109
Boar Farm Ct 20112
Boar Run Ct 20112
Bodensee Ln 20112
Boltonia Dr 20109
Bonair Dr 20109
Bond Ct 20110
Bonham Cir 20110
Bosbury Ct 20111
Bosna Ct 20110
Botsford Rd 20109
Boundary Ave 20111
Boundbrook Ter 20109
Boutilier Ln 20112
Bow Hunter Ct 20112
Bowmans Folly Dr 20112
Boyer Ln 20112
Bracken Ct 20111
Brackets Ford Cir 20110
Braden Dr 20109
Bradford Ln 20112
Bradley Ct 20111
Bradley Forest Rd 20112
Bradley Forge Dr 20112
Bragg Ln 20110
Bramble Ct 20110
Branchview Ct & Ln 20110
Brandon St 20111
Brandon Way 20109
Braxted Ln 20110
Brechin Way 20109
Breeden Ave 20110
Breezy Knoll Dr 20111
Bren Forest Way 20112
Brendel Way 20110
Brendon Dr 20112
Brenmill Ln 20112
Brent St 20110
Brentsville Rd 20112
Brentsville Run Ct 20112
Brentwood Dr 20111
Bretton Woods Dr 20110
Brewer Creek Pl 20109
Brewer Spring Rd 20109
Brian Ct 20111
Briarmont Ln 20112
Brickshire Ln 20112
Bridge Ave 20112
Bridle Post Pl 20112
Brierly Forest Ct 20112
Brigade Ct 20110
Brigantine Ln 20110
Bright Pond Way 20111
Brighton Way 20109
Brinkley Ln 20110
Brinn Ct 20112
Bristow Rd 20112
Broken Branch Ln 20109
Brookmead Dr 20112
Brooks Ln 20111
Brookstone Ct 20109
Brookview Ct 20109
Brothers Ct 20112
Browning Ct 20110
Browns Ln 20111

Broz Ct 20110
Bruce Ct 20110
Bruin Ct 20111
Brunger St 20112
Bruton Parish Ct 20110
Buckeye Ct 20110
Buckeye Timber Dr 20109
Buckhall Rd 20111
Buckhall Farm Ct 20111
Buckner Rd 20110
Bucyrus Ct 20110
Bugle Ct 20112
Bull Run Rd 20111
Bull Run Overlook Ct 20109
Bulloch Dr 20109
Burlington Ct 20110
Burnet Ct 20110
Burnside Ct 20111
Burnt Tree Dr 20111
Burrell Ln 20109
Business Way 20110
Business Center Ct 20110
Buttercup Pl 20109
Butterfield St 20109
Butternut Cir & St 20110
Buttonbush Ct 20110
Buttress Ln 20110
Byrd Dr 20110
Byrne Pl 20112
Byron St 20111
Cabbel Dr 20111
Cabin Branch Ct 20111
Cabin Ridge Ct 20110
Cabot Ct 20111
Cadet Ct 20109
Caitlin Ct 20110
Caladium Dr 20110
Calder Ct 20111
Calico Ln 20112
Callan Dr 20109
Callie Furnace Ct 20112
Calm Pond Ct 20111
Calvary Ct 20109
Calypso Dr 20110
Camfield Ct 20109
Campaign Ct 20109
Campbell Ct 20109
Camphor Ct 20110
Candy Ct 20110
Cane Brake Mews 20109
Cannon Ball Ct 20109
Cannon Ridge Dr 20110
Cannoneer Ct 20110
Canova Dr 20112
Canova Forest Ct 20112
Canova Springs Pl 20112
Capital Ct 20110
Carapace Ct 20112
Caraway Cir 20109
Caribou Ln 20110
Carlington Valley Ct 20111
Carlton Dr 20110
Carmel Way 20110
Carol Ave 20112
Carolina Dr 20110
E & W Carondelet Dr 20111
Carrageen Dr 20112
Carriage Ln 20110
Carriage Hill Dr 20112
Carrie Ln 20111
Carrington Pl 20109
Carrs Brooke Way 20112
Cartwright Ct 20111
Casablanca Ct 20112
Caspian Way 20110
Cass Pl 20109
Castle Rd 20109
Cather Ave 20110
Caton Pl 20112
Catrock Sluice Way 20112
Cattail Ct 20109
Cavalry Ln 20110
Cecil Rd 20112
Cedar Creek Dr 20112
Cedar Ridge Dr 20110
Cello Way 20111
Celtic Ln 20112
Center St 20110
Center Entrance Ct 20109
Center Point Ln 20110
Centerton Ln 20111
Central Park Dr 20110
Centreville Rd
7200-8399 20111
8400-8549 20111
8550-9399 20110
9401-9499 20110
Century Oak Ct 20112
Century Park Dr 20109
Cerise Ct 20110
Chadds Landing Way 20111
Chaddsford Ter 20112
Champion Ct 20110
Champlain Dr 20112
Champs Mill Ct 20112
Chancellorsville Ln 20110
Chandler Dr 20112
Chandler Farm Ln 20111
Chapman Oak Dr 20110
Chardon Ct 20111
Charles Lacey Dr 20112
Charles Wack St 20112
Charleston Dr 20110
Charnwood Ct 20111
Chase Ct 20109
Chatham St 20110
Chatsworth Dr 20109
Chatterly Loop 20109
Cherry St 20110
Cherry Oak Ct 20109
Cherry Ridge Ct 20112
Cherry Tree Ln 20110
Chervil Ct 20110
Cheshire Ridge Cir 20110
Chestnut St 20111
Cheswick Ct 20110
Chevalle Dr 20112
China Grove Ct 20110
Chinaberry Ct 20112
Chinkapin Dr 20111
Chokecherry Ct 20110
Christian Ln 20112
Christine Pl 20112
Christopher Ln 20111
Church St
8800-9107 20110
9108-9108 20108
9108-9298 20110
9109-9299 20110
Cisler Ln 20111
Claremont St 20110
S Clark Pl 20110
Classic Oaks Ct 20112
Classic Springs Dr 20112
Clawson Ln 20112
Clayton Rd 20109
Clearridge Ln 20110
Cleary St 20110
Clematis St 20110
Clemson Ct 20109
Clifton St 20109
Cloudberry Way 20110
Clouds Hill Pl 20111
Clover Ct 20109
Cloverhill Ct & Rd 20110
Clovertree Ct 20109
Coachcrest Ct 20109
Cobb Rd 20112
Cobble Pond Way 20111
Cobblestone Ct 20112
Cobden Ct 20109
Cockrell Rd 20110
Coffee Tree Ct 20110
Coggs Bill Dr 20110
Coiner House Pl 20112
Colbert Ln 20111
Colburn Dr 20111
Colchester Park Dr 20112
Cold Harbor Loop 20111
Cole Timothy Ct 20112
Coleman St 20112
Coles Dr 20112
Colfax Ct & Dr 20111
Colonel Ct 20110
Colonel Weavers Ct 20111
Colonial Village Loop 20112
Coloriver Rd 20112
Colton Ln 20109
Commerce Ct 20110
Commonwealth Ct 20112
Community Dr 20109
Comptons Ln 20109
Concerto Ct 20112
Confederate Trl 20110
Conner Dr 20111
Constance Pl 20110
Contractors Ct 20109
Conway Dr 20112
Cooke Ct 20109
Coolbrook Ln 20112
Coopers Ln 20112
Copeland Dr 20109
Copperfield Way 20109
Coppermine Dr 20109
Coral Berry Dr 20110
Corbett Cir & Pl 20111
Corbin Hall Ln 20112
Corey Dr 20110
Coriander Cir 20110
Cornwell Dr 20112
Coronado Ct 20112
Corporate Cir 20110
Corryton Ct 20110
Corydalis Ct 20110
Cougar Ct 20111
Counselor Rd 20112
Country Ln 20110
Country Roads Ln 20112
W Courthouse Rd 20110
Courtland Cir 20111
Courtney Dr 20111
Coverstone Dr 20109
Coverstone Hill Cir 20109
Covington Pl 20109
Crawfish Hollow Ct 20112
Crecy Ln 20110
Creek View Ter 20111
Cregger Ln 20111
Crespo Ln 20112
Crestbrook Dr 20112
Crestwood Dr 20109
Crigger Ln 20111
Crigger Point Ct 20111
Croatia Way 20109
Croce Ct 20109
Crooked Branch Ct 20112
Crooked Creek Dr 20112
Crooked Knoll Way 20111
Crossbow Dr 20112
Crossed Sabres Ct 20111
Croydon Pl 20109
Crozet St 20111
Crozier Ct 20110
Crystal Creek Ln 20112
Crystal Lake Ct 20112
Cub Run Ct 20109
Cupids Dart Ct 20109
Curling Rd 20112
Cushing Rd 20109
Custer Ct 20112
Cuyahoga Ct 20112
Cynthia Ct 20112
Cynthia St 20111
Cypress Branch Ln 20110
Dabshire Way 20110
Daffodil Dr 20112
Dahlia Ct 20110
Dairymaid Ct 20111
Daisy Ct 20109
Damascus Dr 20109
Damask Ct 20110
Damview Pl 20112
Danny Ln 20112
Dark Forest Dr 20112
Davidson Pl 20109
Davis Ford Rd
5600-6299 20112
6300-7799 20111
Daylily Ct 20110
Dean Dr 20110
Dean Park Ln 20110
Deblanc Pl 20110
Deborah Ct 20111
Deckert Pl 20110
Declan Ct 20111
Deep Hollow Ln 20112
Deer Path Ct 20112
Delano Ct 20112
Democracy Ln 20109
Den Hollow Ct 20112
Denver Dr 20111
Depot Pl 20112
Developers Dr 20109
Devon Ln 20112
Devonshire Ct 20110
Deward Ct 20109
Diane Ct 20110
Dickinson Ct 20111
Digges Rd 20110
Digital Dr 20111
Diplomat Dr 20109
Discovery Blvd 20109
Ditmars Ct 20110
Dixie Ct 20110
Doane Dr 20109
Donegan Dr 20109
Donnington Ct 20111
Donset Ct 20109
Doolittle St 20112
Dorchester Pl 20110
Dorsey Cir 20110
Doubleday Ln 20109
Doubletree Ct 20109
Douglas St 20110
Dove Tree Ct 20112
Doves Ln 20112
Drake Ct 20111
Drew Ct 20109
Dublin Dr 20109
Duck Pond Ter 20111
Duet Ct 20112
Dumfries Rd
10000-10500 20110
10501-15799 20112
Duneiden Ln 20109
Dunster Ct 20111
Dusty Willow Rd 20112
Dutchman Ct 20110
Duvon Pl 20111
Dylan Pl 20109
Eagle Ct & Ln 20111
Eagles Nest Ct 20112
Eaheart Ln 20112
Early St 20110
East St 20110
Easton Ct 20110
Ebert Dr 20112
Eckley Ct 20112
Eclipse Dr 20112
Edgepark Cir 20109
Egglestetton Ct 20112
Elaine Ave 20112
Elderberry Ct 20110
Eleanor Ct 20112
Elim Pl 20111
Elise Ct 20111
Elizabeth Ct 20111
Elizabeth St 20112
Ellicott Ln 20110
Ellis Ct & Rd 20111
Ellsworth Rd 20109
Elm Ct 20111
Elsinore Dr 20112
Elzey Pl 20111
Ember Ct 20112
Emerald Dr 20109
Emerywood Ct 20112
Englewood Ct 20111
English St 20112
English Oak Ct 20110
Ensenada Ct 20112
Enterprise Ct 20111
Eppes Island Pl 20112
Erika Dr 20112
Erin Ct 20110
Estates Pond Ct 20112
Estates View Ln 20112
Esteppe Dr 20111
Ethel Ct 20111
Etheridge Ln 20112
Etherington Ct 20112
Euclid Ave
8200-8298 20111
8300-8599 20111
8601-8999 20111
8900-8908 20111
9000-9125 20110
9127-9199 20110
Euclid Ct
8100-8199 20111
8201-8299 20111
9126-9132 20110
9134-9138 20110
9140-9198 20110
Evans St 20111
Evans Ford Rd 20111
Evelyn Dr 20112
Ewell St 20110
Ewing Pl 20109
Excalibur Ct 20112
Fair Hill Ln 20112
Fairfax St 20110
Fairmont Ave 20109
Fairview Ave 20110
Fairway Ct 20111
Fairweather Ct 20112
Falcon Point Way 20110
Falkirk Way 20109
Falling Creek Dr 20112
Falls Grove Dr 20111
Fancy Farm Ct 20112
Farmington Ct 20110
Farragut Ct 20109
Farthing Park Rd 20109
Fawnlily Ct 20110
Featherbed Ln 20109
Federal Hill Ln 20112
Feeg Ct 20110
Felicia Ct 20110
Felsted Ln 20110
Fence Post Ct 20112
Fendall St 20110
Fenwood Ct 20109
Fern Oak Ct 20112
Fernwood Ct 20110
Festival Ln 20109
Field Ct 20110
Fincastle Dr 20112
Fingerlake Way 20112
Fiore Ct 20110
Firethorn Ct 20110
Fitzgerald Farms Ct 20110
Five Forks Rd 20109
Flager Cir 20109
Flagtree Pl 20112
Flametree Ct 20110
Flanagan Ct 20110
Flannagan Ct 20112
Flannery Ct 20109
Flatbush Ct 20109
Fletcher Farm Ct 20112
Flint Rock Rd 20112
Flocroft Ln 20112
Flowerden Ln 20110
Flowerree Ln 20110
Folksie Ct 20109
Folkstone Rd 20111
Foneswood Ln 20112
Forest Hill Cir 20110
Forest Oak Ct 20112
Forest Point Cir 20110
Forestview Dr 20112
Forestwood Ln 20110
Forrest St 20111
Forrester Ln 20109
Fort Dr & Pl 20110
Foster Dr 20110
Fostern Ln 20112
Fountain Cir 20110
Fox St 20112
Fox Den Ct & Rd 20112
Foxborough Ct 20110
Frank Ct 20110
Frank Marshall Ln 20110
Freedom Center Blvd 20110
Fringe Tree Ln 20110
Frog Hollow Ct 20111
Frosty Ct 20109
Fruit Wood Ct 20111
Fry St 20110
Furr Ct 20112
Gabe Ct 20109
Gaither St 20110
Gales Ct 20109
Gallaudet Ct 20112
Galveston Ct 20112
Gambril Dr 20109
Gandall Ct 20112
Garden St 20110
Gardenia Ln 20109
Garland Ct 20110
Garner Dr 20109
Garnet Ct 20110
Garrison Rd 20111
Garst Dr 20110
Gary Ct 20111
Gary Rd 20109
Gaskins Way 20109
Gateshead Ln 20109
Gateway Blvd 20110
Gateway Ct 20109
Gatsby Rd 20112
Geist Ct 20110
Geller Cir 20112
General Way 20111
General Longstreets Line 20109
General Mcclellan Rd 20109
General Trimbles Ln 20109
General Warren Ave 20109
Genie Ter 20112
Genna Ln 20112
Gent Ct 20110
George St 20110
George Mason Cir 20110
Georgian Ct 20110
Ghadban Ct 20111
Gholson Bridge Ct 20112
Gibbon Pl 20109
Gilbeth Rd 20112
Ginger Ct 20112
Ginny Way 20110
Glade Ct 20112
Glade Bank Dr 20111
Gladney Dr 20111
Gladstone St 20110
Glen Ct 20110
Glen Forest Ct 20112
Glen Wood Loop 20112
Glencrest Dr 20112
Glenolden Pl 20111
Gloxinia Way 20110
Godwin Ct 20110
Godwin Dr
8900-10456 20110
10457-10599 20112
Gold Cup Trl 20112
Golden Autumn Ct 20112
Golden Leaf Cir 20109
Golden Oak Dr 20109
Goldenberry Hill Ln 20112
Golf Ct 20111
Goodland Ct 20112
Gooseberry Dr 20110
Gopost 20109
Gordon Dr 20112
Goshen Ct 20112
Gracie Dr 20112
Grand Ct 20111
Granite Ln 20111
S Grant Ave 20110
S Grant Connector Rd 20110
Grape Myrtle Ct 20110
Grapewood Ct 20110
Gray Fox Trl 20112
Grays Mill Ct 20110
Great Mere Ct 20112
Green Brook Ct 20110
Greengate Ct 20110
Greenleaf Dr 20110
Greenshire Dr 20111
Greenview Ln 20109
Greenway Ct 20112
Gregory Ct 20109
Gregorys Grove Ct 20110
Gretchen Ct 20110
Greystone Rd 20111
Grist Mill Ct 20110
Grizzly Ct 20111
Groveton Rd 20109
Gum Spring Rd 20109
Guy Dr 20111
Gwendolyn Dr 20112
Haag St 20110
Haggle Ct 20112
Hailees Grove Ln 20110
Haire St 20112
S Hall Ter 20110
Hall Tavern Ct 20112
Hallard Ct 20109
Halsey Ct 20109
Halterpath Trl 20109
Hamilton Ct 20111
Hamowell St 20112
Hampton Rd 20110
Hanback Dr 20111
Handerson Pl 20111
Hanson Grove Ct 20109
Happy Pl 20112
Happy Creek Rd 20112
Hara St 20112
Hard Shale Rd 20111
Hardees Dr 20111
Harnsberger Barn Ct 20112
Harrington Ct 20111
Harry J Parrish Blvd 20110
Harton St 20112
Harvest Pl 20110
Harvey Rd 20112
Hastings Dr 20110
Haw Branch Ct 20112
Hawkins Dr 20109
Hawthorn Hill Ct 20110
Hayden Rd 20109
Hayes Station Way 20109
Hazel Dr 20110
Heather Ct 20111
Heather Green Dr 20112
Heaven Scent Ln 20110
Hedgeford St 20112
Helen St 20112
Helmsdale Pl 20109
Hemlock Ct 20112
Hemlock Hills Ct 20111
Hemlock Ridge Ct 20112
Hencount Rd 20112
Hendley Rd 20110
Henrico St 20109
Henry Ct 20109
Hensley Rd 20112
Heron Ridge Ct 20112
Hersch Farm Ln 20112
Hickory Hill Dr 20112
Hickory Hollow Ct 20112
Hicks Ct 20112
Hidden Creek Rd 20112
Hidden Lake Ct 20112
Hidden Spring Dr 20112
High St 20112
High Bluff Trl 20111
Highland St 20110
Highpoint Ct 20112
Highview St 20112
Hikmat Rd 20111
S Hill Dr 20109
Hill Pl 20110
Hillcrest Dr 20111
Hilliard Dr 20109
Hillis Ct 20112
Hilltop Dr 20112
Hillview Ct 20112
Hinson Mill Ln 20112

Hiram Ct 20109
Hoadly Rd 20112
Hoadly Run Ct 20112
Hobsons Choice Loop 20112
Hogan Pl 20112
Holbrook Ct 20112
Holden Dr 20111
Holland Ct 20110
Hollowbrook Way 20110
Holly Berry Ct 20112
Holly Forest Dr 20112
Holly Glen Ct 20112
Holly Grove Ct 20110
Holmes Pl 20111
Honeysuckle Rd 20112
Hood Rd 20110
Hornbaker Rd 20109
Horsely Ct 20112
Hospital Way 20110
Howar Ct 20112
Howard St 20111
Howell Run Ct 20112
Hudson Crest Dr 20112
Hugh Mullen Dr 20109
Hume School Ct 20112
Humphrey Ln 20109
Hunters Grove Rd 20112
Hunters Ridge Rd 20112
Huntsman Dr 20112
Hutchison Ln 20110
Hyde Ct 20109
Hyla Dr 20112
Hynson Dr 20111
I Beam Ln 20110
Idlebrook Ct 20112
Impalla Dr 20110
Independence Dr 20112
Independent Ln 20112
Independent Hill Dr 20112
Indian Moon Ln 20112
Industrial Ct & Rd 20109
Industry Dr 20111
Infantry Ridge Rd 20109
Inkberry Ct 20110
Innovation Dr 20110
Insignia Way 20109
Inspiration Point Pl 20112
Inyo Pl 20111
Iron Mountain Pl 20112
Irongate Way 20109
Irving St 20110
Isabel Ln 20111
Ivakota Ct 20112
Ivy Glen Ct 20110
J D Reading Dr 20109
Jack Dr 20111
Jackson Ave 20110
Jacksonville Ave 20109
Jacobs Ln 20111
Jacobs Grove Ct 20112
Jacqueline Ave 20112
Jamaica Ln 20109
James Hard Ct 20111
James Payne Ct 20110
James Russell Rd 20112
Jan St 20111
Janet Rose Ct 20111
Janja Ct 20110
Jansen St 20112
Jarvis Ct 20109
Jasmine Ct 20110
Jaspers Branch Ct 20111
Jayeselle Dr 20110
Jayhawk Ter 20110
Jefferson Ct 20111
Jefferson St 20110
Jenkins Ct 20111
Jenna Ct 20111
Jenner Pl 20112
Jeremiah Ct 20111
Jerome Ct 20112
Jerrys Cir 20110
Jessica Dr 20111
Jessica Ridge Way 20112
Jill Brenda Ct 20112
John Ave 20112
John Mark Ct 20112
John Wyatt Dr 20112
Johnson Dr 20110
Jones St 20112
Joplin Rd 20112
Jordon Hollow Ct 20109
Joshua Ct 20111
Joyce Ct 20110
Judiths Grove Ct 20112
Juliet Ln 20109
Junction Dr 20112
June St 20111
Justin Ln 20110
Kahns Rd 20112
Kallenburg Ct 20111
Kamlea Dr 20110
Kao Cir 20110
Karen Ct 20111
Karen Marie Ct 20112
Karlo St 20110
Katelyn Ct 20111
Kathy St 20112
Katy Ann Ct 20112
Keanon Ridge Ct 20112
Keara Ct 20109
Kemper House Ct 20111
Kemps Landing Cir 20109
Kendrick Ct 20112
Kent Dr 20111
Kent Village Sq 20111
Kershaw Ct 20110
Kessler Pl 20109
Kettle Pond Ct 20111
Kevin Ct
8400-8499 20112
9300-9399 20111
Key Commons Ct 20110
Kidd Pl 20112
Kilhaven Ct 20112
Kim Graham Ln 20109
Kimberly St 20112
Kimberton Ct 20111
Kincheloe Dr 20110
King Ct 20109
King Arthurs Ct 20112
King Carter St 20110
King George Dr 20109
Kings Arm Dr 20112
Kings Forest Ln 20111
Kinship Ct 20109
Kirby St
100-399 20111
8400-8699 20110
Kirkwood Ct 20112
Kittewan Ct 20112
Knightshayes Dr 20111
Knollwood Dr 20111
Knotty Oak Ln 20112
Kodiak Ct 20111
Koman Cir 20109
Kousa Ct 20112
Kris Ct 20111
Kristy Dr 20111
Kurt Kahn Trl 20112
Labrador Loop 20112
Lacy Dr 20109
Lady Jane Loop 20109
Lady Slipper Ln 20111
Lafayette Ave 20109
Laguna Ct 20112
Lake Dr 20111
Lake Forest Dr 20112
Lake Jackson Dr
9900-10105 20110
10106-11300 20111
11302-11398 20111
Lake Occoquan Dr 20111
Lake Shore Dr 20112
Lakeway Dr 20112
Lambert Dr 20111
Lamont Ct 20110
Lanae Ln 20111
Lancers Ct 20112
Landgreen St 20110
Landings Dr 20109
Landview Dr 20112
Lane Scott Ct 20110
Langholm Way 20109
Lantern Ct 20109
Larch Ln 20112
Lariat Ln 20109
Larksong Ct 20111
Launch Cir 20109
Laurel Ln 20112
Laurel Glen Ct 20112
Laurel Highlands Pl 20112
Laurelwood Ct 20110
Laurie Ct 20111
Lava Rock Cir 20111
Lavender Flower Ct 20110
Lavenham Ct 20111
Laws Dr 20110
Layton Ct 20110
Leander Ln 20110
Leatherleaf Ct 20111
Lee Ave 20110
Lee Ave W 20110
Lee Ct 20110
Lee Hwy 20109
Lee Manor Dr 20110
Leesa Dawn Ct 20112
Lehr Ct 20110
Leighlex Ct 20111
Leighton Pl 20110
Leland Rd 20111
Lemon Tree Ct 20110
Lenfant Pl 20112
Lenore St 20110
Leroux Ln 20112
Leslie Pl 20109
Lester Rd 20112
Levity Pl 20111
Lewis Ct 20111
Lexington Valley Dr 20109
Libeau Dr 20110
Liberia Ave 20110
Liberty St & Trl 20110
Light Guard Loop 20109
Lilac St 20112
Lime Tree Ct 20110
Linblake Ct 20111
Lincoln Ave 20110
Linda Pl 20112
Linden Ct 20110
Linden Lake Plz 20109
Linden Wood Rd 20111
Lindera Ct 20112
Lindsey Ln 20111
Lindy Ln 20112
Linette Ln 20111
Lisle Dr 20109
Litho Ln 20110
Livingston Rd 20109
Loblolly Trl 20110
Lochan Ora Ln 20111
Lochmere Dr 20112
Lockerbie Way 20109
Locust Ter 20111
Lodgepole Ct 20111
Lodi Ct 20112
Lomax Forest Dr 20112
Lomond Ct & Dr 20109
Lomond South Dr 20110
Lone Oak Ct 20111
Long Creek Ct 20111
Long Hill Ct 20110
Longstreet Ct & Dr 20110
Longtree Rd 20112
Lost Creek Ct 20112
Loudoun Ave 20109
Lovers Ln 20112
Lowery Ct 20111
Lucasville Rd 20112
Luke Dr 20111
Lute Ct 20109
Luther Dr 20112
Luxberry Ct 20109
Luxor St 20111
Lyceum Ln 20112
Lyndell Ct 20112
Lynncrest Dr 20112
Lyon Cir 20109
Lyre Ct 20112
Macbeth St 20110
Mace Cir, Ct & St 20111
Macgregor Ct 20110
Macnichol Ln 20111
Madera Ct 20111
Madison Ave 20110
Magenta St 20110
Magnolia Ct 20110
Magnolia Grove Dr 20110
Mahogany Ct 20110
Main St 20110
Makelys Way 20110
Malbrook Ct 20112
Mallard Pond Ct 20112
Mallow Ct & St 20110
Malvern Ct 20110
Manassas Dr 20111
Manassas Forge Dr 20111
Manassas Mill Rd 20110
Mandy Ln 20112
Mangione Ct 20109
Manning Rd 20112
Manor Ct 20111
Manor View Pl 20110
Maple St 20110
Maplewood Dr 20111
Margarite St 20112
Margate Ct 20109
Marian Dr 20111
Marie Dr 20112
Mariposa Dr 20112
Market Cir 20110
Market St
100-399 20111
10001-10099 20110
Market Square Ct 20112
Marshall Ct 20112
Martin Dr 20111
Martinique Ct 20109
Mary Jane Dr 20112
Mason King Ct 20109
Massie St 20110
Mastbrook Ln 20112
Mathis Ave 20110
Matthew Dr 20111
Maury Ln 20110
Maxfield Ct 20112
Maxwell Ct 20110
Maya Ln 20112
Mayfield Ct 20110
Mayfield Trace Pl 20112
Mcclellan Cmn 20110
Mcdowell Cmn 20110
Mcgill Ct 20109
Mcgrath Rd 20112
Mckee Way 20111
Mckenzie Cir 20110
Mckinley Ave 20110
Mclean St & Way 20111
Mcrae Ct 20110
Meadow Ct 20109
Meadow Grove Ct 20109
Meadowgate Dr 20112
Meadowlark Ct 20111
Meadowview Dr 20110
Meanderview Ct 20111
Medway Church Loop 20109
Meeker Ct & St 20111
Mente Rd 20112
Mercedes Dr 20110
Mercury Dr 20112
Merit Ct 20110
Merrifield Way 20109
Merrimack Dr 20110
Merrybell Ct 20110
Metcalf Blvd 20110
Michael Ct 20111
Michala Barrett Ct 20112
Michelle Ct 20109
Middle Ave 20112
Middleburg Ct 20109
Mike Garcia Dr 20109
Miken Ct 20112
Miles Pl 20110
Milic St 20110
Mill Race Ct 20112
Miller Dr 20111
Miller School Pl 20112
Millpond Ct 20112
Milroy Ct 20110
Milton Hall Pl 20112
Mine Gap Way 20110
Mineola Ct 20111
Mineral Springs Dr 20112
Minnieville Rd 20112
Minor Hill Rd 20109
Miramar Dr 20109
Mission Ridge Dr 20109
Mock Orange Ct 20110
Mockingbird Ln 20111
Moffitt Ln 20111
Molair Rd 20112
Molly Pitcher Cir 20109
Monitor Ct 20109
Monocacy Way 20112
Monroe Ave 20111
Monterosa Pl 20110
Montgomery Dr 20111
Monticello Dr 20111
Montrose Way 20109
Montyville Dr 20111
Moonglow Ct 20112
Moor Green Dr 20112
Moore Dr 20111
Moore House Ct 20111
Morias Ct 20110
Morning Glory Ct 20109
Morningside Dr 20112
Morrisania Mews 20109
Morton Ct 20111
Mosby Ct 20111
Moseby Ct & Dr 20111
Moselle Ct 20112
Moss Ln 20111
Mount Vernon Dr 20111
Mountwood Dr 20110
Mulder Ct 20111
Mullen St 20112
Nagle St 20110
Nancy St 20111
Nanette Dr 20110
Nantucket Ct 20110
Napa Dr 20112
Nash Dr 20110
Natchez Trail Ct 20110
Nathan Ct 20109
Nathaniel Harris Ct 20111
Natick Dr 20112
Natural Bridge Ct 20110
Navarone Pl 20110
Nelson Ln 20111
New Britain Cir 20110
New Market Ct 20109
Newman Ct 20110
Newood Dr 20111
Newton Pl 20111
Nicol Ln 20110
Niki Pl 20110
Nimitz Ct 20109
Ninebark Ct 20110
Nittany Dr 20110
Noahs Landing Ct 20112
Nodi Ct 20111
Nokesville Rd 20110
Norfolk Ct & St 20109
Normanton Way 20110
Norseman Dr 20112
Norwalk Ct 20112
Notes Dr 20109
Nottingham Dr 20112
Nova Way 20109
Nyack Ct 20112
Oak St 20111
Oak Hollow Ct 20109
Oakenshaw Dr 20110
Oakglen Ct & Rd 20110
Oakgrove Ct 20110
Oakview Dr 20110
Oarlock Ct 20112
Obrien Ct 20112
Observation Rd 20110
Occoquan Forest Dr 20112
Oconnell Ct 20110
Odie Ln 20112
Old Bushmill Ct 20111
Old Centreville Rd
1-2049 20111
2049-2049 20113
2051-2199 20111
7301-7397 20111
7399-7799 20111
7801-8399 20111
Old Compton Rd 20109
Old Dominion Dr 20110
Old Farm Ln 20109
Old Hickory Ct 20110
Old Lewis Ct 20110
Old Settle Ct 20112
Old Wellington Rd 20110
Olde Mill Run 20110
Olde Town Ct 20110
Oldelley Dr 20109
Olden Ct 20110
Olender Park Ct 20112
Olga Ln 20112
Oliver Ct 20110
Olympic Dr 20112
Omega Ln 20112
Opera Aly 20110
Orchard Ln 20110
Orchid Ct 20109
Ordway Ct 20112
Oriley Ct 20112
Oronoco Ln 20109
Outback Ct 20112
Overhill Dr 20111
Overrun Dr 20111
Owens Ct & Dr 20111
Paddle Wheel Ct 20112
Pageland Ln 20109
Paige Ct 20111
Paine Run Pl 20112
Palace Ct 20111
Pamplin Pipe Ct 20112
Panda Ct 20111
Pappas Dr 20112
Paradise Ct 20109
Park Ave & St 20110
Park Center Ct 20111
Parkington Ct 20109
Parkland St 20111
Parkriver Dr 20112
Parkview Dr 20109
Parrish Ln 20111
Partnership Ln 20109
Passage Creek Ln 20112
Patricia St 20112
Patterson Pl 20110
Patton Ln 20111
Paul Dr 20111
Payne Ct 20111
Peabody St 20110
Peachwood Dr 20110
Peak Ct 20112
Peaks Mill Dr 20112
Peakwood Ct 20111
Pearl St 20112
Pebble Ln 20111
Pelham Ct 20109
Pembridge Rd 20112
Pendragon Way 20112
Penhook Ct 20110
Peninsula Ct 20111
Penneyrail Pl 20112
Pennsylvania Ave 20110
Penny Ln 20112
Pennycress St 20110
Peony Ct 20110
Peppertree Ln 20111
Perennial St 20110
Peric Ct 20110
Pershing Dr 20112
Persinger House Ct 20112
Petersburg Ct 20109
Petterson Ln 20112
Pettigrew Way 20109
Pettus Pl 20110
Phipps Farm Way 20109
Phita Ln 20111
Phoenix Dr 20110
Pickens Pl 20111
Pickett Ln 20110
Pierce St 20111
Pine St 20111
Pinehurst Ln 20111
Pineview Rd 20111
Piney Ave 20112
Piney Point Ct 20110
Pinnacle Ridge Dr 20112
Piper Ln 20110
Placid St 20110
Plain Dealing Pl 20112
Plant Pl 20112
Plantation Ln 20110
Pleasant Colony Dr 20112
Plum Ct 20111
Plum Tree Ct 20110
Poe Dr 20110
W Point Ct 20109
N Point Rd 20112
Point Of Woods Dr 20110
Point View Dr 20112
Pointer Ln 20109
Polk Dr 20111
Pompom Ct 20110
Pond Crest Ter 20111
Ponderosa Pine Ct 20110
Pope St 20109
Poplar St 20111
Poplar Ford Trl 20109
Popwicke Ct 20112
Porter Ridge Ln 20109
Portner Ave 20110
Portsmouth Rd 20109
Portwood Turn 20109
Posey Pl 20112
Possum Trot Ct 20112
Post Oak Ter 20110
Postern Ct 20109
Potter Dr 20112
Powers St 20110
Powhatan St 20109
Pranchan St 20110
Prescott Ave 20110
Presidential Ln 20109
Priangto Dr 20111
Price Dr 20111
Primrose Ct 20109
Primrose Ln 20111
Prince Charles Ct 20111
Prince Cole Ct 20111
Prince William Pkwy 20111
Prince William St 20110
Princess Carol Ct 20111
Princeton Park Dr 20110
Pristine Ct 20110
Privates Ct 20109
Priya Ct 20111
Professional Pl 20110
Promenade Ln 20109
Provincial Dr 20109
Pruett Pl 20109
Public Works Dr 20110
Pump Station Way 20109
Purcell Rd 20112
Purcell Branch Ct 20112
Purdue Ct 20109
Purse Dr 20112
Pyramid Pl 20110
Quail Creek Ln 20112
Quail Hollow Dr 20111
Quail Run Ln 20109
Quarry Rd & St 20110
Quayle Ct 20109
Rachell Ct 20110
Racquet Cir 20110
Railroad Dr 20111
Rainwater Cir 20111
Raleigh Tavern Dr 20112
Ramblewood Trl 20112
Ramseur Pl 20109
Ramsey Ct 20110
Randolph Ridge Ln 20109

Raphiel Ct 20112
Rapidan Ln 20109
Ravens Crest Ct 20109
Ravenwood Dr 20111
Ravine Dr 20111
Rayborn Creek Dr 20109
Reb Yank Dr 20110
Rebecca St 20112
Rebel Walk Dr 20109
Red Wine Ct 20112
Redoubt Rd 20110
Reinecke Ct 20111
Remington Rd 20109
Republic Ct 20109
Reserve Ln 20112
Residency Rd 20110
Rettew Dr 20112
Reynolds Pl 20110
Richie Ct 20112
Richmond Ave & St 20110
Rickover Ct 20109
Ridgefield Village Dr 20112
Ridgeway Dr 20112
Rienzi Pl 20109
Rim Rock Ct 20112
River Rd 20111
River Crest Rd 20110
River Ford Ct 20112
River Forest Dr 20112
River Heights Ln 20112
River Run Ct & Dr 20112
Riverdale Pl 20110
Rixlew Ln 20109
Robard St 20109
Robert Pl 20111
Robertson Dr 20109
Robin Lee Ct 20111
Robin Lynn Ct 20110
Robling Ct 20112
Robnel Ave 20110
Robson Dr 20110
Rocky Brooke Ct 20112
Rodes Dr 20109
Rokeby Dr 20109
Rolling Rd 20110
Ronald Rd 20112
Rosbury Ct 20109
Rosebay Ln 20109
Roseberry Farm Dr 20111
Rosebud Ct 20111
Rosemary Dr 20109
Rosewood St 20110
Rosini Ct 20110
Rosita Ct 20112
Roslyn Ct 20109
Rossiter Ct 20112
Round Ln 20111
Round Top Rd 20112
Roxanna Ct 20112
Roxbury Ave 20109
Royal Fern Cir 20111
Ruddle Ct 20111
Ruffin Ct 20109
Rugby Ct & Rd 20111
Rumson Pl 20111
Runaldue Rd 20110
Running Brook Rd 20112
Running Creek Dr 20112
Running Deer Rd 20112
Runyon Ct 20111
Ruskin Ct 20110
Russia Branch View Dr 20111
Rustic Wood Ct 20112
Sabin Dr 20109
Sabre Ct 20109
Saddle Ct 20110
Saddlehorn Ct 20109
Saffron Hill Ct 20110
Sage St 20109
Saint Croix Ln 20109
Saint Johns Ct 20109
Saint Lucia Ct 20109
Saint Marys Ln 20111
Saint Steven Ct 20111
Saint Thomas Loop 20109
Salem St 20110
Salmon Run Ct 20112
Sals Pl 20112
Saltlick Ter 20112
Sam Keys Ln 20112
Samuel Trexler Dr 20110
Sand Bridge Ct 20111
Sandal Wood Ln 20112
Sandalwood Dr 20110
Sanderling Dr 20110
Sandstone Way 20111
Sandy Ct 20110
Santa Rosa Ct 20112
Sarajevo Ct 20110
Saranac Pl 20112
Sassafras Ct 20110
Sawmill Ct 20111
Sawtooth Ct 20111
Saxer Ct 20112
Scarlet St 20110
Scarlet Oak Dr 20110
Scenic Pointe Pl 20112
Scenic View Ct 20112
Schmitt St 20112
School St 20110
Scotland Loop 20109
Scott Dr 20111
Scott Peters Ct 20112
Scully Ct 20111
Sebastian Ct 20110
Sentry Ridge Rd 20109
Sesame Ct 20110
Seymour Rd 20109
Shady Creek Ct 20112
Shady Grove Cir 20110
Shallow Creek Loop 20109
Shallow Ford Rd 20111
Shamrock Rd 20112
Shane Ct 20112
Shane Thomas Ln 20112
Shannon Ln 20110
Shannon St 20111
Sharlee Ln 20111
Sharpsburg Ct 20109
Sharpshooters Ct 20111
Shawnee Ln 20110
Sheldon St 20111
Shelley Ln 20111
Sheraton Dr 20112
Sheridan Ln 20110
Sherman Ct 20110
Shields Way 20109
Shiloh Ct 20109
Shining Wood Ct 20111
Shirley Ave 20112
Shoppers Sq 20111
Short St 20112
Sierra Ct 20111
Sigfield Ct 20112
Signal Ct 20111
Signal Hill Rd
6700-8199 20111
8200-8799 20110
Signal Station Dr 20111
Signal View Dr 20111
Silent Willow Ct 20112
Silent Wolf Dr 20112
Sills Ct 20110
Silo Mill Ct 20112
Silver Fox Trl 20111
Silver Maple Ct 20110
Silver Meteor Ct 20111
Simmons Ridge Ct 20112
Sinclair Ln 20112
Sinclair Mill Rd 20112
Singleton Ter 20109
Six Towers Rd 20112
Slagle Ln 20111
Sly Fox Ln 20112
Smith Ln 20112
Smith Pond Ln 20112
Smithfield Rd 20112
Snowfall Dr 20112
Soldiers Ct 20109
Soldiers Ridge Cir 20109
Somerset Ln 20111
Somersworth Dr 20111
Songer Ln 20112
Sonia Ct 20111
Sorrel River Way 20109
Sorrell Dr 20110
Souza Ln 20111
Sowder Village Sq 20109
Speedwell Ct 20110
Spice Glade Ct 20110
Spicewood Ct 20111
Spiller Ln 20112
Split Rail Dr 20112
Spotsylvania St 20110
Spraggins Ct 20110
Spriggs Rd 20112
Spriggs Ford Ct 20111
Spring Dr & St 20112
Springhouse Ct 20110
Spruance Ct 20109
Spruce St 20111
Squirrels Nest Cir 20112
Stagestone Way 20109
Stanbaugh Ln 20112
Statesboro Ct 20109
Station Rd 20111
Staunton Cir 20109
Stave Ct 20112
Steeple Chase Ln 20111
Steity Ln 20111
Stephanie St 20111
Stethem Ct 20112
Steve St 20111
Stevens Ct 20110
Stillbrooke Rd 20112
Stillwater Pl 20111
Stilson Dr 20110
Stoddard Dr 20110
Stokely Dr 20111
Stone Rd 20111
Stone Hill Ln 20109
Stonebrook Dr 20112
Stoneridge Dr 20111
Stonewall Ct & Rd 20110
Stonewall Brigade Ct 20109
Stoney Ln 20112
Stoney Run Pl 20112
Stoneybrook Dr 20112
Stonington Ln 20109
Strasburg St 20109
Strawflower Ln 20110
Stream Walk Ln 20109
Stuart Ave 20110
Stuart Ct 20111
Sudley Rd
5100-8529 20109
8530-8540 20110
8531-8535 20109
8542-8800 20110
8801-8801 20108
8801-9299 20110
8802-9298 20110
Sudley Manor Dr 20109
Sugarwood Ln 20110
Suheil Rd 20111
Sullivan Ct 20110
Summer Breeze Pl 20112
Summit Ridge Ct 20112
Sumner Lake Blvd 20110
Sumter Ct 20111
Sun Shadow Rd 20112
Sunderman Pl 20112
Sunnygate Dr 20109
Sunnyside Ct 20111
Sunnyslope Dr 20112
Sunrise Ct 20110
Sunset Ct 20111
Sunset Dr 20110
Superior Ct 20112
Surveyor Ct 20110
Swann Ct 20111
Sweetbriar St 20110
Swindon Pl 20112
Tac Ct 20109
Tackett Ave 20110
Tahoe Ct 20112
Talisa Ln 20112
Tall Oaks Ct 20110
Tall Trees Ln 20112
Taney Rd 20110
Tangier Way 20109
Tanglewood Ln 20110
Tapok Dr 20110
Tappen Mill Way 20109
Tarpleys Ct 20111
Tarra Ln 20110
Tarragon Ct 20110
Tarrytown Ct 20109
Tasha Ct 20111
Tasker Dr 20109
Tattersall Dr 20112
Tayloe Dr 20112
Taylor St 20110
Teaberry Ct 20110
Teakwood Ct 20109
Tech Cir 20109
Technology Dr 20110
Temple Loop 20112
Tempo Ct 20110
Tendring Trl 20111
Terminal Rd 20110
Terrace View Ct 20110
Terrapin Dr 20112
Thistlewood Ct 20110
Thomas Dr 20110
Thornwood Ct & Ln 20110
Thrave Ln 20112
Three Otters Pl 20112
Thunder Dr 20112
Thurston Ln 20111
Tifton Ct 20112
Tillett Loop 20110
Timberlane Dr 20112
Timberview Dr 20111
Timberwolf Trl 20112
Timberwood Ct 20110
Tinkling Springs Ct 20112
Tinsley Way 20111
Tito Ct 20110
Todd Pl 20109
Toddsbury Ln 20112
Token Forest Ct & Dr 20112
Token Valley Rd 20112
Tomislav St 20110
Tommy Ct 20112
Tower Pl 20109
Towering Oak Way 20111
Town Ln 20110
Trails End Ct & Rd 20112
Trailway Ter 20111
Transco Ct 20109
Trappers Ct 20111
Traveller St 20110
Travis St 20111
Tree Spring Ct 20112
Treeline Ct 20112
Trellis Ct 20110
Tremont St 20111
Trenton Chapel Way 20109
Trey Fox Ct 20112
Treywood Ln 20112
Trinidad Ct 20109
Trinity Ln 20110
Trio Ln 20110
Trona Ct 20112
Trotwood Meadows Ct 20109
Troutman Ct 20110
Trumpet Vine Ct 20110
Trumpeter Swan Ln 20112
Trundle Pl 20109
Trusler Ct 20110
Tudor Ln 20110
Tudor Oaks Dr 20110
Tulip Poplar Ct 20111
Tullamore Ct 20111
Turkey Run Ct 20112
Twin Beech Ct 20111
Twin Rivers Dr 20112
Tyler Ct 20110
Unbridled Ct 20112
Union Pl 20111
University Blvd 20110
Urbanna Rd 20109
Valcour Island Way 20109
Valley Falls Ct 20112
Van Doren Rd 20112
Vandor Ln 20109
Vanore Pl 20110
Vassau Ct 20111
Venture Ct 20111
Verbena Ct 20110
Veridan Dr 20110
Vermont Pl 20111
Vernon St 20109
Vic Pl 20112
Vicksburg Ct 20109
Vicksburg Ln 20110
Victoria St 20110
Victory Loop 20112
Victory Ridge Pl 20112
Vine Ct 20111
Vinnia Ct 20110
Violet Ct 20109
Virginia Ave 20110
Virginia Meadows Dr 20109
Visionary Ct 20112
Vista Brooke Dr 20112
Vulcan Ln 20109
Wainwright Pl 20109
Wakeman Ct & Dr 20110
Walcott Ct 20111
Walden St 20111
Walker Way 20111
Wall St 20110
Wallace Ln 20109
Waller Dr 20111
Wallwood Dr 20111
Walton Dr 20112
Warfield St 20110
Warm Springs Ln 20112
Washington Ave 20110
Waterbury Ct 20110
Waterford Dr 20110
Waterfront Dr 20111
Waterside Dr 20112
Waterview Dr 20112
Wax Myrtle Way 20110
Waylon Ln 20112
Weatherwood Ct 20109
Webster Tavern Way 20109
Websters Way 20112
Wedgewood Dr 20109
Weems Rd 20110
Weeping Willow Dr 20110
Weir Pl & St 20110
Well St 20111
Wellingford Dr 20109
Wellington Rd
6700-9199 20109
9200-10099 20110
Wellman Ct 20112
Wesley Ave 20110
Wesley Rd 20109
West St 20110
Westchester Dr 20112
Westfield Rd 20112
Westmoreland Ave 20110
Weston Ct 20110
Westside Rd 20112
Westwood Ct 20110
Weyanoke Pl 20112
Wharton Ct 20110
Wheats Way 20111
Whispering Pine Ct 20110
Whispering Wind Ln 20111
White Eagle Dr 20112
White Flint Ct 20112
White Pine Dr 20111
Whitehall Dr 20111
S Whitt Dr 20111
Whitting Dr 20112
Whitworth Ln 20110
Wichita Ct 20109
Wigfall Way 20111
Wigwag Ct 20111
Wilcox Rd 20109
Wilcoxen Dr 20111
Wilcoxen Farm Pl 20111
Wilcoxen Station Way 20111
Wild Acres Way 20112
Wild Ginger Cir 20109
Willa Ln 20110
Willard Ln 20112
William St 20111
Williamson Blvd 20109
Willmans Way 20111
Willoughby Ln 20109
Willow Glen Ct 20110
Willow Grove Trl 20110
Willow Pond Ct 20111
Willowbrook Ct 20110
Wilmington St 20109
Wilson Ave 20110
Wilton Meadows Ct 20109
Wimbledon Ct 20110
Winchester Ct 20109
Windgate Ct 20110
Winding Brook Ct 20111
Windsor Ave 20110
Winfield Ct 20110
Winfield Loop 20109
Winged Elm Cir 20110
Winstead Pl 20109
Winterset Dr 20110
Winterwood Ct 20110
Wisakon Trl 20111
Wisteria Dr 20110
Wistlewood Ct 20110
Witch Hazel Way 20110
Wolf Run Ln 20112
Wolverine Ct 20111
Wood Drift Cir 20110
Woodbine Rd 20112
Woodbrooke Ct 20110
Woodbury Dr 20109
Wooded Acres Ct 20112
Woodhue Ct & Dr 20111
Woodlark Ct 20112
Woodlea Ct 20110
Woodline Ct 20110
Woodmont Ct 20110
Woodrow Dr 20112
Woodstock St 20109
Wooldridge Dr 20111
Wortham Crest Cir 20109
Wycliffe Ct 20109
Yarrow Ln 20110
Yates Trl 20111
Yates Ford Rd 20111
Yellow Lily Dr 20109
Yellow Wood Ct 20110
Yoder St 20110
Yohr Ct 20110
Yola Ln 20111
Yolanda Ln 20112
Yorkshire Ln 20111
Yost St 20111
Yuma Ct 20109
Zachary Ct 20111
Zachary Taylor Ct 20112
Zebedee St 20110
Zimbro Ave 20110

NUMBERED STREETS

All Street Addresses 20110

MARSHALL VA

General Delivery 20115

POST OFFICE BOXES MAIN OFFICE STATIONS AND BRANCHES

Box No.s
All PO Boxes 20116

NAMED STREETS

All Street Addresses 20115

MARTINSVILLE VA

General Delivery 24112

POST OFFICE BOXES MAIN OFFICE STATIONS AND BRANCHES

Box No.s
1 - 1432 24114
1776 - 1776 24115
2001 - 2417 24113
3001 - 5551 24115
7001 - 7060 24112
40001 - 40010 24115

NAMED STREETS

All Street Addresses 24112

NUMBERED STREETS

All Street Addresses 24112

MC LEAN VA

General Delivery 22101

POST OFFICE BOXES MAIN OFFICE STATIONS AND BRANCHES

Box No.s
A - Z 22101
AA - AA 22101
BB - BB 22101
CC - CC 22101
DD - DD 22101
EE - EE 22101
FF - FF 22101
GG - GG 22101
HH - HH 22101
II - II 22101
JJ - JJ 22101
KK - KK 22101
LL - LL 22101
MM - MM 22101
NN - NN 22101
OO - OO 22101
PP - PP 22101
QQ - QQ 22101
RR - RR 22101
SS - SS 22101
TT - TT 22101
1 - 1295 22101
1302 - 1312 22102
1401 - 1520 22101
6001 - 8434 22106
9001 - 50162 22102

NAMED STREETS

Abbey Way 22101
Addington Dr 22101
Adeline Ct 22101
Aerie Ln 22101
Agate Ct 22102
Agin Ct 22102
N Albemarle St 22101
Aldebaran Dr 22101
Algarve St 22102
Alhambra Ct 22101
Alherst Ave 22101
Alicent Pl 22101
Allendale Rd 22101
Alps Dr 22102
Altamira Ct 22102
Alvermar Ridge Dr 22102
Alvord Ct & St 22102
Ambergate Pl 22102

Amethyst Dr 22102
Anderson Rd 22102
Anna Maria Ct 22101
Anthony Crest Sq 22101
Arbor Ln 22101
Ariel Way 22102
Artnauman Ct 22102
Aspen Wood Ct 22101
Atoga Ave 22101
Audmar Dr 22101
Autumn Dr 22101
Aynsley Ln 22102
Baker Crest Ct 22101
Baldwin Dr 22101
Ballantrae Ct & Ln 22101
Ballantrae Farm Dr 22101
Ballestrade Ct 22102
Balls Hill Rd 22101
Balsam Dr 22101
Banbury Ct 22102
Banquo Ct 22102
Banton Cir 22101
Barbee St 22101
Bargo Ct 22101
Baron Rd 22101
Basil Rd 22101
Basswood Ct 22101
Baymeadow Ct 22101
Bayside Ct 22101
Bdm Way 22102
Beall Dr 22101
Beaver Ln 22101
Belgrove Rd 22101
Bellamine Ct 22101
Bellview Pl & Rd 22102
Belton Ct 22101
Benjamin St 22101
Bent Twig Rd 22101
Beresford Ct 22101
Bermuda Ct 22101
Bernane Forest Ct 22102
Berry Pl 22102
Beverly Ave & Rd 22101
Birch Rd 22101
Birch Grove Ct 22101
Birnam Wood Dr 22102
Blaise Trl 22102
Blue Star Dr 22101
Blueberry Hill Rd 22101
Bonheim Ct 22101
Box Elder Ct 22102
Boyle Ln 22102
Bradmore Ct 22101
Brawner St 22101
Brentfield Dr 22101
Briar Hill Ct 22101
Briar Ridge Ct & Rd 22101
Bridle Path Ln 22102
Bright Ave 22101
Bright Mountain Rd 22101
Broad St 22102
Broad Branch Ct 22101
Brook Rd 22102
Brook Valley Ln 22102
Brookewood Ct 22102
Brookhaven Dr 22101
Brookside Rd 22101
Broyhill St 22101
Bruton Ct 22101
Bryan Branch Rd 22101
Bryan Pond Ct 22102
Buchanan St 22101
Buena Vista Ave 22101
Bulls Neck Rd 22102
Burford Dr 22102
Butternut Ct 22101
Byrnes Dr 22101
Byrns Pl 22101
Byrnwood Ct 22102
Calder Rd 22101
Calla Dr 22101
Callista Ln 22101
Calpurnia Ct 22102
Canal Ct & Dr 22102
Candlewick Ct 22101
Capital One Dr 22102
Capitol View Ct & Dr 22102
Capulet Ct 22102
Carlin Ln 22101
Carlton Ct & Pl 22102
Carol Raye St 22101
Carper St 22101
Carriage Hills Dr 22102
Carrie Ct 22101
Cathy Ln 22102
Cawdor Ct 22102
Cecile St 22101
Cedar Ave 22101
Cedrus Ln 22102
Center St 22101
Centrillion Dr 22102
Chadsworth Ct 22102
Chain Bridge Ct 22101
Chain Bridge Rd
100-1725 22101
1726-1999 22102
Chain Bridge Forest
Ct 22101
Chateau Ct 22101
Chelsea Rd 22101
Chequers Way 22102
Chesterbrook Rd 22101
Chesterbrook Vale Ct 22101
Chesterfield Ave & Pl 22101
Chesterford Way 22101
Chilton Ct 22101
Chinquapin Rd 22102
Chowning Pl 22101
Churchill Rd 22101
Claiborne Dr 22101
Clarkewood Ct 22102
Clayborne House Ct 22101
Claymore Ct 22101
Clinton Pl 22101
Cloisters Dr 22101
Clover Dr 22101
Clover Leaf Dr 22102
Cloverlawn Ct 22101
Cola Dr 22101
Colleen Ln 22101
Colonial Ln 22102
Colonial Rd 22101
Colonial Hills Dr 22102
Colshire Dr 22102
Columbus Hall Ct 22101
Congress Ln 22101
Copely Ln 22101
Corbin Ct 22101
Cordelia Ct 22102
Corland Ct 22101
Corliss Ct 22101
Corner Ln 22101
Corporate Rdg 22102
Cottonwood St 22101
Country Meadow Ct 22101
Countryside Ct 22101
Courser Ct 22101
Court Petit 22101
Craig Ln 22101
Crescent Ln 22101
Crest Ln 22101
Crestwood Ln 22101
Crestwood Heights Dr 22102
Cricket Pl 22101
Crimson Ct 22101
Cross St 22101
Crossover Dr 22102
Crownhurst Ct 22102
Crownpointe Ridge Ct 22102
Curran St 22101
Dahlia Ct 22101
Daleview Dr 22102
Dalewood Pl 22101
Dalmation Dr 22101
Danforth St 22101
Darnall Dr 22101
Dartford Dr 22101
Davidson Rd 22101
Davis Ct 22101
Daviswood Dr 22102
Dead Run Dr 22101
Dean Dr 22101
Deer Dr 22101
Deidre Ter 22101
Delf Dr 22101
Dempsey St 22101
Denny Pl 22101
Desdemona Ct 22102
Dewberry Ct 22101
Dillon Ave 22101
Dinneen Dr 22101
Divine St 22101
Dixie Pl 22102
Dogue Hill Ln 22101
Dogwood Dr 22101
Dolley Madison Blvd
700-1799 22101
1800-1899 22102
Dominion Ct 22102
Dominion Crest Ln 22101
Dominion Hill Ct 22101
Dominion Reserve Dr 22102
Douglass Dr 22101
Dower Ln 22102
Dryden Dr 22101
Duchess Dr 22102
Dulany Dr 22101
N Dumbarton St 22101
Dunaway Ct & Dr 22101
Duncraig Ct 22101
Dunningham Pl 22101
Dunsinane Ct 22102
Dunterry Pl 22101
Earnestine St 22101
East Ave 22101
Eastern Red Cedar Ln 22101
Eaton Dr 22102
Edgeralm Dr 22101
Eldorado Ct & St 22102
Elizabeth Dr 22101
Elliott Ave 22101
Elm St
6800-6842 22101
6841-6841 22106
6843-6845 22101
6844-6998 22101
6845-6845 22106
6847-6999 22101
Elnido Dr 22101
Elsinore Ave 22102
Emerson Ave 22101
Engel Dr 22101
Enola St 22102
Enterprise Ave 22101
Espey Ln 22101
Esquire Ln 22101
Evans Farm Dr 22101
Evans Mill Rd 22101
Evermay Ct & Dr 22101
Evers Dr 22101
Fairlawn Dr 22101
Fairview Ave 22101
Fairway St 22101
Falls Run Rd 22102
Falstaff Ct & Rd 22102
Farm Credit Dr 22102
Farm Meadow Ct 22101
Farver Rd 22101
Father John Ct 22101
Felix St 22101
Fern Hill Run 22101
Fern Oak Ct 22101
Fielding Lewis Way 22101
Fleetwood Rd 22101
Fletcher Ln 22101
Fletcher St 22102
Flor Ln 22102
Fonthill Ct 22102
Forest Ln 22101
Forest Villa Ln 22101
Forestwood Ct & Dr 22101
Founders Ridge Ln 22102
Fox Haven Dr 22102
Foxhall Rd 22101
Foxhound Ct & Rd 22102
Franklin Ave 22101
Franklin Park Rd 22101
Frazier Ln 22101
Frome Ln 22102
Furlong Rd 22101
Galium Ct 22102
Gallant Green Dr 22102
Galleria Dr 22102
Galleria At Tysons Ii 22102
Gelston Cir 22102
George Washington
Memorial Pkwy 22101
Georgetown Ct 22102
Georgetown Pike
6200-7199 22101
7300-8999 22102
Georgetown Ridge Ct 22102
Gilliams Rd 22101
Girard St 22101
Glen Head Ct 22101
Glenhaven Ct 22102
Gold Mine Rd 22102
Golden Ct 22101
Gopost 22101
Gordon Ln 22102
Gower Ct 22102
Grace Manor Ct 22101
Grady Randall Ct 22101
Great Cumberland Rd 22102
Great Falls St 22101
Green Oak Dr 22101
Greensboro Dr 22102
Greenwich Woods Dr 22102
Grovemont Dr 22102
Guilford Ct 22101
Gunnell Ct 22102
Hallcrest Dr 22102
Halsey Rd 22101
Hamel Hill Ct 22101
Hampshire Rd 22101
Hampton Hill Cir 22101
Hampton Oak Ct 22102
Hampton Park Ct 22101
Hampton Ridge Dr 22101
Hampton View Pl 22101
Hane St 22101
Hardison Ln 22102
Hardwood Ln 22101
Hardy Ct & Dr 22101
Harvest Crossing Dr 22101
Harvey Rd 22101
Hawthorne St 22101
Hazel Ln 22101
Hazen Pl 22101
Heather Brook Ct 22101
Heather Hill Ct & Ln 22101
Hector Rd 22101
Heidi Ct 22101
Heights Ct 22101
Helga Pl 22102
Hickory Hill Ave 22101
Highland Glen Pl 22101
Highwood Dr 22101
Hilldon St 22101
Hitt Ave 22101
Holland St 22101
Holly Ct 22101
Holly Leaf Dr 22102
Holly Ridge Dr 22102
Holmes Pl 22101
Holsing Ln 22101
Holyrood Dr 22101
Homeric Ct 22101
Honeywood Ct 22102
Hooking Rd 22101
Horatio St 22102
Hornet Ln 22101
Hunters Grove Ct 22102
Hunting Ave 22102
Hunting Hill Ln 22102
Hunting Ridge Ct & Ln 22101
Huntmaster Ct & Ln 22102
Huntover Ct 22101
S Huntress Ct 22102
Hyannis Ct 22102
Ina Ln 22102
Ingeborg Ct 22101
Ingleside Ave 22101
International Dr 22102
Ironwood Dr 22101
Ivy Hill Dr 22101
James Payne Cir 22101
Jarvis Ct 22101
Jefferson Pl 22101
Jerry Pl 22101
Jill Ct 22101
Jones Branch Dr 22102
Jossie Ln 22102
Julia Ave 22101
Karen Forest Dr 22102
Karlson St 22101
Kedleston Ct 22101
Kellogg Dr 22101
Kenbar Ct 22101
Kennedy Dr 22102
N Kensington Rd & St 22101
Kilcullen Dr 22101
Kimberwicke Rd 22102
Kinglet Ct 22101
Kinyon Pl 22101
Kirby Rd 22101
Kirkley Ave 22101
Kurpiers Ct 22101
Kurtz Rd 22101
Kyleakin Ct 22101
La Salle Ave 22102
Laburnum St 22101
Lady Bird Dr 22101
Lamson Pl 22101
Lancia Ct & Dr 22102
Langdon Ct 22101
W Langley Ln & Pl 22101
Langley Fork Ln 22101
Langley Hill Dr 22101
Langley Ridge Rd 22102
Langley Springs Ct 22101
Lansing Ct 22101
Laughlin Ave 22101
Laurelwood Dr 22102
Lawson Ln 22101
Lawton St 22101
Layman St 22101
Lear Rd 22102
Legere Ct 22102
Lemon Rd 22101
Lessard Ln 22101
Lewinsville Rd 22102
Lewinsville Mews Ct 22102
Lewinsville Park Ct 22101
Lewinsville Square Pl 22101
Lincoln Cir, Ln & Way 22102
Lincoln Center Ct 22101
Linden Hurst Ave 22101
Linganore Ct & Dr 22102
Linway Ter 22101
Linway Park Dr 22101
Linwood Pl 22101
Little Leaf Linden Ln 22101
Litton Ln 22101
Live Oak Dr 22101
Loch Raven Dr 22101
Long Meadow Rd 22101
Longfellow Ct & St 22101
Lorraine Ave 22101
Loughran Rd 22102
Lowell Ave 22101
Lucy Ln 22101
Lumsden St 22101
Lupine Ln 22101
Lynton Pl 22102
Lynwood Hill Rd 22101
Lysander Ct 22102
Macarthur Dr 22101
Macbeth St 22102
Mackall Ave 22101
Mackall Farm Ln 22101
Macon St 22101
Maddux Ln 22101
Madison Ct 22101
Madison Mclean Dr 22101
Malta Ln 22101
Mangered Dr 22102
Margie Dr 22101
Marion Ave 22101
Market Square Dr 22101
Martha Jane St 22101
Martingale Dr 22102
Mary Ellen Ct 22101
Massachusetts Ave 22101
Matthew Mills Rd 22101
Maugh Rd 22101
Maxwell Ct 22101
Mayflower Dr 22101
Mayhurst Blvd 22102
Mccay Ln 22101
Mcfall Pl & St 22101
Mclean Ct & Dr 22101
Mclean Commons Ct &
Ln 22101
Mclean Corner Ln 22101
Mclean Crest Ct 22101
Mclean Mews Ct 22101
Mclean Park Manor Ct 22101
Mclean Ridge Dr 22101
Mcneer St 22101
Meadow Green Ln 22102
Meadowbrook Ave 22101
Meca Ct 22101
Melbourne Dr 22101
Melrose Dr 22101
Menlo Rd 22101
Mercer Ln 22101
Merchant Ln 22101
Merecourt Ln 22102
Meric Rd 22101
Meritage Ln 22102
Merrie Ridge Rd 22101
Merriewood Ln 22102
Merrimac Dr 22101
Merryhill Pl 22101
Meyer Ct 22101
Mill Rdg 22102
Mill Pond Valley Dr 22102
Mintwood Dr 22101
Mirador Pl 22102
Monique Ct 22101
Montcalm Dr 22102
Montvale Way 22102
Monza Rd 22101
Mori St 22101
Morrill Ct 22101
Moss Wood Ln 22101
Mottrom Dr 22101
Mount Pleasant Dr 22101
Moyer Pl 22101
Mulroy St 22102
Munhall Ct 22101
Natalie Joy Ln 22101
Nathaniel Ln 22101
Nelway Ct & Dr 22101
Nesbitt Pl 22101
Nethercombe Ct 22101
Nicole Marie Ct 22101
Nielson Ct 22102
Nina Ct 22101
Noble Dr 22101
Northwoods Trl 22102
Northwyck Ct 22102
N Nottingham St 22101
Oak Ln 22101
Oak Meadow Way 22101
Oak Ridge Ave 22101
Oakdale Rd 22101
Oakview Dr 22101
Oberon Way 22102
Odricks Ln 22102
Old Cedar Ct & Rd 22102
Old Chain Bridge Rd 22101
Old Chesterbrook Rd 22101
Old Dominion Dr
6661A-6661D 22101
6100-7499 22101
7500-9299 22102
7513-4-7513-4 22102
7515-5-7515-5 22102
Old Falls Rd 22102
Old Gate Ct 22102
Old House Rd 22101
Old Maple Dr & Sq 22102
Old Mclean Village Dr 22101
Old Meadow Ln & Rd 22102
Old Springhouse Rd 22102
Old Stable Rd 22102
Old Stage Ct 22102
Old Tolson Mill Rd 22102
Olson Ct 22102
Onyx Dr 22102
Opalocka Dr 22101
Orlo Dr 22102
Ormond Ct 22101
Orris St 22101
Overlook Rd 22102
Ozkan St 22101
Panarama Ct 22101
Panda Ln 22101
Parham Ct 22102
Park Ave & Rd 22101
Park Run Dr 22102
Pathfinder Ln 22101
Patton Ter 22101
Peacock Station Rd 22102
Peridot Dr 22102
Perlich St 22101
Perry William Dr 22101
Peter Pl 22102
Pettit Ct 22102
Pine Creek Ct 22101
Pine Crest Ave 22101
Pine Hill Rd 22101
Pine Tree Rd 22101
Pinnacle Dr 22102
Polk St 22102
Poole Ln 22101
Poplar Pl 22101
Poppy Dr 22101
Portia Pl 22102
Portland Pl 22102
Portobello Rd 22101
Potomac Fall Rd 22102
Potomac Knolls Dr 22102
Potomac River Rd 22102
Potomac School Rd 22101
Powhatan St 22101
Preserve Crest Way 22102
Prestwould Pl 22102
Priory Pl 22101
Providence Ter 22101
Provincial Dr 22102
Purdue Pl 22101
Quail Hollow Ct 22101
Rachel Rd 22101
Rail Ct 22102
Ramshorn Dr & Pl 22101
Randolph Rd 22101
Randwood St 22102
Ranleigh Rd 22101
Ranleigh Manor Dr 22101
Raymond Ave 22101
Rector Ln 22102
Red Twig Ln 22101
Redmond Dr 22101
Rhode Island Ave 22101
Ridge Dr & St 22101
Ridgedale Ct 22101
N Ridgeview Cir & Rd 22101
Riding Ridge Pl 22102
Ridings Ct 22102
Rigby Ln 22101
N River St 22101
River Oaks Dr 22101
Rivercrest Dr 22101
Roberta Ct 22101
Rockingham St 22101
Rockland Ter 22101
Rocky Run Rd 22102
Romeo Ct 22102
Rosamora Ct 22101
Rosemont Ct & Dr 22101
Round Oak Ct 22101
Royal Oak Dr 22102
Rupert St 22101
Saddleback Ct 22102
Saic Dr 22102
Saigon Cir & Rd 22102
Saint Albans Rd 22101
Salt Meadow Ln 22101
Saluja Hill Ct 22102

Sandy Knoll Ct 22101
Santa Maria Ct 22101
Savile Ln 22101
Sawyer Pl 22101
Sconset Ln 22102
Scotts Run Rd 22102
Sea Cliff Rd 22101
Selwyn Dr 22101
Seneca Ave 22102
Seneca Ridge Dr 22102
Sharon Ct 22101
Sheridan Ct 22101
Shetland Ct 22102
Shipman Ln 22101
Silent Ridge Ct 22102
Simmons Ct & Dr 22101
Sinclair Dr 22101
Skipwith Rd 22101
Smith St 22101
Smoot Dr 22101
Snow Meadow Ln 22102
Snowpine Way 22102
Softwood Trl 22101
Solitaire Ln & Way 22101
Solitude Ct 22102
Somerset Dr 22101
Somerville Dr 22101
Sorrel St 22101
Sothoron Rd 22101
Southridge Dr 22101
Sparger St 22102
Sparrow Point Ct 22101
Spencer Ct & Rd 22102
Spoleto Ln 22102
Spring Gate Dr 22102
Spring Hill Ln 22102
Spring Hill Rd
801-897 22102
899-1545 22102
1544-1544 22103
1546-1576 22102
1547-1575 22102
Spring Hill Farm Dr 22102
Spring Side Way 22101
Spring Vale Ave 22101
Springhaven Garden Ln 22102
Stable Gate Ct 22102
Statendam Ct 22101
Still Water Way 22102
Stirrup Cup Ln 22102
Stoneham Ct & Ln 22101
Stony Point Ct 22102
Strata St 22101
Strine Dr 22101
Stuart Robeson Dr 22101
Suffield Dr 22101
Sugarstone Ct 22101
Summerwood Ct & Dr 22102
Summit Rd 22101
Sunny Hill Ct 22101
Sunny Side Ln 22102
Sunstone Dr 22102
Susquehannock Dr 22101
Swinks Ct 22102
Swinks Mill Ct & Rd 22102
Symphony Ct 22101
Teague Dr 22101
Tebbs Ln 22102
Tennyson Dr 22101
Terri Knoll Ct 22101
Theresa Ann St 22101
Thompson Crest Ct 22101
Thrasher Pl & Rd 22101
Tilden Pl 22101
Timberly Ct & Ln 22102
Timon Dr 22102
Tina Ln 22101
Tintagel Ln 22101
Titania Ln 22102
Tompkins Dr 22101
Topeka Rd 22101
Torregrossa Ct 22101
Touchstone Ter 22102
Towlston Rd 22102
Towne Lane Ct & Rd 22101
Tremayne Pl 22102
Tucker Ave 22101
Turkey Run Rd 22101
Turning Leaf Ln 22102
Twincrest Ct 22102
Twisting Tree Ln 22101
Tyndale St 22101
Tysons Blvd 22102
Tysons Corner Ctr 22102
Tysons Landing Ct 22102
Tysons Mclean Dr 22102
Tysons One Pl 22102
Union Church Rd 22102
N Upland St 22101
Upton St 22101
Ursline Ct 22101
Valley Ave 22101
Valleywood Rd 22101
Van Fleet Dr 22101
Van Ness Ct 22101
Vermont Ave 22101
Vernon Palmer Ct 22101
Victor Ct 22102
Vincent Pl 22101
Vinita Ln 22102
Virginia Ave 22101
Vista Dr 22102
Vistas Ln 22101
Waggaman Cir 22101
Walden Dr 22101
Walden Woods Ct 22101
Warbler Ln & Pl 22101
Warner Ave 22101
Washburn Ct 22101
Wasp Ln 22101
Watson St 22102
Waverly Way 22101
Weatheford Ct 22101
Weaver Ave 22101
Weller Ave 22102
Wemberly Way 22101
Wendy Ln 22101
Westbranch Dr 22102
Westbury Rd 22101
Westby Ct 22101
Westerly Ln 22101
Westmont Ln 22102
Westmoreland St 22101
Westpark Dr 22102
Westwind Way 22102
Whann Ave 22101
Whitehall Pl 22101
Whittier Ave 22101
Wilson Ln 22102
Wimbledon Dr 22101
Windrock Dr 22102
Windy Creek Way 22102
Windy Hill Ct & Rd 22102
Windy Ridge Way 22102
Winter Hunt Rd 22102
Wise St 22101
Woburn Ct 22102
Wolfram Ct 22101
Woodacre Ct & Dr 22101
Woodbranch Ct 22102
Woodgate Ln 22101
Woodhurst Blvd 22102
Woodland Ter 22101
Woodlea Mill Ct & Rd 22102
Woodley Rd 22101
Woodman Dr 22101
Woodmoor Ln 22101
Woodside Ct & Dr 22102
Woodsong Ct 22101
Wrightson Dr 22101
Xavier Ct 22101
Yates Ct 22101
Youngblood St 22101

NUMBERED STREETS

All Street Addresses 22101

MECHANICSVILLE VA

General Delivery 23111

POST OFFICE BOXES MAIN OFFICE STATIONS AND BRANCHES

Box No.s
1 - 1200 23111
1501 - 5002 23116
10000 - 20000 23111

NAMED STREETS

Aaroe Dr 23116
Abatis Ct 23116
Abingdon Manor Ct 23116
Academy Dr 23116
Academy Creek Ln 23116
Access Rd 23111
Adaline Ln 23111
Adams Ln 23111
Adams Farm Rd 23111
Addie Dr 23111
Agape Ln 23111
Agecroft Manor Ct 23116
Aldingham Pl 23116
Aldwych Dr 23116
Alexgarden Ct 23116
Alpen Ln 23111
Alpha St 23116
Althea Bend Ct 23116
Ambrose Dr 23111
Amelia Manor Ct 23116
Amesbury Cir 23111
Amf Dr 23111
Ancient Oak Dr 23111
Anderson Ct 23116
Angela Grace Ct 23111
Angela Nicole Ln 23111
Angler Trl 23116
Ann Cabell Ct & Ln 23111
Annex Ln 23116
Ansley Hollow Ct 23116
Antique Ln 23116
Antler Ln 23116
Anton Trce 23111
Anvil Ln 23111
Apiary Ct 23116
Appaloosa Trl 23116
Apple Blossom Dr 23116
Apricot Ln 23111
Aquarius Dr & Loop 23111
Aragon Dr 23116
Armstrong Dr 23111
Arnoka Ct & Rd 23111
Arnold Rd 23111
Arrowstone Rd 23111
Ashby Ridge Pl 23111
Ashcake Station Pl 23116
Ashking Dr 23116
Ashlar Pl 23116
Ashley Manor Ln 23116
Aspen Grove Ter 23116
Assembly Way 23116
Atlee Rd
7200-8162 23111
8163-8169 23116
8164-8170 23111
8171-9499 23116
Atlee Branch Ln 23116
Atlee Lake Ct 23116
Atlee Ridge Rd 23116
Atlee Springs Dr 23116
Atlee Station Rd 23116
Auburn Grove Ct 23116
Autumn Park Way 23116
Autumn Ridge Ln 23111
Avenel Pl 23116
Avondale Dr 23116
Ayersby Dr 23111
Aynhoe Ct & Ln 23116
Azalea Pl 23111
Babbling Brooke Ln 23111
Bagby Ln 23111
Balducci Pl 23116
Bama Rd 23111
Baneberry Dr 23111
Banndoe Ln 23111
Banshire Ct & Dr 23111
Barbette Ct 23116
Barden Acres Ln 23111
Barkers Mill Rd 23111
Barley Ct 23111
Barncroft Cir 23116
Barnescrest Dr 23116
Barnette Ave 23111
Barrett Center Rd 23116
Barricade Ln 23116
Barrowden Ct 23116
Bartletts Bluff Rd 23111
Bartram Springs Dr 23116
Battalion Dr 23116
Battle Hill Dr 23111
Battleline Dr 23111
Bayrock Ct 23116
Bealeton Ct 23116
Bear Grass Ln 23111
Beattiemill Ct & Dr 23111
Beatties Mill Rd 23111
Beatty Farm Dr 23116
Beaver Pond Ct 23116
Beaverdam Trl 23116
Beech Forest Ln 23116
Beechwood Dr 23116
Beeline Dr 23111
Bell Creek Rd
7200-8299 23111
8300-8600 23116
8602-8798 23116
Belle Farm Ter 23116
Bellflower Cir 23111
Bellspring Dr 23111
Bellswood Dr 23111
Belton Cir 23116
Berea Ct 23116
Berkeley Forest Ct 23116
Berkeley Manor Dr 23116
Berkwood Ct & Dr 23116
Berry Farm Ct 23116
Berry Patch Ln 23116
Berry Pond Ln 23116
Betron Way 23111
Beulah Church Rd 23111
Billingswood Dr 23111
Bink Pl 23111
Birch Ln 23111
Birch Tree Trce 23111
Birchbark Ct & Ln 23116
Bird Dog Dr 23111
Birds Reach Ct 23116
Birdsong Creek Ct 23116
Black Creek Dr 23111
Blackbear Trl 23116
Blackbird Ln 23111
Blacksmith Ct & Dr 23116
Blagdon Dr 23116
Blakeridge Ave 23116
Blakewood Dr 23116
Blueberry Hill Ln 23111
Bluebird Way 23111
Boatswain Ln 23111
Bobcat Ln 23111
Bonniefield Ct & Dr 23111
Bosher Dr 23116
Boundary Run Dr 23111
Bracey Mill Pl 23111
Braden Pl 23116
Bradford Cottage Ct 23111
Brahma Dr 23116
Brampton Dr 23116
Brandy Ct 23111
Brandy Branch Mill Rd 23111
Brandy Creek Dr 23111
Brandy Hill Ter 23111
Brandy Run Dr 23111
Branner Woods Ct 23116
Brashier Blvd 23111
Braxton Ct & Way 23116
Breeders Cup Pl 23116
Brentwood Dr 23116
Brevet Ln 23116
Brian Ct 23111
Briarthorn Ct 23116
Brickerton Dr 23116
Bridgerun Pl 23116
Bridle Ct & Path 23111
Brigadier Rd 23116
Brittewood Cir 23116
Bronco Ln 23111
Brook Dr & Way 23111
Brook Way Ct 23111
Brooking Ct & Way 23111
Brooks Farm Rd 23111
Brooks Hollow Pkwy 23111
Bruce Blvd 23111
Bruce Academy Ct & Ln 23111
Buck Trl 23116
Buckard Dr 23111
Bucket Dr 23111
Buckeye Rd 23116
Buckley Ct 23111
Buckwood Ln 23116
Buffridge Dr 23111
Bugle Ln 23116
Bultaco Trl 23111
Bunker Hill Dr 23111
Bunsworthy Pl 23111
Burkes Garden Pl 23116
Burkwood Club Dr 23116
Burnett Field Dr 23111
Burnside Ct & Dr 23116
Burr Cir & Dr 23111
Butternut Ln 23116
Cabell Pl 23111
Cabin Ct 23111
Cactus Ct & Rd 23111
Caleb Dr 23116
Calmar Dr 23111
Camille Cir & Dr 23111
Campaign Trl 23111
Camptown Ct 23116
Candleberry Dr 23111
Canyon Ct 23111
Caraway Ln 23111
Cardinal Way 23111
Cardinal Creek Dr 23116
Carneal Ln 23111
Caro Trce 23111
Carolyn Ln 23111
Carrolton Ridge Pl 23111
Carter Ln 23111
Carywood Ct 23116
Castle Grove Dr 23111
Castle Tower Pl & Rd 23116
Catlin Rd 23111
Cattail Run Dr 23111
Cattail Run Farm Dr 23111
Catterson Ln 23111
Catwalk Ct 23111
Cavalin Ct 23116
Cavalry Ln 23111
Cavalry Run Dr 23111
Cedar Ln 23116
Cedar Berry Rd 23111
Cedar Point Farm Dr 23116
Cedar Springs Ln 23116
Cedarview Ct 23116
Center Oak Ct 23116
Center Path Ln 23116
Chamberlayne Rd 23116
Chance Trce 23111
Charlbury Cir 23116
Charleston Rd 23116
Charter Crossing Dr 23116
Charter Gate Dr 23116
Charter Lake Dr 23116
Charter Point Ct 23116
Chartwell Ct & Dr 23116
Chenault Way 23111
Cheraw Rd 23116
Cherise Ct 23116
Cherry Ln 23111
Cherrygrove Ln 23111
Chestnut Church Rd 23116
Chestnut Grove Ln 23111
Chestnut Grove Ter 23116
Chime Ct 23111
Christian Ln 23111
Christian Field Dr 23111
Christian Ridge Dr 23111
Christopher Paul Dr 23111
Cindy Ct 23111
Cinnamon Ct 23111
Civil Rd 23111
Clark Cir 23111
Clarynton Ln 23116
Clay Farm Way 23116
Clay Hills Ct 23111
Claybird Ln 23111
Clear Run Ct 23111
Clearstream Ter 23116
Clipit Ct 23111
Cloverlea Ct 23116
Cobbs Farm Rd 23111
Coberly Ct 23111
Codel Ct 23111
Codygrove Dr 23116
Cohart Ln 23111
Cold Cv 23111
Cold Harbor Rd 23111
Coleman Rd 23116
Coleman Place Dr 23111
Colemanden Dr 23111
Colesbury Ct & Dr 23116
Colincroft Dr 23116
Colmar Dr 23116
Colonel Crump Dr 23111
Colonial Ln 23111
Colony Cir & Dr 23111
Colony Bee Pl 23116
Colts Neck Rd 23111
Colvincrest Dr 23116
Combs Dr 23116
Compass Ct & Dr 23116
Compass Point Ln 23116
Confederate Hills Dr 23111
Connor Rd 23111
Constance Hill Ln 23116
Cool Autumn Dr 23116
Cool Hive Pl 23116
Cool Spring Rd 23116
Cool Summer Dr 23111
Cool Well Ter 23116
Coolwater Ln 23116
Corbin Braxton Ln 23111
Cornfield Ct & Ln 23111
Cornthwaite Ct 23111
Cory Lee Ct 23111
Cosby Ln 23116
E & W Cottage Dr 23111
Cottleston Cir 23116
Count Kristopher Ct & Dr 23116
Country Quay Ln 23111
Country Walk Ln 23111
Countryside Ct & Ln 23116
Covebrook Ln 23116
Covenant Woods Dr 23111
Covington Ridge Ct 23116
Craigwood Cir 23116
Craney Island Rd 23116
Cranwell Cir 23116
Crato Ln 23116
Creek Bluff Ln 23111
Creekside Bluffs Ln 23111
Creekside Meadow Way 23111
Creekside Village Dr 23111
Creekway Ct 23111
Creighton Pkwy & Rd 23111
Crescent View Dr 23116
Crestfield Dr 23116
Crestline Ln 23111
Cricket Creek Ct 23111
Crocus Ct 23111
Croftwood Dr 23111
Crossdale Ct & Ln 23116
Crossing Oaks Trl 23111
Crossover Dr 23116
Crown Colony Pkwy 23116
Crown Hill Rd 23111
Crump Dr 23111
Crump Creek Trl 23116
Cudlipp Ave 23116
Culley Dr 23116
Curnow Dr 23111
Cutty Sark Cir 23116
Cypresstree Ln 23111
Daffodil Rd 23111
Dahlia Ct & Rd 23111
Dairy Dr 23111
Dandy Ct 23111
Danes Run 23111
Dark Ridge Rd 23116
Darva Gln 23111
Davis Ave 23111
Deborah Dr 23111
Deep Bottom Rd 23111
Deep Creek Dr 23111
Deer Coon Ln 23111
Deer Oak Ln 23116
Deer Run Rd 23116
Deer Stream Dr 23116
Deerhunters Xing 23111
Delkin Cir & Ct 23111
Dell Ray Dr 23116
Denise Lynn Ct 23111
Derwent Dr 23116
Devils Den Ln 23111
Devils Three Jump Rd 23111
Dewitt Dr 23116
Diamond Ct 23111
Dickey Dr 23116
Dijon Dr 23111
Dillionshire Ct 23116
Dixie Ln 23116
Dixie Ridge Ln 23111
Dodsworth Ln 23111
Doe Trl 23116
Doe Run Pl 23116
Dogwood Pl 23111
Dogwood Garth Ln 23116
Dominion Park Dr 23111
Doncastle Ct 23116
Doolittle Dr 23111
Doral Pl 23116
Dorothy Ln 23116
Double Five Dr 23116
Douglas Farm Ln 23111
Dove Way 23111
Dove Creek Pl 23116
Drakes Landing Ct 23111
Draperfield Rd 23111
Drawbridge Ct & Rd 23116
Dress Blue Cir & Dr 23116
Dressage Way 23111
Drewce Ct 23111
Drinkard Ct & Way 23111
Duck Dr 23111
Dugout Ter 23111
Duling Rd 23116
Dun Roamin Ln 23116
Dunfee Ln 23111
Dunwoody Rd 23111
Durhams Ferry Pl 23116
Dusty Ln 23116
Dutch Lily Ct 23116
Eagle Creek Pl 23116
Early Dr 23111
Earthworks Dr 23111
East Blvd 23111
Eastern View Ln 23111
Eaves Way 23116
Ebaugh Ln 23116
Edgewater Cir 23116
Edgewood Rd 23111
Edgeworth Rd 23111
Elde Ln 23111
Elder Trl 23116
Elder Creek Ln 23116
Elder Ridge Ln 23111
Eleanor Dr 23111
Elizabeth Ann Dr 23111
Ellendale Dr 23116
Ellerson Dr 23111

Ellerson Farm Dr 23111
Ellerson Green Cir, Ct, Pl & Ter 23116
Ellerson Green Close 23116
Ellerson Mill Cir & Rd 23111
Ellerson Station Dr 23111
Ellerson Wood Ct & Dr 23111
Elliott Dr 23111
Elm Dr 23111
Elm Tree Ter 23111
Elon Oaks Ln 23111
Elvira Ct 23111
Elwin Dr 23111
Emerald Pool Ct 23111
Emerald Rock Ln 23116
Emerald Woods Ln 23116
Empresstree Ln 23111
Epps Rd 23111
Erle Rd 23116
Essex Cir 23111
Ettington Ln 23111
Eula St 23111
Evanston Ln 23116
Evergreen Ln 23111
Ewell Cir & Rd 23111
Fair Hill Ct & Pl 23116
Fairview Dr 23111
Falcon Dr 23116
Falling Leaf Ct 23111
Falling View Ln 23111
Falling Water Ct 23111
Fallman Dr 23116
Farmer Dr 23111
Fascine Ct 23116
Fast Ln 23111
Fawn Park Ln 23116
Fayemont Dr 23116
Feather Ln 23116
Fenholloway Dr 23116
Fenne Farm Dr 23116
Fenway Dr 23116
Fetlock Dr 23116
Fieldshire Ct & Dr 23111
Figuly Rd 23111
Finlandia Ln 23116
Fire Ln 23116
Fishermans Way 23116
Fishing Cir 23111
Fishtail Pond Ct 23111
Flag Ln 23111
Flaherty Dr 23111
Flannigan Mill Rd 23111
Florida Farm Ln 23111
Fondale Rd 23111
Ford Ave 23111
Forest Haze Ct 23116
Forrest Patch Dr 23116
Fort Myers Rd 23116
Founders Pl 23116
Fourscore Dr 23111
Fox Hill Farm Rd 23116
Fox Hill Race Ct 23116
Fox Hound Ct 23116
Fox Hunter Ln 23111
Foxal Rd 23116
Foxbernie Cir & Dr 23111
Foxlair Ct & Dr 23111
Foxridge Ln 23116
Foxrock Ln 23111
Foxworth Ln 23111
Fraley Ct & Dr 23111
Franklin Ln 23111
Freel Trce 23111
Fullview Ave 23111
Gaines Mill Cir & Rd 23111
Garden Creek Ct 23111
Garden Park Ln 23111
Garden Terrace Ct 23116
Gardenbrook Way 23111
Garthright Ct 23111
Gary Ln 23111
Gathright Valley Ct 23116
Gaulding Rd 23111
Gemstone Pl 23111
General Smith Dr 23111
Generals Dr 23111
Georgetown Rd 23116
Georgie Ct & Dr 23116
Gerljean Dr 23116
Gerry Ct 23116
Gethsemane Ct 23116
Gettysburg Ln 23111
Gibbsdown Pl 23111
Giles Farm Rd 23116
Gittings Ct 23111
Glade Run Ct 23116
Glastonburg Dr 23116
Glebe Hill Rd 23116
Glenbrook Ct & Dr 23111
Glendale Ln 23116
Glenharbor Ln 23111
Glympse Rd 23111
Gobbler Glen Pl 23111
Gold Coast Ln 23111
Gold Pebble Way 23111
Gold Ridge Ln 23116
Golden Oak Ln 23111
Goodfellow Ln 23111
Goodlife Ct 23111
Goodman Forest Ln 23111
Goose Ln 23116
Gooseneck Ln 23111
Grace Ln 23111
Grace Manor Ct 23116
Graff Ct 23116
Granbury Cir 23116
Grand Hickory Dr 23111
Grant Dr 23111
Grantham Dr 23116
Grapevine Bridge Dr 23111
Graycourt Dr 23116
Great Meadows Ct & Dr 23116
Green Haven Dr 23111
Green Retirement Ln 23111
Green Top Ct 23111
Greenback Dr 23111
Greenlake Cir 23116
Greenlands Cir 23116
Greenline Ct 23116
Greenview Rd 23111
Grendel Ct 23116
Greyhawk Ct 23116
Greystone Creek Rd 23111
Greywood Dr 23116
Gristmill Ct 23116
Grove Rd 23116
Guenevere Ct & Pl 23116
Gum Ball Ln 23111
Habeas Ct 23111
Hakala Dr 23111
Hall Ct 23111
Hallwood Way 23111
Halycon Ln 23111
Hambleton Way 23116
Hanna Dr 23111
Hanover Crossing Dr 23116
Hanover Green Dr 23111
Hanover Grove Blvd & Ln 23111
Hanover Meadow Dr 23111
Hanover Town Rd 23116
Hanover Wayside Rd 23116
Happy Hill Ln 23111
Harbor Dr 23111
Harbor Hill Dr 23111
Harbor Light Way 23111
Harbour Mist Ln 23111
Hardtack Rd 23116
Harpe Ct 23116
Harriet Ln 23111
Harris Field Rd 23111
Hartford Oaks Cir, Ct, & Dr 23116
Hartpine Ct 23111
Harver Ct & Way 23111
Harvest Ln 23111
Harvest Honey Rd 23116
Harvey Hollow Dr 23116
Havenview Dr 23111
Haversack Ln 23116
Hawks Hill Ln 23111
Haws Ct 23116
Haynes Dr 23111
Haystack Dr 23111
Hazelgrove Dr 23111
Heatherwood Dr 23116
Hebner Ln 23111
Henderson Hall Rd 23116
Hendree Ln 23111
Henrietta Ct 23111
Hepburn Ct 23116
Hermleigh Ln 23111
Hertfordshire Way 23111
Hickory Ln 23111
Hidden Lake Cir 23111
Hidden Lake Estate Dr 23111
Higgins Ln 23111
Highbury Dr 23116
Highlander Pl 23111
Hill Meadows Ct 23116
Hill View Dr 23111
Hillcrest Ln 23116
Hillis Way 23111
Hillstone Ct 23111
History Ln 23111
Hobbs Crossing Rd 23116
Hobby Horse Ct & Ln 23111
Hoke Hollow Way 23111
Holly Ln 23111
Holly Rd 23116
Holly Bluffs Dr 23116
Holly Branch Dr 23111
Holly Ridge Rd 23116
Hollycroft Ct 23116
Hollyhedge Ln 23116
Holstein Ln 23111
Homehills Rd 23111
Homeplace Ct 23111
Honey Meadows Rd 23116
Honeymoon Cottage Way 23116
Hoof Cir 23116
Hoofprint Ln 23111
Hope Glen Ct 23116
Hope Haven Rd 23111
Hope Valley Rd 23111
Hopewell Rd 23111
Hopkins Branch Way 23116
Horsham Dr 23111
Howard Dr 23116
Hudnall Ln 23111
Hudnalls Rd 23111
Hughes Rd 23111
Hughesland Rd 23116
Hunt Club Ln 23111
Hunter Cir 23111
Hunter Dr 23111
Hunter Xing 23116
Hunterbrook Cir & Dr 23111
Hunters Chase Ct & Dr 23116
Hunters Club Ct 23116
Huntington Woods Dr 23116
Husker Ct 23111
Hyacinth Ct 23111
Immanuel Trl 23111
Indian Trails Ct 23111
Indianfield Dr 23116
Industrial Park Rd 23116
Ingleside Farm Ln 23111
Irish Rose Ct 23111
Ironclad Dr 23111
Ironwood Ln 23111
Ironworks Ct 23111
Ivanhoe Dr 23116
Ivy Banks Dr & Pl 23116
Ivy Hill Ct 23116
Ivy Springs Pl 23116
J David Ln 23111
Jackson Ave 23111
Jackson Arch Dr 23111
Jamie Ct 23111
Jane Lee Cir 23116
Janet Ln 23111
Janice Ave 23111
Jasmac Ln 23116
Jasmine Ct 23111
Jay Way 23111
Jayto Dr 23111
Jeans Grove Ln 23116
Jeff Dr 23111
Jennifer Cir & Ln 23111
Jennings Branch Ct 23116
Jersey Ct 23111
John Henry Ln 23111
Johnson Oak Dr 23111
Johnsonville Way 23111
Jordan Woods Dr 23111
Jordans Journey Ct 23116
Joshua Aaron Ct 23111
Joshue Tree Ln 23111
Joyce Ln 23116
Julie Way 23116
Jump Cir 23116
Jupiter Dr 23116
Kaitlin Ct 23116
Kaye Dr 23116
Keck Cir 23116
Keitts Corner Rd 23111
Kella Way 23111
Kelley Dr 23111
Kelly Oak Dr 23111
Kelshire Trce 23111
Kendrick Dr 23111
Kenebeck Cir 23111
Kenmore Dr 23111
Kenna Way 23116
Kennedy Ct 23111
Kennon Ct 23116
Kentford Cir 23116
Kerrick Trce 23111
Kersey Ln 23116
Kevin Wanda Rd 23111
Kiblercrest Dr 23116
Kilby Ct 23116
Kim Shelly Ct 23111
King Richard Ct 23116
Kings Charter Dr 23116
Kingsrock Ln 23116
Kirby Cove Ln 23116
Kiwi Ln 23111
Knight Dr 23111
Knightly Rd 23116
Knollwood Ct 23116
Korona Dr 23116
Kristy Star Ln 23111
La Gorce Pl 23111
Labrador Ln 23111
Ladiestown Rd 23111
Lady Elizabeth Ct & Ln 23116
Lake Haven Dr 23111
Lake Point Dr 23111
Lake Terrell Dr 23111
Lake View Rd 23111
Lake Willow Way 23111
Lakevista Cir, Ct & Dr 23111
Lakeway Dr 23111
Landover Dr 23111
Lansdowne Rd 23116
Lantana Ln 23111
Lark Cir, Ct & Way 23111
Laurale Cir 23111
Laurel Ln 23116
Laurel Branch Cir 23116
Laurel Grove Rd 23116
Laurel Meadows Dr 23111
Leaf Ln 23116
Learning Ln 23116
Lee Ave 23111
Lee Davis Rd
7200-8399 23111
8400-9199 23116
Lee Park Rd 23111
Left Flank Rd 23116
Legacy Ln 23111
Legacy Park Dr 23111
Leighfield Way 23116
Leon Dr 23116
Lereve Cir & Dr 23116
Lesfield Ct 23116
E Lex Ct 23111
Lexington Dr 23111
Liberty Cir 23111
Lighthouse Pl 23111
Lilac Ln 23111
Lincoln Rd 23116
Linderwood Dr 23116
Lindsay Meadows Dr 23116
Linev Ln 23116
Linneys Ct 23116
Little Florida Rd 23111
Little Garden Way 23116
Little Joselyn Dr 23116
Little Sorrel Dr 23111
Littlerock Ct 23116
Lockwood Blvd 23116
Locust Ln 23116
Locust Green Ln 23116
Lodge View Dr 23111
Lodgepole Dr 23111
Loganberry Ct 23111
Lone Cedar Ct & Dr 23111
Long Ln 23116
Longhorn Dr 23111
Loralea Dr 23111
Lou Ln 23111
Lovings Trl 23111
Lucille Rd 23111
Luck Ave 23111
Lucord Ln 23116
Lunette Ln 23116
Luther Bosher Ln 23111
Lyndon Cir 23116
Lynk Ln 23111
Lynmar Ln 23111
Lynnhill Ct 23116
Lynnroy Way 23111
Lynnshire Ct 23111
Madison Estates Dr 23111
Madison Leigh Ct 23111
Madonna Rd 23111
Magazine Dr 23111
Magnolia Cottage Dr 23111
Magnolia Green Ln 23111
Mahixon Trl 23116
Malabar Cir 23116
Malboro Rd 23116
Mallard Way 23111
Mandeville Trl 23111
Mann Dr 23116
Manor View Dr 23116
Manorwood Dr 23116
Mantilo Creek Rd 23116
Mantlo Ct 23111
Marc Gregory Ct 23116
Marie Ln 23111
Marimel Ct & Ln 23111
Market Rd 23116
Markow Ct 23111
Marl Branch Ct 23116
Marlbourne Way 23116
Marley Dr 23116
Marlinco Rd 23116
Mars Dr 23116
Marshall Arch Dr 23116
Martin Field Dr 23116
Mary Ann Ln 23116
Mary Esther Ln 23111
Mary Mundie Ln 23111
Matadequin Ln 23111
Mater Ln 23116
Matroka Rd 23111
Mattaponi Rd 23116
Mattawan Trl 23116
Matthews Grove Ln 23116
Mayetta Dr 23116
N & S Mayfield Ln 23111
Mccaul Ct 23111
Mccauley Ln 23111
Mcclellan Rd 23111
Mcfaye Ave 23116
Mcghee House Rd 23111
Mcgregor Rd 23116
Mcgregor Farm Dr 23116
Mckenzie Dr 23116
Mead Hall Ct 23116
Meadow Dr 23111
Meadow Haven Cir 23111
Meadow Pond Dr 23116
Meadowbridge Rd 23116
Meadowlake Rd 23111
Meadowsweet Dr 23116
Meadowview Ln 23111
Mechanicsville Tpke 23111
Mechanicsville Elementary Dr 23111
Medley Mill Ct 23116
Melecole Dr 23111
Melinda Kay Ct 23111
Melissa Paige Cir 23111
Memory Ln 23111
Mendenhall Pl 23111
Mentz Manor Dr 23111
Mercury Ct 23116
Meredith Farms Dr 23111
Merle Smith Ln 23111
Merrilake Ct 23116
Miami Ln 23111
Michael Ann Ct 23111
Michael Heather Ct 23111
Midday Ln 23111
Midnight Dr 23111
Mike Mundie Ln 23111
Mildale Rd 23111
Milestone Dr 23116
Mill Pond Trl 23111
Mill Valley Ct & Rd 23111
Mill Waye Dr 23111
Millpond Ln 23116
Mills Ln 23116
Mimosa Hill Ln 23116
Minglewood Ln 23116
Minie Ball Ave 23116
Mintawood Ct & Ln 23111
Molly Ln 23116
Mook Ct 23111
Morella Pl 23116
Morgan Wray Ln 23111
Moritz Ln 23111
Morning Breeze Dr 23111
Morning Dew Ln 23116
Morning Glory Ct & Rd 23111
Moss Rose Ct 23111
Mossybrook Rd 23116
Mount Storm Ct 23111
Mountain Lily Ln 23111
Moving Star Rd 23116
Muzzle Ct 23111
Napper Dr 23116
Narragansett Ct 23111
Nedam Ln 23116
Nells Trce 23111
Neptune Dr 23116
Nesslewood Cir 23116
New Ashcake Rd 23116
New Bethesda Rd 23116
New Britton Rd 23116
New Holland Ln 23116
New Hunter Rd 23111
New London Rd 23116
New Worshams Way 23111
Newcastle Dr & Way 23111
Newman Dr 23116
Niccole Ln 23111
Nina Ct 23116
Nolandwood Dr 23116
Northfall Creek Pkwy 23111
Nuck Trce 23111
Oak St 23111
Oak Bower Ln 23111
Oak Branch Pl 23111
Oak Cottage Dr 23116
Oak Hill Camp Rd 23116
Oak Shade Ct 23116
Oakfield Ln 23116
Oakham Dr 23116
Oaklawn Dr 23116
Oakley Hill Ln 23111
Oatman Ct 23111
Odey Dr 23116
Old Bay Ct 23116
Old Cavalry Ct & Dr 23111
Old Church Rd 23111
Old Coach Trl 23111
Old Cold Harbor Rd 23111
Old Dutch Ln 23111
Old Elijah Ln 23116
Old Estates Way 23111
Old Gainsmill Ln 23111
Old Grove Gln 23111
Old Hickory Dr 23111
Old House Rd 23116
Old Ivy Trce 23116
Old Lafayette Rd 23111
Old Lansdown Rd 23116
Old Lantern Trl 23111
Old Meadow Ct 23111
Old Millstone Dr 23111
Old Oaklawn Dr 23116
Old Quaker Rd 23111
Old Reflection Dr 23111
Old Richfood Rd 23116
Old Spring Garden Ln 23116
Old Thomas Ct 23116
Old Track Ln 23111
Old Traveller Ln 23111
Open Meadows Ln 23116
Orchard Ln 23111
Orchard Meadow Rd 23116
Ordinary Keepers Way 23111
Overlook Dr 23111
Oxfordshire Pl 23111
Pa Pa Ln 23111
Palmwood Cir 23116
Pamela Louise Rd 23111
Pamunkey Rd 23116
Pamunkey Crest Dr 23111
Pamunkey River Farms Dr 23111
Pantego Ln 23116
Park Dr 23111
Parkridge Rd 23116
Parrish Place Ln 23111
Parsley Ct 23111
Parsleys Mill Rd 23111
Patrick Henry Blvd 23116
Peace Rd 23111
Peach Orchard Ln 23111
Peachtree Rd 23111
Peanut Ln 23116
Peashark Rd 23111
Pebble Lake Dr 23111
Pebblebrook Dr 23116
Pebblepath Pkwy 23111
Pecan Trl 23111
Pecan Tree Ct 23116
Pegway Ln 23111
Pelot Pl 23116
Pembridge Dr 23116
Penningcroft Ln 23116
Penrith Dr 23116
Pepper Ln 23111
Peppertown Rd 23111
S Peridot Ct 23116
Perrincrest Pl 23116
Perrins Mill Ln 23116
Perryville Ct, Dr & Ter 23111
Philbunny Ct 23111
Piabads Ct 23111
Pickett Ave 23111
Pimlico Dr 23111
Pine Dr 23111
Pine Creek Ct 23116
Pine Hill Dr & Rd 23116
Pine Ridge Rd 23116
Pine Slash Rd 23116
Pinta Ct 23116
Piping Tree Ferry Rd 23111
Pistil Pl 23116
Placida Cir 23116
Plateau Pl 23116
Pleasant Grove Rd 23116
Pleasant Oaks Ln 23116
Pleasant Run Ln 23111
Plum Grove Cir, Ct & Dr 23111
Plum Rose Ct 23111
Plymouth Pl 23116

Pohite Cir & Dr 23111
Pointe Pl 23116
Pole Green Rd 23116
Pole Green Park Dr & Ln 23116
Pollard Creek Rd 23116
Pollen Dr 23116
Polo Pony Ct 23116
Pond Way 23111
Pond Edge Ct 23111
Pond Grass Rd 23111
Pond Place Way 23111
Poplar Hall Ct 23116
Poppy Seed Ln 23111
Port Ln 23111
Possum Trl 23116
Possum Trot Dr 23111
Pot Hole Ln 23111
Poteet Ln 23111
Power Rd 23111
Powhickery Ct & Dr 23116
Powhite Farm Dr 23111
Princess Anne Dr 23111
Prism Ct 23111
Prolonge Ln 23116
Prospect Hill Rd 23116
Prospectors Bluff Ln 23116
Public Ln 23111
Puller Dr 23111
Quail Way 23111
Quail Creek Dr 23116
Quail Haven Ln 23116
Quail Run Ln 23116
Quailfield Ct & Rd 23116
Queen Carolyn Ln 23116
Queens Lace Cir, Ct & Rd 23111
Quiet Caper Ct 23111
Rabbit Trl 23111
Radford Mill Ter 23116
Rainey Dr 23116
Rainier Dr 23116
Rampart Cir 23111
Ranch Acres Trl 23116
Range Rd 23111
Raspberry Ct 23111
Raven Run Dr 23111
Ravensworth Ct 23116
Red Cloud Ct 23111
Red Deer Ct 23116
Red Finch Ct 23116
Red Hill Cir 23116
Red Sash Dr 23116
Redberry Ln 23116
Redgate Ln 23111
Redvine Ln 23111
Reeds Grove Ln 23116
Retreat Dr 23111
Retreat Farm Ln 23111
Retreat Hill Ln 23111
Reunion Dr 23111
Revolutionary Pl 23116
Richfood Rd 23111
Ridge Ln & Way 23111
Ridge Hill Ln 23111
Ridgebrook Dr 23116
Ridgerun Pl 23116
Ridgeview Rd 23111
Rie Bob Ct & Ln 23111
Right Flank Rd 23116
Rimfire Rd 23111
Rinker Ct & Dr 23116
River Rd 23116
River Holly Rd 23111
River Pine Ct & Dr 23111
River Valley Rd 23111
Roberta Rd 23116
Robin Rd & Way 23111
Robin Ridge Dr 23116
Robins Nest Ln 23116
Rochdale Ct 23116
Rock Hollow Ct 23111
Rockhill Rd 23111
Rockingham Rd 23116
Rockytop Ct 23116
Rodeo Dr 23116
Rolling Forest Cir 23111
Rolling Lawn Ct 23111
Rolling Stone Ln 23111
Rollins Ln 23116
Roosevelt Ave 23111
Rose Dr 23111
Rose Cottage Ln 23116
Rose Garden Path 23116
Rose Hill Dr 23111
Rose Stable Ct 23111
Roseland Ct 23116
Rosemary Dr 23111
Rotherham Dr 23116
Rouzie Ct 23116
Royal Grant Dr 23116
Ruffin Ridge Rd 23116
Rum Hill Ct 23111
N Run Medical Dr 23116
Rural Crosse Dr 23116
Rural Point Ct, Dr & Rd 23116
Rushbrooke Ln 23116
Russet Ln 23116
Rustic Ln 23116
Rustins Rest Dr 23111
Ruth Wood Ct 23116
Rutland Rd 23116
Rutland Center Blvd 23116
Rutland Commons Dr 23116
Rutland Greens Way 23116
Rutlandshire Dr 23116
Ryegate Pl 23111
Saber Ct 23111
Saddle Ct 23116
Saddle Crest Dr 23111
Safflower Ct 23116
Saint Dillons Pl 23116
Salem Creek Pl 23116
Salient Ln 23116
Sandy Cir & Ln 23111
Sandy Creek Ln 23116
Sandy Valley Rd 23111
Santa Maria Dr 23116
Sarah Shelton Ln 23116
Saratoga Dr 23111
Sawyer Ln 23111
Scarecrow Rd 23111
Scooter Ln 23111
Scots Landing Rd 23116
Scott Carter Ln 23111
Seatoncroft Ct 23116
Sedgehill Ct 23116
Sedgemoor Cir 23116
Selborne Cir 23116
Selby Ln 23111
Seminole Rd 23116
Senn Way 23111
Sentry Station Rd 23116
Sesuit Ln 23111
Seven Springs Rd 23111
Seward Way 23116
Shadow Lands Ct 23111
Shady Grove Rd
7200-8240 23111
8241-9299 23116
Shady Knoll Ln 23111
Shady Oak Ct 23111
Shady Ridge Ln 23111
Shady Woods Ln 23111
N & S Shall Dr 23111
Shane Edmonds Ln 23111
Shannon Rd 23116
Shannondale Ct & Rd 23116
Shannonwood Ct 23111
Shauna Ct 23111
Shawns Grove Pl 23116
Shea Tree Cir 23111
Shelley Dr 23116
Shelton Pl 23116
Shelton Pointe Dr 23116
Sherrington Dr 23111
Sherton Ct & Dr 23116
Sherwood Crossing Pl 23111
Shiloh Pl 23111
Ships Ln 23111
Shire Ct & Pkwy 23111
Siege Rd 23111
Signal Hill Rd 23111
Signal Hill Apartment Dr 23111
Silktree Pl 23111
Silkwood Ct & Dr 23116
Silo Ln 23111
Silverbell Ln 23111
Silverstone Dr 23116
Silverthorn Ct 23116
Simi Ct 23111
Simmons Farm Rd 23116
Simpkins Ct 23111
Simpkins Forest Ln 23111
Sinclair Ct & Rd 23111
Sir Bradley Ct 23116
Sir Michael Ln 23116
Six Pound Ln 23111
Skipjack Ct 23111
Skirmish Ln 23111
Sledd Dr 23111
Sledds Lake Rd 23111
Slidingrock Dr 23116
Smallwood Ct 23116
Smithport Dr 23116
Smithy Ct 23111
Smoothbore Ln 23116
Smythes Cottage Way 23116
Snaffle Ct & Ln 23111
Snap Dragon Rd 23116
Snowshed Ln 23111
Snowstraw Pl 23116
Soft Wind Ct, Dr & Ln 23111
Softmoss Ct 23111
Solitude Ln 23111
Sonny Meadows Ln 23116
Southard Ln 23116
Southern Trl 23111
Southern Watch Pl 23111
Spawn Run Ln 23116
Spicewood Cir, Ct, Dr & Pl 23111
Spillway Ln 23111
Sporting Ln 23111
Spotslee Cir 23111
Spring Garden Ct 23111
Spring Ivy Ln 23116
Spring Run Rd
3400-3599 23111
3600-4399 23116
Spring Set Ln 23111
Spring Valley Rd 23116
Springhill Rd 23116
Springton Rd 23111
Squires Passage Dr 23111
Squirrel Cir 23116
Stags Leap Dr 23116
Stallion Dr 23111
Stand Cir 23111
Staple Ln 23116
N Star Dr 23111
Star Ln 23111
Starke Ct 23111
Starling Creek Ct 23116
Steeplebush Pl 23111
Stephens Manor Dr 23111
Stewarts Retreat Ln 23111
Still Creek Ln 23116
Still Spring Ct 23116
Stockade Cir, Ct & Dr 23111
Stone Spring Dr 23116
Stonefield Ct 23116
Stonewall Dr & Pkwy 23111
Straight Oak Ct 23111
Strain Ave 23111
Stratford Hall Ct 23116
Strawbank Dr 23116
Strawhorn Dr 23116
Stronghold Dr 23116
Stuart Dr 23111
Stuart Home Dr 23111
Stuarts Hollow Ln 23111
Studley Rd 23116
Studley Acres Ln 23116
Studley Farms Dr & Ln 23116
Studley Pines Ln 23116
Studley Plantation Dr 23116
Studley Site Dr 23116
Stywalt Ln 23116
Sugar Oak Ct 23111
Sugar Wood Dr 23116
Sugarloaf Dr 23116
Sugarpine Rd 23111
Sujen Ct 23111
Sullivan Dr 23116
Summer Grove Rd 23116
Summer Hill Rd 23116
Summer Oak Dr 23116
Summer Plains Ct & Dr 23116
Summer Walk Ct, Pkwy & Ter 23116
Sunglow Dr 23116
Sunmark Dr 23111
Sunny Oak Dr 23116
Sunnyhill Dr 23111
Sunnyside Dr 23111
Sunset Ct & Dr 23111
Sunshine Ct 23111
Surrey Ct 23111
Sussex Rd 23111
Sutlers Ln 23116
Suzanne Dr 23116
Swamp Ln 23111
Swan Ln 23111
Swannanoa Trl 23116
Swayback Ln 23116
Sweet Hall Way 23116
Sweetbay Ln 23111
Swindale Ct 23116
Sword Ct 23116
Sycamore Hill Pl 23116
Sydnor Ln 23111
Syringa Ct 23111
Tack Room Dr 23111
Tadcaster Cir 23116
Talbot Green Ln 23111
Tall Cedar Ln 23111
Tall Oaks Ln 23116
Talley Farm Rd 23116
Talley Pond Rd 23116
Tally Ho Dr 23111
Tammy Ct & Ln 23111
Tangle Oaks Ct & Dr 23111
Tangle Pond Ln 23111
Tangle Ridge Dr 23111
Tanglewood Ct 23111
Tarleton Dr 23116
Tarragon Dr 23111
Tate Ln 23116
Taunrae Ct 23111
Tavenor Ct 23111
Tavern Keepers Way 23111
Tazewell Green Dr 23116
Teddington Ln 23111
Thaxton Dr 23111
Thebrix Ct 23111
Thelma Lou Rd 23111
Thicket Run Way 23111
Thistle Crown Ct 23111
Thistleberry Ct 23111
Thistleton Ct 23116
Thor Ln 23116
Thrasher Ct & Way 23111
Thrush Way 23111
Thunderbird Ln 23111
Thyme Dr 23111
Tiffany Ln 23111
Timberlake Ln 23111
Timberlake Green Dr 23111
Times Dispatch Blvd 23116
Tippling House Dr 23111
Toms Dr 23116
Topfield Ct 23116
Torbert Pl 23111
Tow Hook Pl 23116
Track Rd 23116
Travelers Rest Dr 23111
Travellers Way 23111
Treasure Ct 23111
Trench Trl 23111
Trenchline Rd 23116
Trimiew Estate Ln 23111
Trinity Way Ct 23111
Triple Trl 23116
Tripps Ln 23116
Troub Ln 23111
Trudi Pl 23111
Truex Pl 23111
Truman Rd 23116
Trumpet Ct 23116
Trumpetvine Ln 23111
Tuckerman Ct 23116
Turkey Hill Trl 23111
Turkey Hollow Pl 23111
Turnage Ln 23111
Turners Mill Dr 23111
Turnout Ct 23116
Turtle Creek Ln 23116
Tusing Ave 23116
Twig Ln 23116
Twin Cedar Ln 23111
Twin Creek Trl 23111
Twin Girls Ln 23111
Twin Oaks Rd 23116
Tyndall Dr 23116
Valeview Pl 23116
Valley Creek Dr 23111
Vanguard Dr 23111
Vaughan Dr 23111
Ventor Cir 23116
Venus Dr 23116
Verdi Ln 23111
Via Farm Dr 23111
Vidette Ln 23116
Violet Cir 23111
Virginia Manor Dr 23111
Wagon Ct 23116
Wagon Trail Ln 23111
Wahoo Ct 23111
Waldelock Pl 23116
Waldron Way 23111
Walgrove Ct 23111
Walker Rd 23116
Walking Horse Dr 23111
Walking Stick Ln 23111
Walnut Branch Dr 23111
Walnut Grove Ct, Dr & Rd 23111
Walnut Spring Pl 23116
Wanchese Way 23116
Wanda Dr 23116
Wanzer Hill Rd 23116
War Horse Ln 23111
Warren Ave 23116
Washington Arch Dr 23111
Washington Henry Dr 23116
Water Way Dr 23111
Watt House Rd 23111
Waxcomb Pl 23116
Weathered Oak Ln 23111
Wedgewood Rd 23111
Wendellshire Way 23111
E & W Wenlock Dr 23116
Wenton Cir 23116
Wesbeam Dr 23111
West Blvd 23111
Westchester Dr 23116
Westhaven Dr 23111
Westone Rd 23116
Westwood Rd 23111
Westwood Farms Ct 23111
Westwood Hill Rd 23111
Wetherden Dr 23111
Wheeling Rd 23116
Wheelwright Way 23111
Whipper Ln 23111
Whippoorwill Rd 23116
Whiskey Hill Ln 23111
White Oak Ridge Dr 23111
White Pine Ct & Ln 23111
Whitlock Farms Rd 23111
Wild Rose Ct 23116
Willdosh Ct 23111
Williams St & Trl 23116
Williamsville Rd 23116
Willow Ave 23111
Willow Brook Ln 23111
Willow Dance Rd 23111
Wilmore Dr 23116
Wilpat Rd 23111
Wilt Ln 23111
Win Ct 23111
Windermere Dr 23116
Windflower Ct 23111
Winding Hills Dr 23111
Winding Knoll Ln 23111
Winding Wood Rd 23111
Windmill Watch Dr 23116
Windsor Dr 23111
Windsor Shade Dr 23116
Windsor Walk Ln 23116
Windy Knoll Dr 23116
Winnepeg Ct 23116
Winsmith Dr 23116
Winston Dr 23116
Winter Spring Dr 23116
Winterham Dr 23116
Wistrom Way 23111
Witheridge Dr 23116
Wolf Hound Dr 23116
Wonderland Ln 23111
Wood Valley Rd 23111
Woodberry Dr 23111
Woodbridge Rd 23111
Woodfield Acres Dr 23111
Woodglen Dr 23116
Woodlawn Dr 23116
Woodlawn Farm Dr 23116
Woods Farm Rd 23111
Woodsage Ct 23116
Woody Ln 23111
Wormleys Ln 23116
Wren Ct 23116
Wren Way 23111
Wren Creek Ct 23116
Wrenwood Dr 23116
Wrexham Cir 23116
Wyattwood Rd 23116
Wychwood Dr 23116
Wynbrook Ln 23111
Wyndale Dr 23116
Wyngate Ln 23116
Yellowrose Ln 23111
York St 23111
Zinnia Ct 23111
Zip Dr 23111
Zorbas Ln 23111

MERRIFIELD VA

General Delivery 22116

POST OFFICE BOXES MAIN OFFICE STATIONS AND BRANCHES

Box No.s
All PO Boxes 22116

NAMED STREETS

Gopost 22116
Lee Hwy
8403-A-8403-A 22081
Northern Virginia District 22081
Shingerm 22081

MIDDLEBURG VA

General Delivery 20117

POST OFFICE BOXES MAIN OFFICE STATIONS AND BRANCHES

Box No.s
All PO Boxes 20118

RURAL ROUTES

01 20117

NAMED STREETS

All Street Addresses 20117

MIDDLETOWN VA

General Delivery 22645

POST OFFICE BOXES MAIN OFFICE STATIONS AND BRANCHES

Box No.s
All PO Boxes 22645

RURAL ROUTES

01 22649

NAMED STREETS

Arlene Ct 22645
Ascalon Dr 22645
Belle Grove Rd 22645
Belle View Ln 22645
Bowmans Mill Rd 22645
Boyers Mill Ln 22645
Buckhorn Rd 22645
N & S Buckton Rd 22645
Buffalo Marsh Rd 22645
Carolyn Ave 22645
Carriage Ln 22645
Catlett Ln 22645
Catletts Ford Rd 22645
Cauthorn Mill Rd 22645
Cedar Creek Ln 22645
Cedar Creek Grade 22645
Chapel Ln & Rd 22645
Chase Ct 22645
Chimney Cir 22645
Church St 22645
Claven Ln 22645
Cockle Ln 22645
Comforter Ln 22645
Commerce St 22645
Confidence Ln 22645
Cooley Dr 22645
Cougill Rd 22645
Creekview Ln 22645
Crest River Dr 22645
Cypress Way 22645
Darterjo Dr 22645
Dependence Ln 22645
Douglas Dr 22645
Drover Ln 22645
Ethan Ct 22645
Fifth St 22645
First St 22645
Flya Way 22645
Forest Grove Rd 22645
Fourth St 22645
Gafia Lodge Rd 22645
Gobbler Ln 22645
Great Lake Dr 22645
Greatland Farm Dr 22645
Greenbriar Rd 22645
Grelare 22649
Guard Rd 22645
Guard Hill Rd 22645
Hazel Mill Ln 22645
Headley Rd 22645
Hidden Valley Ln 22645
High St 22645
High Bluff Rd 22645
Hillside Dr 22645
Hites Rd 22645
Huttle Rd 22645

Idewild St 22645
Jackson Pl 22645
Jacksons Chase Dr 22645
Karleys Way 22645
Katie Ln 22645
Klines Mill Ln & Rd 22645
Lakeland Cir 22645
Larrick Ln 22645
Laurel Ln 22645
Liberty Ln 22645
Little Sorrel Dr 22645
Long Meadow Rd
200-5799 22645
5704-5704 22649
Long Meadows Ln 22645
Lost Pond Ct 22645
Lusitano Ln 22645
Main St 22645
Mark Dr 22645
Marsh Brook Ln 22645
Maslin Valley Ln 22645
Massanutten Dr 22645
Mccune Rd 22645
Mcdaniel Ln 22645
Meadow Branch Rd 22645
Meadow Mills Rd 22645
Meadow Trace Ln 22645
Mercys Dr 22645
Middle Rd 22645
Minebank Rd 22645
Mineral St 22645
Minie Ball Ct 22645
Molly Campbell Ln 22645
Murrays Dr 22645
Mustang Ln 22645
Newell Dr 22645
Ogden Ln 22645
Old Jack Dr 22645
Pappy Ct 22645
Pence Land Rd 22645
Pershing Mill Ln 22645
Plantation Rd 22645
Pleasant View Ave 22645
Quarter Horse Ln 22645
Quincey Mill Ct 22645
Rectors Ln 22645
Red Hawk Rd 22645
Reliance Ln 22645
Reliance Rd
1-4899 22645
1258-1316 22649
1318-2138 22649
2140-2238 22649
Reliance Woods Dr & Ln 22645
Ridgemont Rd 22645
Ridings Mill Rd 22645
Riley Mill Ln 22645
Ritenour Hollow Rd 22645
N River Rd 22645
River Ridge Dr 22645
Senseney Ave 22645
Serenity View Ln 22645
Shawn Dr 22645
Signal Hill Ln 22645
Silliani Rd 22645
Sixth St 22645
Skirmisher Ln 22645
Sulphur Springs Rd 22645
Third St 22645
Thomas Dr 22645
Turkey Ln 22645
Valley Pike 22645
Veterans Rd 22645
Water Plant Rd 22645
Wayside Mill Ln 22645
Westernview Dr 22645
Woods Way 22645

MIDLOTHIAN VA

General Delivery 23113

POST OFFICE BOXES MAIN OFFICE STATIONS AND BRANCHES

Box No.s
1 - 2680 23113
4001 - 9000 23112

NAMED STREETS

Abbey Village Cir 23114
Abbots Ridge Ct 23113
Abbots Wood Ter 23113
Abbotts Mill Way 23114
Abelway Dr 23114
Aberdeen Landing Ln & Ter 23113
Abrahams Ln 23114
Academy Dr 23112
Acorn Hill Ct 23112
Acorn Ridge Ct, Pl & Rd 23112
Affirmed Dr 23112
Agee Ln & Ter 23114
Alanthus Rd 23112
Albion Rd 23113
Alcorn Ter & Way 23114
Aldengate Ct, Rd & Ter 23114
Alsdell Rd 23112
Alsdell Turn 23112
Altimira Ct & Ln 23112
Alverser Dr & Plz 23113
Alysheba Ln 23112
Amajess Ln 23113
Amber Forest Dr 23114
Amber Meadows Ct, Ln & Pl 23114
Ambergate Dr & Ter 23113
Amfit Way 23114
Anita Ave 23112
Anna Park Dr 23112
Annakay Ter & Xing 23113
Ansbauch Dr 23112
Arborcraft Dr 23113
Ardara Ln 23114
Arrandell Rd 23113
Arrowood Ct & Rd 23112
Arsenal Dr 23113
Ascot Dr 23112
Ashbrook Landing Ct, Rd & Ter 23114
Ashley Wilkes Ln 23112
Ashleyville Ln & Mews 23112
Ashleyville Turn 23112
Ashton Cove Ct & Dr 23113
Ashton Village Ct & Ln 23114
Ashtree Pl & Rd 23114
Assault Dr 23112
Astley Ct & Ter 23114
Auger Ln & Pl 23113
Autumn Woods Cir, Ct & Rd 23112
Autumnfield Rd 23113
Avocado Dr 23112
Avon Lake Cir 23114
Aylesford Ct & Dr 23113
Bach Ct, Ln & Ter 23114
Back Bay Ct 23112
N Bailey Bridge Rd 23112
Bailey Creek Rd 23112
Bailey Mountain Trl 23112
Bailey Oak Ct, Dr & Pl 23112
Bailey Woods Dr 23112
Baltrey Ln 23112
Banstead Rd 23113
Bantry Ct, Dr, Loop & Ter 23114
Barkham Ct & Dr 23112
Barnack Rd 23112
Barnes Spring Ct, Rd & Ter 23112
Baronsmede Rd 23113
Barrow Pl 23113
Bass River Ct 23112
Battlecreek Dr 23112
Bay Ct, Dr, Pl & Rd 23112
Bay Knolls Ct, Ter & Trl 23112
Bay Landing Ct 23112
Baycraft Ter 23112
Bayfront Pl & Way 23112
Baymill Ct 23112
Bayport Landing Ct, Rd & Ter 23112
Bayreuth Ct 23112
Bayside Ln 23112
Beacon Hill Ct & Dr 23112
Beauridge Ct 23114
Beaver Brook Rd 23114
Beaver Falls Ct & Rd 23112
Beaver Hollow Ct 23112
Beaver Point Dr 23112
Beaver Spring Ct, Pl & Rd 23112
Bedwyn Ct & Ln 23112
Beechwood Point Cir, Ct & Rd 23112
Beedon Dr 23112
Behetra Dr 23113
Bel Bridge Cir & Ct 23113
Bel Crest Cir & Ter 23113
Bellona Arsenal Rd 23113
Bellson Park Dr 23112
Belmont Stakes Ct, Dr & Pl 23112
Bending Oak Dr 23112
Bent Creek Ct, Pl & Rd 23112
Big Oak Ln 23113
Bigelow Rd 23112
Biggin Pond Ct, Ln, Mews, Pl & Rd 23114
Billstone Dr & Pl 23112
Birch Glen Ct 23112
Bircham Ct, Loop & Ter 23113
Birdsong Ln 23112
Birnam Woods Ct, Dr, Pl, Rd & Ter 23112
Black Heath Rd 23113
Black Seam Ct 23113
Blackbird Dr 23112
Blossom Loop & Pl 23112
Bluegrass Rd 23114
Boggs Cir 23114
E & W Bogie Rd 23113
Bold Forbes Ct & Ln 23112
Bolton Estates Ln 23113
Bon Secours Dr 23114
Bosham Ct & Ln 23113
Boswell Rd 23113
Boundary Ct, Rd & Ter 23112
Boxford Ln 23114
Boyces Cove Dr 23112
Brad Mcneer Pkwy 23112
Bradenshire Ct 23114
Brading Ct, Ln & Mews 23112
Braemar Ct 23113
Brafferton Rd 23112
Brancaster Ct 23113
W Branch Rd 23112
Branched Antler Cir, Ct, Dr, Pl & Ter 23112
Brandenburg Dr 23112
Brandermill Pkwy 23112
Brandermill Woods Trl 23112
Brayfield Pl 23113
Bream Dr 23113
Breezewood Ct 23113
Brewton Ter & Way 23113
Brian Ray Ct 23112
E, N, S & W Briar Patch Dr 23113
Briarmoor Ln 23113
Briars Cir & Ct 23114
Bridge Creek Ct & Dr 23112
Bridge Spring Dr 23112
Bridgewood Ct & Rd 23112
Brightstone Cir, Ct, Dr, Mews & Ter 23112
E & W Brigstock Rd 23113
Brimfield Ln 23114
Bristol Village Dr 23114
Broad Oaks Ct & Rd 23112
Brocket Ct & Dr 23112
Broncroft Ct 23113
Brookforest Ct, Rd & Ter 23112
Brookview Dr 23112
Broughton Rd 23113
Browns Hill Ct 23114
Browns Way Rd 23114
Buck Rub Cir, Ct, Dr, Ln & Pl 23112
Buckhead Ct, Rd & Ter 23113
Buckingham Station Dr 23113
Bucktail Ct 23112
Buffalo Nickel Ct, Dr & Pl 23112
Buffalo Nickel Turn 23112
Buffalo Springs Dr 23112
Bullock Ct 23112
Burlwood Ct 23113
Caddington Ct, Dr, Mews & Ter 23113
Calcutt Dr 23113
Call Federal Dr 23112
Camack Pl & Trl 23114
Camberly Ct 23113
Cambria Cove Blvd 23112
Camelia Cir 23112
Cameron Bay Dr & Ter 23112
Cameron Bridge Ct, Dr & Pl 23112
Camouflage Ct 23112
Campbellridge Ct & Dr 23112
Candlewick Ct & Rd 23112
Canford Loop 23112
Cannon Ridge Ct 23113
Cannonade Ct & Ln 23112
Capwell Dr 23113
Carbon Hill Ct, Dr & Pl 23113
Carefree Ct 23114
N & S Carriage Ln 23114
Carriage Creek Ct, Pl & Rd 23112
Cascade Meadows Dr 23112
Cascade Ridge Ln 23112
Cassaway Rd 23113
Castle Hill Rd 23113
Castle Hollow Ct, Rd & Ter 23114
Castle Rock Rd 23112
Castlebridge Rd 23113
Castleford Ct, Dr & Ter 23113
Castlestone Rd 23113
Castleway Rd 23114
Cedar Crossing Cir, Ct, Dr, Pl, Ter & Trl 23114
Center Pointe Pkwy 23114
Central Pointe Rd 23112
Chalkwell Dr 23113
Charlemagne Ct & Rd 23114
Charles Towne Rd 23112
Charrington Dr 23113
Charter Dr 23113
Charter Club Way 23114
Charter Colony Pkwy 23114
Charter Landing Ct & Dr 23114
Charter Park Dr 23114
Charter Walk Ct, Ln & Pl 23114
Charterhouse Dr 23113
Charters Bluff Pl & Trl 23113
Chartridge Ln 23113
Chartstone Ct & Dr 23113
Chase Ct, Pl & Rd 23112
Chastain Ln 23113
Chateaugay Ln 23112
Chatmoss Ct & Rd 23112
Chattanooga Plz 23112
Chatwell Rd 23113
Chepstow Ct, Rd & Ter 23113
Cherokee Rd 23113
Chestnut Bluff Pl, Rd & Ter 23112
Chestnut Creek Dr 23112
Chimney House Ct, Pl, Rd & Ter 23112
Chislet Ct, Dr & Mews 23112
Chital Dr 23112
Christendom Dr 23113
Church Bay Rd 23114
Citation Dr 23112
City View Dr 23113
Clayborne Ct & Ln 23114
Claypoint Rd 23112
Clear Ridge Ct, Dr & Ter 23112
Clearwater Dr 23114
Clemons Cir, Dr & Way 23114
Clintwood Ct, Rd & Ter 23112
Clipper Cove Ct & Rd 23112
E & W Coal Hopper Ln 23113
Coalbrook Dr 23114
Coalfield Rd 23114
Coalfield Commons Pl 23114
Coby Way 23112
Cohen Trl 23114
Colchester Ln 23113
Colehollow Dr 23113
Colgrave Rd 23112
Collington Cir, Ct & Dr 23112
Collington Turn 23112
Colony Crossing Pl 23112
Colony Forest Ct, Dr & Pl 23114
Colony Oak Ln & Ter 23114
Colton Creek Rd 23113
Colwyn Bay Dr 23112
Commodore Point Cir, Ct, Pl & Rd 23112
Commonwealth Centre Pkwy 23112
Concrete Pl 23114
Cone Ln 23112
Conte Dr 23113
Copper Hill Ct, Pl & Rd 23112
Copperfield Pl 23113
Coralview Ct, Rd & Ter 23114
Corianna Ln 23113
Corner Rock Rd 23113
Cotesworth Way 23113
Cottage Mill Cir, Pl, Rd, Ter & Way 23114
Cottage Oaks Ct 23112
Count Fleet Dr 23112
Country Walk Ct & Rd 23112
W County Line Rd 23112
Court Ridge Rd & Ter 23112
Courthouse Rd 23112
Courthouse Acres Dr 23114
Cove Ridge Cir, Ct, Pl, Rd, Ter & Trce 23112
Cove View Cir & Ln 23112
Cradle Hill Ct & Rd 23112
Craig Rath Blvd 23112
Cranborne Rd 23113
Crawford Wood Dr, Pl & Ter 23114
Craystone Cir 23113
Creek Crossing Dr 23112
Creek Heights Dr 23112
Creekbrook Dr, Pl & Ter 23113
Creekfall Way 23114
Creekglen Ln, Pl & Way 23114
Creekpointe Cir & Ct 23114
Creekwillow Dr 23113
Crescent Grn 23113
Crescent Park Dr 23114
Crossings Way 23113
Crossings Ridge Dr 23113
Crossings Way Cir, Ct & Ter 23113
Crosstimbers Ct, Pl, Rd & Ter 23112
Crowder Dr 23113
Crowne Creek Dr 23112
Crowne Ridge Loop 23112
Dalmore Dr & Ln 23113
Danbury Dr 23113
Danhurst Dr 23113
Dannyhill Ct & Rd 23114
Danwoods Rd 23113
Darby Cir & Dr 23113
Darien Cir 23114
Darrell Dr & Ter 23114
Davelayne Rd 23112
Dawnridge Ct 23114
Dawnwood Ct, Rd & Ter 23114
Decidedly Ct & Ln 23112
Deep Hollow Ct 23112
Deer Meadow Ct, Dr, Ln, Pl & Ter 23112
Deer Run Cir, Ct, Dr, Ln & Way 23112
Deer Thicket Ct, Dr & Ln 23112
Deergrove Rd 23112
Deerhill Ln & Rd 23112
Deerhurst Dr 23113
Deerleaf Ct & Way 23112
Deerpark Ct & Dr 23112
Dehaviland Dr 23112
Delfin Rd 23112
Delgado Rd 23112
Denby Ter & Way 23114
Depot St 23113
Derby Ridge Ct, Loop & Way 23113
Dew Ln 23112
Diamond Creek Dr & Ter 23113
Diamond Hill Dr 23113
Diamond Ridge Dr 23112
Dogwood Dell Ln 23113
Domfont Ct 23113
N Donegal Rd 23113
Dorsetshire Ct 23113
Dovercourt Dr 23113
Dragonnade Trl 23113
Drakewood Cir, Ct, Rd & Ter 23113
Draycot Dr 23112
Drifting Cir 23113
Drumone Ct & Rd 23112
Dry Bridge Rd 23114
Ducatus Dr 23113
Duck Cove Ct, Pl & Rd 23112
Duck River Ct & Rd 23112
Duckbill Ct & Dr 23113
Duckridge Ct & Ter 23112
Dumaine Dr 23112
Dunkeld Ter 23113
Dunleith Ct & Ter 23113
Dunlin Ct 23114
Duns Tew Dr 23112
Durhamshire Ct, Ln & Pl 23113
Duxbury Ct & Pl 23114
Earlswood Rd 23113
Eastbluff Ct & Rd 23112
Easthampton Dr 23113
Echo Ridge Ct, Dr & Pl 23112
Edenfield Ct & Rd 23113
Edenhurst Ct 23114
Edenshire Rd 23113
Edgetree Ct & Ter 23114
Edgeview Ln 23113
Edmiston Ct & Way 23114
Edmonthorpe Rd 23113
Edmonton Dr 23113
Elderberry Ln 23112
Elkwood Ct & Rd 23112
Ellerton Ct, Dr & Ter 23113
Ellesmere Dr 23113
Elmstead Rd 23113
Elmstone Rd 23113
Elshur Rd 23112
Enclave Dr 23114
Enclave Creek Ln 23114
Engerston Rd 23113
Erika Hill Ct, Dr, Pl & Way 23112
Erika Marie Ct 23112
Ethelred Ct 23113
E Evergreen Pkwy 23114
Evershot Cir, Ct & Dr 23112
Exbury Ct, Dr & Ter 23114
Explorer Ct, Dr & Ter 23114
Fairgate Rd 23112
Fairlington Ln 23113
Faline Ct 23112
Farcet Ct, Dr, Pl & Ter 23112
Farm Brook Ct 23112
Farm Crest Ct 23112
Farnborough Dr 23112
Farringdon Rd 23113
Fawley Rd 23112
Fawnview Dr 23113
Featherstone Ct & Dr 23113
Felbridge Ct & Way 23113
Fennimore Rd & Ter 23114
Feraderm Rd 23114
Ferdinand Ln 23112
Fern Meadow Loop 23114
Fernvale Ct 23113
Fiddlers Ridge Ct, Ln, Pl & Rd 23112
Fincastle Ct 23113
Fircrest Pl 23113
Five Springs Ct & Rd 23112
Flag Tail Dr & Way 23112
Flour Mill Ct & Dr 23112
Foggy Mill Dr 23112
Foliage Ct 23112
Follensbee Dr 23113
Forest Creek Dr 23113
Forest Mill Dr 23112
Forest Row Trl 23112
Forest Wood Ct, Ln & Rd 23112
Forestwind Dr 23112
Fort Sumter Ct & Rd 23112
Fortunes Ridge Ct & Rd 23112
Founders Bridge Blvd, Ct, Rd & Ter 23113
Founders Creek Ct 23113
Founders Crest Ct 23113
Founders Grant Pl 23113
Founders Hill Ct 23113
Founders Knoll Ter 23113
Founders View Dr & Ln 23113
Fountain View Dr 23112
Fox Branch Ct & Ln 23112
Fox Briar Cir, Ct, Ln, Rd & Way 23112
Fox Chase Ct, Dr, Ln, Rd & Ter 23112
Fox Club Ct, Ln, Pkwy & Way 23112
Fox Crest Cir, Ct, Ln, Pl & Way 23112
Fox Gate Ct, Ln & Pl 23112
Fox Grove Ct, Ln & Pl 23112
Fox Haven Ct, Ln, Pl & Ter 23112
Fox Hurst Ct, Dr, Pl & Ter 23113
Foxstone Ct & Rd 23113
Foxvale Ct & Way 23112
Framar Dr 23113
Frameway Rd 23113
Frederick Farms Cir, Ct & Dr 23112
French Creek Trl 23114
Fribble Way 23112
Fulbrook Dr 23113
Fulford Ct 23113
Full Rack Cir, Ct, Dr & Pl 23112

Gable Way 23112
Gainsborough Ct 23114
Gallant Fox Ct, Dr, Pl & Ter 23112
Galloway Ct & Ter 23113
Gamecock Rd 23112
Gamelaw Ct 23113
Garden View Pointe 23113
Gardengate Rd 23112
Garnett Ln 23114
Garrison Place Ct, Dr, Rd & Ter 23112
Gate Post Ct 23112
Gates Mill Ct, Pl & Rd 23112
Genito Pl & Rd 23112
Genuine Risk Ct & Ln 23112
Gildenborough Ct & Dr 23113
Gladstone Glen Pl 23114
Glamorgan Ln 23113
Glen Ridge Ct 23112
Glen Tara Ct & Dr 23112
Glendower Cir, Ct & Rd 23113
Glengate Rd 23114
Glenmeadow Ct, Rd & Ter 23114
Glenpark Cir, Ct & Ln 23114
Glenshade Dr 23114
Goby Ct 23112
Goddingham Ct 23113
Goldengate Pl 23112
Goode Ln 23113
Gorham Ct & Ln 23114
Goswick Ln & Way 23114
Goswick Ridge Ct, Pl & Rd 23114
Grace Wood Ct & Pl 23113
Grackle Ct 23112
Gradyhill Pl 23114
Graeme Hall Cir 23112
Grangewood Rd 23113
Grantly Ct 23113
Gravatt Ct & Way 23114
Gravier Rd 23112
Gravity Hill Ln, Rd & Trl 23114
Gray Oaks Ln 23113
Greenway Crossing Dr 23114
Gregwood Rd 23112
Grendon Dr 23113
Grey Friars Ln 23113
Greyhound Ct 23112
Groton Ct 23114
Grove Rd 23114
Grove Forest Ct & Rd 23112
Grove Hill Rd 23114
Grove Park Ct 23114
Grove Pond Dr 23114
Groveton Cir, Ct & Ter 23114
Gum Fork Pl & Rd 23112
Hailey Crescent Dr 23112
Hailsham Cir 23113
Half Moon Bay Ct 23114
Hallford Ct 23114
Hallsboro Holw & Rd 23112
Hancroft Dr 23113
Handley Ct, Ln & Rd 23113
Hanwell Ct 23113
Happy Hollow Dr 23113
Harbour Ln 23112
Harbour Bluff Ct, Pl & Ter 23112
Harbour Hill Pl 23112
Harbour Park Dr 23112
Harbour Pointe Pkwy & Rd 23112
Harbour Ridge Rd 23112
Harbour View Ct 23112
Harbourside Ct & Dr 23112
Harbourside Centre Ct & Loop 23112
Harbourwood Ct, Pl & Rd 23112
Harburn Ct 23113

Hardwood Ct, Dr, Pl & Ter 23114
Harrington Mnr 23113
Hartlepool Ln 23113
Hasty Ln 23112
Havens Oak Cir 23114
Haveridge Ct & Dr 23112
Haversham Dr 23113
Hawkins Park Rd 23114
Hawkins Wood Cir, Ct & Ln 23114
Hayden Run 23112
Hazelnut Branch Ct, Pl, Rd & Ter 23112
Headwaters Ct, Pl & Rd 23113
Heathbrook Ct, Dr, Rd & Ter 23112
Heather Glen Rd 23112
Heathland Dr & Ter 23113
Heathmere Cres & Ct 23112
Heaths Way Rd 23114
Hedgeway Pl 23113
Heidi Ct, Dr, Mews, Pl & Ter 23112
Heidi Turn 23112
Helmsley Ct & Rd 23113
Hendricks Rd 23112
Henlow Dr 23113
W Hensley Rd 23112
E, W, N & S Heritage Woods Ct, Ln, Pl, Rd, Rdg, Ter & Trl 23112
Heth Ct, Dr & Pl 23114
Hickory Grove Dr & Pl 23112
Hickory Nut Ct, Pl & Pt 23112
Hidden Nest Ct & Dr 23112
Highberry Woods Ct, Dr, Pl, Rd & Ter 23112
Highbridge Dr 23113
Hillandale Dr 23113
Hillanne Dr 23113
Hillcreek Cir, Ct, Dr, Mews, Pl & Ter 23112
Hillcreek Turn 23112
Hinshaw Dr 23113
Hockliffe Cir, Ln & Loop 23112
Holding Pond Ct & Ln 23112
Hollow Oak Ct, Dr, Rd & Ter 23112
Holly Bark Dr 23112
Holly View Ct, Pl & Ter 23112
Hollyglen Ct 23112
Hollypark Dr 23114
Horseshoe Bay Ct 23114
Houndmaster Cir, Rd & Ter 23112
W Huguenot Rd & Trl 23113
Huguenot Hundred Ct & Dr 23113
Huguenot Springs Rd 23113
Hull Street Rd 23112
Hullow Village Loop 23112
Hunt Master Dr 23112
Huntgate Woods Rd 23112
Hunts Bridge Ct & Rd 23112
Idstone Way 23112
Ionis Ln 23112
Iron Forge Dr 23113
Island Park Ct 23112
Iverson Ct & Rd 23112
James River Rd 23113
Jefferson Green Cir 23113
Jeffries Pl, Ter & Way 23114
Jennys Pl 23114
Johanna Bay Ct & Dr 23114
Justice Rd 23113
Kanbaugh Ct 23114
Keith Ln 23113
Kelham Rd 23113
Kelly Green Ln 23112
Kellynn Dr 23112
Kenmont Dr & Ter 23113

Kentford Rd 23113
Kentucky Derby Ct, Dr & Pl 23112
Kerri Cove Ct & Way 23113
Kettlewell Ct 23113
Kevinmeade Dr 23114
Key Deer Cir, Ct & Dr 23112
Kidbrook Ln 23113
Kilrenny Rd 23113
King Cotton Ct & Ln 23112
King William Woods Ct, Rd & Ter 23113
Kingfisher Ter 23112
Kingham Cir, Dr & Pl 23114
Kings Farm Ct & Dr 23113
Kings Lynn Rd 23113
Kingscross Ct & Rd 23114
Kingsmill Rd 23113
Kirkgate Ln 23114
Kirkham Rd 23113
Knightcross Rd 23113
Knights Run Ct & Dr 23113
Knobhill Ct 23114
Krim Point Ct, Ln, Loop, Rd, Trl & Way 23114
Lady Allison Ln 23113
Lady Ashley Ct & Rd 23114
Lady Jean Ct 23114
Lady Marian Ct, Ln & Pl 23113
Ladybank Ct 23113
Lake Harbour Dr 23112
Lake Point Dr 23112
Lake Rest Cir 23114
Lakebluff Pkwy 23112
Lakestone Dr 23114
Lambourne Rd 23112
Lancaster Gate Dr & Ln 23113
Lancey Ct & Dr 23114
Lander Ct & Rd 23113
Langford Dr 23113
Lansdowne Ct, Rd & Ter 23113
Lansgate Ct & Rd 23112
Larkin Ln 23112
Lastingham Dr 23112
Latham Blvd, Ct & Pl 23113
Laurel Top Ct, Dr & Pl 23114
Laurel Trail Ct, Pl & Rd 23112
Lauren Cir, Ct, Ln & Pl 23114
Lavenham Ln 23112
Lavenham Turn 23112
Lawford Ln 23114
Le Gordon Dr 23114
Leafield Dr & Ter 23113
Learning Place Loop 23114
Leatherwood Way 23113
Leesburg Cir & Ct 23112
Leiden Ln 23112
Lenox Forest Ct & Dr 23112
Leovey Ln 23113
Letchworth Ln 23113
Liberty Oaks Cir, Ct & Rd 23112
Liberty Point Ct, Dr & Pl 23112
Liberty Walk Dr 23112
Lifestyle Ln 23112
Limbeck Ln 23112
Lintel Ln 23113
Lintz Ln 23112
Linville Ct 23113
Little Hawk Ct, Dr & Pl 23114
Little Horn Rdg 23112
Little Pond Ln 23113
Littlecroft Pl 23113
Live Oak Cir, Ct, Dr & Ln 23113
Lochmere Cir 23114
Lockett Ridge Ave, Ct, Pl & Rd 23114
Logan Trace Ct & Rd 23114

Lomond Dr 23114
Lonas Pkwy 23112
London Park Dr 23113
Long Cove Ct, Pl & Rd 23112
Long Gate Ct & Rd 23112
Long Hill Ct & Rd 23112
Long Oaks Rd 23112
Long Shadow Ct, Dr & Ter 23112
Longfellow Ct, Dr & Pl 23112
Longtown Dr & Pl 23112
Lookout Point Cir & Rd 23112
Lothian Trl 23114
Lowery Bluff Way 23112
Lucks Ln 23114
Lucky Debonair Ln 23112
Lundy Ter 23114
Lynngate Ln 23113
Lynport Ct 23112
Mabry Mill Dr 23113
Madrona St 23114
Magnolia Grove Way 23113
Mallard Creek Cir 23112
Mallard Landing Cir 23112
Manakin Rd 23113
Manakintown Ferry Rd 23113
Manders Knoll Ct & Ter 23114
Mandolin Dr 23113
Manor Gate Ct, Dr & Pl 23112
Mansfield Cir, Lndg & Ter 23114
Maple Brook Ct & Dr 23112
Maple Hall Ct & Dr 23113
Marigold Ct 23114
Mariners Pl & Way 23112
Market Square Ln 23112
Markey Cir & Rd 23112
Markfield Dr 23112
Martin Glen Pl, Rd & Ter 23112
Marva Way 23112
Marylebane Ln 23113
Master Stag Dr 23112
Matyiko Ct 23114
Mcallen Ct 23114
Mcennally Rd 23112
Mckenna Cir & Ct 23112
Mcmanaway Ct & Dr 23112
Mctyres Cove Ct, Ln, Pl, Rd & Ter 23112
Meadow Chase Ln & Rd 23112
Meeting Gate Ct & Rd 23112
Meis Ln 23112
Merit Grove Ct 23112
Meyer Cove Dr 23112
Michaels Ridge Rd 23113
Michaux Bluff Dr 23113
Michaux Branch Ter 23113
Michaux Creek Pl 23113
Michaux Crossing Ln 23113
Michaux Glen Dr 23113
Michaux Ridge Ct 23113
Michaux Run Ct 23113
Michaux View Ct, Ter & Way 23113
Michaux Wood Way 23113
Middlewood Cir, Ct, Pl, Rd & Ter 23113
Midlothian Tpke 23113
Mill Bluff Dr 23112
Mill Flume Ct & Dr 23112
Mill Forest Ct & Dr 23113
Mill Lock Ter 23113
Mill Manor Ct, Dr & Pl 23112
Mill Meadow Ct & Dr 23112
Mill Shed Dr 23112
Mill Spring Cir, Ct, Dr, Ln & Rd 23112
Mill Walk Dr 23112
Millcreek Ct 23112
Millcrest Ter 23112

Millridge Pkwy 23112
Millridge Pkwy E
4800-4943 23112
4944-4948 23112
4944-4944 23113
4945-4999 23112
Millside Ter 23114
Millspray Ct 23112
Millstep Ter 23112
Millwood School Ln 23112
Miners Trail Rd 23114
Mirror Pond Way 23114
Misty Lake Ct & Way 23114
Misty Ridge Ct 23113
Misty Spring Ct, Dr & Pl 23112
Mistyhollow Rd 23112
Mitford Dr & Pl 23114
Mockingbird Ln 23112
Monday Way 23112
Moravia Rd 23112
Morley Rd 23112
Morning Dove Mews 23112
Morning Hill Ct & Ln 23112
Mortemer Rd 23113
Moss Creek Ct, Pl & Rd 23112
Mount Hill Cir, Ct & Dr 23113
Mount Pisgah Dr 23113
Moven Ct, Dr & Pl 23114
Mt Hermon Rd 23112
Muirfield Green Ct, Dr, Ln, Pl & Ter 23112
Mulberry Row Rd 23113
Mulligan Ct 23113
Murray Hill Dr 23113
Murray Olds Ct & Dr 23114
Musical Ln 23113
Musket Dr 23113
Nahant Rd 23112
Nailor Cir & Way 23114
Nashua Ct, Dr, Pl & Ter 23112
Nashua Turn 23112
Native Dancer Dr 23112
Needham Market Rd 23112
Needle Rush Way 23114
S Netherfield Dr 23113
Nevis Ct & Dr 23114
New Forest Ct & Trl 23112
Newberg Ln 23114
Newgate Rd 23113
Nicholas Trace Ct 23113
Nicolay Pl & Way 23114
Nighthawk Ct 23112
Normandstone Dr 23113
Northern Dancer Ct 23112
Northwich Ct, Dr, Rd & Ter 23112
Norwood Pond Ct, Ln & Pl 23112
Nuttree Woods Ct, Dr, Ln, Pl & Ter 23112
Oak Ln 23113
Oak Creek Ct & Ter 23114
Oak Glade Dr 23113
Oak Knoll Cir, Ln & Rd 23112
Oak Lake Blvd, Ct & Trl E 23112
Oak Meadow Ln 23112
Oak Timber Ct 23114
Oakengate Ln 23113
Oaklake Crest Way 23112
Old Bailey Bridge Rd 23112
Old Barn Ct 23112
Old Brick School Rd 23113
Old Buckingham Rd 23113
Old Buckingham Station Dr 23113
Old Chestnut Cir & Dr 23112
Old Confederate Cemet Rd 23113
Old Country Ct, Ln & Ter 23114
Old Exchange Pl 23112

Old Fort Dr & Pl 23113
Old Fox Ct & Trl 23112
Old Gun Rd & Trce 23113
Old Hundred Rd 23114
Old Hundred Rd S 23112
Old Lyme Ln 23114
Old Otterdale Rd 23114
Old Well Ln & Ter 23112
Oldbury Ct & Rd 23113
Olde Coach Dr 23113
Olde Coalmine Ct & Rd 23113
Olde King Cir & Ln 23113
Olde Lynne Ct 23114
Olde Queen Ct & Ter 23113
Olde Stone Cir & Rd 23113
Olde Stonegate Rd 23113
Orchard Grove Ct, Dr & Ln 23112
Otterdale Rd
100-298 23114
300-1799 23114
1800-3999 23112
N Otterdale Rd 23113
Otterdale Woods Rd 23114
Overcliff Ct 23114
Overcreek Ln 23112
Overlea Ct & Dr 23112
Owlsnest Ct 23114
Paddington Dr 23114
Paddle Creek Ct & Dr 23113
Paddock Dr 23113
Paddock Wood Ter 23112
Page Rd 23113
Pagehurst Dr & Ter 23113
Paget Ct 23114
Paigewood Ct & Rd 23114
Painted Post Ln 23112
Palomino Way 23112
Pamplin Dr 23114
Pari Way 23112
Park Ridge Rd 23113
Park West Cir 23114
Parracombe Ln 23112
Parrish Branch Cir & Rd 23112
Parrish Creek Dr & Ln 23112
Pasture Hill Rd 23112
Paulbrook Blvd & Dr 23112
Pavilion Pl 23112
Peartree Ct 23112
Pease Rd 23112
Pebble Creek Ct, Ln, Rd & Ter 23112
Pecan Ter 23112
Pegwell Dr 23113
Pembrooke Dock Ct, Ln & Pl 23112
Pencader Rd 23112
Penhurst Rd 23113
Penny Ln 23112
Penny Bridge Ct, Dr, Mews & Pl 23112
Penny Oak Dr 23112
Pensive Pl 23112
Peppercorn Pl 23112
Perdido Ct & Dr 23112
Perimeter Dr 23113
Petty Ct & Rd 23113
Pharlap Ct 23112
Pharlap Turn 23112
Pike View Dr 23113
Pine Bark Ln 23113
Pine Vale Pl 23113
Pinemist Rd 23112
Pineridge Ln 23114
Pinery Way 23112
Pinifer Park Ct 23113
Pipers Ter 23114
Planters Row Ct & Dr 23113
Planters Walk Ct & Dr 23113
Pleasant Grove Ct & Ln 23112
Point Ct & Rd 23112
Point Landing Ct 23112
Point Placid Dr 23112

Point Sunrise Ct 23112
Point Trace Ct 23112
Pointer Ridge Rd & Ter 23112
Polo Cir, Pkwy & Pl 23113
Poly Pl 23112
Pomfret Ct 23114
Pond Chase Ct, Dr & Pl 23113
W Poplar Grove Ct, Pl, Rd & Ter 23112
Port Elissa Lndg 23114
Port Savage Dr 23112
Port Side Dr 23112
Porters Mill Ct, Ln, Pl, Rd & Ter 23114
Porters Mill Turn 23114
Post Mill Dr, Pl & Ter 23113
Post Office Rd 23112
Powderham Ln 23113
Powell Grove Dr, Rd & Ter 23112
Preakness Ct 23112
Preservation Dr & Rd 23113
Price Club Blvd 23112
Prince Brians Ct 23113
Prince William Dr 23114
Promenade Pkwy 23113
Promontory Pl 23112
Promontory Pointe Rd 23112
Proud Clarion Ln 23112
Puckett Ct & Pl 23112
Quail Hill Ct & Dr 23112
Quail Hollow Ct & Ln 23112
Quail Hunt Ct 23112
Quail Meadows Ct, Ln & Pl 23112
Quailwood Rd 23112
Queens Pl 23114
Queens Crown Dr 23113
Queens Grant Dr 23113
Queensgate Ct & Rd 23114
Queenswood Rd 23113
Quiet Lake Loop 23114
Quisenberry St 23112
Quito Rd 23112
Radnor Pl 23113
Radnor Forest Ct 23113
Radstock Rd 23113
Raftersridge Ct, Dr & Ter 23113
Railey Hill Ct & Dr 23114
Railroad Ave 23113
Raised Antler Cir 23112
Ramshorn Rd 23113
Ratling Dr 23112
Red Chestnut Ct & Dr 23112
Red Fern Ct 23112
Redborne Ct 23114
Redwick Dr 23112
Reed Grass Ln 23114
Reeds Bluff Ln 23113
Reeds Landing Cir & Rd 23113
Regatta Pointe Ct & Rd 23112
Regiment Ter 23113
Reginald Ct 23112
Respess Rd 23112
Ridge Cir, Dr & Ter 23112
Ridge Creek Ct & Rd 23112
Ridge Point Ct, Dr & Rd 23112
Ridgemoor Ct, Dr, Ln & Pl 23114
Rigney Dr 23113
Rimswell Ct, Mews, Pl & Ter 23112
Rimswell Turn 23112
Ripon Rd 23112
Rise Shaft Rd 23114
Rittenhouse Dr 23112
River Breeze Ln 23113
River Hills Cir, Ct, Dr, Ln & Ter 23113
River Oaks Dr 23113

Riverbelle Ct & Way 23113
Riverbirch Trace Ct & Rd 23112
Riverdowns North Ct, Dr, Mews, Pl & Ter 23113
Riverdowns South Dr 23113
Rivermist Ct, Rd & Ter 23113
Riverstone Rd 23113
Riverton Ct & Dr 23113
Roberts Mill Ct 23113
Robious Rd 23113
Robious Crossing Dr 23113
Robious Forest Way 23113
Robious Station Cir 23113
Robys Way 23113
Rochester Ct 23113
Rock Harbour Rd 23112
Rockport Landing Ct, Pl & Rd 23112
Rocky River Dr 23114
Roderick Ct 23113
Roedeer Dr 23112
Roll Dr 23114
Rolling Spring Dr 23114
Rose Family Dr 23112
Rose Glen Dr & Pl 23112
Rose Glen Turn 23112
Rose Mill Cir 23112
Rosebay Forest Dr, Pl & Rd 23112
Rosehall Ter 23114
Rossmere Cir, Ct & Dr 23114
Royal Crest Ct & Dr 23113
Royal Ridge Rd 23114
Royenwood Rd 23113
Rue Noelle Ct 23114
Running Brook Cir & Ln 23113
Ryanwood Ct 23113
Saddle Hill Dr 23112
Safewings Pl 23112
Sagebrook Ct, Pl & Rd 23112
Sagecreek Cir & Ct 23112
Sagegrove Cir & Rd 23112
Sagewood Rd & Trce 23112
Sailboat Cir, Ct, Dr, Ln & Pl 23112
Sailview Ct & Dr 23112
Sainsbury Ct & Dr 23113
Saint Stephens Pl & Way 23113
W Salisbury Dr & Rd 23113
Salles Ridge Ct 23113
Salten Ct 23112
Sanbury Ln 23114
Sandbag Cir, Rd, Ter & Way 23113
Sandgate Rd 23113
Sandhurst Ln 23113
Sandstone Ridge Ct, Rd & Ter 23112
Sandy Brook Ln 23112
Sapphire Dr 23112
Sarah St 23112
Sarsen Ct 23113
Sarum Ter 23113
Savage View Ct, Dr & Pl 23112
Schofield Dr 23113
Scotter Hills Ct, Dr, Ln & Pl 23114
Scottwood Rd 23112
Seabird Dr 23112
Seabright Ter 23114
Seattle Slew Ln & Ter 23112
Secretariat Ct & Dr 23112
Sedberry Ln 23114
Sedgefield Rd & Ter 23112
Senlac Ct 23113
Seven Oaks Ct, Rd & Ter 23112
Shadow Oaks Rd 23112
Shadow Ridge Ct, Ln, Pl & Rd 23112
Shadowhill Ct 23114
Shady Pointe Ct 23112
Shadyglen Ct & Dr 23114
Shallowford Trce 23112
Shallowford Landing Ct, Rd & Ter 23112
Shawhan Ct & Pl 23114
Shefford Dr 23112
Shelter Cove Cir & Rd 23112
Shelter Cove Pointe 23112
Sherfield Ct 23113
Shiloh Church Rd 23112
Shipborne Rd 23112
Ships Watch Ln 23112
Shirlton Ct & Rd 23114
Shore Ct, Ln & Rd 23112
Shorewood Ct & Pl 23112
Sika Ct & Ln 23112
Silbyrd Dr 23113
Silver Birch Ct & Ln 23112
Silver Creek Ct 23113
Silver Lake Ter 23112
Singer Rd 23112
Skyline Ridge Dr 23112
Sodbury Ct & Dr 23113
Solebury Pl & Ter 23112
Solstice Close 23113
Somerville Grove Cir, Pl & Ter 23114
Sommerville Ct 23113
Southbridge Dr 23113
Southernbelle Ct & Ln 23112
Southshore Ct, Dr & Rd 23112
Southshore Pointe Rd 23112
Southwell Ct, Pl & Ter 23113
Southwick Blvd, Ct, Pl & Ter 23113
Sovereign Grace Dr 23114
Spaldwick Ln 23113
Spectrim Ln 23112
Speeks Ct & Dr 23112
Spinnaker Cove Dr & Rd 23112
Spotted Coat Ct & Ln 23112
Spreading Oak Ct & Rd 23112
Spring Bluff Rd 23112
Spring Creek Ct & Dr 23113
Spring Cress Ct 23114
Spring Gate Ct, Pl, Rd & Ter 23112
N Spring Run Rd 23112
Spring Trace Ct, Dr, Mews, Pl & Ter 23112
Spring Trace Turn 23112
Springford Pkwy 23112
St Cecelia Ct & Dr 23112
St Croix Pl 23114
St Elizabeth Dr 23112
St Francis Blvd 23114
St Regina Ct 23112
St Thomas Ct & Dr 23114
Stableside Ct 23113
Staffordshire Ct & St 23113
Stallion Way 23112
Stamford Cir & Rd 23112
Standing Oak Ct, Pl & Rd 23112
Stanford Ct 23113
Starcross Rd 23113
Steeple Chase Ct, Rd & Ter 23112
Steeplestone Dr 23113
Sterlingheath Dr 23112
Sterlings Bridge Ct, Pl, Rd & Ter 23112
Stetson Ct 23114
Stigall Ct, Dr & Way 23112
Stone Harbor Dr 23113
Stone Village Way 23113
Stonegate Ct & Rd 23113
Stonehenge Farm Rd 23113
Stonemill Lake Ct & Ter 23112
Stoney Ridge Ct, Rd & Trl 23112
Sugar Hill Ct & Dr 23112
Sugarberry Ln 23113
Summerhouse Ct & Ln 23112
Summerhurst Dr 23113
Suncrest Dr 23112
Sunday Silence Ct & Ln 23112
Sunfield Ct, Dr & Pl 23112
Sunnys Halo Ct 23112
Sunrise Bluff Ct & Rd 23112
Sunset Point Ct 23112
Sutters Mill Cir, Ct, Rd & Ter 23112
Swale Ln 23112
Swallowtail Pl 23113
Swamp Fox Rd 23112
Swanhurst Cir & Dr 23113
Sweet Willow Dr 23114
Sweetspire Rdg 23113
Swift Cir & Ln 23114
Swift Crossing Ct, Dr & Pl 23112
Swindon Ct & Way 23112
Sycamore Sq 23113
Sycamore Mews Cir 23113
Sycamore Ridge Ct 23114
Sycamore Square Dr 23113
Sycamore Village Dr & Ter 23114
Tackley Pl 23114
Tadley Ct & Dr 23112
Tall Hickory Ct & Dr 23112
Tall Pine Rd 23112
Tamhaven Ln 23113
Tammaway Dr 23112
Tanager Wood Ct & Trl 23114
Tanglebrook Rd 23112
Tannery Cir 23113
Tanya Ter 23112
Taplow Cir, Rd & Ter 23112
Tealby Ct & Dr 23112
Temie Lee Pkwy 23112
Tennessee Plz 23112
Terrace Arbor Cir 23112
Terrybluff Dr 23112
Tevis Ln 23112
Thomassette Dr 23112
Thorncrag Ln 23112
Thorney Ct 23113
Thorngate Rd 23113
Thornleigh Rd 23113
Thornridge Ct & Ln 23112
Thoroughbred Cir 23113
Three Bridges Rd 23112
Thynne Rd 23114
Tidal Dr 23112
Timber Bluff Pkwy 23112
Timber Ridge Ct, Pl & Rd 23112
Timber Trail Ct & Dr 23112
Timbercrest Ct 23112
Timberlake Ct 23114
Timbernorth Ct & Trl 23112
Time Square Dr 23112
Tipple Point Rd 23114
Tollcross Rd 23114
Tomahawk Creek Rd 23114
Tomahawk Meadows Dr, Ln & Pl 23112
Tomahawk Ridge Dr & Pl 23112
Toronette Way 23112
Torrington Dr 23113
Tower Light Rd 23113
Trails End Rd 23113
Tredegar Lake Pkwy 23112
Tremelo Trl 23113
Trenadier Cir 23113
Trilithon Rd 23113
Triple Crown Dr 23112
Trisha Trl 23112
Triton Springs Dr 23114
Troon Bay Dr 23114
Trophy Buck Ct 23112
Trophy Club Dr 23113
Trotters Ln 23113
Troywood Rd 23112
Trumbull Ct 23114
Tunsberg Ter 23113
Turnberry Ct & Ln 23113
Turnerville Rd 23112
Turnley Ln 23113
Turtle Hill Cir, Ct, Ln, Pl & Rd 23112
Twelveoaks Ct & Rd 23112
Twin Team Ln 23113
Two Notch Ct, Pl & Rd 23112
Unison Dr 23113
Upperbury Ct, Dr & Ter 23114
Valerie Ct & Dr 23114
Valley Crest Dr 23112
Valley Overlook Dr 23112
Velvet Antler Cir, Ct, Dr, Ln, Pl, Run, Trl & Way 23112
Venita Rd 23113
Viburg Ct 23113
Victoria Cir & Ln 23113
Victoria Crossing Ln 23113
Village Gate Dr & Pl 23114
W Village Green Dr 23112
Village Mill Dr 23114
Village Place Dr 23114
Village Ridge Dr 23114
Village School Ln 23112
Village Square Pl 23112
Village View Dr 23114
Vincent Ln 23114
Vistapoint Rd 23113
Wadebridge Rd 23113
Wagonwheel Ct & Rd 23113
Walden Springs Dr 23114
Walkers Ferry Ct & Rd 23112
Walking Path Ct & Ln 23112
Wallingham Ct, Dr & Loop 23114
Walmart Way 23113
Walnut Bend Ct, Dr, Rd & Ter 23112
Walnut Creek Cir, Ct & Rd 23112
Walnut Hollow Ct 23112
Walnut Wood Ct & Dr 23112
Walton Bluff Cir, Ct, Pkwy, Pl & Ter 23114
Walton Creek Dr 23114
Walton Lake Dr 23114
Walton Park Ln & Rd 23114
Walton Ridge Ln 23114
War Admiral Dr 23112
Warbro Rd 23112
Warminster Ct & Dr 23113
Watch Pt E & W 23114
Watch Harbour Ct & Rd 23112
Watch Hill Ct, Rd & Ter 23114
Water Creek Ct 23112
Water Horse Ct 23112
Water Overlook Blvd 23112
Water Pointe Ct & Ln 23112
Water Race Ct, Dr & Ter 23112
Water Willow Dr 23114
Watercove Rd 23112
Watercrest Ct, Pl & Rd 23112
Waterford Pl & Way 23112
Waterford Lake Dr 23112
Waterlily Ct 23114
Watermill Lake Trl 23112
Waters Edge Cir, Ct, Rd & Ter 23112
Waters Shore Dr 23112
Waterswatch Ct & Dr 23113
Waterton Dr 23113
Waterwheel Dr 23112
Watkins Centre Pkwy 23114
Watkins Glen Rd 23112
Watkins Landing Rd 23113
Wave Ln 23112
Wc Commons Dr & Way 23113
Wc Main St 23113
Welby Ct, Dr, Mews, Pl & Ter 23113
Welby Turn 23113
Welrose Ct 23113
Wesanne Ln & Ter 23114
Westbury Dr 23114
Westbury Bluff Dr 23114
Westbury Knoll Ln 23114
Westbury Ridge Ct & Dr 23114
Westchester Commons Way 23113
Westcreek Dr 23114
Westfield Rd 23113
Westwood Village Ln & Way 23114
Whirlaway Ct, Dr, Mews, Pl, Ter, Trl & Way 23112
Whirlaway Turn 23112
Whispering Way 23113
Whispering Oaks Ct, Pl, Rd & Ter 23112
Whisperlake Ct 23114
Whistlers Cove Ct & Dr 23112
Whistlewood Ct 23113
White Cap Dr 23112
White Manor Ct & Ln 23112
Whitecastle Dr 23113
Whitechapel Rd 23113
Wiesinger Ln 23113
Wilcot Dr 23113
Wildercroft Rd 23113
Wiley Cir 23114
Wilfong Ct & Dr 23112
Willow Glen Rd 23112
Wilson Wood Ct & Rd 23114
Wiltstaff Ct, Dr & Pl 23112
Winamack Ct & Rd 23114
Winbury Ct, Dr & Ter 23114
Windjammer Dr 23112
Windy Ridge Ct, Dr, Rd & Ter 23112
Winfore Ct & Dr 23113
Wing Haven Pl 23112
Winning Colors Ct, Ln & Pl 23112
Winter Ridge Ln 23113
Winterberry Ct, Rdg & Ter 23112
W Winterfield Ln & Rd 23113
Winterhaven Ct & Rd 23112
Winterpock Rd 23112
Witton Turn 23113
Wivenhall Dr 23112
Wivenhaust Rd 23112
Wood Sage E & W 23114
Woodbriar Ct & Rdg 23112
Woodbridge Crossing Ct, Dr & Way 23112
Wooded Oak Pl 23113
Woodlake Commons Loop 23112
Woodlake Village Cir, Ct & Pkwy 23112
Woodland Creek Way 23114
Woodmont Dr 23113
Woods Walk Ct, Ln & Rd 23112
Woodsong Dr 23112
Woodthrush Ct 23112
Wooferton Ct, Dr & Pl 23112
Worchester Ct & Rd 23113
Worsham Green Ct, Pl & Ter 23114
Wycombe Rd 23112
Wylderose Ct & Dr 23113
Wylderose Commons 23113
Wynn Ln 23112
Yarcombe Rd 23112
Yatesbury Ln 23113
Young Manor Dr 23113

NEWPORT NEWS VA

General Delivery 23601
General Delivery 23602
General Delivery 23603
General Delivery 23605
General Delivery 23606
General Delivery 23607
General Delivery 23608

POST OFFICE BOXES MAIN OFFICE STATIONS AND BRANCHES

Box No.s
A - P 23605
967A - 967A 23607
1 - 980 23607
18 - 18 23605
1001 - 1999 23601
2001 - 2999 23609
3001 - 3368 23603
5001 - 5945 23605
6001 - 6700 23606
9998 - 9998 23612
9998 - 9998 23607
11001 - 11316 23601
12001 - 12994 23612
14001 - 16238 23608
22200 - 22709 23609
120001 - 120674 23612

NAMED STREETS

Abaco Dr 23605
Abbey Ct 23602
Abbitt Ln 23606
Aberdeen Ave 23607
Aberthaw Ave 23601
Abingdon Ct 23608
Abraham Ct & Ln 23605
Academy Ln 23602
Achievement Way 23606
Acorn Ave 23607
Ada Ter 23608
Adams Dr 23601
Adams Wood Ln 23602
Adelaide St 23605
Adena Ct 23605
Adrienne Pl 23602
Advocate Ct 23608
Adwood Ct 23605
Agusta Dr 23601
Alan Dr 23602
Albemarle Cir 23605
Alberta Dr 23602
Alexander Dr 23602
Allison Rd 23602
Almond Dr 23601
Alpine St 23606
Alta Cres 23608
Alva Cir 23608
Amber Ct 23606
American Legion Dr 23608
Americana Dr 23606
Amesbury Ln 23606
Amherst Ave 23605
Amy Brooks Dr 23606
Anchor Bay Cv 23602
Anchorage Dr 23602
Anderson Cir 23606
Andover Ct 23608
Andover Dr 23605
Andrew Pl 23605
Angelo Dr 23608
Anne Dr 23601
Anne Burras Ln 23606
Annette Ct 23601
Antrim Dr 23601
Apex Dr 23601
Appaloosa Ln 23602
April Ln 23601
Aqua Vista Dr 23607
Aqueduct Dr 23602
Arbor Ct 23606
Arboretum Way 23602
Arcadia Dr 23608
Arch St 23605
Archer Rd 23606
Arden Cir 23608
Arden Dr 23601
Argall Pl 23608
Arline Dr 23608
Arlington Ave 23605
Arnett Dr 23608
Arnold St 23605
Arony St 23605
Arrowhead Dr 23601
Arthur Way 23602
Artillery Pl 23608
Ash Ave 23607
Ashford Pl 23602
Ashland Ct 23606
Ashley Pl 23608
Ashridge Ln 23602
Ashton Green Blvd 23608
Ashway Cv 23606
Ashwood Dr 23602
Aspen Dr 23608
Assembly Ct 23606
Astor Dr 23608
Atkins Ln 23602
Atkinson Way 23608
Austin Ct 23605
Autry Pl 23606
Autumn Cir 23606
Avella Ct 23601
Avenue Of The Arts 23606
Avery Cres 23606
Avis Cir 23608
Avondale Ln 23602
Avora Ct 23608
Aylesbury Dr 23608
Ayrshire Way 23602
Azalea Dr 23602
Backspin Ct 23602
Bacon Ct 23602
Baez Ct 23608
Bailiff Ct 23608
Baker Blvd & Cres 23605
Baldwin Pl 23606
Ballard Dr 23603
Ballard Rd 23601
Balthrope Rd 23608
Banks Ln 23608
Barbara Ct 23608
Barbour Cir & Dr 23606
Barclay Rd 23606
Barksdale Dr 23608
Barney Ct 23605
Barrie Cir 23608
Barrister Pl 23608
Barron Dr
1-99 23608
1500-1599 23603
Basswood Dr 23601
Batson Dr 23602
Battery Pl 23608
Baughman Ct 23607
Baxter Ln 23602
Bay Cliff Ct 23602
Bayberry Dr 23601
Baylor Ct 23602
Beacon Ct 23601
Beacon Way 23606
Beaconsdale Ln 23601
Beamer Pl 23602
Beauregard Way 23603
Bedford Rd 23601
Beech Dr 23601
Beechmont Dr 23608
Beechwood Ave 23607
Beechwood Hls 23608

Belgrave Rd 23602
Belinda Dr 23601
Bell King Rd 23606
Bellamy Pl 23608
Belle Cir 23608
Belle Meade Ct 23602
Bellfield Dr 23608
Bellgate Ct 23602
Bellows Way 23602
Bellwood Rd
400-599 23601
600-699 23605
Belmont Rd 23601
Belray Dr 23601
Belton Pl 23608
Belvedere Dr 23607
Belvoir Cir 23608
Benns Rd 23601
Bent Branch Ln 23608
Bentley Dr 23602
Berger Pl 23606
Berkeley Pl 23608
Berkshire Dr 23602
Bernard Dr 23602
Bernardine Dr 23602
Bethany Ct 23608
Bethel Rd 23608
Bethune Dr 23606
Betty Lee Pl 23602
Beverly Hills Dr 23606
Bexley Park Way 23608
Bickerton Ct 23608
Big Ben Ct 23608
Biltmore Ct 23606
Binnacle Dr 23602
Birch Dr 23601
Birchwood Ct 23608
Bird Ln 23601
Birdella Dr 23605
Birdie Ln 23602
Birdsong Way 23602
Bishop Ct 23602
Black Twig Dr 23602
Blackberry Ln 23608
Blacksmythe Ln 23602
Blackwater Way 23606
Blair Ave 23607
Blake Loop 23606
Bland Blvd 23602
Blanton Dr 23608
Blazer Ct 23608
Blenheim Ct 23608
Blount Point Rd 23606
Bloxom Dr 23608
Blue Heron Trl 23606
Blue Point Ter 23602
Bluebird Ln 23605
Bluecrab Rd 23606
Bluff Ter 23602
Blunt Ct 23606
Bond Cir 23602
Bonita Dr 23602
Bonnie Ln 23606
Bonnie Lee Pl 23605
Boone Pl 23605
Booth Cir & Rd 23606
Bosch Ln 23606
Boston Cv 23606
Bosun Ct 23602
Botetourt Rd 23601
Boucher Dr 23603
Boulder Dr 23608
Bowie Ct 23608
Bowman Ln 23606
Boxley Blvd 23602
Boxwood Ln 23602
Boyd Cir 23608
Boykin Ln 23602
Brackin Ln 23608
Brad Ct 23608
Bradford Cir 23602
Bradmere Loop 23608
Brandon Rd 23601
Brandsby Ct 23608
Brandywine Dr 23602
Brassie Way 23602
Breakwater Dr 23606
Breezy Tree Ct 23608
Brenda Rd 23601
Brennhaven Dr 23602
Brentmoor Ct 23608
Brentwood Dr 23601
Bret Harte Dr 23602
Brewer St 23605
Briar Patch Pl 23606
Briarfield Rd 23605
Brick Kiln Blvd 23602
Bridgewater Dr 23603
Bridle Ln 23608
Brighton Cir & Ln 23602
Brigstock Cir 23606
Britnie Ct 23602
Broad Bay Cv 23602
Brody Pl 23602
Brompton Ct 23608
Brooke Dr 23603
Brooke St 23605
Brookfield Dr 23602
Brookside Dr 23602
Brunswick Pl 23601
Bruton Ave 23601
Bryan Ct 23606
Bryson Ct 23608
Buchanan Dr 23608
Buck Cir 23608
Buckingham Grn 23602
Bulkeley Pl 23601
Bunker Hill Cir 23602
Burcher Rd 23606
Burghley Ct 23608
Burke Ave 23601
Burnham Pl 23606
Burns Ave & Dr 23601
Burwell Cir & Ct 23606
Butler Pl 23606
Butte Cir 23608
Buttercup Ln 23602
Buxton Ave 23607
Cabell Dr 23602
Cades Ct 23606
Caldroney Dr 23602
Cale Cir 23606
Calla Ct 23608
Callahan Walk 23601
Calm Branch Ct 23602
Calvert Dr 23601
Cambertree Way 23608
Cambridge Ct 23602
Camellia Dr 23602
Camelot Ct 23602
Cameron Dr 23606
Campbell Ln & Rd 23602
Campside Ln 23603
Campton Pl 23608
Candle Ln 23608
Candlewood Way 23606
Cannon Dr 23602
Canon Blvd 23606
Canter Ct 23602
Canterbury Run 23602
Canvasback Trl 23602
Captain John Smith
Rd 23606
Captains Ln 23602
Cardinal Ln 23601
Carla Dr 23608
Carleton Rd 23603
Carmella Cir 23602
Carnation Dr 23608
Carnegie Dr 23606
Carolyn Dr 23606
Carriage Ln 23606
Carson Cir 23606
Carver Dr 23605
Carywood Ln 23602
Cascade Dr 23608
Casey Ter 23601
Casey Marie Ln 23605
Casper Ln 23602
Castle Keep Ct 23608
Catalina Dr 23608
Catalpa Dr 23601
Cathy Dr 23608
Catina Way 23608
Cavalier Dr 23608
Cay St 23605
Cebaf Blvd 23606
Cedar Ave 23607
N Cedar Ct 23608
S Cedar Ct 23608
Cedar Ln 23601
Cedar Glen Ct 23602
Cedarwood Way 23608
Center Ave
100-699 23601
700-1099 23605
Center St 23606
Central Pkwy 23606
Cesare Ct 23608
Chad Ln 23605
Chadwick Pl 23606
N & S Chalice Ct 23608
Chambers Rd 23602
Chanco Dr 23606
Chandler Pl 23602
Chanticlar Ct 23608
Chapin Wood Dr 23608
Chapman Way 23608
Charity Ln 23602
Charlemagne Ct 23608
Charles St 23608
Charleston Way 23606
Charlotte Dr 23601
Charter Cir 23606
Charter Oak Dr 23608
Chartwell Dr 23608
Chase Ct 23608
Chatham Dr 23602
Chatsworth Dr 23601
Cheeseman Ct 23608
Chelmsford Way 23606
Chelsea Pl 23603
Cherbourg Dr 23606
Cherokee Ct 23608
Cherokee Dr 23602
Cherry Creek Dr 23608
Cherrywood Ct 23608
Cheryl Cir 23602
Chesapeake Ave 23607
Cheshire Ct 23608
Chester Rd 23608
Chestnut Ave
1600-4999 23607
5000-8299 23605
Cheyenne Dr 23608
Childress Dr 23602
Chinkapin Trl 23608
Chinook Ct 23608
Chipley Dr 23602
Chisom Cir 23608
Chiswick Cir 23608
Choice Ln 23602
Choptank Ln 23602
Chowan Pl 23608
Christian St 23608
Christine Cir 23608
Christopher Pl 23607
Christopher Newport
Dr 23601
Christy Ln 23608
Church Rd 23606
Churchill Ln 23608
Cindy Cir 23602
Circle Dr 23605
Circuit Ln 23608
Citation Dr 23602
Citizens Ln 23602
City Farm Rd 23602
City Line Rd 23607
Civil Ct 23608
Claiborne Pl 23606
Claire Ln 23602
Clay Dr 23606
Claymill Dr 23602
Clearbrook Rd 23608
Clearwater Ct 23602
Clemson Dr 23608
Cleveland Ave 23606
Clifton Ct 23608
Clinton Dr 23605
Clipper Dr 23602
Cloverleaf Ln 23601
Club Ter 23606
Clubhouse Way 23608
Coach Trl 23608
Coachman Cir 23608
Cobb Cir 23602
Cobbler Way 23608
Cobblestone Cir 23608
Cobham Hall Cir 23608
Colberts Ln 23601
Colleen Dr 23608
N College Blvd & Dr 23606
Collette Ct 23602
Collins Dr 23601
Collinwood Pl 23602
Coloma Dr 23608
Colombia Dr 23608
Colonial Pl 23601
Colony Rd 23602
Colony Pines Dr 23608
Colony Square Ct 23602
Columbus Way 23606
Comfort Cv 23606
Commerce Dr 23607
Commercial Pl 23606
E & W Commodore Dr 23601
Community Ln 23608
Compass Way 23606
Compton Pl 23606
Concord Cres 23606
Congress St 23608
Connors Dr 23608
Constance Dr 23601
Continental Pkwy 23602
Converse Ct 23608
Conway Rd 23606
Cooper Ct 23602
Copeland Ln 23601
Copley Pl 23602
Coral Ct 23606
Coral Key Pl 23606
Corbin Dr 23606
Corinthia Dr 23608
Cornell Dr 23608
Cornwallis Pl 23608
Corporate Dr 23602
Costigan Dr 23608
Cottage Ln 23603
Cottonwood St 23608
Country Club Rd 23606
Court House Dr 23608
Courtney Ave 23601
Cove Rd 23608
Coventry Ln 23602
Cowgirl Ln 23608
Cox Lndg 23608
Crafford Rd 23603
Craig Ave 23601
Cranbrook Ct 23602
Crane Cir 23608
Cranefield Pl 23602
Creasy Ave 23601
Creekmere Cv 23603
Creekpoint Cv 23603
Creekshire Cres 23603
Creekstone Dr 23603
Cremona Dr 23608
Crescent Way 23608
Crestmont Pl 23606
Crestwood Dr 23601
Cristal Dr 23608
Criston Dr 23602
Crittenden Ln 23606
Croatan Rd 23606
Cromwell Ct 23606
Crosland Ct 23608
Cross Rd 23606
Crossbow Ct 23602
Crossings Ct 23608
Croswell Pl 23605
Crown Ct 23608
Crown Point Dr 23602
Crutchfield Dr 23602
Cub Ln 23602
Culpepper Ave 23606
Cumberland Dr 23608
Cursors Way 23606
Curtis Dr 23603
Curtis Tignor Rd 23608
Custer Pl 23608
Cynthia Ct 23608
N & S Cypress Ct &
Ter 23608
D Lane Dr 23608
Dabney Dr & Pl 23602
Dahlia Ct 23608
Daisy Cir 23608
Dallas Dr 23608
Dana Cir 23602
Dana Rae Ct 23605
Daniel Dr 23601
Daphia Cir 23601
Darden Dr
700-799 23602
800-804 23608
806-899 23608
Darlene Ln 23608
Darrington Ct 23601
Dartmoor Dr 23608
David Cir 23602
Davis Ave 23601
Davis Park Dr 23605
Dawn Ter 23601
Day Cir 23608
Day One Ct 23602
Daybreak Cir 23602
Daylight Ct 23602
Daylily Ln 23608
De Gaule St 23605
De Laura Dr 23608
De Wald Cir 23602
Deal Dr 23608
Dean Ray Ct 23605
Deans Cir 23606
Deauville Cir 23606
Debbie Ln 23602
Deborah Ln 23605
Decatur St 23605
Deencout Dr 23602
Deep Creek Rd 23606
Deep Spring Dr 23602
Deep Water Cv 23606
Deer Path Trl 23608
Deer Run Trl 23602
Deidre Ln 23602
Dellwood Dr 23602
Delmar Ln 23602
Deloice Cres 23602
Delois Ave 23606
Delta Cir 23601
Denbigh Blvd 23608
Denbigh Park Dr 23608
Dendron Pl 23602
Depriest Downs 23608
Deputy Ln 23608
Derry Ct 23602
Deshazor Dr 23608
Devol Dr 23608
Devon Pl 23606
Diane Trl 23601
Digges Dr 23602
Diligence Dr 23606
Dillwyn Dr 23602
Dilts Dr 23608
Dimmock Ave 23601
Dinwiddie Pl 23608
Diplomat Ct 23608
Dixie Pl 23601
Doe Ln 23602
Doewood Ln 23608
N Dogwood Ct 23608
S Dogwood Ct 23608
Dogwood Dr 23606
Dominion Dr 23602
Don Eve Ct 23602
Don Rett Cir 23608
Donna Pl 23606
Dora Dr 23602
Doral Dr 23602
Dorchester Ct 23601
Dorene Pl 23608
Dorothys Dr 23608
Dorsey Rd 23606
Douglas Dr 23601
Dove Ct 23606
Downing Pl 23606
Dozier Rd 23603
Drake Ct 23606
Draper Ln 23606
Dresden Dr 23601
Drivers Ln 23602
Drum Pointe 23603
Dublin Ct 23601
Dubois Dr 23602
Duke St 23607
Duncombe Ln 23608
Dundee Way 23608
Dunhill Way 23602
Dunmore Dr 23602
Dunnavant Ln 23606
Durant Trl 23603
Dusk Ct 23606
Dutchess Ln 23608
Duxbury Cir 23602
Dwight Rd 23601
Eads Ct 23608
Eagle Ln 23605
Earle Ct 23608
Eastfield Ln 23602
Eastnor Ct 23608
Eastwind Cv 23606
Eastwood Dr 23602
Ebb Cove Ct 23602
Echo Ridge Ct 23603
Eclipse Ct 23606
Ed Wright Ln 23606
Edgemoor Dr 23603
Edgewater Dr 23602
Edgewood Dr 23606
Edith Wharton Sq 23606
Edmond Dr 23606
Edney Dr 23602
Edsyl St 23602
Edwards Ct 23608
Edythe St 23605
Effingham Pl 23608
Egret Ct 23608
Elaine Dr 23602
Elder Rd 23608
Eleanor Ct 23602
Electra Dr 23602
Elizabeth Ct 23605
Ellen Rd 23605
Elliffe Rd 23601
Elm Ave 23601
N Elm Ct 23608
S Elm Ct 23608
Elmhurst St 23603
Elowro Rd 23602
Elsie Dr 23608
Elton Hall Cir 23608
Emerald Ct 23608
Emerson Cir 23602
Emily Dickinson N & S 23606
Emma Dr 23605
Emma Kate Ct 23605
Empire Ct 23608
Emrick Ave 23601
Enos Ct 23608
Enterprise Dr 23603
Erin Ln 23605
Erin Leigh Cir 23602
Estelle Ct 23608
Etna Dr 23608
Eton Cv 23608
Eubank Cir 23601
Eugene Oneil St S 23606
Eureka Loop 23601
Eva Ct 23601
Evelyn Ct 23605
Evelyn Dr 23602
Everett Dr 23602
Evergreen Dr 23606
Excalibur Pl 23602
Executive Dr 23606
Exeter Rd 23602
Export Cir 23601
F Scott Fitzgerald St 23606
Fairfax Ave 23605
Fairfield Ct 23602
Fairview Rd 23606
Fairway Ln 23606
Faith Ave 23602
Falcon Dr 23606
Falls Reach Pkwy 23603
Falmouth Cir 23602
Faubus Dr 23605
Fauquier Pl 23608
Fawn Ln 23602
Fawn Lake Dr 23608
Fay Cir 23608
Fenwood Cres 23608
Ferguson Ave 23601
Ferguson Cv 23606
Ferguson Ln 23601
Ferinere Rd 23603
Fern Dr 23606
Ferndale Dr 23606
Field Stone Ln 23602
Filson Ct 23608
Fincastle Dr 23601
Finch Pl 23608
First Light Ct 23602
Fischer Dr 23602
Fishers Lndg 23606
Fishing Point Dr 23606
Fitzhugh Dr 23602
Flag Stone Way 23608
Flagship Dr 23608
Flannery Oconner St 23606
Flat Rock Rd 23605
Flax Mill Rd 23602
Fleming Cir & Ct 23606
Flint Dr 23602
Flora Dr 23608
Flowers Ter 23608
Flume Run 23602
Fluvanna Rd 23601
Folsom Ct 23606
Fontaine Rd 23601
Ford Ct 23608
Forest Lake Ct 23605
Forest View Rd 23608
Forrest Dr
1-99 23606
700-799 23601
800-899 23606
Forrestal Cir 23608
Fort St 23608
Fountain Way 23606
Foxboro Dr 23602
Frances St 23601
Francisco Way 23602
Frank Ln 23606
Franklin Rd 23601
Frederick Dr 23601
Freedom Blvd & Way 23602
Friar Cir 23602
Friedman Pl 23608
Friendly Dr 23605
Friendship Rd 23602
Frigate Dr 23608
Fundy Ct 23608
G Ave 23602
Gabriel Ln 23608
Gaelic Ct 23606
Gail Ct 23605
Gainsborough Pl 23608
Galahad Dr 23608
Galleon Dr 23608
Gallery Ct 23601
Gallop Pl 23608
Gambol St 23601
Garden Dr 23607
Garden State Dr 23602
Garfield Dr 23608
Garland Ct & Dr 23606
Garner Ter 23607
Garnett Cir 23602
Garrow Rd
1-199 23602

800-999 23608
Gary Rd 23601
Gate St 23602
Gate House Rd 23608
Gateway Ct 23602
Gatewood Rd 23601
Gawain Dr 23602
Gay Dr 23606
Gaylor Ln 23602
Gena Ct 23602
General Ct 23608
Genneys Way 23602
Georgetown Loop 23608
Georgia Ct 23606
Gilford Ct 23608
Ginger Trl 23608
Gingerwood Ct 23608
Giovanni Ct 23602
Glade Rd 23606
Glen Allen Ct 23603
Glendale Rd 23606
Gleneagles Dr 23602
Gloucester Dr 23605
Godfrey Dr 23602
Goldsboro Dr 23605
Goldsmith Pl 23606
Goode Dr 23602
Goodwin Rd 23606
Goose Cir 23608
Gosnold Pl 23606
E & W Governor Dr 23602
Grace Dr 23602
Graham Dr 23606
Granada Ct 23608
Grand Bay Cv 23602
Grant Dr 23608
Granville Dr 23606
Graves Cir 23602
Grayson Ave 23605
Great Oak Cir 23606
Great Park Dr 23608
Green Ct 23601
N Green Dr 23602
Green Glen Dr 23602
Green Grove Ln 23608
Green Meadows Dr 23608
Green Oaks Rd 23601
Green Tree Cv 23606
Greenway Ave 23605
Greenwich Ln 23601
Greenwood Rd 23601
Greer Pl 23608
Gregg Ct 23602
Gregorys Way 23601
Gresham Cir 23608
Gretna Way 23608
Greystone Trce 23602
Grissom Way 23608
Groome Rd 23601
Grossman Pl 23605
Grove Ct 23608
Guenevere Ct 23602
Gulfstream Dr 23602
Gum Grove Dr 23601
Gum Rock Ct 23606
Gunby Rd 23601
Gunston Ct 23608
Guy Ln 23602
Gwynn Cir 23602
Habershaw Rd 23602
Hadley Pl 23608
Hahn Pl 23602
Hailsham Pl 23608
Halifax Pl 23602
N & S Hall Way 23608
Hallmark Dr 23606
Halperin Walk 23601
Halyard Dr 23608
Hamder Way 23602
Hamilton Dr 23602
Hamlin St 23601
Hammond St 23601
Hampton Ave & Dr 23607
Hanbury Pl 23608
Hancock Dr 23602
Hanover Way 23608

Hanson Dr 23602
Happiness Pl 23608
Happy Creek Pl 23602
Harbor Ln & Rd 23607
Harbor Access Rd 23607
Harbor Watch Pl 23606
Harborview Ln 23602
Harcourt Pl 23602
Hardwick Rd 23602
Hardwood Trl 23608
Harlech Pl 23608
Harpers Dr 23601
Harpersville Rd 23601
Harrell Ct 23602
Harrington Rd 23602
Harris Rd 23606
Harrison Rd 23601
Harry Ct 23605
Harston Ct 23602
Harvest St 23608
Harwood Dr 23603
Hatchland Pl 23608
Hatfield Pl 23608
Haughton Ave & Ln 23606
Haven Ct 23602
Haviland Dr 23601
Hawkeye Ct 23608
Hawksbill Ln 23601
Hawthorne Dr 23602
Hayes Dr 23602
Haystack Landing Rd 23602
Hazelwood Ct 23608
Hazelwood Rd 23605
Heacox Ln 23608
Healey Dr 23608
Hearthstone Way 23608
Heath Pl 23606
Heather Ln 23606
Heatherwood Loop 23602
Heathland Dr 23602
Helen Dr 23602
Helena Dr 23608
Helm Dr 23602
Hemisphere Cir 23601
Hemlock Rd 23601
Henrico Ct 23608
Henry Clay Rd 23601
Hensley Ct & Dr 23602
Heritage Way 23602
Herman Melville Ave 23606
Hermitage Rd 23606
Heron Dr 23608
Hertzler Rd 23602
Hickory Ave 23607
Hickory Point Blvd 23608
Hidden Glen Ct 23608
Hidden Lake Pl 23602
Hiden Blvd 23606
Hidenwood Dr 23606
Hidenwood Shopping Ctr 23606
Highland Ct 23605
Highlands Pkwy 23603
Highwood Cir 23608
Hillard Cir 23602
Hillcrest Dr 23606
Hillsboro Ct 23605
Hillside Ter 23602
Hilltop Dr 23603
Hilmar Pl 23605
Hilton Blvd 23605
Hilton Ter 23601
Hines Ave 23607
Hingeback Cir 23601
Hitchens Ln 23601
Hodges Ln 23606
Hofstadter Rd 23606
Hogan Dr 23606
Holbrook Dr 23602
Holden Ct 23606
Holland Ct 23608
Hollins Ct 23608
Holloway Rd 23602
Holly Dr 23601
Hollymeade Cir 23602
Honeysuckle Ln 23608

Hoopes Rd 23602
Hope Ct 23602
Hopemont Dr 23606
Hopkins St 23601
Horandel Dr 23608
Horizon Ln 23602
Hornet Cir 23607
Hornsby Ln 23602
Horse Pen Rd 23602
Horse Run Gln 23602
Horseshoe Ct 23608
Hosier St 23601
Howard Ct 23601
Huber Rd 23601
Hudson Cir & Ter 23605
Hughes Dr 23608
Huguenot Rd 23606
Hull St 23601
N & S Hunt Club Run 23608
Hunter Rd 23601
Hunters Glenn 23606
Huntgate Cir 23606
Huntington Ave 23607
Huntstree Pl 23602
Hurley Ave 23601
Hussey Ct 23606
Hustings Ln 23608
Huxley Pl 23606
Hyacinth Cir 23608
Hyatt Pl 23606
Idlewood Cir 23606
Ilene Dr 23608
Impala Dr 23606
Indian Springs Dr 23606
Indigo Dam Rd 23606
Industrial Park Dr 23608
Inland View Dr 23603
Iris Ln 23608
Irongate Ct 23602
Isaac Cir 23608
Isham Pl 23608
Island Quay 23602
Island View Dr 23602
Ivy Ave 23607
Ivy Farms Rd 23601
Ivystone Way 23602
J Clyde Morris Blvd
400-999 23601
1000-1099 23602
J Farmer Ct 23601
J William Ct 23601
Jacinth Cir 23608
Jack Shaver Dr 23608
Jacks Pl 23608
Jacobs Ln 23606
Jakes Ln 23608
James Dr 23605
James Baldwin St 23606
James Landing Rd 23606
James River Dr 23601
James River Ln 23606
Jamestown Dr 23606
Jamie Ct 23608
Janet Cir 23601
Jarvis Pl 23605
Jasmine Cir 23608
Jean Ct 23608
Jebs Pl 23607
Jefferson Ave
11719-B-11719-B 23606
1-4999 23607
5000-10499 23605
10500-11599 23601
11600-11708 23606
11710-12099 23606
12100-12799 23602
12800-13549 23608
13550-13554 23603
13551-13555 23608
13556-14599 23603
14601-15099 23603
Jefferson Point Ln 23602
Jefferys Dr 23601
Jenness Ln 23602
Jennifer Pl 23608
Jessica Cir 23606

Jessie Cir 23608
Jester Ct 23608
Joan Cir 23601
Joanna Pl 23606
Joel Ct 23608
John Rolfe Dr 23602
Johnson Ln 23608
Jolama Dr 23602
Jonathan Ct 23608
Jones Rd 23601
Jonquil Ln 23606
Jordan Dr 23606
Jouett Dr 23608
Joyce Cir 23601
Judges Ct 23608
Judy Dr 23608
Jules Cir 23601
Julia Ter 23608
June Ter 23603
Juniper Dr 23601
Jury Ln 23608
Justin Ln 23605
Karen Dr 23608
Kass Ct 23608
Kates Trace Cir 23608
Kathann Dr 23605
Katherine Ct 23601
Katies Cir 23606
Kearny Ct 23608
Keel Ct 23608
Keith Rd 23606
Kelly Pl 23602
Kelso Dr 23601
Kelvin Dr 23606
Kemper Ave 23601
Kendall Dr 23601
Kenilworth Dr 23606
Kennedy Dr 23605
Kenneth Ct 23602
Kensington Dr 23602
Kentwell Ct 23608
Keppel Dr 23608
Kerlin Rd 23601
Kerry Lake Dr 23602
Kestrel Ct 23606
Keswick Cir 23602
Ketch Ct 23608
Kevin Ct 23602
Kidd Ln 23606
Kiln Creek Pkwy 23602
Kimberly Ct 23602
Kindelde Ave 23605
King Arthur Ct 23608
King Forest Ln 23608
King Richard Pl 23602
Kings Ct 23606
Kings Creek Ln 23602
Kings Grant Ct 23608
Kings Ridge Dr 23608
Kingsbury Dr 23606
Kingsman Dr 23608
Kingsmill Dr 23601
Kingstowne Dr 23606
Kingwood Dr 23601
Kinsale Cres 23602
Kirk Dr 23608
Kittywake Dr 23602
Knolls Dr 23602
Knollwood Dr 23608
Kohler Cres 23606
Kristy Ct 23602
Lackey Dr 23606
Lacon Dr 23608
Lacy Cove Ln 23602
Lafayette Dr 23603
Lafayette Ter 23605
Lake Dr 23602
Lake Forest Dr 23602
Lake Pointe Dr 23603
Lakecrest Ct 23602
Lakefront Cmns 23606
Lakeland Dr 23605
Lakeshore Dr 23608
Lakeside Dr 23606
Lakeview Dr 23602
Lakewood Park Dr 23602

Lambert Dr 23602
Lamphier Ln 23606
Lancaster Ln 23602
Lance Dr 23601
Lancelot Ct 23602
Landing Ln 23602
Landmark Ct 23608
Landridge Ct 23608
Lands End Ln 23608
Lanelle Pl 23608
Langhorne Cir & Rd 23606
Langley Ave 23601
Lantern Cir 23606
Lanyard Rd 23602
Laramie Ct 23608
Larchmont Cres 23606
Larissa Dr 23601
Lark Cir 23601
Larson Ct 23602
Lassiter Dr 23607
Lateen Ct 23608
Latham Dr
111-113 23605
116-120 23605
200-599 23601
Latitude Ln 23601
Laurel Ct 23605
Laurel Wood Rd 23602
Laurent Cir 23608
Lawrence Rd 23606
Laydon Cir 23606
Lear Cir & Dr 23602
Lebanon Church Rd 23603
Lee Rd 23605
Leeds Way 23608
Lees Mill Dr 23608
Leeward Way 23601
Leland Pl 23608
Lennon Dr 23601
Lenora Dr 23601
Lentz Pl 23602
Leo Ct 23606
Leonard Ln 23601
Leslie Dr 23606
Lester Rd 23601
Lewallen Dr 23608
Lewis Dr 23606
Lexington Cir 23602
Liberty Cir 23602
Lighthouse Way 23606
Ligon Pl 23608
Lilac Ct 23601
Limetree Ct 23608
Linbrook Dr 23602
Linda Dr 23608
Linden Ave 23606
Lipton Dr 23608
Lisa Dr 23606
Lisbon Dr 23601
N & S Lismore Ct 23602
Little Bluff Rd 23606
Little Dean Cir 23608
Little Gum Rd 23602
Little John Pl 23602
Live Oak Ln 23602
Loch Ness Dr 23602
Lochaven Dr 23602
Lochview Dr 23602
Lockspur Cres 23608
Lockwood Ave 23602
Lodge Ct 23608
Loftis Blvd 23606
Logan Pl 23601
Loggerhead Dr 23601
Lois Ln 23608
Lolas Dr 23606
Lombardy Ave 23606
Long Bridge Way 23608
Longbow Ct 23608
Longfellow Dr 23602
Longleaf Ln 23608
Longmeadow Dr 23601
Longstreet Rd 23606
Longwood Dr 23606
Lookout Cir 23606
Loraine Cir & Dr 23608

Lori Cir 23602
Lost Cv 23606
Lou Mac Ct 23602
Loudon Ln 23601
Louise Dr 23601
Lowell Pl 23602
Lowry Pl 23608
Loyal Ln 23602
Luanita Ln 23606
Lucas Creek Rd
1-13 23602
15-733 23602
735-799 23602
800-999 23608
Lucerne Cir 23606
Lucinda Dr 23608
Lula Carter Rd 23603
Lyliston Ln 23601
Lynchburg Dr 23606
Lyndon Cir 23605
Lynn Dr 23606
Lyon Dr 23601
Lyttle Dr 23606
Mac Neil Dr 23602
Macirvin Dr 23606
Macon Ave 23601
Madeline Pl 23606
Madison Ave
1600-4999 23607
5000-7499 23605
Madison Cir 23606
Madison Ln N 23606
Madison Ln S 23606
Magistrate Ln 23608
Magna Carta Dr 23608
Magnolia Dr 23605
Magruder Rd S 23605
Maid Marion Cir 23602
Main St
1-399 23601
600-899 23605
Mainsail Dr 23608
Mainship Ct 23602
Majestic Ct 23606
Malbon Ave 23601
Malden Ln 23602
Malibu Pl 23608
Mall Pkwy 23602
Mallard Ln 23605
Mallicotte Ln 23606
Mammoth Oak Rd 23606
Mandy Trl 23601
Maney Dr 23605
Manor Rd 23608
Maple Ave 23607
N Maple Ct 23608
S Maple Ct 23608
Maplewood Ct 23608
Marcus Dr 23602
Mare Cir 23608
Margaux Cir 23608
Marie Ct 23601
Marilea Cir 23606
Marina Dr 23608
Marina Ln 23602
Mariner Row 23606
Mariners Ct 23606
Mark Twain Dr 23602
Mark Twain St N 23606
Mark Twain St S 23606
Market Dr 23607
Marlboro Rd 23602
Marlin Dr 23602
Marly Ct 23608
Marquette Ct 23602
Marrow Dr 23606
Marshall Ave
1300-1398 23607
1400-4999 23607
5001-5097 23605
5099-8299 23605
Marshall Pl 23607
Marshview Dr 23608
Martha Cir 23605
Martin Rd 23606
Martire Cir 23601

Marty Ln 23605
Marvin Dr 23608
Mary Robert Ln 23608
Maryle Ct 23602
Mashie Ct 23602
Massell Ct 23606
Massey Ln 23606
Mast Cir 23602
Masters Trl 23602
Matoaka Ln 23606
Matthew Rd 23601
Mattie Cir 23608
Mattmoore Pl 23601
Mattox Dr 23601
Maureen Dr 23602
Maury Ave 23601
Maxwell Ln 23606
May Ct 23602
Mayfield Pl 23608
Mayland Dr 23601
Maymont Dr 23606
Maynard Dr 23601
Maywood Cir 23608
Mccrae Dr 23608
Mcguire Pl 23601
Mckinley Dr 23608
Mcknew Ct 23608
Mclaw Dr 23608
Mclawhorne Dr
500-599 23601
600-799 23605
Mcmanus Blvd 23602
Mcmorrow Dr 23608
Mcstay Ln 23606
Meade Dr 23602
Meadow Dr 23606
Meadow Creek Dr 23608
Meadowlark Ln 23602
Meagan Ct 23608
Mears Cir 23602
Meeting Rd 23606
Meghan Kay Cv 23606
Melena Ct 23601
Mellon St 23606
Melrose Ter 23608
Melville Dr 23602
Menchville Ct & Rd 23602
Mennonite Ln 23602
Mercantile Dr 23607
Merchants Walk 23606
Mercury Blvd 23605
Meredith Way 23606
Merle Dr 23602
Merlyn Walk Pl 23602
Merrimac Ln 23605
Merry Cir & Ln 23606
Merry Oaks Dr 23608
Merry Point Ter 23606
Meta Cir 23608
Mews Ln 23608
Michael Irvin Dr 23608
Michelle Dr 23601
Middle Ground Blvd 23606
Middlesex Rd 23606
Mikes Ln 23605
Miles Cary Rd 23606
Milford Rd 23601
Mill Pond Ct 23602
Mill Run Ct 23603
Miller Rd 23602
Miller Creek Ln 23602
Millers Cove Rd 23602
Millgate Ct 23602
Millwood Dr 23602
Milstead Rd 23606
Mimosa Dr 23606
Minnie Cir 23608
Minton Dr 23606
Minuteman Dr 23602
Mistletoe Dr 23606
Misty Creek Ct 23608
Misty Point Ln 23603
Mitchell Point Rd 23602
Mobile Pl 23606
Mobjack Pl 23606
Mohea Cir 23602

Moline Dr 23606
Mona Dr 23608
Monarch Dr 23602
Monarda Ct 23608
Monica Dr 23606
Monitor Ct 23605
Monroe Ave 23608
Montclare Pl 23606
Monterry Pl 23608
Monticello Ct 23602
Mookie Ct 23602
Moores Ln N & S 23606
Morgan Dr 23606
Moring Ct 23608
Morris Dr 23605
Morrison Ave 23601
Mortar Loop 23603
Motoka Dr 23602
Mount Airy Pl 23608
Moyer Rd 23608
Mulberry Ave 23607
Muller Ln 23606
Municipal Ln 23601
Mura Ct 23608
Museum Dr
  1-99 23601
  100-399 23606
Museum Pkwy 23606
Musika Ct 23602
Musket Ct 23602
Musket Rd 23603
Myles Ct 23602
Myrtle Ct 23608
Mytilene Dr 23605
Nadine Pl 23601
Nancy Ct 23602
Nansemond Dr 23605
Nantucket Pl 23606
Nat Turner Blvd S 23606
Natalie Cir 23608
Nature Way 23602
Nelms Ave 23607
Nelson Dr 23601
Neptune Pl 23602
Nesbitt Ct 23606
Nettles Dr
  12600-12950 23606
  12951-12999 23602
New Haven Ct 23608
New Kent Ct 23602
Newbury Cir 23608
Newcastle Ct 23602
Newday Ct 23602
Newman Dr 23601
Newmarket Dr, Plz & Sq
N 23605
Newmarket Fair Mall 23605
Newport Ave 23601
Newsome Dr 23607
Niblik Way 23602
Nicewood Dr 23602
Nichols Pl 23606
Nicklaus Dr 23602
Nicks Ln 23606
Nicole Pl 23601
Nina Ct 23602
Ninebark Ct 23608
Norma Ct 23602
Normandy Ln 23606
Normill Lndg 23602
North Ave
  100-699 23601
  700-1099 23605
Nottingham Trl 23602
Nurney Dr 23601
Nutmeg Quarter Pl 23606
Oak Ave 23607
S Oak Ct 23608
Oak Mill Ln 23602
Oak Ridge Dr 23603
Oak Springs Ct 23602
Oakland Dr 23601
Oakleaf Ct 23608
Oakwood Pl 23608
Odum Ct 23605
Ohara Ln 23603

Old Ave 23605
Old Bridge Ct & Rd 23608
Old Chestnut Ave 23605
Old Coach Ln 23608
Old Colonial Way 23608
Old Courthouse Way
  14200-14344 23602
  14346-14350 23602
  14351-14699 23608
Old Denbigh Blvd 23602
Old Dominion Cir 23608
Old Fort Eustis Blvd 23608
Old Grist Mill Ln 23602
Old Harpersville Rd 23601
Old Lucas Creek Rd 23602
Old Marina Ln 23602
Old Menchville Rd 23602
Old Mill Ct 23602
Old Oak Dr 23602
Old Oyster Point Rd 23602
Olde Towne Run 23608
Oldham Way 23608
Olin Dr 23602
Olive Dr 23601
Omni Blvd 23606
Onancock Trl 23602
Oneonta Dr 23602
Opal Dr 23602
Opal Pl 23606
Operations Dr 23602
Orangewood Ct 23608
Orchard Cir 23602
Orchendo Dr 23606
Orcutt Ave
  1100-4599 23607
  5500-8599 23605
  8601-8699 23605
Oriana Rd 23608
Orkney Pl 23608
Oscar Loop 23606
Osprey Way 23608
Otsego Dr 23602
Ottis St 23602
Overlook Cv 23602
Owens Rd 23602
Oxburgh Pl 23608
Oxford Rd 23606
Oyster Point Rd 23602
Pacifica Ct 23608
Paddington Ct 23608
Paddock Dr 23606
Padgett Ct 23606
Page Pl 23608
Pagewood Dr 23602
Paine St 23608
Palace Ct 23608
Palen Ave 23601
Palladium Pl 23601
Palmer Ln 23602
Palmerton Dr 23602
Palomino Dr 23602
Pam Ln 23602
Pamela Dr 23601
Pan Ct 23601
Paradise Way 23603
Parish Ave 23607
Park Ave 23607
Park Pl 23601
Park Hill Cir 23602
Parker Ave 23606
Parkside Dr 23608
S Parkview Dr 23605
Parkway Dr 23606
Parliament Ln 23608
Parma Ct 23608
Patel Way 23601
Patricia Dr 23608
Patrick Ln 23608
Patrick Henry Dr &
Mall 23602
Patrick Henry Airport 23602
Patriot Cir 23602
Pats Ln 23605
Patton Dr 23606
Paul St 23605
Paula Dr 23608

Paula Maria Dr 23606
Paulette Dr 23608
Pauline Cir 23602
Pauls Park Cir 23608
Pavilion Pl 23606
Peach Tree Cres 23602
Peachwood Ct 23608
Pear Ave 23607
Pear Ridge Cir 23602
Pear Tree Ct 23608
Pearl Cir 23602
N & S Pecan Ct 23608
Peebles Dr 23602
Peirsey Pl 23608
Pelham Dr 23608
Pelican Cv 23608
Pendleton St 23606
Peninsula Dr 23605
Penn Cir 23606
Pennington Ave 23606
Penrith Ln 23602
Pentrain Dr 23601
Pepper Rd 23608
Pescara Ln 23601
Peters Ln 23606
Petersburg Ct 23606
Peterson Pl 23607
Petes Ln 23605
Petworth Ln 23608
Philip Roth St 23606
Phillips Ln 23602
Picard Dr 23602
Picketts Line 23603
Piez Ave 23601
Pilot House Dr 23606
Pin Oak Rd 23601
Pinckney Ct 23601
Pine Ave 23607
N Pine Ct 23608
S Pine Ct 23608
Pine Bluff Dr 23602
Pine Grove Rd 23601
Pine Mill Ct 23602
Pine Tree Ct 23608
Pineland Cir 23608
Pinewood Ct 23608
Pinnacle Cir 23601
Piper Ln 23602
Pitman Cir 23602
Plainfield Dr 23602
Planetree St 23602
Plantation Rd 23602
Player Ln 23602
Pleasant Ct 23602
Plum Ct 23608
Plymouth Cir 23602
Pocahantas Dr 23608
Pocahontas Dr 23602
Poindexter Pl 23606
Point Heron Dr 23606
Pointe Ct 23601
Pointer Cir 23602
Pointers Gln 23606
Pollard Dr 23601
Polly Ct 23602
Pond View Ct 23602
Pony Ct 23608
Poplar Ave 23607
Port Lndg 23601
Poseidon Dr 23602
Post St 23601
Post Canyon Ct 23608
Potomac Ave 23605
Powder House Dr 23608
Powellville Ln 23601
Powers Ct 23601
Preakness Dr 23602
Prescott Cir 23602
Prestige Ct 23602
Prestwick Ln 23602
Price Cir 23606
Prince Ct 23608
Prince Drew Rd 23606
Prince Edward Cir 23608
Prince George Ln 23608
Prince William Rd 23608

Princess Ct 23608
Princess Anne Cir 23608
Princess Margaret Dr 23602
Prior Rd 23602
Progress Ct 23602
Providence Blvd 23602
Pueblo Rd 23606
Purdey Ct 23608
Purlieu Dr 23606
Putney Ln 23602
Pyes Cir 23601
Quail Pl 23608
Quarter Trl 23608
Quarterfield Rd 23602
Queens Ct 23606
Queensbury Ct 23608
Quillen Ter 23606
Quince Cir 23608
Racine Dr 23608
Radcliff Ln 23602
Radford Pl 23608
Radius Way 23602
Rainbow Ct 23608
Raleigh Rd 23601
Ramshaw Ln 23602
Ranch Dr 23608
Randolph Rd
  1-599 23601
  600-799 23605
Randy Ln 23605
Ratcliffe Pl 23606
Ratley Rd 23606
Raymond Dr 23602
Rebecca Pl 23601
Red Hill Rd 23602
Red Maple Dr 23605
Red Oak Cir 23608
Redbud Ln 23602
Redcedar Way 23608
Reddick Rd 23608
Redwood Ct 23608
Regal Way 23602
Regency Sq 23601
Regents Cv 23606
Renee Ct 23601
Republic Rd 23603
Reserve Way 23602
Reservoir Cir, Ln &
Rd 23608
Revelle Dr 23608
Revermede Ct 23602
Revolution Ln 23608
Revolution Way 23602
Rexford Dr 23608
Reyano Rd 23608
Reynolds Dr 23606
Rhoda Dr 23608
Richland Dr 23608
Richmond Cir 23606
Richneck Rd 23608
Ricks Ln 23605
Ridgeview Dr 23608
Ridgewood Pkwy
  2-8 23602
  9-199 23608
Ridley Cir 23607
Rilee Pl 23606
Ringo Dr 23606
Ripley St 23603
Ripon Way 23608
River Rd
  1-999 23601
  5101-5197 23607
  5199-7699 23607
  9300-9999 23601
River Bend Ct 23602
River Birch Ct 23602
River Mews Dr 23608
River Palms Rd 23608
River Point Cir 23602
River Rock Way 23608
River Trace Way 23602
Riverlands Dr 23605
Rivermont Dr 23601
Rivers Ridge Cir 23608
Riversedge Rd 23606

Riverside Dr 23606
Riverwood Cir 23606
Roam Ct 23605
Roanoke Ave
  1300-4899 23607
  5000-8299 23605
Robbs Ct 23608
Robert Frost St 23606
Roberto Dr 23601
Roberts Rd 23606
Robin Dr 23606
Robin Ln 23605
Robinhood Ln 23602
Robinson Dr 23601
Rochester Ct 23607
Rock Crest Ct 23602
Rock Landing Dr 23606
Rockingham Dr 23601
Rodeo Cir 23608
Roffman Pl 23602
Rogol Ct 23608
Rolfe Pl 23607
Rollingwood Pl 23606
Romayne Dr 23601
Ronald Dr 23602
Ronda Cir 23602
Roosevelt Dr 23608
Rose Ct 23601
Roseman Ct 23608
Rosewood Ln 23602
Roslyn Rd 23601
Ross Dr 23601
Rotunda Cir 23608
Round Table Ct 23602
Rouse Rd 23608
Rouvalis Cir 23601
Royal Springs Ct 23608
Royall Pl 23606
Rugby Rd 23606
Rumson Ave 23601
Rushlake Ct 23602
E & W Russell Ct 23605
Ruston Dr 23602
Ruth Ct 23608
Rutledge Rd 23601
Ryans Run 23608
Saddle Dr 23602
Saddler Dr 23608
Saint Andrews Ln 23608
Saint Croix Dr 23602
Saint Egnatios Dr 23601
Saint Francis Dr 23602
Saint George St 23602
Saint Ives Cir 23601
Saint James Pl 23602
Saint Johns Rd 23602
Saint Lo Ct 23606
Saint Michaels Way 23606
Saint Stephens Dr 23602
Saint Thomas Dr 23606
Saint Tropez Dr 23602
Sally Ann Pl 23602
Salt Pond Pl 23602
Salters St 23607
Samuelson Ct 23605
San Jose Dr 23606
Sandhurst Cir 23601
Sandlewood Dr 23606
Sandpebble Cir 23606
Sandpiper St 23602
Sandra Dr 23608
Sandstone Ct 23608
Sandy Bay Cv 23602
Sanford Dr 23601
Sanlin Dr 23602
Sarah Ct 23606
Sarazen Ct 23602
Satinwood Ln 23602
Satterfield Dr 23606
Saunders Rd 23601
Savage Dr 23602
Savannah Ct 23606
Saxon Ln 23601
Saybrooke Ct 23606
Scenic Ct 23603
Schooner Dr 23602

Scotch Pine Ct 23608
Scott Rd 23606
Scottland Ter 23606
Scufflefield Rd 23602
Sea Pine Ln 23608
Sea Turtle Way 23601
Seagull Ct 23608
Sean Paul Ct 23602
Searalin Ave 23607
Seasons Trl 23602
Seasons Walk Ct 23603
Secluded Pl 23608
Sedgefield Dr 23605
Selden Rd 23606
Selkirk Dr 23602
Settlement Ln 23608
Settlers Rd 23606
Severn Rd 23602
Shade Tree Dr 23601
Shadwell Ct 23601
Shady Ter 23608
Shadywood Dr 23602
Shamrock Ln 23606
Shannon Dr 23608
Shapiro Ct 23606
Sharon Dr 23602
Shasta Dr 23608
Shawn Cir 23602
Sheffield Way 23602
Sheila Cir 23608
Shelby Dr 23608
Shelter Cir 23608
Shenk Rd 23602
Sherbrooke Dr 23602
Sherry Cir 23608
Sherwood Pl 23602
Sherwood Shopping
Plz 23602
Shields Rd 23608
Shiloh Pl 23607
Ships Lndg 23606
Shipyard Dr 23607
Shire Chase 23602
Shirley Rd 23601
Shoe Ln 23606
Shoemaker Cir 23602
Shore Dr 23607
Shore Park Dr 23602
Shoreline Pt 23602
Short St 23607
Sibby Ct 23602
Sidney Pl 23601
Sierra Dr 23606
Signi Hi Ct 23601
Silversmith Cir 23608
Silverwood Dr 23608
Simon Cir 23606
Simone Ct 23601
Sinton Rd 23601
Sir Albert Ct 23608
Sir Arthur Ct 23602
Sir Francis Wyatt Pl 23606
Sir Lionel Ct 23608
Skelton Way 23608
Skiffs Creek Landing
Rd 23603
Skipjack Rd 23602
Skipper Ct 23602
Sloane Pl 23606
Smith Ln 23601
Smokey Trl 23602
Smucker Rd 23602
Snead Dr 23602
Snidow Blvd 23608
Snug Harbor Ln 23606
Sojourner Ct 23602
Somerset Pl 23602
South Ave
  100-699 23601
  700-999 23605
Southgate Rd 23602
Southlake Pl 23602
Sparrow Ct 23608
Spaulding Dr 23602
Spencer Cir 23605
Spinnaker Rd 23602

Split Rail Cir 23602
Spottswood Ln 23606
Spratley Cir 23602
Spring Rd 23606
Spring Trace Ln 23601
Springdale Dr 23608
Springhouse Way 23602
Springmont Ct 23608
Springwell Pl 23608
N Spruce Ct 23608
S Spruce Ct 23608
Spruce Rd 23601
Spur Ct & Dr 23606
Squires Pl 23606
St Clair Dr 23602
Stacis Ln 23602
Stag Ter 23602
Stage Rd 23606
Stallings Ct 23608
Stanley Dr 23608
Stanton Ct & Rd 23606
Starboard Cir 23602
Stardust Cir 23608
States Dr 23605
Steffi Pl 23606
Sterling St 23605
Stevens Rd 23608
Stillwater Ct 23602
Stone Cv 23602
Stonegate Ct 23602
Stonewall Pl 23606
Stoney Creek Ln 23608
Stoneybrook Ln 23608
Stony Dr 23608
Stony Ridge Ct 23608
Stratford Rd 23601
Strawberry Ln 23602
N & S Stuart Rd 23605
Sue Cir 23605
Suite Life Cir 23606
Summer Dr 23606
Summer Day Ct 23601
Summerglen Rdg 23602
Summerlake Ln 23602
Summitt Ln 23601
Sumter Dr 23608
Sun Ct 23605
Sun Haven Ct 23608
Sun Valley Ct 23608
Sundance Pl 23608
Sundown Ln 23606
Sunnywood Rd 23601
Sunrise Ct 23608
Sunset Rd 23606
Superior Ct 23608
Sura Rd 23606
Surry Ave 23605
Susan Constant Dr 23608
Sussex Pl 23602
Swamp Gate Rd 23602
Sweetbriar Dr 23606
Sycamore Ave 23607
Sylvia Ln 23602
Symantec Way 23606
T S Eliot St 23606
Tabbs Ln 23602
Tack Ct 23608
Tahiska Ln 23602
Tahoe Dr 23602
Taliaferro Rd 23603
Tall Pines Way 23606
Talley Pl 23608
Tamara Path 23601
Tanbark Dr 23601
Tangier Ln 23602
Tara Ct 23608
Tarry Pl 23601
Tarrytown Ct 23601
Taylor Ave 23607
Tazewell Rd 23608
Teakwood Dr 23601
Teardrop Ln 23608
Teepee Dr 23602
Telford Dr 23602
Temple Ln 23605
Terminal Ave 23607

Terrace Cir 23605
Terrace Dr 23601
Terrell Rd 23606
Terri Beth Pl 23602
Terri Sue Pl 23608
Thalia Dr 23608
Thimble Shoals Blvd
600-738 23606
739-799 23606
739-739 23612
740-798 23606
Thimbleby Dr 23608
Thisdell Ln 23607
Thorncliff Dr 23608
Tidal Dr 23606
Tiffany Ln 23608
Tillerson Dr 23602
Timberline Cres 23606
Timberneck Ln 23602
Timothy Cir 23608
Tindall Ct 23602
Tinsley Ct 23608
Tipton Rd 23606
Tivoli Pl 23605
Todd Trl 23602
Tokay Rd 23601
Topsider Ct 23608
Tower Ln 23608
Town Center Dr 23606
Town Pointe Way 23601
Towne Square Dr 23607
Tradewind Cir 23602
Trails Ln 23608
Transit Ln 23601
Traverse Rd
1-99 23606
100-199 23601
Treasure Ct 23608
Tree Dr 23606
Treeland Ct 23608
Treetop Pl 23608
N & S Trellis Ct 23608
Trent Cir 23602
Tricia Ln 23601
Triton Ct 23606
Trouville Ct 23606
Troy Dr 23606
Troy Pl 23608
Trumble Ln 23608
Truswood Ln 23608
Truxtun Ct 23608
Tuckahoe Dr 23606
Tucker Ln 23606
Tudor Ct 23603
Tug Boat Ln 23606
Tukaway Ct 23601
Tulip Dr 23608
Turlington Rd 23606
Turnberry Blvd
500-680 23602
682-698 23602
685-685 23608
Turpin Pl 23602
Tuscon Ct 23605
Twig Ln 23608
Twin Lake Cir 23608
Tyler Ave 23601
Tyndall Dr 23606
Tyner Dr 23608
Union St 23607
University Pl 23606
Valentine Ct 23606
Valley Forge Dr 23602
Van Dyke Ln 23606
Vantage Ct 23602
Venetia Ct 23608
Ventnor Dr 23608
Ventura Way 23608
Vera Cir 23601
Verlander Ct 23608
Verline Ct 23608
Vernon Pl 23605
Vicky Ct 23602
Victoria Sta 23608
View Pointe Dr 23603
Viking Dr 23602

Villa Rd 23601
Village Pkwy 23601
Village Green Pkwy 23602
Virginia Dr 23602
Viscount Dr 23602
Vista Dr 23608
Vivian Cir 23602
Von Steuben Dr 23603
Wade Cir 23602
Wakefield Rd 23606
Walden Pond Ct 23608
Wallace Cir 23606
Walnut Ave 23607
Walnut Grv 23606
Walt Whitman Ave 23606
Walters Rd 23602
Waltham Cir 23608
Wanger Cir 23602
Ward Ct 23602
Ware Ln 23602
Warner Hall Pl 23608
Warren Dr 23608
Warwick Blvd
2500-9299 23607
9300-12241 23601
12250-12298 23606
12300-12950 23606
12951-14105 23602
14104-14104 23609
14106-14398 23602
14107-14399 23602
14400-15999 23608
16800-17499 23603
17501-17699 23603
Warwick Cres 23601
Warwick Landing Pkwy 23608
Warwick Moose Ln 23606
Warwick Springs Dr 23602
Warwick Village Shop Ctr 23601
Warwickshire Ct
500-599 23601
600-699 23605
Washington Ave 23607
Washington Dr 23603
Water Oak Ct 23602
Waterfowl Ln 23602
Waterfront Cir 23607
Watergate Ter 23606
Waterman Dr 23602
Watermill Run 23606
Waters Edge Dr 23606
Waterview Dr 23608
Waterworks Way 23608
Watson Dr 23602
Waverly Pl 23608
Wayfin Cir 23606
Weatherford Way 23602
Wedgewood Dr N 23601
Weldun Ct 23608
Welford Ln 23606
Wellesley Dr 23606
Wellie Ct 23602
Wellington Cir 23603
Wells Rd 23602
Wendfield Cir 23601
Wendwood Dr 23602
Wendy Ct 23601
Wesley Pond Ct 23608
Wesleyan Ct 23602
West Ave 23607
Western Dr 23608
Westgate Ct 23602
Weston Ct 23608
Westover Rd 23601
Westport Cres 23602
Westwind Dr 23602
Weyanoke Ln 23608
Whaler Dr 23608
Wheeler Dr 23608
Whisley Ct 23608
Whisperwood Dr 23602
Whitaker Ct 23603
White House Cv 23602
White Oak Dr 23601

White Stone Ct 23603
Whitebrook Ln 23602
Whites Ln 23606
Whitewater Dr 23608
Whitman Rd 23602
Whits Ct 23606
Whittier Ave 23606
Wickham Ave
900-3699 23607
5900-8299 23605
Wickham Pl 23607
Widgeon Cir 23602
Wilcox Ln 23605
Wilderness Way 23608
Wildwood Ct 23602
Willard Pl 23606
Willbrook Rd 23602
William Faulkner N & S 23606
William Styron Sq N & S 23606
Williams St 23607
Williamsburg Ct 23606
Williamson Dr 23608
Williamson Park Dr 23608
Willis Dr 23606
N Willow Ct 23608
S Willow Ct 23608
Willow Cv 23602
Willow Dr 23605
Willow Pt 23602
Willow Bend Ct 23608
Willow Green Dr 23602
E & W Willow Point Pl 23602
Wilmont Ln 23608
Wilson Cir 23606
Wiltshire Cres 23608
Windbrook Cir 23602
Windemere Rd 23602
Winder Cres 23606
Windjammer Cres 23602
Windsor Ct 23608
Windsor Castle Dr 23608
Windsor Pines Way 23608
Windward Way 23601
Windy Way 23602
Windy Ridge Ln 23602
Windy Tree Ln 23608
Winslow Dr 23608
Winston Ave & Pl 23601
Winterhaven Dr 23606
Winthrope Dr 23602
Witness Ln 23608
Wolf Dr 23601
Wolftrap Ct 23605
Wood Duck Ln 23602
Wood Post Ct 23608
Woodall Ct 23608
Woodbridge Dr 23608
Woodbrook Run 23606
Woodburne Ln 23602
Woodbury Ct 23602
Woodcreek Dr 23608
Woodfin Rd
1-599 23601
600-799 23605
Woodhaven Rd 23608
Woodlake Cir 23606
Woodland Dr 23606
Woodnote Ln 23608
Woodroof Rd 23606
Woods Rd
100-799 23601
800-899 23606
Woodside Ln
12700-12799 23602
12801-12899 23602
13400-13499 23608
Woodstock Dr 23606
Woolridge Pl 23601
Worcester Way 23602
Wreck Shoal Dr 23606
Wrenn Cir 23608
Wright Dr 23605
Wyemouth Dr 23602
Wyn Dr 23608

Wyndham Ct 23608
Wynstone Ct 23602
Wythe St 23608
Yarmouth Cir 23602
Yeardley Dr 23601
Yoder Ln 23602
York Cir 23605
York River Ln 23602
Yorkshire Ln 23608
Yorktown Rd 23603
Youngs Rd 23602
Youngs Mill Ln 23602
Yves Cir 23605
Zenith Loop 23601
Zipp Dr 23605
Zoeller Ct 23602

NUMBERED STREETS

5th St 23607
6th St 23607
9th St 23607
11th St 23607
12th St 23607
13th St 23607
14th St 23607
15th St 23607
16th St 23607
17th St 23607
18th St 23607
19th Pl & St 23607
20th St 23607
21st St 23607
22nd St 23607
23rd St 23607
24th St 23607
25th St 23607
26th St 23607
27th St 23607
28th St 23607
29th St 23607
30th St 23607
31st St 23607
32nd St 23607
33rd St 23607
34th St 23607
35th St 23607
36th St 23607
37th St 23607
38th St 23607
39th St 23607
40th St 23607
41st St 23607
42nd St 23607
43rd St 23607
44th St 23607
45th St 23607
46th St 23607
47th St 23607
48th St 23607
49th St 23607
50th St 23607
600-699 23605
51st St 23607
52nd St 23607
53rd St 23607
54th St 23607
55th St 23607
56th St 23607
5501-5599 23605
57th St 23607
58th St 23607
500-599 23605
59th St 23607
60th St 23607
1300-1398 23605
61st St 23607
62nd St 23607
63rd St 23607
64th St 23607
65th St 23607
66th St 23607
67th St 23607
68th St 23607
69th St 23607
70th St 23607

71st St 23607
72nd St 23607
600-1299 23605
73rd St
200-399 23607
600-1299 23605
74th St 23605
75th St 23607
75th St 23607
1000-1299 23605
76th St 23605
77th St 23605
78th St 23605
79th St 23605
80th St 23605
81st St 23605
82nd St 23605

NOKESVILLE VA

General Delivery 20181

POST OFFICE BOXES MAIN OFFICE STATIONS AND BRANCHES

Box No.s
All PO Boxes 20182

NAMED STREETS

All Street Addresses 20181

NORFOLK VA

General Delivery 23501

POST OFFICE BOXES MAIN OFFICE STATIONS AND BRANCHES

Box No.s
1 - 2914 23501
3000 - 3996 23514
4501 - 4814 23523
6001 - 6398 23508
7001 - 7996 23509
8001 - 8960 23503
8990 - 9007 23501
9000 - 9000 23509
9161 - 9915 23505
9998 - 9998 23519
10001 - 10944 23513
11001 - 11786 23517
12000 - 12954 23541
13001 - 13754 23506
14001 - 14560 23518
15000 - 15539 23511
18000 - 18500 23501
41001 - 41504 23541
55001 - 55600 23505
99001 - 99158 23509

NAMED STREETS

A Ave
700-999 23504
1800-1999 23511
A St 23511
A View Ave 23503
Abbey Rd 23509
Abbott Ln 23505
Abilene Ave 23502
Abingdon Cir 23513
Adair Ave 23502
Adderley St 23502
Addison St 23510
Adele Ct & Dr 23518

Admiral Taussig Blvd S 23511
Afton Ave 23505
Air Cargo Rd 23511
Airway Ln 23502
Alabama Ave 23513
Alabama Rd 23503
Alarranc Ave 23509
Albemarle Dr 23503
Albert Ave 23513
Alden Pl 23523
Alder St
1500-1599 23502
2300-2799 23513
Aldow Dr 23518
Alexander St 23513
Alfred Ln 23503
Algonquin Rd 23505
Alida Ct & Dr 23518
Allen St 23505
Alma Dr 23518
Almeda Ave 23513
Almond Ave 23502
Alpine Ct & St 23503
Alsace Ave 23509
Alson Dr 23508
Amarillo Ave 23502
Ambler Ave 23513
Amelia St 23504
Amherst St 23513
Anderson St 23504
Andes Ct 23502
Andrea Dr 23518
Andrew Ln 23505
Anglewood Ct 23518
Anita Ct 23518
Anna St 23502
Anne St 23504
Apex St 23503
Appleton Dr 23502
Appletree Ln 23505
Appomattox St 23523
Ara St 23503
Arbor Ave 23513
Arcadia St 23502
Archcove Ct 23502
E Arden Cir 23505
Ardmore Rd 23518
Argall Ave & Cres 23508
Argonne Ave 23509
Argyle Ave 23505
Arizona Ave 23513
Arkansas Ave
1500-1599 23502
2300-2799 23513
Arlington Ave 23523
Armfield Ave & Cir 23505
Armistead Bridge Rd 23507
Arrowwood Ct & St 23518
Arthur Cir 23502
Asbury Ave 23513
Asfari Ct 23513
Ashby Ct & St 23502
Ashland Ave & Cir 23509
Ashlawn Dr 23505
Aspin St
1500-1599 23502
2300-2499 23513
Astor Cir 23505
Atlans St 23503
Atlanta Ln 23503
Atlantic St
100-125 23510
126-128 23514
127-199 23510
130-198 23510
Atterbury St 23513
Atwater Cir 23509
Atwood Ave 23503
Auburn Ave 23513
Austin St 23503
Avenue E 23513
Avenue F 23513
Avenue G 23513
Avenue H 23513
Avenue I 23513

Avenue J 23513
Avionics Loop 23511
Avon Rd 23513
Avory Ave 23523
Ayliff Rd 23513
Aylwin St 23511
Azalea Ct
900-999 23517
1000-1099 23507
1101-1499 23507
Azalea Garden Rd
1100-1599 23502
2300-3499 23513
5700-7999 23518
W Azalea Point Rd 23518
B Ave
700-899 23504
1800-1999 23511
B St 23511
Bacon Ave 23511
Baecher Ln & Rd 23509
Bagnall Rd 23504
Bailey St 23518
Bainbridge Ave 23511
Bainbridge Blvd 23523
Baker St
100-399 23505
1800-1899 23511
Baldwin Ave
600-899 23517
900-1099 23507
Ball Ave & Ct 23518
Ballentine Blvd
700-2199 23504
2200-3099 23509
Baltimore St 23505
E & W Balview Ave 23503
Bancker Rd
601-699 23505
701-797 23518
799-899 23518
Bangor Ave 23502
Bank St 23510
Bankhead Ave 23513
Banning Rd 23518
Bapaume Ave 23509
Barbara Dr 23518
Barberry Ln 23505
Barcliff Rd 23505
Barharbor Dr 23502
Barkwood Dr 23518
Barney St 23504
Barnhollow Cir & Rd 23502
Barraud Ave 23504
Barre St 23504
Bartee St 23502
Bartin St 23513
Barton St 23523
Batan Ct 23518
Battersea Rd 23503
Baxter St 23504
E & W Bay Ave 23503
Bay Dunes Dr 23503
Bay Front Dr 23518
Bay Oaks Pl 23518
Bay Point Dr 23518
Bayberry Dr & Ln 23502
Baychester Ave 23503
Bayne Ave 23504
Bayonne St 23505
Bayside Ave 23518
E & W Bayview Blvd 23503
Bayville Ct & St 23503
Baywood Ct & Dr 23518
Beach Ave 23504
E Beach Dr 23518
Beach View St 23503
Beachmont Ave 23504
Beacon Hill Cir & Ct 23502
Beamon Ct & Rd 23513
Bearden Rd 23503
Beatty St 23518
Beaumont Ct & St 23503
Beauregard St 23513
Beck St 23503
Becket St 23518

Street	ZIP
Beckner St	23509
Bedford Ave	23508
Beechwood Ave	23505
Beechwood Pl	23507
Beekman St	23502
Belgrave Ave	23503
Bell St	23513
Bellamy Ave	23523
Bellefield Rd	23502
Bellevue Ave	23509
Bellinger Blvd	23511
Bellmore Ave	23504
W Belvedere Rd	23505
Benjamin Ave	23518
Benningfield Ct	23503
Benton St	23502
Benwood Rd	23502
Bergen St	23518
E & W Berkley Ave & Plz	23523
Berkley Avenue Ext	23523
Berry Hill Rd	23502
Bertha St	23513
Bess St	23513
Bessie St	23513
Beth Ct	23502
Betty Ct	23502
Beverly Ave	23505
Bi County Rd	23518
Biak Ave	23511
Bill St	23518
Billings St	23504
Biltmore Rd	23505
Birch St	
1500-1599	23502
2301-2305	23513
2307-2500	23513
2502-2898	23513
Birmingham Ave	23505
Bison Ave	23518
Bivens Ct	23518
Blackstone St	23502
Blackwood Ave	23513
Blades St	23503
Blair Ave	23509
Blake Rd	23505
Bland St	23513
Blanford Cir & Rd	23505
Blow St	23507
Blueberry Rd	23518
Bluestone Ave	23508
Boissevain Ave	23507
Bolling Ave	23508
Bolton St	23504
Bond St	23504
Bondale Ave	23505
E & W Bonner Dr	23513
Bonnot Dr	23513
Booth St	23504
Borb Ave	23518
Bordeaux Pl	23509
E Botetourt Ct	23507
N Botetourt Ct	23507
S Botetourt Ct	23507
W Botetourt Ct	23507
Botetourt Gdns	
600-1199	23507
1200-1399	23517
Botetourt St	
300-599	23510
700-899	23507
Boulder Ln	23502
Bourbon Ave	23509
Boush St	23510
Boush Way	23502
Boush Creek Ave	23505
Bowdens Ferry Rd	23508
Bowe Pl	23504
Bower St	23504
Bowwood Ln	23518
Boxwood Cir	23518
Boyce Ct & Dr	23509
Bracey St	23504
Brackenridge Ave	23505
S Braden Cres	23502
Bradford Ave	23505
Bradley Ave	23518
E Brambleton Ave	
201-297	23510
299-699	23510
700-1900	23504
1902-2098	23504
W Brambleton Ave	23510
Branch Rd	23513
Branchwood Ct & St	23518
Brandon Ave	
800-999	23517
1000-1499	23507
N Brandon Ave	23507
Breezy Point Cres & Dr	23511
Brennan Ave	23502
Brentwood Dr	23518
Brest Ave	23509
Briar Hill Rd	23502
Briarwood Cir	23518
Brickby Rd	23505
Brickell Rd	23502
Brickhouse Ave	23504
Bridgette Ln	23518
Bridle Way	23518
Brightley Rd	23509
Brighton St	23503
Brinda Ave & Ct	23502
Bristol Ave	23502
N & S Briston Ct	23505
Broadfield Rd	23503
Broadway St	23504
Brock Cir	23502
Brockwell Ave	23502
Bromley Ct	23518
Brooke Ave	23510
Brookfield Rd	23518
Brookneal Ct	23513
Brookside Ct	23502
Brookville Rd	23502
Brookwood Ct & Rd	23518
Broughton St	23502
Brown Ave	23504
Bruce St	23513
Brunswick Ave	23508
Buchanan St	
1001-1099	23523
1700-1799	23511
Buck Rd	23504
Buckingham Ave	23508
Buckingham St	23513
Buckman Ave	23503
Budd Ct & Dr	23518
Buffalo Ave & Ct	23518
Bull Run Ct	23518
Bunker Hl	23511
Bunsen Ct	23513
Burbank Ct	23502
Burgoyne Rd	23503
Burksdale Rd	
501-597	23505
599-699	23505
700-1299	23518
Burleigh Ave	23505
Burrage Rd	23503
Burrell Ave	23518
Burton Station Rd	23502
E & W Bute St	23510
Buttercup Cir	23518
Butterworth St	23505
Buxby Ct	23505
C Ave	
700-899	23504
1800-1999	23511
C St	23505
E C St	23511
W C St	23511
C V Towway	23511
Cabot Ave	23502
Calhoun St	23504
Caliente St	23518
Calla Ave	23503
Calvin Ave & Ct	23518
Cambridge Cres & Pl	23508
Camellia Ln	23505
Camellia Rd	23518
Campbell Ave	23508
Campos Pl	23523
Campostella Rd	23523
Canton Ave	23523
Cap Ln	23503
Cape Henry Ave	
2800-2998	23509
3000-3100	23509
3102-3298	23509
3300-3498	23513
3500-5499	23513
5501-5599	23513
6100-6199	23502
S Cape Henry Ave	
2900-3198	23504
3200-3299	23504
3301-5199	23502
Capella Dr	23505
Capeview Ave	
8300-8399	23518
8400-9699	23503
Capeview Cres	23503
Capeview Ct	23518
Capitol Ave	23503
Captains Way	23518
Caribou Ave	23518
Carillo Ave	23508
Carl St	23505
Carlisle Way	23505
Carlton Ct	23503
Carlton St	
7900-8416	23518
8417-8427	23503
8418-8428	23518
8429-8599	23503
Carmichael Ave	23504
Carolina Ave	
400-799	23508
9500-9599	23511
Caroline St	23505
Carona Ave	23504
Carr St	23504
Carraway Ct	23505
Carrene Dr	23518
Carriage Ln	23518
Carroll Pl	23508
Carswell St	23504
Cary Ave	23504
Cass St	23523
Castleton Pl	23505
Catalpa St	23508
Catherine St	23505
Caton St	23505
Cavern Ct	23518
Cecelia St	23504
Cedar Ln	23508
Cedar Level Ave	23505
Cedarwood Ct	23513
N Center Dr	23502
Central Ave	23513
Central Business Park Dr	23513
Chalfin Ave	23513
Chambers St	23502
Chanelka Rd	23503
Chapel Rd	23511
Chapel St	23504
Chapin St	23503
Charleston St	23505
Charlney Ave	23502
Charlotte St	23504
E Charlotte St	23510
W Charlotte St	23510
Charnwood Ct	23513
Chatham Cir	23513
Chela Ave	23503
Chelsea Ave	23503
Cherry St	23503
Chesapeake Blvd	
2600-3299	23509
3300-7299	23513
7301-7699	23513
7900-7916	23518
7918-8499	23518
8500-9699	23503
Chesapeake St	23503
Cheshire Ave	23504
E & W Chester St	23503
Chesterfield Blvd	23504
Chevy Cir	23505
Child Care Ct	23502
Childrens Ln	23507
Chipping Rd	23505
Chironna Pl	23518
Christopher Ct	23513
Chryslon Ln	23513
Church St	
600-602	23501
601-601	23510
603-1199	23510
1200-3099	23504
Circle Ct & Dr	23503
Citadel Rd	23518
E City Hall Ave	
201-497	23510
499-899	23510
1000-1198	23504
W City Hall Ave	23510
Claiborne Ave	23504
Clare Rd	23513
Claremont Ave	23507
Clarence St	23502
Clarion Ln	23513
Clark Cir	23509
Claud Ln	23505
Clay Ave	23504
Clayton Dr	23513
Clements Ave	23513
Clemson Ave	23518
Cleveland St	23502
Clifton St	23523
Cloncurry Rd	23505
Cloverleaf St	23502
Coach Way Dr	23502
Coburn Cres	23509
Cohoon Rd	23505
Coinbrook Ave	23518
Colane Rd	23518
Colchester Cres	23504
Cold Storage Rd	23511
Coleman Ave	23503
Colgate Ave	23518
Colin Dr	23518
College Pl	23510
College Cross	23510
Colley Ave	
1-199	23510
201-299	23510
400-1199	23507
1200-2799	23517
2800-5299	23508
Colmar Quarter	23509
Colon Ave	23523
Colonial Ave	
200-1199	23507
1200-2799	23517
2800-5099	23508
6600-7399	23505
Colony Point Rd	23505
Colson Pl	23504
Columbia Ave	23509
Columbus Ave	23504
Commander Pkwy	23502
Commercial Pl	23510
Commodore Dr & Pl	23503
Commodore Overlook	23503
Commonwealth Ave	23505
Comstock St	23502
Condor Ave	23518
Congress Rd	23503
Connecticut Ave	23508
Conoga St	23523
Console Ave	23518
Conway Ave	23505
Cooke Ave	23504
Corbell Ave	23502
Corbett Ave	23518
Corbin Rd	23502
Core Ave	23517
Cornell Ave	23518
Cornick Rd	23502
Cornwall Pl	23508
Cornwallis Ln	23502
Corporate Blvd	23502
Corprew Ave	23504
Corregidor Ave & St	23511
Cortlandt Pl	23505
Cottage Ave	23504
Cottage Pl	23503
Cougar Ave & Ct	23518
Count Basie Ln	23504
County St	
3401-3499	23513
3500-3599	23509
Courtney Ave	23504
Covel St	23523
Covenant St	23504
Coventry Ln	23518
Covington Ln	23508
Cowan St	23511
Cowand Ave	23502
Coyote Ave	23518
Crafford Ave	23518
Craig St	23523
Crane Ave & Cres	23518
Craten Rd	23513
Craven Cir	23513
Creamer Rd	23503
Creekwood Ct & Rd	23518
Crescent Rd	23505
Crescent Way	23513
Croft St	23513
Cromwell Dr	23509
Cromwell Pkwy	23505
Cromwell Rd	
2100-2199	23504
2300-3099	23509
Crosman Ave	23523
Croyden Rd	23503
Culfor Cres	23503
Culpepper St	23523
Cumberland St	23510
Curie Ct	23513
Curlew Dr	23502
Curtis St	23523
Cypress St	23523
W D Ave & St	23511
D View Ave	23503
Daisy Ct	23518
Dakota Ave	23505
Dale Ave	23511
Dallas St	23505
Dan Ct	23518
Dana St	23509
Danbury Ct & Dr	23518
Daniel Ave	23505
Danwood Dr	23513
Darden St	23502
Dare Cir	23513
David Ave & Ct	23518
Davidson St	23513
Davis St	
2800-3099	23509
3101-3199	23509
3700-3999	23513
Dayton Ct	23513
Dean Dr	23518
Debbie Cir	23518
Debree Ave	
1300-2799	23517
2800-3400	23508
3402-3698	23508
Decatur Ave	23511
Decker St	23523
Decreny Cir	23505
Deepdale Dr	23502
Deerfield Rd	23518
Defoe Ave	23513
Degrasse Ave	23509
Dehlman Ave	23505
Delano St	23503
Delaware Ave	
100-299	23504
400-799	23508
Delevan St	23523
Dell St	23518
Dellwood Ct & Dr	23518
Denby Ln	23510
Denhart St	23504
Denison Ave & Ct	23513
Densmore Pl	23503
Denver Ave	23513
Devon St	23503
Devonshire Rd	23513
Dewberry Ln	23502
Dey St	23513
Dickson Dr	23518
Diesel Ct	23513
Diggs Rd	23505
Dillingham Blvd	23511
Dillon Ave	23513
Dinwiddie St	23523
Diven Ln & St	23505
Dixie Dr	23505
Dogan St	23504
Dogwood Ter	23502
Dolphin Ave	23513
Dolphin Run	23518
Dominion Ave	23518
Don Ct & Dr	23518
Dora Cir	23513
Doris Dr	23505
Dorwin Cir & Dr	23502
Douglas St	23509
Doummar Ct & Dr	23518
Dove St	23513
W Dover Cir	23505
Dovercourt Rd	23518
Draper Dr	23505
Driftwood Ct & Dr	23518
Druid Cir	23504
Drummond Pl	23507
Dubose Dr	23504
Duck Pond Rd	23502
Dudley Ave	23503
Duffys Ln	23503
Duke St	23510
Dulwich Cres	23503
Dumont Ave	23505
Dunbar St	23504
Dundaff St	23507
Dundale Ave	23513
Dune St	23503
Dunfield Pl	23505
Dungee St	23504
Dunkirk Ave	23509
Dunmore St	23510
Dunn Pl	23504
Dunning Rd	23518
Dunway St	23513
Dupont Cir	23509
Dupre Ave	23503
Dure Rd	23502
Duvall St	23503
Eagle Ave	23518
Earies Way	23502
Earl St	23503
Earlscourt Ave	23504
Early St	
1500-1599	23502
2301-2305	23513
2307-2899	23513
Eason Cir	23509
East St	23510
Easton Ave	23502
Eastover Cir & Rd	23502
Eastwood Ter	23508
Easy St	23505
Eden St	23504
Edgewater Dr	23508
Edgewood Ave	23503
Edison Ave	23502
Edward St	23513
Edwin Dr	23505
Effie Ave	23502
Eilers St	23505
El Paso Ave	23505
Elaine Ave & Ct	23518
S Eleanor Ct	23508
Elgo St	23502
Elizabeth Ave	23502
Elizabeth River Cir	23502
Elk Ave	23518
Elkhorn Ave	23508
Elkin St	23523
Elliott St	23505
Ellsmere Ave	23513
Elm Ct & St	23502
Elm View Ave	23503
Elmhurst Ave	23513
Elmore Pl	23509
Elmwood Ave	23504
Elnora St	23503
Elon Ct	23513
Elsie Cir	23518
Eltham Ave	23513
Elvin Ct & Rd	23505
Elwood Ave	23505
Emeash Ave	23504
Emmett Pl	23523
Emory Pl	23509
E End Ave	23504
Enfield Ave	23505
Engine Test Ave	23511
Enterprise Rd	23502
Escadrille Pt	23508
Esquire St	23503
Essex Cir	23513
Ester Ct	23518
Ethan Allen Ln	23502
Ethel Ave	23504
Etheridge Ave	23502
Eustis Ave	23523
Euwanee Pl	23503
Eva Cir	23509
Evangeline St	23502
E & W Evans St	23503
Evelyn St	23518
Evelyn T Butts Ave	23513
Everglades Rd	23518
Evergreen Ave	23505
Ewing St	23503
Executive Dr	23503
Exeter Rd	23503
Faber Rd	23518
Factory St	23504
Fairbanks Ave	
1500-1599	23502
2300-2399	23513
Fairfax Ave	23507
Fairfield St	23523
N & S Fairwater Dr	23508
Fala Cir	23518
Faraday Ct	23513
Fargo Ave	23505
Faris St	23513
Farkendi St	23505
Farragut Ave	
1700-1899	23509
9400-9699	23511
Farrell St	23503
Faulk Rd	23502
Fauquier St	23523
Fawn Cres	23505
Fawn St	23504
Fayton Ave	23505
Fayver Ave	23505
Fearer Ave	23509
Fechteler Rd	23505
Fenchurch St	
400-598	23504
501-599	23510
Fenner St	23505
Fenton Cir	23509
Fentress Ct	23503
Ferncliff Rd	23518
Fernwood Dr	23518
Fife Ln & St	23505
Filbert St	23505
Filer St	23504
Finch Ave	23518
Finney St	23502
Fishermans Rd	23503
Flanders Ave	23509
Fleetwood Ave	23502
Fletcher Dr	23518
Flicker Pt	23505
Flondowe Ave	23502
Florida Ave	
1500-1599	23502

2300-2398 23513
2400-2700 23513
2702-2798 23513
Flowerfield Ct & Rd 23518
Fluvanna St 23523
Fontaine Ave 23502
Fontainebleau Cres 23509
Foot Of Claiborne Ave 23504
Forbes St 23504
Ford Dr 23523
Fordwick Dr 23518
Foresttown Dr 23502
Forge St 23504
Forrest Ave 23505
Forrestal Dr 23505
Forsythe St 23505
Fort Worth Ave 23505
Foxdale Dr 23518
Foxhound Ln 23518
Foxs Lair Ct & Trl 23518
Foxwell Dr & Ln 23502
Frament Ave 23502
Francis St 23523
Frank St 23518
Franklin St 23511
Frederick St 23523
E & W Freemason St 23510
Fremont St 23504
Fresh Meadow Rd 23503
Friden Ct & St 23518
Frizzell Ave 23502
Front St 23510
Fulcher Ave 23518
Fulton St 23504
Gabriel Ct & Dr 23502
Gail Dr 23518
Gainor Pl 23502
Galt St 23504
Galveston Blvd 23505
Gamage Ct & Dr 23518
Gambols Ln 23505
Gardner Dr 23518
Garfield Ave 23502
Garfield Dr 23503
Garland Cir 23509
Garren Ave 23509
Garrett Ave 23503
N Gate Dr 23513
Gate House Rd 23504
Gates Ave
800-806 23517
808-999 23517
1000-1499 23507
Gatling Ave 23502
Gazel St 23504
Geneva Way 23513
George St 23502
Georgetown Ct & Rd 23502
Georgia Ave 23508
Ghent Commons Ct & Dr 23517
Gifford St 23518
Gilbert St 23511
Giles Cir 23513
Gilmer Rd 23502
E & W Gilpin Ave 23503
Glade Rd 23518
Gladstone Rd 23505
Glen Ave 23513
E Glen Rd 23505
W Glen Rd 23505
Glen Echo Dr 23505
Glen Myrtle Ave 23505
Glencove Pl 23505
Glendale Ave 23505
Glendon Ave 23518
Gleneagles Rd 23505
Glenhaven Cres 23508
Glenoak Dr 23513
Glenrock Rd 23502
Glenroie Ave 23505
Glerelde Ave 23511
Gloucester Ave 23505
Godfrey Ave 23504
Goff St
600-699 23510
700-1499 23504
Goochland St 23504
Goodman St 23523
Gordon Ave 23504
Gornto Ave 23509
Gosnold Ave
2300-2799 23517
2800-5099 23508
E & W Government Ave 23503
Gowrie Ave 23509
Grace St 23510
Gramel St 23503
Granby Park 23505
Granby St
100-1699 23510
1700-2799 23517
2800-4299 23504
5501-5597 23505
5599-7800 23505
7802-8498 23505
8500-9699 23503
Grandy Ave
2100-2199 23504
2300-3099 23509
Granite Arch 23504
Grantham Rd 23505
Graydon Ave & Pl 23507
Grayfalcon Dr 23518
Grayson St 23523
Green St 23513
Green View Ln 23503
Greenbrier Ave 23505
Greendale Ave 23518
Greenleaf Dr 23523
Greenplain Rd 23502
Greenway Ct 23507
Greenwich Ave 23502
Greenwood St 23513
Gregory Dr 23513
Gresham Dr 23507
Greyfalcon Ct 23518
Grimes Ave & Ct 23518
Grove Ave & Ct 23503
Guam Pkwy 23518
Guestwick Cres 23505
Gunn Ct 23505
Gurley St 23505
Guy Ave 23505
Gygax Rd 23505
H St 23511
Hacienda St 23518
Hadley Rd 23502
Hadlock Ave 23509
Hagan Ave 23502
Hale St 23504
Halifax St 23523
Halprin Ct & Dr 23518
Halstead Ave 23502
Halter Ln 23502
Hammett Ave & Pkwy 23503
Hammock Ln 23518
Hammond Ct 23503
Hampshire Ave & Ct 23513
Hampton Blvd
900-1100 23507
1102-1198 23507
1200-2799 23517
3601-3607 23508
3609-6599 23508
7001-7097 23505
7099-7799 23505
7800-7854 23511
7801-9899 23505
7856-9298 23505
Hanbury St
3100-3199 23509
3300-3499 23513
Hancock Ave 23509
Hank Ave 23505
Hannah St 23505
Hanover Ave 23508
Hansford Pl 23503
Hanson Ave 23504
Hanyen Dr 23502
Harbor View Ln 23518
Harbor Walk Ave 23518
Hardwood Ct & Ln 23518
Hardy Ave 23523
Hargrove St 23502
Hariton Ct 23505
Harmon St 23518
Harmony Rd 23502
Harmott Ave 23509
Harold St 23518
Harper St 23513
Harrell Ave
2100-2199 23504
2200-2899 23509
Harrington Ave
800-999 23517
1000-1099 23507
Harrisons Rd 23505
Hartford Dr 23518
Hartwick Ct & Dr 23518
Harvard St 23505
Harvey Ct 23513
Hastings St 23503
Hatton St 23523
Haven Dr 23503
Hayes St 23504
Head St 23505
Hedgewood Ln 23505
Helena Ave 23505
Helmick St 23505
Helsley Ave 23518
Hemlock St
1500-1599 23502
2300-2499 23513
Henneman Dr 23513
Henrico St 23513
Henry St
600-699 23510
700-999 23504
Herbert St 23513
Herbert Collins Way 23504
Heron Ln 23505
Hethersett Rd 23505
Heutte Dr 23518
Hibie St 23523
Hickory St 23503
Hicks Ave 23502
Highland St 23518
Hillandale Rd 23502
Hillside Ave 23503
Hilton St 23518
Hoggard Rd 23502
Holland Ave 23509
Hollister Ave 23504
Holly Ave 23504
Holly Ln 23505
Holly Point Rd 23509
Hollybriar Pt 23518
Holt St 23504
Honaker Ave 23502
Honeysuckle Rd 23518
Hooper St 23513
Hornet St 23511
Horton Cir 23513
Hough Ave 23523
Houston Ave 23502
Howard Pl 23504
Howe St 23503
Hudson Ave 23502
Hughart St 23505
Hugo St 23513
Hull St 23511
Hullview Ave 23503
Humboldt St 23513
Hummel Dr 23502
Hunt Rd 23518
Hunter St 23504
Hunters Ct & Trl 23518
Hunters Chase 23518
Huntington Cres & Pl 23509
Huntsman Rd 23502
Hurley Ave 23513
Hyde Cir 23513
Hyde Park Rd 23503
Hydro St 23504
Illinois Ave 23513
Inca Ct 23513
Inchon Rd 23511
E & W Indian River Rd 23523
Inez Ave 23502
Ingersol St 23505
Ingle Cir 23502
N Ingleside Dr 23502
Ingleside Rd
600-1599 23502
2300-2599 23513
N Ingleside Rd 23502
E & W Ingram Ct, Loop & St 23505
Inlet Rd 23503
Inlet Point Rd 23503
International Blvd 23513
International Terminal Blvd 23505
Inventors Rd 23502
Inwood Ave & Ct 23503
Iowa Ave 23513
Iron Monger Rd 23511
Irving St 23523
Irwin Ave 23518
Isaac St 23523
Ivaloo St 23513
Ivor Ave 23502
Jacob St 23504
Jacquelyn Ct 23513
Jamaica Ave 23504
Jamestown Cres 23508
Jana Ct 23503
Janaf Pl 23502
Janaf Executive Bldg 23502
Janaf Office Bldg 23502
Janaf Shopping Ctr
1-191 23502
190-190 23541
192-298 23502
193-199 23502
Jane Way 23503
Janet Dr 23513
Jarrett Rd 23502
Jasmine Ave 23502
Jason Ave 23509
Jasper Cir & Ct 23518
Jay Ct 23505
Jean Ct 23505
Jefferson Ct 23513
Jeffrey Dr 23518
Jenifer St 23503
Jenny Ct 23503
Jernigan Ave 23513
Jerome Ave 23518
Jerry Ct & Rd 23502
Jerrylee Ct & Dr 23518
Jersey Ave 23513
Jett St 23502
Joan Dr 23502
Joe Austin Dr 23504
John Foster Ln 23504
Johnnie Branch St 23504
Johns St 23513
Johnson Ave 23504
Johnstons Rd
800-1399 23513
1401-1499 23513
1500-1699 23518
1701-1999 23518
Jolima Ave 23518
Jolliff Ct 23518
Jonathan Ct 23513
Joseph St 23504
Joseph Greene Ln 23504
Joyce St 23523
Joyner St 23513
Jubilee St 23523
Julianna Dr 23502
Juniper St
1500-1599 23502
2300-2799 23513
Kane St 23513
Kansas Ave 23513
Kanter Ave 23518
Karen Marie Ct 23509
Karlin Ave & Cir 23502
Kathy Ct 23518
Kearney Rd 23503
Kearsarge Pl 23503
Keene Rd 23505
Kegagie Dr 23518
Keller Ave
2100-2199 23504
2200-3099 23509
Kempsville Cir & Rd 23502
Kenlake Ct & Pl 23518
E & W Kenmore Dr 23505
Kennebeck Ave, Cir & Ct 23513
Kennedy St 23513
Kennon Ave
1500-1599 23502
2300-2599 23513
Kenosha Ave 23509
Kenova St 23508
Kenton Ave 23504
Kentucky Ave 23502
Kenwood Dr 23518
Kerrey Ave 23502
Kersey Ave 23503
Keswick Dr 23518
Kevin Ct & Dr 23518
Kidd Blvd 23502
Killam Ave
2300-2700 23517
2702-2798 23517
3300-3498 23508
3500-5099 23508
Kilmer Ct & Ln 23502
Kimball Cir, Ct, Loop & Ter 23504
Kimberly Ln 23502
Kincaid Ave 23502
King St 23511
Kings Lynn Dr 23505
Kingsley Ln 23505
Kingston Ave 23503
Kingsway Rd 23518
Kingswell Dr 23502
Kingwood Ave 23502
Kirby Cres 23505
Kirby Haigh Cir 23518
Kirkland Ave 23513
Kitchener Ave 23509
Kittrell St 23513
Knox Rd 23513
Kostell Ct 23513
Krick St 23513
La Valette Ave 23504
Ladd Ave 23502
Lafayette Ave 23503
Lafayette Blvd
1201-1297 23509
1299-3299 23509
3300-3799 23513
Lafayette Dr 23504
Lagoon Rd 23505
Lake Herbert Dr 23502
Lake Ridge Cir 23502
Lake Taylor Dr 23502
Lake Terrace Cir 23502
Lake Wright Dr 23502
Lakebridge Dr 23504
N & S Lakeland Dr 23518
Lakeside Dr 23503
Lakewood Dr 23509
Lambert Pl 23505
Lamberts Point Rd 23508
Lamesa Ave 23518
Lamont St 23504
Lancaster St 23523
Lance Rd 23502
Land St 23502
Landale Rd 23503
Landing St 23504
Langley Rd 23507
Lankford Ave 23505
Lansing St 23523
Larchmont Cres 23508
Larkin St 23513
Larrymore Ave & Ct 23518
Lasalle Ave 23509
Lasser Dr 23513
Lathan Rd 23502
Latimer Cir 23513
Laurel Ave & Cres 23505
Lawson Ave 23503
Layton St 23502
Lea View Ave 23503
Lead St 23504
Leafwood Dr 23518
Leake St 23523
Leander Dr 23504
Leclair St 23503
Leepoint Rd 23502
E & W Leicester Ave 23503
Leigh St 23507
Lembla St 23503
Lena St 23518
Lenoir Cir 23513
Lenox Ave 23503
Lens Ave 23509
Leo St 23504
Leonard Rd
500-599 23505
701-799 23518
Lepage Rd 23513
Leslie Ave & Ct 23518
Lesner Ave 23518
Lesselle Dr 23502
Leutz St 23511
Levine Ct 23502
Lewis Rd 23502
Lex St 23505
N & S Lexan Ave & Cres 23508
E Lexington St 23504
Leyte Ave 23511
Liberia Dr 23504
E & W Liberty St 23523
Light St 23523
Lighthouse Cv 23518
Lightwood Ln 23518
Ligon St 23523
Lilac Ct 23518
Limestone Arch 23504
Lincoln St 23510
Lind St 23513
Lindale Ln 23503
Lindenwood Ave 23504
Lindsay Ave 23504
Lines Dr 23511
Link St 23504
Lion Ave 23518
Lisa Dr 23518
Little Bay Ave 23503
E Little Creek Rd
100-600 23505
602-698 23505
700-4300 23518
4302-4398 23518
W Little Creek Rd 23505
Little John Dr 23513
Llewellyn Ave
1000-1098 23507
1100-1199 23507
1200-2799 23517
2801-3197 23504
3199-4299 23504
Llewellyn Mews 23507
Loam St 23518
Lockamy Ln 23502
Locust Ave 23513
Logan St 23505
Lois Ln 23513
London St 23503
Longdale Dr
1300-1499 23513
1500-1899 23518
Longwood Dr 23508
Lontrenw St 23513
E & W Lorengo Ave 23503
Lorraine Ave 23509
Louisa St 23523
Louisiana Dr 23505
Louvett St 23503
Louvick St 23503
Lovitt Ave 23504
Lowery Ct & Rd 23502
Lucas Ave 23502
Lucian Ct 23502
Lucile Ave 23504
Ludlow St 23504
Lunenberg St 23523
Luxembourg Ave 23509
Lydia Ave 23502
Lyndhurst Ave 23502
Lynn St 23513
Lynn River Rd 23503
Lynnbrook Ct & Dr 23518
Lyons Ave 23509
Macarthur Sq 23510
Macdonald Cres & Rd 23505
Mace Ave 23503
Mace Arch 23503
Macon Ct 23513
Madison Ave 23504
Madison Mews 23510
Magnolia Ave 23508
Mahone Ave 23523
Maiden Ln 23518
E Main Plz 23510
E Main St 23510
S Main St 23523
W Main St 23510
Majestic Ave 23504
Major Ave 23505
Malbon Ave 23502
E Malden Ave 23518
Mall Dr 23511
Mallard Dr 23505
Mallory Ct 23507
Malmgren Ct 23502
Maltby Ave & Cres 23504
Malvern Dr 23518
Mamie Blvd 23513
Manassas Ct 23518
Manchester Ave 23508
Mangrove Ave 23502
Manson St 23523
Manteo St
800-1199 23507
1200-1298 23517
1300-2099 23517
Maple Ave 23503
Mapleshade Ave 23505
Mapleton Ave 23504
Maplewood Ave 23503
Mapole Ave 23503
Marathon Ave 23504
Marchant Rd 23505
Marcy St 23505
Margaret Ave 23503
Marietta Ave 23513
Mariner St 23504
Mariners Cv & Way 23503
Mariners Point Rd 23518
Marion St 23505
Marius St 23502
Market St 23510
Marlboro Ave 23504
Marlette Dr 23505
Marlfield Dr 23502
Marlina Ct 23503
Marlow Ave 23503
Marne Ave 23509
Marsh St 23523
Marshall Ave 23504
Martins Ln 23510
Martone Rd 23518
Marvin Ave 23518
Mary Ave 23502
Maryland Ave
200-298 23504
400-799 23508
9400-9799 23511
Masi St 23504
Mason Ave 23518
Mason Creek Rd 23503
Massachusetts Ave 23508
Massey Hughes Dr 23511
Matoaka St 23507
Matthew Henson St 23505
Maurice Dr 23518

Maury Ave
600-899 23517
9600-9799 23511
Maury Cres 23509
Maury Arch 23505
May Ave 23504
Maycox Ave 23505
Mayfield Ave 23518
Mayflower Rd 23508
Maymont Ave 23513
Maysville Ave 23504
Mccloy Rd 23505
Mcclure Rd 23502
Mcdowell Rd 23518
Mcfarland Rd 23505
E & W Mcginnis Cir & Ct 23502
Mckann Ave 23509
Mclean Ave 23508
Mclemore St 23509
Mcneal Ave 23502
Mcnutt Ct 23513
Meadow Brook Ln 23503
Meadow Creek Rd 23518
Meadow Lake Ct & Dr 23518
Meadowlawn Dr 23518
Meads Rd 23505
Mellwood Ct 23513
Melon St 23523
Melrose Pkwy 23508
Memorial Pl 23510
Mercer Dr 23505
Meridian Ln 23502
Merrimac Ave & Ct 23504
Merritt St
7500-7700 23513
7702-7898 23513
7900-8199 23518
Mervis Ct & St 23518
Michael Dr 23505
Michigan Ave 23508
Middle Ave 23504
Middle Towne Cres 23504
Middlesex St 23523
Middleton Pl 23513
Midfield St 23505
Midge Cres 23502
Midland St 23523
Mildred St 23518
Miles End 23509
N Military Hwy
201-297 23502
299-2599 23502
2700-7899 23518
S Military Hwy 23502
Military Circle Mall 23502
Mill St 23507
Millard St 23518
Millbrook Rd 23505
Miller St 23505
Miller Store Rd
2701-3399 23518
6001-6097 23502
6099-6199 23502
Miltate Ave 23502
Milton St 23505
Mimosa Rd 23518
Mindoro St 23511
Minnesota Ave
1500-1599 23502
2300-2599 23513
2601-2699 23513
Minnie Ave 23513
Mission St 23504
Mississippi Ave 23502
Missouri Pl 23503
Modlin Ct 23518
Modoc Ave 23503
Moffett Ave 23511
Mohawk St 23513
Mona Ave 23518
Monaco Ct 23502
Monarch Way 23508
Monitor Way
2800-2899 23504
8700-8999 23503
Monroe Pl 23508
Monrovia Dr 23504
Montague St 23518
Montana Ave 23513
Montclair Ave 23523
Monterey Ave 23508
Montgomery St 23513
Monticello Ave
200-1699 23510
1700-2799 23517
2800-2999 23504
Montpelier Ct 23509
Montserrado Pl 23504
Monty Ct 23518
Mooring Dr 23518
Moose Ave 23518
Moreell Cir 23505
Morris Ave 23509
Morris Cres 23509
Morris St 23511
Morton Ave 23517
Morwin St 23503
Moultrie Ave 23509
Mount Pleasant Ave 23505
Mount Vernon Ave 23523
E & W Mowbray Ct 23507
Mowbray Arch 23507
Muirfield Rd 23505
Mulberry St 23523
Munden Ave 23505
Munson St 23517
Murray Ave & Ct 23518
Muskogee Ave 23509
Myers Rd 23513
Myrtle Ave 23504
Myrtle Park 23508
Nancy Ct & Dr 23518
Nansemond Cir 23513
Nansemond Arch 23503
Nashville Quay 23518
Nathan Ave & Ct 23518
Natrona Ave 23509
Naval Base Rd 23505
Nella Ct 23518
Nelms Ave 23502
Nelson St 23523
Neoma Dr 23503
Nesbitt Dr 23505
Nevada Ave
1500-1599 23502
2300-2799 23513
New St 23503
New Hampshire Ave 23508
New Jersey Ave 23508
New York Ave 23508
Newark Ave 23502
Newell Ave 23518
Newport Ave
2300-2799 23517
2900-5199 23508
6000-7799 23505
Newport Cres 23505
Newport Pt 23505
S Newtown Rd 23502
Niagara Cir 23509
Nichal Ct 23508
Nicholson St 23510
Nickoles Ln 23513
Nipsic Ln 23503
Nissan Dr 23505
Noble St 23518
Noemfoor Rd 23511
Norchester Ave 23504
Norcova Ave
1400-1599 23502
2300-2400 23513
2402-2498 23513
Norcova Ct 23502
E Norcova Dr 23502
W Norcova Dr 23502
Norfolk Ave 23503
Norfolk Sq 23502
Norfolk Crossing Ave 23505
Norfolk International Arpt 23518
Norfolk Southern Terminal Dr 23508
Norland Cir & Ct 23513
Norman Ave 23518
Normandy Lndg 23518
Norristown Dr 23518
Northampton Blvd 23502
Northgate Rd 23505
Norva Park 23505
Norvella Ave & Ct 23513
Norview Ave
800-849 23509
850-1599 23513
1600-2299 23518
Norview Arch 23513
Norway Ct & Pl 23509
Nottaway St 23513
Oak Ave 23502
Oak St 23511
Oak Grove Rd 23505
Oak Park Ave 23503
Oakfield Ave 23523
Oaklawn Ave 23504
Oakmont Ct, Dr & Pl 23513
Oakwood St 23523
Obendorfer Rd 23523
E Ocean Ave 23503
W Ocean Ave 23503
Ocean Way 23518
E Ocean View Ave
100-2099 23503
2100-4799 23518
4801-4899 23518
W Ocean View Ave 23503
Ocella Ave 23503
Oconnor Cres 23503
Odell St 23504
Oetjen Blvd 23502
Ogden Ave 23505
Okeefe St 23504
Oklahoma Ave 23513
Old Brandon Ave 23507
Old Court Dr 23502
Old Dominion Universi 23508
Old Mill Rd 23518
Old Ocean View Rd
7900-8499 23518
8500-8999 23503
9001-9099 23503
Old Phillips Rd 23502
Olean St 23513
Oleo Rd 23518
Olinger St 23523
E Olney Rd
100-699 23510
700-1599 23504
W Olney Rd
100-299 23510
300-1399 23507
Omohundro Ave
1900-2799 23517
2800-2898 23504
2900-4099 23504
Oneida Cir 23509
Orange Ave 23503
Orange St 23513
Orangewood Ave 23513
Orapax St 23507
Orchard St 23505
Orchid Ave 23518
N & S Oriole Dr 23518
Orion Ave 23502
Orleans Cir 23509
Orleans St 23503
Osborne Rd 23503
Otis Cir 23509
Outten Ln 23504
Overbrook Ave 23513
Owens Rd 23505
Oxford St 23505
Pace Rd 23518
Paddock Rd 23518
Painter St 23505
Palem Rd 23513
Pall Mall St 23513
Pallister Rd 23518
Palmer Turn 23505
Palmetto St
1500-1599 23502
2300-2599 23513
Palmyra St
1500-1599 23502
2300-2599 23513
Pamela Pl 23509
Pamlico Cir 23513
Parish Rd 23504
Park Ave
100-199 23510
300-1199 23504
Park Cres
400-599 23511
2701-2899 23504
Parkdale Dr 23505
Parker Ave 23508
Parktown Rd 23518
Parkview Ave 23503
Partridge St 23513
Pasadena Ct 23505
Pascal Pl 23502
Pasteur Ct 23513
Pastinde Ave 23507
Patent Rd 23502
Patrician Rd 23518
Patrick St 23523
Patrol Rd 23511
Paul St 23505
Paulin Ct 23513
Peace Haven Dr 23502
Peachtree St 23503
Peake Rd 23502
Pearl St 23523
Pebble Ln 23502
Pecan Point Rd 23502
Peddars Way 23505
Pefley Ct & Dr 23502
Pelham St 23505
Pembroke Ave 23507
Pender Ct 23517
Pendleton St 23523
Pennington Rd 23505
Pennsylvania Ave
100-200 23504
202-214 23504
400-799 23508
Pepper Mill Ct & Ln 23502
Perch Ln 23518
Peronne Ave 23509
Pershing Ave 23509
Peterson St
2900-3399 23509
3700-3999 23513
Phillip Ave 23503
Philpotts Rd 23513
Picadilly Sq & St 23513
Pickett Rd 23502
Pierce St 23513
Piersey Ct & St 23511
Pike St 23523
Pilot Ave 23513
Pine Grove Ave 23502
Pine Harbor Dr 23502
Pine Hollow Rd 23502
Pine Tree Rd 23503
Pinecroft Ln 23505
Pinedale St 23503
Pinehurst Ave 23513
Pineridge Rd 23502
Pineview Ave 23503
Pinewell Dr 23503
Piney Branch Cir & Ct 23502
Piping Rock Rd 23502
Plearald Ave 23517
Pleasant Ave 23518
Pleasant Point Cir & Dr 23502
Plerelan St 23510
E & W Plume St 23510
Plymouth Cres 23508
Plymouth St 23503
Pocahontas St 23511
Poe Ct 23513
Pollard St 23504
Pomona St 23513
Pomroy Ave 23509
Pontante St 23523
Pope Ave 23509
Poplar Ave 23523
Poplar Hall Cir & Dr 23502
Poppleton St 23523
Poppy Ct 23503
Porielaw Ave 23518
Porpoise Ln 23518
Portal Rd 23503
Porter Rd 23511
Portview Ave 23503
Poston Ln 23513
Potomac Pl 23503
Powder Horn Dr 23518
Powhatan Ave 23508
Powhatan Ct 23508
Powhatan Pl 23508
Powhatan St 23511
Preble St 23511
Presidential Pkwy 23504
Pretty Lake Ave 23518
Pretty Walk Ln 23518
Primrose St 23503
Prince Ave 23502
Prince Edward Way 23517
E Princess Anne Rd
100-699 23510
700-3299 23504
3300-5699 23502
W Princess Anne Rd
101-197 23517
199-899 23517
900-1499 23507
Princeton Ave 23523
Priory Pl 23505
Pritchard St 23502
Production Rd 23502
Proescher St 23504
Progress Rd 23502
Pugh St 23513
Pulaski St 23504
Purdy Ct 23518
Pythian Ave 23518
S Quail St 23513
Queens Way 23517
Quill Rd 23502
Quincy St
8201-8297 23518
8299-8440 23518
8441-8599 23503
Raby Rd 23502
Racine Ave 23509
Rader St 23510
Radford St 23513
Radnor Rd 23503
Rainey Dr 23504
Raleigh Ave 23507
Rallston St 23503
Ralph St 23505
Ramblewood Rd 23513
Ramsey Rd 23503
E & W Randall Ave 23503
Randolph St 23510
Rankin Ave & Ct 23518
Ransom Rd 23518
Ray St 23502
Rebel Rd 23505
Red Brook Ct & Rd 23518
Red Mill Rd 23502
Redgate Ave 23507
Redmon Ct & Rd 23518
Redwing Ave 23503
Redwood Cir 23518
Reel St 23502
Reeves Ave 23504
Regent Rd 23505
Reilly St 23504
Remsen St 23505
Reservoir Ave & Cres 23504
Restmere Rd 23505
Revere Dr 23502
Rhode Island Ave 23508
Rialto St 23504
Rich Ave 23518
Richardson St 23503
Richmond Cres & Pl 23508
Richview St 23503
Riddick St 23518
Ridgefield Ct & Dr 23518
S Ridgeley Cir, Pt & Rd 23505
Ridgewell Ave & Cir 23503
Rippard Ave 23503
Ripplemeade Ln 23502
Ritzcraft Dr 23505
S & W River Cres & Rd 23505
River Edge Rd 23502
River Oaks Ct & Dr 23502
River Road Pt 23505
Rivers Edge Lndg 23502
Riverside Dr 23502
Riverview Ave 23510
Riverwood Rd 23502
Roberts Rd 23504
Robin Hood Rd
3600-5499 23513
5501-5599 23513
5701-5897 23518
5899-6000 23518
6002-6098 23518
Rockbridge Ave 23508
Rockingham St 23523
Rodman Rd 23503
Rogers Ave 23505
Rogers Ave N 23511
Rogers Ave S 23511
Rogers Rd 23511
Roland Dr 23509
Rolfe Ave 23508
Rolleston Ave 23502
Ronald Rd 23502
Roper Dr 23518
Rose Ave 23504
Roseclair St 23523
Rosefield Ct & Dr 23513
N Rosemont Ct & Dr 23513
Roslyn Dr 23502
Rosmar Ct 23503
Rosso Ct 23509
Roswell Ave 23504
Round Bay Cir, Ct & Rd 23502
Roxboro Rd 23505
Royal Windsor Ct & Loop 23505
Royale Park & Ter 23509
Ruffin St & Way 23504
Ruffner St 23504
Rugby St 23504
Rugosa Rose Ct 23518
Runnymede Rd 23505
Rush St
1500-1599 23502
2300-2499 23513
2501-2599 23513
Ruthven Rd 23505
Saban Ave 23518
Sabre Rd 23502
Saddle Rock Rd 23502
Saint Denis Ave 23509
Saint Francis Ln 23505
Saint George Ave 23503
Saint Julian Ave 23504
Saint Louis Ave 23509
Saint Mihiel Ave 23509
Saint Paul St 23510
Saint Pauls Blvd 23510
Saipan Blvd 23518
Sairells Ave 23508
Salem St 23503
San Antonio Blvd 23505
Sandpiper Cir & Ln 23502
Sandy St 23518
Sangamon Ave 23509
Santos St 23513
Saranac Ave 23509
Scope Plz 23510
Scott St 23502
Sea Wolf Dr 23518
Seabee Rd 23511
Seabreeze Rd 23503
Seafarer Ave 23518
W Seaview Ave 23503
Seay Ave 23502
Security Ln 23502
Sedgefield Dr 23513
Sedgewick St 23504
Seekel St 23505
Selby Pl 23503
Selden Arc 23510
Selden Ave 23523
Sellger Dr 23502
Selma Ave 23513
Semmes Ave 23503
Serro Ct 23505
E & W Severn Rd 23505
Sewells Point Rd
1400-1599 23502
2300-7699 23513
Shadywood Rd 23513
Shafer St 23513
Shanks St 23504
Sharon Cir 23518
Sharpley Ave 23513
Shasta Dr 23505
Shaw Pl 23509
Shelton Ave 23502
Shenandoah Ave & Ct 23509
Sheppard Ave 23518
Sherman Ln 23523
Sherwood Pl 23503
Sherwood Forest Ln 23513
Sheryl Dr 23505
Ship Watch Rd 23503
Shipp Ave 23504
Ships Crossing Rd 23518
N Shirland Ave 23505
Shirley Ave
200-930 23517
931-1099 23507
Shoop Ave 23509
Shore Dr 23518
N Shore Rd 23505
Shorewood Ct, Dr, Ln & Pl 23502
Shoshone Ct 23513
Shreveport Cres 23518
Sigmon St 23502
Silbert Rd 23509
Silverwood Ct 23513
Silvey Dr 23502
Simms Rd 23518
Simons Dr 23505
Simpson Ct 23503
Simpson Ln 23523
Sinclair St 23505
Sinoe Pl 23504
Sir Oliver Rd 23505
Skyline Dr 23518
Sloane St 23503
Smith St 23510
Somerset Ln 23518
Somme Ave 23509
Sorby Ct 23513
South Ave 23513
Southampton Ave 23510
Spartan Ave 23518
Spaulding Dr 23513
Spotswood Ave
400-999 23517
1000-1299 23507
Springfield Ave 23523
Springhill Rd 23502
Springmeadow Blvd 23518
Springwood Ct & St 23518
Spruce St
1500-1599 23502
2300-2799 23513
Spy Glass Dr 23518
Stafford St 23523
Stanart St 23502
Standard St 23504
Stanhope Ave 23504
Stanwix Sq 23502
Stapleton St 23504

State St 23523
Staten St 23503
Statler St 23503
Steiner Way 23502
Stephan Ct 23513
Stephens Ln 23503
Stephenson Ave 23502
Sterling Ct & St 23505
Stockley Gdns
600-899 23507
1200-1399 23517
1401-1499 23517
Stockton Rd 23505
N & S Stonebridge Dr 23504
Stoney Pt N & S 23502
Stony Run Rd 23518
Stow St 23523
Stowbridge Ln 23505
Strand St 23513
Stratford St 23503
Strathmore Ave 23504
Stribling Ln 23518
Stuart Cir & Ct 23502
Studeley Ave 23508
Sturgis Rd & St 23503
Suburban Pkwy 23505
Suburban Arch 23505
Summers Dr 23509
Summit Ave 23504
Sunny Ct 23513
Sunset Dr 23503
Sunshine Ave 23509
Surrey Cres 23508
Sussex Pl 23508
Sutton St 23504
Swan Arch 23513
Swanson Rd 23503
Sweet Briar Ave 23509
Sycamore Ln & St 23523
Sylvan St 23508
Tabb St 23504
Tabor Ct 23518
Tait Ct 23509
Tait Ter
1700-3299 23509
3300-3799 23513
Talbot Hall Rd 23505
Tallwood Ct & St 23518
Tallyho Ter 23518
Tanager Pkwy 23518
E & W Tanners Creek Dr 23513
Tapley Ave 23505
Tappahannock Dr 23509
Tarpon Ct & Pl 23518
Tarrall Ave 23509
Tarrallton Dr 23518
Tarrant St 23509
E Taussig Blvd 23505
Taylor Dr 23502
Taylors Ln 23503
E & W Tazewell St 23510
Teal Ct 23513
Templar Blvd 23518
Tennessee Ave 23502
Terry Ct & Dr 23518
Texas Ave 23513
Thaxton St 23513
Thayor St 23504
Thistle St 23504
Thole St 23505
Thomas St 23513
Thompson Rd 23518
Thrasher Ln 23518
Thurgood St 23523
Thurston St 23513
Tidal Rd 23518
Tides Ct 23518
Tidewater Dr
100-2590 23504
2591-2597 23509
2592-2598 23504
2599-6599 23509
6601-6999 23509
7400-8299 23505
8300-8499 23518
8500-9299 23503
Tifton Ct & St 23513
Tillman Rd 23513
Timothy Ave 23505
Toby Ln 23503
Todd St 23523
Toler Pl 23503
Tower St 23511
Townley Ave & Ct 23518
Townsend Ct & Pl 23502
Trafalgar Ct 23513
Trant Ave & Cir 23502
Tree Chop Rd 23513
Trice Ter 23502
Trinity Ave 23518
Trouville Ave 23505
Troy St 23503
Truxton St 23511
Tucker Ave 23505
Tulane Rd 23518
Tullibee Dr 23518
Tunstall Ave 23504
Turner Rd 23518
Tuttle Ave 23502
Twilley St 23503
Tyler St 23504
Tyndale Ct 23505
Typo Ave & Ln 23502
Underwood Ave 23513
Union St 23510
University Dr 23513
Upper Brandon Pl 23508
Upshur St 23513
Usaa Dr 23502
Utah Ave 23502
Vaiden St 23513
Valleau Rd 23502
Valley Dr 23502
Van Patten Rd 23505
Van Wyck Mews 23517
Vantring St 23503
N & S Veaux Loop 23509
Vendome Pl & Ter 23509
Ventura Ct 23518
Verdun Ave 23509
Vernon Dr 23523
Vero St 23518
Versailles Ave 23509
Vick St 23504
Vicksburg Ct 23518
Victoria Ave 23504
Victory Dr 23505
N View Blvd 23518
Villa Cir 23504
Village Ave 23502
Vimy Ridge Ave 23509
Vincent Ave
2100-2199 23504
2200-3099 23509
Vine St 23523
Virgilina Ave 23503
Virginia Ave
401-415 23508
417-799 23508
8900-9799 23511
9301-9397 23511
E Virginia Beach Blvd
101-297 23510
299-699 23510
700-3199 23504
3400-6699 23502
W Virginia Beach Blvd 23510
Virginian Dr 23505
Vista St 23504
Vivian St 23513
Vulcan Dr 23502
Waco St 23505
Wade St 23502
Wailes Ave 23502
Wake Cir 23513
Wakefield Ave 23502
Walke St 23504
Walker Ave 23523
Wall St 23504
Walmer Ave 23513
Walnut Hill St 23508
Walsingham Way 23505
Walters Ct & Dr 23518
Waltham St 23523
Walton Ave 23508
Wapiti Ave 23518
Warbler Ln 23518
Warehouse Rd 23505
Warehouse St 23511
Warner Cir 23509
Warren Cres 23507
Warren St 23505
Warrington Ave 23507
Warwick Ave 23503
S Warwick Cir 23513
Washington Ave 23504
Washington Park 23517
E Water St 23510
Water Works Rd 23502
Waterfront Dr 23508
Waterside Dr 23510
Watson St 23523
Waukesha Ave 23509
Waverly Way 23504
Waycross Rd 23513
Wayland St 23503
Waylon Ave 23509
Wayman St 23523
Wayne Cir & Cres 23513
Webb Ct 23518
Webster Ave 23509
Wedgefield Ave & Ct 23502
Wedgewood Dr 23518
Weems Rd 23502
Weiss Ln 23502
Welaka Rd 23502
Wellington Ct 23513
Wellington Rd 23505
Wellington St 23513
Wellman St 23502
Wells Pkwy 23503
Wesleyan Dr 23502
West Ave 23504
Westcliff Dr 23518
Westcove Ct 23502
Westminster Ave
2300-3532 23504
3533-3599 23502
E Westmont Ave 23503
Westmoreland Ave 23508
Westover Ave & Mews 23507
Westwood Ter 23508
Weyanoke St 23507
Whaley Ave & Ct 23502
Wharton Ave & Ct 23518
Wheeling Ave 23523
While Ln 23518
Whit Ave 23503
Whitaker Ln 23510
White Chapel Rd 23509
White Hall Rd 23518
Whitehead Ave 23523
Whitehorn Dr 23513
Whiting St 23505
Whitney Blvd 23502
Whittier Dr 23513
Wide St 23504
Widgeon Rd 23513
Wilby St 23505
Wildwood Dr 23518
Wiley Dr 23504
Wilkie Rd 23503
Willard Pl 23509
Willben St 23518
Willingham St 23505
Willoughby Ave 23504
Willoughby Bay Ave 23503
Willow Ct & Ter 23503
Willow Grove Ct 23505
Willow Wood Dr
100-198 23505
1300-2299 23509
Wilmington St 23505
Wilson Ave 23510
Wilson Rd 23523
Winburne Ln 23502
Windermere Ave 23513
Windham Rd 23505
Windsor Point Rd 23509
Wingfield Rd 23518
Winshire St 23503
Winstead Ct & Rd 23518
Winston St 23518
Winthrop St 23513
Winward Rd 23513
Wise St 23518
Wisteria Pl 23518
Withers Ave 23509
Wolcott Ave 23513
Wolfe St 23502
Wolferton St 23504
Wood St 23504
Woodall Rd 23518
Woodbine Rd 23502
Woodbury Ave 23508
Woodcock St 23503
Woodfin Ave 23505
Woodford St 23503
Woodis Ave 23510
Woodland Ave 23504
Woodridge Dr 23518
Woodrow Ave
900-999 23517
1000-1499 23507
Woodview Ave 23505
Woodway Ln 23505
Woody Ct & Dr 23518
Woolsey St 23513
Workwood Rd 23513
World Trade Ctr 23510
Woronoca Ave 23503
Worth St 23503
Wyngate Dr 23502
Wyoming Ave
1500-1599 23502
2300-2799 23513
Wythe Pl 23508
Yarmouth St 23510
Yoder Ave 23502
W York St 23510
Yorktown Dr 23505

NUMBERED STREETS

1st Ave & St 23511
1st Bay St 23518
1st View St 23503
2nd St 23511
2nd Bay St 23518
3rd Ave 23511
3rd St 23510
3rd Bay St 23518
3rd View St 23503
4th Ave & St 23511
4th Bay St 23518
4th View St 23503
5th Ave 23511
5th Bay St 23518
6th Ave 23511
6th Bay St 23518
6th View St 23503
7th Ave & St 23511
7th Bay St 23518
8th Ave & St 23511
8th Bay St 23518
8th View St 23503
9th Bay St 23518
9th View St 23503
10th Ave 23511
10th Bay St 23518
10th View St 23503
E 11th St 23510
11th Bay St 23518
11th View St 23503
12th Bay St 23518
12th View St 23503
E 13th St 23510
13th Bay St 23518
13th View St 23503
14th St 23505
14th Bay St 23518
14th View St 23503
E 15th St 23510
15th Bay St 23518
15th View St 23503
E 16th St 23510
16th Bay St 23518
E 17th St 23517
17th Bay St 23518
E 18th St 23517
E 18th St 23517
400-498 23504
500-599 23504
18th Bay St 23518
E & W 19th 23517
19th Bay St 23518
E 20th St 23517
E 20th St 23517
400-699 23504
W 20th St 23517
20th Bay St 23518
E & W 21st 23517
21st Bay St 23518
E & W 22nd 23517
22nd Bay St 23518
E 23rd St 23504
W 23rd St 23517
23rd Bay St 23518
E 24th St 23517
200-399 23504
W 24th St 23517
24th Bay St 23518
E 25th St 23517
200-899 23504
W 25th St
100-1099 23517
1200-1400 23508
1402-1498 23508
25th Bay St 23518
E 26th St 23517
200-1199 23504
W 26th St
100-1099 23517
1200-1499 23508
26th Bay St 23518
E 27th St 23517
200-899 23504
W 27th St
100-1099 23517
1200-1212 23508
1214-1499 23508
27th Bay St 23518
E 28th St 23504
W 28th St
100-299 23504
300-799 23508
28th Bay St 23518
E 29th St 23504
100-299 23504
300-799 23508
29th Bay St 23518
E 30th St 23504
100-299 23504
300-499 23508
30th Bay St 23518
E 31st St 23504
100-299 23504
300-999 23508
W 32nd St
100-299 23504
300-499 23508
W 33rd St
100-299 23504
300-499 23508
W 34th St
100-299 23504
300-1099 23508
W 35th St
100-299 23504
300-1399 23508
W 36th St
100-299 23504
300-1099 23508
W 37th St
100-299 23504
300-1499 23508
W 38th St
100-299 23504
300-1599 23508
E 39th St 23504
100-199 23504
800-1599 23508
E 40th St 23504
W 40th St 23508
E 41st St 23504
W 41st St 23508
E 42nd St 23504
W 42nd St 23508
43rd St 23508
44th St 23508
45th St 23508
46th St 23508
47th St 23508
48th St 23508
49th St 23508
50th St 23508
51st St 23508
52nd St 23508
53rd St 23508
105th St 23511

PETERSBURG VA

General Delivery 23801

POST OFFICE BOXES MAIN OFFICE STATIONS AND BRANCHES

Box No.s
All PO Boxes 23801

NAMED STREETS

A Ave 23801
Aachen Rd 23801
Access Rd
1000-1099 23801
2900-2900 23805
Accomack St 23803
Adair Pl 23803
N & S Adams St 23803
Addison Way 23805
Albemarle St 23803
Aleta Ln 23805
Algiers Rd 23801
Allen Ave 23805
Als St 23803
Amelia St 23803
Amherst Dr 23805
Anchor Ave 23803
Anderson St 23805
Ann St 23803
Anzio Cir & Rd 23801
Apperson St 23803
Arch St 23805
Ardennes Rd 23801
Argonne Ct 23801
Arlington St 23803
Armistead Ave 23803
Ash St 23803
Atlee Station Ct 23801
Augusta Ave 23803
Avon Way 23805
N & S Azalea Rd 23805
B Ave 23801
E & W Bank St 23803
Bannister Rd 23805
Bartow Aly 23803
Bastogne Rd 23801
Bataan Rd 23801
Battle Cir, Ct & Dr 23801
Baxter Rd 23803
Bayberry Ct 23803
Baylors Ln
1200-1499 23803
1800-1898 23805
Bear Aly 23803
Beauregard Ave 23805
Beazley St 23803
Bedford St 23803
Beech St 23803
Beechwood Dr 23805
Belleau Wood Rd 23801
Bellevue Ave 23803
Belmead St 23805
Bennington Ct 23801
Berkeley Ave 23805
Bermuda Dr 23805
Bessemer Rd 23805
Betty Ct 23803
Bishop St 23805
Bishop Loop Rd 23801
Bizerte Cir & Rd 23801
Blackwater Dr 23805
Blair Rd 23805
Bland St 23803
Blanks Aly 23803
Blick St 23803
Blossum Ln 23803
Bluefield St 23803
Bogese Dr 23805
Boisseau Dr 23803
Bolling St 23803
Bollingbrook St 23803
E & W Booker Cir 23803
Botany Bay Cir 23803
Boxwood Ct 23803
Boydton Plank Rd 23805
Bradford Ln 23805
Brandon Ave 23805
Brandywine Ct 23801
Breckenridge Ave 23803
Brickhouse Ave 23803
Brierwood Rd 23805
Brigade Loop 23801
Bristol Ct 23803
Britton St 23803
Brookside Ave 23805
Brown St 23803
Buckner St 23805
Budd Rd 23805
Buna Cir & Rd 23801
Bunker Ct 23805
N & S Burch St 23803
Burks St 23805
Burma Rd 23801
Busby St 23803
Byrd Ave 23801
Byrne St 23803
C Ave 23801
C St 23803
Cam Rahn Ct 23801
Camelot Rd 23805
Cameron Ct & St 23803
Campbell Dr 23805
Canal St 23803
N Carolina Ave 23803
Carrington St 23803
Carroll Dr 23803
Carter St 23803
Cassino Rd 23801
Cedar Mountain Dr 23801
Cedarcroft Ct 23805
Center St 23803
Central Ave 23801
Central Park 23803
Centre Hill Ave & Ct 23803
Century Dr 23805
Chanticleer Dr 23805
N & S Chappell St 23803
Cherbourg Rd 23801
Cherry St 23803
Chestnut St 23803
Chris Rd 23803
Chuckatuck Ave 23805
Church St 23803
Circle Dr 23803
W Clara Dr 23803
Claremont St 23805
Clarke St 23803
Clayton St 23803
Clinton St 23803
Cockade Aly 23803
Coggin St 23805
Cold Harbor Ct 23801
College Pl 23803

Street	ZIP
Colston St	23805
Columbia Rd	23803
Commerce St	23803
Concord Dr	23803
Confederate Ave	23803
Cool Spring Dr	23803
Coral Sea Cir & Dr	23801
Corling St	23803
Corporate Rd	23805
Cottonwood Dr	23803
Country Ln	23805
Country Lane Ct	23805
County Dr	23803
Court St	23803
Courthouse Ave & Rd	23803
Cox Rd	23803
Crater Cir	23805
N Crater Rd	23803
S Crater Rd	
1-699	23803
701-899	23803
900-3999	23805
Crater Woods Ct	23805
Crestfall Ct	23805
Crestwood Ave	23805
Croatan Dr	23803
Cross St	23803
Culpepper Ave	23803
Cumberland Ave	23805
Custer St	23803
Cypress Ct	23803
Dakar Dr	23803
Dalewood Ave	23803
Dalton Ave	23803
Darby Dr	23803
Darcy St	23803
N Davis St	23803
Deerfield Dr	23805
Defense Rd	23805
Delaware Dr	23801
Delmar Ave	23803
Denise Rd	23805
Dering Rd	23805
Desert Storm Ct	23801
Diamond St	23803
Dinwiddie Ct	23803
Doans Aly	23803
Dock St	23803
Dodson Rd	23805
Dogwood Ct	23805
Dolan Dr	23805
Drury Rd	23805
Duke Dr	23803
Dunedin Dr	23803
N & S Dunlop St	23803
Dupuy Rd	23803
Dutch Gap Ct	23801
E Ave	23801
Early Ct	23801
Early St	23803
East Blvd	23805
Eastover Ave	23803
Edar St	23803
Edgewater Dr	23805
Edgewood Rd	23801
Edmonds Ave	23803
Elaine Dr	23803
Elliott Ave	23805
Elm St	23803
Ewell Ct	23801
Exchange Aly	23803
Factory Ln	23803
Fairfax St	23805
Fairgrounds Rd	23803
Farmer St	23803
Federal St	23803
Fern Ct	23803
Ferndale Ave	23803
Field Rd	23805
E & W Fillmore St	23803
Finance Rd	23801
Flank Rd	23805
Fleet St	23803
Fleur De Hundred St	23805
Flower Cir	23803
Floyd St	23803
Flynn Ln	23805
N & S Foley St	23803
Forest Ln	23805
Forest Hills Rd	23805
Forsythia Way	23805
Fort Bross Dr	23805
Fort Hayes Ct	23805
Fort Henry St	23803
Fort Lee	23801
Fort Lee Rd	23803
Fort Mahone St	23805
Fort Rice St	23805
Francis St	23805
Franck Ave	23803
Franklin St	
1-28	23803
29-29	23804
29-399	23803
30-298	23803
Front Access Rd	23801
Frontage Rd	23805
Gates Ln	23803
George St	23805
Gibbons Ave	23803
N & S Gillfield Dr	23803
Gilliam St	23803
Gladstone St	23803
Glendale Ave	23805
Glenwood Ct	23803
Gloucester Cir	23803
Goodrich Ave	23805
Gordon Dr	23805
Gracie White Cir	23803
Graham Rd	
1-297	23803
299-300	23803
302-398	23803
401-497	23805
499-600	23805
602-698	23805
Grant Ave	
1200-1499	23803
1201-1299	23801
Grant Ct	23803
Grayson St	23803
Greensville Ave	23803
Greenwood Dr	23805
Gressett St	23803
Grigg St	23803
Grimes Rd	23803
Grove Ave	23803
Guarantee St	23803
Gustavo Ln	23805
N & S Halcun Dr	23803
Halifax Rd	23805
Halifax St	23803
Hamilton St	23803
Hampton Ct & Rd	23805
Hannon St	23803
Hanover St	23803
Harding St	23803
Harrison Ct	23801
Harrison St	23803
Harrison Creek Blvd	23803
Hartley St	23803
Hastings Rd	23805
Hatchett Rd	23803
Hawk St	23803
Hayden Dr	23803
Haygood Rd	23805
Hazel St	23803
Hazel Grove Ct	23801
Hemlock Cir	23803
Henrico St	23803
Henry St	23803
Heth Rd	23805
Hickory Ct	23803
Hickory Hill Rd	23803
W High St	23803
High Pearl St	23803
Hill St	23803
Hillcrest Rd	23805
Hillside Dr	23803
Hilltop Way	23805
Hilton Pl	23803
Hinton St	23803
Hoke Dr	23805
Holland Dr	23805
Holly Hill Dr	23805
Homestead Dr	23805
Hurt St	23803
Inchon Rd	23801
Independence Ave	23803
Indiana Ln	23803
Industrial Dr	23803
Industrial Rd	23805
Industry Pl	23805
Irving St	23803
Isabella Ct	23803
Ivy Ln	23805
Jackson Cir	23801
Jackson Ct	23805
James Rd	23803
N Jamestown Dr	23803
Jarratt Ct	23803
Jean Ct	23803
N & S Jefferson Ln, Pl & St	23803
Jerusalem Ave	23803
Johnson Ave & Rd	23805
N & S Jones St	23803
Juniper Rd	23803
Kabul Ct	23801
Kelisti Rd	23801
Kenmore Dr	23805
Kennedy Ct	23803
Kentucky Ave	23803
Khe Sahn Ct	23801
King Ave	23805
Kings Rd	23805
Kirkham St	23803
Kutchen St	23805
Lafayette St	23803
Lakeshore Ct	23805
Lakewood Dr	23805
Lamar Ave	23803
Lancelot Rd	23805
Laurel Rd	23805
Laurel Hill Ct	23801
Lawrence St	23803
Layne Cir	23805
Leavenworth St	23803
Ledo Rd	23801
Lee Ave	
500-900	23801
807-897	23803
899-1099	23803
902-4398	23801
Leefield Dr	23803
Lester Ave	23803
Lexington Ct	23803
Lexington Dr	23801
Liberty St	23803
Lieutenants Run Dr	23805
Lily Way	23805
Lincoln St	23803
Linda Ln	23803
Linden St	23805
N & S Little Church St	23803
Lock Ln	23805
Locust Ct	23803
Logan St	23803
Longstreet Dr	23805
Louisa Dr	23803
Low St	23803
Lumsden St	23803
N Madison St	23803
Magazine Rd	23803
Magnolia St	23803
Magnolia Farms Dr	23803
Mahone Ave	23801
Mainsail Ave	23803
Manila Rd	23801
Maria Ct	23803
N & S Market St	23803
Marks Aly	23803
Marne Rd	23801
Mars St	23803
Marseilles St	23803
Marshall St	23803
Matoax Ave	23805
Maycox St	23805
Mckeever St	23803
Mckenney St	23803
Mckenzie St	23803
Meadowbrook St	23803
Mecklenburg St	23803
Medical Park Blvd	23805
Mekong Rd	23801
Melville St	23803
Mercer St	23803
Mercury St	23803
Merryoaks Ave	23805
Metz Rd	23801
Midland Rd	23805
Midway Ave	23803
Mill St	23803
Miller St	23803
Mingea St	23803
Mistletoe St	23803
Mitchell Ct	23803
Monroe St	23803
Montgomery Ave	23803
Montibello St	23805
Monticello St	23805
Montpelier St	23805
Monument Ave	23803
Morton Ave	23805
Mount Airy St	23803
Mount Vernon St	23805
Mulberry St	23805
Myrick Ave	23805
Myrtle Dr	23803
Nance Dr	23803
Nansemond St	23803
Naples Rd	23801
Nash St	23803
Navajo Ct	23803
Nelson Ct	23803
New St	23803
New Guinea Rd	23801
New Market Ct	23801
New Millennium Dr	23805
New Wagner Rd	23805
New York Dr	23801
Newport Ave	23805
Nivram Rd	23805
Norman St	23803
Normandale Ave E & W	23803
Normandy Dr	23805
N Normandy Dr	23805
Normandy Rd	23801
North Blvd	23805
Northampton Rd	23805
Nottoway St	23803
Oak Ln	23803
Oak Hill Rd	23805
Oakdale Ave	23803
Oakland St	23803
Oakmont Dr	23805
Oakridge Rd	23805
Oakwood Cir & Ct	23805
Okinawa Rd	23801
Oklahoma St	23803
E & W Old St	23803
N & S Old Church St	23803
Old Wagner Rd	23805
Old Wythe St	23803
Orange Ln	23803
Osage Rd	23803
Overbrook Rd	23805
Park Ave & Dr E, N, S & W	23805
Parkview Ave	23803
Parkwood Ct	23805
Patrick St	23803
Patterson St	23803
Paul St	23803
Peakside Way	23805
Pecan St	23805
Pegram St	23803
Pender Ave	23803
Perry St	23803
Persimmon Ct	23803
Petty Ct & St	23805
Pike St	23803
Pin Oak Dr	23803
Pine St	23803
Pine Ridge Rd	23805
Pine View Cir	23803
Pinehill Blvd	23805
Pinehurst Dr	23805
Pinetree Dr	23803
N & S Plains Dr	23805
Pleasants Ln	23803
Plum St	23803
Pocahontas St	23803
Poe Ln	23803
Pointer St	23803
Poplar Dr	23805
Poplar St	23803
Port Dr	23803
Porterville St	23803
Powhatan Ave	23805
Prairelm Rd	23803
Priam St	23803
Prince Ave	23803
Prince George St	23803
Princess Ct	23803
Princeton Dr	23801
E Princeton Rd	23805
W Princeton Rd	23805
Progress Pl	23803
Puddledock Rd	23803
Pusan Rd	23801
Quality Dr	23805
Quartermaster Rd	23801
Quarters Rd	23801
Raleigh Ave	23805
Ramblewood Rd	23805
Randolph Ave	23803
Ransom St	23803
Ravine St	23803
Rawlings Ln	23803
Rear Access Rd	23801
Redwood Ct	23803
Regal Ct	23803
Regency Ct	23803
Reservoir Ave & Hts	23803
Retnag Rd	23805
Rhiems Rd	23801
Rhineland Rd	23801
Richland Rd	23805
Richmond Ave	23803
Ridgeview Ln	23805
Ridgewood Dr	23805
River Rd	23801
River St	23803
Rives Rd	23805
Roberson St	23803
Roberts Ave	23805
Rochell Ln	23803
Rock St	23803
Rocky Springs Ct	23801
Rohoic St	23803
Rolfe St	23803
Rollingwood Rd	23805
Rolyart Rd	23805
Rome St	23803
Rosemont St	23803
Rosewood Ter	23805
Ross Ct	23803
Roundtop Ave	23803
Rusty Ct	23805
Saddleback Ln	23805
Sage Ln	23805
Saint Andrew St	23803
Saint Lo Rd	23801
Salem Ct	23803
Salerno Rd	23801
Sandalwood Ct	23805
Sandy Ln	23803
Sapony St	23803
Saratoga Dr	23801
Savage St	23803
School Ct & St	23803
Scott St	23805
Seaboard St	23803
Seaton Rd	23805
Sedgwick St	23805
Selbon Ave	23805
Service Rd	23805
Seyler Dr	23805
Shady Hill Ln	23803
Sherwood Rd	23805
Shields St	23803
Shirley Ave	23805
Shop Rd	23801
Shore St	23803
W Short St	23803
Sicily Rd	23801
Siege Rd	23803
Sisisky Blvd	23801
Slagle Ave	23803
Solomons Rd	23801
South Ave	23803
E South Blvd	23805
W South Blvd	23805
N South St	23803
S South St	23803
Southampton St	23803
Southwood Dr	23805
Spotswood Dr	23805
Spring Ct & St	23803
Spruce St	23803
Squaw Aly	23803
Squirrel Dr	23805
Squirrel Level Rd	
1900-1998	23803
2000-2198	23805
2200-7620	23805
7622-7698	23805
St Andrew St	23803
St James St	23803
St John Ct & St	23803
St Luke St	23803
St Marks St	23803
St Matthew St	23803
Stainback St	23803
Stark St	23803
Starke St	23803
Stately Ct	23803
N Stedman Dr	23803
Steel St	23803
Sterling St	23803
Stratford Ave	23803
Stuart Ave	23803
Summit St	23803
Sunset Ave	23805
Surry Ln	23803
Sussex St	23803
N Sycamore St	23803
S Sycamore St	
1-19	23803
21-900	23803
902-998	23803
1501-1549	23805
1551-2099	23805
E & W Tabb St	23803
Talley Ave	23803
Taylor St	23803
Terrace Ave	23803
Terrell Ct	23803
Texas Ave	23803
Toll Gate Ln	23805
Tora Bora Rd	23801
Townes Rd	23805
Trarich Rd	23805
Travis Ln	23803
Trenton Dr	23801
Triad Pkwy	23803
E & W Tuckahoe St	23805
Tudor Ln	23805
Tulip Aly	23803
Tyler Rd	23805
N & S Union St	23803
Upper Appomattox St	23803
Valley Dr	23805
Valley Forge Ln	23801
E, N & S Valor Dr	23803
Van Buren Dr	23803
Van Dorn St	23805
Varina Ave	23805
Vaughan Rd	23805
Vesonder Rd	23805
Virginia Ave	23803
Wagner Rd	23805
Wakefield Ave	23805
Walker Ave	23803
Walkover St	23803
Walnut Blvd	23805
Walnut Ln	23803
Walnut St	23803
Walsh Ave	23803
Walta Cir	23805
Walton St	23805
Warehouse Rd	23801
Warner Rd	23805
Warren St	23805
E & W Washington St	23803
Weaver Ave	23803
Webster St	23803
Wells Rd	23805
Wells St	23803
Wesley St	23803
N & S West Ct, Ln & St	23803
N & S Westchester Dr	23805
Westover Ave	23805
Westwood Dr	23805
Weyanoke St	23805
Wheelhouse Ct	23805
N & S Whitehill Dr	23803
Wilcox St	23803
William St	23803
Wills Rd	23803
Wilson St	23803
Wilton Rd	23805
Windham St	23803
Windsor Rd	23805
Winfield Rd	23803
Wise Ave	23803
Wisteria Ln	23805
Witten St	23803
Woodland Rd	23805
Woodmere Dr	23805
Wright Rd	23805
E & W Wythe St	23803
Yorktown Dr	23801
Young Ave	23803
Youngs Rd	23803

NUMBERED STREETS

Street	ZIP
1st St	23803
1st St	23801
2nd St	23803
3rd St	23803
3rd St	23801
4th St	23803
5th St	23803
6th St	23803
7th St	23803
8th St	23803
11th St	23801
13th St	23801
16th St	23801
19th St	23801
20th St	23801
22nd St	23801
24th St	23801
27th St	23801
31st St	23801
39th St	23801
40th St	23801
41st St	23801

PORTSMOUTH VA

General Delivery	23705
General Delivery	23707

POST OFFICE BOXES MAIN OFFICE STATIONS AND BRANCHES

Box No.s	ZIP
C9001 - C9001	23705
C - J	23705
1 - 1521	23705
2005 - 2477	23702

3001 - 4178 23701
5001 - 6944 23703
7001 - 8016 23707
9998 - 9998 23705
50001 - 50158 23703

NAMED STREETS

A St 23704
Abbey Ct 23707
Abbott Pl 23702
Academy Ave 23703
Accolade St 23701
Ace Parker Rd 23701
Acorn St 23704
Acres Cir & Rd 23703
Adams St 23703
Admiral Ct 23703
Adriatic St 23707
Aft Ct 23703
Afton Pkwy 23702
Ahoy Ct 23703
Airline Blvd
500-1899 23707
1900-3799 23701
Alabama Ave 23702
Albany Dr 23702
Albemarle St 23707
Alcindor Rd 23701
Alden Ave 23702
Alexander St 23701
Algonquin St 23707
Allard Rd 23701
Allen Rd 23702
Ambler Ave 23707
Amelia Ave 23707
Amherst Dr 23703
Anchor St 23702
Angler St 23703
Ann St 23704
Anndora Rd 23701
Ansell Ave 23702
Apache Rd 23701
Apm Terminals Blvd 23703
Apple St 23704
Appomattox Ave 23702
Arcadia Ave 23704
Arden St 23703
Argyle St 23704
Arizona St 23701
Arlington Pl 23707
Armistead Dr 23704
Armstrong St 23704
Arnold Palmer Dr 23701
Arthur Ave 23703
Ash St 23707
Ashburn Rd 23702
Aspin St 23703
Astor Ave 23704
Atlanta Ave 23704
Attwater Ln 23702
Augusta Ave & Ter 23707
Augustine Cir 23703
Avendong Dr 23703
Avocet Ct 23703
Avondale Rd 23701
Axson St 23702
Aylwin Cres & Rd 23702
Azalea Ave 23704
Aztec Dr 23702
Bagley St 23704
Bailey Pl 23701
Bain St 23704
Bainbridge Ave 23702
Bald Eagle Ct 23703
Baldwin Ave 23702
Ballard Ave 23701
Ballast Ct 23703
Bamboo Rd 23703
Banister River Reach 23703
Barberry Ln 23703
Barbour Dr 23704
Barclay Ave
2400-2799 23702
2800-3099 23701
Bardot Ct & Ln 23701
Barlow Dr 23707
Barney Pl 23702
Barron St 23704
Bart St 23707
Barton Ave 23708
Basie Cres 23701
Baskerville Ln 23701
Bay St 23704
Bayview Blvd 23707
Baywood Ln 23701
Beachfront Ter 23707
Beacon Rd 23702
Beaton Dr 23701
Beazley Dr 23701
Bedford Ct 23701
Beech St 23704
Beechdale Rd
1-99 23702
100-599 23701
Beechwood Ct 23702
Belafonte Ct & Dr 23701
Belle St 23707
Bellhaven Rd 23702
Bellport Ave 23704
Belmont Ave 23701
Ben Hogan Dr 23701
Bender Ct 23702
Benton Ave 23702
Berkley Ave 23707
Berkshire Rd 23701
Bertha Ln 23701
Bertrand St 23703
Bickford Ln & Pkwy 23703
Bide A Wee Ln 23701
Bidgood Dr 23703
Biltmore Pl 23702
Bingham Dr 23703
Birch Rd 23703
Bird Ln 23702
Bishops Pl 23703
Bismarck Myrick Cres & St 23704
Bittern Ct 23703
Blaine St 23703
Blair St 23704
Blanche Dr 23701
Blue St 23702
Blue Heron Pt 23703
Bluegill Ave 23702
Boat St 23702
Bob White St 23701
Bobby Jones Ct & Dr 23701
Bold St 23701
Bolling Rd 23701
Bon Secours Way 23703
Bonney Ter 23704
Boston St 23704
Bouie Ct 23704
Bowden St 23703
Boyd St 23701
Bradford Ter 23704
Bradley Ave 23701
Branch St 23703
Braxton Ave 23701
Breakwater Dr 23703
Breezewood Ct 23703
Brent Cres 23703
Briarwood Ln 23703
Bridges Ave 23703
Brierdale Pl 23702
Brighton St
800-899 23704
3100-3899 23707
Broad St 23707
Broadway St 23703
Broda Ct 23701
Brookmere Ln 23703
Brookside Ln 23703
Brookwood Dr 23703
Broomhill Ave 23701
Brown Ct 23701
Bruce Pl 23707
Brunswick Rd 23701
Buchanan Ave 23704
Buckingham Dr 23703
Bunche Blvd & Ct 23701
Burnham Dr 23703
Burr Ln 23703
Burrland Rd 23703
Burtis St 23702
Burtons Point Rd 23704
Butler St 23704
Byers Ave 23701
Cabot St 23702
California Ave 23701
Callis Rd 23701
Calvary Ct 23704
Calvin St 23701
Cambridge Ave & St 23707
Camden Ave 23704
Camellia Dr 23703
Cammy Cir 23703
Campbell St 23703
Campus Dr 23701
Candlelight Ln 23703
Canoe Ct 23703
Canterbury Ct & Dr 23703
Capelle Rd 23703
Cardinal Ln 23703
Carey Cir 23701
Carisbrooke Ln 23703
Carlton Ct 23703
Carney St 23703
Carney Farm Ln 23703
Carol Ln 23701
Carolina Ave 23707
Caroline Ave
3800-4299 23701
4301-4397 23707
4399-5199 23707
Carrington Cres N 23701
Carson Cres E & W 23701
Carter Rd 23703
Carver Cir 23701
Cassell Ave 23704
Castle Way 23703
Castlewood Rd 23702
Catamaran Ct 23703
Catawba Trl 23701
Cavalier Blvd & Ct 23701
Cedar Ln 23703
Cedarcrest Ln 23701
Cenchams St 23702
Centenary Dr 23703
Centre Ave 23704
Centre Port Cir 23703
Century Dr 23701
Chancellor St 23707
Chandler Harper Dr 23701
Channel Ave 23703
Channing Ave 23702
Charles Ave 23702
Charles Martin St 23708
Charleston Ave 23704
Charlotte Dr 23701
Chartom Ct 23702
Chatham Rd 23702
Chautauqua Ave 23707
Cheaderm Rd 23708
Chelsea St 23704
Cherokee Rd 23701
Cherry Rd 23701
Chesapeake Ave 23704
Chestnut St 23704
Cheyenne Trl 23701
Chicago Ave 23704
Chippewa Trl 23701
Chisholm Cir & Cres 23704
Choate St 23707
Choctaw Dr 23702
Chowan Dr 23701
Christiana Cir 23703
Christopher Cleborne Cir 23708
Chumley Rd 23701
Churchill Dr 23703
Churchland Blvd 23703
Cinnamon Teal Ct 23703
City Park Ave & Dr 23701
Claremont Dr 23702
Clay St 23701
Cleveland St 23707
Clifford St
700-798 23704
1401-1599 23704
3401-3497 23707
3499-4799 23707
4801-4899 23701
Clintwood Dr 23703
Clipper Ln 23703
Clover Hill Dr 23703
Coast Guard Blvd 23703
Cobble Hill Rd 23703
Cole Ct & Rd 23701
N Colin Dr 23701
College Dr 23703
Colonial Ln 23703
Colony Rd 23703
Colorado Ave 23701
Coltrane Ct & Dr 23701
Columbia Ct 23704
Columbia St
300-2199 23704
3300-4699 23707
Columbus Ave 23704
Commerce St 23707
Commonwealth Ave 23707
Compass Ct 23703
Concord Rd 23701
Condor Cir 23703
Confederate Ave 23704
Connor Pl 23702
Constitution Ave 23704
Coolidge St 23704
Cooper Dr 23702
Corell Ct 23701
Cornick Rd 23701
Cornwall Rd 23701
Corprew Dr 23707
Cosby Ct 23701
Cotton Pl 23702
County St
100-2299 23704
2301-2399 23704
3300-4799 23707
Court St 23704
Courtney Rd 23703
Cove Ter 23702
Cpl J M Williams Ave 23701
Crabapple St 23704
Crabtree Ct & Pl 23703
Craford Pl 23704
Craney Island Fuel 23703
Craneybrook Ln 23703
Crawford Cir 23704
Crawford Ct 23704
Crawford Pkwy 23704
Crawford St
300-432 23704
431-431 23705
434-898 23704
501-901 23704
Creekside Ct & Dr 23703
Creig St 23707
Croatan Trl 23701
Crocker Ave 23703
Croft Ct 23703
Cross St 23702
Crystal Lake Dr 23701
Culpepper Rd 23704
Cumberland Ave 23707
Cushing St 23702
Cutherell St 23707
Cypress Cir & Rd 23701
Dahlgren Ave 23702
Dahlia St 23704
Daisy Dr 23703
Dakota Dr 23701
Dale Dr 23704
Damon Ct 23701
Dandridge Dr 23701
Daniel Way 23701
Danvers Ct & Rd 23703
Darby Close 23703
Darden Ter 23701
Darren Cir & Dr 23701
Dartmouth St 23707
David Ln 23701
Davis St 23702
Deal Dr 23701
Debra Ln 23702
Decatur St 23702
Deep Creek Blvd
1500-3100 23704
3102-3298 23704
3300-5199 23702
Dekalb Ave
1-199 23702
200-999 23701
Dekalb Ct 23701
Delham Rd 23701
Denver Dr 23701
Depot Dr 23707
Derby Rd 23702
Des Moines Ave 23704
Detroit St 23707
Dewey St 23704
Dinwiddie St 23704
Dixie Ave 23707
Dixon Rd 23701
Dock St 23702
Doerr Rd 23703
Dogwood Dr & Trl 23703
Dominion Rd 23701
Dorset Ave 23701
Douglas Ave 23707
Dovenshire St 23701
Dover St 23702
Downes St 23704
Duce St 23701
Duchess Rd 23707
Duke Dr 23703
Duke St 23704
Dumont Ave 23701
Dunedin Rd 23701
Dunkin St 23703
Dunkirk St 23703
Dwight Dr 23701
Eagle Pt 23703
Early Dr 23701
East Rd 23707
Easton St 23702
Eaver Ct 23703
Ebbtide Ln 23703
Echo Ct 23703
Edgewood Rd 23701
Edison Ave 23702
Edward May Rd 23708
Edwards St 23704
Edwin Rd 23703
Effingham St
100-199 23708
201-297 23704
299-2699 23704
Egrets Landing Rd 23703
Eisenhower Cir 23701
Ekstine Dr 23701
Eleanor Ct N & S 23701
Elizabeth Pl 23704
Ellington Sq 23701
Elliott Ave
2201-2597 23702
2599-3599 23702
3600-4199 23701
Elm Ave 23704
Elmhurst Ct & Ln 23701
Emerson St 23701
Emmons Pl 23702
Endicotte Rd 23702
Enterprise Way 23704
Eric St 23703
Ericsson St 23702
Estates Ct, Ln & Way 23703
Eustis St 23701
Evergreen Pl 23704
Faber Rd 23703
Fable Ave 23703
Faigle Rd 23703
Fairfax Ave 23707
Fairview Cir & Ln 23702
Fairway Dr 23701
Falling River Reach 23703
Faro Ln 23703
Farragut St 23702
Fauquier Ave 23707
Fawkes St 23703
Fayette St 23704
Felton Rd 23701
Ferguson Dr 23703
Ferry Rd 23701
Feudist Dr 23703
Fifth St 23704
Fillmore St 23704
Fin Ct 23703
Finchley Rd 23702
Fir St 23703
Firehouse Ln 23704
Fiske St 23702
Flagship Way 23703
Flanders Cir 23707
Fleet Ct 23703
Florida Ave 23707
Floyd St 23707
Forestdale Dr 23703
Forrest Ct 23707
Forrest Haven Ln 23703
Forresthills Dr 23703
Fort Ln 23704
Fortune Ln 23703
Founders 23707
Foxgrape Rd 23701
Frailey Pl 23702
Francis St 23702
Franklin Ave 23702
Frederick Blvd
500-1900 23707
1902-1998 23707
2000-3399 23704
Freedom Ave & Ct 23701
Freemason Dr 23703
Fresnel Ave 23703
Fruitwood Ct 23703
Fulton Ave 23702
Gail Ct 23703
Gannon Rd 23703
Garfield St 23704
Garland Dr 23703
Garner Ave 23703
Garrett St 23702
Garwood Ave 23701
Gary Player Rd 23701
Gateway Dr 23703
Gatling Ct 23701
Gay Ave 23701
Gee St 23702
Gendreau Rd 23708
Gentle Rd 23703
George Washington Hwy
2900-3098 23704
3100-3699 23704
3700-5200 23702
5202-5298 23702
Georgia Ct 23703
Gertrude St 23703
Gibney St 23707
Gibson St 23703
Giles St 23707
Gillis Rd 23702
Gilmerton Ave 23704
Gladstone Ave 23701
Glasgow St
200-699 23704
3100-3599 23707
Gleep St 23701
Glencove Dr 23703
Glenwood Dr 23701
Gloucester Ave 23702
Godwin St 23704
Goff St 23703
Golden Eagle Pt 23703
Goode Way 23704
Goose Bay Dr 23703
Gort Ct 23701
Goshawk Ct 23703
Gothic St 23707
Graham St 23704
Granada Rd 23703
Grand St
1-99 23701
100-199 23702
Grayson St 23707
Graystone Way 23704
Green St 23704
Green Acres Pkwy 23703
Green Meadow Dr 23701
Green Point Ln 23702
Greenbrier Rd 23707
Greenbrook Dr 23703
Greenefield Dr N & S 23703
Greeneland Blvd 23701
Greenleaf Trl 23703
Greenway Ct E 23707
Greenwood Dr
2000-2799 23702
2800-4699 23701
Gregory Ct 23703
Griffin St
1600-1698 23704
3400-4799 23707
Grouse Ct 23703
Grove St 23701
Guardian Ct 23704
Gum Dr 23707
Gust Ct & Ln 23701
Guthrie St 23704
Gwaltney Ct 23702
Gwin St 23704
Gygax Ave 23701
Hale Ct 23701
Halifax Ave 23707
Hamilton Ave 23707
Hampshire Grn 23703
Hampton Pl 23704
Hanbury Ave 23702
Hancock Ave 23701
Hanley Ave 23703
Hanover Ave 23707
Hansen Ave
100-150 23702
151-3599 23701
Harbor Ct 23704
Harbor Dr
100-199 23707
500-698 23704
700-799 23704
Harding St 23703
Hardwood Ct & Ln 23703
Hardy Pl 23707
Harley Ave 23704
Harmony Dr 23701
Harper Rd 23707
Harrell St 23704
Harris Rd 23702
Harrower Ct 23701
Hartford St 23707
Harvard Rd 23701
Harvest Ct 23703
Harvey St 23703
Hatton St 23704
Hatton Point Rd 23703
Havenwood Ct 23703
Hawthorne Ln 23703
Haysom St 23701
Haywood Dr 23703
Headwind Ln 23703
Heath Ln 23701
Heather Rd 23703
Hedge Ln 23701
Hedgerow Cir & Ln 23703
Henderson St 23701
Henry St 23704
Hentrinc St 23707
Herbert Ct 23703
Hermitage Dr 23703
Heron Pt 23703
Hertford St 23702
Hickory St 23707
High St
1-2499 23704
2501-2597 23707
2599-3999 23707
4500-6199 23703
High Point Dr 23703
N & S Highgate Cir 23703
Highland Ave 23704
Hightower Rd 23703

Hillwood St 23703
Hobson St 23704
Hodges Ferry Rd 23701
Hodges Manor Rd 23701
Holcomb Rd 23708
Holladay St 23704
Holloway Dr 23701
Holly Rd 23703
Holly Cliff Ln 23703
Holly Hill Cres, Ct & Ln 23702
Holston River Reach 23703
Holt Dr 23701
Honeysuckle Ln 23703
Hoover St 23704
Hopi Ct 23701
Horne Ave 23701
Hosiers Oaks Dr 23703
Howard St 23707
Howell Ln 23701
Hull St 23704
Hunters Cir 23703
Hunters Point Dr 23703
Huron Dr 23702
Hyde Ct 23701
Hyde Rd 23703
Ibis Ct 23703
Idlewood Ave 23704
Independence St 23701
Inland Ln 23701
Irwin St 23702
Island Rd 23703
Ivey St 23701
Jackson St 23703
Jacquelyn Dr 23701
Jamal Ct & Ln 23701
Jamestown Ave 23704
Jarman Ave 23701
Jeffers St 23702
Jefferson St 23704
Jenkins Pl 23702
Jester Ct 23701
Jewell Ave 23701
Jo Ann Dr 23703
John Bean St 23703
John Paul Jones Cir 23708
Johnson Ave 23701
Jordan Ln 23703
Jouett St 23702
Joyce Ct 23703
Julien Dr 23702
Kalona Ct & Rd 23703
Kansas Ave 23701
Kay Rd 23701
Kearney Way 23701
Keel Ct 23703
Keeper St 23703
Kelly Dr 23702
Kemp Dr 23703
Kennedy Dr 23702
Kenny Ct & Ln 23703
Kent Dr 23702
Keswick Ct 23703
Ketch Dr 23703
Keville Rd 23701
Killian Ave 23704
Kilty St 23704
King St
 400-498 23704
 500-2299 23704
 2301-2399 23704
 3201-3397 23707
 3399-4899 23707
Kingman Ave
 3500-3699 23707
 3700-3999 23701
Kings Gate Dr 23701
Kirby St 23702
Kitt Ct 23701
Knight Rd 23701
Knightsbridge Way 23703
Knox St 23704
Laigh Cir & Rd 23701
Lake Cir 23703
Lake Forest Ct & Dr 23701
Lake Shores Dr 23707
Lakeside Dr 23701
Lakeview Dr 23701
Lamper Rd 23701
Lamplighter Ct 23703
Lancaster Ave 23707
Lancer Dr 23701
Lands End Rd 23701
Lane Pl 23704
Langley Cir & Ct 23701
Lanier Cres 23707
Lansing Ave 23704
Lantern Way 23703
Larkspur Rd 23703
Larosa Ct 23701
Lasalle Ave 23704
Laurel Ln 23703
Laurie Ln 23701
Lawrence Cir 23707
Leavell Rd 23701
Leckie St 23704
Lee Ave 23707
Leedale Ave 23701
Lenah Higbee St 23708
Lenora Ave 23707
Lent Ct 23701
Leonard Rd 23701
Leslie Ct & Dr 23703
Lester Ct 23707
Lewis Rd 23701
Lewis Minor St 23708
Lexington Dr 23704
Liberty St 23701
Lighthouse Dr 23703
Lilac Cres & Dr 23703
Lincoln St 23704
Linda Rd 23701
Linden Ave 23704
Lindsay Ave 23704
Linnet Ln 23703
Liston Ln 23701
Little Church Rd 23703
Littlefield Way 23702
Liverpool St 23704
Llewellyn St 23707
Lockport St 23704
Locust Ln 23701
Logan Dr 23701
London Blvd
 700-798 23704
 800-1899 23704
 1901-2199 23704
 2700-2898 23707
 2900-3199 23707
London St 23704
Long Point Blvd 23703
Loon Ct 23703
Loren Cres 23701
Louder Ct 23701
Loudoun Ave 23707
Louisa Ave 23707
Loxley Rd 23702
Luger Ct 23701
Lynn Dr 23707
Lyontine Ln 23701
Macarthur Ave 23704
Madden Ter 23703
Madison St 23704
Magnolia Dr 23703
Magnolia St 23704
Main St 23701
Mallard Cir & Cres 23703
Manchester Rd 23703
Manly St 23702
Manor Ave 23703
Manteo St 23701
Maple Ave 23704
Marciano Dr 23701
Marcy St 23701
Margaret Ave 23707
Mariner Ave 23703
Marion Ave 23707
Market St 23707
Markham St 23707
Marlboro Rd 23702
Marlyn Rd 23703
Marsh Wren Cir 23703
Marsha St 23703
Marshall Ave 23704
Martin Ave 23701
Martin Luther King Fwy 23704
Maryland Ave 23707
Mascott St 23707
Mast Ct 23703
Mathews Ter 23704
Maupin Ave & Ct 23702
Maurice Ave 23701
Maxwell Ave 23702
May St 23702
Mayfair Way 23703
Mayflower Rd 23701
Mcdaniel St 23704
Mclean St 23701
Meadowview Rd 23703
Meander Rd
 400-500 23704
 502-798 23704
 800-898 23707
Median Cir, Ct & Pl 23701
Meherrin River Reach 23703
Melvin Dr 23701
Meredith Dr 23703
Merlerli Rd 23701
Merrifields Blvd 23703
Merrimac Dr 23704
Michael Ln 23703
Mid City Shopping Ctr 23707
Middle St 23704
Midfield Ct & Pkwy 23703
Milan Dr 23703
Military Rd 23702
Mimosa Rd 23701
Mineo Ln 23701
Mintanto St 23704
Misty Ct 23703
Mohawk Dr 23701
Mohican Ct & Dr 23701
Monitor Rd 23707
Monroe St 23703
Montclair Ave 23701
Montgomery St 23707
Moonlit Ave 23703
Moore Rd 23703
Morgate Ln 23703
Morning Side Dr 23702
Morris St 23702
Morro Blvd 23703
Moss St 23701
Moton St 23707
Mount Pleasant Dr 23707
Mt Vernon Ave 23707
Muckle Ct 23701
Mulberry St 23704
Nansemond Cres & St 23707
Nashville Ave 23704
Nathan Ct 23701
Nautico Way 23703
Navajo Ct & Trl 23701
Naval Ave 23704
Nelson St
 600-999 23704
 3300-3599 23707
Neptune Ct 23703
Nero Dr 23701
Nevada St 23701
Neville St 23701
New River Reach 23703
Newby Rd 23701
Newport Ave 23704
Niagra St 23702
Nicholson St 23702
Nnsy Quarters 23704
Nob Ct 23701
Noble St 23702
Norcum Cir 23701
W Norfolk Rd 23703
Norfolk Naval Shipyard 23709
Norman Rd 23703
Normandy St 23701
North St
 200-2199 23704
 2201-2399 23704
 2700-3000 23707
 3002-3098 23707
Nottingham Rd 23701
Oak St 23704
Oakcrest St 23702
Oakhill Ave 23703
Oakhurst Rd 23703
Oakland St 23707
Oakleaf Pl 23707
Oakley Hall Rd 23703
Occoquan River Reach 23703
Old Church Cir & Ln 23703
Old Farm Ct & Rd 23703
Oneal Ct 23701
Oregon Ave 23701
Oriole Rd 23701
Orleans Dr 23703
Orton St 23701
Osprey St 23702
Owens St 23704
Oxford Dr 23701
Pacific Ave 23707
Paddle Ct 23703
Palm Ct 23703
Palmer St 23704
Palmett St 23702
Pamunkey River Reach 23703
Paradise Dr 23701
Parish Ln 23703
Park Rd 23707
Park Manor Rd 23701
Parker Ave 23704
Parkside Pl 23702
Parkview Ave 23704
Patnor Dr 23701
Patrick St 23707
Patriot Way 23707
Paul Jones St 23702
Pawnee Dr 23702
Peace Way 23703
Peach St 23704
Peach Orchard Cir 23703
Peachtree Ct & Ln 23703
Peachwood Dr 23703
Peake Ln 23703
Pearl St 23704
Pebble Point Ct 23703
Pecan St 23703
Pelican Pt 23703
Pembroke Ave 23707
Pendleton Rd 23703
Peninsula Ave 23704
Pennington Blvd & Cir 23701
Pennock St 23702
Pepperwood Ct, Ln & Pl 23703
Perry St 23704
Phelps Pl 23702
Phillips Ave 23707
Phoebus St 23704
Picadilly Ln 23703
Picot Ct 23703
Piedmont Ave 23704
Pierce St 23703
Pine Blf 23701
Pine Cres 23704
Pine Rd 23703
Pine Needles Cir 23703
Pinebark Rd 23703
Pinecrest Dr 23701
Pinecroft Ln 23703
Pinewell St 23704
Pinners Ave 23707
Pleasant Woods Ct 23703
Plover Dr 23704
Pocahontas St 23701
N Point Dr 23703
Point Of View Arch 23703
Point West Dr 23703
Polk St 23703
Pollux Cir E & W 23701
Pond Ln 23703
Ponderosa St 23701
Poplar Ln 23701
Port Centre Pkwy 23704
Porter Rd 23707
Portland St 23707
Portsmouth Blvd
 400-898 23704
 900-3099 23704
 3101-3997 23701
 3999-6599 23701
Potomac Ave 23707
Power St 23707
Powhatan Ave 23707
Premier Pl 23704
Prentis Ave 23704
Preston Ave 23707
Primrose St 23704
Princeton Pl 23707
Progress Ave 23703
Prospect Pkwy 23702
Pueblo Dr 23702
Pulaski Ct & St 23704
Pullman Ave 23707
Quackenbush Pl 23702
Quail Pt 23703
Quantico St 23701
Quebec St 23707
Queen St
 300-2299 23704
 3500-3599 23707
Queenswood Dr 23703
Quiet Ct 23701
Quince Rd 23703
Race St
 601-699 23704
 3400-4799 23707
Radcliff Cir 23703
Radford St 23701
Railroad Ave 23707
Raintree Ln 23703
Randolph St 23704
Rapidan St 23701
Raven St 23702
Raylaine Dr 23703
Raymond Ct 23703
Red Barn Ct & Rd 23703
Redgate Dr 23702
Reef Ct 23703
Reese Dr 23703
Reflection Way 23703
Regent Dr 23703
Reid St 23702
Renshaw Ave 23704
Replica Ct & Ln 23703
Rex Ave 23702
Rexford Rd 23701
Richmond Ave 23704
Riddick Dr 23701
Rivanna River Reach 23703
River Cv 23703
River Green Ct 23703
River Point Cres 23707
River Pointe Dr S 23703
River Reach Close 23703
River Shore Rd 23703
Rivercrest Ct & Dr 23701
Riveredge Dr 23703
Rivermill Cir & Ct 23703
Riverside Dr 23707
Riverview Ave 23704
Rixey Pl 23708
Roanoke Ave 23704
Roberta St 23707
Roberts Ct E & W 23701
Robin Rd 23701
Robinson Rd 23701
Rockbridge Rd 23707
Rodgers Pl 23702
Rodman Ave 23707
Rolen Dr 23703
Rolfe Ter 23707
Romanesque St 23707
Roosevelt Blvd 23701
Rose Ave 23704
Ross Ct & Dr 23701
Rotunda Rd 23701
Royal St 23702
Russell St 23707
Ruth Ln 23701
Rutter St 23704
Sacony St 23701
Sagewood Dr 23703
Sail Ct 23703
Sailfish St 23703
Saint Juliens Crk 23702
Saint Juliens Crk Qtrs 23702
Sampson Pl 23702
Sandie Point Ln 23701
Sandpiper Dr 23704
Sandra Ln 23702
Sarazen Dr 23701
Saunders Dr 23701
Savage Ct 23703
Sawgrass Ln 23703
Schoolhouse Path 23703
Scott St
 800-899 23704
 3101-3297 23707
 3299-4399 23707
Seaboard Ave 23707
Seaboard Ct 23701
Seagrove Rd 23703
Seaguard Ave 23701
Sean Sykes Ave 23704
Sebago Dr 23702
Sedgewyck Cir & Ct 23703
Selfridge St 23702
Seminole Dr 23702
Seneca Trl 23701
Sequoia Rd 23701
Shady Ln 23701
Shamrock Dr 23701
Shannon Rd 23703
Shea St 23701
Shelby St 23701
Shelton Rd 23703
Shenandoah St 23707
Shipwright St 23703
Shirley Rd 23703
Shoal Ct 23701
Shore Dr 23701
Shoreline Dr 23703
Silver Maple Dr 23703
Smith Ave 23701
Smithfield Rd 23702
Snead Fairway 23701
South St
 400-598 23704
 600-2599 23704
 3100-4699 23707
Southampton Ln 23703
Southampton Arch 23703
Spandau Ct 23701
Spectator St 23701
Spence Rd 23703
Spratley St 23704
Springbloom Dr 23703
Springwood Dr 23703
Spruce St
 2300-2499 23704
 2500-2598 23707
Stamford Rd 23703
Stanley Rd 23701
Starboard St 23702
Starling Ct 23703
Stateflower Ct 23703
Stauffer Way 23701
Staunton Ave 23704
Sterling Way 23703
Sterling Cook St 23708
Sterling Point Cir, Dr & Is 23703
Sterling Point Island Rd 23703
Stevens Pl 23702
Stowaway Ln 23703
Stratford St 23701
Sturbridge Way 23703
Suburban Cir & Pkwy 23702
Sugar Creek Cir 23703
Sullivan Ct 23701
Summers Pl 23702
Summerset Dr 23703
Summit Ave 23704
Sumter St 23702
Sunnyfields Rd 23703
Sunnyside Ave 23703
Sunrise Ave 23701
Sunset Ct 23703
Sunset Ln 23701
Sunset Pt 23703
Surry St 23707
Susan St 23701
Sussex Dr 23707
Swan Ct 23703
Swannanoa Dr 23703
Swanson Pkwy 23704
Sweetbriar Cir 23703
Swimming Point Walk 23704
Sycamore Rd 23707
Syer Rd 23707
Sykes Ave & Ct 23701
Taft Dr 23701
Talley Cir 23704
Tanbark Ln 23703
Tanner Pl 23702
Tareyton Ln 23701
Tarnywood Dr 23703
Tatem Ave 23701
Tazewell St 23701
Teal St 23701
Tejo Ln 23703
Templar Ct & Dr 23703
Temple Ct 23707
Temple St 23702
Terry St 23703
Thelmar Ln 23701
Thistle Dr 23703
Thomas Cir 23704
Thorne Ave 23701
Thornwood St 23703
Tidal Ct 23703
Tides Ct 23703
Tigerlilly Dr 23701
Timberland Ct & Dr 23703
Towne Point Rd 23703
Trafalgar Arch 23703
Travis Pl 23702
Treakle Ter 23702
Treemont Ct 23701
Trexler Ave 23704
Trotman Cir 23703
Trucker St 23703
Truman Cir 23701
Truxton Ave 23701
Tucker St 23702
Tudor Rd 23701
Tunnel Facility Dr 23707
Turnpike Rd
 2101-2197 23704
 2199-2499 23704
 2500-3699 23707
 3700-4099 23701
Twin Pines Rd 23703
Twine Ave 23704
Two Oaks Ct & Rd 23703
Tyler Cres E & W 23707
Tyre Neck Rd 23703
Tyron Pl 23702
University Blvd 23703
Upshur Pl 23702
Utah St 23701
Vacation Ln 23703
Vail Pl 23702
Valhalla Dr 23707
Van Buren St 23703
Van Patton Pl 23701
Vaughn Ct 23701
Veneer Rd 23704
Vermont Ave 23707
Verne Ave 23703
Vessell Ct 23703
Vick St 23701
Vickers Ct 23701
Victory Blvd
 2-798 23702
 800-3299 23702
 3300-4099 23701
Victory Ct 23702
Viking St 23701

Village St 23703
Vine St 23703
Viola Ter 23703
Virginia Ave 23707
Vista Ct 23703
Wake Forest Rd 23703
Wakefield Dr 23703
Wall St 23702
Wallace Cir 23707
Walnut St 23704
Ward Ter 23704
Warfield Ct & Dr 23701
Warren Dr 23701
Warwick St 23707
Washington St 23704
Watah Ct 23702
Watch Water Close 23703
Water St 23704
Water Lilly Rd 23701
Waterview Ct 23703
Watson St 23707
Watts Ave 23704
Waverly Blvd 23704
Wavy St 23704
Wayland Dr 23703
Weaver Cir 23701
Webster Ave 23704
Welcome Ct & Rd 23701
Welk St 23701
Wesley St 23707
West Rd 23707
Westcott Rd 23703
Western Branch Blvd 23707
Westgate Plaza Shop Ctr 23701
Westminster Dr 23707
Westmoreland Ave & Ter 23707
Weston St 23702
Westwood Cres 23703
Weyanoke Dr 23703
Whaley Rd 23703
Wheatfield Ct 23703
Wherry Ct 23702
White Heron Pt 23703
Whitestone Ave 23701
Widgeon Cir 23703
Wilcox Ave 23704
Wild Duck Ln 23703
Wilkins Ct 23701
Willett Dr 23707
Williams St 23704
Williamsburg Ave 23704
Williamson Dr
100-199 23708
500-599 23704
600-899 23708
Williamson Rd 23707
Willow St 23701
Willow Way 23707
Willow Bend Ct 23703
Willow Breeze Ct & Dr 23703
Wilshire Rd 23703
Wilson Dr 23707
Wilson Pkwy 23707
Wilson St 23701
Winchester Dr 23707
Windrose Ct 23703
Windsor Rd 23701
Windy Pines Bnd, Cres, Ct & Lndg 23703
Windymille Dr 23703
Winston Rd 23703
Wirt Ave 23704
Wise Rd 23703
Witch Hazel Ct 23703
Woodland St 23702
Woodmere Ct & Dr 23703
Woodmill Ct 23703
Woodrow St 23707
Woodside Cir & Ln 23703
Woodstock St 23701
Wool Ave 23707
Worden Pl 23702
Worthington Sq 23704
Wren Cres 23703
Wright Ave 23702
Wright Rd 23703
Wyatt Dr 23703
Wycliff Rd 23703
Wyndybrow Dr 23703
Wyngate Ct 23703
Wynn Cir & St 23701
Wyoming Ave 23701
Wythe St 23704
Yaupon St 23703
York Dr 23702
Yorkshire Ct & Rd 23701
Yorktown Ave 23704

NUMBERED STREETS

All Street Addresses 23704

PURCELLVILLE VA

General Delivery 20132

POST OFFICE BOXES MAIN OFFICE STATIONS AND BRANCHES

Box No.s
All PO Boxes 20134

RURAL ROUTES

01, 02 20132

NAMED STREETS

All Street Addresses 20132

NUMBERED STREETS

All Street Addresses 20132

RADFORD VA

General Delivery 24141

POST OFFICE BOXES MAIN OFFICE STATIONS AND BRANCHES

Box No.s
1 - 3792 24143
5001 - 9100 24142

NAMED STREETS

Adams St 24141
Adventure Base Rd 24141
Alakeree St 24141
Allen Ave 24141
Altizer Sugar Run Rd 24141
Amber Rd 24141
Annie Akers Rd 24141
Appalachian Rd 24141
Archway Ln 24141
Arlington Ave 24141
Arnold Ave 24141
Arsenal Cir 24141
Auburn Ave 24141
Augusta National Dr 24141
Bains Chapel Rd 24141
Baldwin St 24141
Barberry Rd 24141
Barton St 24141
Bay Hill Ct 24141
Beach Dr 24141
Belspring Rd 24141
Belspring Camelot 24141
Belview Dr 24141
Berkley St 24141
Beth Nelson Dr 24141
Beverly St 24141
Bird St 24141
Blackfish Rd 24141
Blair Rd 24141
Blantana 24142
Bleak Ridge Rd 24141
Blue Springs Rd 24141
Bluff View Dr 24141
Bolling St 24141
Booker Branch Rd 24141
Bradford Ln 24141
Bradley Rd 24141
Brandon Rd 24141
Briarfield Ave 24141
Brooklyn Rd 24141
Buckeye Ln 24141
Burlington St 24141
Burma Rd 24141
Buzzards Roost Rd 24141
Byrd Lodge Rd 24141
Cabin Land Dr 24141
Calhoun St 24141
Camelot Rd 24141
Camelot Apartments 24141
Camelot Farms 24141
Camper Ave 24141
Carden Dr 24141
Carson St 24141
Carter Ln & St 24141
Cedar Grove Ln 24141
Cedar Ridge Dr 24141
Centerville Cir 24141
Centre Ct 24141
Charles Coles Dr 24141
Charlton Ln 24141
Charmont Dr 24141
Cherry Ct 24141
Cherry Branch Rd 24141
Chesley St 24141
Christy Rd 24141
Church St 24141
Circle Dr 24141
Clay St 24141
Clement Ln & St 24141
Cold Mountain Rd 24141
College Park Dr 24141
Copper Beech Dr 24141
Cora Ln 24141
Cornbread Rd 24141
Corporate Dr 24141
Cowan St 24141
Crabapple Rd 24141
Crapemyrtle Ct 24141
Crestview Dr 24141
Crooked Stick Way 24141
Crouse Ct 24141
Crown Dr 24141
Custis St 24141
Dalton Dr 24141
Dana Ln 24141
Davis St 24141
Deerwood Dr 24141
Denby St 24141
Dent Dr 24141
Depot Rd 24141
Divers Rd 24141
Dobbins Ln 24141
Dogwood Ct & Ln 24141
Doral Dr 24141
Downey St 24141
Dry Valley Rd 24141
Dudley Ferry Rd 24141
Duncan Ln 24141
Dundee Dr 24141
Elmwood St 24141
Fairfax St 24141
Fairlawn Ave 24141
Fairway Dr 24141
Falling Branch Rd 24141
Farragut Dr 24141
Federal St 24141
Ferry Point Farm Rd 24141
Fieldale Dr 24141
Fletcher Ave 24141
Flower Land Ln 24141
Forest Ave 24141
Foundry Pl 24141
Frazier Rd 24141
Fulk Dr 24141
Fuqua St 24141
Garland Dr 24141
Gate 10 Rd 24141
George St 24141
Gibsondale Dr 24141
Gilbert St 24141
Glen View Ln 24141
Glenmore Ln 24141
Grandview Dr 24141
Graysontown Rd 24141
Greenbrier Dr 24141
Greenfield Ct 24141
Grove Ave 24141
Hammett Ave 24141
Harbor Town Dr 24141
Harbour Town Dr 24141
Harris Ln 24141
Harrison St 24141
Harry L Brown Rd 24141
Harvey St 24141
Haven Dr 24141
Hazel Hollow Rd 24141
Heather Glen Dr 24141
Heavener Rd 24141
Henry St 24141
Hercules St 24141
Herons Landing Dr 24141
Hickman Cemetery Rd 24141
Hickory Rd 24141
Hidden Valley Dr & Ln 24141
High Meadow Pkwy 24141
Highland Rd & St 24141
Hillcrest Ave 24141
Hillside Ln 24141
Hiwassee Rd 24141
Holly Dr & Ln 24141
Horton Rd 24141
Howe St 24141
Hubbard Way 24141
Hylton Rd 24141
Indian Valley Rd NW 24141
Ingles St 24141
Inglewood Dr 24141
Izaak Walton League Rd 24141
Jackson Ave, Cir & St 24141
Jade Dr 24141
James Way 24141
Jefferson St 24141
Jeffries Dr 24141
Jolliff Ln 24141
Jordan Ave 24141
Joyce Way 24141
Kent St 24141
Kings Hill Ln 24141
Kingsmill Ct 24141
Kinnaird Cir 24141
Kirkwood Dr 24141
Knoll Ct 24141
Lake Dr 24141
Lantern Rd 24141
Last Rd NW 24141
Lawrence St 24141
Lee Ave, Hwy & St 24141
Lester St 24141
Lewis Ln 24141
Little River Rd 24141
Little River Dam Rd 24141
Lone Oak Rd 24141
Long Way 24141
Long Way Home Dr 24141
Longs Ridge Rd 24141
Lovely Mount Dr 24141
Lowes Dr 24141
Lyle St 24141
Mac Arthur Ave 24141
Madison St 24141
Madison Street Ext 24141
E Main St
1-800 24141
801-801 24142
802-2098 24141
803-2099 24141
W Main St 24141
Manns Dr 24141
Maple Branch Rd 24141
Mariners Point Ln 24141
Marshall Ln 24141
Martin Ave & Rd 24141
Mason St 24141
Mcconnell Ave & Cir 24141
Mccormick Rd 24141
Mcghees Trailer Park 24141
Meadow Rdg 24141
Meadowview Dr 24141
Merry Point Rd 24141
Midkiff Ln 24141
Miller St 24141
Mills Ave 24141
Milton Ln 24141
Monroe St 24141
Montgomery St 24141
Morgan Farm Rd 24141
Morning Glory Dr 24141
Morris Rd 24141
Morris Farm Rd 24141
Morton St 24141
Mountain Dr 24141
Mountain Pride Rd 24141
Mountain View Ln 24141
Mystic Rock Ct 24141
New River Dr & Rd 24141
Nicewander Way 24141
Noblin St 24141
North Dr 24141
Nrv Corporate Center Dr 24141
Oak Ln & Pl 24141
Oakland Ave 24141
Oakwood Ct 24141
Old Pagelyn Rd 24141
Old Peppers Ferry Loop 24141
Old Route 11 24141
Old Stage Rd 24141
Onyx Dr 24141
Orchard Rd 24141
Our Place Ln 24141
Overlook Ln 24141
Owens Rd 24141
Oxford Ave 24141
P T Travis Ave 24141
Page Ln & St 24141
Park Rd 24141
Parker Ln NW 24141
Pendleton St 24141
Peppers Ferry Blvd & Rd 24141
Pershing Ave 24141
Peterson Dr 24141
Phillips Farm Rd 24141
Pickett St 24141
Pine St 24141
Pine Tree Ln 24141
Pinehurst Pl 24141
Pineview Dr 24141
Piney Woods Rd 24141
Plantation Estates Rd 24141
Polk St 24141
Preston St 24141
Price Station Rd 24141
Prices Fork Rd 24141
Pulaski Ave 24141
Rakes Trailer Ct 24141
Raleen Court Apartment 24141
Randolph St 24141
Randy Ln 24141
Raven Ln 24141
Ridge Ln & Rd 24141
Ridgecrest Ln 24141
Ridgefield Ln 24141
Ridgewood Ln 24141
Ritter Farm Rd 24141
River St 24141
River Course Dr 24141
River Front Dr 24141
River Hills Dr 24141
River Pointe 24141
Riverbend Dr & Rd 24141
Riverbluff Rd 24141
Riverhaven Dr 24141
Riverlawn Ct 24141
Riverview Dr 24141
Riviera Ct 24141
Roberts St 24141
Robertson St 24141
Robey St 24141
E & W Rock Rd 24141
Rocky Top Ln 24141
Roosevelt Ave 24141
Rose Ln 24141
Round Hill Dr 24141
Round House St 24141
Russell Ave 24141
Sagefield Ave 24141
Sahalee Cir 24141
Sale Selu Ln 24141
Sanford Cir & St 24141
Sawgrass Way 24141
School House Ln 24141
Schooler Hill Dr 24141
Schoolfield Ave 24141
Scott Cir & St 24141
Shadow Land Dr 24141
Shamrock Cir 24141
Shanklin Dr 24141
Shelburne Rd 24141
Sheppard Ave 24141
Shire Cir 24141
Sierra Ln 24141
Simpkins Rd 24141
Slowly Ln 24141
Smith Ave 24141
Smyth Dr 24141
South Dr 24141
Spooky Hollow Ln 24141
Spring Ave & St 24141
Staff Vlg 24141
Staples St 24141
State St 24141
Stevens Trailer Park 24141
Stockton St
501-501 24142
900-998 24141
1000-1100 24141
1102-1198 24141
Stump St 24141
Sullivan St 24141
Summit Rdg 24141
Sunset Terrace Ln 24141
Sutherland Dr 24141
Sutphin Ln 24141
Sutton St 24141
Taylor St 24141
Teeth Of The Dog Dr 24141
Tilia Ct 24141
Timberlane Dr 24141
Todd St 24141
Tree House Ln 24141
Twin Coves Rd 24141
Tyler Ave & Rd 24141
U Cir 24141
University Park Dr 24141
Unruh Dr 24141
Valley Center Dr 24141
Valley Fields Ln 24141
Valley View St 24141
Victoria Ln 24141
Vienna Ave 24141
Village Oaks Shopping Ctr 24141
Virginia Ave 24141
Viscoe Rd 24141
Vista Rdg 24141
Wadsworth St 24141
Walker Dr & St 24141
Walker Farms Dr 24141
Walnut Ave & Ln 24141
Walton Rd 24141
Warden Ct 24141
Warren Newcomb Dr 24141
Washington Ave 24141
Waterview Ln 24141
Waterworks Rd 24141
Watts St 24141
West St 24141
Whiffletree Ln 24141
Whistler Rd 24141
Whistling Straits Dr 24141
White Birch Ln 24141
White Rock Rd NW 24141
Wild Partridge Ln 24141
Wilderness Rd 24141
Williams Ave 24141
Wilson St 24141
Windsor St 24141
Windstream Ct 24141
Winesap Rd 24141
Wintergreen Dr 24141
Wirt St 24141
Wisteria Dr 24141
Wood St 24141
Wood Duck Ln 24141
Woodland Way 24141
Woods On The Lake Rd 24141
Woods View Ct 24141
Yiengling St 24141
Zola Ln 24141

NUMBERED STREETS

All Street Addresses 24141

RESTON VA

General Delivery 20190

POST OFFICE BOXES MAIN OFFICE STATIONS AND BRANCHES

Box No.s
All PO Boxes 20195

NAMED STREETS

Abercorn Ct 20191
Abercromby Ct 20190
Abington Hall Pl 20190
Acton Dr 20191
Aintree Ln 20191
Albot Rd 20191
Aldbury Ct & Way 20194
Aldenham Ln 20190
Alexander Bell Dr 20191
Alsop Ct 20191
Alston Pl 20194
Amberjack Ct 20191
Ambleside Ct 20190
American Dream Way 20190
Andorra Pl 20191
Angel Wing Ct 20191
Ansdel Ct 20191
Antiqua Ct 20191
Appaloosa Ct 20191
Approach Ln 20191
Apricot Ct 20190
Arbor Glen Way 20194
Archdale Rd 20191
Arctic Fox Way 20191
Ascot Way 20190
Association Dr 20191
Auburn Grove Ct & Ln 20194
Autumn Ridge Cir 20194
Autumnwood Dr 20194
Bachan Ct 20190
Ballycairne Ct 20191
Barnstead Dr 20194
Baron Cameron Ave 20190
Barrel Cooper Ct 20191
Barton Hill Ct & Rd 20191
Basset Ln 20191

S Bay Ln 20191
Bayard Dr 20191
Bayfield Ct & Way 20194
Beacon Pl 20191
Beacon Heights Dr 20191
Beaver Cir 20190
Beaver Trail Ct 20191
Becontree Ln 20190
Becontree Lake Dr 20190
Bedfordshire Cir 20191
Belcastle Ct 20194
Belmont Ridge Ct 20191
Bennington Hollow Ln 20194
Bennington Woods Ct & Rd 20194
Bentana Way 20190
Bingham Ct & Ter 20191
Birdfoot Ct & Ln 20191
Bishopsgate Ct & Way 20194
Black Cap Ln 20191
Black Fir Ct 20191
Blaze Dr 20190
Blue Flint Ct 20190
Blue Smoke Trl 20191
Blue Spruce Rd 20191
Bluemont Way 20190
Boathouse Ct 20191
Bowman Green Dr 20190
Bowman Towne Ct & Dr 20190
Bracknell Dr 20194
Bradbury Ln 20194
Bramblebush Ct 20191
Brandon Hill Way 20194
Branleigh Park Ct 20191
Brass Lantern Ct & Way 20194
Brenton Point Dr 20191
Breton Ct 20191
Briar Mill Ln 20194
Briary Branch Ct 20191
Bridoon Ln 20191
Bright Pond Ln 20194
Bromley Village Ln 20194
Brookshire Ct 20190
Brown Fox Way 20191
Brussels Ct 20191
Buckthorn Ln 20191
Bugle Ln 20191
Burgee Ct 20191
Burywood Ln 20194
Business Center Dr 20190
Buttermilk Ln 20190
Buttonwood Ct 20191
Cabots Point Ln 20191
Cameron Crescent Dr 20190
Cameron Glen Dr 20190
Cameron Heath Dr 20194
Cameron Pond Dr 20194
Campus Commons Dr 20191
Canter Ln 20191
Captiva Ct 20191
Cartwright Pl 20191
Castle Rock Sq 20191
Catalpa Ct 20191
Cavesson Ct 20191
Cedar Cove Ct 20191
Cedar Hollow Way 20194
Centennial Park Dr 20191
Center Harbor Pl & Rd 20194
Center Post Ct 20194
Chadds Ford Dr 20191
Chancery Station Cir 20190
Chapel Cross Way 20194
Charlestown Ln 20191
Charter Oak Ct 20190
Chatham Colony Ct 20190
Checkerberry Ct 20191
Chessington Pl 20194
Chesterfield Ct 20190
Chestnut Burr Ct 20191
Chestnut Grove Sq 20190
Chimney House Rd 20190
Church Hill Pl 20194
Citation Ct 20191

Clay Ln 20190
Clipstone Ln 20191
Cloudcroft Sq 20191
Clover Hunt Ct 20194
Club Pond Ln 20191
Clubhouse Ct & Rd 20190
Cobblestone Ln 20191
Cocquina Dr 20191
Coleraine Ct 20191
Colts Brook Ct & Dr 20191
Colts Neck Ct & Rd 20191
Commerce Park Dr 20191
Compass Point Ln 20191
Concord Point Ln 20194
Coopers Ct 20191
Copenhagen Ct 20191
Coppersmith Sq 20191
Covent Gardens Ct 20191
Cranberry Ln 20191
Creekbend Dr 20194
Crescent Park Dr 20190
Crippen Vale Ct 20194
Cross Country Ln 20191
Cross School Rd 20191
Crossbeam Ct 20194
Crosswind Ct 20194
Crows Nest Ln 20191
Cutwater Ct 20191
Cypress Point Ct 20190
Darius Ln 20191
Dark Star Ct 20191
Dasher Ln 20190
Dayflower Ct 20191
Decade Ct 20191
Deep Run Ln 20190
Deer Forest Rd 20194
Deer Point Way 20194
Deerdell Ln 20191
Democracy Dr 20190
Discovery St 20190
Dockside Cir 20191
Dorrance Ct 20190
Dosinia Ct 20191
Double Eagle Ct 20191
Dressage Dr 20190
Drop Forge Ln 20191
Dry River Ct 20191
Duke Of Bedford Ct 20191
Dunlop Ct 20191
Durand Dr 20191
Eakins Ct 20191
Earlsgate Ct 20191
Earnshaw Ct 20190
Edgemere Cir 20190
Edmund Halley Dr 20191
Elk Point Dr 20194
Embers Ct 20191
Emerald Heights Ct 20191
Equestrian Ct 20190
Escalante Ct 20191
Esplanade Ct & Dr 20194
Explorer St 20190
Fairfax County Pkwy 20190
Fairway Ct & Dr 20191
Fairwind Way 20190
Fan Shell Ct 20191
Farrier Ln 20191
Farsta Ct 20190
Fauquier Ln 20191
Fawn Ridge Ln 20194
Fieldstone Ln 20191
Fieldthorn Ct & Dr 20194
Fieldview Dr 20194
Fireside Pl 20190
Forest Edge Dr 20190
Fountain Dr 20190
Fowlers Ln 20191
Fox Fire Ct 20191
Fox Mill Rd 20191
Fox Trot Ter 20191
Fox View Way 20191
Foxclove Rd 20191
Foxcroft Way 20191
Freedom Dr 20190
Freetown Ct & Dr 20191
French Horn Ln 20191

Frensour Dr 20190
Gallant Fox Ct 20191
Garden Wall Cir & Ct 20194
Gas Light Ct 20190
Gate Hill Pl 20194
Gatesborough Ln 20191
Gatesmeadow Way 20194
Geddys Ct 20191
Generation Ct & Dr 20191
Glade Ct & Dr 20191
Glade Bank Way 20191
Glencourse Ln 20191
Goldcup Ln 20191
Golden Eagle Dr 20194
Golden Sands Ln 20191
Goldenrain Ct 20190
Golf Course Dr & Sq 20191
Golf View Ct 20190
Granby Ct 20191
Great Meadow Dr 20191
Great Owl Cir 20194
Green Run Ln 20190
Green Watch Way 20191
Greenbriar Cir & Ct 20190
Greenbush Ct 20191
Greenkeepers Ct 20191
Greenmont Ct 20190
Greenwich Point Rd 20194
Grey Birch Pl 20191
Grey Squirrel Ln 20194
Greywing Ct & Sq 20191
Grovehampton Ct 20194
Guildmore Rd 20191
Gunsmith Sq 20191
Halter Ln 20191
Halyard Ln 20191
N Hampton Ave 20194
Handlebar Rd 20191
Harbor Ct 20191
Harborside Cluster 20191
Harleyford Ct 20191
Harpers Cove Ln 20194
Harpers Square Ct 20191
Harvest Green Ct 20194
Headlands Cir & Ct 20191
Hearthstone Ct 20191
Heath Pl 20191
Heathcliff Ln 20191
Heathcote Ct 20191
Hemingway Ct & Dr 20194
Heritage Commons Ct & Way 20194
Heritage Oak Ct & Way 20194
Hickory Cluster 20190
Hitchcock Ct & Dr 20191
Hollow Timber Ct & Way 20194
Hollowwind Ct 20194
Homer Ter 20191
Hook Rd 20190
Horseferry Ct 20191
Hounds Ln 20191
Howland Dr 20191
Hunt Club Dr & Rd 20190
Hunter Gate Way 20194
Hunters Green Ct 20191
Hunters Run Dr 20191
Hunters Square Ct 20191
Hunters Woods Plz 20191
Hunting Horn Ln 20191
Hurlingham Ln 20191
Indian Ridge Rd 20191
Inlet Ct 20190
Insha Ct 20191
Isaac Newton Sq E 20190
Ivy Bush Ct 20191
Ivy Oak Sq 20190
Ivystone Ct 20191
Ivywood Rd 20191
Jackstay Ter 20191
Jester Ct 20191
Jonathan Way 20190
Karbon Hill Ct 20191
Kemble Ct 20190
Killingsworth Ave 20194

Kings Lake Dr 20191
Kinsley Pl 20190
Knights Bridge Ct 20190
Lagoon Ln 20191
Lake Audubon Ct & Dr 20191
Lake Chapel Ln 20191
Lake Fairfax Dr 20190
Lake Forest Ct & Dr 20194
Lake Newport Rd 20194
Lake Shore Crest Dr 20190
Lakebreeze Way 20191
Lakeport Way 20191
Lakes Ct & Dr 20191
Lakespray Way 20191
Lakewinds Dr 20191
Lamplighter Way 20194
Laurel Glade Ct 20191
Lawyers Rd 20191
Leatherwood Dr 20191
Ledura Ct 20191
Library St 20190
Lima Ln 20191
Links Ct & Dr 20190
Lirio Ct 20191
Little Compton Dr 20191
Lofty Heights Pl 20191
Logan Manor Dr 20190
Longwood Grove Dr 20194
Lovedale Ln 20191
Maple Ridge Rd 20190
Marchmont Ct 20190
Marginella Dr 20191
Markell Ct 20194
Market St 20190
Meadowlook Ct 20194
Mediterranean Ct 20190
Melmark Ct 20191
Mercator Dr 20191
Metro Center Dr 20190
Michael Faraday Ct & Dr 20190
Middle Creek Ln 20191
Midsummer Dr 20191
Milburn Ln 20191
Millennium Ln 20191
Millrace Ln 20191
Mock Orange Ct 20191
Moorings Dr 20190
Moss Point Ln 20194
Mossy Creek Ln 20191
Mountain Laurel Pl 20191
Murray Downs Ct & Way 20194
Myrtle Ln 20191
Nashua Ct 20191
New Bedford Ln 20194
New Dominion Pkwy 20190
Newbridge Ct 20191
Newport Cove Ln 20194
Newport Spring Ct 20194
Night Star Ct & Way 20194
Noble Victory Ct & Ln 20191
Nordic Fox Way 20191
Northgate Sq 20190
Northpoint Village Ctr 20194
Northwind Ct & Dr 20194
November Ln 20191
Nutmeg Ln 20191
Oak Spring Way 20190
Oaktree Ct 20194
Old Bayberry Ln 20194
Old Brookville Ct 20194
Old Club Ln 20191
Old Eaton Ln 20194
Old Quincy Ln 20194
Old Reston Ave 20190
Old Trace Ln 20191
Old Trail Dr 20191
Olde Crafts Dr 20191
Olde English Dr 20190
Olde Tiverton Cir 20194
Oldfield Dr 20191
Oldwick Ct 20191
Oracle Way 20190
Orchard Ln 20190

Orchard Green Ct 20190
Owls Cove Ln 20191
Paddock Ln 20191
Panama Rd 20191
Park Garden Ln 20194
Park Glen Ct 20190
Park Lake Dr 20190
Park Overlook Dr 20190
Parkcrest Cir 20190
Parkridge Blvd 20191
Paterest Dr 20194
Pavilion Club Ct & Way 20194
Pegasus Ln 20191
Pelham Manor Pl 20194
Penny Royal Ln 20191
Peppermint Ct 20191
Pepperridge Ln 20191
Pine Cone Ct 20191
Pinecrest Rd 20191
Pinoak Ln 20191
Players Pond Ln 20191
Plaza America Dr 20190
Plerald Ct 20191
Point Ct & Dr 20194
Pond View Ct 20191
Pony Ln 20191
Pony Club Ct 20190
Poplar Grove Dr 20194
Port Pl 20194
Post Mills Ln 20194
Post Oak Trl 20191
Presidents St 20190
Preston White Dr 20191
Providence Cir 20190
Purple Beech Dr 20191
Purple Sage Ct & Dr 20194
Putter Ln 20190
Putting Green Ct 20191
Pyrenees Ct 20191
Quail Ridge Ct & Dr 20194
Quartermaster Ln 20191
Quietree Dr 20194
Quimby Point Ln 20191
Quorn Ln 20191
Raccoon Ridge Ct 20191
Ramstead Ln 20191
Random Stone Ct 20190
Ravensdon Ct 20191
Red Clover Ct 20191
Red Hawk Cir 20194
Red Leaf Ct 20191
Red Lion Ct 20191
Red Maple Ln 20191
Red Oak Cir 20190
Redtree Way 20194
Regatta Ln 20194
Reston Pkwy
1600-1700 20194
1701-1757 20190
1759-1800 20190
1802-1898 20190
2100-2599 20191
Riders Ln 20191
Ridge Heights Rd 20191
Ridgehampton Ct 20191
Ring Rd 20190
River Basin Ln 20191
Roark Ct & Dr 20191
Robert Fulton Dr 20191
Roger Bacon Dr 20190
Roland Clarke Pl 20191
Rolling Green Ct 20191
Rosedown Dr 20191
Round Pebble Ln 20194
Roundleaf Ct 20190
Royal Fern Ct 20191
Running Cedar Rd 20191
Saffold Way 20190
Sagewood Ln 20191
Saint Bedes Ct 20191
Saint Francis St 20190
Saint Johnsbury Ct 20191
Saint Trinians Ct 20191
Sallie Mae Dr 20190
Salt Kettle Way 20191

Samuel Morse Dr 20190
San Jose Dr 20191
Sanibel Ct & Dr 20191
Sarazen Pl 20191
Sawbridge Way 20194
Scandia Cir 20190
Scotch Bonnet Ct 20191
Seagull Ct 20194
Sentinel Point Ct 20191
Shadbush Ct 20191
Shagbark Cir 20190
Shire Ct 20191
N & S Shore Ct, Dr & Rd 20190
Short Ridge Rd 20191
Sierra Woods Ct & Dr 20194
Silentwood Ln 20191
Silver Fox Ln 20191
Sloane Ct 20191
Soapstone Dr 20191
Soft Wind Ct 20191
Solaridge Ct & Dr 20191
Sourwood Ln 20191
Southgate Sq 20191
Spanish Moss Ct 20191
Spectrum Ctr 20190
Spinnaker Ct 20191
Springhouse Pl 20194
Springwood Dr 20191
Spyglass Cove Ln 20191
Square Sail Ct 20191
Stable Farm Ct 20194
Staley Rd 20191
Stamford Way 20194
Starboard Dr 20194
Steeplechase Dr 20191
Stillbrook Ct 20191
Stirrup Rd 20191
Stirrup Iron Ln 20191
Stockbridge Ln 20194
Stone Wheel Dr 20191
Stoneledge Ct 20191
Stones Throw Dr 20194
Stoneview Sq 20191
Stowe Ct & Rd 20194
Stratford House Pl 20190
Stratford Park Pl 20190
Stuart Rd 20194
Sugarberry Ct 20191
Summer House Ct 20194
Summer Meadow Ln 20194
Summerchase Cir & Ct 20194
Sundance Ct & Dr 20194
Sunder Ct 20190
Sundial Ct & Dr 20194
Sunrise Valley Dr 20191
Sunset Hills Rd
10600-11111 20190
11110-11110 20195
11112-12298 20190
11113-12299 20190
Swans Neck Way 20191
Swaps Ct 20191
Sweetbay Ln 20191
Sycamore Valley Dr 20190
Tack Ln 20191
Taffrail Ct 20191
Taliesin Pl 20190
Tanbark Dr 20191
Thanlet Ln 20190
Thomas View Rd 20191
Thrush Ridge Rd 20191
Thunder Chase Dr 20191
Tigers Eye Ct 20191
Timberhead Ct & Ln 20191
Toddsbury Pl 20191
Tommye Ln 20194
Torrey Pines Ct 20190
Tottenham Ct & Ln 20194
Tournament Dr 20191
Towering Oak Way 20194
Town Center Dr & Pkwy 20190
Town Square St 20190
Trails Edge Ln 20194

Travistock Ct 20191
Tree Fern Ct 20191
Triple Crown Rd 20191
Trophy Ln 20191
Trotter Ln 20191
Trumbull Way 20190
Tryton Way 20190
Tumbletree Way 20191
Tunwell Stable Ct 20194
Turf Ln 20191
Turkey Wing Ct 20191
Turnbridge Ln 20194
Turnmill Ln 20191
Turtle Pond Dr 20191
Turtle Rock Ln 20194
Twisted Oak Dr 20194
Underoak Ct 20191
Upper Lake Dr 20191
Valencia Way 20190
Vantage Hill Rd 20190
Venetian Ct 20191
N Village Rd 20194
Villaridge Ct & Dr 20191
Vintage Pl 20194
Virgate Ln 20191
Wainwright Dr 20190
Wakerobin Ln 20191
Walnut Branch Rd 20194
Wanda Way 20191
Washington Plz W 20190
Water Pointe Cir & Ln 20194
Waterfront Rd 20194
Waterhaven Ct & Dr 20190
Watermans Dr 20191
Waters Edge Ln 20190
Waterside View Dr 20194
Waterview Cluster 20190
Weatherstone Ct 20194
Wedge Dr 20190
Wedgewood Manor Way 20194
Welbury Ct 20194
Westglade Ct 20191
Westhills Ln 20190
Wethersfield Ct 20191
Weybridge Ln 20191
Wheelwright Ct 20191
Whip Rd 20191
Whisper Way 20191
Whisperhill Dr 20194
Whisperwood Glen Ln 20191
White Cornus Ln 20191
Whitetail Ct 20191
Whitstone Pl 20194
Wiehle Ave 20190
Wild Bramble Way 20194
Wild Cherry Pl 20191
Wild Hawthorn Ct & Way 20194
Wild Pine Way 20194
Wilder Point Ln 20191
Wildlife Center Dr 20190
Windbluff Ct 20191
Windleaf Ct & Dr 20194
Winged Foot Ct 20191
Winstead Ln 20194
Winter Corn Ln 20191
Wintergreen Ct 20191
Winterport Cluster 20194
Winterthur Ct & Ln 20191
Wood Fern Ct 20191
Woodbrook Ct & Ln 20194
Woodcrest Dr 20194
Woodcutter Ct 20191
Woodhollow Ct 20191
Woodstock Ln & Way 20194
Yellowwood Ct 20190
York Mills Ln 20194

RICHMOND VA

General Delivery 23219
General Delivery 23220
General Delivery 23221
General Delivery 23222
General Delivery 23223
General Delivery 23224
General Delivery 23225
General Delivery 23226
General Delivery 23227
General Delivery 23230
General Delivery 23232
General Delivery 23235
General Delivery 23236

POST OFFICE BOXES MAIN OFFICE STATIONS AND BRANCHES

Box No.s
90201C - 90212C 23227
90035C - 90162C 23218
90001C - 90001C 23226
92713C - 92713C 23226
90001C - 90003C 23222
90009C - 90016C 23225
1 - 2560 23218
4201 - 5779 23220
6001 - 6179 23222
6201 - 6992 23230
6203 - 6204 23226
7001 - 7475 23221
7901 - 8180 23223
8201 - 8772 23226
8801 - 9094 23225
9101 - 9398 23227
11001 - 11836 23230
12001 - 12535 23241
13001 - 14148 23225
14501 - 14860 23221
15001 - 15898 23227
16001 - 16181 23222
17001 - 18986 23226
23001 - 23270 23223
23284 - 23284 23284
23298 - 23298 23298
24001 - 24978 23224
25001 - 26432 23260
26441 - 27995 23261
42001 - 42240 23224
50001 - 50503 23250
61001 - 61055 23261
62001 - 62388 23226
85000 - 85870 23285
90002 - 90002 23221
90004 - 90019 23225
90013 - 90015 23226
90300 - 90346 23230
91004 - 91027 23220
842000 - 844000 23284
980001 - 981865 23298

NAMED STREETS

Abbey Rd 23235
Abbotsford Way 23227
Aberdare Dr 23237
Aberdeen Rd 23237
Abingdon Cir, Ct & Rd . 23236
Accomac St 23231
Accommodation St 23223
Acorn Ln 23225
Adair Ave 23230
Adams Rd 23222
N Adams St 23220
S Adams St 23220
Addington Ave 23234
S Addison St 23220
Adelaide Ave 23234
Adkins Rd 23236
Adkins Ridge Pl 23236
Adler Rd 23224
Admiral St 23220
Admiral Gravely Blvd ... 23231
Afton Ave 23224
Afton Overlook 23227
Agency Ave 23225
Agincourt Cir, Ln & Ter 23237
Aiko Ct 23223
Ainsworth Ln 23223
Air Express Rd 23250
Airfield Dr 23237
Airleigh Ct 23235
S Airport Dr 23250
Akron St 23222
Alan Dr 23234
Alaska Dr 23224
Albany Ave 23224
Albemarle Ave 23226
Albemarle St 23220
Alberene Rd 23224
Alcott Rd & Ter 23237
Alden Aaroe Ln 23223
Aldersbrook Ct 23224
Aldersgate Dr 23223
Aldersmead Ct, Pl & Rd 23236
Aldwell Dr 23225
Aldwych Ct 23226
Alexander Ave 23234
Alfalfa Ln 23237
Alfaree Rd 23237
Algoma St 23226
Allandale Dr 23224
Allecingie Pkwy 23235
N & S Allen Ave 23220
Allence Blvd 23223
Allerton St 23234
N Allison St 23220
Allwood Ave 23224
Alma Ave 23222
Almond Ave 23231
Alms Ct & Ln 23237
Alpine St 23222
Altamont Ave 23230
Althea Pkwy & St 23222
Alton St 23222
Alvis Ave 23222
Amalfi Ct & Dr 23227
Amanda Dr 23224
Amasis Ct 23234
Amberdale Dr 23236
Amberhill Loop 23236
Amberleigh Blvd & Cir .. 23236
Amberly Rd 23234
Ambler St 23219
Ambleside Dr 23236
Ambrose St 23223
Amelia St 23220
Amesbury Ln 23227
Amherst Ave 23227
Ammonett Dr 23235
Ammons Ave 23223
Ampthill Rd 23226
Amster Rd 23225
Anbern Dr 23235
Ander Ct 23225
Andersons Forge Ct, Dr & Pl 23225
Andrews Ridge Dr 23236
Andria St 23223
Andros Rd 23225
Angela Dr 23224
Angus Rd 23234
Anne St 23225
Anniston St 23223
Antas Ln 23237
Antigo Rd 23223
Antionette Dr 23227
Antler Rd 23226
Antrim Ave
200-998 23221
1000-1099 23221
1400-1599 23230
Antwerp Rd 23235
Anwell Dr 23235
Apache Ct, Pl & Rd 23235
Apdon Ct 23238
Apex Rd 23235
Apollo Rd 23223
Apperson St 23231
Apple Grove Ct & Ln ... 23223
Apple Orchard Ct, Rd & Ter 23235
Appleleaf Ct 23234
Applewood Rd 23234
Appomattox St 23220
Aqua Ct 23230
Aracoma Dr 23234
Arbor Dr 23222
Arbor Glen Ct & Pl 23227
Arbor Ridge Ln 23223
Arboretum Pkwy & Pl ... 23236
Arborgrove Ct 23223
Arcadia St
200-299 23225
5100-5199 23231
N & S Arch Rd 23236
Arch Hill Ct, Dr & Pl .. 23236
N Arch Village Ct 23236
Archangle Ct 23236
Archdale Rd 23235
Archer Ave 23225
Archgrove Ct 23236
Archway Rd 23236
Archwind Ct 23236
Archwood Rd 23234
Arden Rd 23222
Ardendale Rd 23225
Argent Ln 23237
Argus Ln 23230
Argyle Ter 23225
Arizona Ct, Dr & Pl ... 23224
Arkay Dr 23236
Arklow Rd 23235
Arkwright Rd 23236
Arlie St 23226
Arlington Dr 23225
Arlington Rd 23230
Armfield Rd 23225
Armour Ct 23223
Arnold Ave 23222
Arnwood Rd 23234
Arran Rd 23235
Arrow Point Trl 23236
Arrowhead Rd 23235
Arthurwood Pl 23223
Arundel Ave 23234
Arvin Dr 23237
Ashburn Rd 23235
Ashbury Hills Ct, Dr & Ter 23227
Ashcroft Way 23236
Ashdown Rd 23235
Ashfield Hills Ter 23227
Ashington Pl & Way 23236
Ashland Rd 23233
N & S Ashlawn Dr 23221
Ashley Dr 23238
Ashley St 23231
Ashton Ct 23235
Ashton Woods Ct & Dr 23237
Ashwood Rd 23237
Ashworth Dr 23236
Astor Rd 23235
Astoria Dr 23235
Astral Ct 23234
Athens Ave 23227
Atlantic Ave 23234
Atmore Dr 23225
Atwell Dr & Ln 23234
Aubuchon Rd 23223
N & S Auburn Ave 23221
Auburn Chase Rd 23237
Audley Ln 23227
Augusta Ave 23230
Austin Ave
2500-2599 23223
3200-4499 23222
Autumn Ln 23234
Autumn Way 23235
Autumn Glen Ct & Ln ... 23223
Autumn Point Dr 23234
Autumnleaf Ct & Dr 23234
Avalon Heights Rd 23237
Avebury Dr 23236
Avella Ln 23236
Avella Springs Ct 23235
Avenue Of Champions . 23230
Avignon Dr 23235
Avon Rd 23221
Avondale Ave 23227
Axtell St 23220
Ayshire Ct 23225
Ayton Ct 23234
Azalea Ave
100-199 23222
201-297 23227
299-1399 23227
Azalea Mall 23227
Babbler Ln 23235
Backwater Dr & Ter 23234
W Bacon St 23222
Bagette Rd 23235
Bagwell Dr 23235
Bailey Ave & Dr 23231
Bainbridge St
300-2099 23224
2100-2999 23225
E Baker St 23219
W Baker St 23220
Balfour St 23231
Balsam Rd 23225
Balustrade Blvd 23226
Banbury Rd 23221
Banchanc Rd 23237
Bancroft Ave 23222
Bandy Rd 23226
Bangle Dr 23224
Bank St 23219
Bannister Ln 23235
Bannockbarn Dr 23225
Bannon Rd 23235
Banton Ct & St 23234
Barboursville Ln 23234
Barcroft Ln 23226
Bardot Ct 23234
Bareback Ter 23234
Bargrove Rd 23235
Barker Ave 23223
Barkstone Ct 23238
Barlen Dr 23225
Barleycorn Dr 23227
Barlow Ln 23223
Barnacle Ct 23234
Barningham Rd 23235
Barnwell Cir 23236
Barnwood Dr & Ter 23234
Barnwood Turn 23234
Baronet Dr 23234
Barony Ct 23225
Barriedale Rd 23225
Barrington Rd 23222
Barry St 23225
Bartee Rd 23224
Barth Rd 23234
Barton Ave 23222
Barwick Ln 23238
Bashford Ln 23234
Bassett Ave 23225
E Bates St 23219
Bath St 23225
Bathgate Rd & Ter 23234
Bathurst Rd 23234
Battenburg Ct & Pl 23236
Battersea Ct, Ln & Pl . 23223
N & S Battery Dr 23222
Battery Brooke Pkwy ... 23237
N & S Battlebridge Dr .. 23224
Battlewood Rd 23234
Baume Cir 23237
Baxter Bridge Dr & Pl .. 23237
Bay St 23226
Bay Coat Dr 23223
Bayard Rd 23223
Bayberry Ct 23226
Bayfield Dr 23235
Bayham Dr 23235
Bayliss Dr 23235
Baylor Rd 23226
Bayview Dr 23234
Baywood Ct 23226
Beacon Ln 23230
Beale St 23222
Bearbox Ct 23237
Beatrice Ln 23236
Beattie St 23225
Beau Ln 23223
Beauchamp Ct 23225
Beaudet Ln 23235
Beaufont Ct & Ter 23225
Beaufont Hills Ct & Dr .. 23225
Beaufont Springs Dr 23225
Beaumont Ave 23237
Becar Rd 23236
Beck Dr 23223
Beck Rd 23225
Beckford Ln 23238
Beckham Dr 23235
Beckwith Rd 23234
Beddington Rd 23234
Bedrock Ln 23224
S Beech St 23220
Beecham Dr 23227
Beechdale Rd 23235
Beechmont Rd 23235
Beechtree Ct 23234
Beethoven Ct 23234
Belasco Dr 23225
Belcroft Ct 23234
Belfair Dr 23234
Belfield Cir, Ct, Rd & Ter 23237
Belfry Ct 23225
Belgreen Ct 23234
Belker Ct 23234
Bellaverde Cir 23235
Bellbluff Dr 23237
Bellbrook Dr 23237
Belle Glade Dr 23230
Belle Pond Dr 23234
Belleau Dr 23235
Bellemeade Rd 23224
Bellerive Ct 23236
Belleville St 23230
Bellevue Ave 23227
Bellingham Ln 23235
Bellmeadows Ct, Rd & Ter 23237
Bellows Dr 23225
Bells Rd 23234
Bellwood Rd 23237
Bellwood Farms Rd 23237
Belmar Dr 23234
N Belmont Ave 23221
S Belmont Ave 23221
Belmont Ct 23234
Belmont Rd 23234
S Belmont Rd 23234
W Belmont Rd 23234
Belrun Ct, Pl & Rd 23234
Belston Ct 23234
Belt Blvd 23234
E Belt Blvd 23224
W Belt Blvd 23225
Belvedere Vista Ln 23235
N Belvidere St
1-299 23220
100-106 23284
200-298 23220
S Belvidere St 23220
Bemiss Ct & Rd 23234
Ben Nevis Dr 23235
Benbow Ct & Rd 23235
Benchmark Ct 23236
Bendahl Valley Dr & Ter 23237
Bendemeer Rd 23235
Bending Branch Ct & Dr 23223
Benika Dr 23234
Bennington Rd 23225
Bensley Rd 23237
Bensley Commons Blvd & Ln 23237
Bensley Park Blvd 23237
Bent Wood Ct & Ln 23237
Bentley St 23227
Benton Ave 23222
Berclair Ave 23234
Bergen Dr 23225
Berkeley Estates Ln ... 23226
Berkley Dr 23238
Berkley Rd 23224
Berkshire Rd 23221
Berrand Rd 23236
Berrington Ct 23221
Berry Rd 23234
Berrybrook Dr 23234
Berrywood Rd 23224
Bertram Rd 23224
Berwick Rd 23225
Berwyn St 23234
Besler Ln 23223
Best Plz 23227
Bethany Dr 23220
Bethany Ridge Ct, Rd & Ter 23236
Bethel St 23223
Bethlehem Rd 23230
Betty Ln 23226
S Beulah Rd 23237
Beulah Oaks Cir & Ln .. 23234
Bevridge Rd 23226
Bewdley Rd 23226
Bexley Farms Ct & Dr .. 23236
Bicknell Rd 23235
Big Meadows Ct & Ter 23236
Biggs Rd 23224
Billingsly Ct 23227
Biloxi Rd 23223
Bimini Ct 23234
Binford Ct & Ln 23223
Bingham Rd 23234
Binns Ave 23225
Biotech Dr 23235
Birch St 23220
Birchs Bluff Rd 23237
Birdwood Rd 23234
Birkdale Ln 23236
Bishop Rd 23230
Bittersweet Rd 23235
Black Oak Rd 23237
Black Walnut 23238
Blacker St 23230
Blackjack Oak Ct 23234
Blackrock Dr 23225
Blaine Rd 23235
Blair Rd 23238
Blair St 23220
E Blake Ln 23224
W Blake Ln 23225
Blakemore Rd 23225
Blakeston Ct & Dr 23236
Bland St 23225
Blandwood Rd 23226
Blandy Ave 23225
Blanton Ave 23221
Blarney Ln 23236
Blendwell Rd 23224
Blenheim Dr 23225
Blest Ln 23237
Bliley Rd 23225
Blithewood Dr 23225
Bloom Ln 23223
Bloomfield Rd 23225
Bloomsherry Dr 23235
Blue Oak Ct 23237
N & S Blue Tick Ct 23235
Bluefield Rd 23236
Blueridge Ave 23231
Bluespruce Dr 23237
Bluestone Dr 23223
Bluff Dr 23225
Bluffside Dr 23237
Bluffton Dr 23235
Bluffwood Ct 23234
Boatwright Dr 23226
Bobwhite Ln 23227
Bogart Rd 23223
Bolling Ct, Rd & Ter 23223
Bollingbrook Ct, Dr & Pl 23236
Bolton Rd 23225
Bon Air Rd 23235
Bon Air Crest Dr & Pl .. 23235
Bon Air Crossings Dr ... 23235
Bon Air Station Ct & Ln 23235
Bon Oaks Ln 23235
N & W Bon View Dr 23235
Boncreek Pl 23235
Bondsor Ln 23225
Bondurant Ct, Dr & Pl .. 23236
Bonita Rd 23227
Bonmark Dr 23234
Bonneau Rd 23227
Bonney Lea Ct 23236
Bonnie Brae Ct & Rd ... 23234
Bonniebank Rd 23234
Bonnington Ct & Rd 23234
S Boones Trail Rd 23236
Boonesboro Cir, Ct & Dr 23236
Bordeaux Way 23234
Boroughbridge Rd 23225
Boscobel Ave 23225
Boston Ave 23224
Bostwick Ln 23226
Botany Ct 23235
Botetourt St 23220
Botone Ave 23237
Boulder Creek Rd 23225
Boulder Springs Dr 23225
Boulder View Dr & Ln .. 23225
Boulders Pkwy 23225
Boulevard W 23230
N Boulevard
1-899 23220
N Boulevard
900-3399 23230
S Boulevard 23220
Bowe St
600-1098 23220
601-699 23284
701-1099 23220
Bowen St 23224
Bowers Ln 23227
Bowitch Ct & Pl 23223
Bowland Rd 23234
Bowlin Ct 23235
Boxelder 23238
Boyd St 23220
Boyle Ave 23230
Boynton Pl 23225
Bracken Rd 23236
Braddock Rd 23223
Bradford Rd 23234
Bradley Ln 23225
Bradwill Rd 23225
Brady St 23234
Braeside Dr 23225
Braidwood Rd 23225
Brambleton Rd 23234
Brame St 23223
Brampton Way 23234
Bramwell Rd 23225
Branch Ave 23222
Branchs Woods Ln 23237
Branchway Rd 23236
Branchwood Dr 23234
Brander St 23224
Brandon Rd 23224
Brandon Bluff Way 23223
Brandywine Ave 23237
Brantley Rd 23235
Brauers Ln 23223
Braxton Club Way 23234
Braxton Hills Ter 23227
Bray Ave 23223
Breckenridge Rd 23225
Breckstone Pl 23234
Breezy Ct 23234
Breezy Point Cir 23235
Bremo Rd
1800-2098 23226

2100-2199 23230
5801-5897 23226
5899-6199 23226
Brentford Dr 23225
Brenton St 23222
Brentwood Cir 23237
Brentwood Rd 23222
Bressingham Dr 23223
Brewster Ct 23234
Briarcliff Rd 23225
Briarcrest Dr 23236
Briarhurst Rd 23236
Briarmont Rd 23235
Briaroak Rd 23234
Briarwick Dr 23236
Briarwood Cir 23238
Briarwood Dr 23234
Brickland Ct & Rd 23236
Bridgeport Ave 23227
Bridgeside Ct, Dr & Pl 23234
Bridget Ct 23234
Bridgeton Rd 23234
Bridgeway Rd 23226
Bridle Run Ln 23223
Briel St 23223
Brigham Rd 23226
Brighton Dr 23235
Brightwood Ave 23237
Brimley Pl 23234
Brinkley Rd 23237
Brinkwood Ct & Dr 23224
Brinser St 23224
Brisbane Dr 23225
Britannia Rd 23234
Brittons Hill Rd 23230
Brittonwood Ct & Dr 23237
Brittwood Dr 23225
Brixham Dr 23235
Broach Dr 23225
E Broad St
--- 23219
1-1099 23219
1100-1298 23298
1101-1401 23219
1400-1606 23219
1700-3699 23223
9000-9000 23219
1-1 23220
3-521 23220
523-561 23220
600-600 23284
621-621 23284
623-697 23220
699-808 23220
809-809 23284
810-904 23220
811-815 23220
817-817 23284
819-1099 23220
906-906 23284
908-998 23220
1000-1098 23284
1100-1106 23220
1101-1105 23284
1107-1109 23284
1110-1110 23220
1111-1199 23284
1112-1314 23284
1205-1315 23220
1317-2739 23220
2741-2753 23220
2800-6999 23230
Broad Rock Blvd
1200-3337 23224
3400-3428 23234
3430-3513 23234
E Broad Rock Rd 23224
W Broad Rock Rd 23225
Broad Street Rd 23233
Broadgate Dr 23223
Broadingham Rd 23234
Broadstone Rd 23236
Brockenbrough Ln 23221
Brockway Ln 23223
Bromley Ln
4100-4599 23221
4600-5799 23226
Brompton Sq 23234
Bromwich Ct & Dr 23236
Brook Rd
300-1800 23220
1801-1801 23232
1801-1801 23260
1801-1801 23261
1802-2998 23220
2001-2999 23220
3001-3197 23227
3199-8399 23227
Brook Hill Cir & Rd 23227
Brook Hill Shp Ctr 23227
E & W Brook Run Dr 23238
Brookbury Blvd 23234
Brookfield Rd 23227
Brookfield St 23222
Brookhaven Rd 23224
Brooking Meadow Dr 23223
Brookland Pkwy 23227
E Brookland Park Blvd 23222
W Brookland Park Blvd
7-13 23222
15-600 23222
602-706 23222
1013-1013 23220
Brookline St 23225
Brooks Cir & Rd 23223
Brookshire Dr 23234
Brookside Blvd 23227
Brookside Rd 23225
Brookwood Rd 23235
Brown Rd 23235
Brown St 23219
Brown Summit Rd 23235
Brownleaf Dr 23225
Broyhill Ct 23234
Bruce St 23224
Brucewood Ct & Dr 23235
Brundidge Cir & Rd 23236
N Brunswick St
2-6 23220
10-10 23284
25-99 23220
S Brunswick St 23220
Bruterr Ln 23231
Bryan Rd 23227
Bryan St 23223
Bryanbell Dr & Ln 23234
Bryanwood Rd 23234
Bryce Ln 23224
Brynmore Dr 23237
Buck Branch Dr 23238
Buckhill Rd 23225
Buffalo Rd 23223
Buford Ave 23234
Buford Ct 23235
Buford Rd 23235
Buford Commons 23235
Buford Oaks Cir, Dr &
Ln 23235
Buford Square Pl 23235
Buggy Dr & Pl 23225
Bullington Rd 23235
Bunche Pl 23223
Bundy Ave 23224
Bunn Ave 23231
Bunratty Ct & Rd 23236
Bur Oak Ct & Ln 23237
Burfoot Rd 23233
Burfoot St 23224
Burgain Rd 23234
Burge Ave 23237
Burgess House Ln 23236
Burgundy Rd 23235
Burke Rd 23223
Burlington Rd
1300-1399 23236
5300-5399 23250
Burnham Rd 23234
Burns St 23222
Burnt Oak Cir, Dr &
Ter 23234
Burnwick Rd 23227
Burroughs Ct & St 23235
Burrundie Dr 23225
Burton St 23223
Burtwood Ln 23224
Business Center Dr 23236
Busy St 23236
Bute Ln 23221
Buteshire Rd 23236
Butte Rd 23235
Buttermint Dr 23237
Buttonbush 23238
Byrd Ave
1201-1299 23226
1700-1999 23230
E Byrd St 23219
Byrd Park Ct 23220
Byron St
1100-1298 23222
1300-2399 23222
2400-2899 23223
Byswick Ln 23225
Bywood Ln 23224
Cabell Ridge Ct 23230
Cabin Creek Dr 23234
Cabinmill Rd 23234
Caddie Ln 23223
Cadillac Trl 23236
Cadosia Rd 23235
Cakebread Ct 23234
Calais Rd 23236
Calander Ct 23235
Calavetti Ct, Dr &
Loop 23234
Caldwell Ave 23234
Caledonia Rd 23225
Calhoun St 23220
Call St 23222
Calumet Rd 23226
Calvert Dr 23224
Calverton St 23234
Calycanthus Rd 23221
Camberwell Rd 23234
Camborne Ct & Rd 23236
Cambridge Rd 23221
Camelback Rd 23236
Cameo St 23220
Campbell Ave 23231
Camshire Pl 23236
E Canal St 23219
W Canal St 23220
Canasta Dr 23234
Candidate Ct, Rd &
Ter 23223
Candigan Cir 23235
Candlegrove Ct 23223
Candletree Ct 23223
Cane Mill Ln 23236
Caniff Rd 23223
Canna Lily Ln 23223
Cannington Dr 23237
Canterbury Rd 23221
Canute Dr 23234
Capelwood Ct & Dr 23235
Capistrano Dr 23227
Capital One Dr 23238
Capitol Sq & St 23219
Capp Rd 23223
Carafe Dr 23234
Carbe Ct & Rd 23236
Cardiff Ct
2200-2231 23236
5500-5599 23227
Cardiff Pl 23236
Cardiff Rd 23236
Cardiff Way 23236
Cardiff Loop Rd 23236
Cardington Rd 23236
Cardova Cir, Ct & Rd 23227
Cardwell Rd 23234
Cargreen Rd 23225
Carillon Ct 23221
Carldan Ct & Rd 23227
Carleigh Ct 23227
Carlisle Ave 23231
Carlton Rd 23223
Carlton St 23230
Carmen Ln 23223
Carmia Way 23235
Carmine St 23223
Carnaby Ct 23225
Carnation St 23225
Carneal St 23223
Carnegie Dr 23226
Carnoustie Ln 23236
Carolee Ct & Dr 23223
Carolina Ave 23222
Carpenter Rd 23222
Carr Ln 23230
Carriage House Ct 23236
Carriage Pines Dr 23225
Carriageway Ct & Ln 23234
Carrie Ridge Ct 23234
Carrington St 23223
Carroll Ln 23237
Carroll St 23223
Carrolton St 23221
Carryback Dr 23234
Carson St 23225
Carswell St 23237
Carter St
1400-1450 23220
1452-1520 23220
1491-1515 23222
1501-1521 23220
1512-1598 23222
1600-1699 23222
1700-1999 23220
2200-2298 23222
Carter Creek Rd 23224
Carters Mill Rd 23231
Carver St 23223
E Cary St
1-1599 23219
1700-2799 23223
W Cary St
1-899 23220
900-908 23284
901-909 23220
910-912 23284
913-999 23220
914-1098 23284
1001-1099 23284
1100-2799 23220
2800-3699 23221
Cary Street Rd
3700-3898 23221
3900-4599 23221
4600-4698 23226
4700-5699 23226
E & N Caryhurst Rd 23223
Cascade St 23234
Casey Savannah Ln 23234
Caseycurn Ct 23223
Caskie St 23230
Castle Glen Cir, Ct, Dr &
Ter 23236
Castleburg Dr 23236
Castleton Rd 23225
Castlewood Rd 23234
Catalina Dr 23224
Catawba Ln 23226
Catchpenny Rd 23223
Cathedral Pl
802-808 23220
807-807 23284
809-818 23284
820-898 23284
821-899 23220
S Cathedral Pl 23220
Catherine St 23220
Cathlow Cir 23234
Catterick Rd 23224
Caulder Ct 23224
Cauthan Ct 23236
Cavalier Cir 23224
Cavendish Ln 23227
Caymus Way 23234
Cecil Rd 23220
Cedar Ln 23225
Cedar St 23223
Cedar Acres Ct 23223
Cedar Colony Ct & Rd 23223
Cedar Commons Rd 23223
Cedar Crest Ct & Rd 23235
E Cedar Fork Rd &
Ter 23223
Cedar Grove Rd 23235
Cedar Haven Rd 23223
Cedar Manor Pl & Rd 23223
Cedar Park Rd 23223
Cedar Seed Rd 23223
Cedar Summit Ct &
Rd 23223
Cedarbend Ln 23237
Cedardale Ln 23234
Cedarhurst Dr 23225
Celia Cres 23236
Celona Dr 23227
Center View Dr 23235
Central Ave
2600-2699 23225
4700-4999 23231
Centralia Rd 23237
Cersley St 23224
Chadwell Dr 23236
Chainmaile Rd 23235
Chalfont Dr 23224
Chalkley Rd 23237
Chamberlayne Ave
1000-1199 23220
1400-2999 23222
3000-7799 23227
Chamberlayne Pkwy 23220
Chamberlayne Rd 23227
Chambers St 23224
Chancellor Pl & Rd 23235
Channing Cir & Ln 23235
Chanson Rd 23237
Chantecler Ave 23226
Chantilly St
1200-1299 23226
1800-1899 23230
Chapel Dr 23224
Charing Cross Loop &
Pt 23236
E Charity St 23219
W Charity St 23220
Charles St 23226
Charlevoix Ct 23224
Charlise Rd 23235
Charmian Rd 23226
Chasnell Rd 23236
Chateau Dr 23224
E Chatham Dr 23222
N Chatham Dr 23222
W Chatham Dr 23222
Chatham Rd 23227
Chatham Sq 23226
Chatham Grove Ln &
Pl 23236
Chatsworth Ave 23235
Chatsworth Dr 23234
Chatteris Pl 23237
Cheatham St 23234
Cheatwood Ave 23222
Checkers Ct 23235
Chellowe Rd 23225
Chelmford Rd 23235
Chelsea St 23223
Cheltenham Dr 23235
Cherokee Rd
2900-8099 23225
8100-10679 23235
10681-10685 23235
S Cherry St
1-699 23220
2-8 23284
10-698 23220
Cherry Hill Park Ave &
Pl 23237
Cherrybark Rd 23237
Cherrytree Ln 23235
Cherylann Rd 23236
Chesbay Ct 23236
Chesco Rd 23234
Chessington Rd 23236
Chesswood Cir & Dr 23237
Chester Rd 23237
Chester Forest Ct &
Ln 23237
Chester Hill Cir 23234
Chesterfield Dr 23224
Chesterfield St 23225
Chesterman Ave 23224
N Chesterwood Dr 23234
Chestnut St 23222
Chevelle Dr 23235
Cheverly Rd 23225
Chevy Chase St 23227
Cheyenne Ct & Rd 23235
Cheyney Cir 23236
Chicago Ave 23224
Chickadee Ln 23231
Chickahominy Ave 23222
Chickahominy Bluffs Ct &
Rd 23227
Chickasaw Rd 23235
Chickview Ct 23223
Chicora Dr 23234
Chieftain Trl 23236
Chilham Ct 23235
Chimborazo Blvd 23223
China St 23220
Chinaberry Dr 23225
Chippendale Ct & Dr 23234
Chippenham Pkwy
2000-2099 23234
7200-7899 23225
8201-8299 23235
Chippenham Rd 23235
Chippenham Crossing
Ctr 23234
Chipping Dr 23237
Chipplegate Dr 23227
Chiswell Dr 23284
Chiswick Rd 23235
Choctaw Rd 23235
Christie Rd 23226
Christopher Ln 23226
Chuck Rd 23223
Chuckatuck Ave 23224
Church View Ln 23223
Cimmaron Ct 23225
Cinderwood Dr 23234
Cindiwood Dr & Ter 23236
Circlewood Dr 23224
Claiborne St 23220
Clairidge Ct 23235
Clairton Rd 23234
Claremont Ave 23227
Clarence St 23225
Clarendon Dr 23235
Clarendon Rd 23223
Clarke Rd 23226
Clarkson Ct 23224
Clarkson Rd
1400-1498 23224
1500-4499 23224
5600-5799 23250
Claudehart Rd 23234
Clauson Rd 23227
Clay St 23284
E Clay St
--- 23219
1-899 23219
901-1211 23219
1000-1000 23298
1002-1006 23219
1008-1008 23298
1010-1014 23219
1016-1016 23298
1018-1110 23219
1112-1112 23298
1114-1198 23219
1200-1200 23298
1210-1298 23219
1213-1213 23298
1700-3599 23223
W Clay St
1-2099 23220
2801-2897 23230
2899-5099 23230
Claybar Trl 23236
Claypool Ct, Rd & Ter 23236
Clayton Dr 23224
Clearfield St 23224
Clearlake Ct & Rd 23236
Clearview Ct & Dr 23234
Cleary Rd 23223
Cleo Rd 23223
N Cleveland St 23221
Cliff Ave 23222
Cliffbrook Cir & Ln 23227
Cliffwood Rd 23234
Clifton Ave 23222
Clinton Ave 23227
Clisby Rd 23225
Clivendon Ct 23236
Clodfelter Dr 23237
E Clopton St 23224
W Clopton St 23225
Clovelly Rd 23221
Clover Rd 23230
Cloverfield Ct & Ln 23223
Cloverleaf Dr 23225
Cloverpatch Ter 23237
Clovertree Ct 23235
Clovis St 23237
W Club Ln 23226
Clydewood Ave 23234
Coach Rd 23237
Coalter St 23223
Coastal Blvd 23224
Cobblestone Cir 23238
Cobblewood Dr & Ter 23227
Cochise Trl 23237
Cofer Rd 23224
Cogbill Rd 23234
Colby Ln 23234
Coldstream Dr 23234
Cole Mill Rd 23237
Colebrook Rd 23227
S Coleman Ln 23225
Coleman Rd 23230
Coles St 23234
Colgate Ave 23226
College St
207-307 23298
300-306 23219
308-315 23219
316-316 23298
317-399 23219
318-398 23219
401-401 23298
Collier Hill Rd 23234
Collindale Rd 23234
Collingbourne Rd 23235
Collins Rd 23223
N & S Colonial Ave 23221
Colonworth Dr 23236
Colony Trace Dr 23235
Colony Village Ter &
Way 23237
Colorado Ave 23220
Colter Dr 23223
Colton Dr 23235
Columbia St
1300-2199 23224
2200-3199 23234
Columbine Rd 23234
Columbus Dr 23222
Colwyck Ct & Dr 23223
Comanche Dr 23225
Commander Rd 23224
Commerce Rd
200-1999 23224
2000-5299 23234
W Commerce Rd 23224
Commonwealth Ave
1-399 23221
1200-1298 23221
1700-1799 23230
Comstock Dr 23236
Concho Rd 23237
Concord Ave 23234
N Concord Ave 23227
Condie St 23221
Condrey Ridge Ct &
Dr 23236
Confederate Ave 23227
Congress Rd 23237
Conifer Rd 23237

Coniston Ave 23225
Conley Rd 23227
Conrad St 23223
Conway St 23222
Cooks Rd 23224
Cool Ln 23223
Cooper Rd 23225
Copelin Rd 23230
Copperglow Rd 23235
Copperwood Ct 23236
Cora Dr 23223
Coralberry Dr & Way 23236
Corbin St 23222
Corey Ave 23220
Cornell Ave 23226
Cornerstone Blvd 23234
Cornith Dr 23227
Corryville Cir, Ct, Rd & Ter 23236
E & W Cosby Farm Ln 23235
Cosmic Rd 23234
Cotfield Rd 23237
Cottingham Rd 23225
N Cottonwood Rd 23236
Cottrell Rd 23234
Country Ln 23237
Country Club Ln 23238
Country Manor Cir, Ct, Ln, Pl, Ter & Way 23234
Country Spring Ln 23236
County Park Pl 23223
Court St 23222
N Courthouse Rd 23236
Courthouse Three Ln 23237
Courtland St 23234
W Coutts St 23220
Coventry Rd 23221
Covington Rd 23225
Cowan Rd 23235
Cowardin Ave 23224
Cowper Ct 23223
Cozy Ln 23225
Crabtree Rd 23234
Crafton Ln 23222
Craig Ave 23222
Craigie Ave 23222
Cranbeck Cir, Ct, Rd & Ter 23235
Crane St 23219
Cranford Ave 23224
W Crawford St 23222
Creasman Dr 23237
E Credarin St 23219
Creedmore St 23231
W Creek Pkwy 23238
Creek Bottom Ct, Pl, Ter & Way 23236
Creek Meadow Cir 23234
Creek Side Ct & Rd 23235
Creek Summit Cir 23235
Creek Top Way 23236
Creekmore Rd 23238
Creekrun Dr 23234
Creeks Crossing Blvd 23235
Creekview Dr, Rd & Ter 23237
Creekwood Ct 23237
Creighton Rd 23223
Crenshaw Ave 23227
N Crenshaw Ave 23221
S Crenshaw Ave 23221
Crenshaw Rd 23227
Crescent Pkwy 23226
Cresswell Rd 23237
Crestmoor Ct 23236
Crestview Rd 23223
N Crestwood Ave 23230
S Crestwood Ave 23226
Crestwood Rd 23227
Cricklewood Dr 23234
W Crieff Rd 23225
Cripple Creek Dr 23236
Crispin Ct 23234
Croatan Rd 23235
Croft Crossing Ct & Dr 23237

Cromwell Rd 23235
Cronin Dr 23234
Crooked Branch Ter 23237
Crooker Dr 23235
N & S Cropper Cir & Ct 23235
Cross St 23237
Cross Blades Ln 23237
Crosscreek Rd 23223
Crossmill Ct 23235
Crossvine Dr 23237
Croydon Rd 23223
Crump St 23223
Crumpets Ct & Ln 23235
Crumpton Dr 23224
Crutchfield St 23225
Csx Rd 23230
Cullen Rd 23224
Cullenwood Dr 23234
Culpar Ln 23236
Culver Rd 23224
Cumberland St 23220
Cumbermeade Rd 23237
Cummings Dr 23220
Cupula Dr 23223
Currie St 23220
Cushing Dr 23223
Custer St 23222
Custis Rd 23225
Cutshaw Ave
3000-4999 23230
5200-5799 23226
Cutshaw Pl 23226
Cutter Dr 23235
Cypress St 23222
Cypressleaf Dr 23234
Cyrus St 23234
Dabbs House Rd 23223
Dabney Rd 23230
Dade Rd 23227
Dahlgren Rd 23238
Dakins Dr 23236
Dakota Ave 23220
Dale Ave 23234
Dalebluff Ct 23237
Dalebrook Dr
5500-6599 23234
6600-6700 23237
6702-7698 23237
Daleshire Dr 23234
Dalglish Rd 23223
Dalinern 23232
Damascus Dr 23227
Damon Dr 23234
Dana St 23234
Danbury Rd 23234
Dance St 23220
Daniel Bluff Ln 23223
Danray Dr 23227
Danwood Manor Ct & Ter 23227
Danzler Cir 23224
Dapple Grey Dr 23223
Darbytown Rd 23231
Darlene St 23237
Darlington Rd 23234
Darnley Dr 23235
Dartmouth Ave 23226
Darton Ct, Dr & Ter 23223
Darylann Ct 23236
Dauphin Dr 23236
Davee Rd 23234
N & S Davis Ave 23220
Dawn St 23222
Dawnshire Rd 23237
Dawson Rd 23234
Daytona Dr 23225
Deanwood Dr 23237
Deauville Rd 23235
Debbie Ln 23222
Debbs Ln 23235
Debora Dr 23225
Decatur St 23224
Decker Rd 23225
Deensout Ave 23226
Deep Forest Rd 23237

Deepwater Terminal Rd 23234
Deer Keep 23238
Deertrail Dr 23234
Deerwater Ct, Rd & Ter 23237
Deerwood Rd 23234
Deforrest St 23223
Delano St 23234
Delaware Ave 23222
Delft Rd 23234
Dell Dr 23235
Delmonico Dr 23223
Delmont St 23222
Deloak Ave 23224
Delores Ln 23235
Delrio Dr 23223
N & S Den Bark Cir, Ct, Dr, Pl & Ter 23235
Denbigh Dr 23235
Dendron Dr 23223
Denton Dr 23235
Dermotte Ct & Ln 23237
Derrymore Ct & Rd 23225
Derwent Rd 23225
Deter Rd 23225
Detroit Ave 23222
Devara Ct 23235
Devenwood Rd 23235
Devers Rd 23226
Devonshire Ct & Rd 23225
Dexter Rd 23226
Dianawood Dr 23236
Diane Ln 23227
Dickens Pl & Rd 23230
Dickens Glen Ct & Ln 23230
Dill Ave & Rd 23222
Dillon Rd 23235
Dillwyn Rd 23226
Dillyn Ct 23222
Dimock Dr 23236
Dinneen St 23220
Dinwiddie Ave 23224
Dirk Dr 23227
Distributor Dr 23225
Ditchley Rd 23226
Dixie Rd 23223
Dixon Dr 23224
Dmv Dr 23220
Doanld May Jr Dr 23225
Dobson St 23220
Dock St
1500-1699 23219
1700-3099 23223
Dodds Ridge Dr 23236
Dolfield Dr 23235
Dollard Dr 23230
Dominion Townes Cir, Ct, Ln, Pl & Ter 23223
Domino Rd 23235
Donachy Dr 23235
Donald St 23226
Donald May Jr Dr 23225
Donnan St 23222
N & S Dooley Ave 23221
Dorchester Rd 23225
Dorel Cir, Ct & Ln 23236
Dorius Dr 23234
Dorking Rd 23236
Doron Ln 23223
Dorothy Ln 23233
Dorset Ct & Rd 23234
Dorsey Rd 23237
Double Tree Ln 23236
Douglas Ave 23234
Douglasdale Rd 23221
Doulton Rd 23225
Dove Cv 23238
Dove St 23222
Dover Pl 23238
Dover Rd 23221
Dovershire Rd 23235
Dowd Ct & Ln 23235
Downland Rd 23234
Dragonfly Ln 23235
Drake St 23234

Drakeshire Rd 23234
Drayson Ct, Dr & Way 23226
Drewry St 23224
Drewry Oaks Ln 23237
Drewrys Bluff Rd 23237
Driftwood Rd 23235
Druid Dr 23235
Drumheller Dr 23225
Drummond Dr 23222
Drysdale Dr 23236
Duberry Dr 23223
Dubet Ln 23234
Dubois Ave 23220
Duffton Rd 23225
Duke Rd 23222
Dulles Ct & Dr 23235
Dulverton Cir 23237
Dulwich Dr 23234
Dumbarton Rd 23227
Dunaway Dr 23238
Dunbar St 23226
Dunbrook Rd 23235
Duncan Rd 23223
Duncaster Rd
7700-7799 23225
8100-8199 23235
Dundas Rd 23237
Dundee Ave 23225
Dunford Rd 23225
Dunn Ave 23222
Dunnshire Rd 23234
Dunraven Ct & Rd 23236
Dunston Ave 23225
Dunwick Rd 23230
Dupont Ave 23234
Dupont Cir 23222
Duquesne Ave 23226
Durham St 23220
Durrette Dr 23237
Durrington Cir, Ct, Dr & Pl 23236
Duryea Ct, Dr & Pl 23235
Dustin Dr 23226
E Duval St 23219
W Duval St 23220
Dwayne Ln 23235
Dwight Ave 23237
Dyer Ln 23225
Dylisdale Dr 23234
Eagle Run Ct & Ln 23236
Eagle Trace Ct & Ter 23223
Eagles Roost Ct & Rd 23223
Earlwick Rd 23230
Early Settlers Rd 23235
Eastcliff Dr 23236
Eastman Ct & Rd 23236
Eastwood Ct, Dr & Ter 23236
Eaton Rd 23226
Echo Ave 23223
Echo Ho Ln 23235
Echoway Rd 23234
Eddy Way 23226
Eddystone Ct 23225
Edenberry Ct & Dr 23236
Edge Hill Rd
600-899 23222
1000-1099 23220
Edgebrook Ct 23235
Edgefield Cir, Ct & St 23227
Edgehill Rd 23226
Edgemere Blvd 23234
Edgemont Dr 23225
Edgeton Cir 23222
Edgewood Ave
2600-3799 23222
7100-7899 23227
Edinger Rd 23234
Edington Dr 23237
Edmonstone Ave 23226
Edward Holland Dr 23230
Edwards Ave 23224
Effingham Dr 23224
Egee Dr 23237
Eggleston St 23220
Eisenhower Dr 23227

Elaine Ave 23235
Elberon Ct 23222
Elderslie Pl 23226
Elfstone Ct & Ln 23223
Elgar Rd 23234
Elgin Rd 23223
Elgin Ter 23225
Elizabeth St 23220
Elk Rd 23224
Elk Grove Dr 23237
Elkhardt Ln 23224
Elkhardt Rd
6400-6599 23225
6600-7599 23225
7600-8399 23235
Elkridge Cir & Ln 23223
Elkton Rd 23224
Elkview Dr 23236
Ellen Rd 23230
Ellensview Ct 23226
Elliham Ave 23237
Ellington St 23224
Elliott St 23223
Ellis Woods Way 23225
Ellsworth Rd 23235
Ellwood Ave 23221
Elm Rd 23235
Elm St 23223
Elm Crest Dr 23236
Elmart Ct & Ln 23235
Elmbridge Rd 23225
Elmdale Ave 23224
Elmfield Dr 23227
Elmleaf Ct 23234
Elmore Ln 23234
Elmsmere Ave 23227
Elmswell Dr 23223
Elokomin Ave 23237
Elora Rd 23223
Embassy Dr 23230
Emberwood Ct & Dr 23223
Emblem Dr 23234
Emerald Ln 23236
Emerson St 23223
Emory Oak Ln 23237
Empearl Dr 23225
Enchanted Ln 23237
Enfield Ave 23224
Engel Rd 23226
Engleside Cir, Ct & Dr 23222
English Oak Ct 23234
English Setter Ct 23237
Ennismore Ct 23224
Enslow Ave 23222
Epic Rd 23235
Epperson Ave 23234
Epsilon Rd 23235
Erhart Rd 23225
Erich Ct & Rd 23225
Ermavedo Dr 23235
Ernest Rd 23234
Esquire Rd 23235
Essex Pl 23222
Esskay Rd 23234
Essling Rd 23234
Estates Village Ln 23226
Etching St 23237
Ethridge Dr 23226
Euclid Ave 23231
Euclid Rd 23222
Eureka Dr 23225
Eustace Dr 23234
Evansway Ln 23235
Evelake Rd 23237
Evelyn Byrd Rd 23225
Everett St 23224
Everglades Dr 23225
Evergreen Ave
1-399 23223
1100-1399 23224
Evergreen Rd 23223
Evergreen Oak Ct 23234
Evert Ave 23224
Everview Rd 23226
Evon Ave 23235
Ewell Rd 23235

Ewes Ct 23236
Ewing Ct 23222
Excalibur Pl 23237
Exchange Aly 23219
Exeter Rd 23221
Exmore Ct 23222
Exmouth Dr 23225
Express Ln 23237
Exwick Ct & Ln 23237
Fahey Cir & Ct 23236
Fairbank Ln 23225
Fairfax Ave 23224
Fairfield Ave & Way 23223
Fairlee Rd 23225
Fairmount Ave 23223
Fairpines Ln & Rd 23234
Fairwood Dr 23235
Falcon Rd 23235
Falconway Ln 23237
Falkirk Dr 23236
Fallbrooke Ct & Dr 23235
Falling Arrow Rd 23223
Falling Creek Ave & Cir 23234
Falmouth St 23230
Falstone Rd 23234
Farm Creek Dr & Ter 23223
Farmleigh Dr 23235
Farnham Cir, Ct & Dr 23236
Farnley Ct 23223
Farr Ln 23235
Farrand St 23231
Farrar Ct 23236
Faulkner Dr 23234
Fauquier Ave 23227
Fawn Ln 23233
Faye St 23225
Fayette Ave & Cir 23222
Featherwood Way 23223
Federal Rd 23250
E Federal St 23219
W Federal St 23220
Felixstowe Dr 23225
Fells St 23222
Fellsway Cir & Rd 23225
Felton Rd 23224
Fendall Ave
1500-3599 23222
7400-7499 23227
Fenestra Cir 23237
Fenton St 23231
Fenwick St 23222
Ferapont Dr 23234
Ferebee St 23222
Ferguson Ln 23234
Fergusson Rd 23226
Fernbrook Dr, Pl & Ter 23224
Ferncliff Rd 23225
Ferncreek Pl 23235
Fernleaf Dr 23235
Fernleigh Dr 23235
Fernridge Ct 23236
Ferrylanding Dr 23236
Fieldcrest Rd 23235
Fieldrun Dr 23234
Fieldstone Ct & Rd 23234
Fillmore Cir & Rd 23235
Finch Ct 23237
Finchley Pl 23225
Finial Ave 23226
Finworth Ln 23237
Firethorne Ct & Ln 23237
Fishers Run 23231
Fitzhugh Ave
4000-5299 23230
5300-6700 23226
6702-6798 23226
Fitzroy Rd 23234
Flag Station Rd 23238
Flagler Rd 23237
Flat Field Ter 23223
Flicker Dr 23227
Flint St 23234
Flinthill Dr 23227
Flintridge Rd 23235

Flodden Cir 23235
Flora Springs Ln 23234
Floral Ave 23224
Florida Ave 23222
Flower Ave 23230
Floyd Ave
900-920 23284
921-931 23220
922-932 23284
933-999 23220
1000-1000 23284
1001-1013 23220
1002-1126 23220
1015-1015 23284
1017-1199 23220
1128-1128 23284
1130-2798 23220
1311-1315 23284
1317-2799 23220
2800-3999 23221
Floyd Row 23220
Fluvanna Ave 23234
Flynn Rd 23225
Folsom Rd 23234
Fonda St 23237
Fontana Run 23235
Ford Ave 23223
Fordham Ct, Pl & Rd 23236
Fordwych Dr 23236
Forest Ave
1-400 23223
402-404 23223
6900-6920 23230
7000-7398 23226
7001-7099 23230
7101-7399 23226
Forest Cir 23225
Forest Acres Ln 23237
Forest Brook Dr 23230
Forest Haven Dr 23234
Forest Hill Ave
3000-8099 23225
8100-9099 23235
9100-9299 23235
Forest Lawn Dr 23227
Forest View Dr 23225
Forest View School Dr 23225
Forestdale Dr 23235
Forester Ct 23227
Forkland Dr 23235
Formex Rd 23224
Fort Darling Rd 23237
Fort Hill Dr 23226
Foster Rd 23226
Four Vines Dr 23234
Fourqurean Ln 23222
N & S Foushee St 23220
Fox Rd 23250
Fox Gate Ln 23238
Fox Harbor Ct 23235
Fox Hollow Dr 23237
Fox Run Dr 23237
Fox Trotter Dr 23223
Foxberry Cir, Ct & Dr 23235
Foxcatcher Ct 23235
Foxden Dr 23223
Foxfire Ln 23223
Foxglove Rd 23235
E & N Foxhill Rd 23223
Foxpaw Dr 23223
Foxtail Ln 23223
Francill Ct & Dr 23236
Francine Rd 23235
Franconia Rd 23227
Frank Rd 23234
E Franklin St
1-1699 23219
1700-3099 23223
W Franklin St
1-599 23220
600-600 23284
601-815 23220
602-720 23220
800-814 23284
816-817 23284
818-818 23220
819-827 23284

Street	ZIP
820-820	23284
822-824	23220
826-828	23284
829-900	23220
901-907	23284
902-908	23220
909-925	23284
926-1000	23220
927-1001	23284
1002-1013	23220
1014-1014	23284
1015-1299	23220
1016-1298	23220
3100-4599	23221
4600-7399	23226
Frankmont Rd	23234
Fredonia Rd	23227
Freedom Ln	23234
Freeman Rd	23221
French St	23221
Friar Ridge Dr	23237
Friar Tuck Ct	23237
Friend Ave	23237
Fritz St	23220
W Fritz St	23222
Front St	23222
Frontier Dr	23225
Frostick Ct	23227
Fulham Cir, Ct & Dr	23227
Fulton St	23231
Fuqua Ave	23237
Fuqua Farms Dr	23231
Gaffney Ct & Rd	23237
Gaines Rd	23222
Gainford Cir & Rd	23234
Galena Ave	23237
Gallatin Rd	23236
Garber St	23231
Garden Rd	23235
Gardenwood Ct & Ter	23227
Garfield Rd	23235
Garland Ave	23222
Garrett St	23221
S & W Garthdale Rd	23234
Gary Ave	23222
Gatebridge Ct, Pl & Rd	23234
Gateline Dr	23234
Gateshead Dr	23235
Gateway Centre Pkwy	23235
Gaulding Ln	23223
Gavestone Ct	23225
Gavilan Ct	23225
Gawain Ct & Dr	23223
Gay St	23223
Gayland Ave	23237
Gem St	23235
Genacre Ln	23222
S General Blvd	23237
Geneva Ct & Dr	23224
Georgetown Dr	23230
Georgia Ave	23220
Georgiana Ct E	23236
Germain Rd	23224
German School Cres	23225
German School Rd	23225
E German School Rd	23224
Germont Ave	23237
Gettings Ln	23237
Giant Dr	23224
Gilbert St	23220
Giles Ave	23222
Gilling Rd	23234
Gilmer St	23220
Givens Ct	23227
E Gladstone Ave	23222
Gladys Ln	23223
Glascock Ct	23227
Glasgow St	23234
Glass Rd	23236
Gleaming Dr	23237
Glebe Close	23227
Glen Center St	23223
Glen Forest Dr	23226
Glenan Dr	23234
Glenbeigh Rd	23234
Glenburnie Rd	23226
Glencove Ln	23225
Glendye Rd	23235
Glenfield Ave	23224
Glenhaven Ct & Rd	23236
Glenhurst Ave & Ct	23236
Glenlea Ave	23223
Glenmont Rd	23236
Glenoa Rd	23223
Glenside Dr	23226
Glenspring Rd	23223
Glenthorne Rd	23222
Glenview Rd	23222
Glenway Ct & Dr	23225
Glenwilton Dr	23223
Glenwood Ave	23223
Glenwood St	23230
Glenwood Ridge Dr	23223
Glericks St	23223
Glidewell Rd	23227
Glinhurst Rd	23223
Glisson Rd	23237
Global Ct	23234
Gloryvine Ct & Dr	23234
Gloucester Rd	23227
Gloucestershire St	23236
Glyndon Ln	23225
Goddin Cir, Ct & St	23231
Goins Ln	23235
Golden Rd	23230
Golden Leaf Rd	23237
Goldfinch Dr	23234
Goodell Rd	23223
Goodes St	23224
Goodes Bridge Rd	23224
Goodward Ct, Pl, Rd & Ter	23236
Goodwood Ct & Rd	23225
Goolsby Ave & Ct	23234
Gordon Ave	23224
Gordon Ln	23223
Gordon School Ct, Pl & Rd	23236
Goshen St	23220
Gotham Rd	23235
Government Rd	
3600-4099	23223
4300-5099	23231
Governor St	23219
E Grace St	
1-1699	23219
1700-3199	23223
W Grace St	
1-699	23220
700-702	23284
701-2799	23220
704-910	23220
912-912	23284
914-934	23220
936-944	23284
946-2798	23220
2800-3499	23221
3900-4999	23230
5200-7199	23226
W Graham Rd	
1-899	23222
1000-1399	23220
Grahamwood Dr	23234
N & S Grambling Ct & Rd	23223
Grammarcy Cir & Ct	23227
Granada Rd	23235
N & S Granby St	23220
N & S Grand Brook Cir, Ct & Dr	23225
Grand Glen Rd	23223
Grand Meadows Ct	23223
Grand Summit Cir, Ct & Rd	23235
Grandel Dr	23234
Grandview Dr	23225
Grandway Rd	23226
Granite Ave	23226
Granite Hall Ave	23225
Granite Hill Cir	23225
Granite Springs Rd	23225
Grant St	23221
Grantlake Rd	23234
Grantland Dr	23221
Grantwood Ct & Rd	23225
Grapeleaf Dr	23234
Grassmere Rd	23234
Grassy Knoll Ln	23236
Gravel Hill Rd	23225
Gravelbrook Dr	23234
Grayash	23238
Grayfox Cir & Dr	23223
Grayland Ave	
1100-2799	23220
2900-3200	23221
3202-3598	23221
Graymoss Ct & Rd	23234
Grayson Ave & St	23222
Greatbridge Ct, Rd & Ter	23237
Green Aly	
700-914	23220
916-1198	23220
917-917	23284
1101-1199	23220
Green Acres Ave	23224
Green Cedar Ct & Ln	23237
Green Cove Dr	23225
Green Oaks Ct	23234
Green Ridge Dr	23225
Green Spring Rd	23235
Greenbank Rd	23225
Greenbay Rd	23234
Greenbrier Ave	23222
Greencastle Rd	23236
Greenfield Ct & Dr	23235
Greenfinch Rd	23237
Greenleaf Ln	23235
Greenleigh Rd	23223
Greenmoss Dr	23225
Greenock Dr	23235
Greenpine Rd	23237
Greenvale Ct & Dr	23225
Greenville Ave	23220
Greenway Ln	23226
Greenwood Ave	23222
Greer Ave	23234
Greglynn Rd	23236
Gregory Ave	23234
Gregory Dr	23236
Gregory Pond Rd	23236
Gregorys Charter Ct & Dr	23236
Gresham Ave	23237
Greshamwood Pl	23225
Gretna Ct	23223
Grey Birch Dr	23225
Grey Oak Dr	23236
Greycourt Ave	23227
Greyhaven Dr	23234
Greystone Ave	23224
Griffin Ave	
2700-3699	23222
7400-7599	23227
Griffin French Aly	23219
Grimsby Rd	23235
Grinell Ct & Dr	23236
Grinton Rd	23234
Grist Mill Dr	23234
Groomfield Rd	23236
Gross Ave	23236
Groundhog Dr	23235
Grove Ave	
1001-1001	23284
1003-1013	23220
1015-1015	23284
1017-1097	23220
1099-2799	23220
2800-4599	23221
4600-6099	23226
Grove Crest Ct	23236
Groveland Ave	23222
Grovewood Rd	23234
Grubbs Ln	23234
Guilder Ln	23234
Guilford Rd	23235
Gulfstream Rd	23250
Gun Club Rd	23221
Gunn St	23224
Gunnsboro Ct	23223
Gunshop Ln	23237
Gunsight Ct, Ln & Ter	23237
E & W Gurney Ct	23237
Guthrie Ave	23226
Gwynn Ave	23237
Gwynnbrook Rd	23235
H Whiting Cir	23231
Hackney Cir, Ct, Loop, Pl, Rd & Ter	23234
Haddington Ct	23224
Haden Ave	23234
Hagueman Dr	23225
Halesworth Rd	23235
Halidan Dr	23235
Halifax Ave	23224
Hallmark Cir, Ct, Dr & Ter	23234
Hallwood Farms Dr, Ln & Rd	23223
Halrose Ct & Ln	23234
Halsey Ln	23225
Halstead Rd	23235
N Hamilton St	
200-999	23221
1001-1199	23221
1300-2199	23230
Hamlet St	23222
Hammerstone Ct	23223
Hamner Ct & Ter	23234
Hampstead Ave	
900-998	23226
2100-2399	23230
5900-6199	23226
Hampton St	23220
Hampton Commons Ter	23226
Hampton Hills Ln	23226
Hanchind	23298
Hancock St	23220
N Handel Ct	23234
Handy Ln	23226
Hanes Ave	23222
Hann Rd	23236
Hanover Ave	
1501-1597	23220
1599-2799	23220
3001-3097	23221
3099-4599	23221
4600-6800	23226
6802-6898	23226
Hansdale Rd	23224
Hard Rock Ct & Pl	23230
Hardy Rd	23220
Hargrave Hill Ln	23235
Hargrove Ave	23222
Hargrove St	23225
Harierid Rd	23234
Harlan Cir	23226
Harlow Rd	23226
Harmad Ct & Dr	23235
Harold Ave	23222
Harris Ave	23223
N Harrison St	
1-1	23220
3-100	23220
101-125	23284
102-1098	23220
127-323	23220
325-325	23284
327-1099	23220
S Harrison St	23220
Harrods Ln	23225
Harrow Rd	23225
Hartford Ct & Ln	23236
Hartman St	23223
Hartwell Dr	23234
Harvard Rd	23226
Harvest Crest Ct, Dr & Pl	23223
Harvest Grove Ln	23223
Harvette Cir, Ct & Dr	23237
Harvie Pl	23220
Harvie Rd	23223
N Harvie St	23220
S Harvie St	23220
Harwick Dr	23236
Harwood St	23224
Haskell Ct	23236
Hastings Dr	23235
Hatcher St	23231
Hathaway Rd	
200-299	23221
2800-2999	23225
Haupts Ln	23231
Haven Ave	23237
Haverford Cir	23235
Haverford Ln	23236
Haverhill Rd	23227
Hawk Nest Ct & Dr	23227
Hawkbill Cir, Ct & Rd	23237
Hawkes Ln	23223
Haworth Rd	23234
Hawthorne Ave	
2300-2798	23222
2800-3899	23222
5400-7899	23227
Haxall Pt	23219
Hayden Dr	23236
Haymarket Ln	23234
Hazelhurst Ave	23222
Hazelmere Dr	23236
Hazeltine Ct	23236
Hazelwood St	23230
Hazen St	23235
Hazleton Dr	23236
Heartwood Rd	23225
Heath Ave	23224
Heather Rdg	23237
Heatherhill Dr	23234
Hechler St	23223
Hedgelawn Dr	23235
Hedges Ct & Rd	23224
Heflin St	23231
Helen Ln	23224
Hempstead Way	23236
Hempwood Pl	23237
Henderson Rd	23230
Hendon Way	23224
Henri Rd	23226
Henrico Blvd & Dr	23222
N Henry St	23220
Henson Rd	23236
Heppel Rd	23236
Herbert St	23225
Herbert Hamlet Aly	23220
Hermitage Rd	
800-2999	23220
3201-3397	23227
3399-4899	23227
Hey Rd	23224
Heybridge Ct	23224
Heywood Rd	23224
Hickory Rd	23235
Hickory St	
1000-1299	23220
1500-1799	23222
Hickory Knoll Ln & Pl	23230
Hickory Tree Dr	23227
Hickorywood Cir	23223
Hicks Rd	23235
Hickstead Rd	23236
Hiden Rd	23224
High St	23220
High Meadow St	23223
Highgate Rd	23236
Highland St	23222
Highland Meadow Ct	23223
Highland View Ave	23222
Highpoint Ave	23230
Highstream Way	23235
Hilda Ave	23237
Hildreth St	23223
Hill Dr	23225
Hill Rd	23234
E Hill St	23219
W Hill St	23220
Hill Monument Pkwy	23227
Hill Point Ct, Rd & Way	23238
Hill Top Dr	23225
E Hillcrest Ave	23226
W Hillcrest Ave	23226
Hillcrest Cir	23225
Hillcrest Rd	23225
Hillcrest Farms Dr	23223
Hillwood Ave & Rd	23226
Hilmar Dr	23234
Hioaks Rd	23225
Hixson Ct, Dr & Pl	23236
Hobbs Ln	23231
Hobby Hill Rd	23235
Hobson Ln	23223
Hodges Rd	23225
Hokie Ct	23234
Holbein Pl	23225
Holborn Rd	23224
Holcombe Rd	23234
Holdcroft Dr	23225
Holden Rd	23234
Holiday Bowl Rd	23237
Holliday Rd	23225
Hollingsworth Ct & Dr	23235
Hollister Ave	23224
Holly St	
600-899	23220
1900-2299	23223
Holly Grove Ln	23235
Holly Spring Ave	23224
Hollyberry Dr	23237
Hollybrook Ridge Ct & Ln	23223
Hollyleaf Ct	23234
Hollymead Ct & Dr	23223
Hollywood Dr	23234
Holyoake Dr	23224
Home St	23222
Homestead Ct	23235
Homeward Rd	23234
Honaker Ave	23226
Honey Locust	23238
Honey Tree Rd	23235
Hood Dr	23227
Hoof Cir	23234
Hopkins Ct	
3900-3913	23234
8101-8199	23237
Hopkins Rd	
1300-2599	23224
2600-4399	23234
4400-6999	23234
7100-7198	23237
7101-8797	23237
7200-9699	23237
8799-9400	23237
9402-9498	23237
N Hopkins Rd	23224
Hopper St	23222
Hopton Ct	23226
Horne St	23226
Horner Ln	23224
Horsepen Rd	23226
Hospital St	
200-799	23219
2300-2399	23223
Houston Ave	23222
Howard Rd	
3400-3899	23223
6000-6199	23226
Howard St	23223
Howell Dr	23234
Howlett Rd	23237
Huband Ave	23234
Huddersfield Dr	23236
Hudswell Ln	23234
Huguenot Rd	
1900-2099	23235
5000-5099	23226
N Huguenot Rd	23235
W Huguenot Rd	23235
Hull St	23224
Hull Street Rd	
3800-6599	23224
6600-7099	23224
7100-8599	23235
8600-10101	23236
8800-9000	23236
9002-9898	23236
Hummingbird Rd	23227
Hunt Ave	23222
Hunter Ln	23237
Hunters Trce	23223
Hunters Mill Cir, Ct & Dr	23223
Hunters Run Ct, Dr & Pl	23223
Huntersdell Ln, Pl & Ter	23235
Hunterstand Ct & Ln	23237
Huntingcreek Cir, Ct, Dr, Pl & Ter	23237
Huntington Ave	23227
Huntland Rd	23225
Huntley Rd	23226
Hunton Cir & Ct	23235
Huntshire Dr	23236
Huntsman Rd	23250
Huntwood Ct & Rd	23235
Hurtsborne Ct	23223
Hussey Ln	23223
Huth Rd	23224
Huxley St	23221
S Hyannis Dr	23236
Hybla Rd	23236
Hylton Rd	23238
Hyte Cir	23223
Hyth Pl	23237
Ian Pl	23234
Idlewood Ave	
600-2500	23220
2502-2798	23220
2800-3098	23221
3201-3699	23221
Idlewyld Rd	23225
Ilex Ave	23234
Inca Ct & Dr	23237
Indian Point Rd	23237
Indian Springs Rd	23237
Indigo Rd	23230
Industry Ave	23234
Inge Wood Cir	23237
Ingelnook Ct	23225
Ingleton Ln	23238
Inglewood St	23230
Ingram Ave	23224
Inspiration Dr	23235
International Dr	23236
Irby Dr	23225
Iredell Rd	23235
Iris Ln	23226
Iron Bridge Pl	23234
Iron Bridge Rd	
3500-4399	23234
4400-7399	23234
7400-8799	23237
Iron Mill Rd	23235
Iron Ore Way	23234
Irondale Rd	23235
Irongate Dr & Sq	23234
Ironhorse Ct & Rd	23234
Ironington Ct, Rd & Ter	23227
Ironside Dr	23234
Ironstone Ct & Dr	23234
Ironwood Rd	23236
Irvington St	23234
Ives Ln	23235
Ivybridge Xing	23236
Ivymount Rd	23225
Jackie Ln	23234
Jackson Ave	23222
E Jackson St	23219
W Jackson St	23220
Jacob Way Ct	23235
Jacobs Bend Dr & Ter	23236
Jacobs Glenn Ct & Dr	23236
Jacobs Ridge Ct	23236
Jacque St	23230
Jacquelin St	23220
Jade Rd	23236
Jahnke Rd	
1200-7299	23225

7300-7799 23225
7800-8599 23235
Jalee Dr 23234
James Ctr 23219
James Falls Dr 23221
James Riverwatch Dr 23235
Jamestown Ave 23231
W Jamson Rd 23234
Janlar Dr 23235
Jarman Ln 23235
Jarvis Rd 23224
Jason Rd 23235
Jasonwood Ct 23225
Jasper Ave 23222
Jaymont Dr 23237
Jean Dr 23237
Jeffers Dr 23235
Jefferson Ave 23223
Jefferson St 23223
N Jefferson St 23220
S Jefferson St
1-99 23220
100-100 23284
103-113 23284
106-114 23220
116-199 23220
Jefferson Davis Hwy
1-2299 23224
2300-4799 23234
4800-6499 23234
6500-10700 23237
6800-7798 23237
7800-11199 23237
10702-11498 23237
11201-11499 23237
Jeffrey Rd 23226
Jennie Scher Rd 23231
Jennifer Scott Ct 23227
Jervie Dr 23234
Jessamine St 23223
Jessup Rd 23234
Jessup Meadows Dr 23234
Jessup Pond Ln 23234
Jessup Station Ct, Dr & Pl 23234
Jeter Ave 23222
Jimmy Ridge Dr 23236
Jimmy Winters Rd 23235
Jireh Dr 23231
Jodie Ter 23236
John Christopher Ct 23226
John Tyler Memorial Hwy 23231
Johnson Ct 23223
Johnson Pl 23223
Johnson Rd 23223
Johnson St 23234
Johnston Willis Dr
600-999 23236
700-898 23236
1001-1197 23235
1199-1499 23235
Joindre Ct 23237
Joliette Rd 23235
Jonlow Cir 23234
Jonquil Ter 23235
Joplin Ave 23224
Joshua St 23222
Jousting Ln 23235
Jowin Ln 23223
Juanoak Dr 23235
Jubra Dr 23237
Judah St 23220
Judson Rd 23225
N & W Junaluska Cir, Ct & Dr 23225
June Dr 23225
Juniper St
1101-1197 23222
1199-1299 23222
6600-6699 23230
Kahlua Dr 23227
Kaki Dr 23225
Kalanchoe Dr 23237
Kanawha Rd 23226
Kane St 23223

Kansas Ave 23220
Karl Linn Dr 23225
Kawneer Dr 23222
Kay Rd 23234
Kayvee Rd 23236
Keaneland Dr 23225
Kedleston Ave 23234
Keeton Rd 23227
Keichtee Dr 23225
Keighly Rd 23234
Keithwood Ct & Pkwy 23236
Kellington Ln 23238
Kelly Rd 23230
Kelmont Ct 23236
Kelnor Ave 23224
Kelrae Dr 23234
Kelston Ct 23238
Kemper St 23220
Kenbury Ct 23235
Kenbury Rd
2700-2899 23225
2900-3099 23235
Kendall Rd 23224
Kendelwick Dr 23236
Kendrick Ct & Rd 23236
Kenley Sq & Way 23226
Kenmare Loop 23234
Kenmore Cir 23225
Kenmore Rd
2600-3999 23225
5200-5299 23226
5301-5399 23226
S Kenmore Rd 23225
Kennebec Rd 23227
Kennerly Rd 23235
Kennesaw Ct & Rd 23236
Kennondale Ln 23226
Kenova Dr 23237
Kensington Ave
2400-2799 23220
2800-4599 23221
4600-6899 23226
Kent Rd 23221
Kentberry Rd 23236
Kenton Dr 23234
Kentwood Rd 23235
Kenway Ave 23223
Kenwick Ct 23238
Kenwin Rd 23235
Kenyon Ave 23224
Kern St 23223
Kernel Ct 23236
Kerrydale Dr 23234
Kerwin Rd 23237
Keswick Ave 23224
Keswick Ct 23234
Keswick Ln 23234
Keswick Pl 23234
Ketch Ct 23235
Kettering Dr 23235
Keuka Rd 23235
Kevken Dr 23237
Kewbridge Ct 23236
Key Ave 23237
Keydet Ct 23234
Keystone Dr 23226
Kildare Dr 23225
Kim Ct & Dr 23224
Kimberly Cir & Dr 23225
Kimrod Rd 23224
Kimwood Rd 23236
King St 23222
King And Queen Dr 23223
King Arthurs Ct 23235
King Charles Ct 23236
King George Ct 23223
King Henry Ct 23223
King James Ct 23223
King William Rd 23225
Kingcrest Pkwy 23221
Kingman Rd 23236
Kings Crown Rd 23236
Kings Point Ct & Dr 23223
Kings Reach Rd 23223
Kings Tower Pl 23223
Kingsbury Rd 23226

Kingsdale Rd 23237
Kingsland Rd 23237
Kingsport Ln 23225
Kingsridge Rd 23223
Kingstree Ct 23236
Kingsway Ct 23226
Kingsway Rd 23225
Kingswood St 23224
Kingussie Ln 23236
Kinney St 23220
N & S Kinsley Ave 23224
Kipling Ct 23224
Kirby Rd 23224
Kirkland Dr 23227
Kirkstone Cir & Ln 23227
Kirkwall Ct & Dr 23235
Kirkwood St 23230
Klondike Rd 23235
Knight Ct, Dr & Ter 23223
Knighthood Ct 23227
Knightsbridge Rd 23236
Knightsmanor Ct 23227
Knob Rd 23235
Knollwood Dr
400-499 23238
1300-1999 23235
Knox Ct 23234
Koch Ave 23223
Koger Center Blvd 23235
Korth Ln & Pl 23223
Koufax Ct & Dr 23234
Kristenleaf Ct 23225
Krossridge Cir, Ct, Rd & Ter 23236
Krouse St 23234
Krueger Dr 23230
Kwantre Park Ave 23237
La Crosse Ave 23223
La Mesa Dr 23225
La Veta Dr 23225
La Von Dr 23227
Labine Ct 23234
Labrook Dr 23225
Labrook Concourse 23224
E Laburnum Ave
1-1700 23222
1702-2298 23222
2318-3299 23223
500-2-500-2 23222
N Laburnum Ave 23223
S Laburnum Ave 23223
W Laburnum Ave
100-699 23222
1000-1002 23227
1004-2317 23227
2319-2399 23227
Laconia Dr 23223
Lacy Ln 23230
Ladbroke Ct 23234
E & W Ladies Mile Rd 23222
Ladino Ln 23236
Ladue Ct & Rd 23237
Lady St 23220
Lady Blair Ln
7500-7798 23235
7501-7551 23236
7601-7699 23235
Lady Sarah Ct 23236
Lady Slipper Ln 23236
Lafayette St
700-998 23221
1000-1099 23221
1400-1499 23230
Lair Dr 23237
Lake Ave
1100-1699 23226
2100-2299 23230
N Lake Ave 23223
S Lake Ave 23223
Lake Rd 23220
Lake Crest Ct & Way 23227
Lake Hills Ct & Rd 23234
Lake Shore Ct & Dr 23235
Lake Surrey Dr 23235
Lake Terrace Ct 23235
Lake Village Dr 23235

Lakeforest Dr 23235
Lakemere Ct & Dr 23234
Lakent Ln 23236
Lakeshire Ct 23235
Lakeside Blvd 23227
Lakeview Ave 23220
Lamar Dr 23225
Lamb Ave 23222
Lamberts Ave 23234
Lambeth Rd 23225
Lamont St 23227
Lamplighter Ct & Dr 23234
Lancashire Ct, Dr & Pl 23235
W Lancaster Rd 23222
Lancelot Ave 23234
Lancers Blvd & Cir 23224
Lancraft Rd 23235
Land Grant Rd 23236
Landing Cir & Ct 23236
Landis Dr 23226
Landria Dr 23225
Laneview Dr 23225
Lanewood Dr 23234
Langdon Ct & Dr 23225
Langhorne Ave 23222
Langston Ave 23220
Langton Ct 23226
Lansdale Rd 23225
Lansing Ave 23225
Lantern Way 23236
Lanvale Ave 23230
Laporte Rd 23224
Larchmont Ln 23224
Lark Dr 23227
Larkhill Ln 23235
Larkspur Rd 23235
Larne Ave 23225
Larry St 23222
Larrymore Ct & Rd 23225
Larsen Mews 23234
Larus Ct 23235
Lasalle Dr 23225
Latane Dr 23236
Laudeen Dr 23234
Laumic Dr 23235
Lauradale Ln 23234
Lauradale Lane Connector Ln 23234
Laureate Ct & Ln 23236
Laureate Turn 23236
N Laurel St
2-10 23220
14-18 23284
20-198 23220
200-206 23220
207-207 23284
208-398 23220
301-399 23220
S Laurel St 23220
Laurel Fork Dr 23225
Laurel Oak Cir, Ct & Rd 23237
Laurelbrook Dr 23224
Laurelwood Ct & Rd 23234
Laurie Ln 23223
Lavelle Rd 23234
Lawndale St 23237
Lawnwood Ct & Dr 23234
Lawson St 23224
Leadenhall Dr 23234
Leafcrest Ct & Ln 23235
Leafycreek Dr 23237
Leah Rd 23230
Leake Ave 23224
Lear Rd 23235
Leatherhead Ct & St 23223
Leconbury Rd 23234
Lee Ave 23226
Legion Ave 23224
Lehigh Cir 23230
Leicester Rd 23225
E Leigh St
1-899 23219
900-900 23298
901-999 23219
902-998 23219

1100-1198 23298
2100-3499 23223
W Leigh St
1-1600 23220
1601-1699 23284
1602-2498 23220
1701-2499 23220
2900-5099 23230
Leisure Ct, Ln & Ter 23237
Lemoine Ln 23236
Lenmore St 23224
Leno Pl 23236
Lenora Ln 23230
Leonard Pkwy
4400-4599 23221
4600-4899 23226
Leonards Run Dr & Pl 23236
Leopold Cir 23234
Leslie Ann Dr 23223
Letcher Ave 23222
Lethbridge Rd 23235
Level Green Ln 23227
Leveret Ln 23235
Levering Ln 23226
Lexington Rd 23226
Libbie Ave
1-2000 23226
2002-2098 23226
2100-2699 23230
Libbie Lake East St 23230
Libby Ter 23223
Libby Mill Ave E 23230
Liberty Ave 23223
Libwood Ave 23237
Lilac Ln 23221
Lilly Dr 23235
Limerick Dr 23225
Limestone Dr 23224
Lincoln Ave 23222
Lindell Rd 23236
N Linden St
1-11 23220
13-199 23220
100-108 23284
110-128 23220
S Linden St
1-5 23220
6-10 23284
7-99 23220
12-98 23220
101-117 23284
119-121 23284
123-199 23284
130-198 23220
200-299 23220
Lindenhurst 23238
Lindlaw Ave 23234
Lindy Ln 23224
Lingle Ct & Ln 23234
Lingstorm Ln 23225
Linwood Ave 23224
Lipes Ct & Dr 23223
Lipscomb St 23224
Lipton Rd 23225
Lisle Rd 23250
Lisson Cres 23225
Listerbrook Ct 23230
Little Creek Ln 23234
Little John Rd 23227
Littlecote Ln 23236
Littlepage St 23223
Llama Ln 23236
Loch Banif Rd 23236
Loch Braemar Dr 23236
Loch Lomond Ct & Ln 23221
Lochaven Blvd 23234
Lochinvar Dr 23235
Lochness Rd 23235
E Lock Ln S 23226
Lockberry Ridge Ct, Dr & Loop 23237
W Locke Ln 23226
Lockgreen Cir, Ct & Pl 23226
Lockhart Rd 23235
Lockshire Ct & Dr 23236
Locksley Ln & Pl 23236

Lodge St 23220
Logan St 23235
Logan Hill Ct & Pl 23223
Logandale Ave 23224
Lombardy Aly 23219
N Lombardy St
1-599 23220
600-620 23284
601-2599 23220
622-2598 23220
S Lombardy St 23220
Lone St 23224
Long Ln 23221
Longview Ct & Dr 23225
Looking Glass Rd 23235
Lookout Dr 23225
Lordley Ln 23224
Lords Ln 23231
Lorieville Ln 23225
Lorraine Ave 23227
Lost Ln 23224
Lost Forest Ct & Dr 23237
Lothaire Ct 23234
Lotus Dr 23235
Loudon St 23222
Louisiana St 23231
Loumour Ave 23230
Lovells Rd 23224
Lowell St 23223
Lower Tuckahoe Rd 23238
Lowes Pl 23227
Lowry St 23226
Loxley Rd 23227
Lucinda Ln 23234
Luckylee Cres 23234
Ludwig Rd 23225
Lumkin Ave 23234
Lumlay Rd 23236
Lunar Ct 23234
Lunenburg St 23220
Luray Ave 23231
Luray Dr 23227
Luton Ct 23235
Luton Ln 23225
Luton Rd 23235
Lynaire Dr 23235
Lynbrook Ln 23237
Lynchester Dr 23236
Lyndale Cir, Ct, Dr, Pl & Ter 23235
Lyndover Rd 23222
Lynette Rd 23237
Lynhaven Ave
1300-1999 23224
2200-4499 23234
Lynton Ln 23221
Lynview Dr 23235
Lyric Ct 23236
Lythgoe Ave 23234
M St 23223
Macarthur Ave 23227
Macbeth Ct 23234
Mactavish Ave 23230
Maddox St 23223
Madge Ln 23223
N & S Madison St 23220
Madumbie Ln 23220
Magellan Pkwy 23227
Maggie Walker Ave 23222
Maginoak Ct 23236
Magnolia Ct 23223
Magnolia Rd 23223
Magnolia St
1200-1899 23222
2000-2502 23223
2504-2808 23223
Magnus Ln 23223
E Main St
1-699 23219
700-700 23218
700-1598 23219
701-1599 23219
1700-3199 23223
3200-4799 23231
W Main St
1-9 23220

10-40 23284
11-299 23220
100-1018 23220
301-699 23284
701-799 23220
801-901 23284
903-999 23220
1001-1015 23284
1017-2799 23220
1020-1020 23284
1022-1312 23220
1314-1314 23284
1316-2798 23220
Major Ginter Ct 23227
Majorica Dr 23237
Malcott Ct & Dr 23237
Mall Ct & Dr 23235
Mallory Dr 23226
Malone St 23231
Malvern Ave 23221
Manchester Dr 23224
Mandalay Dr 23224
Mandy Ln 23224
Mango Ct 23223
Mann Ave 23226
Manor Cir & Dr 23230
Manorcrest Rd 23234
Mansard Ave 23226
Mansfield Dr 23223
Mansfield Crossing Ct, Ln, Rd & Ter 23236
Mansion Ave 23224
Mantua Ln 23236
Manuel Ct & St 23234
Maple Ave 23226
Maple St 23223
Maple Green Cir 23226
Maple Shade Ln 23227
Maplegrove Dr 23223
Maplested Ln 23235
Maplewood Ave
1800-2499 23220
3000-3500 23221
3502-3598 23221
Marble Rd 23236
Marble Head Ct 23235
Marbleridge Ct & Rd 23236
Marblethorpe Rd 23236
Marbrett Dr 23225
Marc Manor Ct 23225
March Hare Dr 23235
Marcy Pl 23224
Mardick Rd 23224
Margate Dr 23235
Marian St 23226
Marilea Rd
7500-7999 23225
8000-8099 23235
Marina Dr 23234
Marion Mashore St 23224
Maris Rd 23237
Mark Rd 23234
Markel Rd 23230
Markview Ct & Ln 23234
Marlboro Ct & Dr 23225
Marlin Dr 23223
Marlowe Rd 23225
Marquette Rd 23234
E Marshall St
1-999 23219
1000-1399 23298
1500-1699 23219
1700-3699 23223
1/2-1/2 23219
W Marshall St
1-1100 23220
1101-1103 23284
1102-1218 23220
1109-2099 23220
1220-1250 23284
1300-2098 23220
2800-5699 23230
Marston Ln 23221
Martha Ln 23234
Marthaven Dr 23235
Martin Ave 23222

E & W Martins Grant Cir 23235
Marty Blvd 23234
Marvin Dr 23223
Marwood Dr 23235
Marx St 23224
Mary View Dr 23226
Marybrooks Ct & Ln 23234
Maryland Ave 23222
Marylou Ln 23236
Mason Crest Dr 23234
Mason Dale Cir, Ct, Dr, Pl, Ter & Way 23234
Mason Hollow Dr 23234
Mason Rest Ct 23234
Mason Run Ct & Dr 23234
Mason Valley Ct & Dr 23234
Mason Way Ct 23234
Mason Woods Ct & Dr 23234
Masonic Ln & Ter 23223
Massie Rd 23221
Mast Dr 23224
Mastin Ln 23230
Matisse Ln 23224
Matoaka Rd 23226
Matthews St 23222
Mauldin St 23223
Maurice Ave 23224
Maury St 23224
Maverick Ave 23231
Maxwell Rd 23226
May Apple Ter 23236
Mayfair Ave 23226
Mayflower Dr 23235
Mayhew St 23224
Maywill St 23230
Maywood St 23237
Mcaden Pl 23236
Mccarty Ave 23234
Mccauliff Ct & Dr 23236
Mccaw Dr 23235
Mcdonald Rd 23222
Mcdonough St
  900-1599 23224
  2200-3299 23225
Mcdowell Rd 23225
Mcguire Cir & Dr 23224
Mchoward Rd 23237
Mckay Ave 23224
Mckesson Ct & Dr 23235
Mcleod Rd 23224
Mcnair Cir 23236
Mcrae Rd 23235
Mcrand St 23224
Meade St 23220
N & S Meadow St 23220
Meadow Farm Dr 23225
Meadow Glen Ln & Pl 23234
Meadow Oaks Blvd 23234
Meadow Park Cir, Dr & Ter 23225
Meadoway Rd 23234
Meadowbridge Rd 23222
Meadowburm Dr 23234
Meadowburn Dr 23237
Meadowcreek Dr 23236
Meadowdale Blvd 23234
Meadowmont Ln 23223
Meadowood Ct, Ln & Pl 23237
Meadows Run 23223
Meadowspring Rd 23223
Meadowview Ln 23223
Meadwood Cir 23234
Mebane St 23227
Mechanicsville Tpke 23223
Mecklenburg St 23223
Medallion Ct 23237
Medford Ave 23226
Media Rd 23225
Medina Rd 23235
Melaralm Rd 23227
Melba St 23237
S & W Melbeck Cir, Ct, Rd & Ter 23234
Melbourne Dr 23225
Melbourne St 23223
Melbury Way 23226
Melissa Mill Rd 23236
Melmark Ct & Rd 23225
S Melody Ct & Rd 23234
Melrose Ave 23227
Melton Ave 23223
Menokin Rd 23225
Meredith Hill Ter 23237
Meridale Rd 23225
Meridian Ave 23234
Meriwether Ave 23222
Merriewood Rd 23237
Merriewood Ridge Ct & Dr 23237
Merrifield Dr 23225
Merrigan Rd 23235
Merrimac Rd 23235
Merry Oaks Ave 23224
Merryman Rd 23222
Mervine Rd 23225
Metcalf Dr 23227
Metro Ct 23237
Metropolitan Ct 23236
Miami Ave 23226
Michael Gray Way 23225
Micheline Ct & Ter 23223
Middle Cir, Loop & Rd 23235
Midfield Rd 23236
Midlothian Tpke
  2600-4899 23224
  5000-5046 23225
  5048-6999 23225
  7100-7599 23225
  7600-11599 23235
Mike Rd 23234
Milbrae Ct, Pl & Rd 23236
Milbrook Ct & Dr 23235
Milburn Ave 23223
Milfax Rd 23224
Mill Race Cir & Rd 23234
Millcreek Ct & Dr 23235
Millenbeck Rd 23224
Miller Ave 23222
Millers Run Rd 23236
Millhiser Ave 23226
Mills Rd 23233
Millsap Ln 23235
Milo Rd 23225
Milton St 23222
Mimosa St 23224
Mindalin Ave 23220
Minefee St 23224
Minor St 23222
Minuet Ct 23236
Missouri Ave 23222
Misty Oak Ct 23234
Mistyhill Rd 23234
Mistywood Rd 23236
Mitchell St 23222
Mitcheltree Blvd 23223
Mobrey Dr 23236
Mohawk Dr 23235
Monacan Dr 23238
Monath Rd 23236
Monet Ct 23224
Monitor Rd 23225
N Monroe St 23220
Montague Rd 23225
Montaigne Dr 23235
Montauban Cir 23235
Montauk Dr 23225
Montbrook Cir & Ln 23227
Montclair Ct & Rd 23223
Montebello Cir 23231
Montecrest Ave 23234
Monteiro Ave 23222
Monteith Rd 23235
Montezuma Ave 23223
Monticello St 23227
Montour Dr 23236
Montrose Ave
  2601-2797 23222
  2799-3899 23222
  7400-7699 23227
Montvale Ave 23222
Monument Ave
  1600-2799 23220
  2800-3499 23221
  3600-5199 23230
  5200-7299 23226
Monument Park 23230
Monumental Ave & St 23226
Monza Ct & Dr 23234
Moody Ave 23225
Moon Ln 23234
Moonlight Dr 23234
Moore St 23230
W Moore St 23220
Moorefield Park Dr 23236
Moorwood Ridge Cir, Ct, Dr & Ter 23236
Morelock Ct & Dr 23236
Morhaven Trl 23237
Morningmist Cir, Ct, Dr & Pl 23234
Morningside Dr 23226
N & S Morris St 23220
Morrison Rd 23230
Morton Dr 23223
Mosby St 23223
Moss Gate Ct & Ter 23227
Moss Side Ave
  2800-4099 23222
  5600-7899 23227
Mosswood Ct & Rd 23236
N & W Mount Bella Rd 23235
Mount Erin Dr 23231
Mount Vernon St 23227
Mountain Laurel Ct & Dr 23236
Mountain Pine Blvd & Ter 23235
Mt Gilead Blvd 23235
Mt Zion Ct 23223
Muirfield Ct 23236
N & S Mulberry St 23220
Mule Barn Aly 23220
Muncie Rd 23223
Munford St 23220
Murchies Hill Rd 23234
N Myers St 23230
Mylan Rd 23223
Myra Dr 23234
Myron Ave 23237
Myrtle St 23222
Mystic Rd 23238
N St 23223
Nambe Cir 23237
Nancy Dr 23236
N & S Nansemond St 23221
Nantucket Ct 23236
Napoleon St 23222
Narbeth Ave 23234
Natchez Rd 23223
Nathan Ln 23235
Natick Ct 23236
National St 23231
Natural Bridge Ct & Rd 23236
Navaho Rd 23225
Navarone Ave 23234
Navy Hill Dr 23219
Neale St 23223
Necho Ct 23234
Nelson St 23231
Nelwood Dr 23231
Neptune Dr 23235
Nesbitt Dr 23225
Nestle Ave 23224
Netherwood Rd 23225
Nevada Ave 23220
New Kent Ave & Rd 23225
New Park Rd 23237
New York Ave 23220
Newbourne St 23223
Newbridge Cir, Rd & Ter 23223
Newbury Ave 23222
Newbys Bridge Rd 23235
Newbys Crossing Dr 23235
Newell Rd 23225
Newhaven Dr 23234
Newington Ct & Dr 23224
Newkirk Dr 23224
Newman Rd 23231
Newport Dr 23227
Newquay Ln 23236
Newstead Dr 23235
Newton Rd 23231
Nicholson St 23231
Nicolet Cir & Rd 23225
Niles Rd 23234
Nine Mile Rd 23223
Noble Ave
  2900-3899 23222
  7400-7899 23227
Noel Ct & St 23237
Nokomis Rd 23225
Norborne Rd 23234
Norcliff Rd 23237
Norcroft Cir & Ter 23225
Norcross Rd 23225
Nordic Ln 23237
Norfolk St 23230
Norincor Rd 23225
Norman Dr 23227
Normandale Ave 23237
Norris Ln 23226
North Ave 23222
North Rd 23227
Northampton St 23231
Northborough Ct & Ln 23236
Northcliff Ct & Pl 23236
Northcreek Dr 23236
Northfield Ln 23236
Northgate Ct 23236
Northland Dr 23236
Northridge Ct & Rd 23235
Northrop St 23225
Northside Ave 23222
Northumberland Ave 23220
Northview Pl 23225
Norton St 23220
E & W Norwood Ave & Ct 23222
Nottingham Rd 23221
Nottinghill Rd 23234
Nottoway Ave 23227
Nunnally Ave 23230
Nutmeg Ct 23225
O St 23223
Oak Ln 23226
Oak St 23220
Oak Center Dr 23237
Oak Glen St 23225
Oak Hill Ln 23223
Oak Lawn St 23237
Oak Park Ave 23222
Oak Vista Ct 23237
Oak Water Ct & Rd 23235
Oakcliff Ave 23236
Oakcrest Dr 23235
Oakdale Ave 23227
Oakdell Ct, Dr & Pl 23237
Oakford Ct 23236
Oakhurst Ln 23225
Oakland Ave & Pl 23224
Oakleaf Rd 23235
Oakleys Ct, Ln & Pl 23223
Oakridge Ave 23223
Oakshire Ln & Ter 23237
Oakside Cir, Ct & Dr 23237
Oakwood Ave 23223
Oberlin Rd 23234
Obrien Rd 23227
Observation Ave 23234
Oconto Rd 23230
Octagon Dr 23234
October Rd 23234
Okehampton Dr 23237
Olan Ct 23223
Old Bon Air Pl & Rd 23235
Old Brook Cir & Rd 23227
Old Camp Rd 23235
Old Canal Rd 23221
Old Cannon Rd 23237
Old Carnation St 23225
Old Carrollton Ct, Rd & Trce 23236
Old Courthouse Rd 23236
Old Denny St 23231
Old Dominion St 23224
Old Farm Rd 23235
Old Glen Cir 23223
Old Holly Rd 23235
Old Hopkins Rd
  3900-4199 23234
  4201-4299 23234
  7700-7798 23237
  7701-7797 23237
  7799-7900 23237
  7902-7998 23237
Old Indian Rd 23235
Old Jahnke Rd 23225
Old Lewiston Pl & Rd 23236
Old Locke Ln 23226
Old Log Trl 23235
Old Magnolia Rd 23223
Old Main St 23231
Old Masonic Ln 23223
Old Mesa Dr 23237
Old Midlothian Tpke 23224
Old Mill Rd 23226
Old Nicholson St 23231
Old Orchard Ln 23226
Old Orchard Rd 23227
Old Plantation Rd 23237
Old Post Rd 23234
Old Quarry Rd 23225
Old Richmond Ave 23226
Old Salem Church Rd 23237
Old Sellers Way 23227
Old Spring Rd 23235
Old Union Rd 23231
Old Warson Dr 23237
Old Warwick Rd
  3900-4699 23234
  4800-6399 23224
  6500-6599 23225
Old Westham Rd 23225
Old Willow Ct 23225
Old Zion Hill Rd 23234
Olde Liberty Rd 23236
Oldenburg Cir 23223
Oldfield Dr 23235
Oldham Ct & Rd 23235
Olive Ave 23234
Oliver Hill Way
  300-999 23219
  1000-1098 23298
  1001-1799 23219
  1100-1798 23219
Olney Dr 23222
Olympic Ct & Rd 23235
Omaha St 23237
Omalley Dr 23234
Omo Rd 23234
Ontario Dr 23235
Opaline Rd 23223
Orams Ln 23223
Orangewood Rd 23235
Orchard Rd 23226
Orchard Glen Dr 23223
Orchardhill Dr 23234
Orcutt Ln 23224
Ordway Ave 23222
Oregon Creek Dr 23234
Oregon Oak Ct, Dr & Pl 23234
Oreilly Ln 23235
Orinda Dr 23223
Oriole Ave 23234
Orlando Rd 23224
Orleans St 23231
Oronoco Ave 23222
Orville Rd 23230
Osoge Rd 23225
Oster Dr 23227
Osterbind Ln 23237
Ottawa Rd 23225
Overbrook Rd
  1-899 23222
  1000-1699 23220
Overbury Rd 23227
Overlook St 23224
Ownby Ln 23220
Oxbridge Cir, Pl & Rd 23236
Oxer Ct & Rd 23235
Oxford Cir E 23221
Oxford Cir W 23221
Oxford Pkwy 23235
Oxford Rd 23221
Oxnard Rd 23223
P St 23223
Pachanda Rd 23250
Packer Xing 23235
Paddenswick Ct 23236
Pagebrook Dr 23238
Paisley Ln 23236
Palmerston Rd 23236
Palmyra Ave 23227
Palomill Cir 23223
Pamela Ln 23233
Pams Ave 23237
Pamworth Ln 23224
Pano Ct & Dr 23237
Panola Rd 23234
Pantela Dr 23235
Paradise Cove Rd 23237
Paragon Pl 23230
E Parham Rd 23227
Park Ave
  500-599 23223
  800-815 23220
  816-824 23284
  817-899 23220
  826-898 23220
  900-901 23284
  902-921 23220
  922-922 23284
  923-2799 23220
  924-2798 23220
  2800-4599 23221
  4600-7099 23226
Park Dr 23221
Park Ln 23230
Park Rd 23237
Park Central Dr 23227
Parkdale Rd 23234
Parker St 23231
Parkerstown Rd 23237
Parkline Dr 23226
Parkview Ave 23222
Parkway Ln 23225
Parkwood Ave
  1000-2799 23220
  2900-3499 23221
Parliament Rd 23224
Parlow Dr 23222
Parrish St 23226
Partingdale Cir 23224
Partridge Ln 23236
Partridge Hill Rd 23238
Partridge Hill Farm Rd 23238
Pat Ln 23234
Pate Ave 23234
Patrick Ave 23222
Patromdale Dr 23237
Patsy Ann Dr 23234
Patterson Ave
  2800-4599 23221
  4600-7099 23226
  12200-12999 23238
Paulhill Rd 23236
Pauls Ln 23224
Pawnee Rd 23225
Pawpans Ct & Pl 23237
Paxford Rd 23234
Paxton Rd & St 23226
Peabody Ln 23223
Peace Lily Ln 23223
Peach Grove Rd 23237
Peachtree Blvd 23226
Pear St 23223
Pebble Ct 23224
Pebblespring Dr 23234
Peck Rd 23235
Peebles St 23223
Pelham Dr 23222
Pember Ln 23224
Pemberton Ave 23222
Pembroke Ct 23238
Pembroke Ln 23238
Pembroke St 23234
Pendleton Pl 23236
Pennway Dr 23236
Penobscot Rd 23227
Penrose Dr 23235
Pensacola Ave 23222
Penshurst Rd 23221
Pepper Ave 23226
Pepperidge Rd 23236
Percheron Ct 23227
Perdue Ave 23224
Peregrine Rd 23237
Periwinkle Dr 23237
Perl Rd 23230
Perlock Rd 23237
Perry St
  600-1799 23224
  2100-2699 23225
Perrymont Rd 23237
Peter Paul Blvd 23223
Petoskey Ave 23224
Pettus Rd 23234
Pewter Ave 23224
Peyton Ave 23224
Phaup St 23223
Philbrook Rd 23234
Phildavid Ct 23236
Phillips Ln 23234
Philray Ct & Rd 23236
Phobus Ct & Dr 23234
Piccolo Dr 23223
Pickens Rd 23224
Pickering Blvd 23223
Piels Rd 23237
Pierpont Rd 23225
Pilgrim Ct, Ln & Ter 23227
E Pilkington St 23224
W Pilkington St 23225
Pillow Bluff Ln 23237
Pilots Ln 23222
Pinalto Dr 23222
Pinchot St 23235
Pine St 23223
N Pine St 23220
S Pine St 23220
Pine Crest Ave 23225
Pine Glade Ln 23237
Pine Lake Dr 23223
Pine Ridge Rd 23226
Pinebrook Dr 23225
Pineland Ct & Rd 23234
Pineleaf Dr 23234
Pinetree Dr 23230
N & W Pinetta Dr 23235
Pineville Ct & Rd 23236
Pineway Dr 23225
Pinewood Glen Ln 23223
Piney Rd 23222
Piney Branch Rd 23225
Piney Grove Ct 23238
Piney Ridge Ct & Dr 23223
Pink St 23223
Pinoak Rd 23223
Pioneer St 23237
Pippin Ln 23234
Pittaway Dr 23235
Plainfield Rd 23234
Planet Rd 23234
Plantation Dr 23227
Platinum Rd 23234
Playground Cir, Ct & Dr 23237
Plaza Dr 23233
Plazaview Rd 23224
Pleasant St 23223
Pleasant Ridge Rd 23237
Pleasanthill Ct & Dr 23236
Pleasantview Rd 23236
Plerierm Ave 23221
Plestrai Rd 23235
Plotkin Rd 23234

Plowfield Ct 23223
Plum Cir 23237
Plum Ct 23237
Plum St 23237
N Plum St 23220
S Plum St 23220
Plymouth Dr 23222
Pocahontas Ave 23226
Poco Dr 23235
Pocono Dr 23236
Pocosham Dr 23224
Pocoshock Blvd, Pl &
Way 23235
Poe St 23222
Poindexter Rd 23234
W Point Ct 23235
Point Hollow Ct, Dr &
Pl 23227
Pointer Cir, Dr & Ter ... 23237
Polaria St 23223
Polk St 23235
Pollard Dr 23226
Pollock St 23222
Pomona Rd 23223
Pompey Springs Rd ... 23234
Ponce De Leon Rd 23237
Pondera Rd 23235
Pony Cart Dr 23225
Pony Farm Dr 23227
Pool Rd 23236
Pope Ave 23227
Poplar Ln 23226
Poplar St 23223
Poplar Cove Way 23223
Poplar Haven Ct 23223
Poplar Hollow Ter &
Trl 23235
Poplar Ridge Rd 23236
Poplar Way Ct 23223
Port Leon Rd 23237
Porter St
600-1999 23224
2100-3299 23225
Portico Pl 23234
Portland Pl 23221
Portrait Pl 23234
Portugee Rd 23250
Post Cedar Ct & Pl 23223
Post Horn Dr 23237
Post Oak Rd 23235
Potomac St 23231
Potters Ct 23225
Powell Rd 23224
Powhatan St 23220
Poyntelle Rd 23235
Prairie Rd 23225
Pratt St 23226
Presson Blvd 23224
E Preston St 23219
E & S Prestonwood
Ave 23234
Pretty Ln 23234
Price St 23220
Pride Rd 23224
Primrose Pl 23225
Prince Arthur Rd 23225
Prince David Dr 23223
Prince Edward Rd 23225
Prince George Rd 23225
Prince Hall Dr 23224
Prince Robert Ct 23223
Princess Anne Ave 23223
Princess Ella Ln 23225
Princess Grace Ct 23223
Princess Margaret Ct &
Pl 23236
Princeton Rd 23227
Pritchard Ter 23235
Privet Dr 23237
Proctors Rd 23237
Proctors Bluff Ln 23237
Proctors Run Dr 23237
Professional Rd 23235
Prospect St 23226
W Providence Ct 23236
W Providence Mews 23236
Providence Pl 23236
N Providence Rd 23235
S Providence Rd 23236
W Providence Rd 23236
Providence Ter 23236
Providence Creek Cir, Ct,
Mews, Pl, Rd, Ter &
Trl 23236
Providence Forest Ct ... 23235
Providence Glen Turn .. 23236
Providence Knoll Dr &
Mews 23236
Providence Ridge Ct &
Ter 23236
Providence Ridge Turn . 23236
Provincetown Dr 23235
Pulaski Ave & St 23222
Pullbrooke Cir, Ct &
Dr 23236
Pulliam Ct 23235
Pulliam St
100-199 23220
1200-2599 23235
Pump House Dr 23221
Pumpkin Pl 23236
Purcell St 23223
Purvis Rd 23223
Pusey Ln 23234
Q St 23223
Quail Oaks Ave 23237
Quaker Ln 23235
Quarterstaff Ct & Rd ... 23235
Queen Anne Dr 23224
Queen Charlotte Rd 23221
Queen Elizabeth Ave ... 23236
Queen Mary Ct 23223
Queen Scot Dr 23235
Queens Thorpe Ct 23227
Queensbury Rd 23226
Queensway Ct & Rd ... 23236
Quinnford Blvd 23237
Quite Ln 23235
R St 23223
Rabbit Foot Ct, Ln &
Pl 23236
Rachael Corrine Ct 23227
Rachel Rd 23223
Racrete Rd 23230
Radborne Rd 23236
Radford Ave 23230
Rady Ct & St 23222
Ragsdale Rd 23235
Rainwater Ct & Rd 23237
Rainwood Rd 23237
Ralph Blvd 23223
Rambling Rd 23235
Ramona Ave 23237
Rams Cir, Ct & Xing ... 23236
Rams Crossing Ct 23236
Ramsgate Ln & Sq 23236
Randall Ave 23231
Randolph Rd 23236
Randolph St 23220
Randolph Square Ln &
Pkwy 23238
Ransco Ct & Rd 23235
Ransom Hills Ct, Pl, Rd
& Ter 23237
Ransom Hills Turn 23237
Rasper Ct 23235
Ratcliffe Ave 23222
Rattlesnake Rd 23235
Raven St 23223
Ravenscroft Dr 23236
Ravenswood Rd 23222
Ravindale Ave 23237
Rawlings St 23231
Rayanne Dr 23235
Rayburn Rd 23235
Raynor Dr 23235
Reading Rd 23222
Ready Rd 23250
Reams Ct & Rd 23236
Rebecca Rd 23234
Red Ash Dr 23225
Red Barn Rd 23238
Red Leaf Rd 23237
S Red Lion Ct & Pl 23235
Red Oak Ln 23224
Red Queen Ct & Rd ... 23235
Redbridge Cir, Ct, Rd &
Ter 23236
Redbud Rd 23235
Redd St 23223
Redington Ct & Dr 23235
Redman Rd 23226
Redmead Ln 23236
Redpine Rd 23237
Redwood Ave 23223
Reed Rd 23230
Reedy Ave 23225
Regent Cir 23225
Regent Rd 23230
Regester Pkwy 23226
Regina Ln 23238
Reigate Rd 23236
Remora Dr 23237
Remuda Dr 23234
Rendale Ave 23221
Renfro Rd 23235
Rennie Ave 23227
Renovo Ln 23236
Republic Dr 23225
Resaca Rd 23236
Rescue Ave 23223
Research Ct 23236
Research Rd
500-999 23236
1000-1299 23235
Research Plaza Way ... 23236
Reserve St 23220
Reservoir Ln 23234
Restingway Ln 23234
Retriever Rd 23237
Rettig Rd 23225
Reuben Rd 23236
Reveille St 23221
Rex Ave 23222
Rexmoor Ct, Dr, Pl &
Ter 23236
Reycan Rd 23237
Reykin Dr 23236
Reymet Ct & Rd 23237
Reynolds Ct & Rd 23223
Reynolds Ridge Ter 23223
Rhoadmiller St 23220
Rhudy St 23222
Richard E Byrd Terminal
Dr 23250
Richdale Rd 23224
Richeson Ave 23224
Richmond Rd & St 23223
Richmond Henrico Tpke
1501-3097 23222
3099-4500 23222
4502-4598 23222
5000-5399 23227
Richwine Rd 23234
Ridarrin Ave 23230
Ridge Rd 23227
Ridgecliff Dr 23224
Ridgedale Pkwy 23234
Ridgemont Rd 23224
Ridgeway Rd 23226
Riding Place Rd 23223
Rigsby Rd 23226
Rio Vista Ln 23226
Ritter St 23234
Rivanna Dr 23235
Rivendell Ter 23234
River Rd
1-6199 23226
12200-13199 23238
River Bluffs Ct & Pl 23223
River City Court Way ... 23221
Rivercrest Rd 23235
Rivergate Dr 23238
Riverside Ct 23238
Riverside Dr
2000-8099 23225
8100-8999 23235
8813-8899 23235
N Riverside Dr 23225
Riverside Park 23220
Riverview Dr 23225
Roads End Ln 23238
Roane St 23222
E Roanoke St 23224
W Roanoke St 23225
Robcurn Dr 23223
Roberson Ln 23224
N Robert Bruce Dr 23235
Robert Earl Cir 23235
Robert Moore Cir 23222
E Roberts St 23222
W Roberts St
301-399 23222
1000-1099 23220
1101-1199 23232
Robin Ave 23223
Robin Rd 23226
Robin Hood Rd
1300-1399 23227
1501-1597 23220
1599-1799 23220
Robindale Ct & Rd 23235
N & S Robinson St 23220
Robinview Dr 23224
Robious Rd 23235
Robmont Rd 23236
Rochelle Rd 23238
S & W Rock Spring Ct &
Dr 23234
Rockaway Rd 23235
Rockbridge St 23230
Rockcrest Ct & Rd 23235
Rockdale Rd 23236
Rockfalls Dr 23225
Rockfield Rd 23237
Rockland Rd 23225
Rockledge Rd 23235
Rockmont Ct 23236
Rockwood Rd 23226
Rodman Rd 23224
Rodney Rd 23230
Rodophil Rd 23237
Roehampton Ct 23236
Rogers St 23223
Rois Rd 23227
Rolfe Rd 23226
Rollback Dr 23234
Rolling Rd 23226
Rolling Oaks Ct 23234
Ronaldton Rd 23236
Ronnie Ave 23222
Ronson Rd 23234
Rosanell Ln 23234
Rose Ave 23222
Rosecrest Ave 23224
Rosedale Ave
3200-3399 23230
3900-3999 23227
Rosegill Rd 23236
Roselawn Rd 23226
Rosemont Rd 23224
Rosenblum Ct 23234
Roseneath Rd
200-499 23221
501-999 23221
1100-1999 23230
Rosetta St 23223
Rosewell Ct 23235
Rosewood Ave
1800-2499 23220
3200-3599 23221
Roslyn Rd 23226
Rosser Rd 23223
Rossford Rd 23227
Rossmore Rd 23225
Rothbury Dr 23236
Rothesay Cir & Rd 23221
Rowen Ave 23219
N & S Rowland St 23220
Roxbury Rd 23226
Royal Cresent Ct, Dr &
Way 23236
Royal Oak Dr 23234
Royall Ave 23224
Rubimont Rd 23235
Rubis Ter 23235
Rucker Ct & Ln 23234
Ruddy Creek Dr 23234
Rudi Dr 23223
Rudyard Rd 23224
Rueger St 23221
Ruffin Rd 23234
Rugby Rd 23221
E & S Run Ct 23234
Running Pne 23238
Rural Dr 23222
Ruritan Pl 23234
Rushton Rd 23237
Rusk Ave & Ct 23234
Ruslander Ct 23223
Russell Rd 23237
Russell St 23222
Rustic Rd 23235
Rutherford Rd 23225
Ruthers Rd 23235
Ruthwin Ln 23234
Ryburn Rd 23234
Rycliff Ave 23237
Ryder Rd 23235
Ryecove Ln 23235
Ryefield Rd 23238
Ryland St 23220
S St 23223
Sabine St 23226
Sabot St 23226
Saddleback Dr 23225
Saddlebred Dr 23223
Saint Andrews Cir &
Ln 23226
Saint Anns Dr 23225
Saint Christophers Rd .. 23226
Saint Davids Ln 23221
Saint James Ct 23225
Saint James St 23222
Saint Joan Ave & Ct ... 23236
Saint Johns Wood Dr ... 23225
Saint Moritz Ct & Dr 23224
Saldale Dr 23237
Sale St 23223
Salem St
5100-5499 23231
6000-6098 23234
Salem Church Rd 23237
Salem Oaks Ct, Dr, Pl &
Ter 23237
Saline Dr 23224
Sanborn Dr 23225
Sandler Ct, Dr & Way .. 23235
Sandlewood Ct & Dr ... 23235
Sandpiper Dr 23227
Sandrock Ct & Dr 23234
Sandy Ln 23223
Sandy Grove Ct 23223
Saponen Dr 23237
Sara Ln 23224
Sara Kay Ct & Dr 23237
Saratoga Rd 23235
Satinwood Dr 23234
Sauer Ave
801-997 23221
999-1099 23221
1400-1699 23230
Sauna Ct & Dr 23236
Saunders Ave 23227
Sausiluta Dr 23227
Savannah Ave 23222
Savoy Rd 23235
Sawston Rd 23225
Saxony Rd 23235
Saybrook Ct & Dr 23236
Scarlet Oak Rd 23235
Scarsborough Dr 23235
Schenley Dr 23235
Scherer Dr 23235
Schloss Rd 23225
School St
400-498 23222
500-599 23222
1001-1001 23232
1201-1297 23220
1299-1399 23220
Schutte St 23225
Scotford Rd 23236
Scotlow Cir 23234
Scott Rd 23227
Scott St 23231
Scottdale St 23234
Scottingham Ct, Dr &
Ter 23236
Scottview Dr 23225
Seacliff Cir, Ct & Ln 23236
Seagrave Ave 23234
Sealing Wax Way 23235
Seaman Rd 23225
Seamore St 23223
Seasons Ln 23223
Seasons Mill St 23230
Seaton Ct & Dr 23223
Seddon Rd 23227
Seddon Way 23230
Seibel Rd 23223
Selden St 23223
Selma Ln & Pl 23223
Selwood Rd 23234
Seminary Ave
2000-2999 23220
3000-8299 23227
E Seminary Ave 23227
W Seminary Ave 23227
Seminary Pl 23227
Seminole Ave 23237
Semmes Ave
99-697 23224
699-1599 23224
1800-3499 23225
Senate St 23237
Seneca Rd 23226
Sequoyah Rd 23225
Serafim Ln 23227
Sesame St 23235
Seti Ct 23234
Seville Dr 23235
Sewell St 23222
Sexton Dr 23224
Shackleford Rd 23234
Shadowberry Ct & Pl ... 23227
Shady Ln 23234
Shady Creek Rd 23234
Shadybrook Ln 23224
Shadycrest Ln 23225
Shadymist Ct, Dr &
Ter 23235
Shafer St
200-299 23284
300-310 23220
301-399 23284
312-398 23284
400-499 23220
Shagbark Ct 23227
Shallot Rd 23223
Shallow Ct & Way 23224
Shamrock Dr 23237
Shannon Rd 23236
Shanto Ct 23237
Sharon Ct 23225
Sharonridge Dr 23236
Shasta Rd 23235
Shaun Ct 23237
Shaw Ln 23224
Shawnee Rd 23225
Shearwater Ct 23227
Sheffey Ln 23235
Sheffield Rd 23224
Sheffield Forest Rd 23237
Sheila Ln 23225
Shelby Dr 23224
Sheldeb Ct & Dr 23235
Shell Rd 23237
Shenandoah Ave 23226
N Sheppard St
2-4 23221
6-899 23221
901-999 23221
1000-1199 23230
S Sheppard St 23221
Sherbourne Rd 23237
Sherbrook Ct & Rd 23235
Sheridan Ln 23225
Sheringham Rd 23236
Sherman Ct, Pl, Rd &
Ter 23234
Sherwood Ave 23220
Sherwood Forest Dr &
Ter 23237
Shetland Ct 23227
N & S Shields Ave 23220
Shillcutt Rd 23237
Shillingford Dr 23223
Shiloh Dr 23237
Shingle Oak Rd 23237
Shirley Rd 23225
Shockoe Ln & Plz 23219
Shockoe Slip 23219
Shore Dr 23225
Shoreham Dr 23235
Shoremeade Ct & Rd .. 23234
Short St 23234
Short Decatur St 23224
Shreveport Rd 23223
Shrubbery Hill Rd 23227
Sibley Ave 23227
Silbury Rd 23234
Silver Ave 23224
Silver Mews Ln 23237
Silver Mist Ave 23237
Silver Oak Ct & Ln 23234
Silverfox Ln 23223
Silverleaf Ct & Ter 23236
Silverwood Dr 23225
Simons Dr 23234
Simpson Ave 23231
Sinclair Rd 23233
Singletary Ct 23223
Sioux Rd 23235
Sir Dinnadan Ct & Dr ... 23237
Sir Lionel Ct & Pl 23237
Sir Sagamore Ct & Dr .. 23237
Sisco Ave 23234
Sizer Rd 23222
Skelton St 23223
Skilift Ct & Ln 23225
Skipping Rock Ct, Pl &
Way 23234
Skipton Rd 23225
Sledd St 23220
Sleepy Hill Rd 23236
Sloan Ct 23234
Slumber Ln 23234
Smith St 23220
Smithdeal Ave 23225
Smoketree Cir, Ct, Dr, Pl
& Ter 23236
Snead Ct & Rd 23224
Snowden Ln 23226
Snowflake Dr 23237
Snowhill Rd 23235
Snyder Rd 23235
Somerset Ave 23226
Sonnet Hill Ct & Dr 23236
Sora Dr 23227
Souder Ct 23227
Sourwood Ln 23237
South Dr 23225
Southall Ave 23234
Southam Dr 23235
Southampton Ave 23220
Southampton Rd 23235
Southaven Rd 23235
Southcliff Rd 23225
Southern Pine Ct & Dr . 23225
Southgate St 23234
Southlake Blvd & Ct 23236
Southlawn Ave 23224
Southmoor Rd 23234
Southport Dr 23235
E Southside Plz 23224
N & W Southside Plaza
St 23224
Southwood Pkwy 23224
Southwood Rd 23237
Space Rd 23234
Spaine St 23224

Spencer Rd 23230
Spicer Rd 23226
Spiers Ct 23223
Spirea Ct & Rd 23236
Split Rail Rd 23223
Spoke Ct 23234
Spotsylvania St 23223
Spottswood Rd 23220
Spratling Ct & Way 23237
Spring St
100-199 23220
500-599 23219
600-899 23220
Spring Grove Dr 23225
Spring Hollow Dr 23227
Spring Lake Rd 23225
Spring Meadow Rd & Ter 23235
Spring Mill Rd 23236
Springdale Rd 23222
Springforest Dr 23223
Springhill Ave 23225
Springleaf Ct 23234
Springs Rd 23234
Springshire Dr 23237
Springtime Ct 23223
Springton Rd 23222
Springview Dr 23234
Springwood Rd 23237
Spruance Rd 23225
Spruce St 23222
Spruce Pine Dr 23235
Sprucewood Ave 23234
E & W Square Ct, Dr, Ln & Pl 23238
Squire Hill Ct 23234
St Charles Rd 23227
St Claire Ln 23223
St George St
6400-6499 23234
6500-6600 23237
6601-6699 23237
6602-6698 23237
St James St 23220
St John St 23220
St Lo Dr 23227
St Matthews Ln 23233
St Paul St 23220
St Peter St 23220
St Regis Ct, Dr & Ter 23236
Stacie Rd 23224
N Stafford Ave 23220
S Stafford Ave 23220
Stafford Pl 23226
Stanbrook Dr 23234
Stanhope Ave 23227
Stanley Dr 23234
Stanmore Ct, Pl, Rd & Sq 23236
Stansbury Ave 23225
Stanwix Ln 23234
Staples Mill Rd 23230
Starbuck Ct 23223
Starlight Ln 23235
Starmont Rd 23235
Starview Ct & Ln 23225
State St 23231
Stately Oak Rd 23234
Station Rd 23234
Staunton Ave 23226
Steeple Ln 23223
Stegge Ave 23224
Stella Ct & Rd 23234
Stemwell Blvd, Cir, Ct, Ln, Pl, Pt & Ter 23236
Steppeway Ln 23223
Sterling St 23221
Sterling Forest Pkwy 23227
Sterncroft Dr 23225
Steven Hill Ct & Dr 23234
Stiles Ct & Rd 23235
Stillbrook Ct & Rd 23236
Stilwell Rd 23226
Stockton Ln 23221
Stockton St 23224
Stokes Ln 23226

Stone Ln 23227
Stone Dale Ct & Dr 23223
Stone River Ct & Rd 23235
Stone Throw Ct & Ter 23223
Stonebridge Plaza Ave 23225
Stonecrest Ct & Rd 23236
Stonecrop Ct & Pl 23236
Stonehenge Dr 23225
Stonehill Dr 23236
Stonehurst Grn 23226
Stonetree Dr 23235
Stonewall Ave 23225
Stoney Run Pkwy 23223
Stony Crest Cir 23235
E & W Stony Hill Ct 23235
Stony Lake Ct & Dr 23235
Stony Point Dr, Pkwy & Rd 23235
Stony Valley Ct & Dr 23223
Stonybrook Dr 23225
Stornoway Dr 23234
Stowe Dr 23234
Stowmarket Ct 23225
Strasburg Rd 23223
Stratford Ave 23227
Stratford Cres 23226
Stratford Ct 23225
Stratford Pl 23235
Stratford Rd 23225
Stratford Townes Dr, Pl & Way 23225
Strathcona St 23234
Strathmore Ct 23237
Strathmore Rd
6000-6399 23234
6600-6698 23237
6601-6699 23237
6700-6899 23237
W Strathmore Rd 23237
Stratton Rd 23225
Strawberry St 23220
Stroud Ln 23236
Stuart Ave
1901-1997 23220
1999-2799 23220
3000-3098 23221
3100-4599 23221
4600-6899 23226
Stuart Cir 23220
Stukeley Ln 23227
Sturbridge Dr
900-998 23236
901-999 23236
1000-1199 23235
10501-10599 23236
Sturgis Dr 23236
Stuts Ln 23236
Suburban Ave 23230
Suburban Village Cir, Ct, Dr, Ln, Loop, Trl & Way 23235
Sue Jean Dr 23234
Suffolk Rd 23227
Sugar Maple Dr 23225
Sugarbush Dr 23225
Sulgrave Rd 23221
Summer Hill Ave 23234
Summerbrooke Ct & Dr 23235
Summerleaf Ct & Dr 23234
Summertree Ct & Dr 23234
Summit Ave 23230
Summit Ln 23221
Summit Acres Dr 23235
Sumpter St 23220
Sunbeam Rd 23234
Sunbury Rd 23224
Sunflower Ln 23236
Sunkist Ave 23235
Sunora Ct & Dr 23234
Sunrise Five Way 23236
Sunset Ave & Ln 23221
Sunset Hills Ct, Dr & Ter 23236
Sunset Knoll Rd 23237
Sunview Ct & Ln 23235

Surreywood Ct & Dr 23235
Sussex St 23223
Susten Ct & Ln 23224
Sutherland Rd 23236
Swan Ct & Dr 23234
Swanage Rd 23236
Swanhaven Dr 23234
Swansea Rd 23236
Swanson Rd 23225
Swathmore Rd 23235
Sweetback Ln 23238
Sweetbriar Dr 23238
Sweetwood Dr 23225
Swineford Rd 23237
Sydelle Dr 23235
Sykes Rd 23235
Sylvan Ct & Rd 23225
T St 23223
Tacoma St 23230
Tacony Dr 23225
Taft St 23223
Talbert Dr 23224
Tall Grass Ct 23223
Talon Ln 23237
Tamarind Ct, Dr & Pl 23227
Tamiani Ave 23227
Tanbark Rd 23235
Tanby Rd 23235
Tandem Ct & Dr 23234
Tanglewood Rd 23225
Tanners Way 23224
Tapoan Pl & Rd 23226
Tappahannock St 23237
Tarkington Dr 23227
Tarpley Rd 23225
Tarry Ln 23230
Tate St 23223
Tatterton Trl 23223
Taw St 23237
Taylor Ave 23225
Taylor Rd 23223
Taylor Brook Ct & Ln 23234
Taylor Pointe Ct 23225
Tazewell St 23222
Teaberry Dr 23236
Teakwood Ave 23227
Teddington Dr 23235
Tee Cir 23225
Telbury St 23237
Telstar Dr 23237
Temple St 23220
Tempsford Ln 23226
Tennyson Ave 23225
Terenerm Rd 23236
Terminal Ave
2200-3499 23234
3501-3699 23234
3800-4399 23224
Terminal Pl 23220
Terrace View Ln 23235
Terri Lynn Ct 23235
Texas Ave 23220
Thalbro St 23230
Thalen St 23223
Thayer Ct 23226
Thayer St 23224
The Plz & Ter 23222
The Loop Rd 23231
Thierry Ct & St 23234
Thimble Ln 23222
Thomas Dr 23222
Thomas St 23220
Thompson St 23222
N Thompson St
1-499 23221
900-1199 23230
S Thompson St 23221
Thorndale Ln 23225
Thornhurst Ct & St 23223
Thornington Dr 23237
Thornloe Ct 23235
Threadneedle St 23235
Three Chopt Rd
1600-1899 23233
5800-5898 23226
5900-7499 23226

Thrush Ln 23227
Thunderbolt St 23250
Thurloe Dr 23235
Thurman St 23224
Thurston Rd 23237
Tiber Ln 23226
Tiffany Cir 23235
Tiffanywoods Ct & Ln 23223
Tifton Ct 23224
Tiger Lily Ln 23223
Tighe Ct 23223
Tignor Rd 23224
Tilden St 23221
Tilehurst Ct 23237
Tilford Rd 23225
Tillers Ridge Ct, Dr & Ter 23235
Tilton Ct 23224
Tim Price Way 23225
Timbercreek Ct & Dr 23237
Timbers Hill Rd 23235
Tinsley Dr 23235
Titan Dr 23225
Tithonia Cir 23237
Titus St 23224
Tivoli Cir 23227
Toddsbury Rd 23226
Toledo Ave 23234
Tomacee Rd 23221
Tomlynn St 23230
Tonbridge Rd 23221
Tonoka Ct & Rd 23223
Torquay Loop 23236
Totila Ct 23234
Tow Path Cir, Ct & Ln S & W 23221
Towana Rd 23226
Tower Rd 23237
Townes Rd 23226
Trabue Rd 23235
Trace Ct 23234
Trade Ct & Rd 23236
Trafton St 23222
Tranquil Ln 23234
Transport St 23234
Traway Ct & Dr 23235
Traylor Dr 23235
Traymore Rd 23235
Treadwood St 23237
Trebeck Rd 23236
Treboy Ave & Ct 23226
Tredegar St 23219
Treehaven Dr 23224
Treewood Ln 23224
Trefoil Way 23235
E & W Tremont Ct 23225
Trent Rd 23235
Trenton Ave 23234
Trevillian Rd 23235
Trevor Ter 23225
Trickling Creek Rd 23236
Trio St 23223
Triton Cir & Dr 23235
Trout Ln 23236
Troy Ct & Rd 23224
Troycott Pl & Rd 23237
Tuckahoe Ave & Blvd 23226
Tuckahoe Creek Pkwy 23238
Tucker Rd 23234
Tuckers Landing Rd 23236
Tudor Ln 23235
Tulane Ave 23226
Tulip St 23223
Turf Ln 23225
Turkey Oak Rd 23237
Turnaway Ln 23234
Turner Rd
2-98 23225
100-2399 23225
2400-2999 23224
4400-5299 23234
Turngate Rd 23234
Turnmill Ct & Dr 23235
Turpin St 23298
Tuscora Rd 23235
Tutti Dr 23234

Tuxedo Blvd 23223
Tuxford Rd 23236
Twain Ct & Ln 23224
Twila Ln 23234
S Twilight Ln 23235
Twin Crest Dr 23236
Twin Valley Rd 23235
Twining Ln 23223
Twinridge Ln 23235
Twyman Rd 23234
Tyler St 23222
Tyme Rd 23234
Tyndale Rd 23227
Tynick St 23224
Tyrone St 23234
U St 23223
Ullswater Ave 23225
Unicorn Ln 23235
Upham Dr 23227
Upland Dr 23227
Upp St 23234
Uppingham Ct, Rd & Ter 23235
Upshur Ct & Dr 23236
Upton Rd 23237
Utah Pl 23222
V St 23223
Vaden Dr 23225
Vaga Ln 23223
Vale St 23234
Valley Rd 23222
Valley Side Ct, Dr & Ter 23223
Van Ave 23227
Van Buren Ave 23226
Van Hoy Dr 23235
Vanderbilt Ave 23226
Vantage Ct & Pl 23236
Vauxhall Ct & Rd 23234
Vawter Ave 23222
Vayo Ave 23234
Velda Rd 23237
Venable St 23223
Venango Ln 23236
Veranda Ave 23222
W Verennew Pkwy 23238
Veritas Way 23234
N & S Verlinda Ct & Dr 23237
Vesper Rd 23225
Vestry Rd 23237
Vevadel Dr 23225
Vial Rd 23234
N Vickilee Ct & Rd 23236
Victor St 23222
Victoria Way 23238
Victoria Park Ter & Way 23234
Vida Ln 23225
Vietor St 23235
Viewmere Cres 23235
Village Lake Ct & Dr 23234
Ville Ponteaux Ln 23238
N & S Vine St 23220
Vineland Rd 23235
Vinings Dr 23234
Vinita Rd 23238
Vintner Dr & Ln 23234
Vinton St 23231
Virginia Ave 23226
N Virginia Ave 23223
Virginia St 23219
Virginia Pine Ct 23237
Vista St 23231
Vista Ridge Ln 23237
Vivian Ct 23224
Vixen Cir & Ln 23235
Vollie Rd 23236
Waddington Dr 23224
E & W Wadsworth Ct, Dr, Pl & Way 23236
Wagner Ave 23230
N & S Wagstaff Cir 23236
Wainfleet Dr 23235
Wainwright Dr 23225
Wake Ave 23225

Wake Forest Dr 23226
Wakefield Rd
200-299 23221
3600-4499 23235
Wakehurst Dr 23236
Walcott Pl 23223
Walderbrook Ct & Rd 23234
Waldor Dr 23234
Walford Ave 23226
Walhala Cir, Dr & Pt 23236
Walker St 23220
Walkerton Ct & Rd 23236
Wall St 23224
Wallace St 23220
Waller Rd 23230
Wallingford Ln 23227
Walmsley Blvd
2000-4799 23234
2901-3399 23234
4800-6099 23224
6100-6899 23224
6900-8299 23235
Walnut Aly 23223
Walnut Ave 23222
Walpole St 23221
Walton Ave 23222
Walworth Dr 23237
Wannee Way 23237
Wareham Ct & Pl 23237
Warielac St 23224
Warkendi Ave 23222
Warm Springs Way 23223
Warner Rd 23225
Warren Ave 23227
N Warriner Rd 23231
Warrior Trl 23236
Warson Ct 23237
Warwick Ave 23224
Warwick Rd
3900-4699 23234
4800-6200 23224
6201-6299 23225
6202-6398 23224
6301-6399 23224
6500-6899 23225
Warwick Village Dr 23224
Watchhaven Cir & Ln 23237
Watchlight Rd 23234
Watchrun Ct & Dr 23234
Watchspring Ct & Dr 23234
Water St 23223
Water Oak Ct 23237
Waters Mill Cir & Pt 23235
Watkins St 23227
Watson Ave 23234
Watson Ln 23223
Watts Ct & Ln 23223
Waumsetta Rd 23235
Waverly Ave 23231
Waverly Blvd 23222
Waving Meadow Rd 23223
Waxford Rd 23235
Waxwing Dr 23227
Waycrest Ter 23234
Wayland St 23223
Wayne St 23221
Wayside Dr 23235
Weatherfield Way 23223
Weatherford Rd 23224
Weaver Ct 23224
Webber Ave 23224
Webster St 23220
N & S Wedgemont Dr & Pl 23236
Welford Ave 23234
Welford St 23222
Welhaven Dr 23236
Wellington St 23222
Welsh Cir 23223
Welton Ave 23224
Wenatchee Ct, Rd & Ter 23236
Wendell Ln 23234
Wendover Ln 23230
Wentbridge Rd 23227

Wentworth St
6400-6499 23234
6500-6999 23237
7000-7198 23237
7001-7199 23237
Wesley Rd 23226
Wessex Ln 23226
West Ave 23220
Westbourne Dr 23230
Westbrook Ave & Ct 23227
Westchester Cir & Rd 23225
Westcliffe Ave 23222
Westcott Dr 23225
Westcreek Cir, Ct & Dr 23236
Western Rd 23235
Westfield Rd 23226
Westgate Dr 23235
Westham Station Rd 23226
Westhampton Sta & Way 23226
Westhill Rd 23226
Westmeath Ln 23227
Westminster Ave 23227
Westminster Canterbury Way 23227
Westmoreland Pl 23226
Westmoreland St
2-198 23226
200-299 23226
301-1799 23226
1900-2499 23230
Westover Ave 23223
Westover Rd 23220
Westover Gardens Blvd 23225
Westover Hills Blvd 23225
Westover Pines Dr 23223
Westover Village Dr 23225
Westover Woods Cir 23225
Westower Ct & Dr 23225
Westview Ave 23226
Westwick Dr 23225
Westwood Ave
301-797 23222
799-999 23222
1000-1198 23227
1200-1999 23227
2000-2599 23230
Westwood St
6400-6499 23234
6700-6999 23237
6800-6899 23237
Westwood Trl 23230
Wexford Ln 23225
Wexwood Ct, Dr & Pl 23236
E & W Weyburn Rd 23235
Weymouth Dr 23235
Whale Rock Rd 23234
Wharf St 23223
Wharton Rd 23224
Whatley St 23222
Wheaton Rd 23225
Wheelwood Ct & Way 23223
Whetstone Rd 23234
Whiffletree Ct & Rd 23236
Whippoorwill Rd 23233
Whisperwood Dr 23234
Whistler Ct & Rd 23227
Whistling Well Ct 23234
Whitaker Cir & Dr 23235
Whitby Rd 23227
Whitcomb St 23223
White Cedar Ct & Ln 23235
White Cross Ct 23234
White Oak Dr 23224
White Pickett Cir, Ct & Ln 23237
White Rabbit Rd 23235
Whitebark Ter 23237
Whitehall Rd 23235
Whitehead Rd 23225
Whitehorse Rd 23235
Whitepine Rd 23237
Whitesand Dr 23225
Whitestone Ct & Dr 23234

Whitewater Ct 23234
Whitewood Rd 23235
Whitlock Ave 23223
Whitlone Dr 23225
Whittington Dr
7400-7799 23225
7900-8299 23235
Whitworth Rd 23235
Wickham St
100-299 23222
301-699 23222
1000-1098 23220
1101-1199 23220
Wickham Glen Dr 23238
Wicklow Ln & Loop 23236
Wighton Dr 23235
Wigmore Ct 23227
Wilaka Ln 23227
Wild Life Trl 23238
Wildplum 23238
Wilkes Ln 23223
Wilkes Ridge Pl 23233
Wilkinson Ct & Rd 23227
Wilkinson Estates Dr 23227
Willamar St 23234
Willesden Rd 23234
Willetta Dr 23221
Williamsburg Ave
2900-3599 23223
4400-5100 23231
Williamsburg Rd 23231
Williamsdale Dr 23235
Williamstowne Dr 23235
Williamswood Rd 23235
Willis Rd 23237
Willis St 23224
Willomett Ave 23227
Willoughby Ct 23224
Willow St 23222
Willow Creek Ln & Way 23225
Willow Lawn Dr
900-1299 23226
1400-1999 23230
Willow Oaks Dr 23225
Willow Oaks Rd 23238
Willowbranch Ct & Dr 23234
Willtee Ln 23236
Willway Ave 23226
Wilma Ln 23231
Wilmer Ave 23227
Wilmington Ave 23227
Wilmont Dr 23222
Wilmoth Dr 23234
Wilson Ave 23223
Wilton Rd 23238
N Wilton Rd 23226
S Wilton Rd 23226
Wimbledon Dr 23224
Wimbly Way 23234
Winber Dr 23224
Winchell St 23231
Wind Pl 23236
Wind Grove Ct 23236
Windcroft Rd 23225
Winder St 23220
Winding Way 23235
Winding Trail Ln 23223
Windingbrook Rd 23230
Windingrun Ln 23237
Windmoor Ct 23235
Windomere Ave 23227
Windrift Rd 23236
Windrow Ct 23223
Windrush Ct 23234
Windsor Ave 23227
Windsor Way 23221
Windsorview Dr 23225
Windwood Ct & Ln 23237
Windy Oaks Ln 23234
Winford Ln 23225
Wingfield St 23231
Winnetka Ave 23227
Winslow Rd 23235
Winston St 23222
Winter Rd 23225
Winterleaf Ct & Dr 23234
Winters Hill Cir, Ct & Pl 23236
Winterslow Rd & Ter 23235
Winterstick Pl 23223
Wise St 23225
Wishsong Ct 23223
Witchduck Ct & Ln 23223
Wolfberry Rd 23236
Wonderview Dr 23237
Wood St 23223
Wood Bluff Loop 23236
Wood Vale Ct 23236
Woodberry Ln 23225
Woodbine Rd 23225
Woodburn Ct & Rd 23225
Woodcliff Ave 23222
Woodcock Ct 23223
Woodcroft Rd 23235
Woodfern 23238
Woodfield Ct & Rd 23234
Woodfin Dr 23237
Woodhaven Dr 23224
Woodlawn Ave 23221
Woodmere Dr 23234
Woodmill Pl 23236
Woodmont Dr 23235
Woodrow Ave 23222
Woodshill Ct 23235
Woodson Ave 23222
Woodstock Rd 23224
Woodward Ct & Dr 23236
Woodworth Rd 23237
Woody Dr 23222
Woodys Ct & Ln 23234
Woodyshade Cir 23235
Worsham Rd 23235
Worth St 23225
Worthington Ct & Rd 23225
Wren Rd 23223
Wrens Nest Ct & Rd 23235
Wright Ave 23224
Wuthering Hts 23234
Wyandotte Dr 23225
Wyck St 23225
Wycliff Ct & Rd 23236
Wyncliff Dr 23235
Wyndham Dr 23235
Wynfield Ter 23223
Wynnewood Ct & Dr 23235
Wyntrebrooke Ct & Dr 23235
Wythe Ave
3400-4599 23221
4600-5799 23226
X St 23223
Y St 23223
Yale Ave 23224
Yancey St 23222
Yarmouth Cir & Dr 23225
Yarrow Ln 23236
Yates Ct, Ln & Ter 23223
Yeadon Rd 23222
Yeardley Dr 23225
Yellowleaf Ct & Dr 23234
Yellowpine Cir 23225
Yerger Rd 23223
Yondota Ln 23227
W Yorenerl St 23284
York Rd 23226
Yorkdale Ct & Dr 23235
Yorkshire Dr
600-799 23224
2200-2299 23230
Yorktown Ave 23234
Young St 23222
Yucca Ct, Dr & Ln 23236
Yukon Rd 23235
Yuma Rd 23235
Zephyer Rd 23222
Zimalcrest Ct 23225
Zion St 23234
Zion Hill Church Rd 23234
Zion Ridge Ct, Dr & Ter 23234
Zoe Ct 23223
Zurich Dr 23224

NUMBERED STREETS

1st Ave 23222
1st St 23223
E 1st St 23224
N 1st St 23219
S 1st St 23219
2nd Ave 23222
2nd St 23223
E 2nd St 23224
N 2nd St
1-17 23219
19-204 23219
205-205 23241
206-1298 23219
301-1299 23219
S 2nd St 23219
3rd Ave 23222
3rd St 23223
E 3rd St 23224
N 3rd St 23219
S 3rd St 23219
4th Ave 23222
4th St 23223
E 4th St 23224
N 4th St 23219
S 4th St 23219
5th Ave 23222
5th St 23223
E 5th St 23224
N 5th St 23219
S 5th St 23219
6th St 23223
E 6th St 23224
N 6th St 23219
S 6th St 23219
W 6th St 23224
7th St 23223
E 7th St 23224
N 7th St 23219
S 7th St 23219
W 7th St 23224
8th St 23223
E 8th St 23224
N 8th St
1-599 23219
600-601 23298
602-614 23219
615-615 23298
616-798 23219
641-641 23298
643-657 23219
659-659 23298
661-799 23219
S 8th St 23219
W 8th St 23224
E 9th St 23224
N 9th St
1-400 23219
401-499 23298
402-798 23219
501-799 23219
S 9th St 23219
W 9th St 23224
E 10th St 23224
N 10th St
300-512 23219
514-518 23219
515-517 23298
519-699 23298
S 10th St 23219
W 10th St 23224
E 11th St 23224
N 11th St
400-402 23219
403-497 23298
404-498 23219
499-522 23298
526-598 23219
610-610 23298
S 11th St 23219
W 11th St 23224
E 12th St 23224
N 12th St
1-322 23219
323-323 23298
324-398 23219
400-402 23298
403-409 23219
404-410 23298
411-499 23219
500-536 23298
S 12th St 23219
W 12th St 23224
E 13th St 23224
N 13th St
400-598 23219
403-403 23298
405-513 23219
515-515 23298
517-599 23219
S 13th St 23219
W 13th St 23224
E 14th St 23224
N 14th St 23219
S 14th St 23219
W 14th St 23224
E 15th St 23224
N 15th St 23219
S 15th St 23219
W 15th St 23224
E 16th St 23224
E 17th St 23224
N 17th St 23219
S 17th St 23219
E 18th St 23224
N 18th St 23223
S 18th St 23223
19th St 23223
E 19th St 23224
N 19th St 23223
S 19th St 23223
W 19th St
1-399 23224
500-799 23225
20th St 23223
E 20th St 23224
N 20th St 23223
S 20th St 23223
W 20th St
1-99 23224
500-799 23225
E 21st St 23224
N 21st St 23223
S 21st St 23223
W 21st St 23225
E 22nd St 23224
N 22nd St 23223
S 22nd St 23223
W 22nd St 23225
23rd St 23223
N 24th St 23223
W 24th St 23225
E 25th St 23224
N 25th St 23223
S 25th St 23223
W 25th St 23225
N 26th St 23223
S 26th St 23223
W 26th St 23225
N 27th St 23223
W 27th St 23225
E 28th St 23224
N 28th St 23223
W 28th St 23225
E 29th St 23224
N 29th St 23223
W 29th St 23225
E 30th St 23224
N 30th St 23223
W 30th St 23225
E 31st St 23224
N 31st St 23223
W 31st St 23225
E 32nd St 23224
N 32nd St 23223
W 32nd St 23225
E 33rd St 23224
N 33rd St 23223
W 33rd St 23225
E 34th St 23224
N 34th St 23223
W 34th St 23225
E 35th St 23224
N 35th St 23223
E 36th St 23224
N 36th St 23223
E 37th St 23224
N 37th St 23223
N 38th St 23223
N 39th St 23223
W 41st St 23225
W 42nd St 23225
W 43rd St 23225
W 44th St 23225
W 45th St 23225
W 46th St 23225
W 47th St 23225
W 48th St 23225
W 49th St 23225

ROANOKE VA

General Delivery 24022

POST OFFICE BOXES MAIN OFFICE STATIONS AND BRANCHES

Box No.s
K92 - K92 24022
1 - 301 24002
7 - 10 24022
311 - 571 24003
581 - 841 24004
851 - 1111 24005
1121 - 1300 24006
1301 - 1600 24007
1601 - 1951 24008
1961 - 2030 24009
2021 - 2021 24022
2101 - 2281 24009
2291 - 2611 24010
2701 - 2904 24001
3001 - 4847 24015
6001 - 6678 24017
7001 - 7998 24019
8001 - 8996 24014
9000 - 10340 24020
10441 - 12115 24022
12121 - 12234 24023
12201 - 12203 24022
12241 - 12354 24024
12361 - 12474 24025
12481 - 12594 24026
12500 - 12500 24025
12601 - 12714 24027
12700 - 12700 24022
12721 - 12834 24028
12841 - 12954 24029
12900 - 12900 24022
12961 - 13074 24030
13081 - 13194 24031
13201 - 13314 24032
13321 - 13434 24033
13441 - 13514 24034
13521 - 13634 24035
13641 - 13754 24036
13761 - 13874 24037
13881 - 14234 24038
18001 - 18254 24014
19001 - 19712 24019
20001 - 29800 24018
40000 - 40053 24022
47000 - 47002 24017
49500 - 49500 24019
50010 - 50022 24022

NAMED STREETS

Abbott St NW 24017
Aberdeen Ave SW 24018
Abney Rd 24012
Acorn Trl 24019
Adair Cir 24018
Adams St NW 24017
Adrian St SE 24014
Aerial Way Dr SW 24018
Aerospace Rd 24014
Afton Ln 24012
Airport Rd
5301-5397 24012
5399-5401 24012
5403-5727 24012
6100-6299 24019
Airport Rd NW 24012
Airview Rd NW 24017
Airview Rd SW 24018
Ajax Ave NW 24017
Aker Ln 24019
Alamo Cir NE 24012
Albemarle Ave SE 24013
Albemarle Ave SW 24016
Albert Rd 24019
Alberta Ave SW 24015
Alcoa Rd 24014
Alder St NW 24017
Alexander Dr 24019
Alexandra Ct 24012
Allendale St SW 24014
Allison Ave SW 24016
Almond Rd 24018
Alpine Rd 24019
Altamira Dr 24019
Alton Rd SW 24014
Alview Ave NW 24012
Amanda Ln 24014
Ambassador Dr 24019
Amber Ct SW 24018
Amber Way Cir SW 24018
Amberwood Ct 24019
American Tire Blvd 24019
Amherst St SW 24015
Anchor Dr 24012
Anderson Hollow Rd 24019
Andover Ct 24018
Andrews Rd NW
1000-1099 24012
1500-2299 24017
Angel Ln 24019
Angell Ave NW 24012
Angle Ln NE 24019
Angus Rd NW 24017
Ann Ln SW 24018
Anna Ave NE 24012
Annie Holland Dr 24018
Antietam Dr 24018
Apollo Dr 24019
Apple Ln 24019
Apple Blossom Cir 24019
Apple Blossom Ln 24018
Apple Grove Ln 24018
Apple Harvest Dr 24012
Apple Tree Rd 24019
Appleton Ave NW 24017
Appletree Dr
4700-4799 24012
4800-4899 24019
4900-4999 24012
5000-5399 24019
Applewood Dr & St NE 24019
Apricot Trl 24012
April Ln 24012
Arbor Ave SE 24014
Arbutus Ave SE 24014
Arcadia Dr NW 24017
Archbold Ave NE 24012
Archer Dr 24018
Arcturus Dr 24018
Arden Rd SW 24015
Ardmore Dr 24019
Arlington Rd SW 24015
Arlington Hills Dr 24018
Arnold Dr NE 24019
Arrington Dr NE 24012
Arrington Ln 24019
Arrowhead Ln 24019
Arthur Rd 24019
Arthur St 24018
Ashburn Rd 24019
Ashbury Ct & Dr 24012
Ashby St SW 24015
Ashebrook Dr 24014
Ashlawn St SW 24015
Ashley Ln 24018
Ashmeade Dr 24018
Ashmont Dr 24018
Ashton Ln 24019
Ashwood Cir NE 24012
Aspen St NW 24017
Aspen Grove Ct NW 24017
Aster St 24019
Atherly St NE 24012
Atwater St NW 24017
Audrey Dr 24019
Audubon Rd SW 24014
Austin Ave 24019
Autumn Dr 24012
Autumn Ln NW 24017
Autumn Park 24018
Autumn Wood Ln 24019
Avalon Ave NW 24012
Avendale Ave NE 24012
Avenel Ave SW 24015
Avenham Ave SW 24014
Averett St NW 24012
Avery Row 24012
Aviation Dr NW 24012
Avon Rd SW 24015
Ayrshire Dr 24018
Azalea Rd 24014
Azusa St 24019
Back St 24019
Back Creek Orchard Rd 24018
Bainbridge Rd NW 24017
Baird St SW 24015
Baker Ave NW 24017
Baker Hill Ln 24019
Baldwin Ave NE 24012
Baldwin Ct 24019
Ballard St 24014
Bally Hack Trl 24014
Balsam Dr 24018
Baltimore Ave SE 24014
Banbury Ln 24018
Bancroft Dr SW 24014
Bandy Rd SE 24014
Barbara Cir 24018
Barbara Ln 24019
Barberry Ave NW 24017
Barclay Sq SW 24018
Barham Rd SW 24015
Barkley Ave NW 24012
Barn Owl Cir 24018
Barn Swallow Cir 24018
Barnaget Dr 24012
Barnett Cir & Rd 24017
Barnhart Dr SW 24018
Barnhart St NW 24017
Barnhill Ln SW 24018
Barns Ave 24019
Barrens Rd 24019
Barrens Village Ct & Ln 24019
Barrington Dr NW 24017
Barton St SE 24014
Basham Ln 24019
N & S Battery Dr 24019
Bauman Dr 24019
Bayberry Ct 24018
Beacon Dr 24018
Bean St NW 24012
Bear Rd SE 24014
Bear Ridge Cir 24018
Bearing Rd 24018
Beasley Trl 24018
Beaufort Ct 24019
Beaumont Rd 24019
Beckys Pl SW 24018
Beech St NW 24017
Beechnut Rd 24018
Beechwood Dr SW 24014
Belcroft Ct 24018
Belford St SW 24018
Belle Ave NE 24012

Belle Aire Cir & Ln 24018
Belle Haven Rd 24019
Belle Meade Dr 24018
Belleview Ave SE 24014
Belleville Rd SW 24015
Belmont Ct 24012
Belshire Ct SW 24014
Ben St NW 24017
Benbrook Cir NE 24012
S Bend Dr 24019
Bennett Dr NW 24017
Bennington St SE 24014
Benois Rd 24018
Bent Mountain Rd 24018
Berganblick Ln 24018
Berkely Pl 24018
Berkley Ave SW 24015
Berkley Rd NE 24012
Berkshire Cir 24019
Bermuda Rd NW 24017
Bernard Ave SE 24013
Bernard Dr 24018
Berry Ln 24018
Berryhill Dr 24018
Beverly Blvd SW 24015
Bibb St NE 24012
Bighorn Dr 24018
Biltmore Dr NW 24017
Birch Ct 24018
Birchlawn Ave NW 24012
Birchwood Ave NE 24012
Birkdale Dr 24019
Biscayne Rd 24019
Bishop Dr 24019
Black Bear Ln 24018
Black Walnut Ct 24019
Blackhorse Ln 24018
Blair Rd SW 24015
Blaney St NW 24012
Blanton Ave SE 24014
Blenheim Rd SW 24015
Bloomfield Ave 24012
Blue Bird Cir 24018
Blue Heron Cir 24018
Blue Hills Cir & Dr 24012
Blue Hills Village Dr NE 24012
Blue Jay Cir 24018
Blue Ridge Blvd 24012
Blue Ridge Dr SW 24018
Blue View Dr 24012
Bluebell Ln 24012
Blueberry Rdg 24012
Bluefield Blvd SW 24015
Bluemont Ave SW 24015
Bluestone Ave NE 24012
Bluff Ave SW 24016
Bluff Rd 24014
Bobby Dr 24019
Bobolink Ln 24018
Bobwhite Dr 24018
Bohon St NE 24012
Bohon Farm Rd 24018
Bolejack Blvd 24019
Bond St 24018
Bonhill Dr NW 24012
Bonlyn Cir SE 24014
Bonny View Ln 24019
Bonsack Rd 24012
Bonsall Ln 24014
Bosworth Dr SW 24014
Boulevard St SW 24016
Bounty Ct 24019
Bower Rd 24018
Bowman St NW 24012
Boxley Rd 24019
Boxwood Cir & Dr 24018
Bradford Cir 24018
Bradley Ln & St NE 24012
Brahma Rd 24018
Bramble Ln SW 24014
Brambleton Ave 24018
Brambleton Ave SW 24015
Branch Rd 24014
Branderwood Dr 24018
Brandon Ave SW
600-3000 24015
3002-3098 24015
3200-8499 24018
Brandon Ln SW 24015
Brandywine Ave 24018
Branico Dr 24018
Bratton Lawn Dr NE 24012
Braxton Rd NE 24012
Brazo Ct 24019
Breckenridge Ave NW 24017
Brent Cir 24019
Brentwood Ct 24018
Brethren Rd 24014
Briar Hill Ct 24012
Briar Ridge Cir 24018
Bridge St SW 24015
Bridgeport Ln 24012
Bridle Ln 24018
Bridlewood Dr 24018
Brighton Rd SW 24015
Brightwell St NE 24012
Brightwood Pl SW 24014
Bristol Rd SW 24014
Britaney Rd 24012
British Woods Dr 24019
Broad St NW 24012
Broadlawn Rd NW 24017
Broadway Ave SW 24014
Bromley Rd 24018
Brook St 24019
Brook St NE 24012
Brookfield Dr 24018
Brookfield Ln 24012
Brookfield Rd 24019
Brookhaven Ct 24018
Brooklyn Dr NW 24017
Brookridge Rd 24014
Brookrun Cir NE 24012
Brooks Ave SE 24014
Brookside Ln SE 24014
Brookview Rd 24019
Brookwood Cir 24019
Brookwood Dr 24018
Broughton Dr 24018
Brown Rd 24019
Brownlee Ave SE 24014
Brownwood Dr NW 24017
Broyles Ln 24012
Brubaker Dr 24019
Bruceton Rd SW 24018
Brunswick St SW 24015
Bryan Rd 24014
Bryant Cir & Rd 24019
Brymoor Rd SW 24018
Buck Ln 24012
Buck Crossing Dr 24018
Buck Mountain Rd 24018
Buck Run Ct, Dr & Sq 24018
Buckeye Rd 24018
Buckhorn Rd 24018
Buckingham Cir 24018
Buckingham Ct 24019
Buckingham Dr 24018
Buckland Mill Rd 24019
Buckner Rd SW 24015
Buena Vista Blvd SE 24013
Buford Ave SW 24015
Bullington Cir 24019
Bullitt Ave SE 24013
Bullitt Ave SW 24011
Bunche Dr NW 24012
Bunker Cir & Ln 24019
Bunker Hill Dr 24018
Burchette St 24017
Burks St SW 24015
Burkwood Cir 24018
Burlington Dr 24019
Burnham Rd 24018
Burnleigh Rd SW 24014
Burrell St NW 24012
Burton Ave NW 24012
Bushdale Rd 24014
Butternut Rd 24018
Byers Rd 24019
Byrd Ave NE 24012
Byrne St SW 24015
Byron Cir & Dr 24019
Cabel Ct 24019
Cabin Creek Dr 24018
Caldwell St NW 24017
Calloway St NW 24012
Calvary Rd NW 24017
Cambridge Ave SW 24015
Camilla Ave SE 24014
Camille Ave NW 24017
Campbell Ave SE
1-199 24011
200-1799 24013
Campbell Ave SW
1-299 24011
300-1899 24016
Campbell View Aly 24018
Candlelight Cir 24019
Cannaday Rd NE 24012
Canter Cir & Dr 24018
Canterbury Cir 24019
Canterbury Ln SW 24014
Canterbury Rd SW 24015
Cantle Ln 24018
Canyon Rd 24018
Capito St 24019
Capulet Ct 24018
Cardinal Rd SW 24014
Cardington Dr 24019
Carefree Ln 24019
Carlisle Ave SE 24014
Carlos Dr 24019
Carlsbad Cir 24012
Carlton Rd SW 24015
Carner Ln 24019
Carol Ln 24014
Carolina Ave SW 24014
Carolina Trl 24019
Carolyn Cir 24018
Carolyn Dr 24019
Caron View Ln 24014
Carr Rouse Rd 24014
Carriage Dr 24018
Carriage Hills Dr 24018
Carriage Park Dr 24019
Carrington Ave SW 24015
Carroll Ave NW
800-899 24016
1300-2199 24017
Carson Rd 24012
Carter Rd SW 24015
Carter Grove Cir & Ln 24012
Cartwright Dr 24018
Carver Ave NE & NW 24012
Carvin St 24019
Carvin St NE 24012
Casper Dr NE 24019
Cassell Ln SW 24014
Castle Hill St 24018
Castle Rock Rd 24018
Castle View Ct & Ln 24018
Catawba St SE 24014
Cavalier Ct & Dr 24018
Cave Spring Cir & Ln 24018
Cedar Hl 24019
Cedar Ln 24018
Cedar St SE 24013
Cedar Bluff Ave SE 24013
Cedar Crest Rd 24019
Cedar Edge Rd 24018
Cedar Meade Dr 24014
Cedar Ridge Rd 24018
Cedarhurst Ave NW 24012
Cee St 24019
Cell Tower Dr 24018
Center Hill Dr SW 24015
Centre Ave NW
1-1099 24016
1100-2999 24017
Centurion Rd 24019
Century Dr 24019
Ceylon St NE 24012
Cezanne Ct 24018
Chadsworth Ct 24018
Chadwick Cir 24012
Chagall Cir & Dr 24018
Challenger Ave 24012
Chaparral Dr 24018
Chapman Ave SW 24016
Charing Cross Dr 24018
Charleswood Rd 24014
Charlevoix Ct SW 24015
Charnwood Cir 24012
Chateau Ct 24012
Chatham Cir 24019
Chatham St NW 24012
Chatham Hill Rd NW 24017
Chatsworth Dr 24018
Chaucers Ct 24018
Chelsea Dr 24019
Chelsea St 24018
Chelsea Stuart Trl 24019
Cheraw Lake Rd NW 24017
Cherokee St NE 24012
Cherry Ave NW 24016
Cherry Blossom Cir 24019
Cherryhill Cir & Rd 24017
Cheshire Ln 24018
Chester Ave & Dr 24019
Chesterfield St SW 24015
Chesterton St SW 24018
Chestnut Ave NW 24016
Chestnut Hill Trl 24012
Chestnut Oak Ct SW 24018
Chip Cir 24018
Chip Dr NE 24012
Chippenham Dr 24018
Chivas Dr 24019
Christian Ave NE & NW 24012
Christie Ln 24018
Christopher Dr 24018
Chukar Dr 24018
Church Ave SE
1-16 24011
18-198 24011
300-1799 24013
Church Ave SW
1-100 24011
101-101 24001
101-101 24002
101-101 24003
101-101 24004
101-101 24005
101-101 24006
101-101 24007
101-101 24008
101-101 24009
101-101 24010
101-299 24011
102-298 24011
300-599 24016
Churchill Dr NW 24012
Churchland Rd NW 24017
Cider Mill Ct 24012
Circle Dr SW 24018
Circle Brook Dr 24018
Circle View Dr 24014
Clairmont St SW 24018
Clara Ave SW 24018
Clarendon Ave NW 24012
Clarke Ave SW 24016
Clay St SE 24013
Clayton Dr 24019
Clearbrook Ln 24014
Clearbrook Village Ln 24014
Clearfield Rd SW 24015
Clearview Dr 24018
Clearwater Ave 24019
Clearwood Dr 24014
Clemons Rd 24019
E & W Cleo Ln 24019
Cleveland Ave SW 24016
Clifton St NW 24017
Cline St NE 24012
Clinton Ave SE 24013
Clinton Cir NW 24017
Clover Ave NE 24012
Clover Dr 24019
Cloverdale Rd 24019
Clovis St NW 24017
Club Ln 24018
Clubhouse Dr 24019
Clyde St NE 24012
Clydesdale St SW 24014
Coachman Cir & Dr 24012
Coleman Rd 24018
Colgate St NE 24012
College Dr 24019
College View Ct 24019
Collingwood St NE 24012
Colonial Ave 24018
Colonial Ave SW
2000-3199 24015
3200-3399 24018
Colonial Court Dr 24018
Colonial Green Cir SW 24018
Colonial Place Dr 24018
Colonnade Dr 24018
Colony Ct & Ln 24018
Columbia St NE 24019
Columbine Ln 24019
Comer St NW 24017
Commander Dr 24012
N Commerce St 24019
Commonwealth Ave NE 24016
Commonwealth Dr 24018
Compton St NE 24012
Concord Pl 24018
Concourse Dr 24019
Connecticut Ave NE 24012
Connie Dr 24019
Consul Dr 24019
Conway St NE 24012
Cook Ave 24019
Cook Ave NE 24012
Cook Creek Rd 24012
Cooper St 24019
Copper Cir 24019
Coral Ridge Rd SW 24018
Corbieshaw Rd SW 24015
Corbin Cir NW 24017
Cordell Dr 24018
Cornell Dr NW 24012
Corntassel Ln 24018
Cornwallis Ave SE 24014
Corporate Cir SW 24018
Cortland Rd 24019
Cottage Rose Ln 24012
Cotton Hill Ln & Rd 24018
Cougar Dr 24019
Coulter Dr NW 24012
Country Ln 24018
Country Club Dr NW 24017
Country Cottage Ln 24018
Country Homes Rd 24018
Country View Rd 24018
Countryside Rd NW 24017
Countrywood Dr 24018
Court St NW 24012
Courtland Rd NE & NW 24012
Courtney Ave NE 24012
Cove Rd 24019
Cove Rd NW
1100-4899 24017
4900-5300 24019
5302-5498 24019
Coveland Dr NW 24017
Coventry Ln SW 24014
Covington Ct 24018
Cowman Rd 24014
Cox Hopkins Rd 24014
Coyner Springs Rd 24012
Craig Rd NE 24012
Craig Robertson Rd SE 24014
Craun Ln 24019
Cravens Creek Ln & Rd 24018
Crawford Rd 24018
Crawley St NW 24012
Creek Cir 24018
Creekside Cir 24019
Creekview Ct 24018
Crescent Blvd 24018
Crescent St NW 24017
Crescent Ridge Dr SW 24018
Crest St 24018
Cresthill Dr 24018
Crestland Dr 24019
Crestline Cir NW 24017
Crestmoor Dr SW 24018
Creston Ave SW 24015
Crestwood Dr 24018
Crispin St 24019
Crittendon Ave NE & NW 24012
Crockett Ave NW 24012
Cromwell Ct 24018
Cross Rd 24012
Crossbow Cir 24018
Crosstimbers Trl 24019
Crotts Ln 24019
Crowell Gap Rd 24014
Crowmoor St NW 24017
Crown Rd 24018
Crown Point Rd SE 24014
Crumpacker Cir 24019
Crumpacker Dr
5000-5499 24019
5801-5897 24012
5899-6299 24012
Crutchfield St 24019
Crystal Anne Ln 24019
Crystal Creek Dr 24018
Crystal Spring Ave SW 24014
Cuff Town Rd 24019
Cumberland St NW 24012
Cundiff Dr 24012
Curtis Ave NW 24012
Custis Ave 24018
Cynthia Dr 24018
Cypress Ct 24019
Cypress Park Dr 24018
Dairy Rd 24019
Dakota Ave NW 24017
Dale Ave SE 24013
Daleton Ave & Blvd 24012
Daleview Dr 24014
Daleville St NW 24012
Dallas Rd 24019
Dan Ln 24019
Dancing Tree Ln 24019
Daniel Rd 24014
Dansbury Dr NW 24017
Danton Rd SE 24014
Darby Cir & Rd 24012
Darlington Rd SW 24018
Darwin Rd SW 24014
Davenport Ave SE 24014
David Palmer Ln 24012
Davis Ave 24015
Davis Rd 24012
Davis St NE 24012
Dawn Cir & Ln SW 24018
Dawnwood Rd 24018
Day Ave SW 24016
Daytona Rd 24019
Dean Rd SW 24018
Deaner Dr NW 24017
Deaton Rd SE 24014
Deepwoods Dr 24018
Deer Branch Dr & Rd 24019
Deer Crossing Dr 24019
Deer Haven Dr 24012
Deer Hollow Dr 24014
Deer Park Dr 24019
Deer Path Trl 24014
Deer Ridge Trl 24019
Deer Run Rd 24019
Deerfield Ct SE 24014
Deerfield Rd 24018
Deerfield Rd SW 24015
Deerwood Rd 24019
Delano St NE 24012
Delavan St 24018
Delaware Ave NW 24017
Dell Ave NE 24012
Delmar Ln 24014
Delray St NW 24012
Delta Dr NW 24017
Denise Cir 24012
Denniston Ave SW 24015
Densmore Rd NW 24017
Dent Ave SE 24013
Dent Rd 24019
Dentrade Ave SE 24013
Deputy Dr 24019
Derby Dr 24012
Derwent Dr SW 24015
Desi Rd NW 24017
Destinee Ln 24014
Devon Rd SW 24015
Dexter Rd 24019
Deyerle Rd SW 24018
Dickerson Rd 24014
Dillard Rd SW 24014
Diplomat Dr 24019
Dodson Rd NW 24017
Doe Dr 24012
Doe Run Rd 24018
Dogan Ln 24019
Dogwood Ln SW 24015
Dogwood Acres Dr 24019
Dogwood Hill Rd NE 24012
Domaca Dr 24019
Dona Dr NW 24017
Donagale Dr 24012
Dorchester Dr NW 24012
Dorset Dr 24018
Douglas Ave NW 24012
Dove Dr 24018
Dover Dr SW 24018
Dovetail Cir 24018
Downing St
1-4299 24019
5300-5398 24018
5400-5599 24018
1400-1899 24012
Drake Cir 24019
Dresden Cir & Ln 24012
Drew Ave NE 24012
Driftwood Ln SW 24018
Dudding St SW 24015
Dudley St NW 24017
Duke Of Gloucester St SW 24014
Dunbar St NW 24012
Dundee Ave SE 24014
Dunkirk Ave NE 24012
Dunmore St SW 24015
Dupont Cir SW 24015
Dupree St NW 24012
Durham St NW 24012
Duval St SW 24015
Dwight St 24019
Dyer Ct 24018
Eagle Cir 24018
Eagle Rdg 24012
Eagle Crest Dr 24018
Eanes Rd SE 24014
East Dr 24019
East Dr SW 24015
Eastdale Cir 24019
Eastern Ave NE 24012
Eastgate Ave NE 24012
Easthill Dr 24018
Eastland Ave SE 24013
Eastland Rd 24014
Eastpark Dr 24019
Eastshire Ct 24018
Eastview Dr SW 24018
Eddington Rd SE 24014
Eden Ave 24018
Eden Dr NW 24012
Edenshire Rd 24014
Edgelawn Ave NW 24017
Edgerton Ave SE 24014
Edgewood St SW 24015
Edinburgh Dr NW 24012
Edison St NE 24012
Edmund Ave NE 24012
Elbert Dr 24018
Elden Ave 24019
Electric Rd 24018

N Electric Rd 24019
Elena Vista Dr 24018
Elizabeth Rd NE 24012
Elk Hill Dr 24018
Ellerbee St NE 24012
Ellington St 24014
Ellsworth St NE 24012
Elm Ave SE 24013
Elm Ave SW 24016
Elm View Rd 24018
Elmcrest St NE 24019
Elva Rd NW 24017
Elwood St 24019
Embassy Cir 24019
Embassy Dr 24019
Embassy Dr NW 24017
Emearen Ave SW 24016
Emerald Ln 24019
Emerald Court Dr 24019
Emissary Dr 24019
Empire Ln 24018
Empress Dr NW 24012
Enchanted Ln 24018
Encina Ct 24019
Endicott St 24019
Enon Dr 24019
Envoy Dr 24019
Epperley Ave NW 24012
Equestrian Dr 24018
Essex Ave NW 24017
Estates Rd SE 24014
Estes St 24019
Esther Cir SW 24016
Estrada Ln 24012
Ethel Rd SE 24014
Eton Rd SW 24018
Eugene Dr NW 24017
Eureka Cir NW 24017
Eva Ave 24018
Evan Ln 24012
Eveningwood Ln 24019
Evergreen Ln 24018
Evergreen Ln SW 24015
Executive Cir 24012
Exeter St SW 24014
Faineriv Rd 24019
Fair Oaks Rd 24019
Fairburn Dr 24018
Faircrest Ln 24018
Fairfax Ave NW
  300-1099 24016
  1100-1399 24017
Fairfax Pl 24018
Fairfield Dr NE 24012
Fairhope Rd NW 24017
Fairhurst Dr 24012
Fairland Rd NW 24017
Fairview Rd NW 24017
Fairway Dr SW 24015
Fairway Estates Dr 24018
Fairway Forest Dr 24018
Fairway Ridge Rd 24018
Fairway View Trl 24018
Fairway Woods Ct 24018
Falcon Ridge Rd 24018
Faldo Cir NE 24019
Fallon Ave SE 24013
Fallowater Ln 24018
Falwell Dr 24018
Fareham Rd SW 24015
Farm Hill Dr 24018
Farmer Brown Ln 24019
Farmhouse Ct & Ln 24019
Farmington Cir & Dr 24018
Farmington Place Ct 24018
Farmwood Dr 24018
Fauquier Ave & St 24015
Fawn Ct 24012
Fawn Rd SW 24015
Fawn Dell Rd 24018
Fence Post Cir 24019
Fentress St NW 24017
Fenwick Dr 24012
Ferdinand Ave SW 24016
Ferguson Dr 24014
Ferguson Valley Rd 24014

Ferncliff Ave NW 24017
Ferndale Dr NW 24017
Fernway Dr 24018
Fidelity Rd SE 24014
Fieldale Rd NE 24012
Fieldcrest Ln 24012
Fielding Ave NW 24017
Fields Cir & St 24017
Fieldview Dr 24019
First Crossing Dr 24012
Fishpond Rd 24018
Five Oaks Rd 24018
Flag Ln 24019
Flagler Dr 24019
Flamingo Dr 24018
Flanders Ln NW 24017
Fleetwood Ave SW 24015
Fleming Ave NE & NW 24012
Flintlock Ln & Rd 24018
Flippo Rd 24019
Flora Ln NW 24017
Floradale Cir 24019
Floraland Dr NW 24012
Florida Ave NW 24017
Florist Rd NW 24012
Floyd Ave SW 24015
Fontaine Cir & Dr 24018
Fordham Rd SW 24014
Fordwick Dr 24018
Forest Ct 24018
Forest Rd 24014
Forest Rd SW 24015
Forest Creek Dr 24018
Forest Edge Dr 24018
Forest Hill Ave NE & NW 24012
Forest Oak Dr 24012
Forest Park Blvd NW 24017
Forest Ridge Rd 24018
Forest View Rd 24018
Forester Rd SW 24015
Fort Mason Dr 24018
Fox Chase Ct 24018
Fox Croft Cir 24018
Fox Den Rd 24018
Fox Grape Rd 24018
Fox Ridge Rd 24018
Foxhall Cir 24018
Foxtail Ln 24019
Fralin Rd NW 24012
France Dr 24019
Frances Dr NW 24017
Franklin Rd
  4101-4399 24018
  5501-5897 24014
  5899-6199 24014
  6201-6299 24014
  2-98 24011
  1-17 24011
  19-703 24011
  704-708 24016
  705-799 24011
  710-798 24011
  800-1699 24016
  1701-1799 24016
  1801-1897 24014
  1899-5499 24014
Franwill Ave NW 24017
Freeborn Cir 24014
Fremont Cir NW 24017
Fresno St NW 24017
Friends Way 24012
Friendship Ln 24019
Frontage Rd NW
  2701-2799 24017
  4800-4999 24019
Frontier Rd NE & NW 24012
Fugate Rd NE 24012
Futurama Dr 24014
Gabriels Mountain Trl 24019
Gainsboro Rd NW 24016
S Gala Cir & Dr 24019
Gallatin St 24018
Galloway Cir & Dr 24018
Gander Way 24019

N Gandy Dr & Rd 24012
N Garden Ln 24019
Garden City Blvd SE 24014
Gardendale Cir 24012
Gardens Rd SW 24014
Garfield Ln 24019
Garland Cir 24019
Garman Dr 24019
Garner Rd 24018
Garrett Ln 24019
Garst Cabin Dr 24018
Garst Mill Rd SW 24018
Garstland Dr NW 24017
Garstview Cir 24018
Gaston Dr 24019
Gates Cir 24019
Gatewood Ave SW 24018
Gatling Ln NW 24017
Gaugin Cir 24018
Gaye Ln 24018
Gayle St NW 24012
Gaylord Rd 24018
Gaymol Ave NW 24017
Gaymont St SW 24015
Gean St SW 24015
Gearhart Rd SE 24014
Geneva Cir 24019
Georgetown Rd 24018
Georgia Ave NE 24012
Gieser Rd 24018
Gil Haven Dr 24019
Gilbert Rd NW 24017
Gilford Ave NW 24017
Gillette Ave SE 24014
Gilmer Ave NE 24016
Gilmer Ave NW
  1-1099 24016
  1100-1799 24017
Girard Dr 24018
Glade St NE 24012
Glade Creek Blvd & Rd NE 24012
Glade Hill Cir 24012
Glade View Dr NE 24012
Gladies St NW 24017
Gladstone Ave SE 24013
Glen Haven Dr 24019
Glen Heather Cir & Dr 24018
Glen Ivy Cir & Ln 24018
Glen Meadow Dr 24018
Glen Rock Ln 24014
Glenbrook Dr 24018
Glendale Ave NW 24017
Glengary Ave NW 24017
Glenmont Dr 24018
Glenn Ridge Rd NW 24017
Glenoak St SE 24014
Glenrose Ave NW 24017
Glenroy St NW 24017
Glenwood Cir & Dr 24014
Gloster Dr 24019
Gloucester Ct 24018
Goff Rd 24019
Golden Cir & Ct 24012
Golden Eagle Ln 24018
Golden Ivy Dr 24012
Golden Oak Ln 24019
Golfside Ave NW 24017
Golfview Dr NE 24019
Goodland Ave 24019
Goodland Dr NE 24012
Goodman Rd 24014
Goodview Ave 24018
Gordon Ave SE 24014
Gordonbrook Dr 24014
Governor Dr 24019
Grace St SW 24015
Graceland Dr 24018
Granby St NE 24012
Grand Ave NW 24017
Grandin Rd 24018
Grandin Rd SW
  1300-2799 24015
  3001-3197 24018
  3199-4999 24018
Grandin Road Ext SW 24018

Grandview Ave NW 24012
Grape Holly Ln 24018
Grape Tree Ln 24018
Graybill St NW 24017
Grayson Ave NW
  700-999 24016
  1000-1899 24017
Green Meadow Rd 24018
Green Ridge Cir, Ct & Rd NW 24019
Green Spring Ave NW 24017
Green Tree Ln 24019
Green Valley Dr 24018
Greenbrier Ave SE 24013
Greencliff Rd 24018
Greenfield St SW 24018
Greenhurst Ave NW 24012
Greenland Ave NW 24012
Greenlane Rd NW 24017
Greenlawn Ave NW 24012
Greenlee Rd SW 24018
Greenmont Ct 24012
Greenview Rd 24018
Greenville Pl 24019
Greenway Dr 24019
Greenway Dr SW 24018
Greenwich Dr 24019
Greenwood Rd SW 24015
Greggin Dr 24012
Gregory Ave NE 24016
Greyholme Ln 24019
Griffin Rd SW 24014
Grimes St 24019
Grove Ln 24012
Grubb Rd 24018
Guernsey Ln NW 24017
Guildhall Ave NW 24017
Guilford Ave SW 24015
Gum Spring St SE 24014
Gun Club Rd NW 24017
Gus W Nicks Blvd NE 24012
Hackley Ave NW 24016
Hackney Ln 24018
Halcun Dr 24019
Halevan Rd 24018
Hamilton Ave SW 24015
Hamilton Ter SE 24014
Hamlet Trl 24018
Hammond Ln 24018
Hampshire Dr 24018
Hampton Ave SW 24015
Hancock St NE 24012
Hannah Cir SW 24016
Hanover Ave NW
  300-999 24016
  1000-2599 24017
Harford Cir NW 24012
Harmon Cir 24019
Harmony Dr 24014
Harmony Ln 24018
Harmony Rd 24018
Harris Dr 24019
Harris St 24015
Harrison Ave NW 24016
Hartland Rd SW 24015
Hartley Cir 24018
Hartman Ct 24019
Hartman Ln SE 24014
Hartsook Blvd SE 24014
Harvard St SW 24015
Harvest Ln NW 24017
Harvest Hill Rd 24018
Harvest Ridge Rd 24019
Hastings Rd 24018
Hathaway Dr 24018
Hawkbill Cir 24018
Hawthorne Rd NW 24012
Hazel Dr 24018
Hazelridge Rd NW 24012
Hearthstone Rd NW 24012
Heath Cir 24019
Heather Dr SW 24018
Heather Hill Dr 24019
Heatherton Rd SW 24014
Hebert St NW 24012
Hedgelawn Ave 24019

Hedgewood Rd NW 24017
Hemingway Rd 24014
Hemlock Rd NW 24017
Hemlock Rd SW 24014
Henry St NW 24016
Henry Farms Rd 24018
Hereford Rd 24018
Heritage Cir & Rd 24015
Hershberger Rd 24012
Hershberger Rd NW
  200-398 24012
  400-1700 24012
  1702-1798 24012
  2500-4399 24017
Heywood Ave SW 24015
Hickory St NE 24012
Hickory Hill Dr 24018
Hickory Ridge Ct 24018
Hickory Woods Dr NE 24012
Hidden Ln 24018
Hidden Forest Ct 24018
Hidden Hill Cir 24018
Hidden Oak Rd SW 24018
Hidden Valley Dr 24018
Hidden Valley School Rd 24018
Hidden View Rd SW 24015
Hidden Woods Ct & Dr 24018
High Acres Rd NW 24017
High Crest Ct 24012
Highfield Ln 24019
Highfields Rd 24018
Highfields Farm Cir, Dr & Trl 24018
Highland Ave SE 24013
Highland Ave SW 24016
Highland Dr 24019
Highland Rd 24014
Highland Farm Rd NW 24017
Highwood Rd NW 24012
Hildebrand Rd NW 24012
Hill Ave 24014
Hill Cir 24014
Hill Dr 24012
Hillandale Dr 24018
Hillbrook Cir & Dr 24018
Hillcrest Ave NE & NW 24012
Hillendale Dr NW 24017
Hillside Rd 24014
Hilltop Dr 24018
Hilltop Rd 24014
Hillview Ave 24014
Hillview Ave SE 24014
Hillview Dr 24019
Hinchee Ln 24019
Hiram St SE 24014
Hite St SW 24014
Hitech Rd 24019
Hogan Cir 24014
Holland Rd 24018
Hollins Rd 24019
Hollins Rd NE 24012
Hollins Court Cir & Dr 24019
Hollowdale Dr 24018
Hollowell Ave SW 24015
Holly Rd NE 24012
Hollyberry Cir & Rd 24018
Hollyfield Cir 24018
Hollyhock Rd NW 24012
Holmes St NE 24012
Homestead Ln 24012
Homewood Cir 24018
Honeywood Ln 24018
Hoover St NW 24017
Hope Rd SW 24018
Hornes St NW 24012
Horse Shoe Bend Rd 24014
Horseman Dr NE 24019
Hostetler Ct 24018
Hounds Chase Ln SW 24014
Houston Ave NE 24012
Howard Ave NE 24012
Howard Rd SW 24015
Howbert Ave SW 24015

Hubbard Rd SW 24018
Hubert Rd NW 24012
Huff Ln NW 24012
Huff St 24014
Huffman Ln 24014
Hugh Ave 24019
Hummingbird Ln 24018
Hunt Ave NW 24012
Hunt Camp Rd 24018
Hunters Ln 24019
Hunters Rd SW 24015
Hunters Trl 24019
Hunting Hills Cir, Ct, Dr & Sq 24018
Huntington Blvd NE & NW 24012
Huntmaster Cir 24018
Huntridge Rd
  4600-5500 24012
  5502-5798 24012
  5800-5898 24019
  5900-5999 24019
Huntwood St 24018
Hurst Ave NE 24012
Hyde Park Dr 24018
Ichabod Cir NE 24019
Idavere Rd SW 24015
Idlewild Blvd NE 24012
Imlay Rd SE 24014
Indian Rd 24019
Indian Grave Rd 24018
Indian Rock Rd 24014
Indian Village Ln SE 24013
Indiana Ave NE 24012
Indigo Ln 24012
Industrial Dr 24019
Industry Ave & Cir 24013
Ingleside Dr 24018
Inglewood Rd SW 24015
Integrity Dr 24012
Iredell Ave 24018
Irondale Cir 24019
Irvine St SW 24015
Ivy St SE 24014
Ivy Green Ct 24018
Ivy Mountain Dr 24018
Ivyland Dr 24014
Ivywood St SE 24014
Jack St NE 24012
Jacklin Cir & Dr 24019
Jackson Ave SW 24016
Jae Valley Rd 24014
James St SW 24015
Jamison Ave SE 24013
Janda Dr 24019
Janette Ave SW 24016
Janney Ln 24018
Jasmine Cir 24019
Jeana Ln 24012
Jefferson St SE 24014
Jefferson St SW 24014
N Jefferson St 24016
S Jefferson St
  1-699 24011
  700-1899 24016
Jeffrey Dr 24018
Jennings Ave SE 24013
Jerome St SE 24014
Jerry Ln 24012
Jersey Ave NW 24017
John Richardson Rd 24019
Johns Ln SW 24018
Johnsbury Ct NE 24019
Johnson Ave NW 24017
Jonamac Pl 24019
Jonathan Ln & Rd 24019
Joplin Rd SW 24014
Jordan Cir 24012
Journeys End Ln 24014
Juliet Ct 24018
June Dr 24019
Juniper Dr 24012
Juniper St NW 24017
Kaiden Ct NW 24017
Kanter Rd NE 24012
Kathryn Dr 24014

Kay St NW 24017
Keagy Ln & Rd 24018
Keaton Dr 24019
Keats St NW 24017
Keefer Rd 24018
Keene St NW 24017
Kefauver Rd SE 24014
Keffield St 24019
Keithwood Dr SW 24018
Kellington Ct 24012
Kellogg Ave NW 24012
Kelly Ln 24018
Kelly Lane Ext 24018
Kenmore Ave 24018
Kennedy Ln 24018
Kennedy St NE 24012
Kensington Ct SE 24014
Kent Rd SE 24014
Kentland Dr 24018
Kentmere Cir 24012
Kentucky Ave NW 24017
Kenwick Trl 24018
Kenwood Blvd SE 24013
Kenworth Rd 24019
Kepplewood Rd SE 24014
Kermit Ave NE 24012
Kerns Ave SW 24015
Kershaw Rd NW 24017
Kessler Rd NE 24012
Keswick Ave NE 24012
Kettering Ct 24018
Kildeer Cir 24018
Kilgore Ave NE 24012
Kim Ct 24018
Kimball Ave NE 24016
King St NE 24012
King Arthurs Ct NW 24019
King Charles Ave SE 24014
King George Ave SW 24016
King James St SW 24014
Kings Chase Dr 24018
Kings Court Dr 24018
Kingsbury Cir 24014
Kingsmen Rd 24019
Kingston Rd NW 24017
Kingswood Dr 24018
Kipling St SW 24018
Kirk Ave SE
  100-199 24011
  1100-1699 24013
Kirk Ave SW 24011
Kirk Ln 24018
Kirkland Dr NW 24017
Kirkwood Cir & Dr 24018
Knights Ct 24018
Knightsbridge Dr 24018
Knoll Rd
  1-99 24012
  200-299 24019
Knollwood Rd SW 24018
Knowles Dr 24018
Koogler Dr NW 24017
Korte St SW 24015
Kyle Ave NE 24012
La Marre Dr 24019
Laban Rd 24019
Labellevue Dr 24012
Labradore Dr 24012
Laburnum Ave SW 24015
Laconia Ave NE 24012
Lafayette Blvd NW 24017
Lake Dr SW 24018
N Lake Dr 24019
S Lake Dr SW 24018
Lake St 24014
Lake Back O Beyond Dr 24012
Lakecrest Ct SW 24018
Lakedale Rd 24018
Lakeland Dr 24018
Lakemont Dr 24018
Lakeview Cir 24019
Lakeview Dr 24012
Lakeview Dr NW 24017
Lakeview Pl 24019
Lakewood Dr SW 24015

Lamplighter Dr 24019
Lanasey Dr 24019
Lancaster Dr NW 24017
Lancelot Ln NW 24019
Landmark Cir 24018
Landview Dr 24018
Lanewood Dr 24018
Lanford St NW 24012
Langdon Rd SW 24015
Lange Ln 24018
Langhorne St SE 24013
Langley Pl 24019
Lansing Dr SW 24015
Lantern St 24019
Larchwood St NE 24012
Lark Cir 24018
Larkview Cir SW 24015
Larson Ln 24018
Larson Oaks Dr 24018
Laryn Ln 24018
Laura Rd NW 24017
Laurel Cir 24018
Laurel Dr 24018
Laurel St SE 24014
Laurel Hill Rd 24018
Laurel Ridge Dr 24019
Laurel Ridge Rd NW 24017
Laurelwood Dr 24018
Lawndale Rd 24018
Lawnhill St SW 24015
Lawrence Ave SE 24013
Lawrence Ln SW 24018
Layman Rd & St NW 24012
Layne Ct 24019
Leawood Cir 24018
Ledgewood Ave 24018
Lee Ave NE 24012
Lee Hwy 24019
Lee Hi Rd SW 24018
Leffel Rd 24018
Leffler Ln 24018
Legate Dr 24019
Lela Ave NE 24019
Lemon Ln 24014
Lenora Rd 24018
Lenox Cir 24019
Leon St NW 24017
Leslie Ln
2-98 24019
2901-2999 24018
Leslie Ln NW 24017
Lester Ave NE 24012
Levi Rd 24018
Lewis Rd SE 24014
Lewiston St NW 24017
Lexington Ave SW 24015
Liberty Rd NE & NW 24012
Libra Ln 24019
Light St NE 24012
Lila Dr 24019
Lilac Ave NW 24017
Lilly Hill Rd 24018
Lincoln Ave SW 24015
Linda Ln 24018
Lindbergh Ln NE 24012
Linden St SE 24014
Link St NE 24012
Linn Dr 24019
Linn Cove Ct 24018
Linn Spring Ct 24018
Linwood Rd NW 24017
Lipps Rd 24018
Little Bend Rd 24019
Little Hoop Rd 24019
Little Walk Rd 24019
Littlehorn Dr 24018
Littleton Rd 24012
Livingston Rd SW 24015
Loblolly Dr 24019
Loblolly Ln SW 24018
Loch Haven Dr 24019
Loch Haven Lake Dr 24019
Lockhart Dr 24014
Lockridge Rd SW 24014
Locust Grove Cir & Ln
NE 24012
Lodi Ln 24018
Lofton Rd 24018
Lofton Rd SW 24015
Logan St NW 24017
Lois Ln 24019
Loman Dr 24019
Lombardy Ave NW 24017
London Cir 24018
Londonderry Ct 24018
Londonderry Dr SW 24014
Londonderry Ln 24018
Lone Oak Ave NE 24012
Long Acre Dr NE 24019
Long Meadow Ave
NW 24017
Longhorn Rd 24018
Longleaf Dr 24019
Longridge Cir & Dr 24018
Longstreet Rd 24012
Longview Ave SW 24014
Longview Rd 24018
Longwood Ave NW 24017
Lonna Dr NW 24019
Lonsdale Rd 24018
Lori Dr 24014
Lorraine Rd NW 24017
Lost Dr 24018
Lost Mountain Rd 24018
Lost View Ln 24018
Loudon Ave NW
500-1099 24016
1100-2399 24017
Louise Wells Dr 24019
Love View Ln 24012
Lowland Ln 24018
Lucerne St NW 24017
Luck Ave SW
1-199 24011
300-599 24016
Luckett St NW 24017
Lukens St NE 24012
Lula Ave 24019
Luna Ct 24019
Luray St NE 24012
Luwana Dr 24018
Lyndhurst St NW 24012
Lynn Ave SW 24014
Lynn St NW 24017
Lynn Brae Dr NE 24012
Lynn Dell Rd 24018
Lynnhope Dr NW 24017
Lynnson Dr 24018
Lytham Dr SW 24018
Mabry Ave SE 24014
Mack Chick Rd SE 24014
Maddock Ave NE 24012
Madison Ave NE &
NW 24016
Magnolia Rd 24019
Maiden Ln SW 24015
Mailleas Ave NE 24012
Main St SW 24015
Maine Ave NW 24017
Maitland Ave NW 24012
Malcomb St SW 24015
Mallard Dr 24018
Mallard Lake Ct & Dr 24018
Malvern Rd 24012
Malvern Rd SW 24015
Manassas Dr 24018
Manning Rd NE 24012
Manor St 24019
Mansfield St NE 24012
Maple Ave SW 24016
Maple Ct 24018
Maple Hill Way 24019
Maple Leaf Ct & Dr 24018
Maplelawn Ave NE &
NW 24012
Mapleton Ave NE 24012
Marie Dr 24018
Market Sq & St 24011
Markham Cir SE 24014
Marlian Ave NW 24012
Marr St NW 24012
Marsh Wren Ln 24018
Marshall Ave SW 24016
Marson Rd 24019
Martha Dr 24019
Martin Ln SW 24015
Martindale Ave 24019
Martinell Ave 24018
Martins Creek Rd 24018
Marvin St SE 24014
Mary B Pl 24018
Mary Linda Ave NE 24012
Maryland Ave NW 24017
Mason Knob Trl 24018
Mason Mill Rd NE 24012
Mason Park Dr 24019
Masons View Ln 24018
Massachusetts Ave
NW 24017
Masters Cir NW 24017
Matisse Ln 24018
Mattaponi Dr NW 24017
Mattie Dr 24012
Maycrest St NW 24012
Mayfield Dr 24014
Mayfield St 24019
Mayland Rd 24014
Mayo Dr NW 24017
Maywood Rd SW 24014
Mc Spetz Ln 24018
Mcclanahan St SW 24014
Mcconnell Rd 24019
Mcdowell Ave NE
500-599 24016
901-1097 24012
1099-1300 24012
1302-1398 24012
Mcdowell Ave NW 24016
Mcfarland Rd 24019
Mcintosh Rd 24019
Mckinney St 24019
Mcmillian Ct NW 24019
Mcneil Dr SW 24015
Mcvitty Rd SW 24018
Mcvitty Forest Dr 24018
Meadewood Dr 24019
Meador Ln 24012
Meadow Ln 24014
Meadow Creek Dr 24018
Meadow Crossing Ln
NE 24019
Meadow Valley Cir 24018
Meadowbrook Dr 24012
Meadowbrook Rd NW 24017
Meadowcrest St 24019
Meadowlark Rd 24018
Meadowood Rd 24014
Meadowrun Dr NE 24012
Meadows St NW 24012
Meadowview Ct 24019
Meadowview Dr NW 24017
Mecca St NE 24012
Medallion Cir SE 24014
Medmont Cir SW 24018
Melcher St SE 24014
Melinda Ln 24014
Melody Ave 24018
Melrose Ave NW 24017
Memorial Ave SW 24015
Memory Ln 24019
Memphis St SE 24013
Mercer Ave NW 24017
Merino Dr 24018
Merriman Rd 24018
Mews Hill Dr 24018
Mexico Way NE 24012
Meyers Dr 24019
Miami St SE 24013
Michael St NW 24017
Michelle Ln 24019
Michigan Ave NW 24017
Mickey Ln 24019
Middle Valley Dr 24012
Middleton St 24019
Midsummer Ln 24018
Midvale Ave SW 24016
Midway Dr 24018
Midway St NE 24012
Milk A Way Dr 24019
Mill Run Cir 24018
Mill View Ct 24018
Millcrest Ct 24018
Millers Lndg 24019
Milton St NW 24017
Mississippi Ave NE 24012
Missouri Ave NE 24012
Misty Mountain Ln 24012
Mockingbird Hill Rd 24012
Mohawk Ave NE 24012
Moir St NE 24012
Moncap Trl 24018
Monet Dr 24018
Monroe St NW 24017
Montague Way 24018
Montauk Rd NW 24017
Montclair Dr 24019
Monterey Ave NE 24012
Monterey Cir 24019
Monterey Rd NE 24019
Montgomery Ave SW 24015
Monticello Ave NE 24012
Montrose Ave SE 24013
Montvale Rd SW 24015
Moomaw Ave NW 24017
Moonlight Ln 24018
Moonsong Rd 24018
Moore St SE 24013
Moorman Ave NW
500-1099 24016
1100-2199 24017
Moran St SE 24014
Morehead Ave SE 24013
Morgan Ave SE 24013
Morning Dove Rd 24018
Morning Glory Dr 24012
Morningside St SE 24013
Morrill Ave SE 24013
Morrison St SE 24014
Morton Ave SE 24013
Morwanda Ave NW 24017
Mount Chestnut Rd 24018
Mount Holland Dr SW 24018
Mount Laurel Rd 24018
Mount Pleasant Blvd
SE 24014
Mount Vernon Rd SW 24015
Mountain Ave SE 24013
Mountain Ave SW 24016
S Mountain Dr 24018
Mountain Rd NW 24017
Mountain Brook Dr 24012
Mountain Spring Ct &
Trl 24018
Mountain View Dr NW 24017
Mountain View Ter
SW 24015
Mountain Village Dr 24018
Mountainaire Ave NW 24017
Mudlick Rd SW 24018
Muirfield Cir 24019
Mulberry St NW 24017
Mulholland Cir 24012
Munford Ave SE 24013
Municipal Rd NW 24012
Murray Ave SE 24013
Murray Ct 24019
Murray Farm Rd 24019
Murrell Rd NE 24012
Murry Rd SW 24018
Musical Ln 24018
Mystique Ct 24012
Naho St NW 24017
Najjum Ln 24019
Nancy Cir & Dr 24017
Nandina Dr 24018
Narrows Ln SW 24014
Neil Dr 24019
Nell Cir & Dr 24019
Nelms Ln 24012
Nelms Ln NE 24019
New Barrens Ct 24019
New Spring Branch Rd
SE 24014
New York Ave NW 24017
Newland Rd 24019
Nicholas Ave & Ct NE 24012
Nicholas Hill Ln 24019
Noble Ave NE 24012
Norfolk Ave SE 24013
Norfolk Ave SW
1-299 24011
300-1199 24016
Norman St 24019
Normandy Ln 24018
Normandy St NE 24012
Norris Dr NW 24017
Norseman Dr 24019
North Ave NE 24012
North Rd NW 24017
North St NW 24017
Northcross Rd 24018
Northland Dr 24019
Northminster Rd NW 24012
Northmont Ave 24019
Northridge Ln 24019
Northridge St NE 24012
Northshire Ct 24014
Northside Rd 24019
Northside High School
Rd 24019
Northview Dr SW 24015
Northwalk Dr 24019
Northway Dr 24019
Northwood Dr NW 24017
Norton Ave NE 24012
Norway Ave NW 24017
Norwood St SW 24018
Nottingham Rd SE 24014
Nover Ave 24019
Oak Ct 24018
Oak Rd NW 24017
Oak St SW 24015
Oak Crest Ave SW 24015
Oak Grove Blvd NW 24017
Oak Hill Ln SW 24015
Oak Park St SW 24015
Oak Ridge Rd SW 24018
Oakcliff Dr 24018
Oakdale Rd 24018
Oakland Blvd
4701-4797 24012
4799-5199 24012
5300-5899 24019
Oakland Blvd NW 24012
Oaklawn Ave NE &
NW 24012
Oakleaf Dr NW 24017
Oakleigh Ave SW 24018
Oakmont Cir 24019
Oakshire Ln 24014
Oakwood Dr SW 24015
Ogden Rd 24018
Ohio St NE 24019
Old Barn Cir 24018
Old Bent Mountain Rd 24018
Old Black Horse Rd 24019
Old Carriage Rd 24019
Old Cave Spring Rd 24018
Old Country Club Rd
NW 24017
Old Court Ln SW 24015
Old Dominion Dr 24019
Old Farm Rd
1-97 24019
99-299 24019
6500-6699 24018
Old Garst Mill Rd 24018
Old Locke Ct 24018
Old Manor Ct & Dr 24019
Old Mill Ct 24019
Old Mill Dr 24019
Old Mill Rd 24018
Old Mill Forest Cir &
Dr 24018
Old Mill Plantation Dr 24018
Old Mountain Rd NE 24019
Old Rocky Mount Rd
SW 24014
Old Salem Rd SW 24018
Old Spanish Trl NW 24017
Old Stevens Rd NW 24017
Old Tavern Rd 24019
Old Towne Rd 24018
Old Valley Rd 24019
Old Vinton Mill Rd NE 24012
Old Virginia St NE 24019
Old Virginia Springs
Rd 24014
Olde Oak Rd SE 24014
Oleander Cir 24019
Oleva St NW 24017
Olive Ave NW 24017
Oliver Rd NE 24012
Olivette St NW 24017
Olsen Rd 24019
Olyvia Pl 24018
Omar Ave NE 24012
One Oak Rd 24018
Orander Dr 24018
Orange Ave NE
1-799 24016
800-3599 24012
3601-3699 24012
Orange Ave NW
100-1099 24016
1100-2499 24017
Orchard Cir 24019
Orchard Rd SW 24014
Orchard Hill Dr 24019
Orchard Hill Rd SW 24018
Orchard Park Dr 24019
Orchard Tree Ct 24019
Orchard Valley Cir 24018
Orchard View Ln 24018
Orchard Villas Cir 24019
Ordway Dr NW 24017
Oregon Ave SW 24015
Oriole Ln 24018
Orlando Ave & Ct 24019
Othello Cir 24018
Otter Park Ct 24018
Otterview Dr 24019
Ould Dr 24019
Our St SW 24015
Overbrook Dr 24018
Overbrook Dr SW 24018
Overbrook St NW 24017
Overdale Rd 24018
Overhill Trl 24018
Overland Ave SW 24018
Overland Dr 24018
Overland Rd SW 24015
Overlook Rd NE 24012
Overlook Trail Dr 24018
Owen Dr SE 24014
Oxford Ave SW 24015
Padbury Ave SE 24014
Paddington Ct 24018
Palenced Ave SW 24015
Palm Ave NW 24017
Palm Valley Rd 24019
Palmer Ave NE 24019
Palmer Green Cir 24012
Palmer Mountain Ln 24018
Palmetto Ave NW 24017
Palmyra Dr 24012
Pamlico Dr 24018
Panorama Ave NW 24017
Parham Dr 24014
S Park Cir 24018
Park Dr 24012
Park Ln SW 24015
Park Manor Dr 24014
Park Place Ln 24018
Parkcrest St SW 24014
Parkway Dr 24018
Parkway Place Dr 24018
Parkwood Dr 24018
Parliament Rd SW 24014
Partridge Cir 24018
Partridge Ln NW 24017
Pasley Ave SW 24015
Past Times Ln 24019
Patrick Rd NE 24012
Patterson Ave SW 24016
Patton Ave NE & NW 24016
Pawling St NW 24012
Peace Ln 24018
Peach Tree Cir 24018
Peach Tree Dr NW 24017
Peachtree Ct 24012
Peachtree Valley Dr 24012
Peakwood Dr SW 24014
Pearl Ave NE 24012
Pebble Dr 24014
Pechin Ave SE 24013
Peck St NW 24017
Peebles Ln SW 24018
Pelham Dr 24018
Penarth Rd SW 24014
Pencheck Cir 24018
Pendleton Ave 24019
Penguin Dr 24018
Penmar Ave SE 24013
Penn St SW 24015
Penn Forest Blvd & Pl 24018
Pennsylvania Ave NE 24019
Penny Ln 24018
Penrod Ave SE 24013
Penwood Dr 24018
Peppervine Ct 24019
Peregrine Crest Cir 24018
Periwinkle Ln 24014
Persinger Rd SW 24015
Peters Creek Rd 24019
Peters Creek Rd NW
601-697 24017
699-2699 24017
2700-2799 24019
2801-5399 24019
Peters Creek Road Ext
SW 24018
Pettit Ave 24018
Petty Ave 24019
Peyton St 24019
Pheasant Ridge Rd 24014
Pheasant Run Cir 24018
Phyllis Rd 24012
Piccadilly Ln 24018
Piedmont St SE 24014
Pike Ln SE 24014
Pilot Blvd 24018
Pilot St NW 24017
Pin Oak Dr 24019
Pine Ct 24018
Pine St NW 24017
Pine Acres Ln 24018
Pine Flat Ln 24019
Pine Glen Rd NE 24019
Pine Hill Ln 24019
Pine Hurst Cir 24019
Pineland Rd SW 24018
Pinetree Ln 24019
Pinevale Rd 24018
Pinewood Dr 24012
Pinewood Dr NW 24017
Piney Ridge Dr 24018
Pinnacle Ridge Rd NE 24012
Pioneer Dr & Rd NW 24012
Pippin Ln 24018
Pippin St 24019
Pittsfield Ave & Cir 24017
Pitzer Rd 24014
Plain View Ave 24019
Plantation Cir 24019
Plantation Rd 24019
Plantation Rd NE 24012
Plantation Grove Ln 24012
Plateau Rd SE 24014
Player Dr NE 24019
Pleans Ave NW 24017
Pleasant Hill Dr 24018
Pleasant View Ave
NW 24012
Plymouth Dr 24019
Poage Valley Rd 24018
Poage Valley Road
Ext 24018
Poages Mill Dr 24018
Pocahontas Ave NE 24012
Poff Ln 24018
Poindexter Ln 24019

Polk St NW 24017
Pollyhill Ln 24019
Pomeroy Rd NW 24017
Pommel Dr 24018
Ponderosa Cir 24018
Ponderosa Dr 24019
Poplar Dr 24018
Poplar Ln SW 24014
Poplar Springs Ln 24018
Poplar View Rd 24014
Portland Ave NW 24017
Post Rd 24019
Post Oak Dr 24019
Postal Dr 24018
Potomac Ave 24018
Power St SE 24013
Praline Pl 24012
Preakness Ct 24012
Precision Cir 24012
Preston Ave NE & NW 24012
Prillaman Ave NW 24017
Primrose Ave SE 24014
Princeton Cir NE 24012
Production St SE 24013
Progress Dr SE 24013
Prospect Rd SE 24014
Purcell Ave NE 24012
Purple Finch Rd 24018
Quail Dr NW 24017
Quail Pl 24019
Quail Hollow Cir 24019
Quail Ridge Cir & Ct 24018
Quarry Dr 24014
Queen Ave NW 24012
Queen Ann Ct & Dr SE 24014
Rabbit Run Rd 24018
Rachel Dr 24019
Radford Rd NE 24012
Rainelle St 24014
Raintree Rd 24018
Rakes Rd 24014
Ram Dr 24019
Ran Lynn Dr 24018
Ranch Rd NW 24017
Ranchcrest Dr 24018
Randall Dr 24014
Rasmont Rd 24018
Raspberry Ln 24018
Raven Rock Rd 24014
Ravenwood Ave NW 24012
Ray Rd SE 24014
Ray St 24019
Raymond Ave 24012
Read Mountain Rd NE 24019
Read View Rd 24019
Red Barn Ln 24012
Red Bird Cir 24018
Red Cedar Cir 24019
Red Fox Dr NW 24017
Red Oak Ln SW 24018
Red Rock Rd 24015
Red Stag Rd 24018
Redcort Dr 24019
Redwood Rd SE 24014
Reed Rd SE 24014
Reedland Rd 24019
Regency Cir 24018
Remington Rd 24018
Renee Ln 24018
Renfield Rd SW 24018
Renfro Blvd NW 24017
Renoir Ln 24018
Reserve Ave SW 24016
Reserve Point Ln 24018
Reservoir Rd 24019
Return Rd 24019
Rex Rd NE 24012
Reynolds Rd SE 24014
Rhodes Ave NE 24012
Rhododendron Trl 24018
Richard Ave NE 24012
Richards Blvd 24018
Richardson Dr 24019
Richelieu Ave SW 24014
Richland Ave NW 24012
Ridge Cir & Rd 24014
Ridgecrest Dr & Ln 24019
Ridgefield St NE 24012
Ridgelea Rd 24018
Ridgelea Estates Dr 24018
Ridgerun Dr NE 24012
Ridgeview Cir & Dr 24019
Ridgewood Ln SW 24014
Ripplebrook Rd 24018
River Ave SE 24013
River Birch Ln SW 24014
Riverdale Rd SE 24014
Riverland Rd SE 24014
Riverside Blvd SW 24016
Riverside Cir 24016
Riverside Ter SE 24014
Riverview Rd 24014
Roanoke Ave SW 24015
Roberta Rd 24019
Roberts Rd SW 24014
Robertson Ln 24019
Robin Hood Cir 24019
Robin Hood Rd SE 24014
Robin Lynn Rd 24019
Robin View Dr SW 24015
Robyn Rd SW 24015
Rock Garden Ln 24018
Rock Hill Dr 24014
Rock Hill Ln 24019
Rockbridge Ct 24018
Rockingham Blvd 24014
Rockland Ave NW 24012
Rolfe St SW 24015
Rolling Hill Ave NW 24017
N Rome Dr 24019
Rorer Ave SW 24016
Rosalind Ave SW 24014
Rosamae Dr 24019
Rose Ave SE 24014
Rosecliff Rd 24018
Rosecrest Rd 24018
S Roselawn Rd 24018
Roselawn Court Dr 24018
Rosemary Ave SE 24014
Rosevale Rd 24018
Rosewalk Ln 24014
Rosewood Ave SW 24015
Ross Ln SW 24015
Roundhill Ave NW 24012
Roundtop Rd NW 24012
Routt Rd NW 24017
Rowe Ridge Rd NW 24017
Roxbury Ln 24018
Roy Dr SW 24014
Royal Oak Dr SW 24018
Roycroft Dr 24018
Rugby Blvd NW 24017
Running Deer Ln 24019
Runnymeade Ln 24018
Ruritan Rd 24012
Rush St NW 24012
Rushwood St NW 24012
Russell Ave SW 24015
Ruston St NE 24012
Rutgers St NW 24012
Rutherford Ave NE
400-502 24016
419-419 24022
419-419 24023
419-419 24024
419-419 24025
419-419 24026
419-419 24027
419-419 24028
419-419 24029
419-419 24030
419-419 24031
419-419 24032
419-419 24033
419-419 24034
419-419 24035
419-419 24036
419-419 24037
419-419 24038
501-599 24016
Rutherford Ave NW 24016
Rutherford Ct NW 24016
Rutrough Rd SE 24014
Ryan Ln 24018
Saddleridge Cir, Ln & Rd 24018
Saint David Ct 24018
Saint Ives Ct 24018
Saint James Cir 24018
Salem Ave SE 24011
Salem Ave SW
1-299 24011
300-2199 24016
Salem Tpke NW 24017
Salisbury Dr 24018
Samantha Cir 24019
Sample Ave SE 24014
Sand Rd NE 24012
Sanders Dr NE 24019
Sanderson Dr 24019
Sandhurst Dr 24018
Sandlewood Rd 24018
Sandpiper Dr 24018
Sanford Ave SW 24014
Santa Anita Ter 24012
Santa Fe Trl 24018
Santee Rd 24019
Santo Ct 24019
Saul Ln 24014
Savannah Dr 24012
Scarlet Oak Ct & Dr 24019
Scenic Hills Dr 24018
Scotch Pine Ln 24019
Scotford Ct 24018
Scott Rd NE 24012
Sedgefield Rd SW 24015
Sedgewick Dr 24018
Seibel Dr NE 24012
Seneca Dr 24019
Sequoia Dr 24019
Serpentine Rd SW 24014
Service Ave SE 24013
Setter Rd 24012
Sewell Ln SW 24015
Sha Al Rd 24014
Shadeland Ave NW 24012
Shadow Ln 24019
Shadwell Dr 24019
Shady Acres Dr 24014
Shady Side Dr 24018
Shadylawn Ave NW 24012
Shamrock St NW 24017
Shannon St SE 24014
Shanta Ln 24012
Sharmar Rd 24018
Sharolyn Dr 24018
Sharon Rd NE 24012
Shaver Rd 24018
Sheffield Rd SW 24015
Shelby Dr 24018
Sheldon Dr 24018
Shelia Ln 24018
Shenandoah Ave NE 24016
Shenandoah Ave NW
1-1099 24016
1100-4599 24017
Shenandoah Valley Ave NE 24012
Sherman Dr NW 24017
Sherry Rd 24019
Sherwood Ave SW 24015
Shingle Ridge Rd SW 24018
Shirley Ave SW 24015
Shore Dr 24012
Short St NW 24012
Shorthorn Dr 24018
Showalter Rd NW 24017
Shrewsbury Ct 24018
Shull Rd NE 24012
Siden Cir NW 24017
Sidetrack Rd 24012
Sierra Ct 24019
Sierra Dr 24012
Sigmon Rd NW 24017
Signal Hill Ave NW 24017
Silver Fox Rd 24018
Silverwood Rd NW 24017
Simsmore Ave 24014
Singing Hills Cir & Rd 24014
Sioux Ridge Rd NW 24017
Skylar Ct 24012
Skylark Cir 24018
Sleepy Dr NE 24012
Sleepy Hollow Dr 24018
Sloan Rd NW 24017
Slusser Ln 24019
Smith Ford Rd 24012
Smoke Rise Ct 24014
Smokey Ridge Rd 24018
Snead Rd SE 24014
Snow Owl Dr 24018
Snowberry Cir 24019
Snowbird Cir 24018
Snowgoose Cir 24018
Soft Dr 24019
Solonevich Rd 24018
Somercroft Ct 24014
Somerset St SW 24014
Sorrel Ln 24018
Sourwood St 24012
South Dr 24019
Southall Pl SW 24015
Southern Hills Dr SW 24014
Southern Pines Dr 24018
Southlawn Cir SW 24018
Southmont Dr SW 24014
Southview Ter SW 24014
Southway Dr SW 24014
Southwick Cir 24018
Southwood Manor Ct 24014
Southwood Village Ct 24014
Southwoods Dr 24018
Sparks Rd 24018
Spencer Dr 24018
Spessard Ave SW 24015
Split Oak Rd 24018
Split Rail Ln 24018
Spradlin Dr 24014
N Spring Dr 24019
Spring Rd SW 24015
Spring Hollow Ave NW 24012
Spring Meadow Ct & Dr 24018
Spring Run Dr 24018
Spring Willow Ln NW 24017
Springbeauty St 24012
Springbrook Rd NW 24017
Springer Rd 24012
Springfield Ave NW 24017
Springfield Dr 24012
Springhill Dr NW 24017
Springlawn Ave 24018
Springtree Cir & Dr 24012
Springvale St SE 24014
Sprucewood Rd SW 24015
Squires Ct 24018
Stable Rd 24014
Stallion Cir 24018
Stanley Ave SE 24014
Starkey Ln & Rd 24018
Starlight Ln 24018
Starmount Ave 24019
Staunton Ave NW
600-999 24016
1000-2699 24017
Stayman Dr 24012
Stayman Rd 24019
Stearnes Ave 24018
Steele Rd 24018
Steeplechase Dr 24018
Stephenson Ave SW 24014
Sterling Pl 24012
Sterling Rd 24014
Stewart Ave SE 24013
Stickley Ln 24018
Stiltner Rd 24019
Stokes Dr 24019
Stone Manor Dr 24018
Stone Mountain Rd 24018
Stonecreek Way 24019
Stonecroft Ct 24018
Stonegate Dr 24019
Stonehenge Sq 24018
Stonehouse Ln 24019
Stoneledge Dr 24019
Stonelyn Cottage Ct 24019
Stoneridge Rd SW 24014
Stonewall Rd NW 24017
Stoney Corner Ln 24019
Stoney Point Rd 24018
Stoney Ridge Dr 24012
Stoneybrook Dr 24018
Stoneybrook Rd 24019
Stonington Rd 24019
Strand Rd NE 24012
Stratford Pl SW 24015
Stratford Way 24018
Stratford Park Dr SW 24018
Strathmore Ln 24019
Strawberry Ln 24018
Strawberry Hill Rd 24019
Strawberry Mountain Dr 24018
Strother Rd SW 24015
Suburban Ave SW 24015
Sudley Rd 24019
Sugar Loaf Dr 24018
Sugar Loaf Mountain Rd 24018
Sugar Maple Ct 24019
Sugar Ridge Dr 24018
Sugar Rum Ridge Rd 24018
Sulgrave Rd 24018
Sullivan Ln 24012
Summer Dr 24019
Summer View Dr 24019
Summerdean Ave 24019
Summerfield Ct 24019
Summerfield Dr 24012
Summers Way 24019
Summerset Cir & Dr 24018
Summerville Ln 24019
Summit Ave SW 24015
Summit Dr NW 24017
Summit Ln NW 24017
Summit Way SW 24014
Summit Ridge Rd 24012
Sumpter Pl 24019
Sun Valley Ln 24014
Sunberry Cir 24018
Sunbreeze Cir 24018
Sunchase Ct & Ln 24018
Suncrest Dr 24014
Sundance Cir 24019
Sunhaven Ct 24018
Sunny Side Dr 24018
Sunnybrook Dr 24019
Sunnycrest Ln & Rd 24018
Sunnyvale Rd 24018
Sunnyvale St 24014
Sunridge Ln 24018
Sunrise Ave NW 24012
Sunrise Ridge Ct 24012
Sunscape Ct & Dr 24018
Sunset Ave NE 24012
Sunset Dr 24014
Surrey Ave NW 24017
Surrey Ln 24012
Sussex Ct 24018
Sutton St NE 24012
Swarthmore Ave NW 24017
Sweet Cherry Ct 24019
Sweetbrier Ave SW 24015
Sweetenberg Ln 24019
Sweetfern Dr 24019
Sycamore Ave NE 24012
Sydnor Cir NW 24016
Sylvan Rd SE 24014
Sylvan Brook Rd 24018
Syracuse Ave NW
1000-1199 24012
1200-1899 24017
Tacoma Ave NE 24019
Tahoe Ln 24019
Tall Oak Ln 24018
Tallwood Dr 24018
Tamarack Trl 24018
Tamarisk Cir 24019
Tamitann St SW 24011
Tampa Dr 24019
Taney Dr 24019
Tanglewood Dr & Ln 24018
Tannehill Dr 24018
Tayloe Ave SE 24013
Tazewell Ave SE 24013
Technical St SE 24013
Tellico Rd NW 24017
Temple Dr NW 24017
Templeton Ave NE 24012
Tennessee Ave NW 24017
Teresa Ln 24019
Terminal Rd 24018
Terrace Rd SW 24015
Terrapin Trl 24018
Terry Walters Dr 24018
Thames Dr 24018
The Peaks Dr 24018
Thelma St NW 24017
Thirlane Rd NW 24019
Thomas Ave NW 24017
Thomason Rd SE 24014
Thompson Memorial Dr 24019
Thompsons Ln 24018
Thorndale St SW 24015
Thornrose Rd 24012
Three Chop Ln SW 24014
Thrush Dr NW 24017
Thurman Ave NW 24012
Thurston Ave NE 24012
Tillett Rd SW 24015
Timber Bridge Rd 24018
Timberland Trl 24014
Timberlane Ave 24018
Timberline Cir & Trl 24018
Timberview Rd 24019
Timberwolf Cir 24018
Timothy Ln NW 24017
Tinker Dr NE 24012
Tinker Creek Ln NE 24019
Tinkerbell Ln 24019
Tinkerdale Rd 24019
Tinkerview Rd 24019
Tiny Trl 24019
Tipton Ave SE 24014
Titan Trl 24018
Toad Hollow Rd 24019
Tolman Cir 24012
Tom Andrews Rd NW 24019
Tomaranne Dr 24018
Tomi Ln SE 24013
Tomley Dr 24018
Tompkins Ave SE 24013
Top Hill Dr NW 24017
Topping St 24019
Topping Hill Dr 24018
Towne Dr 24018
Towne Square Blvd NW 24012
Townsend Rd 24019
Townside Rd SW 24014
Traders Path 24014
Trail Dr 24012
Trane Dr NW 24017
Trapper Cir NW 24012
Tree Swallow Rd 24018
Tree Top Ln 24018
Trelawny Trl 24018
Tremont Dr NW 24017
Trent Rd SE 24014
Trevilian Rd 24019
Trevino Cir & Dr 24019
Trillium Ln 24012
Trinity Ct 24018
Trinkle Ave NE & NW 24012
Trout St NW 24017
Troutland Ave NW 24017
Troxell Rd SE 24014
Troy Ave NE & NW 24012
Tuck St NE 24012
Tuckawana Cir NW 24017
Tudor Ln NW 24012
Tully Dr 24019
Turkey Hollow Rd 24018
Turkey Ridge Rd 24014
Turnstile Dr 24018
Twelve Oclock Knob Rd 24018
Twilight Rd 24019
Twin Forks Dr 24019
Twin Views Ct 24012
Two Ford Rd 24018
Two Tree Ln NE 24019
Tyler Ave NW 24017
Tyree Rd NW 24017
Underhill Ave 24014
Unincham Rd 24018
Union St SW 24015
Updike Ln 24019
Updike Rd 24014
Upland Game Rd 24018
Vale Ave NE 24012
Valentine Rd SW 24018
Valley Ave 24018
Valley Ave SW 24015
Valley Dr 24018
Valley Forge Ave & Cir 24018
Valley Gateway Blvd 24012
Valley Pike Rd SE 24014
Valley Stream Dr 24014
Valley View Ave NW 24012
Valley View Blvd NW 24012
Valley View Cir 24019
Valley View Rd 24014
Valley View Rd SE 24014
Valleypark Dr 24019
Valleypointe Pkwy 24019
Van Buren St NW 24017
Van Winkle Rd SW 24014
Vance St SE 24014
Vancouver Dr NW 24012
Varnell Ave NE 24012
Vauxhall Rd 24018
Vela Cir 24019
Ventnor Rd SE 24014
Ventura Ct 24019
Vermont Ave NW 24017
Verndale Dr 24019
Vernon St SE 24013
Verona Trl 24018
Vest Dr 24018
Viangt Rd 24014
Victor Ave NE 24012
Victoria St NW 24017
Victory Rd SE 24014
View Ave 24018
Viewmont St NW 24017
Viking Dr 24019
Village Dr 24018
S Village Dr 24018
Village Ln 24019
Village Run 24018
Village Way 24018
Village Court Ln NE 24012
Village Green Dr 24019
Vincent St NW 24012
Vinton Mill Ct NE 24012
Vinyard Ave NE 24012
Vinyard Rd 24018
Virginia Ave NW 24017
Virginia Deer Rd 24019
Vista Ave & Dr 24019
Vista Forest Dr 24018
Vistamont Dr 24019
Vivian Ave 24019
Wade Rd 24018
Wade St 24019
Wades Cir 24012
Wakefield Ave 24018
Wakefield Rd SW 24015
Wales Ct 24018
Walhalla Ct 24019
Wall St SE 24011
Wallace Ave NE 24012
Walmann Rd SW 24018
Walnut Ave SE 24014
Walnut Ave SW 24016
Walrond Dr 24019

Walton Ln 24018
Ward St NW 24017
Warring Ln 24014
Warrington Rd SW 24015
Warwick St SW 24015
Warwood Dr 24018
Wasena Ave SW 24015
Wasena Ter SW 24016
Washington Ave SW 24016
Water Oak Rd 24019
Waterfall Dr 24019
Waterford Dr SE 24014
Waterstone Dr 24018
Wautauga St SW 24015
Waxmyrtle Dr 24019
Waxwing Cir 24018
Wayburn Dr 24019
Wayland St NE 24012
Wayne St NE 24012
Waypoint Dr NW 24012
Weaver Rd SW 24015
Webb Rd NE 24012
Webster Dr 24019
Webster Rd 24012
Webster Heights Rd 24012
Wedgewood Rd SW 24015
Welch Rd SW 24015
Welcome Valley Rd SE 24014
Wellington Dr SE 24014
Wellington Rd 24018
Wells Ave NW 24016
Wellsley St NW 24017
Welton Ave SW 24015
Wembley Pl SW 24018
Wendover Rd 24019
Wentworth Ave NE & NW 24012
Wertz Rd NE 24012
Wertz Orchard Rd 24018
West Dr SW 24015
Westbriar Ct 24018
Westchester Ave SW 24018
Westdale Rd NW 24017
Westfield Pl 24019
Westhampton Ave SW 24015
Westhill Dr 24018
Westland Rd SW 24018
Westmont St NW 24012
Westmoreland Dr 24018
Westover Ave SW 24015
Westport Ave SW 24016
Westshire Ct 24018
Westside Blvd NW 24017
Westvale Rd NE 24019
Westview Ave SW 24016
Westwood Blvd NW 24017
Wesvan Dr 24012
Wexford Ct 24018
Whippletree Dr 24018
Whipplewood Ct & Dr 24018
Whispering Ln 24014
Whispering Willow Ln NW 24017
Whistler Dr 24018
White Ave SE 24013
White Dove Ln 24018
White Oak Rd SW 24014
White Pelican Ln 24018
White Tail Dr 24012
Whitehall Cir 24018
Whiteside St NE 24012
Whitman St SE 24014
Whitmore Ave SW 24016
Whitney Ave NW 24012
Whittaker Ave NE 24012
Whitten Ave NW 24012
Whittle St NE 24012
Whittler Ct 24019
Whitwell Dr 24019
Wilbur Rd SW 24015
Wild Cherry Ct 24019
Wild Oak Dr 24014
Wildflower Ln 24018
Wildhurst Ave NE 24012
Wildwood Rd SW 24014

Wiley Dr SW 24015
Will Carter Ln 24014
Willetta Dr 24018
William Ct 24018
Williamsburg Ct 24018
Williamson Rd
5001-5297 24012
5299-6099 24012
6300-7999 24019
7916-7916 24020
8001-8299 24019
8100-8298 24019
Williamson Rd NE
1-1199 24016
1200-2599 24012
Williamson Rd NW 24012
Williamson Rd SE
1-299 24011
900-1499 24013
Willingham Dr 24018
Willis St NW 24017
Willow Rd NW 24017
Willow Creek Dr 24019
Willow Leaf Cir 24018
Willow Oak Cir & Dr 24014
Willow Park Dr NW 24017
Willow Ridge Rd 24019
Willow Spring Rd 24018
Willow Valley Rd 24018
Willow Walk Dr NW 24017
Willow Wood Dr 24012
Willowbrook Dr & Ln 24012
Willowlawn St 24018
Willowrun Dr NE 24012
Wilmont Ave NW 24017
Wilshire Ave SW 24015
Wilson Rd NW 24017
Wilson St SE 24013
Wilson Mountain Rd 24014
Wilton Rd SW 24014
Wimbledon Ct 24018
Winborne St SW 24015
Winchester Ave SW 24015
Windcrest Ln 24012
Winding Way Rd SW
3400-3999 24015
4001-4099 24018
Windrush Ln 24012
Windsor Ave SW 24015
Windsor Ct 24019
Windsor Rd SW 24018
Windsor Oaks Cir SW 24018
Windward Dr SW 24018
Windy Gap Dr 24014
Windy Hill Circle Dr 24019
Wineberry Trl 24018
Winesap Dr & Rd 24019
Wing Commander Dr 24018
Wingfield Ave NE 24012
Winifred Dr SW 24018
Winnbrook Ct, Dr & Ln 24018
Winona Ave SW 24015
Winsloe Dr NW 24012
Winston Ave SW 24014
Winter Park Dr 24019
Winterberry Ct 24018
Winterberry Dr 24018
Winterberry Ln 24014
Winterberry Sq 24018
Winterset Dr 24018
Winterwood Trl 24018
Winthrop Ave SW 24015
Wipledale Ave 24019
Wise Ave SE 24013
Wisteria Place Ct 24012
Wood Rd 24014
Wood Haven Rd 24019
Wood Warbler Ln 24018
Woodbine St SE 24014
Woodbridge Ave NW 24017
Woodbrook Dr 24018
Woodbury St NW 24012
Woodchuck Ln 24018
Woodcliff Rd SE 24014
Woodcock Cir 24018

Woodcreeper Dr 24019
Woodcrest Rd NW 24012
Woodland Dr SW 24015
Woodland Ln 24018
Woodland Rd SE 24014
Woodland Hills Ln SW 24014
Woodlawn Ave SW 24015
Woodlawn Rd NW 24017
Woodleigh Rd NW 24017
Woodley Dr 24018
Woodmar Dr SW 24018
Woodmont Dr 24018
Woodoak Rd SE 24014
Woodridge Dr 24018
Woodrow Ave SE 24013
Woods Ave SW 24016
Woods Crossing Dr 24018
Woods End Ln 24014
Woodthrush Cir & Dr 24018
Woodvale Cir & Dr 24018
Woodvalley Dr 24012
Woodview Rd 24018
Woodway Rd 24014
Wormack Rd 24019
Wren Rd 24018
Wright Rd SW 24015
Wycliffe Ave SW 24014
Wyndale Ave 24018
Wynmere Dr 24018
Wynne Rd 24018
Wyoming Ave NW 24017
Yardley Dr NW 24012
Yeager Ave NE 24012
Yellow Mountain Rd SE 24014
York Rd SW 24015
York St 24019
Yorker Dr SW 24015
Yorkshire Ct 24019
Yorktown Pl SW 24015
Youngwood Dr NW 24017

NUMBERED STREETS

1st St NW 24016
207-699 24011
700-1199 24016
2nd St NE 24016
1-699 24011
800-1499 24016
3rd St NW 24016
3rd St SE 24013
3rd St SW
100-499 24011
500-1499 24016
4 1/2 St SW 24016
4th St NE 24016
4th St NW 24016
4th St SE 24013
4th St SW 24016
5th St NE 24016
5th St NW 24016
5th St SE 24013
5th St SW 24016
6 1/2 St SE 24013
6th St NE 24012
6th St NW 24016
6th St SE 24013
6th St SW 24016
7th St NE 24012
7th St NW 24016
7th St SE 24013
7th St SW 24016
8 1/2 St SE 24013
8th St NW 24016
8th St SE 24013
8th St SW
1-799 24016
801-899 24016
1300-1399 24015
9th St NW 24016
9th St SE 24013
9th St SW 24016
10th St NE 24012
10th St NW
500-1399 24016

1400-2999 24012
10th St SE 24013
10th St SW
1-599 24016
1000-1399 24015
11th St NE 24012
11th St NW
100-1399 24017
1700-1799 24012
11th St SE 24013
11th St SW
1-699 24016
1000-1399 24015
12th St NW 24017
12th St SE 24013
12th St SW
1-799 24016
1000-1600 24015
1602-1698 24015
13th St NE 24012
13th St NW 24017
13th St SE 24013
13th St SW 24016
14th St NW 24017
14th St SE 24013
14th St SW 24016
15th St NE 24012
15th St NW 24017
15th St SE 24013
15th St SW 24016
16th St NE 24012
16th St NW 24017
16th St SE
100-1299 24013
1400-1698 24014
1700-1799 24014
16th St SW 24016
17th St NE 24012
17th St NW 24017
17th St SE 24013
17th St SW 24016
18th St NE 24012
18th St NW 24017
18th St SE
100-699 24013
1600-1698 24014
1700-1799 24014
18th St SW 24016
19th St NE 24012
19th St NW 24017
19th St SE 24013
19th St SW 24016
20th St NE 24012
20th St NW 24017
20th St SW 24016
21st St NE 24012
21st St NW 24017
21st St SW
600-698 24015
601-699 24014
22nd St NE 24012
22nd St NW 24017
22nd St SW 24014
23rd St NE 24012
23rd St NW 24017
23rd St SE 24014
23rd St SW
1-499 24014
1000-1098 24015
1101-1199 24015
24th St NE 24012
24th St NW 24017
24th St SE 24014
24th St SW 24014
25th St NW 24017
25th St SW 24014
26th St SE 24014
26th St SW
1-300 24014
1000-1199 24015
27th St NW 24017
27th St SE 24014
27th St SW 24014
28th St SW 24014
29th St NW 24017
30th St NW 24017

31st St NW 24017
35th St NW 24017
36th St NW 24017
10 1/2 St SE 24013
12 1/2 St SW 24016
13 1/2 St SE 24013

ROUND HILL VA

General Delivery 20141

POST OFFICE BOXES MAIN OFFICE STATIONS AND BRANCHES

Box No.s
All PO Boxes 20142

NAMED STREETS

All Street Addresses 20141

SMITHFIELD VA

General Delivery 23430

POST OFFICE BOXES MAIN OFFICE STATIONS AND BRANCHES

Box No.s
All PO Boxes 23431

NAMED STREETS

Acacia Cir 23430
Acorn Ln 23430
Alvins Dr 23430
W Andrews Xing 23430
Apache Trl 23430
Appaloosa Way 23430
Applewhite St 23430
Arabian Trl 23430
Artists Way 23430
Ashlee Dale Ln 23430
Astrid St 23430
Autumn Ct 23430
Azalea Dr 23430
Back River Ln 23430
Bailey Ave 23430
Barclay Cres 23430
Barcroft Dr 23430
Barlow Ln 23430
Bartons Landing Rd 23430
Battery Park Rd 23430
Beale Ave 23430
Bears Crossing Ln 23430
Bee St 23430
Beech Ct 23430
Beechwood Ln & Pt 23430
Bellwood Ave 23430
Benns Church Blvd 23430
Berry Hill Farm Ln 23430
Berryhill Rd 23430
Berryman Ct 23430
Bethany Church Rd 23430
Bethel Church Ln 23430
Bettys Ln 23430
Bishop Cir 23430
Bishops Reach 23430
Black Oak Dr 23430
Blairs Creek Dr & Way 23430
Blounts Corner Rd 23430
Bob White Rd 23430
Boogie Ln 23430
Boone Ct 23430
Bowden Ln 23430

Bowling Green Rd 23430
Boykin Ln 23430
Bradbys Ln 23430
Breann Ct 23430
Breezy Hill Ln 23430
Brewer Pl 23430
Brewers Neck Blvd 23430
Bristol St 23430
Bubs Ln 23430
Buckingham Way 23430
Bunkley Ln 23430
Burton Dr 23430
Burwells Bay Rd 23430
Butlers Pointe Ln 23430
E & W Byron Dr 23430
Calvary Way 23430
Canteberry Ln 23430
Captains Walk 23430
Captains Point Ln 23430
Carl Pt 23430
Carnoustie 23430
Carol Dr 23430
Carroll Bridge Rd 23430
Carver Ave 23430
Cary St 23430
Casper Cir 23430
Cathedral St 23430
Cattail Ln 23430
Cedar Ln & St 23430
Chalmers Row 23430
Cherry Grove Cir & Rd N 23430
Chrisfield Cir 23430
Christopher Ct & Dr 23430
N & S Church St 23430
Cindale Dr 23430
Clay St 23430
Clifton Ln 23430
Clipper Creek Cir, Ct & Ln 23430
Cockes Ln 23430
Colonial Ave & Trl E 23430
Comet Rd 23430
Commerce Ln & St 23430
Commodore Ln 23430
Country Way 23430
Courthouse Hwy 23430
Cranford Rd 23430
W Creek Pl 23430
Creekside Dr 23430
Creekway Dr 23430
Crescent Dr 23430
Crest Cir 23430
Croatan Ct 23430
Crook Ln 23430
Curtis Dr 23430
Cypress Ave, Way & Xing 23430
Cypress Creek Pkwy 23430
Cypress Knoll Ln 23430
Cypress Run Dr 23430
Darden Farm Ln 23430
Dashiell Dr 23430
Davis Ln 23430
Days Neck Rd 23430
Days Point Ln & Rd 23430
Deer Creek Trl 23430
Deer Run Dr 23430
Deer Spring Ln 23430
Deerfield Dr 23430
Denson Bailey Ct 23430
Dockside Dr 23430
Dogwood Ln 23430
Dover Ct 23430
Drummonds Ln 23430
Duff Ct 23430
Dunhill 23430
Durham St 23430
Eagle Nest Ln 23430
Eagle Watch 23430
East St 23430
Easton Pl 23430
Easy St 23430
Echo Lake Dr 23430
Edgewood Dr 23430
Edinburgh Ct 23430

Edwards Cir 23430
Emmanuel Church Rd 23430
English Oak Dr 23430
Ennisdale Dr 23430
Evergreen Way 23430
Fair Hills Ln 23430
Farah Ct 23430
Farm Rd 23430
Fawn Ct 23430
Faye Dr 23430
Fenwood Ct 23430
Fergusons Wharf Way 23430
Field Dr 23430
Field Of Dreams Rd 23430
Fishermans Way 23430
Fleetney Cir 23430
Forest View Ln 23430
Fort Boykin Trl 23430
Fort Huger Dr 23430
Founders Way 23430
Foursquare Rd 23430
Fox Ridge Ln 23430
Fulgham Ln 23430
Gateway Dr 23430
Gatling Pointe Pkwy S 23430
Georgia Ln 23430
Ginger Loop 23430
Gleneagles 23430
Goodrich Ln 23430
Goose Hill Way 23430
Grace St 23430
Grandville Arch 23430
Great Oak Cir 23430
Great Spring Rd 23430
Green Crossing Ln 23430
Green Run Ln 23430
Greenbrier Ln 23430
Griffin Ln 23430
Gullane 23430
Gumwood Dr 23430
Gurwen Dr 23430
Halltown Rd 23430
Harbour Rdg 23430
Hardy Cir 23430
Hardys Pl 23430
Harrison Dr 23430
Harry Wilson Rd 23430
Hatchers Ln 23430
Haverty Ln 23430
Havlow Ln 23430
Hayes Ln 23430
Hayloft Ln 23430
Hearn Dr 23430
Heather Ln 23430
Hemlock Ct 23430
Heptinstall Ave 23430
Heritage Ln 23430
Hickory Cres & Ct 23430
Hill St 23430
Hillcrest Dr 23430
Hilltop Ln 23430
Holloway Dr 23430
Holly Dr & Rdg 23430
Holly Point Way 23430
Hollydale Ln 23430
Holmes Ln 23430
Horseshoe Point Ln 23430
Hummingbird Ln 23430
Hunter Way 23430
Huntington Way 23430
India Ln 23430
Institute St 23430
Inverness 23430
Irvin Dr 23430
Isle Of Wight Industrial Par Rd 23430
Jakes Ln 23430
James St & Way 23430
N & S James Landing Cir & Ct 23430
James River Way 23430
James Wilson Way 23430
Jamestown Ave 23430
Jamesview Cir 23430
Jefferson Dr 23430
Jenkins Ln 23430

Jericho Rd 23430
John Rolfe Dr 23430
Jones Dr 23430
Jordan Ave & Dr 23430
Josephines Xing 23430
Joshua Cir & Rd 23430
Juniper Ct 23430
Kathleen Dr 23430
Kendall Hvn 23430
Kenmere Ln 23430
Kerr Pl 23430
Keswick Pl 23430
Kindred Pl 23430
King Ct 23430
Kingbrook Ln 23430
Kings Landing Ln 23430
Kings Point Ave, Ct & Ln 23430
Lakeside Cir 23430
Lakeview Cv 23430
Lane Cres 23430
Lankford Ln 23430
Latimer Ct 23430
Laurel Ln 23430
Laurel Oak Dr 23430
Lauren Dr 23430
Lawne St 23430
Lawnes Ct & Dr 23430
Lawnes Creek Rd 23430
Lawnes Neck Dr 23430
Lawson Creek Ln 23430
Ledford Ln 23430
Lenora Cv 23430
Leonard St 23430
Locherbie 23430
Lochview 23430
Longview Cir & Dr 23430
Longwood Dr 23430
Lumar Rd 23430
Lytham 23430
Madison Ct 23430
Magnet Dr 23430
E & W Magnolia Ct & Pl 23430
Magruder Rd 23430
Main St
1-235 23430
234-234 23431
236-598 23430
237-599 23430
W Main St 23430
Manchester Ct 23430
Maple Ct 23430
Maple Grove Ln 23430
Maplewood Ct 23430
Mariners Cir & Ct 23430
Mariners Point Ln 23430
Martha Cir 23430
Martin St 23430
N & S Mason St 23430
Maxie Ln 23430
Meadow Dr 23430
Meadowbrook Ln 23430
Melissa Dr 23430
Mercer St 23430
Middle St 23430
Mill Swamp Rd 23430
Mimosa Ct 23430
Minton Way 23430
Mitch Ln 23430
Mokete Trl 23430
Monette Ln & Pkwy 23430
Monticello Ct 23430
Montpellier Way 23430
Moone Dr 23430
Moone Creek Cir 23430
Moonefield Dr 23430
Moonlight Rd 23430
Moore Ave 23430
Morgarts Beach Ln & Rd 23430
Mount Castle Ln 23430
Mount Vernon Ct 23430
Mt Holly Creek Ln 23430
Muddy Cross Dr 23430
Muirfield 23430
Nairn Ln 23430
New Castle Way 23430
Nike Park Rd 23430
North St 23430
Nottingham Pl 23430
Oak Aly 23430
Oak Tree Ln 23430
Oakwood Ln 23430
Old Stage Hwy 23430
Olde Towne Ct & Pl 23430
Oliver Dr 23430
Orchard Garden Ln 23430
Osprey Ln 23430
Owens Ln 23430
Oxford Ave, Ct & Pl 23430
Pagan Ave, Rd & Rdg 23430
Paleo Point Ln 23430
Park Pl 23430
Parkers Three Ln 23430
Pasture Ln 23430
Penotha Dr 23430
Peterson Ave 23430
Peyton Ln 23430
Pine Cir 23430
Pinehurst Dr 23430
Pinewood Dr 23430
Plantation Ln 23430
Pleasant Ln 23430
Pocahontas Ct 23430
Pole Rd 23430
Poplar Ct & Dr 23430
Poplar Point Ln 23430
Powell Trce 23430
Prestwick 23430
Private Stock Ln 23430
Purdie Ave 23430
Purvis Ln 23430
Quail St 23430
Queen Ct 23430
Quiet Way 23430
Quillens Point Ln 23430
Raynor Rd 23430
Red Oak Ct & Dr 23430
Red Point Dr 23430
Regal Ct 23430
Regatta Ln 23430
Richmond Ave 23430
Riddick Rd 23430
Ridgeland Dr 23430
River Rd 23430
River Bend Pl 23430
River Landing Trl 23430
River Oaks Ln 23430
Rivers Edge Trl W 23430
Rivers Ridge Ln 23430
Riverside Dr 23430
Riverview Ave & Rd 23430
Robertson Ln 23430
Robin Ln 23430
Rockbridge St 23430
Rocks Landing Rd 23430
Roff Ln 23430
Rolling Acres Ln 23430
Royal Aberdeen 23430
Royal Dornoch 23430
Royal Portrush 23430
Ryder 23430
Saint Charles Dr 23430
Saint George 23430
Salisbury Ct 23430
Salter Ct 23430
Sandpiper Dr 23430
Schooner Cir 23430
Scotts Factory Rd 23430
Seahawk Lndg 23430
Shallowford Cir 23430
Shelter Cv 23430
Sherwood Ln 23430
W, N & S Shore Cir & Dr 23430
Shore Point Ln 23430
Six Ponds Ln 23430
Smith Dr 23430
Smithfield Blvd & Plz 23430
Smithfield Apts Ln 23430
Smithfield Heights Dr 23430
Smithfield Square Shop Ctr 23430
Southampton Ct 23430
Southern Way 23430
Southport Landing Dr & Pl 23430
Spady Ln 23430
Spinnaker Run Ct & Ln 23430
Spratley Ln 23430
Spring Dr 23430
Spring Lake Dr 23430
St Andrews 23430
St James Ave 23430
St Pauls Ave 23430
Stallings Ln 23430
Stallings Creek Dr & Ln 23430
Stallion Ct 23430
Stonehouse Ln 23430
Sue Bee Cir 23430
Sullivans Ct 23430
Sunrise Bluff Ct & Ln 23430
Sunshine Ln 23430
Sycamore Springs Ct 23430
Sykes Ct 23430
Talbot Dr 23430
Tallie Ln 23430
Tallwood Cir 23430
Tan Rd 23430
The Machrie 23430
The Oaks Ln 23430
Thomas St 23430
Thomas Park Ln 23430
Thompson Ln 23430
Thurston Cir 23430
Tillery Ln 23430
Tormentors Ln 23430
Track Ln 23430
Troon 23430
Trumpet Rd 23430
Tucker Ln 23430
Tulip Poplar Ct 23430
Turnberry 23430
Turner Dr 23430
Tylers Beach Rd 23430
Tynes Ln 23430
Underwood Ln 23430
Uzzell Church Rd 23430
Vernon Ln 23430
Vichalin Rd 23430
Villa Dr 23430
Vincents Xing 23430
Vineyard Ln 23430
Virginia Ave 23430
Vista Ct 23430
Vivian Dr 23430
Wainwright Dr 23430
Walnut Ridge Ln 23430
Wariner Ln 23430
Washington St 23430
Watch Harbour Cir 23430
Water Oak Dr 23430
Water Pointe Ln 23430
Waterford Xing 23430
Waterview Cir 23430
Waterworks Rd 23430
Watson Dr 23430
Webb Ln 23430
Wellington Cir 23430
Wells King Ln 23430
Wenley Cir 23430
West St 23430
Westminster Reach 23430
Whisper Ln 23430
White House Rd 23430
White Oak Dr 23430
Whitehead Farm Ln 23430
Whites Point Way 23430
Widgeon Ct 23430
Wilderness Ln 23430
Wildwood Cir 23430
Williams St 23430
Williamsburg Ave 23430
Willow Oak Dr 23430
Willow Wood Ave 23430
Wilson Ct & Rd 23430
Wimbledon Ln 23430
Winchester Pl 23430
Windjammer Ct 23430
Windsor Ave 23430
N & S Winterberry Cir, Ct & Ln 23430
Woodcreek Ln 23430
Woody Acres Way 23430
Wrenn Ct & Rd 23430
Wrenns Mill Rd 23430

NUMBERED STREETS

All Street Addresses 23430

SPOTSYLVANIA VA

General Delivery 22553

POST OFFICE BOXES MAIN OFFICE STATIONS AND BRANCHES

Box No.s
All PO Boxes 22553

RURAL ROUTES

02, 05, 08, 10, 14 22551
04, 06, 09, 11 22553

NAMED STREETS

Acorn Ln 22551
Agnes Ln 22553
Aldrich Ct 22553
Allie Cat Way 22553
Alsop Dr 22553
Alsop Way 22551
Alsop Town Rd 22551
Alta Vista Ln 22551
Alva Brooks Ct & Ln 22551
America Ln 22551
Amie Meagan Ln 22553
Andrews Ln 22551
Angle Way 22553
Anna Pine Ln 22551
Anna Woods Ct 22551
Appaloosa Dr 22551
Appomattox Way 22551
Arabian Trl 22551
Arbor Mill Ct 22551
Armand Ct 22553
Arsenal Ct 22551
Asdee Ln 22551
Ashley Ct 22553
Ashy Petral Ct 22553
Aspen Ln 22551
Aspen Highlands Dr 22553
Aster Ct 22551
Atchison Rd 22551
Atwood Ln 22553
Audrey Oakes Dr 22551
Autumn Ln 22553
Autumn Wood Dr 22553
Avocet Way 22553
Babe Boy Schooler Dr 22551
Baileys Rd 22551
Baldy Ewell Way 22551
Balmartin Ct 22553
Bar Harbor Ln 22553
Bareford Ct 22551
Barrister Ct 22553
Battiste Ln 22551
Battle Park Dr 22551
Battle Trace Ln 22553
Battlefield Dr 22553
Battleground Ct 22553
Bayberry Ln 22553
Bayonet Cir 22551
Beagle Ln 22551
Bearlake Dr 22551
Beau Ct 22553
Beaver Ln 22551
Beaver Dam Dr 22551
Beck Creek Ln 22553
Bell Grove Ln 22551
Belmont Rd & Way 22551
Benning Way 22551
Bentwood Ct 22553
Berkshire Ln 22551
Bernly Ct 22553
Berry Ln 22551
Best Way 22551
Beverlys Ford Ct 22551
Big Oaks Ct 22553
Bivouac Ct 22551
Black Meadow Rd 22553
Black Rock Dr 22551
Black Snake Ct 22551
Black Walnut Ln 22551
Blanton Rd 22551
Blaydes Corner Rd 22551
Bleasdell Dr 22551
Block House Rd 22551
Bloomfield Ct 22553
Bloomsbury Ln 22553
Blue Herron Cir 22553
Blue Star Ln 22551
Bluebird Ln 22553
Bluffs Rdg & Vw 22551
Boathouse Pt 22551
Bob White Ln 22553
Boston Ivy Ln 22553
Boulder Ct 22553
Boulevard Of The Generals 22553
Bradford St 22553
Bradley Ct 22553
Bradley Ln 22551
Bran Derose Dr 22551
Branch Bluff Ct 22551
Brandermill Park 22551
Breawick Ct 22553
Breckenridge Dr 22553
Brenda Way 22553
Brentwood Ridge Dr 22553
Bridgewater Ln 22551
Bridle Creek Ln 22551
Bridlerein Ct 22553
Brittany Commons Blvd 22553
Broadfield Ln 22553
Broadmore Ln 22553
Brock Pt 22551
Brock Rd 22553
Brock Woods Ln 22553
Brokenburg Rd 22551
Brooke Ridge Ln 22551
Brookrun Ct 22553
Browns Farm Rd & St 22553
Bruces Ln 22551
Bugle Ct 22551
Buglenote Way 22553
Burnleigh St 22553
Burnside Pl 22553
Cabin View Ln 22551
Cameron Cir 22553
Camp Town Rd 22551
Canonbury Ct 22553
Canvasback Ct 22553
Carneal Ln 22551
S Carolina Ct 22553
Carriage Rd 22551
Catharines Furnace Ct 22553
Catharpin Rd
9600-10699 22551
10700-10704 22553
10706-11999 22553
W Catharpin Rd 22551
Catharpin Landing Rd 22553
Cavalry Ct 22551
Cedar Creek Ct & Dr 22551
Cedar Plantation Rd 22553
Cedar Post Ln 22553
Chance Dr 22551
Chancellor West Blvd 22553
Chancellorsville Dr 22553
Chancery Ct 22553
Chase Ct 22551
Chatham Ridge Way 22551
Cheetah Ln 22553
Cherokee Ln 22553
Cherylington Ln 22551
Chesney Dr 22553
Chester Ct 22553
Chesterwood Dr 22553
Childs Cove Dr 22551
Chivalry Chase Ct & Ln 22551
Cindy Ln 22551
Cinnamon Teal Dr 22553
Clarendon Ct 22553
Clearview Dr 22551
Cloudy Way 22551
Clover Green Dr 22551
Cloverhill Ct & Rd 22551
Clydesdale Ct 22551
Coalsons Ln 22551
Cobble Run 22551
Cobblestone Dr 22553
Colby Ter 22553
Colise Ln 22553
Colonial Ct 22553
Commodore Ct 22551
Commons Cir 22553
Conaty Cir 22553
Cooktown Rd 22553
Cooper St 22551
E & W Copper Mountain Dr 22553
Corbin Ln 22553
Corene Rd 22551
Countryside Ln 22551
Courthouse Rd
4800-8699 22551
8700-10699 22553
Courthouse Commons Blvd 22553
Courtneys Ln 22551
Coventry Ct 22553
Craigs Church Ln 22551
Creeping Willow Ln 22551
Crestfield Ln 22553
Crestwood Dr 22553
Crismond Ln 22551
Cromwell Ct 22551
Crooked Creek Rd 22551
Crooked Tree Ln 22553
Cross Creek Ln 22551
Crown Grant Dr 22553
Crutchfield Cir 22551
Crystal Palace Ln 22553
Cullin Stone Way 22553
Culpeper Ct 22551
Cunningham Ct 22553
Curtis Ln 22551
Custers Trce 22553
Dalton Ln 22551
Dana Ct 22553
Danbury Cir 22551
Dandelion Dr 22551
Daniels Ct 22553
Danielville Dr 22551
Darden Ct 22553
Darkstone Pl 22551
Deer Park Dr 22551
Deer Path Ln 22551
Deer Ridge Way 22551
Deer Run Rd 22551
Deer Track Rd 22551
Dixon Ln 22551
Dock Luck Ln 22551
Dominique Dr 22551
Dorothy Ln 22551
Dover Ct 22553
Dovey Rd 22551
Dowd Farm Rd 22551
Downstream Ct 22551
Driftwood Ln 22553
Dubin Dr 22551
Duck Cir 22553
Eagle Ridge Dr 22551
Eastridge Way 22551
Eden Brook Dr 22553
Edgewood Farm Ln 22551
Edinburgh Dr 22553
Ellen Dr 22551
Ellis Ln 22553
Elmore Lawson Ln 22551
Elnora Brooks Ln 22551
Emma Dr 22551
Emmitts Rd 22551
Engleman Ct & Ln 22551
Everette Ct & Dr 22553
Farmview Way 22551
Faulconers Ct 22551
Fauntleroy Ln 22551
Fawn Lake Pkwy 22551
Feather Edge Ct 22553
Fenton Rd 22551
Field Cir 22551
Finney Rd 22551
Fireside Ln 22551
Fisher Dr 22551
Flank March Ln 22551
Flintlock Dr 22551
Flock Ct 22551
Foremost Farm Ln 22551
Forest Walk Dr 22551
Foster Rd 22553
Fountain Ln 22551
Fox Trl 22551
Fox Chase Ln 22553
Fox Gate Dr 22553
Fox Hole Ln 22551
Fox Hunt Trl 22551
Fox Ridge Rd 22551
Fox Run Dr 22551
Fox Trot Ct 22551
French Acors Rd 22551
Friendship Way 22551
Furnace Rd 22553
Gabriel Ct 22551
Gannett Ln 22553
Gardner Farm Rd 22551
Garners Way 22553
Garrett Bakers Way 22553
Garrison Ln 22551
Gayle Ct & Ln 22553
Gayle Farm Ln 22553
Gen Jenkins Dr 22551
General Dr 22551
General Wadsworth Dr 22551
Georgetown Dr 22553
Geris Ln 22551
Getty Ln 22551
Gibbs Dr 22551
Gibson Ln 22551
Glady Fork Rd 22551
Godwin Dr 22553
Gold Leaf Cir 22553
Goldfinch Cir 22553
Gordon Rd 22553
Grace Hl 22551
Grady Ln 22553
Grand Brooks Rd 22551
Grand Hill Rd 22551
Granite Rd 22553
Granite Springs Rd 22551
Grant Ct 22551
Gravel Dr 22551
Gray Fox Pt 22551
Green Branch Farm Rd 22551
Greenbriar Ln 22553
Greenwood Dr 22553
Grenade Ln 22551
Gristmill Ct 22553
Guard Post Ln 22551
Gumtree Ct 22551
Gunnery Hill Rd 22551
H D Trl 22551
Hadamar Rd 22551
Hairfields Cv 22551
Haleys Mill Rd 22551
Halls Dr 22551
Halsey Ct 22551

Hampton Dr 22551
Hams Ford Rd 22551
Hancock Rd 22553
Happy Hollow Ln 22553
Hard Rock Way 22551
Hardee St 22551
N & S Harris Farm Rd 22553
Harrison Way 22551
Hartley Ln 22551
Harts Run 22551
Harvest Gold Ln 22551
Hathaway Ln 22551
Hawkins Ln 22551
Hayden Rd 22551
Heather Greens Cir & Ct 22553
Heathermore Pl 22553
Heatherwood Dr 22553
Heavenly Way 22551
Heavenwood Ct 22553
Hebron Church Rd 22551
Helena Ter 22553
Henegan Pl 22551
Henkins Ln 22551
Heritage Commons Ln 22551
Heritage Village Ct 22551
Herndon Rd 22553
Heron Pointe Ct & Way 22551
Herricks Ford Rd 22553
Heths Salient St 22553
Hickory Ridge Rd 22551
Hicks Rd 22551
Hidden Cv 22551
Hidden Creek Ln 22551
Hidden Lake Trl 22553
E & W Hildy Ct 22553
Hill Ewell Dr 22551
Hilliard Ct 22553
Hilltop Farm Ln 22553
Hilltop Plaza Way 22553
Hillwood Ct 22553
Hines Ct 22551
Hockaday Hill Ln 22551
Holladay Ln 22551
Holleybrooke Dr 22553
Holmes Ct 22551
Honor Bridge Farm Ct, Dr & Pl 22551
Hook Ct 22551
Hoppe Ln 22551
Horseshoe Dr & Spur 22551
Horton Ln 22551
Houston Ln 22551
Hunter Cove Dr 22551
Hunters Creek Dr 22551
Hunters Lodge Dr 22551
Hunters Pond Dr 22551
S Hunters Trace Way 22551
Hyde Park Dr 22553
In The Woods Way 22551
Infantry Dr 22551
Investors Pl 22553
Irish Ln 22551
Irvine St 22551
Isle Of Laurels 22551
J R Montgomery Ln 22551
Jackson Trl E & W 22553
Jacksons Ford Rd 22551
Jarrell Ln 22551
Jarretts Way 22553
Jeans Dr 22551
Jefferson Davis Hwy 22551
Jennifer Rd 22551
Jennings Ln 22551
Jett Way 22551
Joe Brooks Ln 22551
Joeys Ln 22551
Johnnie Mills Ln 22551
Jones Powell Rd 22551
Journeys End Rd 22551
Judiciary Dr 22553
Kelsey Cir 22553
Kenrow Ln 22551
Kensal Way 22553
Kerrydale Ct 22551
Kershaw Ct 22553
Kidwell Ln 22551
King Eider Ct 22553
Kings Ln 22553
Kings Cove Ct 22553
Kirk Ln 22553
Kirkland Dr 22551
Kirtley Ln 22553
Kleineidam Way 22551
Knightsbridge Ct 22553
Knob Hill Ct 22553
Knolls End 22551
Knotty Pine Cir & Ct 22553
Lacy Mill Rd 22551
W Lake Cir 22553
Lake Anna Ct & Pkwy 22551
Lake Anna Village Dr 22551
Lake Front Way 22551
Lake Haven Way 22551
Lake Wilderness Ln 22551
Lakewood Ln 22551
Landmark Ct 22553
Lando Dr 22551
Landon Ln 22551
Landrum Rd 22553
Landview Ln 22551
Lanes Corner Rd 22551
Langdon Ct 22553
Lanning Rd 22551
Lares Ln 22551
Laurel Hill Farm Dr 22551
Laurel Point Ln 22551
Lawyers Rd 22551
Lazy Acres Ln 22551
Leaf Ln 22553
Lee Dr 22553
Lee Jackson Cir 22553
Lee Lake Dr 22551
Legato Ln 22551
Legion Ct 22553
Liam Ln 22553
Linden Hall Ct 22551
Lismore Ln 22551
Litchfield Dr 22553
Little Bay Harbor Dr & Way 22551
Little Odd Ln 22551
Livingston Ct & Dr 22551
Locklear Landing Dr 22551
Logan Heights Cir 22551
Loggers Ln 22551
Lonesome Pine Rd 22551
Long Acres Ln 22551
Longmont Ct 22553
Longstreet Dr 22553
Longview Ln 22553
Lunar Ct 22553
Lyndhurst Ct 22553
Lyons Ln 22553
Macfaden Dr 22551
Mackay Ct 22553
Macklin Dr 22553
Magnolia Harbour Dr 22551
Maguire Ct 22553
Mahone Ct 22551
Mahone Dr 22553
Mallard Point Ln 22553
Maple Ridge Dr 22553
Marathon Pl 22553
Marble Arch Way 22553
Marble Hills Dr 22551
Marc Dr 22551
Marengo Ct 22553
Margo Rd 22551
Marigold Ln 22551
Marrilley Ct 22551
Marrywood Ct 22551
Marshall Park Ln 22551
Marshall Tract Ct 22551
Marye Rd 22551
Maslock Ln 22551
Massaponax Church Rd 22551
Massey Rd 22551
Mastin Ln 22551
Matta Way 22551
Matta Way Ct 22551
Matthew Maury Ct 22553
Maxie Lee Ct 22551
Maxson Ct 22553
Mccalls Way 22553
Mccracken Ct 22551
Mcgee Ct 22553
Mchenry Ct 22551
Mckinney Ct 22551
Mclaws Dr 22553
Mcleod Ln 22551
Mcmillian Dr 22551
Meade Pt 22551
Meadow Valley Dr 22551
Meadowlark Ln 22553
Meadows Run 22551
Meadowview Rd 22551
Meeting St 22553
Melton Ln 22553
Memorial Rd 22553
Mi Way 22551
Military Ct 22553
Mill Creek Dr 22553
Mill Pond Rd 22551
Millbrook Ln 22551
Miller Ln 22551
Millridge Ln 22553
Millstream Dr 22551
Millwood Ct & Dr 22551
Mockingbird Ln 22553
Monument Ct 22553
Moore Ct 22553
Moorgate Ave 22553
Morgan Ln 22551
Morris Rd 22551
Mortar Ln 22551
Mount Holly Ln 22551
Mountain Laurel Ct 22553
Mountain View Dr 22553
Mueller Ln 22551
Musket Ct 22553
Mustang Ct 22553
Mystic Ln 22551
Natures Trl 22551
Nellies Ln 22551
Nestling Rdg 22551
Newell Ln 22551
Newton Ln 22551
Next To Never Ln 22551
Ni River Dr 22553
Ni South Ln 22553
Northlake Dr 22551
Nottoway Ln 22551
Old Battiste Ln 22553
Old Battlefield Blvd 22553
Old Block House Ct & Ln 22551
Old Brook Rd 22553
Old Carter Rd 22553
Old Courthouse Rd 22551
Old Elm Ct 22551
Old Hickory Ct 22551
Old Mill Ln 22551
Old Robert E Lee Dr 22551
Old Travelers Rd 22551
Old Virginia Dr 22553
Olde Kent Dr 22551
Olde Meadow Way 22551
Olive Ln 22553
Orange Plank Rd
9800-10599 22553
10600-11999 22551
Orange Springs Rd 22551
Orchard Ln 22551
Osprey Trl 22551
Our Pl 22553
Out Back Rd 22551
Paddington Pl 22553
Palmer Ct 22553
Palomino Ct 22551
Pamela Ct 22553
Pamunkey Rd 22551
Panier Rd 22551
Paradise Ct 22551
Partlow Rd 22551
Pathfinders Ct 22553
Pauls Ln 22551
Paxton Dr 22551
Payne Cir 22551
Paynes Ln 22551
Peanut Rd 22551
Pebble Ln E & W 22553
Pelham Dr 22553
Pembroke Cir 22551
Pepperidge Dr 22551
Peppertree Rd 22553
Percy Sacra Ln 22551
Perrin Cir 22551
Perry Ln 22551
Piccadilly Cir 22553
Pickett Ct 22551
Pigeon Trl 22551
Pigeon Cove Ln 22551
Piltzer Ct 22551
Pine Acres Way 22551
Pine Hollow Ln 22551
Pine Ridge Dr 22551
Pineberry Ct 22553
Pinehurst Ln 22551
Piney Branch Rd 22553
Pinnacle Dr 22551
Pintail Pt 22553
Pioneer Ct 22551
Plank Rd 22553
Plantation Dr 22551
Plantation Forest Dr 22553
Platoon Dr 22553
Plentiful Creek Ln 22551
Po River Dr 22551
E & N Point Cir & Dr 22551
Polk Dr 22551
Pond View Ln 22553
Pond Walk Ln 22551
Pool Dr 22551
Post Ln 22551
Post Oak Rd 22551
Powder Keg Ln 22551
Powder Mill Ct 22553
Powderhorn Dr 22553
Prayer Way 22551
Preston Ln 22551
Preswick Ln 22553
Pritchett Rd 22551
Prosperity Dr 22551
Pryor Ln 22553
Purcell Ln 22551
Quail Meadows Dr 22551
Quarter Charge Dr 22551
Quicks Way 22551
Quince Rd 22551
Radcliff Ter 22551
Rainbow Ln 22551
Ramseur Ct 22553
Randolph Brooks Ln 22551
Raven Cir 22553
Ravenscourt Dr 22553
Rebel Rd 22551
Red Faulconer Way 22553
Red Feather Ln 22551
Red Fox Dr 22551
Red Hill Rd 22553
Redbird Ln 22553
Renée Korie Ln 22553
Renfield Ct 22553
Resurrection Way 22551
Richmond Rd 22551
W Ridge Ct 22553
Ridge Rd 22551
Ridge Top Ct 22553
Rising Fawn Ln 22553
River Valley Ln 22551
River Will Rd 22553
Robert E Lee Ct & Dr 22551
Robin Ln 22551
Robin Woods Cir 22551
Robinson Rd 22551
Rock Hill Rd 22551
Rockaway Ct 22553
Rockinghorse Ln 22553
Rolling Ridge Dr 22553
Ronnie Ct 22551
Ronquest Ln 22551
Rope Swing Ct 22551
Rosenhart Cor 22551
Rosewood Ln 22551
Round Hill Rd 22551
N & S Roxbury Mill Ct & Rd 22551
Rumsey Ln 22551
Ryan Ct 22551
Ryland Payne Rd 22551
Sabre Ct 22551
Saddle Ct 22551
Saddlebrooke Dr 22551
Saint Julian Ct 22551
Saint Pauls Ln 22551
Sale Greene Ln 22551
Salient Ln 22551
Salisbury Dr 22553
San Mar Pl 22553
Sanderling Ct 22553
Sandy Hill Ct 22553
Santee Dr 22551
Sawhill Blvd 22553
Sawick Ct 22553
Sawmill Cir 22551
Saxony Cir 22553
Scabbard Ct 22551
Scotts Dale Ln 22551
Scotts Farm Rd 22553
Seay Breeze Ln 22553
Seays Rd 22551
Seven Oaks Ct 22553
Seven Oaks Dr 22553
Seven Oaks Rd 22553
Seymour Ln 22551
N & S Shade Tree Ln 22551
Shadow Ln 22551
Shady Ln 22551
Shady Grove Ct 22551
Shallow Creek Ct 22553
Shannon Meadows Ln 22551
Shaw Dr 22553
Shawnee Ln 22553
Sheridan Dr 22553
Sherrie Ln 22551
Shetland Ct 22551
Shiloh Springs Rd 22551
Shirley Rd 22551
Shot Ct 22553
Sickles Ln 22551
Silas Hicks Dr 22551
Silver Creek Ct 22553
Silverbrook Dr 22553
Simpsons Ln 22551
Singing Wood Ct & Ln 22553
Skyline Ct 22553
Smith Ct 22551
Smith Mill Ct 22551
Smith Station Rd 22553
Smoke Rise Ln 22551
Snow Drift Ln 22551
Snow Hill Dr 22551
Snowy Egret Ct 22553
Solon Dr 22551
Sourwood Ct 22551
South Ct 22551
Southlake Dr 22551
Southridge Ct 22553
Spano Ln 22551
Sparrow Ln 22553
Spotslee Dr 22551
Spotsylvania Baptist Rd 22553
Spring Creek Dr 22553
Springbrook Ter 22553
Springwood Dr 22553
Stafford Ln 22553
Stanfield Rd 22551
Stanley Ct 22553
State Park Ln 22551
Stephen Dr 22551
Stewart Rd 22553
Stockade Dr 22551
Stonebridge Ct 22551
Stonewall Jackson Dr 22551
Stonewood Ct 22551
Stuarts Flank Ct 22553
Stubbs Bridge Rd 22551
Stubbs Cove Ln 22551
Sullivan Rd 22551
Sumner Glen Dr 22551
Sun Ray Ln 22553
Sunlight Mountain Rd 22553
Sunnybrooke Farm Rd 22551
Sunset Rd 22551
T J Wright Ln 22551
T Pat Rd 22551
Ta River Dr 22551
Tall Oaks Dr 22551
Talley Rd 22553
Talley Farm Ln 22553
Tanglewood Rd 22551
Tapp Pt 22551
Tarrington Way 22551
Taverneer Ln 22551
Taylor Ln 22551
Taylor Ridge Way 22551
Teal Ct 22553
Telluride Ln 22553
Terembes Ln 22553
Thiel Ct 22551
Thompson Ln 22551
Thoriang St 22553
Timber Trl 22551
Timberbrook Ln 22551
Todds Tavern Dr 22551
Toll House Rd 22551
Toney Ln 22553
Towles Mill Rd 22551
Tracy Ln 22553
Tranquility Ct 22551
Trapp Dr 22551
Travellers Rest Rd 22551
Treaty Ct 22553
Tree Haven Ln 22551
Treemont Ln 22553
Trideli Rd 22551
Tupelo Dr 22551
Turning Leaf Ct & Ln 22551
Twilight Ln 22551
Twin Ln 22551
Twin Oaks Dr 22551
Tyler Ln 22551
U S Grant Ct 22553
Valley Po Rd 22551
Valor Bridge Ct & Dr 22551
Vanderbilt Cv 22551
Vanreenan Way 22551
Verrey Ct 22551
Vintage Ln 22551
Virginia Cir 22551
Volunteer Ln 22551
Wadsworth Ln 22551
Walnut Farm Ln 22551
Ware Rd 22551
Warren Ln 22551
Warwick Plantation Ln 22551
Waterford Dr 22551
Watermill Ct 22551
Waterstone Pl 22551
Waucoma Trl 22551
Westfield Ln 22553
Westgate Way 22551
Westmont Dr 22551
Wheeler Rd 22551
Whiperwhill Ct 22553
White Rock Trl 22551
Whitehall Blvd 22553
Whites Ln 22551
Wild Flower Ln 22551
Wild Turkey Dr 22553
Wildbrooke Ct 22551
Wilderness Ct 22551
Wilderness Park Dr 22551
Wildwood Knoll Farm Ln 22551
Wilkshire Way 22553
Williams Ln 22551
Willies Ln 22551
Willoughby Dr 22551
Willow Creek Ct 22553
Willow Ridge Ln & Way 22553
Windfield Oaks Dr 22553
Windtree Ct & Dr 22553
Windy Oaks Ln 22551
Winston Ln 22551
Winter Park Ln 22553
Wise Ct 22553
Wood Ibis Ct 22553
Woodcock Ln 22553
Woodcrest Way 22551
Woodfield Dr 22553
Woodlake Ct 22553
Woodward Dr 22553
Woolfolk Rd 22551
Wyndham Hill Ln 22551
Yakama Trl 22551
Young Ln 22553

SPRINGFIELD VA

General Delivery 22150

POST OFFICE BOXES MAIN OFFICE STATIONS AND BRANCHES

Box No.s
1 - 875 22150
1001 - 1960 22151
2001 - 2954 22152
5000 - 6694 22150
8003 - 8265 22151
57000 - 57000 22150
523001 - 524364 22152

NAMED STREETS

Abilene St 22150
Accomac St 22150
Accotink Park Rd 22150
Adair Ln 22151
Adrienne Glen Ave 22152
Ainsworth Ave 22152
Alamo St 22150
Alarandi Dr 22152
Alban Rd
7900-8499 22150
8500-8599 22153
Alban Station Blvd & Ct 22150
Alberta Ct & St 22152
Aldrich Ln 22151
Alexis Ct & Ln 22152
Alloway Ct 22152
Alma Ln 22151
Alvarado Ct 22153
Ambrose Ct 22153
Amelia St 22150
Amherst Ave 22150
Anders Ter 22151
Andrew Matthew Ter 22150
Angus Ct 22153
Anola Ct 22151
Anson Ct 22152
Antelope Pl 22153
Antrican Dr 22150
Apache St 22150
Applecross Ln 22153
Aquary Ct 22153
Arley Dr
8600-8699 22152
8700-9099 22153
Arley Pl 22153
Armendown Dr 22152
Arundel Pl 22153
Ash Dr 22150
Ashbury Dr 22152
Ashford Ct 22152
Ashlawn Ct 22150
Ashley Pl 22150
Ashtonbirch Dr 22152
Ashview Dr 22153
Asterella Ct 22152

Astongale Ct 22152
Athena St 22153
Atlee Pl 22151
Atteentee Rd 22150
Attleboro Dr 22153
Augusta Dr 22150
Ava St 22152
Avon Ct 22151
Axton St 22151
Ayers Meadow Ln 22150
Backlash Ct 22153
Backlick Ct 22151
Backlick Rd
5411C1-5411C1 22151
5415B2-5415B2 22151
6651AA-6651AA 22150
5200-5729 22151
5730-7999 22150
Backlick Woods Ct 22151
Ballston Ct & Dr 22153
Ballyshannon Ct 22153
Barb Anne Ct 22152
Barcarole Ct 22153
Bardu Ave & Ct 22152
Bark Tree Ct 22153
Barkers Ct 22153
Barnack Dr 22152
Barrington Ct 22152
Bath St 22150
Bauer Cir & Dr 22152
Bayshire Rd 22152
Beachway Ct & Ln 22153
Bear Ct 22153
Beatrice Ct 22152
Bedstraw Ct 22152
Beech Hollow Ln 22153
Beech Monarch Ct 22153
Beechwood Dr 22153
Belfast Ln 22150
Belfast Pl 22151
Belinger Ct 22150
Bellamy Ave 22152
Belleflower Dr 22152
Bellington Ave & Ct 22151
Ben Franklin Rd 22150
Bent Arrow Ct 22153
Bentley Village Dr 22152
Berry Hill Ct 22153
Bertito Ln 22153
Bethelen Woods Ln 22153
Bethnal Ct 22150
Beverly Ln 22150
Beverly Park Dr 22150
Bienville Ct 22152
Birchtree Ct 22152
Bird Dog Ct 22153
Birmingham Ln 22152
Bison St 22150
Blackford St 22151
Blacksburg Rd 22151
Blairton Rd 22152
Bland St 22150
Blarney Stone Ct & Dr 22152
Bloomington Ct 22150
Blue Jasmine Ct 22153
Blue Oak Ct 22153
Bluecurl Cir 22152
Bluefield Ct 22152
Bona Vista Ct 22150
Bonniemill Ln 22150
Boston Blvd 22153
Bostwick Dr 22151
Botsford Ct 22152
Boudinot Dr 22150
Boulder St 22151
Bowie Dr 22150
Boyd Ct 22152
Bracken Ct 22152
Braddock Rd 22151
Braddock Mews Pl 22151
Bradgen Ct 22151
Bradwood Ct & St 22151
Braemar Way 22153
Brainerd Ct 22153
Brandeis Way 22153
Brandon Ave 22150
Brentford Dr 22152
Brian Michael Ct 22153
Brian Run Ct & Ln 22153
Briarcliff Dr
7100-7199 22152
7200-7399 22153
Bridge Creek Ct 22152
Bridgeport Ct 22153
Bridgeton Ct 22152
Bridle Wood Dr 22152
Brisbane St 22152
Bristlecone Pl 22153
Bristol Square Ct 22153
Brixton St 22152
Brocton Ct 22150
Brompton St 22152
Brookfield Plz 22150
Brookvale Ct 22153
Brunswick St 22150
Brutus Ct 22153
Bubbling Brook Cir 22153
Buckskin St 22150
Bullock Ln 22151
Burke Lake Rd 22151
Burling Wood Dr 22152
Burlington Pl 22152
Burning Forest Ct 22153
Burton Hill Ct 22152
Burwell St 22150
Byeforde Ct 22150
Byron Ave 22150
Cabell Ct 22150
Cabin John Rd 22150
Cabot Ct 22152
Calamo St 22150
Calico Ct 22153
Callander Dr 22151
Calvin Ct 22151
Camberly Ave 22150
Cambridge Dr 22152
Cameo Sq 22152
Cameron Brown Ct 22153
Camilla St 22152
Camp David Dr 22153
Camrose Pl 22151
Camus Pl 22152
Candytuft Ct 22153
Caneel Ct 22152
Canima Spring Ct 22152
Cantering Pl 22153
Canyon Oak Dr 22153
Carath Ct 22153
Carawood Ct 22150
Carbondale Way 22153
Cardinal Brook Ct 22152
Cardinal Hill Pl 22152
Carla Ct 22153
Carmela Cir 22153
Carnation Ct 22152
Carolina Pl 22151
Carr Pl 22152
Carriage Hill Rd 22152
Carrick Ln 22151
Carrleigh Pkwy 22152
Carrsbrook Ct 22150
Carters Grove Ct 22153
Castine Ln 22150
Castle Hill Rd 22153
Castlefield Way 22150
Cather Rd 22151
Catia Ln 22153
Catlett St 22151
Caton Woods Ct 22150
Cedar Falls Ct 22153
Center Rd 22152
Cervantes Ct & Ln 22153
Chancellor Way 22153
Chaney Ct 22152
Channing Rd 22150
Chapman Oak Ct 22153
Charles Goff Dr 22150
Charlotte St 22150
Charlottesville Rd 22151
Charnwood St 22152
Chars Ln 22153
Chars Landing Ct 22153
Chatham St 22151
Cherry Heights Ct 22153
Cherry Orchard Ct 22153
Chester Grove Ct 22153
Chillum Ct 22153
Cimarron St 22150
Cissna Rd 22153
Clarkson Dr 22150
Clearbrook Dr 22150
Clelia Ct 22152
Cliff Rock Ct 22153
Clifforest Dr 22153
Cliffside Ct 22153
Cliffview Ave 22153
Clifton St 22151
Clive Pl 22151
Cloud Ct 22153
Cloud Dr 22150
Clowser Ct 22150
Cluny Ct 22153
Clydesdale Rd 22151
Coachman Dr 22152
Cold Plain Ct & Ln 22153
Colony Point Rd 22152
Colorado Springs Dr 22153
Columbia Rd 22151
Comet Cir 22150
Commack Ct 22152
Commerce St 22150
Commercial Dr 22151
Conservation Dr &
Way 22153
Constance Dr 22150
Constantine Ave 22150
Conway Ct 22150
Copperfield Ct 22151
Cork County Ct 22152
Cork Glen Way 22153
Corporate Ct 22153
Cory Pl 22150
Cosgrove Pl 22151
Cottontail Ct 22153
Countrywood Ct 22151
Covington Woods Ct 22153
Craig St 22150
Creedmor Dr 22153
Creek Crest Way 22150
Creekside Way 22153
Creekside View Ln 22153
Creekview Dr 22153
Crestmont Cir 22153
Crockett Pl 22150
Cromwell Dr 22151
Crozet Ct 22150
Crystal Creek Ct 22153
Cumberland Ave 22150
Cumbertree Ct 22153
Curving Creek Ct 22153
Cushing Ct 22153
Custer St 22150
Cuttermill Pl 22153
Cutting Horse Ct 22153
Cyril Pl 22153
Dabney Ave & Ct 22152
Daffodil Ct 22152
Dakine Cir 22150
Dalhouse St 22151
Dalton Rd 22151
Dampier Ct 22153
Dana Ave 22150
Danbury Rd 22150
Danbury Forest Dr 22151
Danford Ct, Ln & Pl 22152
Dante Ct 22152
Danville St 22151
Darby Ln 22150
Dark Den Cir 22153
Darlington St 22152
Daum Ct 22153
Davis Field Ln 22153
Dawley Ct 22152
Dayspring Ct 22153
De Arment Ct 22153
Deansgate Ct 22150
Deavers Run Ct 22152
Deborann Ct 22152
Debra Lu Way 22150
Deep Valley Ct 22153
Deepford St 22150
Deer Ridge Trl 22150
Deer Ridge Trail Ct 22150
Deercreek Pl 22153
Deerlee Dr 22153
Deland Ct & Dr 22152
Delong Dr 22153
Delozier Ct 22153
Demme Pl 22150
Denison Pl 22151
Denton Ct 22152
Derby Ct 22151
Devers St 22150
Dianne Pl 22152
Dickenson St 22150
Dina Leigh Ct 22153
Dinwiddie St 22150
Diving Cliff Ln 22153
Doane Ave & Ct 22152
Dominican Dr 22152
Doncaster Ct & St 22150
Donegal Ln 22153
Donna Dean Dr 22153
Donnelly Ct 22151
Donset Dr 22152
Dorchester St 22150
Dormont St 22150
Dorothy Ct & Ln 22153
Double Creek Ct 22153
Drayton Ln 22151
Dreyfuss St 22151
Dryburgh Ct 22152
Dublin Ave 22151
Duck Ct 22152
Dudrow Ct 22150
Dulciana Ct 22153
Dunham Ct 22152
Dunn Ct 22150
Dunston St 22151
Duntley Ct & Pl 22152
Durer Ct 22153
Durham Ct 22151
Dyer Ct 22150
Dynatech Ct 22153
Eagle Rock Ln 22153
Earlehurst St 22151
Earthstar Ct 22152
Eastbourne Dr 22151
Eastleigh Ct 22152
Easton Dr 22151
Edgebrook Dr 22150
Edgerton Ln 22150
Edinburgh Dr 22153
Edmonton Ct 22152
Edsall Rd 22151
Eggar Woods Ln 22153
Eighteenth Century Ct 22150
Elder Ave 22150
Electronic Dr 22151
Elgar St 22151
Elk Dr 22153
Elkton Dr 22152
Ellet Rd 22151
Ellwood Pl 22150
Emporia Ct 22152
English Ivy Ct & Way 22152
Erska Woods Ct 22153
Erving St 22150
Essex Ave 22150
Essex Ct 22152
Estaban Pl 22151
Etta Dr 22152
Eucalyptus Ct 22153
Euclid Way 22153
Evangel Dr 22153
Evanston Rd 22150
Everett Ct 22152
Exmore St 22150
Fairburn Dr 22152
Falling Leaf Rd 22153
Falmouth St 22150
Fargo St 22150
Farley St 22152
Farnum St 22151
Felecity Ct 22153
Fenwood Dr 22152
Ferber Pl 22151
Fern Leaf Ct 22153
Ferncliff Ct 22153
Ferndale St 22151
Fernholly Ct 22150
Fernleigh Blvd 22152
Field Master Dr
6500-6599 22152
6800-6899 22153
Filbert Ct 22152
Finlay Ct 22153
Fishermans Ln 22153
Fisteris Ct 22152
Flag Run Dr 22151
Flanders St 22150
Flax St 22152
Flemingwood Ln 22153
Flint St 22153
Flora St 22150
Floridon Ct 22150
Flower Tuft Ct 22153
Floyd Ave 22150
Fontana Pl 22151
Foote Ln 22151
Forbes Pl 22151
Forest Breeze Ct 22152
Forest Creek Ct & Ln 22152
Forest Dew Ct 22152
Forest Hunt Ct 22153
Forest Lawn Ct 22152
Forest Path Way 22153
Forest View Dr 22150
Forman Ct 22151
Forrest Hollow Ln 22152
Forrester Blvd 22152
Forsythia St 22150
Fountain Spring Ct 22150
Fox Grape Ln 22152
Fox Hill St 22150
Fox Ridge Rd 22152
Foxe Pl 22151
Franconia Ct & Rd 22150
Frederick St 22150
Fremont St 22151
Freshaire Dr 22153
Front Royal Rd 22151
Frontier Dr 22150
Fullerton Ct 22153
Fullerton Rd
7659A-7659C 22153
7719K1-7719K2 22153
7644L2-7644L2 22153
7721A1-7721A1 22153
7721A2-7721B2 22153
7647A-7647E 22153
7649C-7649G 22153
7653A-7653F 22153
7655E-7655G 22153
7666I1-7666I3 22153
7721A-7721C 22153
7100-7299 22150
7400-7799 22153
Gainesville Rd 22151
Galax Ct 22151
Galbreth Ct 22153
Galgate Dr
7000-7199 22152
7200-7299 22153
Galla Knoll Cir 22153
Gambel Oak Dr 22153
Gambrill Ct, Ln & Rd 22153
Gambrill Woods Way 22153
Game Lord Dr 22153
Gamid Dr 22153
Garden Rd 22152
Gardner Pl 22151
Garfield Ct 22152
Garner St 22151
Gary St 22150
Gateside Pl 22150
Gavelwood Ct 22153
Gentian Ct 22152
Geoint Dr 22150
Getty Ct 22153
Gilbert St 22150
Giles Pl 22150
Giles St 22153
Gillings Rd 22152
Gilpin Dr 22151
Giltinan Ct 22153
Gist Ct 22153
Glen Oaks Ct 22152
Glenallen St 22151
Glendower Ct 22153
Glenister Dr 22152
Glenville Ct 22153
Gloucester Ave 22150
Glover Ct 22152
Godolphin Dr 22153
Goins St 22153
Gold Sky Ct 22153
Golden Aspen Ct 22153
Golden Ball Tavern Ct 22153
Golden Horseshoe Ct 22153
Golden Iris Ct 22153
Golden Leaf Ct 22153
Golden Sunset Ln 22153
Gopost
212-212 22150
Gopost
5001-5023 22150
5212-5212 22152
Gormel Dr 22150
Gormley Pl 22152
Gosport Ln 22151
Grace St 22150
Grainger Ct 22153
Gralnick Pl 22153
Granberry Way 22151
Grandstaff Ct 22153
Grandview Ct 22153
Grantham St 22151
Grass Valley Ct 22153
Grayson St 22150
Great Lake Ln 22153
Greeley Blvd & Ct 22152
Green Ash Ct & Dr 22152
Green Garland Dr 22153
Green Hollow Ct 22152
Greenlawn Ct 22152
Greenleaf St 22150
Greenview Ln 22152
Greenville Pl 22150
Gregory Ct 22152
Grenoble Ct 22152
Gresham St 22151
Grey Fox Dr 22152
Griffin Pond Ct 22153
Grigsby Dr 22152
Gromwell Ct 22152
Groveland Dr & Sq 22153
Groveland Heights Ct 22153
Gutman Ct 22153
Guy Pl 22151
Gwynedd Way 22153
Hackberry St 22150
Hadlow Ct & Dr 22152
Halifax Pl 22150
Hall St 22152
Halleck Pl 22151
Hallmark Pl 22150
Hamlet St 22151
Hamor Ln 22153
Hampton Creek Way 22150
Hampton Manor Pl 22150
Hanks Pl 22153
Hanover Ave 22150
Hansford Ct 22151
Harland Dr 22152
Harmon Pl 22152
Harness Horse Ct 22153
Harrow Way 22151
Harrowgate Cir 22152
Harwood Ct & Pl 22152
Hastings St 22150
Hathaway St 22152
Hatteras Ln 22151
Haute Ct 22150
Havelock St 22150
Havenbrook Way 22153
Haverhill Ct 22152
Hayload Ct 22153
Healy Dr 22150
Heather Point Dr 22152
Hechinger Dr 22151
Heller Loop & Rd 22150
Heming Ave, Ct & Pl 22151
Hempstead Way 22151
Heston Ct 22151
Hibbling Ave 22150
Hickory Glen Way 22153
Hickory Ridge Ct 22153
Hidden Bridge Dr 22153
Hidden Knolls Ct 22153
Hidden Ridge Ct 22152
Hidden Woods Ct 22152
Highgrove Park Ct 22150
Highland St 22150
Hill Stream Ct 22153
Hillmead Ct 22150
Hillside Rd 22152
Hillside Manor Dr 22152
Hilltopper Ct 22153
Hinton St 22151
Hofstra Ct 22152
Hogarth St 22151
Holford Ln 22152
Hollow Hill Ln 22152
Hollow Knoll Ct 22152
Homestead Pl 22151
Hooes Rd
7000-7648 22150
7649-8399 22152
8400-8851 22153
Hopewell Ave 22151
Hopkins Ct 22153
Hornbuckle Dr 22153
Houndmaster Rd 22152
Howe Pl 22150
Hubbardton Way 22150
Hudson Falls Way 22153
Hundsford Ln 22153
Hunt Square Ct 22153
Hunters Oak Ct 22150
Huntsman Blvd
6600-6899 22152
6900-7899 22153
Husky Ln 22151
Huxley Ct 22153
Independence Ave 22151
Industrial Dr & Rd 22151
Ingle Pl 22151
Inishmore Ct 22153
Innisfree Dr 22153
Inverchapel Rd 22151
Inverness Dr 22150
Inwood Dr 22150
Inzer St 22151
Irene Ct 22153
Iron Pl 22151
Iron Stove Ct 22150
Itte Ln 22150
Ives Pl 22151
Ivor St 22151
Ivy Mint Ct 22153
Ivybridge Ct 22152
Jackie Deneese Ct 22152
James Creek Dr 22152
Janphil Ln 22153
Jansen Ct & Dr 22152
Japonica St 22150
Jenna Ct & Rd 22153
Jenner Ct 22153
Jennings Ln 22150
Jenny Dee Pl 22152
Jerome St 22150
Jervis St 22151
Jewelweed Ct 22152
Jillspring Ct 22152
Jiri Woods Ct 22153
Joffa Pl 22150
John Ryland Way 22150
Joplin St 22151
Joshua Tree Ln 22152
Journey Ln 22153
Jovin Cir 22153

Joyce Phillip Ct 22153
Julian Pl & St 22150
Juliet St 22151
Junction Blvd 22150
June St 22150
Juxon Pl 22151
Kalmia St 22150
Katherine Ann Ln 22150
Kathleen Pl 22151
Kedron St 22150
Keene Dr 22152
Kelvin Pl 22151
Kempsville St 22151
Kempton Dr 22151
Kenilworth Dr 22151
Kenmont Pl 22152
Kenova Ln 22153
Kensal Ct 22152
Kentford Dr 22152
Kentland St 22150
Kenwood Ave 22152
Kepler Ln 22151
Kerkam Ct 22152
Kerr Dr 22150
Kerry Ln 22152
Kerrydale Ct & Dr 22152
Kesley Ct 22153
Kevin Ct 22151
Kilworth Ln 22151
Kings Charter Ln 22152
Kings Park Dr 22151
Kings Point Ct 22153
Kings Ridge Ct 22153
Kingsford Rd 22152
Kingsgate Rd 22152
Kingsview Ct 22152
Kingsway Ct 22152
Kinsdale Ct 22150
Kipling St 22151
Kirkham Ct 22151
Kitchener Dr 22153
Kite Flyer Ct 22150
Kittiwake Ct 22153
Kousa Ln 22152
Kroy Ct & Dr 22150
Kyles Lndg 22150
Lackawanna Dr 22150
Lady Lewis Ct 22153
Lake Pleasant Dr 22153
Lakeland Valley Ct & Dr 22153
Lakinhurst Ln 22152
Lamar Dr 22150
Lamese Ct 22152
Lamont Ct 22152
Lancashire Dr 22151
Landgrave Ln 22151
Landor Ln 22152
Langbrook Rd 22152
Langport Dr 22152
Langsford Ct 22153
Larrick Ct 22153
Larrlyn Dr 22151
Laural Valley Way 22153
Lauralin Pl 22150
Laurel Creek Ct & Ln 22150
Laurel Oak Ct & Dr 22153
Lauren Dr 22153
Lavant Dr 22152
Lavell Ct 22152
Lavender Ln 22150
Law Ct 22152
Layton Dr 22150
Lazy Creek Ct 22153
Lee Brooke Pl 22152
Lee Valley Dr 22150
Leebrad St 22151
Leestone Ct & St 22151
Leesville Blvd 22151
Leewood Forest Dr 22151
Lehigh Ln 22151
Lemoyne Ln 22153
Levi Ct 22150
Lexton Pl 22152
Leyton Pl 22152
Light St 22151

Lignum St 22150
Limerick Ct 22152
Linden Tree Ln 22152
Lindside Pl & Way 22153
Little Ann Ct 22152
Littleford St 22151
Lobelia Ln 22152
Log Cabin Ct 22153
Lois Dr 22150
Loisdale Ct & Rd 22150
London Ct 22151
Long Pine Dr 22151
Lonsdale Dr 22151
Lorcom Ct 22152
Loretto St 22150
Loudoun Ln 22152
Loughboro Ln 22150
Louis Edmund Ct 22152
Lovejoy Ct 22152
Loving Forest Ct 22153
Lovingston Cir 22150
Lowmoor Ct & Rd 22153
Luce Ct 22153
Lureta Ann Ln 22150
Lyles Rd 22150
Lynbrook Dr 22150
Lynn Susan Ct 22152
Macswain Pl 22153
Madley Ct 22152
Magic Leaf Rd 22153
Magic Tree Ct 22153
Mallow Ct 22152
Manley Pl 22152
Maple Glen Ct 22153
Maple Ridge Ave 22153
Maple Tree Ln 22153
Mapleleaf Ct 22153
Marconi Ct 22153
Marcy Ave 22152
Margate St 22151
Maritime Ct & Ln 22153
Marsh Ct 22153
Martel Pl 22152
Marysia Ct 22153
Matisse Way 22153
Matthew Pl 22151
Mayo Ct 22150
Mazzello Pl 22153
Mcweadon Ln 22150
Meadowforest Ct 22151
Meadwood Forest Ct 22151
Melia St 22150
Mendota Pl 22150
Meriwether Ln 22150
Merryvale Ct 22152
Meteor Pl 22150
Metropolitan Center Dr 22150
Michael Robert Dr 22150
Middle Run Dr 22153
Middle Valley Ct & Dr 22153
Middleford Dr 22153
Middlesex Ave 22150
Middlewood Pl 22153
Miles Ct 22151
Milford Ct 22152
Milland St 22151
Millbury Dr 22152
Millwood Cir, Ct, Dr & Pl 22152
Milva Ln 22150
Mineola Ct 22152
Mineral Spring Ct 22153
Ming Tree Ct 22152
Minutemen Rd 22153
Misty Blue Ct 22153
Mitcham Ct 22151
Modisto Ln 22153
Moline Pl 22153
Monroe Dr 22151
Montgomery St 22151
Monticello Blvd 22150
Moose Ct 22153
Morning Dew Ct 22153
Morning Star Ct 22153
Morrissette Dr 22152
Moultrie Rd 22151

Mountain Ash Ct & Dr 22153
Moverly Ct 22152
Mulberry Bottom Ct & Ln 22153
Mullingar Ct 22153
Mulvaney Ct 22152
Murillo St 22151
Nancemond St 22150
Nanlee Dr 22152
Narcissus Ct 22152
Nassau Dr 22152
Neuman St 22150
New Hope Dr 22151
New London Dr 22153
Newby Ct 22152
Newell Ct 22153
Newington Forest Ave & Ct 22153
Newington Woods Dr 22153
Newport Ct 22153
Noblestown Rd 22152
Northanna Dr 22150
Northedge Ct & Dr 22153
Northern Oaks Ct 22153
Northumberland Rd 22153
Norview Ct 22152
Nottoway Pl 22150
Nutting Dr 22151
Oak Field Ct 22153
Oakford Dr 22152
Octavia Ct 22153
Odell Ct & St 22153
Ohara Ct 22152
Ohara Pl 22153
Okeith Ct 22152
Old Keene Mill Ct 22152
Old Keene Mill Rd
6900-7599 22150
7600-9199 22152
Old Oaks Ct & Dr 22152
Old Scotts Ct 22152
Old Tree Ct 22153
Oldcastle Ln 22151
Olde Lantern Way 22152
Oldham Leeds Way 22150
Omega Ct 22152
Ontario St 22152
Orange Plank Rd 22153
Oriole Ave 22150
Orono Ct 22152
Oshad Ln 22153
Over See Ct 22152
Overton Ct 22153
Paige Glen Ave 22152
Painted Daisy Dr 22152
Palamino St 22150
Paloma Ct & Ln 22153
Panola Ct 22151
Park Forest Dr 22152
Park Hunt Ct 22153
Park View Ct 22152
Parkdale Ct 22153
Parklane Ct 22153
Parkway Pl 22151
Parliament Dr 22151
Parthian Ct 22153
Peaceful Ct 22151
Pebble Brook Ct 22153
Penley Pl 22151
Penn Manor Ct 22153
Penshurst Dr 22152
Peoria Ct 22153
Perth Ct 22151
Petunia St 22152
Phillip Ct 22152
Piccadilly Pl 22151
Pillow Ln 22151
Pin Oak Dr 22153
Pinto Pl 22150
Pioneer Dr 22150
Plandome Ct 22153
Pohick Rd 22153
Pohick Creek Vw 22153
Pohick Forest Ct 22153
Pohick Ridge Ct 22153
Pohick Stream Pl 22153

W Point Dr 22153
Port Royal Rd 22151
Portree Ct 22152
Powder Horn Rd 22152
Powderbrook Ln 22153
Prince George Dr 22152
Prince James Dr 22152
Princoma St 22151
Pyracantha Ct 22153
Quebec Ct 22152
Queensberry Ave 22151
Queenston St 22152
Quicksilver Ct 22150
Quincy Hall Ct 22153
Racetec Ct & Pl 22150
Rainbow Bridge Ln 22153
Raindrop Way 22153
Ramsey Ct 22151
Raspberry Plain Pl 22153
Rathbone Pl 22151
Rathlin Dr 22152
Ravenel Ct & Ln 22151
Ravensworth Rd 22151
Readington Ct 22152
Red Ash Ct 22153
Red Fox Estates Ct 22152
Red Hill Dr 22153
Red Horse Tavern Ln 22153
Red Jacket Rd 22152
Red Lion Tavern Ct 22153
Red Tulip Ct 22153
Redbridge Ct 22153
Redman St 22153
Regal Oak Ct & Dr 22152
Renshaw Ct 22153
Research Way 22153
Reseca Ln 22152
Reservation Dr 22153
Reservoir Rd 22150
Retriever Rd 22153
Revenna Ln 22153
Rexford Ct & Dr 22152
Reynard Dr 22152
Reza Ct 22152
Rhodell Ln 22153
Rhoden Ct 22153
Riata Ct 22153
Richfield Ct & Rd 22153
Ridge Rd 22153
Ridge Creek Way 22153
Ridge Crossing Ln 22152
Ridge Hollow Ct 22152
Ridge Oak Ct 22153
Ridgebrook Dr 22153
Ridgepark Ct 22153
Ridgeway Dr 22150
Ringold Pl 22151
Rippled Creek Ct 22153
Rising Creek Ct 22153
Rivanna Dr 22150
Rivermont Ct 22153
Rives Ct 22150
Rivington Rd 22152
Robin Rd 22150
Rochambeau Pl 22153
Rock Island Rd 22150
Rockdale Ln 22153
Rockefeller Ln 22153
E & W Rockglen Ct & Dr 22152
Rockledge Ct 22152
Rockwood Ct 22153
Rocky Forge Ct 22153
Rolling Rd
5201-5699 22151
5800-7299 22152
7300-8399 22153
Rolling Forest Ave 22152
Rolling Knoll Ct 22153
Rolling Mill Pl 22152
Rolling Oak Ln 22153
Rolling Spring Ct 22152
Rolling View Ln 22153
Rolling Woods Ct 22152
Rookings Ct 22153
Rose Garden Ct & Ln 22153

Rosewall Ct 22152
Roso St 22150
Rothery Ct 22153
Rotunda Ct 22150
Roundabout Way 22153
Roxbury Ave 22152
Royal Azalea Ct 22153
Royal Ridge Dr 22152
S Run Vw 22153
Running Creek Ct 22153
Rural Plains Pl 22153
Rushing Creek Ct & Dr 22153
Ruskin St 22150
Ruxton Dr 22153
Saddlemount Ct 22153
Sagebrush Pl 22150
Saint David Ct 22153
Saint Dennis Dr 22153
Saint George Ct 22153
Salisbury Ct 22151
Samos Ct 22153
Sampal Pl 22153
Sandover Ct 22152
Saratoga Ridge Ct 22153
Scarborough St 22153
Scott Ct & St 22153
Seabright Rd 22152
Seabrook Ln 22153
Seacraft Ct 22153
Seatrend Way 22150
Sedgwick Ln 22151
Selger Dr 22153
Selwood Pl 22152
Serenade Pl 22150
Seton Ct 22152
Setter Pl 22153
Shadeway Pl 22153
Shadowcreek Ter 22153
Shadowlake Way 22153
Shady Palm Dr 22153
Shamrock Ct 22152
Shannon Station Ct 22152
Shaundale Dr 22152
Shepherd Ridge Ct 22153
Sherborn Ln 22152
Sherbrooke Ct 22152
Sheridan Farms Ct 22152
Ships Curve Ln 22153
Shootingstar Dr 22152
Shotgun Ct 22153
Side Saddle Rd 22152
Silver Oak Ct 22153
Silver Pine Dr 22153
Silver Sage Ct 22153
Simmer Cir 22150
Skibbereen Pl 22153
Skyles Way 22151
Skyron Pl 22153
Sleepy Brook Ct 22153
Sleepy View Ln 22153
Slidell Ln 22151
Smithfield Ave 22152
Smyth St 22152
Snowden Ct 22150
Solomon Seal Ct & Dr 22152
Sontag Way 22153
Southampton Dr 22151
Southern Dr 22150
Southern Oak Dr 22153
Southrun Rd 22153
Southstream Run 22153
Southwater Ct 22153
Spaniel Rd 22153
Spelman Dr 22153
Spring Rd 22150
Spring Beauty Ct 22152
Spring Creek Ct 22153
Spring Forest Ct 22152
Spring Garden Dr 22153
Spring Mall Rd 22150
Spring Summit Rd 22150
Spring Tree Dr 22153
Spring View Ct 22153
Spring Village Dr 22150

Springfield Blvd, Mall & Plz 22150
Springfield Center Dr 22150
Springfield Hills Dr 22153
Springfield Oaks Dr 22153
Springfield Village Ct & Dr 22152
Springville Ct 22150
Sprouse Ct 22153
Spur Rd
6800-6899 22152
6900-8999 22153
Squirrel Run Ct & Rd 22152
Stagecoach St 22150
Stagg Ct 22150
Steel Mill Dr 22150
Steeple Chase Ct 22153
Sterling Grove Dr 22150
Steven Irving Ct 22153
Stone Hill Pl 22153
Stoneygate Ct 22152
Strand Ct 22151
Strause Ct 22153
Stream Way 22152
Stream Bluff Way 22153
Stringer Ct 22150
Sue Paige Ct 22152
Sugar Creek Ln 22153
Summer Breeze Ln 22153
Summer Grape Ct 22152
Summerton Ct & Way 22150
Sumpter Ln 22150
Sunset Ter 22153
Sunset Path Ct 22153
Suntralt St 22150
Supreme Ct 22150
Surrey Hill Pl 22152
Surveyors Pl 22152
Sweet Birch Ct 22152
Sweet Dale Ct 22152
Sweet Gum Pl 22153
Sweet Maple Ct 22152
Sweet Oak Ct 22152
Sweet Pine Ct 22153
Sweet Spice Ct 22152
Swope Ln 22153
Sydenstricker Rd 22152
Tailcoat Ct 22153
Talford Ct 22152
Tall Trees Ct & Ln 22152
Tanager St 22150
Tangier Dr 22153
Tanglewood Ct 22152
Tanner Robert Ct 22153
Tanworth Ct & Dr 22152
Tara Heights Pl 22153
Taunton Pl 22152
Teddy Rae Ct 22152
Tender Ct 22151
Terra Grande Ave 22153
Terra Woods Dr 22153
Terry Dr 22150
Terry Lynn Ct 22152
Thames St 22151
Thomas Dr 22150
Thorncliff Ln 22153
Thornhill Ct 22150
Tiburon Ct 22152
Tiffany Park Ct 22152
Timber Brook Ln 22153
Timber Hollow Ln 22152
Tiros Dr 22151
Tiverton Dr 22152
Tobey Ct 22150
Tomcris Ct 22153
Topsails Ln 22150
Torington Dr 22152
Tory Rd 22152
Tower Woods Dr 22153
Trafalgar Ct 22151
Traford Ln 22152
Trailside Dr 22150
Tralee Woods Ct 22153
Trappers Pl 22153
Treasure Tree Ct 22153
Treeside Ct 22152

Treetop Hill Ln 22152
Trefor Ct 22152
Triad Way 22151
Tributary Ct 22153
Trillium Ln 22152
Trips Way 22150
True Ln 22150
Truro Ct 22152
Turlock Rd 22153
Tuttle Rd 22152
Twin Ct 22150
Twist Ln 22153
Tyner St 22152
Tyrolean Way 22153
Utica St 22150
Uxbridge Ct 22151
Valleyfield Dr 22153
Vancouver Rd 22152
Velliety Ln 22152
Ventnor Ln 22151
Veranda Dr 22152
Versar Ctr 22151
Vervain Ct 22152
Viceroy Ct & St 22151
Victoria Rd 22151
Vienna Ct 22152
Villa Del Rey Ct 22150
Villa Park Rd 22150
Viola St 22152
Vogels Way 22153
Wadebrook Ter 22153
Wagon Trail Ln 22153
Wainfleet Ct 22152
Walking Horse Ct 22153
Walnut Knoll Dr 22153
Ward Park Ln 22153
Water Valley Ct 22153
Waterbury Ct 22152
Wayles St 22150
Waynesboro Cir 22150
Webbwood Ct 22151
Wendy Way 22151
Wentworth Pl 22152
Wesley Rd 22150
Westbury Oaks Ct 22152
Westcreek Ct 22153
Western Oak Dr 22153
Westhaven Ln 22150
Westmeath Ct 22152
Westmore Ct & Dr 22150
Westover Ct 22152
Weymouth Dr 22151
Whisperwood Ct 22153
White House Dr 22153
White Star Ct 22153
White Stone Ln 22153
White Willow Ct 22153
Whitlers Creek Ct & Dr 22152
Whitson Ct & Dr 22153
Wickham Rd 22152
Wilbur Ct 22153
Wild Rose Ct 22152
Wild Spruce Dr 22153
Willow Bend Ct 22152
Willow Forge Rd 22152
Willow Oak Pl 22153
Willowdale Ct 22153
Willowfield Way 22150
Willowick Ln 22152
Willshire Hunt Ct 22153
Wimsatt Rd 22151
Wind Fall Rd 22153
Wind Song Ct 22153
Winding Hollow Way 22152
Winding Way Ct 22153
Windy Point Ct 22153
Winslow Ave 22152
Winter Blue Ct 22153
Wintercress Ln 22152
Wintrank Ct 22153
Wold Den Ct 22153
Woodland Dr 22151
Woodland Estates Way 22151
Woodlawn Way 22153

Woodruff Ct 22151
Woodstown Ct & Dr 22153
Woodstream Ct 22153
Woodview Dr 22153
Woolin Pl 22150
Wren Dr 22150
Wrenford Ct 22152
Wyngate Dr 22152
Wyoma Ct 22152
Wythe Ln 22152
Yarnwood Ct 22153
Yellow Leaf Ct 22153
Yorkshire St 22151
Young Ct 22153
Zekan Ln 22150
Zephyr Ln 22150

STAFFORD VA

General Delivery 22554

POST OFFICE BOXES MAIN OFFICE STATIONS AND BRANCHES

Box No.s
All PO Boxes 22555

NAMED STREETS

Abraham Ct 22554
Abrahms Ct 22556
Acadia St 22554
Accokeek Furnace Rd 22554
Addison Ct 22556
Admiral Cv & Dr 22554
Affirmed Dr 22556
Agnes Way 22556
Alda Rae Ct 22554
Alder Dr 22554
Alderwood Dr 22556
Alf Ln 22556
Algrace Blvd 22556
Alice Ct 22556
Allatoona Ln 22554
Allegheny Dr 22556
Almond Dr 22554
Alvin Ct 22556
Aly Sheba Ln 22556
Amsonia Ct 22556
Anchor Cv 22554
Andrew St 22556
Andrew Chapel Rd 22554
Anita Dr 22556
Annalisa Ln 22556
Antietam Loop 22554
Apache Ln 22556
Appalachian Dr 22554
Apple Blossom Ct 22554
Appletree Ln 22554
Appling Rd 22554
Apricot St 22554
Aquia Ave 22556
Aquia Dr 22554
Aquia Bay Ave 22554
Aquia Creek Rd 22554
Aquia Crest Ln 22554
Aquia Towne Ctr Dr 22554
Arbor Ln 22554
Archwood Cir 22556
Arden Ln 22556
Arkendale Rd 22554
Arla Ct 22554
Arrowhead Dr 22556
Arthurs Ln 22554
Ash Ln 22556
Ashbrook Rd 22554
Ashley Ct 22554
Asmead Pl 22554
Aster Ln 22554
Aston Ct 22554
Atina Dr 22554
Atlantic Dr 22554
Augusta Dr 22556
Augustine Rd 22554
Austin Ct 22554
Austin Dr 22556
Austin Park Dr 22554
Austin Run Blvd 22554
Autumn Dr S 22556
Aylor Ct 22554
Aztec Dr 22554
B Vue Ave 22556
Babcock Rd 22556
Bailey Ct 22556
Bainbridge Ct 22556
Ballantrae Ct 22554
Ballister Pl 22554
Bankston Ct 22554
Banner Spring Cir 22554
Bannon Ln 22556
Barbara Ann Dr 22554
Barclay Ln 22554
Barge Ln 22554
Barksdale Pl 22554
Barley Corn Dr 22556
Barley Mill Ct 22554
Barlow House Ct 22554
Barnswallow Ln 22556
Barnum Dr 22556
Baron Ct 22554
Barrett Ct 22554
Barrett Heights Rd 22556
Barrington Ct 22554
Barrington Woods Blvd 22556
Basket Ct 22554
Bass Dr 22554
Battle Ridge Ln 22556
Battleship Cv 22554
Bay Cv 22554
Bayview Overlook 22554
Beacon Cv 22554
Beau Ridge Dr 22556
Beaumont Ln 22554
Beaver Lodge Rd 22556
Beaver Ridge Rd 22556
Beavers Ct 22556
Beech Dr 22556
Beech Tree Ct 22554
Belcroft Dr 22554
Bell Towers Ct 22554
Bella Vista Ct 22554
Belladonna Ln 22554
Bellingham Dr 22556
Bells Hill Rd 22554
Bells Ridge Dr 22554
Bent Creek Ct 22556
Bentley Ct 22554
Bergamot Dr 22556
Berkshire Dr 22554
Bertram Blvd 22556
Betts Rd 22554
Big Cliffs Ln 22554
Big Spring Ln 22554
Birch Ln 22554
Birkenhead Ln 22554
Biscoe Ct 22556
Bishop Ln 22554
Bismark Dr 22554
Black Oak Ln 22556
Blackbeard Dr 22554
Blackgum Ct 22554
Blacksmith Ct 22554
Blake Way 22556
Blast Furnace Way 22554
Blessed Ct 22554
Blizzard Ct 22556
Bloomington Ln 22554
Blossom Ln 22554
Blossom Tree Ct 22554
Blossom Wood Ct 22554
Blue Spruce Cir 22554
Blueberry Ct 22554
Bluebird Ln 22554
Blueridge Ct 22554
Boathouse Way 22554
Bob White Ln 22554
Bombay Ct 22554
Bonnie Lee Ct 22556
Boondocks Ln 22554
Booth Ct 22554
Bosun Cv 22554
Boulder Dr 22554
Boundary Dr 22556
Bow Cv 22554
Bowling Ct 22554
Boxwood Ct & Dr 22556
Boyd Dr 22556
Boyette Ln 22554
Bradbury Way 22554
Bradstreet Ct 22556
Braewood Dr 22556
Brafferton Blvd 22554
Branch Creek Way 22556
Brandice St 22554
Brandons Blf 22554
Brannigan Dr 22554
Brantford Dr 22554
Breakers Edge Ct 22554
Breezy Hill Dr 22556
Brent Point Rd 22554
Brentsmill Dr 22554
Brenwick Ct 22556
Brian Ct 22556
W Briar Dr 22556
Bridgecreek Ct 22554
Bridgeport Cir 22554
Bridgewood Ct 22554
Brighton Way 22554
Bristol Ct 22556
Brittany Ln 22554
Brittany Manor Way 22554
Brixham Ct 22554
Brooke Rd 22554
Brooke Crest Ln 22554
Brookesmill Ln 22554
Broomfield Dr 22554
Broyhill Ct 22554
Bruce St 22554
Brush Everard Ct 22554
Bryant Blvd & St 22556
Buck Rd 22554
Buckingham Ln 22556
Buckner Ln 22554
Bulkhead Cv 22554
Bullrush Ct 22554
Buoy Dr 22554
Burhead Ln 22556
Burley St 22554
Burningbush Ct 22554
Burns Rd 22554
Burwell Pl 22554
Buttercup Ln 22554
Buttgens Ln 22554
Cabell Rd 22554
Cabin Ct 22554
Cabinet Maker Ct 22554
Caldwell Ln 22554
Caledon Ct 22556
Calvary Ct 22556
Calvin Ct 22554
Camp Geary Ln 22554
Campbell Ct 22556
Canaan Ct 22554
Candleridge Ct 22554
Candlestick Dr 22554
Cannon Bluff Dr 22554
Canter Pl 22556
Canterbury Dr 22554
Cape Cod Dr 22554
Captain Johns Cv 22554
Carissa Ct 22554
Carlsbad Dr 22554
Carnaby St 22554
Carolyn Ct 22554
Carroll Dr 22554
Carter Ln 22556
Castings Ln 22554
Castle Ct 22554
Castle Garden Ct 22556
Castlebury Ct 22554
Catbird Ct 22556
Cathedral Ln 22554
Catherine Ln 22554
Cattail Ct 22554
Caval Cade Ln 22556
Cedar Ln 22554
Cedar Hill Ln 22556
Cedar Ridge Dr 22554
Center St 22556
Century St 22554
Chadwick Dr 22556
Champion Way 22554
Channel Cv 22554
Charleston Ct 22554
Charlies Ln 22556
Chelsea Ct 22554
Chelsea Manor Ln 22554
Cherry Blossom Ln 22554
Cherry Hill Dr 22556
Chesapeake Cv & Dr 22554
Cheshire Dr 22554
Chesterbrook Ct 22554
Chesterfield Ln 22556
Chesterwood Ln 22556
Chestnut Dr 22554
Chestnut Ln 22556
Chichester Dr 22554
Choptank Rd 22556
Christina Ct 22556
Christopher Way 22554
Chriswood Ln 22556
Churchill Ln 22556
Citation Ct 22556
Clara St 22556
Clark Ln 22554
Clarke Hill Rd 22554
Clearview Ln 22554
Clearwater Ct 22554
Clement Dr 22556
Cliff Cir 22556
Clifton Chapel Ln 22554
Clippership Cv & Dr 22554
Clore Dr 22556
Clover Hill Dr 22554
Club Dr 22554
Coachman Cir 22554
Coal Landing Rd 22554
Coast Guard Dr 22554
Cobblers Ct 22554
Cobham Ct 22554
Coldspring Dr 22554
Colfax Ct 22554
Collingsworth St 22554
Collins Ct 22556
Colonel Colin Ct 22554
Colonial Forge Rd 22554
Columbia Way 22554
Columbus Cv & Dr 22554
Comfort Ln 22554
Commander Cv 22554
Commodore Cv 22554
Compass Cv 22554
Concord Dr 22556
Confederate Way 22554
Constitution Dr 22554
Cookson Dr 22556
Coopers Ln 22554
Coral Reef Ct 22554
Corduroy Ct 22554
Coriander Way 22554
Cork St 22554
Cornerstone Dr 22554
Corporate Dr 22554
Cory Ct 22554
Cottonwood Ct 22554
Country Ct 22554
Courage Ln 22554
Courthouse Rd 22554
Cove Ct 22554
Craftsman Ct 22554
Craig Ct 22554
Cranston Ln 22556
Crater Ln 22556
Crawford Ln 22556
Creek Run Rd 22556
Creekside Ct 22554
Crescent Blvd 22554
Crestview Dr 22556
Crestwood Ln 22554
Cromwell Ct 22554
Crossridge Ct 22554
Crosswood Pl 22554
Crown Manor Dr 22556
Crows Nest Cv 22554
Cruiser Dr 22554
Cummings Dr 22554
Curving Branch Way 22556
Cutstone Dr 22554
Cutter Cv 22554
Dacey Ln 22556
Daffodil Ln 22554
Dallhan Ct 22554
Daly Ct 22556
Danbury Ct 22554
Danbury Forest Ln 22554
Dandridge Ct 22554
Darbywood Ct 22554
Darden Ct 22554
Dartmouth Ave 22554
Davenport Dr 22554
Daventry Pl 22554
David Ct 22554
Davidson St 22554
Day Dr 22556
Debra Dr 22556
Decatur Rd 22554
Decatur Woods Ln 22554
Declaration Dr 22554
Decoy Ln 22556
Deene Ct 22556
Deer Run Rd 22556
Delaware Dr 22554
Delewinski Ln 22556
Delphinium Way 22556
Demian Ct 22556
Democracy Cir 22554
Den Rich Rd 22554
Denali Dr 22554
Denise St 22554
Dent Rd 22554
Derrick Ln 22554
Deshields Ct & Ln 22556
Destroyer Cv 22554
Devonshire Ln 22554
Dewey Dr 22554
Dewitt Rd 22554
Dinas Way 22554
Dishpan Ln 22554
Dittmann Way 22556
Dobe Point Rd 22554
Doc Stone Rd 22556
Dog Hollow Ln 22556
Dog Patch Ln 22554
Dolphin Cv 22554
Donelson Loop 22554
Donovan Ln 22556
Dorchester Ct 22554
Dorothy Ln 22554
Dottie Ln 22556
Doug Ct 22554
Douglas Dr 22554
Dover Pl 22556
Doyle Pl 22554
Drake St 22554
Draper Cir 22554
Drayman Ln 22554
Dream Ln 22556
Driftwood Ln 22554
Drum Ct 22556
Drummers Cv 22554
Duffey Dr 22556
Dun Rovin Ln 22556
Dunbar Dr 22556
Dunkirk Ln 22556
Dunn Dr 22554
Dutch Brandy Rd 22556
Earley Ct 22554
Eastbrook Ct 22554
Easter Dr 22554
Eaton Ct 22554
Ebenezer Church Rd 22556
Edgecliff Ln 22554
Edgemere Ct 22554
Edrington Ct 22554
Egret Ct 22554
Ella Ct 22554
Ellers Way 22554
Elliott Ln 22554
Embrey Mill Rd 22554
Emerson Ct 22554
Endicott Ln 22554
Enfield Dr 22556
England Dr 22554
Engles Ct 22554
English Rd 22556
Equestrian Dr 22556
Erin Dr 22556
Ervin Overlook 22556
Eskimo Hill Rd 22554
Essex St 22554
Estate Row 22554
Eternity Ct 22554
Eustace Rd 22554
Evans Ln 22556
Evelyn Ln 22554
Everglades Ln 22554
Evergreen Ln 22554
Executive Cir 22554
Exeter Ln 22554
Fair Oaks Ave 22554
Fairfield Ct 22554
Falcon Ct 22554
Faleantr Loop 22554
Falling Creek Dr 22554
Fallsway Ln 22554
Farmers Ln 22556
Farmview Dr 22554
Farragut Dr 22554
Fathom Cv 22554
Favour Ct 22554
Fence Post Rd 22556
Ferguson Dr 22554
Fern Ln 22556
Fern Oak Cir 22554
Fiddlers Ct 22554
Fieldstone Ct 22554
Fife St 22554
Finch Ct 22556
Fireberry Blvd 22554
Firehawk Dr 22554
Flatford Rd 22554
Fleet Cv 22554
Flewellen Dr 22554
Flint Ct 22554
Flippo Rd 22554
Floyd Ln 22554
Foresail Cv 22554
Forest Dr 22556
Forest Hill Ln 22556
Forest Vista Ln 22554
Foreston Woods Dr 22554
Fort Sumter Ln 22554
Founders Way 22554
Foundry Ln 22554
Fountain Dr 22554
Fox St 22556
Foxwood Dr & Rd 22556
Francis Ct 22554
Frank Ct 22554
Franklin St 22556
Frasier Dr 22556
Frederick Pl 22554
Freesia Ln 22554
Freya Ln 22556
Fritters Ln 22556
Fulton Dr 22554
Furnace Rd 22556
Gallery Rd 22554
Galt Way 22554
Galway Ln 22554
Garden Ln 22554
Gardenia Dr 22554
Garfield St 22556
Garrison Woods Dr 22556
Garrisonville Rd
1-899 22554
2-98 22556
100-898 22554
900-2899 22556
Gavins Ln 22556
Geddy Way 22554
George St 22554
George Mason Rd 22554
George Walker Dr 22556
Germanna Way 22554
Gettysburg Ct 22554
Giles Ct 22554
Ginger Ln 22554
Glacier Way 22554
Glade Dr 22556
Glendale Dr 22556
Glenwood Ave 22554
Gloucester Way 22554
Goal Ct 22554
Goose Pond Rd 22556
Grace Ct 22556
Grand Garden Ln 22556
Grants Ct 22554
Grapevine Ln 22556
Grassland St 22554
Gray Birch Ln 22554
Green Acre Dr 22556
Green Bell Ln 22554
Green Leaf Ter 22556
Greenbriar Dr 22556
Greenfield Rd 22556
Greenhaven Ct 22554
Greenhow Ln 22554
Greenridge Dr 22554
Greenspring Dr 22554
Greystone Pl 22554
Griffis Ln 22554
Gristmill Dr 22554
Grosvenor Ln 22556
Grouse Pointe Dr 22556
Groves Ln 22556
Guinns Ln 22554
Gulf Cv 22554
Gull Cv 22554
Gunston Rd 22554
Guy Ln 22554
Halcomb Ln 22556
Halifax Ct 22554
Hamearre Rd 22556
Hamn Ln 22554
Hampshire Ct 22554
Hampton Park Rd 22554
Hanson Ln 22556
Harbour Cv & Dr 22554
Harley Ct 22556
Harmony Ct 22554
Harpoon Cv & Dr 22554
Harris Ln 22554
Harry Ct 22554
Harvest Green Ct 22556
Harwill Ct & Dr 22556
Hatchers Run Ct 22554
Haven Ct 22554
Hawthorne Ct 22554
Hay Barn Rd 22556
Hayes St 22556
Healy Ct 22554
Heatherbrook Ln 22554
Hedgeapple Ct 22554
Heflin Rd 22556
Helm Ct 22556
Hemlock Dr 22554
Hemming Dr 22554
Hempstead Ln 22554
Hermitage Dr 22556
Hickory Ln 22556
Hidden Ln 22556
Hidden Lake Dr 22556
Hidden Springs Ln 22554
High St 22556
High Ridge Dr 22554
Highpointe Blvd 22554
Hilda Dr 22556
Hill Ln 22556
Hillcrest Dr 22556
Hillside Ct 22554
Hollister Ln 22556
Holly Ct, Dr & Ln 22556
Holly Brooke Ct 22554
Holly Knoll Ct 22554
Hollywood Ave 22554
Holmes St 22554

Honey Ln 22554
Honor Ct 22554
Hoot Owl Rd 22554
Hoovler Ln 22556
Hope Rd 22554
Hope Springs Ln 22554
Hope Valley Ln 22554
Hospital Center Blvd 22554
Hot Springs Way 22554
Hoy Rd 22556
Hubbard Ct 22554
Huckstep Ave 22556
Hulvey Dr 22556
Hunter Trl 22554
Hunting Creek Ln 22556
Hyde Park 22556
Idylwood Pl 22554
Ilona Ct 22554
Independence Dr 22554
Indian Ln 22556
Indian Point Rd 22554
Indian View Ct 22554
Inez Way 22554
Inheritance Pl 22556
Inman Overlook 22556
Innsbrook Ct 22556
Iris Ln 22554
Ironside Cv 22554
Irving Ct 22556
Isabella Dr 22554
Ivywood Dr 22554
Jam Parrell Dr 22556
Jamall Cv 22554
James Ln 22556
Jamestown Ct 22554
Jane Ct 22554
Jason Ct & Ln 22554
Jaymar Ct 22554
Jefferson Davis Hwy
1501-1529 22554
1531-2649 22554
2650-2650 22555
2650-2650 22430
2650-2650 22554
2651-4099 22554
2652-4098 22554
Jennifer Ln 22554
Jib Dr 22554
Jody Ct 22556
John Paul Jones Dr 22554
Johnson Ct 22556
Johnsons Pride Ln 22554
Jolly Roger Cv 22554
Jonnycake Ct 22554
Jonquil Pl 22554
Joplin Ct 22554
Joseph Ct 22556
Josh Pl 22556
Joshua Rd 22556
Joyce St 22556
Juggins Rd 22556
Jumping Branch Rd 22554
Justin Ct 22554
Kane Way 22556
Kassy Ln 22556
Katrine Ct 22556
Keating Cir 22554
Keith Ct 22554
Kellogg Mill Rd
987-999 22556
1000-1199 22554
Kelly Way 22556
Kelsey Rd 22554
Kelvin Dr 22554
Kenmore Ln 22554
Kennesaw Dr 22554
Keswick Rd 22556
Kettlebrook Ct 22556
Keystone Dr 22556
Kimberly Dr 22554
Kimberwick Ln 22556
Kincaid Ln 22556
Kings Crest Dr 22554
Kingsland Dr 22556
Kingsley Ct 22554
Kinross Dr 22554

Kinser Way 22556
Kip Ct 22556
Kirby Ln 22556
Kline Ct 22556
Knapp Rd 22554
Knightsbridge Way 22554
Knoll Ct 22554
Knollside Ct 22554
Knollwood Ct 22554
Knoxville Ct 22554
Krismatt Ct 22554
Kristen Rd 22556
Lafayette St 22554
Lake Dr 22554
Lake View Ln & Ter 22556
Lakeland Rd 22556
Lakesedge Ln 22554
Lakeside Dr 22554
Lakeview Ct 22554
Lakeview Dr 22556
Lakewind Ln 22554
Lakewood Dr 22554
Lamplighter Ln 22554
Landmark Dr 22554
Langley Ct 22554
Langley Oaks Ct 22554
Lark Ln 22556
Larkwood Ct 22554
Latham Ln 22554
Laurel Ln 22556
Laurel Haven Dr 22554
Lawhorn Rd 22554
Leaf Miner Ct 22554
Leather Bark Ct 22554
Lee Ct 22554
Legal Ct 22554
Leisure St 22556
Leslie Dr 22556
Lieutenant Howard Ln 22556
Lightfoot Dr 22554
Lighthouse Cv 22554
Lincoln Dr 22554
Lindsey Ln 22556
Little Branch Ln 22554
Little Forest Church Rd 22554
Little Rocky Run Ln 22554
Live Oak Ln 22554
Loblolly Ln 22556
Locust Ln 22556
London Way 22554
Long Branch Ln 22556
Longfellow Ct 22556
Longview Dr 22556
Longwood Dr 22556
Lotus Ln 22554
Louie Ln 22554
Lovelace Ln 22556
Ludwell Ln 22554
Lunesford Ct 22554
Lupine Dr 22556
Lusitania Dr 22554
Lusterleaf Ct 22554
Lynhaven Ln 22556
Lyons Den Way 22554
Macgregor Ridge Rd 22554
Mack Ln 22556
Macon Dr 22554
Madeline Ln 22556
Madison Ct 22556
Madrid Ln 22554
Magnes Pl 22556
Magnolia Dr 22556
Maidenhair Way 22556
Main St 22556
Mallard Rd 22554
Malvern Hill Ct 22554
Manila Cv 22554
Mantle Ct 22556
Maple Dr 22554
Maple Ln 22556
Maple Hill Ln 22556
Maple Leaf Ct 22554
Maplewood Dr 22554
Marine Cv 22554
Mariposa Ln 22554

Marjorie Ln 22556
Markham Way 22556
Marla Ct 22556
Marlborough Point Rd 22554
Marquis Ct 22554
Marshall Ct & Ln 22554
Martha Ct 22554
Martin St 22556
Mary Dr 22556
Maryanne Ave 22554
Mason Ln 22554
Mast Cv 22554
Masters Dr 22554
Masters Mill Ct 22556
Matio Cv 22554
Matthew Ct 22554
Mavel Pl 22554
Mayfair Pl 22556
Mccormick Ct 22556
Mclaughlin St 22556
Mcmillion Dr 22554
Meade Ct 22554
Meadow Ln 22556
Meadow View Ct 22554
Meadowbrook Ln 22554
Meadowood Dr 22554
Mediterranean Dr 22554
Melody Ln 22554
Melville Ct 22556
Menne Dr 22554
Meridan Ln 22556
Merrill Ct 22554
Merrimac Dr 22556
Mews Ct 22556
Meyer Ln 22556
Mica Way 22554
Mickelson Ln 22554
Midshipman Cir & Dr 22554
Midway Rd 22554
Mill Ln 22556
Mill Race Rd 22554
Millbrook Rd 22554
Millers Crossing Ln 22554
Millstone Dr 22556
Mine Rd 22554
Minor Dr 22554
Minuteman Ct 22554
Mirage Dr 22556
Mistro Ct 22554
Misty Ln 22556
Mockingbird Ln 22556
Monarch Ct 22554
Moncure Ln 22556
Monitor Cv & Dr 22554
Monna Lee Dr 22556
Montague Loop 22554
Montgomery Dr 22556
Monticello Dr 22556
Montpelier Dr 22556
Monument Dr 22554
Moores Ln 22556
Mooring Ct 22554
Morrissey Stone Ct 22554
Mosby Ln 22556
Moss Dr 22556
Mount Ararat Ln 22554
Mount Hope Church Rd 22554
Mount Olive Rd 22556
Mount Perry Dr 22554
Mountain Ash Ct 22554
Mountain View Rd
1275-1899 22554
1900-1916 22556
1901-1917 22554
1918-3099 22556
Mourning Dove Dr 22554
Mt Hope Church Rd 22554
Munsons Hill Ct 22554
Murray Cir 22554
Muster Dr 22554
Mynell St 22554
Naples Rd 22554
Nassau Ct 22554
Natures Ln 22554
Nautical Cv 22554

Neil Ct 22554
Nestors Pl 22556
Neupauer Ln 22554
Neville Ct 22554
New Bedford Ct 22554
New Brunswick Ct 22554
Newbury Dr 22556
Newland Cv 22554
Newport Ct 22554
Niday Dr 22556
Niles St 22554
Nina Cv 22554
Noahs Ct 22554
Nob Hill Dr 22556
Norman Rd 22554
Northampton Blvd 22554
Northedge Ct 22554
Novak Dr 22554
Nugent Dr 22554
Nulls Ln 22554
Oak Dr 22554
Oak Ln 22554
Oak Rd 22556
Oak Grove Ln 22556
Oakbrook Ct 22554
Oaklawn Rd 22554
Oakridge Dr 22554
Oakview Ct 22554
Oakwood Dr 22554
Oakwood Farm Ln 22554
Ocala Way 22556
Old Bridge Rd 22554
Old English Way 22554
Old Fort Ln 22554
Old Mineral Rd 22554
Old Mount Rd 22554
Old Potomac Church Rd 22554
Olde Concord Rd 22554
Oleander Dr 22554
Olympic Dr 22554
Ontell Ct 22554
Onville Rd 22556
Onyx Ct 22554
Orchard Ln 22556
Orchid Ln 22554
Orion Way 22556
Ortega St 22556
Osprey View Ln 22554
Ottinger Ln 22556
Owen St 22556
Oxen Ct 22554
Oyster Bay Cv 22554
P G A Dr 22554
Palace Ln 22554
Palisades Dr 22554
Palladio Dr 22554
Palmer Ct 22554
Paradise Ct 22554
Paris Ln 22556
W Park Dr 22554
Park Rd 22556
Park Brook Ct 22554
Park Cove Dr 22554
Park Ridge Ct 22554
Parkside Ln 22556
Parkway Blvd 22554
Parkwood Ct 22554
Partridge Ln 22554
Pasture Ln 22556
Patriot Way 22554
Patton Dr 22556
Paynes Ln 22554
Peaceful Ct 22556
Peachy Ct 22554
Peake Ln 22554
Pear Blossom Rd 22554
Pear Tree Ln 22554
Pebble Beach Dr 22554
Pelham Way 22556
Pelican Cv 22554
Pembroke Ln 22554
Pepper Tree Ln 22554
Peregrine Ct 22554
Pergola Dr 22554
Perkins Ln 22554

Persevere Dr 22554
Pewter Ln 22554
Picadilly Ln 22556
Pickett Ln 22556
Pickos Pl 22556
Piedmont Dr 22554
Pike Pl 22556
Pilgrim Cv 22554
Pilot Knob Loop 22554
Pin Oak Ct 22554
Pine Tree Ln 22556
Pinecrest Ct 22554
Pinehurst Ln 22554
Pinkerton Ct 22554
Pinnacle Dr 22554
Pinta Cv 22554
Pinto Ln 22556
Pita Pl 22554
Plantation Ln 22556
Planters Pl 22554
Pleasure Ct 22556
Plymouth Dr 22554
Pocahontas Ln 22556
Poe Pl 22556
Pond View Ct 22554
Pondsedge Ct 22554
Popes Creek Ln 22556
Poplar Dr & Rd 22556
Poplar View Dr 22554
Porter Hill Rd 22556
Portugal Cv & Dr 22554
Potomac Dr 22554
Potomac Hills Dr 22554
Potomac Overlook Ln 22554
Potomac View Ln 22554
Potter Ln 22554
Power Way 22554
Powhatan Ct 22556
Presidential Ln 22554
Primrose Ln 22554
Prince Ct 22554
Princess St 22556
Pritchard Ct 22554
Prosperity Ln 22556
Providence St 22554
Puller Pl 22556
Puri Ln 22554
Puritan Pl 22554
Quail Ridge Ln 22556
Quail Run Dr 22554
Quarry Rd 22554
Quarry Oaks Rd 22554
Quarter Horse Ct 22554
Queens Mill Ct 22554
Quiet Brook Ct 22554
Raft Cv 22554
Raines Ct 22554
Raintree Blvd 22556
Raleigh Ln 22556
Ralphs Way 22554
Ram Ln 22554
Ramoth Church Rd 22554
Ramsey Dr 22556
Randall Rd 22554
Rapidan Dr 22556
Raspberry Ln 22556
Raven Rd 22554
Raynar Ct 22554
Rectory Dr 22554
Red Cedar Cir 22554
Red Fern Ln 22554
Red Hill Dr 22556
Red Maple Ct 22554
Red Oak Dr 22554
Redbud Cir 22554
Redoubt Ct 22554
Regal Ct 22554
Regatta Ln 22554
Regency Dr 22554
Rehoboth Dr 22554
Reids Rd 22554
Remington Ct 22554
Renee Rd 22556
Renwick Ct 22556
Republic Way 22554
Revere Ct 22554

Richmond Cv & Dr 22554
Ridge Rd 22556
Ridgecrest Ct 22554
Ridgeway Rd 22556
Ridgewood Dr 22556
Ridings Ln 22556
Ripley Rd 22556
Rippling Water Ct 22554
Riva Ridge Ln 22556
River Oak Dr 22554
Riverton Dr 22554
Robert St 22554
Robin Rd 22554
Rock Hill Church Rd 22556
Rockdale Rd 22554
Rockhill Ln 22556
Rocky Stone Dr 22556
Rocky Way Dr 22554
Roger Wayne Dr 22554
Roles Ln 22554
Rolling Rd 22556
Rolling Brooke Ct 22554
Rolling Hill Ct 22554
Rollinswood Ln 22554
Rome Dome Ct 22556
Rosa Ct 22556
Rose St 22554
Rose Hill Farm Dr 22556
Rosedale Dr 22556
Rosehaven St 22556
Rosemary Ln 22554
Rosepetal St 22556
Roseville Ct 22556
Ross Ct 22554
Rover Ct 22554
Roxanne Rd 22556
Royce Ct 22556
Ruby Dr 22556
Ruffian Dr 22556
Runyon Dr 22554
Rushmore Ln 22554
Ryan Way 22554
Rye Creek Dr 22554
Ryland Rd 22556
Sable Ln 22554
Saginaw Dr 22556
Sail Cv 22554
Saint Adams Dr 22556
Saint Albans Blvd 22556
Saint Anthonys Ct 22556
Saint Charles Ct 22556
Saint Christophers Dr 22556
Saint Claires Ct 22556
Saint Davids Ct 22556
Saint Elizabeths Ct 22556
Saint Georges Dr 22556
Saint Ives Ct 22556
Saint Jacquelyns Ct 22556
Saint James Ct 22556
Saint Johns Ct 22556
Saint Lisas Ct 22556
Saint Marks Ct 22556
Saint Marys Ln 22556
Saint Patricks Ct 22556
Saint Peters Ct 22556
Saint Phillips Rd 22556
Saint Randalls Ct 22556
Saint Richards Ct 22556
Saint Roberts Dr 22556
Saint Sebastian Ct 22556
Saint Stephens Ct 22556
Saint Thomas Ct 22556
Saint Vincent Ct 22556
Saint Williams Way 22556
Salem Ln 22554
Salisbury Dr 22554
Salma Way 22554
Sanctuary Ln 22554
Sand Dollar Cv 22554
Sandpiper Ter 22554
Sandy Ln 22554
Sandy Level Dr 22554
Santa Maria Dr 22554
Sarasota Dr 22554
Sarrington Ct 22554
Sassafras Ln 22554

Savannah Ct 22554
Sawgrass Ct 22554
Scarborough Ct 22554
Scarlet Flax Ct 22556
Scarlet Oak Cir 22554
Scarsdale Dr 22554
Scattered Pines Ln 22556
Schooner Dr 22554
Scotland Cir 22554
Scroggins Ln 22554
Seasons Ln 22556
Seaspray Ter 22554
Secretariat Dr 22556
Sedgwick Ct 22554
Seneca Ln 22556
Sentinel Ridge Ln 22554
Sentry Ct 22554
September Ln 22554
Sequester Dr 22556
Serene Ct 22556
Serenity Ln 22554
Settlers Way 22554
Sevier St 22556
Seymour Ct 22556
Shadow Bridge Rd 22554
Shady Ln 22554
Shady Cove Ln 22554
Shady Hill Ln 22554
Shallow Creek Ln 22554
Shamrock Dr 22556
Shannon Ct 22554
Sharon Ln 22554
Sharp Ct 22556
Shawnee Way 22556
Shelton Dr 22556
Shelton Shop Rd 22554
Shenandoah Ln 22554
Shepherds Way 22556
Shields Rd 22556
Shiloh Way 22556
Shore Dr 22554
Short Branch Rd 22556
Signal Way 22554
Silverleaf Ct 22554
Silverthorn Ct 22554
Sky Ter 22556
Skyview Ct 22554
Skywood Ct 22556
Sloop Cv 22554
Small Bear Ct 22554
Smelters Trace Rd 22554
Smith Lake Dr 22556
Smokewood Ct 22554
Snapdragon Dr 22556
Snow Dr 22554
Snow Meadow Ln 22554
Snowbird Ln 22554
Soaring Eagle Dr 22556
Somerset Ln 22554
Somerville St 22554
Sons Ct 22554
Southampton Ct 22554
Southern View Dr 22554
Spain Dr 22554
Sparky Ct 22556
Spartan Dr 22554
Spindle Top Ct 22556
Spinnaker Way 22554
Spotswood St 22554
Spring Lake Dr 22556
Springhill Rd 22556
Spyglass Ln 22556
Squirrel Hollow Ln 22554
Stable Cv 22554
Stafford Ave 22554
Stafford Glen Ct 22554
Stafford Manor Way 22556
Stafford Market Pl 22556
Stafford Mews Ln 22556
Stafford Ridge Rd 22554
Stafford Stone Dr 22554
Stallings Ln 22554
Stanhope Ct 22554
State Room Dr 22554
State Shop Rd 22554
Staunton Ct 22554

Stefaniga Rd 22556
Stefaniga Farms Dr 22556
Sterling Ct 22554
Stern Cv 22554
Stevens Cir & Dr 22556
Stingray Ct 22554
Stolen Will Ct 22554
Stonegate Pl 22554
Stoneridge Ct 22554
Stones Throw Way 22554
Stonewall Dr 22556
Stoney Brook Ct 22554
Stratford Pl 22556
Strathmore Ln 22556
Strother Ln 22554
Sturbridge Ln 22554
Sulgrave Way 22554
Summer Lake Ct 22554
Summerwood Dr 22554
Sunbury Ln 22556
Sundance Dr 22556
Sunningdale Dr 22556
Sunny Hill Ct 22554
Sunnybrooke Ln 22554
Sunnyside Dr 22554
Sunrise Valley Ct 22554
Sunrise View Ln 22554
Sunset Dr 22554
Sunshine Dr 22556
Surry Ln 22556
Susa Dr 22554
Susan St 22556
Susies Ln 22554
Sutton Ct 22554
Swansea Cv 22554
Swedish Elm Cir 22554
Sweetgum Ct 22554
Sweetwater Ct 22554
Sydney Ln 22554
Taber Ct 22556
Tacketts Mill Rd 22556
Taft Dr 22554
Tall Oaks Ct 22556
Tamar Creek Ln 22554
Tamerlane Dr 22554
Tamis Ct 22554
Tanglewood Ln 22554
Tanterra Dr 22556
Tapestry Ct 22554
Tara Ln 22554
Tarleton Way 22554
Tavern Rd 22554
Tech Pkwy 22556
Telegraph Rd 22554
Temple Dr 22554
Tenbrooke Ct 22556
Terrace Dr 22554
Thames Ct 22554
Thaxton Ct 22556
Thayer Ct 22556
Theresa Dr 22554
Thornberry Ln 22556
Thorny Point Rd 22554
Timber Lake Ct 22554
Timberlake St 22554
Timberland Dr 22556
Timberwood Ct 22554
Timothy Ln 22556
Tinder Ct 22554
Titanic Dr 22554
Tolbelt Ct 22554
Toliver Ln 22554
Tolson Ln 22556
Toluca Rd 22556
Tom Ct 22554
Torbert Loop 22554
Torey Ct 22554
Tracey St 22554
Tradewinds Ter 22554
Travis Ln 22556
Treasure Ln 22554
Tree Haven Ln 22556
Trellis Dr 22554
Trillium Dr 22556
Triumph Ln 22554
True Rd 22556
Tudor Ct 22554
Turner Dr 22556
Turnstone Ct 22556
Twain Ct 22556
Twin Brook Ln 22554
Twin Hill Ln 22554
Twin Oaks Dr 22554
Twinleaf Dr 22556
Tyll Ct 22556
Tyson Dr 22554
Union Camp Dr 22554
Upper Mill Way 22556
Upton Ln 22554
Valdosta Dr 22554
Valley Ridge Dr 22554
Van Horn Ln 22556
Vanburgh Ct 22554
Vargas Ct 22556
Varone Dr 22554
Venture Dr 22554
Vessel Dr 22554
Via De Rosa Dr 22556
Victoria Dr 22554
Viking Ln 22554
Vincent Ln 22554
Vine Pl 22554
Vineyard Ct 22554
Vista Woods Rd 22556
Voyage Cv & Dr 22554
Vulcan Quarry Rd 22556
Wagoneers Ln 22554
Wakerobin Dr 22556
Walker Way 22554
Wallace Ln 22554
Waller Point Dr 22554
Walmsley Ct 22554
Walnut Ridge Dr 22556
Walpole St 22554
Walt Whitman Blvd 22556
Warbler Ct 22556
Warwick Way 22554
Washington Dr 22554
Washington And Lee Blvd 22556
Water Way 22556
Waterbury Ct 22554
Waterfall Ln 22554
Watermill Ct 22554
Waters Lndg 22554
Waters Cove Ct 22554
Waterside Ter 22554
Waterview Dr 22554
Wave Dr 22554
Wayside Ct 22554
Webb Ct 22556
Wedman Way 22554
Wellington Dr 22554
Wells Rd 22556
Wendover Ct 22554
Wendy St 22554
Wesberry Ct 22556
Westbrook Ln 22554
Westchester Ct 22554
Westhampton Ct 22554
Westminster Ln 22556
Wet Rock Ln 22554
Wexwood Ct 22554
Whaler Cv 22554
Whaling Ln 22554
Wheelwright Ln 22554
Whetstone Ct 22554
Whetzel Ln 22554
Whirlaway Dr 22556
Whispering Pines Ln 22556
White Pine Cir 22554
Whitestone Dr 22554
Whitson Ridge Dr 22554
Whitsons Run 22554
Wicomico Dr 22554
Widewater Rd & Trl 22554
Wilbur Ln 22554
Wild Oak Ln 22554
Wild Plum Ct 22554
Wild Turkey Dr 22556
Wilderness Ct 22556
Wildflower Ct 22554
William And Mary Ln 22554
Williamsburg Ln 22556
Willies Ln 22556
Willingham Ct 22554
Willow Ln 22556
Willow Glen Ct 22554
Willow Landing Rd 22554
Willowmere Ct 22556
Willowmere Pond Rd 22556
Wilson Cv 22556
Wiltshire Dr 22554
Wimbeldon Ct 22556
Wind Ridge Dr 22554
Windermere Dr 22554
Winding Creek Rd 22554
Windjammer Ct 22554
Windrush Ct 22554
Windsong Way 22556
Windsor Way 22556
Windwhistle Ln 22556
Winning Colors Rd 22556
Wintergreen Ln 22554
Winthrop Way 22554
Wizard Ct 22554
Wood Dr 22556
Wood Rd 22554
Woodbourne Ln 22554
Woodflower Ct 22554
Woodland Dr 22556
Woodleigh Ln 22556
Woodlot Ct 22554
Woodmont Ct 22554
Woodrow Dr 22554
Woods Edge Ct 22554
Woodside Ln 22556
Woodstock Ln 22554
Woodstream Blvd & Cir 22556
Worth Ave 22556
Wren Way Ct 22554
Wyche Rd 22554
Wyncotte Ln 22554
York Ct 22554
Yorkshire Ct 22554
Yosemite Rdg 22554
Young Ct 22556
Zachary Ln 22554

STAUNTON VA

General Delivery 24402

POST OFFICE BOXES MAIN OFFICE STATIONS AND BRANCHES

Box No.s
All PO Boxes 24402

RURAL ROUTES

01, 02, 03, 04, 05, 06, 07, 08, 09, 10 24401

HIGHWAY CONTRACTS

32, 33 24401

NAMED STREETS

A St 24401
Academy St 24401
Adams St 24401
Aiken St 24401
Aintree Pl 24401
Albemarle Ave 24401
Alden St 24401
Alexander St 24401
Alextine Dr 24401
Alleghany Ave 24401
Alpine Rd 24401
Alta St 24401
Ames St 24401
Amherst Rd 24401
Anderson St 24401
Anderson School Ln 24401
Ann St 24401
Annandale Farm Ln 24401
Annex Rd 24401
Anthony St 24401
Apple Jack Ln 24401
Apple Orchard Ln 24401
Apple Wood Ln 24401
Arborhill Rd 24401
Archer St 24401
Archery Ln 24401
Arlington St 24401
Armstrong Ave 24401
Ashby St 24401
Audubon St 24401
N Augusta St
6-12 24401
14-1499 24401
1430-1430 24402
1500-3098 24401
1501-3099 24401
S Augusta St 24401
Augusta Woods Dr 24401
Austin Ave 24401
Avenue Of Trees 24401
B St 24401
Back Ln 24401
Back Meadow Ln 24401
Bagby St 24401
Baker Ln 24401
Baldwin Dr, Ln, Pl & St 24401
Balsley Rd 24401
Baltimore Ave 24401
Bangor Hl 24401
Baptist St 24401
Bare St 24401
Barrenridge Rd 24401
Barristers Row 24401
Barterbrook Rd 24401
Bartley St 24401
Bath St 24401
Battlefield Rd 24401
Baylor St 24401
Beaver Creek Rd 24401
Bell St 24401
Bell Creek Dr 24401
Belle Vista Dr 24401
Bells Ln 24401
Bellview St 24401
Belmont Dr 24401
N Belmore Ave 24401
Bennington Dr 24401
Benson St 24401
Berkeley Pl 24401
Berry Ln 24401
Berry Farm Rd 24401
Berry Moore Rd 24401
Bessie Weller Dr 24401
Bessies Ln 24401
Bethel Green Rd 24401
Betsy Bell Rd 24401
Beulah St 24401
E & W Beverley Ct & St 24401
Biltmore St 24401
Birch St 24401
Birchwood Rd 24401
Bird Haven Ln 24401
Bishop Ln 24401
Bittersweet Ln 24401
Blackberry Ln 24401
Blackburn St 24401
Blair St 24401
Blair Hill Ln 24401
Blandford St 24401
Blue Bird Ln 24401
Blue Ridge Dr 24401
Bobbys Way 24401
Bocock Ln 24401
Boddington Rd 24401
Bolling Heights Ln 24401
Bon Lea Dr 24401
Bowie St 24401
Bowling St 24401
Bowman Springs Rd 24401
N & S Braeburn Pl 24401
Bramble Ln 24401
Breezewood Dr 24401
Briarwood Cir 24401
Briarwood One 24401
Briarwood Two 24401
Bridge St 24401
Bridle Path 24401
Brinkley Dr 24401
Brooke St 24401
Brookewood Ave 24401
Brookmere Ct & Dr 24401
Brookside Ln 24401
Brookwood Rd 24401
Brown Bear Path 24401
Brushy Knob Ln 24401
Buchanan St 24401
Buckingham St 24401
Buick St 24401
Bull Run 24401
Burnett St 24401
Burnley Dr 24401
Burwell Ave 24401
Business Way 24401
Butler St 24401
Buttermilk Spring Rd 24401
Byers St 24401
C St 24401
C And O Flt 24401
C Bo G Ln 24401
Cabot Cv 24401
Callahans Aly 24401
Calvert St 24401
Campbell St 24401
Candlelight Dr 24401
Carann St 24401
Cardinal St 24401
Caribou Ln 24401
Caroline St 24401
Carriage Dr 24401
Carrs Brook Dr 24401
Carter St 24401
Carterlee Ln 24401
Cedar St 24401
Cedar Green Rd 24401
N & S Central Ave 24401
Charles St 24401
Cherry Hill Dr 24401
Chesapeake St 24401
Chesley Pl 24401
Chestnut Dr, Rd & St 24401
Chestnut Ridge Rd 24401
Cheyenne Ln 24401
Christian Hill Dr 24401
Christians Creek Rd 24401
Church St 24401
Churchmans Mill Rd 24401
Churchville Ave 24401
Circle Dr 24401
Clem Ln 24401
Clemmer Ln 24401
Clemmer Knoll Ln 24401
Clifford St 24401
Clover Ln 24401
N & S Coalter St 24401
Cochran St 24401
Cole Ave 24401
College Cir 24401
Collinswood Dr 24401
Commerce Rd 24401
Commodore St 24401
Community Way 24401
Copeland Dr 24401
Corey Hill Dr 24401
Cotton Wood Ln 24401
Country Acres Ln 24401
Country Boy Ln 24401
Country Club Ln 24401
Court Sq 24401
Cow Pasture Ln 24401
Crabtree Cir 24401
Craftons Park Ln 24401
Craig Dr 24401
Craigmont Rd 24401
Crescent Dr 24401
Crestwood Dr 24401
Crestwood Apartments 24401
Cricket Rd 24401
Crossing Ln 24401
Croyden Ln 24401
D St 24401
Dale St 24401
Dandelion Ln 24401
David St 24401
Davis St 24401
Deer Haven Ln 24401
Deer Hill Ln 24401
Deer Run Ln 24401
Deer Springs Dr 24401
Deer View Ln 24401
Dennison Ave 24401
Desarno Ln 24401
Desper Hollow Rd 24401
Devon Rd 24401
Docs Haven Ln 24401
Dogwood Rd 24401
Donaghe St 24401
Donovans Ln 24401
Douglas Dr 24401
Dove Hill Ln 24401
Dover St 24401
Driscoll St 24401
Drury St 24401
Dudley Ln 24401
Dupont Ave 24401
Dynamite Rd 24401
Eagle Rock Ln 24401
Eakle Rd 24401
Earl St 24401
Early Ln 24401
Early Vista Ln 24401
East Ave 24401
Eastwood Dr 24401
Edelweiss Ln 24401
Edgefield Ln 24401
Edgewood Rd 24401
Eidson Creek Rd 24401
Elizabeth Miller Gdns 24401
Ellen St 24401
Ellendin Ave 24401
Elliot St 24401
Elm St 24401
Emilys Ln 24401
Englewood Dr 24401
Equestrian Dr 24401
Essex Dr 24401
Estate Ln 24401
Eston Dr 24401
Eureka Mill Rd 24401
Evans Ln 24401
F St 24401
Fairfield Ct & Dr 24401
Fairmont Dr 24401
Fairview Ln 24401
Fairway Ln 24401
Fallon St 24401
Farm Kids Ln 24401
Farmington Dr 24401
Farrier Ct 24401
Fauber Ln 24401
Fawn Meadow Trl 24401
Fayette Ct & St 24401
Federal St 24401
Ferguson Ln 24401
Fieldhaven Pl 24401
Fielding Pl 24401
Fieldstone Ln 24401
Fillmore St 24401
Finch Ln 24401
First St 24401
Fisher Cir 24401
Fleetwood Rd 24401
Florida Ave 24401
Folly Rd 24401
Folly Mills Station Rd 24401
Forest Ln & St 24401
Forest Ridge Rd 24401
Fox Crest Rdg 24401
Fox Hill Dr & Pl 24401
Foxfield Dr 24401
Franks Mill Rd 24401
Fraser Ln 24401
Frazier St 24401
E Frederick St 24401
W Frederick St
1-200 24401
123-123 24402
201-699 24401
202-698 24401
Freeport Ln 24401
Friends Ln 24401
Frog Pond Rd 24401
Frontier Dr 24401
Frontier Ridge Ct 24401
G St 24401
Gaddy View Ln 24401
Galena Rd 24401
Galloping Hills Rd 24401
Garber St 24401
Garland Dr 24401
E & W Gay St 24401
Gaymont Pl 24401
Geoffrey St 24401
George St 24401
Georgetown St 24401
Gibson Ct 24401
Gilmer Ln 24401
Gilnochie Ln 24401
Gish Ln 24401
Glebe School Rd 24401
Glen Ave 24401
Gloria Pl 24401
Glory Ln 24401
Glover Cir 24401
Gooch St 24401
Gordon St 24401
Gosnell Xing 24401
Grand Vw 24401
Grandon Rd 24401
Grasty St 24401
Gray Ave 24401
Gray Fox Ln 24401
Grayson St 24401
Green St 24401
Greenview Dr 24401
Greenville Ave 24401
Greenville Farm Ln 24401
Greenway Rd 24401
Greenwood Rd 24401
Griner Rd 24401
Grove Ln 24401
Grower Ln 24401
Grubert Ave 24401
Guernsey Ln 24401
Guilford Ave 24401
Guthrie Rd 24401
Guy St 24401
Gypsy Ave 24401
Gypsy Hill Park 24401
Hackberry Trl 24401
Haile St 24401
Hall St 24401
Hammond Ln 24401
E & W Hampton St 24401
Hamrick St 24401
Hancock St 24401
Hanger St 24401
Hannah Cir 24401
Hanover St 24401
Hardwood Ln 24401
Harper Ct 24401
Hays Ave 24401
Hearns Dr 24401
Heather Ln 24401
Hebron Rd 24401
Henderson St 24401
Hendren Ave 24401
Herlock Rd 24401
Hermitage Rd 24401
Hessian Ln 24401
Hevener St 24401
Hewitt Rd 24401
Heydenreich St 24401
Hickory St 24401

Hickory Nut Ln 24401
Hidden Ln 24401
Hidden Hollow Ln 24401
High St 24401
Highland Ave 24401
Highview Cir 24401
Hildebrand Cir 24401
W Hill Rd 24401
W Hill Farm Dr 24401
Hill Haven Ln 24401
Hillandale Dr 24401
Hillcrest Dr 24401
Hillside Pl 24401
Hillsmere Ln 24401
Hilltop Dr 24401
Hilltop Terrace Rd 24401
Hillview Ln 24401
Hite Ln 24401
Holiday Ct 24401
Homes Ln 24401
Hook Ln 24401
Hoover St 24401
Hope St 24401
Hotchkiss St 24401
Houston St 24401
Howard St 24401
Howardsville Rd 24401
Hudson Ave 24401
Hull St 24401
Hull Hills Ln 24401
Hundley Mill Rd 24401
Hunter Rd 24401
Hunters Ln 24401
Ichabod Ln 24401
Idlewood Blvd 24401
Imboden Ln 24401
Imperial Dr 24401
Indian Mound Rd 24401
Industry Way 24401
Institute St 24401
International Ln 24401
Ivey Ln 24401
Jackson St 24401
N & S Jefferson Ct, Hwy & St 24401
Jericho Rd 24401
Jersey St 24401
Joan Cir 24401
E & W Johnson St 24401
Jones St 24401
Jordan St 24401
Kable St 24401
Kalorama St 24401
Karman Hill Dr 24401
Kasey Lee Dr 24401
Kellsye Way 24401
Kellwood Ln 24401
Kelsey Ln 24401
Kerry Ln 24401
King St 24401
Kings Sq 24401
Kinzley Ct 24401
Kittery Pt 24401
Knollwood Dr 24401
Koogler Hill Ln 24401
Lake Ave 24401
Laketree Dr 24401
Lambert St 24401
Lammermoor Dr 24401
Lamplighter Ln 24401
Lancaster Ave 24401
Lancelot Ln 24401
Lariat Cir 24401
Laurel Hill Rd 24401
Lawyers Row 24401
Lebanon Church Rd 24401
Lee St 24401
Lee Jackson Hwy 24401
N & S Lewis St 24401
E & W Liberty St 24401
Lickliter St 24401
Lime Rock Ln 24401
Lincoln Ave & Ln 24401
Linden Dr & St 24401
Little Bear Path 24401
Loch Dr 24401
Locust Ave & St 24401
Lone Oak Ln 24401
Long Ridge Ln 24401
Lorway Farm Ln 24401
Luck Stone Rd 24401
Lumber Yard Ln 24401
Lyle Ave 24401
Lynn Ln 24401
N & S Lynnhaven Dr 24401
Mactanly Pl 24401
Mader Ln 24401
N & S Madison Pl & St 24401
Maine Cir 24401
Manchester Dr 24401
Maple St 24401
Maple Leaf Dr 24401
Marian Pl 24401
Markels Ln 24401
N & S Market St 24401
Marquis St 24401
Marr St 24401
Marshall St 24401
Martha Ln 24401
Mary Gray Ln 24401
Mason St 24401
Maxwell Dr 24401
Mcarthur St 24401
Mccombs Mill Ln 24401
Mcmahon St 24401
Mcpheeters Rd 24401
Meadow Glen Dr 24401
Meadow Knolls Ln 24401
Meadowbrook Rd 24401
Middle River Rd 24401
Middlebrook Ave & Rd 24401
Middlebrook Village Rd 24401
Midvale Xing 24401
Milky Way Ln 24401
Mill Ln & St 24401
Mill Creek Ln 24401
Miller St 24401
Miller Farm Rd 24401
Mineola St 24401
Mint Spg 24401
Mint Springs Cir 24401
Miss Phillips Rd 24401
Misty Dawn Ln 24401
Mitchell Ln 24401
Mona Cir 24401
Monroe St 24401
Montgomery Ave & Rd 24401
Monument Dr 24401
Moore St 24401
Morris St 24401
Morris Mill Rd 24401
Mount Elliot Ave 24401
Mount Ida Ln 24401
Mountain View Dr 24401
Mt Tabor Rd 24401
Mulberry St 24401
Myers Corner Dr 24401
Myrtle St 24401
National Ave 24401
Nature Trail Ln 24401
Nelson St 24401
N & S New St 24401
New Hope Rd 24401
Niswander Rd 24401
Noon St 24401
Norfolk Ave 24401
North Dr 24401
Norwood Rd 24401
Nottingham Rd 24401
Oak Ave, Ln & Ter 24401
Oak Hill Rd 24401
Oak Ridge Cir & Ln 24401
Oak Springs Ln 24401
Oakenwold St & Ter 24401
Oakerrel St 24401
Oakmont Dr 24401
Old Churchville Rd 24401
Old Greenville Rd 24401
Old Greenville Farm Rd 24401
Old Mill Rd 24401
Old White Hill Rd 24401
Olive St 24401
Opie St 24401
Orange St 24401
Orchard Ave, Ln & Rd 24401
Orchard Hills Cir & Sq 24401
Oriole St 24401
Osage Pl 24401
Overbrook St 24401
Overlook Rd 24401
Oxford Cir 24401
Packard St 24401
Paige Dr & St 24401
Palmer Mill Ln 24401
Park Blvd 24401
Park Hill Rd 24401
E & W Park View Ln 24401
Parkersburg Tpke 24401
Parkview Ave 24401
Parkwood Ln 24401
Partlow St 24401
Partridge Ct 24401
Patton St 24401
Paul St 24401
Payne Ln 24401
E & W Peabody St 24401
Peaceful Valley Ln 24401
Peach St 24401
Pear Tree Dr 24401
Peck St 24401
Penrose Ln 24401
Perry St 24401
Perryville Ct 24401
Peyton St 24401
Phillip St 24401
Pierce St 24401
Pine St 24401
Pine Glen Rd 24401
Pine Hill Cir 24401
Pine Tree Ln 24401
Pinehurst Rd 24401
Pioneer Ln 24401
Plaza Apt Dr 24401
Pleasant Ter 24401
Pleasant Grove Rd 24401
Pleasant View Rd & St 24401
Plunkett St 24401
Pocahontas St 24401
Point St 24401
Poplar St 24401
Powell St 24401
Powhatan St 24401
Preston Dr 24401
Price Ln 24401
Prospect St 24401
Pump St 24401
Purviance St 24401
Quarry St 24401
Quicks Mill Rd 24401
Railroad Ave 24401
Rainbow Dr 24401
Ralston Ln 24401
Ramsey Rd & St 24401
Randolph St 24401
Ranson St 24401
Reaper Rd 24401
Red Oaks Dr 24401
Red Sunset Ln 24401
Redbud Hollow Ln 24401
Reid St 24401
Reservoir St 24401
Richardson St 24401
Richmond Ave 24401
Ridge Rd 24401
Ridgecrest Cir 24401
Ridgemont Dr 24401
Ridgeview Rd 24401
Ridgeway Dr 24401
Ridgewood Dr 24401
Riley Ln 24401
Ritchie Blvd 24401
Riverhead Dr 24401
Robertson St 24401
Robin St 24401
Robinhood Rd 24401
Rockport Dr 24401
Rockway St 24401
Rocky Hill Ln 24401
Rolling Green Dr 24401
Rolling Thunder Ln 24401
Roman Rd 24401
Rome Ave 24401
Root Ln 24401
Rose St 24401
Rose Hill Cir 24401
Rosebud Ln 24401
Rosen Ln 24401
Rowe Rd & St 24401
Royal Dr & St 24401
Rutherford St 24401
Sage Rd 24401
S Saint Clair St 24401
Sandy Ln 24401
Sangers Ln 24401
Sears Hill Rd 24401
Second St 24401
Seldom Seen Rd 24401
Selma Blvd 24401
Seth Dr 24401
Seymour Cir 24401
Shady Hollow Ln 24401
Shady Oaks Ln 24401
Shaner Ln 24401
Shannon Pl 24401
N & S Sharlaine Dr 24401
Sharon Ln 24401
Shawn Cir 24401
N Sheets St 24401
Shelley Ln 24401
Shenandoah St 24401
Shenandoah West Apts 24401
Sheperd Ln 24401
Sherwood Ave & Ln 24401
Shirey Rd 24401
Shover Ln 24401
Shutterlee Mill Ln & Rd 24401
Silver Creek Dr 24401
Singing Pines Ln 24401
Sky Manor Rd 24401
Skyeast Rd 24401
Skyland Dr 24401
Skyline Ave 24401
Skyline View Dr 24401
Skymont Cir & Rd 24401
Sleepy Hollow Trl 24401
Smiley Ln 24401
Smithleigh Cir 24401
Smoky Row Rd 24401
Spaulding St 24401
Spottswood Rd 24401
Spring Mdws 24401
Spring Crest Ln 24401
Spring Hill Rd 24401
Spring View Dr 24401
Springfield Ln 24401
Springleigh Dr 24401
Sproul Ln 24401
Spruce St 24401
Stack St 24401
Stafford St 24401
Stagecoach Rd 24401
Stanley St 24401
State St 24401
Statler Blvd 24401
Stayman Ln 24401
Steffey St 24401
Sterling St 24401
Stevens Ln 24401
Stiles Cir 24401
Stingy Hollow Rd 24401
Stocker St 24401
Stone Branch Rd 24401
Stoneburner St 24401
Stonewall Cir 24401
Stonewall Jackson Blvd 24401
Straith St 24401
Stuart St 24401
Stuarts Draft Hwy 24401
Sudbury St 24401
Sugar Loaf Rd 24401
Sullivan St 24401
Summerson St 24401
Summerson Row St 24401
Sunnyside St 24401
Sunset Blvd 24401
Sunset Acres Ln 24401
Surrey Rd 24401
Sussex Dr 24401
Swartzel Shop Rd 24401
Swisher Rd 24401
Swisher Truck Ln 24401
Sycamore St 24401
Sycamore Creek Ln 24401
Tams St 24401
Tannehill St 24401
Taylor St 24401
Technology Dr 24401
Terrace St 24401
Terry Ct & St 24401
Thomas St 24401
Thompson St 24401
Thornrose Ave 24401
Tilt Hammer Cir 24401
Timber Scott Ln 24401
Tinkling Spring Rd 24401
Tisdale Farm Ln 24401
Tivoli Ln 24401
Topside Cir 24401
Trace Cir & Dr 24401
Trenary St 24401
Trinity Ln 24401
Triple Ridge Dr 24401
Troll Bridge Ln 24401
Trout St 24401
Troxell Ln 24401
Tuxedo Rd 24401
Twin Maples Ln 24401
Two Wood Ln 24401
Tyler St 24401
Udder Ln 24401
Union Church Rd 24401
Va Institute Way 24401
Valley Center Dr 24401
Valley View Dr & Rd 24401
Van Fossen Ln 24401
Vickers Way 24401
Victoria Dr 24401
Villa View Dr 24401
W Village Dr 24401
Village Green Dr 24401
Vine St 24401
Vinson St 24401
Violet Ct 24401
Virginia Ave & Dr 24401
Virginia Angus Ln 24401
Vista Ln 24401
Vista View Ln 24401
Voilet Ct 24401
Wakefield Cir 24401
Walnut St 24401
Walnut Creek Dr 24401
Walnut Hills Rd 24401
Walnut Ridge Ln 24401
Walters Mountain Ln 24401
Warwick Dr 24401
N & S Washington St 24401
Waterford Loop 24401
Waterton St 24401
N & S Waverley Grn & St 24401
Wayne Ave 24401
Wayt St 24401
Welcher Ln 24401
Wendell Ln 24401
West Ave 24401
Westmoreland Dr 24401
Weston Dr 24401
Westover Dr 24401
Westside Dr 24401
Westview Dr 24401
Westwood Blvd 24401
Wetherwood Dr 24401
Wexford St 24401
Wheat St 24401
Whispering Oaks Dr 24401
White Hill Rd 24401
White Oak Ln 24401
White Oak Gap Rd 24401
Whitehall Ave 24401
Wild Rose Ln 24401
Wilfong Ln 24401
William Cousins Rd 24401
Williams St 24401
Willoughby Ln 24401
Wilson Ln & Loop 24401
Winchester Ave 24401
Windemere Dr 24401
Windjammer Ln 24401
Windsor Ln 24401
Windy Knoll Ln 24401
Winthrop St 24401
Wood Lotts Ln 24401
Woodbrook Ln 24401
Woodcliff Ln 24401
Woodcrest Rd 24401
Woodland Dr 24401
Woodlawn Dr 24401
Woodlee Rd 24401
Woodmont Dr 24401
Woodrow Ave 24401
Woodrow Wilson Pkwy 24401
Woodvale Dr 24401
Woodward St 24401
Wren St 24401
Wythe St 24401
Yardley Sq 24401
York Ave & Ct 24401
Young St 24401
Yount Ave 24401

NUMBERED STREETS

All Street Addresses 24401

STERLING VA

General Delivery 20164

POST OFFICE BOXES MAIN OFFICE STATIONS AND BRANCHES

Box No.s
1 - 3816 20167
1003 - 1227 20166
5000 - 8000 20167
65100 - 65993 20165
636000 - 636000 20163
650001 - 655066 20165

RURAL ROUTES

05 20164
03, 04, 06, 08, 11 20165
01, 09, 12, 17 20166

NAMED STREETS

Aaron Ct 20164
Abbey Cir 20164
Abigail Ter 20165
Abington Ter 20165
Acacia Ln 20166
Acorn Ct 20164
Adelphi Ter 20166
Air Freight Ln 20166
Aisquith Ter 20165
Albemarle Rd 20164
Alberta Ter 20166
Alcott Way 20164
Alden Ct 20165
N & S Alder Ave 20164
Aldridge Ct 20165
Algonkian Pkwy 20165
Allegheny Cir 20165
Allsbrook Pl 20165
Almey Ct 20164
Almond Ct 20164
N Amelia St 20164
Amersham Ct 20165
W & E Amhurst Pl & St 20164
Amin Ct 20164
Amy Ct 20164
Anchorage Cir 20165
Andrew Pl 20164
Angela Sq 20166
Ankers Shop Cir 20164
Antioch Pl 20164
Antler Ct 20164
Aol Way 20166
Applegate Dr 20164
Arbor Ct 20165
Arcola Rd 20166
N Argonne Ave 20164
Argus Pl 20164
Asbury Way 20165
Ascot Sq 20164
N & W Ash Ct & Rd 20164
Ashcroft Ter 20165
Ashgrove Ct 20166
Ashleaf Ct 20165
Ashley Ter 20165
Ashmere Sq 20165
Askegrens Ln 20165
N Aspen Ave 20164
Aster Ter 20164
Atlantic Blvd 20166
Atwood Sq 20164
N Auburn Dr 20164
Augusta Dr 20164
Austen Ct 20165
Auto World Cir 20166
Autopilot Dr 20166
Autumn Leaf Ct 20165
Autumn Olive Way 20164
Avalon Ct 20165
Aviane Way 20166
Aviation Dr 20166
Avondale Dr 20164
Awsley Ct 20165
Azalea Ln 20166
Backwater Dr 20164
Baggett Ter 20166
Bailey Ct 20164
Bainbridge Pl 20165
Baker Ln 20164
Baldwin Sq 20164
W Balsam Rd 20164
Banbury Sq 20165
Bank Way 20165
Barcroft Way 20164
Barnswallow Ct 20164
Bartholomew Fair Dr 20164
Bartlet Sq 20164
Baskin Ct 20164
Bayberry Ct 20164
N Baylor Dr 20164
Bayswater Ter 20166
Beacon Dr 20164
Bears School Rd 20166
Beaufort Ct 20165
Beaver Meadow Rd 20166
Bedford Dr 20165
E & W Beech Rd 20164
Beecher Pl 20164
N Belfort St 20164
Belwood Ct 20165
Benedict Dr 20164
Bennington Ct 20165
Benson Ter 20166
Bentgrass Ter 20165
Bentley Dr 20165
Bentmoor Ct 20165
Benton Ct 20165
Berkeley Ct 20165
Berwick Ct 20165
Bickel Ct 20165
Biltmore Ct 20165
N & S Birch Ct & St 20164

Street	ZIP
Birchfield Pl	20165
Biscayne Ct & Pl	20164
Blackberry Ct	20164
Blackbird Ct	20164
Blackthorn Sq	20166
Blackwater Falls Ter	20165
Blackwood Ct	20166
Blawnox Ter	20165
Blockhouse Point Pl	20165
Blossom Dr	20166
Blossom Landing Way	20165
Blue Heron Ter	20165
Blue Jay Ct	20164
Bluemont Junction Sq	20164
Bluestem Ct	20165
Bobwhite Ln	20165
Bonfire Peach Ter	20164
Boston Ter	20166
Bowline Ter	20165
Box Car Sq	20166
Boxelder Ct	20164
Bradford Ct	20164
Bramble Ct	20164
Branchwood Way	20164
Brandeis Ter	20166
N Brandon Ave	20164
Brandy Station Ct	20165
Brandywine Ct	20165
Brasswood Pl	20165
Bravo Rd	20166
Brawner Pl	20165
Braxton Dr	20165
Breezy Point Ter	20165
Brentmeade Ter	20165
Brethour Ct	20164
Briar Oak Ln	20164
Briarcliff Ter	20165
Briarcroft Plz	20164
Briarwood Ct	20164
Bridalveil Falls Ter	20165
Bridgeport Ct	20165
W & N Brighton Ave & Ct	20164
Brightwater Pl	20165
Brinks Ct	20165
Brisbane Sq	20165
Brixton Ct	20164
Broad Run Dr	20165
Broadleaf Sq	20164
Broadmore Dr	20165
Broadspear Ter	20165
Broadwater Ct	20165
Broderick Dr	20166
Brondesbury Park Ter	20166
Brookfield Cir	20164
Brookmeade Ct	20165
Brookside Ln	20165
Brownwood Sq	20164
E & N Brunswick St	20164
Bryant Ct	20166
Buckeye Ct	20164
Buckingham Ct & Rd	20164
Buckskin Pl	20164
Buckthorn Ct	20164
Bullfinch Sq	20164
Bullrush Pl	20164
Burbank Ter	20166
Burgess Ter	20165
Burning Branch Ter	20164
Burnley Sq	20165
Bushwood Ct	20164
Business Ct	20166
Butternut Way	20164
Butterwood Falls Ter	20165
Byron Ct	20165
Cabin Branch Dr	20164
Caboose Ter	20166
Calamary Cir	20164
Calvert Ct	20164
Cambers Trail Ter	20164
N & S Cameron Ct & St	20164
Camerons Point Ct	20166
Campus Dr	20164
Canal Crossing Ct	20165
Canberra Dr	20165
Candleberry Ct	20164
Canfield Ter	20164
Canopy Ter	20164
Capelwood Ct	20165
Caragana Ct	20164
Caraway Ter	20166
Cardinal Glen Cir	20164
Cargo Dr	20166
Carlyle Ct	20165
Carnwood Ct	20165
Carolina Ct	20164
Carousel Ct	20164
Carpenter Dr	20164
Carriage Ct	20164
Carrollton Rd	20165
Carter Ct	20165
Cascades Pkwy	
20200-20299	20165
21501-21999	20166
21600-21998	20164
Catalina Ct	20166
Catalpa Ct	20164
Cavendish Sq	20165
Cecil Ter	20165
Cedar Ct	20164
Cedar Dr	20164
Cedar Ln	20166
Cedar Green Rd	
22100-22371	20164
22372-22799	20166
22801-22899	20166
Cedar Lake Plz	20164
Cedarhurst Dr	20165
Center Brook Sq	20165
Center Oak Plz	20166
Chambliss Ct	20165
Chamois Ct	20166
Chandler Ct	20164
Channel Ct	20165
Chapin Ct	20165
Charing Ct	20164
E & W Charlotte St	20164
Chase Heritage Cir	20164
Chase View Ter	20164
Chelmsford Ct	20165
Cherokee Ter	20165
Cherry Tree Ct	20164
Cherrywood Ct	20165
Chesapeake Sq	20165
Cheshire Ct	20164
Chester Ter	20165
Chestnut Ct	20164
Chestnut Oak Ter	20166
Cheswick Park Ct	20166
Cheval Ct	20164
Cheyenne Ter	20165
Chimney Ridge Pl	20165
Chinkapin Oak Ter	20166
Chippoaks Forest Cir	20165
Christopher Ln	20165
E & W Church Rd	20164
Cindy Ct	20164
Cinnamon Ct	20164
Circle Dr	20164
City Center Blvd	20166
Clapham Ct	20165
Clarion Ter	20164
Clarkes Crossing Sq	20164
Clear Spring Ter	20165
Clearview Ter	20164
Cliff Haven Ct	20164
Cliftons Point St	20165
Clinton Ct	20165
Clover Field Ter	20165
Clydesdale Ct	20164
Cockpit Ct	20166
Coffee Tree Ct	20164
Colby Ct	20164
Coldspring Pl	20165
Coleman Ln	20165
N College Dr	20164
S Collier Ct	20164
Collingwood Ter	20165
Coloma Ct	20164
Colonel Young Way	20165
Colonial Ave	20164
Colonnade Ter	20166
Colorado Dr	20166
Columbia Pl	20166
Comer Sq	20165
Commerce St	20164
Commerce Center Ct	20166
Community Plz	20164
Compass Ct	20166
Compton Cir	20165
Comstock Cir	20164
E, N, S & W Concord Ct	20164
Concrete Plz	20166
Conductor Ter	20166
Connemara Dr	20164
Conoy Ct	20165
Cooperative Way	20166
Copilot Way	20166
Copper Ct	20165
Corkwing Sq	20164
Corkwood Dr	20165
E Cornell Dr	20164
Cosworth Ter	20165
N & S Cottage Rd	20164
Cottonwood Ct	20164
Cottswold Ter	20165
Country Rd	20165
Countryside Blvd	20165
Courtney Ln	20165
Courtyard Sq	20164
Coventry Sq	20164
Coyote Ct	20165
N Craig St	20164
Cranston St	20165
Crescent Ct	20164
Crestmont Ter	20165
Crisswell Ct	20165
Crouch St	20165
N Croydon Ct & St	20164
Crystal Ct	20164
S Culpeper Rd	20164
Cumberland Ct	20165
Cutwater Pl	20165
N & S Cypress Ct & Rd	20164
Cypress Valley Ter	20166
Dairy Ln	20165
Danbury Ct	20164
Danforth Pl	20165
Darian Ct	20165
Darkhollow Falls Ter	20165
E Dartmouth Dr	20164
Darus Ct	20164
Davenport Dr	20165
Davis Dr	20164
Debhill Ter	20166
Deepwater Ter	20165
Deerwood Ct	20165
Delta Rd	20166
Denizen Plz	20165
Derby Ave & Ct	20164
Derrydale Sq	20165
Devenshire Ct	20165
Devon Ct	20165
S & E Dickenson Ave & Ct	20164
N Dinwiddie St	20164
Dockside Ter	20165
N & S Dogwood Ct & St	20164
Domain Ter	20165
Dominick Ter	20166
Dominion Ln	20166
Doncaster Ter	20165
Dorrell Ct	20165
Douglas Ct	20166
Dove Tree Ct	20164
Drazenovich Epoch Ter	20166
Dresden St	20165
Drew Ct	20165
Driftwood Ter	20165
Drury Cir	20164
Drysdale Ter	20165
Ducksprings Way	20164
Dudley Ct	20165
N Duke Dr	20164
Dulany Ct	20165
Dulles Plz	20166
Dulles Center Blvd	20166
Dulles Crossing Plz	20166
Dulles Eastern Plz	20166
Dulles Landing Dr	20166
Dulles Retail Plz	20166
Dulles Summit Ct	20166
Dulles Town Cir	20166
Dunbar Way	20165
Dunkirk Sq	20165
Dupont St	20164
Eaglewood Ct	20166
Eaker St	20165
Earhart Pl	20165
Earle Wallace Cir	20166
Eastlake Ct	20165
Eaton Ter	20164
Echo Rd	20166
Edds Ln	20165
Eden Dr	20166
Edenberry Ct	20164
Edgewood Ct	20165
Edinburgh Sq	20164
Edwards Ter	20166
Eland Pl	20166
Elizabeth Ct	20164
Elkins Ter	20166
Ellicott Sq	20165
Elm Tree Ln	20164
Elmwood Ct	20166
Emerald Point Ter	20165
Emerson Ct	20164
N Emory Dr	20164
Enterprise St	20164
Environs Rd	20165
Epoch Ter	20166
W Erving Pl	20164
Eskridge Ct	20165
Essex Sq	20164
Esterbrook Cir	20165
Ethan Ct	20164
Evening Way	20164
Evergreen St	20164
Evergreen Mills Rd	20166
Executive Dr	20166
Exeter Ct	20165
Export Dr	20164
Fairchild Ter	20165
Fairgrove Sq	20164
Fairhills Ct	20165
Fairmont Pl	20165
Fairwater Pl	20165
Fairway Dr	20165
Falcon Pl	20166
Falcons Landing Cir	20165
Falke Plz	20166
Fallsway Ter	20165
Farmington Ct, Ln & Ter	20164
Fathom Pl	20165
Fellows St	20165
Felsted Ct	20165
Fenton Wood Dr	20165
Ferguson Ct	20165
Fernbank Ct	20165
Fessenden Ter	20166
Fielding Ter	20164
S Filbert Ct	20164
N & S Fillmore Ave	20164
Finchingfield Ct	20165
N Fir Ct	20164
Fireside Ct	20164
Fitzhugh Ct	20165
Five Oaks Ct	20165
Flatboat Ct	20165
Flatwood Pl	20164
Fleet Ter	20166
Fletcher Rd	20164
Flicker Ter	20164
Flight Crew Dr	20166
Fontwell Sq	20166
Footed Ridge Ter	20166
Forest Overlook Ct	20165
Forest Ridge Dr	20164
Forester Ct	20165
S Fork Ct	20166
Formosa Sq	20164
Forum Ter	20166
S Fox Rd	20164
Fox Hall Ter	20165
Foxmore Ct	20165
Foxstone Pl	20165
E & W Frederick Dr	20164
Free Ct	20164
Freeport Pl	20166
Freistadt Sq	20166
E Furman Dr	20164
Gable Sq	20164
Gallion Forest Ct	20165
Gannon Way	20165
N & S Garfield Rd	20164
Garrett Pl	20165
Gary Ct	20164
Gateway Fountain Plz	20166
Geneva Ter	20165
Gentry Dr	20166
Giles Pl	20164
Glade St	20165
Gladstone Dr	20164
Glenaire Ct	20165
Glenbrook Ter	20165
Glengyle Ct & Ln	20165
Glenmere Sq	20165
Glenn Dr	20164
Glide Slope Dr	20166
Global Plz	20166
Gold Thorn Way	20164
Golden Spike Ter	20166
Goldstone Ter	20164
E Gordon St	20164
Graham Cove Sq	20165
Grammercy Ter	20166
Grand Central Sq	20166
Grandview Pl	20165
Grant Ct	20164
Grayson Pl	20164
Great Falls Plz	20165
Great Falls Forest Dr	20165
Great Trail Ter	20164
Greencastle Rd	20164
Greenfield Ct	20164
Greenoak Way	20166
S & W Greenthorn Ave	20164
Greentree Ter	20164
Griffith Pl	20165
Grisdale Ter	20165
Grissom St	20165
Griswold Ct	20165
Guilford Station Ter	20166
W Gum Ct	20164
Gum Spring Rd	20166
Gunflint Way	20164
Halcyon Pl	20165
Haleybird Dr	20166
Halifax Ct	20165
E Hall Rd	20166
Halleark Ct	20164
Hamilton Ct & Rd	20165
Hammerstone Way	20165
Hampshire Station Dr	20165
Hanford Ct	20165
W Hanover Pl	20164
Harbert Ct	20165
Harding Ct	20164
Hardwood Forest Dr	20165
Harlow Meadows Ter	20166
N & S Harrison Rd	20164
Harrow Ct	20165
Harry Byrd Hwy	20164
Harvest Ln	20164
Hatenback Ct	20164
Haven Ter	20165
Hawick Ter	20165
Hawkins Ln	20165
Hawthorne Ct	20164
Haxall Ct	20165
Hayloft Ct	20164
Hazelnut Sq	20164
Heather Glen Rd	20165
Helen Ct	20164
Hemlock Ct	20164
Hemmingford Cir	20166
Heritage Farm Ln	20164
Heritage Trail Sq	20164
Herring Pond Ter	20165
N Hickory Rd	20164
Hidden Acres Way	20165
Hidden Cove Ct	20165
Highbrook Ct	20165
Highwood Ct	20165
Hillsdale Dr	20164
Hilltop Oaks Ct	20165
Hobblebush Ter	20164
Hobbs Sq	20165
Hoga Rd & St	20164
Holborn Ct	20164
Holiday Dr	20166
Holiday Park Dr	20166
Hollow Falls Ter	20165
Hollow Mountain Pl	20164
E & W Holly Ave	20164
Hollymead Pl	20165
Homestead Rd	20164
Hopeland Ct & Ln	20164
Hopton Ct	20165
Horseshoe Dr	20166
Howard Pl	20164
Hummer Ct	20164
Huntington Sq	20166
Huntley Ct	20165
Hutchens Sq	20166
Hutchinson Farm Dr	20166
E Iberia Rd	20164
Ibex Dr	20166
Idle Brook Ter	20165
Image Ct	20164
Indian Creek Dr	20166
Indian Summer Ter	20166
Ingomar Ter	20166
International Dr	20166
Inwood Ct	20165
Iris Dr	20165
Iron Horse Ter	20166
Iron Oak Ter	20166
Ironstone Ter	20164
Ironwood Ct & Rd	20164
N & S Irving Rd	20164
Island View Ct	20165
Ithaca Ct & Rd	20164
W Ivy Ave	20164
Jackpine Ct	20164
Jackrabbit Ct	20165
Jaclyn Pl	20166
Jason Ct	20164
W Jasper Ct	20164
E Jefferson Ct	20164
Jefferson Dr	20165
E Jefferson Rd	20164
Jenkins Leaf Ter	20166
Jennings Farm Dr	20164
Jeremy Ct	20165
Jermyn Ct	20165
Jesse Ct	20166
N & S Johnson Rd	20164
Johnson Oak Ter	20166
Jona Dr	20165
Jonathan Dr	20164
Joseph Ter	20166
N Joshua Ct	20164
Juneberry Ct	20164
E & W Juniper Ave	20164
Kale Ave & Ct	20164
E Kennedy Rd	20164
Kentwell Pl	20165
Kenyon Ct	20164
Kerrisdale Way	20166
Keswick Sq	20165
Keyes Ct	20164
Kingschase Ct	20165
E Kingsley Ave	20164
Kingston Ct	20165
Knight Ter	20166
Kojun Ct	20164
Lacey Oak Ter	20166
Lacroys Point Ter	20165
Ladbroke Grove Ct	20166
Ladbrook Dr	20166
Lagrande Ct	20165
Lake Dr	20164
Lake Center Plz	20165
Lake Haven Ter	20165
Lakeland Dr	20164
Lakemont Sq	20165
Lakeside Dr	20165
Lancaster Sq	20164
Landau Ct	20164
Lane Ct	20166
Langford Ct	20165
Langley Dr	20165
N Larch Ct	20164
N Laura Anne Ct & Dr	20164
E & W Laurel Ave	20164
Lawnes Creek Ter	20165
League Ct	20165
Leatherleaf Cir & Ct	20164
E & S Lee Ct & Rd	20164
Leechecker Ct	20165
N Leesburg Ct	20164
Lennoxville Way	20166
Leopards Chase Ter	20165
Leslie Ct	20164
Levee Way	20165
Lewins Ct	20165
Lillard Rd	20164
N & S Lincoln Ave	20164
Linden Ct	20164
Lindenwood Ct	20165
Lindsay Ct	20164
Lipscomb Ct	20165
Lisa Gaye Dr	20164
Livingstone Station St	20166
Loblolly Ct	20164
Lock Ct	20165
Lockridge Rd	20166
Locomotive Ter	20166
Locust Ln	20166
Logan Way	20165
Lonetree Ct	20165
Longbank Ct	20165
Longford Way	20165
Longpier Way	20165
Longwood Ct	20165
Lost Trail Ter	20164
Loudoun Park Ln	20164
Loweland Ter	20165
Lowell Ct	20164
N & S Lowery Ct	20165
Lowes Island Blvd	20165
Ludwell Ct	20165
Lyndhurst Ct	20165
E Lynn Ct	20164
Lynnhaven Sq	20165
Macaw Sq	20164
Macgill Ct	20165
E Madison Ct	20164
Magnolia Ct & Rd	20164
Majestic Dr	20166
Major Beckham Way	20165
Malibu Ter	20166
Mallard St	20165
Mallard Point Ter	20165
Manchester Ter	20165
Manekin Plz	20166
Manning Sq	20166
E, W & S Maple Ave & Ct	20164
Maple Hollow Ct	20164
Maple Leaf Pl	20164
Marble Ter	20166
Marcum Ct	20164
Margate Ct	20164
Marguritte Sq	20165
Marian Ct	20165
Maries Rd	20166
Marigold Cir	20164
Mariner Ct	20165
Markborough Ter	20166
Markey Ct	20166
Markwood Dr	20165
Marlane Ter	20166
Marsden Ct	20164

Marsh Ct 20165
Martingale Sq 20165
Mason Oak Ct 20165
Matador Ter 20166
Materials Rd 20166
Mayapple Pl 20164
Mayfield Cir, Sq, Ter &
Way 20164
Maywood Ter 20164
Mccarthys Island Ct 20165
Mccarty Ct 20165
Mcclellan Way 20165
Mcfadden Sq 20165
Mcgees Ferry Way 20165
Mcpherson Cir 20165
Meadow Island Pl 20165
Meadow Ridge Ct 20165
E & W Meadowland
Ln 20164
Meadowvale Glen Ct ... 20166
Meanders Run Ct 20165
Melrose Ct 20164
Memory Ln 20165
Mercer Ct 20165
Mercure Cir 20166
Meskill Ct 20165
Mid Surrey Sq 20165
Midday Ln 20164
Middle Bluff Pl 20165
Middlecreek Ct 20165
Middlefield Dr 20165
Middleton Ln 20164
N & S Midland Ave 20164
Millard Ct 20165
Millwood Sq 20165
Milthorn Ter 20165
Minor Rd 20165
Mint Springs Ct 20165
Miranda Falls Sq 20165
Mirror Ridge Pl 20164
Monarch Dr 20164
Monocacy Sq 20165
Monterey Pl 20166
Montgomery Pl 20165
Moran Rd 20166
Morgan Way 20164
Morning Way 20164
Morningside Ter 20165
Mornington Cresent
Ter 20166
Mosbey Ct 20165
Moss Rd 20165
Mossgrove Ct 20164
Mountain Falls Ter 20165
Mountain Laurel Ter 20164
Mountain Pine Sq 20166
Mucklehany Ln 20165
Muddy Harbour Sq 20165
Muirfield Cir & Ct 20164
Mycroft Ct 20164
Myrtlewood Sq 20164
Nalls Ct 20164
Navigation Rd 20166
Nerine Ct 20165
W Nettle Tree Rd 20164
Newbury Pl 20164
Newfield Pl 20165
Newland Ct 20165
Newman Ct 20164
Newport Ct 20164
Nicholson Ct 20165
Noble Ter 20165
Nokes Blvd 20166
Noland Woods Ct 20165
Northbrook Way 20164
Norwood Ct & Pl 20164
Nutmeg Ct 20164
Oak Ln 20165
Oak Branch Ln 20164
Oak Shade Rd 20164
Oak Trail Sq 20164
Oak Tree Ln 20164
Oakbrook Ct 20166
Oakdale Ct 20165
Oakgrove Rd 20166
Oakhurst Ct 20165
Oakmere Ter 20165
Oakspring Sq 20165
Ocean Ct 20166
Ogden Pl 20166
Old Ox Rd 20166
Old River Way Ct 20164
Old Vestals Gap Rd 20164
Overland Dr 20166
Overmountain Sq 20164
Overton Ct 20165
Owens Ct 20165
Ox Bow Cir 20165
Pacific Blvd 20166
Package Ct 20166
Paddington Station
Ter 20166
Palace Ter 20166
Palmer Ct 20165
Paragon Ter 20164
Parc Dulles Sq 20166
Parisville Ct 20166
Park Hill Ct & Ln 20164
Parkside Cir 20165
Paulsen Sq 20165
Paxton Ct 20165
Peach Oak Ter 20166
Pebble Run Pl 20166
Pebblebrook Pl 20165
Pembridge Ct 20165
Pennrun Way 20165
Penny Ln 20164
Penny Oak Ter 20164
Pepperidge Pl 20164
Persimmon Ln 20165
Peyton Rd 20165
Pheasant Run Ct 20164
Pidgeon Hill Dr 20165
Pin Oak Ct 20164
Pine Ln 20166
Pine Trail Ter 20164
Pine Tree Ct 20164
Pinewood Ct 20164
Piney Branch Way 20165
Pitt Ter 20165
Planetree Forest Ct 20165
Plum Tree Ct 20164
Pomegranate Ct 20164
E & W Poplar Ct &
Rd 20164
Porter Ter 20165
Potomac Hill Sq 20166
Potomac Landing Ter ... 20165
Potomac Ridge Ct 20164
Potomac Run Plz 20164
Potomac View Rd
1600-21299 20165
21300-21500 20164
21502-21998 20164
Powers Ct 20166
Prentice Dr 20166
Prescott Ct 20165
Price Cascades Plz 20164
Pridalls Rd 20166
Prielak Ct 20165
Primavera Cir 20165
Primula Ct 20165
Prince Lowes Ter 20165
Prologis Plz 20166
Promontory Sq 20165
Propeller Ct 20166
Prophecy Ter 20166
Providence Sq 20164
Providence Village Dr .. 20164
Pryor Sq 20165
Pullman Ct 20164
Quarterpath Trace Cir .. 20165
Quay Ln 20165
Queens Quilt Sq 20165
Quicksilver Dr 20166
Quiet Brook Pl 20165
Quincy Ct 20165
Rabbitrun Ter 20164
Rafter Ct 20165
Railway Ter 20166
Ramsgate Ct 20164
Ramshead Ter 20165
Randolph Dr 20166
Ravenwood Ct 20165
Rawlston Ct 20165
Reading Ter 20166
Rector St 20164
Red Lake Ter 20166
Red Oak Ln 20164
Red Wing Ct 20164
Redbark Pl 20165
Redfox Ct 20165
Redlin Ct 20165
Redrose Dr 20165
W Redwood Rd 20164
Reef Ter 20165
Reflection Way 20164
Regal Plz 20165
Regent Ter 20166
Regents Park Cir 20166
Regina Dr 20165
Regis Cir 20164
Relocation Dr 20166
Reserve Falls Ter 20165
Rheims Ct 20164
Rhyolite Pl 20165
Richland Cir 20164
Ridgehaven Ter 20165
Ridgetop Cir 20166
Rippling Dr 20165
Riptide Sq 20165
River Bank St 20165
River Crest St 20165
River Falls Dr 20165
River Meadows Ter
46500-46583 20165
46585-46599 20164
River Oaks Dr 20165
River Ripple Sq 20165
Riverbank Forest Pl 20165
Riverbend Sq 20165
Riverbirch Pl 20165
Rivercliff Ct 20165
Riverland Pl 20165
Riverview Ct 20164
Riverwood Ter 20165
S & E Roanoke Ct &
Rd 20164
Rock Falls Ter 20165
Rock Haven Way 20166
Rock Hill Rd 20166
Rockforest Ct 20166
Rockingham Ter 20165
Rockwood Ter 20164
Rogerdale Pl 20165
Rolling Woods Pl 20164
Rosemallow Ct 20165
Rosewood Pl 20165
Rotunda Ter 20166
Royal Burnham Ter 20165
Royal Palace Sq 20165
Royal Villa Ter 20165
Rudder Rd 20166
Ruislip Manor Way 20166
Running Brook Ln 20164
Rupert Island Pl 20165
Ruritan Cir & Rd 20164
Russell Ct 20165
Rusty Blackhaw Sq 20164
Rutherford Cir 20165
Rutledge Ct 20165
Saarinen Cir 20166
Saffron Ct 20165
Saint Charles Sq 20164
Saint Johns Sq 20164
Salisbury Ct 20164
Sally Ride Dr 20164
Samantha Dr 20164
Sandalwood Sq 20164
Sandbank Sq 20165
Sanderson Dr 20164
Sandian Ter 20165
Sandstone Sq 20165
Saulty Dr 20165
Saynamkhan Ct 20164
Scotsborough Sq 20165
Scott Dr 20164
Sedgemoor Sq 20164
Selden Ct 20165
Selden Island Way 20164
Semblance Dr 20164
Seneca Chase Ct 20164
Seneca Ridge Dr 20164
N Sequoia Ct 20164
Serenity Ct 20165
NW Service Rd 20166
Settlers Point Pl 20165
Severn Way 20166
Sexton Ct 20164
Shadow Woods Ct 20165
Shady Point Sq 20164
Shagbark Ter 20166
Shallow Rock Sq 20164
Sharpskin Island Sq 20165
Shaw Rd
100-599 20166
21900-22099 20164
22100-23299 20166
Sheel Ter 20165
Shepard Dr 20164
Sherwood Ct 20164
Shoal Pl 20165
Shoreline Ter 20165
Shumard Oak Ln 20164
Signal Ct 20164
Signal Hill Plz 20164
Silhouette Sq 20164
Silo Mill Ct 20164
Silver Pond Sq 20165
Silver Ridge Dr 20164
Silverbrook Center Dr .. 20166
Silverleaf Ct & Dr 20164
Simeon Ln 20164
Sinegar Pl 20165
Sisler Ct 20165
Skidmore Ter 20166
Sky Ln 20165
Smithfield Ct 20165
Smithwood Ct 20165
Smoketree Ter 20166
Snow Hill Way 20165
Solomons Ct 20165
Sommersworth Ct 20165
Sonoma Way 20165
Sound Ter 20165
Southall Ct 20165
Southampton Ct 20165
Southbank St 20165
Southern Magnolia Sq .. 20164
Southern Oaks Ter 20164
Southward Ter 20165
Sparrow Pl 20165
Spectrum Way 20164
Spring Ridge Ct 20164
Springlake Ct 20166
Springwood Ct 20165
Spruce Ct 20164
Squire Ct 20166
Stablehouse Dr 20164
Stablemates Ct 20164
Stafford Ct 20165
Stanford Sq 20166
Stanmoor Ter 20165
E Staunton Ave 20164
Steed Pl 20165
Sterdley Falls Ter 20165
N Sterling Blvd 20164
S Sterling Blvd
150-272 20164
150-150 20167
274-906 20164
908-1700 20164
1800-1899 20166
22200-22599 20164
Sterling Plz 20164
Sterling Bridge Pl 20164
Sterling Park Shopping
Mall 20164
Stillhouse Branch Pl 20165
Stillwood Pl 20165
Stone Skip Way 20165
Stonebrook Ct 20164
Stonehelm Ct 20165
Stonehouse Pl 20165
Stonetree Ct 20166
Stoney Creek Ct 20164
Stonington Sq 20164
Straham Way 20165
Stratton Ter 20165
Stukely Dr 20166
Sudbury Sq 20164
Sue Ann Ct 20164
Sugarland Rd 20164
Sugarland Oaks Sq 20164
Sugarland Run Dr 20164
Sugarland Square Ct ... 20164
Sulgrave Ct 20165
Sully Rd 20166
Summer Breeze Ct 20165
Summerhill Pl 20165
Summers Ct 20164
Summerstown Pl 20166
Summit Ter 20164
Sunrise Ter 20165
Surrey Way 20164
Sutherlin Pl 20165
Swan Creek Ct 20165
Swecker Farm Pl 20165
Sweet Birch Ter 20164
Sycamore Ct & Rd 20164
Tag Way 20166
Tamarack Ct & Ln 20164
Tamarack Ridge Sq 20164
Tanglewood Way 20165
Tappahannock Pl 20165
Tavenner Ct 20164
E Tazewell Rd 20164
Teasdale Ct 20165
Temple Ct 20164
Tenfoot Island Ter 20165
Terminal Dr 20166
Terrie Dr 20165
Thales Way 20165
Thayer Rd 20166
Thomas Jefferson Dr ... 20164
Thompson Sq 20166
Thoreau Ct 20164
Thornwood Ct 20165
Thorton Ct 20165
Three Oaks Ct 20164
Thrush Rd 20164
Tidewater Ct 20165
Tilden Ct 20165
Timber Trail Sq 20164
Timberland Pl 20165
Toms Ln 20165
Tottenham Ct 20164
Tottenham Hale Ct 20166
Towlern Pl 20166
Towncenter Plz 20164
Traction Pl 20166
Trade Center Pl 20166
Trade West Dr 20166
Trail Ct 20164
Trail Ridge Ct 20164
Trail Run Ter 20164
Trailside Sq 20165
Trailwood Pl 20165
Tramore Ct 20164
Tranquil Ct 20165
Transamerica Plz 20166
Traskwood Ct 20165
Trefoil Ln 20166
Trestle Ter 20166
Trillum Sq 20165
Trinity Sq 20165
Tripleseven Rd 20165
Trumpet Cir 20164
Tufts Ter 20166
Tupelo Ct 20165
Turner Ln 20165
Turnham Green Ct 20166
Turnstone Sq 20164
Twinridge Sq 20164
Tyler Ln 20165
Underwood Ln 20166
N Upton St 20164
Utica Sq 20165
W Valery Ct 20164
Vandercastel Rd 20165
Vassar Ter 20166
Vermont Maple Ter 20164
W & N Vernon Ct &
St 20164
Victoria Pl 20164
Victoria Falls Sq 20165
Victoria Station Dr 20166
View Glass Ter 20164
Villa Sq 20165
Vinson Ct 20165
Vintage Park Plz 20166
Vista Ct 20165
Volcano Island Dr 20165
Vortac Rd 20166
Wake Ter 20165
Wakefield Ct 20164
Wales Ter 20165
Wallingford Sq 20165
Walpole Ter 20165
Waltham Ct 20165
Warburton Bay Sq 20165
Warden Dr 20166
Warp Dr 20166
Warwick Ct 20164
Warwickshire Ter 20165
Water Mark Pl 20165
Water Valley Ct 20165
Waterbeach Pl 20165
Waterfall Branch Ter ... 20165
Waterloo Station Sq 20166
Waterview Plz 20166
Watford Ct & St 20164
Watkins Island Sq 20165
Waxpool Rd 20166
Weather Service Rd 20166
Weatherburn Ter 20165
Webley Ct 20165
Wedgedale Dr 20164
Wellesley Ter 20166
Welton Ter 20165
Wembley Central Ter ... 20166
Wendy Ln 20165
Wesleyan Ct 20164
West Ct 20165
Westgate Ct 20164
Westlake Dr 20165
Westminster Pl 20164
Westmoreland Dr 20165
Westover Ter 20165
Westridge Dr 20165
Westwick Ct 20165
Westwood Pl 20165
Whaley Ct 20165
Wharf Ct 20165
Whirlpool Sq 20165
Whistle Stop Sq 20164
Whistling Ter 20166
Whitcomb Sq 20166
White Oak Dr 20165
Whitechapel Way 20165
Whitehall Ter 20166
Whitewater Dr 20165
Whitfield Pl 20165
Whittingham Cir 20165
Wicker Ct 20164
Wickham Ct 20165
Wideoak Ct 20164
Wilder Ct 20166
Willesden Junction Ter . 20166
N & S Williamsburg Ct &
Rd 20164
Willoughby Sq 20165
Willow Pl & Ter 20164
Willow Pond Plz 20164
Willowmere Ct 20165
Willowood Pl 20165
Wiltshire Ct E & W 20165
Winchester Dr 20164
Wind Sock Dr 20166
Windemere Ct 20165
Winding Rd 20165
Winding Branch Ter 20166
Windrift Ter 20165
Windrush Ct 20165
Windsor Ct 20164
Winfield Pl 20165
Winsbury West Pl 20166
Winter Frost Ct 20165
Winterset Ct 20165
Winterwood Way 20165
Wood Owl Ct 20164
Woodboro Ter 20165
Woodgate Ct 20164
Woodhaven Ct 20165
Woodlake Pl 20165
Woodland Rd 20166
Woodmere Ct 20165
Woodmint Ter 20164
Woodshire Dr 20166
Woodson Dr 20164
Woodstone Ter 20164
Woodthrush Ct 20165
Woolcott Sq 20165
Worthington Ct 20165
Wren Ct 20164
Wrightwood Pl 20164
Wyatt Ct 20165
Yew Ct 20164
N York Rd 20164
Youngs Cliff Rd 20165

STRASBURG VA

General Delivery 22657

POST OFFICE BOXES MAIN OFFICE STATIONS AND BRANCHES

Box No.s
All PO Boxes 22657

RURAL ROUTES

01 22641

NAMED STREETS

Abby Ln 22657
Aden Dr 22657
E Afton Pl 22657
Aileen Ave 22657
Alsberry St 22657
Amos Ln 22657
Andrews Rd 22657
Angel St 22657
Anna Mae Ct 22657
Artz St 22657
Ash St 22657
Back Rd 22657
Banks Fort Rd 22657
Barn Owl Ln 22657
Battlefield Rd 22657
Beacon St 22657
Beeler Dr 22657
Bethel Rd 22657
Big Sky Rd 22657
Blue Bell Ln 22657
Bluff Rd 22657
Bobcat Ln 22641
Borden Mowery Dr 22657
Borum St 22657
Bowman Mill Rd 22657
Branch St 22657
Brandy Ct 22657
Breckenridge Ct 22657
Brill Dr 22657
Brooks Ln 22657
Brown St 22657
Bruebeck Ln 22657
Bucks Mill Rd 22657
Burgess St 22657
Calamus Ln 22657
Cannon Ct 22657
Capon Rd & St 22657
Capon Heights Ln 22657
Cardinal St 22657
Carrier Dr 22657

Catlett Farm Rd 22657
Cavalry Ct 22657
Cedar Ln & Rd 22657
Cedar Berry Dr 22657
Cedar Crossing Ln 22657
Cedar Hill Rd 22657
Cedar Lake Ct 22657
Cedar Spring Ln 22657
N & S Charles St 22657
Chester St 22657
Chickory Ln 22657
Christiansen Dr 22657
Church Hill Ln 22657
Clary Rd 22657
Clear View Ln 22657
Coal Mine Rd 22657
Colley Block Rd 22657
Company House Ln 22657
Cool Spring Rd 22657
Copp Rd 22657
Cottontown Rd 22657
Courtney Cir 22657
Cozy Acres Ln 22657
Crawford St 22657
Crim Dr 22657
Crystal Ln & Pl 22657
Crystal Hill Ct 22657
Cullers Ln 22657
Daniel Ct 22657
Deaken Cir 22657
Deep Hollow Ln 22657
Deer Meadow Dr 22657
Deer Place Ct 22657
Deer Rapids Rd 22657
Dellinger Dr 22657
Depot Rd & St 22657
Devine Dr 22657
Dickerson Ln 22657
Dixie Ln 22641
Dower Ln 22657
Duke Cir 22657
Dutchess Cir 22657
N & S Eberly St 22657
Edith Ln 22657
Ellen Dr 22657
E & W Fairchild Dr 22657
Forest Dr 22657
Forest Glen Ct 22657
N & S Fort St 22657
Fort Bowman Rd 22657
Fort Valley Rd 22657
Founders Way 22657
Fox Den Rd 22657
Fox Ridge Dr 22657
N & S Franklin St 22657
Fravel Park 22657
Front Royal Rd 22657
Frontier Fort Ln 22657
Fulton Dr 22657
N & S Funk Rd & St 22657
Gap Rd 22657
Gardner Ln 22657
Green Acre Dr 22657
Greenleaf Rd 22657
Hailey Ln 22657
Hall Ln 22657
Helsley Hts 22657
Hidden Ln 22657
High St 22657
Hilltop Farm Ln 22657
Hite Ln 22657
Hockman Rd 22657
N & S Holliday St 22657
Hollis Cir 22657
Homewood Way 22657
Hope St 22657
Horseshoe Ln 22657
Howard Ln 22657
Hupp St 22657
Hupps Hill Ct 22657
Indian Rock Rd 22641
Indian Run Ln 22657
Island Farm Rd 22657
Island Ford Ln 22657
Jackson St 22657
Jenkins Ln 22657
Jenny Ct 22657
Jesse Ln 22657
John Marshall Hwy
5307A-5307B 22641
200-5299 22657
5300-5352 22641
5353-5353 22657
5354-10198 22641
5355-9399 22641
Julius Keller Rd 22657
Junction Rd 22657
Junction Overlook 22657
Kanter Dr 22657
Keller Ln 22657
E & W King St 22657
Koy Ct 22657
Lake Ridge Rd 22657
Lakes Valley Rd 22657
Laurel Hill Way 22641
Laurie Dr 22657
Lee St 22657
Lee Rae Ct 22657
Lemley St 22657
Lincoln St 22657
Lindamood Ln 22641
Lineburg Ln 22657
Little Sorrel Dr 22657
Locust Dr 22657
Locust Grove Rd 22657
Logan Cir 22657
N & S Loudoun St 22657
Loving Ln 22657
Lower Ct 22657
Lower Valley Rd 22657
Lower View Rd 22657
Macs Mountain Rd 22657
Mallewo Rd 22657
E & W Maphis St 22657
N & S Marshall St 22657
N & S Massanutten Hts, Mnr & St 22657
Massanutten Manor Cir 22657
Mathison Ct 22657
Maynard Ln 22657
Mcdonald Ln 22641
Meadow Mills Rd 22657
Meadow View Ln 22657
Messick Rd 22657
Middle Rd
7900-9999 22657
10100-10199 22641
Mile Ridge Ests 22641
Miller Dr 22657
Millner Rd 22657
Minebank Rd 22657
Mineral St 22657
Mitchell Dr 22657
Moores Ford Rd 22657
Moose Ridge Dr 22657
Mountain Rd 22657
Mountain Pond Rd 22657
Mt Hebron Rd 22657
Mulberry St 22657
Mumaw Rd 22657
Musket Ln 22657
Natures Way Ln 22657
Neff Ln 22657
Nelson Rd 22657
Newman St 22657
E & W North St 22657
Oak Cir 22657
Old Factory Rd 22657
Old Grade Rd 22657
Old Valley Pike 22657
Oranda Rd 22657
Orchard St 22657
Orndorff Rd 22657
Oxbow Dr 22657
Pangle Ln 22657
Passage Manor Dr 22657
Peach Orchard Rd 22657
Pendleton Ln 22657
Penny Ln 22657
Penny Ann Ln 22657
Philips Ct 22657
Pike St 22657
Pine Cir 22657
Pine Grove Rd 22657
N Place Ln 22657
Pleasant View Dr 22657
Pontzer Rd 22657
Posey Hollow Ln 22657
Post Office Rd 22641
Potters Cir 22657
Pouts Hill Rd 22657
Powhatan Rd 22657
Quarry Ln 22657
E & W Queen St 22657
Racey Ln 22657
Radio Station Rd 22657
Ram Dr 22657
Red Bud Rd 22657
Richardson Rd 22657
River Lakes Dr 22657
Rocky Ln 22657
Rocky Bluff Rd 22657
Rocky View Dr 22657
Rogers Mill Rd 22657
Rose Ln 22657
Royal Ave 22657
Ruth Ct 22657
Rutz Ln 22657
Sadlick Rd 22657
Sager Holw 22657
Sandy Hook Rd 22657
Savannah Dr 22657
Seldon Dr 22657
Settlers Way 22657
Shady Ln 22657
Sharpe St 22657
Shenandoah Valley Dr 22657
Shepherds Rd 22657
Shopping Center Rd 22657
Signal Ct 22657
Signal Knob Dr 22657
Signal Knob Cottage Dr 22657
Signal View Rd 22657
Southern Dr 22657
Speelman Ln 22657
Spiker Ln 22657
Stickley Loop & St 22657
Stone Cir 22657
Stonewall St 22657
Stoney Mountain Dr 22657
Stony Pointe Way 22657
Stover Ave 22657
Strasburg Rd 22657
Strasburg Reservoir Rd 22657
Stuart Ct 22657
Sunflower Ln 22657
Sunset St 22657
Taylor St 22657
Thompson St 22657
Timberlake Rd 22657
Tracy Dr 22657
Triplett Rd 22657
Tumbling Run Ln 22657
Tyler Cir 22657
Valley Lake Dr 22657
Valley Overlook Ct 22657
Valley Park Ct & Rd 22657
Valley View Dr 22657
Varghese Dr 22657
Vincond Hwy 22641
N & S Virginia Cir, Dr & St 22657
Walnut Hill Ln 22657
Walton St 22657
E & W Washington St 22657
N Water St 22657
Waverly Dr 22657
Waxwing Ln 22657
White Deer Ln 22657
White Ox Ln 22657
White Rock Ln 22657
Williams Ln 22641
Wise Ave 22657
Woods Ln 22657
Wren Ln 22657
Zea St 22657

SUFFOLK VA

General Delivery 23432
General Delivery 23433
General Delivery 23434
General Delivery 23435
General Delivery 23437
General Delivery 23438

POST OFFICE BOXES MAIN OFFICE STATIONS AND BRANCHES

Box No.s
1 - 1978 23439
2001 - 2617 23432
3001 - 4320 23439
5001 - 5620 23435
6001 - 6152 23433
7001 - 7414 23437
8001 - 8237 23438
8990 - 18000 23439

NAMED STREETS

Abercorn Dr 23435
Aberdeen Pl 23435
Abingdon Cir 23434
Abraham St 23434
Adams Dr E 23433
Adams Dr W 23436
Adams St 23434
Adams Swamp Rd
3300-4499 23434
4501-4503 23434
4502-4594 23438
4596-4699 23438
Adderly Pl 23434
Adkins Cir 23434
Adorn Ct 23434
Afton Ct 23435
Ainslie Ct N & S 23434
Airport Ct & Rd 23434
Alabama Ave 23434
Alder Pl 23435
Alexander Ct 23434
Amberly Cir & Ct 23435
Amedeo Ct 23434
Ames Cove Dr 23435
Anderson Ave 23435
Anna Goode Way 23434
Anthony Pl 23432
Appaloosa Ct 23434
Apple St 23435
Applewood Ct 23434
Arabian Pl 23435
Arbor Ct & Rd 23435
W Arbor Arch 23433
Arbor Bluff Cv 23435
Arcanum Ln 23434
Archers Dr 23434
Archers Mill Rd 23434
Arizona Ave 23434
Armor Way 23435
Armstead Rd 23435
Armstrong Ave 23435
Arrington St 23435
Arrow Head Ct 23435
Art Ct 23434
Art Ray Dr 23434
Arthur Dr 23438
Ashburn Rd 23434
Ashby Ct 23435
Ashcrest Ct 23435
Ashford Dr 23434
Ashley Ave 23434
Ashmeade Ct 23435
Ashwood Dr 23434
Aspen Ct 23434
Atlantic Coastline Ave 23434
Auburn Ct 23434
Audubon Rd 23434
Augusta Ct 23435
Austin Dr 23434
Autumn Cir 23434
Avery Ct 23434
Ayers Creek Ln 23434
Azalea Ct 23434
B St 23434
Babbtown Rd 23434
Badger Rd 23434
Bailey Cir 23434
Baker St 23434
Baltic St 23434
Bank St 23434
Bank Street Ext 23434
Barbara Dr 23434
Barclay Pl 23435
Barka Dr 23434
Barn Owl Ct 23434
Barnes Rd 23437
Baron Blvd 23435
Barrett Dr 23434
Bartons Creek Ct 23435
Battery Ave 23434
Bay Cir 23435
Bay Breeze Dr 23435
N & S Bay Hill Ct 23435
Bay Shore Ln 23435
Bayberry Ln 23433
Bayport Lndg 23435
Beamons Mill Trl 23434
Bearadia Rd 23438
Beaton St 23434
Bedford Pl 23434
Beech St 23434
Beech Grove Ln 23435
Beech Tree Ct 23433
Beechwood Ave & Dr 23434
Bell St 23434
Belle Orchard Ln 23435
Belleharbour Cir 23435
Ben St 23434
Benham Ct 23434
Bennetts Creek Ln & Lndg 23435
Bennetts Creek Park Rd 23435
Bennetts Meadow Ln 23435
Bennetts Pasture Rd 23435
Benson Ct 23435
Bent Pine Ln 23434
Bentley Dr 23435
Benton Rd 23434
Berkshire Blvd 23434
Bernhowe Manor Ln 23435
Berry Ridge Ln 23435
Berwyn Way 23435
Bethlehem St 23434
Bidwell St 23434
Billings Dr 23435
Birdie Dr 23434
Biscayne St 23434
Bishop Pl 23434
Black Oak Ct 23435
Black Pine Ct 23435
Blackstone Way 23435
Blair St 23434
Blair Brothers Rd 23435
Blaze Ct 23435
Bleakhorn Rd 23433
Blossom Ct 23434
Blue Heron Pt 23435
Blue Stem Ct 23435
Blue Teal Ct 23435
Blue Wing Ln 23435
Bluebill Dr 23435
Bluegrass Rd 23435
Blythewood Ln 23434
Boat St 23434
Bob Foeller Dr 23434
Bob White Ln & Pkwy 23435
Bogie Dr 23434
Bond Ln 23434
Boonetown Rd 23438
Bosley Ave 23434
Bott Ln 23437
Boundary Dr 23434
Bowen Pkwy 23435
Box Elder Rd 23437
Boxwood Ct 23434
Boynton Pl 23435
Bracey Dr 23434
Brackley Ct 23434
Bradford Dr 23435
Braebourne Ct 23435
Bravo Ct 23434
Breezeport Way 23435
Breleigh Ln 23435
Brent St 23435
Brentwood Rd 23437
Brewer Ave 23434
Brians Ln 23434
Bridge Rd
1400-2299 23433
2500-4899 23435
Bridge Point Trl E 23432
Bridgewater Ct 23434
Bridle Path Ln 23435
Bridlewood Ln 23434
Briggs St 23434
Bright Dr & Ln 23434
Brighton Mews 23435
Brittany Ln 23435
Brittle Dr 23434
N & S Broad St 23434
Brook Ave 23434
Brookline Dr 23434
Brookstone Way 23435
Brookwood Ct & Dr 23435
Bruce St 23434
Bruce Farm Dr 23435
Buchanan St 23435
Buckhorn Dr
100-1599 23437
1600-2199 23434
Buckhorne Cres & Ct 23435
Buckingham Rd 23435
Bullock St 23434
Bunch Ave 23434
Buoy Ct 23435
Burbage Dr 23435
Burbage Acres Dr 23435
Burbage Lake Cir 23435
Burbage Landing Cir 23435
Burlington St 23435
Burnetts Ct & Way 23434
Burning Tree Ct & Ln 23435
Burr Oak Pl 23435
Bute St 23434
Butler Ave 23434
Butler Dr 23437
Butternut Ct 23434
Byrd St 23434
C St 23434
Cabaret Ln 23435
Cain Ct 23435
Calvert Ct 23435
Calvin St 23435
Cambridge Dr W 23435
Camel Back Ct 23434
Camellia Dr 23435
Camero Ct 23434
Cameron Xing 23434
Camp Pond Rd 23437
Campbell Ct 23435
Canaan Cir 23435
Canal Turn Ct 23435
Canine Trl 23434
Cannon St 23434
Canterbury Ln 23435
Canterbury Crest Ln 23436
Cantering Ct 23435
Cantor St 23434
Canvasback Dr 23435
N & S Capital St 23434
Capps Creek Dr 23435
Captains Walk 23435
Cardinal Ln 23434
Carlisle Ct 23435
Carolina Ave & Rd 23434
Caroline Cres 23435
Carr Ln 23437
Carriage Ct 23434
Carriage House Dr 23434
Carroll St 23434
Carter Ln 23435
Carters Cove Rd 23433
Carver Ave 23434
Casper Ct 23434
Cassidy Ct 23434
Castle Ct 23434
Castlewood Cir 23435
Catalina Ave 23434
Catalpa Ct 23435
Catapult Ct 23434
Cathedral Dr 23434
Cattail Cove Ct 23435
Catterick Cv 23435
Causey Ave 23434
Cavaletti Chase 23435
Cavalier Rd 23435
Cedar Ct & St 23434
Cedar Creek Ln 23432
Cedar Crest Ln 23436
Cedar Lake Dr 23434
Cedar Street Ext 23434
Cedarwood Ln 23434
Cencoria Dr 23433
Centerbrooke Ln 23434
Centerpoint Dr 23434
Central Ave 23434
Chambers Ln 23435
Champions Way 23435
Chancellor Ct 23434
Chandler Pl 23435
Chapel Hill Ct 23434
Chappell Dr 23437
Charlemagne Dr 23435
Charles St 23434
Charlotte Ave 23434
Chatham Rd 23435
Chelsea Mews 23435
Chenango Cres & Ct 23434
Chenti Rd 23437
Cheriton Ln 23434
Cherokee Ct & Dr 23434
Cherry St 23434
Cherry Blossom Dr 23434
Cherry Grove Rd 23438
Cherry Grove Rd N 23432
Cherry Hill Ln 23435
Cherry Point Rd 23436
Cheshire Dr 23435
Chestnut St 23434
Chisholm Ln 23434
Church St 23434
Cider Ln 23435
Claremont Dr 23434
Clarys Dr 23434
Clay St 23434
Clay Hill Rd 23434
Clearbrook Ln 23434
Clearcreek Rd 23434
Clifton St 23435
Clipper Cove Ln 23435
Clover Ln 23434
Club Rd 23435
Clubhouse Dr 23433
Coachhouse Ct 23435
Coachman Dr N & S 23435
Cog Hill Ct 23435
Cogic Sq 23434
Cole Ave 23435
College Ct 23434
College Dr 23435
Collier Cres 23434
Collins Rd 23438
Colonel Meade Dr 23434
Colonial Ave 23434
Colonial Dr 23435
Coltrane Ave 23435
Columbus Ave 23434
Commerce St 23434
Commercial Ln 23434
Commodore Blf 23435
Compass Ct 23435
Compton Ct 23435

Concord Dr 23435
E & W Constance Rd 23434
Constance Woods Dr 23434
Contonde Rd 23434
Cook Rd 23435
Cooper Ln 23435
Copeland Rd 23434
Coral Ct 23434
Corinth Chapel Rd 23437
Cornus Ct 23433
Corporate Ln 23434
Corral Cv 23435
Cortland Ct 23434
Cottage Ct 23434
Cotton Farm Ln 23432
Cottondale Pl 23435
Cottonwood Ct 23434
Count Cres 23435
Country Club Dr 23435
County St 23434
Cove St 23435
Cove Point Dr 23434
Coxley Ln 23435
Craftsman Cir 23434
Craig Dr 23434
W Creek Ct 23435
Creekside Ct 23435
Crestwood Dr 23437
Cripple Creek Ln 23434
Crittenden Rd
6000-8099 23432
8100-8999 23436
Crocker Ln & St 23434
Crooked Stick Way 23435
Cross St 23433
Cross Ter 23434
Cross Landing Dr 23434
Crosswinds Ct 23435
Crowdy Blvd 23435
Crown Arch 23435
Crumpler Ln 23432
Crystal Bay Cir 23435
Cullen Ln 23435
Culloden St 23434
Culpepper Ln 23434
Cumberland Ln 23437
Cummings Dr 23434
Curry Comb Pt 23435
Cushing St 23435
Custis Rd 23434
Cutspring Trce 23434
Cuttysark Ln 23435
Cypress Cir 23434
Cypress Chapel Rd
100-599 23438
600-1899 23434
Cypress Cove Ln 23434
Cypresswood Ln 23434
Dallerne Rd 23436
Dana Dr 23434
Darby Ct 23435
Darden Ave 23434
Darden Ln 23435
Darden Farm Ln 23435
Darlington Ct 23434
Davenport Ct 23434
David Ln 23434
Davis Blvd 23434
Dawn Ln 23432
Day St 23434
Dayle Acres Rd 23435
Deal Trl 23434
Deanes Station Rd 23435
Deborah Dr 23434
Deer Forest Rd 23434
Deer Path Rd
2900-4899 23434
4900-4904 23437
4901-4905 23434
4906-5299 23437
Deer Run Ct 23434
Deerfield Ct & Dr 23435
Delaney Dr 23434
Delaware Ave 23434
Dennis Pl 23435
Derby Cv 23435
Desert Rd 23434
Devonshire Ct 23434
Dickens Ct E & W 23435
Diggs Ct 23435
Dill Rd 23434
N & S Division St 23434
Dixon Dr 23433
Dock Ct 23435
Dock Landing Ct 23435
Dockside Cres 23435
Doe Run Ct 23434
Dogwood Ln 23434
Dominion Dr 23435
Donald Ave 23435
Doncaster Dr 23435
Doral Woods Ct 23435
Dorothy Ln 23435
Dorset Way 23434
Douglas Ct 23434
Dove Ct 23434
Dover Ct 23434
Dover Dr 23435
Driver Ln 23435
Driver Pointe Ct 23435
Driver Station Way W 23435
Drum Hill Rd 23438
Duck Landing Ct 23435
Duckwood Ct 23435
Dudley Dr 23434
Duke St 23434
Duke Of Glouchester Dr 23434
Duke Of Norfolk St 23434
Duke Of York St 23434
Dumpling Ct 23435
Dumville Ave & Ln 23434
Dunbar Dr 23434
Dutch Rd 23437
Dutchess Way 23435
Dutchland Trl 23434
Dykes Park Ln 23434
Eagle Ln 23432
Eagle Point Cres 23434
Eagles Nest Trce 23435
Earl Ct 23434
Eberwine Ln 23435
Eclipse Dr 23433
Edgefield Ct 23435
Edgewater Ln 23435
Edgewood Ave 23434
Edinburgh Ct 23434
Edward Ave 23434
Egret Cir 23436
Elderberry Rd 23435
Elenor St 23438
Eley Ct & St 23434
Elizabeth St 23434
Ellen St 23434
Ellington Ave 23435
Ellis Rd 23437
Elm St 23434
Elm Tree Ct 23435
Elmington Way 23434
Elmore Cir 23434
Elwood Rd 23437
Emerald Ct 23434
Emma Ave 23434
English Oak Dr 23434
Ennis Mill Rd 23434
Eola Ave 23434
Equinox Lndg 23434
Eric Ct 23434
Erin Dr 23435
Eugenia St 23434
Everets Rd 23434
Everhart Ct 23434
Exchange Rd 23434
Executive Ct 23434
Exeter Dr 23434
Factory St 23434
Fair Oaks Ln 23432
Fairfield Ave 23434
Fairview Dr 23437
Fairway Dr 23433
W Falcon St 23434
Fallawater Way 23434
Farmview Ln 23434
Farrier Cv 23435
Faulk Rd 23434
Fawn Ct 23435
Fayette St 23434
Fdr Ct 23434
Fennell Ct & Ln 23435
Ferguson Pl 23435
Fern Ln 23434
Fernwood Ct 23434
Ferry Rd 23435
Ferry Point Rd 23432
Festival Ct 23434
Fieldbrook Pl 23434
Fieldcrest Ct 23435
Fieldstone Ln 23434
Film Way 23434
Fincastle Ct 23435
Finish Line Arch 23435
W Finney Ave 23434
Five Mile Rd 23434
Flick Ct 23434
Florida Ave 23434
Fontwell Ct 23435
Ford Dr 23435
Forest Glen Cir & Dr 23434
Forest Hill Cres 23434
Forest Lake Ct 23435
Forest Oak Ln 23434
Forrest St 23434
Forsythia Ct 23435
Fort St 23434
Fox Run Pl 23434
Fox Wood Run Pl 23434
Foxcroft Rd 23435
Foxwood Pl 23435
Foxworth Cir & Ct 23435
Frank St 23434
Franklin St 23434
Frazier Ave 23435
Frederick St 23435
Freeman Ave 23435
Freeman Mill Rd 23438
Freeney Ave 23434
Friar Ct 23434
Fulcher St 23434
Fuller St 23434
Galiceno Ct 23434
Garden Ln 23434
Gardenbrook Pl 23434
Gardenia Ct 23435
Gardenstone Cir 23434
Gardner Ln 23434
Garfield Ave 23434
Gaskins Ln 23435
Gates Rd 23437
Gates Run Rd 23438
Gatewood Ave 23434
Gauntlet Way 23434
Gays Row 23434
Gene Ave 23434
Gene Bolton Dr 23434
General Early Dr 23434
General Pickett Dr 23434
Gentry St 23435
Georgia Ave 23434
Ginkgo Ct 23435
Girl Scout Dr 23434
Gittings St 23434
Glasgow St 23435
Glebe Point Rd 23435
E Glen Haven Dr 23437
Gleneagles Way 23435
Glenrose Dr 23435
Glenwood Dr 23434
Gloucester St 23434
Godwin Blvd
2400A-2400F 23434
2300-5699 23434
5700-6599 23432
Gold Cup Pt 23435
Golden Maple Dr 23434
Golden Sunset Ln 23435
Goldeneye Ct 23435
Goodlin Dr 23434
Goodman St 23434
Goodwin St 23434
Goose Creek Ln 23434
Goshawk Ct 23435
Governors Ln 23436
Governors Pointe Dr 23436
Governors Wharf 23432
Grace St 23434
Grainery Rd 23437
Granby St 23434
Grant St 23435
Gray Ct 23434
Grayson Ct 23434
Graystone Trce 23435
Great Fork Rd 23438
Great Oak Ct 23434
Green Ash Ct 23435
Green Spring Dr 23435
Green Wing Ct & Dr 23434
Greene Chapel Rd 23434
Greenfield Cres 23434
Greenway Rd
100-1099 23434
1200-3399 23438
Greenwood Cir 23435
Greenwood Rd 23437
Gresham Ln 23435
Griffin Ln 23435
Griggs St 23434
Grove Ave 23434
Gum Ct 23435
Gunston Dr 23434
Hackberry Ct 23435
Halifax St 23434
Hall Ave 23434
Halter Cv 23435
Hamer Rd 23434
Hamilton Ct 23435
Hampton Roads Pkwy 23435
Hannah Hunt Blvd 23434
Happys Dr 23434
N Harbor Rd 23435
Harborwood Pl 23436
Harbour Pointe Dr 23435
Harbour Towne Pkwy 23435
Harbour View Blvd 23435
Hardy Ct & Dr 23435
Hare Rd 23437
Harewood Ln 23435
Hargrove Lndg & Trce 23435
Harlan Dr 23436
Harrell Dr 23434
Harrison St 23434
Harvest Dr 23437
Harvest Reach Ln 23434
Haskins Dr 23434
Hastings Pl 23436
Haverhill Ct 23434
Hawk Ln 23432
Hawks Nest Ln 23435
Haydock Ct 23435
Hazelcroft Dr 23435
Heath Dr 23434
Heather Glen Dr 23435
Hedrick Ct 23434
Helen St 23435
Henderson Ct 23434
Hennesy Cup Way 23435
Henry St 23434
Heritage Dr 23435
Herman Ct 23438
Heron Ct 23433
Hickory Neck Ln 23437
Hickorywood Dr 23434
Highfield Rd 23434
Highland Ave 23434
Hill St 23434
Hillpoint Blvd & Rd 23434
Hillside Ave 23434
Hobson Dr 23436
Hoffler St 23435
Hogans Way 23435
Holbrook Arch 23434
Holiday Point Dr 23435
Holladay St 23434
Holland Rd
1548A-1548C 23434
1100-1198 23434
1200-4199 23434
4200-6699 23437
Holland Corner Rd 23437
Holly Rd 23435
Holly Hill Ln 23434
Holly Point Ln 23436
Hollywood Ave 23434
Holston Ct 23435
Holy Neck Rd 23437
Homestead Ln 23437
Hopemont Ln 23434
Horseback Ln 23437
Horseshoe Point Rd 23432
Hosier Rd 23434
Howard Pl 23434
Howell Blvd 23434
Hubbard Ave 23435
Hudgins Cir 23436
Hull St 23434
Humphreys Dr 23435
Huntclub Chase 23435
Hunter St 23434
Hunters Ct 23435
Hunters Creek Pl 23435
Huntersville Pl 23435
Huntsman Ct 23435
Ibis Blvd 23434
Indian Trl
2100-5926 23434
5927-5941 23437
5928-5942 23434
5943-7699 23437
Indian Point Rd 23434
Industrial Dr 23435
Inlet Pl 23435
Integra Ct 23434
Island Park Cir 23435
Ithaca Trl 23435
Ivanhoe Ct 23435
Jackson Rd & St 23434
N James Ave & Dr 23435
James Point Ct 23435
Jasmine Ln 23437
Jefferis Ct 23434
Jefferson St 23434
Jehu St 23435
Jenkins Mill Rd 23437
Jennifer Ct 23434
Jericho Ditch Ln 23434
Jester Cir 23434
Jfk Ct 23434
Jib Ct 23435
John St 23435
John Deere St 23434
John T Mullen Rd 23438
Johnson Ave & Ln 23434
Jolly Ln 23437
Jonathans Way 23434
Jones St 23434
Jordan Ave & Cir 23434
Joshua Ln 23434
Jouster Way 23434
Joyner Ct & St 23434
Judah Ln 23435
Judkins Ct 23434
Juniper Ln 23435
Justin Ct 23434
Kansas St 23434
Katherine St 23434
Keaton Way 23434
Kelso Ct & St 23435
Kemp Lndg 23434
N & S Kemper Lakes Ct 23435
Kempton Park Rd 23435
Kendal Ct & Way 23435
Kenmore St 23434
Kennedy Ct 23434
Kennet Dr 23434
Kensington Blvd 23434
Kent Ct 23435
Kentucky Ave 23434
Kenyon Ct & Rd 23434
Keswick Ct 23435
Ketches Ct 23435
Kilbourne Way 23435
Kilby Ave, Ct & Ln 23434
Kilby Shores Dr 23434
King Ct & St 23434
King Charles Ct 23435
King Fisher Dr 23435
King Of France Ct 23435
Kings Hwy
100-1516 23432
1518-1598 23432
1700-3199 23435
Kings Fork Cir & Rd 23434
Kings Grant Cir 23434
Kings Point Dr 23434
Kings Reach 23435
Kingsale Rd 23437
Kingsboro St 23434
Kingsdale Rd 23434
Kingston Pkwy 23434
Kingsway Ct 23435
Kinnards Ct 23434
Kinsey Ln 23434
Kippling Ct 23434
Kirk Rd 23434
Kissimmee Ave 23434
Knight St 23434
Knotts Creek Ln 23435
Knotts Neck Rd 23435
Kristen Ln 23434
Kyle Ct 23434
Labrador Ct & Ln 23434
Lake Dr 23434
Lake Rd 23435
Lake Cohoon Pt & Rd 23434
Lake Cove Ct 23435
Lake Front Dr 23434
Lake Kennedy Dr 23434
Lake Kilby Rd 23434
Lake Meade Dr 23434
Lake Point Ln & Rd 23434
Lake Prince Dr 23434
Lake Speight Dr 23434
Lake View Pkwy 23435
Lakeland Ave & Trl 23434
Lakes Edge Dr 23434
Lakeside Ct 23435
Lakeside Dr 23435
Lakeside St 23434
Lakeview Ct 23434
Lakewood Dr 23434
Lamb St 23434
Lambeth Pl 23435
Lamplight Ct 23435
Lance Ct 23435
Lancelot Dr 23434
Landing Ct 23434
Lane St 23438
Larry Anne Dr 23434
Lassiter Ln 23434
Laucks Trl 23434
Laurel Ave 23434
Laurel Lake Ln 23433
Lawson Cir 23434
Laxey Ct 23434
Leafwood Rd 23437
Lee St 23434
Lee Farm Ln 23435
Lee Hall Ave 23435
Leefield Ct 23435
Leesville Rd 23437
Legends Way 23435
Lenox Ct 23434
Lewis Ave 23434
Lexington Ave 23434
Leyton Pl 23435
Liberty St 23434
N & W Liberty Spring Rd 23434
Lida Ave 23434
Lighthouse Dr 23435
Lincoln Ave 23434
Linden Ave 23434
Lingfield Cv 23435
S Links Cir 23435
Linkside Ct 23435
Lipton Cir 23434
Little Creek Rd 23434
Little Fork Rd 23438
Little John Rd 23435
Little Pond Ct 23434
Litton Ln 23434
Liverpool Ln 23435
Livery St 23435
Livingston St 23435
N & S Lloyd St 23434
Loblolly Ct 23435
Lockwood Cir 23434
Locust Ct & St 23434
Longstreet Ln
100-4499 23437
7900-8499 23438
Longvue Cir 23436
Longwood Ave 23434
Lookout Cir 23435
Loxley Ct 23435
Loyal Ln 23437
Lucerne Ave 23434
Lucy Cross Rd 23438
Ludlow Cv 23435
Lummis Rd
100-699 23434
700-1699 23437
Lynn Dr 23435
Macarthur Dr 23434
Macedonia Dr 23436
Madison Ave 23434
Magnolia Dr 23435
Magnolia St 23434
Mahan St E 23434
Mahlon Ave 23434
Maiden Ct 23435
N Main St
100-444 23434
445-2299 23434
445-445 23439
446-2298 23434
S Main St 23434
Mainsail Ln 23435
Majestic Dr 23434
Mallard Dr 23434
Mann Rd 23435
Manning Rd
100-3499 23434
3500-5199 23434
5201-5299 23437
Manning Bridge Rd 23434
Mansfield Rd 23434
Maple St 23434
Maple Leaf Cres 23434
Maplewood Dr 23435
March Dr 23434
Marina Dr 23435
Mariners Cv 23435
Market Ct & St 23434
Marlin Ave 23435
Marsh Landing Ln 23435
Marsh Ridge Ct 23435
Marshall Ave 23434
Martin Rd 23433
Martingale Ct 23435
Maryland Ave 23434
Mason Ave 23434
Matoaka Rd 23434
Matthews Ct 23434
Matthews Ln 23435
Maury Pl 23434
Mayflower Dr 23434
Mcintosh Ct 23434
Mckinley Ave 23434
Meade Dr & Pkwy 23434
Meadow Country Rd 23434
Meadow View Blvd 23435
Meadowbrook Trl 23434
Meadows Ct 23434
Meadows Reach Cir 23434
Meeting Rd 23435
Megan Ln 23434
Melrose Ct 23434
Michael Dr 23432
Middlecoff Ln 23434
Miles Ave 23435
Milford Ln 23434

Military Rd 23434
Mill Ln 23438
Mill St 23434
Mill Brook Ct 23434
Mill Cove Ct 23434
Mill Dam Ct 23434
Mill Lake Rd 23434
Mill Landing Ct 23434
Mill Lane Quarter 23434
Mill Oak Ct 23434
Mill Point Ct 23434
Mill Pond Ct 23434
Mill Run Ct 23434
Mill Wood Way 23434
Millers Ct 23434
Millstone Ct 23434
Millwheel Ct 23434
Milners Rd 23434
Milum Ln 23434
Mineral Spring Rd
100-6099 23438
6100-6799 23437
Mintonville Point Dr 23435
Missouri Dr 23434
Mistral Ter 23434
Misty Ridge Ln 23434
Mize Ln 23435
Mockingbird Ln 23434
Mondavi Ln 23435
Monticello Vw 23434
Moonlight Pt 23434
Moore Ave 23434
Moore Farm Ln 23434
Moores Point Rd 23436
Moreland St 23435
Morgan St 23434
Morning Tide Cv 23434
Moss Side Ct 23435
Mount Horeb St 23434
Mount Lebanon Ave 23436
Mount Pleasant Dr 23434
Mount Sinai St 23434
Mountainside Ave 23434
Muirfield Loop 23435
Mulberry St 23434
Murphys Mill Rd 23434
Mustang Trl 23432
Myava Ln 23434
Myrick Ave 23434
Myrtle St 23434
Nancy Dr 23434
Nansemond Ave 23434
Nansemond Cres 23435
N Nansemond Dr 23435
S Nansemond Dr 23435
Nansemond Pkwy
1000-3399 23434
3400-5499 23435
Nansemond Pointe Dr 23435
Nansemond River Dr 23435
Nathaniel St 23435
Neal Ct 23434
Netherland Dr 23437
Nevada St 23434
New Rd 23437
Newbury Ct 23435
Newington Pl 23435
Newport St 23434
Newtown Ct 23434
Niblick Cir 23434
Nicklaus Dr 23435
Nixon Dr 23434
Nora Ln 23434
Norfolk Western Ave 23434
Normandy Dr 23434
North St 23434
Northbrooke Ave 23434
Northgate Ln 23434
Northgate Commerce Pkwy 23435
Northpoint Dr 23434
Nottingham Blvd 23434
Oak St 23434
Oak Grove Ct 23434
Oak Island Ln 23434
Oak Manor Ct 23434
Oakdale Ter 23434
Oakengate Dr 23435
Oakglen Dr 23435
Oakwood Ave 23434
Obici Industrial Blvd 23434
Obrien Ct 23434
Ocentren Rd 23432
Ocklawaha Ave 23434
Okelly Dr 23437
Old College Dr 23435
Old E Pinner St 23434
Old Mill Rd 23434
Old Myrtle Rd 23434
Old Somerton Rd 23434
Old South Quay Rd 23437
Old Townpoint Rd 23435
Old Westham Dr N & S 23435
Old Wharf Rd 23435
Olde Bullocks Cir 23435
Olde Mill Creek Dr 23434
Oliver St 23434
Olympia Ct 23435
Orchard Ave 23434
Orchard Cove Ct 23435
Oregon Ave 23434
Oriole Rd 23435
Orkney Ct 23435
Oscar Babb Ln 23434
Osceola Ave 23434
Osprey Ct 23435
Outland St 23434
Outlaw Ln 23435
Overlook Ct 23435
Owls Ct 23434
Oxford St 23434
Oyster Bay Ln 23436
Oyster Creek Dr 23435
Pacers Pl 23435
Paddock Cir 23435
Page Pl 23435
Palmer Ct 23435
Palmyra Dr 23434
Palomino Trl 23432
Pamlico Cir 23434
Park Rd 23434
Parker Dr 23434
Parker Store Rd 23437
Parkside Cir 23435
Parkview Ct 23434
Parkway St 23434
Partridge Pl 23433
Partridge Point Rd 23436
Pasture Cv 23435
Patrick Dr 23435
Peachtree Dr 23434
Peachwood Ct 23434
Peafowl Ct 23435
Peanut Dr 23437
Pear Orchard Way 23435
Pearl St 23434
Pebble Creek Ct & Dr 23435
Pecan Ct 23434
Pecks Mill Ct 23434
Pelham Pl 23434
Pelican Cres N & S 23435
Pelican Reach 23435
Pelican View Ct 23435
Pembroke Ln 23434
Pender St 23434
Pennsylvania Ave 23434
Peppercorn Ln 23432
Person St 23435
Pheasant Cir 23434
Philhower Dr 23434
Piedmont Rd 23435
Pike St 23433
Pin Oak Dr 23434
Pine St 23434
Pine Acres 23432
Pine Tree Ct & Way 23434
Pine Valley Dr 23434
Pinehurst Dr 23434
Pineview Rd 23437
Pinewood Cir 23435
E Pinner St 23434
Pintail Dr 23435
Pinto Ct 23435
Pioneer Rd 23437
Pippin Dr 23434
Pitchkettle Rd 23434
Pitchkettle Farm Ln 23434
Pitchkettle Point Cir & Dr 23434
Pitt Rd 23434
Pittmantown Rd 23438
Planters Dr 23434
Planters Club Rd 23435
Player Ct 23435
Pleasant St 23434
Pleasant Ridge Ct 23435
Plover Dr 23434
Plummer Blvd 23435
W Point Dr 23434
Polk St 23434
Pond Dr 23434
Pontiac Cir 23434
Pony Club Pt 23435
Poplar Grove Cres 23434
Poplarwood Ln 23434
Porter Cir 23434
Porterfield Ln 23437
Porthole Pl 23435
Portsmouth Blvd 23434
Preakness Cir 23435
Prentis St 23434
Prescott Ct 23434
Presley Ct 23435
Prestwick St 23435
Pricesfork Blvd 23435
Prince Ct 23434
Princess Arch 23435
Princeton Rd 23434
Princeview Dr 23434
Pritchard St 23435
Privet Ct 23435
Proctor St 23434
Progress Rd 23434
Prospect Rd 23434
Providence Rd 23434
Pruden Blvd 23434
Pughsville Rd 23435
Purple Martin Ln 23435
Quail Holw 23433
Quail Run Ct 23434
Quaker Dr 23437
Quaker Ridge Ct 23435
Quarter Horse Ln 23434
S Quay Rd 23437
Queen St 23435
Queen Annes Ct 23434
Queens Point Dr 23434
Quince Rd 23437
Qvc Dr 23434
Rabey Farm Rd 23435
Rachels Dr 23434
Railroad Ave W 23434
Raintree Cir 23435
Raleigh Ave & Dr 23434
Ram Ct 23434
Randolph St 23434
Raniand Rd 23435
Raven St 23434
Ravine Gap Dr 23434
Red Duck Cir 23434
Red Oak Ln 23434
Red Top Ct 23434
Redgate Dr 23434
Redwood Ct 23434
Reed Ct 23434
Regatta Pointe Rd 23435
Regency Dr 23434
Reid St 23434
Reids Ferry Rd 23434
Remus Ln 23434
Reno St 23434
Resource Dr 23434
Respass Beach Rd 23435
Reynard Rd 23433
Richard Ave 23434
Richardson St 23434
Riddick Cir & Dr 23434
Ridgecrest Dr 23434
Ridley St 23434
Rilee Dr 23434
River Cres 23433
River Rd 23434
N River Rd 23435
River Birch Rd 23434
River Breeze Rd 23435
River Club Dr 23435
N & S River Creek Cres, Dr & Lndg 23434
River Inlet Rd 23434
River Park Dr 23434
River Point Dr 23434
River Watch Dr 23434
Riverbluff Dr 23435
Rivercliff Cres E & W 23435
Riverfront Dr 23434
Rivers Bend Pl 23435
Rivershore Dr 23433
Riverside Dr 23435
E & W Riverview Ct & Dr 23434
Riverwood Trce 23434
Roanoke Ave 23434
Robbie Rd 23438
Roberts Ct 23434
Robertson St 23438
Robin Ln 23434
Robinhood Trl 23435
Robs Dr 23434
Rochdale Ln 23434
Rockcreek Ln 23434
Rockland Ter 23434
Rockport Lndg 23435
Rockwood Pl 23435
Rodney Ln 23434
Rodset Ct 23434
Roland St 23434
Rollingwood St 23435
Romans Rd 23434
Ronald Dr 23434
Roosevelt Dr 23434
Rosemary St 23435
Rosemont Ave 23434
Rosewood Dr 23434
Round Table Arch 23435
Rountable Ct 23434
Rountree Cres 23434
Roy St 23434
Royal Oak Ct 23434
Ruby Ct 23434
Ruger Ct 23434
Ruritan Blvd 23437
Rushwood Ct 23435
Russett Ct 23434
Ryan Arch 23434
Sack Ct 23435
Sack Point Rd 23434
Sadler Dr 23434
Saint Andrews Dr 23435
Saint Anne Ave 23434
Saint Brie E & W 23435
Saint James Ave 23434
Saint Martin Dr 23434
Salt Marsh Way 23435
Sandgate Dr N & S 23435
Sandown Cv 23435
Sandstone Ct 23435
Sandtrap Ct 23434
Sandy Cres 23437
Sandy Beach Ct 23435
Sandy Lake Dr 23435
Sandy Spring Ln 23434
Santoro Pl 23435
N & S Saratoga St 23434
Saunders Dr 23434
Savoy Ct 23434
Sawgrass Ct 23435
Sawmill Point Rd 23436
Sawtooth Dr 23434
Schoolhouse Ln 23435
Schooner Blvd 23435
Scotch Pine Rd 23435
Scottsfield Dr 23435
Scuppernong Dr 23435
Seabreeze Ln 23435
Seasons Cir 23434
Sedgefield St 23435
Seminole Dr 23434
Sentry Way N & S 23435
Settlers Landing Rd 23435
Shady Grove Ln 23432
E & W Shallowford Ct 23435
Shannon Ln 23435
Sharpe Dr 23435
Sheffield Ct N & S 23435
Shellito Ln 23437
Shelter Cove Ct 23435
Shelton Ct 23434
Shepherd St 23434
Sherwood Dr 23434
Sherwood Pl 23435
Sheryl Lyn Ct 23435
Shingle Creek Rd 23434
Shirley Dr 23434
Shoal Creek Rd 23435
Shore Dr 23434
N Shore Dr 23435
Short Ln 23438
Shoulders Hill Rd 23435
Shropshire Ln 23434
Sierra Dr 23434
Silver Charm Cir 23435
Silver Poplar Ct 23435
Simons Dr 23434
Skeet Rd 23435
Skeetertown Rd 23434
Skiffs Landing Ln 23435
Skimmers Ln 23434
Sleepy Hole Rd 23435
Sleepy Lake Pkwy 23433
Sleepy Point Way 23435
Sleepy Ridge Ct 23435
Smalleys Dam Cir 23434
Smith St 23434
Snead Dr 23434
Snire Arch 23434
Soundings Crescent Ct 23435
Southwestern Blvd 23437
Spencer Ct 23434
Spinnaker Cove Ct 23435
Spirit Cir E 23434
Spivey Farm Ln 23438
Spivey Run Rd 23438
Spoon Ct 23434
Sport Club Run 23435
Sportsman Blvd 23435
Spring Meadow Ln 23432
Springfield Ter 23434
Springhill Way 23435
Spruce St 23434
Sprucewood Ln 23434
Squire Reach 23434
Stacey Dr 23434
Staley Dr 23434
Star Creek Ct 23435
Starcher Ct 23434
Steeple Dr 23433
Steeplechase Ln 23435
Sterling Ct 23434
Stone Cv 23435
Stone Creek Dr 23434
Stone Harbour Ct 23435
Stonegate Way 23435
Stonehenge Dr 23434
Stonewall Ct 23435
Stoney Brook Ct 23435
Stoney Ridge Ave 23435
Stowe Dr 23435
Strata Ct 23434
Stratford Dr 23435
Stuart Ave 23434
Stuart Dr 23437
Stumpy Lake Ct 23434
Suburban Dr 23434
Suffolk St 23434
Suffolk Meadows Blvd 23435
Suffolk Plaza Shop Ctr 23434
Summer Garden Pl 23434
Summer Harvest Ln 23434
Summerfield Ct 23434
Summerhouse Dr 23435
Sumner Ave 23434
Sumner St 23438
Sunrise Ct 23435
Sunset Ave 23434
Sunset Manor Dr 23438
Sussex Ct 23434
Swansea Cir 23435
Sweatt Rd 23438
Sweetbriar Ln 23435
Sweetwood Dr 23434
Sycamore St 23434
Tanglewood Ct 23435
Tanoak Ct 23434
Tason Dr 23434
Tautog Rd 23433
Taylor Ave & St 23435
Teal Ct 23434
Tee Box Ln 23434
Terrace Ct 23434
Teton Cir 23435
Tieman Trl 23434
Timber Trl 23433
Timberlake Dr 23434
Timberneck Arch 23434
Tindalls Ct 23436
Toddsbury Ct 23434
Topsail Ct 23435
Torrey Pines Ln 23434
Torrington Cir 23436
Tournament Ct 23434
Townpoint Rd 23435
Townsend Pl 23435
Tracy Dr 23434
Tradd St 23434
Trade Winds Dr 23435
Trapfalls Ct 23434
Traverse Cir 23435
Tree Ln 23437
Trilogy Loop 23435
Trotman Wharf Dr 23435
Truman Rd 23434
Trumpet Dr 23437
Tucker Dr 23435
Tuliptree Cir 23435
Tupelo Way 23434
Turlington Ct & Rd 23434
Turnberry Ct 23435
Turner Dr 23435
Turnstone Dr 23435
Turtle Pond Ct 23434
Twin Pines Ct 23434
Tynes St 23434
Unity Ct 23434
University Blvd 23435
Upton Ln 23434
Upton Pl 23433
Valor Ct 23434
Van Buren Ave 23434
Vaughan Ave 23438
Vermont Ave 23434
Vernon Dr 23435
Vicksburg Rd 23437
W View Ct 23435
Village Square Pl 23435
Vine Ave 23433
Viney Vis 23436
Vineyard Pl 23435
Vinyard Ln 23435
Virginia Ave 23434
Virginia Ham Dr 23434
Virginia Regional Dr 23434
Wake Forest Ct 23434
Walden Rd 23435
Walker Ct 23435
Walkers Ferry Ln 23435
Walnut St 23434
Walnut Park Dr 23434
Walter Earl Ln 23435
Warren St 23434
Warrington Dr 23435
Warwick St 23434
E & W Washington St 23434
Watch Harbour Ct 23435
Water Pointe Way 23434
Waterbury Cv 23434
Waterford Pl 23435
Waterjump Cres 23435
Waters Ave 23434
Waters Edge Ln 23435
Waterview Rd 23435
Waterway Ct 23434
Waterwheel Cres 23434
Waterwood Way 23434
Watts St 23435
Wavey Ct E & W 23435
Wayne Ave 23435
Weatherby Way 23435
Webb St 23434
Wedgewood Dr 23438
Wekiva Ave 23434
Welch Pkwy 23434
N Wellons St 23434
Wentworth Ct 23436
West Rd 23436
Western Ave 23434
Westfalen Ct 23434
Westgate Ave 23434
Westwood Dr 23434
Wet Marsh Ct 23435
Wexford Dr E & W 23434
Whaley St 23438
Whaleyville Blvd
1300-4549 23434
4551-4599 23434
4700-9199 23438
Whichard Rd 23434
Whimbrel Dr 23435
White Dr 23434
White Ash Ct 23435
White Dogwood Trl 23433
White Elm Ct 23435
White Hall Arch 23434
White Herons Ln 23434
White Marsh Rd 23434
White Oak Ln 23434
Whitewood St 23435
Whitfield Way 23435
Widgeon Ct 23434
Wiggins Rd 23434
Wigneil St 23433
Wildwood Dr 23437
Wilkie Ct 23434
Wilkins Dr 23434
Willet Ct 23435
William Penn Ln 23435
William Reid Dr 23434
Williams Cir & Rd 23434
Willow Ln & St 23434
Willow Glenn Cir 23435
Willow Ridge Ct 23434
Willowbrook Dr 23434
Wilroy Rd 23434
Wilson Ct, Ln & St 23434
Wimbleton Ct 23435
Winborne Dr 23435
Wincanton Cv 23435
Windemere Ct 23434
Windjammer Rd 23435
Windmill Ln 23437
Windsor Ct 23435
Windward Ln 23435
Windy Pines Ln 23432
Windy Point Dr 23435
Wing Foot Ct 23435
Winona Trl 23434
Winterview Dr 23434
Winthrope Dr 23435
Wise St 23435
Withers St 23434
Wonderland Dr 23435
Wood Creek Ct 23434
Wood Duck Ct 23434
Wood Duck Rd 23433
Woodberry Cres 23435
Woodhaven Dr 23435
Woodlake Ter 23434
Woodland Cir 23436
Woodland Rd 23436
Woodland Trl 23434
Woodlawn Dr 23434

Woodrow Ave 23434
Woodruff St 23434
Woods Pkwy 23434
Woods Edge Cir 23434
Woodshire Way 23434
Woodspath Ln 23433
Worcester Way 23435
Word Ter 23434
Wyanoke Trl 23437
Yeates Dr 23435
York Ct & St 23434
Yorkshire Dr 23435
Zebulon Ct 23435

NUMBERED STREETS

All Street Addresses 23434

UPPERVILLE VA

General Delivery 20184

POST OFFICE BOXES MAIN OFFICE STATIONS AND BRANCHES

Box No.s
All PO Boxes 20185

NAMED STREETS

All Street Addresses 20184

VIENNA VA

POST OFFICE BOXES MAIN OFFICE STATIONS AND BRANCHES

Box No.s
All PO Boxes 22027

RURAL ROUTES

13 22027

NAMED STREETS

Abbey Glen Ct 22182
Abbey Oak Dr 22182
Abbotsford Dr
1800-2199 22182
2200-2299 22181
Academy St 22180
Acorn Cir 22180
Adahi Rd SE 22180
Adams Hill Rd 22182
Addison St 22180
Adelman Cir SW 22180
Admirals Hill Ct 22182
Ainstree Ct NE 22180
Albea Ct NE 22180
Albrecht Cir SW 22180
Allard Ln 22180
Alma St SE 22180
Alto Ct 22182
Amanda Ct & Pl 22180
Amber Meadows Dr 22182
Amberwood Manor Ct 22182
Andiron Ln 22180
Angelico Way 22181
Annies Way 22182
Antioch Cir 22180
Aponi Ct & Rd 22180
Apple Blossom Ct 22181
Arabian Ave 22182
Arcadian Cir SW 22180
Arden Ct & St 22027
Arrowleaf Dr 22182
Arroyo Ct 22181
Aryness Dr 22181
Ashgrove Ln 22182
Ashgrove House Ln 22182
Ashgrove Meadows Way 22182
Ashgrove Plantation Cir 22182
Asoleado Ln 22182
Atwood Rd 22182
Aubrey Place Ct 22182
Audreys Ct SE 22180
Augustus Ct 22180
Avenir Pl 22180
Avery Ct SW 22180
Avis Ct 22182
Ayito Rd SE 22180
Ayr Hill Ave NE & NW 22180
Babcock Rd 22181
Balliett Ct 22180
Ballycor Dr 22182
Baritone Ct 22182
Barkham Ln 22182
Barnwood Ter 22181
Baronhurst Dr 22181
Bartholomew Ct 22182
Baton Dr 22182
Batten Hollow Rd 22182
Battery Park St 22182
Battle Ct & St 22180
Beekay Ct 22181
Bell Ln 22182
Bellforest Ct 22180
Benedictine Ct 22182
Bent Creek Ln 22182
Berea Ct & Dr 22180
Bermudez Ct 22182
Berry St SE 22180
Besley Rd 22182
Best Bower Ct 22182
Bethany Ct 22182
Betterton Ct 22182
Beulah Rd 22182
Beulah Rd NE 22180
Bickley Ct 22181
Birch St SW 22180
Bird Rd 22181
Bixler Ln 22182
Black Eyed Susan Ln 22182
Black Stallion Pl 22182
Blackstone Ter NW 22180
Blair Ct & Rd 22180
Blairstone Dr 22182
Blake Ln 22181
Blandfield Ct 22182
Blevins Way Ct 22182
Blitz Ct 22027
Blythe Dale Ct 22182
Bobbyber Dr 22182
Bois Ave 22182
Bonaventure Dr 22181
Boone Blvd 22182
Boss St 22182
Bowdoin Cir 22180
Bowling Green Ct & Dr 22180
Branch Cir & Rd 22180
Brandywine Dr 22182
Brenner Ct 22180
Brenthill Ct & Way 22182
Brentridge St 22182
Brentwood Ct NW 22180
Brian Dr 22180
Briarcliff Ct 22182
Bridleridge Ct 22181
Bright Meadows Ln 22027
Bright Wood Dr 22027
Brightlea Dr 22181
Brighton Ct 22181
Brittenford Ct & Dr 22182
Broadfield Ln 22182
Broadleaf Dr NE 22180
Broadstone Pl 22182
Bronco Ln 22182
Brookdale Ter 22182
Brookhill Ln 22182
Brookmeade Pl 22182
Brookmeadow Ct & Dr 22182
Brookside Ln 22182
Brookstone Ct & Ln 22182
Brooktrail Ct 22182
Broome Ct 22182
Brothers Rd 22182
Browns Mill Rd 22182
Bruton Pl NW 22180
Bucknell Dr 22180
Bull Run Ct 22180
Bunchberry Pl 22181
Burlwood Ct 22182
Burning Tree Dr 22182
Byrd Rd 22182
Cabin Rd SE 22180
Campbell Rd 22182
Cantata Ct 22182
Capo Ct 22182
Cardinal Glen Ct 22182
Carey Ln 22181
Carmichael Dr 22181
Carnegie Dr 22180
Carnegie Hall Ct 22180
Carnot Way 22182
Carole Ct SE 22180
Carpers Farm Ct & Way 22182
Carrhill Ct & Rd 22181
Carriage Ct 22181
Carrington Ln 22182
Carrington Ridge Ln 22182
Carter Ct SW 22180
Carters Glen Ct SW 22180
Cashel Ln 22181
Casmar St SE 22180
Cedar Ln
2200-2380 22182
2381-2900 22180
2902-2906 22180
Cedar Ln SE 22180
Cedar Ln SW 22180
Cedar St 22027
Cedar Crossing Ln 22180
Cedar Meadow Ct 22180
Cedar Mill Ct 22180
Cedar Pond Dr 22182
Celesta Ct 22182
Cello Ct 22182
Center St 22181
Center St N 22180
Center St S 22180
Centerboro Dr 22181
Central Ave 22182
Ceret Ct SW 22180
Cerritos Ct 22182
Chain Bridge Rd
2000-2199 22182
2201-2299 22182
2500-2900 22181
Chamberlain Dr 22182
Chamberlain Woods Way 22182
Chanbourne Way 22181
Chappell Ln 22181
Charles Cir & St SW & SE 22180
Charles Dunn Dr 22180
Charnita Ct 22182
Chase Hill Ct 22182
Chathams Ford Dr & Pl 22182
Cheddar Dr 22182
Cheriton Ct 22181
Cherry Cir & St 22180
Chestertown Dr 22182
Chestnut Farm Dr 22182
Chestnut Oak Ct 22182
Chilcott Ct 22181
Chilcott Manor Way 22181
Chintow St 22027
Chopin St 22182
Church St NE & NW 22180
Cinnamon Creek Dr 22182
Circle Dr SE 22180
Citadel Pl 22180
Clachan Ct 22182
Clarks Crossing Rd 22182
Clarks Glen Pl 22182
Claudia Ct 22180
Claves Ct 22182
Clearfield Ave 22181
Clifdale Ct 22182
Clovelly Ct 22182
Clover Glen Dr 22181
Cloverdale Pl 22182
Clovermeadow Dr 22182
Clyde Ct 22181
Coach Rd 22181
Coal Train Dr 22027
Cobble Mill Rd 22182
Cobble Pond Way 22182
Cody Ct & Rd 22181
Colby Ct & St 22180
Cold Creek Ct 22182
Coldstream Pl 22182
Colin Ln NW 22180
Colonade Dr 22181
Colony Ct NW 22180
Colvin Forest Dr 22182
Commons Dr NW 22180
Concert Ct 22181
Concerto Cir 22182
Connirae Ln 22182
Contralto Ct 22182
Cooper Ct SE 22180
Coral Bells Ct 22182
Coral Crest Ln 22182
Coral Gables Ln 22182
Cornerside Blvd 22182
Cornflower Ct 22182
Corsica St 22181
Corsini Ct 22182
Cottage St
8100-8199 22027
8200-8699 22180
Cottage St SW 22180
Council Ct & Dr 22180
Counsellor Dr NW 22181
Country Club Dr NE 22180
Country View Ct 22182
Course St NE 22180
Courthouse Cir SW 22180
Courthouse Rd 22181
Courthouse Rd SW 22180
Courthouse Commons Rd 22181
Courthouse Oaks Rd 22181
Courthouse Woods Ct 22181
Coving Cross Ln 22182
Cowberry Ct 22182
Craigo Ct 22182
E Creek Ct 22180
Creek Crossing Rd 22182
Creek Crossing Rd NE 22180
Creekside Ct 22182
Crianza Pl 22182
Criaza Branch Ct 22182
Cricklewood Ct 22182
Crossbow Ct 22181
Crossing Gate Way 22181
Crowell Rd 22182
Cunningham Park Ct SE 22180
Curzon Ct 22181
Cy Ct 22182
Cymbal Dr 22182
Cynthia Ln NE 22180
Dale Ct SE 22180
Dale Ridge Ct 22181
Daniel Lewis Ln 22181
Darnley Pl 22181
Darrow Ct 22181
Dawson St 22182
Days Farm Dr 22182
Decree Ln 22181
Deed Ct 22181
Deercrest Meadow Pl 22182
Delancey Dr 22182
Delano Dr SE 22180
Delilah Dr SW 22180
Dellway Ln 22180
Dellwood Dr 22180
Delta Glen Ct 22182
Dennis Dr 22180
Depaul Dr 22180
Deramus Farm Ct 22182
Desale St SW 22180
Devonshire Dr NE 22180
Difficult Run Ct 22182
Docket Ln 22181
Dogwood St SW 22180
Dominion Rd NE & SE 22180
Donal Ln 22181
Doral Ct 22182
Dove Cir SW 22180
Dove Point Ct 22182
Doveton Cir 22182
Downey Dr 22182
Drake St SW 22180
Dreamweaver Ct 22182
Drewlaine Dr 22182
Drexel St 22180
Druid Hill Rd NE 22180
Dulcimer Ct 22182
Dumont Dr 22180
Dunfries Rd 22181
Dunn Meadow Ct & Rd 22182
Earls Ct 22181
East St NE & SE 22180
Echols St SE 22180
Edgefield Ln 22182
Edgelea Rd 22181
Edgepark Rd 22182
Edwin Ln NE 22180
Elaine Cir SE 22180
Electric Ave
1000-1099 22180
8100-8599 22182
Elgin Dr 22182
Elm Pl 22027
Elm St SW 22180
Elm Grove Ct 22182
Elm Shade Ct 22182
Elmar Dr SE & SW 22180
Eluna Ct 22182
Ermantrude Ct 22182
Esquire Crossing Ln 22180
Evelyn Ct 22180
Fairfax Metro Ln 22181
Fairoaks Rd 22181
Fairway Dr NE 22180
Falcone Pointe Way 22182
Fallbrook Ln 22182
Fardale St SE 22180
Fariba Ct 22181
Farley Ct SE 22180
Farmside Pl 22182
Faust Dr 22182
Fawncrest Ct 22182
Fellini Ct SE 22180
Fernwood Dr 22181
Ferol Dr 22182
Filene Ct 22182
Finian Ct 22181
Firth Ct 22181
Five Oaks Rd 22181
Flint Hill Ct & Rd 22181
Follin Ln SE 22180
Fonda Dr 22182
Forest Maple Rd 22182
Forestree Ct 22182
Fosbak Ct & Dr 22182
Fox Rest Ln 22181
Fox Run Ct 22182
Foxmoor Dr 22027
Foxstone Dr 22182
Francis Young Ln 22182
Frank St 22182
Freda Dr 22181
Frederick St SW 22180
Fremont Ln 22182
Frick Way 22027
Gables Ln 22182
Galesburg Pl 22027
Galloping Way 22181
Galloway Dr 22182
Gallows Rd
2240A-2240F 22182
1900-2130 22182
2130-2599 22027
2132-2240 22182
2600-2802 22180
2804-2896 22180
Gallows Oak Ct 22182
Gallows Tree Ct & Ln 22182
Gamba Ct 22182
Garnett Ct 22180
Garrett St 22181
Gelding Ln 22182
George St SW 22180
George Washington Ct & Rd 22182
Gerken Ave 22181
Gettysburg Sq 22181
Gibson Cir & Dr 22180
Gina Pl 22182
Gingerwood Ct 22182
Glade Vale Way 22181
Glen Ave SW 22180
Glencoe Dr 22181
Glencroft Ct & Rd 22181
Glendevy Ct 22181
Glengyle Dr 22181
Glenoak Ct 22181
Glenridge Ct 22182
Glyndon Ln & St 22180
Gold Dust Ct 22181
Goldentree Way 22182
Goldstream Ct 22182
Gopost 22182
Gosnell Rd 22182
Grace Forest Pl 22180
Grampion Pl 22182
Grand Ct 22182
Grand Oaks Ct 22181
Greenbrier Way 22182
Gretna Pl 22181
Grovemore Ln 22180
Gunnell Farms Dr 22181
Halcyon Ln 22181
Hambletonian Pl 22182
Haney Ln
2100-2198 22027
2108-2199 22182
Harithy Dr 22027
Harmony Dr SE & SW 22180
Harte Pl 22180
Hartland Rd 22180
Harvest Oak Dr 22182
Hatmark Ct & St 22181
Hawthorne Ridge Ct 22182
Heatherton Ln 22180
Helena Dr 22027
Helmwood Ct 22181
Heritage Ln NW 22180
Hichinti St SW 22180
Hickory Cir SW 22180
Hicks Dr 22182
Hidden Rd 22181
Hidden Estates Cv 22181
Hidden Fox Way 22182
Hidden Hill Ln 22182
Hidden Oaks Ct 22181
Hidden Valley Rd 22181
Higdon Dr 22182
High Dr 22182
Highland St NW 22180
Hill Rd 22181
Hill Top Rd NE 22180
Hillcrest Dr SW 22180
Hillington Ct 22182
Hillside Cir SW 22180
Hilltop Ave 22182
Hilltop Rd 22180
Hine St SE 22180
Hollis Ln 22182
Holloway Ct NE 22180
Holmes Ct & Dr 22180
Holt St 22180
Horse Shoe Ct & Dr 22182
Horseback Trl 22182
Howard Ave 22182
Howard Manor Dr 22182
Hull Rd 22182
Hunt Country Ln 22182
Hunt Valley Dr 22182
Hunter Ct SW 22180
Hunter Mill Rd
1200-1999 22182
2000-2499 22181
2501-2501 22181
Hunter Station Rd 22181
E Hunter Valley Rd 22181
Hunter View Rd 22181
Hunter View Farms 22182
Hunters Pl 22181
Hunters Crest Way 22181
Hunters Den Ln 22181
Hunters Run Ct 22181
Hunters Valley Rd 22181
Hunting Crest Ln & Way 22182
Hunting Lodge Ct 22182
Huntrace Way 22182
Hunts End Ct 22182
Hursley Ct 22182
Idylwood Rd
7816-8199 22027
8200-8599 22182
Idylwood Mews Ct & Ln 22182
Idylwood Valley Pl 22182
Iliff Dr 22027
Irvin St 22182
Ithaca St 22027
Ivy Ln 22181
Jackson Pkwy 22180
Jade Ct NW 22180
James Dr SE & SW 22180
James Madison Dr 22181
Janet Ln 22180
Jarrett Valley Dr 22182
Jawed Pl 22027
Jean Pl NE 22180
Jeffersonian Ct & Dr 22182
Jerry Ln NW 22180
Jessica Ct 22181
John Marshall Dr NE & NW 22180
Johns Hollow Rd 22182
Johnson St SW 22180
Journet Dr 22027
Joy Ln 22181
Judge Ct 22181
Judy Witt Ln 22182
Jumper Ct 22182
Katie Bird Ln 22181
Kearney Ct SW 22180
Kedge Ct & Dr 22181
Kelleher Rd 22027
Kelley St SW 22180
Kelly Sq 22181
Kenbrooke Ct 22181
Kentsdale Ln 22182
Kerge Ct SE 22180
Key West Ln 22182
Keystone Ln 22180
Kibler Cir SW 22180
Kidwell Ct & Dr 22182
Kidwell Hill Ct 22182
Kidwell Town Ct 22182
Kilbarry Ct 22182
Kilby Glen Dr 22182
Kildownet Ct 22182
Killarney Ct 22182
Kilport Ct 22182
Kings Way Ct SW 22180
Kingsley Rd SE & SW 22180
Knoll St NW 22180
Knollside Ln 22180
Kohoutek Ct 22182
Kramer Ct & Dr 22180
Labbe Ln 22182
Labrador Ln 22182

Lafora Ct 22180
Lagersfield Cir 22181
Lakeside Dr 22182
Lakevale Dr 22181
Lakewood Dr SW 22180
Landon Hill Rd 22182
Langholm Pl 22181
Larkin Ln 22182
Larkmeade Dr 22182
Laura Gae Cir 22180
Laurel Hill Ct & Rd 22182
Laurel Ridge Rd 22181
Lauren Ln SE 22180
Laurlin Ct 22182
Lawyers Rd
9600-10899 22181
100-201 22180
200-200 22183
202-598 22180
203-599 22180
Layminster Ln 22182
Leamoore Ln 22181
Lee Ln 22182
Leeds Castle Dr 22182
Leemay St 22182
Leesburg Pike 22182
Lellah Ct 22027
Lemontree Ln 22181
Lewis St NW 22180
Liberty Tree Ln 22182
Lieuvin Ct 22182
Limb Tree Ln 22182
Lincoln St NW 22180
Lindel Ln 22181
Little Fox Ln 22181
Little Run Farm Ct 22182
Little Sorrel Ct 22180
Litwalton Ct 22182
Livingstone Ln 22180
Loch Lomond Dr 22181
Lochalsh Ln 22181
Lochmoore Ln 22181
Lochness Ct 22181
Lockerbie Ln 22182
Locust Dr & St 22180
Logway Rd 22181
Lomond Ct 22181
Longford Ct 22181
Longview Ct NE 22180
Lord Fairfax Ct & Rd 22182
Lovers Ln NW 22180
Lozano Dr 22182
Luckett Ave 22180
Lucky Estates Dr 22182
Ludlow Ln 22027
Lullaby Ln SE 22180
Lupine Den Ct & Dr 22182
Lydia Pl 22181
Lynn St SW 22180
Lynnhill Ct NE 22180
Macarthur Ave NE 22180
Macy Ave 22182
Madrigal Way 22181
Madrillon Ct & Rd 22182
Madrillon Creek Ct 22182
Madrillon Estates Dr 22182
Madrillon Oaks Ct 22182
Madrillon Springs Ct & Ln 22182
Madron Ln 22182
Majestic Knolls Ct 22182
Malcolm Rd NW 22180
Malraux Dr 22182
Mamie Dyer Ln 22182
Manassas Cir 22180
Mandolin Ct 22182
Manhattan Pl 22180
Manor Dr NE 22180
Mansion View Ct 22182
Manvell Rd SE 22180
Maple Ave E & W 22180
Marcliff Ct 22181
Marian Cir SW 22180
Marjorie Ln SE 22180
Marlistr Rd 22182
Marquette St 22180

Marshall Rd SW 22180
Martinhoe Dr 22181
Marymount Ln 22180
Marywood Rd 22181
Marywood Oaks Ln 22181
Mashie Dr SE 22180
Massonoff Ct 22182
Masterworks Dr 22181
Matt Ct 22027
Maya Ct 22182
Maymont Dr 22182
Mcchesney Ct 22181
Mcclintic Ct 22181
Mcduff Ct 22181
Mcgregor Ct 22182
Mcguire Ct 22182
Mchenry St SE 22180
Mckinley St NE 22180
Mcneil St 22180
Meadow Ln SW 22180
Meadow Dale Ct 22181
Meadow Glen Dr 22182
Meadow Knoll Ct 22181
Meadow Springs Ct & Dr 22182
Meadow Valley Dr 22181
Meadowlark Rd 22182
Meadowlark Gardens Ct 22182
Meadowmere Dr 22182
Meadowood Dr 22181
Melody Ln SE & SW 22180
Memory Ct 22182
Mendon Ln SW 22180
E & W Meredith Dr 22181
Merry Oaks Ct & Ln 22182
Mervis Way 22182
Michael Schar Ct 22181
Middleton Ct 22182
Middleton Ridge Rd 22182
Midlothian Ct 22182
Mildred Ct 22182
Miles Stone Ct & Dr 22181
Mill St NE & SE 22180
Mill Race Estates Dr 22182
Mill Wheel Ln 22182
Miller Ln 22182
Millfarm Dr 22182
Millwood Ct SW 22180
Minerva Ct 22182
Minuet Ct 22181
Montafia Ln 22182
Montague Dr 22182
Montclair Ct 22181
Montmorency Dr 22182
Moonac Ct 22182
Moore Ave & Pl 22180
Moorefield Rd SW 22180
Moorefield Creek Rd SW 22180
Moorefield Hill Ct, Grv & Pl 22180
Morada Ct 22180
Morgan Ln 22027
Mossy Stone Ct 22182
Motley Ln 22181
Mount Sunapee Rd 22182
Mountfort Ct SW 22180
Mountington Ct 22182
Murnane St 22181
Murray Ln NE 22180
Myers Cir SW 22180
Nadine Dr 22181
Nanterry Cir SW 22180
Narragansett Pl 22180
Nelson Dr NE 22180
Nevar Ct 22182
Newcombs Farm Rd 22182
Newkirk Ct 22182
Newton St 22181
Niblick Dr SE 22180
Nicholas Cir SE 22180
Nigel Ct 22182
Night Shade Ct 22182
Ninovan Rd SE 22180
Nobehar Dr 22181

Noory Ct 22182
Northern Neck Dr 22182
Notre Dame Dr 22182
Nursery Ln 22181
Nutley St NW & SW 22180
W Oak Pl 22182
Oak St 22027
Oak St SW 22180
Oak Branch Dr 22181
Oak Knoll Rd NE 22180
Oak Valley Ct & Dr 22181
Oakcroft Way 22181
Oakdale Woods Ct 22181
Oakledge Ct 22181
Oakley Ct 22181
Oakmont Ct NE 22180
Oakton Crest Pl 22181
Oakton Glen Dr 22181
Oakton Park Ct 22181
Oakton Plantation Ct & Ln 22181
Oakvale Ct NW 22181
Occidental Dr 22180
Old Ash Grv 22182
Old Courthouse Rd 22182
Old Courthouse Rd NE 22180
Old Gallows Rd 22182
Old Hunt Rd 22181
Oleander Ave 22181
Olympia Fields Ln 22182
Olympian Cir SW 22180
Onondio Cir SE 22180
Orchard Ct & St 22180
Orleans Cir SW 22180
Orrin St SE 22180
Otis Ct 22180
Overlook St 22182
Owaissa Ct & Rd 22180
Paisley Ct 22182
Paisley Blue Ct 22182
Palace Green Way 22181
Palm Springs Dr 22182
Paris Ct SW 22180
N Park Ct 22027
Park St 22180
Park St NE 22180
Park St SE 22180
N Park St 22027
Park Terrace Ct SE 22180
Park Tower Dr 22180
Parsons Grove Ct 22027
Patrick Cir & St SW & SE 22180
Patty Ln 22180
Pearl Fog Way 22027
Pebble Beach Dr 22182
Pekay St SW 22180
Pembroke Pl 22182
Pembsly Dr 22181
Pennington Pl 22181
Pennycress Ln 22182
Pepperdine Dr 22180
Peppermill Pl 22182
Pepperwood Ct 22181
Percussion Way 22182
Periewoo Rd 22181
Pickett Pl SW 22180
Pieris Ct 22182
Pillory Dr 22182
Pine St SE 22180
Pine Bough Pl 22181
Pine Cluster Cir 22181
Pine Knot Dr 22181
Pine Needles Ct 22182
Pine Valley Dr 22182
Pinstripe Ct 22182
Pleasant St NW & SW 22180
Pleasantdale Rd 22180
Plum St SW 22180
Plum Tree Ct 22181
Podium Dr 22182
Pollard Ter 22182
Polly St SE 22180
Polo Pointe Dr 22181
Poplar Glen Ct 22182

Post Rd 22181
Potterton Cir SW 22180
Powdermill Ln 22181
Prelude Ct & Dr 22182
Prescott Cir & Dr SE 22180
Prichards Ct 22027
Princess Ct SW 22180
Princeton Ter SW 22180
Proffit Rd 22182
Promontory Ct 22027
Pruitt Ct SW 22180
Quaint Ln 22182
Quarter Ct 22182
Quartet Cir 22182
Quinn Ter 22180
Rachel Ln SW 22180
Rachelle Pl 22182
Raglan Rd 22182
Railroad St 22027
Rainbow Rd 22182
Raleigh Hill Rd 22182
Rambling Ct & Rd 22181
Red Rock Ct 22182
Red Vine Dr 22182
Redwood Dr SE 22180
Reflection Ln 22182
Regency Crest Dr 22181
Regency Forest Dr 22181
Rehoboth Ct 22182
Rensselaer Ct 22181
Reprise Ct 22182
Reserve Way 22182
Revatom Ct 22027
Rhapsody Dr 22182
Richelieu Dr 22182
Richview Ct 22182
Ridge Ln 22182
Ridge Rd SW 22180
Ridgewood Ct NE 22180
Riesley Ln 22182
Riviera Dr 22181
Robarge Ct 22027
Roberts Dr NW 22180
Robin Way Ct 22182
Robnel Pl 22182
Rockbridge St 22180
Rockport Rd 22180
Rocky Branch Rd 22181
Roesh Way 22181
Roland Ct & St 22180
Roosevelt Ct NE 22180
Rosaleigh Ct 22182
Rosewood Hill Cir & Dr 22182
Ross Dr SW 22180
Round Springs Dr 22181
Roundhouse Rd 22181
Royal Estates Dr 22182
Rustic Rail Ln 22181
Sabrina Dr 22182
Saddle Rd 22181
Saddle Ridge Ct 22182
Saddleview Ct 22182
Sagarmal Ct 22027
Saint Andrews Dr NE 22180
Saint Bernard Dr NE 22180
Saint Boniface St 22182
Saint Croix Dr 22180
Saint Roman Dr 22182
Sandburg Ct & St 22027
Sandburg Hill Ct 22027
Sandburg Ridge Ct 22027
Sanoey Cir SE 22180
Santillane Cir 22182
Sarah Woods Ct 22182
Saratoga Waye NE 22180
Satinwood Ct 22182
Savannah Crossing Ct 22182
Sawdust Rd 22181
Sawtooth Oak Ct 22182
Saybrook Ct 22180
Scarab St 22182
Scenic View Ter 22182
Schafflind Ct 22180
Schubert Ct 22182
Schuman Ct 22182

Science Applications Ct 22182
Scotch Haven Dr 22181
Scotch Pine Ct 22181
Scott Cir SW 22180
Sebon Dr 22180
Security Pl 22180
Sereno Ct 22182
Shady Dr SE 22180
Shahraam Ct SE 22180
Sharon Ln NW 22180
Shawn Ct 22027
Shawn Leigh Dr 22181
Shelford Ct 22182
Shenandoah St 22180
Shepherdson Ln NE 22180
Sheriff Ct 22181
Sherwood Dr NE 22180
Short Ct 22181
Short St NW 22180
Shouse Dr 22182
Shreve Hill Rd 22027
Sibelius Dr 22182
Sideling Ct NE 22180
Silentree Dr 22182
Silk Oak Dr 22182
Silverberry Way 22182
Sioux Ct SE 22180
Skidmore Cir 22180
Skokie Ln 22182
Skyline Ct NE 22180
Snowberry Ct 22181
Snowbound Ct 22181
Snughill Ct 22182
Southern Pines Ct 22182
Southwind Ct 22182
Spice Ct 22181
Spinet Ct 22182
Spring St 22027
Spring St SE 22180
Spring Branch Dr 22181
Spring Hill Rd 22182
Spring Leaf Ct 22182
Spring Ridge Ln 22182
Springwood Ct NE 22180
Squaw Valley Dr 22182
Squires Crest Ln 22182
Stanbridge Pl 22182
State St 22182
Statute Ln 22181
Steeple Run 22181
Stefan Dr 22027
Stenhouse Pl 22027
Stephen Cir SW 22180
Stokley Way 22182
Stone Hollow Dr 22180
Stone Meadow Way 22182
Stone Ridge Ln 22182
Stone Vale Dr 22181
Stonewall Dr 22180
Strathaven Pl 22181
Stream Side Ct 22182
Streamview Ln 22182
Stryker Ave 22181
Sugar Ln 22181
Suncrest Ln 22182
Sunny Creek Cv 22182
Sunny Meadow Ln 22181
Sunrise Rd 22181
Surrey Ln SE 22180
Surveyors Ct SW 22180
Sutton Rd 22181
Sutton Green Ct 22181
Sutton Oaks Ln 22181
Sutton Woods Ct 22181
Sweet Mint Dr 22181
Swift Run St 22180
Symphony Cir SW 22180
Symphony Meadow Ln 22182
Syracuse Cir 22180
Talahi Ct & Rd 22180
Talisman Dr 22182
Tamarack Dr 22182
Tamerisk Ct 22182
Tanglevale Dr 22181
Tannin Pl 22182

Tapawingo Rd SE & SW 22180
Tartan Ct 22181
Tazewell Rd NW 22180
Teel Dr 22182
Teets Ln 22182
Telfer Ct 22182
Terra Ridge Dr 22181
Tetterton Ave 22182
Thelma Cir SW 22180
Thistle Ridge Ln 22182
Thompson Run Ct 22182
Thunderbird Ct 22182
Timber Ln SW 22180
Timber Valley Ct 22027
Timberview Ct 22182
Timberwolf Ct 22182
Timmark Ct 22181
Tipperary Pass 22181
Tire Swing Rd 22027
Tower Forest Dr 22180
Towers Crescent Dr & Plz 22182
Towers Plaza Dr 22182
Towlston Rd 22182
Towney View Ct 22180
Toyon Way 22182
Trailridge Ct 22182
Trailwood Ct 22182
Train Ct 22027
Trap Rd 22182
Trapline Ct 22182
Trevor Pl 22182
Tricia Ct 22181
Trombone Ct 22182
Trosby Ct 22181
Trott Ave 22181
Trowbridge Ln SW 22180
Troy Ct SE 22180
Truman Cir SW 22180
Trumpet Ct 22182
Trumpeter Ct 22182
Tuba Ct 22182
Tulip Poplar Ln 22182
Tweed Ct 22182
Tyco Rd 22182
Tyson Oaks Cir 22182
Tysons Ct 22182
Tysons Crest Ln 22182
Tysons Executive Ct & Ln 22027
Tysons Trace Ct & Dr 22182
Tyspring St 22182
Tyvale Ct 22182
Upham Pl NW 22180
Vale Rd NW 22181
Valera Ct 22181
Valeview Ct NW 22180
Valley Dr SE 22180
Valley Creek Ln 22182
Van Arsdale Dr 22181
Vance Pl 22182
Vanetta Ln 22182
Verdict Dr 22181
Verrier Ct 22182
Verveille Dr 22182
Vesper Dr 22182
Vickers Dr 22181
Victoria Ct NW 22180
Victoria Farms Ln 22182
Vigne Ct 22182
Village Spring Ln 22181
Villanova Ct & Dr 22180
Virginia Center Blvd 22181
Wade Hampton Dr SW 22180
Walker Cir & St 22180
Wall St 22182
Walnut Ln NW 22180
Walter Thompson Dr 22181
Walters Glen Way 22027
Wandering Creek Rd 22182
Ware St SW 22180
Wareham Ct 22180
Water Falls Ln 22182
Waterford Ct 22181

Watervale Way 22182
Weatherwood Ct 22182
Wedderburn Ln 22180
Wedderburn Station Dr 22180
Welles St SE 22180
Wellingham Ct 22182
Wendover Dr 22181
Wesleyan St 22180
West Ct & St 22180
Westbriar Ct & Dr 22180
Westchester Dr 22182
Westerholme Way 22182
Westford Dr 22182
Westglen Ct 22182
Westmanor Ct SE 22180
Westown Way 22182
Westview Ct NE 22180
Westwood Dr 22182
Westwood Dr NE 22180
Westwood Ter 22182
Westwood Center Dr 22182
Westwood Forest Dr & Ln 22182
Westwood Mews Ct 22182
Wexford Dr & Way 22182
Weycroft Pl 22182
Wheystone Ct & St 22182
Whipping Post Way 22182
Whippoorwill Rd 22181
Whispering Wind Ct SE 22180
White Beech Way 22182
White Pine Dr 22182
Whitecedar Ct 22181
Whitley Dr 22182
Wickens Rd 22181
Wild Olive Ct 22181
William Terry Dr 22181
Williams Ave
2200-2399 22182
2400-2499 22180
Willow Dr 22181
Willow Branch Ct 22181
Willow Crest Ct 22182
Willowmere Dr 22180
Willowmere Woods Dr 22180
Wilmar Pl NW 22180
Winchester Cir 22180
Wind Haven Way 22182
Winder St 22180
Winding Brook Ln 22182
Winding Creek Ln 22182
Windover Ave & Ct 22180
Windsor Hunt Ct 22182
Windsor Meadows Ln 22182
Windstone Dr 22182
Windy Knoll Ln 22182
Wintercress Ct 22182
Witness Ct NW 22181
Wolftrap Ct 22182
Wolftrap Rd
8000-8079 22027
8080-8700 22182
8702-8798 22182
Wolftrap Rd SE 22180
Wolftrap Oaks Ct 22182
Wolftrap Run Rd 22182
Wolftrap Vale Ct 22182
Woodcroft Ct 22027
Wooded Way 22182
Woodford Ct & Rd 22182
Woodford Forest Pl 22182
Woodland Ct 22027
Woodland Ct NW 22180
Woodland Glen Ct 22182
Woodnor Dr NE 22180
Woodrow St 22181
Woodview Cir SW 22180
Woodwind Way 22182
Wooster Ct 22180
Wynhurst Ln 22182
Yarmouth Forest Pl 22180
Yearling Ct 22182
Yellow Pine Dr 22182
Yeonas Cir & Dr SE & SW 22180

Yvonnes Way 22027
Zinc Ct 22182

NUMBERED STREETS

1st Ave 22182
2nd Ave 22182
4th Pl 22027

VIRGINIA BEACH VA

General Delivery 23450
General Delivery 23455
General Delivery 23457
General Delivery 23459
General Delivery 23462
General Delivery 23464

POST OFFICE BOXES MAIN OFFICE STATIONS AND BRANCHES

Box No.s
C2600 - C2600 23450
C6000 - C6000 23466
C2200 - C2200 23450
C8600 - C8600 23450
C9000 - C9000 23450
C2700 - C2700 23466
C2800 - C2800 23466
C61010 - C61030 23466
C61247 - C61247 23466
C62200 - C62200 23466
C62600 - C62600 23466
C66300 - C66300 23466
C62500 - C62500 23466
C66200 - C66220 23466
C2200 - C2200 23466
500 - 1736 23451
2000 - 2976 23450
3001 - 4976 23454
5001 - 5990 23471
6001 - 6990 23456
7001 - 7160 23457
8001 - 10656 23450
55001 - 55470 23471
56001 - 56700 23456
57001 - 57055 23457
59011 - 59064 23459
61001 - 62999 23466
64001 - 65640 23467
66001 - 67005 23466
68001 - 68920 23471

NAMED STREETS

A St
900-999 23451
1000-1298 23459
1001-1099 23455
1001-1099 23459
1101-1297 23455
1299-1399 23455
Abbey Ct & Dr 23455
Abbey Arch 23455
Abbot Rd 23459
Abbot Muse 23452
Abbotsbury Ct & Way 23453
Abbotsleigh Ct 23452
Abelia Way 23454
Aberdeen Ct 23453
Abilene Ln 23456
Abingdon Rd 23451
Aborfield Ct 23464
Absalom Dr 23451
Academy Ct & Rd 23462
Acapulco Ct 23456
Accomac Sq 23455
Ace Ct 23462
Achilles Ct & Dr 23464
Ackiss Ave 23451
Aclare Ct 23462
Acorn Cv 23455
Acredale Rd 23464
Adair Ct & Dr 23456
Adam Rd 23455
Adam Keeling Rd 23454
Adanka Ln 23451
Addington Rd 23454
Addison Ct & St 23462
Adelia Dr 23455
Adelphi Cir & Rd 23464
Adirondack Ct 23452
Adkins Arch 23462
Adler Ave 23462
E & W Admiral Cir & Dr 23451
Admiral Wright Rd 23462
Admiration Dr 23464
Admissions Ct 23462
Adobe Ct 23456
Adonis Ct 23456
Adrian Ct & Dr 23452
Advance Rd 23452
Advent Ct 23454
N & S Adventure Ct & Trl 23454
Aegean Ct 23464
Aeries Way 23455
Affirmed Way 23456
Afton Ct 23462
Agate St 23462
Agecroft Ct & Rd 23454
Agnes Ct 23454
Aiken Ct 23456
Ainsley Pl 23462
Air Rail Ave 23455
Air Station Dr 23454
Ajax Ct 23464
Akinbury Rd 23456
Al Jubayl Rd 23459
Alabama Rd 23452
Alabaster St 23462
Alamance Cir 23456
Alameda Dr 23456
N Alanton Dr 23454
Albacore Ky 23452
Albany Ct 23456
Albemarle Ave 23455
Albert Ct 23456
Alberthas Dr 23452
Albright Ct & Dr 23464
Albuquerque Dr 23456
Alcon Ct 23456
Alcott Rd 23452
Aldea Cir 23456
Alden Ct 23462
Alder Cir 23462
Aldrich Ln 23454
Alewife Ct 23454
Alexis Ct 23454
Alfriends Trl 23455
Alger Ct 23454
Algiers Rd
500-598 23459
501-599 23451
Algonac Ave 23455
Algonquin Ct 23452
Alicia Dr 23462
Alishire Ct 23464
Alister Ct 23453
All Saints Ct 23454
Allaben Ct & Dr 23453
Allearri Dr 23464
Alleghany Loop 23456
Allendale Dr 23451
Allenwood Ave 23454
Allerson Ln 23455
Alliance Dr 23454
Allman Ct 23464
Alloway Ct & Dr 23454
Allyne Rd 23462
Almandine Ave 23462
Aloma Ct & Dr 23453
Alphine Ct & Rd 23451
Alsab Cir 23462
Alton Dr & Rd 23464
Alvena Ln 23464
Alwood Ct 23454
Amador Dr 23456
Ambassador Dr 23462
Amber Way 23462
Amber Bay Ct 23456
Amberbrooke Way 23464
Amberbrooke Arch 23464
Amberjack Ct & Dr 23464
Amberley Forest Pl & Rd 23453
Amberly Rd 23462
Amboy Ct 23462
American Elm Ct 23453
Americus Ave 23451
Amerigroup Way 23464
Amersham Ct 23454
Amesbury Rd 23464
Amethyst Cir 23456
Amherst Cir & Ln 23464
Amhurst Ct 23462
Amigo Ct 23456
Amish Ct 23462
Amphibious Dr
1100-1198 23459
1101-1197 23455
1199-2099 23455
2100-2498 23459
2101-2499 23455
2500-2798 23455
2501-2599 23459
2601-2799 23455
2800-2999 23459
N & S Amsterdam Ct 23454
Amy Dr 23464
Anderson Way 23464
Andover Ct & Rd 23464
Andre Ct 23456
Andrew Jackson Ln 23455
Angel Ct 23455
Angela Ct 23455
Angelfish Ln 23456
Angler Ln 23451
Anglia Ct 23464
Angus Ct & Dr 23464
Ann Arbor Ln 23464
Annandale Ct & Dr 23464
Annefield Ct 23454
Annie Ln 23452
Anoka Ave 23455
Ansol Ln 23452
Anson Ln 23452
Antelope Ct & Pl 23456
Anthony Rd 23455
Anthony Wayne Ct & Rd 23462
Antietam Ct 23454
Antioch Cir, St & Way 23464
Antler Cir 23464
Antonick Ln 23464
Anvers Rd 23462
Apasus Trl 23452
Apiary Ct 23454
Appalachian Ct 23452
Appaloosa Ct 23464
Appian Ave 23452
Apple Blossom Ct 23464
Apple Orchard Ct 23455
Apple Tree Cres 23456
Apple Valley Ct 23464
Appleby Ct 23462
Appleton Ct 23464
Applewood Ln 23452
April Ave & Ct 23464
Aqua Ln 23451
Aquamarine Dr 23456
Aquarius Ct 23464
Aqueduct Ct 23464
Arabian Dr 23456
Aragon Dr 23455
Aragona Blvd
100-699 23462
700-1099 23455
Aragona Cir 23455
Arapahoe Trl 23464
Arboretum Ave 23455
Arbre Ct 23451
Archdale Ct & Dr 23456
Archer Ct & Dr 23452
Archives Ct 23464
Archway Ct 23455
Arctic Ave, Cir & Cres 23451
Arcturus Ln 23456
Ardito Ct 23453
Ardmore Ln 23456
Ardsley Sq 23464
Argo Ct 23453
Arkley Dr 23462
Arklow Rd 23456
Arleen Ct 23453
Arlington Arch Ct & Dr 23464
Arlo Ct 23464
Arlynn Ln 23451
Armistine Ct 23462
Armon Ave 23452
Arnold Cir 23454
Arnold Palmer Dr 23456
Arrow Cir 23452
Arrowfield Rd 23454
Arrowhead Dr 23462
Arrowhead Pt 23455
Arrowhead Point Ct 23455
Arrowstone Ct 23456
Artesia Way 23456
Arthur Ave 23452
Articles Ln 23462
Arvida Ct & Ln 23462
Arvin Rd 23464
Ascot Ct 23452
Ash Ave 23452
Ashaway Ct & Rd 23452
Ashbrook Ct 23464
Ashburnham Arch 23456
Ashbury Ln 23462
Ashforth Ct 23462
Ashland St 23455
Ashlawn Ter 23452
Ashley Dr 23454
Ashmeade Ct 23464
Ashmont Dr 23456
Ashmore Dr 23454
Ashton Dr 23464
Ashwood Ln 23453
Aspen Cir, Ct & Dr 23464
Assembly Dr 23454
Aston Ln 23454
Astor Ct & Ln 23464
Astoria Ct 23453
Athens Blvd 23455
Athol Ct 23456
Atkinson Close 23456
Atlanta Dr 23453
Atlantic Ave
2-16 23451
18-600 23451
601-609 23459
602-702 23451
613-8899 23451
704-704 23459
706-8898 23451
S Atlantic Ave 23451
Atlantic Shores Dr 23454
Atlantis Dr 23451
Atley Ln 23452
Atmore Ln 23455
Atterbury Ct 23462
Attica Ave 23455
Attu Rd 23459
Atwater Arch 23456
Atwoodtown Rd 23456
Au Sable Cir, Ct & Pl 23453
Aubrey Dr 23462
Auburn Dr 23464
Audley Way 23452
Audubon Ct 23454
Augusta Cir 23453
Aura Dr 23457
Aurora Dr 23455
Austin Ln 23455
Automne Cir 23451
Autumn Harvest Ct & Dr 23464
Autumn Lakes Ct 23451
Autumn Leaf Ct 23456
Autumn Woods Ln 23454
Ava Way 23456
Avalon Ave 23464
Avalon Woods Cir, Ct & Dr 23464
Avant Ct 23454
Avatar Dr 23454
Avella St 23464
Avenger Dr 23452
Averadia Dr 23462
Averham Dr 23455
Avery Way 23464
Aviator Dr 23453
Avilla Ct 23455
Avon Lndg 23464
Axis Ct 23454
Aydlette Ct 23454
Aylesbury Dr 23462
Azalea Ct 23452
Aztec Ct 23454
B Ave 23460
B St
900-999 23451
1000-1499 23455
Baal Ct 23464
Babbling Brook Dr 23462
Babney Ct 23462
Babson Way 23464
Baccalaureate Dr 23462
Bach Ln 23456
Back Acres Ct & Rd 23454
Back Bay Cres 23456
Back Bay Landing Rd 23457
Back Cove Rd 23454
Backwoods Rd 23455
Bacon Ct 23462
Baden Ave 23464
Baez Ct 23464
Bagelwood Ct 23456
Baggett Ln 23451
Bagpipers Ct & Ln 23464
Bailey Ln 23451
Baileywick Dr 23455
Baillio Dr 23454
Baja Ct 23456
Baker Ct 23462
Baker Rd
400-899 23462
900-1499 23455
Bakerfield Rd 23453
Balboa Dr 23464
Balch Pl 23454
Bald Eagle Bnd & Rd 23453
Balderton Ct 23455
Baldwin St 23452
Balereli Ave 23461
Balfor Ct & Dr 23464
Ballard Ct 23462
Ballylinn Ct & Rd 23464
Balsam Pine Ct 23452
Balston Ct 23464
Baltic Ave & Walk 23451
Bamberg Pl 23453
Bamboo Ln 23452
Banbury Ct 23462
Bancroft Dr 23452
Bangor Sq 23455
Banister Ct 23454
Bank St 23462
Banks Ln 23456
Bannock Rd 23462
Bantry Ln 23455
Bantry Cross 23452
Banyan Dr 23462
Banyan Grove Ln 23462
Baptist Cir 23464
Bar Harbor Way 23455
Barbara Lee Ct 23464
Barberry Ct & Ln 23453
Barberton Ct & Dr 23451
Barbour Dr 23456
Barcelona Ct & Ln 23452
Barclay Sq 23451
Barco Dr 23464
Bardith Cir 23455
Barham Ct 23454
Bark Ln 23455
Barkading Ct & Ln 23464
Barkie Ct 23464
Barkingdale Dr 23462
Barkleaf Dr 23462
Barksdale Dr 23456
Barkwood Ct 23464
Barlborough Way 23453
Barn Brook Ct & Rd 23454
Barn Owl Ct 23456
Barn Stall Ln 23456
Barn Swallow Ct 23456
Barnaby Ct 23455
Barnacle Ct 23451
Barnard Way 23464
Barnards Cove Rd 23455
Barnet Ct 23456
Barnsely Ct 23456
Barnstable County Rd 23459
Barnstable Quay 23452
Barrett St 23452
Barrington Ct & Dr 23452
Barrison Way 23462
Barrs Rd 23455
Barry St 23452
Barten Ct 23464
Bartholomews Xing 23456
Bartlett Oaks Ct 23456
Bartow Pl 23454
Barwood Ct 23456
Basilica Cir & Ct 23464
Basin Ct & Rd 23451
Bassett Ave 23452
Basswood Ct 23453
Bastion Ct 23454
Bates Way 23464
Bathley Pl 23455
Bathurst Rd 23464
Battery Rd 23455
Battle Creek Ct 23464
Battle Royal Cir 23455
Battleford Dr 23464
Baugh Ct 23454
Baum Rd 23457
Baxter Rd 23462
Bay Dr & Rd 23451
Bay Breeze Cir, Ct, Cv & Dr 23454
Bay Bridge Ln 23455
Bay Colony Dr 23451
Bay Cove Quay 23462
Bay Island Quay 23451
Bay Landing Dr 23455
Bay Point Ct & Dr 23454
Bay Quarter Ct 23455
Bay Ridge Ct 23451
E Bay Shore Dr 23451
Bay Winds Ct 23455
Bayberry St 23451
Baycliff Cir, Ct, Dr & Ln 23454
Bayhead Dr 23453
Baylake Rd 23455
Baylor Way 23464
Bayne Dr 23454
Baynebridge Dr 23464
Bays Edge Ave 23451
Bayshire Ct 23462
Bayside Rd 23455
Bayview Ave 23455
Bayville Rd 23455
Bayway Rd 23451
Beach Dr 23455
Beach Bay Ct 23455
Beach Castle Ln 23451
Beach Cove Pl 23455
Beach Haven Dr 23451
Beach Landing Ct 23455
Beach Town Dr 23451
Beachview Dr 23464
Beacon Ln 23452
Beacons Reach Ct & Dr 23454
Beaden Ct & Dr 23456
Beagle Way 23453
Bear Trl 23456
Bearcroft Ct 23464
Beasley Ct 23462
Beaton St 23464
Beaufain Blvd 23464
Beaufort Ave 23455
Beaumeade Ct 23462
Beaumont Dr 23464
Beautiful St 23451
Beauty Way 23456
Beaver Dr 23452
Beaver Creek Ct 23464
Beaver Falls Ct 23464
Beaver Pond Ct 23464
Beckman Ct & Cv 23454
Becks Ct 23464
Becontree Ct 23462
Becton Pl 23452
Bedford Ln 23452
Bee St 23454
Beech St 23451
Beecher Ct 23456
Beechwalk Dr 23464
Beechwood Cv 23464
Beethoven Ct & Dr 23454
Behl Ct 23464
Bel Air Ln 23455
Beldover Ct & Ln 23452
Belingham Rd 23462
Bellamy Ct 23462
Bellamy Manor Dr 23464
Belle Ct 23453
Belle Haven Dr 23452
Belleza Ct 23456
Bellows Ln 23455
Bells Rd
1000-1099 23451
1100-1399 23454
Bellview Ct 23454
Belmeade Dr 23455
Belmont Ct 23452
Belmont Stakes Dr 23456
Belspring Ct 23464
Belspring Dr
900-1099 23456
1100-1299 23464
Belvidere Rd 23454
Belvoir Ln 23464
Belwood Ct 23455
Ben Ky 23452
Ben Bow Dr 23464
Ben Franklin Ln 23462
Ben Gunn Rd 23455
Ben Hogan Dr 23462
Bending Birch Trl 23456
Bendix Rd 23452
Benecia Dr 23456
Benedict Ct 23454
Benertho Rd 23455
Benjamin Pl 23454
Benjamin Harrison Dr 23452
Benlar Ct 23456
Benlea Cir & Ct 23454
Bennett Ln 23462
Bennington Cir & Rd 23464
Benns Church Pl 23455
Bent Branch Dr & Ln 23452
Bente Way 23451
Bentley Ct 23462
Bentley Gate Way 23452
Bentley Heath Cmn 23452
Benton Ct 23453
Bergen Ct 23451
Beringer Pl 23454
Berkley Ct & Pl 23452
Berkshire Ln 23451
Bernadotte Ct & St 23456
Bernice Pl 23452
Bernstein Ct & Dr 23454
E & W Berrie Cir & Rd 23455
Berry Garden Way 23453
Berrypick Ln 23462
Berrywood Ct & Rd 23464
Bertrum Ct 23455
Berwick Cres & Ct 23452

Berwyn Rd 23464
Beryl Ave 23464
Bessie Walk 23451
Bethesda Ct 23464
Bethune Dr 23452
Betsy Cres 23453
Betsy Ross Rd 23462
Betula Ct 23456
Beverly Pl 23452
Bexley Cir 23455
Bibb Ct 23456
Bierce Dr 23454
Big Bear Ct 23456
Big Ben Rd 23452
Big Boulder Dr 23456
Big Leaf Cir & Ct 23454
Big Oak Ct 23456
Big Pine Dr 23452
Big Springs Pl 23453
Biltmore Ct & Dr 23454
Binford Ct 23456
Bingham St 23451
Birch Ct & Rd 23462
Birch Bark Dr 23452
Birch Forest Ct 23464
Birch Lake Cres & Rd 23451
Birch Tree Ct 23451
Birchridge Ct 23462
Birchwood Rd 23455
Birchwood Park Dr 23452
Birdhaven Ct 23462
Birdie Ct 23462
N & S Birdneck Cir & Rd 23451
Birdneck Lake Dr 23451
Birdsong Ln 23455
Birks Ln 23464
Birnam Lndg 23464
Birnam Woods Ct & Dr 23464
Biscayne Dr 23455
Bishop Ct & Dr 23455
Bishop Thoroughgood Ave 23451
Bishopsgate Ct & Ln 23452
Bitter Root Ct 23456
Bivens St 23464
Bizet Ct 23454
Bizzone Cir 23464
Black Angus Ct 23453
Black Cove Rd 23455
Black Duck Ct 23451
Black Watch Ln 23464
Blackbeard Rd 23455
Blackburn Ct & Ln 23454
Blackfoot Cir, Cres & Ct 23462
Blackfriars Dr 23455
Blackpoole Ln 23462
Blacksmith Ct 23464
Blackstone Ct & Trl 23453
Blackthorne Ct 23455
Blackwatch Ct 23455
Blackwater Loop & Rd 23457
Blackwell Ct 23464
Blackwood Ct 23456
Blair Cir 23452
Blairmore Dr 23454
Blairmore Arch 23454
Blake St 23456
Blakely Sq 23464
Blakemore Ct 23464
Blanding Ct 23464
Blasters Cv 23451
Bleecker St 23462
Blitz Ct 23453
Bliven Ln 23455
Bloomfield Ct & Dr 23453
Bloomsbury Cres & Ln 23454
Blossom Cir 23456
Blossom Hill Ct 23457
Blue Bonnet Dr 23453
Blue Castle Ct & Ln 23454
Blue Heron Ct & Rd 23454
Blue Jay Dr 23453
Blue Knob Ct & Rd 23464

Blue Lagoon Ct 23456
Blue Lake Ct 23462
Blue Marlin Cir 23452
Blue Pete Rd 23451
Blue Ridge Ct 23452
Blue Spring Ct & Ln 23452
Blueberry Rd 23451
Bluebill Dr 23456
Bluebird Dr 23451
Bluecher Ct 23454
Bluefish Ln 23456
Bluemont Ct 23462
Bluff Ct 23462
Blythe Dr 23456
Boagie Ct 23456
Boardwalk Way 23451
Bob Ln 23454
Bob Jones Dr 23462
Bob White Ln 23464
Bobolink Dr 23451
Bobtail Ct 23456
Bodie Ct 23456
Bodnar Ln 23456
Boerum Ct 23452
S Boggs Ave 23452
Bogus Ln 23456
Bohnhoff Ct & Dr 23454
Bold Ruler Dr 23454
Bolero Ct 23462
Boles Pl 23454
Bombay Lndg 23456
Bonfield Ct 23454
Bonita Ln 23456
Bonney Rd
3600-4375 23452
4376-5199 23462
Bonneydale Rd 23464
Bonneys Quay 23462
Booty Ln 23451
Bordeaux Ct 23456
Border Ct & Way 23456
Borg Ct 23464
Bosco Ct 23453
Boston Ct 23456
Boswell Ct 23452
Bosworth Rd 23462
Botanical Dr 23455
Botany Park Dr 23462
Botetourt Ct 23453
Bottino Ln 23455
Boughton Way 23453
Boulder Ct 23455
Bound Brook Ct 23462
Bounty Rd 23455
Boush Quarter 23452
Bouthol Ave 23451
Bow St 23464
Bow Creek Blvd 23452
Bowden Ave 23455
Bowery St 23462
Bowland Pkwy 23454
Bowling Green Ct & Dr 23452
Bowman Rd 23462
Bowsprit Cir 23453
Box Elder Arch 23454
Boxford Ct & Rd 23456
Boxhill Ct & Rd 23464
Boxley Dr 23456
Boxwood Ln 23452
Boyd Rd 23452
Boyle Ct 23462
Boynton Ct 23452
Boysenberry Ct 23456
Bracken Ct 23453
Bracston Rd 23456
Brad Dr 23464
Braddock Ave 23455
Bradford Pt & Rd 23455
Bradley Way 23464
Bradpointe Ln 23455
Bradston Rd 23455
Bragg Ct 23462
Brahms Dr 23454
Braileigh Ln 23455
Bramcote Pl 23455

Branch Cir 23454
Branchwood Way 23464
Brandon Blvd 23464
Brandon Rd 23451
Brandy Station Ct 23464
Brandywine Dr 23464
Brannon Dr 23456
Brant Rd 23451
Brantingham Dr 23464
Brantley Pl 23452
Brasileno Ct & Dr 23456
Braswell Cir 23462
Brattleboro Arch 23464
Bray Rd 23452
Breakers Ct 23451
Breakwater Ct 23462
Breccia Ln 23462
Breck Ave & Ct 23464
Breckenridge Cir 23453
Breeds Hill Rd 23462
Breezewood Arch 23464
Breezy Rd 23451
Breezy Pines Ln 23456
Breezy Point Cir & Rd 23453
Brendle Ct 23464
Brenland Cir 23464
Brentwater Rd 23452
Brentwood Cir, Cres & Ct 23452
Breslaw Ct 23453
Brestwick Cmns 23464
Breton Ct 23454
Brian Ave 23462
Briar Ct 23452
Briarbush Ln 23453
Briarwood Pt 23452
Brices Ln 23464
Brickell Ct 23454
Brickhaven Dr 23462
Brickhouse Ct 23452
Brideshead Ct 23464
Bridge Landing Ct 23454
Bridge Port Pl 23464
Bridge Side Pl 23455
Bridgeford Ct 23456
Bridgehampton Ln 23455
Bridgeman Ct & Ln 23455
Bridges Pl 23464
Bridgeview Ct 23452
Bridgewater Arch 23462
Bridle Way 23456
Bridle Creek Blvd & Ct 23464
Bridlepath Ln 23456
Bridlewood Ct 23456
Briercliff Pt 23455
Brigadoon Ct & Dr 23455
Brigands Way 23453
Brigantine Ct 23454
Brighton Ct 23464
Brighton Beach Pl 23451
Brightwell Pl 23456
Brightwood Dr 23456
Brigita Ct 23453
Brigstock Ct 23454
Brinker Dr 23462
Brinsley Ln 23455
Brinson Ln 23455
Brinson Arch 23455
Britannica Pl 23454
Britt Ter 23452
Brittany Ct 23454
Brittingham Ct 23464
Brittlebank Dr 23462
Brixton Dr 23462
Broad St 23462
Broad Bay Cir 23454
Broad Bay Rd 23451
Broad Meadows Blvd & Ct 23462
Broadacres Ct & Way 23453
Broadholme Pl 23455
Broadlawn Rd 23454
Broadleaf Ct 23453
Broadmoor Ct 23452
Broadwindsor Ln 23464
Brock Ct 23462

Brockie Cir & St 23464
Brockway Ct 23464
Brodeur Ln 23456
Bromfield Ave & Ct 23455
Bromley Ct 23454
Brompton Ct & Dr 23456
Bronte Trce 23462
E Brook Cir 23454
Brook Meadow Ct 23462
Brookbridge Rd 23452
Brookbury Ct 23464
Brooke Rd 23454
Brookeway Ct & Dr 23464
Brookfield Cv & Dr 23464
Brookhill Ct 23454
Brooklyn Ave & Ct 23451
Brookside Ct & Ln 23452
Brookstone Ln 23455
Brookwood Cres & Pl 23453
Broomsedge Ct & Trl 23456
Brotman Ct 23464
Browning Dr 23456
Brownshire Trl 23456
Brownstone Ct 23456
Brunick Ct 23462
Brush Creek Ln 23454
Brush Hill Ln 23456
Brushwood Ter 23456
Bruton Ln 23451
Bryan Ln 23452
Bryce Ln 23464
Brynmawr Ln 23464
Buccaneer Rd 23451
Buchanan Dr 23453
Buck Ct 23464
Buckboard Ct 23456
Buckeye Ct 23462
Buckhorn Ct & Pl 23456
Buckhurst Ln 23462
N & S Buckingham Ct 23462
Buckley Arch 23453
Buckminister Ln 23462
Bucknell Cir 23464
Buckner Blvd 23453
N & S Budding Ave 23452
Buenos Aires Ct 23454
Buffer Ct & Dr 23462
Bull Run Ct 23464
Bullock Trl 23454
Bullpup St 23461
Bulls Bay Dr 23462
Bunker Dr 23462
Bunker Hill Ln 23462
Bunnell Ct 23464
Bunsen Dr 23454
Bunyan Ct & Rd 23462
Burford Ave 23451
Burgesses Ln 23452
Burlington Rd 23464
Burns Ct 23462
Burnt Mill Rd 23452
Burr Oak Cir & Ct 23454
Burroughs Rd 23455
Burton Dr 23454
Burton Station Rd 23455
Burwillow Dr 23464
Busher Rd 23462
Bushnell Ct & Dr 23451
Business Park Dr 23462
Busky Ln 23454
Butler Ln 23456
Butterchurn Ct 23456
Butterfly Arch 23456
Buttermilk Ct 23456
Butternut Dr 23454
Butternut Ln 23452
Button Bush St 23456
Buttonwood Ct 23462
Butts Ln 23451
Buyrn Cir & Ct 23453
Buyrn Farm Rd 23453
Buzzard Neck Rd 23457
Byrd Ln 23454
Byrn Brae Dr 23464
C Ave 23451

C St
200-299 23451
1200-1399 23455
Cabin John Dr 23464
Cabot Ct 23453
Cabrini Pl 23464
Cabriole Mews 23455
Cacapon Ct 23454
Cachet Ct 23456
Cadbury Cir 23454
Caddoan Rd 23462
Caddoan Turn 23462
Caddwind Ct 23456
Caddy Ct 23462
Cadence Way 23456
Cadiz Ct 23454
Cainhoy Ln 23462
Caitlan Loch Ln 23456
Calash Way 23454
Calgary Ct 23464
Calhoun Ct 23456
Calico Ct 23464
Calistoga Ct 23456
Callahan Ct 23453
Callandish Ct 23464
Calm Wood Ln 23453
Calumet Dr 23456
Calvert St 23451
Calverton Cir & Ln 23455
Calypso Ln 23454
Cam Ranh Bay 23459
Camarillo Ln 23456
Cambell Ct 23453
Cambelton Dr 23462
Camberwell Ct 23453
Cambria Cir, Ct & St 23455
Cambridge Dr 23454
Camden Ct 23457
Camelback Pl 23464
Camellia Ct 23452
Camelot Dr 23454
Cameron Ln 23452
Camino Ct 23456
Camino Real S 23456
Campbells Landing Rd 23457
Campion Ave & Ct 23462
Campus Dr 23462
Canadian Ct 23453
Canadian Arch 23453
Canal Rd 23451
Canary Dr 23453
Canavos Ct 23456
Canberry Ct 23454
Cancun Ct 23456
Candle Pine Ln 23456
Candlewood Dr 23464
Candy Ct 23455
Candytuft Ct 23456
Canebrake Ct 23456
Canisbay Ct 23464
Cannan Valley Ave 23464
Cannes Ct 23456
Cannich Ct 23464
Cannon Dr 23454
Cannonade Trl 23454
Cannonbury Cmn 23452
Canoe Lndg 23464
Canopy Ct 23455
Canter Ct 23456
Canterbury Rd 23452
Canterford Ct & Ln 23464
Canterwood Ct 23462
Cantwell Rd 23453
Canvasback Way 23451
Cape Ann Ct & Way 23453
Cape Arbor Dr 23451
Cape Cod Cir 23455
Cape Henry Cir 23451
Cape Henry Ct 23451
Cape Henry Dr 23451
Cape Henry Rd
1-100 23451
102-198 23451
300-399 23459
500-599 23451
Cape Joshua Ln 23462

Cape Levi Ln 23462
Capehart Ct 23464
Capel Manor Way 23456
Capital Pl 23464
Capital Hill Ln 23452
Capot Rd 23462
Capstone Xing 23455
Captain Adams Ct 23455
Captains Ct & Run 23464
Carabao Cir 23464
Cardamon Ct & Dr 23464
Cardiff Rd 23455
Cardinal Rd 23451
Cardington Ct 23456
Cardini Pl 23453
Cardo Pl 23453
Cardston Ct 23454
Caren Dr 23452
Carew Rd 23462
Caribbean Ave 23451
Caribe Ct & Pl 23462
Caribou Ct 23456
Carisbrooke Ct 23464
Carissa Ct 23451
Carlisle Sq 23464
Carlsbad Ct 23456
Carlson Ln 23452
Carlton E & W 23454
Carmel St 23457
Carnaby Ct & Dr 23454
Carnation Ave 23462
Carnegie Ct & Rd 23452
Carnelian St & Way 23462
Caroga Ct 23453
Carolanne Dr & Ter 23462
Carolanne Point Cir 23462
Carolina Ave 23451
Carolyn Dr 23451
Carothers Arch 23464
Carrara Ct 23456
Carrene Dr 23455
Carriage Dr 23462
Carriage Hill Rd 23452
Carriage House Ct & Dr 23462
Carrington Ave 23464
Carter Hall Rd 23455
Carteret Arch 23464
Cartwell Dr 23452
Carver Ave 23451
Casa Ct 23456
Casa Verde Way 23456
Casablanca Rd 23455
Casanova Dr 23454
Cascade Ct 23453
Casey Ct 23454
Cason Ln 23462
Casper Ct 23462
Caspian Ave 23451
Cassady Ave 23452
Cassatt Ct 23464
Casselberry Ln 23452
Cassell Ct & St 23454
Cassena Ct 23453
Castilian Dr 23462
Castle Rd 23464
Castle Gate Ln 23456
Castle Hill Ct 23454
Castlefield Rd 23456
Castlerea Ct 23455
Castleton Ct 23454
Castleton Commerce Way 23456
Castlewood Dr 23456
Casual Ct 23454
Catalina Ave 23452
Catamaran Ct 23451
Catano Ct 23462
Caterpillar Ct 23456
Catesby Cir 23456
Catfish Rd 23457
Cathedral Dr 23455
Catherine Ct 23454
Catina Arch 23462
Caton Dr 23454
Catskill Ct 23451

Cattail Ln 23456
Cattayle Run 23452
Cattingham Ln 23456
Catworth Dr 23456
Caussome Mews 23455
Cavalier Dr 23451
Cavan Ct 23462
Cavelletti Ct 23454
Cavendish Dr 23455
Caversham Mews 23455
Cavesson Ct 23464
Cawdor Cir 23464
Caxton Ct 23462
Cayenne Ct 23462
Cayman Ln 23456
Caymus Ct 23454
Cayuga Ct & Rd 23462
Cebu Island Rd 23451
Cedar Ln 23452
Cedar Bark Rd 23454
Cedar Bridge Cir & Rd 23452
Cedar Crescent Ct 23457
Cedar Forest Dr 23464
Cedar Glen Ct 23462
Cedar Grove Cir 23452
Cedar Lake Ct 23462
Cedar Point Dr 23451
Cedar Springs Ct 23462
Cedarhurst Ct 23454
Cedarwood Ct 23454
Celbridge Ct 23452
Cellar Door Way 23456
Centell Rd 23451
Centerfield Pl 23464
Centerville Tpke 23464
Central Dr 23454
Central Park Ave 23462
Centre Pointe Dr 23462
Century Ct & Dr 23462
Cereta Way 23453
Cerino Ct 23464
Cessna Dr 23452
Chabot Way 23464
Chadwick Ct 23464
Chadwick Dr 23454
Chain Bridge Rd 23464
Chaka Ct & Ln 23454
Chalet Pl 23462
Chalfont Dr 23464
Chalk Ct 23462
Challedon Dr 23462
Chamberino Dr 23456
Chamberlayne Ct 23452
Chamberling Ky 23454
Chambers Dr 23456
Champion Cir 23456
Champlain Ln 23452
Chancellor Dr 23452
Chancellor Walk Ct 23454
Chancery Ln & Sq 23452
Chandler Ln 23455
Chandler Creek Rd 23453
Chandler Scott Ct 23464
Chandon Cres 23454
Channel Points Ln 23454
Channing Ln 23456
Chantilly Ct 23451
Chaparal Ct 23462
Chapel Lake Dr 23454
Chapel Lawn Dr 23454
Chapel Wood Dr 23454
Chapham Cross 23452
Chappell Pl 23452
Charing Cross Rd 23456
Charisma Ct 23456
Charity Dr 23455
Charity Farm Ct 23457
Charity Neck Rd
3300-3799 23456
3800-4499 23457
Charla Lee Ln 23455
Charlan Pl 23464
Charlecote Cir & Dr 23464
Charlemagne Dr 23451
Charles Ct 23462
Charlestown Dr 23464

Charmont Ct 23455
Charnell Dr 23451
Charter Ct 23454
Charter Oak Rd 23452
Chartfield Ct 23456
Chartwell Dr 23464
Chase Ct 23462
Chase Arbor Cmn & Ct 23462
Chase Pointe Cir 23454
Chaseway St 23462
Chateau Run Ct 23456
Chatham Ct 23455
Chatham Hall Dr 23464
Chatham Lake Dr 23464
Chatmoss Ct & Dr 23464
Chatsworth Ct 23454
Chatterton Dr 23454
Chattingham Dr 23464
Chaucer Ct & St 23462
Chayote Ct 23462
Chelmsford Ct 23464
Chelsea St 23455
Chelsea Green Dr 23456
Cheltenham Ct & Dr 23454
E & W Cheltingham Pl 23452
Chelwood Ln 23452
Cherbourg Rd 23455
Cherie Dr 23453
Cherokee Rd 23462
N & S Cherokee Cluster 23462
Cherry Ct & Ln 23454
Cherry Blossom Ct 23464
Cherrywood Ln 23453
Cheshire Forest Ct 23456
N & S Chesire Ct 23454
Chesopeian Pt & Trl 23452
Chessie Ct 23464
Chessington Ct 23464
Chester St 23452
Chester Forest Ct 23452
Chesterbrook Dr 23464
Chesterfield Ave 23455
Chesterton Ct 23453
Chestnut Ave 23452
Chestnut Ct 23464
Chestnut Hill Rd 23464
Chestnut Oak Way 23453
Chestwood Bnd & Dr 23453
Cheswick Ln 23455
Cheswick Arch 23455
Cheval Cir 23451
Cheverly Ct 23464
Chewink Ct 23451
Cheyenne Cir & Rd 23462
Cheyne Walk 23454
Chichester Ct 23464
Chickadee Ct & Ln 23454
E & W Chickasaw Ct & Rd 23462
Chicken Valley Rd 23454
Chicks Beach Ct 23455
Chicory Ct & St 23453
Chief Trl 23464
Chigwell Ct & Rd 23454
Childeric Rd 23456
Chilhowie Cir 23464
Chilton Pl 23456
Chilworth Ct 23464
Chimney Creek Dr 23462
Chimney Hill Ct & Pkwy 23462
Chimney Hill Shopping Ctr 23452
Chimo Ct 23454
Chinaberry Cir & Ct 23454
Chinook St 23462
Chinquapin Ln 23451
Chippendale Ct & Dr 23455
E Chippenham Rd 23455
Chippewa Rd 23462
Chipping Ct & Ln 23455
Chippokes Ct 23454
Chipstead Ln 23464
Chirnside Ct 23464
Chisholm Dr 23452
Chisman Ct 23464
Chloe Ln 23456
Choctaw Ct & Dr 23464
Chopin Dr 23454
Chownings Dr 23462
Christa Ct 23462
Christian Cir & Ct 23464
Christine Dr 23451
Christopher Arch 23464
Christopher Farms Dr 23453
W Chubb Lake Ave 23455
Chumley Rd 23451
Church 23457
Church St 23464
Church Point Ct, Ln, Pl & Rd 23455
Churchill Ct & Dr 23464
Churchside Ln 23454
Cindy Ct 23464
Cinnabar Ct 23456
Cinnamon Ridge Dr 23462
Cinta Ct 23456
Circle Ln 23451
Circuit Ct 23454
Citadel Ct 23464
Citation Ct & Dr 23462
Citrine Ave 23462
City Of Virginia Bch 23456
Claiborne Pl 23454
Clairmont Ct 23462
Claridge Ct 23454
Clarion Ct 23464
Clarke Dr 23456
Claudia Dr 23455
Claudia May Rd 23457
Clay Ave 23454
N & S Claypool Ct 23464
Clayton Ct 23464
Clear Lake Cir 23464
Clear Springs Ct, Ln & Rd 23464
Clearbrook Ln 23464
Clearfield Ave 23462
Clearwater Pl 23464
Clearwood Ct 23453
Cleary Ct 23464
Cleeve Abbey 23462
Clemsford Ct & Dr 23456
Cleveland Pl & St 23462
Clevhamm Cmn 23456
Clevhamm Common Ct 23456
Cliff Cir 23455
Cliff Cutter Dr 23454
Cliffony Dr 23464
Cliffwood Dr 23456
Clifton Rd 23457
Clifton Bridge Dr 23456
Clinton Ct & St 23464
Clintwood Ln 23452
Clipper Bay Dr 23455
Cloquet Ct 23454
Close Ave 23451
Clover St 23462
Cloverlawn Ct 23464
Clovis Ct 23454
Club Head Ct & Rd 23455
S Club House Cir, Ct & Rd 23452
Clyde St 23455
Clydesdale Ln 23464
Clymer Ct 23455
Clyne Ln 23452
Coach Cir 23462
Coach Dr 23462
Coach Ln 23454
Coach House Ct & Ln 23452
Coachman Ct 23462
Coast Artillery Rd 23459
Coastal Dr 23451
Coastal Walk Pl 23451
Coastaway Dr 23451
Coastview Ct 23464
Coatbridge Ct 23464
Cobblestone Dr 23452
Cobden Rd 23455
Cocoa Cir 23454
Coconut Ln 23452
Cocowalk Ln 23462
Coffee Ct 23462
Coggeshall Ct 23452
Coker Ct 23464
Cokesberry Ct 23453
Colbeck Ct 23456
Colby Way 23464
Cold Harbor Ct 23464
Cold Spring Rd 23454
Cold Stream Pl 23452
Coldingham Ct 23464
Coldwell St 23456
Cole Ct 23454
Colebrook Dr 23464
Colechester Rd 23456
Coleridge Ct 23462
Colgin Dr 23455
Coliss Ave 23462
Collection Creek Way 23454
Colleen Ct 23464
College Cres 23453
College Park Blvd & Sq 23464
Collier Ln 23455
Collingswood Trl 23464
Collins Ln 23452
Cologne Ct 23464
Colonel Cir 23452
W Colonial Pkwy 23452
Colonial Acres Ct 23456
Colonial Arms Cir 23454
Colonial Meadows Way 23454
Colonial Medical Ct 23454
Colonnade Cres & Dr 23451
Colony Dr 23453
Colony Pines Ct & Dr 23452
Colorado Cir 23453
Colson Ct 23454
Colt Ct 23453
Coltan Ave 23462
Colter Ct 23462
Coltfield Ln 23455
Columbia Rd 23454
Columbus Ctr 23462
Columbus St
4500-4830 23462
4831-4899 23462
4831-4831 23466
4832-4898 23462
Colwyck Ct 23464
Comaired Cv 23453
Comanche Ct & Rd 23462
S Comanche Cluster 23462
Commerce Pkwy 23454
Commerce St 23462
Commodore Ct & Dr 23454
Commons Ct 23462
Commonwealth Dr & Pl 23464
Communications Cir 23455
Commuter Dr 23462
Compass Cir 23451
Compass Hill Ct 23456
Competitor Ct 23453
Compton Cir 23464
Comte Ct 23453
Concert Dr
1800-1899 23453
2000-2099 23456
Concord Bridge Rd 23452
Concordia Way 23453
Condor St 23462
Conestoga Rd 23462
Confederate Cres 23453
Conference Ct 23462
Congress St 23452
Conifer Ct 23453
Coniston Muse 23452
Connie Ln & Way 23462
Connors Dr 23464
Conrad Ln 23454
Conservatory Ave 23455
Consolvo Ct & Dr 23454
Constance Ct 23462
Constitution Ct & Dr 23462
Consul Ave 23462
Continental St 23452
Convention Ct & Dr 23462
Convoy Ct 23454
Conway Cir & Ct 23453
Coolspring Way 23464
Cooper Cir & Rd 23454
Coopers Arch 23456
Cooperstown Ct 23451
Copper Kettle Dr 23464
Copperfield Rd 23455
Copperhawke Dr 23456
Coquina Ln 23451
Coquina Chase 23451
Coral Ky 23452
Coral Bay Ct 23455
Coral Gables Ct 23452
Coral Reef Ln 23455
Corbett Rd 23456
Cordova Ct 23456
Coriander Ct 23462
Cormith Ct 23453
Corn Husk Rd 23456
Cornerstone Ct 23456
Cornfield Ct 23464
Cornick Dr 23454
Corning Ct 23451
Cornsilk Cir 23456
Cornstalk Ct 23456
Cornwall Ct 23464
Cornwallis Dr 23452
Cornwell Ln 23454
Coronet Ave 23455
Corporate Landing Pkwy 23454
Corporate Woods Dr 23462
Corporation Ln 23462
Corral Ct 23464
Corrente Ln 23456
Corrine Ln 23452
Corsair Dr 23454
Cortland Ln 23452
Corvette Ct & Ln 23452
S Corwood Ave 23452
Costa Grande Dr 23456
Cotswold Lndg 23464
Cottage Ct & Way 23462
Cottenham Ln 23454
Cotton Creek Dr 23455
Cottontail Ct 23464
Cottonwood Ct 23462
Cougar Ct 23456
Counselor Ln & Sq 23452
Count Fleet Cir 23462
Count Turf Rd 23462
Country Pl 23452
Country Club Cir 23455
Country Glen Ct 23453
Country Manor Ln 23456
Country Mill Rd 23454
Countryside Ln 23454
County Pl 23456
Couples Ct 23456
Course View Cir 23455
Court Cir 23453
Court Plaza Dr 23456
Courthouse Dr 23456
Courtney Arch 23452
Courtview Dr 23452
Courtyard Ln 23455
Cove Rd
1800-1899 23459
1900-1999 23455
2000-2099 23451
Cove Point Pl 23454
Covenant Ct 23464
Covent Garden Rd 23456
Coventry Cir & Rd 23462
Coverdale Cir, Ct & Ln 23452
Covered Bridge Way 23454
Covert Ct 23464
Covey St 23454
Covington Ct 23453
Cowan Ct 23456
Cowbridge Ct 23464
Coyote Cir 23456
Crabapple Rd 23452
Crabbers Cove Ln 23452
Crabtree Ln 23452
Craftsman Dr 23464
Crags Cswy 23457
Craig Ct 23452
Cranberry Ct 23456
Cranborne Ct 23453
Cranbrook Ct 23464
Crane Cres 23454
Cranston Ln 23452
Crashaw St 23462
Crawford Pl 23452
Crawley Cir 23464
Credle Rd 23454
Cree Arch 23464
Creek Way 23454
Creek Cove Ct 23455
Creekmore Ct 23464
Creeks Edge Dr 23451
Creekside Ct & Dr 23453
Creekstone Ct 23453
Creekview Dr 23464
Creekview Ridge Ct 23464
Creekwood Ct & Dr 23456
Crepe Myrtle Ct & Ln 23455
Crescent Moon Ct 23456
Crescent Pointe Ln 23453
Cresthaven Ct & Ln 23464
N & S Crestline Dr 23464
Creston Ct 23464
Crestview Lndg 23454
Crestwood Ln 23453
Cretan Ct 23454
Crew Ct 23454
Cricket Ct 23454
Cricklewood Quay 23452
Crimson Holly Ct & Ln 23453
Criollo Dr 23453
Cripple Creek Ct 23452
Crisfield Rd 23452
Crist Pl 23454
Croatan Ct & Rd 23451
Croatan Hills Ct & Dr 23451
Crocus Ln 23453
Crofts Pride Dr 23453
Croix Ct & Dr 23451
Cromarty Ct 23464
Cromwell Ct 23452
Cromwell Park Dr 23456
Cronin Rd 23452
Croonenbergh Way 23452
Crosby Rd 23452
Crossborough Ct & Rd 23455
Crossbow Cir 23452
Crossett St 23452
Crossfield Rd 23464
Crossing Ct 23455
Crossroad Trl 23456
Crosstimber Way 23456
Crossway Rd 23454
Crow Wing Dr 23456
Crown Grant Ct & Way 23455
Crown Point Ln 23462
Crows Nest Ct 23456
Crowsfoot Ct 23464
Croydon Ct & Dr 23454
Crusader Cir 23453
Crystal Dr, Ln & Pkwy 23451
Crystal Creek Dr 23455
Crystal Lake Cir & Dr 23451
Crystal Point Ct & Dr 23455
Crystal Springs Ct 23462
Crystalline Pl 23462
Crystalwood Ct 23464
Cullen Rd 23455
Cully Farm Rd 23456
Culmer Ct & Dr 23454
Culpepper St 23456
Culver Ln 23454
Culver Quay 23454
Cumberland Pkwy 23452
Cummings Rd 23452
Cunningham Rd 23462
N Curcon Ct 23452
Curlew Dr & Pl 23451
Curling Rd 23455
Curry Cir 23462
Curry Comb Ct 23453
Curtis Breathwaite Ln 23462
Curtiss Ct & Dr 23455
Custom Cir & St 23454
Cutler Rdg 23454
Cutter Ln 23457
Cutter Pt 23454
Cutty Sark Rd 23454
Cypress Ave 23451
Cypress Point Cir & Way 23455
Cypress Vine Ct & Ln 23456
Cypresswood Ct 23454
D Ave 23460
D St
1000-1099 23455
1100-1198 23459
1101-1199 23455
1200-1299 23459
1300-1399 23455
1400-1499 23459
1500-1799 23455
Da Nang Rd 23451
Da Vinci Dr 23454
Dabney Ct 23456
Dadson Ct 23455
Daffodil Cres 23453
Dagan Ct 23456
Dahlia Dr 23453
Dailey Dr 23455
Daimler Dr 23454
Daiquiri Ct 23456
Daiquiri Ln 23456
Daiquiri Rd 23451
Daisy Cres 23453
Dakota Ct 23464
Dale Dr 23452
Dalebrook Ct & Dr 23454
Dallas Ct 23464
Dalrymple St 23464
Dalsbury Ln 23456
Dalwood Mews 23455
Dam Neck Rd
400-1599 23454
2700-3699 23453
4000-4499 23456
Dam Neck Station Rd 23454
Damascus Ct & Trl 23453
Damson Way 23456
Dana Ln 23452
Danali Ln 23456
Danbury Cir 23464
Dancers Ct 23464
Dandelion Cres 23453
Dandy Ct 23462
Daniel Maloney Dr 23464
Daniel Smith Rd 23462
Dannemora Dr 23453
Dante Pl 23453
Danville Ct 23453
Daphne Ct 23464
Darby Ct & Rd 23464
Darden Ct & Dr 23456
Darga Dr 23455
Darien Ct 23464
Dark Star Run 23454
Darnell Dr 23455
Darrow St 23456
Dartford Mews 23452
Dartmoor Ct 23453
Dartmouth Cir & Way 23464
Darwood Ct 23453
Dasa Leo Ct 23456
Daton Rd 23455
Dauntless Run 23453
Dauphin Ln 23452
Davenport Ln 23451
Daventry Pl 23455
Davies Ct 23462
Davis St & Way 23462
Dawes Ct 23455
Dawley Rd 23457
Dawn Ave 23451
Dawson Rd 23451
Daytona Dr 23452
De Ford Rd 23462
De Gaul Ct 23462
De La Fayette Ct 23455
De Laura Cir & Ln 23455
Deacons Ln 23455
Dean Dr 23452
Dearborn Dr 23451
Deary Ln 23451
Debaca Ct 23454
Debussy Ct 23454
Decathlon Cres & Dr 23453
Decatur Dr 23454
Declaration Rd 23462
Dedham Cir 23456
Dedi Ct 23453
Deepwater Way 23456
Deer Lake Ct & Dr 23462
Deer Park Dr 23452
Deere Ct 23457
Deerfield Ln 23455
Deerpond Ln 23464
Deerwood Ct 23452
Deford Rd 23455
Degas Cir 23456
Degree Ct 23462
Dehart Ct 23456
Dekolta Ct 23453
Del Haven Ct 23455
Del Park Ave & Ct 23455
Delaney St 23464
Delaware Ave 23451
Delaware Xing 23453
Delco Rd 23455
Delk Ct 23462
Dellwood Dr 23454
Delmar Dr 23455
Delray Ct & Dr 23455
Demille Ct 23453
Deming Ct 23462
Dendron Dr 23451
Denn Ln 23462
Denny Dr 23464
Densewoods Ln 23464
Denver Dr 23464
Depaul Cir & Way 23464
Derby Run 23454
Derby Wharf Dr 23456
Derbyshire Ct 23464
Derken Ct 23464
Dermott Ave 23455
Desert Point Rd 23455
Destination Ln 23454
Detroiter Ct & Dr 23462
Devastator Run 23453
Devereaux Dr 23462
Devon Way 23456
Devonfield Rd 23456
Devonshire Ct 23462
Devore Ct 23451
Dewberry Ln 23456
Dewey Rd 23454
Dewitt Way 23456
Dey Cove Dr 23454
Diamond Ln 23456
Diamond Grove Ct 23454
Diamond Plum Cir 23452
Diamond Springs Rd 23455
Diana Lee Ct 23452
Dickens Ct & Dr 23452
Dickinson Way 23464
Diggs Ln 23452
Dighton Ct 23464
Dillard Pl 23464
Dillaway Ct 23456
Dillingham Rd 23456
Dillon Dr 23452
Dills Ct 23454
Dingle Dr 23455
Dinwiddie Rd 23455
Diploma Ct 23462

Discovery Cir, Cres & Rd 23451
Distribution Dr 23451
Ditas Ct 23456
Ditchley Rd 23451
Ditmas Ct 23452
Dix Inlet Rd 23452
Dixie Dr 23452
Dober Ct 23453
Dock Lndg 23456
Dockside Ct 23453
Doctor Dr 23452
Dodd Dr 23454
Dodge Dr 23452
Dodington Ct 23462
Doe Ct 23464
Doewood Ct 23455
N & S Dogwood Rd 23451
Dolina Dr 23464
Dolly Madison Ln 23455
Dolphin Rd 23451
Dolton Dr 23462
Dominion Ct 23453
Donalbaine Dr 23464
Donald Way 23451
Donation Dr 23455
Doncaster Ct, Pt & Rd 23452
Donegal Dr 23455
Donelson Rd 23455
Donham Ct 23452
Donna Blvd 23454
Donna Dr 23451
Donnawood Ct & Dr 23452
Donne Ct 23462
Donnington Ct & Dr 23456
Dool Ct 23464
Doon Ct & St 23464
Doppler Ct & Dr 23454
Dora Ct 23462
Dorchester Ln 23464
Dorian Ct 23454
Dorset Ave 23462
Dory Dr 23453
Doubles Ct 23462
Dougherty Ct 23455
Douglas Ct 23464
Dove Dr 23454
Dove St 23461
Dove Ridge Dr 23464
Dove View Dr 23464
Dover Ct 23454
Dovetail Ct 23464
Downeast Ct 23455
Downey Dr 23462
Downing Cres, Ct & Ln 23452
Downs Ln 23455
Downshire Chase 23452
Doyle Way 23452
Dozier Ln 23454
Drake Ct 23452
Drakesmile Rd 23453
Draketail Ln 23451
Drawbridge Cir 23453
Drew Dr 23464
Drexel Cir 23464
Drift Tide Dr 23464
Driftwood Cir, Ct & Rd 23452
Driskill Ct 23464
Driver Ct 23462
Drum Ln 23455
Drum Castle Ct 23455
Drum Point Rd 23457
Drumheller Ct & Dr 23464
Drury Cir 23455
Dry Creek Ct 23456
Dryden Ct & St 23462
Drylie Ct & Ln 23464
Dublin Ct 23453
Dubois Pl 23453
Duck Hunter Ct 23451
Duck Pond Dr 23464
Duck Run Ct 23455
Ducking Point Trl 23455
Dudley Ct 23457
Duffy Dr 23462
Duke Of Norfolk Quay 23454
Duke Of Suffolk Dr 23454
Duke Of Windsor Rd 23454
Duke Of York Quay 23454
Dukes Ln 23454
Dulcie Ave 23455
Dulles Ct 23464
Dulwich Pl 23456
Dumas Ct 23454
Dunbarton Dr 23454
Duncan Ln 23455
Duncannon Ln 23452
Dundee Ln 23464
Dunderdale Ct 23462
Dunhill Dr 23464
Dunkirk Ct 23452
Dunlace Way 23454
Dunloe Dr 23455
Dunmoor Ct 23452
Dunn Ct 23464
Dunn Loring Ct 23464
Dunnbury Ct 23453
Dunnebrook Ct & Dr 23453
Dunneman Dr 23462
Dunstan Cir & Ln 23455
Dunway Ct 23462
Dunwood Ct 23456
Duplin St 23452
Dupont Cir 23455
Dupree Ln 23456
Duquesne Pl 23464
Durango Ct 23464
Durbin Pl 23453
Durham E & W 23454
Dutch St 23452
Dwyer Ct & Rd 23454
Dyer Pl 23464
Dylan Ct & Dr 23464
E Ave 23460
E St
1200-1399 23455
1400-1499 23459
1500-1699 23455
Eagle Ave 23453
Eagle Way 23456
Eagle Nest Pt 23452
Eagle Point Dr 23456
Eagle Ridge Ct 23456
Eagle Rock Ct & Rd 23456
Eagle Run Rd 23464
Eagles Lake Rd 23456
Eagleton Ln 23455
Eaglewood Dr 23454
Ealing Cres 23454
Eamon Ct 23452
Earhart Cir 23464
Earl Of Balfon Cir & Ct 23454
Earl Of Chatham Ln 23454
Earl Of Chesterfield Ct & Ln 23454
Earl Of Essex Ct & Dr 23454
Earl Of Essex Arch 23454
Earl Of Warwick Ct 23454
Earlston Ln 23464
Earlton Ct 23464
Early Ct 23454
Earnhardt St 23464
East Rd 23454
Eastborne Dr 23454
Eastchester Ct & Dr 23454
Eastern Shore Rd 23454
Eastgate Ct 23452
Eastham Rd 23453
Eastover Ct 23464
Eastport Rd 23464
Eastwind Ct & Rd 23464
Eastwood Cir 23454
Eastwood Villa Ln 23454
Eaton Ct 23462
Ebb Tide Rd 23451
Echingham Dr 23464
Echo Cv 23454
Eddystone Dr & Ln 23464
Eden Way 23454
Eden Roc Cir 23451
Edenberry Ct 23452
Edenham Ct 23464
Edenton Ct 23456
Edenwood Cir 23452
Edgartown Ct 23456
Edge Brook Ct 23454
Edgehill Ave & Ct 23454
Edgelake Dr 23464
Edgestone Ct 23453
Edgevale Ct 23451
Edgeware Ct 23464
Edgewater Dr 23464
Edgewood Ct 23452
Edinburgh Ct, Dr & Pl 23452
Edison Rd 23454
Edisto Ct 23462
Edith Ct 23464
Edmenton Dr 23456
Edmonds Rd 23451
Edna Way 23464
Edon Hall Ln 23464
Edwardian Ct 23455
Edwin Dr
300-799 23462
800-999 23464
Eggleston Ct 23455
Egham Ct 23464
Ego Dr 23454
Egret Lndg & Pt 23454
Egton Ct 23464
Egyptian Ln 23456
Einstein Dr 23456
Eksdale Ct 23464
Elam Ave 23462
Elba St 23452
Elbow Rd 23456
Elco Ct 23456
Elder Rd 23451
Elderberry Ln 23456
Elderwood Ct 23462
Eldon Ct 23462
Electric Ct 23451
Elegance Ln 23456
Eleni Ct 23453
Elgin Rd 23464
Elizabeth Ct
800-899 23451
5600-5699 23455
Elk Ct 23464
Elkins Cir 23453
Elkinson Ct 23454
Elkstone Ct 23456
Ellerbeck Ct 23456
Ellesmere Ct 23464
Ellington Ct 23456
Elliott Rd 23464
Ellis Ave 23455
Elloree Ct 23464
Ellsberg Ct 23464
Ellswood Ct 23453
Elm Forest Dr 23464
Elm Grove Ct 23462
Elm Tree Ct 23452
Elmington Cir 23454
Elmont Rd 23452
Elmore St 23456
Elmwood Ct 23454
Elon Ct & Dr 23454
Elson Green Ave
2200-2499 23456
2500-2599 23454
2600-2799 23456
Elson Green Ct 23454
Elston Ln 23455
Elton Ct 23464
Embassy Ct 23454
Embassy Row Dr 23464
Embers Ct & Dr 23456
Emelita Dr 23456
Emerald Cv 23452
Emerald Lake Dr 23455
Emerson Cir 23456
Emmerton Ct 23456
Emmy Pl 23455
Emory Ct & Pl 23464
Empire Passage Ct 23456
Emporia Ave 23464
Enchanted Forest Ln 23453
Enchanting Cir 23456
Encounter Ct 23453
Endicott Ct & Ln 23464
Energy Dr 23456
Enfield Chase 23452
Engagement Ct 23453
Englehard Dr 23462
Englewood Ct & Dr 23462
English Ct 23454
English Cedar Cir 23451
English Oak Ct 23453
Eniwetok Rd 23451
Enon Ct 23454
Enterprise Blvd 23453
Enterprise Ct 23454
Entrada Dr 23456
Eppington Ct & Dr 23454
Eriksen Ct 23451
Erin Ct 23454
Erle Cres 23451
Ershire Ct 23462
Erskine St 23462
Escorial Ct 23456
Esher Ct 23464
Eskers Ct 23456
Esplanade Cir, Ct & Dr 23456
Esquiana Ct 23456
Essex Ct 23454
Essex Pond Quay 23462
Estates Ct & Dr 23454
Estevan Ct 23454
Estrella Ct 23456
Estuary Ct 23451
Etheridge Cir & Ct 23464
Ettington Ln 23456
Etworth Ln 23464
Euclid Rd 23462
Eunice Ct 23454
Eureka Ave 23452
Eustis Ct 23462
Evangelines Way 23451
Evar Pl 23454
Evelear Ave 23455
Everest Cir 23454
Evergreen Ct 23453
Evert Dr 23464
Everton Ln 23456
Evesham Cir & Dr 23464
Ewell Rd 23455
Ewing Ct & Pl 23456
Excalibur Ct 23454
Executive Blvd 23462
Exeter Lndg 23464
Exmoor Ct 23464
Expiry Ky 23454
Expressway Ct 23462
Expressway Dr 23452
Eydon Ct 23464
Eyre Hall Way 23456
F Ave
600-699 23454
800-899 23460
900-1899 23454
F St 23455
Faculty Blvd 23453
Fair Lady Pl & Rd 23454
Fair Meadows Rd 23462
Fair Oaks Dr 23464
Fairbank Ct 23464
Fairborn Cir & Ct 23464
Fairfax Dr 23453
Fairfax County Rd
1100-1198 23459
1101-1199 23455
Fairfield Blvd & Ct 23464
Fairfield Shopping Ctr 23464
Fairford Ln 23464
Fairhill Ct 23464
Fairlawn Ave 23455
Fairlight Ct 23464
Fairmeade Dr 23464
Fairview Ln 23455
Fairway Ave 23462
Fairweather Ct 23456
Fairwood Ln 23455
Faith Ct 23456
Falcon Ave 23462
Falcon Cres 23454
Falkirk Ct 23456
Fall Meadow Ct 23456
Fallbrook Bnd 23455
Falling Ln 23454
Falling Sun Cir & Ln 23454
Fallmouth Ct 23464
Fallon Dr 23464
Falls Church Ct 23464
Fallsmead Downs 23464
Fallsway Ct 23456
Family Ln 23454
Fancy Ct 23454
Fanshaw Ct 23462
Fanwood Ct 23456
Faraday Ln 23452
Faraid Ln 23464
Fareham Ln 23455
Farley Ct 23456
Farmers Ct 23456
Farmhouse Ct 23453
Farmingdale Cir 23453
E & W Farmington Ct & Rd 23454
Farmwood Ct 23456
Farmwood Creek Ct 23456
Farmworth Trl 23456
Farnham Ln 23455
Farnworth Ct 23452
Farragut Cir 23454
Farrar St 23451
Farrcroft Way 23455
Farrington Dr 23455
Faulkner Rd 23454
Faversham Ct 23464
Fawkes Ct 23453
Fawn Lake Ct 23462
Fawnwood Rd 23455
Fayette Ct & Dr 23456
Fayson Ct 23464
Feather Ridge Dr 23456
Featherbed Ct 23456
Featherstone Ct 23462
Federal Ct 23462
Feldspar Ct 23456
Feldspar St 23462
Fellowship Ln 23455
Fence Post Ct 23453
Fenrose Ct 23454
Fenton St 23464
Fentress Ave 23455
Fenwick Way 23453
Ferdinand Cir 23462
Ferebee Dr 23454
Ferguson Ct 23456
Fern Ct 23451
Fern Lake Ct 23462
Fern Mill Ct 23464
Fern Oak Ct 23462
Fern Ridge Rd 23452
Ferncliff Ct 23456
Ferndale Ct 23464
Fernside Ct 23464
Fernwood Ct 23454
Ferrell Pkwy 23464
Ferrier Ct 23464
Ferry Rd 23455
Ferry Farm Ln 23452
W Ferry Plantation Cir & Rd 23455
Ferry Point Rd 23464
Fetsch Pl 23453
Fiddlers Green Ct 23454
Field Flower Rd 23464
Fielding Ln 23451
Fieldstone Cir & Pl 23453
Fieldstone Glen Way 23454
Fighter Dr 23454
Filbert Way 23462
Filly Ct 23453
Filmore Rd 23452
Fincastle Ct 23453
Finch Ave 23453
Finchdale Cir 23464
Finchley Ln 23455
Finespun Last 23455
Finn Rd 23455
Finney Cir 23455
Finsbury Cir & Ln 23454
Fiona Ln 23464
N & S Fir Ave & Ct 23452
Firefall Ct & Dr 23454
Fireside Ct & Ln 23464
First Colonial Ct 23454
First Colonial Rd
100-499 23454
500-599 23451
550-550 23454
600-898 23451
601-899 23451
900-1299 23454
1301-1399 23454
S First Colonial Rd 23454
First Colony Way 23453
First Court Rd 23455
First General Pkwy 23454
First Landing Ln & Rd 23451
First Settlers Ave 23453
Firth Ln 23464
Firview Ct 23462
Fishbrooke Ct 23464
Fisher Arc 23456
Fishermans Bnd 23451
Fitztown Rd 23457
Five Forks Cir, Ct & Rd 23455
Five Gait Trl 23453
Five Hill Trl 23452
Five Point Ct & Rd 23454
Flagler Ct 23464
Flagstaff Ct 23462
Flammarion Ct & Dr 23454
Flanagans Ln 23456
Flanders Ct 23454
Flatrock Ct 23456
Flax Mill Dr 23456
Fleet Dr & Ter 23454
Fleming Cir & Dr 23451
Fletcher Mews 23455
Fletchers Arch 23462
Flicka Ct 23455
Flicker Way 23454
Flint Ct 23452
Flobert Dr 23464
Floral St 23462
Florence St 23452
Flores Ct 23464
Floridays Way 23452
Flower St 23455
Flowerdew Ct 23454
Fluridy Rd 23457
Flurry Ct 23454
Fluvanna Cir 23456
Flyfisher Ct 23456
Folkstone Way 23462
Fontstown Ct 23464
Fordham Dr 23464
Forehand Ln 23454
Foreman Trl 23456
Foreneri St 23455
Forest St 23462
Forest Trl 23452
Forest Brook Cir 23456
Forest Fern Cir 23454
Forest Glen Ct & Rd 23452
Forest Green Dr 23453
Forest Hills Ct 23454
Forest Lake Dr 23464
Forest View Dr 23455
Forestwood Ct 23453
Formosa Dr 23462
Forrester Ct, Ln & Way 23452
Fort Belvoir Ct & Dr 23464
Fort Raleigh Dr 23451
Fort Story 23459
Fort Sumter Ct 23453
Foster Ln 23451
Fountain Ct 23462
Fountain Dr 23454
Fountain Hall Dr 23464
Fountain Lake Dr & Pl 23451
Four Seasons Ct 23451
Foursome Ct & Ln 23455
Fowler Ct 23453
Fox Creek Ct 23462
Fox Grove Ct E & W 23464
Fox Hollow Ln 23452
Fox Run Rd 23452
Foxboro Lndg 23464
Foxglenn Ct 23464
Foxglove Ct 23453
Foxhound Ln 23454
Foxmoore Ct 23462
Foxon Ct & Rd 23464
Foxwood Ct & Dr 23462
Fraford Ct 23455
Francis Land Ct 23452
Francis Lee Dr 23452
Franklin Dr 23454
Fraternity Ct 23462
Frazee Ln 23451
Frazier Ln 23456
Freedom Ct 23455
Freehold Close 23455
Freelon Ct 23456
Freewood Ct 23456
Freight Ln 23462
Fremac Dr 23451
N & S French Ct 23454
Fresh Meadow Ct 23453
Freshwater Cir 23464
Friendship Sq 23451
Frizzell Dr 23455
Frog Pond Ln 23455
Front St 23455
Front Cove Ct 23454
Front Royal Rd 23453
Frost Rd 23455
Frostburg Ln 23455
Fuller Ln 23455
Fulton Ct 23454
Fulwood Ct 23455
Fundy Ct 23464
Funnell St 23455
Furman Ct 23462
Furrow Reach 23455
Fury Way 23456
G Ave 23460
G St 23455
Gable Way 23455
Gadsby Ct 23464
Gadwall Ct & Pl 23462
Gafney Ln 23455
Gaineford Ct 23464
Gaines Lndg 23454
Gaines Mill Dr 23456
Gainsborough Ct & Rd 23462
Galaxy Ct 23456
Gale Ct & Dr 23464
Galeforce Ct 23455
Gallahad Dr & Way 23456
Gallant Fox Rd 23462
Galleon Dr 23451
Gallery Ave & Ct 23454
Galvani Ct & Dr 23454
Gambrill Ct 23462
Gammon Rd 23464
Gampoint Ct 23454
Gamston Ln 23455
Gannet Run 23451
Gara Rd 23464
Garcia Dr 23454
Garden Dr 23454
Garden Grove Ct 23452
Gardenia Rd 23452
Gardenwood Pkwy 23455
Garfield Ave 23452
Garita Ct 23456
Garland Way 23453
Garner Ln 23464
N Garnett Point Rd 23462
Garnett Pointe Ct 23462
Garrett Dr 23462

Street	ZIP
Garrison Pl	23452
Garth Ct	23454
Garwood Ave	23455
Gary Ave	23454
Gas Light Ln	23462
Gaskin Cir & Ct	23464
Gassett Ct	23464
Gaston Ln	23456
Gate Tree Ct	23454
Gatehouse Way	23455
Gates Landing Rd	23464
Gateshead Ct	23456
Gateway Pl	23452
Gatewood Ave	23454
Gator Blvd	
1000-1099	23455
1100-1198	23459
1101-1199	23455
1200-1249	23459
1250-1299	23455
1300-1498	23459
1301-1499	23455
1500-1699	23459
1700-1799	23455
1800-1999	23459
2000-2199	23455
2200-3098	23459
2201-2299	23455
3100-3103	23459
3105-3199	23459
Gator Ct	23455
Gator Rd	23452
Gatwick Dr	23462
Gauguin Dr	23454
Gawain Ct	23464
Gay Dr	23451
Gaymont Ct	23456
Gazebo Arch	23455
Gedney Ct	23456
Geico Lndg	23454
Gela Ct & Dr	23455
Gelding Ct	23453
Gem Ct	23462
Gemstone Ln	23462
Gene Ct	23455
General St	23464
General Beauregard Dr	23454
General Booth Blvd	
400-1299	23451
1301-1399	23451
1400-2199	23454
2200-2399	23456
General Clark Ct	23462
General Forrest Cir	23454
General Gage Ct & Rd	23462
General Hill Dr	23454
General Jackson Dr	23454
General Lee Dr	23454
General Longstreet Dr	23454
General Stuart Dr	23454
Genesee Ct & Way	23456
Genius Pl	23456
Genoa Cir	23462
Gentle Fawn Ct	23456
Gentry Rd	23452
George Mason Dr	23456
Georgetown Pl	23455
Geranium Cres	23453
Gershwin Ct & Dr	23454
Gettysburg Ct & Rd	23464
W Gibbs Rd	23457
Gibraltar Ct	23454
Gibson Ct	23456
Gideon Rd	23454
Gilbert Cir	23454
Gilda Ct	23464
Giles Ct	23453
Gill Ct	23451
Gilling Ct	23464
Gills Pl	23464
Gimbert Dr	23452
Ginger Cres	23453
Ginger Ridge Ct	23462
Gladiola Cres	23453
S Gladstone Dr	23452
S Gladstone Arch	23452
Glamis Ct	23464
Glanmire Dr	23464
Glasgow Ct	23452
Glassy Lake Dr	23453
Glastonbury Cir & Dr	23453
Gleaning Close	23455
Glebe Rd	23456
Glen Rd	23452
Glen Arden Rd	23464
Glen Burnie Ct	23454
Glen Canyon Dr	23462
Glen Eden Quay	23452
Glen Ellert Ct	23456
Glen Falls Ct	23451
Glen Lake Path	23462
Glen Lochen Dr	23464
Glen Ray Ct	23454
Glen View Ct & Dr	23464
Glen Willow Ct & Dr	23462
Glenbrook Ct	23452
Glencoe Ln	23464
Glendale Dr	23454
Gleneagle Dr	23462
Glenfield Ct	23454
Glengarry Ct & Way	23451
Glenmont Ct & Ln	23464
Glenmore Hunt Trl	23456
Glenn Mitchell Dr	23456
Glenn Regis Way	23452
Glenridge Ct	23452
Glenrose Ct	23456
Glenshire Dr	23462
Glenside Dr	23464
Glenville Cir	23464
Glenwood Way	23456
Glenwood Links Ln	23464
Gloria Pl	23454
Gloucester Ln	23454
Glyndon Dr	23464
Gneiss Ave	23462
Godfrey Ln	23454
Godfrey Farm Rd	23454
Golden Maple Ct & Dr	23452
Golden Oak Ct	23452
Goldeneye Ct	23462
Goldenrod Ct	23456
Goldfinch Ln	23454
Goldleaf Ct	23464
Goldner Ct	23451
Goldsboro Ave	23451
Golfwatch Ln	23456
Good Adams Ln	23455
Good Hope Rd	23452
Goodard Dr	23454
Goodspeed Rd	23451
E & W Goodview Dr	23464
Goolagong Dr	23464
Goose Lndg	23451
Goose Creek Ct & Rd	23462
Goose Pond Ln	23455
Gooseberry Dr	23453
Goosehill Ct	23456
Gordon Walk	23451
Goshen Dr	23454
Gosling Ct	23462
Gosnold Ct	23451
Gossman Ct & Dr	23452
Gotham Rd	23452
Governors Way	23452
Gower Pl	23462
Grace Ave	23451
Grace Hill Dr	23455
Graduate Ct	23462
Grafton Ct	23456
Graham Rd	23454
Granada Ct	23456
Grand Cir	23455
Grand Bay Dr	23456
Grand Cypress Sq	23455
Grand Lake Cres	23462
Grand Oak Ln	23455
Grandon Loop Rd	23456
Granite Trl	23452
Grant Ave	23452
Grantham Ct	23464
Grapevine Cir	23456
Grassland Ct	23462
Grassmere Ct	23464
Grassy Hollow Pl	23454
Gravatt Ln	23454
Gravenhurst Cir & Dr	23464
Gray Slate Ct	23456
Graylyn Ct & Rd	23464
Grayson Rd	23462
Graystone Ct	23464
Grazing Ct	23464
Great Hall Ct	23452
Great Lakes Dr	23462
Great Meadows Ct	23452
Great Neck Cir	23454
N Great Neck Rd	23454
S Great Neck Rd	23454
W Great Neck Rd	23451
Great Neck Sq	23454
Great Neck Vlg	23454
Great Pine Rd	23454
Great View Ct	23453
Grebe Cres	23456
Greeley Ct	23456
Green Cedar Ln	23453
Green Garden Cir	23453
Green Hill Rd	23454
Green Holly Cres	23452
Green Kemp Rd	23462
Green Lakes Cir, Ct & Dr	23452
Green Meadows Dr	23462
Green Pine Ln	23452
Green Run Sq	23452
Green Springs Ct	23452
Green Valley Dr	23462
Greencastle Ln	23452
Greendale Rd	23452
Greenhouse Rd	23455
Greenlaw Dr	23464
Greensboro Ave	23451
Greensward Quay	23454
Greentree Dr	23452
Greentree Arch	23451
Greenview Dr	23462
N Greenwell Ct & Rd	23455
Greenwich Rd	23462
Greenwood Ln	23452
Greer Ct	23456
E Gregory Ln	23451
Grenfell Ave	23462
Gresham Ct	23452
Gretna Rd	23455
Grey Dove Ct & Ln	23456
Grey Fox Ln	23456
Grey Friars Chase	23456
Greyedge Dr	23462
Greystone St	23456
Griffin Rd	23462
Griggs Ct	23453
Grimstead Rd	23457
Grindstone Ct	23456
Grinnell Ct	23454
N & S Grosvenor Ct	23462
Grouse Run Ct	23464
Grove Ct	23462
Grove Hill Ct	23456
E Groveland Rd	23452
Grumman Sq	23452
Guadalcanal Rd	
300-2499	23459
2500-2699	23455
Guam St	23455
Guardhouse Cir & Way	23456
Guardian Ln	23452
Guernsey Way	23456
Guest Dr	23454
Guilford Ct	23464
Gulfstream Cir	23464
Gull Ln	23456
Gulls Quay	23455
N & S Gum Ave	23452
Gum Bridge Ct & Rd	23457
Gumwood Ct	23456
Gunn Hall Dr	23454
Gunsmith Ct	23464
Gunston Rd	23451
Gunston Hall Rd	
1000-1199	23455
1200-1300	23459
1302-2498	23459
Gunter St	23455
Gunter Hall Dr	23454
Guther Pl	23453
Guthrie St	23464
Gwinnett Arch	23455
Habitat Ln	23455
Haby Ln	23464
Hackberry Rd	23451
Hackensack Rd	23455
Hackney Brief	23455
Haden Rd	23455
Hadley Ct	23456
Hafford Rd	23464
Hagen Dr	23462
Haig Cir	23453
Haley Ct & Dr	23452
Halfmoon Cres	23454
Halifax Dr	
4800-4818	23456
4820-4898	23456
5200-5299	23464
Hall Haven Dr	23454
Hallowed Halls Rd	23462
Halsey Rd	23454
Halter Dr	23464
Halwell Dr	23464
Halyard Ct	23453
Halycon Ct	23454
Hamer Ct	23464
Hamill Ct	23453
Hamilton Ln	23462
Hamlet Rd	23464
Hammerhead Cir & Ln	23464
Hammerstone Ct	23453
Hampden Ln	23452
Hampshire Ln & Pl	23462
Hampstead Ct	23462
Hampton Way	23462
Hancock Ct	23464
Handcross Way	23456
Handel Ct & Dr	23454
Hannah Ln	23451
Hannibal St	23452
Hanover Ct & Dr	23464
Hanson Way	23454
Happy St	23452
Harbinger Rd	23453
Harbor Ct & Ln	23454
Harbor Oaks Way	23455
Harbor Springs Trl	23462
Harbor View Cv	23464
Harbour Pt	23451
Hardwick Ct	23454
Harewood Ct	23456
Hargrove Blvd	23464
Harlesden Dr	23462
Harlie Ave & Ct	23464
Harmony Sq	23451
Harness Ct	23462
Harnessmaker Ct	23464
Harpers Rd	
1301-1799	23454
1800-2399	23453
Harpers Ferry Dr	23464
Harrier St	23462
Harrington Ct	23464
Harris Rd	23452
Harris Creek Ct	23456
Harris Point Dr	23455
Harrow Cross	23452
Harshaw Ct & Dr	23456
Hartford Ct & Dr	23464
Hartland Ct	23455
Hartley St	23456
Harton Cir, Ct & Rd	23452
Hartsdale Rd	23462
Hartwood Ave	23454
Harvest Ct	23464
Harvest Bend Ct	23464
Harvest Farms Ln	23455
Harvest Moon Cir & Ct	23453
Hassell St	23455
Hassett Ct	23464
W Hastings Ct	23462
E & W Hastings Arch	23462
Hathern Ct	23464
Hatick Ct	23456
Hatteras Ct & Rd	23462
Hattie St	23457
Hatton St	23451
Haven Rd	23452
Haverhill Ct & Dr	23453
Havering Ct	23454
Haversham Ky	23454
Haversham Close	23454
Haviland Dr	23454
Hawaiian Dr	23454
Hawk Ave	23453
Hawkeye Ct	23452
Hawkins Ln	23462
Hawks Bill Ct & Dr	23464
Hawks Nest Way	23451
Hawksworth Ct	23455
Hawser Ct	23453
Hawthorne Ct	23456
Hawthorne Farm Ter	23454
Hay Bale Ln	23456
Hayes Ave	23452
Haygood Cir & Rd	23455
Haygood Estate Ln & Way	23455
Haygood Point Ct & Rd	23455
Hayloft Ln	23456
Haymarket Dr	23462
Haystack Dr	23453
Hayton Way	23455
Haywards Heath	23456
Hazel Ct	23456
S Head River Rd	23457
Headdress Ct	23464
Heald Way	23464
Healey Dr	23464
Healthy Way	23462
Hearth Cir, Ct & Dr	23464
Hearthside Ln	23453
Heathcliff Ct & Dr	23464
Heather Dr	23462
Heather Wood Way	23456
Heatherton Ct	23462
Heatherwood Ct & Dr	23455
Heathglen Cir	23456
Heathmoor Ct	23452
Heathrow Dr	23464
Heathwood Ct	23464
Hebden Cv	23452
Hecate Dr	23454
Hedgefield Ct & Ln	23453
Hedgelawn Way	23454
Hedgerow Dr	23455
Heffington Dr	23456
Helicopter Rd	
1000-1299	23455
1300-1400	23459
1401-1497	23455
1402-1498	23459
1499-1599	23455
Helmsley Ct	23464
Hemingway Rd	23456
Hemlock Ave, Cres & Ct	23464
Hempstead Ct	23451
Hen House Dr	23453
Henderson Pl	23462
Hendrix Dr	23464
Henley Lndg	23464
Henri Pl	23456
Hepplewhite Mews	23455
Herbert Pl	23454
Herbert Moore Rd	23462
Herford Way	23454
Heritage Ave	23464
Heritage Park Dr	23456
Hermes St	23452
Hermit Thrush Ln	23455
Hermitage Pt	23455
Hermitage Rd	
1000-1098	23459
1001-1097	23455
1099-1100	23455
1101-1199	23459
1102-4798	23455
4159-4799	23455
Herndon Rd	23462
Heron Point Cir & Ct	23452
Heron Ridge Dr & Ln	23456
Herons Gate	23452
Herrmann Ct	23453
Hershridge Rd	23452
N & S Hessian Ct & Rd	23462
Hester Dr & Ln	23462
Heston Rd	23451
Hewitt Dr	
1200-1399	23455
1400-1499	23459
1500-1650	23455
1651-1699	23459
1652-1698	23455
Hexall Ct	23454
Hialeah Dr	23464
Hiawatha Dr	23464
Hickman Dr	23452
Hickman Arch	23454
Hickory Ln	23452
Hickory Rdg	23455
Hickory Nut Loop	23453
Hickory Ridge Ct	23455
Hickorywood Ct	23453
Hidden Cv & Way	23454
Hidden Creek Ct	23454
Hidden Pointe Cv	23452
Hidden Shores Ct & Dr	23454
Hidden Valley Dr	23464
High Borough	23452
High Falls Ct	23453
High Gate Cir & Mews	23452
High Plains Dr	23464
High Point Ave	23451
Highcliff Ct	23454
Highfield Ct	23454
Highgate Greens Blvd	23456
Highland Ct & Dr	23456
Highland Cape Ln	23456
Highland Meadows Way	23456
Highnoon Pl	23462
Highway Ln	23454
Hilber St	23452
Hill Rd	23451
Hill Breeze Rd	23452
Hill Gail Rd	23462
Hill Meadow Ct & Dr	23454
Hill Prince Rd	23462
Hillcrest Ln	23464
Hillcrest Farms Blvd & Cir	23456
Hillcrest Meadows Ln	23456
Hillingdon Ct	23462
Hillock Xing	23455
Hillridge Ct	23452
Hillsboro Ct	23456
Hillsboro Quay	23456
Hillshire Way	23454
Hillswick Dr	23464
N Hilltop Plz & Rd	23454
Hilltop East Shopping Ctr	23451
Hilltop North Shopping Ctr	23451
Hilltop West Shopping Ctr	23451
Hillview Blvd & Ct	23464
Hinsdale Ct & St	23462
Hinton Ct	23464
Historyland Dr	23452
Hitching Post Ct	23462
Hiteshew Pl	23454
Hiwassee Cir	23464
Hobart Ave	23451
Hobbs Rd	23464
Hoby Ct	23462
Hockman Ct	23456
Hodges Pl	23464
Hoffman Ave	23464
Hogge Ct	23464
Holborn Ct	23455
Holbrook Rd	23452
Holcomb Pl	23462
Holder Ct	23452
Holgate Cres	23452
Holladay Ct	23455
Holladay Ln	23455
Holladay Pt	23451
Holladay Rd	23455
Holland Ct	23462
Holland Dr	23462
Holland Rd	
2000-3299	23453
3300-3398	23452
3400-4499	23452
W Holland Rd	23459
Holland Lake Shopping Ctr	23452
Holland Office Park	23452
Holland Plaza Shopping Ctr	23452
Hollingsworth Ln	23456
Hollins College Ct	23455
Hollis Rd	23455
W Holly Blvd, Cres, Mews & Rd	23451
Holly Dune Ln	23451
Holly Farms Dr	23462
Holly Hedge Ave	23452
Holly Point Rd	23454
Hollybriar Ct	23464
Hollygreen Cir & Dr	23452
Holm Oak Ct	23453
Holmes Ct	23456
Homer Ct	23454
Homespun Ave	23452
Homestead Dr	23464
Homeward Dr	23464
Honaker Cir	23453
Honey Flower Ct	23456
Honeybrook Ct & Dr	23462
Honeycutt Ct & Way	23464
Honeygrove Ct & Rd	23455
Honeysuckle Ct	23454
Honeytree Ln	23452
Honorary Ct	23454
Hood Cir, Ct & Dr	23454
Hoof Ct	23453
Hook Ln	23455
Hope Ave	23451
Hopedale Ct	23456
Hopemont Dr	23454
Hopi Ct	23464
Hopkins Rd	23452
Hopwood Ln	23455
Horace Ave	23462
Horn Point Rd	23456
Hornbeam Ct & Dr	23452
Hornell Ln	23452
Hornet Ct	23454
Hornet Dr	23460
Horse Pasture Rd	23453
Horse Point Ct	23454
Horseshoe Bnd	23455
N Horseshoe Cir	23451
Horseshoe Ct	23451
Horton Pl	23454
Hospital Dr	23452
Hospital Rd	
800-1052	23459
1053-1069	23451
1054-1070	23459
1071-1079	23451
1080-1088	23459
1081-1089	23451
1090-1092	23459
1094-1098	23459
W Hospital Rd	23459
Hosskine Mews	23455

Houdon Ln 23455
Hound Ct 23453
Housman Ct............ 23462
Houston Cir 23453
Howell Pl & St 23464
Hoylake Dr 23462
Hubbell Ct & Dr 23454
Huckleberry Trl 23456
Hudgins Ct & Dr 23455
Huey Ct............ 23456
Huggins Path 23452
Hughes Ave 23451
Hummingbird Ln 23454
Hungarian Rd 23457
Hungers Parish Ct 23455
Hunley Dr 23462
Hunt Ct 23452
Hunt Club Dr 23462
Hunt Meet Cir 23454
Hunter Ct 23451
Hunters Chase Dr 23452
Hunters Run Trl 23456
Hunters Wood Way 23454
Hunting Hill Ct & Ln 23455
Hunting Horn Way 23456
Huntington Ct & Dr 23462
Hunts Neck Ct & Trl 23456
Hunts Pointe Dr 23464
Huntwick Ln 23451
Hurds Rd 23452
Hurlingham Ct 23454
Hustings Court Ln 23452
Hutton Cir & Ln 23454
Huxley Ct 23462
Huybert Pl 23462
Hyde Ln 23456
Hymans Ln 23451
I St
200-299 23459
1300-1499 23455
Ichabod Ct 23454
Icon Ct 23456
Idylwood Ct 23456
Inca Ct 23456
Independence Blvd
100-661 23462
662-1054 23455
1053-1053 23471
1055-2199 23455
1056-2198 23455
S Independence Blvd
100-188 23462
300-599 23452
1400-1899 23462
1900-2099 23453
2100-5099 23456
Independence Cir 23455
Indian Ave, Cir & Rd ... 23451
Indian Creek Ct & Rd .. 23457
Indian Hill Rd 23455
Indian Lakes Blvd 23464
Indian Orchard Ct 23456
Indian Plantation Dr 23456
Indian River Rd
1500-4899 23456
4900-6699 23464
Indian Run Rd 23454
Indian Summer Ln 23462
Indiana Ave 23454
Indies Ct 23462
Industrial Park Rd 23451
Industry Ln 23454
Infanta Cir 23456
Inglewood Ct & Ln 23456
Ingram Rd 23452
Inland Cv 23454
Inlet Rd 23454
Inlet Shore Ct 23451
N Inlynnview Rd 23454
Innsbruck Cir 23453
Integrity Way 23451
Intercove Rd
1300-1599 23455
1801-1899 23459
International Pkwy 23452
Intervale Ct 23456

Intrepid Ct 23454
E & W Intruder Cir 23454
Inverness Rd 23452
Inverrary Ct 23456
Investors Pl 23452
Iola Ct 23456
Iredell Ct 23455
Iris Ct & Ln 23462
Irish Bank Dr 23454
Iron Bridge Dr 23462
Iron Leige Run 23454
Irongate Ct 23456
Ironstone Ct 23456
Ironwood Dr 23462
Iroquois Rd 23462
Irvington Ct 23453
Isabella Ln 23462
Island Ct 23462
Island Ln 23454
Islander Ct 23455
Ithaca Ct 23451
Ivanroad Ct 23456
Ives Rd 23457
Ivy Dr 23451
Ivywood Rd 23453
Iwo Jima Rd
2300-2399 23455
2400-2498 23459
2401-2499 23455
Jack Frost Rd 23455
Jack Rabbit Rd 23451
Jackson St 23451
Jacob Ct 23464
Jacqueline Ave 23462
Jade Ct & St 23451
Jagged Rock Dr 23456
Jagger Ct 23464
Jake Sears Cir & Rd 23464
Jakeman St 23455
Jamaica Ave 23454
James Ct 23455
James Madison Dr 23456
Jameson Dr 23464
Jamestown Landing
Rd 23464
Jamestowne Dr 23464
Jamesville Dr 23454
Janet Ct & Dr 23464
Janke Rd 23455
Jared Ct 23462
Jarvis Rd 23456
Jasmine Ct 23464
Jasper Ct 23462
Javelin Ct 23456
Jax Pl 23455
Jay Are Ct 23462
Jeanne St 23462
Jefferson Ave 23451
Jefferson Blvd 23455
Jeffreys Ln 23464
Jenan Rd 23454
Jenkins Dr 23464
Jennings St 23464
Jensen Dr 23451
Jeremy Ct 23454
Jeri Ct 23464
Jericho Rd
700-799 23455
4600-4899 23462
Jermyn Ln 23454
Jersey Ave 23462
Jessamine Ct 23456
Jessica Ct & Ln 23456
Jesters Ct 23454
Jet Cir 23454
Jib Cir 23451
Joan Ter 23452
John Alden Rd 23455
John Brown Ln 23464
John Hancock Dr 23452
John Jay Ln 23462
John Parker Ln 23462
John Silver Rd 23455
John Smith Ct 23464
Johnson St 23452
Johnston Ct 23454

Johnstown Ln 23464
Joliet Ct 23456
Jolor Way 23462
Jonas St 23462
Jonathan Ct 23462
Jonathans Cove Ct &
Dr 23464
Jonquil Ct 23456
Joplin Ct & Ln 23464
Joppa Ln 23456
Jordans Parish Pl 23455
Joseph Pl 23454
Josephine Cres 23464
Joshua Ct & Dr 23462
Joslin St 23455
Jousting Arch 23456
Jovett Ln 23462
Juanita Ct 23456
Jude Ct 23464
Judge Ln 23455
Judicial Pkwy 23456
Judith Ct 23464
Judson Ct 23456
Jules Ct 23456
Julie Ct & Dr 23454
Juniper Ln 23456
Juno Rd 23455
Jupiter St 23452
Jurgen Ct 23456
Justice Walk Ln 23453
Justin Ct 23462
Justis St 23464
Kabler Rd 23456
Kaders Rd 23457
Kamichi Ct 23451
Kanawha Ct 23464
Kanturk Ct 23456
Kara Ct 23454
Karen Ln 23454
Kasba Ct 23464
Kashiwa Ct 23456
Kashmir Ave 23462
Kaster Arch 23455
Kathleen Ct 23464
Katie Brown Dr 23462
Kaw Ln 23462
Kearney Pl 23462
Kearsarge Ct 23454
Keaton Ct 23456
Keats Cir 23462
Keelboat Cir 23453
Keeler Ln 23455
Keeling Rd 23455
Keelings Landing Rd 23455
Keelingwood Ct & Ln 23454
Keene Mill Run Ct 23464
Keener Ln 23452
Kela Cres 23451
S Kellam Ct & Rd 23462
Keller Ct 23456
Kelley Ct 23462
Kellie Ann Ln 23452
Kelsey Bay Ln 23453
Kelso Ct 23464
Kelvin Ct 23454
Kemper Dr 23454
Kemps Farm Pl 23464
Kemps Lake Dr 23462
Kempshire Ln 23462
Kempsriver Dr 23464
Kempsville Ct 23464
Kempsville Rd
401-567 23464
569-1226 23464
1225-1225 23467
1227-2299 23464
1228-2298 23464
Kempsville Crossing
Ln 23464
Kempsville Greens Ct &
Pkwy 23462
Kenai Ct 23456
E & W Kendall Cir &
St 23451
Kenelm Ct 23464
Kenley Rd 23462

Kennedy Ave 23451
Kennesaw Ct 23464
Kenneth Rd 23462
Kensal Green Dr 23456
Kensington St 23452
Kenstock Dr 23454
Kent Ln 23454
S Kentucky Ave 23452
Kentucky Derby Dr 23456
Kenwood Ct & Dr 23454
Kenya Ct & Ln 23451
Keokirk Ln 23456
Kepler Bnd 23454
Kern Ct 23456
Kerr Dr 23454
Kerry Ln 23451
Kerswick Ct 23452
Kestons Cross 23452
Kestrel Ln 23456
Ketch Ct 23451
Ketch Pt 23454
Ketchikan Ct 23454
Kew Grn 23452
Key West Ct 23454
Keydet Dr 23462
Keystone Pl 23464
Kiawah Ct 23462
Kidder Dr 23462
Kilburton Priory Ct 23456
Kildeer Ct 23451
Killarney Ct 23455
Killey Ct & St 23453
Killington Cv 23453
Kilt St 23464
Kim Ter 23452
Kimball Cir 23455
Kimbleton Ct 23453
Kinderly Ln 23464
Kindlewood Dr 23455
Kindling Hollow Rd 23456
Kindly Ln 23455
Kindness Ct 23456
King Arthur Dr 23464
King Charles Ct 23454
King Christian Cir &
Rd 23462
King Edward Ct 23454
King George Rd 23462
King Henry Ct 23454
King James Ct 23452
King John Ct 23454
King Richard Ct & Dr ... 23452
King William Rd 23455
Kingbird Ln 23455
Kingdom Ct 23452
Kingfisher Ct 23451
E Kings Rd 23452
Kings Arms Dr 23452
Kings Creek Dr 23464
Kings Cross 23452
Kings Grant Ct & Rd 23452
Kings Grove Dr 23452
Kings Lake Ct & Dr 23452
Kings Landing Cir 23452
Kings Neck Cv & Dr 23452
S Kings Point Cir, Ct &
Rd 23452
Kings Point Arch 23452
Kings Row Ct 23452
Kings Way Dr 23455
Kingsgrove Cir 23452
Kingsland Ln 23456
Kingsman Ln 23453
Kingsman Arch 23453
Kingsmill Walk 23452
W Kingston Cir, Ct, Dr &
Ln 23452
Kingswood Pl 23452
Kiowa Ln 23462
Kipling St 23452
Kirkby Ln 23456
Kirkwood Ln 23452
Kirton Ct 23455
Kistler Ct 23454
Kitimal Ct & Dr 23454
Kittery Dr & Lndg 23464

Kittiwake Ct 23451
Kittridge Dr 23456
Kiwanis Ct & Loop 23456
Klamath Rd 23462
Kleen St 23451
Kline Dr 23452
Kneeland St 23456
Knights Bridge Ln 23455
Knob Hill Dr 23464
Knollwood Ct 23464
Knorr Ct 23455
Knotts Island Rd 23457
Knox Ct 23453
Knox Rd
2100-2199 23455
2200-2298 23459
2201-2299 23455
Kriste Ct 23454
Kumbaya Ct 23456
Kwaja Lein Rd 23451
Kwajalein Rd 23459
La Jolla Ct 23451
La Mirage Ct 23456
La Moure County Rd 23455
La Ray Ct & Dr 23462
La Rue Cir 23455
La Tierra Cir & Ct 23456
Laconia Ct 23464
Lacrosse Ct & Dr 23464
Lady Ginger Ln 23455
Lady Victoria Way 23464
Ladysmith Mews 23455
Lagrange Bnd 23454
Lake Dr
201-297 23451
299-699 23451
4500-4598 23455
4600-4899 23455
E Lake Dr 23454
N Lake Rd 23455
S Lake Rd 23455
W Lake Rd 23455
Lake Bradford Ln 23455
Lake Christopher Dr 23464
Lake Conrad Ct 23454
Lake Destiny Ct 23464
Lake Edward Dr 23462
Lake Front Cir & Pl 23452
Lake Geneve Dr 23464
Lake Havasu Ct & Dr .. 23454
Lake Huron Dr 23464
Lake James Dr 23464
Lake Lawson Rd 23455
Lake Point Cir 23451
Lake Ridge Cir & Pl 23452
Lake Shores Rd 23455
Lake Smith Ct & Dr 23455
Lake Tahoe Trl 23453
Lake Victoria Arch 23464
Lakecrest Rd 23452
Lakeland Ct 23464
Lakeport Ct 23464
Lakesedge Cv 23455
Lakeside Ave 23451
N Lakeside Dr 23454
Lakeside Rd 23455
Lakeview Dr 23455
Lakeville Ct 23456
Lakewood Cir 23451
Lamb Ct 23456
Lambdin Arch 23455
Lambeth Ln 23455
Lambourne Ln 23462
Lambs Creek Ct & Ln .. 23455
Lamerton Ct 23453
Lamorelle Ct & Ln 23452
Lampl Ave & Ct 23452
Lamplight Ln 23452
Lanark Ct 23454
Lancaster Ct 23452
Lancelot Ct & Dr 23464
Lancke Ln 23453
Lanckfield Mews 23455
Land Of Promise Rd 23457
Landfall Dr 23462
Landfall Arch 23462

Landing Rd 23457
N Landing Rd 23456
W Landing Rd 23456
Landings Crst 23464
Landmark Sq 23452
Landola Dr 23462
Lands End Way 23451
Landstown Ct 23453
Landstown Rd
1700-2099 23453
2100-3799 23456
Landstown Centre
Way 23456
Landvale Rd 23453
Landview Cir 23454
Langhorne Ct 23456
Langley Ct 23453
Langston Ct & Rd 23464
Lankford Ct 23453
Lansglen Ct 23462
Lansing Ct 23456
Lansonso Rd 23459
Lantana Ct & Pl 23456
Lapis Ln 23456
Laplaca Ln 23464
Lapstone Ct 23453
Larch Ct 23453
Larchwood Cv & Dr 23456
Larder Post 23455
Largo Dr 23464
Larimar Ave 23462
Larissa Ct 23464
Lark St 23452
Lark Lake Ct 23462
Larkaway Ct 23464
Larkhaven Ln 23452
Larkins Lair Ct 23464
Larkspur Ct 23462
Larkspur Square Shop
Ctr 23462
Larkview Dr 23454
Larkwood Ct & Dr 23464
Larry Ave 23462
Las Brisas Dr 23456
Las Corrales Ct 23456
Las Cruces Ct & Dr 23454
Lasalle Dr 23453
Laser Rd 23460
Laskin Rd
200-1699 23451
1700-2200 23454
2202-2298 23454
Lateener Ct 23455
Latham Ct 23464
Latuque Cir 23456
Lauderdale Ave 23455
Laughing Creek Ct 23456
Laurel Ln 23451
Laurel Cove Cir & Dr .. 23454
Laurel Green Cir 23456
Laurel Oak Ln 23453
Laurel View Dr 23451
Laurelfield Ct 23454
Laurelwood Ln 23452
Laurie Ct 23464
Lavender Ln 23462
Lavergne Ln 23454
Lawrence Ct & Dr 23462
Lawrence Grey Dr 23455
Lawson Rd 23455
Lawson Cove Cir 23455
Lawson Hall Ky & Rd .. 23455
Layden Cove Way 23454
Layton St 23462
Le Cove Ct & Dr 23464
Leamore Square Rd 23462
Lear Ln 23452
Learning Cir 23462
Leatherneck Rd 23455
Leatherwood Ct & Dr ... 23462
Ledge Hill Ct 23456
Ledura Rd 23462
Lee Ave 23455
Lee Ct 23455
Lee Rd 23451

Lee Highlands Blvd &
Ct 23452
Leedom Rd 23464
Leeds Ln 23455
Leesburg Dr 23462
Leeward Shore Ct &
Dr 23451
Leeway Ct 23455
Leffler Ln 23452
Legacy Lndg 23464
Legacy Way 23462
Legare Ct & Ln 23464
Legendary Dr 23456
Lehman Dr 23462
Leicester Ct 23462
Leisure Sq 23451
Leland Cir 23464
Lemans Way 23456
Lemming Ct 23456
Lenoir Ct 23456
Lenox Dr 23455
Leominster Ct 23456
Leroy Rd 23456
Leslie Ter 23452
Lesner Cres 23451
Lethbridge Ct 23454
Lettie St 23457
Level Green Blvd & Ct . 23464
Level Loop Rd 23456
Levy Ct & Loop 23454
Lewis Dr 23454
Lewisham Way 23454
Lexington Ct 23464
Leyte Cir 23451
Leyte Ct 23454
Leyte Rd
600-730 23459
731-799 23451
Leyte St 23451
Liberal Arts Ct 23462
Liberty Ct 23462
Liberty Bell Ct & Rd 23462
Liberty Ridge Rd 23452
Lifetime Cir 23456
Light Horse Loop 23453
Lighthouse Pt 23451
Lila Ln 23464
Lilac Ln 23464
Lillian Ave 23452
Lillipond Ln 23456
Lilyturf Ct 23456
Limerick Ln 23455
Limestone Ave 23462
Linbay Dr 23451
Lincoln Ave 23452
Lincolnshire Pl 23464
Linda Ct 23455
Lindberg Pl 23453
Linden Ct 23462
Lindenwood Ct 23453
Lindsley Dr 23454
Lineberry Ct & Rd 23452
Linehan Ct & St 23454
Linganyan Gulf 23459
Lingayan Gulf Rd 23451
Link Ct 23462
Linkhorn Cir & Dr 23451
Linkhorn Bay 23451
Linlier Dr 23451
Linshaw Ln 23455
Linwood Ct 23464
Lippizan Cir 23464
Lisa Ct 23464
Lisa Sq 23454
Lisbon Ct & Ln 23462
Lishelle Pl 23452
Litchfield Ct 23452
Litchfield Rd 23452
Litchfield Way 23453
Little Acorn Ct 23456
Little Haven Rd 23452
Little Horseshoe Dr 23451
Little Island Rd 23456
Little John Ct & Rd 23455
Little Lake Ct & Dr 23454
W Little Neck Pt & Rd .. 23452

Little Pine Ct 23452
Little River Ln 23464
Little Rock Ct 23456
Live Oak Trl 23456
Liverpool Ct & St 23455
Livery Brief 23455
Livingston Ct & Loop 23456
Livingston Oak Dr 23464
Livorno Ct 23454
Lobaugh Dr 23464
Loblolly Ln 23462
Lochness Ct 23452
Locke Ct & Ln 23464
Lockhaven Cres 23455
Lockheed Ave 23451
Lockridge Ct 23454
Locksley Arch 23456
Lockwood Ct & Ln 23464
Locust Cres 23455
Locust Grove Ln 23456
Lodgepole Dr 23462
Loflin Way 23462
Loganberry Ct 23453
Lois Cir 23452
Lola Cir & Dr 23464
Lolly Cir & Ln 23453
Lombard Ct & Dr 23453
Londale Ct 23456
London St 23454
London Bridge Rd
123-599 23454
601-899 23454
1000-1999 23453
2000-2499 23456
London Bridge Shop Ctr 23454
London Pointe Ct & Dr 23454
Londonderry Ct 23462
Lone Holly Ln 23462
Lone Oak Ct 23454
Lone Pine Pt & Rd 23451
Lonesome Pine Ct 23456
Lonewillow Ln 23455
Long Beach Ct 23464
Long Bridge Ln 23454
Long Creek Dr & Rd 23451
Long Hill Dr 23452
Long Meadow Pl 23464
Long Ship Ct 23455
Longfellow Ave 23462
Longlac Rd 23464
Longleaf Ct & Rd 23454
Longmont Rd 23456
Longstreet Ave 23451
Longwood Rd 23453
Longworth Ct 23456
Looking Glass Ct 23456
Lookout Ct & Rd 23455
Loran Ct 23451
Lord Bowman Rd 23464
Lord Byron Dr 23452
Lord Dunmore Ct & Dr 23464
Lord Felton Ln 23455
Lord George Dr 23464
Lord Harrison Ct 23464
Lord Leighton Ct & Dr 23454
Lord Nelson Dr 23464
Lord North Rd 23462
Lord Seaton Cir 23454
Lord Tennyson Arch 23462
Lords Ct 23452
Lords Lndg 23454
Loretta Ln 23451
Lorierie Dr 23456
Loring Rd 23456
Lorton Ct 23452
Los Colonis Dr 23456
Los Conaes Way 23456
Lotus Dr 23456
Lotus Creek Ct & Dr 23456
Loudoun St 23456
Lough Ln 23455
Louisa Ave 23454
Lourdes Ct 23456
Love Ct 23464

Loveland Ln 23454
Loveliness Ct 23456
Lovell Dr 23454
Lovetts Pond Ln 23454
Lower Church Ct 23455
Lower Greens Pl 23456
Lowery Downs 23464
Lowland Cottage Ln 23454
S Lowther Dr 23462
Loxham Ct & Way 23456
Loyalist Ct 23452
Lubao Ln 23456
Lucia Ct 23455
Luck Ln 23464
Ludington Dr 23464
Ludlow Dr 23456
Ludway Ct 23454
Ludwick Ln 23452
Luke Dr 23464
Lumberjack Dr 23462
Luna Ave 23462
Lusk St 23464
Luxford Cir & Ln 23455
Luxor Ave 23464
Luzerne Cir 23453
Luzon Rd 23451
Lym Dr 23464
Lyme Regis Quay 23452
Lynbrook Lndg 23462
Lynch Cir & Ln 23455
Lyndhurst Pl 23464
Lyndora Rd 23464
Lynn Rd 23451
Lynn Acres Rd 23452
Lynn Cove Ln 23454
Lynn Hill Rd 23451
E, W & S Lynn Shores Cir & Dr 23452
Lynndale Rd 23452
Lynnfield Dr 23452
Lynnhaven Cir 23451
Lynnhaven Dr 23451
Lynnhaven Mall 23452
Lynnhaven Pkwy
100-298 23452
300-1199 23452
1200-1999 23453
2000-2153 23456
2155-2299 23456
2300-2398 23464
2400-5299 23464
5301-5799 23464
N Lynnhaven Rd 23452
S Lynnhaven Rd 23452
Lynnhaven Xing 23452
Lynnhaven Exec Park 23452
Lynnhaven Green Shopping Ctr 23453
Lynnhaven Mall Loop 23452
N Lynnriver Dr 23452
Lynnville Cres 23452
Lynnwood Dr 23452
Lynx Ct & Dr 23456
Lyon Cir 23453
Lyons Head 23452
Maat Ct 23456
Mable Ln 23454
Mac St 23462
Macalpin Ct 23464
Macarthur Rd 23453
Macchonanchy St 23464
Macdonald Ct & Rd 23464
Macduff Cir 23464
Mace Hill St 23451
Macgregory Ct & St 23464
Macguffie Ct & St 23464
Machen Ave 23455
Mackenzie Bay Ln 23453
Macleigh Ct 23464
Macnean Cir 23464
Macon St 23456
Macqueen Dr 23464
Macroger Ct 23464
Madeira Rd 23455
Madison Ave 23455
Madison Mews 23456

Madison Crossing Ln 23453
Madras Ct 23454
Mae Pl 23454
Magellan Dr 23454
Magic Hollow Blvd 23453
Magma Ct 23456
Magnolia St 23462
Magnolia Chase Way 23464
Magnolia Run Cir 23464
Magwood Ct 23462
Maharis Rd 23455
Maid Marian Cir 23454
Maidstone Cir 23452
Main St 23462
Mainsail Ct 23453
Maison Ct 23451
Maitland Dr 23454
Maitland Arch 23454
Maize Ct & Dr 23464
Majestic Cir 23452
Majestic Oak Ct 23456
Majesty Ln 23456
Major Andre Rd 23462
Malaga Ct & Ln 23456
Malbon Rd 23456
Malcom Ct 23464
Malcoms Way 23464
Maldon Cir 23464
Malen Rd 23454
Malibu Dr 23452
Malibu Palms Dr 23452
N Mall Dr 23452
Mallard Ln 23455
Mallory Ct 23464
Malta Ct 23454
Manassas Run 23464
Manatee Dr 23464
Manchester Ln 23452
Mandan Rd 23462
Mango Dr 23452
Manila Rd 23451
Manitowoc Rd 23455
Mannings Ln 23462
Manoomin Pl 23451
Manor Dr 23464
Manor Glenn Ct 23453
Mansards Ct 23455
Mansfield Ln 23457
Mansion Cross Ln 23456
Mantane Arch 23454
Mantle Ln 23452
Maple St 23451
Maple Cluster Ct 23462
Maple Forest Dr 23464
Maple Ridge Ln 23452
Maple Shade Ct & Dr 23453
Maple Terrace Ct 23455
Maplehurst Ct & Rd 23462
Mapleton Rd 23452
Maplewood Ct 23452
Marabou Ln 23451
Maracas Arch 23462
Maralon Dr 23464
Marble Trl 23464
Marble Walke Way 23455
Marblehead Ct & Dr 23453
Marchris Ct 23455
Marcia Ct 23464
Mare Ln 23453
Marengo Dr 23456
Margaret Cir & Dr 23456
Margate Ave 23462
Margin Ct 23456
Marian Ln 23462
Marigold Cir 23464
Marilyn Ln 23452
Marina Bay Cv 23451
Marina Lake Rd 23452
Marina Shores Dr 23451
Mariner Ct 23454
Mariners Mark Way 23451
Mario Ct 23456
Mariposa Ct 23455
Market St 23462
Markham Ct 23453
Marlborough Cir & Dr 23464

Marlene St 23452
Marlin Ln 23456
Marlin Bay Ct & Dr 23455
Marlinton Dr 23462
Marlwood Way 23462
Marmora Rd 23464
Marque Ct 23464
Mars St 23452
Marseilles Ct 23454
Marseilles Rd 23451
Marsh Creek Ct 23451
Marsh Duck Way 23451
Marshall Cir 23454
Marshall Ct 23455
Marshall Ln 23455
Marshview Ct & Dr 23451
Marta Ct 23454
Martine Ct 23454
Martingale Ct 23454
Martinique Ct 23455
Martlet Ln 23456
Marvell Rd 23462
Marvin Rd 23457
Mary Lou Ct 23464
S Maryland Ave & Ct 23451
Marylebone Ct 23454
Marymount Arch 23464
Maryus Ct 23454
Masada Dr 23464
Masefield Cir 23452
Mason St 23455
Mason Neck Ct & Ln 23464
Massanutten Ct 23453
Masters Ave 23462
Masury Ct 23451
Match Point Dr 23462
Mathews Grn 23456
Mathews Green Rd 23456
Mathis Pl 23462
Matoaka Pl 23452
Matt Ln 23454
Mattaponi Rd 23456
Matunuck Ct 23452
Matyiko Dr 23464
Maury Cir 23454
Maverick St 23452
Maxey Dr 23454
Maxey Manor Ct 23454
Maximus Sq 23451
Maxine Ct 23452
Maxwell Ct 23453
Maxwood Ct 23462
May Ct 23453
Maybach Rd 23455
Mayberry Dr 23456
Maycox Ct 23453
Maycraft Rd 23455
Mayfair Ct 23452
Mayfield Dr 23453
Maymont Ct 23454
Mayo Rd 23462
Mayport Ct 23454
Mayview Pl 23452
Maywood Blvd 23455
Maze Hill Mews 23455
Mccauley Ct 23453
Mclannan Ln 23456
Mccluskey Pl 23453
Mccomas Way 23456
Mccullough Ln 23454
Mcgregor Ct & Dr 23462
Mckenzie Dr 23455
Mclean Ct 23464
Mcnelly Ln 23456
Meade Cir & Ln 23455
Meadow Crest Way 23456
Meadow Grove Trl 23455
Meadow Lake Cir & Rd 23454
Meadow Pines Pl 23464
Meadow Ridge Ln 23456
Meadow Sage Ln 23464
Meadowbridge Ct & Ln 23452
Meadowbrook Ct 23453
Meadowburn Cir 23452

Meadowglen Cir & Rd 23453
Meadowood Dr 23452
Meadows Dr 23462
Meadowside Dr 23455
Meadowview Pl 23464
Meals Gate Ct 23464
Mecklen Ln 23464
Meckley Ct 23454
Medcap Ct 23453
Medford Ct 23456
Mediterranean Ave 23451
Medwin Ct 23462
Meer St 23451
Meeting House Ln & Rd 23455
Meighan Dr 23464
Melinda Pl 23452
Melody Ct 23464
Melrose Cir 23452
Melstone Ct & Dr 23456
Melton Ct 23464
Memorial Dr 23455
Mendelssohn Ct 23454
Mendon Ct 23453
Menteith Ct 23464
Mercedes Ct 23455
Merchants Hope Ct 23455
Mercury Ct 23456
Meredith Rd 23455
Meridian Way 23454
Merion Ct 23452
Merl Cir 23455
Merlin Ct 23456
Merner Ln 23455
Meroe Ct 23453
Merrifield Lndg 23464
Merrimac Ln 23455
Merry Oaks Ct 23451
Merton Ct 23464
Miami Ct & Rd 23462
Mica Ave 23462
Michael Ct 23454
Michaelwood Dr 23452
Michaux Ct & Dr 23464
Michelle Ct 23464
Michigan Ave 23454
Middle Ln 23454
Middle Plantation Quay 23452
Middlebrook Ct & Ln 23464
Middleburg Rd 23454
Middleground Run 23454
Middleham Dr 23456
Middlemost Ky 23454
Middlesboro Ct 23464
Middleton Pl 23456
Middlewood Ct & Dr 23456
Midhurst Cir & Ct 23464
Midlands Grn 23452
Midtowne Way 23464
Midway Rd
2400-2499 23455
2500-2598 23459
2501-2599 23455
2601-2699 23459
Mikie Ct 23453
Milan Ct 23456
Milburne Dr 23464
Mile Course Walk 23455
Miles Standish Ct & Rd 23455
Milford Ln 23452
Milissa Ct & St 23464
S Military Hwy 23464
Mill Creek Dr 23456
Mill Crossing Dr 23454
Mill Dam Rd 23454
Mill Landing Rd 23457
Mill Oak Dr 23464
Mill Pond Ct 23464
Mill Stream Ct & Rd 23452
Millay Ct 23454
Millbrook Ct 23453
Milldale Ct 23456
Miller Store Rd 23455
Millers Ln 23451

Millhaven Ct 23454
Millington Ct & Dr 23464
Millpoint Ln 23456
Millwheel Ct 23456
Millwood Rd 23454
Mima Cir 23464
Mimosa Ct 23453
Minden Ct & Rd 23464
Mineola Dr 23464
Miner Dr 23462
Minion Brief 23455
Minnard Ct 23462
Minneapolis Dr 23453
Minnows Ct 23456
Mintwood Ct 23452
Minute Men Rd 23462
Mirassou Ln 23454
Mirror Lake Cir, Ct & Dr 23453
Mission Ave 23462
Mistral Ln 23456
Misty Pl 23452
Misty Dawn Ct 23456
Misty Harbor Ct 23454
Misty Hollow Way 23454
Misty Meadow Ct 23456
Mitcham Ct 23464
Mitchell Cir 23454
Mitchell Ct 23453
Mizzen Ln 23454
Moate Cir 23462
Mobile St 23456
Mockingbird Dr & Pl 23451
Moffat Ct & Ln 23464
Mogulbear Ct 23453
Mohawk Trl 23454
Mojave Ct & Rd 23462
Molly Cooper Rd 23456
Monaco Ct 23454
Monarch Dr 23462
Mondrian Ct & Loop 23453
Monet Ct & Dr 23453
Monitor Ct 23453
Monmouth Ln 23464
Monmouth Castle Rd 23455
Monroe Ave 23451
Monroe Ct 23464
Monsarat Ln 23456
Montague Cir 23464
Montcliff Ct 23452
Montecito Dr 23456
Monterrey Ct 23453
Montford Ct 23452
Montgolfier Arch 23455
Montgomery Pl 23452
Monticello Dr 23464
Montour Ct 23453
Montpelier Ct 23454
Montrose Dr 23464
Monument Dr 23464
Moody Rd 23455
Moon Valley Dr 23453
Moonraker Ln 23454
Moonstone Dr 23456
Moorefield Ct 23454
Mooregate Ct 23462
Moores Ln 23455
Moores Pond Rd 23455
Mooring Pl 23451
Moorland Dr 23452
Moosewood Ct & Dr 23462
Morado Ct 23456
Moraine Ct 23455
Morea Ct 23454
Morgan Trl 23464
Morgan Meadow Ct 23453
Morgan Mill Ct & Way 23454
Morgans Point Dr 23456
Morning Light Ln 23456
Morning Mist Ct 23456
Morning View Dr 23456
Morningside Ct 23462
Morningwood Ct 23453
Morris Neck Rd 23457
Morrison Ave 23452
Mortons Rd 23455

Mosby Rd 23455
Moss Rd 23451
Mossy Hollow Pl 23454
Mossy Oaks Ct 23454
Mossycup Ct & Dr 23462
Moultrie Cir & Ct 23455
Mount Airy Ct 23456
Mount Holly Muse 23462
Mount Jackson Ct 23462
Mount Marcy Cir 23453
Mountain Dr 23453
Mountain Laurel Trl 23454
Mountainleaf Ct 23462
Mowbray Ct 23454
Mozart Cir & Dr 23454
Muddy Creek Rd
3400-3899 23456
3900-4499 23457
N Muddy Creek Rd 23456
Mulberry Loop 23456
Mulberry Grove Ct 23452
Mulch Landing Rd 23453
Mulkerin Ct 23456
Muller Ln 23452
Mullholand Ct & Dr 23454
Mulligan Dr 23462
Munden Rd 23457
Munden Point Rd 23457
Municipal Ctr 23456
Munson Ct 23456
Murdock Ct 23464
Murmur Ct 23454
Murphy Ln 23464
Murray Rd 23455
Mustang Trl 23452
Muth Ct & Ln 23462
Myers Ct & Dr 23464
Myrica Pl 23454
Myrtle Ave 23451
Myrtle Oak Ct 23453
Mystic Ct 23455
Mystic Cove Ct & Dr 23455
Na Trang Rd 23451
Nader St 23464
Nahant Ct 23454
Nanneys Creek Ct & Rd 23457
Nansemond Loop 23456
Napa Ct 23456
Naples Ct 23454
Napton Ct 23452
Narbonne Ct 23456
Narragansett Ct & Dr 23462
Nashe Ct 23462
Nashua Rd 23462
Nathaniel Ct 23454
Natoma Dr 23456
Nature Ln 23455
Naugatuck Dr 23455
Nauticus Cir 23454
Navarre Way 23456
Navigator Ct 23454
Navy Dr 23459
Naxera Cir 23464
Neal Ct 23453
W Neck Rd 23456
Needham Ct 23456
Needle Ct 23456
Nellie Ct 23464
Nelms Ln 23462
Nelson Ct 23464
Nemo Ct 23452
Neptune Ave 23464
Nesbitt Ct & Dr 23453
Nestlebrook Ct & Trl 23456
Netherland Ct 23453
Nettle St 23453
Nettleford Way 23453
Nevan Rd 23451
New Bridge Rd 23456
New Colony Dr 23464
New Guinea Rd
500-599 23459
600-699 23451
700-799 23459
New Hanover St 23456

New Kent St 23456
New Lake Ct 23462
New Land Dr 23453
New London Ct & Pl 23454
New Orleans Way 23453
New York Ave 23454
Newall Ln 23454
Newbern Ln 23451
Newberry Ct 23462
Newburgh Ct 23451
Newcastle Rd 23452
Newcombe Dr 23464
Newgate Ct 23455
Newman St 23453
Newmarket Dr 23464
Newmill Ct 23456
Newport Cir 23453
Newport Ct
1200-1299 23455
1400-1499 23453
Newsome Cir 23455
Newstead Ct & Dr 23454
S Newtown Rd 23462
Newtown Arch 23462
Niagara Way 23456
Nicewood Ct 23456
Nichols Ridge Rd 23462
Nicholson Ct 23453
Nicklaus Ct 23462
Nider Blvd
1000-1298 23455
1001-1199 23459
1201-1299 23455
Nighthawk Pl 23451
Nightingale Way 23454
Niland Ct 23464
Nimitz Dr 23454
Nimmo Pkwy
800-899 23456
1000-1099 23454
1100-2500 23456
2502-2598 23456
Nina Dr 23462
Nine Elms 23452
Nipigon Ct 23454
Noank Ct 23455
Noble Walk Ct 23454
Nolan Ave 23464
Norchester Cres 23456
Nordic Ct 23464
Norfeld Ct 23453
Norfleet Rd 23464
Norfolk Ave 23451
Norham Pl 23462
Norlina Rd 23455
Norman Ln 23452
Normandy Ave & Ct 23464
Norrington Ct 23454
Northampton Blvd 23455
Northern Dancer Run 23454
Northface Ct 23462
Northgate Ct & Dr 23452
Northmoor Ct 23452
Northtree Cir & Pl 23453
Northvale Dr 23464
Northwood Ct & Dr 23452
Norton Ct 23454
Norwalk Dr 23455
Norwell Ln 23455
Norwich Ave 23455
Norwood Ct 23454
Notley Ct & Dr 23456
Notre Dame Ct 23455
Nottingham Dr 23452
Nottinghill Park 23452
Nottoway Ln 23456
Nuthall Dr 23455
Nuttfield Ln 23455
Nutting Ct 23456
Oak St 23451
Oak Creek Ct 23452
Oak Forest Ct 23464
Oak Grove Ct & Ln 23452
Oak Hill Ct 23454
Oak Hill Rd 23455
Oak Hurst Ct 23462
Oak Knoll Ct & Ln 23464
Oak Lake Dr 23462
Oak Leaf Ln 23455
Oak Lynn Path 23452
Oak Pointe Ln 23454
Oak Spring Ct 23452
Oak Terrace Dr 23464
Oakdale Ct 23455
Oakehampton Ct 23464
Oakengate Dr 23462
Oakengate Turn 23462
Oakland Ave 23451
Oaklawn Ct 23454
Oakmears Cres 23462
Oakridge Cir 23451
Oakshire Dr 23454
Oakton Mews 23464
Oakum Creek Dr & Ln 23457
Obsidian St 23462
Ocean Bay Dr 23454
Ocean Cut Ln 23451
Ocean Front Ave 23451
Ocean Garden St 23454
Ocean Hills Ct & Rd 23451
Ocean Lakes Ct & Dr 23454
Ocean Mist Ct 23454
Ocean Pebbles Way 23451
Ocean Shore Ave &
Cres 23451
Ocean Side Ct 23451
Ocean Tides Dr 23455
Ocean Trace Ln 23451
Ocean Trace Arch 23451
Ocean View Ave 23455
Ocean Villas Way 23451
Ocean Woods Ct 23454
Oceana Blvd
100-500 23454
502-1398 23454
601-699 23460
801-1599 23454
N Oceana Blvd 23454
Oconee Ave 23454
Odessa Dr 23455
Odin Pl 23451
Office Square Ln 23462
Oglesby Ct 23464
Ohare Dr 23453
Ohio Ave 23454
Ojibwa Ln 23462
Okinawa Rd
800-1099 23459
1100-1199 23455
Old Bay Ct 23454
Old Canterbury Dr 23455
Old Carolina Rd 23457
Old Clubhouse Rd 23453
Old Colony Cir & Ln 23452
Old Cutler Rd 23454
Old Dam Neck Rd 23454
Old Dominion Ln 23451
Old Donation Pkwy 23454
Old English Cir 23455
Old Farm Ln 23452
Old Forge Cir, Ct &
Rd 23452
Old Gate Muse 23452
Old Glory Rd 23453
Old Great Neck Rd 23454
Old Guard Cres 23462
Old Harris Ln 23455
Old Hickory Rd 23455
Old Homestead Ln 23464
Old House Ln 23452
Old Kempsville Rd 23464
Old Kirkwood Dr 23452
Old Landing Rd 23457
Old Lyne Rd 23453
Old Mill Ct 23452
Old Oak Arch 23453
Old Pewter Cir 23455
Old Pine Ct 23452
Old Point Ferry Ln 23464
Old Post Ct & Rd 23452
Old Princess Anne Rd 23462
Old Providence Rd 23464
Old Pungo Ferry Rd 23457
Old Ridge Rd 23464
Old Shell Rd 23452
Old Tree Ln 23452
Old Virginia Beach Rd
800-898 23451
900-1099 23451
1101-1299 23451
1300-1699 23454
Olde Town Trl 23455
Oldfield Cir 23453
Oldham Rd 23464
Olds Ln 23451
Oldwick Ct 23462
Ole Towne Ct & Ln 23452
Oleander Cir 23464
Olive Rd 23464
Olive Grove Cir & Ln 23455
N & S Oliver Dr 23455
Olivewood Ct 23464
Olivia Ct 23454
Olivieri Ct & Ln 23455
Olivine Ave 23462
Olmstead Ln 23456
Olympia Ln 23452
Olympic Ct & Dr 23453
Omaha Rd 23462
Omaha Beach Rd
500-599 23451
700-799 23459
800-899 23451
Oneida Ct 23453
Onondaga Rd 23462
Onyx Ln 23456
Opal Ave 23462
Open Greens Ct & Dr 23462
Operations Dr 23460
Opus Ct 23456
Oralearl Rd 23457
Orangewood Dr 23453
Orantani Dr 23454
Orchard Ln 23464
Orchard Hill Ln 23456
Orchard Spring Way 23456
Orchid Ct 23454
Ordsall Pl 23455
Orillia Rd 23464
Oriole Cir & Dr 23451
Orkney Dr 23464
Orleans Way 23456
Ormond Ct 23464
Ornamental Way 23455
Osage St 23462
Osprey St 23462
Osprey Landing Ct 23456
Osprey Point Dr 23455
Osprey Point Trl 23451
Osprey Villa Ct 23451
Osterly Ct 23456
E, N, S & W Ottawa
Rd 23462
Outer Dr 23462
Outerbridge Quay 23464
Outlands Way 23456
W Overholt Ct & Dr 23462
Overland Ct & Rd 23452
Overlook Ct 23454
Overman Ave 23455
Owl Ct 23464
Owls Creek Ln 23451
Oxbow Dr 23464
Oxen Ct 23454
Oxford Cir & Dr 23452
Oxford Trace Way 23464
Oxgate Ln 23462
Oyster Ln 23456
Oyster Bluff Ln 23455
Oyster Point Quay 23452
Paca Ln 23462
Pacific Ave 23451
Paddock Ln 23464
Padma Ct 23462
Page Ave, Ct & Cv 23451
Page Harbor Lndg 23451
Paine Ln 23455
Painters Ln 23456
Paisley Ct 23464
Paiute Rd 23462
Palace Pl 23452
Palace Green Blvd 23452
Paladin Dr 23452
Palermo Ct 23456
Pallets Ct & Rd 23454
N & S Palm Ave 23452
Palm Beach Pl 23452
Palmer St 23456
Palmetto Ave 23454
E, N, S & W Palmyra Ct
& Dr 23462
Pamlico Loop 23456
Pandoria Ave & Ct 23455
Paperwhite Ln 23455
Par Dr 23462
Paragon Ct 23455
Paramore Dr 23454
Pardue Ct 23464
Paris St 23454
Parish Rd 23455
Parish Cove Ct 23456
Parish Turn Ct & Pl 23455
Park Lake Ct 23464
Park Landing Ct 23456
Park Place Dr 23451
Parker Ln 23454
Parkland Ct & Ln 23464
Parks Ave 23451
Parkside Ct & Pl 23454
Parkview Ct 23456
Parkway Ct 23452
Parkwood Ct 23452
S Parliament Dr 23462
Parry Rd 23462
Parsonage Ct 23455
Parsons Ln 23455
Parthenon Dr 23462
Partlet Ct 23451
Partridge Dr 23464
Parvathi Ct 23462
Pascal Ct 23462
Pastern Brief 23455
Pasture Ln 23453
S Pastures Ln 23456
Pateshall Ct 23464
Pathfinder Ct & Dr 23454
Patience Pl 23453
Patrick Henry Way 23455
Patriot Ln 23462
Pattie Ln 23464
Pattington Cir 23454
Patton Ln 23452
Paul Jones Cir 23454
Paul Jones Ln 23462
Paul Revere Rd 23455
Pavilion Dr 23451
Pawleys Arch 23462
N Pawnee Rd 23454
Paxford Dr 23462
Peace Sq 23451
Peachcreek Ln 23455
Peachtree Ct 23456
Peachwood Ln 23452
Peak Ct 23462
Pearl St 23455
Peartree Arch 23453
Pebble Pl 23456
Pebblebrook Way 23464
Pebblewood Dr 23464
Pecan Ct 23453
Pecan Grove Rd 23455
Peele Ct 23453
Pefley Ln 23457
Peggy Cir 23464
Pelham Pl 23453
Pelican Ln 23452
Pemberton St 23455
Pembroke Blvd 23455
Pembroke Lake Cir 23455
Pembroke Mdws Shop
Ctr 23455
Pencil Box Way 23462
Pender Ct & Dr 23456
Pendergrass Ct 23454
Pendleton Ave 23455
Penguin Cir & Pl 23451
Penhook Ct 23464
Peninsula Rd 23451
Pennsylvania Ave 23462
Penny Ct 23464
Pennywhistle Arch 23464
Penrith Close 23452
Penrose Arch 23453
Pensacola Pl 23453
Pensacola St 23455
Penshurst Way 23456
Pensive Ct 23462
Pentathlon Arch 23453
Peony Arch 23453
Peoples Way 23451
Pepper Pl 23464
Pepper Mill Pl 23464
Peppercorn Ct 23453
Pepperell Dr 23464
Percheron Ln 23464
Peregrine St 23462
Perez Ct & Way 23456
Performance Ct 23453
Peridot Dr & Pl 23456
Perimeter Pkwy 23454
Peritan Rd 23454
Periwinkle Ct 23456
Perkins Ct 23464
Perrel St 23455
Perrins Chase 23452
Perry Ct 23456
Perry Shores Ct 23451
Pershing Ct 23453
Persimmon Ct 23452
Perth Ln 23455
Petite Ct 23451
Petree Dr 23456
Petrell Ct & Dr 23454
Petunia Cres 23453
Pewter Rd 23452
Peyton Way 23456
Pheasant Run 23452
Pheasant Hill Ct 23464
Philbate Ter 23452
Phillip Ave 23454
Phoenix Dr 23452
Phyllis Ct 23452
Piankatank Ln 23454
Picardy Ct 23454
Picasso Ct & Dr 23456
Pickerel Ln 23456
Pickering St 23462
Pickett Cir 23454
Pickle Barn Ct 23454
Pickwick Rd 23455
Piedmont Cir 23455
Pier Ct 23462
Pier Point Pl 23455
Pierce Ln 23453
Pierside Ct 23453
Pike Cir & Ln 23456
Pilgrims Mews 23455
Pillar Ct 23462
Pillow Ct & Dr 23454
Pimlico Cir 23464
Pin Oak Ct 23464
Pine Rd 23451
Pine Acre Cir 23451
Pine Cone Cir 23453
Pine Forest Ct 23464
N & S Pine Grove Ln &
Rd 23452
Pine Hill Rd 23452
Pine Knob Way 23451
Pine Lake Dr 23462
Pine Neck Ct 23454
Pine Needles Cir 23453
Pine Oak Cir 23452
Pine Ridge Ln 23452
Pine Shore Ct 23455
Pine Song Ln & Pl 23451
Pine Tops Ct 23451
Pine View Ave & Ct 23456
Pinebrook Ct & Dr 23462
Pinecrest Rd 23464
Pinehurst Pt 23464
Pineland Ln 23454
Pinetree Cir & Dr 23452
Pinewood Ct 23464
Pinewood Dr
400-699 23451
2801-2809 23452
2811-3099 23452
Pinewood Rd 23451
Pinewood Sq 23451
Piney Bark Ct & Dr 23456
E Piney Branch Ct, Dr &
Ln 23451
Piney Marsh Ct 23454
Piney Point Rd 23452
Piney Ridge Ct & Rd 23452
Piney Woods Ct & Ln 23456
Pink Star Ct 23454
Pinnacle Dr 23462
Pinon Ct 23456
Pinta Ln 23462
Pintail Cres 23456
Pinter Ct 23452
Pinto Dr 23456
Pinyon Dr 23462
Pipers Cres 23454
N & S Piping Rock Ln &
Rd 23452
Pirata Pl 23462
Pissarro Cir & Dr 23456
Pitch Pine Ct 23452
Pitchfork Way 23456
Pittsburg Lndg 23464
Placid Cir, Ct & Pl 23453
Plainsman Cir, Ct &
Trl 23452
Plane Cir 23454
E, N & W Plantation Ct,
Dr & Rd 23454
Planters Ct 23457
Planting Ct 23453
Plateau Ct 23464
Platen Brief 23455
Play Ct & Dr 23462
Player Ln 23462
N Plaza Trl 23452
S Plaza Trl
100-4120 23452
4122-4198 23452
4200-4299 23462
4301-4541 23462
Plaza Trail Ct 23452
Pleasant Cir 23464
Pleasant Acres Ct &
Dr 23453
Pleasant Hall Ct & Dr 23464
Pleasant Lake Dr 23453
Pleasant Pond Ln 23455
Pleasant Ridge Ct 23457
Pleasant Ridge Rd
1300-1599 23456
1600-2499 23457
Pleasant Valley Rd 23464
Pleasure Ave 23455
Pleasure House Ct &
Rd 23455
Plowshare Brief 23455
Plowshares Ct 23453
Plum Cres 23453
Plumstead Dr 23462
Plymouth Ln 23451
Pocahontas Club Rd 23457
Pocasset Ct 23452
Pocono Pl 23464
Poincare Bnd 23454
Poinciana Dr 23451
Poinsetta Arch 23453
N Point Ct 23455
W Point Ct 23452
N Point Ln 23452
Point Way 23462
Point Hollow Ct 23455
Polaris St 23461
Polk Dr 23456
Pollard Pl 23464
Pollock Dr 23462
Pollypine Dr 23452
Polo Ct 23451
Pompano Ln 23456
Pompey Ct & St 23464
Ponca Cir & Rd 23462
Pond Cypress Dr 23455
Ponderosa Arch 23453
Pondview Cir 23452
Pons Dr 23456
Pontiac Rd 23462
Pony Ct 23453
Pool Side Pl & Rd 23455
Pope St 23464
Pope Valley Ct 23456
Popes Head Arch 23464
Poplar Bnd 23452
Poplar Breeze Ct 23452
Poplar Point Ct & Rd 23454
Poppy Cres 23453
Poquoson Cir 23452
Porpoise Ln 23456
Port Ct 23462
Port Au Prince Rd 23459
Port Hudson Ct 23464
Port Lyautey Ct & Dr 23455
Port Royal Dr 23462
Porter Ct 23451
Porter Rd 23454
Porters Island Rd 23456
Portland Ct
1000-1025 23453
1300-1399 23455
Portnoy Ct 23456
Portofino Ct 23456
Portules Ct 23454
Poseidon Ct 23451
Post Canyon Rd 23451
Post Oak Ct & Dr 23464
Potomac St 23462
Potters Rd
1700-2198 23454
2200-2599 23454
2600-2698 23452
Poughkeepsie Ct 23451
Powder Ridge Ct 23453
Powderhorn Trce 23464
Powells Point Rd 23455
Powhatan Ave 23455
Poyner Ln 23454
Prairie Ct 23464
Pratt Ct 23452
Preakness Way 23464
Precision Dr 23454
Prescott Ave 23452
Preserve Dr 23451
Presidential Blvd, Cir &
Ct 23452
Prestige Ln 23462
Preston Dr 23456
Prestwick St 23464
Price Cir 23455
Price St 23462
Priddy Ln 23455
Prince Albert Ct 23454
Prince Allen Ct 23454
Prince Andrew Ct &
Ln 23452
Prince Arthur Ct 23454
Prince Charles Cir, Ct &
Ln 23452
Prince Edward Ct 23452
Prince Frederick Ct 23454
Prince George Ct 23454
Prince James Ct 23454
Prince John Ct 23452
Prince Michael Ct 23454
Prince Of Wales Ct &
Dr 23452
Prince Phillip Cir, Ct &
Dr 23452
Prince William Ct 23452
Princess Ave 23464
Princess Anne Ct 23457
Princess Anne Ln 23456
Princess Anne Rd
100-1399 23457

1400-4399 23456
4400-5799 23462
Prior Ct 23462
Priscilla Ln 23455
Pritchard Rd 23452
Prodan Ln 23453
Production Rd 23454
Professional Cir 23455
Professor Ct 23462
Progress Ln 23454
Prominence Pl 23452
Prospect Ct & Ln 23462
Prosperity Rd
900-1000 23451
1001-1039 23454
1002-1398 23451
1101-1299 23451
Proteus Ct 23464
Proud Clarion Run 23454
Proust Rd 23454
Providence Rd 23464
Providence Sq Shopping Ctr 23464
Provincetown Ct 23456
Public Landing Rd 23457
Pulaski Loop 23456
Pulley Ct 23452
Pungo Ferry Rd 23457
Pungo Ridge Ct 23457
Purchase Arch 23454
Purebred Dr 23453
Purple Martin Ln 23455
Purpose Dr 23453
Purrington Ct 23454
Putnam Cir, Ct & Rd 23462
Pylon Ct 23462
Quail Covey Way 23451
Quail Hollow Ct & Pl 23454
Quail Point Rd 23454
Quail Pointe Cv 23454
Quail Roost Ct 23451
Quail Run Quay 23452
Quailridge Ct 23464
Quality Ct 23454
Quarry Ct & Ln 23464
Quarter Way 23464
Quarterhorse Ct 23453
Quarterpath Gate 23455
Quartz Ln 23456
Queen Anne Rd 23452
Queen Catherine Ct 23454
Queen City Rd 23464
Queen Elizabeth Dr 23452
Queen Mary Ct 23454
Queen Victoria Ct 23454
Queens Way 23454
Queens Elm Pl 23454
Queensbury Dr 23452
N & S Queensgrove Cir, Cres & Ct 23452
Quesnel Dr 23454
Quick Pl 23454
Quimby Ct & Rd 23452
Quinwood Ln 23455
Rachel St 23462
Radcliff Lndg 23464
Radford Ct 23455
Radisson Ct 23464
Raeford Ct 23456
Raff Ct & Rd 23462
Rainbow Ct & Dr 23456
Rainey Ct & Rd 23452
Rainier Ct 23452
Raintree Rd 23452
Raleigh Ave 23455
Rally Ct & Dr 23454
Ramapo Ct & Rd 23462
Ramblewoods Ct 23453
Rampart Ave 23455
Ramsay Ct 23464
Ramshorn Way 23462
Ranchero Rd 23456
Rand Ct 23464
Randall Ct 23464
E & W Randolph Ct 23464
Ranger Ct & St 23464
Rapahannock Rd 23462
Rapidan Ct 23454
Rapids Ct 23456
Raton Ct 23454
Ravel Dr 23454
Raven Ave 23453
Ravencroft Ct & Ln 23454
Ravenel Ct 23454
Ravenswood Rd 23462
Ray Pl 23454
Ray Way 23457
Rayburn Ln 23453
Raycraft Dr 23462
Raymond Ct 23464
Raynor Ct & Dr 23456
Reading Ct & Rd 23451
Reads Rd 23457
Reagan Ave 23454
Realty Ln 23454
Reardon Cir 23453
Reasor Ct & Dr 23464
Rebel Run Ct 23453
Rechter Ct 23454
Recreation Dr 23456
Red Barn Dr 23453
Red Coat Ct & Rd 23455
Red Duck Ct 23462
Red Horse Dr 23451
Red Horse Ln 23462
Red Lion Rd 23452
Red Maple Ln 23452
S Red Mill Blvd & Ct 23454
Red Oak Rd 23452
Red Robin Rd 23451
Red Rooster Ct 23453
Red Tide Rd 23451
Redbird Ct 23451
Redbud Ct 23452
Redgrove Ct 23453
Redhead Way 23451
Redkirk Ln 23462
Redtree Ct 23451
Redwood Cir 23464
Redwood Farm Ct & Dr 23452
Reedtown Rd 23455
Reef Ct 23451
Reef Ky 23452
Reef Ln 23452
Reflections Dr & Way 23452
Refuge Ct 23454
Regal Ct 23452
Regatta Cir 23454
Regency Dr 23454
Regent Park Walk 23452
Regent University Dr 23464
Regina Ln 23455
Registry Ln 23452
Regret Ln 23453
Regulus Ave
1600-1700 23461
1702-1702 23461
1703-1799 23454
1800-2199 23461
Rein Ln 23456
Reliance Dr 23452
Rellen Ct 23464
Rembrandt Ct 23453
Remington Ct 23453
Remus Ln 23452
Renaissance Way 23456
Renfrew St 23464
Rennie Ct & Dr 23454
Renoir Ct 23454
Renwood Ct 23462
Reon Ct & Dr 23464
Republic Rd 23454
Resort Ct 23462
Reston Ct 23464
Retreat Ct 23454
Reuben St 23454
Revelstroke Ct 23454
Revere Dr 23456
W Revere Point Rd 23455
Rex Ln 23456
Rexmore Ln 23453
Rexton St 23454
Reynard Cres & Dr 23451
Reynolds Dr 23455
Rhodes Ct 23456
Rica Ct & Dr 23453
Rich Ct 23464
Richard Rd 23462
Richard Lee Ct 23452
Richardson Rd 23455
Richland Dr 23464
Richwood Ct 23464
Ricker Rd 23455
Riddick Ln 23456
Riddle Ave 23454
Riddlesworth Dr 23456
Riders Ln 23453
Ridge Ct 23464
Ridge Rd
100-199 23451
1600-1699 23464
Ridge End Rd 23454
Ridgecrest Ct 23456
Ridgedale Ct 23453
Ridgely Manor Blvd 23455
Ridgemont Ct 23456
Ridgeview Ct & Rd 23452
Ridgeway Ct 23453
Ridley Pl 23454
Rifton Ct 23455
Rightmier Pl 23452
Riner Ct 23453
Ringfield Ct & Rd 23454
Rio Bravo Bnd 23456
Rio Grande Ct & Dr 23456
Rio Rancho Dr 23456
Rip Rap Ct 23456
Ripplemead Ct & Dr 23464
Rippling Rock Ct & Dr 23456
Riptide Ct 23451
Risher Ct 23464
Rising Sun Ct 23454
Rising Sun Arch 23454
Rittenberg Cir 23462
Rittman Rd 23464
Ritzcraft Dr 23462
Riva Ridge Run 23454
N River Ct & Rd 23454
River Birch Ct 23451
River Breeze Cv 23452
River Forest Rd 23454
River Lake Loop 23456
River Oak Cir & Dr 23456
River Rock Arch 23456
River Shores Ct 23454
Riveranne Ct 23462
Riverbend Rd 23452
Riverfront Ct 23451
Rivers Edge Cv 23452
Rivers Post Ct 23454
Rivers Reach 23452
Riverside Cir, Ct & Dr 23453
Riverstone Dr 23464
Riverton Pt 23464
Riverwood Ct 23454
Riviera Dr 23464
Riviera Arch 23464
Roadstead Ct 23462
Roan Trl 23456
Roanoke Ave 23455
Roaring Springs Dr 23454
Robbins Ct & Ln 23452
Robens Rd 23452
Robert Jackson Dr 23452
Roberts Pt 23454
Roberval Ct & Dr 23454
Robin Dr 23454
Robins Nest Arch 23456
Robinson Rd 23456
Robinswood Ct 23453
Rochelle Rd 23464
Rochelle Arch 23464
Rock Ln 23456
Rock Creek Ct & Ln 23462
Rock Lake Loop 23456
Rock Spring Ct 23462
Rockbridge Rd 23455
Rockbrook Ln 23464
Rockingchair Ln 23456
Rockingham Ct 23464
Rockland Ct 23454
Rockport Ln 23454
Rockwater Cir & Way 23456
Rockwell Ln 23455
Rockwood Ct 23464
Rocky Mount Rd 23452
Rocky Run Ct 23462
Rodeo Dr 23464
Rodin Ln 23455
Rodney Ln 23464
Rodriquez Dr 23452
Roebling Ln 23452
Roehampton Vale 23452
Roenker Ln 23455
Rolfe Ln 23451
Rolleston Ct & Dr 23464
Rolling Point Ct 23456
Rollingview Ct 23456
Rollingway Ct 23456
Rollingwood Arch 23464
Rollins Ct 23454
Rolo Ln 23464
Roman Dr 23456
Romney Ln 23455
Ronald Ct 23455
Rondeau Ct 23462
Rookery Way 23455
Roosevelt Ave 23452
Rope Ln 23452
Rosaer Cir, Ct, Ln & Pl 23464
Rosalie Ct 23462
Rose Ln 23451
Rose Galaxy Lndg 23456
Rose Garden Way 23456
Rose Hall Dr 23454
Rose Marie Ave 23462
Rose Petal Ct & Dr 23453
Rosebay Ct 23453
Rosebriar Ct 23452
Rosecroft St 23464
Rosedale Cir 23464
Rosegate Ct & Pl 23452
Roselynn Ln 23454
Rosemead Ct 23464
Rosemont Rd 23453
N Rosemont Rd 23452
S Rosemont Rd
100-899 23452
1100-1199 23453
Rosewell Dr 23454
Rosewood Ct 23464
Rossburn Ct & Dr 23455
Rossini Ct & Dr 23454
Rota Cir 23456
Rothesay Rd 23451
Rothwell Ct & Dr 23456
Round Hill Dr
1400-1499 23456
2000-2099 23464
2101-2299 23464
Roundtable Ct 23464
Roundtree Ct 23456
Rouse Dr 23462
Roves Ct & Ln 23464
Rowan Pl 23456
Roxbury Pl 23462
Royal Cove Ct & Way 23454
Royal Haven Crst 23454
Royal Oak Close 23452
Royal Palm Ct & Dr 23452
Royal Palm Arch 23452
Royal Park Ct 23454
Royal Tern Way 23451
Royale Walk Dr 23456
Royster Ct 23454
Ruby Cir 23456
Rudder Rd 23454
Ruddy Cres 23456
Ruddy Oak Ct 23453
Rudee Ave & Ct 23451
Rudee Point Rd 23451
Rudyard Ln 23464
Rueger St 23464
Rugby Rd 23464
Rumford Ln 23452
Runaway Bay Dr 23452
Rundel Ln 23452
Runey Dr 23462
Runners Way 23454
Running Brook Dr 23462
Running Creek Ct 23454
Runnymede Cir & Ct 23452
Rupert Ct 23464
Ruritan Ct 23462
Rushmere Dr 23464
Russell Ct 23464
Russet Leaf Ln 23456
Rust Dr 23455
Rustic Ct 23455
Rustic Arbor Way 23455
Ruth Rd 23464
Rutherford Rd 23455
Rutherglen Muse 23452
Rutland Dr 23454
Rutledge Ct & Rd 23464
Ryan Ct 23456
Rycroft Ct 23455
Rydale Ct 23464
Ryder Cup Ln 23462
Ryegate Ct 23464
Rylands Rd 23455
Sabal Palm Ct 23462
Sabina Way 23456
Sabre St 23452
Sac Ln 23462
Sacandaga Ct 23453
Sacramento Dr 23456
Saddle Ct 23453
Saddle Rock Rd 23452
Saddlebred Dr 23464
Saddlebrook Ct 23462
Sadie Ln 23462
Sadler Ct 23454
Safe Harbour Way 23462
Safi Cir 23455
Sagamore Ct 23464
Sage Rd 23456
Sages Ct 23456
Sagewood Ct & Dr 23455
Saginaw Ct 23464
Saginaw Bay Ct 23453
Sailboat Lndg 23452
Sailfish Ln 23456
Saint Cir 23454
Saint Albans Cmn 23452
Saint Albans St 23455
Saint Andrews Pl 23452
Saint Bernards Sq 23454
Saint Catherines Way 23452
Saint Charles Ave 23456
Saint Clement Rd 23455
Saint Davids Pl 23452
Saint Denis Ct 23455
Saint George Ct 23452
Saint Giles Grn 23452
Saint Gregorys Way 23452
Saint James Cir, Ct & Dr 23455
Saint John Ct 23455
Saint Lukes St 23455
Saint Marie Ct 23464
Saint Mark Ct & Rd 23455
Saint Marshall Dr 23454
Saint Martin Ct & Dr 23455
Saint Matthews Sq 23454
Saint Nicholas Sq 23454
Saint Pauls St 23454
Saint Regis Cir & Ln 23453
Sajo Farm Rd 23455
Sale Dr 23464
Salem Rd & Ter 23456
Salem Lakes Blvd 23456
Salem Springs Way 23456
Salisbury Dr 23453
Salisbury Grn 23452
Salk St 23455
Salmon Ln 23456
Salmons Rd 23457
Salt Aire Ct 23451
Salt Pond Ct 23456
Saltmeadow Bay Dr 23451
Saltmeadow Bay Arch 23451
Salty Marsh Ct 23454
Sam Bates Ct 23462
Sam Snead Ct & Ln 23462
Sammy St 23455
Sampson Ln 23462
Samuelson Ct 23464
San Jose Ct 23456
San Lorenzo Quay 23456
San Marco Cir, Ct & Rd 23456
San Marcos Ct & Ln 23451
San Marino Ct 23456
San Miguel Ct 23456
San Remo Ct 23454
Sancillio Dr 23455
Sanctuary Ct 23454
Sand Bend Rd 23456
Sand Pine Rd 23451
Sandalwood Rd 23451
Sandbridge Rd 23456
Sandburg St 23462
Sandee Cres 23454
Sanderlin Ln 23464
Sanderson Ln 23456
Sandfiddler Rd 23456
Sandollar Ct 23451
Sandoval Dr 23454
Sandpiper Rd 23456
Sandpit Rd 23455
Sandra Ln 23464
Sandstone Ct 23464
Sandusky Ave 23456
Sandy Ct 23451
Sandy Bay Dr 23455
Sandy Lake Ct 23454
Sandy Narrows Ct 23454
Sandy Point Ky & Ln 23452
Sandy Springs Ct & Ln 23452
Sandy Valley Ct & Rd 23452
Sandy Woods Cir & Ln 23456
Sandyfalls Way 23456
Sandyville Ct & Dr 23454
W Sanford Ave 23455
Sangaree Cir 23464
Sanibel Cir 23462
Sansapor Rd 23451
Santa Clara Ct 23456
Santa Fe Ct & Dr 23456
Santa Fe Arch 23456
Santa Marta Ct 23456
Santiago Pt 23456
Santiago Rd 23451
Sarah Cir & Ct 23464
Saranac Ct 23453
Sarasan Ct 23452
Saratoga Cir 23464
Sarsfield Ct & St 23456
Sassafras Ct 23452
Saturn St 23452
Saunders Dr 23464
Savannah Trl 23456
Saville Garden Ct & Way 23453
Savin Ct 23455
Savona Quay 23456
Savoy Ct 23455
Saw Grass Bnd 23451
Saw Mill Ct 23453
Saw Pen Point Cir & Trl 23455
Saxon Pl 23453
Saybrook Cv 23464
Scallop Rd 23451
Scarborough Ct & Way 23453
Scarlet Oak Ct & Dr 23452
Scarlotti Ct 23454
Schilling Pt 23455
Schofield Rd
2200-2298 23459
2201-2299 23455
Scholarship Dr 23462
School Rd 23455
Schoolhouse Rd 23464
N & S Schooner Ln 23454
Schooner Strait Ct 23453
Schroeder Ct 23453
Schubert Ct & Dr 23454
Schumann Dr 23454
Schuyler Rd 23462
Scotch Ct 23453
Scotchtown Dr 23454
Scotland St 23456
Scott Ln 23454
Scott Bend Ln 23454
Scottish Ct 23464
Sea St 23451
S Sea Breeze Cir & Trl 23452
Sea Breeze Point Trl 23452
Sea Chest Rd 23455
Sea Cove Ct 23451
Sea Gull Rd 23452
Sea Gull Bluff Dr 23455
Sea Holly Ct 23454
Sea Horse Way 23452
Sea Oaks Ct 23451
Sea Oats Way 23451
Sea Pines Ct & Rd 23451
Sea Pointe Ct 23451
Sea Scape Rd 23456
Sea Shell Rd 23451
Sea Trace Ct 23451
Seabee Dr
1600-1698 23459
1800-1998 23455
1801-1899 23459
1901-1999 23455
Seaboard Rd 23456
Seabridge Rd 23451
Seabright Ct 23454
Seabury Cir 23456
Seafarer Ct, Cv & Ln 23454
Seaford Cv 23464
Seahawk Cir 23452
Seal Dr 23455
Seancou Dr 23452
Seashore Cv & Pt 23454
Seashore Shoppes 23451
Seaside Ln 23462
Season Ln 23455
Seaton Dr 23464
Seaview Ave 23455
Seawall Ct 23462
Seawatch Cv 23451
Seawinds Ln 23451
Sebastian Dr 23452
Sechrist Ct 23454
Secotan Rd 23451
Secretariat Run 23454
Secure Ct 23455
Seddon Cir 23454
Sedgefield Ave 23462
Sedgemoor Rd 23455
Sedgewick Ct & Dr 23454
Sedley Ct & Rd 23462
Seedling Grove Ct 23456
Seeman Ct & Rd 23452
Segovia Ct 23462
Seine Ct 23455
Selden St 23454
Selma Dr 23455
Selwood Ct & Dr 23464
Semmie Dr 23457
Senators Ct 23464
Senior Ct 23456
Senora Ct 23456
Sentara Way 23452
Sentinec Ct 23453
Sequoia Way 23451
Serapis Ln 23462
Sergin Ct 23452
Sessile Oak Ct 23456
Settlers Lndg 23453
Settlers Park Dr 23464
Seven Kings Rd 23456

Seven Pines Way 23464
Seven Springs Ct 23453
Severance Ct 23453
Severn Ct & Dr 23455
Sevilla Ct 23456
Seward Ln 23451
Shad Ln 23456
Shadblow Ct 23454
Shade Tree St 23456
Shadow Ln 23452
Shadow Point Ct 23456
Shadow Ridge Ct 23456
Shadow Tree Way 23452
Shadowlake Ct 23454
Shadowwood Ct & Dr 23455
Shady Ln 23456
Shady Grove Ln 23462
Shady Hollow Ln 23452
Shady Oaks Cir & Dr 23455
Shady Pines Ln 23456
Shagbark Rd 23454
Shakespeare Ct & Dr 23452
Shallowford Cir 23462
Shaman Cres 23455
Shamrock Ave 23455
Shane Ct 23462
Shannon Ct 23452
Sharbot Cir & Dr 23464
Sharon Dr 23464
Sharp St 23452
Sharpie Ct 23456
Shasta Ct 23452
Shawn Ct & Dr 23453
Shea Cir 23453
Sheafe Ct 23454
Shearwater Cv 23454
Sheepshead Ln 23452
Sheffield Ct & Dr 23455
Shelborne Ct 23456
Shelby Ln 23464
Sheldon Dr 23455
Shelford Ct 23454
Shell Rd 23455
Shelley Ct 23452
Shelter Dr 23462
Sheltered Woods Ln 23451
Shelton Rd 23455
Shenandoah Ct 23452
Shenstone Cir, Ct & Dr 23455
Shenvalee Dr 23464
Shepham Ct 23452
Shepherds Ln 23454
Shepherds Quarter 23452
Shepparton Way 23455
Sheraton Ct & Dr 23452
Sherbrooke Cir 23454
Sherburne Ct 23464
Sheringham E & W 23454
Sherluck Ct & Rd 23462
Sherman Oaks Ave 23456
Sherry Ave & Ct 23464
Sherwood Ln 23455
Shetland Ct 23464
Shiflett Ct 23453
Shinfield Dr 23464
Shingle Wood Way 23456
Shinglemaker Ct 23464
Ship Chandlers Wharf 23453
Ship Shoal Way 23451
Shipley Ct 23456
Shippen Ct 23455
Shipps Ln 23454
Shipps Cabin Rd 23457
Shipps Corner Rd 23453
Ships Lndg 23464
Ships Watch Ct 23451
Shire Reach 23455
Shirley Ln 23457
Shirley Landing Dr 23457
Shooting Star Dr 23456
Shore Dr
2500-3399 23451
3500-5599 23455
5601-5799 23455
7600-7698 23459
Shore Sands Ct 23451
Shore View Ct 23451
Shorebreeze Ct 23464
Shorecrest Ct 23464
Shoreham Ct 23451
Shorehaven Ct & Dr 23454
Shoreline Cir 23452
Shoreside Way 23452
Shoreway Ln 23454
Short Line Rd 23451
Shortleaf Ct 23452
Shoveller Ave 23454
Shrew Trl 23456
Shrewsbury Ct 23456
Shurney Ln 23462
Sibley Ct 23454
Siboney Rd 23451
Sicily Quay 23456
Sidney Cir & Ct 23464
Siena Ct 23456
Sierra Dr 23453
Sierra Arch 23453
Signal Point Rd 23455
Signature Cir & Dr 23456
Silina Cir, Ct & Dr 23452
Silo Ct 23456
Silver Lake Ct & Dr 23464
Silver Maple Cir & Dr 23452
Silver Oaks Ct 23456
Silver Sands Cir 23451
Silver Springs Ct 23456
Silverbrook Ln 23462
Silvercrest Ln 23464
Silveria St 23464
Silverleaf Ct & Dr 23462
Silversmith Ct 23464
Silvertree Ct 23452
Simi Ct 23454
Simon Ct & St 23464
Simpkins Ct & Ln 23454
Simsbury Ln 23455
Singer Ct 23456
Singing Wood Trl 23452
Singleton Way 23462
Sinking Creek Ct & Dr 23464
Sioux Dr 23462
Sir Barton Dr 23462
Sir George Cir 23452
Sir Johns Ln 23455
Sir Leslie Ct 23464
Sir Michael Ln 23464
Sir Richard Ct & Rd 23455
Sir Timothy Dr 23452
Sir Walter Cir 23452
Sir Wilfred Cir & Pl 23452
Sir William Osler Dr 23454
Sirine Ave 23462
Sisters Walk Ct 23454
Ski Lodge Rd 23453
Ski Slope Cres 23453
Skipjack Ct 23464
Skipper Dr 23452
Skipwith Rd 23464
Skyhawk Cir 23454
Skylark Dr 23453
Skymont Ct 23456
Slalom Dr 23453
Sleeper Ct 23456
Slidell Ln 23454
Sligo Ct 23462
Sloane Ct 23456
Sloop Pt 23454
Smallbrooke Ct 23454
Smith Cove Cir & Ct 23455
Smith Farm Cir & Rd 23455
Smiths Ln 23452
Smoke Rise Ln 23452
Smoke Tree Ln 23452
Smokehouse Rd 23456
Smokey Chamber Dr 23462
Smokey Lake Dr 23462
Smyrna Cir 23464
Smythe Ct 23452
Snow Cres 23453
Snow Goose Ln 23451
Snowbird Ct & Ln 23454
Snowdrift Cir 23462
Snowflake Cir 23453
Snowmass Ct 23464
Snug Harbor Dr 23453
Society Ct & Ln 23464
Soho Ct 23455
Solar Ln 23456
Solomons Ave 23451
Solomons Rd 23459
Solway Ct 23454
Somersby Ln 23456
Somerton Pl 23464
Sonic Dr 23453
Sonnet Ln 23456
Sonoma Ct 23456
Sonora Ct 23456
Soria Cir 23456
Sorrel Ct 23464
Sotheby Ct 23464
Sour Gum Ct 23453
South Blvd 23452
Southampton Cir 23454
Southaven Dr 23464
Southcross Ct & Dr 23456
Southern Blvd
1001-1299 23451
1400-1500 23454
1502-1798 23454
2600-2698 23452
2700-4399 23452
4900-5799 23462
Southern Pines Dr 23462
Southern Points Cir & Ct 23454
Southfield Pl 23452
Southgate Ave 23462
Southleaf Ct & Dr 23462
Southmoor Dr 23455
Southport Cir 23452
Southside Rd 23451
Southwick Rd 23451
Souverain Ln 23454
Spain Ln 23464
E Sparrow Rd 23464
Sparrow St 23461
Sparsewoods Ct 23453
Spartan St 23462
Speckled Rock Ln 23456
Spence Cir 23462
Spence Farm Ct 23457
Spence Gate Cir 23456
Spencer Ct 23451
Spiceberry Ct 23456
Spider Ct 23455
S Spigel Ct & Dr 23454
Spindle Xing 23455
Spindrift Rd 23451
Spinel St 23462
Spinnaker Cir & Ct 23451
Spinning Wheel Ct 23456
Spinweb Arch 23464
Spire Ct 23462
Spirit Ct 23462
Split Rail Dr 23453
Spooner Rd 23462
Spot Ln 23456
Spring Ct 23462
Spring Cove Way 23464
Spring Garden Ln 23452
Spring House Trl 23455
Spring Lake Cres 23451
Spring Meadows Ct 23456
Spring Run Ct 23454
Springbreeze Ct 23452
Springhaven Dr 23456
Springs Edge Ct 23456
Springside Ct 23456
Springtree Ct 23455
Springwater Ct 23456
Springwood Ct 23455
Spruce Cir, Ct & St 23452
Spruce Knob Ct & Rd 23456
Spruce Pine Rd 23453
Squadron Ct 23453
Square Dance Ct 23453
Squaw Valley Trl 23464
Stable Rd 23456
Stace Ct 23453
Stacey Pl 23464
Staceywood Ct 23452
Stadium Ct 23454
Stagecoach Trl 23464
Staghorn Dr
4600-4682 23456
4683-4699 23464
Stalls Way 23453
Stalwart Rd
2400-2498 23455
2401-2499 23459
Stamford Dr 23455
Stamp Act Ln 23462
Stancil Ct & St 23452
Stanfield Rd 23455
Stanhope Ct 23464
Stanten Ln 23464
Staple Inn Dr 23456
Stapleford Chase 23452
N Star Ct 23456
Star Grass Rd 23454
Star Lake Dr 23453
Starboard Ct 23454
Starfish Rd 23451
Starlighter Ct & Dr 23452
Starling Ct 23451
Starr Way 23454
Starwood Arch 23456
State Cir 23456
State Ct 23455
State St 23455
Station Ct 23462
Station House Ln 23455
Steamboat Ct 23464
Stedwick Ct 23455
Steeplechase Ct & Dr 23464
Steinbeck Ct 23456
Steinem Ct 23464
Stell Ct & Ln 23455
Stephanie Ct 23462
Stephens Rd 23454
Stephenson Ct 23456
Stepney Ln 23452
Stepping Stone Ln 23452
Sterling Ct & Rd 23464
Sterling Cove Ct 23456
Sterncroft Ct & Dr 23456
Steve Ln 23454
Stewards Way 23453
Stewart Ct & Dr 23464
Still Breeze Ct 23456
Still Harbor Ln 23464
Stillmeadow Ct 23456
Stillwood Ct & Ln 23456
Stirrup Way 23453
Stockbridge Dr 23464
Stockton Dr 23464
Stokes Ct 23455
Stone Rd 23457
Stone Church Ct & Mews 23455
Stone Gap Dr 23456
Stonebridge Ln 23462
Stonecypher Ct 23464
Stonehall Ct 23462
Stonehaven Dr & Ln 23464
Stonemoss Ct 23462
Stoneshore Rd 23452
Stonewall Ct 23452
Stonewood Dr & Xing 23456
Stoney Brook Pl 23464
Stoney Creek Cir 23452
Stonington Ct & Ln 23464
Storm Bird Loop 23453
Storm Lake Dr 23454
Stormy Ct 23456
Stowe Rd 23457
Strand Dr 23462
Stratem Ct 23451
E & W Stratford Rd 23455
Stratford Chase Dr 23464
Stratford Hall Dr 23452
Strathmoor Cir 23452
Strauss Ct & Dr 23454
Strawberry Ln 23454
Strawbridge Rd 23456
Strawflower Ct 23453
N & S Streamline Dr 23454
Streatham Ct 23454
Strickland Blvd 23464
Stringfellow Ct 23464
Stuart Rd 23456
Studio Dr 23452
Stumpy Lake Ct & Ln 23456
Sturbridge Ct 23453
Sturgeon Ln 23456
Styron Ct & Ln 23464
Suber Ct & Dr 23452
Sudbury Ct 23464
Suffield Cir 23456
Suffolk Cir, Ct & Ln 23452
Sugar Creek Dr 23452
Sugar Maple Dr 23453
Sugar Oak Dr 23462
Sugar Pine Ct 23456
Sugarleaf Ct 23462
Suhtai Ct 23451
Sullins Ct 23455
Sullivan Blvd, Cir & Ct 23455
Sully Trce 23456
Summer Cres 23462
Summer Pl 23453
Summer Lake Ct & Ln 23454
Summerhaven Rd 23451
Summerhedge Close 23456
Summerset Ln 23452
Summerside Ct 23456
Summerville Ct 23451
Summerwalk Dr 23456
Summerwind Cir & Rd 23454
Summit Ct 23462
Summit Arch 23462
Sumter Rd 23455
Sun Ave 23464
Sun Valley Dr 23464
Sunbeam Ct 23456
Sundance Ct 23464
Sundevil Dr 23464
Sunfish Ln 23456
Sunflower Ct 23454
N & S Sunland Dr 23464
Sunninghill Ct 23451
Sunny Cir 23455
Sunnybrook Ln 23452
Sunnyfield Ct 23454
Sunnyside Dr & Sq 23464
Sunnywood Cir & Dr 23455
Sunrise Dr 23455
Sunset Ct & Pt 23454
Sunshine Ct 23456
Sunstates Ct 23451
Sunstream Pkwy 23456
Sunview Ct 23454
Sunvista Dr 23455
Surf Scoter Ct 23462
Surfside Ave 23451
Surry Rd 23455
Susan Constant Dr 23451
Susan Lee Ln 23464
Susquehanna Dr 23462
Sussex Ct & Rd 23464
Sutter St 23462
Sutton Pl 23464
Swain Hill Ct 23452
Swaine Ct 23455
Swainsons Ln 23456
Swallow Dr 23453
Swallow Ln 23454
Swallowburg Ct 23456
Swan Lake Dr 23455
Swanton Ct 23464
Swapscott Ct 23454
Swaying Limb Ct & Ln 23456
Sweeney Rd 23452
Sweet Bay Ct & Ln 23464
Sweet Cherry Cir 23452
Sweet Gum Ct 23456
Sweetbriar Ct 23453
Sweetwater Ct 23462
Sweetwood Ct 23462
Sword Ct 23464
Sword Rd 23455
Sword Dancer Dr 23454
Swordfish Ln 23456
Sycamore Rd 23452
Sydenham Ct & Trl 23464
S Sykes Ave 23454
Sylvan Ct & Ln 23453
Table Rock Ct, Ln & Rd 23452
Tabor Ct & Ln 23451
Taft Ave 23452
Tahitian Dr 23454
Tait Close 23456
Tajo Ave 23455
Talbot Ct 23456
Taldan Ave & Ct 23462
Talisman Cir 23464
Tall Oak Ct & Dr 23462
Tall Pines Bnd & Ct 23456
Tallwood Trl 23456
Tallwood Manor Ct 23464
Talon Ct 23453
Talos St 23461
Tamara Ct 23453
Tamarack Ct 23462
Tamer Ave 23464
Tamworth Pl 23455
Tanager Trl 23451
Taneva Ct 23454
Tanglewood Trl 23454
Tanner Ct 23464
Tanning Reeve Way 23453
Tanoak Ct 23462
Tappanzee Ct 23451
Tapscott Ct 23456
Tar Heel Ct 23464
Taranto Ct 23454
Tarawa Ct
2600-2698 23459
2601-2699 23455
Tarawa Rd 23455
Tarington Lndg 23464
Tarkill Run 23452
Tarleton Oaks Dr 23464
Tarlton Ct 23456
Tarpon Ln 23456
Tarragon Ct 23462
Tartan Trl 23456
Tartar Ave 23461
Tartingers Quay 23456
Tattershall Ct 23462
Taureau Ct 23451
Taylor Rd 23464
Taylor Farm Ct & Rd 23453
Taylors Point Rd 23454
Taylors Walke Ln 23462
Tazewell Rd 23455
Teaberry Ct 23456
Teach Ln 23454
Teakwood Dr 23452
Teal Cres 23456
Teal Duck Ct 23462
Tealwood Ct & Dr 23453
Teasdale Dr 23454
Tee Ct 23462
Teets Ln 23455
Telac Ct 23456
Telfair Pl 23462
Tempest Ct & Way 23455
Temple Ct 23455
Templeton Ct & Ln 23454
Tenbee Ln 23451
Tenbury Pl 23455
Tendril Last 23455
Tennyson Ct & Rd 23454
Tenure Ln 23462
Tepee Ct 23464
Tern Rd 23455
Terra Firma Ct 23452
Terrace Ave & Ct 23451
Terrazzo Trl 23452
Terret Ct 23464
Terrier Ave 23461
Terrywood Dr 23456
Teslin Ct 23464
Tether Keep 23454
Tewksbury Ct 23456
Thackeray Ct & Ln 23454
N & S Thalia Dr & Rd 23452
Thalia Forest Ln 23452
Thalia Point Rd 23452
Thalia Station Cir, Ct & Dr 23452
Thalia Trace Ct & Dr 23452
Thalia Village Shoppes 23452
Thames Dr 23452
Thamesford Dr 23464
Thatcher Way 23456
Thaxton Ln 23452
The Midway 23451
Theodorus Ct 23453
Thicket Wynd 23455
Thirza Pl 23454
Thistle Cir 23462
Thomas Ln 23454
Thomas Bishop Ct & Ln 23454
Thomas Jefferson Dr 23452
Thomas Moore Cir 23452
Thomas Nelson Dr 23452
Thompkins Ct & Ln 23464
Thompson Way 23464
Thoresby Way 23464
Thornbury Ln 23462
Thorndike Ct 23455
Thornhill Pl 23462
Thornton Rd 23455
Thoroughbred Dr 23453
Thoroughgood Dr 23455
Thoroughgood Ln 23455
Thoroughgood Rd
2100-2199 23455
2109-2109 23471
Thoroughgood Sq 23455
Thoroughgood Shop Ctr 23455
Thorwood Ct 23456
Thousand Oaks Dr 23454
Three Gait Trl 23453
Three Oaks Dr 23456
Three Pine Ln 23457
Three Ships Lndg 23455
Thresher Ct 23464
Thrush Ct 23451
Thule Dr & Rd 23451
Thunderbird Dr 23454
Thurston Ave 23455
Tibberton Ct 23464
Tibbetstown Ct & Dr 23454
Tice Ct 23462
Ticonderoga Rd 23462
Tidal Bay Ln 23451
Tidemark Ct 23464
Tideswell Ln 23456
Tideway Ct 23455
Tieback Trl 23464
Tierra Monte Arch 23456
Tierra Roja Dr 23455
Tiffany Ct & Ln 23456
Tiger Eye Ct 23456
Tigertail Rd 23454
Tijuana Arch 23456
Tilden Pl 23454
Tiller Cir 23451
Tillman Dr 23452
Tim Rd 23455
Tim Tam Run 23454
Timber Ct 23454
Timber Run 23456
Timber Creek Pl 23464
Timber Mist 23456
Timber Neck Trl 23452
Timber Ridge Ct & Dr 23455
Timber Valley Way 23464
Timberdale Ct 23456
Timberhill Pl 23452
Timberlake Dr 23464
Timberlake Shopping Ctr 23462
Timberland Trl 23452

Street	ZIP
Timberwood Ct & Ln	23454
Timon Ct	23462
Timanog Cv	23451
Titian Ln	23455
Tiverton Dr	23452
Tivoli Cres	23453
Tobin Arch	23452
Todd St	23464
Toddsbury Ln	23454
Toledo Pl	23456
Toler Ln	23456
Tolstoy Ct & Dr	23454
Tolworth Dr	23454
Tomahawk Trl	23454
Tomcat Blvd	23460
N Tomcat Ct	23454
S Tomcat Ct	23454
Tono Ct	23456
Tony Lema Ln	23462
Top Seed Dr	23462
Topaz Cir & Ln	23456
Topgallant Ct	23454
Topiary Pl	23455
Torenia Ct	23464
Torero Ct	23456
Torngat Ct	23454
Toro Ct	23456
Torpedo Way	23453
Torrey Ct & Pl	23454
Tortuga Rd	23455
Tory Rd	23462
Totem Trl	23454
Tottenham Ln	23454
Totteridge Ln	23462
Toulon Ct	23454
Tourmaline Ct	23462
Tournament Dr	23456
Towanda Rd	23464
Tower Dr	23462
Town Center Dr	23462
Townfield Ln	23454
Townsend Dr	23452
Toy Ave	23462
Trace Ct	23452
Tradd Dr	23462
Tradewinds Ct & Rd	23464
Trading Pl	23452
Trading Point Ln	23452
Trafalgar Ct	23462
Trafton Arch	23456
Tranquil Ct	23454
Tranquility Ln	23455
Trant Lake Dr	23454
Trantwood Ave	23454
Trapelo Ct	23456
Trappings Wynd	23455
Trapshooter Ct	23456
Travertine Ave	23462
Travis Pkwy	23454
Trawler Ct	23454
Treasure Island Dr	23455
Treble Ct	23462
Tree Chop Cir	23455
Tree Garden Way	23456
Tree Line Rd	23454
Tree Trunk Ct	23453
Treefern Dr & Pl	23451
Treemont Ct	23454
Treesong Trl	23456
Treetop Dr	23451
Trelawney Rd	23455
Trellis Way	23462
Trellis Arch	23462
Tremerton Ct	23456
Tres Ln	23456
Tressle View Pl	23452
Trestman Ave	23464
Trevino Ct	23456
Trevor Rd	23454
Trewey Ct	23453
Treyson Trl	23456
Tribell Ct	23456
Trieste Ct	23454
Trigger Ct	23456
Trillium Pl	23464
Triner Ct	23462
Trinity Ct	23455
Trio Ln	23452
Troon Chase	23462
Trooper Ct	23451
Tropical Ct & Dr	23464
Trowbridge Ct	23464
Truitt Ct	23454
Truman Ln	23455
Trumbull Ct	23464
Trumpet Vine Ct	23462
Truro Ct	23452
Tuckahoe Ct	23454
Tucson Rd	
700-799	23462
800-899	23464
Tudor Ct	23452
Tufton Ct	23454
Tufts Ct	23456
Tuition Ct & Dr	23462
Tulip Dr	23455
Tuna Ln	23456
Tunlaw Ct	23462
Tupelo Trl	23452
Tupper Ct	23453
Turf Dr	23452
Turnberry Ct & Cv	23454
Turnbridge Close	23452
Turnstone Quay	23454
Turquoise Ct	23456
Turtle Cove Ct & Rd	23452
Turtle Pond Ln	23455
Turtle Rock Dr	23452
Tuscany Dr	23456
Tutbury Ct	23456
Tuttle Creek Ct	23462
Tuza Ct & Ln	23464
Twain Ln	23455
Tweed Ct	23464
Tweedbrook Pl	23452
Tweedsmuir Ct	23456
Twilight Ln	23451
W Twin Cove Rd	23454
Twin Fern Ct	23462
S Twin Lake Rd	23454
Twin Oaks Ln	23454
Twinbrook Ct	23452
Twinflower Ct & Ln	23453
Two Farms Ln	23456
Two Woods Rd	23455
Tyburn Ct	23462
Tyler Ct	23456
Tyson Rd	23462
Ulverston Quay	23452
Unbridled Ln	23456
Underwood Ct	23456
Unicorn Dr	23454
Union Pl	23456
University Dr	23453
University Pl	23462
Upland Rd	23452
Upper Bishops Ct	23455
Upper Chelsea Reach	23454
Upper Greens Pl	23456
Upper Hastings Way	23452
Upper James Ct	23454
Upper Palace Grn	23452
Upperville Ct & Rd	23462
Upton Dr	23454
Urban Ct	23464
Urchin Rd	23451
Vadito Way	23456
Vail Cres	23453
Vail Ct	23464
Valencia Ct	23454
Valentine Ln	23462
Valhalla Arch	23454
Valiant Ave	23452
Valiente Ct	23456
Valle Rio Way	23456
Valley Forge Ln	23462
Valley Stream Ct	23464
E & W Valleyside Ct	23464
Van Buren Ct & Dr	23452
Van Dyck Dr	23456
Van Gogh Ct	23456
Van Loen Dr	23453
Van Ness Dr	23462
Vance Way	23456
Vanderbilt Ave	23451
Vanderhorst Dr	23462
Vanderpool Ct	23453
Vantage Pt	23455
Vaso Ct	23456
Vasser Dr	23462
Vaughan Rd	23457
Vaughan Town Ct	23457
Veau Ct	23451
Vedalia Ct	23454
Velvet Ct	23456
Venice Ct	23456
Venture Ct	23455
Venus St	23452
Vera Cruz Ct	23454
Vera Cruz Rd	
101-397	23451
399-456	23451
457-459	23459
458-498	23451
461-499	23451
Verano Cir & Ct	23456
Verde St	23462
Vermeer Dr	23453
Vermilya Ct	23454
Verona Quay	23456
Veronica Dr	23464
Vest Ct	23464
Vestry Ct & Dr	23464
Victor Rd	23454
Victoria Dr	23452
Victorian Cres	23454
Victory Rd	23455
Vienna Ct	23464
Viking Ave	23461
Viking Dr	
400-500	23452
501-501	23450
501-599	23452
502-598	23452
Village Dr & Rd	23454
Village Square Ct	23455
Villas Ct	23456
N & S Villier Ct	23452
Vince Rd	23464
Vincent Ct	23453
Vindale Dr	23462
Vine Ct	23452
Vineyard Ln	23455
Vinland Cir	23456
Vintage Ct	23454
Vintage Pointe Pl	23455
Vintage Quay	23454
Violet Ln	23464
Violet Bank Dr	23464
Virgil St	23455
Virginia Ave	23451
W Virginia Ave	23452
Virginia Ct	23451
Virginia Beach Blvd	
200-1199	23451
1300-2499	23454
2500-4351	23452
4352-5699	23462
Virginia Dare Dr	23451
Virginia Tech Ct & Trl	23455
Virginius Ct & Dr	23452
Vista Cir & Pt	23451
Vogel Ct	23456
Volsung Ct	23462
Volunteer Trl	23456
Voss Ct	23454
Voyager Ct	23462
Vung Tau Rd	23451
Waff Rd	23464
Wagons Way	23462
Wahoo Ct	23464
Wake Forest St	23451
Wakefield Cir, Ct & Dr	23455
Wakehurst Ct	23453
Walden Ct	23453
Wales Dr	23452
Walke St	23451
Walker Rd	23464
Walkers Grant Ln	23455
Waller Ct	23464
Wallingford Arch	23464
Wallington Way	23456
Walnut Ln	23452
Walnut Hill Rd	23452
Walpole St	23456
Walsh Ct	23454
Walt Whitman Way	23455
Waltham Cir	23452
Waltmar Dr	23464
Walton Ct & Dr	23464
Wanda Cir	23464
Wandsworth Dr	23454
War Admiral Rd	23462
Ward Ave & Ct	23455
Ware Neck Dr	23456
Ware Parish Ct	23455
Wareham Ct	23452
Waring Ct	23464
Warm Springs Ct	23454
Warminster Dr	23455
Warner St	23464
Warner Hall Dr	23454
Warning St	23464
Warren Pl	23452
Warwick Dr	23453
Washington Ave	23451
Wasserman Ct & Dr	23454
Water Mill Cir	23454
Water Oak Ln, Pl & Rd	23452
Waterbury Pl	23453
Watercrest Ct & Pl	23464
Waterford Pl	23464
Waterfront Cv & Dr	23451
Watergate Ln	23452
Waterman Rd	23452
Waterpump Cir	23456
Waters Dr	23462
Watersedge Ct & Dr	23452
Waterside Ct	23452
Waterspoint Pl	23455
Watertown Ct	23451
Waterview Pl	23452
Waterway Pl	23452
Waverly Dr	23452
Waxham Ct	23462
Waxhaws Ln	23455
Wayman Ln	23454
Waymart Ct	23464
Wayne St	23452
Weak Branch Ct	23453
Weather Vane Ct	23464
Weatherstone Dr	23456
Weaver Dr	23462
Webb Ct	23464
Weblin Dr	23462
Weblin Farm Rd	23455
Webster Pl	23454
Wedge Dr	23462
Weeping Willow Ln	23453
Weich Ln	23455
Welbeck Ln	23456
Welch Cir	23452
Welcome Sq	23454
Weldon St	23455
Well Water Ln	23456
Weller Blvd	23462
Wellesley Ct	23456
Wellfleet Ct	23464
Wellingborough Reach	23455
Wellings Ct	23455
Wellingsworth Ct	23464
Wellington Ct	23454
Wellsford Ct & Dr	23454
Wellston Ct	23462
Welsh Dr	23456
Welwyn Muse	23452
Wembly Ln	23456
Wendfield Dr	23453
Wenlock Ct	23456
Wentworth Dr	23453
Wesley Dr	23452
Wesleyan Dr	23455
Wesmere Dr	23462
Wessex Ln	23464
Wessington Dr	23454
West Ct & Ln	23454
Westbriar Dr	23455
Westbrook Ct	23455
Westbury Rd	23455
Westchester Cir	23452
Westerfield Rd	23455
Westerly Dr & Trl	23464
Westerwald Pl	23462
S Westgrove Cir, Ct & Rd	23455
Westham Woods Ct & Pl	23454
Westhaven Cres	23464
Westminster Ln	23454
Westmoreland Ct	23453
Westover Ln	23464
Westport Pl	23464
Westsail Ln	23455
Westview Ct	23454
Westward Dr	23464
Westwell Ln	23455
Westwind Pl	23452
Westwood Cir	23454
Wetherington Dr	23453
Wexford Ct & Dr	23462
Wexler Ct	23462
Weybridge Cir & Dr	23454
Weyburn Ct	23464
Weymouth Ct	23462
Whaler Ct	23451
Whales Run Ct	23454
Wharf Ct	23462
Wharton Brief	23455
Wheathusk Ct	23453
Wheatsheaf Ct	23464
Wheatstone Ct	23456
Wheatstraw Ct	23453
Wheelgate Ln	23455
Whindark Ave	23460
Whipaway Ln	23464
Whipple Ct	23464
Whippoorwill Pt	23452
Whirlaway Rd	23462
Whisper Cir, Ct & Dr	23454
Whispering Oaks Pl	23455
Whispering Pines Ct	23454
Whispering Sands Ln	23455
Whispering Waters Way	23454
Whispering Willow Ct	23462
Whispering Woods Ct	23456
Whistler Ln	23455
Whistling Swan Dr	23464
Whitaker Pl	23462
Whitbeck Ct	23464
White Acres Ct & Rd	23455
White Beam Ct	23462
White Birch Ln	23453
White Blaze Ct	23464
White Cap Ln	23456
White Dove Ln	23455
White Hall Ln	23462
White Heron Rd	23451
White Hill Rd	23451
White House Ln	23455
White Marlin Ln	23464
White Marsh Ct	23464
White Oak Dr	23462
White Pine Ct	23453
White Water Dr	23456
Whitechapel Cir, Ct & Dr	23455
Whiteface Cir & Ct	23453
Whitehaven Ln & Rd	23451
Whitehurst Arch	23464
Whitehurst Landing Ct & Rd	23464
Whiteside Ln	23454
Whitestone Way	23454
Whitetail Ct	23464
Whitethorne Rd	23455
Whitewash Ct	23456
Whitewater Ct	23456
Whitewood Ln	23464
Whiting Ln	23456
Whitley Abbey Ct & Dr	23456
Whitley Park Ct & Dr	23456
Whitlow St	23464
Whitman Ct & Ln	23455
Whitney Ct	23453
Whittier Rd	23454
Whittington Ct	23464
Whitton Way	23453
Whooping Crane Cir	23455
Wickford Lndg	23464
Wickham Ct	23464
Wicklow Pl	23452
Wicomico Ct & Ln	23464
Widener Ct	23464
Widgeon Ln	23456
Wier Cir	23464
Wigton Ct	23452
Wiigwaas Ln	23451
Wilbraham Dr	23456
Wilcher Way	23462
Wilchester Glen Dr	23456
Wilcox Ct & Dr	23456
Wild Cherry Ct	23453
Wild Duck Ky	23452
Wild Oak Cres	23456
Wildcat Ln	23456
Wildcat Way	23453
Wilde Ct	23462
Wilder Rd	23451
Wilderness Ln	23456
Wildflower Ct	23452
Wildwood Dr	23454
Wildwood Square Ct	23454
Wiley Pl	23452
Wilhelm Dr	23456
Wilkes Dr	23456
Will O Wisp Dr	23454
Will Scarlet Pl	23454
Willberry Dr	23462
William And Mary Ct	23455
William Penn Blvd	23452
William Pitt Ln	23462
Williams Ct	23462
Williams Farm Rd	23457
Williams Ridge Ct	23457
Williamsburg Ct & Rd	23462
Willimantic Ct & Dr	23456
Williston Ct & Dr	23453
Willow Dr	23451
Willow Creek Ct	23464
Willow Croft Dr	23462
Willow Lake Cir	23452
Willow Oak Cir	23451
Willow Pointe Ct & Ln	23464
Willowbrooke Ct	23464
Willowdale Ct	23464
Willowlawn Way	23456
Willowood Ln	23454
Willray Ct	23451
Willway Cir	23455
Willwood Ct	23464
Wilmington Ct & Rd	23453
Wilshire Dr	23456
Wilson Creek Rd	23464
Wilsonia Way	23453
Wilton Ln	23451
Wimbledon Way	23453
Wimbledon Point Dr	23454
Winchester Ln	23452
Wind Branch Cir	23456
Windbrooke Ct & Ln	23462
Windermere Ct	23455
Windfall Ct	23462
Winding Way	23462
Winding Bank Rd	23455
Winding Lake Ct	23456
Winding Trail Cir	23456
Winding Wood Ct	23456
Windjammer Ct	23454
Windlass Cir	23453
Windmill Dr	23453
Windmill Point Cres	23453
Windom Pl	23454
Windridge Rd	23452
Windship Cv & Pt	23454
Windshore Dr	23455
Windsong Ct & Dr	23455
Windsor Ln	23464
Windsor Rd	23451
Windsor Castle Ct	23452
Windsor Gate Cir, Pl & Rd	23452
Windsor Lake Pl	23452
Windsor Oaks Blvd	
600-698	23452
900-999	23462
Windsor Oaks Arch	23452
Windsor Woods Blvd & Ct	23452
Windward Ln	23455
Windward Shore Cir & Dr	23451
Windway Ln	23455
Windy Rd	23455
Windy Leaf Ct	23456
Windy Pines Bnd & Ct	23456
Windy Ridge Pt	23454
Windy Willow Ct	23453
Wingate Ct & Way	23464
Winners Cir	23456
Winston Ave	23456
Winston Salem Ave	23451
Winter Rd	23455
Winter Forest Ct	23453
Winter Park Ct	23453
Winter Wheat Ct	23453
Winterberry Ct & Ln	23453
Winterhaven Dr & Ln	23456
Winterville Ct	23451
Winthrope Cir & Dr	23452
Winwick Way	23456
Winwood Dr	23451
Wisdom Arch	23456
Wise Pl	23456
Wishart Rd	23455
Wishart Lake Dr	23455
Wishart Point Rd	23455
Wisteria Ln	23456
Witch Point Trl	23455
Witchduck Ct	23462
N Witchduck Rd	
100-699	23462
4000-4849	23455
4851-4899	23455
S Witchduck Rd	23462
Witchduck Bay Ct	23455
Witchgate Ct	23455
Witham St	23464
Wittie Cir	23464
Wivenhoe Ct & Way	23454
Woburn Ln	23462
Wolf St	23454
Wolf Creek Ct	23464
Wolfpack Ct	23462
Wolfs Neck Trl	23452
Wolfsnare Cres	23454
S Wolfsnare Ct	23454
N Wolfsnare Dr	23454
S Wolfsnare Dr	23454
Wolfsnare Rd	
1500-1699	23451
1700-2299	23454
Wolftrap Ln	23462
Wonderland Ct	23456
Wood Beach Lndg	23455
Wood Duck Dr	23456
Wood Gate Ln	23452
Wood Hollow Cv	23454
Wood Ibis Way	23455
Woodberry Ct	23453
Woodbine Ln	23452
Woodbox Dr	23462
Woodbridge Pl & Trl	23453
Woodburne Ct & Dr	23452
Woodcliff Cir	23454
Woodcock Ln	23454
Woodcrest Ln	23452
Woodenshoe Ct	23453
Woodfence Ct	23456
Woodfern Pl	23451
Woodglen Ct	23462

Woodgreen Rd 23455
Woodgrove Ct & Ln ... 23464
Woodhaven Ct 23464
Woodhill Rd 23464
N & S Woodhouse Rd .. 23454
Woodhue Ct 23452
Woodhurst Dr 23454
Woodlake Ct & Rd 23452
Woodland Ct 23456
Woodlawn Ave 23455
Woodmark Ct 23452
Woodport Cir 23452
Woodridge Ct 23464
Woodruff Cir 23464
Woods Edge Ct & Rd .. 23462
Woods Hole Ct 23456
Woodscape Ln 23462
Woodshire Way 23454
S Woodside Ln 23454
Woodsman Ln 23452
Woodstock Ct, Pt & Rd 23464
Woodtide Shopping Ctr 23462
Woodway Ln 23462
Woodwind Way 23455
Woody Ct 23464
Woolard Cres 23462
E Worcester Dr 23455
Wordsworth Ln 23462
Worship Ct 23464
Worthington Ct & Ln ... 23464
Wren Pl 23451
Wright Ln 23451
Wyandotte Rd 23462
Wyckoff Dr 23452
Wyden Dr 23462
Wye Ln 23451
Wyncliff Ct 23456
Wynd Crest Way 23456
Wyndham Ct 23464
Wynne Ct 23462
Wysong Ct 23454
Wythe Ln 23451
Yadkin Dr 23456
Yancey Cir 23454
Yaqui St 23462
Yarbrough Way 23455
Yardley Lndg 23464
Yarmouth Ct 23455
Yawl Pt 23454
Yearling Ct 23464
Yeates Ln 23452
Yellow Knife Ct & Trl ... 23464
Yellowfin Ct 23452
Yoder Ln 23462
York Ln 23451
Yorkborough Way 23453
Yorkshire Dr 23452
Yorktown Ave 23452
Yorktown Blvd 23453
Youlous Ave 23455
Young St 23455
Young Cedar Ct 23462
Yountville Ct 23456
Zamani Ct 23455
Zephyr Ct 23462
Zia Ct & Dr 23456
Zimmerman Ct 23464
Zinia Ct 23464
Zircon Ct 23462
Zivo Ct 23455
Zodiac Ln 23456
Zoisite Ln 23462
Zurich Arch 23452

NUMBERED STREETS

1st St 23460
3rd St
200-299 23451
1100-1398 23455
1101-1199 23459
1201-1399 23455
1700-1799 23460
4th St
200-399 23451
1000-1099 23455
5th St
200-299 23451
1100-1298 23459
1101-1199 23455
1201-1399 23459
1300-1498 23455
1500-1799 23455
1800-2099 23460
6th St
200-299 23451
1300-1399 23455
1900-1999 23460
7 1/2 St 23451
7th St
200-299 23451
1100-1399 23455
1400-1498 23459
1401-1499 23455
1500-1599 23459
1600-1699 23455
1900-1999 23460
8th St
100-299 23451
1300-1398 23459
1301-1399 23455
9th St
200-899 23451
1400-1499 23455
10th St
200-598 23451
600-799 23451
1300-1400 23455
1402-1798 23455
1701-1799 23459
2100-2199 23460
11th St
205-299 23451
1300-1399 23459
1400-2100 23455
2101-2199 23459
2102-2198 23455
12th St 23451
13th St 23451
14th St 23451
15th St 23451
16th St 23451
17th St 23451
18th St 23451
19th St 23451
20th St 23451
21st St 23451
22nd St 23451
23rd St 23451
24th St 23451
25th St 23451
26th St 23451
27th St 23451
28th St 23451
29th St 23451
30th St 23451
32nd St 23451
33rd St 23451
34th St 23451
35th St 23451
36th St 23451
37th St 23451
39th St 23451
40th St 23451
42nd St 23451
43rd St 23451
44th St 23451
45th St 23451
46th St 23451
48th St 23451
49th St 23451
50th St 23451
51st St 23451
52nd St 23451
53rd St 23451
54th St 23451
55th St 23451
56th St 23451
57th St 23451
58th St 23451
59th St 23451
60th St 23451
61st St 23451
62nd St 23451
63rd St 23451
64th St 23451
65th St 23451
66th St 23451
67th St 23451
68th St 23451
69th St 23451
70th St 23451
71st St 23451
72nd St 23451
73rd St 23451
74th St 23451
75th St 23451
76th St 23451
77th St 23451
78th St 23451
79th St 23451
80th St 23451
81st St 23451
82nd St 23451
83rd St 23451
84th St 23451
85th St 23451
86th St 23451
87th St 23451
88th St 23451
89th St 23451
11 1/2 St 23451
15 1/2 St 23451
20 1/2 St 23451
21 1/2 St 23451
22 1/2 St 23451
23 1/2 St 23451
24 1/2 St 23451
25 1/2 St 23451
26 1/2 St 23451
27 1/2 St 23451
32 1/2 St 23451
33 1/2 St 23451
34 1/2 St 23451
35 1/2 St 23451
37 1/2 St 23451
43 1/2 St 23451
45 1/2 St 23451
49 1/2 St 23451
51 1/2 St 23451
54 1/2 St 23451
55 1/2 St 23451
57 1/2 St 23451

WARRENTON VA

General Delivery 20186

POST OFFICE BOXES MAIN OFFICE STATIONS AND BRANCHES

Box No.s
1 - 4006 20188
9998 - 9998 20187

RURAL ROUTES

01, 02, 05 20186
04, 06, 07, 08, 11, 12 .. 20187

NAMED STREETS

Abingdon Pl 20187
Academy Rd 20187
Academy Hill Rd
1-399 20186
6200-6499 20187
Acorn Ct
1-799 20186
6500-6599 20187
Acorn Farm Ln 20187
Admiral Nelson Dr 20186
Afton Ln 20187
Aiken Dr 20187
Airlie Rd 20187
Akers Ln 20187
Albemarle St 20187
Albrecht Ln 20187
Alex Ct 20186
Alexander Ln 20187
Alexandria Pike 20186
Alleghany St 20187
Allison Marshall Dr 20187
Alwington Blvd 20186
Amber Cir 20186
Amberview Ln 20186
Ambler Ct & Dr 20187
Amy Ct 20187
Angus Hill Dr 20187
Applewood Ln 20187
Appomattox Dr 20187
Arbor Ct 20186
Argyll Ct 20187
Armstrong St 20186
Artillery Rd 20187
Ashby St 20186
Ashley Dr 20187
Ashton Way 20187
Atlee Rd 20187
Auburn Mill Rd 20187
Aurora Ave 20187
Autumn Wind Ct 20186
Avatar Ln 20187
Avatar Way 20187
Avenel Dr 20187
Averbach Ct 20187
Aviary St 20186
Bailey Rd 20187
Baileys Joy Ln 20186
Bainbridge Ln 20187
Baker Ct 20187
Bald Eagle Dr 20187
Baldwin St 20187
Baldwin Ridge Rd 20187
Barn Owl Ct 20187
Basswood Ln 20186
Bayfield Ln 20187
Beach Rd 20187
Beach St 20187
Beaconsfield Ln 20187
Bear Wallow Dr & Rd .. 20186
Bears Ln 20187
Beauregard Ct 20187
Beckham St 20186
Beech Ln 20186
Beecham Ln 20186
Beechnut Cir 20187
Beechtree Dr 20187
Belair Dr 20186
Belle Air Ln 20186
Belle Grove Ln 20186
Bellevue Farm Rd 20186
Benner Dr 20186
Bethany Ln 20187
Bethel Dr E & W 20187
Beverly Ct 20187
Bill Ct 20187
Bingham Rd 20187
Birch Ct 20187
Black Snake Ln 20186
Black Sweep Rd 20186
Blackwell Rd
1-899 20186
6200-7399 20187
Blackwell Park Ln 20186
Blantyre Rd 20187
Bludau Dr 20187
Blue Heron Ln 20187
Blue Ridge St 20186
Boathouse Rd 20187
Bob White Dr 20187
Botha Rd 20186
Boundary Ln 20186
Bramble Way 20187
Branch Dr 20186
Breezewood Dr 20186
Breezy Dr 20187
Brenda Ct 20186
Brewster Ln 20187
Bridle Path 20187
Briggs Rd 20187
Brighton Ct 20187
Brittany Ln 20186
Brixton Ln 20186
Broad Run Church Rd .. 20187
Broadview Ave 20186
Broken Hills Rd 20187
Brookmoor Dr 20187
Brookshire Dr 20186
Bruce Dr 20186
Brydon Ct 20187
Buckingham Ct 20187
Buckminster Ln 20187
Buena Vista Dr 20186
Burke Ln 20187
Burrough Dr 20187
Business Blvd 20187
Butler Grant Ln 20187
Butterfly Way 20187
Cadet Ln 20187
Caitlin Ct 20187
N & S Calhoun St 20186
Cambridge Way 20186
Camdent Cir 20186
Camellia Ct 20187
Camelot Ct 20187
Candy Meadow Ln 20186
Cannon Dr 20187
Cannon Way 20187
Cannonball Gate Rd ... 20186
Cannonball Ridge Ln ... 20186
Cannoneer Ct 20186
Canter Ln 20187
Canterbury Dr 20186
Cardinal Ln 20186
Carib Way 20186
Carriage Chase Cir 20186
Carriage House Ln 20186
Carter Ct 20187
Carters Run Rd 20186
Casanova Rd 20187
Castle Ln 20187
Castle Kingston Ln 20187
Castlebury Ct 20186
Cattail Ct 20187
Cavalry Dr 20187
Cedar Brook Ln 20187
Cedar Crest Dr 20186
Cedar Hill Ln 20187
Cedar Knolls Dr 20187
Cedar Run Dr 20187
Chappell St 20186
Chasewood Ln 20186
Chelsea Dr 20186
Cherry Tree Ln 20186
Chesapeake Pl 20186
Cheshire Ln 20187
Chesterfield Dr 20187
Chestnut Ct 20186
N Chestnut St 20186
S Chestnut St 20186
Chestnut Oak Ln 20187
Chestnut Wood Ln 20187
Chicory Ln 20187
Chittenden Dr 20187
Christa Ct 20187
Christopher Ln 20186
Church St 20186
Claire Ct 20187
Claston Ct 20187
Cleveland St 20186
Cliff Mills Rd 20186
Club House Ln 20187
Cobblestone Dr 20186
Coblentz Ave 20187
Col Edmonds Ct 20186
College St 20187
Colonel Dr 20187
Colonial Rd 20187
Colonnades Dr 20187
Colony Ct 20186
Colt Ln 20187
Comfort Inn Dr 20187
Commerce Ct 20187
Comrie Ct 20187
Constantine Ct 20186
Cooks Ct 20186
Coopers Hawk Dr 20187
Coppermill Dr 20186
Corbin Ln 20186
Cornerstone Ct 20187
Corral Rd 20187
Cosner Ct 20187
Country Ln 20187
Country Club Ln 20186
Country View Dr 20187
Court St 20186
Courthouse Sq 20186
Covey Rd 20187
Cray Dr 20187
Creedmore South Dr ... 20187
Creekside Xing 20187
N Crest Ct 20187
Crew Ct 20187
Crown Ln 20187
Culpeper St 20186
Culver Dr 20187
Cumberland Dr 20187
Curtis St 20186
Daisy Ln 20187
Danielle Ln 20187
Dapple Ln 20187
Dawn Ct 20187
Deborah Dr 20187
Deer Hollow Ln 20186
Dell Ct 20187
Della St 20186
Den Haag Rd 20187
Denning Ct 20186
Derby Way 20186
Derrymore Ct 20186
Devon Dr 20186
Diagonal St 20186
Diamond Hill Rd 20186
Dinwiddie Ct 20186
Dizzy Ln 20186
Dogwood Dr 20187
Dorset Ln 20186
Double Poplars Ln 20187
Douglas St 20186
Dover Rd 20186
Dovetail Ln 20187
Drake Dr 20187
Driftwood Ct 20186
Dublin Ln 20186
Duhollow Rd 20187
Duke Ln 20186
Dumfries Rd 20187
Dunnottar Ln 20186
Earlys Rd 20187
East St 20186
Eastwood Dr 20187
Echols Ct 20187
Eckert Ct 20187
Edgebrook Dr 20187
Edgehill Dr 20187
Edington Dr 20187
Eiseley Ct 20187
Electric Ave 20187
Elm St 20186
Elmores Ln 20187
Elway Ln 20186
Emerson Ln 20187
Emily Anne Ct 20187
Emma Ct 20187
English Chase Ln 20186
Equestrian Rd 20186
Erin Dr 20186
Essex Ct 20187
Estate Ave 20186
Evan Ct 20187
Evans Ave 20186
Executive Ct 20187
Fairfax St 20186
Fairfield Dr 20186
Falcon Glen Rd 20186
Fallen Leaf Ct 20186
Falmouth Ct & St 20186
Family Ln 20187
Fargo Ln 20186
Farm Ln 20186
Farmingdale Dr 20187
Fauquier Rd 20186
Fenton Farm Ln 20186
Fernwood Pl 20186
Filly Ln 20186
Finch Ln 20187
Fincham Ct 20187
Finchingfield Rd 20187
Fishback Ct 20186
Fisher Ln 20186
Fleetwood Ct 20187
Fletcher Dr 20186
Fletchers Mill Rd 20186
Flikeid Ln 20186
Fluvana Ct 20187
Flycatchers Ct 20187
Forbes Ct 20186
Forest Ct 20186
Forrest Ct & Rd 20187
Fosters Fork Rd 20187
Fox Trl 20186
Fox Call Ln 20186
Fox Chase St 20186
Fox Haven Ln 20187
Foxboro Ln 20187
Foxcroft Rd 20186
Foxtail Ln 20186
Foxview Dr 20186
Foxville Rd 20186
E Franklin St 20186
Frazier Rd 20186
Frederick Ct 20187
Freemont Hill Ct 20187
Friendly Pl 20187
Friendship Ln 20187
Frost Ave 20186
Frys Ln 20187
Frytown Rd 20187
Fusilier Rd 20186
Gaines St 20186
Gale Ct 20186
Galina Way 20186
Garden St 20186
Garland Dr 20187
Garnet Ct 20186
Garrett St 20186
Gates Rd 20187
Gay Rd 20186
General Wallace Ct 20186
Gerber Ln 20186
Ghadban Ct 20187
Glanamman Way 20187
Glen Curtiss Ln 20187
Gloucester Ct 20187
Glouchester St 20187
Gold Cup Dr 20186
Goochland St 20187
Grapewood Dr 20187
Gray Ct 20187
Gray Sentry Ln 20187
Grays Mill Rd 20187
Graystone Rd 20187
Great Arne Ln 20186
Great Oak Way 20187
Great Run Ln 20186
Green Rd 20187
Green St 20186
Green Meadows Rd 20187
Green Springs Dr 20187
Greenbrier Rd 20187
Greenbush Ln 20186
Greenpark Ln 20187
Greenview Ln 20187
Greenway Ct 20186
Group Rd 20187
Haiti St 20186
Halifax Ct 20187
Hampton Ct 20187
Harbor Ct 20187
Harrow Rd 20187
Harts Mill Rd 20186
Hastings Ln
600-799 20186
7200-7299 20187

Hatch Dr 20187
Haven Ct 20187
Hazelwood Ct 20187
Heather Ct 20187
Heritage Pl 20187
Heron Pl 20187
Hersmans Way 20186
Hesperides Dr 20186
Hi Rock Ridge Rd 20187
Hidden Creek Ln 20186
Hidden Hollow Ln 20187
High Ct 20187
High St 20186
Highland Ct 20187
Highland Towne Ln 20186
Highmeadow Pl 20187
N Hill Dr 20186
S Hill Dr 20186
Hills Ln 20187
Hillsbourough Ln 20186
Hillside Ct & Dr 20187
Hilly Ln 20187
Holiday Ct 20186
Hollerith Ct 20187
Holly Farm Ln 20187
Holly Hill Dr 20187
Holtzclaw Rd 20186
Homestead Ct 20187
Honeysuckle Ct & Ln 20187
Hope Ln 20187
Horn Ln 20187
Horner St 20186
Horseshoe Ln 20186
Hospital Dr 20186
Hot Springs Ln 20186
Hotel St 20186
Hummingbird Ln 20187
Hunsberger Dr 20187
Hunt Trl 20187
Hunting Ln 20186
Hunton St 20187
Huntsmans Dr 20186
Hyde Ln 20186
Imagination Way 20187
Industrial Rd 20186
Institute Ln 20186
Iron Bit Dr 20186
Ironwood Ln 20186
Ivy Hill Dr 20187
Jackson Ct 20187
Jackson St 20186
Jaclyn Dr 20187
James Madison Hwy
700-900 20186
902-10098 20186
6101-7299 20187
8201-8499 20186
8501-10099 20187
Jamison Rd 20187
Jamisons Farm Dr 20187
Jefferson St 20186
Jeffries Ln 20187
Jocelyn Ct 20187
Joffa Cir 20187
John Ct 20186
John E Mann St 20186
John Marshall St 20186
Johnson Dr 20187
Jordan Dr 20187
Joshua Tree Cir 20187
Juniper Pl 20186
Kathryn Ln 20187
Keith Rd & St 20186
Keiths Chapel Ln 20186
Kelly Rd 20187
Kennedy Rd 20187
Kensington Ln 20187
Kimberly Ct 20186
Kines Rd 20187
King St 20186
King William St 20187
Kingsbridge Ct 20186
Kirk Ln 20187
Kirkland Dr 20187
Knights Ct 20186
Knightsbridge Ln 20187
Lake Dr 20187
Lake Ashby Ct 20187
Lake Brittle Rd 20187
Lake Wesley Ct 20187
Lake Willow Ct 20187
Lakeview Dr 20187
Lakewood Dr 20187
Lancaster Dr 20187
Lancrel Rd 20186
Langston Ln 20186
Lapis Ct 20186
Lee Hwy
5171-1A-5171-1A 20187
4100-6499 20187
7700-8020 20186
8022-18599 20186
E Lee Hwy 20186
W Lee Hwy 20186
E Lee St 20186
W Lee St 20186
Lee Highway Access Dr 20187
Leeds Ct 20186
Leeds Manor Rd 20186
Lees Mill Rd 20186
Lees Ridge Rd 20186
Leeton Ct 20186
Leeton Forest Ln 20186
Leeton Hill Dr 20186
Leeton Lake Dr 20186
Leeton Ridge Rd 20186
Legion Dr 20186
Leigh Rd 20186
Leighton Forest Rd 20186
Leland Dr 20187
Liberty St 20186
Lilly Ln 20187
Linden Ct 20187
Linden St 20186
Lineweaver Rd 20187
Little Ct 20187
Little Tree Ln 20187
Lock Ln 20186
Locust St 20186
Loudoun Ct 20187
Louis St 20186
Lovers Ln 20186
Low Ct 20187
Lower Waterloo Rd 20186
Lowpond Dr 20187
Lunsford Rd 20187
Lynn Dr 20187
Macintosh Dr 20187
Mackenzie Ct 20187
Madell Ln 20187
Madison St 20186
Main St
1-54 20186
53-53 20188
55-299 20186
56-298 20186
Mallard Ct 20187
Maloney Way 20187
Manchester Ct 20187
Mangum Ct 20187
Manor Ct 20186
Manor House Dr 20187
Maple Ct 20187
Maple Tree Ln 20187
March Wales Rd 20186
Marigold Ct & Ln 20187
Marlow Ct 20187
Marr Dr 20187
Mason Ln 20187
Mauchley Ct 20187
Maxwell Ave 20187
Mayfield Ln 20187
Mcculla Blvd 20187
Mcraes Rd 20187
Meadow Ct 20186
Meadow Ln 20187
Meadow St 20187
Meadows Rd 20186
Meadowvale Dr 20187
Meadowview Ln 20186
Meaghan Ln 20187
Mecklenburg Dr 20187
Medallion Ave 20187
Medlock Way 20187
Meetze Rd 20187
Menlough Dr 20186
Merchant Pl 20187
Mes Enfants Ct 20186
Miles Ln 20187
Mill House Ln 20187
Mill Run Dr 20187
Mill Valley Dr 20187
Millers Ct 20186
Millfield Dr 20187
Millpond Ct 20187
Millstead Ln 20186
Millwood Dr 20187
Minder Ln 20186
Mint Springs Dr 20187
Moccassin Ln 20186
Mockingbird Ln 20186
Moffett Ave 20186
Moffett Dr 20187
Molloy Way 20186
Mongoose Ct 20187
Monroe St 20186
Montreux Rd 20187
Moonlight Ct 20187
Moonstone Dr 20186
Moorhead Dr 20186
Morton Rdg 20186
Mosby Cir 20186
Mosby Dr 20187
Moser Rd 20186
Moss Ln 20187
Mount Sterling Farm Rd 20187
Mountain Rd 20186
Mourningdove Ln 20187
Movern Ln 20187
Mull Ct 20187
Myers Ct 20187
Myriah Ct 20187
Nancy Ln 20187
Nelson Ln 20186
New Kensington Ct 20187
Newbury St 20187
Nordix Dr 20187
Norfolk Dr 20187
North St 20186
Northampton St 20187
Norwich Ct 20187
Nuthatch Ct 20187
Oak Leaf Ct 20186
Oak Springs Dr 20186
Oak Tree Ln 20186
Oakmont Dr 20187
Oaks Rd 20186
Oakwood Dr 20186
Oatlands Ln 20187
Old Alexandria Tpke 20187
Old Auburn Rd 20187
Old Culpeper Rd 20186
Old Dominion Ct 20187
Old Forest Ln 20187
Old Foxville Rd 20186
Old Meetze Rd
500-699 20186
6300-6499 20187
Old Mill Ln 20187
Old Mill Estates Ln 20187
Old Orchard Ln 20186
Old Waterloo Rd 20186
Old Zion Rd 20187
Oliver City Rd 20186
Oliver Farm Rd 20187
Onyx Way 20186
Opal Ct & Rd 20186
Opal Tower Ln 20186
Orchard Ln 20187
Orchid Ln 20187
Osborne Dr 20187
Over The Dam Ln 20186
Overlook Trl 20186
Oxford Way 20186
Oyster Pond Ln 20186
Paddock Way 20186
Pahlson Ct 20187
Palmer Ct 20187
Panorama Ct 20187
Paradise Rd 20186
Parkside Ct 20187
Pavilion St 20187
Pebble Run Rd 20187
Pebblebrook Ln 20187
Pelham St 20186
Pembrooke Ct 20187
Pendleton Ln 20187
Pepper Tree Ct 20186
Periwinkle Ct 20187
Phoenix Hill Ln 20187
Piccadilly Dr 20186
Piedmont St 20186
Pigeon Hill Ln 20187
Pignut Mountain Dr 20187
Pilcher St 20186
Pilgrims Rest Rd E 20187
Pine Tree Ct 20186
Pinehurst Dr 20187
S Pines Rd 20186
Pineview Ct 20186
Pinewood Ln 20187
Piney Mountain Rd 20186
Pinn Turn 20186
Pinnacle Ct 20186
Plain Rd 20186
Plantation Ln 20187
Pleasant Colony Ln 20187
Pleasant Valley Dr 20187
E & W Pointe Ln 20187
Pond Ln 20186
Poplar Pl 20187
Poplar Grove Dr 20187
Poplar Point Ln 20186
Porch Rd 20187
Portman Ln 20186
Potomac Ct 20187
Powhatan Ct 20187
Preston Dr 20186
Princess Anne Ct 20187
Pump House Ct 20187
Quarterpole Ct 20186
Quarters 20187
Race Course Rd 20186
Raider Dr 20187
Railroad St 20186
Rapidan Ct 20187
Rappahannock St 20186
Ray Ct 20187
Rayquick Ct 20186
Rebel Dr 20187
Red Brick Rd 20187
Red Fox Ln 20186
Red Maple Ct 20187
Red Oak Ct 20187
Redfield Ln 20187
Redturn Ln 20187
Redwinged Blackbird Dr 20187
Reese Ct 20187
Reeves Ct 20186
Retreat Ln 20186
Richards Dr 20186
Richlands Dr 20187
Rider Rd 20187
Ridge Ct 20186
W Ridge Ct 20186
Ridge Ln 20187
Ridgecrest Ave 20187
Ridgedale Dr 20187
Ridgeline Ln 20187
Riley Rd 20187
Robert Hunt Ct 20187
Robin Ln 20187
Robinson Ln & St 20186
N Rock Ln 20186
Rock Pointe Ln 20186
Rock Springs Rd 20187
Rockbridge St 20187
Rockingham Rd 20186
Rocky Ln 20187
Roebling St 20186
Rogues Rd 20187
Rosedale Ct 20186
Rosehaven Ct 20187
Routs Ridge Ln 20186
Routts Hill Rd 20186
Royal Ct 20186
Ruby Ct 20186
S Run Rd 20187
Saint Leonards Ln 20186
Sandstone Ct 20187
Sapphire Ct 20186
Scenic Dr 20187
Scondara Rd 20187
Seaton Ln 20187
Secretariat Ct 20186
Semington Rd 20186
Servants Quarters Way 20187
Settlers Ridge Rd 20187
Shady Oak Ct & Ln N 20187
Shamrock Ct 20187
Shannon Ct 20187
Sharp St 20186
Shepherdstown Rd 20187
Sherry Lynn Ln 20187
Shipmadilly Ln 20186
E & W Shirley Ave 20186
Sholes Ct 20187
Short St 20186
Shrayer Ct 20187
Shugart Ct 20187
Shumates Mill Ln 20187
Side Hill Dr 20187
Sigler Rd 20187
Silver Beech Ln 20187
Silver Cup Dr 20186
Silver Maple Ct 20187
Sinclair Dr 20187
Singleton Cir 20186
Sir Topas Dr 20186
Sire Way 20186
Skyland Dr 20187
Smith St 20186
Solgrove Rd 20186
Split Oak St 20186
Spotsylvania St 20187
Spring Ln 20186
Spring Branch Dr 20187
Spring Hill Ln 20187
Spring Run Rd 20187
Springdale Dr 20187
Springs Dr & Rd 20186
Springs Hollow Rd 20186
Springs Way Pl 20186
Spruce Hill Ct 20187
Spy Plane Ln 20187
Squires Ln 20187
Squirrel Nest Ln 20187
Stable Gate Rd 20186
Stafford St 20187
Stag Ln 20187
N & S Starcrest Dr 20187
Starling Dr 20186
Starting Point Ct 20186
Steeplechase Rd 20186
Stephens Ln 20187
Sterling Ct 20186
Stewart St 20186
Stonefield Ln 20187
Stonehouse Ln 20187
Stonehurst Ct 20187
Stonelea Ln 20186
Stoneridge Ct 20187
Stream View Ln 20187
Stuart Cir 20187
Sturgis Ln 20186
Stuyvesant St 20186
Suffield Ln 20187
Sullivan St 20186
Summer Breeze Rd 20186
Summerfield Ln 20186
Summerfield Hills Dr 20186
Summit Pl 20187
Suncrest Dr 20187
Sundance Dr 20187
Sunrise Ct 20187
Sunset Ct 20187
Surry Ct 20187
Sutherland Ct 20187
Swain Dr 20187
Sweetgum Ct 20187
Swift Xing 20187
Sycamore Ln & St 20186
Sycamore Springs Dr 20187
Tanglewood Dr 20187
Tapscott Ter 20187
Taylor St 20186
Tazewell St 20187
Telephone Rd 20187
Terranova Dr 20187
Terrapin Ct 20187
The Mountain Rd 20186
Tidewater Ln 20187
Tiffany Ct 20186
Timber Ln 20187
Timothy Ln 20187
Tollhouse Ln 20186
Topaz Ct 20186
Tournament Rd 20186
Trafalgar Pl 20186
Travelers Way 20187
Trinity Ln 20187
Tucan Ct 20187
Tulip Hill Dr 20187
Turkey Run Dr & Rd 20187
Turnbull Rd 20186
Twilight Ct 20187
Twin Poplar Ln 20187
Uninerie Rd 20186
University Ct 20187
Us Army 20187
Vale View Dr 20186
Valle Doro Ct 20186
Valley Dr 20187
Van Roijen St 20186
Veterans Dr 20186
Victoria Dr 20187
Victory Ln 20187
N View Cir 20186
View Point Ln 20186
View Tree Turn 20186
Viewtree Dr 20186
Vint Hill Pkwy, Rd & Sta 20187
Von Neuman Cir 20187
Wade Ct 20187
N Wales Rd 20186
Walker Dr 20186
Wall St 20186
Walnut Ct 20187
Walnut Heights Dr 20186
Warren Ct 20186
Warrenton Blvd 20186
Warrenton Industrial Park 20186
Warwick Ln 20187
Washington St 20186
Waterford Ln 20187
Waterloo Rd & St 20186
Waterloo Farm Rd 20186
Waters Pl 20187
Watery Mountain Ln & Rd 20186
Watson Ct 20187
Waverly Dr 20186
Wayland Dr 20187
Weeks Dr 20187
Welding Ln 20186
Well House Dr 20187
Wellington Dr 20186
Wellspring Ct 20187
Wemberly Dr 20187
Westbury Dr 20186
Westfield Ct 20187
Westmoreland Dr 20187
Wheeler Cir 20187
Whippoorwill Dr 20187
Whirlaway Ln 20187
Whisperwood Dr 20187
Whitehall Farm Ln 20187
Whites Mill Ln 20187
Wickie Ct 20187
Wide Oak Ct 20186
Wildcat Mountain Rd 20186
Wildfire Ct 20187
Wildrose Ln 20186
Wilkes Ct 20187
William Dr 20187
Williams Ln 20186
Willow Ct 20186
Willow Dr 20187
Willowmeade Dr 20187
Willowspring Ln 20186
Wilshire Ct & Dr 20187
Wilson Rd & St 20186
Wince Ln 20187
Winchester St 20186
Winchester Mews Dr 20186
Windhaven Ln 20187
Winding Oak Ln 20187
Windsor Ct 20186
Windsor Retreat 20187
Windward Ct 20186
Winners Cir 20186
Wintergreen Ct 20187
Wirth Ln 20187
Withers Mill Way 20186
Wood Ct 20187
Wood Thrush Ct 20187
Woodberry Ct 20187
Woodbourne Ln 20186
Woodlake Ct 20187
Woodlawn Ln 20187
Woodley Heights Dr 20186
Woods Edge Ct 20187
Woodstone Ct 20187
Wythe Ct 20187
Yellowrose Ln 20187
York Ct 20187
Zellas Rd 20187

NUMBERED STREETS

All Street Addresses 20186

WILLIAMSBURG VA

General Delivery 23081

NAMED STREETS

Abbitt Ln 23185
Abbotsford Mews 23188
Aberdeen 23188
Abigail Ln 23185
Abington Park 23188
Acacia Ct 23185
Acoma Cir 23188
Acorn St 23188
Adams 23188
Adams Rd 23185
Adams St 23185
Adams Hunt Dr 23188
Addingtons 23188
Aden Ct 23188
Ainsdale 23188
Aintree 23188
Airport Rd 23188
Alabama Ln 23188
Albemarle Dr 23185
Alderwood Dr 23185
Alesa Dr 23188
Alexander Pl 23185
Alexander Lee Pkwy 23185
Alexander Walker 23185
Algonquin Trl 23185
Alice St 23185
Allegheny Ct & Rd 23188
Allendale Pl 23185
Allyson Dr 23188
Alwoodley 23188
Ambassador Cir 23188
Ambrose Hl 23185
Amendment Ct 23188
Andersons Ordinary 23185
Andre Esteve 23185

Andrew Lindsey 23185
Andrews Cir 23185
Angel Ct 23185
Angus Ln 23188
Ann Johnson Ln 23185
Annamary Way 23188
Anns Ct 23188
Ansley 23188
Anthony Wayne Rd 23185
Apothecary Pl 23185
Archers Ct 23185
Archers Hope Rd 23185
Archers Mead 23185
Arden Dr 23185
Arena St 23185
Argall Town Ln 23185
Armistead Ave 23185
Armstrong Dr 23185
Arran Thistle 23188
Arthur Hls 23188
Arthur Hills Dr 23188
Artillery St 23188
Ascot 23188
Ash Vw 23185
Ashby Ln 23188
Ashford Mnr 23188
Ashington Way 23188
Ashley Way 23185
Ashmont 23188
Ashwood Dr 23185
Aspen Ct 23185
Astrid Ct & Ln 23188
Attleborough Way 23188
Auburn Ln 23188
Audley Green Ter 23188
Augusta 23188
Autumn Cir & Trce 23188
Avery Cir 23188
Avon Ave 23185
Ayrshire Reach 23188
Back Forty Loop 23188
Back River Ln 23185
Bacon Ave 23185
Bailey Dr 23188
Bald Eagle Way 23188
Ballard Ln 23185
Ballycastle 23188
Balmoral 23188
Baltusrol 23188
Banneker Dr 23185
Baptista Ct 23188
Barfleur Pl 23188
Barley Mill Pl 23185
Barlow Rd 23188
Barlows Run 23188
Barn Elm Rd 23188
Barnstaple Way 23188
Barons Ct 23188
Barrets Pointe Rd 23185
Barrett Pl 23185
Barretts Ferry Dr 23185
Barrows Mt 23185
Basswood Way 23188
Bastille Ct 23185
Bates Ct 23188
Battlefield Dr 23188
E Bay 23185
W Bay 23185
Bay Hl 23188
Bay Club Ct 23185
Bayberry Ln 23185
Beacon Hill Dr 23188
Beamers Rdg 23188
Beaver Run E 23188
Beckenham Ct 23188
Beckie Ln 23185
Beechnut Ct 23188
Beechtree Ln 23188
Beechwood Dr 23185
Beeston Flds 23188
Beler Rd 23188
Belleview 23188
Benjamin Ct 23188
N & S Benjamin Howell St 23188
Bennett Cir 23185

Bennetts Pond Rd 23185
Benomi Dr 23185
Bent Creek Rd 23185
Bergen Cir 23188
Berkeley Cir, Dr & Ln 23185
Berkeleys Grn 23185
Berkshire Rd 23188
Bermuda Cir 23188
Berrow 23188
Bertier Ct 23185
N Berwick 23188
Bethune Dr 23185
Betsy Ross Ct 23185
Betty Ln 23188
Big Gap Rd 23188
Bigler Mill Rd 23188
Birch Cir 23188
Birdella Dr 23188
Birdie 23188
Birkdale 23188
Birmingham 23188
Black Oak Dr 23185
Blackheath 23188
Blacklake 23188
Blair Ct 23185
Blakemore Ter 23188
Blalock Dr 23185
Blassingham 23185
Blenheim 23188
Bliss Armstead 23188
Blockade Reach 23185
Blow Flats Rd 23185
Blue Bill Run 23188
Blue Cat Way 23188
Blue Lake Ct 23185
Blue Ridge Ct 23188
Bluffs Cir 23185
Boatwright Cir 23185
Boca Raton Cir 23185
Bogey 23188
Bolling Rd 23185
Bonyman Ct 23188
Booker T Rd 23185
Bordeaux Ct 23185
N Botetourt St 23185
Boulder Way 23185
N Boundary St
100-499 23185
425-425 23187
S Boundary St 23185
Bournemouth Bnd 23188
Bow Ln 23185
Bowstring Dr 23185
Boxwood Ln 23188
Braddock Ct & Rd 23185
Bradford 23188
Bradinton 23188
Bradshaw Dr 23188
Brady Dr 23188
Braemar Crk 23188
Braemore 23188
Brafferton Rd 23188
Brancaster 23188
Brandon Cir 23185
Brannan Ln 23188
Branscome Blvd 23185
Bransford Ct 23188
Braxton Ct 23185
Bray Wood Rd 23185
Brennans Ln 23185
Brentmoor 23188
Brettwood Ct 23185
Brewhouse Ave 23185
Brian Ct 23185
Brian St 23188
Briar Ln 23188
Briarwood Ave 23185
Brick Bat Rd 23185
Brickhampton 23188
Bridgewater Dr 23188
Bridlington Way 23188
Brigstock Ct 23188
Bristol Cir 23185
Bristol Cmn 23188
Brittania Dr 23185
Brittany Way 23188

E & W Brittington 23185
Brixton Rd 23185
Broadmead Ct 23188
Broadmoor 23188
Broadwater 23188
Broadway St 23185
Brockton Ct 23185
Bromley Dr 23185
Bronze Ct 23185
Brook View Ln 23188
Brooke Ct 23188
Brookhaven Dr 23188
Brookmeade 23188
Brooks St 23185
Brookwood Dr 23185
Broomfield Cir 23185
Bruton Dr 23185
Bucktrout Ln 23185
Buford Rd 23188
Bulifants Blvd 23188
Bulwell Frst 23188
Bunche Dr 23185
Bunker Arch 23188
Burbank St 23185
Burgess St 23185
Burgh Crse 23188
Burgundy Rd 23185
Burlington Ct & Ln 23188
Burma Rd 23188
Burnham 23188
Burnham Rd 23185
Burnley Dr 23188
Burns Ln 23185
Burnwether Ln 23188
Burrows Ct 23185
Burtcher Ct 23185
Burton Ct 23188
Burton Woods Dr 23188
Burwell Ct 23185
Busch Gardens Blvd 23185
Bush Neck Rd 23188
Butler 23188
Bypass Rd 23185
Cabell Ct 23185
Cabernet Rd 23185
Cactus Rd 23188
Callahan Dr 23185
Calvin St 23188
Camberley Cir 23188
Cambridge Ln 23185
Camden Cir 23185
Camellia Ct 23188
Cameron Cir 23188
Campbell Close 23188
Camrose Dr 23185
Candleberry Way 23188
Candlestick Pl 23185
Canham Rd 23188
Cannonball Ct 23185
Canterbury Ln 23185
Canterbury Pl 23188
Canvas Back Run 23188
Capitol Ct 23185
Capitol Landing Rd 23185
Captain Drew 23188
Captain John Smith Rd 23185
Captain Newport Cir 23185
Captain Wynne Dr 23185
Captaine Graves 23188
Captains Ct 23185
Caran Rd 23185
Cardinal Ct 23185
Cardinal Acres Dr 23185
Carlas Hope Rd 23188
Carlisle Mews 23188
Carlton Ct 23185
Carlton House Cres 23188
Carmel Vly 23188
Carnoustie 23188
Carol Ln 23185
Carriage Rd 23188
Carriage House Way 23188
Carrs Hill Rd 23185
Carters Neck Rd 23188
Cartgate 23188

Cary St 23185
Cascades 23188
Casey Blvd 23188
Castel Pnes 23188
Castle Ln 23185
Castlerock 23188
Castleside Cir 23188
Castling Xing 23185
Catalpa Dr 23188
Catawba Ct 23185
Catesby Ln 23185
Cavendish Ct 23188
Cedar Br 23188
Cedar Cir 23188
Cedar Ct 23185
Cedar Run 23185
Cedar Point Ln 23188
Cedar Rock 23188
Cedarwood Ln 23188
Cemetery Ln 23185
Center St 23188
Centerville Rd 23188
Chadsworth Cir 23188
Chancery Ln 23188
Chanco Rd 23185
Chandler Ct 23185
Channel House Ct 23185
Chanteraine Close 23185
Chanticleer Ct 23185
Chapel Xing 23188
Chapel Hill Ln 23188
Chardonnay Rd 23185
Charles Dillard Ln 23185
Charles River Landing Rd 23185
Charleston Pl 23185
Charter House Ln 23188
Chartstone Cres 23188
N & S Chase 23185
Chateau Dr 23188
Cheeseman Rd 23185
Chelmsford Ct 23188
Chelsea Cres & Lndg 23188
Chelsford Way 23185
Cherry Walk 23188
Cherrywood Ct 23185
Cherwell Ct 23188
Chesdale Ct 23188
Chestnut Dr 23185
Chestnut Hill Ct 23185
Chickahominy Bluff Rd 23185
Chickasaw Ct 23188
Chinkapin Ln 23188
Chisel Run Rd 23188
Chiswick Park 23188
Chorley 23188
Christopher Wren Rd 23185
Church St 23185
Claiborne Dr 23185
Clara Croker 23185
Claremont 23185
Clarendon Ct 23188
Clark Ln 23188
Clarke Ct 23188
Clay Cir 23188
Cliffside Dr 23188
Cliftons Blf 23188
Clipper Ct 23185
Cloverleaf Ln 23185
Club Dr 23185
Cluster Way 23188
Clydeside 23188
Coach House Rd 23188
Cobble Stone 23185
Cokes Ln 23188
Col Frederick Jones 23185
Col Philip Johnson 23185
Cold Spring Rd 23188
Cole Ln 23185
Coleman Dr 23185
College Ter 23185
College Creek Pl 23185
Colonels Way 23185
Colonial Ave 23185
Colonial Cres 23188

Colonial Pkwy
1300-1367 23185
1368-1369 23081
Colonial St 23185
Colonies Xing 23188
Colony Cir & Sq 23185
Colony Point Rd 23185
Commanders Ct 23185
Commerce Blvd 23185
Commons Way 23185
Commonwealth Ave 23185
Concord 23188
Congress Hall 23188
Congressional 23188
Conies Run 23185
Conservancy 23185
Constance Ave 23185
Constitution 23188
Continental St 23185
Conway Dr 23185
Cooley Rd 23188
Cooper Nace 23185
Copperfield 23185
Copse Way 23185
Corbin Close 23185
Corbridge Crse 23188
W Cornwall 23188
Coronation 23188
Corvette Dr 23185
Cotswold Ct
100-121 23185
4800-4899 23188
Cottage Cove Ln 23185
Counselors Way 23185
Country Club Ct & Dr 23185
Court St 23185
Courthouse St 23188
S Cove Ct 23188
Cove Rd 23185
N Cove Rd 23188
Cove Point Ln 23185
Coventry Rd 23188
Coxmoor 23188
Craggy Oak Ct 23185
Craig End 23188
Crail 23188
Creedmoor Ct 23185
Creek Ct 23185
Creek Vw E 23188
Creek Vw W 23188
Creek Point Cir 23188
Creekside Loop 23188
Crescent Dr 23185
Crestwood Dr 23185
Croaker Cir & Rd 23188
Crocker Pl 23185
Cromwell Ln 23185
Crooked Stick 23188
Cross Creek Rd 23188
Crosscut Ct 23188
Crossover Rd 23188
Crowe Creek Rd 23188
Crown Ct 23185
Crownpoint Rd 23185
Cruden Bay 23188
Crump Ln 23185
Crystal Ln 23188
Culpeper Ct 23188
Curles Cir 23188
Curls Neck Ct 23185
Curry Dr 23188
Custis Dr 23185
Cutspring Arch 23185
Cypress Crk 23188
Cypress Isle 23185
Cypress Point Rd 23185
Daingerfield Rd 23185
Dam Lake Ct 23185
Danbury Pl 23185
Dancy Pl 23185
Danesbury Park 23188
Darbi Ln 23188
Darden Pl 23188
Dartmoor Ct 23185
Davis Dr 23185
Deal 23188

Debra Dr 23188
Deepwoods Trl 23188
Deer Path Rd 23188
Deer Run Cir 23188
Deer Spring Rd 23188
Deere Cir 23188
Deerfield Ct 23188
Deerhurst Grn 23188
Deerlope Trl 23188
Deerwood Dr 23188
Degrasse St 23188
Dehaven Ct 23188
Del Lago Dr 23185
Delafayette Pl 23188
Delaware Ave 23185
Deliverance Dr 23185
Dena Dr 23185
Dennis Dr 23185
Derby Ln 23185
Desmonde Ln 23185
Devon Rd 23188
Devonshire Dr 23188
Dewitt Dr 23188
Digges Ct 23188
Discovery Ln 23185
Discovery Park Blvd 23188
Dodge Dr 23185
Dogleg Dr 23188
Dogwood Dr 23185
Domino Dr 23185
Doral 23188
Dornoch 23188
Dorset Mews 23188
Douglas Dr & Ln 23185
Dovedale Dr 23188
Dover Rd 23185
Down Patrick Way 23188
Downing Ct & St 23185
Drammen Ct 23185
Drew Rd 23185
Driftwood Way 23188
Druid Ct & Dr 23185
Drummond Ct 23188
Duer Dr 23188
Duffie Dr 23185
E & W Duke Of Gloucester St 23185
Dunbarton Cir 23188
Duncan 23188
Duncan Dr 23185
Dundee 23188
Dunes 23188
Dunning St 23185
Duntrune Gln 23185
Durfeys Mill Rd 23185
Durham Ct 23185
Dutchess 23188
Dyke 23188
Eagle 23188
Eaglebrook Dr 23188
Eaglecliffe 23188
Eagles Watch 23188
Eaglescliffe 23188
Earl Dr 23188
Earl Lee Cv 23188
Earls Ct 23185
Eastbury 23188
Easter Cir 23188
Edale Ave 23185
Eden Riv 23185
Edenbridge 23188
Edgewood Ln 23185
Edinburgh Dr 23188
Edward Grindon 23185
Edward Harrington Rd 23185
Edward Wakefield 23185
Edward Wyatt Dr 23188
Efford Ct 23188
El Sombrero Ct 23185
Elbow Beach Ln 23185
Eleanors Way 23188
Elie 23188
Elizabeth Champion Ct 23185
Elizabeth Davis Blvd 23188
Elizabeth Harrison Ln 23188
Elizabeth Killebrew 23188

Elizabeth Meriwether 23185
Elizabeth Page 23185
Ellinson Ct 23185
Elmwood Ln 23188
Eltham 23188
Embers Ln 23185
Emma Rose Ct 23185
Empress Ct 23185
Endeavor Dr 23185
England Cir & St 23185
English Garden Way 23188
Ensign John Utie 23185
Ensign Spence 23185
Entry Hl 23188
Erin Leigh Ct 23185
Ernest Ln 23188
Ernestine Ave 23188
Essex Ct 23188
Evensong Ln 23188
Evergreen Way 23185
Evesham Ct 23185
Ewell Pl & Rd 23188
Exbury Ln 23188
Executive Dr 23188
Exeter Ct 23185
Exmoor Ct 23185
F St 23185
Fair Chase 23185
Fairfax Way 23185
Fairmont Dr 23188
Fairview Dr 23188
Fairway Lookout 23188
Fairways Reach 23188
Falcon Creek Dr 23188
Falkirk Mews 23188
Fall E 23188
Falling Creek Cir 23188
Farmville Ln 23188
Felix Dr 23188
Fenn Ct 23188
Fenton Croft 23188
Fenton Mill Rd 23188
Fenwyck Ct 23188
Fern Ct 23188
Ferncliff Dr 23188
Fernwood 23185
Ferrell Dr 23185
Fiddlers Ridge Pkwy 23185
Fieldcrest Ct 23185
Fifth Ave 23185
Fillmore Dr 23185
Firestone 23188
Firethorn Pl 23185
First St 23185
First Patent Ct 23188
Fithian Ln 23185
Fitzhugh Bacon Dr 23188
Flavias Ct 23188
Fleetwood Ln 23188
Flintlock Rd 23185
Flowerdew Ct 23185
Foley Dr 23188
Fords Colony Dr 23188
Forest Ct & Ln 23188
Forest Glen Dr 23188
Forest Heights Rd 23188
Forest Hill Dr 23185
Formby 23188
Forth Riv 23188
Foundation St 23185
Founders Hl N & S 23185
Four Mile Tree 23188
N Fowlers Close 23185
Fowlers Lake Rd 23185
Fox Holw & Run 23188
Fox Den 23188
Fox Hill Rd 23188
Fox Hunt Trl 23188
Foxcroft Rd 23188
Foxridge Rd 23188
Frances Berkeley 23188
Frances Thacker 23185
E & W Francis St 23185
Francis Chapman N & W 23185
Francis Jessup 23185

Franklin St 23185
Freedom Dr 23185
S Freeman Rd 23185
Frenchmens Ky 23185
Friars Ct 23185
Frond Ct 23188
Fyfe Ct 23185
Galleon Ct 23185
Gallo Ct 23185
Galverneck 23188
Garden Vw 23188
Gardner Ct 23188
Garrison Dr 23185
Gaslight Way 23188
Gate House Blvd 23185
Gatehouse Rd 23188
General Gookin Ct 23185
Gentry Ln 23188
George Mason 23188
George Perry 23185
George Sandys 23185
George Wilson Ct 23188
George Wythe Ln 23188
Georgetown Cres 23188
Gersham Pl 23185
Giles Bland 23188
Gilley Dr 23188
Ginger Ct 23188
Gladys Dr 23188
Glasgow 23188
Glen Nevis Trce 23188
Glenburnie Rd 23188
Glencoe Way 23188
Gleneagles 23188
Glenn Cir 23185
Glenwilton Ln 23188
Glenwood Dr 23185
Glisan Ct 23188
Glory Ln 23188
Glynn Springs Dr 23185
Godspeed Ln 23185
Goering Dr 23188
Gold Knight Ct 23185
Golden Dr 23185
Golf Club Rd 23185
Goodrich Durfey 23185
Goodwin St 23185
Government Rd 23185
Governor Berkeley Rd 23185
Governor Edward Nott Ct 23188
Governor Yeardley Ln 23185
Governors Dr 23185
Governors Sq 23188
Governors Landing Rd 23185
E & W Grace Ct 23188
Grand Strand Dr 23188
Granite Pl 23185
Graves Ordinary 23185
Gray Gables Dr 23185
Grays Deed 23185
Great Gln 23188
Greate Way 23185
Green St 23185
Green Mount Pkwy 23185
Green Swamp Rd 23188
Greenbrier 23185
Greencastle Dr 23188
Greendale Dr 23188
Greenleigh Ct 23185
Greens Way 23185
Greensprings Rd 23185
Greenway Cir 23188
Greenwich Mews 23188
Greenwood Dr 23185
Greg Ln 23188
Grenelefe 23188
Grey Abbey Cir 23188
Grey Fox Cir 23188
Griffin Ave 23185
Grist Mill Ct 23188
Gristmill Plz 23185
Grove Ave 23185
Grove Gate Ln 23188
Grove Heights Ave 23185
Grovewood Way 23188
Guesthouse Ct 23188
Guildford Ln 23188
Gullane 23188
Gunlock Rd 23188
Gwens Way 23188
Hadlock Ct 23185
Hague Close 23185
Halstead Ln 23185
Hamilton St 23185
Hamlin Ct 23188
Hampton Ky 23185
Hangmans Ln 23185
Haradd Ln 23188
Harbin Ct 23185
Harbor Rd 23185
Harbour Town 23188
Harbourside 23188
Harding Rd 23188
Harlech 23188
Harpers Ml 23185
Harpoon Ct 23185
Harrells Ct 23185
Harriett Tubman Dr 23185
Harrington Cmns 23188
Harrison Ave 23185
Harrop Ln 23185
Harrop Parrish Ct 23188
Harrops Gln 23185
Hartwell Perry Way 23185
Harvest Cir 23185
Harwood Cir 23185
Hastings Ln 23188
Hatton Cross 23188
Hawks Nest Dr 23185
Hawthorn Ln 23188
Hawtree Landing Rd 23188
Haymaker Pl 23185
Haymarket Ln 23188
Haynes Dr 23185
Hearthside Ln 23185
Hearthstone Rd 23185
Heather Ct 23188
Heathery 23188
Heaths Ln 23188
Helen Potts Pl 23188
Helmsdale Ct 23188
Helmsley Rd 23185
Hempstead Ct & Rd 23188
Henderson St 23185
N & S Henry St 23185
Henry Tyler Dr 23188
Heritage Landing Rd 23185
Heritage Pointe 23188
Hermitage Rd 23188
Herndon Jenkins Dr 23188
Heron Ct 23188
Herstad Ct 23188
Hiawatha Ct 23185
Hickory Ct & Ln 23188
Hickory Hills Dr 23185
Hickory Signpost Rd 23185
Hidden Lake Dr 23185
Higginson Ct 23188
High St 23185
High Point Rd 23185
Highgate Grn 23188
Highland 23188
Hill Grove Ln 23188
Hillside Ln & Way 23185
Holcomb Dr 23185
Holdsworth Rd 23185
Holland Dr 23188
Hollingsworth 23188
Hollinwell 23188
Holloway Dr 23188
Holly Grv & Rd 23185
Holly Brook Dr 23185
Holly Hills Dr 23185
Holly Point Rd 23185
Holly Ridge Ln 23185
Holman Rd 23185
Horan Ct 23188
Hornes Lake Rd 23188
Horseshoe Dr 23185
House Of Burgess Way 23185
House Of Lords 23188
Howard Dr 23188
Hoylake 23188
Hubbard Ln 23188
Hudson Dr 23188
Hunstanton 23188
Hunter Ln 23188
Huntercombe 23188
Hunters Rdg 23188
Hunting Cv 23185
Hunting Towers Ct 23185
Huntingdon Rd 23185
Huntington Dr 23188
Hurlston 23188
Hurst St 23185
Hutchinson Pl 23185
Idaho Cir 23188
Idlewood Ln 23188
Indian Cir 23185
Indian Path 23188
Indian Springs Ct & Rd 23185
Indian Summer Ln 23188
Indiana Ln 23188
Indigo Ter 23188
Indigo Dam Rd 23188
Information Center Dr 23185
Ingram Rd 23188
Inverness 23188
Ireland St 23185
Iris St 23188
Ironbound Rd
100-1198 23188
101-199 23185
201-1199 23188
2701-2897 23185
2899-3199 23185
3200-4699 23188
4701-5299 23188
Ironwood Dr 23185
E & W Island Rd 23185
Isle Of Wight Ct 23185
Ivey Ln 23188
Ivy Ct 23185
J Farm Ln 23188
Jackson Dr & St 23185
Jacobs Rd 23185
James Sq 23185
James Bray Dr 23188
James Longstreet 23185
Jamestown Rd 23185
Jameswood 23185
Jan Rae Cir 23185
Jason Dr 23185
Jefferson St 23185
Jeffersons Hundred 23185
Jerdone Rd 23185
Jesters Ln 23188
Jib Ct 23185
Jockeys Neck Trl 23185
John Bratton 23185
John Browning 23185
John Fowler 23185
John Hancock 23185
John Jackson Rd 23185
John Jefferson Rd 23185
John Paine 23185
John Pinckney Ln 23185
John Pott Dr 23188
John Proctor E & W 23185
John Ratcliffe 23185
John Rolfe Ln 23185
John Shropshire 23185
John Twine 23185
John Tyler Hwy & Ln 23185
John Vaughan Rd 23185
John Wickham 23185
John Wythe Pl 23185
Jolly Pond Rd 23188
Jonas Profit Trl 23185
Jones Dr 23185
Jones Mill Ln 23185
Jones Mill Rd 23188
Jordans Journey 23185
Jubal Pl 23185
Jubilee 23188
Judy Dr 23185
Julies Way 23188
Juniper Ct 23185
Juniper Hls 23188
Justice Grice 23185
Katherine Shaye Ln 23185
Kathleen Way 23188
Kathryn Ct 23185
Keaton Ln 23188
Kelsey Rd 23185
Kempe Dr 23188
Kensington Ct 23188
Kersten 23188
Kestrel Ct 23188
Keswick Pl 23188
Ketch Ct 23185
Keystone 23188
W Kilbride 23188
Killarney 23188
Killington 23188
Kilton Frst 23188
Kinde Cir 23188
King Henry Way 23188
King James 23188
King Richard Ct 23185
King Rook Ct 23185
King William Dr 23188
Kingdom Of Fife 23188
Kings Ct & Way 23185
Kings Gate Pkwy 23185
Kings Manor Dr 23185
Kings Oak Ln 23188
Kingsgate Rd 23185
Kingsmill Rd 23185
Kingspoint Dr 23185
W Kingswood Dr 23185
Kirkcaldy Ct 23188
Kirkland Ct 23185
Kitchums Close 23185
Kitchums Pond Rd 23185
N Knob Hl 23188
Knollwood Dr 23188
Knott Pl 23188
Knox Rd 23188
Kristiansand Dr 23188
Kristos Ct 23185
Kroken Ct 23188
Lady Slipper Path 23188
Ladybank 23188
Lafayette Blvd 23185
Lafayette St 23185
Lafiete Ln 23188
Lake Dr 23185
Lake Powell Rd 23185
Lake Powhatan 23188
Lakepoint Ct 23188
Lakeshead Dr 23185
Lakeside Cir 23185
Lakeside Dr 23188
Lakewood Dr 23185
Lamplighter Pl 23185
W Lancashire 23188
Lancaster Ct 23185
Lancaster Ln 23188
Landfall Dr 23185
E Landing 23185
W Landing 23188
Landing Cir 23185
Lands End Dr 23185
Landsdown 23185
Lane Place Dr 23188
Langman Pl 23185
Lantern Pl 23185
Larkspur Run 23185
Las Brisas Ct 23185
Laurel Ct 23185
Laurel Ln
101-113 23185
7400-7499 23188
Laurel Keep 23185
Lauren Ct 23188
Lavelle Ct 23185
Lawnes Cir 23185
Lawnes Creek Rd 23185
Leafwood Ln 23188
Lee Dr 23185
Leeds 23188
Leicester N & S 23188
Lely 23188
Leon Dr 23188
Leslie Faye Overlook 23188
Lethbridge Ln 23185
Leven Links 23188
Levingston Ln 23188
Levinson Pass 23188
Lewis Cir 23188
Lewis Burwell Pl 23185
Lewis Robert Ln 23188
Lexington Dr 23188
Liberty Ridge Pkwy 23188
Lightfoot Rd 23188
Lillie St 23188
Lily Ln 23188
Lincolnshire 23188
Linden Ln 23185
Lindrick 23188
Linfoot Ct 23185
W Links 23188
Links Of Leith 23188
Linwood Dr 23188
Little Aston 23188
Little Deer Run 23188
Little John Rd 23185
Littletown Quarter 23185
Liverpool 23188
Liza Ln 23188
Lloyds Ln 23188
Loch Haven Dr 23188
Locust Pl 23185
Lodge Rd 23185
Logan Pl 23188
London Company Way 23185
Londonderry Ln 23188
Long Pt 23188
Longboat 23188
Longhill Rd
100-299 23185
3700-5399 23188
Longhill Gate Rd 23188
Longhill Station Rd 23188
Longhorn Ct 23185
Longleaf Cir 23188
Longview Lndg 23188
Lopez Pl 23188
Lorac Ct & Rd 23185
Lord Dunmore Dr 23185
Lori Mahone Overlook 23188
Lothian 23188
Low Ridge Rd 23188
Loxley Ln 23185
Ludin Links 23188
Ludwell Pkwy 23188
Luffness New 23188
Lusk Way 23188
Luther Dr 23185
Lydias Dr 23188
Lynette Dr 23188
Macaulay Rd 23185
Mace St 23185
Machrie 23188
Macon Cir 23185
Madison Rd 23185
Magazine Rd 23185
Magnolia Dr 23185
Magruder Ave 23185
Magruder Ln 23185
Magruder Park 23188
Magruder Rd 23188
Mahogany Ln 23185
Mahogany Run 23188
Maid Marion Pl 23185
Main St 23188
Majesties Mews 23185
Makah Ct 23188
Mal Mae Ct 23188
Mallard Cv 23185
N Mallard Run 23185
S Mallard Run 23185
Mallard Creek Run 23185
Malvern Cir 23185
Manchester 23188
Manion Dr 23185
Manor Blvd 23185
Manor Gate Dr 23188
Manufacture Dr 23185
Maple Ln 23185
Maplewood Pl 23185
Mara Park Pl 23185
Marble Run 23185
Marclay Rd 23185
Margaret Jones Ln 23185
Marina Pt 23188
Marion 23188
Market Street Ct 23185
Marks Pond Way 23188
Marmont Ln 23185
Marquis Pkwy 23185
Marshall Way 23185
Marstons Ln 23188
Martin Ct 23185
Martins Rdg 23188
Mary Ln 23188
Mary Byrd 23188
Marywood Dr 23185
Massacre Hill Rd 23185
Massena Dr 23188
Masters Ln 23188
Mathew Brown 23185
Mathew Scrivener 23185
Mathews Grant 23185
Matoaka Ct 23185
Mattaponi Trl 23188
Matthew Cir 23185
Maupin Pl 23185
Maxton Ln 23185
Maxwell Pl 23185
N & S Mayfair Cir & Ln 23188
Mayfield St 23185
Mayflower Dr 23188
Maynard Dr 23188
Maynor Dr 23188
Mclaws Cir 23185
Meadow Cir 23185
Meadow Grove Way 23188
Meadow Rue Ct 23185
Meadowbrook 23188
Meadowcrest Trl 23188
Melanies Way 23188
Melissa Ln 23188
Menife Ct 23185
Merchant Man Ct 23185
Meredith Way 23188
Meriwether Ct 23185
Merlot Dr 23185
Merrimac Trl 23185
Mesa Riv 23188
Michael Ct 23185
Mid Ocean 23188
Middle St 23185
Middle Woodland Close 23185
Midlands Rd 23185
Milden Rd 23185
Mildred Ct & Dr 23188
Mile Crse 23185
Miles Mahone 23185
Mill Dam Ct 23188
Mill Neck Rd 23185
Mill Stream Way 23185
Mill View Cir 23185
Miln House Rd 23185
Mimosa Dr 23185
Minor Ct 23188
Minutemen Way 23188
Mirror Lake Dr 23185
Misty Ct 23188
Mobile Ln 23188
Mockingbird Dr 23185
Molesey Hurst 23188
Monifieth 23188
Montague Cir 23185
Montgomerie Arch 23188
Monticello Ave
100-399 23185
2800-5699 23188
Montpelier Dr 23188
Montrose 23188
Monument Dr 23185
Monumental Ave 23185
Moodys Run 23185
Moore Dr 23188
Mooretown Rd
2001-2099 23185
3000-3098 23185
4600-5128 23188
5130-6799 23188
Moray Firth 23188
Morgan Dr 23185
Mosby Dr 23185
Mosel Ct 23185
Moses Ln 23185
Moses Harper 23185
Moss Side Ln 23188
Mossock 23188
Mossy Creek Dr 23185
Mott Ln 23185
Mount Laurel Rd 23188
Mount Pleasant Dr 23188
Mount Vernon Ave 23185
Mounts Bay Rd 23185
Muirfield 23188
Mulberry Ln 23188
Murcar 23188
Musket Dr 23185
Nairn 23188
Nappa Ct 23185
Nathaniell Powell Rd 23185
Nathaniels Grn & Run 23185
Nathaniels Close 23185
National Ln 23185
Natures Way 23188
Neal Ct 23185
Neck O Land Rd 23185
Neighbors Dr 23185
Nelms Ln 23185
Nelson Ave & Dr 23185
Nevada Cir 23188
Nevalou Ct 23188
Nevis Xing 23188
New Ct 23188
New Castle Dr 23185
New Hope Rd 23185
New Market 23188
New Point Rd 23188
New Quarter Dr 23188
New Town Ave 23188
New Wilkinson Way 23188
Newman Ct & Rd 23188
Newport Ave 23185
Newport Frst 23188
News Rd 23188
Ney Ct 23188
Nice Dr 23188
Nicholas Ct 23188
E & W Nicholson St 23185
Nina Cir & Ln 23188
Noland Blvd 23188
Norfolk St 23185
Norge Ln 23188
North Ct 23185
North Trce 23185
Northpoint Dr 23185
Norwyk Ln 23188
Nottingham Rd 23185
Nottinghamshire 23188
Nuthatch Dr 23185
O L Taylor Dr 23185
Oak Dr 23185
Oak Holw 23188
Oak Rd 23185
Oak Hill Dr 23185
Oak Ridge Ct 23185
Oak Tree Crst & Ln 23185
Oakland Dr 23185
Oakmere Park 23188
Oakmont Cir 23188
Oaktree Rd 23185
Oakwood Dr 23185
October Breeze Ln 23185
Ohio Ln 23188
Oholloran Way 23188
Old Carriage Way 23188
Old Cart Rd 23188

Old Church Rd 23188
Old Colonial Dr 23188
Old Colony Ln 23185
Old Field Rd 23188
Old Glory Ct 23185
Old Hollow Rd 23185
Old Lock Rd 23188
Old Meadows Rd 23188
Old Mill Ln 23188
Old Mooretown Rd 23188
Old News Rd 23188
Old Regency Dr 23188
Old Stage Coach Rd 23188
Old Taylor Rd 23188
Old Tomahund Dr 23185
Old Woods Ct 23185
Olde Jamestown Ct 23185
Olde Towne Rd 23188
Oldham Ct 23188
Olivers Way 23188
Olympic 23188
Opportunity Way 23188
Orange Dr 23185
Ormskirk 23188
Oslo Ct 23188
Outrigger Ct 23185
Overlook Dr 23185
Owl Crk 23188
Owl Creek Cir 23188
Oxford Cir & Rd 23185
Oxmor Ct 23188
Packets Ct 23185
Paddock Ln 23188
Padgetts Ordinary 23185
Page St 23185
Palace Ln 23185
Palace Green St 23185
Palisade Ct 23185
Palmer Ln 23188
Panmure 23188
Panther Paw Path 23185
Par Dr 23188
Parchment Blvd 23185
Park Cir & Pl 23185
Parke Ct
1-99 23188
200-299 23185
Parker View Ct 23188
Parkside Ln 23185
Parkway Dr 23185
Pasbehegh Dr 23185
Pasture Cir 23188
Pates Crk 23185
Patrick Henry Dr 23185
Patricks Xing 23185
Patriot Ln 23185
Patriots Colony Dr 23188
Paynes Rd 23185
Peacepipe Pl 23185
Peach St 23188
Peachtree 23188
Peale Ct 23188
Pearl St 23188
Pearl Harbor Rd 23188
Pebble Bch 23188
Pebble Beach Ln 23185
Pelegs Way 23185
Pelhams Ordinary 23185
Pemberton Ln 23188
Peninsula St 23188
Penn Dr 23188
Penniman Rd 23185
Pennington Pl 23188
Penrith Ct 23185
Penzance Pl 23188
Percussion Rd 23185
Perdido 23188
Persimmon Pl 23185
Peter Lyall 23185
Peter Van Wirt Way 23188
Pettus Ordinary 23185
Pewter Ct 23185
Peyton Rd 23185
Pheasant Run 23188
Pheasant Springs Rd 23188
Philip Ludwell 23188

Phoenix Cir 23188
Pierces Ct 23185
Pierpoint 23188
Pierside Reach 23188
Pine Vly 23188
Pine Bluff Ct 23188
Pine Hollow Path 23185
Pinebrook Rd 23188
Pinedell Ln 23185
Pinehurst 23188
Pinepoint Rd 23185
Pineside Dr 23188
Pinetree Rd 23185
Pinewood Dr 23188
Pinewood Rd 23185
Piney Creek Dr 23185
Pinnacle Arch 23188
Pintail Trce 23188
Pipe Kiln Ct 23185
Pitlochry 23188
Plains View Rd 23188
Plantation Dr & Rd 23185
Pleasant Pt 23188
Pleasant View Dr 23188
Pocahontas St & Trl 23185
Poggio Fld 23188
Poindexter Ct 23188
Point Rd 23185
Point Laurel Pl 23185
Point O Woods 23188
Pollard Park 23185
Pond St 23188
Popeley Ct 23188
Poplar Creek Ln 23188
Port Royal 23188
Portland 23188
Portmarnoch 23188
Portofino Ct 23185
Portstewart 23188
Powell St 23185
Powhatan Dr 23188
Powhatan Pkwy 23188
Powhatan St 23185
Powhatan Xing 23188
Powhatan Overlook 23188
Powhatan Secondary 23188
Powhatan Springs Rd 23188
Powie Cir 23185
Powner Ct 23188
Prentis Pl 23185
Prescott Dr 23188
Presidents Ct 23188
Preston Grange Crse 23188
Prestwick 23188
Prince Charles Rd 23185
Prince George St 23185
Prince Trevor Dr 23185
Princess Ln 23188
Princess Pl 23185
Princeville 23188
Priorslee Ln 23188
Pristine Vw 23188
Proctor Cir 23185
Professional Cir & Dr 23185
Prosperity Ct 23188
E & W Providence Rd 23188
Puffin Ln 23185
Quail Holw 23185
Quaker Rdg 23188
Quaker Meeting House
Rd 23188
N Quarter 23185
Quarterpath Rd 23185
Queen Anne Dr 23185
Queen Bishop Ln 23185
Queen Mary Ct 23188
E & W Queens Cres,
Dr, Path, Way & Xing 23185
Queens Creek Rd 23185
Queensbury Ln 23185
Quill Pl 23185
Railroad St 23185
Raintree Way 23185
Raleigh St 23185
Randolph St 23185
Randolphs Grn 23185

Rannock Moor 23188
Raven Ter 23185
Reades Way 23185
Red Berkshire 23188
Red Dirt Rd 23188
Red Fox Cir 23188
Red Oak Dr 23185
Red Oak Landing Rd 23185
Red Wing Ct 23188
Redbud Ln 23185
Reed Ct 23185
Reflection Dr 23188
Regency Ct 23188
Regents Park 23188
Rembold Way 23185
Renick Ln 23188
Reserve Dr & Way 23185
Revolutionary Way 23188
Rexford Ln 23188
Rhine Ct 23185
Rhoda Ln 23188
Rich Neck Rd 23185
Richard Grv N & S 23185
Richard Bolling 23185
Richard Brewster 23185
Richard Buck N & S 23185
Richard Burbydge 23185
Richard Pace N & S 23185
Richards Rd 23188
Richards Patent 23185
Richardson Ln & Run 23188
Richmond Rd
100-2300 23185
2302-3052 23185
3053-7699 23188
7421-1-7421-3 23188
Richmond Hill Ct 23185
Richmonds Ordinary 23185
Richpress Dr 23188
Richwine Dr 23185
Ridge Xing 23188
Ridgecrest Cir 23185
Ridings Cv 23185
Riesling Rd 23188
Rileys Pl 23188
Ringfinger Ct 23185
Ripley Rd 23185
River Blfs & Rdg 23185
River Don 23188
River Moor 23188
River Oaks Rd 23188
River Reach 23185
Rivers Edge 23185
Riverview Cir & Rd 23188
Riverview Plantation
Dr 23188
Riviera 23188
Road Hole 23188
Robert Cole Ct 23185
Robert Elliffe Rd 23185
Robert Fenton Rd 23185
Robert Hunt N & S 23185
Robert Miles 23185
Robertson St 23185
Robins Way 23185
Robinson Ln 23188
E Rochambeau Dr 23188
Rock Landing Way 23188
Rockingham Dr 23188
Roffinghams Way 23185
Roger Smith 23185
Roger Webster 23185
Rogers Ct 23185
Roland St 23188
Rolfe Rd 23185
Rolling Hills Dr 23185
Rolling Reach 23185
Rolling Woods Dr 23185
Rollison Dr 23188
Ron Springs Dr 23185
Rondane Pl 23188
Rook Pawn Reach 23188
Rose Ln 23188
Rosemount 23188
Rosewood Ct 23188
Rothbury Dr 23185

Roy Ln 23188
Royal Ct 23185
Royal Adelaide 23188
Royal County Down 23188
Royal Dublin 23188
Royal Grant Dr 23185
Royal Melbourne 23188
Royal Musselburgh 23188
Royal North Devon 23188
Royal Orleans Ct 23185
Royal Portrush 23188
Royal Saint Georges 23188
Royal Sydney 23188
Royal West Norfolk 23188
Royal Worlington 23188
Roycroft St 23185
Rudder Ct 23185
Running Cedar Way 23185
Rustads Cir 23188
Rusty Ct 23185
Ruth Ln 23188
Rye 23188
Sabre Dr 23185
Saddle Brk 23188
Saddletown Rd 23188
Sagamore 23188
Saint Annes 23188
Saint Johns Ct 23185
Saint Jude Cir 23185
Saint Simone Ct 23185
Salisbury Mews 23188
Samoset 23188
Samuel Mathews 23185
Samuel Sharpe 23185
San Angel Ct 23185
Sanctuary Dr 23185
Sand Dr W 23188
Sand Hill Rd 23188
Sanda Ave 23185
Sandstad Ct 23185
Sandy Bay Rd 23185
Sandy Point Rdg 23188
Sanford Arms 23185
Sarah Spence 23185
Sasha Ct 23185
Sassafras Ct 23185
Saunders Brg 23188
Saunton Links 23188
Saw Mill Rd 23188
Saxon Rd 23185
Scarborough Mews 23188
Scenic Ct 23185
Schenck Dr 23185
School House Ln 23188
Schooner Blvd 23185
Scotland St 23185
Scotscraig 23188
Scott Dr 23185
Scotts Pond Dr 23185
Seasons Ct & Trce 23188
Second St 23185
Sedwick Ct 23188
Selby Ln 23185
Seminole 23188
W Semple Rd 23185
Sentara Cir 23188
Seton Hill Rd 23188
Settlement Dr 23188
Settlers Ln 23188
Settlers Market Blvd 23188
Seven Oaks 23185
Shackleton Ln 23188
Shadow Ln
150-160 23185
4000-4099 23188
Shadwell 23188
Shady Ln 23188
Shady Bluff Pt 23188
Shady Grove Cir 23188
Shaindel Dr 23185
Sharps Ln 23185
Sharps Rd 23188
Shea Ln 23185
Sheffield Rd 23188
Shellbank Dr 23185
Shenandoah Ct & Dr 23188

Sheppard Dr 23185
Sheriffs Pl 23185
Sheringham Grn 23188
Sherwood Dr 23185
Sherwood Frst 23188
Shields Poynt 23188
Shinnecock 23188
Shirley Ave 23185
Shirley Dr 23188
Shoal Crk 23188
Shore Dr 23185
Shoreham Ln 23185
Shoreline Ct 23185
Short Hole 23188
Shotley Way 23188
Shrewsbury Sq 23188
Sidewinder Ct 23185
Silver Fox Ln 23185
Silverado Trl 23188
Silverwood Dr 23185
Sir George Percy 23185
Sir Gilbert Loop 23185
Sir John Randolph Ter 23188
Sir Thomas Way 23185
Sir Thomas Lunsford
Dr 23185
Sixpence Ct 23185
Skalak Dr 23188
Skewer Ct 23185
Skiffes Blvd 23185
Skiffes Creek Cir 23185
Skimino Rd 23188
Skimino Landing Dr 23188
Sloane Sq 23188
Sloop Ct 23185
Smallpage Trce 23185
Smokehouse Ln 23185
Somerset Ct 23188
Sommersby Ct 23185
Sommerset Ln 23188
Sonoma Ct 23185
South Ct 23185
Southbury Sq 23188
Southeast Trce 23185
Southern Hls 23185
Southpoint Dr 23185
Southport 23188
Southport Trl 23185
Southwold Ct 23188
Sparks Ct 23185
Sparrow Ct 23185
Spinnaker Way 23185
Spotswood St 23185
Spotswood Cay 23185
Spring E 23188
Spring W 23188
Spring Br 23188
Spring Rd 23188
Spring Trce 23188
Springfield Dr & Rd 23185
Springhill Dr 23188
Sprucemont 23188
Spur Ct 23188
Spyglass 23188
S Square 23188
St Albans 23188
St Andrews Dr 23188
St Cuthbert 23188
St Erics Turn 23185
St Georges Blvd 23188
St James Park 23188
St Johns Wood 23188
St Marys Cir 23185
Stafford Ct 23185
Staffordshire Ln 23188
Stanford Pl 23185
Stanley Dr 23188
Staples Rd 23185
Starboard Ct 23185
Starling Dr 23185
Statesman 23188
Staunton Ct 23188
Stavenger Ct 23188
E & W Steeplechase
Way 23188
Sterling Manor Dr 23185

Stewart Dr 23185
N & S Stocker Ct 23185
Stoke Poges 23188
Stone Brg 23188
Stone Path 23185
Stonehouse Rd 23188
Stonewood Ln 23188
Stoney Creek Dr W 23185
Stowe 23188
Stoweflake 23188
Strategy Ct 23185
Stratford Dr & Rd 23185
Stratton 23188
Strawberry Plains Rd 23188
Stuart Cir 23185
Stylers Mill Xing 23188
Sugar Bush 23188
Sugarloaf Run 23188
N & S Sulgrave Ct 23185
Summer E 23188
Summit Loop 23188
Sunningdale 23188
Sunrise Ct 23185
Suri Dr 23185
Surry Dr 23188
Susan Dr 23185
Sussex Ct 23188
Swan Rd 23188
Sweet Gum Ln 23185
Swilkens Brg 23188
Swinley Frst 23188
Sycamore Landing Rd 23188
Taber Park 23188
Tadich Dr 23185
Tadworth 23188
Tahoe Trl 23188
Tam O Shanter Blvd 23185
Tampa Cir 23188
Tanbark Ln 23188
Tanglewood Cv 23185
Tantallon Dr 23185
Tanyard St 23185
Taps Neck Loop 23188
Tara Ct 23188
Tarleton Bivouac 23185
Tarpleys Tavern Rd 23188
Tay Riv 23188
Tayloe Cir 23188
Tayside 23188
E & W Tazewells Way 23185
Teakwood Dr 23188
Teal Way 23188
Telemark Dr 23188
Tempsford Ln 23188
Tendril Ct 23188
Tetbury Ln 23185
Tettington Ct 23188
Tewkesbury Way 23188
Tewning Rd 23185
The Grn & Mall 23185
The Colony 23185
The Foxes 23188
The Maine W 23185
The Palisades 23188
Theodore Allen Rd 23185
Theresas Way 23188
Thomas Ct 23188
Thomas Dl 23188
Thomas Dr 23188
Thomas Bransby 23185
Thomas Brice 23185
Thomas Cartwright 23185
Thomas Gates 23185
Thomas Nelson Ln 23185
Thomas Paine Dr 23185
Thomas Smith Ln 23185
Thompson Ln 23188
Thorngate Dr 23188
Thorpe Ct 23188
Thorpes Parish 23185
Thunderbird Ln 23185
Tilghman Ct 23188
Timber Ln 23188
Timber Rdg 23185
Timberwood Dr 23185
Tims Ln 23188

Titan Ct 23188
E & W Tiverton 23185
Toddington Cir 23188
Tolers Rd 23185
Tom Thomas Rd 23188
Tomahund Dr 23185
Topping Cir 23185
Torbay Bnd 23188
Torea Ct 23188
Torrington Trl 23188
Tower Hl 23188
Town Creek Dr 23188
Tracy Ct 23185
Trafalgar Ct 23185
Trails End Dr 23188
Tralee 23188
Tranquility Dr 23185
Travis Ln 23188
Travis Close 23188
Travis Pond Rd 23185
Treasure Island Rd 23185
Treyburn Dr 23185
Trolls Path 23188
Troon 23188
Trudy Ln 23188
Tudor Dr 23188
Tufton 23188
N & S Turnberry Dr 23188
Tutters Nck 23185
Two Rivers Pt & Rd 23185
Tyler Dr & St 23185
Tyler Brooks Dr 23185
Tyndal Ct 23188
Tynemouth Way 23188
Underwood Rd 23185
Vaiden Dr 23188
Vail Rdg 23188
Valley Grn 23188
Valor Ct 23185
Vass Ln 23185
Vaughan Ln 23185
Venture Ln 23188
Verde Mdws 23188
Vernon Hall 23188
Victoria Ct 23185
Viking Rd 23188
Village Park Dr E & W 23185
Vineyard Ln 23185
Vintage Ct 23188
Virginia Ave 23185
Visitor Center Dr 23185
Wadebridge 23188
Wadsworth St 23185
Wake Robin Rd 23185
Walker Dr 23188
Wallace Rd 23185
N & S Waller St 23185
Waller Mill Rd 23185
Walnut Hills Cir & Dr 23185
Walton Heath 23188
Waltrip Ln 23185
Waltz Farm Dr 23185
War Hill Grn 23188
Warbler Pl 23185
Ware Ln 23185
Ware Rd 23185
Ware Creek Rd 23188
Warehams Pt 23185
Warehams Pond Rd 23185
Warhill Trl 23185
Warwick Ct 23185
Warwick Hls 23188
Washington St 23185
Water Country Pkwy 23185
Water Oak Ct 23188
Waterford Ct 23188
Waterloo Pl 23188
Waters Edge Dr 23185
Waterside Ln 23188
Waterton 23188
Watford Ln 23188
Watson Dr 23188
Wax Myrtle Dr 23185
Weathersfield Way 23188
Weaver Rd 23185
Weavers Cottage 23188

Wedgewood Dr 23188
Welarint Rd 23185
Wellesley Blvd 23185
Wellington Cir & Dr 23185
Wentworth 23188
Wessex Hundred 23185
West Cir 23185
Westberry Ct 23188
Westbury Hls 23188
Westchester 23188
Western Gailes 23188
Westgate Cir 23185
Westhampton 23188
Westlake Ct 23185
Westminster Pl 23188
Westmoreland Dr 23188
Weston Ct 23185
Westover Ave 23185
Westover Dr 23185
Westover Rdg 23188
Westward Ho 23188
Wetherburn Ln 23188
Wexford Run 23185
Whistle Walk 23188
Whistling Swan Ct 23188
Whitaker Ct 23188
Whitby Ct 23185
Whitby Mews 23188
White Ct 23188
White Acre Rd 23188
Whitehall Ct 23188
Whitehaven Cir 23188
Whitehouse Cir 23188
Whithorn Cir 23188
Whiting Ave 23185
E & W Whittaker Close 23185
Whittaker Island Rd 23185
Whittakers Trce 23185
Whittakers Mill Rd 23185
Whittles Wood Rd 23185
Wichita Ln 23188
Wickre St 23185
Wiffet Way 23188
Wilderness Ln 23188
Wildwood Ln 23185
Wilkins Dr 23185
Wilkinson Dr 23188
N Will Scarlet Ln 23185
William Way S 23185
William Allen 23185
William Barksdale 23185
William Bedford 23185
William Carter Rd 23185
William Claiborne 23185
William Hodgson 23188
William Lee 23188
William Richmond 23185
William Spencer 23185
William Tankard Dr 23185
Williams Cir 23188
Williamsburg Ave 23185
Williamsburg Rd 23188
Williamsburg Glade 23185
Williamsburg Landing Dr 23185
Williamsburg West Dr 23188
Williamson Dr 23188
Willoughby Dr 23185
Willow Dr 23185
Willow Spring Ct 23185
Wilson Cir & Dr 23188
Wiltshire Rd 23188
Wimbledon Way 23188
Wind River Run 23188
Windbrook Ln 23185
Windjammer Ct 23185
Windmill Rd 23188
Windsor Ln 23185
Windsor Rdg 23188
Windsor Rdg S 23188
Windsor Way 23188
Windsor Hall Dr 23188
Windsormeade Way 23188
Windstar 23188
Wingate Dr 23185
Winged Foot 23188
Wingerma Rd 23188
Wingfield Close 23185
Wingfield Lake Rd 23185
Winster Fax 23185
Winston Dr 23185
Winter E 23188
Winterberry Ct 23188
Winterset Pass 23188
Winthrop Cir 23188
Winthrop Rd 23185
Wisteria Garden Dr 23185
Wm Ludwell Lee 23188
Woburn 23188
Wolf Crk 23188
Wood Duck Commons 23188
Wood Pond Cir 23185
Wood Violet Ln 23188
Woodbine Ct & Dr 23185
Woodbury Dr 23188
Woodhall Spa 23188
Woodland Rd 23188
Woodmere Ct & Dr 23185
Woodmont Pl 23188
Woods Dr 23185
Woods Walk Ct 23185
Woodside Dr 23185
Workington 23188
Worksop 23188
Worplesdon 23188
Wrenfield Dr 23188
Wyatt Cir 23185
Wyndham Way 23188
Wythe Ave & Ln 23185
Yacht Ct 23185
Yancey Ct 23188
Yardarm Ct 23185
Yarrow Ct 23188
Yeardley Loop 23185
Yeardleys Grant 23185
York St 23185
York River Rd 23188
York River Park Rd 23188
Yorkshire Dr 23185
Zelkova Rd 23185
Zinfandel Rd 23185

NUMBERED STREETS

All Street Addresses 23185

WINCHESTER VA

General Delivery 22601

POST OFFICE BOXES MAIN OFFICE STATIONS AND BRANCHES

Box No.s
All PO Boxes 22604

RURAL ROUTES

05 22603

NAMED STREETS

Abbey Rd 22602
Aberdeen Pl 22603
Abington Dr 22602
Abrams Creek Dr 22601
Abrams Pointe Blvd 22602
Academy Cir & Ln 22601
Adams Dr 22601
Adams Rd 22603
Admiral Byrd Dr 22602
Agri Ct 22603
Airport Rd 22602
Albert Cir 22603
Allegiance Dr 22603
Allen Dr 22601
Allison Ave 22601
Alloy Ln 22602
Allston Cir 22601
Alpine Meadow Rd 22602
Alta Vista Dr 22602
Amberwood Ln 22602
Ambrose Dr 22603
Amherst St 22601
Amoco Ln 22603
Amy Ave 22603
Anderson Ave & St 22602
Andrew Ave 22603
Angels Way 22603
Angus Hill Ln 22603
Anna Margaret Dr 22602
Anne Glass Rd 22602
Antelope Trl 22602
Apache Trl 22602
Apple Blossom Dr 22601
Apple Pie Ridge Rd 22603
Apple Valley Rd 22602
Applecroft Rd 22601
Appleseed Ct 22601
Arbor Ct 22602
Archwood Trl 22602
Ardeyth Ln 22602
Armel Rd 22602
Armistead St 22601
Armour Dl 22601
Armstrong Cir & Pl 22602
Arrowhead Trl 22602
Arthur Ln 22602
Artifact Ave 22603
Artillery Rd 22602
Asbury Ct & Rd 22602
Ash Hollow Dr 22602
Ashburn St 22601
Ashland Dr 22603
Ashley Cir & Dr 22602
Ashton Dr 22603
Ashwood Trl 22602
Aspen Trl 22602
Assateague Trl 22602
Astoria Ct 22602
Atoka Dr 22602
Atwell Ave 22601
Aulee Ct 22603
Aurora Ln 22602
Autumn View Ln 22603
Averrell Ave 22603
Aviation Dr 22602
Aviator Pl 22602
Avon Ct 22601
Azalea Ln 22602
Aztec Trl 22602
Babbs Mountain Rd 22603
Babbs Run Ln 22603
Back Mountain Rd 22602
Back Ridge Rd 22602
Baileys Ford Rd 22603
Baker Ln
500-700 22601
701-1499 22603
Baker St 22601
Baldwin Cir 22603
Baldwin St 22601
Ballygar Dr 22602
Balmoral Ln 22603
Banbury Ter 22601
Banks Dr 22602
Barksdale Ln 22601
Barley Ln 22602
Barney Ln 22603
Barnston Ct 22602
Barr Ave 22601
Barracks Ln 22602
Barrington Ln 22601
Bass Ln 22603
Battaile Dr 22601
Battery Dr 22601
Battle Ave 22601
Battlefield Dr 22602
Bay Ct 22602
Baybreeze Ct 22602
Beans Pond Ln 22602
Bear Trl 22602
Bear Run Rd 22602
Beau St 22601
Beaver Trl 22602
Beaver Dam Ln 22603
Bedford Dr 22602
Beechcroft Rd 22601
Beecher Pl 22603
Beehive Way 22601
Beeler Ln 22603
Bell Hollow Rd 22603
Belleville Ct 22602
Bellview Ave 22601
Bentley Ave 22602
Bentpath Ct 22602
Berkshire Cir 22601
Berryville Ave 22601
Berryville Pike 22603
Bethany Hill Dr 22603
Bethel Grange Rd 22603
Beverly Dr 22602
Bing Ct 22602
Birch Trl 22602
Bittersweet Ct 22601
Black Bear Dr 22602
Blackfeet Trl 22602
Blackpowder Ct 22603
Blanche Cir 22602
Blossom Dr 22602
Blue Ridge Ln 22602
Blue Ridge Ter 22601
Bluebell Ct 22602
Bluebird Dr & Trl 22602
Bobcat Ct & Trl 22602
Boggess Ln 22603
E & W Bond St 22601
Bonnings Dr 22603
E & W Boscawen St 22601
Boundary Ave 22602
Bowman Ln 22602
Bowwood Trl 22602
Boxwood Trl 22602
Boyd Ave 22601
N & S Braddock St 22601
Bradford Ct 22601
Braeburn Dr 22601
Bramble Ct 22602
Branch Banking Dr 22602
Brandon Dr & Pl 22601
Branner Ave & Cir 22601
Brannon Ford Rd 22603
Brass Kettle Ct 22603
Braveheart Trl 22602
Braxton Ct 22602
Breckinridge Ln 22601
Breezy Acres Ln 22602
Brenda Ct 22601
Briarmont Dr 22601
Briarwood Dr & Ln 22603
Brick Kiln Rd 22601
Bridgeport Ln 22602
Bridle Path Rd 22602
Brigstock Dr 22602
Brimstone Ln 22602
Bristol Dr 22603
Broad Ave 22602
Broadview St 22601
Brockham Ct 22602
Bronze Manor Ct 22603
Brookdale Ct 22601
W Brooke Rd 22603
Brookfield Dr 22601
Brookland Ct, Ln & Ter 22602
Brookneil Dr 22602
Brown St 22602
Bruce Dr & St 22601
Brush Creek Rd 22603
Bryarly Rd 22603
Bucher Run Ln 22602
Buckhorn Ln 22602
Buckner Dr 22601
Bucksaw Ln 22603
Buckskin Trl 22602
Buckwood Ln 22602
Buffalo Trl 22602
Bufflick Rd 22602
Bumble Bee Ln 22602
Buntline Dr 22602
Burnt Church Rd 22603
Bush Dr 22602
Butler Ave 22601
Butterhouse Way 22602
Butterscotch Ct 22602
C W Cir 22602
Cabin Ln 22603
Cahille Dr 22602
Caldwell Ln 22603
Caliber Ct 22603
Calico Ct 22602
Cambridge Pl 22601
Camden Dr 22602
Cameo Ter 22603
N & S Cameron St 22601
Campfield Ln 22602
Campus Blvd 22601
Candlewick Dr 22602
Cannon Cir 22602
Canter Ct 22603
Canterbury Ln 22603
Canyon Rd 22602
Capitol Ln 22602
Cardinal Dr & Ln 22602
Caribou Trl 22602
Carlos Ct 22603
Cammore Dr 22602
Caroline St 22601
Carpers Dr 22603
Carpers Valley Rd 22602
Carrollton Ln 22602
Carter Cir & Pl 22602
Carters Ln 22602
Cassidy Ct 22601
Cast Iron Ct 22602
Castlebridge Ct 22602
Castleman Dr 22601
Catalpa Rd 22603
Cather Ave 22601
Cather Ln 22602
Cattail Rd 22603
Cavalry Dr 22602
Cecil Ln 22603
E Cecil St 22601
W Cecil St 22601
Cedar Cir 22601
Cedar Creek Forest Ln 22602
Cedar Creek Grade
500-999 22601
Cedar Creek Grade
1002-5900 22602
5902-5998 22602
1207-1-1207-1 22602
Cedar Grove Rd 22603
Cedar Hill Rd 22603
E & W Cedarmeade Ave 22601
Center St 22601
Century Ln 22603
Chalcedony Ln 22602
Chalybeate Springs Rd 22603
Chamberlain Ct 22603
Champlain Pl 22603
Chandler Ct 22603
Channing Dr 22603
Chapman Ln 22603
Charles St 22601
Charlton Rd 22602
Charming Ct 22603
Charmwood Ln 22602
Chase St 22601
Chatham Sq 22601
Cheifton Pl 22602
Chelan Pl 22603
Chelsea Dr 22601
Cherokee Ct & Trl 22602
Cherry Hill Cir 22602
Cheshire Ct 22602
Chestnut St 22601
Chestnut Grove Rd 22603
Cheyenne Trl 22602
Chickadee Ln 22603
Chipmonk Ct 22603
Chipmonk Trl 22602
Chippewa Trl 22602
Christopher Dr 22601
Cidermill Ln 22601
Circle Dr 22601
Circle St 22603
Cives Ln 22603
Clarendon Ct 22602
Clark St 22601
Clarkville Dr 22603
Clayhill Dr 22602
Clayton Dr 22603
Clayton Ridge Dr 22601
Clevenger Ct 22601
E & W Clifford St 22601
Cliffwood Trl 22602
Clocktower Ridge Dr 22603
Cloverdale Ct 22602
Cluseret Ct 22603
Cobble Stone Dr 22602
Cochise Trl 22602
Cody Dr 22602
Cole Ln 22602
Colin Ct & Dr 22601
Colston Pl 22601
Comanche Trl 22602
Combe Dr 22602
Commerce St 22601
W Commercial St 22601
Commonwealth Ct 22602
Comstock Ct 22603
Confederate Dr 22603
Conner Ln 22602
Conrad Ct 22603
Contented Ct 22603
Conway St 22601
Coolfont Ln 22602
Coopers Ln 22602
Copperfield Ln 22602
Copperhead Ln 22602
E & W Cork St 22601
Cornerstone Cir 22601
Cornstalk Trl 22602
Cornwallis Ct 22601
Costello Dr 22602
Cottage Dr 22603
Cotton Ridge Rd 22603
Cottonwood Dr 22603
Cougar Trl 22602
Country Club Cir 22602
Country Park Dr 22602
Country Squire Ln 22603
Court Sq 22601
Courtfield Ave 22601
Coverstone Dr 22602
Covington Ln 22601
Cranberry Ct 22602
Creekside Ln 22602
Creepy Crow Ln 22603
Creola Dr 22603
Crescent Dr 22601
Crest Cir 22602
Crestleigh Dr 22602
Crestview Ter 22601
Crestwood Ln 22602
Cricket Ln 22602
Crimson Dr 22603
Crinoline Ln 22603
Crisman Ave 22601
Crispin Trl 22603
Crock Wells Mill Dr 22603
Cromwell Ct 22602
Crosscreek Ln 22602
Crossing Paths Ln 22602
Crossway Dr 22603
Crow Dr 22602
Crystal Ct 22601
Cub Trl 22602
Curt Wood Ln 22603
Custer Ave 22602
Cutshaws Ct 22603
Dairy Corner Pl 22602
Dakota Trl 22602
Dale Ct 22602
Dalton Pl 22601
Daniel Ter 22601
Darby Dr 22602
Darlington Dr 22603
Darrview St 22601
Dawn Heights Trl 22603
Dawson Dr 22602
Day Dr 22603
De Sant Cir 22603
Deer Trl 22602
Deer Creek Ct & Rd 22602
Deer Haven Pl 22602
Deer Run Dr 22602
Delaware Trl 22602
Delco Plz 22602
Dell Ct 22602
Delmas Trl 22602
Denny Ln 22603
Development Ln 22602
Devland Dr 22603
Dewberry Dr 22602
Diamond Ct 22602
Diamondback Ln 22602
Dicks Hollow Rd 22603
Diehl St 22601
Dinkle Dr 22601
Dixie Belle Dr 22602
Dodge Ave 22602
Doe Ct & Trl 22602
Dogwood Rd & Trl 22602
Dolan Ct 22603
Donegal Ct 22602
Donna Cir 22602
Doobeg Ct 22602
Doolin Ave 22602
Dots Way 22602
Double Hitch Ln 22603
Douglas St 22601
Dover Dr 22602
Dowell J Cir 22602
Draper Ave 22603
Dreamcatcher Dr 22603
Dry Creek Ln 22603
Dulles Cir 22601
Dunbar Ln & St 22603
Duner Ct 22602
Dunlap St 22601
Durham Way 22602
Dustin Dr 22603
Dusty Ln 22602
Dutch Apple Dr 22602
Dutton Pl 22601
Duwamish Trl 22602
Dwayne Pl 22603
Eagle Dr 22601
Eagle Pl 22601
Eagle Trl 22602
Eagle Way 22602
Early Dr 22603
N & S East Ln & St 22601
Easter Ridge Ln 22603
Eastside Ln 22602
Ebert Rd 22603
Echo Ln 22603
Echota Trl 22602
Eckard Cir 22602
Eddys Ln 22602
Edgewood Dr 22602
Edmonson Ln 22602
Edwards Ln 22603
Elaine Dr 22602
Elderberry Ct & Dr 22603
Eleanor Ln 22602
Elk Trl 22602
Elm St 22601
Elmwood Rd 22602
Emily Ln 22602
Enchanting Dr 22603
Enfield Dr 22602
Erie Trl 22602
Estate Dr 22603
Etnam St 22602
Ettawah Trl 22602
N & S Euclid Ave 22601
Evans Farm Ln 22603
Evening Ln 22603

Everette Pl 22602
Evette Pl 22602
Ewell Dr 22602
Ewell St 22601
Exeter Dr 22603
Fair Ln 22603
E & W Fairfax Ln 22601
Fairfield Dr 22602
Fairmont Ave 22601
Fairview Ave 22601
Fairway Dr 22602
Falcon Dr & Trl 22602
Fall Run Ln 22602
Farmer Jebs Ln 22603
Farmington Blvd 22602
Farrier Ln 22602
Farris Ln 22603
Farwood Trl 22602
Fawcetts Run Ln 22602
Fawn Dr & Trl 22602
Fay St 22602
Featherbed Ln 22601
Fenwick Ct 22602
Fern Ct 22602
Fiddler Ave 22603
Fieldstone Dr 22603
Files Chapel Dr 22603
Finicky Ln 22602
Fir Trl 22602
Fire Tower Trl 22602
Firelock Ct 22602
Firewood Trl 22602
First St 22601
First Woods Dr 22603
Fishel Rd 22602
Flanagan Dr 22602
Flathead Trl 22602
Fleetwood Ln 22602
Flegal Ln 22602
Flicker Ct 22602
Flint Ridge Ln 22602
Flowers Ln 22603
Foggy Mountain Dr 22603
Footstone Ln 22603
Foreman Ln 22603
Forest Ridge Rd 22602
Forest Valley Ct & Rd 22602
Forianda Rd 22603
Forked Horn Trl 22602
Forrest Dr 22603
Fort Braddock Ct 22601
Fort Collier Rd
100-499 22603
500-598 22601
501-599 22603
600-799 22601
Fortress Dr 22603
Four Wheel Dr 22602
Fout Ln 22603
W Fowler Dr 22603
Fox Ct 22603
Fox Dr
100-613 22601
614-899 22603
Fox Trl 22602
Fox Meadow Ln 22602
Fox Run Ln 22602
Foxbury Ln 22602
Foxglove Dr 22602
Foxridge Ln 22603
Frances Cir 22602
Franklin St 22601
Frederick Ave 22601
N Frederick Pike 22603
Freedom Cir 22602
Fremont St 22601
Fries Ln 22603
Fries Loop Rd 22602
Frog Hollow Rd 22603
Frogale Ct 22602
Fromans Rd 22602
Front Dr 22602
Front Royal Pike 22602
Frontage Rd 22601
Full House Dr 22603
Furnace Dr & Rd 22602
Furrow Field Ct 22602
Gainesboro Rd 22603
Gannentaha Trl 22602
Garber Ln 22602
Garden Ct 22601
Gateway Dr 22603
Gatling Dr 22602
Gazelle Trl 22602
Gemstone Dr 22602
Genesee Trl 22602
Geneva Pl 22603
George Dr 22602
George St 22601
E & W Germain St 22601
Germany Rd 22602
Geronimo Trl 22602
E & W Gerrard St 22601
Getty Ln 22603
Gibbens St 22601
Gilmore Trl 22602
Ginger St 22602
Glaize Ave 22601
Glaize Orchard Rd 22603
Glass Spring Ln 22602
Glen Lea Ct 22601
Glen Ridge Rd 22602
Glendale Cir 22602
Glendobbin Ln & Rd 22603
Glengary Rd 22603
Glenridge Dr 22602
Glentawber Dr 22603
Gloucester Dr 22603
Gobblers Knob Ln 22602
Godwin Ct 22602
Goldenfield Ln 22601
Goldenrod Rd 22603
Golds Hill Rd 22603
Gooseberry Dr 22602
Gordon Pl 22601
Gough Rd 22602
Graber Ln 22603
Grace St 22601
Grange Ln 22602
Grannies Ln 22603
Granville Ct 22602
Gray Ave 22601
Graystone Ln 22603
Graywolf Trl 22602
Great Mountain Ln 22602
Great Pond Way 22603
Green St 22601
Green Park Ct & Dr 22602
Green Spring Ct, Dr & Rd 22603
Greenfield Ave 22602
Greenfield Dr 22603
Greenway Ct 22602
Greenwood Ave & Rd 22602
Gregory Pl 22603
Greyhawk Dr 22602
Greystone Ter 22601
Grindstone Dr 22602
Grocery Ave 22602
Grouse Dr 22602
Grove St 22601
Guildhall Way 22603
Gun Barrel Ln 22603
Haddox St 22601
Haines Dr 22603
Hammack Ln 22602
Hampton Ct 22601
Handley Ave 22601
Handley Blvd 22601
Handley Dr 22603
Hanging Tree Rd 22603
Hannah Ct 22603
Hardwood Trl 22602
Harold Ct 22602
Harpers Hollow Ln 22603
Harrelson Pl 22603
Harrison Ln 22602
Harrison St 22601
Harrow Ln 22603
E Hart St 22601
W Hart St 22601
Hart Trl 22602
Harvard Dr 22602
Harvest Dr 22601
Harvest Ridge Dr 22601
Hastings St 22601
Haven Ter 22602
Hawk Trl 22602
Hawthorne Dr 22601
N Hayfield Rd 22603
S Hayfield Rd 22602
Heartwood Dr 22602
Heath Ct 22602
Heather Hill Ln 22603
Heathrow Ln 22601
Hedrick Ln 22602
Heishman Ln 22602
Helen Cir 22602
Hemlock Trl 22602
Henry Ave 22601
Henry Dr 22602
Herman Lewis Ln 22603
Heth Pl 22601
Hiatt Rd 22603
Hiawatha Trl 22602
Hickory Ln 22603
Hickory Trl 22602
Hidden Valley Ln 22603
High Tail Ln 22603
Highland Ave 22601
Highpointe Ct 22602
Highview Cir 22602
W Hill Ln 22603
Hill Valley Dr 22602
Hillandale Rd 22602
Hillman Dr 22601
Hillside Ter 22601
Hilltop Ter 22602
Hites St 22602
Hockman Ave 22601
Hockman Ct 22602
Hodges Ln 22603
Hogue Creek Ln 22603
Holiday Rd 22603
Holliday Dr 22601
Hollingsworth Dr & Pl 22601
Homeplace Ct 22602
Homer Dr 22602
Homestead Farm Ln 22602
Honeysuckle Ln 22601
Hood Way 22602
Hope Dr 22601
Horizon Dr 22602
Hornet Dr 22602
Horseshoe Ct 22602
Howards Chapel Rd 22603
Hudson Ave 22603
Huffman Hollow Ln 22602
Hunsper Ln 22603
Huntcrest Cir 22602
Hunter Run Rd 22602
Huntersridge Rd 22602
Hunting Rd 22603
Hunting Ridge Rd 22603
Huron Trl 22602
Ideal Pl 22603
Idylwood Dr 22602
Imboden Dr 22603
Imperial St 22601
Inca Trl 22602
Independence Rd 22602
N & S Indian Aly 22601
Indian Hollow Rd 22603
Indian Lake Rd 22603
Indiana Trl 22602
Industrial Dr 22602
Iris Ln 22602
Iroquois Trl 22602
Isaac St 22601
Ithaca Dr & Trl 22602
Ivy St 22601
Jackson Ave 22601
Jackson Dr 22602
Jalapa Trl 22602
E & W James St 22601
Janes Way 22602
Jeb Dr 22602
Jefferson St 22601
Jeni Ct 22602
Jennifer Ct 22603
Jessica Ln 22603
Jigsaw Pl 22601
Jireh Ln 22603
Johnston Ct 22601
Johnston Dr 22603
Joist Hite Pl 22601
Jones Rd 22602
Jones St 22601
Jordan Dr 22602
E & W Jubal Early Dr 22601
Judy Dr 22601
Julasar Dr 22602
Julee Dr 22602
Julie Ct 22602
Junco Ln 22602
Juniper Trl 22602
Kapok Cir 22602
Kassie Ln 22602
Kathleen Ct 22602
Kathy Ct 22601
Katie Ln 22602
Katydid Dr 22603
Kay Ct 22602
Keating Dr 22601
Kennedy Dr 22601
Kenny Ln 22602
N & S Kent Cir & St 22601
Kentmere Ct 22603
Kern St 22601
Kerns Aly 22601
Kernstown Ct 22601
Kernstown Commons Blvd 22602
Kershaw Ln 22601
Keswick Ct 22602
Keval Gyan Way 22603
Kevin Ct 22601
Killaney Ct 22602
Killbuck Trl 22602
Kimball Ct 22603
Kimberly Way 22601
Kinderal Rd 22602
King Ln 22602
Kingsland Ct 22602
Kingsley Dr 22602
Kingston Ct 22601
Kinross Dr 22602
Kinzel Dr 22601
Knight Dr 22602
Knollwood Ct 22602
Krag Dr 22602
La Costa Ct 22602
Lacewood Ln 22602
Ladderback Ct 22602
Ladyslipper Dr 22602
Lafayette Pl 22601
Lake Dr 22601
Lake Saint Clair Dr 22603
Lake Serene Dr 22603
Lake Sever Dr 22603
Lake Wisdom Dr 22603
Lakeville Cir 22603
Lamaster Ln 22602
Lambden Ave 22601
Landfill Rd 22602
Lanny Cir & Dr 22601
Larue Ln 22602
Latane St 22601
Lauck Dr 22603
Launchris Dr 22602
Laurel Grove Rd 22602
Laurelwood Dr 22602
Lavender Hills Ln 22603
Lay Cir 22602
Layside Dr 22602
Leafield Ct 22602
Leaning Oak Rd 22603
Lee Ave & St 22601
Legge Blvd 22601
E & W Leicester St 22601
Lemming Ln 22602
Lenoir Dr 22603
Lewis Cir 22602
Lewis St 22601
Liberty Ave 22601
Lickskillet Ln 22602
Light Rd 22603
Lighthouse Ln 22602
Lightwood Ct 22602
Likens Way 22602
Lilac Ln 22602
Lilys Way 22602
Limestone Ct 22601
Limestone Ln 22602
Lincoln St 22601
Linden Dr 22601
Lisas Dr 22603
Little Mountain Church Rd 22603
Little Pond Ln 22603
Little River Dr 22602
Liza Kates Ln 22603
Llama Ln 22603
Lloyds Rd 22602
Lockhart Cir 22603
Locust Ave 22601
Locust Trl 22602
Lodge Ln 22603
Lomax Dr 22601
Long Green Ln 22603
Longcroft Rd 22602
Longstreet Ave 22603
Longview Ave 22601
Longview Ln 22602
N Loudoun St
1-199 22601
132-132 22604
201-901 22601
202-798 22601
S Loudoun St 22601
Loy Cir 22602
Loyalty Ct 22601
Ludlow Dr 22602
Lugano Pl 22603
Lunette St 22603
Lynnehaven Dr 22602
Madigan Ln 22602
Magic Mountain Rd 22602
Magruder Ct 22601
Mahlon Dr 22603
Mahone Dr 22601
Maitland Ct 22602
Mala Ln 22602
Mall Barn Ln 22602
Maloy Dr 22602
Manito Trl 22602
Manitou Ct 22603
Manor Dr 22602
Maple St 22601
Maple Trl 22602
Mara Ln 22603
Maranto Manor Dr 22602
Marathon Dr 22602
Marcel Dr 22602
Mareth Ct 22602
Margaret Ln 22603
Margate Ct 22602
Margies Way 22603
Marion Dr 22603
Marion St 22601
Market St 22603
Marlin Dr 22602
Marlise Ln 22602
Marple Rd 22603
Marquis Ct 22603
Marriott Dr 22603
Marshall Ln 22602
Martin Dr 22602
Martinsburg Pike
900-1039 22601
1040-2400 22603
2402-2498 22603
1305-1-1305-2 22603
Mason St 22602
Massanutten Ter 22601
Massie Dr 22602
Masterpiece Ln 22602
Masters Ln 22601
Mate Ct 22602
Matthew Ct 22603
Mauser Dr 22602
May Cir 22602
Mccanns Rd 22603
Mccarty Ln 22602
Mcclure Way 22602
Mccubbin Rd 22603
Mcdonald Rd 22602
Mcfarland Rd 22602
Mcghee Rd 22603
Mcguire Rd 22603
Mcneil Pl 22603
Meade Dr 22602
Meadow Ct 22601
Meadow Ln 22602
Meadow Branch Ave 22601
Meadowbrooke Pl 22602
Meadowlark Ct 22602
Meadowview Ct 22602
Medical Cir 22601
Meeting House Dr 22602
Melissa Ave 22602
Melvor Ln 22601
Memory Ln 22603
Mercedes Ct 22603
Merchant St 22603
Merrifield Ln 22602
Merrimans Ln
1-761 22601
762-998 22602
763-799 22601
1000-1699 22602
Merrimans Pl 22601
Mesquite Ct 22602
Mews Ln 22601
Middle Rd
2201-2297 22601
2299-2882 22601
2883-5899 22602
Mikey Ct 22601
Milam Dr 22602
Milburn Rd 22603
Milhon Ln 22602
Mill Race Dr 22602
Mill Stone Cir 22602
Millbrook Rd 22603
Miller Rd 22602
Miller St 22601
Millwood Ave 22601
Millwood Pike 22602
Milroy Ct 22601
Milroy Dr 22602
Mimosa Trl 22602
Miracle Way 22603
Missy Brock Dr 22603
Misty Meadow Dr & Ln 22603
Mockingbird Ln 22603
Moffett Dr 22601
Mohawk Trl 22602
Molden Dr 22601
Monarch Ln 22603
Monet Ter 22602
E & W Monmouth St 22601
Monroes Cir 22602
Montague Ave & Cir 22601
Monticello Sq 22602
Monticello St 22601
Monument Dr 22603
Moon Ridge Ln 22603
Moonshine Run Dr 22602
Moorecroft Ln 22602
Moreland Dr 22601
Morgan St 22601
Morgan Mill Rd 22603
Morning Glory Dr 22602
Morningside Dr 22601
Mosby St 22601
Mount Olive Rd 22602
Mount Vista Dr 22602
Mount Williams Ln 22602
Mountain Falls Blvd & Rd 22602
Mountain Laurel Ln 22603
Mountain Lodge Dr 22602
Mountain View Ct 22603
Mountain View Dr 22603
Mountain View Ln 22602
Mountain View Rd 22603
Mulligan Ln 22603
Mummert Cir 22601
Murphy Ct 22602
Muse Dr 22603
Musket Dr 22602
Muskoka Ct 22602
Myers Ln 22603
Myersons Dr 22602
Myrtle Ave 22601
Nain Ln 22603
Narrow Ln 22602
Nassau Dr 22602
Nathaniel Dr 22603
National Ave 22601
National Lutheran Blvd 22603
Navajo Trl 22602
Nazarene Dr 22601
Neil Dr 22602
Nescliffe Ct 22602
Nester Dr 22601
Netherfield Ct 22602
Nettle Ln 22603
Newlins Hill Rd 22603
Norfolk Ct 22602
E North Ave 22601
W North Ave 22601
North Dr 22603
Northwestern Pike 22603
Nulton Ln 22603
Nutmeg Ln 22602
Oak Dr 22603
W Oak Ln 22602
Oak Ridge Ln 22602
Oak Side Ln 22603
Oakmont Cir 22602
Oakwood Ct 22601
E & W Oates Ave 22601
Obriens Cir 22602
Ohio Ave 22601
Okeefe Dr 22602
Old Baltimore Rd 22603
Old Bethel Ln 22603
Old Bethel Church Rd 22603
Old Dominion Dr 22603
Old Forest Cir 22602
Old Fort Rd 22601
Old Middle Rd 22602
Old Wagon Rd 22602
Omps Dr 22601
Opequon Ave & Ct 22601
Opequon Church Ln 22602
Opossum Trl 22602
Orchard Ave 22601
Orchard Dr 22602
Orchard Ln 22602
Orchard Hill Dr 22601
Orchard View Ln 22602
Orchid Ct 22602
Orion Ct 22602
Orkney Dr 22602
Otter Trl 22602
Outback Ln & Trl 22602
Overseer Ln 22602
Pack Horse Rd 22603
Packer St 22601
Pactiv Way 22603
Page Ct 22602
E & W Pall Mall St 22601
Panarama Dr 22603
Pangborne Ct 22602
Panther Dr 22602
Papermill Rd
2200-3217 22601
3218-3799 22602
Park Center Dr 22603
Parkins Ln 22602
E & W Parkins Mill Rd 22602
Parkside Dr 22602
Parkview Ave 22601
Parkway St 22601
Parkwood Cir 22602
Parrish Ln 22601
Parson Ct 22603
Passage Rd 22602

Pasture Ln 22602
Patsy Cline Blvd 22601
Patterson Ave 22601
Paw Paw Ct 22603
Payne Rd 22603
Peace Field Ln 22603
Peach Orchard Ln 22602
Pebble Brook Ln 22602
Peeper Ln 22603
Pegasus Ct 22602
Pemberton Dr 22601
Pembridge Dr 22602
Pendleton Dr 22602
Pennsylvania Ave 22601
Peppermint Spring Ln 22603
Peppertree Ln 22601
Perry Rd 22602
Peyton St 22601
Phalen Dr 22603
Pheasant Dr 22602
Phelpsmore Ln 22602
Philpot St 22601
E & W Piccadilly St 22601
Pierenco Ave 22601
Pikeside Ln 22603
Pileated Ln 22603
Pilot Cir 22602
Pin Oak Ln 22601
Pine St 22601
Pine Trl 22602
Pine Crest Ln 22603
Pinehill Dr 22603
Pingley Ln 22602
Pinnacle Ridge Rd 22602
Pinto Trl 22602
Pioneers Rd 22602
Pitcock Ln 22602
Plainfield Dr 22602
Plantation Dr 22602
W Plaza Dr 22601
N Pleasant Valley Rd
1-7 22601
9-341 22601
340-340 22604
343-699 22601
400-698 22601
S Pleasant Valley Rd 22601
Pocahontas Trl 22602
Pond View Ln 22603
Pondview Dr 22601
Poorhouse Rd
100-199 22602
200-999 22603
Poplar Trl 22602
Possum Draw Pl 22603
Potomac Pl 22602
Potomak Trl 22602
Powhatan Trl 22602
Precision Dr 22603
Premier Pl 22602
Price Dr 22602
Primrose Pl 22602
Prince Frederick Dr 22602
Prince George Pl 22601
Princess Ct 22601
Princeton Dr 22602
Pritchards Hill Ct 22601
Procession Way 22603
Proclamation Dr 22603
Prominence Cir 22603
Prosperity Dr 22602
Providence Dr 22602
Puma Trl 22602
N Purcell Ave 22601
S Purcell Ave 22601
Purcell Ln 22603
Purdue Dr 22602
Pyramid Dr 22603
Quail Dr 22602
Quail Run Ln 22602
Quaker Ln 22603
Quartzite Cir 22601
Quiet Meadow Ln 22603
Quigley Ct 22602
Rabbit Hill Ln 22603
Raccoon Dr 22602
Race St 22601
Racey Ridge Dr 22602
Rainville Rd 22602
Raleigh Ct 22601
Ramseur Ln 22601
Randolph Pl 22601
Range Ct 22602
Ranger Ct 22602
Rappahannock Trl 22602
Rawlings Ave 22603
Reardon Rd 22602
Reaves St 22601
Rebecca Dr 22602
Rebels Cir 22602
Red Fox Trl 22602
Redbud Rd 22603
W Redoubt Ln 22603
Redwood Ln 22603
Regency Lakes Dr 22603
Remey Ave 22602
Remington Dr 22602
Renee Ln 22602
Rest Church Rd 22603
Retreat Ln 22603
Richards Ave 22601
Ricketts Dr 22601
Ridge Ave 22601
Ridge Ct 22603
Ridge Rd 22602
Ridgecrest Ct 22602
Ridgetop Ct 22601
Riflemen Ln 22601
Riggers Dr 22603
Ritter Rd 22602
Rivendell Ct 22603
Roanoke Ln 22602
Roberts Ln 22603
Roberts St 22601
Robin Hood Cir 22603
Robinson Dr 22602
Robyn Ter 22601
Rock Harbor Dr 22602
Rockland Dr 22601
Rockwall Trl 22602
Rockwood Trl 22602
Rocky Top Ln 22603
Rodes Cir 22601
Rolling Ridge Ln 22603
Ronner Ln 22603
Roosevelt Blvd 22601
Rosa Ln 22602
Rose Hill Cir 22602
Rosenberger Ln 22602
Rosewood Ln 22602
Ross St 22601
Rosser Ln 22602
Rossmann Blvd 22602
Rossum Ln 22602
Roszel Rd 22601
Round Hill Rd 22602
Rouss Ave 22601
Royal Ave 22602
Royal St 22601
Rubinette Way 22602
Rugby Pl 22603
Russelcroft Rd 22601
Rustic Wood Ln 22602
Ryco Ln 22602
Saddleback Ln 22602
Saint Andrews Ct 22602
Saint Clair Rd 22603
Salvo Ct 22603
Samary Ln 22602
Sanctuary Dr 22603
Sarah Anns Mountain Rd 22603
Saratoga Dr 22601
Savage Dr 22602
Sawyer Ln 22602
Scarlet Maple Dr 22603
Scenic Cir 22602
Schoolmarm Ln 22602
Scirocco Ln 22602
Scott St 22601
Seabreeze Ln 22602
Second St 22601
N Sector Ct 22601
Security Dr 22602
See Ln 22602
Seldon Dr 22601
Selma Dr 22601
Seneca Trl 22602
Senseny Rd 22602
Senseny Glen Dr 22602
Sentinel Dr 22603
Sentry Ct 22603
Serenity Ln 22602
Sesar Ct 22602
Settlers Cir 22602
Shadow Brook Ln 22603
Shadow Glen Ct 22603
Shady Elm Rd 22602
Shaffer Ln 22602
Shagbark Ridge Ln 22602
Shane Ln 22603
Shannon Ct 22602
Sharon Dr 22602
Sharp St 22601
Shawnee Ave 22601
Shawnee Ct 22602
Shawnee Dr
3078-A-3078-B 22601
2900-3103 22601
3105-3133 22601
3134-3399 22602
3078-1-3078-5 22601
3082-2-3082-3 22601
Shawnee Trl 22602
Sheffield Ct 22601
Shelby Ct 22602
Shenandoah Ave 22601
Shenandoah Pl 22601
Shenandoah Trl 22602
Sheridan Ave 22601
Sherlock Trce 22601
Sherwood Ln 22603
Shields Dr 22602
Shirley Ct 22603
Shirley St 22601
Shockey Cir 22602
Shockey Dr 22603
Shockeysville Rd 22603
Short St 22603
Signal Ridge Ln 22603
Siler Ln & Rd 22603
Silver Lake Ln 22603
Silverrod Ln 22603
Singhass Rd 22602
Skyjes Ln 22602
Skylar Lanes Way 22603
Skyview Ln 22603
Smelter Ln 22602
Smith Dr 22603
Smithfield Ave 22601
Snake Dr 22603
Snappy Ln 22602
Snyder Ln 22601
Sofia Way 22601
Soldiers Rest Ln 22602
Somerset St 22602
Songbird Ln 22603
Sorrel Ln 22602
Sorrell Ct 22601
Sotheby Ct 22602
South St 22601
E & W Southwerk St 22601
Spartan Ct 22603
Spaulding Dr 22603
Spencer Sq 22601
Spinning Wheel Ln 22603
Spirit Hollow Dr 22603
Spring St 22601
Spring Hill Ln 22603
Spring House Ct 22601
Spring Valley Dr 22603
Springdale Rd 22602
Spruce St 22601
Spruce Trl 22602
Stafford Dr 22602
Stag Trl 22602
Stanley Cir & Dr 22602
Star Fort Dr 22601
Steeplechase Ln 22602
Steepwood Ln 22603
Sterling Dr 22601
N & S Stewart St 22601
Stine Ln 22603
Stirrup Cup Cir 22602
Stone House Ct 22601
Stone Meadow Ct 22601
Stone Mill Ct 22601
Stone Ridge Ct 22602
Stonebrake Ln 22603
Stonebrook Rd 22602
Stonecrest Ct 22603
Stonedown Ln 22603
Stonegate Dr 22601
Stonehenge Rd 22601
Stoneleigh Dr 22601
Stoneridge Rd 22601
Stonewall Ave 22601
Stonewall Dr 22602
Stony Hill Rd 22603
Stonymeade Dr 22602
Stratford Dr 22601
Stuart Dr 22602
Sulgrave Ct 22602
Sulky Dr 22602
Sully Ct 22601
Sulphur Spring Rd 22602
Summerfield Dr 22602
Summerfield Ln 22601
Summit Ave 22601
Sunnyside Dr 22603
Sunnyside Plaza Dr 22603
Sunset Dr 22603
Sunshine Dr 22602
Superior Ave 22601
Susquehanna Trl 22602
Sutton Ct 22601
Sweetbriar Ln 22603
Tabbs Ln 22602
Taft Ave & Cir 22601
Taggart Dr 22602
Tailspin Cir 22602
Tamarack Cir 22602
Tanglewood Ln 22602
Tankard Ln 22603
Tanner Pl 22603
Tapestry Ln 22603
Tasker Rd 22602
Tavistock Dr 22602
Taylor Dr 22601
Taylor Grace Ct 22601
Teaberry Dr 22602
Tecumseh Trl 22602
Tennyson Ave 22601
Terrapin Ln 22602
Terrys Ln 22602
E & W Tevis St 22601
Tey Ct 22602
Theodore Dr 22602
Thomas Ct 22601
Thompson Ct 22602
Thrasher Ct 22602
Three Creeks Rd 22603
Throughwood Trl 22602
Thumper Trl 22603
Thunder Ridge Ln 22602
Thwaite Ln 22603
Tick Hill Ln 22602
Tilden Ct 22602
Tilford Dr 22602
Tilghman Ln 22601
Timber Ridge Trl 22602
Tinderbox Ln 22603
Tom Tom Trl 22602
Tomahawk Trl 22602
Tonto Trl 22602
Tori Ln 22603
Tower Ave 22601
Trade Wind Ln 22602
Tranquil Wood Ln 22602
Travis Ct 22602
Treetops Ln 22601
Trefoil Ct 22602
Trent Ct 22602
Treys Dr 22601
Tuckers Valley Dr 22603
Tucks Cir 22602
Tudor Dr 22603
Turtle Meadow Dr 22602
Tuscarora Rd 22603
Twin Hill Cir 22602
Twinbrook Cir 22602
Tyler Dr 22603
Tyson Dr 22603
Umpire Ln 22602
Underwood Ln 22602
Union View Ln 22603
University Dr 22601
Upland Rd 22603
Upper Ridge Rd 22603
Vale Ct 22602
Valley Ave 22601
Valley Pike
3595-A-3595-A 22602
3100-3128 22602
3130-4299 22602
3202-1-3202-2 22602
3223-1-3223-12 22602
3266-1-3266-1 22602
3283-1-3283-9 22602
3303-1-3303-1 22602
3383-1-3383-1 22602
4046-1-4046-3 22602
Valley Mill Rd 22602
Valley View Dr 22603
Valley View Ln 22602
Valley View Trl 22602
Valor Dr 22601
Valpro Dr 22603
Van Buren Ct & Pl 22602
Van Couver St 22601
Van Fossen St 22601
Van Gogh Ter 22602
Vanceright Cir 22601
Vassar Cir 22602
Victory Rd 22602
W View Ln 22601
Village Ct 22602
Vine Ln 22602
Vintage Ln 22602
Violet Ridge Dr 22603
W Virginia Ave & Pkwy 22601
Wal Mart Dr 22603
Wales Ct 22602
Walker Ct 22602
Walker St 22601
Walls Cir 22602
Walnut St 22601
Wandering Ln 22603
Ward Ave 22602
Wardensville Grade 22602
Ware Pl 22602
Warm Springs Rd 22603
Warner Dr 22603
N & S Washington St 22601
Washout Ln 22603
Waterford Ln 22602
Waterloo Ct 22602
Watson Ave 22601
Wayfaring Dr 22602
Wayland Dr 22601
Wayne Dr 22601
Weathervane Dr 22602
Weems Ln 22601
Weitzell Pl 22601
Well Drillers Ln 22603
Welltown Ct & Rd 22603
Wembley Ct 22603
Wentworth Dr 22601
West Ln & St 22601
Westbury Pl 22603
Westminster Canterbury Dr 22603
Westside Station Dr 22601
Westview Dr 22603
Westwood Cir & Dr 22602
Wharton Cir 22601
Wheatfield Ln 22601
Whipp Dr 22602
Whirlwind Dr 22602
Whiskey Bottom Ct 22603
Whispering Knolls Dr 22603
Whissens Ridge Rd 22602
Whistler Ct 22602
Whistlewood Ln 22602
Whitacre St 22601
White Rd 22602
White Clover Dr 22602
White Hall Rd 22603
White Pine Ln 22602
Whites Pl 22602
Whitetail Ln 22603
E & W Whitlock Ave 22601
Whittier Ave 22601
Wickham Ter 22602
Widener Dr 22603
Wild Rose Cir 22602
Wild Wood Dr 22603
Wildflower Ln 22602
Wildlife Ct 22603
Wilkins Dr & Pl 22602
Williams Cir & Pl 22603
Williamson Pl & Rd 22602
Willow Trl 22602
Willowbrook Ct 22602
Wilson Blvd 22601
Wilton Dr 22603
Winchester Dr 22602
Wincrest Dr 22602
Windchime Ln 22602
Windcrest Cir 22602
Winder Ct 22601
Winding Hill Rd 22603
Winding Ridge Ln 22603
Windmill Ln 22602
Windsor Ln 22602
Windstone Dr 22602
Windwood Dr 22601
Windy Hill Ln 22602
Windy Pine Dr & Ln 22603
Wineberry Dr 22603
Wingate Dr 22601
Winnepeg Pl 22603
Winns Cir 22602
Winslow Ct 22602
Winterberry Ct 22602
Wisecarver Ln 22602
Witch Hazel Trl 22602
Wolf Spring Trl 22602
Wolfe St 22601
Wollaston Dr 22603
Wood Ave & Cir 22601
Wood Rise Ln 22601
Woodberry Ln 22601
Woodbury Ct 22602
Woodchuck Ln 22602
Woodcrest Dr 22603
Woodfield Ln 22602
Woodland Ave 22601
Woodman Ct 22602
Woodridge Ln 22603
Woodrow Rd 22602
Woodside Ln 22603
Woodstock Ln
300-1199 22601
1500-1799 22602
Woodys Pl 22602
Wool Card Ln 22602
Worsham Ter 22602
E & W Wyck St 22601
Yale Dr 22602
Yarrow Ct 22602
Yeatras Dr 22602
York Ave 22601
Yorktowne Pl 22601
Youth Development Ct 22602
Zeiger Dr 22602
Zephyr Ln 22602

WOODBRIDGE VA

General Delivery 22191

POST OFFICE BOXES MAIN OFFICE STATIONS AND BRANCHES

Box No.s
A - Z 22194
AA - AF 22194
JK - JK 22194
NO - NO 22194
1 - 700 22194
1001 - 2819 22195
4000 - 5410 22194
6001 - 9998 22195

RURAL ROUTES

01, 02, 03, 04, 05, 06 22192

NAMED STREETS

Abbey Glen Ct 22192
Abbey Knoll Ct 22192
Abbott Ct 22193
Abbottsbury Way 22191
Abilene Way 22193
Abner Ave 22192
Acorn Ct 22193
Adair Ln 22192
Adams St 22193
Addison Ln 22193
Adelman Run Ct 22193
Aderman Ct 22192
Admeasure Cir 22191
Admiral Dr 22192
Adrian Ct 22191
Adrift Ct 22191
Aegean Ter 22192
Aetna Springs Rd 22193
Aiden Dr 22191
Akron St 22191
Alabama Ave 22191
Alaska Ct & Rd 22191
Albany Ct 22193
Alden Ct 22192
Aldrich Pl 22191
Aldrin St 22191
Alexis Ct & Rd 22191
Alford Valley Ln 22192
Alison St 22191
All Saints Pl 22192
Alliance Ln 22193
Allspice Ct 22192
Alps Dr 22193
Altomare Trace Way 22193
Alton Hotel Ct 22192
Altus Ct 22191
Amanda Rose Ln 22193
Amara Pl 22192
Amaranth Ct 22193
Ambergate Dr 22193
American Eagle Blvd 22191
Ames Ct 22191
Amesbury St 22192
Anchor Ct 22192
Anchor Bend Cir 22191
Anchorstone Dr 22192
Anderson Ct & St 22193
Andes Ct 22193
Andorra Dr 22193
Andover Ct 22192
Andover Heights Dr 22193
Andrus Dr 22193
Andy Ct 22193
Ann Arden Ave 22193
Ann Scarlet Ct 22191
Annapolis Way 22191
Anns Brook Ct 22191
Anthony Dr 22193
Antietam Rd 22192
Antwerp Ct 22192
Apollo Dr
12600-12799 22192
12800-12899 22193
Appaloosa Dr 22192
Arabian Pl 22192
Arbor Ct 22193
Archelon Way 22193
Archer Ct 22193
Arden Ct 22191
Ardmore Loop 22193
Aris Ct 22193

Arizona Ave & Ct 22191
Arkansas Ct & St 22191
Arkendale St 22193
Arles Pl 22192
Armada Pl 22192
Armitage Ct 22191
Armstead St 22191
Arrowhead Ct 22192
Artery Ln 22193
Arum Pl 22191
Ascot Ct 22192
Asdee Ln 22192
Ashby Ct 22192
Ashdale Ave & Cir 22193
Ashford Pl 22191
Ashmont Ct 22192
Ashwood Ct 22193
Atwood Dr 22192
Aubrey Glen Ter 22192
Auburn Hills Dr 22193
Augustus Ct 22192
Aurora Dr 22193
Austin Ct 22193
Austra Pl 22193
Averet St 22191
Aviary Way 22192
Avocet Loop 22191
Ayrshire Ln 22191
Azalea Ln 22191
Aztec Pl 22192
Babbitt Ln 22193
Bacon Race Rd 22192
Bacons Castle Ct 22193
Bakersfield St 22193
Bald Eagle Ln 22191
Bali Ct 22192
Ballast Ln 22191
Balls Bluff Ct 22193
Balsam St 22191
Bambi Ct 22193
Bancroft Ln 22192
Banjo Ct 22193
Bannon Way 22193
Bantry Ct 22193
Barcelona Ct 22191
Barge Cir 22191
Barkham Dr 22191
Barksdale St 22193
Barkwood Dr 22193
Barn Swallow Pl 22191
Barnabas Trl 22193
Barnes Ln 22193
Barnes Edge Ct 22193
Barnes Meadows Ct 22193
Barrister Pl 22192
Barrows Ln 22192
Barton Ct 22193
Basin St 22191
Basin View Ln 22191
Basque Pl 22192
Bateman Ct 22192
Bath Ct 22193
Batley Pl 22192
Battery Hill Cir 22191
Baxter St 22191
Bay Cir & St 22191
Bay Vista Dr 22191
Bayfield Dr 22193
Baylor St 22193
Bayou Wood Cir 22192
Bayside Ave 22191
Bayview Dr 22191
Beachview Creek Dr 22192
Beacon Ridge Dr 22191
Beale Ct 22193
Beau Ridge Dr 22193
Beaufont Spring Ct 22192
Beaumont Rd 22193
Beaver Ford Rd 22192
Beaver Pond Rd 22192
Beaverwood Pl 22192
Bedford Cove Ln 22192
Bedford Glen Way 22192
Beechnut Ct 22192
Beechtree Ln 22191
Beegee Ct 22192
Bel Air Rd 22191
Bel Aire Estates Pl 22193
Belfield Ct 22192
Belfry Ln 22192
Bell Ct 22193
Belle View Rd 22191
Belleville Ave 22193
Bellflower Ct 22193
Bellona Rd 22191
Belmont Dr 22191
Belmont Bay Dr 22191
Belvedere Dr 22193
Belwood Ln 22193
Benbow Ct 22193
Benedict Ct 22191
Benita Fitzgerald Dr 22193
Bentley Cir 22192
Benton St 22193
Berkley Ln 22193
Berkshire Dr 22193
Berlin Ct 22193
Bertram St 22192
Berwick Pl 22192
Bethel Church Dr 22192
Bevanwood Dr 22193
Bicycle Pl 22193
Big Crest Ln 22191
Binder Ct 22193
Birch White Ct 22193
Birchdale Ave & Sq 22193
Bird Watch Ct 22191
Bisbee Ct 22193
Bismark Ave 22193
Bison Ct 22192
Bixby Rd 22193
Bixley Hill Ct 22191
Bjork Ln 22192
Black Forest Ln 22192
Blackburn Rd 22191
Blackjack Oak Ln 22191
Blacksmith Ter 22191
Blair Ct 22193
Blasius Ct 22193
Blazer Loop 22193
Bloomfield Dr 22193
Bloomsbury Ct 22192
Blue Jay Ct 22193
Blue Pool Dr 22191
Bluefin Dr 22193
Bluff View Ct 22192
Blysdale Ln 22192
Blyth Ct 22193
Boaters Cove Pl 22191
Boatswain Cir 22191
Bobcat Ct 22193
Bobolink Dr 22191
Bobster Ct 22191
Bogner Dr 22193
Bolling Brook Ct 22191
Bolton Overlook Ct 22192
Bombay Way 22192
Bonita Ct 22193
Bonneville Ln 22193
Bonny Rd 22192
Bordeaux Pl 22192
Bottner Ct 22191
Botts Ave 22191
Bountiful Ln 22193
Bowes Ln 22193
Bowline Loop 22192
Bowman Ct 22193
Box Turtle Ct 22193
Boyd Ct 22193
Bracknell Dr 22192
Braddock Dr 22193
Bradford St 22193
Bradiant Dr 22193
Brahms Dr 22193
Bramblewood Ln 22191
Brandon Ct 22193
Brandy Moor Loop 22191
Brazil Cir 22193
Brazilnut Ct 22193
Breckinridge Ln 22192
Breezy Ridge Way 22191
Bremen Ct 22191
Bremerton Dr 22193
Brentwood Ct 22193
Brewster Cir 22192
Briar Rose Ln 22192
Brice St 22191
Brice House Ct 22192
Brickert Pl 22192
Brickwood Dr 22193
Bridge View Dr 22191
Bridgeton Ct 22192
Bridle Creek Rd 22193
Brier Pond Cir 22191
Briggs Way 22193
Brightleaf Ct 22193
Brightwood Ln 22193
Bristol Cir 22192
Bristol Ct 22193
Briton Ct 22192
Brittany Ct 22192
Broker Ln 22193
Bromley Ct 22192
Bronco Way 22193
Bronson Ct 22193
Brook Dr 22193
Brooke Farm Ct 22192
Brookmoor Ln 22191
Brookside Ct 22191
Brookville Ln 22192
Brookway Ct 22192
Brunswick Ct 22191
Brussels Way 22192
Bryan Ct 22193
Buchanan Ct 22192
Buck Board Ct 22192
Buckley Ct 22192
Buena Ct 22193
Buffalo Ct 22193
Bufflehead Ct 22193
Build America Dr 22191
Bulkhead Dr 22191
Buoy Ct 22191
Burbank Ln 22193
Burgundy Pl 22192
Burke Dr 22191
Burleigh Ln 22193
Burning Ridge Ct 22192
Burntwood Ct 22191
Burrough Hill Ln 22191
Burton St 22191
Bushey Dr 22193
Buttonwood Ct 22193
Bybrook Ln 22192
Cadbury Way 22191
Cagney Ct 22193
Cairo Pl 22192
Caisson Ct 22192
Caleb Ct 22192
Caledonia Cir 22192
Calexico Ln 22193
California St 22191
Calla Ct 22191
Callao Ct 22191
Callee Way 22192
Calloway Ct 22192
Caloosa Way 22193
Calvert St 22191
Cambridge Dr 22192
Campbell Ln 22193
Canada Goose Loop 22191
Canary Ct 22193
Candlewood Ct 22191
Cannon Bluff Dr 22192
Cannons Ct 22191
Cantania Pl 22192
Cantilever Ct 22192
Canvasback Ct 22191
Cape Cod Ct 22192
Caperton Ct 22193
Capon Tree Ln 22191
Captains Ct & Cv 22192
Cara Dr 22192
Cardamom Dr 22192
Cardiff Ct 22192
Cardin Pl 22193
Cardinal Dr 22193
Cardinal Crest Dr 22193
Cardinal Ridge Ct 22192
Carlsbad Rd 22193
Carly Ln 22192
Carmody Pl 22193
Caroline Ct & St 22191
Carolyn Forest Dr 22192
Carroll Ave 22191
Carson Dr 22193
Carter Ln 22191
Carthage Dr 22191
Carveth Pl 22191
Cascabel Ct 22192
Cascade Way 22192
Cass Brook Ln 22191
Cassandra Ct 22192
Cast Off Loop 22191
Castile Ct 22192
Castle Ct 22193
Castle Hill Dr 22193
Castlebridge Ln 22193
Catalpa Ct 22193
Catawba Dr 22192
Catbrier Ct 22193
Catenary Dr 22191
Cathedral Dr 22192
Catoctin Dr 22192
Caton Hill Rd 22192
Cavalier Dr 22193
Cavallo Way 22192
Cave Ct 22192
Cebu Island Ct 22192
Cecilia Ct 22191
Cedar Cove Way 22191
Cedar Crest Ct 22192
Cedarwood Ct 22192
Celestial Dr 22191
Centerpointe Way 22193
Central Loop 22193
Central Park Dr 22193
Chablis Cir 22192
Chadwick Ct 22192
Chalet Ct 22192
Chamberlain Pl 22191
Chambord Ln 22193
Chanceford Dr 22192
Chancellor Dr 22192
Chandon Cross Rd 22193
Chaparral Dr 22192
Chapel Hill Ct 22191
Charing Ct 22192
Charity Ct 22193
Charles Ct 22191
Charles Ewell Ln 22193
Charlton Ct 22193
Charmed Ct 22192
Charter Ct 22192
Chase Eagle Ln 22191
Chaste Tree Pl 22192
Chatsford Ct 22191
Chattanooga Ln 22191
Chaucer Ln 22192
Chelmer Ct 22192
Chelsea Dr 22192
Chelson Ln 22192
Cheltenham Ct 22192
Cherborg Pl 22192
Cherrydale Dr 22193
Cherrywood Dr 22192
Cheshire Station Plz 22193
Chesley Pl 22191
Chester Cir 22193
Chesterfield Dr 22191
Cheswald Ct 22192
Chetham Way 22192
Chevington Ct 22191
Chevoit Hill Ct 22191
Chicacoan Dr 22193
Chickadee Ct 22193
Chickasaw Ct 22192
Chico Ct 22193
Chicory Ct 22193
Chimera Pl 22191
Chimney Rock Ter 22193
Chincoteague Ct 22193
Chinkapin Oak Ln 22191
Chinn Park Dr 22192
Chippendale Cir 22193
Choate Ct 22193
Choctaw Ridge Ct 22192
Choir St 22192
Chopawamsic Ct 22191
Chowning Ct 22191
Christopher Pl 22192
Christy Ln 22193
Chrysler Ct 22193
Chula Pl 22193
Church Hill Dr 22191
Churchman Way 22192
Cinnamon St 22192
Cismont Ct 22192
Claremont Ln 22193
Clarinet Ct 22191
Clarkford Ct 22192
Classic Ct 22192
Cleburne Ln 22192
Cleeve Hill Ct 22191
Clipper Dr 22192
Clore Pl 22192
Cloverdale Rd 22193
Cloyd Way 22193
Club Ct 22192
Coachman Ter 22191
Cobb Ct 22191
Cobia Ct 22193
Code Way 22192
Cohasset Ln 22192
Colby Dr 22192
Colchester Rd 22191
Colchester Ferry Pl 22191
Colder Ln 22193
Colebrook Ct & Ln 22192
Colfax Rd 22191
Colgate Ct 22192
Collington Ct 22191
Collingwood Ct 22192
Colonel Tansill Ct 22193
Colonial Dr 22192
Colonnade Ct 22192
Colony Pl 22191
Colony Creek Ct 22193
Colorado Ave 22191
Colt Foot Ct 22193
Columbia Rd 22191
Comeash Ct 22192
Commission Ct 22192
Commitment Ct 22193
Compass Cir 22191
Comus Ct 22193
Concord Dr 22193
Condor Ln 22192
Congress St 22191
Conquest Ct 22192
Conrad Ct 22191
Constellation Pl 22191
Constitution Cir 22192
Copper Turtle Pl 22193
Coppersmith Ter 22191
Corbett Pl 22191
Corbin Ct 22191
Corcyra Ct 22192
Cordelia Ct 22192
Cordell Ave 22193
Corinthia Ct 22192
Cornell Ct 22192
Cornice Pl 22192
Corona Ln 22193
Corsair Dr 22193
Costa Dr 22193
Cotton Ln 22193
Cotton Mill Dr 22192
Cotton Tail Ct 22191
Cottonwood Ct 22191
County Complex Ct 22192
Courage Dr 22193
Course View Way 22191
Courtlandt Heights Rd 22193
Cove Landing Dr 22191
Coventry Glen Dr 22192
Covered Bridge Ln 22192
Cowes Mews 22193
Coxcomb Mews 22193
Crabapple Ct 22192
Crag Mews 22193
Cranes Bill Way 22191
Cranmer Mews 22193
Creek Moor Ct 22191
Creekview Cir 22192
Creel Ct 22192
Crescent St 22193
Cressida Pl 22192
Crest Ct & Dr 22191
Crest Maple Dr 22192
Crest Ridge Way 22192
Cricket Ln 22192
Cridercrest Pl 22191
Cristina Ct 22192
Critton Cir 22192
Croaker Ln 22193
Cromwell Ct 22192
Cronin Dr 22191
Crossfield Way 22191
Crossing Pl 22192
Crosswater Ct 22192
Crotona Ct 22193
Crown Ct 22193
Cuddy Loop 22193
Culbreth Ct 22192
Cullers Ct 22192
Culpeper Dr 22191
Cumberland Dr 22191
Cummings Ct 22193
Custis Sq & St 22191
Cutter Way 22191
Cyclamen Ct 22193
D St 22191
Dabney Rd 22191
Daisy Reid Ave 22192
Dale Blvd 22193
Daley Ln 22193
Danbury Ct 22193
Dandridge Pl 22191
Dane Ridge Cir 22193
Daniel K Ludwig Dr 22191
Daniel Stuart Sq 22191
Danville Rd 22193
Dapple Gray Ct 22192
Dara Dr 22192
Darby Brook Ct 22192
Darbydale Ave 22193
Darden Dr 22192
Darlington Loop 22191
Darnley Rd 22192
Darrowby Mews 22192
Darwin Ct 22191
Dashiell Pl 22192
David Ct 22191
Davis St 22191
Davis Fairfax Ln 22192
Davis Ford Rd 22192
Dawson Ct 22191
Dawson Beach Rd 22191
Daybreak Ln 22193
Daytona Ct 22193
Decatur Dr 22193
Decoy Ct 22191
Deepford Dr 22192
Deer Ct 22193
Deerfield Ln 22191
Del Mar Dr 22193
Delaney Rd 22193
Delano Dr 22193
Delaware Dr 22191
Delta Ct 22193
Densmore Ct 22192
Dent Ln 22192
Derby Ct 22193
Derriford Ct 22192
Desoto Ct 22193
Dettingen Pl 22191
Devil Ln 22192
Devils Reach Rd 22192
Devoe Ct 22193
Devonwood Way 22192
Dexter Ct 22193
Diamond View Way 22191
Diamondback Rd 22193
Diamondleaf Oak Ln 22191
Diehl Ct 22193
Dillingham Sq 22192
Dillon Ave 22193
Dillwyn Ct 22193
Diloreta Dr 22191
Dinghy Way 22191
Dining Way 22191
Directors Loop 22192
Divided Sky Ct 22193
Dixon Ct 22193
Dockside Ct 22192
Dodson Dr 22193
Dogues Ter 22191
Dolly Madison Cir 22192
Donald Curtis Dr 22191
Donna Ln 22191
Dorian Dr 22193
Doris Ct 22191
Dover Ct 22192
Doverhill Ct 22192
Downey Ct 22193
Drew Hunt Ct 22192
Drexel St 22192
Driftwood Ln 22191
Dubois Ct 22193
Duckling Pl 22191
Dulcinea Pl 22192
Dunbar Ln 22193
Dundee Ct 22193
Dunleigh Ct 22192
Dunnington View Ct 22193
Duran Dr 22193
Dutch Elm Ct 22193
Duxbury Ct 22192
Dyer Dr 22193
Dyers Rd 22193
Dyers Mill Ct 22191
Dynasty Loop 22192
E St 22191
Eagle Beak Cir 22191
Eagle Feather Dr 22191
Eagle Flight Cir 22191
Eagle Ridge Dr 22191
Eagle Rock Ct 22192
Eagle Talon St 22191
Eames Ln 22193
Earlham Ct 22193
Easley Way 22193
Eastbourne Dr 22191
Eastham Ct 22192
Eastlawn Ave 22193
Eastman St 22193
Easy St 22191
Eaton Ct 22193
Echo Ct 22193
Eddystone Ct 22192
Eden Ln 22192
Edgemoor Ct 22192
Edgewater Dr 22193
Edinborough Ct 22193
Edinburg Dr 22193
Edison Ct 22193
Edsall Dr 22193
Edward Rd 22192
Effie Rose Pl 22192
Effingham Ct 22192
Efty Ct 22191
Egret Ct 22191
Eiderdown Ct 22191
Eike Ln 22191
Eileen Ct 22193
Eisenhower Cir 22191
El Rio Ct 22193
Elba Ct 22193
Eldorado Dr 22193
Eliff Way 22192
Elizabeth Burbage Loop 22191
Elkwood Ct 22193
Elliot Ct 22193
Elm Farm Rd 22192
Elmira Ct 22193
Elmwood Dr 22193
Ely Ct 22193
Embassy Dr 22193
Emberdale Dr 22193
Emil Ct 22191

Emmet Ct 22192
Emory Ln 22193
Empire St 22193
Emporia St 22191
Endsley Turn 22193
Ensbrook Ln 22193
Ensign Ct 22192
Ensor Ct 22193
Enterprise Ln 22191
Ermine Ct 22193
Eskew Ct 22192
Esquarre Ct 22193
Essex Dr 22191
Estate Dr 22193
Evansdale Rd 22193
Evansport Pl 22192
Everest Peak Ln 22192
Everett Ave 22191
Evergreen Dr 22193
Evesham Ct 22192
Evey Turn 22193
Ewells Mill Way 22193
Exmore Ct 22191
Express Dr 22191
F St 22191
Fairfield Ln 22193
Fairhope Rd 22193
Fairmont Ct 22193
Fairview Ln 22193
Faith Ct 22193
Falcon Dr 22192
Fall Ridge Ct 22192
Fallbrook Ln 22193
Fallen Leaf Ct 22192
Fallway Ln 22193
Falmouth Ct 22192
Falmouth Dr 22193
Farm Creek Dr 22191
Farmberry Ct 22192
Farmer Ct 22193
Farrabow Ln 22192
Farrington Ct 22192
Fascia Ct 22192
Faversham Way 22192
Fawn Hollow Ln 22191
Fawnridge Ct 22193
Fayette Ct 22193
Featherstone Rd 22191
Feeder Ln 22193
Felmore Ct 22193
Felty Pl 22193
Fennegan Ct 22192
Ferguson Ct 22191
Fern Pl 22191
Ferndale Rd 22193
Fernleaf Ct 22192
Ferrara Ter 22193
Ferry Landing Ln 22191
Fig Ct 22193
Filarete St 22193
Fillmore Dr 22193
Financial Loop 22192
Finch Ct 22193
Findley Rd 22193
Fir Ct 22191
Fireside Ct 22191
Fish Hawk Ct 22191
Fisher Ave 22191
Fitchburg Ct 22193
Fitzhugh Ln 22191
Five Fathom Cir 22191
Flagship Dr 22192
Flatback Ln 22193
Fleet St 22191
Fletcher Ct 22193
Flint Ct 22193
Flint Hill Pl 22192
Flint Tavern Pl 22192
Flintlock Ter 22191
Flodden Ct 22192
Florence Ct 22193
Florida Ave 22191
Flotilla Way 22191
Flotsam Ln 22191
Folsome Ct 22193
Fontaine Ct 22193
Fontana Ct 22193
Foothill St 22192
Forecastle Ct 22192
Forest Ln 22191
Forest Glen Rd 22191
Forest Grove Dr 22191
Forest Hill Rd 22192
Forest Park Dr 22192
Forestdale Ave & Ct 22193
Forge Ct & Dr 22193
Forsythia Ter 22193
Fort Craig Dr 22192
Fort Lyon Dr 22192
Fortuna Ct 22193
Foster Pl 22191
Foulger Sq 22192
Fountainbrook Ct 22192
Fowke Ln 22192
Fox Glove Ct 22193
Fox Haven Ct 22193
Fox Lair Dr 22191
Fox Ridge Ct 22192
Fox Run Pl 22191
Fox Tail Ct 22192
Foxhall Dr 22192
Frances Dr 22191
Frankfurt Ct 22191
Franklin St 22191
Fraser Ct 22191
Freda Pl 22193
Freemont Pl 22193
Freeport Ct 22193
Freestone Ct 22192
Freshes Ln 22191
Fresno Dr 22193
Frisco Ct 22193
Frishman Ct 22193
Frontier Ln 22192
Fruit Tree Ct 22193
Fullerton Rd 22193
Fulton Pl 22191
G St 22191
Gableridge Turn 22191
Gailemont Ct 22192
Galapagos Pl 22193
Galley Ct 22192
Galt Ct 22191
Gangplank Ln 22191
Garber Way 22192
Gardensen Dr 22193
Gardenview Loop 22191
Garfield Pl 22191
Garsdale Pl 22192
Gascony Pl 22192
Gate Post Ct 22193
Gatehouse Ter 22191
Gatlin Ct 22191
Gazebo Ct 22192
Geddy Ct 22191
Gemstone Dr 22191
General Washington
Dr 22193
Genesee Pl 22192
George Frye Cir 22193
George Page Pl 22191
Georges Knoll Ct 22192
Georgetown Rd 22191
Georgia Ct & Rd 22191
Geraldine Ct 22193
Geranium Ct 22193
Germander Way 22192
Germyn Rd 22191
Gerry Ln 22193
Getty Ln 22192
Gettysburg Ct 22192
Gibson Ct 22193
Gideon Dr 22192
Gilbert Rd 22193
Giles Ct & St 22191
Gilroy Ct 22193
Gina Pl 22193
Ginko Ct 22193
Gladiolus Ct 22193
Glendale Rd 22193
Glenriver Way 22191
Glory Ct 22193
Gloucester Ct 22191
Goa Pl 22192
Golansky Blvd 22192
Golden Ct 22193
Golden Eagle Ct 22192
Golf Side Cir 22192
Gopher Turtle Way 22193
Gopost 22193
Gordon Blvd
1-12899 22192
13000-13399 22191
Gorham Way 22192
Governors Ct 22192
Grace St 22193
Gracelyn Ct 22193
Grady Ln 22192
Grambell Ct 22192
Gran Deur Dr 22193
Granada Way 22192
Granby Rd 22193
Grand Masters Way 22192
Grand Targee Dr 22192
Grandview Ave 22191
Grantley Ct 22193
Granville Ct 22191
Grassy Knoll Ct 22193
Grayson Rd 22191
Grayton Ln 22191
Greatbridge Rd 22192
Greco Ct 22192
Green Dr 22191
Green Ash Loop 22192
Greenacre Dr 22191
Greenbriar Dr 22193
Greendale Dr 22191
Greenhall Dr 22192
Greenmount Dr 22193
Greenvale Rd 22192
Greenwood Dr 22193
Gregg St 22193
Gresham Ct 22193
Greywing St 22191
Grindle Ln 22191
Grist Mill Ter 22191
Groom Pl 22192
Grosbeak Ct 22191
Groupe Dr 22192
Grouse Ct 22192
Grove Ct & Ln 22193
Grover Glen Ct 22192
Grundy Rd 22191
Guilford Ln 22193
Gull Ct 22191
Gullane Dr 22191
Gum Ln 22193
Gunner Ct 22192
Gunsmith Ter 22191
Gunston Ct 22193
Gunston Hall Dr 22193
Gunwale Pl 22192
Gustus Dr 22193
Habrown Ct 22192
Hackwood St 22191
Haddock Rd 22193
Haddon Ln 22192
Hadwin Pl 22193
Hale Ct 22191
Half Moon Ln 22192
Halifax Rd 22191
Hall St 22192
Halleck Trl 22192
Hallow Way Ct 22193
Halter Pl 22192
Hamilton Dr 22193
Hampshire Ct 22193
Hampstead Ln 22192
Hanco Center Dr 22191
Hanover Ct 22193
Hanson Ln 22191
Harbor Dr 22192
Harbor Side St 22191
Harborview Ct 22192
Harding Ct 22192
Hardy Ct 22193
Hardy Ridge Dr 22192
Hargrett Way 22192
Harpers Hill Way 22192
Harrison St 22191
Harry Allen Pl 22193
Hartfield Ct 22191
Hartford Ct 22193
Hartlake St 22192
Harvard St 22192
Harvest Ct 22193
Harvest Moon Ln 22193
Harvest Sun Rd 22193
Harwich Ct 22192
Hatchway Ct 22192
Hatteras Ct 22191
Haverford Loop 22191
Havering Way 22193
Haversack Ln 22192
Haviland Ct 22193
Hawfinch Ct 22193
Hawk Ct 22193
Hawksbill Ct 22193
Hawkwatch Ct 22191
Hawthorn Ln 22193
Hayes Ln 22191
Hazelnut Ct 22193
Hazelton Dr 22193
Headway Dr 22191
Hearthstone Ter 22191
Heathcliffe Ct 22192
Heather Glen Ct 22191
Heatherbrook Ct 22192
Heathfield Dr 22193
Hedges Run Dr 22192
Hedgewood Dr 22193
Hedrick Ln 22193
Hedrow Mews 22192
Helm Ct 22192
Helmsman Ln 22191
Hemingway Dr 22193
Hendricks Dr 22193
Henry Watts Loop 22191
Herbert Dr 22192
Hercules Ln 22193
Hereford Rd 22192
Herndon Dr 22192
Heron Way 22191
Herons Run Ln 22191
Hersand Ct 22193
Hetten Ln 22193
Highams Ct 22191
Highbourne Dr 22191
Hildas Way 22191
Hill Ct 22191
Hill Meade Ln 22192
Hillendale Dr 22193
Hingham Ct 22192
Hoadly Rd 22192
Hoffman Dr 22193
Holiday Ct 22193
Hollow Ridge Ct 22192
Hollow Wind Way 22191
Holly Leaf Ct 22192
Holly Oak Ct 22192
Holly View Dr 22192
Hollyhock Ct 22192
Home Guard Dr 22192
Honey Locust Ct 22193
Honor Ct 22193
Hope Ct & St 22191
Hope Hill Ave 22193
Hopton Rd 22191
Horizon Ct 22191
Horner Rd
1100-2099 22191
2200-3199 22192
Hornet Way 22191
Horseshoe Ln 22191
Howitzer Ln 22192
Hummel Way 22192
Hummock Pl 22192
Hunter Ln & Pl 22192
Hunter Crest Rd 22193
Hunterbrook Dr 22192
Huntington Ln 22193
Huntley Ct 22192
Hyannis Ln 22193
Hyatt Pl 22191
Hyden Pl 22191
Hydrangea Ct 22193
Hylton Ave 22191
Ice Ct 22193
Idaho St 22191
Illinois Ct & Rd 22191
Imperial Eagle Ct 22191
Indiana Ave 22191
Indus Dr 22191
Industry Ct 22191
Inglebrook Dr 22192
Inland Loop 22192
Inverness Way 22192
Iowa Ct 22191
Irene Ct 22191
Ironhorse Dr 22192
Ironwood St 22191
Island House Loop 22193
Ivy Ct 22191
Ivy League Ct 22192
Ivy Stone Pl 22191
Jacks Dr 22192
Jadestone Way 22192
James St 22191
Jamestown Ct 22192
January Ct 22193
Jarrell Pl 22193
Jato Ct 22192
Javins Pl 22192
Jeans Ct 22193
Jed Forest Ln 22191
Jedburg Ln 22192
Jefferson Plz 22191
Jefferson Davis Hwy 22191
Jeffries Rd 22191
Jellico Ct 22191
Jennerette Ln 22193
Jennings St 22191
Jenny Ln 22192
Jessup Ln 22192
Jetty Loop 22191
Jib Ln 22192
Joanna Ct 22193
Jocelyn Dr 22192
Jodhpur Pl 22193
Jody Ct 22192
John Coffee Ct 22192
John Diskin Cir 22191
John Hancock Ct 22192
Jonah Cove Pl 22192
Josephine Ct 22193
Jousters Way 22192
Joyce Rd 22191
Kaiser Ct 22193
Kale Ct 22193
Kamet Ct 22193
Kapel Dr 22193
Kaplan Ct 22193
Kapp Ln 22193
Karen Rd 22193
Karoly Pl 22193
Kaslo Ct & Dr 22193
Kassel Cir 22193
Katherine Ct 22191
Kaye Rd 22193
Kaywood Dr 22193
Keating Dr 22193
Keelingwood Cir 22191
Kelley Farm Ct 22193
Kellogg Dr 22193
Kelly Rd 22193
Kelmont Ct 22193
Kelsey Ct 22193
Kelso Ct 22193
Kempair Ct & Dr 22193
Kemper Dr 22193
Kempston Ln 22192
Kenbury Dr 22193
Kendale Ct 22193
Kendall Dr 22193
Kenilworth Ct 22191
Kenmar Dr 22193
Kenmont Ct 22193
Kennedy St 22191
Kenneweg Ct 22191
Kenny Ct & Rd 22193
Kensington Park Dr 22191
Kenslow Ct 22193
Kentbury Ct 22193
Kentland Ct & Dr 22193
Kentmore Dr 22193
Kentshire Dr 22191
Kentucky Ave 22191
Kentwood Ln 22193
Kenwood Dr 22193
Kenyon Ct 22193
Kephart Ln 22193
Kerr Ct 22193
Kerrman Ct 22193
Kerry Ln 22193
Kerrydale Pl & Rd 22193
Kestral Ct 22193
Keswick Mews 22192
Ketch Ct 22193
Ketchum Ct 22193
Ketterman Ct & Dr 22193
Kettler Ct 22193
Kew Gardens Dr 22191
Keystone Dr 22193
Keytone Rd 22193
Kidwell Dr 22193
Kilbane Rd 22193
Kilburn Pl 22193
Kilby Ct 22193
Kiley Ct 22193
Killarney Dr 22192
Kim Ct 22193
Kimbrough Ln 22192
King Elm Ct 22192
King Iron Ct 22192
Kings Mountain Rd 22191
Kingsbury Ct & Ln 22192
Kingsley Rd 22193
Kingsman Rd 22193
Kingston Rd 22193
Kingswell Dr 22193
Kingswood Ct 22192
Kinkade Ln 22193
Kinnicutt Dr 22192
Kirkdale Ct & Dr 22193
Kirkland Ct 22193
Kirwyn Ct 22193
Kitten Ct 22193
Kittredge Ct 22193
Kitty Hawk Way 22191
Klein Ct 22193
Knickerbocker Dr 22193
Knightsbridge Dr 22192
Knoll Ct & Dr 22193
Knoll Top Ln 22191
Knowles St 22191
Knox Ct 22193
Koester Ct & Dr 22193
Kogan Dr 22193
Kolman Ct 22193
Kona Noe Ct 22193
Korvett Dr 22193
Koval Ln 22192
Kraft Ct 22193
Kramer Pl 22193
Kramer Estate Dr 22191
Kristin Ct 22193
Kumar Ct & Rd 22193
Kurt Ct 22193
Kurtz Rd 22193
Kushner St 22193
La Harve Pl 22192
Labourn Dr 22193
Lacebark Elm Ct 22192
Laconia Cir 22191
Lacrosse Ct 22193
Ladino Ct 22193
Ladue Ct 22191
Ladymeade Ct 22192
Lake Ridge Dr 22192
Lake Terrapin Dr 22193
Lakeland Ct 22193
Lakeside Ct 22192
Lakewood Dr 22192
Lakota Dr 22192
Lamar Rd 22191
Lambsgate Ln 22193
Lancashire Dr 22191
Lancaster Dr 22191
Landings Point Loop 22191
Landon Ln 22193
Landover Ct 22193
Langer Ln 22193
Langford Ct 22193
Langley Ct 22193
Langstone Dr 22193
Langtree Ln 22193
Lanyard Ln 22192
Lapene Ct 22192
Large Oak Ct 22192
Larkmeade Ln 22193
Larry Ct 22193
Lashmere Ct 22192
Laurel St 22191
Laurel Hills Dr 22192
Lea Meadow Ct 22193
Leaf Lawn Ln 22192
Leatherback Rd 22193
Leatherwood Ln 22192
Lebourget Ct 22193
Leeds Hill Way 22191
Leesburg Ct 22193
Leeway Ct 22192
Leewood Ct 22192
Legere Ct 22193
Lehigh Ct 22193
Leicestershire St 22191
Leilani Dr 22193
Leith Ct 22192
Lenox Ln 22192
Leocrie Pl 22191
Leopard Tortoise Way 22193
Lestric Ln 22193
Lexington Ct 22192
Liberty Manor Cir 22193
Liberty Woods Ln 22193
Lighthouse Ln 22192
Limoux Pl 22192
Linden St 22191
Linden Knoll Ct 22191
Lindendale Rd 22193
Linfield Dr 22193
Linsey Ct 22193
Linwood Ln 22192
Litza Way 22192
Lock Loop 22192
Lockleven Ln 22192
Lockwood Ln 22193
Lodge Ter 22191
Logan Ct 22193
Loggerhead Pl 22193
Lolly Post Ln 22192
Lomax Way 22193
Lombard Ln 22193
Londonderry Ct 22193
Long Shadows Ct 22192
Longbow Ct 22192
Longbranch Ln 22192
Longfellow Ct 22192
Longhorn Dr 22193
E & W Longview Dr 22191
Longwood Ct 22193
Longwood Manor Ct 22191
Lord Culpeper Ct 22191
Lost Canyon Ct 22191
Lost Colony Dr 22193
Lotte Dr 22192
Louisa St 22191
Louise St 22191
Louisville Pl 22191
Luca Station Way 22192
Luckland Way 22191
Lupine Turn 22192
Lupino Ct 22193
Luther Allen Pl 22193
Lutz Ct 22193
Lynbrook Ct 22193
Lynhurst Dr 22193
Lynn Ct & St 22191
Lynway Ct 22193
Lynwood Dr 22193
Lyon Park Ct 22192
Macdonald Rd 22193

Macedonia Dr 22191
Mackenzie Pl 22191
Macomb Ct 22193
Macrina Ct 22192
Macwood Dr 22193
Maddox Ct 22193
Madeira Ct 22192
Madelyn Ct 22192
Madison Ct 22191
Madison Farm Dr 22192
Madrigal Dr 22193
Mahoney Dr 22193
Maidstone Ct 22192
Maine Ct 22191
Malta St 22193
Manchester Way 22192
Mandolin Ln 22192
Manet Ct 22193
Manitoba Dr 22192
Manor House Ct 22193
Mansfield Ct 22193
Mantle Ct 22193
Maple Leaf Ln 22191
Maple Ridge Dr 22192
Mapledale Ave & Plz 22193
Mapleton St 22191
Marblestone Dr 22192
Marbury Ln 22191
Marcel Ct 22193
Marfield Ct 22191
Margaret St 22191
Margraf Cir 22191
Maribelle Pl 22193
Marigold Ct 22192
Marilyn Ct 22193
Marina Way 22191
Marina Landing Ln 22191
Mariner Ln 22192
Marisa Ct 22192
Markhams Grant Dr 22191
Marlboro Ct 22192
Marline Ct 22192
Marquis Pl 22192
Marr Ct 22193
Marsala Ct 22192
Marseille Ln 22191
Marsh Overlook Dr 22191
Marumsco Dr 22191
Mary St 22191
Maryland Ave 22191
Marys Way 22191
Mason Creek Cir 22191
Mathews Dr 22191
Mattapony Dr 22193
Matura Ln 22192
Maurice Dr 22191
Mauti Ct 22192
Maverick Ct 22193
Mayfair Ct 22193
Mayflower Dr 22192
Mcguffeys Ct & Trl 22191
Mcintire Dr 22192
Mcnamera Ct 22191
Mead Ter 22191
Meadowbrook Rd 22193
Meandering Way 22192
Meckon Ct 22193
Medwick Ct 22193
Meeting Pl 22193
Meherrin Way 22191
Melbourne Ave 22191
Melcombe Ct 22192
Mellott Rd 22191
Mellowdew Ct 22193
Melvin Ct 22193
Mendoza Ln 22191
Mercer Hill Ct 22192
Merchant Plz 22192
Merganser Ln 22192
Meridian Ct & Dr 22191
Merrily Way 22193
Merrywood Ct 22192
Merseyside Dr 22191
Metro Plz 22192
Michie Ct 22192
Michigan Rd 22191
Midnight Ct 22193
Midsummer Ln 22192
Midway Ct 22193
Milan Ct 22192
Milbank Rd 22191
Miles Ct 22193
Mill Brook Ct 22192
Mill House Ct 22192
Millet St 22192
Millwood Dr 22191
Milstead Way 22192
Miniclier Ct 22192
Minion St 22192
Minnie Ct 22193
Minnieville Rd
12700-13599 22192
13600-14899 22193
Mintwood Ct 22192
Mipalsal Ct 22193
Miranda Ct & Ln 22191
Misty Ln 22192
Mizzen Pl 22192
Mobilia Ct 22192
Moccasin Ct 22193
Mohican Rd 22192
Mojave Ln 22192
Monarch Ct 22192
Monroe Dr 22191
Montega Dr 22192
Montgomery Ave 22191
Montoclair Ln 22193
Montpelier Ct 22192
Montreal Ct 22192
Monument Ave & Sq 22191
Moon Way 22193
Moonbeam Dr 22193
Morning Dew Dr 22192
Morrison Ct 22193
Morse Ln 22192
Moss Point Pl 22192
Mosser Mill Ct 22192
Mount Airy Ct 22192
Mount Burnside Way 22192
Mount High St 22192
Mount Pleasant Dr 22191
Mountain Ash Ct 22192
Mountain Eagle Ct 22191
Mouser Pl 22192
Muddy Creek Ct 22193
Mulberry Ct 22192
Murray Pl 22191
Muscogee Ln 22192
Musket Ct 22193
Nadia Loop 22193
Nancy Ct 22193
Nanticoke Way 22191
Narrow Glen Way 22192
Nascoby Ln 22193
Nassau Dr 22193
Nates Pl 22192
Nationville Ln 22193
Nautilus Pl 22192
Navigation Dr 22191
Naylor Ct 22193
Neabsco Rd 22191
Neabsco Beach Way 22191
Neabsco Church Way 22193
Neabsco Creek Ct 22191
Neabsco Mills Rd 22191
Neabsco Overlook 22193
Neath Dr 22193
Neddleton Ave 22193
Nellings Pl 22192
Nettlecreek Pl 22192
Nevada St 22191
New Bedford Way 22192
Newberry Ct 22193
Newbold Ct 22192
Newcastle Loop 22192
Newgate Rd 22193
Newtone Ct 22193
Nexus Ct 22192
Nibbs Ct 22193
Nickleson Dr 22193
Nightfall Ln 22193
Nimes Ct 22191
Noble Fir Ct 22192
Noble Pond Way 22193
Noblewood Plz 22193
Noland Rd 22193
Norbury Ct 22192
Normandy Ct 22191
Norris Point Way 22191
Northton Ct 22193
Norwood Ln 22191
Nottingdale Dr 22193
Nutmeg Ct 22192
Nuttal Oak Pl 22191
Nystrom Ct 22193
Oak Farm Dr 22192
Oak Leaf Ct 22192
Oak Tree Ln 22191
Oak Valley Dr 22191
Oakham Ct 22193
Oakhurst Ln 22192
Oakland Ct & Dr 22193
Oaklawn Ln 22193
Oakwood Dr 22193
Oat Ct 22193
Oberlin Dr 22191
Observer Ln 22192
Occoquan Rd
12600-12698 22192
12700-13003 22192
13000-13499 22191
Occoquan Club Dr 22192
Occoquan Oaks Ln 22192
Occoquan Overlook 22192
Occoquan View Ct 22192
Odion Ln 22192
Office Pl 22192
Ogilvie Ct 22192
Ohio Ave 22191
Old Bridge Ln & Rd 22192
Old Coach Rd 22191
Old Delaney Rd 22193
Old Horner Rd 22192
Old Ironsides Ct 22192
Old Landing Way 22191
Old Marsh Rd 22191
Old Post Ter 22191
Old Salem Ct 22192
Oleander Ct 22193
Olive Ct 22193
Olmstead Ln 22191
Omisol Rd 22192
Omni Ct 22193
Opal Ln 22193
Opey Ln 22193
Opitz Blvd
1800-2550 22191
2600-2699 22192
Optimist Mews 22193
Orange Ct 22191
Orangewood Dr 22193
Orchard Dr 22191
Oregon Ave 22191
Oriskany Way 22191
Orkin Ln 22193
Orkney Ct 22192
Orleans St 22193
Osage Dr 22193
Oscar Ct 22193
Osprey Ct 22193
Ospreys View Pl 22191
Ottawa Ct 22192
Otter Mews 22193
Otto Rd 22193
Oust Ln 22193
Overleigh Dr 22192
Overlook Dr 22191
Owl Eagle Ct 22191
Oxbow Ct 22193
Oxbridge Inn Ct 22193
Ozack Ct 22193
Pace Ct 22193
Packard Dr 22193
Paddle Boat Ln 22192
Paducah Ct 22191
Page St 22191
Painted Turtle Way 22193
Paisley Ct 22191
Palermo Ter 22191
Palisades St 22191
Palm Rd 22193
Palmcrest Ct 22193
Palomino Pl 22192
Pamela Ct 22193
Pancreek Ct 22193
Panorama Dr 22191
Pansy Ct 22193
Papillon Pl 22193
Paramount Ln 22193
N & S Park Ct 22193
Park Shore Ct 22192
Parliament Dr 22192
Parson Weems Loop 22193
Partree Ct 22191
Patamon Way 22192
Patrick St 22191
Patrick Henry Dr 22191
Paula St 22191
Pauls Ct 22192
Paxton St 22192
Peachtree Ct 22192
Peacock Ct 22193
Pearlberry Ct 22193
Pearson Dr 22193
Pebble Brooke Ct 22192
Pecan Ct 22193
Pelican Rd 22193
Pemberley Ct 22193
Pembroke Ct 22192
Penacle Ct 22193
Penbury Ct 22191
Penfold Ct 22192
Pennington Ln 22192
Penshurst Ln 22192
Pepco Ct 22193
Pepper Ct 22193
Pepperidge Ct 22192
Perch Branch Way 22193
Perchance Ter 22192
Peregrine Ct 22193
Peregrine Ridge Ct 22192
Periwinkle Ln 22192
Persian Ct 22193
Persimmon Pl 22192
Persistence Dr 22191
Pewter Pl 22192
Pfitzner Ct 22192
Pheasant Ln 22191
Pheasant Hunt Rd 22192
Phillipp Ct 22193
Photo Dr 22193
Picadilly Ct 22193
Piccolo Ln 22191
Pickering Ln 22193
Pickwick Ln 22192
Piedmont Pl 22193
Pierre Ct 22193
Pilgrim Dr 22192
Pilgrims Inn Dr 22193
Pine Ln 22191
Pine Shadows Way 22192
Pineneedle Ct 22192
Pinetree Ct & Dr 22191
Pinewood Ct 22191
Pineyridge Ln 22193
Pinnacle St 22191
Pinon Ct 22191
Pintail Rd 22192
Pinwheel Ct 22193
Plainville Ln 22193
Plastron Ct 22193
Plumage Eagle St 22191
Plumwood Ln 22193
Plymbridge Ln 22193
Plymouth Ct 22192
Pocomoke Ct 22192
Pocono Ct 22193
Pohick Creek Ct 22192
Point Longstreet Way 22192
Polar Ct 22193
Pomander Loop 22192
Pond Way 22192
Pond Run Dr 22192
Ponderosa Ct 22191
Pondwater Ct 22192
Ponhill Dr 22193
Pontiac Dr 22193
Poplar Ln 22192
Poppy Ct 22192
Port Potomac Ave 22191
Portal Ct 22193
Portland Dr 22193
Post Office Rd
3300-3360 22193
3360-3360 22195
3362-3398 22193
Postillion Ter 22191
Potomac Branch Dr 22191
Potomac Club Pkwy 22191
Potomac Heights Pl 22191
Potomac Mills Cir &
Rd 22192
Potomac Path Dr 22191
Potomac Town Pl 22191
Potomac View Ave 22191
Potomac Vista Dr 22191
Powder Horn Ter 22191
Powell Dr 22191
Powells Crossing Ct 22193
Powells Landing Cir 22191
Prather Pl 22193
Pratt St 22191
Prendons Dr 22191
Presidio Way 22192
Prestige Dr 22193
Preston Ct 22193
Primer Ct 22192
Prince William Pkwy
1500-1699 22191
2400-3000 22192
3002-5098 22192
3101-3199 22193
3901-5099 22192
Princedale Dr 22193
Princess Anne Ln 22191
Princeton St 22192
Profit Ct 22191
Prospect Ct 22193
Ps Business Center
Dr 22192
Pulpit Hill Ct 22191
Purdham Dr 22191
Putnam Cir 22191
Pyxie Way 22192
Quade Ln 22193
Quaint Dr 22193
Qualey Pl 22193
Qualls Ln 22193
Quance Ln 22193
Quander Ct 22193
Quann Ln 22193
Quantas Pl 22193
Quarles Ct 22193
Quarterhorse Ln 22192
Quate Ln
13000-13199 22192
13200-13599 22193
Quay Ct 22193
Que Pl 22193
Quebec Pl 22193
Queen Chapel Rd 22193
Queensbury Ct 22192
Queensdale Dr 22193
Quell Ct & Ln 22193
Query Ln 22193
Quest Ct 22193
Quick Pl 22193
Quiet Pl 22193
Quiet Creek Ct 22192
Quiller Ct 22193
Quince Ct 22193
Quinlan Dr 22193
Quinn Ln 22193
Quixote Ct 22193
Rabson Ct 22193
Race Pointe Pl 22193
Racine Ct 22193
Radburn St 22191
Radcliffe Ln 22191
Raddock Ct 22193
Radford Ct & Dr 22191
Raft Cove Ct 22193
Rahill Ct 22193
Railroad Ave 22191
Rainbow Ct 22192
Rainer Ct 22193
Rainswood Ln 22191
Ralston Ct 22193
Ramos Ct 22193
Ramrod Rd 22192
Randall Ct & Dr 22191
Randolph Ct 22193
Ranger Loop 22191
Rapid Ln 22193
Raptor Ct 22191
Ravenbrook Ct 22193
Rawls St 22191
Rayburn Ct 22193
Raywood Ct 22193
Razorback Pl 22193
Reagon Ct 22193
Reardon Ln 22193
Reaves Ln 22193
Rector Dr 22193
Red Bird Ln 22193
Red Wing Ln 22193
Redbud Ct 22191
Reddy Dr
1800-1811 22191
1810-1810 22194
1812-1998 22191
1813-1999 22191
Redford Ln 22193
Redgate Ln 22191
Redskin Ct 22193
Redstone Dr 22193
Redwood Ct 22192
Reef Knot Way 22191
Reese Ct 22192
Refuge Ct 22191
Regal Ct 22193
Regatta Ln 22191
Regency Ct & Rd 22191
Regent Ct 22193
Regents Park Dr 22191
Regiment Ct 22193
Rehfield Ct 22193
Rehnquist Ct 22193
Relay Ct 22193
Renate Dr 22192
Renegade Ct 22193
Renley Ct 22193
Research Ct 22192
Revillo Loop 22191
Rexburg Ct 22193
Rhapsody Ct 22193
Rhode Island Dr 22193
Rhumfield Ct 22193
Ribbon Ct 22193
Richmond Ave 22191
Ridge View Ct 22192
Ridgedale Dr 22193
Ridgefield Village Dr 22193
Ridgewood Center Dr 22192
Riggs Ct 22191
Right Ct 22193
Ringgold Ct 22192
Rio Ct 22193
Ripple Creek Ct 22192
Rippon Blvd 22191
Rippon Landing Blvd 22191
Rising Eagle Ct 22191
Rivanna Ct 22192
River Basin Ln 22191
River Bend Way 22192
River Oak Ct 22192
River Ridge Blvd 22191
River Walk Way 22191
Riverside Dr 22193
Riverton Ct 22193
Riverview Ln 22192
Riviera Ct 22193
Rizdon Ct 22193
Roanoke St 22191
Robey Way 22192
Robin Glen Way 22191
Robinson Ct 22191
Rochelle Ct 22192
Rock Bridge Ct 22191
Rock Ridge Ln 22191
Rockcliff Ln 22193
Rockford Ct 22193
Rockinghorse Dr 22193
Rockledge Ter 22192
Rocksbury Ln 22193
Rockwood Ln 22192
Roeburn Ct 22192
Roland Ct 22193
Rolling Brook Dr 22192
Rollingwood Dr 22192
Rolok Ct 22192
Romney Mews 22192
Rope Ct & Dr 22191
Rosa Dr 22191
Rosedale Ct 22191
Rosewood Dr 22193
Roth Ct 22193
Rotterdam Loop 22191
Roundtree Dr 22193
Rowser Dr 22193
Royal Ct 22191
Ruby Ridge Ct 22192
Ruler Ct 22193
Rumford Ct 22192
Rush Dr 22192
Rushbrook Ct 22191
Ruskin Row Pl 22193
Russell Rd 22192
Russett Leaf Ct 22193
Rusty Rudder Dr 22191
Rutgers Ct 22193
Rutherford Dr 22193
Rutland Ct 22191
Ruxton Dr 22193
Rycroft Ct 22193
Rye St 22193
Ryecliff Ct 22192
Ryon Ct 22193
Sabine Hall Pl 22193
Sable Ct 22193
Saddler Ln 22193
Saffron Ln 22193
Sagamore Ct 22192
Sailstone Ln 22193
Saint Andrews Ct 22192
Saint Charles Dr 22193
Saint Davids Ct 22192
Saint Ives Ct 22192
Salemtown Dr 22193
Salemway Ct 22192
Salsbury Ct 22193
Salt Pond Pl 22193
Samantha Ct 22193
San Ysidro Ct 22192
Sandal Ct 22193
Sandra Dr 22191
Sandy Ridge Ct 22191
Saphire Ct 22193
Saratoga Ln 22193
Satterfield Dr 22193
Savannah Dr 22193
Saxon St 22191
Saxophone Way 22191
Schalk Ct 22192
Scotch Ct 22191
Scotch Heather Pl 22192
Scuppers Ln 22191
Sea Lawn Pl 22191
Sea Ray Ln 22192
Sea View Ave 22191
Seabury Ct 22193
Seaford Ct 22193
Seeton Sq 22192
Selma Ct 22193
Seminole Rd 22192
Seneca Ct 22193
Sentry Ln 22193
Sentry Falls Way 22191
Sequoia Ct 22191
Serendipity Rd 22193
Seville Cir 22192
Shackleford Way 22191

Shadwell Ct 22192
Shady River Ct 22192
Shadybrook Dr 22193
Shagwood Ct 22192
Shamus Ct 22193
Shandor Rd 22193
Shannon Ct 22193
Sharp Dr 22191
Shaw Ct 22193
Shearwater Ct 22192
Sheffield Hill Way 22191
Shelby Ct 22193
Shenandoah Ct 22192
Sherbrooke Cir 22192
Sherry Ct 22193
Sherwood Pl 22191
Shetland Ct 22193
Shingle Oak Dr 22191
Shipping Point Pl 22191
Shoppers Best Way 22192
Shorewood Ct 22192
Shotwell Ct 22193
Shumard Oak Ln 22191
Sidney Way 22192
Silent Tree Pl 22191
Silk Tree Ct 22193
Silverdale Dr 22193
Silversmith Ct 22191
Silvia Loop 22192
Simmons Ln 22193
Simpson Mill Way 22192
Sindlinger Way 22191
Single Oak Hill Ct 22192
Skipfare Ct 22192
Skipjack Ct 22192
Skipper Cir 22192
Sleaford Ct 22192
Sleepy Creek Way 22192
Slippery Elm Ct 22193
Sloop Ct 22193
Sluice Channel Pl 22192
Small Oak Ct 22192
Smallwood Ct 22193
Smoketown Rd 22192
Snapper Ct 22193
Soffit Pl 22192
Softwood Ln 22193
Sonnette Ct 22193
Sonora St 22193
Sophia Ct 22193
Sourwood Way 22192
Southampton St 22191
Southgate Ct 22193
Space More Cir 22191
Spangler Ln 22193
Spanish Dollar Ct 22193
Sparrow Ct 22193
Spindle Tree Ct 22193
Spinnaker Ct 22192
Spirea Ct 22193
Spoonbill Ct 22191
Sport And Health Dr 22192
Spotted Eagle Ct 22191
Spotted Turtle Ct 22193
Spriggs Rd 22193
Spriggs Branch Rd 22193
Spriggs Meadow Dr 22193
Spriggs Tree Ln 22193
Spriggs Valley Ct 22193
Springbrook Ct 22193
Springwoods Dr 22192
Square Tiller Mews 22191
Stacys Ridge Ct 22193
Stafford St 22191
Staggs Ct 22191
Stallion Ct 22192
Standing Eagle Ct 22191
Standish Ct 22192
Staples Ln 22193
Staples Mill Plz 22193
Starboard Pl 22192
Stargrass Ct 22192
Starling Ct 22193
Starry Night Ct 22193
Statler Dr 22193
Steamboat Landing Ct 22191
Steeple Pl 22192
Steerage Cir 22191
Steidel Ln 22193
Stella Ct 22193
Stevens Rd 22191
Stevenson Ct 22192
Still Pl 22193
Stirrup Ct 22192
Stockholm Way 22191
Stockton Ct 22193
Stone Lined Cir 22192
Stoneford Dr 22192
Stonehurst Dr 22192
Stratford Dr 22193
Stretton Farm Ct 22192
Strickland Ct 22191
Sturbridge Rd 22192
Sudberry Ln 22193
Sugar Hill Dr 22192
Sugar Pine Ct 22192
Sulky Ct 22192
Summer Ridge Ct 22192
Summerton Ln 22193
Summit School Rd 22192
Sunflower Ct 22192
Sunny Brook Ct 22192
Sunny Ridge Ct 22191
Sunshine Ct 22192
Surrey Dr 22191
Surrydale Dr 22193
Sussex Ct 22191
Sutter Ln 22193
Sutton Pl 22191
Swallow Ct 22193
Swan Point Rd 22192
Sweeney Ln 22191
Sweet Gum Ct 22192
Swift Stream Ct 22192
Swinksville Ct 22191
Sylvan Moor Ln 22191
Tabor Ct 22191
Tacketts Mill Dr 22192
Tadmore Ct 22193
Tadworth Pl 22193
Taffrail Way 22191
Taffy Ct 22193
Taft Ct 22193
Tag Ct 22193
Talent Way 22193
Talk Pl 22193
Tally Ho Ct 22192
Talmadge Dr 22193
Tamarack Pl 22191
Tamborine Ct 22193
Tango Ln 22193
Tanterra Ct 22191
Tanyard Hill Rd 22192
Tapestry Dr 22193
Tarberry Pl 22193
Target Ct 22192
Tarpon Ln 22193
Tassia Ln 22191
Tassleford Ln 22191
Taverner Loop 22192
Taxi Dr 22193
Tazanari Way 22192
Tazewell Ct 22191
Teal Way 22191
Team Pl 22193
Teasel Ct 22193
Tecumseh Ct 22192
Telegraph Rd 22192
Telfair Ct 22193
Tendril Ct 22192
Tenor Ct 22193
Terminal Way 22193
Terranova Ln 22192
Thackery Ter 22192
Thenia Pl 22192
Thin Leaf Pl 22193
Three Dormers Ct 22193
Thrift Ln 22193
Thyme Ln 22192
Ticket Way 22193
Tides St 22191
Tideswell Mill Ct 22192
Tidewater Ct 22191
Tiger Ct 22192
Tiger Lily Cir 22192
Tilbury Way 22193
Tilletson Pl 22191
Tilney Ct 22192
Tina Ln 22193
Tipton Ln 22192
Titania Way 22192
Tobacco Way 22193
Tolson Pl 22192
Tomlinson Dr 22192
Tonbridge Pl 22193
Tonka Ct 22193
Topsail Ln 22191
Torbay Way 22191
Torchlight Dr 22193
Torrence Pl 22193
Torrey Pine Ct 22193
Torrington St 22192
Tortoise Pl 22193
Tory Loop 22192
Totten Rd 22191
Touchstone Cir 22192
Tournai Ct 22191
Towhee Ct 22193
Town Center Rd 22192
Trafalgar Ln 22192
Transom Pl 22191
Travailer Ct 22193
Traverser Ct 22193
Trawler Dr 22193
Tree House Dr 22192
Treetop Ct 22191
Trentdale Dr 22193
Trethaway Dr 22191
Trevor Ln 22192
Triad Ct 22192
Trident Ln 22193
Trimaran Way 22191
Troika Ct 22192
Trotter Ct 22192
Troupe St 22192
Trowbridge Dr 22192
Truffle Oak Pl 22191
Trunnion Trl 22192
Tumbling Brook Ln 22192
Tupelo Ct 22192
Turnbuckle Ln 22191
Tuscany Ct 22192
Two Chimneys Ct 22193
Tyler Cir 22191
Ulysses St 22191
Undercliff Ct 22193
Uppsala Ct 22191
Ursula Ct 22191
Vale Ct 22192
Valley Dr 22191
Valley Stream Dr 22191
Valleyhill St 22192
Valleywood Dr 22192
Vanderbilt Ct 22192
Vantage Dr 22191
Vantage View Ln 22192
Varsity Dr 22191
Veronica Ln 22192
Vestal St 22191
Veterans Dr 22191
Village Dr 22191
Vineyard Way 22191
Vireo Ct 22193
Vista Forest Dr 22192
Vonnies View Ct 22192
Wabash Pl 22193
Wade Ln 22192
Wadsworth Way 22192
Wagon Wheel Ln 22192
Wainscott Pl 22192
Wakewater Way 22191
Walnut St 22191
Walsh Way 22193
Waltham Forest Mews 22192
Wanda Ct 22192
Warbler Ct 22193
Warren Dr 22191
Warwick Pl 22192
Wasp Way 22191
Water Birch Ct 22192
Water Oak Ct 22192
Watermans Dr 22191
Watermill Ter 22191
Waters End Trl 22192
Waterwheel Ter 22191
Watson Ln 22193
Waynesboro Ct 22193
Weathervane Ter 22191
Weeburn Way 22191
Weldin Dr 22193
Wellesley Dr 22192
Wellspring Way 22192
Welsh Ln 22193
Welton Mews 22192
Wensley Ct 22192
Wentwood Ln 22191
Wermuth Way 22192
Wertz Dr 22193
Wessex Ct 22191
Westminister Ln 22193
Westport Ln 22192
Westway Ln 22193
Westwind Dr 22193
Wet Rock Ct 22193
Wetherburn Ct 22191
Weymouth Ct 22192
Wheatfield Rd 22193
Wheel Cog Pl 22192
Whips Run Dr 22193
Whistling Swan Way 22191
Whitaker Pl 22193
White Birch Ct 22192
Whitely Ct 22193
Whiting Ct 22193
Whitmer Dr 22193
Whittier Loop 22193
Wicker Ct 22193
Wicklow Ct 22191
Wide Oak Ct 22192
Widebranch Ln 22193
Wigan Dr 22193
Wigeon Way 22191
Wigglesworth Way 22191
Wilderness Ln 22193
Wildflower Ct 22192
Wildlife Way 22191
Wildwood Ct 22191
William And Mary Cir 22192
William Bayliss Ct 22191
William Harris Way 22191
Williamsburg Ct 22191
Willow Ln 22191
Willowood Dr 22192
Wimbley Ln 22192
Windermere View Pl 22192
Windflower Ct 22192
Winding Loop 22191
Windjammer Dr 22192
Windy Leaf Ct 22192
Winewood Ln 22193
Wingfield Rd 22191
Wink Way 22193
Winona Dr 22192
Winsford Mews 22192
Winslow Ct 22191
Winston Ct & Ln 22191
Wintergreen Ct 22192
Wisley Turn 22192
Wits End Dr 22193
Wolf Run Shoals Rd 22192
Wood St 22191
Wood Duck Ct 22191
Wood Hollow Dr 22192
Wood Lilly Ct 22192
Woodbridge St 22191
Woodburn Ct 22192
Woodfern Ct 22192
Woodhaven Ct 22192
Woodie Ct 22193
Woodlawn Ct 22192
Woodmark Dr 22191
Woods Cove Ln 22192
Woodside Dr 22191
Woodsman Ln 22193
Woodvale Ct 22191
Woodway Pl 22193
Worchester Dr 22193
Wordsworth Ct 22192
Worth Ave 22192
Worthy Ct 22191
Wrangler Ln 22193
Wren Ct 22191
Wyatt Rd 22191
Wyndale Ct 22192
Wythe Ct 22191
Yale Ct 22192
Yardarm Pl 22192
Yardley Ln 22191
Yarmouth Ct 22192
Yawl Ct 22193
Yellow Turtle Pl 22193
York Dr 22191
Yosocomico Ln 22191

YORKTOWN VA

General Delivery 23692

POST OFFICE BOXES MAIN OFFICE STATIONS AND BRANCHES

Box No.s
1 - 718 23690
701 - 2680 23692
6501 - 6860 23690
8001 - 8180 23693

RURAL ROUTES

09 23690
01, 02, 03, 04, 05, 06, 07, 08, 10, 11, 12 23692

NAMED STREETS

Aberfeldy Way 23693
Accomac Turning 23693
Acorn Ln 23692
Ada Dr 23693
Adele Ct 23693
Alanna Ct 23690
Albacore Dr 23692
Alexia Ln 23690
Alfred Ct 23693
Alice Ct 23692
Allen Harris Dr 23692
Allens Mill Rd 23692
Ambler St 23690
Ambrits Way 23693
Ambrose Ln 23690
Amelia Ct 23693
Amersham Dr 23693
Amory Ln 23692
Anacostia Turn 23693
Anchor Dr & Ln 23692
Anderson Ln 23692
Andover Ct 23693
Andrews Xing 23692
Anne Cir 23693
Appaloosa Dr 23693
Apple Ln 23693
Aquia Turn 23693
Arabian Cir 23693
Arcadia Loop 23692
Arrow Ct 23693
Artillery Rd 23692
Ascot Dr 23693
Ashley Cir 23692
Ashton Dr 23690
Aspen Blvd 23692
Atoka Turn 23693
Austins Pt 23692
Autumn Way 23693
Azalea Dr 23692
Bailey Dr & Rd 23692
Baldric Pl 23692
Ballard St 23690
Baptist Rd 23690
Barbee Cir 23692
Barcanmore Ln 23692
Barclay Rd 23693
Barcroft Dr 23692
Barfleur Pl 23692
Barham Blvd 23690
Barn Swallow Rdg 23692
Barncord Way 23690
Barrington Ln 23693
Basta Dr 23692
Battery Cir 23692
Battle Rd 23692
Bayberry Ln 23693
Bayview Dr 23692
N Beach Rd 23692
Beatties Landing Rd 23692
Beecham Dr 23692
Beechwood Dr 23692
Beechwood Ln 23693
Bell Hill Dr 23692
Bellows Pl 23693
Belmont Cir 23693
Belvin Ln 23692
Bennington Ct 23693
Bentley Ct 23693
Berrys Lndg 23692
Bethany Ter 23693
Big Bethel Rd 23693
Bill Sours Dr 23693
Birkdale Ct 23693
Blackberry Bnd 23693
Blacksmith Arch 23693
Blackwood Ct 23693
Blair Dr 23692
Blevins Run 23693
Blue Heron Dr 23692
Boathouse Cv 23692
Bolivar Dr 23692
Bonito Dr 23692
Borden Way 23690
Boundary Rd 23690
N Bowman Ter 23693
Bradley Dr 23692
E Branch Ln & Rd 23692
Brandon Way 23692
Brandywine Dr 23692
Brantley Ct 23693
Brassie Dr 23693
Breezy Point Dr 23692
Brenda Ct 23693
Brentmeade Dr 23693
Brian Wesley Ct 23693
Briarwood Pl 23692
Brick Church Rd 23692
Bridge Ln & Xing 23692
Bridge Wood Dr 23693
Brigade Dr 23692
Brightwood Ter 23690
E & W Bristol Ln 23693
Brock St 23690
Brokenbridge Rd 23692
Brook Ln 23692
Brook Rd 23692
Brook Run 23693
Brookstone Ct 23693
Browns Ln 23690
Bryon Rd 23692
Buckingham Dr 23692
Buckner St 23690
Bucktail Run 23692
Buffie Rd 23693
Bugle Ct 23693
Bunting Point Rd 23693
Burcher Rd 23692
Burnt Run 23692
Burnt Bridge Way 23692
Burts Rd 23692
Buttonwood Ln 23693
Byrd Ln 23693
Cabot Dr 23690
Calthrop Neck Rd 23693
Calumet Turn 23693
Camden Way 23693
Camelot Cres 23693
Camille Ct 23693
Cannon Rd 23690
Cape Lndg 23693
Captain Jims Way 23693
Cardinal Ln 23693
Carlton Dr 23692
Carnoustie Ct 23693
Carol Dr 23692
Carpenter Dr 23693
Carraway Ter 23692
Carver Pl 23692
Carys Trce 23693
Carys Chapel Rd 23693
Castellow Ct 23692
Castlewood Ct 23692
Cattail Ln 23693
Cavalier Dr 23692
Cedar Point Cres 23692
Chadds Cir 23692
Chadwick Ct 23693
Champions Path 23693
Chandler Ln 23690
Chaney Ct 23693
Chanticlair Dr 23693
Chaptico Run 23693
Charlene Ct 23692
Charles Rd 23692
Charter Dr 23692
Chase Oak Ct 23693
Chatham Ct 23692
Cheltenham Way 23693
Chennault Cir 23690
Cherry Point Dr 23692
Chestnut Ct 23692
Cheswick Cir 23693
Chinaberry Way 23692
Chinquapin Orch 23693
Chippenham Dr 23693
Chippokes Turn 23693
Chischiak Watch 23690
Choisy Cres 23692
Choptank Turn 23693
Chowan Turn 23693
Chowning Pl 23693
Chris Ct 23693
Chris Slade Chase 23693
Chuckatuck Turn 23693
Church Rd & St 23690
Clairmont Way 23692
Clarden Ct 23692
Clayton Dr 23693
Clearbrooke Lndg 23692
Clearwater Ct 23692
Clements Ln 23692
Clydesdale Dr 23693
Coach Hovis Dr 23693
Coachman Dr 23693
Cobia Dr 23692
Coburn Ct 23690
Cockletown Rd 23692
Cody Pl 23693
Coinjock Run 23693
Colberts Trce 23692
Colleen Dr 23692
Collington Run 23693
Collins Ln 23693
Colonna Pt 23692
Comarthe Rd 23690
Combs Loop 23693
Commerce Cir 23693
Commonwealth Dr 23693
Compass Ct 23693
Connor Dr 23692
N Constitution Dr 23692
Conway Ct 23693
Cook Rd 23690
Cool Ct 23690
Coopers Ln 23692
Copeland Ln 23692
Corbett Pl 23692
Cornwallis Rd 23690
Corrotoman Run 23693
Country Ln 23692
Court Rd 23692
Cove Cres & Ct 23692

Coventry Blvd 23693
Cox Dr 23692
Crandol Dr 23693
Cranwood Ct 23693
Crate Ct 23692
Creek Ter 23693
Crescent Ct 23693
Crest Lake Ct 23693
Crestwood Ct 23692
Crimson Ct 23693
Criner Ln 23693
Crossing Waters Way 23690
Crosspointe Ct 23693
Crystal Lake Dr 23692
Cub Ct 23693
Cybernetics Way 23693
Cypress Xing 23692
Daisy Ln 23693
Dale Hollow Dr 23692
Dalzell Ct 23693
Dandy Haven Ln 23692
Dandy Loop Rd 23692
Dandy View Ln 23692
Daniels Dr 23690
Daphne Dr 23692
Darby Rd 23693
Dare Rd 23692
Darrells Cir 23692
Dartmouth Dr 23693
Davids Way 23692
Dawn Pl 23693
Declaration Dr 23692
Delray Dr 23692
Denbigh Blvd 23692
Denise Dr 23693
Derby Run 23693
Dillard Ln 23693
Dockside Way 23693
Dogwood Ct 23692
Dogwood Dr 23693
Dogwood Rd 23690
Dolphin Dr 23692
Don Juan Cir 23693
Donovan Ct 23693
Dorothy Dr 23692
Doyle Ct 23693
Driftwood Ct 23693
Dryden Ln 23693
Duff Dr 23692
Durham Ct 23693
Eagle Ln 23692
Edgehill Ln 23692
Edgewood Ct 23692
Edith Ln 23692
Edwards Ct 23693
Egret Ct 23692
Elise Pl 23693
Elizabeths Quay 23692
Ella Taylor Rd 23692
Elliott Rd 23693
Ellis Dr 23692
Elm Dr 23693
Elm Lake Way 23693
Emerald Ct 23693
Emily Ln 23690
Enchanted Forest Ln 23693
Englewood Dr 23692
Eric Nelson Run 23693
Estons Run 23693
Fairfield Dr 23692
Fairway Ln 23693
Fairwinds Dr 23693
Falcon Rd 23690
Falling Spring Run 23692
Farelarb Rd 23692
Farmstead Pl 23692
Faulkner Rd 23692
Fay Cir 23692
Feathergrass Park 23692
Ferguson Bnd 23693
N & S Fern Cove Ct 23693
Fernwood Bnd 23692
Ferrier Pl 23693
Fielding Lewis Dr 23692
Fieldstone Ct 23693
Firby Rd 23693
First St 23692
Fishermans Cv 23692
Fishneck Landing Rd 23692
Flag Creek Rd 23692
Flamingo Pl 23692
Fleming Way 23692
Forgotten Parcel Ln 23693
Fort Eustis Blvd 23692
Fortune Pl 23692
Foster Rd 23690
Foundry Ct 23693
Fountain Trce 23693
Foxfield Pl 23692
Frances Cir 23693
Frances Dr 23692
Franklin Rd 23692
Freedom Blvd 23692
Freemans Trce 23693
Fullenwinder Rd 23691
Gaines Way 23692
Galaxy Way 23693
Gardenville Dr 23693
Garman Loop 23690
George Emerson Ln 23693
George Washington Mem Hwy
1100-1210 23693
1212-3699 23693
3800-3898 23692
3900-9399 23692
10000-11899 23690
Giles Ln 23690
Glebe Spring Ln 23693
Glenkinchiey Ct 23693
Gnarled Oak Ln 23692
Goodwin Neck Rd 23692
Goosley Rd 23690
Gordon Ln 23693
Gorham Ct 23693
Grafton Dr 23692
Grafton District Rd 23692
Grafton Station Ln 23692
Granger Cir 23692
Grant Ct 23692
Gray Ln 23692
Grayson Way 23693
Greene Dr 23692
Greenland Dr 23693
Greystone Walk 23692
Griffin St 23693
Grindstone Turn 23693
Hailsham Pl 23692
Hale Cir 23690
Halles Run 23693
Hamlet Ct 23693
Hampton Hwy 23693
Harbour Dr 23692
Harlan Dr 23692
Harrigan Way 23693
Harris Ln 23692
Harris Grove Ln 23692
Harrod Ln 23692
Harvest Way 23693
Harwood Dr 23692
Hatcher Ct 23693
Hautz Way 23693
Haverstraw Ct 23692
Hawthorne Pt 23692
Hearthstone 23692
Heath Pl 23693
Heather Way 23692
Heatherwood Ln 23692
Heavens Way 23693
Hedgerow Ln 23693
Helen Crafford Rd 23690
Hemlock Ct 23693
Henry Lee Ln 23692
Heron Ct 23692
Hidden Hbr 23692
Hilda Holw 23693
Hillburne Ln 23692
Hobbs Way 23690
Hodges Cove Rd 23692
Holden Ln 23692
Hollingsworth Ct 23693
Holly Pl 23692
Holly Point Rd 23692
Hollywood Blvd 23692
Holmes Blvd 23692
Homestead Pl 23693
Honeysuckle Ln 23693
Horatio Gates Dr 23690
Hornsbyville Rd 23692
Hounds Chase 23693
Hudgins Farm Dr 23692
Hunters Ln 23692
Hyde Ln 23693
Ibis Pl 23692
Idlewood Cir 23693
Ilex Dr 23692
Indian Summer Dr 23693
Industry Dr 23693
Ironwood Dr 23693
Ivy Arch 23693
Jackson Cir 23693
Jacobs Run 23692
Janis Dr 23692
Jara Ln 23693
Jean Pl 23693
Jefferson Ln 23692
Jeffrey Kenneth Pl 23693
Jenkins Ct 23693
Jennie Dr 23692
Jennifer Dr 23693
Jennings Dr 23692
Jerdone Pl 23692
Jernigan Ln 23692
Jesse St 23693
Jessica Dr 23693
Jethro Ln 23692
Joel Ln 23692
John Carl Dr 23692
Jonadab Rd 23692
Jonathan Jct 23693
Jonquil Ct 23693
N & S Joshuas Way 23692
Jotank Turn 23693
Joy Ct 23693
Judith Cir 23693
Justice Ln 23692
Kaitlyn Ct 23693
Kanawah Run 23693
Karley Pl 23692
Katalina Way 23693
Kathleen Pl 23692
Kay Cir & Ln 23693
Kayla Ct 23693
Kelly St 23690
Kenmar Dr 23692
Kensington Pl 23693
Kent Taylor Dr 23693
Kentucky Dr 23693
Kerr Ln 23693
Kevin Ct 23692
Key Cir 23692
Kicotan Turn 23693
Killarnock Ct 23693
Kiln Creek Pkwy 23693
Kimberly Ct 23692
Kings Grant Dr 23692
Kings Pointe Xing 23693
Kingsbridge Ln 23692
Kingston Ct 23693
Kinnakeet Run 23693
Kirby Ln 23693
Kiskiac Turn 23693
Kiskiak Cir 23691
Kitty Dr 23692
Knoll Crst 23692
Kraft Ct 23693
Kristin Ct 23692
Kubesh Ct 23693
Kyle Cir 23693
Lackey Rd 23691
Lafayette Rd 23690
Lake Dale Way 23693
Lake Herrin Ct 23693
N Lakeland Cres 23693
Lakepoint Pl 23692
Lakeside Dr 23692
Lakeview Dr 23692
Lakewood Cir 23692
Lambs Creek Dr 23693
Lambs Rest Ln 23693
Lance Way 23693
Land Grant Rd 23692
Langston Pt 23693
Larchwood Rd 23692
Larkin Run 23692
Larkspur Holw 23692
Latta Ln 23693
Laura Ln 23692
Laurel Acres 23692
Laurel Path Rd 23692
Lawson Dr 23693
Laydon Way 23692
Leanne Ct 23692
Leigh Rd 23690
Lenox Ct 23693
Leroy Dr 23692
Leslie Ln 23693
Levelfield Park 23692
Lexington Ct 23693
Leyland Ct 23693
Liberty Dr 23693
Lilburne Way 23693
Linden Ct 23693
Lindsay Landing Ln 23692
Link Rd 23692
Little Bay Ave 23693
Loblolly Ct & Dr 23692
Lochmere Ct 23693
Locust Ln 23693
Lone Oak Dr 23692
Long Green Blvd 23693
Longwood Cir 23692
Lookout Pt 23692
Loon Ct 23692
Lord North Ct 23693
Lord Pelham Way 23693
Lorna Doone Dr 23692
Lotz Dr 23692
Lynns Way 23692
Madeira Dr 23693
Madison Ct 23692
Magnolia Ln 23690
Main Rd 23691
Main St 23690
Malcolm Ct 23693
Mallard Ln 23692
Manassas Loop 23693
Manchester Way 23692
Manhoac Run 23693
Manokin Turn 23693
Manor House Ct 23692
Mansion Rd 23693
Maple Rd 23690
S Maple Rd 23693
N & S Maragret Ct 23692
Marcy Dr 23693
Marine Cir 23692
Marl Ravine Rd 23692
Marlbank Dr 23692
Marlin Cir 23692
Marshland Vw 23693
Martiau St 23690
Marty Lee Dr 23693
Marvin Ln 23693
Mary Bierbauer Way 23693
Mason Ct 23692
Mason Row 23691
Massie Ln 23693
Matoaka Turn 23693
Maurice Ct 23690
Mays Lndg 23690
Mcclellan Ct 23692
Mcdonald Cir 23693
Meadowfield Rd 23692
Meadowlake Rd 23693
Meadowview Dr 23693
Medford Ct 23693
Meherrin Run 23693
Melbourne Ct 23693
Melinda Ln 23693
Melody Ln 23693
Melvins End 23693
Meredith Ln 23692
Messongo Run 23693
Michael Pl 23692
Mid Atlantic Pl 23693
Middle Rd 23692
Middlewood Ln 23692
Militia Ct 23693
Mill Ln 23692
Mill Rd 23693
Mill Xing 23693
Millside Way 23692
Millstone Ct 23693
Mimado Ct 23693
Mindy Ln 23693
Misty Dr 23692
Mitchells Method 23693
Mobjack Loop 23693
Monarch Glade 23692
Monty Mnr 23693
Monument Ct 23693
Moore House Rd 23690
Moores Creek Dr 23693
Mount Vernon Dr 23693
Moyock Run 23693
Muirfield Ct 23693
Mulberry Ct 23690
Muse Ln 23690
Myers Ct & Rd 23693
Nancy Ct 23690
Nandua Run 23693
Nansemond Turn 23693
Nanticoke Turn 23693
Nathan Pl 23692
Naurene Ct 23693
Nelson Rd & St 23690
Nelson District Rd 23692
Newsome Dr 23692
Nobles Landing Rd 23692
Nottoway Turn 23693
Oak Ln & St 23693
Oak Point Dr & Ln 23692
Oakwinds Pt 23692
Oakwood Dr 23693
Occoquan Turning 23693
Ocean Breeze Dr 23693
Ocracoke Ln 23693
Old Dare Rd 23692
Old Dominion Rd 23692
Old House Point Cir 23692
Old Lakeside Dr 23692
Old Landing Rd 23692
Old Railway Rd 23692
Old Williamsburg Rd 23690
Old Wormley Creek Rd 23692
Old York Hampton Hwy 23692
Olde Pond Ln 23693
Oleander Ct 23693
Onancock Turning 23693
Orchard Vw 23692
Oriana Rd 23693
Orion Ct 23693
Osprey Pt 23692
Ottis St 23693
Overlook Pt 23693
Owen Davis Blvd 23693
Oyster Cove Rd 23692
Pageland Dr 23693
Palmer Ct 23692
Pamlico Run 23693
Pamunkey Turn 23693
Paradise Point Rd 23692
Parkwood Dr 23693
Parrish Church Ln 23693
Paspeheghe Run 23693
Pasture Ln 23693
Paths Ridge Ct 23690
Patricks Creek Rd 23692
Patriot Way 23693
Patuxent Turn 23693
Paula Ct 23693
Pawpaw Pl 23693
Peachtree Ln 23693
Pecan Ter 23693
Pelican Pl 23692
Penny Ln 23692
Penrith Xing 23692
Perdue Ct 23692
Periwinkle Dr 23692
Perlie Ct 23692
Persimmon Dr 23693
Peyton Randolph Dr 23692
Pheasant Watch 23692
Phillips Ln 23693
Piankatank Turn 23693
Piccadilly Loop 23692
Pickett Pl 23693
Pine St 23693
Pine View Ct 23693
Pinehurst Dr 23692
Pinetree Ln 23692
Pinewood Cres 23693
Piney Point Rd 23692
Pintail Pl 23692
Pinyon Pnes 23693
Pioneer Ln 23692
Pleasant Dale Ln 23693
Pocomoke Run 23693
Pohick Run 23693
Polaris Dr 23693
Pond Vw 23692
Ponsonby Dr 23693
Poplar Point Rd 23692
Poridend Rd 23691
Port Cv 23693
Post Oak Rd 23692
Potapsco Turn 23693
Potomac Run 23693
Potter Ln 23693
Preamble Ln 23692
Prestwick Ct 23693
Prince Arthur Dr 23693
Prince Henry Ct 23693
Production Dr 23693
Providence Ln 23692
Pulaski St 23690
Pungo Turn 23693
Quail Rd 23692
Quantico Loop 23693
Quarter Trak 23693
Quartermarsh Dr 23692
Quest Ct 23692
Quincy Ct 23693
Rachel Ln 23692
Railway Rd 23692
Rainbrook Way 23692
Randolph St 23692
Ravenwood Ln 23692
Read St 23690
Red Bud Ln 23692
Redoubt Rd 23692
Resolution Dr 23692
Rhetts Run 23692
Rich Rd 23693
Richard Run 23693
Richter Ln 23693
Riva Ct 23690
River Point Dr 23693
Rivermeade Ct 23690
Riverside Dr 23692
Robert Rd 23693
Robin Hood Dr 23693
Robs Rd 23692
Rock Creek Ct 23693
Rockmor Ln 23693
Rocky Rd 23692
Rollins Way 23692
Rosetta Dr 23693
Rosewood Ln 23692
Royal Colven Dr 23693
Runaway Ln 23692
Runey Way 23693
Running Cedar Ct 23690
Running Man Trl 23693
Rural Retreat Rd 23692
Russell Ln 23693
Rustling Oak Rdg 23692
Ryans Way 23693
Saint Clair Cir 23693
Saint George Dr 23693
Salem Ct 23692
Salisbury Way 23693
Sallys Way 23692
Sanctuary Cv 23693
Sandalwood Ln 23693
Sandbox Ln 23692
Sanderling Walk 23692
Sandpiper Cv 23692
Sangaree Twist 23692
Sawgrass Turn 23692
Schembri Dr 23693
N School Ln 23692
Scotch Tom Way 23692
Scuttle Ln 23693
Seagrams Ct 23693
Seagull Pt 23692
Seasons Walk Ct 23690
Second St 23692
Seekright Dr 23693
Sentry Cir 23692
Seth Ln 23693
Seven Hollys Dr 23692
Shackleford Rd 23693
Shallow Lagoon 23693
Shamrock Ave 23693
Shanna Ct 23692
S Shannon Dr 23693
Sheep Ln 23693
Sheffield Ln 23693
Sheilas Way 23692
Sheild Ln 23692
Sheldon Ct 23693
Sherman Cres 23693
Ship Point Rd 23692
Shirley Dr 23693
Shorewood Trce 23693
Showalter Rd 23692
Shrewsbury Sq 23692
Shupper Dr 23691
Siege Ln 23692
Silkwood Turn 23693
Silver Fox Trce 23693
Sinclair Ln 23693
Skipper Ln 23693
Sleepy Hollow Ln 23692
Smith St 23690
Solebay St 23692
Somerset Cir 23692
Songbird Trl 23692
Sonshine Way 23690
Souverain Lndg 23692
Spencer Ln 23692
Spoon Ct 23693
Spring Rd 23690
Spruce Dr 23693
Stadium Vw 23690
Stagecoach Watch 23692
Stallion Ct 23693
Steckys Twist 23692
Stellar Cir 23693
Stephanie Ln 23692
Sterling Ct 23693
Stevens Ct 23693
Stillwater Ln 23692
Stone Lake Ct 23693
Sudbury Way 23693
Sulik Ln 23692
Sun Rise Way 23693
Susan Newton Ln 23693
Sussex Ct 23693
Swain Ln 23693
Swan Tavern Rise 23692
Swanson Ct 23693
Sweetbay Arbour 23692
Sycamore Ln 23690
Sylvia Dr 23693
Tabb Ln 23693
Tabb Lakes Dr 23693
Tabb Smith Trl 23693
Tall Pine Cir 23693
Talliaferro Rd 23690
Tallyho Dr 23693
Tannin Bark Trl 23692
Tarpon Dr 23692
Taurus Ct 23693
Taylor Farm Ln 23693
Tee Reach 23693
Tern Ct 23692
Terrance Cir 23693

Terrebonne Rd 23692
Terrys Run 23693
Terrywood Ct 23692
Tewkesbury Quay 23692
Theatre Rd 23693
Thoreau Cir 23693
Thornrose Dr 23692
Three Notched Rd 23692
Three Point Ct 23692
Tide Mill Rd 23693
Tides Run 23692
Tiger Run 23693
Tiger Paw Path 23692
Timber Ct 23693
Timberline Loop 23692
Tinnette Dr 23693
Todd Ct 23692
Townley Ct 23690
Tradewinds Dr 23693
Trebor Ln 23693
Treis Trl 23693
Trevor Trce 23692
Trinity Dr 23693
Tristen Dr 23693
Trivalon Ct 23693
Tuckahoe Trce 23693
Tue Marsh Ln 23692
Tui Pl 23693
Tulipwood Turn 23693
Tully Cove Trl 23692
Turnbridge Ln 23693
Tutelo Turn 23693
Two Turkey Run 23692
U S Coast Guard Trn Ctr 23690
Uppershire Way 23693
Us Navy 23691
Valentine Cir 23692
Van Curen Ct 23693
Victory Blvd 23693
Victory Rd 23692
View Hallo Way 23693
Villa Way 23693
Village Ave 23693
Vine Dr 23692
Virginia Ln 23692
Vivian Ct 23690
Vixen Ct 23693
Vreeland Dr 23692
Wainwrights Bnd 23692
Walden Dr 23692
Wallace Ct 23693
Walnut Dr 23690
Walters Ln 23692
Waltons Approach 23693
Wandering Doe Trl 23693
Warehouse Crse 23692
Washington Rd 23690
Water St 23690
Water Fowl Dr 23692
Watermans Way 23692
Waterside Pl 23692
Waterview Rd 23692
E & W Wedgwood Dr 23693
Wesley Ct 23692
Weston Rd 23692
Wethersfield Park 23692
Wexford Ct 23693
Wharf Row 23692
Wheeley Cir 23692
Whispering Way 23692
Whispering Pine Dr 23692
White Cedar Ln 23693
White Ridge Ln 23693
Whites Rd 23692
Whitt Ct 23690
Wicomico Turn 23693
Wilderness Vw 23692
Wildwood Dr 23692
Willards Way 23693
Willow Leaf Dr 23692
Willowood Dr 23693
Wilson Farm Ln 23693
Wiltons Way 23693
Wind Forest Ln 23692
Winder Rd 23693
Winders Ln 23692
Windsong Ln 23693
Windy Shore Dr 23693
Winfree Ln 23692
Winstead Dr 23693
Winter Ct 23693
Wolf Trap Rd 23692
Woodhaven Dr 23692
Woodlake Run 23692
Woodland Dr & Rd 23692
Woods Edge Ln 23693
Worley Farm Trl 23693
Wormley Creek Dr 23692
Wrought Iron Bnd 23693
Wynne Rd 23692
Wynterset Cir 23692
Yearling Ct 23693
York Dr 23690
York Ln 23692
York Crossing Rd 23692
York Downs Dr 23693
York Warwick Dr 23692
Yorkshire Dr 23693
E Yorktown Rd 23693
Yorkview Rd 23692
Yorkville Rd 23692
Yorkwood Ln 23692
Zachary Pl 23693
Zanca Turn 23693

Washington

People QuickFacts	Washington	USA
Population, 2013 estimate	6,971,406	316,128,839
Population, 2010 (April 1) estimates base	6,724,543	308,747,716
Population, percent change, April 1, 2010 to July 1, 2013	3.7%	2.4%
Population, 2010	6,724,540	308,745,538
Persons under 5 years, percent, 2013	6.4%	6.3%
Persons under 18 years, percent, 2013	22.9%	23.3%
Persons 65 years and over, percent, 2013	13.6%	14.1%
Female persons, percent, 2013	50.0%	50.8%
White alone, percent, 2013 (a)	81.2%	77.7%
Black or African American alone, percent, 2013 (a)	4.0%	13.2%
American Indian and Alaska Native alone, percent, 2013 (a)	1.9%	1.2%
Asian alone, percent, 2013 (a)	7.9%	5.3%
Native Hawaiian and Other Pacific Islander alone, percent, 2013 (a)	0.7%	0.2%
Two or More Races, percent, 2013	4.4%	2.4%
Hispanic or Latino, percent, 2013 (b)	11.9%	17.1%
White alone, not Hispanic or Latino, percent, 2013	71.0%	62.6%
Living in same house 1 year & over, percent, 2009-2013	82.7%	84.9%
Foreign born persons, percent, 2009-2013	13.2%	12.9%
Language other than English spoken at home, pct age 5+, 2009-2013	18.5%	20.7%
High school graduate or higher, percent of persons age 25+, 2009-2013	90.0%	86.0%
Bachelor's degree or higher, percent of persons age 25+, 2009-2013	31.9%	28.8%
Veterans, 2009-2013	582,265	21,263,779
Mean travel time to work (minutes), workers age 16+, 2009-2013	25.7	25.5
Housing units, 2013	2,928,217	132,802,859
Homeownership rate, 2009-2013	63.2%	64.9%
Housing units in multi-unit structures, percent, 2009-2013	25.6%	26.0%
Median value of owner-occupied housing units, 2009-2013	$262,100	$176,700
Households, 2009-2013	2,629,126	115,610,216
Persons per household, 2009-2013	2.54	2.63
Per capita money income in past 12 months (2013 dollars), 2009-2013	$30,742	$28,155
Median household income, 2009-2013	$59,478	$53,046
Persons below poverty level, percent, 2009-2013	13.4%	15.4%

Business QuickFacts	Washington	USA
Private nonfarm establishments, 2012	175,553	7,431,808
Private nonfarm employment, 2012	2,361,697	115,938,468
Private nonfarm employment, percent change, 2011-2012	0.3%	2.2%
Nonemployer establishments, 2012	412,542	22,735,915
Total number of firms, 2007	551,340	27,092,908
Black-owned firms, percent, 2007	S	7.1%
American Indian- and Alaska Native-owned firms, percent, 2007	1.2%	0.9%
Asian-owned firms, percent, 2007	6.8%	5.7%
Native Hawaiian and Other Pacific Islander-owned firms, percent, 2007	0.2%	0.1%
Hispanic-owned firms, percent, 2007	3.2%	8.3%
Women-owned firms, percent, 2007	28.7%	28.8%
Manufacturers shipments, 2007 ($1000)	112,053,283	5,319,456,312
Merchant wholesaler sales, 2007 ($1000)	76,790,966	4,174,286,516
Retail sales, 2007 ($1000)	92,968,519	3,917,663,456
Retail sales per capita, 2007	$14,380	$12,990
Accommodation and food services sales, 2007 ($1000)	12,389,422	613,795,732
Building permits, 2012	28,118	829,658

Geography QuickFacts	Washington	USA
Land area in square miles, 2010	66,455.52	3,531,905.43
Persons per square mile, 2010	101.2	87.4
FIPS Code	53	

(a) Includes persons reporting only one race.
(b) Hispanics may be of any race, so also are included in applicable race categories.
FN: Footnote on this item for this area in place of data
NA: Not available
D: Suppressed to avoid disclosure of confidential information
X: Not applicable
S: Suppressed; does not meet publication standards
Z: Value greater than zero but less than half unit of measure shown
F: Fewer than 100 firms
Source: US Census Bureau State & County QuickFacts

Washington

3 DIGIT ZIP CODE MAP

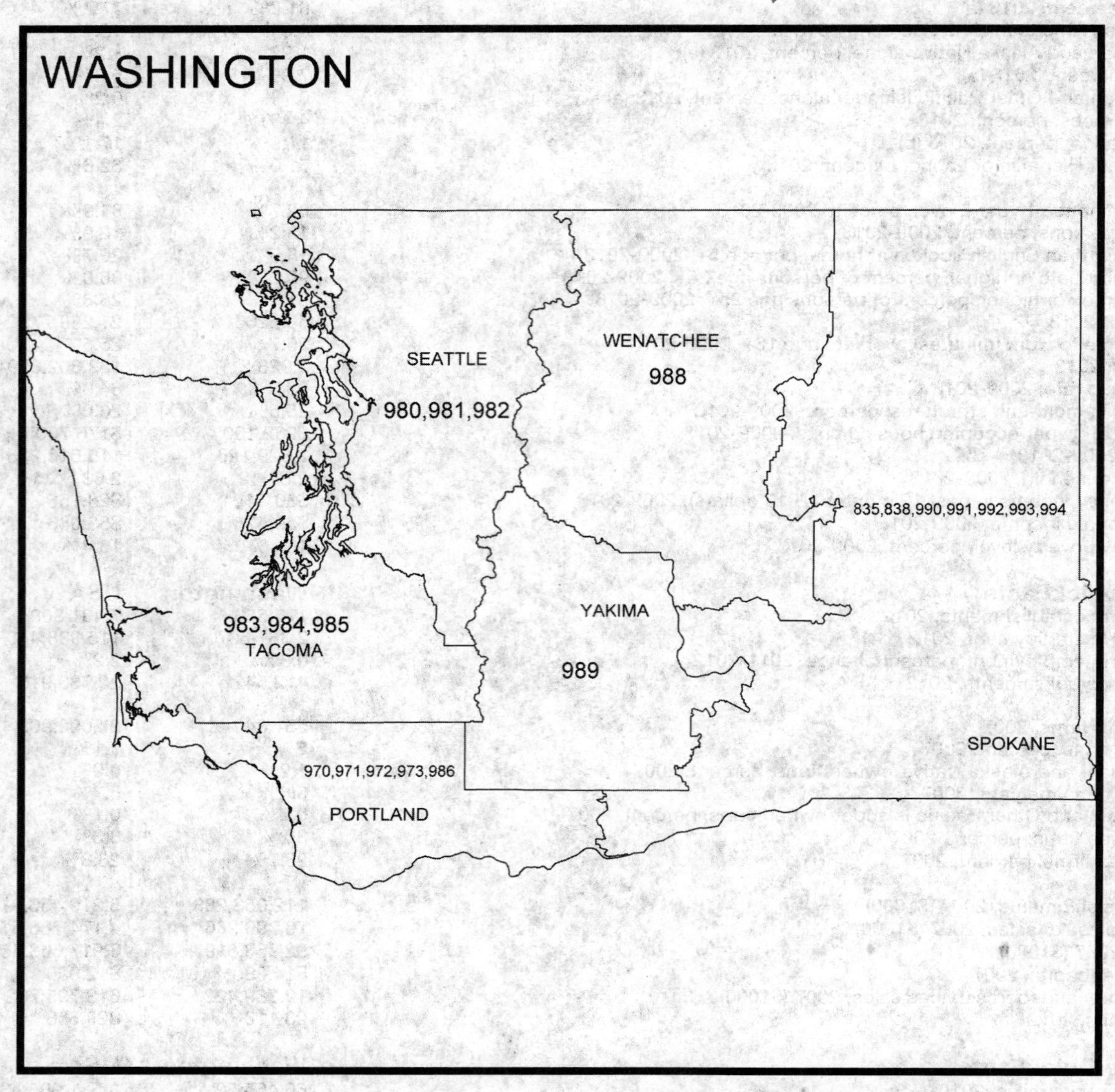

Washington

(Abbreviation: WA)

Places with more than one ZIP code are listed in capital letters, See pages indicated.

Post Office, County	ZIP Code
Aberdeen, Grays Harbor	98520
Acme, Whatcom	98220
Addy, Stevens	99101
Adna, Lewis	98522
Airway Heights, Spokane	99001
Albion, Whitman	99102
Algona, King	98001
Allyn, Mason	98524
Almira, Lincoln	99103
Amanda Park, Grays Harbor	98526
Amboy, Clark	98601
Anacortes, Skagit	98221
Anacortes, San Juan	98222
Anatone, Asotin	99401
Anderson Island, Pierce	98303
Appleton, Klickitat	98602
Ardenvoir, Chelan	98811
Ariel, Cowlitz	98603
Arlington, Snohomish	98223
Ashford, Pierce	98304
Asotin, Asotin	99402
AUBURN, King (See Page 4211)	
Bainbridge Island, Kitsap	98110
Baring, King	98224
Battle Ground, Clark	98604
Bay Center, Pacific	98527
Beaux Arts, King	98004
Beaver, Clallam	98305
Belfair, Mason	98528
BELLEVUE, King (See Page 4212)	
BELLINGHAM, Whatcom (See Page 4215)	
Belmont, Whitman	99104
Benge, Adams	99105
Benton City, Benton	99320
Bethel, Pierce	98387
Beverly, Grant	99321
Bickleton, Klickitat	99322
Bingen, Klickitat	98605
Black Diamond, King	98010
BLAINE, Whatcom (See Page 4218)	
Blakely Island, San Juan	98222
Bonney Lake, Pierce	98391
BOTHELL, King (See Page 4218)	
Bow, Skagit	98232
Boyds, Ferry	99107
BREMERTON, Kitsap (See Page 4220)	
Brewster, Okanogan	98812
Bridgeport, Douglas	98813
Brier, Snohomish	98036
Brinnon, Jefferson	98320
Brownstown, Yakima	98920
Brush Prairie, Clark	98606
Buckley, Pierce	98321
Bucoda, Thurston	98530
Buena, Yakima	98921
Burbank, Walla Walla	99323
Burien, King	98062
Burley, Kitsap	98322
Burlington, Skagit	98233
Burton, King	98013
Camano Island, Island	98282
Camas, Clark	98607
Camp Murray, Pierce	98430
Carbonado, Pierce	98323
Carlsborg, Clallam	98324
Carlton, Okanogan	98814
Carnation, King	98014
Carrolls, Cowlitz	98609
Carson, Skamania	98610
Cashmere, Chelan	98815
Castle Rock, Cowlitz	98611
Cathlamet, Wahkiakum	98612
Centerville, Klickitat	98613
Centralia, Lewis	98531
Chattaroy, Spokane	99003
Chehalis, Lewis	98532
Chelan, Chelan	98816
Chelan Falls, Chelan	98817
Cheney, Spokane	99004
Chewelah, Stevens	99109
Chimacum, Jefferson	98325
Chinook, Pacific	98614
Cinebar, Lewis	98533
City Of Spokane Valley, Spokane	99027
Clallam Bay, Clallam	98326
Clarkston, Asotin	99403
Clayton, Stevens	99110
Cle Elum, Kittitas	98922
Clearlake, Skagit	98235
Clinton, Island	98236
Clyde Hill, King	98004
Colbert, Spokane	99005
Colfax, Whitman	99111
College Place, Walla Walla	99324
Colton, Whitman	99113
Colville, Stevens	99114
Conconully, Okanogan	98819
Concrete, Skagit	98237
Connell, Franklin	99326
Conway, Skagit	98238
Cook, Klickitat	98605
Copalis Beach, Grays Harbor	98535
Copalis Crossing, Grays Harbor	98536
Cosmopolis, Grays Harbor	98537
Cougar, Cowlitz	98616
Coulee City, Grant	99115
Coulee Dam, Okanogan	99116
Coupeville, Island	98239
Covington, King	98042
Cowiche, Yakima	98923
Creston, Lincoln	99117
Creston, Lincoln	99147
Curlew, Ferry	99118
Curtis, Lewis	98538
Cusick, Pend Oreille	99119
Custer, Whatcom	98240
Dallesport, Klickitat	98617
Danville, Ferry	99121
Darrington, Snohomish	98241
Davenport, Lincoln	99122
Dayton, Columbia	99328
Deer Harbor, San Juan	98243
Deer Meadows, Lincoln	99122
Deer Park, Spokane	99006
Deming, Whatcom	98244
Des Moines (See Seattle)	
Desert Aire, Grant	99349
Diamond, Whitman	99111
Dixie, Walla Walla	99329
Doty, Lewis	98539
Dryden, Chelan	98821
Dupont, Pierce	98327
Duvall, King	98019
East Olympia, Thurston	98540
East Wenatchee, Douglas	98802
Easton, Kittitas	98925
Eastsound, San Juan	98245
Eatonville, Pierce	98328
Edgewood (See Puyallup)	
EDMONDS, Snohomish (See Page 4222)	
Edwall, Lincoln	99008
Elbe, Pierce	98330
Electric City, Grant	99123
Elk, Spokane	99009
Ellensburg, Kittitas	98926
Ellensburg, Kittitas	98950
Elma, Grays Harbor	98541
Elmer City, Okanogan	99124
Eltopia, Franklin	99330
Endicott, Whitman	99125
Entiat, Chelan	98822
Enumclaw, King	98022
Ephrata, Grant	98823
Espanola, Spokane	99022
Ethel, Lewis	98542
Evans, Stevens	99126
EVERETT, Snohomish (See Page 4223)	
Everson, Whatcom	98247
Everson, Whatcom	98276
Fairchild Air Force Base, Spokane	99011
Fairfield, Spokane	99012
Fall City, King	98024
Farmington, Whitman	99104
Farmington, Whitman	99128
FEDERAL WAY, King (See Page 4225)	
Ferndale, Whatcom	98248
Fife, Pierce	98424
Fircrest, Pierce	98466
Ford, Stevens	99013
Forks, Clallam	98331
Fort Lewis, Pierce	98433
Four Lakes, Spokane	99014
Fox Island, Pierce	98333
Freeland, Island	98249
Friday Harbor, San Juan	98250
Fruitland, Stevens	99129
Ft Lewis, Pierce	98433
Galvin, Lewis	98544
Garfield, Whitman	99130
George, Grant	98824
George, Grant	98848
Gifford, Stevens	99131
GIG HARBOR, Pierce (See Page 4226)	
Gleed, Yakima	98904
Glenoma, Lewis	98336
Glenwood, Klickitat	98619
Gold Bar, Snohomish	98251
Goldendale, Klickitat	98620
Goose Prairie, Yakima	98937
Gorst, Kitsap	98337
Graham, Pierce	98338
Grand Coulee, Grant	99133
Grandview, Yakima	98930
Granger, Yakima	98932
Granite Falls, Snohomish	98252
Grapeview, Mason	98546
Grayland, Grays Harbor	98547
Grays River, Wahkiakum	98621
Greenacres, Spokane	99016
Greenbank, Island	98253
Hamilton, Skagit	98255
Hansville, Kitsap	98340
Harrah, Yakima	98933
Harrington, Lincoln	99134
Harrington, Lincoln	99154
Hartline, Grant	99135
Hatton, Adams	99344
Hay, Whitman	99136
Heisson, Clark	98622
Hobart, King	98025
Home, Pierce	98349
Hoodsport, Mason	98548
Hooper, Whitman	99333
Hoquiam, Grays Harbor	98550
Humptulips, Grays Harbor	98552
Hunters, Stevens	99129
Hunters, Stevens	99137
Hunts Point, King	98004
Husum, Klickitat	98623
Ilwaco, Pacific	98624
Inchelium, Ferry	99138
Index, Snohomish	98256
Indianola, Kitsap	98342
Ione, Pend Oreille	99139
ISSAQUAH, King (See Page 4228)	
Joyce, Clallam	98343
Kahlotus, Franklin	99335
Kalama, Cowlitz	98625
Kapowsin, Pierce	98344
Keller, Ferry	99140
Kelso, Cowlitz	98626
Kenmore, King	98028
KENNEWICK, Benton (See Page 4229)	
KENT, King (See Page 4231)	
KETTLE FALLS, Ferry (See Page 4234)	
Keyport, Kitsap	98345
Kingston, Kitsap	98346
KIRKLAND, King (See Page 4234)	
Kittitas, Kittitas	98926
Kittitas, Kittitas	98934
Klickitat, Klickitat	98628
Klickitat, Klickitat	98670
La Center, Clark	98629
La Conner, Skagit	98257
La Grande, Pierce	98348
La Push, Clallam	98350
LACEY, Thurston (See Page 4235)	
Lacrosse, Whitman	99143
Lake Forest Park, King	98155
Lake Stevens, Snohomish	98258
Lake Tapps, Pierce	98391
Lakebay, Pierce	98349
Lakebay, Pierce	98351
LAKEWOOD, Pierce (See Page 4237)	
Lamona, Lincoln	99144
Lamont, Whitman	99017
Langley, Island	98260
Latah, Spokane	99018
Laurier, Ferry	99146
Leavenworth, Chelan	98826
Lebam, Pacific	98554
Liberty Lake, Spokane	99016
Liberty Lake, Spokane	99019
Lilliwaup, Mason	98555
Lincoln, Lincoln	99147
Lind, Adams	99341
Littlerock, Thurston	98556
Long Beach, Pacific	98631
Longbranch, Pierce	98351
Longmire, Pierce	98397
Longview, Cowlitz	98632
Loomis, Okanogan	98827
Loon Lake, Stevens	99148
Lopez Island, San Juan	98261
Lowden, Walla Walla	99360
Lummi Island, Whatcom	98262
Lyle, Klickitat	98635
Lyman, Skagit	98263
Lynden, Whatcom	98264
LYNNWOOD, Snohomish (See Page 4238)	
Mabton, Yakima	98935
Madigan Hospital, Pierce	98431
Malaga, Chelan	98828
Malden, Whitman	99149
Malo, Ferry	99150
Malone, Grays Harbor	98559
Malott, Okanogan	98829
Manchester, Kitsap	98353
Mansfield, Douglas	98830
Manson, Chelan	98831
Maple Falls, Whatcom	98266
Maple Valley, King	98038
Marblemount, Skagit	98267
Marcus, Stevens	99151
Marlin, Grant	98832
Marshall, Spokane	99020
MARYSVILLE, Snohomish (See Page 4239)	
Matlock, Mason	98560
Mattawa, Grant	99349
Mazama, Okanogan	98833
Mcchord Afb, Pierce	98438
Mcchord Afb, Pierce	98439
Mccleary, Grays Harbor	98557
Mckenna, Pierce	98558
Mead, Spokane	99021
Medical Lake, Spokane	99022
Medina, King	98039
Menlo, Pacific	98561
Mercer Island, King	98040
Mesa, Franklin	99343
Metaline, Pend Oreille	99152
Metaline Falls, Pend Oreille	99153
Methow, Okanogan	98834
Mica, Spokane	99023
Mill Creek, Snohomish	98012
Mill Creek, Snohomish	98082
Millwood, Spokane	99212
Milton, Pierce	98354
Mineral, Lewis	98355
Moclips, Grays Harbor	98562
Mohler, Lincoln	99154
Monitor, Chelan	98836
Monroe, Snohomish	98272
Montesano, Grays Harbor	98563
Morton, Lewis	98356
Moses Lake, Grant	98837
Mossyrock, Lewis	98564
MOUNT VERNON, Skagit (See Page 4240)	
Mountlake Terrace, Snohomish	98043
Moxee, Yakima	98936
Mukilteo, Snohomish	98275
Naches, Yakima	98937
Nahcotta, Pacific	98637
Napavine, Lewis	98532
Napavine, Lewis	98565
Naselle, Pacific	98638
Neah Bay, Clallam	98357
Neilton, Grays Harbor	98566
Nespelem, Okanogan	99155
Newcastle (See Renton)	
Newman Lake, Spokane	99025
Newport, Pend Oreille	99156
Nine Mile Falls, Spokane	99026
Nooksack, Whatcom	98276
Nordland, Jefferson	98358
Normandy Park (See Seattle)	
North Bend, King	98045
North Bonneville, Skamania	98639
North Lakewood, Snohomish	98259
Northport, Stevens	99157
Oak Harbor, Island	98277
Oakbrook, Pierce	98497
Oakesdale, Whitman	99158
Oakville, Grays Harbor	98568
Ocean City, Grays Harbor	98569
Ocean Park, Pacific	98640
Ocean Shores, Grays Harbor	98569
Odessa, Lincoln	99144
Odessa, Lincoln	99159
Okanogan, Okanogan	98840
Olalla, Kitsap	98359
Olga, San Juan	98279
OLYMPIA, Thurston (See Page 4241)	
Omak, Okanogan	98841
Onalaska, Lewis	98570
Orcas, San Juan	98280
Orient, Ferry	99160
Orondo, Douglas	98843
Oroville, Okanogan	98844
Orting, Pierce	98360
Othello, Adams	99344
Otis Orchards, Spokane	99027
Outlook, Yakima	98938
Oysterville, Pacific	98641
Pacific, King	98047
Pacific Beach, Grays Harbor	98571
Packwood, Lewis	98361
Palisades, Douglas	98845
Palouse, Whitman	99161
Paradise, Pierce	98398
Paradise Inn, Pierce	98398
Parker, Yakima	98939
Parkland (See Tacoma)	
PASCO, Franklin (See Page 4246)	
Pateros, Okanogan	98846
Paterson, Benton	99345
Pe Ell, Lewis	98572
Peshastin, Chelan	98847
Plaza, Whitman	99170
Plymouth, Benton	99346
Point Roberts, Whatcom	98281
Pomeroy, Garfield	99347
PORT ANGELES, Clallam (See Page 4248)	
Port Gamble, Kitsap	98364
Port Hadlock, Jefferson	98339
Port Hadlock, Jefferson	98365
Port Ludlow, Jefferson	98365
PORT ORCHARD, Kitsap (See Page 4250)	
Port Townsend, Jefferson	98368
Poulsbo, Kitsap	98370
Prescott, Walla Walla	99348
Preston, King	98050
Prosser, Benton	99350
Pullman, Whitman	99163
PUYALLUP, Pierce (See Page 4252)	
Quil Ceda Village, Snohomish	98271
Quilcene, Jefferson	98376
Quinault, Grays Harbor	98575
Quincy, Grant	98848
Rainier, Thurston	98576
Randle, Lewis	98377
Ravensdale, King	98051
Raymond, Pacific	98577
Reardan, Lincoln	99029
REDMOND, King (See Page 4255)	
RENTON, King (See Page 4257)	
Republic, Ferry	99166
Retsil, Kitsap	98378
Rice, Stevens	99167
RICHLAND, Benton (See Page 4260)	
Ridgefield, Clark	98642
Ritzville, Adams	99169
Riverside, Okanogan	98849
Roche Harbor, San Juan	98250
Rochester, Thurston	98579
Rock Island, Douglas	98850
Rockford, Spokane	99030
Rockport, Skagit	98283
Rollingbay, Kitsap	98061
Ronald, Kittitas	98940
Roosevelt, Klickitat	99356
Rosalia, Whitman	99170
Rosburg, Wahkiakum	98643
Roslyn, Kittitas	98941
Roy, Pierce	98580
Royal City, Grant	99357
Ruston, Pierce	98407
Ryderwood, Cowlitz	98581
Saint John, Whitman	99171
Salkum, Lewis	98582
SAMMAMISH, King (See Page 4261)	
Satsop, Grays Harbor	98583
Seabeck, Kitsap	98380
Seahurst, King	98062
Seatac (See Seattle)	
SEATTLE, King (See Page 4262)	
Seaview, Pacific	98644
Sedro Woolley, Skagit	98284
Sekiu, Clallam	98381
Selah, Yakima	98942
Sequim, Clallam	98382
Seven Bays, Lincoln	99122
Shaw Island, San Juan	98286
Shelton, Mason	98584
Shoreline (See Seattle)	
Silvana, Snohomish	98287
Silver Creek, Lewis	98585
SILVERDALE, Kitsap (See Page 4271)	
Silverlake, Cowlitz	98645

Skamokawa, Wahkiakum 98647
Skokomish Nation, Mason ... 98584
Skykomish, King 98288
SNOHOMISH, Snohomish
(See Page 4271)
Snoqualmie, King 98065
Snoqualmie Pass, Kittitas ... 98068
Soap Lake, Grant 98851
South Bend, Pacific 98586
South Cle Elum, Kittitas 98943
South Colby, Kitsap 98384
South Hill
(See Puyallup)
South Park Village, Kitsap ... 98366
South Prairie, Pierce 98385
Southworth, Kitsap 98386
Spanaway, Pierce 98387
Spangle, Spokane 99031
SPOKANE, Spokane
(See Page 4273)
Spokane Valley, Spokane 99016
Sprague, Whitman 99017
Sprague, Lincoln 99032
Springdale, Stevens 99173
Stanwood, Island 98282
Stanwood, Snohomish 98292
Starbuck, Columbia 99359
Startup, Snohomish 98293
Stehekin, Chelan 98852
Steilacoom, Pierce 98388
Steptoe, Whitman 99174
Stevenson, Skamania 98648
Stratford, Grant 98853
Sultan, Snohomish 98294
Sumas, Whatcom 98295
Sumner, Pierce 98390
Sunnyside, Yakima 98944
Sunset Hill, Spokane 99219
Suquamish, Kitsap 98392
TACOMA, Pierce
(See Page 4279)
Taholah, Grays Harbor 98587
Tahuya, Mason 98588
Tekoa, Whitman 99033
Tenino, Thurston 98589
Thornton, Whitman 99176
Thorp, Kittitas 98946
Tieton, Yakima 98947
Tokeland, Pacific 98590
Toledo, Lewis 98591
Tonasket, Okanogan 98855
Toppenish, Yakima 98948
Touchet, Walla Walla 99360
Toutle, Cowlitz 98649
Tracyton, Kitsap 98393
Tri Cities, Franklin 99302
Trout Lake, Klickitat 98650
Tukwila
(See Seattle)
Tulalip, Snohomish 98271
Tumtum, Stevens 99034
Tumwater
(See Olympia)
Twisp, Okanogan 98856
Underwood, Skamania 98651
Union, Mason 98592
Union Gap
(See Yakima)
Uniontown, Whitman 99179
University Place, Pierce 98464
Usk, Pend Oreille 99180
Vader, Lewis 98593
Valley, Stevens 99181
Valleyford, Spokane 99023
Valleyford, Spokane 99036
VANCOUVER, Clark
(See Page 4285)
Vantage, Kittitas 98950
Vashon, King 98013
Vashon, King 98070
Vaughn, Pierce 98394
Veradale, Spokane 99037
Wahkiacus, Klickitat 98670
Waitsburg, Walla Walla 99361
Waldron, San Juan 98297
Walla Walla, Walla Walla 99362
Wallula, Walla Walla 99363
Wapato, Yakima 98951
Warden, Grant 98857
Washougal, Clark 98671
Washtucna, Adams 99371
Waterville, Douglas 98858
Wauconda, Okanogan 98859
Wauna, Pierce 98329
Wauna, Pierce 98395
Waverly, Spokane 99039
Wellpinit, Stevens 99040
WENATCHEE, Chelan
(See Page 4292)
West Richland, Benton 99353
Westport, Grays Harbor 98595
Whidbey Island Naval Air,
Island 98278
White Salmon, Klickitat 98672
White Swan, Yakima 98952
Wilbur, Lincoln 99185
Wilkeson, Pierce 98396
Wilson Creek, Grant 98860
Winlock, Lewis 98596
Winthrop, Okanogan 98862
Wishram, Klickitat 98673
WOODINVILLE, King
(See Page 4293)
Woodland, Cowlitz 98674
Woodway, Snohomish 98020
Yacolt, Clark 98675
YAKIMA, Yakima
(See Page 4294)
Yarrow Point, King 98004
Yelm, Thurston 98597
Zillah, Yakima 98953

AUBURN WA

General Delivery 98002

POST OFFICE BOXES MAIN OFFICE STATIONS AND BRANCHES

Box No.s
All PO Boxes 98071

NAMED STREETS

A Pl SE 98002
A St NE 98002
A St NW 98001
A St SE
1-11 98002
13-4500 98002
4502-4598 98002
4900-5198 98092
5200-5300 98092
5302-5698 98092
A St SW 98001
Aaby Dr 98001
Academy Dr SE 98092
Alexander Ave & Pl 98092
Algona Blvd N & S 98001
Alpine Dr, Pl & St 98002
Annette Ave & Ct 98092
Auburn Ave 98002
Auburn Way N 98002
Auburn Way S
1-2800 98002
2801-5899 98092
SE Auburn Black Diamond Rd
1600-1738 98002
2800-12798 98092
12800-22399 98092
Auburn Enumclaw Rd SE 98092
B Pl NW 98001
B St NE 98002
B St NW 98001
B St SE 98002
B St SW 98001
Beendari Ave SE 98092
Bennett Ave SE 98092
Boundary Blvd 98001
Bridget Ave SE 98092
Broadway Blvd 98001
C Ct SE 98002
C Pl SE 98002
C St NE 98002
C St NW 98001
C St SE 98002
C St SW 98001
Cedar Dr SE 98002
Celery Ave 98001
Charlotte Ave SE 98092
Chicago Ave 98001
Clay St NW 98001
Coal Ave 98001
Cross St SE 98002
D Pl SE 98002
D St NE 98002
D St NW 98001
D St SE 98002
D St SW 98001
S Dave St 98001
Diana Ct SE 98092
N & S Division St 98001
Dogwood Dr & St 98092
Douglas Ave & Ct 98092
Duncan Ave SE 98092
E St NE 98002
E St SE 98002
E St SW 98001
Elaine Ave & Ct 98092
Elizabeth Ave & Loop 98092
Ellingson Rd 98001
Elliot Ct SE 98092
Elm St SE 98092
Emerald Downs Dr 98001
Evan Ct SE 98092
Evergreen Loop & Way 98092
F Ct SE 98002
F Pl NE 98002
F St NE 98002
F St NW 98001
F St SE 98002
F St SW 98001
Fir Pl & St 98092
SE Flaming Geyser Rd 98092
Forest Ridge Dr SE
2100-2799 98002
2801-2899 98092
Forest Ridge Pl SE 98092
Foster Ave SE 98092
Francis Ave, Ct & Loop 98092
Franklin Ave SE 98092
Frontage Rd NW 98001
G St NW 98001
G St SE 98002
G St SW 98001
Ginkgo St SE 98092
Grace Ct SE 98092
Grady Ct SE 98092
Green Acres Pl 98001
Green River Rd SE 98092
SE Green Valley Rd 98092
H St NE 98002
H St NW 98001
H St SE 98002
Harvey Rd 98002
Hazel Ave, Ln, Loop & Pl SE 98092
Heather Ave SE 98092
Hemlock Dr & St 98092
Henry Rd 98002
Hi Crest Dr 98001
Highland Ct & Dr 98092
Howard Rd 98002
SE Husky Way 98092
I Pl NE 98002
I St NE 98002
I St NW 98001
I St SE 98002
Industry Dr N & SW 98001
Irene Ave SE 98092
Iron Ave 98001
Isaac Ave & Ct 98092
J Ct & St 98002
James Ave & Pl 98092
Jasmine Ave SE 98092
Jordan Ave SE 98092
Junction Blvd 98001
Juniper Ct & Ln 98092
K St NE & SE 98002
Katherine Ave SE 98092
Kennedy Ave SE 98092
Kent Black Diamond Rd SE 98092
Kersey Way SE 98092
Knickerbocker Dr 98001
L Ct, Pl & St NE & SE 98002
E & SE Lake Holm Dr & Rd SE 98092
SE Lake Moneysmith Rd 98092
Lake Tapps Dr & Pkwy 98092
Lakeland Hills Way SE 98092
Lea Hill Rd 98092
Lemon Tree Ln 98092
Lilac St SE 98092
Lindsay Ave SE 98092
Lund Rd 98001
M Dr NE 98002
M Pl NE 98002
M Pl SE 98002
M St NE 98002
M St NW 98001
M St SE 98002
Main St 98001
E Main St 98002
W Main St 98001
Main Street Pl 98002
Maple Dr 98092
Marshall Ave & Pl 98092
Military Rd S 98001
Mill Pond Dr & Loop 98092
Milwaukee Ave & Blvd N & S 98001
Montevista Dr SE 98092
Mountain View Dr 98001
N Ct & St 98002
Nathan Ave, Loop, Pl & Way SE 98092
Noble Ct SE 98092
O Ct NE 98002
O Ct SE 98002
O Pl NE 98002
O St NE 98002
O St SE 98002
O St SW 98001
Olive Ave SE 98092
Olympic St SE 98002
Oravetz Pl & Rd 98092
Orchard Pl & St 98092
Outlet Collection Dr SW 98001
Palerens Ave S 98001
Panorama Dr SE 98092
Park Ave 98002
Pearl Ave SE 98092
Peasley Canyon Rd & Way S 98001
Perimeter Rd 98001
Perry Ave, Dr & Pl 98092
Pike Pl NE 98002
Pike St NE 98002
Pike St NW 98001
Pike St SE 98002
Poplar St SE 98092
Pullman Ave 98001
Q St NE 98002
Quincy Ave SE 98092
R Pl NE 98002
R Pl SE 98002
R St NE 98002
R St NW 98001
R St SE 98002
Randall Ave SE 98092
Rebecca Ave, Ct & Pl 98092
Redwood Ct 98092
Riverview Dr NE & SE 98002
Riverwalk Dr SE 98002
S St SE 98002
Scenic Dr & Pl 98092
Seattle Blvd N & S 98001
Skyway Ln
2300-2799 98002
2800-2899 98092
Skyway Pl 98092
Stanley Ave & Ct 98001
S Star Lake Rd 98001
Stuart Ave & Pl 98092
Stuck River Dr 98092
T St NE 98002
T St NW 98001
T St SE 98002
Tacoma Blvd 98001
Terrace View Ln SE 98092
Thomas Ct, Pl & Rd 98092
U Ct NW 98001
U Pl NE 98002
U St NE 98002
U St NW 98001
U St SE 98002
Udall Ave, Ct & Pl 98092
V Ct SE 98002
V Pl SE 98002
V St NW 98001
V St SE 98002
Valearel St SE 98002
E Valley Hwy E 98092
W Valley Hwy N 98001
W Valley Hwy S 98001
SE Victoria Ave, Ct & St SE 98092
W Ct SE 98002
W Pl NW 98001
W St NW 98001
Ward Ave SE 98092
Warde St 98001
Washington Blvd 98001
Wesley Pl SE 98092
Western Ave 98001
Wyman Dr 98092
Z St SE 98002

NUMBERED STREETS

1st Ave N 98001
1st St NE 98002
1st St NW 98001
1st St SE 98002
1st St SW 98001
2nd Ave N 98001
2nd Ave S 98001
2nd St NE 98002
2nd St NW 98001
2nd St SE 98002
2nd St SW 98001
3rd Ave N 98001
3rd Ave S 98001
3rd Ct SE 98002
3rd Pl S 98001
3rd St NE 98002
3rd St NW
1-99 98002
10-11 98071
100-114 98001
116-298 98001
3rd St SE 98002
3rd St SW 98001
4th Ave N 98001
4th Ave S 98001
4th Pl NE 98002
4th Pl SE 98002
4th St NE 98002
4th St SE 98002
4th St SW 98001
5th Ave N 98001
5th Ave NE
118-120 98047
400-498 98001
5th Ave NW 98001
5th St NE 98002
5th St NW 98001
5th St SE 98002
5th St SW 98001
6th Ave N 98001
6th Pl NE 98002
6th St NE 98002
6th St NW 98001
6th St SE 98002
7th NE & SE 98001
7th NE & SE 98002
8th Ave N 98001
8th St NE 98002
8th St NW 98001
8th St SE 98002
8th St SW 98001
9th Ave N 98001
9th Ct NW 98001
9th St NE 98002
9th St SE 98002
10th Ave N 98001
10th Ct NW 98001
10th Pl SE 98002
10th St NE 98002
10th St SE 98002
11th NE & SE 98001
11th NE & SE 98002
12th Ct NW 98001
12th Pl NE 98002
12th St NE 98002
12th St SE 98002
13th NE & SE 98002
14th Pl NE 98002
14th Pl SE 98092
14th St NE 98002
14th St NW 98001
14th St SE
100-198 98002
200-299 98002
2900-3099 98092
15th St NE 98002
15th St NW 98001
15th St SE
100-399 98002
2900-3099 98092
15th St SW 98001
16th St NE 98002
16th St NW 98001
16th St SE
100-399 98002
3000-3299 98092
17th Ct SE 98002
17th Dr SE 98002
17th St NE 98002
17th St SE
101-297 98002
299-2799 98002
2900-3099 98092
18th Pl NE 98002
18th St NE 98002
18th St SE
1000-2799 98002
2900-3099 98092
19th Dr NE 98002
19th Pl SE
1900-1999 98092
2500-2598 98002
2600-2799 98002
19th St SE
600-698 98002
700-1099 98002
2801-3097 98092
3099-3499 98092
20th Ct SE 98002
20th St NE 98002
20th St NW 98001
20th St SE
1000-1100 98002
1102-1198 98002
3200-3499 98092
21st Pl SE 98002
21st St NE 98002
21st St NW 98001
21st St SE
100-1599 98002
3000-3499 98092
22nd St NE 98002
22nd St NW 98001
22nd St SE
400-1599 98002
2800-3099 98092
22nd Way NE 98002
23rd Pl SE 98002
23rd St NE 98002
23rd St NW 98001
23rd St SE 98002
24th Pl SE 98002
24th St NE 98002
24th St NW 98001
24th St SE 98002
25th Pl & St 98002
26th Pl NE 98002
26th Pl SE 98002
26th St NE 98002
26th St NW 98001
26th St SE 98002
27th Pl SE
2300-2399 98002
2900-2999 98092
27th St SE
400-2399 98002
2900-2999 98092
28th Ct SE 98002
28th Pl SE 98002
28th St NE 98002
28th St SE
601-697 98002
699-2299 98002
2900-3099 98092
29th St NW 98001
29th St SE 98002
30th Ct S 98001
30th Pl S 98001
30th St NE 98002
30th St NW 98001
30th St SE 98002
30th Way S 98001
31st Ct S 98001
31st Pl S 98001
31st St NE 98002
31st St SE 98002
32nd Ave S 98001
32nd Pl NE 98002
32nd Pl S 98001
32nd St NE 98002
32nd St SE
1200-1599 98002
5300-5398 98092
33rd Ave S 98001
33rd Ln S 98001
33rd Pl S 98001
33rd Pl SE 98002
33rd St SE
1100-1198 98002
1200-1999 98002
5300-5499 98092
34th Ave S 98001
34th Ct S 98001
34th Ln S 98001
34th Pl S 98001
34th St SE 98002
35th Ave S 98001
35th Ct SE 98002
35th Pl S 98001
35th Pl SE 98092
35th St NE 98002
35th St SE 98002
35th Way S 98001
35th Way SE 98092
36th Ave S 98001
36th Pl S 98001
36th St SE
1500-2099 98002
6100-6399 98092
37th Ave S 98001
37th Ct SE 98092
37th Pl S 98001
37th Pl SE
201-399 98002
6301-6315 98092
37th St NE 98002
37th St NW 98001
37th St SE
200-398 98002
5400-6399 98092
37th Way SE 98002
38th Ave S 98001
38th Pl S 98001
38th St SE 98092
39th Ave & Pl 98001
40th Ave S 98001
40th Pl S 98001
40th St NE 98002
41st Ave, Ct & Pl 98001
42nd Ave S 98001
42nd Ct NE 98002
42nd Pl S 98001
42nd St NE 98002
42nd St NW 98001
43rd Ave S 98001
43rd Ct NE 98002
43rd Ct S 98001
43rd Pl S 98001
43rd St NE 98002
44th Ave, Ct, Pl & St S & NW 98001
45th Ave S 98001
45th Ct S 98001
45th Pl S 98001
45th St NE 98002
46th Ave, Ct & Pl 98001
47th Ave S 98001
47th Ct S 98001
47th Pl S 98001
47th St SE 98092
48th Ave S 98001
48th Ct S 98001
48th Ct SE 98092
48th Pl S 98001
49th Ave S 98001
49th Ct S 98001
49th Ln S 98001
49th Pl S 98001
49th St NE 98002
49th St NW 98001
49th St SE 98092
50th Ave S 98001
50th Ct S 98001
50th Ln S 98001
50th Pl S 98001
50th St NE 98002
50th St NW 98001
50th St SE 98092
51st Ave S 98001
51st Ct S 98001
51st Pl NE 98002
51st Pl S 98001
51st St NE 98002
51st St SE 98092
52nd Ave S 98001
52nd Pl S 98001
52nd St NE 98002
52nd St SE 98092
53rd Ave S 98001
53rd Pl S 98001
53rd St SE 98092
54th Ave S 98001
54th Ct S 98001
54th Pl S 98001
54th St SE 98092
55th Ave S 98001
55th Ct SE 98092
55th Pl S 98001
55th St SE 98092
55th Way SE 98092
56th Ave S 98001
56th Ct S 98001
56th Ct SE 98092
56th Pl S 98001
56th St SE 98092
57th Ave S 98001
57th Ct SE 98092
57th Dr SE 98092
57th Pl S 98001
57th Pl SE 98092
57th St SE 98092
58th Ave S 98001
58th Ct S 98001
58th Pl S 98001
58th Pl SE 98092
58th Way SE 98092
59th Ave S 98001
59th Ct SE 98092
59th Pl S 98001
59th Pl SE 98092
59th St SE 98092
60th Ct S 98001
60th Pl S 98001
60th St SE 98092
61st Ave S 98001
61st Pl SE 98092
61st St SE 98092
62nd Ct SE 98092
62nd Loop SE 98092
62nd Pl S 98001
62nd Pl SE 98092
62nd St SE 98092
63rd Ct S 98001
63rd Ct SE 98092
63rd Pl S 98001
63rd Pl SE 98092
63rd St SE 98092
64th Ave S 98001
64th Ct SE 98092
64th St SE 98092
65th Ave S 98001
65th Ct SE 98092
65th St SE 98092
66th Ave S 98001
66th Pl SE 98092
66th St SE 98092
67th Ct, Ln & St 98092
68th Loop & St 98092
69th Ct & St 98092
71st St SE 98092

72nd Ct & St 98092
73rd St SE 98092
80th Ave S 98001
100th Ave N 98001
100th Ave SE 98092
101st Ave & Pl 98092
102nd Ave SE 98092
103rd Ct SE 98092
104th Ave & Pl 98092
105th Ave & Pl 98092
106th Pl SE 98092
107th Ave & Pl 98092
108th Ave & Pl 98092
109th Ave & Pl 98092
110th Ave & Pl 98092
111th Ave, Ct & Pl 98092
112th Ave & Pl 98092
113th Ave, Ct, Pl & Way SE 98092
114th Ave, Ln, Pl & Way SE 98092
115th Ave, Ct, Ln & Pl SE 98092
116th Ave SE 98092
117th Ave & Pl 98092
118th Ave, Ct & Pl 98092
119th Ave & Pl 98092
120th Ave, Ct, Ln, Pl & Way SE 98092
121st Ave, Ln, Pl & Way SE 98092
122nd Ave, Ct, Ln, Pl & Way SE 98092
123rd Ave, Ln & Way 98092
123 Pl SE 98092
124th Ave & Pl 98092
125th Ave, Ct & Pl 98092
126th Ave & Ct 98092
127th Pl & Way 98092
128th Ct & Pl 98092
129th Ave, Pl & Way 98092
130th Ave & Way 98092
132nd Ave, Ct & Pl 98092
133rd Ave SE 98092
134th Ave, Ct & Pl 98092
135th Ave, Ct & Pl 98092
136th Ave SE 98092
137th Ave SE 98092
138th Ave & Pl 98092
139th Ter SE 98092
140th Ave SE 98092
141st Pl SE 98092
142nd Ave & Ln 98092
143rd Ct & Pl 98092
144th Ave SE 98092
145th Pl SE 98092
146th Ave SE 98092
147th Ave SE 98092
148th Ave & Way 98092
149th Ave SE 98092
150th Pl SE 98092
151st Ave SE 98092
152nd Ave SE 98092
154th Ave SE 98092
156th Ave SE 98092
157th Ave SE 98092
158th Ave & Pl 98092
159th Ave SE 98092
160th Ave, Dr & Pl 98092
161st Ave, Dr, Ln & Pl SE 98092
162nd Ave, Ct & Pl 98092
164th Ave SE 98092
165th Ave & Pl 98092
166th Ln & Way 98092
168th Ave & Way 98092
169th Ave SE 98092
170th Ave & Pl 98092
171st Ave SE 98092
172nd Ave & Ct 98092
173rd Ave, Ln & Pl 98092
174th Ave, Ln & Pl 98092
175th Ln SE 98092
176th Ave, Pl & Way 98092
177th Ave & Pl 98092
178th Pl SE 98092
179th Ave & Pl 98092
180th Ave SE 98092
181st Ave SE 98092
182nd Ave SE 98092
183rd Ave SE 98092
184th Ave SE 98092
186th Ave SE 98092
188th Ave SE 98092
190th Ave SE 98092
191st Ave SE 98092
192nd Ave SE 98092
196th Ave SE 98092
198th Ave SE 98092
200th Ave SE 98092
202nd Pl SE 98092
204th Ave SE 98092
205th Ave SE 98092
206th Ave & Pl 98092
207th Pl SE 98092
208th Ave SE 98092
210th Ave SE 98092
211th Pl SE 98092
212th Ave & Way 98092
213th Pl SE 98092
214th Ave SE 98092
215th Ave SE 98092
216th Ave SE 98092
217th Ave SE 98092
218th Ave SE 98092
221st Ave SE 98092
227th Ave SE 98092
240th Ave SE 98092
243rd Ave SE 98092
252nd Ave SE 98092
253rd Ave SE 98092
S 272nd Pl 98001
273rd Pl & St 98001
S 274th St 98001
275th Ct & Pl 98001
S 276th St 98001
277th Pl & St 98001
278th Pl & St 98001
279th Pl & St 98001
S 280th Pl 98001
S 280th St
3400-8099 98001
8201-8397 98002
S 281st St 98001
SE 281st St 98092
S 282nd St 98001
SE 282nd St 98092
S 282nd Way 98001
S 283rd Ct 98001
S 283rd Ln 98001
S 283rd Pl 98001
S 283rd St 98001
SE 283rd St 98092
S 284th Pl 98001
S 284th St 98001
SE 284th St 98092
S 285th Pl 98001
S 285th St 98001
SE 285th St 98092
S 286th Ct 98001
SE 286th Pl 98092
S 286th St 98001
SE 286th St 98092
S 287th St 98001
SE 287th St 98092
S 288th Pl 98001
SE 288th Pl 98092
S 288th St 98001
SE 288th St 98092
S 289th Pl 98001
SE 289th St 98092
S 290th Pl 98001
SE 290th Pl 98092
S 290th St 98001
SE 290th St 98092
S 291st St 98001
SE 291st St 98092
S 292nd Pl 98001
S 292nd St 98001
SE 292nd St 98092
SE 292 Way 98092
S 293rd Pl 98001
S 293rd St 98001
SE 293rd St 98092
SE 294 Ct 98092
S 294th Pl 98001
SE 294th Pl 98092
S 294th St 98001
SE 294th St 98092
S 295th Ct 98001
SE 295 Ct 98092
S 295th Pl 98001
S 295th St 98001
SE 295th St 98092
S 296th Ct 98001
S 296th Pl 98001
S 296th St 98001
SE 296th St 98092
SE 296th Way 98092
SE 297th Ct 98092
S 297th Pl 98001
SE 297th Pl 98092
S 297th St 98001
SE 297th St 98092
S 298th Ct 98001
S 298th Pl 98001
SE 298th Pl 98092
S 298th St 98001
SE 298th St 98092
S 299th Ct 98001
SE 299th Ct 98092
S 299th Pl 98001
SE 299th Pl 98092
S 299th St 98001
SE 299th St 98092
S 300th Pl 98001
SE 300th Pl 98092
S 300th St 98001
SE 300th Way 98092
S 301st Ct 98001
SE 301st Ct 98092
S 301st Dr 98001
S 301st Pl 98001
SE 301st Pl 98092
S 301st St 98001
SE 301st St 98092
SE 301st Way 98092
SE 302nd Ct 98092
S 302nd Ln 98001
S 302nd Pl 98001
SE 302nd Pl 98092
S 302nd St 98001
SE 302nd St 98092
S 303rd Ct 98001
SE 303rd Ct 98092
S 303rd Pl 98001
S 303rd St 98001
SE 304th Ct 98092
SE 304th Pl 98092
S 304th St 98001
SE 304th St 98092
SE 304th Way 98092
SE 305th Ct 98092
S 305th Pl 98001
SE 305th Pl 98092
S 305th St 98001
SE 305th St 98092
SE 306th Ct 98092
S 306th Pl 98001
SE 306th Pl 98092
SE 306th St 98092
S 307th Pl 98001
SE 307th Pl 98092
S 307th St 98001
SE 307th St 98092
SE 308th Ct 98092
SE 308th Ln 98092
S 308th Pl 98001
SE 308th Pl 98092
S 308th St 98001
SE 308th St 98092
SE 309th Pl 98092
S 309th St 98001
SE 309th St 98092
SE 310th Ln 98092
S 310th Pl 98001
S 310th St 98001
SE 310th St 98092
S 311th Ct 98001
SE 311th Pl 98092
SE 311th St 98092
S 312th Ln 98001
SE 312th Ln 98092
S 312th Pl 98001
SE 312th Pl 98092
S 312th St 98001
SE 312th St 98092
SE 312th Way 98092
SE 313th Ln 98092
S 313th Pl 98001
SE 313th Pl 98092
S 313th St 98001
SE 313th St 98092
S 314th Ct 98001
S 314th Pl 98001
SE 314th Pl 98092
S 314th St 98001
SE 314th St 98092
SE 315th Ct 98092
S 315th Pl 98001
SE 315th Pl 98092
S 315th St 98001
SE 315th St 98092
SE 316th Ct 98092
SE 316th Pl 98092
S 316th St 98001
SE 316th St 98092
SE 317th Ct 98092
SE 317th Pl 98092
S 317th St 98001
SE 317th St 98092
SE 318th Ct 98092
S 318th Pl 98001
SE 318th Pl 98092
S 318th St 98001
SE 318th St 98092
SE 318th Way 98092
SE 319th Ct 98092
SE 319th Pl 98092
S 319th St 98001
SE 319th St 98092
SE 320th Pl 98092
S 320th St 98001
SE 320th St 98092
SE 321st Pl 98092
S 321st St 98001
S 322nd Pl 98001
SE 322nd Pl 98092
SE 322nd St 98092
323rd Pl, St & Way 98092
SE 324th Ln 98092
S 324th Pl 98001
S 324th St 98001
SE 324th St 98092
325th Ct, Pl & St 98092
S 326th Ln 98001
SE 326th Pl 98092
S 326th St 98001
SE 326th St 98092
327th Pl & St 98092
SE 328th Pl 98092
S 328th St 98001
SE 328th St 98092
S 329th Pl 98001
SE 329th St 98092
SE 330th Pl 98092
SE 330th St
10400-10499 98002
18200-20599 98092
SE 330th Way 98092
SE 331st Ct 98092
S 331st St 98001
SE 331st St 98092
332nd Pl & St 98092
333rd Ct & Pl 98092
334th Pl & St 98092
SE 335th St 98092
S 336th Pl 98001
SE 336th Pl 98092
S 336th St 98001
SE 336th St 98092
S 337th St 98001
SE 337th St 98092
S 338th St 98001
SE 338th St 98092
339th Ct & St 98092
S 340th Pl 98001
S 340th St 98001
SE 340th St 98092
SE 342nd Pl 98092
S 342nd St 98001
SE 342nd St 98092
S 343rd St 98001
S 344th Ct 98001
S 344th St 98001
SE 344th St 98092
S 345th St 98001
SE 345th St 98092
S 346th St 98001
SE 346th St 98092
S 347th Pl 98001
S 347th St 98001
SE 347th St 98092
S 348th Pl 98001
S 348th St 98001
SE 348th St 98092
349th Pl & St 98001
350th Pl & St 98001
S 351st St 98001
SE 351st St 98092
S 352nd Ln 98001
S 352nd St 98001
SE 352nd St 98092
SE 353rd St 98092
SE 354th Pl 98092
S 354th St 98001
SE 354th St 98092
S 355th St 98001
S 356th St 98001
SE 356th St 98092
SE 357th St 98092
S 358th St 98001
SE 358th St 98092
S 359th St 98092
S 360th St 98001
362nd Pl & St 98001
SE 363rd St 98092
S 364th St 98001
SE 364th St 98092
SE 366th Pl 98092
S 366th St 98001
S 367th Pl 98001
S 368th Pl 98001
SE 368th Pl 98092
S 368th St 98001
SE 368th St 98092
S 369th Pl 98001
SE 369th St 98092
SE 370th Pl 98092
S 370th St 98001
S 371st St 98001
S 372nd Pl 98001
S 372nd St 98001
SE 372nd St 98092
SE 373rd St 98092
S 374th St 98001
S 375th Pl 98001
S 376th Pl 98001
S 376th St 98001
SE 376th St 98092
S 378th St 98001
SE 378th St 98092
S 379th Ct S 98001
SE 379th St 98092
S 380th Pl 98001
S 380th St 98001
SE 380th St 98092
S 381st Ct 98001
S 381st Pl 98001
SE 381st Pl 98092
S 381st Way 98001
SE 382nd Pl 98092
S 382nd St 98001
383rd Pl & St 98092
S 384th St 98001
SE 384th St 98092
SE 385th Ct 98092
386th Pl & Way 98092
387th Pl & St 98092
SE 388th St 98092
SE 389th Ave 98092
SE 391st St 98092
SE 392nd St 98092
SE 393rd St 98092
SE 394th St 98092
SE 396th St 98092
SE 400th St 98092
SE 408th St 98092
SE 411th Ln 98092

BELLEVUE WA

General Delivery 98009

POST OFFICE BOXES MAIN OFFICE STATIONS AND BRANCHES

Box No.s
B - J 98009
1 - 5072 98009
6001 - 7976 98008
9998 - 9998 98009
40001 - 53594 98015
70001 - 70554 98007
85001 - 85024 98015
90000 - 99596 98009

NAMED STREETS

SE Allen Rd 98006
Bel Red Rd
2400-2498 98007
2601-2799 98008
3400-3698 98008
11800-11998 98005
12000-13999 98005
14000-15199 98007
15201-15599 98007
15601-15697 98008
15699-15700 98008
15702-15798 98008
Belfair Ln & Rd 98004
Bellefield Park Ln 98004
Bellevue Sq 98004
Bellevue Way NE
3-25 98004
27-1170 98004
1171-1171 98009
1172-3098 98004
1199-3699 98004
Bellevue Way SE 98004
Blarney Pl SE 98004
Cascade Ky 98006
Catheani Ave NE 98004
Cedar Crest Ln 98004
Chelan Ky 98006
SE Cliff Pl 98004
Clyde Ln 98004
SE Coal Creek Pkwy 98006
Columbia Ky 98006
Cougar Mountain Dr & Way 98006
Crescent Ky 98006
Decatur Ky 98006
Detwiller Ln 98004
Diamond S Rnch 98004
SE Eastgate Dr 98006
SE Eastgate Way
13200-13999 98005
14200-14700 98007
14702-15098 98007
15800-16298 98008
Enatai Dr 98004
Evergreen Dr 98004
Factoria Blvd SE 98006
Factoria Square Mall SE 98006
Fairweather Pl 98004
Glacier Ky 98006
Hazelwood Ln SE 98006
NE Hendarel St 98007
Highland Dr 98006
Hilltop Rd 98004
Huntint Ave SE 98006
Hunts Point Cir, Ln, Pl & Rd 98004
Kamber Rd 98007
Kaylen Pl 98007
Killarney Dr & Way 98004
SE Kilmarnock St 98004
SE Lake Rd 98004
Lake Bellevue Dr 98005
Lake Heights St 98006
Lake Hills Blvd
100-299 98008
14200-15300 98007
15302-15598 98007
15600-16699 98008
W Lake Sammamish Ln & Pkwy NE & SE 98008
Lake Washington Blvd NE 98004
Lake Washington Blvd SE 98006
Lakehurst Ln SE 98006
Lakemont Blvd SE 98006
Landerholm Cir SE 98007
Larson Ln SE 98004
Literann Ave NE 98008
Lopez Ky 98006
Lummi Ky 98006
Main St
10000-11300 98004
11302-11498 98004
11600-11998 98005
12000-13899 98005
14200-14598 98007
14600-15100 98007
15102-15298 98007
15600-16499 98008
Meydenbauer Way SE 98004
Mistowes Ave NE 98005
Newcastle Way 98006
SE Newport Ky & Way SE 98006
Northside Rd 98004
Northup Way
200-298 98008
300-1099 98008
2601-2697 98004
2699-11599 98004
11800-12999 98005
15701-15797 98008
15799-17000 98008
17002-17298 98008
Orcas Ky 98006
Park Rd 98004
Parkridge Ln 98004
Phantom Way 98008
Pleasure Point Ln SE 98006
Points Dr NE 98004
Richards Rd 98005
SE Ridge St 98004
SE Roanoke Pl 98006
SE Shoreland Dr SE 98004
Skagit Ky 98006
SE Somerset Ave, Blvd, Dr, Ln & Pl SE 98006
Sucia Ky 98006
Sunset Ln & Way 98004
Tatoosh Ky 98006
Tulalip Ky 98006
Vashon Ky 98006
Village Park Dr SE 98006
Vineyard Crst 98004
Wolverine Way 98004
Woodhaven Ln 98004

NUMBERED STREETS

NE 1st Ln 98007
NE 1st Pl
10200-10299 98004
13800-13999 98005
14700-15299 98007
15600-16599 98008

SE 1st Pl
11100-11199 98004
15200-15299 98007
16801-16897 98008
NE 1st St
8900-9799 98004
11701-11897 98005
14200-14899 98007
15600-16599 98008
SE 1st St
10900-10999 98004
11601-13597 98005
15200-15399 98007
15600-16499 98008
NE 2nd Pl
10800-11406 98004
11405-11405 98007
11405-11405 98015
11407-11499 98004
13601-13799 98005
14200-14599 98007
16500-17199 98008
SE 2nd Pl
15200-15299 98007
16701-16797 98008
NE 2nd St
10400-11199 98004
12301-12397 98005
14100-14199 98007
16000-16299 98008
SE 2nd St
10601-10797 98004
12800-13899 98005
16000-16499 98008
NE 3rd Pl
11001-11097 98004
12200-13099 98005
15200-15499 98007
16000-16299 98008
SE 3rd Pl
13600-13999 98005
16801-16899 98008
NE 3rd St
12500-12700 98005
14500-15599 98007
16000-16299 98008
SE 3rd St
10101-10197 98004
12800-12899 98005
15800-16099 98008
NE 4th Pl
12400-12899 98005
14500-15299 98007
17200-17599 98008
SE 4th Pl
11800-13099 98005
15400-15499 98007
16600-16699 98008
NE 4th St
9800-10999 98004
12600-12698 98005
14100-14599 98007
15700-17299 98008
SE 4th St
10600-11199 98004
12800-12899 98005
14001-14197 98007
15600-16399 98008
NE 5th Pl
12800-13999 98005
16700-17199 98008
SE 5th Pl
9900-9906 98004
12900-12999 98005
15800-15899 98008
NE 5th St
9200-9900 98004
12001-12247 98005
14000-14599 98007
16500-17199 98008
SE 5th St
9300-9498 98004
11600-13999 98005
16000-16199 98008
NE 6th Pl
12400-12499 98005
14000-15499 98007
16700-17299 98008
12900-12999 98005
15400-15499 98007
NE 6th St
10501-10897 98004
10899-11100 98004
11102-11198 98004
12101-12597 98005
12599-12699 98005
14800-14899 98007
14901-15499 98007
15600-17099 98008
10000-10098 98004
10100-11300 98004
11302-11498 98004
14000-14098 98007
14100-14299 98007
14301-14399 98007
15601-15697 98008
15699-15899 98008
15901-15999 98008
SE 7th Ct 98004
NE 7th Pl
12300-12599 98005
14100-15399 98007
17200-17299 98008
SE 7th Pl
12501-12597 98005
15400-15499 98007
NE 7th St 98005
SE 7th St
9600-10299 98004
13600-13999 98005
16000-16700 98008
NE 8th Pl
15000-15199 98007
17100-17899 98008
NE 8th St
9601-10097 98004
11600-13900 98005
14000-15300 98007
15600-17299 98008
SE 8th St
10000-11499 98004
11700-11999 98005
14000-14098 98007
15600-16699 98008
NE 9th Pl
10600-10699 98004
12601-13597 98005
14800-15199 98007
16800-16899 98008
SE 9th Pl
12101-12199 98005
14400-14899 98007
NE 9th St
9100-9198 98004
12900-12999 98005
16600-17799 98008
SE 9th St
10900-10998 98004
15400-15599 98007
15600-16699 98008
SE 10th Ct 98004
NE 10th Pl
12301-12497 98005
12499-13705 98005
13707-13799 98005
14100-15100 98007
15102-15198 98007
16400-16499 98008
10900-10999 98004
14200-14899 98007
NE 10th St
8800-8898 98004
8900-11003 98004
11005-11511 98004
13000-13799 98005
14400-14799 98007
14801-15599 98007
16000-18099 98008
10100-10998 98004
11000-11099 98004
12000-13900 98005
13902-13998 98005
14000-15599 98007
15600-16699 98008
NE 11th Pl
14400-15099 98007
16800-16899 98008
NE 11th St
8714-11098 98004
13600-13900 98005
15200-15598 98007
16100-17398 98008
SE 11th St
9501-10397 98004
12000-12099 98005
15400-15499 98007
15600-16700 98008
NE 12th Ct 98008
NE 12th Pl
10400-10700 98004
13400-13599 98005
14100-14198 98007
16201-17997 98008
SE 12th Pl 98008
NE 12th St
10001-10197 98004
11700-13800 98005
14800-15199 98007
16100-17899 98008
SE 12th St
10801-10899 98004
12200-12299 98005
14300-14398 98007
16300-16598 98008
SE 13th Ln 98004
NE 13th Pl
14600-15499 98007
16200-17999 98008
SE 13th Pl
10200-10299 98004
14000-14198 98007
NE 13th St
8401-8497 98004
13600-13700 98005
14800-15099 98007
16400-18099 98008
SE 13th St
10400-10499 98004
12100-12199 98005
15800-15899 98008
NE 14th Ct 98008
NE 14th Ln 98004
SE 14th Ln 98008
NE 14th Pl
12800-12899 98005
14400-14499 98007
16221-16797 98008
SE 14th Pl 98007
NE 14th St
8600-9799 98004
13601-13897 98005
14300-14398 98007
16100-16898 98008
SE 14th St
10400-10899 98004
12100-12599 98005
14200-15099 98007
16400-16799 98008
NE 15th Pl
8800-8899 98004
12700-12798 98005
14800-15410 98007
17200-18599 98008
SE 15th Pl 98007
NE 15th St
8500-9199 98004
14800-15300 98007
15600-15698 98008
SE 15th St
9500-9599 98004
12100-12599 98005
14300-14398 98007
16300-16699 98008
NE 16th Pl
9900-10499 98004
14300-15299 98007
15900-16398 98008
SE 16th Pl
10100-10199 98004
12100-12199 98005
14600-14639 98007
NE 16th St
8801-8897 98004
13200-13500 98005
14640-14648 98007
17900-18699 98008
SE 16th St
9600-10899 98004
12500-12599 98005
14301-14397 98007
15800-16799 98008
NE 17th Pl
8400-8699 98004
14800-14899 98007
16400-17399 98008
SE 17th Pl
12100-12200 98005
14000-14198 98007
16600-16699 98008
NE 17th St
8600-9499 98004
15300-15598 98007
SE 17th St
10800-10899 98004
12300-13799 98005
14300-15599 98007
16400-16699 98008
NE 18th Pl
10900-11099 98004
17200-17399 98008
SE 18th Pl
12200-12299 98005
14000-14899 98007
NE 18th St
9400-9500 98004
15301-15397 98007
15609-16197 98008
SE 18th St
10600-10699 98004
12100-13799 98005
14200-14398 98007
16501-16799 98008
NE 19th Pl
8400-8699 98004
16000-16204 98008
SE 19th Pl
12900-12999 98005
14400-14699 98007
NE 19th St
8800-9399 98004
16201-16209 98008
SE 19th St
10400-10499 98004
12100-13699 98005
16500-16799 98008
SE 20th Ln 98007
NE 20th Pl 98004
SE 20th Pl
12100-12899 98005
14500-15499 98007
NE 20th St
8400-9499 98004
13000-13900 98005
14000-15499 98007
16400-17099 98008
SE 20th St
10400-10699 98004
12000-13900 98005
14000-15499 98007
NE 21st Pl
8400-9499 98004
12800-12899 98005
14000-14099 98007
16400-16499 98008
SE 21st Pl
13000-13099 98005
14000-15499 98007
16400-16699 98008
NE 21st St
8600-8699 98004
14000-14399 98007
16400-17099 98008
SE 21st St
10100-10899 98004
12100-13899 98005
14600-15399 98007
NE 22nd Pl
8400-9100 98004
16900-16999 98008
SE 22nd Pl
12800-12899 98005
15301-15397 98007
NE 22nd St
9800-10099 98004
16700-17099 98008
SE 22nd St
10400-10699 98004
12100-13999 98005
14200-15399 98007
16400-16499 98008
SE 23rd Ln 98005
NE 23rd Pl
8600-8699 98004
12400-12599 98005
16700-17100 98008
SE 23rd Pl
12300-12399 98005
14400-14499 98007
16600-16799 98008
NE 23rd St
9800-10299 98004
16600-16699 98008
SE 23rd St
10200-10899 98004
12100-13999 98005
14200-15399 98007
16400-16499 98008
NE 24th Pl 98008
SE 24th Pl 98004
NE 24th St
8600-9700 98004
11900-11998 98005
14000-15599 98007
15600-15798 98008
SE 24th St
13400-13799 98005
14100-15599 98007
15600-16500 98008
NE 25th Pl
8800-9199 98004
12900-13199 98005
15700-16599 98008
SE 25th Pl
10800-10899 98004
12400-12799 98005
NE 25th St
8500-9699 98004
12501-13397 98005
16200-16899 98008
SE 25th St
10001-10297 98004
12200-12799 98005
15300-15599 98007
15700-17099 98008
NE 26th Pl
8600-8699 98004
12000-12098 98005
16900-16999 98008
SE 26th Pl
12400-12999 98005
16600-16699 98008
NE 26th St
8500-9799 98004
15901-15997 98008
SE 26th St
10900-11099 98004
12100-13699 98005
14400-14599 98007
15600-16899 98008
NE 27th Pl
8400-8599 98004
13400-13499 98005
15800-16599 98008
SE 27th Pl
10600-10699 98004
13400-13499 98005
NE 27th St
9300-9398 98004
12400-12499 98005
14000-14399 98007
16000-16999 98008
SE 27th St
10000-10599 98004
12100-12699 98005
15300-15599 98007
16300-16699 98008
NE 28th Pl
9200-9299 98004
13000-13099 98005
17000-17199 98008
SE 28th Pl
10000-10299 98004
12400-12499 98005
16200-16299 98008
NE 28th St
8000-8098 98004
12100-13799 98005
15801-15897 98008
SE 28th St
10100-10599 98004
15200-15299 98007
16500-16899 98008
SE 29th Ct 98008
NE 29th Pl
10000-10099 98004
13400-13598 98005
14400-14799 98007
17000-17199 98008
SE 29th Pl
11000-11198 98004
12901-12999 98005
16200-17199 98008
NE 29th St
9600-9799 98004
12400-12999 98005
16100-16799 98008
SE 29th St
10201-10297 98004
12400-12899 98005
16200-16800 98008
NE 30th Pl
9400-9699 98004
11600-11899 98005
14000-14699 98007
17100-17199 98008
SE 30th Pl
11000-11099 98004
15301-15397 98007
NE 30th St
9300-9599 98004
12500-13799 98005
14640-14660 98007
16200-16700 98008
SE 30th St
10100-11299 98004
12400-13499 98005
16500-16799 98008
NE 31st Ct 98008
NE 31st Pl
10000-10299 98004
12200-12998 98005
17100-17199 98008
SE 31st Pl 98008
NE 31st St
9200-9699 98004
12900-12999 98005
14400-14598 98007
16700-16898 98008
SE 31st St
10800-11099 98004
12100-12499 98005
16000-16799 98008
NE 32nd Ln 98005
NE 32nd Pl
9000-9099 98004
12800-13899 98005
14000-14199 98007
SE 32nd Pl 98008
NE 32nd St
9001-9097 98004
12200-12899 98005
14401-14597 98007
16600-17199 98008
SE 32nd St
10500-10699 98004
11801-11997 98005
SE 33rd Cir 98008
NE 33rd Ln 98005
SE 33rd Ln 98008
NE 33rd Pl
10900-11098 98004
11100-11199 98004
16700-16799 98008
NE 33rd St
8900-9099 98004
9800-10099 98004
12100-13199 98005
16800-16899 98008
NE 34th Pl
9800-9900 98004
12800-13999 98005
17000-17099 98008
NE 34th St
8800-9099 98004
11700-11798 98005
14601-14699 98007
SE 34th St
11000-11098 98004
16200-16298 98008
SE 35th Ct 98008
NE 35th Pl
9600-10999 98004
12600-12899 98005
16800-16899 98008
SE 35th Pl 98008
NE 35th St
14400-14498 98007
16700-17199 98008
SE 35th St
12200-12299 98006
16400-17199 98008
NE 36th Pl
11200-11399 98004
11600-13899 98005
SE 36th Pl 98006
NE 36th St
8800-9199 98004
12200-13499 98005
14400-14498 98007
14500-14699 98007
14701-14799 98007
17000-17198 98008
SE 36th St 98006
NE 37th Ct 98004
NE 37th Pl
9000-9499 98004
13400-13899 98005
14400-14599 98007
16900-17199 98008
SE 37th Pl 98006
NE 37th St
12200-12499 98005
16300-16399 98008
SE 37th St
12200-15899 98006
16300-16399 98008
NE 38th Pl
9000-9099 98004
13100-13199 98005
16900-17099 98008
SE 38th Pl
12100-15399 98006
16801-16897 98008
NE 38th St
9200-9299 98004
14400-14698 98007
SE 38th St
12200-12299 98006
12400-12400 98015
12400-12400 98007
16601-16697 98008
NE 39th Pl 98004
SE 39th Pl
12200-12299 98006
16400-16699 98008
NE 39th St
11600-13000 98005
13002-13098 98005
14401-14697 98007
14699-14799 98007
SE 39th St
12200-15299 98006
15301-15399 98006
16900-16999 98008
SE 40th Cir 98006
SE 40th Ct
12800-12899 98006
17000-17299 98008
SE 40th Ln 98006

NE 40th Pl
9000-9100 98004
14200-14299 98007
SE 40th Pl
12800-15199 98006
16600-18099 98008
NE 40th St
9200-9499 98004
12901-13197 98005
14000-14799 98007
SE 40th St 98006
SE 41st Ln
12300-14599 98006
18100-18199 98008
SE 41st Pl 98006
NE 41st St 98004
SE 41st St
12000-15499 98006
16900-17199 98008
SE 42nd Ct 98006
SE 42nd Ln 98006
NE 42nd Pl
9500-9598 98004
14200-14300 98007
14302-14698 98007
SE 42nd Pl 98006
NE 42nd St
9000-9199 98004
13600-13899 98005
SE 42nd St 98006
SE 43rd Ct 98006
NE 43rd Pl 98007
SE 43rd Pl 98006
SE 43rd St 98006
SE 44th Ct 98006
NE 44th Pl
13800-13899 98005
14701-14799 98007
SE 44th Pl 98006
NE 44th St 98007
SE 44th St 98006
SE 44th Way 98006
SE 45th Ct 98006
SE 45th Ln 98006
SE 45th Pl 98006
NE 45th St
13200-13398 98005
13400-13499 98005
14501-14597 98007
14599-14699 98007
SE 45th St 98006
SE 45th Way 98006
46th Ct, Ln, Pl, St & Way 98006
SE 47th Ct 98006
SE 47th Ln 98006
SE 47th Pl 98006
NE 47th St
9000-9199 98004
13200-13499 98005
SE 47th St 98006
SE 47th Way 98006
SE 48th Ct 98006
SE 48th Dr 98006
NE 48th Pl 98005
SE 48th Pl 98006
SE 48th St 98006
49th Pl & St 98006
NE 50th Pl 98007
SE 50th Pl 98006
NE 50th St 98005
SE 50th St 98006
NE 51st Pl
13200-13298 98005
13300-13400 98005
13402-13498 98005
14600-14700 98007
14702-14798 98007
SE 51st Pl 98006
SE 51st St 98006
52nd Pl & St 98006
53rd Pl & St 98006
SE 54th Ct 98006
NE 54th Pl 98005
SE 54th Pl 98006
SE 54th St 98006
NE 55th Pl 98005

SE 55th Pl 98006
NE 55th St 98007
SE 55th St 98006
56th Pl & St 98006
SE 57th Pl 98006
NE 57th St 98007
SE 57th St 98006
SE 58th Pl 98006
NE 58th St 98007
SE 58th St 98006
59th Pl & St 98006
60th Ct, Pl & St 98006
61st Ct, Ln, Pl & St 98006
62nd Ct, Pl & St 98006
63rd Ct, Ln, Pl & St 98006
64th Pl & St 98006
65th Pl & St 98006
66th Pl & St 98006
67th Pl & St 98006
68th Pl & St 98006
69th Pl, St & Way 98006
SE 70th St 98006
80th Ave NE 98004
84th Ave NE 98004
84th Pl NE 98004
85th Ave NE 98004
86th Ave NE 98004
87th Ave NE 98004
88th Ave & Pl 98004
89th Ave NE 98004
89th Pl NE 98004
90th Ave NE 98004
91st Ave & Ln 98004
91st Ave & Ln 98004
92nd Ave NE 98004
92nd Pl NE 98004
93rd Ave NE 98004
94th NE & SE 98004
95th Ave NE 98004
95th Pl NE 98004
96th NE & SE 98004
97th Ave & Pl 98004
98th NE & SE 98004
99th NE & SE 98004
100th Ave & Pl NE & SE 98004
101st Ave, Ct, Ln & Pl NE & SE 98004
102nd Ave & Pl NE & SE 98004
103rd Ave & Pl 98004
104th Ave & Pl 98004
105th NE & SE 98004
106th Ave & Pl 98004
106th Ave & Pl 98004
107th Ave & Pl NE & SE 98004
108th Ave NE 98004
108th Ave SE
100-3599 98004
6200-6499 98006
108th Pl NE 98004
109th Ave & Pl 98004
110th Ave NE 98004
110th Ave SE
1-3251 98004
3253-3299 98004
5700-6199 98006
110th Pl NE 98004
110th Pl SE 98004
111th Ave NE 98004
111th Ave SE
100-3299 98004
5700-5899 98006
111th Pl SE
801-897 98004
899-1099 98004
5800-5899 98006
112th Ave NE 98004
112th Ave SE
101-297 98004
299-3299 98004
6217-6397 98006
6399-6600 98006
6602-6698 98006
113th Ave NE 98004

113th Ave SE 98004
113th Pl SE 98006
114th Ave NE 98004
114th Ave SE
400-1800 98004
1802-1898 98004
6300-6799 98006
114th Pl SE 98006
115th Ave NE 98004
115th Ct SE 98006
115th Pl SE 98006
116th Ave NE 98004
116th Ave SE
2-98 98004
100-399 98004
4500-6699 98006
116th Pl SE 98006
117th Ave & Pl 98006
118th Ave NE 98005
118th Ave SE
100-3299 98005
4600-6699 98006
119th Ave NE 98005
119th Ave SE 98006
119th Pl SE 98006
120th Ave NE 98005
120th Ave SE 98006
120th Pl SE 98005
121st Ave SE
900-998 98005
1000-2699 98005
4600-6799 98006
121st Pl NE 98005
121st Pl SE 98006
122nd Ave NE 98005
122nd Ave SE
1000-2599 98005
3500-6299 98006
122nd Pl NE 98005
122nd Pl SE 98006
123rd Ave NE 98005
123rd Ave SE
1200-2799 98005
4200-6899 98006
123rd Pl NE 98005
123rd Pl SE
2300-2399 98005
4800-6799 98006
124th Ave NE 98005
124th Ave SE
2700-2799 98005
3800-3998 98006
4000-4200 98006
4202-4298 98006
124th Pl NE 98005
125th Ave NE 98005
125th Ave SE
1400-3199 98005
4500-6599 98006
125th Pl SE 98006
126th Ave NE 98005
126th Ave SE
1700-2899 98005
4900-6599 98006
126th Pl NE 98005
126th Pl SE 98006
127th Ave NE 98005
127th Ave SE
1400-2599 98005
6200-6799 98006
127th Pl NE 98005
127th Pl SE
2700-2799 98005
2801-3099 98005
4900-6799 98006
128th Ave NE 98005
128th Ave SE
2-398 98005
400-3099 98005
5100-6899 98006
128th Pl NE 98005
128th Pl SE 98006
129th Ave NE 98005
129th Ave SE
1-2999 98005
5600-6699 98006
129th Ln SE 98006
129th Pl NE 98005

129th Pl SE
1800-1900 98005
1902-3298 98005
3900-6899 98006
130th Ave NE 98005
130th Ave SE
2-198 98005
4400-4899 98006
130th Ln SE 98006
130th Pl NE 98005
130th Pl SE
401-2097 98005
4300-4699 98006
131st Ave NE 98005
131st Ave SE 98006
131st Ln SE 98006
131st Pl NE 98005
131st Pl SE 98006
132nd Ave NE 98005
132nd Ave SE
1839-1897 98005
1899-2500 98005
2502-2504 98005
3600-4799 98006
132nd Pl SE 98005
133rd Ave NE 98005
133rd Ave SE 98006
133rd Pl SE 98006
134th Ave NE 98005
134th Ave SE
1500-1598 98005
1600-2599 98005
3600-5899 98006
134th Ln NE 98005
134th Pl NE 98005
134th Pl SE
1800-1999 98005
4300-5999 98006
135th Ave NE 98005
135th Ave SE 98006
135th Pl SE
2000-2299 98005
2301-2399 98005
4100-5999 98006
136th Ave NE 98005
136th Ave SE
100-199 98005
3700-4799 98006
136th Pl NE 98005
136th Pl SE
1800-1999 98005
3600-5599 98006
137th Ave NE 98005
137th Ave SE
2400-2499 98005
4400-4599 98006
137th Pl SE
800-1998 98005
2000-2399 98005
5200-5799 98006
138th Ave NE 98005
138th Ave SE
2100-2499 98005
3800-4699 98006
138th Pl SE
1800-1899 98005
3700-6399 98006
139th Ave NE 98005
139th Ave SE
2400-3299 98005
3700-5399 98006
139th Ct NE 98005
139th Pl NE 98005
139th Pl SE
2000-2299 98005
3700-3798 98006
3800-6399 98006
140th Ave NE 98005
140th Ave SE
100-1899 98005
3700-6099 98006
140th Ct SE 98007
140th Ln SE 98007
140th Pl NE 98007
140th Pl SE
1400-1842 98007
4600-5799 98006

140th Ter SE 98007
140th Way SE 98007
141st Ave NE 98007
141st Ave SE
500-599 98007
4400-6400 98006
141st Ct SE
601-699 98007
4600-4699 98006
141st Ln SE 98007
141st Pl NE 98007
141st Pl SE
800-899 98007
4400-5899 98006
142nd Ave NE 98007
142nd Ave SE
500-2399 98007
3800-6399 98006
142nd Ct SE 98006
142nd Pl NE 98007
142nd Pl SE
700-2999 98007
3800-6099 98006
143rd Ave NE 98007
143rd Ave SE
1-1599 98007
4400-5599 98006
143rd Pl NE 98007
143rd Pl SE
700-1799 98007
5700-5899 98006
5901-5999 98006
144th Ave NE 98007
144th Ave SE
1200-2300 98007
2302-2398 98007
4400-4599 98006
144th Ln SE 98006
144th Pl NE 98007
144th Pl SE
800-1099 98007
4600-6199 98006
145th Ave NE 98007
145th Ave SE
200-2699 98007
3800-6099 98006
145th Pl NE 98007
145th Pl SE
1-1899 98007
1901-2699 98007
4500-6199 98006
146th Ave NE 98007
146th Ave SE
1-797 98007
799-2699 98007
3600-5899 98006
146th Pl NE 98007
146th Pl SE
1800-1898 98007
1900-3399 98007
4600-6299 98006
147th Ave NE 98007
147th Ave SE
1-1899 98007
3700-6299 98006
147th Ln NE 98007
147th Pl NE 98007
147th Pl SE
1700-1999 98007
4000-6299 98006
148th Ave NE 98007
148th Ave SE
1-97 98007
99-3299 98007
3700-6599 98006
148th Dr SE 98007
148th Pl SE
1000-1299 98007
4000-4699 98006
149th Ave NE 98007
149th Ave SE 98006
149th Pl SE
1000-1699 98007
4100-4199 98006
150th Ave NE 98007
150th Ave SE
1200-1900 98007

1902-2098 98007
3600-3698 98006
3700-6399 98006
150th Pl NE 98007
150th Pl SE
800-1299 98007
4500-6599 98006
151st Ave NE 98007
151st Ave SE
1000-2099 98007
3900-6399 98006
151st Ct SE 98006
151st Pl NE 98007
151st Pl SE
1-100 98007
102-2498 98007
4800-6599 98006
152nd Ave NE 98007
152nd Ave SE
1600-2099 98007
3900-6599 98006
152nd Ct SE 98006
152nd Ln SE 98006
152nd Pl NE 98007
152nd Pl SE
1-97 98007
4400-5699 98006
153rd Ave NE 98007
153rd Ave SE
1600-2699 98007
2701-2799 98007
3900-6599 98006
153rd Ct SE 98006
153rd Pl NE 98007
153rd Pl SE
100-1499 98007
5300-6799 98006
154th Ave NE 98007
154th Ave SE
400-2599 98007
3800-5599 98006
154th Pl NE 98007
154th Pl SE
200-299 98007
4400-6799 98006
155th Ave NE 98007
155th Ave SE
200-2599 98007
3800-6599 98006
155th Pl NE 98007
155th Pl SE
400-2599 98007
4200-6799 98006
156th Ave NE 98007
156th Ave SE
100-3299 98007
3301-3399 98007
3600-3798 98006
3800-6799 98006
156th Ln SE 98006
156th Pl NE 98008
156th Pl SE 98006
157th Ave NE 98008
157th Ave SE
1-2599 98008
4300-5099 98006
157th Pl SE
2100-2399 98008
4300-4399 98006
158th Ave SE
1200-2599 98008
2601-3299 98008
4100-6199 98006
158th Ct NE 98008
158th Pl NE 98008
158th Pl SE
1-1399 98008
4300-4899 98006
159th Ave NE 98008
159th Ave SE
1-2500 98008
2502-2598 98008
4200-4699 98006
159th Pl NE 98008
159th Pl SE
100-1099 98008
4800-4898 98006

4900-6199 98006
160th Ave NE 98008
160th Ave SE
100-3399 98008
4200-6299 98006
160th Ct SE 98006
160th Pl NE 98008
160th Pl SE
100-399 98008
4505-6399 98006
161st Ave NE 98008
161st Ave SE
2400-3400 98008
3402-3498 98008
3900-6799 98006
161st Ct SE 98006
161st Pl NE 98008
161st Pl SE
400-3439 98008
6400-6599 98006
162nd Ave NE 98008
162nd Ave SE
100-2999 98008
4000-4699 98006
162nd Ct SE 98006
162nd Ln NE 98008
162nd Ln SE 98006
162nd Pl NE 98008
162nd Pl SE
3000-3400 98008
4800-6299 98006
162nd Way SE 98006
163rd Ave NE 98008
163rd Ave SE
600-3799 98008
4100-4299 98006
163rd Ct SE 98006
163rd Ln NE 98008
163rd Ln SE 98006
163rd Pl SE
100-3599 98008
4400-6899 98006
164th Ave NE 98008
164th Ave SE
1-1299 98008
1301-1849 98008
4100-6799 98006
164th Ln SE 98006
164th Pl NE 98008
164th Pl SE
3200-3699 98008
6400-6499 98006
164th Way SE 98006
165th Ave NE 98008
165th Ave SE
1-3299 98008
4500-4799 98006
165th Ct SE 98008
165th Pl NE 98008
165th Pl SE
1900-3899 98008
4100-6499 98006
166th Ave NE 98008
166th Ave SE
400-3899 98008
5800-6099 98006
166th Ln SE 98006
166th Pl NE 98008
166th Pl SE
3300-3399 98008
5500-6899 98006
166th Way SE 98006
167th Ave NE 98008
167th Ave SE
400-3999 98008
4300-6399 98006
167th Ct SE 98006
167th Ln SE 98006
167th Pl NE 98008
167th Pl SE 98006
168th Ave NE 98008
168th Ave SE
200-2999 98008
4500-7399 98006
168th Pl NE 98008
168th Pl SE
700-3399 98008

5500-6599 98006
169th Ave NE 98008
169th Ave SE
2600-4099 98008
4500-7399 98006
169th Pl NE 98008
169th Pl SE
2400-2499 98008
4500-7399 98006
170th Ave NE 98008
170th Ave SE
2600-4099 98008
4400-7399 98006
170th Pl NE 98008
170th Pl SE
900-3099 98008
4300-6799 98006
171st Ave NE 98008
171st Ave SE
2400-4099 98008
4600-7399 98006
171st Pl NE 98008
171st Pl SE 98006
172nd Ave NE 98008
172nd Ave SE 98006
172nd Ct NE 98008
172nd Ct SE 98006
172nd Pl NE 98008
172nd Pl SE
4000-4099 98008
4600-5999 98006
173rd Ave NE 98008
173rd Ave SE 98006
173rd Ln SE 98006
173rd Pl NE 98008
173rd Pl SE
4000-4099 98008
4700-4999 98006
174th Ave NE 98008
174th Ave SE 98006
174th Ct SE 98006
174th Pl NE 98008
174th Pl SE 98006
175th Ave SE 98006
175th Pl NE 98008
175th Pl SE 98006
176th Ave NE 98008
176th Ave SE
4000-4099 98008
4600-4699 98006
176th Ln NE 98008
176th Pl NE 98008
176th Pl SE 98006
177th Ave NE 98008
177th Ave SE
4000-4099 98008
4500-4699 98006
177th Ln NE 98008
178th Ave NE 98008
178th Ave SE 98006
178th Ct SE 98008
178th Ln SE 98008
178th Pl NE 98008
179th Ave NE 98008
179th Ave SE 98006
179th Ct NE 98008
179th Ln SE 98008
179th Pl NE 98008
180th Ave & Pl 98008
181st Ave SE 98008
183rd Ave NE 98008
184th Ave NE 98008
185th Ave NE 98008
186th Ave NE 98008
187th Ave NE 98008
SE 3 Ln 98007

BELLINGHAM WA

General Delivery 98225

POST OFFICE BOXES MAIN OFFICE STATIONS AND BRANCHES

Box No.s
AB - AC 98227
E - X 98227
1 - 9798 98227
28001 - 95001 98228
95000 - 229180 98229

NAMED STREETS

A St 98225
Aaron Ct 98226
Abbey Pl 98229
Abbott St 98225
Acacia Pl 98225
Academy Rd & St 98226
Acorn Pl 98229
Adams Ave
3100-3198 98225
3700-4399 98229
Agate Rd 98226
Agate Bay Ln 98226
Agate Heights Ln & Rd 98226
Airport Dr & Way 98226
Akron Ct 98226
Alabama St
100-999 98225
1001-3899 98226
1100-3898 98229
Alder Ct 98229
Alder St 98225
Alderwood Ave 98225
Aldrich Rd 98226
Aletha Ln 98226
Alice St 98226
Allen Ave 98225
Allison Rd 98226
Alpha Way 98226
E & W Alpine Dr & Way 98226
Alta Vista Pl 98226
Altair Ct 98226
Alvarado Dr 98229
Alyssa Ct 98226
Amberland Way 98229
Amy Ct 98226
Anderson Way 98226
Andrea Ct 98226
Andy Ct 98226
Angela Ct 98229
Ankar Park Dr 98226
Ann Ct 98229
Appaloosa Ct & Ln 98229
Applejack Ln 98226
Aquila Ct 98226
Arabian Way 98229
Arbor Ct & St 98229
Arbutus Pl 98225
Archer Dr 98226
Arrowroot Pl 98229
Arroyo Ln 98229
Ashbrooke Ln 98226
S Ashley St 98229
Astor St 98225
Aurora Loop 98226
Austin Ct, Ln & St 98229
Austin Creek Ln 98229
Autumn Ln 98229
Autumn Vista Pl 98229
Autumnwood Ct 98229
Ava Ln 98226
Avalon Ct 98226
E & W Axton Rd 98226
Azalea Pl 98225
Azure Way 98229
B St 98225
Baker St 98225
Baker Creek Pl 98226
E & W Bakerview Rd & Spur 98226
Bakerview Valley Rd 98226
Balch Rd 98226
Bamboo Ln 98225
Bancroft Rd & St 98225
Barkley Blvd 98226
Barkley Grove Loop 98226
Barkley Meadows Cir 98226
Barleen Rd 98229
Barnes Rd 98226
Barnview Ct 98229
Barrell Springs Ln & Rd 98229
Bartlett Ave 98226
Basin View Cir 98229
Bass St 98229
Bay St 98225
Bay Shore Dr 98226
Bayon Rd 98225
Bayside Pl & Rd 98225
Bayview Ave 98229
Bayview Dr 98226
Baywood Ct 98229
Beach Pl 98226
E & W Beachview Pl 98226
Beacon Rd 98229
Beal St 98225
Bear Creek Ln & Rd 98229
Beaumont Dr 98226
Beazer Ct & Rd 98226
Bedford Ave 98226
Beecher St 98229
Bel West Dr 98226
Belfern Dr 98226
Bellaire Dr & Way 98226
Bellevue Pl 98226
Bellinger Rd 98226
E Bellis Fair Pkwy 98226
Belltown Ct 98226
Bellwether Ln 98226
Bellwether Way 98225
Bennett Ave
1100-1200 98225
1202-1298 98225
3800-3999 98229
Bennett Ct 98229
Bennett Dr 98225
Bennett Rd 98229
Benton Ct 98229
Berry Wood Pl 98229
Best Ln & Rd 98226
Bevan St 98226
Bigleaf Ln 98229
Bill Mcdonald Pkwy 98225
Birch Cir 98229
Birch St
1200-2499 98229
2500-2699 98226
E Birch St 98229
W Birch St 98229
Birch Falls Dr 98229
Birchwood Ave & Ct 98225
Birdie Ln 98229
Birnamwood 98225
Black Bear Ct 98229
Blackberry Ln 98229
Blake Ln 98226
Blakely Ct 98229
Bloor St 98229
Blueberry Ln 98229
Bluebonnet Trl 98226
Boardwalk Dr 98226
Bogey Ln 98229
Bonanza Way 98229
Bonnie Ln 98225
Boulevard 98225
Bowline Ct 98229
Boxwood Ave 98225
Boyer Rd 98226
Bracken Pl 98229
Braden Way 98226
Bradley Ln 98225
Bramble Way 98229
Brandywine Ct & Way 98226
Bray Way 98226
Briar Rd 98225
Briarcliffe Ct 98226
Bridlewood Ct 98226
Brier Ln 98225
Brighton Crest Dr & Ln 98229
Bristol Pl, St & Way 98226
Britton Cir, Ct & Rd 98226
Britton Loop Rd 98226
Briza Ct 98229
Broad St
1200-1499 98229
2500-3199 98225
3400-4400 98229
4402-4798 98229
Broadway St 98225
Brookedge Ct 98226
Brookings Pl 98229
Brookline Ct 98229
Brookview Ct & Pl 98229
Brownsville Dr & Pl 98226
Bryant St 98225
Buchanan Towers 98225
Buena Vista Pl 98226
Burnhaven Ln 98226
Burns St 98226
Byron Ave 98229
Byron St 98225
C St 98225
Cable St 98229
Caddie Ln 98229
Cagey Rd 98226
California St 98229
Calluna Ct 98226
Cammack Rd 98226
Canby Ct 98229
Canterbury Ln 98225
Canterbury Rd 98229
Canyon Ct 98229
Canyon View Dr 98225
Carolina St
100-999 98225
1101-1297 98229
1299-2300 98229
2302-2398 98229
Carpenter Rd 98226
Carrington Way 98226
Carter Dr 98225
Cascade Ave, Ln & Pl 98229
Cascadia Ln 98225
Catkin Ct 98229
Cayuse Ct 98229
Cedar Pl 98229
Cedar St 98225
Cedar Acres St 98229
Cedar Creek Ln 98229
Cedar Hills Ave & Ct 98229
Cedarbrook Ct 98229
Cedarside Ct 98226
Cedarsong Ln 98226
Cedarville Rd 98226
Cedarwood Ave 98225
Celia Way 98226
Celtic Ln 98226
Central Ave 98225
E & W Champion St 98225
Chance Rd 98226
Chandler Pkwy 98226
Chautaqua Ave 98226
Cheeskin Trail Rd 98226
Cherry Ln 98229
Cherry St 98225
Cherrywood Ave 98225
E & W Chestnut St 98225
Chief Martin Rd 98226
Christian Way 98229
Chuckanut Ave, Dr & Ln N 98229
Chuckanut Crest Dr & Ln 98229
Chuckanut Heights Ct, Dr & Rd 98229
Chuckanut Point Rd 98229
Chuckanut Shore Rd 98229
Chum Cir 98226
Church St 98225
Cimarron Ln 98229
Cindy Ln 98226
Cinema Pl 98226
Civic Circle Dr 98229
Civic Field Way 98229
Clark Rd 98225
S Clarkwood Dr 98225
Claudia Ct 98229
Clear Lake Ct 98229
E & W Clearbrook Dr & Pl 98229
Clearwater Ct 98229
Cleator Rd 98229
Clematis Ln 98229
Cliffside Dr 98225
Clinton St 98225
Clover Ln 98226
Clubhouse Cir 98229
Coast Way 98226
Cody Ave
2000-2999 98225
3400-3899 98229
Cody Cir 98225
Cody Ln 98226
Coho Way 98225
N & S Colby Ct 98229
Cold Spring Ln 98229
College Ave 98225
College St 98229
Colony Ct 98229
Columbine Dr 98229
Columbus Ave 98229
N Commercial St 98225
Concord Ct 98226
E Connecticut St
400-498 98225
801-899 98225
2600-3999 98226
W Connecticut St 98225
Connelly Ave
2000-3199 98225
3300-3999 98229
Consolidation Ave
1700-1798 98229
3400-3799 98225
3800-4498 98229
Coolidge Dr 98225
Copper Crst 98229
Coral Ln 98226
Cordata Pkwy 98226
Cordero Dr 98229
Cornerstone Ln 98226
Cornwall Ave 98225
Corona Ct 98226
Coronado Ave & Ln 98229
Cottonwood Ave & Pl 98225
Cougar Rd 98226
Country Ln 98225
Cove Rd 98229
Cowgill Ave
401-1997 98225
1999-2999 98225
3001-3199 98225
3601-3799 98229
Coyote Ln 98226
Coyote Creek Dr 98226
Crabapple Ln 98226
Cranberry Ct 98226
Creekbend Ln 98226
Creekside Ln 98229
Creekwood Ln 98229
Crescent Pl 98225
Crest Ct 98226
Crest Ln 98229
Crestline Dr
100-2499 98229
2500-3299 98226
E Crestline Dr 98226
W Crestline Dr 98226
Crestline Pl 98226
Cross St 98229
Crown Ln 98229
Crystal Ct 98226
Crystal Springs Ln 98226
Curtis Rd
4100-4298 98225
4300-4699 98229
Cyclone Dr 98225
Cypress Dr 98226
Cypress Rd 98225
D St 98225
Dakin St
1700-1798 98229
1800-1999 98229
2500-2900 98226
2902-2998 98226
Dale Rd 98226
Dana St 98225
Daniels Ct 98229
Darby Dr 98226
Darcy Ct 98226
Davis St 98226
Dawn Break Ct 98229
Dean Ave 98225
Decatur St 98229
Deemer Rd 98226
Deer Creek Ln 98226
Deer Pointe Ct 98226
Deer Run Ln 98229
Defiance Dr 98226
Del Bonita Ct & Way 98226
Dellesta Dr 98226
Democrat St 98229
Desmond St 98229
Dewey Ln & Rd 98226
Diamond Loop 98226
Dike Rd 98226
Dinkle Rd 98226
Discovery Heights Dr 98226
Division St 98226
Dlinda St 98226
Doe Ct 98229
E Dolphin Pl 98229
Donald Ave 98226
Dondee Ct 98229
Donovan Ave
400-3299 98225
3400-3800 98229
3802-3998 98229
Douglas Ave 98225
E Douglas Ave 98229
Dove Ct 98229
Dover St 98226
Drummer Boy Ln 98226
Dumar Ln 98229
Dumas Ave 98229
Dupont St 98225
Durbin Ct 98225
E St 98225
W Eagle Ave 98226
Eagle Crest Ct 98229
Eagle Flyway 98226
Eagleridge Dr & Way 98226
Eaglewood Ln 98229
East Rd 98226
Easton Ave 98225
Eberly Pl & Rd 98226
Edens Ave 98225
Edens Hall N 98225
Edgefield Dr 98229
Edgewater Ln 98226
Edgewood Ln 98226
Edwards Ct 98229
Edwards St
400-598 98225
1201-1397 98229
1399-3299 98229
El Dorado Way 98226
Eldridge Ave 98225
Electric Ave 98229
Eliza Ave 98226
Elizabeth St 98225
Ellis St 98225
Ellsworth St 98225
Elm St 98225
Elwood Ave 98225
Emerald Lake Way 98226
Emma Rd 98226
Equestrian Way 98229
Erie St
1901-1997 98229
1999-2499 98229
2500-2899 98226
Erie Ter 98229
Espana Pl 98225
Ethan Ct 98226
Euclid Ave 98229
Evening Star Ln 98229
Everglade Rd 98225
Evergreen Ave & Dr 98226
Everson Goshen Rd 98226
Express Dr 98229
F St 98225
Fairhaven Ave 98229
Fairhaven Residence 98225
Fairview St 98229
Fairway Ln 98229
Falcon Ct 98229
Falls Dr & Loop 98229
Far Summit Pl 98229
Farragut St 98225
Fat Dog Ln 98226
Fawn Ct 98229
Fazon Rd 98226
Fern Rd 98225
Ferry Ave 98225
Festival Blvd 98226
Fielding Ave
3200-3398 98225
3600-3999 98229
Fields Park Pl 98229
Fieldston Rd 98225
Fillmore Ave 98225
Finch Ct 98229
Finkbonner Rd 98226
Finnegan Way 98225
Finney Creek Ln 98229
Fir St
2100-2499 98229
2500-2599 98226
2601-2799 98226
4000-4098 98229
Fir Tree Way 98229
Firelane Rd 98229
Firwood Ave 98225
Flint St 98226
Flora St 98225
Flower Ct 98229
Flynn St 98229
N & S Forest Ct, Ln & St 98225
Forest View Dr 98229
Fort Bellingham Rd 98225
Fowles Ln 98226
Frances Ave 98226
Franklin St 98225
Fraser St
801-899 98225
1000-1198 98229
1200-3999 98229
Fremont St 98229
Friday Creek Rd 98229
Fruitland Dr 98226
Fuchsia 98226
G St 98225
Gablecrest Ct 98226
Gabriola Ct 98229
Gala Ct & Loop 98226
N Galbraith Ln 98229
Gallop Ln 98229
Gambier Ave 98225
N & S Garden St & Ter 98225
Garden Springs Ln 98226
Garland Dr & Ln 98226
Geneva St 98229
Geneva Hills Rd 98229
Geneva Shore Ln 98229
Gentlebrook Ln 98226
Gerard Dr 98226
Gerity Rd 98229
Giarde Ln 98226
Gilbert Dr 98226
Gilliam Dr 98226
Gilligan Way 98225
Ginger Pl 98226
Girard St 98225
Glacier Ridge Dr 98229
Gladstone St
300-799 98225
900-1799 98229
Glen Meadows Pl 98226
Glencove Ln 98226
Glengary Rd 98226
Gloria Ln 98226
Golden Ct 98226
Gooding Ave 98226

Gooseberry Cir 98229
Goshen Rd 98226
Governor Pl & Rd 98229
N & S Grace Ln 98226
Grady Way 98226
Granada Way 98225
Grand Ave 98225
Grand Blvd 98229
Grand View Ln 98229
Granite Cir 98229
Grant St 98225
Graveline Rd 98226
Gray Birch Ln 98229
Green St 98229
Green Hill Rd 98229
Greene Point Rd 98229
Greenville Ct, Dr, Pl & St 98226
Greenwood Ave 98225
Griffith Ave 98225
Grove Rd 98226
Grove St 98225
Guide Meridian 98226
Gumel Pl 98226
H St 98225
Hackett Rd 98226
Hadley St 98226
Haggin Rd & St 98226
S Halestri Cir N 98229
Halleck St 98225
Hallmark Ln 98226
Hammer Dr 98226
Hampton Pl 98225
Hannah Ct 98226
Hannegan Rd 98226
Hansen Ln 98229
Happy Ct 98225
Harbor Ln & Pl 98226
N & S Harbor Loop Dr 98225
Harbor View Dr 98229
Harmony Rd 98226
Harnden Rd 98226
Harris Ave 98225
Harrison St
3000-3199 98225
3600-3698 98229
3700-4599 98229
Harvest Way 98226
Hawk Way 98229
Hawks Hill Pl 98229
Hawthorne Rd 98225
Haxton Way 98226
Hayward Ct, Dr & St 98226
N & S Heather Pl 98226
Heights Dr & Pl 98226
Hel Lyn Pl 98226
E & W Hemmi Ln, Pl & Rd 98226
Henderson Rd 98226
Henry St 98225
Heritage Hills Ct 98226
Herlerin St 98225
Heron Point Ln 98229
Higginson Hall 98225
High St 98225
High Cliff Ln 98229
High Noon Rd 98226
Highfield Ct 98226
Highland Dr 98225
Highland Hall 98225
Highwood Cir 98229
Hiline Rd 98229
Hillcrest Way 98225
Hilliard St 98226
Hills Dr & Pl 98229
Hillsdale Rd 98226
Hillside Pl 98229
Hillspring Rd 98226
Hilltop Ln 98226
Hilton Ave 98225
Hoff Rd 98225
Holland Ave 98226
Holly Ct 98226
E Holly St 98225
W Holly St 98225
Holly View Way 98229
Hollywood Ave 98225
Home Rd
3600-3799 98225
3900-4099 98226
Honeycomb Ln 98229
Honeysuckle Pl 98229
Horizon Hill Ln 98229
Horseshoe Cir 98229
E & W Horton Rd & Way 98226
Howard Ave 98225
Howard Ln 98226
Howe Pl 98226
Huckleberry Ct 98229
Humboldt St 98225
Hunsicker Rd 98226
Hunters Pointe Dr 98225
Huntington St 98226
Huntley Rd 98226
Huron St
2000-2499 98229
2500-2899 98226
Husky Dr 98226
I St 98225
Idaho St 98229
Idell Dr 98226
Illinois Ln 98226
E Illinois St
101-297 98225
299-799 98225
801-899 98225
1000-2999 98226
W Illinois St 98225
Indian St & Ter 98225
Indian Meadow Ct 98229
Indian Ridge Ct 98229
Indiana St 98226
E Indiana St 98226
W Indiana St 98225
Inglewood Pl 98229
Inlet Cir 98229
Inverness Ln 98229
Iowa Dr 98229
Iowa St
300-999 98225
1001-1097 98225
1099-2200 98229
2202-2298 98229
Iris Ln 98229
Iron St 98225
Irongate Rd 98226
Irving St & Way 98225
Irwin Dr 98226
Isaacson Rd 98226
Island View Dr 98225
E Ivy St 98225
J St 98225
Jade Pl 98226
Jaeger St 98225
James St
1400-2999 98225
3401-3597 98226
3599-4299 98226
Jasper Pl 98226
Jasper Ridge Ln 98229
Jefferson Ave 98229
Jefferson Ln 98226
Jefferson St 98225
Jenkins St 98225
Jensen Rd 98226
Jerome St 98229
Jerry Garcia Way 98226
Jersey St 98225
Jills Ct 98226
Jimi Hendrix Way 98226
Jones Ln 98225
Jorgensen Pl 98226
Jubilee Ln 98229
Judy Way 98226
Julia Ave
2000-2200 98225
2202-2298 98225
3600-3699 98229
Kaitlyn Ct 98226
Kale Ln 98226
Kansas St
401-499 98225
3600-3900 98229
3902-4398 98229
Kathryn Ln 98229
Kearney St 98225
Keel Ct 98229
Keesling St 98225
Kelbay Ave 98226
Kelley Ridge Ct 98229
E Kellogg Rd 98226
W Kellogg Rd 98226
Kellogg St 98225
Kelly Rd 98225
Kenoyer Ct & Dr 98229
Kent Dr 98226
Kentucky St
201-497 98225
499-999 98225
1400-1498 98229
1500-2799 98225
Key St 98225
Keystone Way 98226
King Ave 98226
King St
1300-1400 98229
1402-1498 98229
1601-1697 98225
1699-2799 98225
2801-3099 98225
N King Mountain Rd 98226
W King Tut Rd 98226
Kinglet Ct 98229
Kings Ln 98226
Kingsmill St 98229
Kingswood Ct 98226
Kinley Way 98226
Kirkview Pl 98226
W Kline Rd 98226
Knight Rd 98226
Knox Ave
1001-1497 98225
1499-2300 98225
2302-2398 98225
3601-3799 98229
Kramer Ln 98226
Krystal Pond 98226
Kulshan St 98225
Kwina Rd 98226
La Vista Pl 98226
Lady Rose Ct 98226
Lafayette St 98225
Lahti Ct & Dr 98226
Laine Ct 98226
Lake Rd 98226
Lake Crest Dr 98229
Lake Louise Dr & Rd 98229
E, N & W Lake Samish Dr & Rd 98229
Lake Whatcom Blvd 98229
Lake Whatcom Shore Ct 98229
Lakehill Ln 98229
Lakemont Rd 98226
Lakeridge Ln 98226
Lakeshore Rd 98226
Lakeside Ave & Ln 98229
Lakeview St 98229
Lakeway Dr
300-699 98225
700-798 98229
800-4700 98229
4702-4798 98229
Lakeway Pl 98229
Lakewood Ln 98229
Lamberto Pl 98226
Lamoureaux Ln 98226
Landon Ave 98226
Langara Cir 98229
Lange Rd 98226
Larkspur Ct 98229
Larrabee Ave
400-998 98225
1000-2399 98225
3500-3700 98229
3702-3798 98229
Larrabee Rd 98226
W Larson Rd 98226
Lasalle Ave 98229
E Laurel Rd 98226
W Laurel Rd 98226
E Laurel St 98225
W Laurel St 98225
Laurel Meadows Dr 98226
Laurel Ridge Way 98226
Laurelwood Ave 98225
Lazer Ln 98226
Lee Ct & Way 98226
Leeward Pl & Way 98226
Legacy Ln 98226
Leland St 98226
Lemon Grove Dr 98226
Lena Rd 98226
Lenora Ct 98225
Leroy Pl 98226
Levitt St 98226
Lewis St 98229
Liberty St 98225
Lightning Bird Ln 98226
Likely Ct & Dr 98229
Lilly Ln 98226
Lincoln St
600-798 98229
800-1700 98229
1702-1798 98229
2001-2699 98225
2800-3098 98226
Lindbergh Ave 98225
Linden Rd
400-498 98226
500-699 98225
700-799 98229
Lindquist Rd 98226
Lindsay Ave
2001-2197 98225
2199-3199 98225
3300-3999 98229
Lindshier Ave 98226
Lingbloom Rd 98226
Lisa Ln 98229
Little Beaver Rd 98226
Little Palimino Ct 98229
Little Strawberry Ln 98229
Locust Ave 98225
Logan St 98225
Loganberry Ln 98229
Lohink Pl 98229
Lone Eagle Cir 98226
Lone Tree Ct 98229
Lone Wolf Ln 98226
Longeets Ln 98229
Longshore Ln 98229
Lookout Ave 98229
Lookout Mountain Ln 98229
Lopez Ct & St 98229
Lorraine Ellis Ct 98225
Lost Creek Ln 98229
Lost Fork Ln 98229
Lost Lake Ln 98229
Lottie St 98225
Lotus Ct 98229
Louise View Dr 98229
Lowe Ave 98229
Lowell Ave 98225
Lummi Rd 98226
Lummi Shore Rd 98226
Lummi View Dr 98226
Lyla Ln 98225
Lyle St 98225
Lynn St 98225
Mackenzie Rd 98226
Madison St 98225
Madrona St 98225
E Magnolia St 98225
W Magnolia St
101-101 98225
103-105 98225
104-104 98227
107-199 98225
114-298 98225
Magrath Rd 98226
Mahogany Ave 98226
N & S Mahonia Dr & Pl 98229
Majestic Dr 98226
Malachite Rd 98226
Mandarin Ct 98229
Manley Rd 98229
Manor Ln 98229
Manthey Rd 98226
E Maple 98225
Maple Ct 98229
Maple Ln 98229
E Maple St
100-198 98225
200-1499 98225
1701-1799 98229
Maple Ridge Ct 98229
E Maplewood Ave 98225
W Maplewood Ave
2600-3299 98225
4101-4299 98225
Maralee Ln 98226
Marblemount Ln 98226
Marie Ct 98226
Marietta Ave 98226
Marigold Dr 98229
Marigold Ln 98225
Marina Dr 98229
Marine Dr
600-1600 98225
1602-1698 98225
1700-2399 98226
Marine Way 98225
Marionberry Ct & Ln 98229
Market Rd 98226
Marriott Ln 98229
Martin Rd & St 98226
Maryland Pl 98226
E Maryland St
301-397 98225
399-800 98225
802-898 98225
1000-4999 98226
W Maryland St 98225
Mason St 98225
Masonry Way 98226
Mathes Hall 98225
Matheson Ln 98226
Mayflower Ln 98226
Maynard Pl 98226
Mcabee Ln 98226
Mcalpine Rd 98225
Mckenzie Ave 98225
Mcleod Rd
1200-1499 98226
2600-3230 98225
E Mcleod Rd 98226
W Mcleod Rd 98225
Meador Ave
500-700 98225
702-798 98225
1001-1197 98229
1199-1499 98229
Meadow Ct 98229
Meadowbrook Ct 98226
Medcalf Rd 98226
Megan Ln 98226
Mercer Ave 98225
Meridian St
2301-2397 98225
2399-3799 98225
3900-3998 98226
4000-4599 98226
Merlin Ct 98229
Mertz Rd 98226
Michael Rd 98226
Michigan St
2000-2499 98229
2500-2999 98226
Middlefield Rd 98225
Midnight Ct 98229
Midway Ln 98226
Midwood Ct & Ln 98229
Miles Rd 98226
Mill Ave
1000-2799 98225
3701-3797 98229
3799-4199 98229
Mill St 98226
Milton St 98229
Milwaukee Loop & Rd 98226
Minot St 98226
Mission Rd 98226
Misty Ln 98226
Misty Ridge Ct 98229
Mitchell Way 98226
Mockingbird Ln 98226
Modoc Dr 98229
Moena Dr 98229
Monroe St 98225
Montgomery Rd 98226
Moonstone Ln 98229
Moore St
1000-1398 98229
1400-2499 98229
2500-2999 98229
Morey Ave 98225
Morgan St 98229
Morning Beach Dr 98229
Morning Glory Dr 98229
Morning Mist Way 98229
Morning Star Dr 98226
Morris St 98225
Mossop Dr 98229
Mountain Ash Ct 98229
Mt Baker Hwy 98226
Mulberry Rd 98225
Muriel Dr 98226
Murphy Pl 98226
Murray Rd 98226
Mustang Way 98226
E Myrtle St 98225
Nash Hall 98225
Nelson Cove Rd 98229
Nequalicum Ave 98225
Nettle Ln 98226
Nevada St
800-2499 98229
2500-2999 98226
New St 98225
New Haven Pl 98226
Newell St 98225
Newmarket St 98226
Newton St 98229
Niagara Dr 98229
Niagara Pl 98229
Niagara St
2401-2499 98229
2700-3099 98226
Nigel Rd 98226
Nighthawk Dr 98229
Noahs Way 98226
Nome St 98225
Noon Rd 98226
Noon Valley Rd 98226
E North St
100-999 98225
1000-5299 98226
W North St 98225
Northgate Rd 98226
Northridge Pl & Way 98226
Northwest Ave
2600-3599 98225
3600-4099 98226
Northwest Dr 98226
Northwind Cir & Ct 98226
Northwood Ct 98226
Not Assigned Ct 98229
Nulle Rd 98229
Nulle Woods Ct 98229
Oak St 98225
Oakcrest Cir 98229
Offshore Ct 98229
Ohio St
100-298 98225
300-799 98225
801-899 98225
1800-3798 98229
3800-3899 98229
Okanogan St 98229
Old Fairhaven Pkwy 98225
Old Guide Rd 98226
Old Highway 99 N 98229
Old Highway 99 North Rd 98229
Old Lake Samish Rd 98229
Old Lakeway Dr 98229
Old Marine Dr 98225
Old Samish Rd 98229
Older Ln 98229
Olivia Ct 98226
Olympic Pl 98229
Olympic Way 98225
Om Ln 98226
Omega Hall 98225
Ontario St
2100-2499 98229
2500-2899 98226
Opal Ter 98226
Orange Blossom Ct 98226
E Orchard Dr 98226
W Orchard Dr 98225
Orchard Pl 98225
Orchid Ct 98229
Orchid Pl 98226
Oregon Pl 98226
E Oregon St 98226
W Oregon St 98225
Oriental Ave & Ln 98229
Orion Way 98226
Orleans St
1100-2298 98229
2300-2499 98229
2500-3151 98226
3150-3150 98228
3152-3298 98226
3153-3199 98226
Otis St 98225
Oval Ct 98229
Overlake Ct 98229
Owens Ct 98225
Pacific Hwy
100-499 98229
4000-4899 98226
Pacific St
1300-2499 98229
2500-3099 98226
Pacific Rim Ct, Ln & Way 98226
E & W Pacificview Ct & Dr 98229
Padden Hills Ct 98229
Palisade Way 98226
Palm St 98225
Palmer Rd 98229
Paloma Ln 98226
Pana Vista Dr 98226
Papetti Ln 98226
Par Ln 98229
N Park Dr 98225
S Park Dr 98225
Park Pl 98226
Park St 98225
Parker St 98225
Parkhurst Dr 98229
Parkridge Rd 98225
N & S Parkstone Ct, Ln & Way 98229
Parkview Cir 98229
Parnell St 98229
Partridge Cir 98229
Partridge Ln 98225
Pasco St 98225
Patrick Ct 98226
Patrick Ln 98229
Pattle St 98225
Patton Rd 98226
Patton St 98225
Peabody St 98225
S Pebble Pl 98226
Pebble Beach Trl 98226
Pence Ave 98226
Pennington Way 98229
Penny Ln 98226
Pickett Rd 98226
Piedmont Pl 98229
Pincher Ct & St 98226
Pine St 98225
Pinedrop Pl 98229
Pinehurst Ct 98226
Pinewood Ave 98225
Pinto Creek Ln 98229

Street	ZIP
Pleasant Ln	98226
Pleasant Bay Rd	98226
Plum Ln	98229
Plymouth Dr	98225
N Point Dr	98229
Polo Park Dr	98229
Ponderosa Ct & Dr	98229
Poplar Dr	98226
Portal Dr	98229
Postal Ave	98226
Potter St	
300-699	98225
900-998	98229
1000-1299	98229
Powell St	98229
Prescott Ln	98229
Primrose Ln	98226
Prince Ave	98226
Princeton Ct	98229
Private Dr	98226
Probert Pl	98225
Prospect St	
1-299	98225
301-315	98225
315-315	98227
317-399	98225
Prospect Way	98229
Puget St	98229
Pullman St	98226
Pyeatt Pl	98226
Quartz Ridge Ln	98229
Queen St	
800-2499	98229
2500-2899	98226
Quinault St	98229
Quinn Ct	98226
W Racine Pl	98229
Racine St	
600-2499	98229
2500-3399	98226
E Racine St	98229
W Racine St	98229
Railroad Ave	98225
Rainier Ave	98229
Ranchos Rd	98226
Raptor Ln	98229
Rauch Dr	98226
Raven Crst	98226
Ravenwood Ct	98229
Raymond St	98229
Red Tail Ln	98226
Red Tree Ln	98229
Redondo Way	98226
Redwing Ct	98226
Redwood Ave	98225
Repeater Rd	98229
Reveille St	98229
Rhododendron Way	98229
NW Ridge Ln	98226
Ridge Crest Way	98229
Ridgemont Ct & Way	98229
Ridgeway Dr	98225
Ridgeway Alpha	98225
Ridgeway Beta	98225
Ridgeway Delta	98225
Ridgeway Gamma	98225
Ridgeway Kappa	98225
Ridgeway Omega	98225
Ridgeway Sigma	98225
Ridgewood Ave	98229
Riley St	98229
Rimland Dr	98226
River Ridge Loop	98229
Robby Ct	98226
Roberts Rd	98226
Robertson Rd	98226
Rocky Rd	98226
Rocky Ridge Dr	98229
Roeder Ave	98225
Roland St	98229
Roma Ct & Rd	98226
Ronnona Ln	98226
Rosario Ct	98229
Rose St	98225
Rose Ridge Loop	98229
Rosebud Ln & Pl	98229
Rosette Ct	98226
Rosewood Ln	98225
Roslyn Pl	98226
Ross Rd	98226
Roy Rd	98229
Ruby Pl	98226
Rural Ave	98226
E & W Rusley Ct & Dr	98225
Russell St	98225
Ruston Way	98226
Rusty Ln	98229
Ruth Rd	98226
Ryzex Way	98226
Saddlestone Dr	98226
Saffron Ct	98229
Sagewood Ct	98229
Salakanum Way	98226
Salal Cir	98229
Salmon Rd	98226
Salmonberry Ln	98229
Samish Ln	98229
Samish Way	98229
N Samish Way	98225
S Samish Way	98225
Samish Crest Dr, Ln & Way	98229
San Juan Blvd	98229
Sand Rd	98226
Sandalwood Cir	98229
Sandstone Way	98229
Sandy Cir	98225
Sanwick Point Ct	98229
Sapphire Trl	98226
Sara Ct	98226
Scenic Ave	98229
Schickler Ln	98226
Schultz Dr	98226
Scott Rd	98226
Sea Pines Ln & Rd	98229
Seaview Cir	98225
Sedona Ln	98229
Seeley St	98226
Sehome Ave	98229
Sentinel Ct	98229
Sequoia Dr	98226
Setting Sun Cir	98226
Shady Ln	98229
Shady Tree Ln	98226
Shallow Shore Ln & Rd	98229
Shaw Rd	98229
Shellfish Cove Ln	98226
Shepardson St	98226
Sheridan Trl	98226
Shetland Ct	98229
Shooting Star Ct	98229
Shore Dr, Ln & Rd	98226
Shorewood Dr	98225
Shorewood Ln	98226
Shum Cir	98226
Sierra St	98226
Sierra Vista Pl	98226
Sigma Cir	98229
Silesia Ln	98226
Silver Ln	98225
Silver Beach Ave	98226
Silver Beach Rd	98229
Silver Oak Ct	98226
Silver Run Ln	98229
E & W Silverado Ct	98226
Silverbell Way	98226
Silvern Ln	98226
Silverstar Rd	98226
Sitka Ct	98226
Skagit St	98226
Skyland Ct	98229
Skylark Loop	98226
Slater Rd	98226
Sleepy Hollow Ln	98226
E & W Smith Rd & Way	98226
Smokehouse Rd	98226
Sommerset Ct	98226
Sound Way	98226
Soundview Rd	98229
South Ave	
2900-2998	98225
3400-3599	98229
South St	98225
Southbend Pl	98226
Southern Ct	98229
Southgate Rd	98226
Sparrow Ct	98229
Spieden Ln & Pl	98229
Spinnaker Ln	98229
Spokane St	98229
Spring Ct	98226
Spring Rd	98229
Spring St	98229
Spring Coulee Rd	98226
Spring Creek Ln	98226
Spring Valley Ave	98229
N & S Springfield Ct	98229
Springhill Pl	98226
Springland Ct & Ln	98226
Spruce St	98225
Spur Ridge Ln	98226
Spyglass Dr	98226
Squalicum Pkwy & Way	98225
Squalicum Creek Dr	98226
Squalicum Lake Rd	98226
Squalicum Mountain Rd	98226
Squires Rd	98229
St Andrews Way	98229
St Clair Pl	98226
St Clair St	
2000-2098	98229
2100-2499	98229
2500-3199	98226
St Paul Ln	98229
St Paul St	
1100-2499	98229
2500-3099	98226
Stable Ln	98229
Stangroom Rd	98229
Star View Ln	98229
Starflower Ct	98226
Starry Rd	98226
Starrybrook Ln	98226
N & S State St	98225
Steller Ct	98226
Stephens Dr	98226
Sterk Ln	98226
Sterling Dr	98226
Stommish Ln	98226
Stone Crest Ct	98226
Stonecrest Ln	98226
Stonecrop Ln & Way	98226
Stoney Brook Ln	98229
Stoney Ridge Dr	98226
Stoneycreek Ln	98226
Stormus Way	98226
Strawberry Pl, Pt & Rd	98229
Strawberry Canyon Ct	98229
Strawberry Pt Ct	98229
Strawberry Shore Dr	98229
Strider Ln	98226
Strider Loop Rd	98226
Stromer Rd	98226
W Stuart Rd	98226
Studio Ln	98226
Sudden Vly	98229
Sudden Valley Dr SE	98229
Sugarpine Pl	98229
Summer St	98225
Summer Bell Ln	98229
Summerland Rd	98229
Summit Ct	98226
N Summit Dr	98225
Summit St	98229
Sundew Ct	98229
Sundown View Ln, Ter & Way	98226
Sunflower Cir	98229
Sunflower Ln	98229
Sunny Cove Ct	98226
Sunnybrook Ln	98226
Sunnyside Ln	98229
Sunset Ave	98226
Sunset Dr	98225
E Sunset Dr	
300-730	98225
732-898	98225
1000-3000	98226
3002-3098	98226
Sunset Ln	98229
Sunset Way	98226
Sunset Pond Ln	98226
Superior St	
2000-2098	98229
2100-2499	98229
2500-2999	98226
Susan Ct	98229
Sussex Dr	98226
Swallow Cir	98229
Swamp Creek Ln	98226
Sweetbay Ct & Dr	98229
Sweetclover Cir	98229
Sycamore St	98225
Sydney Ct	98226
Sylvan Pl & St	98226
Taku Dr	98229
Tamarack Rd	98226
Tanglewood Ln	98226
Tawny Cir	98229
Taylor Ave	
1100-2600	98225
2602-3198	98225
3300-3899	98229
Taylor Pl	98229
Teal Ct	98229
Tee Pl	98229
Telegraph Rd	98226
N Terrace Ave	98229
Terrace Pl	98225
Terressa Ln	98226
Texas St	
101-197	98225
199-299	98225
301-999	98225
1200-3099	98229
Thimbleberry Pl	98229
Thomas Rd	98226
Thomas J Glenn Dr	98225
Thunder Peak Way	98229
Timber Creek Ln	98226
Timberlake Ct & Way	98229
Timberline Dr	98226
Timothy Ct	98226
Tiopi Loop	98226
Toad Lake Rd	98226
Toledo Ct	98229
Toledo St	
1100-2099	98229
2101-2499	98229
2500-2899	98226
E Toledo St	98229
W Toledo St	98229
Topaz Ct	98226
Topper Dr	98226
Topside Ct	98229
Totem Trl	98226
Track St	98226
Tree Farm Ct & Ln	98226
Tremont Ave	98226
Trickle Creek Blvd	98226
Trout Lake Dr	98226
Tulip Rd	98225
Tull Rd	98226
Tumbling Water Dr	98229
Tut Ter	98226
Tweedsmuir Ct	98226
Twin Flower Cir	98229
Twin Lakes Dr	98229
Underhill Rd	98225
Undine Ln	98226
Undine Pl	98226
Undine St	
1100-1499	98229
1501-2499	98229
2500-2899	98226
Unity St	98225
University Ave	98225
Utter St	98225
Vacca Ln	98226
Valencia St	
1600-2499	98229
2500-2899	98226
Valhalla Ln & St	98226
Vallette St	98225
Valley Crest Way	98229
Valley View Cir	98229
Valleybrook Ln	98229
Van Horn Ln	98226
Van Wyck Ln & Rd	98226
Varsity Pl	98225
Velma Rd	98226
Vendovi Ln	98229
Verbena	98226
Vermont St	98226
Verona St	
1100-1198	98229
1200-2499	98229
2500-2899	98226
E Victor St	98225
Victoria Pl	98226
Victoria St	98225
View Ridge Dr	98229
Viewcrest Rd	98229
Viewhaven Ln	98229
Viewmont Ct	98229
Villa Ln	98225
E, N & W Village Dr & Ln	98226
Vine St	98229
Vineyard Dr & Pl	98226
Vining Dr	98229
Vining Pl	98226
Vining Rd	98226
Vining St	
2000-2298	98229
2300-2499	98229
2500-3799	98226
Virginia St	98225
Vista Dr	98229
Voltaire Ct	98229
Wade St	98226
Wahl Rd	98226
Waldron Rd	98226
Wall St	98229
Walnut St	98225
Warchief Cir	98226
Warrior Loop	98226
Waschke Rd	98226
Washington St	98225
Water Tower Ct	98229
Waterside Ln	98229
Wayside Ct	98226
Wekes Ln	98226
Welleari St	98226
Welling Ct & Rd	98226
West St	98225
Westbrook Ct	98229
Westerly Rd	98226
Western Ln	98229
Westhills Pl	98226
Westridge Pl	98226
Whatasen Ln	98226
Whatcom Ln	98229
Whatcom St	
300-599	98225
1100-3399	98229
Wheatstone Way	98229
Whipple Ct	98226
Whisper Way	98226
Whispering Cedars Ct	98229
Whistling Swan Pl	98229
White Mountain Ln	98229
Whitecap Rd	98229
Whitewater Dr	98229
Whitney Ct & St	98229
Whitsonville Way	98226
Whitworth Ct	98229
Wilderness Ridge Rd	98229
Wildflower Ct & Way	98229
Wildhaven Crst	98226
Wildlife Ln	98226
Wildrose Ct	98229
Wildwood Ave & Dr	98229
Wilkin St	98229
Wilkins St	98225
Williams St	98225
Williamsburg Ct	98226
Williamson Way	
3600-3699	98225
3700-4099	98226
Willis St	
2600-2899	98225
2901-2999	98225
4600-4799	98229
Willow Ct N	98225
Willow Ct S	98225
Willow Ln	98226
Willow Rd	98225
Willow Road Pl	98225
Willowbrook Ln & Pl	98229
Willowwood Ave	98225
Wilson Ave	98225
Wiltse Ln	98226
Windtree Ct	98229
Windward Dr	98229
Winter Creek Pl	98229
Wintercress Way	98229
Wintergreen Cir & Ln	98226
Wisteria Ln	98229
Woburn St	
1200-2400	98229
2402-2498	98229
2500-3499	98226
Wood Crst	98226
Woodbine Pl & Way	98229
Woodcliff Ln	98229
Woodfern Way	98226
Woodlake Rd	98226
Woodpecker Pl	98229
Woodridge Dr	98229
Woodrush Ct	98229
Woodside Ct & Way	98226
Woodstock Way	98226
Wynn Rd	
3900-4099	98225
4101-4299	98225
4500-4799	98226
Xenia Ln	98229
Xenia St	
1100-1198	98229
1200-2499	98229
2500-2899	98226
Y Rd	98226
Yearling Pl	98229
Yellow Brick Rd	98226
Yew St	
800-2499	98229
2500-2900	98226
2902-2998	98226
Yew Street Rd	98229
York St	
201-397	98225
399-499	98225
501-899	98225
900-4199	98229
Young St	98225
Zander Dr	98226
Zeta Rd	98226

NUMBERED STREETS

Street	ZIP
E 3rd Rd	98226
4th St	98225
E 5th Ave	98226
6th St	98225
8th St	98225
10th St	98225
11th St	98225
E 12th Dr	98226
12th St	
500-1502	98225
1501-1501	98227
1503-1699	98225
1504-1798	98225
E 13th Crst	98226
13th St	98225
14th St	98225
15th St	98225
E 16th Pl	98226
16th St	
400-1899	98225
2500-2999	98229
E 17th Crst	98226
17th St	98225
E 18th Ave	98226
E 18th Crst	98226
18th St	
1100-1999	98225
3200-3699	98229
E 19th Crst	98226
19th St	
800-1299	98225
3600-3699	98229
20th St	98225
E 21st Dr	98226
E 21st Pl	98226
21st St	
800-1699	98225
3200-3299	98229
22nd St	98225
E 23rd Ave	98226
E 23rd Crst	98226
E 23rd Pl	98226
23rd St	98225
24th Ave	98226
24th St	98225
25th St	98225
E 26th Ave	98226
E 26th Dr	98226
26th St	98225
27th St	98225
28th St	98225
30th St	98225
31st Pl & St	98225
W 32nd Ln	98225
32nd St	
100-1799	98225
3200-3399	98229
W 32nd Ter	98225
33rd St	
100-199	98225
3200-3299	98229
34th St	98229
N 34th St	98225
S 34th St	98225
35th St	
100-198	98225
1400-1498	98229
E 36th Ln	98226
36th St	
200-498	98225
700-2400	98229
2402-2498	98229
E 36th Ter	98226
37th St	
100-198	98225
400-2399	98229
38th St	98229
39th Pl	98229
39th St	98229
S 39th St	98229
E 39th Ter	98226
40th Pl & St	98229
41st St	98229
S 41st St	98229
E 41st Ter	98226
S 42nd St	98229
43rd St	98229
S 44th St	98229
S 46th	98229
47th St	98229
48th St	98229
51st St & Ter	98226
E 52nd Ter	98226
W 53rd Vis	98226
E & W 54th Ln & Ter	98226
55th Ln & Ter	98226
56th Pl & Vis	98226
E 57th Pl	98226

BLAINE WA

General Delivery 98230

POST OFFICE BOXES MAIN OFFICE STATIONS AND BRANCHES

Box No.s
All PO Boxes 98231

NAMED STREETS

A St 98230
Abalone Way 98230
Adelia St 98230
Aerie Ln 98230
Alder St & Way 98230
Alderson Rd 98230
Allan St 98230
Anchor Pkwy 98230
Anderson Rd 98230
Arnie Rd 98230
Ashbury Ct 98230
B St 98230
Bald Eagle Dr 98230
Baldwin Pl 98230
Bay Cir & Rd 98230
Bay Ridge Dr 98230
Bayshore Dr 98230
Bayview Ave & Ct 98230
Bayvue Rd 98230
Beach Lamar Dr 98230
Beach Rock Loop Dr 98230
Beach Way Dr 98230
Beachcomber Dr 98230
Beanblossom Ln 98230
Bell Rd 98230
Belted Kingfisher Rd 98230
Bennett Ave 98230
Birch Ct, Dr & Ln 98230
Birch Bay Dr 98230
Birch Bay Lynden Rd 98230
Birch Bay Square St 98230
Birch Point Loop & Rd 98230
Blaine Ave & Rd 98230
Blossomberry Ln 98230
Blue Grouse Way 98230
Boblett Rd & St 98230
Boone Rd 98230
Boundary Ct & Ln 98230
W Boundry Rd 98230
Breeze Loop 98230
Bridge Way 98230
Bridger Rd 98230
Broadway St 98230
Brown Rd 98230
Bufflehead Ct 98230
Burbank Cres 98230
Burk Rd 98230
C St 98230
California Trl 98230
Camas Dr 98230
Camber Ln 98230
Cambridge Loop 98230
Canada View Dr 98230
Canoe Ct 98230
Canvasback Loop & Rd 98230
Carson Rd 98230
Carstan Loop 98230
Castlerock Dr 98230
Catalina Ct 98230
Cedar Ave, Ln, St & Way 98230
Cedarwood Ln 98230
Charel Dr 98230
Chehalis Pl & Rd 98230
Cherry St 98230
Cherry Tree Ln 98230
Chickadee Way 98230
Chilliwack Rd 98230
Chinook Way 98230
Clamdigger Dr 98230
Clark St 98230
Clubhouse Point Dr 98230
Clyde St 98230
Coastal Loop 98230
Cody Rd 98230
Comfort Ln 98230
Comox Loop & Rd 98230
Coquitlam Dr & Pl 98230
Cormorant Dr 98230
Cotterill Blvd 98230
Cottonwood Ct & Dr 98230
Cowichan Rd 98230
Crest Dr 98230
Crockett Rd 98230
Custer Rd 98230
D St 98230
Dahl Ln 98230
Davit Ct 98230
Dearborn Ave 98230
Deer Trl 98230
Delta Line Rd 98230
Deltop Dr 98230
Dodd Ave 98230
Donald Way 98230
Dory Ct 98230
Dournerm Rd 98230
Drayton Ct 98230
Drayton Harbor Rd 98230
Dunlin Ct 98230
Dupree Dr 98230
E St 98230
Earls Ct 98230
East St 98230
Elaine St 98230
Elm Ave 98230
Elmwood Dr 98230
Evans Dr 98230
Evergreen Ln 98230
F St 98230
Fawn Cres 98230
Fern St 98230
Fir Ave, Dr, St & Way 98230
Firtree Ln 98230
Fishermans Bend Ln 98230
Flambeau Rd 98230
Fleet Rd 98230
Forsberg Rd 98230
Fortune Ln 98230
Fox Hurst Ct 98230
Francis Ln 98230
G St 98230
Garfield Ave 98230
Gemini St 98230
Georgia St 98230
Giles Rd 98230
Glendale Dr 98230
Gleneagle Dr 98230
Golden Eagle Ln 98230
Goldenbrook Way 98230
Goldeneye Ln 98230
Goldfinch Way 98230
Goldstar Dr 98230
E, N, S & W Golf Course Dr 98230
Goshawk Rd 98230
Grandview Rd 98230
Grant Ave 98230
Great Blue Heron Ln 98230
Great Horned Owl Ln 98230
Grouse Cresent Dr 98230
H St 98230
H Street Rd 98230
Haida Way 98230
Halibut Dr 98230
Hall Rd 98230
Halverson Ln 98230
Harbor Ct, Dr & Pl 98230
Harbor Side Dr 98230
Harborview Dr & Rd 98230
Harlequin Ct 98230
Harrison Ave
  701-1499 98230
  701-705 98231
N Harvey Rd 98230
Hayley Ln 98230
Haynie Rd 98230
Hazel Ln 98230
Helweg Ln & Rd 98230
Henley St 98230
Heronswood Dr 98230
Highland Dr 98230
Hillvue Rd 98230
Hinkley St 98230
Hogan Dr 98230
Hoier Rd 98230
Holeman Ave 98230
Holiday Dr 98230
Holly Ln 98230
Holtzheimer Trail Rd 98230
Horizon Dr 98230
Hoyt Rd 98230
Hughes Ave 98230
Ironwood Ct 98230
Jackson Rd 98230
James Tree Ln 98230
Jerome St 98230
Karber Rd 98230
Kayak Way 98230
Kettle Way 98230
Key St 98230
Kickerville Rd 98230
Kildeer Way 98230
Kispiox Rd 98230
Kitamat Way 98230
Knorr Ct 98230
Koehn Rd 98230
Lateener Ln 98230
Lee Ln 98230
Leeside Dr 98230
Legion Dr 98230
Leighton St 98230
Lighthouse Dr 98230
Lillian Way 98230
Lincoln Ln & Rd 98230
Loft Ln 98230
Loomis Trail Rd 98230
Lora Ln 98230
Ludwick Ave 98230
Madison Ave 98230
Makah Rd 98230
Mallard Rd 98230
Maple St & Way 98230
Maplecrest St 98230
Marine Dr 98230
Markworth Rd 98230
Martin St 98230
Mary Ave 98230
Masterson Rd 98230
Matsqui Pl 98230
Mayfair Pl 98230
Mcgee Rd 98230
Mcmillan Ave 98230
Merganser Ct 98230
Merle Pl 98230
Mitchell Ave 98230
Molers Ln 98230
Montfort Ave 98230
Moonglow Ct & Pl 98230
Moonlight Way 98230
Morgan Dr 98230
Morningside Dr 98230
Morris Rd 98230
Morrison Ave 98230
Mountvue Way 98230
Nakat Way 98230
Natures Path Way 98230
Nautical Ct 98230
Nemo Ct 98230
Night Heron Dr 98230
Nightingale Ct 98230
Niska Rd 98230
Nitinat Way 98230
Nootka Loop 98230
Normar Pl 98230
Oakridge Dr 98230
Ocean Mist Dr & Loop 98230
Odell St 98230
Oertel Dr 98230
Osprey Rd 98230
Ostrich Trl 98230
Outrigger Loop 98230
Owl Ln 98230
Oyster Dr 98230
Pacific Hwy 98230
Park Ln 98230
Parkland Dr 98230
Parkside Pl 98230
Parkview Pl & St 98230
Peace Rd 98230
Peace Arch Ct 98230
Peace Portal Dr 98230
Pearl St 98230
Pemberton Pl 98230
Peregrine Way 98230
Petticote Dr & Ln 98230
Pheasant Dr 98230
Pine Dr 98230
Pine Sisken Rd 98230
Pine Tree Ln 98230
Piney Ln 98230
Pintail Loop 98230
Pipeline Rd 98230
Plover Ct 98230
Point Whitehorn Rd 98230
Pointe Rd N 98230
Poplar Dr 98230
Poplar View Rd 98230
Portal Way 98230
Puffin Pl 98230
Quail Run 98230
Quinault Rd 98230
Red Cedar Rd 98230
Rene Ct 98230
Richard Way 98230
Richmond Cres 98230
Richmond Park Rd 98230
Ritchie Ln 98230
Roblee Dr 98230
Rock Crab Dr 98230
Roger Rd 98230
Ronald Dr 98230
Roseview St 98230
Ruby St 98230
Runge Ave 98230
Sage St 98230
Sagebrush Ln 98230
Salish Ln & Rd 98230
Salmon Creek Ln 98230
Sandcastle Dr 98230
Sanderling Way 98230
Sandpiper Ln 98230
Sawgrass Way 98230
Scenic Ridge Dr 98230
School Dr 98230
Sea Breeze Ct 98230
Seafair Ct & Dr 98230
Seashell Way 98230
Seaside Dr 98230
Seaview Dr 98230
Seavue Rd 98230
Seawan Pl 98230
Sehome Ct & Rd 98230
Selder Rd 98230
Semiahmoo Dr, Ln, Pkwy & Rdg 98230
Shady Ln 98230
Shearwater Rd 98230
Sherwood Dr 98230
Shintaffer Rd 98230
Shipyard Ln & Rd 98230
Shoreline Ct 98230
E & W Shoreview 98230
Siena Ct 98230
Sigurdson Ave 98230
Skagit Pl & Way 98230
Skeena Way 98230
Skyline Dr 98230
Skyvue Rd 98230
Snohomish Rd 98230
Snow Goose Ln 98230
Snowy Owl Ln 98230
Sole Dr 98230
Spooner Creek Ln 98230
Stadsvold Rd 98230
Starfish Ln 98230
Sterling Ave 98230
Stillwater Ln 98230
Sunburst Dr & Pl 98230
Sunrise Rd & Way 98230
Sunset Dr & St 98230
Surf Pl 98230
Sweet Rd 98230
Tananger Rd 98230
Tarte Rd 98230
Terrace Ave 98230
Terrill Dr 98230
Tidal Way 98230
Timber Ln 98230
Titan Ter 98230
Tracy Pl 98230
Treevue Rd 98230
Tsawwassen Loop 98230
Twilight Pl 98230
Valentine Ln 98230
Valley View Rd 98230
Vista Ave & Ter 98230
Washington Ave 98230
Watervue Way 98230
Wedgewood Ct 98230
Welkers Rd 98230
West Rd 98230
White Rd 98230
Whitehorn Way 98230
Wigeon Ct 98230
Willow Dr & Way 98230
Wilson Ave 98230
Windlass Ln 98230
Winged Teal Ct 98230
Wood Duck Way 98230
Woolridge Ave 98230
Yellow Fin Ct 98230
Yew Ave 98230
Yvonne Way 98230

NUMBERED STREETS

All Street Addresses 98230

BOTHELL WA

General Delivery 98011

POST OFFICE BOXES MAIN OFFICE STATIONS AND BRANCHES

Box No.s
All PO Boxes 98041

NAMED STREETS

Atlas Rd 98021
Balder Ln 98011
Baldwin Rd 98012
Barker Rd 98021
Bartlett Rd 98012
Beardslee Blvd
  10400-10501 98011
  10500-10500 98041
  10502-19198 98011
  10503-19199 98011
Beardslee Pl 98011
S Bellflower Rd 98012
SE Berwick Dr 98011
NE Bothell Way NE 98011
Bothell Everett Hwy
  13200-16800 98012
  16802-17598 98012
  16901-17697 98012
  17699-20799 98012
  20800-24399 98021
Brickyard Rd 98011
Brook Blvd 98012
Campus Way NE 98011
Carter Rd 98021
Cascadian Way 98012
Castle Dr 98021
Circle Dr 98011
Clover Rd 98012
Country Club Dr 98012
N Creek Dr 98012
N Creek Pkwy 98011
N Creek Pkwy N 98011
N Creek Pkwy S 98011
Damson Rd 98021
Dantontr St SE 98012
SW Downfield Way 98011
Duchess Rd 98012
Dumas Rd 98012
Eason Ave 98011
Filbert Dr & Rd 98012
Fitzgerald Rd 98021
Grannis Rd 98012
Gravenstein Rd 98012
Gredare Ave NE 98011
Greening Rd 98012
Grimes Rd 98012
Hall Rd 98011
Harvest Rd 98012
Heatherwood Dr 98012
Hoeder Ln 98011
NE Hollyhills Dr NE 98011
W Interurban Blvd 98012
Jewell Rd 98012
John Bailey Rd 98012
E Jonathan Rd 98012
Juanita Woodinville Way NE 98011
Lake Cir & Dr 98021
Lake View Cir 98021
Lockwood Rd 98021
Locust Way 98021
Main Pl 98011
Main St
  10000-10399 98011
  14600-15799 98012
Maltby Rd
  2000-2098 98021
  2100-2199 98021
  2300-4699 98012
Meridian Ave S
  16400-16599 98012
  21600-24399 98021
Meridian Dr SE
  19200-19299 98012
  21300-21599 98021
Meridian Pl W
  18800-19499 98012
  21100-23799 98021
Mill Creek Blvd
  1100-15900 98012
  15833-15833 98082
  15901-16399 98012
  15902-16398 98012
Mill Creek Rd 98012
Mill Fern Dr SE 98012
Mill Green Ct SE 98012
Mill Pointe Dr SE 98012
Monte Villa Pkwy 98021
Nellis Rd 98012
Newton Rd 98012
North Rd 98012
Odin Way 98011
Ormbreck St 98011
Palomino Dr 98012
Park Cir 98021
N Pointe Cir 98012
Poppy Rd 98012
Reder Way 98011
Richmond Rd 98012
W Richmond Rd 98021
Riverbend Dr 98011
E & W Riverside Dr & Pl 98011
Rock Cir 98021
Ross Rd 98011
Royal Anne Rd 98021
Sage Rd 98021
Seattle Hill Rd 98012
Silver Crest Dr 98012
Simonds Rd NE 98011
Sprague Dr 98012
Stafford Ln & Way 98012
Strumme Rd 98012
Sunrise Dr 98011
Sunset Rd 98012
Timber Trl 98012
Trillium Blvd SE 98012
Valhalla Dr & Way 98011
Valley Circle Dr 98012
Valley View Rd 98011
Village Green Dr 98012
Vista View Ave 98021
Wandering Creek Dr 98021
Waxen Rd 98012
Waynita Way NE 98011
Willow Cir 98021
Willow Ln SE 98012
W Winesap Ln & Rd 98012
Woodcrest Dr NE 98011
Woodinville Dr 98011
Woodland Dr 98012
Yorins Ave SE 98021
York Rd 98012

NUMBERED STREETS

1st Ave SE 98012
1st Ave W
  18700-19799 98012
  19801-19899 98012
  21100-23899 98021
1st Dr SE
  16400-19599 98012
  22100-22799 98021
1st Park SE 98012
1st Pl W
  16200-19399 98012
  21800-24299 98021
2nd Ave SE
  16100-20499 98012
  21300-23999 98021
2nd Ave W 98021
2nd Dr SE
  16200-20599 98012
  21300-21600 98021
2nd Park SE 98012
2nd Pl SE 98021
2nd Pl W
  18200-19799 98012
  21700-24399 98021
3rd Ave SE
  15600-19899 98012
  21600-23999 98021
3rd Ave W
  18700-19399 98012
  21200-21299 98021
3rd Dr SE
  14400-15599 98012
  15600-20499 98012
  21700-23999 98021
3rd Pl W
  17000-17199 98012
  21200-24399 98021
4th Ave SE
  16000-20599 98012
  20900-24399 98021
4th Ave W 98021
4th Dr SE
  16400-19799 98012
  21900-21999 98021
4th Pl W
  17600-17799 98012
  21300-24399 98021
5th Ave SE 98012
5th Ave W
  17200-17699 98012
  21100-23999 98021
5th Dr SE
  19200-19399 98012
  22001-22097 98021
  22099-22299 98021
5th Pl W
  17200-17499 98012
  22200-22599 98021
6th Ave SE 98012
6th Ave W
  17600-17999 98012
  21300-22099 98021
6th Dr SE
  19300-19799 98012
  22300-22499 98021

6th Pl SE 98012
6th Pl W 98021
7th Ave SE
19400-20199 98012
22800-24399 98021
7th Ave W
17200-17999 98012
21100-24399 98021
7th Dr SE 98021
7th Pl W 98021
8th Ave SE
14800-14899 98012
18300-19999 98012
21700-23899 98021
8th Ave W 98012
8th Dr SE
14800-14899 98012
18300-20399 98012
22600-23899 98021
8th Pl W 98021
9th Ave SE
16400-17299 98012
20000-20199 98012
20800-23599 98021
9th Ave W 98021
9th Dr SE
14800-14899 98012
19600-19799 98012
20800-22599 98021
9th Pl W 98021
10th Ave SE
14800-17699 98012
18600-20299 98012
20800-23299 98021
10th Ct SE 98021
10th Dr SE
13200-13299 98012
18300-20399 98012
21600-21699 98021
10th Pl W 98021
11th Ave W 98021
11th Ct SE 98021
11th Dr SE
14100-15299 98012
21200-21699 98021
12th Ave SE 98012
12th Ave W 98021
12th Dr SE
13800-15299 98012
23000-23199 98021
12th Pl W 98021
13th Ave SE
14500-14799 98012
17300-19199 98012
23300-23499 98021
13th Dr SE
13901-14797 98012
14799-14999 98012
17300-20799 98012
23000-23099 98021
13th Pl W 98021
14th Ave SE 98012
14th Ave W 98021
14th Ct SE 98012
14th Dr SE
13500-15600 98012
23100-23599 98021
14th Pl W 98021
15th Ave SE
15100-17999 98012
22800-24299 98021
15th Ct SE 98012
15th Dr SE 98012
15th Pl SE 98021
15th Pl W 98021
16th Ave SE
14601-14697 98012
14699-15299 98012
17100-19199 98012
24100-24199 98021
16th Ave W 98021
16th Ct SE 98012
16th Dr SE
16900-17399 98012
21400-21699 98021
16th Pl SE 98021
17th Ave SE
16300-16399 98012
16800-17199 98012
22000-22200 98021
22202-22298 98021
17th Ave W 98021
17th Ct SE 98012
17th Dr SE 98012
17th Ln W 98021
17th Pl W 98021
18th Ave SE
16300-16399 98012
17200-17399 98012
17401-17499 98012
22300-22499 98021
18th Ct SE 98012
18th Dr SE 98012
18th Ln SE 98012
18th Pl W 98021
18th St SE 98012
19th Ave SE
14800-14898 98012
14900-16399 98012
17800-17999 98012
22300-24399 98021
19th Ave W 98021
19th Dr SE
14000-14199 98012
18100-18900 98012
18902-20298 98012
22900-23799 98021
19th Pl W 98021
20th Ave SE
17700-18999 98012
21200-23599 98021
20th Ave W 98021
20th Cir SE 98012
20th Dr SE
14100-14499 98012
16900-19199 98012
22600-22739 98021
21st Ave SE
13401-15697 98012
15699-15900 98012
15902-15998 98012
16800-17299 98012
22900-23399 98021
21st Ave W 98021
21st Cir SE 98012
21st Ct SE 98012
21st Dr SE
14100-16399 98012
17200-17229 98012
23800-24299 98021
22nd Ave SE
13400-13599 98012
16600-19599 98012
23400-23599 98021
22nd Ave W 98021
22nd Ct SE 98021
22nd Dr SE
16201-16399 98012
18000-18799 98012
22700-23999 98021
22nd Pl W 98021
23rd Ave SE
13600-14010 98012
16400-17899 98012
20800-24399 98021
23rd Ave W 98021
23rd Dr SE
13900-14199 98012
18300-19899 98012
21501-21697 98021
21699-23999 98021
23rd Ln SE 98012
24th Ave SE 98012
24th Ave W 98021
24th Ct SE 98012
24th Dr SE
14100-16299 98012
23800-23999 98021
25th Ave SE
13400-16399 98012
24200-24299 98021
25th Ct SE 98012
25th Dr SE
15300-16299 98012
21000-23999 98021
25th Ln SE 98012
26th Ave SE
13600-16399 98012
22000-24299 98021
26th Ct SE 98012
26th Dr SE
14400-16399 98012
24000-24099 98021
27th Ave SE
17900-20499 98012
23000-23198 98021
23200-23299 98021
27th Dr SE
13200-13298 98012
13300-16399 98012
18000-20199 98012
22900-23299 98021
28th Ave SE
13201-13297 98012
13299-13599 98012
17400-20499 98012
20800-21099 98021
28th Dr SE
13600-16199 98012
29th Ave SE
13200-15699 98012
18000-20700 98012
20702-20798 98012
20800-21099 98021
29th Ct SE 98012
29th Dr SE
13200-16399 98012
16400-19999 98012
22300-22799 98021
30th Ave SE
14100-15799 98012
18000-19599 98012
21400-21599 98021
30th Ct SE 98021
30th Dr SE
13200-16399 98012
16400-20099 98012
20800-24099 98021
31st Ave SE
13200-14899 98012
14901-14999 98012
18000-18399 98012
18401-18599 98012
21100-22699 98021
31st Dr SE
13407-15199 98012
16400-20799 98012
21600-21899 98021
31st St SE 98012
32nd Ave SE
15300-16399 98012
20801-20897 98021
32nd Dr SE 98012
33rd Ave SE
13400-16399 98012
20800-20999 98021
33rd Dr SE
13400-15399 98012
20800-23999 98021
34th Ave SE
13400-15999 98012
18200-20099 98012
22200-23999 98021
34th Dr SE
13900-16399 98012
35th Ave SE
13401-14613 98012
14615-15100 98012
15102-16198 98012
15801-16497 98012
16499-19899 98012
20900-24099 98021
35th Dr SE
14600-14899 98012
15200-19699 98012
20700-23199 98021
35th Park SE 98012
36th Ave SE
14600-14899 98012
22300-23099 98021
36th Dr SE
15100-19599 98012
21200-23199 98021
37th Ave SE
14700-14799 98012
20600-22623 98021
37th Dr SE
16300-19699 98012
20700-21999 98021
38th Ave SE
13400-13499 98012
21200-23199 98021
38th Dr SE
14500-14799 98012
20600-22799 98021
39th Ave SE
13400-20799 98012
20800-24299 98021
39th Ct SE 98021
39th Dr SE
13400-14099 98012
17100-18599 98012
20800-22099 98021
39th Ln SE 98021
40th Ave SE
13400-14599 98012
16100-18599 98012
21000-24199 98021
40th Dr SE
13700-14099 98012
15300-18399 98012
20700-23999 98021
40th Ln SE 98021
41st Ave SE
13400-14299 98012
21500-24099 98021
41st Dr SE
13800-14299 98012
22800-23949 98021
42nd Ave SE
13600-14199 98012
16400-18599 98012
20700-24099 98021
42nd Dr SE
14600-18400 98012
18402-20398 98012
22800-23099 98021
43rd Ave SE 98012
43rd Dr SE 98021
44th Ave SE
13700-13799 98012
24000-24099 98021
44th Ct SE 98012
44th Dr SE
13500-13599 98012
21800-23099 98021
45th Ave SE
13200-19999 98012
20800-24199 98021
45th Dr SE 98012
46th Ave SE
13200-17899 98012
20800-21199 98021
46th Dr SE 98012
47th Ave SE
13200-13399 98012
21200-21600 98021
21602-24398 98021
47th Dr SE
21000-21199 98021
48th Ave SE
17600-20399 98012
23600-23799 98021
49th Ave SE
15400-15599 98012
21000-23709 98021
49th Dr SE 98012
50th Ave & Dr 98021
51st Ave SE 98012
52nd Ave SE 98021
53rd Ave SE 98021
54th Ave SE 98012
57th Ave SE 98021
58th Dr SE 98021
59th Ave SE 98021
61st Ave SE 98021
84th Ave & Pl 98011
85th Ave & Pl 98011
86th Ave & Pl 98011
88th Ave & Pl 98011
89th Ave, Ct & Pl 98011
90th Ave & Pl 98011
91st Ave & Pl 98011
92nd Ave, Ct & Pl 98011
93rd Ave, Blvd, Ct & Pl
NE 98011
94th Ave, Dr & Pl 98011
95th Ave & Pl 98011
96th Ave & Ct 98011
97th Ave & Ct 98011
98th Ave & Ct 98011
99th Ave, Ct & Pl 98011
100th Ave & Pl 98011
101st Ave & Pl 98011
102nd Ave & Ct 98011
103rd Ave, Ct & Pl 98011
104th Ave NE 98011
105th Ave & Pl 98011
106th Ave & Pl 98011
107th Ave & Pl 98011
108th Ave & Pl 98011
109th Ct & Pl 98011
110th Ave & Pl 98011
111th Ave NE 98011
112th Ave, Ln & Pl 98011
113th Ave NE 98011
115th Ave NE 98011
116th Ave NE 98011
117th Ct NE 98011
118th Ave, Ct, Ln & Pl
NE 98011
119th Ave, Ct, Ln, Pl &
Ter NE 98011
120th Ave NE 98011
121st Ave & Pl 98011
122nd Ave, Ct & Pl 98011
123rd Ave & Pl 98011
124th Ave NE 98011
125th Ave NE 98011
126th Ave NE 98011
127th Ave, Ct & Pl 98011
128th Ave, Ct & Pl 98011
129th Ave, Ct, Ln & Pl
NE 98011
130th Ave, Ct & Pl 98011
131st Ct NE 98011
132nd Pl SE 98012
133rd Pl SE 98012
134th Pl SE 98012
135th Pl SE 98012
136th Pl SE 98012
137th Pl SE 98012
138th Pl SE 98012
139th Pl SE 98012
140th Pl SE 98012
141st Ct SE 98012
142nd Ct SE 98012
143rd Pl SE 98012
144th Ct SE 98012
145th Ct, Pl & St 98011
145th Ct, Pl & St 98012
146th Cir & St 98011
146th Cir & St 98012
147th Ln & St 98011
147th Ln & St 98012
148th Ct, Ln & St 98012
148th Ct, Ln & St 98011
149th Ct & St 98012
149th Ct & St 98011
150th Cir SE 98012
150th Ct SE 98012
NE 150th Ct 98011
NE 150th Dr 98011
150th Ln SE 98012
150th Pl SE 98012
150th St SE 98012
NE 150th St 98011
151st Dr, Pl & St 98011
151st Dr, Pl & St 98012
152nd Pl SE 98012
NE 152nd Pl 98011
152nd St SE 98012
NE 152nd St 98011
153rd Pl & St 98012
153rd Pl & St 98011
NE 154th Ct 98011
154th Pl SE 98012
NE 154th Pl 98011
154th St SE 98012
NE 154th St 98011
155th Pl SE 98012
NE 155th Pl 98011
155th St SE 98012
NE 155th St 98011
156th Pl SE 98012
156th Pl SW 98012
NE 156th Pl 98011
156th St SE 98012
NE 156th St 98011
157th Pl SE 98012
NE 157th Pl 98011
NE 157th St 98011
158th Pl SE 98012
158th St SE 98012
NE 158th St 98011
159th Ct SE 98012
NE 159th St 98011
160th Pl SE 98012
NE 160th Pl
9100-9199 98028
11100-11199 98011
160th St SE 98012
NE 160th St 98011
161st Pl SE 98012
NE 161st Pl 98011
161st St SE 98012
NE 161st St 98011
NE 162nd Ct 98011
NE 162nd Ln 98011
162nd Pl SE 98012
NE 162nd Pl 98011
162nd St SE 98012
NE 162nd St 98011
163rd Dr SE 98012
163rd Pl SE 98012
NE 163rd Pl 98011
163rd St SE 98012
NE 163rd St 98011
NE 164th Ln 98011
164th Pl SE 98012
NE 164th Pl 98011
164th St SE 98012
164th St SW 98012
NE 164th St 98011
165th Pl SE 98012
NE 165th Pl 98011
NE 165th St 98011
166th Ct SE 98012
NE 166th Ct 98011
166th Pl SE 98012
NE 166th Pl 98011
166th St SE 98012
NE 167th Ct 98011
167th Pl SE 98012
167th Pl SW 98012
167th St SE 98012
167th St SW 98012
NE 167th St 98011
NE 168th Ct 98011
168th Pl SE 98012
NE 168th Pl 98011
168th St SE 98012
168th St SW 98012
NE 168th St 98011
169th Pl SE 98012
169th Pl SW 98012
169th St SE 98012
169th St SW 98012
NE 169th St 98011
170th Pl SE 98012
170th Pl SW 98012
NE 170th Pl 98011
170th St SE 98012
NE 170th St 98011
171st Pl SE 98012
NE 171st Pl 98011
171st St SE 98012
172nd Pl SE 98012
172nd Pl SW 98012
NE 172nd Pl 98011
172nd St SE 98012
NE 172nd St 98011
173rd Pl SE 98012
173rd Pl SW 98012
NE 173rd Pl 98011
173rd St SE 98012
173rd St SW 98012
NE 173rd St 98011
174th Pl SE 98012
NE 174th Pl 98011
174th St SE 98012
174th St SW 98012
NE 174th St 98011
175th Pl SE 98012
175th Pl SW 98012
175th St SE 98012
175th St SW 98012
NE 175th St 98011
176th Pl SE 98012
176th Pl SW 98012
176th St SE 98012
NE 176th St 98011
NE 177th Ct 98011
177th Pl SE 98012
NE 177th Pl 98011
177th St SE 98012
NE 177th St 98011
178th Pl SE 98012
178th Pl SW 98012
178th St SE 98012
178th St SW 98012
NE 178th St 98011
179th Pl SE 98012
NE 179th Pl 98011
179th St SE 98012
180th Pl SE 98012
180th Pl SW 98012
180th St SE 98012
NE 180th St 98011
NE 181st Ln 98011
181st Pl SE 98012
181st Pl SW 98012
181st St SE 98012
181st St SW 98012
NE 181st St 98011
NE 182nd Ct 98011
182nd Pl SE 98012
182nd Pl SW 98012
NE 182nd Pl 98011
182nd St SE 98012
182nd St SW 98012
NE 182nd St 98011
NE 183rd Ct 98011
183rd Ln SE 98012
183rd Pl SE 98012
183rd St SE 98012
183rd St SW 98012
NE 183rd St 98011
NE 184th Ct 98011
184th Pl SE 98012
NE 184th Pl 98011
184th St SE 98012
184th St SW 98012
NE 185th Ct 98011
185th Pl SE 98012
185th Pl SW 98012
185th St SE 98012
NE 185th St 98011
186th Pl SE 98012
NE 186th Pl 98011
186th St SE 98012
NE 186th St 98011
187th Pl SE 98012
187th St SE 98012
NE 187th St 98011
NE 188th Ct 98011
188th Pl SE 98012
NE 188th Pl 98011
188th St SE 98012
NE 188th St 98011
189th Pl SE 98012
189th Pl SW 98012
NE 189th Pl 98011
189th St SE 98012

NE 189th St 98011
NE 190th Pl 98011
190th St SE 98012
NE 190th St 98011
191st Pl SE 98012
NE 191st Pl 98011
191st St SE 98012
NE 191st St 98011
192nd Pl SE 98012
NE 192nd Pl 98011
192nd St SE 98012
192nd St SW 98012
NE 192nd St 98011
NE 193rd Ct 98011
193rd Pl SE 98012
193rd Pl SW 98012
193rd St SW 98012
NE 193rd St 98011
194th Pl SE 98012
194th St SE 98012
194th St SW 98012
NE 194th St 98011
NE 195th Cir 98011
195th Pl SE 98012
195th Pl SW 98012
NE 195th Pl 98011
195th St SE 98012
NE 195th St 98011
NE 195th Way 98011
196th Pl SE 98012
196th Pl SW 98012
196th St SE 98012
NE 196th St 98011
NE 197th Ct 98011
197th Pl SE 98012
197th Pl SW 98012
NE 197th Pl 98011
197th St SE 98012
197th St SW 98012
NE 197th St 98011
NE 198th Ct 98011
198th Pl SE 98012
198th Pl SW 98012
NE 198th Pl 98011
198th St SE 98012
NE 198th St 98011
199th Pl SE 98012
199th St SE 98012
199th St SW 98012
NE 199th St 98011
200th Pl SE 98012
NE 200th Pl 98011
200th St SE 98012
NE 200th St 98011
201st Pl SE 98012
NE 201st Pl 98011
201st St SE 98012
NE 201st St 98011
202nd Pl SE 98012
NE 202nd Pl 98011
202nd St SE 98012
NE 202nd St 98011
NE 202nd Way 98011
203rd Pl SE 98012
NE 203rd Pl 98011
203rd St SE 98012
NE 203rd St 98011
204th Pl SE 98012
NE 204th Pl 98011
204th St SE 98012
NE 204th St 98011
205th Pl SE 98012
205th St SE 98012
NE 205th St 98011
206th Pl & St 98012
207th Pl SE
 700-3499 98012
 3700-3999 98021
207th St SE
 1200-1299 98012
 2300-2399 98021
208th Pl SE 98021
208th St SE
 300-1799 98012
 3600-4999 98021
209th Pl & St 98021
210th Pl & St 98021
211th Pl & St SE & SW 98021
212th Pl & St 98021
213th Pl & St SE & SW 98021
214th Pl & St 98021
215th Pl & St 98021
216th Pl & St 98021
217th Pl & St SE & SW 98021
218th Pl & St SE & SW 98021
219th Pl & St 98021
220th Pl & St 98021
221st Pl & St SE & SW 98021
222nd Pl & St SE & SW 98021
223rd Pl & St SE & SW 98021
224th Pl & St SE & SW 98021
225th Pl & St SE & SW 98021
226th Pl & St 98021
227th Pl & St 98021
228th Pl & St SE & SW 98021
229th Pl SE 98021
230th Pl SE 98021
231st Pl & St 98021
232nd Pl & St SE & SW 98021
233rd Pl & St SE & SW 98021
234th Pl & St SE & SW 98021
235th Pl & St SE & SW 98021
236th Pl & St 98021
237th Pl & St 98021
238th Pl & St SE & SW 98021
239th Pl & St 98021
240th Pl & St SE & SW 98021
241st Pl & St 98021
242nd Pl & St SE & SW 98021
243rd Pl & St 98021
244th SE & SW 98021

BREMERTON WA

General Delivery 98337

POST OFFICE BOXES MAIN OFFICE STATIONS AND BRANCHES

Box No.s
931A - 935A 98337
A7 - A9 98337
1 - 1497 98337
2001 - 3281 98310
4001 - 6998 98312
6000 - 6000 98310

NAMED STREETS

Abalone St 98312
Acorn St 98310
Addie Pl NW 98312
Adele Ave 98312
W Admiralty Heights Ln 98312
Aegean Blvd & Ct 98311
Alder St 98310
Alexis Dr NE 98311
Allview Blvd NE 98311
Almira Ct 98310
Almira Dr 98310
Almira Dr NE 98311
Alnus Way 98310
Alpenglow Dr NW 98312
NW Alta Dr 98310
NE Ambleside Ln 98311
Anderson St 98312
Anoka Ave 98337
Apache Pl NE 98311
Appaloosa Way 98310
Apple St 98310
NW Apple Blossom Loop 98311
NE Aquarius Ln 98311
Aquene Loop NE 98311
Arcade Pl NW 98311
Archie Ave W 98312
Argyle Ct NW 98312
NE Arizona St 98311
Armstrong Ln NE 98310
NE Arrowhead Dr 98311
W Arsenal Way 98312
NE Arta Ct 98311
Arvon Ave 98312
Ascot Ln NE 98310
Ash Pl & St 98310
Athens Ct & Way 98311
Audree Ln NE 98310
Audrey Ave 98312
Auklet Ct & Pl NE 98311
Austin Dr 98312
Auto Center Blvd & Way 98312
Autumn Hills Pl NE 98311
Aviator Ln NW 98312
Avon Ct NE 98311
B St 98312
Baer Blvd 98312
NE Bahia Vista Dr 98310
Baird Ct NW 98311
Barclay St 98337
Barefoot Ln NW 98312
NW Barker Creek Rd 98311
E Barlow Ct E 98310
Barnard Way NW 98312
Barnes St W 98312
Barnett St 98310
SW Barney White Rd 98312
Bartolatz Rd W 98312
Bay Vista Blvd 98312
Baymont Pl 98312
Bayview Dr W 98312
Beach Dr 98312
Beachside Dr NE 98311
Beacon Pl NE 98311
NE Beaumont Ln 98311
W Belfair Valley Rd 98312
NE Bellpark Dr 98310
NE Belmont Pl 98311
Bender Cir NE 98311
NE Benita Pl 98310
NE Bentley Cir & Dr NE 98311
Berkeley Pl NE 98311
Bertha Ave NW 98312
Big Beef Xing NW 98312
Bill Evans Rd 98312
Birch Ave 98310
N Birch Ave W 98312
Black Walnut Ln NE 98310
Blackbird Dr NE 98311
NW Blackhawk Ct 98312
Blake Ct NW 98311
Bledsoe Ave 98310
Bloomington Ave 98312
NE Blossom Pl 98311
Blue Heron Pl 98312
Blue Oak Pkwy NE 98311
NE Bonair Pl 98310
Bonkla Ln NW 98312
Boone Rd 98312
Bootleg Hill Pl NE 98310
Boundary Trl NW 98312
Boundry Ln NE 98311
Bowen St 98310
Bowwood Cir NE 98310
Bradley St 98310
NW Braemar Dr 98312
Brashem Ave 98310
NE Breakwater Ct 98311
Bree Dr 98312
Breeze Way NW 98312
NE Breezewood Ln 98311
Bremerton Blvd W 98312
Brentridge Pl NE 98311
Brentwood Dr 98312
Brewster Pl 98310
Bridge Pl NE 98311
Bridgeview Ln 98337
Bridle Ridge Blvd & Pl 98311
Bridle Tree Dr NW 98312
Bridle View Ct & Pl 98311
Bridlevale Blvd & Pl 98311
NW Bright Way St 98312
Bristlecone Dr 98310
Broad St N 98312
Broad St W 98312
E Broad St 98310
NE Broadleaf Ct 98311
Broadmoor Loop NE 98310
Broadway Ave 98337
Bronco Pl NW 98311
Brook Ln NW 98312
NE Brookdale Ln 98311
NW Brookwood Ln 98311
Broussard Ln W 98312
Brownsville Hwy NE 98311
Bruenn Ave 98312
Brunswick Pl NE 98311
Bryan Ave & Rd NW 98312
Brygman St 98312
NE Buckeye Ln 98311
NW Bucklin Ct 98311
NW Bucklin Hill Rd 98311
Buckthorn Dr NE 98311
Bullard Ave 98310
NW Bumpy Way 98312
Bunker St NW 98312
Burchfield Dr 98312
NE Burrett St 98310
Burwell Pl 98312
Burwell St
 200-1999 98337
 2200-2298 98312
 2300-4000 98312
 4002-5098 98312
Bye Rd 98312
W C St 98312
NE Cady St 98310
Calamity Ln NW 98312
Caledonia Ct NW 98312
NE Calhoun St 98310
NE California St 98311
Callahan Dr 98310
N Callow Ave 98312
Calumet Dr NW 98312
Camano Ct NW 98311
N & S Cambrian Ave 98312
Cameron Ln NW 98312
Camp Sundown Rd NW 98312
Campbell Way 98310
NE Campus Ln 98311
Canoe Trl NE 98311
Cantershire Ave, Ct & Pl 98311
Canvasback Ct NW 98312
NW Canyon Trl 98312
Canyon Vista Pl NE 98311
Capewind Ln 98312
Capricorn Ln NE 98311
Capstone Ave 98310
NE Carlson Ct 98311
Carnival Pl NW 98311
NW Carolina Ln 98312
Carr Blvd 98312
NW Carter Farms Ct 98310
Cartier Dr 98312
Carver St W 98312
Casad Ave 98312
Cascade Trl & Vw 98310
Cathedral Pl NW 98312
Caymans Pl NE 98311
NE Cecilia Ln 98310
NW Cedar Terrace Ln 98312
Cedargrove St 98310
NE Center St 98310
Central Valley Rd NE & NW 98311
NW Champagne Ln 98312
NE Chantel Ct 98311
Chantrin Ave 98337
NE Charise Ct 98311
NE Charity Ct 98311
N & S Charleston Ave & Blvd W 98312
Charleston Beach Rd W 98312
N Charlotte Ave W 98312
Charmont Ln NE 98310
NE Chaudie Ct 98311
NE Chelsea Ln 98310
NW Chena Rd 98311
Cherry Ave, Ct & Pl 98310
NE Cheryl St 98310
Chester Ave 98337
Chestnut St 98310
Chico Way NW 98312
Chico Beach Dr NW 98312
Chinook Cir NW 98312
Chinook Ct NE 98311
Chinook Pl NW 98312
Chinook Way NE 98311
NW Chrey Ln 98312
Christie Pl 98312
Christine Ln NW 98312
Chum Ln NW 98312
Churchill Ln NE 98311
NE Cimeron Ct 98311
Circle Dr & Way 98312
Clare Ave 98310
NE Clark St 98311
Classic Ave NE 98310
NE Clearview Ln 98310
NE Clemens St 98310
Clogston Ave NE 98310
Clough Pl NW 98312
Clover Blossom Ln NE 98311
Cloward Way 98312
Club Car Pl NE 98311
NW Coastal Ct 98312
Cobblestone Ln NE 98310
Cobi Pl NW 98312
NE Coco Ct 98311
Coffee Pl NW 98312
Cogean Ave 98337
Coghlan St 98337
NW Coho Run 98312
Colby Ct NE 98311
NE Coley Ln 98310
Colony Ct NE 98311
NE Colorado St 98311
Comfort Ln NW 98311
Conch St 98312
Concord Ln NE 98311
Conifer Ct & Dr 98311
Constance Dr SW 98312
N Constitution Ave 98312
Cook Ln 98312
Coontz St 98312
Coralie Pl NW 98311
Corbet Dr 98312
Corey Ct NW 98312
Corfu Blvd NE 98311
Cormorant Pl 98312
Cornell Ct NW 98311
Cortez Pl NW 98311
Cottage Ln 98310
Cottage Pl NE 98311
Cottman Ave 98312
NE Cottonwood Dr 98311
NW Country Ln 98312
Courtyard Ln 98310
NE Coventry Pl 98311
Covina Loop NE 98311
Crane Ave 98310
Crawford Dr 98312
Creek Wood Pl NE 98311
NW Creekside Ln 98311
Crestview Dr 98312
W Critter Creek Ln 98312
NE Cromwell St 98311
Crossharbor Ln 98312
Cruiser Loop SW 98312
NE Crystal Peak Ln 98311
NW Cutthroat Ct 98312
D St 98312
Daniels Ave, Ct & Ln 98312
Darling Rd NW 98311
NE Dartmouth Ct 98311
NE David Dr 98310
David Rd NW 98312
W Davis St 98312
NE Dawn Rd 98311
Decatur Ave 98337
Deerhorn Trl NW 98312
NE Delphi Ct & Loop NE 98311
Denise Pl NE 98311
NE Denny Way 98310
NE Derek Dr 98311
Deville Dr NW 98312
Diane Ct NE 98311
Dibb St 98310
Dickerson Dr NW 98312
Dill Way 98312
Discovery Ave SW 98312
Dishman Rd NW 98312
Division Ave W 98312
Dockside Ave 98312
Dodge St NE 98310
Dogwood Dr NE 98310
Dolan St 98310
Dolly Varden Ln NW 98312
Doncee Dr NW 98311
Donida Dr 98312
Dora Ave 98312
Dorado Ln NW 98312
Dorothy Ave NW 98312
NE Double Hitch Ct 98311
Dowell Rd 98312
Doyen St 98337
Driftwood St 98312
NW Drury Ln 98312
NW Durango Ct 98311
NW Duryea Rd 98312
Dyes Inlet Ln & Rd 98312
NW Dyes View Ct 98311
W E St 98312
Eagle Ave 98310
Earendel Ave 98310
Earhart St 98312
East Blvd NE 98311
Easthaven Ave 98310
Eastlake Dr 98312
Eastview Ave NE 98310
NE Echo Dr 98311
Echo Valley Rd NW 98312
Eden Rd W 98312
NE Edgar Rd 98311
Edgewood Dr 98310
NW Eells Rd 98311
NW El Camino Blvd 98312
Elaine Ct 98312
Eldorado Blvd & Pl NW 98312
Elizabeth Ave 98337
Elkhorn Trl NW 98312
NE Ellen Ln 98311
Elm St 98310
Elwood Point Rd 98312
Emereend Ln NE 98311
Enetai Beach Dr 98310
Engine Ln NE 98311
NW English Hill Ct 98312
NW Erlands Ct 98312
Erlands Point Rd NW 98312
Essex St NW 98310
Ethan Ct 98312
NE Eton Ln 98311
Evans Ave W 98312
Everett St 98312
W F St 98312
NE & NW Fairgrounds Rd 98311
Fairside Pl NW 98311
NW Fairway Ln 98312
NW Fairwood Way 98311
Faith Pl NW 98312
Falcon Ct & Pl NE 98311
NE Fallon Ct 98311
Farragut St 98312
Fenner Pl 98312
Fern Ave NE 98311
Fern Ln W 98312
NW Fern Leona Rd 98312
Fernwood Ct NE 98310
Fidalgo Ct NW 98311
Filbert Ave 98310
Fir Ave, Ct & Dr 98310
NW Firglade Ct & Dr NW 98311
NW Firway Ln 98311
Fischer Ct & Pl 98310
Fischer Park Ave NE 98310
Fitz Dr 98312
Fitzwater Ln 98312
NE Flagstone Ln 98310
Fleenor Dr 98312
N Ford Ave 98312
Forest Dr NE 98310
NE Forest Ridge Dr & Ln NE 98311
NE Foster Ln & Rd NE 98311
Foster Grove Ct NE 98311
NW Fox Run 98311
W Francis Ave & St NW 98312
NE Franklin Ave 98311
Franklin Ct NE 98310
Franklin St 98310
NE Franklin St 98310
Freddies Ln NW 98312
Fredrickson Rd NW 98312
Freeman Pl 98312
Freeport Ln NE 98311
W Frone Dr 98312
Front Ave W 98312
Fruitland Dr & St 98310
E Fulton Way 98310
NE Furneys Ln 98311
NE Fuson Rd 98311
W G St 98312
Galyan Dr 98312
Garinger St NE 98310
Garland Ln NE 98310
Gatestone Ct 98310
Gateway Ln NE 98311
Gatewood Ave 98337
Gemigahi Ln NE 98311
Gentile Ln NE 98311
Gerard Pl E 98310
NW Gillespie Way 98311
Gillette Ave 98310
NW Glade Ct 98311
NE Glenridge Ct 98310
Gleu Ridge Ct 98310
NE Gluds Pond St 98311
Gold Creek Rd NW & W 98312
Gold Medal Blvd NW 98312
Goldenrod Ave, Cir & Pl 98311
NE Goldstone Ln 98311
Golf Club Rd 98312
NW Golf Club Hill Rd 98312
Graceland Ave NE 98311
NE Grady 98311
Grahns Ln NE 98311
Grand Pine Loop NE 98311
NW Grandstand St 98311
NW Green Rd 98312
NE Green Glen Ln 98311
NW Green Hill Ct 98311
Green Mountain Rd NW 98312
Greenhaven Pl NW 98312
Greenwood Dr NE 98310

Gregory Way 98337
Grevena Ave NE 98311
Griffin Pl 98312
NW Gross Rd 98312
Grove St 98310
NW Grover Ln 98312
W H St 98312
NE Hackamore Ct 98311
Halifax Ln NE 98311
Halsey Ln 98310
Halverson Ave 98310
Hamilton Rd W 98312
Hamlet Shire Ave NW 98311
Hamling Ln NW 98311
Hamma Hamma Ln NE 98311
Hampshire Ln NE 98311
Haneberg Ln NE 98311
Hanford Ave 98310
Hansberry St NW 98311
Harbel Dr NE 98310
W Harbor Dr 98312
Harbor Ridge Dr 98312
Hardt Ave NE 98311
Harkins Pl & St 98310
Harlow Dr 98312
Harrow Pl NW 98311
Hart St NW 98311
S Hartford Ave 98312
Harvard Ct NW 98311
Haven Ct & Rd 98312
Hawthorne Ave W 98312
Haynes Ln NE 98311
Haystack Rock Pl NW 98311
Hayton St 98310
Hayward Ave 98310
Hazel Ave NW 98312
NE Hazelwood Pl 98311
Heather Ln 98312
Hefner Ave 98310
Heider Dr 98310
Helena Ct & Dr NE 98311
Helm St 98310
Hemlock St 98310
Henry Ave 98337
Heritage Ln NE 98311
Herren Ave 98310
Hewitt Ave 98337
Hickory Pl NE 98311
Hickory St 98310
Hickory St NE 98311
Hicks Ave NE 98311
NE Hidden Firs Ln 98311
Hideaway Ln 98312
High Ave 98337
High View Ln NW 98312
Highland Ave 98337
E Highlands St 98310
NW Highpoint Ct 98312
Hill Ct 98310
Hillrise Ct & Pl 98311
W Hills Blvd 98312
Hillside Dr NE 98310
Hilltop Ln NW 98312
NE Hilstad Rd 98311
NW Hogan Ln 98311
Holiday Pl NW 98312
Holland Rd NW 98311
Hollis St 98310
NW Holly Rd 98312
NW Holly Beach Ct 98312
NE Holly Leaf Ln 98311
Holly Park Ct & Dr 98312
Holly Tree Pl NW 98312
Hollywood Ave 98310
Holman St 98310
NW Holmberg St 98311
Homer Dr 98310
Homer R Jones Dr 98310
Hoogenraad Pl NE 98311
Hope St 98312
E Hope St 98310
Houston Ave 98312
NW Huckle Dr 98311
Hume Ln NE 98311
Humphrey Ave W 98312

NE Hyak Way 98311
Hylen Ave NE 98311
W I St 98312
Ida St W 98312
Illahee Rd NE
 3900-4399 98310
 4500-9599 98311
Imperial Way SW 98312
NW Inverness Ct 98312
NE Iron Mountain Ln 98311
Ironsides Ave 98310
Isis Ct NE 98311
NW Iskra Blvd 98312
Island Dr NW 98312
NE Island View Dr 98310
NE Ivy Rd 98310
W J St 98312
Jack Pine Dr 98310
Jackson Dr 98312
Jacobsen Blvd 98310
Jagger Pl NE 98311
W Jarstad Dr 98312
NE Jasmine Ln 98311
Jenner Ave 98310
Jennifer Ln NE 98311
NE Jensen Ave 98310
Joanne Ln NE 98311
NW Joels Ct 98311
John St 98310
NE John Carlson Rd 98311
Johnny Hoss Rd NW 98312
Johnson Rd NE 98311
Johnson St NW 98311
Johnson Way NW 98312
Jones St 98312
Juanita Cir NE 98311
Jungle Ct NW 98311
Juniper St 98310
Kari Ln NW 98311
Karolena Pl NE 98311
Kaster Ct & Dr 98311
Katherine St NW 98311
Katy Penman Ave 98312
Kean Blvd 98312
Kearney Rd NW 98312
Keel Ave 98310
Kellum Ranch Rd NW 98312
Kelly Rd 98312
NW Kennedy Dr 98312
Kent Ave W 98312
Kestrel Ct 98312
Kid Haven Ln NW 98312
Kimberly Pl NW 98311
Kimi Ct NE 98311
Kingfisher Ct 98312
Kingsway NW & W 98312
NW Kint Dr 98311
Kiowa Ave NE 98311
Kitsap Dr & Way 98312
Kitsap Lake Rd NW 98312
Kittyhawk Dr NW 98312
NW Klahanie Pl 98312
NW Klahowya Trl 98312
Kloshi Ct NW 98312
NE Knights Ct 98311
Kokanee Ln NW 98312
Kristi Ct NW 98311
Kristine Dr NW 98311
W L St 98312
Laddie Pl NE 98310
N & S Lafayette Ave 98312
Lake Dr 98312
SW Lake Flora Rd 98312
Lake Tahuyeh Rd NW 98312
Lakehurst Dr NW 98312
Lakemont Ln 98312
NW Lakeview Ave, Ct, Dr & Pl NW 98312
Lamotte Ave NE 98310
Lansing Ave W 98312
Larado Pl NW 98311
Larch Pl 98310
Lariat Trl NW 98311
NE Larkin Ln 98311
Larkspur Pl NW 98311
Lars Dr NE 98311

Laurel Pl 98312
Laurelhurst Dr NW 98311
Lazy S Ln NE 98311
Leber Ln NW 98312
Lebo Blvd 98310
NW Leisure Ln 98311
Lenea Dr NW 98312
NW Lester Ct 98311
Lewis Ave 98310
Lewis Dr NE 98311
NE Lexington Dr 98311
NE Libra Ln 98311
Lilac Ln 98312
Lincoln Ave 98337
Lind Dr 98312
Lindberg Pl 98310
NW Linden Ln 98312
NE Liverpool Ct & Dr NE 98311
Livingstone Ct 98310
NW Loboz Ct 98311
NW Lois Ln 98311
NE Lombard Ct 98311
Londonderry Loop NW 98312
Lone Eagle Pl NW 98312
Lone Star Ln NW 98312
Longfellow Pl NW 98312
Longhorn Dr NW 98312
Longshaw St 98337
NW Lopez Ln 98311
NE Loretta Ln 98310
Lost Creek Ln NW 98312
Louann Ct NE 98311
Lower Marine Dr 98312
Lower Oyster Bay Dr 98312
W Loxie Eagans Blvd 98312
NE Loyola St 98311
NE Luxury Ln 98311
Lyle Ave 98312
W M St 98312
Madlin Ranch Rd NW 98312
Madrona Ave NE 98311
Madrona St 98312
Madrona Point Dr 98312
Magnolia Dr 98310
NE Magnum Ct 98311
Magnuson Ct & Way 98310
Mahan Ave 98337
NE Makah Ct 98311
Maple Ave & St 98310
Maple Valley Rd 98310
Maple View Dr 98312
Marguerite Ave 98337
NE Mariah Ln 98311
Marine Dr 98312
Marine Drive Pl 98312
Marine View Pl 98312
S Marion Ave & Ct N, S & W 98312
Marissa Ln NW 98311
Maritime Dr SW 98312
Marks Rd NW 98312
NE Marlene Ct 98311
Marlow Ave 98310
NE Marric Ct 98311
NE Marwood Dr 98311
E Mathews Dr NW 98312
Mathisen Ln NW 98312
NW Maui Ln 98312
May St NW 98311
Mayheu Ln NE 98311
Mccall Blvd W 98312
Mcclain Ave 98310
Mccollom Ave W 98312
Mcintyre Ln NE 98311
Mckenna Falls Rd W 98312
Mckenzie Ave 98337
Mcwilliams Ct & Rd 98311
N Mead Ave 98312
NW Meadow Ln 98311
NE Meadowlark Cir 98311
NE Melanie Ct 98311
NE Melia Ln 98311
NE Melissa Pl 98310
Merastone Ln NE 98311
NE Mercer Ct 98311

NW Merideth St 98312
Merlie Ave NE 98310
Merlin Ln NW 98312
Merrill Pl W 98312
NE Mesa Ln 98310
Meyerwood Ln NE 98311
NE Michelle Ct 98311
NW Millglade Ln 98312
NE Millwood Ct 98311
NE Milton Ct 98311
Minard Rd W 98312
NE Miramar Cir 98311
N & S Mission Rd 98312
Mission Lake Shore Dr W 98312
Monaco Pl NW 98312
NE Monarch Ln 98310
Monroe St 98312
Monte Vista Ln NW 98311
N Montgomery Ave 98312
Monticola Dr 98310
Montwood Ln 98312
NE Moonrise Way 98311
Morgan Ln & Rd NW 98312
Morning View Ave NE 98311
Morong Rd 98337
Morris St 98310
Morrison Ct 98310
NW Mosher Canyon Rd 98311
Mount Buckhorn Ln NE 98311
NE Mount Constance Ln 98311
NE Mount Lacrosse Ln 98311
NE Mount Olympus Ln 98311
Mountain View Dr 98310
NE Mulberry Ln 98311
Murphy Ln 98310
Mustang Ln 98312
Myers Rd 98312
NW Myles Ct 98312
N St 98312
Nakoosa Ln NW 98312
Naomi Ave 98310
Naomi St NW 98311
Narrows View Ln NE 98310
Nathan Adrian Dr 98310
National Ave N 98312
SW Nautical St 98312
Navajo Trl NE 98311
Naval Ave
 100-598 98337
 101-697 98312
 699-1199 98312
 1300-1499 98337
 1500-1600 98312
 1602-1998 98312
Navy Yard Hwy 98312
Needle Ct NE 98310
Nels Nelson Rd NW 98311
NE Nevada St 98311
New Hope Cir 98312
Newaukum Pl NE 98311
Newberry Ln & Pl 98312
NE Newcastle Ct 98311
Newport Ct NW 98312
Newton Pl NE 98311
Nicholas St NW 98312
NW Nichols Ave 98311
Nikomis Ln NW 98312
Nimitz Ln 98310
Nipsic Ave & Pl 98310
NE Nittney Ln 98311
SW Nixon Loop 98312
NE Nobles Ln 98310
Nollwood Ln 98312
Nome Dr 98310
Nora St NW 98311
Norfolk Ave NE 98311
Normandy Dr 98310
Northlake Way NW 98312
Northpark Ln 98310
NW Northridge Ln 98312
O St 98312

Oak St 98310
Oak Park Dr & Pl 98311
NW Oakmont Way 98311
Ocasta St NE 98311
NE Oceangate Ln 98311
Oceanside Pl NE 98311
Oceanview Blvd NE 98311
Ogle Rd NE 98311
Ohana Pl NE 98311
Ohio Ave 98337
Old Military Rd NE 98311
Old Sawmill Pl NW 98312
Olding Rd 98312
Olive Ave NE 98311
N Olson Rd 98311
Olympic Ave, Dr & Pl 98312
Olympus Dr NE 98310
Oneida Cir NW 98311
NE Opal Ct 98311
Orcas Pl NW 98311
Oregon St NE 98311
NE Oriole Way 98311
Orrfelt Dr NW 98311
Osiris Ct NE 98311
Osprey Cir 98312
Otter Run NW 98312
Overland Trl NW 98312
Overlook Cir NE 98311
Oxbow Ave NE 98311
Oxford Ct NW 98311
Oyster Bay Ave & Ct N & S 98312
Pacific Ave 98337
NW Pacific Jewell Rd 98312
Pahrmann Pl NW 98311
Painter St NW 98311
Palmer Ln & Pl NW 98311
NE Panther Lake Rd W 98312
NE Papoose Pl 98311
Park Ave & Dr 98337
Parkdale Dr NW 98311
Parker Ln & Pl 98310
Parkhurst Dr NE 98310
Parklane Dr NE 98310
Parkside Dr 98310
Parkway Ct NE 98311
Partridge Holw NE 98310
Patten Ave 98312
NW Paul Benjamin Rd 98312
Pawnee Dr 98310
NW Paxford Ln 98311
Payne Ln NW 98311
Pearl Pl & St 98310
Pecan Ln NE 98311
Pendergast St 98312
Pennie Ln 98310
Pennsylvania Ave 98337
Peppard Ln NE 98310
Percheron Ln NW 98312
Peregrine Ct 98312
Perry Ave 98310
Perry Ave NE 98310
Perry Ct NE 98311
Pershing Ave 98312
Peters Rd 98312
NW Peterson Dr 98311
Petersville Rd NE 98310
Pheasant Cir NE 98311
Phillips Ave 98310
E & NW Phinney Bay Dr & Pl 98312
Pickering Ave & Pl 98310
Pine Ave NE 98310
Pine Ct NE 98310
E Pine Dr 98310
Pine Rd NE
 2700-4399 98310
 4800-4898 98311
 4900-6399 98311
Pinecone Ct & Dr 98310
NE Pinecrest Dr 98311
W Pinehurst Way 98312
Pineneedle Dr 98310
Pineridge Ct, Dr & Pl 98311
Pinewood Dr 98310

Pitt Ave 98310
Pleasant Ave 98337
Pleasant Dr 98312
Plum St 98310
Poindexter Ave W 98312
Porter St 98312
Preble St 98312
Premier Pl NW 98312
Price Rd NW 98312
Prince Pine Ln NW 98312
W Prospect St 98312
Prosperity Pl NE 98311
Provost Rd NW 98312
Puller Ln 98310
Quarry St 98312
NW Quarterhorse Way 98312
Quatermass Ave NE 98310
NE Quinault Ct & Dr NE 98311
Radcliff Ave NE 98311
Rail Ln NE 98311
Rainbow Ct NW 98312
N Rainier Ave 98312
Rainstone Ln NE 98311
NW Rampart Ridge Ct 98311
Rankin Rd 98312
Rasmussen Ln 98310
Raven Creek Ct, Dr & Pl 98311
Reagan Ave 98310
W Reba Way 98312
NW Red Oaks Ct 98311
NE Redbud Ct & Ln NE 98311
Redwing Trl NW 98312
NE Reeds Meadow Ln 98311
NE Regal Ct 98311
Regatta Pl NE 98311
Reid Ave 98310
Reintree Ct NW 98311
Rest Pl NE 98311
NW Rhododendron Ct 98312
NW Rhododendron Dr 98312
Rhododendron Pl NW 98311
Rhododendron Way NW 98312
Richardson Rd NW 98311
Rickey Rd NE 98310
NE & NW Riddell Rd 98310
Ridge Ln NE 98311
Ridgecrest Dr W 98312
Ridgemont Ct & Dr 98311
Ridgetop Ct NE 98310
NE Ridgeview Dr & Pl NE 98310
Ridgeway Cir, Dr & Pl 98312
Rim View Ct NW 98312
NE Rimrock Dr 98311
NW Rinacke Ct 98311
Rita Rd NE 98311
Rivenhurst Ct & St 98310
Riverview Dr W 98312
Roanoke Rd NE 98311
Robbie Ct NE 98311
Robin Ave 98310
Robinson Rd NE 98310
Rocklin Ave NE 98311
E Rocky Dr NW 98312
Rocky Point Rd NW 98312
Rodgers St 98312
Roosevelt Ave 98337
Roosevelt Blvd 98312
NE Roosevelt St 98311
Root Ct 98312
NE Roseway Ln 98311
Roswell Dr 98310
Roy Rd NE 98311
NE Rozene Way 98311
Rozewood Dr 98310
Rue Villa St NE 98310
S Russell Rd 98312
NE Rustic Ln 98310
Ryan Ave 98310
NW Rydan Ct 98312
Sabbatical Loop NE 98311
Saddle Trl NW 98311

NW Saenz Ln 98311
Sagebrush Ln NW 98312
Sahali Dr 98310
Saint Charles Ln NE 98311
Saint Johns Pl NE 98311
Sam Christopherson Ave W 98312
Samara St 98310
NW San Juan Dr 98311
Sand Dollar Rd & St W 98312
Sand Spit Ln NW 98312
Sanders Ave 98310
Sandpiper Ct 98312
Sandra Ln NE 98311
Sandy Ct & Rd NE 98311
NE Sarai Ct 98310
NE Saturn Ln 98311
NW Sawmill Ct 98311
Sawtooth Ridge Ln NE 98311
Schlagel Ln 98310
Schley Blvd & Way 98310
School St NE 98311
Schuett Ln NW 98312
Schultz Rd NW 98312
NW Schuyler Rd 98311
Scorpio Ln NE 98311
Scott Ave & Pl 98310
Seabeck Hwy NW 98312
NE Seahurst Ct 98311
NW Selbo Rd 98311
SW Sentinel Peak Way 98312
Sereno Circle Dr 98312
Seringa Ave 98310
Shadden Ln NW 98312
NE Shady Ln 98311
NE Shady Brook Ct 98311
Shady Forest Pl NE 98311
Shady Hollow Ln NW 98312
Shamrock Dr NW 98312
NW Shaw Island Way 98312
NE Sheeler Ln 98310
NE Sheffield Ct & Pl NE 98311
Sheldon Blvd 98337
Shepler Rd NE 98311
Sheridan Rd 98310
W Sherman Heights Rd 98312
NW Sherwood St 98311
Shilohwood Pl NW 98311
W Shipview Ct 98312
Shire Estate Pl NE 98311
Shirehill Ct & St 98310
S Shore Ct 98312
Shore Dr 98310
S Shore Rd 98312
NE Shore Cliff St 98311
Shorecliff Rd 98312
Shorewood Dr 98312
Shorthorn Dr NW 98312
Sidney Ave 98337
Sierra Rd 98310
Signal Ln NE 98311
Silver Ln NW 98312
NW Silver St 98311
Silver Beach Dr NW 98311
Silver Creek Ln NW 98311
NW Silver Glen Ln 98311
NW Silver Meadow Ln 98311
NE Silver Pine Dr 98311
Sinclair Way 98312
NE Sipes Ln 98311
NW Siren Way 98311
Skipping Stone Ln 98312
Skylark Dr W 98312
Skyline Ln NW 98312
Skyview Pl NW 98311
NW Snow Creek Way 98311
Snowberry Ln NE 98311
Snyder Ave 98312
Sol Duc Dr NE 98311
Solid Ln W 98312
Solie Ave 98310

NW Solnae Pl 98311
Solstice Ave NW 98311
Songbird Ln NW 98312
Sound Ridge Dr 98312
Soundview Ave NE 98310
NW Sparrow Way 98312
NE Spartacus St 98311
NW Spectrum Ct 98312
Spice Ln NE 98311
Spring St NE 98310
Springhill Pl NE 98311
Spruce Ave & Pl 98310
Spur Ct NW 98311
Stampede Blvd NW 98311
Stanford Ct NW 98311
Starflower Pl NW 98312
State Ave 98337
State Highway 16 W 98312
State Highway 3 SW &
W 98312
State Highway 303 NE 98311
Steele Creek Dr & Loop
NE 98311
Steelhead Dr NW 98312
NE Steeple Rock Ln 98311
NE Steinman Ln 98310
Stephenson Ave 98310
Stevens Dr 98312
Stewart Rd 98310
Stingle St NW 98311
Stirrup Ct NW 98311
NE Stone Way 98310
Stonewood Pl 98310
Stourbridge Pl NE 98311
NE Strand Rd 98311
Strassburg St NE 98310
Sucia Pl NW 98311
Sugar Pine Dr 98310
Sullivan Pl 98312
Sulphur Springs Ln 98310
Sumac St 98310
N & S Summit Ave 98312
Sundown Dr 98312
Sunflower Ln NE 98311
Sungate Pl NE 98311
W Sunn Fjord Ln 98312
Sunnyhill Rd W 98312
NE Sunrise Dr 98310
Sunrise Ter NE 98311
Sunset Ave NE 98311
Sunset Ln 98310
Sunset Vis 98310
NW Susie Ln 98312
NE Sutton Pl 98311
NE Sweet Birch Ct 98311
NW Swiftshore Ct 98312
Sycamore Ln NE 98311
NE Sylvan Way 98310
Sylvan Pines Cir & Ln 98310
Sylvester Pl 98312
Symes Rd NW 98312
Symington Pkwy NW 98312
Taffinder Pl 98312
Taft Ave 98312
W Tahuyeh Ct, Dr & Pl
NW & W 98312
Takota Pl NE 98311
Tanbark Dr NE 98311
NW Tanda Ave & Pl 98312
Tara Ct 98310
Targett Beach Ln 98337
Tate Pl NE 98311
NW Taterbug Ct 98312
Taurus Ln NE 98311
NW Taylor Rd 98312
Taynic Pl NW 98312
Teepee Cir NE 98311
Tenino Dr W 98312
NE Teri Ct 98311
Terrace St 98310
NW Terrace View Dr 98312
Terrell Ave 98312
Thasos Ave NE 98311
That A Way Rd NW 98312
The Cedars 98312
Thebes St NE 98311

This A Way Rd NW 98312
Thompson Dr 98337
Thompson Ln NE 98310
Thorson Rd W 98312
Tibardis Ct & Rd NW 98311
Tiger Mission Rd W 98312
Times Ave 98312
Timothy Pl W 98312
NW Tinkam Ct 98311
NE Totem Pl 98311
Towne Ct, Pl & Rd
NE 98311
Townsend Ln NE 98311
NE Tracy Ave 98311
NW Tracy Ave 98311
Tracy Way 98312
NE Tracy Hill Way 98311
Tracyton Blvd NW 98311
Tracyton Beach Rd 98310
Trails End Rd NW 98312
Treemont Ct & Ln NE 98311
Trenton Ave NE 98310
Trica Ave NE 98311
Trillium Ln NW 98312
Tristen Ln NW 98312
NE Trout Brook Ln 98311
Troy Ln NE 98311
NE Trudi Ct 98310
NE Trussel Ct 98311
NE Tucannon Ct 98311
Turnquist Ct & Rd 98312
Tweed Ln NW 98312
Twin Maple Ln W 98312
Twin View Pl 98312
Tyee Ct, Pl & Way 98311
S U St 98337
Union Ave W 98312
University Point Cir
NE 98311
Upper Corbet Dr 98312
Utah St NE 98311
Valley Dr 98312
NE Valley Oak Ct & Dr
NE 98311
Valley Wood Pl NE 98311
Vandalia Ave 98310
Vanderbilt Ln NE 98311
NW Vanishing Way 98311
Vantanin St 98312
Vantrins Ave 98310
Varsity Ln NE 98311
Veldee Ave 98312
Vena Ave, Ct & St 98311
Veneta Ave 98337
NW Vermont Ct 98311
Veska Ave 98310
Victoria Ave 98337
View Dr SE 98312
Viewcrest Dr NE 98310
NW Viewpoint Ln 98312
Viking St W 98312
Vincent Way 98312
Vineyards Ln NE 98311
Virginia St 98310
Virgo Ln NE 98311
Vista Ln W 98312
Von Ruks Ln NE 98310
Vue Ct 98310
NE Waaga Way 98311
Wade Rd NW 98312
Wallin St 98310
Walnut Ct & St 98310
Ward Ave 98310
Warner St 98310
Warren Ave 98337
SW Warrior Ave 98312
Washington Ave 98337
Washington Ave NE 98311
Washington Beach
Ave 98337
Waterside Ln 98312
Watson Ct & Pl NE 98311
Weatherstone Ln NE 98311
Webster Pl & St W 98312
NW Wedgewood Ln 98312
Wellington Ln NE 98311

NE Wellsly Pl 98311
Wembly Ave NE 98311
Wencker Cir & Way 98312
Werner Rd 98312
Weslon Pl 98312
NE Westchester St 98311
NW Westmont Ln 98311
Westview Dr NE 98310
Wheaton Way 98310
Whisper Dr NW 98312
Whistle Ln NE 98311
White Peaks Ln NW 98311
White Pine Dr 98310
Whitney Ave 98312
Whittle Pl W 98312
Widgeon Ct 98312
Wilbert Ave 98312
Wild Eagle Ln W 98312
Wild Ridge Ln NW 98312
NW Wildcat Lake Rd 98312
Wildflower Ln NE 98311
NW Wildwood Ln 98311
Wilkes Ave 98312
Wilkinson Rd W 98312
NE William E Sutton
Rd 98311
Willow St 98310
Wilmont St 98312
NE Wilshire Ct 98311
Wilson Blvd 98312
Winchester Ct NW 98311
NE Windermere Dr 98310
Windfall Pl NW 98312
NW Windjammer Ct 98312
NE Windsor Ct 98311
Windward Pl NW 98312
Winfield Ave 98310
NE Winston Dr 98311
NE Winters Rd 98311
NE Wise St 98311
Wisteria Ln NE 98311
Withers Pl NW 98311
Woodland Ct NE 98311
NW Woodland Dr 98312
Woodlawn Ct & Dr
NW 98311
NW Woodridge Ln & Pl
NW 98311
Woods Ct & Pl 98311
Woodstone Ln NW 98312
Worrall Dr 98310
NW Wrangler Ct 98311
Wright Ave 98310
N & S Wycoff Ave 98312
Wynoochee Ln NE 98311
Wyoming St 98310
Yacht Haven Way 98312
NE Yale Way 98311
S Yantic Ave 98312
Yates Ln NW 98312
Yew St 98310
Yoder Ln NE 98311
NW Young Pl 98311
Zeeden Way 98310
W Zircon Ln 98312
NE Zodiac Ln 98311
Zoey Pl NW 98312

NUMBERED STREETS

1st Ave W 98312
1st St
100-299 98337
2100-3098 98312
3100-5299 98312
NE 1st St 98311
W 1st St 98312
2nd Ave W 98312
2nd St 98337
3rd Ave W 98312
NE 3rd St N 98311
4th St 98337
2101-2299 98312
5th Ave NE 98311
5th St
200-1999 98337
2100-5399 98312
6th Ave NE 98311
6th St
100-2099 98337
2100-3900 98312
7th St 98337
2100-2399 98312
8th St
500-2099 98337
2101-2297 98312
9th St
200-2099 98337
2300-3599 98312
E 9th St 98310
10th St
800-2099 98337
2100-2298 98312
E 10th St 98310
11th St
500-2099 98337
2100-3499 98312
E 11th St 98310
11th Street Pl 98337
12th St 98337
2101-2199 98312
13th St
300-2099 98337
2400-3199 98312
E 13th St 98310
14th St 98337
E 14th St 98310
15th St
800-2099 98337
2100-2298 98312
E 15th St 98310
E 16th St 98310
17th St 98337
2800-2898 98312
E 17th St 98310
18th St 98337
E 18th St 98310
NW 18th St 98312
19th St 98312
E 19th St 98310
NW 19th St 98312
20th St 98312
21st St 98312
E 21st St 98310
E 22nd St 98310
E 23rd St 98310
24th St 98312
E 24th St 98310
25th St 98312
26th St 98312
E 28th St 98310
E 29th St 98310
NW 29th St 98312
E & NE 30th 98310
E 31st St 98310
E 32nd St 98310
E 33rd St 98310
NE 40th Pl 98310
NW 64th St 98311
NE 72nd St 98311
NE & NW 73rd 98311

EDMONDS WA

General Delivery 98020

POST OFFICE BOXES MAIN OFFICE STATIONS AND BRANCHES

Box No.s
1 - 2016 98020
2002 - 91000 98026

NAMED STREETS

A Ave S 98020
Admiral Way 98020
Alan A Dale Pl 98020
Alder St 98020
Algonquin Rd 98020
Aloha Pl, St & Way 98020
Andover St 98026
B Ave S 98020
Beach Pl 98020
Beeson Pl 98026
Bell St 98020
Bella Coola Rd 98020
Bendongt Ave W 98020
Berry Ln 98020
Bertola Rd 98026
Beverly Park Rd 98026
Birch Pl & St 98020
Blake Pl 98020
Bowdoin Way
8400-9199 98026
9200-9599 98020
Braemar Dr 98026
Brookmere Dr & St 98020
C Ave S 98020
Carol Way 98020
Cary Rd 98020
Cascade Dr
1000-1099 98020
9100-9199 98026
9200-9299 98020
Cascade Ln 98020
Caspers St 98020
Cedar Pl & St 98020
Central Ave 98026
Cherry St 98020
Chinook Rd 98020
Clearview Dr 98026
Coronado Pl 98020
Crawford Dr 98020
Cyrus Pl 98026
Daley Pl & St 98020
W Dayton St 98020
N & S Deer Dr 98020
Dellwood Dr 98026
N & S Dogwood Ln &
Pl 98020
Driftwood Ln & Pl 98020
Durbin Dr 98020
Eagle Ln 98020
Edmonds St 98020
Edmonds Way
500-23199 98020
23200-24099 98026
Elm Pl, St & Way W 98020
Emerald Hills Dr 98020
Euclid Ave 98020
Excelsior Pl 98020
Fir Pl & St 98020
Firdale Ave 98026
Fisher Rd 98026
Forest Dell Dr 98020
Forsyth Ln 98020
Frederick Pl 98026
Friar Tuck Ln 98020
Giltner Ln 98020
Glen St 98020
Grandview St 98020
E & W Greystone Ln 98020
Hanna Park Rd 98020
Hemlock St & Way 98020
Herentra St SW 98026
High St 98020
Highland Dr 98020
Highway 99 98026
Hillcrest Pl 98026
Hindley Ln 98020
Holly Dr 98020
Holly Ln 98026
Homeland Dr 98020
Homeview Dr 98026
Howell Way 98020
Humber Ln 98020
James St 98020
Kairez Dr 98026
Kulshan Rd 98020
Lake Ballinger Way 98026
Laurel Ln, St & Way 98020
Lindsay Pl 98020
Little John Ct 98020
Madrona Ln 98026
Magnolia Ln 98020
Main St
100-1199 98020
8400-9100 98026
9102-9198 98026
Makah Rd 98020
Maple Ln 98026
Maple St 98020
Maple Way 98020
Maplewood Ave, Dr &
Ln 98026
Marine View Dr 98026
Mcaleer Way 98026
N Meadowdale Rd 98026
Meadowdale Beach
Rd 98026
Melody Ln 98020
Monticello Dr 98026
Mountain Ln 98020
Nootka Rd 98020
Norma Beach Rd 98026
Northstream Ln 98020
Nottingham Rd 98020
Ocean Ave 98020
Olympic Ave 98020
Olympic View Dr
1200-1599 98020
7001-7517 98026
7519-9199 98026
9200-9399 98020
9401-19399 98020
17400-17998 98026
18200-19398 98020
Orchard Ln 98020
Paradise Ln 98020
Park Pl 98026
Park Rd
9000-9199 98026
9200-9299 98020
Picnic Pl 98026
Picnic Point Rd 98026
Pictorial Ave 98026
Pine St 98020
Pioneer Way 98026
Point Edwards Pl 98020
Poplar Way 98020
Possession Ln 98026
Puget Dr, Ln & Way 98020
Puget Sound Blvd 98026
Quail Ln 98020
Railroad Ave 98020
Ridge Way 98026
Robin Hood Dr 98020
Salal Dr 98026
Sater Ln 98020
Scenic Dr 98026
Sea Vista Pl 98020
Sealawn Dr & Pl 98026
Seamont Ln 98020
Shell Pl 98026
Shell Valley Rd &
Way 98026
Sierra Dr 98026
Sierra Pl 98020
Sierra St
9100-9199 98026
9200-9299 98026
Skyline Dr 98020
Somerset Ln 98020
Sound View Pl 98020
Soundview Dr & Ln 98026
Sprague St 98020
Spruce Pl & St 98020
Summit Ln 98026
Sunset Ave 98020
Sunset Ave N 98020
Sunset Way 98026
Talbot Rd 98026
Timber Ln 98020
Totem Pole Ln 98020
View Pl 98020
Viewland Way 98020
Viewmoor Pl 98020
Vista Pl & Way 98020
Vista Del Mar Dr 98026
Wachusett Rd 98020
Walnut St 98020
Water St 98020
Wharf St 98020
Whitcomb Pl 98020
Willowick Ln 98020
Woodhaven Pl 98020
Woodlake Dr 98026
W Woodway Ln 98020
Woodway Park Rd 98020

NUMBERED STREETS

2nd N & S 98020
3rd N & S 98020
4th N & S 98020
5th N & S 98020
6th Ave & Pl 98020
7th Ave & Pl 98020
8th Ave & Pl 98020
9th N & S 98020
10th Ave & Pl N & S 98020
11th Pl N 98020
12th Ave & Pl 98020
13th Way SW 98020
14th St & Way 98020
15th St & Way 98020
46th Ave W 98026
47th Ave & Pl 98026
48th Ave & Pl 98026
49th Ave & Pl 98026
50th Ave & Pl 98026
51st Ave & Pl 98026
52nd Ave & Pl 98026
53rd Ave & Pl 98026
54th Ave & Pl 98026
55th Ave & Pl 98026
56th Ave & Pl 98026
57th Ave & Pl 98026
58th Pl W 98026
59th Ave & Pl 98026
60th Ave & Pl 98026
61st Ave & Pl 98026
62nd Ave & Pl 98026
63rd Ave & Pl 98026
64th Ave & Pl 98026
65th Ave & Pl 98026
66th Ave & Pl 98026
67th Ave W 98026
68th Ave W 98026
69th Ave & Pl 98026
70th Ave & Pl 98026
71st Ave & Pl 98026
72nd Ave & Pl 98026
73rd Ave & Pl 98026
74th Ave & Pl 98026
75th Ave & Pl 98026
76th Ave & Pl 98026
77th Ave & Pl 98026
78th Ave & Pl 98026
79th Ave & Pl 98026
80th Ave, Ct, Ln, Pl &
Way W 98026
81st Ave & Pl 98026
82nd Ave & Pl 98026
83rd Ave & Pl 98026
84th Ave & Pl 98026
85th Ave & Pl 98026
86th Ave & Pl 98026
87th Ave & Pl 98026
88th Ave & Pl 98026
89th Ave & Pl 98026
90th Ave & Pl 98026
91st Ave & Pl 98026
92nd Ave & Pl 98020
93rd Ave & Pl 98020
94th Ave & Pl 98020
95th Ave & Pl 98020
96th Ave & Pl 98020
97th Ave & Pl 98020
98th Ave & Pl 98020
99th Ave & Pl 98020
100th Ave W 98020
101st Ave & Pl 98020
102nd Ave & Pl 98020

04th Ave & Pl 98020
05th Ave & Pl 98020
06th Ave & Pl 98020
07th Pl W 98020
08th Ave W 98020
10th Pl W 98020
11th Pl W 98020
12th Pl W 98020
13th Pl W 98020
14th Ave W 98020
15th Pl W 98020
16th Ave W 98020
16th St SW 98026
28th Pl & St 98026
33rd Pl & St 98026
34th Pl SW 98026
35th Pl SW 98026
36th Pl & St 98026
37th Pl SW 98026
38th Pl & St 98026
39th Pl SW 98026
40th Pl & St 98026
41st St SW 98026
42nd Pl & St 98026
43rd Pl & St 98026
44th Pl & St 98026
45th Pl & St 98026
46th Pl & St 98026
47th Pl & St 98026
48th Pl & St 98026
49th Pl & St 98026
50th Pl SW 98026
51st Pl & St 98026
52nd St SW 98026
53rd Pl & St 98026
54th Pl & St 98026
55th Pl & St 98026
56th Pl & St 98026
57th Pl & St 98026
58th Pl & St 98026
59th Pl & St 98026
60th Pl & St 98026
61st Pl SW 98026
62nd Pl & St 98026
63rd Pl SW 98026
64th Pl & St 98026
65th Pl SW 98026
68th Pl SW 98026
69th Pl SW 98026
70th Pl SW 98026
171st St SW 98026
172nd Pl & St 98026
173rd St SW 98026
174th St SW 98026
175th Pl & St 98026
176th Pl & St 98026
177th St SW 98026
178th Pl SW 98026
179th Pl & St 98026
180th Pl & St 98026
181st Pl SW 98026
182nd Pl & St 98026
183rd Pl SW 98020
184th Pl & St 98026
185th Pl & St 98026
186th Pl & St 98026
187th Pl SW 98026
187th St SW
8100-8499 98026
9200-9399 98020
188th St SW 98026
189th Pl SW 98026
190th Pl SW 98020
190th St SW
8000-8499 98026
9200-9399 98020
191st Pl & St 98026
192nd Pl SW 98026
9200-9399 98020
192nd St SW 98026
193rd Pl SW 98026
194th Pl & St 98026
195th St SW 98026
196th Pl & St 98026
197th St SW 98026
198th Pl & St 98026
199th Pl & St 98026
200th St SW 98026
201st Pl & St 98026
202nd Pl & St 98026
203rd Pl & St 98026
204th Pl & St 98026
205th Pl & St 98026
206th Pl & St 98026
207th Pl & St 98026
208th Pl & St 98026
209th Pl & St 98026
210th Pl & St 98026
211th Pl SW 98026
212th St SW 98026
213th Pl & St 98026
214th Pl SW 98026
9600-9799 98020
215th Pl SW
8000-8199 98026
9600-9699 98020
215th St SW
7300-8599 98026
9200-9899 98020
216th Pl SW 98020
216th St SW
7300-9199 98026
9200-9599 98020
217th Pl SW 98020
217th St SW
8600-9099 98026
9200-9599 98020
218th Pl SW 98020
218th St SW 98026
219th St SW
7500-8199 98026
9600-9699 98020
220th Pl SW 98026
220th St SW
7200-9199 98026
9200-9999 98020
221st Pl & St 98026
222nd Pl & St 98026
223rd Pl & St 98026
224th Pl SW 98026
224th St SW
7100-9199 98026
9200-9999 98020
225th Pl SW
7800-8999 98026
9800-9999 98020
225th St SW 98026
226th Pl SW
8900-8999 98026
9600-10499 98020
226th St SW
8000-8699 98026
10400-10799 98020
227th Pl SW
7800-7999 98026
9700-9999 98020
227th St SW 98026
228th Pl SW 98020
228th St SW
7203-7305 98026
9200-10799 98020
229th Pl SW
8700-8999 98026
10600-10799 98020
229th St SW 98026
230th St SW 98026
231st Pl SW 98026
9500-9799 98020
231st St SW
8400-8899 98026
9200-10799 98020
232nd Pl SW
8800-9099 98026
10100-10199 98020
232nd St SW
7600-9099 98026
9200-9999 98020
233rd Pl SW 98026
233rd St SW
8300-8399 98026
9500-9599 98020
234th Pl SW 98020
234th St SW
7600-8399 98026
9300-9999 98020
235th Pl SW
8400-8499 98026
9400-10799 98020
235th St SW 98020
236th Pl SW 98020
236th St SW
7400-9199 98026
9200-9899 98020
237th Pl SW 98020
237th St SW 98026
238th Pl SW 98026
238th St SW
7700-9199 98026
9600-10399 98020
239th Pl SW
7600-7799 98026
9800-9999 98020
239th St SW 98020
240th Pl SW
7600-7699 98026
9600-10799 98020
240th St SW
7800-9199 98026
9200-9999 98020
241st Pl SW
8700-8799 98026
9600-10299 98020
241st St SW 98026
242nd Pl SW
7400-7599 98026
9600-10699 98020
242nd St SW
7600-9199 98026
9200-9299 98020
243rd Pl SW 98020
244th St SW 98026
9201-10197 98020

EVERETT WA

General Delivery 98201

POST OFFICE BOXES MAIN OFFICE STATIONS AND BRANCHES

Box No.s
A - K 98206
1 - 1995 98206
2001 - 3996 98213
4001 - 4478 98204
5001 - 13438 98206

NAMED STREETS

Adams Ave 98203
Admiralty Way 98204
Airport Rd 98204
Alden Pl 98203
Alder St 98203
Alexander Rd 98204
Alger Ave 98203
Alki Dr 98203
Alpine Dr 98203
Alta Dr 98203
Alverson Blvd 98201
Andrew Sater Rd 98208
Angle Ln 98201
Ash Way 98204
Associated Blvd 98203
Avondale Rd & Way 98204
Bailey Ave 98203
Baker Ave 98201
Baker Dr 98203
Ballew Ave 98203
Balsam Ln 98201
Barbara Ln 98203
Baring Way 98208
Basswood Dr 98203
Bayside 98201
Bayview Ln & Pl 98203
Beaumont Dr 98203
Bedal Ln 98208
Bedrock Dr 98203
E & W Beech St 98203
Bell Ave 98201
Belmont Dr 98208
Belmonte Ln 98201
Belvedere Ave 98203
Berkshire Dr 98203
Beverly Blvd & Ln 98203
Beverly Park Rd 98204
Bigelow St 98203
Black Forest Ln 98203
Bluff Pl 98203
N & W Boeing Perimeter Rd 98204
Bomarc Rd 98204
Bond St 98201
Bothell Everett Hwy 98208
Brentwood Pl 98203
Bridge Way 98201
Broadway
901-997 98201
999-3900 98201
3902-3998 98201
4500-4598 98203
4600-8299 98203
8301-8399 98203
8400-8499 98208
N Broadway 98201
Brookridge Blvd 98203
Bruin Blvd 98203
Bruskrud Rd 98208
Burl Pl 98203
Burley Dr 98208
Butler St 98201
Cabot Rd 98203
Cadet Way 98208
E Cady Rd 98203
California St 98201
Capri Pl 98203
Carlton Rd 98203
Carson Rd 98203
Cascade Dr 98203
Cascadia Ave 98208
Cascadian Way 98208
E Casino Rd
1-599 98208
601-699 98208
700-798 98203
800-7800 98203
7802-7898 98203
W Casino Rd 98204
Castle Ln 98203
Cedar St 98201
Center Pl 98203
Center Rd 98204
Charles Ave 98201
Cherry Ave 98201
Chestnut Ct & St 98201
Chinook Dr 98203
Claremont Way 98203
Clerendi Ave SE 98208
Cleveland Ave 98201
Cliff Dr 98203
Clinton Pl 98201
Colby Ave
500-4099 98201
4100-4398 98203
4400-7099 98203
College Ave 98203
Columbia Ave & Ct 98203
Commando Rd W 98204
Commercial Ave 98203
Corbin Dr 98204
Craftsman Way 98201
Crescent Ave 98203
Crest Ln 98203
Crown Dr 98203
Cypress St 98203
Dakota Way 98204
Darlington Ln 98203
Del Campo Dr 98208
Delaware Ave & Ln 98203
Dexter Ave 98203
Dogwood Dr 98203
Donovan Ln 98201
Dorn Ave 98208
Douglas Ave 98201
Dover St 98203
Dull Pl 98203
Earl Ave 98201
East Dr 98203
Eastview Ave 98208
Easy St 98203
Edgemoor Ln 98203
Edwards Ave 98201
El Capitan Way 98208
El Charlee St 98203
Elgin Way SE 98208
Elliott Way 98203
Elm St 98203
Emerson Pl 98208
England Ave 98203
Euclid Ave 98203
Everett Ave 98201
SE Everett Mall Way 98208
SW Everett Mall Way 98204
Evergreen Way
4500-4598 98203
4600-8199 98203
8400-8899 98208
8901-8999 98208
9000-11804 98204
11806-11898 98204
Fairfax Ave 98203
Fairview Ave 98203
Falcon Dr 98204
Federal Ave
2600-2698 98201
2700-4099 98201
4100-4599 98203
Fern Rd 98203
Fir St 98201
Firland Pl 98203
Firwood Pl 98203
Fleming St 98203
Florida Dr 98203
Forest Ct & Dr 98203
Forest Glade 98203
Forest View Dr 98203
Fowler Ave 98203
Franklin St 98203
Freeway Pl 98208
Friday Ave 98201
Fulton St 98201
Gale Pl 98203
Gardner Ave 98203
Gateway Ter 98203
Gedney St 98201
Geyer Ln 98203
Gibson Pl 98203
Gibson Rd 98204
E Gibson Rd 98204
Glacier Ln 98203
Glacier Peak Ave 98208
E & W Glen Dr 98203
W Glenhaven Dr 98203
Glenwood Ave 98203
Goblin Ln 98208
Gold Way 98208
Gorin Dr & Pl 98208
Gothic Way 98208
Grand Ave
700-4099 98201
4100-4599 98203
E Grand Ave 98201
Grandview Dr 98203
Grant Dr 98203
Greely St 98203
Hamlet Ln 98203
Harbor Ln 98203
Harborview Ln 98203
Hardeson Rd 98203
Harrison Ave 98201
Hawthorne St 98201
Hayes St 98201
E Heather Rd & Way 98203
Helena Ln 98208
Hemlock St 98201
Herencon St 98201
Hewitt Ave 98201
High St 98201
Highland Ave 98201
Highland Dr 98203
Highland Rd 98203
W Highland Rd 98203
Highway Pl 98203
Highway 99 98204
Hill Ave 98201
Hillside Ln 98203
Hilltop Rd 98203
Holbrook Ave 98203
Hollow Dale Pl 98204
Holly Dr
8401-8597 98208
8599-8699 98208
8701-8999 98208
9100-10999 98204
Home Pl 98203
Howard Ave 98203
Hoyt Ave
600-3099 98201
3101-4099 98201
3102-4098 98201
3102-3102 98206
3102-3102 98213
4100-4699 98203
E & W Ibberson Dr 98208
Idaho Ave 98204
Industry St 98203
E Intercity Ave 98208
W Intercity Ave 98204
Jackson Ave 98203
Jade Ave 98201
Jefferson Ave & Pl 98203
Juniper Dr 98203
Kasch Park Rd 98204
Kenilworth Pl 98203
Kenwood Dr 98203
Kings Pl 98203
Kirby Pl 98203
Kossuth Ave 98203
Kromer Ave 98201
Lake Heights Dr 98208
Lane Pl 98203
Larch St 98201
Larimer Rd 98208
Larlin Dr 98203
Laurel Dr 98201
Legion Dr 98201
Leland Dr 98203
Leonard Dr 98201
Lexington Ave 98203
Lincoln St 98203
Linden St 98201
Locust St 98201
Lombard Ave
800-3699 98201
5600-7099 98203
Lowell Rd 98203
Lowell Larimer Rd 98208
Lower Ridge Rd 98203
Madison St 98203
Madrona Ave 98203
W Magnolia Ave 98203
Main St 98203
Malerich Ave 98203
W Mall Dr 98208
Manor Pl 98203
Manor Way 98204
Maple St 98201
Marble Ln 98203
E Marilyn Ave 98208
W Marilyn Ave 98204
E & W Marine View Dr 98201
Marino Ave 98204
Maryland Ave 98203
Maulsby Ln 98201
Mcdougall Ave
1300-3899 98201
6000-7499 98203
E Mcgill Ave 98208
W Mcgill Ave 98204
Meadow Ln 98203
Meadow Pl SE 98208
Meadow Pl SW 98208
Meadow Rd 98208
Meadow Way 98208
Medora Way 98201
Melrose Ave 98203
Melvin Ave 98203
Merchant Way 98208
Meridian Ave
6000-8099 98203
10100-10399 98208
Meridian Ave S 98208
Meridian Ct SW 98204
Meridian Dr SE 98208
Meridian Pl W
11000-11199 98204
13301-13497 98208
13499-13899 98208
Mermont Dr 98203
Merrill Creek Pkwy 98203
Minuteman Dr 98204
Monroe Ave 98203
Montana Rd 98204
Monte Cristo Dr 98208
Morgan Ct & Rd 98203
E & W Mukilteo Blvd 98203
Narbeck Ave & Rd 98203
Nassau Pl & St 98201
Navajo Rd 98204
Nels Peters Rd 98208
Nichols Pl 98203
Niles Ave 98201
Norton Ave 98201
Oakes Ave
900-3799 98201
5800-6399 98203
Ocean Ave 98203
Oklahoma Ave 98201
Olive St 98203
Olympic Blvd & Dr 98203
Orca View Ln 98203
Pacific Ave 98201
Paine Ave 98201
Paine Field Way 98204
Palm Ave 98203
Panaview Blvd 98203
N Park Dr & Pl 98203
Parkview Ln 98203
Pebble Pl 98203
Pecks Dr 98203
Peters Pl 98208
Pilchuck Path 98201
Pine St 98201
Pinehurst Ave 98203
Pinkerton Ave 98203
Polk Pl 98203
Poplar St 98201
Puget Dr 98203
Puget Park Dr 98208
Railway Ave 98201
Rainier Ave 98201
Rainier Dr 98203
Rancho Pl 98204
Ravenna St 98203
Ridgemont Dr 98203
Ridgewood Dr 98203
Rim Dr 98208
Rivercrest Ave 98208
Riverside Ave & Rd 98201
Riverview Blvd 98203
Rockefeller Ave
301-397 98201
399-3799 98201
5300-6399 98203
Rose Way 98203
Rosewood Ave 98204
Ross Ave 98201
Rucker Ave
700-4099 98201
4100-5199 98203
Ruggs Lake Rd 98208
Russell Way 98204
Sabre St 98204
Sanincor St SW 98204
Saratoga Ln 98203
Scenic Dr 98203

Scorpion Rd 98204
Seabreeze Way 98203
Seahurst Ave 98203
Seaview Way 98203
Seaway Blvd 98203
Sevenich Dr 98201
Shadow Wood Dr 98208
Sharon Crst 98201
Sharon Dr 98204
Shore Ave 98203
Short St 98201
Shuksan Way 98203
Sievers Duecy Blvd 98203
Silver Way 98208
Silver Firs Dr 98208
Silver Lake Dr & Rd 98208
Silvertip Ln 98203
Skyline Dr 98201
Sloan Dr 98208
Smith Ave 98201
Smith Island Rd 98201
Snohomish Ave 98201
Sound Ave 98203
Sperry Ln 98203
Spire Ln 98203
Spokane Dr 98203
Spring St 98203
Starfire Rd 98204
State St 98201
Summit Ave 98201
Sumner Ln 98203
Sumner Pl 98201
Sunset Ln 98203
Sycamore Pl 98203
Sydney Ln 98203
Tamarack Dr 98203
Taylor Dr 98203
Temple Dr 98201
Terminal Ave 98201
Terrace Dr 98203
Thomson Ave 98203
Timber Cir 98203
Timber Hill Dr 98203
Tower St 98201
Trenton Pl 98208
Ttereve Dr 98203
Tulalip Ave 98201
Tyee Rd 98203
Upland Ave 98203
Upper Ridge Rd 98203
Valhalla Dr 98208
Veralene Way SW 98203
Vesper Dr 98203
Victor Pl 98201
W View Dr 98203
E View Ridge Dr 98203
Viewcrest Ave 98203
Virginia Ave 98201
Vista Pl 98203
Vistarama Ave 98208
Wall St 98201
Walnut St 98201
Waltham Dr 98208
Warren Ave 98201
Washington Ave 98203
Washington Way 98204
Wave Dr 98203
Waverly Ave 98201
Wayne Ave 98201
West Dr 98203
Westmere Dr 98201
Westminster Cir 98203
Wetmore Ave
400-4099 98201
5200-7499 98203
Whitechuck Dr 98208
Whitehorse Trl 98201
Willow Rd 98203
Wilmington Ave 98203
Winton Ave 98201
Wood Pl 98203
Woodlawn Ave 98203
Xavier Way
8000-8399 98203
8400-8699 98208
E Xavier Way 98208
Yew St 98203
York Rd 98204

NUMBERED STREETS

1st Ave SE
5400-5799 98203
9200-9298 98208
1st Ave W
11200-11299 98204
13300-14199 98208
S 1st Ave 98203
1st Dr SE
6000-6399 98203
9100-12199 98208
1st Dr W 98203
1st Pl W
9800-11399 98204
13400-13899 98208
2nd Ave SE 98208
2nd Ave W 98208
S 2nd Ave
4800-5198 98203
5200-5799 98203
5800-5899 98208
2nd Dr SE
6200-7499 98203
9401-11697 98208
11699-14299 98208
2nd Pl W 98204
3rd Ave SE 98208
3rd Ave W
11000-11199 98204
13900-14299 98208
S 3rd Ave 98203
3rd Dr SE 98208
3rd Dr W 98203
3rd Pl SE 98208
3rd Pl W 98204
4th Ave SE 98208
4th Ave W 98204
S 4th Ave 98203
4th Dr SE 98208
4th Dr W 98203
4th Pl SE 98208
4th Pl W
12200-12399 98204
14000-14299 98208
5th Ave SE 98208
5th Ave W
4600-8399 98203
8500-8798 98204
5th Dr SE
4500-4599 98203
12400-12599 98208
5th Pl 98203
5th Pl W
5100-5199 98203
9000-12399 98204
14000-14199 98208
5th St 98201
6th Ave SE 98208
6th Ave W
7200-7299 98203
10800-11699 98204
6th Dr SE 98208
6th Pl W 98204
6th St 98201
7th Ave SE 98208
7th Ave W 98204
7th Dr W 98203
7th Pl W 98204
7th St 98201
8th Ave W
5800-5999 98203
8400-12999 98204
13001-13099 98204
8th Dr SE 98208
8th Dr W 98203
8th Pl SE 98208
8th Pl W 98204
8th St 98201
9th Ave SE 98208
9th Ave W
4900-5099 98203
10000-13799 98204
9th Dr SE 98208
9th Dr W 98203
9th Pl W 98204
9th St 98201
10th Ave SE 98208
10th Ave W 98204
10th Dr SE 98208
10th Dr W 98203
10th Pl W
5000-5099 98203
9000-11799 98204
10th St 98201
11th Ave W
5800-5899 98203
9300-13499 98204
11th Dr SE 98208
11th Dr W 98204
11th Pl W 98204
11th St 98201
12th Ave SE 98208
12th Ave W
5600-5899 98203
9800-11899 98204
12th Dr SE 98208
12th Pl W 98204
12th St 98201
12th St NE 98201
12th St SE 98201
13th Ave SE 98208
13th Ave W
5400-5599 98203
10400-11799 98204
13th Dr SE 98208
13th Pl W 98204
13th St 98201
14th Ave W 98204
14th Dr SE 98208
14th Dr W 98203
14th St 98201
15th Ave W
5100-5299 98203
12100-12799 98204
15th Pl W 98204
15th St 98201
16th Ave SE 98208
16th Ave W 98203
16th Dr W 98204
16th Pl W 98204
16th St 98201
17th Ave SE
7400-7599 98203
12400-12599 98208
17th Ave W 98204
17th Ct W 98204
17th Pl W 98204
17th St 98201
18th Ave W 98204
18th Dr SE 98208
18th Pl W 98204
18th St 98201
19th Ave SE 98208
19th Pl W 98204
19th St 98201
20th Ave SE 98208
20th Dr SE 98208
20th Pl W 98204
20th St 98201
21st Ave SE 98208
21st Ave W 98204
21st Dr SE 98208
21st Dr W 98203
21st Pl W 98204
21st St 98201
22nd Ave SE 98208
22nd Dr SE 98208
22nd St 98201
23rd Ave SE 98208
23rd Ave SW 98204
23rd Ave W
4900-5799 98203
10001-10097 98204
10099-12299 98204
23rd Dr SE 98208
23rd Dr W 98203
23rd Pl W 98204
23rd St 98201
24th Ave SE 98208
24th Ave W 98203
24th Dr SE
8000-8199 98203
9800-13199 98208
24th Pl W 98204
24th St 98201
25th Ave SE 98208
25th Ave W 98203
25th Dr SE 98208
25th Pl W 98204
25th St 98201
26th Ave SE 98208
26th Ave W 98204
26th Dr SE 98208
26th Pl 98201
26th Pl W 98204
26th St 98201
27th Ave SE 98208
27th Ave W
4900-5199 98203
11300-12599 98204
27th Dr SE 98208
27th Pl NE 98201
27th Pl W 98204
28th Ave SE 98208
28th Ave W 98204
28th Dr SE 98208
28th Pl NE 98201
28th Pl W 98204
28th St NE 98201
29th Ave SE 98208
29th Ave W 98204
29th Dr SE 98208
29th Pl W 98204
30th Ave SE 98208
30th Ave W 98204
30th Dr SE 98208
31st Ave SE 98208
31st Ave W 98204
31st Dr SE 98208
31st Pl W 98204
32nd Ave NE 98201
32nd Ave SE 98208
32nd Ave W 98204
32nd Dr SE 98208
32nd Dr W 98204
32nd St 98201
33rd Ave SE 98208
33rd Ave W 98203
33rd Dr SE 98208
33rd Pl W 98204
33rd St 98201
34th Ave NE 98201
34th Ave SE 98208
34th Dr SE 98208
34th St 98201
35th Ave NE 98201
35th Ave SE 98208
35th St 98201
36th Ave SE 98208
36th Ave W 98203
36th Dr SE 98208
36th Pl NE 98201
36th Pl W 98204
36th St 98201
37th Ave SE 98208
37th Dr SE 98208
37th St 98201
38th Ave SE 98208
38th Dr SE 98208
38th St 98201
38th St SE 98201
39th Ave SE 98208
39th Dr SE 98208
39th St 98201
40th Ave SE 98208
40th Dr SE 98208
40th Pl 98201
40th Pl NE 98201
40th St 98201
41st Ave SE 98208
41st Dr SE
5300-5699 98201
10800-11399 98208
41st Pl 98201
41st St
1100-1599 98201
1601-1799 98201
1800-1802 98203
42nd Ave SE 98208
42nd Dr SE 98208
42nd St SE 98203
42nd St SW 98203
43rd Ave SE 98201
43rd Dr SE 98208
43rd St SE 98203
44th Ave SE 98208
44th Dr SE 98208
44th St SE 98203
45th Ave SE
5300-5799 98201
10600-12899 98208
45th Dr SE 98208
45th St SE 98203
45th St SW 98203
46th Ave SE 98208
46th Dr SE 98208
46th St SE 98203
46th St SW 98203
47th Ave SE 98208
47th Dr SE 98208
47th St SE 98203
47th St SW 98203
48th Ave SE 98208
48th Dr SE 98208
48th Pl SE 98203
48th St SE 98203
48th St SW 98203
49th Ave SE 98208
49th Dr SE 98208
49th Pl SW 98203
49th St SE 98203
49th St SW 98203
50th Ave SE
5300-5599 98201
11000-15299 98208
50th Dr SE 98208
50th St SE 98203
50th St SW 98203
51st Ave SE
1500-1999 98201
10900-14799 98208
51st Dr SE 98208
51st Pl SW 98203
51st St SW 98203
52nd Ave SE 98208
52nd Dr SE 98208
52nd Pl SW 98203
52nd St SE
700-2399 98203
3800-5299 98201
52nd St SW 98203
53rd Ave SE 98208
53rd Dr SE 98208
53rd St SE 98203
53rd St SW 98203
54th Ave SE 98208
54th Dr SE 98208
54th St SW 98203
55th Ave SE
1200-1299 98201
12800-15299 98208
55th Dr SE 98208
55th Pl SW 98203
55th St SE 98203
55th St SW 98203
56th Ave SE 98208
56th Dr SE 98208
56th Pl SE 98203
56th Pl SW 98203
56th St SE 98203
56th St SW 98203
57th Ave SE 98208
57th Dr SE 98208
57th St SE 98203
57th St SW 98203
58th Ave SE 98208
58th Dr SE 98208
58th Pl SE 98203
58th Pl SW 98203
58th St SE 98203
58th St SW 98203
59th Ave SE 98208
59th Dr SE 98208
59th Pl SE 98203
59th Pl SW 98203
59th St SW 98203
60th Ave SE 98208
60th Dr SE 98208
60th Pl SE 98203
60th St SE 98203
60th St SW 98203
61st Ave SE
900-999 98201
13200-14399 98208
61st Pl SE 98203
61st St SE 98203
62nd Ave SE 98208
62nd Dr SE 98208
62nd St SE 98203
63rd Ave SE 98201
63rd St SE 98203
65th Pl SE 98203
66th Pl SE 98203
69th Pl & St 98203
70th Pl SE 98203
71st Pl SE 98203
72nd Pl & St 98203
73rd SE & SW 98203
74th Pl & St 98203
75th Pl & St 98203
76th Pl & St 98203
77th Pl & St SW &
SE 98203
78th SE & SW 98203
79th SE & SW 98203
80th Pl & St 98203
81st Pl & St SE & SW 98203
82nd Pl SW 98203
84th St SE 98208
85th Pl SW 98204
85th St SE 98208
86th St SE 98208
87th St SE 98208
88th Pl SW 98204
88th St SE 98208
88th St SW 98204
89th St SE 98208
89th St SW 98204
90th Pl SE 98208
90th St SE 98208
90th St SW 98204
91st Pl SE 98208
91st Pl SW 98204
91st St SE 98208
92nd Pl SE 98208
92nd St SE 98208
92nd St SW 98204
93rd Pl SE 98208
93rd Pl SW 98204
93rd St SE 98208
93rd St SW 98204
94th Pl SE 98208
94th St SE 98208
94th St SW 98204
95th Ct SE 98208
95th Pl SE 98208
95th Pl SW 98204
95th St SE 98208
95th St SW 98204
96th Pl SE 98208
96th St SE 98208
96th St SW 98204
97th Pl SE 98208
97th Pl SW 98204
97th St SE 98208
98th Pl SE 98208
98th Pl SW 98204
98th St SE 98208
98th St SW 98204
99th Pl SE 98208
99th Pl SW 98204
99th St SE 98208
99th St SW 98204
100th Ct SE 98208
100th Pl SE 98208
100th St SE 98208
100th St SW 98204
101st Pl SE 98208
101st Pl SW 98204
101st St SE 98208
102nd Pl SE 98208
102nd Pl SW 98204
103rd Pl SE 98208
103rd Pl SW 98204
103rd St SE 98208
103rd St SW 98204
104th Pl SE 98208
104th Pl SW 98204
104th St SE 98208
104th St SW 98204
105th Pl SE 98208
105th St SE 98208
105th St SW 98204
106th Pl SE 98208
106th Pl SW 98204
106th St SE 98208
106th St SW 98204
107th Pl SE 98208
107th Pl SW 98204
107th St SE 98208
107th St SW 98204
108th Pl SE 98208
108th St SE 98208
108th St SW 98204
109th Pl SE 98208
109th St SE 98208
109th St SW 98204
110th Pl & St 98208
111th Pl SE 98208
111th Pl SW 98204
111th St SE 98208
111th St SW 98204
112th Pl SE 98208
112th St SE 98208
112th St SW 98204
113th Pl SE 98208
113th Pl SW 98204
113th St SE 98208
113th St SW 98204
114th Pl SE 98208
114th St SE 98208
114th St SW 98204
115th Pl SE 98208
115th Pl SW 98204
115th St SE 98208
115th St SW 98204
116th Pl SE 98208
116th Pl SW 98204
116th St SE 98208
116th St SW 98204
117th Pl SE 98208
117th Pl SW 98204
117th St SE 98208
117th St SW 98204
118th Pl SE 98208
118th Pl SW 98204
118th St SE 98208
119th Pl SE 98208
119th St SE 98208
119th St SW 98204
120th Pl SE 98208
120th Pl SW 98204
120th St SE 98208
120th St SW 98204
121st Pl SE 98208
121st Pl SW 98204
121st St SE 98208
121st St SW 98204
122nd Pl SE 98208
122nd Pl SW 98204
122nd St SE 98208
122nd St SW 98204
123rd Pl SE 98208
123rd Pl SW 98204
123rd St SE 98208
123rd St SW 98204
124th Pl SE 98208
124th Pl SW 98204
124th St SE 98208
124th St SW 98204
125th Pl SE 98208
125th Pl SW 98204

125th St SE 98208
126th Pl SE 98208
126th Pl SW 98204
126th St SE 98208
126th St SW 98204
127th Pl SE 98208
127th Pl SW 98204
127th St SE 98208
128th Pl SE 98208
128th Pl SW 98204
128th St SE 98208
128th St SW 98204
129th Pl SE 98208
129th St SE 98208
129th St SW 98204
130th Pl SE 98208
130th St SE 98208
130th St SW 98204
131st Pl SE 98208
131st Pl SW 98204
131st St SE 98208
132nd Pl SE 98208
132nd St SE 98208
132nd St SW 98204
133rd St SE 98208
134th Pl SE 98208
134th Pl SW 98208
134th St SE 98208
134th St SW
200-299 98208
700-1199 98204
135th Pl SE 98208
135th St SE 98208
135th St SW 98204
136th Pl SE 98208
136th St SE 98208
136th St SW 98204
137th Pl SE 98208
137th St SE 98208
137th St SW
1-9 98208
11-499 98208
800-898 98204
900-999 98204
138th Pl & St 98208
139th Pl & St 98208
140th Pl & St 98208
141st Pl SE 98208
142nd Pl & St SE & SW 98208
143rd St SE 98208
144th St SE 98208
145th St SE 98208
146th Pl & St 98208
147th Pl & St 98208
148th Pl & St 98208
149th Pl & St 98208
150th Pl & St 98208
151st Pl & St 98208
152nd Pl & St 98208
153rd Pl SE 98208
156th St SE 98208

FEDERAL WAY WA

POST OFFICE BOXES MAIN OFFICE STATIONS AND BRANCHES

Box No.s
3001 - 9800 98063
23001 - 27616 98093
90301 - 90301 98063

NAMED STREETS

S Beamera St 98003
SW Campus Dr
100-1900 98023
1815-1815 98093
1901-2099 98023
1902-2004 98023
S Commons 98003
Conerin Ave SW 98023
S Dash Point Rd 98003
SW Dash Point Rd 98023
Enchanted Pkwy S 98003
S Gateway Center Blvd & Pl S 98003
Hoyt Rd SW 98023
S Marine Hills Way 98003
Marine View Dr SW 98023
Military Rd S
27700-30599 98003
32000-33299 98001
Milton Rd S 98003
Mirror Lake Park 98023
Old Military Rd S 98003
Pacific Hwy S
27200-32900 98003
32829-32829 98063
32901-37499 98003
32902-37698 98003
Redondo Way S 98003
S Star Lake Rd 98003
Weyerhaeuser Way S 98001

NUMBERED STREETS

1st Ave S 98003
1st Ave SW 98023
1st Cir S 98003
1st Ct SW 98023
1st Ln S 98003
1st Ln SW 98023
1st Pl S 98003
1st Pl SW 98023
1st Way S 98003
1st Way SW 98023
2nd Ave S 98003
2nd Ave SW 98023
2nd Ct S 98003
2nd Ln S 98003
2nd Ln SW 98023
2nd Pl S 98003
2nd Pl SW 98023
3rd Ave S 98003
3rd Ave SW 98023
3rd Ct S 98003
3rd Ct SW 98023
3rd Ln SW 98023
3rd Pl S 98003
3rd Pl SW 98023
4th Ave S 98003
4th Ave SW 98023
4th Ct SW 98023
4th Ln S 98003
4th Pl S 98003
4th Pl SW 98023
5th Ave S 98003
5th Ave SW 98023
5th Pl S 98003
5th Pl SW 98023
5th Way S 98003
6th Ave S 98003
6th Ave SW 98023
6th Ct SW 98023
6th Pl S 98003
6th Pl SW 98023
7th Ave S 98003
7th Ave SW 98023
7th Ct SW 98023
7th Pl S 98003
7th Pl SW 98023
7th Way SW 98023
8th Ave S 98003
8th Ave SW 98023
8th Ct S 98003
8th Ct SW 98023
8th Pl S 98003
8th Pl SW 98023
9th Ave S 98003
9th Ave SW 98023
9th Ct SW 98023
9th Pl S 98003
9th Pl SW 98023
10th Ave S 98003
10th Ave SW 98023
10th Ct SW 98023
10th Pl S 98003
10th Pl SW 98023
11th Ave S 98003
11th Ave SW 98023
11th Ct SW 98023
11th Pl S 98003
11th Pl SW 98023
12th Ave S 98003
12th Ave SW 98023
12th Ct SW 98023
12th Ln SW 98023
12th Pl S 98003
12th Pl SW 98023
13th Ave S 98003
13th Ave SW 98023
13th Ct SW 98023
13th Pl S 98003
13th Pl SW 98023
13th Way SW 98023
14th Ave S 98003
14th Ave SW 98023
14th Ct S 98003
14th Pl S 98003
14th Pl SW 98023
14th Way SW 98023
15th Ave S 98003
15th Ave SW 98023
15th Ct S 98003
15th Ct SW 98023
15th Pl S 98003
15th Pl SW 98023
16th Ave S 98003
16th Ave SW 98023
16th Ct SW 98023
16th Pl SW 98023
17th Ave S 98003
17th Ave SW 98023
17th Ct SW 98023
17th Ln S 98003
17th Pl S 98003
17th Pl SW 98023
18th Ave S 98003
18th Ave SW 98023
18th Ct SW 98023
18th Ln S 98003
18th Pl S 98003
18th Pl SW 98023
19th Ave S 98003
19th Ave SW 98023
19th Ct SW 98023
19th Ln S 98003
19th Ln SW 98023
19th Pl S 98003
19th Pl SW 98023
19th Way S 98003
20th Ave S 98003
20th Ave SW 98023
20th Ct S 98003
20th Ct SW 98023
20th Ln SW 98023
20th Pl S 98003
20th Pl SW 98023
20th Way S 98003
21st Ave S 98003
21st Ave SW 98023
21st Ct S 98003
21st Ln S 98003
21st Pl S 98003
22nd Ave S 98003
22nd Ave SW 98023
22nd Ct S 98003
22nd Ct SW 98023
22nd Ln S 98003
22nd Pl S 98003
22nd Pl SW 98023
23rd Ave S 98003
23rd Ave SW 98023
23rd Ct S 98003
23rd Dr S 98003
23rd Ln S 98003
23rd Pl S 98003
24th Ave S 98003
24th Ave SW 98023
24th Ct S 98003
24th Ct SW 98023
24th Pl S 98003
24th Pl SW 98023
25th Ave S 98003
25th Ave SW 98023
25th Ct S 98003
25th Dr S 98003
25th Ln S 98003
25th Ln SW 98023
25th Pl S 98003
25th Pl SW 98023
26th Ave S 98003
26th Ave SW 98023
26th Ct S 98003
26th Ct SW 98023
26th Dr S 98003
26th Pl S 98003
26th Pl SW 98023
27th Ave S 98003
27th Ave SW 98023
27th Ct S 98003
27th Pl S 98003
27th Pl SW 98023
28th Ave S 98003
28th Ave SW 98023
28th Ln S 98003
28th Pl S 98003
28th Pl SW 98023
29th Ave S 98003
29th Ave SW 98023
29th Ct S 98003
29th Ct SW 98023
29th Pl S 98003
29th Pl SW 98023
30th Ave S 98003
30th Ave SW 98023
31st Ave S 98003
31st Ave SW 98023
31st Ct SW 98023
31st Pl S 98003
31st Pl SW 98023
32nd Ave S 98001
32nd Ave SW 98023
32nd Ct SW 98023
32nd Pl SW 98023
33rd Ave SW 98023
33rd Pl S 98001
33rd Pl SW 98023
34th Ave & Pl 98023
35th Ave S 98001
35th Ave SW 98023
35th Pl SW 98023
36th Ave, Ct & Pl 98023
37th Ave SW 98023
37th Ct SW 98023
37th Pl S 98001
37th Pl SW 98023
38th Ave S 98001
38th Ave SW 98023
38th Ct SW 98023
38th Pl SW 98023
39th Ave S 98001
39th Ave SW 98023
39th Ct SW 98023
39th Pl SW 98023
40th Ave S 98001
40th Ave SW 98023
40th Ct SW 98023
40th Pl SW 98023
41st Ave SW 98023
41st Ln S 98001
41st Pl S 98001
41st Pl SW 98023
41st Way S 98001
42nd Ave S 98001
42nd Ave SW 98023
42nd Ct S 98001
42nd Pl S 98001
42nd Pl SW 98023
43rd Ave SW 98023
43rd Pl S 98001
43rd Pl SW 98023
44th Ave S 98001
44th Ave SW 98023
44th Pl SW 98023
45th Ct SW 98023
45th Pl SW 98023
45th Way S 98001
46th Ave, Ct & Pl 98023
47th Ave, Ln & Pl 98023
48th Ave, Cir, Ct, Ln & Pl SW 98023
49th Ave, Ct, Ln, Pl & Ter SW 98023
50th Ave, Ct, Ln, Pl & Ter SW 98023
51st Ave, Ln & Pl 98023
52nd Ave & Pl 98023
53rd Ave & Pl 98023
54th Ave SW 98023
55th Ave SW 98023
S 272nd St 98003
273rd Pl & St 98003
S 274th Pl 98001
S 275th Pl 98003
276th Pl & St 98003
277th Pl & St 98003
278th Ct & St 98003
279th Pl & St 98003
S 280th Pl 98003
281st Pl & St 98003
282nd Pl & St 98003
283rd Pl & St 98003
284th Ct, Ln, Pl & St 98003
285th Pl & St 98003
286th Ln, Pl & St 98003
287th Pl & St 98003
288th Ln, Pl & St 98003
289th Pl & St 98003
290th Pl & St 98003
S 291st Pl 98003
S 291st St 98003
SW 291st St 98023
S 292nd St 98003
SW 292nd St 98023
S 293rd Pl 98003
S 293rd St 98003
SW 293rd St 98023
S 294th Pl 98003
SW 294th Pl 98023
SW 294th St 98023
S 295th Pl 98003
SW 295th Pl 98023
SW 295th St 98023
S 296th Pl 98003
S 296th St 98003
SW 296th St 98023
S 297th Pl 98003
S 297th St 98003
SW 297th St 98023
SW 298th Pl 98023
S 298th St 98003
SW 298th St 98023
S 299th Pl 98003
SW 299th Pl 98023
S 299th St 98003
SW 299th St 98023
S 300th Pl 98003
SW 300th Pl 98023
S 300th St 98003
SW 300th St 98023
S 301st Ln 98003
S 301st Pl 98003
SW 301st Pl 98023
S 301st St 98003
SW 301st St 98023
S 302nd Pl 98003
SW 302nd Pl 98023
S 302nd St 98003
SW 302nd St 98023
SW 303rd Pl 98023
S 303rd St 98003
SW 303rd St 98023
S 304th Pl 98003
S 304th St 98003
SW 304th St 98023
S 305th Pl 98003
SW 305th Pl 98023
S 305th St 98003
SW 305th St 98023
SW 306th Ln 98023
S 306th Pl 98003
SW 306th Pl 98023
S 306th St 98003
SW 306th St 98023
307th Pl & St 98023
S 308th Ct 98003
SW 308th Ct 98023
S 308th Ln 98003
SW 308th Pl 98023
S 308th St 98003
SW 308th St 98023
S 309th Ct 98003
SW 309th Ct 98023
S 309th Pl 98003
SW 309th Pl 98023
S 309th St 98003
SW 309th St 98023
S 310th Ct 98003
SW 310th Ct 98023
S 310th Pl 98003
SW 310th Pl 98023
S 310th St 98003
SW 310th St 98023
SW 311th Ct 98023
S 311th Pl 98003
SW 311th Pl 98023
S 311th St 98003
SW 311th St 98023
SW 312th Pl 98023
S 312th St 98003
SW 312th St 98023
SW 313th Ct 98023
SW 313th Pl 98023
S 313th St 98003
SW 313th St 98023
S 314th Pl 98003
SW 314th Pl 98023
S 314th St 98003
SW 314th St 98023
S 315th Ln 98003
S 315th Pl 98003
SW 315th Pl 98023
S 315th St 98003
SW 315th St 98023
SW 316th Ct 98023
S 316th Ln 98003
S 316th Pl 98003
SW 316th Pl 98023
S 316th St 98003
SW 316th St 98023
SW 317th Ct 98023
SW 317th Ln 98023
S 317th Pl 98003
SW 317th Pl 98023
S 317th St 98003
SW 317th St 98023
SW 318th Ct 98023
S 318th Pl 98003
SW 318th Pl 98023
S 318th St 98003
SW 318th St 98023
SW 319th Ct 98023
SW 319th Ln 98023
S 319th Pl 98003
SW 319th Pl 98023
SW 319th St 98023
SW 320th Ct 98023
SW 320th Pl 98023
S 320th St 98003
SW 320th St 98023
SW 321st Ln 98023
S 321st Pl 98003
SW 321st Pl 98023
S 321st St
500-999 98003
3700-3899 98001
SW 321st St 98023
SW 322nd Ct 98023
S 322nd Pl 98003
SW 322nd Pl 98023
S 322nd St 98001
SW 322nd St 98023
S 323rd Pl 98003
S 323rd St 98003
SW 323rd St 98023
SW 324th Ct 98023
S 324th Pl
100-1999 98003
4100-4299 98001
SW 324th Pl 98023
S 324th St 98003
SW 324th St 98023
SW 325th Ct 98023
S 325th Ln 98003
S 325th Pl
100-499 98003
3900-3999 98001
SW 325th Pl 98023
S 325th St
500-1699 98003
3800-4399 98001
SW 325th St 98023
SW 325th Way 98023
SW 326th Ct 98023
S 326th Pl 98001
SW 326th Pl 98023
S 326th St 98003
SW 326th St 98023
S 327th Ln 98003
S 327th Pl 98003
SW 327th Pl 98023
S 327th St 98003
SW 327th St 98023
SW 328th Ct 98023
S 328th Ln 98003
S 328th Pl 98003
SW 328th Pl 98023
S 328th St
400-1599 98003
3800-3999 98001
SW 328th St 98023
S 329th Ct 98003
SW 329th Ct 98023
S 329th Ln 98003
S 329th Pl 98003
SW 329th Pl 98023
S 329th St 98001
SW 329th St 98023
SW 329th Way 98023
SW 330th Ct 98023
S 330th Pl
200-699 98003
4100-4599 98001
SW 330th Pl 98023
S 330th St 98003
SW 330th St 98023
S 331st Pl
100-699 98003
4000-4199 98001
SW 331st Pl 98023
S 331st St
1900-2099 98003
4200-4299 98001
SW 331st St 98023
SW 332nd Ct 98023
S 332nd Pl
100-199 98003
4100-4499 98001
SW 332nd Pl 98023
S 332nd St 98003
SW 332nd St 98023
SW 333rd Ct 98023
S 333rd Ln 98003
S 333rd Pl 98001
SW 333rd Pl 98023
S 333rd St
100-2299 98003
4200-4499 98001
SW 333rd St 98023
SW 334th Ct 98023
S 334th Ln 98003
SW 334th Pl 98023
S 334th St
100-699 98003
3300-3799 98001
SW 334th St 98023
SW 335th Ct 98023
S 335th Pl 98001
SW 335th Pl 98023
SW 335th St 98023
SW 336th Ct 98023
SW 336th Pl 98023
S 336th St
100-2299 98003

2500-2515 98001
2525-2599 98003
3400-3599 98001
SW 336th St 98023
S 337th Ln 98003
SW 337th Pl 98023
S 337th St 98001
SW 337th St 98023
S 338th Pl 98003
SW 338th Pl 98023
S 338th St 98003
SW 338th St 98023
S 339th Cir 98003
SW 339th Pl 98023
SW 339th St 98023
SW 340th Pl 98023
S 340th St 98003
SW 340th St 98023
SW 341st Ct 98023
S 341st Pl 98003
SW 341st Pl 98023
SW 341st St 98023
SW 342nd Ct 98023
S 342nd Pl 98003
SW 342nd Pl 98023
SW 342nd St 98023
SW 343rd Pl 98023
S 343rd St 98003
SW 343rd St 98023
SW 344th Pl 98023
S 344th St 98003
SW 344th St 98023
S 344th Way 98001
345th Ct, Pl & St 98023
SW 346th Ct 98023
S 346th Ln 98003
SW 346th Pl 98023
SW 346th St 98023
SW 347th Ct 98023
S 347th Pl 98003
SW 347th Pl 98023
SW 347th St 98023
SW 347th Way 98023
SW 348th Ct 98023
S 348th Pl 98003
SW 348th Pl 98023
S 348th St 98003
SW 348th St 98023
SW 349th Pl 98023
S 349th St 98003
SW 349th St 98023
SW 349th Way 98023
SW 350th Ct 98023
SW 350th Pl 98023
S 350th St 98003
SW 350th St 98023
SW 351st Ct 98023
SW 351st Pl 98023
S 351st St 98003
SW 351st St 98023
SW 352nd Ct 98023
SW 352nd Pl 98023
S 352nd St 98003
SW 352nd St 98023
SW 353rd Ct 98023
S 353rd Pl 98003
SW 353rd Pl 98023
S 353rd St 98003
SW 353rd St 98023
S 354th Ln 98003
SW 354th Pl 98023
S 354th St 98003
SW 354th St 98023
SW 355th Ct 98023
S 355th Pl 98003
SW 355th Pl 98023
S 355th St 98003
S 356th Pl 98003
SW 356th Pl 98023
S 356th St 98003
SW 356th St 98023
S 357th Ct 98003
SW 357th Ct 98023
S 357th Pl 98003
S 357th St 98003
SW 357th St 98023
SW 358th Ct 98023
S 358th St 98003
SW 358th St 98023
S 359th St 98003
SW 359th St 98023
S 360th St 98003
SW 360th St 98023
S 361st Pl 98003
S 361st St 98003
SW 361st St 98023
S 362nd Ct 98003
S 362nd Pl 98003
SW 362nd Pl 98023
S 362nd St 98003
SW 363rd Ct 98023
S 363rd Pl 98003
SW 363rd Pl 98023
S 363rd St 98003
S 364th Pl 98003
SW 364th Pl 98023
S 364th St 98003
S 364th Way 98003
S 365th Ct 98003
S 365th Pl 98003
SW 365th Pl 98023
SW 365th St 98023
S 366th Ct 98003
S 366th Pl 98003
SW 366th St 98023
S 367th Ct 98003
SW 367th Ct 98023
S 367th Pl 98003
S 368th Ln 98003
S 368th Pl 98003
S 368th St 98003
SW 368th St 98023
S 369th St 98003
SW 369th St 98023
370th Ct, Pl & St 98003
S 371st Ct 98003
S 371st Pl 98003
S 371st St 98003
SW 371st St 98023
S 372nd Ct 98003
S 372nd Pl 98003
S 372nd St 98003
SW 372nd St 98023
S 372nd Way 98003
373rd Ct, Pl & St 98003
S 374th Ct 98003
S 374th Pl 98003
S 374th St 98003
SW 374th St 98023
375th Ct, Pl & St 98003
376th Pl & St 98003
S 377th St 98003
379th Pl & St 98003
380th Pl & St 98003

GIG HARBOR WA

General Delivery 98335

POST OFFICE BOXES MAIN OFFICE STATIONS AND BRANCHES

Box No.s
All PO Boxes 98335

NAMED STREETS

A St NW 98335
Alastra Ln 98335
Alder Dr NW 98335
Allen Point Rd NW 98332
Amber Ct NW 98332
Anne Marie Ct 98335
Aqua Drive Kp N 98329
Aqua Vista Ct & Dr 98335
Arnold Ln 98335
Artena Ln 98332
Artondale Dr NW 98335
Baker Way NW 98335
Baltic St NW 98332
Barkley Ln NW 98332
E Bay Dr NW 98335
Bay View Ln 98332
Bayridge Ave 98332
Beach Ln NW 98332
Beachwood Dr NW 98332
Bear Creek Ln 98335
Beardsley Ave NW 98335
Beaver Creek Ln 98335
Benson St 98332
Berg Ct & Dr 98335
Bering St NW 98332
Berk Ln 98335
Birch Tree Ln NW 98335
Bliss Cochrane Road Kp N 98329
Borgen Blvd & Loop NW 98332
Boulder Ct 98332
Bowman Ln NW 98332
Bracken Fern Dr NW 98332
Bridlepath Dr NW 98332
Bristol Ct & Pl 98332
Bujacich Rd NW 98332
Burnham Dr NW 98332
Butler Dr 98335
C St NW 98335
Cabrini Dr NW 98335
Camp Rd NW 98335
Canterwood Blvd & Dr 98332
Cartier Ln NW 98335
Cascade Ave 98335
Cascade Pl NW 98332
Castelan Ln 98335
Cedar Ct NW 98332
Cedar Ln NW 98335
Cedarwood Ln NW 98335
Chapman Dr NW 98332
Cherry Ln NW 98335
Chinook Ave 98335
Cliffside Ln NW 98335
Clorindi Cir NW 98335
Coatsworth Dr NW 98335
Coho St 98335
Coleman Camp Rd NW 98335
Colvos Dr NW 98332
Comte Dr NW 98335
Craig Ln 98335
Cramer Road Kp N 98329
Creek Ln & Loop 98335
Crescent Cove Pl 98332
Crescent Lake Dr NW 98332
Crescent Valley Dr NW 98332
Creviston Dr NW 98329
Creviston Drive Kp N 98329
Crews Road Kp N 98329
Cromwell Dr NW 98335
Cromwell Beach Dr NW 98335
Dana Dr NW 98332
Danforth St NW 98329
Darby Ct 98335
David Day Dr NW 98332
Dawson Dr NW 98335
Debbie Ct 98335
Deer Creek Ln 98335
Defiance Ln 98332
Dogwood Ln NW 98335
Dogwood Court Kp N 98329
Dorotich St 98332
Drake Ln NW 98332
Driftwood Cv NW 98332
Drummond Dr NW 98332
Duggan Jahns Drive Kp N 98329
Dunbar Dr NW 98335
Dylan Ct 98335
Eagle Creek Ln 98335
Eantria N 98329
Easy Street Kp N 98329
Edgewood Dr NW 98332
Edwards Dr 98335
Elk Creek Ln 98335
Emerald Dr NW 98329
Emerald Ln 98335
Englewood Drive Kp N 98329
Erickson St 98335
Evergreen Lane Kp N 98329
Fairwind Ln NW 98335
Fawn Ct & Dr 98332
Fennimore St 98332
Fern Ln NW 98335
Fir Dr & Ln 98335
Firdrona Dr NW 98332
Firgrove Pl NW 98335
Ford Dr NW 98335
Forest Beach Dr NW 98335
Forest Glen Ct 98335
Foster St 98335
Fox Dr NW 98332
N Foxglove Dr 98332
Franklin Ave 98332
Fuller Ct & St 98332
Garden Pl NW 98335
Gig Harbor Dr NW 98332
Glacier Pl NW 98332
Glencove Road Kp N 98329
Goldman Dr NW 98329
Goodman Ave & Dr NW 98332
Goodnough Dr NW 98332
Goodrich Ct & Dr 98329
Grace Court Kp N 98329
Grandview Pl & St 98335
Granite Dr NW 98329
Greyhawk Ave 98335
Griffin Pl NW 98332
Gustafson Dr NW 98335
Hallstrom Dr NW 98335
Harbor Pl NW 98335
Harbor Country Dr 98335
Harbor Hill Dr NW 98332
Harbor Sunset Ln & Pl 98335
Harborcrest Ct NW 98332
Harborview Bch 98335
Harborview Dr
2800-3219 98335
3220-4399 98332
N Harborview Dr 98332
Harborview Pl 98332
Harmony Ln 98332
Heather Pl 98332
Hemlock Dr & Ln 98335
Hidden Ln NW 98335
Hidden Haven Ln NW 98335
High Acres Dr NW 98332
Hill Ave 98335
Hilltop Rd NW 98335
Holiday Drive Kp N 98329
Hollemgay Ct 98335
Holly Ct & Ln 98335
Holly Bluff Ct 98335
Hollyburn Lane Kp N 98329
Hollycroft St 98335
Homestead Ln 98335
Honeysuckle Ln NW
5300-5499 98335
11300-11499 98332
Horsehead Bay Dr NW 98335
Huckleberry Ln NW 98335
Huckleberry Lane Kp N 98329
Hudson Ln NW 98332
Hunt St NW 98335
Hunt Highlands Loop & Pl 98335
Hunter Ln NW 98332
Huntwick Dr NW 98335
Insel Ave 98335
Islandview Ct & Ter 98335
Jacobsen Ln 98332
Jade Pl NW 98329
Jahn Ave NW 98335
Johnson Ln 98332
Judson St 98335
Kauppila Ln 98335
Kelsey Ln 98335
Key Peninsula Hwy N 98329
Kimball Dr 98335
Kinglet Ln NW 98332
Knorieli Ct NW 98335
Kooley Drive Kp N 98329
Kopachuck Dr NW 98335
Lagoon Ln NW 98335
Lakeview Way Kp N 98329
Lamphere Ln 98335
Larellia Ct NW 98332
Larkspur Ct 98335
Leon Ln NW 98332
Leonie Ln NW 98335
Lewis St 98335
Lombard Dr NW 98335
Lucille Pkwy NW 98335
Lupine Ct 98335
Lybecker Dr NW 98332
Madrona Dr NW 98335
Madrona Ln NW 98335
Madrona Way NW 98332
Magnolia Ln 98335
Main Sail Ln 98335
Maple Ln NW 98335
E & W Maple Lane Cir 98335
Marble Beach Dr, Ln & Rd 98332
Mcallister Ave NW 98335
Mccormick Dr NW 98332
Mcdonald Ave 98335
Meadowlark Drive Kp N 98329
Michael Ln NW 98332
Milton Ave 98332
Minterwood Drive Kp N 98329
Mitts Ln 98332
Moller Dr NW 98332
Moorelands Ave, Dr & St 98335
Moose Trl NW 98335
Morris Ln N 98329
Mountainview Pl 98332
Muir Dr NW 98332
Murphy Dr NW 98335
Myers Ln 98335
Narrows View Cir NW 98335
Neel Ct 98335
Nuthatch Dr NW 98332
Old Stump Dr NW 98332
Olson Dr NW 98335
Olson Drive Kp N 98329
Olympic Dr NW 98335
Olympic View Dr NW 98335
Olympic Vista Ct NW 98332
Olympus Way 98332
Osprey Dr NW 98332
Overlook Ct 98332
Pacific Ave 98332
Packard Road Kp N 98329
Park Ave & Ln 98335
Parkdale Drive Kp N 98329
Paul Dr NW 98335
Peacock Hill Ave NW 98332
Peantria N 98329
Pelton Ct 98332
Picnic Point Ct & Dr 98335
Pinehurst Lane Kp N 98329
Pioneer Way 98335
Plant Dr NW 98335
Point Fosdick Cir, Dr, Pl & Ter NW 98335
Point Richmond Dr & Rd 98332
Point Richmond Beach Rd NW 98332
Point View Pl NW 98335
Port Ln 98335
Portage Pl NW 98332
Powell Dr NW 98335
Prentice Ave 98332
Purdy Dr & Ln 98332
Raft Island Dr & Rd 98335
Rainier Ave 98335
Randall Dr NW 98332
Ray Nash Ct & Dr 98335
Regatta Ct 98335
Reid Dr NW 98335
Reliance Ridge Ln 98335
Rhododendron Dr NW 98335
Ridgeway Dr 98332
Roby St NW 98335
Rocky Creek Road Kp N 98329
Rosedale St NW 98335
Rosedale Bay Ct NW 98335
Rosemont Dr NW 98335
Ross Ave 98332
Rust St 98332
Ryan Ln & St 98335
Saddle Back Dr NW 98332
Salmon Creek Ln 98335
Sandin Packard Rd NW 98335
Sandy Point East Kp N 98329
Sandy Point West Kp N 98329
Sari Ln 98332
Schoolhouse Ave NW 98335
Sea Cliff Dr NW 98332
Sea View Ct NW 98332
Secore Pl 98335
Sehmel Dr NW 98332
Sellers St 98332
Serena Ln NW 98335
Shaw Ln 98335
Shawnee Ct, Dr & Pl 98335
Sherman Dr NW 98332
Shirley Ave 98332
Shore Dr NW 98332
Short St 98335
Shyleen St 98335
Silver Springs Dr NW 98335
Skansie Ave
7400-7999 98335
8100-8599 98332
Slippery Hill Dr NW 98332
Snug Harbor Ln 98335
Snyder Ln 98335
Sorrel Ct 98335
Sorrel Run NW 98332
Soundview Ct & Dr 98335
Spadoni Ln 98335
Spinnaker Ln 98335
Springbrook Ln NW 98329
Springfield Dr NW 98329
Spruce Ln NW 98335
Stanich Ave & Ln 98335
Starboard Ln 98335
Starlet Ln NW 98335
State Game Access NW 98332
State Route 16 NW 98332
State Route 302 NW 98329
State Route 302 Kpn 98329
Stinson Ave
7100-7999 98335
8000-8299 98332
Stone Dr NW 98335
Stonebridge Dr NW 98332
Sullivan Dr NW 98335
Sunny Bay Dr NW 98335
Sunrise Pl NW 98335
Sunrise Beach Dr NW 98332
Sunset View Dr NW 98332
Sutherland Ct & St 98332
Swanson Dr NW 98332
Talmo Dr NW 98332
Tanager Dr NW 98332
Tarabochia St 98335
Taylor Pl 98332
Thomas Road Kp N 98329
Timber Ln NW 98335
Towhee Dr NW 98332
Tyee Dr NW 98332
Uddenberg Ln 98335
Valley Dr NW 98335
Valley View Dr NW 98335
Vernhardson Pl & St 98332
View Dr NW 98332
View Place North NW 98332
View Point Dr NW 98335
Vipond Dr NW 98329
Wagner Way NW 98335
Warren Dr NW 98335
Weather Glass Ln 98335
Weatherswood Dr NW 98335
Wheeler Ave 98332
Whispering Pine Dr NW 98332
White Cloud Ave NW 98335
Whitmore Dr NW 98335
Wilkes Ln 98332
Wilkinson Ln 98335
Willow Ln NW 98335
Willow Tree Lane Kp N 98329
Wind And Tide Dr NW 98329
Windlass Ln 98335
Wollochet Dr NW 98335
Woodhill Dr NW 98332
Woodworth Ave 98332
Wright Bliss Road Kp N 98329

NUMBERED STREETS

1st St NW 98335
2nd Avenue Ct NW 98332
2nd Street Ct NW 98335
3rd Ave NW 98332
3rd Avenue Ct NW 98332
4th St NW 98335
4th Avenue Ct NW 98332
5th St NW 98332
5th Street Ct NW 98335
6th Ave NW 98332
6th St NW 98335
6th Avenue Ct NW 98332
7th St NW 98335
7th Avenue Ct NW 98332
8th St NW 98335
9th Ave NW 98332
9th Avenue Ct NW 98335
9th Avenue Ct NW 98335
13600-13799 98332
9th Street Ct NW 98335
10th Ave NW 98332
10th St NW 98335
10th Avenue Ct NW 98332
11th Ave NW 98335
13600-13899 98332
11th Avenue Ct NW
3200-3399 98335
13500-13599 98332
12th Ave NW 98335
13600-13899 98332
12th Avenue Ct NW
2800-3799 98335
11100-11999 98332
13th Ave NW 98335
13300-13899 98332
13th Avenue Ct NW 98335
14th Ave NW
2001-2097 98335
2099-3999 98335
4001-4199 98335
14000-15999 98332
15th Ave NW 98335
11600-11899 98332
15th Avenue Ct NW 98335
16th Ave NW 98335
11600-11899 98332
16th Avenue Ct NW
1900-3999 98335
11300-11499 98332
17th Ave NW 98335
11700-11999 98332
17th St NW 98335
17th Avenue Ct NW
3000-4399 98335
11200-15999 98332
17th Street Ct NW 98335
18th Ave NW 98332
18th St NW 98335

18th Avenue Ct NW
2600-4399 ... 98335
10200-10299 ... 98332
18th Street Ct NW ... 98335
19th Ave NW ... 98335
15210-15399 ... 98332
19th St NW ... 98335
19th Avenue Ct NW
2400-3099 ... 98335
15100-15209 ... 98332
19th Street Ct NW ... 98335
20th Ave NW ... 98335
15400-15999 ... 98332
20th St NW ... 98335
20th Avenue Ct NW ... 98335
20th Street Ct NW ... 98335
21st Ave & St ... 98335
21st Avenue Ct NW ... 98335
22nd Ave NW ... 98335
9400-10399 ... 98332
22nd Avenue Ct NW ... 98335
23rd Ave & St ... 98335
24th Ave NW ... 98335
8305-9399 ... 98332
24th St NW ... 98335
24th Avenue Ct NW
3400-3599 ... 98335
8300-8310 ... 98332
24th Street Ct NW ... 98335
25th Ave NW ... 98335
25th Avenue Ct NW ... 98335
8300-8399 ... 98332
25th Street Ct NW ... 98335
26th Ave NW ... 98335
7900-15499 ... 98332
26th St NW ... 98335
26th Avenue Ct NW
1200-3999 ... 98335
13600-13999 ... 98332
26th Street Ct NW ... 98335
27th Ave NW ... 98335
10400-15199 ... 98332
27th St NW ... 98335
27th Street Ct NW ... 98335
28th Ave NW ... 98335
28th Ave NW ... 98335
9100-15999 ... 98332
28th St NW ... 98335
28th Street Ct NW ... 98335
29th Ave & St ... 98335
29th Street Ct NW ... 98335
30th Ave NW ... 98332
30th St NW ... 98335
30th Avenue Ct NW
3600-4199 ... 98335
15200-15599 ... 98332
30th Street Ct NW ... 98335
31st Ave NW ... 98335
13400-15599 ... 98332
31st St NW ... 98335
31st Avenue Ct NW
4000-4299 ... 98335
9500-15199 ... 98332
31st Street Ct NW ... 98335
32nd Ave NW ... 98335
13700-15399 ... 98332
32nd St NW ... 98335
32nd Avenue Ct NW ... 98335
32nd Street Ct NW ... 98335
33rd Ave NW ... 98335
14500-15199 ... 98332
33rd St NW ... 98335
33rd Avenue Ct NW
1-4999 ... 98335
10600-14399 ... 98332
33rd Street Ct NW ... 98335
34th Ave & St ... 98335
34th Avenue Ct NW ... 98335
9700-9798 ... 98332
34th Street Ct NW ... 98335
35th Ave NW ... 98335
14400-15099 ... 98332
35th St NW ... 98335
35th Avenue Ct NW
1-4699 ... 98335
11200-13499 ... 98332
35th Street Ct NW ... 98335

36th Ave NW ... 98335
11000-11716 ... 98332
36th St NW ... 98335
36th Avenue Ct NW
1100-5099 ... 98335
11500-13499 ... 98332
36th Street Ct NW ... 98335
37th Ave NW ... 98335
11000-11199 ... 98332
37th St NW ... 98335
37th Avenue Ct NW ... 98332
37th Street Ct NW ... 98335
38th Ave & St ... 98335
38th Avenue Ct NW ... 98335
10300-12399 ... 98332
38th Street Ct NW ... 98335
39th Ave NW ... 98332
39th St NW ... 98335
39th Avenue Ct NW
300-4299 ... 98335
13300-13399 ... 98332
39th Street Ct NW ... 98335
40th Ave NW ... 98335
11701-11703 ... 98332
40th St NW ... 98335
40th Avenue Ct NW
5700-5799 ... 98335
9600-11999 ... 98332
40th Street Ct NW ... 98335
41st Ave NW ... 98335
9700-15999 ... 98332
41st St NW ... 98335
41st Avenue Ct NW
5700-5899 ... 98335
11200-15299 ... 98332
41st Street Ct NW ... 98335
42nd Ave NW ... 98335
15000-15299 ... 98332
42nd St NW ... 98335
42nd Avenue Ct NW
6800-6999 ... 98335
14000-14999 ... 98332
42nd Street Ct NW ... 98335
43rd Ave NW ... 98335
9700-9999 ... 98332
43rd St NW ... 98335
43rd Avenue Ct NW
6400-7399 ... 98335
12800-12999 ... 98332
43rd Street Ct NW ... 98335
44th Ave NW ... 98335
9600-15199 ... 98332
44th St NW ... 98335
44th Avenue Ct NW ... 98332
44th Street Ct NW ... 98335
45th Ave NW ... 98335
15200-15399 ... 98332
45th St NW ... 98335
45th Avenue Ct NW
6800-6999 ... 98335
12000-15199 ... 98332
45th Street Ct NW ... 98335
46th Ave & St ... 98335
46th Avenue Ct NW ... 98335
14500-14899 ... 98332
46th Street Ct NW ... 98335
47th Ave NW ... 98335
12800-14999 ... 98332
47th St NW ... 98335
47th Avenue Ct NW
3700-3799 ... 98335
11900-13999 ... 98332
47th Street Ct NW ... 98335
48th Ave NW ... 98335
14600-14899 ... 98332
48th St NW ... 98335
48th Avenue Ct NW
3600-3699 ... 98335
14400-14699 ... 98332
48th Street Ct NW ... 98335
49th Ave NW ... 98335
49th St NW ... 98335
49th Avenue Ct NW
4000-4299 ... 98335
9300-14399 ... 98332
49th Street Ct NW ... 98335

50th Ave NW ... 98335
10000-10899 ... 98332
50th St NW ... 98335
50th Avenue Ct NW ... 98332
50th Street Ct NW ... 98335
51st Ave NW ... 98335
11300-14399 ... 98332
51st St NW ... 98335
51st Avenue Ct NW
3800-5599 ... 98335
14400-14699 ... 98332
51st Street Ct NW ... 98335
52nd Ave NW ... 98335
13600-14099 ... 98332
52nd Pl ... 98335
52nd St NW ... 98335
52nd Avenue Ct NW
4000-4199 ... 98335
11600-11699 ... 98332
52nd Street Ct NW ... 98335
53rd Ave NW ... 98335
12800-13699 ... 98332
53rd St NW ... 98335
53rd Avenue Ct NW ... 98332
53rd Street Ct NW ... 98335
54th Ave NW ... 98335
9200-14599 ... 98332
54th St NW ... 98335
54th Street Ct NW ... 98335
55th Ave NW ... 98335
13400-14199 ... 98332
55th St NW ... 98335
55th Ave Ct NW ... 98332
55th Avenue Ct NW ... 98335
55th Street Ct NW ... 98335
56th Ave NW ... 98335
13800-14399 ... 98332
56th St NW ... 98335
56th Avenue Ct NW ... 98335
56th Street Ct NW ... 98335
57th Ave NW ... 98335
8000-14399 ... 98332
57th St NW ... 98335
57th Avenue Ct NW ... 98335
57th Street Ct NW ... 98335
58th Ave NW ... 98335
58th Ave NW ... 98335
8000-14599 ... 98332
58th St NW ... 98335
58th Street Ct NW ... 98335
59th Ave NW ... 98335
12200-12599 ... 98332
59th St NW ... 98335
59th Avenue Ct NW ... 98332
59th Street Ct NW ... 98335
60th Ave NW ... 98335
10800-11199 ... 98332
60th St NW ... 98335
60th Avenue Ct NW
1600-2999 ... 98335
12900-12999 ... 98332
60th Street Ct NW ... 98335
61st Ave NW ... 98335
8000-11199 ... 98332
61st St NW ... 98335
61st Ave Ct NW ... 98332
61st Avenue Ct NW ... 98335
61st Street Ct NW ... 98335
62nd Ave NW ... 98335
12800-15999 ... 98332
62nd St NW ... 98335
62nd Avenue Ct NW ... 98335
62nd Street Ct NW ... 98335
63rd Ave NW ... 98335
10600-11199 ... 98332
63rd St NW ... 98335
63rd Avenue Ct NW
2400-6117 ... 98335
10800-10899 ... 98332
63rd Street Ct NW ... 98335
64th Ave NW ... 98335
8500-11699 ... 98332
64th St NW ... 98335
64th Avenue Ct NW
3200-3999 ... 98335
10600-12399 ... 98332

64th Street Ct NW ... 98335
65th Ave NW ... 98335
10600-11499 ... 98332
65th St NW ... 98335
65th Avenue Ct NW
2800-3599 ... 98335
10400-13999 ... 98332
65th Street Ct NW ... 98335
66th Ave NW ... 98335
8100-16099 ... 98332
66th St NW ... 98335
66th Avenue Ct NW
2900-7999 ... 98335
11000-15599 ... 98332
67th Ave NW
4101-4197 ... 98335
4199-7799 ... 98335
11223-15899 ... 98332
67th St NW ... 98335
67th Avenue Ct NW
2800-3999 ... 98335
11200-15699 ... 98332
67th Street Ct NW ... 98335
68th Ave NW ... 98335
8900-14399 ... 98332
68th St NW ... 98335
68th Avenue Ct NW
2500-3999 ... 98335
11500-11599 ... 98332
68th Street Ct NW ... 98335
69th Ave NW ... 98335
8800-10199 ... 98332
69th St NW ... 98335
69th Avenue Ct NW ... 98335
69th Street Ct NW ... 98335
70th Ave NW ... 98335
10200-11899 ... 98332
70th St NW ... 98335
70th Avenue Ct NW ... 98335
71st Ave NW ... 98335
8800-11899 ... 98332
71st St NW ... 98335
71st Avenue Ct NW
2400-6399 ... 98335
11600-11699 ... 98332
71st Street Ct NW ... 98335
72nd Ave NW ... 98335
8200-10399 ... 98332
72nd St NW ... 98335
72nd Avenue Ct NW ... 98335
73rd Ave NW ... 98335
73rd Avenue Ct NW ... 98335
9000-9199 ... 98332
73rd Street Ct NW ... 98335
74th Ave NW ... 98335
9200-11299 ... 98332
74th Avenue Ct NW
3600-6399 ... 98335
9700-9799 ... 98332
74th Street Ct NW ... 98335
75th Ave NW ... 98335
8800-9099 ... 98332
75th Avenue Ct NW ... 98335
76th Ave NW ... 98335
8100-8199 ... 98332
76th St NW ... 98335
76th Avenue Ct NW ... 98335
76th Street Ct NW ... 98335
77th Ave NW ... 98335
77th Avenue Ct NW ... 98335
77th Street Ct NW ... 98335
78th Ave NW ... 98332
78th Ave NW ... 98335
14100-14199 ... 98329
78th St NW ... 98335
78th Avenue Ct NW
2700-6699 ... 98335
14100-14199 ... 98329
78th Street Ct NW ... 98335
79th Ave NW ... 98335
14300-14499 ... 98329
79th St NW ... 98335
79th Avenue Ct NW
2500-4709 ... 98335
10100-10199 ... 98332
13400-14199 ... 98329
79th Street Ct NW ... 98335

80th Ave NW ... 98335
10200-10399 ... 98332
80th St NW ... 98335
80th Avenue Ct NW
3000-3499 ... 98335
10100-10199 ... 98332
81st Ave NW ... 98335
81st St NW
2400-2599 ... 98332
7300-7499 ... 98335
81st Avenue Ct NW ... 98335
81st Street Ct NW
2600-5899 ... 98332
7200-7299 ... 98335
82nd Ave NW
6800-7299 ... 98335
8800-10899 ... 98332
13300-16199 ... 98329
82nd St NW ... 98332
82nd Avenue Ct NW
9600-9799 ... 98332
13200-13299 ... 98329
82nd Street Ct NW ... 98332
83rd Ave NW ... 98335
13400-14999 ... 98329
83rd St NW ... 98332
83rd Avenue Ct NW
4000-4299 ... 98335
10000-10099 ... 98332
83rd Street Ct NW ... 98332
84th Ave NW ... 98335
84th St NW ... 98332
84th Avenue Ct NW
7400-7799 ... 98335
9600-9699 ... 98332
14100-15299 ... 98329
84th Street Ct NW ... 98332
85th Ave NW ... 98335
9600-9699 ... 98332
85th St NW ... 98332
85th Avenue Ct NW ... 98329
86th Ave NW ... 98335
86th Ave NW ... 98335
13600-13799 ... 98329
86th St NW ... 98332
86th Avenue Ct NW ... 98335
86th Street Ct NW ... 98332
87th Ave NW ... 98335
14000-14199 ... 98329
87th St NW ... 98332
87th Avenue Ct NW
3700-7299 ... 98335
14000-14199 ... 98329
87th Street Ct NW ... 98332
88th Ave NW ... 98335
13300-15099 ... 98329
88th St NW ... 98332
88th Avenue Ct NW
3000-3199 ... 98335
13600-13999 ... 98329
88th Street Ct NW ... 98332
89th Ave NW ... 98335
8600-8699 ... 98332
89th St NW ... 98332
89th Avenue Ct NW ... 98335
89th Street Ct NW ... 98332
89th Street Court Kp
N ... 98329
90th Ave NW ... 98335
8500-10099 ... 98332
90th Street Ct NW ... 98332
90th Street Court Kp
N ... 98329
90th Street Kp N ... 98329
91st Ave NW ... 98335
13800-14799 ... 98329
91st Avenue Ct NW
2900-3999 ... 98335
13000-13599 ... 98329
92nd Ave NW
3600-4899 ... 98335
14200-14599 ... 98329
92nd St NW ... 98332
92nd Avenue Ct NW
7000-7099 ... 98335
13600-13799 ... 98329
92nd Street Ct NW ... 98332

92nd Street Kp N ... 98329
93rd Ave NW ... 98332
13600-14599 ... 98329
93rd St NW ... 98332
93rd Street Ct NW ... 98332
94th Ave NW ... 98332
12800-15799 ... 98329
94th St NW ... 98332
94th Street Ct NW ... 98332
94th Street Kp N ... 98329
95th Ave NW ... 98329
95th Street Ct NW ... 98332
96th Ave NW ... 98329
96th St NW ... 98332
96th Avenue Ct NW ... 98329
96th Street Kp N ... 98329
97th Ave NW ... 98335
12600-14399 ... 98329
97th St NW ... 98332
97th Avenue Ct NW ... 98329
97th Street Ct NW ... 98332
97th Street Kp N ... 98329
98th Ave NW ... 98335
98th Avenue Ct NW ... 98335
12200-13999 ... 98329
98th Street Ct NW ... 98332
98th Street Court Kp
N ... 98329
99th Ave NW ... 98335
13200-13299 ... 98329
99th St NW ... 98332
99th Avenue Ct NW
5000-5199 ... 98335
13700-13999 ... 98329
99th Street Ct NW ... 98332
99th Street Court Kp
N ... 98329
100th Street Kp N ... 98329
100th Street Court Kp
N ... 98329
100th Ave NW
5200-5599 ... 98335
13200-15899 ... 98329
100th Street Ct NW ... 98332
100th Avenue Ct NW
4200-4899 ... 98335
13800-13899 ... 98329
101st Street Kp N ... 98329
101st Avenue Ct NW ... 98335
101st Street Ct NW ... 98332
101st Avenue Ct NW
12500-13999 ... 98329
101st St NW ... 98332
102nd Street Kp N ... 98329
102nd Ave NW ... 98335
102nd Avenue Ct NW ... 98329
102nd Street Ct NW ... 98332
102nd St NW ... 98332
103rd Street Court Kp
N ... 98329
103rd Street Kp N ... 98329
103rd Avenue Ct NW ... 98335
103rd Street Ct NW ... 98332
103rd Avenue Ct NW
13900-14299 ... 98329
104th Street Court Kp
N ... 98329
104th Street Kp N ... 98329
104th Avenue Ct NW ... 98335
13300-14399 ... 98329
104th St NW ... 98332
105th Street Court Kp
N ... 98329
105th Street Kp N ... 98329
105th Ave NW ... 98335
12500-13799 ... 98329
105th Street Ct NW ... 98332
105th Avenue Ct NW
4824-5199 ... 98335
13300-13499 ... 98329
105th St NW ... 98332
106th Street Court Kp
N ... 98329
106th Street Kp N ... 98329
106th Ave NW ... 98335
106th Avenue Ct NW ... 98329

106th Street Ct NW ... 98332
106th St NW ... 98332
107th Street Kp N ... 98329
107th Street Court Kp
N ... 98329
107th Street Ct NW ... 98332
107th Avenue Ct NW ... 98329
107th St NW ... 98332
108th Street Court Kp
N ... 98329
108th Avenue Ct NW ... 98329
108th St NW ... 98332
109th Street Court Kp
N ... 98329
109th Street Kp N ... 98329
109th Ave NW ... 98329
109th Street Ct NW ... 98332
109th St NW ... 98332
110th Street Kp N ... 98329
110th Street Court Kp
N ... 98329
110th Ave NW ... 98329
110th Street Ct NW ... 98332
110th St NW ... 98332
111th Street Court Kp
N ... 98329
111th Avenue Ct NW ... 98329
111th Street Ct NW ... 98332
111th St NW ... 98332
112th Street Kp N ... 98329
112th Ave NW ... 98329
112th Avenue Ct NW ... 98335
112th Street Ct NW ... 98332
112th St NW ... 98332
113th Street Kp N ... 98329
113th Ave NW ... 98329
113th Street Ct NW ... 98332
114th Street Kp N ... 98329
114th Street Court Kp
N ... 98329
114th Street Ct NW ... 98332
114th Avenue Ct NW ... 98329
114th St NW ... 98332
115th Street Court Kp
N ... 98329
115th Street Kp N ... 98329
115th Ave NW ... 98335
12800-13999 ... 98329
115th Street Ct NW ... 98332
115th St NW ... 98332
116th Street Court Kp
N ... 98329
116th Street Kp N ... 98329
116th Ave NW ... 98329
116th Avenue Ct NW ... 98335
116th Street Ct NW
1100-6399 ... 98332
116th Avenue Ct NW
11100-11399 ... 98329
116th Street Ct NW
12300-12599 ... 98329
117th Street Court Kp
N ... 98329
117th Street Kp N ... 98329
117th Ave NW ... 98335
11800-13399 ... 98329
117th Street Ct NW ... 98332
117th St NW ... 98332
118th Street Kp N ... 98329
118th Ave NW ... 98329
118th Street Ct NW ... 98332
118th St NW ... 98332
119th Avenue Court Kp
N ... 98329
119th Street Kp N ... 98329
119th Street Court Kp
N ... 98329
119th Street Ct NW ... 98332
119th St NW ... 98332
120th Street Court Kp
N ... 98329
120th Street Kp N ... 98329
120th Avenue Court Kp
N ... 98329
120th Avenue Kp N ... 98329
120th Street Ct NW ... 98332

120th St NW ... 98332
121st Avenue Kp N ... 98329
121st Street Kp N ... 98329
121st Avenue Court Kp N ... 98329
121st Street Ct NW ... 98332
121st St NW ... 98332
122nd Avenue Kp N ... 98329
122nd Street Kp N ... 98329
122nd Avenue Court Kp N ... 98329
122nd Street Ct NW ... 98332
122nd St NW ... 98332
10200-10599 ... 98329
123rd Street Court Kp N ... 98329
123rd Street Kp N ... 98329
123rd Avenue Kp N ... 98329
123rd Street Ct NW ... 98332
11600-11699 ... 98329
123rd St NW ... 98332
10200-10599 ... 98329
124th Avenue Court Kp N ... 98329
124th Street Kp N ... 98329
124th Avenue Kp N ... 98329
124th Street Ct NW ... 98332
124th St NW ... 98332
11100-11399 ... 98329
125th Avenue Kp N ... 98329
125th Street Kp N ... 98329
125th Street Ct NW ... 98332
125th St NW ... 98332
10200-10299 ... 98329
126th Avenue Kp N ... 98329
126th Street Kp N ... 98329
126th Street Ct NW ... 98332
9600-9699 ... 98329
126th St NW ... 98332
10200-10399 ... 98329
127th Avenue Kp N ... 98329
127th Street Ct NW ... 98332
9600-10099 ... 98329
127th St NW ... 98329
128th Street Kp N ... 98329
128th Street Court Kp N ... 98329
128th Avenue Court Kp N ... 98329
128th Avenue Kp N ... 98329
128th Street Ct NW ... 98329
128th St NW
2200-3699 ... 98332
9400-10499 ... 98329
129th Street Court Kp N ... 98329
129th Avenue Kp N ... 98329
129th Street Kp N ... 98329
129th Street Ct NW ... 98332
9300-9399 ... 98329
129th St NW ... 98332
9700-9799 ... 98329
130th Street Court Kp N ... 98329
130th Avenue Kp N ... 98329
130th Street Kp N ... 98329
130th Street Ct & St ... 98332
130th St NW
3500-3799 ... 98332
10600-10899 ... 98329
131st Street Court Kp N ... 98329
131st Avenue Court Kp N ... 98329
131st Street Kp N ... 98329
131st Street Ct NW ... 98332
131st St NW ... 98332
8300-10999 ... 98329
132nd Street Court Kp N ... 98329
132nd Avenue Kp N ... 98329
132nd Street Kp N ... 98329
132nd Street Ct NW ... 98329
132nd St NW ... 98332
9300-9999 ... 98329
133rd Street Court Kp N ... 98329
133rd Avenue Kp N ... 98329
133rd Street Ct NW ... 98332
133rd St NW ... 98332
10000-11199 ... 98329
134th Street Court Kp N ... 98329
134th Avenue Court Kp N ... 98329
134th Avenue Kp N ... 98329
134th Street Kp N ... 98329
134th Street Ct NW ... 98332
9400-11499 ... 98329
134th St NW ... 98332
135th Street Court Kp N ... 98329
135th Street Kp N ... 98329
135th Avenue Kp N ... 98329
135th Street Ct NW ... 98332
7800-7999 ... 98329
135th St NW ... 98332
8100-10499 ... 98329
136th Street Court Kp N ... 98329
136th Avenue Kp N ... 98329
136th Avenue Court Kp N ... 98329
136th Street Ct NW ... 98332
9100-9499 ... 98329
136th St NW ... 98332
10600-11199 ... 98329
137th Avenue Kp N ... 98329
137th Street Kp N ... 98329
137th Street Ct NW ... 98332
9100-9199 ... 98329
137th St NW ... 98332
8600-11099 ... 98329
138th Street Court Kp N ... 98329
138th Avenue Kp N ... 98329
138th Street Kp N ... 98329
138th Street Ct NW ... 98332
9600-9699 ... 98329
138th St NW ... 98332
9000-11699 ... 98329
139th Street Court Kp N ... 98329
139th Avenue Kp N ... 98329
139th Street Ct NW ... 98332
7500-7699 ... 98329
139th St NW ... 98332
9800-10199 ... 98329
140th Street Kp N ... 98329
140th Avenue Court Kp N ... 98329
140th Avenue Kp N ... 98329
140th Street Ct NW ... 98332
11600-11699 ... 98329
140th St NW ... 98332
9600-9799 ... 98329
141st Street Court Kp N ... 98329
141st Avenue Kp N ... 98329
141st Avenue Court Kp N ... 98329
141st Street Kp N ... 98329
141st Street Ct NW ... 98332
11400-11799 ... 98329
141st St NW ... 98332
142nd Street Kp N ... 98329
142nd Avenue Kp N ... 98329
142nd Street Ct NW ... 98329
142nd St NW ... 98332
9600-9699 ... 98329
143rd Avenue Court Kp N ... 98329
143rd Street Court Kp N ... 98329
143rd Street Ct NW ... 98332
7800-11799 ... 98329
143rd St NW ... 98332
7500-8399 ... 98329
144th Avenue Kp N ... 98329
144th Street Kp N ... 98329
144th Street Ct NW ... 98332
9000-9399 ... 98329
144th St NW ... 98332
7500-11699 ... 98329
145th Avenue Kp N ... 98329
145th Street Kp N ... 98329
145th Street Ct Kp N ... 98329
145th Street Ct NW ... 98332
7900-9699 ... 98329
145th St NW ... 98332
7600-8799 ... 98329
146th Avenue Court Kp N ... 98329
146th Avenue Kp N ... 98329
146th Street Kp N ... 98329
146th Street Ct NW ... 98332
146th St NW ... 98332
9000-9399 ... 98329
147th Street Kp N ... 98329
147th Avenue Kp N ... 98329
147th Street Ct NW ... 98332
9000-9299 ... 98329
147th St NW ... 98332
8804-8917 ... 98329
148th Avenue Kp N ... 98329
148th Avenue Court Kp N ... 98329
148th Street Ct NW ... 98332
7500-7599 ... 98329
148th St NW ... 98332
8600-8799 ... 98329
149th Avenue Court Kp N ... 98329
149th Avenue Kp N ... 98329
149th Street Ct NW ... 98332
9400-9699 ... 98329
149th St NW
3000-4999 ... 98332
7900-11799 ... 98329
150th Avenue Kp N ... 98329
150th Street Kp N ... 98329
150th Street Ct NW ... 98332
150th St NW
3500-4599 ... 98332
8300-8799 ... 98329
151st Avenue Kp N ... 98329
151st Street Ct NW ... 98332
8100-8199 ... 98329
151st St NW ... 98332
7900-8099 ... 98329
152nd Street Kp N ... 98329
152nd Street Court Kp N ... 98329
152nd Street Ct NW ... 98332
153rd Street Court Kp N ... 98329
153rd Street Ct NW ... 98332
153rd St NW ... 98332
8200-8599 ... 98329
154th Street Kp N ... 98329
154th Avenue Kp N ... 98329
154th Street Ct NW ... 98332
154th St NW ... 98332
8500-8599 ... 98329
155th Street Kp N ... 98329
155th Street Ct NW ... 98332
155th St NW ... 98332
8400-8499 ... 98329
156th Avenue Kp N ... 98329
156th Avenue Court Kp N ... 98329
156th Street Kp N ... 98329
156th St NW ... 98332
157th Street Ct NW ... 98332
7900-8099 ... 98329
157th St NW ... 98332
158th Avenue Kp N ... 98329
158th Street Kp N ... 98329
158th Street Ct NW ... 98329
158th St NW
4400-4599 ... 98332
9700-9799 ... 98329
159th Street Kp N ... 98329
159th Avenue Kp N ... 98329
159th St NW ... 98332
9500-10099 ... 98329
160th Street Kp N ... 98329
160th Avenue Kp N ... 98329
160th St NW ... 98332
8000-8399 ... 98329
161st Avenue Kp N ... 98329
161st St NW ... 98329
162nd Avenue Kp N ... 98329
162nd St NW ... 98329
163rd Avenue Kp N ... 98329
163rd Avenue Court Kp N ... 98329
163rd St NW ... 98329
164th Avenue Kp N ... 98329
164th St NW ... 98329
166th Avenue Kp N ... 98329
166th Street Ct NW ... 98329
166th St NW ... 98329
167th Avenue Kp N ... 98329
168th Avenue Kp N ... 98329
169th Avenue Kp N ... 98329
171st Avenue Kp N ... 98329
172nd Avenue Court Kp N ... 98329
172nd Avenue Kp N ... 98329
173rd Avenue Kp N ... 98329
174th Avenue Kp N ... 98329
175th Avenue Kp N ... 98329
176th Avenue Kp N ... 98329
176th Avenue Court Kp N ... 98329
177th Avenue Kp N ... 98329
178th Avenue Kp N ... 98329
179th Avenue Kp N ... 98329
180th Avenue Kp N ... 98329
180th Avenue Court Kp N ... 98329
182nd Avenue Court Kp N ... 98329
182nd Avenue Kp N ... 98329
184th Avenue Kp N ... 98329
186th Avenue Kp N ... 98329
187th Avenue Kp N ... 98329
188th Avenue Court Kp N ... 98329
188th Avenue Kp N ... 98329
189th Avenue Court Kp N ... 98329
189th Avenue Kp N ... 98329
190th Avenue Kp N ... 98329
191st Avenue Kp N ... 98329
192nd Avenue Court Kp N ... 98329
193rd Avenue Kp N ... 98329
194th Avenue Kp N ... 98329
196th Avenue Kp N ... 98329

ISSAQUAH WA

General Delivery ... 98027

POST OFFICE BOXES MAIN OFFICE STATIONS AND BRANCHES

Box No.s
All PO Boxes ... 98027

NAMED STREETS

Aires Pl NW ... 98027
NW & NE Alder Ct, Pl & St ... 98027
Almak Ct NW ... 98027
Alpen Glow Pl NW ... 98027
NW Alpine Crest Way ... 98027
Alpine Ridge Pl NW ... 98027
SE Andrews St ... 98027
Bear Ridge Ct & Dr ... 98027
NW Bernina Ct ... 98027
Big Bear Pl NW ... 98027
Big Tree Dr NW ... 98027
NW & NE Birch Pl & St ... 98027
SE Black Nugget Rd ... 98029
NE Blakely Dr ... 98029
NW Boulder Pl ... 98027
NW Boulder Way Dr ... 98027
NE Brooklyn Loop ... 98029
Brookside Dr SE ... 98027
SE Bush St ... 98027
Cabin Creek Ln SW ... 98027
Capella Ct & Dr ... 98027
Cedar Grove Rd SE ... 98027
SW Cedarglade Dr ... 98027
NW Cervinia Ct ... 98027
Champery Pl NW ... 98027
Chelsea Ave NE ... 98029
NW Cherry Pl ... 98027
Circle SE ... 98029
SE & SW Clark St ... 98027
Col De Vars Pl NW ... 98027
Cougar Mountain Dr & Ln NW ... 98027
Cougar Ridge Rd NW ... 98027
NW Coyote Creek Ln ... 98027
NE Creek Way ... 98029
Crenchar Ave SE ... 98027
NE Crescent Dr ... 98029
SE Croston Ln ... 98027
SE Crystal Creek Cir ... 98027
Cyprus Ct NW ... 98027
NE Daphne St ... 98029
NE Darby Ln ... 98029
SE Darst St ... 98027
NW Datewood Ct & Dr NW ... 98027
NE Davis Loop ... 98029
NE Dayton Ct ... 98029
NE Denny Way ... 98029
NE Discovery Cir, Dr & Walk NE ... 98029
NE & NW Dogwood St ... 98027
SE Donnelly Ln ... 98027
Dorado Dr NW ... 98027
Douglas Ct SW ... 98027
SE Duthie Hill Rd ... 98029
NE Eagle Way ... 98029
NE Eaton Ln ... 98029
SW Edgewood Ct ... 98027
Eiger Pl NW ... 98027
SW Ellerwood St ... 98027
NE Ellis Dr ... 98029
Evans Ln & St ... 98027
NW Everwood Ct & Dr NW ... 98027
NW Fall Line Ln ... 98027
NE Falls Dr ... 98029
NW Far Country Ln ... 98027
SW Fernwood St ... 98027
NW Firwood Blvd ... 98027
Forest Dr & Pl ... 98027
SW Francis Ln ... 98027
NE Franklin Dr ... 98029
Front St N & S ... 98027
SW Gibson Ln ... 98027
NE & NW Gilman Blvd ... 98027
Glenwood Ct & Pl ... 98027
NW Goode Pl ... 98027
Gran Paradiso Pl NW ... 98027
SE Grand Ridge Dr ... 98029
Greenwich Ave NE ... 98029
Greenwood Blvd SW ... 98027
NW Harmony Way ... 98027
NE Harrison Ct, Dr, St & Way NE ... 98029
Hawthorne Sq & St ... 98029
SW Hepler Ln ... 98027
NE Hickory Ln ... 98029
NW Hidden Ln ... 98027
NE High St ... 98029
SE High Point Way ... 98027
Highland Cir, Ln & Ter ... 98029
Highlands Dr NE ... 98029
NE Highmoor Ct ... 98029
Highwood Dr SW ... 98027
Hillside Dr SE ... 98027
NW Holly St ... 98027
Honeywood Ct & Pl ... 98027
NE Huckleberry Cir, Ct & Ln ... 98029
Idylwood Dr SW ... 98027
Indigo Pl NW ... 98027
NE Ingram St ... 98029
Inneswood Dr & Pl ... 98027
NE Iris St ... 98029
Isola Pl NW ... 98027
SE Issaquah Fall City Rd ... 98029
Issaquah Hobart Rd SE ... 98027
Issaquah Pine Lake Rd SE ... 98029
NE Iverson Ln ... 98029
NE Ivy Way ... 98029
NE Jade St ... 98029
James Bush Rd NW ... 98027
NE Jared Ct ... 98029
Jasmine Pl NW ... 98027
NE Jewell Ln ... 98029
NE Jonquil Ln ... 98029
NE Joshua Tree Ln ... 98029
Judson Ln NE ... 98029
NE Julep St ... 98029
NE Juneberry Ct, Ln & St NE ... 98029
Jung Frau Pl NW ... 98027
NE & NW Juniper St ... 98027
Kalmia Ct & Pl ... 98027
NE Katsura St ... 98029
NE Kelsey Ln ... 98029
NE Kenilworth Ln ... 98029
NE Kensington Ct ... 98029
NE Kenyon Ct ... 98029
NE Keystone Ct ... 98029
NE Killian Ln ... 98029
Kincaid Walk ... 98029
Kirkwood Pl ... 98029
Klahanie Blvd & Dr SE ... 98029
NW Konigs Ct ... 98027
SE Kramer Pl ... 98027
NE Kyle Ct ... 98029
NW Lac Leman Dr ... 98027
Lake Dr ... 98027
E Lake Sammamish Pkwy SE ... 98029
W Lake Sammamish Pkwy SE ... 98027
E Lake Sammamish Shore Ln SE ... 98075
NE Larchmount Dr & St NE ... 98029
NE Larkspur Ln ... 98029
NE Laurel Ct ... 98029
NE Laurel Crest Ln ... 98029
NE Laurel Wood Ln ... 98029
SE Lewis Ln & St SE ... 98027
Lingering Pine Ct, Dr & Ln ... 98027
NW Locust St ... 98027
NE Logan St ... 98029
Longmire Ct NE ... 98029
NE Madison Way ... 98029
NE Magnolia St ... 98029
NW Mall St ... 98027
NW Maple St ... 98027
NE Marion Ln ... 98029
NE Marquette Way ... 98029
NW Marseille Ct ... 98027
Matterhorn Pl NW ... 98027
SE May Valley Rd ... 98027
NE Meadow Way ... 98029
Mine Hill Rd SW ... 98027
Mirrormont Blvd, Dr, Pl & Way ... 98027
Mont Blanc Pl NW ... 98027
NE Monterey Ln ... 98029
NW Montreux Dr ... 98027
NW Moraine Pl ... 98027
NE Morgan Ln ... 98029
SW Mount Baker Dr ... 98027
SW Mount Cedar Dr ... 98027
Mount Defiance Cir SW ... 98027
Mount Everest Ln SW ... 98027
Mount Fury Cir SW ... 98027
Mount Grenville Pl SW ... 98027
Mountain View Ln NW ... 98027
Mountainside Dr SW ... 98027
Mt Hood Dr SW ... 98027
Mt Index Pl SW ... 98027
Mt Jupiter Dr SW ... 98027
Mt Kenya Dr SW ... 98027
Mt Logan Dr SW ... 98027
SW Mt Markham Pl ... 98027
Mt Mckinley Dr SW ... 98027
Mt Olympus Dr NW & SW ... 98027
Mt Park Blvd SW ... 98027
SW Mt Pilchuck Ave & Pl NW & SW ... 98027
Mt Quay Dr NW ... 98027
Mt Rainier Pl NW ... 98027
Mt Si Pl NW ... 98027
Mt View Pl SW ... 98027
Mulberry St & Walk NE ... 98029
NE Natalie Way ... 98029
NE Nelson Ln ... 98029
SE & SW Newport Way NW & SW ... 98027
NE Newton Ln ... 98029
NE Noble St ... 98029
NE Northstar Ln ... 98029
NE Norton Ln ... 98029
Oakcreek Pl NW ... 98027
NW Oakcrest Dr ... 98027
Oakhill Pl NW ... 98027
Oakwood Pl NW ... 98027
Oberland Pl NW ... 98027
SE Old Black Nugget Rd ... 98029
NW Pacific Elm Dr ... 98027
NW Pacific Yew Pl ... 98027
NE Park Dr ... 98029
NW Pebble Ln ... 98027
Pickering Pl NW ... 98027
Pine Cone Dr & Pl ... 98027
Pine Crest Cir NE ... 98029
Pine View Dr NW ... 98027
NW Poplar Way ... 98027
SE Preston Way ... 98027
Preston Fall City Rd SE ... 98027
Providence Point Dr & Pl ... 98029
Quinalt Ct SW ... 98027
Rainier Blvd N & S ... 98027
Renton Issaquah Rd SE ... 98027
Ridge View Ave NE ... 98029
Ridgewood Cir & Pl ... 98027
Saddleback Loop Way NW ... 98027
NW Sammamish Rd ... 98027
Shangrila Way NW ... 98027
Shy Bear Way NW ... 98027
Sierra Ct SW ... 98027
Sky Country Way NW ... 98027
Skyridge Rd NW ... 98027
NW Spring Fork Ln ... 98027
Squak Mountain Loop & Rd SW & SE ... 98027
NW Stoney Creek Dr ... 98027
SE Summerhill Ln ... 98029
Summerhill Ridge Dr NW ... 98027
Sunrise Pl SE & SW ... 98027
E & W Sunset Ct & Way NW ... 98027
SE Sycamore Dr, Ln & Pl SE ... 98027
SE Sycamore Creek Ln ... 98027
NW Talus Dr ... 98027
SE Tiger Mountain Rd SE ... 98027
Tiger View Ct NW ... 98027
Timber Creek Dr NW ... 98027
Timber Ridge Way NW ... 98027
Timberview Ct SW ... 98027
Upper Preston Rd SE ... 98027
Valley View Pl SW ... 98027

NW Varese Ct 98027
NW Village Park Dr 98027
Wilderness Peak Dr NW 98027
Wildwood Blvd SW 98027
NE Williamsburg Loop .. 98029
Yorindel Ave SE 98029

NUMBERED STREETS

1st Ave & Pl NE, NW & SE 98027
2nd Ave & Pl NE, NW & SE 98027
3rd Ave NE
2-198 98027
200-399 98027
800-999 98029
3rd Ave NW 98027
3rd Ct NE 98029
3rd Ct NW 98027
3rd Pl NE 98029
3rd Pl NW 98027
4th Ave NE 98029
4th Ave NW 98027
4th Pl SE 98027
5th Ave NE 98027
5th Ave NW 98027
5th Ave SE 98027
5th Pl NE 98029
6th Ave NE
2-198 98027
700-899 98029
6th Ave NW 98027
6th Ave SE 98027
7th Ave NW 98027
8th Ave NE 98029
9th Ct & Pl 98029
10th Ave NE 98029
10th Ave NW 98027
10th Ct NE 98029
10th Ln NE 98029
10th Loop NE 98029
10th Pl NE 98029
10th Way NE 98029
11th Ave NE 98029
11th Ave NW 98027
11th Ln NE 98029
11th Pl NW 98027
12th Ave NE 98029
12th Ave NW 98027
12th Ct NE 98029
14th Ave, Ct, Ln & Pl NE 98029
15th Ave NE 98029
15th Pl NW 98027
16th Ave, Ct & Ln 98029
17th Ave NE 98029
17th Ave NW 98027
17th Ct NE 98029
17th Pl NE 98029
18th Ave NE 98029
18th Ave NW 98027
18th Pl NE 98029
19th Ave NW 98027
20th Ave NE 98029
22nd Ave & Ct 98029
23rd Ln & Pl 98029
24th Ave, Ct & Pl 98029
25th Ave, Pl & Walk 98029
26th Ave, Ct & Walk 98029
27th Ln NE 98029
28th Ave & Pl 98029
29th Ave, Ct, Ln & Pl NE 98029
30th Ave, Ct, Ln & Pl NE 98029
31st Ave & Ln 98029
SE 32nd Ave, St & Way NE 98029
SE 33rd Ave & St NE 98029
SE 34th Ave & Pl NE 98029
SE 35th Ave, Pl & St NE 98029
36th Ct, Ln & Pl 98029
37th Pl, St, Ter & Way 98029
38th Ct, Pl, St & Ter 98029
39th Ct, Pl, St & Way 98029
40th Ct, Dr, Ln, Pl & St 98029
SE 41st Ct
18600-18699 98027
25500-25999 98029
SE 41st Dr 98029
SE 41st Ln
18131-18167 98027
22100-24399 98029
SE 41st Pl
18150-18166 98027
18168-18199 98027
23900-25899 98029
SE 41st St 98029
SE 42nd Ct 98029
SE 42nd Dr 98029
SE 42nd Ln 98029
SE 42nd Pl
18100-18999 98027
21200-25499 98029
SE 42nd St
18700-18899 98027
23900-26299 98029
SE 42nd Ter 98029
SE 42nd Way 98029
SE 43rd Ct
18200-18299 98027
22700-24299 98029
SE 43rd Ln 98029
SE 43rd Pl
18200-19299 98027
24200-25199 98029
SE 43rd St
18700-19299 98027
24900-24999 98029
SE 43rd Way 98029
SE 44th Ct
18900-18999 98027
23800-24699 98029
SE 44th Ln 98029
SE 44th Pl
18700-18999 98027
22600-24499 98029
SE 44th St
18400-18799 98027
24200-24699 98029
SE 44th Way 98027
SE 45th Ct
19200-19299 98027
24700-24799 98029
SE 45th Ln 98029
SE 45th Pl
18700-19299 98027
22500-24799 98029
SE 45th St
18500-19199 98027
22500-24599 98029
SE 45th Way 98029
SE 46th Ct 98029
SE 46th Pl
19200-19299 98027
23800-24799 98029
SE 46th St
19200-19299 98027
24400-24699 98029
SE 46th Ter 98029
SE 46th Trce 98029
SE 46th Way
18800-19299 98027
24200-24399 98029
SE 47th Ct 98029
SE 47th Pl
19100-19199 98027
23800-24299 98029
SE 47th St
19200-19399 98027
24000-24399 98029
SE 48th Pl
19200-19299 98027
22400-22699 98029
SE 48th St 98029
SE 49th Pl 98029
SE 49th St
19200-19299 98027
23400-23599 98029
SE 50th St 98029
SE 51st Pl 98029
SE 51st St
19500-19599 98027
22000-22799 98029
52nd Ln & St 98029
SE 53rd St 98029
SE 54th Pl 98029
SE 54th St 98027
SE 56th St
19000-22199 98027
22400-24799 98029
SE 57th Pl 98027
SE 57th St 98029
SE 58th Pl 98029
SE 58th St
18400-18699 98027
23000-23299 98029
28400-28599 98027
SE 59th St
23800-23899 98029
28400-28699 98027
SE 60th St
17900-22099 98027
24200-24299 98029
28400-28599 98027
SE 61st St 98027
62nd Pl & St 98027
63rd Pl & St 98027
64th Pl, St & Way 98027
SE 65th Pl 98027
SE 66th St 98027
SE 67th St 98027
SE 68th St 98027
SE 74th St 98027
SE 75th St 98027
SE 76th Pl 98027
SE 78th St 98027
SE 79th St 98027
SE 82nd St 98027
SE 83rd Pl 98027
SE 84th St 98027
SE 86th St 98027
SE 87th St 98027
SE 88th St 98027
SE 93rd St 98027
SE 95th St 98027
SE 97th St 98027
SE 98th Pl 98027
SE 102nd St 98027
103rd Pl & St 98027
SE 104th St 98027
SE 105th Pl 98027
SE 106th Pl 98027
SE 108th St 98027
SE 109th St 98027
SE 110th St 98027
111th Pl & St 98027
SE 113th St 98027
114th Pl & St 98027
SE 115th St 98027
SE 116th Pl 98027
SE 118th St 98027
119th Ct & St 98027
SE 121st St 98027
SE 122nd St 98027
SE 123rd St 98027
SE 124th St 98027
125th Pl & St 98027
SE 126th St 98027
SE 127th St 98027
128th Pl & Way 98027
SE 130th St 98027
132nd Pl, St & Way 98027
133rd St & Way 98027
SE 134th St 98027
135th Ct & St 98027
136th Ct & St 98027
137th Pl & St 98027
138th Pl & St 98027
SE 139th Ct 98027
SE 141st Ct 98027
SE 144th Pl 98027
SE 146th St 98027
147th Pl & St 98027
SE 148th St 98027
SE 149th St 98027
SE 150th St 98027
SE 152nd St 98027
SE 153rd Pl 98027
154th Pl & St 98027
SE 155th Pl 98027
156th Pl & St 98027
SE 157th St 98027
SE 158th St 98027
159th Pl & St 98027
160th Pl & St 98027
162nd Pl & St 98027
SE 163rd Pl 98027
164th Pl & St 98027
SE 165th St 98027
166th Pl & St 98027
167th Pl & St 98027
SE 168th St 98027
SE 169th St 98027
SE 170th St 98027
SE 171st St 98027
SE 172nd St 98027
SE 175th Pl 98027
181st Ave & Pl 98027
182nd Ave & Pl 98027
184th Ave SE 98027
185th Ave & Pl 98027
186th Ave & Pl 98027
187th Ave & Pl 98027
SE 188th Ave & St SE 98027
189th Ave & Pl 98027
190th Ave SE 98027
191st Ave & Pl 98027
SE 192nd Ave, Ct, Ln, Pl & St SE 98027
SE 193rd Ave, Pl & St SE 98027
194th Ave & Ln 98027
195th Pl SE 98027
SE 196th Pl 98027
198th Ave SE 98027
199th Ave & Pl 98027
200th Ave SE 98027
201st Ave SE 98027
202nd Ave & Pl 98027
204th Pl SE 98027
205th Ct & Pl 98027
206th Ct & Pl 98027
207th Ave & Ct 98027
208th Pl SE 98027
209th Ave SE 98027
210th Ct & Pl 98027
212th Ave SE 98027
213th Pl SE 98029
214th Pl SE 98029
217th Ave SE 98027
218th Ave SE 98027
219th Ave SE 98027
220th Ave SE 98029
220th Pl SE
4000-4299 98029
5800-5999 98027
221st Ct SE 98029
221st Pl SE
4100-4299 98029
5600-6099 98027
223rd Ave SE 98027
223rd Pl SE 98029
224th Ave SE 98027
224th Ct SE 98029
224th Ln SE 98029
224th Pl SE 98029
225th Pl SE 98029
226th Pl SE 98029
6500-6599 98027
226th Ter SE 98029
227th Ave SE 98029
228th Ave SE 98029
14000-14299 98027
229th Ave SE
5100-6499 98029
12900-15399 98027
229th Dr SE 98027
230th Ave SE 98029
6600-12798 98027
231st Ave SE
5300-5699 98029
12900-15499 98027
231st Pl SE 98027
232nd Ave SE
5000-5799 98029
13800-14099 98027
233rd Ave, Pl & Way 98027
234th Ave SE 98027
235th Ave SE 98029
16700-16799 98027
235th Pl SE
5100-5299 98029
13200-13299 98027
236th Ave SE
4900-4999 98029
10400-16399 98027
236th Pl SE 98027
237th Ave SE 98027
237th Pl SE 98027
237th Ter SE 98029
238th Ave SE
5600-5799 98029
15100-15199 98027
238th Ct SE 98029
238th Ln SE 98029
238th Pl SE 98029
238th Way SE
4600-4699 98029
9600-10599 98027
239th Ave SE
3200-5899 98029
12800-16799 98027
239th Ln SE 98027
239th Pl SE
4000-4396 98029
14700-14999 98027
240th Ave SE 98029
9200-14199 98027
240th Pl SE
3700-5099 98029
10300-10499 98027
241st Ave SE
3200-4799 98029
16400-16499 98027
241st Ct SE 98029
241st Pl SE
3400-3699 98029
13600-14199 98027
242nd Ave SE
3800-4999 98029
13200-13299 98027
242nd Pl SE
4300-4399 98029
13200-13299 98027
243rd Ave, Cir, Ct, Ln & Pl SE 98029
244th Ave SE 98027
244th Ln SE
4100-4199 98029
13300-13398 98027
244th Pl SE
4100-4899 98029
16600-16699 98027
245th Ave SE
3700-4399 98029
14600-15099 98027
245th Ct SE 98029
245th Ln SE 98029
245th Pl SE 98029
246th Ave SE
3600-4599 98029
12900-12900 98027
12902-13799 98027
246th Ct SE 98029
246th Pl SE
3600-4699 98029
14200-16699 98027
247th Ave SE 98029
247th Pl SE
4500-5499 98029
14700-14799 98027
248th Ave SE
3600-3799 98029
13100-13899 98027
248th Ct SE 98029
248th Ln SE 98029
248th Pl SE
3601-5599 98029
14200-14299 98027
249th Ave SE
4000-4399 98029
13300-15799 98027
249th Ct SE 98029
249th Ter SE 98029
250th Ave SE 98029
250th Pl SE
4200-4299 98029
13000-14899 98027
251st Ave SE 98027
251st Pl SE
4000-4099 98029
14900-14999 98027
252nd Ave SE
4000-4699 98029
13300-16699 98027
252nd Pl SE
3500-4399 98029
13800-14099 98027
253rd Ave SE 98027
253rd Ct SE 98029
254th Ave SE
3500-3699 98029
14400-17199 98027
254th Pl SE 98029
255th Ave SE 98027
255th Ln SE
3500-3699 98029
14600-14699 98027
255th Pl SE 98029
256th Ave SE
4400-4499 98029
14900-15899 98027
257th Ave, Ct & Pl 98029
258th Ave SE 98029
258th Ave SE 98029
14300-16399 98027
258th Pl SE 98027
258th Way SE 98029
259th Ave SE
3900-4199 98029
15900-16099 98027
260th Ave SE 98029
14400-16699 98027
261st Ave SE 98027
262nd Ave SE 98029
14400-15199 98027
262nd Pl SE 98029
263rd Ave SE 98027
264th Pl SE 98027
266th Ave SE 98027
266th Ct SE 98029
268th Ave SE 98027
268th Pl SE 98029
269th Ave SE 98027
270th Ave SE 98029
270th Ave SE 98029
7900-17499 98027
270th Pl SE 98029
271st Ave SE
2400-2699 98029
7500-7599 98027
272nd Ave SE 98027
273rd Ave SE 98029
14500-14599 98027
274th Ave SE
3600-3999 98029
14500-14799 98027
276th Ave SE 98027
277th Way SE 98027
280th Ave & Dr 98027
282nd Ave SE 98027
284th Ave SE 98027
285th Ave SE 98027
286th Ave SE 98027
288th Ave SE 98027
289th Ave & Pl 98027
290th Ave SE 98027
293rd Ave SE 98027
297th Ave SE 98027
299th Pl SE 98027
300th Ave & Pl 98027
302nd Ave SE 98027
303rd Pl SE 98027
304th Ave & Pl 98027
308th Ave & Pl 98027
309th Ave & Pl 98027
312th Ave, Pl & Way 98027
314th Ave & Pl 98027
315th Ave SE 98027
316th Ln & Pl 98027
324th Pl SE 98027
325th Ave SE 98027
329th Ct SE 98027

KENNEWICK WA

General Delivery 99336

POST OFFICE BOXES MAIN OFFICE STATIONS AND BRANCHES

Box No.s
All PO Boxes 99336

NAMED STREETS

E Access Pr SE 99337
S Agua Mansa Ct 99338
E & W Albany Ave & Ct 99336
S Alder Loop 99337
S Alder Pl
501-699 99336
1000-1099 99337
S Alder St
1-999 99336
1300-1399 99337
E Alhambra Rd 99338
E Alice St 99337
S Amon Rd 99338
S Anderson Pl 99337
S Anderson St
100-899 99336
2400-4099 99337
W Arrowhead Ave 99336
S Arthur Ct 99338
S Arthur Loop 99338
N Arthur Pl 99336
S Arthur Pl 99336
N Arthur St 99336
S Arthur St
100-399 99336
1700-2099 99338
S Auburn Pl 99337
N Auburn St 99336
S Auburn St
1-999 99336
1500-4299 99337
E Badger Rd 99338
S Badger Meadows Dr 99338
Badger View Dr 99338
Beck Rd 99337
S Beech Ct 99337
N Beech St 99336
S Beech St
100-298 99336
300-999 99336
1000-4699 99337
S Belfair Ct 99338
S Belfair Pl
200-299 99336
1200-1299 99338
N Belfair St 99336
S Belfair St
100-899 99336
1000-1199 99338
N & S Bent Rd 99338
S Benton Pl 99337
N Benton St 99336
S Benton St
1-299 99336

1000-3699 99337
N & S Bermuda Rd 99338
E Bernath Rd 99337
Bofer Canyon Rd 99337
Bonnie Ave & Pl 99336
E Bowles Rd 99337
E Brandon Dr 99338
Brent Ln 99338
Brian Ln 99338
Brighton Ct 99338
W Brinkley Rd 99338
E Brooklyn Dr 99338
Bruce Lee Ct & Ln 99338
E & W Bruneau Ave &
Pl 99336
E Bryson Brown Rd 99337
S Buchanan Ct 99336
S Buchanan Pl
400-599 99336
1400-1499 99338
N Buchanan St 99336
S Buchanan St
400-999 99336
1800-1999 99338
S Buntin Ct 99337
S Buntin Loop 99337
N Buntin Pl 99336
N Buntin St 99336
S Buntin St
400-999 99336
1900-3499 99337
C Williams Pr & Rd
SE 99338
E & S Caballo Pl &
Rd 99338
Calico Ct 99338
Cambridge Ct 99338
W Canal Dr 99336
Cantera St 99338
Canterbury Ct & Rd 99338
W Canyon Ave 99336
E Canyon Dr 99337
W Canyon Pl 99336
W Canyon Lakes Dr 99337
Canyon Meadows Dr 99338
Canyon View Dr 99338
S Carlson Rd 99337
W Carmichael Dr 99336
S Carrol Pr SE 99337
S Cascade Pl 99337
N Cascade St 99336
S Cascade St
1-199 99336
1300-4299 99337
4301-4399 99337
S Cedar Pl
800-999 99336
1400-1499 99337
N Cedar St 99336
S Cedar St
700-798 99336
1000-3999 99337
N Center Pkwy 99336
S Cerda Rd 99338
Charity Ct 99338
E Chelsea Rd 99338
E Chemical Dr
800-898 99336
900-999 99336
1600-1699 99337
E Christenson Rd 99338
E Christine Dr 99338
Cindy Rd 99338
S Clear View Loop 99338
W Clearwater Ave
1600-10699 99336
11500-12299 99338
W Clearwater Dr 99336
W Clearwater Pl 99336
S Cleveland Ct 99338
N Cleveland St 99336
S Cleveland St
300-999 99336
1400-2399 99338
S Clodfelter Rd
500-999 99336
1000-110399 99338
Clover Is 99336
E Clover Rd 99338
N Clover Rd 99338
Clover Island Dr 99336
E Cochran Rd 99337
N & S Colorado St 99336
E & W Columbia Ctr &
Dr 99336
N Columbia Center
Blvd 99336
S Columbia Center Blvd
309-714 99336
716-912 99336
1300-1399 99338
Columbia Park Trl 99336
S Conway Ct 99337
S Conway Dr 99337
N Conway Pl 99336
S Conway Pl
100-599 99336
3436-3598 99337
N Conway St 99336
S Conway St
400-800 99336
802-898 99336
1000-2699 99337
Cottonwood Blvd & Dr 99338
Cottonwood Creek
Blvd 99338
Cottonwood Springs
Blvd 99338
E Cougar Rd 99337
S Coulee Vista Dr 99338
Country Heights Dr 99338
S Country Meadows
Ln 99338
S Coyote Cross Pr SE 99337
S Dague Rd 99337
S Date Pl 99337
N Date St 99336
S Date St
100-999 99336
1300-4399 99337
S Dawes Ct 99338
N Dawes St 99336
S Dawes St
1-999 99336
1000-3199 99338
S Dayton Ct 99337
S Dayton Pl 99337
N Dayton St 99336
S Dayton St
1-999 99336
2000-5299 99337
N Delaware St 99336
S Delaware St
500-599 99336
1200-1299 99338
S Dennis Ct 99337
N Dennis Pl 99336
S Dennis Pl
400-499 99336
1500-1699 99337
N Dennis St 99336
S Dennis St
400-799 99336
1500-4099 99337
Deschutes Ave, Dr &
Pl 99336
E Donelson Rd 99337
S Dunham Rd 99337
E Eastlake Dr 99337
S Edison Ct 99338
N Edison Pl 99336
S Edison Pl
400-499 99336
2400-3199 99338
N Edison St 99336
S Edison St
1-999 99336
1200-2499 99338
S Elm Ct 99337
N Elm St 99336
S Elm St
200-999 99336
1400-4399 99337
S Elma St 99338
N Ely Pl 99336
N Ely St 99336
S Ely St
100-999 99336
1600-5099 99337
Entiat Ave & Pl 99336
E Erickson Rd 99337
Escolar Rd 99338
S Etiwanda Ct 99338
S Everett Ct 99337
S Everett Pl 99337
N Everett St 99336
S Everett St
600-899 99336
1200-4599 99337
E Fairbanks Pr SE 99338
S Fairview Loop 99338
W Falenern Ave 99336
Falls Ave & Pl 99336
S Fescue St 99338
S Fillmore Ct 99338
N Fillmore Pl 99336
S Fillmore Pl 99338
N Fillmore St 99336
S Fillmore St
100-599 99336
1600-2199 99338
E & S Finley Rd 99337
S Fir St
201-397 99336
399-899 99336
1400-4299 99337
S Fisher Ct 99337
N Fisher Pl 99336
S Fisher Pl 99337
N Fisher St 99336
S Fisher St 99337
Florida Pl & St 99336
S Fremont Rd 99337
N Fruitland St 99336
S Fruitland St
1-999 99336
1600-5099 99337
W Gage Blvd 99336
E Game Farm Rd 99337
S Garfield Ct 99337
S Garfield Pl 99337
N Garfield St 99336
S Garfield St
1-999 99336
1000-5499 99337
N & S Georgia Pl &
St 99336
S Gerards Rd 99337
S Gertrude St 99337
S Glen Miller Rd 99338
E Granada Ct 99338
E Grand Bluff Loop 99338
Grand Ronde Ave, Ct &
Pl 99336
W Grandridge Blvd 99336
Grandview Ln 99338
S Grant Ct 99338
N Grant Pl 99336
N Grant St 99336
S Grant St
100-516 99336
518-520 99336
1100-3199 99338
S Green Loop 99337
N Green Pl 99336
S Green Pl
400-499 99336
3200-4699 99337
N Green St 99336
S Green St
800-999 99336
3600-4199 99337
N Gum St 99336
S Gum St
2-98 99336
100-999 99336
1001-1297 99337
1299-4499 99337
S H Smith Rd 99338
S Haney Rd 99337
S Harrison Ct 99338
S Harrison Pl 99338
N Harrison St 99336
S Harrison St
100-799 99336
1100-2399 99338
S Hartford Pl 99337
N Hartford St 99336
S Hartford St
600-999 99336
1900-4799 99337
S Havana St 99337
N & S Hawaii Pl & St 99336
S Hawks Tree Pr SE 99337
S Hawthorne Pl 99336
S Hawthorne St
500-899 99336
1300-18799 99337
Heather Dr 99338
E Hedges Rd 99337
Highland Dr & Pl 99337
S Hildebrand Blvd 99338
W Hildebrand Blvd
4800-5598 99338
4801-4899 99337
5201-5599 99338
W Hildebrand Rd 99338
Hillview Dr 99338
E Holly Rd 99338
S Honeysuckle St 99338
Hood Ave, Ct & Pl 99336
E Hover Rd 99337
S Huntington Ct 99337
S Huntington Loop 99337
S Huntington Pl
400-498 99336
500-999 99336
1600-1899 99337
N Huntington St 99336
S Huntington St
800-999 99336
1600-3399 99337
N & S Idaho Pl & St 99336
Imnaha Ave & Ct 99336
S Ione Pl 99337
N Ione St 99336
S Ione St
600-999 99336
1600-4499 99337
S Irby Ct 99337
S Irby Loop 99337
N Irby St 99336
S Irby St
1-599 99336
1000-1399 99338
3400-4299 99337
N Irving Pl 99336
S Irving Pl
400-599 99336
1100-1899 99338
N Irving St 99336
S Irving St
100-399 99336
2400-2799 99338
S Ivy St 99338
Jacob Ct 99338
S Janelle Ln 99338
S Jean Pl 99337
N Jean St 99336
S Jean St
500-799 99336
1600-4899 99337
S Jefferson Ct 99338
N Jefferson Pl 99336
S Jefferson Pl 99338
N Jefferson St 99336
S Jefferson St
1-999 99336
1200-5799 99338
Jenna Ln & Rd 99338
John Day Ave & Pl 99336
S Johnson Ct 99337
S Johnson Pl 99337
N Johnson St 99336
S Johnson St
1-999 99336
1000-1299 99338
2500-3799 99337
N & S Joliet Pl & St 99336
Joshua Ct & Rd 99338
N & S Juniper Pl & St 99336
N & S Jurupa St 99336
E Kaitlyn Rd 99338
N & S Kansas St 99336
E Kase Blvd 99338
Kash Loop 99338
Katie Ct & Rd 99338
Keewaydin Dr 99336
S Keller Pl 99337
N Keller St 99336
S Keller St
300-999 99336
2100-4199 99337
S Kellogg Pl 99338
N Kellogg St 99336
S Kellogg St
1-999 99336
1100-2699 99338
W Kencoman Ave 99336
E & W Kennewick Ave &
Ct 99336
N Kent Pl 99336
N Kent St 99336
S Kent St
1-699 99336
1600-4899 99337
Kentbrook Ct 99338
S Keystone St 99337
Kimberly Dr 99338
N Kingwood St 99336
S Kingwood St
500-899 99336
3900-4399 99337
Kirby Pr & Rd SE 99337
E Kirk Rd 99337
Klamath Ave, Ct & Pl 99336
Kristen Ln 99338
Kyle Rd 99338
Lapierre Canyon Dr 99338
S Larch Pr SE 99337
S Larch St 99336
E Law Ln 99337
E Lechelt Rd 99337
S Ledbetter Ct 99337
S Ledbetter Pl 99337
N Ledbetter St 99336
S Ledbetter St
300-399 99336
2102-4699 99337
S Lemon Dr 99337
Lesa Marie Ct & Ln 99338
W Leslie Rd 99338
S Lexington St 99337
Lilliann Dr 99338
N Lincoln St 99336
S Lincoln St
1-99 99336
1100-3899 99338
39700-40099 99337
S & E Locust Ln & Pr
SE 99337
E Locust Grove Rd 99338
Lorayne J Blvd 99338
N & S Louisiana Ct, Pl &
St 99336
Lower Blair Rd 99337
N Lyle St 99336
S Lyle St
1-99 99336
1700-4199 99337
E Main St 99337
Manuel Dr 99338
S Manzanita Ct 99338
E Mary Pr SE 99337
Mata Rd 99338
E Matzat Rd 99337
S Mayfield Ct 99337
N Mayfield St 99336
S Mayfield St
300-399 99336
1800-4199 99337
S Mckinley Ct 99338
S Mckinley Pl 99336
N Mckinley St 99336
S Mckinley St
1-599 99336
3700-6099 99338
S Meals Rd 99337
Metaline Ave & Pl 99336
E Michelle Dr 99338
N & S Montana Ct, Pl &
St 99336
N Morain Loop 99336
S Morain Loop 99337
S Morain Pl 99337
N Morain St 99336
S Morain St
2-198 99336
200-999 99336
1000-1498 99338
1500-1599 99338
3400-4899 99337
S Morton Rd 99337
S Mountain Ridge Ct 99338
S Myrtle St
400-599 99336
2401-20199 99337
S Neel Ct
800-999 99336
1800-1899 99338
4100-4299 99337
N Neel Loop 99336
S Neel Pl 99337
N Neel St 99336
S Neel St
200-399 99336
1900-2099 99338
4600-4799 99337
S Nelson Ct 99338
S Nelson St
500-999 99336
1600-1699 99338
N & S Nevada Ct, Pl &
St 99336
S Newport Pl 99337
N Newport St 99336
S Newport St 99337
S Newport Place Pr 99337
Nicole Dr 99338
Nicoson Rd 99338
S Nine Canyon Rd 99337
S Nutmeg St 99336
S Oak St 99337
Okanogan Ave, Ct, Loop
& Pl 99336
N & S Oklahoma Ct, Pl
& St 99336
S Olson Ct 99337
S Olson Pl 99337
N Olson St 99336
S Olson St
200-899 99336
1500-1899 99338
4100-4899 99337
S Olympia Pl 99337
N Olympia St 99336
S Olympia St
101-197 99336
199-899 99336
1200-37199 99337
S Osborne St 99336
S Palouse Ct 99337
S Palouse Pl 99337
N Palouse St 99336
S Palouse St 99337
W Park Hills Dr 99337
Payette Ave & Ct 99336
S Penn Pl
400-799 99336
1600-1799 99338
S Penn St
100-999 99336
1100-1799 99338
E Perkins Rd 99337
S Perry Ct
500-699 99336
1500-1799 99338
N Perry Loop 99336
S Perry Pl 99336
N Perry St 99336
S Perry St 99338
Pico Dr 99338
E Pidcock Rd 99337
S Piert Rd 99337
E Pine Hollow Pr SE 99338
N & S Pittsburg Ct &
St 99336
Plaza Way 99338
Postage Due St
1-99 99337
1-99 99338
2-98 99337
2-98 99338
S Power Line Pr SE 99337
S Prichame St 99337
S Pullman Rd 99337
S Quay Ct 99338
S Quay Pl 99336
N Quay St 99336
S Quay St
1-429 99336
1200-1399 99338
Quebec Ct & St 99336
N Quillan Ct 99336
S Quillan Ct
1400-1499 99338
3500-3599 99337
S Quillan Pl 99336
N Quillan St 99336
S Quillan St
1-499 99336
1500-2699 99338
2700-2799 99337
W Quinault Ave 99336
S Quince Pl 99337
S Quincy Ct 99337
N Quincy Pl 99336
S Quincy Pl 99337
N Quincy St 99336
S Quincy St
1-599 99336
1900-4099 99337
S Quinn St 99337
Rachel Rd 99338
W Railroad Ave 99336
S Rainier Ct 99337
S Rainier Pl 99337
S Rainier St
1-999 99336
1300-1498 99338
1500-3899 99337
E Reata Rd 99338
S Redwood St 99337
S Reed Ct
1500-1599 99338
3500-4099 99337
N Reed Pl 99336
N Reed St 99336
S Reed St
1-399 99336
1100-2199 99338
4500-4899 99337
E Reese Rd 99338
Rhode Island Ct & St 99336
S Rialto Ct 99338
S Ridge View Ln 99338
Ridgeline Dr 99338
Ridgeview Ct & Dr 99338
E Riek Rd 99337
Rio Grande Ave & Ct 99336
S Roosevelt Pl
100-399 99336
1500-1699 99338
S Roosevelt St
100-899 99336
1000-1499 99338
S Rosena Ct 99338
S Ruff Pr SE 99337
Ryanick Rd 99338
S Sagebrush Rd 99338
S Sandlewood Pr SE 99338
Sarah Ct & Rd 99338
E Schuster Rd 99337
S Sharron Ct 99337
S Sharron St
1-999 99336

1100-1698 99337
1700-4299 99337
N Sheppard Pl 99336
S Sheppard Pl 99338
N Sheppard St 99336
S Sheppard St
300-399 99336
1500-2199 99338
S Sherman Pl 99336
N Sherman St 99336
S Sherman St 99338
S Short Ave 99337
E Sidibe Pr SE 99338
Skagit Ave & Ct 99336
Sloan Ct & Rd 99337
Southridge Blvd 99338
Spirit Ln 99338
S Spruce St 99337
E Sr 397 99337
N Steptoe St 99336
S Stevens Dr 99337
E Straightbank Rd 99337
Summit View Dr 99338
E Sundown Pr SE 99338
S Sunnyvale Dr 99338
E & S Sunset Meadows Loop 99338
S Tacoma Ct 99337
S Tacoma Pl
701-799 99336
2700-4299 99337
S Tacoma St
400-799 99336
1300-3599 99337
S Taft St
401-999 99336
1000-1999 99338
S Tamarack Pr SE 99337
E Terril Rd 99337
N & S Texas St 99336
E Tierney Pr SE 99337
Timothy Ln 99338
E Toothaker Rd 99337
Toro Ct, Pl & Rd 99338
S Tranquility Pr SE 99338
Travis Ct & Ln 99338
S & E Tripple Vista Ct & Dr 99338
W Tucannon Ave 99336
S Tweedt Ct 99338
N Tweedt Pl 99336
S Tweedt Pl 99336
N Tweedt St 99336
S Tweedt St
100-899 99336
1900-2699 99338
3200-3499 99337
W Umatilla Ave 99336
S Underwood Ct 99337
S Underwood Pl 99337
N Underwood St 99336
S Underwood St
1-599 99336
1300-3699 99337
S Union Ct 99338
N Union St 99336
S Union St
1-999 99336
1400-2599 99338
4101-4299 99337
S Upper Blair Rd 99337
N & S Utah St 99336
E Vaca Rd 99338
E Valencia Dr 99338
S Valley Vista Pr SE 99338
N Van Buren Ct 99336
S Van Buren Ct 99336
S Van Buren Pl 99338
S Van Buren St 99336
S Vancouver Pl 99337
N Vancouver St 99336
S Vancouver St
1-900 99336
902-998 99336
1000-4399 99337
S Verbena St 99337
N & S Vermont Loop & St 99336
W Victoria Ave 99336
W Vineyard Dr 99336
Vista Way 99336
N Volland Ct 99336
S Volland Ct
1800-1899 99338
3200-3299 99337
N Volland St 99336
S Volland St
1-899 99336
3300-3599 99337
Walnut Ridge Pr 99338
E Walter Pr SE 99337
N Washington Pl 99336
S Washington Pl 99337
N Washington St 99336
S Washington St
1-999 99336
1000-4999 99337
5001-5599 99337
S Waverly Ct 99337
N Waverly Pl 99336
S Waverly Pl 99337
S Waverly St
1-299 99336
2700-4099 99337
S Whitney Rd 99337
W Willamette Ave 99336
S Williams Pr SE 99337
N Williams St 99336
S Williams St
1-399 99336
1900-2099 99338
3300-3599 99337
S Willow Pr SE 99338
S Wilson Ct
100-999 99336
1500-1599 99338
S Wilson St 99336
E Windigo Pr SE 99337
E Windward Ln 99338
Wiser Pkwy 99338
Wiser Park Way 99338
S Wyoming St 99336
W Yellowstone Ave 99336
S Yelm Ct 99337
S Yelm Pl
700-799 99336
1100-1199 99337
N Yelm St 99336
S Yelm St
1-499 99336
1500-3199 99337
S Yew St 99337
S Yolo St 99336
S Yost Pl 99338
N Yost St 99336
S Yost St 99336
S Young Ct
600-699 99336
1400-1499 99338
S Young Pl
100-899 99336
1400-1499 99338
N Young St 99336
S Young St
100-899 99336
1000-1299 99338
S Zillah Ct 99337
N Zillah St 99336
S Zillah St
300-699 99336
1200-4099 99337
N Zinser St 99336
S Zinser St
100-699 99336
1900-2199 99338
S Zintel Way 99337

NUMBERED STREETS

E & W 1st Ave & Pl 99336
E & W 2nd Ave & Pl 99336
E 3rd Ave
1-799 99336
1300-199999 99337
W 3rd Ave 99336
W 3rd Pl 99336
E & W 4th Ave, Ct & Pl 99336
E & W 5th Ave, Ct & Pl 99336
E & W 6th Ave & Pl 99336
E 7th Ave
100-1199 99336
1501-1597 99337
1599-202199 99337
W 7th Ave 99336
W 7th Ct 99336
W 7th Pl 99336
E & W 8th Ave, Ct & Pl 99336
E & W 9th Ave, Ct & Pl 99336
E 10th Ave
1-1499 99336
197900-207399 99337
W 10th Ave 99336
W 10th Pl 99338
E 11th Ave 99337
W 11th Ave
300-1899 99337
3200-7399 99338
W 11th Ct 99338
W 11th Pl
1200-1299 99337
5700-5899 99338
W 12th Ave
200-2300 99337
2302-2398 99337
3200-7899 99338
W 12th Pl
2300-2399 99337
6700-6899 99338
E 13th Ave 99337
W 13th Ave
500-2299 99337
3200-7799 99338
W 13th Ct 99338
E 14th Ave 99337
W 14th Ave
1-1799 99337
4400-5999 99338
W 14th Ct 99338
E 14th Pl 99337
W 14th Pl 99337
E 15th Ave 99337
W 15th Ave
1400-2699 99337
3600-7399 99338
W 15th Pl 99337
E 16th Ave 99337
W 16th Ave
1-3199 99337
5300-6799 99338
W 16th Ct 99338
W 16th Pl
1000-1299 99337
3600-3799 99338
E 17th Ave 99337
W 17th Ave
700-2099 99337
3800-6099 99338
W 17th Ct 99338
W 17th Pl
1100-1299 99337
3600-6899 99338
W 18th Ave
400-2099 99337
4000-5799 99338
W 18th Ct
700-899 99337
4200-4299 99338
W 18th Pl 99338
E 19th Ave 99337
W 19th Ave
1-3299 99337
3300-5899 99338
W 19th Ct 99338
W 19th Pl 99337
W 20th Ave
300-2499 99337
3600-8099 99338
W 20th Ct 99338
W 21st Ave
101-107 99337
109-3299 99337
3700-8099 99338
W 21st Ct 99337
W 21st Pl
400-2099 99337
5900-5999 99338
E 22nd Ave 99337
W 22nd Ave
700-3399 99337
3600-5499 99338
W 22nd Ct 99338
W 22nd Pl 99337
E 23rd Ave 99337
W 23rd Ave
600-3499 99337
5300-5899 99338
W 23rd Pl 99337
W 24th Ave
1-3399 99337
4200-5699 99338
W 24th Loop 99337
W 24th Pl
600-2399 99337
4800-5099 99338
E 25th Ave 99337
W 25th Ave
700-1799 99337
5300-6099 99338
W 25th Ct 99337
W 25th Pl 99337
E 26th Ave 99337
W 26th Ave
700-2099 99337
5100-6099 99338
W 26th Pl 99337
E 27th Ave 99337
W 27th Ave
1-4099 99337
4100-5100 99338
5102-5198 99338
W 27th Pl
400-1699 99337
4300-4399 99338
W 28th Ave
100-1899 99337
5100-5399 99338
W 28th Pl 99337
29th Ave & Ct 99337
E & W 30th Ave, Ct & Pl 99337
W & E 31st Ave & Ct 99337
W 32nd Ave
300-4299 99337
4900-5599 99338
W 32nd Ct 99337
W 32nd Pl 99337
33rd Ave & Pl 99337
34th Ave, Ct & Pl 99337
35th Ave, Ct, Loop & Pl 99337
E 36th Ave 99337
W 36th Ave 99337
W 36th Ct 99337
W 36th Loop 99337
E 36th Pl 99337
W 36th Pl
100-2099 99337
5500-5599 99338
W 37th Ave 99337
W 37th Pl
400-1699 99337
5700-6199 99338
W 38th Ave
3300-3599 99337
6000-6199 99338
W 38th Ct 99337
W 38th Pl 99337
39th Ave & Ct 99337
40th Ave & Pl 99337
W & E 41st Ave & Pl 99337
E & W 42nd Ave & Pl 99337
E & W 43rd Ave, Ct & Pl 99337
E & W 44th Ave & Pl 99337
E & W 45th Ave & Pl 99337
W & E 46th Ave & Pl 99337
E & W 47th Ave & Pl 99337
W 48th Ave 99337
E & W 49th 99337
W & E 50th Ave, Ct & Pl 99337
W 51st Ave 99337
W 52nd Ave 99337
W 53rd Ave 99337
E 59th Ave 99337
E 73rd Ave 99337
S 1005 Pr SE 99338
S 1018 Pr SE 99338
E 1023 Pr SE 99338
E 1035 Pr SE 99338
E 1045 Pr SE 99338
E 1049 Pr SE 99338
162 Pr SE 99338
E 163 Pr SE 99337
S 1877 Pr SE 99337
S 1884 Pr 99337
E 193 Pr SE 99337
E 194 Pr SE 99337
S 1942 Pr SE 99337
S 1977 Pr SE 99337
S 1987 Pr SE 99337
S 1996 Pr SE 99337
S 1998 Pr SE 99337
S 2001 99337
E 200 Pr SE 99337
S 2009 Pr SE 99337
E 2013 Pr SE 99337
S 2021 Pr SE 99337
S 2034 Pr SE 99337
S 2047 Pr SE 99337
S 2048 Pr SE 99337
S 2058 Pr SE 99337
S 2054 Pr SE 99337
S 2060 Pr SE 99337
S 2066 Pr SE 99337
S 2079 Pr SE 99337
S 2083 Pr SE 99337
S 2085 Pr SE 99337
S 2090 Pr SE 99337
S 2093 Pr SE 99337
S 2099 Pr SE 99337
S 2106 Pr SE 99337
S 2100 Pr SE 99337
S 2138 Pr SE 99337
S 2154 Pr SE 99337
S 2156 Pr SE 99337
S 2157 Pr SE 99337
S 2161 Pr SE 99337
E 217 Pr SE 99338
S 2174 Pr SE 99337
S 2175 Pr SE 99337
S 2179 Pr SE 99337
S 2180 Pr SE 99337
S 2184 Pr SE 99337
S 2187 Pr SE 99337
S 2181 Pr SE 99337
S 2198 Pr SE 99337
S 2200 Pr SE 99337
S 2209 Pr SE 99337
E 223 Pr SE 99337
S 2243 Pr SE 99337
S 2289 Pr SE 99337
S 2299 Pr SE 99337
E 239 Pr SE 99337
S 2410 Pr SE 99337
E 245 Pr SE 99338
E 247 Pr SE 99337
E 249 Pr SE 99338
E 252 Pr SE 99338
E 292 Pr SE 99337
E 297 Pr SE 99338
E 302 Pr SE 99337
S 302 Pr SE 99338
E 304 Pr SE 99337
E 315 Pr SE 99337
E 350 Pr SE 99337
E 355 Pr SE 99337
E 361 Pr SE 99337
E 382 Pr SE 99338
E 403 Pr SE 99337
E 421 Pr SE 99337
E 45 Pr SE 99337
E 479 Pr SE 99337
E 490 Pr SE 99337
E 491 Pr SE 99337
E & W 528 99337
E 54 Pr SE 99337
E 549 Pr SE 99337
E 654 Pr SE 99337
E 672 Pr SE 99337
S 816 Pr SE 99338
S 823 Pr SE 99338
E 83 Pr SE 99338
S 855 Pr SE 99338
S 875 Pr SE 99338
S 887 Pr SE 99338
S 89 Pr SE 99338
S 903 Pr SE 99338
S 918 Pr SE 99338
S 930 Pr SE 99338
S 932 Pr SE 99338
S 944 Pr SE 99338
S 952 Pr SE 99338
S 959 Pr SE 99338
E 973 Pr SE 99338
S 984 Pr SE 99338

KENT WA

General Delivery 98031

POST OFFICE BOXES MAIN OFFICE STATIONS AND BRANCHES

Box No.s
1 - 1795 98035
3001 - 4639 98089
5001 - 6655 98064
7001 - 96010 98042
97002 - 97074 98064

NAMED STREETS

Adarinda Ave S 98032
Alder Ln 98030
Alexander Ave 98030
Alpine Way 98030
Alvord Ave N
200-699 98030
700-899 98031
Arden Ct 98032
Avon Ct 98032
Benson Rd SE 98031
Bridges Ave S 98032
Bristol Ct 98032
Burke Ave 98030
Cambridge Ct, Dr & Pl 98032
Canterbury Ln 98032
Canyon Dr 98030
Cardiff Ave 98032
Carlench Ave SE 98031
Carnaby St & Way 98032
Carter Pl 98030
E Cedar St 98030
Central Ave N 98032
Central Ave S 98032
Central Pl S 98030
E Cherry Hill St 98030
E Chicago St 98030
Clark Ave N
300-398 98030
400-699 98030
700-798 98031
Clearview Pt 98030
W Cloudy St 98032
W Cole St 98032
W Concord St 98032
Covington Way SE 98042
SE Covington Sawyer Rd 98042
Crest Ave 98030
Crest Pl 98031
W Crow St 98032
E Dean St 98030
Dover Ct 98032
Downing Ave 98032
Eaton Ct 98032
Ellis Pl 98030
SE Falcon Way 98042
Feigley Rd W 98032
Fenwick Ct 98032
E Filbert St 98030
Frager Rd S 98032
Garfield Ave 98030
E George St 98031
Glenwood Ln 98030
E Gowe St
200-299 98032
300-398 98030
400-499 98030
W Gowe St
200-215 98032
216-216 98035
217-699 98032
300-698 98032
Green River Rd 98030
E Guiberson St 98030
Hampton Ct & Way 98032
W Harrison St 98032
Hawley Rd 98032
Hazel Ave N
300-699 98030
700-899 98031
E Hemlock St 98030
Highland Ave 98032
Hillcrest Ave 98030
Hilltop Ave 98031
Howestri Ave SE 98042
Ives Ave 98032
W James Ct 98032
W James Ln 98032
W James Pl 98032
E James St
201-299 98032
501-797 98031
799-900 98031
902-1398 98031
W James St 98032
Jason Ave N
300-398 98030
400-699 98030
700-799 98031
Kennebeck Ave N & S 98030
Kenosia Ave S 98030
Kensington Ave S 98030
Kent Ct 98032
Kent Black Diamond Rd SE 98042
S Kent Des Moines Rd 98032
SE Kent Kangley Rd 98030
W Kent Station St 98032
Kimberly Ave 98030
Kirkwood Ave 98030
Lake Fenwick Rd S 98032
E & W Lake Morton Dr 98042
Lakeside Blvd 98032
E Lane Ave 98030
E Laurel St 98030
Lenora Ave N 98031
Lincoln Ave 98032
E Maclyn St 98030
Madison Ave 98032
Manchester Ave, Ct & Way 98032
E Maple Ln & St 98030
Maplewood Ave 98030
Marion Pl & St 98030
E Mcmillan St 98030
E Meeker St
200-215 98032
217-217 98032
300-499 98030

W Meeker St 98032
Military Rd S 98032
E & W Morton St 98032
Naden Ave S 98032
E Novak Ln 98032
Olympic Pl & Way 98030
Orillia Rd S 98032
W Overlock St 98032
Pacific Hwy S
23200-23417 98032
23418-23418 98089
23419-25399 98032
23420-27198 98032
E Pintontr Ave N 98030
Pioneer St 98032
Princeton Ave 98032
Prospect Ave N
400-699 98030
700-899 98031
Rachael Pl 98032
Railroad Ave N & S 98032
Ramsay Way 98032
Reiten Rd 98030
Reith Rd 98032
Ridgeview Dr 98032
E Russell Rd & St 98032
W Saar St 98032
W Sam St 98032
Saxon Ct 98032
Scenic Way 98030
E Seattle Pl & St 98030
W Smith Ct 98032
E Smith St
200-298 98032
300-1299 98030
W Smith St 98032
Somerset Ct & Ln 98032
Spring Ave N 98030
Stanford Ct 98032
State Ave N
100-499 98030
700-799 98031
State Ave S 98030
Stetson Ave 98031
Stoneburner Ln 98030
Strattford Ct 98032
Summit Ave N 98030
E Tacoma St 98030
E Temperance St 98030
Thomas Rd SE 98042
Tilden Ave 98030
Timberlane Blvd, Dr & Way 98042
E Titus St
100-198 98032
201-299 98032
300-699 98030
701-799 98030
W Titus St 98032
Titusville Aly 98032
Todd Blvd 98032
E Valley Hwy 98032
W Valley Hwy 98032
W Valley Hwy S 98032
Valley Pl 98031
Van De Vanter Ave 98030
View Pl 98030
E Walnut St 98030
E Ward St 98030
Washington Ave N & S 98032
W Waterman St 98032
SE Wax Rd 98042
Weiland St 98030
Westview Ct 98031
E & W Willis St 98032
Woodford Ave N 98031
Woodland Way S 98030
Wynwood Dr 98030
Yale Ct 98032

NUMBERED STREETS

1st N & S 98032
2nd Ave & Pl 98032
3rd N & S 98032
4th N & S 98032
5th N & S 98032
6th N & S 98032
20th Ave & Pl 98032
21st Ave & Pl 98032
22nd Ave S 98032
23rd Ave & Pl 98032
24th Pl S 98032
25th Ave & Ln 98032
26th Pl S 98032
27th Ave & Pl 98032
28th Ave S 98032
29th Ave S 98032
30th Ave S 98032
31st Ave S 98032
32nd Pl S 98032
33rd Ave & Pl 98032
34th Ave & Pl 98032
35th Ave, Ln & Pl 98032
36th Ave, Ct, Ln & Pl S 98032
37th Ave & Pl 98032
38th Ave & Pl 98032
39th Ave & Pl 98032
40th Ave & Pl 98032
41st Ave & Pl 98032
42nd Ave & Pl 98032
43rd Ave & Pl 98032
44th Ave, Ct & Pl 98032
45th Ave, Ct & Pl 98032
46th Ave & Pl 98032
47th Ave, Ct & Pl 98032
48th Ave, Ct & Pl 98032
49th Ave S 98032
50th Ave & Pl 98032
51st Ave, Ct & Pl 98032
52nd Ave, Ln, Pl & Way S 98032
53rd Ave & Pl 98032
54th Ave S 98032
55th Ave & Pl 98032
56th Ave, Ct & Pl 98032
57th Ave & Ct 98032
58th Ave, Ct & Pl 98032
59th Ct & Pl 98032
60th Ave, Ct & Pl 98032
61st Ave & Pl 98032
62nd Ave, Pl & Way 98032
63rd Ave, Pl & Way 98032
64th Ave & Pl 98032
65th Ave & Pl 98032
66th Ave S 98032
67th Ave & Pl 98032
68th Ave S 98032
70th Ave S 98032
71st Ave & Pl 98032
72nd Ave S 98032
74th Ave S 98032
76th Ave S 98032
77th Ave & Pl 98032
78th Ave S 98032
79th Ave S 98032
80th Ave, Ct & Pl 98032
81st Ave S 98032
83rd Ave S 98032
84th Ave S 98032
84th Pl S 98031
85th Ave S
19801-19997 98031
19999-21699 98031
28101-28197 98032
28199-28499 98032
85th Pl S 98031
86th Ave S
21500-22999 98031
26800-26899 98030
86th Pl S 98031
87th Ave S
19800-20699 98031
25800-25898 98030
88th Ave S
21300-23100 98031
23102-23298 98031
25800-25899 98030
88th Pl S 98031
89th Ave & Pl 98031
90th Ave, Pl & Way 98031
91st Ave, Pl & Way 98031
92nd Ave & Pl 98031
93rd Ave S 98031
94th Ave S 98031
24000-24799 98030
94th Ct S 98031
94th Pl S
20200-22899 98031
26400-26899 98030
95th Ave S 98031
95th Ct S 98031
95th Pl S
20000-21999 98031
24200-24299 98030
96th Ave S
20100-23099 98031
24000-24899 98030
96th Pl S 98031
96th Way S 98031
97th Ave S
20400-23799 98031
24600-26499 98030
26501-26699 98030
97th Ct S 98031
97th Pl S
20300-21299 98031
24200-25499 98030
98th Ave S
21000-23999 98031
24000-25499 98030
25501-25623 98030
98th Pl S
20400-22899 98031
25000-25699 98030
99th Ave S 98031
99th Pl S
22100-22199 98031
24800-26599 98030
99th Pl SE 98031
100th Ave SE 98031
24200-24599 98030
100th Ct SE 98031
100th Pl SE
21200-21899 98031
24200-25799 98030
101st Ave SE
20400-23499 98031
25300-25799 98030
101st Ct SE 98031
101st Pl SE
21800-23799 98031
24200-24999 98030
102nd Ave SE
20100-23899 98031
23901-23999 98031
24301-26697 98030
26699-26899 98030
102nd Ct SE 98031
102nd Pl SE
20000-23699 98031
24200-25899 98030
103rd Ave SE
20400-22899 98031
24400-26499 98030
103rd Ct SE 98031
103rd Pl SE
20000-22599 98031
27200-27299 98030
104th Ave SE
20000-23999 98031
24000-27299 98030
104th Pl SE 98031
105th Ave SE
20100-23399 98031
27000-27999 98030
105th Ct S 98031
105th Pl SE
20400-23699 98031
24400-27199 98030
106th Ave SE
20000-23699 98031
24400-27999 98030
106th Pl SE
20300-22999 98031
26000-26799 98030
107th Ave SE
21800-22099 98031
24800-26899 98030
107th Pl SE
21800-23299 98031
27300-27899 98030
108th Ave SE
19200-19998 98031
24500-27999 98030
108th Pl SE
21700-23626 98031
24000-24599 98030
109th Ave SE
21200-23999 98031
24900-26899 98030
109th Ct SE 98030
109th Ln SE 98031
109th Pl SE
20900-23299 98031
24000-26999 98030
110th Ave SE
20400-23999 98031
24400-27399 98030
110th Ct SE
22600-22699 98031
24800-27099 98030
110th Ln SE 98031
110th Pl SE
20143-23599 98031
24000-26499 98030
110th Ter SE 98031
111th Ave SE
20300-22499 98031
24200-27699 98030
111th Ct SE
21400-22699 98031
26800-27099 98030
111th Pl SE
22100-23999 98031
24000-27399 98030
111th Way SE 98031
112th Ave SE
19200-21298 98031
21300-23999 98031
24100-26899 98030
112th Ct SE 98031
112th Pl SE
22100-23222 98031
24400-26699 98030
113th Ave SE
19300-22899 98031
25200-25999 98030
113th Ct SE 98031
113th Pl SE
19300-23999 98031
24000-27299 98030
114th Ave SE
22600-23899 98031
24800-27899 98030
114th Ln SE 98030
114th Pl SE
19300-23999 98031
24000-26599 98030
114th Way SE 98031
115th Ave SE
22611-23299 98031
24800-27199 98030
115th Ct SE 98031
115th Pl SE
19300-23399 98031
24200-27099 98030
116th Ave SE
19200-23700 98031
23701-24197 98030
23702-23798 98031
24199-27699 98030
116th Pl SE
22500-22599 98031
22601-23799 98031
24200-27599 98030
117th Ave SE
20000-23899 98031
24200-27599 98030
117th Ct SE 98030
117th Pl SE
19201-19797 98031
19799-23799 98031
24600-27100 98030
27102-27198 98030
118th Ave SE
19800-22299 98031
24300-28019 98030
118th Ct SE 98030
118th Pl SE
20900-23999 98031
24000-27199 98030
118th Way SE 98030
119th Ave SE
19700-23499 98031
24300-26899 98030
119th Ct SE
21600-21699 98031
25100-25999 98030
119th Dr SE 98030
119th Ln SE 98031
119th Pl SE
21100-23799 98031
24100-25899 98030
120th Ave SE
19200-23899 98031
24100-27599 98030
120th Pl SE
19400-22099 98031
25100-27699 98030
121st Ave SE
19500-19899 98031
26000-28199 98030
121st Ct SE 98031
121st Pl SE
19200-21899 98031
24800-27899 98030
121st Way SE 98031
122nd Ave SE
20201-20297 98031
20299-22399 98031
25800-27499 98030
122nd Ct SE
20310-20399 98031
26300-26399 98030
122nd Pl SE
19400-21899 98031
25300-28199 98030
123rd Ave SE
21500-23699 98031
26100-27699 98030
123rd Ct SE 98031
123rd Pl SE 98030
20500-23699 98031
25500-28199 98030
124th Ave SE 98031
24800-27899 98030
124th Pl SE 98030
125th Ave SE
20800-23299 98031
27000-27699 98030
125th Ct SE
22200-22299 98031
27400-27499 98030
125th Pl SE
20200-23899 98031
25900-27999 98030
126th Ave SE
20800-23699 98031
25200-27999 98030
126th Ct SE
22000-22099 98031
27700-27799 98030
126th Ln SE 98030
126th Pl SE
20200-23799 98031
25600-27999 98030
127th Ave SE
22400-23499 98031
25200-27699 98030
127th Ct SE 98031
127th Ln SE 98031
127th Pl SE 98031
128th Ave SE
20100-23699 98031
25300-26699 98030
128th Ct SE
23500-23599 98031
28100-28199 98030
128th Pl SE
22000-23499 98031
24500-27900 98030
27902-27998 98030
129th Ave SE
21400-23699 98031
24100-26900 98030
26902-27398 98030
129th Ct SE
21700-21799 98031
24000-27699 98030
129th Pl SE
21400-22799 98031
24500-28099 98030
130th Ave SE
20100-23799 98031
24000-28299 98030
130th Ct SE 98031
130th Pl SE
20400-23099 98031
24400-25999 98030
131st Ave SE
21000-23699 98031
27400-27998 98030
28000-28099 98030
131st Ct SE
21400-21499 98031
27700-27799 98030
131st Pl SE
20300-22099 98031
24200-26699 98030
132nd Ave, Ct & Pl 98042
133rd Ave, Ct & Pl 98042
134th Ave, Ct, Ln & Pl SE 98042
135th Ave, Ln & Pl 98042
136th Ave & Pl 98042
137th Ave, Ct & Pl 98042
138th Ave, Ct, Ln & Pl SE 98042
139th Ave, Ct, Pl & Way SE 98042
140th Ave, Ct, Ln & Pl SE 98042
141st Ave, Ln & Pl 98042
142nd Ave & Pl 98042
143rd Ave, Ct & Pl 98042
144th Ave & Pl 98042
145th Ave, Ct, Ln & Pl SE 98042
146th Ave & Pl 98042
147th Ave & Pl 98042
148th Ave, Ln, Pl & Way SE 98042
149th Ave & Pl 98042
150th Ave & Ln 98042
150th Ave & Ln 98042
151st Ave SE 98042
151st Pl SE 98042
152nd Ave SE 98042
153rd Ave & Pl 98042
154th Ave & Pl 98042
155th Ave, Ln & Pl 98042
156th Ave SE 98042
156th Pl SE 98042
157th Ave SE 98042
158th Ave SE 98042
159th Ave & Ln 98042
159th Ave & Ln 98042
160th Ave SE 98042
160th Pl SE 98042
161st Ave SE 98042
162nd Ave SE 98042
163rd Ave SE 98042
164th Ave SE 98042
164th Pl SE 98042
165th Ave SE 98042
165th Pl SE 98042
166th Ave SE 98042
166th Pl SE 98042
167th Ave & Pl 98042
168th Ave SE 98042
168th Pl SE 98042
169th Ave SE 98042
170th Ave SE 98042
170th Pl SE 98042
171st Ave SE 98042
172nd Ave SE 98042
172nd Pl SE 98042
173rd Ave SE 98042
174th Ave & Pl 98042
175th Ave SE 98042
175th Pl SE 98042
176th Ave SE 98042
176th Pl SE 98042
177th Ave SE 98042
177th Pl SE 98042
178th Ave, Loop & Pl 98042
179th Ave SE 98042
179th Pl SE 98042
180th Ave SE 98042
180th Pl SE 98042
S 180th St 98032
181st Ct & Pl 98042
181st Ct & Pl 98042
182nd Ave SE 98042
S 182nd St 98032
183rd Ave & Ct 98042
183rd Ave & Ct 98042
184th Ave SE
24100-26199 98042
184th Ct SE
24400-26199 98042
184th Pl SE
24700-26399 98042
S 184th St
7800-7999 98032
8801-8899 98031
185th Ave SE 98042
NE 185th St 98042
186th Ave SE 98042
186th Ct SE 98042
186th Pl SE 98042
S 186th Pl 98032
187th Ave SE
25800-26599 98042
187th Ct SE
24100-26399 98042
187th Pl SE
26200-26299 98042
S 187th St
8000-8099 98032
8600-8999 98031
188th Ave SE 98042
188th Pl SE 98042
S 188th St 98032
189th Ave SE 98042
190th Ave SE
23500-27099 98042
190th Pl SE
24400-26299 98042
S 190th St
6000-6198 98032
6200-7699 98032
7701-7999 98032
8400-8498 98031
8500-8899 98031
8901-8999 98031
191st Pl SE 98042
S 191st Pl 98032
192nd Ave SE 98042
192nd Pl SE 98042
S 192nd St
6600-8299 98032
8600-8899 98031
SE 192nd St 98031
193rd Ave SE 98042
193rd Ct SE 98042
193rd Pl SE
24000-26299 98042
S 193rd Pl 98032
SE 193rd Pl
11300-11799 98031
S 193rd St 98032
SE 193rd Ter 98031
194th Ave SE 98042
194th Pl SE 98042
S 194th St 98032
SE 194th St 98031
195th Ave SE 98042
SE 195th Pl 98031
196th Ave SE 98042
196th Pl SE 98042

S 196th St
5800-8000 98032
8400-8498 98031
SE 196th St 98031
197th Ave SE 98042
SE 197th Pl 98031
198th Ave SE 98042
198th Ct SE
26400-26499 98042
11900-11999 98031
198th Pl SE
25700-25799 98042
12100-12499 98031
S 198th St 98032
SE 198th St 98031
199th Ave SE 98042
SE 199th Ct 98031
199th Pl SE 98042
S 199th Pl 98032
SE 199th St 98031
200th Ave SE 98042
200th Ct SE 98042
200th Pl SE 98042
S 200th St
4300-8399 98032
9000-9198 98031
9200-9900 98031
9902-9998 98031
SE 200th St
10001-10097 98031
10099-12299 98031
13400-14699 98042
201st Ave SE 98042
201st Ct SE 98042
201st Pl SE
26000-26699 98042
11000-12699 98031
SE 201st St
10700-12999 98031
13700-14299 98042
202nd Ave SE 98042
SE 202nd Ct
11100-11199 98031
13700-13799 98042
202nd Ln SE 98031
SE 202nd Pl
10400-12999 98031
13700-13799 98042
S 202nd St
7200-7900 98032
9201-9297 98031
SE 202nd St
10000-10199 98031
14000-14399 98042
S & SE 203rd Pl & St
SE 98042
S & SE 203rd Pl & St
SE 98031
204th Ave SE 98042
S 204th Ct 98031
204th Pl SE
29300-29399 98042
S 204th Pl 98031
SE 204th Pl
10500-13199 98031
14300-20299 98042
S 204th St
4300-7199 98032
9200-9299 98031
SE 204th St 98031
S & SE 205th Ct, Pl &
St 98031
206th Ave SE 98042
206th Ct SE 98042
S 206th Pl 98031
SE 206th Pl 98031
S 206th St 98032
SE 206th St 98031
207th Ave SE 98042
S 207th Ct 98032
S 207th Pl 98031
SE 207th Pl 98031
SE 207th St 98031
208th Ave SE 98042
208th Ct SE 98042
SE 208th Pl 98031

S 208th St
6400-8399 98032
8401-8597 98031
8599-9799 98031
SE 208th St
10000-12499 98031
12501-13099 98031
13200-14699 98042
209th Ave SE 98042
SE 209th Ct 98031
SE 209th Ln 98031
SE 209th Pl 98031
S 209th St 98032
SE 209th St
12000-12499 98031
13400-13499 98042
210th Ave SE 98042
SE 210th Ct 98031
S 210th Pl 98031
SE 210th Pl 98031
S 210th St 98032
SE 210th St 98031
211th Ave SE 98042
211th Ct SE
28700-28799 98042
12600-12699 98031
SE 211th Ln 98031
SE 211th Pl 98031
S 211th St 98032
SE 211th St 98031
212th Ave SE 98042
S 212th Ct 98031
SE 212th Ct 98031
SE 212th Ln 98031
SE 212th Pl
11600-12699 98031
13200-13399 98042
S 212th St
5001-5197 98032
8401-8597 98031
SE 212th St 98031
213th Ave SE 98042
213th Ct SE
28800-28899 98042
10600-12099 98031
S 213th Pl 98031
SE 213th Pl 98031
S 213th St
5200-5299 98032
9500-9999 98031
SE 213th St
10500-12699 98031
14200-14699 98042
213th Way SE 98042
214th Ave SE 98042
SE 214th Ct 98031
S 214th Pl
4600-5099 98032
9400-9599 98031
SE 214th Pl 98031
S 214th St
5000-5099 98032
9600-9699 98031
SE 214th St
11000-12699 98031
14400-14799 98042
S 214th Way 98032
SE 214th Way 98031
215th Ave SE 98042
215th Pl SE
29000-29399 98042
S 215th Pl 98032
SE 215th Pl
12500-12599 98031
SE 215th Pl SE 98042
S 215th St 98032
SE 215th St 98031
215th Ter SE 98042
216th Ave SE 98042
SE 216th Ct 98031
SE 216th Ln 98031
216th Pl SE
29700-29799 98042
S 216th Pl
4200-4599 98032
9300-9399 98031

SE 216th Pl
12900-12999 98031
S 216th St
4100-8299 98032
9600-9999 98031
SE 216th St
10000-13199 98031
13200-14799 98042
SE 217th Ct 98031
217th Pl SE
29700-29799 98042
S 217th Pl 98032
SE 217th Pl
10200-12999 98031
S 217th St 98032
SE 217th St 98031
SE 218th Ct 98031
218th Pl SE
29700-29799 98042
S 218th Pl 98032
SE 218th Pl
10000-13199 98031
S 218th St
4500-8399 98032
8401-8597 98031
8599-9799 98031
SE 218th St
10400-11299 98031
14800-17599 98042
SE 219th Ct 98031
S 219th Pl 98031
SE 219th Pl 98031
S 219th St 98032
SE 219th St
10400-10599 98031
17600-17899 98042
SE 220th Ct 98031
S 220th Ln 98031
S 220th Pl
4001-4097 98032
9201-9917 98031
SE 220th Pl 98031
S 220th St
4300-7100 98032
9800-9999 98031
SE 220th St
10000-10600 98031
14400-14699 98042
221st Ave SE 98042
S 221st Pl
4200-4299 98032
9500-9699 98031
SE 221st Pl 98031
S 221st St
4401-4497 98032
4499-4599 98032
9500-9699 98031
SE 221st St 98031
222nd Ave SE 98042
SE 222nd Ct 98031
S 222nd Pl
3300-4599 98032
9300-9399 98031
SE 222nd Pl 98031
S 222nd St
4500-8299 98032
8400-9899 98031
SE 222nd St
10100-10198 98031
14600-14699 98042
223rd Ave SE 98042
S 223rd Ct 98031
SE 223rd Ct 98031
SE 223rd Dr 98031
SE 223rd Ln 98031
S 223rd Pl 98031
SE 223rd Pl 98031
S 223rd St 98032
SE 223rd St 98031
224th Ave SE 98042
S 224th Pl 98032
SE 224th Pl
10700-11299 98031
13300-13399 98042
S 224th St
6400-8099 98032
9400-9499 98031

SE 224th St
10000-10425 98031
10427-10499 98031
13400-18599 98042
225th Ave SE 98042
SE 225th Ct 98031
S 225th Pl 98032
SE 225th Pl
9300-12599 98031
13200-13399 98042
SE 225th St
10300-10698 98031
10700-11899 98031
16400-16499 98042
226th Ave SE 98042
226th Pl SE
13400-13499 98042
10000-12899 98031
13000-13199 98030
13501-13599 98042
S 226th St
5400-6100 98032
9900-9999 98031
SE 226th St
10400-12699 98031
13200-13399 98042
227th Ave SE 98042
SE 227th Ct 98031
227th Pl SE
32200-32299 98042
S 227th Pl 98032
SE 227th Pl
10900-12099 98031
13200-13499 98042
SE 227th St
10000-12899 98031
13200-15699 98042
SE 228th Ct 98031
S 228th Pl 98031
SE 228th Pl 98031
S 228th St
5600-5998 98032
6000-8299 98032
8400-9599 98031
SE 228th St
10000-10899 98031
14101-17197 98042
17199-17699 98042
SE 229th Ct 98031
SE 229th Pl
10000-11999 98031
14600-22899 98042
SE 229th St 98031
S 230th Pl 98031
SE 230th Pl 98031
S 230th St 98031
SE 230th St
10800-12599 98031
13200-13499 98042
SE 231st Ct 98031
S 231st Pl 98032
SE 231st Pl 98031
S 231st St
5800-6699 98032
9800-9899 98031
SE 231st St
10800-12699 98031
13200-16399 98042
SE 231st Way 98031
S 232nd Ct 98032
SE 232nd Ct 98031
S 232nd Pl 98032
SE 232nd Pl
10500-13099 98031
13300-15599 98042
S 232nd St
5000-5799 98032
9300-9699 98031
SE 232nd St
10400-12899 98031
13600-17499 98042
SE 233rd Ct 98031
S 233rd Pl
4900-6099 98032
9400-9499 98031
SE 233rd Pl 98031
S 233rd St 98032

SE 233rd St
10000-11498 98031
11500-12599 98031
13200-13799 98042
S 234th Pl
5100-5999 98032
9500-9799 98031
SE 234th Pl
10300-11799 98031
14400-15499 98042
S 234th St 98032
SE 234th St
11200-13199 98031
13200-15499 98042
S 235th Pl 98031
SE 235th Pl 98031
S 235th St
5600-6099 98032
8621-8999 98031
SE 235th St
10000-12699 98031
13200-16799 98042
SE 236th Ct 98031
S 236th Pl
5400-6599 98032
8400-9699 98031
SE 236th Pl
10400-13199 98031
13200-18999 98042
S 236th St
3900-6399 98032
9800-9999 98031
SE 236th St
10101-10197 98031
14900-16699 98042
SE 237th Ct 98031
S 237th Pl
5100-5599 98032
9200-9999 98031
SE 237th Pl
11200-12999 98031
13700-14099 98042
19000-19099 98042
S 237th St
5600-6299 98032
9900-9999 98031
SE 237th St
10200-10799 98031
13400-13499 98042
S 238th Ct 98032
SE 238th Ln 98042
S 238th Pl 98032
SE 238th Pl
11100-12499 98031
13900-13999 98042
S 238th St 98032
SE 238th St
10000-11799 98031
17200-17699 98042
S 239th Pl
3500-6799 98032
9200-9799 98031
SE 239th Pl 98031
S 239th St
3501-3697 98032
9200-9299 98031
SE 239th St
10200-10300 98031
13400-13498 98042
S 240th Ct 98032
S 240th Pl 98030
SE 240th Pl
10800-11999 98030
13400-18599 98042
S 240th St
2701-2997 98032
9245-9247 98031
SE 240th St
10000-10198 98031
10612-10612 98064
10614-13198 98031
13200-17899 98042
SE 241st Pl
10800-11099 98030
13400-14499 98042
19400-19599 98042

S 241st St
3600-3999 98032
9400-9699 98030
SE 241st St
12800-12899 98030
13400-14099 98042
18600-18699 98042
S 242nd Ct 98030
SE 242nd Ct
12800-12899 98030
18400-18499 98042
S 242nd Pl
6100-6399 98032
9800-9926 98030
SE 242nd Pl
10000-10299 98030
13900-13999 98042
S 242nd St
3600-4199 98032
9400-9498 98030
SE 242nd St
10700-11799 98030
13400-13499 98042
S 243rd Pl 98032
SE 243rd Pl 98042
S 243rd St
3600-4199 98032
9600-9699 98030
SE 243rd St
10100-12999 98030
14000-17499 98042
19000-19499 98042
SE 244th Ct
10000-10099 98030
13700-13799 98042
SE 244th Ln 98042
244th Pl SE
10800-10899 98030
S 244th Pl 98030
SE 244th Pl
17200-18299 98042
S 244th St
2801-3497 98032
9200-9399 98030
SE 244th St
10000-12999 98030
14600-14799 98042
S 245th Ct 98032
SE 245th Ct 98042
245th Pl SE
10800-10899 98030
S 245th Pl 98030
SE 245th Pl
10000-11999 98030
18500-18599 98042
SE 245th St
12800-13199 98030
13200-17899 98042
S 246th Ct 98032
SE 246th Ct 98042
S 246th Pl 98030
SE 246th Pl
10000-12899 98030
14600-14799 98042
18500-18599 98042
SE 246th St
12900-13099 98030
13700-13899 98042
18000-18399 98042
S 247th Ct
4200-4299 98032
9800-9899 98030
S 247th Pl 98030
SE 247th Pl
10000-13099 98030
18400-18499 98042
S 247th St
4200-4299 98032
9400-9499 98030
SE 247th St 98042
SE 248th Ct 98030
S 248th Pl
3300-4599 98032
9900-9911 98030
SE 248th Pl
11100-11799 98030
13300-13399 98042

S 248th St
2101-2597 98032
9400-9999 98030
SE 248th St
10104-13099 98030
18000-18099 98042
SE 249th Ct 98030
S 249th Pl
2100-3599 98032
9900-9999 98030
SE 249th Pl
12000-12099 98030
13500-13599 98042
16000-16299 98042
S 249th St 98032
SE 249th St
10000-11799 98030
13200-13399 98042
SE 250th Ct
10900-11899 98030
13400-13499 98042
16000-16799 98042
S 250th Pl 98032
SE 250th Pl
10400-12099 98030
16200-16399 98042
S 250th St 98032
SE 250th St
12900-12999 98030
13500-13599 98042
S 251st Ct 98032
SE 251st Ct 98030
S 251st Pl 98032
SE 251st Pl
10900-12499 98030
13500-14499 98042
16700-17099 98042
S 251st St 98032
SE 251st St
11000-13199 98030
13600-14099 98042
15200-17199 98042
SE 252nd Ct 98042
S 252nd Pl 98032
SE 252nd Pl
10900-12799 98030
13800-14599 98042
15300-16999 98042
S 252nd St
2100-2498 98032
2500-4299 98032
9600-9899 98030
SE 252nd St
10500-12999 98030
13200-19699 98042
13400-17799 98042
SE 253rd Ct 98030
S 253rd Pl 98032
SE 253rd Pl
10400-11299 98030
13200-13999 98042
15000-16799 98042
S 253rd St 98032
SE 253rd St
11600-12000 98030
12002-12298 98030
13700-13899 98042
SE 254th Ct 98030
S 254th Pl 98032
SE 254th Pl
10600-10898 98030
10900-12799 98030
13600-16999 98042
S 254th St 98032
SE 254th St
11800-12899 98030
14100-15499 98042
15900-18199 98042
S 255th Pl 98032
SE 255th Pl
10900-11799 98030
11801-12699 98030
13700-14399 98042
15600-16999 98042
S 255th St 98032
SE 255th St
11800-11899 98030

13200-14199 98042
15500-15999 98042
S 256th Ct 98032
S 256th Pl 98032
SE 256th Pl
10900-13000 98030
13700-14499 98042
S 256th St 98032
SE 256th St
10000-10098 98030
13200-18500 98042
SE 257th Ct 98042
S 257th Pl 98032
SE 257th Pl
11400-11599 98030
14200-14499 98042
17000-17099 98042
S 257th St 98032
SE 257th St
10900-12999 98030
13500-13599 98042
15800-18999 98042
S 258th Pl
2700-4699 98032
8700-8799 98030
SE 258th Pl
10000-12399 98030
13700-14499 98042
18500-20199 98042
S 258th St 98032
SE 258th St
11400-13199 98030
13500-13599 98042
15800-20299 98042
S 259th Ct 98032
SE 259th Ct 98042
S 259th Ln 98032
S 259th Pl 98032
SE 259th Pl
11700-13199 98030
14100-17799 98042
S 259th St
2700-7899 98032
8101-8297 98030
SE 259th St
10900-12899 98030
13700-14099 98042
SE 260th Ct 98042
S 260th Ln 98032
SE 260th Ln 98042
SE 260th Pl
10700-12399 98030
16200-20199 98042
S 260th St 98032
SE 260th St
10200-11999 98030
13200-15899 98042
15700-20799 98042
SE 261st Ct
12100-12199 98030
15900-20299 98042
S 261st Pl 98032
SE 261st Pl
10601-11797 98030
11799-13199 98030
15500-20599 98042
S 261st St 98032
SE 261st St
12200-13199 98030
13200-14599 98042
16600-19799 98042
SE 262nd Ct 98030
S 262nd Pl
4000-4199 98032
9600-9899 98030
SE 262nd Pl
10600-12899 98030
15600-18299 98042
S 262nd St 98032
SE 262nd St
12300-12399 98030
14300-14799 98042
16900-20899 98042
SE 263rd Ct 98030
SE 263rd Pl
13000-13099 98030
13101-13199 98030
13200-13399 98042
15600-20899 98042
S 263rd St 98032
SE 263rd St
12000-12299 98030
12301-12399 98030
14400-20599 98042
16400-19299 98042
SE 264th Ct 98042
SE 264th Pl
11018-13199 98030
15600-19799 98042
SE 264th St
10200-12699 98030
13500-15099 98042
SE 265th Ct
11800-12599 98030
15800-16299 98042
SE 265th Pl
11200-12699 98030
13500-20399 98042
S 265th St
3000-3099 98032
9801-9899 98030
SE 265th St
11400-12899 98030
15600-19899 98042
SE 266th Ct
11600-11699 98030
19800-19899 98042
SE 266th Pl
10500-13199 98030
16300-19799 98042
S 266th St
8001-8099 98032
8400-8498 98030
SE 266th St
11100-12699 98030
13200-14699 98042
16100-20199 98042
SE 267th Ct 98042
SE 267th Pl
11200-11299 98030
13600-13699 98042
16100-20099 98042
S 267th St 98030
SE 267th St
10000-10399 98030
14600-14699 98042
14800-19499 98042
SE 268th Ct 98042
SE 268th Ln 98042
S 268th Pl 98032
SE 268th Pl 98042
S 268th St 98032
SE 268th St
10000-12999 98030
13200-13799 98042
SE 269th Pl
11700-12099 98030
16900-19599 98042
S 269th St 98032
SE 269th St
10100-11699 98030
16400-21099 98042
SE 270th Ct
11000-11099 98030
19000-19099 98042
SE 270th Pl
10100-12299 98030
14200-14999 98042
16600-19599 98042
S 270th St 98032
SE 270th St
10900-12699 98030
13200-13800 98042
13802-14898 98042
17600-20999 98042
SE 271st Ct 98042
S 271st Pl 98032
SE 271st Pl
10500-10599 98030
14900-14999 98042
18800-19699 98042
S 271st St 98032
SE 271st St
10500-11399 98030
13800-13899 98042
16700-21199 98042
SE 272nd Ct 98042
S 272nd Pl 98032
SE 272nd Pl 98030
S 272nd St 98032
SE 272nd St
10400-10799 98030
13200-19899 98042
15601-16197 98042
16199-17700 98042
17702-20798 98042
19901-20599 98042
SE 273rd Ct
10600-12999 98030
13600-14499 98042
S 273rd Pl 98032
SE 273rd Pl
10300-12900 98030
12902-12998 98030
15200-15399 98042
SE 273rd St
12900-12998 98030
13300-13799 98042
SE 274th Ct
13100-13199 98030
14400-14799 98042
SE 274th Ln 98042
S 274th Pl 98032
SE 274th Pl 98042
SE 274th St
11200-12699 98030
12701-13199 98030
13300-14999 98042
SE 275th Pl
12300-12599 98030
13700-14699 98042
SE 275th St
10800-11798 98030
11800-12999 98030
13700-15499 98042
17200-17299 98042
SE 275th Way 98042
SE 276th Ct 98030
SE 276th Pl
12000-12899 98030
14400-15599 98042
SE 276th St
10500-12199 98030
13200-20699 98042
SE 276th Way 98030
SE 277th Ct
12700-12799 98030
14600-14699 98042
SE 277th Pl
10500-13199 98030
15200-18699 98042
S 277th St
8000-8098 98032
9200-9498 98030
SE 277th St
10700-12999 98030
18801-19097 98042
19099-19999 98042
SE 278th Ct
12700-12799 98030
18600-18699 98042
SE 278th Pl
12400-13199 98030
14400-15199 98042
16800-16899 98042
SE 278th St
10600-12999 98030
13200-19299 98042
16500-16599 98042
SE 279th Ct 98030
SE 279th Pl
12500-13199 98030
13200-18499 98042
16600-16699 98042
279th St SE
15400-15499 98042
10600-10699 98030
15400-15599 98042
SE 280th Ct
12100-12199 98030
13500-13699 98042
SE 280th Pl
13000-13099 98030
13600-18099 98042
SE 280th St
10400-12899 98030
13500-19399 98042
SE 281st Ct
12000-12099 98030
13600-17999 98042
SE 281st Pl 98042
SE 281st St 98042
SE 282nd Ct 98042
SE 282nd Pl 98042
SE 282nd St
12410-12648 98030
13200-18799 98042
SE 282nd Way 98030
283rd Ct, Pl & St 98042
SE 284th Ct 98042
SE 284th Pl 98042
S 284th St 98032
SE 284th St 98042
285th Pl & St 98042
286th Ct, Pl & St 98042
SE 287th St 98042
288th Ln, Pl & St 98042
289th St & Way 98042
290th Pl & St 98042
291st Pl & St 98042
292nd Ct, Pl & St 98042
293rd Ct, Pl & St 98042
294th St & Way 98042
SE 295th St 98042
SE 296th St 98042
297th Ct, Pl, St & Ter 98042
298th Pl & St 98042
299th Ct, Pl & Way 98042
300th Pl & St 98042
SE 301st St 98042
302nd Ct, Pl & St 98042
303rd Pl & St 98042
304th Pl & St 98042
306th Pl & St 98042
307th Ln, Pl & St 98042
SE 308th St 98042
SE 309th St 98042
310th Ct, Pl & St 98042
SE 311th Ct 98042
SE 314th Pl 98042
316th Pl & St 98042
SE 319th St 98042
SE 320th St 98042
321st Pl & St 98042
322nd Pl & St 98042
SE 323rd St 98042
SE 324th St 98042
328th Pl & St 98042

KETTLE FALLS WA

General Delivery 99107

POST OFFICE BOXES MAIN OFFICE STATIONS AND BRANCHES

Box No.s
All PO Boxes 99107

RURAL ROUTES

02 99107

NAMED STREETS

All Street Addresses 99107

KIRKLAND WA

General Delivery 98033

POST OFFICE BOXES MAIN OFFICE STATIONS AND BRANCHES

Box No.s
1 - 4988 98083
8001 - 8626 98034
97000 - 97115 98083

NAMED STREETS

Alexander Ave 98033
Bridlewood Cir 98033
Carillon Pt 98033
Cedar St 98033
Central Way 98033
NE Champagne Point Ln, Pl & Rd NE 98034
Forbes Creek Dr 98033
Garendal Ave NE 98034
Holiday Dr NE 98034
Holmes Point Dr NE 98034
NE Juanita Dr & Ln NE 98034
Juanita Woodinville Way NE 98034
Kirkland Ave, Cir & Way 98033
Kirkwood Mall 98033
Lake Ave & St 98033
Lake Shore Plz 98033
Lake Washington Blvd NE 98033
Lakeview Dr 98033
Main St S 98033
Market St 98033
North Ave 98033
Northup Way 98033
Observation Dr 98033
Ohde Ave & Cir 98033
Park Ln 98033
Parkplace Ctr 98033
NE Points Dr 98033
Rose Point Ln 98033
Simonds Rd NE 98034
Slater Ave NE
9000-11499 98033
11600-12099 98034
12101-12421 98034
Slater St 98033
Slater St S 98033
State St S 98033
NE Totem Lake Blvd & Way NE 98034
Trichean Ave NE 98033
Waverly Way 98033
Waverly Park Way 98033
Willows Rd NE 98034
NE Woodland Cove Dr 98034

NUMBERED STREETS

1st Ave & St 98033
2nd Ave & St S & W 98033
3rd Ave, Ln, Pl & St S & W 98033
4th Ave
1-722 98033
721-721 98083
723-799 98033
724-798 98033
4th Ave S 98033
4th Pl 98033
4th St 98033
4th St S 98033
4th St W 98033
5th Ave, Ln, Pl & St S & W 98033
6th Ave, Ct, Pl & St S & W 98033
7th Ave & St S & W 98033
8th Ave, Ln & St S & W 98033
9th Ave, Ln & St S & W 98033
10th Ave, Pl & St S & W 98033
11th Ave & Pl 98033
12th Ave 98033
13th W 98033
14th Ave & Pl W 98033
15th Ave & Pl 98033
16th Ave & Ln 98033
17th Ave & Pl 98033
18th Ave & Pl 98033
19th Ave, Ln & Pl 98033
20th Ave & Pl 98033
21st Pl 98033
37th Cir & Ct 98033
38th Ct, Pl & St 98033
41st Dr, Ln & St 98033
NE 42nd Pl 98033
43rd Pl & St 98033
NE 44th St 98033
NE 45th St 98033
NE 46th St 98033
47th Pl & St 98033
48th Pl & St 98033
NE 49th St 98033
NE 50th Pl 98033
NE 52nd St 98033
NE 53rd St 98033
NE 55th St 98033
NE 57th St 98033
58th Pl, St & Way 98033
59th Pl & St 98033
60th Ln & St 98033
61st Pl & St 98033
62nd Ave NE 98034
NE 62nd St 98033
63rd Ave NE 98034
NE 63rd St 98033
64th Ave NE 98034
64th Ct NE 98034
64th Pl NE 98034
NE 64th St 98033
64th Ter NE 98034
NE 65th Ct 98033
NE 65th Ln 98033
65th Pl NE
13800-13899 98034
10500-12422 98033
NE 65th St 98033
66th Ave NE 98034
NE 66th Ln 98033
66th Pl NE
13000-13199 98034
10900-12699 98033
NE 66th St 98033
67th Ave NE 98034
NE 67th Pl 98033
NE 67th St 98033
68th Ave NE 98034
68th Pl NE
13200-13399 98034
10200-12699 98033
NE 68th St 98033
69th Ave NE 98034
NE 69th Pl 98033
70th Ave NE 98034
NE 70th Ct 98033
NE 70th Dr 98033
70th Ln NE 98034
70th Pl NE
13300-13399 98034
11600-13199 98033
NE 70th St 98033
71st Ave NE 98034
NE 71st Ct 98033
NE 71st Ln 98033
71st Pl NE 98034
NE 71st St 98033
72nd Ave NE 98034
NE 72nd Ln 98033
72nd Pl NE 98034
NE 72nd St 98033
73rd Ave NE 98034
73rd Pl NE
11600-12300 98034
12300-12399 98033
NE 73rd St 98033
74th Ave NE 98034
74th Pl NE 98034
NE 74th St 98033
75th Ave NE 98034
NE 75th Pl 98033
NE 75th St 98033
76th Ave NE 98034
76th Ct NE 98034
76th Pl NE 98034
NE 76th St 98033
77th Ave NE 98034
NE 77th Ct 98033
78th Ln NE 98034
78th Pl NE
12000-13499 98034
12900-12999 98033
NE 78th St 98033
79th Ave, Ct, Pl & Way NE 98034
80th Ave NE 98034
NE 80th Ln 98033
80th Pl NE
10900-12599 98034
12500-12599 98033
NE 80th St 98033
NE 80th Way 98033
81st Ave NE 98034
NE 81st Cir 98033
81st Ct NE 98034
NE 81st Dr 98033
81st Pl NE
10900-14199 98034
12600-12799 98033
82nd Ave NE 98034
NE 82nd Ln 98033
82nd Pl NE 98034
83rd Ave NE 98034
83rd Ct NE
12700-12799 98034
12700-12799 98033
83rd Ln NE
12700-12799 98034
12700-12799 98033
83rd Pl NE 98034
NE 83rd St 98033
84th Ave NE 98034
84th Ct NE 98034
NE 84th Ln 98033
84th Pl NE 98034
NE 84th St 98033
85th Ave NE 98034
85th Pl NE 98034
NE 85th St 98033
86th Ave NE 98034
86th Pl NE 98034
NE 86th St 98033
NE 86th Way 98033
87th Ave NE 98034
87th Ct NE
12300-14299 98034
12500-12599 98033
NE 87th Ln 98033
87th Pl NE
11900-14199 98034
12600-12699 98033
NE 87th St 98033
88th Ave NE 98034
88th Ct NE 98034
NE 88th Ln 98033
88th Pl NE 98034
NE 88th St 98033
89th Ave, Ct & Pl 98034
90th Ave NE 98034
90th Ct NE 98034
90th Pl NE 98034
NE 90th St 98033
91st Ave NE 98034
91st Ct NE 98034
91st Ln NE
11600-11699 98034

11100-12999 98033
91st Pl NE 98034
NE 91st St 98034
92nd Ave NE 98034
NE 92nd Ln 98033
92nd Pl NE
13400-14299 98034
12700-12799 98034
NE 92nd St 98033
93rd Ave, Ct, Ln & Pl
NE 98034
94th Ave NE 98034
NE 94th Ct 98033
94th Pl NE
12100-13499 98034
11600-12399 98033
NE 94th St 98033
NE 94th Way 98033
95th Ave NE 98034
NE 95th Ln 98033
95th Pl NE 98034
NE 95th St 98033
96th Ave NE
3601-3697 98033
3699-3799 98033
12000-12899 98034
96th Pl NE
12200-13099 98034
13000-13099 98033
NE 96th St 98033
97th Ave NE
3800-3999 98033
11800-14199 98034
97th Ln NE
11600-11899 98034
11600-11699 98033
97th Pl NE
12200-12899 98034
12700-12799 98033
NE 97th St 98033
98th Ave NE
11200-11499 98033
11600-14098 98034
98th Pl NE
12700-12899 98034
13000-13099 98033
NE 98th St 98033
99th Ave NE 98034
NE 99th Ln 98033
99th Pl NE 98033
100th Ave NE
11000-11198 98033
11200-11499 98033
11600-14499 98034
100th Ln NE 98034
100th Pl NE
13200-13399 98034
11000-12799 98033
NE 100th St 98033
101st Ave NE
10800-11399 98033
12000-12099 98034
101st Ct NE
6200-6299 98033
12300-12399 98034
101st Ln NE
13000-13399 98034
12300-12399 98033
101st Pl NE
10800-11599 98033
11600-14499 98034
11600-13099 98033
NE 101st St 98033
101st Way NE
3700-3799 98033
12500-12599 98034
102nd Ave NE
6500-10999 98033
12600-14499 98034
102nd Ct NE
11400-11599 98033
12000-14099 98034
102nd Ln NE
4400-5099 98033
12300-13399 98034
12300-12399 98033

102nd Pl NE
6200-6699 98033
11600-14099 98034
11100-13099 98033
NE 102nd St 98033
102nd Way NE 98034
103rd Ave NE
6400-11299 98033
11700-14399 98034
NE 103rd Ct 98033
103rd Ln NE
4500-4699 98033
13300-13399 98034
12201-12216 98033
103rd Pl NE
11400-11599 98033
12700-13199 98034
11200-13099 98033
NE 103rd St 98033
104th Ave NE
5500-11299 98033
11600-14499 98034
104th Pl NE
13000-14199 98034
13000-13099 98033
NE 104th St 98033
NE 104th Way 98033
105th Ave NE
4200-11199 98033
11900-14499 98034
105th Ct NE
11400-11499 98033
13900-14499 98034
11700-12799 98033
NE 105th Ln 98033
105th Pl NE
11400-11599 98033
12100-13099 98034
12400-12999 98033
NE 105th St 98033
106th Ave NE
4700-11399 98033
11600-14399 98034
106th Ct NE 98033
106th Ln NE
13100-13199 98034
11400-12799 98033
106th Pl NE
4100-10699 98033
12400-14499 98034
11100-12899 98033
NE 106th St 98033
107th Ave NE
5100-5199 98033
12100-14699 98034
NE 107th Ln 98033
107th Pl NE
4100-11499 98033
12300-14499 98034
10600-12899 98033
NE 107th St 98033
108th Ave NE
4500-11499 .... 98033.
11600-14299 98034
108th Ct NE 98033
NE 108th Ln 98033
108th Pl NE
6200-11099 98033
14400-14499 98034
12100-12899 98033
NE 108th St 98033
109th Ave NE
4700-11499 98033
11900-14399 98034
109th Ct NE 98034
NE 109th Ln 98033
109th Pl NE
4400-11199 98033
12200-13199 98033
NE 109th St 98033
NE 109th Way 98033
110th Ave NE
4500-11499 98033
11600-14399 98034
NE 110th Ct 98033
110th Ln NE
12400-12499 98034

12200-12299 98033
110th Pl NE
9300-9499 98033
13400-14099 98034
8000-8699 98034
12400-13199 98033
NE 110th St 98033
111th Ave NE
4800-11099 98033
11600-14699 98034
111th Ct NE
10700-10899 98033
13200-13299 98034
111th Ln NE
5200-5299 98033
12400-12499 98034
111th Pl NE
5900-11599 98033
12900-14799 98033
10100-13199 98033
NE 111th St 98033
112th Ave NE
4500-11199 98033
11700-14799 98034
112th Ct NE 98033
112th Dr NE 98033
112th Ln NE 98033
112th Pl NE
5800-11599 98033
12800-14299 98034
10100-12699 98033
NE 112th St
7300-8099 98034
10000-13199 98033
112th Way NE 98034
113th Ave NE
6100-6599 98033
12000-14899 98034
113th Ct NE
10300-10999 98033
12600-12699 98033
113th Ln NE 98033
113th Pl NE
5300-11599 98033
11600-14499 98034
10100-12799 98033
NE 113th St
8100-8199 98034
12800-13099 98033
113th Way NE 98033
114th Ave NE
4900-10005 98033
11600-14999 98034
114th Ct NE
11500-11599 98033
11500-11599 98033
114th Dr NE 98034
114th Ln NE
13100-13199 98034
10500-10599 98033
114th Pl NE
10006-10599 98033
11700-11799 98034
7900-7999 98034
10300-12699 98033
NE 114th St
8000-8099 98034
10400-12799 98033
115th Ave NE
11100-11199 98033
11800-11998 98034
115th Ct NE
10800-11099 98033
8100-8199 98034
11400-11599 98033
115th Ln NE
11400-11599 98033
10000-10599 98033
115th Pl NE
5800-11299 98033
8200-8299 98034
10400-12399 98033
NE 115th Way 98034
116th Ave NE
4600-11199 98033
12200-13999 98034
116th Ct NE 98034

NE 116th Ln 98034
116th Pl NE
6500-11399 98033
13200-15299 98034
8800-11499 98034
NE 116th St 98034
117th Ave NE
4100-9599 98033
13300-14399 98034
NE 117th Ct 98034
117th Dr NE 98033
NE 117th Ln 98034
117th Pl NE
4700-11399 98033
13000-15299 98034
8100-12599 98033
NE 117th St 98034
118th Ave NE
4100-8299 98033
11700-15299 98034
118th Ct NE 98033
NE 118th Ln 98033
118th Pl NE
6700-11099 98033
13000-14299 98034
7300-10399 98033
NE 118th St 98034
119th Ave NE
6700-10399 98033
13200-15199 98034
NE 119th Ct 98034
119th Pl NE
4800-4898 98033
4900-4999 98033
13000-14899 98034
7200-10599 98033
NE 119th St 98034
NE 119th Way 98034
120th Ave NE
6000-11499 98033
11600-14099 98034
120th Ct NE 98034
120th Ln NE
14435-14436 98034
10000-13199 98034
120th Pl NE
6100-6199 98033
11800-14499 98034
7200-10599 98034
NE 120th St 98034
121st Ave NE 98034
121st Ct NE
14700-14799 98034
9200-9399 98034
121st Ln NE
7300-7399 98033
9600-13099 98034
121st Pl NE
10700-12199 98033
14400-14499 98034
7200-9499 98034
NE 121st St 98034
121st Way NE 98034
122nd Ave NE
6100-8999 98033
13400-14299 98034
122nd Ct NE
9200-9299 98033
15100-15199 98034
122nd Ln NE
9600-11200 98033
13000-13199 98034
7700-12999 98034
122nd Pl NE
6800-6899 98033
13200-15099 98034
7800-9699 98034
NE 122nd St 98034
NE 122nd Way 98034
123rd Ave NE
6100-10799 98033
13400-15099 98034
NE 123rd Ct 98034
123rd Ln NE
8700-11299 98033
13000-14499 98034
10900-11199 98034

NE 123rd Pl 98034
NE 123rd St 98034
124th Ave NE
6400-11599 98033
11600-14524 98034
124th Ct NE
5800-8099 98033
13200-13599 98034
10500-10599 98034
124th Ln NE
12800-12899 98034
11000-11199 98034
124th Pl NE
7500-7599 98033
14100-14199 98034
8200-10199 98034
NE 124th St 98034
125th Ave NE
6400-10599 98033
13200-14199 98034
NE 125th Ct 98034
125th Dr NE
12800-13199 98034
10000-10199 98034
125th Ln NE
5600-8999 98033
12800-14299 98034
9800-11199 98034
125th Pl NE
7500-8299 98033
14000-14199 98034
8200-10699 98034
NE 125th St 98034
NE 125th Way 98034
126th Ave NE
6000-11399 98033
13900-14399 98034
126th Ct NE 98034
126th Pl NE
8100-10999 98033
13200-14199 98034
8000-13799 98034
NE 126th St 98034
126th Way NE 98034
127th Ave NE
5500-11499 98033
13500-14599 98034
NE 127th Ct 98034
127th Dr NE 98034
127th Ln NE
6500-6599 98033
11600-14599 98034
127th Pl NE
7900-11399 98033
13300-14099 98034
8800-10099 98034
NE 127th St 98034
128th Ave NE
6000-11299 98033
13200-14299 98034
128th Ln NE
12400-12498 98034
9100-9399 98034
128th Pl NE
7500-11099 98033
13400-14299 98034
12900-13199 98034
NE 128th St 98034
NE 128th Way 98034
129th Ave NE
7300-10499 98033
12800-14524 98034
129th Ct NE
13100-13199 98034
8700-12799 98034
NE 129th Dr 98034
129th Ln NE
12000-12299 98034
10200-10299 98034
129th Pl NE
9900-11099 98033
13200-14499 98034
6400-13599 98034
NE 129th St 98034
130th Ave NE
6100-11099 98033
12800-14499 98034

130th Ct NE
12800-13999 98034
12400-12799 98034
130th Ln NE
12000-13199 98034
6600-13199 98034
130th Pl NE
13200-14399 98034
6000-13299 98034
NE 130th St 98034
NE 130th Way 98034
131st Ave NE
7700-11099 98033
12900-14399 98034
131st Ct NE
12500-12599 98034
8000-12499 98034
131st Ln NE
12000-13099 98034
11200-11299 98034
131st Pl NE
7400-10099 98033
12200-14499 98034
7200-13299 98034
NE 131st St 98034
NE 131st Way 98034
132nd Ave NE
6000-10699 98033
10701-11299 98033
11601-12397 98034
12399-14299 98034
14301-14599 98034
NE 132nd Ct 98034
NE 132nd Ln 98034
NE 132nd Pl 98034
NE 132nd St 98034
133rd Ave NE
6100-10399 98033
13400-13699 98034
NE 133rd Ct 98034
133rd Ln NE
13400-13499 98034
10200-10299 98034
133rd Pl NE
12800-13899 98034
7700-12999 98034
NE 133rd St 98034
134th Ave NE
6600-10699 98033
13000-13799 98034
134th Ct NE
13600-13699 98034
9900-12199 98034
NE 134th Ln 98034
134th Pl NE
9500-9599 98033
9700-13399 98034
NE 134th St 98034
135th Ave NE
6100-6399 98033
12500-13799 98034
NE 135th Ct 98034
NE 135th Ln 98034
NE 135th Pl 98034
NE 135th St 98034
136th Ave NE
6000-10399 98033
12800-13799 98034
136th Ct NE 98034
136th Pl NE
13200-13299 98034
9200-13799 98034
NE 136th St 98034
137th Ct, Pl & St NE 98034
138th Ave NE 98033
NE 138th Ct 98034
NE 138th Pl 98034
NE 138th St 98034
NE 139th Ave, Ct, Pl &
St NE 98034
140th Ct, Pl & St 98034
NE 141st Ave, Ct, Pl,
St & Way NE 98034
142nd Ct, Ln, Pl, St &
Way 98034
143rd Ct, Pl & St 98034

144th Ct, Ln, Pl, St &
Way 98034
145th Pl & St 98034
NE 146th St 98034
147th Ct, Pl & St 98034
148th Ct, Pl & St 98034
149th Ct, Pl & St 98034
150th Ct, Pl & St 98034
151st Pl & St 98034
153rd Pl & St 98034
NE 155th St 98034

LACEY WA

POST OFFICE BOXES MAIN OFFICE STATIONS AND BRANCHES

Box No.s
All PO Boxes 98509

NAMED STREETS

Abbey Way SE 98503
Acorn Ct SE 98503
Afflerbaugh Ct & Dr 98503
Agate Ct SE 98503
Alabaster Ln & St 98503
Alanna Dr SE 98503
Aldea Ct SE 98503
Alder St SE 98503
Alderwood Ct SE 98503
Alexander Dr NE 98516
Alexandria Ln SE 98503
Alice Ct SE 98503
Allegheny Ct SE 98503
Alpha St SE 98503
Angela St SE 98503
Annette Ct SE 98503
Apollo St SE 98503
Arbor Ct & Dr 98503
Arcarro Ct SE 98503
Asia Ct SE 98503
Asotin Ln SE 98503
Athena Ct SE 98503
Atlenso Ave SE 98503
Aurora St NE 98516
Austin Ln SE 98503
Avery Ln SE 98503
Avonlea Dr SE 98503
Axis St SE 98513
Bacchus Ct SE 98503
Bailey St SE 98513
Bainbridge Ct & Loop 98516
Balata Ct NE 98516
Balboa Ln SE 98503
Bali St NE 98516
Balustrade Blvd SE 98513
Banbury Pl SE 98503
Barklay Dr NE 98516
Barstow Ln SE 98513
Baylor Ct SE 98503
Beaumont Ln SE 98503
Becket St NE 98516
Beckonridge Ln &
Loop 98513
Beemer Ct NE 98516
Belair Dr SE 98503
Beltway Loop SE 98513
Bend Ct & Dr 98516
Bentley Ct NE 98516
Beta St SE 98503
Beth Ct NE 98516
N & S Bicentennial
Loop 98503
Bismark Ln SE 98503
Blackberry Ct SE 98503
Blade St SE 98513
Blakley Loop NE 98516
Blue Finch Ct SE 98503
Blue Jay Ct SE 98503
Blueberry Ct SE 98503

Boardwalk St SE 98503
Boat Launch St SE 98503
Bobcat Dr SE 98503
Bonanza Ct & Dr 98516
Boone St SE 98503
Boulevard Park Ln SE 98503
Bowker St SE 98503
Breccea Ln SE 98503
Brentwood Dr & Pl 98503
Bretherton Ave NE 98516
Breton Ln SE 98503
Brillshire Ln SE 98503
Brittany Ln NE 98516
Britton Ln NE 98516
Bruno Ln SE 98503
Brunswick St SE 98503
Bryanston Ln SE 98513
Bucknell Ct SE 98503
Budd Ct NE 98516
Bulldog St SE 98503
Butterball Ln NE 98516
Callison Rd NE 98516
Calypso Ct SE 98503
Camano Ct & Loop 98516
Camaro Ct SE 98503
Cameron Dr & Ln 98516
Campus Dr NE 98516
Campus Glen Dr NE 98516
Campus Green Ct, Dr & Loop 98516
Campus Highlands Dr NE 98516
Campus Meadows Loop NE 98516
Campus Prairie Loop NE 98516
Candace Ct SE 98513
Candlewood Ct & Dr 98503
Canonbury Ln SE 98513
Cantabella Ct 98503
Capstan Dr NE 98516
Cardinal Ln SE 98503
Carmel Ct & Ln 98503
Carnegie Dr SE 98503
Carpenter Ct SE 98503
Carpenter Loop SE 98503
Carpenter Rd NE 98516
Carpenter Rd SE 98503
Carpenter Hills Loop SE 98503
Carson Ln SE 98503
Cascade Ct SE 98503
Cashmere Dr NE 98516
Catalina Dr SE 98503
Cedar Ct SE 98503
Cedar Hills Ct SE 98503
Cedarbaough Ct NE 98516
Century Ct NE 98516
Chambers Lake Dr & Ln 98503
Channel View Ln SE 98503
Chardonnay Dr SE 98513
Chelan Ln SE 98503
Cherokee Loop SE 98513
Chetshire Ln SE 98513
Chinook St NE 98516
Choker St SE 98503
Christa Dr NE 98516
Christine Ct NE 98516
Church St SE 98503
Circle Ct, Ln & Loop 98503
Citadel Ct SE 98503
Clarendon Ln SE 98513
Classic Dr NE 98516
Clearbrook Dr SE 98503
Clearwater Ct, Dr & Loop 98503
Colebrooke Ln SE 98513
Colleen Ct & St 98503
College Ln NE 98516
College Ln SE 98503
College St NE 98516
College St SE 98503
College Glen Loop SE 98503
Cologne Ct SE 98503
Colorado Ave SE 98513
Columbia Way NE 98516
Columbine Ct SE 98513
Commerce Place Dr NE 98516
Compass St SE 98513
Compton Blvd & Loop 98513
Concordia Ln SE 98503
Cook Ct NE 98516
Cora St SE 98503
Cornell Ct SE 98503
Corona Ct & St 98516
Corporate Center Ct, Dr, Ln & Loop SE 98503
Corvette Ct NE 98516
Cory Ct SE 98513
Cottage Ln SE 98503
Cottonwood Ct SE 98503
Cougar St SE 98503
Cranberry Ln SE 98503
Craney Ct SE 98503
Creighton Ct SE 98503
Crestone St NE 98516
Cricket Ln SE 98503
Crimson Ct SE 98513
Crowe St SE 98503
Crystal Ct SE 98513
Cuddy Ln NE 98516
Curtis Ct SE 98503
Cypress Dr & Loop 98516
Danials Loop SE 98513
Darlington Ln SE 98513
Dartmouth Dr SE 98503
David St SE 98503
Davis Ct NE 98516
Daylily Ln SE 98503
Delaware Ave SE 98513
Deni Dr NE 98516
Denton Ln SE 98503
Derby Ln SE 98503
Desmond Dr SE 98503
Detlefsen Pl SE 98503
Diamond Ct, Loop & Rd 98503
Diana Ct SE 98503
Dogwood St SE 98503
Dominion Ave NE 98516
Donegal Ct SE 98503
Draham Rd NE 98516
Drake Ct NE 98516
Dudley Ct & Dr 98516
Duke Ct SE 98503
Durham St SE 98503
East St SE 98503
Edgewater Blvd NE 98516
Edsel Ct NE 98516
Eld Ct NE 98516
Electra Ct SE 98503
Ellsworth Ct NE 98516
Elm Ct SE 98503
Emerald St SE 98513
Enterprise Dr NE 98516
Essex Pl NE 98516
Everest Ct SE 98503
Fagan Ct NE 98516
Fairhill Dr NE 98516
Fir Ct SE 98503
Firpark Dr SE 98503
Flute St SE 98513
Fordham Ct SE 98503
Forest Ct SE 98503
Forrestal Pl NE 98516
Fortman Dr NE 98516
Foxglove Ct SE 98513
Frances Dr SE 98503
Franklin Pl NE 98516
Franz St SE 98503
Freedom Ct SE 98503
Freedom Ln NE 98516
Fresco Dr SE 98513
Galaxy Dr NE 98516
Galena St SE 98503
Gator Ct SE 98503
Gem Ct SE 98513
Gemini St SE 98503
Glacier Ct SE 98503
Glen Ct SE 98503
Glen Mary Dr & Ln 98503
Glen Terra Ct & Dr 98503
Glenalda Ct SE 98503
Goldfinch Ct & Dr 98503
Golf Club Pl & Rd 98503
Gonzaga Ct SE 98503
Gravel Ln NE 98516
Gray Ct NE 98516
Green Ct SE 98503
Greenbriar St SE 98503
Greenlawn St SE 98503
Greenview Dr NE 98516
Gresham Ln SE 98513
Grizzly Ct SE 98503
Gwinn Ln SE 98503
Hall St SE 98503
Hancock Ct SE 98503
Hanna Ct NE 98516
Hanover Dr SE 98503
Harvard Ct & Dr 98503
Hawaiian Ct SE 98503
Hazelwood Ln SE 98503
Helena Ave SE 98503
Hemlock Ct SE 98503
Hicks Lake Ln & Rd 98503
Hidden Springs Loop SE 98503
Hidden Valley Dr SE 98503
Hilmes Ct SE 98503
Hogum Bay Ln & Rd 98516
Hogum Bay Road Ext NE 98516
Hoh St NE 98516
Holladay Park Loop SE 98503
Hollyhock Ln SE 98503
Holmes Island Rd SE 98503
Homann Dr SE 98503
Hornet Dr & Pl 98516
Huntamer Ln SE 98503
Huntington Ln SE 98503
Husky Ct & Way 98503
Hydra St NE 98516
Ida Jane Rd & Way 98503
Illinois Ln SE 98513
Impala Dr SE 98503
Ingleside Dr & Loop 98503
Inlay St SE 98513
Intelco Loop SE 98503
Ipsut Ct SE 98503
Irene St SE 98503
Ivy Hill Ln SE 98513
Jackson Farm Loop SE 98503
Jacobson Ct SE 98513
Jaguar Ct NE 98516
James St SE 98513
Jamestown Ln SE 98503
Jeffrey Ct SE 98513
Jeri Dr NE 98516
Jessica Ct SE 98513
Jim Ct SE 98503
Josephine Ct SE 98503
Judd St SE 98503
Juliann Ct SE 98513
Juniper Ct SE 98503
Kapalea Way SE 98503
Karla Ln SE 98503
Keegan St NE 98516
Kelly Ct NE 98516
Ken Jan Ct SE 98503
Kendra Ct SE 98513
Kenneth Ct SE 98503
Kenya Ct SE 98503
Keystone Ave NE 98516
Kialynn Ct SE 98503
Kingham St SE 98503
Kinwood Ct & St 98503
Kinwood Park Ln SE 98503
Koala St SE 98503
Komachin Loop SE 98513
Kona St NE 98516
Kyro Rd SE 98503
Lacey Blvd SE
4101-4397 98503
4399-5799 98503
5801-5815 98503
5815-5815 98509
5817-5899 98503
Lacey St SE 98503
Lackland Ct NE 98516
Lafayette Ln SE 98503
Laguna Ln SE 98503
Lake Forest Ct & Dr 98503
Lake Hills St SE 98513
Lakecrest St SE 98503
Laker Ct SE 98503
Lakeridge Ct & Dr 98503
Lakeside Dr SE 98503
Lakeview Ct, Dr & Ln 98503
Lambeth Ln SE 98513
Lana Lee Ct SE 98503
Langley Pl NE 98516
Lanier Ct SE 98503
Lanyard Dr NE 98516
Larch St SE 98503
Leah Ct SE 98503
Lebanon St SE 98503
Leisure Ln & Way 98503
Lewis Dr NE 98516
Lexington Pl NE 98516
Lilac St SE 98503
Lintel Ln SE 98513
Lisa Ln SE 98503
Livingston Ct & St 98516
Logan Dr NE 98516
Logger Ct & St 98503
London Loop NE 98516
Long Lake Ct, Dr & Loop 98503
Lopez Ct NE 98516
Lorna Ct & Dr 98503
Lupine St NE 98516
Lynn Ct NE 98516
Madera Ct SE 98503
Madora Ct & Dr 98503
Madrid St NE 98516
Madrona Ct SE 98503
Magnolia Ct & St 98503
Malibu Dr SE 98503
Maple Hills Dr SE 98503
Maricite St SE 98503
Marietta Ct NE 98516
Marina Ln SE 98503
Marquette Dr & St 98503
Martin Way E 98516
Marvin Rd NE 98516
Marvin Rd SE 98503
Mary Lou St SE 98503
Masters Ln SE 98513
Maxine St SE 98503
Mayes Rd SE 98503
Mcdaniel Ln SE 98503
Mckinley Loop & St 98516
Meade Ln SE 98503
Meadow Dr SE 98503
Meadow Lake St SE 98503
Meadowbrook Ln SE 98503
Melody Dr SE 98503
Mercedes Dr NE 98516
Mercer Ct NE 98516
Meridian Rd NE 98516
Meriwood Dr NE 98516
Merlot Ln SE 98513
Merrill Ct NE 98516
Mesplay Ave SE 98503
Messenger Ct & St 98503
Mia St NE 98516
Michelle Ct SE 98503
Midway Dr NE 98516
Mill Ct & Dr 98503
Mills Landing Ct SE 98503
Monique Ct SE 98503
Montclair Ct & Dr 98503
Monterey Ln SE 98503
Mount Adams St SE 98503
Mount Baker St SE 98503
Mount Hood Ct SE 98503
Mount Olympus St SE 98503
Mount Rainier St SE 98503
Mount Saint Helens St SE 98503
Mount Tahoma Ct & Dr 98503
Mountain Aire Ct, Dr, Loop & Way SE 98503
Mowich Ct SE 98503
Mt Green Ln SE 98503
Muir Ct SE 98503
Mullen Rd SE 98503
Muriel Ct SE 98503
Narada Ct SE 98503
Natalee Dr SE 98503
Nelson Rd SE 98503
Noble Firs Ct SE 98503
Northridge Pl SE 98503
Northwest Ln SE 98503
Notre Dame Ct SE 98503
Notter Ln SE 98503
Nottingham Ct & Dr 98503
Nova St NE 98516
Oakcrest Ct, Dr & St 98503
Oklahoma St SE 98513
Opal Ct SE 98513
Orion Dr NE 98516
Oslo Ln NE 98516
Oxford Ave, Ct, Dr & Loop SE 98503
Pacific Ave SE 98503
Pacific Park Dr SE 98503
Paddington Ln SE 98503
Paine Ct SE 98503
Pamela Ct & Dr 98503
Paradise Ct SE 98503
Park Pl SE 98503
Park Center Ave NE 98516
Park Place Loop SE 98503
Parkside Dr SE 98503
Patricia Ct SE 98503
Penguin Ct SE 98503
Pennsylvania St SE 98513
Pilatus Ave SE 98503
Pine Creek Ln SE 98503
Pleasanton Ct SE 98503
Poppy Ln SE 98503
Preston St NE 98516
Princeton Ct SE 98503
Prism St SE 98513
Quail Dr SE 98503
Quinault Dr NE 98516
Radcliff Ct SE 98503
Radius Loop SE 98513
Rainier Loop SE 98513
Ram Ct SE 98503
Ranger Dr SE 98503
Red Cedar Ct SE 98503
Redcoat Ct SE 98503
Redwing Ln SE 98503
Reed Ct SE 98503
Remington Ln SE 98503
Revere Ct SE 98503
Richmond Ln SE 98503
Ridge St SE 98503
Rigi St SE 98503
River Ridge Dr SE 98513
Rochelle St SE 98503
Rohr Ct SE 98503
Rosemont Ct SE 98503
Rossberg St SE 98503
Roxanna Ct & Loop 98503
Royal Oak Dr SE 98503
Royce Ct NE 98516
Ruddell Loop & Rd 98503
Rumac St SE 98513
Rushmore Ave & Way 98516
Rustin Ct SE 98513
Ryan St SE 98503
Sadie St NE 98516
Samurai Ct & Dr 98503
San Juan St NE 98516
Sandstone Ave SE 98503
Sandy Ln NE 98516
Santis Loop SE 98503
Saratoga Pl NE 98516
Sawgrass Ln SE 98503
Scarlet Oaks Dr SE 98503
Scenic Ct SE 98503
School Ct & St 98503
Scoria Ln SE 98503
Seahawk St SE 98503
Sebastian Dr NE 98516
Selma St SE 98503
Sentinel Dr NE 98516
Seville Dr & Ln 98503
Shady Ln SE 98503
Shadywood Ct SE 98503
Shale St SE 98503
Shangrila Pl NE 98516
Shasta Ct SE 98503
Shaw Ln NE 98516
Shelby Ct & Ln 98503
Shepard Way NE 98516
Sheridan Dr SE 98503
Sherwood Ln SE 98513
Shirley St SE 98503
Shorewood Ct & Ln 98503
Sidney St SE 98503
Sierra Ct & Dr 98503
Silver Maple Ct SE 98503
Sinclair Loop NE 98516
Skyridge St SE 98503
Sleater Kinney Rd SE 98503
Snowberry St NE 98516
Sorrel Ln SE 98503
Southlake Dr SE 98503
Spartan Ct SE 98503
Spinnaker Ln SE 98503
Spokane Ct & St 98516
Springfield Ln SE 98503
Stanfield Rd SE 98503
Stanford Ct SE 98503
Starlite Ct SE 98503
Steamer Dr SE 98513
Steilacoom Rd SE 98503
Steinerberg St SE 98503
Stephan Ct SE 98503
Stevens Ct & Dr 98516
Stikes Ct, Dr & Loop 98503
Stockholm Ln NE 98516
Stockton Ct, Ln & St 98513
Stonegate St SE 98503
Strawberry Ct SE 98513
Sulky Dr SE 98503
Summerwalk St SE 98503
Sunny Ln SE 98503
Sunset Dr SE 98503
Sunview Ct SE 98513
Sutter Ln SE 98503
Sutton Ln SE 98503
Switchback Loop SE 98513
Sycamore St SE 98503
Tallon Ln NE 98516
Tanager Ct SE 98503
Tarawa Pl NE 98516
Teakwood Ct SE 98503
Terri Ct SE 98503
Thornbury Ct, Dr & Pl 98513
Thunderbird Ct & St 98503
Ticonderoga Pl NE 98516
Tiffani Ln SE 98503
Timberlake Ct & Dr 98503
Timberline Ct & Dr 98503
Timothy St SE 98503
Titan Ct & Dr 98503
Titus Ct SE 98503
Topaz St SE 98513
Tracy Ln SE 98503
Traditions Ave NE 98516
Trail View Ln SE 98503
Trailblazer Ct, Loop & St 98503
Trestrin Dr NE 98516
Trillium St SE 98503
Trojan Ct SE 98503
Turf Ln SE 98513
Tyler Ct SE 98513
Ulery St SE 98503
Union Mills Rd SE 98503
Vancouver Dr NE 98516
Vashon Dr NE 98516
Vassar Loop SE 98503
Ventura Ln SE 98503
Vicwood Ln NE 98516
Viking St SE 98503
Villa Ct SE 98503
Vincent Ct SE 98513
Vine Maple Dr SE 98503
Violet St SE 98503
Virginia St SE 98513
Wade Ct SE 98513
Wales Ln SE 98503
Wallaby Ct SE 98503
Wallingford Ct & Ln 98516
Walthew Ct, Dr & St 98503
Warrior St SE 98503
Water Lily Ct SE 98503
Waterford Ln SE 98503
Webb Ln & St 98503
Webster Dr NE 98516
Wellington Loop SE 98503
Westlake Dr SE 98503
Westminster Ct & Dr 98516
White Fir Dr NE 98516
White Top Ave NE 98516
Whitman Ln SE 98513
Whitney Ave NE 98516
Wildcat St SE 98503
Wildspitz St SE 98503
Willamette Dr NE 98516
Willow St SE 98503
Wilshire Ct SE 98503
Windflower Ln SE 98503
Windham Ct NE 98516
Wonderwood Ln SE 98503
Woodland Ct & Loop 98503
Woodland Square Loop SE 98503
Woodmere Ct & Ln 98503
Woodridge Ct SE 98503
Yakima Ln SE 98503
Yelm Hwy SE
4700-5199 98503
5201-5399 98503
5600-6198 98513
Yonkers Dr SE 98503
Zenith Ct NE 98516

NUMBERED STREETS

3rd Ave & Way 98503
4th Ct, Ln & Way 98503
5th Ave, Ct & Way 98503
6th Ave NE 98516
6th Ave SE 98503
6th Way SE 98503
7 Oaks Rd SE 98503
7th Ave NE 98516
7th Ave SE 98503
8th Ave NE 98516
8th Ave SE 98503
9th Ave & Ct 98503
10th Ave & Way 98503
11th Ave & Ct 98503
12th Ave & Ct 98503
13th Ave & Ct 98503
14th Ave, Ct & Way 98503
15th Ave NE 98516
15th Ave SE 98503
15th Ct SE 98503
15th Ln SE 98503
15th Way NE 98516
16th Ave & Ct 98503
17th Ave & Ct 98503
18th Ave & Ln 98503
19th Ave, Ct & Ln 98503
20th Ave & Ln 98503
21st Ave, Ct & Ln 98503
22nd Ave, Ct & Ln 98503
23rd Ave SE 98503
24th Ave SE 98503
25th Ave, Ct & Loop 98503
26th Ave, Ct & Loop 98503
27th Ave NE 98516
27th Ave SE 98503
27th Ct SE 98503
27th Ln SE 98503
28th Ave SE 98503
28th Ct NE 98516
29th Ave NE 98516
29th Ave SE 98503

29th Ct SE 98503
30th Ave NE 98516
30th Ave SE 98503
30th Ct SE 98503
31st Ave NE 98516
31st Ave SE 98503
31st Ct SE 98503
32nd Ave, Ct & Ln 98503
33rd Ave NE 98516
33rd Ave SE 98503
33rd Ct SE 98503
33rd Loop SE 98503
33rd Way NE 98516
34th Ave NE 98516
34th Ave SE 98503
34th Ct SE 98503
35th Ave & Ct 98503
36th Ave, Ct & Ln 98503
37th Ave, Ct & Ln 98503
38th Ave, Ct, Dr & Loop SE 98503
39th Ave & Ct 98503
40th Ct & Ln 98503
41st Ave & Ln 98503
42nd Ln SE 98503
43rd Ave, Ct, Ln & Loop SE 98503
44th Ct SE 98503
45th Ave SE 98503
46th Ave NE 98516
46th Ave SE 98503
46th Ln SE 98503
47th Ave SE 98503
48th Ave, Ln & Loop 98503
50th Ave & Ct 98503
51st Ln SE 98503
52nd Ln SE 98503
53rd Ave SE
5200-5399 98503
6000-6099 98513
54th Ave SE
5200-5799 98503
5900-6198 98513
6200-6900 98513
6902-8298 98513
54th Ct SE 98513
54th Way SE 98513
55th Ave SE 98503
55th Ct SE 98513
55th Ln SE 98513
55th Way SE 98513
56th Ave, Ln & Loop 98503
57th Ave SE
5601-5799 98503
6000-6699 98513
57th Ct SE 98513
57th Loop SE 98503
58th Ave & Ct 98513
59th Loop SE 98513
60th Ave, Ct & Loop 98513
61st Ave & Loop 98513
66th Ave & Way 98513

LAKEWOOD WA

POST OFFICE BOXES MAIN OFFICE STATIONS AND BRANCHES

Box No.s
39001 - 39820 98496
97001 - 97427 98497
98001 - 99998 98496

NAMED STREETS

Addison St SW 98499
Agate Dr SW 98498
Alameda Ave SW 98498
Alderwood Ct SW 98498
Alfaretta St SW 98499
Alva Ave SW 98498
Amber Dr & Ln 98498
American Ave SW 98498
Amethyst Ct SW 98498
Angle Ln SW 98498
Ardmore Dr SW 98499
Arrowhead Rd SW 98499
Avalon St SW 98499
Avenue Dubois SW 98499
Avondale Rd SW 98499
Barleark St SW 98498
Barlow Rd SW 98499
Beach Ln SW 98498
Becker Dr SW 98499
Bellwood Dr SW 98499
Berkeley Ave SW 98498
Bernese Rd SW 98498
Beverly Dr SW 98499
Blackhawk Ct SW 98499
Blossom Ln SW 98499
Boat St SW 98498
Bocott Ln SW 98499
Boston Ave SW 98499
Boundary Rd SW 98498
Briar Rd SW 98499
Bridge Ln SW 98498
Bridgeport Way SW & W 98499
Briggs Ln SW 98498
Bristol Ave SW 98499
Brook Ct & Ln 98499
Burgess St W 98499
Butte Dr & Ter 98498
Cadillac Ave & Ln 98499
Cameo Dr SW 98498
Candlewyck Dr W 98499
Caraway Dr SW 98499
Carol Ave S 98499
Cecile Ct SW 98499
Cedrona St SW 98498
Chapel St S 98499
Chase Ln 98498
Cherry Ln SW 98499
Chicago Ave SW 98499
Citrine Ln SW 98498
Clara Blvd SW 98498
Clover Creek Dr SW 98499
Clover Crest Dr SW 98499
Clover Park Dr SW 98499
Cloverdale Ct SW 98499
Cochise Ln SW 98499
Cody St W 98499
Columbia Cir SW 98499
Commercial Ave & St 98498
Community Pl SW 98499
Coral Dr, Ln & Pl 98498
Country Club Cir, Dr, Ln & Rd SW 98498
Cournera St SW 98499
Creekside Dr SW 98499
Creekwood Ln SW 98499
Crescent Cir & Ln 98499
Crestwood Dr SW 98499
Cronins Dr SW 98499
Cross Ln & Rd 98498
Custer Rd SW & W 98499
Dalton Dr SW 98498
Dalwood Rd SW 98498
Dalwyn Ct SW 98498
David Ln SW 98499
Davisson Rd SW 98499
De Floer Ln SW 98498
Dean Ct SW 98498
Dean St W 98499
Deepwood Dr SW 98498
Dekoven Dr SW 98499
Delwood Dr SW 98498
Detroit Ave SW 98499
Diamond Blvd SW 98499
Docken Ln SW 98499
Dolly Madison Ct & St 98498
Doten Dr SW 98499
Douglas Dr & St SW & W 98499
Dowerdell Ln W 98499
Dresden Ln SW 98498
Drum Ln SW 98499
Durango St SW 98499
Eagle Point Loop Rd SW 98498
Earley Ave SW 98499
Edgemere Dr SW 98499
Edgewater Dr SW 98499
Edgewood Ave & Ln 98498
Elm St SW 98439
Elwood Dr SW 98498
Emerald Dr SW 98498
Evergreen Ter SW 98498
Fairlawn Dr SW 98499
Fairway Dr SW 98498
Farwest Dr SW 98498
Fern St SW 98498
Filbert Ln SW 98499
Filbert St SW 98498
Fir Glen Dr SW 98498
Flanegan Rd W 98499
Flora St SW 98499
Forest Ave, Ct & Rd 98498
Forest Glen Ln SW 98498
Forest Lake Rd SW 98498
Foster St SW 98499
Frances Folsom St SW 98498
Freiday St SW 98499
Front St S 98499
Garnet Ln SW 98498
N Gate Rd SW 98498
Gayle Ave S 98499
Gerlings Dr SW 98499
Glen Echo Ln SW 98499
Glenwood Ave SW 98498
Glenwood Dr SW 98498
Gramercy Pl SW 98498
Grange St W 98499
Grant Ave SW 98498
Gravelly Lake Dr SW 98499
Green Ln SW 98499
Greendale Dr SW 98498
Greengate Ln SW 98498
Greystone Dr SW 98499
Haman Ln W 98499
Harmony Pl SW 98499
Haviland Ave SW 98498
Hayden St SW 98499
Hemlock St SW 98498
Highland Ave SW
8700-9400 98498
9402-9498 98498
11101-11199 98499
Hill Ter SW 98498
Hillcrest Dr SW 98499
Hillgrove Ln SW 98499
Hilltop Ln SW 98499
Hipkins Rd SW 98498
Holden Rd SW 98499
Holly Ln SW 98499
Holly Hedge Ln SW 98499
Hudson Pl SW 98499
Hudson St W 98499
Huggins Meyer Rd SW 98498
Idlewild Rd SW 98498
Idlewood Dr SW 98498
Interlaaken Dr SW
7100-7299 98499
7900-12399 98498
Irene Ave & Ln 98499
Jade Dr SW 98498
John Dower Rd SW & W 98499
Judith Ct SW 98498
Juniper St SW 98439
Kendrick St SW 98499
Kenwood Dr SW 98498
Kirkwood Dr SW 98498
Kline St SW 98499
Lagoon Lane North SW 98498
Lagoon Lane South SW 98499
Lake Ave SW 98499
N Lake Dr SW 98498
Lake St SW 98498
Lake City Blvd SW 98498
Lake Grove St SW 98499
Lake Louise Dr & Ln 98498
Lake Steilacoom Dr SW 98498
Lake Steilacoom Point Rd SW 98498
Lakeholme Rd SW 98498
Lakeland Ave SW 98498
Lakeside Country Clb SW 98498
Lakeview Ave SW 98499
Lakewood Blvd & Dr 98498
Lakewood Oaks Dr SW 98499
Lakewood Towne Center Blvd SW 98499
Langlow St SW 98498
Lasalle St SW 98499
Laurel Crest Ln SW 98498
Lawndale Ave SW 98498
Lenox Ave SW 98498
Leona Way SW 98499
Leschi Rd SW 98498
Lexington Ave SW 98499
Lila Ln SW 98499
Lincoln Ave SW 98499
Lincoln Blvd SW 98439
Lindale Ln SW 98499
Linwood Ln SW 98499
Loch Ln SW 98499
Loch Lea Dr SW 98499
Lochburn Ln SW 98499
Loma Pl SW 98499
Lorraine Ave S 98499
Lucerne Rd SW 98498
Lundstrom Dr SW 98498
Luzader Ln SW 98499
Lyris Ct SW 98498
Maas Ln SW 98498
Madera Cir & Dr 98499
Madera Gardens Dr SW 98499
Main St SW 98499
Maple Ave SW 98499
Maple St SW
3200A-3216A 98439
3205A-3299A 98439
3200B-3216B 98439
3209B-3299B 98439
3200-3217 98439
3219-3299 98439
8100-8699 98498
Mary Ln SW 98498
Masonic Rd SW 98499
Maury Ln SW 98498
Maybelle Ln SW 98498
Mcchord Dr SW 98499
Meadow Rd SW 98499
Meadow Park Rd W 98499
Melody Ln SW 98499
Military Rd SW 98498
Mills Dr SW 98499
Montclair Ave SW 98499
Montgrove Ave SW 98499
Montrose Ave SW 98499
Moreland Ave SW 98498
Motor Ave SW 98499
Mount Tacoma Dr SW
5600-7000 98499
7002-7098 98499
8000-8699 98498
Mountbrook Ln SW 98499
Mullen St SW 98409
Murray Rd SW 98439
Naomilawn Dr SW 98498
Newgrove Ave SW 98498
Newman Ave SW 98498
Nixon Ave SW 98498
North St & Way 98498
Northstar Way SW 98498
Norwood Dr SW 98498
Nottingham Rd SW 98499
Nyanza Rd SW 98499
Nyanza Park Dr SW 98499
Oak Ln SW 98499
Oak Park Dr SW 98499
Oak Tree Pl SW 98498
Oakbrook Ln SW 98498
Oakridge Dr SW 98498
Occident St SW 98499
Okanogan Ave SW 98499
Old Byrd School Ave SW 98499
Onyx Ct & Dr 98498
Opal Ct & Ln 98498
Orchard St SW 98498
Orient St SW 98499
Pacific Hwy & St 98499
Paine St SW 98499
Patton Ave SW 98499
Pawnee Dr SW 98499
Perkins Ln SW 98499
Phillips Ln & Rd 98498
Pine St S 98499
Pine St SW 98498
Pleasant St SW 98499
Point Ln SW 98499
Ponce De Leon Crk & Ter 98499
Portland Ave SW 98498
Proctor St SW 98498
Rainier Ave SW 98499
Rebecca Dr SW 98499
Rembert Ct SW 98498
Rips Ln SW 98499
Rose Rd SW 98498
Rowland Ave SW 98499
Ruby Dr SW 98498
Russell Rd SW 98499
Rustic Ln SW 98499
Sacramento St SW 98499
Saint Francis St SW 98499
Sales Rd S 98499
San Francisco Ave SW 98499
Sapphire Ct & Dr 98498
Sardonyx Dr SW 98498
Schencom St SW 98439
School St SW 98499
Scottsdell Ct SW 98499
Seattle Ave SW 98499
Seeley Lake Dr SW 98499
Seminole Rd SW 98499
Shadywood Ln SW 98499
Sharon St SW 98498
Sharondale St SW 98499
Sherwood Dr SW 98498
Sherwood Forest St SW 98498
W Shore Ave SW 98498
Shore Acres Rd SW 98498
Short Ln SW 98498
Silcox Dr & Is SW 98498
Solberg Dr SW 98499
South Way SW 98499
Southgate Ave SW 98499
Spring St SW 98439
Springbrook Ln SW 98499
Spruce St SW 98498
Steele St S 98499
Steilacoom Blvd SW
3600-7499 98499
7501-7697 98498
7699-8699 98498
8701-9699 98498
Steilacoom Crest Ln SW 98498
Sunnybrook Ln SW 98498
Superior St SW 98498
Sylvia Blvd S 98499
S Tacoma Way 98499
Tacoma Mall Blvd 98499
Tepee Ln SW 98498
Terrace Rd SW 98498
Terry Lake Rd SW 98498
Thomas Ct SW 98498
N & W Thorne Ln 98498
Thornewood Ln SW 98498
Thunderbird Pkwy SW 98498
Tomahawk Rd SW 98499
Topaz Ct & Dr 98498
Tower Rd SW 98498
True Ln SW 98499
Tucka Way Dr SW 98499
Turquoise Ct & Dr 98498
Twilight Ln SW 98498
Tyler St SW 98499
Union Ave SW 98498
Vernon Ave SW 98498
Veterans Dr SW 98498
Villa Ln SW 98499
Villa Madera Dr SW 98499
Vine Maple Dr SW 98499
Wadsworth St SW 98498
Walnut St SW 98498
Washington Ave & Blvd 98498
Wauna St SW 98498
Waverly Dr SW 98498
Wedgewood Ct SW 98498
Weller Rd SW 98498
Westlake Ave SW 98498
Westmont Pl SW 98498
Westshore Dr SW 98498
Westview Dr SW 98498
Westwood Dr SW 98499
Whisper Ln SW 98499
Whitman Ave SW 98499
Wildaire Ct & Rd 98499
Wildwood Ave SW 98498
Williams Way SW 98498
Willowood Cir & Pl 98498
Winona St SW 98498
Woodbine Ln SW 98499
Woodbourne Dr & Rd 98499
Woodbrook Dr SW 98439
Wooddale Ln SW 98498
Woodholme Rd SW 98498
Woodlawn Ave SW 98499
Woodlawn Pl SW 98498
Woodlawn St SW 98498
Yew Ln SW 98499
Zircon Ct & Dr 98498

NUMBERED STREETS

25th Ave S 98499
25th Avenue Ct S 98499
26th Ave S 98499
26th Avenue Ct S 98499
27th Avenue Ct S 98499
28th Ave S 98499
29th Avenue Ct S 98499
30th Ave S 98499
30th Avenue Ct S 98499
31st Ave S 98499
31st Avenue Ct S 98499
32nd Ave S 98499
32nd Avenue Ct S 98499
33rd Ave S 98499
33rd Avenue Ct S 98499
34th Ave S 98499
34th Avenue Ct S 98499
35th Ave S 98499
36th Avenue Ct SW 98499
38th Ave SW 98499
39th Ave SW 98499
39th Avenue Ct SW 98499
40th Ave SW 98499
41st Ave SW 98499
43rd Avenue Ct SW 98499
44th Avenue Ct SW 98499
45th Ave SW
8000-8099 98409
9600-9699 98499
46th Ave SW 98409
47th Ave SW 98499
48th Ave SW 98499
49th Ave SW 98499
50th Avenue Ct SW 98499
51st SW & W 98499
51st Avenue Ct W 98499
52nd SW & W 98499
52nd Avenue Ct W 98499
53rd Ave W 98499
55th Ave SW 98499
56th Ave SW 98499
56th Avenue Ct SW 98499
57th Ave SW 98499
57th Avenue Ct SW 98499
58th Ave SW 98499
58th Avenue Ct SW 98499
59th SW & W 98499
59th Avenue SW & W 98499
60th Avenue Ct W 98499
62nd SW & W 98499
62nd Avenue Ct W 98499
63rd SW & W 98499
64th SW & W 98499
65th Ave W 98499
65th Avenue Ct SW 98499
66th Ave W 98499
67th Ave W 98499
68th SW & W 98499
68th Avenue Ct SW 98499
69th Ave SW
7500-7598 98498
8000-8499 98499
69th Avenue Ct SW 98439
69th Street Ct SW 98498
70th Ave SW 98499
14605-14616 98439
70th St SW 98498
70th St W 98499
70th Avenue Ct SW
8000-8100 98499
14500-14612 98439
70th Street Ct SW 98498
70th Street Ct W 98499
71st St SW 98498
71st Avenue Ct SW
7400-7499 98498
8301-8397 98499
71st Street Ct SW 98498
71st Street Ct W 98499
72nd St SW 98498
72nd Avenue Ct SW 98499
72nd Street Ct SW 98498
72nd Street Ct W 98499
73rd St SW 98498
73rd Street Ct SW 98498
73rd Street Ct W 98499
74th St SW 98498
74th St W 98499
75th St SW 98498
75th St W 98499
76th Ave SW 98498
76th St SW 98498
76th St W 98499
76th Street Ct SW 98498
76th Street Ct W 98499
77th Ave SW 98498
77th St SW 98498
77th St W 98499
77th Avenue Ct SW 98498
77th Street Ct SW 98498
78th Ave SW 98498
78th St SW 98498
78th St W 98499
78th Street Ct W 98499
79th St SW 98498
79th St W 98499
79th Street Ct W 98499
80th Ave SW 98498
80th St SW
4400-4499 98409
4801-4897 98499
4899-6800 98499
6802-6998 98499
S 80th St 98499
80th Avenue Ct SW 98498
80th Street Ct S 98499
81st Ave SW 98498
81st St S 98499
81st St SW
4900-7099 98499
8700-9399 98498
81st Avenue Ct SW 98498
81st Street Ct S 98499
82nd Ave SW 98498
82nd St S 98499
82nd St SW
4600-4699 98409

5400-6899 98499
8300-8699 98498
82nd Avenue Ct SW 98498
82nd Street Ct S 98499
82nd Street Ct SW 98498
83rd Ave SW 98498
83rd St S 98499
83rd St SW
4700-4898 98499
4900-6299 98499
8310-8316 98498
83rd Avenue Ct SW 98498
83rd Street Ct SW 98499
83rd Street Ct SW 98499
8500-8699 98498
84th Ave SW 98498
84th Ct SW 98499
84th St S 98499
84th St SW
3800-6098 98499
6100-6299 98499
8401-8497 98498
8499-8599 98498
84th Street Ct S 98499
84th Street Ct SW 98498
85th S & SW 98499
85th Street Ct S 98499
86th Ave SW 98498
86th St S 98499
86th St SW
5700-7199 98499
7500-7598 98498
86th Street Ct S 98499
87th Ave SW 98498
87th St S 98499
87th St SW 98499
87th Avenue Ct SW 98498
87th Street Ct SW 98499
88th Ave SW 98498
88th St S 98499
88th St SW 98499
88th Avenue Ct SW 98498
88th Street Ct SW 98499
7900-8299 98498
89th Ave SW 98498
89th St S 98499
89th Avenue Ct SW 98498
90th Ave SW 98498
90th St S 98499
90th Avenue Ct SW 98498
91st Ave SW 98498
91st St S 98499
91st St SW 98499
91st Avenue Ct SW 98498
92nd Ave SW 98498
92nd St S 98499
92nd St SW 98498
92nd Avenue Ct SW 98498
92nd Street S & SW 98499
93rd Ave SW 98498
93rd St SW 98499
93rd Avenue Ct SW 98498
93rd Street S & SW 98499
94th Ave SW 98498
94th St S 98499
94th St SW
3601-6297 98499
6299-6599 98499
8500-8699 98498
94th Avenue Ct SW 98498
95th Ave SW 98498
95th St SW
4201-4297 98499
4299-5899 98499
5901-6799 98499
8300-8699 98498
95th Avenue Ct SW 98498
96th Ave SW 98498
96th St S 98499
96th St SW 98499
97th Ave SW 98498
97th St S 98499
97th St SW 98498
97th Avenue Ct SW 98498
97th Street Ct S 98499
98th Ave & St 98498
98th Avenue Ct SW 98498
98th Street Ct SW 98499
99th Ave SW 98498
99th St SW
5901-5997 98499
5999-6199 98499
9900-10100 98498
10102-10198 98498
99th Avenue Ct SW 98498
99th Street Ct SW 98499
100th Ave SW 98498
100th Street Ct SW 98498
100th Avenue Ct SW 98498
100th St SW
3600-3798 98499
3800-5410 98499
5409-5409 98496
5411-6999 98499
5412-6998 98499
8700-9898 98498
9900-9999 98498
10001-10025 98498
101st Ave SW 98498
101st Avenue Ct SW 98498
101st Street Ct SW 98498
101st St SW
3700-5299 98499
8500-10198 98498
102nd Ave & St 98498
102nd Avenue Ct SW 98498
103rd Avenue Ct SW 98498
103rd St SW 98498
104th Ave SW 98498
104th Street Ct S 98499
104th Avenue Ct SW 98498
104th Street Ct SW
8111-10299 98498
104th St SW
5200-5499 98499
8001-8297 98498
8299-9199 98498
9201-9499 98498
105th Ave SW 98498
105th Street Ct SW 98498
105th Avenue Ct SW 98498
106th Street Ct SW 98499
106th Avenue Ct SW 98498
106th Street Ct SW
8700-8899 98498
106th St S 98499
107th Ave SW 98498
107th Street Ct SW
4400-4499 98499
10100-10599 98498
107th St S 98499
107th St SW 98498
108th Street Ct SW
5206-5598 98499
5600-5799 98499
10300-10499 98498
108th St S 98499
108th St SW
3600-3798 98499
3800-5899 98499
8300-8598 98498
8600-10299 98498
109th Street Ct SW 98498
109th St SW
4001-4097 98499
8400-9900 98498
110th Street Ct SW 98498
110th St S 98499
4100-5799 98499
8700-10699 98498
111th Street Ct SW 98498
111th St SW 98499
112th Street Ct SW 98498
112th St S 98499
112th St SW
3601-4797 98499
4799-5900 98499
5902-6298 98499
7401-7597 98498
7599-10500 98498
10502-10598 98498
113th St SW 98499
9100-9199 98498
114th Street Ct SW 98499
8700-9199 98498
114th St SW 98498
115th Street Ct SW
4701-4797 98499
4799-4999 98499
8600-10399 98498
115th St SW
5100-5299 98499
9900-10199 98498
116th Street Ct SW 98498
116th St SW
5500-5699 98499
8300-10400 98498
117th Street Ct SW 98498
117th St SW 98499
9200-9299 98498
118th Street Ct SW 98499
8201-8299 98498
118th St SW 98499
119th St SW
5200-6199 98499
9500-10199 98498
120th St SW
4700-5598 98499
5600-6299 98499
9900-10299 98498
121st St SW
4701-4797 98499
8100-9899 98498
122nd St SW 98499
123rd St SW 98499
124th Street Ct SW 98499
127th Street Ct SW 98499
127th Street Ct SW 98499
9101-9199 98498
127th St SW 98499
128th Street Ct SW 98499
128th St SW 98498
130th St SW 98498
146th St SW 98439
148th St SW 98439
150th St SW 98439

LYNNWOOD WA

General Delivery 98046

POST OFFICE BOXES MAIN OFFICE STATIONS AND BRANCHES

Box No.s
C2170 - C2170 98036
1 - 1999 98046
2001 - 2739 98036
3001 - 7018 98046
80001 - 80003 98036
97000 - 97027 98046

NAMED STREETS

Admiralty Way 98087
Alaska Rd 98036
Alder Way 98037
Alderwood Mall Blvd 98036
Alderwood Mall Pkwy
3000-3099 98036
16400-18799 98037
18801-18899 98037
19200-19699 98036
Allview Way 98036
Ash Way
13820-16299 98087
16400-17999 98037
Barker Rd 98036
Beverly Park Rd 98087
Bing Rd 98036
Birch Way 98036
Blue Ridge Dr 98037
Brier Rd & Way 98036
Butternut Rd 98037
Canchari 98087
Cascadian Way 98087
N & S Castle Way 98036
Cedar Valley Rd 98036
Cobblestone Dr 98037
Crawford Rd 98036
W Cypress Way 98036
Dale Way 98036
N Damson Rd 98036
N & S Danvers Rd 98036
Darben Pl 98087
Elberta Rd 98036
Elm Dr 98036
Fender Dr 98087
Fieldstone Dr 98037
Filbert Rd 98036
Firwood Dr 98036
Floral Way 98036
Granite Dr 98037
Graystone Dr 98037
Halls Lake Way 98036
Heinz Pl 98036
Hickory Way 98036
Highway 99
13700-16399 98087
Highway 99
16400-18699 98037
18701-18799 98037
18800-21015 98036
21017-21709 98036
Hillpointe Cir 98037
Hubbard Rd 98036
Hurst Rd 98037
Jefferson Way 98087
Jeryl Ann Pl 98037
Kentish Rd 98036
King Pl 98087
Lake Rd 98087
N & S Lake Stickney Dr 98087
Lakeview Rd 98087
Larch Way
1700-3799 98036
14800-16399 98087
16400-18999 98037
20400-20900 98036
20902-21098 98036
Lawton Rd 98036
Lincoln Way 98087
Locust Pl & Way 98036
Logan Rd 98036
Madison Way 98087
Magnolia Rd 98036
Manor Way 98087
Maple Rd 98037
Meadow Rd 98087
N Meadowdale Dr & Rd 98037
Meridian Ave S 98036
Meridian Dr SE 98087
Meridian Pl W 98087
Motor Pl 98087
Mukilteo Speedway 98087
Nike Manor Rd 98036
North Rd 98087
Oak Rd 98087
Oak Way 98036
Old Manor Way 98087
Old Poplar Way 98036
Olympic Pl 98036
Olympic View Dr 98037
Park Way 98036
Penny Ln 98036
Pitner Dr 98087
Poplar Way 98036
Quartz Dr 98037
River Rock Dr 98037
Russell Way 98087
Russet Ln & Rd 98036
Scriber Lake Rd 98036
Serene Way 98087
Shelby Rd 98087
E Shore Dr 98087
Spruce Way 98037
Stonebridge Way 98037
Tonya Ln 98036
Vine Rd 98036
Wigen Rd 98087

NUMBERED STREETS

1st Ave & Pl 98036
2nd Ave W
14800-15499 98087
20200-20999 98036
2nd Pl W 98087
3rd Ave W 98036
3rd Pl W
15200-15599 98087
20200-20799 98036
4th Ave W
14300-15399 98087
19400-21099 98036
4th Pl W
14600-14799 98087
20200-20399 98036
5th Ave W
14300-14399 98087
19900-20999 98036
5th Pl W 98036
6th Ave W
14500-15399 98087
16400-17299 98037
6th Pl W 98036
7th Ave W 98036
7th Pl W
16400-17199 98037
20100-20399 98036
8th Ave W 98036
8th Pl W
14900-14999 98087
15001-15099 98087
17600-18299 98037
19300-21599 98036
9th Ave W
18400-18599 98037
19900-20599 98036
9th Pl W
14900-15499 98087
19600-21400 98036
21402-21598 98036
10th Ave W 98087
19200-20399 98036
10th Pl W
16700-16799 98037
18700-21399 98036
11th Ave W
18400-18599 98037
19500-20699 98036
11th Pl W
14000-14899 98087
17000-17799 98037
19200-21399 98036
12th Ave W 98037
19500-21599 98036
12th Pl W
17200-18099 98037
20400-20499 98036
13th Ave W 98087
13th Ave W 98037
19500-20999 98036
13th Pl W
15900-15999 98087
17500-18399 98037
19700-21399 98036
14th Ave W 98087
14th Ave W 98037
20300-20599 98036
14th Pl W
13300-15499 98087
17600-18099 98037
20700-22099 98036
15th Ave W 98087
15th Ave W 98037
20400-20599 98036
15th Park W 98087
15th Pl W
13800-15299 98087
17500-17799 98037
16th Ave W 98087
16th Ave W 98037
17800-17999 98037
16th Park W 98087
16th Pl W
14100-15099 98087
17600-18399 98037
21500-21699 98036
17th Ave W 98087
16900-17999 98037
17th Pl W
13800-14999 98087
18200-18499 98037
20900-21899 98036
18th Ave W 98087
18th Ave W 98037
18700-20799 98036
18th Pl W
14500-15999 98087
17000-17199 98037
18800-19899 98036
19th Ave W 98087
19000-21799 98036
19th Pl W
14000-15199 98087
20100-20299 98036
20th Ave W 98087
16400-17099 98037
20th Pl SW 98037
20th Pl W
13700-15999 98087
17100-17199 98037
18900-20499 98036
21600-21799 98036
21st Ave W 98087
18900-21199 98036
21st Pl W
13200-15099 98087
20200-20699 98036
22nd Ave W 98037
22nd Ave W 98087
20400-21199 98036
22nd Pl W
14500-15499 98087
17800-17999 98037
22500-22699 98036
23rd Ave W 98036
23rd Pl W
14800-15399 98087
22500-22999 98036
24th Ave W 98087
18800-22599 98036
24th Pl W 98036
25th Ave W
13500-15899 98087
20500-23299 98036
25th Pl W
13900-14999 98087
20300-20499 98036
26th Ave W
13900-15799 98087
18100-18199 98037
20400-20499 98036
26th Pl W 98087
27th Ave W 98036
27th Pl W 98087
28th Ave W 98087
18800-21099 98036
28th Pl W
13000-13199 98087
20400-20499 98036
29th Ave W
12900-15299 98087
18900-20499 98036
20501-21099 98036
22800-24299 98036
29th Pl W
13000-13199 98087
20700-21199 98036
30th Ave W
13100-13199 98087
20400-20699 98036
30th Pl W
17900-17999 98037
20700-21199 98036
31st Ave W
15300-15399 98087
20800-20899 98036
31st Pl W
17500-17599 98037
20700-20899 98036
32nd Ave W
15100-15299 98087
16700-17899 98037
20000-20199 98036
21600-24399 98036
32nd Pl W
13400-14799 98087
17600-17799 98037
20700-20899 98036
21400-21699 98036
33rd Ave W
16400-18799 98037
18800-20899 98036
33rd Ct W 98036
33rd Pl SW 98087
33rd Pl W
13400-14799 98087
17000-18099 98037
20100-21199 98036
22300-22399 98036
34th Ave W
15800-15899 98087
21800-24200 98036
34th Pl W
15600-15799 98087
17200-17899 98037
20200-20299 98036
35th Ave W
14800-15999 98087
16500-16599 98037
20000-20199 98036
35th Pl W
15800-15999 98087
21500-21599 98036
36th Ave W
13200-16399 98087
16400-18799 98037
18800-18998 98036
19000-21099 98036
21501-21697 98036
21699-21999 98036
22001-22099 98036
36th Pl W
13500-13799 98087
20600-21099 98036
23600-23699 98036
37th Ave W
13700-13799 98087
17000-17499 98037
20100-20399 98036
37th Pl W
16500-17899 98037
20600-21099 98036
21600-23699 98036
38th Ave W
13700-13899 98087
17000-18899 98037
20200-20399 98036
21900-21999 98036
38th Ct W 98036
38th Pl W
14600-14799 98087
17800-17899 98037
21200-23499 98036
39th Ave W
16800-17899 98037
22900-23599 98036
39th Pl W
13700-14999 98087
17000-17899 98037
21200-23699 98036
40th Ave W
13600-15799 98087
16900-18799 98037
18800-19999 98036
40th Pl W 98037
41st Ave W 98087
41st Pl W
16400-18799 98037
18800-20499 98036
42nd Ave W
14300-14799 98087
16400-17699 98037
42nd Pl W 98037
43rd Ave W
14200-16499 98087

16500-18199 98037
18800-18899 98036
43rd Pl W
16400-16499 98087
17000-18599 98037
44th Ave W
14200-16099 98087
16400-18799 98037
18901-19097 98036
19099-21000 98036
21002-21198 98036
44th Pl W
15100-15699 98087
18000-18099 98037
20900-20999 98036
45th Ave W 98087
45th Pl W
14100-15599 98087
20900-20999 98036
46th Ave W
18700-18799 98037
18800-20199 98036
46th Pl W
14400-15599 98087
17800-18599 98037
47th Ave W
14500-14598 98087
17800-17999 98037
18800-21199 98036
47th Pl W
14400-15399 98087
18400-18499 98037
48th Ave W
16600-16698 98037
16700-18799 98037
18800-21099 98036
48th Pl W 98036
49th Ave W 98036
49th Pl W
18000-18699 98037
18900-19199 98036
50th Ave & Pl 98036
51st Pl W 98036
52nd Ave W 98037
18800-20999 98036
52nd Pl W 98036
53rd Ave W 98036
53rd Pl W
17400-17599 98037
19200-20099 98036
54th Ave W
16400-17899 98037
20000-21199 98036
54th Pl W 98037
55th Ave W 98036
55th Pl W 98037
56th Ave W
16400-18299 98037
19100-20799 98036
56th Pl W 98037
57th Ave, Ct & Pl 98037
58th Ave W 98037
19500-19599 98036
58th Pl W
16400-18499 98037
19400-20899 98036
59th Pl W
16600-18299 98037
20800-21099 98036
60th Ave W
16400-18799 98037
18800-20799 98036
61st Ave W 98036
61st Pl W
17200-18599 98037
19100-20599 98036
62nd Ave & Pl 98037
63rd Ave W 98037
19600-21099 98036
63rd Pl W
18000-18499 98037
20400-20599 98036
64th Ave W
16400-18799 98037
18600-20099 98036
65th Ave W 98037
65th Pl W
17600-17899 98037
18800-18999 98036
66th Ave W
16200-18799 98037
19300-21399 98036
66th Pl W
17600-18499 98037
18900-20199 98036
67th Ave W
16400-18799 98037
19000-21499 98036
67th Pl W 98037
68th Ave W
16401-18297 98037
18800-21599 98036
68th Pl W 98036
69th Pl W
16800-18399 98037
19100-19799 98036
70th Ave W
18500-18699 98037
19300-20900 98036
20902-20998 98036
70th Pl W
16600-16899 98037
19400-19599 98036
71st Ave W 98037
71st Pl W
16600-16899 98037
19200-19799 98036
72nd Pl W 98036
73rd Ave & Pl 98036
74th Ave & Pl 98036
75th Ave & Pl 98036
76th Ave W 98037
18801-19597 98036
121st St SW 98087
122nd Pl SW 98087
128th Pl SW 98087
132nd Pl & St 98087
133rd St SW 98087
134th Pl & St 98087
135th Pl & St 98087
136th Pl & St 98087
137th Pl SW 98087
138th Pl & St 98087
139th Pl & St 98087
140th Pl & St 98087
141st Ln, Pl & St 98087
142nd Pl & St 98087
143rd Ln, Pl & St SW & SE 98087
144th Pl & St 98087
145th Pl & St 98087
146th Pl & St 98087
147th Pl & St 98087
148th Pl & St 98087
149th Pl & St 98087
150th Pl & St SE & SW 98087
151st Pl & St 98087
152nd Pl & St 98087
153rd Pl & St 98087
154th Pl & St 98087
155th SE & SW 98087
156th Pl & St 98087
157th Pl & St 98087
158th Pl & St 98087
159th Pl & St 98087
160th Pl & St 98087
161st Pl & St 98087
162nd Pl SW 98087
6600-6799 98037
162nd St SW 98087
163rd Pl SW
2100-2199 98087
6600-6799 98037
163rd St SW 98037
164th Pl SW
3900-4099 98037
4300-4399 98087
5800-5999 98037
164th St SW
200-4799 98087
5700-6799 98037
165th Pl SW 98037
166th Pl & St 98037
167th Dr, Pl & St 98037
168th Pl & St 98037
169th Pl & St 98037
170th Pl & St 98037
171st Pl & St 98037
172nd Pl & St 98037
173rd Pl & St 98037
174th Pl & St 98037
175th Pl & St 98037
176th Pl & St 98037
177th Pl & St 98037
178th Pl & St 98037
179th Pl & St 98037
180th Pl & St 98037
181st Pl & St 98037
182nd Pl & St 98037
183rd Pl & St 98037
184th Pl & St 98037
185th Pl & St 98037
186th Pl & St 98037
187th Pl SW
900-1199 98036
6000-7100 98037
188th Pl SW 98036
188th St SW 98037
189th Pl & St 98036
190th Pl & St 98036
191st Pl & St 98036
192nd Pl & St 98036
193rd Pl & St 98036
194th Pl & St 98036
195th Pl & St 98036
196th Pl & St 98036
197th Pl & St 98036
198th Pl & St 98036
199th Pl & St 98036
200th Pl & St 98036
201st Pl & St 98036
202nd Pl & St 98036
203rd Pl & St 98036
204th Pl & St 98036
205th Pl & St 98036
206th Pl & St 98036
207th Pl & St 98036
208th Pl SW 98036
208th St SW
1000-6700 98036
6702-7098 98036
6817-7599 98036
6817-6817 98046
209th Pl & St 98036
210th Pl & St 98036
211th Pl & St 98036
212th Pl & St 98036
213th Pl SW 98036
213th St SW 98036
214th Pl & St 98036
215th Pl & St 98036
216th Dr SW 98036
216th St SW 98036
217th Pl SW 98036
218th Pl & St 98036
219th Ct SW 98036
219th Pl SW 98036
220th Pl SW 98036
221st Pl SW 98036
222nd Pl SW 98036
223rd Pl SW 98036
224th Ct SW 98036
225th Pl SW 98036
226th Pl SW 98036
227th Pl SW 98036
228th Pl SW 98036
229th Pl SW 98036
230th Pl SW 98036
231st Pl SW 98036
231st St SW 98036
232nd Ct SW 98036
233rd Pl SW 98036
234th Pl SW 98036
235th Pl SW 98036
236th St SW 98036
237th Pl SW 98036
238th Pl SW 98036
239th Pl SW 98036
240th Pl SW 98036
241st Pl SW 98036
242nd Pl SW 98036
243rd Pl SW 98036
244th St SW 98036

MARYSVILLE WA

General Delivery 98270

POST OFFICE BOXES MAIN OFFICE STATIONS AND BRANCHES

Box No.s
All PO Boxes 98270

NAMED STREETS

Alder Ave 98270
Alfred Sam Dr 98271
Alla Madison Dr 98271
Alphonsus Bob Loop Rd 98271
Ambrose Pkwy 98271
Ambrose Bagley Rd 98271
Arcadia Rd 98271
Armar Rd 98270
Ash Ave 98270
S Bayview Dr 98271
Beach Ave 98270
Birch Dr NW 98271
Cedar Ave 98270
Cedar Loop Rd 98271
Columbia Ave 98270
Delia Jimicum Pl NW 98271
Delta Ave 98270
Densmore Rd 98270
Donald Campbell Rd 98271
Ed Williams Rd 98271
Edward Beatty Rd 98271
Elliott Brown Sr Pl 98271
Ellison James Dr 98271
Ernie Cladoosby Jr St 98271
Ernie Cladoosby Sr St 98271
Ezra Hatch Rd 98271
Fir Dr NW 98271
Frank Madison Pl 98271
Gays Dr 98271
George C Jones Jr Pl 98271
George Comenote Ln 98271
Grove St 98270
Gus Smith Dr 98271
Harold Joseph Rd 98271
Hemlock Dr NW 98271
Hermosa Beach Rd 98271
Jack George Dr 98271
Joseph Charles Jr Dr & Pl 98271
Joseph Charles Jr Loop Rd 98271
Kelarlia Ave NE 98271
Lager Ln 98271
S Lake Crabapple Rd 98271
Larry Price Loop Rd 98271
Levi Lamont Rd 98271
Liberty Ln 98270
Lloyd Hatch Sr Dr 98271
Lois Madison Dr 98271
Lower Shoemaker Rd 98271
Madrona Dr NW 98271
Maple Dr NW 98271
Marine Dr NE 98271
Marysville Mall 98270
Meridian Ave N 98271
Mission Ave 98271
Mission Beach Ln, Rd & Walk 98271
Mission Beach Heights Rd 98271
Mission Hill Rd 98271
Old Tulalip Rd 98271
Park Way NW 98271
Parkside Dr 98270
Percival Rd 98271
Potlatch Beach Rd 98271
Priest Point Dr NE & NW 98271
Quil Ceda Blvd 98271
Quil Scenic Dr 98271
Quinn Ave 98270
Ray Fryberg Dr 98271
Reuben Shelton Dr 98271
Richard Madison Pl 98271
Sandra Madison Loop Rd 98271
Scenic Dr NW 98271
Sdodohobc Pl 98271
Shoemaker Rd 98271
Short St 98270
Shoultes Rd 98270
Smokey Point Blvd 98271
Soper Hill Rd 98270
Spring Lane Ave 98271
Spruce Blvd NW 98271
State Ave
1-9999 98270
10100-14599 98271
State Route 529 98270
Steve Williams Dr 98271
Sturgeon Dr 98271
Sunny Shores Rd 98271
Sunnyside Blvd 98270
E Sunnyside School Rd 98270
Teralint St NE 98270
Thomas Gobin Ln 98271
Timberbrook Dr 98271
Tom Reeves Rd 98271
Totem Beach Rd 98271
Totem Beach Loop Rd 98271
Tulalip Bay Dr 98271
Tulalip Shores Rd 98271
Tulare Way W 98271
Turk Dr & Rd 98271
Twin Lakes Ave 98271
Union Ave 98270
Verle Hatch Dr 98271
Walter Moses Jr Dr 98271
Water Works Rd 98271
Wesley Charles Ln 98271
Wildwood St 98270
Willow Dr 98271
Woodgate Ave 98270

NUMBERED STREETS

1st Ave NE 98271
1st St 98270
2nd Ave NE 98271
2nd Ave NW 98271
2nd Dr NE 98271
2nd St 98270
3rd Ave NE 98271
3rd St 98270
4th Ave NE 98271
4th St 98270
5th Ave NE 98271
5th Ave NW 98271
5th Dr NW 98271
5th St 98270
6th Ave NE 98271
6th St 98270
7th Ave NE 98271
7th St 98270
8th Ave NE 98271
8th Ave NW 98271
8th Dr NW 98271
8th St 98270
9th St 98270
10th Ave NW 98271
10th Dr NW 98271
10th St 98270
11th Ave NE 98271
12th Ave NW 98271
14th Ave NE 98271
15th Dr NW 98271
16th Ave NW 98271
16th Dr NE 98271
17th Ave NW 98271
18th Ave NW 98271
19th Ave NE 98271
19th St NE 98271
20th Dr NE 98271
20th Dr NW 98271
21st Ave NE 98271
22nd Ave NW 98271
22nd Dr NE 98271
23rd Ave NE 98271
24th Ave NE 98271
25th Ave & Dr 98271
26th Ave NE 98271
26th Dr NE 98271
27th Ave & Dr 98271
27th Ave & Dr 98270
28th Ave NE 98271
28th Ave NW 98271
28th Dr NE 98271
28th Dr NW 98271
28th Pl NE 98270
28th St NE 98270
29th Pl & St 98271
29th Pl & St 98270
30th Pl & St 98271
30th Pl & St 98270
31st Pl & St 98271
31st Pl & St 98270
32nd Pl & St 98271
32nd Pl & St 98270
33rd Pl & St 98271
33rd Pl & St 98270
34th Pl & St 98271
34th Pl & St 98271
34th Pl & St 98270
35th Ave NE
6600-7399 98271
8800-9999 98270
12003-12113 98271
35th Dr NE 98270
35th Pl NE 98270
35th St NE 98270
36th Ave NE 98270
36th Ave NW 98271
36th Dr NE 98271
36th Dr NW 98271
36th Pl NE 98270
36th St NE 98270
37th Ave NE
9200-9499 98270
11500-11599 98271
37th Ave NW 98271
37th Pl NE 98270
37th St NE 98270
38th Ave NE 98271
38th Ave NW 98271
38th Dr NE
8000-9699 98270
10500-11599 98271
38th Pl NE 98270
38th St NE 98270
39th Ave NE 98271
39th Dr NE
9800-10099 98270
10400-12099 98271
39th Dr NW 98271
39th Pl NE 98270
39th St NW 98271
40th Ave NE 98271
40th Dr NE 98270
40th Dr NW 98271
40th St NE 98270
41st Ave NE 98271
41st Ave NW 98271
41st Dr NE
8400-8499 98270
11200-11599 98271
41st Pl NW 98271
41st St NE 98270
42nd Ave NE 98271
42nd Dr NE
8400-9100 98270
9102-9198 98270
12100-12399 98271
42nd Dr NW 98271
42nd Pl NE 98270
42nd St NE 98270
43rd Ave NE
7200-8299 98270
11300-14799 98271
43rd Dr NE 98271
43rd Pl NW 98271
43rd St NW 98271
44th Ave NE
7200-7799 98270
12600-15199 98271
44th Dr NE
8401-8597 98270
8599-9399 98270
10700-15099 98271
44th Dr NW 98271
44th Pl NE 98270
44th St NE 98270
45th Ave NE 98271
45th Dr NE
8400-9599 98270
12400-15199 98271
45th Dr NW 98271
45th Pl NE 98270
45th St NE 98270
46th Ave NE 98271
46th Ave NW 98271
46th Dr NE
8400-9399 98270
10700-14599 98271
46th Pl NE 98270
46th St NE 98270
47th Ave NE
5000-8399 98270
10700-15999 98271
47th Ave NW 98271
47th Dr NE
8400-9599 98270
11600-13599 98271
47th Pl NE 98270
47th St NE 98270
48th Ave NE 98271
48th Dr NE
5600-10599 98270
11200-14499 98271
48th St NE 98270
49th Ave NE
8100-8299 98270
13000-13299 98271
49th Dr NE
6300-6302 98270
6304-10399 98270
13600-14799 98271
49th Dr NW 98271
49th Pl NE 98270
49th St NE 98270
50th Ave NE
8200-9799 98270
13000-14799 98271
50th Dr NE
6400-7999 98270
12600-14899 98271
50th Pl NE 98270
50th St NE 98270
51st Ave NE
6000-10199 98270
10201-10299 98270
10900-16399 98271
51st Dr NE 98271
51st Pl NE 98270
51st St NE 98270
52nd Ave NE
5700-10799 98270
11200-13899 98271
52nd Ave NW 98271
52nd Dr NE
7800-10299 98270
10800-14099 98271
52nd Pl NE 98270
52nd St NE 98270
53rd Ave NE
5900-10399 98270
11200-13899 98271
53rd Dr NE
8000-9999 98270
10800-14199 98271
53rd Pl NE 98270

53rd St NE 98270
54th Ave NE
5600-10799 98270
12500-12899 98271
54th Dr NE
6100-10299 98270
10800-14699 98271
54th Pl NE 98270
54th St NE
400-599 98271
6800-6899 98270
55th Ave NE
6100-10799 98270
11600-14799 98271
55th Dr NE
6500-9499 98270
12900-14599 98271
55th Pl NE 98270
55th St NE
1-199 98271
6700-7399 98270
56th Ave NE
6701-8997 98270
8999-10799 98270
11600-14799 98271
56th Dr NE
6200-10699 98270
12100-14699 98271
56th Pl NE 98270
56th St NW 98271
57th Ave NE
6100-9199 98270
11600-14299 98271
57th Dr NE
4600-10799 98270
12400-13999 98271
57th Dr NW 98271
57th Pl NE 98270
57th St NE 98270
58th Ave NE
6501-10099 98270
11600-13199 98271
58th Dr NE
4300-10799 98270
11600-14599 98271
58th Pl NE 98270
58th St NE
100-199 98271
5600-7999 98270
59th Ave, Dr, Pl & St NE 98270
59th Ave, Dr, Pl & St NE 98271
60th Ave NE 98270
60th Dr NE
4400-9599 98270
13300-13499 98271
60th Pl NE
3400-3499 98271
5200-7499 98270
60th St NE 98270
61st Ave, Dr, Pl & St NE 98270
62nd Ave, Dr, Pl & St NE 98270
62nd Ave, Dr, Pl & St NE 98271
63rd Ave, Dr, Pl & St NE 98270
64th Ave, Dr, Pl & St NE 98270
64th Ave, Dr, Pl & St NE 98271
65th Ave, Dr, Pl & St NE 98270
65th Ave, Dr, Pl & St NE 98271
66th Ave, Dr, Pl & St NE 98270
66th Ave, Dr, Pl & St NE 98271
67th Ave, Dr, Pl & St NE 98270
67th Ave, Dr, Pl & St NE 98271
68th Ave, Dr, Pl & St NE 98270
69th Ave, Dr, Pl & St NE 98270
70th Ave, Dr, Pl & St NE 98270
70th Ave, Dr, Pl & St NE 98271
71st Ave, Dr & St 98270
71st St NE
1900-2199 98271
72nd Ave, Dr, Pl & St NE 98270
72nd Ave, Dr, Pl & St NE 98271
73rd Ave, Dr, Pl & St NE 98270
74th Ave, Dr, Pl & St NE 98270
74th Ave, Dr, Pl & St NE 98271
75th Ave, Dr, Pl & St NE 98270
76th Ave NE 98270
76th Ave NW 98271
76th Dr NE
3200-10699 98270
10800-10899 98271
76th Pl NE 98270
76th Pl NW 98271
76th St NE 98270
76th St NW 98271
77th Ave, Dr, Pl & St NE 98270
77th Ave, Dr, Pl & St NE 98271
78th Ave NE
3200-8599 98270
10800-11199 98271
78th Ave NW 98271
78th Dr NE 98270
78th Pl NE 98270
78th Pl NW 98271
78th St NE
2000-2099 98271
7200-7599 98270
79th Ave, Dr, Pl & St NE 98270
79th Ave, Dr, Pl & St NE 98271
80th Ave, Dr, Pl & St NE 98270
80th Ave, Dr, Pl & St NE 98271
81st Ave NE
9800-10299 98270
11200-12199 98271
81st Dr NE 98270
81st Pl NE 98270
81st St NE
2800-3099 98271
5400-7799 98270
82nd Ave, Dr, Pl & St NE 98270
82nd Ave, Dr, Pl & St NE 98271
83rd Ave NE
2800-9799 98270
11100-11199 98271
83rd Dr NE 98270
83rd Pl NE 98270
83rd Pl NW 98271
83rd St NE 98270
83rd St NW 98271
84th Ave, Dr, Pl & St NE 98270
84th Ave, Dr, Pl & St NE 98271
85th Ave, Dr, Pl & St NE 98270
86th Ave, Dr, Pl & St NE 98270
86th Ave, Dr, Pl & St NE 98271
87th Ave NE
2800-10799 98270
10800-11499 98271
87th Pl NE 98270
87th St NE 98270
88th Pl & St 98270
88th Pl & St 98271
89th Pl & St 98270
90th Pl & St 98270
90th Pl & St 98271
91st Pl & St 98270
92nd Pl & St 98270
92nd St NE
1-399 98271
92nd St NW
1-1199 98271
93rd Pl & St 98270
94th Pl & St 98270
94th Pl & St 98271
95th Pl & St 98270
95th Pl & St 98271
96th Pl & St 98270
96th Pl & St 98271
97th Dr, Pl & St 98270
98th Pl & St 98270
98th Pl & St 98271
99th Pl & St 98270
100th Pl & St 98270
101st Pl NE 98270
102nd Pl & St 98270
103rd Pl NE
4800-8299 98270
103rd St NE
3700-4199 98271
5600-6699 98270
104th Pl NE
4300-4699 98271
4800-5699 98270
104th St NE
3800-4199 98271
5000-5099 98270
105th Ave NE 98271
105th Pl NE
3900-4699 98271
5600-6499 98270
105th St NE 98270
106th Pl NE
4300-4699 98271
5800-5999 98270
106th St NE 98270
107th Pl NE
3800-4699 98271
4900-6499 98270
107th St NE 98270
108th Pl & St 98271
109th Pl & St 98271
110th Pl & St 98271
112th Pl NE 98271
113th Pl & St 98271
114th NE & NW 98271
114th NE & NW 98271
115th Pl NE 98271
115th St NW 98271
116th St NE 98271
117th Pl & St 98271
118th Pl NE 98271
118th St NE 98271
119th Pl & St 98271
120th Pl & St 98271
121st Pl & St 98271
122nd Pl NE 98271
122nd St NE 98271
123rd Pl & St 98271
124th Pl & St 98271
124th Pl & St 98271
125th Pl NE 98271
125th Pl NW 98271
126th Pl & St 98271
126th Pl & St 98271
127th Pl & St 98271
128th Pl NE 98271
128th St NE 98271
129th Pl & St 98271
129th Pl & St 98271
130th Pl NE 98271
130th St NE 98271
131st Pl & St 98271
131st Pl & St 98271
132nd Pl & St 98271
133rd Pl NE 98271
134th Pl NE 98271
134th St NE 98271
135th Pl & St 98271
135th Pl & St 98271
136th Pl & St 98271
136th Pl & St 98271
138th Pl NE 98271
138th St NE 98271
139th Pl & St 98271
139th Pl & St 98271
140th Pl & St 98271
140th Pl & St 98271
141st Pl & St 98271
142nd Pl & St NE & NW 98271
143rd Pl & St NE & NW 98271
144th Pl & St 98271
145th Pl & St 98271
146th Pl & St 98271
147th Pl & St 98271
148th Pl & St 98271
149th Pl & St 98271
150th Pl & St 98271
151st Pl & St 98271
152nd NE & NW 98271
154th St NW 98271
156th St NE 98271
158th St NW 98271
162nd St NW 98271
168th Pl NE 98271
169th Pl & St 98271
171st Pl NE 98271
172nd St NE 98271
174th St NE 98271
175th Pl NE 98271
176th NE & NW 98271
177th Pl NE 98271
178th Pl & St 98271
179th Pl NE 98271
180th St NE 98271
188th St NE 98271

MOUNT VERNON WA

General Delivery 98273

POST OFFICE BOXES MAIN OFFICE STATIONS AND BRANCHES

Box No.s
All PO Boxes 98273

NAMED STREETS

Addison Pl 98273
Aemmer Pl & Rd 98274
Alder Ln 98273
Alder Brook Ln 98274
Allison Ave 98273
Alpine Crest Loop 98274
Alpine View Dr & Pl 98274
Alverson Rd 98273
Amber Ln 98273
Amick Rd 98274
S Andal Ln & Rd 98274
Anderson Rd
200-399 98273
1200-1399 98274
1401-19899 98274
1700-1726 98273
2800-19898 98274
Apache Dr 98273
Arapaho Pl 98273
Arbor Ln 98274
Arbor St 98273
Arthur Pl 98273
Ascension Way 98273
Austin Ln & Rd 98273
Avalon Hide Away Rd 98274
Avon St 98273
Avon Allen Rd 98273
B St 98273
Babcock Rd 98273
N & S Baker St 98273
Baker Heights Rd 98273
Bakerview Ct 98274
Bakerview Pl 98273
S Ball Rd & St 98273
Balsam Ln 98274
Bamboo Ln 98274
N & S Barker St 98273
Barrett Rd 98273
Barry Loop & Pl 98274
Bay Creek Ln 98273
Bayview Rd 98273
Bayview Cemetery Rd 98273
Bayview Edison Rd 98273
Beasheld Rd 98273
Beaver Lake Rd 98273
Beaver Marsh Rd 98273
Beaver Pond Dr N & S 98274
Becky Pl & St 98274
Behrens Millett Rd 98273
E & N Belair Dr 98273
Bella Vista Ln 98274
Belmont Ter 98274
Benham Rd 98273
Bennett Ln & Rd 98273
Benson Rdg 98274
Bernice St 98274
Bernie Morris Ct 98274
Best Rd 98273
Big Fir Pl 98274
W Big Lake Blvd 98274
Big Lake Ridge Pl 98274
Birch Ct 98274
Blackberry Ct 98274
Blackberry Dr 98273
Blackberry Ln 98274
E Blackburn Rd
100-329 98273
331-399 98273
1000-3399 98274
W Blackburn Rd 98273
Blodgett Rd 98274
Blue Jay Pl 98274
Bonney Ln 98273
Bonnie Pl 98274
Bonnieview Ln & Rd 98273
Boyd Rd 98274
Bradshaw Rd 98273
Brentwood Ln 98274
Briarwood Cir 98273
Briarwood Ct 98274
Bridgeview Way 98273
Brigham Ln 98274
Britt Rd 98273
Brittany St 98274
Broad St 98274
E Broadway 98274
W Broadway 98273
Broadway St 98274
Brook Ct 98274
Brookstone St 98273
Brotherhood Rd 98274
Brunswick St 98273
Bruun Rd 98273
Buchanan Ln, Pl & St 98273
Buck Way 98274
Buckhorn Way 98273
Bulltrout Ln 98274
W Bulson Rd 98274
Bumblebee Ln 98273
Burkland Rd 98274
Burlingame Rd 98274
C St 98273
Calhoun Rd 98273
Calvary Way 98273
Cameron Way 98273
W Campus Pl 98273
Cardinal Ln 98274
Caribou Pl 98273
Carlson Pl 98274
Carmel Ave 98273
Carol Pl 98273
Carpenter St 98274
Cascade Ave & St 98273
Cascade Ridge Ct & Dr 98274
Cascade View Dr 98274
Cavanaugh Ct & Rd 98274
E Cedar Ct, Ln & St 98273
E & S Cedar Hills Dr & Pl 98274
Cedardale Rd 98274
Cedarwood Ct & Pl 98273
Chantrelle Ln 98274
Chenoweth St 98273
Cherie Ln 98274
Cherokee Ln 98273
Cherry Pl 98273
Chestnut Ct 98274
Chestnut Loop 98274
Chestnut Pl 98273
Chilberg Ln & Rd 98273
Chilberg Heights Way 98273
Chinook Ct 98274
Chippewa St 98273
Cindy Pl 98273
Claremont Pl 98274
Clarence Ln 98273
Clearwater Ct 98273
Cleveland Ave 98273
Cliff Rd 98274
Clifftop 98273
Club Ct 98273
Cody St 98274
Coho Ct 98274
E & W College Way 98273
Columbine Ct 98273
Colvin Pl 98274
Comanche Dr 98273
Comet Ln 98274
Commercial St
400-499 98273
22800-22999 98274
Continental Pl 98273
Conway Rd 98273
E Conway Hill Ln & Rd 98274
Cooma Pl 98274
Coots Cove Ln 98274
Copper River Ct 98274
Cosgrove St 98273
Cottonwood Ln 98274
W Cove Ln 98274
Coyote Ln 98274
Craig Rd 98274
Creek Pl 98273
Crested Butte Blvd 98273
Crestview Dr & Ln 98273
Crestwood Way 98274
Criddle Ln 98274
Crosby Dr 98274
Crow Ln 98273
Cultus Ct 98274
Curran Pl 98274
Curtis St 98273
Cygnus Ln
1700-1799 98274
19500-19699 98273
Cypress St 98274
Daisy Ln 98274
Dakota Dr 98274
Dalacey Ln 98274
Dale Ln 98274
Daleway St 98274
Dallas St 98274
David Pl 98274
Day Lumber Ln 98274
Dealo Ln 98274
Debays Island Rd 98274
Deer Creek Rd 98274
Deer Park Ln 98274
Denny Pl 98274
Deschutes Ct 98274
Devil Mountain Rd 98274
Devils Creek Rd 98274
Devils Lake Rd 98274
Digby Ln, Pl & Rd 98274
Dike Rd 98273
E Division St 98274
W Division St 98273
Dodge Valley Rd 98273
Doe Ln 98273
Dogwood Ln 98273
Dogwood Pl 98274
Donnelly Rd 98273
Douglas St 98273
Drawbridge Ln 98273
Dry Slough Rd 98273
Dunbar Ct, Ln & Rd 98273
E St 98273
Eagle Point Ln 98274
Eagle Ridge Dr & Ln 98274
Eaglemont Dr & Pl 98274
Earl Ct 98273
Earle Dr 98273
Eastwind Dr & St 98274
Edgemont Dr 98274
Edgemont Pl 98273
Egbers Kalso Rd 98273
Egret Pl 98274
Eleanor Ln 98273
Elegant Heights Rd 98273
Elfin Ln 98273
Elk Dr 98273
Elliott Pl 98273
Ellison Rd 98274
Emerald Ct 98273
N English Rd 98274
Eric St 98274
Erika Ln 98273
Ervine Ln 98274
Estate Ct & Dr 98274
Evergreen St 98273
F Stevens Rd 98273
Falcon Ct 98274
Family Ct 98273
Farm To Market Rd 98273
Farnham St 98273
Fawn Ln 98273
Fieldstone Ln 98274
Finch St 98273
Finlan Pl 98274
E & W Fir Ln & St 98273
Fir Island Rd 98273
Fire Mountain Ln 98274
Firwood Ln 98274
S Flantrin St 98274
Florence St 98273
Fonk Rd 98273
Forest Dr 98273
Forest Hill Ln 98274
Forest Ridge Pl 98273
Four Jay Ln 98274
Fowler Pl & St 98274
Fox Rd 98273
E Fox Hill St 98273
Foxglove Cir 98273
Foxglove Ln 98274
Francis Ln & Rd 98273
Franklin Rd 98273
Frans Ridge Ln 98274
Fraser Ave 98274
S Fredonia Rd 98273
Freeway Dr 98273
Fremali Ln 98274
Front St 98274
S Front St 98273
E & W Fulton St 98273
Garden St 98274
Garden Ridge Ln 98274
Garfield St 98273
Gaspard Ln 98274
W Gates St 98273
Gaven Dr 98274
Gem Ln 98274
Geneva Aly 98273
Ginthner Dr 98273
Glacier St 98273
Glenn Rd 98273
Glenn Allen Pl 98274
Glenwood Dr 98273
Glory To Glory Ln 98273
Goldie Ln 98273
Grand Ave 98274
Granite Ln 98274

Granite St 98273
Granstrom Rd 98274
Greenacres Rd 98273
Grouse Ln 98274
Gunderson Rd 98273
Gunderson Ridge Dr & Ln 98273
Gunn Rd 98273
Habitat Pl 98273
Hall Pl 98273
Harmony Ln 98274
Harrison St 98273
Hawthorne Pl 98274
E Hazel St
100-199 98274
200-399 98273
1300-1799 98274
W Hazel St 98273
Heather Cir 98273
Heather Ln
1900-1999 98273
20400-20499 98274
Hemlock Pl 98273
Henson Rd 98273
Hermway Heights Dr, Pl & Rd 98274
Hickory Pl 98274
Hickox Rd
1726-1799 98274
18200-18799 98273
E Hickox Rd
400-599 98273
900-20499 98274
Hidden Lake Loop 98273
E & W Highland Ave & St 98273
Hill Creek Ln 98274
Hillcrest Loop & Pkwy 98274
Hoag Rd 98273
Holly Ln 98273
Hollydale Acres Ln 98273
Holmstrom Rd 98274
Holyoke St 98274
Homewood Pl 98274
Honey Ln 98273
Honeysuckle Dr 98273
Hopi Ln 98273
Horizon St 98273
Horton Ln 98273
Hulbert Rd 98273
Hull Rd 98274
Humpy Pl 98274
Irene Pl 98273
Iroquois Dr 98273
J J Pl 98273
Jackpot Ln 98273
Jacks Ln 98273
Jacob Pl 98274
Jacqueline Pl 98273
James St 98274
Jasmine Pl 98273
Jason Ln 98273
Jay Way 98273
Jeff St 98274
Jefferson St 98274
Jessica Pl 98273
Jewel Ln 98274
Jillian 98274
E Johnson Rd 98274
Josh Green Ln 98273
Josh Wilson Rd 98273
Junco Pl 98274
Jungquist Rd 98273
Juniper Pl 98273
W Kamb Rd 98273
Kamloop Ct 98274
Kanako Ln 98274
Karla Ct 98274
Karli St 98274
Kato Ln 98274
Kay Ln 98274
E Kincaid St
100-199 98273
300-2499 98274
W Kincaid St 98273
King Ln 98273
Kingfisher Cove Ln 98274
Kiowa Dr 98273
Knapp Rd 98273
Knudson Ln 98273
Kokanee Ct 98274
Krause Pl 98274
Kristine Ln 98273
Kulshan Ave 98273
Kulshan View Dr 98273
Kylee 98274
Laconner Whitney Rd 98273
Lake Cavanaugh Rd 98274
Lake Mcmurray Ln 98274
Lake Sixteen Rd 98274
Lake Terrace Ln & Pl 98274
Lake View Blvd 98274
Lake View Pl 98274
Lakeside Ln 98273
W Lakeview Blvd & Ln 98274
Landing Rd 98273
Landmark Dr 98274
Lange Rd 98273
Lanyard Ln 98274
Larrabee Way 98273
Larson Ln 98273
Laurel Ct 98274
N Laventure Rd 98273
S Laventure Rd 98274
E & W Lawrence St 98273
Leann Ln & St 98274
Lee Ln & Rd 98274
Legge Rd 98274
Leigh Way 98273
Leslie Ln 98273
Lesourd Ln 98273
Lilac Dr 98273
Lilly Ln 98274
Lincoln St 98273
Lind St 98273
Lindberg Ln 98274
Lindgren Rd 98273
Lindsay Cir, Loop & Pl 98274
Little Mountain Ln, Pl & Rd 98274
Locken Hill Ln 98274
Lost Island Ln 98274
Lucky Ln 98274
Lupine Dr 98273
Maddox Creek Ln & Rd 98274
Madison Park Dr 98273
Magnolia Ln 98273
Mahonia Ln 98274
Main St
300-13699 98273
23500-23699 98274
Majestic Ridge Ln 98274
Mallard Ln 98274
Mallard Cove Ln 98274
Mallard View Dr 98274
Malloree Ln 98273
Manito Dr 98274
Mann Ln & Rd 98274
Maple Ave & Ln 98273
Maple Hill Ln 98274
Marble Crk 98273
Marde Pl 98274
Margaret Pl 98273
Marie St 98274
Marihugh Pl & Rd 98273
Mariposa Ln 98273
Market St 98273
Marsh Rd 98273
E Martin Rd 98273
Mason Ct 98274
Maupin Rd 98273
Mccormick Ln 98273
W Mccorquedale Rd 98273
Mcfarland Ln & Rd 98273
Mclaughlin Rd 98273
Mclaughlin Extension Rd 98273
Mclean Rd 98273
Mcmurray Ridge Ln 98274
Mcmurray Shore Dr 98274
E Meadow Blvd 98273
W Meadow Blvd 98273
Meadow Dr 98273
Meadow Ln 98274
Meadowlark Ln 98274
Melody Ln 98274
Memorial Hwy 98273
Michael St 98274
Milltown Rd 98273
Milwaukee St 98273
Moberg Rd 98273
Mobile Dr 98273
Mohawk Ct & Dr 98273
Mohican Pl 98273
Molly Ln 98274
Monarch Blvd 98273
Monica Dr 98273
Montborne Rd 98274
Monte Vista Dr & Pl 98273
Montgomery Ct 98274
Montgomery Pl 98274
E Montgomery St
100-199 98273
300-398 98274
400-3399 98273
W Montgomery St 98273
Montpiliar Pl 98274
Moody Ct, Pl & St 98274
Moore Rd 98273
Moores Garden Rd 98273
Morning Star Ln 98274
Morrison Rd 98273
Mount Baker Loop 98273
Mount Vernon Big Lake Rd 98274
Mountain Ridge Dr 98274
Mountain Springs Ln 98274
Mountain View Dr 98274
Mountain View Rd 98274
Mud Lake Rd 98273
Myrtle St 98273
Nathan Ln 98274
Nelson Rd 98273
New Woods Pl 98274
Nez Perce Dr 98273
Nilson Rd 98273
Noble Ave 98274
Nookachamp Hills Dr 98274
Nookachamps Rd 98274
Nooksack Loop 98273
Norman Pl 98273
Northridge Way 98273
Northview Ct 98274
Northwoods Loop Rd 98273
Nylin Ct 98273
Oak Pl 98273
Oakland Ln 98273
Odessa Dr 98274
Okerlund Dr 98273
Old Highway 99 S Rd 98273
Oleary Rd 98273
Olive St 98274
Olympic Ln & Pl 98274
Osborne Dr 98274
Osprey Ct 98274
Otter Pond Dr
2000-2099 98274
15700-15899 98273
16600-16899 98274
Ovenell Rd 98273
Pacific Hwy & Pl 98273
Padilla Bay Ln 98273
Palm Crest Pl 98273
Pamela St 98274
Panorama Rdg 98273
Park Ave 98273
Park Ln 98274
Park St 98273
Parker Way 98273
Parkhurst Ln 98273
Parkside Ln 98273
Parkside Ter 98274
Parkview Ln 98274
E & W Parkway Dr 98273
Paul Pl 98273
Pavilion Dr 98273
Pawnee Ln 98273
Pedersen Pl 98273
Pederson Ln 98273
Penn Rd 98273
Peregrine Ln 98274
Periwinkle Ln 98274
Peter Burns Rd 98274
Peter Johnson Rd
1700-1899 98274
18200-18999 98273
Phipps Dr 98274
Pine St 98273
Pine Creek Dr 98273
Pintail Ln 98273
Pioneer Hwy 98273
Polson Rd 98273
Poplar Ln 98273
Porter St 98273
Priscilla Ln 98274
Produce Ln 98273
Pueblo Hts 98273
Pulver Rd 98273
Pyramid Peak Pl 98273
Quail Dr 98274
Quentin Ave 98274
Railroad Ave 98273
Rainbolt Pl 98274
Rawlins Rd 98273
Razor Peak Dr 98273
Rector Rd 98273
Red Hawk Ct 98274
Rexville Grange Rd 98273
Ridge Ct 98274
W Ridge Ln 98274
Ridge Way 98274
Ridgewood Dr 98274
Riley Rd 98274
Rindal Ln 98274
River Bend Rd 98273
River Rock Rd 98274
River Vista Ct, Ln, Loop & Pl 98273
Rivers Ct 98273
Riverside Dr & Ln 98273
Riverview Ln 98273
Roosevelt Ave & Ln 98273
Rose Ct 98273
Rose Rd 98274
Rosewood St 98273
Ruby Peak Ave 98273
Rudene Rd 98274
Rufous Ln 98273
Ruth Ln 98274
Sagers Ln 98273
Sahale Dr 98273
Sandalwood Ct & St 98273
Sandstone Ln 98274
Sarah St 98273
Schalyce Pl 98274
Schuller Pl 98274
Scotts Aly 98274
Seabird Ln 98273
Seaview Ln 98274
E Section St
100-399 98273
1100-3399 98274
W Section St 98273
Seneca Dr 98273
Seths Aly 98274
Shady Ln
500-599 98273
21900-22599 98274
Shalyce Pl 98274
Shantel St 98274
Shawnee Pl 98273
Shelly Hill Rd 98274
Sherman Ln 98273
Sherry Ln 98274
Shirley Pl 98274
N Shore Dr 98274
Short Rd 98273
Shoshone Dr 98273
Shuksan 98273
Sicklesteel Ln 98274
Sigmar Ln 98273
Signe Rd 98273
Silver Ln 98273
Silver Loop 98274
Silvernail Rd 98273
Sinnes Rd 98274
Sioux Dr 98273
Skagit St 98274
Skagit City Rd 98273
Skagit River Pl 98273
Skydda Ln 98273
Skylers Aly 98274
S & W Skyridge Ct, Dr & Rd 98274
Slow Ln 98274
Smiley Dr 98274
Snoqualmie St 98273
Snowden Ln 98274
Sockeye Dr 98274
Soundview Rd 98274
Spring Hill Ln 98274
E & W Spruce Ct & St 98273
E Stackpole Rd 98274
W Stackpole Rd 98273
Staffanson Ln 98273
Stanford Dr 98273
Star View Rd 98273
N Starbird Rd 98274
Starbird Creek Ln 98274
Starbrook Ln 98274
Stargate Pl 98274
Starvation Ridge Ln 98273
State Route 20 98273
State Route 534 98274
State Route 536 98273
State Route 9
1549-1618 98274
State Route 9
12200-15430 98273
15431-25199 98274
Staudt Rd 98273
Steves Aly 98274
Stewart Rd 98273
Stonebridge Way 98274
Stonewood Dr 98274
Streeter Pl 98274
Sulfur Springs Rd 98274
Sumac Pl 98274
Summers Ct, Dr & Ln 98273
Sundance Ln 98274
Sunday Ln 98274
Sunray Ct 98274
Sunrise Dr & Pl 98273
Sunset Ln & Pl 98273
Suzanne Ln 98273
Swan Ct & Rd 98273
Swift Creek Dr 98273
Sycamore Ct 98274
Tahoma St 98273
E Taylor Rd & St 98273
Teak Ln 98274
Tellesbo Ln 98273
Ten Acres Ln 98273
Terra Ln 98274
Theodorson Ln 98273
Thillberg Ln & Rd 98273
Tiffany Way 98274
Timber Ridge Dr 98273
Timothy Pl 98273
Tomahawk Dr 98273
Torset Rd 98273
Traci Pl 98274
E Tree Bark Ln 98274
Triple Creek Ln 98274
Tristan Pl 98274
Trophy Ln 98274
Trout Dr 98274
N Trumpeter Ct, Dr, Ln & Pl 98273
Tundra Ct & Loop 98273
Tyee Rd 98274
Union St 98273
Unison Pl 98274
Upland Dr & Pl 98273
Urban Ave 98273
Valentine Rd 98273
Valley Rd 98273
Valley Mall Way 98273
Valley Ridge Ln 98274
Valley View Dr 98273
Van Pelt Ln 98273
Vaughn Rd 98273
Vera Ct & St 98273
View Ave 98274
View Moor Dr 98273
E & N Viewmont Dr 98273
Village Ct 98273
Vintage Ln 98273
Virginia St 98273
Walden Ln 98274
Walker Rd 98273
Walker Valley Rd 98274
Walking M Ln 98273
N & S Wall St 98273
Walter St 98273
Warren St 98273
Washington Ln 98274
E Washington St
100-199 98273
201-297 98274
299-599 98274
W Washington St 98273
N Waugh Rd 98273
S Waugh Rd 98274
Webster Ln 98273
Wellspring Ln & Rd 98273
West St 98273
N & S West View Rd 98274
White Hawk Ln 98273
W Whitmarsh Rd 98273
Widnor Dr 98274
Wildflower Ct 98273
Willabelle Pl 98274
Willett St 98274
William Way 98273
Willow Ln 98273
Wilson Dr & Ln 98273
Windsor Dr 98273
Wiseman Ln 98273
Withers Pl 98274
N & S Woodland Dr & Pl 98274
Woodridge Ave 98273
Wylie Rd 98273
Young Rd 98273
Zoya Dr 98274
Zylstra Aly 98274

NUMBERED STREETS

N & S 1st 98273
S 2nd 98273
3rd St 98273
4th St 98273
N 4th St 98273
S 4th St 98274
N 5th St 98273
S 5th St 98274
N 6th St 98273
S 6th St
2-98 98274
100-400 98274
402-498 98274
801-897 98273
899-1999 98273
N 7th St 98273
S 7th St
100-599 98274
1101-1297 98273
N 8th St 98273
N 9th St 98273
S 9th St 98274
N 10th St 98273
S 10th St 98274
N 11th St 98273
S 11th St 98274
N 12th Pl 98273
N 12th St 98273
S 12th St 98274
S 13th St 98274
N 14th Pl 98273
N 14th St 98273
S 14th St 98274
N 15th St 98273
S 15th St 98274
N 16th St 98273
S 16th St 98274
N 17th Pl 98273
N 17th St 98273
S 17th St 98274
N 18th Pl 98273
N 18th St 98273
S 18th St 98274
N 19th Pl 98273
N 19th St 98273
S 19th St 98274
N 20th Pl 98273
N 20th St 98273
S 20th St 98274
S 21st Ct 98274
S 21st Pl 98274
N 21st St 98273
S 21st St 98274
22nd Ct & Pl 98274
N 23rd St 98273
N 24th Pl 98273
S 24th St 98274
N 25th Pl 98273
S 25th St 98274
N 26th St 98273
N 27th St 98273
S 27th St 98274
S 28th St 98274
N 29th Pl 98273
S 29th Pl 98274
S 29th St 98274
S 30th Pl 98274
N 30th St 98273
S 30th St 98274
N 32nd Pl 98273
S 32nd Pl 98274
N 33rd Pl 98273
N 34th Pl 98273
35th Pl & St 98273
N 38th Pl 98273
S 38th Pl 98274
N 39th Pl 98273
S 39th Pl 98274
N 40th Pl 98273
N 42nd Pl 98273
N 43rd Pl 98273

OLYMPIA WA

General Delivery 98501

POST OFFICE BOXES MAIN OFFICE STATIONS AND BRANCHES

Box No.s
WSECU - WSECU 98507
CCI - CCI 98507
TCCU - TCCU 98507
VERISIGN - VERISIGN 98507
1 - 2958 98507
4001 - 4460 98501
6001 - 9910 98507
11001 - 13878 98508
19002 - 19022 98507
29001 - 29001 98508
50600 - 50600 98506

NAMED STREETS

Abelia Ct SE 98513
Aberdeen Ct SE 98501
Abernethy Rd NE 98516
Abigail Ct & Dr 98516
Abington Loop SE 98513
Acacia Ct SE 98513
Accalia St SE 98513
Ad El Rd SE 98513
Adams Ln NW 98502
Adams St NE 98501

Street	ZIP
Adams St SE	98501
Affermer Ct SW	98512
Airport Ct SE	98501
Alban Pl NW	98502
Alder Glen Ct & Dr	98513
Alderview Ln SE	98501
Alki St NE	98516
Allegro Dr SE	98501
Allen Rd SE	98501
Allison Springs Ln SW	98502
Alma Ln SE	98513
Alonda Ln NE	98516
Alonna Dr & Pl	98506
Alpine Dr SW	98512
Alta St SW	98502
Alta Vista Dr SE	98501
Alternate Ln SE	98513
Alyssa Ct SE	98501
Amanda Dr NE	98516
Amber Ct SE	98501
Amelia Ct NE	98516
American St SW	98502
Ames Rd NE	98506
Amethyst St SE	98501
Amhurst Ct, Pl & St	98501
Anchor Ln NW	98502
Andover Ln SE	98501
Andress St NE	98516
Andrews Beach Rd NE	98516
Angelo Ct SW	98512
Ann Ln & St	98506
Anthem Ln SW	98512
Anthony Ct SW	98512
Anton Ct SE	98501
Antsen Rd SW	98512
Apple Valley Rd SW	98512
Applehill Ct NE	98506
Appletree Ln NE	98506
Aqua Ct NW	98502
Arab Ct & Dr	98501
Arbutus St NE	98506
Arcadia St NW	98502
Archer Dr SE	98513
Archwood Dr SW	98502
Arena Ct SE	98501
Arietta Ave & Pl	98501
Arledge Ln SW	98502
Arlington Ct SE	98501
Armour Dr, Loop & St	98513
Armstrong Ave SE	98501
Armstrong Rd SW	98512
Arnesen Ln SW	98512
Arrow Ct NE	98516
Ascension Ave NW	98502
Ash Ln NW	98502
Ashbourne Ln SE	98501
Ashdown Ln SE	98513
Ashford Ct SE	98501
Ashley Dr NE	98506
Ashley Ln SW	98512
Ashlynn Ct & Dr	98502
Ashram Ln NW	98502
Ashwood Downs Ln SE	98501
Aspinwall Ct & Rd	98502
Astaire St NE	98516
Aster St SE	98501
Atchinson Ct, Dr & Ln	98513
Athens Beach Rd NW	98502
Auklet Dr SE	98513
Autumn Ct & Pl	98513
Autumn Gold Ct SE	98513
Autumn Line Dr & Loop	98513
Autumn Park Dr SE	98513
Autumnwood Ct SE	98501
Avalon Ct SE	98513
Avondale Ct SE	98501
Ayer St SE	98501
Azalea Ct SE	98501
Aztec Dr NW	98502
B St SW	98512
Ba Kwom Dr SE	98513
Bacall St NE	98516
Baird Rd NE	98516
Baker Rd SW	98512
Baker Ter SE	98501
Baker Ames Rd NE	98506
Bald Eagle Ln SW	98512
Ballantine Dr SE	98501
Balsam Ave NE	98506
Bamberg Ln SE	98513
Banbridge Loop SE	98501
Banks Ln SW	98512
Barboullat St SW	98512
Barclift Ln SE	98501
Barley Dr SE	98513
Barnes Blvd SW	98512
Barrington Ct NE	98506
Barrington Ln SE	98513
Basin Dr NE	98516
Basswood Ct SE	98513
Bates St SE	98501
Bates St SW	98512
Bavarian Ln SE	98513
E Bay Dr NE	98506
W Bay Dr NW	98502
Bay Loop SW	98512
S Bay Loop NE	
3800-3899	98506
3900-3999	98516
S Bay Rd NE	
300-398	98506
400-3899	98506
3900-4099	98516
Bay St SW	98512
S Bay Ter NE	98516
Bayberry Ln NW	98502
Bayenes Ct SE	98513
Bayshore Ln NW	98502
Bayside Pl NE	98506
Bayview Dr NE	98506
Beach Way NE	98516
Beacon Ave SE	98501
Beam St SE	98513
Beatty Ct SW	98512
Beaver Creek Dr SW	98512
Becker Dr SE	98501
Bedford Ln SE	98501
Bedington Dr SE	98513
Bedstone Dr SE	98513
Bee Dee Dr NE	98516
Beechwood Ct SW	98502
Bel Mor Ct SW	98512
Bell Ct, Ln & St	98501
Bella Ct SE	98513
Bellerive Way SE	98501
Bellevista Dr & Pl	98502
Bellhaven Ct SE	98501
Bellwood Dr NE	98506
Belmore St SW	98512
Benjamin Ct SE	98501
Benson Rd SW	98512
Bent Arrow Ln SW	98512
Berger Ct, Dr & Pl	98513
Berkshire Ct & Loop	98513
Berne Ln SE	98513
Berry St NE	98506
Berwick Ln SE	98501
Bethel St NE	98506
Bethel Park Ct NE	98506
Bette Ln NE	98506
Beverly Ct & Dr	98516
Beverly Beach Dr NW	98502
Big Bear Ct SE	98501
Bigelow Ave NE	98506
Bing Ct & St	98502
Birch St NW	98502
Birch St SE	98501
Birchwood Dr SW	98502
Birdie St NE	98506
Birkdale Ln SE	98501
Biscay Ct & St	98502
Bishop Rd SW	98512
Bittern Ct SE	98513
Bittersweet St SE	98501
Black Hills Ln SW	98502
Black Lake Blvd SW	
401-597	98502
599-1516	98502
1518-1698	98502
1800-6099	98512
2401-2497	98512
2499-3999	98512
Black Lake Belmore Rd SW	98512
Black Rock Loop SE	98501
Blackberry Ln NW	98502
Blacksmith St SE	98501
Blackstone Ct & Dr	98512
Blacktail Ct NE	98516
Blass Ave SE	98501
Blomberg St SW	98512
Bloomingdale Ln SW	98512
Blooms Ct SW	98512
Blossomwood Ct NW	98502
Blowers St SW	98512
Blubyrd Ln NW	98502
Blue Heron Ln NW	98502
Blue Jay Ln NW	98502
Blue Mountain Ln SW	98512
Blue Sky Dr SW	98512
Bo Ct SE	98501
Boardman Ct & Rd	98502
Bobb Ct SE	98513
Bona Vista Ct & Dr	98512
Bonnie Ln SW	98501
Bonniewood Dr SE	98501
Bonniview Ct SW	98512
Bonshaw Ct SE	98501
Bordeaux Loop & Rd	98512
Bordeaux Vista Ln SW	98512
Boston St SE	98501
Boston Harbor Rd NE	98506
Boston Harbor Ext Rd NE	98506
Boulder Ln SE	98501
Boulevard Ct, Loop & Rd	98501
Boulevard Extension Rd SE	98501
Boulevard Heights Loop SE	98501
Boulevard Park Ct SE	98501
Boundary St SE	98501
Bowman Ave NW	98502
Box Elder Ct & Dr	98512
Brandon Ct NE	98506
Brassfield Dr SE	98501
Bravado Dr SE	98501
Brawne Ave NW	98502
Braywood Ln SE	98513
Brech St SE	98501
Breen Ln SW	98512
Breeze Dr SE	98513
Brenner Rd NW	98502
Brianna Ct SE	98513
Briar Lea Loop SE	98501
Briarwood Ct NW	98502
Briarwood Ct SE	98501
Bridle Ct & Dr	98501
Brigadoon Dr SE	98501
Briggs Dr SE	98501
Bright Ct SW	98512
Bright Star Way NE	98506
Brighton Way SE	98501
Brinkwood St NE	98506
Bristol Ct SW	98502
Britt St SE	98513
Brittany Ln SW	98512
Bromley Ln NE	98506
Bronington Dr SW	98512
Brooks Ln SE	98501
Brooks St SW	98512
Brookside Rd SW	98512
Brookstone Ln SE	98513
Brown Rd SW	98512
Brown St SE	98501
Brown Farm Rd NE	98516
Brownell Ln SW	98512
Bryan Loop SE	98513
Brycen Ln SW	98512
Buckeye Ct SW	98512
Buckingham Ct & Dr	98501
Buckthorn Ct NW	98502
Budd St NW	98502
Buker St SE	98501
Bungalow Dr NW	98502
Burbank Ave NW	98502
Burnaby Ave SE	98501
Burnaby Park Loop SE	98501
Burns Dr SW	98512
Burr Rd SE	98501
Bush Ave NW	98502
Bush Mountain Ct & Dr	98512
Butler Ct NW	98502
Buttercup St SE	98501
Butternut Ct SE	98513
Buttonwood Ln NE	98516
Byron St NE	98506
C St SW	98512
Cabot St SE	98501
Cain Rd SE	98501
Caitlin Ct SE	98501
Calais Ln NW	98502
Caleb Ct SE	98513
Caledonia St SE	98513
Cali Ln SE	98513
Calistoga St SE	98513
Callaway Ln SW	98512
Callen Ct NE	98516
Calvary Ct SE	98501
Camberton Ct NW	98502
Cambridge Ln SW	98512
Camden Cir & Pl	98512
Camden Park Dr SW	98512
Camelot Dr & Park	98512
Cameo Ct NW	98502
Cameron Ct NE	98516
Camillia Ln SW	98512
Campus Park Dr NE	98516
Campus Willows Loop NE	98516
Camus St NW	98502
Canady Ct SE	98501
Candlestick Ln SW	98512
Canna Ct SE	98513
Canning Ct SW	98512
Canter Ln NE	98506
Canterbury Pl SW	98512
Canterwood Dr SE	98513
Canton Ave NE	98516
Canyon Ct SW	98512
Capital Mall Dr SW	98502
Capitol Blvd & Way S, SE, SW & N	98501
Capitol Auto Mall Dr SW	98502
Capitol Creek Ln SW	98512
Capitol Forest Ct, Dr & Loop	98512
Capitol View Ln SW	98512
Capri Ct NE	98516
Cardigan Loop & St	98502
Cardinal Dr NW	98502
Carly Ct SE	98501
Carlyon Ave SE	98501
Carnbee Ct SE	98513
Carney Dr SE	98501
Carnoustie Ln SE	98501
Carole Dr NE	98516
Carolina St SE	98513
Carpenter Rd NE	98516
Carpenter Rd SE	98513
Carriage Dr, Loop & St	98502
Carson Ln NW	98502
Carver St SE	98501
Cascade Loop NE	98516
Case Rd SW	98512
Case Extension Rd SW	98512
Cassie Ct & Dr	98512
Castlewood Ct SE	98501
Cate Farm Ct & Dr	98513
Cathy Ct SE	98501
Catkin Ct SW	98512
Caton Way SW	98502
Cattail Ln SW	98512
Cavalier Ct, Loop & St	98512
Cedar Ln NW	98502
Cedar Flats Rd SW	98512
Cedar Lake Ct & Dr	98501
Cedar Park Loop SE	98501
Cedarbury Ln SW	98512
Cedrona Ct, Dr & Pl	98502
Celesta Ln	98512
Centennial Ct SE	98501
Center Ln NE	98516
Center St SW	98501
Centerwood Ct & Dr	98501
W Central Pl SE	98501
Central St NE	98506
Central St SE	98501
Century Ct SE	98501
Chalco Pl NW	98502
Chambers St NE	98506
Chambers St SE	98501
Chambers Creek Loop SE	98501
Chamfer Dr NW	98502
Champion Ct & Dr	98512
Chancery Ln SE	98513
Chandler Ct SW	98502
Channel Dr NW	98502
Chapperel Dr SW	98512
Charlie St & Way	98506
Charmont Ln SW	98512
Charter Ln SW	98512
Chatham Ct & Dr	98513
Chaucer St SE	98501
Chelsea Ct NW	98502
Chelsea Ln SW	98512
Chelsie Ln SW	98512
Cheri Estates Dr SE	98501
Cherie Dr SE	98513
Cherry Ln & St	98501
Cherry Blossom Dr NE	98506
Cherrywood Dr SW	98502
Chestnut St SE	98501
Chestnut Hill Dr & Ln	98513
Chickaman Ct SE	98513
Childress Ct SW	98512
Chukar Ct SE	98513
Cimmaron Ln & St	98502
Clairmont Cir SW	98512
Clar Mar Ln SE	98501
Claridge Dr SE	98501
Clark Pl SE	98501
Clark St SW	98512
Claussen Ct SW	98512
Clay Ct SE	98513
Cleanwater Dr SW	98501
Clearfield Ct & Dr	98501
Clearwood Ct SW	98512
Cleveland Ave SE	98501
Cliff Ct SE	98513
Cliffs Ln NE	98506
Clover Dr SE	98513
Clover Loop SE	98513
Clover St NE	98516
Cloverfield Dr SE	98501
Clubhouse Ln SE	98513
Coachman Ln SE	98501
Coho Ln NE	98506
Colbalt Dr SW	98512
Colby Ct SE	98501
Cole Ct SE	98501
Coleman Ave NW	98502
College St NE	98516
Colonial Ct SW	98512
Columbia St NW & SW	98501
Comanche Ln SW	98512
Comiskey Ln SW	98512
Commercial St NE	98506
Compton Ct SW	98512
Concolor Ct SW	98512
Condor Loop NE	98516
Conger Ave & Ct	98502
Congressional Dr SE	98513
Conifer Ct SE	98513
Conine Ave & St	98513
Cooper Crest Dr, Ln, Pl & St NW	98502
Cooper Point Est NW	98502
Cooper Point Loop SW	98502
Cooper Point Pl SW	98502
Cooper Point Rd NW	98502
Cooper Point Rd SW	
400-598	98502
400-400	98508
600-2299	98502
Cooperfield Dr NW	98502
Coos Dr SE	98513
Corral Ln SE	98501
Correa Ct SW	98512
Cortez Loop SW	98512
Cotton Dr SE	98513
Cottondale Ln SE	98501
Cougar Ln SW	98512
Coulter St NE	98506
Country Club Ct, Dr, Loop & Rd NW	98502
Country Village Dr SW	98512
Countryside Beach Dr NW	98502
Countryview Ct SW	98512
Countrywood Dr SE	98501
Courtney St SE	98513
Courtside St SW	98502
Cove Ln NW	98502
Coventry Ln SW	98512
Covey St SE	98501
Covington Ct NE	98516
Cowlitz Ct & Dr	98501
Coyote Ln SW	98512
Cozy Dr NW	98502
Craftsman Dr NW	98502
Craig Rd SE	98501
Craincou Ave NE	98506
Crancour Rd SW	98512
Creekview Ln NW	98502
Creekwood Ct SE	98501
Creekwood Dr SW	98512
Cressida St SE	98513
Crestline Blvd & Dr	98502
Crestmont Ln SW	98512
Crestridge Dr NW	98502
Crestview Loop NE	98516
Crestwood Ln & Pl	98502
Crete St SE	98501
Crisman Ct SE	98501
Cristen Ct SW	98512
Crites St SW	98512
Crockett St SW	98512
Crosby Blvd & Ct	98512
Cross Cut Ln SW	98512
Cuda Ln	98512
Cumberland Ave SW	98512
Cunningham Dr NE	98516
Cushing Ct & St	98502
Cushman Rd NE	98506
Custer Way SE & SW	98501
Cypress Pl SE	98501
Cyrene Dr NW	98502
D St SW	
100-198	98501
200-299	98512
W D St SW	98512
D Milluhr Dr NE	98516
Daffodil Ln SE	98513
Dahlia Ln SW	98512
Dairy Ct NE	98506
Daisy Ln SW	98512
Dana St NE	98506
Danbury Ct SE	98501
Danbury Ln SW	98512
Dandelion Dr SE	98501
Danico Ln SE	98513
Darby Ct SE	98501
Darcy Ln SE	98501
Darian St SE	98501
Dawn Hill Dr & Ln	98513
Day Ct & Dr	98513
Daycrest Ct & Dr	98513
Dayton St SE	98501
Debbie Ct SE	98501
Decatur St NW & SW	98502
Deencome Ave NW	98502
Deer Trail Ln SW	98512
Deerbrush Ct, Dr & Loop	98513
Deerfield Park Ct & Dr	98516
Defiance St SE	98501
Dehart Dr SE	98501
Dellrose Rd SW	98512
Delores Ct & Dr	98516
Delphi Rd NW	98502
Delphi Rd SW	
200-298	98502
700-10999	98512
Delta Ln SE	98501
Demarie Ct SE	98501
Dempsey Ln SW	98512
Dena Ct SE	98501
Denali Ave NE	98516
Dennis Ct, Pl & St SE & SW	98501
Dent Rd SW	98512
Derby Ln SE	98501
Deschutes Ct SE	98501
Deschutes Pkwy SW	98502
Deschutes Way SW	98501
Desoto Ave	98512
Desperado Dr SE	98501
Deuce Ct NE	98516
Devoe St NE	98506
Devoe St SE	98501
Devon Dr & Loop	98506
Devonshire St SE	98501
Diagonal Rd SE	98501
Diann St NE	98516
Dickinson Ave NW	98502
Digby St SE	98513
Division St NW	98502
Division St SW	
200-298	98512
300-499	98512
1500-1699	98502
Dodge Ln	98512
Dodjatree Ln SE	98501
Doe St SE	98501
Dolphin Ln NW	98502
Donna Ct SE	98513
Donnelly Ct & Dr	98501
Donovan Dr & Loop	98501
Dorchester Dr SW	98512
Doris Ct SE	98513
Douglas St SW	98512
Dove Ln NE	98506
Dover Ct SE	98501
Dover Pt NE	98506
Dowcor Ln SW	98512
Dowel Dr NW	98502
Draham Rd NE	98516
Dream St SW	98512
Driver St SW	98512
Dublin Dr NW	98502
Duckabush Ct SE	98501
Dunbar Ct SE	98513
Dundee Pl & Rd	98502
Dunlin Ct SE	98513
Durango Ct NW	98502
Durell Rd SE	98501
Durgin Rd SE	98513
Dutterow Rd SE	98513
E St SW	
100-198	98501
300-400	98512
402-598	98512
Eagle Dr NE	98516
E Eagle Ln SW	98512
W Eagle Ln SW	98512
Eagle Loop NE	98516
Eagle Bend Dr SE	98501
Eagle Lake Ln NE	98506
Eagle Ridge Ln SE	98513
Earhart St NE	98516
Earling St NE	98506
Early Spring Dr SE	98513
Easthill Ct & Pl	98502
Eastland Cir SE	98501
Eastside St NE	98506
Eastside St SE	98501
Eastview Ct NW	98502
Eastwood Dr & Pl	98501

Ebb Tide Ter NW 98502
Ebbets Dr SW 98512
Ebony Ct SE 98513
Edelweiss Ln SE 98513
Edgewood Cir & Dr 98501
Edgeworth Dr SE 98501
Edinburgh Dr SE 98501
Edison St NE 98506
Edison St SE 98501
Edith Ct SW 98512
Egret Dr SE 98513
Eklund Ct SE 98501
Eld Ln NW 98502
Elders Ln & Loop 98513
Elegy Pl SE 98513
Elizabeth St SE 98501
Elizan Dr NW 98502
Elliott Ave & Cir 98502
Ellis St SE 98501
Ellison Loop NW 98502
Elm St SE 98501
Emberwood Ct SE 98501
Emerald Ln SW 98512
Emerson St SW 98512
Emily Ln SW 98512
Emma Ct SE 98501
End Ct & St 98502
Endicott Rd SW 98512
Englewood Dr SE 98513
Ensign Rd NE 98506
Ensley Ln SE 98501
Entrada Ct & Dr 98506
Entree View Dr SW 98512
Equus Ln SE 98513
Erie St SE 98501
Erik Ct SE 98513
Eskridge Blvd & Way 98501
Espirit Ct SE 98513
Estate Ln SW 98512
Esther St SW 98501
Ethan Ct SW 98512
Ethel St 98502
Ethridge Ave & Ct 98506
Etude Loop SE 98513
Evanston Ct NE 98506
Evergreen Dr NE 98506
Evergreen Park Ct, Dr &
Ln 98502
Evergreen Valley Rd
SE 98513
Excelsior Dr SE 98501
W F St 98512
Fadling Rd SW 98512
Fair Oaks Loop & Rd 98513
Fairfield Rd SE 98501
Fairmont Ln NW 98502
Fairview Rd SW 98512
Fairview St NE 98506
Fairview St SE 98501
Fairway Dr SW 98512
Fairway Ln SE 98501
Fairweather St NE 98516
Falcon Dr SE 98501
Falcon Way NE 98516
Fallbrook St 98502
Farina Loop SE 98513
Farman Ln SE 98513
Farmer Ln & Way 98501
Farwell Ave & Ct 98502
Fassett St SW 98512
Fast Ln SW 98512
Fawn Ct SW 98512
Fellowship Ln NW 98502
Fenske Dr NE 98506
Fenway Ln SW 98512
Fenwick Loop SE 98513
Ferguson Ct, Ln & St 98512
Fern Ct SW 98512
Fern St SW 98502
Ferndale Ct SE 98501
Fernleaf Ct SE 98513
Fernwood St NE 98516
Ferry St SE 98501
Ferry St SW 98512
Field Ln NW 98502
Fiesta St SW 98512
Filly Ct SE 98501
Finch Dr SE 98513
Fir St NE 98506
Fir St SE 98501
Fir Tree Rd SE
4100-5299 98501
5300-6899 98513
Fire Ct SE 98501
Firewillow St & Way 98502
Firland St SW 98512
Firwood Loop SE 98501
Fish Pond Creek Dr
SW 98512
Fisher Ct SE 98501
Fishtrap Loop & Rd 98506
Fitz Hugh Ct & Dr 98513
Fleetwood Ct SE 98513
Flora Vista Rd NE 98506
Fones Rd SE 98501
Foote St NW & SW 98502
Foothill Ct, Dr & Loop 98512
Forest Glen Ct & Dr 98513
Forest Hill Cir & Dr 98501
Forest Park Ct, Dr &
St 98502
Forest Shores Dr NW 98502
Forestbrook Way SW 98502
Forrest Parse Ln NE 98506
Fortner Dr SW 98512
Foster Ct & Dr 98512
Fox Ave SE 98501
Fox Ridge Ln SE 98513
Fox Run Dr NW 98502
Foxfire Dr SE 98513
Foxhall Ct & Dr 98516
Foxtail Ct SE 98501
Foxtrail Ct & Dr 98516
Francesca Ln SW 98512
Franklin St NE & SE 98501
Frederick Ln NE 98506
Frederick St NE 98506
Frederick St SE 98501
Freeman Ln NE 98506
Freemont St NE 98516
French Ln, Loop & Rd 98502
Friday Ln SW 98512
Friendly Cove Ln 98513
Friendly Grove Rd NE 98506
Frog Leap Ln NE 98506
Frontier Ct & Dr 98501
Frye Way NW 98502
Fuchsia Ln SW 98512
Fuller Ln SE 98501
G St SW 98512
Gadwell Ct SE 98513
Gael Ct SE 98501
Gainsborough Ct & Dr 98501
Galenta Ct & Dr 98512
Gallagher Ct & Way 98502
Gallagher Cove Rd
NW 98502
Gallea St NE 98516
Galloway St SE 98501
Gallup Ct & Dr 98513
Gannet Ct SE 98513
Garden Ln NW 98502
Gardenia Ln SW 98512
Gardner Ct SE 98513
Garfield Ave NW 98502
Garnet St SE 98501
Garrett Ct NE 98506
Garrison St NE 98506
Gaston Ln SW 98501
Gate Rd SW 98512
Gateway Blvd NE 98516
Gelding Ct & Dr 98501
Gem Dr SE 98513
Gene Dr SE 98513
Geneco Ct SE 98501
Geneva Ln SE 98513
Gentle Ridge Dr SE 98513
Gentry Ct SW 98512
Georgetowne Dr NE 98516
Gerth St SW 98501
Gibraltar Ct SE 98501
Gifford Rd SW 98512
Giles Ave NW 98502
Giles Rd NE 98506
Gina Ct SE 98513
Glacier View Ln SE 98513
Glacis Dr NE 98516
Glass Ave NE 98506
Glen Annie Ct & Ln 98512
Glen Ayre Ln NW 98502
Glen Kerry Ct SE 98513
Glendale Ct & Dr 98501
Glenmore Ct & Dr 98501
Glenmore Village Dr
SE 98501
Glenwood Dr SW 98512
Glory Dr SE 98513
Gold Ct SW 98512
Gold Dust Ct SW 98512
Gold Ridge Ln SW 98512
Goldcreek Ct & Dr 98512
Goldcrest Dr & Hts 98502
Golden Eagle Ct SE 98513
Golden Eagle Ln SW 98512
Golden Eagle Loop
SE 98513
Golden Maples Ct NW 98502
Golden Oak Ct SE 98513
Goldeneye Ln SE 98513
Goldenrod Dr SE 98513
Goldsby St SW 98512
Golson Rd SE 98513
Gopher Ct SE 98501
Goss Ln SE 98513
Governor Ln SE 98501
Governor Stevens Ave &
Ct 98501
Grace Ave NW 98502
Graham Dr SE 98513
Grampin Ct SE 98501
Grand Fir Ln NW 98502
Grandview Ave NW 98502
Granite Ln NE 98516
Grant Ln & St 98512
Grantree Ct SE 98513
Grass Ct SE 98513
Grass Lake Ln & St 98502
Gravelly Beach Loop &
Rd 98502
E & W Gray Sea Eagle
Ln 98512
Grayhawk Ln NE 98516
Green Ct SW 98512
Green Cove Ct & St 98502
Greendale Ct SW 98512
Greenfield Ct NE 98506
Greenfield Ct SE 98501
Greenfield St SE 98501
Greenlie Ln SW 98512
Greenridge Loop & St 98512
Greenvalley Ct SW 98512
Greenway Ln SE 98513
Greenwood Dr SW 98502
Greg Ct SE 98513
Gregory Way SE 98513
Griffin Ln SE 98501
Grindstone Dr SE 98513
Grotto Ct SW 98512
Grove Rd & St 98502
Groves Ave NW 98502
Guerin St SW 98512
Gull Harbor Dr & Rd 98506
Gunstone St SW 98512
Gunvor Ct & Dr 98516
H St SW 98512
Haig Ct & Dr 98501
Halcyon Ave NW 98502
Hale Pl NE 98506
Hallie Ct NW 98502
Halokuntux Ln SW 98512
Hamelin Ln SE 98513
Hamma Hamma Ct
SE 98501
Hammersley Way NW 98502
Hampshire Ct SE 98513
Hampton Ct SE 98501
Hampton Dr SW 98512
Hamptons St SE 98501
Handicap Ct SW 98512
Hansen St SE
700-999 98501
5800-5898 98513
5900-6199 98513
Harbor View Dr NW 98502
Hargis St NW 98502
Harmony Ln SW 98512
Haro Ct SE 98513
Harrier St NE 98516
Harriman Ln NE 98506
Harrington Ln 98506
Harrison Ave NW 98502
Harstene St NE 98516
Hart Rd SE 98501
Hartman Ct SE 98501
Hartman Rd SE 98513
Hartman St SE 98501
Hartwood Ct SE 98513
Harvest Ave, Ct & Dr 98501
Havencrest Ct SE 98513
Hawks Glen Dr &
Loop 98513
Hawks Prairie Rd NE 98516
Hawksridge Ct & Dr 98513
Hawthorne Pl & St 98501
Hayes St SW 98512
Hayko Ln SE 98513
Hays Ave NW 98502
Hayworth Ave NE 98516
Hazard Lake Pl SE 98501
Hazelhurst Dr SE 98501
Heather Ct NE 98516
Heather Ln SW 98501
Heavenly Ct SE 98501
Hedera Ct SE 98513
Heights Ln NE 98506
Helen Ave NE 98516
Helm Ct SW 98512
Hemphill Dr SE 98513
Hendershot St NE 98516
Henderson Blvd & Ct 98501
Henry St NE 98506
Henry St SE 98501
Hensley St NE 98516
Henslin Ct & Dr 98513
Hepburn St NE 98516
Herb Ct SE 98513
Heritage Ct & St NW &
SW 98502
Herman Rd SE 98501
Hewitt Lake Dr SE 98501
Hibiscus Ct SE 98513
Hickory Ct SE 98501
Hidden Cove Ln NW 98502
Hidden Forest Dr SE 98513
Hidden Lake Ln SE 98501
Hidden Meadows Ln
SW 98512
Highland Dr SW 98501
Highlands Dr NE 98516
Highline Dr SE 98501
Hill Ct & St 98516
Hillcrest Dr SE 98501
Hillside Dr SE 98501
Hilltop Ct SW 98512
Hillview Ct NW 98502
Hilton Ln & Rd 98516
Hixon Dr SE 98501
Hoadly Loop & St 98501
Hoffman Ct & Rd 98501
Hogan Dr SE 98513
Hogum Bay Rd NE 98516
Holiday Cir & Dr 98501
Holiday Valley Ct & Dr 98502
Holland Ct SE 98513
Hollis Dr SE 98513
Holloway Ln NE 98516
Holly Ct NE 98516
Holly Ln SE 98501
Hollywood Dr NE 98516
Hollywood Park Ct SE 98513
Homestead Ave NE 98516
Homestead Ln NE 98506
Honeysuckle Ln SW 98512
Horne St NE 98516
Horse Haven St SE 98501
Horseshoe Ct SE 98501
Horsetail Ct SE 98513
Houston Dr NW 98502
Howard Ave NE 98506
Howe Rd NW 98502
Huber Ln NE 98506
Huckleberry Rd NW 98502
Hudson Ct NW 98502
Hudson Ln SE 98513
Hudson St NW 98502
Huetter Ct SW 98512
Hummingbird Ln NW 98502
Humphrey St SE 98501
Hunter Ln SW 98512
Hunter Mill Ln NE 98516
Hunter Point Rd NW 98502
Hunters Ln SE 98513
Huntington Loop SE 98513
Hyak Ct NE 98516
I St SW 98512
Ian Ct SE 98501
Ida Ct NE 98516
Illahee Ln NE 98516
Illahee Ln SW 98512
Incline Ct & Dr 98513
Indian Rd NE 98506
Indian Crest Ln NE 98516
Indian Summer Ct &
Dr 98513
Indiana St SE 98513
Iris Ln SW 98512
Iron Ct SW 98512
Irving St SW 98512
Island Dr NW 98502
Island View Ct & Dr 98506
Israel Rd SE
100-199 98501
200-398 98501
200-200 98511
201-299 98501
600-698 98501
Israel Rd SW
100-298 98501
300-1199 98501
1500-1899 98512
Ivy St NE 98516
Jabbok Way NE 98506
Jacki Ct NE 98506
Jacksnipe Ct SE 98513
Jackson Ave NW 98502
Jacob Ct SW 98512
James Pl SE 98501
Jamieson Ct SW 98512
Jamison Ln SE 98513
Jana Ln SE 98501
Janet Dr SW 98501
Janis Ct SE 98513
Jasmine St NW 98502
Jason Ct SE 98513
Jasper Ave NE 98506
Jayden Ln NE 98516
Jayhawk Ln SW 98512
Jefferson St NE 98501
Jefferson St SE
400-498 98501
500-899 98501
900-1798 98501
900-900 98507
901-1799 98501
Jenni St NE 98506
Jennifer Ln NW 98502
Jericho Ln SW 98512
Jester Ct NW 98502
Jett Ln NE 98516
Jill Ct SE 98513
Joanie Ln NW 98502
Joann Ave NE 98516
Jody Ct SW 98512
Joelle Ln SE 98513
John Luhr Rd NE 98516
Johns Pl NE 98516
Johnson Rd SE 98513
Johnson Point Loop &
Rd 98516
Jon Ct SE 98513
Jones Rd SW 98512
Jonquil Ln NW 98502
Joppa St SW 98512
Jorgenson Rd NE 98516
Joseph St SE 98501
Joshua Way SE 98501
Joy Ave NE 98506
Judd St NE 98516
Jude Ct 98516
Judy Ln SE 98513
Juli Ct SE 98501
Jump A Stump Ln SE 98501
Juniper Dr SE 98513
Kaelin Elise Ln SE 98501
Kagy St SE 98513
Kaiser Rd NW 98502
Kaiser Rd SW
400-699 98502
901-997 98512
999-1500 98512
1502-1698 98512
Kamerlyn Hill Ln SE 98513
Kamerlyn Prairie Ln
SE 98513
Karat Ct SW 98512
Karen Frazier Rd SE 98501
Karenna Ln SE 98501
Katie St NW 98502
Kdee Ln SE 98501
Keating Rd NW 98502
Kegley Meadows Ct
NE 98506
Kellogg Dr NE 98516
Kelly Beach Rd SE 98513
Kelsey St SE 98501
Kempton St SE 98501
Ken Lake Dr SW 98512
Kennedy Creek Rd
SW 98512
Kensington Ct SE 98501
Kensington Ln SW 98512
Kenton Ln SE 98501
Kenwood Pl SE 98501
Kenyon St NW 98502
Kenzi St SE 98513
Kerbaugh Rd NE 98516
Kerrysdale Dr SE 98513
Kiel Ct SE 98513
Kiely Dr SE 98501
Kildane Way 98501
Killarney Ct NW 98502
Kimmie Rd & St 98512
Kimtah Ct NE 98516
Kingfisher Ct SE 98513
Kingham St NE 98516
Kings Way SE 98501
Kingsbury Ln SE 98501
Kingston Ln SW 98512
Kingswood Dr SW 98512
Kinney Rd SW 98512
Kinsale Ln SE 98501
Kirkaldy Ct SE 98501
Kirsop Ln & Rd 98512
Kirsop Village Dr SW 98512
Kittiwake Ct, Dr & St 98513
Kiwa Dr SE 98513
Kiwi Ct NW 98502
Klahanie Dr NW 98502
Klahowya Ln SW 98512
Klein St NW 98502
Klipsun Ln SW 98512
Knight Ct SE 98501
Kodiak Ave NE 98516
Koskie Ct SW 98512
Kuhlman Rd SE 98513
Kwan Tupso Ln SW 98512
Kyle St SE 98501
Kylee Ln SE 98501
L St SW 98512
La France Rd SW 98512
La Vista Ct & Dr 98512
Lachman Ln SW 98502
Lady Fern Loop NW 98502
Laguna Dr SW 98512
Lake Cove Loop SE 98501
Lake House Ln SE 98513
Lake Lucinda Dr SW 98512
Lake Park Dr SW 98512
Lake Saint Clair Dr
SE 98513
Lake Terrace Dr SW 98512
Lakehills Dr SE 98501
Lakehurst Dr SE 98501
Lakemont Ct & Dr 98513
Lakemoor Cir, Dr, Ln,
Loop & Pl SW 98512
Lakeridge Dr & Way 98502
Lakeshore Ln SE 98513
Lakeside St SW 98512
Lakeview Ct SW 98512
Lakewood Cir & Dr 98501
Lambskin St SW 98512
Lana Ln SW 98512
Lancelot Ct & Dr 98512
Landau Ave NE 98506
Langridge Ave, Ct &
Loop 98502
Lansdale Rd SE 98501
Lapush Way NE 98516
Laredo Dr SE 98513
Lark St SW 98512
Larkspur Dr SE 98513
Lashi St SE 98513
Lathrop Industrial Dr
SW 98512
Latigo St SE 98513
Laura Ct & St 98501
Laurelhurst Dr SE 98501
Laurelwood Ln NW 98502
Lawson Ct & St 98513
Lazy Ct & St 98512
Leach Ct SE 98501
Leapfrog Ave NE 98506
Leavelle St NW 98502
Leavenworth Ave NE 98506
Lee St SE & SW 98501
Leeward Ct NW 98502
Legacy Dr NE 98516
Legion Way SE & SW 98501
Leingang Ln NE 98506
Lemon Rd NE 98506
Lenox Ct NW 98502
Lento Pl SE 98513
Leprechaun Dr NW 98502
Leschi Cir SE 98513
Leslie Ct SE 98501
Lewis Rd NW 98502
Libby Rd NE 98506
Liberal St NW 98502
Liberty St SW 98512
Lido Ct SW 98512
Lighthouse Ln NE 98506
Lilly Rd NE 98506
Lilly Rd SE 98501
Lilly Jo Ct SE 98501
Limited Ln NW 98502
Limpkin Ct SE 98513
Lincoln Ave SE 98501
Linda St SE 98501
Lindell Rd NE 98506
Linderson Way SW 98501
Lindsley St SE 98506
Link Ct SW 98512
Linwood Ave SW 98512
Lister Rd NE 98506
Little St SW 98512
Little Bear Ct SE 98501
Littlerock Rd SW 98512
Littlestone Ln SW 98512
Lively St SW 98512
Lloyd St SE 98501
Lochton Ct SE 98513
Loete Ct SE 98501
Log Cabin Rd SE 98501
Logez Ct SW 98512
Lohman Ct SE 98512
Lohrer Ln NE 98516
Lone Tree Ln SW 98512
Longhorn Ct & Loop 98501
Longinaker Dr SE 98501
Lookout Dr NW 98502
Loon Ct SE 98513

Lords Ln SW 98512
Loren St NE 98516
Lorne St SE 98501
Lorraine Dr SE 98501
Louise St SW 98512
Lovejoy Ct NE 98506
Lovely Ln NE 98516
Loyola St NE 98516
Lubbers Ln NW 98502
Lucerne Ln SE 98513
Lucinda Ct SW 98512
Luhr Rd NE 98516
Ly Rhon Ct SW 98512
Lybarger St NE 98506
Lybarger St SE 98501
Lyon Crest Ln NE 98506
M St SE 98501
Mac Ln SE 98513
Macadam Ct SE 98501
Macintosh Ct SE 98513
Madison Ave NW 98502
Madison Heights Ct SE 98501
Madrona Pl NE 98506
Madrona Beach Rd NW 98502
Magnolia Dr SE 98501
Main St NE 98516
Makah St NE 98516
Malcolm St SE 98501
Malia Ln SE 98513
Malin Ln SW 98501
Mallard Ct & Dr 98513
Mamook Ct NE 98516
Manchester Ln SE 98513
Mandy Pl NE 98516
Manito Dr NE 98516
Manning Ln NW 98502
Manzanita Dr NW 98502
Maple St SE 98501
Maple Beach Ln NW 98502
Maple Creek Ln SE 98501
Maple Park Ave SE 98501
Maple Valley Rd SW 98512
Maplecrest Ct NE 98506
Mapleleaf Ct NE 98506
Mapleridge Ct & Dr 98506
Mapleview Ct & Dr 98506
Maplewood Ct SW 98512
Maplewood Ln SE 98501
Marantha Ln SW 98512
Marcus Ln SE 98513
Mare Ct SE 98501
Margaret Mckenny St SE 98501
Margo Pl SE 98501
Mari Ln SE 98513
Marian Dr NE 98516
Marie St SE 98501
Marigold St NW 98502
Marilyn Ct SW 98512
Marine Dr NE 98501
Mariner Dr NW 98502
Maringo Rd SE 98501
Marion St NE 98506
Mark St NE 98516
Market St NE 98501
Marksman St SW 98512
Marla Ct NE 98506
Marland St SW 98502
Marlbrook Ct & Loop 98513
Marlene Ct SW 98512
Marshall Dr SE 98501
Martin Way E
2600-4099 98506
4100-10399 98516
Marvin Rd NE 98516
Marwood Ln SW 98502
Mary Ann Ct SE 98501
Mary Bobb Dr & Loop 98513
Mary Elder Rd NE 98506
Mason St SW 98512
Mason Way NW 98502
Massey Ave NE 98506
Matsu St NW 98502
Maya Ln SE 98501

Mayfair Dr SW 98512
Maytown Rd SW 98512
Mazama Ct & St 98512
Mcallister Ct SE 98513
Mccorkle Rd SE 98501
Mccormick Ct SE 98501
Mccormick St NE 98506
Mccormick St SE 98501
Mcdonald St SE 98501
Mcgill Ct SE 98501
Mciver Ct SW 98512
Mckena St SW 98512
Mckenny Ln SW 98512
Mckenzie Rd SW 98512
Mclane Ct SW 98512
Mclane Creek Ct SW 98512
Mcphee Rd SW 98502
Meadow View Ct NE 98516
Meadowood Ln NE 98506
Meadowwood Dr SW 98502
Meagan Ct SE 98501
Meander Ln NW 98502
Medallion Ct & Loop 98502
Medicine Bend Ln SE 98513
Meixner St NE 98506
Melichar Ln NW 98502
Melinda Ct NE 98516
Memory Ct SE 98513
Mercantile Ln NE 98506
Mercury Cir SE 98501
Meridian Ct SE 98513
Meridian Rd NE 98516
Meridian Rd SE 98513
Meriwood Dr NE 98516
Merkel Pl, St & Way 98516
Merryman Pl SE 98501
Mesa Dr SE 98501
Mett St NE 98516
Michael Ct NE 98516
Middle St SE 98501
Middleridge Ct NE 98516
Midway St NW 98502
Mike Ct NE 98506
Milano Ct SE 98513
Milas Ave NE 98506
Milbanke Ct & Dr 98513
Milburn Loop SE 98513
Mill Bight Rd NE 98516
Miller Ave NE 98506
Miller Rd NW 98502
Miller St SW 98512
Millstone Ln SE 98513
Milroy St NW & SW 98502
Milton Ln NE 98516
Mima Rd SW 98512
Mima Vista Rd SW 98512
Miner Ct & Dr 98512
Mink St NW 98502
Mirada Dr NW 98502
Mirasett St SW 98512
Mirimichi Dr NW 98502
Mirror Ct SE 98513
Mission Dr NE 98506
Mitchell Ave NE 98506
Miter Dr NW 98502
Mix St NW 98502
Mockingbird Dr SE 98513
Monaco Ct & Dr 98501
Monroe Ln NE 98516
Monta Vista St SE 98501
Montague Ln SE 98513
Monterey St SW 98512
Montrose Ct SE 98501
Moore St SE 98501
Morgan Ln SW 98512
Morse Ct & Rd 98501
Morse Merryman Rd SE 98501
Morton Ct SE 98501
Mossy Rock Ave NE 98516
Mottman Ct & Rd 98512
Mountain Ln SW 98512
Mountain View Pl SE 98501
Muck Creek Dr SE 98513
Mud Bay Rd NW & W 98502
Mugho Dr & St 98513

Muirfield Ln SE 98501
Muirhead Ave NW 98502
Muk Sut Wei Dr SE 98513
Mullen Rd SE 98513
Mullen Heights Dr SE 98513
Mulligan Ct NE 98516
Munn Lake Dr SE 98501
Munson Ct & Rd 98512
Murray Ct NW 98502
Musser Ln SW 98512
Mykonos St NW 98502
Myra Ln SE 98501
Myrtle Pl SE 98501
N St SE 98501
Narnia Ln NW 98502
Natasha Ln SW 98512
Nathan Ct & Ln 98501
Natooka Ct SE 98513
Neil St NE 98516
Nels St SW 98512
Nepean Dr SE 98513
Nettot Ct NW 98502
New Market St SW 98501
New View Ct NE 98506
Newberry Ln SE 98513
Newbury Ct SE 98501
Newport Ct SW 98512
Newport St NE 98506
Newton Dr SE 98513
Neylon Dr SW 98512
Nicholas Ln SE 98513
Nighthawk Ct SE 98513
Nikolas St SE 98501
Nine Bark St NW 98502
Nisqually Ct & Dr 98513
Nisqually Cut Off Rd SE 98513
Nisqually Park Ct, Dr & Loop 98513
Nisqually View Loop NE 98516
Nisqually Vista Ct NE 98516
Nissing Way SE 98501
Noble St SW 98512
Noble View Ln NW 98502
Nooksack Ct SE 98501
Norcross Ct SE 98501
Norfolk Ct SE 98501
Normandy Dr, Pl & St 98501
North Ct & St 98501
Northcote St NW 98502
Northill Dr & Loop 98512
Northland Ln SE 98513
Northwood Ct & Dr 98513
Norunn Ct NE 98516
Noschka Rd SW 98512
Nugget Ct SW 98512
Nunn Rd SW 98512
Nut Tree Ct & Loop 98501
Nyla Ln SE 98501
O St SE 98501
Oak Ave NE 98506
Oakbrook Ct & Dr 98513
Oakmont Pl SE 98513
Oakview Ct SE 98513
Octave Ct SE 98513
Odegard Rd SW 98512
Ofarrell Ave SE 98501
Ogden Rd SE 98501
Old Forest Ln SE 98501
Old Highway 101 NW 98502
Old Highway 410 SW 98512
Old Highway 99 SE & SW 98501
Old Israel Rd SW 98512
Old Morse Rd SE 98501
Old Oak St SE 98501
Old Olympic Hwy NW 98502
Old Olympic Hwy SW 98512
W Old Olympic Hwy 98502
Old Oregon Trl SW 98501
Old Pacific Hwy SE 98513
Old Port Ct, Dr & Ln 98502
Old Reservation Rd SE 98513

Old Steamboat Island Rd NW 98502
Oldstead Ct SE 98501
Oleary St NW 98502
Olmstead Ln SW 98512
Oly Bar Ln NW 98502
Olympia Ave NE
100-499 98501
800-2500 98506
2502-2598 98506
Olympic Dr NE 98506
Olympic St NW 98502
Olympic Way NW 98502
Olympic Way SW 98502
Ontario St SE 98501
Onyx Ct & St 98501
Orange St SE 98501
Orbit Pl SE 98501
Orcas Ct, Loop & St 98516
Orchard Dr NW 98502
Orchid Ln SW 98512
Oriental Dr NE 98506
Oriole Ln NW 98502
Orvas Ct SE 98501
Osborn St SW 98512
Oso Berry St & Way 98502
Osprey Dr NE 98516
Ostrander Ct SE 98501
Ostrich Dr SE 98513
Otis St SE 98501
Otis Beach St NE 98516
Overhulse Rd NW 98502
Overlook Dr NW 98502
Overton Ct SE 98513
Owl Ln NE 98516
Oxbow St NE 98516
Oxford Ct SE 98501
Oyster Bay Rd NW 98502
Pacific Ave SE
2000-2198 98506
2201-2297 98501
2299-3799 98501
8300-9199 98513
Pacific Hwy SE 98513
Pacific Ridge Dr SE 98513
Paddock Ct SE 98501
Palermo Ave SE 98501
Palermo Dr SW 98512
Palomino Ct & Dr 98501
Pamela Ln NE 98506
Par Ct SW 98512
Park Cir SW 98512
Park Dr SW 98512
Park Ln SW 98501
Park Place Ln SE 98501
Parkmont Ln SW 98502
Parkridge Dr SE 98501
Parkview Ct SW 98512
Parkwood Dr SE 98501
Parrish Rd SW 98512
Parrot St SE 98501
Partridge Dr NW 98502
Pat Kennedy Way SW 98501
Patrick Ct SE 98501
Patsy Dr SE 98501
Pattison St NE 98506
Pattison St SE 98501
Pattison Lake Dr SE 98513
Peach Ave NW 98502
Pear Ct NE 98506
Pear St NE 98506
Pear St SE 98501
Pearl Ct SE 98501
Pearl Beach Dr NW 98502
Peninsula Dr SE 98513
Pennant Ct NW 98502
Percival St NW & SW 98502
Peregrine Ct, Dr & Loop 98513
Periwinkle Loop NE & SE 98516
Permapl Dr SE 98513
Perry St NW 98502
Perry Creek Rd SW 98512
Perry Falls Ln SW 98512
Perth Ct SE 98501

Peter Kalama Dr SE 98513
Pheasant Ln NW 98502
Pheasant Ln SE 98513
Phelps Ln NW 98502
Phoenix St NE 98506
Phoenix St SE 98501
Pickering Ln NW 98502
Piedra Dr SW 98512
Pifer Ct & Rd 98501
Pike Ave NE 98516
Pilchuck Ct SE 98501
Pine Ave NE 98506
Pinebrook Dr SE 98501
Pinecrest Dr SE 98513
Pinedrop Ct, Dr & Loop 98513
Pinehurst Dr SE & SW 98501
Pioneer Ave NE 98506
Pioneer St SW 98512
Piperhill Dr SE 98513
Pippit Ct SE 98513
Placid Ave NW 98502
Planer Ct SE 98513
Plaza Ct SE 98513
Pleasant Glade Rd NE 98516
Pleasant Hill Ct & Dr 98516
Pleasure Dr SE 98501
Plum St SE 98501
Plummer St SE 98501
Plymouth Ct & St 98502
Pneumonia Gulch Ln NW 98502
Point Ct SE 98513
Point View St NE 98516
Polar Pl SE 98501
Polaris Ln NE 98516
Polo Club Ln SE 98501
Poole Dr SE 98513
Poplar St SE 98501
Poppy Ln SW 98512
Porta Ct NW 98502
Portstewart Ln SE 98501
Powder Ridge St SE 98501
Prairie Ct SE 98513
Prairie Pkwy SW 98512
Prairie Park Ln SW 98512
Prairie Ridge Dr NE 98516
Prestwick Ln SE
3600-4409 98501
4410-4799 98513
Primrose Ln SE 98501
Prine Dr SW 98512
Prine Villa Ln SW 98512
Prosik Ln SW 98512
Prospect Ave NE 98506
Prospector Pl SW 98512
Providence Ln NE 98506
Puffin Ct SE 98513
Puget Rd NE 98516
Puget St NE 98506
Puget Beach Rd NE 98516
Quail Ln SW 98512
Quail Creek Ln NE 98516
Quail Run Loop NW 98502
Quartz Ln NE 98516
Quasar Way NE 98506
Queens Ct SE 98513
Queets Dr NE 98516
Quiemuth Ct & St 98513
Quinault Dr & Loop 98516
Quince St NE 98506
Quince St SE 98501
R W Johnson Rd SW 98512
Racca Ct & Dr 98513
Raccoon Valley Rd SE 98513
Raft St NW 98502
Rainbow Ln SE 98501
Rainier Ave SE 98501
Rainier Rd SE 98513
Raintree Ct SE 98501
Rainwater Ct SW 98512
Rainwood Dr NW 98502
Ramblewood Ln SE 98513
Ramona Ct SW 98512

Randall Ln SW 98512
Random Ln SW 98512
Raptor Ave NE 98516
Ravenna Ln SE 98501
Ravine Ln SE 98513
Reading St SE 98501
Rechet Ct SE 98501
Red Alder Dr NE 98516
Red Fern Dr NW 98502
Red Maple Ct NE 98506
Redstart Dr SE 98513
Redtail Ct & Dr 98513
Redwood Pl SE 98501
Regal Park Ln SW 98512
Regency Loop SE 98513
Regents Ln SE 98513
Rehklau Rd SE 98513
Rein St SE 98501
Rejoice Way SE 98501
Renata Ln SW 98512
Renee Ct SE 98513
Reservation Rd SE 98513
Restawhile Ct SW 98512
Rhododendron Ct NE 98516
Rhondo Ct & St 98512
Rich Rd SE 98501
Richardson Ln NW 98502
Richardson Ln SE 98501
Ridge Ct SE 98513
Ridge High Ct SW 98512
Ridge Top Ln NW 98502
Ridge View Dr & Loop 98513
Ridgefield Ave NE 98516
Ridgegate Ln SW 98512
Ridgemont Ct & Dr 98513
Ridgeview Ct & Loop 98512
Ridgeway Ct SW 98512
Ridgewood Ct & Ln 98502
Riki Ln SE 98501
Riley Dr SE 98513
Rimrock Ct SW 98512
River Dr SE 98501
River St SW 98512
River Bend Ln SE 98513
Riverdale Dr SE 98501
Riverlea Ct & Dr 98501
Rivers Ct SE 98513
Riverside Dr & Pl 98513
Riverview Ct & Dr 98501
Riverwood Dr SE 98501
Riviera Ct SE 98513
Rixie Ct & St 98501
Road 65 NW 98502
Roberts Rd SE 98501
Robin Ct SE 98513
Robin Ln NW 98502
Robin Hill Ct SW 98502
Rock Candy Mountain Rd SW 98512
Rock Maple Ln NW 98502
Rockcreek Ln SW 98512
Rockcress Dr SE 98513
Rockrose Ct SE 98513
Rocky Ln SE 98513
Rocky Mountain Dr SW 98512
Rogers Ct & St 98502
Rolling Hills Ter NW 98502
Ronlee Ln NW 98502
Roosevelt St NE 98506
Rosario Ct SE 98513
Rose St NE 98506
Rosewood Dr SW 98502
Ross Cir SE 98501
Roth Rd SW 98512
Rothenberg Dr SW 98512
Rough Ct SW 98512
Rowen Dr SE 98501
Rowland Dr SE 98513
Roxburg Ct SE 98513
Royal St SE 98501
Roycroft Dr NW 98502
Ruby St SE 98501
Ruddell Rd SE 98513
Rumac Dr & St 98513
Run Cir, Ct & Dr 98513

Runner Stone Ct SE 98513
Rural Rd SW 98512
Ruth Ct SE 98513
Ryan Ln SE 98513
Sa Sada Wa St SE 98513
Sable Ln NE 98506
Saddle Ct SE 98501
Saint Andrews Dr SE 98513
Saint Charles Ct, Dr & Loop 98516
Saint Clair Cut Off Rd SE 98513
Saint James Ct NW 98502
Salal Ln NW 98502
Salmon Ln SE 98513
Salmon Creek Ln SW 98512
Salt Chuck Ln NE 98506
Salty Dr NW 98502
Salzburg Ln SE 98513
San Francisco Ave NE 98506
San Mar Dr NE 98506
Sandalwood Dr SW 98502
Sandpiper Ct NW 98502
Sandra Lee Ct & St 98513
Sandtrap Ct SW 98512
Sandy Point Beach Rd NE 98516
Sanford Cir SE 98501
Sapp Rd SW 98512
Sapphire Ln NE 98516
Sarah Ct NW 98502
E & W Sarazen Ct & St SE 98513
Saskatoon Ln SE 98513
Satsop Ct SE 98501
Sawmill Ct SE 98513
Sawyer St NE 98506
Sawyer St SE 98501
Scammell Ave NW 98502
Scenic Dr NE 98516
Schirm Rd NW 98502
Schirm Loop Rd NW 98502
Schmidt Pl SW 98501
Schonberg Ln SE 98513
Schoth Rd SW 98512
Schuetz Ln SW 98512
Scotch Meadows Ct SE 98501
Scotlac Ct & Dr 98512
Scott Rd NW 98502
Scott St SE 98501
Scott Creek Dr & Loop 98512
Seaton Ct SE 98513
Seaview Dr NW 98502
Select Ct SE 98501
Seneca St SE 98501
Serenity Ln SW 98512
Serry Lee Ln SW 98512
Sevedge Ct NE 98506
Sexton Dr NW 98502
Shadberry Ct & Dr 98513
Shadlewood Ct SE 98501
Shadow Cir, Ln & Pl 98506
Shadowbrook Dr SW 98512
Shadybrook Ln SE 98501
Shadycrest Ct SW 98512
Shaker Church Rd NW 98502
Shalom Ct & Dr 98512
Shana Ct SE 98501
Shawn Dr SW 98512
She Nah Num Dr SE 98513
Shea Ln SW 98512
Shelburne Ct & Way 98501
Sheldon Rd SE 98501
Shellridge Rd NW 98502
Shelly St SW 98512
Sherman St NW & SW 98502
Sherman Valley Rd SW 98512
Shermer Ln SE 98513
Sherwood Dr SE 98501
Shincke Rd NE 98506
Shore St NE 98506

Shore Acres Dr NE 98506
Shoreview Dr SW 98512
Short Ct SE 98513
Shy Bear Dr SE 98501
Sid Snyder Ave SW 98501
Sienna Dr SE 98501
Silo Ct SE 98501
Silvan View Ct SW 98512
Silver Ln SW 98512
Silver Fox Ct SW 98512
Silver Oaks Ct SE 98501
Silver Ridge Ct, Dr & Way 98501
Silverleaf Ct NW 98502
Silverspot Ct & Dr 98501
Simmons Rd NW 98502
Simmons St NW 98501
Simmons Heights Ln SW 98512
Simmons Mill Ct SW 98512
Simon Ln NE 98506
Siskin Ct & Dr 98513
Siskiyou Loop & St 98501
Sitka Ct & Dr 98513
Sitkum Dr SE 98513
Skagit Ct & Dr 98501
Ski View Ln SW 98512
Skillman Ln NW 98502
Skokomish Way NE 98516
Skooter Ln NE 98506
Skyline Ter NW 98502
Skyline Ridge Ln SW 98512
Slate Ct SE 98501
Sleater Kinney Rd NE 98506
Sleepy Creek Ln NE 98506
Sleepy Hollow Ln NE 98516
Smith St SE 98501
Snow Grass Pl NE 98516
Snug Harbor Ct & Rd 98506
Sockeye Ln SE 98513
Solar Ct NE 98516
Solitude St SE 98501
Sophie Way NW 98502
Soroya Ct & Dr 98502
Soundview Ln NW 98502
South St SE 98501
Southall Ct NW 98502
Southampton Ct SE 98501
Southerness Ct & Ln 98513
Southglen Ave & Pl 98501
Southwick Ct SW 98512
Sparrow Ct SE 98513
Spencer Ave NE 98516
Sportsman Ln SE 98513
Springer Ln NE 98506
Springer Hills Ln SE 98501
Springer Lake Ln SE 98501
Springfield Ct & Pl 98506
Springview Dr NE 98506
Springwood Ave NE 98506
Spruce St SE 98513
Sprucecrest Dr SW 98512
Spurgeon Creek Rd SE 98513
Spurgeon Meadow Ct SE 98513
St George Ln SE 98501
Stable Ct SE 98501
Stadium Ln SE 98501
Stafford Ln SE 98513
Stagecoach Ct SE 98501
Stahi Ct SE 98513
Stanhope St NE 98506
Stanton Ct SW 98501
Stanwick Ln SE 98513
Star Ct SE 98501
Stardust Ln SE 98501
Stark Ln NE 98516
Starling Dr NW 98502
Starview Ln NW 98502
State Ave NE
101-109 98501
111-499 98501
501-699 98501
700-2500 98506
2502-2698 98506
State Ave NW 98501
State Route 8 W 98502
Stead Ln NE 98506
Steamboat Is & Loop 98502
Steamboat Island Rd NW 98502
Stedman Rd SE 98513
Steele St NE 98506
Steele St SE 98501
Steilacoom Ct & Rd 98513
Stellar Ln SE 98513
Stetson Ct NW 98502
Stibgen Rd NW 98502
Stillwater Ave NW 98502
Stillwell St NE 98516
Stirling Ct & St 98501
Stirrup Ct SE 98501
Stoll Rd SE 98501
Stone St SE 98513
Stonecrest Ln NW 98502
Stonehaven Ln SE 98501
Stoner Ln SE 98513
Stonewood Dr SE 98513
Stoney Creek Ln SW 98512
Stratford Ln SE 98501
Stratford Ln SW 98512
Strathmore Cir SW 98512
S Street Ct SE 98501
Streld St SE 98501
Stuart St NE 98506
Sugar Maple St SE 98513
Sugarloaf Ln & St 98501
Sulenes Loop SE 98501
Sullivan St NE 98506
Summerfield Ct, Dr & Loop 98513
Summerhill Ct SW 98512
Summerset Ct & Dr 98513
Summerwood Dr SE 98513
Summit Ct SW 98512
Summit Lake Cir & Rd 98502
Summit Lake Shore Rd NW 98502
Sundrop Ln SE 98501
Sunflower Ln SW 98512
Sunny Beach Ln NE 98516
Sunnyvale Ct NW 98502
Sunrise Beach Rd NW 98502
Sunrise Heights Ln NW 98502
Sunrise Ridge Ln NW 98502
Sunrise Vista Ln SW 98512
Sunset Ct NE 98516
Sunset Dr NW 98502
Sunset Way SE 98501
Sunset Beach Dr NW 98502
Sunset Point Ln NW 98502
Sunset Ridge Ln NW 98502
Supreme Ct SW 98512
Surrey Ct SE 98501
Surrey Dr NE 98506
Surrey Trce SE 98501
Susan Ct SE 98501
Susitna Ln SW 98512
Swa Wa Ct SE 98513
Swallow Ln NW 98502
Swanee Pl SE 98501
Swayne Dr NE 98516
Swecker Ave SE 98501
Sweetbrier Ln & Loop 98513
Sweetens Ln SE 98513
Sweetiron Ln SE 98501
Sweetwater Loop SW 98512
Swift Creek Ln SW 98512
Swordfern Dr NW 98502
Sylvester St SW 98501
T St SE & SW 98501
Tabitha Ct NW 98502
Tag Ln NW 98502
Tahoe Dr SE 98501
Tamoshan Dr NW 98502
Tanbark St SE 98513
Tandem Ct SE 98501
Taner Ln SW 98512
Tanwax Dr SE 98513
Tartan Dr SW 98501
Taryn Ln NE 98516
Taylor St SW 98512
Tellkamp Rd NE 98506
Tempo Lake Dr SE 98513
Tenby Ln SE 98513
Tennis Ct SW 98512
Terminal St SW 98501
Tern Ct & Dr 98513
Terrace Ln SW 98502
Texas Ave SE 98513
Thelma Ct SE 98513
Thomas St NW & SW 98502
Thompson Ln SE 98513
Thomsen Rd SE 98513
Thornburg St SW 98512
Thornhill Ct SE 98513
Thornton Rd SE 98513
Thornton St NW 98502
Thoroughbred Ln SE 98513
Thorpe Dr SW 98512
Three Sisters Ct NE 98506
Threshing Dr SE 98513
Thrulake Cir SE 98513
Thrush Dr SE 98513
Thurston Ave NE
101-197 98501
199-299 98501
900-2599 98506
Thurston Ave NW 98501
Tiahalish Ave SE 98513
Tierney St SW 98512
Tiger Lilly Ln SE 98513
Tiger Tail Dr SW 98512
Tilley Rd S 98512
Tilley Rd SE 98501
Tillicum Ct NE 98516
Timber Ct, Dr & Loop 98513
Tina Ct SE 98513
Titleist Ln SE 98513
Tobacco Ln SE 98513
Todderjen Ln SW 98512
Todtkarle Rd SE 98513
Tolmie Ct & Dr 98516
Tolo Ct NE 98516
Toltec Ct NW 98502
Tom Evans Rd NE 98506
Tonya Ct SE 98513
Torden Ln SE 98513
Torrey St SE 98513
Totten Ct NW 98502
Toulliere Ln SW 98512
Toulouse Ct SW 98512
Toutle Ct SE 98501
Tracie Ct SW 98512
Tradewind Dr SE 98501
Trails End Ct & Dr 98501
Tralee Dr NW 98502
Tranquil Ave NW 98502
SW Treasure River Trl 98512
Trenton Loop SE 98501
Trevue Ave SW 98512
Tri Lake Ct, Dr & Loop 98513
Trillium Ln SE 98513
Trimble Ln SE 98501
Troon Ln SE 98501
Trosper Rd SW
100-198 98501
201-299 98501
501-597 98512
599-2400 98512
1727-1797 98512
1799-1800 98512
1802-1998 98512
2402-5298 98512
Trosper Lake St SW 98512
Trowbridge Ln & Rd 98513
Tsuga Ct SW 98512
Tucker Rd SE 98513
Tulip Ln SW 98512
Tullis St NE 98506
Tumwater Blvd SE 98501
Tumwater Blvd SW
100-198 98501
200-399 98501
401-799 98501
2400-2499 98512
Tumwater Valley Dr SE 98501
Turkey Rd NW 98502
Turnberry Ln SE 98501
Turner St NE 98506
Tuscany Ln SW 98512
Twin Cedar Ln SE 98501
Twisted Tree Ln NE 98516
Tyee Dr SW 98512
Tyndell Cir SW 98512
U St SE 98501
Union Ave SE & SW 98501
Urquhart St NW 98502
Us Highway 101 NW 98502
V St SE & SW 98501
Vacation Dr SW 98512
Vale Ct SE 98513
Valley Green Ct & Dr 98513
Valley View Dr SE 98513
Van Epps St SE 98501
Vantage Ave & Ct 98512
Vantage Terrace Ct SE 98513
Venus Cir SE 98501
Vermont Ave SE 98513
Verna St SE 98513
Vicki Ct NE 98506
Victoria Ct & Dr 98501
View Hill Rd NE 98506
View Point Ct SW 98512
Viewridge Dr SE 98501
Village Cir, Ct & Dr 98501
Villanova St NE 98516
Vine Ave SW 98502
Vine Ct NE 98516
Vineyard Ave SE 98501
Viola St SE 98501
Vireo Ct SE 98513
Vista Ave SE 98501
Vista Loop SW 98512
Vista Pl SE 98501
Vista Verde Ln SW 98512
Von St SE 98501
Vue St SW 98512
W St SE & SW 98501
Waddell Creek Ct, Ln & Rd 98512
Wagon Wheel St SE 98501
Wakeman Ct & Dr 98513
Waldon Dr SE 98513
Waldrick Rd SE 98501
Walker Ct SE 98501
Walnut Loop NW 98502
Walnut Rd NE 98516
Walnut Rd NW 98502
Walona St SE 98501
Walter Ct SW 98512
Wapato Ct NE 98516
Warbler Ct SE 98513
Ward Lake Ct SE 98501
Warner St NE 98516
Warren Ln SW 98512
Washington St NE & SE 98501
Water St NW & SW 98501
Wedgewood Ct & Dr 98501
Well Dr SE 98513
Wendy Dr SE 98513
Wentworth Ave 98502
Wesley Dr & Loop 98502
Westchester St 98502
Westcott Ln SE 98501
Western Ct SE 98501
Western Ct SW 98512
Westhampton Ln SW 98512
Westhill Ct & Dr 98512
Westmoor Ct SW 98502
Westpark Ct NW 98502
Westridge Ln NW 98502
Westside Dr NW 98502
Westview Pl NW 98502
Westwind Dr NW 98502
Westwood Ct, Dr & St 98502
Wexford Loop SE 98501
Wheatberry Dr SE 98513
Wheeler Ave SE 98501
Whisler St NE 98516
Whispering Firs Ln 98506
Whispering Pines St NE 98516
White Hawk Ln SE 98501
Whitecap Dr NW 98502
Whitehall Ln SE 98501
Whitetail Ct SE 98513
Whitmore Dr 98501
Whittaker Rd NW 98502
Wickie Ct & Pl 98501
Widgeon Ct SE 98513
Wier St SE 98501
Wiggins Rd SE 98501
Wild Goose Ln NW 98502
Wild Horse Ln SE 98513
Wild Moose Ct SE 98501
Wild Rose Ln SW 98512
Wilda Ln NE 98516
Wilderness Ct, Dr & Loop 98501
Wildflower St SE 98501
Wildrye Ln SE 98501
Wildwood Ln SE 98513
Wilkins Pl SE 98501
Willa St NE 98516
Willow Dr NE 98506
Wilmer Ln SE 98501
Wilson Rd NW 98502
Wilson St NE 98506
Wilson St SE 98501
Wily St NW 98502
Windemere Dr SE 98501
Windjammer Ct NW 98502
Windolph Ln & Loop 98502
Windsor Ln NE 98516
Windsor Ln SW 98512
Windward Dr NW 98502
Windwood Pl NE 98506
Winesap Ln SE 98501
Wingate Dr SE 98513
Winlock Ct SE 98513
Winners Ct SE 98513
Winnwood Ct, Dr & Loop 98513
Winslow Dr SW 98512
Winter Bright Dr SE 98513
Wintergarden Dr SE 98501
Winthrop Cir SW 98512
Wisley Ln SE 98513
Wisteria Ct & Dr 98513
Wood Ct SW 98512
Wood Ibis Dr SE 98513
Wood Trails Dr 98502
Woodard Ave & Ct 98502
Woodard Bay Rd NE 98506
Woodard Green Dr NE 98506
Woodcrest Cir & Dr 98501
Woodduck Dr SW 98502
Woodfield Loop SE 98501
Woodglen St NE 98516
Woodgrove Ct & St 98513
Woodland Ct & Dr 98512
Woodland Creek St NE 98516
Woodlawn Dr SE 98501
Woodmont Ln SE 98501
Woods Estate Ln NE 98506
Woodside Ct NE 98506
Wooduck Dr SW 98502
Woodwind Dr SW 98502
Woolworth Ct NE 98506
Wrangler Dr SE 98501
Wrigley Ln SW 98512
Wynoochee Pl NE 98516
X St SE & SW 98501
Y St SE & SW 98501
Yakima St NE 98516
Yantis St NW 98502
Yarrow Ct SE 98501
Yauger Way NW & SW 98502
Yearley Dr NE 98516
Yelm Hwy SE
800-998 98501
1500-1598 98501
1600-3999 98501
4001-4099 98501
6600-6998 98513
7000-13299 98513
Yelm Creek Ct SE 98513
Yew Ave NE 98506
Yew Trails Dr NW 98502
Yew Wood Ct SE 98513
Yolanda Dr SW 98512
Yorkshire Ct & Dr 98513
Young Rd & St 98502
Z St SE 98501
Zangle Rd NE 98506
Zenda Dr SE 98501
Zephyr Ln SW 98512

NUMBERED STREETS

1st Ln SE 98513
2nd Ave NW 98502
2nd Ave SW 98512
N 2nd Ave SW 98512
S 2nd Ave SW 98512
2nd Ln SE 98513
3rd Ave NW 98502
3rd Ave SE 98513
3rd Ave SW 98501
N 3rd Ave SW 98512
S 3rd Ave SW 98512
3rd Ct SE 98513
3rd Way SE 98513
4th Ave E
100-198 98501
700-2599 98506
4th Ave NE 98516
4th Ave NW 98502
4th Ave W
100-599 98501
701-797 98502
N 4th Ave SW 98512
S 4th Ave SW 98512
4th Way SW 98502
5th Ave NE 98506
5th Ave NW 98502
5th Ave SE 98501
5th Ave SW
101-197 98501
301-497 98512
302-498 98501
499-611 98512
612-616 98501
613-999 98512
1000-1799 98502
N 5th Ave SW 98512
SW 5th Ave
800-899 98502
5th Ct SE 98513
5th Way SW 98502
6th Ave NW 98502
6th Ave SE 98513
6th Ave SW
1000-1799 98502
1801-1899 98502
5701-6597 98501
6599-6999 98501
N 6th Ave SW 98512
S 6th Ave SW 98512
6th St SE 98501
6th Way SE 98513
7th Ave NW 98502
7th Ave SE
101-401 98501
403-2399 98501
10700-11099 98513
7th Ave SW
1200-4799 98502
6401-6497 98501
6499-6599 98501
N 7th Ave SW 98512
S 7th Ave SW 98512
7th Ct NW 98502
8th Ave NE 98506
8th Ave SE 98501
8th Ave SW
801-899 98512
1200-1298 98502
1300-1899 98502
1901-1999 98502
N 8th Ave SW 98512
S 8th Ave SW 98512
8th Ct SE 98513
8th Ct SW 98502
8th Way SE 98513
9th Ave NW 98502
9th Ave SE
200-298 98501
300-2599 98501
8400-8699 98513
9th Ave SW 98502
N 9th Ave SW 98512
9th Ln NW 98502
9th Way SE 98513
10th Ave NE
2800-2826 98506
7200-7299 98516
10th Ave NW 98502
10th Ave SE 98501
10th Ave SW
100-199 98501
1200-1298 98502
10th Ct SE 98501
10th Way SE 98501
11th Ave NE 98516
11th Ave NW 98502
11th Ave SE 98501
11th Ave SW
100-298 98501
1400-1800 98502
1802-1898 98502
11th Ct SW 98502
11th Ln SE 98513
12th Ave NE
1901-1997 98506
7200-7699 98516
12th Ave SE 98501
12th Ave SW
401-499 98501
824-898 98512
1400-1999 98502
5400-5699 98512
12th Ct SW 98502
12th Way NE 98516
12th Way SE 98501
12th Way SW 98502
13th Ave NE 98516
13th Ave SE
500-1899 98501
8300-8499 98513
13th Ave SW
500-599 98501
1400-1999 98502
2001-2199 98502
3400-5599 98512
13th Ct NE 98516
13th Way NE 98516
14th Ave NE 98516
14th Ave NW 98502
14th Ave SE
300-698 98501
700-3799 98501
8400-8499 98513
14th Ave SW
200-299 98501
1300-2099 98502
14th Ct NE 98506
14th Loop NE 98516
15th Ave NE 98516
15th Ave SE
700-2198 98501
2200-2899 98501
8300-8699 98513
15th Ave SW
201-415 98501
500-598 98501
1400-2099 98502
15th Ct NE 98506
15th Way SE 98501
16th Ave SE
500-3399 98501
8300-8499 98513

16th Ave SW ... 98501
16th Ln NE ... 98506
16th Ln SW ... 98512
16th Trl NE ... 98516
17th Ave NE ... 98516
17th Ave NW ... 98502
17th Ave SE ... 98501
17th Ave SW ... 98501
17th Ct NE ... 98506
17th Ln NE ... 98516
17th Way NE ... 98516
17th Way SE ... 98501
18th Ave NE ... 98506
18th Ave NW ... 98502
18th Ave SE ... 98501
18th Ave SW
100-299 ... 98501
6200-6399 ... 98512
18th Ct NE
1700-1799 ... 98506
5600-5699 ... 98516
18th Ln NW ... 98502
19th Ave NE ... 98506
19th Ave SE ... 98501
19th Ave SW ... 98501
19th Ct NE ... 98506
19th Ct NW ... 98502
19th Ln NW ... 98502
19th Ln SE ... 98501
19th Way NW ... 98502
20th Ave NE ... 98506
20th Ave NW ... 98502
20th Ave SE ... 98501
20th Ave SW ... 98501
20th Ct NE ... 98506
20th Ln NE ... 98516
20th Ln NW ... 98502
20th Way NE ... 98516
21st Ave SE ... 98501
21st Ave SW
100-199 ... 98501
201-399 ... 98501
2501-2599 ... 98512
3300-3398 ... 98512
21st Ct NE ... 98516
21st Ct SE ... 98501
21st Way SE ... 98513
22nd Ave NE ... 98516
22nd Ave SE
101-111 ... 98501
113-3899 ... 98501
8200-8298 ... 98513
8300-8399 ... 98513
22nd Ave SW ... 98501
22nd Way NE ... 98506
22nd Way SE ... 98513
23rd Ave NE ... 98516
23rd Ave SE ... 98501
23rd Ave SW ... 98501
23rd Ln NE ... 98506
23rd Ln SW ... 98512
23rd Way SE ... 98513
24th Ave NE ... 98506
24th Ave NW ... 98502
24th Ave SE ... 98501
24th Ave SW ... 98501
24th Ct SE ... 98513
24th Ln ... 98502
24th Way SW ... 98502
25th Ave NW ... 98502
25th Ave SE
100-199 ... 98501
201-299 ... 98501
11500-12199 ... 98513
25th Ave SW ... 98512
25th Ct NE ... 98506
25th Ct SW ... 98512
25th Ln NE ... 98506
25th Ln NW ... 98502
25th Way SE ... 98501
26th Ave NE
900-4099 ... 98506
4101-4297 ... 98516
4299-4399 ... 98516
26th Ave NW ... 98502
26th Ave SW
100-198 ... 98501
2900-2999 ... 98512
26th Ct SW ... 98512
26th Ln NW ... 98502
27th Ave NW ... 98502
27th Ave SE
300-4099 ... 98501
8500-8999 ... 98513
27th Ave SW ... 98512
27th Ct NE ... 98506
27th Ln NE ... 98506
28th Ave NW ... 98502
28th Ave SE ... 98501
28th Ave SW ... 98512
28th Ct SE ... 98501
28th Ln NE ... 98506
28th Way SE ... 98513
29th Ave NE ... 98506
29th Ave NW ... 98502
29th Ave SW ... 98512
29th Ct NW ... 98502
29th Ln NE ... 98506
29th Way SE ... 98513
30th Ave SE ... 98501
30th Ct SE ... 98501
30th Ln SE ... 98513
30th Way SE ... 98501
31st Ave NE ... 98516
31st Ave NW ... 98502
31st Ct NE ... 98506
31st Ct SE ... 98501
31st Ln NE ... 98516
31st Ln NW ... 98502
32nd Ave NE ... 98516
32nd Ave NW ... 98502
32nd Ave SW ... 98512
32nd Ct NE ... 98516
32nd Ct NW ... 98502
32nd Ct SE ... 98501
32nd Ct SW ... 98512
32nd Way NW ... 98502
33rd Ave NE ... 98506
33rd Ave NW ... 98502
33rd Ct NE ... 98516
33rd Ln NE
601-697 ... 98506
699-3399 ... 98506
6100-6299 ... 98516
33rd Ln NW ... 98502
33rd Trl NE ... 98506
33rd Way NW ... 98502
34th Ln NE ... 98506
35th Ave NE ... 98506
35th Ln NE ... 98506
35th Ln SE ... 98513
36th Ave NE
700-3399 ... 98506
4100-4400 ... 98516
36th Ave NW ... 98502
36th Ave SE ... 98501
36th Ct SE
1700-1799 ... 98501
9700-9799 ... 98513
36th Ln NE ... 98506
36th Loop NW ... 98502
37th Ave SE ... 98501
37th Ave SW ... 98512
37th Ct NW ... 98502
37th Ct SE ... 98513
37th Ln NW ... 98502
38th Ave NE ... 98506
38th Ct SE
1200-1299 ... 98501
9600-9699 ... 98513
38th Ln NE ... 98506
38th Ln NW ... 98502
38th Way NE ... 98516
39th Ave NE ... 98506
39th Ct SE ... 98501
39th Ln NW ... 98502
39th Loop NE ... 98516
39th Way NE ... 98506
40th Ave SE ... 98501
40th Ave SW ... 98512
40th Ct NE ... 98516
40th Ct SE ... 98513
40th Ln NW ... 98502
41st Ave NE ... 98506
41st Ave NW ... 98502
41st Loop SE ... 98501
41st Trl SE ... 98513
41st Way NW ... 98502
41st Way SE ... 98501
42nd Ave SE ... 98501
42nd Ct NE ... 98516
42nd Ct SE ... 98501
42nd Ln SW ... 98512
43rd Ave NW ... 98502
43rd Ave SE ... 98501
43rd Ct NE ... 98516
43rd Ct NW ... 98502
43rd Ln NE ... 98516
43rd Ln SW ... 98512
43rd Trl NW ... 98502
44th Ave NE ... 98516
44th Ave NW ... 98502
44th Ave SE ... 98513
44th Ln NE ... 98516
44th Ln NW ... 98502
44th Ln SW ... 98512
44th Way NE ... 98516
45th Ave, Ct & Loop ... 98501
45th Ave, Ct & Loop ... 98512
46th Ave NE
200-3599 ... 98506
4500-9900 ... 98516
9902-9998 ... 98516
46th Ave NW ... 98502
46th Ave SE ... 98513
46th Ct NE ... 98516
46th Ct SE ... 98501
47th Ave NE
900-998 ... 98506
1001-1099 ... 98506
6601-6797 ... 98516
6799-7399 ... 98516
47th Ave SE ... 98501
47th Ln NE ... 98516
47th Ln NW ... 98502
47th Ln SE ... 98513
47th Loop NE ... 98516
48th Ave SW ... 98512
48th Ct NE ... 98516
48th Ct NW ... 98502
48th Ct SE ... 98501
48th Ln NE ... 98506
48th Way NE ... 98516
48th Way NW ... 98502
49th Ave NW ... 98502
49th Ave SE ... 98513
49th Ave SW ... 98512
49th Ct NE ... 98516
49th Ct SE ... 98513
49th Ln NW ... 98502
49th Loop SE ... 98513
49th Trl NW ... 98502
50th Ave NE ... 98516
50th Ave SE
3300-3399 ... 98501
7500-7799 ... 98513
50th Ave SW ... 98512
50th Ct SE
2600-2699 ... 98501
6700-6799 ... 98513
50th Ln NE ... 98516
50th Ln NW ... 98502
51st Ave NE ... 98516
51st Ave NW ... 98502
51st Ave SE
1800-2699 ... 98501
9400-9499 ... 98513
51st Ct SE ... 98501
51st Ln NW ... 98502
52nd Ave NW ... 98502
52nd Ave SE ... 98501
52nd Ave SW ... 98512
52nd Ln NE ... 98516
52nd Way SE ... 98501
53rd Ave SE ... 98501
53rd Ln NE ... 98506
53rd Loop SE ... 98501
53rd Way NE ... 98506
53rd Way SE ... 98501
54th Ave NE ... 98516
54th Ave NW ... 98502
54th Ave SE
3000-3299 ... 98501
8201-8297 ... 98513
8299-8499 ... 98513
54th Ave SW ... 98512
54th Ln SE ... 98501
55th Ave NW ... 98502
55th Ave SE
2300-2599 ... 98501
8100-8499 ... 98513
55th Ct SE ... 98501
55th Loop SE ... 98513
56th Ave NE
3300-3999 ... 98506
7000-7799 ... 98516
56th Ave SW ... 98512
56th Ct SE ... 98501
56th St NW ... 98502
56th Trl SE ... 98501
57th Ave SE ... 98501
57th Ln NE ... 98516
57th Ln SE ... 98501
57th Trl SE ... 98501
57th Way NW ... 98502
58th Ave NE ... 98516
58th Ave NW ... 98502
58th Ave SE
1600-1699 ... 98501
4600-9499 ... 98513
58th Ct SE ... 98501
58th Ln NW ... 98502
58th Ln SW ... 98512
59th Ave NW ... 98502
59th Ave SW ... 98512
59th Ct SE
3000-3199 ... 98501
8100-8299 ... 98513
59th Ct SW ... 98512
60th Ave SE ... 98501
60th Ave SW ... 98512
60th Ct NE ... 98516
60th Ct NW ... 98502
60th Ct SE ... 98501
60th Ln NW ... 98502
60th Ln SE
2800-2999 ... 98501
8300-9799 ... 98513
60th Ln SW ... 98512
60th Loop SE ... 98501
61st Ave NE ... 98516
61st Ave NW ... 98502
61st Ave SE ... 98513
61st Ct SE ... 98501
61st Ct SW ... 98512
62nd Ave NW ... 98502
62nd Ave SE ... 98513
62nd Ave SW ... 98512
62nd Ct SE ... 98501
62nd Ln SW ... 98512
63rd Ave NE ... 98516
63rd Ave NW ... 98502
63rd Ave SE ... 98513
63rd Ct SW ... 98512
63rd Ln SW ... 98512
64th Ave NW ... 98502
64th Ave SE ... 98513
64th Ct SE ... 98513
64th Way SE
1800-1899 ... 98501
5500-5599 ... 98513
65th Ave NE ... 98516
65th Ave SE
1401-1697 ... 98501
5200-5599 ... 98513
65th Ave SW ... 98512
65th Ct SE ... 98501
65th Ct SW
200-299 ... 98501
2200-2499 ... 98512
65th Ln NW ... 98502
65th Ln SE ... 98513
65th Way NE ... 98516
65th Way SW ... 98501
66th Ave NE ... 98506
66th Ave NW ... 98502
66th Ave SE ... 98513
66th Ave SW ... 98512
67th Ave NE
1200-1399 ... 98506
5600-6099 ... 98516
67th Ave NW ... 98502
67th Ave SE ... 98513
67th Ct SW ... 98512
67th Ln SW ... 98512
68th Ave NE
600-799 ... 98506
4300-4999 ... 98516
68th Ave NW ... 98502
68th Ave SE
1200-1298 ... 98501
1300-1399 ... 98501
7900-8099 ... 98513
68th Ave SW ... 98512
68th Ct SW ... 98512
68th Loop SE ... 98513
69th Ave NW ... 98502
69th Ave SE ... 98501
69th Ave SW ... 98512
69th Ct SE ... 98501
69th Way SE ... 98501
70th Ave NE ... 98516
70th Ave NW ... 98502
70th Ave SW ... 98512
70th Way SE ... 98513
70th Way SW ... 98512
71st Ave SE
1201-1397 ... 98501
5000-5099 ... 98513
71st Ave SW ... 98501
71st Ct SW ... 98512
71st Dr SE ... 98501
71st Ln SW ... 98512
71st Way NE
300-599 ... 98506
5000-7299 ... 98516
71st Way SW ... 98512
72nd Ave NE
300-599 ... 98506
4500-4999 ... 98516
72nd Ave SE ... 98501
72nd Ln NE
500-599 ... 98506
5000-5599 ... 98516
72nd Ln SE ... 98513
72nd Way NE ... 98506
72nd Way SE ... 98501
73rd Ave NE
200-1199 ... 98506
5000-6799 ... 98516
73rd Ave SE ... 98501
73rd Ave SW
400-498 ... 98501
801-899 ... 98501
2401-2599 ... 98512
73rd Ln SW ... 98512
73rd Way NE ... 98506
74th Ave NW ... 98502
74th Ave SE
3100-4799 ... 98501
6900-6999 ... 98513
74th Ave SW
1600-1698 ... 98501
5000-5199 ... 98512
74th Ln NE ... 98516
75th Ave NE ... 98516
75th Ave NW ... 98502
75th Ave SE
3100-3399 ... 98501
6400-6899 ... 98513
75th Ave SW ... 98512
75th Ct SW ... 98512
75th Ln SE ... 98513
75th Way NE ... 98506
76th Ave NE
400-3199 ... 98506
4700-6999 ... 98516
76th Ave SE ... 98513
76th Ave SW
701-799 ... 98501
2701-2899 ... 98512
76th Ct SW ... 98512
76th Ln SW ... 98512
76th Way NE ... 98506
77th Ave NE ... 98506
77th Ave SE ... 98501
77th Ave SW ... 98512
77th Ct SE ... 98501
77th Ct SW ... 98512
77th Ln SE ... 98513
77th Trl SE ... 98501
77th Way NE ... 98506
78th Ave NE ... 98516
78th Ave NW ... 98502
78th Ave SE ... 98501
78th Ave SW
101-797 ... 98501
799-899 ... 98501
4200-4599 ... 98512
78th Ct SW ... 98512
78th Ln SE ... 98513
78th Loop NW ... 98502
79th Ave NE ... 98516
79th Ave NW ... 98502
79th Ave SE ... 98501
79th Ave SW ... 98512
79th Ct SE ... 98501
79th Ct SW ... 98512
80th Ave SE
1800-3999 ... 98501
8100-8499 ... 98513
80th Ave SW ... 98512
80th Ct SW ... 98512
80th Ln SE ... 98513
81st Ave NE ... 98506
81st Ave NW ... 98502
81st Ave SE ... 98501
81st Ave SW ... 98512
81st Ct SE ... 98513
82nd Ave SE ... 98501
82nd Ln SE ... 98513
83rd Ave SE
3400-3799 ... 98501
8300-8499 ... 98513
8501-9099 ... 98513
83rd Ave SW ... 98512
83rd Ct NE
2600-2799 ... 98506
5000-5099 ... 98516
83rd Ln SE ... 98513
84th Ct NE ... 98506
84th Ln SW ... 98512
85th Ave NE
2400-2499 ... 98506
5700-6199 ... 98516
85th Ave NW ... 98502
85th Ave SE ... 98501
85th Ave SW ... 98512
85th Ct NE ... 98506
85th Ln SE ... 98513
85th Ln SW ... 98512
86th Ave NE ... 98516
86th Ave NW ... 98502
86th Ave SE ... 98513
86th Ct SW ... 98512
87th Ave SE
3800-5099 ... 98501
5600-5699 ... 98513
87th Ct SW ... 98512
88th Ave NE ... 98516
88th Ave SE ... 98501
88th Ave SW ... 98512
89th Ave SE
1200-5399 ... 98501
5400-5899 ... 98513
89th Ave SW ... 98512
89th Ln SE ... 98513
90th Ave NW ... 98502
90th Ave SE ... 98501
90th Ln SW ... 98512
90th Way SE ... 98501
91st Ave SE ... 98513
91st Ave SW ... 98512
91st Ln SE ... 98513
92nd Ave NE ... 98516
92nd Ct SE ... 98501
92nd Ln SE ... 98513
93rd Ave NW ... 98502
93rd Ave SE
100-2299 ... 98501
5400-5799 ... 98513
93rd Ave SW ... 98512
93rd Ln SE ... 98513
93rd Trl SE ... 98513
95th Ave SW ... 98512
95th Ln SE ... 98501
96th Ln SE ... 98501
97th Ct SW ... 98512
97th Ln SE ... 98501
98th Ln SE ... 98501
98th Ln SW ... 98512
99th Ave SW ... 98512
99th Ln SE ... 98501
99th Ln SW ... 98512
100th Ave & Ln ... 98501
101st Ave SE ... 98501
101st Ave SW ... 98512
101st Ln SW ... 98512
103rd Ave SE ... 98513
103rd Ave SW ... 98512
103rd Ln SW ... 98512
104th Ave SW ... 98512
104th Ln SE ... 98501
105th Ave SW ... 98512
105th Ln SE ... 98501
106th Ln SE ... 98501
107th Ave SW ... 98512
107th Ln SE ... 98501
110th Ave SW ... 98512
113th Ave SE ... 98501
113th Ave SW ... 98512
113th Way SW ... 98512
114th Ave SW ... 98512
114th Ln SE ... 98501
114th Ln SW ... 98512
114th Way SW ... 98512
115th Ave SW ... 98512
116th Ave SE ... 98501
117th Ave SW ... 98512
118th Ave, Ct & Loop ... 98512
119th Ct & Ln ... 98512
123rd Ave SW ... 98512
124th Way SW ... 98512
125th Ln SW ... 98512
127th Ave SW ... 98512
128th Ave SW ... 98512
129th Ln SW ... 98512
130th Ln SW ... 98512
131st Ave SW ... 98512
146th Ln SW ... 98512
152nd Ave SW ... 98512

PASCO WA

General Delivery ... 99301

POST OFFICE BOXES MAIN OFFICE STATIONS AND BRANCHES

Box No.s
A - K ... 99302
C1900 - C1900 ... 99302
1 - 1051 ... 99301
2 - 630 ... 99302
1101 - 1760 ... 99301
1525 - 1525 ... 99302
1800 - 1800 ... 99301
1900 - 5920 ... 99302

NAMED STREETS

E & W A St ... 99301
Acacia Ct ... 99301
Adams Dr ... 99301
E Adelia St ... 99301
Adler Rd ... 99301
Adobe Ct & Dr W ... 99301
W Agate St ... 99301
E & W Ainsworth St ... 99301

Aintree Dr 99301
Alan Rd 99301
Alder Rd 99301
Alderman Rd 99301
Alderson Rd 99301
Allen Rd 99301
Alpine Lakes Dr 99301
Alta Ln 99301
E Alton St 99301
E & N Alvina Ct & St 99301
Amber Rd 99301
Anaconda Ave 99301
Andorra Ct 99301
Andrea Ave 99301
Angelo Ln 99301
Angus Dr 99301
Antigua Dr 99301
Anza Borrego Ct 99301
Apeldorn Ct 99301
Appaloosa Ct & Ln 99301
Aquarius Dr 99301
Aqueduct Ln 99301
Arabian Ln 99301
Arbutus Ave & Ct 99301
Argent Pl & Rd 99301
Aries Dr 99301
Armstrong Rd 99301
Arousa Rd 99301
Artesia Dr 99301
Arthur Ln 99301
Aspen Loop 99301
Astor Way 99301
Atlanta Ln 99301
Atom Dr 99301
Auburn Rd 99301
Augusta Ln 99301
Austin Ct & Dr 99301
N Autoplex Way 99301
N Avery Ave 99301
Avion Dr 99301
E & W B Cir & St 99301
Baja Dr 99301
E Baker St 99301
Bakerloo Ln 99301
Balflour Ln 99301
Balmoral Ct 99301
Barcelona Ct 99301
Basalt Fls 99301
Bayview Ln 99301
Beacon Rock Ln 99301
Bedford St 99301
N & S Beech Ave 99301
Belgian Ln 99301
Bell St 99301
Bellerive Ln 99301
Bellevue Dr & Rd 99301
Belmont Dr 99301
Bengen Ln 99301
Berkshire Ln 99301
Bermuda Dunes Dr 99301
Bilbao Dr 99301
Birch Rd 99301
Blasdel Rd 99301
Blue Jay Dr 99301
Blue Sage Dr 99301
Blue Star Ct 99301
W Boeing St 99301
Boise Dr 99301
Bonanza Dr 99301
Bond Ln 99301
Bonilla Dr 99301
W Bonneville St 99301
Bosch Ct 99301
Bragueta Ct 99301
Brahman Ln 99301
Branch Rd 99301
Brewster Ln 99301
Broadmoor Blvd 99301
Broadway Pl & St 99301
Brooklyn Ln 99301
Brothers Dr 99301
Broughton Dr 99301
Brown Pl & St 99301
Buchanan Ln 99301
Buckingham Dr 99301
Buena Ct 99301
Bulldog Ln 99301
W Bumpaous Rd 99301
Burden Blvd 99301
N Burlington Loop & St 99301
Burns Rd 99301
Burr Canyon Rd 99301
E Butte Ct & St 99301
Buttercreek Ct 99301
Buttercup Ct 99301
Butternut Cir 99301
Byers Rd 99301
W C St 99301
Cabernet Ct 99301
Cabrillo Ct 99301
Cactus Ct 99301
Cadboro Ln 99301
Calder Ln 99301
N California Ave 99301
Camano Dr 99301
Camargo Ln 99301
Cambridge Ln 99301
Camden Dr 99301
Campolina Ln 99301
Canada Ct 99301
Candellia Ct 99301
Candlestick Dr 99301
Canterbury Ln 99301
Canyon Dr 99301
N Capitol Ave 99301
Carbon Ct 99301
E Cargo St 99301
Carnation Ct 99301
Carr Rd 99301
Cartmell St 99301
Case Ln 99301
Cashmere Ln 99301
Catalonia Ct & Dr 99301
Cathedral Dr 99301
Cavendish Ct 99301
N & S Cedar Ave & Rd 99301
Cereza Ct 99301
Chapel Hill Blvd 99301
Chardonnay Dr 99301
N Charles St 99301
Chehalis Dr & Ln 99301
Chelan Ct 99301
Cherry Dr & Ln 99301
Cheshire Ct 99301
S Chestnut Ave 99301
Chiwana Dr 99301
Cholla Ct & Dr 99301
Christina Ct 99301
Christopher Ln 99301
Churchill Downs Ln 99301
Clara Dr 99301
E & W Clark Rd & St 99301
Clarwalt Rd 99301
Clearview Rd 99301
Clemente Ln 99301
Cleveland Ln 99301
Clover Ln 99301
Clydesdale Ln 99301
Coachella Ct 99301
Cochins Ln 99301
Colby Ct 99301
Coltsfoot Rd 99301
E & W Columbia St 99301
N Columbia River Rd 99301
Comiskey Dr 99301
E Commerce St 99301
N Commercial Ave 99301
NW Commons Dr 99301
Concordia Ct 99301
Convention Dr & Pl 99301
Coolidge Ct 99301
Cooperstown Ln 99301
Coppercap Mountain Ln 99301
Coral Ct 99301
Cord Dr 99301
Cordero Dr 99301
Cordova Ct 99301
Cornish Ln 99301
Coronado Dr 99301
Cottonwood Dr 99301
Coulee Rd 99301
Country Haven Loop 99301
W Court St
300-3499 99301
3500-11598 99301
3500-3500 99302
3501-11599 99301
Coventry Ln 99301
Cowlitz Ln 99301
E Crane St 99301
Crescent Rd 99301
Crestloch Ln & Rd 99301
Cross Rd 99301
Crystal Dr 99301
Curlew Ln 99301
Custer Ct 99301
Cypress Ct, Dr & Ln 99301
Daffodil Ct 99301
Dahlia Ct 99301
Daisy Ct 99301
Damon Point Dr 99301
Dartmoor Ln 99301
Dayton Dr & Rd 99301
Decker Rd 99301
Del Mar Ct 99301
Dent Rd 99301
Denver Dr 99301
Des Moines Ln 99301
Deschutes Dr 99301
Deseret Dr 99301
Desert Ct, Dr, Pl & St 99301
Desert Meadow Ln 99301
Desert Plateau Dr 99301
Desoto Dr 99301
Devon Ct 99301
Diamond Dr 99301
Dietrich Rd 99301
E Dock St 99301
Dodger Dr 99301
Dogwood Rd 99301
Dorchester Ct 99301
N & S Douglas Ave & Ct 99301
W Dougville Rd 99301
W Dradie St 99301
Dunbarton Ave 99301
Dundas Ln 99301
Dunsmuir Dr 99301
Durham Ct & Dr 99301
Duroc Ln 99301
Dusty Rd 99301
Eagle Reach Ct 99301
Easy St 99301
Ebbets Dr 99301
Eisenhower Ct 99301
El Paso Dr 99301
Eldorado Dr 99301
Ella Ct & St 99301
N & S Elm Ave, Ln & Rd 99301
Elmwood St 99301
Eltopia Rd 99301
Emerald Downs Ln 99301
Empire Dr 99301
Entiat Ct 99301
Enzian Falls Dr 99301
Erin Rd 99301
Esperanza Ct 99301
Essenprise Rd 99301
Estevan Dr 99301
Estrella Dr & Ln 99301
W Ethan Ct 99301
Everett Rd 99301
Exeter Ln 99301
W Fairchild St 99301
Fairfield Dr 99301
Fallon Ct 99301
Falls Rd 99301
Famville Ct 99301
Fanning Rd 99301
N Feed Lot Rd 99301
Fenway Dr 99301
Fernwood Ln 99301
Fiesta Ct 99301
Fillmore Dr 99301
Finnhorse Ln 99301
Fir Ln, Rd & Way 99301
Fleming Ln 99301
Flores Ln 99301
E & W Foster Wells Rd 99301
Franklin Ave & Rd 99301
Fraser Dr 99301
W Frontage Rd 99301
E Frontier Dr, Ln, Loop & Rd 99301
Galiano Dr 99301
Galicia Ct 99301
Galloway Rd 99301
Galway Ln 99301
Garden Dr 99301
Garland St 99301
Gatwick Ct 99301
Gehrig Dr 99301
Geiger Dr 99301
Gemini Dr 99301
E George St 99301
Gertler Rd 99301
Giesler Rd 99301
Glacier Peak Dr 99301
N Glade Rd 99301
Glendive Ct & St 99301
Glenwood Rd 99301
Gobi Ct 99301
Goose Hollow Rd 99301
Grant Ln 99301
Graystone Ln 99301
Green Rd 99301
S Grey Ave 99301
W Grumman St 99301
Guemes Ln 99301
Gum Dr 99301
E Hagerman St 99301
Hampshire Ct 99301
Harris Rd 99301
Harvest Ct 99301
W Hassola St 99301
Haugen Rd 99301
W Havstad St 99301
Haworth Rd 99301
Hawthorne Ln 99301
Hayden Ln 99301
Hayes Ln 99301
Heathrow Ct 99301
E Helena St 99301
Helm Dr 99301
Henley Dr 99301
Henry Pl & St 99301
Highland St 99301
Hilbert Ln 99301
Hillcrest Dr 99301
E Hillsboro St 99301
Hilltop Dr 99301
Hiram Ct 99301
Hockett Ln 99301
Holborn Loop 99301
Holland Ln 99301
Hollyhock Ct 99301
Homerun 99301
Homestead Dr 99301
Honeysuckle Rd 99301
W Hopkins St 99301
Horizon Ct & Dr 99301
Hornby Ln 99301
Hovley Ln 99301
W Howard St 99301
Hudson Ct & Dr 99301
N & S Hugo Ave 99301
Hummel Ln 99301
Hunt Rd 99301
Ice Harbor Rd 99301
N & S Idaho Ave 99301
Indian Ridge Dr 99301
N Industrial Way 99301
Innisbrook Ln 99301
Inverness Way 99301
Ione Rd 99301
Iris Ct & Ln 99301
W Irving St 99301
Ivy Ln & Rd 99301
Jackson Ln 99301
Jacob Ln 99301
Jake Rd 99301
E James St 99301
W Jan St 99301
Janet Rd 99301
Jasmine Ln 99301
N Jason Ave 99301
Jasper Ct 99301
Jay Ct & St 99301
Jayleen Way 99301
Jefferson Dr 99301
Jersey Dr 99301
Jessica Rd 99301
John Deere Ln 99301
Johnson Dr 99301
Joshua Dr 99301
Joyce Rd 99301
Judemein Ct 99301
Juneau Ln 99301
Kalahari Dr 99301
Kalispell Ct 99301
Kariba Ct 99301
E Kartchner St 99301
Kathemein Ct 99301
Kau Trl 99301
Keeneland Ln 99301
Kennedy Way 99301
Kensington Ct 99301
Kent Ln 99301
Kepps Rd 99301
Killdeer Ln 99301
King Ave 99301
Kingsbury Dr 99301
Klickitat Ln 99301
Klundt Rd 99301
Knightsbridge Ln 99301
Kohler Rd 99301
Kootenay Ct 99301
Koufax Dr & Ln 99301
Kruse Rd 99301
Kubota Ln 99301
La Porte Dr 99301
Ladbroke Ln 99301
Laguna Ct 99301
Lancaster Dr 99301
Landsdowne Ct 99301
Langara Dr 99301
Lansing Dr & Ln 99301
Lantana Dr 99301
Laredo Dr 99301
Larkspur Dr 99301
Larrabee Ln 99301
Lasalle Dr & Ln 99301
Latimer Ct 99301
Laurie Ln 99301
Lavender Ct 99301
Leicester Ln 99301
W Leola St 99301
Leon Ct 99301
Leopard Dr 99301
Levey Rd 99301
E & W Lewis Pl & St 99301
Libertad Ct 99301
Lincoln Dr 99301
Lindemein Ct 99301
S Lindsay St 99301
Lisa Ln 99301
W Livingston Rd 99301
Lobelia Ct 99301
W Lockheed St 99301
Locust Ln 99301
Locust Water Rd 99301
Lopez Dr 99301
Louisville Dr 99301
Lucena Dr 99301
Lummi Dr 99301
E Lytle St 99301
Madeira Dr 99301
Madrid Ln 99301
Madrona Ave 99301
W Magnolia Ct 99301
N & S Main Ave 99301
S Maitland Ave 99301
Majestia Ln 99301
Malaga Dr 99301
Maltese Dr 99301
Manassas Ct 99301
Manzanita Ln 99301
W Maple Dr 99301
Marbella Ln 99301
W Margaret St 99301
Marie Ct & St 99301
Marigold Loop 99301
Mariner Ln 99301
Mariola Ct & Ln 99301
Mariposa Ct 99301
Market Ct & Dr 99301
Marlin Ln 99301
Martindale Rd 99301
E Marvin St 99301
Maryhill Ln 99301
Massey Dr 99301
Matia Ln 99301
Maverick Ct 99301
Mayne Dr 99301
Mays Ln 99301
Mcclenny Rd 99301
Mcdonald Dr 99301
Mckinley Ct 99301
Meadow Ct 99301
Meadow Beauty Dr 99301
Meadowsweet St 99301
Meadowview Ct & Dr 99301
W Mearinte St 99301
Meeker Rd 99301
Melody Ln 99301
W Melville Rd 99301
W Mercedes Ct 99301
Merlot Dr 99301
Merrick Dr 99301
Mesquite Dr 99301
Messara Ln 99301
Metcalf Rd 99301
Mia Ln 99301
Michelle Rd 99301
Midland Ln 99301
Milagro Dr 99301
Minorca Ln 99301
Mission Ridge Dr 99301
Mojave Ct & Dr 99301
Moline Ln 99301
Monrovia Ct & Ln 99301
Montague Ln 99301
Monterey Dr 99301
Montgomery Ln 99301
Montpelier Dr 99301
Moore Rd 99301
Moulton Ln & Rd 99301
Muirfield Ln 99301
Mukilteo Dr 99301
Mulberry Rd 99301
Muris Ln 99301
Murphy Ln & Rd 99301
Mustang Dr 99301
S Myrtle Ave 99301
Naches Ct 99301
Nash Dr 99301
Nauvoo Ln 99301
Neff Jones Rd 99301
Nicole Rd 99301
Nisqually Dr 99301
W Nixon St 99301
Norfolk Dr 99301
Nottingham Dr 99301
Oak Ct & Ln 99301
Obrian Rd 99301
Ochoco Ln 99301
W Octave St 99301
Okanogan Ln 99301
Old Airport Building 99301
Oliver Dr 99301
W Olivia Ct 99301
Opal Pl & St 99301
Orcas Dr 99301
Orchard Rd 99301
N & S Oregon Ave & St 99301
Oriole Dr & Ln 99301
Osprey Pointe Blvd 99301
Outlet Dr 99301
Overland Ct 99301
Overton Rd 99301
Overturf Rd 99301
N & S Owen Ave 99301
Oxford Ln 99301
Pacific Pines Dr 99301
Packard Dr 99301
Paddington Ln 99301
Page Rd 99301
Palo Verde Ct 99301
Palomino Dr 99301
Pamplona Dr 99301
Panther Ln 99301
Park Pl & St 99301
E Parkview Blvd 99301
Parley Ct & Dr 99301
Pasco Kahlotus Rd 99301
Paz Ct 99301
W Pearl St 99301
Pederson Rd 99301
Pelican Ct, Ln & Rd 99301
Pender Dr 99301
Pennie Ave 99301
Penrose Point Dr 99301
Peppertree Ct 99301
Percheron Dr 99301
Peterson Rd 99301
Peyote Dr 99301
Ph 15 99301
Pheasant Ct, Ln & Run 99301
Pheasant Run Rd 99301
Phend Ln & Rd 99301
Phoenix Ln 99301
Piccadilly Dr 99301
Piekarski Rd 99301
Pilgrim Rd 99301
Pimlico Dr 99301
Pine Ct 99301
Pisces Dr 99301
Polk Ct 99301
Polo Ln 99301
Polson Ct 99301
Pooler St 99301
Porlier Ln 99301
Powerline Rd 99301
Pradera Ct 99301
Prairie Ln 99301
Prestwick Ln 99301
Providence Ln 99301
Quadra Ct & Dr 99301
Quail Rd 99301
Quail Bluff Run 99301
Quail Run Rd 99301
Quatsino Dr 99301
Queensbury Dr 99301
N & S Railroad Ave 99301
N Rainier Ave 99301
Ramus Ln 99301
Reagan Way 99301
Red Roan Ct 99301
Redonda Dr 99301
Reynolds Rd 99301
W Richardson Rd 99301
Richmond Rd 99301
Richview Dr 99301
Rickenbacker Dr 99301
Ricky Ct & Rd 99301
Ridgeview Dr 99301
Riesling Ct 99301
Ringold Rd 99301
River Blvd & St 99301
Riverhaven St 99301
Riverhawk Ln 99301
Riverhill Ct & Dr 99301
Rivershore Dr 99301
Riverview Dr 99301
Riverward Ct & St 99301
Road 100 99301
Road 101 99301
Road 103 99301
Road 104 99301
Road 105 99301
Road 106 99301
Road 107 99301
Road 108 99301
Road 109 99301
Road 110 99301

Road 111 99301
SE Road 18 E 99301
N Road 27 99301
N & S Road 28 99301
N Road 30 99301
N Road 32 99301
N & SE Road 33 99301
N Road 34 99301
N Road 35 99301
N Road 36 99301
N Road 37 99301
N Road 38 99301
N Road 39 99301
N & S Road 40 E 99301
N Road 41 99301
N Road 42 99301
N Road 44 99301
N Road 45 99301
N Road 46 99301
N Road 47 99301
N Road 48 99301
N Road 49 99301
N Road 50 99301
N Road 51 99301
N Road 52 99301
N Road 54 99301
N Road 55 99301
N Road 56 99301
Road 57 Pl 99301
N Road 58 99301
N Road 59 99301
N Road 60 99301
N Road 61 99301
Road 62 99301
N Road 64 99301
N Road 67 99301
N Road 68 99301
Road 70 Pl 99301
N Road 72 99301
Road 76 99301
N Road 77 99301
N Road 79 99301
N Road 80 99301
N Road 84 99301
N Road 88 99301
Road 90 99301
N Road 92 99301
N Road 94 99301
N Road 96 99301
N Road 97 99301
Robert Wayne Dr 99301
Roberta Rd 99301
Roberts Dr 99301
Robinson Dr 99301
Rocket Ln 99301
Rocky Rd 99301
Rogers Rd 99301
Roosevelt Ct & Dr 99301
Rose Ct 99301
Rose Creek Ct 99301
W Ruby Ct & St 99301
Rush Creek Dr 99301
Ruth Dr 99301
Rye Grass Coulee 99301
Ryeland Dr 99301
Sacajawea Park Rd 99301
Sacramento Dr 99301
Saddle Creek Ln 99301
Saffron Ct 99301
E & W Sagemoor Ln & Rd 99301
Saguaro Dr 99301
Sahara Dr 99301
Saint Andrews Loop 99301
E Saint Helens St 99301
Saint Paul Ct & Ln 99301
Saint Thomas Dr 99301
Salem Dr 99301
Salmon Dr 99301
E Salt Lake St 99301
Salvia Ct 99301
Samuel Brown Trl 99301
Sandifur Pkwy 99301
Sandy Ridge Rd 99301
Santa Anna Loop 99301
Santa Fe Ln 99301
Santa Rosa Ct 99301
Saratoga Ln 99301
Saturna Dr 99301
Savary Dr 99301
Scenic View Dr 99301
Schultz Rd 99301
Schuman Ln 99301
W Seabrook Ct 99301
Sedona Ct & Dr 99301
Sego Lily Ct 99301
Segovia Dr 99301
Selph Landing Rd 99301
Serena Ln 99301
Seville Dr 99301
Shady Ln 99301
E Sheppard St 99301
Shetland Dr 99301
Shire Dr 99301
Shoreline Ct & Rd 99301
W Shoshone St 99301
Shumway Rd 99301
Sidon Ct & Ln 99301
Sierra Dr 99301
Sierra Gold Dr 99301
Silver Crest Ct 99301
Sinai Ct & Dr 99301
Sirocco Dr 99301
Skagit Dr 99301
Snake River Rd 99301
Snoqualmie Dr 99301
Snowcrest Ct 99301
Socas Ct 99301
Somerset Ln 99301
Sonora Dr 99301
Sorento Ct 99301
Spieden Dr 99301
E Spokane St 99301
Springfield Dr 99301
Spruce St 99301
Sr 395 99301
Star Ln 99301
Stearman Ave 99301
Sterling Rd 99301
Stinson Ave 99301
Stone Ct 99301
Studebaker Dr 99301
Sturgis Rd 99301
Stutz Dr & Ln 99301
Sun Willows Blvd 99301
Sunflower Ct 99301
Sunnybank Rd 99301
Sunset Ln, Loop & Trl 99301
Sunset View Ln 99301
N Sunview Ave 99301
N & S Sycamore Ave & Ct 99301
W Sylvester St 99301
Syrah Ct & Dr 99301
N & S Tacoma St 99301
Taft Dr 99301
Tamarisk Dr 99301
Tamarron Ln 99301
Tamworth Ln 99301
Tank Farm Rd 99301
Tarragona Ct 99301
Taylor Flats Rd 99301
Ter Ray Ct 99301
Terrace Dr 99301
Teruel Ln 99301
Texada Ln 99301
Thetis Dr 99301
Thistledown Dr 99301
Three Rivers Dr 99301
Tierra Vida Ln 99301
Tieton Ln 99301
Tiger Ln 99301
Tippet Ln 99301
Topaz Rd 99301
Topeka Dr 99301
Tottenham Ct 99301
Tracie Rd 99301
Travel Plaza Way 99301
Tree Farm Rd 99301
Truman Ln 99301
Tucker Ct 99301
Tulip Ct 99301
Turf Paradise Dr 99301
Turquoise Ct 99301
Tusayan Ct & Dr 99301
Tuscany Dr 99301
Twilight Ct 99301
Tyler Ct 99301
Tyre Dr 99301
Valdez Ln 99301
Valencia Dr 99301
Valley View Pl 99301
Vendovi Dr 99301
Ventura Dr 99301
Verbena Ct 99301
Victoria Ct 99301
View Ct & Ln 99301
Vincenzo Dr 99301
E & W Vineyard Dr & Ln 99301
Vista Pl 99301
Voss Rd 99301
Wade Ct 99301
N & S Waldemar Ave 99301
W Walker Way 99301
Wallace Walker Rd 99301
S Walnut Ave 99301
E & W Washington St 99301
Washougal Ln 99301
Waters Edge Dr 99301
N & S Wehe Ave 99301
Weisner Way 99301
Wellington Dr 99301
Welsh Ct & Dr 99301
Wembley Dr 99301
Wenatchee Ct & Dr 99301
W Wernett Rd 99301
Westminster Ln 99301
Westmorland Ln 99301
Westport Ln 99301
Whidbey Dr 99301
Whipple Dr & Rd 99301
White Bluff Ct 99301
Whitetail Ct 99301
W Wilcox Dr 99301
Wildcat Ln 99301
Wildflower Ct 99301
Willington Dr 99301
W Willow Cir, Ct & Way 99301
Wilshire Dr 99301
Windsor Ln 99301
Winthrop Dr 99301
Woodbine Dr 99301
Wrigley Dr 99301
W Yakima St 99301
Yankee Dr 99301
Yucatan Ct 99301
Yuma Dr 99301
Zafra Ct 99301
Zayas Dr 99301
Zephyr Ct 99301
Zinnia Ct 99301

NUMBERED STREETS

All Street Addresses 99301

PORT ANGELES WA

General Delivery 98362

POST OFFICE BOXES MAIN OFFICE STATIONS AND BRANCHES

Box No.s
1 - 3260 98362
4001 - 4085 98363
62001 - 62002 98362

NAMED STREETS

S A St 98363
Abbott Rd 98362
E Acorn Ln 98362
Adams Ave 98363
Afternoon Hill Ln 98362
Agate Beach Rd 98363
Agnew Pkwy 98362
E & W Ahlvers Rd 98362
S Airport Rd 98363
Albert St 98362
N & S Alder Ln & St 98362
Alderview Dr 98362
Alderwood Cir 98362
Alderwood Creek Dr 98362
Alice Rd 98363
Alpine Rd 98362
Alpine View Ln 98362
Alta Vista Rd 98363
Amarillo Rd 98362
E Angeles Ridge Rd 98362
Angels Lair Ln 98363
Apple Ln 98362
Apple Tree Ln 98363
Arbutus St 98363
Arcadia Pl 98363
E & W Arnette Rd 98362
Ash St 98362
Ashas Ct 98363
Ashley Ln 98363
N Aurora Ct 98363
S Aviation Pl 98363
Avis St 98362
Ayers Ln 98363
S B St 98363
E & W Bachelor Rock Dr 98363
Bagley Bluff Trl 98362
N & S Bagley Creek Rd 98362
N Baker St 98362
Baker Farm Rd 98362
Bald Eagle Way 98363
W Baldy View Dr 98363
Bantowel Rd 98363
Barnacle Dr 98363
Barnes Point Rd 98363
N & S Barr Rd 98362
Baskins Rd 98363
E Bay St 98363
N & S Bayview Ave 98362
Bayview Park Ln 98362
E Beach Rd 98363
S Bean Rd 98363
Bear Creek Rd 98363
Bear Meadow Rd 98362
Bear Tracts Rd 98362
Bear Valley Rd 98363
N Beech St 98362
Belbrook Ln 98362
Benjamin St 98362
Benson Crst & Rd 98363
Bent Cedars Way 98362
Bigelow Rd 98362
Billy Smith Rd 98362
Birdsong Ln 98362
Bishop Rd 98363
Black Bear Trl 98362
Black Diamond Rd 98363
Black Hawk Loop 98362
Blackberry Ln 98362
Blue Jay Pl 98362
Blue Mountain Rd 98362
Blue Ridge Rd 98362
Blue Shadow Ln 98362
Blue Valley Rd 98362
S Blue Water Vw 98362
E & W Bluff Dr 98363
Bluff View Dr 98363
Boardwalk Rd 98362
Boathaven Dr 98362
W Boathaven Dr 98363
Bobcat Hollow Rd 98362
Bonita Ln 98362
Boulder Rd 98363
Boulevard Ct 98362
Boundary Ln 98363
N Bourchier St 98362
Bower Ln 98362
Bravo Rd 98362
Break View Rd 98363
N & S Breakerpoint Pl 98363
Breeze Way 98362
Breezy Ln 98362
Bridge Ln 98362
Brierwood Ln 98363
N & S Brook Ave 98362
Brown Rd 98362
Bryson Ave 98362
Buchanan Dr 98362
Bumpy Rd 98362
Burch Ave 98362
S Butler St 98363
Bytha Way 98363
S C St 98363
C Street Ext 98363
Cagey Rd 98363
Cain Ln 98363
Calbert Rd 98362
Cameron Rd 98363
Camp David Junior Rd 98363
Camp Hayden Rd 98363
Campbell Ave 98363
Cannon Ball Rd 98363
S Canyon Cir 98362
Canyon Edge Dr 98362
Canyon View Dr 98362
N Carne St 98362
Caroline St 98362
Cathleen St 98363
S Cayanus Rd 98363
N Cedar St 98363
S Cedar St 98362
Cedar Glen Ln 98363
Cedar Grove Ln 98363
Cedar Hollow Dr 98363
S Cedar Mill Rd 98363
Cedar Park Dr 98362
N & S Chambers Rd & St 98362
Champion Rd 98362
Charles Rd 98362
Charles Hopie Ln 98363
S Chase St 98362
Chasewood Dr 98363
S Cherry St 98362
Cherry Tree Ln 98362
Chessie Ln 98363
Chickaree Ln 98363
Chinook Ln 98363
Christman Pl 98362
Christmas Tree Ln 98363
Church Ave 98362
Circle Dr 98362
City Light Pl 98362
Cline Cabin Ln 98362
Clipper Cv 98363
Coho Run Ct 98362
Columbia St 98362
Columbine Way 98362
Columbus Ave 98362
Colville Rd 98363
Conner Rd 98362
Coppertop Trl 98362
Cosmos Ln 98362
Cottonwood Ln 98362
Cougar Ln 98362
Cougar Ridge Rd 98363
Country Meadow Ln 98363
Country View Dr 98363
W Courtney Rd 98363
S Coyote Run Ln 98362
Cozy Cove Ln 98363
Crabapple St 98362
Craig Ave 98362
Crescent Bay Ln 98363
Crescent Beach Rd 98363
Crestview Dr 98362
S Critchfield Rd 98363
Critter Xing 98363
Crosby Ln 98363
Crown Z Water Rd 98363
S Currier Ct 98362
Cypress Cir 98362
S D St 98363
Dan Kelly Rd 98363
Daniel Pond Way 98363
Davis St 98363
Deer Run 98362
Deer Meadows Dr 98362
Deer Park Ln & Rd 98362
Deer Tracks Rd 98363
E Defrang St 98362
Del Guzzi Dr 98362
Delores Pl 98363
Dempsey Rd 98363
Derrick Rd 98362
W Devanny Ln 98363
W Dew Knot Enter Rd 98363
Diamond View Dr 98363
Diamond Vista Dr 98363
Dietz Rd 98362
Dodger Ln 98363
Dogwood Pl 98363
Dolan Ave 98363
S Doss Rd 98362
Doyle Rd 98363
Draper Rd 98362
Draper Valley Rd 98362
Driftwood Pl 98363
S Dry Creek Rd 98363
Duce Ln 98362
Dun Rollin Ln 98362
Dunker Dr 98363
Dunmire Rd 98362
Durrwachter Rd 98363
Dutch Dr 98363
W Duval Pl 98363
Dylan Rd 98363
S E St 98363
Eagle Hts 98363
Eagle Ridge Rd 98363
Eagle Tree Rd 98363
Eagle View Ln 98363
Eagles Nest Ln 98363
Easy St 98362
Ebb Tide Ln 98363
Eckard Ave & Pl 98362
Eclipse Industrial Pkwy 98363
Eclipse West Dr 98363
E Eddy Ln 98362
Eden Valley Rd 98363
W Edgewood Dr 98363
Edgewood Ln 98363
Edgewood Pl 98362
Ediz Vw 98363
Ediz Hook 98362
W Edwards Rd 98363
E Elderberry Ln 98362
Elizabeth Pl 98362
Elk Run Trl 98362
E Elliott Creek Rd 98363
Elwha Rd 98362
Elwha Bluff Rd 98363
Elwha Dike Rd 98363
Elwha Rim Trl 98363
Elwha River Rd 98363
Emery Ln & Rd 98362
Emily Ln 98363
N & S Ennis St 98362
E Ennis Creek Rd 98362
Erving Jacobs Rd 98362
Estates Way 98363
Estes Ct 98363
Euclid Ave 98363
N & S Eunice St 98362
Eva Cove St 98363
Evans Ave 98363
Everett Rd 98362
N & S Evergreen Dr 98363
Evergreen View Pkwy 98363
S F St 98363
Fairchild Airport Rd 98363
Fairmont Ave 98363
Farrell Pl 98362
Farrington Rd 98363
Fawn Haven Rd 98362
Fern Rd 98362
Ferne Meadows Ln 98362
Fernwood Ln 98362
Festina Lente Ln 98363
S Fey Rd 98363
Fielding Creek Dr 98363
Findley Rd 98362
Finn Hall Rd 98362
Flores St 98363
Fogarty Ave 98362
Forest Trl 98362
Forrest Ave 98362
Fors Rd 98363
Forsberg Rd 98363
Forsell Dr 98362
Fountain St 98363
Four Winds Rd 98362
Fox Run 98363
Fox Point Rd 98363
Foxglove Ln 98363
N & S Francis St 98362
Franklin Ln 98362
Franson Rd 98362
Frederickson Rd 98363
Freedom Pl 98363
Freshwater Park 98363
Freshwater Bay Rd 98363
Frog Creek Dr 98362
E & W Front St 98362
Full Moon Trl 98363
S G St 98363
Gagnon Rd 98363
Gakin Rd 98363
Galaxy Pl 98362
N Gales St 98362
Gandalf Rd 98363
Garling Rd 98362
Gasman Rd 98362
Gehrke Rd 98362
Gellor Rd 98362
Georgiana St 98362
Gerber Rd 98363
Glacier Ln 98363
Glass Rd 98362
Glen Ln 98363
Glenbrook Cir 98362
Glenwood St 98362
Goa Way 98362
Goldfinch Ln 98363
S Golf Course Rd 98362
Gossett Rd 98363
Grand Ridge Way 98362
Granite 98363
Grant Ave 98362
Grants View Ln 98362
Grauel Ramapo Rd 98363
Gravel Pit Rd 98362
Graystone Ln 98362
Green Belt Dr 98363
E Greentree Ln 98362
Gregory Pl 98362
Gretchen Way 98362
Grouse Dr 98362
Grouse Rdg 98363
Grouse Glen Way 98363
Gunn Rd 98363
Guy Kelly Rd 98362
S H St 98363
E Half Mile Rd 98362
Hamilton Way 98363
Hancock Ave 98362
Hansen Rd 98362
Hanusa Ln 98362
Harbor Crest St 98362
Harbor Heights Rd 98362
Harbor View Dr 98363
Harmony Ln 98362
Harrington Rd 98362
Harrison Beach Rd 98362
Harry Brown Rd 98363
Hart Rd 98363
Harvel Ln 98362
Hatchery Rd 98362
Hauk Rd 98363
Hawthorne Pl 98362
Hazel St 98363
Headwaters Ln 98362
Heather Cir 98362
Heather Park Rd 98362

Street	ZIP
Hebeisen Rd	98362
Heckel Rd	98363
S Hedin Rd	98363
Heitsch Ln	98362
E Helm Dr	98362
N & S Hemlock Ln	98362
Hennessy Ln	98363
Henry Boyd Rd	98362
Heritage Ct	98363
Heron Cove Rd	98363
Herrick Rd	98363
Heuhslein Rd	98362
E Hickory St	98362
Hidden Cv	98363
Hidden Highlands Dr	98362
Hidden Valley Rd	98362
Hidden View Dr	98362
E Hidden Way Rd	98362
High Country Dr	98362
Highland Ave	98362
Highland Crest Dr	98362
Highway 101	
204800-238999	98363
253100-258099	98362
E Highway 101	98362
W Highway 101	98363
Highway 112	98363
Hill Cir	98362
Hillcrest St	98362
Hillstrom Rd	98363
Hilts Trl	98363
Hoare Rd	98363
Hobby Ln	98362
Hoffman Rd	98363
Holly Cir & St	98362
Holly Hill Rd	98363
Home Ln	98362
Homestead St	98362
Howard Rd	98363
Howe Rd	98362
Huckleberry Hill Dr	98363
Hudson Rd	98363
Hughes Rd	98362
Hulse Rd	98362
Hunt Rd	98363
Hunters Gate Ln	98362
Hupt Ln	98363
Hurricane Ridge Rd	98362
Hurricane View Ln	98362
S I St	98363
Indigo Eagle Way	98362
Island View Rd	98362
Island Vista Way	98362
Ivy Ln	98362
J Shea Way	98362
W Jackson Alley Rd	98363
W Jakes Rd	98363
James Page Rd	98362
N & S Jensen Rd	98362
Jeri Lynn St	98363
Jnell Ln	98363
John Jacobs Rd	98362
John Mike Rd	98363
Johnson Rd	98363
N & S Jones St	98362
Jonquille Pl	98362
Joshua St	98363
Joyce Piedmont Rd	98363
Juan De Fuca Way	98362
Juma Ct	98363
Juniper Ln	98362
S K St	98363
Kacee Way	98363
Karpen Rd	98363
Karvellis Ln	98363
Kates Ct	98362
Kayda Ln	98362
E Keller Dr	98362
Kemp St	98362
Kenchead Rd	98362
Key Rd	98362
Killer Whale Ln	98363
King St	98363
Kingo Ridge Rd	98363
Klahanie View Ln	98363
Klahanne Ridge Dr	98362
E Kolonels Way	98362
Kreaman Rd	98363
Kruse Rd	98362
Kweynesen Rd	98363
Kwitsen Dr	98363
S L St	98363
La Paloma Ln	98363
Lady Of The Lake Ln	98363
Ladybug Ln	98362
Laird Rd	98363
Lake Aldwell Rd	98363
Lake Crescent Rd	98363
Lake Cresent Rd	98363
Lake Dawn Rd	98362
Lake Farm Rd	98362
Lake Sharon Ln	98362
Lake Sutherland Rd	98363
E Lambert Ln	98362
Lancaster Ln	98362
N Larch Ave	98362
Largent Ln	98362
Larry Bennett Rd	98363
N & S Laurel St	98362
E Lauridsen Blvd	98362
W Lauridsen Blvd	
100-599	98362
800-898	98363
900-1899	98363
Lawrence Rd	98363
Lawrence Forest Rd	98363
Lawrence Point Rd	98363
Leda Ln	98363
N Lees Creek Rd	98362
Leighland Ave	98362
Leisure Ln	98362
Lemmon Rd	98362
Leo Ln	98363
Leprechaun Ln	98362
Levig Rd	98362
Lewallen Rd	98363
Lewis Rd	98362
N & S Liberty St	98362
N Lilac Ave	98362
Liljedahl Rd	98363
Lilly Rd	98362
Lilu Ln	98363
N & S Lincoln St	98362
Linda Ln	98363
E & S Lindberg Rd	98362
Linderman Rd	98362
Lisel Ln	98362
Little Loop Dr	98362
Little Pond Rd	98363
Little River Rd	
100-3499	98363
6300-7299	98362
Loafer Ln	98362
Lockerbie Pl	98362
Lone Pine Rd	98363
Longfellow Rd	98363
Lopez Ave	98362
Lorilee Ln	98363
Louisa Ln	98363
Low Point Rd	98363
Lower Dam Rd	98363
Lower Elwha Rd	98363
E & W Lyre River Rd	98363
S M St	98363
E Maddock Rd	98362
Madeline St	98363
Madrona St	98363
Maharaj Ln	98362
E Mahogany St	98362
Majerle Rd	98363
Majesty Way	98362
Maletti Hill Rd	98363
Mallard Cove Rd	98363
Maloney Ct	98363
N & S Maple Ln & St	98362
Maple Grove Rd	98363
Maple Ridge Rd	98363
Mapleton Way	98363
Mar Vista Way	98362
Mariah Winds	98362
Marie View St	98363
Marine Dr	98363
Maritime Dr	98362
Markuson Rd	98363
Marmot Loop	98362
W Marquam St	98363
Marsden Rd	98362
Marsh Hawk Ln	98362
E & N Masters Rd	98362
Matson Rd	98362
Mcblair Ln	98362
Mccarver Rd	98362
S Mccrorie Rd	98362
Mcdonald St	98363
Mcdougal St	98362
Mcgarvie Rd	98363
Mcgill Ave	98362
Mcnally Ln	98363
Meadow Cir	98362
Meadow Ridge Ln	98362
W Meagher Rd	98363
Melody Cir & Ln	98362
Melton Rd	98363
Merrill Way	98362
E Mesa View Ln	98362
Miles Rd	98362
Miletich Ln	98362
Mill Creek Ct	98362
Miller Rd	98363
Miller Creek Rd	98362
Milwaukee Dr	98363
Mimwhetten Way	98362
E & W Misty Ln	98362
Misty Creek Ln	98363
Misty Hollow Rd	98362
Monroe Rd	98362
Monterra Dr	98362
Montrose Pl	98362
Morning Ct	98362
Morse Ln	98362
Morse Homestead Rd	98362
N Moss St	98362
Motor Ave	98362
S Mount Angeles Rd	98362
Mount Mcdonald Rd	98363
Mount Pleasant Rd	98362
Mount Pleasant Crest Rd	98362
Mount Pleasant Estates Rd	98362
Mount Pleasant Heights Ln	98362
Mount Pleasant Summit Rd	98362
Mountain Home Rd	98362
Mountain Shadow Dr	98362
Mountain Springs Ln	98362
S Mountain Terrace Way	98362
Mountain Valley Ln	98363
Mountain View Cir	98362
E Myrtle St	98362
S N St	98363
E Nancy Ln	98362
Nellie Ln	98363
Nelson Creek Ln	98363
New Haven Ln	98362
Newell Rd	98363
Nicholas Rd	98363
Nordstrom Rd	98363
Northwood Ln	98363
Ns Klallam Dr	98363
Nygren Pl	98362
S O St	98363
N & S Oak Ln & St	98362
Oakcrest Ave, Loop & Way	98362
N Oakridge Dr	98363
Obrien Rd	98362
E Ocean Breeze Ln	98362
Ocean Cove Ln	98363
Ocean View Dr	98362
Octane Ln	98362
Okerman Rd	98363
Olallie Trl	98363
Old Rd	98362
Old Black Diamond Rd	98363
Old Deer Park Rd	98362
Old Joe Rd	98363
Old Mill Rd	98362
E Old Mill Mountain Rd	98362
N Old Nelson Rd	98362
Old Olympic Hwy	98362
Old Raven Way	98363
Old State Rd	98363
S Old Time Pl	98363
Olympian Ct & Way	98362
Olympic Ln	98362
Olympic Hot Springs Rd	98363
Olympus Ave	98362
One Horse Ln	98362
Onella Rd	98363
Orcas Ave	98362
N & S Orchard Ln	98362
Orvis St	98362
Osborn Rd	98362
Owen Ave	98362
Oxenford Rd	98363
P St	98363
S Pacific Vis	98363
E Panorama Ln	98362
E & W Park Ave & Ln	98362
Park Forest Dr	98362
Park Knoll Dr	98362
Park View Ln	98363
Parkway Heights Dr	98362
S Pastoral Dr	98363
Patterson Rd	98363
Pauline Rd	98362
N & S Peabody St	98362
Peach Ct	98363
Pearce Rd	98363
Peele Rd	98363
Pelikan Rd	98363
Pendley Ct	98363
Penn St	98362
Percival Rd	98362
Peters Rd	98363
Peterson Rd	98363
Pew Ln	98363
Phillips Pkwy	98362
Phinn Rd	98362
S Pine St	98362
E Pioneer Rd	98362
Place Rd	98363
Plaza St	98362
Plum Ct	98363
N & S Point Rd	98363
W Pollow Rd	98363
Porter St	98362
Poulsen Point Rd	98363
Poverty Ln	98363
Power Plant Rd	98363
Prawn Rd	98363
Pristine Rd	98362
Prospect Pl	98362
Pyramid Pl	98363
Quail Run Rd	98362
N & S Race St	98362
E & W Railroad Ave	98362
Raleigh Rd	98363
Ram Hill Rd	98363
Ramona Rd	98362
Ranger Rd	98363
Rebel Ln	98362
Red Cedar Ln	98362
Red Deer Dr	98362
S Reddick Rd	98363
S Regent St	98362
Reich Ln	98362
Reservoir Rd	98363
Reyes St	98363
Reynold Rd	98363
Rhodes Rd	98362
Rhody Ln	98363
Rickarla Cir	98363
N & S Ridge View Dr	98362
Rife Rd	98363
Ripplebrook Dr & Ln	98362
Riverside Rd	98363
Robinson Rd	98362
Rocky Rd	98363
Roll Inn Park Dr	98362
Rolling Hills Ct & Dr	98363
Roman Rd	98362
Rook Dr	98362
Rose St	98363
Rosewood Ln	98362
Ross Ln	98363
Round Mountain Rd	98362
Roundtree Rd	98362
Roy St	98362
Ruby Rd	98362
Runamuck Ln	98362
Rustic Ln	98363
Rustic Fields Way	98362
E Ryan Dr	98362
Ryan Wayne Pl	98362
Saddle Club Ln	98363
Saghalie Trl	98363
Salmon St	98363
Salt Creek Rd	98363
Sam Ulmer Rd	98363
Samara Dr & Pl	98363
Sampson Rd	98363
San Juan St	98362
Sandhagen Rd	98363
Sands Rd	98363
Sandstone Pl	98362
Sawtooth Rd	98363
Saydee Ln	98362
Scenic View Ln	98362
Schilke Way	98362
Schmitt Rd	98363
School House Ln	98362
Schultz Dr	98362
E Scrivner Rd	98362
Sea Bluff Ln	98362
Sea View Dr	98362
Sea Wind Dr	98363
Seabreeze Pl	98363
Seagull Dr	98362
Seal Rock Rd	98363
Seamit Rd	98363
Seamount Dr	98363
Seaview Cir	98363
Sentinal Ct	98363
Shade Tree Ln	98362
Shadow Ln	98363
Shady Creek Ln	98362
Shaffer Rd	98363
Shale Rd	98362
Shamrock Ln	98362
Shimko Rd	98363
Shire Ln	98363
Shirley Ct	98363
Shore Rd	98362
N Shore Rd	98363
S Shore Rd	98363
Short Rd	98362
Sieberts Creek Rd	98362
Silver Ln	98363
Silverado Dr	98363
E Simmons Rd	98362
Sisson Rd	98363
Sky Ln	98362
Sky View Dr	98362
Skyline Dr	98362
Sleepy Hollow Ln	98363
Sleepy Meadow Ln	98363
E & W Snider Rd	98363
Snow Ln	98362
Snowcaps Ln	98363
E Snowline Dr	98362
Snowridge Ln	98362
Snug Harbor Ln	98363
Soaring Hawk Ln	98362
Sockeye Way	98363
Sol Duc Hot Springs Rd	98363
Solar Ln	98362
E & W Sorrel Ln	98362
Southridge Rd	98363
Southview Dr	98363
Sparrow Ln	98363
Sponberg Ln	98363
Sportsman Rd	98363
Spring Rd	98362
Springhaven Ln	98363
Spruce St	98363
Stanley Way	98362
Stephanie Lee Pl	98362
Storm King Rd	98363
Storman Pl	98363
Stormy Windy Ln	98363
Strait View Dr	98362
Straitland Rd	98363
Stratton Rd	98363
Striped Peak Rd	98363
Stuart Dr	98362
Summit View Pl	98362
Sunflower Rd	98363
Sunny Point Ln	98363
Sunnybrook Meadow Ln	98362
Sunrise Pl	98362
Sunset Hts	98363
Sutter Rd	98362
Swede Rd	98363
Sylvan Way	98362
Tac Dale Dr	98363
Tacoma Ave	98362
Tamarack Ln	98362
N & S Tara Ln	98362
Terry Mills Rd	98362
Thistle St	98362
Thistledown Ln	98362
Thompson Rd	98363
Thompson Point Rd	98363
Thors Rd	98363
Three Sisters Way	98363
Thunder Rd	98362
S Tiller Rd	98362
Tonda Vista Rd	98362
Township Line Rd	98362
Treasure Ct	98363
Tumwater Truck Rd & Rte	98363
Twin Cedars Dr	98362
Twin Firs Pl	98362
Twin Firs Estates Dr	98362
S Tyler Rd	98363
Uphill Dr	98362
Upland Ln	98362
Valhallas Dr	98362
S Valley St	98362
Valley Creek Rd	98362
Vashon Ave & St	98362
Verns Ln	98362
Vert Rd	98363
Victoria St	98362
View Ridge Dr	98362
View Vista Park	98362
Viewcrest Ave	98362
Village Cir & Pl	98362
N & S Vine St	98362
E Vinup St	98362
Vista Ln	98362
Vista View Dr	98362
Vogt Rd	98362
E Wabash St	98362
Walgren Rd	98363
Walgren Hts Dr	98363
Walkabout Way	98363
Walker St	98363
Walker Ranch Rd	98363
Walker Valley Rd	98362
Wall St	98362
E Walnut St	98362
Wanner Rd	98363
Wapiti Way	98363
Wasankari Rd	98363
N & S Washington St	98362
Water St	98362
Watershed Rd	98362
Watkins Rd	98362
Weiler Rd	98362
Wellman Rd	98363
Westridge Rd	98363
Westview Dr	98363
Westwind Dr	98362
Whidby Ave	98362
Whiskey Creek Beach Rd	98363
Whispering Firs	98363
E White Creek Dr	98362
Whitesbrook Ln	98362
N Whitney Way	98362
N Wid Rd	98362
Wild Blackberry Ln	98363
Wild Currant Way	98362
Wild Orchid Ln	98362
Wildcat Rd	98363
Wildflower Ln	98362
Willes Way	98362
Willow Ave & Ln	98362
Winddancer Ln	98363
N & S Windflower Ln	98362
Winter Rd	98362
Winterhaven Dr	98362
Wisen Creek Rd	98363
Wolcutt St	98362
E Woodhaven Ln	98362
Woodside Dr	98363
Wye Rd	98363
Wynn Ln	98362
Yellow Rock Ln	98362
Yew Tree Dr	98363

NUMBERED STREETS

Street	ZIP
E & W 1st	98362
E & W 2nd Ave & St	98362
E 3rd Ave	98362
E 3rd St	98362
W 3rd St	
100-625	98362
627-799	98363
E 4th Ave	98362
E 4th St	98362
W 4th St	
100-599	98362
700-2199	98363
E 5th Ave	98362
E 5th St	98362
W 5th St	
100-599	98362
700-2099	98363
E 6th Ave	98362
E 6th St	98362
W 6th St	
100-699	98362
700-2299	98363
E 7th Ave	98362
E 7th St	98362
W 7th St	
100-699	98362
700-2199	98363
E 8th St	98362
W 8th St	
100-699	98362
700-2199	98363
E 9th St	98362
100-699	98362
700-1799	98363
E 10th St	98362
100-699	98362
800-2699	98363
E 11th St	98362
100-699	98362
700-2299	98363
E 12th St	98362
100-699	98362
700-2499	98363
E 13th St	98362
100-699	98362
700-2999	98363
E 14th St	98362
100-699	98362
700-2999	98363
W 15th St	
200-599	98362
700-2599	98363
W 16th St	
400-599	98362
800-2599	98363
W 17th St	98363
W 18th St	98363

W 19th St ... 98363

PORT ORCHARD WA

General Delivery ... 98366

POST OFFICE BOXES MAIN OFFICE STATIONS AND BRANCHES

Box No.s
All PO Boxes ... 98366

NAMED STREETS

Abbey Ln SW ... 98367
Abdula Pl SE ... 98366
SE Abernathy Ct ... 98366
Abigail Way ... 98366
Ada St ... 98366
Adair Rd SE ... 98366
Advantage Ave ... 98366
E Aguilar Ct ... 98366
Ahern Ct W ... 98367
Ahlstrom Rd E ... 98366
Aiken Rd SE ... 98366
Alameda St SW ... 98367
Alaska Ave E & SE ... 98366
Albright Ave SE ... 98366
Alder Ln ... 98366
E Alder St ... 98366
W Alder St ... 98367
E Alki View Ct ... 98366
Allison Way SE ... 98367
Alonah Pl SE ... 98367
Alpenridge Pl SE ... 98367
Alpha Ln ... 98366
Alpine Dr SW ... 98367
SW Alpine Lake Rd ... 98367
Alropa Pl SW ... 98367
SE Alson Ct ... 98366
SW Alta Vista Dr ... 98367
Amberly Pl SE ... 98367
SE Amelia Ct ... 98366
American Pl SE ... 98367
Anderbar Rd SE ... 98367
Anderson Ave & Rd SE ... 98366
Anderson Hill Rd SW ... 98367
SW Andrews Ln ... 98367
Annies Pl ... 98366
Antrim Ln SW ... 98367
Apple Orchard Ln SW ... 98367
SE April Ln ... 98367
SE Ardenwald Pl ... 98366
SE Arie Ct ... 98366
Arlington Pl SE ... 98367
Arnold Ave E & N ... 98366
SE Arthur Ct ... 98367
Arvick Rd SE ... 98366
SW Asberry Way ... 98367
Ash Ave & St ... 98366
Ashridge Ave SW ... 98367
SW Ashton Ct ... 98367
Aspen Ct & St ... 98366
SW Atkinson St ... 98367
SE Auburn St ... 98367
Austin Ave ... 98366
SE Azalea Ave ... 98366
SE Aztec Ct ... 98367
Baby Doll Rd E & SE ... 98366
SW Bachelor Flat Ln ... 98367
SE Badger Ln ... 98367
Bag End Way ... 98367
SE Baker Rd ... 98367
SE Bakken Ct ... 98366
Balsam Blvd SE ... 98366
Baltray Pl SW ... 98367
Bancroft Rd E ... 98366
SE Bandera Ct ... 98367
Banner Rd SE
2800-4799 ... 98366
4800-9599 ... 98367
E Barsay Ln ... 98366
SE Basil Ct ... 98366
SE Basswood Ct & Ln SE ... 98366
Bay St ... 98366
Bay Crest Ct ... 98366
Bayview Ave E ... 98366
Bayview Dr SE ... 98367
Beach Dr E ... 98366
SE Bean Rd ... 98366
Bear Lake Dr SW ... 98367
Bear Track Ln SW ... 98367
SE Bear Tree Ln ... 98367
E Beaver Creek Rd ... 98366
SE Beck St ... 98366
Becky Ave ... 98366
Bedrock Pl SE ... 98367
SE Beech Ct ... 98366
SE Beechcrest Ct ... 98366
SE Belford Ln ... 98366
Bellingham Ave SE ... 98367
W Bens Ln ... 98366
SE Bentwood Ln ... 98366
Berger Ln & Pl SE ... 98366
SE Berry St ... 98366
SW Berry Lake Rd ... 98367
Berwick Pl SW ... 98367
Bethel Ave ... 98366
Bethel Rd SE
1901-2197 ... 98366
2199-4699 ... 98367
4800-6799 ... 98367
Bethel Burley Rd SE ... 98367
SE Bethel Valley Ln ... 98366
SE Bielmeier Rd ... 98367
Big Timber Pl SE ... 98367
Bill Ave ... 98366
Bingo Ln SE ... 98366
SW Birch Ave & Rd W ... 98367
SW Birt Dr ... 98367
SW Bishop Ct ... 98367
SW Black Jack Ln ... 98367
Blackstone Ct ... 98366
E Blaisdell Rd ... 98366
SE Blakeview Dr ... 98366
SE Blueberry Rd ... 98366
SW Bob Ct ... 98367
SE Bobcat Ln ... 98366
Bodle Rd SE ... 98367
Bonnieville Pl SE ... 98367
Bothwell St ... 98366
Bowe Ln SE ... 98367
Brady Pl SE ... 98366
Brame Ln SE ... 98366
Branson Ct & Dr SE ... 98366
Brasch Rd SE ... 98367
Bravo Ter ... 98366
Briarwood Dr SE ... 98366
Broadstone Pl SW ... 98367
SE Brook St ... 98366
SE Brookside Ct ... 98367
SE Brookwood Ct & Dr SE ... 98367
SE Buchannen St ... 98366
Buckhaven Ct E ... 98366
SE Buckingham Dr SE ... 98366
Builder Ln SW ... 98367
Bull Frog Ave SW ... 98367
Bulman Rd SE ... 98366
Burchard Dr SW ... 98367
Burley Ave SE ... 98367
SE Burley Olalla Rd ... 98367
Butler Ave SW ... 98367
Buttercup Ln SE ... 98367
SW Caboose Ct ... 98367
Cabrini Dr SE ... 98367
SE Cain Ln ... 98366
SE Calaveras ... 98366
Caleb Pl SE ... 98366
California Ave E & SE ... 98366
E Calistoga Ct ... 98366
SE Calle Bonita Ln ... 98367
Calvinwood Rd SW ... 98367
SW Camas Ln ... 98367
SE Cambridge Rd ... 98366
E Camellia Way ... 98366
SE Cameron Pl ... 98366
E Cammer Rd ... 98366
Campbell Ln ... 98366
Canterbury Pl SE ... 98366
Canyon Ct & Ln ... 98366
E Caraway Rd ... 98366
Cardon Pl SW ... 98367
Carefree Ln SW ... 98367
SE Carl Pickel Dr ... 98366
Carla Ct SE ... 98366
Carlson Ln SE ... 98366
SE Carmae Dr ... 98366
Carnation Ct ... 98366
Carney Lake Rd SW ... 98367
Carol Ln SE ... 98366
SE Carousel Ln ... 98366
Carr Ln SE ... 98366
Carson Ave SE ... 98366
Carter Ave SW ... 98367
Casandra Loop ... 98366
Cascade Ct & Dr ... 98366
Caseco Ln ... 98366
SE Cashmere St ... 98367
SE Castlewood Dr ... 98366
Catalpa Dr SE ... 98366
SW Caulfield Ln ... 98367
SE Cavalry Way ... 98367
SE Cedar Ct ... 98366
Cedar Ln SE ... 98366
SE Cedar Rd ... 98367
Cedar St E ... 98366
Cedar Canyon Pl ... 98366
Cedar Crescent Dr SE ... 98366
Cedar Ridge Ct ... 98366
SW Cedarvale Ct ... 98367
SE Celebrity Ct ... 98366
Celeste Ct SE ... 98366
E Center St ... 98366
Chanting Cir SW ... 98367
Chase Rd SE ... 98366
SE Chasewood Ct ... 98366
Chatterton Ave SW ... 98367
SW Chawla Ct ... 98367
Cheantra Rd SE ... 98366
SE Cheetah Ln ... 98367
SE Cherry St SE ... 98366
Cherub Pl ... 98366
Chester Rd & St ... 98366
SW Chipmunk Hill Ln ... 98367
Chive Pl SE ... 98366
SW Chowchilla Way ... 98367
SW Christmas Tree Ln ... 98367
SW Cimarron Ln ... 98367
SW Circle Dr ... 98367
SE Cisco Rd ... 98367
SE City View Way ... 98366
Clair Rd SW ... 98367
E Clam Bay Ct ... 98366
Clay Ln ... 98366
Clayton Rd SE ... 98367
Clearwater Ln SE ... 98367
SE Cleveland Ave ... 98366
SW Cleveland St ... 98367
SW Clevenger Ln ... 98367
SW Cliff Ridge Way ... 98367
Cline Ave ... 98366
Clover Valley Rd SE ... 98367
SW Club House Ct ... 98367
SW Colbert Way ... 98367
Colchester Dr E & SE ... 98366
Cole Loop & St ... 98366
Coles Ln ... 98366
E Collins Rd ... 98366
Colonial Ln SE ... 98366
Colony Ave SE ... 98366
SE Colusa Ave ... 98366
SE Colvea Dr ... 98366
E Commons Ct ... 98366
SE Compass Ln ... 98366
SE Concept Ln ... 98367
SE Condor Ln ... 98367
SW Conifer Ln ... 98367
SE Conifer Park Dr ... 98366
Connecticut Pl E ... 98366
Connery Ln E ... 98366
SE Constitution Ct ... 98367
Converse Ave SE
2500-2799 ... 98366
2801-2899 ... 98366
5400-5499 ... 98367
SE Converse Cir ... 98366
SE Converse Ct ... 98367
SE Converse Cv ... 98367
SE Converse Pl ... 98367
Conwhit Ln SW ... 98367
SW Cook Rd ... 98367
Cooper Ave SW ... 98367
Copper Creek Dr SE ... 98366
SE Cornell Rd ... 98366
Coronet Pl SE ... 98366
E Cosmo Ln ... 98366
Cottage Path Way ... 98367
SE Cottonwood Dr SE ... 98366
SE Cougar Ln ... 98367
Country Club Way SE ... 98367
SW County Line Rd ... 98367
Cove Way SE ... 98367
SW Cozy Ln ... 98367
SE Crabb Ct ... 98366
Crane Ave E ... 98366
SE Crawford Rd ... 98366
Creek View Ct SE ... 98366
Creek View Dr SW ... 98367
Crest Dr SE ... 98367
E Crestwood Ct ... 98366
E Cricket Ln ... 98366
Crossing Pl SW ... 98367
SW Crossway Ct ... 98367
Cub Dr SW ... 98367
Cynthia Ln SW ... 98367
Cypress Ct SE ... 98366
SW Daffodil St ... 98367
SW Dahlia Way ... 98367
SW Daisy St ... 98367
E Dakota St ... 98366
SE Dalea Pl ... 98367
Dallas St ... 98366
Dana Dr SE ... 98366
E Daniels Loop ... 98366
Darla Ln SE ... 98366
SE Darrell Ln ... 98366
SE Dean Ct ... 98366
Deanna Ln SE ... 98366
Decatur Ave & St ... 98366
SE Deep Lake Rd ... 98367
Deer Crest Dr SW ... 98367
Deeridge Pl SE ... 98366
Dekalb St ... 98366
Del Tormey Pl SE ... 98366
Delia Ln SW ... 98367
SE Delta Pl ... 98367
Demars Ln SE ... 98367
Denniston Ln E ... 98366
Denny Ave SW ... 98367
SW Depot Ct ... 98367
Desoto Ct SW ... 98367
SE Devonshire Pl ... 98366
SE Dews Ln ... 98367
SE Diamond Pl ... 98366
Diaz Pl SW ... 98367
SE Disney Way ... 98367
Division St ... 98366
Dogwood Rd SE ... 98367
Dogwood Hill Rd SW ... 98367
SE Donato Ln ... 98367
Donna St ... 98366
SE Dorlane Ct ... 98367
Dormar Dr SE ... 98367
SE Dover Ct ... 98367
SE Downing Pl ... 98366
SE Driftwood Dr ... 98367
SE Duchess Ct ... 98367
SW Dundee Ct ... 98367
SW Dunraven Ln ... 98367
Dunrobin Ln E ... 98366
Durand Pl SE ... 98367
SW Durfey Ln ... 98367
SE Dusty Ln ... 98367
Dutchess Pl SE ... 98366
Dwight St ... 98366
Eagle Crest Pl ... 98366
SE Earls Ct ... 98366
Eastbrook Dr SW ... 98367
Eastview Dr SW ... 98367
Eastway Dr SE ... 98366
Eastwood Ave SE ... 98366
SE Easy Street Ln ... 98367
Ebbert Dr SE ... 98366
Echo Ct ... 98366
SE Edmonds St ... 98367
Edwards Ct E ... 98366
SW Egret St ... 98367
Ehlert Woods Pl SW ... 98367
Eisenhower Ave SE ... 98367
Elder Ave SW ... 98367
Eliot Pl SE ... 98367
SE Ellis Ct ... 98367
SE Elwood Ct ... 98366
SE Emelia Ln ... 98367
Emerald Ct, Dr & Pl ... 98367
SE Empress Ct ... 98367
Endsley Ln SE ... 98366
SE Engledow Ln ... 98367
Eric Pl SE ... 98367
Essex Ct SW ... 98367
Estonia Ct SE ... 98367
Evergreen Ave SE ... 98366
Fairview Blvd SW ... 98367
Fairview Lake Rd SW ... 98367
SE Fairway Cir ... 98367
SW Falls Ct ... 98367
Fantail Pl SW ... 98367
Farmer Dell Rd E ... 98366
Farragut Ave N & S ... 98366
SE Fauna Ln ... 98367
SW Fawn Ln ... 98367
SE Fay Ct ... 98367
Feigley Rd SW & W ... 98367
SE Fenton Rd ... 98367
Ferate Ave SE ... 98366
Fern Ct SE ... 98366
Fern Meadows Loop SE ... 98366
Fern Vista Pl SW ... 98367
SE Fernbrook Ln ... 98366
Fernwood Ln ... 98366
E Fillmore St ... 98366
E & SE Fir St ... 98366
Fircrest Dr & Pl ... 98366
Firdrona Ln N & S ... 98367
E Firefly Ct ... 98366
Fireweed Ln ... 98366
SE Firmont Dr ... 98367
SW Fiscal St ... 98367
E Fish On Way ... 98366
SE Flaiz Ct ... 98366
SE Flint St ... 98366
S Flower Ave ... 98366
Flower Meadows St ... 98366
Forest Glen Rd SW ... 98367
Forest Haven Ln SE ... 98366
SE Forest Villa Ct ... 98366
Forrest Park St ... 98366
SE Foss Rd ... 98366
Fox Glove Ct SE ... 98366
Foxwood Dr SE ... 98366
Franway Ln SW ... 98367
Fraser Rd SE ... 98367
Frederick Ave ... 98366
Friends Ln SE ... 98367
SE Frog Pond Rd ... 98366
W Frontage Rd ... 98367
Fry Ave SW ... 98367
Gable Ave SW ... 98367
SE Galeel Ct ... 98366
SW Galway Ct ... 98367
SE Game Trail Way ... 98367
Garden Dr ... 98366
SE Garfield Ave, Pl & St SE ... 98366
Garrison Ave ... 98366
Gazebo St ... 98366
Geiger Rd SE
4401-4697 ... 98366
4699-4700 ... 98366
4702-4798 ... 98366
4800-5099 ... 98367
Gemstone Ln SE ... 98367
Genesis Ln SE ... 98367
Gertsch Rd SE ... 98367
Gillette Dr SE ... 98366
SE Gillio Ct ... 98367
Gilman Pl SW ... 98367
Ginger Pl E ... 98366
Givens St ... 98366
Glacier Ridge Pl SE ... 98367
Glendale Ave & St ... 98366
Gleneagle Ave SW ... 98367
Glenmore Loop ... 98366
Glenn Ct SE ... 98366
Glenwood Rd SW ... 98367
SE Goat Trail Rd ... 98367
Golden Pond St ... 98366
Goldenrod St ... 98366
SE Goldmaur Ct ... 98366
SW Grace St ... 98367
Granada Pl SE ... 98367
Granat Rd ... 98366
Grand Fir Pl SE ... 98366
SE Grandhaven St ... 98367
Grandridge Dr SE ... 98367
E & SE Grandview St ... 98366
SE Grant Ave & St ... 98366
Gravelly Ln SW ... 98367
SW Grebe Way ... 98367
Green Leaf Ln SW ... 98367
Greenacres Pl SW ... 98367
SE Greenbriar Pl ... 98366
Greendale Dr SE ... 98366
Greengate Pl SE ... 98366
SE Greenridge Ct ... 98367
SE Greenshores Dr ... 98367
Greentree Dr SE ... 98366
Gregory Ln E ... 98366
Griffith Ln SE ... 98366
SW Grotto Ct ... 98367
SE Grovewood St ... 98367
Guildfore Ct SE ... 98366
SE Guise Pl ... 98367
Guthrie St ... 98366
Guy Wetzel Rd ... 98366
SE Haida Dr ... 98367
SE Halfmoon Ln ... 98367
SW Hanson Rd ... 98367
Harbor Heights Dr & Ln E ... 98366
Harding Ave SE ... 98366
Harland Ln SE ... 98367
SW Harmon St ... 98367
Harold Dr SE ... 98366
SW Harper Rd ... 98367
Harper Hill Rd SE ... 98366
SE Harriet St ... 98366
Harris Rd SE ... 98366
E Harrison Ave & St SE ... 98366
Harvey St SE ... 98366
SE Hastings Ln ... 98367
SE Hathaway Ct ... 98367
Haughton Ln SW ... 98367
Haven Ln SE ... 98367
Havenwood Rd SW ... 98367
SW Hawk Ridge Way ... 98367
Hawkstone Ave SW ... 98367
Hawthorne Ave W ... 98367
Hayward St SW ... 98367
SW Hayworth Dr ... 98367
SW Headlands Way ... 98367
SW Heartwood Ln ... 98367
SE Heather Ct & Ln SE ... 98366
Helena Trl SW ... 98367
E Hemlock St ... 98366
Henry Hanson Rd SE ... 98366
Heron Ridge Ave ... 98366
SE Hershey Way ... 98367
Hickory Ln SE ... 98366
Hidden Acres Pl SW ... 98367
Hidden Terrace Ln SE ... 98366
Higgins Rd SE ... 98366
High Ct SW ... 98367
High St ... 98366
SE High Ridge Ct ... 98367
Higher Ground Ln ... 98366
Hill Ave ... 98366
Hillandale Ct & Dr E ... 98366
E Hillcrest Dr ... 98366
E Hilldale Rd ... 98366
Hillington Ct SE ... 98366
Hillridge Pl SE ... 98367
Hillwood Ln SE ... 98367
SE Hillyrock Ln ... 98367
Hinkley Rd SE ... 98367
SW Hipkins Ct ... 98367
SE Holly Ct ... 98366
SE Holman Rd ... 98367
Holmes Ave SE ... 98366
Hoover Ave SE ... 98366
SE Hoquiam St ... 98367
Horizon Ln SE ... 98367
Horizon Lane East SE ... 98367
Horizon Lane West SE ... 98367
Horseshoe Ave SW ... 98367
E & SE Horstman Rd ... 98366
Hoskin Hill Ln SE ... 98367
SW Hovde Rd ... 98367
Howard Ave ... 98366
SW Huckleberry Rd ... 98367
SW Hudson Dr ... 98367
SW Huge Creek Ln ... 98367
Hull Ave ... 98366
Hummingbird Ln SW ... 98367
Hunter Ln & Rd ... 98366
Huntington St ... 98366
Hutchins Ave SE ... 98366
E Idaho St ... 98366
E Illinois St ... 98366
Independence Pl SW ... 98367
E Indiana St ... 98366
E Indianwood Ct ... 98366
Indigo Point Pl ... 98366
Inlet Ln SE ... 98366
SE Inwood Ln ... 98367
SE Irish Ct ... 98367
Isabelle Ln SE ... 98367
SE Ives Mill Rd ... 98367
SW J H Rd ... 98367
J M Dickenson Rd SW ... 98367
SW Jabirin Way ... 98367
Jackie Ln SE ... 98367
Jackson Ave SE ... 98366
Jacobs Ln SE ... 98367
Jacqueline Ln E ... 98366
Jason Ln SE ... 98367
Jasper Pl SE ... 98367
E Jeanine Ln ... 98366
Jefferson Ave SE ... 98366
SE Jerry Ln ... 98367
E Jessica Way ... 98366
Jimi Pl SW ... 98367
SE John St ... 98366
Joletta Ave SW ... 98367
Jones Dr ... 98366
Joslin Ave SE ... 98366
Journey Ln SE ... 98367
Joy Ln SW ... 98367
SE Joyce Ct ... 98367
Julian Rd SW ... 98367
E Juneau Ct ... 98366
SW Junette Ln ... 98367
SE Juniper Ct ... 98366
SE Kansas Ave ... 98366
Kara Ln SE ... 98367
Karcher Rd SE ... 98367
E Karen Ln ... 98366
SE Karli Way ... 98367
SE Kazac Ln ... 98366
Kc Pl SE ... 98367
Kegel Ln SE ... 98366
SE Kelby Cir ... 98366
Kells Ln SW ... 98367
Kelowna Pl SE ... 98366
Kelp Pl E ... 98366
SE Kelsey Ct ... 98367
SE Kemp Ln ... 98367

Street	ZIP
Kendall St	98366
SW Kendora Rd	98367
Kenfig Pl SW	98367
SW Kenmore Ct	98367
Kentridge Pl SE	98367
SE Kerri Ct	98366
Kerry Ln SE	98367
SE Keystone Ct	98367
Kidd Ave SE	98366
Killeen Pl SW	98367
Kimble Rd E	98366
SE King Rd	98367
Kings End Pl SE	98367
SE Kira St	98367
Kitsap Blvd & St	98366
Klondike Ct & Trl E	98366
Knight Dr SE	98367
Koda Cir SE	98366
Kodiak Pl SW	98367
Kona Ln SE	98367
Kowalski Ln SE	98367
SE Krista St	98367
Kristin Ln SE	98367
Krystal Woods Way	98366
SE La Donna Ct	98366
La Linda Ct SE	98366
E La Salle St	98366
Laburnum Ln SE	98367
SW Lafollette St	98367
Laguna Ln SE	98366
SW Lake St	98367
SW Lake Flora Rd	98367
SW Lake Helena Rd	98367
SE Lake Valley Rd SE	98367
SE Lakefront Pl	98367
Lakeview Dr SE	98366
Lakeview Pl SE	98367
SE & SW Lakeway Blvd	98367
Lancashire Ct SE	98366
SE Lancaster Ln	98366
SE Land Summit Ct	98366
Landing Ln SE	98367
Landis Ct SW	98367
Landover Pl	98366
SE Larch Ln	98366
SE Larksprings Ln	98366
Lars Hansen Rd SE	98367
Lasada Ln SE	98366
E Last Refuge Way	98366
Laura Ln SE	98367
SE Laurel Ct	98366
Lawrence Dr SE	98367
Lawrence St	98366
SE Layton Ct	98367
SW Lazuli St	98367
Leader International Dr	98367
SW Legacy Ln	98367
SE Legrande St	98366
E Leighton Rd	98366
SE Lela Ln	98367
E Leola Ln	98366
SE Leopard Ln	98367
Leora Park St	98366
SE & SW Lider Rd	98367
Lidstrom Pl & Rd	98366
E Lidstrom Hill Rd	98366
Lieseke Ln	98367
Lieske Ln SW	98367
E Lighthouse Dr	98366
SE Lilla Lund Ln	98367
Lillehei Ln SE	98367
Lilly Pond Ln SW	98367
SE Lincoln Ave SE	98366
Lindi Ln SW	98367
SE Linlou Ln	98367
Lippert Dr W	98366
Little Tree Cir & Pl SW	98367
Lloyd Pkwy	98367
Locker Rd SE	98366
Lodgepole Ct & Dr SE	98366
Log Cabin Ln SE	98367
SW Logan Rd	98367
Lone Bear Ln SW	98367
Lonely Owl Pl SW	98367
Long Lake Rd SE	
1600-4799	98366
4800-8899	98367
Longbranch Pl	98366
Longview Ave	98366
SW Loop Dr	98367
SE Lori Linda Ct	98366
Lorsten Ln SE	98367
SW Lotus Ct	98367
SE Lovell St	98366
Lovely Ln SE	98367
Lowren Loop	98366
Lucas Ln SW	98367
Lucero Pl E	98366
Lucille Ln SE	98367
Lumsden Rd	98367
SE Lund Ave & St SE	98366
Lyons Ln SW	98367
Maccubbin Ln SE	98366
SW Madeline Ln	98367
Madrona Dr SE	98366
Madrona Rd SW	98367
E Madrone Ave E	98366
SE Mahali Ct & Ln SE	98366
Mahan St	98366
E Main St	98366
Malibu Ct SE	98366
Mallard Dr SW	98367
Malott Pl SE	98366
Maloya Ln SE	98367
Maltese Ct	98366
E Manchester Ct	98366
E Manders Way	98366
Mansfield Ct SW	98367
Maple Ave	98366
Maple Ave E	98366
Maple Rd SE	98367
E Maple St	98366
SE Maple St	98366
Maple Crest Ln SE	98366
SW Marion Dr	98367
SE Marion St	98366
Mariposa Ln SE	98367
Marjorie Ln SE	98367
Marlin Dr SE	98367
Marlyce Ct SE	98366
Martin Ave & Ln E & SE	98366
Maryland Way E	98366
Marymac Dr SW	98367
Massachusettes Pl E	98366
Matrix Ln & Loop	98367
May St W	98366
May Ranch Ln SW	98367
Mayfair Ave SW	98367
Mayhill Ct, Dr & Rd	98366
SE Mayvolt Rd	98366
SE Mcbreen Ln	98367
Mccary Rd SW	98367
Mccool Pl SW	98367
Mccormick Woods Dr SW	98367
Mcgregor Rd SE	98366
SE Mckinley Pl & St SE	98366
Meadow Pl SE	98367
Medallion Pl E	98366
Megan Ct E	98366
W Melcher St	98366
Meline Rd SE	98367
SW Melrose Ln	98367
Memory Ln SW	98367
Menzies Rd SE	98366
Merganser Ln SE	98367
Meri Ln SE	98366
E Michigan St	98366
SE Mile Hill Dr	98366
SW Miller Rd	98367
SE Miller Creek Rd	98367
Minter Ln SW	98367
SW Minterbrook Rd	98367
Miracle Mile Dr E	98366
Missouri St E	98366
SE & SW Misty Ct & Ln	98367
Mitchell Ave & Rd SE	98366
SE Modoc Ct	98367
SW Moffett Ln	98367
E Montana St	98366
SE Monte Bella Pl	98366
SE Moon Beam Ct	98367
SW Moorea Ln	98366
SE Moose Hill Ct	98367
SE Moritz Way	98366
SE Morning Light Ct	98367
SE Morning Mist Rd SE	98366
Morton St	98366
Mountain Beaver Rd SW	98367
Mountain View Rd E	98366
Muir Ct SE	98366
Muirkirk Ln SW	98367
SE Mullenix Rd	98367
Murrelet Ave SW	98367
Mystery Ln	98366
Nanette Ln SE	98366
SE Natchez Ct	98366
E Nautical Cove Way	98366
SE Navigation Ln	98366
Nebraska St SE	98366
SE Ness Ln	98366
E Nevada Ave & St E & SE	98366
SE Nicole Ct	98367
SE Nina Ln	98366
Nokomis Rd SE	98366
SW Norpoint Ct	98367
SE North St	98367
SW Northview Dr	98367
SE Northway Pl	98366
Novak Dr SW	98367
Nubling Ave E	98366
SE Nyanza Ln	98367
SE Nylace Ln	98367
SE & SW Oak Rd	98367
Oakhurst Ln SW	98367
Oakridge Dr SW	98367
Obrian Ave W	98367
SW Odell St	98367
SE Ofarrell Ln	98367
Okanogan Dr SE	98366
SE Olalla Valley Rd SE	98367
Old Banner Rd SE	98367
SW Old Clifton Rd	98367
SW Old Farm Rd	98367
Olney Ave & St	98366
SE Olympia St	98367
SE Olympiad Dr SE	98367
Olympic Ct SE	98366
Olympic Dr SE	98366
Opdal Rd E	98366
Orchard Ave SE	98366
E Orchard Ln	98366
SE Orchard Ln	98366
Orchard St	98366
Oregon St E	98366
SE Oregon St	98367
SE Orlando St	98367
Our Pl SW	98367
SE Overaa Rd	98367
Owl Pl SW	98367
Pacific Ave E	98366
Pacific Firs Pl SE	98366
SE Palisades Ln	98367
Palm Ct SE	98366
Palo Alto Ln SE	98367
Pancho Villa Pl SE	98366
Par Fore Dr SE	98367
SW Paradise Ln	98367
SE Parakeet Ln	98367
Parent Ave SW	98367
Park Ave E	98366
Park Dr SE	98367
Parkington Pl SE	98366
Parkstone Ln SW	98367
Parkwood Dr SE	98366
SE Parsons Green Ct	98367
E Party Place Ln	98366
E Patricia St	98366
Patrosa Ln SE	98367
Payseno Ln SE	98366
SE Peabody Ct	98367
SW Peace Ln	98367
Pebble Pl SE	98367
Pelican Ln SE	98367
Pembrook Pl SE	98366
SE Penguin Ln	98367
Peninsula Pl SW	98367
SE Pennswood Ct	98367
Peppermill Pl SE	98366
Perdemco Ave SE	98367
E Perelli Ln	98366
SW Perkins Ct	98367
Perry Ave N	98366
Peru Ave E	98366
Peterson Rd SE	98367
E Pheasant Hill Ln	98366
Phillips Rd SE	
3801-3997	98366
3999-4699	98366
4701-4799	98366
4800-9799	98367
SW Phipps Way	98367
Pickford Pl SW	98367
SE Pierson St	98366
Pike Pl SE	98367
SE & SW Pine Rd	98367
Pine Cone Ct SE	98366
SE Pine Tree Dr SE	98366
Pioneer Ln & Pl	98366
Piperberry Way SE	98366
Pirates Cove Ave SW	98367
Placid Pl SE	98367
W Pleasant St	98367
Plisko Ln SE	98367
SE Plymouth Way	98366
Point Glover Ln E	98366
SE Polar Star Way	98366
E Polk Ave	98366
Ponderosa Dr SE	98366
Poplar St	98366
Porani Rd SW	98367
Port Orchard Blvd	98366
Portland Ave	98366
Pot Hole Pl SW	98367
Pottery Ave	98366
Powell Pl SE	98367
SE Prairie Ct	98366
Prestwick Ln SW	98367
Primrose Ln SW	98367
Pristine Beach Ln SE	98367
Pritchard Rd E	98366
SE Promenade Ln	98367
Prospect Aly & St	98366
SE Providence Ct	98367
SE Puffin Ln	98367
Puget Dr E & SE	98366
SE Puget Heights Ln	98367
Pullman Pl SW	98367
Quail Ridge Rd SW	98367
SE Quarter Mile Way	98367
SE Quartz Ct	98367
Rabbit Ln SW	98367
Radey St	98367
SE Rae Ct	98366
SW Ragle Ct	98367
Rainbow Ridge Ln SW	98367
Rainier Ridge Ave SE	98367
SE Rainshadow Ct	98366
E Raintree Ln	98366
Raintree Pl SE	98367
Rama Dr E	98366
Ramblewood Ct & St	98366
Ramiller Ln SE	98367
Ramsey Rd SE	98366
Ranch Dr SW	98367
Ranch Ridge Ct SW	98367
E Randall Ln	98366
SW Rapids Dr	98367
SE Ravenridge Ct	98367
Ray Rd SE	98367
SE Raymond Ct	98367
Red Fox Pl SE	98367
SE Red Hawk Ln	98366
Red Spruce Dr SE	98366
Redemption Ave SE	98366
Redwood Dr	98366
SW Reese Ln	98367
Reflection Ln E	98366
Regency Ct & Dr SE	98367
Reindeer Ln SW	98367
SE Renee Ct	98367
Retsil Rd E & SE	98366
SE Rhapsody Dr	98366
SW Rhododendron Dr	98367
Rich Cove Ln E	98366
Rich View Dr E	98366
Richards Ave SE	98367
SE Richmond Ln	98367
Ricky Ct E	98366
Ridge Rim Trl SE	98367
Ridgecrest Way SE	98366
Ridgeway Pl E	98366
Riflebird Pl SW	98367
SE Rim Ln	98367
SW Ritchie Dr	98367
Ritz Ct SE	98366
Riverside Ave W	98367
SE Rocket Ln	98367
Rockwell Ave	98366
Rocky Creek Ln SE	98366
Rodstol Ln SE	98366
Roland Ave	98366
Roosevelt Ave SE	98366
Roosevelt Ave SW	98367
Rosalee Ln SE	98367
SE Rose Ct	98366
SE Rose Rd	98367
Rosedale Ln SW	98367
Ross St	98366
Roth Pl SE	98367
Row Ln SE	98367
Rowan Ln E	98366
Roxburghe Pl SW	98367
SW Royal Spruce Dr	98367
E Royalview Ln	98366
SE Royalwood Ct & Pl SE	98367
Ruby Ct SE	98366
SW Running Deer Way	98367
Russell Ave SE	98366
Rustlewood Ln SE	98366
Rutherford Cir SW	98367
Saber Ln SE	98367
Saddle Club Rd SE	98367
SE Safe Haven Way	98367
Sage Ct & St	98366
Saint Andrews Dr SW	98367
SE Saint Anns Ct	98367
SE Saint James Ct	98367
SE Saint Matthews Ct	98367
Saint Nick Pl SW	98367
SE Saint Patrick Ct	98367
SE Saint Pauls Ct	98367
Salal St E	98366
SW Salma Ln	98367
SE Salmonberry Dr & Rd SE	98366
Salt Point Pl E	98366
SW Sam Nichols St	98367
SE Sanctuary Way	98367
E Sandbar Ct	98366
SE Santa Maria Ln	98366
Sarann Ave E	98366
SE Saxon Ct	98366
SE Scatterwood Ln	98366
SE Scenic View Ln	98367
Schermerhorn Pl SE	98366
Schweitzer Pl SW	98367
SE Scofield Rd	98367
Scotland Ct	98366
Seamont Ct E	98366
Seattle Ave	98366
E Seaview Dr	98366
SE Sedgwick Rd	98366
SW Sedgwick Rd	98367
SW Sedona Ct	98367
Seiford Ave SE	98366
SE Sequoia St	98366
SE Serenade Way	98366
SE Shadowood Ct & Dr SE	98367
Shamrock Ln	98366
SW Shannon Dr	98367
Shawn St SW	98367
SE Shelton Ln	98366
Sherlyn Ave SE	98367
Sherman Ave	98366
SW Shirey St	98367
Short Ave	98366
Siana Pl SE	98366
Sidney Ave	98366
Sidney Ln	98366
Sidney Pkwy	98366
Sidney Rd SW	98367
SW Sidney Heights Ln	98367
Silver Ln SW	98367
Silverleaf Ct E	98366
SE Sinclair View Dr	98366
SW Siskin Cir	98367
E Sitka Ct	98366
Sky Ln SW	98367
SE Skycrest Ln	98366
SE Skyhawk Ln	98367
SE Sleepy Hollow Ct	98366
Sleigh Ave SW	98367
Smalley Ln	98366
Smith St	98366
Snowridge Ave	98366
SE Soholt Ln	98367
SE Somerset Ct	98366
Sonoma Ter SE	98366
SE South St	98366
Southgate Dr SW	98367
SE Southworth Dr	98366
SE Spencer Ave	98367
SE Spicewood Ct	98366
Spindrift Ln SW	98367
Spokane Ave	98366
Sprague St	98366
Spring St E	98366
SE Spring Creek Rd	98367
E Spring Hill Rd	98366
SE Spruce Rd	98367
SW Spruce Rd	98367
E Spruce St	98366
Spurling Ln SE	98367
Square Lake Rd SW	98367
Sroufe St	98366
E Stable Ln	98366
E Stanley Ln	98366
SW Stanwick Way	98367
Starboard Ln SE	98366
Starlet Ln	98366
Starview Dr SW	98367
W State Highway 16 SW	98367
SW Station Circle Rd	98367
Steamboat Loop E	98366
SE Steinway Ln	98367
E Stellar Way	98366
Stetson St	98366
Stevens Ct SE	98367
SW Stewburner Way	98367
Stockton St	98366
Stohlton Rd SE	98366
Stoney Ridge Ln SW	98367
SE Stormy Ln	98367
SE Stornelli Way	98366
Strathmore Cir SW	98367
SE Summer Pl	98366
E Summit Ave	98366
W Summit St	98367
Sunburst Ct SE	98366
Sunflower Pl SW	98367
Sunnyslope Rd SW	98367
Sunset Ln	98366
SW Sunshine Way	98367
Sunshine Glenn Ct SW	98367
Surrey Ct SE	98366
SW Susan Ln	98367
Sutton Ln	98366
Sweany St	98366
SE Sweethome Ln	98366
Swift Ave SW	98367
SE Swofford Ln	98367
SW Sylvan St	98367
SE Sylvis Ln	98366
Tacoma Ave	98366
SW Taft Blvd	98367
Tall Firs Ln SW	98367
SE Tamarack Dr	98366
Tania Ln SW	98367
Tanner Ln SW	98367
Tartan Ln E	98366
Taylor St	98366
SW Tenby Ct	98367
SE Tennis Ct	98366
SE Terrace Ln	98367
Terrace Way SE	98366
Texas Pl SE	98366
Thane Ln SE	98367
SE Tharp Pl	98367
Thimbleberry Pl SE	98366
SE Tiburon Ct	98366
Tidepool Pl E	98366
SE Tiffany Ln	98366
Timber Trail Rd E	98366
SE Timberidge Ct	98367
Timberwood Pl SW	98367
SE Timmerman Ct	98367
Toad Rd SW	98367
Tobermory Cir SW	98367
SE Tola Rd	98366
Tracy Ave	98366
Transue Ln SE	98367
SE Travera Dr	98366
SW Treehouse Way	98367
Tremont Pl & St	98366
SE Triviere Trl SE	98366
Troon Ave SW	98367
SE Truman St	98366
SE Tucci Pl	98367
Tufts Ave E	98366
Tumbleweed Ln SE	98366
Turley Loop Rd SE	98366
Turnberry Pl SW	98367
SE Upchurch Way	98366
Upton Park Pl SE	98367
Vale Ct & Rd	98366
Valentine Ln SE	98366
SE Vallair Ct	98366
Valley Ave E	98366
Valley View Ln SE	98367
Van Buren Ave & St	98366
N Van Decar Rd	98367
SE Van Skiver Rd	98367
SE Vashon Vista Dr	98367
Vaughn Ln E	98366
Vernon Ln SE	98367
Verona Ct SW	98367
Vesper Pl SE	98366
Victory Dr & Pl	98367
SW & SE View Dr & Pl SE & N	98367
SE View Park Rd	98367
Viewsound Ln SE	98366
Villa Ct SE	98366
SE Villa Carmel Dr	98366
Village Ln & Way	98366
Vintage Dr SW	98367
Violet Ct	98366
Virginia Ave E	98366
Vista Rama Dr E	98366
Vista Ridge Ln SE	98367
Vivian Ct	98367
Wales Ct	98366
SW Warbler Way	98367
Warner Ave SE	98366
E Washington St SE	98366
Watauga Beach Dr E	98366
Water Ln SE	98366
Waterman Ridge Ln E	98366
SW Wava Ln	98367
SE Way Dr	98367
Wayne Pl SE	98367
Weathers Ct SE	98366
Wendell Ave SE	98366
Wentworth Ave SW	98367
West Ave	98366
Westbrook Dr & Pl	98367

Westland Ct SE 98366
Westminster Dr SE 98366
Westview Dr SW 98367
Westway Dr SE 98366
Westwood Pl SE 98366
Wexford Ave SW 98367
Weyers Ln SW 98367
SE Wheatland Ct 98366
White Cedar Dr SE 98366
Whittier Ave SE 98366
Wicks End Ln SW 98367
Wicks Lake Rd SW 98367
Widgeon Point Pl SE 98367
Wigeon Ave SW 98367
SW Wildaire Dr 98367
SW Wildwood Rd 98367
Wilkins Dr & Pl SW 98366
William Heights Ln SW 98367
E Williams Ln 98366
SE Willow Ln 98366
Willow Rd SE 98367
Wilson Creek Rd SE
4000-4699 98366
5300-7299 98367
SE Windsor Ct 98366
Windy Cedar Ln SW 98367
SW Windy Song Way 98367
Winona St SW 98367
SW Winter Springs Ln 98367
SE Wolf Ln 98367
Wolves Rd 98366
Woodchuck Ln SE 98367
SE Woodland Ct 98366
Woodridge Dr SE 98366
Woods Rd E & SE 98366
Woodside Ln SW 98367
SW Wycoff Rd 98367
Wye Lake Blvd SW 98367
Wynn Jones Rd E 98366
Wynstone Way 98367
E Wyoming St 98366
Wyvern Dr SE 98367
SE Yakima St 98366
SW Yellow Bloom Ct 98367
SE Yeshua Ln 98367
Yorkshire Ct & Dr 98366
SE Yosemite 98367
SW Young Rd 98367
Young Hill Ln SE 98366
SW Youwood Way 98367
SE Yucca Ct 98366
Yukon Harbor Rd SE 98366
SE Zachary Ln 98367
SW Zimmerman Ln 98367
SE Zion Pl 98367

NUMBERED STREETS

E 1st St 98366
E 2nd Ave & St E 98366
E 3rd Ave & St E 98366
E 4th St 98366
SW 44th St 98367

PUYALLUP WA

General Delivery 98371

POST OFFICE BOXES MAIN OFFICE STATIONS AND BRANCHES

Box No.s
1 - 37199 98371
73001 - 732198 98373

NAMED STREETS

Acadia Ct 98374
Admiralty Street Pl 98371
Alderbrook Ct N & S 98374
Amber Blvd 98372
Bath Rd E 98374
Benston Dr E 98372
Bentley Rd 98371
Big Bend Ct 98374
Bonnie Brae Ct 98372
Bowman Hilton St E 98372
Briarwood Ct N & S 98374
Bridge Ave 98372
Brookmonte Dr SE 98372
Bryce Canyon Ct 98374
Caldwell Rd E 98372
Camden Dr E 98375
Canyon Rd E
7100-7198 98371
7200-9599 98371
9600-9600 98373
9602-14199 98373
14201-14299 98373
14500-19299 98375
Canyon Lands Ct 98374
Carlsbad Ct 98374
Chateau Dr 98373
Cherokee Blvd 98374
Chrisella Rd E 98372
Clachenn Ct E 98375
Columbia St 98371
Commencement Ave 98371
Corwin Rd 98371
Country Hollow Dr E 98375
County Line Rd 98372
Crater Lake Ct 98374
Crown Dr E 98375
Crystal Lane Loop SE 98372
Crystal Ridge Dr SE 98372
Cypress Dr 98372
Dana Ln E 98373
Dechaux Rd E 98371
Discovery Dr 98371
Dunhill Dr 98372
Eagle Ridge Dr E 98374
Eastwood Ave E 98375
Edgewood Dr E 98372
Everglades Ct 98374
Fairview Dr 98371
Firland Dr 98371
Firlane Dr E 98375
Forest Green Blvd 98374
Forest Park Ct N 98374
Forest Ridge Ct N & S 98374
Forest Rim Ct N & S 98374
Forest View Ct N & S 98374
Freeman Rd E 98371
S Fruitland
501-599 98371
S Fruitland
601-2299 98371
2301-2997 98373
2999-3099 98373
3101-3409 98373
Fruitland Ave E
7501-8697 98371
8699-9500 98371
9502-9598 98373
9600-11000 98373
11002-11098 98373
Garden Way 98371
Gem Heights Dr E 98375
Glacier Ct 98374
Graham Rd E 98374
Greenwood Ct S 98374
Griffin Dr E 98375
Heather Ct 98372
Highland Dr 98372
Highlands Blvd 98372
S Hill Park Dr 98373
Historic Way 98371
Houston Rd E 98372
Industrial Park Way 98371
Inter Ave 98372
Jennifer Ct E 98374
John Bananola Way E 98374
Jovita Blvd E 98372
Karshner Rd E 98372
Kilt Ct 98372
Kings Canyon Ct 98374
La Grande Blvd 98373
Larichig Ave E 98372
Larkspur Ct & Dr SE 98374
Lassen Ct 98374
N Levee Rd 98371
Linden Ln 98372
E Main 98372
W Main 98371
Mammoth Cave Ct 98374
Manorwood Dr SE 98374
Marion Ln SE 98372
Mcelroy Pl 98372
E Meeker 98372
W Meeker 98371
Meridian E
11401-11597 98373
Meridian E
11599-14300 98373
14302-14398 98373
14400-19199 98375
N Meridian 98371
S Meridian
100-2299 98371
2301-2497 98373
2499-4499 98373
4501-4699 98373
Meridian Ave E 98371
Mesa Verde Ct 98374
Military Rd E 98374
Milwaukee Ave E 98372
Monta Vista Dr E 98372
Moradenc Ave E 98373
Morning Side Dr E 98372
Mt Mckinley Ct 98374
Olympic Blvd 98374
Park Ave 98372
Parkwood Blvd 98374
Peach Park Ln 98371
Pintren Ave E 98371
E Pioneer 98372
W Pioneer 98371
Pioneer Way E
5400-5498 98371
5500-7700 98371
7702-7798 98371
12601-13097 98372
13099-14899 98372
14901-14999 98372
Pipeline Rd E
9233-9297 98371
9299-9499 98371
10000-10098 98373
10100-10999 98373
11001-11699 98373
Platte Ct 98374
Prospect Ave 98371
Prospect Avenue Ct 98371
Rainier Blvd 98374
Rainier St 98372
Rampart Dr E 98374
Reservoir Rd E 98374
Richardson Dr 98371
River Rd E 98371
Rocky Mountain Ct 98374
Rodesco Ct & Dr 98374
Rose Pl 98371
Ross Ln 98371
Sandy Glen Ln E 98375
Shaw Rd
801-897 98372
899-2100 98372
2102-2298 98372
2301-2497 98374
2499-2599 98374
2601-3299 98374
Shaw Rd E
8113-8821 98372
11200-12699 98374
Shawnee Rd E 98374
Sierra Dr E 98374
Silver Creek Ave E 98375
Spencer Rd 98372
Spring St 98372
St Andrews Ct 98372
State Route 162 E
8100-8398 98372
State Route 162 E
8400-9500 98372
9502-9598 98372
9600-9798 98374
9800-12799 98374
W Stewart 98371
Stewart Ave E
6201-6297 98371
100-199 98372
Sumner Heights Dr E 98372
Sunridge Way E 98374
Sunrise Blvd E 98374
Tacoma Rd E 98371
Tartan Ct 98372
Tatoosh Rd E 98374
Taylor St E 98371
Terrace Dr 98372
Thornhill Ct & Rd 98374
Todd Rd E 98372
Todd Rd NE 98372
Todd Rd NW 98371
Valley Ave E
8201-8399 98371
8801-8899 98371
10701-10797 98372
10799-12400 98372
12402-12618 98372
Valley Ave NE 98372
Valley Ave NW 98371
W Valley Hwy E 98372
Valley View Dr 98372
Victoria Lane Ct SE 98372
Vista Dr 98372
Westmore Dr E 98374
Wildflower Ct 98374
Wildwood Park Dr 98374
Wilson Dr 98371
Winchara Ct E 98374
S Woodland 98371
Woodland Ave E
7200-9599 98371
9600-13000 98373
13002-14398 98373
14800-15600 98375
15602-15998 98375

NUMBERED STREETS

2nd Ave NE 98372
2nd Ave NW 98371
2nd St E 98372
2nd St NE 98372
2nd St NW 98371
2nd St SE 98372
2nd St SW
101-197 98371
199-899 98371
4300-4499 98373
3rd Ave NE 98372
3rd Ave NW 98371
3rd St NE 98372
3rd St NW 98371
3rd St SE
201-297 98372
299-2199 98372
2201-2299 98372
3800-3898 98374
3rd St SW 98371
4th Ave NE 98372
4th Ave NW 98371
4th Ave SE 98372
4th Ave SW 98371
4th St E 98372
4th St NE 98372
4th St NW 98371
4th St SE 98372
4th St SW 98371
4th Street Pl SE 98374
4th Street Pl SW 98373
5th Ave NE 98372
5th Ave NW 98371
5th Ave SE 98372
5th Ave SW 98371
5th St NE 98372
5th St NW 98371
5th St SE
200-2299 98372
2601-2797 98374
5th St SW
100-298 98371
2301-2397 98373
5th Avenue Ct SW 98371
5th Street Ct E 98372
6th Ave NW 98371
6th Ave SW 98371
6th St E 98372
6th St NW 98371
6th St SE 98374
6th St SW 98371
6th Street Ct E 98372
6th Street Pl SE 98374
7th Ave NE 98372
7th Ave NW 98371
7th Ave SE 98372
7th Ave SW 98371
7th Pl SE 98372
7th St E 98372
7th St NE 98372
7th St NW 98371
7th St SE
100-310 98372
2301-2497 98374
7th St SW
100-2099 98371
3900-4199 98373
7th Street Pl SE
1500-1699 98372
4300-4499 98374
8th Ave NE 98372
8th Ave NW 98371
8th Ave SE 98372
8th Ave SW 98371
8th St E 98372
8th St NW 98371
8th St SE
900-2099 98372
2700-2799 98374
8th St SW
100-1598 98371
2500-2599 98373
8th Avenue Ct NW 98371
8th Avenue Ct SE 98372
8th Avenue Pl NW 98371
8th Street Ct E 98372
8th Street Ct SW 98371
9th Ave NE 98372
9th Ave NW 98371
9th Ave SE 98372
9th Ave SW 98371
9th St E 98372
9th St NE 98372
9th St NW 98371
9th St SE
923-1007 98372
2700-2899 98374
9th St SW
100-2100 98371
2300-3899 98373
9th Avenue Ct SE 98372
9th Street Pl SE 98374
10th Ave E 98372
10th Ave NW 98371
10th Ave SE 98372
10th Ave SW 98371
10th St E 98372
10th St SE
100-198 98372
200-899 98372
3900-4299 98374
10th St SW
100-499 98371
2500-2699 98373
10th Avenue Ct NE 98372
10th Avenue Ct NW 98371
10th Avenue Ct SE 98372
10th Street Ct E 98372
10th Street Ct SE 98374
10th Street Pl NW 98371
10th Street Pl SW
1900-2199 98371
3100-3199 98373
11th Ave NW 98371
11th Ave SE 98372
11th Ave SW 98371
11th St E 98372
11th St NW 98371
11th St SE
500-999 98372
2800-2999 98374
11th St SW 98371
11th Avenue Ct SE 98372
11th Street Ct E 98372
11th Street Pl SW 98371
12th Ave NW 98371
12th Ave SE 98372
12th Ave SW 98371
12th Pl SE 98374
12th St E 98372
12th St NW 98371
12th St SE
100-1199 98372
2800-2999 98374
12th St SW 98371
12th Street Ct NW 98371
12th Street Ct SW 98371
12th Street Pl SW 98373
13th Ave NW 98371
13th Ave SE 98372
13th Ave SW 98371
13th Pl NW 98371
13th Pl SE 98372
13th St E 98372
13th St NW 98371
13th St SE
300-598 98372
2300-2999 98372
13th St SW
300-2299 98371
2300-3499 98373
13th Avenue NW & SW 98371
13th Street Ct E 98372
13th Street Ct NW 98371
13th Street Pl SW 98373
14th Ave NW 98371
14th Ave SE 98372
14th St E 98372
14th St NW 98371
14th St SE
301-597 98372
599-699 98372
2800-2999 98374
14th St SW 98371
14th Avenue NE & SE 98372
14th Street Ct E 98372
14th Street Pl NW 98371
14th Street Pl SE 98374
14th Street Pl SW 98373
15th Ave SE 98372
15th Ave SW 98371
15th St E 98372
15th St NW 98371
15th St SE
100-899 98372
901-1099 98372
2300-2800 98374
2802-2898 98374
15th St SW 98371
15th Street Pl NW 98371
15th Street Pl SW 98373
16th Ave NW 98371
16th Ave SE 98372
16th Ave SW 98371
16th Ct SE 98372
16th St E 98372
16th St NW 98371
16th St SE
400-498 98372
2801-2897 98374
16th St SW 98371
16th Avenue Ct SE 98372
16th Avenue Ct SW 98371
16th Street Pl NW 98371
16th Street Pl SW 98373
17th Ave SE 98372
17th Ave SW 98371
17th St E 98372
17th St NW 98371
17th St SE 98372
17th St SW
100-1199 98371
2400-3499 98373
3501-3899 98373
17th Avenue Ct SW 98371
17th Street Ct E 98372
17th Street Pl NW 98371
17th Street Pl SE 98374
18th Ave SW 98371
18th St E 98372
18th St NW 98371
18th St SE
100-2098 98372
2100-2299 98372
2301-2397 98374
2399-3000 98374
3002-3098 98374
18th St SW
300-999 98371
2900-2999 98373
18th Avenue Ct SW 98371
18th Street Ct E 98371
18th Street Pl SE 98372
18th Street Pl SW 98373
19th Ave SE 98372
19th Ave SW 98371
19th St NW 98371
19th St SE 98372
19th Avenue Ct SE 98372
19th Street Ct E 98372
19th Street Ct NW 98371
19th Street Pl NW 98371
19th Street Pl SE 98374
19th Street Pl SW 98373
20th Ave SE 98372
20th Ave SW 98371
20th St E
7900-8098 98371
8100-9199 98371
10800-10898 98372
10900-12499 98372
20th St NW 98371
20th St SE
900-2199 98372
2300-2899 98374
20th St SW 98373
20th Avenue Ct SE 98372
20th Avenue Ct SW 98371
20th Street Ct E 98371
20th Street Pl SE 98374
20th Street Pl SW
300-399 98371
2700-3099 98373
21st Ave SE 98372
21st Ave SW 98371
21st St E 98372
21st St NW 98371
21st St SE
600-1899 98372
2300-3799 98374
21st St SW
900-1499 98371
2300-2999 98373
21st Avenue Ct SE 98372
21st Street Ct E 98372
21st Street Pl NW 98371
21st Street Pl SE 98374
22nd Ave SE 98372
22nd Ave SW 98371
22nd Ct SE 98372
22nd St E
9301-9399 98371
10301-10499 98372
22nd St NW 98371
22nd St SE
1200-2199 98372
2400-4399 98374
22nd St SW 98371
22nd Avenue Ct SE 98372
22nd Avenue Ct SW 98371
22nd Street Ct E 98372
22nd Street Pl NW 98371
22nd Street Pl SW 98373
23rd Ave SE 98372

23rd Ave SW ... 98371
23rd St E ... 98372
23rd St NW ... 98371
23rd St SE ... 98372
23rd St SW
700-1099 ... 98371
3200-3499 ... 98373
23rd Avenue Ct SE ... 98374
23rd Avenue Ct SW ... 98371
23rd Street Ct E ... 98372
23rd Street Pl NW ... 98371
23rd Street Pl SE ... 98372
24th Ave SE ... 98374
24th Ave SW ... 98373
24th St E
9200-10099 ... 98371
10101-10199 ... 98371
10200-12499 ... 98372
24th St NW ... 98371
24th St SE
2100-2199 ... 98372
2600-4699 ... 98374
24th Avenue Ct SE ... 98374
24th Avenue Ct SW ... 98373
24th Street Ct E ... 98372
24th Street Pl SE ... 98372
25th Ave SE ... 98374
25th Ave SW ... 98373
25th St E
8300-8398 ... 98371
8400-8599 ... 98371
12300-12498 ... 98372
25th St SE
700-798 ... 98372
800-1499 ... 98372
2500-4699 ... 98374
25th St SW ... 98373
25th Avenue Ct SE ... 98374
25th Street Ct E ... 98372
25th Street Pl SE ... 98372
25th Street Pl SW ... 98371
26th Ave SE ... 98374
26th Ave SW ... 98373
26th Pl SE
2000-2298 ... 98372
3400-3499 ... 98374
26th St NW ... 98371
26th St SE ... 98374
26th Avenue Ct SE ... 98374
26th Avenue Ct SW ... 98373
26th Street Pl SW ... 98371
27th Ave SE ... 98374
27th Ave SW ... 98373
27th Pl SE
1900-2299 ... 98372
3400-3499 ... 98374
27th St E
8600-8898 ... 98371
12300-12500 ... 98372
27th St NE ... 98372
27th St SE
1200-1500 ... 98372
3201-3297 ... 98374
27th St SW ... 98371
27th Avenue Ct NW ... 98371
27th Avenue Ct SE ... 98374
27th Avenue Ct SW ... 98373
27th Street Ct E ... 98372
27th Street Pl SW ... 98371
28th Ave SE ... 98374
28th Pl SE ... 98374
28th St E
8601-8797 ... 98371
8799-9399 ... 98371
11000-11100 ... 98372
11102-12198 ... 98372
28th St SE
1500-2299 ... 98372
3200-3399 ... 98374
28th St SW ... 98371
28th Avenue Ct SW ... 98373
28th Street Ct E ... 98371
29th Ave SE ... 98374
29th Ave SW ... 98373
29th Pl SE ... 98374
29th St E ... 98372
29th St NE ... 98372
29th Avenue Ct SW ... 98373
29th Street Ct E
8400-9999 ... 98371
10200-10399 ... 98372
29th Street Ct SE ... 98374
29th Street Pl NW ... 98371
30th Ave SE ... 98374
30th Ave SW ... 98373
30th Pl SE ... 98374
30th St E
8400-8599 ... 98371
10200-12099 ... 98372
30th St SE ... 98374
30th Avenue Ct SW ... 98373
30th Street Ct E
10500-10999 ... 98372
2000-2199 ... 98372
2500-2699 ... 98374
31st Ave SE ... 98374
31st Ave SW ... 98373
31st St E
9200-10199 ... 98371
10300-12399 ... 98372
31st St NW ... 98371
31st St SE ... 98374
31st Street Ct & Pl ... 98371
31st Street Ct & Pl ... 98374
32nd Ave SE ... 98374
32nd St E ... 98371
32nd Avenue Ct SE ... 98374
32nd Avenue Ct SW ... 98373
32nd Street Ct E ... 98372
32nd Street Pl ... 98372
32nd Street Pl SE ... 98374
33rd Ave SE ... 98374
33rd Ct E ... 98372
33rd St E ... 98371
33rd Avenue Ct SW ... 98373
33rd Street Ct E ... 98371
34th Ave SE ... 98374
34th St E
8200-9199 ... 98371
11400-11498 ... 98372
1300-1899 ... 98372
2300-3099 ... 98374
34th Avenue Ct SW ... 98373
34th Street Ct E ... 98371
35th Ave SE ... 98374
35th St E ... 98372
35th Street Ct E ... 98371
35th Street Pl SE ... 98372
36th Ave SE ... 98374
36th Pl SE ... 98374
36th St E
8201-8297 ... 98371
10200-10498 ... 98372
36th St SE
2001-2299 ... 98372
2300-3199 ... 98374
37th Ave SE ... 98374
37th St SE ... 98372
37th Street Ct E ... 98371
37th Street Pl SE ... 98372
38th Ave & St ... 98374
38th Ave & St ... 98371
38th Street Ct E ... 98371
39th Ave SE ... 98374
39th Ave SW ... 98373
39th St E ... 98372
39th St SE ... 98372
39th Avenue Ct SE ... 98374
39th Street Ct E ... 98372
40th St E ... 98371
40th St SE
1400-1999 ... 98372
2001-2199 ... 98372
2700-2898 ... 98374
2900-3000 ... 98374
3002-3098 ... 98374
40th Street Ct E ... 98372
41st St E ... 98371
41st St SE ... 98374
41st Street Pl SE ... 98372
42nd St E ... 98371
42nd Avenue Ct SW ... 98373
42nd Street Ct E ... 98371
43rd Ave SE ... 98374
43rd Ave SW ... 98373
43rd St E ... 98372
43rd St SE
1800-2299 ... 98372
2300-2629 ... 98374
2631-2799 ... 98374
43rd Avenue Ct SE ... 98374
43rd Street Ct E ... 98371
44th St E ... 98372
44th St E ... 98371
44th Street Ct E ... 98371
45th St E ... 98372
45th Street Ct E ... 98372
46th Ave SE ... 98374
46th St E ... 98372
46th Street Ct E ... 98372
47th St E ... 98372
47th Street Ct E ... 98372
48th St E
6200-6398 ... 98371
6400-6500 ... 98371
6502-6598 ... 98371
10301-10697 ... 98372
10699-12699 ... 98372
48th Street Ct E ... 98372
49th St E ... 98371
49th St E ... 98372
49th Street Ct E ... 98372
50th Street Ct E ... 98372
50th Street Ct E ... 98371
51st St E ... 98372
51st Street Ct E ... 98372
52nd St E ... 98372
52nd St E ... 98371
52nd Street Ct E ... 98371
53rd Street Ct E
7100-7298 ... 98371
10800-10999 ... 98372
11800-13199 ... 98372
54th St E ... 98372
55th Ave E ... 98373
55th St E
7701-7799 ... 98371
13100-13299 ... 98372
55th Avenue Ct E
8000-8699 ... 98371
10900-13799 ... 98373
55th Street Ct E ... 98371
56th Ave E
4100-7699 ... 98371
7701-8499 ... 98371
10600-10698 ... 98373
10701-10799 ... 98373
15300-15400 ... 98375
15402-15498 ... 98375
56th St E
6600-7599 ... 98371
12900-13420 ... 98372
56th Avenue Ct E
6000-8399 ... 98371
10900-11099 ... 98373
15900-16099 ... 98375
56th Street Ct E ... 98371
56th Street Ct E ... 98372
57th Ave E
6301-6397 ... 98371
6399-9099 ... 98371
11600-13799 ... 98373
16100-19899 ... 98375
57th St E
7800-7999 ... 98371
10800-10999 ... 98372
57th Avenue Ct E
7201-7397 ... 98371
7399-7400 ... 98371
7402-7498 ... 98371
10800-11199 ... 98373
15900-15999 ... 98375
57th Street Ct E ... 98372
58th Ave E
4301-6497 ... 98371
6499-9199 ... 98371
11400-12799 ... 98373
14501-14597 ... 98375
14599-15899 ... 98375
15901-16199 ... 98375
58th St E ... 98371
58th Avenue Ct E
8800-9399 ... 98371
9800-13799 ... 98373
15903-16197 ... 98375
58th Street Ct E ... 98372
59th Ave E
8200-8799 ... 98371
10400-14099 ... 98373
16200-16399 ... 98375
59th St E
6400-6599 ... 98371
10500-10599 ... 98372
59th Avenue Ct E
8400-8499 ... 98371
9800-11299 ... 98373
15801-15897 ... 98375
59th Street Ct E ... 98372
60th Ave E
7700-9000 ... 98371
13300-14399 ... 98373
60th St E ... 98371
60th Avenue Ct E
8300-9198 ... 98371
12600-12698 ... 98373
60th Street Ct E ... 98372
61st Ave E
7700-8699 ... 98371
8701-8799 ... 98371
9701-9797 ... 98373
9799-11099 ... 98373
61st St E
5200-6499 ... 98371
6501-6599 ... 98371
10500-10799 ... 98372
61st Avenue Ct E ... 98371
61st Street Ct E ... 98372
62nd Ave E
4500-9399 ... 98371
10100-10298 ... 98373
10300-13500 ... 98373
13502-13598 ... 98373
14500-15999 ... 98375
62nd St E ... 98372
62nd Avenue Ct E
8700-8798 ... 98371
8800-9500 ... 98371
9502-9598 ... 98371
9600-11099 ... 98373
16200-16299 ... 98375
62nd Street Ct E ... 98372
63rd Ave E
7800-8999 ... 98371
10900-12599 ... 98373
63rd St E ... 98372
63rd Avenue Ct E
9100-9299 ... 98371
9600-10399 ... 98373
15900-16399 ... 98375
63rd Street Ct E ... 98372
64th Ave E
7700-8899 ... 98371
10400-12799 ... 98373
17200-17899 ... 98375
64th Avenue Ct E
9200-9399 ... 98371
9900-11599 ... 98373
15700-15899 ... 98375
65th Ave E
8000-9399 ... 98371
10400-14198 ... 98373
15600-15699 ... 98375
65th Avenue Ct E ... 98375
65th Street Ct E ... 98372
66th Ave E
4800-4898 ... 98371
4900-6399 ... 98371
6401-8699 ... 98371
9600-11199 ... 98373
11201-11599 ... 98373
14401-14497 ... 98375
14499-16399 ... 98375
66th Avenue Ct E
8100-9099 ... 98371
12200-13199 ... 98373
14800-17999 ... 98375
67th Ave E
6000-8298 ... 98371
10100-13599 ... 98373
15100-17999 ... 98375
67th Avenue Ct E
9000-9499 ... 98371
9700-12499 ... 98373
15200-17699 ... 98375
68th Ave E
5800-8299 ... 98371
12000-12798 ... 98373
12800-14199 ... 98373
14201-14399 ... 98373
14800-17999 ... 98375
68th Avenue Ct E
8400-9399 ... 98371
10400-13999 ... 98373
14400-16199 ... 98375
69th Ave E
7800-8999 ... 98371
17708-17999 ... 98375
69th Avenue Ct E
5200-8399 ... 98371
9800-13598 ... 98373
14400-17999 ... 98375
70th Ave E
5100-5198 ... 98371
5200-5299 ... 98371
5301-5899 ... 98371
13601-13999 ... 98373
16000-16198 ... 98375
16200-17799 ... 98375
70th Avenue Ct E
5200-5998 ... 98371
14200-14399 ... 98373
14400-18699 ... 98375
71st Ave E
5201-5201 ... 98371
5203-9599 ... 98371
13801-13897 ... 98373
13899-13999 ... 98373
15000-18399 ... 98375
71st Avenue Ct E
5201-5203 ... 98371
5205-5300 ... 98371
5302-5498 ... 98371
10200-14399 ... 98373
18400-19199 ... 98375
72nd Ave E
5200-9599 ... 98371
10700-14199 ... 98373
14700-18399 ... 98375
72nd St E ... 98371
72nd Avenue Ct E
6000-6299 ... 98371
9700-14399 ... 98373
14400-19099 ... 98375
73rd Ave E
5200-9599 ... 98371
10100-10498 ... 98373
14800-18399 ... 98375
73rd Avenue Ct E
13000-13099 ... 98373
14500-18399 ... 98375
74th Ave E
9600-9698 ... 98373
9700-13499 ... 98373
13501-13899 ... 98373
14900-18899 ... 98375
74th St E
6401-6599 ... 98371
13401-13499 ... 98372
74th Avenue Ct E
11200-14399 ... 98373
17600-17699 ... 98375
75th Ave E
8400-8999 ... 98371
9001-9099 ... 98371
9901-9997 ... 98373
9999-11299 ... 98373
17700-18499 ... 98375
75th St E ... 98371
75th Avenue Ct E
9100-9199 ... 98371
13000-13199 ... 98373
15400-19199 ... 98375
76th Ave E
5400-5598 ... 98371
5600-6000 ... 98371
6002-6398 ... 98371
12300-14399 ... 98373
15000-18199 ... 98375
76th Avenue Ct E
9000-9199 ... 98371
11300-13599 ... 98373
14600-14698 ... 98375
76th Street Ct E ... 98371
77th Ave E
9000-9199 ... 98371
11300-14399 ... 98373
15300-18999 ... 98375
19001-19099 ... 98375
77th St E ... 98371
77th Avenue Ct E
5801-7997 ... 98371
7999-8299 ... 98371
13700-13799 ... 98373
13801-13999 ... 98373
14400-19099 ... 98375
77th Street Ct E
6800-6999 ... 98371
14400-14498 ... 98372
78th Ave E
10001-10097 ... 98373
10099-12999 ... 98373
13001-14399 ... 98373
15200-19199 ... 98375
78th St E
5400-6399 ... 98371
14100-14199 ... 98372
78th Avenue Ct E ... 98375
78th Street Ct E ... 98371
79th Ave E
11100-12599 ... 98373
15200-18199 ... 98375
79th St E ... 98371
79th Avenue Ct E
5601-5799 ... 98371
12800-13499 ... 98373
17600-19199 ... 98375
79th Street Ct E ... 98371
80th Ave E
5500-5699 ... 98371
10500-13599 ... 98373
14500-18899 ... 98375
80th St E
5500-6900 ... 98371
6902-7698 ... 98371
13401-13797 ... 98372
13799-15900 ... 98372
15902-15998 ... 98372
80th Avenue Ct E
5500-5598 ... 98371
12400-14399 ... 98373
14800-18999 ... 98375
80th Street Ct E ... 98371
81st Ave E
5600-5698 ... 98371
10200-14399 ... 98373
14500-19199 ... 98375
81st St E
5500-6399 ... 98371
15700-15899 ... 98372
81st Avenue Ct E
12800-13599 ... 98373
14700-18399 ... 98375
81st Street Ct E
6600-6999 ... 98371
14700-14799 ... 98372
82nd Ave E
9601-9697 ... 98373
9699-12799 ... 98373
14401-14997 ... 98375
14999-19199 ... 98375
82nd St E ... 98371
82nd Avenue Ct E
10000-13099 ... 98373
17700-18799 ... 98375
82nd Street Ct E ... 98371
83rd Ave E
10400-10498 ... 98373
15600-18799 ... 98375
83rd St E ... 98371
83rd Avenue Ct E
10000-10399 ... 98373
18700-18799 ... 98375
83rd Street Ct E ... 98371
84th Ave E
10400-10499 ... 98373
15200-18499 ... 98375
84th St E
5501-5797 ... 98371
5799-7500 ... 98371
7502-7606 ... 98371
13701-13799 ... 98372
84th Avenue Ct E
2900-3798 ... 98371
3800-4199 ... 98371
10200-12999 ... 98373
15200-18699 ... 98375
85th Ave E
4100-4199 ... 98371
5000-5098 ... 98371
5100-5899 ... 98371
10500-13299 ... 98373
14700-18616 ... 98375
85th St E ... 98371
85th Avenue Ct E
11500-11599 ... 98373
14600-19199 ... 98375
85th Street Ct E
6200-7799 ... 98371
15000-15200 ... 98372
86th Ave E
2401-2897 ... 98371
2899-3299 ... 98371
3301-3399 ... 98371
4300-4798 ... 98371
9600-9698 ... 98373
9700-13900 ... 98373
13902-14298 ... 98373
14400-16900 ... 98375
16902-16998 ... 98375
86th St E
5400-5898 ... 98371
5900-7699 ... 98371
15000-15299 ... 98372
86th Avenue Ct E
2000-2199 ... 98371
10400-13599 ... 98373
15400-18699 ... 98375
86th Street Ct E ... 98371
87th Ave E
3201-3299 ... 98371
14800-18299 ... 98375
87th St E
5900-7699 ... 98371
15018-15299 ... 98372
87th Avenue Ct E
1801-1897 ... 98371
1899-3199 ... 98371
10400-13499 ... 98373
16100-19199 ... 98375
87th Street Ct E ... 98372
88th Ave E
2001-2197 ... 98371
2199-3299 ... 98371
11200-11599 ... 98373
15600-18999 ... 98375
88th St E
6400-6900 ... 98371
6902-7098 ... 98371
15000-15699 ... 98372
88th Avenue Ct E
10000-13400 ... 98373
15200-16699 ... 98375
88th Street Ct E ... 98371
89th Ave E
1900-3299 ... 98371
10000-13299 ... 98373
15400-15498 ... 98375
89th St E ... 98371
89th Avenue Ct E
11200-12299 ... 98373
14400-18199 ... 98375
89th Street Ct E ... 98371
90th Ave E
2600-3999 ... 98371
4001-4499 ... 98371
9600-12700 ... 98373
12702-12798 ... 98373
15700-18999 ... 98375

90th St E
5600-6999 98371
15000-15199 98372
90th Avenue Ct E 98371
90th Avenue Ct E 98375
90th Street Ct E 98371
91st Ave E
2600-3599 98371
10400-11698 98373
16000-18999 98375
91st St E 98371
91st Avenue Ct E
3601-3799 98371
10200-10399 98373
14901-15097 98375
91st Street Ct E 98371
92nd Ave E
1801-1897 98371
11200-14399 98373
14800-15398 98375
92nd St E 98371
92nd Avenue Ct E
3300-3399 98371
9800-11899 98373
15600-17499 98375
92nd Street Ct E 98371
93rd Ave E
2800-3099 98371
11300-13698 98373
14800-18999 98375
93rd Avenue Ct E
2200-2299 98371
11800-11899 98373
17400-17899 98375
93rd Street Ct E 98371
94th Ave E
1600-1798 98371
1800-3699 98371
3701-3799 98371
9800-11598 98373
11600-14399 98373
14400-14598 98375
14600-18999 98375
94th Ln E 98375
94th St E 98371
94th Avenue Ct E
2101-2399 98371
13300-13399 98373
14900-18799 98375
94th Street Ct E
7000-7098 98371
14800-14999 98372
95th Ave E
2600-2698 98371
11600-13599 98373
14900-18499 98375
95th Avenue Ct E
1700-2799 98371
12300-12598 98373
15200-18799 98375
96th Ave E
3400-3699 98371
3701-4599 98371
13400-13799 98373
18100-18699 98375
96th St E
5400-7700 98371
7702-9298 98371
14600-14698 98372
14700-15599 98372
15601-15799 98372
96th Avenue Ct E
1900-2799 98371
12400-13399 98373
14800-19199 98375
97th Ave E
3200-3899 98371
12600-13799 98373
14800-18599 98375
97th Ln E 98375
97th St E 98373
97th Avenue Ave E 98373
97th Avenue Ct E
1501-1597 98371
13600-13612 98373
15101-15597 98375
97th Street Ct E 98373

98th Ave E
2400-2499 98371
11600-12699 98373
15400-18699 98375
98th St E 98373
98th Avenue Ct E
2401-2499 98371
13000-13599 98373
15000-19199 98375
98th Street Ct E 98373
99th Ave E
1601-3397 98371
13400-13600 98373
15400-15599 98375
99th St E 98373
99th Avenue Ct E
11600-13599 98373
15000-19199 98375
99th Street Ct E 98373
100th Ave E
2601-2697 98371
2699-3399 98371
15400-18599 98375
100th Street Ct E 98373
100th Avenue Ct E
1600-1799 98371
11600-13099 98373
15800-19199 98375
100th St E 98373
101st Ave E
11600-11899 98373
18400-19199 98375
101st Street Ct E 98373
101st Avenue Ct E
12800-12899 98373
18525-18617 98375
101st St E 98373
102nd Ave E 98371
102nd Street Ct E 98373
102nd St E
6200-7800 98373
15000-15499 98374
103rd Ave E
2401-2497 98372
13400-19099 98374
103rd Street Ct E 98373
103rd Avenue Ct E 98372
103rd Avenue Ct E 98374
103rd St E
5400-8399 98373
15001-15199 98374
104th Ave E
400-500 98372
12100-14698 98374
104th Avenue Ct E 98374
104th Avenue Ct E 98372
104th Street Ct E
8300-8399 98373
14000-14099 98374
104th St E 98373
105th Ave E
201-497 98372
12800-12898 98374
105th Street Ct E 98373
105th Avenue Ct E
1401-1701 98372
12100-15399 98374
105th St E 98373
106th Ave E
2400-3500 98372
3502-4698 98372
5900-5999 98372
13400-13499 98374
13501-15699 98374
106th Street Ct E 98373
106th Avenue Ct E
300-398 98372
12000-14799 98374
106th St E
5401-5497 98373
5499-8999 98373
13501-13597 98374
13599-15899 98374
15901-15999 98374
107th Ave E 98372
107th Avenue Ct E
200-4699 98372
4701-4799 98372
5300-5399 98372
12000-15399 98374
107th St E
5701-5797 98373
13000-13100 98374
108th Ave & St 98372
108th Ave & St 98374
108th Avenue Ct E
600-799 98372
5200-5899 98372
108th Street Ct E
7200-7398 98373
108th Avenue Ct E
12000-14599 98374
108th Street Ct E
13700-13798 98374
109th Ave E
400-599 98372
14800-14899 98374
109th Avenue Ct E
300-1900 98372
1902-1998 98372
5300-5599 98372
6200-7700 98373
109th Avenue Ct E
12100-14399 98374
12900-12998 98374
109th St E
5500-8599 98373
15000-15298 98374
110th Ave E
901-1097 98372
1099-4500 98372
4502-4698 98372
11600-18699 98374
110th Avenue Ct E
1-5199 98372
6200-6298 98372
110th Street Ct E
6300-8499 98373
110th Avenue Ct E
12900-18999 98374
110th Street Ct E
13400-13799 98374
110th St E 98373
111th Ave E
400-2099 98372
11600-18799 98374
111th Avenue Ct E
2200-2399 98372
111th Street Ct E
5900-5999 98373
111th Avenue Ct E
13000-18899 98374
111th Street Ct E
13400-13899 98374
111th St E 98373
112th Ave E
1600-3099 98372
3101-3399 98372
5400-6899 98372
11600-18699 98374
112th Avenue Ct E
5000-5198 98372
5510-5799 98372
8000-8100 98373
8102-8198 98373
112th Avenue Ct E
11700-18899 98374
13320-13398 98374
13400-15500 98374
15502-15598 98374
112th St E
5500-5598 98373
5600-11299 98373
12600-12698 98374
13301-13399 98374
113th Ave E
5025-5199 98372
5500-5799 98372
12200-18399 98374
113th Avenue Ct E
5000-5025 98372
5027-5299 98372
5501-5597 98372
5599-5600 98372
5602-5698 98372
6900-8111 98373
12000-12198 98374
12200-17099 98374
13500-13598 98374
113th St E
7600-9399 98373
13300-13398 98374
14701-14799 98374
114th Ave E
1-397 98372
11600-18499 98374
114th Avenue Ct E
5500-6799 98372
7000-7599 98373
114th Avenue Ct E
12000-17199 98374
12600-14999 98374
114th St E
6800-9199 98373
12701-12799 98374
115th Ave E
2500-2598 98372
2600-2699 98372
13200-18899 98374
115th Avenue Ct E
2401-2797 98372
115th Street Ct E
7200-7399 98373
115th Avenue Ct E
12000-12098 98374
115th Street Ct E
12600-14799 98374
115th St E
5900-9199 98373
12800-12898 98374
12900-13200 98374
13202-14998 98374
116th Ave E
2100-2298 98372
4401-4799 98372
12000-18799 98374
116th Avenue Ct E 98374
116th Avenue Ct E 98372
116th Street Ct E
6200-7899 98373
12201-12597 98374
116th St E
6601-9400 98373
9402-10198 98373
10900-11598 98373
11600-15600 98374
15602-15698 98374
117th Ave E
200-2600 98372
12200-17299 98374
117th Avenue Ct E
2800-2898 98372
2900-3199 98372
117th Street Ct E
5400-8800 98373
117th Avenue Ct E
5700-5999 98372
117th Street Ct E
11000-13399 98374
117th Avenue Ct E
12000-18899 98374
117th St E
9300-9499 98373
12800-12898 98374
118th Ave E
300-2399 98372
2401-4699 98372
12200-16498 98374
16500-16599 98374
118th Avenue Ct E
800-5399 98372
118th Street Ct E
7801-7899 98373
118th Avenue Ct E
12200-18499 98374
118th Street Ct E
12500-13199 98374
118th St E
5500-6198 98373
6200-9999 98373
12000-13599 98374

119th Ave E
400-3298 98372
3300-3399 98372
3401-3499 98372
5601-5697 98372
5699-6600 98372
6602-6698 98372
11900-16205 98374
119th Avenue Ct E 98374
119th Street Ct E
5500-8999 98373
12000-12598 98374
119th St E
6200-7800 98373
7802-9298 98373
11000-11098 98374
11100-13599 98374
120th Ave E
800-5099 98372
11400-11498 98374
11500-18399 98374
120th Avenue Ct E
5700-5899 98372
120th Street Ct E
6200-8999 98373
11000-13099 98374
120th Avenue Ct E
12001-12197 98374
120th St E
6700-10000 98373
10002-10198 98373
10300-11498 98373
11500-13999 98374
121st Ave E
4800-5099 98372
12800-18399 98374
121st Avenue Ct E
500-699 98372
5500-5599 98373
121st Street Ct E
5500-7399 98373
5600-5611 98372
5612-5699 98373
5613-5699 98372
121st Street Ct E
10901-11897 98374
11600-16899 98374
121st St E
5500-8999 98373
12300-12398 98374
12400-14899 98374
14901-14999 98374
122nd Ave E
801-897 98372
899-5499 98372
11700-11998 98374
12000-16799 98374
122nd Avenue Ct E 98374
122nd Avenue Ct E 98372
122nd Street Ct E 98373
122nd St E
5400-6598 98373
6600-10099 98373
10101-10199 98373
10200-15000 98374
15002-15098 98374
123rd Ave E
100-5499 98372
6300-6399 98372
11600-16999 98374
123rd Avenue Ct E 98372
123rd Avenue Ct E 98374
6000-6400 98373
10200-12799 98374
123rd St E
8200-8800 98373
8802-8998 98373
12200-13799 98374
124th Ave E
800-5499 98372
11801-13397 98374
13399-17199 98374
124th Avenue Ct E
2700-4799 98372
124th Street Ct E
5800-9499 98373
124th Avenue Ct E
5800-6199 98372

124th Street Ct E
11000-14399 98374
124th Avenue Ct E
12000-17099 98374
124th St E
6501-6797 98373
6799-9999 98373
10001-10099 98373
11101-11697 98374
11699-12599 98374
125th Ave & St 98372
125th Ave & St 98374
125th Avenue Ct E
800-4799 98372
125th Street Ct E
5800-9499 98373
125th Avenue Ct E
5800-5898 98372
125th Street Ct E
10201-10997 98374
125th Avenue Ct E
12000-15999 98374
126th Ave E
1300-4799 98372
13000-17099 98374
126th Avenue Ct E 98372
126th Avenue Ct E 98374
126th Street Ct E
8600-8699 98373
11000-12199 98374
126th St E
6200-10199 98373
11300-12399 98374
127th Ave E
4300-5199 98372
14100-15600 98374
127th Avenue Ct E 98374
127th Street Ct E
6500-7799 98373
11000-13299 98374
127th St E 98374
128th Ave E
5100-5299 98372
16200-17199 98374
128th Avenue Ct E 98374
128th Street Ct E
10100-10199 98373
11401-12399 98374
128th St E
5500-10099 98373
10101-10199 98373
10201-10497 98374
10499-15099 98374
129th Ave E
4600-4799 98372
12400-16899 98374
129th Avenue Ct E 98372
129th Avenue Ct E 98374
129th Street Ct E
8000-10199 98373
12100-12399 98374
129th St E
7601-9397 98373
9399-9499 98373
11301-13500 98374
13502-13598 98374
130th Ave E 98374
130th Avenue Ct E 98374
130th Street Ct E
6600-9999 98373
10800-13200 98374
130th St E
7301-8397 98373
8399-8599 98373
11300-11414 98374
11416-12199 98374
131st Ave E
5400-5699 98372
14500-17099 98374
131st Avenue Ct E 98372
131st Avenue Ct E 98374
131st Street Ct E
6800-9799 98373
11302-13300 98374
131st St E
6600-6799 98373
10401-10497 98374

132nd Ave E
5300-5499 98372
11800-16999 98374
132nd Avenue Ct E 98374
132nd Street Ct E
6800-9999 98373
10200-12599 98374
132nd St E
5900-9999 98373
10500-12199 98374
133rd Ave E 98374
133rd Avenue Ct E 98374
133rd Street Ct E
6800-8999 98373
10800-12699 98374
133rd St E
6600-9999 98373
11200-12199 98374
134th Ave E
6701-7297 98372
7299-7399 98372
7401-7599 98372
10600-15899 98374
134th Avenue Ct E 98374
134th Street Ct E
5700-8799 98373
11500-12699 98374
134th Ln E 98374
134th St E
6700-9999 98373
11600-11998 98374
12000-12299 98374
135th Ave E 98374
135th Avenue Ct E 98374
135th Street Ct E
6700-9910 98373
11000-12499 98374
135th Ln E 98374
135th St E
6700-9999 98373
11001-11397 98374
11399-12699 98374
136th Ave E
8400-8499 98372
10900-11198 98374
11200-17399 98374
136th Street Ct E 98373
136th Avenue Ct E 98374
136th St E
5400-5498 98373
5500-9600 98373
9602-9998 98373
10201-10297 98374
10299-12699 98374
137th Ave E 98374
137th Avenue Ct E 98374
137th Street Ct E
7400-8599 98373
10300-12599 98374
137th St E
9001-9297 98373
10300-10599 98374
138th Ave E 98374
138th Avenue Ct E 98374
138th Street Ct E
7200-7699 98373
11500-12499 98374
138th St E 98373
139th Ave E 98374
139th Street Ct E
7200-7699 98373
139th Avenue Ct E
7900-7999 98372
139th Street Ct E
10201-10297 98374
139th Avenue Ct E
17100-17299 98374
140th Ave & St 98374
140th Avenue Ct E 98374
140th Street Ct E
6900-10199 98373
10300-12599 98374
141st Ave E
7800-7999 98372
17400-17599 98374
141st Avenue Ct E 98372

141st Street Ct E
7000-7399 ... 98373
10500-12099 ... 98374
141st St E
5400-5498 ... 98373
5500-6099 ... 98373
6101-9999 ... 98373
10300-12599 ... 98374
12601-12799 ... 98374
142nd Ave E
7601-7697 ... 98372
7699-7999 ... 98372
10400-12398 ... 98374
12400-12800 ... 98374
12802-13098 ... 98374
142nd Street Ct E
7100-7399 ... 98373
142nd Avenue Ct E
8200-8399 ... 98372
142nd Street Ct E
12000-12099 ... 98374
142nd Avenue Ct E
12600-12799 ... 98374
143rd Ave E
8200-8398 ... 98372
12400-12499 ... 98374
143rd Avenue Ct E
7900-8799 ... 98372
143rd Street Ct E
8500-8599 ... 98373
10300-10599 ... 98374
143rd Avenue Ct E
12400-12499 ... 98374
143rd St E ... 98374
144th Ave E ... 98372
144th Avenue Ct E ... 98372
144th Street Ct E ... 98375
11000-11099 ... 98374
144th St E
5400-9799 ... 98375
9801-10199 ... 98375
10201-10297 ... 98374
10299-13500 ... 98374
13502-13598 ... 98374
145th Street Ct E
6800-9499 ... 98375
13700-13799 ... 98374
145th St E
8000-8099 ... 98375
11800-13399 ... 98374
146th Ave E ... 98372
146th Avenue Ct E ... 98372
146th Street Ct E ... 98375
12000-13799 ... 98374
146th St E
8100-8199 ... 98375
10201-12497 ... 98374
147th Avenue Ct E ... 98372
147th Street Ct E ... 98375
147th Street Ct E ... 98375
12000-12399 ... 98374
147th St E
6000-9399 ... 98375
9401-9599 ... 98375
10301-10697 ... 98374
148th Ave E ... 98372
148th Avenue Ct E ... 98372
148th Street Ct E ... 98375
148th Street Ct E ... 98375
10300-10599 ... 98374
148th St E
7000-7499 ... 98375
11000-12899 ... 98374
149th Avenue Ct E ... 98374
149th Street Ct E ... 98375
10300-11500 ... 98374
149th St E
7000-10000 ... 98375
10200-13707 ... 98374
150th Ave E ... 98374
150th Street Ct E
5600-9599 ... 98375
150th Avenue Ct E
8500-8798 ... 98372
10300-10399 ... 98374
150th Street Ct E
10300-12099 ... 98374

150th St E
7000-9299 ... 98375
10800-12199 ... 98374
151st Ave E ... 98374
151st Street Ct E ... 98375
151st Avenue Ct E ... 98374
151st Street Ct E
12000-12199 ... 98374
151st St E
7900-9499 ... 98375
10900-13199 ... 98374
152nd Ave E ... 98372
152nd Street Ct E
6600-8199 ... 98375
10800-13599 ... 98374
152nd St E
5401-5597 ... 98375
10200-13599 ... 98374
153rd Ave E ... 98372
153rd Street Ct E
6600-9999 ... 98375
10400-11999 ... 98374
153rd St E
7601-8397 ... 98375
12000-12699 ... 98374
154th Avenue Ct E ... 98374
154th Street Ct E ... 98375
11000-11999 ... 98374
154th St E
7400-8599 ... 98375
12601-12697 ... 98374
155th Street Ct E ... 98375
11800-12399 ... 98374
155th St E ... 98375
156th Street Ct E
5900-8899 ... 98375
11800-13599 ... 98374
156th St E
6701-9497 ... 98375
9499-10099 ... 98375
10200-10599 ... 98374
157th Ave E ... 98372
157th Street Ct E
5800-5898 ... 98375
5900-8799 ... 98375
10300-13599 ... 98374
157th St E ... 98375
158th Street Ct E ... 98375
158th Avenue Ct E ... 98372
158th Street Ct E
12100-13599 ... 98374
158th St E ... 98375
159th Ave E
8200-8299 ... 98372
10800-10898 ... 98374
10900-11000 ... 98374
11002-18098 ... 98374
159th Street Ct E
7600-9799 ... 98375
13400-13599 ... 98374
159th Pl E ... 98375
159th St E
6600-9199 ... 98375
11800-13199 ... 98374
160th Street Ct E
7000-9599 ... 98375
10200-12310 ... 98374
160th St E
5401-5697 ... 98375
5699-10099 ... 98375
10426-11798 ... 98374
161st Street Ct E
5700-9799 ... 98375
13200-13399 ... 98374
161st St E
5500-5798 ... 98375
11800-12199 ... 98374
162nd Street Ct E
5800-10099 ... 98375
11200-13799 ... 98374
162nd St E
6000-7799 ... 98375
11800-11999 ... 98374
163rd Street Ct E ... 98375
11800-13399 ... 98374
163rd St E ... 98375

164th Street Ct E
8400-8811 ... 98375
13200-13899 ... 98374
164th St E
6800-9799 ... 98375
11200-13199 ... 98374
16400-16499 ... 98375
165th Street Ct E
7900-9799 ... 98375
13600-13699 ... 98374
165th St E
9000-9099 ... 98375
13200-13699 ... 98374
166th Street Ct E
8409-9799 ... 98375
12000-12999 ... 98374
166th St E
7401-7497 ... 98375
7499-9700 ... 98375
9702-9798 ... 98375
12000-13399 ... 98374
167th Street Ct E
8400-10199 ... 98375
12700-12999 ... 98374
167th St E
6601-7297 ... 98375
7299-7399 ... 98375
13200-13599 ... 98374
168th Street Ct E
8700-9699 ... 98375
12800-13799 ... 98374
168th St E
9900-9999 ... 98375
12000-13015 ... 98374
169th Street Ct E
8800-9099 ... 98375
11600-13599 ... 98374
169th St E
8700-9499 ... 98375
13400-13599 ... 98374
170th Street Ct E
8900-10099 ... 98375
12800-12999 ... 98374
170th St E
7000-9299 ... 98375
12000-13899 ... 98374
171st Street Ct E
8500-10199 ... 98375
12800-12999 ... 98374
171st St E
9300-9499 ... 98375
11100-13899 ... 98374
172nd Street Ct E
8400-9399 ... 98375
11500-14099 ... 98374
172nd Pl E ... 98374
172nd St E
8700-9399 ... 98375
10400-13499 ... 98374
172nd Street St E
13900-13998 ... 98374
173rd Street Ct E ... 98375
173rd St E
8200-8799 ... 98375
11700-13699 ... 98374
174th Street Ct E
7800-9099 ... 98375
13500-14199 ... 98374
174th St E ... 98375
11600-13599 ... 98374
175th Street Ct E ... 98375
13600-13699 ... 98374
175th St E ... 98374
176th Street Ct E ... 98375
176th Pl E ... 98375
176th St E
5400-9599 ... 98375
13800-14199 ... 98374
177th Street Ct E ... 98375
177th St E ... 98375
178th Street Ct E ... 98375
178th St E ... 98375
179th Street Ct E ... 98375
179th St E ... 98375
180th Street Ct E ... 98375
180th St E ... 98375

181st Street Ct E
7600-9699 ... 98375
11100-11299 ... 98374
181st St E ... 98375
11800-12099 ... 98374
182nd Street Ct E ... 98375
182nd St E
7400-8899 ... 98375
11100-11999 ... 98374
183rd Street Ct E ... 98375
183rd St E ... 98375
11300-12099 ... 98374
184th Street Ct E
7000-8799 ... 98375
11400-11499 ... 98374
184th St E ... 98375
11100-12899 ... 98374
185th Street Ct E
7800-9599 ... 98375
11500-11699 ... 98374
185th St E
9400-9999 ... 98375
11100-12099 ... 98374
186th Street Ct E
7600-9699 ... 98375
11200-11299 ... 98374
186th Pl E ... 98375
186th St E
2000-10199 ... 98375
11400-11499 ... 98374
187th Street Ct E ... 98375
187th St E
9400-9600 ... 98375
9602-10098 ... 98375
10400-11299 ... 98374
188th Street Ct E
7000-8799 ... 98375
10200-10299 ... 98374
188th St E ... 98375
10301-11699 ... 98374
189th Street Ct E
7000-9699 ... 98375
10201-10299 ... 98374
189th St E
5400-10099 ... 98375
11200-11799 ... 98374
190th Street Ct E ... 98375
10301-10399 ... 98374
190th St E ... 98375
191st Street Ct E ... 98375
191st St E ... 98375

REDMOND WA

General Delivery ... 98052

POST OFFICE BOXES MAIN OFFICE STATIONS AND BRANCHES

Box No.s
All PO Boxes ... 98073

NAMED STREETS

NE Adair Rd ... 98053
Adair Creek Way NE ... 98053
Alder Crest Dr & Ln ... 98053
E, W & NE Ames Lake Dr, Ln & Rd NE ... 98053
Ames Lake Carnation Rd NE ... 98053
Avondale Pl, Rd & Way NE ... 98052
Bear Creek Pkwy ... 98052
Bel Red Rd ... 98052
Big Leaf Way NE ... 98053
Brown St ... 98052
NE Cascara Cir ... 98053
NE Cedar Park Cres NE ... 98053
Cleveland St ... 98052
Dave Rd ... 98052
NE Devon Way ... 98053
Eastridge Dr & Ln ... 98053
Elliston Way NE ... 98053
Ferianco Ave NE ... 98053
NE Fern Reach Cir ... 98053
Gilman St ... 98052
NE Greens Crossing Rd ... 98053
E & W Lake Sammamish Pkwy ... 98052
NE Leary Way NE ... 98052
Mahonia Pl NE ... 98053
E Main St ... 98053
NE Marketplace Dr ... 98053
Microsoft Way ... 98052
Morgan Dr NE ... 98053
Muirwood Way NE ... 98053
NE Novelty Hill Rd
18600-18899 ... 98052
19100-23599 ... 98053
Old Redmond Rd ... 98052
NE Patterson Way ... 98053
Quail Creek Dr & Way NE ... 98053
NE Redmond Rd ... 98053
Redmond Way ... 98052
Redmond Fall City Rd NE ... 98053
Redmond Ridge Dr NE ... 98053
Redmond Woodinville Rd NE ... 98052
NE Salal Pl ... 98053
Sheridan Cres NE ... 98053
Sunbreak Way NE ... 98053
Trilogy Pkwy NE ... 98053
NE Twinberry Way ... 98053
NE Union Hill Rd
17401-17497 ... 98052
17499-18300 ... 98052
18302-18702 ... 98053
19100-28099 ... 98053
NE Vine Maple Way ... 98053
Wasteri Ave NE ... 98052
E Whidbey Ave ... 98052
Willows Rd NE ... 98052
Woodinville Redmond Rd NE ... 98052

NUMBERED STREETS

NE 1st St ... 98053
NE 4th Pl ... 98053
NE 5th St ... 98053
NE 9th St ... 98074
NE 10th St ... 98074
NE & SE 11th Pl & St ... 98074
NE 15th St ... 98053
NE 16th St ... 98074
NE 17th St ... 98053
NE 18th St ... 98074
NE 19th St ... 98074
20th Ct, Pl & St ... 98052
NE 21st St ... 98052
NE 22nd Ct ... 98052
NE 22nd St
17300-18199 ... 98052
24400-24699 ... 98074
27400-27499 ... 98053
NE 22nd Way ... 98052
NE 23rd Ct ... 98052
NE 23rd St
18100-18199 ... 98052
26800-27099 ... 98053
NE 24th St
14333-14797 ... 98052
14799-18799 ... 98052
26001-26097 ... 98053
26099-26699 ... 98053
NE 25th Ct ... 98052
NE 25th St
17800-18699 ... 98052
25800-26399 ... 98053
NE 25th Way ... 98052
NE 26th Ct
17200-17399 ... 98052
24200-24399 ... 98074
NE 26th St
17700-18599 ... 98052
24400-24799 ... 98074
27900-27999 ... 98053
NE 26th Way ... 98052
NE 27th Ct ... 98052
NE 27th Dr ... 98053
NE 27th Pl ... 98074
NE 27th St ... 98052
NE 27th Way ... 98052
NE 28th Ct ... 98053
NE 28th St ... 98052
NE 29th Ct ... 98053
NE 29th Pl ... 98053
NE 29th St ... 98052
NE 30th Ct ... 98053
NE 30th Pl ... 98052
NE 30th St
18000-18199 ... 98052
27700-27899 ... 98053
NE 30th Way ... 98053
NE 31st Cir ... 98052
NE 31st Ct
17300-17599 ... 98052
27500-27599 ... 98053
NE 31st Pl
17600-17699 ... 98052
27200-27299 ... 98053
NE 31st St ... 98052
NE 31st Way ... 98052
NE 32nd St
17200-17299 ... 98052
25900-25999 ... 98053
NE 33rd Ct ... 98052
NE 33rd Pl ... 98052
NE 33rd St
17200-18099 ... 98052
27800-28099 ... 98053
NE 34th Ct
16600-17699 ... 98052
28900-28999 ... 98053
NE 34th St
17200-17899 ... 98052
22500-25898 ... 98053
25900-27799 ... 98053
NE 35th Ct ... 98052
NE 35th Pl ... 98052
NE 35th St ... 98053
36th Ct, St & Way ... 98052
NE 37th St
16500-16799 ... 98052
27700-27799 ... 98053
38th Ct & St ... 98052
NE 39th Ct ... 98052
NE 39th St ... 98052
NE 39th Way
16600-16699 ... 98052
22400-25899 ... 98053
NE 40th Ct ... 98052
NE 40th Pl ... 98052
NE 40th St
14901-15117 ... 98052
15119-17599 ... 98052
26000-28299 ... 98053
NE 40th Way ... 98053
NE 41st Ct ... 98052
NE 41st Ln ... 98053
NE 41st Pl ... 98053
NE 41st St ... 98052
NE 42nd Ct ... 98052
NE 42nd Pl ... 98053
NE 42nd St
15900-17399 ... 98052
17401-19599 ... 98052
22800-22899 ... 98053
22901-22999 ... 98053
NE 43rd Ct ... 98052
NE 43rd St ... 98053
NE 43rd Ter ... 98052
NE 44th Ct ... 98053
NE 44th St ... 98053
NE 44th Way ... 98052
NE 45th Ct
16200-16299 ... 98052
25000-25099 ... 98053
NE 45th Pl ... 98053
NE 45th St
15300-17499 ... 98052
24000-27699 ... 98053
NE 46th Ct ... 98052
NE 46th St
16200-16298 ... 98052
22200-22999 ... 98053
NE 47th Ct
15800-15899 ... 98052
25100-25199 ... 98053
NE 47th Pl ... 98053
NE 47th St
16600-16699 ... 98052
22800-28099 ... 98053
48th Ct & St ... 98052
NE 49th Ct ... 98052
NE 49th St
15800-15899 ... 98052
27700-28099 ... 98053
NE 50th Ct ... 98052
NE 50th St
16200-16298 ... 98052
16300-16599 ... 98052
19600-27199 ... 98053
NE 50th Way ... 98052
NE 51st Ct ... 98053
NE 51st St
15200-16353 ... 98052
22800-26499 ... 98053
NE 52nd Pl ... 98053
NE 52nd St ... 98052
NE 53rd Pl
15500-15599 ... 98052
24000-24099 ... 98053
NE 53rd St
15600-18699 ... 98052
26400-27599 ... 98053
NE 54th Pl
15400-15599 ... 98052
23600-26399 ... 98053
NE 54th St ... 98053
NE 54th Way ... 98052
NE 55th Pl ... 98053
NE 55th St ... 98052
NE 55th Way ... 98052
NE 56th Ct ... 98052
NE 56th St ... 98053
NE 56th Way ... 98052
NE 57th Ct ... 98053
NE 57th St
5100-18621 ... 98052
18623-18633 ... 98052
22800-23199 ... 98053
NE 57th Way ... 98052
NE 58th Ct ... 98052
NE 58th Pl ... 98053
NE 58th St ... 98053
NE 59th Ct ... 98052
NE 59th Ln ... 98053
NE 59th St ... 98052
NE 59th Way ... 98052
NE 60th Ct ... 98052
NE 60th Pl ... 98053
NE 60th St
13700-15599 ... 98052
22100-22799 ... 98053
NE 60th Way ... 98052
NE 61st Ct
14700-18699 ... 98052
20300-20399 ... 98053
NE 61st Ln ... 98053
NE 61st Pl
14800-14899 ... 98052
19600-19899 ... 98053
NE 61st St
14000-15899 ... 98052
21000-23899 ... 98053
NE 61st Way ... 98052
NE 62nd Ct ... 98052
NE 62nd Pl ... 98053
NE 62nd St
14000-14299 ... 98052
25100-25599 ... 98053
NE 62nd Way ... 98052
NE 63rd Ct ... 98052
NE 63rd Pl ... 98053
NE 63rd St ... 98053

NE 63rd Way 98052
NE 64th Ct
14200-15399 98052
24000-24099 98053
NE 64th Pl 98053
NE 64th St
14400-15099 98052
22700-23299 98053
NE 64th Way 98052
NE 65th Ct 98052
NE 65th Pl 98053
NE 65th St 98052
NE 65th Way 98052
NE 66th Ct
14400-15399 98052
20400-20499 98053
NE 66th Pl
15700-15899 98052
20600-22299 98053
NE 66th St
13800-15099 98052
20500-21199 98053
NE 66th Way 98052
NE 67th Ct 98052
NE 67th Pl
15100-15899 98052
24500-25799 98053
NE 67th St
14800-14899 98052
20800-21699 98053
NE 67th Way 98052
NE 68th Ct
15500-15599 98052
21400-21499 98053
NE 68th St
14800-19099 98052
20400-20799 98053
NE 68th Way 98052
NE 69th Ct 98053
NE 69th Pl
14000-14099 98052
23900-23999 98053
NE 69th St
13600-13899 98052
21800-21899 98053
NE 69th Way 98052
NE 70th Ct 98052
NE 70th Pl
13700-13999 98052
20700-20799 98053
NE 70th St
13201-13297 98052
13299-17699 98052
21700-26500 98053
26502-26598 98053
NE 71st Ct 98052
NE 71st Pl 98052
NE 71st St
14100-14399 98052
20400-23399 98053
NE 72nd Ct 98052
NE 72nd Pl
13700-14199 98052
23000-23599 98053
NE 72nd St
13300-15299 98052
23500-24699 98053
NE 72nd Way 98052
NE 73rd Ct 98052
NE 73rd Pl
13700-13999 98052
21600-21799 98053
NE 73rd St
13300-18799 98052
21900-23499 98053
NE 73rd Way 98052
NE 74th Ct 98052
NE 74th Pl 98053
NE 74th St
13300-16699 98052
22800-22999 98053
NE 74th Way 98052
NE 75th Ct 98052
NE 75th Pl
13700-13799 98052
20600-20699 98053
NE 75th St
13200-14899 98052
22000-23798 98053
23800-24199 98053
NE 76th Ct 98052
NE 76th Pl
13700-13799 98052
20600-20699 98053
NE 76th St
13400-18499 98052
21600-25999 98053
NE 77th Ct 98052
NE 77th Pl
13700-13799 98052
24400-24599 98053
NE 77th St
13300-14599 98052
20900-23099 98053
NE 78th Ct 98052
NE 78th Pl 98052
NE 78th St 98053
NE 78th Way
14800-14899 98052
23201-23297 98053
23299-23699 98053
NE 79th St
16400-16999 98052
20600-22799 98053
NE 80th Pl 98052
NE 80th St
13200-13298 98052
19200-26099 98053
NE 81st Ct 98052
NE 81st St
13700-16399 98052
21300-23099 98053
NE 81st Way 98052
NE 82nd Ct 98052
NE 82nd Pl 98053
NE 82nd St
15000-16999 98052
23000-23099 98053
83rd Ct, St & Way 98052
84th Ct NE
14000-14099 98052
13600-16999 98052
NE 84th Pl 98053
NE 84th St
13400-18899 98052
19000-21899 98053
NE 84th Way 98052
NE 85th Ct 98052
NE 85th Pl 98052
NE 85th St
13200-16200 98052
16135-16135 98073
16201-16699 98052
16202-16698 98052
19900-25799 98053
NE 86th Ct 98052
NE 86th Pl 98052
NE 86th St 98053
NE 87th Pl 98053
NE 87th St 98052
88th Pl & St 98052
NE 89th Ct 98052
NE 89th Pl 98053
NE 89th St
13200-16899 98052
20800-23699 98053
NE 90th Ct 98052
NE 90th Pl 98053
NE 90th St
14900-17999 98052
20600-20799 98053
NE 90th Way 98052
NE 91st Ct 98052
NE 91st Pl 98052
NE 91st St
14500-18299 98052
20800-21099 98053
NE 91st Way
15600-16099 98052
22500-22799 98053
NE 92nd Ct 98052
NE 92nd Pl 98053
NE 92nd St
15100-17199 98052
21000-22599 98053
NE 92nd Way 98052
NE 93rd Ct 98052
NE 93rd Pl 98053
NE 93rd St
13200-13799 98052
22100-22999 98053
NE 93rd Way 98052
NE 94th Ct 98052
NE 94th St 98052
NE 94th Way
16000-16099 98052
22700-22799 98053
NE 95th Ct 98052
NE 95th St
14500-18999 98052
19000-19499 98053
NE 95th Way 98052
NE 96th Ct 98052
NE 96th Pl
15300-17199 98052
24100-24299 98053
NE 96th St 98053
NE 96th Way 98052
NE 97th Ct 98052
NE 97th Pl
16000-16599 98052
21000-22999 98053
NE 97th St 98052
NE 97th Way 98052
NE 98th Ct 98052
NE 98th Pl
16700-18399 98052
22500-24199 98053
NE 98th St
15900-16399 98052
22300-22399 98053
NE 98th Way 98052
NE 99th Ct 98052
NE 99th St 98052
NE 99th Way
15600-18399 98052
22500-22599 98053
NE 100th Ct 98052
NE 100th Pl
16900-17099 98052
22800-22899 98053
NE 100th St
16100-17099 98052
23900-25699 98053
NE 100th Way
15600-15799 98052
22300-22599 98053
NE 101st Ct
15600-18399 98052
21300-24398 98053
NE 101st Pl
16000-17099 98052
22300-23999 98053
NE 101st St
16000-16099 98052
21500-22499 98053
NE 102nd Ct 98052
NE 102nd Pl
16700-16799 98052
22400-23999 98053
NE 102nd St 98053
NE 102nd Way 98052
NE 103rd Ct
15600-18399 98052
21300-21399 98053
NE 103rd Pl
16700-16799 98052
23500-23899 98053
NE 103rd St
16000-18999 98052
19000-21999 98053
NE 103rd Way 98052
NE 104th Ct 98052
NE 104th Pl 98053
NE 104th St 98052
NE 104th Way 98052
NE 105th Ct 98052
NE 105th Pl
16400-16599 98052
21700-21799 98053
NE 105th St 98052
NE 105th Way 98052
NE 106th Ct 98052
NE 106th Pl
16400-16499 98052
19800-19899 98053
NE 106th St 98052
NE 106th Way 98052
NE 107th Ct 98052
NE 107th Ln 98053
NE 107th Pl 98052
NE 107th St
15400-18399 98052
20401-20499 98053
NE 107th Way 98052
NE 108th Ct 98052
NE 108th Pl
15100-16699 98052
23700-23799 98053
NE 108th St
13200-13398 98052
13400-13499 98052
20300-25499 98053
NE 108th Way 98052
NE 109th Ct
17800-18099 98052
23600-23699 98053
NE 109th Pl
13200-13299 98052
23700-23799 98053
NE 109th St
15600-18999 98052
24600-24699 98053
NE 109th Way 98052
NE 110th Ct 98052
NE 110th Pl
15100-15399 98052
23600-23699 98053
NE 110th St
15600-18299 98052
24200-24299 98053
NE 110th Way
17000-18199 98052
23500-23699 98053
NE 111th Ct 98052
NE 111th Pl 98053
NE 111th St
15700-18399 98052
23500-23699 98053
NE 111th Way 98052
NE 112th Cir 98053
NE 112th Ct 98052
NE 112th Ln 98053
NE 112th Pl
13200-13399 98052
23900-23999 98053
NE 112th St
15600-16199 98052
20700-20899 98053
NE 112th Ter 98053
NE 112th Way 98052
NE 113th Ct 98052
NE 113th Ln 98053
NE 113th Pl 98053
NE 113th St
16500-18399 98052
19301-19397 98053
19399-19599 98053
NE 113th Way 98052
NE 114th Ct 98052
NE 114th St
13200-13299 98052
20900-24099 98053
NE 115th Ct 98052
NE 115th Ln 98053
NE 115th St 98053
NE 115th Way 98052
NE 116th Ct 98052
NE 116th Pl 98053
NE 116th St
14500-15198 98052
15200-18899 98052
19200-20899 98053
NE 116th Way 98052
NE 117th Ct 98052
NE 117th St
15700-17199 98052
20900-21099 98053
NE 117th Way 98052
NE 118th Ct 98052
NE 118th Pl 98053
NE 118th St 98053
NE 118th Way 98052
119th Ct & Way 98052
NE 120th Pl 98053
NE 120th St
15700-17200 98052
17202-18998 98052
19400-20398 98053
20400-20799 98053
NE 120th Way 98052
121st Ct, St & Way 98052
NE 122nd Ct
16900-17799 98052
23500-23599 98053
NE 122nd St
16400-17799 98052
20500-24199 98053
NE 123rd Ln 98053
NE 123rd St
16900-18099 98052
23100-23299 98053
NE 123rd Way 98053
NE 124th Pl 98053
NE 124th St 98052
NE 124th Ter 98053
NE 125th St 98052
NE 126th Ct 98052
NE 126th Pl
12600-12699 98053
17100-17499 98052
23800-23899 98053
NE 126th St 98053
NE 127th Pl 98053
NE 127th St
17600-19299 98052
23700-23999 98053
NE 127th Way 98053
NE 128th Pl
17600-17799 98052
22800-23199 98053
NE 128th St 98052
NE 128th Way 98052
NE 129th Ct
17000-17099 98052
23400-23499 98053
NE 129th Pl
17600-18199 98052
22800-22899 98053
NE 129th St 98052
NE 130th Ct 98052
NE 130th Pl
18100-18199 98052
24200-24299 98053
NE 130th St
16200-19199 98052
22800-23099 98053
NE 131st Pl
16900-17799 98052
23400-23499 98053
NE 131st St 98052
NE 131st Ter 98053
132nd Ave NE 98052
132nd Ct NE 98052
132nd Pl NE
6900-11999 98052
17200-17299 98052
22800-22999 98053
NE 132nd St
15701-16397 98052
16399-18699 98052
18701-18799 98052
22800-22999 98053
133rd Ave NE 98052
133rd Ct NE
6900-9299 98052
16400-16499 98052
NE 133rd Pl
17200-17299 98052
22900-22999 98053
NE 133rd St 98052
134th Ave NE 98052
134th Ct NE 98052
134th Pl NE
8100-11799 98052
16500-17899 98052
23700-23799 98053
NE 134th St
15700-15799 98052
23700-23799 98053
135th Ave NE 98052
135th Ct NE
6700-6899 98052
17000-17099 98052
135th Pl NE
7500-9499 98052
22900-22999 98053
NE 135th St 98052
NE 135th Way 98053
136th Pl & St 98052
NE 137th Ave, Ct, Pl &
St NE 98052
138th Ave NE 98052
138th Ct NE
8300-9399 98052
17800-17899 98052
22800-22899 98053
138th Ln NE 98052
138th Pl NE
7100-7799 98052
15300-18199 98052
NE 138th St 98052
139th Ave NE 98052
139th Ct NE
9300-9399 98052
17700-17799 98052
23000-23099 98053
139th Pl NE
6300-11599 98052
17400-17499 98052
NE 139th St 98052
NE 140th Ave, Ct, Pl &
St NE 98052
NE 141st Ave, Ct, Pl &
St NE 98052
NE 142nd Ave, Ct, Pl &
St NE 98052
NE 143rd Ave, Ct, Pl &
St NE 98052
NE 144th Ave & St
NE 98052
145th Ave & Ct 98052
146th Ave & Ct 98052
147th Ave, Ct & Pl 98052
148th Ave, Ct & Pl 98052
149th Ave, Ct, Pl & Way
NE 98052
150th Ave & Ct 98052
151st Ave, Ct & Pl 98052
152nd Ave & Ct 98052
153rd Ave & Ct 98052
154th Ave & Pl 98052
155th Ave & Pl 98052
156th Ave, Ct, Dr, Ln &
Pl NE 98052
157th Ave, Ct, Dr & Pl
NE 98052
158th Ave, Ct, Pl, St &
Way NE 98052
159th Ave, Ct & Pl 98052
160th Ave, Ct & Way 98052
161st Ave, Ct & Pl 98052
162nd Ave, Ct & Pl 98052
163rd Ave, Ct & Pl 98052
164th Ave, Ct & Pl 98052
165th Ave, Ct, Ln & Pl
NE 98052
166th Ave, Ct & Pl 98052
167th Ave, Ct & Pl 98052
168th Ave, Ct & Pl 98052
169th Ave, Ct & Pl 98052
170th Ave, Ct & Pl 98052
171st Ave, Ct & Pl 98052
172nd Ave, Ct & Pl 98052
173rd Ave, Ct & Pl 98052
174th Ave, Ct & Pl 98052
175th Ave, Ct & Pl 98052
176th Ave, Cir, Ct & Pl
NE 98052
177th Ave, Ct & Pl 98052
178th Ave, Ct & Pl 98052
179th Ave, Ct & Pl 98052
180th Ave, Ct, Ln & Pl
NE 98052
181st Ave, Ct, Ln & Pl
NE 98052
182nd Ave, Ct & Pl 98052
183rd Ave, Ct & Pl 98052
184th Ave, Ct & Pl 98052
185th Ave NE
2400-7300 98052
7241-7241 98073
7302-7798 98052
7501-7799 98052
185th Ct NE 98052
185th Pl NE 98052
186th Ave, Ct & Pl 98052
187th Ave, Ct & Pl 98052
188th Ln & Pl 98052
189th Ct & Pl 98052
190th Ave NE 98052
191st Pl NE 98052
192nd Ave NE 98053
192nd Pl NE
5001-5097 98074
5099-5100 98074
5102-5398 98074
6400-6799 98052
193rd Pl NE 98052
194th Ave NE 98053
194th Pl NE 98052
195th Ave NE 98053
195th Pl NE 98052
196th Ave NE 98053
197th Ct NE 98053
198th Ave NE 98053
199th Ave NE 98053
200th Ave NE 98053
201st Pl NE 98053
203rd Ave NE 98053
204th Ave, Dr & Pl 98053
205th Ave NE 98053
206th Ave & Pl 98053
207th Ave & Pl 98053
208th Ave & Ct 98053
209th Ave NE 98053
210th Ave & Pl 98053
211th Ave & Pl 98053
212th Ave NE 98053
213th Ave & Pl 98053
SE 214th Ave & Ct
NE 98053
215th Ave, Ct & Pl 98053
216th Ave, Ct & Pl 98053
217th Ave, Ct & Pl 98053
218th Ave, Ct & Pl 98053
219th Ave, Ct & Pl 98053
220th Ave & Pl 98053
221st Ave, Ln & Pl 98053
222nd Ave & Ct 98053
223rd Ave & Pl 98053
224th Ave, Ct & Pl 98053
225th Ave, Ct, Ter &
Way NE 98053
226th Ave & Pl 98053
227th Ave, Pl & Way 98053
228th Ave, Pl, Ter &
Way NE 98053
229th Ave, Dr, Ln & Pl
NE 98053
230th Ave, Pl & Way 98053
231st Ave, Ln, Pl & Way
NE 98053
232nd Ave, Pl, Ter &
Way NE 98053
233rd Ave & Pl 98053
234th Ave, Ct & Pl 98053
235th Ave & Pl 98053
236th Ave & Pl 98053
237th Ave, Pl & Way 98053
238th Ave, Pl & Ter 98053
239th Ave, Ln, Pl & Way
NE 98053
240th Ave, Ct, Pl, Ter &
Way NE 98053

241st Ln, Pl & Ter 98053
242nd Ave, Pl & Way .. 98053
243rd Ave, Ct, Pl & Ter NE 98053
244th Ave NE 98074
244th Ave NE 98074
244th Ave NE 98074
4000-11400 98053
11402-11598 98053
244th Pl NE
2400-2499 98074
6700-9999 98053
245th Ave NE
1100-1199 98074
5300-5699 98053
245th Pl NE
600-2499 98074
5800-5999 98053
245th Way NE 98053
246th Ave NE 98053
246th Ln NE 98053
246th Pl NE
2200-2499 98074
5800-5899 98053
247th Ave NE 98053
247th Ct NE 98074
247th Pl NE 98074
248th Ave NE 98053
248th Pl NE 98074
248th Ter NE 98074
249th Ct NE 98053
250th Ave NE
800-1599 98074
8100-10999 98053
250th Ln NE 98074
250th Pl NE 98074
251st Ave, Ct & Way ... 98053
252nd Ave & Pl 98053
254th Ave NE 98074
4101-4197 98053
255th Ave NE 98053
256th Ave NE 98053
258th Ave NE 98053
259th Ave, Pl & Way ... 98053
260th Ave NE 98053
261st Ave & Ct 98053
262nd Ave NE 98053
263rd Ct NE 98053
264th Ave & Ct 98053
265th Ave NE 98053
266th Ave NE 98053
268th Ave NE 98053
269th Ave NE 98053
270th Ave NE 98053
272nd Ave NE 98053
273rd Ave NE 98053
274th Ave NE 98053
275th Way NE 98053
276th Ave & Ct 98053
277th Ave & Pl 98053
278th Ave & Pl 98053
279th Ave & Ct 98053
280th Ave, Ln & Pl 98053
281st Ave & Pl 98053
288th Ave NE 98053
289th Ave NE 98053
290th Way NE 98053

RENTON WA

General Delivery 98058

POST OFFICE BOXES MAIN OFFICE STATIONS AND BRANCHES

Box No.s
1 - 1996 98057
2001 - 3558 98056
4001 - 9811 98057
50010 - 50010 98058
56990 - 56990 98059
58001 - 60274 98058

NAMED STREETS

Aberdeen Ave NE 98056
Aberdeen Ave SE 98055
Aberdeen Ct SE 98055
Aberdeen Pl NE 98056
Aberdeen Pl SE 98055
Airport Way 98057
Anacortes Ave, Ct & Pl N, NE & SE 98059
Beacon Way S 98057
Beacon Way SE 98058
Benson Dr & Rd 98055
Birch Dr 98058
Blaine Ave NE 98056
Blaine Ave SE 98055
Blaine Cir SE 98055
Blaine Ct NE 98056
Blaine Ct SE
200-259 98056
1600-1699 98055
Blaine Dr SE 98056
Bremerton Ave, Ct & Pl NE & SE 98059
Bronson Pl NE 98056
Bronson Way N 98057
Bronson Way NE 98056
Bronson Way S 98057
N Brooks St 98057
Burnett Ave N
200-400 98057
402-598 98057
2800-3500 98056
3502-3598 98056
Burnett Ave S
1-97 98057
99-699 98057
1800-1899 98055
Burnett Ct S 98055
Burnett Pl S
1-99 98057
101-199 98057
2100-2199 98055
Camas Ave NE 98056
Camas Ave SE 98056
Camas Cir SE 98055
Camas Ct SE 98055
Camas Pl NE 98056
Capri Ave NE 98056
S & SE Carr Rd 98055
Cedar Ave S
300-899 98057
2600-3199 98055
3201-3599 98055
SE Cedar Mountain Pl .. 98058
Chelan Ave, Ct & Pl NE & SE 98059
Coal Creek Pkwy SE ... 98059
Dansou Ave NE 98056
Davis Ave & Pl 98055
Dayton Ave NE 98056
Dayton Ave SE 98056
Dayton Ct NE 98056
Dayton Ct SE 98055
Dayton Dr SE 98055
Dayton Pl NE 98056
Duvall Ave & Pl 98059
Eagle Ln S 98055
Eagle Ridge Dr S 98055
Earlington Ave SW 98057
Edmonds Ave NE 98056
Edmonds Ave SE
200-399 98056
1701-1709 98058
1711-1899 98058
1901-2207 98058
Edmonds Ct NE 98056
Edmonds Ct SE 98058
Edmonds Dr SE 98055
Edmonds Pl NE 98056
Edmonds Way SE 98058
Elma Ave, Ct & Pl NE & SE 98059
Factory Ave & Pl 98057
SE Fairwood Blvd 98058
Ferndale Ave NE 98056
Ferndale Ave SE
100-399 98056
1500-1899 98058
Ferndale Cir NE 98056
Ferndale Ct NE 98056
Ferndale Pl NE 98056
Field Ave & Pl 98059
Garden Ave N
101-197 98057
199-1099 98057
3100-3198 98056
Garden Ct N 98056
Glennwood Ave, Ct & Pl NE & SE 98056
Glennwood Ave SE 98058
S & SW Grady Way 98057
Graham Ave NE 98059
Grandey Way NE 98056
Grant Ave S
500-1099 98057
1200-1900 98055
1902-2098 98055
Hardie Ave NW & SW .. 98057
Harrington Ave NE 98056
Harrington Ave SE
200-298 98056
300-399 98056
1300-1632 98058
1634-1698 98058
Harrington Cir NE 98056
Harrington Ct SE 98056
Harrington Pl NE 98056
Harrington Pl SE 98058
Hayes Pl SW 98057
High Ave NE 98056
High Ave S 98057
Hillcrest Ln NE 98056
Hoquiam Ave, Ct & Pl NE & SE 98059
Houser Way N & S 98057
Ilwaco Ave & Pl 98059
Index Ave NE 98056
Index Ave SE
100-198 98056
200-399 98056
1400-1699 98058
Index Ct NE 98056
Index Ct SE 98058
Index Pl NE 98056
Index Pl SE 98056
Jefferson Ave NE 98056
Jefferson Ct SE 98058
Jericho Ave & Pl 98059
Jones Ave NE 98056
Jones Ave S
701-1099 98057
2401-2699 98055
Jones Cir SE 98055
Jones Ct SE 98055
Jones Dr SE 98055
Jones Pl SE
2100-2299 98055
14600-15099 98058
SE Jones Rd 98058
Kennewick Ave NE 98056
Kennewick Ave S 98055
Kennewick Cir SE 98055
Kennewick Ct SE 98055
Kennewick Pl NE 98056
Kirkland Ave NE 98056
Kirkland Ave SE
300-399 98056
1000-1899 98058
Kirkland Ct SE 98058
Kirkland Pl NE 98056
Kirkland Pl SE 98056
Kitsap Ave & Pl 98059
Lake Ave S
100-198 98057
1500-5006 98055
5008-5012 98055
Lake Pl S 98055
W & E Lake Desire Ct & Dr SE 98058
E & W Lake Kathleen Dr & Rd SE 98059
Lake Washington Blvd N 98056
SE Lake Youngs Ct, Rd & Way SE 98058
N Landing Way 98057
Langston Pl & Rd 98057
SE Licorice Way 98059
Lincoln Ave NE 98056
Lincoln Ave SE 98057
Lincoln Cir SE 98055
Lincoln Ct NE 98056
Lincoln Ct SE 98055
Lincoln Dr NE 98056
Lincoln Pl NE 98056
Lincoln Pl SE 98055
Lind Ave NW & SW 98057
Logan Ave S 98057
Lynnwood Ave NE 98056
Lynnwood Ave SE 98056
Lynnwood Ct SE 98058
Lyons Ave & Pl 98059
Main Ave S
100-399 98057
401-599 98057
901-3097 98055
3099-4999 98055
Main Ct S 98055
Maple Ave NW 98057
Maple Ave SW 98057
Maple Dr 98058
Maple Valley Hwy
1701-1797 98057
1799-1899 98057
1901-2499 98057
2501-2897 98058
2899-16499 98058
N Marion St 98057
SE May Creek Park Dr 98056
SE May Valley Rd 98059
Meadow Ave N
100-399 98057
2201-2397 98056
2399-4099 98056
Meadow Pl N 98056
Mill Ave S
100-300 98057
302-698 98057
2500-3699 98055
3701-3899 98055
Mill Pl S 98055
Monroe Ave NE 98056
Monroe Ave SE 98058
Monroe Ct NE 98056
Monroe Ct SE 98058
Monster Rd SW 98057
Monterey Ave NE 98056
Monterey Ct NE 98056
Monterey Ct SE 98055
Monterey Dr NE 98056
Monterey Ln NE 98056
Monterey Pl NE 98056
Morris Ave S
200-699 98057
1301-1397 98055
1399-4799 98055
4801-4999 98055
Moses Ln S 98057
Mountain View Ave N .. 98056
Mt Baker Ave & Pl 98059
Naches Ave SW 98057
Newcastle Way
11201-12797 98056
12799-12899 98056
12901-12999 98056
13013-13015 98059
13018-13398 98059
13031-13051 98056
13201-13399 98059
Newcastle Golf Club Rd 98059
Newport Ave NE 98056
Newport Ave SE 98059
Newport Ct NE 98056
Newport Ct SE 98058
Nile Ave & Pl 98059
Nishiwaki Ln 98057
Oak Dr 98058
Oakesdale Ave SW 98057
SE Old Petrovitsky Rd .. 98058
Olympia Ave NE 98056
Olympia Ave SE 98058
Orcas Ave & Pl 98059
Park Ave N
100-1056 98057
1058-1098 98057
2601-2797 98056
2799-3999 98056
4001-4099 98056
Park Pl N
200-298 98057
2400-2599 98056
Parkside Way SE 98058
Pasco Ave, Dr & Pl 98059
Patriot Way SE 98059
Pelly Ave N 98057
E & W Perimeter Rd 98057
Peter Grubb Rd SE 98058
SE Petrovitsky Rd
10800-11599 98055
11600-19200 98058
19202-19498 98058
Pierce Ave NE 98056
Pierce Ave SE 98058
Pierce Ct NE 98056
Pierce Pl NE 98056
Pine Dr 98058
SE Pipeline Rd 98058
Powell Ave SW 98057
S Puget Dr 98055
Queen Ave, Ct & Pl 98056
Quincy Ave & Pl NE & SE 98059
Rainier Ave N & S 98057
Raymond Ave & Pl NW & SW 98057
Redmond Ave, Ct & Pl 98056
Renton Ave S 98057
Renton Center Way SW 98057
SE Renton Issaquah Rd 98059
SE Renton Maple Valley Rd 98058
S Renton Village Pl 98057
Ripley Ln N & SE 98056
N Riverside Dr 98057
Rolling Hills Ave SE 98055
Rosario Ave & Pl NE & SE 98059
Royal Hills Dr SE 98058
Seahawks Way 98056
Seneca Ave, Ct & Pl NW & SW 98057
Shadow Ave & Pl NE & SE 98059
Shattuck Ave S
1-699 98057
1300-3699 98055
Shattuck Ct S 98055
Shattuck Pl S 98055
Shelton Ave NE 98056
Shelton Ave SE 98058
Shelton Ct NE 98056
Shelton Pl NE 98056
Smithers Ave S
300-699 98057
1300-4799 98055
Smithers Ct S 98055
Smithers Pl S 98055
E & W Spring Lake Dr . 98058
Stevens Ave & Ct 98057
Sunset Blvd N 98057
Sunset Blvd NE
600-1199 98056
2601-2797 98056
2799-4099 98056
4100-5599 98059
SW Sunset Blvd 98057
Sunset Ln NE 98056
Tacoma Ave & Pl 98056
Talbot Pl & Rd 98055
Talbot Crest Dr S 98055
Taylor Ave & Pl 98057
Thomas Ave SW 98057
Thomas Ln 98055
S Tillicum St 98057
S Tobin St 98057
Toledo Ave SE 98059
Underwood Pl NE & SE 98059
Union Ave & Ct 98059
E Valley Rd 98057
Vashon Ave, Ct & Pl NE & SE 98059
Verair Ave SE 98059
Vesta Ave NE & SE 98059
SW Victoria St 98057
Vuemont Pl NE 98056
Wells Ave N
2-98 98057
100-599 98057
3600-4199 98056
Wells Ave S
1-599 98057
3100-3699 98055
Wells Ct S 98055
Wells Pl S 98055
Whitman Ave, Ct & Pl .. 98059
Whitworth Ave S
200-599 98057
1300-4899 98055
Whitworth Ct S 98055
Whitworth Ln S 98057
Whitworth Pl S 98055
Williams Ave N
100-100 98057
102-599 98057
2600-4299 98056
Williams Ave S
1-599 98057
601-699 98057
2201-2299 98055
Windsor Pl & Way 98056
Woodside Dr SE 98058
Yakima Ave & Pl 98059
Zillah Pl SE 98059

NUMBERED STREETS

NE 1st Cir 98059
NE 1st Ct 98059
NE 1st Pl
4000-4098 98056
4100-6899 98059
SE 1st Pl 98059
N 1st St 98057
NE 1st St
2500-2599 98056
2601-2899 98056
4600-6699 98059
NE 2nd Ct 98059
SE 2nd Ct
2201-2297 98056
5500-6099 98059
NE 2nd Ln 98059
SE 2nd Ln 98059
NE 2nd Pl
2500-2699 98056
3900-4098 98059
NW 2nd Pl 98057
SE 2nd Pl
2100-2499 98056
4100-6799 98059
N 2nd St 98057
NE 2nd St
2500-3599 98056
4100-6099 98059
NW 2nd St 98057
S 2nd St 98057
SE 2nd St 98059
SW 2nd St 98057
NE 3rd Cir 98059
NE 3rd Ct
3800-4099 98056
4600-6100 98059
NW 3rd Ct 98057
SE 3rd Ct 98056
NE 3rd Ln
4000-4098 98056
4400-5600 98059
NE 3rd Pl
3800-4099 98056
4700-5799 98059
NW 3rd Pl 98057
S 3rd Pl 98057
SE 3rd Pl 98059
SW 3rd Pl 98057
N 3rd St 98057
NE 3rd St
1801-2797 98056
5000-5899 98059
NW 3rd St 98057
S 3rd St 98057
SE 3rd St
2200-3200 98056
4200-6799 98059
SW 3rd St 98057
NE 4th Cir
3900-3999 98056
6200-6299 98059
NE 4th Ct
2700-2899 98056
5100-6299 98059
NE 4th Pl
4000-4099 98056
4900-6199 98059
NW 4th Pl 98057
S 4th Pl 98057
SE 4th Pl 98059
SW 4th Pl 98057
N 4th St 98057
2201-2897 98056
2899-4099 98056
4100-4300 98059
4301-4301 98056
4301-6627 98059
4302-6298 98059
NW 4th St 98057
S 4th St 98057
2101-2697 98056
2699-3299 98056
4100-6799 98059
NE 5th Cir 98059
NE 5th Ct
2600-2799 98056
4101-4197 98059
SW 5th Ct 98057
NE 5th Pl
2500-4099 98056
4500-5699 98059
NW 5th Pl 98057
S 5th Pl 98057
SE 5th Pl
3600-3799 98058
6500-6799 98059
SW 5th Pl 98057
N 5th St 98057
NE 5th St
3700-3999 98056
4100-5999 98059
NW 5th St 98057
S 5th St 98057
SE 5th St
2900-2998 98058
6700-6899 98059
6 Penny Ln 98059
NE 6th Cir 98056
NE 6th Ct
2100-4099 98056
4300-5499 98059
NE 6th Pl
2100-3999 98056
4100-5699 98059
S 6th Pl 98057
N 6th St 98057
NE 6th St
2900-4099 98056
4900-5899 98059
NW 6th St 98057
S 6th St 98057
SE 6th St 98058
NE 7th Ct
3301-3997 98056
5100-6299 98059

SE 7th Ct 98057
NE 7th Pl
3300-3700 98056
4300-6299 98059
NE 7th St
2000-4099 98056
4100-5999 98059
NW 7th St 98057
S 7th St 98057
SE 7th St
3201-3599 98058
6700-6899 98059
SW 7th St 98057
NE 8th Ct
3800-3899 98056
5100-5299 98059
SE 8th Dr 98055
NE 8th Pl
2100-2198 98056
5000-5699 98059
SE 8th Pl
1800-1899 98057
2000-2499 98055
2800-2999 98058
N 8th St 98057
NE 8th St
2100-3699 98056
4100-5899 98059
SE 8th St
1700-1899 98057
2800-3099 98058
6700-6899 98059
NE 9th Cir 98059
NE 9th Ct
2000-3899 98056
4100-4198 98059
4200-4299 98059
NE 9th Pl
2100-4099 98056
4100-5299 98059
NE 9th St
2000-3799 98056
4400-5699 98059
S 9th St 98057
NE 10th Ct 98056
NE 10th Ln 98056
N 10th Pl 98057
NE 10th Pl
2200-3599 98056
4100-5299 98059
SE 10th Pl 98058
N 10th St 98057
NE 10th St
900-999 98059
2200-4099 98056
4100-5699 98059
S 10th St 98057
SE 10th St 98058
SW 10th St 98057
NE 11th Ct
2300-3999 98056
5100-5499 98059
NE 11th Ln 98059
NE 11th Pl
3100-3999 98056
5300-5599 98059
SE 11th Pl 98058
NE 11th St
3300-3999 98056
4100-5299 98059
SE 11th St 98058
NE 12th St
1801-1897 98056
1899-3700 98056
3702-4098 98056
4400-5299 98059
SE 12th St 98058
SW 12th St 98057
NE 13th Pl
1300-1399 98059
2201-2297 98056
2299-3799 98056
4700-5599 98059
NE 13th St
2400-3199 98056
5400-5599 98059
SW 13th St 98057

NE 14th Pl
3700-3899 98056
3901-4099 98056
4100-4199 98059
NE 14th St
1700-3899 98056
4700-4799 98059
S 14th St 98055
NE 15th Pl 98056
NE 15th St
2001-2997 98056
2999-3099 98056
3101-3199 98056
4100-4199 98059
S 15th St 98055
SE 16th Ct 98055
SE 16th Pl
1700-1999 98055
3300-3499 98058
NE 16th St
1700-3199 98056
5100-5300 98059
5302-5498 98059
S 16th St 98055
SE 16th St 98058
SW 16th St 98057
NE 17th Ct 98056
SE 17th Ct
1900-2099 98055
3100-3199 98058
NE 17th Pl
1800-3599 98056
4500-5399 98059
NE 17th St
3300-4099 98056
4100-5599 98059
S 17th St 98055
SE 17th St 98058
NE 18th Cir 98059
NE 18th Ct 98059
SE 18th Ct
1900-1998 98055
3600-3699 98058
NE 18th Pl
1700-2099 98056
4700-4899 98059
SE 18th Pl
1701-1797 98055
2800-2899 98058
NE 18th St
2100-4099 98056
4500-4899 98059
S 18th St 98055
SE 18th St 98058
NE 19th Ct 98059
SE 19th Ct
1900-1999 98055
3100-3699 98058
NE 19th Pl 98056
NE 19th St
2400-4099 98056
4100-5199 98059
S 19th St 98055
SE 19th St 98055
SW 19th St 98057
NE 20th Ct 98059
SE 20th Ct
2100-2199 98055
3100-3399 98058
NE 20th Pl
3130-3199 98056
4800-4999 98059
S 20th Pl 98055
N 20th St 98056
NE 20th St
1700-3128 98056
4100-5199 98059
S 20th St 98055
NE 21st Ct 98059
SE 21st Ct 98055
NE 21st Pl 98059
SE 21st Pl 98055
NE 21st St
1800-4099 98056
4700-5199 98059
S 21st St 98055
SE 21st St 98055

NE 22nd Ct 98059
S 22nd Ct 98055
NE 22nd Pl
3700-4099 98056
4100-4699 98059
S 22nd Pl 98055
SE 22nd Pl 98055
NE 22nd St
2300-2498 98056
2500-4099 98056
4100-4199 98059
NE 23rd Ct
3500-3699 98056
4400-5399 98059
NE 23rd Pl
2500-4099 98056
4700-4799 98059
NE 23rd St
1700-2599 98056
2601-2899 98056
4500-5199 98059
S 23rd St 98055
NE 24th Ct
2600-3999 98056
5300-5599 98059
NE 24th Pl 98056
N 24th St 98056
NE 24th St
1601-1697 98056
1699-3799 98056
4000-5699 98059
NE 25th Ct 98059
NE 25th Pl
1800-2099 98056
4100-4400 98059
4402-4498 98059
NE 25th St
2400-3299 98056
4900-5399 98059
S 25th St 98055
NE 26th Ct
3200-3299 98056
4500-4599 98059
S 26th Ct 98055
NE 26th Pl 98056
N 26th St 98056
NE 26th St 98059
S 26th St 98055
N 27th Ct 98056
NE 27th Ct 98056
S 27th Ct 98055
N 27th Pl 98056
NE 27th Pl
1700-1799 98056
4100-4299 98059
S 27th Pl 98055
NE 27th St 98056
S 27th St 98055
SW 27th St 98057
S 28th Ct 98055
N 28th Pl 98056
NE 28th Pl 98056
S 28th Pl 98055
N 28th St 98056
NE 28th St 98056
S 28th St 98055
NE 29th Ct 98056
S 29th Ct 98055
S 29th Pl 98055
N 29th St 98056
SE 29th St 98055
SW 29th St 98057
S 30th Ct 98055
S 30th Pl 98055
SE 30th Pl 98055
N 30th St 98056
NE 30th St 98056
S 31st Ct 98055
N 31st St 98056
NE 31st St
2100-2398 98056
2401-2499 98056
4900-5399 98059
S 31st St 98055
S 32nd Pl 98055
N 32nd St 98056
NE 32nd St 98056

S 32nd St 98055
N 33rd Pl 98056
NE 33rd Pl 98056
S 33rd Pl 98055
N 33rd St 98056
NE 34th Pl 98056
S 34th Pl 98055
N 34th St 98056
S 34th St 98055
SW 34th St 98057
NE 35th Pl 98056
N 35th St 98056
S 35th St 98055
S 36th Pl 98055
N 36th St 98056
NE 36th St 98056
S 36th St 98055
NE 37th Pl 98056
S 37th Pl 98055
N 37th St 98056
S 37th St 98055
S 38th Ct 98055
NE 38th Pl 98056
N 38th St 98056
NE 38th St 98056
N 39th Pl 98056
N 39th St 98056
SW 39th St 98057
N & NE 40th 98056
N 41st Pl 98056
SW 41st St 98057
N 42nd Pl 98056
NE 43rd St 98056
S 43rd St 98055
SW 43rd St 98057
NE 44th St 98056
S 46th Pl 98055
47th Pl & St 98055
NE 48th St 98056
S 48th St 98055
49th Pl & St 98055
S 50th Pl 98055
NE 50th St 98056
S 50th St 98055
51st Ct & St 98055
S 52nd St 98055
S 53rd Pl 98055
S 55th St 98055
SE 64th St 98056
SE 66th Ct 98056
SE 66th St 98056
SE 68th St 98056
SE 69th Pl 98056
SE 70th St 98056
SE 71st Ct 98059
SE 72nd Pl 98059
SE 73rd Ct 98056
SE 74th Ct 98056
SE 75th Pl 98056
SE 76th Ct 98056
SE 77th Ct 98056
SE 78th Ct 98056
SE 79th Ct 98056
SE 80th Ct 98059
SE 81st Ct 98056
SE 81st Pl 98059
SE 82nd Ct 98059
SE 83rd Ct 98059
SE 84th Ct 98059
SE 85th Ln 98056
SE 86th Pl 98056
87th Ave & Pl 98057
87th Ave & Pl 98056
88th Ave S 98057
SE 88th Pl 98056
89th Ave S 98057
SE 89th Pl 98056
90th Ave S 98057
SE 90th Pl 98059
91st Ave S 98057
SE 91st St 98056
92nd Ave S 98055
SE 92nd Pl 98056
SE 93rd St 98056
95th Ave S 98055
SE 95th Pl 98056

SE 95th Way
12200-13198 98056
13200-13498 98059
SE 96th Pl 98056
97th Ave S 98055
98th Ave S 98055
98th Pl S 98055
SE 98th St 98056
SE 99th Ct 98059
99th Pl S 98055
SE 99th St
12500-12599 98056
14700-14799 98059
SE 100th Pl 98059
SE 100th St
12400-12699 98056
13800-17199 98059
101st Ave SE 98055
101st Pl SE 98055
SE 101st St 98056
102nd Ave SE 98055
SE 102nd St
12800-13099 98056
14700-18099 98059
103rd Ave, Ct & Pl 98055
104th Ave SE 98055
104th Pl SE 98055
SE 104th St 98056
105th Ave SE 98055
105th Pl SE
17701-17899 98055
12600-12699 98056
14400-14798 98059
106th Ave SE 98055
106th Pl SE 98055
SE 106th St 98059
107th Ave SE 98055
107th Ct SE 98055
107th Pl SE
18100-18499 98055
13600-14599 98059
SE 107th St 98059
108th Ave SE 98055
108th Ln SE 98055
108th Pl SE 98055
SE 108th St 98059
109th Ave, Ln & Pl 98055
109th Pl SE
6600-6699 98056
110th Ave SE
7900-7999 98056
17600-18399 98055
110th Ct SE 98055
110th Ln SE 98055
110th Pl SE
17000-19199 98055
14600-14699 98059
SE 110th St 98059
111th Ave SE 98055
111th Pl SE
7300-7799 98056
16100-18199 98055
14800-17699 98059
SE 111th St 98059
112th Ave SE
6401-6797 98056
17600-18699 98055
112th Pl SE
8800-8899 98056
18800-19099 98055
14400-14599 98059
SE 112th St 98059
113th Ave SE
7600-8799 98056
16000-18199 98055
113th Ln SE 98055
113th Pl SE
6800-6999 98056
17600-17899 98055
16100-16199 98059
SE 113th St 98059
113th Way SE 98055
114th Ave SE
7000-8899 98056
16000-18699 98055
114th Ct SE
7600-7699 98056

18900-19099 98055
114th Ln SE 98055
114th Pl SE
7600-7699 98056
17600-19199 98055
14500-14599 98059
SE 114th St 98059
115th Ave & Ln 98056
115th Ave & Ln 98055
116th Ave SE
6900-8999 98056
15500-19100 98058
19102-19198 98058
116th Ct SE 98056
116th Pl SE
16410-16699 98058
16400-16500 98059
SE 116th St 98059
117th Ave SE
8200-9299 98056
15700-17499 98058
117th Ct SE 98056
117th Ln SE 98058
117th Pl SE
7300-8099 98056
19100-19199 98058
SE 117th St 98059
118th Ave SE
7400-8999 98056
15600-18899 98058
118th Ct SE 98056
118th Ln SE 98058
118th Pl SE
9200-9299 98056
15700-15799 98058
SE 118th St 98059
119th Ave SE
8000-8699 98056
16100-16899 98058
119th Ct SE 98056
119th Ln SE 98058
119th Pl SE
6900-7599 98056
15700-15799 98058
17500-17699 98059
120th Ave SE
7901-9097 98056
9099-9299 98056
15700-19099 98058
120th Ln SE 98058
120th Pl SE
7500-8299 98056
17300-17499 98059
SE 120th St 98059
120th Ter SE 98058
121st Ave SE
6900-9199 98056
15700-16999 98058
121st Ln SE 98058
121st Pl SE
6900-7299 98056
18300-19199 98058
17300-18299 98059
SE 121st St 98059
122nd Ave SE
7000-8099 98056
9600-9699 98056
16100-17799 98058
122nd Ct SE
8800-8899 98056
17800-17899 98058
122nd Ln SE 98058
122nd Pl SE
7401-7497 98056
7499-9199 98056
17600-17699 98058
14500-14599 98059
SE 122nd St 98059
123rd Ave SE
6900-8899 98056
9600-9699 98056
15600-17099 98058
123rd Ct SE 98058
123rd Pl SE
16000-17899 98058
17600-17999 98059
SE 123rd St 98059

124th Ave SE
8700-8999 98056
9600-9899 98056
15800-19199 98058
124th Pl SE
15800-15899 98058
14600-17799 98059
SE 124th St 98059
125th Ave SE
6900-7499 98056
10300-10399 98056
16400-17399 98058
125th Ct SE 98056
125th Pl SE
7300-8899 98056
9500-9598 98056
9600-9699 98056
16900-17199 98058
S 125th St 98057
SE 125th St 98059
126th Ave SE
7500-8099 98056
9800-10599 98056
16000-17499 98058
126th Pl SE
7300-8599 98056
9500-9599 98056
16100-18799 98058
SE 126th St 98059
127th Ave SE
7300-8499 98056
16300-18499 98058
127th Pl SE
7000-8499 98056
16300-19099 98058
16000-16099 98059
128th Ave SE
8000-8499 98056
16100-17699 98058
128th Ln SE 98056
128th Pl SE 98058
SE 128th St 98059
129th Ave SE
7200-8999 98056
16300-17499 98058
129th Ct SE
8600-8699 98056
15600-15699 98058
129th Pl SE
7500-8999 98056
15600-19099 98058
14200-14399 98059
130th Ave SE
10100-10199 98056
14800-19199 98058
130th Pl SE
8400-8599 98059
15800-15899 98058
16200-16299 98059
S 130th St 98057
SE 130th St 98059
131st Ave SE 98058
SE 131st Ln 98059
131st Pl SE
15800-18999 98058
16300-16399 98059
SE 131st St 98059
132nd Ave SE
9500-9999 98059
10001-10299 98059
15000-19699 98058
132nd Pl SE
6800-9099 98059
15800-19899 98058
15800-15899 98059
S 132nd St 98057
SE 132nd St 98059
133rd Ave SE
7800-9099 98059
14900-19999 98058
SE 133rd Ct 98059
133rd Ln SE 98058
133rd Pl SE
16000-19899 98058
15800-19199 98059
S 133rd St 98057
SE 133rd St 98059

134th Ave SE
7200-7799 98059
14900-19599 98058
134th Ct SE
6900-8199 98059
19600-19699 98058
134th Ln SE 98058
134th Pl SE
19700-19899 98058
15900-18899 98059
S 134th St 98057
SE 134th St 98059
135th Ave SE
7500-8599 98059
14800-19599 98058
135th Pl SE
6900-8299 98059
16800-18699 98058
15900-16399 98059
SE 135th St 98059
136th Ave SE
6800-8899 98059
13000-13499 98059
18000-18299 98058
SE 136th Ln 98059
136th Pl SE
17000-19699 98058
13901-13999 98059
SE 136th St 98059
137th Ave SE
7500-8999 98059
11200-11699 98059
17200-19999 98058
137th Ct SE 98058
137th Pl SE
7400-8999 98059
16200-17099 98058
15200-16299 98059
SE 137th St 98059
SE 137th Ter 98059
138th Ave SE
7000-9099 98059
10000-13599 98059
16100-19999 98058
138th Ct SE 98059
138th Pl SE
7500-8799 98059
12000-12199 98059
15601-16997 98058
16999-17099 98058
14600-19599 98059
SE 138th St 98059
139th Ave SE
7900-9999 98059
15400-15499 98058
139th Ct SE
15600-15699 98058
14800-16399 98059
139th Pl SE
13500-14399 98059
16100-17299 98058
14400-19699 98059
SE 139th St 98059
139th Way SE 98058
140th Ave SE
8600-9100 98059
9102-9298 98059
10000-14299 98059
16201-16997 98058
16999-19899 98058
140th Ct SE 98058
140th Pl SE
13600-13699 98059
15600-19399 98058
14600-15146 98059
SE 140th St 98059
140th Way SE 98058
141st Ave SE
8000-9299 98059
10000-14499 98059
16200-19499 98058
141st Ct SE 98059
141st Pl SE
14400-14499 98059
15400-15499 98058
15100-15199 98059
SE 141st St 98059

142nd Ave SE
8500-8699 98059
11000-14699 98059
16200-19899 98058
142nd Pl SE
14400-14499 98059
15700-19999 98058
14400-16099 98059
SE 142nd St 98059
142nd Way SE 98059
143rd Ave SE
7700-9199 98059
9500-14299 98059
15700-18299 98058
143rd Ct SE
8300-8399 98059
18400-18499 98058
143rd Pl SE
14400-14499 98059
16200-19799 98058
14400-16499 98059
SE 143rd St 98059
144th Ave SE
7900-8899 98059
10900-14599 98059
16200-16999 98058
144th Ct SE 98058
144th Pl SE
8000-8899 98059
14400-14599 98059
19400-19899 98058
15400-18299 98058
SE 144th St 98059
145th Ave SE
7900-7999 98059
11200-14099 98059
15300-19699 98058
145th Ct SE 98059
145th Pl SE
10400-14299 98059
14600-16299 98059
SE 145th St 98059
146th Ave SE
9501-9597 98059
9599-14099 98059
16500-19499 98058
146th Ct SE 98058
146th Pl SE
7800-8599 98059
12400-14499 98059
15300-15499 98058
15600-16199 98059
SE 146th St 98059
147th Ave SE
8000-8499 98059
10200-12399 98059
16500-19799 98058
147th Ct SE 98058
147th Pl SE
11000-14299 98059
18300-18399 98059
SE 147th St 98059
148th Ave SE
7900-8099 98059
9600-12699 98059
16400-19899 98058
148th Ln SE 98058
148th Pl SE 98059
SE 148th St
13101-13599 98058
15500-16599 98059
149th Ave SE
12300-12499 98059
14800-18399 98058
149th Ln SE 98058
149th Pl SE 98059
SE 149th St
13000-13399 98058
16000-19699 98059
150th Ave SE
10700-14499 98059
16900-18399 98058
150th Ct SE 98058
150th Ln SE 98058
150th Pl SE 98059
SE 150th St
13100-13299 98058
19600-19999 98059
151st Ave SE
10300-10799 98059
16900-17600 98058
17602-17798 98058
151st Ct SE 98059
151st Pl SE 98059
SE 151st St
12900-13499 98058
20100-20198 98059
20200-20399 98059
152nd Ave SE
11200-14199 98059
15700-18399 98058
152nd Ct SE 98058
152nd Pl SE
13700-14599 98059
17500-17899 98058
SE 152nd St 98059
153rd Ave SE 98058
153rd Ct SE 98058
153rd Pl SE
13600-13799 98059
18300-18399 98058
14500-14699 98058
154th Ave SE
8200-8399 98059
13600-14299 98059
16700-17899 98058
154th Ct SE 98058
154th Pl SE
10700-10899 98059
14600-18299 98058
14100-14199 98059
SE 154th St 98058
155th Ave SE
7800-8098 98059
8100-8299 98059
11500-12699 98059
17400-17899 98058
155th Pl SE
16800-18399 98058
13900-15499 98058
20700-21199 98059
SE 155th St 98059
156th Ave SE
11900-14699 98059
17000-18200 98058
18202-18298 98058
156th Ct SE
15500-15599 98058
14000-15899 98058
156th Pl SE 98058
SE 156th St
13800-16199 98058
20300-20399 98059
157th Ave SE 98058
157th Ct SE 98058
157th Pl SE
14400-14699 98059
16900-17599 98058
11800-14299 98058
SE 157th St
11600-15799 98058
20200-20599 98059
158th Ave SE
12829-12897 98059
12899-14799 98059
15600-17499 98058
158th Ct SE 98058
158th Pl SE
13700-14499 98059
16600-18099 98058
11700-12999 98058
SE 158th St
12300-14099 98058
20500-20699 98059
159th Ave SE 98058
159th Ct SE 98058
159th Pl SE
13700-13799 98059
16000-17099 98058
13000-14099 98058
SE 159th St
12900-13099 98058
20400-21099 98059

160th Ave SE
11600-14699 98059
17000-18299 98058
160th Ct SE 98058
160th Pl SE
14700-14899 98059
15200-18399 98058
11500-11599 98055
13000-15899 98058
SE 160th St
11200-11499 98055
11600-12999 98058
161st Ave SE
11400-14699 98059
15600-17899 98058
161st Ct SE
14800-14899 98059
18000-18099 98058
161st Pl SE
13600-13799 98059
12200-13899 98058
SE 161st St 98058
162nd Ave SE
10500-14499 98059
15200-17899 98058
162nd Ct SE 98059
162nd Pl SE
16500-18099 98058
13100-14499 98058
SE 162nd St
10901-11097 98055
11099-11499 98055
12600-18699 98058
SE 162nd Way 98059
163rd Ave SE 98059
163rd Ct SE
14900-14999 98059
15300-15399 98058
163 Pl SE 98059
16500-17899 98058
14200-19399 98058
SE 163rd St 98058
164th Ave SE
10900-14399 98059
16500-16699 98058
164th Pl SE
14400-14999 98059
16500-16599 98058
12500-16099 98058
SE 164th St
10800-11499 98055
11600-19399 98058
164th Way SE 98058
165th Ave SE
12800-14699 98059
17000-17099 98058
165th Pl SE
14300-14999 98059
16900-16999 98058
14200-14799 98058
SE 165th St
10600-11599 98055
11600-16399 98058
SE 165th Way 98058
166th Ave SE
11800-13599 98059
16100-16199 98058
SE 166th Ct 98058
166th Pl SE
14300-14599 98059
16700-17099 98058
11100-11299 98055
11600-15999 98058
SE 166th St
10400-10800 98055
12200-16199 98058
SE 166th Ter 98058
167th Ave SE 98058
167th Pl SE
14400-14899 98059
12700-16099 98058
SE 167th St 98058
168th Ave SE 98059
168th Ct SE 98058
SE 168th Pl 98058
SE 168th St
10801-10897 98055
11600-11798 98058
168th Ter SE 98058
168th Way SE 98058
169th Ave SE
10300-14799 98059
18000-18299 98058
169th Pl SE
16600-16699 98058
10900-10999 98055
11900-16099 98058
SE 169th St
11300-11599 98055
12600-16699 98058
170th Ave SE 98059
SE 170th Ct
11500-11599 98055
16000-16099 98058
170th Pl SE
18000-18299 98058
11600-16199 98058
SE 170th St
10700-10999 98055
12600-19499 98058
171st Ave SE
9900-14799 98059
18000-18299 98058
171st Ct SE 98058
SE 171st Ln 98058
171st Pl SE
11800-12399 98059
11401-11499 98055
12700-16899 98058
SE 171st St
11400-11499 98055
12500-15899 98058
SE 171st Way 98058
172nd Ave SE
10300-13499 98059
18200-18299 98058
172nd Ct SE
10500-10599 98059
18400-18499 98058
16200-16299 98058
172nd Ln SE
18500-18599 98058
11800-11898 98058
172nd Pl SE
11700-11999 98059
18600-19199 98058
13400-16099 98058
SE 172nd St
10400-10999 98055
12101-12197 98058
173rd Ave SE 98059
SE 173rd Pl 98058
SE 173rd St
10800-11599 98055
12700-16799 98058
173rd Way SE 98058
174th Ave SE
9700-12799 98059
16700-21499 98058
SE 174th Ln 98058
174th Pl SE
11800-11899 98059
18532-18599 98058
SE 174th St
10400-10500 98055
10502-10798 98055
12700-19499 98058
SE 174th Way 98058
175th Ave SE
10700-11098 98059
11100-14999 98059
18600-18699 98058
SE 175th Ct 98058
SE 175th Ln 98058
SE 175th Pl 98058
SE 175th St
11500-11599 98055
11900-19099 98058
176th Ave SE 98059
SE 176th Ct 98058
SE 176th Ln 98058
176th Pl SE
18600-18699 98058
15100-16299 98058

SE 176th St 98058
177th Ave SE 98059
SE 177th Ct 98058
177th Pl SE
12400-12699 98059
11400-11499 98055
14900-15699 98058
S 177th St 98055
SE 177th St 98058
178th Ave SE 98059
SE 178th Ct 98058
SE 178th Pl
11400-11599 98055
14200-19399 98058
S 178th St 98055
SE 178th St 98058
179th Ave SE 98059
179th Pl SE
18600-18699 98058
10900-10999 98055
12200-14299 98058
SE 179th St
11200-11499 98055
14801-14997 98058
14999-16299 98058
180th Ave SE 98059
SE 180th Ct 98058
180th Pl SE
14701-14799 98059
10600-10798 98055
10800-11499 98055
14100-17099 98058
SE 180th St
11000-11199 98055
11600-18699 98058
181st Ave SE
13200-14699 98059
18800-18999 98058
SE 181st Pl 98058
SE 181st St
10800-11299 98055
12300-15099 98058
182nd Ave SE
13400-14699 98059
16000-16299 98058
182nd Pl SE
14700-14799 98059
15700-16999 98058
SE 182nd St
10800-10898 98055
10900-11499 98055
12501-13397 98058
13399-15499 98058
183rd Ave SE 98059
SE 183rd Ct
10900-10999 98055
15000-15099 98058
SE 183rd Dr 98058
SE 183rd Pl
10900-11199 98055
16900-17099 98058
SE 183rd St
11200-11299 98055
13200-19599 98058
183rd Way SE 98058
184th Ave SE
12400-14399 98059
16000-21899 98058
SE 184th Ln 98055
SE 184th Pl
11000-11199 98055
12600-19299 98058
SE 184th St
11402-11410 98055
11412-11599 98055
11600-19699 98058
184th Way SE 98058
185th Ave SE 98058
SE 185th Ct 98058
SE 185th Pl
10200-11499 98055
12600-20299 98058
SE 185th St 98058
185th Way SE 98059
186th Ave SE
13300-13399 98059
16200-22699 98058

SE 186th Ln 98055
186th Pl SE
12400-12498 98059
10400-11034 98055
11800-13899 98058
SE 186th St
10200-11499 98055
11800-12999 98058
SE 186th Way 98058
187th Ave SE 98058
SE 187th Ct
10400-11099 98055
13100-14799 98058
SE 187th Ln 98055
187th Pl SE
17300-17599 98058
10300-10499 98055
12600-13499 98058
SE 187th St
10000-10699 98055
14000-19899 98058
188th Ave SE 98058
SE 188th Ct 98055
188th Ln SE 98059
SE 188th Pl
11200-11299 98055
12500-19999 98058
SE 188th St
10100-10199 98055
11600-19499 98058
SE 188th Way 98058
189th Ave SE 98059
SE 189th Ct
10400-11299 98055
13000-13099 98058
SE 189th Ln 98055
SE 189th Pl
11100-11199 98055
11600-19699 98058
SE 189th St
10901-11099 98055
12700-12799 98058
190th Ave SE 98058
SE 190th Ct 98055
SE 190th Ln 98055
SE 190th Pl
10301-11299 98055
12700-12999 98058
SE 190th St
10000-10899 98055
14000-14099 98058
14101-19599 98058
191st Ave SE
13300-13499 98059
21300-21499 98058
SE 191st Ct 98055
191st Pl SE
13300-13499 98059
17800-21499 98058
12700-12799 98058
SE 191st St 98058
192nd Ave SE 98058
SE 192nd Dr 98058
SE 192nd Pl 98055
S 192nd St 98055
SE 192nd St
10000-10700 98055
10702-11498 98055
11600-12598 98058
12600-20700 98058
20702-20798 98058
193rd Ave SE 98058
193rd Ln SE 98059
SE 193rd St 98058
194th Ave SE 98058
SE 194th Ct 98058
SE 194th Pl
10300-10499 98055
20400-20499 98058
S 194th St 98055
SE 194th St
10600-10699 98055
14000-14499 98058
SE 195th Ct 98058
195th Pl SE
17400-17699 98058
14000-18499 98058

SE 195th St
10400-10499 98055
13200-13399 98058
196th Ave SE
13300-14899 98059
14901-14999 98059
16600-23099 98058
SE 196th Ct 98058
SE 196th Dr 98058
S 196th Pl 98055
SE 196th Pl 98058
SE 196th St
10200-10799 98055
12800-19299 98058
197th Ave SE 98059
SE 197th Ct 98058
SE 197th Pl 98058
S 197th St 98055
SE 197th St 98058
SE 198th Ct 98058
S 198th Pl 98055
SE 198th Pl 98058
S 198th St 98055
SE 198th St 98058
199th Ct SE 98059
199th Pl SE
13800-14999 98059
13700-13799 98058
S 199th St 98055
SE 199th St 98055
200th Ave SE
14200-14899 98059
19200-19299 98058
SE 200th St 98058
201st Ave SE 98059
202nd Ave SE 98059
SE 202nd St 98058
203rd Ave & Pl 98059
204th Ave SE 98059
204th Pl SE 98059
SE 204th St 98058
205th Ave, Ln & Pl 98059
206th Ave SE 98059
SE 206th St 98058
207th Pl SE 98059
SE 207th St 98058
208th Ave SE 98058
209th Ave SE 98059
209th Pl SE
14400-14799 98059
18400-19499 98058
212th Ln & St 98058
SE 213th St 98058
SE 214th St 98058
SE 215th St 98058
SE 216th Ave & St
SE 98058
SE 220th St 98058
227th Pl & St 98058
SE 228th St 98058
SE 232nd St 98058
SE 234th Pl 98058

RICHLAND WA

General Delivery 99352

POST OFFICE BOXES MAIN OFFICE STATIONS AND BRANCHES

Box No.s
1 - 2458 99352
3001 - 3100 99354
5200 - 5220 99352

NAMED STREETS

Aaron Dr 99352
Abbot St 99352
Abert Ave 99352
Acacia Ave 99354
Ada St 99352
Adair Ct & Dr 99352
Adams St 99352
Agier Dr 99352
Agnes St 99352
Aileron Ln 99354
Aimee Dr 99352
Airport Way 99354
Alameda Ct 99354
Alamosa Ave 99352
Albany Ct 99354
Albemarle Ct 99354
Alder Ave 99354
Alexander Ave & Ct 99354
Alice St 99352
Alla Vista St 99352
Allegheny Ct 99354
Allenwhite Dr 99352
Allison Way 99352
Aloe Ct 99352
Amon Ct & Dr 99352
Amon Park Dr 99352
Andrea Ln 99352
Anna Ave 99352
Anthony Dr 99352
Apollo Blvd 99354
Appaloosa Way 99352
Apple Cider Ct 99352
April Loop 99354
Arbor St 99352
Arena Rd 99352
Argon Ln 99354
Armistead Ave 99352
Arroyo St 99352
Ash St 99352
Ashwood St 99352
Atkins Ave 99352
Austin Ct, Pl & St 99354
Aviator St 99354
Azalea Ave 99352
Badger Mountain Loop 99352
Baker Ave 99354
Banyon St 99352
Barber Ct & Pl 99352
Barth Ave 99352
Bartlett Rd 99352
Basswood Ave 99352
Battelle Blvd 99354
Baum St 99352
Bay Ct 99354
Baywood Ave 99352
Bear Dr 99352
Bebb Ct 99352
Beech Ave 99354
Belle Meade Ct 99352
Bellerive Dr 99352
Benham Ct & St 99352
Benton Ave 99354
Berkshire Pl & St 99354
N Bermuda Rd 99352
Bernard Ave 99352
Big Sky Dr 99352
Birch Ave
400-999 99352
1000-1999 99354
Bismark St 99354
Bitterroot Dr 99352
Black Ct 99354
Blalock Ct 99352
Blue Ave & St 99354
Blue Hill Ct 99352
Blue Mountain Loop 99352
Bluebell St 99352
Bluffs Dr 99354
Boise St 99352
Bolleana Ave 99352
Boros Ct 99352
Boston St 99354
Boulder St 99352
Bradley Blvd 99352
Bramasole Dr 99354
Brantingham Rd 99352
Breakwater Ct 99354
Bremmer St 99352
Brentwood Ave 99352
Bretz Rd 99352
Briarwood Ct 99354
Bridle Dr 99352
Brittlebush Ln 99352
Broadmoor St 99352
Bronco Ln 99354
Brookwood Ave &
Loop 99352
Bruce Lee Ln 99352
Buckboard Ct 99354
Buckskin Loop Ln 99354
Buena Ct 99354
Butler Loop 99354
Butternut Ave 99354
By Pass Hwy 99352
Cabela Ct 99352
Cactus Loop 99352
Caliente Sands Ct 99352
Calle Del Sol St 99352
Camas Ave 99354
Camden St 99352
Cameo Dr 99352
Camy Ct & St 99352
Canyon Ave, Ct & St 99352
Canyon Rim Ct 99352
Carner Ct & St 99352
Carolina Ave 99352
Carondelet Dr 99354
Carriage Ave 99354
Carson St 99352
Casa Sueno Ct 99352
Cascade Ave, Ct & St 99354
Casey Ave 99352
Castillo Ct 99352
Catalina Ct 99354
Catskill St 99354
Cedar Ave
600-999 99352
1000-1399 99354
Cedarwood Ct 99352
Center 99354
Center Blvd 99352
Center Pkwy 99352
Chad Ct 99352
Chadwick St 99352
Chamnaview Ln 99352
Chaparral St 99352
Charbonneau Dr 99352
Chardonnay Dr 99352
Chateau Ct 99352
Cherokee St 99352
Cherry Ln 99354
Cherry Blossom Loop 99352
Cherrywood Loop 99354
Chester Rd 99352
Chestnut Ave 99352
Cimarron Ave, Pl & St 99352
Citrus Ave 99352
City View Dr 99352
Clearview Ave 99354
Clermont Dr 99352
Cliffrose Pl 99352
Clipper Dr 99354
Clovernook St 99352
Clubhouse Ln 99354
Coast St 99354
Cobblestone Ct 99352
Colley Dr 99352
N Columbia Center
Blvd 99352
Columbia Park Trl 99352
Columbia Point Dr 99352
Compton Ln 99354
Comstock St 99352
Concord St 99352
Copperbrook Ct 99354
Copperbutte St 99354
Coppercreek St 99354
Copperhill St 99354
Copperleaf St 99354
Coppermist Ct 99354
Copperstone St 99354
Coppertree Ct 99354
Cordoba Ct 99354
Cortland Ave 99354
Cosmic Ln 99354
Cottontail Ln 99352
Cottonwood Dr
1-999 99352
1000-1098 99354
1100-1599 99354
Cottonwood Loop 99352
Coulter Ct 99352
Country Ct 99352
Country Club Pl 99352
Country Ridge Dr 99352
Covina Ct 99354
Cowiche Ct 99352
Craighill Ave 99352
Crestview Ave 99354
Crestwood Dr 99352
Crimson Way 99354
Criterion Dr 99352
Cromwell Ave 99352
Crosswater Loop 99354
Cullum Ave 99352
Curie Ave 99354
Cypress Pl 99354
Dakota Ave 99352
Dallas Rd & St 99352
Dalton St 99354
Daly Dr 99352
Darby Pl 99352
Darcie Ct 99352
Davenport St 99352
Davison Ave 99354
Dawn Hill Ct 99352
De Palma Ct 99352
Deanna Ct 99352
Del Cambre Loop 99352
Del Mar Ct 99354
Delafield Ave 99352
Delaware Ave 99352
Delle Celle Dr 99354
Denver St 99352
Desert Springs Ave 99352
Dogwood Pl 99354
Dolphin Ct 99354
Dornoch Pl 99354
Dos Palos Ct 99354
Doubletree Ct 99354
Douglass Ave 99352
Dover St 99352
Downing St 99352
Driftwood Ct 99354
Duluth St 99354
Duportail St 99352
Dusky Ct 99352
Eagle Ridge Ct 99354
Eagle Watch Loop 99354
Easton Ave 99354
Eastwood Ave 99352
Eaton Ct 99352
Edgewood Dr 99352
Einstein Ave 99354
El Monte Ct 99354
Elder Ct 99352
Elementary St 99352
Elizabeth Ct 99352
Elm Ave 99354
Emerald St 99352
Endress St 99352
Englewood Dr 99352
Enterprise Dr 99354
Erica Dr 99352
Evanslee Ct 99352
Everest Ave 99354
Fairway Ct & Dr 99352
Fairwood Ct 99352
Falconcrest Loop 99352
Falconridge St 99352
Falley St 99352
Farrell Ln 99354
Fermi Dr 99354
Ferndale Ave 99354
Ferry Rd 99354
Firerock Ave 99352
Fitch St 99352
Florida Ave 99352
Fontana Ct 99354
Ford Pr 99352
Forest Ave 99354
Fort St 99352
Fowler St 99352
Foxglove Ave 99352
Foxtrot Ln 99352
Frankfort St 99352
Franklin St 99354
Franz Ct 99352
French St 99352
Fries St 99352
Fuji Way 99352
Fuller St 99354
Gage Blvd 99352
Gaillard Pl 99354
Gala Way 99352
Galaxy Ln 99354
Garlick Blvd 99354
Geneva St 99352
George Washington Way
101-397 99352
399-1299 99352
1300-3399 99354
Georgia Ave 99352
Gigi Ct 99352
Gillespie St 99352
Gillmore Ave 99352
Glen Rd 99354
Glen Eagles Ct 99352
Glenbriar Ln 99352
Glenwood Ct 99352
Goethals Dr
1-1198 99352
1300-1699 99354
Golden Dr 99352
Gomer Rd 99354
Gowen Ave 99352
Granada Ct 99354
Gray St 99352
Greenbriar E & W 99352
Greenbrook Blvd & Pl 99352
Greentree Ct 99352
Greenview Dr 99352
Gulf Ct 99354
Gunnison Ct 99354
Guyer Ave 99352
Hains Ave 99354
Hall Rd 99354
Halter Ct 99352
Hamilton Ave & Ct 99354
Hanford St 99354
Hanstead St 99352
Harding St 99352
Harris Ave 99354
Hartford St 99352
Hartwood St 99352
Harvest Lane Pr NE 99352
Haupt Ave 99354
Hawk Haven Ct 99352
Hawkstone Ct 99354
Hazelwood Ave 99352
Heather Ln 99352
Heidi Pl 99352
Helena St 99352
Henderson Loop 99354
Heritage Hills Dr 99352
Hetrick St 99354
High Meadows St 99352
Highview St 99352
Hills St 99354
Hills West Way 99352
Hillview Dr 99352
Hillwood St 99352
Hodges Ct 99354
Hoffman St 99352
Hogan Ct 99352
Holly St 99354
Hood Ave 99354
Horizon View Ln 99352
Horn Ave 99354
Horn Rapids Rd 99354
Horseshoe Ct 99352
Houston Ct 99354
Howell Ave 99354
Hoxie Ave 99354
Hudson Ave 99354
Humphreys St 99352
Hunt Ave & Pt 99354
Hunter St 99352
Hyde Rd 99354
Indian Ct 99354
Innovation Blvd 99354
Inverness Ct 99352
Iry St 99352
Isola Vista Ct 99352
Jackson Ct 99352
Jadwin Ave
1-1299 99352
1300-1999 99354
Jason Loop 99352
Jasper St 99352
Jefferson St 99352
Jericho Ct & Rd 99352
Jewett St 99352
Johnston Ave 99354
Jonagold Dr 99352
Jones Rd 99354
Jordan Ln 99352
Jubilee St 99352
Judson Ave 99354
Kambeth Ct 99352
Kapalua Ave 99352
Karlee Dr 99352
Keene Ct & Rd 99352
E Kellachi St NE 99352
Keller Ave 99354
Kennedy Rd 99352
Kensington Way 99352
Kentwood Ct 99352
Kimball Ave 99354
Kimberly St 99352
Kingsgate Way 99354
Kingston Rd 99354
Knight St 99352
Knollwood Ct 99352
Kona Ct 99352
Kranichwood Ct & St 99352
Kuhn St 99352
Kurtview Ct 99352
Lacey St 99352
Lago Vista Dr 99352
Lakerose Loop 99352
Lakeview Ct 99352
Lamb Ave 99352
Lantana Ave 99352
Larch Ct 99352
Lariat Ln 99352
Larkhaven Ct 99352
Larkspur Dr 99352
Lasiandra Ct 99352
Lassen Ave 99354
Laurelbrook Ct 99352
Laurelwood Ct 99352
Lavender Ct 99354
Lee Blvd 99352
Leopold Ln 99352
Leslie Rd 99352
Lethbridge Ave 99352
Liberty Ln 99352
Lily St 99352
Limar Ct 99352
Limestone Ct 99352
Linda Ct 99352
Lindberg Loop 99354
Littler Ct 99352
Llandwood Ave & Ct 99352
Lodi Loop 99352
Log Ln 99354
Logston Blvd 99354
Lombardy Ln 99352
Lonetree Ln 99352
Long Ave
900-999 99352
1000-1199 99354
Longfitt St 99352
Lorayne J Blvd 99352
Louisiana Ave 99352
Lucca Ln 99352
Luther Pl 99354
Lynnwood Ct & Loop 99354
Macarthur St 99354
Mackenzie Ct 99352
Magnolia Ct 99354
Mahan Ave & Ct 99354
Maidstone St 99354
Mainmast Ct 99354
Malibu Pr 99352
Manchester St 99352
Mansfield St 99352
Maple Pl 99354
Marine Ct 99354
Mark Ave & Ct 99352
Marshall Ave & Ct 99354
Mateo Ct 99354
Mattis Dr 99352
Maui Dr 99352
Mcclellan St 99352
Mcintosh Ct 99352
Mcmurray Ave & St 99354
Mcpherson Ave
900-999 99352
1000-1999 99354
Meadow Hills Ct & Dr 99352
Meadow Ridge Loop 99352
Meadows Dr E 99352
Meleina Ct 99352
Melissa St 99352
Mercury Dr 99354
Meriwether Ave 99352
Merlot Ct 99352
Merrill Ct 99354
Mesa Dr 99352
Mesquite Ct 99352
Michael Ave 99352
Mickelson Ct 99352
Miller Ct 99352
Millwood Ct 99354
Mint Loop 99352
Molly Marie Ave 99352
Molokai St 99352
Monarch Ln 99354
Monrean Loop 99352
Mont Blanc Way 99352
Montana Ave 99352
Montgomery Ave 99354
Moonstone Ct 99352
Morency Ct & Dr 99352
Morning Side Pkwy 99352
Mountain View Ln 99352
Mowry Sq 99354
Mullet Ct 99354
Muret Ct 99352
Muriel Ct & St 99352
Naches Ave & Ct 99352
Napa Ct 99352
Naples Ln 99352
Nastacia St 99352
Nevada Ave 99352
Newcomer Ave & St 99354
Newhaven Ct, Loop &
Pl 99352
Nicklaus Ct 99352
Norris St 99352
Northgate Dr 99352
Norwood Ct 99354
Nottingham Dr 99352
Nova Ln 99352
Nuclear Ln 99354
Nuvola Vista Ct 99352
Oahu St 99352
Oak St 99354
Oak Hill Ct 99352
Oakland St 99352
Oakmont Ct 99352
Oconnor St 99352
Odessa St 99352
Ogden St 99352
Olympia St 99354
Ontario Ct 99352
Orchard Ct & Way 99352
Orchid Ct 99354
Oregon St 99352
Ottawa Ct 99352
Oxford Ave 99352
Pacific Ct 99352
Palm Dr 99352
Palmer Ct 99352
Palomino Ct 99352
Park St 99354
Patricia Ct 99352
Patton St 99354

Pattyton Ln 99352
Pauling Ave 99354
Peachtree Ln 99352
Penny Ln 99352
Penny Royal Ave 99352
Peppergrass Ct 99352
Percheron Pl 99352
Perkins Ave 99354
Perry Ct 99354
Pershing Ave 99354
Pike Ave 99354
Pine St 99354
Pinetree Ct & Ln 99352
Pinionwood Ct 99352
Pinot Ct 99352
Pinto Loop 99352
Piper Ct & St 99352
Plateau Dr 99352
Platt Ave 99354
Player Ct 99352
Pompano Ct 99354
Poplar St 99354
Port Of Benton Blvd 99354
Postage Due St 99354
Potter Ave 99354
Prestwick Dr 99354
Proton Ln 99354
Provo St 99354
Pullen St 99354
Punkie Ln 99352
Purple Sage St 99352
Putnam St 99354
Q Ave & St 99354
Quailwood Pl 99352
Quarterhorse Way 99352
Queensgate Dr 99352
Railroad Ave 99352
Rainier Ave 99354
Raintree Ln 99352
Raleigh St 99354
Rand Dr 99352
Rathwood Ave 99352
Rau St 99352
E Reata Rd 99352
Redrock Ridge Loop 99354
Redwood Ct & Ln 99354
Regent St 99352
Richardson Rd 99354
Riche Ct 99354
Richmond Blvd 99354
Ridgecliff Dr 99352
Ridgeview Ct 99352
Riesling St 99352
Rimrock Ave & Ct 99352
Rio Senda Ct 99354
River Valley Dr 99354
Riverbend Dr 99354
Riverhaven Ct 99354
Riverstone Dr 99352
Riverwood St 99352
Roberdeau St 99354
Robert Ave 99352
Robertson Dr 99354
Rochefontaine St 99354
Rockcreek Ct 99354
Rockwood Dr 99352
Rocky Mountain Ct 99352
Rome Ct 99352
Rosemary St 99352
Rosewood Ct 99354
Rossell Ave 99352
Rowan Ct 99352
Royal Ann Ct 99352
Rue Ct 99352
Sacajawea Ave 99352
Sacramento Blvd 99354
Saddle Way 99352
Sage Ct 99352
Sagewood Loop & St 99352
Saguaro Way 99354
Sailfish Ct 99354
Saint Ct & St 99354
Salk Ave 99354
Sand Dunes Rd 99354
Sandpiper Loop 99354
Sandstone Ln 99354
Sanford Ave
300-999 99352
1000-1699 99354
Saratoga Ct 99352
Satus Ct & St 99352
Sauvignon Ct 99352
Sawgrass Loop 99354
Scarlet Pl 99352
Scot St 99354
Scottsdale Pl 99352
Scouler Ct 99352
Seaside Ct 99354
Seattle Ct & St 99354
Sedgwick Pl 99352
Sedona Cir 99354
Selah Ct 99352
Sell Ln 99352
Sequoia Ave 99352
Shasta Ave 99354
Shaw St 99354
Sheridan Pl 99352
Sherman St 99354
Sherwood St 99352
Shockley Rd 99352
Shoreline Ct 99354
Short St 99352
Sibert St 99354
Sicily Ln 99352
Sierra St 99354
Silver Ct 99352
Silver Meadows Dr 99352
Silverleaf Ct 99352
Silverwood Ct & Dr 99352
Singletree Ct 99354
Sirron Ave 99352
Sitka Ct 99352
Skagit St 99354
Skamania St 99354
Sky Meadow Ave 99352
Skyline Dr 99352
Smart Park 99354
Smith Ave
400-999 99352
1000-1099 99354
Smoketree Pl 99352
Snohomish Ave 99354
Snow Ave
400-999 99352
1000-1099 99354
Snyder St 99354
Soaring Hawk St 99352
Somerset St 99354
Sonoran Ct & Dr 99354
Southwell St 99352
Spartan Ct 99352
Spaulding Park 99352
Spengler St 99352
Spokane St 99354
Spring St 99354
Springfield St 99354
Sprout Rd 99354
Stagecoach Ct 99354
Stallon Pl 99352
Stanley St 99354
Stanton Ave 99352
Steptoe St 99352
Stevens Dr
700-999 99352
1100-3400 99354
3402-3798 99354
Stevens Center Pl 99354
Stewart Dr 99352
Stonecreek Dr 99354
Stonehaven Dr 99352
Strange Dr 99352
Strawberry Ln 99352
Summit St 99352
Sundance Dr 99352
Sunset St 99354
Sunshine Ridge Rd 99352
Sunstone Ct 99352
Sunterra Ct 99352
Surrey Ct 99354
Swift Blvd 99352
Sycamore Ct 99352
Symons St 99354
Talon Ct 99352
Tamarisk Ln 99352
Tami St 99352
Tanglewood Dr & Ln 99352
Tapteal Dr 99352
Taylor St 99354
Temple Meadow Ln 99352
Terminal Dr 99354
Thayer Dr
100-999 99352
1000-1999 99354
The Pkwy 99352
Thomas St 99354
Thompson St 99354
Thoroughbred Way 99352
Thyme Cir 99352
Tieton Ct, Pl & St 99354
Tiger Ln 99352
Tilden Ct 99354
Timmerman Dr 99352
Tinkle St 99354
Tomich Ave 99352
Torbett St 99354
Torrey Pines Way 99354
Torthay Ct & Pl 99354
Totten Ave 99354
Townsend Ct 99354
Travis Ln 99352
Trevino Ct 99352
Trippe St 99354
Troon Ct 99354
Truman Ave 99352
Tulip Ln 99352
Tunis Ave 99354
Turner St 99354
Tuscanna Dr 99354
Tuscany Pl 99352
Twin Bridges Rd 99354
Tyler Ct 99352
Valdez Ct 99352
Valencia Dr 99352
Valleyview Cir & Dr 99352
Valmore Pl 99352
Van Dyke Ct 99352
Van Giesen St 99354
Vantond St 99354
Venice Ln 99352
Venturi Ct 99352
Venus Cir 99352
Vienna Ct 99354
View Dr 99352
View Meadows Ct 99352
Viewmont Ct 99352
Viewmoor Ct 99352
Vintage Ave 99354
Violet Ct 99354
Vista Ct 99354
Wagon Ct 99354
Waldron St 99354
Wallace St 99354
Warehouse St 99352
Warren Ct 99354
Waterford St 99352
Wazzu Ave 99354
Weiskopf Ct 99352
Wellhouse Loop 99352
Wellsian Way 99352
Wenas Ct & Pl 99352
Westcliffe Blvd 99352
Westgate Way 99352
Westmoreland Dr 99354
Westwood Ct 99354
White Bluffs St 99354
Whitetail Dr 99352
Whitten St 99354
Whitworth Ave 99352
Wildwood Ct 99352
Willard Ave
700-899 99352
901-999 99352
1000-1299 99354
Williams Blvd 99354
Willis St 99354
Willow Pointe Dr 99354
Willowbrook Ave & Pl 99352
Wilson St 99354
Windhaven Ln 99352
Windsor Ct 99352
Windwood Ln 99352
Winesap Ct 99352
Winslow Ave
400-999 99352
1000-1399 99354
Wisteria St 99352
Wolverine Ct 99352
Woodbury St 99354
Woods Dr 99352
Woodvine Ln 99352
Wordrop St 99354
Wright Ave
200-999 99352
1000-1599 99354
Wyman St 99352
Yucca Rd 99352
Yuma Ln 99352

NUMBERED STREETS

1st St 99354
6th St 99354
E 210 Pr NE 99352
E 260 Pr NE 99352
E 266 Pr NE 99352
E 279 Pr NE 99352
E 669 Pr NE 99352
E 680 Pr NE 99352
E 685 Pr NE 99352
E 710 Pr NE 99352
E 713 Pr NE 99352
E 715 Pr NE 99352

SAMMAMISH WA

NAMED STREETS

Audubon Park Dr SE 98075
E & W Beaver Lake Dr 98075
SE Duthie Hill Rd 98075
NE Inglewood Hill Rd 98074
SE Issaquah Beaver Lake Rd 98075
Issaquah Pine Lake Rd SE 98075
Kellinso Ave NE 98074
E Lake Sammamish Pkwy NE 98074
E Lake Sammamish Pkwy SE
1-799 98074
1000-4299 98075
E Lake Sammamish Pl SE 98075
E Lake Sammamish Shore Ln NE 98074
E Lake Sammamish Shore Ln SE 98075
Lancaster Way SE 98075
Louis Thompson Rd NE & SE 98074
Main Dr & St 98074
Peregrine Point Way SE 98075
E Plateau Dr 98074
Pleashit Ave SE 98075
Sahalee Dr & Way 98074
NE Sahalee Country Club Dr 98074
Trossachs Blvd SE 98075
Windsor Blvd & Dr SE 98074

NUMBERED STREETS

NE & SE 1st Ct, Pl & St 98074
NE & SE 2nd Ct, Pl, St & Way 98074
SE & NE 3rd Ct, Pl, St & Way 98074
SE & NE 4th Ct, Ln, Pl & St 98074
SE & NE 5th Ct, Ln, Pl & St 98074
NE & SE 6th Ct, Pl & St 98074
NE & SE 7th Ct, Ln, Pl & St 98074
SE 8th Ct 98075
NE 8th Pl 98074
SE 8th Pl 98075
NE 8th St 98074
SE 8th St
19600-20499 98074
21000-21100 98075
21102-21198 98075
21200-23599 98074
SE 9th Ct 98075
NE 9th Dr 98074
NE 9th Pl 98074
SE 9th Pl
24600-24699 98074
27001-27297 98075
27299-27399 98075
NE 9th St 98074
SE 9th St 98075
SE 9th Way 98075
SE 10th Ct 98075
NE 10th Pl 98074
SE 10th Pl 98075
NE 10th St 98074
SE 10th St 98075
NE 11th Ct 98074
NE 11th Pl 98074
SE 11th Pl 98075
NE 11th St 98074
SE 11th St 98075
NE 12th Ct 98074
SE 12th Ct 98075
SE 12th Ln 98075
NE 12th Pl 98074
SE 12th Pl 98075
NE 12th St 98074
SE 12th St 98075
SE 12th Way 98075
NE 13th Ct 98074
SE 13th Ct 98075
SE 13th Ln 98075
NE 13th Pl 98074
SE 13th Pl 98075
NE 13th St 98074
SE 13th St 98075
SE 13th Way 98075
NE 14th Ct 98074
SE 14th Ct 98075
NE 14th Dr 98074
NE 14th Pl 98074
SE 14th Pl 98075
NE 14th St 98074
SE 14th St 98075
NE 15th Ct 98074
SE 15th Ct 98075
NE 15th Ln 98074
NE 15th Pl 98074
SE 15th Pl 98075
NE 15th St 98074
SE 15th St 98075
SE 16th Ct 98075
NE 16th Pl 98074
SE 16th Pl 98075
NE 16th St 98074
SE 16th St 98075
NE 17th Ct 98074
NE 17th Pl 98074
SE 17th Pl 98075
NE 17th St 98074
SE 17th St 98075
NE 18th Ct 98074
SE 18th Ct 98075
NE 18th Pl 98074
SE 18th Pl 98075
NE 18th St 98074
SE 18th St 98075
NE 18th Way 98074
SE 19th Ct 98075
NE 19th Dr 98074
NE 19th Pl 98074
SE 19th Pl 98075
NE 19th St 98074
SE 19th St 98075
NE 20th Ct 98074
SE 20th Ct 98075
NE 20th Pl 98074
SE 20th Pl 98075
NE 20th St 98074
SE 20th St 98075
NE 20th Way 98074
NE 21st Ct 98074
SE 21st Ct 98075
NE 21st Pl 98074
SE 21st Pl 98075
NE 21st St 98074
SE 21st St 98075
NE 21st Way 98074
NE 22nd Ct 98074
SE 22nd Ct 98075
NE 22nd Pl 98074
SE 22nd Pl 98075
NE 22nd St 98074
SE 22nd St 98075
SE 22nd Way 98075
NE 23rd Ct 98074
SE 23rd Ct 98075
NE 23rd Pl 98074
SE 23rd Pl 98075
NE 23rd St 98074
SE 23rd St 98075
NE 24th Ct 98074
NE 24th Pl 98074
SE 24th Pl 98075
NE 24th St 98074
SE 24th St 98075
SE 24th Way 98075
NE 25th Ct 98074
SE 25th Ct 98075
NE 25th Pl 98074
NE 25th St 98074
SE 25th St 98075
NE 25th Way 98074
SE 25th Way 98075
NE 26th Ct 98074
SE 26th Ct 98075
NE 26th Pl 98074
SE 26th Pl 98075
NE 26th St 98074
SE 26th St 98075
SE 26th Way 98075
SE 27th Ct 98075
NE 27th Pl 98074
SE 27th Pl 98075
NE 27th St 98074
SE 27th St 98075
SE 27th Way 98075
NE 28th Ct 98074
SE 28th Ct 98075
SE 28th Ln 98075
NE 28th Pl 98074
SE 28th Pl 98075
NE 28th St 98074
SE 28th St 98075
NE 29th Ct 98074
SE 29th Ct 98075
NE 29th Pl 98074
SE 29th Pl 98075
NE 29th St 98074
SE 29th St 98075
NE 30th Ct 98074
SE 30th Ct 98075
NE 30th Pl 98074
SE 30th Pl 98075
NE 30th St 98074
SE 30th St 98075
SE 31st Ct 98075
SE 31st Pl 98075
NE 31st St 98074
SE 31st St 98075
NE 31st Way 98074
NE 32nd Ct 98074
32nd Pl SE
3100-3199 98075
NE 32nd Pl 98074
SE 32nd Pl
21300-25799 98075
SE 32nd St 98075
SE 32nd Way 98075
NE 33rd Ct 98074
NE 33rd Pl 98074
SE 33rd Pl 98075
SE 33rd St 98075
NE 34th Ct 98074
NE 34th Pl 98074
SE 34th Pl 98075
SE 34th St 98075
NE 35th Ct 98074
NE 35th Ln 98074
NE 35th Pl 98074
SE 35th Pl 98075
NE 35th St 98074
SE 35th St 98075
SE 35th Way 98075
SE 36th Ct 98075
NE 36th St 98074
SE 36th St 98075
SE 37th Pl 98075
SE 37th St 98075
NE 37th Way 98074
NE 38th Ct 98074
NE 38th Pl 98074
SE 38th Pl 98075
NE 38th St 98074
SE 38th St 98075
NE 39th Ln 98074
SE 39th Pl 98075
NE 39th St 98074
SE 39th St 98075
NE 40th Ct 98074
SE 40th Ct 98075
SE 40th Pl 98075
NE 40th St 98074
SE 40th St 98075
SE 41st Ct 98075
SE 41st Pl 98075
NE 41st St 98074
NE 42nd Ct 98074
SE 42nd Ct 98075
NE 42nd Pl 98074
NE 42nd St 98074
SE 42nd St 98075
NE 42nd Way 98074
NE 43rd Ct 98074
NE 43rd Pl 98074
SE 43rd Pl 98075
NE 43rd St 98074
NE 44th Ct 98074
NE 44th Pl 98074
NE 44th St 98074
SE 44th St 98075
SE 45th Ct 98075
NE 45th Pl 98074
SE 45th Pl 98075
NE 46th Ct 98074
SE 46th Pl 98075
47th Ct, Pl, St & Way 98075
NE 48th St 98074
SE 48th St 98075
NE 49th Pl 98074
NE 50th St 98074
51st Ct & St 98074
NE 54th Pl 98074
NE 55th St 98074
188th Pl NE 98074
189th Ave NE 98074
190th Pl NE 98074
190th Pl SE 98075
191st Ct SE 98075
191st Pl NE 98074
192nd Ave SE 98075
192nd Dr NE 98074
192nd Pl NE 98074
193rd Ave SE 98075
194th Ave SE 98075
194th Pl NE 98074
194th Pl SE 98075
194th Way NE 98074
195th Ave SE 98075
196th Ave NE 98074

196th Ave SE 98075
197th Ave SE 98075
198th Ave SE 98075
198th Ct NE 98074
198th Pl SE 98075
199th Ave SE
700-799 98074
1800-3199 98075
200th Ave SE 98075
201st Ave NE 98074
201st Ave SE 98075
201st Ct SE 98075
201st Pl NE 98074
201st Pl SE 98075
202nd Ave NE 98074
202nd Ave SE 98075
202nd Pl SE 98075
203rd Ave NE 98074
203rd Ave SE 98075
203rd Pl NE 98074
204th Ave NE 98074
204th Ave SE 98075
204th Ct NE 98074
204th Ln NE 98074
204th Pl NE 98074
204th Ter NE 98074
205th Ave NE 98074
205th Ave SE 98075
205th Ct NE 98074
205th Pl NE 98074
206th Ave NE 98074
206th Ave SE 98075
206th Pl NE 98074
206th Ter NE 98074
206th Way NE 98074
207th Ave NE 98074
207th Ave SE 98075
207th Pl NE 98074
208th Ave NE 98074
208th Ave SE
400-899 98074
1200-2699 98075
208th Pl NE 98074
208th Pl SE 98075
209th Ave & Pl NE & SE 98074
210th Ave NE 98074
210th Ave SE 98075
210th Cir NE 98074
210th Ct NE 98074
210th Ct SE
300-399 98074
900-999 98075
210th Pl NE 98074
210th Pl SE
1-799 98074
2000-2099 98075
211th Ave NE 98074
211th Ave SE 98075
211th Ct NE 98074
211th Pl NE 98074
211th Pl SE
1-399 98074
800-3599 98075
211th Way NE 98074
212th Ave NE 98074
212th Ave SE
400-799 98074
800-3899 98075
212th Ct SE 98075
212th Pl NE 98074
212th Pl SE 98075
212th Way SE 98075
213th Ave NE 98074
213th Ave SE 98075
213th Pl NE 98074
213th Pl SE
400-499 98074
2600-3399 98075
214th Ave NE 98074
214th Ave SE
1-799 98074
2600-2699 98075
214th Ct SE 98075
214th Pl NE 98074
214th Pl SE
100-199 98074
3100-3499 98075
215th Ave NE 98074
215th Ave SE 98075
215th Ct SE 98075
215th Ln SE 98075
215th Pl NE 98074
215th Pl SE
1-199 98074
1600-1999 98075
216th Ave NE 98074
216th Ave SE 98075
216th Ct SE 98075
216th Pl NE 98074
216th Pl SE
200-299 98074
3300-3699 98075
217th Ave NE 98074
217th Ave SE 98075
217th Pl NE 98074
217th Pl SE 98075
218th Ave NE 98074
218th Ave SE
200-799 98074
2900-3299 98075
218th Ct SE 98075
218th Ln SE 98075
218th Pl NE 98074
218th Pl SE 98074
219th Ave NE 98074
219th Ave SE 98075
219th Ln SE 98075
219th Pl NE 98074
219th Pl SE 98075
220th Ave NE 98074
220th Ave SE
100-399 98074
1500-3399 98075
220th Pl NE 98074
220th Pl SE 98075
221st Ave NE 98074
221st Ave SE 98075
221st Ct NE 98074
221st Pl NE 98074
221st Pl SE 98075
222nd Ave NE 98074
222nd Ave SE 98075
222nd Ct SE 98075
222nd Pl NE 98074
222nd Pl SE
1-699 98074
2800-2999 98075
223rd Ave NE 98074
223rd Ave SE 98075
223rd Ct NE 98074
223rd Pl NE 98074
224th Ave NE 98074
224th Ave SE
100-399 98074
3000-22399 98075
224th Ct NE 98074
224th Pl NE 98074
224th Pl SE
100-399 98074
2900-2999 98075
225th Ave NE 98074
225th Ave SE 98075
225th Ct NE 98074
225th Ln NE 98074
225th Pl NE 98074
225th Pl SE
200-399 98074
1200-1599 98075
226th Ave NE 98074
226th Ave SE 98075
226th Ct NE 98074
226th Ct SE 98075
226th Ln NE 98074
226th Pl NE 98074
227th Ave NE 98074
227th Ave SE 98075
227th Ct NE 98074
227th Ln NE 98074
227th Ln SE 98075
227th Pl NE 98074
227th Pl SE 98075
227th Ter SE 98075
228th Ave NE 98074
228th Ave SE
1-699 98074
800-3699 98075
228th Ct NE 98074
228th Pl NE 98074
229th Ave NE 98074
229th Ave SE 98075
229th Ct SE 98075
229th Pl NE 98074
229th Pl SE 98075
230th Ave NE 98074
230th Ave SE 98075
230th Ct NE 98074
230th Ct SE 98075
230th Ln SE 98075
230th Pl NE 98074
230th Pl SE 98075
230th Ter SE 98075
230th Way SE 98075
231st Ave NE 98074
231st Ave SE 98075
231st Ct NE 98074
231st Ct SE 98075
231st Ln SE 98075
231st Pl NE 98074
231st Pl SE 98075
232nd Ave NE 98074
232nd Ave SE 98075
232nd Ct NE 98074
232nd Ln NE 98074
232nd Pl NE 98074
232nd Pl SE 98075
233rd Ave NE 98074
233rd Ave SE 98075
233rd Pl NE 98074
233rd Pl SE 98075
234th Ave NE 98074
234th Ave SE
600-799 98074
2600-4699 98075
234th Ct NE 98074
234th Ct SE 98075
234th Pl NE 98074
234th Pl SE 98075
235th Ave NE 98074
235th Ave SE 98075
235th Ct NE 98074
235th Pl NE 98074
235th Pl SE 98075
236th Ave NE 98074
236th Ave SE 98075
236th Ct NE 98074
236th Pl NE 98074
237th Ave, Ct, Ln & Pl SE & NE 98074
238th Ave NE 98074
238th Ave SE
200-399 98074
1200-3099 98075
238th Ct NE 98074
238th Pl NE 98074
239th Ave NE 98074
239th Ave SE
500-599 98074
2401-2497 98075
239th Ct SE 98074
239th Ln SE 98074
239th Pl NE 98074
239th Pl SE
700-799 98074
2000-3199 98075
239th Way SE 98074
240th Ave NE 98074
240th Ave SE
500-699 98074
2000-2299 98075
240th Pl SE 98074
240th Way SE
600-799 98074
1000-1499 98075
241st Ave SE 98075
241st Ln SE 98074
241st Pl SE
100-199 98074
1300-1499 98075
100-199 98074
242nd Ave SE
100-199 98074
1600-2699 98075
242nd Ct SE
100-199 98074
900-999 98075
242nd Pl NE 98074
242nd Pl SE 98075
242nd Way SE 98074
243rd Ave NE 98074
243rd Ave SE
200-399 98074
2900-3099 98075
243rd Pl SE
100-499 98074
900-1299 98075
244th Ave NE 98074
244th Ave SE 98075
244th Ct SE 98075
245th Ave SE
400-499 98074
1800-3099 98075
245th Pl NE 98074
245th Pl SE
100-199 98074
2800-2899 98075
246th Ave SE 98075
246th Ct NE 98074
246th Way SE 98074
247th Ave SE
100-199 98074
1400-3199 98075
247th Pl NE 98074
247th Pl SE 98075
248th Ave SE 98075
248th Pl NE 98074
248th Pl SE 98075
249th Ave NE 98074
249th Ave SE 98075
249th Pl NE 98074
249th Pl SE 98075
250th Ct & Pl 98075
251st Ave & Pl 98075
252nd Ave & Pl 98075
253rd Pl SE 98075
254th Ave & Pl 98075
255th Ave SE 98075
256th Ct SE 98075
257th Ct & Pl 98075
258th Ave NE 98074
258th Ave SE 98075
258th Ct SE 98075
258th Pl SE 98075
259th Ave NE 98074
259th Ct NE 98074
259th Ct SE 98075
259th Pl NE 98074
259th Pl SE 98075
260th Ct & Pl 98075
261st Ave SE 98075
262nd Ave & Pl 98075
263rd Ave, Ct, Ln & Pl SE 98075
264th Ave & Pl 98075
265th Ave SE 98075
266th Ave, Ct, Pl & Way SE 98075
267th Ct & Pl 98075
268th Pl & Way 98075
269th Ave & Ct 98075
270th Ct, Ln, Pl & Way SE 98075
271st Ave, Ct & Pl 98075
272nd Ct, Pl & Way 98075
273rd Ct & Pl 98075
274th Ct, Pl & Way 98075
275th Ave, Ct & Pl 98075
277th Ave, Pl & Ter 98075
278th Ave & Ct 98075
279th Dr SE 98075

SEATTLE WA

General Delivery 98101

POST OFFICE BOXES MAIN OFFICE STATIONS AND BRANCHES

Box No.s
G - G 98166
1 - 1316 98111
787 - 787 98124
1701 - 2477 98111
2310 - 2310 98122
2501 - 2934 98111
3001 - 3494 98114
3501 - 3998 98124
4001 - 4999 98194
5000 - 5395 98145
9001 - 9998 98109
11007 - 11050 98111
12001 - 12274 98102
12275 - 12275 98112
12275 - 12275 98122
12301 - 12939 98111
13001 - 13903 98198
14001 - 14975 98114
15101 - 15991 98115
16001 - 16799 98116
17001 - 17980 98127
18001 - 18998 98118
19001 - 19888 98109
20001 - 20838 98102
21001 - 21994 98111
22000 - 22999 98122
23001 - 23398 98102
24001 - 24999 98124
25001 - 27999 98165
28001 - 28998 98118
30001 - 30974 98113
31001 - 31998 98103
33000 - 33992 98133
34000 - 35199 98124
45001 - 45898 98145
46001 - 47983 98146
48001 - 48980 98148
50009 - 50040 98145
50013 - 50023 98105
50095 - 50096 98145
51001 - 51255 98115
55001 - 55999 98155
58001 - 58999 98138
60001 - 60298 98160
61001 - 61418 98141
65001 - 65274 98155
66001 - 66999 98166
68001 - 69814 98168
70101 - 70897 98127
75001 - 75999 98175
77001 - 77818 98177
78001 - 78690 98178
79000 - 79030 98119
80001 - 81463 98108
84001 - 84999 98124
85001 - 85900 98145
88001 - 88994 98138
91000 - 91342 98111
94001 - 94794 98124
95001 - 95998 98145
97050 - 97050 98124
98000 - 98999 98198
98185 - 98185 98145
99001 - 99836 98139
180801 - 180801 98118
200202 - 200202 98102
221001 - 222000 98122
300303 - 300328 98103
300407 - 300408 98113
330300 - 330333 98133
389662 - 389681 98138
440408 - 440408 98114
550501 - 550516 98155
900898 - 900999 98109

NAMED STREETS

Academy Pl 98109
Adams Ln NE 98105
S Adams St
800-2798 98108
2800-3199 98108
3500-5199 98118
SW Adams St 98126
SW Admiral Way
3000-3899 98126
4000-6699 98116
Aikins Ave SW 98116
Air Cargo Rd 98158
Airentri Ave SW 98106
Airport Way S
1000-3799 98134
3800-6099 98108
6101-6299 98108
Alamo Pl S 98144
Alaska Ave 98199
S Alaska Pl 98108
S Alaska St
2-100 98134
600-3199 98108
3400-5399 98118
5401-5499 98118
SW Alaska St
1500-2399 98106
2401-2499 98106
3500-3799 98126
3801-3899 98126
3900-5099 98116
Alaska Service Rd S 98158
Alaskan Way
600-798 98104
800-1099 98104
1101-1197 98101
1199-1500 98101
1502-1998 98101
2000-2198 98121
2200-2799 98121
2801-2899 98121
Alaskan Way S
100-399 98104
401-499 98104
1201-1799 98134
Alaskan Way W 98119
Albion Pl N 98103
S Albro Pl 98108
Alder St 98104
E Alder St 98122
Alderbrook Pl NW 98177
Alki Ave SW 98116
Allachal Ave W 98199
N Allen Pl 98103
E Allison St 98102
Aloha St 98109
E Aloha St
700-1300 98102
1302-1398 98102
1400-2699 98112
2701-2899 98112
W Aloha St 98119
Alonzo Ave NW 98117
Alpine Way NW 98177
Altavista Pl W 98199
Alton Ave & Pl 98125
Alvin Pl NW 98117
Ambaum Blvd S 98148
Ambaum Blvd SW 98146
NE Ambleside Rd 98105
S Americus St
2500-2599 98108
3900-3999 98118
Amgen Ct W 98119
Amherst Pl W 98199
Andover Park E 98188
Andover Park W
2-198 98188
200-216 98188
218-18398 98188
225-225 98138
225-18399 98188
S Andover St
601-647 98108
649-3099 98108
3600-3698 98118
3700-4699 98118
SW Andover St
1900-2400 98106
2402-2498 98106
2601-2997 98126
2999-3800 98126
3802-3898 98126
3900-4098 98116
4100-5899 98116
5901-5999 98116
S Angel Pl 98118
S Angeline St
1200-2699 98108
2701-3099 98108
3700-5449 98118
SW Angeline St 98116
S Angelo St 98108
Ann Arbor Ave NE
5500-5899 98105
6000-6099 98115
Anthony Pl S 98144
S Apple Ln 98198
Aqua Way S 98168
Arapahoe Pl W 98199
Arboretum Dr & Pl 98112
Arch Ave & Pl 98116
W Argand St 98119
N Argyle Pl 98103
W Armory Way 98119
W Armour Pl 98199
Armour St 98109
W Armour St
1-1399 98119
2101-2297 98199
2299-4500 98199
4502-4598 98199
Arrowsmith Ave S
9700-9999 98118
10000-10099 98178
Arroyo Ct & Dr 98146
Arroyo Beach Pl SW 98146
E Arthur Pl 98112
Ashworth Ave N
3500-9700 98103
9702-9798 98103
10000-14399 98133
14500-19900 98133
19902-19998 98133
Ashworth Pl N 98133
S Atlantic St
51-1097 98134
1099-1199 98134
1400-3099 98144
SW Atlantic St 98116
Atlas Pl SW 98136
Auburn Ave S 98178
Auburn Pl E 98112
Augusta Pl S 98108
S Augusta St 98178
Aurora Ave N
100-2599 98109
3800-9899 98103
9901-9999 98103
10000-14399 98133
14500-19999 98133
20001-20499 98133
SW Austin Pl 98106
S Austin St
200-3099 98108
3201-3297 98118
3299-4899 98118
SW Austin St
700-1799 98106
3500-3799 98126
3900-4600 98136
4602-4698 98136
Autumn Ln SW 98136
SW Avalon Way 98126
S Avon St 98178
S Avon Crest Pl 98108
Bagley Ave N
3500-8299 98103
10600-14399 98133
19000-19099 98133
Bagley Dr N 98133
Bagley Ln N 98133

Bagley Pl N 98133
S Bailey St 98108
Bainbridge Pl SW 98136
Baker Ave NW 98107
Baker Blvd 98188
NW Ballard Ave & Way
NW 98107
Ballinger Pl & Way NE 98155
Bangor Ct & St 98178
Banner Pl & Way NE 98115
E Barclay Ct 98122
Barnes Ave NW 98107
W Barrett Ln 98199
W Barrett St
300-398 98119
400-1399 98119
2000-4200 98199
4202-4298 98199
Bartlett Ave NE 98125
S Barton Pl 98118
SW Barton Pl 98106
S Barton St
300-398 98108
801-899 98108
3600-3798 98118
3800-3900 98118
3902-4898 98118
SW Barton St
1200-1498 98106
1500-2299 98106
2301-2599 98106
2600-3899 98126
3901-4899 98136
SW Bataan Pl & St
SW 98126
S Bateman St
2300-2899 98108
4200-4899 98118
Battery St 98121
Bay St 98121
Bayard Ave NW
9800-9900 98117
9902-9998 98117
10001-10099 98177
S Bayview St
900-999 98134
1300-1398 98144
1400-3199 98144
Beach Dr NE 98155
Beach Dr NW 98177
Beach Dr SW
3300-3598 98116
3600-4899 98116
5000-7099 98136
7101-7199 98136
SW Beach Drive Ter 98116
Beacon Ave S
2100-2199 98134
2300-3499 98144
3501-3699 98144
3801-4697 98108
4699-7341 98108
7343-7399 98108
7400-9999 98118
10000-12699 98178
10401-10797 98178
10799-10899 98178
Beacon Coal Mine Rd
S 98178
Bedford Ct NW 98177
Belgrove Ct NW 98177
Bell St 98121
Bella Vista Ave S 98144
Bellevue Ave 98122
Bellevue Ave E 98102
Bellevue Ct E 98102
Bellevue Pl E 98102
Belmont Ave 98122
Belmont Ave E 98102
Belmont Pl E 98102
Belvidere Ave SW 98126
NE Belvoir Pl 98105
S Benefit St 98118
S Bennett Dr 98108
S Bennett St
100-198 98108
200-3100 98108
3102-3198 98108
3500-4799 98118
Benton Pl SW 98116
SW Bernice Pl 98126
W Bertona St
101-297 98119
299-1500 98119
1502-1598 98119
2000-4799 98199
SW Beveridge Pl SW 98136
Beverly Ln & Rd 98166
Bigelow Ave N 98109
Birch Ave N 98109
Bishop Pl W 98199
Bitter Pl N 98133
Blaine St 98109
E Blaine St
101-197 98102
199-1099 98102
1900-4199 98112
4201-4299 98112
W Blaine St
1-1199 98119
2600-3499 98199
Blair Ter S 98118
Blake Pl SW 98136
NE Blakeley St 98105
Blakely Ct & Pl NW 98177
Blanchard St 98121
Blenheim Dr E 98112
S Blockhouse Dr 98198
NW Blue Ridge Dr 98177
NE Boat St 98105
Bonair Dr & Pl 98116
S Bond St 98118
Boren Ave
400-1099 98104
1101-1197 98101
1199-1900 98101
1902-1998 98101
2000-2099 98121
100-699 98109
100-398 98144
Boston St 98109
E Boston St
1-1399 98102
1400-3999 98112
W Boston St
1-1599 98119
2200-2999 98199
E Boston Ter 98112
Bothell Way NE 98155
W Bothwell St 98119
Boundary Ln NW 98177
N Bouninso St 98103
S Bow Lake Dr 98188
N Bowdoin Pl 98103
NW Bowdoin Pl 98107
Bowen Pl S 98118
Bowlyn Pl S 98118
Boyd Pl SW 98116
Boyer Ave E
1600-2499 98112
2500-2899 98102
Boylston Ave
801-897 98104
899-1099 98104
1101-1197 98101
1199-1299 98101
1400-1899 98122
100-1099 98102
S Bozeman St 98118
SW Brace Point Dr 98136
S Bradford Pl 98108
S Bradford St
800-2998 98108
3000-3099 98108
4600-4699 98118
SW Bradford St
3000-3099 98126
3900-4098 98116
4100-5599 98116
5601-5799 98116
Bradner Pl S 98144
S Brandon Ct 98108
S Brandon Pl 98108
S Brandon St
2-48 98134
100-2600 98108
2602-3198 98108
3201-3297 98118
3299-5599 98118
SW Brandon St
1500-2499 98106
2501-2599 98106
2600-3699 98126
3900-3998 98136
4000-4700 98136
4702-4898 98136
W Briarcliff Ln W 98199
Bridge Way N 98103
Briereld Ave NW 98117
NW Bright St 98107
Brighton Ln S 98118
S Brighton St
501-2997 98108
2999-3099 98108
4200-5299 98118
Brittany Dr SW 98166
Broad St
2-48 98121
200-300 98109
201-349 98121
302-998 98109
351-599 98109
Broadmoor Dr E 98112
Broadway 98122
Broadway E 98102
Broadway Ct 98122
NE Brockman Pl 98125
Brook Ave SW 98126
Brooklyn Ave NE
3700-5699 98105
5701-5999 98105
6101-6297 98115
6299-8099 98115
Brookside Blvd NE 98155
SW Bruce St 98136
Brygger Dr W 98199
NW Brygger Pl 98107
S Budd Ct 98118
Burke Ave N
3300-9099 98103
10701-11697 98133
11699-14399 98133
14500-20399 98133
Burke Pl N 98133
S Burns St 98118
Burton Pl W 98199
S Bush Pl 98144
S Byron St 98144
E Calhoun St 98112
California Ave SW
1101-1297 98116
1299-4899 98116
5000-9899 98136
10000-10300 98146
10302-10698 98146
California Dr SW 98136
California Ln SW 98116
California Way SW 98116
S Camano Pl 98118
S Cambridge St
800-899 98108
5000-5098 98118
SW Cambridge St
900-998 98106
1000-1899 98106
2900-3799 98126
4300-4399 98136
SW Campbell Pl 98116
NE Campus Pkwy 98105
SW Canada Dr 98136
N Canal St 98103
NW Canal St 98107
Canfield Pl N 98103
NW Canoe Pl 98117
Canterbury Ln E 98112
Canton Aly S 98104
Carkeek Dr S 98118
NW Carkeek Park Rd 98177
Carleton Ave S 98108
Carlyle Hall Rd N 98133
Carlyle Hall Rd NW 98177
Caroline Ave N 98103
Carr Pl N 98103
Carranso Ave NE 98125
SW Carroll St 98116
S Carstens Pl 98108
S Carver St 98118
Cascade Ave S 98188
NW Cascade Dr 98177
Cascadia Ave S
2500-3799 98144
3800-4599 98118
Cecil Ave S 98118
Cedar St 98121
NW Central Pl 98107
SW Channon Dr 98166
Chapel Ln 98177
Chapin Pl N 98103
S Charles St
700-899 98134
1800-3499 98144
S Charlestown St
600-1299 98108
2700-3600 98144
3602-3698 98144
SW Charlestown St
1901-2099 98106
2900-3799 98126
3801-3899 98126
3900-3998 98116
4000-5999 98116
6001-6099 98116
Chatham Dr S 98118
Cheasty Blvd S
3200-3600 98144
3602-3798 98144
3800-3898 98108
3900-4200 98108
4202-4398 98108
Chelan Ave SW 98106
NW Cherry Loop 98177
Cherry St 98104
E Cherry St 98122
Cherrylane Ave & Pl 98144
Chicago Ct S 98118
SW Chicago Ct 98106
S Chicago St
200-498 98108
500-3099 98108
3200-4899 98118
Chilberg Ave & Pl 98116
Christensen Rd 98188
SW City View St 98126
Claremont Ave S 98144
Clay St 98121
Cleantr Ave SW 98116
Cleopatra Pl NW 98117
Cliff Ave S 98198
Clise Pl W 98199
N Clogston Way 98103
S Cloverdale Pl 98118
S Cloverdale St
301-397 98108
399-1499 98108
3400-5599 98118
5601-5699 98118
SW Cloverdale St
400-2499 98106
2501-2599 98106
2901-2997 98126
2999-3799 98126
4001-4297 98136
4299-4699 98136
SW Colewood Ln 98166
S College St 98144
SW College St 98116
College Way N
9201-9597 98103
9599-9699 98103
9701-9799 98103
10001-10099 98133
Colorado Ave 98199
Colorado Ave S 98134
Columbia Dr S 98108
Columbia St 98104
E Columbia St 98122
S Columbian Way
1400-1499 98144
1600-2999 98108
W Commodore Way 98199
Comstock Pl 98109
Comstock St 98109
W Comstock St 98119
S Concord St 98108
SW Concord St 98136
Condon Way W 98199
Coniston Rd NE 98105
Conkling Pl W 98119
E Conover Ct 98122
S Conover Way 98118
Constance Dr W 98199
Convention Pl 98101
S Cooper St 98118
S Corgiat Dr S 98108
Corliss Ave N
3600-9100 98103
9102-9198 98103
11001-11197 98133
11199-14399 98133
14501-14597 98133
14599-19499 98133
Corliss Pl N 98133
Cornell Ave S 98178
Corporate Dr S 98188
Corson Ave S 98108
Coryell Ct E 98112
Costco Dr 98188
Cottage Pl SW 98106
Country Club Ln S 98168
S Court St 98144
Courtland Pl N 98133
Courtland Pl S
3600-3699 98144
3800-4098 98118
Covello Dr S 98108
Cowen Pl NE 98105
Cowlitz Rd NE 98105
W Cramer St 98199
Crane Dr W 98199
Crawford Pl 98122
W Cremona St 98119
E Crescent Dr 98112
SW Crescent Rd 98166
Crest Dr NE 98115
Crest Pl S 98108
Crestmont Pl W 98199
S Creston St 98178
Crestwood Dr S 98178
Crista Ln N 98133
Crockett St 98109
E Crockett St
1200-1298 98102
3800-3899 98112
W Crockett St
1-1099 98119
2300-3399 98199
NE Crown Pl 98115
NW Culbertson Dr 98177
Culpeper Ct NW 98177
Cycle Ct & Ln SW 98126
Cyrus Ave NW 98117
S Dakota St
100-199 98134
600-3199 98108
3700-5099 98118
SW Dakota St
1800-1899 98106
1901-2599 98106
2600-2798 98126
2800-3799 98126
3801-3899 98126
3901-3997 98116
3999-5599 98116
Dalendia Ave S 98134
Dalestin Ave N 98109
Dallas Ave S 98108
Daniel Pl NE 98125
Darnerli Ave NE 98105
Dartmouth Ave W 98199
Davis Pl S 98144
S Dawson St
1-59 98134
61-99 98134
101-197 98108
199-3099 98108
3200-3498 98118
3500-5799 98118
SW Dawson St
1600-1698 98106
1700-1999 98106
3501-3797 98126
3799-3899 98126
3901-3997 98136
3999-5099 98136
S Day St 98144
Dayton Ave N
3600-9799 98103
10100-14399 98133
14500-20499 98133
Dayton Pl N 98133
S Dean Ct 98108
S Dean St 98144
Dearborn Pl S 98144
S Dearborn St
1-900 98134
902-1198 98134
1200-1398 98144
1400-3499 98144
Decatur Pl S 98108
S Dedham St 98118
S Delappe Pl 98144
Delmar Dr E 98102
Delridge Way SW 98106
Denny Way 98109
E Denny Way 98122
W Denny Way 98119
E Denny Blaine Pl 98112
Densmore Ave N
3400-9799 98103
10000-14399 98133
14500-20299 98133
Dentiney Ave 98164
Denver Ave S
4700-4800 98134
4802-4898 98134
5200-5298 98108
5300-5499 98108
Des Moines Memorial Dr
9600-9999 98108
10000-12699 98168
14200-14698 98168
20000-20798 98198
20101-20797 98198
20799-21299 98198
21301-21399 98198
15000-17998 98148
Detroit Ave SW 98106
Dewey Pl E 98112
Dexter Ave & Way 98109
Diagonal Ave S 98134
Dibble Ave NW
6500-9799 98117
10000-10399 98177
SW Director Pl 98136
S Director St
500-1406 98108
1408-1498 98108
4200-4598 98118
4600-5199 98118
SW Director St 98136
Discovery Park Blvd 98199
Division Ave NW 98117
Dixon Dr S 98178
Dock Ave 98198
NW Dock Pl 98107
SW Donald St 98116
S Donovan St
500-1499 98108
3401-3499 98118
SW Donovan St
1400-1499 98106
3600-3799 98126
4000-4399 98136
S Doredalm St 98158
Dorffel Dr E 98112
S Doris St 98108
N Dorothy Pl 98103
S Dose Ter 98144
SW Douglas Pl 98116
Dravus St 98109
W Dravus St
1-1699 98119
2000-4600 98199
4602-4698 98199
Dumar Way SW 98106
Duncan Ave S 98118
Durland Ave & Pl 98125
Duwamish Ave S 98134
Earl Ave NW 98117
SW Eastbrook Rd 98166
Eastern Ave N 98103
Eastlake Ave
1801-1899 98101
101-397 98109
399-1199 98109
1200-3299 98102
Eastmont Way W 98199
S Eastwood Dr 98178
E Eaton Pl 98112
W Eaton St 98199
Echo Lake Pl N 98133
Eddy Ct S
6300-6399 98118
3300-3399 98118
S Eddy St
900-2600 98108
2602-2898 98108
3800-6099 98118
SW Eddy St 98136
E Edgar St 98102
Edgecliff Dr SW 98166
Edgemont Pl W 98199
Edgewater Ln NE
14050-14100 98125
14102-14398 98125
14500-14798 98155
E Edgewater Pl 98112
Edgewest Dr NW 98117
Edgewood Ave SW 98116
S Edmunds St
601-1297 98108
1299-3099 98108
3200-3999 98118
SW Edmunds St
2300-2400 98106
2402-2498 98106
3700-3799 98126
4001-4097 98116
4099-5499 98116
NW Elford Dr 98177
S Elizabeth St 98108
NE Elk Pl 98115
Elleray Ln NE 98105
Elliott Ave 98121
Elliott Ave W 98119
Ellis Ave S 98108
Elm Pl SW 98116
S Elmgrove St
501-697 98108
699-1099 98108
3900-5099 98118
SW Elmgrove St
800-998 98106
1000-1900 98106
1902-2298 98106
2700-3799 98126
3900-4199 98136
Elmore Pl & St 98199
S Elmwood Pl 98144
NE Elshin Pl 98125
W Emerson Pl
1800-1900 98119
1902-1998 98119
2100-2198 98199
W Emerson St
500-598 98119
600-1399 98119
2200-2298 98199
2300-3599 98199
3601-4799 98199
Emmett Ln S 98198
SW Englewood St 98136
Erickson Pl NE 98125
Erie Ave 98122
Erskine Way SW
4800-4999 98116

5000-5299 98136
5301-5399 98136
NW Esplanade 98117
S Estelle St 98144
Etruria St 98109
W Etruria St 98119
Euclid Ave 98122
Evans Black Dr 98188
Evanston Ave N
3400-9799 98103
10101-10197 98133
10199-14399 98133
14500-19599 98133
Evanston Pl N 98133
Everett Ave E 98102
Evergreen Pl 98122
Ewing Pl & St 98119
Exeter Ave NE 98125
Eyres Pl W 98199
S Fairbanks St 98118
Fairmount Ave SW
1900-2299 98126
2700-2798 98116
2901-3099 98116
Fairview Ave 98121
Fairview Ave E 98102
Fairview Ave N 98109
Fairview Pl N 98109
Fairway Dr NE 98115
S Farrar St 98118
Farwell Pl SW 98126
Fauntlee Crst SW 98136
Fauntleroy Ave SW 98126
Fauntleroy Pl SW 98136
Fauntleroy Way SW
3400-4599 98126
4700-4899 98116
5000-9699 98136
Federal Ave E 98102
S Ferdinand St
1101-1297 98108
1299-3199 98108
3200-5599 98118
S Ferris Pl 98144
Ferry Ave SW 98116
S Fidalgo St 98108
Fill Stand Rd S 98158
S Findlay St
100-3099 98108
3501-3597 98118
3599-5199 98118
SW Findlay St
1500-2398 98106
2400-2599 98106
2801-3797 98126
3799-3899 98126
4000-4098 98136
4100-4899 98136
E Fir St 98122
Firlands Way N 98133
Fischer Pl NE 98125
N Fish Singer Pl 98133
S Fisher Pl 98118
S Fletcher St 98118
SW Fletcher St 98136
Flora Ave S 98108
E Florence Ct 98112
W Florentia Pl 98119
Florentia St 98109
W Florentia St 98119
SW Florida St
1100-1199 98134
2900-2999 98126
S Fontanelle Pl 98118
S Fontanelle St
301-2897 98108
2899-2999 98108
4600-4899 98118
SW Fontanelle St 98136
E Ford Pl 98112
Forest Ave S 98178
Forest Ct SW 98136
Forest Dr NE 98115
S Forest St
400-698 98134
700-799 98134
1201-1397 98144
1399-2399 98144
SW Forest St 98116
Forest Hill Pl NW 98117
Forest Park Dr NE 98155
Forinte Ave N 98133
SW Forney St 98116
W Fort St 98199
Fort Dent Way 98188
Fort Lawton St 98199
Fountain Pl & St 98178
Fox Ave S 98108
Francis Ave N 98103
Franklin Ave & Pl 98102
Frater Ave SW 98116
Frazier Pl NW 98177
Fremont Ave N
3400-9799 98103
9801-9899 98103
10000-10098 98133
10100-14399 98133
14500-20399 98133
Fremont Ln N 98103
Fremont Pl N
3401-3497 98103
3499-3520 98103
3522-3598 98103
14800-16399 98133
Fremont Way N 98103
S Front St 98108
S Frontenac St
2800-3098 98108
3100-3199 98108
4200-5199 98118
5201-5599 98118
SW Frontenac St 98136
Fuhrman Ave E 98102
Fullerton Ave 98122
Fulton St 98109
W Fulton St
1-1099 98119
2500-3799 98199
Fun Center Way 98188
G Ter E 98102
Gale Pl S 98144
Galer Pl N 98109
Galer St 98109
E Galer St
200-1099 98102
1400-1498 98112
1500-4199 98112
W Galer St
1-1600 98119
1602-1698 98119
2600-2899 98199
2901-3199 98199
Garden Pl S 98178
S Garden St 98118
S Garden Loop Rd 98118
Garfield St 98109
E Garfield St
201-299 98102
1000-1098 98102
1500-4299 98112
W Garfield St
1-1499 98119
1501-2099 98119
2800-3099 98199
Garieria Ave SW 98126
Garlough Ave SW 98116
Gateway Dr S 98168
Gatewood Rd SW 98136
Gay Ave W 98199
S Gazelle St 98118
S Genesee St
2800-3199 98108
3200-3498 98118
3500-5099 98118
SW Genesee St
1900-2300 98106
2302-2598 98106
2600-3098 98126
3100-3300 98126
3302-3698 98126
4000-4098 98116
4100-5599 98116
5601-5999 98116
Gilman Ave W 98199
Gilman Dr W 98119
Gilman Pl W 98199
S Glacier St 98188
E Glen St 98112
Glen Acres Dr S 98168
Glendale Way S 98168
W Glenmont Ln 98199
Glenn Way SW 98116
Glenridge Way SW 98136
Glenwilde Pl E 98112
Gold Ct SW 98136
Golden Dr & Pl 98117
Golden Gardens Dr
NW 98117
Goodwin Way NE 98125
Gould Ave S 98108
W Government Way 98199
S Graham St
1500-1598 98108
1600-3199 98108
3200-5299 98118
5301-6399 98118
SW Graham St
1600-2500 98106
2502-2598 98106
2800-3899 98126
3900-3998 98136
4000-4799 98136
4801-4899 98136
Gralett Ave E 98112
Grand Ave 98122
S Grand St 98144
Grandview Pl E 98112
S Grattan Pl & St S 98118
SW Grayson St
3700-3799 98126
4001-4997 98116
4999-5199 98116
Green Lake Ave N 98103
Green Lake Dr N 98103
E Green Lake Dr N
7100-7499 98115
7500-7948 98103
W Green Lake Dr N 98103
Green Lake Way N 98103
E Green Lake Way N
5500-5698 98103
5700-5800 98103
5802-6798 98103
6800-6998 98115
W Green Lake Way N 98103
NW Greenbrier Way 98177
Greenwood Ave N
3600-8399 98103
8306-8306 98113
8400-9798 98103
8401-9799 98103
10000-14499 98133
14500-15498 98133
15500-20399 98133
N Greenwood Cir 98103
N Greenwood Dr 98133
Greenwood Pl N 98133
W Grover St 98199
E Gwinn Pl 98102
Hahn Pl S 98144
Halladay St 98109
W Halladay St
300-999 98119
1001-1099 98119
2200-2799 98199
Halleck Ave SW 98116
Hamerthe Ave NE 98155
Hamlet Ave S 98118
Hamlin Rd NE 98155
E Hamlin St
2-98 98102
100-1299 98102
1800-2199 98112
Hampton Rd S 98118
S Hanford St
1-699 98134
701-799 98134
1200-1298 98144
1300-3899 98144
SW Hanford St
1101-1399 98134
3001-3697 98126
3699-3750 98126
3900-5899 98116
Haraden Pl S 98118
Harbor Ave SW
1001-1399 98116
1600-3499 98126
SW Harbor Ln 98126
W Harley St 98199
S Harney St 98108
Harold Pl NE 98105
Harris Pl S 98144
Harrison St 98109
E Harrison St
300-1399 98102
1400-3499 98112
3501-3699 98112
W Harrison St 98119
Harvard Ave 98122
Harvard Ave E 98102
Hawaii Cir 98199
S Hawthorn Rd 98118
Hayes St 98109
W Hayes St 98199
Hazel Ct & St 98178
Heights Ave & Pl 98136
SW Heinze Way 98136
E Helen St 98112
SW Hemlock Way 98136
Henderson Pl SW 98106
S Henderson St
100-198 98108
200-1499 98108
4001-4197 98118
4199-4899 98118
SW Henderson St
800-2199 98106
3001-3097 98126
3099-3699 98126
3701-3799 98126
3900-3998 98136
4000-4599 98136
Hiawatha Pl S 98144
E High Ln 98112
High Point Dr SW 98126
Highland Dr 98109
E Highland Dr
600-700 98102
702-998 98102
1500-1598 98112
1600-4299 98112
NW Highland Dr 98177
W Highland Dr 98119
Highland Ln NW 98177
Highland Park Way
SW 98106
Highlands 98177
S Hill St 98144
SW Hill St
3700-3798 98126
4000-4099 98116
4100-4899 98116
4901-4999 98116
Hillcrest Ave SW 98116
Hillman Pl NE 98115
Hillside Dr E 98112
Hillside Dr NE 98155
Hilltop Ln NW 98177
S Hinds St
1-397 98134
399-699 98134
701-999 98134
1400-3699 98144
SW Hinds St
3000-3800 98126
3802-3898 98126
3901-3997 98116
3999-6499 98116
Hiram Pl NE 98125
Hobart Ave SW 98116
Holden Pl SW 98126
S Holden St
200-3099 98108
3200-4899 98118
SW Holden St
701-797 98106
799-2499 98106
2600-3899 98126
3900-4399 98136
S Holgate St
1-197 98134
199-999 98134
1200-2999 98144
SW Holgate St 98116
Holly Pl SW 98136
S Holly Pl
3000-3099 98108
3300-3499 98118
S Holly St
2400-3119 98108
3121-3199 98108
3200-3598 98118
3600-5599 98118
SW Holly St
1201-1497 98106
1499-1999 98106
3000-3098 98126
3100-3499 98126
3501-3699 98126
3920-3998 98136
4000-4599 98136
4601-4799 98136
Holly Ter S 98118
S Holly Park Dr S 98118
Holman Rd N 98133
Holman Rd NW
8700-9799 98117
9801-9999 98117
10000-10199 98177
10201-10399 98177
Holyoke Way S 98178
S Homer St 98108
W Hooker St 98199
Horichi Ave E 98102
S Horton St
1-999 98134
1301-1697 98144
1699-3899 98144
SW Horton St 98116
Host Rd S 98158
Howe St 98109
E Howe St
200-1099 98102
1500-3899 98112
W Howe St
1-1199 98119
1201-1499 98119
2300-3599 98199
Howell Pl 98122
Howell St 98101
E Howell St 98122
Hubbell Pl 98101
Huckleberry Ln NW 98177
S Hudson St
1-299 98134
1101-1297 98108
1299-3199 98108
3200-5500 98118
5502-5598 98118
SW Hudson St
2300-2400 98106
2402-2598 98106
3900-3998 98116
4000-5199 98116
Hughes Ave SW 98116
Humes Pl W 98119
Hunter Blvd S 98144
E Huron St 98122
Iago Pl S 98118
SW Ida St
3500-3799 98126
3900-4199 98136
S Idaho St 98134
S Industrial Way 98108
Industry Dr 98188
S Ingersoll Pl 98144
Innis Arden Dr & Way 98177
Interlake Ave N
3500-9599 98103
10000-14399 98133
14500-17899 98133
Interlake Ct 98133
E Interlaken Blvd
1300-1398 98102
1401-1497 98112
1499-2899 98112
Interlaken Dr E 98112
Interlaken Pl E 98112
International Blvd
15201-15997 98188
15999-17699 98188
17800-17803 98158
17804-17898 98188
17805-17899 98158
17900-19999 98188
20000-21200 98198
21201-21499 98198
21202-21498 98198
Interurban Ave & Pl 98168
Inverness Ct & Dr 98115
NW Ione Pl 98107
S Irving St 98144
Island Dr S 98118
Ithaca Pl S 98118
Ivanhoe Pl NE 98105
S Jackson Pl 98144
S Jackson St
1-100 98104
91-91 98194
101-1099 98104
102-1098 98104
1200-3599 98144
SW Jacobsen Rd 98116
E James Ct 98122
James St 98104
E James St 98122
E James Way 98122
W Jameson St 98199
E Jansen Ct 98112
Jefferson St 98104
E Jefferson St 98122
Jill Pl S 98108
S Joers Way 98198
John St 98109
E John St
400-898 98102
900-1399 98102
1400-3899 98112
W John St 98119
Jones Ave & Pl 98117
S Judkins St 98144
S Juneau St
1601-1997 98108
1999-3099 98108
3200-5299 98118
SW Juneau St
2400-2498 98106
2501-2599 98106
3000-3700 98126
3702-3898 98126
4000-4198 98136
4200-4899 98136
Juneau Ter S 98118
S Juniper St 98178
Keen Way N 98103
NE Kelden Pl 98105
Kenilworth Pl NE 98105
S Kenny St
2100-2200 98108
2202-2298 98108
4200-4899 98118
SW Kenny St 98126
Kensington Pl N 98103
S Kent Des Moines
Rd 98198
Kenwood Pl N 98103
SW Kenyon Pl 98136
S Kenyon St
100-899 98108
3200-5399 98118
SW Kenyon St
400-1900 98106
1902-2498 98106
2600-3699 98126
3701-3899 98126
3900-4399 98136
4401-4415 98136
S Keppler St 98118
NE Keswick Dr 98105
Keystone Pl N 98103
Kilbourne Ct SW 98136
S King St
1-1099 98104
1200-3699 98144
Kings Garden Dr N 98133
W Kinnear Pl 98119
Kirkwood Pl N 98103
SW Klickitat Ave & Way
SW 98134
Knox Pl E 98112
Lafayette Ave S 98144
Lafern Pl S 98118
Lago Pl NE 98155
S Lago Pl 98118
Lake City Way NE
7400-7498 98115
7500-9899 98115
10000-14399 98125
Lake Dell Ave 98122
Lake Park Dr S 98144
Lake Ridge Dr S 98178
Lake Shore Blvd NE
9500-9799 98115
10000-10199 98125
10201-10399 98125
15500-15599 98155
Lake Shore Dr S 98118
Lake Washington Blvd 98122
Lake Washington Blvd E
100-2599 98112
Lake Washington Blvd S
200-498 98144
500-1999 98144
3800-5999 98118
E Lake Washington Blvd
2201-2499 98112
Lakemont Dr NE 98115
S Lakeridge Dr 98178
Lakeside Ave 98122
Lakeside Ave NE 98125
Lakeside Ave S 98144
Lakeside Pl NE 98125
Lakeview Blvd E 98102
Lakewood Ave S 98144
SW Lander Pl 98116
S Lander St
51-799 98134
1200-3499 98144
SW Lander St
1301-1597 98134
1599-1699 98134
3600-3750 98126
3752-3898 98126
3900-5800 98116
5802-5898 98116
S Lane St
600-899 98104
1200-1598 98144
1600-3499 98144
3501-3599 98144
S Langston Rd S 98178
SW Lanham Pl & Way
SW 98126
Laradert Ave S 98108
NE Latimer Pl 98105
Latona Ave NE
3800-5999 98105
6000-9099 98115
E Laurel Dr NE 98105
W Laurel Dr NE 98105
Laurel Ln S 98178
S Laurel St 98178
NE Laurelcrest Ln 98105
E & W Laurelhurst Dr 98105
S Lawrence Pl 98118
W Lawton Cir, Ln, Pl &
St W 98199
NW Leary Ave & Way
NW 98107
SW Ledroit Ct & Pl
SW 98136
Lee St 98109
E Lee St 98112
W Lee St 98119
Lenora Pl N 98133
Lenora St 98121
S Leo St 98178
Leroy Pl S 98118

S Leschi Pl 98144
Letitia Ave S 98118
Lewis Pl SW 98116
Lexington Pl S 98118
Lexington Way E 98112
S Lilac St
2800-2899 98108
3501-3599 98118
Lima Ter S 98118
Lincoln Park Way SW 98136
Linden Ave N
3600-9899 98103
10000-10098 98133
10100-14399 98133
14500-19999 98133
Lindsay Pl S 98118
Logan Ave W 98199
NE Longwood Pl 98115
Lorelach 98161
Lorentz Pl N 98109
E Loretta Pl 98102
Lotus Ave SW 98126
Lotus Pl S 98178
E Louisa St
1-299 98102
1900-1998 98112
2000-2499 98112
Loyal Ave & Way 98117
N Lucas Pl 98103
S Lucile St
2-80 98134
100-3099 98108
3101-3199 98108
3200-5499 98118
Luther Ave S 98178
W Lynn Pl 98199
Lynn St 98109
E Lynn St
1-1299 98102
1301-1399 98102
1400-4299 98112
W Lynn St 98199
S Lyon Ct 98118
Macadam Rd S
13001-13097 98168
13099-14600 98168
14602-14998 98168
15000-15399 98188
SW Macarthur Ct & Ln SW 98126
Madison St 98104
E Madison St
950-1108 98122
1110-2099 98122
2100-2198 98112
2200-4300 98112
4302-4398 98112
Madrona Dr 98122
NW Madrona Ln 98177
Madrona Pl E 98112
Magnolia Blvd, Ln & Way 98199
Maiden Ln E 98112
S Main St
1-599 98104
601-699 98104
1200-3599 98144
Malden Ave E 98112
S Malerado St 98188
SW Manning St
3000-3599 98126
3601-3749 98126
4200-5699 98116
W Manor Pl 98199
W Mansell St 98199
SW Maple Way 98136
NE Maple Leaf Pl 98115
Maplewood Pl SW 98146
Marcus Ave S 98118
Marginal Pl SW 98106
W Marginal Pl S 98168
E Marginal Way S
1901-3397 98134
3399-5999 98134
6000-6498 98108
6500-7400 98108
7402-7598 98108
7700-9499 98108
9501-9799 98108
10000-13099 98168
13101-13299 98168
W Marginal Way S 98108
W Marginal Way SW 98106
SW Marguerite Ct 98116
W Marina Pl 98199
Marine Ave SW 98116
Marine View Cir SW
18900-18999 98166
800-1099 98166
Marine View Dr S 98198
Marine View Dr SW
9601-9697 98136
9699-9899 98136
10000-11699 98146
17700-21099 98166
21101-21399 98166
Marine View Pl SW 98146
Marion St 98104
E Marion St 98122
N Market St 98103
NW Market St 98107
Marmount Dr NW 98117
Mars Ave S 98108
Marshall Ave SW 98136
E Martin St 98102
Martin Luther King Jr Way
100-110 98122
101-109 98112
118-314 98144
316-3499 98144
3501-3699 98144
3800-4899 98108
4900-4998 98118
5000-9899 98118
10000-13499 98178
10401-10401 98178
10403-10499 98178
Mary Ave NW
6700-9799 98117
10000-10399 98177
Mary Gates Memorial Dr NE 98105
SW Maryland Pl 98116
Mashench Ave S 98148
S Massachusetts St
1-900 98134
902-1100 98134
1200-1298 98144
1300-3599 98144
SW Massachusetts St
1100-1198 98134
3800-3898 98126
4001-4197 98116
4199-4699 98116
Matthews Ave & Pl 98115
Mayes Ct S 98118
Mayfair Ave N 98109
S Mayflower St 98118
Maynard Aly S 98104
Maynard Ave S
300-799 98104
800-900 98134
902-998 98134
5401-5499 98108
S Mcclellan St 98144
Mcclintock Ave S 98144
W Mccord Pl 98199
Mccoy Pl S 98108
E Mcgilvra Blvd & St E 98112
Mcgraw Pl 98109
W Mcgraw Pl 98119
Mcgraw St 98109
E Mcgraw St 98112
W Mcgraw St
1-1099 98119
2400-3210 98199
3211-3211 98139
3211-3599 98199
3212-3698 98199
Mckinley Pl N 98103
W Mclaren St 98199
S Mead St
100-498 98108
500-2299 98108
3300-5299 98118
NE Meadow Pl 98155
Mearkerl Ave W 98119
S Medley Ct 98118
Melrose Ave 98122
Melrose Ave E 98102
N Menford Pl 98103
W Mercer Pl 98119
Mercer St 98109
E Mercer St
300-398 98102
400-1308 98102
1310-1398 98102
1400-3699 98112
W Mercer St 98119
Meridian Ave N
3300-3398 98103
3400-9099 98103
10300-14399 98133
14500-19099 98133
19101-20399 98133
Meridian Ct N 98133
Meridian Pl N
9000-9099 98103
20000-20099 98133
Merton Way S 98118
S Michigan St 98108
SW Michigan St 98106
Midalto Ave 98122
Midland Dr 98188
Midvale Ave N
3900-8900 98103
8902-9698 98103
10300-14350 98133
15500-18899 98133
N Midvale Pl 98103
NW Milford Way 98177
Military Rd S
6901-7097 98108
7099-7500 98108
7502-8398 98108
11200-11398 98168
11400-12799 98168
12800-12998 98168
12801-12899 98168
13000-14899 98168
15000-15798 98188
15001-15997 98188
15800-15900 98188
15902-16408 98188
15999-19999 98188
20001-20097 98198
20099-22899 98198
E Miller St
900-998 98102
1000-1099 98102
1900-2599 98112
SW Mills St 98136
Minkler Blvd 98188
Minor Ave
501-697 98104
699-1099 98104
1100-1999 98101
2000-2599 98102
100-600 98109
S Mission Dr 98178
Mithun Pl NE 98105
S Monroe St
500-799 98108
3200-3599 98118
SW Monroe St
3500-3799 98126
3900-4699 98136
Montana Cir 98199
Montavista Pl W 98199
W Montfort Pl 98199
E & W Montlake Blvd & Pl E 98112
Montvale Ct & Pl 98199
S Moore St 98178
S Morgan Pl 98118
S Morgan St
2400-3099 98108
3201-3297 98118
3299-5599 98118
SW Morgan St
1501-1599 98106
2800-3800 98126
3802-3898 98126
4001-4897 98136
4899-4999 98136
5001-5099 98136
Morley Pl W 98199
E Morley Way 98112
Morse Ave S
3200-3399 98144
3900-3998 98108
Moss Rd NW 98177
N Motor Pl 98103
Mount Adams Pl S 98144
Mount Baker Blvd & Dr S 98144
Mount Claire Dr S 98144
Mount Rainier Dr S 98144
Mount Saint Helens Pl S 98144
Mount View Dr S 98108
Murray Ave SW 98136
Myers Way S
9401-9999 98108
10000-10899 98168
S Myrtle Pl 98118
S Myrtle St
500-598 98108
600-2899 98108
2901-3099 98108
3700-5299 98118
SW Myrtle St
1200-2699 98106
2900-2998 98126
3000-3899 98126
3901-3997 98136
3999-4699 98136
Nagle Pl 98122
NE Naomi Pl 98115
S Nebraska St 98108
Nelson Pl 98188
NW Neptune Pl 98117
Nesbit Ave N 98103
S Nevada St
1-26 98134
28-98 98134
600-3099 98108
SW Nevada St 98126
Newell St 98109
W Newell St 98119
Newport Way 98122
Newton St 98109
E Newton St
52-198 98102
200-1299 98102
2000-4299 98112
W Newton St
1300-1399 98119
2300-2999 98199
Nickerson St 98109
W Nickerson St 98119
Nicklas Pl NE 98105
SW Niesz Ct 98116
Nob Hill Ave & Pl 98109
NW Norcross Way 98177
S Norfolk St 98118
S Norman St 98144
Normandy Rd & Ter 98166
Normandy Park Dr SW 98166
E North St 98112
NW North Beach Dr 98117
N Northgate Way 98133
NE Northgate Way 98125
N Northlake Pl 98103
NE Northlake Pl 98105
N Northlake Way 98103
NE Northlake Way 98105
Northrop Pl SW 98136
Northshire Rd NW 98177
NW Northwood Pl & Rd NW 98177
Norwood Pl 98122
S Nye Pl 98144
Oakhurst Pl & Rd S 98118
S Oaklawn Pl 98118
Oakwood Ave S 98178
Oberlin Ave NE
5800-5899 98105
6000-6099 98115
Occidental Ave S
100-599 98104
800-898 98134
900-2000 98134
2002-3298 98134
6401-7897 98108
7899-9899 98108
10000-12699 98168
19200-19699 98148
Ocean Ct SW 98136
SW Ocean View Dr 98146
Ohio Ave S 98134
W Ohman Pl 98199
Oldeldel Ave NW 98177
SW Olga St
3601-3797 98126
3799-3800 98126
3802-3898 98126
5000-5199 98116
E Olin Pl 98112
E Olive Ln 98122
E Olive Pl 98122
E Olive St 98122
Olive Way 98101
E Olive Way
1300-1549 98122
1550-1598 98102
1600-1899 98102
Olson Pl SW 98106
Olympic Ave S 98188
Olympic Dr NW 98177
W Olympic Pl 98119
Olympic Way W 98119
Orange Pl N 98109
S Orcas St
1-97 98108
99-2900 98108
2902-3098 98108
3200-5799 98118
Orchard Pl S 98118
S Orchard St
100-698 98108
700-799 98108
4600-5199 98118
SW Orchard St
1200-1900 98106
1902-2298 98106
3600-3798 98126
3800-3899 98126
3900-4199 98136
S Orchard Ter 98118
S Oregon St
1101-1197 98108
1199-3199 98108
3300-5099 98118
SW Oregon St
3600-3798 98126
3800-3899 98126
4000-4599 98116
4601-4999 98116
Orillia Rd S 98198
Orin Ct N 98103
SW Orleans St
3000-3099 98126
5100-6099 98116
S Orr St 98108
Oswego Pl NE 98115
S Othello St
600-2798 98108
2800-3099 98108
3200-5599 98118
SW Othello St
600-1299 98106
3500-3699 98126
3900-4899 98136
4901-4999 98136
Ovenes Ave S 98144
Pacific Hwy S 98198
N Pacific St 98103
NE Pacific St 98105
Padilla Pl S 98108
Paisley Dr & Pl 98115
Palatine Ave N
3600-9799 98103
10500-14099 98133
15500-20099 98133
Palatine Ln N 98133
Palatine Pl N
5600-5699 98103
18500-18599 98133
Palm Ave SW 98116
Palmer Dr NW 98107
S Pamela Dr 98178
Par Pl NE 98125
Pareenso Ave 98121
N Park Ave N 98133
E Park Dr E 98112
NW Park Dr 98177
W Park Dr E 98112
N Park Pl N 98133
NE Park Pl 98115
Park Rd NE
5600-5699 98105
2100-2199 98105
Park Point Dr, Ln, Pl & Way NE 98115
Parker Ct NW 98117
S Parkland Pl 98144
W Parkmont Pl 98199
Parkside Dr E 98112
Parkview Ave S 98178
Parshall Pl SW 98136
Pasadena Pl NE 98105
Patten Pl W 98199
Peach Ct E 98112
S Pearl St
1100-2199 98108
3900-5299 98118
Peashang Ave NE 98115
NE Penrith Rd 98105
Perimeter Rd S 98108
Perkins Ln W 98199
Perkins Pl NE
18600-18699 98155
1800-1899 98155
NE Perkins Way 98155
S Perry St 98118
Phinney Ave N
3400-9799 98103
10500-14400 98133
14402-14498 98133
14500-19798 98133
19800-19899 98133
Piedmont Pl W 98199
Pierinew Ave SW 98146
Pike Pl 98101
Pike St 98101
E Pike St 98122
S Pilgrim St 98118
Pine St 98101
E Pine St 98122
S Pinebrook Ln 98198
Pinehurst Way NE 98125
W Pleasant Pl 98119
S Plum St
900-998 98134
1200-3399 98144
S Plummer St 98134
W Plymouth St 98199
Point Pl SW 98116
Pontius Ave N 98109
Poplar Pl S 98144
Pomeric Ave SW 98136
Portage Bay Pl E 98102
SW Portland Ct 98106
S Portland St
201-497 98108
499-3099 98108
3200-3599 98118
SW Portland St
900-1000 98106
1002-1098 98106
3900-4399 98136
Post Aly 98101
Post Ave
600-700 98104
702-898 98104
1100-1199 98101
Powell Pl S 98108
Power Ave 98122
Prefontaine Pl S 98104
S Prentice St 98178
SW Prescott Ave & Pl SW 98126
Priantat Ave 98101
Pridaran 98131
SW Prince St 98116
Princeton Ave NE
5400-5498 98105
5500-5899 98105
6000-6099 98115
NE Princeton Way 98115
SW Pritchard St 98116
Prosch Ave W 98119
Prospect St 98109
E Prospect St
701-797 98102
799-1399 98102
1400-4100 98112
4102-4198 98112
W Prospect St 98119
W Prosper St 98199
Puget Blvd SW 98106
NW Puget Dr 98177
Puget Way SW 98106
Pullman Ave NE 98105
Purdue Ave NE 98105
Queen Anne Ave & Dr N 98109
Radford Ave NW 98177
NE Radford Dr 98115
Railroad Ave NE 98105
S Rainbow Ln 98198
Rainier Ave S
401-497 98144
499-3799 98144
3800-9999 98118
10000-11699 98178
11701-11799 98178
Rainier Pl S 98118
Randolph Ave & Pl 98122
Ravenna Ave NE
4501-4697 98105
4699-5399 98105
5401-5599 98105
6100-9899 98115
10000-10599 98125
NE Ravenna Blvd
400-999 98115
1000-2199 98105
Ravenna Pl NE 98105
Raye St 98109
W Raye St
1-1300 98119
1302-1498 98119
2101-2197 98199
2199-4600 98199
4602-4698 98199
S Raymond Pl 98118
S Raymond St
1700-1998 98108
2000-3000 98108
3002-3198 98108
3200-3598 98118
3600-5199 98118
SW Raymond St
2800-3599 98126
3601-3799 98126
3900-4899 98136
Redondo Way S 98198
Redondo Beach Dr S 98198
Redondo Shores Dr S 98198
S Redwing St 98118
E Remington Ct 98122
Renton Ave S
3600-3700 98144
3702-3798 98144
3800-4599 98108
5000-9900 98118
9902-9998 98118
10000-13099 98178
Renton Pl S 98144
Republican St 98109
E Republican St
300-1299 98102
1301-1399 98102

1400-3699 98112
W Republican St 98119
Restrai Ave 98104
Restrali Ave 98154
Richmond Beach Dr
NW 98177
N Richmond Beach
Rd 98133
NW Richmond Beach
Rd 98177
Richwood Ave NW 98177
Ridge Dr NE 98115
Ridgefield Rd NW 98177
Ridgemont Way N 98133
S Ridgeway Pl 98144
S River St 98108
Riverside Dr 98188
S Riverside Dr 98108
Riviera Pl NE 98125
Riviera Pl SW
17900-18400 98166
1100-1199 98166
E Roanoke St
1-1000 98102
1002-1198 98102
2000-2599 98112
S Roberto Maestas
Festival St 98144
W Roberts Way 98199
Rockery Dr S 98118
S Ronald Dr 98118
Ronald Pl N 98133
Roosevelt Way N 98133
Roosevelt Way NE
4001-4097 98105
4099-5999 98105
6000-9828 98115
9830-9898 98115
10000-13399 98125
S Rose Ct 98118
S Rose St
700-1299 98108
3300-3798 98118
3800-5299 98118
SW Rose St
3500-3799 98126
3900-4699 98136
Roseberg Ave S 98168
Rosemont Pl W 98199
Roslyn Pl N 98133
NW Roundhill Cir 98177
Rowan Rd S 98178
SW Roxbury Pl 98136
S Roxbury St 98118
SW Roxbury St
200-2499 98106
2501-2599 98106
2600-2798 98126
2800-3699 98126
4200-4298 98136
4300-4599 98136
Roy St 98109
E Roy St
301-397 98102
399-1299 98102
1400-2899 98112
W Roy St 98119
Royal Ct E 98112
S Royal Brougham
Way 98134
W Ruffner St
1000-1400 98119
1402-1498 98119
2100-4799 98199
S Ruggles St 98178
Russell Ave NW 98107
S Rustic Rd S 98178
Rutan Pl SW 98116
Ryan St & Way 98178
Saint Luke Pl N 98133
Salt Aire Pl 98198
Sand Point Pl NE 98105
Sand Point Way NE
4500-5899 98105
6000-6122 98115
6124-9799 98115
10000-12399 98125

Sander Rd S 98144
Saxon Dr 98188
NW Scenic Dr 98177
Schmitz Ave SW 98116
E Schubert Pl 98122
Seanchig Ave S 98198
Seattle Blvd S 98134
SW Seattle St 98116
Seaview Ave NW
5500-6499 98107
6500-8099 98117
Seaview Ter SW 98136
Seelye Ct S 98108
Segale Park Drive B 98188
Segale Park Drive C 98188
Segale Park Drive D 98188
W Semple St 98199
Seneca St 98101
E Seneca St 98122
SW Seola Ln 98146
Seola Beach Dr SW 98146
NE Serpentine Pl 98155
Seward Park Ave S 98118
Shaffer Ave S 98108
Shearedg Ave S 98178
E Shelby St
800-1299 98102
1800-2199 98112
Shell Ave S 98118
S Shelton St 98108
Shenandoah Dr E 98112
W Sheridan St 98199
Sherman Rd NW 98177
Sherwood Rd NW 98177
Shilshole Ave NW 98107
Shinkle Pl SW 98106
Shiteren Ave 98174
Shore Dr NE 98155
E Shore Dr 98112
NE Shore Pl 98155
SW Shore Pl 98136
SW Shorebrook Dr 98166
Shoreland Dr S 98144
Shoreline Park Dr NW 98177
SW Shoremont Ave 98166
Sierra Dr S 98144
Slade Way 98188
NW Sloop Pl 98117
Smith Pl 98109
Smith St 98109
NE Smith St 98131
W Smith St
1-600 98119
602-698 98119
2300-3599 98199
S Snoqualmie St
601-997 98108
999-1599 98108
1601-2999 98108
4300-4398 98118
4400-5099 98118
SW Snoqualmie St 98116
Sound View Dr S 98198
Sound View Dr W 98199
Southcenter Blvd, Mall &
Pkwy 98188
S Southern St 98108
SW Southern St
3500-3799 98126
3900-4399 98136
Spear Pl S 98118
S Spencer St
2300-2499 98108
4200-5199 98118
Sperry Dr 98188
S Spokane St
1-300 98134
302-698 98134
1200-3699 98144
SW Spokane St
900-1199 98134
1201-1399 98134
2300-2398 98106
3001-3097 98126
3099-3499 98126
4200-6200 98116
6202-6298 98116

Sports Field Dr NE 98115
Spring Dr NW 98177
Spring St 98104
E Spring St 98122
NW Springdale Ct & Pl
NW 98177
Spruce St 98104
E Spruce St 98122
E St Andrews Way 98112
S Stacy St 98134
Stanford Ave NE 98105
Stanley Ave S 98108
Stanton Pl NW 98117
Starfire Way 98188
Starling Rd 98158
S State St 98144
Stendall Dr & Pl 98133
S Stevens St 98144
SW Stevens St
3601-3697 98126
3699-3700 98126
3702-3798 98126
3901-3997 98116
3999-6500 98116
6502-6598 98116
Stewart St
2-98 98101
100-1299 98101
1300-1399 98109
Stone Ave N
4500-9699 98103
10000-10298 98133
10300-14399 98133
14500-19299 98133
19301-19599 98133
Stone Ct N 98133
Stone Ln N 98133
Stone Way 98103
Stone Way N 98103
Strander Blvd 98188
Stroud Ave N 98103
Sturgus Ave S 98144
Sturtevant Ave S 98118
S Sullivan St
500-1299 98108
3800-3999 98118
SW Sullivan St
1400-1499 98106
3700-3799 98126
4200-4299 98136
Summit Ave
1100-1299 98101
1301-1399 98101
1400-1899 98122
100-1100 98102
Sumner Ave SW 98126
S Sunnycrest Rd 98178
Sunnyside Ave N
3635-3697 98103
3699-8099 98103
8101-8299 98103
11300-14099 98133
14101-14399 98133
14500-19099 98133
Sunnyside Ct N 98133
Sunnyside Dr N 98133
S Sunnyview Dr 98118
NE Sunrise Vis 98115
Sunset Ave SW 98116
Sunwood Blvd 98188
E Superior St 98122
NE Surber Dr NE 98105
Swift Ave S 98108
Sycamore Ave NW
6000-6299 98107
6500-7299 98117
Sylvan Ln SW 98136
Sylvan Pl NW 98117
Sylvan Way SW
6400-6498 98126
6500-6599 98126
6900-7199 98106
SW Sylvan Heights Dr 98106
Sylvester Rd SW 98166
S Taft St 98178
Tallman Ave NW 98107
Taylor Ave N 98109

SW Teig Pl 98116
Temple Pl 98122
Teradelm Ave SW 98166
Terrace Ct SW 98166
Terrace Dr NE 98105
Terrace St 98104
E Terrace St 98122
Terry Ave
200-1099 98104
1101-1197 98101
1199-1999 98101
2000-2099 98121
2101-2199 98121
100-899 98109
Texas Way W 98199
Thackeray Pl NE 98105
S Thayer St 98178
S Thistle Pl 98118
S Thistle St
800-1499 98108
3400-4999 98118
5001-5099 98118
SW Thistle St
401-897 98106
899-2200 98106
2202-2498 98106
2600-3799 98126
3900-4399 98136
4401-4699 98136
Thomas St 98109
E Thomas St
300-1300 98102
1302-1398 98102
1400-1498 98112
1500-2899 98112
2901-3399 98112
W Thomas St 98119
Thorndyke Ave W
1500-2899 98199
3401-3699 98119
Thorndyke Pl W 98199
NE Thornton Pl 98125
Thunderbird Dr S 98198
W Thurman St
1501-1599 98119
2300-2398 98199
2400-3599 98199
W Tilden St 98199
Tillicum Rd SW 98136
SW Tillman St 98126
S Todd Blvd 98188
Tower Pl 98109
Treck Dr 98188
S Trenton St
201-297 98108
299-1499 98108
3801-4197 98118
4199-4599 98118
SW Trenton St
800-2599 98106
2601-2799 98126
2721-2721 98146
2801-2897 98126
2899-3799 98126
3900-4600 98136
4602-4698 98136
Triland Dr 98188
Triton Dr NW 98117
Troll Ave N 98103
Tukwila Pkwy 98188
Tukwila International Blvd
10601-10997 98168
10999-14899 98168
15000-15100 98188
15102-15898 98188
15200-15298 98188
NE Tulane Pl 98105
Turner Way E 98112
Twin Maple Ln NE 98105
Ual Service Dr 98158
Union St
84-300 98101
301-301 98111
302-1098 98101
303-907 98101
E Union St 98122
Union Bay Pl NE 98105

University St 98101
University Vlg NE
4601-4623 98105
2500-2700 98105
University Way NE
3900-4243 98105
4244-5698 98105
4244-4244 98145
4245-5699 98105
University View Pl NE 98105
NE University Village
Ct, Pl, Plz & St NE 98105
Upland Dr 98188
S Upland Rd 98118
Upland Ter S 98118
Ursula Pl S 98108
Utah Ave 98199
Utah Ave S 98134
Valdez Ave S 98118
S Vale St 98108
Valentine Pl S 98144
W Valley Hwy 98188
Valley St 98109
E Valley St 98112
Valmay Ave NW 98177
S Van Dyke Rd 98118
Vashon Pl & Vw 98136
Vassar Ave NE
5700-5899 98105
6000-6299 98115
Veredalm Ave NW 98107
S Vern Ct 98108
NW Vernon Pl 98107
Viburnum Ct S 98108
S Victor St 98178
Victoria Ave SW 98126
Victory Ln NE 98125
View Ave NW 98117
View Ln SW 98136
W View Pl 98199
W Viewmont Way 98199
NE Village Ct, Ln & Ter
NE 98105
Vine St 98121
Vinerlea Ave S 98168
Vinton Ct NW 98177
Virginia St 98101
Vista Ave S 98108
Wabash Ave S 98118
S Waite St 98144
SW Waite St 98116
S Walden St 98144
S Walker St
101-1199 98134
1200-3099 98144
SW Walker St 98116
Wall St 98121
S Wallace St 98178
Wallingford Ave N
3300-9799 98103
10001-10297 98133
10299-14399 98133
14500-20399 98133
Walnut Ave SW 98116
Ward Pl 98109
Ward St 98109
E Ward St 98112
Warlerth Ave S 98118
Warren Ave & Pl N 98109
S Warsaw St
801-897 98108
899-2699 98108
3800-4899 98118
SW Warsaw St 98126
Washington Ave 98199
Washington Pl E 98112
S Washington St
65-65 98104
67-1099 98104
1400-1598 98144
1600-3300 98144
3302-3398 98144
Waters Ave S
9200-9298 98118
9300-9999 98118
10000-10499 98178
Waverly Pl N 98109

Waverly Way E 98112
Wayne Ave & Pl 98133
S Webster St
200-3000 98108
3002-3098 98108
3201-3297 98118
3299-4599 98118
SW Webster St
901-1197 98106
1199-2499 98106
2700-3799 98126
3900-4599 98136
Webster Point Rd NE 98105
Weedin Pl NE 98115
S Weller St
500-1099 98104
1200-2099 98144
Wellesley Way NE 98115
Wellington Ave 98122
Western Ave
600-1099 98104
1100-1198 98101
1200-1599 98101
2000-3199 98121
100-200 98119
Westlake Ave
1600-1998 98101
2000-2299 98121
Westlake Ave N 98109
Westminster Way N 98133
Westmont Way W 98199
Westview Dr W 98119
Westwood Pl NE 98125
Wetmore Ave S 98144
Whalley Pl W 98199
Wheeler St 98109
W Wheeler St
700-1599 98119
2300-3198 98199
3200-3299 98199
3301-3499 98199
Whitman Ave N
3600-4999 98103
10500-10999 98133
14500-20300 98133
20302-20498 98133
Whitman Pl N 98133
Whitney Pl NW 98117
Wickstrom Pl SW 98116
S Wildwood Ln 98118
SW Wildwood Pl 98136
Willard Ave W 98119
Williams Ave W 98199
S Willow St
700-3099 98108
3101-3299 98108
3700-5699 98118
SW Willow St
2200-2398 98106
3401-3697 98126
3699-3899 98126
3900-4599 98136
Wilson Ave S 98118
SW Wilton Ct 98116
Windermere Dr E 98112
NE Windermere Rd
5400-6599 98105
6600-6699 98115
Wingard Ct N 98133
Winona Ave N 98103
Winslow Pl N 98103
Winston Ave S 98108
S Winthrop St 98144
SW Winthrop St 98116
Wolcott Ave S 98118
Wolfe Pl W 98199
Woodbine Pl & Way 98177
Woodland Pl N 98103
Woodland Park Ave N 98103
Woodlawn Ave N 98103
Woodlawn Ave NE 98115
Woodley Ave S 98178
Woodmont Dr S 98198
Woodmont Beach Rd
S 98198
Woodrow Pl E 98112
Woodside Pl SW 98136

Woodward Ave S 98178
Wright Ave SW 98136
Yakima Ave & Pl 98144
Yale Ave 98101
Yale Ave E 98102
Yale Ave N 98109
Yale Pl E 98102
Yale Ter E 98102
SW Yancy St 98126
Yesler Way 98104
E Yesler Way 98122
York Rd S 98144
Yukon Ave S 98118

NUMBERED STREETS

1st Ave
600-1099 98104
1100-1999 98101
2000-3099 98121
1st Ave N 98109
1st Ave NE
3906-3906 98105
6003-6003 98115
11000-11514 98125
14513-14513 98155
1st Ave NW
3500-6299 98107
6500-9799 98117
10119-10197 98177
1st Ave S
100-599 98104
800-5099 98134
5200-7249 98108
10000-12699 98168
17401-19999 98148
20001-21099 98198
1st Ave SW 98146
1st Ave W 98119
1st Ct S 98198
1st Ln SW 98146
1st Pl S 98198
1st Pl SW 98166
2nd Ave
500-900 98104
901-999 98174
902-1098 98104
1100-1999 98101
2000-2699 98121
2nd Ave N 98109
2nd Ave NE
3801-3897 98105
6500-9199 98115
11000-13999 98125
15401-15401 98155
2nd Ave NW
3600-6299 98107
6500-9799 98117
10500-14099 98177
2nd Ave S
200-404 98104
3300-5099 98134
5200-5298 98108
10000-12699 98168
19200-19899 98148
20000-21099 98198
2nd Ave SW
9200-9598 98106
10000-12799 98146
16400-20799 98166
2nd Ave W 98119
2nd Ct SW 98146
2nd Ln SW 98146
2nd Pl NE 98155
2nd Pl SW
10400-13399 98146
16600-20899 98166
2nd Avenue Ext S 98104
3rd Ave
501-507 98104
1100-1999 98101
2000-2899 98121
2901-2999 98121
3rd Ave N
700-3099 98109
3rd Ave NE
9500-9799 98115

10100-10998 98125
11000-13700 98125
13702-13798 98125
14501-15097 98155
15099-19200 98155
19202-19298 98155
3rd Ave NW
3900-4098 98107
4100-6299 98107
6500-9799 98117
10000-10098 98177
10100-14499 98177
17100-17798 98177
17800-20399 98177
3rd Ave S
100-299 98104
301-399 98104
1201-2697 98134
2699-4999 98134
5001-5099 98134
5300-5498 98108
5500-9099 98108
10200-12100 98168
12102-12298 98168
19200-19599 98148
20000-21499 98198
21600-21699 98198
3rd Ave SW
7901-8997 98106
8999-9999 98106
10000-12499 98146
16400-20099 98166
3rd Ave W
300-398 98119
3rd Ln SW
9900-9999 98106
3rd Pl NE
16600-16699 98155
3rd Pl NW
11534-11536 98177
3rd Pl S
19800-19899 98148
3rd Pl SW
17600-20099 98166
4th Ave
400-598 98104
900-998 98164
1000-1098 98104
1001-1099 98154
1100-1214 98101
1215-1215 98161
1216-1998 98101
1217-1999 98101
2000-2799 98121
2801-2899 98121
4th Ave N 98109
4th Ave NE
3800-4799 98105
6000-9899 98115
11500-11512 98125
11514-13999 98125
14001-14299 98125
15400-17299 98155
4th Ave NW
4200-6299 98107
6500-9799 98117
10100-13299 98177
17800-20399 98177
4th Ave S
101-197 98104
199-200 98104
202-598 98104
820-1198 98134
1200-2421 98134
2420-2420 98124
2422-4698 98134
2423-5099 98134
5200-9400 98108
9402-9498 98108
10220-10698 98168
10700-12799 98168
19200-19999 98148
20000-21499 98198
21600-21899 98198
4th Ave SW
7901-8097 98106
8099-9500 98106
9502-9998 98106
10000-12699 98146
17100-20699 98166
4th Ave W 98119
4th Pl S
11200-11299 98168
20000-28999 98198
21600-21999 98198
4th Pl SW
9600-9700 98106
9702-9998 98106
10000-11400 98146
11402-11498 98146
19300-19499 98166
5th Ave
300-398 98104
400-900 98104
901-999 98164
902-1098 98104
1100-1298 98101
2000-2699 98121
5th Ave N 98109
5th Ave NE
3801-3997 98105
6000-9899 98115
10000-12500 98125
14500-14698 98155
5th Ave NW
4200-6299 98107
6500-7299 98117
10700-10799 98177
5th Ave S
100-611 98104
5201-5597 98108
10800-12499 98168
18100-18899 98148
20000-22299 98198
5th Ave SW
7900-9899 98106
10000-12399 98146
17800-17900 98166
5th Ave W 98119
5th Ct NW 98177
5th Ln SW 98146
5th Pl S
2400-2499 98134
6500-6599 98108
21400-28799 98198
5th Pl SW
9601-9697 98106
10800-10999 98146
18600-18799 98166
6th Ave
601-999 98104
1101-1197 98101
2000-2399 98121
6th Ave N 98109
6th Ave NE
3801-3897 98105
6000-7699 98115
14500-20199 98155
6th Ave NW
3900-4098 98107
6500-9799 98117
11500-13299 98177
6th Ave S
100-298 98104
414-414 98114
500-798 98104
800-998 98134
3800-3998 98108
10400-10798 98168
19201-19297 98148
20000-23999 98198
6th Ave SW
7300-9899 98106
10000-12799 98146
16646-16798 98166
6th Ave W 98119
6th Cir SW 98106
6th Pl NE
11536-11599 98125
20100-20199 98155
6th Pl NW 98177
6th Pl S
2700-2742 98134
21619-28799 98198
6th Pl SW
9600-9899 98106
11800-13099 98146
17100-18199 98166
7th Ave
600-998 98104
1500-1999 98101
2000-2499 98121
7th Ave NE
4000-5399 98105
9600-9699 98115
11500-11512 98125
17501-17997 98155
7th Ave NW
5500-6299 98107
6500-9799 98117
10000-13299 98177
7th Ave S
400-700 98104
800-3598 98134
3801-3897 98108
19600-19699 98148
20200-26499 98198
7th Ave SW
7300-9999 98106
10200-10398 98146
17400-17499 98166
7th Ave W 98119
7th Pl NW 98177
7th Pl S
11000-11099 98168
19200-19699 98148
20200-27299 98198
7th Pl SW
7301-9597 98106
12100-12200 98146
17400-17899 98166
8th Ave
100-1099 98104
1100-1999 98101
2000-2399 98121
8th Ave N 98109
8th Ave NE
4000-5999 98105
6000-9899 98115
10000-11037 98125
11036-11036 98175
11038-13098 98125
14501-14697 98155
8th Ave NW
4200-4498 98107
6500-9799 98117
10000-13599 98177
8th Ave S
100-799 98104
1000-1698 98134
7100-9999 98108
10100-12699 98168
17800-19398 98148
20000-28199 98198
8th Ave SW
7500-9999 98106
10001-10397 98146
16800-18999 98166
8th Ave W 98119
8th Ct NE 98125
8th Ln NE 98155
8th Pl S
11100-11199 98168
16800-16898 98148
24000-25299 98198
8th Pl SW 98106
8th Pl W 98119
9th Ave
201-497 98104
499-1000 98104
1002-1098 98104
1100-1198 98101
2000-2299 98121
9th Ave N 98109
9th Ave NE
4000-5399 98105
6100-6198 98115
10500-12299 98125
14600-18399 98155
9th Ave NW
4200-6399 98107
6500-9799 98117
10000-13299 98177
9th Ave S
3700-3799 98134
3801-4099 98108
10200-12799 98168
19300-19999 98148
20100-28299 98198
9th Ave SW
7900-9999 98106
10000-12399 98146
9th Ave W 98119
9th Ct NE 98155
9th Ct SW 98146
9th Pl NE 98155
9th Pl NW 98177
9th Pl S 98198
9th Pl SW 98106
10th Ave 98122
10th Ave E 98102
10th Ave NE
12600-13100 98125
14500-15198 98155
10th Ave NW
6500-8599 98117
12000-13099 98177
10th Ave S
100-499 98104
4200-4498 98108
10201-11197 98168
16600-16699 98148
20100-28199 98198
10th Ave SW
7700-9999 98106
10000-12199 98146
16801-16899 98166
10th Ave W 98119
10th Ct S 98148
10th Ln SW 98146
10th Pl NE 98125
10th Pl NW 98177
10th Pl S
19300-19399 98148
22200-27399 98198
10th Pl SW
9700-9999 98106
20200-20398 98166
10th Pl W 98119
10th Ter NW 98177
11th Ave 98122
11th Ave E 98102
11th Ave NE
4100-5699 98105
7300-7498 98115
10400-13399 98125
14501-15097 98155
11th Ave NW
4300-6400 98107
6500-9799 98117
10000-12799 98177
11th Ave S
1500-1798 98134
4200-4599 98108
10100-11798 98168
19800-19999 98148
20600-26099 98198
11th Ave SW
2400-2498 98134
7500-9999 98106
10000-11499 98146
11th Ave W 98119
11th Pl NE 98155
11th Pl NW 98177
11th Pl S
19200-19298 98148
22200-23298 98198
11th Pl SW
11800-11898 98146
16800-16898 98166
12th Ave
100-1850 98122
12th Ave E
100-2399 98102
12th Ave NE
3900-4098 98105
4100-5700 98105
5702-5998 98105
6100-9799 98115
9801-9899 98115
10000-13400 98125
13402-14398 98125
14500-20199 98155
12th Ave NW
6500-9799 98117
10000-13099 98177
17000-20499 98177
12th Ave S
200-3199 98144
3900-4098 98108
4100-8800 98108
8802-9098 98108
10000-12699 98168
20200-20398 98198
20400-20799 98198
20900-27199 98198
12th Ave SW
6701-7497 98106
7499-9499 98106
9501-9899 98106
10000-10598 98146
10600-11499 98146
16800-17699 98166
12th Ave W
1600-1798 98119
12th Ln S
19800-19999 98148
12th Pl NE
16800-16999 98155
12th Pl NW
19000-20499 98177
12th Pl S
14000-14099 98168
19600-19699 98148
20000-20699 98198
21100-27599 98198
12th Pl SW
15801-16997 98166
13th Ave
100-448 98122
13th Ave E
100-2299 98102
13th Ave NE
17000-17099 98155
13th Ave NW
6700-9799 98117
10000-10599 98177
10601-13099 98177
16900-20499 98177
13th Ave S
1300-3799 98144
3800-6299 98108
10200-10299 98168
19900-19999 98148
20000-20799 98198
20800-28099 98198
13th Ave SW
1701-1797 98134
1799-3499 98134
6700-9899 98106
10001-10099 98146
11300-11398 98146
17201-17397 98166
17399-17599 98166
13th Ave W
1900-3899 98119
13th Ct S
23800-23999 98198
13th Pl NW
20000-20099 98177
13th Pl S
18800-19599 98148
23700-26399 98198
14th Ave 98122
14th Ave E 98112
14th Ave NE
6300-8100 98115
10700-12599 98125
15500-20199 98155
14th Ave NW
4400-6499 98107
6700-9799 98117
10000-10599 98177
14th Ave S
300-1298 98144
3800-9999 98108
10000-12699 98168
20000-20799 98198
14th Ave SW
4601-4797 98106
10000-11499 98146
14th Ave W 98119
14th Ct NE 98155
14th Ct NW 98177
14th Ct S
9900-9999 98108
24800-24899 98198
14th Ln NW 98177
14th Ln S 98198
14th Pl NE 98125
14th Pl NW 98177
14th Pl S
12600-12699 98168
24100-27599 98198
15th Ave 98122
15th Ave E 98112
15th Ave NE
3701-4197 98105
6200-9899 98115
10000-14399 98125
14500-20399 98155
15th Ave NW
4400-6499 98107
6500-9999 98117
10000-10599 98177
15th Ave S
101-1297 98144
3900-5600 98108
10000-10199 98168
19600-19699 98148
20000-20799 98198
15th Ave SW
4601-4797 98106
9900-9998 98146
15th Ave W 98119
15th Pl NE
13500-13599 98125
18300-18499 98155
15th Pl S
9100-9199 98108
25800-27699 98198
15th Pl W 98119
16th Ave
100-1899 98122
16th Ave E
100-2399 98112
16th Ave NE
4500-5899 98105
6300-8599 98115
11500-11506 98125
11508-13599 98125
16501-16797 98155
16799-19299 98155
16th Ave NW
6500-8799 98117
16700-19199 98177
16th Ave S
200-298 98144
300-3499 98144
5300-8699 98108
8701-9999 98108
10000-12699 98168
12701-14699 98168
18800-19099 98188
19101-19199 98188
22000-27099 98198
27101-27899 98198
16th Ave SW
1801-2497 98134
2499-3300 98134
3302-3498 98134
3800-9837 98106
9839-9899 98106
10000-11499 98146
16800-17099 98166
16th Ave W
1200-2998 98119
16th Ln S
23600-23899 98198
16th Pl NE
19700-19799 98155
16th Pl NW
20400-20499 98177
16th Pl S
23500-27899 98198
17th Ave 98122
17th Ave E 98112
17th Ave NE
4500-5899 98105
6200-9899 98115
10000-13800 98125
14501-14597 98155
17th Ave NW
4700-4898 98107
5706-5706 98127
5712-6498 98107
6500-9999 98117
17700-20399 98177
17th Ave S
100-198 98144
4900-5999 98108
10400-10499 98168
20800-26899 98198
17th Ave SW
3801-3997 98106
10000-11099 98146
17th Ave W 98119
17th Ct S 98198
17th Pl NE
8500-8599 98115
17400-17499 98155
17th Pl NW 98177
17th Pl S
10000-10099 98168
22001-23197 98198
18th Ave 98122
18th Ave E 98112
18th Ave NE
4500-5799 98105
6300-8299 98115
12300-12399 98125
16500-19299 98155
18th Ave NW
6500-6698 98117
19600-19798 98177
18th Ave S
101-397 98144
5300-6099 98108
10400-10699 98168
22600-26199 98198
18th Ave SW
3800-9899 98106
10000-10008 98146
18th Ave W 98119
18th Ct NE 98155
18th Pl NW 98117
18th Pl S 98198
18th Pl SW 98146
19th Ave 98122
19th Ave E 98112
19th Ave NE
4500-5299 98105
6200-9799 98115
10500-14399 98125
19600-20399 98155
19th Ave NW
6501-6697 98117
19800-19899 98177
19th Ave S
800-3499 98144
4800-6099 98108
10400-10699 98168
22200-26799 98198
19th Ave SW
3601-3697 98106
10000-11099 98146
16800-16899 98166
19th Ct NE 98155
19th Ct S 98198
19th Pl S
5200-5298 98108
24800-26599 98198
19th Pl SW 98146
20th Ave 98122
20th Ave E 98112
20th Ave NE
4500-5699 98105
6200-9899 98115

10000-14399 98125
14500-19598 98155
20th Ave NW
4800-6499 98107
6500-9299 98117
19000-20300 98177
20th Ave S
200-398 98144
4800-5999 98108
10400-12699 98168
22901-22997 98198
20th Ave SW
3700-9899 98106
10000-11599 98146
20th Ave W 98199
NW 20th Ave
6500-6599 98117
20th Ln S 98168
20th Pl NE
7000-7099 98115
17500-20299 98155
20th Pl S 98144
20th Pl SW 98146
21st Ave 98122
21st Ave E 98112
21st Ave NE
4500-5599 98105
6100-8399 98115
10000-10099 98125
16500-20399 98155
21st Ave NW
6500-9899 98117
19000-20299 98177
21st Ave S
201-1097 98144
5200-6000 98108
12000-12700 98168
22900-24799 98198
21st Ave SW
3700-9899 98106
10000-11499 98146
21st Ave W 98199
21st Ct NE 98155
21st Ct S 98198
21st Pl NE 98155
21st Pl NW 98177
21st Pl S 98198
21st Pl SW 98146
22nd Ave 98122
22nd Ave E 98112
22nd Ave NE
4500-4598 98105
6200-8299 98115
11500-11506 98125
14501-14697 98155
22nd Ave NW
5300-6499 98107
6500-9399 98117
19000-19599 98177
22nd Ave S
100-198 98144
5400-5498 98108
12000-12699 98168
24000-25499 98198
22nd Ave SW
3600-9899 98106
10400-11100 98146
22nd Ave W 98199
22nd Ct NW 98117
22nd Ln S 98168
22nd Pl NE
8200-8299 98115
17700-17730 98155
22nd Pl NW 98177
22nd Pl S
10400-10598 98168
23200-24499 98198
22nd Pl SW 98146
23rd Ave 98122
23rd Ave E 98112
23rd Ave NE
6200-9799 98115
10200-14099 98125
14500-19599 98155
23rd Ave NW
6500-9899 98117
19200-20299 98177

23rd Ave S
100-3499 98144
5400-6499 98108
12000-12699 98168
23400-24499 98198
23rd Ave SW
3600-3798 98106
11300-11398 98146
23rd Ave W 98199
23rd Ct NE
8100-8199 98115
17900-17998 98155
23rd Ct SW 98146
23rd Ln NE 98155
23rd Pl NE 98125
23rd Pl NW 98177
23rd Pl S
13201-13299 98168
22800-23499 98198
24th Ave 98122
24th Ave E 98112
24th Ave NE
4700-5799 98105
6000-7800 98115
10500-14399 98125
17800-20300 98155
24th Ave NW
5300-6499 98107
6500-9999 98117
19600-20299 98177
24th Ave S
100-3500 98144
3800-4798 98108
10801-11597 98168
20600-21098 98198
24th Ave SW
6300-9899 98106
10000-10899 98146
24th Ave W 98199
24th Ln NE 98155
24th Pl NE
14300-14399 98125
17801-17845 98155
24th Pl S
4000-5036 98108
14700-14799 98168
24th Pl SW 98146
24th Pl W 98199
25th Ave 98122
25th Ave E 98112
25th Ave NE
4500-5799 98105
6000-9600 98115
11300-14399 98125
14500-20399 98155
25th Ave NW
6500-9599 98117
19100-19298 98177
25th Ave S
100-3499 98144
3801-3897 98108
11600-11899 98168
20700-20798 98198
25th Ave SW
4100-9899 98106
10000-11399 98146
25th Ave W 98199
25th Ct S 98168
25th Ln S 98198
25th Pl NE
8700-8799 98115
16300-16399 98155
25th Pl S
13400-13799 98168
20400-20599 98198
25th Pl W 98199
26th Ave 98122
26th Ave E 98112
26th Ave NE
4600-5799 98105
6000-8999 98115
11500-14399 98125
14500-16399 98155
26th Ave NW
5300-6499 98107
6500-9699 98117
19500-19999 98177

26th Ave S
100-2399 98144
4700-4898 98108
10800-12199 98168
15030-15098 98188
20601-20799 98198
26th Ave SW
4000-9899 98106
10000-11499 98146
26th Ave W 98199
26th Ct S 98168
26th Ln S
13500-14198 98168
15000-15199 98188
26th Pl NW 98117
26th Pl S
13600-14300 98168
20500-20599 98198
26th Pl SW 98126
26th Pl W 98199
27th Ave 98122
27th Ave E 98112
27th Ave NE
4501-5097 98105
6000-9799 98115
10500-10798 98125
14500-16599 98155
27th Ave NW
6500-9899 98117
19401-19799 98177
27th Ave S
100-3399 98144
3900-6999 98108
10700-10798 98168
19400-19999 98188
22701-22797 98198
27th Ave SW
7000-7199 98106
7300-9499 98126
10600-11599 98146
27th Ave W 98199
27th Ln S 98168
27th Pl S
14500-14599 98168
14900-14999 98188
20500-20599 98198
27th Pl SW 98146
27th Pl W 98199
28th Ave 98122
28th Ave E 98112
28th Ave NE
5500-5799 98105
6000-8399 98115
10700-14099 98125
14500-16330 98155
28th Ave NW
5300-6499 98107
6500-9699 98117
28th Ave S
100-2399 98144
4300-6999 98108
12000-12499 98168
18601-18799 98158
18800-19899 98188
20200-20499 98198
28th Ave SW
4000-9999 98126
10000-11500 98146
28th Ave W 98199
28th Ct S 98198
28th Ln S
14400-14499 98168
14900-15099 98188
28th Pl NE 98155
28th Pl S
13600-13699 98168
21900-22099 98198
28th Pl W 98199
29th Ave 98122
29th Ave E 98112
29th Ave NE
5100-5799 98105
6000-8699 98115
10000-10100 98125
17800-18599 98155
29th Ave NW 98117

29th Ave S
100-198 98144
4000-4098 98108
13800-14699 98168
15000-15299 98188
21200-21499 98198
29th Ave SW
5400-9999 98126
11200-11599 98146
29th Ave W 98199
29th Ct S 98198
29th Ln S
14600-14699 98168
14900-15199 98188
29th Pl NE 98155
29th Pl S 98168
29th Pl SW 98146
30th Ave 98122
30th Ave E 98112
30th Ave NE
4701-4997 98105
6000-9600 98115
10500-14399 98125
14500-15899 98155
30th Ave NW
5300-5498 98107
6500-9199 98117
30th Ave S
100-3199 98144
4000-6999 98108
14400-14499 98168
15000-15500 98188
20000-21499 98198
30th Ave SW
3200-9500 98126
10000-10300 98146
30th Ave W 98199
30th Pl S
13200-14199 98168
22000-22099 98198
30th Pl SW 98146
31st Ave 98122
31st Ave E 98112
31st Ave NE
5500-5799 98105
6000-8499 98115
10000-13399 98125
14500-14799 98155
31st Ave NW 98117
31st Ave S
100-2899 98144
3900-6599 98108
13200-13399 98168
16600-18199 98188
21100-21299 98198
31st Ave SW
3200-9999 98126
10000-11099 98146
31st Ave W 98199
31st Ln S 98198
31st Pl NE 98125
31st Pl S
6900-6999 98108
15100-17219 98188
31st Pl SW 98126
32nd Ave 98122
32nd Ave E 98112
32nd Ave NE
4900-4998 98105
6000-9899 98115
10000-14399 98125
14500-15599 98155
32nd Ave NW
5400-6499 98107
6500-9399 98117
32nd Ave S
100-2899 98144
4700-7899 98118
13000-13198 98168
15200-15249 98188
15250-15250 98168
15250-19898 98188
20000-21299 98198
32nd Ave SW
4000-9999 98126
10000-11399 98146
32nd Ave W 98199

32nd Ln S
14600-14698 98168
15100-15200 98188
20800-20899 98198
32nd Pl NE 98155
32nd Pl S
14800-14999 98168
15001-15099 98188
20400-21899 98198
32nd Pl SW 98146
33rd Ave 98122
33rd Ave E 98112
33rd Ave NE
4700-5599 98105
6000-7799 98115
11500-12799 98125
15500-20499 98155
33rd Ave NW 98117
33rd Ave S
500-3699 98144
4400-7398 98118
4401-4499 98108
4501-7399 98118
13000-14099 98168
16200-19999 98188
21100-21498 98198
33rd Ave SW
3001-3297 98126
10000-10299 98146
33rd Ave W 98199
33rd Ct NE 98155
33rd Pl NE 98125
33rd Pl NW 98117
33rd Pl S 98168
NE 33rd St 98105
34th Ave 98122
34th Ave E 98112
34th Ave NE
4700-5600 98105
6000-8399 98115
11000-11599 98125
15600-19599 98155
34th Ave NW
5300-6499 98107
6500-7799 98117
34th Ave S
400-1898 98144
4000-8500 98118
12600-14499 98168
16000-19799 98188
20300-22099 98198
34th Ave SW
3000-3298 98126
10000-11499 98146
34th Ave W 98199
34th Ct S 98118
34th Ct W 98199
34th Ln S 98188
34th Pl S
6700-6799 98118
14100-14199 98168
17400-19199 98188
20400-20499 98198
34th Pl SW 98146
N 34th St 98103
35th Ave 98122
35th Ave E 98112
35th Ave NE
4500-5799 98105
6000-9899 98115
10000-14399 98125
14700-19799 98155
35th Ave NW
6000-6099 98107
6700-7199 98117
35th Ave S
300-3699 98144
4500-7800 98118
12501-12597 98168
15400-15499 98188
20000-21899 98198
35th Ave SW
3200-9999 98126
10000-11500 98146
35th Ave W 98199
35th Ln S
11600-11699 98168

19700-19999 98188
35th Pl NE 98155
35th Pl NW
6000-6099 98107
6700-6799 98117
35th Pl S
6700-6799 98118
18200-18399 98188
N 35th St 98103
NE 35th St 98105
36th Ave 98122
36th Ave E 98112
36th Ave NE
4100-5799 98105
6000-8499 98115
10000-14399 98125
15600-19699 98155
36th Ave NW
5900-6499 98107
6500-6899 98117
36th Ave S
1400-3699 98144
4101-4197 98118
18000-18098 98188
36th Ave SW
1900-9499 98126
10000-11099 98146
36th Ave W 98199
36th Ct NE 98155
36th Ln S 98188
36th Pl NE 98155
36th Pl S 98188
N 36th St 98103
NE 36th St 98105
NW 36th St 98107
37th Ave 98122
37th Ave E 98112
37th Ave NE
4100-5799 98105
6000-8299 98115
12500-14399 98125
14500-20499 98155
37th Ave NW
6100-6499 98107
6500-6799 98117
37th Ave S
3100-3799 98144
3800-9499 98118
12601-12797 98168
16601-16797 98188
37th Ave SW
2200-9999 98126
10000-11499 98146
37th Ave W 98199
37th Ln S 98188
37th Pl E 98112
37th Pl S
3100-3399 98144
15200-15299 98188
20900-20999 98198
37th Pl SW 98146
N 37th St 98103
38th Ave 98122
38th Ave E 98112
38th Ave NE
4401-4493 98105
6000-9899 98115
10000-14399 98125
14500-19599 98155
38th Ave S
3600-3799 98144
3800-9499 98118
13000-14899 98168
17600-18599 98188
38th Ave SW
2600-9299 98126
10200-10299 98146
38th Ave W 98199
N 38th Ct 98103
38th Ln S
13000-13099 98168
15400-15499 98188
38th Pl E 98112
38th Pl NE 98155
38th Pl S
13200-13224 98168
15800-15898 98188

20900-20999 9819
N 38th St 98103
NE 38th St 9810
38th Ter S 98188
39th Ave 98122
39th Ave E 9811
39th Ave NE
5000-5799 9810
6000-8299 98115
10000-13799 98125
14700-18899 98155
39th Ave S
3700-3799 98144
3800-9499 98118
11600-11699 98168
18200-19499 98188
39th Ave SW
2501-2597 98116
5900-9999 98136
10000-11099 98146
39th Ave W 98199
39th Ln S 98188
39th Pl NE 98155
39th Pl S 98188
N 39th St 98103
NE 39th St 98105
NW 39th St 98107
39th Way S 98198
40th Ave 98122
40th Ave E 98112
40th Ave NE
3800-5899 98105
6000-9800 98115
10000-14399 98125
14501-14697 98155
40th Ave S
6700-9899 98118
11400-11498 98168
15200-15499 98188
40th Ave SW
3200-4899 98116
5000-9899 98136
10000-10499 98146
40th Ave W 98199
40th Ct NE 98155
40th Ln S 98188
40th Pl NE 98155
40th Pl S
11700-11798 98168
15801-15899 98188
21000-21499 98198
N 40th St 98103
NE 40th St 98105
NW 40th St 98107
40th Way S 98198
41st Ave E 98112
41st Ave NE
3700-4799 98105
6000-9899 98115
10000-14100 98125
15900-19799 98155
41st Ave S
3700-3799 98144
3800-9799 98118
11301-12997 98168
17600-19799 98188
41st Ave SW
1700-4899 98116
5000-9899 98136
10000-10499 98146
41st Ave W 98199
41st Pl NE
9700-9799 98115
10500-10800 98125
18600-20299 98155
41st Pl S
14900-14999 98168
20900-21099 98198
N 41st St 98103
NE 41st St 98105
NW 41st St 98107
42nd Ave E 98112
42nd Ave NE
3600-4199 98105
6500-9699 98115
10300-13799 98125
19600-20399 98155

42nd Ave S
3700-3799 98144
3800-9899 98118
11500-12598 98168
15000-15900 98188
21201-21599 98198
42nd Ave SW
1300-4899 98116
5000-9899 98136
10000-10899 98146
42nd Ave W 98199
42nd Ln S 98188
42nd Pl NE 98125
42nd Pl S 98118
N 42nd St 98103
NE 42nd St 98105
NW 42nd St 98107
43rd Ave E 98112
43rd Ave NE
3200-5899 98105
6000-8699 98115
18400-18498 98155
43rd Ave S
3801-4597 98118
12200-12299 98178
13401-13497 98168
15800-15899 98188
43rd Ave W 98199
43rd Ln S 98188
43rd Pl NE
9800-9899 98115
10000-10099 98125
43rd Pl S
13700-13799 98168
15000-15099 98188
43rd Pl SW 98136
N 43rd St 98103
NE 43rd St 98105
NW 43rd St 98107
44th Ave NE
3800-5059 98105
6000-9899 98115
10000-10399 98125
17000-20200 98155
44th Ave S
4600-8699 98118
11600-12299 98178
13100-13698 98168
15600-15699 98188
44th Ave SW
1100-1298 98116
5200-9899 98136
10000-10098 98146
44th Ave W 98199
44th Ct S 98188
44th Ln S 98188
44th Pl NE
6800-9499 98115
19600-19699 98155
44th Pl S
7900-7999 98118
11800-11820 98178
15500-15599 98188
44th Pl SW 98136
N 44th St 98103
NE 44th St 98105
NW 44th St 98107
45th Ave NE
3401-3497 98105
6000-9800 98115
10000-12599 98125
16501-16697 98155
45th Ave S
3800-4598 98118
12200-12299 98178
13700-13800 98168
16000-16299 98188
45th Ave SW
1400-1498 98116
5200-9899 98136
45th Ave W 98199
45th Ct NE 98155
45th Pl NE
18501-18697 98155
45th Pl S
13601-13699 98168
16300-16399 98188

NE 45th Pl
3200-3400 98105
N 45th St 98103
NE 45th St 98105
NW 45th St 98107
46th Ave NE
3300-5199 98105
6500-9800 98115
10000-10399 98125
18700-18798 98155
46th Ave S
3801-3897 98118
10001-11997 98178
13600-14999 98168
16000-16299 98188
46th Ave SW
1500-1598 98116
5000-9899 98136
46th Ave W 98199
46th Ln S
14800-14899 98168
16700-16899 98188
46th Pl NE
10000-10098 98125
20300-20399 98155
46th Pl S 98188
46th Pl SW 98136
N 46th St 98103
NE 46th St 98105
NW 46th St 98107
47th Ave NE
3301-3397 98105
6500-7399 98115
17000-20199 98155
47th Ave S
3900-9999 98118
10400-10899 98178
13300-14598 98168
15600-16399 98188
47th Ave SW
1700-4899 98116
5000-9899 98136
10000-10499 98146
47th Ln S 98188
47th Pl NE
3700-3799 98105
18200-19199 98155
47th Pl S 98188
47th Pl SW 98136
N 47th St 98103
NE 47th St 98105
NW 47th St 98107
48th Ave NE
3700-5199 98105
6500-9799 98115
10000-10399 98125
48th Ave S
3901-3997 98118
10800-12198 98178
12800-14314 98168
15900-16299 98188
48th Ave SW
1900-4899 98116
5000-9699 98136
48th Pl NE 98105
48th Pl S
13430-13440 98168
16300-16399 98188
N 48th St 98103
NE 48th St 98105
NW 48th St 98107
49th Ave NE
3600-3798 98105
6500-9799 98115
10000-10099 98125
49th Ave S
4000-9799 98118
10700-11098 98178
16200-16299 98188
49th Ave SW
2100-4899 98116
5000-9899 98136
49th Pl NE 98155
N 49th St 98103
NE 49th St 98105
NW 49th St 98107

50th Ave NE
3600-5299 98105
6000-7399 98115
18700-18799 98155
50th Ave S
4000-9699 98118
10701-10897 98178
17900-18199 98188
50th Ave SW
2100-2198 98116
5000-9800 98136
50th Ct S 98188
50th Pl S 98178
N 50th St 98103
NE 50th St 98105
NW 50th St 98107
51st Ave NE
3800-4599 98105
6000-7599 98115
18800-20199 98155
51st Ave S
4001-4097 98118
10000-10400 98178
13400-13798 98168
15000-16499 98188
51st Ave SW
2300-4899 98116
5000-9899 98136
10000-10199 98146
51st Pl NE 98155
51st Pl S
5900-6100 98118
12200-12599 98178
51st Pl SW 98116
N 51st St 98103
NE 51st St 98105
NW 51st St 98107
52nd Ave NE
4300-4599 98105
6000-7499 98115
18800-18899 98155
52nd Ave S
4501-4697 98118
13500-14299 98168
15101-15197 98188
52nd Ave SW 98116
52nd Pl S 98168
52nd Pl SW 98116
N 52nd St 98103
NE 52nd St 98105
NW 52nd St 98107
53rd Ave NE
4200-4298 98105
6000-8599 98115
18000-20199 98155
53rd Ave S
4700-9699 98118
10600-11700 98178
13500-14299 98168
15401-15797 98188
53rd Ave SW 98116
53rd Ct NE
8500-8599 98115
19200-19299 98155
53rd Pl S 98188
N 53rd St 98103
NE 53rd St 98105
NW 53rd St 98107
54th Ave NE
4300-5499 98105
6200-8599 98115
54th Ave S
4700-9699 98118
11600-11899 98178
13601-13699 98168
16200-16499 98188
54th Ave SW 98116
54th Ln NE 98155
54th Pl NE 98155
54th Pl S
14200-14298 98168
17800-17899 98188
54th Pl SW 98116
N 54th St 98103
NE 54th St 98105
NW 54th St 98107

55th Ave NE
4000-5899 98105
6200-6498 98115
18701-20099 98155
55th Ave S
4800-9899 98118
10001-10197 98178
13901-13997 98168
55th Ave SW 98116
55th Pl NE
7500-7599 98115
20400-20499 98155
1700-1798 98105
N 55th St 98103
NE 55th St 98105
NW 55th St 98107
56th Ave NE
5600-5899 98105
6900-7799 98115
56th Ave S
5200-9699 98118
10200-11200 98178
13700-14799 98168
56th Ave SW 98116
56th Pl NE 98115
56th Pl S
11800-12499 98178
13900-13999 98168
56th Pl SW 98116
N 56th St 98103
NE 56th St 98105
NW 56th St 98107
57th Ave NE
5600-5899 98105
6000-7799 98115
57th Ave S
5000-9899 98118
10000-12699 98178
14000-14999 98168
57th Ave SW 98116
57th Pl NE 98115
57th Pl SW 98116
NW 57th Pl 98107
N 57th St 98103
NE 57th St 98105
NW 57th St 98107
58th Ave NE
5700-5799 98105
6300-7799 98115
58th Ave S
9400-9699 98118
14000-14999 98168
58th Ave SW 98116
58th Pl S 98178
58th Pl SW 98116
N 58th St 98103
NE 58th St 98105
NW 58th St 98107
59th Ave NE 98105
59th Ave S
9501-9597 98118
9599-9999 98118
10000-12100 98178
12102-12298 98178
14200-14799 98168
59th Ave SW 98116
N 59th St 98103
NE 59th St 98105
NW 59th St 98107
60th Ave NE
5301-5397 98105
6000-6100 98115
60th Ave S
9600-9899 98118
10400-12699 98178
60th Ave SW 98116
60th Ln S 98178
60th Pl S 98118
N 60th St 98103
NE 60th St 98115
NW 60th St 98107
61st Ave NE 98105
61st Ave S
9601-9697 98118
9699-9899 98118
10000-12299 98178
61st Ave SW 98116

61st Pl S 98178
N 61st St 98103
NE 61st St 98115
NW 61st St 98107
62nd Ave NE 98115
62nd Ave S
9700-9899 98118
10000-12099 98178
14701-14897 98168
14899-14999 98168
15100-15499 98188
62nd Ave SW 98116
N 62nd St 98103
NE 62nd St 98115
NW 62nd St 98107
63rd Ave NE
5700-5799 98105
6000-7398 98115
63rd Ave S
9701-9797 98118
10000-10799 98178
63rd Ave SW 98116
N 63rd St 98103
NE 63rd St 98115
NW 63rd St 98107
64th Ave NE 98105
64th Ave S
9900-9999 98118
10000-13199 98178
15300-15399 98188
64th Ave SW 98116
64th Ln S 98178
64th Pl S 98178
64th Pl SW 98116
N 64th St 98103
NE 64th St 98115
NW 64th St 98107
65th Ave NE
5700-5799 98105
6001-6097 98115
65th Ave S
9901-9999 98118
10000-12900 98178
15100-15499 98188
65th Ave SW 98116
NW 65th Ct 98117
N 65th St
100-2499 98103
2401-2499 98115
NE 65th St 98115
NW 65th St 98117
66th Ave S 98178
66th Ave SW 98116
66th Ln S 98178
N 66th St 98103
NE 66th St 98115
NW 66th St 98117
67th Ave S 98178
67th Pl S 98178
N 67th St 98103
NE 67th St 98115
NW 67th St 98117
68th Ave S 98178
68th Pl S 98178
N 68th St 98103
NE 68th St 98115
NW 68th St 98117
69th Ave S 98178
69th Pl S 98178
NE 69th St 98115
NW 69th St 98117
70th Ave S 98178
70th Pl S 98178
N 70th St 98103
NE 70th St 98115
NW 70th St 98117
71st Ave S 98178
71st Pl S 98178
N 71st St 98103
NE 71st St 98115
NW 71st St 98117
72nd Ave S 98178
72nd Pl S 98178
N 72nd St 98103
NE 72nd St 98115
NW 72nd St 98117

73rd Ln S 98178
NE 73rd Pl 98115
N 73rd St 98103
NE 73rd St 98115
NW 73rd St 98117
74th Ave S 98178
74th Ln S 98178
74th Pl S 98178
NE 74th Pl 98115
N 74th St 98103
NE 74th St 98115
NW 74th St 98117
75th Ave S 98178
N 75th St 98103
NE 75th St 98115
NW 75th St 98117
76th Ave S 98178
N 76th St 98103
NE 76th St 98115
NW 76th St 98117
77th Ave S 98178
N 77th St 98103
NE 77th St 98115
NW 77th St 98117
78th Ave S 98178
N 78th St 98103
NE 78th St 98115
NW 78th St 98117
79th Ave S 98178
79th Pl S 98178
N 79th St 98103
NE 79th St 98115
NW 79th St 98117
80th Ave S 98178
N 80th St 98103
NE 80th St 98115
NW 80th St 98117
81st Ave S 98178
81st Pl S 98178
NE 81st Pl 98115
N 81st St 98103
NE 81st St 98115
NW 81st St 98117
82nd Ave S 98178
82nd Pl S 98178
N 82nd St 98103
NE 82nd St 98115
NW 82nd St 98117
83rd Ave S 98178
N 83rd St 98103
NE 83rd St 98115
NW 83rd St 98117
84th Ave S 98178
N 84th St 98103
NE 84th St 98115
NW 84th St 98117
85th Ave S 98178
N 85th St 98103
NE 85th St 98115
NW 85th St 98117
86th Ct S 98178
N 86th St 98103
NE 86th St 98115
NW 86th St 98117
87th Ave S 98178
N 87th St 98103
NE 87th St 98115
NW 87th St 98117
88th Ave S 98178
NE 88th Pl 98115
N 88th St 98103
NE 88th St 98115
NW 88th St 98117
NW 89th Pl 98117
N 89th St 98103
NE 89th St 98115
NW 89th St 98117
NE 90th Pl 98115
NW 90th Pl 98117
N 90th St 98103
NE 90th St 98115
NW 90th St 98117
N 91st St 98103
NE 91st St 98115
NW 91st St 98117
S 92nd Pl 98108

N 92nd St 98103
NE 92nd St 98115
NW 92nd St 98117
N 93rd St 98103
NE 93rd St 98115
NW 93rd St 98117
S 93rd St 98108
N 94th St 98103
NE 94th St 98115
NW 94th St 98117
N 95th St 98103
NE 95th St 98115
NW 95th St 98117
SW 96th Cir 98106
NE 96th Pl 98115
SW 96th Pl 98106
N 96th St 98103
NE 96th St 98115
NW 96th St 98117
S 96th St 98108
SW 97th Ct 98126
SW 97th Pl 98106
N 97th St 98103
NE 97th St 98115
NW 97th St 98117
SW 97th St
500-700 98106
3000-3098 98126
3900-5099 98136
SW 98th Pl 98106
N 98th St 98103
NE 98th St 98115
NW 98th St 98117
SW 98th St
1201-1297 98106
1299-2499 98106
2501-2599 98106
3500-3799 98126
3900-5199 98136
S 99th Pl 98108
NW 99th St 98117
S 99th St 98108
SW 99th St
500-999 98106
2800-3799 98126
NW 100th Pl 98177
SW 100th Pl 98146
N 100th St 98133
NE 100th St 98125
NW 100th St 98177
S 100th St 98168
SW 100th St
1-4699 98146
700-998 98106
1200-4598 98146
N 101st St 98133
NW 101st St 98177
S 101st St 98168
SW 101st St 98146
SW 102nd Ln 98146
N 102nd St 98133
NE 102nd St 98125
S 102nd St 98168
SW 102nd St 98146
NE 103rd Pl 98125
N 103rd St 98133
NE 103rd St 98125
NW 103rd St 98177
S 103rd St 98168
SW 103rd St 98146
NE 104th Pl 98125
S 104th Pl 98178
N 104th St 98133
NE 104th St 98125
NW 104th St 98177
S 104th St 98168
SW 104th St 98146
NE 104th Way 98125
NE 105th Pl 98125
SW 105th Pl 98146
N 105th St 98133
NE 105th St 98125
NW 105th St 98177
S 105th St 98168
SW 105th St 98146
NE 106th Pl 98125

N 106th St 98133
NE 106th St 98125
NW 106th St 98177
S 106th St
100-1799 98168
7700-7898 98178
SW 106th St 98146
SW 107th Pl 98146
N 107th St 98133
NE 107th St 98125
NW 107th St 98177
S 107th St
100-300 98168
302-2198 98168
4700-4999 98178
SW 107th St 98146
SW 107th Way 98146
NE 108th Pl 98125
S 108th Pl 98168
SW 108th Pl 98146
NE 108th St 98125
NW 108th St 98177
S 108th St 98168
SW 108th St 98146
SW 109th Pl 98146
N 109th St 98133
NE 109th St 98125
S 109th St 98178
SW 109th St 98146
S 110th Ct 98178
SW 110th Ln 98146
S 110th Pl 98168
SW 110th Pl 98146
N 110th St 98133
NE 110th St 98125
NW 110th St 98177
S 110th St 98168
SW 110th St 98146
SW 111th Ln 98146
S 111th Pl 98168
SW 111th Pl 98146
NE 111th St 98125
S 111th St 98168
SW 111th St 98146
S 112th Pl 98178
SW 112th Pl 98146
N 112th St 98133
NE 112th St 98125
NW 112th St 98177
S 112th St
100-2399 98168
2900-2999 98168
4901-5099 98178
6401-7397 98178
7399-8599 98178
SW 112th St 98146
N 113th Pl 98133
NW 113th Pl 98177
SW 113th Pl 98146
N 113th St 98133
NE 113th St 98125
S 113th St
2000-2058 98168
2060-2098 98168
3900-3999 98168
4001-4199 98168
4900-4998 98178
5000-5099 98178
7600-8799 98178
SW 113th St 98146
NW 114th Pl 98177
S 114th Pl 98168
N 114th St 98133
NE 114th St 98125
NW 114th St 98177
S 114th St
3900-3998 98168
4000-4199 98168
4900-5099 98178
7400-8599 98178
8601-8799 98178
SW 114th St 98146
S 115th Ln 98178
S 115th Pl 98178
N 115th St 98133
NE 115th St 98125
NW 115th St 98177
S 115th St
1000-1299 98168
3900-4298 98168
6900-8599 98178
SW 115th St 98146
S 116th Pl
2305-2327 98168
6700-8899 98178
SW 116th Pl 98146
N 116th St 98133
NE 116th St 98125
NW 116th St 98177
S 116th St
100-132 98168
6001-6197 98178
SW 116th St 98146
S 116th Way 98168
S 117th Pl
900-4099 98168
6000-8799 98178
SW 117th Pl 98146
N 117th St 98133
NE 117th St 98125
NW 117th St 98177
S 117th St
1000-2399 98168
5100-8799 98178
SW 117th St 98146
S 118th Ct 98168
S 118th Pl 98178
SW 118th Pl 98146
NE 118th St 98125
NW 118th St 98177
S 118th St
1800-2599 98168
4400-4998 98178
SW 118th St 98146
NW 119th St 98177
4000-4099 98168
5500-8599 98178
SW 119th St 98146
S 120th Pl
3301-3499 98168
6800-8799 98178
N 120th St 98133
NE 120th St 98125
NW 120th St 98177
S 120th St
101-129 98168
131-2599 98168
5301-5897 98178
5899-12099 98178
SW 120th St 98146
SW 121st Ct 98146
S 121st Pl 98168
SW 121st Pl 98146
N 121st St 98133
NW 121st St 98177
S 121st St
2400-2499 98168
5600-8999 98178
SW 121st St 98146
S 122nd Ln 98178
N 122nd Pl 98133
S 122nd Pl 98168
N 122nd St 98133
NE 122nd St 98125
NW 122nd St 98177
S 122nd St
2600-2699 98168
4200-4298 98168
4300-4698 98178
4700-5899 98178
6700-8500 98178
8502-8998 98178
SW 122nd St 98146
S 123rd Pl 98178
SW 123rd Pl 98146
NE 123rd St 98125
S 123rd St
2500-2699 98168
6800-6898 98178
6900-8699 98178
S 124th Pl
1000-1099 98168
8400-8499 98178
NE 124th St 98125
S 124th St
100-2399 98168
3600-4198 98168
4200-4299 98168
4300-4398 98178
4400-4598 98178
4600-8599 98178
SW 124th St 98146
S 125th Ct 98168
S 125th Pl 98168
N 125th St 98133
NE 125th St 98125
NW 125th St 98177
S 125th St
2600-2627 98168
4601-4697 98178
SW 125th St 98146
NW 126th Pl 98177
S 126th Pl 98178
SW 126th Pl 98146
NE 126th St 98125
NW 126th St 98177
S 126th St
200-2399 98168
3400-3498 98168
3500-4099 98168
6000-8399 98178
SW 126th St 98146
S 127th Pl 98178
N 127th St 98133
NE 127th St
500-3100 98125
3019-3019 98165
3102-3998 98125
NW 127th St 98177
S 127th St
2800-2802 98168
7000-7499 98178
SW 127th St 98146
N 128th St 98133
NE 128th St 98125
S 128th St
101-197 98168
199-1499 98168
1600-1998 98168
2000-2699 98168
2800-4099 98168
6600-8299 98178
SW 128th St 98146
129th Pl & St 98178
NE 130th Pl 98125
S 130th Pl
2400-2499 98168
2600-2699 98168
5701-5799 98178
N 130th St 98133
NE 130th St 98125
NW 130th St 98177
S 130th St
3200-4199 98168
6900-8299 98178
S 131st Ct 98178
NE 131st Pl 98125
S 131st Pl
2400-2499 98168
4300-4400 98168
4402-4498 98168
6601-6605 98178
6607-6621 98178
6623-6699 98178
N 131st St 98133
NW 131st St 98177
S 131st St
2701-2799 98168
4100-4199 98168
6413-6415 98178
6417-7299 98178
S 132nd Pl 98168
N 132nd St 98133
NW 132nd St 98177
S 132nd St
2000-2499 98168
3200-3298 98168
3300-3599 98168
3601-3899 98168
6500-6604 98178
6606-8099 98178
8101-8299 98178
S 133rd Ln 98168
S 133rd Pl 98178
N 133rd St 98133
NE 133rd St 98125
S 133rd St
2400-2799 98168
2801-2897 98168
2899-4599 98168
5600-5798 98178
6700-6798 98178
6800-6999 98178
7001-7399 98178
S 134th Ln 98168
S 134th Pl
4401-4497 98168
4499-4799 98168
7801-7897 98178
7899-7999 98178
8001-8099 98178
N 134th St 98133
NE 134th St 98125
NW 134th St 98177
S 134th St
2000-2299 98168
7400-8100 98178
8102-8698 98178
N 135th Pl 98133
NE 135th Pl 98125
NW 135th Pl 98177
N 135th St 98133
NE 135th St 98125
S 135th St
2400-2899 98168
2900-3499 98168
7101-7197 98178
7199-7899 98178
N 136th St 98133
NE 136th St 98125
NW 136th St 98177
S 136th St 98168
S 137th Pl 98168
N 137th St 98133
NE 137th St 98125
NW 137th St 98177
S 137th St 98168
N 138th St 98133
NE 138th St 98125
S 138th St 98168
NE 139th St 98125
S 139th St 98168
N 140th St 98133
NE 140th St 98125
NW 140th St 98177
S 140th St 98168
141st Ct & St 98133
141st Ct & St 98168
141st Ct & St 98168
S 142nd Ln 98168
S 142nd Pl 98168
N 142nd St 98133
NE 142nd St 98125
S 142nd St 98168
NE 143rd Pl 98125
S 143rd Pl 98168
N 143rd St 98133
NE 143rd St 98125
NW 143rd St 98177
S 143rd St 98168
N 144th St 98133
NE 144th St 98125
NW 144th St 98177
S 144th St 98168
N 145th Ct 98133
N 145th Ln 98133
N 145th St
101-929 98133
929-929 98177
1201-2399 98133
NE 145th St 98155
NW 145th St 98177
S 145th St 98168
NE 146th Ct 98155
S 146th St 98168
N 147th St 98133
S 147th St 98168
N 148th Pl 98133
S 148th St 98168
N 149th Ct 98133
S 149th Ln 98168
NE 149th Pl 98155
NE 150th Ct 98155
S 150th Pl 98188
S 150th St 98188
S 151st Pl 98188
NE 151st St 98155
S 151st St 98188
S 152nd Pl 98188
N 152nd St 98133
S 152nd St 98188
NE 153rd Ct 98155
S 153rd St 98188
N 154th Ct 98133
S 154th Ln 98188
S 154th St 98188
NE 155th Pl 98155
N 155th St 98133
N 156th Ct 98133
S 156th St 98158
S 156th St 98188
N 157th Ct 98133
NE 157th Ln 98155
NE 158th Ln 98155
S 158th Ln 98188
N 158th Pl 98133
S 158th St 98148
S 159th Ln 98188
N 159th St 98133
S 160th Ln 98188
N 160th Pl 98133
S 160th St 98188
S 161st Ct 98148
N 161st Pl 98133
S 161st St 98188
S 161st St 98158
N 162nd St 98133
S 162nd St 98188
N 163rd Pl 98133
S 163rd Pl 98188
S 163rd St 98158
N 164th Pl 98133
SW 164th Pl 98166
S 164th St 98188
N 165th Pl 98133
S 165th St 98158
N 166th Ct 98133
S 166th Ln 98188
NE 166th Pl 98155
S 166th St 98188
N 167th St 98133
S 167th St 98188
S 168th Ln 98188
SW 168th Pl 98166
N 168th St 98133
S 168th St 98188
NE 169th Ct 98155
N 169th St 98133
S 169th St 98188
N 170th Ct 98133
S 170th Ln 98188
NE 170th Pl 98155
S 170th St 98188
SW 170th St 98166
NE 171st Pl 98155
SW 171st Pl 98166
S 171st St 98188
NE 172nd Ct 98155
S 172nd Ln 98188
SW 172nd St 98166
S 173rd Ln 98188
N 173rd St 98133
N 174th Pl 98133
NE 174th Pl 98155
SW 174th Pl 98166
S 174th St 98148
NW 175th Ct 98177
SW 175th Pl 98166
S 175th St 98188
NE 176th Pl 98155
SW 176th Pl 98166
NE 176th St 98155
S 176th St 98188
S 177th Ct 98188
NW 177th Ln 98177
S 177th Pl 98148
SW 177th St 98166
N 178th Ct 98133
S 178th St 98188
SW 178th St 98166
NE 179th Ct 98155
SW 179th Ct 98166
N 179th Pl 98133
S 179th Pl 98188
180th Ct & Pl 98155
180th Ct & Pl 98148
180th Ct & Pl 98155
180th Ct & Pl 98188
180th Ct & Pl 98166
N 181st Ct 98133
S 181st Pl 98188
SW 181st Pl 98166
NE 181st St 98155
S 181st St 98148
N 182nd Ct 98133
S 182nd Pl 98188
S 182nd St 98148
SW 182nd St 98166
NE 183rd Ct 98155
S 183rd Pl 98188
SW 183rd St 98166
N 184th Ct 98133
S 184th Pl 98188
SW 184th St 98166
N 185th Ct 98133
SW 185th Pl 98166
S 185th St 98188
186th Ln & St 98148
186th Ln & St 98133
186th Ln & St 98188
186th Ln & St 98166
NE 187th Ct 98155
S 187th Pl 98188
N 187th St 98133
SW 187th St 98166
S 188th Ln 98188
N 188th St 98133
S 188th St 98148
NE 189th Ct 98155
NE 189th Pl 98155
S 189th Pl 98188
SW 189th Pl 98166
S 189th St 98148
N 190th Ct 98133
NE 190th Ct 98155
S 190th Ct 98188
NW 191st Ln 98177
S 191st Pl 98188
SW 191st St 98166
S 192nd Ln 98188
NE 192nd Pl 98155
NW 192nd Pl 98177
S 192nd Pl 98148
SW 192nd St 98166
N 193rd Ct 98133
NE 193rd Pl 98155
S 193rd Pl 98148
S 193rd Pl 98148
SW 193rd Pl 98166
S 194th Ct 98148
NE 194th Pl 98155
NW 194th Pl 98177
SW 194th Pl 98166
S 194th St 98148
N 195th Ct 98133
NE 195th Pl 98155
S 195th Pl 98188
S 195th Pl 98148
N 196th Ct 98133
NE 196th Ct 98155
S 196th Pl 98148
SW 196th Pl 98166
S 196th St 98148
N 197th Ct 98133
NE 197th Ln 98155
SW 197th Pl 98166
S 197th St 98148
NE 198th Ct 98155
S 198th Pl 98148
S 198th St 98188
NE 199th Ct 98155
SW 199th Pl 98166
S 199th St 98148
NE 200th Ct 98155
NE 200th Pl 98155
S 200th St 98198
SW 200th St 98166
NE 201st Ct 98155
S 201st St 98198
SW 201st St 98166
NW 202nd Ln 98177
S 202nd St 98198
SW 202nd St 98166
N 203rd Ct 98133
NE 203rd Ct 98155
S 203rd St 98198
SW 203rd St 98166
N 204th Pl 98133
NE 204th Pl 98155
S 204th Pl 98198
S 204th St 98198
S 205th Pl 98198
N 205th St 98133
SW 205th St 98166
S 206th St 98198
SW 206th St 98166
SW 207th Pl 98166
S 207th St 98198
S 208th St 98198
SW 208th St 98166
S 209th Pl 98198
S 209th St 98198
S 210th St 98198
S 211th Pl 98198
SW 211th St 98166
S 212th Ct 98198
S 212th St 98198
S 213th Ct 98198
S 213th St 98198
S 214th St 98198
S 215th Pl 98198
S 216th St 98198
S 218th St 98198
S 219th St 98198
S 220th St 98198
S 221st St 98198
S 222nd Ln 98198
S 222nd St 98198
S 223rd St 98198
S 224th Pl 98198
S 225th Ln 98198
S 226th Pl 98198
S 227th Pl 98198
S 228th Pl 98198
S 229th Pl 98198
S 230th St 98198
S 231st Pl 98198
S 232nd Ct 98198
S 233rd Ct 98198
S 234th Pl 98198
S 235th Pl 98198
S 236th Pl 98198
S 237th Ct 98198
S 238th Ln 98198
S 239th Pl 98198
S 240th Pl 98198
S 241st St 98198
S 242nd St 98198
S 243rd Ct 98198
S 244th Pl 98198
S 245th Pl 98198
S 246th Pl 98198
S 247th St 98198
S 248th St 98198
S 249th Pl 98198
S 250th Pl 98198
S 251st Ct 98198
S 252nd Pl 98198
S 253rd Pl 98198
S 254th Ct 98198
S 255th Pl 98198
S 256th Pl 98198
S 257th Pl 98198
S 258th Ct 98198

S 259th Pl ... 98198
S 260th Pl ... 98198
S 261st Ct ... 98198
S 262nd Ct ... 98198
S 263rd Pl ... 98198
S 264th Pl ... 98198
S 265th Pl ... 98198
S 266th Pl ... 98198
S 268th St ... 98198
S 269th Ct ... 98198
S 270th St ... 98198
S 272nd St ... 98198
S 273rd Ct ... 98198
S 274th Pl ... 98198
S 275th Pl ... 98198
S 276th Pl ... 98198
S 277th Pl ... 98198
S 278th Ct ... 98198
S 279th Pl ... 98198
S 280th Pl ... 98198
S 281st St ... 98198
S 282nd St ... 98198
S 284th St ... 98198
S 287th St ... 98198
S 288th St ... 98198
80 Pl S ... 98178

SILVERDALE WA

General Delivery ... 98383

POST OFFICE BOXES MAIN OFFICE STATIONS AND BRANCHES

Box No.s
1 - 4058 ... 98383
5961 - 7030 ... 98315

NAMED STREETS

NW Aileron Ct ... 98383
NW Airpark Ct ... 98383
Alabama Ct ... 98315
Albacore Cir ... 98315
NW Alexandria Ct ... 98383
NW Amanda Loop ... 98383
NW Ambercrest Way ... 98383
Amethyst Loop NW ... 98383
NW Amron Ct ... 98383
Anderson Lndg NW ... 98383
NW Anderson Hill Rd ... 98383
Andrea Ln NW ... 98383
Apex Rd NW ... 98383
NW Arriva Way ... 98383
Ashley Cir & Dr ... 98383
NW Atwater Loop ... 98383
Avante Dr NW ... 98383
Avellana Cir NW ... 98383
Bach Ln NW ... 98383
NW Bandit Way ... 98383
Barb St ... 98315
Barbel St ... 98315
Bartlett Ct NW ... 98383
Bayshore Dr NW ... 98383
Bearist Rd NW ... 98383
Bennington Dr NW ... 98383
NW Bernard St ... 98383
Berry Ridge Ln & Rd ... 98383
Bessie Pl NW ... 98383
NW Big Bird Dr ... 98383
NW Bison Ln ... 98383
Blarney Stone Pl ... 98383
Boardwalk Pl NW ... 98383
NW Bobwhite Ln ... 98383
NW Bogard Rd ... 98383
NW Bondale Ln ... 98383
Bonefish Cir ... 98315
NW Bramble Ct ... 98383
Breckenridge Ln NW ... 98383
Brian Ln NW ... 98383
NW Brinkley Ct ... 98383
NW Bryce Ct ... 98383
Buccaneer Pl NW ... 98383
NW Bucklin Hill Rd ... 98383
Bushlac Ln NW ... 98383
NW Byron St ... 98383
NW Cairo St ... 98383
Calico Pl NW ... 98383
NW Calypso Cir ... 98383
Canova Ave NW ... 98383
Capelin Dr ... 98315
Capewind Ln NW ... 98383
Capitola Pl NW ... 98383
Carina Pl NW ... 98383
NW Carlton St ... 98383
NW Cascade Pl & St NW ... 98383
Celtic Loop NW ... 98383
NW Chad Ct ... 98383
Chagnon Pl NW ... 98383
Chambana Pl NW ... 98383
Chance Pl NW ... 98383
NW Chancery Ct ... 98383
Chickadee Ln NW ... 98383
Clear Creek Ct & Rd ... 98383
NW Clearbrook Ln ... 98383
Clearidge Ave NW ... 98383
Clipper Pl NW ... 98383
NW Cloninger Ct ... 98383
Cloudy Peak Ln NW ... 98383
NW Concrete Blvd ... 98383
Connor Loop NW ... 98383
Contact Ct NW ... 98383
Cookie Monster Ln NW ... 98383
Copper Pl NW ... 98383
Country Meadows Ln NW ... 98383
NW Covey Ct ... 98383
Cranberry Ln NW ... 98383
Cranway Ln NW ... 98383
Crestview Cir & Ct ... 98383
NW Crista Shores Ln ... 98383
Crocus Pl NW ... 98383
Crossridge Ave NW ... 98383
Crown Point Pl NW ... 98383
Crystal Manor Ln NW ... 98383
Cutter Pl NW ... 98383
NW Dabob Ln ... 98383
Dahl Rd NW ... 98383
Daniel Pl NW ... 98383
Danskin Ln NW ... 98383
Danwood Ln NW ... 98383
Daphne Ln NW ... 98383
Davis Pl NW ... 98383
Daybreak Pl NW ... 98383
Deer Park Ln NW ... 98383
Delta Refit Pier ... 98315
NW Derryfield Dr ... 98383
Dickey Pl & Rd ... 98383
NW Discovery Ridge Ct ... 98383
Doyle Ln NW ... 98383
Drago Ct NW ... 98383
NW Dream Ct ... 98383
Drum St ... 98315
NW Duckabush Ln ... 98383
NW Duesenberg Ct ... 98383
Durham Pl NW ... 98383
Ebbtide Ln NW ... 98383
NW Ebony Ct ... 98383
NW Eldorado Blvd ... 98383
Eldridge Pl NW ... 98383
Emery Blvd NW ... 98383
Enchantment Ave NW ... 98383
Enterprise Ln NW ... 98383
Erie Ave NW ... 98383
Esther Pl NW ... 98383
NW Estrellita Ln ... 98383
Finback Cir ... 98315
Fishhook Ln NW ... 98383
NW Flintwood Ct ... 98383
Florida Dr ... 98315
Foothills Pl NW ... 98383
NW Forest Creek Dr ... 98383
NW Foxhall Ln ... 98383
NW Francis Dr ... 98383
Frontier Dr, Ln & Pl ... 98383
NW Fuschia Ct ... 98383
Garons View Ln NW ... 98383
Gato St ... 98315
Georgia Ct ... 98315
Gildar Ln NW ... 98383
Glacier View Dr NW ... 98383
NW Gladiola Ct ... 98383
NW Glen Ct ... 98383
NW Glenn Firs Ln ... 98383
Golden Ridge Pl NW ... 98383
NW Goldfern Ct ... 98383
NW Gooseberry Ct ... 98383
Grafton Pl NW ... 98383
Grandpeak Ln NW ... 98383
Granite Ln NW ... 98383
Grayback Cir, Ct & Dr ... 98315
Graystone Loop & Way ... 98383
Graytail Pl NW ... 98383
Greenfish Ct & Dr ... 98315
Gregory Ln NW ... 98383
Grenadier Dr ... 98315
Grouse Ln NW ... 98383
Growler Cir ... 98315
Guardfish St ... 98315
Gudgeon Ave ... 98315
NW Gumtree Ln ... 98383
NW Gustafson Rd ... 98383
NW Half Mile Rd ... 98383
Hamilton Pl NW ... 98383
Hammerhead Ct ... 98315
Hampton Ave NW ... 98383
NW Happy Hollow Ln ... 98383
Happy Valley Rd ... 98383
Harder Rd ... 98315
NW Harlequin Ct ... 98383
NW Harrington Ln ... 98383
NW Herried Rd ... 98383
NW Hidden Pl ... 98383
Hide A Way Ln NW ... 98383
High Sierra Ln NW ... 98383
NW Highland Ct ... 98383
Hillsboro Dr NW ... 98383
Honeyset Ln NW ... 98383
Hood Canal Farms Rd NW ... 98383
Hoot Ridge Ln NW ... 98383
NW Hosman Cir ... 98383
Hunley Rd ... 98315
Huntley Pl NW ... 98383
Hurricane Ct NW ... 98383
NW Hydrangea St ... 98383
Icicle Pl NW ... 98383
NW Illich Rd ... 98383
Impasse Pl NW ... 98383
Inlet View Ct NW ... 98383
Ioka Dr & Way NW ... 98383
NW Iris Ln ... 98383
NW Island Lake Rd ... 98383
Ivy Ln NW ... 98383
Jace Ln NW ... 98383
Jeatran Pl NW ... 98383
Jeffery Ln NW ... 98383
NW Jessie Mae Way ... 98383
Jetty Pl NW ... 98383
NW Jupiter Trl ... 98383
Kayla Pl NW ... 98383
Kegley Rd NW ... 98383
NW Kensington Ln ... 98383
Kildare Loop NW ... 98383
Kingscross Cir NW ... 98383
Kiptree Ln NW ... 98383
Kirkland Ln NW ... 98383
Kitsap Ct & Pl ... 98383
Kitsap Mall Blvd NW ... 98383
Klipsan Ln NW ... 98383
Knute Ln NW ... 98383
Knute Anderson Rd NW ... 98383
NW Kyle Ct ... 98383
NW Lakehill Cir ... 98383
Lakeridge Cir NW ... 98383
Lathrop Ln NW ... 98383
NW Latigo Ln ... 98383
NW Lause Way ... 98383
NW Lawstad Pl ... 98383
Leeway Ave NW ... 98383
Left Wing Ct NW ... 98383
Legarto Ct ... 98315
NW Lenox Ln ... 98383
Lester Rd NW ... 98383
Levin Rd NW ... 98383
Linder Way NW ... 98383
NW Littlewood Ln ... 98383
Lobelia Ave NW ... 98383
NW Lois Dr ... 98383
Long Point Ln NW ... 98383
Lorie Ct NW ... 98383
NW Lowell St ... 98383
NW Lucky Ln ... 98383
Lupine Ln NW ... 98383
Luquasit Trl NW ... 98383
Mahogany Ln NW ... 98383
Majestic Ln NW ... 98383
Marigold Dr NW ... 98383
Marmot Cir & Ct ... 98383
NW Martha Ln ... 98383
Martin Ave NW ... 98383
NW Mathwig Ln ... 98383
NW Mayfield Blvd ... 98383
Mcauliffe Ln NW ... 98383
Mcconnell Ave NW ... 98383
NW Melody Ln ... 98383
Michigan Dr ... 98315
Mickelberry Rd NW ... 98383
NW Mirage Ln ... 98383
NW Misty Ridge Ln ... 98383
Miz Malia Ln NW ... 98383
Mockingbird Dr NW ... 98383
NW Monopoly St ... 98383
NW Montery Ct ... 98383
Morning Side Dr NW ... 98383
NW Mount Vintage Way ... 98383
Mount Worthington Loop NW ... 98383
Mountain Cruiser Ln NW ... 98383
Mountain Vista Cir & Ln ... 98383
NW Mountain Vw Rd ... 98383
NW Munson St ... 98383
Myhre Pl & Rd ... 98383
NW Mystic Ct ... 98383
New Haven Ln NW ... 98383
NW Newberry Hill Rd ... 98383
Nika Trl NW ... 98383
Nite Owl Ln NW ... 98383
Norbert Pl NW ... 98383
NW Norhinkle Ln ... 98383
NW Northstar Dr ... 98383
NW Nuthatch Way ... 98383
Ohio St ... 98315
Old Cedars Pl NW ... 98383
Old Frontier Rd NW ... 98383
NW Olympic Circle Dr ... 98383
Olympic View Ct & Rd NW ... 98383
Olympic View Loop Rd NW ... 98383
Orchid Pl NW ... 98383
Oslo Ln NW ... 98383
Outback Ave NW ... 98383
Owlet Pl NW ... 98383
Pacific Ave NW ... 98383
NW Paddington Ct ... 98383
Page Rd NW ... 98383
Pansy Pl NW ... 98383
NW Peace And Quiet Way ... 98383
Peach Tree Pl NW ... 98383
Peakview Pl NW ... 98383
Peony Pl NW ... 98383
Perch Cir NW ... 98315
Peridot Pl NW ... 98383
Petersen Ln NW ... 98383
Pickerel Cir NW ... 98315
Pillar Point Ln NW ... 98383
NW Pinnacle Ct ... 98383
Pintail Ln NW ... 98383
NW Piper Ct ... 98383
Plateau Cir NW ... 98383
NW Plaza Rd ... 98383
Poplars Ave NW ... 98383
NW Poppy Ct ... 98383
Porellak St ... 98315
Prescott Pl NW ... 98383
NW Princeton Ln ... 98383
Provost Rd NW ... 98383
NW Puddingstone Ln ... 98383
Quail Run Dr NW ... 98383
Queets Ln NW ... 98383
NW Quiet View Ln ... 98383
Rainier View Ln NW ... 98383
NW Randall Way ... 98383
NW Ranger Way ... 98383
Ravena Pl NW ... 98383
NW Redfern Ct ... 98383
Remington Ln NW ... 98383
NW Reo Pl ... 98383
NW Ridge Lane Ct ... 98383
Ridgelane Dr NW ... 98383
Ridgepark Pl NW ... 98383
Ridgepoint Cir & Dr ... 98383
Ridgetop Blvd NW ... 98383
Right Wing Ct NW ... 98383
Rising Hill Ln NW ... 98383
Robalo Ct & Dr ... 98315
Rock Port Ln NW ... 98383
NW Rockford Cir ... 98383
Rocky Ridge Rd NW ... 98383
NW Romero Ln ... 98383
Rooney Rd NW ... 98383
Rosewood Ln NW ... 98383
Roundup Ln NW ... 98383
Rubicon Trail Pl NW ... 98383
Rudder Pl NW ... 98383
Salem Ln NW ... 98383
Sam Houston Dr ... 98315
Sandhill Ln NW ... 98383
Sandy Isle Ln NW ... 98383
NW Santa Fe Ln ... 98383
Sargo Cir ... 98315
Savannah Ct NW ... 98383
NW Scarlet Ct ... 98383
Schold Pl & Rd NW ... 98383
Scorpion Ave ... 98315
Sea Isle Ln NW ... 98383
NW Sea Mist Ln ... 98383
Sea Scape Ln NW ... 98383
Seabeck Hwy NW ... 98383
Seadragon Ct ... 98315
NW Seal Point Ln ... 98383
Sealion Rd ... 98315
Seasons Ln NW ... 98383
NW Seastar Ln ... 98383
NW Segerman Ln ... 98383
NW Sequim Ln ... 98383
Sesame St NW ... 98383
Settlers Ln NW ... 98383
NW Shadow Glen Blvd ... 98383
NW Shelley Ct & Dr NW ... 98383
Shipside Ln NW ... 98383
NW Shontel Ct ... 98383
Shore Pl NW ... 98383
NW Sid Uhinck Dr ... 98383
Silver Sound Ln NW ... 98383
Silverdale Way NW ... 98383
Silverdale Loop Rd NW ... 98383
Silverhill Pl NW ... 98383
Silversides Rd ... 98315
Sirocco Cir NW ... 98383
Skate St ... 98315
NW Skiff Ln ... 98383
Skipjack Cir ... 98315
Skymont Pl NW ... 98383
NW Slate Ln ... 98383
Spinnaker Blvd NW ... 98383
Spirit Ct E & W ... 98383
Spirit Ridge Dr NW ... 98383
NW Springer Way ... 98383
NW Springtree Ct ... 98383
Starpoint Ln NW ... 98383
Stoli Ln NW ... 98383
Sturgeon St ... 98315
NW Stutz Pl ... 98383
NW Summer Beach Ln ... 98383
Sunde Rd NW ... 98383
Sunfish Dr ... 98315
Swordfish Ct ... 98315
NW Tahoe Ln ... 98383
Tanager Ln NW ... 98383
Tautog Cir ... 98315
Templeton Ave NW ... 98383
Thackery Pl NW ... 98383
Thayer Ln NW ... 98383
Thielbar Ln NW ... 98383
Thomas Dr NW ... 98383
NW Thornwood Cir ... 98383
Thresher Ave ... 98315
Tides Ln NW ... 98383
Tieton Pl NW ... 98383
NW Timber Shadow Ct ... 98383
NW Timberview Ct ... 98383
Topsail Pl NW ... 98383
NW Toroni Way ... 98383
NW Tower View Cir ... 98383
Town Summit Pl NW ... 98383
NW Tradewinds St ... 98383
Trailwood Pl NW ... 98383
Trident Ave ... 98315
Trident Ln NW ... 98383
Trigger Ave ... 98315
Trout Cir ... 98315
Tulip Pl NW ... 98383
Tullibee Cir ... 98315
Tunny St ... 98315
Tuscola Pl NW ... 98383
Twilight Pl NW ... 98383
Twin Brooks Ln NW ... 98383
NW Uff Da Ln ... 98383
Vanessa Pl NW ... 98383
Vantage Vista Pl NW ... 98383
NW Vasquez Way ... 98383
NW Velvet Ln ... 98383
Verissimo Ln NW ... 98383
NW View Ln ... 98383
NW Viewmont Ct ... 98383
Voyager Ln NW ... 98383
Wahoo St ... 98315
NW Walgren Dr ... 98383
Wallingford Pl NW ... 98383
NW Warehouse Way ... 98383
Warren Rd NW ... 98383
Washington Ave NW ... 98383
Wenatchee Pl NW ... 98383
NW Westgate Rd ... 98383
Westridge Ct, Dr & Pl ... 98383
Whaling Ave NW ... 98383
Wharf Pl NW ... 98383
NW Whisper St ... 98383
NW White Tail Pl ... 98383
NW Wilkes Ct & St NW ... 98383
Willamette Meridian Rd NW ... 98383
Willowberry Ave NW ... 98383
Windcove Ln NW ... 98383
Windish Ln NW ... 98383
NW Windsprint Ct ... 98383
Windswept Ln NW ... 98383
NW Windy Beach Ln ... 98383
NW Windy Ridge Rd ... 98383
Winter Creek Ave NW ... 98383
Woodcrest Ct & Loop NW ... 98383
Yvonne Pl NW ... 98383
Zephyr Ln NW ... 98383

NUMBERED STREETS

All Street Addresses ... 98383

SNOHOMISH WA

General Delivery ... 98290

POST OFFICE BOXES MAIN OFFICE STATIONS AND BRANCHES

Box No.s
All PO Boxes ... 98291

NAMED STREETS

Adams Log Cabin Rd ... 98290
Airport Way ... 98296
Alder Ave ... 98290
Alger Pl ... 98290
Alice Ave ... 98290
Ash Ct ... 98290
Aspen Way ... 98296
Austin Ave ... 98290
Avenue E ... 98290
Avenue A ... 98290
Avenue B ... 98290
Avenue C E ... 98290
Avenue D
100-1324 ... 98290
1323-1323 ... 98291
1325-1699 ... 98290
1326-1398 ... 98290
Avenue F ... 98290
Avenue G ... 98290
Avenue H ... 98290
Avenue I ... 98290
Avenue J ... 98290
Avenue K ... 98290
Avenue L ... 98290
Badke Rd ... 98290
Baird Ave ... 98290
Beach Dr ... 98290
Bickford Ave ... 98290
Birch Ln ... 98290
Blackman Shores Pl ... 98290
Bluff Ave ... 98290
Bonneville Ave ... 98290
Bosworth Dr ... 98290
Bowen St ... 98290
Broadway Ave ... 98296
Brookside Pl ... 98290
Bunk Foss Rd ... 98290
Butler Rd ... 98290
Cairns Rd ... 98290
Carlson Rd ... 98290
N & S Carpenter Rd ... 98290
Cascade Dr SE ... 98296
Cathcart Way ... 98296
Cedar Ave ... 98290
Chain Lake Rd ... 98290
Clark Ave ... 98290
Cleveland Ave ... 98290
Cole Ave ... 98290
Commercial St ... 98290
Connelly Rd ... 98296
Connors Rd ... 98290
Cottage Ave ... 98290
Covington Ct ... 98290
Creswell Rd ... 98290
Cypress Ave & Ln ... 98290
Division St ... 98290
Downes Rd ... 98296
Dubuque Rd ... 98290
E, N & S Echo Lake Rd ... 98296
Elliott Rd ... 98296
Emerson St ... 98290
Emory Dr ... 98290
Fales Rd ... 98296
Ferguson Park Rd ... 98290
W Flowing Lake Rd ... 98290
Fobes Rd ... 98290
Ford Ave ... 98290
Foster Slough Rd ... 98290
Frank Monsen Dr ... 98290
Galdend St SE ... 98296

- Garden Ct 98290
- Gemmer Rd 98290
- Glen Ave 98290
- Glenwood Foss Rd 98290
- Grant Pl 98290
- Grove St 98290
- Hamitand Ave SE 98290
- Harrison Ave 98290
- High Bridge Rd 98296
- Hill Pl 98290
- Hillcrest Dr 98290
- Holiday St 98290
- Holly Vista Dr 98290
- Home Ave 98290
- Home Acres Rd 98290
- Ingraham Rd 98290
- Interurban Blvd 98296
- James St 98296
- Kendall Ct 98290
- Kenwanda Dr 98296
- Lake Ave & Pl 98290
- Lake Bosworth Dr & Ln 98290
- Lake Crest Dr 98290
- Lake Mount Dr 98290
- N, NW, S & SW Lake Roesiger Dr & Rd 98290
- Lake View Ave & Pl 98290
- Lakewood Dr 98290
- Lerch Rd 98290
- Lincoln Ave & Pl 98290
- Long St 98290
- Lost Lake Rd 98296
- E Lowell Larimer Rd 98296
- Lowell Snohomish River Rd 98296
- Ludwig Rd 98290
- N & S Machias Rd 98290
- Machias Cut Off 98290
- Madrona Dr 98290
- Maltby Rd 98296
- Maple Ave 98290
- Maple Rd 98296
- Market St 98296
- Marquette Ave 98290
- Marsh Rd 98296
- Mcallister Rd 98290
- Mcdonald Ave 98290
- Meadow Dr & Pl 98290
- E & W Meadow Lake Dr & Rd 98290
- Mero Rd 98290
- Middle Shore Rd 98290
- Mill Ave 98290
- Miller St 98290
- Monroe Camp Rd 98290
- Nevers Rd 98290
- Newberg Rd 98290
- Northlake Ave 98290
- Northridge Dr 98290
- Northshore Pl 98290
- Ok Mill Rd 98290
- Old Machias Rd 98290
- Old Siler Logging Rd 98296
- Old Snohomish Monroe Rd 98290
- Old Tester Rd 98290
- Orchard Ave 98290
- Panther Lake Dr & Rd 98290
- Paradise Lake Rd 98296
- Park Ave 98290
- Pearl St 98290
- Pilchuck Ave & Way 98290
- Pilchuck Tree Farm Rd 98290
- Pine Ave 98290
- Pipeline Rd 98290
- Price Rd 98290
- Puget Park Dr 98296
- Pulliam Pl 98290
- Railroad Ave 98290
- Railroad Way 98296
- Rainbow Pl 98290
- Rainier St 98290
- Ridge Ave 98290
- River Park Pl 98290
- Rivershore Rd 98290
- Riverview Ln & Rd 98290
- Riviera Blvd 98290
- Robinhood Ln 98290
- Robinson Rd 98296
- Roosevelt Rd 98290
- Root Ave 98290
- Russell Rd 98290
- Ryan Ct 98290
- Sanders Rd 98290
- Seattle Hill Rd 98296
- Seneca Ave 98290
- Sexton Rd 98290
- W Shore Loop Rd 98290
- Short St 98290
- Shorts School Rd 98290
- Silva St 98290
- Simon Rd 98290
- Sinclair Ave 98290
- Skipley Rd 98290
- Sky Meadows Ln 98290
- Smithson Pl 98290
- Snohomish Ave 98296
- Snohomish Cascade Dr 98296
- S Spada Rd 98290
- Springhetti Rd 98296
- State Ave 98290
- State St 98296
- State Route 2 98290
- State Route 9 SE 98290
- Stone Ridge Dr 98290
- Storm Lake Rd 98290
- Summit St 98290
- Suncrest Dr 98290
- Swans Slough Rd 98290
- Swans Trail Rd 98290
- Taylor St 98290
- Terrace Ave 98290
- Tester Rd 98290
- S Tom Marks Rd 98290
- Treosti Rd 98290
- Trombley Rd 98290
- N & S Tulloch Rd 98290
- Union Ave 98290
- Utley Rd 98290
- Vanjan St 98290
- Vaughn Ct 98290
- Victor Ave 98290
- Villa Dr 98296
- Virginia St 98290
- Wagner Rd 98290
- Wall St 98296
- Walsh Rd 98290
- Washington Ave 98290
- Waverly Dr 98296
- Weaver Rd & Way 98290
- Weber Rd 98290
- Welch Rd 98296
- Westwick Rd 98290
- Wheeler St 98296
- Wildwood Dr 98296
- Willow Ave 98290
- E Wishon Rd 98290
- Wonderland Rd 98290
- Wood St 98290
- Woods Pl 98296
- Woods Creek Rd 98290
- Yew Way 98296

NUMBERED STREETS

- 1st St 98290
- 2nd St 98290
- 3 Lakes Rd 98290
- 3rd SE 98290
- 4th Pl & St NE & SE 98290
- 5th St 98290
- 6th St 98290
- 7th Pl & St 98290
- 8th SE 98290
- 9th Pl & St 98290
- E 10th Pl & St SE 98290
- E 11th 98290
- 12th NE & SE 98290
- 13th St 98290
- 14th Pl & St 98290
- 15th St 98290
- 16th SE 98290
- 17th Ct & Pl 98290
- 18th Pl & St 98290
- 19th St 98290
- 20th SE 98290
- 21st Pl & St SE 98290
- 22nd Pl & St 98290
- 23rd Pl & St 98290
- 24th Pl & St 98290
- 25th Pl SE 98290
- 27th Pl & St 98290
- 28th Pl & St NE & SE 98290
- 29th Pl NE 98290
- 30th SE 98290
- 32nd St SE 98290
- 33rd Pl SE 98290
- 34th NE & SE 98290
- 35th Dr SE 98296
- 36th Ave SE 98296
- 36th Dr SE 98296
- 36th St SE 98290
- 37th St SE 98290
- 38th Pl & St 98290
- 40th Pl NE 98290
- 41st St SE 98290
- 42nd Dr SE 98296
- 42nd Pl SE 98290
- 42nd St NE 98290
- 42nd St SE 98290
- 43rd Ave SE 98296
- 43rd Dr SE 98296
- 43rd St NE 98290
- 44th Dr SE 98296
- 44th Pl SE 98296
- 44th St SE 98290
- 45th Dr SE 98296
- 45th Pl SE 98290
- 46th Ave SE 98296
- 46th Dr SE 98296
- 46th St SE 98290
- 47th Dr SE 98296
- 47th St SE 98290
- 48th Ave SE 98296
- 48th Dr SE 98290
- 48th St NE 98290
- 48th St SE 98290
- 49th Ave SE 98296
- 49th Pl SE 98290
- 50th Dr SE 98296
- 50th St NE 98290
- 50th St SE 98290
- 51st St SE 98290
- 52nd St SE 98290
- 53rd St SE 98290
- 54th Ave SE 98296
- 54th Dr SE 98296
- 54th St NE 98290
- 54th St SE 98290
- 55th Ave SE 98296
- 55th Dr SE 98296
- 55th St SE 98290
- 56th Pl & St 98290
- 57th Ave SE
  - 6400-6799 98290
  - 11600-16899 98296
- 57th Dr SE 98296
- 57th Pl SE 98290
- 58th Ave SE 98296
- 58th Dr SE 98296
- 58th Pl SE 98290
- 58th St SE 98290
- 59th Ave SE 98296
- 59th Dr SE 98296
- 59th St SE 98290
- 60th Ave SE 98296
- 60th Dr SE 98296
- 60th St SE 98290
- 61st Ave SE
  - 5600-7299 98290
  - 11800-20399 98296
- 61st Dr SE 98296
- 61st Pl SE 98290
- 62nd Ave SE 98296
- 62nd Pl SE 98296
- 62nd St SE 98290
- 63rd Ave SE 98296
- 63rd Dr SE 98296
- 63rd Pl SE 98290
- 63rd St SE 98290
- 64th Ave SE 98296
- 64th Dr SE 98296
- 64th St SE 98290
- 65th Ave SE
  - 6000-7599 98290
  - 13000-20399 98296
- 65th Dr SE
  - 6100-6299 98290
  - 14600-14799 98296
- 66th Ave SE
  - 5400-5999 98290
  - 12700-15599 98296
- 66th Dr SE 98290
- 66th Pl SE 98290
- 66th St SE 98290
- 67th Ave SE
  - 7600-7999 98290
  - 12400-19699 98296
- 67th Dr SE
  - 5500-5599 98290
  - 12500-15999 98296
- 68th Ave SE
  - 5500-7599 98290
  - 12400-15999 98296
- 68th Dr SE 98296
- 68th St SE 98290
- 69th Ave SE
  - 5500-8099 98290
  - 13500-17699 98296
- 69th Dr SE 98296
- 69th St SE 98290
- 70th Ave SE 98296
- 70th Dr SE
  - 5400-7299 98290
  - 13200-14199 98296
- 70th St NE 98290
- 70th St SE 98290
- 71st Ave SE 98296
- 71st Dr SE 98296
- 71st Pl SE 98290
- 72nd Ave SE
  - 7300-7399 98290
  - 21000-21199 98296
- 72nd Dr SE
  - 5000-5199 98290
  - 12700-20299 98296
- 72nd Pl SE 98290
- 72nd St NE 98290
- 72nd St SE 98290
- 73rd Ave SE 98296
- 73rd Dr SE 98296
- 73rd Pl SE 98290
- 74th Dr SE 98296
- 74th St SE 98290
- 75th Ave SE 98296
- 75th St SE 98290
- 76th Ave SE 98296
- 76th Dr SE
  - 6000-6699 98290
  - 20900-21199 98296
- 76th St SE 98290
- 77th Ave SE
  - 6500-7599 98290
  - 12800-15099 98296
- 77th Dr SE 98290
- 77th Pl SE 98290
- 77th St SE 98290
- 78th Ave SE
  - 8000-8099 98290
  - 13300-20799 98296
- 78th Dr SE 98296
- 78th Pl SE 98290
- 78th St SE 98290
- 79th Ave SE
  - 5200-8299 98290
  - 13300-16799 98296
- 79th Dr SE 98296
- 79th Pl SE 98290
- 80th Ave SE 98296
- 80th Dr SE 98296
- 80th St SE 98290
- 81st Ave SE
  - 6700-7599 98290
  - 13200-15099 98296
- 81st Pl SE 98290
- 81st St SE 98290
- 82nd Ave SE
  - 7800-7899 98290
  - 19700-20499 98296
- 82nd Dr SE 98296
- 82nd Pl SE 98290
- 82nd St SE 98290
- 83rd Ave SE
  - 3900-7699 98290
  - 14800-18599 98296
- 84th St SE 98290
- 85th Ave SE
  - 6400-8299 98290
  - 18600-20499 98296
- 85th St SE 98290
- 86th Ave SE 98296
- 86th Pl SE 98290
- 86th St SE 98290
- 87th Ave SE
  - 3200-7199 98290
  - 16100-21199 98296
- 87th Pl SE 98290
- 87th St SE 98290
- 88th Ave SE 98296
- 88th Dr SE 98290
- 88th Pl SE 98290
- 88th St SE 98290
- 89th Ave SE
  - 6500-7799 98290
  - 14000-19799 98296
- 89th St SE 98290
- 90th Ave & Pl 98290
- 91st Ave SE
  - 4900-7999 98290
  - 15200-21399 98296
- 92nd Pl & St 98290
- 93rd Ave SE
  - 5200-5499 98290
  - 13100-14099 98296
- 93rd Dr SE 98290
- 93rd St SE 98290
- 94th Dr SE 98290
- 95th Ave SE 98296
- 95th Dr SE
  - 5500-6199 98290
  - 19400-19599 98296
- 95th St SE 98290
- 96th Ave SE 98296
- 96th Dr SE
  - 5400-6299 98290
  - 18000-18499 98296
- 96th St SE 98290
- 97th Ave & Dr 98296
- 98th Ave SE
  - 6800-6899 98290
  - 16000-19899 98296
- 98th Dr SE 98290
- 99th Ave SE
  - 5200-6599 98290
  - 10600-21999 98296
- 99th St SE 98290
- 100th Ave SE 98296
- 100th St SE 98290
- 101st Pl SE 98290
- 102nd Ave & Dr 98296
- 103rd Ave SE 98290
- 103rd Dr SE
  - 6000-6199 98290
  - 22400-22499 98296
- 103rd St SE 98290
- 104th Ave SE 98296
- 104th St SE 98290
- 105th Ave SE 98296
- 105th Dr SE 98290
- 105th St SE 98290
- 106th Ave SE 98296
- 106th Dr SE
  - 11400-11499 98290
  - 13300-13899 98296
- 107th Ave SE
  - 4900-6300 98290
  - 6302-6398 98290
  - 17100-21499 98296
- 107th Pl SE 98290
- 107th St SE 98290
- 108th Ave SE 98296
- 108th Dr SE 98296
- 108th St SE 98290
- 109th Ave SE
  - 3600-5099 98290
  - 18000-21099 98296
- 109th Pl SE 98290
- 109th St SE
  - 10000-10199 98296
  - 20100-20299 98290
- 110th Dr SE 98296
- 111th Ave SE 98296
- 111th Pl SE 98290
- 111th St SE 98296
- 112th Dr SE
  - 9000-9199 98290
  - 19500-20099 98296
- 112th St SE 98290
- 113th Ave SE 98290
- 113th Dr SE
  - 3800-9199 98290
  - 20400-20498 98296
  - 20500-20699 98296
- 113th St SE 98290
- 114th Ave SE 98296
- 114th Pl SE 98290
- 115th Ave SE 98290
- 116th Dr SE 98290
- 116th St SE
  - 5900-5999 98296
  - 16800-21799 98290
- 117th Ave SE 98296
- 117th Dr SE 98290
- 117th St SE
  - 5900-5999 98296
  - 17900-18199 98290
- 118th Dr SE 98290
- 118th St SE
  - 6200-6299 98296
  - 19300-20699 98290
- 119th Ave SE
  - 5000-5199 98290
  - 22200-23499 98296
- 119th Dr SE 98290
- 119th Pl SE 98296
- 119th St SE 98296
- 120th Ave SE
  - 6900-7699 98290
  - 18100-18399 98296
- 120th Dr SE 98296
- 120th Pl SE 98296
- 120th St SE 98296
- 121st Ave SE
  - 5000-15199 98290
  - 20400-21199 98296
- 121st Dr SE 98290
- 121st St SE
  - 5800-5999 98296
  - 17600-18399 98290
- 122nd Ave SE 98290
- 123rd Ave SE
  - 5300-15299 98290
  - 18400-20399 98296
- 123rd Pl SE 98296
- 123rd St SE 98290
- 124th Ave SE 98290
- 124th Dr SE 98296
- 124th Pl SE 98296
- 124th St SE
  - 5700-5799 98296
  - 17900-18199 98290
- 125th Ave SE 98290
- 125th Pl SE
  - 5400-5731 98296
  - 5795-5799 98290
- 125th St SE
  - 5400-5899 98296
  - 17100-17499 98290
- 126th Pl SE 98296
- 126th St SE
  - 5500-6799 98296
  - 18100-18999 98290
- 127th Ave SE
  - 2500-15499 98290
  - 19900-24399 98296
- 127th Pl SE 98296
- 127th St SE 98290
- 128th Pl SE
  - 5700-6599 98296
  - 17500-18299 98290
- 128th St SE 98296
- 129th Ave SE 98296
- 129th Dr SE 98290
- 129th Pl SE
  - 6300-6799 98296
  - 18000-18099 98290
- 129th St SE
  - 6400-7099 98296
  - 11000-11099 98290
- 130th Dr SE 98290
- 130th Pl SE
  - 6000-6699 98296
  - 17800-19499 98290
- 130th St SE
  - 6400-7299 98296
  - 17500-18099 98290
- 131st Ave SE
  - 3800-9199 98290
  - 23000-24399 98296
- 131st Dr SE 98296
- 131st Pl SE
  - 5700-6799 98296
  - 17700-18199 98290
- 131st St SE
  - 6700-6999 98296
  - 17500-17699 98290
- 132nd Ave SE 98290
- 132nd Pl SE
  - 6700-8299 98296
  - 18100-18199 98290
- 132nd St SE
  - 6900-7299 98296
  - 12800-18099 98290
- 133rd Ave SE
  - 5600-6799 98290
  - 19600-24399 98296
- 133rd Dr SE
  - 6800-6899 98290
  - 20100-20299 98296
  - 20301-22811 98296
- 133rd Pl SE
  - 4900-10399 98296
  - 12300-18099 98290
- 133rd St SE 98296
- 134th Ave SE 98296
- 134th Dr SE 98290
- 134th Pl SE 98296
- 134th St SE 98296
- 135th Ave SE 98290
- 135th Dr SE
  - 5400-9199 98290
  - 23700-23899 98296
- 135th Pl SE 98296
- 135th St SE 98296
- 136th Dr SE 98290
- 136th Pl SE 98296
- 136th St SE 98296
- 137th Ave SE 98290
- 137th Dr SE
  - 2000-2199 98290
  - 23600-23899 98296
- 137th Pl SE 98296
- 137th St SE 98296
- 138th Ave SE 98296
- 138th Dr SE
  - 5200-9699 98290
  - 23600-23999 98296
- 138th Pl SE 98296
- 138th St SE 98296
- 139th Ave SE 98290
- 139th Dr SE 98296
- 139th Pl SE 98296
- 140th Ave SE 98290
- 140th Pl SE 98296
- 140th St SE
  - 4700-6499 98296
  - 12300-12699 98290
- 141st Ave SE
  - 14100-15399 98290
  - 22000-22399 98296
- 141st Dr SE
  - 2500-15599 98290

23800-23999 98296
141st Pl SE
4700-4799 98296
12700-12999 98290
141st St SE
4228-6999 98296
14000-14799 98290
142nd Ave SE 98290
142nd Dr SE
6800-7799 98290
23700-23899 98296
142nd Pl SE 98296
142nd St SE 98296
143rd Ave SE
3000-4399 98290
22400-24399 98296
143rd Pl SE 98296
143rd St SE 98296
144th Dr SE 98290
144th Pl SE 98296
144th St SE
4100-7099 98296
14200-14699 98290
145th Ave SE 98290
145th Dr SE 98290
145th Pl SE 98296
145th St SE 98296
146th Ave SE
14800-15799 98290
23600-32699 98296
146th Dr SE 98296
146th Pl SE
4200-9899 98296
12700-13399 98290
146th St SE 98296
147th NE & SE 98290
148th Ave, Pl & St 98296
149th Ave SE
1600-4399 98290
22400-22699 98296
149th Pl SE 98296
149th St SE 98296
150th Ave NE 98290
150th Pl SE 98296
150th St SE
6000-9599 98296
12900-12999 98290
151st Ave SE 98290
151st Pl SE 98296
151st St SE 98296
152nd Ave SE 98290
152nd Dr NE 98290
152nd Pl SE
6100-6299 98296
11900-12299 98290
152nd St SE 98296
153rd Ave SE
2000-7299 98290
22200-22799 98296
153rd Dr SE 98290
153rd Pl SE 98296
153rd St SE 98296
154th Dr NE 98290
154th Dr SE 98290
154th Pl SE 98296
154th St SE 98296
155th Ave NE 98290
155th Ave SE
1600-9299 98290
22800-24399 98296
155th Pl SE 98296
155th St SE 98296
156th St SE 98296
157th Ave SE
2000-17599 98290
22000-22899 98296
158th Ave SE 98290
158th Pl SE 98296
158th St SE 98296
159th Ave NE 98290
159th Ave SE 98290
159th Dr SE 98290
159th Pl SE 98296
159th St SE 98296
160th Ave SE 98290
160th St SE 98296
161st NE & SE 98290

162nd Dr SE 98290
162nd St SE 98296
163rd Ave & Dr 98290
164th Ave SE 98290
164th Dr SE 98290
164th St SE 98296
165th Ave & Dr 98290
166th St SE 98290
167th Ave SE 98290
167th St SE 98296
168th St SE 98296
169th Ave & Pl 98290
170th St SE 98296
171st NE & SE 98290
172nd Ave NE 98290
172nd Ave SE 98290
172nd St SE
5900-9599 98296
15900-16099 98290
173rd Ave & Dr 98290
174th Ave SE 98290
174th Pl SE 98296
174th St SE 98296
175th Ave NE 98290
175th Ave SE 98290
175th Dr SE 98290
175th Pl SE 98296
176th Ave SE 98290
176th Dr SE 98290
176th Pl SE 98290
176th St SE 98296
177th NE & SE 98290
178th Ave SE 98290
178th Dr SE 98290
178th St SE 98296
179th Ave SE 98290
180th Pl SE 98296
180th St SE 98296
181st Ave & Dr 98290
182nd Ave & Dr 98290
183rd Ave SE 98290
183rd Dr SE 98290
183rd Pl SE 98296
183rd St SE 98296
184th Dr SE 98290
184th St SE 98296
185th Ave NE 98290
185th Ave SE 98290
185th Dr SE 98290
185th Pl SE 98296
185th St SE 98296
186th Dr SE 98290
187th Ave SE 98290
187th Dr SE 98290
187th St SE 98296
188th Dr SE 98290
188th St SE 98296
189th Ave & Dr 98290
190th Ave SE 98290
190th St SE 98296
191st Dr SE 98290
191st St SE 98296
192nd Dr SE 98290
192nd St SE 98296
194th St SE 98296
195th Ave & Dr 98290
196th St SE 98296
197th Ave SE 98290
197th St SE 98296
198th Ave NE 98290
198th Dr SE 98290
198th Pl SE 98296
198th St SE 98296
199th Ave SE 98290
199th Pl SE 98296
199th St SE 98296
200th Ave SE 98290
200th Pl SE 98296
200th St SE 98296
201st Ave NE 98290
201st Ave SE 98290
201st Dr SE 98290
201st St SE 98296
202nd Ave SE 98290
202nd Pl SE 98296
202nd St SE 98296

203rd Ave NE 98290
203rd Ave SE 98290
203rd Dr SE 98290
203rd St SE 98296
204th Ave SE 98290
204th Dr SE 98290
204th Pl SE 98296
204th St SE 98296
205th Ave SE 98290
205th Dr SE 98290
205th St SE 98296
206th Ave SE 98290
206th Dr SE 98290
206th St SE 98296
207th Ave SE 98290
207th St SE 98296
208th Ave SE 98290
208th Pl SE 98296
208th St SE 98296
209th Ave SE 98290
210th St SE 98296
211th Ave SE 98290
211th Pl SE 98296
211th St SE 98296
212th Ave SE 98290
212th Dr SE 98290
212th St SE 98296
213th Ave SE 98290
214th Pl & St 98296
215th Ave SE 98290
215th Pl SE 98296
216th St SE 98296
217th Ave SE 98290
217th St SE 98296
218th Pl SE 98296
219th Ave SE 98290
219th Pl SE 98296
219th St SE 98296
220th Pl SE 98296
221st Pl & St 98296
223rd St SE 98296
224th St SE 98296
226th St SE 98296
228th St SE 98296
230th St SE 98296
231st Ave NE 98290
232nd Ave NE 98290
233rd Ave SE 98290
233rd St SE 98296
234th St SE 98296
235th St SE 98296
236th Pl SE 98296
238th Pl & St 98296
239th Ave NE 98290
239th Pl SE 98296
240th St SE 98296
241st St SE 98296
242nd St SE 98296

SPOKANE WA

General Delivery 99210

POST OFFICE BOXES MAIN OFFICE STATIONS AND BRANCHES

Box No.s
A - B 99219
C1900 - C1900 99220
1 - 2485 99210
2501 - 4856 99220
4000 - 4000 99210
4921 - 4996 99220
5351 - 5500 99205
5577 - 5577 99220
6000 - 6880 99217
7101 - 7660 99207
8000 - 8760 99203
9000 - 10915 99209
11000 - 11000 99211
15108 - 15108 99215
18001 - 18979 99228
19001 - 19478 99219
21001 - 21789 99201
24000 - 24000 99219
28001 - 28998 99228
30001 - 31556 99223
40001 - 40499 99220
48001 - 48840 99228

RURAL ROUTES

02 99217

NAMED STREETS

N A St
900-1399 99201
1401-1499 99201
3101-4797 99205
4799-6299 99205
6401-6697 99208
6699-6799 99208
6801-6899 99208
S A St 99224
S Abbott Rd 99224
W & N Abigail Ave, Ct & Ln 99208
S Abrams Ct 99203
S Achilles St 99223
Acoma Ct, Dr & St 99208
N Adams Rd 99217
N Adams St
801-1197 99201
1199-1599 99201
1601-1997 99205
1999-6100 99205
6102-6298 99205
6800-7010 99208
S Adams St
101-199 99201
501-697 99204
699-1399 99204
1400-2099 99203
2101-2499 99203
N Addison Ct 99208
E Addison Dr 99208
N Addison St
1300-1400 99202
1402-1498 99202
1700-5499 99207
5900-6899 99208
12800-12999 99218
13100-13599 99208
E Adirondack Ct 99223
W Aero Rd 99224
Aimee Ave & Ct 99208
W Airport Dr 99224
N Airport Rd 99212
E Alakerid Ave 99202
N Alameda Blvd 99205
N Alberta Cir 99208
N Alberta Ct 99208
N Alberta Ln 99218
N Alberta Rd 99208
N Alberta St
2701-2797 99205
2799-6299 99205
6400-7899 99208
N Alcan St 99218
W Alcott Ct 99208
Alder Cir, Ct & Dr 99223
E Alderman Ln 99223
W Alderwood Ave
200-599 99218
5200-5299 99208
E Aldridge Ln 99223
E Alexa Ct 99208
E Alexandra Ln 99223
W Alice Ave 99205
W Alison Ave 99208
E Alki Ave 99202
N Allen Pl 99205
W Allman Rd 99224
N & W Alpine Ct, Dr & Ln 99208
N Alpine Fir 99217
W Alta Ct 99218

S Altamont Blvd 99202
S Altamont Ct 99223
S Altamont Ln 99223
E Altamont Pl 99202
N Altamont St
100-1300 99202
1302-1498 99202
1500-3399 99207
4700-7999 99217
S Altamont St
1-97 99202
99-799 99202
3301-3397 99223
3399-4599 99223
Ambassador Way 99224
S Amberstone Ct 99224
E & S Amberwood Ct & Ln 99223
W Amherst Ct 99205
N Andrew St 99218
E Angela Ct 99223
E Ann Marie Ln 99223
N Anna J Dr 99218
S Antelope Ave 99224
N Antietam Dr 99208
Apache Pass Ln & Rd 99206
S Apollo St 99223
S Apple Tree Ct 99203
N Appomattox Ct 99208
N Arabian Ln 99224
N Arapaho Ct 99208
W Ardea Ln 99208
W Ardmore Dr 99218
N Argonaut Rd 99208
E Argonne Ln 99212
N Argonne Ln 99212
N Argonne Rd
2700-5599 99212
5700-8999 99217
W Armstrong Dr 99224
W Arrow Ln 99208
W & N Arrowhead Ct, Ln & Rd 99208
E Arrowleaf Ln 99206
S Arthur St
100-1200 99202
1202-1298 99202
1700-1798 99203
1800-4200 99203
4202-4398 99203
5400-5500 99223
5502-5598 99223
N Ash Ln 99208
N Ash Pl 99205
N Ash St
1-1599 99201
1600-6299 99205
6300-9099 99208
S Ash St
430-432 99201
500-1399 99204
1400-1700 99203
1702-1798 99203
S Ashland Ct 99224
W Ashley Ave 99208
N Ashley Cir 99208
W Ashley Cir 99208
N Ashley Ln 99218
S Ashton Ct 99223
E Aspen Ln 99206
S Aspen Rd 99224
E Aspen Bluff Ln 99217
W Aspen View Ave 99224
S Assembly Rd 99224
N Assembly St
4500-6100 99205
6102-6298 99205
6300-6698 99208
6700-6799 99208
S Assembly St 99224
E Astor Dr 99208
N Astor St
1100-1499 99202
1600-2500 99207
2502-2898 99207
5900-6297 99208

6299-6299 99208
N Atlantic Dr 99205
N Atlantic St
1000-1198 99201
1200-1400 99201
1402-1498 99201
1600-6099 99205
6101-6299 99205
6301-6797 99208
6799-8599 99208
9300-12099 99218
S Atwood Ln 99224
N Aubrey L White Pkwy
3400-3499 99224
4401-4499 99205
6400-6699 99208
W Auburn Crest Ct 99224
S Audubon Ct 99224
N Audubon Dr 99208
N Audubon St
3100-3298 99205
3300-6200 99205
6202-6298 99205
6600-7298 99208
7300-7799 99208
S Audubon St 99224
S Auer St 99223
E Augusta Ave 99207
W Augusta Ave 99205
N Austin Ln 99208
N Austin Rd 99208
S Austin Rd 99224
W Austin Rd 99208
Autumn Rd & St 99224
W Aviation Rd 99224
W Avon Ave 99208
S Azalea Dr 99224
N Azure Dr 99208
W Baird Ave 99224
E Baldwin Ave 99207
N Balerene St 99208
S Ball Rd 99224
W Ballard Rd 99208
S Ballou Rd
1200-1399 99202
1400-1499 99203
W Balmer Rd 99224
S Baltimore Rd 99223
N & W Banbury Dr 99218
E Barley Brae Ct 99208
N Barnes Rd 99208
W Barnes Rd
200-699 99218
4900-5499 99208
S Basalt St 99224
W Basalt Ridge Ct 99224
S Bates Rd 99206
E Baycourt Ln 99223
Baymont Ct & St 99224
W Baywood Ct 99208
E Beacon Ave 99208
W Beacon Ave 99208
E Beacon Ln 99217
Bedford Ave & Ct 99208
E & N Bedivere Dr 99218
E Belle Terre Ave 99206
E Bellerive Ln 99223
S Bellgrove Ln 99223
W Bellwood Dr 99218
N & W Belmont Dr 99208
N Belt St
1200-1300 99201
1302-1498 99201
1601-2197 99205
2199-6299 99205
6500-6798 99208
6800-7099 99208
N Bemis St 99205
S Bemis St 99224
E Ben Burr Blvd 99223
S Ben Burr Blvd 99202
S Ben Burr Rd 99223
S Ben Franklin Ln 99224
W Bencoria Ave 99204
W Bennett Ave 99201
N Benton Dr 99218
W Bentwood Ct 99208

N Bernard St 99201
S Bernard St
200-299 99201
401-497 99204
499-1399 99204
1400-1498 99203
1500-3999 99203
5900-5999 99224
W Bernhill Rd 99208
N Berridae Rd 99208
N Bessie Rd 99212
S Best Ln 99206
E Big Rock Rd 99223
E Big Springs Rd 99223
E Bigelow Gulch Rd 99217
S Bighorn Ln 99206
W Bing Ct 99208
E Birch Ave 99217
N Birch Ct 99208
N Birch Pl 99205
E Birch Rd 99218
E Birkdale Ln 99223
E Bismark Ave
600-2500 99208
2502-2998 99208
3704-3899 99217
W Bismark Ave
1100-3999 99205
5300-5399 99208
E Bismark Ct 99217
W Bismark Pl 99205
E Bitteroot Ln 99206
E Black Bear Ln 99217
E Black Oak Ln 99217
W Blackfoot Ave 99208
E Blackhawk Dr 99208
S Blackwing Ct 99224
S & E Blackwood Ct & Ln 99223
S Blake St 99224
S Blue Fern Ln 99223
E Blue Fox Ln 99217
E Blue Grass 99217
E Blue Heron Ct 99208
N Blue Raven Ln 99224
N Blue Spruce Ln 99217
W Blueberry Ln 99218
W Bluebird Ln 99224
N Bluecoat Ct 99208
N Bluegrass St 99217
S Bluegrouse Ln 99224
S Blueridge Dr 99224
S Bluff Rd 99224
E Boardwalk Ln 99212
N Boeing Rd 99206
S Bogart Ct 99223
W Bolan Ave 99224
W Bonnie Dr 99224
E Boone Ave 99202
W Boone Ave 99201
W Borden Rd 99224
N Boulder Park Ln 99208
S Bowdish Rd 99206
W Bowie Rd 99224
W Bowling Rd 99218
S Boxwood Ln 99223
W Boy Scout Way 99201
N & W Bradbury St 99208
W Bradford Ct 99203
E Bradley Ln 99223
N Bradley Rd 99217
E Brady Ct 99208
N Braeburn Dr 99205
W Braeden Ln 99208
N Brannon Ln 99208
N Brenda Ct 99208
E & N Brentwood Dr 99208
E Brevier Rd 99217
E Briant Ln 99217
W Briar Ln 99208
W & N Briar Cliff Ct & Dr 99218
W Briarcliff Ln 99208
W Bridge Ave 99201
E Bridgeport Ave
1-3099 99207

3100-3999 99217
8300-9099 99212
Bridget Ct & St 99208
W Bridle Ln 99224
Bridlewood Ct & Ln 99224
W Brierwood Ave 99218
E Brierwood Ct 99218
E Brierwood Dr 99218
E Brierwood Ln 99218
W Brierwood Ln 99208
S Brighton Ln 99223
W Bristol Ave 99224
E & W Brita Ave 99208
E Broad Ave
300-1799 99207
2900-3828 99217
W Broad Ave 99205
E Broad Ct 99212
E Broad Ln 99212
W Broad Pl 99205
E Broadway Ave 99202
W Broadway Ave 99201
W Broken Arrow Ct 99208
N Brook Terrace St 99224
W Brookfield Ave 99208
W Brookfield Ct 99208
E Brookfield Ln 99223
S Brookhaven St 99224
E Brooklawn Dr 99208
E Brooklyn Ave 99217
N Brooks Rd 99224
S Brookshire Ct 99223
W Brown Hollow Ln 99224
N Browne St 99201
S Browne St
100-299 99201
401-497 99204
499-1399 99204
2101-2397 99203
2399-3800 99203
3802-3998 99203
N Brownsville Ct 99208
E Bruce Ave 99217
W Bruce Ave 99208
N Bruce Rd 99217
E Buckeye Ave
1701-1897 99207
1899-2699 99207
2701-2799 99207
3700-5099 99217
8100-8799 99212
9200-9298 99206
W Buckeye Ave 99205
E Buckeye Ct 99217
N Buell Ct 99205
S Buell Ln 99224
S Buena Vista Dr 99224
N Buffalo St 99205
E Bull Pine Ln 99217
E Bull Run Ct 99208
E Burnett Rd 99217
N Burnett Rd 99224
W Burnett Rd 99224
W Burns Pl 99224
Butler Ln 99223
N Butler Rd 99206
S Buttercup Ln 99224
N C St 99205
W Caden Ave 99208
N Calispel Ct
8100-8199 99208
11200-11299 99218
13400-13499 99208
N Calispel Ln 99208
N Calispel St
1000-1399 99201
1401-1499 99201
1601-1697 99205
1699-6299 99205
6300-7899 99208
8700-8898 99218
E Calkins Dr
501-697 99208
699-900 99208
902-970 99208
1200-1899 99217
N Calkins Dr 99208
N Calvert Ln 99224
N Cambridge Dr 99208
E Cambridge Ln 99203
N Cambridge Ln 99208
N Camilla Marie Ct 99208
E Campanile Ln 99223
W Campus Dr 99224
W Candlewood Ct 99218
Candy Ln 99208
N Cannon Ct 99208
S Cannon Pl 99204
N Cannon St
600-1299 99201
1301-1499 99201
1800-1998 99205
2000-6299 99205
7001-7099 99208
S Cannon St
101-135 99201
137-599 99201
601-697 99204
699-800 99204
802-998 99204
W Cannon Place Ln 99204
W Canyon Dr 99224
E Canyon Ln 99212
S Canyon Woods Ln 99224
N Capri Ln 99217
S Carillon Pl 99223
W Carl J Ln 99218
E Carlisle Ave
400-1499 99207
1501-3199 99207
3201-3297 99217
3299-4299 99217
W Carlisle Ave 99205
Carlson Ct & Ln 99208
E Carmella Ct 99223
S Carmella Ln 99224
S Carnahan Ln 99223
S Carnahan Rd 99212
N Carnahan St 99217
S Carnation Rd 99224
W & N Carolina Ct &
Way 99208
E Caroline Ct 99218
S Carousel Ln 99224
E Carriage Ct
400-499 99218
1300-1399 99208
E Carroll Ln 99223
S Carter Ln 99224
E & W Cascade Ct, Pl &
Way 99208
E Casper Dr 99223
N Castlebrook Ln 99208
E Castlerock Ln 99208
N Castor Ridge Ln 99217
E Cataldo Ave 99202
W Cataldo Ave 99201
N Catherine St 99208
S Cattail Ln 99224
N Cedar Rd 99208
S Cedar Rd 99224
N Cedar St
1-1599 99201
1600-6299 99205
S Cedar St
1-399 99201
500-1299 99204
1400-1999 99203
S Cedar Rim Ln 99224
E Cedarwood Ct 99223
E Celesta Ave 99202
E Center Ln 99208
S Center Ln 99224
W Center Ln 99208
E Center Rd 99208
N Center Rd 99212
W Center St 99208
E Central Ave
1-197 99208
199-2999 99208
3001-3099 99208
3700-10699 99217
W Central Ave 99205
Chadwick Ct & Ln 99208
E Challis Ct 99223
N Chance Ln 99218
S Chandler St 99202
E Chantel Dr 99218
S & W Chaperon Peak
Ct & Dr 99224
W Charlene Ct 99208
Charlton Ave & Cir 99208
E Chaser Ln 99223
E & W Chatham Ave &
Ct 99218
W Chaucer Ave 99208
S Cheatham Rd 99224
W Chelan Ave 99205
S Chelsea Ct 99203
E Chelsea Ln 99217
S Cheney Spokane
Rd 99224
Cherry Ln 99208
S Cherry Ln 99223
S Cherry St
1001-1199 99204
2100-2499 99224
E & S Cherry Tree Ln 99203
W Cherrywood Ct 99218
S Chester Creek Rd 99206
N Chestnut St 99201
S Chestnut St
100-142 99201
144-499 99201
1200-1298 99224
1300-2899 99224
Chicha Ct 99224
E Chilton Ave 99218
W Chippewa Ct 99208
E Chisholm Ln 99223
N Chrisalan Ln 99217
N Christensen Rd 99224
W Christi Dr 99208
E Christmas Tree Ln 99203
S Chronicle Ln 99223
N Chronicle St 99217
W Cimarron Ln 99208
N Cincinnati Ct 99208
N Cincinnati St
700-1399 99202
1600-1698 99207
1700-4499 99207
4501-5419 99207
6001-6397 99208
6399-15600 99208
15602-15698 99208
W Cinnibar Ln 99224
W Circle Pl 99205
Cirrus Ct & Rd 99208
W & N Claire Ave &
Ct 99208
N Clallam Ct 99208
N & W Claney Ct 99208
E Clark Rd 99223
W Clarke Ave 99201
N Clatsop Ct 99208
W Clearelm Ave 99205
E Clearview Ln 99217
E Clements Ln 99217
E Cleveland Ave
101-197 99207
199-3099 99207
3101-3197 99217
3199-4399 99217
W Cleveland Ave 99205
Cleveland Bay Ln 99208
W Cliff Dr 99204
S Cliff View Ln 99224
W Cliffwood Ct 99218
Clover Ave & Ct 99217
E Club Ct 99203
N Cochran Rd 99208
N Cochran St
600-1599 99201
3100-6199 99205
6900-7599 99208
S Cochran St 99224
S Coeur Dalene St
100-198 99201
200-599 99201
900-1098 99224
1100-1399 99224
S Coleman Ln 99223
N Colfax Rd 99218
W College Ave 99201
N College Cir 99218
N College Rd 99218
N College Place Dr 99218
N Colton Ln 99212
N Colton Pl 99208
N Colton St
6101-6117 99208
6119-8699 99208
8700-9399 99218
E Columbia Ave
300-2999 99208
3001-3099 99208
3600-6999 99217
W Columbia Ave 99205
N Columbia Cir 99205
E Columbia Ct 99212
E Columbia Dr
6900-7099 99217
7300-8600 99212
8602-9102 99212
E Columbia Park Dr 99212
N Columbus Dr 99208
N Columbus St
700-898 99202
900-1399 99202
1401-1499 99202
2000-2599 99207
14300-15399 99208
N Colville Rd 99224
W & N Comanche Ave &
Dr 99208
S Comax Ct 99224
E Commellini Rd 99208
E Commerce Ave 99212
W Comstock Ct 99203
W & N Conestoga Ave,
Ln & St 99208
E Congress Ave 99223
S Conklin St
500-799 99202
1601-4097 99203
4099-4399 99203
W Connaught Dr 99208
S Connor Ln 99224
W Conrad Ct 99208
S Cook Ct 99223
N Cook St
101-697 99202
699-1499 99202
1500-4499 99207
4700-5199 99217
5201-5499 99217
5501-5697 99208
5699-6299 99208
S Cook St
500-598 99202
600-1399 99202
1400-6299 99223
E Coplen Ave 99217
N Copper Canyon Ln 99208
S Copper Ridge Blvd 99224
E Copper River Ln 99206
Cora Ave & Ct 99205
E Coral Ln 99223
N Corey Ct 99208
E Corkery Rd 99223
S Corkery Road Ext 99223
S Corrisa Ct 99223
W Cotta Ave 99204
W Cougar Ln 99224
W Coulee Creek Rd 99224
W Coulee Hite Rd 99224
W & N Country Club Ct
& Dr 99218
E Country Hill Ct 99208
W Country Hills Ln 99208
N Country Homes Blvd
6700-8699 99208
8700-9199 99218
W Country Hunt Ln 99224
N Country Ridge Ln 99208
N Coursier Ln 99208
E Courtland Ave
1-3099 99207
3201-3215 99217
3217-3999 99217
8300-8699 99212
W Courtland Ave 99205
E Courtview Ln 99217
N & W Coventry Ln 99205
S Covey Run Ln 99224
S Cowley St 99202
N Cowlitz Ct 99208
E Cozza Dr 99208
S Craftsman Ct 99223
N Craig Rd 99224
E Crandall Ct 99223
W Crandall Ln 99208
S Crawford Ln 99224
W Cree Ct 99208
S Cree Dr 99206
E Creek Way 99208
S & W Creekstone St 99224
E Creekview Ln 99224
W Crescent Ct 99205
N Crest Ct 99218
E Crest Rd 99203
S Crest Rd 99203
S & W Crest View Ave &
St 99224
S Cresthill Dr 99203
N Crestline St
100-1200 99202
1202-1498 99202
1500-5499 99207
5700-6199 99208
6201-6299 99208
6300-6498 99217
6500-8799 99217
12700-13599 99208
S Crestline St
1-1199 99202
1201-1399 99202
1401-2297 99203
2299-4399 99203
4401-5697 99223
5699-6499 99223
Crestmont Ln 99217
Creston Ln 99208
S & W Crestview Rd 99224
W Crestwood Ct 99218
N Cristy Ln 99212
E Crooked Arrow Ln 99224
W Crosby Ct 99208
W Crowchief Ct 99208
E Crown Ave
1-1799 99207
3500-3899 99217
W Crown Ave 99205
W Crown Pl 99205
S Croydon Ct 99203
N Cuba St 99217
S Cuba St
901-1399 99202
2100-2198 99223
2200-7999 99223
S Cumberland Rd 99224
S Custer Ct 99223
W Custer Dr 99224
E Custer Ln 99223
N Custer Rd 99217
S Custer Rd 99223
S Custer St 99223
E Cypress Ln 99217
E Cyprus Ln 99223
N D St 99205
S D St 99224
W & N Daisy Ave &
Pl 99205
N Dakota Ct 99208
N Dakota Ln 99218
N Dakota St
1104-1198 99202
1200-1499 99202
1701-1797 99207
1799-2999 99207
6800-8200 99208
8202-8298 99208
12401-12697 99218
12699-12799 99218
12800-15099 99208
N Dale Rd 99212
E Dalke Ave
100-198 99208
200-2499 99208
3700-4199 99217
W Dalke Ave 99205
E Dalton Ave
18-2099 99207
8500-8999 99212
9001-9099 99212
9600-10199 99206
W Dalton Ave 99205
N Dalton Rd 99208
N Danbury St 99208
S Dandy Ct 99224
N Darknell Rd 99217
N Dartford Dr 99208
E Dave Ct 99208
N Davis Rd 99206
S Davison Blvd 99224
W Dawn Ave
200-299 99218
1200-4099 99208
N Dawn Ct 99208
S Daystar Ln 99224
W Dean Ave 99201
S Deanna Ct 99223
S Dearborn Ct 99223
S Dearborn Ln 99223
N Dearborn Rd 99217
S Dearborn Rd 99223
S Dearborn St 99223
N Debby Ln 99208
N Debby Lynn Ct 99208
W Deborah Ln 99208
S Decamp Dr 99223
E Decatur Ave
600-2499 99208
2501-2939 99208
3700-3799 99217
W Decatur Ave 99205
S Deer Heights Rd 99224
S Deercrest Ln 99224
S Deerview Ln 99223
E Deerwood Ct 99223
S Degray Ln 99224
W Delbert Ave 99208
S Delfino Ln 99224
W Dell Dr 99208
S Denny Ct 99202
W Deno Rd 99224
N Denver Ct 99208
N Denver Dr 99218
N Denver St
500-598 99202
2200-2599 99207
S Denver St
500-598 99202
600-699 99202
2600-2699 99203
N Deschutes Dr 99208
W Deska Dr 99224
E Desmet Ave 99202
Devoe Ave & Ln 99217
S Devonshire Ct 99223
E Diamond Ave
2100-2299 99207
2300-3199 99217
E Diamond Ln 99212
E Diane Ct 99223
N Dick Rd 99212
S Dishman Mica Rd 99206
N Division St
3-1499 99202
1600-5499 99207
5500-5698 99208
5700-8699 99208
8700-12899 99218
S Division St
100-1399 99202
1400-3500 99203
3502-3598 99203
5900-5999 99224
N Doak Rd 99217
W Dogwood Ln 99224
S Donald Ct 99223
E Donegal Ave 99223
E Donna Ct 99218
Donnatella Ln 99224
E & S Donora Ct & Dr 99223
W Dorothy Ct 99208
N Dorset Rd 99208
S Dorset Rd 99224
N Douglas Dr 99205
N Douglass St 99208
W Dover Ct 99203
N Dover Rd 99224
N Dowdy Rd 99224
S Downing Ct 99203
N Driscoll Blvd 99205
N Drumheller St
5500-5999 99205
6500-7599 99208
E Dunbar Ln 99223
N Dusk Ct 99208
S Dyer Rd 99223
W Dynamite Ln 99224
N E St
2801-3397 99205
3399-5899 99205
7500-7699 99208
S E St 99224
N Eagle Bluff Ln 99208
E Eagle Feather Ln 99224
W Eagle Ridge Blvd 99224
Eagle View Ln 99208
S Eaglecrest Dr 99206
W Eagles Nest Ln 99208
N East Bluff Ct 99208
N East Oval St 99205
N Eastern Rd 99217
S Eastern Rd 99223
S Eastgate Ct 99203
W Eastmont Way 99208
E Eastview Dr 99208
S Easy Ln 99223
E Eaton Ave 99218
S Echo Ct 99223
Echo Glen Dr & Ln 99223
S Echo Ridge St 99224
W Eddy Ave 99208
N Edencrest Dr 99208
E Edenderry Ct 99223
W Edgehill Rd 99218
Edgemont Rd 99217
S Edgerton Ln 99212
W Edgewood Ct 99208
S Edison St 99224
N Edmond St 99217
N Edna Ln 99218
N Edna St 99208
W Eichenberger Pl 99224
W & E Elcliff Ave &
Rd 99218
E Elde Dr 99212
W Elderberry Ave 99208
W Electric Ave 99224
N Elgin St
3900-3998 99205
4000-6299 99205
6300-6998 99208
7000-7099 99208
N Elizabeth St 99208
S Elk Ridge Ln 99223
S Elk Run Ln 99224
N Ella Rd 99212
N Ella St
5700-5999 99212
6000-6399 99217
S Ellis Rd 99223
E Ellsworth Ln 99223
E Elm Rd 99218
N Elm St
400-1199 99201
1201-1399 99201
1601-1997 99205
1999-6299 99205
8700-9399 99208
S Elm St
1-200 99201
202-598 99201

600-1200 99204
1202-1298 99204
N Elma Dr 99218
W & N Elmhurst Ave &
St 99208
W Elmwood Ct 99218
W Eloika Ave 99205
E Elto Ave 99208
N Elton Ct 99212
N Elton Dr 99217
N Elton Ln 99212
N Elton Rd 99212
Elwood Ct & Dr 99218
Ely Ct & Rd 99212
N Emerald Ln 99212
E Emily Ln 99208
E Empire Ave
1-2499 99207
3401-3528 99217
9600-10499 99206
N Entiat Ct 99208
E Erica Ct 99208
N Erie St 99202
E Ermina Ave
1-97 99207
99-3199 99207
3700-4299 99217
N Espe Rd 99217
N Essex Ct 99208
E Estates Rd 99224
Ethan Ln 99208
E Euclid Ave
1-3099 99207
3100-3699 99217
3701-4499 99217
8300-9099 99212
W Euclid Ave 99205
W Euclid Rd 99224
N Evening Ct 99208
E Everett Ave
1-2299 99207
2300-3899 99217
W Everett Ave 99205
W Everett Pl 99205
N Evergreen Rd 99217
N Evergreen St 99201
E Excaliber Ave 99218
W Excell Ave 99208
N Excell Ct 99208
N Excell Dr
7100-8199 99208
9800-10099 99218
W Excell Dr 99208
W Excell Ln 99208
E Excelsior Rd 99224
W Ezra 99208
N F St
3600-5498 99205
5500-6199 99205
6700-7899 99208
S F St 99224
E Fairmont Ln 99217
N Fairmount Pl 99205
E Fairview Ave
2-198 99207
200-3099 99207
3100-5199 99217
W Fairview Ave 99205
E Fairview Ct 99206
N Fairview Rd 99217
W Fairway Dr 99218
S Fairway Ridge Ln 99224
N Fairwood Dr 99218
N Fairwood Ln 99208
E & W Falcon Ave 99218
E Falling Springs Ln 99224
W Falls Ave 99201
S Fan Rd 99224
S Fanazick Pl 99224
S Fancher Rd 99223
N Farainde St 99218
S Farm Rd 99223
N Farmdale St 99208
N & S Farr Rd 99206
N Farrel Rd 99217
E Farwell Rd
100-499 99218

900-1699 99208
13100-16099 99217
N Felts St 99217
W Fernwood Ct 99208
S Ferrall Ct
1200-1299 99202
6200-6299 99223
N Ferrall St 99217
S Ferrall St
1-1399 99202
1400-4798 99223
4800-5799 99223
S Ferris Ct 99202
E Ferry Ave 99202
Fircrest Cir & Ct 99208
E Fireside Ln 99208
N Fischer Ct 99208
N Fiske St
2-498 99202
500-1300 99202
1302-1498 99202
1501-1511 99207
S Fiske St
1-1299 99202
1301-1399 99202
1400-3599 99223
N & W Five Mile Rd 99208
E Flagstone Ln 99206
Fleetwood Ct & St 99208
W Fleming Pl 99205
N Fleming St
5500-6199 99205
6400-7199 99208
W Flight Dr 99224
W Flightline Blvd
6800-7298 99224
6801-6801 99219
6801-7299 99224
N & S Flint Ln & Rd 99224
Florence Ave & Ln 99218
N Florida St 99217
S Florida St 99202
S Flying Goose Ln 99224
N Foal Ct 99208
E & N Foothills Ln &
Rd 99217
N Forest Blvd
5500-6299 99205
6300-8799 99208
N Forest Ct 99208
S Forest Estates Dr 99223
N & W Forest Hill Dr &
Ln 99218
N Forker Rd
5600-6299 99216
6301-6397 99217
6399-15999 99217
E Forker Ridge Ln 99216
W Fort George Wright
Dr 99224
E Fort Henry Ct 99208
S Fosseen Rd 99224
N Fotheringham St
5500-5899 99205
5901-5999 99205
6301-6397 99208
6399-9999 99208
W Fountain Ave 99224
W Four Mound Rd 99224
N Fowler Rd 99206
N Fox Point Dr 99208
N Fox Wood Ct 99208
W Foxtail Ln 99224
E Foxwood Dr 99223
E Francis Ave
31-77 99208
79-2999 99208
3001-3199 99208
3500-13899 99217
W Francis Ave
100-4299 99205
4301-4399 99205
4800-5399 99208
W Franklin Ave 99208
N Franklin Ct 99208
W Franklin Ct 99205
W Franklin Rd 99224

N Franklin St 99208
E Fraser Ct 99206
E Frederick Ave
3600-5199 99217
5201-5399 99217
8600-9099 99212
9100-9699 99206
W Frederick Ave 99205
E Frederick Rd 99217
N Fredericksburg Ct 99208
W Fremont Rd 99224
S Freya Rd 99223
N Freya St
201-297 99202
299-1199 99202
2100-8599 99217
S Freya St
100-1100 99202
1102-1398 99202
1400-1698 99223
1700-6299 99223
N Freya Way 99202
E Front Ave 99202
W Front Ave 99224
S Fruit St 99223
E Fruit Hill Rd 99206
N Fruit Hill Rd 99217
E Funk Ave 99223
S Funseth Dr 99223
N G St
3000-3698 99205
3700-6299 99205
6700-6798 99208
6800-7899 99208
S G St 99224
W Gail Jean Ln 99218
S Gaiser Ct 99223
N Galahad Dr 99218
S Gandy St 99203
E Garden Ave 99208
W Garden Ct 99208
S Garden Ln 99224
S & W Garden Springs
Rd 99224
W Gardner Ave 99201
N Garfield Rd 99224
S Garfield Rd 99203
W Garfield Rd 99224
S Garfield St
500-1399 99202
1401-2797 99203
2799-4299 99203
4301-4399 99203
5400-5599 99223
E Garland Ave
1-2900 99207
2902-3098 99207
9700-10499 99206
W Garland Ave
200-298 99205
300-1904 99205
1903-1903 99209
1906-3798 99205
2001-3699 99205
E Garnet Ave
3000-3099 99207
3100-3699 99217
E Garnet Ln 99212
W Garwood Ct 99208
Gary Ln 99218
N Gates Ln 99217
S & W Geiger Blvd 99224
N General Grant Way 99208
N General Lee Way 99208
S George Rd 99224
N Gerlach Rd 99217
W Geronimo Dr 99208
E Gertrude Dr 99206
Gettysburg Ct & Dr 99208
E Gibbs Rd 99224
S Gibbs Rd 99223
W Gibbs Rd 99224
N Girard Ln 99212
S Girard Ln 99223
E Girard Pl
2100-2198 99203
2200-2299 99203

2300-2699 99223
E Glass Ave
1-2299 99207
2301-2499 99207
3100-3599 99217
W Glass Ave 99205
W Glass Ln 99224
E & N Glencrest Ct &
Dr 99208
N Glendale Ct 99208
Glendora Dr & Ln 99223
E Gleneagle Ln 99223
Gleneden Dr & St 99208
E Glenn Ct 99223
N Glenn Rd 99206
E Glennaire Dr 99223
S & E Glenngrae Ct &
Ln 99223
S Glenrose Rd 99223
S Glenview Ln 99223
Glenwood Ct & Dr 99208
S Godfrey Blvd 99224
Golden Ct & Rd 99208
N Golden Pond Ln 99218
W Goldenrod Ave 99224
N Golfview Ln 99208
E Gordon Ave
1-2999 99207
3100-3300 99217
3302-3420 99217
3422-3518 99217
W Gordon Ave 99205
N Gordon Ct 99217
N Gordon Rd 99224
N Government Way 99224
E Grace Ave
1701-1997 99207
1999-2999 99207
3200-5199 99217
8500-9099 99212
9100-9599 99206
W Grace Ave 99205
Gramps Ln 99208
E Granary Ct 99208
S Grand Blvd
900-1399 99202
1400-4299 99203
W Grandview Ave 99224
N Granite Dr 99218
S Granite Hills Dr 99224
N & S Grant St 99202
S Grape Tree Dr 99203
E Grassland Ct 99217
E Graves Rd 99218
W Graves Rd
1-699 99218
2600-2899 99208
W Gray Ct 99205
W Gray Heron Ln 99208
N Graycoat Ct 99208
W Grayson Ct 99224
N Green Hollow Ct 99218
N Greene St
100-199 99202
201-1499 99202
1800-2099 99217
S Greene St
2-98 99202
100-1399 99202
1900-1918 99223
1920-1998 99223
E Greenleaf Dr 99208
N Greenwood Blvd
4700-6299 99205
6300-7099 99208
N Greenwood Ct 99208
N Greenwood Pl 99208
W Greenwood Rd 99224
N Greenwood St 99208
E, W & N Greta Ave, Ct
& Ln 99208
S Greyhawk Ln 99224
S Greystone Ln 99223
W Grouse Ave 99208
E Grouse Mountain Ln 99206
N Grove Rd 99224
S Grove Rd 99224

W Grove Rd 99208
S Grove St 99204
N Guinevere Dr 99218
Gunning Dr & Ln 99212
W Gunthers Rd 99224
N Gustavus St 99205
N H St
3501-3599 99205
7600-7899 99208
S H St 99224
S Hailee Ln 99223
W Hailey Ln 99218
E Hallet Rd 99206
Hallett Ln & Rd 99224
N Hamilton Ct 99208
N Hamilton St
601-697 99202
699-1499 99202
1601-1697 99207
1699-3099 99207
6800-7499 99208
12600-12799 99218
12800-16699 99208
E Hampton Ln 99208
E Hangman Ln 99224
E Hangman Creek Ln 99224
E Hangman Valley Rd 99223
S Hangman Valley Rd 99224
W Harder Pl 99224
E Harding Dr 99218
S Hargreaves Ct 99223
E Harmon Rd 99223
S Harmon Extension
Rd 99223
N Harms Ln 99208
N Harpers Ferry St 99208
S Harrison St 99224
N Hartley St
4500-4699 99205
5900-6699 99208
E Hartson Ave 99202
W Hartson Ave 99224
E Harvest Ct 99217
E & W Hastings Rd 99218
S Hatch Rd
5301-6397 99223
6399-6499 99223
7200-12399 99224
S Hatch St
201-497 99202
499-999 99202
1700-1898 99203
1900-4299 99203
Havana St S
2200-2299 99223
N Havana St
200-1299 99202
2600-7199 99217
S Havana St
1-1399 99202
2000-2098 99223
2100-4800 99223
4802-4898 99223
S Havana Yale Rd 99223
N Haven St
100-1399 99202
2500-3299 99207
3301-4299 99207
4800-5499 99217
5500-5599 99208
5601-5799 99208
7200-7299 99217
S Haven St 99202
E Hawk Ct 99208
W Hawkcrest Ct 99224
S Hawthorne Pl 99202
E Hawthorne Rd 99218
W Hawthorne Rd
1-97 99218
99-1199 99218
1201-1299 99218
2400-3099 99208
N Hawthorne St 99205
W Hayden Ln 99208
N & S Hayford Rd 99224
N Hayley Ct 99208
N & W Hazard Rd 99208

E Hazelwood Ln 99212
S Hazelwood Rd 99224
N Hazelwood Terrace
Ln 99212
W Heath Ave 99208
N Heatherglen Ct 99208
W Heavenly Horse Ln 99224
W Heidi Ln 99208
E Helena Ct 99217
N Helena Ct 99218
S Helena Ct 99203
S Helena Ln 99223
N Helena St
100-298 99202
300-1300 99202
1302-1398 99202
3300-5499 99207
5500-5800 99208
5802-5998 99208
6300-7399 99217
12900-13099 99208
S Helena St
100-999 99202
1001-1299 99202
1400-4399 99203
4400-6599 99223
W Helens Ln 99208
N Hemlock Ct
7300-8399 99208
12016-12016 99218
12018-12025 99218
N Hemlock St
1800-5899 99205
11701-11797 99218
11799-12099 99218
S Hemlock St 99201
N Herald Rd 99206
E Heritage Ln 99208
E Heroy Ave
1-2999 99207
3001-3099 99207
7800-8099 99212
9100-9699 99206
W Heroy Ave 99205
E Heroy Ct 99206
E Heroy Ln 99212
W Hiawatha Dr 99208
E High Dr 99203
E Highgrove Ln 99223
E Highland Blvd 99203
S Highland Park Dr 99223
E Highland View Ct 99223
W Highline Ln 99201
W Highpeak Dr 99224
N Highview Ln 99217
S Highway 195 99224
W Highway 2 99224
S Highway 27 99206
N Highway 395 99218
N Highwood Ct 99218
S Hilby Rd 99223
S Hilda Ct 99202
W Hill Ln 99224
N Hill N Dale St
8500-8599 99208
8601-8699 99208
8701-8899 99218
Hillmont Ln 99217
E Hills Ct 99202
N Hillsdale Ct 99208
E Hodin Dr 99212
E & W Hoerner Ave 99218
E Hoffman Ave
1-3099 99207
3101-3199 99217
W Hoffman Ave 99205
E Hoffman Ln
4200-4899 99223
9500-9699 99206
W Hoffman Pl 99205
N Hogan Ct 99217
S Hogan Ct 99223
N Hogan Ln 99208
S Hogan Ln 99223
N Hogan St
400-598 99202
600-1099 99202

2400-3099 99207
3101-3499 99207
7100-7299 99217
S Hogan St
200-299 99202
1401-1497 99203
1499-4399 99203
4400-5099 99223
E & W Holland Ave 99218
N Hollis St 99201
N Holliston Rd 99201
S Holly Rd 99224
E Holman Rd 99206
Holmberg Ln & Rd 99218
E Holyoke Ave
600-999 99208
1400-1899 99217
W Holyoke Ave 99208
E Honorof Ln 99223
W Hood River Ave 99224
N Hooper Rd 99218
S Hoot Owl Ln 99224
N Hope Ln 99208
W Hope Rd 99224
W Hopi Ct 99208
E Hopper Rd 99217
W Horizon Ave 99208
S Horizon Hill Ln 99206
W & N Horizon Ridge Ct
& Ln 99208
N Hough St 99212
E Houghton Ave
100-299 99208
1800-2899 99217
E Houghton Ct 99217
W Houston 99224
E Houston Ave
600-999 99208
1400-3099 99217
W Houston Ave 99208
N Houston Rd 99224
N Howard Ct 99218
N Howard Ln 99208
N Howard St
100-1599 99201
1600-6199 99205
6201-6299 99205
6300-8399 99208
9300-9599 99218
9601-9699 99218
S Howard St
1-133 99201
135-200 99201
202-298 99201
500-699 99204
2700-2799 99203
2801-3299 99203
N Howe Rd 99212
Howesdale Ct & Dr 99208
W Howsdale Ct 99208
E Huckleberry Ln 99224
E Hudlow Ln 99217
N Hughes Dr 99208
E & N Humboldt Ave &
Dr 99218
N Huntington Ln 99224
N Huntington Rd 99218
E & N Huron Ct & Dr 99208
Hutchinson Ln & Rd 99212
E Hutton Ave 99212
E Hutton View Ln 99212
W Huxley Dr 99224
N I Ct 99208
N I St 99205
E Illinois Ave
700-1599 99207
1601-2999 99207
3200-3299 99217
N Indian Bluff Rd 99224
N & W Indian Trail Rd 99208
E Indiana Ave 99207
W Indiana Ave 99205
N Inland St 99224
S Inland Empire Way 99224
E Inverness Ln 99223
N Iron Ct 99202
N Iron Bridge Way 99202

N & W Iroquois Dr 99208
N & W Ivanhoe Rd 99218
S Ivory St
100-1399 99202
1400-1498 99203
1500-4199 99203
4201-4299 99203
5400-5499 99223
S Ivy Glen Ln 99223
W Iwan Ct 99208
N J Ct 99208
N J St 99205
E Jackpine Ct 99208
E Jackson Ave
100-498 99207
500-3199 99207
3200-4299 99217
8300-8499 99212
W Jackson Ave 99205
E Jacobs Ln 99217
E Jacobs Rd 99217
W Jacobs Rd 99224
W Jade Ave 99224
James Ct & Dr 99208
W Jamie Ct 99208
E Jamieson Rd 99223
W Jamieson Rd 99224
W Janes Ln 99224
W Janice Ave 99208
S Jaques St 99202
W Jared Ct 99208
N Jared Ln 99224
E Jason Hill Ln 99223
W Jay Ave
300-699 99218
1800-1899 99208
W Jay St 99208
E Jean Ave 99217
W Jedi Ln 99224
W Jefferson Ct 99203
N Jefferson Dr 99208
S Jefferson Dr 99203
N Jefferson St
1300-1599 99201
1700-5999 99205
6400-7099 99208
S Jefferson St
100-199 99201
400-598 99204
600-1399 99204
1400-3299 99203
E Jennie Ln 99212
N Jensen Rd 99217
N Jesse Ct 99208
W Jillian Ct 99208
E Joanne Ct 99218
W Johannsen Rd 99208
W John Gay Dr 99224
S Jordan Ln 99224
E Joseph Ave
300-2999 99208
3700-4399 99217
13200-13299 99216
W Joseph Ave 99205
E Joseph Ln 99217
N Joyce Ct 99205
N Juanita Rd 99218
E & N Judkins Ln &
Rd 99217
S Julia Ct 99223
N Julia St
1-100 99202
102-498 99202
2400-8499 99217
S Julia St 99223
W Juliann Ct 99208
N Juliann Dr 99218
W Juliann Dr 99218
N Juneberry Dr 99208
W Juniper Ln 99208
W Justin Ln 99208
E Justine Ln 99224
E Juul Ct 99223
N K Ct 99208
N K St
4100-4699 99205
9100-9499 99208

E Kaelin Ln 99217
S Kahuna Dr 99223
W Kamayley Ct 99208
N Kamiah Ct 99208
Kammi Ave & Ct 99208
S Kaniksu Ct 99206
N Karen Ln 99208
W Katelyn Ln 99224
W Kathleen Ave 99208
Kathy Dr & Ln 99218
E Katie Ln 99223
S Katy Ct 99224
E Kaywood Way 99208
E Kedlin Ave 99218
W Kedlin Ct 99218
Kedlin Ln 99208
W Keely Ct 99224
W Keenan Ln 99208
S Keeney Rd 99224
N Kelly Ct 99208
N Kelsey Dawn Ln 99217
S Kendall St 99224
W Kens Ct 99208
N Kensington Ct 99218
N Kensington Dr 99208
S Kenyon Rd 99224
S Kenzie Ln 99224
N Kettle Ct 99208
S Keyes Ct 99224
E Keystone Ct 99223
E Kiernan Ave 99207
W Kiernan Ave 99205
S Kiesling Rd 99223
E Kiko Ln 99206
N Kimberly Ct 99208
N King Ct 99205
N King Arthur Dr 99218
W Kingsford Ave 99208
E Kiowa Ct 99206
N Kiowa Ct 99208
S Kip Ln 99224
W Kitsap Dr 99208
W Kittitas Ct 99208
N Klamath Ct 99208
N Klickitat Ct 99208
E Knorindo Ave 99223
Knox Ave & Ct 99205
W Koda Ct 99208
N Korey Ln 99218
S Krell Rdg 99223
E Kronquist Rd 99217
E Krueger Ln 99217
N Kyle Ct 99208
N Kynan Rd 99224
N L Ct 99208
N La Tiara Ln 99208
S Labrador Ln 99223
S Lacey Ct 99223
S Lacey Ln 99223
N Lacey St
2-1298 99202
1500-4500 99207
4502-4598 99207
4700-5400 99217
5402-5498 99217
5501-5697 99208
5699-6299 99208
S Lacey St
1-597 99202
599-1399 99202
4000-4099 99223
E Lacrosse Ave
1-2299 99207
8100-8400 99212
8402-8498 99212
11100-11499 99206
W Lacrosse Ave 99205
E Lacrosse Ln 99206
Laird Rd 99224
E Lakerley Ave 99212
E Lakeview Ln 99208
W Lamar Ave 99208
S Lamonte St 99203
N Lancelot Dr 99218
N Langley St 99212
N Lantern Ln 99208

N Lapis Ln 99208
W & N Larchwood Ct &
St 99208
S Latah Ln
6000-6099 99224
10600-11099 99223
S Latah Hills Ct 99224
S Latawah St 99203
N Laura Rd 99212
S Laura St
700-799 99202
1400-4199 99203
Laurelcrest Ct & St 99224
S Laurelhurst Ct 99223
N Laurelhurst Dr 99208
W Lawrence Dr 99218
W Lawton Rd 99224
S Lee Cir 99223
S Lee Ct 99223
N Lee St
100-1399 99202
1401-1499 99202
1500-5099 99207
6300-6699 99217
S Lee St
301-597 99202
599-629 99202
2700-4399 99203
5700-5798 99223
5800-5999 99223
S Leeway Ct 99223
E Legacy Ln 99208
N Lehman Rd
5300-5399 99206
5400-10299 99217
E Leisure Ln 99223
E Leona Dr 99208
E Lewis Ln 99212
S Lewis St 99224
E Liberty Ave
1-2999 99207
3001-3099 99207
3100-4599 99217
8300-9026 99212
9028-9098 99212
W Liberty Ave 99205
N Lidgerwood Ct 99208
N Lidgerwood St
1301-1397 99202
1399-1400 99202
1402-1498 99202
1600-5200 99207
5202-5410 99207
5500-7499 99208
7501-7599 99208
11301-11399 99218
W Lincoln Blvd 99224
N Lincoln Ct 99218
S Lincoln Dr 99203
E Lincoln Ln 99217
W Lincoln Ln 99224
S Lincoln Pl 99204
W Lincoln Pl 99204
E Lincoln Rd
1-299 99208
1700-16300 99217
16302-16498 99217
W Lincoln Rd
3100-3899 99208
12700-16099 99224
16101-16499 99224
N Lincoln St
500-698 99201
700-1599 99201
1600-1698 99205
1700-6299 99205
6600-6999 99208
S Lincoln St
100-132 99201
134-299 99201
600-1099 99204
1400-2899 99203
S Lincoln Way 99224
N Lindeke Ct 99208
N Lindeke Rd 99208
N Lindeke St
600-1499 99201
2800-6099 99205
6401-7597 99208
7599-7999 99208
S Lindeke St 99224
Lindgren Ln & Rd 99217
E Lindsey Ln 99208
W Lisa Ct 99208
N Lisa Ln 99218
W Litchfield Pl 99205
W Little Rock St 99224
N Little Spokane Dr 99208
E Little Spokane
Connection Rd 99208
S & E Littler Dr & Ln 99223
S Lloyd Ct 99223
S Lloyd Ln 99223
S Lloyd Rd 99223
S Lloyd St
1200-1799 99212
5400-5699 99223
N Lloyd Charles Ln 99218
Lochsa Dr & Ln 99206
N Locust Rd 99206
N Logan Ln 99208
N Loganberry Ct 99208
N Lola Ln 99218
N Lolo Ln 99217
N Loma Ct 99208
N Loma Dr 99205
W & N Londale Ct &
Dr 99208
S London Ct 99203
Lonewolf Ave & Ct 99208
E Longfellow Ave
1-2999 99207
3700-4599 99217
7900-9099 99212
W Longfellow Ave 99205
S Lookout Ln 99224
W Lookout Mountain
Ln 99208
W Lountrid Ave 99201
W Lowell Ave 99208
N Lower Crossing St 99201
N Lucia Ct 99208
S Luck Ln 99224
W Luke Ave 99224
E Lydia Ct 99223
Lynwood Dr & St 99208
E Lyons Ave
200-1300 99208
1302-1398 99208
1500-6699 99217
W Lyons Ave 99208
W Lyons Ct 99208
E Lyons Ln 99217
N Lyons Rd 99224
E Maas Ln 99223
S Mack Rd 99224
E Macmahan Rd 99217
N Madelia Ct 99217
S Madelia Ln 99223
N Madelia St
100-1399 99202
2400-3399 99207
7100-7299 99217
S Madelia St
100-399 99202
1600-3998 99203
4000-4399 99203
4400-6500 99223
6502-6598 99223
N Madeline Ln 99208
N Madison Ct 99208
N Madison Rd 99217
N Madison St
1-1197 99201
1199-1599 99201
1601-1697 99205
1699-5999 99205
11200-11899 99218
S Madison St
100-199 99201
500-516 99204
518-1399 99204
1401-1497 99203
1499-2899 99203

E Magnesium Rd
101-597 99208
599-800 99208
802-1198 99208
1400-2899 99217
N Magnolia Ct 99217
S Magnolia Ct 99203
N Magnolia St
101-197 99202
199-1499 99202
1501-1513 99207
1515-5299 99207
5301-5499 99207
5600-5698 99208
7300-7499 99217
S Magnolia St
2-98 99202
100-499 99202
1500-2398 99203
2400-4399 99203
4400-6199 99223
N Mahr Ct 99208
E Main Ave 99202
W Main Ave 99201
W Mallard Ave 99208
E Mallon Ave 99202
W Mallon Ave 99201
N Mallory Ct 99208
W Malstrom Dr 99224
S Mamer Rd 99206
N Manassas Ct 99208
E Mandalay Ln 99217
S & E Manito Blvd &
Pl 99203
W Manor Crest St 99205
Mansfield Ave & Ct 99205
E Maple Ave 99217
S Maple Blvd 99203
N Maple Ct 99206
N Maple Rd 99206
S Maple Rd 99224
N Maple St
1-1599 99201
1600-1698 99205
1700-6299 99205
6300-8899 99208
S Maple St
150-398 99201
400-499 99201
500-1399 99204
1401-1411 99203
1413-1599 99203
N Mapleleaf Ln 99217
W Marc Dr 99218
W Marchand Rd 99224
N Marguerite Rd 99212
E Marie Ct 99223
E Marietta Ave
801-897 99207
899-3199 99207
3200-3298 99217
3300-4299 99217
8300-8599 99212
E Maringo Dr
8000-9099 99212
9100-9899 99206
N Maringo Dr 99212
E Marion Ct 99223
E Marissa Ct 99208
Marjorie Ct & St 99208
W Mark Ct 99208
N Market St
2400-4699 99207
4700-5400 99217
5402-5498 99217
5500-6299 99208
6300-9399 99217
9401-9499 99217
S Markwell Ct 99223
S Marquette St 99224
E Marshall Ave 99207
S Marshall Rd 99224
N Martin St
2600-5499 99207
7500-7899 99217
S Martin St
1700-4399 99203
4800-6299 99223
6301-6399 99223
E Martingale Ct 99224
W Mary Lee Ln 99208
W Matts Ln 99224
E Maxine Ave 99218
W Maxine Ave
300-499 99218
1800-3999 99208
W Maxine Ct 99208
W Maxs Ln 99224
W Maxwell Ave 99201
N Mayberry Dr 99218
E Mayfair Ct 99208
N Mayfair Ln 99208
N Mayfair Rd 99218
N Mayfair St
2700-4299 99207
4301-4499 99207
5901-5997 99208
5999-6200 99208
6202-8698 99208
11100-11399 99218
S Mayflower Rd 99224
S Mcclellan St
101-199 99201
800-1399 99204
1900-1998 99203
S Mcdonald Ln 99206
E Mcelhaney Rd 99217
N Mcintosh Ct 99206
Mckenzie River St 99224
E Mead St 99218
S Meadow St 99224
S Meadow Mist Ln 99224
W Meadow Ridge Ln 99208
E Meadowcreek Ln 99208
N Meadowglen Ct 99208
E & S Meadowlane
Rd 99224
W Medical Lake Rd 99224
N Meghan St 99208
W Melinda Ln 99203
W Melrose Ln 99208
S Menaul Ct 99224
E Mercer Ln 99217
N Merlin Dr 99218
E Merrimac Ct 99208
S Merryweather Rd 99224
W Methow Ct 99208
Metler Dr & Ln 99218
N Miami Ct 99217
S Miami St 99223
Mica Ct & Ln 99206
N Middleton Dr 99218
W Midwick Ave 99205
N Milbrath Ln 99208
W Milford Pl 99201
N Mill Rd
12000-12199 99218
12700-13799 99208
N Mill Pond Ln 99217
W Millbury Ave 99208
W Miller Ave 99224
N Millview Dr 99212
N Milton Ct 99208
N Milton St
2800-3698 99205
3700-6099 99205
7700-7899 99208
S Milton St 99224
N Minihdoka Trl 99208
W Mirage Ln 99224
E Mission Ave 99202
W Mission Ave 99201
W Mission Rd 99224
S Mitchel Ln 99223
S Mitchell Pl 99224
E Moffat Rd 99217
Mohawk Dr & Ln 99206
N Monroe Ct 99218
N Monroe Rd 99208
W Monroe Rd 99208
N Monroe St
1-1500 99201
1502-1598 99201
1600-6299 99205
6301-6399 99208
6325-6325 99228
6400-7099 99208
7101-7499 99208
S Monroe St
100-134 99201
136-199 99201
600-1399 99204
1400-2899 99203
S Montavilla Dr 99224
N Montevista Pl 99205
E Montgomery Ave
1-1399 99207
3300-4299 99217
W Montgomery Ave 99205
W & N Monticello Pl &
St 99205
S Monument Ln 99224
Moonlight Ave & Ct 99208
N Moore Ct 99208
N Moore St
5500-6199 99205
6400-10299 99208
Moran Ct & Dr 99223
S & W Moran View Ave
& St 99224
E Moran Vista Ln 99223
E Morgan Rd 99217
W Morning Ln 99224
E Morrill Ct 99223
S Morrill Ct 99223
S Morrill Dr 99223
S Morrill Ln 99223
N Morrill St 99217
S Morrill St 99223
N Morrison Rd 99217
S Morrow Ln 99206
S Morrow Park Rd 99206
N Morton Ct 99218
N Morton Dr
11900-12299 99218
12301-12399 99218
16400-16699 99208
N Morton St
1601-1697 99207
1699-5399 99207
5401-5499 99207
5500-5598 99208
5600-7899 99208
N Moss Ln 99208
N Mossy Rock Ct 99208
E Mount Vernon Ct 99223
E Mount Vernon Dr 99223
S Mount Vernon Dr 99223
S Mount Vernon St
1300-1399 99202
1400-6899 99223
N Mountain Ln 99218
E Mountain High Ln 99223
N Mountain Home Ln 99217
S Mountain Springs
Rd 99223
W Mountain View Ave 99218
N Mountain View Ln
8400-8699 99208
8701-8897 99218
8899-9399 99218
E Mt Baldy Ln 99217
S Muirfield Ln 99223
S Mullen Hill Rd 99224
N Mulvaney Ct 99212
E Myrtle Ct 99223
S Myrtle Ln 99223
N Myrtle St 99217
S Myrtle St
201-1197 99202
1199-1399 99202
1600-1898 99223
1900-4900 99223
4902-4998 99223
W Myrtlewood Ct 99208
N Mystic Ct 99208
W Nadine Ct 99208
S Nancy Ln 99223
N Napa Ct 99217
N Napa Ln 99208

N Napa St
1-1400 ... 99202
1402-1498 ... 99202
1500-5299 ... 99207
5500-6199 ... 99208
6500-7899 ... 99217
S Napa St
1-1399 ... 99202
2300-2398 ... 99203
2400-4399 ... 99203
4400-6199 ... 99223
6201-6299 ... 99223
N Nathan Ct ... 99208
W & N Navaho Ave, Ct & Dr ... 99208
E Nebraska Ave
301-497 ... 99208
499-3000 ... 99208
3002-3098 ... 99208
3600-4299 ... 99217
W Nebraska Ave ... 99205
N Nelson Rd ... 99218
N Nelson St
900-1199 ... 99202
1201-1399 ... 99202
1500-3299 ... 99207
4700-5099 ... 99217
S Nelson St ... 99202
N Nettleton Ct ... 99208
N Nettleton Ln ... 99208
S Nettleton Ln ... 99224
N Nettleton St
600-1198 ... 99201
1200-1599 ... 99201
2300-2398 ... 99205
2400-6199 ... 99205
N Nevada Ct
12100-12299 ... 99218
16500-16699 ... 99208
N Nevada St
2400-5499 ... 99207
5500-8699 ... 99208
9200-10299 ... 99218
10301-10499 ... 99218
14400-14699 ... 99208
N New York Ln ... 99212
E Newark Ave ... 99202
Newbury Ct & Dr ... 99208
W Newell Ct ... 99208
W Newkirk Rd ... 99224
N Newport Hwy ... 99218
N Nez Perce Ct ... 99208
E Nez Perce Ln ... 99206
Nicklaus Ave, Ct & Pl ... 99223
E Nina Ave ... 99202
N & W Nine Mile Rd ... 99208
S Nola Ct ... 99223
E Nora Ave ... 99207
W Nora Ave ... 99205
E Nordin Ave ... 99218
W Norman Ct ... 99218
N Norman Rd ... 99217
E Norman Ridge Ln ... 99217
N Normandie Ln ... 99218
N Normandie St
1000-1499 ... 99201
1700-6199 ... 99205
6201-6299 ... 99205
6300-8016 ... 99208
8018-8098 ... 99208
11100-12299 ... 99218
E North Ave ... 99207
E North Altamont Blvd ... 99202
N North Center St ... 99207
E North Crescent Ave ... 99207
S North Dearborn Ct ... 99223
W North Five Mile Rd ... 99208
E North Foothills Dr ... 99207
E North Glenngrae Ln ... 99223
W North Loop Ave ... 99224
S North Morrill Ct ... 99223
E North Rim Ln ... 99217
W North River Dr ... 99201
W Northridge Ct ... 99208
W Northstar Ln ... 99208
Northview Ct, Ln & Rd ... 99208
W Northwest Blvd ... 99205

N Northwood Dr ... 99212
E Notting Hill Ln ... 99223
S Oak Rd ... 99224
N Oak St
600-1599 ... 99201
1600-6299 ... 99205
8900-9499 ... 99208
S Oak St
1-199 ... 99201
201-399 ... 99201
600-698 ... 99204
700-1299 ... 99204
2701-2997 ... 99224
2999-3099 ... 99224
S Oakridge Dr ... 99224
E Offmy Ln ... 99217
W Ohio Ave ... 99201
W Okanogan Ct ... 99208
N Old Argonne Rd ... 99217
N & W Old Fort Ct & Dr ... 99208
N Old Lyons Rd ... 99224
N Old Trails Rd ... 99224
E Olive Ave ... 99202
E Olmsted Rd ... 99223
E Olympic Ave
300-1799 ... 99207
2900-3799 ... 99217
W Olympic Ave ... 99205
W Olympic Pl ... 99205
S Olympus Ct ... 99223
S Oneida Pl ... 99203
E Onyx Ln ... 99217
W Orangewood Ct ... 99208
N Orchard Ln
9200-10299 ... 99208
11300-11399 ... 99218
E Orchard Rd ... 99217
N Orchard Prairie Rd ... 99217
N Orchard View Ln ... 99217
S Orlando Ct ... 99223
W Osage Way ... 99208
N Osprey Ln ... 99218
S & W Osprey Heights Ct & Dr ... 99224
E Ostrander Ave ... 99207
S & E Overbluff Ct & Rd ... 99203
E Overbluff Estates Ln ... 99203
N Overview Dr ... 99217
Oxford Dr & Ln ... 99208
E Pacific Ave ... 99202
W Pacific Ave
1-2499 ... 99201
3400-3799 ... 99224
W Pacific Park Dr ... 99208
N Palisades ... 99224
N Palm Pl ... 99208
N Palmer Rd ... 99217
E Palomino Ln ... 99206
N Palomino Ln ... 99208
E & S Palouse Hwy ... 99223
Pamela Ct & St ... 99208
W & N Panorama Ave, Ct & Dr ... 99208
Pantops Ln ... 99223
W Paradise Rd ... 99224
N Park Blvd ... 99205
S Park Dr ... 99203
W Park Dr ... 99224
E Park Ln ... 99203
S Park Ln
2000-2099 ... 99203
2300-3199 ... 99212
4400-6099 ... 99223
W Park Pl ... 99205
S Park Rd ... 99212
S Park Ridge Blvd ... 99224
N & W Park View Ln ... 99205
W Park West Ct ... 99208
E Parkhill Dr ... 99208
S Parkside Ct ... 99223
E Parkside Ln ... 99217
E Parkwater Ave ... 99212
N & W Parkway Dr ... 99208
S Parkwood Cir ... 99223

W Parkwood Ct ... 99218
N Pasadena Ln ... 99212
E Patrick Ln ... 99224
S Paula Ct ... 99223
Pawnee Ct & Ln ... 99206
W Payton Ln ... 99218
E Peach Tree Ct ... 99203
E Peak Ln ... 99217
N Pearl St ... 99202
N Peck Rd ... 99217
S Pendell Ln ... 99224
S Pender Ln ... 99224
N Penn Ave ... 99206
W Pepper Ln ... 99218
S Pepper Tree Ln ... 99224
E Percival Ave ... 99218
S Perennial Ln ... 99224
N Perrine Rd ... 99217
N Perry Ln
9100-9299 ... 99217
15200-15299 ... 99208
N Perry St
1-999 ... 99202
1701-1997 ... 99207
1999-5000 ... 99207
5002-5498 ... 99207
5501-5597 ... 99208
5599-5799 ... 99208
5801-6199 ... 99208
6400-7599 ... 99217
10800-12599 ... 99218
12700-13399 ... 99208
S Perry St
100-1399 ... 99202
1400-4399 ... 99203
4400-5799 ... 99223
5801-5899 ... 99223
W Persimmon Ln ... 99224
N Petersburg Ct ... 99208
N Pettet Dr ... 99205
S Phalon Ln ... 99223
W Pheasant Bluff Ct ... 99224
S Pheasant Ridge Dr ... 99224
N Phoebe Dr ... 99208
S Phoebe St ... 99224
E, N & S Pierce Ln & Rd ... 99206
W Pilot Dr ... 99224
W Pima Ct ... 99208
N Pine Ct ... 99205
N Pine St ... 99202
S Pine St ... 99202
E Pine Glen Ct ... 99208
Pine Rock Pl & St ... 99208
E & N Pine Tree Dr ... 99208
S Pinebrook Ct ... 99206
E Pinecone Ct ... 99208
N Pinecrest Dr ... 99218
W Pinecrest Dr ... 99218
W Pinecrest Ln ... 99218
E Pinecrest Rd ... 99203
W Pinedale Ct ... 99208
E Pinegate Ln ... 99224
S Pinegrove Ln ... 99223
E Pinehill Ln ... 99224
W Pinehill Rd ... 99218
E Pineridge Ct ... 99208
N Pineview Cir ... 99208
S Pineview Ln ... 99206
N Pineview Rd ... 99208
W Pinewood Rd ... 99218
N Pioneer Ln ... 99217
E Piper Rd ... 99217
W Pirate Ln ... 99218
Pirates Ct ... 99224
N Pittsburg Ln ... 99208
N Pittsburg St
2-98 ... 99202
100-1100 ... 99202
1102-1298 ... 99202
2400-5300 ... 99207
5302-5398 ... 99207
5601-6197 ... 99208
6199-6299 ... 99208
6300-7599 ... 99217
12301-12599 ... 99218
12800-13699 ... 99208

S Pittsburg St
1-197 ... 99202
199-1399 ... 99202
1400-4399 ... 99203
4400-6599 ... 99223
E Plateau Rd ... 99203
E & S Player Dr ... 99223
W Pleasant Ln ... 99208
N Pleasant Hill Ln ... 99217
E & N Pleasant Prairie Rd ... 99217
S Plumrose Ln ... 99224
S Plymouth Rd ... 99224
S Polk St ... 99224
N Pond Ln ... 99224
W Ponderosa Dr ... 99224
S Ponderosa Ln ... 99206
S Pony Ct ... 99224
S Poplar St
100-199 ... 99201
201-299 ... 99201
1400-1499 ... 99224
E Poreens Ave ... 99207
E Portico Ct ... 99223
N Portsmouth Ct ... 99208
N Post St
1-1500 ... 99201
1502-1598 ... 99201
1600-6299 ... 99205
6600-7099 ... 99208
11201-11297 ... 99218
11299-11599 ... 99218
S Post St
1-299 ... 99201
1900-2900 ... 99203
2902-3098 ... 99203
N Prairie Dr ... 99208
W Prairie Breeze Ave ... 99208
N Prairie Crest Rd ... 99224
E Prairie Lane Ct ... 99223
S Prairie View Ln ... 99223
N Prairie Vista Ln ... 99224
E Pratt Ave ... 99202
E Prentanc Ave ... 99217
N Prescott Ct & Rd ... 99208
W Price Ave ... 99208
S Primrose Ln ... 99224
E Princeton Ave
1-1399 ... 99207
3600-4399 ... 99217
7700-7999 ... 99212
9300-9899 ... 99206
W Princeton Ave ... 99205
E Princeton Ln ... 99212
W Princeton Pl ... 99205
N Progress Rd ... 99216
E Prospect Rd ... 99223
W Prosperity Ln ... 99208
E Providence Ave ... 99207
W Providence Ave ... 99205
E & S Quail Creek Ln ... 99224
W Quail Crest Ave ... 99224
S Quail Meadows Ln ... 99224
Quail Ridge Cir & Ct ... 99223
Qualchan Dr & Ln ... 99224
S Quamash Ct ... 99224
N Quamish Dr ... 99208
N Quanah Ct ... 99208
Quartz Rd ... 99208
E Queen Ave
1-2299 ... 99207
2300-4499 ... 99217
W Queen Ave ... 99205
W Queen Pl ... 99205
N Quinault Ct ... 99208
N Quincy Ct ... 99208
S Quincy Ln ... 99203
S Radio Ln ... 99223
W Radley Ln ... 99224
N Rahland Rd ... 99218
Railroad Aly & Ave ... 99201
W Rain Ln ... 99208
N Rainbow Dr ... 99208
Rainier Ct & Way ... 99208
N Ralph St
1-1100 ... 99202

1102-1198 ... 99202
2600-3724 ... 99217
S Ralph St ... 99202
Rambo Ct & Rd ... 99224
Ramona Ln & Rd ... 99224
S Ranch Park Ln ... 99206
W Randolph Rd ... 99224
E Random Point Ln ... 99223
E Raptor Ln ... 99208
W Raven Ln ... 99224
Ravencrest Cir & Dr ... 99224
S Ray Ct ... 99223
S Ray St
1-1399 ... 99202
1601-1697 ... 99223
1699-3199 ... 99223
3201-3599 ... 99223
N Raymond Rd ... 99206
S Rebecca Ln ... 99223
N Rebecca St ... 99217
S Rebecca St
200-598 ... 99202
600-1099 ... 99202
1701-2097 ... 99223
2099-5999 ... 99223
W Red Cloud Ct ... 99208
S Red Fir Ln ... 99223
N Red Hawk Ln ... 99217
E Red Oak Dr ... 99217
E Red Roan Dr ... 99217
E Redwood Ln ... 99217
W Reese Ct ... 99208
S Regal Ct ... 99223
S Regal Rd ... 99223
N Regal St
700-1499 ... 99202
1501-1897 ... 99207
1899-4699 ... 99207
4700-5499 ... 99217
5500-6299 ... 99208
6300-8399 ... 99217
S Regal St
1-397 ... 99202
399-1199 ... 99202
1400-1798 ... 99223
1800-6399 ... 99223
W Regency Ln ... 99205
W Regent Ct ... 99203
E & W Regina Ave & Ln ... 99218
E Renwick Ct ... 99223
W Rhoades Ave ... 99208
S Rhyolite Rd ... 99203
N Riblet View Ln ... 99212
E Rich Ave
1-2999 ... 99207
3601-3697 ... 99217
3699-4399 ... 99217
8400-8499 ... 99212
E Rich Ln ... 99206
S Richard Allen Ct ... 99202
W Richland Ln ... 99224
E Riderrel Ave ... 99203
N & W Ridgecrest Dr ... 99208
N Ridgeview Pl ... 99205
Rifle Club Ct & Rd ... 99208
N Rim View St ... 99224
N Rimrock Dr ... 99224
S Rimrock Dr ... 99224
E Rimrock Ln ... 99206
Ritchey Ln & Rd ... 99224
River Edge Ln ... 99224
N River Ridge Blvd ... 99224
N River Vista St ... 99224
N Riverbluff Ln ... 99208
N Riverpoint Blvd ... 99202
E Riverside Ave ... 99202
W Riverside Ave
1-999 ... 99201
904-904 ... 99210
1000-2498 ... 99201
1001-2299 ... 99201
W Riverview Dr ... 99205
N Riverwood Dr ... 99218
N Rivilla Ln ... 99208
N Roanoke Rd ... 99218
N Robbins Rd ... 99217

W Rock Bluff Ct ... 99208
N Rock Ridge Dr ... 99208
N Rockaway Dr ... 99218
E Rockcrest Ln ... 99206
N Rockview Ln ... 99212
E Rockwell Ave
1-2499 ... 99207
2501-2999 ... 99207
8500-8699 ... 99212
9600-11099 ... 99206
W Rockwell Ave ... 99205
E Rockwood Blvd
2-198 ... 99202
200-599 ... 99202
600-2299 ... 99203
S Rockwood Blvd
1000-1099 ... 99202
1400-2299 ... 99203
W Rockwood Blvd ... 99204
E Rockwood Pines Rd ... 99203
E Rocky Top Ln ... 99217
N Rodenbough Ln ... 99224
W Rogers Ct ... 99208
W Rogers Dr ... 99218
W Rolland Ave ... 99218
S Rosa Butte Ln ... 99224
W Rosamond Ave ... 99224
E Roscoe Ct ... 99224
N Rose Eva Ct ... 99217
N Rosebury Ln ... 99208
E Rosedale Ln ... 99223
E Rosewood Ave
600-999 ... 99208
1400-1799 ... 99217
W Rosewood Ave ... 99208
W Rosewood Ct ... 99208
E Ross Ct ... 99207
N Rossmoor Ct ... 99208
Rougue River St ... 99224
E Roundtable Cir ... 99218
E Rowan Ave
1-2299 ... 99207
2300-4399 ... 99217
W Rowan Ave ... 99205
E Rowan Ln ... 99217
S Rowan Terrace Ln ... 99206
W Rowand Rd ... 99224
N Royal Ct ... 99205
N Royal Dr ... 99208
N Royal Ln ... 99208
S Royal St ... 99224
N Royal Crescent Ln ... 99205
E Roycroft Ct ... 99223
E Ruby Ln ... 99212
N Ruby Rd ... 99218
N Ruby St
800-1499 ... 99202
1600-2600 ... 99207
2602-2898 ... 99207
5901-5997 ... 99208
5999-6000 ... 99208
6002-6098 ... 99208
Russell Ln & Rd ... 99224
W & N Russett Ct & Dr ... 99208
N Rustic Ln ... 99208
N Rustle ... 99208
N Rustle St ... 99205
S Rustle St ... 99224
E Rutter Ave ... 99212
W Rutter Pkwy ... 99208
N Rye Ct ... 99208
N Saddle Ln ... 99224
W Sagewood Ct ... 99224
S Sagewood Rd ... 99223
S Saint Andrews Ln ... 99223
S Saint Annes Ln ... 99223
N Saint James Pl ... 99212
N Saint Michaels Rd ... 99217
E Saint Thomas Moore Way ... 99208
W Saint Thomas More Way ... 99208
E Salisbury Ln ... 99223
S Salish Ct ... 99224
N Sally Ct ... 99208

E & W Salmon Ave ... 99218
S San Diego Rd ... 99224
N Sand Brook St ... 99224
E Sandlewood Ln
8000-8099 ... 99212
8300-8799 ... 99217
E Sandstone Ln ... 99206
S Sandstone St ... 99224
E Sanson Ave
1-2299 ... 99207
2300-3799 ... 99217
12700-13799 ... 99216
W Sanson Ave ... 99205
W Sanson Pl ... 99205
E Sanzy Ln ... 99217
E Saphire Ln ... 99212
E Sapphire Ln ... 99208
E Sara Ln ... 99223
W Sarah Ct ... 99208
N Sargent Rd ... 99212
N Sarkis Ln ... 99208
Sarkis Lance Rd ... 99208
S Savannah Ln ... 99223
N Sawbuck Ln ... 99224
S & W Saxon Ct & Dr ... 99203
S Saybrook Ln ... 99223
N Scarlet Sky Dr ... 99208
S Scenic Blvd ... 99224
N Scenic Ln ... 99217
W Schafer Rd ... 99208
S Schafer Branch Rd ... 99206
S Schnug Ct ... 99224
N Scott Rd ... 99217
S Scott St
1-97 ... 99202
99-799 ... 99202
2600-2798 ... 99203
2800-4399 ... 99203
E & N Scribner Rd ... 99217
E & N Scribner Branch Ln & Rd ... 99217
W Selkirk Ave ... 99208
N Seminole Dr ... 99208
N Seneca Dr ... 99208
W Seven Mile Rd ... 99224
N Shady Slope Rd ... 99208
E Shaker Ct ... 99223
Shane Ct & Ln ... 99212
W Shannon Ave ... 99205
S Sharon Rd ... 99223
E Sharp Ave ... 99202
W Sharp Ave ... 99201
E Sharpsburg Ave
900-999 ... 99208
1001-1099 ... 99208
1300-1699 ... 99217
N Sharpsburg Ct ... 99208
W Shasta Way ... 99208
W Shawnee Ave ... 99208
E Shawnee Dr ... 99206
W Shawnee Ln ... 99208
Shelby Ridge Rd & St ... 99224
E & N Shenandoah Ct & Dr ... 99208
S Sheri Ct ... 99223
N Sheridan Ct ... 99205
S Sheridan St ... 99202
S Sherman Ln ... 99224
S Sherman Rd ... 99224
S Sherman St
100-1099 ... 99202
1600-1698 ... 99203
1700-4299 ... 99203
W & N Sherwood Ave & St ... 99201
E & N Shiloh Hills Ct & Dr ... 99208
Shire Ln ... 99208
E Short Ave ... 99202
W Shoshone Pl ... 99203
N Sicilia Ct ... 99208
W Sienna Ln ... 99208
E & W Sierra Ave, Ct & Way ... 99208
S Silver Ln ... 99223
E Silver Fox Ln ... 99224

S Silver Hill Rd 99223
E Silver Spur Ln 99217
E Sinto Ave 99202
W Sinto Ave 99201
E Sioux Cir 99206
Sipple Ct & Rd 99212
E Sitka Ave 99208
Skagit Ave & Ct 99208
N Skykomish St 99208
N & W Skyline Dr 99208
S Skyview Dr 99203
Slate 99208
E Sleigh Ct 99218
S Smith Ct 99223
W Smith Dr 99224
S Smith Ln 99223
N Smith St
2-98 99202
1301-1399 99202
1500-3299 99207
4700-5099 99217
5900-6299 99208
6300-7999 99217
S Smith St
1-99 99202
700-798 99202
3500-6099 99223
S & W Smythe Rd 99224
E Snead Ave 99223
E Snowberry Ln 99223
N Snyder Rd 99208
S Soda Rd 99224
Sommerset Ct & Dr 99217
N Sorenson Ct 99208
E Sorrel Ave 99217
S Sorrel Ct 99224
W Sound Ave 99204
E South Altamont Blvd 99202
S South Cliff Rd 99224
E South Crescent Ave 99207
S South Dearborn Ct 99223
W South Loop Ave 99224
South Meadows Ln & Rd 99223
S South Morrill Ct 99223
W South Oval Rd 99224
South Ridge Ct & Dr 99223
E South Riverton Ave 99207
N South Riverton Ave 99202
E South Riverway Ave 99212
E Southeast Blvd 99203
S Southeast Blvd
1001-1197 99202
1199-1399 99202
1400-2400 99203
2402-2498 99203
2500-2598 99223
2600-3399 99223
S Southfork Ln 99223
S Southview Ln 99223
W Spofford Ave 99205
S Spokane St 99202
E Spokane Falls Blvd 99202
W Spokane Falls Blvd 99201
N Spokane Falls Ct 99201
N & S Spotted Rd 99224
E Sprague Ave
2-98 99202
100-1699 99202
1602-1602 99220
1700-4298 99202
1701-4299 99202
W Sprague Ave 99201
W Spring Ln 99218
S Spring Creek Ln 99224
N Spring Hill Ln 99224
E Springfield Ave 99202
S Springview St 99224
W Spruce Ct 99218
N Spruce St 99201
S Spruce St
100-399 99201
1100-1199 99224
S Spur St 99223
W Sr 2 Hwy 99224
S Sr 27 Hwy 99206

N Standard St
1218-1398 99202
1400-1499 99202
1601-1697 99207
1699-5400 99207
5402-5436 99207
5901-6297 99208
6299-8599 99208
8800-8898 99218
N Stanton Ct 99208
S Stark Ln 99206
S State St 99201
E States Ln 99212
W Stearns Rd 99208
E Steele Ridge Ln 99217
N Stephanie St 99208
N Stevens Ct 99218
N Stevens Dr 99208
N Stevens Ln 99218
N Stevens St
100-1299 99201
1900-1998 99205
2000-6299 99205
6300-7899 99208
9000-9098 99218
9100-11399 99218
11401-11499 99218
13101-13197 99208
13199-13299 99208
S Stevens St
1-199 99201
600-1299 99204
1301-1399 99204
1700-1898 99203
1900-3299 99203
S Stevens Creek Rd 99223
S & W Stirlingview Dr 99224
S Stone Ct 99223
N Stone Ln 99208
S Stone Ln 99223
N Stone St
1-1399 99202
1401-1499 99202
1500-5299 99207
5500-6299 99208
S Stone St
100-599 99202
601-699 99202
2601-2697 99223
2699-6000 99223
6002-6198 99223
S Stone Crest Ln 99223
W Stonecrest Ave 99224
E Stoneman Rd 99217
N Stoneman Bluff Ln 99217
E & W Stonewall Ave 99208
S Stonington Ln 99223
Stout Ct & Rd 99206
W Stratton Ave 99208
W Strong Rd 99208
N Stuart St 99207
E & W Stutler Rd 99224
E Sugar Pine Ln 99217
N Sullivan Rd 99216
E & S Sumac Dr & Ln 99223
E Summercrest Ave 99223
W Summerhill Ct 99208
S Summerwood St 99224
N Summit Blvd 99201
W Summit Blvd 99201
N Summit Ln
5800-5999 99212
10700-11099 99217
W Summit Pkwy 99201
E Summit Rd 99217
E Sumner Ave 99202
W Sumner Ave 99204
E & N Sumter Ct & Way 99208
E Sunburst Ln 99224
N & W Sundance Dr & Ln 99208
N Sunderland Ct 99206
Sunflower Ct, Dr & Ln 99217
S & W Sunny Creek Cir & Dr 99224

W Sunset Blvd
1801-1897 99201
1899-1900 99201
1902-2098 99201
2601-2697 99224
2699-4399 99224
W Sunset Hwy 99224
W Sunset Frontage Rd 99224
W Sunset View Ln 99224
E Sunview Ln 99217
S Sunward Dr 99223
N Superior St 99202
S Supreme Ct 99223
N Susan Ct 99208
E Susan Ln 99223
W Sussex Ct 99205
W Sutherlin Pl 99208
N Sutherlin St
5600-6299 99205
6300-7499 99208
N Sycamore St
100-599 99202
601-1399 99202
2101-2197 99217
2199-5799 99217
S Sycamore St 99223
N Sylvia Ct 99208
W Sylvian Ct 99208
E Syndicate Blvd 99202
E & S Syringa Rd 99203
S Tacoma St 99203
W Taft Dr 99208
W Talon Dr 99224
S Talon Peak Dr 99224
N Tamarack Ct 99208
E Tamarisk Ln 99223
Tampa Dr & St 99223
W Tanya Ln 99208
W Tapestry Dr 99224
E Tara Dr 99223
W Taryn Ct 99208
E Tate Rd 99217
S Tay St 99224
S & W Taylor Rd 99224
W Teal Ave 99218
S Technology Rd 99224
S Tekoa St 99203
E Temple Rd 99217
S Tenfel Ln 99223
W Tepee Ct 99208
W Tepee Rd 99224
E Terra Ct 99223
S Terre Vista St 99224
N Terry Ct 99208
S Thierman Ln 99223
N Thierman Rd 99217
S Thierman Rd 99223
S Thistle Ln 99223
S Thomas Mallen Rd 99224
S Thor Ct 99223
N Thor St
1001-1099 99202
2600-4399 99217
S Thor St
1-1299 99202
2028-2098 99223
2100-5699 99223
W Thorpe Rd 99224
E Thurston Ave
700-2200 99203
2202-2298 99203
2300-2599 99223
2601-2799 99223
E Tieton Ave 99218
W Tieton Ave
400-699 99218
1600-3999 99208
W Tieton Ct 99208
W Tiffany Ave 99208
E Tilsley Pl 99207
E Timber Ridge Ln 99212
N Timber Rim Dr 99212
N Timberglen Ct 99208
W Timberview Ln 99224
E & N Timberwood Cir & Ct 99208

N Tolt Ct 99208
S Tomaker Ln 99223
W Tomtom Ct 99208
W Toni Rae Dr 99218
E Tony Ct 99217
N Torrey Ln 99208
S Torrino Ct 99223
E Touchmark Ln 99203
W Toutle Ct 99208
E Tower Mountain Ln 99223
E Tracey Ct 99223
N Tracy Rd 99217
W Trail Ridge Ct 99224
W Trails Rd 99224
S Trainor Rd 99224
E Travis Ct 99208
E Treaty Ln 99217
W Tree Ln 99208
E Trent Ave
1-4299 99202
4300-5399 99212
5401-5599 99212
S Trevino Dr 99223
S Tricia Ct 99223
S Trident St 99224
W Trinity Ave 99208
W Trinity Cir 99224
W Trinity Pl 99224
S Troon Ln 99223
N Tucannon St 99208
E Tudor Ct 99208
E Turnberry Ln 99223
W Turner Ave 99224
N Twilight St 99208
E Uhlig Rd 99217
S Ultra St 99224
E Union Ave 99212
N Upper Mayes Ln 99208
E & S Upper Meadow Ln 99224
S Upper Terrace Rd 99203
S Upper Vista Dr 99202
N Upriver Ct 99217
E Upriver Dr
1800-3099 99207
3401-4899 99217
4901-6499 99217
6501-6799 99217
7500-9099 99212
9100-12299 99206
12300-12398 99216
N Upriver Dr 99217
E Upriver Ln 99217
W Upton Ave 99205
N Ute Ct 99208
S Valaneov Ln 99223
S Vale Ct 99224
W Vale Ln 99208
W Valeri Ln 99224
Valerie Ct & St 99208
W Valewood Ct 99218
E Valley Springs Rd 99217
S Valleyview Ln 99212
N Van Marter Rd 99206
S Vandals Ct 99224
Vanetta Ave & Ln 99217
E & N Vantage Ln 99217
W Vel View Dr 99208
Velvet Ct & Ln 99208
E Veranda Ct 99223
W Vernon Ave 99208
Verona Ct & Ln 99223
S Vicari Rd 99206
Vicksburg Ave & Pl 99208
N Victor St 99208
W Victoria Ln 99224
S View Acres Ln 99224
E View Ridge Ln 99206
W Viewmont Rd 99224
N Vista Ct 99212
S Vista Ct 99223
E Vista Ln 99212
N Vista Ln 99212
N Vista Rd 99212
E & N Vista Park Dr 99217
N Vista Ridge Ln 99217

N Vista View Cir 99212
N Vistawood Ct 99218
E Wabash Ave
300-2199 99207
2400-4699 99217
W Wabash Ave 99205
E Wabash Rd 99206
E Wagner Rd 99223
N Waikiki Ct 99218
N Waikiki Rd 99218
W Waikiki Rd
1100-1298 99218
1300-2899 99218
2900-2999 99208
N Waldo Rd 99212
W Walker Ct 99208
N Wall St
100-1599 99201
1600-6299 99205
6300-8500 99208
8502-8598 99208
8600-8698 99218
8700-11800 99218
11802-11998 99218
S Wall St
100-299 99201
1000-1299 99204
1400-1498 99203
1500-2899 99203
N Walnut Ct 99208
S Walnut Pl 99204
N Walnut Rd 99217
N Walnut St
701-897 99201
899-1599 99201
1600-6299 99205
7500-7799 99208
S Walnut St
101-199 99201
500-1299 99204
1301-1399 99204
1400-1699 99203
3001-3099 99224
E Walters Ln 99223
E Walton Ave
1-2299 99207
8500-8598 99212
8600-8799 99212
W Walton Ave 99205
N Wandermere Rd 99208
E & N Wandermere Estates Ln 99208
N Wanderview Ln 99208
E Wanderview Terrace Ln 99208
S Waneta Rd 99223
W Warn Way 99208
N Warren Ln 99208
N Warren St
4700-4899 99205
4901-4999 99205
8700-9399 99208
S Washandi Rd 99224
N Washington Ct
11800-11999 99218
13200-13299 99208
N Washington Dr 99208
E Washington Rd 99224
W Washington Rd 99224
N Washington St
1-97 99201
99-1500 99201
1502-1598 99201
1600-1698 99205
1700-6299 99205
6301-6397 99208
6399-7099 99208
9200-12200 99218
12202-12298 99218
S Washington St
1-135 99201
137-299 99201
400-699 99204
W Water Ave 99201
S Waterford Dr 99203
S Waterford Crest Ln 99203
S Waterlilly Ln 99224

N Waterworks St 99212
W Waverly Pl 99205
E Webster Rd 99217
E Wedgewood Ave
101-197 99208
199-699 99208
3901-3999 99217
W Wedgewood Ave 99208
E Wedgewood Ct 99217
W Wedgewood Ln 99208
E Weile Ave
1-97 99208
99-499 99208
1500-7099 99217
W Weile Ave 99208
E Weile Ct 99217
N Weipert Dr
8200-8699 99208
8700-8800 99218
8802-8898 99218
S & E Welden Ct, Dr & Ln 99223
N Wellen Ln 99218
E Wellesley Ave
2-298 99207
300-2200 99207
2202-2298 99207
2300-2398 99217
2400-4899 99217
7900-8900 99212
8902-9098 99212
9100-9999 99206
17500-17799 99216
W Wellesley Ave 99205
E Wellington Dr 99208
N Wellington Pl 99205
E Wesley Ct 99202
N Wesley Rd 99218
W West Dr 99224
N West Oval St 99205
N West Point Rd 99201
W West Rim Ln 99224
W Westbow Blvd 99224
S Westchester Dr 99223
S Westcliff Pl 99224
W Westera Ct 99224
N Westgate Pl 99208
E Westminster Ln 99223
Westmont Ave & Way 99208
W Westover Ln 99208
W Westover Rd
800-1099 99218
1101-1199 99218
2600-2899 99208
E & W Westview Ave & Ct 99218
N & W Westwood Ln 99224
N Wheat Crest Ln 99217
N Whipple Rd 99217
N Whispering Pines Ln 99224
E & W White Rd 99224
E White Pines Ln 99223
N Whitehouse Ct 99208
N Whitehouse Dr 99208
N Whitehouse St
3900-6299 99205
6300-7099 99208
9001-9097 99218
9099-12299 99218
13100-13399 99208
E Whitetail Ln 99206
E Whitman Ave 99212
E Whitman Ct 99206
N Whittier St 99218
N Whitworth Dr 99218
N Wickiup Ct 99208
N Wieber Dr 99208
W Wigwam Ct 99208
W Wigwam Rd 99224
S Wilcox Ln 99206
E Wildflower Ln 99224
E Wilding Ave
500-699 99208
1300-6199 99217
N Wilding Dr 99208
E Wilding Ln 99217

S Wildwood Ln 99206
Will D Alton Cir & Ln 99224
Willamette Ct, Ln & St 99223
Willapa Ave & Ct 99224
S Williams Ln 99224
S Williamson Ln 99223
N Willow Rd 99206
E Willow Springs Rd 99223
S Willowell Dr 99202
N Willowglen Ct 99208
W Wilson Ave
200-499 99208
1400-1498 99201
1500-1699 99201
W Wilson Ct 99208
W Wilson Ln 99208
Winchester Ave & Ct 99218
E Windemere Ct 99223
W Winder Ln 99224
Windham Ct 99208
S Windmill Dr 99223
W Windriver Dr 99208
E Windsong Ave 99223
N Windsor Dr 99205
S Windsor Rd 99224
W Windsor Rd 99224
N Windsor St 99208
S Windstar St 99224
S Windward Ct 99223
E Winger Rd 99208
W Winston Ct 99205
N Winston Dr
6200-6299 99205
6300-7199 99208
W Winston Dr 99205
S Winthrop Ln 99203
N Wiscomb Ct 99208
N Wiscomb Dr 99208
N Wiscomb Ln 99218
N Wiscomb St
2400-3099 99207
5900-7499 99208
E Wisconsin Ave 99212
Wisher Ln 99224
E Woodcliff Rd 99203
E & N Woodcrest Ct 99208
S Woodfern St 99202
S Woodfield Ln 99223
E Woodglen Ct 99208
W Woodgrove Ct 99208
W Woodland Blvd 99224
S Woodland Ct 99224
E Woodland Ln 99212
E Woodland Park Dr
7900-8199 99212
8200-8999 99217
E Woodland Ridge Ln 99212
Woodridge Ct & Dr 99208
N & S Woodruff Rd 99206
W Woodside Ave 99208
N Woodside Ln 99217
W Woodside Pl 99208
E Woodview Ct 99212
W Woodview Ct 99208
E Woodview Dr 99212
N Woodview Ln 99212
W Woodway Ave 99218
W Woolard Rd 99208
S Wortman Pl 99224
N Wright Dr 99224
S Yale Rd 99223
N Yale St 99217
E York Ave 99212
W York Ave 99205
N Zappone Pl 99207
S Zuni Dr 99206

NUMBERED STREETS

E 1st Ave 99202
W 1st Ave 99201
E 2nd Ave 99202
1-2499 99201
3300-3599 99224
E 3rd Ave 99202

W 3rd Ave
1-2400 99201
2402-2498 99201
3201-3297 99224
3299-3500 99224
3502-3598 99224
E 4th Ave 99202
W 4th Ave
300-599 99204
1500-2199 99201
2201-2299 99201
3100-3499 99224
3501-3599 99224
E 5th Ave 99202
W 5th Ave
1-1599 99204
1801-1897 99201
1899-2299 99201
3100-6399 99224
E 6th Ave 99202
W 6th Ave
1-1799 99204
1801-1899 99204
2900-5399 99224
W 6th Ct 99201
E 6th Ln 99212
E 7th Ave 99202
W 7th Ave
100-1999 99204
2001-2099 99204
2800-3399 99224
3401-3599 99224
E 7th Ln 99212
E 8th Ave 99202
W 8th Ave
1-97 99204
99-1999 99204
2001-2099 99204
2600-3400 99224
3402-3498 99224
E 9th Ave 99202
W 9th Ave
2-98 99204
100-2099 99204
2201-3097 99224
3099-10499 99224
E 10th Ave 99202
W 10th Ave
1001-1097 99204
1099-1999 99204
2001-2099 99204
2200-10499 99224
E 11th Ave 99202
W 11th Ave
800-1999 99204
2200-2499 99224
W 11th Ct 99224
E 12th Ave 99202
W 12th Ave
300-704 99204
706-1899 99204
2100-10699 99224
E 12th Pl 99202
E 13th Ave 99202
W 13th Ave
1-1799 99204
2100-2899 99224
W 13th Ct 99224
E 14th Ave 99202
1-1799 99204
2100-3399 99224
E 15th Ave
1000-2199 99203
2700-4299 99223
W 15th Ave
1-1799 99203
1801-1899 99203
1900-3399 99224
E 16th Ave
1-2099 99203
2101-2199 99203
2700-4299 99223
4301-4399 99223
W 16th Ave
1-1599 99203
1900-4899 99224
E 17th Ave
1-197 99203
199-2299 99203
2301-2397 99223
2399-4300 99223
4302-4398 99223
W 17th Ave
1-1799 99203
1900-4899 99224
E 17th Ct 99223
E 18th Ave
200-2100 99203
2600-3999 99223
7500-8299 99212
W 18th Ave
2-98 99203
2901-3097 99224
E 18th Ct 99223
E 19th Ave
205-1799 99203
2500-4200 99223
4202-4298 99223
W 19th Ave
100-198 99203
200-1399 99203
2900-3199 99224
E 19th Ln 99206
E 20th Ave
300-1799 99203
3200-4300 99223
4302-4498 99223
W 20th Ave
300-398 99203
400-1399 99203
3100-3399 99224
E 21st Ave
300-699 99203
3200-5599 99223
5601-5899 99223
W 21st Ave
1-1300 99203
1302-1398 99203
1600-1698 99224
1700-10599 99224
E 22nd Ave
100-699 99203
3300-4699 99223
W 22nd Ave
100-1299 99203
2900-3199 99224
E 22nd Ct 99223
E 23rd Ave
200-2099 99203
3200-3398 99223
3400-4299 99223
W 23rd Ave
1-1299 99203
1900-3399 99224
E 24th Ave
201-297 99203
299-2099 99203
3200-4299 99223
9400-9698 99206
9700-9899 99206
9901-10199 99206
W 24th Ave 99203
E 24th Ln
8400-8499 99212
9500-9599 99206
E 25th Ave
2-198 99203
200-1999 99203
2800-2898 99223
2900-6699 99223
W 25th Ave
1-1199 99203
1700-4399 99224
E 25th Ln 99223
E 26th Ave
1-1499 99203
3200-4299 99223
W 26th Ave
1-1199 99203
1600-4299 99224
E 26th Ct 99203
E 27th Ave
1-1799 99203
2501-2597 99223
2599-5899 99223
W 27th Ave
1-1199 99203
1700-4399 99224
E 28th Ave
1-1399 99203
2300-4299 99223
9400-10299 99206
W 28th Ave
1-1199 99203
1800-4399 99224
E 29th Ave
1-2238 99203
2240-2298 99203
2301-2397 99223
2399-5499 99223
W 29th Ave
1-1100 99203
1102-1198 99203
3700-4299 99224
E 30th Ave
1-2100 99203
2800-4299 99223
W 30th Ave 99203
E 31st Ave
1-999 99203
2700-5800 99223
W 31st Ave 99203
E 32nd Ave
1-1400 99203
1402-2298 99203
2300-6599 99223
W 32nd Ave 99203
E 32nd Ct 99203
E 32nd Ln 99223
E 33rd Ave
1-1800 99203
2600-4299 99223
W 33rd Ave 99203
E 34th Ave
1-2299 99203
2300-4299 99223
W 34th Ave
1-299 99203
4600-4800 99224
4802-4898 99224
E 34th Ct 99223
E 34th Ln 99223
E 35th Ave
600-2299 99203
2301-2397 99223
E 35th Ct 99223
E 36th Ave
600-2299 99203
2700-4299 99223
W 36th Ave
1-299 99203
4500-4599 99224
E 36th Ct 99223
E 37th Ave
100-2299 99203
2300-2498 99223
2500-6299 99223
W 37th Ave
1-500 99203
502-598 99203
3700-4199 99224
E 38th Ave
400-698 99203
700-1999 99203
2400-4300 99223
4302-4698 99223
E 39th Ave
1-2299 99203
2300-4500 99223
4502-4598 99223
W 39th Ave
1-199 99203
4300-4399 99224
E 40th Ave
1-1999 99203
2300-4599 99223
W 40th Ave
1-299 99203
3900-4399 99224
E 40th Ct 99223
E 41st Ave
500-798 99203
800-1499 99203
3200-4499 99223
11500-13899 99206
W 41st Ave 99224
E 41st Ct 99223
E 42nd Ave
400-938 99203
940-1899 99203
1901-2299 99203
2300-2498 99223
2500-4699 99223
4701-6999 99223
13600-13899 99206
E 43rd Ave
700-1399 99203
1401-1499 99203
3100-4699 99223
13701-13797 99206
13799-13899 99206
E 44th Ave
1400-1598 99203
2400-2498 99223
8600-8900 99206
W 44th Ave 99224
E 44th Ln 99223
W 44th Ln 99224
45th Ave & Ct 99223
E 46th Ave 99223
E 46th Ave 99223
13400-13698 99206
13700-13899 99206
W 46th Ave 99224
E 46th Ct 99223
E 47th Ave 99223
W 47th Ave 99224
E 47th Ct 99223
E 48th Ave 99223
W 48th Ave 99224
E 48th Ct 99223
E 49th Ave 99223
W 49th Ave 99224
E 50th Ave 99223
W 50th Ave 99224
E 51st Ave 99223
W 51st Ave 99224
E 51st Ln 99223
52nd Ave, Ct & Ln 99223
E 53rd Ave 99223
W 53rd Ave 99224
54th Ave & Ln 99223
E 55th Ave 99223
W 55th Ave 99224
56th Ave, Ct & Ln 99223
E 57th Ave 99223
W 57th Ave 99224
58th Ave, Ct & Ln 99223
E 59th Ave 99223
W 59th Ave 99224
E 59th Ct 99223
E 59th Ln 99223
E 60th Ave 99223
E 61st Ave 99223
W 61st Ave 99224
E 61st Ct 99223
62nd Ave, Ct & Ln 99223
E 63rd Ave 99223
64th Ave & Ct 99223
E 65th Ave 99223
E 71st Ave 99223
W 71st Ln 99224
E 73rd Ave 99223
E 77th Ave 99223
E 80th Ave 99223

TACOMA WA

General Delivery 98402

POST OFFICE BOXES MAIN OFFICE STATIONS AND BRANCHES

Box No.s
1 - 3021 98401
2999 - 2999 98424
5001 - 5967 98415
6821 - 7988 98417
8001 - 8999 98419
9001 - 9860 98490
11000 - 11800 98411
12001 - 12309 98412
18000 - 18200 98419
33001 - 33996 98433
44001 - 45999 98448
64001 - 66999 98464
110421 - 119998 98411
331001 - 339571 98433
657771 - 657771 98464

NAMED STREETS

A St
1-1199 98438
700-898 98402
900-1199 98402
1102-1102 98401
1200-2898 98402
1201-1399 98402
3500-4599 98418
4600-8299 98408
8400-9499 98444
11500-11599 98433
9601-9697 98444
A Street Ct NE 98422
Academy Terrace Dr W 98467
Acclamation St E 98424
Acorn Way E 98445
Adams St 98433
N Adams St
600-2599 98406
2600-2698 98407
2700-3899 98407
S Adams St
600-798 98405
800-2199 98405
2900-6899 98409
Agnes Rd NE 98422
Ainsworth Ave S
9601-9797 98444
N Ainsworth Ave 98403
S Ainsworth Ave
500-2599 98405
2700-2898 98409
3300-3999 98418
6100-8399 98408
8400-9399 98444
Alameda Ave 98466
Alameda Ave W 98467
Alameda Way W 98467
E Alangerl St 98421
Alaska Ct 98408
Alaska St S
9800-12199 98444
2100-2200 98405
2202-2598 98405
2700-2898 98409
2900-3000 98409
3002-3098 98409
3301-3497 98418
3499-4500 98418
4502-4698 98418
4701-4797 98408
4799-8399 98408
8401-8797 98444
8799-9499 98444
9501-9599 98444
Alder St NE 98422
N Alder St
700-2599 98406
2600-3300 98407
3302-3398 98407
S Alder St
700-798 98405
800-1699 98405
2900-7299 98409
Alder Way 98407
Alexander Ave E
1201-1297 98424
300-2499 98421
3600-3699 98424
N Alki St 98407
Aloha Ln 98466
Alpine Ln 98466
Alta Vista Pl 98466
Altadena Ave, Ct & Dr 98466
Altheimer St 98405
Alturus St W 98466
Amber Rd NE 98422
American Lake Ave 98433
S American Lake Blvd 98409
Amherst St 98466
N Anderson St 98406
S Anderson St 98405
Anthem St E 98424
Aqueduct Dr E 98445
Arbordale Ave & Ln 98466
Arizona Ave 98433
S Arizona Ave 98409
Arleo Ln 98466
E Arlington Dr 98404
Arondale Dr 98466
Arthur St NE 98422
S Ash St
1900-2400 98405
2402-2598 98405
2700-2799 98409
3500-3799 98418
9000-9298 98444
9300-9502 98444
9504-9598 98444
S Asotin Ct 98408
Asotin St S
9800-9999 98444
2801-2897 98409
2899-2999 98409
3300-4699 98418
4700-7899 98408
8600-8899 98444
Aspen St 98466
Astoria Ct 98433
Atlanta Dr 98433
Augusta Dr 98466
Augusta Dr NE 98422
Augusta Pl 98406
N Aurora Ave 98406
S Aurora Ave 98465
Austin Pl 98433
Austin Rd NE 98422
B St 98438
B St E
9600-16399 98445
B St S 98444
E B St
3400-3498 98404
3500-8299 98404
8400-9499 98445
9501-9599 98445
S Baker St 98402
Balence St E 98445
Baltimore St 98433
N Baltimore St
1400-2199 98406
2600-4845 98407
4900-5099 98407
S Baltimore St 98465
Barber Dr 98433
S Baridern St 98418
Barnes Blvd 98438
Barnes Ln S 98444
Barracks St 98438
Battery Rd 98438
Bay Ln NE 98422
Bay Pl NE 98422
Bay St 98421
Bay Hill Ave 98466
Baylor St 98466
Bayview Dr NE 98422
Bayview Pl W 98466
Beach Dr NE 98422
Beacon Ct NE 98422
Beangeri St 98438
Beaumont Ave 98433
Beckonridge Dr W 98466
Beechwood Dr W 98466
Bel Air Rd 98406
Bel Aire Ct 98466
S Bell St
4000-4599 98418
4600-8299 98408
Bellview St W 98466
S Benchans St 98408
N Bennett St
1000-2199 98406
2600-4399 98407
4401-4599 98407
4901-5097 98407
5099-5200 98407
5202-5398 98407
S Bennett St 98465
Berkeley Ave 98466
E Berleadi St 98404
Berry Ln E 98424
Beverly Ave NE 98422
Bingham Ave E 98446
Birch St 98466
Birch St NE 98422
S Birmingham St 98409
E Bismark St 98404
Bitar Ave 98433
Blaine St 98433
Blossom Dr NE 98422
Boise St 98466
N Borough Rd 98403
Boston St 98433
Boulders Way W 98466
Bowes Dr 98466
N Bradley Rd 98406
Braeburn Dr NE 98422
Brentwood Pl 98466
Bridgeport Way W
1900-4500 98466
4502-4798 98466
4800-5717 98467
5719-6399 98467
Bridgeview Dr
1100-2499 98406
2600-2698 98407
Bridgland Ln 98407
N Bristol St
1800-2299 98406
2600-5399 98407
Bristonwood Dr W 98467
Broad View Ave NE 98422
Broadmoor Dr NE 98422
Broadview Dr 98466
Broadway 98402
N Broadway 98403
Broadway Ave S 98444
Brookdale Rd E
600-2999 98445
3000-5099 98446
5101-5199 98446
S Brookside Ter 98465
Brookside Way W 98466
Brouse Blvd W 98466
Browns Point Blvd NE 98422
Buena Vista Ave 98466
S Burkhart Dr 98409
S Burlington Way 98409
Burning Tree Ln 98406
C St 98438
C St E
9600-10399 98445
C St S
11100-14800 98444
E C St
2400-2499 98421
2501-2699 98421
3700-3998 98404
4000-8299 98404
N C St 98403
S C St
1901-2097 98402
2099-2999 98402
3201-3299 98418
4800-8199 98408
8600-8898 98444
E C Street Ct 98404
Caledonia Rd & Smt 98422
S California Ave 98409
Canoe Ave 98433
Canvas St 98433

Cardinal Ct & Loop 98433
Carolyn Dr W 98466
N Carr St 98403
Carver Rd SW 98498
N Cascade Ave 98406
Cascade Pl W 98466
Cascade St 98433
Casey Cir 98433
Cayuse St 98433
N Cedar St
601-697 98406
699-2500 98406
2502-2598 98406
2601-2697 98407
2699-3299 98407
S Cedar St
600-2299 98405
2301-2699 98405
3000-3098 98409
3100-7299 98409
7301-7499 98409
Cedarcrest St NE 98422
Celebration Ave E 98424
Centennial Way NE 98422
Center St 98409
Central Ave 98407
Chambers Ln W 98467
Chambers Creek Rd W 98467
Chandler St
2900-2999 98409
3001-3099 98409
3300-3399 98418
9800-9999 98444
Chelan Pl 98409
Cherry Ave 98466
Cherry St E 98445
Chesney Rd E 98445
Chestnut Dr W 98466
S Cheyenne Ct 98405
N Cheyenne St
601-697 98406
699-2599 98406
2600-2698 98407
2700-4700 98407
4702-4798 98407
S Cheyenne St 98409
Cheyenne Loop Rd 98409
Chicago Ave 98433
Chinook Ct 98433
Chinook Dr NE 98422
Chokecherry Cir W 98467
Circle Dr E 98424
Circle Way 98465
Cirque Dr W 98467
Claremont Ct 98466
Claremont Dr 98407
Claremont Pl 98407
Claremont St 98466
Clark Pl 98409
Clark Rd 98433
Clarkston St 98404
Clattam St 98433
S Clement Ave 98409
Cliff Ave 98402
Cliff Side Dr NE 98422
Col Joe Jackson Blvd 98438
Colgate Dr W 98466
Colorado Ave 98433
Colter Ave 98433
Columbia Ave
100-300 98466
302-1198 98466
2600-2699 98433
E Columbia Ave 98404
Columbine Cir W 98467
Command Cir 98438
Commencement Bay Dr 98407
Commerce St 98402
N Commercial St 98407
Commissary Dr 98438
Concord St 98433
Contra Costa Ave 98466
Coolidge Ave 98433
Cooper Dr 98433

Copalis St NE 98422
Coral Dr 98466
Corbit Rd W 98466
Cornell St 98466
Corona Dr 98466
Cottonwood Ave 98466
Country Club Dr NE 98422
Court E 98402
N Court St 98407
Court A 98402
Court C 98402
Court D 98402
Court F 98405
Court G 98405
Court Q 98404
Court R 98404
S Crandall Ln 98418
Crary Ave 98433
Crestview Dr W 98466
Crestwood Ln 98466
Croft St S 98444
Cruzatte Cir 98433
Crystal Dr 98433
Crystal Pl W 98466
S Crystal Springs Pl 98465
Crystal Springs Rd W 98466
S Crystal Springs Rd 98465
Curran Ln W 98466
Curtis Pl W 98466
N Cushman Ave 98403
S Cushman Ave
401-497 98405
499-2599 98405
2801-2897 98409
2899-2900 98409
2902-2998 98409
3300-4199 98418
4201-4699 98418
4700-8299 98408
S Cushman Ct 98408
Cypress Point Ave 98466
D St 98438
D St E
9600-11099 98445
200-298 98421
300-2799 98421
3100-8299 98404
8400-9499 98445
N D St 98403
S D St
2800-2999 98402
3001-3099 98402
3200-4599 98418
4600-4798 98408
4800-8299 98408
8400-9499 98444
Dahl Dr 98406
Dale Ln E 98424
Dale St 98407
Dallas Pl 98433
Dammann Rd E 98445
Dandintr Ave E 98443
Daniels Dr 98466
N Darien Dr 98407
Dartmouth St 98466
Dash Point Blvd NE 98422
David Ct E 98424
Davis Ct NE 98422
Davis Ln 98433
E Davis Ln 98404
E Day Island Blvd 98466
Daybreak Ave E 98424
Deers Tongue Cir W 98467
N Defiance St
1500-1900 98406
1902-2298 98406
3300-5399 98407
Deidra Cir 98407
Del Monte Ave 98466
Delin St 98402
Delta Ct 98466
Denver Ave 98433
Destination Ave E 98424
Discovery Ave 98433
Discovery St E 98424
Division Ave 98403

E Division Ct 98404
Division Ln SW 98498
E Division Ln 98404
S Division Ln 98418
N Division St 98433
S Division St 98433
Dock St 98402
Dogwood St NE 98422
Dogwood St SW 98438
Dover Pl 98433
Drake St 98466
Drexler Dr W 98466
Drum Rd W 98467
Duct Cho St 98404
Dumas Cir NE 98422
S Durango St
1200-1999 98405
3000-5699 98409
Duryea Ln S 98444
E St 98438
E E St
900-2499 98421
2501-2699 98421
3208-3304 98404
3306-7699 98404
8400-9599 98445
N E St 98403
Eagle Cir 98433
Earnest S Brazill St 98405
East Rd 98406
Edwards Ave 98466
Eldorado Ave 98466
Electron Way 98466
Elleness Ct W 98467
Elm Tree Ln 98466
Elwood Dr W 98466
Emerald Ridge Rd 98433
Emerson St 98466
Enetai Ave NE 98422
W Entrance Rd 98438
Estate Pl 98466
Everett St 98404
Evergreen Dr & Pl 98466
F St 98438
F St E
9600-10299 98445
200-1099 98421
1101-2699 98421
3201-3497 98404
3499-8099 98404
8400-9100 98445
9102-9398 98445
E Fairbanks St 98404
N Fairview Dr 98406
S Fairview Dr 98465
Fairway Dr 98466
Fairway Rd 98438
Fairwood Blvd NE 98422
Falcon Ct 98433
Farallone Ave 98466
Farwest Dr SW 98498
Fawcett Ave
400-2599 98402
2601-2999 98402
3200-4599 98418
4600-8299 98408
8400-9499 98444
Fawnlilly Cir W 98467
S Ferdinand Dr 98405
N Ferdinand St
1000-2299 98406
2601-2697 98407
2699-4899 98407
4901-4999 98407
S Ferdinand St 98409
N Fernside Dr 98406
S Fernside Dr 98465
S Ferry St 98405
Festival Ave E 98424
Field Ave 98433
N Fife St 98406
S Fife St
600-1799 98405
3000-7699 98409
N Fir St 98406
Fir Park Ln 98466

Fircrest Dr 98466
Firlands Dr 98405
Fitzsimmons St 98433
Five Views Rd 98407
Flora Dr 98466
Flores Pl 98433
Floyd Ave 98433
Fordham Ct 98466
Forrest Park Dr 98466
Foster Pl NE 98422
Fox Ave 98433
N Frace Ave 98407
N Frace St
900-2199 98406
5300-5399 98407
Frances Ave NE 98422
Frank Albert Rd E 98424
Freeman Rd E 98424
Fremont Cir & St 98406
G St 98438
E G St
2600-2699 98421
3200-3298 98404
3300-7499 98404
8400-9399 98445
9401-9599 98445
N G St 98403
S G St
1-2540 98405
2542-2542 98405
3300-3706 98418
3705-3705 98419
3707-4599 98418
3708-4598 98418
4600-8299 98408
8400-9299 98444
Galleon Ct & Dr 98422
S Gallisti St 98405
Garcia Blvd 98433
Garden Cir 98466
Garfield Rd 98403
Garfield St S
200-321 98444
320-320 98448
323-1799 98444
400-598 98444
Gass Ct 98433
S Gate Rd 98438
Gay Rd E 98443
Geiger Cir & St 98465
E George St 98404
E Gilreath St 98404
Glacier Ct 98433
Glass St 98433
Glendale Ct & Dr 98466
Goldau Rd E 98424
Golden Gate Ave 98466
Golden Given Rd E
7000-8399 98404
8400-14499 98445
Goldeye St 98433
Goldfinch Ct 98433
N Gove St 98407
S Gove St 98409
Grand Ave 98407
E Grandview Ave 98404
Grandview Dr W
1900-4700 98466
2700-4499 98466
4702-4798 98466
4901-6297 98467
6299-6399 98467
E Grandview St 98404
N Grant Ave 98403
S Grant Ave 98405
Granville Ave NE 98422
Gratzer Rd E 98443
Green Hills Ave NE 98422
Greenway Ave 98466
Greenwood Ave W 98466
Gregory St W 98466
E Gregory St 98404
S Gregory St 98409
E Gregory Street Ct 98404
Greliana Ave E 98446
Grey Wolf St 98433

S Grove Pl 98409
S Gunnison St 98409
N Hale St 98407
S Hamerail St 98409
Hanger 98438
Hannah Pierce Rd W 98467
Harbor Ridge Rd NE 98422
Harbor View Dr 98422
N Harmon St 98406
Harper St 98404
S Harreend St 98465
E Harrison St 98404
S Harrison St 98418
Harry Smith Rd E 98424
Harvard Ave 98466
Haven Ct 98466
N Hawthorne Dr 98406
Hawthorne Ln 98433
N Hawthorne St 98406
S Hawthorne St 98465
Hawthorne Ter NE 98422
Heather Pl W 98466
Heatherwood Cir 98466
S Hegra Rd 98465
Heitman Way W 98466
Henry Rd 98403
Heritage Ave E 98424
Heritage Ct NE 98422
Heron Ridge Dr NE 98422
Hi Ab La Pl NE 98422
Hidden Beach Rd 98465
Hide A Way Dr 98438
N Highland Ave 98407
S Highland Ave 98465
N Highland St
901-1197 98406
1199-1899 98406
1901-2399 98406
2601-2997 98407
2999-4199 98407
4900-5399 98407
N Highlands Pkwy 98406
Highline Pl NE 98422
E Hill St 98404
Hillside Dr NE 98422
Holgate St 98402
Holiday Park Cir 98438
Holloway St 98433
Holly Ct 98466
Holly Dr
900-999 98466
6300-6999 98433
Holm Ln & Rd 98424
E Home St 98404
Homestead Ave & Ct 98404
Honeysuckle Ln 98433
S Hood St
2300-2399 98402
2401-2599 98402
2601-2699 98409
Horizon St 98433
S Hosmer St
1600-2399 98405
2401-2599 98405
2700-2799 98409
3501-3997 98418
3999-4400 98418
4402-4498 98418
7300-7499 98408
7501-8299 98408
8400-9100 98444
9102-9298 98444
N Howard St 98406
S Howard St 98465
E Howe St 98404
Hume St S 98444
Hummingbird St 98433
Hunianta St W 98466
Hunter St 98433
Huson Dr 98405
N Huson St
600-798 98406
800-2300 98406
2302-2598 98406
2600-4999 98407
S Huson St
601-697 98405

699-1199 98405
3000-6899 98409
Hyada Blvd NE 98422
E I St 98404
N I St 98403
S I St
200-498 98405
500-2599 98405
4800-8399 98408
8800-9499 98444
Idaho Ave 98433
Idaho St 98409
Indian Trl NE 98422
Industry Dr E 98424
Inkwell St 98433
Inspiration Ave E 98424
Inverness Dr NE 98422
Island View Ln W 98466
E J St
1500-1598 98421
1600-1699 98421
3000-7099 98404
N J St 98403
S J St
201-397 98405
399-2599 98405
2700-2799 98409
2801-2999 98409
3301-3497 98418
3499-4599 98418
4600-8100 98408
8102-8399 98408
8400-8798 98444
8800-9499 98444
J Ramp Ln 98438
N Jackson Ave 98406
S Jackson Ave 98465
N James St 98406
Jane Russells Way 98409
Jay St 98433
Jean Ct W 98466
Jefferson Ave 98402
Johns Rd E 98445
Johnson Rd NE 98422
Judson St S 98444
Judson St SW 98498
Julies Ter W 98466
N Junett St
600-2599 98406
2600-3200 98407
3202-3398 98407
S Junett St
600-698 98405
700-1599 98405
3800-7999 98409
Juniper Dr W 98466
N Juniper St 98406
K St 98438
E K St 98404
N K St 98403
S K St
3300-4599 98418
4600-8099 98408
8800-9499 98444
N Karl Johan Ave 98406
S Karl Johan Ave 98465
Kaufman Ave 98433
Keelboat St 98433
Kelsey Ln E 98424
Kennedy Rd NE 98422
King St E 98446
Klapache Ave NE 98422
Kootnai St W 98466
E L St
2501-2699 98421
2800-2998 98404
3000-7199 98404
7201-8299 98404
N L St 98403
S L St
301-497 98405
499-2599 98405
3500-4599 98418
4600-8099 98408
9000-9398 98444
9400-9499 98444
La Hal Da Ave NE 98422

Lafayette St S 98444
Lakewood Dr W 98467
Lantern St 98433
Larchmont Ave NE 98422
Larchmount Ct 98445
S Laural Ln 98465
Laurel Ct 98466
N Laurel Ln 98406
Laurelwood Cir NE 98422
N Lawrence St
601-697 98406
699-2599 98406
2600-3199 98407
S Lawrence St
600-1899 98405
3001-3797 98409
3799-7699 98409
Laymans Ter NE 98422
Le Lou Wa Pl NE 98422
Leif Ericson Dr 98465
Lemons Beach Rd W 98466
E Lennox Pl 98404
Lenore Dr 98406
S Leslie St 98418
Levee Rd E 98424
Levitow Blvd 98438
Lewis Pl 98409
S Lewis Rd 98465
N Lexington St
1700-2199 98406
3800-4298 98407
4300-5399 98407
Ligget Ave 98433
Lighthouse Dr & Ln 98422
Lincoln Ave 98421
Lincoln Blvd 98438
Linden Dr 98433
S Linden Ln 98465
E Linden St 98404
S Linerint St 98402
Linwood Ln 98466
E Lister Dr 98404
Locust Ave W 98466
N Locust Ln 98406
S Locust Ln 98465
Loma Ct NE 98422
Longfellow Ave NE 98422
Longmire Rd 98433
Louise St W 98466
Lowama Ln NE 98422
Lupine Cir W 98467
E M St 98404
N M St 98403
S M St
400-2599 98405
2900-2999 98409
3300-4599 98418
4600-7599 98408
8401-8597 98444
8599-9399 98444
Macarthur St W 98466
S Macarthur St 98465
Madison Ave 98433
N Madison St
600-2300 98406
2302-2498 98406
2700-3899 98407
S Madison St
600-2000 98405
2002-2198 98405
2900-7299 98409
7301-7499 98409
Madrona Ave 98433
Madrona Dr NE 98422
Madrona Rd 98438
Madrona Way 98407
Madrone Cir W 98467
Magnolia Blvd 98433
Magnolia Ct 98466
Magnolia Dr 98466
N Magnolia Ln 98406
S Magnolia Ln 98465
Main St 98407
Mana Wana Pl NE 98422
N Mance St 98407
Manchester St 98433

Manito Ct NE 98422
S Manitou Way 98409
Mann Ave 98433
Manor Dr 98466
Maple St 98466
Maplewood Cir NE 98422
Mar Vista Dr 98466
Marc St 98421
Mare Vista Ter 98403
Marietta St SW 98498
Marine View Dr 98422
Mariner Cir NE 98422
Marinera St 98407
Market Pl W 98466
Market St 98402
Markham Ave NE 98422
Marshall Ave 98421
Martin Luther King Jr Way 98405
N Mason Ave
  601-697 98406
  699-2599 98406
  2600-2698 98407
  2700-4299 98407
S Mason Ave
  600-698 98405
  700-1799 98405
  1801-1899 98405
  3200-3598 98409
  3600-7300 98409
  7302-7398 98409
Mason Rd 98409
Mason Loop Rd 98409
Maywood Ln 98466
Mcbride St 98407
Mccarthy Blvd 98438
Mccarver St 98403
Mcdacer Ave 98404
Mcdonald Rd SW 98498
Mcghee St 98404
Mckinley Ave
  3101-3197 98404
  3199-8399 98404
  8400-8498 98445
  8500-8826 98445
  8828-9598 98445
Mckinley Ave E 98445
E Mckinley Rd 98404
Mckinley Way 98404
Mcmurray Rd NE 98422
Meadows Ct E 98445
Meeker Ave NE 98422
S Melrose St 98405
Memory Ln W 98466
Menlo Dr W 98466
Meriwether Trl 98433
Merry Ln W 98466
N Meyers St 98406
S Meyers St 98465
E Middle Rd 98404
Middle Waterway 98421
Mildred St W 98466
N Mildred St
  600-2199 98406
  2201-2399 98406
  4901-5099 98407
S Mildred St 98465
Military Rd E
  100-2999 98445
  3001-3097 98446
  3099-5399 98446
Military Rd S 98444
Military Rd SW 98498
Mill Park Ave 98433
Milwaukee St 98433
Milwaukee Way 98421
Monfore Dr 98433
N Monroe St
  600-2200 98406
  2202-2598 98406
  2600-2898 98407
  2900-3899 98407
S Monroe St
  600-1699 98405
  2900-2998 98409
  3000-7299 98409
Montana Ave 98409
Monterey Ln 98466
Montgomery St 98433
S Montgomery St 98409
Moorlands Dr 98405
Morrison Rd W 98466
E Morton St 98404
W Mount Dr 98466
Mount Tacoma Dr SW 98498
N Mountain View Ave 98406
S Mountain View Ave 98465
Mr Dahl Dr 98403
Mtn Ash Cir W 98467
Mtn View Ave W 98466
N Mullen St
  600-2199 98406
  2201-2599 98406
  2701-3097 98407
  3099-4899 98407
S Mullen St
  700-1699 98405
  3000-4698 98409
  4700-7919 98409
Munter Ln NE 98422
Musket St 98433
E N St
  2600-2699 98421
  2800-2898 98404
  2900-6199 98404
  6201-6699 98404
Nahane East NE 98422
Nahane West NE 98422
Nanaimo Ct NE 98422
N Narrows Dr
  1500-2599 98406
  2800-3699 98407
Narrows Ln 98407
Narrows Pl 98407
Nassau Ave, Ct & Pl 98422
Nevada Ave 98409
Nevada St 98433
New York Ave 98433
N Newton St 98406
Night Hawk Ave 98433
S Nollmeyer Ln 98402
Norma Rd NE 98422
Norpoint Way NE 98422
North Ln 98404
North Rd N 98406
Northshore Blvd & Pkwy 98422
Northwood Ave & Ct 98422
E O St 98404
N Oakes St
  600-2199 98406
  2900-2998 98407
  3000-3100 98407
  3102-3198 98407
S Oakes St
  600-1799 98405
  4700-7699 98409
Oakmont Pl & St 98422
Oas Dr W 98466
Ohio Ave 98433
Olive Way 98433
Olympia Way 98433
Olympic Blvd W 98466
Olympic Dr NE 98422
Olympic St 98433
Olympus Dr W 98466
Opera Aly 98402
Orca Dr & Pl 98422
Orchard Rd N 98406
Orchard St W
  2100-4798 98466
  5000-5698 98467
  5700-5799 98467
  5801-5999 98467
N Orchard St
  600-2500 98406
  2502-2598 98406
  2600-4899 98407
  4900-5099 98407
S Orchard St
  601-697 98465
  699-999 98465
  1001-1199 98465
  2100-2199 98466
  2201-4799 98466
  4901-5499 98467
  5601-5699 98409
  6000-6499 98467
Orchid Ln 98466
Ordnance Rd 98438
Ordway Blvd 98433
Oregon Ave 98409
Oregon St 98433
Osprey Dr NE 98422
Outer Dr 98438
N Overisou St 98407
Overlook Ave NE 98422
Overview Dr NE 98422
Oxalis Dr W 98467
Oxbow Ave E 98424
S Oxford St 98465
Pacharie St S 98444
Pacific Ave
  601-697 98402
  699-2799 98402
  2801-2899 98402
  3200-4599 98418
  4600-8299 98408
  8400-9999 98444
Pacific Ave S 98444
Pacific Hwy E
  2200-6600 98424
  6602-6998 98424
  6701-6899 98424
  8000-8499 98422
  8501-8599 98422
Palisades Pl W 98466
Palm Dr 98466
Palmer Ln 98433
Panorama Ct 98466
Panorama Dr 98466
Panorama Dr NE 98422
Paradise Ave, Ln & Pkwy 98466
Park Ave S
  9600-14199 98444
N Park Ave 98407
S Park Ave
  3701-3797 98418
  3799-4599 98418
  4600-8300 98408
  8302-8398 98408
  8400-9499 98444
N Park Dr 98403
Park St E 98424
N Park Way 98407
Parkridge Dr W 98467
Parkside Cir NE 98422
N Parkside Ln 98407
Parkview Dr NE 98422
N Parkview Ln 98407
Parkway W 98466
Pasadena Ave 98466
Pasinetti St E 98424
Patrician Ln W 98466
Patterson St S 98444
N Pearl St
  600-998 98406
  1000-2599 98406
  2600-5599 98407
  4901-5399 98407
S Pearl St 98465
Pendleton Ave 98433
Pennsylvania Ave 98433
Perimeter Rd 98438
Perkins St 98407
Pickett Cir 98433
Pierce Ave 98433
Pierce Ln NE 98422
Pierce St 98405
Pierrald 98413
N Pine St
  601-697 98406
  699-900 98406
  902-1798 98406
  3100-3198 98407
S Pine St
  601-697 98405
  699-1599 98405
  3001-3097 98409
  3099-3800 98409
  3802-7998 98409
  4001-4099 98413
  4001-4001 98411
  4201-7999 98409
Pinehurst Dr NE 98422
Pinehurst St 98466
Pinnacle Ct NE 98422
Pioneer Way 98404
Pioneer Way E 98443
Pipeline Rd
  4300-6998 98404
  7600-7698 98443
  7700-8299 98443
  8801-8897 98446
  8899-8900 98446
  8902-9198 98446
Pitsenbarger Blvd 98438
Poe Ave NE 98422
Pointe Woodworth Dr NE 98422
Polk St S 98444
N Poradian St 98406
E Port Center Rd 98421
Port Of Tacoma Rd
  700-1900 98421
  1902-2698 98421
  3600-3698 98424
Port View Pl NE 98422
Portland Ave E
  7400-7498 98404
  7500-8299 98404
  8301-8399 98404
  8500-11018 98445
  11020-11028 98445
  801-1697 98421
  1699-2099 98421
  2101-2699 98421
  2800-7100 98404
  7102-7214 98404
Portland St 98433
Princeton St 98466
N Proctor St
  600-2599 98406
  2600-3900 98407
  3902-3998 98407
S Proctor St
  600-1800 98405
  1802-1998 98405
  2900-6700 98409
  6702-6798 98409
S Prospect Ln 98405
N Prospect St 98406
S Prospect St
  600-1799 98405
  3000-3898 98409
  3900-7499 98409
Pryor Ct 98433
Psc 98438
N Puget Sound Ave
  600-2599 98406
  2600-2798 98407
  2800-3600 98407
  3602-3698 98407
S Puget Sound Ave
  700-1200 98405
  1202-1498 98405
  2901-2997 98409
  2999-7499 98409
Puyallup Ave 98421
E Q St
  2300-2399 98421
  3700-6599 98404
Quincy Ave 98433
E R St 98404
Radiance Blvd E 98424
Railroad St 98409
Rainier 98433
Rainier Ct 98466
Rainier Dr 98466
Rainwater Rd S 98444
Ramsdell St 98466
Raven Ct 98433
S Reade St 98409
Reflection St E 98424
Regents Blvd 98466
Rhode Island Ave 98433
Richmond Pl 98433
Ridge Dr NE 98422
Ridge Ln NE 98422
Ridge Pl NE 98422
Ridge Rd W 98466
Ridgeview Cir W 98466
S Ridgewood Ave 98405
Rimrock Dr 98404
River Rd E
  2600-2999 98404
  3000-5399 98443
E River St 98421
Roanoke Pl 98433
Robin Ct 98433
Robin Rd W 98466
Rochester St W 98466
N Rochester St 98406
S Rochester St 98465
Rock Rd W 98466
E Roosevelt Ave 98404
Rose Ln 98406
Rose St 98466
Rosemary Ln 98433
Rosemont Way 98406
Rosemount Cir 98465
Rosewood Ln 98466
Ross Way 98421
Royal Dr W 98467
N Ruby St 98407
Rust Way 98407
Ruston Way
  2201-3097 98402
  3099-3199 98402
  3201-5099 98402
  4801-4997 98407
  4999-5099 98407
E S St 98404
Sacramento St 98433
Saint Andrews Ct NE 98422
Salem Pl 98433
Sales Rd S 98444
E Salishan Blvd 98404
N Salmon Bch 98407
San Antonio Pl 98433
San Francisco Ave 98433
San Juan Ave 98466
Santa Fe Ave 98433
Sawyer St
  3001-3099 98409
  3300-3399 98418
Scenic Dr NE 98422
N Scenic View Ln 98407
N Schuster Pkwy 98402
Sealawn Ave NE 98422
S Seashore Dr 98465
Seaview St W 98466
N Seaview St 98407
Shannon Ct 98433
Sheffield Ln E 98424
Sheridan Ave S
  9600-12000 98444
N Sheridan Ave 98403
S Sheridan Ave
  400-2599 98405
  3301-3497 98418
  3499-4499 98418
  4501-4599 98418
  4600-8299 98408
  8301-8399 98408
  8800-9500 98444
  9502-9598 98444
E Sherman St 98404
Sherwood Ct E 98445
Sherwood Ln E 98445
E Sherwood St
  8001-8197 98404
  8199-8299 98404
  8400-8998 98445
  9000-9099 98445
Shield Ave 98433
N Shirley St
  900-2200 98406
  2202-2398 98406
  2600-4800 98407
  4802-4898 98407
  5100-5400 98407
  5402-5498 98407
S Shirley St 98465
Shorecliff Dr NE 98422
Shoshone St W 98466
E Side Dr NE 98422
Silver Bow Rd NE 98422
Sitcum Way 98421
Skylark Ct 98433
N Skyline Dr 98406
Skyview Ln & Pl 98406
Slayden Rd NE 98422
Sma Van Autreve Ave 98433
Snowberry Cir W 98467
Sonia St 98404
Soundview Dr NE 98422
Soundview Dr W 98466
South Ln 98404
Southbay Pl NE 98422
Southcreek Ln 98466
Spanaway Loop Rd S 98444
E Spokane St 98404
N Sprague Ave 98403
S Sprague Ave
  600-1899 98405
  1901-2399 98405
  3200-3698 98409
S Sprague Ct 98409
Spring St 98466
Spring St NE 98422
Spruce St 98466
Spyglass Dr NE 98422
St Helens Ave 98402
St Paul Ave
  1100-1600 98421
  1602-1698 98421
  8753-8764 98433
N Stadium Way 98403
S Stadium Way 98402
Stanford St 98466
Starlight St E 98424
N Starr St 98403
N State St 98403
S State St
  600-2398 98405
  2400-2498 98405
  4900-5499 98409
State Route 509 N Frontage Rd 98421
State Route 509 S Frontage Rd 98421
Steele St S
  10501-12299 98444
N Steele St 98406
S Steele St
  600-2500 98405
  2502-2598 98405
  2900-2998 98409
  3000-5400 98409
  5402-5498 98409
  9300-9398 98444
  9501-9799 98444
N Stevens St
  600-698 98406
  700-2599 98406
  2600-4500 98407
  4502-4598 98407
S Stevens St
  600-1699 98405
  1701-1899 98405
  4800-5398 98409
  5400-7400 98409
  7402-7898 98409
Stewart St 98421
Stonegate Ave NE 98422
Stryker Ave 98433
Sturgeon Ave 98433
Summit Ave 98466
Summit Cir 98433
N Summit Rd 98406
S Sunray Dr 98465
Sunrise Cir 98433
Sunrise Ln 98466
Sunset Bch 98466
Sunset Cir W 98466
N Sunset Ct 98406
Sunset Dr W
  1900-2600 98466
  2602-2698 98466
  2700-4799 98466
  4800-5199 98467
N Sunset Dr 98406
S Sunset Dr 98465
Sunset Pl NE 98422
Sunset Ter W 98466
Sunset Beach Rd W 98466
S Suspension Dr 98465
Sutherland Dr 98433
E Swan Creek Dr 98404
Sweet St 98404
Sycamore Ln 98433
Sylvan Dr W 98466
E T St 98404
Tacoma Ave 98433
Tacoma Ave S
  2-198 98402
  200-2799 98402
  3201-3497 98418
  3499-4599 98418
  4600-8299 98408
  8400-9499 98444
N Tacoma Ave 98403
Tacoma Ct 98405
S Tacoma Way
  201-499 98402
  1201-1709 98409
  1711-7899 98409
Tacoma Mall Blvd 98409
Tahoma Pl W 98466
E Tanglewood Ave 98404
Taylor Way 98421
Taylor Way E 98424
Terrace Dr 98406
Texas Ave 98433
S Thompson Ave
  3200-4599 98418
  4600-8100 98408
  8102-8398 98408
  8400-9299 98444
Thorne Rd 98421
S Thurston St 98408
Titlow Rd 98465
Tok A Lou Ave NE 98422
Ton A Wan Da Ave NE 98422
E Tonia St 98404
Topeka St 98433
Tower Dr NE 98422
Tower Ln NE 98422
Tower Pl 98433
Tower Rd 98433
Town Ctr NE 98422
Traderad Ave E 98424
N Trafton St 98403
S Trafton St
  600-1699 98405
  1701-1999 98405
  3000-4998 98409
  5000-7100 98409
  7102-7898 98409
Trendark Ave 98433
Trenton Ave 98433
Tribute Ave & Cir 98424
Trillium Cir W 98467
Tucson Ave 98433
Tulalip St NE 98422
Tule Lake Ave S 98444
Tule Lake Ct S 98444
Tule Lake Dr S 98444
Tule Lake Rd E 98445
Tule Lake Rd S 98444
Tuskegee Blvd E 98438
Twin Berry Ave 98466
Twin Hills Ct & Dr 98467
Tyee Dr W 98466
N Tyler St
  900-2299 98406
  2301-2499 98406
  2601-2697 98407
  2699-3899 98407
S Tyler St
  700-2000 98405
  2002-2598 98405
  3000-7299 98409
Union Ave 98438
N Union Ave
  601-697 98406

699-2599 98406
2600-3799 98407
S Union Ave
600-2500 98405
2502-2698 98405
2900-2998 98409
3000-4599 98409
W Union Ave 98405
Upland Ter NE 98422
Upper Park St 98404
Utah Ave 98433
Valley Ave E 98424
E Valley View Ter 98404
Vanderpool Ct 98433
Varco Rd NE 98422
Vassar St 98466
N Vassault St
1100-2599 98406
2600-5099 98407
5101-5199 98407
S Vassault St 98465
Ventura Dr 98465
N Verde St
601-1097 98406
1099-2499 98406
2700-4699 98407
S Verde St
600-1699 98405
5000-5598 98409
5600-7899 98409
Vickery Ave E
4201-4297 98443
4299-8399 98443
8401-8497 98446
8499-13900 98446
13902-14098 98446
View Dr 98433
View Pl 98433
View St NE 98422
View St W 98466
View Point Cir NE 98422
View Ridge Dr 98407
Viewmont St 98407
N Villard St
900-2299 98406
3100-5099 98407
S Villard St 98465
Violet Meadow St E 98445
Violet Meadow St S 98444
N Visscher St
1501-1699 98406
3300-5200 98407
5202-5398 98407
S Visscher St 98465
Vista Dr 98465
Vista Pl NE 98422
Vista Pl W 98466
Vista View Dr
2300-2599 98406
2700-3099 98407
Wa Tau Ga Ave NE 98422
Waller Rd E
3300-8299 98443
8301-8399 98443
8401-8497 98446
8499-17599 98446
S Walters Rd 98465
Wan I Da Ave NE 98422
Wana Wana Pl NE 98422
S Wapato St 98409
S Wapato Lake Dr 98408
Warehouse Rd 98438
N Warner St
600-698 98406
700-2599 98406
2600-3699 98407
S Warner St
600-798 98405
800-1199 98405
2900-7499 98409
7501-7899 98409
Washington St 98433
N Washington St
700-2599 98406
2700-3899 98407
S Washington St
600-2000 98405

2002-2398 98405
2901-2997 98409
2999-5700 98409
5702-5898 98409
Watchtower Rd NE 98422
Water St NE 98422
N Waterfront Dr 98407
N Waterview St 98407
Wayneworth St W 98466
Weathervane Ct & Dr 98466
N Welarist St 98403
West Rd 98406
West St
200-799 98404
1214-1315 98438
Westgate Blvd 98406
S Westley Dr 98465
Westridge Ave W 98466
Westwood Sq W 98466
Wheeler St S 98444
White St 98407
Whitman St NE 98422
N Whitman St
1000-2299 98406
3000-5099 98407
S Whitman St 98465
Whittier St NE 98422
Wild Rose St 98466
Wilkeson St S
10000-10500 98444
1900-2098 98405
2100-2400 98405
2402-2598 98405
2901-3099 98409
3500-4699 98418
4800-7899 98408
8801-8899 98444
Willow Ln W 98466
Willow Lane Rd 98466
Willows Rd E 98424
Wilson Ave 98433
Wilton Ln E 98424
S Wilton Rd 98465
Winchester Dr E 98445
S Windom St 98409
S Winnetka St 98408
N Winnifred Pl 98407
N Winnifred St
900-2399 98406
2600-4799 98407
4900-5399 98407
S Winnifred St 98465
Winona Ct NE 98422
Woodlake Dr W 98467
S Woodland Glen Dr 98444
N Woodlawn St 98406
S Woodlawn St 98465
Woodside Ct & Dr 98466
N Woodworth Ave 98406
E Wright Ave 98404
S Wright Ave
201-297 98418
299-1000 98418
1002-1698 98418
2400-3798 98409
3800-4049 98409
Wright Cir 98433
Yacht Club Rd 98407
Yakima Ave
600-2548 98405
2550-2550 98405
2700-2798 98409
3700-4599 98418
4600-8399 98408
8400-8598 98444
8600-9499 98444
Yakima Ave S 98444
N Yakima Ave
101-197 98403
199-1300 98403
1302-1398 98403
2401-2497 98406
2499-2799 98406
Yakima Ct 98405
Yale St 98466
Yellowstone Ct 98433
Yorneria Ave NE 98422

NUMBERED STREETS

1st Ave E 98445
1st St 98438
1st St E 98424
N 1st St 98403
1st Avenue Ct E 98445
1st Avenue Ct S 98444
1st Street Ct E 98424
1st Street Ct NE 98422
2nd Ave E 98445
2nd St 98438
2nd St NE 98422
N 2nd St
500-999 98403
5000-5099 98433
S 2nd St
600-698 98405
2300-2399 98433
2nd Avenue Ct E 98445
2nd Street Ct E 98424
3rd Ave E 98445
3rd St 98438
3rd St NE 98422
N 3rd St
501-597 98403
5000-5399 98433
S 3rd St 98433
3rd Avenue Ct E 98445
3rd Street Ct E 98424
4th Ave E 98445
4th St 98438
4th St E 98424
4th St NE 98422
N 4th St
300-1299 98403
1301-1399 98403
5000-5599 98433
S 4th St
201-299 98402
900-1198 98405
1200-1300 98405
1302-1398 98405
2300-2699 98433
4th Avenue Ct E 98445
4th Avenue Ct S 98444
4th Street Ct NE 98422
5th Ave E 98445
5th Ave S 98444
5th St 98438
5th St E 98424
5th St NE 98422
N 5th St
301-897 98403
899-1499 98403
1501-1599 98403
5000-5599 98433
S 5th St
900-1500 98405
1502-1598 98405
2300-2699 98433
5th Avenue Ct E 98445
5th Avenue Ct S 98444
5th Street Ct E 98424
5th Street Ct NE 98422
6th Ave
300-599 98402
600-898 98405
2000-2198 98403
2400-7799 98406
8300-8500 98465
6th Ave E 98445
6th Ave S 98444
6th St E 98424
6th St NE 98422
N 6th St
201-397 98403
5600-5699 98433
S 6th St 98433
6th Avenue Ct E 98445
6th Avenue Ct S 98444
6th Street Ct & St 98422
7th Ave E 98445
7th Ave S 98444
N 7th Pl 98406
7th St 98438
7th St E 98424

7th St NE 98422
N 7th St
400-1599 98403
2900-7999 98406
5400-5699 98433
S 7th St
300-599 98402
601-797 98405
2400-2499 98433
7th Avenue Ct E 98445
7th Street Ct E 98424
7th Street Ct NE 98422
8th Ave E 98445
8th Ave S 98444
8th St 98438
8th St E 98424
N 8th St
600-2399 98403
2400-2498 98406
5445-5499 98433
8002-8398 98406
S 8th St
100-199 98402
601-697 98405
2500-2599 98433
5100-6598 98465
8th Avenue Ct E
7301-8197 98404
11200-15799 98445
8th Avenue Ct S 98444
9th Ave E
7401-8197 98404
8500-15599 98445
9th Ave NE 98422
N 9th Pl
5861-5864 98433
7900-7999 98406
N 9th Rd 98433
9th St E 98424
N 9th St
600-1700 98403
2900-8399 98406
5859-5876 98433
S 9th St
100-399 98402
601-797 98405
5100-5499 98465
9th Avenue Ct E
7200-7700 98404
7702-8322 98404
8400-8514 98445
8516-15999 98445
9th Avenue Ct S 98444
9th Division Dr 98433
9th Street Ct E 98424
9th Street Ct NE 98422
10th Ave E 98445
10th Ave S 98444
10th St E 98424
10th St NE 98422
N 10th St
300-1699 98403
2400-7999 98406
5700-5999 98433
S 10th St
100-199 98402
900-4599 98405
2400-2599 98433
5100-7499 98465
10th Avenue Ct E
7500-7599 98404
9400-15599 98445
10th Avenue Ct S 98444
11th Ave E 98445
11th Ave S 98444
11th St E
6600-6799 98424
11th St NE 98422
E 11th St
300-1000 98421
N 11th St
300-398 98403
2401-3097 98406
5100-5999 98433
S 11th St
301-399 98402
600-698 98405

2500-2599 98433
5100-5499 98465
11th Avenue Ct E 98445
11th Avenue Ct S 98444
11th Street Ct E 98445
12th Ave E
7201-7297 98404
9201-9297 98445
12th Ave S 98444
12th St 98438
12th St E 98424
12th St NE 98422
N 12th St
700-1199 98403
2400-2598 98406
5100-5999 98433
S 12th St
2000-4599 98405
2500-2899 98433
4601-5099 98405
5101-5197 98465
12th Avenue Ct E 98445
12th Avenue Ct S 98444
S 12th Street Ct 98405
13th Ave E 98445
13th Ave S 98444
N 13th St
800-898 98403
900-999 98403
2900-7600 98406
7602-7798 98406
S 13th St
400-500 98402
502-598 98402
600-3599 98405
13th Avenue Ct E
7200-7399 98404
10100-16299 98445
13th Avenue Ct S 98444
13th Street Ct NE 98422
14th Ave E
8000-8399 98404
8400-16399 98445
14th Ave S 98444
14th St 98438
N 14th St 98406
S 14th St
601-697 98405
699-4199 98405
4201-4999 98405
8100-8199 98465
14th Avenue Ct E
8000-8099 98404
10000-15499 98445
14th Avenue Ct S 98444
14th Street Ct NE 98422
15th Ave E 98445
15th Ave S 98444
15th St E
4401-4497 98424
15th St NE 98422
E 15th St
401-497 98421
N 15th St
2600-2898 98406
2900-7699 98406
5900-5999 98433
S 15th St
401-599 98402
600-4199 98405
5600-8299 98465
15th Avenue Ct E
8300-8399 98404
9900-15999 98445
15th Avenue Ct S 98444
16th Ave E 98445
16th Ave S 98444
16th St E 98424
16th St NE 98422
N 16th St 98406
S 16th St
600-4600 98405
4602-4898 98405
7300-8499 98465
16th Avenue Ct E 98445
16th Avenue Ct S 98444
16th Street Ct NE 98422

17th Ave E 98445
17th Ave S 98444
N 17th St 98406
S 17th St
600-4299 98405
7200-8499 98465
17th Avenue Ct E
7200-7399 98404
15200-15298 98445
17th Street Ct NE 98422
18th Ave E
7300-7399 98404
8501-8597 98445
18th Ave S 98444
18th St E
6300-6498 98424
18th St NE 98422
E 18th St
400-500 98421
N 18th St 98406
S 18th St
600-4899 98405
5701-8297 98465
18th Avenue Ct E
7500-8399 98404
13800-13898 98445
18th Avenue Ct S 98444
19th Ave E
8000-8399 98404
8800-15999 98445
19th Ave S 98444
19th St 98433
19th St NE 98422
19th St W 98466
E 19th St 98421
N 19th St 98406
S 19th St
600-4899 98405
5501-9099 98466
19th Avenue Ct E
7500-8399 98404
10401-10417 98445
19th Avenue Ct S 98444
19th Street Ct W 98466
20th Ave E
7200-7398 98404
7400-8399 98404
9300-14999 98445
20th Ave S 98444
20th St E 98424
20th St NE 98422
20th St W 98466
N 20th St 98406
S 20th St 98405
20th Avenue Ct E 98445
20th Avenue Ct S 98444
20th Street Ct W 98466
21st Ave E
7900-7999 98404
8500-16199 98445
21st Ave NE 98422
21st Ave S 98444
21st St E
5300-5398 98424
21st St NE 98422
21st St W 98466
E 21st St
600-1298 98421
N 21st St 98406
S 21st St 98405
21st Avenue Ct E 98445
21st Avenue Ct NE 98422
21st Avenue Ct S 98444
21st Street Ct W 98466
22nd Ave E 98445
22nd Ave NE 98422
22nd St 98433
22nd St W 98466
N 22nd St 98406
22nd Avenue Ct E
7700-7899 98404
10801-16699 98445
22nd Avenue Ct S 98444
22nd Street Ct NE 98422
22nd Street Ct W 98466
23rd Ave E 98445
23rd Ave NE 98422

23rd St E
5400-5500 98424
23rd St NE 98422
23rd St W 98466
E 23rd St
501-599 98421
N 23rd St 98406
S 23rd St
100-198 98402
600-3499 98405
3501-3899 98405
23rd Avenue Ct E 98445
23rd Avenue Ct S 98444
23rd Street Ct W 98466
24th Ave E
8100-8399 98404
8400-15799 98445
24th Ave NE 98422
24th St E 98424
24th St NE 98422
24th St W 98466
N 24th St 98406
S 24th St 98402
24th Avenue Ct E 98445
24th Avenue Ct S 98444
24th Street Ct NE 98422
24th Street Ct W 98466
25th Ave E
7200-7298 98404
10400-19199 98445
25th St NE 98422
25th St W 98466
E 25th St 98421
N 25th St 98406
S 25th St
101-199 98402
701-997 98405
25th Avenue Ct E 98445
25th Avenue Ct S 98444
26th Ave E
1300-1399 98424
10401-10497 98445
10499-18699 98445
26th Ave S 98444
26th St E
5000-7399 98424
26th St NE 98422
26th St W 98466
E 26th St
100-1500 98421
N 26th St
1100-2399 98403
2700-6399 98407
S 26th St 98402
26th Avenue Ct E 98445
26th Street Ct W 98466
27th Ave E 98445
27th St E
5000-5199 98424
27th St NE 98422
27th St W
6700-6898 98466
6817-6817 98464
6900-8900 98466
E 27th St
401-1499 98421
N 27th St
1100-2399 98403
2800-2898 98407
3801-3801 98417
3802-7298 98407
S 27th St
200-298 98402
601-697 98409
27th Avenue Ct E 98445
27th Street Ct W 98466
28th Ave E
2401-3597 98404
8500-11298 98445
28th St E
5700-7299 98424
28th St NE 98422
28th St W 98466
E 28th St
1300-1998 98404
N 28th St
1100-2399 98403

2900-6799 98407
S 28th St
100-399 98402
800-1000 98409
28th Avenue Ct E 98445
28th Street Ct E 98443
29th Ave E
2500-2600 98404
17300-19100 98445
29th Ave NE 98422
29th St E
3000-3099 98443
5700-5799 98424
29th St NE 98422
29th St W 98466
E 29th St
1000-1198 98404
N 29th St
1900-2399 98403
2401-2697 98407
S 29th St
201-297 98402
3800-3898 98409
29th Avenue Ct E
3700-3999 98404
14600-16299 98445
29th Street Ct E 98424
30th Ave E
2600-2698 98443
13300-18399 98446
30th Ave NE 98422
30th St NE 98422
30th St W 98466
E 30th St 98404
N 30th St
2000-2098 98403
2400-6499 98407
S 30th St
300-500 98402
1000-1198 98409
30th Avenue Ct E
2800-2899 98443
14900-18399 98446
30th Street Ct W 98466
31st Ave E
2601-2799 98443
18901-18997 98446
18999-19100 98446
19102-19198 98446
31st St NE 98422
31st St W 98466
E 31st St 98404
N 31st St
2300-2399 98403
2400-6499 98407
S 31st St 98409
31st Avenue Ct E
2700-2898 98443
17100-17299 98446
31st Street Ct W 98466
32nd Ave E
3600-8399 98443
16400-16798 98446
16800-18099 98446
18101-18199 98446
32nd St NE 98422
32nd St W 98466
E 32nd St 98404
N 32nd St 98407
S 32nd St 98418
32nd Avenue Ct E 98446
32nd Division Dr 98433
32nd Street Ct W 98466
33rd Ave E
1501-1599 98424
5601-6197 98443
6199-6299 98443
15200-16799 98446
33rd Ct NE 98422
33rd St NE 98422
33rd St W 98466
N 33rd St 98407
33rd Avenue Ct E
4801-5497 98443
8800-15899 98446
33rd Street Ct NE 98422
34th Ave E
1301-1499 98424
5600-8399 98443
10100-19099 98446
34th Ave NE 98422
34th Ct NE 98422
34th St E
5200-5399 98424
34th St NE 98422
34th St W 98466
E 34th St
100-2299 98404
N 34th St 98407
S 34th St
201-297 98418
3601-3797 98409
34th Avenue Ct E
2800-4999 98443
16800-16899 98446
34th Street Ct E 98443
34th Street Loop NE 98422
35th Ave E
2901-5722 98443
15200-17999 98446
35th Ave NE 98422
35th St E
5000-5399 98424
35th St NE 98422
35th St W 98466
E 35th St
100-2299 98404
N 35th St 98407
S 35th St
300-1799 98418
2001-2197 98409
35th Avenue Ct E 98443
35th Street Ct E 98443
35th Street Ct NE 98422
35th Street Ct W 98466
36th Ave E
2900-3098 98443
12000-19099 98446
36th Ave NE 98422
36th St E
7200-7498 98424
36th St NE 98422
36th St W 98466
E 36th St
101-197 98404
N 36th St 98407
S 36th St
101-397 98418
3001-3197 98409
36th Avenue Ct E
3100-3199 98443
10800-14999 98446
36th Avenue Ct NE 98422
36th Street Ct W 98466
37th Ave E 98446
37th Ave NE 98422
37th St NE 98422
37th St W 98466
E 37th St 98404
N 37th St 98407
S 37th St
101-197 98418
2100-2198 98409
37th Avenue Ct E 98446
37th Street Ct W 98466
38th Ave E 98446
38th Ave NE 98422
38th St E
4000-4198 98443
38th St NE 98422
38th St W 98466
E 38th St
100-1799 98404
N 38th St 98407
S 38th St
100-1749 98418
2500-4199 98409
38th Avenue Ct E
4700-4799 98443
15300-17598 98446
38th Street Ct NE 98422
38th Street Ct W 98466
39th Ave E 98446
39th Ave NE 98422
39th St E
6200-6299 98424
39th St NE 98422
39th St W 98466
E 39th St
1700-2199 98404
N 39th St 98407
S 39th St
700-1899 98418
2500-2598 98409
39th Avenue Ct E 98446
39th Street Ct NE 98422
40th Ave E
3600-3898 98443
9001-9097 98446
40th Ave NE 98422
40th St E
2600-3099 98404
5100-5198 98443
6252-6457 98424
40th St NE 98422
40th St W 98466
E 40th St
100-1899 98404
N 40th St 98407
S 40th St
100-1999 98418
2500-2898 98409
40th Avenue Ct E 98443
40th Avenue Ct E 98424
40th Street Ct E 98424
40th Street Ct W 98466
E 40th Street Ct 98404
41st Ave E
5600-6399 98443
8800-15499 98446
15501-18299 98446
41st St E
6200-6999 98424
41st St NE 98422
41st St W 98466
E 41st St
1100-2199 98404
N 41st St 98407
S 41st St
700-1999 98418
2200-2498 98409
2500-4399 98409
41st Avenue Ct E
7200-7899 98443
8900-8999 98446
41st Division Dr S 98433
41st Street Ct W 98466
42nd Ave E
7701-7897 98443
10101-12997 98446
42nd Ave NE 98422
E 42nd Ct 98404
42nd St NE 98422
42nd St W 98466
E 42nd St 98404
N 42nd St 98407
S 42nd St
1400-1999 98418
2501-2599 98409
42nd Avenue Ct E 98446
42nd Street Ct E 98424
42nd Street Ct NE 98422
42nd Street Ct W 98466
43rd Ave E
5500-5700 98443
16300-17999 98446
43rd Ave NE 98422
43rd Pl NE 98422
43rd Pl W 98466
43rd St E
6300-6599 98424
43rd St NE 98422
43rd St W 98466
E 43rd St
100-2099 98404
N 43rd St 98407
S 43rd St
151-1999 98418
3000-3098 98409
43rd Avenue Ct E 98446
43rd Avenue Ct NE 98422
43rd Street Ct W 98466
E 43rd Street Ct 98404
44th Ave E
1500-6598 98424
4300-4498 98443
6600-6699 98424
7101-7199 98443
10101-10197 98446
44th Ave NE 98422
44th St E
3000-5399 98443
44th St NE 98422
44th St W 98466
E 44th St
400-2299 98404
N 44th St 98407
S 44th St 98418
44th Avenue Ct E
5201-5299 98443
15600-15899 98446
44th Street Ct E 98443
44th Street Ct NE 98422
44th Street Ct W 98466
45th Ave E
6201-6499 98443
10000-10100 98446
45th Ave NE 98422
E 45th Ct 98404
45th St E
6500-6599 98424
45th St NE 98422
45th St W 98466
E 45th St
100-1200 98404
N 45th St 98407
S 45th St
100-198 98418
2900-3599 98409
45th Avenue Ct E 98443
45th Street Ct E 98424
45th Street Ct W 98466
46th Ave E
1200-1499 98424
6600-6798 98443
9800-10398 98446
46th Ave NE 98422
46th St E
3200-3499 98443
46th St NE 98422
46th St W 98466
E 46th St
100-1799 98404
N 46th St 98407
S 46th St 98418
46th Avenue Ct E 98443
46th Street Ct NE 98422
46th Street Ct W 98466
47th Ave E
1200-1499 98424
4000-7999 98443
8900-11898 98446
47th Ave NE 98422
47th St NE 98422
47th St W 98466
E 47th St 98404
N 47th St 98407
S 47th St
200-1749 98408
2600-2898 98409
47th Avenue Ct E
6600-6799 98443
17000-17099 98446
47th Street Ct E 98443
47th Street Ct W 98466
48th Ave E
5500-7999 98443
8800-16400 98446
48th Ave NE 98422
48th St E
2900-2998 98404
3101-3497 98443
7101-7597 98424
48th St NE 98422
48th St W
5100-5899 98467
7100-7199 98466
9901-10099 98467
E 48th St
200-1399 98404
N 48th St 98407
S 48th St
100-1799 98408
2100-2598 98409
48th Avenue Ct E 98424
48th Avenue Ct NE 98422
48th Street Ct E
3200-4599 98443
7100-7398 98424
48th Street Ct W 98467
S 48th Street Ct 98409
49th Ave E
1300-1399 98424
6301-6797 98443
49th Ave NE 98422
49th St E
3800-3898 98443
7000-7399 98424
49th St NE 98422
49th St W 98467
E 49th St
501-597 98404
N 49th St 98407
S 49th St
400-1699 98408
2200-4298 98409
49th Avenue Ct E
5300-6399 98443
15800-17499 98446
49th Avenue Ct NE 98422
49th Street Ct E
4400-4599 98443
49th Street Ct W 98467
400-512 98404
50th Ave E
3700-7999 98443
9600-9698 98446
50th Ave NE 98422
50th St E
7800-8199 98424
50th St NE 98422
50th St W 98467
E 50th St
100-198 98404
N 50th St 98407
S 50th St
100-1600 98408
2101-2197 98409
50th Avenue Ct E
5701-5997 98443
8800-16398 98446
50th Street Ct E
3400-3600 98443
50th Street Ct W 98467
200-299 98404
51st Ave E
1600-1799 98424
6600-6999 98443
13600-14100 98446
51st St NE 98422
51st St W 98467
E 51st St 98404
N 51st St 98407
S 51st St
100-1699 98408
2401-2497 98409
51st Avenue Ct E
5701-7799 98443
8800-8898 98446
51st Avenue Ct W 98467
51st Street Ct E 98443
51st Street Ct W 98467
52nd Ave E
1301-1499 98424
7500-7600 98443
9600-17999 98446
52nd Ave NE 98422
52nd Ave W 98467
52nd Pl NE 98422
52nd St E
3400-5398 98443
7800-7998 98424
52nd St NE 98422
52nd St W 98467
E 52nd St
101-497 98404
N 52nd St 98407
S 52nd St
100-1799 98408
2100-4600 98409
52nd Avenue Ct E
3400-3499 98424
7700-7798 98443
8800-9699 98446
52nd Avenue Ct W 98467
52nd Street Ct E 98443
52nd Street Ct W 98467
53rd Ave E
500-699 98424
16000-16199 98446
53rd Ave NE 98422
53rd Ave W 98467
53rd Pl NE 98422
53rd St E
3400-4398 98443
53rd St NE 98422
53rd St W 98467
E 53rd St
400-1499 98404
N 53rd St 98407
S 53rd St
200-1799 98408
2500-2599 98409
2601-2899 98409
53rd Avenue Ct E
4000-4098 98443
8900-16699 98446
6401-6499 98467
53rd Street Ct E 98443
53rd Street Ct NE 98422
53rd Street Ct W 98467
54th Ave E 98424
54th Ave NE 98422
54th St E
3700-3799 98443
54th St W 98467
E 54th St
100-398 98404
N 54th St 98407
S 54th St
100-1799 98408
1901-2447 98409
2449-3699 98409
54th Avenue Ct W 98467
54th Street Ct E 98443
54th Street Ct NE 98422
54th Street Ct W 98467
55th Ave E 98424
55th Ave NE 98422
55th Pl NE 98422
55th St E
3500-3598 98443
55th St NE 98422
55th St W 98467
E 55th St
401-597 98404
S 55th St
200-1799 98408
4600-4699 98409
55th Street Ct W 98467
56th Ave E 98424
56th Ave NE 98422
56th Ave W 98467
56th St E
4400-4799 98443
56th St NE 98422
56th St W 98467
E 56th St
100-1900 98404
S 56th St
100-1699 98408
2101-2597 98409
3503-3503 98490
3504-4998 98409
56th Street Ct E 98443
56th Street Ct W 98467
57th Ave E 98424
57th Ave NE 98422
57th Ave W 98467
57th St E
3000-3198 98443
57th St NE 98422
57th St W 98467
E 57th St
600-2099 98404
S 57th St
200-1799 98408
4300-4398 98409
57th Avenue Ct E 98424
57th Avenue Ct W 98467
57th Street Ct E
2701-2797 98404
2799-2900 98404
2902-2998 98404
4100-4400 98443
4402-4898 98443
57th Street Ct W 98467
58th Ave E 98424
58th Ave NE 98422
58th Ave W
4400-4500 98466
5200-5399 98467
58th St E
4901-4999 98443
58th St NE 98422
58th St W 98467
E 58th St
101-147 98404
S 58th St
100-1799 98408
2601-3197 98409
5100-5199 98467
58th Avenue Ct NE 98422
58th Avenue Ct W 98467
58th Street Ct E 98443
58th Street Ct W 98467
S 58th Street Ct 98408
59th Ave E 98424
59th Ave NE 98422
59th St E
4600-4699 98443
59th St W 98467
E 59th St
800-2099 98404
S 59th St
200-1599 98408
3201-3299 98409
59th Avenue Ct NE 98422
59th Avenue Ct W 98467
59th Street Ct E 98443
59th Street Ct W 98467
60th Ave E 98424
60th Ave W 98466
60th St E
4100-4112 98443
60th St W 98467
E 60th St
100-2199 98404
S 60th St
100-1799 98408
2500-4399 98409
60th Avenue Ct W 98466
60th Avenue Ct W 98467
60th Street Ct E 98443
60th Street Ct W 98467
61st Ave E 98424
61st Ave NE 98422
61st Ave W
4400-4799 98466
5600-5900 98467
5902-5998 98467
61st St E
4100-4199 98443
61st St NE 98422
61st St W 98467
E 61st St
200-2100 98404
S 61st St 98408
61st Avenue Ct W 98467
61st Street Ct E 98443
61st Street Ct W 98467
62nd Ave E 98424
62nd Ave NE 98422
62nd Ave W
4300-4699 98466
5400-6399 98467
62nd St E
2500-2999 98404

62nd St W 98467
E 62nd St
100-2400 98404
S 62nd St
100-1199 98408
2401-2597 98409
2599-5199 98409
62nd Avenue Ct E 98424
62nd Avenue Ct W 98467
62nd Street Ct E 98443
62nd Street Ct W 98467
63rd Ave E 98424
63rd Ave NE 98422
63rd Ave W
3500-3698 98466
4700-4799 98466
4800-5999 98467
63rd St NE 98422
63rd St W 98467
E 63rd St 98404
S 63rd St
201-297 98408
299-1200 98408
1202-1598 98408
3100-3198 98409
63rd Avenue Ct E 98424
63rd Avenue Ct NE 98422
63rd Avenue Ct W 98467
63rd Street Ct W 98467
64th Ave E 98424
64th Ave NE 98422
64th Ave W
1900-4398 98466
4801-4897 98467
64th St E
2600-2698 98404
3001-3197 98443
64th St W 98467
E 64th St
100-2299 98404
S 64th St
100-1200 98408
2000-6299 98409
64th Avenue Ct E 98424
64th Street Ct W 98467
65th Ave E 98424
65th Ave NE 98422
65th Ave W
1900-4699 98466
3500-3699 98466
5000-5999 98467
65th St E
4401-4497 98443
65th St NE 98422
65th St W 98467
E 65th St
100-2299 98404
S 65th St
100-1199 98408
4200-4299 98409
65th Avenue Ct E 98424
65th Street Ct E 98443
65th Street Ct W 98467
66th Ave E 98424
66th Ave NE 98422
66th Ave W
3500-3699 98466
4400-4799 98466
4800-6299 98467
66th St W
5030-5098 98409
5100-5106 98467
5108-5300 98467
5302-5398 98467
E 66th St 98404
S 66th St
2001-2397 98409
2399-5029 98409
5031-5099 98409
5101-5107 98467
66th Avenue Ct E 98424
66th Avenue Ct NE 98422
4400-4599 98466
5000-6099 98467
66th Street Ct E 98443
66th Street Ct W 98467
67th Ave E 98424
67th Ave NE 98422
67th Ave W
2700-3498 98466
3500-4400 98466
4402-4598 98466
5000-5898 98467
67th Pl NE 98422
E 67th St 98404
S 67th St
100-1199 98408
3900-4199 98409
67th Avenue Ct E 98424
67th Avenue Ct W 98466
67th Street Ct E 98404
68th Ave E 98424
68th Ave NE 98422
68th Ave W
2901-2997 98466
2999-4599 98466
3800-3899 98466
5200-5299 98467
68th St E
5000-5099 98443
68th St W 98467
E 68th St
100-2299 98404
S 68th St
100-1399 98408
2701-2897 98409
2899-5099 98409
68th Avenue Ct W 98466
69th Ave E 98424
69th Ave W 98466
69th St E
4800-4900 98443
200-1399 98404
S 69th St 98409
69th Avenue Ct E 98424
69th Avenue Ct W 98466
70th Ave E 98424
70th Ave W
1900-2699 98466
2100-3800 98466
3802-3898 98466
4800-5600 98467
5602-5698 98467
70th St E
5000-5099 98443
70th St W 98467
E 70th St
100-2099 98404
S 70th St
100-1399 98408
2450-3499 98409
3501-5099 98409
70th Avenue Ct W 98466
71st Ave W 98466
E 71st St 98404
71st Avenue Ct W 98466
E 71st Street Ct 98404
72nd Ave W
4300-4699 98466
5800-5899 98467
72nd St E
800-2598 98404
3000-3098 98443
100-1211 98404
S 72nd St
100-1799 98408
2201-2297 98409
72nd Avenue Ct W 98466
72nd Street Ct E 98443
73rd Ave W 98466
73rd St E 98404
S 73rd St
700-798 98408
4300-4899 98409
73rd Avenue Ct E 98424
73rd Avenue Ct W 98466
73rd Street Ct E
800-1799 98404
4600-5299 98443
S 73rd Street Ct 98409
74th St E
800-1807 98404
100-199 98404
S 74th St
400-1699 98408
2201-2397 98409
2399-4699 98409
74th Avenue Ct W 98467
74th Avenue Ct W 98466
74th Street Ct E
1600-1999 98404
5000-5399 98443
75th St E
800-2199 98404
4800-4899 98443
400-699 98404
S 75th St 98408
75th Avenue Ct W 98467
75th Street Ct E
900-911 98404
5101-5199 98443
76th Ave E 98424
76th Ave W
4400-4599 98466
6200-6300 98467
6302-6398 98467
76th St E
900-2399 98404
4000-4999 98443
S 76th St
201-297 98408
299-1799 98408
1801-1899 98408
2400-3300 98409
3302-3398 98409
76th Avenue Ct W 98466
76th Street Ct E
912-998 98404
5200-5298 98443
S 76th Street Ct 98409
77th Ave W 98467
77th St E
5100-5199 98443
400-499 98404
S 77th St
1100-1199 98408
3000-3100 98409
3102-3298 98409
77th Avenue Ct E 98424
77th Avenue Ct W 98466
77th Street Ct E 98404
78th Ave E 98424
78th Ave W 98466
78th St E
4700-4899 98443
400-599 98404
S 78th St
200-1799 98408
2200-2999 98409
78th Avenue Ct W 98466
78th Street Ct E
900-2199 98404
4000-4098 98443
79th Ave E 98424
79th Ave W
3500-3600 98466
4800-4898 98467
79th St E 98443
200-299 98408
2900-4599 98409
79th Avenue Ct E 98424
79th Avenue Ct W 98466
79th Street Ct E
2000-2199 98404
4201-4399 98443
80th Ave W
3800-4399 98466
4800-5199 98467
80th St E
1100-2899 98404
3000-3098 98443
3100-5399 98443
80th St SW 98409
E 80th St
400-500 98404
S 80th St
100-1750 98408
1752-1798 98408
2101-3099 98409
80th Avenue Ct E 98424
80th Avenue Ct W 98467
81st Ave W 98467
S 81st St 98408
81st Avenue Ct W
1901-1997 98466
1999-2000 98466
2002-2098 98466
5400-5800 98467
5802-5898 98467
82nd Ave W
3900-3998 98466
4900-5699 98467
82nd St E
806-826 98404
100-699 98404
S 82nd St 98408
82nd Avenue Ct W 98466
82nd Street Ct E 98404
83rd Ave W 98467
83rd St E
1200-1299 98404
400-499 98404
S 83rd St 98408
83rd Avenue Ct W 98466
83rd Street Ct E 98404
84th Ave W
2900-2999 98466
4800-5400 98467
5402-6398 98467
84th St E
901-1797 98445
1799-2899 98445
3100-5399 98446
100-700 98445
S 84th St 98444
84th Avenue Ct W 98466
84th Street Ct E 98445
85th Ave W 98467
85th St E
800-1899 98445
5100-5199 98446
S 85th St 98444
85th Street Ct E
2000-2199 98445
5100-5198 98446
S 85th Street Ct 98444
86th Ave W
2500-2599 98466
4400-4499 98466
6400-6524 98467
86th St E
1801-1897 98445
1899-2000 98445
2002-2298 98445
3900-3999 98446
4001-4199 98446
400-798 98445
S 86th St 98444
86th Avenue Ct W 98467
86th Street Ct E
1100-1199 98445
5000-5299 98446
87th Ave W
2000-2498 98466
5800-6100 98467
S 87th St 98444
87th Avenue Ct W 98466
87th Avenue Ct W 98466
87th Street Ct E 98446
88th Ave W
1900-2099 98466
4800-4898 98467
4900-6300 98467
6302-6598 98467
88th St E
800-898 98445
900-2200 98445
2202-2798 98445
3100-3198 98446
3200-4199 98446
100-298 98445
S 88th St 98444
88th Avenue Ct W 98467
88th Street Ct E
1100-1199 98445
5100-5199 98446
89th Ave W
4600-4799 98466
5600-6399 98467
89th St E 98446
89th Avenue Ct W 98466
89th Avenue Ct W 98467
90th Ave W 98467
90th St E
800-2900 98445
2902-2998 98445
4701-5197 98446
5199-5399 98446
200-799 98445
S 90th St 98444
90th Street Ct E
1700-1799 98445
5100-5299 98446
S 90th Street Ct 98444
91st Ave W
2100-2198 98466
5000-5099 98467
91st St E
901-959 98445
100-799 98445
S 91st St 98444
91st Avenue Ct W 98467
91st Street Ct E 98446
91st Street Ct SW 98498
92nd Ave W 98467
92nd St E
2400-2498 98445
2500-2999 98445
3000-3700 98446
3702-4998 98446
92nd St SW 98498
E 92nd St
100-199 98445
S 92nd St 98444
92nd Avenue Ct W 98466
92nd Street Ct SW 98498
93rd Ave W 98467
93rd St E
1001-1297 98445
93rd St SW 98498
E 93rd St
400-799 98445
S 93rd St 98444
93rd Street Ct SW 98498
94th St SW 98498
S 94th St 98444
94th Street Ct E 98445
95th Ave W 98467
95th St E 98445
95th St SW 98498
S 95th St 98444
95th Avenue Ct W 98467
95th Street Ct E 98445
96th Ave W 98467
96th St E
100-898 98445
900-2800 98445
2802-2898 98445
3100-3298 98446
3300-5399 98446
96th St S
100-2398 98444
E 96th St
101-799 98445
S 96th St
101-197 98444
96th Avenue Ct W 98467
96th Street Ct S 98444
97th Ave W
4400-4498 98466
4500-4600 98466
4602-4798 98466
4800-4814 98467
97th St E
600-698 98445
700-2399 98445
4801-4897 98446
4899-4999 98446
97th St S 98444
97th St SW 98498
97th Avenue Ct W 98467
97th Street Ct E 98445
97th Street Ct S 98444
98th St E
700-799 98445
3800-3898 98446
3900-3999 98446
98th St S 98444
98th St SW 98498
98th Avenue Ct W 98467
98th Street Ct E
1000-1299 98445
4500-4599 98446
98th Street Ct S 98444
99th St E
201-297 98445
299-2499 98445
2501-2599 98445
3900-4199 98446
4201-4299 98446
99th St S 98444
99th St SW 98498
99th Street Ct E 98445
99th Street Ct S 98444
100th Street Ct E 98445
100th Street Ct S 98444
100th Street Ct SW 98498
100th St E 98446
100th St S 98444
100th St SW 98498
101st Street Ct E 98445
101st Street Ct SW 98498
101st St E
801-1117 98445
1119-1399 98445
1401-1699 98445
3800-4199 98446
4201-5099 98446
101st St S 98444
102nd Street Ct E 98445
102nd Street Ct S 98444
102nd St E
801-897 98445
899-1599 98445
3800-3898 98446
3900-5118 98446
102nd St S 98444
102nd St SW 98498
103rd Avenue Ct SW 98498
103rd St E
1100-2199 98445
3800-4099 98446
4101-4199 98446
103rd St S 98444
103rd St SW 98498
104th Street Ct S 98444
104th Avenue Ct SW 98498
104th Street Ct SW
10700-10799 98498
104th St E
100-2999 98445
3001-3097 98446
104th St S 98444
105th Ave SW 98498
105th Street Ct E 98445
105th Street Ct S 98444
105th Avenue Ct SW 98498
105th Street Ct SW
10700-10799 98498
105th St E
200-2499 98445
4600-4798 98446
105th St S 98444
105th St SW 98498
106th Ave SW 98498
106th Street Ct E 98445
106th Street Ct S 98444
106th Avenue Ct SW 98498
106th St E 98445
106th St S 98444
107th Ave SW 98498
107th Street Ct S 98444
107th St E 98445
107th St S 98444
107th St SW 98498
108th Ave SW 98498
108th Street Ct E 98445
108th Avenue Ct SW 98498
108th Street Ct SW
11000-11399 98498
108th St S 98444
108th St SW 98498
109th Ave SW 98498
109th Street Ct E 98445
109th St E 98445
109th St S 98444
109th St SW 98498
110th Ave SW 98498
110th Street Ct E
400-1099 98445
3601-3799 98446
110th St E 98445
110th St S 98444
110th St SW 98498
111th Ave SW 98498
111th Street Ct E 98445
111th St S 98444
111th St SW 98498
112th Ave SW 98498
112th Street Ct E 98445
112th St E
100-2600 98445
2602-2998 98445
3000-5299 98446
5301-5399 98446
112th St S 98444
112th St SW 98498
113th Ave SW 98498
113th Street Ct E 98445
113th St E 98445
113th St S 98444
114th Ave SW 98498
114th Street Ct E 98445
114th Avenue Ct SW 98498
114th St E 98445
114th St S 98444
115th Ave SW 98498
115th Street Ct E 98445
115th St E 98445
115th St S 98444
116th Ave SW 98498
116th Street Ct E
900-1099 98445
3401-3699 98446
116th St E
100-799 98445
4600-4698 98446
4700-5299 98446
5301-5399 98446
116th St S 98444
117th Street Ct E 98445
117th St E 98445
117th St S 98444
118th Street Ct E 98445
118th St E
101-197 98445
199-1099 98445
3900-3998 98446
4000-4400 98446
4402-4498 98446
118th St S 98444
119th St S 98444
120th St E
2201-2297 98445
2299-2999 98445
3400-3498 98446
3500-3999 98446
120th St S 98444
121st St E 98445
121st St S 98444
122nd Street Ct E 98445
122nd St E
1101-1197 98445
5201-5399 98446
122nd St S 98444
123rd Street Ct E 98445
123rd St E 98445
123rd St S 98444
124th Street Ct E 98445
124th St S 98444
125th Street Ct E 98445
125th St E 98445
125th St S 98444
126th Street Ct E 98445
126th Street Ct S 98444
126th St E 98445
126th St S 98444
127th Street Ct E 98445

127th St E ... 98445
127th St S ... 98444
128th Street Ct E ... 98445
128th St E
601-697 ... 98445
699-2999 ... 98445
3000-5300 ... 98446
5302-5398 ... 98446
128th St S ... 98444
129th Street Ct E ... 98445
129th St E ... 98445
129th St S ... 98444
130th Street Ct E ... 98445
130th Street Ct S ... 98444
130th St E ... 98445
130th St S ... 98444
131st Street Ct E
800-1399 ... 98445
5000-5098 ... 98446
131st St E ... 98445
131st St S ... 98444
132nd Street Ct E ... 98445
132nd Street Ct S ... 98444
132nd St E
100-999 ... 98445
3100-3398 ... 98446
132nd St S ... 98444
133rd Street Ct E ... 98445
133rd Street Ct S ... 98444
133rd St E ... 98445
133rd St S ... 98444
134th Street Ct E ... 98445
134th Street Ct S ... 98444
134th St E ... 98445
134th St S ... 98444
135th Street Ct E ... 98445
135th Street Ct S ... 98444
135th St E ... 98445
135th St S ... 98444
136th Street Ct E
800-2099 ... 98445
2700-3000 ... 98446
136th Street Ct S ... 98444
136th St E
100-298 ... 98445
300-1399 ... 98445
4300-5000 ... 98446
5002-5198 ... 98446
136th St S ... 98444
137th Street Ct E
600-699 ... 98445
4400-4598 ... 98446
137th Street Ct S ... 98444
137th St E
1100-2099 ... 98445
4201-4297 ... 98446
4299-4399 ... 98446
4401-4999 ... 98446
137th St S ... 98444
138th Street Ct E
1800-1999 ... 98445
2701-4797 ... 98446
138th Street Ct S ... 98444
138th St E
100-1913 ... 98445
3000-5399 ... 98446
138th St S ... 98444
139th Street Ct E
601-1797 ... 98445
4600-4698 ... 98446
139th St E ... 98445
140th Street Ct E ... 98446
140th St E
700-2199 ... 98445
5200-5299 ... 98446
140th St S ... 98444
141st Street Ct S ... 98444
141st St E
600-1299 ... 98445
4600-5099 ... 98446
141st St S ... 98444
142nd Street Ct S ... 98444
142nd St E ... 98445
142nd St S ... 98444
143rd Street Ct E ... 98445
143rd St E
100-198 ... 98445
200-1399 ... 98445
4600-4699 ... 98446
4701-5199 ... 98446
143rd St S ... 98444
144th Street Ct E ... 98445
144th Street Ct S ... 98444
144th St E
200-2399 ... 98445
4600-4698 ... 98446
144th St S ... 98444
145th Street Ct E
200-2399 ... 98445
3901-4597 ... 98446
145th St E
201-1997 ... 98445
4100-4199 ... 98446
145th St S ... 98444
146th Street Ct E
2000-2098 ... 98445
4800-5399 ... 98446
146th St E
2600-2699 ... 98445
3800-5198 ... 98446
146th St S ... 98444
147th Street Ct E
1001-1797 ... 98445
4800-5399 ... 98446
147th St E
2601-2613 ... 98445
3201-3299 ... 98446
148th Street Ct E ... 98445
148th St E
1000-1098 ... 98445
1100-2399 ... 98445
3101-3197 ... 98446
3199-3399 ... 98446
3401-5199 ... 98446
149th Street Ct E
800-2904 ... 98445
3100-3400 ... 98446
149th St E ... 98445
149th St S ... 98444
150th Street Ct E
200-2699 ... 98445
3401-3799 ... 98446
150th Street Ct S ... 98444
150th St E
1800-2399 ... 98445
5000-5198 ... 98446
151st Street Ct E
900-2598 ... 98445
3100-3900 ... 98446
151st St E
900-998 ... 98445
4000-4299 ... 98446
151st St S ... 98444
152nd Street Ct E
1100-1399 ... 98445
3800-4099 ... 98446
152nd St E
101-197 ... 98445
3500-5399 ... 98446
153rd Street Ct E ... 98445
153rd St E
100-1799 ... 98445
3801-3897 ... 98446
154th Street Ct E ... 98445
154th St E
101-297 ... 98445
3800-3998 ... 98446
155th Street Ct E ... 98445
155th St E
201-1497 ... 98445
1499-2899 ... 98445
2901-2999 ... 98445
3801-3897 ... 98446
3899-3999 ... 98446
156th Street Ct E ... 98445
156th St E
100-1200 ... 98445
3000-3398 ... 98446
157th Street Ct E ... 98445
157th St E
100-1999 ... 98445
3100-4399 ... 98446
158th Street Ct E
100-1799 ... 98445
3000-3098 ... 98446
158th St E ... 98445
159th Street Ct E
1100-2799 ... 98445
3000-4099 ... 98446
159th St E
100-198 ... 98445
3600-3799 ... 98446
160th Street Ct E ... 98445
160th St E
301-397 ... 98445
4000-4098 ... 98446
161st Street Ct E ... 98445
161st St E
2000-2299 ... 98445
3000-5199 ... 98446
162nd Street Ct E
700-2999 ... 98445
4600-5399 ... 98446
162nd St E
200-2911 ... 98445
3800-4399 ... 98446
163rd Street Ct E ... 98446
163rd St E
1200-2200 ... 98445
3000-3800 ... 98446
164th St E ... 98445
165th Street Ct E ... 98446
165th St E ... 98445
166th Street Ct E
2200-2299 ... 98445
5200-5399 ... 98446
167th Street Ct E ... 98445
167th St E
2300-2499 ... 98445
4800-5202 ... 98446
168th Street Ct E ... 98445
168th St E ... 98445
169th Street Ct E ... 98446
169th St E
2500-2699 ... 98445
3300-3399 ... 98446
170th Street Ct E
2601-2699 ... 98445
3400-3599 ... 98446
170th St E
2201-2297 ... 98445
5101-5399 ... 98446
171st St E
2200-2599 ... 98445
3700-3799 ... 98446
172nd Street Ct E
2500-2599 ... 98445
4700-4899 ... 98446
172nd St E
2201-2297 ... 98445
3400-3499 ... 98446
173rd St E
2500-2699 ... 98445
3400-3599 ... 98446
174th St E
2200-2498 ... 98445
4700-4899 ... 98446
176th St E
2200-2298 ... 98445
2300-2699 ... 98445
2701-2899 ... 98445
3101-3597 ... 98446
3599-4499 ... 98446
4501-4599 ... 98446
177th Street Ct E ... 98445
177th St E
2200-2422 ... 98445
3200-3298 ... 98446
178th St E
2200-2499 ... 98445
3500-3799 ... 98446
179th Street Ct E ... 98445
179th St E ... 98446
180th St E
2200-2799 ... 98445
3500-5399 ... 98446
181st St E ... 98446
182nd St E
2901-2999 ... 98445
3000-3699 ... 98446
183rd Street Ct E
2200-2800 ... 98445
3901-3921 ... 98446
183rd St E ... 98446
184th Street Ct E ... 98445
184th St E
2800-2899 ... 98445
3800-5299 ... 98446
185th Street Ct E
2600-2899 ... 98445
3400-3799 ... 98446
185th St E
2500-2599 ... 98445
3201-3799 ... 98446
186th Street Ct E ... 98445
186th St E ... 98445
187th St E
2500-2999 ... 98445
3600-3799 ... 98446
188th St E ... 98446
189th Street Ct E ... 98445
189th St E
2200-2399 ... 98445
3600-3798 ... 98446
190th Street Ct E ... 98445
190th St E ... 98445
191st Street Ct E ... 98445
191st St E ... 98445
192nd St E
2500-2698 ... 98445
2700-2899 ... 98445
2901-2999 ... 98445
3000-3098 ... 98446
3100-4700 ... 98446
4702-4798 ... 98446
5000 ... 98438

VANCOUVER WA

General Delivery ... 98661

POST OFFICE BOXES MAIN OFFICE STATIONS AND BRANCHES

Box No.s
324C - 324C ... 98666
410C - 410C ... 98666
1147C - 1147C ... 98666
8815C - 8815C ... 98666
8875C - 8875C ... 98666
1 - 1394 ... 98666
1401 - 3503 ... 98668
4269 - 4269 ... 98682
5000 - 5000 ... 98666
5001 - 8811 ... 98668
8811 - 8880 ... 98666
8900 - 8997 ... 98668
9802 - 9830 ... 98666
9901 - 9998 ... 98668
61401 - 61997 ... 98666
65001 - 65958 ... 98665
66001 - 66037 ... 98666
70001 - 70178 ... 98665
87001 - 87998 ... 98687
820001 - 823496 ... 98682
871000 - 874438 ... 98687

NAMED STREETS

Adams St ... 98661
NE Airport Dr ... 98684
Akron Ave ... 98664
Alabama Dr ... 98664
Algona Dr ... 98661
SE Alicia Cir ... 98683
Alki Rd ... 98663
NE Alpine St ... 98664
NW Anderson Ave ... 98665
Anderson St ... 98661
NE Anderson St ... 98665
N Andresen Rd ... 98661
NE Andresen Rd
1700-3099 ... 98661
3101-3199 ... 98661
8501-8799 ... 98665
S Andresen Rd ... 98661
NE Angelo Dr ... 98684
SE Angus St ... 98683
NE Aquilla Ct ... 98682
Arizona Ct & Dr ... 98661
NE Arnold Rd ... 98663
Ash St ... 98661
NW Ashley Heights Dr ... 98685
SE Assembly Ave ... 98661
NE Auto Mall Dr ... 98662
NW Bacon Rd ... 98665
SE Balboa Dr ... 98683
Baltimore Way ... 98664
NE Banton Dr ... 98686
Barnes St ... 98661
NE Barradow St ... 98665
NW & NE Bassel Ct & Rd ... 98685
SE Bay Point Cir ... 98683
SE Baypoint Dr ... 98683
SE Beach Dr ... 98661
Beacon Ave ... 98664
Beech St ... 98661
Bella Vista Cir, Loop, Pl & Rd ... 98683
NE Benton Dr ... 98662
Bergeron Ct ... 98661
Berkeley Way ... 98661
NW Bernie Dr ... 98663
NE Betts Rd ... 98686
SE Biddle Rd ... 98683
Billings Ct ... 98661
NW Birch St ... 98660
Birmingham Way ... 98664
SE Blair St ... 98661
SE Blairmont Dr ... 98683
S Blanford Dr ... 98661
NW Bliss Rd ... 98685
NE Blue Grass Dr ... 98684
Boise Ave & Ct ... 98661
NE Bonner Dr ... 98665
NE Bonnie Dr ... 98686
Boulder Ave ... 98664
NE Bradford Rd ... 98682
Brandt Rd ... 98661
SE Briarwood Dr ... 98683
Bridge St ... 98661
NE Bridgecreek Ave ... 98664
Broadview Ln ... 98661
Broadway St
500-598 ... 98660
600-1099 ... 98660
1101-1399 ... 98660
1400-2499 ... 98663
2501-2899 ... 98663
NE Brookview Dr ... 98686
Bryant St ... 98661
Buena Vista Dr ... 98661
N & S Burdick Ave ... 98661
SE Burlington Dr ... 98664
NE Burton Rd
2501-2597 ... 98662
2599-10500 ... 98662
10502-10598 ... 98662
10701-10997 ... 98682
10999-11099 ... 98682
11101-11199 ... 98682
NE Burtonwood Ct ... 98682
SE Butte Ave ... 98664
C St
600-798 ... 98660
800-899 ... 98660
901-1399 ... 98660
1401-1597 ... 98663
1599-2500 ... 98663
2502-2598 ... 98663
NW Cady Ct ... 98663
California Ct & St ... 98661
NE Campus Dr ... 98661
NW Canyon Crest Loop ... 98665
Capitol St ... 98664
Caples Ave
2700-2700 ... 98661
2700-2700 ... 98668
2800-2999 ... 98661
SE Cardinal Ct ... 98683
Carlson Rd ... 98661
Carolina Ln ... 98664
SE Cascade Ave ... 98683
Cascade Dr ... 98664
SE Cascade Park Dr ... 98683
NE Cassady Ct ... 98685
Cedar Dr & St ... 98661
NE Cedar Ridge Loop ... 98664
Cellars Ave ... 98661
NE Centerpointe Dr ... 98665
Charleston Way ... 98664
Charlotte Way ... 98664
NE Chateau Dr ... 98661
SE Chelsea Ave ... 98664
NE Chendarn St ... 98684
W Chendenn St ... 98660
NE Cherry Ln ... 98663
NE Cherry Rd ... 98663
Cherry St ... 98660
NW Cherry St
4201-4499 ... 98660
4700-4798 ... 98663
4800-6599 ... 98663
Chesapeake Dr ... 98664
Chestnut St ... 98660
NW Chikeric St ... 98665
NE Chkalov Dr ... 98684
SE Chkalov Dr ... 98683
Clair St ... 98661
Clark Ave ... 98661
NW Coach House Ct ... 98685
Coast Pine Ave & Ct ... 98684
Columbia Riv ... 98660
Columbia St ... 98660
NW Columbia St
3900-4499 ... 98660
4500-5199 ... 98663
SE Columbia Way ... 98661
SE Columbia Crest Ct ... 98664
Columbia House Blvd ... 98661
SE Columbia Ridge Dr ... 98664
SE Columbia River Dr ... 98661
SE Columbia Shores Blvd ... 98661
Columbia View Dr ... 98661
NE Columbine Dr ... 98682
NE Conifer Dr ... 98662
NE Corbin Rd ... 98686
Corregidor Rd ... 98664
Council Bluffs Way ... 98661
NE Countryside Dr ... 98684
NE Covington Rd ... 98662
NE Coxley Dr ... 98662
NE Cranbrook Dr ... 98664
NW Creekside Dr ... 98685
NE Crest Ave ... 98685
NW Creston Ave ... 98663
Crestwood Ct, Dr & St ... 98684
NE Crystal Ct ... 98686
SE Cutter Ln ... 98661
D St
1200-1298 ... 98660
1301-1399 ... 98660
1400-1798 ... 98663
1800-2499 ... 98663
2501-2599 ... 98663
NW Dale Rd ... 98665
Dallas Ave ... 98661
Daniels St
800-3898 ... 98660
1211-1211 ... 98666
1501-3999 ... 98660
NW Daniels St
3900-3998 ... 98660
4000-4300 ... 98660
4302-4498 ... 98663
4500-5400 ... 98663
5402-5498 ... 98663
Date St ... 98661
Davis Ave ... 98661
Dayton Ave ... 98664
Deencoll St ... 98663
NE Delancey Ct ... 98682
Delaware Ln ... 98664
NW Demaris Rd ... 98665
Detroit Ave ... 98664
N & S Devine Rd ... 98661
Division Ave ... 98660
NW Division Ave
3900-3998 ... 98660
4001-4199 ... 98660
4500-4598 ... 98663
4600-4800 ... 98663
4802-4898 ... 98663
NW Division St ... 98660
NW Dogwood Dr ... 98663
NE Douglas Way ... 98662
NE Douglas Fir Ct ... 98684
NE Drexel Ave ... 98663
Drummond Ave ... 98661
Dubois Ct & Dr ... 98661
Durham Way ... 98664
E St
1300-1398 ... 98660
1500-1898 ... 98663
1900-2599 ... 98663
SE Eastridge Dr ... 98683
NE Edelweiss Ave ... 98682
Edge Park Dr & Loop ... 98663
Edgewood Dr ... 98661
NE Edmunds Rd ... 98682
Edwards Ln ... 98661
Elevator Way ... 98660
SE Ellsworth Rd ... 98664
NE Emmerson Ct ... 98682
Enid Ave ... 98661
NE Erin Way ... 98686
NW Erwin O Reiger Memorial Hwy ... 98660
Esther St ... 98660
NW Esther St ... 98663
Eureka Way ... 98661
E Evergreen Blvd
100-298 ... 98660
300-499 ... 98660
501-599 ... 98660
601-1697 ... 98661
1699-5800 ... 98661
5802-6698 ... 98661
W Evergreen Blvd ... 98660
SE Evergreen Ct ... 98664
Evergreen Dr ... 98661
SE Evergreen Hwy
6301-6799 ... 98661
6800-6898 ... 98664
6900-11799 ... 98664
11901-12197 ... 98683
12199-19899 ... 98683
F St ... 98663
NW Fair Acres Dr ... 98685
Fairmount Ave ... 98661
NE Fairway Ave ... 98662
SE Fairwinds Loop ... 98661
Falk Rd ... 98661
Farview Dr ... 98661
NE Ferngrove St ... 98664
SE Fernwood Dr ... 98683
NW Fir St ... 98660
W Firestone Ln ... 98660
NW Firwood Dr ... 98665
SE Fisher Dr ... 98661
Flint Ave & Way ... 98664
Florida Dr ... 98664
SE Forest St ... 98683
Fort Vancouver Way
600-699 ... 98661
1200-2399 ... 98663
2500-2699 ... 98661
2701-2899 ... 98661
NE Four Seasons Ln ... 98684
E Fourth Plain Blvd
100-198 ... 98663
200-600 ... 98663
602-698 ... 98663
1000-5799 ... 98661
NE Fourth Plain Blvd
17103A-17133A ... 98682
3300-5698 ... 98661

5700-7199 98661
7200-11600 98662
11602-11698 98662
11700-11998 98682
12000-17089 98682
17091-17103 98682
W Fourth Plain Blvd 98660
NE Fourth Plain Rd 98682
SE Frances Ave 98664
Franklin St 98660
NW Franklin St
3900-4099 98660
4101-4499 98660
4500-5999 98663
N & S Fredericksburg Way 98664
SE French Rd 98664
Friedel Ave 98664
Fruit Valley Rd 98660
NW Fruit Valley Rd
3900-6100 98660
6102-6198 98660
6300-8299 98665
8301-8599 98665
G St 98663
NE Galeadi St 98682
NE Garden Dr 98682
NW Garfield Ave 98663
N & S Garrison Rd & Ter 98664
NW Gateway Ave 98660
General Anderson Rd 98661
NE Gher Rd
5100-5398 98682
5400-5498 98662
5500-5800 98662
5802-5898 98662
Gibbons St 98661
Gillis St 98661
NE Glenwood Dr 98662
NW Golden Ave 98665
Grace St 98661
SE Graham Rd 98683
Grand Blvd & Pl 98661
NW Grant Pl 98663
Grant St 98660
NW Grant St
3900-4299 98660
4301-4499 98660
4500-4799 98663
NW Greenbriar Dr 98665
Greenpark Cir & St 98683
NE Greenwood Dr 98662
NW Gregory Dr 98665
NE Grove Rd 98665
Grove St 98661
NE Grove St 98665
Gulf Dr 98664
H St 98663
SE Halyard Ln 98661
NW Harborside Dr 98660
Harney St 98660
NW Harney St 98663
Harney Way 98661
Harney Heights Ln 98661
Hathaway Rd 98661
NW Hathaway Rd 98685
SE Hawks View Ct 98664
NE Hawthorne Cir 98663
NE Hazel Dell Ave
4700-5899 98663
5900-9899 98665
9900-11499 98685
11501-11699 98685
NE Hazel Dell Way 98665
NW Hazel Dell Way 98665
Hazelwood Dr 98661
NE Hearthwood Blvd 98684
SE Hearthwood Blvd
100-198 98684
301-599 98684
304-304 98687
304-398 98684
NW Heermann Dr 98685
Helena Ave 98661
NE Heron Cir 98664
NE Hickory St 98682
SE Hidden Way 98661
SE Hiddenbrook Dr 98683
SE Higgins Dr 98683
Highland Dr 98661
NE Highland Meadows Dr 98682
NE Highway 99
5400-5499 98663
NE Highway 99
6100-9899 98665
9900-13399 98686
SE Hillcrest Dr 98664
NE Hillside Dr 98682
Holly Ct & St 98664
Howard St 98661
I St 98663
Idaho Ct & St 98661
NE Idell Rd 98686
Image Ln & Rd 98664
NW Indian Spring Dr 98685
Indiana St 98664
Industrial Way 98660
Ingalls St 98660
NE Ingle Rd 98682
Interstate 5 98663
Iowa Ln 98664
NE Issler St 98661
Jefferson St 98660
NW Jordan Way 98665
June Dr 98661
NE Juniper Ave 98684
K St 98663
SE Kaiser Way 98661
Kansas St
5601-5697 98661
5699-6799 98661
6800-6898 98664
6900-7399 98664
Kauffman Ave 98660
NW Kauffman Ave
3900-3999 98660
4500-6199 98663
Kelly Dr & Rd 98665
Kentucky Dr 98664
NE Kerr Rd 98682
Keyes Ct & Rd 98684
King St 98660
NE Klineline Ave 98686
NE Knollcrest Ave 98664
NE Knowles Dr 98685
N & S Knoxville Way 98664
NE Kogan Rd 98665
Kotobuki Way 98660
L St 98663
Laframbois Rd 98660
Lakecrest Ave & Ct 98665
NW Lakeridge Dr 98685
NW Lakeshore Ave
7000-9600 98665
9602-9898 98665
9900-10098 98685
10100-11800 98685
11802-11898 98685
NW Lakeview Rd 98665
NE Landover Dr 98684
Larson Way 98661
Latourell Way 98661
NE Laura Ct 98684
Laurel Pl 98661
NE Laurin Rd 98662
SE Laver St 98683
Lavina St 98660
NW Lavina St
3900-4499 98660
4501-4597 98663
4599-4799 98663
NE Lea View Ct 98663
NE Leaper Rd 98686
NE Leichner Rd 98686
Leverich Ct & Pl 98663
NE Leverich Park Way 98663
Lewis Ave 98661
NE Lewis Dr 98662
SE Lewis And Clark Hwy 98683
Lexington Way 98664
N & S Lieser Ct & Rd 98664
Lieser Point Dr & Rd 98664
Lincoln Ave 98660
NW Lincoln Ave 98663
Linda Ln 98661
Little Rock Way 98664
NE Littler Way 98662
NW Loan Pl 98665
NE Loowit Loop 98662
SE Lorry Ave 98664
SE Louise Ave 98664
Louisiana Dr
6200-6799 98661
6800-7200 98664
7202-7298 98664
Louisville Way 98664
NW Lower River Rd 98660
Lupin St & Way 98663
M St 98663
Macarthur Blvd
801-5297 98661
5299-5800 98661
5802-6798 98661
7300-7598 98664
7600-8399 98664
SE Macwood Dr 98683
NW Madrona St 98665
Main St
500-598 98660
600-2599 98660
2600-4599 98663
4601-4699 98663
NE Maitland Rd 98686
NE Major St 98684
SE Manor Ave 98683
NE Manor Dr 98686
Manor Ln 98661
Manzanita Ct & Way 98661
SE Maple Ave 98664
Maple St 98660
NE Maplewood Dr 98665
SE Maritime Ave 98661
Markle Ave 98660
Martin Ct & Way 98661
NE Mason Dr 98662
SE Maxon Rd 98664
NE May St 98661
NW Mccann Rd 98685
Mcclellan Rd 98661
SE Mcgillivray Blvd 98683
NW Mckinley Dr 98665
Mcloughlin Blvd 98663
E Mcloughlin Blvd
100-198 98663
200-799 98663
801-1799 98663
2001-2097 98661
2099-3999 98661
W Mcloughlin Blvd 98660
NE Mead Rd 98682
SE Meadow Ln 98664
Meadow Park Cir & Dr 98683
NE Meadowbrook Cir 98664
Meadows Ct & Dr 98662
Memphis Way 98664
SE Menlo Dr 98683
Miami Ct & Way 98664
Michigan St 98664
SE Middle Way 98664
E Mill Plain Blvd 98661
NE Minnehaha St
800-2600 98665
2602-2698 98665
2700-3298 98663
3301-3399 98663
3601-4197 98661
4199-5300 98661
5302-5598 98661
Mississippi Dr 98664
Missoula Ave 98661
Missouri Dr
6601-6697 98661
6699-6799 98661
6800-6808 98664
6810-6999 98664
Mobile Way 98664
Montana Ln 98661
Monterey Way 98661
SE Morgan Rd 98664
N & S Morrison Ave & Rd 98664
NE Morrow Rd 98682
NE Mother Joseph Pl 98664
NW Mountlake Way 98665
NE Mountview St 98664
Mt Adams Ave 98664
Mt Baker Ave 98664
Mt Hood Ave 98664
Mt Jefferson Ave 98664
Mt Lassen Ave 98664
Mt Mckinley Ave 98664
Mt Olympus Ave 98664
Mt Rainier Dr 98664
Mt Shasta Dr 98664
Mt Thielsen Ave 98664
Mt Whitney Ave 98664
Multnomah Ave 98661
Murray Ct 98661
Murton St 98661
N St 98663
Nampa Ct 98661
SE Nancy Rd 98664
N & S Nashville Way 98664
SE Nautilus Dr 98683
Neals Ct & Ln 98661
New Mexico St 98661
NE Newhouse Rd 98663
Nicholson Loop & Rd 98661
NE Noble St 98682
SE Norelius Dr 98683
Norris Rd 98661
SE Northgate Ave 98664
Northshore Cir & Dr 98683
NE Notchlog Dr 98685
O St 98663
NE Oak View Dr 98662
NE Oakbrook Cir 98662
NE Oakhurst Dr 98662
NE Oaks Ln 98662
Officers Row 98661
Ogden Ave & Ct 98661
Ohio Dr 98664
Oklahoma Dr 98661
NW Old Lower River Rd 98660
NW Old Orchard Dr 98665
Olive St 98660
NW Olive St
3901-4097 98660
4099-4400 98660
4402-4498 98660
4500-4799 98663
SE Olympia Dr
300-399 98684
500-1400 98683
1402-1698 98683
Omaha Way 98661
NE Orchard Dell Ct 98663
Oregon Dr 98661
NE Orion St 98682
Orlando Way 98664
Oswego Dr 98661
NW Overlook Dr 98665
NW Oxbow Ridge Dr 98685
P St 98663
NE Pacific Ave 98663
NE Pacific Way 98662
Palo Alto Dr 98661
NE Par Ln 98662
SE Park St 98683
SE Park Crest Ave 98683
NE & SE Park Plaza Dr 98684
NE Parkview Dr 98686
NE Parkway Dr 98662
Pasadena Way 98661
SE Patterson Pl 98664
SE Peacehealth Dr 98683
NE Perrault Dr 98684
NW Perthshire Rd 98663
SE Petticoat Hl 98664
NE Petticoat Ln 98661
Phoenix Way 98661
NE Pierce Dr 98662
NE Pietz St 98664
Pine St 98660
Pinebrook Ave & St 98684
NE Pinecreek St 98664
NE Piper Rd 98684
NE Plains Way 98662
NE Plantation Rd 98685
Plomondon Ln & St 98661
NE Pluss Rd 98682
Pocatello Ave 98661
NE Ponderosa Pine Ave 98684
NE Poplar St 98682
Port Way 98660
Porter Cir, Ct & Rd 98664
Postage Due 98660
Potomac Dr 98664
Powers Ct & St 98682
Q St 98663
R St
600-699 98661
2600-3700 98663
3702-3898 98663
NE Rancho Dr 98682
Rankin Dr 98665
NE Regents Dr 98684
NE Repass Rd 98665
E Reserve St 98661
W Reserve St 98663
Rhododendron Dr 98661
NW Ridgecrest Ave 98685
NE Riley Ct 98686
Rivercrest Ave & Dr 98683
SE Riverridge Dr 98683
SE Rivershore Dr 98683
SE Riverside Dr
5600-5698 98661
5700-6699 98661
6701-6799 98661
6800-6898 98664
6900-7000 98664
7002-7098 98664
SE Riverside Ln 98661
SE Riverside Way 98661
SE Riverview Ln 98664
SE Riverwood Ln 98683
NE Rockwell Dr 98686
Roosevelt Ave 98660
NW Rose St 98660
NE Rosewood Ave 98662
Rossiter Ln & Pl 98661
NE Royal St 98662
NE Royal Oaks Dr 98662
NE Royal View Ave 98662
S St
500-598 98661
600-799 98661
2600-2698 98663
2700-3900 98663
3902-3998 98663
Salmon Creek Ave & St 98686
NE Sandpiper Cir 98664
N & S Santa Fe Ct & Dr 98661
SE Scenic Ln 98661
SE Schwind Cir 98664
Scott Ave 98660
SE Sequoia Cir 98683
NW Seward Rd 98685
NE Shanghai Rd 98682
Sheridan Dr 98661
Sherley Ave & Ct 98664
NE Sherwood Dr 98686
SE Shorewood Dr 98661
Shreveport Way 98664
SE Silver Cir 98683
Silver Star Ave 98664
SE Silversprings Dr 98683
Simpson Ave 98660
SE Single Tree Dr 98683
Sleret Ave 98664
NW Sluman Rd 98665
NE Snowberry Loop 98664
SE Solomon Loop 98683
NE Sorrel Dr 98682
SE Spinaker Way 98661
NE Springwood Ct 98682
NW Spruce St 98660
SE Spyglass Dr 98683
St Francis Ln 98660
St Helens Ave 98664
NE St James Rd 98663
St Johns Blvd 98661
NE St Johns Rd
3701-3997 98661
3999-6700 98661
6702-6798 98661
6800-6998 98665
7000-9800 98665
9802-9898 98665
9901-10097 98686
10099-11200 98686
11202-11498 98686
St Louis Way 98664
NE Stapleton Rd 98661
NE Starflower Ct 98664
NW Starkrest Ave 98665
SE Stevenson Dr 98683
SE Stonemill Dr 98684
NE Stoney Meadows Dr 98682
NE Strand Rd 98686
NE Stutz Rd 98685
NW Summit Dr 98665
NE Summit Ridge Dr 98686
Sun Park Ct & Dr 98683
NE Suncrest Ct 98684
NE Sunnyside Dr 98662
NW Sunset Ln 98663
NE Sunset Way 98662
NE Sylvan Ter 98686
T St
700-798 98661
800-2699 98661
2700-3999 98663
SE Talton Ave 98683
NE Tamarack Ct 98684
Tampa Way 98664
NE Tanglewood Dr 98664
Tech Center Dr & Pl 98683
Tennessee Ln 98664
NE Tenney Rd 98685
NE Tenny Creek Dr 98665
Terrace Dr 98661
NW Terrace St 98685
Texas Dr 98661
Thompson Ave 98660
NW Thunderbird Ave 98663
NE Thurston Way 98662
SE Tidewater Pl 98661
NE Tiffany Dr 98684
Todd Rd 98661
Topeka Ln 98664
SE Topper Dr 98664
NW Trillium Ln 98663
Tucson Way 98661
Tulsa Ave 98661
U St
500-798 98661
800-1000 98661
1002-1098 98661
2800-3899 98663
Umatilla Way 98661
Unander Ave 98660
NE Union Rd 98686
Utah St 98661
V St
501-797 98661
799-1299 98661
2800-2898 98663
2900-3899 98663
N V St 98661
S V St 98661
SE Valencia Dr 98683
NE Valley View Ln 98663
NW Vallorth Ave 98685
Van Allman Ave 98660
NE Vancouver Mall Dr
7001-7199 98661
7200-9499 98662
NE Vancouver Mall Loop 98662
NE Vancouver Plaza Dr 98662
SE Victory Ave 98661
NW View Rd 98685
SE Village Loop 98683
NE Village Green Dr 98684
Virginia Ln 98664
NW Vista Ave 98665
W St
1000-1599 98661
1601-1799 98661
3100-3508 98663
3510-3698 98663
Wahclellah Ave 98661
NW Walnut St 98663
NE Ward Rd 98682
Washington St 98660
NW Washington St
3900-4499 98660
4501-4597 98663
4599-5299 98663
Watson Ave 98661
Wauna Vista Dr 98661
Weigel Ave 98660
Westgate Ave & Ct 98665
NW Westridge St 98665
NE Whitman Ave 98662
NW Whitney Rd 98665
Wichita Dr
6600-6699 98661
6701-6799 98661
6800-6899 98664
NE Wilding Rd 98686
NE Wildrose Dr 98682
NW Wildwood Dr 98665
Willamette Ct & Dr 98661
Wilson Ave 98661
Winchell Ave 98661
SE Windward Pl 98661
Wintler Dr 98661
NE Woodridge St 98664
NE Work Ave 98663
Wyoming St 98661
X St
201-997 98661
999-1899 98661
1901-2999 98661
3000-3098 98663
3100-3799 98663
Xavier Ave 98660
Y St
100-998 98661
1000-3099 98661
3200-3498 98663
3500-3699 98663
Yeoman Ave 98660
Z St
700-798 98661
800-3199 98661
3201-3299 98661
3500-3599 98663
3601-3699 98663

NUMBERED STREETS

NE 1st Ave 98685
NW 1st Ave
4900-4999 98663
7300-8199 98665
15000-15299 98685
NE 1st Cir 98684
NE 1st Ct
6700-6799 98665
11500-11599 98685
NW 1st Ct 98685
NE 1st Pl 98685
NW 1st Pl 98665
E 1st St 98661
NE 1st St 98684
SE 1st St 98684
NE 2nd Ave
5002-5498 98663
6800-7200 98665
11400-15399 98685

NW 2nd Ave
6800-7298 98665
10300-12998 98685
NE 2nd Cir 98684
SE 2nd Cir 98684
NE 2nd Ct 98685
NW 2nd Ct 98685
NE 2nd Loop 98684
NE 2nd Pl 98665
E 2nd St 98661
NE 2nd St
9700-10198 98664
11400-17699 98684
SE 2nd St
10500-10699 98664
15600-15698 98684
17300-17499 98683
NE 3rd Ave 98685
NW 3rd Ave
6800-9399 98665
10200-14899 98685
NE 3rd Cir 98684
NE 3rd Ct
6800-6899 98665
13500-14299 98685
NW 3rd Ct 98685
E 3rd Loop 98661
NW 3rd Pl 98685
NE 3rd St
9400-9498 98664
11500-17600 98684
SE 3rd St
10500-10699 98664
15200-17099 98684
17300-17499 98683
SE 3rd Way 98684
NE 4th Ave
5001-5199 98663
6300-6399 98665
10100-14799 98685
14801-14899 98685
6400-9799 98665
9801-9899 98665
9900-13500 98685
13502-15298 98685
NE 4th Cir
9700-9899 98664
15000-17699 98684
NE 4th Ct 98685
7300-9799 98665
11200-14899 98685
NW 4th Pl 98685
E 4th St 98661
9400-10399 98664
11200-11798 98684
11800-17499 98684
10500-10699 98664
15100-17099 98684
W 4th St 98660
NE 4th Way 98684
NE 5th Ave
7600-9899 98665
10901-11097 98685
NW 5th Ave
6500-7799 98665
10800-14799 98685
NE 5th Cir
9700-10499 98664
14000-14199 98684
SE 5th Cir 98684
NE 5th Ct 98685
NW 5th Pl 98685
E 5th St 98661
NE 5th St
8200-10399 98664
11701-11797 98684
SE 5th St
9500-9598 98664
11600-11798 98683
14800-17099 98684
W 5th St 98660
NE 5th Way 98664
NE 6th Ave
5800-8099 98665
9900-14599 98685
6601-6697 98665
6699-8799 98665
8801-8899 98665
10900-10998 98685
11000-15299 98685
NE 6th Cir
9801-9897 98664
9899-10099 98664
14400-17599 98684
NE 6th Ct 98685
E 6th St
100-198 98660
1601-1697 98661
1699-2899 98661
8200-10999 98664
11800-17499 98684
9500-10099 98664
14000-14200 98683
14202-14498 98683
16900-17099 98684
W 6th St 98660
SE 6th Way 98683
NE 7th Ave
9500-9599 98665
9900-14799 98685
8200-8399 98665
10501-10697 98685
10699-15099 98685
NE 7th Cir 98684
NE 7th Ct 98685
NW 7th Ct 98685
NE 7th Pl
12700-12799 98684
13900-14099 98685
NW 7th Pl 98685
E 7th St 98660
8200-10999 98664
11301-11697 98684
11699-17599 98684
9600-9799 98664
11601-11697 98683
11699-14299 98683
14301-14699 98683
W 7th St 98660
NE 7th Way 98684
SE 7th Way 98683
NE 8th Ave
8301-8597 98665
10900-13399 98685
NW 8th Ave
5300-5699 98663
7900-9799 98665
12000-14299 98685
NE 8th Cir
9800-10999 98664
16000-16099 98684
NE 8th Ct
5800-5899 98665
12400-14599 98685
NW 8th Ct 98685
NE 8th Pl 98684
NW 8th Pl 98685
E 8th St
101-199 98660
1900-4000 98661
NE 8th St
9000-10799 98664
11400-17199 98684
SE 8th St 98683
W 8th St 98660
NE 8th Way 98664
NW 8th Way 98685
NE 9th Ave 98685
NW 9th Ave
7400-7498 98665
10900-15099 98685
NE 9th Cir 98684
NE 9th Ct 98685
NW 9th Pl 98685
E 9th St
100-199 98660
1800-2899 98661
NE 9th St
8000-10400 98664
11000-11198 98684
SE 9th St 98683
W 9th St 98660
NE 9th Way 98684
NE 10th Ave
6001-6497 98665
10700-10798 98685
NW 10th Ave
7200-9799 98665
11600-12098 98685
NE 10th Cir 98684
NW 10th Ct
7800-8699 98665
11501-11597 98685
NE 10th Pl 98684
NW 10th Pl 98685
NE 10th St
8301-8397 98664
12201-12297 98684
SE 10th St
9900-11400 98664
12500-12799 98683
NE 10th Way 98684
NE 11th Ave
6200-6299 98665
10600-13399 98685
NW 11th Ave
7300-9700 98665
9900-15800 98685
NE 11th Cir 98684
SE 11th Cir
10500-10799 98664
13600-15399 98683
NE 11th Ct 98685
NW 11th Ct
7901-7997 98665
11700-12499 98685
NE 11th Pl 98685
NW 11th Pl 98685
E 11th St
100-198 98660
1901-1997 98661
NE 11th St
8700-10899 98664
12600-17199 98684
SE 11th St
10000-10599 98664
11900-18799 98683
W 11th St 98660
NE 11th Way 98664
SE 11th Way 98683
NE 12th Ave
13318B-13338B 98685
4300-4599 98663
6300-7100 98665
7102-7198 98665
11200-13319 98685
13321-13399 98685
NW 12th Ave
7800-9899 98665
9900-11499 98685
SE 12th Cir
10400-10499 98664
13900-18399 98683
NE 12th Ct
12400-12499 98685
NW 12th Ct
8600-9599 98665
SE 12th Dr
17500-17899 98683
NE 12th Loop
15800-15899 98684
NE 12th Pl
9500-9699 98664
E 12th St
100-198 98660
200-300 98660
302-398 98660
2000-3599 98661
NE 12th St
7800-8799 98664
12200-12298 98684
12300-17099 98684
SE 12th St
16301A-16333A 98683
16331B-16333B 98683
9500-10399 98664
14000-16299 98683
W 12th St
200-1200 98660
NE 12th Way
9200-9399 98664
9401-10599 98664
12600-15799 98684
SE 12th Way
18800-19099 98683
NE 13th Ave
7101-7497 98665
9901-9997 98686
12300-14599 98685
NW 13th Ave
7400-7498 98665
11900-14799 98685
NE 13th Cir 98684
SE 13th Cir
8800-10499 98664
15200-18699 98683
NE 13th Ct 98685
NW 13th Ct
7300-8699 98665
11300-11899 98685
E 13th Pl 98661
NW 13th Pl 98685
E 13th St
100-500 98660
2000-4599 98661
NE 13th St
8300-8398 98664
12200-12298 98684
SE 13th St
9500-10599 98664
11900-18999 98683
W 13th St 98660
NE 13th Way 98684
NE 14th Ave
4300-4500 98663
6600-6799 98665
11600-13099 98685
NW 14th Ave
7800-9700 98665
10400-15099 98685
NE 14th Cir
10100-10199 98664
12500-16199 98684
SE 14th Cir
10300-10399 98664
11900-18699 98683
E 14th Ct 98661
NE 14th Ct 98665
NW 14th Ct
7900-8499 98665
9900-13499 98685
NE 14th Ln 98664
NW 14th Pl 98685
E 14th St 98661
NE 14th St
7100-7398 98664
11000-11098 98684
SE 14th St
9500-10599 98664
13600-13798 98683
W 14th St 98660
NE 14th Way
8700-9399 98664
15000-15099 98684
SE 14th Way 98683
NE 15th Ave
4201-4597 98663
8700-9399 98665
12400-12900 98685
NW 15th Ave
7500-9800 98665
9900-15099 98685
NE 15th Cir
10200-10299 98664
14300-15699 98684
SE 15th Cir
8500-10699 98664
14200-14399 98683
NE 15th Ct
11200-11399 98685
15600-15699 98686
NW 15th Ct
8000-8499 98665
10500-11499 98685
NE 15th Pl 98686
E 15th St
100-198 98663
3401-3497 98661
NE 15th St
8300-10999 98664
11500-16399 98684
SE 15th St
9500-10799 98664
11800-19199 98683
W 15th St 98660
SE 15th Way 98683
NE 16th Ave
6400-6498 98665
6500-8799 98665
12400-14099 98685
NW 16th Ave
7300-7398 98665
7400-8399 98665
9901-9997 98685
9999-13800 98685
13802-15898 98685
NE 16th Cir
14000-16199 98684
SE 16th Cir
7700-11599 98664
12000-17599 98683
NW 16th Ct
8400-8499 98665
NE 16th Ln
8500-8599 98664
SE 16th Ln
18500-18599 98683
E 16th Pl
2900-2999 98661
E 16th St
4012A-4022A 98661
4012B-4022B 98661
100-198 98663
200-700 98663
702-798 98663
2100-2198 98661
2200-4013 98661
4015-4299 98661
NE 16th St
8000-10799 98664
11300-11498 98684
11500-15099 98684
SE 16th St
9700-10198 98664
10200-10799 98664
12500-19099 98683
W 16th St
200-1099 98660
NE 16th Way
8700-8899 98664
NE 17th Ave
5800-5898 98665
14501-15099 98686
NW 17th Ave
8001-8097 98665
10001-10097 98685
NE 17th Cir
8900-10299 98664
12300-15599 98684
SE 17th Cir
8400-10899 98664
12500-17699 98683
NE 17th Ct 98686
SE 17th Dr 98683
SE 17th Ln 98683
NW 17th Pl 98685
E 17th St
100-298 98663
2101-2197 98661
NE 17th St
8700-9199 98664
12800-13099 98684
SE 17th St
7400-10700 98664
12000-19099 98683
W 17th St 98660
NE 17th Way 98664
SE 17th Way 98683
NE 18th Ave
4900-5299 98663
7900-8398 98665
12100-12798 98685
15000-15899 98686
NW 18th Ave
8600-9699 98665
10500-10998 98685
SE 18th Cir
9701-10797 98664
12500-18699 98683
NE 18th Ct
4100-4799 98663
15600-15899 98686
E 18th St 98661
NE 18th St
6501-6597 98661
10500-10599 98664
11000-11698 98684
SE 18th St
10900-11199 98664
12700-19099 98683
SE 18th Way 98683
NE 19th Ave
4800-4898 98663
6000-9800 98665
10400-15799 98686
NW 19th Ave
7501-7597 98665
10000-10098 98685
NE 19th Cir
7500-8099 98664
11300-17799 98684
SE 19th Cir 98683
NE 19th Ct
7800-7998 98665
15200-15899 98686
NW 19th Ct
9000-9099 98665
11900-12099 98685
NW 19th Loop 98685
NE 19th Pl
7700-7799 98664
9700-9799 98665
E 19th St
100-198 98663
2500-2900 98661
NE 19th St
9200-10799 98664
12400-17099 98684
SE 19th St
10800-11400 98664
13100-18999 98683
W 19th St 98660
NE 19th Way
7700-7899 98664
16900-17099 98684
SE 19th Way 98683
NE 20th Ave
4900-5099 98663
6501-6597 98665
10200-15599 98686
NW 20th Ave
8801-8897 98665
9900-9998 98685
NE 20th Cir
10200-10399 98664
14700-14899 98684
SE 20th Cir 98683
NE 20th Ct
6000-6199 98665
10700-10899 98686
NW 20th Ct
6301-6599 98660
13800-14899 98685
NE 20th Pl
8200-9599 98665
15700-15899 98686
E 20th St
101-197 98663
2400-3099 98661
NE 20th St
7600-10699 98664
12400-18499 98684
SE 20th St 98683
W 20th St 98660
SE 20th Way 98683
NE 21st Ave
4900-4999 98663
6000-9099 98665
NW 21st Ave
8501-8597 98665
9901-10097 98685
SE 21st Cir 98683
NE 21st Ct
9100-9299 98665
10400-10699 98686
NE 21st Pl 98665
E 21st St 98661
NE 21st St
7601-9197 98664
12300-19199 98684
SE 21st St
9200-9298 98664
13200-18999 98683
W 21st St 98660
NE 21st Way
8000-8099 98664
12400-12499 98684
SE 21st Way 98683
NE 22nd Ave
4500-4598 98663
8200-8299 98665
14400-15799 98686
NW 22nd Ave 98685
NE 22nd Cir
9000-9899 98664
17700-17899 98684
SE 22nd Cir 98683
NE 22nd Ct 98665
NW 22nd Ct
9400-9499 98665
11100-12899 98685
SE 22nd Dr 98683
NE 22nd Pl
8300-8399 98665
10400-10899 98686
NW 22nd Pl 98685
E 22nd St
200-298 98663
2600-2699 98661
NE 22nd St
7900-10599 98664
10900-18299 98684
SE 22nd St 98683
W 22nd St 98660
NE 22nd Way 98684
SE 22nd Way 98683
NE 23rd Ave
5400-5699 98663
9100-9699 98665
9900-15799 98686
NW 23rd Ave
8800-9599 98665
10100-14899 98685
NE 23rd Cir 98684
SE 23rd Cir
10700-10899 98664
13800-18699 98683
NE 23rd Ct 98665
NW 23rd Ct
7000-9599 98665
10900-15899 98685
SE 23rd Dr 98683
NE 23rd St
10200-10599 98664
11200-11298 98684
SE 23rd St
10800-10898 98664
13500-19099 98683
W 23rd St 98660
NE 23rd Way 98684
SE 23rd Way 98683
NE 24th Ave
4500-4598 98663
8800-8999 98665
10500-15899 98686
NW 24th Ave
8800-8898 98665
10000-14799 98685
NE 24th Cir
10100-10299 98664
13000-13099 98684
SE 24th Cir 98683
NE 24th Ct 98665
NW 24th Ct 98685
NW 24th Pl 98665

E 24th St
200-298 98663
2800-3200 98661
NE 24th St
10200-10299 98664
10900-18099 98684
SE 24th St 98683
W 24th St 98660
SE 24th Way 98683
NE 25th Ave
7800-9799 98665
10200-15899 98686
NW 25th Ave
6900-6998 98665
11700-15799 98685
NE 25th Cir
8600-9199 98662
15200-18399 98684
SE 25th Cir 98683
NE 25th Ct
4500-4899 98663
9200-9499 98665
15000-15299 98686
NW 25th Ct 98685
NE 25th Pl
5200-5299 98663
8300-8399 98665
10400-10799 98686
E 25th St
100-799 98663
2100-2298 98661
NE 25th St
7501-8397 98662
10300-10400 98664
11200-18599 98684
SE 25th St 98683
W 25th St 98660
NE 25th Way 98684
SE 25th Way 98683
NE 26th Ave
4401-4497 98663
7600-9899 98665
10900-15699 98686
NW 26th Ave 98685
W 26th Ave 98660
SE 26th Cir
11500-11599 98664
13400-13599 98683
NE 26th Ct
4300-4499 98663
8100-9499 98665
13600-15199 98686
NW 26th Ct 98665
SE 26th Dr 98683
W 26th Ext 98660
NE 26th Pl
8300-9598 98665
11800-11899 98686
E 26th St
700-1098 98663
2100-3399 98661
NE 26th St
9900-10099 98662
10800-18399 98684
SE 26th St 98683
NE 26th Way
8701-8799 98662
17200-17699 98684
NE 27th Ave
6800-6898 98665
10000-15399 98686
NW 27th Ave
9100-9198 98665
10000-14699 98685
E 27th Cir 98661
NE 27th Cir
8600-10299 98662
15700-16099 98684
SE 27th Cir 98683
NE 27th Ct
4900-4999 98663
9900-14399 98686
NW 27th Ct 98685
NE 27th Pl 98686
E 27th St
101-197 98663
2101-2197 98661

NE 27th St
7700-10099 98662
12300-18099 98684
SE 27th St 98683
W 27th St 98660
NE 27th Way 98684
NE 28th Ave
4400-4899 98663
6800-8999 98665
10001-10497 98686
NW 28th Ave
9600-9899 98665
10200-13299 98685
NE 28th Cir 98662
SE 28th Cir 98683
NE 28th Ct
5100-5299 98663
8300-8399 98665
10200-15799 98686
NW 28th Ct
9200-9499 98665
10400-14099 98685
NE 28th Pl
8401-8597 98665
9900-10199 98686
NW 28th Pl 98685
E 28th St
100-1899 98663
2200-3200 98661
NE 28th St
7800-9800 98662
11200-18600 98682
SE 28th St 98683
W 28th St 98660
NE 28th Way 98662
SE 28th Way 98683
NE 29th Ave
4200-4398 98663
8200-8799 98665
10400-15699 98686
NW 29th Ave
9100-9899 98665
10000-14399 98685
NE 29th Cir
5400-5499 98661
11400-11499 98682
SE 29th Cir 98683
NE 29th Ct
9400-9499 98665
10701-10797 98686
NW 29th Ct 98685
NW 29th Pl 98685
E 29th St
101-197 98663
2301-2397 98661
NE 29th St
7800-10199 98662
11500-18199 98682
SE 29th St 98683
W 29th St 98660
NE 29th Way 98662
NE 30th Ave
5300-5799 98663
7800-7998 98665
8000-9599 98665
10600-15800 98686
15802-15898 98686
NW 30th Ave 98685
NE 30th Cir
9300-9999 98662
11400-18299 98682
SE 30th Cir 98683
NE 30th Ct
9600-9799 98665
11600-14399 98686
NW 30th Ct 98685
E 30th St
100-498 98663
500-2300 98663
2302-2398 98663
2401-2497 98661
2499-3399 98661
7800-8799 98662
12500-12698 98682
12700-18599 98682
SE 30th St 98683
W 30th St 98660

NE 31st Ave
6801-6897 98665
10400-15799 98686
NW 31st Ave
9601-9697 98665
10400-13199 98685
NE 31st Cir
8600-8699 98662
18100-18199 98682
SE 31st Cir 98683
NE 31st Ct
5100-5199 98663
8400-8799 98665
14000-14299 98686
NW 31st Ct 98685
E 31st St 98663
NE 31st St
9700-9798 98662
11600-17799 98682
SE 31st St 98683
W 31st St 98660
NE 31st Way 98682
SE 31st Way 98683
E 32nd Ave 98661
NE 32nd Ave
8800-9800 98665
11100-11299 98686
NW 32nd Ave 98685
NE 32nd Cir
10300-10499 98662
13700-18599 98682
W 32nd Cir 98660
NE 32nd Ct
4800-4899 98663
10700-11599 98686
NW 32nd Ct 98685
NW 32nd Dr 98685
W 32nd Pl 98660
E 32nd St
100-2499 98663
2501-2697 98661
NE 32nd St
6201-6297 98661
7800-8199 98662
11500-18499 98682
SE 32nd St 98683
W 32nd St 98660
NE 32nd Way 98682
NE 33rd Ave
5600-5698 98663
10100-14299 98686
NW 33rd Ave 98685
NE 33rd Cir
5900-6199 98661
13100-18299 98682
NE 33rd Ct
9400-9599 98665
10200-10399 98686
NW 33rd Ct 98685
E 33rd Pl 98661
NE 33rd Pl 98665
E 33rd St
100-2600 98663
2605-2605 98661
NE 33rd St
6400-6699 98661
8600-8899 98662
11900-18199 98682
SE 33rd St 98683
W 33rd St 98660
SE 33rd Way 98683
W 33rd Way 98660
NE 34th Ave
7500-9198 98665
11500-11599 98686
NW 34th Ave 98685
NE 34th Cir
4300-4399 98661
10200-10399 98662
11000-13399 98682
SE 34th Cir 98683
NE 34th Ct 98686
NW 34th Ct 98685
E 34th St 98663
NE 34th St
4701-4797 98661
8200-8498 98662

12600-12698 98682
SE 34th St 98683
W 34th St 98660
NE 34th Way
4200-4299 98661
8600-8799 98662
SE 34th Way 98683
W 34th Way 98660
NE 35th Ave
4100-6399 98661
8000-9799 98665
11300-14400 98686
NW 35th Ave 98685
NE 35th Cir
3900-6199 98661
11900-17599 98682
SE 35th Cir 98683
NE 35th Ct
8900-8999 98665
12600-12699 98686
NW 35th Ct 98685
SE 35th Loop 98683
E 35th St 98663
NE 35th St
3600-3699 98661
10000-10399 98662
12000-16599 98682
SE 35th St 98683
W 35th St 98660
SE 35th Way 98683
W 35th Way 98660
NE 36th Ave
3401-3497 98661
7400-8498 98665
10500-12699 98686
NW 36th Ave 98685
NE 36th Cir
8400-10299 98662
13100-13199 98682
SE 36th Cir 98683
NE 36th Ct
8100-8399 98665
9900-11699 98686
NE 36th Pl
4200-4299 98661
9500-9799 98665
13100-13399 98686
E 36th St 98663
NE 36th St
8600-8999 98662
12000-17499 98682
SE 36th St 98683
W 36th St 98660
NE 36th Way 98682
SE 36th Way 98683
NE 37th Ave
4101-4199 98661
7000-7298 98665
10500-16699 98686
NW 37th Ave 98685
NE 37th Cir
3700-3703 98665
8400-8599 98662
11000-17199 98682
SE 37th Cir 98683
NE 37th Ct 98686
NW 37th Ct 98685
E 37th St 98663
NE 37th St
3500-6199 98661
8600-10199 98662
11800-18000 98682
SE 37th St 98683
W 37th St 98660
NE 38th Ave
3501-3597 98661
8000-9499 98665
10700-11299 98686
NW 38th Ave 98685
NE 38th Cir 98682
SE 38th Cir 98683
NE 38th Ct
8200-8399 98665
10500-11499 98686
NW 38th Ct 98685
E 38th Loop 98663
E 38th St 98663

NE 38th St
3600-6499 98661
12900-16599 98682
SE 38th St 98683
W 38th St 98660
NE 38th Way 98682
NE 39th Ave
4000-5199 98661
8400-9600 98665
9900-9988 98686
NW 39th Ave 98685
SE 39th Cir 98683
NE 39th Ct 98661
NW 39th Ct 98685
E 39th St 98663
NE 39th St
3200-5999 98661
8600-10199 98662
10900-10998 98682
SE 39th St 98683
W 39th St 98660
SE 39th Way 98683
E 40th Ave 98661
NE 40th Ave
3600-7200 98661
7202-7298 98661
9100-9199 98665
11900-17200 98686
17202-17298 98686
NW 40th Ave 98685
NE 40th Cir
4800-4899 98661
12000-15599 98682
SE 40th Cir 98683
NE 40th Dr 98665
NE 40th Pl
8800-8999 98665
11800-11899 98686
15300-15399 98682
E 40th St 98663
NE 40th St
4200-4698 98661
4700-7099 98661
7101-7199 98661
13800-17500 98682
17502-17698 98682
NW 40th St 98660
SE 40th St 98683
E 41st Ave 98661
NE 41st Ave
5400-5999 98661
8200-9899 98665
10100-10198 98686
NW 41st Ave 98685
NE 41st Cir
1500-1798 98663
5800-6299 98661
14200-17099 98682
SE 41st Cir 98683
NE 41st Ct
3800-6099 98661
9900-13099 98686
SE 41st Dr 98683
SE 41st Loop 98683
E 41st St 98663
NE 41st St
3300-6499 98661
7200-7400 98662
10400-16099 98682
NW 41st St 98660
NE 41st Way 98661
SE 41st Way 98683
NE 42nd Ave
4001-4097 98661
9001-9099 98665
10901-12297 98686
NW 42nd Ave 98685
NE 42nd Cir
2700-2799 98663
5200-5299 98661
SE 42nd Cir 98683
NE 42nd Ct
5100-5199 98661
8700-8799 98665
10400-12099 98686
NW 42nd Ct 98685
NE 42nd Pl 98661
NE 42nd St
2800-3100 98663

3500-6699 98661
10600-10698 98682
NW 42nd St 98660
SE 42nd St 98683
NE 42nd Way 98661
NE 43rd Ave
7000-7399 98661
9100-9899 98665
9900-12799 98686
NW 43rd Ave 98685
NE 43rd Cir 98682
NE 43rd Ct
5500-5699 98661
13200-13799 98686
NW 43rd Ct 98685
SE 43rd Ln 98683
NE 43rd Pl
3300-3399 98661
10500-10599 98686
E 43rd St 98663
NE 43rd St
1300-3199 98663
3500-7199 98661
7200-7499 98662
10400-24899 98682
NW 43rd St 98660
SE 43rd St 98683
NE 43rd Way
5500-5599 98661
7200-7499 98662
15800-16499 98682
SE 43rd Way 98683
NE 44th Ave
3900-4999 98661
9200-9599 98665
12000-13100 98686
NW 44th Ave 98685
NE 44th Cir
6100-7199 98661
14900-15099 98682
NE 44th Ct
9100-9199 98665
9900-12699 98686
NW 44th Ct 98685
SE 44th Ln 98683
E 44th St 98663
NE 44th St
3303A-3321A 98663
3400-3698 98661
10400-241099 98682
NW 44th St 98660
NE 44th Way
6300-6399 98661
7200-7499 98662
SE 44th Way 98683
NE 45th Ave
4100-5999 98661
8800-8900 98665
10300-13100 98686
NW 45th Ave 98685
NE 45th Cir
2300-2499 98663
4100-6499 98661
12600-12699 98682
NE 45th Ct
5001-5099 98661
13400-14199 98686
NW 45th Ct 98685
NE 45th Pl
4600-4699 98661
9100-9799 98665
13700-13799 98686
SE 45th Pl 98661
E 45th St 98663
NE 45th St
1000-3300 98663
3501-5799 98661
7401-7497 98662
10600-16599 98682
NW 45th St 98660
NE 45th Way 98661
NE 46th Ave
5400-5699 98661
10201-11297 98686
NW 46th Ave 98685
NE 46th Cir 98661
NE 46th Ct
9600-9899 98665

12300-12399 98686
NW 46th Ct 98685
NE 46th St
2200-2899 98663
4500-5799 98661
10400-15499 98682
NW 46th St 98663
NE 47th Ave
4000-7600 98661
9400-9599 98665
11200-17899 98686
NW 47th Ave 98685
NE 47th Cir
9300-9399 98665
13200-15499 98682
NE 47th Ct
9800-9899 98665
11400-12099 98686
NE 47th Rd 98665
NE 47th St
2500-3099 98663
4000-6599 98661
10500-16099 98682
NE 47th Way 98682
NE 48th Ave
3800-4098 98661
11200-13799 98686
NW 48th Ave 98685
NE 48th Cir
5100-6599 98661
10800-20499 98682
NW 48th Cir 98663
NW 48th Ct 98685
NE 48th St
1301-1397 98663
4000-5999 98661
10900-15899 98682
NW 48th St 98663
NE 49th Ave 98661
NW 49th Ave 98685
NE 49th Cir 98682
NW 49th Cir 98663
NE 49th Ct
6100-6299 98661
11900-15099 98686
NE 49th Pl 98686
NE 49th St
1201-1497 98663
3500-5599 98661
11201-11297 98682
NW 49th St 98663
NE 49th Way 98682
NE 50th Ave
3300-6999 98661
9400-9698 98665
9900-9998 98686
NW 50th Ave 98685
NE 50th Cir
2600-3199 98663
4100-4899 98661
13100-15599 98682
NE 50th Ct
3400-4899 98661
9200-9399 98665
NW 50th Ct 98685
NW 50th Dr 98685
NE 50th Pl 98661
NE 50th St
4000-4098 98661
12400-24599 98682
NW 50th St 98663
NE 50th Way 98682
NE 51st Ave
4200-7500 98661
7502-7598 98661
8600-9000 98665
9002-9098 98665
10100-10199 98686
10201-10299 98686
NW 51st Ave 98685
NE 51st Cir
5400-6799 98661
10400-11200 98682
11202-11398 98682
NE 51st Ct
3200-5699 98661
10900-11099 98686

NW 51st Ct 98685
NE 51st St
1900-1998 98663
2000-3199 98663
3500-5899 98661
7300-7498 98662
7500-7700 98662
7702-8198 98662
12700-25099 98682
NW 51st St 98663
NE 51st Way 98662
NE 52nd Ave
4600-6699 98661
9001-9097 98665
NW 52nd Ave 98685
NE 52nd Cir
4800-5399 98661
12700-14699 98682
NE 52nd Ct
5600-6099 98661
7900-8099 98665
10300-10599 98686
NW 52nd Ct 98685
NE 52nd Pl 98661
NE 52nd St
201-3300 98663
3400-6799 98661
7500-9399 98662
12400-14499 98682
NW 52nd St 98663
NE 52nd Way 98682
NE 53rd Ave
5800-7700 98661
9500-9599 98665
9900-17899 98686
NW 53rd Ave 98685
NE 53rd Cir
2000-2199 98663
3800-6799 98661
NW 53rd Cir 98663
NE 53rd Ct
5100-5399 98661
10800-18199 98686
NW 53rd Ct 98685
NE 53rd Pl 98661
NE 53rd St
2200-2398 98663
3400-5999 98661
7500-10599 98662
12900-26099 98682
NW 53rd St 98663
NE 53rd Way 98662
NE 54th Ave
3300-3398 98661
11100-11298 98686
NE 54th Cir 98662
NW 54th Cir 98663
NE 54th Ct
5100-6699 98661
9400-9499 98665
9900-11799 98686
NE 54th Pl 98661
NE 54th St
2001-2197 98663
3400-7099 98661
7500-7598 98662
12900-23899 98682
NW 54th St 98663
NE 54th Way
13824A-13834A 98682
7900-7999 98662
13800-13824 98682
NW 54th Way 98663
NE 55th Ave
3800-7799 98661
8300-8799 98665
10100-10199 98686
NE 55th Cir
4600-6199 98661
8500-8599 98662
NE 55th Ct 98661
NW 55th Ct
500-599 98663
14200-14299 98685
NW 55th Loop 98663
NE 55th Pl 98661

NE 55th St
3800-7099 98661
7200-8499 98662
12900-13099 98682
NW 55th St 98663
NE 56th Ave
3900-7499 98661
9401-9499 98665
11400-11498 98686
NW 56th Ave 98685
NE 56th Cir
5900-5999 98661
8500-8599 98662
11800-12000 98682
NW 56th Cir 98663
NE 56th Ct
5900-7399 98661
9500-9699 98665
NE 56th Pl 98661
NE 56th St
3500-7199 98661
7301-7597 98662
12301-12597 98682
NW 56th St 98663
NE 56th Way 98661
NW 56th Way 98663
NE 57th Ave
2900-6799 98661
11400-15799 98686
NE 57th Cir
6200-6299 98661
7600-7799 98662
NE 57th Ct
6100-7699 98661
12600-14899 98686
NE 57th Pl 98661
NE 57th St
2300-2699 98663
3800-3898 98661
7301-8497 98662
13500-13599 98682
NW 57th St 98663
NE 58th Ave
6200-7700 98661
7900-8000 98665
10900-18700 98686
NE 58th Cir 98661
NE 58th Ct 98661
NE 58th Pl
5400-5499 98661
13900-14199 98686
NE 58th St
2301-2397 98663
4400-4498 98661
7200-10499 98662
16200-25599 98682
NW 58th St 98663
NE 58th Way 98662
NE 59th Ave
3800-6299 98661
9600-9698 98665
9900-9999 98686
NE 59th Cir
4900-5899 98661
7600-8699 98662
NE 59th Ct 98661
NE 59th St
100-198 98665
2400-3399 98663
3400-3699 98661
7201-7397 98662
13100-13198 98682
NW 59th St
100-199 98665
500-1699 98663
NE 60th Ave
3700-7199 98661
9701-9799 98665
11700-11899 98686
NE 60th Cir
5900-5999 98661
8001-8099 98662
NE 60th Ct
5401-5406 98661
10600-10699 98686
NE 60th St
1500-2199 98665
3400-6999 98661
7600-10199 98662
16200-26199 98682
NW 60th St 98663
NE 60th Way
7600-7799 98662
11700-12499 98682
NE 61st Ave
3801-3897 98661
10900-11599 98686
NE 61st Cir
1800-1899 98665
5900-5999 98661
7600-10199 98662
13200-13299 98682
NW 61st Cir 98663
NE 61st Ct
3700-5899 98661
9700-9899 98665
NE 61st Pl 98686
NE 61st St
200-799 98665
5000-6998 98661
8000-9999 98662
13700-22999 98682
NW 61st St 98663
NE 61st Way 98662
NE 62nd Ave
3000-7499 98661
8801-9197 98665
NE 62nd Cir
5700-5899 98661
7900-10199 98662
13900-13999 98682
NE 62nd Ct
6700-6899 98661
10600-10699 98686
NE 62nd St
5700-7199 98661
7300-8699 98662
13100-15599 98682
NW 62nd St 98663
NE 62nd Way 98662
NE 63rd Ave 98661
NE 63rd Cir 98682
NE 63rd Ct 98686
NE 63rd St
301-997 98665
5901-5997 98661
7200-10499 98662
12300-23599 98682
NW 63rd St 98663
NE 64th Ave
1700-5799 98661
8600-8799 98665
10901-10997 98686
NE 64th Cir
7400-8499 98662
13701-13797 98682
NE 64th Ct
7000-7399 98661
10000-10099 98686
SE 64th Ct 98661
NE 64th Pl 98661
NE 64th St
1000-1499 98665
3400-3498 98661
7800-10799 98662
13500-13598 98682
NE 65th Ave
2200-2398 98661
10100-17399 98686
NE 65th Cir
8400-10199 98662
16400-16699 98682
NE 65th Ct
4300-7799 98661
9900-17899 98686
NE 65th Pl 98661
NE 65th St
300-398 98665
2901-3097 98663
3400-5599 98661
7200-11899 98662
11900-19499 98682
NW 65th St 98663

NE 66th Ave
3100-3998 98661
12300-13099 98686
NE 66th Cir
200-2199 98665
5600-5699 98661
11100-11699 98662
16300-16399 98682
NW 66th Cir 98663
NE 66th Dr 98661
NE 66th St
3100A-3118A 98663
300-498 98665
3101-3399 98663
7900-10700 98662
13500-13699 98682
NE 66th Way
7400-7799 98662
16300-16699 98682
NE 67th Ave
7400-7499 98661
10400-10599 98686
NE 67th Cir
1600-1699 98665
5600-6699 98661
7800-7899 98662
NE 67th Ct 98661
NE 67th St
1900-1999 98665
5200-7199 98661
7500-11000 98662
13500-16599 98682
NE 67th Way 98661
NE 68th Ave
5100-5699 98661
10400-13099 98686
NE 68th Cir
6600-6699 98661
10700-10899 98662
NE 68th Dr 98661
NE 68th St
100-3100 98665
3400-6599 98661
8901-8997 98662
16300-24799 98682
NW 68th St 98665
NE 68th Way 98682
NE 69th Ave
5500-7499 98661
10400-10599 98686
NE 69th Cir
2800-2899 98665
5200-6399 98661
9900-10699 98662
NW 69th Cir 98665
NE 69th St
100-1499 98665
5600-7199 98661
7200-11499 98662
14100-16599 98682
NW 69th St 98665
NE 70th Ave
7200-7298 98661
11301-11397 98686
NE 70th Cir
100-2799 98665
5300-5499 98661
9100-10999 98662
12400-16499 98682
NW 70th Cir 98665
NE 70th Ct
6100-7499 98661
10400-10499 98686
NE 70th St
1600-1698 98665
5501-5597 98661
7200-10899 98662
14000-15899 98682
NW 70th St 98665
NE 71st Ave
5500-6299 98661
10400-12998 98686
NE 71st Cir
10800-10899 98662
14400-14499 98682
NE 71st Ct
6000-6199 98661
15600-15899 98686
NE 71st Dr 98665
NE 71st Loop 98662
NE 71st St
100-2800 98665
5100-5799 98661
7100-7198 98662
12000-16499 98682
NE 71st Way 98682
NE 72nd Ave
3901-4097 98661
7800-9700 98665
9901-9997 98686
NE 72nd Cir
100-2899 98665
5100-7099 98661
8400-10099 98662
16000-16499 98682
NW 72nd Cir 98665
NE 72nd Dr 98661
NE 72nd Pl 98662
NE 72nd St
900-3299 98665
8800-9699 98662
12100-18199 98682
NW 72nd St 98665
NE 72nd Way 98665
NE 73rd Ave 98662
SE 73rd Ave 98664
NE 73rd Cir
5800-6699 98661
9400-9699 98662
14800-15199 98682
NW 73rd Cir 98665
NE 73rd Ct 98662
NE 73rd St
101-197 98665
6500-7199 98661
7201-8997 98662
12000-22499 98682
NW 73rd St 98665
NE 74th Ave 98662
NE 74th Cir
5100-6099 98661
14800-16499 98682
NE 74th Ct 98662
NE 74th St
3600-3699 98665
6100-6599 98661
8900-10499 98662
12100-16099 98682
NW 74th St 98665
NE 74th Way 98662
NE 75th Ave 98662
NE 75th Cir
5100-5199 98661
9800-9899 98662
12000-21199 98682
NW 75th Cir 98665
NE 75th Ct 98662
SE 75th Ct 98664
NE 75th Pl 98662
NE 75th St
1100-1299 98665
5500-7199 98661
9000-9098 98662
12400-12699 98682
NW 75th St 98665
NE 75th Way 98662
NE 76th Ave 98662
NE 76th Cir
6000-6799 98661
10000-10099 98662
15200-15399 98682
NW 76th Cir 98665
NE 76th St
100-199 98665
5100-6699 98661
8500-8598 98662
11701-11997 98682
NW 76th St 98665
NE 76th Way
9700-9899 98662
13100-16499 98682
NE 77th Ave
2100-2499 98664
4400-4598 98662

NE 77th Cir
5300-5399 98661
10000-11099 98662
15900-16399 98682
NE 77th Ct
1800-1899 98664
5400-5499 98662
SE 77th Ct 98664
NE 77th Pl
1900-1999 98664
6300-6499 98662
NE 77th St
101-199 98665
5700-6198 98661
9100-9299 98662
12000-27199 98682
NW 77th St 98665
NE 77th Way 98662
NE 78th Ave
2100-2399 98664
2700-6499 98662
SE 78th Ave 98664
NE 78th Cir
8900-10099 98662
13500-13599 98682
NE 78th Ct 98664
NW 78th Rd 98665
NE 78th St
100-198 98665
7700-7798 98662
12000-22999 98682
NW 78th St 98665
NE 78th Way 98682
NE 79th Ave
1900-2399 98664
3301-5397 98662
NE 79th Cir
10800-10999 98662
13500-16199 98682
NW 79th Cir 98665
NE 79th Ct
2400-2499 98664
6200-9299 98662
SE 79th Ct 98664
NE 79th St
2400-2499 98665
8700-10299 98662
11700-16599 98682
NW 79th St 98665
NE 79th Way 98682
NE 80th Ave 98662
SE 80th Ave 98664
NE 80th Cir
9200-9399 98662
13500-14899 98682
NE 80th Ct 98662
NE 80th Pl 98664
NE 80th St
2300-3899 98665
8700-8798 98662
11700-11798 98682
NW 80th St 98665
NE 80th Way 98682
NE 81st Ave
2100-2299 98664
2500-15899 98662
NE 81st Cir
3500-3699 98665
14000-18199 98682
NW 81st Cir 98665
NE 81st Ct 98662
NE 81st Loop 98662
NE 81st St
301-397 98665
8900-10699 98662
12300-12398 98682
NE 81st Way
9200-11099 98662
15100-15399 98682
NE 82nd Ave
401-997 98664
5100-16399 98662
NE 82nd Cir
2600-2899 98665
9100-9399 98662
13500-15799 98682
NW 82nd Cir 98665

NE 82nd Ct
1500-1599 98664
5800-9399 98662
SE 82nd Ct 98664
NE 82nd St
100-4399 98665
8800-9198 98662
13800-16599 98682
NW 82nd St 98665
NE 82nd Way 98665
NE 83rd Ave 98662
NE 83rd Cir
3700-3799 98665
9500-9899 98662
13500-16099 98682
NE 83rd Ct
1500-1599 98664
5800-9899 98662
SE 83rd Ct 98664
NE 83rd Pl 98662
NE 83rd St
23621A-23641A 98682
101-197 98665
9800-10399 98662
12100-12198 98682
NW 83rd St 98665
NE 83rd Way
2500-2500 98665
14400-14698 98682
NE 84th Ave
900-998 98664
2400-2598 98662
NE 84th Cir
500-699 98665
10600-11299 98662
17700-18199 98682
NW 84th Cir 98665
NE 84th Ct 98662
NW 84th Ct 98665
SE 84th Ct 98664
NE 84th Loop 98662
NW 84th Loop 98665
NE 84th Pl 98662
NE 84th St
1900-6799 98665
8600-11199 98662
13500-15599 98682
NW 84th St 98665
NE 84th Way
1800-1999 98665
9600-9799 98662
11800-11899 98682
NE 85th Ave
1000-1299 98664
2600-2698 98662
NE 85th Cir
500-2899 98665
10200-11299 98662
14500-15899 98682
NE 85th Dr 98662
NE 85th St
300-3899 98665
10500-11099 98662
12700-22499 98682
NW 85th St 98665
NE 85th Way
500-699 98665
17900-18199 98682
NE 86th Ave
1000-2399 98664
2400-10499 98662
NE 86th Cir
2000-2899 98665
10700-11299 98662
13800-15899 98682
NW 86th Cir 98665
NE 86th Ct 98662
SE 86th Ct 98664
NE 86th St
500-3100 98665
8400-8498 98662
12200-15599 98682
NW 86th St 98665
NE 86th Way 98662
NW 86th Way 98665
NE 87th Ave
400-498 98664

2500-14399 98662
NE 87th Cir
1400-3099 98665
7400-8799 98662
14000-18199 98682
NW 87th Cir 98665
NE 87th Ct 98662
SE 87th Ct 98664
NE 87th Pl
1400-1699 98664
2800-3899 98662
NE 87th St
1501-1599 98665
7500-11299 98662
13000-16199 98682
NW 87th St 98665
NE 87th Way
1500-1599 98665
9000-9099 98662
NE 88th Ave
100-1699 98664
3000-10499 98662
SE 88th Ave 98664
NE 88th Cir
800-1899 98665
11100-11199 98662
13100-14499 98682
NE 88th Ct 98662
NE 88th Pl 98662
NE 88th St
501-1197 98665
7200-11099 98662
13600-23199 98682
NW 88th St 98665
NE 88th Way
4000-4099 98665
16300-16399 98682
NE 89th Ave
100-1299 98664
5400-14199 98662
SE 89th Ave 98664
NE 89th Cir
1800-2799 98665
9000-10599 98662
13800-16399 98682
NW 89th Cir 98665
NE 89th Ct
1500-1599 98664
8100-8199 98662
NE 89th Pl 98664
NE 89th St
2200-6299 98665
10400-10999 98662
13000-16199 98682
NW 89th St 98665
NE 89th Way 98665
NE 90th Ave
100-2300 98664
2400-10499 98662
SE 90th Ave 98664
NE 90th Cir 98665
NW 90th Cir 98665
NE 90th Ct 98662
NE 90th Pl 98662
NE 90th St
2100-5199 98665
8800-11499 98662
14200-16099 98682
NW 90th St 98665
NE 91st Ave
100-1699 98664
5800-10699 98662
SE 91st Ave 98664
NE 91st Cir
1500-4099 98665
11500-11599 98662
13000-22199 98682
NW 91st Cir 98665
NE 91st Ct 98662
NE 91st Pl 98662
NE 91st St
2000-2098 98665
8100-9299 98662
13100-20199 98682
NW 91st St 98665
NE 91st Way 98665
NE 92nd Ave
100-2399 98664
2400-10499 98662
SE 92nd Ave 98664
NE 92nd Cir
2700-2799 98665
8100-11199 98662
NE 92nd Ct 98662
SE 92nd Ct 98664
NE 92nd St
100-4098 98665
9000-11599 98662
13100-16099 98682
NW 92nd St 98665
NE 92nd Way 98682
NE 93rd Ave
100-1100 98664
2400-13399 98662
SE 93rd Ave 98664
NE 93rd Cir
9300-9399 98662
13300-13599 98682
NW 93rd Cir 98665
NE 93rd Ct
1400-2299 98664
6800-6899 98662
NE 93rd Pl 98662
NE 93rd St
100-398 98665
10300-11199 98662
13000-16399 98682
NW 93rd St 98665
NE 94th Ave
100-499 98664
4700-4798 98662
SE 94th Ave 98664
NE 94th Cir
5500-5599 98665
9300-9399 98662
13700-13799 98682
NE 94th Ct
1900-2399 98664
7400-7599 98662
13700-13799 98682
NE 94th Pl 98664
NE 94th St
100-4899 98665
8100-11599 98662
13200-15099 98682
NW 94th St 98665
NE 94th Way 98665
NE 95th Ave
100-2399 98664
5801-10097 98662
SE 95th Ave 98664
NE 95th Cir
2700-4799 98665
14200-14399 98682
NW 95th Cir 98665
NE 95th Ct 98662
SE 95th Ct 98664
NW 95th Pl 98665
NE 95th St
1000-6000 98665
8200-11599 98662
11700-20999 98682
NW 95th St 98665
NE 95th Way 98665
NE 96th Ave
800-2099 98664
2401-2497 98662
SE 96th Ave 98664
NE 96th Cir
2600-5399 98665
13300-13399 98682
NW 96th Cir 98665
NE 96th Ct
2000-2399 98664
2600-2699 98665
SE 96th Ct 98664
NE 96th St
100-2298 98665
8000-8098 98662
13000-23199 98682
NW 96th St 98665
NE 96th Way
2100-2899 98665
13000-13099 98682
NE 97th Ave
100-208 98664
2700-14099 98662
SE 97th Ave 98664
NE 97th Cir
2100-4599 98665
9100-10999 98662
14300-14899 98682
NW 97th Cir 98665
NE 97th Ct 98662
NE 97th St
1600-6099 98665
10400-11599 98662
13000-13699 98682
NW 97th St 98665
NE 97th Way 98665
NE 98th Ave
101-997 98664
2400-2498 98662
SE 98th Ave 98664
NE 98th Cir
700-4599 98665
10900-11499 98662
NW 98th Cir 98665
NE 98th Ct 98664
NE 98th Loop 98664
NE 98th St
1900-5999 98665
11000-11199 98662
13200-16099 98682
NW 98th St 98665
NE 98th Way 98665
NE 99th Ave
1400-1499 98664
2600-12300 98662
SE 99th Ave 98664
NE 99th Cir
4100-4199 98686
8200-8299 98662
15200-15399 98682
NE 99th Ct 98662
SE 99th Ct 98664
NE 99th St
100-6099 98665
7201-7497 98662
11700-22999 98682
NW 99th St 98665
NE 99th Way
2800-2899 98665
13100-13199 98682
NE 100th Ave 98664
5900-10399 98662
SE 100th Ave 98664
NE 100th Cir
3700-5999 98686
8000-8099 98662
13900-22699 98682
NE 100th Ct
500-599 98664
3800-7099 98662
SE 100th Ct 98664
NE 100th St
2400-2799 98686
8100-10699 98662
12800-14599 98682
NW 100th St 98685
NE 100th Way 98662
NE 101st Ave
1500-1999 98664
2600-8199 98662
SE 101st Ave 98664
NE 101st Cir
4900-5699 98686
8000-8099 98662
15300-23199 98682
NW 101st Cir 98685
NE 101st Ct
600-1199 98664
2800-6999 98662
NE 101st Pl 98662
NE 101st St
100-199 98685
3500-5499 98686
7200-11499 98662
12000-16699 98682
NW 101st St 98685
NE 101st Way 98682
NE 102nd Ave
101-597 98664
3600-12199 98662
SE 102nd Ave 98664
NE 102nd Cir 98662
NW 102nd Cir 98685
NE 102nd Ct 98662
SE 102nd Ct 98664
NE 102nd St
100-399 98685
1300-1498 98686
8700-8798 98662
12100-21699 98682
NW 102nd St 98685
NE 102nd Way 98682
NE 103rd Ave 98662
SE 103rd Ave 98664
NE 103rd Cir
6500-6599 98686
9900-9999 98662
NW 103rd Cir 98685
NE 103rd Ct
600-1599 98664
6100-8199 98662
NE 103rd Dr 98682
NE 103rd Loop 98662
NE 103rd St
200-599 98685
4100-5499 98686
9200-11699 98662
12700-14299 98682
NW 103rd St 98685
NE 104th Ave
201-297 98664
4100-4400 98682
6600-12299 98662
SE 104th Ave 98664
NE 104th Cir
3300-3899 98686
8100-10899 98662
14200-14300 98682
NW 104th Cir 98685
NE 104th Ct
6100-9999 98662
14200-14398 98682
SE 104th Ct 98664
NE 104th Loop 98686
NW 104th Loop 98685
NE 104th Pl 98662
NE 104th St
1700-1998 98686
8800-11699 98662
12100-22199 98682
NW 104th St 98685
NE 104th Way 98686
NE 105th Ave
1800-2499 98664
4000-4398 98682
5700-5798 98662
SE 105th Ave 98664
NE 105th Cir
2800-6999 98686
12800-12999 98682
NW 105th Cir 98685
NE 105th Ct 98662
SE 105th Ct 98664
NE 105th St
300-1199 98685
2200-5499 98686
8800-8898 98662
12200-23699 98682
NW 105th St 98685
NE 106th Ave
500-2299 98664
4000-4098 98682
5800-9099 98662
SE 106th Ave 98664
NE 106th Cir
6300-6499 98686
8900-9099 98662
NW 106th Cir 98685
NE 106th Ct 98662
SE 106th Ct 98664
NE 106th Pl 98662
NE 106th St
100-1299 98685
1300-1498 98686
9000-11199 98662
12200-15599 98682
NW 106th St 98685
NE 106th Way 98686
NE 107th Ave
1400-2099 98664
5400-12500 98662
SE 107th Ave 98664
NE 107th Cir 98662
NW 107th Cir 98685
NE 107th Pl 98662
NE 107th St
100-1299 98685
1800-1898 98686
9400-11399 98662
NW 107th St 98685
NE 108th Ave
500-698 98664
3900-4299 98682
5900-6398 98662
NE 108th Cir 98686
NE 108th Ct 98662
NE 108th St
100-1099 98685
2200-3299 98686
23200-23699 98682
NW 108th St 98685
NE 109th Ave
1400-1699 98664
2800-2898 98682
5901-5997 98662
NE 109th Cir
900-999 98685
2100-4199 98686
NW 109th Cir 98685
NE 109th Ct
800-899 98664
2200-2399 98684
5500-10599 98662
NE 109th Avenue
Loop 98682
SE 109th Pl 98664
NE 109th St
300-1299 98685
2100-7199 98686
10900-11399 98662
20900-23199 98682
NW 109th St 98685
NE 109th Way 98685
NE 110th Ave
600-698 98664
2000-2198 98684
4300-4999 98682
5900-5998 98662
SE 110th Ave 98664
NE 110th Cir 98662
NW 110th Cir 98685
NE 110th Ct
2000-2099 98684
10500-10599 98662
SE 110th Ct 98664
NE 110th Pl 98686
NE 110th St
200-1399 98685
2100-2198 98686
7300-7999 98662
12000-12399 98682
NW 110th St 98685
NW 110th Way 98685
NE 111th Ave 98662
NE 111th Cir
3000-5199 98686
12200-12400 98682
NW 111th Cir 98685
NE 111th Ct
2000-2099 98684
10500-11299 98662
SE 111th Ct 98664
NW 111th Loop 98685
NE 111th St
100-1099 98685
2600-5999 98686
10700-11699 98662
12400-13099 98682
NW 111th St 98685
NE 111th Way 98662
NE 112th Ave
301-397 98684
2800-2998 98682
5700-5998 98662
SE 112th Ave 98664
NE 112th Cir
300-499 98685
3100-5499 98686
NW 112th Cir 98685
NE 112th Ct 98662
SE 112th Ct 98664
NE 112th Dr 98662
NE 112th Pl 98662
SE 112th Pl 98664
NE 112th St
1414A-1434A 98685
1600-6700 98686
11000-11299 98662
12400-12999 98682
NW 112th St 98685
NW 112th Way 98685
NE 113th Ave 98662
SE 113th Ave 98664
NE 113th Cir
5500-5599 98686
10200-10599 98662
NW 113th Cir 98685
NE 113th Ct
2300-2499 98684
6100-10899 98662
SE 113th Ct 98664
NE 113th St
1601-2515 98686
10900-12099 98662
22300-23199 98682
NW 113th St 98685
NE 114th Ave
2600-2799 98684
6101-9597 98662
NE 114th Cir
3000-6599 98686
9800-10199 98662
NW 114th Cir 98685
NE 114th Ct
2300-2499 98684
10500-10699 98662
SE 114th Ct 98664
NE 114th St
101-197 98685
2600-6599 98686
8700-9099 98662
12400-23699 98682
NW 114th St 98685
NE 115th Ave
100-298 98684
2900-3199 98682
8900-10399 98662
NE 115th Cir
400-900 98685
3000-3699 98686
23300-23399 98682
NW 115th Cir 98685
NE 115th Ct 98662
SE 115th Ct 98664
NE 115th St
1100-1298 98685
2600-5899 98686
8700-8999 98662
12800-23199 98682
NW 115th St 98685
NE 115th Way 98686
NE 116th Ave
200-298 98684
2800-3199 98682
6400-10399 98662
SE 116th Ave 98683
NE 116th Cir
1300-1399 98685
3100-3199 98686
9900-10199 98662
12800-22399 98682
NW 116th Cir 98685
NE 116th Ct 98662
SE 116th Ct 98683
NE 116th Pl 98662
NE 116th St 98686
NW 116th St 98685
NE 116th Way 98682
NW 116th Way 98685
NE 117th Ave
100-899 98684
6300-14399 98662
SE 117th Ave 98683
NE 117th Cir 98682
NW 117th Cir 98685
NE 117th Ct 98682
NE 117th St
100-1499 98685
1700-5799 98686
8100-8199 98682
NW 117th St 98685
NW 117th Way 98685
NE 118th Ave
300-398 98684
3100-12999 98682
SE 118th Ave
200-298 98684
300-499 98683
NW 118th Cir 98685
NE 118th Ct 98682
SE 118th Ct 98683
NE 118th St
4000-5799 98686
10600-10699 98662
NW 118th St 98685
NW 118th Way 98685
NE 119th Ave
1400-1498 98684
2801-2997 98682
SE 119th Ave 98683
NE 119th Cir 98682
NE 119th Ct 98682
NE 119th Pl 98682
NE 119th St
12731A-13751A 98682
2301-2597 98686
7601-7797 98662
11700-11798 98682
NW 119th St 98685
NE 120th Ave
101-497 98684
2800-11199 98682
SE 120th Ave 98683
NW 120th Cir 98685
NE 120th Ct 98682
NE 120th St 98686
NW 120th St 98685
NE 121st Ave
100-1899 98684
1901-2299 98684
3300-7499 98682
SE 121st Ave
101-199 98684
500-1699 98683
NW 121st Cir 98685
NE 121st Ct 98682
NE 121st St
2100-4599 98686
22700-23199 98682
NW 121st St 98685
NE 121st Way 98686
NE 122nd Ave
300-398 98684
3100-10599 98682
SE 122nd Ave 98683
NE 122nd Cir 98682
SE 122nd Ct 98683
NE 122nd St 98686
NW 122nd St 98685
NE 123rd Ave
300-2100 98684
2102-2498 98684
3501-3897 98682
SE 123rd Ave 98683
NE 123rd Cir
4400-4499 98686
10500-10699 98662
NW 123rd Cir 98685
NE 123rd Ct
2400-2599 98684
4500-10299 98682
NE 123rd Pl 98682
NE 123rd St 98686
NW 123rd St 98685

NE 124th Ave
100-2799 98684
2801-2997 98682
SE 124th Ave
100-299 98684
900-1899 98683
NW 124th Cir 98685
NE 124th Ct 98682
SE 124th Ct 98683
NE 124th St
1300-1499 98685
4201-4297 98686
NW 124th St 98685
NW 124th Way 98685
NE 125th Ave
700-2499 98684
4200-8599 98682
SE 125th Ave 98683
NE 125th Cir
500-599 98685
4600-4999 98686
NW 125th Cir 98685
NE 125th Ct
1801-2597 98684
2800-4099 98682
SE 125th Ct 98683
NE 125th St
1300-1499 98685
2500-5200 98686
NW 125th St 98685
NE 125th Way 98686
NE 126th Ave
200-2799 98684
3100-3198 98682
SE 126th Ave 98683
NE 126th Cir
4500-4899 98686
10400-10699 98662
NW 126th Cir 98685
NE 126th Ct
1500-1599 98684
2800-7599 98682
SE 126th Ct 98683
NE 126th Street Loop 98685
NE 126th Pl 98684
NE 126th St
700-1799 98685
4201-4297 98686
NW 126th St 98685
NE 126th Way 98662
NE 127th Ave 98684
2800-11299 98682
SE 127th Ave 98683
NE 127th Cir
100-199 98685
3700-3899 98686
NE 127th Ct 98682
SE 127th Ct 98683
NE 127th Pl 98684
NE 127th St
200-1499 98685
3400-5499 98686
NW 127th St 98685
NE 127th Way 98686
NE 128th Ave
500-2299 98684
4200-11599 98682
SE 128th Ave 98683
NE 128th Cir 98685
NW 128th Cir 98685
NE 128th Ct 98682
SE 128th Ct 98683
NE 128th Pl 98682
NE 128th St
600-1299 98685
3400-4900 98686
NW 128th St 98685
NE 128th Way 98662
NE 129th Ave
1100-2099 98684
2800-11699 98682
NE 129th Cir 98686
NW 129th Cir 98685
NE 129th Ct 98684
SE 129th Ct 98683
NE 129th Pl 98682
NE 129th St
100-198 98685
1900-6899 98686
7400-7598 98662
NW 129th St 98685
NE 130th Ave
500-1398 98684
1400-2599 98684
2900-11799 98682
SE 130th Ave 98683
NE 130th Cir
1100-1699 98685
4200-4299 98686
11000-11399 98662
NW 130th Cir 98685
NE 130th Ct
800-899 98684
3100-9799 98682
SE 130th Ct 98683
NE 130th Pl 98682
NE 130th St
700-1599 98685
4000-4999 98686
NW 130th St 98685
NE 130th Way 98686
NE 131st Ave
7403A-74023A 98682
400-1398 98684
3900-10299 98682
SE 131st Ave 98683
NE 131st Cir 98685
NW 131st Cir 98685
NE 131st Ct
2400-2599 98684
3800-9799 98682
SE 131st Ct 98683
NE 131st St
3600-4799 98686
10600-10698 98662
NW 131st St 98685
NE 131st Way
4400-4499 98686
7800-7899 98662
NW 131st Way 98685
NE 132nd Ave
500-598 98684
2900-11899 98682
SE 132nd Ave 98683
NE 132nd Cir 98686
NW 132nd Cir 98685
NE 132nd Ct 98682
SE 132nd Ct 98683
NE 132nd Pl 98682
NE 132nd St
300-999 98685
4200-4699 98686
NW 132nd St 98685
NE 132nd Way 98685
NE 133rd Ave 98682
SE 133rd Ave 98683
NE 133rd Cir 98685
NW 133rd Cir 98685
NE 133rd Ct 98682
SE 133rd Ct 98683
SE 133rd Pl 98683
NE 133rd St
800-899 98685
4100-4300 98686
NW 133rd St 98685
NE 134th Ave
1800-2499 98684
3100-3198 98682
SE 134th Ave 98683
NE 134th Cir
300-399 98685
4200-4299 98686
NW 134th Cir 98685
NE 134th Ct 98682
SE 134th Ct 98683
NE 134th St
100-1500 98685
2200-4799 98686
8700-10599 98662
NW 134th St 98685
NE 134th Way 98686
NW 134th Way 98685
NE 135th Ave 98682
SE 135th Ave 98683
NE 135th Cir 98685
NW 135th Cir 98685
NE 135th Ct 98682
SE 135th Ct 98683
NE 135th St
100-599 98685
4500-4999 98686
NW 135th St 98685
NE 136th Ave
100-2199 98684
2800-2898 98682
SE 136th Ave
100-300 98684
400-898 98683
NE 136th Cir 98686
NW 136th Cir 98685
NE 136th Ct 98682
SE 136th Ct 98683
NE 136th St
100-1299 98685
2500-4199 98686
NW 136th St 98685
NE 136th Way
300-599 98685
3300-3499 98686
NE 137th Ave 98682
NE 137th Cir
4100-4199 98686
10700-10999 98662
NE 137th Ct
2000-2299 98684
2800-2899 98682
SE 137th Ct 98683
NE 137th Pl 98682
NE 137th St 98686
NW 137th St 98685
NE 138th Ave
400-2699 98684
2701-2799 98684
2800-2998 98682
SE 138th Ave 98683
NE 138th Cir 98686
NW 138th Cir 98685
NE 138th Ct 98682
SE 138th Ct 98683
SE 138th Loop 98683
NE 138th Pl 98682
NE 138th St 98686
NW 138th St 98685
NE 138th Way 98686
NW 138th Way 98685
NE 139th Ave
400-1699 98684
3900-8800 98682
SE 139th Ave 98683
NE 139th Cir 98686
NE 139th Ct 98682
SE 139th Ct 98683
NE 139th Loop 98682
NW 139th Loop 98685
NE 139th St
100-1200 98685
2100-7099 98686
7200-9299 98662
NW 139th St 98685
NE 140th Ave
1300-1599 98684
3000-9099 98682
SE 140th Ave 98683
NE 140th Cir 98686
NW 140th Cir 98685
NE 140th Ct 98682
SE 140th Ct 98683
NE 140th St 98686
NW 140th St 98685
NW 140th Way 98685
NE 141st Ave
900-1599 98684
2800-2898 98682
SE 141st Ave 98683
NE 141st Cir 98686
NW 141st Cir 98685
NE 141st Ct 98682
SE 141st Ct 98683
SE 141st Pl 98683
NE 141st St
700-798 98685
2900-3399 98686
NW 141st St 98685
NE 141st Way 98686
NW 141st Way 98685
NE 142nd Ave
1000-1499 98684
4500-10200 98682
NW 142nd Cir 98685
NE 142nd Ct
1500-1599 98684
3000-7099 98682
SE 142nd Ct 98683
NE 142nd St 98686
NW 142nd St 98685
NW 142nd Way 98685
NE 143rd Ave
1000-1599 98684
2900-10399 98682
SE 143rd Ave 98683
NE 143rd Cir
4700-4899 98686
9000-9099 98662
NW 143rd Cir 98685
NE 143rd Ct 98682
NE 143rd Pl 98682
NE 143rd St
600-1499 98685
2600-3499 98686
NW 143rd St 98685
NW 143rd Way 98685
NE 144th Ave
300-700 98684
4500-10499 98682
SE 144th Ave 98683
NE 144th Cir
2700-2800 98686
7900-8199 98662
NW 144th Cir 98685
NE 144th Ct
2600-2799 98684
4900-10110 98682
SE 144th Ct 98683
NE 144th St
301-1399 98685
2100-7199 98686
NW 144th St 98685
NE 145th Ave
500-2799 98684
2800-10099 98682
SE 145th Ave 98683
NE 145th Cir
200-299 98685
2400-3499 98686
NW 145th Cir 98685
NE 145th Ct 98682
SE 145th Ct 98683
NE 145th Pl 98682
NE 145th St
400-699 98685
3000-3199 98686
NW 145th St 98685
NE 146th Ave
600-2000 98684
3000-10099 98682
SE 146th Ave 98683
NW 146th Cir 98685
NE 146th Ct
500-2799 98684
3500-3699 98682
SE 146th Ct 98683
NE 146th Pl 98682
SE 146th Pl 98683
NE 146th St
100-1200 98685
5000-5298 98686
NW 146th St 98685
NW 146th Way 98685
NE 147th Ave
300-1399 98684
4300-10299 98682
SE 147th Ave 98683
NE 147th Cir
600-699 98685
2400-2599 98686
NW 147th Cir 98685
NE 147th Ct 98684
SE 147th Ct 98683
SE 147th Pl 98683
NE 147th St
100-199 98685
2600-2899 98686
NW 147th St 98685
NW 147th Way 98685
NE 148th Ave
100-2799 98684
2800-9299 98682
SE 148th Ave
100-198 98684
2900-3099 98683
NW 148th Cir 98685
NE 148th Ct
2300-2599 98684
3601-3697 98682
NE 148th Pl
1200-1399 98684
3100-3200 98682
NE 148th St
100-999 98685
2300-2398 98686
NW 148th St 98685
NE 149th Ave
200-2799 98684
3400-10199 98682
SE 149th Ave 98683
NE 149th Cir 98686
NW 149th Cir 98685
NE 149th Ct
300-398 98684
6800-7099 98682
SE 149th Ct
200-499 98684
2900-3099 98683
NE 149th Pl 98684
NE 149th St
200-398 98685
2300-2399 98686
NW 149th St 98685
NE 150th Ave
500-2299 98684
3100-9799 98682
SE 150th Ave 98683
NE 150th Cir
200-299 98685
1800-1898 98686
NW 150th Cir 98685
NE 150th Ct
700-799 98684
8000-8699 98682
SE 150th Ct 98684
NE 150th Pl 98682
NE 150th St
100-199 98685
1700-2899 98686
15000-15099 98685
NW 150th St 98685
NW 150th Way 98685
NE 151st Ave
200-2799 98684
3100-8199 98682
SE 151st Ave
100-400 98684
2400-2699 98683
NE 151st Cir 98686
NE 151st Ct
2100-2199 98684
3500-9699 98682
SE 151st Ct 98683
NE 151st St
200-299 98685
4800-4899 98686
NW 151st St 98685
NW 151st Way 98685
NE 152nd Ave
101-197 98684
2800-11899 98682
SE 152nd Ave
100-299 98684
800-3799 98683
NE 152nd Cir 98686
NE 152nd Ct 98682
SE 152nd Ct
300-399 98684
1300-3899 98683
NE 152nd Pl
1900-1999 98684
4300-4399 98682
NE 152nd St
100-199 98685
1800-2199 98686
NW 152nd St 98685
NE 153rd Ave
100-2299 98684
4100-10599 98682
SE 153rd Ave 98683
NE 153rd Cir 98686
NE 153rd Ct 98682
SE 153rd Ct
300-399 98684
3800-3899 98683
NE 153rd Pl 98682
NE 153rd St
100-199 98685
1800-1812 98686
NW 153rd St 98685
NE 154th Ave
700-798 98684
3000-15599 98682
SE 154th Ave 98683
NE 154th Cir
2100-2499 98686
7800-7817 98662
NE 154th Ct
2600-2799 98684
4200-7999 98682
SE 154th Ct
200-299 98684
3800-3999 98683
NE 154th Pl 98682
NE 154th St
201-297 98685
1500-2899 98686
7301-7497 98662
NW 154th St 98685
NE 155th Ave
900-1498 98684
2800-10599 98682
SE 155th Ave
100-600 98684
1200-4099 98683
NE 155th Cir
800-999 98685
1900-1999 98686
NW 155th Cir 98685
NE 155th Ct 98682
NE 155th St 98686
NW 155th St 98685
NE 155th Way 98686
NE 156th Ave
600-2599 98684
7300-10599 98682
SE 156th Ave
100-499 98684
1600-3299 98683
NE 156th Ct 98682
SE 156th Ct 98683
NE 156th Pl 98682
NE 156th St 98686
NW 156th St 98685
NE 157th Ave
100-2799 98684
3200-10599 98682
SE 157th Ave
100-198 98684
2300-2998 98683
NE 157th Cir 98686
NW 157th Cir 98685
NE 157th Ct
600-799 98684
2900-8699 98682
SE 157th Loop 98684
NE 157th St 98686
NW 157th St 98685
NE 158th Ave
100-2400 98684
2800-9299 98682
SE 158th Ave
100-200 98684
1600-4099 98683
NE 158th Cir 98686
NE 158th Ct
1400-1699 98684
3000-8200 98682
SE 158th Ct
300-399 98684
2200-4299 98683
SE 158th Loop 98683
NE 158th Pl 98682
NE 158th St 98686
NE 159th Ave
1600-2399 98684
3401-3497 98682
SE 159th Ave
200-399 98684
1200-1499 98683
NW 159th Cir 98685
NE 159th Ct 98684
SE 159th Ct 98683
SE 159th Pl 98683
NE 159th St
5001-5497 98686
7200-8100 98662
15900-15998 98682
NE 160th Ave
400-2300 98684
3400-3698 98682
SE 160th Ave
401-697 98684
801-997 98683
NE 160th Ct 98682
NE 160th Loop 98684
NE 160th Pl 98682
SE 160th Pl 98683
NE 161st Ave
1100-1199 98684
2900-10499 98682
SE 161st Ave
200-498 98684
2900-3199 98683
NE 161st Ct
700-1299 98684
3700-10699 98682
SE 161st Ct 98683
NE 161st Pl
2100-2299 98684
7400-10299 98682
SE 161st Pl 98683
NE 162nd Ave
1900A-1900B 98684
2800-4598 98682
SE 162nd Ave 98683
SE 162nd Ct 98683
NE 162nd Pl 98684
NE 162nd St 98686
NE 163rd Ave
800-2499 98684
3300-9299 98682
SE 163rd Ave 98683
NE 163rd Ct
1200-2699 98684
2800-3899 98682
NE 163rd Pl
2100-2299 98684
7100-7199 98682
SE 163rd Pl 98683
NE 164th Ave
100-2799 98684
6300-9299 98682
SE 164th Ave
100-398 98684
900-4399 98683
NE 164th Ct
1200-1299 98684
3300-7199 98682
NE 164th Pl 98684
NE 164th St 98662
NE 165th Ave
2400-2799 98684
2800-10399 98682
SE 165th Ave 98683
NE 165th Cir 98686
NE 165th Ct
1200-1299 98684
3500-3599 98682
NE 165th Loop 98682
NE 165th Pl 98682

NE 166th Ave
800-2599 98684
3100-8199 98682
SE 166th Ave
300-399 98684
2500-2599 98683
NE 166th Ct 98684
SE 166th Ct 98683
NE 166th Pl
2400-2799 98684
2800-3199 98682
SE 166th Pl 98683
NE 167th Ave 98684
SE 167th Ct 98683
NE 168th Ave
600-2098 98684
2100-2799 98684
3100-3299 98682
SE 168th Ave
600-699 98684
1500-4199 98683
NE 168th Ct 98682
SE 168th Ct 98683
NE 169th Ave
400-2199 98684
3100-8799 98682
SE 169th Ave
200-599 98684
1700-2799 98683
NE 169th Ct 98684
SE 169th Ct 98683
SE 169th Pl 98683
NE 169th St
6900-7199 98686
7400-8099 98662
NE 170th Ave 98684
SE 170th Ave 98683
NE 170th Ct 98684
SE 170th Ct 98683
NE 170th Pl 98682
NE 171st Ave
600-2199 98684
3100-4200 98682
4202-4398 98682
SE 171st Ave
200-599 98684
2700-4299 98683
NE 171st Ct 98684
SE 171st Ct 98683
SE 171st Pl 98683
NE 171st St 98686
NE 172nd Ave
100-198 98684
200-2699 98684
2701-2799 98684
2800-3298 98682
SE 172nd Ave
100-198 98684
2900-3699 98683
SE 172nd Pl 98683
NE 173rd Ave
700-2699 98684
2900-2999 98682
SE 173rd Ave 98683
NE 173rd Ct
2700-2799 98684
2800-2899 98682
SE 173rd Ct 98683
SE 173rd Pl 98683
NE 174th Ave 98682
SE 174th Ave 98683
NE 174th Ct 98682
SE 174th Ct 98683
SE 174th Pl 98683
NE 174th St 98686
NE 175th Ave
100-198 98684
200-799 98684
2800-3599 98682
SE 175th Ave 98683
NE 175th Cir 98686
SE 175th Ct 98683
SE 175th Pl 98683
NE 176th Ave
100-198 98684
200-2699 98684
2800-7199 98682
SE 176th Ave 98683
NE 176th Ct 98684
SE 176th Ct 98683
SE 176th Pl 98683
NE 177th Ave
1800-2799 98684
2800-2899 98682
SE 177th Ave 98683
SE 177th Ln 98683
NE 178th Ave
2000-2099 98684
2800-3099 98682
SE 178th Ave 98683
NE 178th Ct 98682
SE 178th Ct 98683
SE 178th Pl 98683
NE 178th St 98686
NE 179th Ave
2400-2799 98684
2800-2899 98682
SE 179th Ave 98683
SE 179th Ct 98683
NE 179th Pl
1900-2299 98684
8400-8799 98682
NE 179th St 98686
NE 180th Ave
1800-2398 98684
2800-3699 98682
SE 180th Ave 98683
NE 180th Ct 98682
SE 180th Ct 98683
NE 180th Pl 98684
SE 180th Pl 98683
NE 181st Ave
2000-2799 98684
2800-3399 98682
SE 181st Ave 98683
NE 181st Cir 98682
NE 181st Ct 98682
SE 181st Ct 98683
SE 181st Pl 98683
NE 182nd Ave 98682
SE 182nd Ave 98683
NE 182nd Ct 98684
SE 182nd Ct 98683
SE 182nd Pl 98683
NE 183rd Ave 98684
SE 183rd Ave 98683
NE 183rd Ct 98682
SE 183rd Ct 98683
SE 183rd Loop 98683
NE 183rd Pl 98682
SE 183rd Pl 98683
NE 184th Ave
2000-2599 98684
2800-2999 98682
SE 184th Ave 98683
SE 184th Ct 98683
SE 184th Pl 98683
NE 185th Ave
1800-1898 98684
1900-2200 98684
2202-2298 98684
6800-7099 98682
SE 185th Ave 98683
NE 185th Ct 98682
SE 185th Ct 98683
NE 185th Pl 98682
SE 185th Pl 98683
SE 186th Ave 98683
NE 186th Ct 98682
SE 186th Ct 98683
NE 186th Pl 98682
SE 186th Pl 98683
SE 186th Way 98683
NE 187th Ave
1801-1897 98684
1899-2799 98684
2801-7297 98682
7299-7599 98682
SE 187th Ave 98683
SE 187th Loop 98683
SE 187th Pl 98683
SE 188th Ave 98683
NE 189th Ave 98682
SE 189th Ave 98683
SE 189th Ct 98683
SE 189th Pl 98683
190th Ave & Pl 98683
191st Ave & Pl 98683
NE 192nd Ave 98684
6500-6606 98682
SE 192nd Ave 98683
NE 193rd Ct 98684
NE 194th Ave 98682
NE 198th Cir 98686
NE 199th Ave 98682
NE 199th St 98686
NE 201st Ave 98682
NE 202nd Ave 98682
204th Ave & Pl 98682
NE 205th Ave 98682
NE 207th Ave 98682
NE 208th Ave 98682
211th Ave & Ct 98682
NE 212th Ave 98682
NE 213th Ave 98682
NE 214th Ave 98682
215th Ave & Ct 98682
NE 216th Ave 98682
217th Ave & Ct 98682
NE 219th Ave 98682
NE 221st Ave 98682
NE 222nd Ave 98682
NE 223rd Ave 98682
NE 224th Ave 98682
NE 226th Ct 98682
NE 227th Ave 98682
NE 228th Ave 98682
NE 229th Ct 98682
NE 230th Ave 98682
NE 232nd Ave 98682
NE 233rd Ave 98682
NE 237th Ave 98682
NE 238th Ave 98682
NE 241st Ct 98682
NE 242nd Ave 98682
NE 243rd Ave 98682
NE 246th Ave 98682
NE 247th Ave 98682
NE 248th Ave 98682
NE 251st Ave 98682
252nd Ave & Ct 98682
NE 253rd Ct 98682
NE 256th Ave 98682
NE 258th Ave 98682
NE 259th Ave 98682
NE 262nd Ave 98682
NE 269th Ave 98682
NE 270th Ave 98682

WENATCHEE WA

General Delivery 98801

POST OFFICE BOXES MAIN OFFICE STATIONS AND BRANCHES

Box No.s
All PO Boxes 98807

NAMED STREETS

Abby Ln 98801
Academy St 98801
Adams Ave 98801
Agate Pl 98801
Alaska Ave 98801
Alder Ct 98801
Alderwood St 98801
Alexandria Rd 98801
Allison St 98801
Alpine Ct & Dr 98801
Alvista Pl 98801
American Fruit Rd 98801
Amherst Ave 98801
Amy Ct 98801
Angela St 98801
Anna Ln 98801
Antles St 98801
Anton Pl 98801
Apollo Pl 98801
Appleland Dr 98801
Appleridge St 98801
Appleyard Dr 98801
April Dr 98801
Ashley Brooke 98801
Aspen Pl 98801
Aspen Creek Ln 98801
Atwood Rd & St 98801
Austin Ave & Ct 98801
Avalon Ter 98801
Avenida Way 98801
Bartlett Ave 98801
Beacon Rd 98801
Bell Dr 98801
Benoy Ave 98801
Benton St & Way 98801
Berg Ave 98801
Beuzer St 98801
Big Springs Ranch Rd 98801
Black Forest Rd 98801
Blair Slack Rd 98801
Bluegrass Ln 98801
Bohart Rd 98801
Boodry St 98801
Booie Ct 98801
Brandi Ct, Ln & Ter 98801
Bridge St 98801
Britini Dr 98801
Broad St 98801
Broadcrest Ct 98801
Broadhurst Pl 98801
Broadleaf Ct 98801
Broadview 98801
Broadway Pl N 98801
Brookside Way 98801
Brown St 98801
Bryan St & Ter 98801
N & S Buchanan Ave 98801
Burch Mountain Rd 98801
Burchvale Rd 98801
Burns St 98801
N Canal Blvd 98801
Canyon Pl 98801
Canyon Breeze Rd 98801
Canyon Creek Dr 98801
Canyon Crest Dr 98801
Canyon View Pl 98801
Canyonside Rd 98801
Carlson Loop 98801
Carson Ct & Ln 98801
Casandra Dr 98801
Cascade St 98801
Cashmere St 98801
Castle Heights Dr 98801
Castlerock Ave 98801
Castleview Pl 98801
Castlewood Pl 98801
Cedar St 98801
Cedar Wood Ln & Pl 98801
Center Court Dr 98801
Central Ave 98801
Champion Ln 98801
Chapman Dr & Rd 98801
Charles St 98801
Chatham Hill Dr & Rd 98801
Chehalis St 98801
N & S Chelan Ave 98801
Cherry Ct, Ln & St 98801
Chester Kimm Rd 98801
Chiefs Rd 98801
Chinook Dr 98801
Chrisand Ln 98801
Chukar Hills Dr 98801
Cinda Ct 98801
Circle St 98801
Citation Loop 98801
Clark Ct & Dr 98801
N & S Cleveland Ave 98801
College Ct & St 98801
N & S Columbia St 98801
Columbia View Cir & Ct 98801
Columbine St 98801
Concord Pl 98801
Connery Rd 98801
Coolidge Dr 98801
Corbaley Pl 98801
Cordell Ave 98801
Cornell Ave 98801
Cove Ave N & S 98801
Crabapple Ln 98801
Cranmer Dr 98801
Crawford Ave 98801
Crescent St 98801
Crestview St 98801
Crestwood St 98801
Cross Rd & St 98801
Crown St 98801
Cumbo Ct 98801
Cypress Ln 98801
Dago Grade Rd 98801
Dakota St 98801
Dana Ave 98801
Dana Wood 98801
Dartmouth Ave 98801
Dawn Ter 98801
Day Dr & Rd 98801
Debord Dr 98801
Dechand Ln 98801
Deer Haven Ln 98801
N & S Delaware Ave 98801
Denise Cir 98801
Depot St 98801
Dianna Way 98801
Dillon St 98801
Dogwood Ln 98801
Dorner Pl 98801
Douglas St 98801
Downs Rd 98801
S Duke St 98801
Duncan Rd N 98801
Dundas St 98801
Eaglerock Dr & Pl 98801
Eastview Ln 98801
Easy St & Way 98801
E & W Edgemont Dr 98801
Edgewood Ln 98801
Eisenhower Dr 98801
Elijah Rd 98801
Elizabeth Ct 98801
N & S Elliott Ave 98801
Elm St 98801
Elmwood St 98801
Emerald Pl 98801
N & S Emerson Ave 98801
Enchantment Pl 98801
Erika Ln 98801
Erin Pl 98801
Ernie Ct 98801
Euclid Ave 98801
Fairfield Ln 98801
Fairhaven Ave 98801
Fairview Ave 98801
Farrah Ln 98801
Ferry St 98801
Filbeck Pl 98801
Fir Crest Dr 98801
Foothills Ln 98801
Forest Ridge Dr 98801
Fox Run 98801
Frances Ct 98801
N & S Franklin Ave 98801
Fuller St 98801
Furney St 98801
Gabriella Ln 98801
Gallers St 98801
Gardiner St 98801
N & S Garfield Ave 98801
Garnet Pl 98801
Gary St 98801
Gaspar St 98801
Gehr St 98801
Gellatly Ave 98801
George Johnson Ave 98801
Gilcrest St 98801
Glacier Pl 98801
Glenwood Ave 98801
Golden Ln 98801
Golden Crest Dr 98801
Gossman Ln 98801
Grandview Ave & Loop 98801
Greenwalt Pl 98801
Grenz St 98801
Grover Ct 98801
Gs Center Rd 98801
Gudmundson Rd 98801
Hainsworth St 98801
Halvorson Canyon Rd 98801
Hampton Rd 98801
Harbel St 98801
Harlow Ln 98801
Harris Ct 98801
Harrison St 98801
Harvard Ave 98801
Hawley St E 98801
Hawthorne St 98801
Heather Ln 98801
Heritage Dr & Hvn 98801
Hidden Meadow Dr 98801
Hideaway Pl 98801
Highland Dr 98801
Hill St 98801
S Hills Dr 98801
Hilltop Pl 98801
Historic Ln 98801
Holbrook St 98801
W Honeysett Rd 98801
Horan Rd 98801
Horizon Pl 98801
Horselake Rd 98801
Howard St 98801
Huckleberry Ln 98801
Icicle Pl 98801
Idaho St 98801
Indy Ln 98801
Inks Rd 98801
Ione St 98801
Iroquois Ln 98801
Island Vw 98801
Jagla Rd 98801
Jefferson Pl & St 98801
Jeffrey Ct 98801
Jennings St 98801
Jessica Ln 98801
Jim Smith Rd 98801
Joe Miller Rd 98801
John St 98801
Johnson Ct & St 98801
Jolen Dr 98801
Judkins St 98801
Jump Off Rd 98801
Kayla Way 98801
Kearns Ct 98801
N Kelso Ave 98801
Kenaston Dr 98801
Kimberly Ct 98801
King St 98801
Kings Ct 98801
Kirby Ln 98801
Kittitas St 98801
Knowles Rd 98801
Kookaburro Run 98801
Krayike Ct 98801
Kriewald Ct 98801
Kristi Ct 98801
Kyle Mathison Amigos Rd 98801
Lambert St 98801
Lark Brooke 98801
Lars Ln 98801
Lasso Dr 98801
Laurie Dr 98801
Lavender Ct 98801
Laverne Pl 98801
Leanne Pl 98801
Leavenworth Pl 98801
Lemaister Ave 98801
Lester Rd 98801
Lewis St 98801
Lexington Pl 98801
Lilly Ln 98801
Lincoln St 98801
Lincoln Park Cir 98801
Linda Ln 98801
Lindy St 98801
Linville Dr & Ln 98801
Linwood Ave 98801
Lion Pl 98801
Locust St 98801
Lois Pl 98801
Lombard Ln 98801
Loop Rd 98801
Lorena Pl 98801
Love Ln 98801
Lovell Rd 98801
Loves Ct 98801
Lowe St 98801
Lower Hedges Rd 98801
Lower Monitor Rd 98801
Lower Sunnyslope Rd 98801
Lynn St 98801
Madison St 98801
Mahogany Ln 98801
Maiden Ln 98801
Majestic View Dr 98801
Malaga Ave 98801
Malaga Alcoa Hwy 98801
Maple St 98801
Marble St 98801
Marian Ave 98801
N Marie Ave 98801
Marilane Dr 98801
N Marilyn Ave 98801
Marjo St 98801
Marker St 98801
Marr St 98801
Martin Pl 98801
Mathison Cherry Camp Rd 98801
Matthews Rd 98801
Mckittrick St 98801
Mcmullan Rd 98801
Meadow Ridge Dr 98801
Meadows Dr 98801
Medina Pl 98801
Meeks Rd & St 98801
Melissa Way 98801
Melody Ln 98801
S Methow St 98801
Michael Pl 98801
Michael Brooke 98801
N & S Miller St 98801
Millerdale Ave 98801
Millerdale Heights Dr 98801
Mills Ave 98801
N & S Mission St 98801
Mission Ridge Rd 98801
Mission Village Rd 98801
Monitor St 98801
Monroe St 98801
Montana Ct & St 98801
Morning Wind Ln 98801
Morris St 98801
E & W Mountain Brook Ln 98801
Mountain Vista Dr 98801
Mulberry Ln 98801
Mylius Rd 98801
Nelson Ave 98801
Norman St 98801
North Rd 98801
Northfield Pl 98801
Northridge Dr NE 98801
Northwood Rd 98801
Number 1 Canyon Rd 98801
Number 2 Canyon Rd 98801
Oak St 98801
Ohme Rd 98801
Ohme Garden Rd 98801
Okanogan Ave 98801
Olds Station Rd 98801
Olympus Dr 98801
Oneonta Dr 98801
Orchard Ave 98801
Oregon St 98801
Ormiston St 98801
E Orondo Ave 98801

Overlook Dr 98801
Pacific Ct & Ln 98801
Palouse St 98801
Parelarl St 98801
W Park St 98801
Parkway St 98801
Patsue Pl 98801
Peachy St 98801
Pear Ln 98801
Pearl St S 98801
Pearview Cir 98801
Pennsylvania Ave 98801
E & W Penny Rd 98801
Pensione Pl 98801
Pershing St 98801
Peters St E & W 98801
Pheasant Canyon Ct 98801
Pickens St 98801
Piere St 98801
N Pine Ave 98801
Pinehurst Dr 98801
Pinnacle Pl 98801
Pioneer Dr 98801
Pitcher Canyon Rd 98801
Pleasant Ave 98801
Plum St 98801
Poe St 98801
Poplar Ave 98801
Pot O Gold Ln 98801
Princeton Ave N 98801
Quail Hollow Ln 98801
Quail Run Blvd 98801
Queens Ct 98801
Rainbow Ln 98801
Rainbows End 98801
Rainier St 98801
Ramona Ave 98801
Red Apple Rd 98801
Red Fern Rd 98801
Redwood St 98801
Renn Ln 98801
Rex Rd 98801
Ridge Crest Dr 98801
Ridgeview Blvd, Ln & Pl 98801
Ridgeview Loop Dr 98801
Ringold St 98801
Riter St 98801
River Park Ave E 98801
Rivers Edge Pl 98801
Riverside Dr 98801
Riverwalk Dr 98801
Robinswood Ct 98801
Rocklund Dr 98801
N Rogers Dr 98801
W Rolling Hills Ln 98801
Roosevelt Ave 98801
Roper Ln 98801
Rosewood Ave 98801
Ross Ave 98801
Royal Anne Dr 98801
Rue Jolie Ln 98801
Russell St 98801
Saddlehorn Ave & Ln 98801
Saddlerock Dr & Loop 98801
Sage Crest Dr 98801
Sage Grouse Rd 98801
Sage Hills Dr 98801
Saint Joseph Pl 98801
Sally Dr 98801
Samantha Ln 98801
Sandy Brooke 98801
Scenic View Dr 98801
Schafer St 98801
Schons Pl 98801
School St 98801
Seattle St 98801
Seneca Pl & St S 98801
Shade Tree Ln 98801
Shady Ln 98801
Shelby Ct 98801
Silver Ln 98801
Simmons St 98801
Skyline Dr & Pl 98801
Skyview Ct 98801
Sleepy Hollow Hts & Rd 98801
Snohomish St 98801
Solstice Ln 98801
Somerset Dr 98801
Songbird Ln 98801
Sorensen Ave 98801
Southridge Ct 98801
Splett St 98801
Spokane St 98801
Springwater Ave 98801
Squilchuck Rd 98801
State Highway 97a 98801
Steinbach Rd 98801
N Stella Ave 98801
Stemilt Creek Rd 98801
Stemilt Hill Rd 98801
Stemilt Loop Rd 98801
Stephanie Brooke 98801
Stevens St 98801
Stewart St 98801
Stiss Canyon Rd 98801
Stoney Ct 98801
Stoneybrook Ln 98801
Story Ln 98801
Summercreek Pl 98801
Summerhill Pl 98801
Summit View Pl 98801
Sun Valley Dr 98801
Sunburst St 98801
Sunny Meadows Loop 98801
Sunnyslope Heights Rd 98801
Sunridge Ln 98801
Sunrise Cir 98801
Sunset Ave & Dr 98801
Surry Rd 98801
Susan Pl 98801
Sutton Pl 98801
Swakane Rd 98801
N Tacoma Ave 98801
Tamarack Pl 98801
Tanda Ln 98801
Tarn Pl 98801
Teakwood Ln 98801
Technology Center Way 98801
Terminal Ave 98801
Terrea Ct 98801
Thurston St 98801
Tilly Ln 98801
Toaimnic Dr 98801
Trigger Ln 98801
Trip St 98801
Trisha Way 98801
Turtle Ln 98801
Twinpeaks Dr 98801
Tybeau Rd 98801
Tyler St 98801
Upper Hedges Rd 98801
Utah Ct & St 98801
Valley Vue Rd 98801
Vassar Ave 98801
View Pl 98801
View Ridge Cir 98801
S Viewdale St 98801
Viewmont Dr 98801
Vinyard Way 98801
Virginia Way 98801
Vista Pl 98801
Vista Linda Ter 98801
Walker Ave 98801
Walla Walla Ave 98801
Walnut Ct, Pl & St 98801
Warehouse Rd 98801
Warm Springs Dr 98801
Warm Springs Canyon Rd 98801
Washington St 98801
Wedgewood Ave 98801
Welch Ave 98801
Wellington Pl 98801
N & S Wenatchee Ave 98801
Wenatchee Heights Rd 98801
Westchester Dr 98801
N & S Western Ave 98801
Westknoll Ave 98801
Westmorland Dr 98801
Westpoint Pl 98801
Westridge Pl 98801
Westview Dr 98801
Westwick Rd 98801
Westwood Ave 98801
Wetherald St 98801
Wheeler Hill Rd 98801
Whispering Ridge Rd 98801
Whitebirch Pl 98801
N Whitman Way 98801
Willis St 98801
Willow Pl 98801
Willowbrook Dr 98801
Wilson St N & S 98801
Windsor Ct 98801
Woodhaven Pl 98801
Woodland Dr 98801
Woodridge St 98801
Woods St 98801
N Woodward Dr 98801
N & S Worthen St 98801
Yakima St
1-300 98801
301-899 98801
301-301 98807
302-898 98801
Yale Ave 98801
Yarrow St 98801

NUMBERED STREETS

All Street Addresses 98801

WOODINVILLE WA

General Delivery 98072

POST OFFICE BOXES MAIN OFFICE STATIONS AND BRANCHES

Box No.s
All PO Boxes 98072

NAMED STREETS

Avondale Rd NE
13300-17598 98077
13301-17599 98072
17501-18199 98077
Bantint St NE 98077
Bear Creek Ln & Rd 98077
Bear Creek Farm Rd NE 98077
Bostian Rd 98077
W Bostian Rd 98072
Crystal Lake Dr, Pl, Rd & Way 98077
Garden Way NE 98072
Kencens Ave NE 98072
Little Bear Creek Rd 98072
Maltby Rd 98072
Marwood Pl 98072
Mink Rd NE 98077
NE North Woodinville Way 98072
NE Old Woodinville Duvall Rd 98077
Paradise Lake Rd 98077
Saybrook Dr NE 98077
Snohomish Woodinville Rd 98072
State Route 9 SE 98072
NE Woodinville Dr 98072
NE Woodinville Duvall Pl
15600-15699 98072
18000-18316 98077
18318-18498 98077
NE Woodinville Duvall Rd
14000-17721 98072
17723-17899 98072
17800-17898 98077
17900-18000 98077
18002-24198 98077
18201-18899 98072
18801-18899 98077
19101-19199 98072
19201-24199 98077
Woodinville Redmond Rd NE 98072
Woodinville Snohomish Rd NE 98072

NUMBERED STREETS

47th Ave SE 98072
49th Ave & Dr 98072
50th Ave & Dr 98072
51st Ave SE 98072
52nd Ave SE 98072
55th Ave SE 98072
57th Ave SE 98072
58th Ave SE 98072
59th Ave SE 98072
60th Ave SE 98072
61st Ave SE 98072
63rd Ave SE 98072
65th Ave SE 98072
71st Dr SE 98072
73rd Dr SE 98072
75th Ave SE 98072
76th Ave & Dr 98072
77th Ave SE 98072
78th Ave SE 98072
79th Ave SE 98072
80th Ave SE 98072
81st Ave SE 98072
82nd Ave SE 98072
83rd Ave SE 98072
85th Ave SE 98072
87th Ave SE
21200-21899 98072
22400-22799 98077
94th Ave SE 98077
95th Ave SE 98077
99th Dr SE 98077
101st Ave SE 98077
102nd Ave SE 98077
104th Ave SE 98077
105th Ave SE 98077
106th Dr SE 98077
107th Dr SE 98077
110th Ave SE 98077
119th Ave SE 98077
NE 121st St 98077
NE 122nd Pl 98077
NE 123rd Ct 98077
124th Ave NE 98072
124th Ct NE
16000-16499 98072
19800-19899 98077
124th Pl NE
14600-16399 98072
19800-19899 98077
125th Ave NE 98072
125th Ct NE
16400-16499 98072
19600-19699 98077
125th Pl NE
15300-17299 98072
19700-19899 98077
126th Ave NE 98072
NE 126th Ct 98077
126th Pl NE
15700-17299 98072
19800-19899 98077
NE 126th Way 98077
127th Ave NE 98072
NE 127th Ct 98077
127th Pl NE
15300-17299 98072
19700-19799 98077
128th Ave NE 98072
128th Ct NE
15500-15599 98072
19800-19899 98077
128th Ln NE 98072
128th Pl NE 98072
129th Ave NE 98072
NE 129th Ct 98077
129th Pl NE 98077
NE 129th St 98077
NE 129th Way 98077
130th Ave NE 98072
130th Ct NE
20200-20299 98072
21100-21199 98077
130th Pl NE 98072
131st Ave, Ct & Pl 98072
132nd Ave NE 98072
132nd Ct NE
14500-14599 98072
21200-21299 98077
132nd Pl NE 98072
NE 132nd St 98077
133rd Ave NE 98072
133rd Ct NE
19400-19499 98072
19000-19099 98077
133rd Pl NE 98072
NE 133rd St
18400-18899 98072
19501-19597 98077
19599-22799 98077
134th Ave, Ct & Pl 98072
135th Ave NE 98072
135th Ct NE
14600-20299 98072
22700-22799 98077
135th Pl NE 98072
136th Ave NE 98072
136th Pl NE
14600-14698 98072
16100-16199 98072
21700-21799 98077
NE 136th St
18300-18399 98072
19041-19299 98077
137th Ave NE 98072
137th Ln NE 98072
137th Pl NE 98072
NE 137th St
16700-18899 98072
21800-22499 98077
NE 138th Ct 98072
NE 138th St 98077
138th Way NE
14600-14699 98072
23200-23499 98077
139th Ave NE 98072
NE 139th Pl 98072
NE 139th St
18400-18699 98072
21700-21799 98077
NE 139th Way 98077
140th Ave NE 98072
140th Ct NE
17000-17099 98072
16700-16719 98072
20900-20999 98077
140th Ln NE 98072
140th Pl NE
15300-16600 98072
18800-18999 98072
19100-21799 98077
NE 140th St 98077
NE 140th Way 98077
141st Ave NE 98072
141st Pl NE
17000-19899 98072
15600-18399 98072
22100-23299 98077
NE 141st St 98077
142nd Ave NE 98072
142nd Ct NE
18800-18899 98072
19300-19399 98077
142nd Pl NE
17000-17099 98072
22600-23399 98077
NE 142nd St 98077
143rd Ave NE 98072
143rd Ct NE
18600-18899 98072
22600-22699 98077
143rd Pl NE
17000-17499 98072
15700-18599 98072
19100-21599 98077
NE 143rd St
16000-19099 98072
19500-22099 98077
144th Ave NE 98072
NE 144th Ct 98077
NE 144th Pl
15200-15799 98072
19200-21799 98077
NE 144th St
18700-18799 98072
23000-23199 98077
145th Ave NE 98072
145th Ct NE 98072
145th Pl NE
17400-18199 98072
13200-18699 98072
NE 145th St
13600-17099 98072
19900-23199 98077
146th Ave NE 98072
NE 146th Ln 98072
146th Pl NE
17300-17399 98072
12400-15099 98072
21400-21599 98077
NE 146th St
13100-13199 98072
13201-13499 98072
19700-19799 98077
NE 146th Way 98072
147th Ct NE
18300-18399 98072
14900-14999 98072
147th Pl NE
15800-17899 98072
12500-14999 98072
23300-23599 98077
NE 147th St 98072
148th Ave NE 98072
NE 148th Pl 98072
NE 148th St
12500-16499 98072
19700-19798 98077
19800-20300 98077
20302-20338 98077
149th Ave NE 98072
149th Ave SE 98077
149th Pl NE 98072
NE 149th St
12400-13199 98072
19200-21499 98077
150th Ct NE
16700-16799 98072
18800-18899 98072
NE 150th Pl 98077
NE 150th St
16800-18999 98072
20300-23199 98077
151st Ave NE 98072
NE 151st Ct 98077
NE 151st Pl
16600-16799 98072
19900-19999 98077
NE 151st St
12800-19199 98072
21200-21899 98077
151st Way NE 98072
152nd Ave NE 98072
152nd Pl NE
15700-16799 98072
15400-15498 98072
22800-23599 98077
NE 152nd St 98077
NE 153rd Ave, Pl & St NE 98072
154th Ave NE 98072
154th Ct NE 98072
NE 154th Dr 98072
NE 154th Pl 98072
NE 154th St
12500-18299 98072
19800-21999 98077
155th Ave NE 98072
155th Pl NE
17300-17699 98072
12400-18099 98072
19800-21199 98077
NE 155th St
15500-19299 98072
19900-20499 98077
156th Ave NE 98072
NE 156th Ct 98072
156th Pl NE
14000-17599 98072
12600-12699 98072
19600-23499 98077
NE 156th St
12500-18499 98072
20500-21999 98077
157th Ave NE 98072
NE 157th Ct 98077
157th Pl NE
14200-19799 98072
18600-18699 98072
22900-32199 98077
NE 157th St
12400-18899 98072
19900-22599 98077
158th Ave NE 98072
158th Pl NE 98072
NE 158th St
16700-17199 98072
19600-19999 98077
159th Ave NE 98072
159th Ct NE 98072
159th Pl NE
16500-19599 98072
16800-16999 98072
NE 159th St
15600-19199 98072
19200-23199 98077
160th Ave NE 98072
NE 160th Ct 98072
160th Pl NE
14300-14398 98072
12500-17799 98072
19700-22399 98077
NE 160th St
12400-17999 98072
20100-21099 98077
161st Ave NE 98072
161st Ln NE 98072
161st Pl NE
19500-19599 98072
18500-18799 98072
21000-21199 98077
NE 161st St 98077
162nd Ave NE 98072
NE 162nd Ct 98072
162nd Pl NE
16000-16199 98072
19000-19099 98072
NE 162nd St
12400-18999 98072
19400-23199 98077
163rd Ave NE 98072
163rd Ct NE
14800-19499 98072
12400-12499 98072
163rd Pl NE
15200-15299 98072
12400-17699 98072
NE 163rd St
12500-15399 98072
20124-20999 98077
164th Ave NE 98072
164th Pl NE
14800-15815 98072
20100-20399 98077
NE 164th St
12400-12436 98072
12438-17099 98072
19700-23499 98077
165th Ave NE 98072
NE 165th Ct 98077

165th Pl NE
14500-18812 98072
18800-19099 98072
NE 165th St
15400-18999 98072
19001-19199 98072
19200-23199 98077
166th Ave NE 98072
NE 166th Ct 98072
NE 166th Ln 98072
166th Pl NE
15000-17199 98072
17400-17499 98072
19400-19499 98077
NE 166th St
12500-17099 98072
20100-22999 98077
23001-23099 98077
167th Ave NE 98072
167th Ct NE
15000-15099 98072
16600-16699 98072
19700-19799 98077
NE 167th Pl
12500-15699 98072
20700-21399 98077
NE 167th St 98072
168th Ave NE 98072
NE 168th Ct
12500-12599 98072
22000-22099 98077
168th Pl NE
16600-18299 98072
19900-20299 98077
NE 168th St
13700-19199 98072
23700-23799 98077
169th Ave NE 98072
NE 169th Ct 98072
NE 169th Pl
16000-16599 98072
19400-23299 98077
NE 169th St
12400-14799 98072
19600-22699 98077
170th Ave NE 98072
170th Ln NE
14000-14099 98072
12600-12899 98072
170th Pl NE
17500-17699 98072
16400-16499 98072
22000-22299 98077
NE 170th St
18400-18499 98072
23600-23799 98077
171st Ave NE 98072
NE 171st Ct
12400-12499 98072
23200-23299 98077
171st Ln NE
14000-14099 98072
12700-12799 98072
171st Pl NE
16000-19099 98072
12400-12499 98072
NE 171st St
13300-14203 98072
24600-24699 98077
172nd Ave NE 98072
NE 172nd Ct 98072
NE 172nd Ln 98072
172nd Pl NE
16700-17099 98072
16400-17199 98072
NE 172nd St
14800-16399 98072
19200-24299 98077
173rd Ave NE 98072
NE 173rd Pl
12400-12699 98072
23200-23299 98077
NE 173rd St 98072
174th Ave NE 98072
NE 174th St
14300-14899 98072
19800-19899 98077
175th Ave NE 98072
NE 175th Pl 98072
NE 175th St
12700-16299 98072
19900-22399 98077
176th Ave NE 98072
NE 176th Pl
15300-15499 98072
19700-21799 98077
NE 176th St
16700-18299 98072
19600-20499 98077
177th Ave NE 98072
NE 177th Ct 98072
NE 177th Dr 98072
177th Pl NE
15100-16499 98072
13000-17099 98072
NE 177th St
13100-14899 98072
19900-20599 98077
178th Ave NE 98072
178th Ln NE 98072
178th Pl NE
16200-16299 98072
13900-15899 98072
NE 178th St
12600-14799 98072
19700-19899 98077
179th Ave NE 98072
179th Ct NE 98072
179th Pl NE 98072
NE 179th St
14100-18499 98072
19400-20599 98077
180th Ave NE 98072
180th Pl NE
15700-15799 98072
14600-16699 98072
23500-23599 98077
NE 180th St
14500-16399 98072
23900-24399 98077
181st Ave NE
15300-15399 98072
18900-19599 98072
NE 181st Ct 98072
181st Pl NE
14600-15999 98072
18800-20199 98072
14000-14299 98072
20400-21799 98077
NE 181st St
14001-14021 98072
19400-23799 98077
182nd Ave NE
14000-17899 98072
18500-20099 98077
182nd Pl NE
15300-15999 98072
15200-15699 98072
NE 182nd St 98072
183rd Ave NE
14500-15699 98072
19100-19399 98072
183rd Pl NE
15500-17099 98072
19800-20199 98077
17100-17199 98072
22000-22099 98077
NE 183rd St
13200-15999 98072
18500-23699 98077
184th Ave NE 98072
184th Ct NE 98072
184th Pl NE
15100-15599 98072
19100-19999 98077
13200-16099 98072
21400-21499 98077
NE 184th St 98077
185th Ave NE
15300-17999 98072
18001-18199 98072
18600-19099 98077
185th Ct NE
13900-15399 98072
14300-14399 98072
NE 185th Pl 98077
NE 185th St
13000-15099 98072
19400-20100 98077
20102-23098 98077
186th Ave NE
13300-15999 98072
18600-18699 98077
NE 186th Ct
14300-14399 98072
20100-20199 98077
186th Pl NE
14300-14599 98072
18300-20199 98077
13100-14399 98072
18900-18999 98077
NE 186th St
13000-14199 98072
18200-21499 98077
187th Ave NE 98072
187th Ct NE
13300-13399 98072
14200-14299 98072
NE 187th Pl 98072
NE 187th St
16200-16399 98072
21900-22299 98077
188th Ave NE
14300-16599 98072
20200-20299 98077
NE 188th Ct 98072
188th Pl NE
14200-16799 98072
13500-15599 98072
20000-20099 98077
NE 188th St 98072
189th Ave NE
14600-16799 98072
18300-19099 98077
NE 189th Ct
14300-14399 98072
22200-22299 98077
189th Pl NE
18200-19599 98077
14300-14399 98072
NE 189th St
14100-14199 98072
18100-24199 98077
189th Way NE 98072
190th Ave NE
14500-16599 98072
19800-20099 98077
NE 190th Ct 98077
190th Pl NE
18200-18299 98077
13100-13599 98072
20100-20399 98077
NE 190th St
13900-17299 98072
19300-23999 98077
191st Ave NE
14600-17499 98072
20200-20399 98077
NE 191st Ct 98077
191st Pl NE
16500-16799 98072
15200-15299 98072
NE 191st St
15600-15999 98072
18100-19799 98077
192nd Ave NE 98077
192nd Ct NE
15400-15499 98072
22600-22699 98077
NE 192nd St
13000-15199 98072
18300-23799 98077
NE 192nd Way 98072
193rd Ct NE 98077
NE 193rd Pl
13100-15999 98072
24100-24699 98077
NE 193rd St 98072
194th Ave NE 98077
NE 194th Ct 98077
194th Pl NE 98077
NE 194th St
13100-13199 98072
18200-22199 98077
195th Ct NE 98077
195th Pl NE
12900-18199 98077
22200-22299 98077
NE 195th St
13100-17799 98072
17800-22799 98077
196th Ave NE 98077
196th Ct NE
12900-14399 98077
18200-18299 98077
196th Pl NE
15800-15999 98077
13000-13099 98072
18400-18499 98077
NE 196th St
16300-16399 98072
17800-24699 98077
197th Ave NE 98077
197th Ct NE 98077
197th Pl NE
12500-18199 98077
12800-16599 98072
18100-18199 98077
NE 197th St 98072
198th Ave NE 98077
198th Ct NE
12000-12099 98077
13000-13099 98077
198th Dr NE 98077
198th Pl NE
15800-15999 98077
12800-17899 98072
NE 198th St
14800-16399 98072
18300-22199 98077
199th Ave NE 98077
199th Ct NE 98077
199th Pl NE
16600-18399 98077
13400-13499 98072
18300-18399 98077
NE 199th St 98072
200th Ave NE 98077
200th Ct NE
12000-12099 98077
16200-16299 98072
18100-18199 98077
NE 200th Pl 98072
NE 200th St
13500-14399 98072
18200-24399 98077
201st Ave NE 98077
201st Ct NE
12200-12299 98077
13200-13299 98072
21700-21799 98077
NE 201st Dr 98077
201st Pl NE 98077
NE 201st St
12800-15599 98072
23400-23499 98077
NE 201st Way 98072
202nd Ave NE 98077
NE 202nd Ct 98072
202nd Pl NE
17600-17699 98077
13000-17199 98077
19400-19599 98077
NE 202nd St
13500-15699 98072
18600-22999 98077
203rd Ave NE 98077
NE 203rd Ct
12900-12999 98072
19100-19199 98077
203rd Pl NE
16500-19099 98077
13100-16399 98072
19400-21899 98077
NE 203rd St
12900-17899 98072
21700-21799 98077
204th Ave NE 98077
NE 204th Ct 98077
204th Ln NE 98077
204th Pl NE
14500-14799 98077
12900-12999 98072
NE 204th St 98072
NE 204th Way 98072
205th Ave NE 98077
205th Pl NE 98077
NE 205th St
12801-17797 98072
17799-17899 98072
18201-18299 98077
206th Ave & Pl 98077
207th Pl NE 98077
208th Ave & Pl 98077
209th Ave & Pl 98077
210th Ave NE 98077
211th Pl & Way 98077
212th Ave & Dr 98077
213th Ave & Pl 98077
214th Ave NE 98077
214th Pl SE 98072
214th St SE 98072
214th Way NE 98077
215th Pl SE 98072
215th St SE 98072
215th Way NE 98077
216th Ave NE 98077
216th Pl SE 98072
216th St SE 98072
216th Way NE 98077
217th Ave NE 98077
217th Pl NE 98077
217th St SE 98072
218th Ave NE 98077
218th Pl NE 98077
218th St SE 98072
219th Ave NE 98077
219th St SE 98072
220th Ave, Ct & Pl 98077
221st Ave & Pl NE & SE 98077
222nd Ave, St & Way 98077
223rd Ave & Ct 98077
224th Ave NE 98077
224th Ct NE 98077
224th St SE 98072
225th Ave NE 98077
225th Pl NE 98077
225th St SE 98072
226th Ave & St NE & SE 98077
227th Ave NE 98077
227th Pl SE 98077
227th St SE 98072
228th Ave NE 98077
228th Pl NE 98077
228th Pl SE 98077
228th St SE 98072
229th Ave NE 98077
229th Pl SE
7400-8299 98072
10500-10699 98077
229th St SE
7500-7699 98072
10400-10499 98077
230th Ave NE 98077
231st Ct NE 98077
231st Pl SE
5900-6099 98072
9900-10699 98077
232nd Ave NE 98077
232nd St SE
7500-8299 98072
12100-12299 98077
233rd Ave NE 98077
233rd Ct NE 98077
233rd Pl NE 98077
233rd Pl SE 98072
234th Ct NE 98077
234th St SE 98072
235th Ave NE 98077
235th Ct NE 98077
235th Pl NE 98077
235th St SE 98072
236th Ave NE 98077
236th Pl NE 98077
236th Pl SE 98072
237th Ave & Pl 98077
238th Ave NE 98077
238th St SE 98072
239th St SE 98072
240th Ave NE 98077
240th St SE 98072
242nd Ave NE 98077
242nd St SE
8000-8099 98072
12100-12399 98077
243rd Ave NE 98077
243rd St SE 98072
244th Ave NE 98077
244th St SE 98072
246th Ave NE 98077

YAKIMA WA

General Delivery 98903

POST OFFICE BOXES MAIN OFFICE STATIONS AND BRANCHES

Box No.s
1 - 2974 98907
3000 - 3460 98903
4001 - 4149 98904
8001 - 8360 98908
9001 - 11600 98909
9998 - 9998 98904
12500 - 12571 98909
22500 - 22730 98907

NAMED STREETS

W A St 98902
Abbess Ln 98908
Ackerman Ave 98902
W Acre Ct 98903
E Adams St 98901
Adamsview Rd 98901
Aerial Dr 98903
Aeroview 98908
E, S & W Ahtanum Rd 98903
Ahtanum Ridge Dr 98903
Airport Ln 98903
Alder St 98903
E Alder St 98901
Alexandria Ct 98908
Aller Ave 98908
Almo Rd 98901
Alpine Ct & Way 98908
Amber Crest Pl 98908
American Fruit Rd 98903
Andring Way 98901
Angus Ln 98901
Ann Dr 98908
Apple Blossom Ct 98908
N & S Appleview Rd & Way 98908
Aquila Rd 98908
Arboretum Dr 98901
W Arlington Ave 98908
E Arlington St 98901
W Arlington St
1-3799 98902
4000-5399 98908
5401-5799 98908
Arrowhead Rd 98901
Arroyo Dr 98901
Arthur Blvd
1-99 98901
101-1599 98901
200-298 98902
900-1598 98901
Aspen Rd 98903
Aspen Springs Ln 98903
Autumn Dr 98901
Autumn Breeze Ln 98903
Avalanche Ave & Ct 98908
Ayon Ln 98901
Bachelorview Dr 98903
Baggarley Dr 98903
Baker Ct 98901
Baker St 98902
Baldie Way 98902
Bandenew Rd 98908
Bandwagon Ln 98903
Barber Rd 98908
Barge Ct 98908
Barge St
2100-3499 98902
4200-6599 98908
W Barge St 98908
Barnes Rd 98908
Barrett Rd 98908
Bartlett Pl 98901
Basalt Way 98908
Bay St 98903
Beacon Ave 98901
Beaudry Rd 98901
E Beech St 98901
Bel Air Dr 98908
Belgold Dr 98902
Bell Ave 98908
Bell Rd 98901
Bell St 98902
Bellevue Pl 98908
Belmont Ave 98902
Benjamin Dr 98908
Berndt Bluff Rd 98908
Betty Rae Way 98908
Birch St 98901
W Birchfield Rd 98901
Bitterroot Ln & Way 98908
Bittner Rd 98901
Blackburn St 98902
Blackhawk Rd 98908
Bline Rd 98908
Blossom Way 98908
Blue Crane Ln 98901
Blue Hills Pl 98908
Boggess Ln 98901
Bohoskey Dr 98901
Bonnie Ln 98908
Bonnie Doon Ave 98902
Borley Way 98908
Borton Rd 98903
Boucher Ln 98901
Boulder Way 98901
Bowers Rd 98908
Brackett Ave 98902
Braeburn Loop 98903
Breaum Rd 98908
Breezeway 98901
Bridle Ln & Way 98901
Bristol Ct & Way 98908
Bristol Way Ct 98908
Broadview Dr 98901
Brown Ave 98908
Browne Ave 98902
Buckskin Creek Rd 98908
Buds Pl 98901
Burbank Creek Rd 98901
Burman Way 98901
Burnham Rd 98908
Burning Tree Dr 98902
E Burwell St 98901
Business Ln 98901
Business Pkwy 98903
Butterfield Rd 98901
Buwalda Ln 98901
E C St 98901
E & W California St 98903
Callahan Ln 98903
Camelot Way 98908
Cameo Ct & Pl 98903
Camfield Rd 98908
Camp 4 Rd 98908
Campbell Ave 98902
Camus Ln 98901
Canter Ln 98903
Canterbury Ln 98902

Canyon Rd 98901
N Canyon Rd 98901
W Canyon Rd 98908
Canyon Crest Rd 98903
Canyon View Pl 98908
Carey St 98903
Carlson Dr & Rd 98903
Carol Ave
3200-3799 98902
4700-4799 98908
Carriage Hill Dr 98908
Carriage Park Ln 98902
Carson Rd 98903
Carvo Rd 98908
Casa Ct 98902
Cascade Ct 98908
Cascade Dr 98908
Cascade Loop 98902
Cascade Rd 98901
Cascadia Park Dr 98901
Castle Pl 98901
Castle Mountain Ct 98901
Castlevale Rd 98902
Castleview Dr 98908
Cayuse Ln 98901
Cedar Hill Dr 98908
Cedar Hills Ct 98902
Central Ave 98901
Century Ave 98908
Chalmers St 98901
Channel Dr 98901
Charlene Way 98901
Cherry Ave 98902
Cherry Park Ct 98908
N Cherry Ridge Ct 98908
Chesterly Dr 98902
E Chestnut Ave 98901
W Chestnut Ave
301-397 98902
399-3999 98902
4000-9599 98908
Chevelle Ct 98903
Cheviot Dr 98901
Chicago Ave 98902
Chickadee Ln 98908
Chinook Dr 98908
Chisholm Trl 98908
Chuckar Dr 98901
Church Rd 98903
City Reservoir Rd 98908
Clark Ave 98902
N & S Clark Heights Rd 98901
Clasen Ln 98903
Cleman Ave 98902
Clinton Pl 98902
Clinton Way
2400-3700 98902
3702-3898 98902
4700-6899 98908
Clover Ln 98908
Coach Ct & Ln 98908
Cobblestone Pl 98908
E & W Columbus St 98903
Commonwealth Rd 98901
N Conestoga Blvd 98908
Conover Dr 98908
Conrad Ave 98902
Cook Rd 98908
Cook St 98902
Cook Hill Rd 98908
Coolidge Pl & Rd 98903
Coombs Rd 98901
Cornell Ave
600-1700 98902
1702-1898 98902
1900-2299 98903
Corpman Ln 98903
Correy Ln 98901
N & S Corriedale Rd 98901
Corrigan Way 98902
Cottage Way 98908
N Cottonwood Ln & Rd 98908
Cottonwood Canyon Rd 98908

Cougar Ln 98901
Country Crst 98901
Country Ln 98908
Country Club Dr 98901
Country Home Ln 98901
W Court St 98903
Courthouse 98901
Courtney Heights Ln 98908
Covington Ln 98901
Cowden Pl 98908
Cowiche Canyon Ln & Rd 98908
Cowiche Mill Rd 98908
Coyote Creek Rd 98901
Coyote Springs Rd 98901
Crawford Ln 98901
Creekside Loop
1600-3999 98902
4000-4099 98908
Crest Cir & Dr 98908
Crest Acres Ln & Pl 98908
Crestfield Rd 98903
Crown Crest Ave 98903
Culdorn Dr 98903
Custer Ave 98902
Cynthia Ct 98901
Cypress Way 98908
E D St 98901
W D St 98902
Dahl Rd 98908
Dalton Rd 98901
Dammar Ln 98908
Davell Ln 98901
Dazet Rd 98908
Del Mar Ter 98902
Densoury Rd 98903
Desert Rose Dr 98903
Deweese Ln 98901
Ditchbank Rd 98908
Ditter Dr 98902
Division St 98902
Doescher Dr 98908
Donald Dr 98908
Donelson Ln 98908
Dorset Dr 98901
Douglas Ct, Dr & Rd 98908
Douglas View Ln 98908
Dove Trail Ln 98908
Drake Ct 98902
Drake Dr 98908
Draper Rd 98903
Dundee Ct 98908
Durand Ln 98901
Dusty Ln 98903
E E St 98901
Eagle Way 98901
Eagle Crest Dr 98903
Eagle Nest 98903
Eastridge St 98901
Eastview Dr 98902
Easy St 98903
Echo Ct 98908
Echo Glenn Pl 98908
Ehler Rd 98908
Ekelman Rd 98901
El Rio Dr 98908
Eleanor St 98902
Elk Rd 98901
Elnora St 98902
Elton Rd 98901
W Emma Ln & St 98903
Englewood Ave
1600-1698 98902
1700-3699 98902
3701-3999 98902
4000-7999 98908
Englewood Pl 98908
Englewood Ter 98908
Englewood Crest Ct & Dr 98908
Englewood Hill Dr & Pl 98908
Erickson Ln 98901
Eschbach Rd 98908
Eschbach Hill Rd 98908
Estate Way 98908

Estee Ct 98908
Estes Rd 98908
Evergreen Ct 98902
Ewe Dr 98901
E F St 98901
N & S Fair Ave 98901
Fairbanks Ave 98902
Fairbrook Dr 98908
Fairway Dr 98901
Falcon Crest Way 98908
Farenerl Rd 98901
Farm Country Ct 98908
Faucher Rd 98901
Fechter Rd 98908
Fedderly Ln 98908
Fellows Dr 98908
Fenton St 98901
Ferncrest Dr 98901
Fetzer Ln 98903
Firing Center Rd 98901
Fisk Rd 98908
Flintstone Rd 98908
Follow Through Dr 98901
Folsom Ave 98902
Fonara Ave 98903
N & S Fork Rd 98903
Four Hills Dr 98908
W Franklin St 98903
Fraser Way 98902
Frayne Pl 98901
Freeway Ave 98903
Fremont Dr 98908
Fremont St 98902
Fremont Way 98908
Friedline Rd 98908
Fromherz Dr 98908
N & S Front St 98901
Fruitvale Blvd
500-3900 98902
3902-3998 98902
4000-4098 98908
4100-4199 98908
E G St 98901
N Galloway Dr 98908
Gamache Ln 98903
Garden Ave & Dr 98908
Garden Park Way 98908
Garden Terrace Ln 98901
Garfield Ave 98902
Garretson Ln 98908
Garrett Ln & St 98902
Gephart Rd 98901
Ghormley Rd 98908
Gibbler Rd 98908
Gilbert Dr 98902
Gilbert Rd 98903
Glacier Ct & Way 98908
Glaspey Ln 98903
E & N Gleed Pl & Rd 98908
Glenmoor Cir 98908
Glenside Ct 98908
Glessner Ln 98901
Goat Rocks Ct 98901
Golden Ln 98908
Goldfinch Ln 98908
Goodman Rd 98903
Goose Haven Ln 98901
Gordon Rd 98901
Graham St 98902
Grange Rd 98901
Grant St 98902
Graystone Ct 98908
Green Acres Ln 98901
Green Meadows Dr 98908
Green Ridge Dr 98908
Greenview Dr 98908
Greenway 98902
Gregory Ave 98902
Gregory Ct 98902
Gregory Pl 98908
Grissom Ln 98903
Gromore Rd 98908
Grove Ave 98908
Grunewald Rd 98908
Gun Club Rd 98901
E H St 98901

Hackett Rd 98903
Hadley Dr 98908
Hagar Pl 98902
Hahn Rd 98908
Hailey Pl 98901
Hall Ave 98902
Hall Rd 98908
S Hamerrid Ave 98902
Hamilton Ave 98902
Hamm Ave 98902
Hanraty Dr 98902
Harbor Ln 98903
Hardy Rd 98901
Harmony Ln 98908
Hartford Rd 98901
Harvest Dr 98901
Hathaway St 98902
Haven Way 98908
Hawks Lndg 98903
Hawthorn Dr 98908
Haynes St 98902
Hazen Rd 98903
Heathers Ave & Way 98903
Hedge Ln 98903
Hennessy Rd 98908
Henning St 98901
Henry St 98902
Hi Valley View St 98901
Hideaway Rd 98908
High Point Lndg 98901
Highview Dr 98902
Hill Dr 98908
Hillcrest Ct 98902
Hillcrest Dr 98901
E Hillcrest Dr 98901
Hillcroft Way 98901
Hillman Rd 98908
Hillside Dr & Pl 98903
Hillstone Dr 98908
Hilltop Dr 98901
Hilltop Ln 98901
Hilltop Way 98908
Hobby Horse Ln 98901
Holbrook Ct 98902
Holiday Ave 98903
Hollow Creek Ln 98908
Hollow Creek Pl 98902
Holly Ln 98908
Holton Ave 98902
Home Dr 98902
Home Acres Rd 98901
Homesite Dr 98908
Homestead Rd 98908
Honeycrisp Ct 98903
Hope Ln 98903
Hoppis Ln 98908
Horgan St 98901
Horizons Ct 98901
Howard Ave 98902
Hubbard Rd
500-1899 98903
2000-2199 98908
Hughes Rd 98903
Hummingbird Ln 98903
Hunziker Rd 98908
E I St 98901
W I St 98902
Iler Ln 98901
Indian Heaven Ct 98901
Industrial Way 98903
Industry Ln 98901
Iron Horse Ct 98901
Isabella Way 98901
Ivy Ave & Ct 98908
E J St 98901
W J St 98902
Jack Rabbit Rd 98901
Jackson Ct 98908
Jade Pl 98908
Jefferson Ave 98902
Jerome Ave 98902
Jessica Ln 98908
Jonagold Ct 98903
Joyce Pl 98908
Juanita Dr 98908
Judy Ln 98901

Justice Dr 98901
E K St 98901
Kail Dr 98908
Karin Dr 98901
Karr Ave 98902
Kateenah Way 98903
Kelly Ln 98901
Kenny Dr 98902
Kenward Way 98901
Kern Way
3600-3798 98902
3800-3999 98902
4100-4199 98908
N & S Kershaw Dr 98908
Kestrel Ln 98908
Keys Rd 98901
Kilgary Way 98901
Kimberly Pl 98908
W King Ct 98902
E King St 98903
W King St
1-3299 98902
4003-7999 98908
Kittitas Canyon Rd 98901
Klendon Dr 98908
Kloochman Way 98901
Knobel Ave 98902
Knoll Rd 98908
Knox Rd 98908
Koch Dr & Rd 98901
Kona Ln 98908
Kristi Ln 98901
Kroum Rd 98901
La Follett St 98901
La Salle St 98901
Laban Ave 98902
Ladwig St 98903
Lakeata Ave 98903
Lakeside Ct 98902
Lakeview Dr 98902
Lanai Dr 98908
Landon Ave
900-1699 98902
1900-2299 98903
Langell Dr 98903
W Larch Ave 98903
Laredo Ln 98901
Laroca Dr 98901
Larson Rd 98908
Larson Bldg 98901
Latigo Ln 98901
Laura Ln 98908
Laurel St 98902
Lava Way 98903
Leann Pl 98908
Ledwich Ave
1100-1699 98902
2000-2099 98903
Leininger Dr 98901
Leisure Ln 98908
Leisure Hill Dr 98903
Lester Ave 98902
Lewis St 98902
Lightning Way 98903
Lila Ave & Pl 98902
Lilac Ln 98903
E Lincoln Ave 98901
W Lincoln Ave
2-298 98902
300-3909 98902
3911-3999 98902
4000-12699 98908
Lincoln Estates Dr 98908
Lindgren Dr 98908
Lindy Ln 98901
N Lisa Ln 98908
Lockhart Dr 98901
Locust Ave 98901
Locust St 98903
W Logan Ave
2-198 98902
200-3999 98902
6800-6999 98908
Logan Ln 98902
Logan Pl 98908
Lombard Ln 98902

Lone Dove Ln 98903
Lonesome Pine Rd 98903
Long Ln 98908
Longfibre Ave 98903
Loranger Ln 98901
Loren Ave 98902
Loren Ct 98902
Loren Pl 98908
Lost Goose Ln 98901
Low Rd 98908
Lucas Rd 98901
Lupine Dr 98901
Lynch Ln 98903
Lynch Rd 98908
Lynn Pl 98901
Lyons Ln & Loop 98903
Macias Ln 98901
Maclaren Ave 98908
Maclaren Ct 98908
Maclaren Ln 98908
Maclaren St
900-998 98902
1000-2399 98902
5801-7497 98908
7499-7599 98908
Maclaren Way 98908
Madera Way 98908
Madison Ave 98902
Magnolia Ct 98908
Magpie 98908
Mahoney Rd 98908
Mahre Rd 98908
Main St 98903
Majesty Heights Dr 98908
Manor Dr 98901
Manor Way 98908
E Maple Ave, Ct & St 98901
Mapleway Rd 98908
Marble Ct, Ext, Ln & Rd 98908
Maree Ln 98908
Margaret Ct 98908
Marilane St 98908
Marion Ave 98903
Market St 98903
Marks Rd 98903
Marsh Rd 98901
E Martin Luther King Jr Blvd 98901
W Martin Luther King Jr Blvd 98902
Mary Way 98908
Marylin Dr 98908
Matthews Pl 98908
Maui Pl 98908
Mavis Ave 98902
Mcallister Dr 98908
Mcauley Rd 98908
Mccargar St 98908
Mccormick Rd 98908
Mccoy Rd 98908
Mccullough Rd 98903
Mcinnis Ln 98903
Mckinley Ave 98902
Mclaughlin Rd 98908
Mclean Dr
3600-3698 98902
3700-3999 98902
4000-4199 98908
Mclean Pl 98908
Mcnair Ave 98903
E Mead Ave 98903
W Mead Ave
1-2699 98902
2701-3099 98902
7000-7999 98908
Meadow Ct 98908
Meadow Ln
3400-3499 98903
3800-3999 98902
5300-8799 98908
Meadowbrook Rd 98903
Meadowcrest Ln 98903
Meridian Way 98908
Mesa Vista Pl 98901
Messina Dr 98902

Michael Dr 98901
Midvale Rd 98908
Mieras Rd 98901
Mini Pines Rd 98903
N & S Mitchell Dr & Pl 98908
N & S Mize Rd 98908
Mobile Home Ave 98903
Modesto Way 98908
Monroe Ave 98902
Moonlight Ln 98901
Moore Rd 98908
Morningside Ct & Dr 98901
Morrier Ln 98901
Mount Aix Way 98901
Mount Clemens Way 98901
Mount Vernon Ave 98902
Mount Vista Ct 98903
Mountain Shadows Pl 98908
Mountainview Ave 98901
Mulberry Way 98908
Mulder Dr 98902
Murphy Ln 98901
Murray Rd 98908
E N St 98901
N Naches Ave 98901
S Naches Ave 98901
S Naches Rd 98908
Naches Heights Rd 98908
Nelson Rd 98903
E Nob Hill Blvd 98901
W Nob Hill Blvd
52-3999 98902
4000-4298 98908
4300-8299 98908
Noble Hill Rd 98908
Nola Loop Rd 98901
E Norman Rd 98901
Nugent St 98901
E O St 98901
W O St 98902
Oahu Ln 98908
Oak Ave 98903
W Oak Ave 98903
E Oak St 98901
W Oak St 98903
Obrien Vista Ln 98901
Observation Dr 98901
Occidental Rd 98903
Old Naches Hwy 98908
Old Stage Way 98908
Old Town Rd 98903
Oliver Dr 98901
Olmstead Ct 98908
Olson Rd 98908
Orchard Ave 98908
Orchard Rite Rd 98908
Oster Dr 98901
Overbluff Ct, Dr & Ln 98901
E P St 98901
Pacific Ave 98901
Paint Horse Rd 98901
Painted Rocks Dr 98908
Palatine Ave 98902
Palm Ct 98908
Palomino Rd 98908
Panorama Dr 98901
Park Ave
1-7 98903
5-399 98902
9-116 98903
118-118 98903
Park Ln 98902
Park Pl 98908
Parkway Pl 98902
Parsons Ave & Loop 98908
Patnode St 98901
Patricia Ave 98901
Paulson Pl 98908
Peach St 98902
Peach Tree Ln 98908
N & S Pear Ave 98908
Pear Butte Dr 98901
Pear Tree Ct 98908
Pearl St 98901
Pebbles Crest Rd 98908

Pecks Canyon Rd 98908
Peggy Point Rd 98901
Pence Rd 98908
Perry Ct
1300-1399 98902
6900-7099 98908
Perry Loop 98902
Perry St
300-1700 98902
1702-1898 98902
7301-7397 98908
7399-7499 98908
Perry Way 98901
Perry Vista Ln 98901
Phaeton Pl 98908
Pheasant Crest Dr 98908
Pickens Loop & Rd 98908
N Pierce Ave 98902
W Pierce Ct 98908
Pierce St
1400-1598 98903
7200-7399 98908
W Pierce St
1-299 98902
301-1599 98902
6700-6799 98908
Pilot Ln 98901
E Pine St
2-98 98901
6-102 98903
100-899 98901
W Pine St
2-98 98903
100-399 98902
100-1699 98903
401-799 98902
E & W Pine Hollow Rd 98903
Pine Mountain Dr 98903
Pioneer Ln 98903
Pioneer Way 98908
N Pioneer Way 98908
Pitcher St 98901
Plateau Pl 98908
Plath Ave 98908
W Plath Ave
1600-3300 98902
3302-3798 98902
7800-7999 98908
Pleasant Ave
600-1899 98902
2501-2501 98903
2503-2699 98903
Pleasant Hills Dr 98908
Pleasant Valley Pl & Rd 98908
Plum Ln 98908
Polly Ln 98901
Pomona Rd 98901
Pomona Heights Rd 98901
Pond Rd 98901
E Ponderosa Dr 98903
W Ponderosa Dr 98903
Ponderosa Pl 98902
Poplar Ave 98902
Poplar View Way 98908
Postma Rd 98901
Powell St 98901
Powerhouse Rd 98902
W Powerhouse Rd 98908
W Prasch Ave
1-3499 98902
3501-3999 98902
4100-7099 98908
Presson Ln 98902
Presson Pl 98903
Prestige Ct 98908
Prospect Way 98908
E Q St 98901
Quail Run Dr 98908
Queen Ave 98902
Queen Anne Blvd 98902
Quince St 98902
E R St 98901
E Race St 98901
Racquet Ln 98902
E Railroad St 98901
Rainier Pl 98903
Rainier St 98901
Ram Way 98901
Ranch Rite Rd 98901
Rancho Ln 98908
Raven Ln 98901
Ravens Gate Way 98908
Ray Symmonds Rd 98901
Red Sky Dr 98903
Red Tail Rd 98908
Redwood Way 98902
Reed Ln 98901
E Reed Ln 98903
Rest Haven Rd 98901
Richards Cir & Rd 98903
Richartz Rd 98903
Richey Rd
2900-3999 98902
4000-4098 98908
4100-7799 98908
N & W Ridge Ct 98908
Ridgeway Dr 98901
Ridgeway Rd 98903
Rippee Ln 98908
River Rd 98902
Rivers Edge Ln 98901
Riverside Rd & St 98901
Riverview Dr 98901
Roberts Rd 98908
Rock Ave
1000-1699 98902
2000-2100 98903
2102-2198 98903
Rock Garden Ln 98908
Rockstrom Rd 98903
Rocky Top Rd 98908
Rodgers Rd 98908
Rolling Hills Dr 98908
Roosevelt Ave 98902
Rose Pl 98902
Rose St 98903
Rosewood Ln 98901
Ross Ln 98903
Royal Palm Ave 98903
Royale Ct 98901
Royer Ave 98902
Roza Hill Dr 98901
Roza View Dr 98901
Roza Vista Dr 98901
N & S Rozalee Way 98901
Rudkin Rd
1600-1798 98901
1800-2398 98903
2400-2699 98903
2701-2899 98903
Runway Ln 98908
Russell Ln 98903
Rutherford Rd 98903
Ryegrass Rd 98903
E S St 98901
Saddle Brook Ct & Dr 98908
Sage Cove Rd 98903
Sage Trail Rd 98901
Sagebrush Heights Rd 98903
Saint Andrews Pl 98908
Saint Helens St 98902
N Saint Hilaire Rd 98901
Saint Johns St 98902
Saint Martin Ln 98901
Saint Thomas St 98903
Sali Rd 98903
Samantha Ct 98903
Sand Crest Pl 98901
Santa Roza Dr 98901
Sara Loop 98908
N Scenic Dr & Ter 98908
Scenic Bluff Dr 98908
Scenic Canyon Ln 98908
Scenic Crest Dr 98901
Scenic Ridge Loop 98908
Schade St 98901
Schlagel Rd 98903
Schlect Rd 98908
School Rd 98901
Schuller Grade 98908
Scogin Ln 98908
Scott Ct 98908
Scudder Way 98901
Seasons Pkwy 98901
Seattle Slew Run 98908
Section 12 Rd 98903
Segur Rd 98901
E Selah Rd 98901
Selah Creek Dr 98901
Selah Naches Rd 98908
Shadbolt Rd 98908
Shamrock Dr E & W 98908
Shannon Rd 98908
Sharon Way 98902
Sharon View Pl 98908
Sheets Rd 98901
Shelton Ave 98902
Sherwood Forest Ln 98903
Short St 98903
Shotgun Ln 98901
Siegmund Pl 98901
Simpson Ln 98901
Sisotow Belle Ln 98903
Sky Vista Ave & Pl 98901
Skyline Ave & Way 98908
Skyview Ct 98903
W Slavin Hts & Rd 98903
Sliger Rd 98901
Snow Mass Ln 98908
Snowmountain Rd 98908
Snowy Owl Ln 98908
Solar Ln 98901
Songbird Way 98908
Southcreek Dr 98903
Southern Cross St 98903
Sparrow Ln 98908
Spokane St
600-1399 98902
7200-7398 98908
7400-9399 98908
S Sprague Rd 98908
Spring Ave 98903
Spring Creek Rd 98903
Spring View Dr 98901
E Spruce St 98901
W Spruce St 98902
E Staff Sgt Pendleton Way 98901
Stanley Blvd 98902
Stanton Rd 98903
Stark Rd 98908
Starview Rd 98903
State Route 24 98901
State Route 821 98901
Stealth Ln 98903
Stein Rd 98908
Sterling Ct 98908
Stewart St 98902
Stone Rd 98908
Stonewood Ct 98901
Storm Ave 98908
Streif Ln 98908
Stroud Rd 98908
Stump Rd 98908
Summerset 98901
Summit Haven Pl 98908
Summitview Ave
700-3999 98902
4000-10499 98908
Summitview Ext 98908
Summitview Rd 98908
Sun Valley Way 98908
Suncrest Way 98902
Sunnyslope Rd 98908
Sunrise Park Dr 98902
Sunset Dr & Ln 98901
Suntides Blvd 98908
Superior Ln 98902
Surrey Ln 98908
Susan Ave 98902
Sutherland Dr 98903
Swalley Ln 98903
Swan Ave 98902
Swier Ln 98901
Sycamore Dr & St 98901
E T St 98901
T P Rd 98901
Tacoma St 98903
Tah Kin 98902
Tahoma Ave 98902
Tamarack St 98901
Tampico Park Rd 98903
Tanarae Pl 98908
Tashas Ln 98901
Tatum Way 98908
Taylor Way 98902
Temple Ln 98901
Tennant Ln 98901
Terra Cotta Pl 98901
Terrace 98902
E Terrace Heights Dr & Way 98901
Terrace Hill Dr 98901
Terrace Park Dr 98901
Terrace View Dr 98901
Terrett Way 98901
Terry Ave 98908
Thompson Rd 98908
Thornton Ln 98901
Tieton Dr
401-597 98902
599-3999 98902
4001-4197 98908
4199-18999 98908
Tipp Rd 98901
Titleist Ln 98901
Top Ct 98901
Torrey Pines Ln 98908
Tower Ln 98901
Trails End Ln 98908
Treneer Rd 98908
Triple Crown Way 98908
Trout Lake Ct 98901
Tumac Dr 98901
Turner Ln 98901
Udell Ln 98908
Union St 98901
Union View Dr 98901
University Pkwy 98901
Uplands Way 98908
Us Highway 12 98908
E & W Valley Mall Blvd 98903
Valley View Rd 98908
Valley Vista Ln 98908
Valley West Ave 98908
Vaughn Rd 98908
Vendome Ave & Dr 98902
Vertner Rd 98908
Victory Ln 98901
View Haven Dr 98908
View Ridge Dr 98901
Viewcrest Pl & Way 98908
Viewland Dr 98908
Viewmont Dr & Pl 98908
Villa Dr 98901
Vincenta Dr & Way 98902
E Viola Ave 98901
W Viola Ave
1-27 98902
29-3400 98902
3402-3798 98902
4000-5199 98908
Viola Ct 98902
Viola Pl 98908
Violet Ct 98908
Vista Ln 98908
Vista Verde Dr 98901
Voelker Ave
1200-1498 98902
1500-1699 98902
2000-2098 98903
Voltaire Ave 98902
Wagon Trail Dr 98901
Wakatak Rd 98908
Walker St 98901
Walla Walla St 98903
Wallaby Ln 98901
Wally Ln 98902
E Walnut St 98901
W Walnut St
100-198 98902
200-3799 98902
3801-3999 98902
4000-9599 98908
Wapatox Hills Ln 98908
Warren Acres Rd 98901
Warrior Rd 98901
E Washington Ave 98903
W Washington Ave
1-300 98903
205-205 98909
301-7999 98903
302-7998 98903
E Washington St 98903
W Washington St 98903
Watkins Way 98908
Watson Rd 98908
Webster Ave
3201-3497 98902
3499-3599 98902
3601-3999 98902
4400-9099 98908
Webster Ct 98908
Webster Rd 98908
Wedgewood Heights Dr 98908
Weikel Rd 98908
Wellington Dr 98903
Wendt Rd 98901
West Way 98901
Westbrook Ave, Ct, Loop & Pl 98908
Westland Dr 98908
Westover Dr 98908
Westview Dr 98908
W Whatcom Ave & St 98903
Wherry Rd 98908
White Rd 98901
White St 98903
White Pine Ct 98902
Whitish Ln 98903
W Whitman Ave, Pl & St 98903
Wickersham Rd 98908
Wide Hollow Rd 98908
S Wiley Rd 98903
William Ct 98901
Willow Ct 98908
Willow Pl 98908
Willow St 98903
Willowlawn Rd 98908
Wilson Ln & Rd 98901
Winchester Rd 98908
Windcrest Dr 98908
Windy Ln 98903
Wise Acre Rd 98901
Woodland Ave 98902
Woodward West Rd 98901
Woodwinds Way 98908
Woolsey Rd 98903
Wyman Dr 98902
Wyss Ln 98901
E Yakima Ave 98901
W Yakima Ave
1-3499 98902
6100-9599 98908
Yakima Ct 98908
Yakima St 98903
Young Grade Rd 98908
Yule Rd 98908
Zier Rd 98908
Zimmerman Rd 98908

NUMBERED STREETS

N 1st Ave 98902
S 1st Ave
2-98 98902
1901-1997 98903
1st St 98903
N 1st St 98901
S 1st St
1-1732 98901
1800-2499 98903
N 2nd Ave 98902
S 2nd Ave
1-1699 98902
2000-2299 98903
2nd St 98903
N 2nd St 98901
S 2nd St 98901
N 3rd Ave 98902
S 3rd Ave
1-1800 98902
1900-2299 98903
3rd St 98903
N 3rd St 98901
S 3rd St
1-97 98901
112-112 98907
114-698 98901
N 4th Ave 98902
S 4th Ave
2-98 98902
100-1699 98902
1701-1899 98902
2000-2399 98903
4th St 98903
N 4th St 98901
S 4th St 98901
N 5th Ave 98902
S 5th Ave
1-1699 98902
2000-3599 98903
5th St 98903
N 6th Ave 98902
S 6th Ave
1-1699 98902
2100-2299 98903
N 6th St 98901
S 6th St 98901
N 7th Ave 98902
S 7th Ave
1-97 98902
99-1899 98902
1900-2299 98903
N 7th St 98901
S 7th St 98901
N 8th Ave 98902
S 8th Ave
1-1816 98902
1818-1826 98902
1900-3499 98903
N 8th St 98901
S 8th St 98901
N 9th Ave 98902
S 9th Ave
1-97 98902
99-1899 98902
1900-2199 98903
N 9th St 98901
S 9th St 98901
N 10th Ave 98902
S 10th Ave
1-1899 98902
1900-2599 98903
N 10th St 98901
S 10th St 98901
N 11th Ave 98902
S 11th Ave
2-98 98902
100-1899 98902
1904-1998 98903
2000-3399 98903
N 11th St 98901
S 11th St 98903
S 12th Ave
1-1799 98902
1900-1999 98903
S 12th St 98901
S 13th Ave 98902
S 13th St
100-498 98901
1800-1898 98903
N 14th Ave 98902
S 14th Ave
1-197 98902
199-1799 98902
2600-2699 98903
S 14th St
700-798 98901
800-1699 98901
1800-1898 98903
1900-2499 98903
N 15th Ave 98902
S 15th Ave 98902
N 15th St 98901
S 15th St 98901
N 16th Ave 98902
S 16th Ave
1-197 98902
199-1799 98902
1801-1899 98902
1900-2899 98903
S 16th St 98901
N 17th Ave 98902
S 17th Ave 98902
S 17th St
201-1397 98901
1800-1999 98903
N 18th Ave 98902
S 18th Ave 98902
S 18th St
101-197 98901
1800-2099 98903
N 19th Ave 98902
S 19th Ave 98902
S 19th St 98901
N 20th Ave 98902
S 20th Ave 98902
S 20th St 98901
N 21st Ave 98902
S 21st Ave
600-1499 98902
2400-2500 98903
N 22nd Ave 98902
S 22nd Ave 98902
S 22nd St 98901
N & S 23rd 98902
N & S 24th 98902
N & S 25th 98902
N 26th Ave 98902
S 26th Ave
200-1500 98902
2400-2598 98903
N & S 27th 98902
N 28th Ave 98902
S 28th Ave 98902
N 28th St 98901
N & S 29th Ave & Pl 98902
N & S 30th 98902
N 31st Ave 98902
S 31st Ave 98902
N 31st St 98901
N & S 32nd 98902
N 33rd Ave 98902
S 33rd Ave 98902
N 33rd St 98901
N 34th Ave 98902
S 34th Ave
200-1500 98902
1502-1598 98902
2600-2999 98903
N 34th St 98901
N 35th Ave 98902
S 35th Ave
200-899 98902
2900-2999 98903
S 35th Pl 98902
N & S 36th 98902
N 37th Ave 98902
S 37th Ave
200-1299 98902
2600-2999 98903
N 37th St 98901
N 38th Ave 98902
S 38th Ave
400-1399 98902
1401-1499 98902
2200-2298 98903
2300-2500 98903
2502-2598 98903
N 38th St 98901
S 38th St 98901
N 39th Ave 98902
S 39th Ave 98902
N 39th St 98901
S 39th St 98901
N 40th Ave 98908
S 40th Ave
200-1499 98908
1501-1599 98908
1900-3498 98903

3500-3799 98903
N 40th St 98901
S 40th St 98901
N 41st Ave 98908
S 41st Ave
900-1299 98908
1301-1399 98908
1900-1998 98903
2000-2999 98903
N 41st St 98901
S 41st St 98901
N 42nd Ave 98908
S 42nd Ave
900-1499 98908
2600-3099 98903
N 42nd Pl 98908
S 42nd St 98901
N 43rd Ave 98908
S 43rd Ave 98908
S 43rd St 98901
N 44th Ave 98908
S 44th Ave
1-1499 98908
1900-1999 98903
S 44th St 98901
N 45th Ave 98908
S 45th Ave
1-1199 98908
1201-1299 98908
1900-1999 98903
S 45th St 98901
N 46th Ave 98908
1-1299 98908
1900-1999 98903
N 47th Ave 98908
200-499 98908
1900-2099 98903
N & S 48th 98908
N 49th Ave 98908
S 49th Ave 98908
N 49th Ct 98908
S 49th Pl 98908
S 49th St 98901
N & S 50th 98908
N & S 51st 98908
N 52nd Ave 98908
S 52nd Ave 98903
N 53rd Ave 98908
100-1099 98908
2500-2599 98903
N 54th Ave 98908
S 54th Ave
600-711 98908
713-899 98908
2000-3399 98903
N 54th St 98901
N 55th Ave 98908
S 55th Ave
1-99 98908
2000-2099 98903
N 55th St 98901
N 56th Ave 98908
1-899 98908
2000-2099 98903
57th Ave 98903
N 57th Ave 98908
S 57th Ave 98908
N 57th St 98901
S 57th St 98901
58th Ave 98903
N 58th Ave 98908
S 58th Ave 98908
S 58th St 98901
N 59th Ave 98908
200-899 98908
2000-2599 98903
N 60th Ave 98908
200-899 98908
2000-2299 98903
N 61st Ave 98908
1-499 98908
2100-2199 98903
N 62nd Ave 98908
S 62nd Ave
1-299 98908
2600-3599 98903
N 63rd Ave 98908
S 63rd Ave 98908
S 63rd St 98901
N 64th Ave 98908
S 64th Ave
200-1399 98908
1900-1998 98903
2000-2399 98903
2401-2599 98903
S 64th St 98901
N 65th Ave 98908
S 65th Ave
200-499 98908
2100-2299 98903
N 65th Pl 98908
N 66th Ave 98908
1-1899 98908
2200-2599 98903
N 67th Ave 98908
S 67th Ave
200-1699 98908
2100-2299 98903
N 67th Pl 98908
68th Ave 98903
N 68th Ave 98908
S 68th Ave 98908
N 68th Pl 98908
N 69th Ave 98908
200-1899 98908
2100-2299 98903
N 70th Ave 98908
200-1899 98908
2400-2599 98903
N & S 71st 98908
N 72nd Ave 98908
S 72nd Ave
100-1800 98908
1900-2699 98903
N 73rd Ave 98908
S 73rd Ave
701-797 98908
1900-2599 98903
N 74th Ave 98908
200-1799 98908
2000-3199 98903
N 75th Ave 98908
S 75th Ave
600-1504 98908
1900-2299 98903
S 75th Pl 98908
N 76th Ave 98908
S 76th Ave
1-297 98908
1901-2299 98903
N 77th Ave 98908
200-999 98908
2200-2299 98903
N 78th Ave 98908
S 78th Ave
200-1499 98908
1800-2599 98903
S 78th Ct 98908
N 79th Ave 98908
900-1499 98908
2300-3699 98903
N 80th Ave 98908
100-1699 98908
2100-2399 98903
N 81st Ave 98908
S 81st Ave
200-499 98908
2400-2599 98903
S 81st Pl 98908
S 81st St 98901
N & S 82nd 98908
S 83rd Ave 98908
2400-2599 98903
N 84th Ave 98908
S 84th Ave 98903
N 85th Ave 98908
S 85th Ave
900-1099 98908
2300-2799 98903
S 85th Pl 98908
N 86th Ave 98908
S 86th Ave 98903
S 86th Pl 98908
N 87th Ave 98908
S 87th Ave
400-598 98908
600-899 98908
2000-2899 98903
S 87th Pl 98908
N 88th Ave 98908
100-1699 98908
1900-2299 98903
N & S 89th 98908
N & S 89th 98903
N 90th Ave 98908
100-1099 98908
2600-3599 98903
91st Ave 98903
N 91st Ave 98908
S 91st Ave 98908
N & S 92nd 98908
N & S 93rd 98908
N & S 94th Ave & Pl ... 98908
N 95th Pl 98908
N 96th Ave 98908
200-1299 98908
2100-2299 98903
N & S 98th 98908
N 99th Ave 98908
S 99th Ave 98903
N 101st Ave 98908
800-1099 98908
3200-3399 98903
N 112th Ave 98908
S 119th Ave 98908
S 121st Ave 98908
S 123rd Ave 98908

West Virginia

People QuickFacts	West Virginia	USA
Population, 2013 estimate	1,854,304	316,128,839
Population, 2010 (April 1) estimates base	1,852,999	308,747,716
Population, percent change, April 1, 2010 to July 1, 2013	0.1%	2.4%
Population, 2010	1,852,994	308,745,538
Persons under 5 years, percent, 2013	5.5%	6.3%
Persons under 18 years, percent, 2013	20.6%	23.3%
Persons 65 years and over, percent, 2013	17.3%	14.1%
Female persons, percent, 2013	50.6%	50.8%
White alone, percent, 2013 (a)	93.8%	77.7%
Black or African American alone, percent, 2013 (a)	3.6%	13.2%
American Indian and Alaska Native alone, percent, 2013 (a)	0.2%	1.2%
Asian alone, percent, 2013 (a)	0.8%	5.3%
Native Hawaiian and Other Pacific Islander alone, percent, 2013 (a)	Z	0.2%
Two or More Races, percent, 2013	1.5%	2.4%
Hispanic or Latino, percent, 2013 (b)	1.4%	17.1%
White alone, not Hispanic or Latino, percent, 2013	92.7%	62.6%
Living in same house 1 year & over, percent, 2008-2012	87.9%	84.8%
Foreign born persons, percent, 2008-2012	1.4%	12.9%
Language other than English spoken at home, pct age 5+, 2008-2012	2.4%	20.5%
High school graduate or higher, percent of persons age 25+, 2008-2012	83.4%	85.7%
Bachelor's degree or higher, percent of persons age 25+, 2008-2012	17.9%	28.5%
Veterans, 2008-2012	164,979	21,853,912
Mean travel time to work (minutes), workers age 16+, 2008-2012	25.4	25.4
Housing units, 2013	879,449	132,802,859
Homeownership rate, 2008-2012	73.7%	65.5%
Housing units in multi-unit structures, percent, 2008-2012	12.0%	25.9%
Median value of owner-occupied housing units, 2008-2012	$97,300	$181,400
Households, 2008-2012	742,674	115,226,802
Persons per household, 2008-2012	2.43	2.61
Per capita money income in past 12 months (2012 dollars), 2008-2012	$22,482	$28,051
Median household income, 2008-2012	$40,400	$53,046
Persons below poverty level, percent, 2008-2012	17.6%	14.9%

Business QuickFacts	West Virginia	USA
Private nonfarm establishments, 2012	37,906	7,431,808
Private nonfarm employment, 2012	579,583	115,938,468
Private nonfarm employment, percent change, 2011-2012	2.0%	2.2%
Nonemployer establishments, 2012	89,213	22,735,915
Total number of firms, 2007	120,381	27,092,908
Black-owned firms, percent, 2007	S	7.1%
American Indian- and Alaska Native-owned firms, percent, 2007	S	0.9%
Asian-owned firms, percent, 2007	1.3%	5.7%
Native Hawaiian and Other Pacific Islander-owned firms, percent, 2007	0.0%	0.1%
Hispanic-owned firms, percent, 2007	0.7%	8.3%
Women-owned firms, percent, 2007	28.1%	28.8%
Manufacturers shipments, 2007 ($1000)	25,080,573	5,319,456,312
Merchant wholesaler sales, 2007 ($1000)	11,036,467	4,174,286,516
Retail sales, 2007 ($1000)	20,538,829	3,917,663,456
Retail sales per capita, 2007	$11,340	$12,990
Accommodation and food services sales, 2007 ($1000)	2,553,258	613,795,732
Building permits, 2012	2,718	829,658

Geography QuickFacts	West Virginia	USA
Land area in square miles, 2010	24,038.21	3,531,905.43
Persons per square mile, 2010	77.1	87.4
FIPS Code	54	

(a) Includes persons reporting only one race.
(b) Hispanics may be of any race, so also are included in applicable race categories.
FN: Footnote on this item for this area in place of data
NA: Not available
D: Suppressed to avoid disclosure of confidential information
X: Not applicable
S: Suppressed; does not meet publication standards
Z: Value greater than zero but less than half unit of measure shown
F: Fewer than 100 firms
Source: US Census Bureau State & County QuickFacts

West Virginia

3 DIGIT ZIP CODE MAP

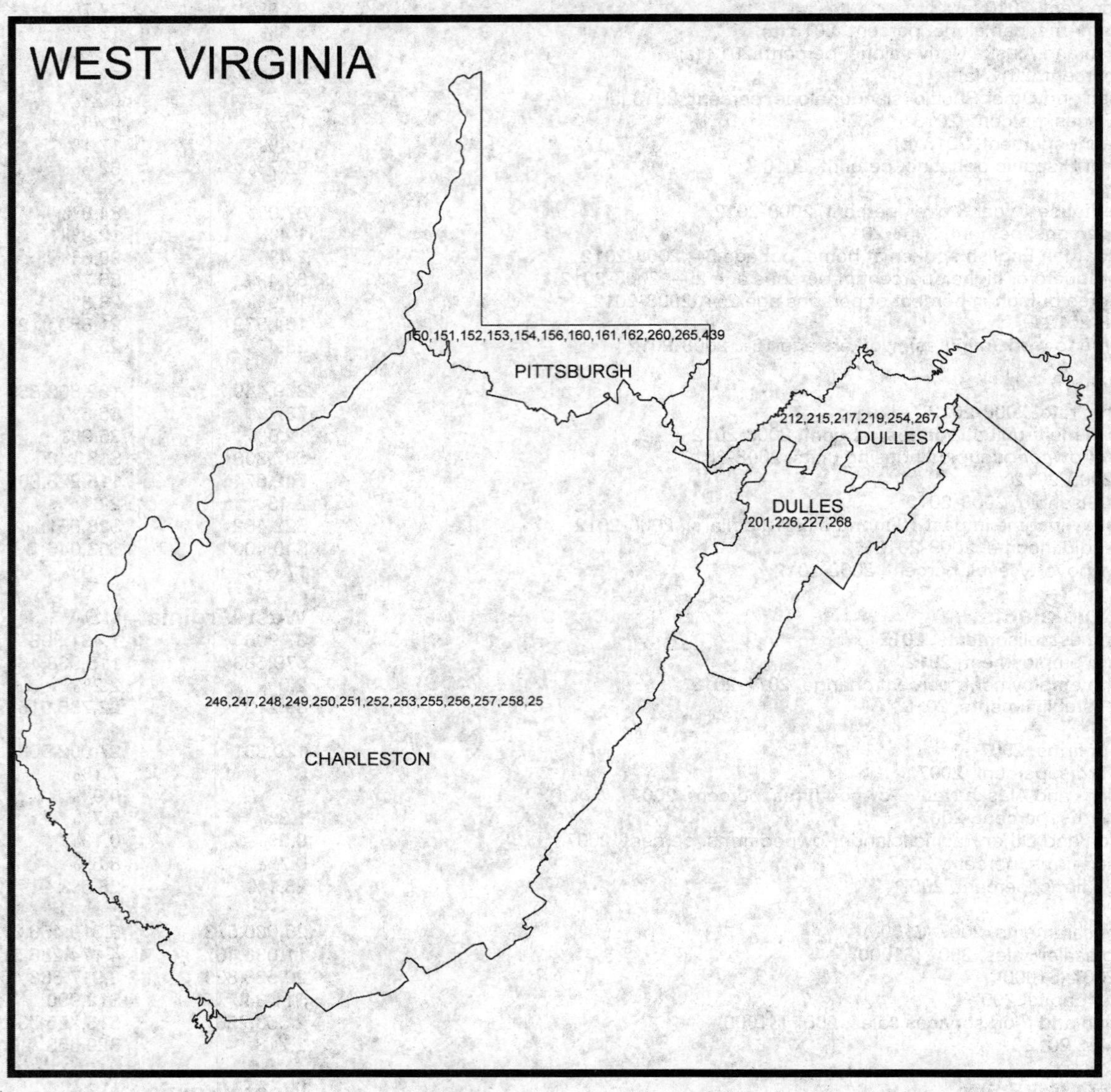

West Virginia

(Abbreviation: WV)

Places with more than one ZIP code are listed in capital letters, See pages indicated.

Post Office, County	ZIP Code
Abraham, Raleigh	25918
Accoville, Logan	25606
Adamsville, Harrison	26431
Adrian, Upshur	26210
Advent, Jackson	25231
Albright, Preston	26519
Alderson, Monroe	24910
Alexander, Upshur	26218
Algoma, Mcdowell	24868
Alkol, Lincoln	25501
Alkol, Boone	25572
Allen Junction, Wyoming	25810
Alloy, Fayette	25002
Alma, Tyler	26320
Alta, Greenbrier	24916
Alum Bridge, Lewis	26321
Alum Creek, Kanawha	25003
Alvy, Wetzel	26377
Amboy, Preston	26705
Ameagle, Raleigh	25060
Amherstdale, Logan	25607
Amigo, Wyoming	25811
Amma, Roane	25005
Anawalt, Mcdowell	24808
Anmoore, Harrison	26323
Annamoriah, Wirt	26141
Ansted, Fayette	25812
Anthony, Greenbrier	24938
Apple Grove, Mason	25502
Arbovale, Pocahontas	24915
Arbuckle, Mason	25123
Arnett, Raleigh	25007
Arnoldsburg, Calhoun	25234
Arthur, Grant	26847
Arthurdale, Preston	26520
Artie, Raleigh	25008
Asbury, Greenbrier	24916
Asco, Mcdowell	24828
Ashford, Boone	25009
Ashland, Mcdowell	24868
Ashton, Mason	25503
Astor, Taylor	26347
Athens, Mercer	24712
Auburn, Ritchie	26325
Augusta, Hampshire	26704
Aurora, Preston	26705
Auto, Greenbrier	24966
Avondale, Mcdowell	24811
Baisden, Mingo	25608
Baker, Hardy	26801
Bakerton, Jefferson	25410
Bald Knob, Boone	25208
Baldwin, Gilmer	26351
Ballard, Monroe	24918
Ballengee, Summers	24981
Bancroft, Putnam	25011
Bandytown, Boone	25204
Barboursville, Cabell	25504
Barnabus, Logan	25638
Barrackville, Marion	26559
Barrett, Boone	25208
Bartley, Mcdowell	24813
Bartow, Pocahontas	24920
Baxter, Marion	26560
Bayard, Grant	26707
Beards Fork, Fayette	25173
Beaver, Raleigh	25813
BECKLEY, Raleigh (See Page 4304)	
Beckwith, Fayette	25840
Beech Bottom, Brooke	26030
Beeson, Mercer	24714
Belgium, Taylor	26354
Belington, Barbour	26250
Bellburn, Greenbrier	25972
Belle, Kanawha	25015
Belleville, Wood	26133
Bellwood, Greenbrier	25962
Belmont, Pleasants	26134
Belva, Nicholas	26656
Bens Run, Tyler	26146
Bentree, Clay	25125
Benwood, Marshall	26031
Berea, Ritchie	26327
Bergoo, Webster	26298
Berkeley Springs, Morgan	25411
Berwind, Mcdowell	24815
Bethany, Brooke	26032
Bethlehem, Ohio	26003
Beverly, Randolph	26253
Bickmore, Clay	25019
Big Bend, Calhoun	26136
Big Chimney, Kanawha	25302
Big Creek, Logan	25505
Big Otter, Clay	25113
Big Run, Wetzel	26561
Big Sandy, Mcdowell	24816
Big Springs, Calhoun	26137
Bim, Boone	25021
Bingham, Greenbrier	25958
Birch River, Nicholas	26610
Blackberry City, Mingo	25678
Blacksville, Monongalia	26521
Blair, Logan	25022
Blandville, Doddridge	26456
Bloomery, Hampshire	26817
Bloomingrose, Boone	25024
Blount, Kanawha	25025
Blue Creek, Kanawha	25026
Blue Goose, Wirt	26160
Blue Jay, Raleigh	25813
Bluefield, Mercer	24701
Bluewell, Mercer	24701
Bob White, Boone	25028
Boggs, Webster	26206
Bolivar, Jefferson	25425
Bolt, Raleigh	25817
Bomont, Clay	25030
Boomer, Fayette	25031
Booth, Monongalia	26505
Borderland, Mingo	25665
Bowden, Randolph	26254
Bozoo, Monroe	24963
Bradley, Raleigh	25818
Bradshaw, Mcdowell	24817
Bramwell, Mercer	24715
Branchland, Lincoln	25506
Brandonville, Preston	26525
Brandywine, Pendleton	26802
Breeden, Mingo	25666
Brenton, Wyoming	24818
Bretz, Preston	26524
Bridgeport, Harrison	26330
Bristol, Harrison	26426
Brohard, Wirt	26138
Brooks, Summers	25951
Brownsville, Fayette	25085
Brownton, Taylor	26347
Bruceton Mills, Preston	26525
Bruno, Logan	25611
Brushy Fork, Harrison	26330
Buckeye, Pocahontas	24924
Buckhannon, Upshur	26201
Bud, Wyoming	24716
Buffalo, Putnam	25033
Bunker Hill, Berkeley	25413
Burlington, Mineral	26710
Burnsville, Braxton	26335
Burnt House, Ritchie	26178
Burnwell, Kanawha	25083
Burton, Wetzel	26562
Cabin Creek, Kanawha	25035
Cabins, Grant	26855
Cairo, Ritchie	26337
Caldwell, Greenbrier	24925
Calvin, Nicholas	26660
Camden, Lewis	26338
Camden On Gauley, Webster	26208
Cameron, Marshall	26033
Camp Creek, Mercer	25820
Canaan Valley, Tucker	26260
Canebrake, Mcdowell	24815
Cannelton, Fayette	25036
Canvas, Nicholas	26662
Capels, Mcdowell	24801
Capon Bridge, Hampshire	26711
Capon Springs, Hampshire	26823
Carbon, Kanawha	25075
Caretta, Mcdowell	24892
Carolina, Marion	26563
Carpendale, Mineral	26753
Cascade, Preston	26542
Cass, Pocahontas	24927
Cassville, Monongalia	26527
Cedar Grove, Kanawha	25039
Cedarville, Gilmer	26611
Center Point, Doddridge	26339
Centralia, Braxton	26601
Century, Upshur	26201
Ceredo, Wayne	25507
Chapel, Braxton	26624
Chapmanville, Logan	25508
Charles Town, Jefferson	25414
CHARLESTON, Kanawha (See Page 4305)	
Charlton Heights, Fayette	25040
Charmco, Greenbrier	25958
Chattaroy, Mingo	25667
Chauncey, Logan	25612
Cherry Run, Berkeley	25427
Chesapeake, Kanawha	25315
Chester, Hancock	26034
Chloe, Calhoun	25235
Circleville, Pendleton	26804
CLARKSBURG, Harrison (See Page 4312)	
Clay, Clay	25043
Clear Creek, Raleigh	25044
Clear Fork, Wyoming	24822
Clem, Braxton	26623
Clendenin, Kanawha	25045
Cleveland, Upshur	26215
Clifftop, Fayette	25831
Clifton, Mason	25260
Clintonville, Greenbrier	24931
Clio, Kanawha	25045
Clothier, Logan	25047
Coal City, Raleigh	25823
Coal Mountain, Wyoming	24823
Coaldale, Mercer	24724
Coalton, Randolph	26257
Coalwood, Mcdowell	24801
Coburn, Wetzel	26562
Colcord, Raleigh	25048
Coldwater Creek (See Mineral Wells)	
Colfax, Marion	26566
Colliers, Brooke	26035
Comfort, Boone	25049
Cool Ridge, Raleigh	25825
Copen, Braxton	26615
Cora, Logan	25614
Core, Monongalia	26541
Corinne, Wyoming	25826
Corinth, Preston	26764
Corley, Braxton	26621
Corliss, Greenbrier	25962
Corton, Kanawha	25045
Costa, Boone	25051
Cottageville, Jackson	25239
Cottle, Nicholas	26205
Country Club, Harrison	26301
Cove Gap, Wayne	25534
Covel, Wyoming	24719
Cowen, Webster	26206
Coxs Mills, Gilmer	26342
Crab Orchard, Raleigh	25827
Craigmoore, Harrison	26408
Craigsville, Nicholas	26205
Crawford, Lewis	26343
Crawley, Greenbrier	24931
Creston, Wirt	26141
Crichton, Greenbrier	25981
Cross Lanes, Kanawha	25313
Crown Hill, Kanawha	25067
Crum, Wayne	25669
Crumpler, Mcdowell	24868
Cucumber, Mcdowell	24826
Culloden, Cabell	25510
Cunard, Fayette	25840
Curtin, Webster	26288
Cuzzart, Preston	26525
Cyclone, Wyoming	24827
Dailey, Randolph	26259
Dallas, Marshall	26036
Danese, Fayette	25831
Daniels, Raleigh	25832
Danville, Boone	25053
Davin, Logan	25617
Davis, Tucker	26260
Davisville, Wood	26142
Davy, Mcdowell	24828
Dawes, Kanawha	25054
Dawmont, Harrison	26301
Dawson, Monroe	24910
Decota, Kanawha	25075
Deep Water, Fayette	25057
Dehue, Logan	25654
Delbarton, Mingo	25670
Dellslow, Monongalia	26531
Delray, Hampshire	26714
Diamond, Kanawha	25015
Diana, Webster	26217
Dille, Clay	26617
Dingess, Mingo	25671
Dixie, Nicholas	25059
Dola, Harrison	26386
Dorcas, Grant	26847
Dorothy, Raleigh	25060
Dothan, Fayette	25833
Dott, Mercer	24736
Drennen, Nicholas	26667
Droop, Pocahontas	24946
Dry Creek, Raleigh	25062
Drybranch, Kanawha	25061
Dryfork, Randolph	26263
Duck, Clay	25063
Duhring, Mercer	24747
Dunbar, Kanawha	25064
Duncan, Jackson	25252
Dunlow, Wayne	25511
Dunmore, Pocahontas	24934
Duo, Greenbrier	25984
Dupont City, Kanawha	25015
Durbin, Pocahontas	26264
Earling, Logan	25632
East Bank, Kanawha	25067
East Gulf, Raleigh	25915
East Lynn, Wayne	25512
Eccles, Raleigh	25836
Eckman, Mcdowell	24829
Edgarton, Mingo	25672
Edmond, Fayette	25837
Eglon, Preston	26716
Elbert, Mcdowell	24830
Eleanor, Putnam	25070
Elgood, Mercer	24740
Elizabeth, Wirt	26143
Elk Garden, Mineral	26717
Elkhorn, Mcdowell	24831
Elkins, Randolph	26241
Elkview, Kanawha	25071
Ellamore, Randolph	26267
Ellenboro, Ritchie	26346
Elm Grove, Ohio	26003
Elmira, Clay	25063
Elton, Fayette	25976
Emmett, Mingo	25650
English, Mcdowell	24892
Enterprise, Harrison	26568
Erbacon, Webster	26203
Eskdale, Kanawha	25075
Ethel, Logan	25076
Eureka, Pleasants	26134
Evans, Jackson	25241
Everettville, Monongalia	26505
Exchange, Braxton	26619
Fairdale, Raleigh	25839
Fairlea, Greenbrier	24902
FAIRMONT, Marion (See Page 4312)	
Fairview, Marion	26570
Falling Rock, Kanawha	25079
Falling Sprg, Greenbrier	24966
Falling Waters, Berkeley	25419
Falls Mill, Braxton	26631
Fanrock, Wyoming	24834
Farmington, Marion	26571
Fayetteville, Fayette	25840
Fenwick, Nicholas	26202
Ferrellsburg, Lincoln	25524
Filbert, Mcdowell	24830
Fisher, Hardy	26818
Five Forks, Calhoun	26136
Flat Top, Mercer	25841
Flatwoods, Braxton	26621
Flemington, Taylor	26347
Floe, Calhoun	25235
Flower, Gilmer	26611
Fola, Clay	25019
Follansbee, Brooke	26037
Folsom, Wetzel	26348
Forest Hill, Summers	24935
Fort Ashby, Mineral	26719
Fort Gay, Wayne	25514
Fort Neal, Wood	26103
Fort Seybert, Pendleton	26802
Fort Spring, Greenbrier	24970
Foster, Boone	25081
Four States, Marion	26572
Frame, Kanawha	25071
Frametown, Braxton	26623
Francis Mine, Harrison	26431
Frankford, Greenbrier	24938
Franklin, Pendleton	26807
Fraziers Bottom, Putnam	25082
Freeman, Mercer	24724
Freeport, Wood	26180
French Creek, Upshur	26218
Frenchton, Upshur	26219
Friars Hill, Greenbrier	24938
Friendly, Tyler	26146
Gallagher, Kanawha	25083
Gallipolis Ferry, Mason	25515
Galloway, Barbour	26349
Gandeeville, Roane	25243
Gap Mills, Monroe	24941
Garrison, Boone	25209
Gary, Mcdowell	24836
Gassaway, Braxton	26624
Gauley Bridge, Fayette	25085
Gauley Mills, Webster	26208
Gay, Jackson	25244
Gem, Braxton	26335
Genoa, Wayne	25517
Gerrardstown, Berkeley	25420
Ghent, Raleigh	25843
Gilbert, Mingo	25621
Gilboa, Nicholas	26671
Gilmer, Gilmer	26351
Given, Jackson	25245
Glace, Monroe	24983
Glade Springs, Raleigh	25832
Glady, Randolph	26268
Glasgow, Kanawha	25086
Glen, Clay	25088
Glen Dale, Marshall	26038
Glen Daniel, Raleigh	25844
Glen Easton, Marshall	26039
Glen Ferris, Fayette	25090
Glen Fork, Wyoming	25845
Glen Jean, Fayette	25846
Glen Morgan, Raleigh	25813
Glen Rogers, Wyoming	25848
Glen White, Raleigh	25849
Glendon, Braxton	26623
Glengary, Berkeley	25421
Glenhayes, Wayne	25514
Glenville, Gilmer	26351
Glenwood, Mason	25520
Gordon, Boone	25093
Gormania, Grant	26720
Grafton, Taylor	26354
Grant Town, Marion	26574
Grantsville, Calhoun	26147
Granville, Monongalia	26534
Grassy Meadows, Greenbrier	24943
Great Cacapon, Morgan	25422
Green Bank, Pocahontas	24944
Green Spring, Hampshire	26722
Green Sulphur Springs, Summers	25966
Green Valley, Mercer	24701
Greenville, Monroe	24945
Greenwood, Ritchie	26415
Griffithsville, Lincoln	25521
Grimms Landing, Mason	25123
Gypsy, Harrison	26361
Hacker Valley, Webster	26222
Halltown, Jefferson	25423
Hambleton, Tucker	26269
Hamlin, Lincoln	25523
Hampden, Mingo	25621
Hancock, Morgan	25411
Handley, Kanawha	25102
Hanover, Wyoming	24839
Hansford, Kanawha	25103
Harman, Randolph	26270
Harmony, Roane	25243
Harmony Grove, Taylor	26354
Harper, Raleigh	25851
Harpers Ferry, Jefferson	25425
Harrison, Clay	25063
Harrisville, Ritchie	26362
Hartford, Mason	25247
Hartford City, Mason	25247
Harts, Lincoln	25524
Harvey, Fayette	25901
Hastings, Wetzel	26419
Havaco, Mcdowell	24801
Haymond, Taylor	26354
Haywood, Harrison	26366
Hazelgreen, Ritchie	26362
Hazelton, Preston	26525
Heaters, Braxton	26627
Hedgesville, Berkeley	25427
Helen, Raleigh	25853
Helvetia, Randolph	26224
Hemphill, Mcdowell	24801
Henderson, Mason	25106
Hendricks, Tucker	26271
Henlawson, Logan	25624
Hensley, Mcdowell	24843
Hepzibah, Harrison	26369
Herndon, Wyoming	24726
Hernshaw, Kanawha	25107
Herold, Braxton	26601
Hewett, Boone	25108
Hiawatha, Mercer	24729
Hico, Fayette	25854
High View, Hampshire	26808
Highland, Ritchie	26346
Hillsboro, Pocahontas	24946
Hilltop, Fayette	25855
Hilton Village, Greenbrier	25962
Hines, Greenbrier	25958
Hinton, Summers	25951
Holden, Logan	25625
Hometown, Putnam	25109
Hopemont, Preston	26764
Horner, Lewis	26372
Horse Shoe Run, Preston	26716
Hughes River, Wirt	26143
Hugheston, Kanawha	25110
Hundred, Wetzel	26575
Hunt, Logan	25635
HUNTINGTON, Cabell (See Page 4315)	
Hurricane, Putnam	25526
Huttonsville, Randolph	26273
Iaeger, Mcdowell	24844
Idamay, Marion	26576
Ikes Fork, Wyoming	24845
Independence, Preston	26374
Indian Mills, Summers	24935
Indore, Clay	25111
Industrial, Harrison	26426
Institute, Kanawha	25112
Inwood, Berkeley	25428
Ireland, Lewis	26376
Isaban, Mcdowell	24846
Itmann, Wyoming	24847
Ivydale, Clay	25113

Jacksonburg, Wetzel 26377
Jane Lew, Lewis 26378
Jefferson, Kanawha 25177
Jeffrey, Boone 25114
Jenkinjones, Mcdowell 24848
Jesse, Wyoming 24849
Job, Randolph 26296
Jodie, Nicholas 26690
Jolo, Mcdowell 24850
Jonben, Raleigh 25823
Jones Springs, Berkeley 25427
Jordan, Marion 26554
Josephine, Raleigh 25857
Julian, Boone 25529
Jumping Branch, Summers 25969
Junction, Hampshire 26852
Junior, Barbour 26275
Justice, Mingo 24851
Kanawha Falls, Fayette 25115
Kanawha Head, Upshur 26228
Kasson, Barbour 26405
Kayford, Kanawha 25075
Kearneysville, Jefferson 25430
Kegley, Mercer 24731
Kellysville, Mercer 24732
Kenna, Jackson 25248
Kenova, Wayne 25530
Kentuck, Jackson 25248
Kerens, Randolph 26276
Kermit, Mingo 25674
Keslers Cross Lanes, Nicholas 26675
Kessler, Greenbrier 25984
Keyser, Mineral 26726
Keystone, Mcdowell 24868
Kiahsville, Wayne 25534
Kieffer, Greenbrier 24931
Kimball, Mcdowell 24853
Kimberly, Fayette 25118
Kincaid, Fayette 25119
Kincheloe, Lewis 26378
Kingmont, Marion 26578
Kingston, Fayette 25917
Kingwood, Preston 26537
Kirby, Hampshire 26755
Kistler, Logan 25628
Knob Fork, Wetzel 26581
Kopperston, Wyoming 24854
Kyle, Mcdowell 24855
Lahmansville, Grant 26731
Lake, Logan 25121
Lake Ridge, Harrison 26330
Lakin, Mason 25287
Lanark, Raleigh 25860
Landes Station, Grant 26847
Landville, Logan 25635
Lanham, Putnam 25159
Lansing, Fayette 25862
Lashmeet, Mercer 24733
Laurel Park, Harrison 26301
Laurel Valley, Harrison 26301
Lavalette, Wayne 25535
Lawton, Fayette 25864
Layland, Fayette 25864
Le Roy, Jackson 25252
Leckie, Mcdowell 24808
Leet, Lincoln 25524
Leewood, Kanawha 25075
Left Hand, Roane 25251
Lehew, Hampshire 26865
Leivasy, Nicholas 26676
Lenore, Mingo 25676
Leon, Mason 25123
Lerona, Mercer 25971
Lesage, Cabell 25537
Leslie, Greenbrier 25972
Lester, Raleigh 25865
Letart, Mason 25253
Letter Gap, Gilmer 25267
Levels, Hampshire 25431
Lewisburg, Greenbrier 24901
Liberty, Putnam 25124
Lilly Park, Greenbrier 25962
Lima, Wetzel 26377
Limestone Hill, Wirt 26143
Linden, Roane 25259
Lindside, Monroe 24951
Linn, Gilmer 26384
Little Birch, Braxton 26629
Little Falls, Monongalia 26508
Littleton, Wetzel 26581
Liverpool, Jackson 25252
Livingston, Kanawha 25083
Lizemores, Clay 25125
Lobata, Mingo 25678
Lochgelly, Fayette 25866
Lockbridge, Fayette 25976
Lockney, Gilmer 25267
Logan, Logan 25601
London, Kanawha 25126
Longacre, Fayette 25186
Lookout, Fayette 25868
Looneyville, Roane 25259
Lorado, Logan 25630
Lorentz, Upshur 26229
Lost City, Hardy 26810
Lost Creek, Harrison 26385
Lost River, Hardy 26810
Lovern, Summers 25979
Lumberport, Harrison 26386
Lundale, Logan 25630
Lyburn, Logan 25632
Lynco, Wyoming 24857
Lynncamp, Wirt 26160
Maben, Wyoming 25870
Mabie, Randolph 26278
Mabscott, Raleigh 25871
Mac Arthur, Raleigh 25873
Macfarlan, Ritchie 26148
Madison, Boone 25130
Mahan, Kanawha 25083
Mahone, Ritchie 26362
Maidsville, Monongalia 26541
Malden, Kanawha 25306
Mallory, Logan 25634
Mammoth, Kanawha 25132
Man, Logan 25635
Manheim, Preston 26425
Mannington, Marion 26582
Maple Lake, Harrison 26330
Maplewood, Fayette 25831
Marfrance, Greenbrier 25981
Marianna, Wyoming 24859
Marlinton, Pocahontas 24954
Marmet, Kanawha 25315
MARTINSBURG, Berkeley (See Page 4317)
Mason, Mason 25260
Masontown, Preston 26542
Matewan, Mingo 25678
Matheny, Wyoming 24860
Mathias, Hardy 26812
Matoaka, Mercer 24736
Maxwelton, Greenbrier 24957
Maybeury, Mcdowell 24861
Maysel, Clay 25133
Maysville, Grant 26833
Mc Comas, Mercer 24747
Mc Connell, Logan 25646
Mc Dowell, Mcdowell 24868
Mc Graws, Wyoming 25875
Mc Graws, Wyoming 25876
Mcalpin, Raleigh 25921
Mcmechen, Marshall 26040
Mcwhorter, Harrison 26385
Mead, Raleigh 25915
Meador, Mingo 25678
Meadow Bluff, Greenbrier 24977
Meadow Bridge, Summers 25966
Meadow Bridge, Fayette 25976
Meadow Creek, Summers 25977
Meadowbrook, Harrison 26404
Medley, Mineral 26710
Metz, Marion 26585
Miami, Kanawha 25134
Middlebourne, Tyler 26149
Middleway, Jefferson 25430
Midkiff, Lincoln 25540
Midway, Raleigh 25878
Milam, Hardy 26838
Mill Creek, Randolph 26280
Mill Point, Pocahontas 24946
Millstone, Calhoun 25261
Millville, Jefferson 25432
Millwood, Jackson 25262
Milton, Cabell 25541
Minden, Fayette 25879
Mineral Wells, Wood 26150
Mingo, Randolph 26294
Minnehaha Springs, Pocahontas 24954
Minnora, Calhoun 25268
Mitchell Hts, Logan 25601
Moatsville, Barbour 26405
Mohawk, Mcdowell 24862
Monaville, Logan 25601
Monongah (See Fairmont)
Montana Mines, Marion 26586
Montcalm, Mercer 24737
Montcoal, Raleigh 25140
Monterville, Randolph 26282
Montgomery, Fayette 25136
Montrose, Randolph 26283
Moorefield, Hardy 26836
MORGANTOWN, Monongalia (See Page 4319)
Morrisvale, Lincoln 25565
Moundsville, Marshall 26041
Mount Alto, Mason 25264
Mount Carbon, Fayette 25139
Mount Clare, Harrison 26408
Mount Gay, Logan 25637
Mount Hope, Fayette 25880
Mount Lookout, Nicholas 26678
Mount Nebo, Nicholas 26679
Mount Olive, Fayette 25185
Mount Storm, Grant 26739
Mount Zion, Calhoun 26151
Mountain, Ritchie 26415
Moyers, Pendleton 26815
Mozart, Ohio 26003
Mullens, Wyoming 25882
Munday, Calhoun 26152
Murraysville, Jackson 26164
Myra, Lincoln 25544
Myrtle, Mingo 25670
Nallen, Fayette 26680
Naoma, Raleigh 25140
Napier, Braxton 26631
Naugatuck, Mingo 25685
Nebo, Clay 25141
Nellis, Boone 25142
Nemours, Mercer 24738
Neola, Greenbrier 24986
Nettie, Nicholas 26681
New Creek, Mineral 26743
New Cumberland, Hancock 26047
New England, Wood 26181
New Haven, Mason 25265
New Manchester, Hancock 26056
New Martinsville, Wetzel 26155
New Milton, Doddridge 26411
New Richmond, Wyoming 24867
Newark, Wirt 26143
Newberne, Ritchie 26362
Newburg, Preston 26410
Newell, Hancock 26050
Newhall, Mcdowell 24866
Newton, Roane 25266
Newtown, Mingo 25686
Newville, Braxton 26601
Nicut, Gilmer 26636
Nimitz, Summers 25978
Nitro, Kanawha 25143
Nobe, Calhoun 26137
Nolan, Mingo 25661
Normantown, Gilmer 25267
North Hills, Wood 26104
North Matewan, Mingo 25688
North Parkersburg, Wood 26104
North Spring, Wyoming 24869
Northfork, Mcdowell 24868
Norton, Randolph 26285
Nutter Fort, Harrison 26301
Oak Hill, Fayette 25901
Oakvale (See Princeton)
Oceana, Wyoming 24870
Odd, Raleigh 25902
Ohley, Kanawha 25075
Old Fields, Hardy 26845
Omar, Logan 25638
Ona, Cabell 25545
Onego, Pendleton 26886
Organ Cave, Greenbrier 24970
Orgas, Boone 25148
Orient Hill, Greenbrier 25958
Orlando, Lewis 26412
Orma, Calhoun 25268
Osage, Monongalia 26543
Ottawa, Boone 25149
Ovapa, Clay 25164
Overbrook, Ohio 26003
Owings, Harrison 26431
Packsville, Boone 25209
Paden City, Wetzel 26159
Page, Fayette 25152
Pageton, Mcdowell 24871
Palermo, Lincoln 25506
Palestine, Wirt 26160
Panther, Mcdowell 24872
Parcoal, Webster 26288
PARKERSBURG, Wood (See Page 4323)
Parsons, Tucker 26287
Patterson Creek, Mineral 26753
Paw Paw, Morgan 25434
Pax, Fayette 25904
Paynesville, Mcdowell 24873
Peach Creek, Logan 25639
Pecks Mill, Logan 25547
Pemberton, Raleigh 25878
Pence Springs, Summers 24962
Pennsboro, Ritchie 26415
Pentress, Monongalia 26544
Peora, Harrison 26431
Perkins, Gilmer 26636
Petersburg, Grant 26847
Peterstown, Monroe 24963
Petroleum, Ritchie 26161
Pettus, Boone 25209
Peytona, Boone 25154
Philippi, Barbour 26416
Pickaway, Monroe 24976
Pickens, Randolph 26230
Piedmont, Mineral 26750
Pigeon, Clay 25164
Pinch, Kanawha 25156
Pine Bluff, Harrison 26431
Pine Grove, Wetzel 26419
Pineville, Wyoming 24859
Pineville, Wyoming 24874
Piney View, Raleigh 25906
Pipestem, Summers 25979
Pleasant Valley, Marion 26554
Pliny, Putnam 25082
Poca, Putnam 25159
Point Pleasant, Mason 25550
Points, Hampshire 25437
Pond Gap, Kanawha 25160
Pool, Nicholas 26684
Porters Falls, Wetzel 26162
Powellton, Fayette 25161
Powhatan, Mcdowell 24868
Pratt, Kanawha 25162
Premier, Mcdowell 24878
Prenter, Boone 25181
Prichard, Wayne 25555
Prince, Fayette 25907
PRINCETON, Mercer (See Page 4325)
Princewick, Raleigh 25908
Procious, Clay 25164
Proctor, Marshall 26055
Prosperity, Raleigh 25909
Pullman, Ritchie 26421
Purgitsville, Hampshire 26852
Pursglove, Monongalia 26546
Quick, Kanawha 25045
Quincy, Kanawha 25015
Quinwood, Greenbrier 25981
Rachel, Marion 26587
Racine, Boone 25165
Radnor, Wayne 25517
Ragland, Mingo 25690
Rainelle, Greenbrier 25962
Raleigh, Raleigh 25911
Ramage, Boone 25114
Ramsey, Fayette 25938
Ranger, Lincoln 25557
Ranson, Jefferson 25438
Ravencliff, Wyoming 25913
Ravenswood, Jackson 26164
Rawl, Mingo 25691
Raysal, Mcdowell 24879
Reader, Wetzel 26167
Red Creek, Tucker 26289
Red House, Putnam 25168
Red Jacket, Mingo 25692
Redstar, Fayette 25901
Reedsville, Preston 26547
Reedy, Roane 25270
Renick, Greenbrier 24966
Replete, Webster 26222
Reynoldsville, Harrison 26422
Rhodell, Raleigh 25915
Richwood, Nicholas 26261
Ridgeley, Mineral 26753
Ridgeview, Boone 25169
Ridgeway, Berkeley 25440
Riffle, Braxton 26619
Rig, Hardy 26836
Rio, Hampshire 26755
Ripley, Jackson 25271
Rippon, Jefferson 25441
Riverton, Pendleton 26814
Rivesville, Marion 26588
Roanoke, Lewis 26447
Robertsburg, Mason 25123
Robinette, Logan 25607
Robson, Fayette 25173
Rock, Mercer 24747
Rock Castle, Jackson 25245
Rock Cave, Upshur 26215
Rock Cave, Upshur 26234
Rock Creek, Raleigh 25174
Rock View, Wyoming 24880
Rocket Center, Mineral 26726
Rockport, Wood 26169
Roderfield, Mcdowell 24881
Romance, Jackson 25248
Romney, Hampshire 26757
Ronceverte, Greenbrier 24970
Rosedale, Gilmer 26636
Rosemont, Taylor 26424
Rossmore, Logan 25601
Rowlesburg, Preston 26425
Runa, Nicholas 26679
Rupert, Greenbrier 25984
Russelville, Fayette 26680
Sabine, Wyoming 25916
Saint Albans, Kanawha 25177
Saint George, Tucker 26287
Saint Marys, Pleasants 26170
Salem, Harrison 26426
Salt Rock, Cabell 25559
Saltwell, Harrison 26431
Sam Black, Greenbrier 24931
Sand Fork, Gilmer 26430
Sand Ridge, Calhoun 25234
Sandstone, Summers 25985
Sandyville, Jackson 25275
Sanoma, Wirt 26160
Sarah Ann, Logan 25644
Sarton, Monroe 24983
Saulsville, Wyoming 25876
Saxon, Raleigh 25180
Scarbro, Fayette 25917
Scherr, Mineral 26726
Scott Depot, Putnam 25560
Secondcreek, Monroe 24974
Seebert, Pocahontas 24946
Selbyville, Upshur 26236
Seneca Rocks, Pendleton 26884
Seth, Boone 25181
Shady Spring, Raleigh 25918
Shanks, Hampshire 26761
Sharples, Logan 25183
Shenandoah Junction, Jefferson 25442
Shepherdstown, Jefferson 25443
Sherman, Jackson 26164
Shinnston, Harrison 26431
Shirley, Tyler 26434
Shively, Logan 25508
Shoals, Wayne 25562
Shock, Gilmer 26638
Short Creek, Brooke 26058
Short Gap, Mineral 26726
Shrewsbury, Kanawha 25015
Sias, Lincoln 25506
Simon, Wyoming 24882
Simpson, Taylor 26435
Sinks Grove, Monroe 24976
Sissonville, Kanawha 25320
Sistersville, Tyler 26175
Skelton, Raleigh 25919
Skygusty, Mcdowell 24801
Slab Fork, Raleigh 25920
Slanesville, Hampshire 25444
Slatyfork, Pocahontas 26209
Slatyfork, Pocahontas 26291
Smithburg, Doddridge 26436
Smithers, Fayette 25186
Smithfield, Wetzel 26437
Smithville, Ritchie 26178
Smoot, Greenbrier 24977
Snowshoe, Pocahontas 26209
Sod, Lincoln 25564
Sommerville Fork, Wirt 26160
Sophia, Raleigh 25921
South Charleston (See Charleston)
Southside, Mason 25187
Spanishburg, Mercer 25922
Spelter, Harrison 26438
Spencer, Roane 25276
Sprague, Raleigh 25802
Sprigg, Mingo 25661
Spring Dale, Fayette 25986
Spring Valley, Wirt 26143
Springfield, Hampshire 26763
Spurlockville, Lincoln 25565
Squire, Mcdowell 24884
Stanaford, Raleigh 25927
Standard, Kanawha 25083
Standing Stone, Wirt 26143
Star City (See Morgantown)
Statts Mills, Jackson 25271
Stephenson, Wyoming 25928
Stickney, Raleigh 25140
Stirrat, Mingo 25670
Stollings, Logan 25646
Stonewood, Harrison 26301
Stony Bottom, Pocahontas 24927
Stouts Mills, Gilmer 26430
Strange Creek, Clay 25063
Streeter, Summers 25969
Stumptown, Gilmer 25267
Sugar Grove, Pendleton 26815
Sumerco, Lincoln 25567
Summerlee, Fayette 25901
Summersville, Nicholas 26651
Summit Point, Jefferson 25446
Sundial, Raleigh 25140
Superior, Mcdowell 24801
Surveyor, Raleigh 25932
Sutton, Braxton 26601
Sweet Springs, Monroe 24941
Sweetland, Lincoln 25523
Swiss, Nicholas 26690
Switchback, Mcdowell 24887
Switzer, Logan 25647
Sylvester, Boone 25193
Tad, Kanawha 25201
Talcott, Summers 24981
Tallmansville, Upshur 26237
Tams, Raleigh 25921
Tanner, Calhoun 26137
Taplin, Logan 25632
Tariff, Roane 25259
Teays, Putnam 25569
Tennerton, Upshur 26201

Post Office	ZIP
Terra Alta, Preston	26764
Terry, Fayette	25864
Tesla, Braxton	26629
Thacker, Mingo	25672
Thomas, Tucker	26292
Thornton, Taylor	26440
Thorpe, Mcdowell	24888
Three Churches, Hampshire	26757
Thurmond, Fayette	25936
Tioga, Nicholas	26691
Toll Gate, Ritchie	26415
Tornado, Kanawha	25202
Triadelphia, Ohio	26059
Trout, Greenbrier	24991
Troy, Gilmer	26443
True, Summers	25951
Tunnelton, Preston	26444
Turtle Creek, Boone	25203
Twilight, Boone	25204
Twin Branch, Mcdowell	24828
Two Run, Wirt	26160
Uler, Roane	25266
Uneeda, Boone	25205
Unger, Morgan	25411
Union, Monroe	24983
Upper Falls, Kanawha	25202
Upper Tract, Pendleton	26866
Upperglade, Webster	26266
Vadis, Lewis	26321
Valley Bend, Randolph	26293
Valley Chapel, Lewis	26452
Valley Fork, Clay	25285
Valley Grove, Ohio	26060
Valley Head, Randolph	26294
Vallscreek, Mcdowell	24815
Van, Boone	25206
Varney, Mingo	25696
Verdunville, Logan	25649
Verner, Mingo	25650
Victor, Fayette	25938
Vienna, Wood	26105
Vivian, Mcdowell	24853
Volga, Barbour	26238
Vulcan, Mingo	25672
Wadestown, Monongalia	26590
Waiteville, Monroe	24984
Walker, Wood	26180
Walkersville, Lewis	26447
Wallace, Harrison	26448
Wallback, Clay	25285
Walton, Roane	25286
Wana, Monongalia	26590
War, Mcdowell	24892
Wardensville, Hardy	26851
Warriormine, Mcdowell	24894
Warwood, Ohio	26003
Washington, Wood	26181
Waverly, Wood	26184
Wayne, Wayne	25570
Wayside, Monroe	24985
Webster Springs, Webster	26288
Weirton, Hancock	26062
Welch, Mcdowell	24801
Wellsburg, Brooke	26070
Wendel, Taylor	26347
West Columbia, Mason	25287
West Hamlin, Lincoln	25571
West Liberty, Ohio	26074
West Logan, Logan	25601
West Milford, Harrison	26451
West Union, Doddridge	26456
Weston, Lewis	26452
Westover (See Morgantown)	
Wharncliffe, Mingo	25651
Wharton, Boone	25208
Wheeling, Ohio	26003
Whitby, Raleigh	25823
White Day, Taylor	26354
White Hall, Marion	26554
White Oak, Raleigh	25989
White Sulphur Springs, Greenbrier	24986
Whitehall, Marion	26555
Whitesville, Boone	25209
Whitman, Logan	25652
Whitmer, Randolph	26296
Whittaker, Kanawha	25083
Wht Sulphur S, Greenbrier	24986
Wht Sulphur Spgs, Greenbrier	24986
Wick, Tyler	26149
Widen, Clay	25211
Wilbur, Tyler	26320
Wilcoe, Mcdowell	24895
Wildcat, Lewis	26376
Wiley Ford, Mineral	26767
Wileyville, Wetzel	26581
Wilkinson, Logan	25653
Williamsburg, Greenbrier	24991
Williamson, Mingo	25661
Williamstown, Wood	26187
Willow Bend, Monroe	24983
Willow Island, Pleasants	26134
Wilsie, Braxton	26623
Wilson, Grant	26707
Wilsondale, Wayne	25699
Winding Gulf, Raleigh	25908
Windsor Heights, Brooke	26075
Winfield, Putnam	25213
Winifrede, Kanawha	25214
Winona, Fayette	25942
Witcher, Kanawha	25015
Wolf Pen, Mcdowell	24801
Wolf Summit, Harrison	26426
Wolfcreek, Monroe	24993
Wolfe, Mercer	24751
Woodville, Boone	25572
Worth, Mcdowell	24868
Worthington, Marion	26591
Wriston, Fayette	25840
Wyatt, Harrison	26463
Wyco, Wyoming	25943
Wymer, Randolph	26254
Wyoming, Wyoming	24898
Yawkey, Lincoln	25573
Yellow Spring, Hampshire	26865
Yolyn, Logan	25654
Yukon, Mcdowell	24892

BECKLEY WV

General Delivery 25801

POST OFFICE BOXES MAIN OFFICE STATIONS AND BRANCHES

Box No.s
1 - 2988 25802
3000 - 5777 25801
6001 - 9008 25802
9992 - 9992 25801

NAMED STREETS

Adair St 25801
Adamos St 25801
Adkins St 25801
Adrian Ct 25801
Aetna Ln 25801
Airdale Ln 25801
Albert Ave 25801
Allegheny Pass 25801
Allen Ave 25801
Aloha Ct 25801
Alvin St 25801
Amber Dr 25801
Amtrak Ln 25801
Andover Ln 25801
Angels Rst 25801
Angle Dr 25801
Ann St 25801
Antonio Ave 25801
Appalachian Dr 25801
Apple St 25801
Applegrove Ave 25801
Arbor Ln 25801
Arlington Rd 25801
Armory Dr 25801
Arnold Ave 25801
Arrow Ln 25801
Arthur Ct 25801
Asbury Ct 25801
Asher Dr 25801
Ashley Dr 25801
Ashwood St 25801
Ashworth Dr 25801
Athey Pl 25801
Augusta Ln 25801
Austin Ave 25801
Auto Plaza Dr 25801
Autumn Ln 25801
Avocet Way 25801
Avon St 25801
Azalea Cir 25801
Azzara Ave 25801
Bailey Ave 25801
Bair St 25801
Baker St 25801
Ball St 25801
Barber Ave 25801
Basin St 25801
Bataan Rd 25801
Bava Dr 25801
Bays St 25801
Bear Crossing Ln 25801
Bear Den Rd 25801
Beaver Ave 25801
Beckett Ct & Dr 25801
E Beckley Ave, Byp & Plz 25801
Beckley Crossing Shpg Ctr 25801
Beckwoods Dr 25801
Beech Ave 25801
Bellevue Ln 25801
Bellewood Ln 25801
Bellwood Dr 25801
Berkley St 25801
Berlin Ct 25801
Bero Ave 25801
Berry St 25801
Beth Ln 25801
Bethel Rd 25801
Beverley St 25801
Bibb Ave 25801
Birch St 25801
Bird Haven Ln 25801
Bishop St 25801
Blackburn St 25801
Blackstone Dr 25801
Blair Ave 25801
Bland Dr 25801
Blinn Ln 25801
Bloodhound Rd 25801
Bluebird Ln 25801
Bluemont Ln 25801
Bluestone Rd 25801
Bluff Rd 25801
Boblett Ave & Hl 25801
Boeing St 25801
Boggs Ct 25801
Bolton Dr 25801
Booker St 25801
Booth Ave 25801
Borneo St 25801
Bostick Ave 25801
Botman Dr 25801
Bouganville Ave 25801
Bowles Ln 25801
Bradford Dr 25801
Bradley Ave 25801
Brady Ln 25801
Brammer St 25801
Branch Rd 25801
Brandon Dr 25801
Bratton St 25801
Braxton Loop 25801
Breezeway Ct 25801
Brethren Church Rd 25801
Briarwood Ln 25801
Brierhill Dr 25801
Brierside Way 25801
Britnae Dr 25801
Brittlewood Dr 25801
Broadway St 25801
Brock Ln 25801
Brooks St 25801
Brookshire Ln 25801
Brookwood Ln 25801
Brown St 25801
Buckland St 25801
Bucks Br 25801
E Bunting Ln 25801
Burgess St 25801
Burkett St 25801
Burning Tree Dr 25801
Burrell Br 25801
Burton St 25801
Business St 25801
By Pass Plaza Shpg Ctr 25801
E & W C St 25801
Cabell Heights Rd 25801
Cajun St 25801
Caldwell St 25801
Cales Ln 25801
Callie St 25801
Calloway St 25801
Campbell St 25801
Candace Ct 25801
Cannaday St 25801
Canterbury Dr 25801
Captain Dunbar Ln 25801
Cardinal Ln 25801
Carl Jones Dr 25801
Carleton St 25801
Carriage Dr 25801
Carson Ave 25801
Carter St 25801
Carver Ln 25801
Cashmere Loop 25801
Catherine St 25801
Catlett St 25801
Cawley St 25801
Cayman Dr 25801
Cedar St 25801
Cedar Ridge Rd 25801
Center St 25801
Central Ave 25801
Cessna St 25801
Chambers Dr 25801
Champion Dr 25801
Chandler St 25801
Char Dr 25801
Charles St 25801
Chase Ave 25801
E & W Cherokee St 25801
Cherry Ave 25801
Cherry Tree Dr 25801
Chert Ln 25801
Chesapeake Ln 25801
Chesla Ln 25801
Chestnut Dr 25801
Chickadee Way 25801
Chicory Ln 25801
Chloe St 25801
Christian Rd 25801
Christie Ln 25801
Christopher Dr 25801
Church St 25801
Cinco St 25801
Circle St 25801
Circle Tree Dr 25801
Circleview Dr 25801
Citizens Dr 25801
City Ave 25801
Clark St 25801
Clay Farm Rd 25801
Clayton Ave 25801
Clear Creek Xing 25801
Clear Fork Rd 25801
Clear Water Ln 25801
Cleveland School Rd 25801
Clifford Dr 25801
Clutch St 25801
Clyburn St 25801
Clyde St 25801
Coal St 25801
Cobalt Ln 25801
Cobblestone Ln 25801
Cochran Ln & St 25801
Cohen St 25801
College Ave 25801
Collie Ln 25801
Collins Dr 25801
Colton Loop 25801
Combs St 25801
Connor St 25801
Conway St 25801
Cook Ave 25801
Coonhound Ct 25801
Coponiti St 25801
Coral Ct 25801
Corregidor Rd 25801
Corvair Rd 25801
Cottonwood Ln 25801
Cova St 25801
Crab Orchard Ave 25801
Craig St 25801
Cranberry Dr 25801
Cranberry Creek Dr 25801
Cranberry Pointe Way 25801
Crane St 25801
Cranston St 25801
Crawford St 25801
Creekview Dr 25801
Creole St 25801
Crescent Rd 25801
Crestview Dr 25801
Crestway Dr 25801
Crestwood Dr 25801
Croft St 25801
Cromwell Pl 25801
Cross St 25801
Crowe St 25801
Crown St 25801
Crystal Ave 25801
Cumberland Pl 25801
Cunningham Ave 25801
S Curtis Ave & St 25801
Cuthrill St 25801
Daisy Ln 25801
Dalton St 25801
Daniel St 25801
Daugherty St 25801
Davis Dr & St 25801
Davis Farm Dr 25801
Dawson Dr 25801
Dayton St 25801
Dean St 25801
Deck Ln 25801
Deegans St 25801
Deepwood Ave 25801
Deerview Ln 25801
Dexter Ave 25801
Diamond Ct 25801
Diane Dr 25801
Dickens Ln 25801
Dickinson Ave 25801
Dillon Crk 25801
Dingess Br 25801
Division St 25801
Dixie Ave 25801
Dixieland Rd 25801
Dixon Ave 25801
Dock St 25801
Dodson Ct 25801
Dogwood Ct & Ln 25801
Don St 25801
Dorcas Ave 25801
Doug Ln 25801
Dove Ln 25801
Downing St 25801
Dreamas Way 25801
Druid Ave 25801
Dry Hill Rd 25801
Dublin Rd 25801
Dunbar Ave 25801
Dunkley St 25801
Dunn Dr 25801
Dutch Ln 25801
Dye Dr 25801
E St 25801
Eagles Rd 25801
Earhart St 25801
Earle St 25801
Earwood St 25801
Easton St 25801
Eastview Ln & St 25801
Eddie Dr 25801
Edgar Dr 25801
Edgell St 25801
Edgewood Dr 25801
Edwards St 25801
N & S Eisenhower Dr 25801
Elco Ln 25801
Electric Ave 25801
Elkins St 25801
Ellen Ave 25801
Ellis St 25801
Ellison Ave 25801
Elm St 25801
Elmridge Ct 25801
Emerald Ct 25801
Emily St 25801
Emory St 25801
Equestrian Ln 25801
Erie St 25801
Ester Ln 25801
Evans St 25801
Evans Farm Rd 25801
Evergreen Ln & Pl 25801
Ewart Ave 25801
F St 25801
Fairlawn Ave 25801
Fairview Ave 25801
Falcon Cir 25801
Farley Ln 25801
N & S Fayette St 25801
Felix Ct 25801
Fern Ln 25801
Fernadez Dr 25801
Fernwood Ln 25801
Fields Way 25801
File Dr 25801
Fitzpatrick Rd 25801
Flannery Rd 25801
Fletcher St 25801
Flicker Ln 25801
Flintstone 25801
Florida Ave 25801
Fondale St 25801
Foote St 25801
Foothill Dr 25801
Ford St 25801
Forestview Dr 25801
N Forrest Ave & Rd 25801
Foster Ave 25801
Fox Run Rd 25801
Fox Sparrow Rd 25801
Francis Ave 25801
Franklin Ave 25801
Freeman St 25801
S French St 25801
Front St 25801
Frontier St 25801
Fulton Ave 25801
G St 25801
Gaines Ave 25801
Galleria Plz 25801
Garden Ter 25801
Gardenia Ct 25801
Garfield St 25801
Garten Pl 25801
Gate St 25801
George St 25801
Georgetown Ct 25801
Georgia Ave 25801
Gillespie 25801
Glendale Rd 25801
Glenn Ave 25801
Glory Ln 25801
Gobbler Ln 25801
Goldcrest Dr 25801
Goodman Dr 25801
Goodys Pl 25801
Goss Ct 25801
Grace St 25801
Grady Ave 25801
Grafton St 25801
Graham St 25801
Grant St 25801
Granville Ave 25801
Grear Ln 25801
Green St 25801
Greenbrier Ct 25801
Greenwood Dr 25801
Gregory St 25801
Grey Flats Rd 25801
Grist Mill Dr 25801
Grove Ave 25801
Guadalcanal Ave 25801
Guam Ave 25801
Gunter Rd 25801
H St 25801
Hager St 25801
Hague St 25801
Halbert Ln 25801
Hale St 25801
Hall St 25801
Hamlin Ct 25801
Hancock Dr & St 25801
Hankwoods Dr 25801
Hargrove St 25801
Harlan Ct 25801
Harold Rd 25801
Harper Ct & Rd 25801
Harper Heights Rd 25801
Harper Park Dr 25801
Harrah Rd 25801
Harris Ct 25801
Hart St 25801
Hartley Ave 25801
Harvell Dr 25801
Harvey St 25801
Hawaii St 25801
Hawksbury Trce 25801
Hawthorne St 25801
Hayes Ct 25801
Haymarket Dr 25801
Hazel St 25801
Heartland Dr 25801
N & S Heber St 25801
Heber Street Cut Off 25801
Hedgerow Ln 25801
Hedrick St 25801
N Heights Dr 25801
Hemlock St 25801
W Hendricks St 25801
Herbert Dr 25801
Heritage St 25801
Hewitt Dr 25801
Hickory Dr 25801
High St 25801
Highland Dr & St 25801
Highpoint Dr 25801
Hill St 25801
Hillcrest Dr 25801
Hillpark Dr 25801
Hilltop Vw 25801
Hilton St 25801
Hodges St 25801
Hoist Rd 25801
Holliday Dr 25801
Holly Ln 25801
Hollywood Dr 25801
Home St 25801
Homewood Dr 25801
Honda Dr 25801
Honey Ln 25801
Honeysuckle Ln 25801
Hoover St 25801
Horseshoe Dr 25801
Houston St 25801
Howard Ave 25801
Howe St 25801
Hubbard St 25801
Huffman St 25801
Hughes St 25801
Hull St 25801
Hume Ct 25801
Hummingbird Ln 25801
Hunt Ave 25801
Hunter St 25801
Hunting Hills Dr 25801
Huntington Ct 25801
Hutchinson St 25801
Hylton Ln 25801
I St 25801
Idlewood Ct 25801
Industrial Dr
100-132 25801
100-198 25802
101-131 25801
133-3799 25801
3801-3899 25801
Itzelt Ct 25801
Jackson Ave & St 25801
Jade Ln 25801
James St 25801
Jamescrest Dr 25801
Jamestown Ct 25801
Jamison St 25801
Jarrell St 25801
Jasper Dr 25801
Jefferson St 25801
Jenkins Dr 25801
Jennings St 25801
Jerome Van Meter Dr 25801
Jerry Ct 25801
Jessup Ln 25801
Jo Ann Pl 25801
Joe Smith Rd 25801
John St 25801
Johnston St 25801
Johnstown Rd 25801
Jonathan Dr 25801
Joseph St 25801
Joyce St 25801
Juliana St 25801
Junction St 25801
Juniper St 25801
Kaluha Ln 25801
N & S Kanawha St 25801
Kansas Ave 25801
Karen Ln 25801
Keaton St 25801
Keller Ln 25801
Kelso Ln 25801
Kent Ave & St 25801
Kentucky Ave 25801
Kessinger St 25801
Kevin Ridge Dr 25801
Kincaid St 25801
King St 25801
Kinglet Pl 25801
Kinzer St 25801
Kipawa Ct 25801
Kiser St 25801
Klaus St 25801
Kona St 25801
Kyle Ln 25801
Lakeview Dr 25801
Lambert Dr 25801
Lanark Pl 25801
Lancaster St 25801
Landmark Ln 25801
Lane Ave 25801
Larew Ave 25801
Lark Pl 25801
Latta Ct 25801
Laurel Ter 25801
Lauren Ave 25801
Lebanon Ln 25801
Lee Ave & St 25801
Lester St 25801
Levels Ln 25801
Lewis St 25801
Light Addition 25801
Lilly Dr & St 25801
Lincoln St 25801
Linden St 25801
Lindy St 25801
Lionel St 25801
Lisa Ln 25801
Little St 25801
Little Farm Addition 25801
Lively St 25801
Locust Dr & St 25801
Lode Dr 25801
Lodi Dr 25801
London Ln 25801
Longspur Way 25801
Longview Ct 25801
Longwood St 25801
Lonnies Ln 25801
Lori St 25801
Lotus Ln 25801
Lovell St 25801
Lower Sandlick Rd 25801
Lucas Dr 25801
Lundy Ln 25801
Lynwood Dr 25801
Lyons St 25801
Macarthur St 25801
Mack St 25801
Mactaggart Dr 25801
Magnolia St 25801
Mahan Ave 25801
E Main St 25801
Majestic Ct 25801
Mallard Ct 25801
Malvern Ln 25801
Mankin Ave 25801
Manor Dr 25801
Mansfield Ct 25801
Maple Ave 25801
Mapleview Dr 25801
Maplewood Ln 25801
Marcella Ln 25801
Marietta Ln 25801
Marigold Ln 25801
Marion St 25801
Market Rd 25801
Marshall Ave & St 25801
Martin Dr & Ln 25801
Maryland Ave 25801
Mason St 25801
Massey St 25801
Mattsville Rd 25801
Maui Ct 25801
Maxwell Hill Rd 25801
Maynor Br 25801
Mcberry St 25801
Mcclure St 25801
Mccool Ln 25801
Mccreery St 25801
Mcculloch Dr 25801

Street	ZIP
Mcdowell Dr & Holw	25801
Mcginnis St	25801
Mcginnis Cemetary Rd	25801
Mcmanamay Ln	25801
Mcnabb Ave	25801
Meadowbrook Ln	25801
S Meadows Ct & St	25801
Megan Cir	25801
Mellon St	25801
Melody Ln	25801
Melrose Ln	25801
Melvin Ln	25801
Melwood Ln	25801
Mercer St	25801
Mercury Rd	25801
Merit Dr	25801
Meritor Dr	25801
Merrywood Ln	25801
Michigan Ave	25801
Midland St	25801
Midway Rd	25801
Miller St	25801
Millers Ln	25801
Milliron Ave	25801
Mills Ave	25801
Millstone Dr	25801
Mindora Ave	25801
Minnesota Ave	25801
Minor Ln	25801
Miramir Ln	25801
Missouri Ave	25801
Mockingbird Ln	25801
Mollohan Dr	25801
Mondorf Ave	25801
Monroe Ave	25801
Montgomery Ct	25801
Moodespaugh Ln	25801
Mool Ave	25801
Morgan St	25801
Morning Star Ln	25801
Morris Ave	25801
Morton Ave	25801
Mount Tabor Cir & Rd	25801
Mountain View Rd	25801
Mulberry St	25801
Mullins St	25801
Munich Ct	25801
Munson Dr	25801
Murray St	25801
Myers Ave	25801
Myles Ave	25801
Nardas Mtn	25801
Nathan St	25801
Nathaniel Ln	25801
Navy Ln	25801
Neal St	25801
Nebraska Ave	25801
Neely St	25801
Nell Jean Sq	25801
Neptune Dr	25801
Neville St	25801
New Caledonia St	25801
New Guinea Ave	25801
New Jersey Ave	25801
New River Dr	25801
New River Town Ctr	25801
Newport Ct	25801
Newtown Rd	25801
Nimitz Ave	25801
Nixon Dr	25801
North Ave & St	25801
Northwestern Ave	25801
Norwood Ln	25801
Oahu St	25801
Oak Grove Ave & Rd	25801
Oak Run Rd	25801
Oakcrest Dr	25801
Oakhurst Dr	25801
Oakley Rd	25801
Oakview Ln	25801
N & S Oakwood Ave	25801
Odell Park	25801
Odessa Ave	25801
Old Eccles Rd	25801
Old Grove Rd	25801
Old Mill Rd	25801
Old Pemberton Rd	25801
Old Soak Rd	25801
Old Turnpike Rd	25801
Oleander Dr	25801
Olympia Dr	25801
Oppie Rd	25801
S Orchard Ave & Ct	25801
Orchard Wood Dr	25801
Oriole Pl	25801
Orlando St	25801
Orwell Ln	25801
Oscar Ct	25801
Osprey Rd	25801
Overlook Dr	25801
Pack Mtn & St	25801
Paint St	25801
Paint Creek Rd	25801
Painter Dr	25801
Palm St	25801
Pardee Ln	25801
Park Ave	25801
Parkway St	25801
Parkwood Dr	25801
Partridge Ln	25801
Patch St	25801
Patteson St	25801
Patton Dr	25801
Peach Ln	25801
Pearl Ln	25801
Pebble Ln	25801
Pebblestone Dr	25801
Pedley St	25801
Pepper Ln	25801
Perch Ln	25801
Perdue St	25801
Peregrine Ln	25801
Periwinkle Ln	25801
Perry St	25801
Pershing St	25801
Persinger St	25801
Peters Dr	25801
Petersburg St	25801
Pheasant Ln	25801
Phil Ave	25801
Phillips St	25801
N & S Pike St	25801
Pikeview Dr	25801
Pin Ct	25801
Pine St	25801
Pine Cove Dr	25801
Pine Park Pl	25801
Pinecrest Dr	25801
Pinelodge Dr	25801
Pineridge Dr	25801
Pinevilla Dr	25801
Pinewood Dr	25801
Piney Ave	25801
Piney View Rd	25801
Pinto Dr	25801
Piper St	25801
Plaza Ctr & Dr	25801
Pleasant Dr	25801
Plumley Ave & Ln	25801
Poplar St	25801
Porter St	25801
Porterfield Ln	25801
Powerline Dr	25801
Preston St	25801
Price St	25801
Prillerman Ave	25801
Primrose Ln	25801
E Prince St	25801
Professional Park	25801
Prosperity Rd	25801
Prudential Dr	25801
Quail Cir	25801
Quarry St	25801
Queen St	25801
Queen Anne Dr	25801
Quesenberry St	25801
Quiet Woods Pl	25801
Quincy Dr	25801
Rachel Ln	25801
Ragland Rd	25801
S Railroad Ave	25801
Rainbow Rdg	25801
Raleigh Ave & Mall	25801
Raleigh Ridge Rd	25801
Rambler Ct	25801
Ramey Ct	25801
Randolph St	25801
Randrick Dr	25801
Range Rd	25801
Rawling St	25801
Raybom Ct	25801
Raymond Dr	25801
Red Berry Dr	25801
Red Gate Rd	25801
Redbud Ct & Dr	25801
Redden Ln	25801
Redford Ln	25801
Renard St	25801
Reservation Ave	25801
Reservoir Rd	25801
Resource Dr	25801
Rhodes St	25801
Rhododendron Trl	25801
Rice St	25801
Richmond Ln	25801
Rider Dr	25801
N Ridge Ave & Rd	25801
Ridgecrest Ave	25801
Ridgelawn Dr	25801
Ridgepark Dr	25801
Riley St	25801
Rimview Dr	25801
Ringleben St	25801
Riverview Ln	25801
Robert C Byrd Dr	25801
Roberts St	25801
Robertson St	25801
Robin Pl	25801
Rocky Ct	25801
Rogar Ln	25801
Rollingwood Dr	25801
Rollyson Dr	25801
Roosevelt St	25801
Rosedale Ct	25801
Roseville Dr	25801
Rubin Dr	25801
Ruby Ln	25801
Rural Acres Dr	25801
Ruskin Dr	25801
Russell St	25801
Ryan St	25801
Sabre Dr	25801
Saddlebred Dr	25801
Sadie Ct & St	25801
Saint Clair Ln	25801
Saint Francis Ln	25801
Saipan Ave	25801
Salem Ct	25801
Salmon Dr	25801
Samoa Dr	25801
Sand Piper Pl	25801
S Sandbranch Rd	25801
Sandlewood Dr	25801
Sandstone Dr	25801
Sapphire Ln	25801
Sarah Ct	25801
Saunders Ave	25801
Schlager Dr	25801
Scott Ave	25801
Seahurst Dr	25801
Serviceberry Ln	25801
Shadow Ln	25801
Shady Ln	25801
Shannontown Rd	25801
Sharon St	25801
Sheffler St	25801
Sheppard St	25801
Sheridan Ave	25801
Sherman Hts	25801
Shore Ln	25801
Sidney St	25801
Sigmund St	25801
Simpkins St	25801
Sisson St	25801
Sizemore St	25801
Skyline Dr	25801
Skyview Dr	25801
Smith St	25801
Smoot Ave	25801
Snow Pl	25801
Snuffer Br & Ln	25801
Soccer Field Rd	25801
Solar Dr	25801
Solo Dr	25801
Solomon Ln	25801
Sour St	25801
South St	25801
Spangler St	25801
Spangler Mill Rd	25801
Sparacino St	25801
Speedwell Dr	25801
Spicewood Hl	25801
Sprague Ave	25801
Spring St	25801
Springdale Ave	25801
Springwood Ln	25801
Sprite Ln	25801
Spruce Ln	25801
Squire Ln	25801
Stadium Dr	25801
Stanaford Rd	25801
Stanaford Mine Rd	25801
Stanhope Ct	25801
Stanley Rd & St	25801
Stansbury St	25801
State St	25801
Station St	25801
Sterling St	25801
Stevens Ln	25801
Stewart Ave	25801
Stiffler Dr	25801
Stone Circle Rd	25801
Stonewall Rd	25801
Stovers Fork Rd	25801
Strawberry Ln	25801
Sumac Ln	25801
Summers St	25801
Summit Dr & Ln	25801
Sunflower Ln	25801
Sunrise Ave	25801
Sunset Dr & Vw	25801
Sunshine Cir	25801
Surprise Valley Rd	25801
Swain St	25801
Sweeneysburg Rd	25801
Sycamore St	25801
Tally Ho Dr	25801
Tamarack Park & Pl	25801
Tanager Pl	25801
Tanglewood Dr	25801
Tanner Dr	25801
Taylor St	25801
Teel Rd	25801
Temple St	25801
Templeview Dr	25801
Terrace Pt	25801
Terrill St	25801
Theater St	25801
Thomas St	25801
Thornton St	25801
Thornwood Ln	25801
Thurmond St	25801
Tifton Ct	25801
Tiljohn Ct	25801
Timber Ridge Dr	25801
Timberland Rd	25801
Timor Ct	25801
Tinnian Ave	25801
Tolbert St	25801
Tolbert Farm Rd	25801
Tolley Dr	25801
Toney Ln	25801
Totten St	25801
Towerview Ln	25801
Travelers Ln	25801
Treetop Ln	25801
Trent Ln	25801
Triangle Ln	25801
Trieste Pl	25801
Truman Ave	25801
Underwood St	25801
Union Hall Rd	25801
Upper Sandlick Rd	25801
Valentine St	25801
Valinda St	25801
Valley View Dr	25801
Valliant Dr	25801
Value City Ctr	25801
Van Voorhis St	25801
N & S Vance Dr	25801
Vankirk Dr	25801
Vass Br	25801
Venus Ave	25801
Verona Ct	25801
Veterans Ave	25801
Vine St	25801
Vintage Ln	25801
W Virginia Ave & St	25801
Waddell Ln	25801
Wade Rd	25801
Walker Ave	25801
Wallace Ct	25801
Walnut St	25801
Walter St	25801
Warbler Ln	25801
Warden St	25801
Warren Ave	25801
Washington Ave	25801
Waybright St	25801
Wc St	25801
Webster Ln	25801
West Ave & Ct	25801
Westfield Ln	25801
Westline Dr	25801
Westmoreland St	25801
Westover Ct	25801
Westview Ln	25801
Westwood Dr	25801
Wheeler Rd	25801
Whippoorwill Pl	25801
Whistler Dr	25801
White Ave	25801
White Oak Dr & Trce	25801
White Pine Dr	25801
Whitestick Rd	25801
Wickham Ave & Rd	25801
Wilderness Ridge Rd	25801
Wildwood Ave	25801
Wilkerson Dr	25801
Wilkes Ave & Rd	25801
Williams St	25801
Willow Ln	25801
Willowood Rd	25801
Wilson Ave & St	25801
Windellwood Way	25801
Windsong Trl	25801
Winger Ave	25801
Winston Ct	25801
Winter Set Rd	25801
Wiseman St	25801
Witherspoon St	25801
Wolf Ln	25801
Wood St	25801
Woodberry Ln	25801
Woodcrest Dr	25801
Woodland Ave & Dr	25801
Woodlawn Ave	25801
Woodthrush Ln	25801
Woodview Ln	25801
Workmans Crk	25801
Worley Rd	25801
Wren Pl	25801
Wright Rd	25801
Wyndmere Ct	25801
Wyoming Ave	25801
Yellow Wood Way	25801
Yorktown Ct	25801

NUMBERED STREETS

Street	ZIP
All Street Addresses	25801

CHARLESTON WV

General Delivery	25301

POST OFFICE BOXES MAIN OFFICE STATIONS AND BRANCHES

Box No.s	ZIP
A - J	25365
1 - 313	25321
321 - 633	25322
641 - 953	25323
961 - 1233	25324
1241 - 1513	25325
1521 - 1793	25326
1801 - 2073	25327
2000 - 2000	25305
2081 - 2393	25328
2300 - 2300	25364
2401 - 2633	25329
2641 - 2993	25330
3001 - 3147	25331
3110 - 3110	25364
3148 - 3284	25332
3200 - 3200	25364
3301 - 3394	25333
3401 - 3469	25334
3481 - 3549	25335
3561 - 3699	25336
3701 - 3786	25337
3801 - 3886	25338
3901 - 3986	25339
4001 - 4999	25364
5001 - 5660	25361
6001 - 6956	25362
7001 - 7949	25356
8001 - 8999	25303
9000 - 9714	25309
10001 - 10694	25357
11000 - 11932	25339
12001 - 12380	25302
13001 - 13980	25360
15001 - 15499	25365
18000 - 18695	25303
20001 - 20640	25362
38000 - 38015	25303
40000 - 40558	25364
50110 - 50919	25305
58001 - 58776	25358
59000 - 59997	25350
60001 - 60100	25306
69004 - 69076	25334
70001 - 70359	25301
75001 - 75480	25375

HIGHWAY CONTRACTS

36	25306

RURAL ROUTES

07, 08	25309
06, 09	25311
01, 03, 04, 05, 10, 13	25312
02	25314
81	25315
68, 69, 83, 84	25320

NAMED STREETS

Street	ZIP
A St	
1-99	25306
100-199	25303
Aarons Fork Rd	25320
Abb Ln	25312
Abbey Rd	25311
Abbeywood Ln	25320
Abby Dr	25314
Abilene Ln	25312
Abney Cir	25314
Acadia Ln	25311
Acorn Dr	
1-99	25312
100-128	25309
101-129	25312
130-799	25309
801-899	25309
Acorn Ridge Rd	25313
Acoustic Dr	25306
Acre Ln	25312
Ada Mae Dr	25302
Adams St	25302
Addison Dr	25309
Addition Rd	25313
Adele St	25302
Adkins Fisher Ln	25320
Adrian Rd	25314
Aerie Est	25302
Affinity Dr	25313
Agnes St	25303
Air View Dr	25302
Airborne Ave	25312
Airport Rd	25311
Alamo Dr	25312
Albert St	25302
Alberta Acres Rd	25312
Alcan Ave	25314
Alcoa Dr	25304
Alden St	25309
Alderwood Dr	25313
Alethia St	25302
Alex Ln	25304
Alexander St	25302
Alexandria Pl	25314
Alexis Ln	25312
Alicia Dr	25309
Aliff Dr	25387
Alleback Ave	25387
Allegheny Dr	25312
Allen Dr	
200-299	25303
400-499	25302
Allen Creek Rd	25320
Allens Rte	25320
Allens Fork Rd	25320
Allison Way	25313
Alliston Dr	25311
Allran Rd	25320
Allview Dr	25309
Almond Bend Ln	25311
Alpine Dr	25313
Alta Rd	25314
Altoona Dr	25311
Alum Creek Rd	25309
Alva Dr	25314
Alynwood Cir	25314
Amanita Dr	25309
Amaron Dr	25302
Amber Rd	25303
Ameila Dr	25313
American Way	25320
Amethyst Dr	25320
Amherst Dr	25302
Amity Dr	25302
Ampere Dr	25313
Amsbury Ln	25320
Amy Rd	25312
Anaconda Ave	25302
Anderson Hts	25314
Andover Cir	25313
Andover Ln	25320
Andover Pl	25311
Andys Way	25309
Angel Dr	25313
Angel Ter	25314
Angel Meadow Rd	25306
Angels Trumpet Rd	25320
Angola Dr	25302
Angus Cir	25312
Angus E Peyton Dr	25303
Anheuser Dr	25312
Animal Ln	25312
Ann Ct	25313
Ann St	25320
Ann Lee Dr	25313
Anna St	25302
Anna Lee Cir	25312
Annabelle Ln	25312
Annie Black Ln	25312
Antelope Ln	25313
Anthem Dr	25313
Antioch Way	25311
Antique Ln	25312
Antler Dr	25314
Antonia Ln	25320
Antwerp Ln	25313
Apex Dr	25313
Apollo Dr	25309
Apple Dr	25314
Apple Tree Ln	25320

Street	ZIP
Applegate Ln	25320
Applehill Ln	25312
Applewood Cir	25320
Applewood Dr	25302
Appomattox Pl	25302
April Cir	25313
April Ln	25312
Aquamarine Dr	25313
Araminta Ln	25320
Arbor Dr	25302
Arcadia Ln	25312
Arch Dr	25309
Archdale Ln	25320
Archibald Dr	25320
Arctic Dr	25311
Arden Gate Dr	25320
Ariel Hts	25311
Arlington Ave	25302
Arlington Ct	25301
Armeda Ln	25311
Arnett Dr	25309
Arney Dr	25312
Arnold Dr	25387
Arrow Dr	25313
Arrowwood Dr	25313
Arthur Dr	25313
N Arthur Dr	25387
Artillery Dr	25309
Asborough Ln	25312
Asbury Heights Rd	25312
Ash St	25302
Ashbrook Dr	25313
Ashby Ave	25314
Asheville Ln	25320
Ashlawn Dr	25303
Ashlee Meadows Dr	25312
Ashley Ave & Ln	25313
Ashmont Ln	25312
Ashwood Rd	25314
Ashworth Dr	25309
Aspen Rd	25304
Assembly Dr	25309
Association Dr	25311
Athens Ave	25306
Atherton Ave	25311
Atkins Dr	25314
Atkinson Ct	25302
Atlantic St	25302
Atlas Rd	25309
Augusta Pl	25309
Aultz Ct	25387
Aurora Dr	25314
Austin Reese Rd	25312
Autumn Ln	
1-99	25314
1-99	25309
2-98	25309
Autumn Rd	25314
Autumn Shadows Ln	25312
Avery Cir	25313
Aviation Dr	25314
Avon St	25302
Avondale Rd	25302
Awesome Ln	25312
Azalea Ln	25306
B St	
1-99	25306
100-399	25303
Babbitt Ln	25313
Backus Rd	25309
Bagado Dr	25313
Bailey Dr	25312
Bainbridge Dr	25312
Baird Dr	25302
Baker Ln	25302
Bakers Fork Rd	25311
Bald Eagle Dr	25306
Bald Knob Rd	25312
Baldwin Dr	25313
Ballard Rd	25309
Balmy Dr	25313
Balsam Cir	25313
Balser Ln	25312
Bam Gilley Rd	25309
Bandit Ln	25311
Baneberry Ln	25309
Banister Dr	25313
Banjo Ln	25311
Banks St	25311
Baptist Mountain Rd	25311
Barbara St	25387
Barber Dr	25302
Barberry Ln	25314
Barbershop Ln	25313
Barbies Dr	25320
Barclay Dr	25311
Bare Ln	25309
Barker Dr	25309
Barley Dr	25312
Barlow Dr	25311
Barn Dance Way	25312
Barnes Pl	25314
Barnett Dr	25313
Barnhouse Way	25312
Barnwood Rd	25312
Barred Owl Dr	25312
Barrett St	25309
Barronwood Ln	25312
Barton St	25302
Basalt Dr	25311
Basil Rd	25314
Bassett Dr	25312
Basswood Rd	25314
Bath Rd	25312
Bauer Ave	25302
Baxter Dr	25302
Baxter Woods Dr	25312
Bay Laurel Dr	25313
Bayberry St	25309
Baybrook Ln	25320
Bayfield Ln	25320
Bayless Dr	25312
Bayou Rd	25313
Bays Dr	
1-199	25309
700-799	25306
Bayshore Ln	25312
Beacon Hl	25311
Beacon Ter	25302
Beagle Run	25313
Beane Rdg	25312
Bear Fork Rd	25312
Bear Tracks Dr	25306
Bear Trap Ln	25313
Beatrice St	25302
Beaumont Rd	25314
Beauregard St	25301
Becca Dr	25313
Bedford Dr	25309
Bedford Rd	25314
Beech Ave	
400-1399	25302
1400-1699	25387
Beech Dr	25320
Beech St	
700-799	25309
1000-1098	25311
1100-1399	25311
Beechcrest Dr	25313
Beechnut Ln	25320
Beechtree Cir	25313
Beechvale Dr	25313
Beechwood Dr	25303
Belcher Ln	25306
Belcher Rd	25311
Belfast Rd	25314
Bellaire Dr	25387
Belle Dr	25313
Bellehaven Dr	25309
Bellevue Dr	25302
Bellhaven Ln	25312
Bellington Dr	25387
N Belmont St	25314
Ben Greene Ln	25312
Bench Rd & Way	25311
Bendcrest Pl	25314
Bendview Dr	25314
Benfield Dr	25320
Bennett Dr	25313
Bennington Dr	25313
Benny St	25320
Bens Fork Rd	25312
Benson Dr	25302
Bentbrook Rd	25313
Berea Rd	25312
Berenger Ln	25306
Berg Dr	25302
Bergen Dr	25312
Berkeley St	25302
Berkshire Pl	25314
Berry Hls	25314
Berry Ln	25312
Berry St	25309
Berry Hills Dr	
2-700	25309
702-798	25309
801-897	25314
899-1000	25314
1002-1298	25314
Berry Hollow Rd	25320
Berrywood Rd	25314
Bessie Ln	25312
Beta Ln	25304
Bethel Ln	25312
Bethel Rd	25314
Betheny Dr	25313
Beuhring Ave	25302
Beulah St	25302
Beverly Dr	25304
Bias Ln	25312
Bibby St	25301
Bible Center Dr	25309
Bickerstaff Rd	25312
Biden Dr	25306
Big Bottom Hollow Rd	25311
Big Coal Fork Dr	25306
Big Hickory Rd	25312
Big Oak Rd	25309
Big Pine Dr	25309
Big Tyler Rd	25313
Bigley Ave	25302
Billy Bob Ln	25309
Birch Rd	25314
Birch St	25309
Birch Tree Ln	25314
Bird Ct	25303
Bird Rd	25314
Biscayne Dr	25306
Black Bear Dr	25312
Black Jack Rd	25312
Black Oak Dr	25313
Black Pine Rd	25309
Black Willow Ln	25306
Black Willow Ln	25306
Blackberry Ln	25304
Blackberry Mtn	25320
Blackshire Ct	25313
Blackstone Dr	25309
Blacktop Rd	25312
Blackwell Dr	25387
Blackwell St	25309
Blaine Blvd	25387
Blankenship Dr	25309
Blazewood Dr	25313
Blockade Rd	25311
Blondwood Ln	25313
Bloomfield Rd	25320
Blossom Hill Rd	25320
Blue Lake Dr	25320
Blue Moon Dr	25320
Blue Ridge Dr	25313
Blue Sky Dr	25309
Blue Spruce Ln	25313
Bluebell Dr	25313
Bluebird Ln	25312
Bluefield Ave	25306
Bobbys Dr	25312
Bobcat Ln	25309
Bobolink Ln	25312
Bode Dr	25302
Boggess Btm	25320
Boggs Branch Rd	25311
Bohemia Dr	25312
Bon Ami Dr	25309
Bona Vista Dr & Pl	25311
Bonham Rd	25312
Bonus Ln	25302
Booker St	25303
Boonville Ln	25302
Bootlegger Ln	25311
Boreman Dr	25312
Bostic Ln	25306
Boston Ln	25312
Bottom Dr	25320
Bougemont Rd	25314
Bow Hunter Rd	25314
Bowen St	25311
Bowers Rd	25314
Bowles Hollow Rd	25311
Bowling Ln	25314
Bowman Ct	25387
Bowne Ave	25303
Bownemont St	25303
Boxwood Dr	25306
Boyz Ln	25320
Brackenrich Dr	25313
Bradchar Dr	25313
Bradford St	25301
Bradley Dr	25313
Bradshaw Dr	25314
Bragg Farm Rd	25312
Braidwood Ln	25302
Brammer Dr	25311
Branch St	25302
Branchfield Dr	25314
Bravo Rd	25306
Brawley Rd	25314
Brawley Walkway	25301
Braxton Dr	25311
Bray Dr	25320
Bream St	25387
Breece St	25302
Breezemont Dr	25302
Breezy Dr	25311
Breezy Peak Rd	25312
Brelyssa Dr	25312
Brenda Ln	25312
Brentwood Rd	25314
Brewer Ave	25303
Brewster St	25302
Briar Rd	25313
Briar Hill Rd	25314
Briar Meadow Rd	25313
Briarwood Rd	25314
Brick Cir & Ln	25313
Brick Lane Ct	25313
Bridge Rd	25314
Bridgeport Ln	25312
Bridgeview Dr	25309
Bridlewood Rd	25314
Brier Rd	25309
Brighton Ln	25311
Bristol Dr	25320
Britt Way	25313
Brittany Woods	25314
Britton St	25302
Britton Ridge Rd	25312
Broad Tree Run	25320
Broadmoor Dr	25313
Brogan Ln	25309
Brook Rd	25309
Brooke Hill Dr	25311
Brookevale Dr	25302
Brooks St	25301
Brooks Range Ln	25309
Brookside Dr	25313
Brookside Ln	25309
Brookside Park Dr	25312
Brookstone Rd	25314
Brookview Dr	25313
Brookwood Blvd	25302
Broom Branch Rd	25309
Brounland Rd	25309
Brown St	25309
Bruce Dr	25302
Brumby Dr	25313
Brushy Knob Way	25309
Bryant Dr	25315
Bryant Rd	25314
Bryant Lake Rd	25313
Brynwood Dr	25302
Buccaneer Rd	25306
Buchanan St	25302
Buck Run Rd	25312
Buckhorn Rd	25314
Buckingham Pointe	25309
Buckner Ln	25311
Bud Hill Rd	25320
Buena Vista Pl	25302
Buffalo Rd	25311
Buffy Dr	25313
Bull Holw	25312
Bullitt St	25301
Bumblebee Ln	25314
Bungalow Rd	25306
Burbank Ln	25320
Burberry Ln	25312
Burd Ln	25311
Burdette Way	25387
Burfords Hilltop Acres	25312
Burgess Dr	25312
Burgess St	25302
Burginater Ln	25314
Burkewood Pl	25314
Burlew Dr	25302
Burton Rd	25314
Bush St	25313
Bushrod Dr	25312
Butler St	25302
Butternut Ln	25312
Butterscotch Ln	25312
Buttonwood Ln	25314
Byng Dr	25303
Byus Dr	25311
C St	25303
Cactus Ln	25313
Cadbury Ln	25312
Cadle Dr	25313
Cairns Ct	25387
Calamity Dr	25313
Caldwell Rd	25312
California Ave	
2-98	25311
100-299	25305
8300-9199	25315
Call Rd	
1-99	25309
2-198	25312
200-799	25312
801-999	25312
Callie Rd	25314
Camargo Ln	25314
Cambrian Way	25312
Cambridge Dr	25314
Cambridge Pointe	25309
Cambronne Ln	25306
Camden Dr	25302
Camelback Ln	25313
Cameo Dr	25311
Cameron Ln	25320
Camp Way	25309
Camp Creek Rd	25320
Camp Virgil Tate Rd	25312
Campbells Creek Dr	25306
Campbells Hollow Rd	25311
Campus Dr	25303
Canal Rd	25312
Candace Dr	25311
Candleberry Ct	25309
Cane Fork Rd	25314
Cannon Creek Rd	25314
Canteen Rd	25309
Cantelope Ln	25313
Canterbury Dr	25314
Canterbury Woods Dr	25312
Cantley Dr	25314
Canyon Dr	25309
Canyon Ln	25312
Canyonview Rd	25314
Canyonwood Ln	25302
Capaci Dr	25309
Capitol Dr	25320
Capitol St	25301
Carbon Ctr	25315
Carbon Dr	25306
Carden Dr	25313
Cardinal Dr	
2-98	25313
4800-5099	25306
Cardinal Rd	25314
Carey Pl	25314
Cargo Rd	25320
Carl Mountain Rd	25320
Carleton Ct	25313
Carlton Dr	25304
Carmen Dr	25303
Carney Dr	25312
Carney Rd	25314
Carolina Ave	25315
Carolina St	25311
Carolyn Rd	25313
Carper St	25303
Carriage Ln & Rd	25314
Carrie Ln	25312
Carrier Ln	25320
Carrington Ln	25312
Carroll Ct	25387
Carroll Rd	25314
Carson St	25302
Carson Way	25309
Carte St	25311
Carter Dr	25306
Cartlyn Dr	25312
Casbuck Ln	25312
Cascade Dr	25311
Casdorph Ln & Rd	25312
Casey Ln	25320
Casper Ln	25312
Casper Rd	25320
Cassondra Ln	25320
Castine Ln	25314
Castle Dr	25313
Castle Pine Ln	25309
Castleberry Hl	25309
Castlegate Rd	25303
Casto Rd	25313
Cat Fish Rd	25311
Cauliflower Ln	25314
Cavelick Rd	25320
Cavender Ln	25312
Cayton Rd	25320
Cecil Dr	25314
Cedar Ln	25309
Cedar Rd	25314
Cedar Cliff Ln	25312
Cedar Flats Addition	25320
Cedar Ridge Rd	25320
Cedar View Dr	25313
Cedele Ln	25309
Celebration Dr	25306
Cellar Dr	25320
Cellular Dr	25320
Centennial Dr	25312
Centers Rd	25311
Central Ave	
100-500	25303
501-597	25302
502-598	25303
599-1199	25302
Centre Way	25309
Centre Court Rd	25314
Chads Cv	25313
Chadwicks Ln	25312
Chafton Rd	25314
Chalet Dr	25309
Challenger Rd	25309
Chamberlain Ct	25311
Champ Dr	25309
Champion Dr	25309
Chancey Ln	25315
Chandler Dr	25387
Chapel Hill Ln	25312
Chappell Rd	25304
Chapps Fork Rd	25312
Charles St	25302
Charleston Rd	25320
Charleston Town Ctr	25389
Charlie Ln	25312
Charlotte Pl	25314
Charmac Dr	25302
Charmont Rd	25312
Charmwood Dr	25302
Chasewood Ln	25302
Chatfield Ln	25312
Chatham Rd	25304
Chatsworth Ln	25314
Chatwood Rd	25304
Chaweva Hts	25313
Cheerful Ln	25314
Chelsea Rd	25303
Cherie Dr	25309
Cherokee Ave	25304
Cherokee Ln	25320
Cherry Ln	25309
Cherry Meadow Ln	25314
Chesapeake Ave	25311
Chesapeake St	25309
Chesswood Dr	25306
Chester Rd	25302
Chester Hill Rd	25320
Chesterfield Ave	25304
Chestnut Ave	25309
Chestnut Rd	
411B-411D	25309
800-999	25314
2600-2998	25309
3000-4999	25309
5001-5299	25309
Chestnut St	
1213A-1213Z	25309
400-500	25309
501-599	25313
502-3798	25309
601-2699	25309
Cheyenne Ln	25312
Chief Dr	25313
Childerss Plz	25309
Childress Ln, Pl & Rd	25309
Childress Farm Rd	25309
Chilton Mnr	25314
Chilton St	25311
Chimney Dr	25302
Chimney Hl	25311
Chinaberry Ln	25304
Chipmunk Ln	25311
Chisholm Ln	25320
Chisum Ln	25320
Chiswell Ln	25320
Chittum Ln	25309
Christa Cir	25309
Christian Dr	25303
Christian Rd	25313
Christine Ln	25302
Christopher St	25301
Chubba Kulu Rd	25312
Church Dr	25306
Church Pl	25313
Church Rd	25302
Churchill Cir & Dr	25314
Churchview Ln	25306
Chyboo Ln	25313
Cicerone Rd	25320
Cicerone Star Rte	25320
Circle Dr	25313
Circle Rd	25314
Circle St	25320
Circle Way	25309
Circle Lake Dr	25311
Civic Center Dr	25301
Claire St	25302
Clara Dr	25312
Claridge Cir	25303
Clarion Dr	25309
Clark Dr	
101-197	25301
199-299	25301
700-799	25315
Clark Rd	25314
Clark Point Ter	25314
Clay Ave	25387
Clay Sq	25301
Clay Lick Branch Rd	25312
Claybank Rd	25313
Clayburn Dr	25313
Clayfield Ln	25311
Claymont Rd	25304
Clearview Hts	25312
Clemmer Dr	25302
Clemson Ave	25306
Clendenin St	25301
Cleon Ferrell Dr	25306
Cleone St	25302

Cleveland Ave 25302
Clifford Rd 25306
Cliffrose Ln 25320
Cliffview Ave 25387
Clifton Rd 25303
Cline Hollow Rd 25306
Clinton Ave 25302
Clintwood Rd 25314
Clover Dr
3200-4599 25306
4601-4699 25306
4701-5199 25311
Cloverfield Ln 25312
Cloverleaf Cir 25306
Clubview Dr 25309
Cluster Oak Ln 25306
Clyde Ct 25387
Coal Rd 25312
Coal Fork Dr 25306
Coal Hollow Rd 25314
Coal Mountain Rd 25312
Coaldale Cir 25320
Cobb St 25309
Cobb Hollow Rd 25312
Cobble Ln 25313
Cobra Ln 25311
Coconut Dr 25306
Coffman Ests 25312
Colan Ct 25314
Colborne Dr 25311
Colby Rd 25314
Coleenas Ln 25320
Coleman St 25311
Colington Dr 25309
Collias Rd 25320
Collindale Cir 25312
Collins Dr 25311
Collins Ln 25309
Colonial Ln & Way 25314
Colonial Park Dr 25309
Colony Dr 25314
Columbia Ave 25302
Columbia St 25309
Columbia Mobile Home Park 25306
Commerce Dr 25306
Commerce Sq 25301
Commercial Dr 25311
Commodity Dr 25312
Community Dr 25306
Comrey Ln 25320
Comstock Pl 25314
Concord St 25302
Conestoga Ln 25312
Connell Ln & Rd 25314
Conner Dr 25302
Constance Way 25312
Conville Dr 25312
Cook Dr 25314
Cooks Hollow Rd 25306
Cool Spgs 25312
Cool Springs Addition Rd 25312
Coolbrook Dr 25320
Coon Creek Rd 25320
Coon Hollow Rd 25312
Coonskin Dr 25311
Cooper Hawk Ln 25313
Coopers Dr 25302
Coopers Creek Rd 25312
Copeland Rd 25320
Copen Dr 25302
Copen Branch Rd 25312
Copenhaver Dr & St W 25387
Copper Stone Dr 25309
Copperhead Ln 25320
Cora St 25302
Coral Dr 25312
Corbina Ln 25309
Cornell St 25302
Corns Dr 25309
Cornwall Ln 25314
Corporate Lndg 25311
Corridor G 25309
Corsicana Dr 25314

Cortona Ln 25320
Corvair Dr 25387
Corvus Dr 25312
Cosine Dr 25312
Cosmic Rd 25311
Cosmos Dr 25387
Costello St 25302
Cotner Dr 25306
Cottage Ave
3700-3898 25304
3900-3999 25304
4001-4099 25304
5300-5399 25309
Cottage Pointe Ln 25311
Cottrell Ln
1-99 25309
2-98 25320
Couch St 25302
Country Ln 25312
Country Rd 25313
Country Club Blvd 25309
Country Oaks Ln 25312
Country Squire Ln 25313
Countrywood Ln 25311
Court St 25301
Courtland Rd 25312
Courtney Dr 25304
Cove Dr & Way 25309
Coventry Ln 25314
E Coventry Rd 25309
W Coventry Rd 25309
Coventry Rdg 25309
Covey Ln 25313
Cox Ln 25309
Coyote Ln 25302
Crack Rock Dr 25312
Cracker Creek Dr 25312
Craddock Ln 25309
Craelyn Ln 25309
Craigmar Rd 25314
Craigo Ln 25311
Craigs Branch Rd 25312
Cranbrook Dr 25311
Crances Dr 25387
Crandall Rd 25312
Cranes Ln 25312
Crash Rd 25320
Crawford Rd 25314
Crawford Hill Rd 25309
Craze Dr 25387
Crazy Ln 25313
Creative Pl 25311
N Crede Dr 25302
Creek Aly 25315
Creekstone Rdg 25309
Creel Ave 25314
Crescent Rd 25302
Crest Dr 25311
Crestlyn Dr 25302
Crestmont Dr 25311
Crestview Dr 25302
Crestwood Rd
400-2999 25302
3201-3297 25312
3299-3399 25312
3401-3599 25312
Crimson Oaks Dr 25320
Crimson Oaks Rd 25312
Crindle Ln 25320
Crockett Ln 25306
Crondine Dr 25311
Crook Rd 25320
Crooked Creek Rd 25309
Cross Dr 25313
Cross Creek Rd 25314
Cross Lanes Dr 25313
Cross Terrace Blvd 25309
Crossfire Rd 25320
Crosshaven Ln 25320
Crouch Hollow Rd 25311
Crowberry Hill Rd 25320
Crowder Ln 25302
Crowder Hager Ln 25320
Crown Dr 25309
Crusade Way 25312
Crystal Dr 25313

Culpepper Dr 25313
Cuma Ln 25320
Cumberland Way 25313
Cunningham Dr 25302
Curney Creek Rd 25312
Curry Dr & Ln 25309
Curtis Price Way 25311
Cyan Dr 25320
Cypress Dr 25306
Cyrus Pt 25314
Cyrus Point Pl 25314
D St
100-401 25303
400-400 25309
403-1099 25303
500-1098 25303
Dabney Dr 25314
Dagger Ln 25311
Daisy Dr 25387
Dakota Dr 25320
Dalewood Dr 25313
Dalewood Mobile Home Park 25313
Daley Branch Rd 25309
Dalton Dr 25311
Dalton Way 25303
Damron Pl 25302
Dan Slater Holw 25320
Dana Pointe 25302
Dancenco Dr 25320
Dandelion Ln 25306
Daniel Boone Dr 25301
Daniels Ave 25303
Danner Rd 25303
Danny Ray Ln 25309
Dapplewood Rd 25309
Darby St 25311
Darien Ln 25309
Darkwood Ln 25315
Dartmouth Ave 25302
Daugherty St 25302
Daverton Rd 25303
David Dr 25313
Davidson Ave 25306
Davis Cir 25387
Davis Ln 25313
Davis Sq 25301
Dawn Pl 25314
Dawn St 25313
Dawnlight Ln 25312
Dawnview Dr 25313
Dawson Ct 25387
Dayton Dr 25302
Daytona Dr 25311
Dead End Rd 25309
Dean Dr 25313
Debord Ln 25309
Dee Dr 25311
Deer Country Ln 25312
Deer Crossing Ln 25320
Deer Oaks Rd 25314
Deer Valley Rd 25312
Deer View Dr 25312
Deere Run 25302
Deerfield Ln 25313
Deerhaven Ln 25313
Deerwalk Ln 25314
Deitrick Blvd & Dr 25311
Delana Ct 25320
Delarma Dr 25312
Delaware Ave 25302
Delford Dr 25387
Dell Way 25309
Dellway Dr 25313
Delmont Rd 25312
Delray Dr 25387
Delsie Ln 25320
Delta Dr 25387
Deming Dr 25314
Dempsey Dr 25313
Demra St 25320
Denali Dr
1-199 25320
400-498 25312
Denmark Dr 25313
Dennison Dr 25311

Dennitt Dr 25313
Denton St 25311
Derricks Creek Rd 25320
Derricks Utah Rd 25320
Derringer Dr 25306
Deseret Dr 25302
Desmond Dr 25314
Devondale Cir 25314
Dewayne Rd 25312
Dewberry Ln 25313
Dewitt Rd 25313
Diagonal Dr 25313
Diamond Stone Dr 25320
Dickens Way 25312
Dickinson St 25301
Dickinson Mobile Home Park 25306
Dickson Ln 25312
Dijon Dr 25313
Dinwiddie St 25311
Diomandback Rd 25320
Disney Ln 25306
Distribution Dr 25306
Divine Ln 25320
Division St 25309
Dixie St 25311
Doberman Ln 25302
Doc Bailey Rd 25313
Doe Meadows Dr 25313
Dogwood Dr 25320
Dogwood Ln 25312
Dogwood Rd 25314
Dogwood Flat Rd 25309
Dolan Rd 25312
Dolaron Ln 25309
Dolin Dr 25309
Dolin Ln 25313
Dollar Dr 25311
Dolman Dr 25314
Dolores Dr 25313
Dolphin Dr 25306
Domingo Dr 25311
Dominion Pl 25301
Dominion Way 25309
Donna Dr 25313
E Donnally Rd 25304
Donnally St 25301
Donnas Dr 25315
Donnie Dr 25309
Donnybrook Rd
1-99 25312
201-299 25320
Dons Dr 25311
Dooley Ln W 25387
Doolittle Ln 25306
Doral Ln 25313
Dorchester Rd 25303
Dorfer Dr 25302
Dormont Dr 25306
Dorothy Dr 25302
Dorothy Ln 25320
Dorsey Rd 25314
Dotson Dr 25309
Doug And Lucy Ln 25320
Doughty Dr 25313
Douglas Dr 25309
Dover Dr 25313
Dovewing Ln 25313
Downing St 25301
Drakesburg Ln 25312
Drakewood Ln 25314
Draper Dr 25306
Dreamview Dr 25314
Dreamwood Dr 25313
Drexel Pl 25313
Driftwood Dr 25306
Drone Ln 25312
Druid Pl 25314
Dry Branch Dr 25306
Dry Branch Rd 25312
Dryden Rd 25309
Dublin Dr 25313
Dudley Dr 25311
Dudley Rd 25314
Dudley Farms Ln 25309
Dugan Rd 25309

Dunbar St 25301
Duncansville Rd 25313
Dunlevy Rd 25314
Dunlop Rd 25320
Dunraven Ln 25320
Dusk Rd 25320
Dustin Dr 25309
Dusty Hollow Rd 25309
Dutch Rd 25302
Dutch Creek Rd 25312
Dutch Hollow Rd 25312
Duvoy Ln 25314
Dye Farm Rd 25320
Dysart Ln 25311
E St 25303
Eagan St 25301
Eager Ln 25313
Eagle Dr & Way 25309
Eagle Mountain Rd 25311
Eagle Rock Dr 25313
Eagle View Way 25306
Earl St 25302
Earley Dr & Ln 25312
Early St 25302
Earthstone Dr 25311
East Ave 25309
Eastcove Ln 25309
Eastern Dr 25311
Eastridge Rd 25312
Eastview Heights Dr 25311
Eastwood Ave 25309
Easy St 25309
Ebert Ln 25313
Ebony Dr 25313
Echo Rd 25303
Edds Ln 25313
Edelweiss Ln 25306
Edens Ests 25312
Edens Fork Rd 25312
Edenview Ln 25312
Edgebrook Dr 25313
Edgell Dr 25313
Edgewood Dr 25302
Edmond Dr 25306
Edview Cir 25313
Edward St 25311
Ehman Dr 25302
Eisenhower Dr 25302
Elaine Dr 25306
Elberta Dr 25306
Elder Dr 25302
Elderberry Ln 25312
Eldorado Dr 25313
Eleanor Ln 25302
Eliza Ln 25313
Elizabeth Ave 25303
Elizabeth Dr 25312
Elizabeth St 25311
Elk Dr 25302
Elk Shore Dr 25302
Elkdale Dr 25302
Elkgrove Ln 25312
Elkhart Dr 25311
Elkhorn Ln 25302
Elkins Ln 25314
Elkmont Dr 25302
Ella Ave 25302
Ellen Dr 25303
Ellette Dr & Pl 25311
Ellison Rd 25314
Ellwood Dr 25309
Elm St
100-199 25303
200-305 25302
306-398 25303
307-499 25302
402-414 25302
402-424 25303
Elmer Ln 25309
Elmhaven Cir 25313
Elmont Dr 25311
Elmore Ave 25302
Elmwood Ave 25301
Elvis Dr 25309
Embassy Dr 25313
Emerald Rd 25314

Emery S Fisher Ln 25320
Emily St 25302
Emma Way 25313
Emmanuel Dr 25313
Emmitt Ln 25313
Emory Ave 25306
Emperor Ln 25320
Empire Dr 25313
Enchantment Rd 25312
Enclave Dr 25313
Energy Dr 25313
Epic Trl 25314
Eric Dr 25312
Erin Ln 25309
Ernest Way 25311
Esta Ln 25312
Estate Ln 25309
Estep Ln 25320
Esther Stone Way 25306
Estill Dr 25314
Estonia Ln 25302
Ethel Ave 25315
Eureka Rd 25314
Evanbrier Rd 25320
Evanwood Rd 25314
Evening Star Rd 25312
Everest Hl 25302
Evergreen Dr & St 25302
F St 25303
Fabird Rd 25302
Fairfax Ln 25313
Fairfax Rd 25303
Fairhaven Dr 25306
Fairhope Ln 25312
Fairview Dr
1-299 25312
300-360 25302
361-399 25312
362-498 25302
401-499 25302
500-698 25312
Fairview Acres 25309
Fairway Dr 25309
Falcon Dr
500-1799 25312
2100-2399 25387
2801-2897 25312
2899-3699 25312
Faleadwa Mall 25387
Fallam Dr 25306
Falls Run Rd 25311
Family Dr 25309
Fannin Mtn 25312
Fantasy Ln 25306
Farmhouse Ln 25302
Farnsworth Dr 25311
Farr Dr 25306
Favorite Ln 25311
Felix Ln 25311
Fellowship Ln 25311
Feltleaf Dr 25320
Fenwick Dr 25314
Ferguson Ave 25302
Fern Rd E 25314
Ferndale Dr 25302
Fernridge Dr 25302
Ferrell Dr 25320
Ferrell Hollow Rd
1-1299 25314
2-12 25311
46-1498 25314
Ferry St 25314
Fielder Dr 25313
Fields Ln 25312
Fields St 25387
Fieldstone Ln 25312
Fieldview Rd 25302
Fiesta Ln 25313
Figgatt Ln 25313
Finesse Dr 25313
Fire Creek Rd 25313
Fishers Branch Rd 25312
Fishers Fork Rd 25312
Fitness Ln 25313
Fitzgerald St 25302
Fitzwater Dr 25303

Five String Dr 25312
Flairwood Dr 25313
Flatwood Dr 25313
Fleck Dr 25306
Fledderjohn Rd 25314
Fleetwood Ln 25312
Fletcher Dr 25309
Flinstone Rd 25312
Flint Lock Rd 25314
Floradale Dr 25313
Florence Dr 25302
Florence Ln 25309
Florida Ave 25315
Florida St
100-700 25302
702-798 25302
5200-5299 25309
Florina Ln 25312
Floyd St 25309
Footpath Ln 25311
Fop Ln 25313
Forbes Dr 25313
Ford St 25309
Fore Dr 25312
Forest Ave 25303
Forest Cir 25303
Forest Dr 25302
Forest Rd 25314
Forest Rdg 25320
Forest Edge Dr 25309
Forest Ridge Rd 25320
Forgotten Rd 25320
Fork Rd 25313
Fort Cir & Dr 25314
Fort Circle Dr 25314
Fort Hill Dr 25314
Forward Pass Ln 25313
Fossil Creek Ln 25314
Fountaincrest Dr 25311
Four Mile Rd 25312
Four Winds Dr 25311
Fowler Pl 25313
Fowler Hollow Rd 25312
Fox Bark Ln 25313
Fox Chase Rd 25304
Fox Hound Ln 25314
Fox Run Rd 25313
Foxborough Ln 25302
Foxcrest Ln 25302
Foxfire Ln 25312
Fraction Ln 25306
Frame St
1206A-1206B 25302
1200-1399 25302
1400-1699 25387
Francis Dr 25311
Francisco Ln 25312
Frank Hill Dr 25387
Franklin Ave 25311
Franks Ct 25311
Frederick Dr 25313
Freehold Ln 25320
Freeland Rd 25320
Freewater Rd 25312
Frentind Dr 25306
Friar Tuck Cir 25314
Friendly Dr 25387
Friendship Dr 25312
Friston Dr 25313
Frogs Creek Rd 25312
Front St 25302
Front Royal Dr 25313
Frontage Rd 25306
Frontier Dr 25313
Frost St 25311
Frosty Rd 25313
Frosty Creek Dr 25306
Fruitwood Ln 25306
Full Moon Dr 25306
Fulton Rd 25302
Furman Dr 25306
Furnace Rd 25313
G St 25303
Gabel Farm Rd 25320
Gable Dr 25309
Gabriel Dr 25303

Street	ZIP
Gail Dr	25314
Gaines Dr	25309
Galen Dr	25302
Galena Rd	25312
Galloway Dr	25313
Galway Cir	25314
Gamewell Dr	25312
Gamma Rdg	25312
Gander Ln	25312
Gandy Mountain Rd	25312
Gap View Dr	25306
Garden St	25302
Garden Grove Ln	25309
Garden Heights Dr	25309
Garden Path Way	25309
Gardenview Ln	25309
Garfield Ave	25387
Garnas Ln	25309
Garnes Dr	25312
Garnes Farm Rd	25312
Garrett St	25309
Garrison Ave	25302
Garvin Ave	25302
Gaston Ln	25302
Gate Pl & Rd	25314
Gatesville Rd	25312
Gatewater Rd	25313
Gateway Rd	25309
Gatewood Ave	25315
Gatha Ln	25312
Gator Ln	25314
Gats Creek Rd	25314
Gavin Ln	25312
Gaylor Ln	25312
Gaylord Ave	25387
Geary Rd	25303
Gelstone Dr	25312
Gemstone Ln	25313
Gencharn St	25303
General Dr	25306
Generation Rd	25313
Genesee Ln	25311
Gentry Ln	25315
Georges Dr	25306
Georges Creek Dr	25306
Georgetown Cir & Pl	25314
Georgia St	25302
Georgian Way	25309
Geraint Rd	25312
Getaway Ln	25311
Gettysburg Rd	25309
Ghannams Building	25309
Giant Oak Ln	25302
Gibson Kees Way	25320
Gideon Rock Dr	25313
Gil Dr	25312
Gilbert Dr	25302
Gilbert Ln	25320
Gilmer St	25303
Girard Dr	25313
Glacial Dr	25313
Glade Ave	25306
Gladeview Ln	25312
Gladstone Dr	25302
Glass Dr	25313
Glen Rd	25314
Glen St	25302
Glen Way	25309
Glen Cove Dr	25304
Glen Oaks Ln	25309
Glendale Ave	25303
Glenfield Ter	25303
Glenlou Ln	25312
Glenn Elk St	25302
Glenridge Rd	25304
Glenview Ln	25312
Glenville Ln	25306
Glenwood Ave	25302
Glimmer Rd	25313
Glory Way	25312
Gloucester Dr	25313
Glover St	25302
Glow Dr	25313
Goff Xing	25313
Goff Mountain Rd	25313
Goins Way	25312
Gold Finch Rd	25312
Gold Meadow Rd	25312
Golden Ln	25314
Golden Oaks Dr	25313
Goldenrod Ln	25306
Goldenvue Ln	25312
Gondola Dr	25313
Good Dog Rd	25312
Goodwin Ln	25312
Goose Creek Rd	25320
Gordon Dr	
600-699	25314
700-1099	25303
Goshorn St	
1-99	25301
500-599	25309
Grace Ave	25302
Graceland Cir	25309
Gracie May Ln	25312
Graff Ln	25304
Graham Dr	25302
Graley Rd	25314
Granada Way	25304
Grand Four Dr	25313
Grand Kids Way	25312
Grandcliff Ln	25312
Grandview Dr	25302
Granite Dr	25309
Granite Rd	25304
Grant Dr	25320
Grant St	25302
Grapevine Rd	25320
Gravity Dr	25306
Green Rd	25309
Green St	25311
Green Acres Dr	25309
Green Hill Dr	25302
Green Knoll Dr	25309
Green Meadow Rd	25314
Green Tree Ln	25312
Greenbottom Rd	25311
Greenbrier Dr	25320
Greenbrier St	25311
Greenbrier Trl	25313
Greendale Dr	25302
Greenland Cir	25309
Greens Paradise Rd	25309
Greenview Dr & Rd	25309
Greenway Ave	25309
Greenwood Ave	25302
Greer Ln	25312
Greg Tan Ln	25313
Gregg Dr	25309
Gregory Ln	25311
Greyhound Dr	25313
Greystone Pl & Rd	25314
Greywood Dr	25313
Griffin Dr	25387
Griffith Ln	25309
Grimm St	25302
Grishaber St	25303
Grosscup Rd	25314
Grouse Cove Rd	25312
Grove Ave	25302
Grovetree Dr	25313
Grubbs Rd	25304
Gunnysack Ln	25313
Gunsmoke Rd	25309
Gus R Douglass Ln	25312
Guthrie Ctr & Rd	25312
Guy Ln	25313
Gwen Dr	25313
Hackberry Ln	25313
Hacker Ln	25309
Hackney Dr	25320
Haddad Ct	25303
Haditha Ln	25320
Haines Br	25320
Haines Branch Rd	25320
Hakeswell Rd	25306
Hale St	25301
Hall St	25302
Halls Fork Rd	25312
Hamblin Ln	25387
Hamdor St	25309
Hamilton Cir	25311
Hamilton Dr	25312
Hamilton Pl	25314
Hamlet Way	25314
Hammond Ln	25312
Hammons Dr	25313
Hampshire Dr	25387
Hampton Rd	25314
Hanna Dr	25387
Hanna Ln	25309
Hannon Ln	25309
Hansford St	
1300-1499	25301
1500-1599	25311
Hanshaw Dr	25387
Hanson Hollow Rd	25311
Happy Hl	25314
Happy Hollow Rd	25320
Happy Hounds Dr	25302
Harainta Dr	25312
Harbert Dr	25312
Harding Hill Rd	25320
Hardman Dr	25311
Hardwood Dr	25313
Harless Ln	25302
Harlow Ln	25312
Harmon Rd	25314
Harmony Ln	25303
Harmony Hollow Rd	25311
Harper Dr	25313
Harpold St	25312
Harpoon Dr	25312
Harriman Rd	25312
Harris St	25309
Harris Hollow Rd	25311
Harry Dr	25320
Hart St	25304
Hartsville Rd	25320
Harvard Ave	25306
Harvest Ln	25312
Harvest Meadow Rd	25311
Harvey Rd	25314
Haskell Dr	25312
Hatfield Dr	25306
Hattie Ln	25320
Havana Dr	25311
Haven Hill Dr	25309
Haversack Hl	25315
Hawes Dr	25306
Hawkesyard Ln	25311
Hawkeye Ln	25311
Hawksburry Ln	25302
Hawthorne Dr	25302
Hayes Ave	25314
Haynes Hl	25312
Haystack Ln	25311
Hayvon Ln	25309
Hazard Dr	25312
Hazel Rd	25314
Hazelton Dr	25313
Hazelwood Ave	25302
Headley Dr	25312
Heaherwood Dr	25309
Heartland Ln	25311
Heath St	25311
Heather Dr & Pl	25313
Heavenly Dr	
1-99	25313
2-98	25309
100-1199	25309
1201-2599	25309
Heavens Hl	25320
Heidi Ln	25312
Helen Ave	25302
Helena Dr	25313
Hemingway Ave	25311
Hemlock Way	25302
Hendrix Ave	25387
Henry Rd	25303
Henry Cadle Ln	25313
Hensey Rd	25314
Hensley Pl	25309
Henson Ave	25303
Heritage Dr	25312
Heritage Ridge Cir	25314
Hermitage Rd	25314
Hershal Dr	25309
Hershey Ln	25311
Hertz Avis Rd	25311
Hess Dr	25311
Hess Mountain Dr	25309
Hickory Dr	25320
Hickory Hts	25320
Hickory Rd	25314
Hickory St	25309
Hickory Hills Pl	25314
Hicks Ln	25306
Hicumbottom Run Rd	25320
Hidden Cv	25313
Hidden Rdg	25302
Hidden Pines Ln	25313
Hidden Valley Dr	25312
Hideout Ln	25309
High St	25311
High Hollow Rd	25312
High Meadow Dr	25311
Highcliff Ln	25302
Highland Ave	25303
Highland Rd	25302
Highline Park	25315
Highmeadows Dr	25302
Hilda Ct	25302
Hildebrand Dr	25313
Hiley Dr	25306
Hill Dr	25311
Hill Rose Ln	25312
Hillary Dr	25320
Hillbilly Ln	25309
Hillbrook Dr	25313
Hillcrest Dr	25302
Hillcrest Dr E	25311
Hillpoint Dr	25302
N Hills Dr	25387
Hills Ln	25312
Hills Plz	25387
Hillsdale Dr	25302
Hilltop Ct	25314
Hilltop Dr	25303
Hillview Dr	
2-98	25312
100-109	25314
111-111	25314
121-127	25312
129-200	25312
202-298	25312
800-899	25315
Hillwood Dr	25312
Hilton Dr	25313
Hinton Ter	25301
Hinzman Ln	25309
Hodges Rd	25314
Holliday Ln	25313
Hollister Dr	25302
Holly Rd	25314
Holly Berry Ln	25309
Holly Berry Rd	25314
Hollywood Dr	25311
Holmes Hollow Rd	25312
Holstein Breeze Ln	25312
Homer St	25302
Homestead Ln	25312
Homewood Dr	25303
S Homewood Dr	25314
Honaker Dr	25312
Honakers Valley Rd	25306
Honeyrose Ln	25312
Honeywell Dr	25312
Honeywood Dr	25313
Honor Dr	25309
Hooper Dr	25313
Hope Ln	25311
Hope Rd	25302
Hopelawn Rd	
2-20	25320
22-198	25309
Hopeville Ln	25312
Hopewell Dr	25313
Horns Ave	25387
Horseshoe Bend Rd	25320
Hotel Cir	25311
Houghton Dr	25311
Houston Rd	25312
Howards Fork Dr	25313
Howelint Rd	25314
Hoytville Ln	25312
Hubbard Dr	25311
Huber Rd	25314
Hudson St	25302
Hudson Valley Dr	25309
Hughart Dr	25320
Hulbert Dr	25313
Humbolt Dr	25312
Hummingbird Ln	25320
Humphreys Ct	25302
Humphreys Hill Rd	25320
Hundred Oaks Ln	25306
Hunt Ave	25302
Hunter Dr	25311
Hunter Ln	25312
Hunter Rd	25311
Hunters Cv	25320
Hunters Point Rd	25314
Hunters Ridge Rd	25314
Hunterwood Rd	25312
Hunting Hills Dr	25311
Huntington Sq	25301
Huntley Ln	25315
Hurley Dr	25313
Huron Ter	25311
Hutchinson St	25387
Hylbert Dr	25312
Ida Mae Way	25301
Imperial Dr & Pl	25313
Inca Way	25313
Indiana Ave	25302
Indiana St	25309
Indianola Dr	25313
Indigo Ln	25309
Industrial St	25302
Industrial Way	25303
Infantry Dr	25311
Ingles Dr	25306
Ingram Dr	25309
Ingram Ln	25313
Inland Ln	25309
Inlet Dr	25311
Inn Brooke Ln	25312
Innovation Cir	25303
Innsbruck Dr	25311
International Dr	25313
Iowa St	25387
Iris Dr	25387
Irongate Ln	25320
Ironton Rd	25312
Irving St	25309
Irwin St	25311
Isabella Dr	25309
Island Branch Rd	25320
Isolation Dr	25309
Ithaca Dr	25302
Ivy Dr	25387
Ivywood Ln	25309
J B Ln	25320
Jacks Mountain Rd	25312
Jackson Ln	25309
Jackson St	
700-798	25309
1400-1499	25301
1500-1599	25311
Jacob St	25301
Jadawn Ln	25320
Jadewood Rd	25312
Jaffa Ln	25313
Jagged Edge Rd	25312
Jain Dr	25313
Jakes St	25303
Jalloh Ln	25309
James Ave	25387
James Dr	
1-99	25302
100-9099	25320
Jamestown Rd	25314
Jane St	25302
Janet Pl	25303
January Dr	25309
Japonica Ln	25313
Jarrell Dr	25387
Jarrett Ct	25302
Jarvis St	25302
Jasmine Ln	25314
Jasmine Fields Ln	25306
Jason Dr	25313
Jay I Dr	25309
Jean St	25302
Jefferson Plz	25309
Jefferson Rd	25309
Jefferson St	
300-399	25311
600-799	25309
Jeffries Ct	25301
Jeniel Dr	25309
S Jenkins Dr	25312
Jenna Way	25320
Jennifer Dr	25313
Jericho Dr	25311
Jerick Cir	25302
Jersey Dr	25306
Jewelstone Ln	25312
Jim Derrick Dr	25320
Jimsonweed Ln	25313
Jody Ln	25311
John Fouts Dr	25309
John Glenn Dr	25309
John Harper Ln	25312
John Robert Dr	25309
John Wesley Dr	25302
Johnson Dr	
1-19	25309
2-18	25306
20-99	25306
100-800	25309
802-1098	25309
Johnson Rd	25314
Johnstone Rd	25309
Jonas Dr	25313
Jones Dr	25320
Jones St	25309
Jones Farm Rd	25314
Jones Ridge Rd	25311
Jonquil Dr	25306
Jonsen Dr	25312
Joplin Pl	25303
Jordan Pl	25314
Jordyn Pl	25302
Joseph St	
100-221	25303
223-299	25303
298-304	25301
306-308	25301
310-316	25301
312-398	25303
313-399	25303
Josh Dr	25309
Journeys Dr	25302
Joy Ln	25313
Juanita Dr	25306
Judd Ln	25311
Judith Dr	25387
Judson Pl	25303
Julesburg Rd	25320
Juniper Ln	25313
Justin Dr	25309
Jw Dr	25313
K Huff Ln	25313
Kalaski Dr	25313
Kama Ln	25313
Kanawha Ave	25315
Kanawha Ave SE	25304
Kanawha Ave SW	25309
Kanawha Blvd E	
2-188	25301
190-190	25305
192-698	25301
700-800	25301
802-1498	25301
1500-1698	25311
1700-1998	25305
2000-2504	25311
2506-3099	25311
3300-5899	25306
1-100	25302
102-1198	25302
1400-1699	25387
Kanawha Ln	25309
Kanawha Mall	25304
Kanawha Tpke	
3200-3299	25303
4001-4097	25309
4099-5299	25309
5301-5799	25309
Kanawha 2 Mile Rd	25312
Kanawha Farm Cir	25312
Kanawha Salines Dr	25306
Kanawha State Forest Dr	25314
Karen Cir	25313
Karen St	25303
Karnes St	25309
Katherine St	25387
Kathy Dr	25309
Kathy Ln	25313
Katie Ln	25313
Kaufmann Rd	25312
Kaufmans Branch Rd	25312
Kay Ln	25302
Kay Neva Ln	25312
Kearse Ave	25387
Keffer Ridge Rd	25309
Keith Dr	25313
Kel Dawn Cir	25313
Kelameg Ln	25312
Keller Dr	25387
Kelly Rd	25313
Kellys Creek Rd	25312
Kelmont Ln	25320
Kelsie Dr	25311
Kemp Ave	25387
Kempway Ln	25312
Kendall Dr	25313
Kendie Dr	25309
Kendra Dr	25311
Kendra Ln	25312
Kenella Dr	25313
Kenna Dr	25309
Kennedy Dr	25302
Kens Ln	25313
Kensey Ln	25312
Kensington Ln	25312
Kent Hall St	25311
Kenton Cir	25313
Kenton Dr	25311
Kentucky St	25309
Kenwood Pl & Rd	25314
Kenyon Ln	25306
Kermit Ln	25312
Kersey Rocks Mtn	25313
Kessell Way	25312
Kessenger Rd	25314
Kessinger Rd	25314
Key Haven Ln	25311
Keystone Dr	25311
Kidd Dr	25320
Kilarney Way	25313
Kilby St	25311
Kilgore Ln	25313
Killen Hollow Dr	25313
Kimberly Rd	25309
Kimeric Ln	25313
Kinder St	25309
King Ave	25387
King St	25303
Kingbrook Est	25312
Kings Row	25314
Kingsport Rd	25309
Kingston Ct	25314
Kingstree Dr	25311
Kingsway Ln	25320
Kingswood Dr	25309
Kingswood Ln	25313
Kingwood Dr	25309
Kinross Rd	25313
Kinsbury Rd	25312
Kinser Rd	25314
Kinship Ln	25313
Kirby St	25309
Kirby Hollow Rd	25314
Kirk Ct	25387
Kirklee Rd	25314
Kirkton Dr	25302
Kirkwood Dr	25311
Kit Rd	25304

Kitts Dr 25309
Kitty Ln 25312
Kiwanis Dr 25309
Klondike Rd 25313
Knightdale Dr 25309
Knob Rd 25314
Knob Way 25309
Knollwood Dr
101-103 25313
104-108 25302
105-109 25313
110-116 25313
130-144 25302
146-399 25302
Knollwood Hts 25302
Knollwood Rd 25302
Knuckles Rd 25309
Koine St 25314
Kokomo Dr 25312
Koontz Dr & Pl 25313
Kori Rd 25304
Kouns Dr 25309
Kramer St 25309
Krb Ln 25312
Kristin Pl 25314
Krystal Dr 25309
Kuhn Dr 25309
La Siesta Ln & Ter 25320
Labelle St 25387
Lacy Hollow Rd 25311
Lacy Oak Dr 25309
Ladybug Ln 25311
Lafayette Ln 25309
Lagrange Ln 25313
Laidley St 25301
Laidley Tower 25301
Lake Shore Dr 25313
Lakeland Cir, Dr & Ter 25320
Lakeland Forest Dr 25320
Lakeview Dr
1-99 25314
100-129 25313
130-198 25314
131-1099 25313
800-1098 25313
Lakewood Dr 25312
Lakin St 25311
Lambert Pl 25314
Lamont Dr 25313
Lancaster Ave 25304
Lance Dr 25311
Landeda Dr 25312
Landers Ln 25320
Landmark Ln 25320
Langford Ln 25320
Lanham Dr 25313
Lanphere Dr 25313
Lansbury Rd 25313
Lansing Dr 25313
Larchmont Dr 25387
Larchwood Rd 25314
Lariat Dr 25320
Laromie Dr 25302
Larter Dr 25311
Larue Ln 25312
Larwood Dr 25302
Lauderdale Rd 25306
Laura Ln 25302
Laura Beth Ln 25312
Laurel Rd 25314
Lawless Ln 25306
Lawndale Ln 25314
Lawnview Rd 25314
Lawrence Dr 25314
Lawrence Ln 25309
Lazy Ln 25309
Lazy Acres Ln 25311
Leadership Ln 25320
Leadville Rd 25312
Leaf Cir 25320
Ledgehill Dr 25387
Lee Ave 25309
Lee Ln 25313
Lee St E
100-1099 25301
1002-1002 25321
1002-1002 25322
1002-1002 25323
1002-1002 25324
1002-1002 25325
1002-1002 25326
1002-1002 25327
1002-1002 25328
1002-1002 25329
1002-1002 25330
1002-1002 25331
1002-1002 25332
1002-1002 25333
1002-1002 25334
1002-1002 25335
1002-1002 25336
1002-1002 25337
1002-1002 25338
1002-1002 25339
1002-1002 25361
1101-1499 25301
1200-1498 25301
1500-1599 25311
Lee St W 25302
Leelo Ln 25312
Left Fork Rd 25315
Left Fork Vw 25313
Left Fork Of Lens Creek Rd 25315
Legend Ln 25312
Legg Ave 25312
Legg Fork Rd 25320
Legg Star Rte 25320
Lego Rd 25313
Lehigh Ter 25302
Lemon Pl 25309
Lemondrop Ln 25313
Lemur Ln 25312
Lennox Dr 25306
Lenora Ln 25314
Lens Creek Rd 25315
Lens Creek Road Ln 25315
Leon St 25387
Leon Sullivan Way 25301
Leonard Ln 25314
Leonard Heights Ln 25312
Leontine Dr 25306
Leslie Ln 25309
Leslie Rd 25314
Lessie Ln 25312
Lester Dr 25309
Letart Ln 25311
Leva Ln 25309
Level Dr 25313
Lewis Dr 25309
Lewis Ln 25306
Lewis St
1000-1499 25301
1500-1599 25311
Lexington Dr 25303
Lexus Dr 25313
Libby Ln 25387
Liberty Ln 25313
Liberty St 25309
Libertyville Rd 25312
Lick Branch Rd 25312
Lighthouse Way 25302
Lightning Bug Ln 25313
Lightsville Ln 25312
Lillian Rd 25309
Lillian Way 25313
Lilly Dr 25387
Lilly Hls 25309
Lilly St 25302
Limeoak Rd 25320
Limestone Rd 25312
Lincoln Cir 25302
Lincoln Dr
1-97 25313
99-799 25313
800-1099 25309
Linda Vista Dr 25313
Linden Rd 25314
Lindenhurst Ln 25320
Lindhurst Dr 25302
Lindway Ave 25303
Lindy Rd 25314
Line Dr 25312
Linhurst Dr 25313
Linton Rd 25312
Linwood Dr 25302
Lional Dr 25309
Lippert St 25387
Lisa Ct 25313
Litansou Ctr 25389
Litha Ln 25309
Little Cherry Tree Ln 25306
Little Debbie Ln 25312
Little Quarry Ln 25314
Litz Dr 25311
Lively Ln & Rd 25309
Liverpool Ln 25320
Livingston Ave
1100-1199 25302
1400-1699 25387
3200-3299 25320
Lloyd Ct 25309
Lockheed Lndg 25311
Locksley Cir 25314
Locust Ave 25303
Locust Ln 25309
Locust Rd 25314
Locust St 25313
Locust Heights Rd 25302
Lodi Ln 25313
Log Cabin Ln 25314
Logan Dr
2-48 25313
50-98 25311
Loma Rd 25314
Lona Ln 25311
Londeree Ave 25303
Londonderry Rd 25314
Lone Pine Ln 25313
Lonesome Rd 25320
Long Branch Rd
1-899 25314
900-1398 25309
901-1097 25309
1099-1300 25309
1302-1598 25309
Longleaf Dr 25309
Longmeadow Dr 25320
Longmont Ln 25312
Longridge Rd 25314
Longview Dr 25313
Longwood Rd 25314
Lookout Rd 25314
Loop Rd 25303
Loop Rd N 25312
Lora Max Ln 25309
Lorane Rd 25312
Lorello Dr 25302
Loretta Ln 25309
Lorien Way 25313
Lory Dr 25312
Lost Creek Way 25313
Lost Gravel Rd 25312
Lostwood Ln 25312
Lotus Dr 25312
Loudendale Ln 25314
Loudon Heights Rd 25314
Louisiana Rd 25313
Lovell Dr 25302
Lowell Dr 25311
Lower Chester Rd 25302
Lower Donnally Rd 25304
Lower Maccorkle Ave SW 25303
Lower Ridgeway Rd 25314
Loxton Rd 25312
Loyal Dr 25306
Luann Dr 25313
Lucado Rd 25314
Lucas Hollow Rd 25311
Lucy Ln 25309
Lude Rd 25309
Luke Dr 25306
Lumari Ln 25314
Lummie Ln 25320
Luna Pt 25302
Luray Ln 25313
Lyell Ln 25306
Lynch Dr 25309
Lyndale Dr 25314
Lynn Pl 25314
Lynn St 25303
Lynn Brooke Pl 25312
Lynn Oak Dr 25313
Lynnhaven Dr 25302
Lynnville Ln 25312
Lynnwood Dr 25313
Mac Ave 25302
Macarthur Ave 25315
Maccorkle Ave
7800-13999 25315
200-1600 25314
1602-1798 25314
2300-3098 25304
3100-4601 25304
4600-4600 25364
4602-7598 25304
4603-7599 25304
1-3999 25303
4000-5799 25309
Macedonian Rd 25313
Macel Dr
1-99 25313
2-98 25309
100-198 25313
Macellar Way 25311
Mackenzie Ln 25312
Mackinaw Dr 25313
Macon St 25303
Madaline Ave 25313
Madison St
600-800 25302
802-1398 25302
1400-1599 25387
Maefair Dr 25314
Maggie Dr 25311
Magnum Dr 25312
Main Dr 25309
Main St 25302
Maineville Ln 25312
Majestic Dr 25313
Malden Dr 25306
Male Ct 25387
Mallard Ln 25312
Mallory Ln 25309
Mallory Airport Rd 25309
Malta Ln 25311
Mandalay Ln 25311
Mandy Ln 25302
Manistee Ln 25313
Manning Dr 25309
Manningham Dr 25306
Manor Pl 25311
Manorhaven Dr 25312
Mansion Dr 25313
Manuel Dr 25313
Maple Dr
101-199 25313
1800-1899 25320
S Maple Dr 25304
Maple Ln 25313
Maple Rd 25302
Maple St 25309
Maple Grove Dr 25312
Maple Hollow Rd 25311
Maple Leaf Ln 25314
Maple Tree Ln 25313
Mapleton Ln 25311
Mapleview Dr 25320
Maranatha Acres 25312
Marauder Rd 25315
Marble Ln 25311
Marble Hill Ln 25312
Marburn Rd 25314
Margaret Ln 25312
Margaret St 25301
Margaux Way 25311
Margy Ln 25309
Mariana St 25302
Marie Ln 25313
Mariel Way 25311
Marigold Rd 25313
Marion Ave 25302
Marion Cir 25314
Marion Ter 25313
Marionview Ln 25312
Marionwood Ln 25312
Mark Dr 25309
Market Dr 25302
Markley Ln 25304
Marlanka Ln 25309
Marlin Dr 25302
Marlow Dr 25312
Marojada Way 25312
Marshall Ave 25306
Marshwood Ln 25312
Martha Rd 25303
Martin Dr 25313
Martins Branch Rd
100-1099 25320
1100-1198 25312
1200-4699 25312
Martins Hollow Rd 25311
Marvin Dr 25309
Mary St 25302
Mary Jackie Ln 25320
Mary Lou Ln 25302
Maryland Ave
100-699 25302
8000-9199 25315
Marysville Ln 25312
Massey Cir 25303
Matchlock Rd 25314
Matheny Dr 25302
Mathews Ave 25302
Mathias Ln 25309
Maude Dr 25309
Maxine Dr 25312
Maxwell St 25311
May Cir 25313
Mayapple Ln 25313
Mayer Dr 25302
Mayfair Ln 25311
Mayflower Dr 25311
Mays Ln 25311
Mayspring Rd 25312
Mayview Ln 25312
Mcadoo Ln 25306
Mccaw Ln 25306
Mcclung St
1600-1699 25311
4400-4899 25309
4901-4999 25309
Mcclure Pkwy 25312
Mccormick St 25301
Mccown Cir 25313
Mccoy Dr 25302
Mccubbin Dr 25311
Mcdavid Ln 25311
Mcdonald Ave 25309
Mcdonald St 25301
Mcfarland St 25301
Mcghee Dr 25309
Mcgovran Rd 25314
Mcgregor Ln 25309
Mcguffin Dr 25302
Mckee Ave 25311
Mckenzie Rd 25309
Mckinley Ave 25314
Mcknoll Rd 25314
Mcleod Way 25309
Mcmann Ct 25303
Mcmillion Ln 25313
Mcqueen St 25302
Mcvey Way 25387
Meadow Dr 25309
Meadow Rd 25314
Meadow Way 25313
Meadow Lark Ln 25312
Meadow Mist Ln 25312
Meadowbrook Dr 25311
Meadowbrook Shopping Plz 25311
Meadowcrest Dr 25314
Meadowview Dr
101-199 25313
2000-2099 25320
Meadville Rd 25312
Medina St 25302
Meg Dr 25320
Mel St 25387
Melinda Rd 25312
Melody Ln 25313
Melrose Dr 25302
Melwood Dr 25313
Memory Ln 25306
Memory Hill Dr 25313
Mercator Way 25312
Mercury Rd 25309
Mercy Ln 25309
Meredith Ct 25301
Meridian Ln 25315
Merlot Dr 25312
Merrimac Dr 25309
Messinger Ln 25309
Meyers Ln 25312
Michael Ave 25387
Michelle Ln 25309
Michigan Ave 25311
Middle Rd 25314
S Middle St 25387
Middle Fork Dr 25314
Middle Ridge Rd 25314
Middle School Ln 25312
Middlelick Br 25314
Midkiff Rd 25309
Midland Dr 25306
Midridge Way 25312
Midway Dr 25312
Milam Dr 25309
Mile Fork Rd 25312
Military Dr 25309
Mill Creek Rd 25311
Miller Ln 25313
Miller Rd 25320
Miller St 25301
Millgrove Rd 25312
Milliken Dr 25311
Milton St
1200-1399 25301
1400-1499 25311
Mimosa Ln 25320
Minden Ln 25309
Mingo Ln 25311
Mini Storage Dr 25313
Miniacres Ln 25311
Mink Ln 25302
Mink Shoals Branch Rd 25302
Minnesota Dr 25313
Minturni Ln 25314
Miquela Ln 25320
Miser Ln 25311
Misfit Ln 25312
Mission Dr 25311
Mississippi Way 25311
Missouri Dr 25309
Misty Mountain Ln 25312
Mitchell Ln 25309
Mockernut Ln 25302
Mockingbird Ln 25312
Moles Dr 25302
Molly Dr 25320
Moms Rd 25312
Monarch Dr 25313
Monk Pl 25314
Monongalia St 25302
Monroe St
100-399 25303
600-699 25302
Monta Vista Dr & Pl 25313
Montana Ests 25313
Montana Rd 25312
Montcalm Dr 25302
Montclair Dr 25311
Monterey Ln 25313
Monticello Pl 25314
Montrose Dr 25303
Montvale Dr 25311
Moon Beam Way 25315
Moon Ridge Dr 25312
Mooney Ln 25314
Moonglo Ln 25314
Moore Rd 25314
Moorland Dr 25311
Moosemont Rd 25304
Morecott Dr 25320
Moreland Ln 25312
Morgan Dr 25313
Morgans Way 25312
Moriah Dr 25313
Moriane Ln 25320
Morierid St 25302
Morning Dove Ln 25313
Morning Glory Dr 25309
Morning Mist Ln 25312
Morning Sun Ln 25320
Morningside Dr 25314
Morris St 25301
Morrison Dr & Pl 25313
Moss Meadows Rd 25320
Moss Valley Ln 25320
Mossburg Dr 25309
Mound Ave 25309
Mount Alpha Rd 25304
Mount Highland Rdg 25309
Mount Olivet Ln 25312
Mount Shadow Rd 25303
Mount Vernon Pl & Rd 25314
Mount View Dr 25314
Mountain Rd 25303
Mountain Spring Ln 25312
Mountain Top Cir 25309
Mountain Vista Dr 25312
Mountaineer Blvd 25309
Mountaineer Ln 25312
Mouse Hill Rd 25302
Mud Suck Blvd 25309
Muggelberg Ln 25309
Muirfield Ct 25304
Mulberry Cir 25314
Mullins Ln 25312
Mullins Rd 25314
Mundy Hollow Rd 25312
Musket Ln 25314
Mustang Vly 25312
Myna Dr 25306
Myrna Ln 25313
Myrtle Rd 25314
Myrtle Tree Rd 25309
Namaste Ln 25314
Nancy Ave 25315
Nancy St
514 1/2A-514 1/2Z 25311
400-599 25311
1500-1599 25303
Nantes Ln 25309
Nascar Ln 25306
Natalie Dr 25309
Nathaniel Dr 25311
Natural Spring Ln 25313
Naughton Way 25313
Navajo Trl 25312
Navigator Ln 25306
Naylor Dr 25302
Nazarene Dr 25309
Nease Dr 25387
Nectarine Dr 25311
Neighbors Dr 25387
Neilan Dr 25306
Nel Ann Ln 25312
Nellie Ln 25320
Nellie Reba Ln 25309
Nelson Dr 25313
Nesbitt Rd 25320
Nesting Way 25313
New Castle Rd 25314
New Goff Mountain Rd & Xing 25313
New Haven Rd 25313
New Wine Ln 25312
Newberry Ln 25320
Newbridge Rd 25309
Newcomer Rd 25309
Newgate Ln 25312
Newhouse Dr 25302
Newman Ln 25309
Newquay Dr 25312
Newstead Ln 25312
Newton Rd 25314
Ngk Dr 25320
Nichols Dr 25306
Nicole Way 25387

Nightingale Ln 25313
Nitro Market Pl 25313
Nittany Dr 25309
Noble Valley Ln 25312
Nocturne Trl 25309
Noonday Dr 25311
Nora Ln 25320
Norma Ln 25309
Norman Dr 25306
Normandy Ln 25311
Normar Rd 25309
North Dr
1-99 25301
1500-1599 25303
Northcrest Ln 25312
Northfield Dr 25312
Northstar Ln 25302
Northview Dr 25311
Northwood Rd 25314
Norton Ave 25311
Norwood Rd 25314
Nottingham Rd 25314
Nova Pl 25309
Nowhere Rd 25314
Noyes Ave 25304
Noyes St 25309
Null Rd 25312
Nunley Dr 25306
Nuttibok Ln 25302
Oak St
600-799 25309
1000-1099 25304
Oak Brooke Ln 25302
Oak Kidd Cv 25313
Oak Knolls Rd 25314
Oak Ridge Rd 25311
Oak Tree Ln 25309
Oakdale Ave 25303
Oakes Ave 25303
Oakhaven Ln 25313
Oakhurst Dr
1011A-1011B 25314
400-498 25309
801-997 25314
999-1799 25314
1800-3400 25309
3402-3898 25309
Oakland Dr 25313
Oakland Walk 25387
Oakmont Dr 25309
Oakmont Rd 25314
Oakridge Dr 25311
Oakvale Rd 25314
Oakview Rd 25309
Oakwood Dr 25320
Oakwood Rd
101-103 25313
103-105 25314
105-124 25313
107-899 25314
126-128 25313
Oasis Dr 25306
Observatory Rd 25314
Octane Ln 25320
October Way 25320
Odell Ave 25302
Odessa Rd 25312
Odyssey Way 25312
Offutt Dr 25302
Ogden Hill Rd 25312
Oglethorpe Rd 25314
Ohara Ln 25309
Ohio Ave
110 1/2A-110 1/2Z 25302
1-699 25302
8501-9797 25315
9799-12999 25315
Ohio St 25309
Okemo Dr 25311
Old Cellar Ln 25312
Old Farmhouse Rd 25309
Old Goff Mountain Rd 25313
Old Horse Hill Rd 25320
Old Hunters Holw 25320
Old Mill Rd 25320
Old Mill Creek Rd 25311
Old Monday Hollow Rd 25312
Old Place Ln 25309
Old Tuppers Creek Rd 25312
Olde Ash Ln 25311
Olde Comfort Ln 25313
Older Rd 25312
Olivewood Dr 25306
Olson Rd 25314
Olympus Rd 25314
Omaha Rd 25312
Ontario Rd 25313
Opal Hill Ln 25312
Opportunity Ln 25311
Orchard Pl 25302
Orchard St
700-1099 25302
4800-4899 25309
Oregon Ave 25315
Oregon St 25387
Otter Ln 25302
Otto Dr 25309
Our Way Rd 25312
Overbrook Rd 25314
Overland Rd 25312
Overlook Dr 25312
Overlook Way 25309
Overview Dr 25313
Ox St 25311
Oxford Cir 25314
Oxley Dr 25309
P S D Dr 25306
Pablo Dr 25309
Pacer Dr 25309
Pacific St 25302
Paddington Ave 25314
Paderborn Dr 25312
Page Rd
101-297 25312
299-599 25312
601-799 25312
1200-1399 25320
Pago Rd 25314
Painter Pl 25313
Paisley Ln 25309
Palm Dr 25312
Palm Crest Dr 25302
Palomino Rd 25312
Pamela Cir 25313
Pansy Dr 25387
Pantego Ln 25309
Papaw Ln 25320
Papaya Ln 25313
Parachute Rd 25313
Paradise Ln
1-99 25312
2-26 25311
28-64 25312
66-98 25311
100-298 25312
Paramount Rd 25320
Park Ave
312A-312Z 25309
1-300 25302
301-301 25309
302-312 25302
303-401 25302
403-405 25302
403-499 25309
407-1299 25302
414-444 25309
500-1298 25302
312 1/2-312 1/2 25309
Park Ct 25302
S Park Ct 25304
Park Dr 25302
S Park Rd 25304
Park St 25309
Parker Dr 25309
Parkstone Ln 25320
Parkview Dr 25309
Parkway Rd 25309
Parkwood Rd 25314
Parlmora Rd 25312
Parsons Ct 25387
Parsons Ln 25309
Partridge Dr 25313
Passage Way 25313
Patricia Way 25309
Patrick St 25387
Patrick Street Plz 25387
Patriot Way 25314
Pattern Dr 25313
Patterson Ln 25311
Patterson St 25302
Paul St 25303
Paul Jo Dr 25309
Paula Rd 25314
Pauley Hts
1-50 25302
51-199 25312
52-98 25302
Pauley Ln
1-299 25314
2-18 25312
20-48 25314
50-88 25312
90-1072 25314
1001-1071 25309
1073-1099 25309
1100-1300 25314
1302-1398 25314
Pauley Rd 25309
Pauley St 25302
Pawnee Dr 25312
Paxton Dr 25313
Peaceful Ln 25309
Peaceful Hills Dr 25313
Peaceful View Ln 25312
Peach Tree Ln 25309
Peachador Ln 25320
Peaksview Rd 25311
Pear Ridge Rd 25306
Pearcy Rd 25314
Pearl Dr 25311
Peasherr Ave 25315
Pebble Dr 25313
Pedal Ln 25320
Pellston Way 25313
Pemberton Ln 25302
Pembroke Sq 25314
Pence St 25303
Pendleton Ln 25312
Pennington Ln 25314
Pennsylvania Ave 25302
Pennsylvania Ave SW 25309
Peppermint Ln 25306
Perkins Way 25313
Perlican Dr 25312
Perrow Dr 25313
Perry Ln 25387
Pershing Dr 25309
Peterson Dr 25302
Pettry Dr 25309
Peyton Way 25309
Phantom Dr 25311
Phillips Rd 25320
Phillips St 25303
Phoenix Pl & Way 25312
Phyllis Dr 25302
Piccadilly St 25302
Pickford Ct 25314
Piedmont Rd
1-1399 25301
1501-1997 25311
1999-2932 25311
2934-3098 25311
3100-3499 25306
Pierce Ln 25312
Pigeon Roost Rd 25320
Pike St 25309
Pillerton Dr 25312
Pilsner Pl 25312
Pin Oak Dr 25309
Pine Rd 25314
Pine St
1-299 25311
700-799 25309
Pine Ter 25313
Pine Trce 25309
Pine Acre Ln 25312
Pine Hill Rd 25314
Pine Manor Rd 25311
Pine Top Pl & Rdg 25314
Pine Valley Dr 25320
Pine View Dr 25313
Pinebluff Rd 25320
Pinecroft Dr 25309
Pinewood Dr 25320
Pinnacle Dr, Pl & Way 25311
Pinnacle Woods Dr 25311
Pioneer Dr 25313
S Pioneer Dr 25313
Pioneer Ln 25312
Pipeline Dr 25313
Piper Cir 25311
Pistore Dr 25309
Pittman Ln & Rd 25311
Placid Dr 25312
Plainview Ln 25312
Plantation Rd 25312
Planters Dr 25306
Plata Pl 25313
Plateau Rd 25314
Platinum Dr 25309
Players Club Dr 25311
Plaza E 25301
Pleasant Ln 25311
Pleasant Rd 25314
Pleasant Bend Ln 25312
Pleasant Valley Dr 25309
Pleasant View Cir 25309
Pleasure Hill Dr 25311
Plermank Dr 25313
Plum Dr 25306
Plumstone Rd 25312
Poca Flats Rd 25320
Poca River Rd
1-99 25320
101-397 25312
399-400 25312
402-498 25312
600-838 25320
839-839 25312
840-898 25320
841-5099 25320
900-948 25312
950-5098 25320
Poe Holw 25315
E Point Dr 25311
Point Lick Dr & Ter 25306
S Pointe Dr 25314
Polaris Dr 25320
Poling Dr 25303
Pond Ln 25309
Pond Fork Dr 25312
Pondview Ln 25320
Pony Ln 25309
Pony Chase Rd 25313
Pope Way 25309
Poplar Rd 25302
Poplar St 25309
Poplar Hill Dr 25311
Poplar Point Rd 25309
Pops Way 25311
Porshe Dr 25311
Port Amherst Dr 25306
Port View Dr 25311
Portella Dr 25314
Porter Rd 25314
Portman Ln 25320
Postwood Ln 25306
Potato Ln 25320
Potomac St 25302
Potterfield Dr 25314
Powder Horn Rd 25314
Power Stroke Rd 25314
Ppsi Cir 25312
Praise Ln 25320
Precious View Addition Rd 25312
Preferred Pl 25309
Prenerel Rd 25309
Prescott Ln 25314
Presidential Dr 25314
Presidio Pl 25313
Presidio Pointe 25313
Presson Dr 25320
Preston St 25302
Prezioso Pl 25387
Price St 25302
Prickley Woods Dr 25320
Primer Rd 25314
Primrose Dr 25313
Princess Dr 25309
Princeton Ln 25320
Principal Rd 25312
Pring Dr 25313
Pritt Ln 25320
Pritt Ford Est 25320
Private Dr 25320
Prodigial Way 25309
Prospect Ave 25303
Prosperity Pl 25313
Proximity Dr 25309
Puckett Dr 25309
Pueblo Ln 25309
Pullman Rd 25312
Puppy Ln 25302
Purdy Dr 25313
Purple Dr 25313
Purple Martin Dr 25320
Putney St 25306
Pyramid Dr 25320
Quadview Ln 25311
Quail Cove Rd 25314
Quail Pointe Dr 25302
Quantz Rd 25315
Quarrier St
1599A-1599Z 25311
100-1499 25301
1500-2099 25311
2000-2004 25305
Quarry Crk, Pt & Rdg E & S 25304
Quarterhorse Ln 25312
Quartz Dr 25313
Quebec Dr 25309
Queens Ct 25313
Queensbury Ln 25313
Questa Dr 25313
Quiet Dr 25302
Quincy Ln 25314
Quincy St 25303
R H L Blvd 25309
R Holmes Rd 25312
Rabel Rd 25309
Rabel Mountain Rd 25309
Racer Dr 25313
Rachel Ln 25309
Radford Rd 25312
Radiance Dr 25313
Radio Way 25313
Rae Pl 25314
Ragland St 25309
Railroad Ave 25302
Railview Ln 25320
Rainbow Dr 25313
Rainbow Acres 25312
Raleigh Pl 25313
Ralph Dr 25309
Rambler Rd 25314
Ramsey Dr 25312
Ramu Rd 25314
Ranch Rd 25303
Ranchland Rd 25312
Randolph St 25302
Ranger Ln 25309
Ratcliff Ln 25309
Rathbone Rd 25306
Rattlesnake Rd 25309
Rattlesnake Run 25314
Rattlesnake Hollow Rd 25306
Raven Dr 25306
Ravenall Ln 25312
Ravenwood Dr 25312
Ravinia Rd 25314
Ray Rd 25309
Rayhill Dr 25387
Rays Branch Rd 25314
Reardon Dr 25306
Rebecca Rd 25313
Rebecca St 25387
Rebekah Ln 25312
Rebel 25311
Recter Ln 25309
Red Autumn Ln 25311
Red Barn Ln 25311
Red Bud Ln 25313
Red Fox Ln 25320
Red Mulberry Way 25306
Red Oak St
1527A-1527Z 25387
700-1399 25302
1400-1699 25387
Redleaf Ln 25302
Redmans Ct 25313
Redmond Ln 25312
Reds Pl 25313
Redstone Rd 25309
Redwood Dr 25302
Reed Dr 25320
Reedridge Rd 25320
Reel Rd 25309
Reflection Ln 25311
Regency Dr 25314
Regina Dr 25311
Relation Rd 25313
Rena Dr 25312
Renaissance Cir 25311
Renard St 25320
Renault Dr 25309
Rensford Star Rte 25306
Reserve Rd 25311
Retiree Ln 25312
Reveal Dr 25387
Revelation Rd 25312
Rexburg Rd 25312
Reynolds Pt 25314
Reynolds St 25301
Rhein Dr 25306
Rhinestone Dr 25306
Rhododendron Ln 25309
Rich Fork Rd 25312
Richards Dr 25309
Richards St 25301
Richfield Ln 25302
Richland Dr 25309
Richmond Cir & Rd 25309
Richview Dr 25309
Ridge Dr
1-999 25313
1000-1399 25309
E Ridge Pl 25314
Ridge Rd 25314
E Ridge Rd 25314
Ridgecross Dr 25313
Ridgedale Ln 25311
Ridgemont Rd 25314
Ridgeview Dr
1-99 25320
3000-3099 25303
Ridgeview Rd 25314
Rigsby Ln 25309
Riheldaffer Ave 25303
Ripple Ln 25312
Ripplewind Way 25309
Ripplewood Dr 25302
Ritenour Dr 25309
River Ave 25309
River Bend Rd 25320
River Walk Mall 25303
Riverdale Dr 25302
Riverfront Pl 25320
Riverlane Dr 25306
Rivermont Ln 25312
Riverside Dr
1-99 25303
300-399 25309
Riverview Cir 25311
Roane St 25302
Roanoke Trce 25314
Robert Rd 25313
Robin Ln 25309
Robin St 25313
Robinhood Rd 25314
Robinson Hollow Rd 25312
Rocco Rd 25312
Rock Holly Rd 25314
Rock Lake Dr 25309
Rock Point Ln 25320
Rock Quarry Ln 25302
Rock Quarry Rd 25314
Rockaway Rd 25302
Rockcrest Dr 25309
Rockdale Dr 25313
Rockford Ct 25314
Rockledge Dr 25302
Rocky Ln 25313
Rocky Fork Rd
5100-5599 25313
5800-6698 25312
6700-7300 25312
7302-8298 25312
Rocky Moore Rd 25309
Rocky Shoals Rd 25320
Rodeo Dr 25302
Rogers Way 25312
Roller Rd 25314
Rollersville Ln 25312
Rolling Hills Cir, Pl & Rd 25314
Rollins Ln 25387
Romans Rd 25309
Romeo Dr 25312
Romie Dr 25312
Ronald Dr 25309
Rondal Dr 25309
Roosevelt Ave 25304
Roper Rd 25320
Rosalie Dr 25302
Roscommon Rd 25314
Rose Ct 25302
Rose Mdws 25309
Rose Hill Dr 25312
Rose Of Sharon Ln 25306
Rosebud Acres 25320
Roselane Dr 25302
Rosemont Ave 25303
Rosetta Ln 25311
Rosewood Rd 25314
Rosewood Way 25312
Ross St 25301
Roswell Ln 25320
Roundhill Rd 25314
Rowlands Farm Way 25311
Roxbury St 25309
Royal Oaks Rd 25314
Rubiola Rd 25302
Ruby Ln 25320
Rubyville Ln 25312
Ruffner Ave 25311
S Ruffner Rd 25314
Ruffner Walk 25311
Rugby St 25311
Ruhl Dr 25313
Rumbaugh Rd 25309
Rummelbrown Dr 25302
Rummell Dr 25302
Rush Creek Rd 25304
Russell Ct 25306
Russell St 25302
Russet Dr 25313
Rust Dr
1-299 25320
5005-5099 25313
Rust Ln 25313
Rustic Hill Rd 25312
N Rustling Rd 25303
Ruth Rd 25309
Ruth St 25302
Ruthdale Rd 25309
Ruthlawn Dr 25309
Rutledge Rd 25311
Ryan Dr 25311
Ryanwood Ln 25312
Rye Hill Ln 25309
Ryelle Rd 25312
Sablewood Rd 25312
Sabol Dr 25312
Saddle Horn Rd 25314
Saddlebred Ln 25309
Saddlecrest Ests 25314
Sage Rd 25312
Sahara Ln 25306
Saint Charles Pl 25314

Saint Francis Pl 25314
Saint Patrick Cir 25313
Salem Dr 25302
Salem Rd 25314
Salemburg Ln 25312
Salines Dr 25306
Sally Ln 25313
Salvador Dr 25306
Samantha Ln
100-148 25314
150-198 25312
Sand Castle Ln 25302
Sand Hill Mobile Park 25312
Sand Plant Rd 25309
Sandhurst Ln 25313
Sandlewood Dr 25313
Sandstone Dr 25313
Saratoga St 25306
Satinwood Ln 25302
Saturn St 25309
Saulton Dr 25313
Savilla Ln 25312
Savory Dr 25387
Sawmill Rd 25309
Saybrooke Dr 25314
Scarberry Ln 25309
Scarborough Dr 25306
Scenic Dr 25311
Schenley Dr 25309
Schenley Ln 25311
Schmidt Dr 25309
School St 25387
School House Branch Rd 25312
Science Park Dr 25303
Scofield Rd 25320
Scotland Dr 25311
Scott Holw 25312
Scott Rd 25314
Scotts Claire Ln 25304
Scraggs Dr 25387
Sean Ln 25306
Sebo Ln 25312
Second Creek Rd 25320
Selbe Ln 25314
Seneca Dr 25302
Seneca Ln 25313
Seneca Valley Est E 25320
Sentry Rd 25312
Serene Dr 25311
Serenity Dr 25311
Serenity Ln 25313
Serls Ln 25320
Serrano Ln 25320
Seymour Ln 25313
Shaded Valley Rd 25320
Shadow Ln 25309
Shadow Wood Ln 25320
Shadowbrook Rd 25313
Shady Ln 25314
Shady Way 25309
Shady Ridge Rd 25320
Shadybrook Rd 25314
Shadyview Ln 25309
Shaker Hts 25309
Shaker Ln 25311
Shale Dr 25312
Shamblin Pl 25314
Shamrock Rd 25314
Shannon Dr 25313
Shannon Pl 25314
Sharon Dr 25314
Sharonville Rd 25312
Sharpsburg Rd 25312
Shasta Dr
1-6099 25312
200-299 25313
Shaw St 25301
Shawnee Cir 25304
Shawver Way 25313
Shearwater Ln 25320
Sheb Kelly Rd 25313
Sheffield Ct 25314
Shelby Dr 25313
Sheldwich Ln 25314
Shellar Dr 25314
Shelly Ln 25313
Shelter Way 25309
Shelton Ave 25301
Shenandoah Dr 25313
Shepherd Ave 25303
Sheridan Cir 25314
Sherlock Ln 25320
Sherry Cir 25313
Sherwood Rd 25314
Shirkey Ln 25320
Shirkey And Johnson Rd 25320
Shirley Ln 25312
Shoemaker Ln 25311
Shoraler St E 25305
Short Dr 25311
Short St
1-99 25306
2-98 25302
600-799 25303
Short Meadow Dr 25320
Short Track Ln 25312
Shrewsbury St 25301
Shuttle Ln 25312
Shyville Dr 25320
Sierra Ln 25313
Sierra Rd 25314
Siesta Dr 25320
Sigman Fork Dr 25320
Sigmon Fork Dr 25320
Silas Dr 25312
Silas Kanawha 2 Mile Rd 25312
Silent Dr 25312
Silkwood Ln 25312
Silo St 25312
Silver Maple Rdg 25306
Silverado Ln
2-98 25312
5201-5299 25313
Silverstone Dr 25315
Silverton Ln 25312
Silverwood Ln 25320
Simmerson Pl 25313
Simms St 25302
Simons Quest Dr 25309
Simual Dr 25320
Sisson Ln & Ter 25320
Sissonville Dr
8311A-8311Z 25320
Sissonville View Dr 25320
Sisters Ln 25320
Skiles Brown Hollow Rd 25311
Skillet St 25312
Skylark Ln 25312
Skyline Dr 25302
Skyline Rd 25314
Skytop Cir 25314
Slack St 25301
Slate Lick Dr 25306
Slater Dr 25309
Slater Farm Rd 25312
Slaughter Dr 25313
Sled Rd 25306
Smallridge Ct 25387
Smallridge Dr 25312
Smiley Dr 25309
Smith Rd 25314
Smith St 25301
Smith Creek Rd 25309
Snapdragon Rd 25312
Snodgrass Dr 25309
Snow Hill Dr 25311
Snowbird Dr 25306
Softwood Ln 25313
Sol Ln 25312
Solace Dr 25302
Soldier Ln 25313
Somerlayton Rd 25314
Somerset Dr 25302
Songer Ln 25309
Sonlight Rd 25311
Sonnys Dr 25313
Sounint Ave SE 25304
Sourdough Ln 25313
Sourwood Ln 25320
South Dr 25301
South St 25303
Southcove Ln 25309
Southern Pines Trl 25309
Southern Woods Dr 25309
Southridge Blvd 25309
Sowards Dr 25309
Sparks Ln 25311
Sparrow Dr 25312
Spartan Dr 25311
Spartanburg Rd 25312
Spence Dr 25311
Spencer St 25303
Spencer Hollow Rd 25320
Spiritwood Ln 25320
Split Rail Dr 25309
Spotswood Ct & Rd 25303
Spotted Horse Ln 25312
Sprigg Dr 25320
Spring Dr
100-199 25387
1800-1899 25303
Spring Rd 25314
Spring St
1-149 25302
150-199 25301
2300-2599 25303
Spring Branch Dr 25312
Spring Branch Rd 25320
Spring Fork Dr 25312
Spring Hill Ave 25309
Spring Valley Dr 25313
Springdale Dr 25302
Springfield Dr 25306
Springfork Dr 25306
Springwood Cir 25320
Spruce Rd
2-98 25306
1000-1199 25314
Spruce Hill Dr 25306
Squeaks Rd 25312
Stable Ridge Rd 25312
Stables Rd 25309
Stacy Dr 25302
Stadium Pl 25311
Staehlin Rd 25314
Stafford Ln 25313
Stagecoach Dr 25309
Stanwix Dr 25306
Starcher Ln 25309
Stardust Ln 25309
Starlight Dr 25320
Starling Dr 25306
Starlite Dr 25320
Staton Dr 25306
Staunton Ave 25303
Staunton Ave SE 25304
Staunton Rd 25314
Steiner Dr 25302
Stephen Way 25313
Stephens Ave 25302
Sterling Ln 25312
Stewart Park 25313
Stockton St 25387
Stogdon Rd 25320
Stone Rd 25314
Stone Acres Rd 25306
Stone Creek Xing 25309
Stone Mountain Ests 25312
Stone Spring Ln 25313
Stonebrook Rd 25314
Stonecove Rd 25309
Stonehenge Rd 25314
Stonewall Dr 25302
Stonewood Rd 25313
Stoney Ln 25309
Stoney Oaks 25312
Stoneybrook Rd 25313
Stony Point Rd 25314
Stowers Ln 25313
Strader Rd 25311
Stranahan Dr 25313
Stratford Pl & Rd 25303
Street Rod Ln 25312
Stricker Rd 25314
Stuart St
1100-1399 25302
1400-1499 25387
Sturm Pritt Rd 25312
Substation Ln 25302
Sugar Creek Dr 25387
Sugar Maple Rd 25320
Sugar Mill Ln 25311
Sugarcamp Br 25314
Sugarpine Ln 25320
Sugarwood Ln 25312
Sultan Rd 25309
Summer Pl & Way 25309
Summers Ave 25303
Summers Dr 25312
Summers St 25301
Summerside Rd 25312
Summit Dr
700-999 25315
1000-1599 25302
Summit Dr W 25302
Summit Ln 25302
Sun Dance Ln 25320
Sun Valley Dr 25313
Suncrest Pl & Rd 25303
Sundown Rdg 25309
Sunflower Ln 25306
Sunlit Dr 25320
Sunnybrook St 25313
Sunnyvale Dr 25302
Sunrise Dr 25302
Sunrise Ln 25313
Sunset Cv 25309
Sunset Dr 25301
Sunset Rdg 25309
Sunset Ridge Rd 25309
Sunsetview Ln 25320
Sunshine Cir 25313
Superior Ave 25303
Surface Dr 25302
Susan Rd 25303
Sutherland Dr 25303
Sutphin Dr 25315
Sutters Mtn 25309
Sutton Cir 25306
Swallow Way 25313
Swan Rd 25314
Swarthmore Ave 25302
Sweet Gum Ln 25306
Sweetbrier Rd 25314
Swinburn St 25302
Swiss Dr 25313
Sycamore Dr 25309
Tackett Cir 25309
Tahoe Rd 25320
Tall Oak Dr 25302
Tamarock Dr 25313
Tanglewood Rd 25313
Tanner Frk 25312
Tanner Rd 25314
Tark Hill Rd 25312
Tarklin Rd 25312
Tarrington Rd 25312
Taryn Ln 25313
Tate Dr 25387
Tate Hollow Rd 25312
Taylor Acres 25312
Taylor Cemetery Rd 25313
Teaberry Cir 25312
Teakwood Dr 25312
Teakwood Rd 25320
Tealeaf Ln 25302
Technology Dr 25309
Teel Hill Dr 25313
Temple St 25387
Tenderheart Ln 25309
Tennessee Ave 25302
Tennessee St 25309
Tenney Dr
1-199 25314
101-199 25309
Tennis Club Rd 25314
Teresa Ln 25320
Terrace Rd 25314
Terrace Rdg 25313
Terry Rd 25309
Teter Rd 25314
Texas Ave 25315
Thaxton Holw 25312
Thaxton Hollow Rd 25309
Thelma St 25302
Thevenin Ln 25309
Thomas Ave 25309
Thomas Cir 25314
Thomas Rd 25303
Thomas Mobile Home Park 25320
Thomas Mountain Rd 25309
Thomasson Rd 25320
Thomosson Rd 25320
Thompson Cir 25387
Thompson St 25311
Thor Dr 25306
Thornapple Ln 25313
Thornberry Ln 25320
Thorne Rd 25303
Thornhill Ln 25309
Thornton Pl 25303
Three Island Dr 25313
Three Star Ln 25313
Thunderbird Dr 25306
Thunderstone Rd 25320
Thurston Dr 25311
Tick Ridge Cir 25309
Ticonderoga Dr 25306
Tiffany Dr 25313
Tiffany Ln 25302
Tiger Mdws 25314
Timber Trail Rd 25304
Timbercrest Dr 25311
Timberland Trl 25309
Timberline Pl 25311
Timbermist Ln 25302
Timberview Dr 25314
Timberwood Dr 25302
Timothy Ln 25309
Timothy Way 25387
Tinder Ave 25302
Tinney Ln 25312
Tinsel Dr 25312
Tinsley Ln 25314
Tipperary St 25313
Tipton Dr 25306
Titan Dr
1-99 25309
3700-3799 25306
Toledo Ave 25304
Toler Dr 25304
Toler Rd 25311
Tolley Dr 25320
Tolley Hollow Rd 25320
Toman St 25303
Tomato Ln 25306
Toolmaker Rd 25314
Topeka Dr 25306
Tori Ln 25312
Tortoise Ln 25309
Tourant Dr 25311
Tower Dr 25306
Town Ct 25387
Townsend Dr 25311
Trace Fork Blvd 25309
Trace Fork Rd
200-350 25309
511-529 25309
531-597 25320
599-1199 25320
1201-1899 25320
1500-1598 25309
1501-1597 25309
1599-3799 25309
1600-1898 25320
1900-1998 25309
2000-2099 25309
2101-2199 25309
2200-2299 25320
2300-2399 25309
2400-2499 25320
2500-2899 25309
3000-3099 25320
3200-3298 25309
3300-3599 25309
3700-3799 25320
3801-3897 25309
3899-4099 25309
4101-4299 25309
Tractor Dr 25309
Tracy Way 25311
Trafford Ln 25302
Trail Dr 25309
Trailridge Ln 25306
Trails End 25313
Tranquil Ln 25320
Trap Post Rd 25309
Trapani Dr 25314
Trappers Pl 25314
Traveler Dr 25309
Traverse Ln 25313
Treadwell Ln 25309
Tree Ln 25311
Treehouse Ln 25314
Treelane Dr 25311
Tremont St 25303
Trinity Cv 25320
Triple A Farm Rd 25320
Triple Oaks Dr 25313
Triple Run Rd 25313
Trotters Ln 25312
Trout Ln 25312
Troy Rd 25303
Truman Rd 25302
Trysting Ln 25312
Tudor Rd 25314
Tulip Tree Rd 25302
Tumbleweed Ln 25306
Tuppers Creek Rd 25312
Turkey Pen Dr 25320
Turley Rd 25314
Turnwood Ln 25302
Turtle Hill Dr 25302
Tuttle Ln 25320
Twilight Dr 25311
Twin Beech Ln 25309
Twin Blessing Ln 25309
Twin Lakes Dr 25313
Two Creek Ln 25311
Tyler Ln 25314
Tyler Pl 25309
Tyler Ridge Rd 25313
Tyler View Dr 25313
Ullalan Dr 25309
Underhill Dr 25320
Unicorn Ln 25312
Union Sq 25302
Union Carbide Dr 25303
United Disciples Dr 25309
United Way Sq 25301
Unity Ln 25313
Upland Dr 25309
Upper Dartmouth Ave 25302
Upper Falcon Dr 25312
Upper Middle Rd 25314
Upper Ridgeway Rd 25314
Upper Vine St 25302
Upshur Ln 25302
Upton Dr 25309
Upton Creek Rd 25309
Urban Dr 25302
Us Highway 119 N 25309
Utah Hollow Rd 25312
Vada Ln 25302
Vadalia Ln 25313
Vala St 25302
Valley Dr 25303
Valley Rd
9-11 25309
13-99 25309
801-897 25302
899-1099 25302
Valley Brook Dr 25312
Valley Grove Rd 25311
Valley Hill Dr 25313
Valley View Dr
600-699 25313
900-999 25309
1000-1199 25313
Van Buren Ave 25314
Vance Holw 25320
Vandall Dr 25309
Vanguard Dr 25306
Varsity Dr 25302
Vaughan Ln 25309
Veazey St 25311
Velma Dr 25302
Veltri Way 25302
Velvet Dr
1-299 25311
2-98 25309
Venable Ave
3500-5499 25304
11500-11998 25315
12000-12500 25315
12502-13698 25315
Ventura Acres 25302
Venus Dr 25306
Vermont Dr 25387
Vest Pl 25314
Veterans Ln 25320
Via Rd 25311
Victoria Ln 25302
Victoria Rd 25313
Victory Ave 25304
Vidalia Ln 25309
Vienna Pointe 25313
Viewmont Dr 25302
Viking Rd 25302
Villa Est 25311
Villa Pike 25313
Villa Oaks Cir 25313
E Village Dr 25309
Vincent St 25302
Vindale Dr 25311
Vine St 25302
Vine St SW 25309
Vinewood Rd 25312
Vintage Ln 25309
Viola Rd 25314
Violet St 25387
Virgie Ln 25312
Virginia Ave 25315
Virginia Ave SE 25304
Virginia St E
100-1499 25301
1500-1699 25311
Virginia St SW 25309
Virginia St W 25302
Vista Dr 25302
Vista Hts 25313
Vogel Dr 25302
Volcano Rd 25309
Wade Dr 25313
Wade St 25311
Wagner Dr 25311
Wagon Wheel Ln 25320
Wakefield 25312
Walbridge Rd 25309
Walker Ave 25302
Walker Dr 25312
Walker Rd
1-99 25309
101-199 25309
700-899 25311
Walker Mountain Rd 25312
Walking Horse Ln 25312
Wallburg Ln 25312
Walnut Dr
1-99 25306
101-199 25306
1600-1699 25387
Walnut Rd 25314
Walnut St
300-699 25309
900-999 25387
7000-7099 25320
Walnut Crossing Ln 25320
Walnut Gap Rd 25311
Walnut Valley Dr 25313
Walters Rd 25314
Walton Dr 25309
Walton Ln 25306
Wanzer Ct 25301
Warner Ln 25311
Warren Pl & St 25302
Warrington Rd 25312

Warsaw Dr 25306
Warwick Pl 25314
Washington Ave 25315
Washington Ave SE 25304
Washington St E
1598A-1598Z 25311
100-1499 25301
1500-1595 25311
1597-1699 25311
1598-1598 25301
1600-1698 25311
1800-2199 25305
2200-2599 25311
Washington St SW 25309
Washington St W
4698A-4698Z 25313
1238 1/2A-1238 1/2Z 25302
100-1399 25302
1400-3999 25387
4000-5199 25313
Watson Ave 25304
Watts St 25302
Waverly Dr 25313
Waybrooke Dr 25320
Waycross Dr 25313
Wayne Dr 25306
Wayne Isaac Ln 25306
Wayside Dr 25303
Weathervane Ln 25320
Weavers Ln 25312
Webb Dr 25309
Weber St 25309
Weberwood Dr 25303
Webster Ter 25301
Wedgebrook Ln 25313
Wedgewood Dr 25309
Weir Dr 25311
Welcome Ln 25306
Weldon Ln 25309
Wellington Way 25313
Wellington Pointe 25309
Wells Dr 25315
Welsh Dr 25311
Wertz Ave 25311
Wesley Dr 25302
West Ave 25302
Westbrook Dr 25313
Westminister Way 25314
Westmont Ln 25320
Westmoreland Dr 25302
Westview Dr 25311
Westwind Way 25302
Westwood Dr 25302
Wet Springs Ln 25312
Wharton Ln 25302
Wheatfield Ln 25312
Wheelersburg Ln 25312
Wheeling Dr 25309
Whimp Dr 25309
Whippoorwill Way 25314
Whispering Way 25303
Whispering Hills Dr 25313
Whispering Oaks 25312
Whispering Pines Rd 25320
Whispering Woods Rd 25304
Whisperwood Ln 25320
White St 25302
White Oak Dr 25320
White Oak Rd 25302
White Pine Dr 25311
N White Tail Ln 25312
White Water Dr 25313
Whiting Dr 25320
Whitlock Dr 25309
Whitney Ln 25304
Whitney St 25302
Whittier Dr 25312
Whittingshire Ln 25312
Whittington Rd N 25312
Wick Ln 25313
Wickline Mountain Rd 25320
Wilbur Dr 25303
Wilcox Farm Ln 25309
Wild Acre Dr 25314
Wild Cherry Ln 25320
Wild Turkey Rd 25304
Wildberry Dr 25312
Wilderness Dr 25312
Wildflower Cv 25312
Wildwood Dr 25302
Wildwood Way 25312
Wildwood Acres Dr 25312
Wiley Rd 25306
Wilkie Dr 25314
Willa Ln 25309
William Ln 25309
William Way 25312
Williams Dr 25313
Williams St 25302
Williamsburg Way 25314
Williamsview Ln 25312
Willow Dr
1-1300 25309
1302-1698 25309
13700-13799 25315
Willow Tree Way 25314
Willow Wood Pl 25314
Willowcrest Dr 25311
Wills Dr 25309
Wilma Ln 25311
Wilmore Ln 25312
Wilshire Pl 25314
Wilson Ave 25309
Wilson Rd 25312
Wilson St 25309
Wilson Way 25311
Wimbleton Dr 25309
Winchester Rd 25303
Windham Rd 25303
Windhaven Ln 25302
Winding Hills Dr 25320
Winding Woods Dr 25311
Windover Way 25302
Windsor Dr & Pl 25311
Windy Hill Farm Rd 25320
Wineberry Ln 25302
Winewood Rd 25312
Winona St 25303
Winston Ct 25387
Winterberry Ln 25313
Winterfell Rd 25314
Wintz Rd 25313
Winwood Dr 25302
Wise Dr 25306
Wise Acres Dr 25311
Wisteria Dr 25309
Witt Hl & Rd 25309
Wizard Dr 25311
Wolf Pen Dr 25312
Wolf Pen Ln 25309
Wolfe Run Rd 25304
Wolverine Dr 25311
Wood Rd 25302
Woodall Dr 25313
Woodberry Ln 25304
Woodbine Ave 25302
Woodbreeze Ln 25304
Woodbridge Dr 25311
Woodchuck Ln 25306
Woodchute Ln 25314
Woodcliff Rd 25314
Woodcrest Ln 25314
Wooded Acres Dr 25312
Woodfield Ln 25314
Woodhaven Dr 25387
Woodland Ave 25303
Woodland Dr 25302
E Woodland Dr 25311
Woodland Height Rd 25312
Woodmere Dr 25314
Woodmont Dr 25309
Woodoak Ln 25314
Woodpath Ln 25387
Woodridge Ln 25314
Woodrow Wilson Pl 25302
Woodrum Ln 25313
Woods Cv 25313
Woodsedge Way 25302
Woodshire Pl 25314
Woodside Cir 25314
Woodstock Pl 25314
Woodsview Hts 25302
Woodvale Dr 25314
Woodward Ct 25302
Woodward Dr
300-399 25312
800-1099 25387
1100-5299 25312
5301-5399 25312
Woolridge Dr 25311
Wooster Ln 25309
Wormwood Ln 25302
Wrangler Dr 25320
Wray Cir 25309
Wwii Blackhawks Rd 25320
Wychwood Rd 25314
Wyman Dr 25312
Wymer Rd 25313
Wynterhall Ln 25309
Wyoming St 25302
Yale Dr 25302
Yancey Cir 25313
Yankeetown Ln 25320
Yarrow Ln 25320
Ymca Dr 25311
York Ave 25387
Yorkshire Dr 25314
Yorktowne Pl 25309
Young Rd
1-20 25320
22-98 25320
89-97 25312
99-100 25312
101-197 25320
102-198 25312
199-1899 25320
Young St
1000-1099 25301
4600-4699 25309
Young Hollow Rd 25320
Younger Dr 25306
Zabel Dr 25387
Zach Summers Ln 25320
Zandale Ln 25320
Zebulon Rd 25309
Zella Dr 25309
Zero Dr 25306

NUMBERED STREETS

1 Valley Sq 25301
1st Ave 25303
900-1299 25302
1400-1699 25387
1st Creek Rd 25320
2nd Ave
100-799 25303
1000-1399 25302
1400-3199 25387
2nd St 25306
W 2nd St 25302
2nd Creek Rd 25320
2nd Creek Church Cir 25320
3 Mile Rd 25312
3 Mile Of Coopers Crk 25312
3rd Ave
102 1/2A-102 1/2Z 25303
100-599 25303
1400-2900 25387
2902-3298 25387
4 Mile Rd 25312
4 Mile Extension Rd 25312
4th Ave 25387
100-499 25303
1400-3000 25387
3002-3398 25387
5 Mile Rd
2-198 25306
1000-2799 25312
5th Ave
234 1/2A-234 1/2Z 25303
1400-3499 25387
6th Ave
100-399 25303
1400-2699 25387
6th St 25302
7th Ave 25303
901-997 25302
999-1300 25302
1302-1398 25302
1400-3799 25387
7th St 25302
8 Mile Hollow Rd 25306
9th Ave 25303
10th Ave 25303
11th Ave 25303
12th Ave 25303
12th St SE 25314
20th St SE 25304
21st St SE 25304
21st St W 25387
22nd St SE 25304
22nd St W 25387
23rd St W 25387
24th St W 25387
25th St W 25387
26th St SE 25304
26th St W 25387
27th St SE 25304
27th St W 25387
28th St SE 25304
28th St W 25387
29th St SE 25304
29th St W 25387
30th St SE 25304
30th St W 25387
31st St W 25387
32nd St W 25387
33rd St SE 25304
33rd St W 25387
34th St SE 25304
34th St W 25387
35th St SE 25304
35th St W 25387
36th St SE 25304
37th St SE 25304
37th St W 25387
38th St SE 25304
39th St SE 25304
40th St SE 25304
41st St SE 25304
42nd St SE 25304
43rd St SE 25304
44th St SE 25304
45th St SE 25304
46th St SE 25304
47th St SE 25304
48th St SE 25304
49th St SE 25304
50th St SE 25304
51st St SE 25304
52nd St SE 25304
53rd St SE 25304
54th St SE 25304
55th St SE 25304
56th St SE 25304
57th St SE 25304
58th St SE 25304
65th St SE 25304
66th St SE 25304
67th St SE 25304
68th St SE 25304
69th St SE 25304
70th St SE 25304
71st St SE 25304
72nd St SE 25304
81st St 25315
82nd St 25315
83rd St 25315
84th St 25315
85th St 25315
86th St 25315
87th St 25315
89th St 25315
90th St 25315
91st St 25315
92nd St 25315
93rd St 25315
94th St 25315
95th St 25315
96th St 25315
97th St 25315
98th St 25315
99th St 25315
100th St 25315
114th St 25315
115th St 25315
116th St 25315
117th St 25315
118th St 25315
119th St 25315
120th St 25315
121st St 25315
122nd St 25315
123rd St 25315
124th St 25315
125th St 25315
126th St 25315
127th St 25315
128th St 25315
129th St 25315
130th St 25315
131st St 25315
132nd St 25315
133rd St 25315
134th St 25315
135th St 25315
136th St 25315
137th St 25315
138th St 25315

CLARKSBURG WV

General Delivery 26301

POST OFFICE BOXES MAIN OFFICE STATIONS AND BRANCHES

Box No.s
All PO Boxes 26302

RURAL ROUTES

01, 02, 03, 04, 05, 06, 07 26301

NAMED STREETS

All Street Addresses 26301

NUMBERED STREETS

All Street Addresses 26301

FAIRMONT WV

General Delivery 26554

POST OFFICE BOXES MAIN OFFICE STATIONS AND BRANCHES

Box No.s
All PO Boxes 26555

RURAL ROUTES

01, 02, 03, 04, 05, 06, 07, 08, 09, 11, 12, 13, 16 26554

NAMED STREETS

Abbey Ln 26554
Abbott St 26554
Abel Rd 26554
Abingdon Rd 26554
Abundance Ln 26554
Acorn Dr 26554
Adams St 26554
Afr Dr 26554
Airport Rd 26554
Alamo Dr 26554
Albert Ct 26554
Alexander Pl 26554
Alexandria Dr 26554
Alice St 26554
Allegheny Ave 26554
Allen Cir 26554
Alpine Ln 26554
Alta Vista Ave 26554
Alza Ln 26554
Amber Ln 26554
American Eagle Dr 26554
Amos St 26554
Anchor Ln 26554
Anderson Ct & St 26554
Anderson Hollow Rd 26554
Angel Ln 26554
Apache Cir 26554
Apollo Ln 26554
Apple Ct 26554
Apple Valley Rd 26554
Appleview Ln 26554
Arcadia Dr 26554
Arch St 26554
Arlie St 26554
Arlington Ct & St 26554
Armstrong St 26554
Artillery Dr 26554
Ash St 26554
Ashbury Ln 26554
Ashgrove Ln 26554
Ashley Ln 26554
Aspen Dr 26554
Astoria Rd 26554
Auborn St 26554
Auburn St 26554
Augusta Ave & Pnes 26554
Avalon Rd 26554
Avery St 26554
Avery Olivia Way 26554
Aviation Dr 26554
Aviator Way 26554
Avondale Rd 26554
Aztec Ct 26554
Babcock Dr 26554
Bailey Cir & Dr 26554
Baker Dr 26554
Bakers Mill Dr 26554
Baldwin St 26554
Balsa Ln 26554
Baltimore St 26554
Barbara St 26554
Barberry Ln 26554
Barbour St 26554
Barnes St 26554
Barry St 26554
Bartrug Rd 26554
Bastille Ln 26554
Bates Rd 26554
Bayberry Ln 26554
Beach Ln 26554
Beacon Ln 26554
Beaver Ln 26554
Beech Ln & St 26554
Bel Air Dr 26554
Bel Manor Dr 26554
Belinda Dr 26554
Bell Run Rd 26554
Bella View Dr 26554
Bellaire St 26554
N Bellview Ave & Blvd 26554
Belmont Dr 26554
Beltline St 26554
Bennett St 26554
Benoni Ave 26554
Benton Ln 26554
Benwood Aly 26554
Berkeley St 26554
Betty St 26554
Betty Ann St 26554
Beverly Cir, Hls, Pike & Rd 26554
Big Rock Ln 26554
Big Timber Ln 26554
Big Tree Dr 26554
Billingslea St 26554
Bind St 26554
Birch Dr 26554
Birchview Dr 26554
Bison St 26554
Black Ave 26554
Black Cherry Dr 26554
Blaine St 26554
Blatha Way 26554
Blissfield Vlg 26554
Blosser St 26554
Bluestone Dr 26554
Bobbeck Ln 26554
Bobcat Rd 26554
Bogey Ln 26554
Bolton Ln & St 26554
Bonanza Ln 26554
Bonasso Dr 26554
Bonneville Dr 26554
Bonview Ave 26554
Booths Creek Rd 26554
Boothsville Rd 26554
Boulevard Ave 26554
Bourbon St 26554
Boxwood Ln 26554
Boyce Ln 26554
Boyd Park Rd 26554
Boydston St 26554
Boyers Dr 26554
Braddock Sq & St 26554
Bradley Ct & Dr 26554
Bramble Ln 26554
Brandywine Dr 26554
Breezy Ln 26554
Brenda Ln 26554
Brentwood Dr 26554
Brewer Ln 26554
Briarwood Ter 26554
Brick Hill Rd 26554
Bridge St 26554
Bridge Street Ext 26554
Brierwood Ln 26554
Bright Dr 26554
Brightwood St 26554
Brinton St 26554
Brittany Oaks Dr 26554
Broadview Ave 26554
Broadway St 26554
Brockway Dr 26554
Brodick St 26554
Brookdale Dr 26554
Brooks Dr & Ln 26554
E Brookside Dr & Vlg 26554
Broomsage Rd 26554
Brown St 26554
Browning Ln 26554
Brummage Cemetery Rd 26554
Bryan Pl 26554
Bryant St 26554
Bub Ln 26554
Buckeye Dr 26554
Buffalo Ave 26554
Bullion St 26554
Bumblebee Ln 26554
Bundy Ln 26554
Bungalow Ave 26554
Bunker Ave 26554
Bunker Hill Ln 26554
N Bunner Ridge Rd 26554
Bunners Run Rd 26554
Burdick Ln 26554
Burgundy Ln 26554
Burke Ave 26554
Burnt Cabin Rd 26554
Business Park Dr 26554
Buttermilk Dr 26554
Butternut Dr & Rd 26554
Buttons Ln 26554
C Anna Sq 26554
Cacapon Cir & Ln 26554
Cadet St 26554
Caldwell Dr 26554

Street	ZIP
Calvary Ln	26554
Calvin St	26554
Camden Ave & Rd	26554
Camelot Mobile Home Park	26554
Camp David Way	26554
Candlewick Rd	26554
Canterbury Ln	26554
Canyon Ln	26554
Cardinal Pl	26554
Carl May Way	26554
Carleton St	26554
Carlone St	26554
Carolyn Rd	26554
Carpenter Dr	26554
Carr Ln	26554
Carriage Dr & Ln	26554
Carter St	26554
Casseday Ct	26554
Catawba Rd	26554
Cathy Ave	26554
Cayman Dr	26554
Cedar Dr, Ln & St	26554
Cedarwood Ln	26554
Celia St	26554
Celtic Way	26554
Center Ave & St	26554
Centerview Dr	26554
Chamberlain Ave	26554
Charity Ln	26554
Charles St	26554
Charleston Way	26554
Chateau Dr	26554
Chelsea Ln	26554
Cherokee Dr	26554
Cherry Ln	26554
Cherry Hill Farms Rd	26554
Cherrybrooke Ln	26554
Chesapeake Rd	26554
Chestnut St	26554
Chew St	26554
Chicago St	26554
Chickadee Ln	26554
Chip Ln	26554
Chipmunk Way	26554
Chris St	26554
Christie St	26554
Christine Ct	26554
Chunks Run Rd	26554
S Church St	26554
Circle Dr & Rd	26554
City View Ter	26554
Clark St	26554
Clay Ave & St	26554
Clearview Ponds Rd	26554
Clermont Rd	26554
Cleveland Ave	26554
Cliff Ave	26554
Clifton Rd	26554
Clinton St	26554
Clover Dr	26554
Cloverdale Hts	26554
Cloverhill Rd	26554
Club Crest Rd	26554
Clubview Dr	26554
Coal Bank Hill Rd	26554
Coal Country Ln	26554
Cobblestone Ln	26554
Cochran St	26554
Cody Ln	26554
Colassesano Dr	26554
Cole St	26554
Coleman Ave	26554
Colfax Rd	26554
Colfax Camp Rd	26554
College Park	26554
Colonial Way	26554
Colton Dr	26554
Columbia Dr & St	26554
Comfort Rd	26554
Commerce St	26554
Commodari Ct	26554
Common Ln	26554
Community Dr	26554
Conaway St	26554
Concord St	26554
Connecticut Ave	26554
Constitution Dr	26554
Coogle St	26554
Coons Hollow Rd	26554
Copeland Dr	26554
Copley Dr	26554
Copperhead Ln	26554
Cora Dr	26554
Coral St	26554
Corbin Pl	26554
Cordelia Ave	26554
Cornstalk Rd	26554
Coronet St	26554
Cory Rd	26554
Cottage Ave	26554
Country Club Mnr & Rd	26554
Country Estates Rd	26554
Courtland St	26554
Cove Rd	26554
Cowger Ln	26554
Cox Rd	26554
Crabapple Ln	26554
Cranbrook Ln	26554
Creek Rd	26554
Creekside Ln	26554
Crescent Loop & St	26554
Crestmont Cir	26554
Crestview Ave & Ln	26554
Crestwood Cir	26554
Cricket Ln	26554
Cross St	26554
Crosswinds Ct & Dr	26554
Crumb Ln	26554
Curtis Ave	26554
Cypress Dr	26554
Daisy Ln	26554
Dakota Ln	26554
E Dale Dr & Rd	26554
Dalewood Dr	26554
Dally Dr	26554
Danbury Ln	26554
Danielle Dr & Ln	26554
David Cir	26554
David Daniels Dr	26554
Davis Ln & St	26554
Davis Ridge Rd	26554
Davisson Ln	26554
Davys Run Rd	26554
Dawn Dr	26554
Dayton St	26554
Dean Dr	26554
Dearborn St	26554
Dearfield Dr	26554
Decker Ln	26554
Dee St	26554
Deepwoods Ln	26554
Deer Ln	26554
Deer Haven Dr	26554
Deerfield Dr	26554
Deerwalk Ln	26554
Delaney Ln	26554
Delaware Ave	26554
Delmar St	26554
Delta St	26554
Delvia Ln	26554
Desire Ln	26554
Deusenberry Way	26554
Dewey St	26554
Diamond Ct & St	26554
Diana Dr	26554
Discovery Ln	26554
Dixie Ave	26554
Dock Ln	26554
Doddridge St	26554
Doe Run Rd	26554
Dogwood Dr & Ln	26554
Domico Dr	26554
Dominion Ln	26554
Dontonto St	26554
Double Eagle Dr	26554
Dover St	26554
Downridge Rd	26554
Downs Dr	26554
Dream River Rd	26554
Drexel Pl	26554
Dry Run Rd	26554
Duffton Way	26554
Dunham Lick Rd	26554
Dunmore St	26554
Dunn Ave	26554
Dustin Dr	26554
Dusty Trl	26554
Dylan Dr	26554
Eagle Ln	26554
Earl Dr	26554
East Ln	26554
Eastwood Dr	26554
Eclipse Dr	26554
Eddies Dr	26554
Eddy St	26554
Edencourt Ln	26554
Edgemont Ter	26554
Edgeway Dr	26554
Edison St	26554
Edman Ln	26554
Eds Cir	26554
Elderbury Ln	26554
Eldora St	26554
Elephant Walk	26554
Elk Ave	26554
Elkins St	26554
Elm Dr	26554
Elmwood Dr	26554
Emerald Ln	26554
Emerson St	26554
Emily Ct	26554
W End Dr	26554
Erdie Ln	26554
Erie Ave	26554
Ermine Pl	26554
Erwin Ln	26554
Estate Rd	26554
Euclid St	26554
Evergreen Dr	26554
Everlasting Dr	26554
Everson Rd	26554
Factory St	26554
Fair Oaks Dr	26554
Fairbrook Ln	26554
Fairfax St	26554
Fairfield Rd	26554
Fairhaven Cir	26554
Fairhills Plz	26554
Fairlane Ave	26554
Fairmont Ave	26554
Fairway Ln	26554
Faith Meadow Rd	26554
Falcon Ln	26554
Falconcrest Ln	26554
Fallen Rd	26554
Family Dr	26554
Faraway Hl	26554
Farms Ct & Dr	26554
Farrell St	26554
Fast Ln	26554
Faust St	26554
Fawn View Dr	26554
Fay St	26554
Fellowship Dr	26554
Fennimore St	26554
Fernwood Ln	26554
Ferry St	26554
Fessler Ave	26554
Fetty Ave	26554
Field St	26554
Fire House Rd	26554
Fitzgerald Ave	26554
Five Forks Rd	26554
Fleming Ave, Ct, Dr, Ln, Pl & St	26554
Floral Ave	26554
Florida Ave	26554
Flower Dr & Ln	26554
Floyd Ln	26554
Foothills Ln	26554
Ford St	26554
W Fork Rd	26554
Fox Ln	26554
Fox Chase Ln	26554
Fox Hill Ln	26554
Foxlair Pl	26554
Frances St	26554
Francis Mine Rd	26554
Francis Mine Tower Rd	26554
Franconia Dr	26554
Franklin Ct & St	26554
Franklin Farms Dr	26554
Franklin Ridge Rd	26554
Frederick Dr	26554
Freedom Hwy & St	26554
Freeland St	26554
Friend Dr	26554
Fritz Cir	26554
Front St	26554
Frosty Holw	26554
Fulton St	26554
Furbee Ln	26554
Gail Dr	26554
Galliher Dr	26554
E Garden Ln	26554
Garner St	26554
Garnet Ln	26554
Garrett Aly & Ave	26554
Garron St	26554
Garvin Dairy Rd	26554
Gary St	26554
Gaston Ave	26554
Gateway Dr	26554
Gemini Dr	26554
Gendel Rd	26554
Georgian Mnr	26554
Gerron St	26554
Gettings Dr	26554
Gilboa Rd	26554
Gilbob St	26554
Gillespie Rd	26554
Ginger Ln	26554
Gladden St	26554
Glade View Ln	26554
Glady Creek Rd	26554
Glenn Ave	26554
Glenwood St	26554
Gloria St	26554
Golf Dr	26554
Goose Run Ln & Rd	26554
E Grafton Rd & St	26554
Graham St	26554
Graham Heights Rd	26554
Grand Ln	26554
Grandview Ave & Dr	26554
Grandview Cemetery Rd	26554
Granite Dr	26554
Grant St	26554
Grape Arbor Ln	26554
Grassy Run Rd	26554
Graves Hill Ln	26554
Green St	26554
Green Gables Rd	26554
Green Oak Ln	26554
Green River Dr	26554
Green View Dr	26554
Greenbrier Hts, Plz & Rd	26554
Greenfield Ln	26554
Greenway Dr	26554
Greenwood Dr	26554
Gristmill Rd	26554
Grove Hill Rd	26554
Grovehill Ln	26554
Guest Dr	26554
Guffey St	26554
Guffey Street Ext	26554
Guyses Run Rd	26554
Halftrack Ln	26554
Halifax St	26554
Hall St	26554
Halleck Rd	26554
Hallhurst Rd	26554
Halo Dr	26554
Hamilton St	26554
Hammond Rd	26554
Hampton Rd	26554
Harlee St	26554
Harlem St	26554
Harlen Ln	26554
Harr St	26554
Harris Ln	26554
Harrison St	26554
Harvest Dr	26554
Harvey Ct	26554
Harwood Ln	26554
Haven Ln	26554
Hawthorne St	26554
Hayhurst Way	26554
Haymond St	26554
Headley Ct	26554
Heatherwood Dr	26554
Heavenly Hls	26554
Hecks Run Rd	26554
Hedge St	26554
Helms Ln	26554
Hemlock Dr	26554
Henderson Ridge Rd	26554
Henry Dr	26554
Herald Dr	26554
Hess Ave & Ct	26554
Heston Ln	26554
Hibbs Ave	26554
Hickman St	26554
Hickman Run Rd	26554
Hickory Ave & Dr	26554
Hidden Ln & Trl	26554
Hiddentimes Ln	26554
Hideaway Ln	26554
High St	26554
High Meadow Pass	26554
High Point Dr	26554
Highland Ave & Dr	26554
Hill St	26554
Hillcrest Rd	26554
S & W Hills Dr	26554
Hillside Dr & Vlg	26554
Hilltop Dr	26554
Hillview Dr	26554
Hite Ave & Cir	26554
Hoglick Holw	26554
Holbert Ave & Rd	26554
Hollen Cir	26554
Hollowtree Ln	26554
Holly Hls & St	26554
Holly Acres Dr	26554
Hollythorn Dr	26554
Home St	26554
Homewood Ave	26554
Honey Bee Dr	26554
Honeyhill Ln	26554
Honeysuckle Rd	26554
Hood St	26554
Hook St	26554
Hope Dr & St	26554
Hopewell Rd	26554
Hoult Rd	26554
Hoult School Rd	26554
Howard Ave & St	26554
Huckleberry Ln	26554
Humanity St	26554
Hummingbird Ln	26554
Hunsaker St	26554
Hunter Zane Rd	26554
Huntington Way	26554
Huskie Dr	26554
Husky Hwy	26554
Hutchinson Dr	26554
Hyacinth Ln	26554
Ice St	26554
Ice Linn Ln	26554
Ices Vlg	26554
Ices Run Rd	26554
Idlebrook Ln	26554
Idlewyle Ln	26554
Independence Dr	26554
Indiana Ave	26554
Industrial Park Rd	26554
Ivy Ln	26554
Jacklin St	26554
Jackson Ln & St	26554
Jacobs St	26554
James St	26554
Jamison St	26554
Janet St	26554
Jarrett Rd	26554
Jason Camp Rd	26554
Jasons Way	26554
Jaynes Dr	26554
Jefferson St	26554
Jeffrey Dr	26554
Jetts Dr	26554
Jim Kennedy Rd	26554
Jo St	26554
Jo Harry Dr	26554
Joe Carrie Dr	26554
Joe Kincaid Rd	26554
Joelyn St	26554
John St	26554
John Deere Dr	26554
John Mary Dr	26554
Johnson Rd	26554
Jordan Rd	26554
Joseph Koon Ln	26554
Joy Ln & Way	26554
Jubilee Ln	26554
June Dr	26554
Juniper Ln	26554
Justin Dr	26554
Kada Ln	26554
Kanawha St	26554
Karen Ct	26554
Katherine St	26554
Katy Ln, Rd & Vlg	26554
Kaufman Dr	26554
Keith St	26554
Kelly Pl & St	26554
Kendall Dr	26554
Kennedy Rd	26554
Kennywood Dr	26554
Kentucky Ave	26554
Kerns Ave	26554
Kevin Ln	26554
Kilarm Ct	26554
Kimber Ln	26554
Kimberly Cir	26554
King Ct & St	26554
Kingdom Hts	26554
Kingfish Dr	26554
Kingmont Rd	26554
Kings Ct & Row	26554
Kingsbury Ct	26554
Kirkway Dr	26554
Kisner Hill Rd	26554
Knicely Hollow Rd	26554
Konnor Ln	26554
Koon Farm Ln	26554
Koons Run Rd	26554
Kramer Ln	26554
Laager Ln	26554
Lady Ln	26554
Lafayette Cir & St	26554
Lake Ave	26554
Lakeview Dr	26554
Lambert Ave & Rd	26554
Lance Dr	26554
Landing Ln	26554
Lanham Ln	26554
Larkin St	26554
Larry Ln	26554
Laurel Dr & Ln	26554
Lavender Ln	26554
Lavigna Vlg	26554
Lawnview Dr	26554
Lawrence St	26554
Lawson Rd	26554
Layman St	26554
Layman School Rd	26554
Lee St	26554
Lee Farms Ln	26554
Lehman Ave	26554
Lemley St	26554
Lemon Ln	26554
Lemont Ct	26554
Leona Ct	26554
Leonard Ave & St	26554
Leonard Avenue Ext	26554
Leopard Ln	26554
Leslie Dr	26554
Levels Rd	26554
Levi Ln	26554
Lewis St	26554
Liberty Ave	26554
Lick Run Rd	26554
Light Dr	26554
Lillie St	26554
Limerick Ln	26554
Lincoln St & Way	26554
Linda Ln	26554
Linden Ln	26554
Lindley Ln	26554
Line Dr	26554
Linear St	26554
Linmar Dr	26554
Linn Ave & St	26554
Linn Ann Dr	26554
Linwood St	26554
Lion Ln	26554
Lions Den	26554
Little Ln	26554
Little Mill Fall Rd	26554
Little Mountain Ln	26554
Little Sycamore Sq	26554
Littlebrook Way	26554
Lloyd St	26554
Local Dr	26554
Lockhaven Dr	26554
Lockview Ave	26554
Locust Ave	26554
Logwood Dr	26554
Lois Ln	26554
Lonesome Ln	26554
Long Run Rd	26554
Longhorn Dr	26554
Loop Park Dr	26554
Loren Ln	26554
Lowell St	26554
Lucinda Ln	26554
Lyndon Ave	26554
Lynmyra Dr	26554
Mabel Dr	26554
Mack St	26554
Madison Ln	26554
Madison St	
100-332	26554
331-331	26555
334-698	26554
401-609	26554
609 1/2-609 1/2	26554
Magnolia Dr	26554
Maidstone Dr & Ln	26554
Main Ave	26554
Mall Loop	26554
Manley Chapel Rd	26554
Manning Dr	26554
Manuel Dr	26554
Maple Ave, Dr, St & Ter	26554
Maple Avenue Ext	26554
Maplewood Dr	26554
Maranatha Dr	26554
Marcella Ln	26554
March Dr	26554
Margaret Ct	26554
Maria Julian Ln	26554
Marigold Ln	26554
Marion Ave, Sq & St	26554
Mark Linn St	26554
Market St	26554
Markley Dr	26554
Markwood Dr	26554
Marshall St	26554
Martha Ave	26554
Mary St	26554
Mary Lou Retton Dr	26554
Maryland Ave	26554
Maset Pl	26554
Mason St	26554
Matthew Dr	26554
Maxwell Vlg	26554
N May St	26554
Mayapple Ln	26554
Mayberry Dr	26554
Mayo Ln & Way	26554
Mazewood Dr	26554
Mcclure St	26554
Mccoy St	26554
Mccue Ave	26554

Mcintyre Ave 26554
Mckinley St 26554
Mckinney St 26554
Mclane Dr 26554
Mcneely St 26554
Meadowdale Rd 26554
Meadowlane Ave 26554
Meadowlark Ln 26554
Memory Ln 26554
Mercer Ln 26554
Merchant St
1-216 26554
215-215 26555
218-898 26554
301-899 26554
Meredith Ln 26554
Merrick Rd 26554
Michael Dr & Ln 26554
Michael Developement Rd 26554
Middlebury Ln 26554
Middletown Cir, Mall & Rd 26554
Mill St 26554
Mill Fall Rd 26554
Miller Ave & St 26554
Millersville Rd 26554
Millstone Rd 26554
Milton St 26554
Mingo Ln 26554
Minor Ave 26554
Misty Ln 26554
Moats St 26554
Mockingbird Ln 26554
Molly St 26554
Monkey Wrench Hollow Rd 26554
Monongah Hts & Rd 26554
Monroe St 26554
Montana Rd 26554
Monterey Ln 26554
Montgomery Ave 26554
Monumental Rd 26554
Moody Run Rd 26554
Moore Pl 26554
Moran Cir 26554
Morgan Rdg & St 26554
N Morgan Ridge Rd 26554
Morgantown Ave 26554
Morningside Dr 26554
Morningstar Ln 26554
Morris Dr 26554
Morrison Dr 26554
Morse St 26554
Mossy Oak Trl 26554
Mound Ave 26554
Mount Harmony Rd 26554
Mount Vernon Ave & St 26554
Mount Zion Rd 26554
Mountain Glen Ln 26554
Mountain Park Dr 26554
Mountainside Dr 26554
Mountainside Trailer Park 26554
Moyer Way 26554
Mt Zion Rd 26554
Mudlick Run Rd 26554
Mulberry Ln & St 26554
Mullenax Ln 26554
Mundell Ferry Rd 26554
Munford St 26554
Murray Ave 26554
Myers Dr 26554
Myra Jean 26554
Mystery Ln 26554
Naomi Ct & St 26554
Nasa Blvd 26554
Nathan Dr 26554
Nearway Dr 26554
Nellie Ln 26554
Neva Blvd & Dr 26554
New St 26554
New England Cir 26554
Newton St 26554
Nichols Dr 26554
Nicki St 26554
Nixon School Rd 26554
No Dak Ln 26554
Noble St 26554
Norman Ln 26554
North St 26554
Northwood Dr 26554
Norval St 26554
Norway Rd 26554
Norway Loop Rd 26554
Nottingham Ln 26554
Nugget Ln 26554
Nutmeg Ln 26554
Nuzum Pl 26554
Oak St 26554
Oak Ridge Rd 26554
Oakdale Pl 26554
Oakwood Rd 26554
Oakwood Mobile Home Park 26554
Ocheltree Ln 26554
Odell St 26554
Ogden Ave 26554
Ogden Avenue Ext 26554
Ohio Ave 26554
Old East Grafton Rd 26554
Old Hickory Dr 26554
Old Monogah Rd 26554
Old Monongah Rd 26554
Olive Ann Dr 26554
Oliver Ave 26554
Olympic Ln 26554
Opal Dr 26554
Opekiska Rd 26554
Opekiska Ridge Rd 26554
Orange Dr 26554
Orchard Rd & St 26554
Orchard Cove Dr 26554
Oregon Ave 26554
Oriole Ln 26554
Orion Ln 26554
Orr St 26554
Ossaway St 26554
Otlahurst Dr 26554
Otter Run Rd 26554
Outlet Dr 26554
Outlook Rd 26554
Overfort Rd 26554
Overhill Rd 26554
Overlook Rd 26554
Owens Ave 26554
Page Dr 26554
Palatine Ave 26554
Palmer Dr 26554
Panola Rd 26554
Panther Path 26554
Papa Bear Ln 26554
E & S Park Ave, Dr, Rd & Vlg 26554
Park Side Est 26554
Parkside Dr 26554
Parkview Dr 26554
Parkway Dr 26554
Pat Addition 26554
Patio Dr 26554
Patrick Dr 26554
Patriot Dr 26554
Patriot Ridge Rd 26554
Pattam Trl 26554
Patty Ln 26554
Peachtree Dr 26554
Peacock Ave & Ln 26554
Pear Tree Ln 26554
Pearl St 26554
Pell St 26554
Pelligran St 26554
Pender Ln 26554
Penlaw Dr 26554
Pennington Ln 26554
Pennsylvania Ave 26554
Penrose St 26554
Pepperbush Ln 26554
Persis Way 26554
Pete Johnson Ln 26554
Pheasant Dr 26554
Phil Ln 26554
Philips Ln 26554
Phillips Ln 26554
Physicians Plz 26554
Pickens Ln 26554
Pierpont Ave 26554
N Pike Dr & St 26554
Pin Oak Ln 26554
Pinchgut Hollow Rd 26554
Pine Ln & St 26554
Pine Grove Rd 26554
Pine Haven Dr 26554
Pine Hill Dr 26554
Pine Lake Est 26554
Pine Lake Apt 26554
Pine Valley Dr 26554
Pineridge Ln 26554
Pineview Ave 26554
Pinewood Dr 26554
Pinnacle Peak Dr 26554
Pipestem Dr 26554
Pittsburgh Ave 26554
Plainview Ave 26554
Plaza Pl 26554
Pleasant St 26554
Pleasant Acres Dr 26554
Pleasant Valley Rd 26554
Pleasant View Cir 26554
Plum Run Rd 26554
Plymouth Ln 26554
Po Corner Ln 26554
Poco Ln 26554
Pointe Ln 26554
Poling Ave 26554
Pond Dr 26554
Pooles Ln 26554
Poplar Dr 26554
Poplar Island Rd 26554
Pople Ave 26554
Potomac Ave 26554
Powder House Rd 26554
Powell Rd & St 26554
Preston St 26554
Price St 26554
Prichard Hill Rd 26554
Pricketts Creek Rd 26554
Pricketts Fort Rd 26554
Pride Ridge Rd 26554
Princeton St 26554
Pristine Ln 26554
Promise Ln 26554
Prospect Ave 26554
Pullman St 26554
Pump Station Rd 26554
Pup Run Rd 26554
Quarry Ave 26554
Queensbury Ct 26554
Quiet Dell Ln 26554
Quincy St 26554
Quint Dr 26554
Rabish Ln 26554
Race St 26554
Raintree Dr 26554
Ralph Cir 26554
Ranch Rd 26554
Random Ln 26554
Raptor Way 26554
Rayford Dr 26554
Raymond Dr 26554
Red Oak Dr 26554
Red Rock Rd 26554
Red Roof Rd 26554
Redwood Dr 26554
Reed Ct 26554
Reeves Ave & Dr 26554
Regency Dr 26554
Reidy St 26554
Rest Haven Rd 26554
Reubens Run Rd 26554
Rhea Ter 26554
Richards Ln 26554
Richmond Ln 26554
Ricron Dr 26554
Ridgely Ave 26554
Ridgeview Dr 26554
Ridgewood Dr & Rd 26554
Riggi Ln 26554
Ringgold Ln 26554
Ritchie Ave 26554
River Rd 26554
River Crest Dr 26554
River Farms Dr 26554
River Rock Dr 26554
River Run Rd 26554
Riveria Rd 26554
Rivershore Dr 26554
Riverside Dr 26554
Riverview Ave, Dr, Est, Ln & St 26554
Riverwood Cir 26554
Robert L Harr Rd 26554
Roberts St 26554
Robin Ln 26554
Robinson St 26554
Rock Dr 26554
Rock Haddon Dr 26554
Rock Lake Rd 26554
Rock Union Rd 26554
Rocky Ln 26554
Rockytop Ln 26554
Rodeo Dr 26554
Rogers Vlg 26554
Rolling Acres Dr 26554
Rollingwood Dr 26554
Rose Ave & Ln 26554
Rosewood Ave 26554
Ross St 26554
Roush Cir 26554
Roxbury Rd 26554
Ruby Dr 26554
Ruskin Dr 26554
Russell Ct & St 26554
Rustic Ln 26554
Ryan Rd 26554
Sabina St 26554
Sable St 26554
Sabraton Ave 26554
Sage St 26554
Saint Barbaras Rd 26554
Saint Charles St 26554
Saint Josephs Trl 26554
Salem St 26554
Saltwell St 26554
Samantha Dr 26554
Samaria Rd 26554
Sand Bank Rd 26554
Sands Dr & St 26554
Sandy Beach Rd 26554
Sanford Rd 26554
Sapphire Dr 26554
Sapps Farm Rd 26554
Sapps Run Rd 26554
Sarrietta Dr 26554
Sassafras Dr 26554
Satterfield St 26554
Sauro Pl 26554
Sawmill Rd 26554
Scenic Ave 26554
Scenic View Dr 26554
Scenicwood Ln 26554
School House Rd 26554
Scott Pl 26554
Scottsdale Rd 26554
Scottswood Dr 26554
Scratches Run Rd 26554
Seastar Ln 26554
Secluded Ln 26554
Serene Ave & Dr 26554
Serenity Ct 26554
Seven Springs Dr 26554
Seymour Rd 26554
Shackleford 26554
Shady Ln 26554
Shady Tree Ln 26554
Shafer Ln 26554
Shamrock Dr & Ln 26554
Shaver St 26554
Shaver Farm Ln 26554
Sheila Ln 26554
Shelby Ave 26554
Shenandoah Dr 26554
Shenasky Ln 26554
Sherbs Dr 26554
Sheridan St 26554
Sheridan Ridge Rd 26554
Sherman St 26554
Sherwood Dr 26554
Shimmey Ln 26554
Shipley Dr 26554
Shirlane Ave 26554
Shirley Ln 26554
Short Ave 26554
Silent Hill Dr & Rd 26554
Silver Maple Ct 26554
Simmons Ln 26554
Singing Pines Dr 26554
Skyhawk Ct 26554
Skyline Dr & Ter 26554
Skyview Dr 26554
Sleepy Hollow Rd 26554
S Smith St 26554
Smithtown Rd 26554
Snapfinger Ln 26554
Snider St 26554
Snoderly Dr 26554
Snow Bound Rd 26554
Snowball Bush Ln 26554
Snowbound Ln 26554
Soccer Rd 26554
Songbird Ln 26554
Southgate Dr 26554
Southland Dr 26554
Southwind Dr 26554
Sparrow Ln 26554
Speedway St 26554
Spence St 26554
Spence Street Ext 26554
Spencer Dr 26554
Spring St 26554
Spring Hill Acres Dr 26554
Spring Hollow Rd 26554
Spring Street Ext 26554
Springston Dr 26554
Spruce St 26554
Squirell Run Rd 26554
Squirrel Run Rd 26554
Stafford Cir 26554
Star Ln 26554
State St 26554
State Park Rd 26554
Steeple Chase Ln 26554
Stemple Ln 26554
Sterling Rd 26554
Stevens St 26554
Stillwater Ln 26554
Stone Ridge Dr 26554
Stonewall Rd 26554
Stoney Rd 26554
Stoney Lonesome Rd 26554
Stoneybrook Ln 26554
Stony Rd 26554
Storage Ln 26554
Straight St 26554
Straights Run Rd 26554
Strolling Ln 26554
Sugarmaple Ln 26554
Summerhill Ln 26554
Summerwind Ln 26554
Summit Ave & Dr 26554
Summitt Ridge Rd 26554
Sunburst Dr 26554
Suncrest Blvd 26554
Sunday Dr 26554
Sunny Croft Ln 26554
Sunnychapel Ln 26554
Sunnyview Ln 26554
Sunrise Ln 26554
Sunset Dr & Est 26554
Sunshine Way 26554
Sutton Dr 26554
Sweeps Run Rd 26554
Swisher Ln & St 26554
Swisher Hill Ct 26554
Sycamore St 26554
Sylvan Ave 26554
Taft St 26554
Tailwind Trl 26554
Talbott Ct 26554
Tall Pines Dr 26554
Tallwood Ln 26554
Tamarack Ln 26554
Tanglewood Ln 26554
Tanner Rd 26554
Tappan Rd 26554
Taylor Ln & St 26554
Teaberry Ln 26554
Technology Dr 26554
Tee St 26554
Terrace Mnr 26554
The Dr 26554
The Credit Union Way 26554
Thistlewood Ln 26554
Thoburn Rd 26554
Thomas Ave 26554
Thunder Rd 26554
Tiano St 26554
Tick Tock Way 26554
Tiger Trl 26554
Timberline Rd 26554
Timothy Ln 26554
Timrod Ln 26554
Tom Moran Ln 26554
Tonkery Dr 26554
Toothman Ln 26554
Tow Truck Ln 26554
Traction Ave & Park 26554
Tranquil Dr 26554
Treetop Dr 26554
Trent Pl 26554
Trenton Dr 26554
Tresara Dr 26554
Trey Ln 26554
Triple P Ln 26554
Trolley St 26554
Troy Ln 26554
Tucker Dr 26554
Tulip Ln 26554
Tunnel Hollow Rd 26554
Turf Ln 26554
Turkey Hollow Rd 26554
Turning Ln 26554
Tuttle Ln 26554
Twin Oaks Dr 26554
Tygart St 26554
Tygart Mall Loop 26554
Tygart Valley Mall 26554
Ullom Ct & St 26554
Union St 26554
Unity Ln & Ter 26554
University Dr 26554
Upland Dr 26554
Utopia Dr 26554
V I P Way 26554
Valley Dr 26554
Valley Falls Rd 26554
Valley Forge Cir 26554
Valley School Rd 26554
Valley View Dr & Ln 26554
Van Kirk Dr 26554
Van Mar Ln 26554
Vandalia Ln 26554
Vandegrift Ln 26554
Vangilder Ln 26554
Vassar Ln 26554
Ventura Dr 26554
Venus Dr 26554
Vermont Ave 26554
Vernon Dr 26554
Victorian Dr 26554
Victory Ct 26554
Vie St 26554
View Ave & Ln 26554
Viking Rd 26554
Village Dr & Way 26554
Vine St 26554
Vinegar Hill Rd 26554
Vineyard Ln 26554
Viola Dr & Rd 26554
Violet St 26554
Virginia Ave 26554
Vista Ln 26554
Vista Mobile Home Park 26554
Vista Oaks Dr 26554
Volunteer Ln 26554
Wabash St 26554
Wakefield Rd 26554
Wallace St 26554
Walnut Ave & St 26554
Walnut Grove Way 26554
Walton Ave 26554
Wannalee Ln 26554
Warren Rd & St 26554
Washington St 26554
Wateman Way 26554
Water Cress Rd 26554
Watercrest Ln 26554
Waterhouse Rd 26554
Watson Ave & Dr 26554
Wayman Dr 26554
Wayside Dr 26554
Weatherwax St 26554
Weaver Ln 26554
Welding Way 26554
Westbrook Dr 26554
Westfield Ct 26554
Westlawn Ave 26554
Westmont Rd 26554
Westview Dr 26554
Westwood Ct & Ln 26554
Wetzel St 26554
Wheeling St 26554
Whisper Ln 26554
Whispering Pines Dr 26554
White Ave 26554
White Day Rd 26554
White Day Creek Rd 26554
White Hall Blvd 26554
White Island Rd 26554
White Pine Dr 26554
Whitehall Blvd 26554
Whitetail Ln 26554
Wildberry Ln 26554
Wildlife Dr 26554
Wildwood Dr 26554
Wiley St 26554
Willetts Ave 26554
William Dr & Rd 26554
Williams St 26554
Williams Cross Roads Way 26554
Williams Crossroads Way 26554
Williamsburg Ln 26554
Willow Ave, Rd & Way 26554
Wilmar Ln 26554
Wilson Ln, Rd & St 26554
Wilson Ridge Rd 26554
Winding Ln 26554
Windward Cir 26554
Wine Dr 26554
Winfield St 26554
Winfield School Rd 26554
Winners Dr 26554
Wintergreen Ln 26554
Wood St 26554
Woodbury Dr 26554
Woodcliff Dr 26554
Woodhaven Ln 26554
Woodland Cres 26554
Woodland Hills Vlg 26554
Woodleaf Dr 26554
Woodline Dr 26554
Woodmaker Ln 26554
Woodmont Way 26554
Woodside Dr 26554
Woody Lea Wilson Ln 26554
Woodys Way 26554
Worthington St 26554
Wright Ave 26554
Yellow Poplar Dr 26554
Yodie St 26554
Zeck Dr 26554

NUMBERED STREETS

All Street Addresses 26554

HUNTINGTON WV

General Delivery 25704

POST OFFICE BOXES MAIN OFFICE STATIONS AND BRANCHES

Box No.s
1 - 179 25706
181 - 299 25707
301 - 414 25708
421 - 494 25709
501 - 610 25710
611 - 730 25711
731 - 940 25712
941 - 1150 25713
1151 - 1330 25714
1331 - 1420 25715
1421 - 1600 25716
1601 - 1700 25717
1701 - 1800 25718
1801 - 1897 25719
1901 - 2078 25720
2081 - 2155 25721
2161 - 2236 25722
2241 - 2276 25723
2281 - 2396 25724
2401 - 2516 25725
2521 - 2714 25726
2721 - 2834 25727
2841 - 2994 25728
3001 - 3440 25702
4001 - 4180 25729
5341 - 5900 25703
6300 - 6300 25771
6451 - 6624 25772
6631 - 6804 25773
6811 - 7054 25774
7061 - 7294 25775
7301 - 7474 25776
7481 - 7654 25777
7661 - 7894 25778
7901 - 7998 25779
8001 - 8556 25705
9001 - 9560 25704
10001 - 10040 25770

NAMED STREETS

A D Lewis Ave 25701
Aaron Ct 25702
Adams Ave
1-799 25701
800-2799 25704
Adkins Ct 25705
Airport Rd 25704
Alabama St 25704
Alexander Hts 25705
Alice Ct 25705
Allen Ave & Ct 25705
N & S Altamont Rd 25701
Altizer Ave & Ct 25705
Amber Rd 25704
Angela Ln 25704
Ann St 25703
Ann Tom Dr 25704
Anton Dr 25704
Apple St 25705
Aracoma Dr & Rd 25705
Arlington Blvd 25705
Arnold Ct 25705
Arthur St 25701
Artisan Ave 25703
Artisan Heights Dr 25705
Ashlee Rd 25704
Aspen Pl & Rd 25705
Auburn Rd 25704
Audra Ln 25705
Augusta Dr 25704
Avondale Rd 25705
S Baer St 25705
Baker Rd 25705
Baltimore St 25702
Barbour Ct 25702
Barkley Pass 25705
Bates Dr 25705
Bayberry Dr 25705
Bayside Dr 25705
Beaupel Ct 25705
Bee Tree Ln 25702
Beech Dr 25705
Beech St 25701
Beechwood Dr 25701
Belford Ave 25701
Belle St 25704
Bellevue Rd 25702
Belmont Dr 25705
Bennetts Point Dr 25701
Benton Ct 25705
Berkley Pl 25705
Bernard St 25704
Berry Mountain Ln 25704
Bethel Rd 25705
Beuhring Dr 25705
Beverly Ct, Dr & Rd 25705
Bevis Cir & Ct 25705
Big 7 Mile Rd 25702
Birch Dr 25705
Birch Ln 25704
Birchfield Branch Rd 25701
Birchwood Cir 25705
Birkewood Rd 25705
Blair Rd & St 25704
Blakeney Rose Ln 25705
Blankenship Rd 25701
Bonnie Blvd 25705
Bostic Rd 25702
Bottom Rd 25705
Boulevard Ave 25701
Bouvier St 25704
Bowalker Ln 25705
Bowden Ln 25705
Bowen Ridge Rd 25701
Bowman Hill Rd 25701
Bradley Rd 25704
Bradley Foster Dr 25701
Braley Rd 25705
Brandi Ln 25704
Brandon Rd 25704
Braxton Dr 25705
Brenda Ct 25705
Brentwood Dr 25701
Brentwood Ter 25704
Brereton Ct 25705
Briar Oaks Dr 25704
Briarcliff Dr & Pt 25704
Briarwood Dr 25704
Bridge St 25702
Brighton Way 25705
Brittany Dr 25704
Broad Hollow Rd 25704
Broadmoor Dr 25705
Bronson Ct 25704
Brookshire Dr 25705
Brookstone Dr 25704
Brown Ln 25701
Brown Rd 25702
Bruce St 25701
Brumfield Branch Rd 25704
Bryn Myrr Dr 25705
Buena Vista Dr 25704
Buffalo Creek Rd 25704
Buffington Ave 25703
Buffington St 25702
Bungalow Ave 25701
Burchette Rd 25701
Burlington Rd 25704
Butterfly Ln 25701
Byard Dr 25704
Cabell Ct 25703
California St 25704
Cambridge Dr 25705
Camden Rd
400-899 25704
900-905 25701
907-907 25701
909-999 25704
Camelot Dr 25701
Camp St 25702
Camp Branch Rd 25701
Camp Creek Rd 25701
Campbell Dr 25705
E Campbell Park Dr 25705
Carlton St 25705
Carriage Ln 25705
Carrington Ct 25701
Carson St 25704
Cascade Dr 25705
Castle Hl 25701
Cavalier Dr 25701
Cedar Pl 25702
Cedar St 25705
N Cedar St 25705
Cedar Crest Dr
1-199 25704
1000-1599 25705
Cedar Grove Ct 25702
Cemetery Dr 25704
Center St 25701
Central Ct 25705
Charles Ct
900-999 25701
3400-3499 25705
Charleston Ave
1200-1999 25701
2000-2099 25703
Chase St 25704
Cherokee Ct & Trl 25705
Cherry Ave & Ln 25701
Cherry Lawn Rd 25705
Chesapeake Ct 25701
Chesapeake St 25702
Cheshire Way 25704
Chesterfield Ave 25702
Chestnut Dr & St 25705
Childers Ct 25705
Chippewa Dr 25705
Chrisandra Dr 25705
Circle Dr 25701
Clarendon Ct 25704
Clark Dr 25705
Clark Est 25702
Clark Graham Holw 25701
Clem St 25705
Clemens Ct 25704
Cleveland Ave 25705
Cliff Woods Dr 25704
Cliffview Dr 25704
Clinton Pl 25705
Cloverdale Ln & St 25704
Club House Dr 25705
Cobblestone Ln 25705
Cole Branch Rd 25704
College Ave 25703
Collins Dr 25704
Collis Ave
2400-2599 25703
2600-2899 25702
Columbia Ave 25701
Commerce Ave
400-1499 25701
1600-1698 25703
Concord Ln 25705
Congressional Way 25705
Connor Ct 25701
Cook School Rd 25701
Coplen Branch Rd 25704
Copper Glen Dr 25701
Cottage St 25705
Country Crk 25701
Country Club Dr 25705
Court St W 25704
Court Side Dr 25705
Crane Ave 25705
Creekwood Dr 25705
Crescent Dr 25704
Crescent Ln 25702
Crescent Rd 25701
Crested Butte Rd 25705
Crestmont Dr 25701
Crestridge Dr 25705
Cross Creek Dr 25705
Crotty St 25705
Crump St 25705
Cummings Ct 25701
Curry Ave 25705
Cypress Ln & St 25701
Dale Ct 25701
Dalvonia Ct 25704
Darnell Rd 25705
Darwin St 25705
Davis St 25705
Deer Run Ct 25705
Deer Run Rd 25704
N Deer Run Rd 25704
Defoe Rd 25701
Delta Dr & Ln 25705
Depot St 25702
Derby Ln 25705
Devon Rd 25704
Division Rd 25705
Division St 25702
Division St W 25701
Dixie Dr 25705
Dogwood Dr 25704
Dogwood Ln 25701
Dogwood Pl 25705
Donald Ave 25701
Donna Hts 25704
Doral Dr 25704
Douglas St 25701
Doulton Ave 25701
Drift Ridge Ln 25701
Dugan St 25705
Duncan Dr 25705
Dylan Dr 25701
Earl Ct 25705
Earl Dr 25701
East Dr 25705
East Rd
300-599 25704
601-699 25705
1500-1699 25701
Eastwood Ave 25701
Eastwood Dr 25705
N & S Edgemont Rd & Ter 25701
Edgewood Dr 25701
Edison Dr 25705
Edwards Dr 25705
Edwards St 25701
Elaine Ct 25703
Elizabeth St 25705
Ellis Dr 25701
Ellis Ln 25704
Elm Ln 25704
Elm St
200-898 25703
301-399 25705
501-899 25703
Elm St E 25701
Elm St W 25704
Elmwood Ave 25702
Eloise St 25704
Elway Dr 25705
Elwood Ave & Dr 25705
Emerson Ave 25705
Emmondale Dr 25705
Emmons Ave 25702
Endicott Ln 25705
N & S Englewood Rd 25701
Ensley St 25703
Enslow Ave & Blvd 25701
Estate Dr 25702
Ethan Way 25701
Euclid Pl 25701
Eutaw Pl 25701
Evamae Ln 25701
Evans St 25704
Everett Rd & St 25702
Evergreen Cir 25705
Fairfax Dr 25705
Fairfield Plz 25701
Fairview Dr 25705
Fairway Dr 25705
Fairwood Rd 25705
Fannin Dr 25704
Farley St 25704
Ferguson Ct 25701
Ferguson Rd 25705
Fern Ct & St 25701
Ferrell Ct 25704
Ferris Ct 25702
Fitzpatrick Dr 25701
Fletcher Scaggs Ln 25704
Flora Ct 25704
Florence Ave 25701
Florence Ct 25704
Florence St 25704
Forensic Science Dr 25701
Forest Hts & Rd 25705
Forest Park Ln 25705
Forest View Dr 25705
Forrest Dr 25701
Foster Ave & Rd 25701
Foster Hollow Rd 25701
Fountain Pl 25701
Fox Run 25705
Fraley Branch Rd 25701
Francis Ct 25701
Francis St 25705
Franklin Ave 25701
Franklin St 25704
Fraziers Ln & Trl 25701
Freeman Ct 25701
Frost St 25705
Frye Ct 25704
Galesway Rd 25701
Gallaher St 25705
Galleries E 25701
Garden Ct 25704
Garden Ln 25705
Garden Park Dr 25705
Garwood Dr 25705
Gary Dr 25705
E Gate Rd 25705
Gator Ln 25701
Gayle Ct 25704
German Ridge Rd 25701
German Valley Ln 25701
Gideon Rd 25705
Giger St 25701
Gilbert St 25705
Gill St 25701
Ginger Dr 25705
Glen Carla Dr 25705
Glenbrier Ln 25702
Glenway Ln 25701
Glenwood Ter 25701
Golden Oak Dr 25701
Goodwill Rd 25704
Goodwill Riverside Dr 25704
Grace St 25705
Grady Dr 25705
Grand Blvd 25705
Grandview Rd 25702
Grant Dr
1101-1199 25701
1327-1397 25704
1399-1499 25704
1600-1698 25701
Grant St 25704
Grapevine Ct E 25705
Grapevine Ct W 25705
Grapevine Dr 25705
Grapevine Rd 25701
Grapevine St 25705
Graystone Dr 25701
Green Oak Dr 25705
Green Spring Dr 25705
Green Valley Rd 25701
Greenbrier Dr 25704
Greenbrier Mt 25705
Greenridge Dr 25704
Greenway Pl 25705
Greenwell Ct 25705
Greystone Dr 25704
Grove St 25701
Guthrie Ct 25703
Guyan Ave
2500-2599 25703
2600-2799 25702
Guyan St 25702
Guyan Oaks Dr 25705
Guyan River Rd 25702
Gwinn Ln 25702
Hagan St 25702
Hal Greer Blvd
200-699 25701
800-899 25703
900-1599 25701
Haleangs St 25702
Hall Ave 25701
Hall St 25705
Hamer Dr 25704
Hamill Rd 25701
Hamlet Ln 25702
Handley Rd 25704
Haneys Branch Rd 25704
Hansford Dr 25705
Hapgood Hl 25705
Harrison Ave 25701
Harrison Ct 25702
Harvest Dr 25705
Harvey Rd
1200-1999 25701
2037-2097 25704
2099-3399 25704
2643-1-2643-5 25704
Harvey St 25702
Haven Ln 25701
Hawthorne Way 25701
Haynie Rd 25704
Hazeldine Dr 25704
Hazelwood Pl 25705
Hearth Ln 25704
Heath Ct 25705
Heather Ct 25705
Heatherwood Ln 25705
Heavenly Pl 25705
Henderson Ln 25705
Henry St 25705
Heritage Dr 25704
Heritage Vlg 25701
Heritage Park Rd 25704
Herman Rd 25704
Hibner Ave 25705
Hickory Dr 25704
Hickory Ln 25705
Hidden Ave & Ln 25705
Hidden Acres Ln 25704
Hidden Park Dr 25705
High Dr 25705
High St 25705
High St W 25704
N High St 25702
S High St 25702
Highland Ct 25705
Highland Dr 25705
Highland Ln 25704
Highland St 25705
Highland Oaks Ln 25705
Highlander Way 25701
Highlawn Ave & Ct 25702
Hill Rd & St 25704
Hillendale Ct & Dr 25705
Hills Ct 25701
E Hills Mall 25705
Hillside Dr 25702
Hilltop Dr 25702
Hilltop Pl 25705
Hilltop Rd 25701
Hillview Dr 25702
Hilmus Rd 25704
Hite Ave 25705
Hite St 25702
Holderby Rd 25701
Holley Ave 25705
Hollywood Pl 25705
Holswade Dr 25701
Homestead Pl 25703
Homewood Ln 25705
Honeysuckle Ln 25701
Hubbards Hts 25704
Hubbards Branch Rd 25704
Hughes Rd 25701
Hughes St 25704
Hughes Branch Rd 25701
Humphrey Rd 25704
Hunting Bow Trl 25705
Huntington Ave 25701
Hutchinson St 25704
Idle Acres 25701
Idlewood Dr 25705
Illinois St 25704
Indiana St 25704
Industrial Ln 25702
Inez Dixon Dr 25704
Inverness Way 25705
E, N & S Inwood Dr 25701
Irvin Ave 25702
Irvin Rd 25705
Irwin Rd 25705
Ives Dr 25705
Ivy Hills Ests 25704
Ivy Woods 25701
Jackie Ct 25704
Jackson Ave 25704
Jackson St 25705
Jacqueline Hts 25702
James Ct & Dr 25705
James River Rd
1501-1797 25701
1799-4399 25701
4500-5599 25704
5601-5699 25704
Jarrell St 25705
Jarrod Dr 25705
Jefferson Ave 25704
E Jefferson Dr 25705
N Jefferson Dr 25701
S Jefferson Dr 25701
Jefferson Rd 25704
Jefferson Park Dr 25705
Jennifer Ln 25704
Jenny Lynn Ln 25705
Jo Lin Dr 25704
John Cir 25705
John Marshall Dr 25703
Johns Ct 25701
Johnson Hts 25702
Johnson Mountain Rd 25704
Johnstown Rd 25701
K Mart Shopping Plz 25705
Kanawha Ter 25701
Kanode Ct 25702
Kay Crest Dr 25705
Keeneland Dr 25705
Kennedy Ct 25705
Kennon Ln 25705
Kensington Ln 25705
Kentucky St 25704
Kessler Ave 25701
Kilgore Farm Rd 25701
Kilowatt Ln 25701
Kinetic Dr 25701
Kings Hwy 25705
Kings Court Est 25704
Kingsbury Dr 25701
Kingston Ter 25702
Kirk Pl 25703
Kite Ave 25701
Knollwood Dr 25705
Kristen Dr 25701
Kyle Ln 25702
Kylemore Rd 25702
La Crissa Ln 25704
Laken Dr 25701
Lakeview Ct, Dr & Hts 25704
Larchmont Dr 25705
Larkspur Dr 25705
Latulle Ave 25702
Laurel Pt & Xing 25705
Lawson Ave, Ct & Hts 25705
Lea Hill Dr 25705
Ledgewood Dr 25705
Lee Ave 25704
Lee Rd 25704
Lee St
1-19 25705
600-699 25704
Leeward Ave 25705
Left Fork Sherwood Dr 25704
Lehi Dr 25705
Leisure Ln 25705
Lewis St 25705
Lewis Subdivision Rd 25704
Liberty Ln 25705
Lincoln Ave 25703

Lincoln Dr 25704
Lincoln Pl 25701
Linden Cir 25705
Little 7 Mile Rd 25702
Little Valley Ln 25704
Locust Ct 25705
Locust Dr 25705
Locust Ln 25704
Locust St 25705
Locust Ter 25705
Logan St & Trce 25705
Lola St 25705
Long Branch Rd 25701
Long Valley Dr 25704
Longwood Rd 25705
Lookout Dr 25704
Lorman Rd 25701
Lorraine Ct 25705
Lorrimel Dr 25705
Lost Valley Dr 25705
Lotus Dr 25704
Louis Ct 25705
Lower Ter 25705
Lower Glendale Ave 25705
Lower Union St 25705
Lucas Hollow Rd 25704
Lucian St 25704
Lynda Ct 25703
Lynn St 25701
Lynn Courtney Dr 25701
Lynn Creek Rd 25704
Lynn Marr Dr 25705
Lynnwood Ct 25704
Lynwood Dr 25701
Lynwood Ter 25705
Madison Ave & Ln 25704
Magazine Ave 25704
Magnolia Ct 25704
Magnolia Ln 25701
Mahola Dr 25704
Mahood Dr & Trce 25705
Main St
100-500 25702
502-598 25702
800-899 25704
200-299 25704
Malcolm Dr & Ln 25704
Mallory Ct 25701
Manchester Ave 25703
Manor Dr 25704
Maple Ave 25703
Maple Ct 25702
Maple Dr 25705
Maple Ln 25704
Maple Ridge Ln 25705
Marcum Ter 25705
Marie St 25705
Marie Arnold Ct 25704
Marion Ct 25703
Marion St 25705
Marisa Ln 25701
Marjon Ln 25701
Marne Dr 25705
Marquis Dr 25705
Marr Park Ln 25701
Marshall Ave 25701
Marshall St 25702
Marshall University Hts 25705
Marti Jo Dr 25702
Mary St 25704
Mary Hill Ln 25705
Mason St 25704
Maupin Rd 25705
May Dr & Rd 25704
Mayfair Way 25705
Mayo Trl 25704
N Maywood Hts 25704
Maywood Hills Rd 25704
Mccoy Rd 25701
Mccoy Hollow Rd 25704
Mccullough Rd 25701
Mcguffin Ave 25701
Mcveigh Ave 25701
Meadow Ln 25704
Meadow Haven Dr 25704
Medical Center Dr 25701

Meixsell Dr 25704
Melody Branch Rd 25704
Memorial Blvd W 25701
Memorial Park Dr 25701
Memory Ln 25704
Merrick Creek Rd 25702
Merrill Ave 25702
Michigan St 25704
Midvale Dr 25705
Midway Ave 25701
Midway Dr 25705
Mildred Pl 25705
Military Rd 25701
Miller Ln 25704
Miller Rd
1900-2499 25701
6000-6199 25702
Miller St
400-499 25702
1500-1599 25701
Mills Ct 25705
Mincoran Rd 25704
Minerva Rd 25702
Minton St 25701
Misty Mnr 25702
Mohawk Ct & Trl 25705
Monel Ave 25705
Monroe Ave 25704
Montrose Pl 25705
Moore Rd & St 25702
Moreland Ave 25705
Morgan Pl 25705
Morris Ct 25701
Morris St 25705
Morrow Rd 25701
Mortimer Pl 25701
Mount Union Rd 25701
Mount Vernon Ridge Rd 25704
Mountain View Dr 25701
Mountwest Way 25701
Mullberry Ct 25701
Mullens Branch Rd 25701
Napier St 25701
Nathan Rd 25705
Navajo Trl 25705
Neel St 25701
New York St 25704
Newcomb Creek Rd 25704
Nicholas Dr 25705
Nickel Plate Dr 25705
Nickel Plate Rd 25702
North Blvd 25701
North Blvd W 25701
North Ter 25705
Northcott Ct 25701
Norway Ave 25705
N Norwood Rd 25705
Nova St 25705
Oak Dr 25704
Oak Ln
1-99 25704
108-148 25701
149-197 25704
150-198 25701
199-500 25704
502-598 25704
2000-2099 25701
Oak St
300-399 25702
3000-3098 25704
Oak Brook Dr 25705
Oak Hill Dr 25704
Oak Point Rd 25701
Oak Ridge Dr 25705
Oak Ridge Ln 25704
Oak Tree Ln
100-199 25701
3000-3099 25701
Oakland Ave 25705
Oakmont Dr 25704
Oakview Dr 25701
Oakwood Dr 25704
Oakwood Rd 25701
Ocean Dr 25705
Ohio Ave 25701

Ohio River Rd 25702
Old Davis Creek Rd 25705
Old Oak Dr
100-198 25704
200-500 25704
502-698 25704
4000-4099 25701
Old Spring Valley Rd 25704
Old Trail Rd 25704
Old Wayne Rd 25701
Old White Dr 25704
Olive St 25705
Oney Ave 25705
Opengate Rd 25701
Orchard Ave
1500-1899 25701
2600-2799 25704
Orchard Dr 25701
Orchard Rd 25705
Overby Rd 25704
Overlook Dr 25705
Owens Branch Rd 25701
Owls Lair Dr 25701
Oxford Dr 25705
Oxley Rd 25701
Palm Dr 25705
Palomar Ct 25705
Pamela Dr 25704
Paradise Ln 25704
Paris Dr & St 25705
Park Ave 25704
Park Cir 25704
Park Dr 25705
S Park Dr 25701
Park Rd 25701
Park St
1-99 25702
100-198 25705
101-699 25702
600-698 25702
1300-1399 25701
Park Pointe Way 25701
Parkland Dr 25705
Parkside Pl 25704
Parkview St 25701
Parkway Dr 25705
Parkwood Rd 25705
Parsons St 25705
Partridge Ct 25705
Paths End Rdg 25704
Patty Ln 25704
E & W Pea Ridge Rd 25705
Pembrooke Ln 25705
Pencomer Dr 25705
Perry Ave, Dr & St 25705
Perry Winkle Ln 25702
Persimmon Ln 25701
Peyton Ct & St 25705
Piedmont Ave 25702
Piedmont Hts 25701
Piedmont Rd 25704
Pine Dr
3100-3110 25704
3112-3198 25704
6200-6399 25705
Pine Ln 25704
Pine St 25705
Pine Cove Ln 25704
Pine Grove Ln 25704
Pine Hills Dr 25705
Pine Ridge Dr 25701
Pine Valley Dr 25704
Pinecrest Dr & Ln 25705
Pinedale Dr 25705
Pinehurst Dr & Ln 25704
Pineview Dr 25705
Plateau Heights Dr 25704
Pleasant Valley Dr 25701
Pleasant View Rd 25701
Plum Tree Ln 25701
Plybon Rd 25701
Plymale Branch Rd 25704
Pogue St 25705
Pontride Ave 25703
Porter Ridge Dr 25704
Porters Fork Rd 25704

Powell Ct 25701
Prandary Rd 25701
Premiere St 25704
Prestera Way 25705
Preston Ct 25704
Price Ct & Ln 25705
Price Industrial Ln 25705
Prices Crk 25701
Prices Creek Rd 25701
Priddie St 25705
Primrose Ave 25701
Prospect Ct 25702
Prospect Dr 25701
Prospect St 25702
Pullman Sq 25701
Pyramid Dr 25705
Quail Ridge Rd 25701
N & S Queens Ct 25705
Ratcliff Rd 25704
Ray Rd & Rdg 25704
Raynell Dr 25704
Rays Rdg 25704
Rebecca Ln 25701
Red Bud Ln 25701
Red Dirt Rd 25701
Red Oak Dr 25704
Reid Ave 25705
Resco Ave 25705
Rice Ave 25705
Rice Branch Rd 25704
Richmond Dr 25705
Richmond St 25702
Ricketts Rd 25705
Ridgeway Dr 25702
Ridgewood Ct & Rd 25701
Right Fork Broad Hollow Rd 25704
Right Fork Buffalo Creek Rd 25704
Right Fork Camp Creek Rd 25701
Right Fork Sherwood Dr 25704
Right Fork West Rd 25701
Right Frk Mount Vernon Ridge Rd 25704
Rissa Ln 25704
Ritchie Dr 25701
Ritter Blvd & Dr 25701
Ritter Park Dr 25701
River Ave 25705
W River Rd 25704
Riverlick Ave 25705
Riverside Dr 25705
Riverview Ave & Ln 25702
Roberto Dr 25705
Roby Rd 25705
Rockford Ln 25705
Roland Park Dr 25705
Romar Ct 25705
Rosalind Ct & Rd 25705
Rosanna Dr 25701
Rosco Dr 25705
Roseland Ct 25705
Rosemont Ct 25705
Roseneath Rd 25705
Rotary Rd 25705
Route 75 25704
Rowland Ct 25702
Rowley Hts 25705
Royal Oaks Ln 25705
Rugby Rd 25705
Rujon Dr 25705
Rural Ave 25701
Russell Ave & St 25705
Rutland Ave 25705
Saint Louis Ave 25705
Saltwell Rd 25705
Sam Collins Rd 25702
Sandalwood Dr 25705
Sara Ct 25705
Saratoga Ln 25705
Sauk Ct 25705
Savanah Dr 25701
Scenic Ln 25702
Segar Hill Rd 25704

Seminole Rd 25705
Seneca Rd 25705
Sequoia Dr 25705
Serenity Hls 25705
Shady Spring Ln 25705
Shamrock Ln 25704
Shawnee Cir & Dr 25705
Shawnee Oaks Dr 25705
Sheppard Dr 25705
Sheri Ln 25704
Sherwood Dr 25704
Shivel Ln 25705
Shockey Dr 25701
Short St 25702
Siders Ave 25702
Sierra Cir 25705
Simpson Dr 25705
Singer St 25702
Sky Oak Dr 25701
Skyview Dr 25701
Slater Ct 25702
Sleepy Acres Ln 25704
Smith Dr 25705
Smith Ln 25704
Smith St W 25704
Smith Branch Rd 25704
Smith Ridge Dr 25704
South Blvd 25701
South Ter 25705
Southview Ln 25705
Southwind Dr 25701
Southwood Dr & Hts 25701
Spears Ln 25701
Spring Dr & Rd 25705
Spring Branch Rd 25705
Spring Run Ln 25704
Spring Valley Cir 25704
Spring Valley Dr
1000-1411 25701
1412-2900 25704
2902-2998 25704
Springdale Ave 25705
Springwood Dr 25705
Stamford Park Dr 25705
Stanley Rd 25702
N & S Staunton Rd & St 25702
Stewart Ave 25701
Stiles Dr 25705
Stonecrest Dr 25701
Stonewood Dr 25705
Stor Mor Dr 25705
Stratford Way 25705
Sturgill Ln 25704
Sturm Rd 25705
Sugarwood Dr 25701
Summit Dr
1-99 25701
100-199 25705
600-699 25701
Summit St 25705
Sumner Ave 25705
Sunny Dr 25704
Sunnycrest Dr 25705
Sunrise Hl 25704
Sunset Dr
1-99 25701
4600-4999 25704
5200-5299 25705
Sunwatch 25705
Sutherland Rd 25705
Sycamore Dr 25704
Sycamore St 25705
Syncor Dr 25705
Tallwood Rd 25705
Taylor Rd 25705
Taylor Ridge Rd 25704
Taylors Village Dr 25701
Taymor Rd 25701
Tecumseh Trl 25705
Teel Branch Rd 25704
Teresa Dr 25702
Terrace Ave 25705
Terrace Dr 25701
Terrace St 25705
Terry Rd 25704

Thistlewood Ln 25705
Thomas Ave 25705
Thompson Branch Rd 25704
Thornburg Rd 25705
Thornburg St 25701
Thunderbird Dr 25704
Thundering Herd Dr 25703
Tiernan St 25702
Timberlake Dr 25705
Timberwolf Ln 25704
Topping Ct 25705
Trailside Acres Ln 25704
Trenton Pl 25701
Tudell St 25704
Turman Ct 25702
Turner Rd 25705
Turner Hagley Memorial Dr 25702
Twelve Oaks St 25705
Twin Oaks Ct 25705
Twin Oaks Dr
1-99 25701
1300-1360 25705
1362-1398 25705
Twin View Ln E 25704
Tyler Ln 25704
Tynes Ln 25705
Underwood Ave 25701
Upland Pl & Rd 25701
Upper Franklin St 25704
Upper Glendale Ave 25705
Upper Union St 25705
Us Route 60 25705
Vagabond Trl 25702
Valentia St 25705
Valley Ct 25704
Valley Dr 25704
Valley Rd 25705
Valley Terrace Rd 25704
Valley View Dr
1-9 25705
10-199 25704
Van Buren Ave 25704
Van Sant St 25704
Vanderpool Gdns 25704
Vernon St 25704
Veterans Memorial Blvd
600-1200 25701
1200-1200 25706
1200-1200 25707
1200-1200 25708
1200-1200 25709
1200-1200 25710
1200-1200 25711
1200-1200 25712
1200-1200 25713
1200-1200 25714
1200-1200 25715
1200-1200 25716
1200-1200 25717
1200-1200 25719
1200-1200 25720
1200-1200 25721
1200-1200 25722
1200-1200 25723
1200-1200 25724
1200-1200 25725
1200-1200 25726
1200-1200 25727
1200-1200 25728
1200-1200 25729
1200-1200 25718
Veterans Memorial Hwy 25705
Victory Ln 25705
Vinson Rd & St 25704
Vinton St 25701
Violet St 25705
Virginia Ave 25701
Virginia Ave W
800-1001 25704
1000-1000 25705
1000-1000 25707
1000-1000 25708
1000-1000 25772
1000-1000 25773
1000-1000 25774
1000-1000 25775
1000-1000 25776
1000-1000 25777
1000-1000 25778
1000-1000 25779
1003-2099 25704
1100-2098 25704
Virginia Ct 25701
Vista Crest Dr 25704
Waco Rd 25701
Wakefield Ct 25702
Wakefield Pl 25705
Walker Ct 25701
Walkers Branch Rd 25704
Wallace Cir 25705
Walmott Dr 25705
Walnut Ln 25704
N Walnut St 25705
S Walnut St 25705
Walnut Gap Rd 25701
Walter Rd 25704
Warren Rd 25704
Washington Ave
1-799 25701
800-2399 25704
Washington Blvd
1200-1699 25701
1701-2099 25701
2100-3299 25705
Washington Ct 25704
Washington Sq 25703
Water St 25702
Waverly Rd 25704
Wayne St 25704
Wellman Ln 25704
Wellswerth Gdns 25704
Wentz St 25705
Wentz Hollow Rd 25702
West Rd 25701
Westchester Dr 25704
Westfield Ct 25702
Westmoreland Rd 25704
Weston Ct 25705
Westpoint Dr 25705
Westview Ave 25701
Westwood Dr 25702
Westwood Ln
1-199 25704
1000-1099 25702
Wetzel Ct 25704
Whaley Ct 25704
Whispering Pines Ct & Ln 25704
Whitaker Blvd W 25701
White Oak Ln & Trl 25701
Whitetail Ln 25702
Wildwood Ln 25701
Wilkinson St 25705
Willard Ct 25703
Williams Ave 25701
Williams Ct 25705
Willoughby Ave 25705
Willow St 25701
Willow Glen Rd 25701
Willowtree Dr 25704
Wilson Ct 25701
Wilson Dr 25705
Wilson Hts 25705
Wilson Pl 25702
Wilson St
2600-2899 25705
3202-3299 25704
Wiltshire Blvd 25701
Windmere Dr 25704
Windsor Dr 25705
Windward Ln 25704
Windy Hl 25704
Winters Rd 25702
Wolf Creek Rd 25704
E Wolfe Dr 25705
Wolfeshire Hts 25701
Wood Dr & Ln 25701
Wood Pointe Ln 25701
Woodhaven Dr 25701
Woodland Dr
100-599 25705

1601-1697 25704
1699-1899 25704
3200-3399 25705
Voodland Ln 25704
Voodland Pl 25705
Voodland Trl 25704
I Woodlomond Pl &
Vay 25705
Voodmont Rd 25701
Voodridge Ct 25705
Voodridge Est 25704
Voodrum Ln 25705
Voodson Ct 25705
Voodview Dr 25705
Voodview Ln 25701
Voodville Dr 25701
Voodward Ter 25705
Vorkman Ln 25704
Vright Ave & Ct 25705
'eich Ave 25705
'oung Ct 25705

NUMBERED STREETS

st Ave
2400-2599 25703
2600-2999 25702
st St
2-98 25705
100-327 25705
329-399 25705
330-330 25701
330-342 25705
400-598 25701
600-1299 25701
nd Ave 25703
nd Ave W 25701
nd St
100-311 25705
312-316 25701
312-342 25705
321-321 25701
321-345 25705
400-1200 25701
nd St W 25701
Mile Creek Rd 25702
rd Ave
100-1599 25701
1800-1898 25703
1900-2599 25703
2600-3999 25702
rd Ave W 25701
rd St
200-328 25705
330-332 25705
400-1199 25701
rd St W 25701
Pole Rd 25701
th Ave
100-1599 25701
2300-2599 25703
2600-3999 25702
th St
100-199 25705
200-299 25701
300-318 25705
319-319 25701
320-398 25705
400-899 25701
th St W 25701
th Ave
100-208 25701
209-209 25702
210-300 25701
215-215 25701
215-221 25702
223-301 25701
301-303 25702
305-307 25702
308-308 25701
309-309 25702
310-312 25702
311-313 25701
315-406 25701
407-409 25702
408-500 25701
411-603 25701
506-508 25702
510-600 25701
602-602 25702
604-607 25702
604-604 25701
609-621 25702
610-612 25702
610-610 25701
618-620 25701
624-624 25702
633-633 25701
635-643 25701
645-701 25701
701-702 25702
703-703 25701
704-714 25702
707-707 25702
711-711 25701
711-711 25702
713-717 25701
717-725 25702
731-747 25701
749-1599 25701
1601-1697 25703
1699-2599 25703
2600-3999 25702
207 1/2-207 1/2 25701
409 1/2-707 1/2 25702
711 1/2-711 1/2 25701
5th Ave W
300-499 25701
700-2699 25704
5th St
100-199 25705
316-398 25701
400-899 25701
901-2219 25701
5th St W 25701
5th Street Rd 25701
6th Ave
101-205 25701
104-106 25702
110-298 25701
207-207 25702
223-297 25701
308-312 25702
328-404 25701
406-408 25702
412-412 25701
412-418 25702
423-427 25701
1600-2199 25703
2900-3099 25702
404 1/2-412 1/2 25701
6th Ave W 25701
6th St
209-213 25705
300-1299 25701
6th St W
200-399 25701
515-799 25704
1000-1099 25701
7th Ave
100-310 25701
315-317 25702
333-401 25701
403-404 25702
405-405 25701
405-405 25702
409-409 25701
416-416 25702
418-418 25701
420-420 25702
422-1598 25701
429-431 25702
435-1599 25701
1600-2199 25703
2900-3099 25702
7th Ave W 25701
7th St
100-199 25705
200-299 25701
300-399 25705
400-1299 25701
7th St W
200-599 25701
600-899 25704
1000-1099 25701
8th Ave
100-332 25701
343-348 25702
400-416 25701
417-417 25702
418-1598 25701
421-421 25702
423-1599 25701
1600-3199 25703
421 1/2-511 1/2 25701
8th Ave W 25701
8th St
100-199 25705
200-400 25701
301-399 25705
401-1399 25701
8th St W 25704
8th Street Rd 25701
9th Ave
101-107 25701
106-106 25702
108-108 25701
110-110 25702
112-114 25701
114-114 25702
128-306 25701
309-311 25702
312-314 25701
313-313 25702
316-317 25701
318-322 25702
319-321 25701
321-321 25702
323-1599 25701
412-412 25702
416-1598 25701
1600-2799 25703
3201-3299 25702
9th Ave W 25701
9th St
1-199 25705
200-1299 25701
9th St W 25704
10th Ave
100-1999 25701
2000-2599 25703
10th Ave W 25701
10th St
200-200 25701
216-224 25705
226-248 25705
250-298 25705
300-1299 25701
10th St W 25704
11th Ave
100-1999 25701
2000-2299 25703
11th Ave W 25701
11th St
1-199 25705
200-1299 25701
11th St W 25704
12th Ave
100-1999 25701
2000-2199 25703
2500-2599 25705
12th Ave W 25701
12th St
100-199 25705
300-1499 25701
1501-1599 25701
12th St W 25704
13th Ave 25701
13th St
1-199 25701
200-217 25705
218-298 25701
219-299 25705
300-1200 25701
1301-1303 25705
1307-1343 25701
1342-1342 25705
1344-1376 25701
1347-1347 25705
1351-1375 25701
13th St W 25704
14th Ave 25701
14th St 25701
14th St W 25704
15th St 25701
15th St W 25704
16th St W 25704
16th Street Rd 25701
17th St 25703
1000-1799 25701
17th St W 25704
18th St
200-899 25703
1100-1999 25701
18th St W 25704
19th St
200-999 25703
1000-1499 25701
19th St W 25704
S 19th St W 25701
20th St 25703
20th St W 25704
21st St 25703
21st St W 25704
22nd St 25703
22nd St W 25704
23rd St 25703
23rd St W 25704
23rd 1/2 St W 25704
24th St 25703
24th St W 25704
25th St
1-1199 25703
1200-1399 25705
25th St W 25704
26th St
1-999 25703
1000-1299 25705
26th St W 25704
27th St
1-599 25702
700-899 25703
900-1099 25705
27th St W
300-599 25704
28th St
1-699 25702
800-1499 25705
28th St W 25704
29th St 25702
29th St W 25704
30th St 25702
31st St 25702
31st St W 25704
32nd St 25702
32nd St W 25704
33rd St 25702
33rd St W 25704
34th St 25702
35th St 25702
36th St 25702
37th St 25702
38th St 25702
39th St 25702
40th St 25702
45th St 25702
10 1/2 Ave 25703
10 1/2 St W 25704
46 1/2 St W 25704

MARTINSBURG WV

General Delivery 25401

POST OFFICE BOXES MAIN OFFICE STATIONS AND BRANCHES

Box No.s
All PO Boxes 25402

RURAL ROUTES

15 25401
01, 06, 19 25403
02, 03, 09, 14 25404
04, 05 25405

NAMED STREETS

Abell St 25401
Abino Hills Way E &
W 25403
Abrahams Way 25404
Academy Dr 25404
Access Dr 25404
Achilla Ter 25404
Acoustic Dr 25404
Adams St 25404
E & W Addition St 25401
Administrative Dr 25404
Adrian Dr 25403
Advantage Dr 25404
Advent Dr 25403
Aero St 25401
Aikens Ctr 25404
Airport Rd 25405
N & S Alabama Ave 25401
E Alancom Ter S 25405
Albert St 25404
Aldershot Ln 25405
Aldrin Ln 25403
Alec Ln 25404
All American Way 25405
Almshouse Rd 25403
Alonzo Dr 25401
Amandas Way 25405
Ambassador Cir 25405
Ambrosia Ln 25405
Amorette Dr 25404
Amos Dr 25404
Andalusian Dr 25405
Anderson Rd 25404
Anita Dr 25401
Ankers Rd 25404
Annies Way 25404
Ansted Way 25404
Anthony Taylor Way 25404
Apache Dr 25401
Apartment Blvd 25401
Apollo Ct 25405
Appian Way 25403
Apple Harvest Dr
8800-8998 25403
9000-14200 25403
14202-14398 25403
14500-14998 25405
14701-14899 25401
Appomattox Dr 25403
Aquarius Way 25405
Aqueduct Ave 25404
Arabian Ln 25404
Arbor Way 25401
Arbutus Ln 25405
Arch St 25401
Arden Nollville Rd 25403
Argon Dr 25405
Arlington Ct 25405
Armstrong Way 25403
Artillery Way 25403
Artisan Way 25401
Aruba Dr 25405
Ascot Dr 25404
Aster Ct 25404
Athletic St 25404
Atlas St 25404
Auburn St 25401
Augusta Ln 25405
Auklet Ct 25404
Austin Dr 25403
Auto Parts Pl 25403
Autumn Leaf Dr 25401
Avenue Jubilee 25403
Avery St 25404
Aviation Way 25405
Avondale Rd 25404
Aylesbury Ln 25403
Azalea Ln 25401
Aztec Dr 25405
Azure Dr 25404
Babbling Brook Ln 25403
Bachman Ln 25404
Backing Cir 25405
Badger Ct 25403
Baker Rd 25405
Balmoral Ln 25404
Baltimore St 25401
Bamboo Ln 25404
Bane Berry Ln 25404
Barbie Ln 25405
Barlow Ct 25403
Baron Dr 25405
Bashore Dr 25404
Basket Dr 25403
Beacon Dr 25403
Beall Rd 25404
Beautiful Ct 25404
Beauty St 25405
Bedget Ln 25404
Bedington Rd 25404
Beefy Dr 25404
Beetle Dr 25403
Belview Dr 25404
Bendheim Cir 25404
Bennett Shade Ln 25403
Bergen Ln 25405
Berkeley Station Rd 25404
Bernice Ave 25405
Berrantr Dr 25401
Berry St 25401
Bertelli Ct 25403
Bertha Ln 25404
Bessemer Ln 25404
Beth St 25404
Betts Way 25404
Bianca Ct 25405
Binkley Dr 25405
Binns Ct 25405
Bird St N 25405
Bittersweet Ln 25404
Bittinger Ct 25405
Blair St 25404
Blairton Rd 25404
Blake Ct 25404
Blanchard Ln 25403
Blessing Ln 25403
Blossom Dr 25405
Bluestone Ct 25401
Boarman Pl 25401
Bogey Dr 25405
Bollinger Dr 25404
Bolton Ct 25405
Bonnies Way 25405
Boston St 25401
Boston Tea St 25404
Botanical Dr 25405
Botany Dr 25404
Botecelli Ct 25403
Boundary Ln 25403
Bovey Ridge Rd 25403
Bowers St 25401
Bowling Ln 25401
Boyd Ave 25401
Braeburn Dr 25403
Bramblewood Ct 25403
Brandewine Cir 25404
Brant Ln 25403
Bravery Way 25405
Breckinridge Dr 25403
Breeze Hill Ln 25405
Brenda Dr 25404
Brentwood St 25404
Breton Dr 25405
Brian Dr 25405
Bridget Rd 25404
Bridle Path Dr 25404
Brigadere Cir 25404
Bright Cherry Ct 25403
Brilliant Stone Dr 25404
Britania Ct 25405
Brockton Ln 25403
Brommell Cir 25405
Bronco Way 25403
Bronze Ct 25403
Brookdale Ave 25401
Brown Rd 25404
Bruce Dr 25404
Brush Dr 25405
Bryce Ln 25405
Buddy Dr 25405
Buena Vista Dr 25405
Bulldog Blvd 25401
Bumble Bee Ln 25404
Bunting Ave 25405
Burdette Dr 25404
E Burke St
100-247 25401
248-250 25404
249-251 25401
252-599 25404
W Burke St 25401
Burkharts Ln 25405
Burr Ridge Rd 25401
Butler Ave 25405
Butlers Chapel Rd 25403
Buttonwood Ln 25404
Buxton St 25401
Byrd Dr 25401
Cabana Ln 25403
Cabriolet Ct 25401
Cacapon Dr 25401
Caddy Dr 25405
Cadet Ln 25404
E & W Calabash Ct 25405
Calder St 25401
Calebs Pt 25403
Caledonia Dr 25405
Callaway Ct 25403
Cambrian Ct 25403
Cambridge Ct 25403
Camden Ct 25403
Cameron Ln 25405
Campolina Way 25404
Campus Dr 25404
Canadian Dr 25404
Candi Ct 25401
Candlewick Ct 25401
Canterbury Dr 25403
Cape Cod Cir 25403
Caperton Blvd 25403
Capital Dr 25401
Caplinger Dr 25405
Capri Ct 25403
Capricorn Dr 25403
Cara Ct 25401
Care Bear Dr 25401
Care Haven Rd 25405
Carib St 25405
Carlyle Rd 25404
Carmody Ln 25404
Carnegie Links Dr 25405
Carolina St 25401
Carot Ct 25403
Carousel Ln 25404
Carrie Way 25401
Carroll St 25404
Cascades Ln 25405
Cashlin Dr 25403
Cashmere Dr 25404
Cass Dr 25401
Castanea Dr 25403
Casteel Dr 25404
Castlerock Ln 25405
Catalina Pt 25403
Catalpa Ct 25404
Catera Ct 25403
Catherine Ct 25404
Catlett Dr 25405
Catonville Rd 25403
Catrow Rd 25403
Cavalier Ave 25403
Cayman Ct 25404
Cearfoss Ave 25404
Cedar Ln 25404
Celadon Dr 25403
Celebrity Cir 25405
Celeste Dr 25405
Celica Ct 25403
Cemetery Rd 25404
Central Ave 25404
N Centre St 25404
Ceramic Dr 25405

Street	ZIP
Chagall Ln	25403
Champion Ct	25404
Chance Ln	25403
Chapel Wood Ct	25403
Chapman Ave	25404
Chardin Ct	25403
Chardonnay Ave	25405
Charge Ct	25404
Charismatic Ct	25404
Charles Town Rd	
100-348	25405
350-360	25401
362-598	25405
600-2899	25405
Charlotte Ct	25405
Checko Ct	25401
Chestnut St	25401
Cheswick Dr	25403
Chew Ct	25403
Chicken Hawk Dr	25404
Childrens Way	25401
Chillingham Ct	25405
Chipped Cedar Ln	25404
Chris Dr	25404
Christian Tabler Rd N & S	25404
Christina Ln	25403
Chub Ct	25404
N & S Church St	25401
Cicada Dr	25403
Cimarron Dr	25405
Cindy Ct	25403
Cinnamon Dr	25404
Circle Dr	25401
Clarion Ct	25403
Classic Vanville Rd	25405
Clay Rock Dr	25404
Cleanview Dr	25403
Clematis Ct	25401
Clendenin Dr	25404
Cleveland Ln	25405
Clifford Dr	25404
Clock Makers Way	25403
Clohan Ave	25404
Close Dr	25404
Cloud St	25404
Clouser Ct	25405
Clover St	25404
Clyde Borum Rd	25403
Coachman Run Rd	25404
Cobblestone Ct	25403
Cobra Ct	25403
Cody Ct	25403
Cogle Ct	25403
Cold Spring Dr	25405
N & S College St	25401
Collins Dr	25403
Colonel Myers Dr	25404
Colonial Vlg	25401
Columbus Ct	25404
Comet Ln	25405
W Commerce St	25401
Compass Pt	25404
Compassion Dr	25405
Compound Cir	25403
Compton Ln	25404
Concorde St	25404
Cone Ct	25405
Confederate Dr	25403
Congressional Ct & Ln	25405
Connector Rd	25405
Connell St	25404
Constable Ln	25401
Constellation Blvd	25405
Constitution Blvd	25405
Cook Ct	25405
Coot Ln	25405
Copperhead Ln	25403
Coralberry Dr	25401
Corbin Heights Way	25404
Cornelius Grv	25404
Cornerstone Dr	25404
Corning Way	25405
Corrina Dr	25404
Corvette Dr	25405
Cosmos Dr	25404
Cotta Ln	25404
Cottage Rd	25404
County Line Dr	25404
Courthouse Dr	25404
Cozy Retreat	25404
Crab Apple Ct	25403
Cracked Walnut Way	25404
Cranberry Ct	25403
Creasey Way	25404
Creekside Dr	25404
Creighton Ct	25404
Crestview Dr	25405
Crimson Cir	25403
Criswell Dr	25403
Crockett Ln	25405
Cromwell Ct	25403
Crooked Oak Way	25405
Crowell Dr	25401
Crown Ct	25401
Crushed Apple Dr	25403
Crystal Brook Ln	25403
Cumberland Valley Pl	25401
Cumbo Rd	25403
Curlew Ct	25404
Cushwa Rd	25403
Cusick Ct	25403
Cutlip Dr	25404
Cypress Way	25401
Dailey St	25404
Daintree Dr	25403
Daisy Ln	25405
Dale Earnhart Ln	25404
Dali Ct	25403
Dancing Leaf Dr	25403
Dandelion Ln	25405
Daniel St	25401
Darden Ct E & W	25403
Darlington Ct	25405
Davinci Ct	25403
Davis Dr	25404
Dawson Ln	25404
Day Lily Ct	25404
Dead End Ln	25403
Dee Dee Ln	25404
Deer Rd	25404
Degas Ct	25403
N & S Delaware Ave	25401
Delia Way	25405
Delicious Ct	25403
Delmar Orchard Rd	25403
Demure Ln	25404
Dennis St	25401
Derby Ct	25403
Derick Ct	25403
Derossi Way	25405
Desert Rose Way	25404
Desota Way	25401
Dexter Dr	25405
Diamond Ave	25404
Diane Dr	25404
Diesel Ave	25404
Dietrick Dr	25404
Dinali Dr	25403
Dip Bridge Ln	25403
Discovery Rd	25403
District Way	25404
Divine Dr	25403
Divot Dr	25405
Dixie Ln	25403
Doctor Oates Dr	25401
Dodson Ln	25405
Dogwood Ct	25401
Doll Baby Ln	25404
Domestic Way	25401
Domino Ct	25404
Donut Dr	25405
Dora Dr	25405
Doral Ln	25405
Dorset Dr	25404
Dos Ln	25405
Dotage Dr	25403
Douglas Ave	25404
Douglas Grove Rd	25405
Dozer Ln	25405
Drawing Arm Ln	25403
Drumwood Dr & Rd	25403
Dry Run Rd	25403
Duchess Way	25403
Duck Woods Rd	25403
Duff Ct	25405
Duke Rd	25404
Dumpling Dr	25404
Dunbar Ln	25403
Dunnview Dr	25405
Dunrobin Dr	25405
Dupont Rd	25404
Durango Ct	25404
Duvall Ln	25403
Dwight Ct	25405
Dyer Way	25404
Eagle School Rd	25404
East Rd	25404
Easy St	25403
Echo St	25404
Eclipse Ct	25404
Eden Ct	25403
Edgemont Ter	25401
Edsel Ave	25405
Edward Dr	25404
Edwin Miller Blvd	25404
Effie Ln	25404
Egyptian Ln	25404
Eiderdown Dr	25404
Einstein Way	25404
El Dorado Dr	25403
Elaine Ave	25404
Electra Ct	25401
Elegant Dr	25403
Elementary Dr	25404
Elestial Way	25404
Elijah St	25401
Elizabeth St	25404
Elliott Dr	25403
Ellis St	25404
Ellsworth Dr	25403
Elmer Ln	25404
Elwood St	25404
Embassy Ct	25405
Emmett Rousch Dr	25401
Energy Dr	25404
Englewood Ter	25403
English St	25401
Entwine Ave	25405
Equestrian Way	25404
Equinox Way E & W	25401
Erving Dr	25405
Escalade Ln	25403
Evans Run Dr	25405
Evelyn Cir	25404
Evening Star Ln	25404
Evergreen Dr	25405
Exchange Pl	25401
Excursion Dr	25405
Expedition Ct	25403
Explorer Ln	25404
Factory St	25404
Fairfax Ave & St	25401
Fancy Filly Cir	25403
Faraway Pl	25405
Farm Pond Ln	25404
Faulkner Ave	25401
Fawn Haven Ct	25405
Featherbed Rd	25404
Federal Dr	25403
Fellowship Ct	25405
Fenwick Dr	25405
Fern Creek Ln	25404
Ferrarri Ct	25404
Fescue Rd	25405
Files Cross Rd	25404
Firefly Ln	25403
Fiser Ln	25404
Five Point Ave	25404
Flagstaff Cir	25405
Fleetwood Ct	25404
Fletcher Ct	25404
Flight O Arrows Way	25403
Florence Ln	25403
Florida Ave	25401
Foal Ln	25405
Foliage Dr	25403
Fontana Cir	25403
Foothill Ln	25403
Forbes Dr	25404
Forgotten Rd	25403
Foundation Way	25401
Founders Ct	25405
Fountain Head Ln	25401
Foxcroft Ave	25401
Francis Dr	25404
Franklin Ave	25403
Frederick St	25404
Fredonia Cir	25405
Freedom Ln	25405
Friendship Dr	25405
Fritts Dr	25404
Fruit Tree Ln	25405
Fulks Ter	25405
G W Orr Dr	25403
Gabriel Dr	25405
Gail Dr	25403
Gainsboro Dr	25403
Galaxy Ct	25404
Gall Dr	25405
Galloway Rd	25403
Gantt Dr	25403
Gap View Dr	25403
Garden Dr	25404
Garett Dr	25404
Gates St	25401
Gathering Pl	25405
Gauguin Dr	25403
Gemini Ct	25404
Gemstone Dr	25401
Generation Dr	25404
Georgetown Sq	25401
N & S Georgia Ave	25401
Gettysburg Dr	25403
Gib St	25404
Given Ln	25405
Globe St	25404
Glossy Ibis Ln	25405
Gloucester Dr	25401
Gloworm Ln	25404
Gm Access Rd	25403
Gnatcatcher Ln	25405
Gobbler Ln	25403
Godby Cir	25404
Golf Course Rd	
100-199	25404
201-1299	25404
1500-1898	25405
1900-4600	25405
4602-4698	25405
Gondola Dr	25404
Good Dr	25405
Goshen Ln	25404
Gosling Marsh Rd	25404
Gotland Cir	25405
Grace Ave	25404
Grant Pl	25401
Grantham Farm Rd	25403
Grapevine Rd	25405
Grazier St	25404
Grebe Ct	25404
Greenbriar Rd	25401
Greensburg Rd	25404
Gregory Dr	25404
Grenadine Ct	25404
Grimes Dr	25403
Grove Farm Ln	25404
Gulkana Glacier Ln	25403
Gussie Ave	25404
Hack Wilson Way	25401
Hadrian Ct	25403
Haines Ct	25404
Half St	25404
Halifax Ct	25403
Hallmark Dr	25403
Halsey Ct	25405
Hamilton Ct	25403
Hammonds Mill Rd	25404
Hanover Pl	25404
Hanshew Ln	25404
Hargrove Cir	25403
Harlan Spring Rd	25403
Harlan Springs Rd	25403
Harness Race Rd	25404
Harpine Dr	25404
Harris Way	25401
Harvest Mountain Rd	25403
Hawthorne Ave	25401
Health Care Ln	25401
Heartwood Cir	25403
Heather Dr	25404
Hedgesville Rd	25403
Hedrick Ave	25405
Heights Ave	25404
Helmet Dr	25404
Hemmingway Ln	25405
Hensell Dr	25404
Herb Ln	25401
Hercules Dr	25405
Herman Ln	25405
Hermitage Dr	25405
Hershey Ct	25404
Hess Ave	25404
Hewitt Dr	25403
Hialeah Pl	25404
Hickory Ct	25401
N & S High St	25404
Hillcrest Dr	25401
Hinton Ct	25404
Hobart Cir	25405
Hoffman Rd	25404
Hogan Dr	25405
Holden Dr	25403
Holland Dr	25403
Hollida Ln	25404
Hollingsworth Ct	25405
Holly Ln	25401
Holstein Rd	25404
Homemeadow Dr	25405
Honeysuckle Dr	25401
Honor Way	25405
Hood Cir	25403
Hooge St	25404
Hook Dr	25405
Horizon Way	25403
Hospital Dr	25401
Hosta Ct	25401
Hot Springs Dr	25403
Hovermale Ct	25405
Humanitarian Way	25401
Hunters Woods Ln	25404
Huttons Vireo Dr	25405
Hyre Ct	25405
Iberian Ct	25405
Icelandic Ct	25405
Iden Ln	25404
N & S Illinois Ave	25401
Impala Ct	25403
Independence Ln	25405
Industrial Cir	25403
Infinity Way	25405
Innisbrook Ln	25405
Insurance Ct	25404
Integrity Ter	25405
International Ct	25403
Iris Dr	25404
Irish Ln	25403
Iroquois Trl	25403
Isadore Ln	25404
Ives St	25405
Ivey Ct	25401
Izaak Walton Rd	25404
Jackson Pl	25401
Jacobs Rd	25405
Jacqueline Dr	25404
Janesa Dr	25403
Janice St	25404
Jasmine Ln	25401
Jeb Stuart Ln	25403
Jefferson St	25401
Jennings Dr	25404
Jenny Wren Dr	25404
Jensen Way E	25401
Jermanda Ct	25405
Jerry Ct	25401
Jersey Farm Ln	25403
Jerson Ave	25404
Jetta Cir	25403
Jewels Ct	25404
E & W John St	25401
Jolly Rancher Dr	25405
Jonquil Ln	25401
Joshua Dr	25404
Joy Ct	25401
Juicy Grape Ct	25403
Jump St	25404
Junkyard Ln	25405
Jupiter Ct	25404
Justice Ct	25405
Kackley Way	25405
Kapalua Ct	25403
Karickhoff Ct	25404
Karla Ct	25404
Karns Ct	25401
Kaufman Ave	25404
Kelly Island Rd	
1-100	25401
102-298	25401
800-2099	25405
2101-2199	25405
Kendig Ln	25404
Kennedy Cir	25404
Kensington Ter	25405
Kent Ct	25403
N & S Kentucky Ave	25401
Kerrigan Ct	25405
Kesecker Ct	25401
Kia St	25403
Kibler Ct	25404
Kilbourne Ave	25401
Killdeer Ln	25405
Kilmer Ct	25401
Kimberly Dr	25404
E King St	
100-299	25401
300-400	25404
402-498	25404
W King St	25401
Kinkade Ct	25403
Kinship Ln	25404
Kisner Ln	25403
Klee Dr	25403
Kline St	25404
Knoll Dr	25405
Kodiak Dr	25404
Koncer Dr	25404
Kristin Ln	25403
Kyle Dr	25401
Labella Ct	25403
Labonte Dr	25404
Lacosta Blvd	25405
Lady Slipper Ct	25404
Lahaye Dr	25405
Laing Dr	25404
Lakeview Dr	25401
Lancelot Dr	25403
Lancer Pl	25404
Landfill Dr	25405
Lanee Way	25403
Langston Blvd	25404
Lantern Ln	25403
Larkspur Ln	25403
Lasalle Way	25404
Laurel Ct	25401
Lawn St	25405
Leaf Ln	25404
Ledge Dr	25401
Lee St	25404
Lefevre Ln	25404
Legado Dr	25403
Legendary Dr	25404
Legion St	25404
Leighton Dr	25404
Lemir Dr	25404
Leo Ln	25405
Leslie Ln	25405
Lewisburg Ln	25403
E Liberty St	25404
Lights Addition Dr	25404
Lilac Ln	25401
Lillian Way	25404
Limestone Ln	25403
Lina Ln	25405
Lincoln Dr	25401
Linden Ln	25401
Lindsey Ter	25404
Lineweaver Ln	25404
Link Dr	25405
Linwood Way	25403
Lippizan Ct	25405
Lisa Ct	25405
Litchfield Ln E & W	25405
Live Oak Ct	25405
Liverpool Ln	25405
Lizs Way	25405
Lofting Ln	25405
Lois Ln	25404
Lola Way	25405
Longbranch Dr	25405
Loop Rd	25403
Lopez Dr	25405
Lost Rd	25403
Lotus Dr	25404
Louie Ln	25404
N & S Louisiana Ave	25401
Lovelace Way	25401
Loweland Dr	25401
Loyalty Ln	25403
Lucas Ln	25403
Lunar Way	25404
Lupton Dr	25401
Lusitano Ln	25405
Luther Ln	25403
Lutz Ave & Dr	25404
Lynn Haven Dr	25404
Mabdarin Dr	25403
Mabel Ln	25404
Madera Dr	25405
Madison Ave	25404
Magellan Dr	25404
Magnolia Ter	25404
Mahogany Ct	25404
Majestic Dr	25401
Malibu Ct	25405
Mall Dr	25401
Mango St	25401
Manor Dr	25403
N & S Maple Ave	25401
Marcley Dr	25401
Margarets Way	25404
Marie Ln	25405
Marks Dr	25404
Marlene Ave	25404
Marlpit Ln	25404
Marquette Dr	25401
Marshall Ave	25404
Marston Dr	25403
Martha Dr	25405
E Martin St	
100-299	25401
300-399	25404
W Martin St	25401
Martins Landing Cir	25401
Marva Ct	25404
Maryland Ave	25401
Mason Ln	25404
Matilda Ct	25404
May Apple Ln	25403
Mccormick Ln	25404
Mcdaniel Ln	25405
Mcmillan Ct	25404
Mcneill Dr	25403
Meadow Ln	25404
Meadowbrook Cir & Dr	25401
Medford Dr	25404
Medical Ct	25401
Melody Dr	25405
Memorial Park Ave	25401
Memory Ln	25405
Mercedes Dr	25404
Merchants Way	25401
Mercury Ct	25404
Meridian Pkwy	25404
Mermaid Way	25405
Metro Dr	25404
Mid Atlantic Pkwy	25404
Midnoon Dr	25404
Mill Race Dr	25401
Mimosa Dr	25404
Minister Dr	25404
Mira Maple Dr	25405

Street	ZIP
Miracle Ln	25403
Miranda Ct	25403
Miss Staci Dr	25404
Misty Dr	25404
Moats Ln	25404
Model T Ln	25405
Moditti Dr	25403
Mojave Dr	25404
E & W Moler Ave	25404
Monarch Ct	25403
Mong Ct	25405
Monocacy St	25404
Monroe St	25404
Moody Dr	25405
Moonlight Ln	25404
Morgan St	25401
Morlatt Ln	25404
Morrison Dr	25404
Morrow Ave	25404
Mosby Ct	25404
Mossy Ln	25404
Motel Dr	25404
Mount Olive Rd	25405
Mountainview Dr	25404
Mouth Of Opequon Rd	25404
Muddler Ct	25405
Mulberry Dr	25401
Mule Skinner Ln	25405
Mullens Cir	25404
Music Ct	25401
Myers Bridge Rd	25404
Myna Ct	25404
Myriah Dr	25405
Nadenbousch Ln	25405
Nailsworth St	25405
Nameless Way	25404
Nanette Dr	25401
Nascar St	25401
Nash Ct	25401
Natalie Ln	25403
Nathaniel Dr	25403
Natural Way	25404
Near Bethels Way	25405
Nedmonton Rd	25404
Needmore Rd	25403
Needy Rd	25405
New York Ave	25401
Niblick Ct	25405
Nipetown Rd	
1-149	25403
151-1400	25403
1402-1498	25403
1600-1799	25404
Noahs Ct	25404
Nobels Way	25405
Nobility Dr	25405
Noel Dr	25404
North St	25401
Norwalk Ave	25401
Nottingham Blvd	25405
Novak Dr	25405
Oak St	25401
Oconnor Ln	25405
Oden Dr	25405
Oflannery Ct	25403
Okeefe Dr	25403
Old Courthouse Sq	25404
Old Mill Rd	25401
Old Shepherdstown Rd	25404
Oliver Ave	25404
Olympic Dr	25404
Opal Ct	25404
Opequon Ln	25405
Ora Lee Ct	25404
Orbit Ct	25403
Orchard Ave	25401
Oregon Trl	25403
Orion Pl	25404
Orr Dr	25403
Orrick Riner Ln	25403
Osage Ln	25403
Osborne Way	25401
Ottis Beck Ln	25404
Ours Dr	25405
Overlook Dr	25401
Owl Ave	25405
Packard Ct	25401
Packhorse Ford Rd	25405
Pakath Ln	25403
Palestine Cir & Way	25404
Panorama Dr	25403
Parallel Ln	25404
Parasol Trl	25405
Pardalote Ct	25404
Parish Dr	25403
Pastoral Ct	25403
Patience Way	25403
Patriot Ct	25405
Paynes Ford Rd	25405
Payton Ter	25405
Pear Shape Dr	25403
Pendleton Dr	25401
Pennsylvania Ave	25404
Peoples Ct	25405
Peregrine Dr	25405
Periwinkle Pl	25403
Peruvian Paso Dr	25405
Petersburg Ln	25403
Phlox Ln	25404
Phyllis Dr	25404
Picasso Ct	25403
Picnic Ln	25405
Picture Mountain Dr	25404
Piedmont Way	25404
Pierce Arrow Way	25401
Pierpoint Ter	25403
Pikeview Dr	25405
Pillar St	25401
Pilot Way	25405
Pimlico Path	25404
Pineway Dr	25405
Pioneer Ct	25405
Pipestem Dr	25401
Piping Plover Way	25405
Pippin Dr	25403
Pisano Dr	25403
Pisces Pl	25405
Pit Ln	25404
Pitzers Chapel Rd	25403
Place Dr	25401
Planet Ct	25404
Plantation Place Dr	25405
Plaza Ct	25404
Pleasant Ct	25404
Pluto Pl	25404
Plymouth Ln	25404
Pochards Ct	25403
Point Cedar Dr	25404
Polo Greene Dr	25401
Pond Ln	25405
N Poneranc Pkwy E	25404
Pony Cir	25405
Poor House Rd	25403
Pope Farm Rd	25405
Poplar St	25401
Pops Pl	25404
Porshe Cir	25404
Porter Ave	25401
Powell Ln	25404
Powers Rockwell Ln	25405
Prairie Ln	25404
Prayer Ln	25405
Preakness Pl	25404
Prentiss Point Pkwy	25401
Price Dr	25404
Primrose Dr	25404
Princeton St	25404
Prodigy Ct	25405
Professional Ct	25401
Prosperity Ct	25405
Prune Ln	25403
Pulpit Ln	25403
Puppy Drum Ln	25405
Purple Finch Dr	25405
Putters Ct	25405
Quaint Swan Dale Dr	25404
Quality Ter	25403
Quartz Rd	25404
N Queen St	
100-399	25401
401-499	25401
501-537	25404
539-1274	25404
1276-1298	25404
S Queen St	25401
Quicksilver Ct	25404
Quince Tree Dr	25403
E Race St	
100-198	25401
300-599	25404
W Race St	25401
Radiant Dr	25404
Radnor Ln	25404
Raider Ln	25403
Railroad Dr	25404
N & S Raleigh St	25401
Ralphs Ct	25404
Ramblin Rose Ln	25404
Ramer Ct	25401
Rams Ln	25403
Ran Rue Dr	25403
Ranchero Dr	25404
Randolph St	25401
Rankin Cir	25404
Raphael Ct	25403
Raven Blvd	25404
Rebeccas Ct	25403
Recurve Ln	25403
N & S Red Hill Rd	25401
Redemption Way	25403
Reflection Ln	25405
Regiment Ln	25403
Reliance Rd	25403
Renaissance Dr	25403
Republic Dr	25405
Restoration St	25404
Retail Commons Pkwy	25403
Retirement Ln	25404
Rhinestone Ct	25405
Rhonda Ln	25404
Richard St	25404
Rick St	25404
Ridge Rd S	25403
Riordan Dr	25403
Ripe Berry Ln	25403
Ritter Dr	25404
Riviera Dr	25403
Roberts Dr	25404
Roca Ln	25401
Rock Cliff Dr	
1-197	25401
199-1999	25401
2001-2099	25401
2400-2498	25403
2501-2599	25403
Rodeo Dr	25403
Rolling Meadows Dr	25403
Rome Dr	25403
Ropp Dr	25403
N & S Rosemont Ave	25401
Rosewood Dr	25401
Rothwell Ave	25404
Rousch Ct	25401
Roving Dr	25403
Royal Crest Dr	25401
Rubens Cir	25403
Ruddy Duck Ln	25405
Rudolph Ct	25404
Rue De Todd	25403
Ruidoso Downs Dr	25404
Rumsey Ter	25403
Rural Hill Ln	25403
Russett Rd	25403
Ryneal St	25401
Sabre Jet Blvd	25405
Safeguard Ln	25405
Sahalee Ct	25403
Saint Andrews Dr	25403
Saint George St	25405
Salem Church Rd	25403
Salvation Rd	25405
Sandy Dr	25404
Saturn Ct	25404
Savannah Sparrow Ln	25405
Scarlet Oak Dr	25405
Scenic Valley Trl	25404
Scholarship Ln	25404
Schuman Blvd	25405
Scotland Dr	25404
Scrabble Rd	25404
Seal Dr	25405
Seascape Ct	25403
Seattle Slew Way	25403
Secretariat Ln	25403
Security St	25404
Sedge Wren Ln	25405
Sedona Ct	25403
Sentry Ln	25401
Sequest Ln	25405
Serpentine Ln	25405
Seurat Ln	25403
Severna Pkwy	25403
Shadow Ln	25403
Shady Ln	25405
Shaftment Way	25403
Shape Charge Rd	25404
Sharons Ln	25403
Shasta Ln	25401
Shearwater Way	25405
Sheerer Dr	25404
Shellbark Ln	25403
Shenandoah St	25405
Shepherdstown Rd	25404
Sheridan Ave	25401
Shetland Hill Rd	25404
Shipper Ct	25404
Shiraz Cir	25405
Shireoaks Dr	25403
Shoal Creek Ct	25405
Shoap Dr	25405
Shooting Star Ln	25404
Shopkeepers Ln	25404
Showers Ln	25403
Shuykill Dr	25403
Sialia Way	25404
Sidehill Rd	25403
Siebert St	25404
Sierra Dr	25403
Silene Ter	25404
Silver Ln	25401
Skylab Ter	25403
Slonaker Ln	25405
Smallwood Dr	25405
Smarty Jones Cir	25404
Snail Kite Rd	25405
Snapp St	25401
Snead Dr	25405
Snipe Ln	25405
Snooks Ln	25405
Snyders Ln	25405
Soaring Eagle Way	25403
Soft Hickory Ct	25404
Solid Oak Dr	25404
Sonoma Ct	25403
Sopwith Way	25401
E & W South St	25401
Sovereign Way	25403
Spaniel Rd	25404
Sparks Dr	25405
Spartan Dr	25403
Sperow Trl	25404
Sperry Ave	25404
Spicy Cedar Ct	25404
Spider Web Ln	25404
Spillway Ct	25405
Spinners Ln	25401
Spreading Oak Dr	25404
N & S Spring St	25401
Springers Mill Rd	25404
Sprinkle Mill Rd	25404
Spruce St	25401
Spur Rd	25404
Spur Cap Park	25404
Spyglass Dr	25403
Squaw Ter	25403
St George St	25405
Stacy St	25401
Stagshead Ct	25404
Stained Cedar Ct	25404
Starbright Ct	25404
State Cir	25401
Station Ter E & W	25403
Steeple Chase Ln	25404
E & W Stephen St	25401
Sterling St	25404
Stewart Ave	25405
Still Meadow Dr	25405
Stinson Ct	25405
Stitchery Ln	25401
Stoic Acres	25404
Stolipher Rd	25403
Stoney Lick Rd	25403
Stork Ln	25405
Stormfield Dr E & W	25404
Stotelmyer Ln	25405
Strada Dr E & W	25403
Strathmore Way E & W	25403
Strawberry Ln	25404
Street Of Dreams	25403
Stribling Rd	25403
Strine Ave	25404
Striper Dr	25405
Strobridge Rd	25405
Stuckey Ct	25401
Studebaker Ct	25401
Sudley Ln	25403
Sue Ct	25405
Summit Dr	25403
Sumter Dr	25403
Sunset Dr	25405
Supreme Ct	25403
Surrey Ct	25405
Susan Ln	25404
Sushruta Dr	25401
Swan Pond Rd	25404
Swartz St	25404
Sweetbriar Rd	25405
Swinging Bridge Rd	25403
Sycamore Ln & St	25401
Sylvia Ct	25404
Symington Dr	25404
Syracuse Ct	25405
Tabler Station Rd	25403
Talbott Ave	25405
Talisman Dr	25403
Taljen Ave	25403
Tamarack St	25404
Tammy Ln	25405
Tamsens Ct	25403
Tanbridge Dr	25401
Tanglewood Dr	25405
Tanner Ln	25405
Tara Dr	25403
Tarkay Pl	25403
Tarleton Dr	25403
Tasha Ct	25405
Tasker Ln	25404
Tasley Ct	25403
Tather Dr	25405
Taurus Dr	25405
Tavern Rd	
1-97	25401
99-199	25401
200-298	25404
1000-2098	25401
Taylor Way	25404
Teague Ln	25404
Teal Rd N	25405
Temptation Dr	25403
Tenacious Hts	25404
Teneno St	25404
N & S Tennessee Ave	25401
Terrace St	25404
Tersky Ct	25405
Tevis Cir	25404
Texas St	25401
Thanes Way	25403
Thatcher Rd	25403
Thayers Gull Dr	25405
Thistle Ln	25405
Thomas Ln	25401
Thompson St	25401
Thornberry Dr	25403
Thorpe Ln	25404
Tie Run Rd	25405
Tilburg Ln	25405
Timberleaf Ln	25401
Timothy Dr	25405
Tinsman Ln	25403
Titan Pl	25401
Toledo Ln	25404
Topflite Dr	25403
Toronado Dr	25403
Tottenham Cir	25404
Toulouse Ln	25403
Towerview Dr	25404
Trackside Ter	25403
Traders Way	25401
Trafalgar Cir	25404
Train Crossing Dr	25404
Tranines Ct S	25403
Tranquility Ave	25405
Treasure Dr	25403
Trees Bottom Rd	25404
Trent Arden Ct	25405
Trevino Dr	25405
Trevor Ct	25403
Trianigas Dr	25404
Trillium Ct	25401
Trimble Ave	25404
Trinity Church Rd	25403
Trooper Dr	25404
Troy Ave	25404
Trumpet Ln	25404
Truth Way	25405
Turf Dr N & S	25405
Turnbuckle	25405
Turner Dr	25404
Tuscarora Pike	25403
N & S Tuskegee Dr	25401
Twigg Dr	25404
Twin Lakes Cir	25405
Twisting Run Ln	25405
Two Sisters Way	25404
Tyler Way	25404
Union Ave	25404
Universe Dr	25404
Upper Rd	25404
Utica Ct	25405
Valentine Dr	25405
N & S Valley St	25401
Van Clevesville Rd	25405
Vane Dr	25403
Vaquero Dr	25403
Variform Dr	25405
Vast St	25404
Vaughndom Way	25404
Verbena Ter	25404
Verde Dr	25404
Verity Dr	25405
Vermeer Ln	25401
Veronica Dr	25404
Vestal Gap Way	25404
Veterans Way	25405
Vicksburg Ct	25404
Vicky Bullett St	25404
Victoria Dr	25403
Vienna Way	25404
View Creek Ct	25405
S Viking Way	25401
Vine Cir	25405
Vintage Ct	25401
W Virginia Ave	25401
Virginia Avenue Ext	25401
Virgo Ln	25404
N & S Vista Ln	25401
Volkswagen Rd	25405
Vonette Dr	25405
Wager Ln	25404
Wagley Dr	25404
Wagner Dr	25405
Wakeman Dr	25403
Wall St	25401
Walnut St	25401
Walter Dr	25403
Waltson Dr	25403
Warm Springs Ave	25404
Warren Clark Dr	25403
Washington Ave	25401
Wasser Dr	25403
S Water St	25401
Watkins Ferry Way	25404
Waverly Ct	25403
Waxed Cherry Ct	25404
Wayne Ave	25404
Weatherburn Ter	25403
Weaver Ln	
2-198	25404
200-298	25403
300-1000	25403
1002-1498	25403
Webb Ct	25405
Weller Dr	25403
Welltown School Rd	25403
N Western Ave	25404
Wheatland St	25405
Whippet Ct	25401
Whirlwind Dr	25404
Whitacre Ave	25404
White Ave	25401
White Oaks Dr	25404
Whitings Neck Rd	25404
Whitney Way	25401
Whitonia Way	25404
Wildflower Creek Dr	25404
Wilkins Ct	25404
Williamsport Pike	25404
Willingham Way	25404
Wilson St	25401
Wilt Dr	25405
Winchester Ave	
200-1120	25401
1122-1128	25401
1200-5599	25405
5601-5699	25405
Winchester Pike	25405
Winebrenner Rd	25404
Winslow Dr	25404
Woodbury Ave	25404
Woolen Mill Rd	25403
Working Deere Dr	25403
Worthy Dr	25401
Wr Caskey Dr	25404
Wren St N	25405
Wycliff Dr	25403
Yardley Ct	25405
Yarrow Cir	25404
Yeakley Dr	25403
Yoakum Ave	25404
York Rd	25403
Yorktown St	25404
Yountz Dr	25405
Zaharias Dr	25405
Zeiler Dr	25404

NUMBERED STREETS

Street	ZIP
All Street Addresses	25404

MORGANTOWN WV

General Delivery	26505

POST OFFICE BOXES MAIN OFFICE STATIONS AND BRANCHES

Box No.s	ZIP
1 - 1900	26507
2001 - 2776	26502
4001 - 4760	26504
5001 - 5240	26507
6000 - 6897	26506
7000 - 7000	26507
8000 - 9897	26506
18001 - 18238	26507

NAMED STREETS

Street	ZIP
Aarons Creek Rd	26508
Abby Ln	26508
Abigail Ct	26508
About Town Pl	26508
Ackerman Rd	26508
Adam Heights Rd	26508
Adams St	26501

Adeline Ave 26501
Afton St 26505
Agronomy Farm Rd 26508
Airport Blvd 26505
Alamosa Ct 26508
Albany St 26501
Alcova 26505
Alderman Dr 26508
Alexander Dr 26508
Alicia St 26501
Allamong Ln 26508
Allegheny Ct 26508
Allen Ave 26505
Allison St 26501
Alma St 26501
Almost Heaven Way 26508
Alpine St 26505
Alum St 26505
Amarillo St 26508
Amber Rdg 26508
Amherst Rd 26505
Amy Dr 26501
Anchorage Ln 26508
Anderson Ave & Pl 26505
Andmore St 26505
Andover St 26505
Andrew Dr 26508
Angel Falls Way 26508
Animal Science Farm Rd 26505
Anini Dr 26508
Ann St 26501
Ann Marie Dr 26508
Anna Furnace Cir 26508
Anthony Dr 26508
Antietam Dr 26508
Apolla Dr 26501
Apple Ln 26505
Apple Meadow Ln 26508
Appleway Dr 26505
Arabela Ct 26508
Arbogast Ln 26508
Arcadia Dr 26508
Arch St
300-599 26501
1100-1199 26508
Arena Rd 26501
Arkwright Ave 26505
Arlington St 26501
Arnold Hall 26506
Arrowwood Dr 26508
Arwick Ave 26508
Ash St 26501
Ashbrooke Sq 26508
Ashebrooke Sq 26508
Ashland Ave 26505
Ashley Oaks 26505
Ashton Dr & Pl 26508
Ashwood Ln 26508
Ashworth Ln 26508
Aspen St 26505
Astor Ave 26501
Auburn Dr 26501
Augusta Ave 26501
Aurora Dr 26508
Austin Way 26508
Autumn Ave 26508
Avalon St 26501
Avery Dr & Knl 26508
Axel Ave 26505
Babbling Brooke Ests 26508
Bailes Ave 26505
Bailey Cir 26508
Baird St 26505
Baker St 26508
Bakers Dr, Lndg & Pt 26505
Bakers Cemetary Dr 26508
Bakers Ridge Rd
100-1221 26508
1222-1399 26505
Baldwin St 26505
Baltimore St 26501
Bancroft Dr 26508
Banner Pl 26508
Barberry Ln 26508
Barbour Rd 26508
Barclay Dr 26508
Barker Ave 26508
Barker St 26501
Barrickman St 26501
Bartges Rd 26508
Bartlow St 26505
Bates Rd 26505
Battelle Ave 26505
Bayberry Ter 26508
Beaumont Dr 26508
Beaver Ave 26505
Beaver Cove Way 26508
Beech St 26501
Beechurst Ave 26505
Beechwood Ave 26505
Beekman Ln 26508
Bell Ln 26508
Bellaire Dr 26505
Belle View Dr 26508
Belmar Ave 26505
Bendview Ave 26501
Bennett Dr 26508
Bennett Tower 26506
Bent Tree Ct 26505
Benten Grv 26508
Bergamont St 26505
Berkshire Dr 26508
Bernard Ln 26508
Bernerth Rd 26508
Bernita Way 26508
Berwood Dr 26505
Bethel Rd 26501
Betty St 26501
Beulah Rd 26508
Beverly Ave 26505
Bierer Ln 26508
Big Buck Ln 26508
Big Mountain Dr 26508
Big Rock Rd 26508
Bill Willard Rd 26501
Birch Ln & St 26505
Birch Hollow Rd 26508
Birchfield Run Rd 26501
Birds Eye View Dr 26501
Bishop Dr 26505
Bitonti St 26505
Black Bear Ln 26508
Black Hawk Dr 26508
Blackberry Ln 26508
Blackberry Ridge Dr 26508
Blackstone Dr 26508
Blanchita Pl 26508
Blaney Ln 26508
Blaney Hollow Rd 26508
Bloody Run Rd 26508
Blossom Dr & Ln 26508
Blue Grass Vlg 26501
Blue Horizon Dr 26501
Blue Ridge Ln 26508
Blue Sky Ln 26508
Blue Stone Dr 26501
Blueberry Hills Dr 26508
Bluebird Cir 26508
Bob White Ln 26508
Bobcat Run 26508
Bonasso St 26508
Bonfili Ln 26501
Booth Rd 26501
Boreman Hall 26506
Bortz Mine Rd 26508
Boston St 26508
Boughner Ln 26505
Boulder Rd 26508
Bounds Cir 26501
Bowers Ln 26508
Bowlby Hill Rd 26501
Boy Scout Camp Rd 26508
Boyers Ave 26505
Braddock St 26505
Bradford Ln 26508
Bradley St 26505
Braewick Dr 26505
Brains Run Rd 26508
Brand Rd 26501
Brandon St 26501
Brandonville Ter 26508
Brands Run Rd 26501
Brandywine Est 26508
Brandywine Estates Dr 26508
Braxton Tower 26506
Breakiron Hill Rd 26508
Breezewood Ln 26508
Breezy Dr 26501
Bretton Ct 26508
Bretton Woods 26508
Brettwald Dr 26508
Brettwood Ln 26508
Bretz St 26505
Brewer Rd 26508
Brian Pl 26505
Briar Lea Ln 26508
Briar Patch Ln 26505
Briarwood Ct & St 26505
Brickyard Ave 26505
Bridge Rd 26508
Broadmore Ln 26508
Broadview Dr 26505
Broadway Ave 26505
Brockton Dr 26508
E Brockway Ave 26501
Brook Vw 26508
Brook Ridge Ln 26508
Brookdale Dr 26508
Brooke Ave 26505
Brooke Tower 26506
Brookhaven Rd 26508
Brookings Dr 26508
Brookline Rd 26508
Brooks St 26508
Brookside Ln & Pl 26505
Brookstone Plz 26508
Brookwood Dr 26508
Brown St 26505
Brown Chapel Rd 26508
Brown Haron Rd 26508
Brownstone Dr 26505
Bruce Sliger Rd 26508
Brunswick Ct 26508
Bryan Dr 26508
Bryanna Ct 26508
Bryant St 26501
Bryson Ave 26505
Brytes Way 26508
Bubbys Ln 26508
Buck Cool Rd 26501
Buckhannon Ave
2-8 26501
10-400 26501
402-498 26501
1100-1799 26508
Buckhannon St 26501
Buckingham Rd 26508
Bucy Rd 26508
Bull Run Rd 26508
Bunker Rd 26501
Burke St 26505
Burns St 26505
Burns Church Rd 26508
Burnt Meeting House Rd 26501
Burroughs St 26505
Butler Dr 26508
Buxton Ln 26508
Cable Ln 26508
Caddell St 26501
Cadet Ct 26508
Cain St 26505
Callen Ave 26501
Cambridge Ave 26505
Camby Rd 26508
Camden St 26501
Camp Mountaineer Rd 26508
Camp Run Rd 26508
Campus Dr 26505
Candlelight Dr 26508
Canfield St 26505
Canterberry Dr 26505
Cantis Hilltop Villas 26508
Canton Ave 26505
W Canyon Cv, Dr, Rd & Vlg 26508
Canyon Gorge Rd 26508
Canyon School Rd 26508
Cardiff Dr 26508
Cardinal Cir 26508
Carlisle Ave 26505
Carmell Ct 26505
Carnegie St 26505
Carolina Ave 26501
Caroline Ln 26508
Carrol Rd 26508
Carrol Sawmill Rd 26508
Carson St 26505
Casey Ln 26508
Cass St 26505
Cassina Dr 26505
Cassville Mount Morris Rd 26501
Castle Ct 26508
Catalpa St 26505
Caterpillar Rd 26508
Cathy Dr 26505
Cave Rock Rd 26508
Cayton St 26505
Cedar Cir 26508
Cedar Ct 26505
Cedar Ln 26508
Cedar St 26501
Cedarstone Ct & Rd 26505
Cedarwood Dr 26505
Center Aly 26505
Center St
2-98 26501
400-699 26505
1100-1199 26508
Centerhill Ave 26505
Central Ave 26505
Chalfant Ln 26505
Champagne Dr 26508
Chancery Row 26505
Chaplin Rd 26501
Chardonnay Dr 26508
Charles Ave & St 26505
Charleston Ave 26501
Chase St 26508
Chasewood Ln 26508
Chateau Royale Ct 26505
Cheat Rd 26508
Cheat Canyon Park Dr 26508
Cherokee Dr 26508
Cherry Ln 26505
Cherry St
200-299 26501
2100-2199 26505
Cherry Hill Rd 26508
Cherry Wood Dr 26508
Chestnut Hls & St 26505
Chestnut Ridge Rd 26505
Chicago Ave 26501
Chickadee Ln 26508
Chico Dr 26505
Chipps Holw 26505
Christy St 26505
Church Hill Dr 26505
Cimarron Pl 26508
Circle Dr 26505
Citadel Rd 26505
Cityview Dr 26501
Civitan St 26505
Claremont Ct 26501
Clark Rd 26508
Clark St 26501
Clay St 26501
Clayton Dr 26508
Clear Mountain Way 26505
Clear Spring Dr 26508
Clearview Ave 26505
Clearwood Dr 26508
Clemmer Ct 26508
Cleveland Ave 26501
Cliffside Ln 26501
Clinton Ave 26505
Clover St 26505
Clover Meadow Ln 26508
Cobblestone Cir 26505
Cobun Ave 26501
Cobun Rdg 26508
Cobun Creek Rd 26508
Cobun Valley Ln 26508
Cody Dr 26508
Cold Springs Rd 26501
Coles Ct 26508
College Ave 26505
Collins Ferry Rd 26505
Colonial Dr 26505
W Colony Est 26501
Colorado Ave 26501
Columbia St 26505
Columbus St 26501
Comfort Inn Rd 26508
Commerce Dr 26501
Community Dr 26505
Congress Ave 26505
Conn St 26501
Connecticut Ave 26501
Cool Rd 26501
Coombs Rd 26501
Cooms Farm Rd 26508
Cooper St 26501
Cooper Beach Dr 26508
Coopers Rock Incline 26508
Copper Beach Way 26508
Copper Creek Ct 26505
Copperfield Ct 26505
Corbin Vlg 26508
Corfu Ln 26508
Cornell Ave 26505
Cornerstone Vlg 26508
Corona Dr 26508
Corporate Dr 26501
Corton Pl 26508
Corvet Ave 26505
Cottage St 26501
Cottagewood Ln 26508
Cottonwood Ct & St 26505
Cottrell Ln 26508
Country Club Dr 26505
Country Squire Vlg 26508
Country View Ln 26505
Court St 26505
Courtney Ave 26501
Cove Point Dr 26508
Cowell St 26501
Cox Pl 26501
Crammys Run Rd 26508
Cranberry Sq 26508
Crawford Ave 26505
Creek Rd 26508
Creekside Dr 26508
Creekview Ln 26508
Crescent Heights Trailer Ct 26505
Cress Ln 26508
Crest Dr 26501
Creston Ave 26505
Crestview Dr 26505
Crestwood Dr 26505
Crimson Sky Dr 26508
Crosby Rd 26508
Cross Ln 26508
Crowl St 26501
Crown Point Dr 26508
Cryster Ln 26508
Cub Ln 26508
Curtis Ave 26501
Cypress St 26505
Dadisman Hall 26506
Daffodil Rd 26501
Dairy Ln 26508
Dallas St 26505
Dalton Rd 26508
Dana Ln 26508
Dandelion Ln 26501
Daniel Paul Dr 26501
Darlington Rd 26501
Darnell Dr 26508
Darnell Hollow Rd 26508
Darrah Ave & Ct 26508
Darst St 26505
Dartmouth St 26505
Davis Ave 26501
Davis Rd 26508
Davis St 26501
Davis Hill Ln & Rd 26501
Dawn Dr 26501
Dawson Rd 26501
Dayton St 26505
December Ln 26508
Deckers Creek Blvd
1-599 26501
1400-1499 26508
1500-1699 26505
Deer Run 26508
Deer Ridge Ct 26508
Deerfield Ct 26508
Deerwood Dr 26508
Deland Ave 26505
Delaware Ave 26501
Delbert Ln 26508
Dellslow Ln 26508
Delphi Ln 26508
Delrose Dr 26508
Demain Ave & Ct 26501
Dents Run Rd 26501
Denver Ave 26505
Des Moines Ave 26505
Detroit St 26501
Devin Ln 26508
Devon Rd 26505
Dewey St 26501
Dewitt Farm Rd 26508
Diamond Ave & Ct 26505
Digman Gln 26508
Dille St 26505
Discovery Pl 26508
Distributor Dr 26501
District Dr 26505
Dmr Rentals 26508
Dobbs St 26501
Dockview Ln 26508
Dogwood Ave 26505
Dogwood Est 26508
Domain Dr 26501
Don Knotts Blvd
2-99 26508
101-697 26501
699-900 26501
902-966 26501
Donaldson Ct 26508
Donaldson Addition 26508
Donley St 26501
Donna Ave 26505
Doris Rd 26501
Dormont St 26501
Dorsey Ave & Ln 26501
Dorsey Knob Rd 26508
Douglas Ave 26505
Dove Dr 26508
Downs Ave 26505
Downwood Manor Dr 26508
Doyle St 26505
Dream Catcher Cir 26508
Drummond St 26505
Dudley St 26505
Dug Hill Rd 26508
Dunkard Ave 26501
Dunn St 26505
Dunn Cemetary Rd 26508
Dupont Hts & Rd 26501
Duquesne St 26505
Durham Ln 26508
Dustin Ln 26501
Duvall Ln 26501
Eagle Run 26508
Earl C Atkins Dr 26501
Earl L Core Rd
1200-1999 26505
2001-2099 26505
3000-5399 26508
East St 26501
Eastern Ave 26505
Eastern Trl 26508
Eastgate Dr, Mnr & Plz 26508
Eastlake Dr 26508
Eastland Ave 26505
Easton Ave 26501
Easton Hl 26505
Easton Mill Rd 26508
Eastwood Ln 26508
Ebenklein Ln 26508
Eclipse Dr 26508
Ed Dunn Rd 26508
Eddy Rd 26501
Eden Church Rd 26508
Edgehill St 26501
Edgewood St 26501
Edna Gas Rd 26501
Edward St 26501
Edwin St 26501
Eisenhower St 26505
El Paso Ave 26508
Eldon Ln 26508
Eleanor Dr 26508
W Electric Dr 26508
Elgin St 26501
Elizabeth Valley Rd 26508
Eljadid St 26505
Elk St 26505
Elk Mountain Ave 26501
Elkins Dr 26505
Ellen Ln 26505
Elm St 26501
Elm Crest Ct 26508
Elmer Prince Dr 26505
Elmhurst St 26505
Elmina St 26501
Elyse Ln 26508
Elysian Ave 26501
Emerald Ct 26505
Emil Dr 26508
Emma Kaufman Camp Rd 26508
E End Ave 26505
Engineering Blvd 26501
England Rd 26508
Ensign Ave 26505
Eric St 26501
Erow Ave 26505
Estate Dr 26508
Euclid Ave 26501
Eugeniva Ave 26505
Eureka Dr 26505
Evans St 26505
Everettville School Rd 26501
Evergreen Ln 26505
Everhart Dr 26508
Everlasting Ln 26505
E Everly St 26505
Excalibur Dr 26508
F St 26501
Fairchance Rd 26508
Fairfax Dr 26505
Fairfield Mnr & St 26505
Fairlawns Ave 26505
Fairmont Rd 26501
Fairmor Dr 26501
Fairview Ave 26505
Fairview Rd 26508
Fairway Dr 26508
Falcon Run 26508
Falcon Crest Way 26508
Fallen Oak Rd 26508
Falling Run Rd 26505
Falling Water Ln 26508
Falls Ave 26505
Far Mdws 26508
Farm View Rd 26505
Farrell St 26505
Fawn Ln 26508
Fawnhaven Way 26508
Fayette St 26505
Fcx Ln 26501
Fenwick Ave 26505
Fern St 26501
Ferry St 26501
Fieldcrest Hall 26506
Fields Park Rd 26508
Fife St 26505
Finch Rd 26508
Finnell St 26505
Fire Department Rd 26508
Flagel St 26505
Flaggy Meadow Rd 26501
Flat Field Ln 26501
Flatts Ln 26505

Fleming Rd 26501
Florida Ave 26501
Folger St 26505
Foothills Ln 26508
Ford St 26501
Forest Ave & Dr 26505
Forest Heights Dr 26505
Forks Of Cheat Forest Rd 26508
Forman Dr 26508
Fort Pierpont Dr 26508
Fortney St 26505
Founders Way 26508
Foundry St 26505
Fountain Vw 26505
Fox Ln 26508
Fox Run Ct 26508
Foxchase Way 26508
Foxtown Dr 26508
Foxtrot Dr 26508
Frank Burchinal Rd 26508
Franklin Dr & St 26501
Fredd St 26501
Frederick Ln 26508
Frederick Ice Cir 26508
Fredrick St 26501
Freestone Way 26508
French Quarters Dr 26505
Friend Dr 26508
W Front Ave & St 26501
Frontier Ave 26505
Frum St 26505
Frymyer Ln 26501
Fullmer St 26505
G St 26501
Gabbertville Rd 26501
Gainer St 26508
Gallatin Ave 26505
Galloway Dr & Ln 26508
Gallus Rd 26501
Galusky Ln 26501
Gamble Rd 26501
Gans St 26501
Garden Ln 26501
Garfield St 26501
Garlow Dr 26508
Garrett St 26505
Garrison Ave 26505
Garrison St 26501
W Gaston St 26501
Gem St 26505
George Rd 26508
George St 26505
Georgia Ave 26501
Georgian Ln 26508
Ghuste Dr 26508
Gibbons St 26505
Gibson St 26508
Gifford Ave 26501
Gilmore St 26505
Giuliani Ln 26501
Gladesville Rd 26508
Glen Abbey Ln 26508
Glen Oaks Dr 26508
Glencoe Ln 26508
Glendon St 26505
Glenmark Ave & Ct 26505
Glenn St 26505
Globe Ave 26501
Glory Barn Rd 26501
Gobblers Run 26508
Goff St 26501
Gold Pt 26508
Golden Acres 26501
Golden Eagle Dr 26508
Golden Leaf Way 26508
Goodwin St 26501
Goodwin Hill Rd 26508
Goose Holw 26508
Goose Hollow Rd 26508
Gordon St 26501
Goshen Rd 26508
Grace Ln 26508
Grafton Rd 26508
Grand St 26501
Grand Central Station Dr 26505
Grandview Ave 26501
Grant Ave 26505
Grants Dr 26505
Grapevine 26505
W Green Dr 26508
Green St 26501
Green Acres Dr 26501
Green Apple Ln 26501
Green Valley Vlg 26501
Greenbag Rd
1-300 26501
302-498 26501
401-499 26508
501-599 26501
600-1500 26508
1502-2198 26508
3200-5099 26501
Greenbrier St 26501
Greentree Dr 26508
Greenview Dr 26508
Greenway Ave 26508
Greenwood Dr 26505
N Greystone Cir & Dr 26508
Grove St
100-199 26501
400-799 26505
Gully Ln 26508
Gum Springs Rd 26508
Guston Run Rd 26501
Guthrie Ln 26508
H St 26501
Hagans Rd & St 26501
Hailey Ln 26505
Halleck Rd 26508
Halpine St 26505
Hampton Ave & Ctr 26505
Hampton North Vlg 26508
Hanalei Dr 26508
Hanna Ln 26505
Harbor Dr 26508
Hard Rock Rd 26508
Harding Ave 26505
Hardy St 26505
Hare Ln 26508
Harewood Dr & Mnr 26508
Harley Dr 26508
Harner Run 26508
Harner St 26501
Harrison St
1-99 26501
800-899 26505
Hart Field Rd 26505
Hartford St 26501
Hartman St 26505
Hartman Run Rd 26505
Harvard Ave 26505
Harvatis St 26508
Harvest Dr 26508
Harvest Ridge Ln 26508
Harvey St 26501
N & S Harwich Cir 26508
Haskell Ln 26508
Hatfield Pl 26505
Haven Ct 26508
Hawks Nest Dr 26508
Hawks Run Rd 26508
Hawley Ln 26505
Hawthorne Ave 26505
Hawthorne Vlg 26508
Hayden Ln 26505
Hayes St 26501
Hayfield St 26508
Headlee Ave 26505
Healthy Heights Vlg 26508
Heather Dr & St 26505
Heaven Hill Rd 26508
Heavy Rd 26508
Heavy Haul Rd 26508
Helmick Rd 26501
Hemlock Ct 26508
Henry Clay Dr 26508
Heritage Pl & Pt 26505
Herman Ave 26505
Herrington Manor Dr 26508
Hertzog Ln 26508
Hess St 26501
Hickory Dr 26508
Hickory Ln 26505
Hickory St 26505
Hickory Hills Dr 26508
Hickory Park Vlg 26508
Hickory Ridge Rd 26508
Hidden Point Trl 26508
Hidden Valley Rd 26501
Hidden View Way 26508
High St 26505
N High St 26505
S High St 26501
W High St 26501
Highland Ave 26505
Highland St 26501
Highview Pl 26505
Hildebrand Lock And Dam Rd 26501
Hill Ln 26508
Hill St 26505
Hillary Dr 26508
W Hillcrest Ave 26501
Hillcrest St 26505
Hilling Ln 26508
S & W Hills Dr & Plz 26501
Hilltop Ln 26508
Hillview Dr 26505
E Hillview Dr 26508
Hillview Ests 26501
Hillwood Dr 26508
Hinton St 26501
Hirshman St 26501
Hite St 26501
Hoard Rd 26508
Hobson St 26501
Hodges St 26505
Hoffman Ave 26505
Hogue St 26501
Holland Ave 26501
Holly Ln
100-104 26505
106-298 26508
300-499 26508
Holly Ridge Dr 26508
Honeysuckle Hl 26501
Hoot Owl Ln 26508
Hoover Aly 26505
Horizon Dr 26508
Hornbeck Rd 26508
Horsemans Trl 26508
Horseshoe Rd 26508
Horton Ln 26508
Houndstooth Ln 26508
Houston Dr 26505
Huckleberry Ln 26508
Hudson St 26501
Hummingbird Ln 26508
Humphreys Rd 26508
Hunter Ln 26505
Hunters Way 26505
Huntington Ave 26501
Hurley St 26501
Husgavarna Dr 26508
Hyatt Ave 26505
Ices Ferry Dr 26508
Idacore Ln 26505
Idlewood St 26505
Impala Ct 26501
Imperial Dr & Vw 26508
Imperial Woods Dr 26508
Independence St 26505
Independence Hills Vlg 26505
Industrial Ave 26505
Inglewood Blvd 26505
Iris Ln 26501
Irish Rd 26501
Iron Bridge Cir 26508
Iron Mountain Dr 26508
Iroquois Way 26508
Irving Ct 26508
Irwin St 26505
Itty Bitty Vl 26508
Ivy St 26501
J D Anderson Dr 26505
Jacks Auto Ln 26508
W Jackson Ave & St 26501
Jaco Dr 26505
Jacobs Dr & St 26505
Jade Dr 26508
James St
700-899 26505
900-999 26508
Jamestown Dr 26508
Janice Dr 26508
Jayden Dr 26508
Jeff Hayden Rd 26508
W Jefferson Ct & St 26501
Jeffrey Vlg 26501
Jenny Lynn Ct & Est 26508
Jeremy Ln 26508
Jerome St 26505
Jersey Ave 26505
Jester Ct 26508
Jewel Dr 26508
Jo Glen Dr 26508
Joe Bridge Dr 26508
Joes Run Rd 26508
John Fox Rd 26501
John Poole Rd 26508
Johnathan Ln 26508
Johns St 26505
Johnson Ave 26505
Johnson Ln 26508
Johnson Way 26508
Jones Ave 26505
Jordan Ln 26501
Joshua Way 26508
Junction St 26505
June Ln 26508
Junior Ave 26505
Kanar Dr 26508
Kansas St 26501
Karen Ln 26501
Katelyn Ln 26501
Kathryn Dr 26508
Kaustin Dr 26501
Kay St 26501
Kaylan Dr 26508
Keener Rd 26508
Keener St 26501
Kelly Rd 26505
Kendall Mill Rd 26508
Kendall Ridge Pl 26501
Kenmore St 26505
Kennedy Dr 26508
Kennedy Store Rd 26508
Kenneth Ln 26501
Kensington Ave 26505
Kentucky St 26501
Kenwood Pl 26505
Kenyon Vlg 26508
Kermit Pl 26501
Keyser Ave 26505
Killarney Dr 26505
King Rd 26508
King St 26501
Kings Rd 26508
Kingsland Cir 26508
Kingston Dr 26505
Kingwood Pike 26508
Kingwood St 26501
Kirk St 26505
Kisner Cove Rd 26508
Kiwanis Ave 26505
Knob St 26505
Koehler Dr 26508
Kolbe St 26508
Koontz Ave 26505
Krepps Ave & St 26505
Kuykendall Ln 26508
Lafollette Dr 26508
Laguna Dr 26508
Lake Pt 26508
Lake St
500-599 26505
1000-1098 26501
Lake Crest Ln 26508
Lake Lynn Dr 26508
Lakeland Ave 26505
Lakeside Dr, Ests & Vlg 26508
Lakeside Village Dr 26508
Lakeview Dr & Mnr 26508
Lakeview Estate Townhomes 26508
Lakewood Ctr 26508
Lambert St & Vlg 26501
Lamesa Vlg 26508
Lamplighter Dr & Ln 26508
Lancaster Dr 26508
Landfill Rd 26505
Landis Ln 26501
Lane St 26501
Langford Ave 26501
Lashley St 26505
Lassie Ln 26508
Laura Lee Ests 26508
Laurel Ct 26508
Laurel St 26505
Laurel Ridge Dr 26508
Laurel Wood Dr 26508
Law Center Dr 26505
Lawless Rd 26501
Lawnview Dr 26505
Lawnwood St 26501
Lawrence St 26508
Lazzelle Union Rd 26501
Leah Dr 26508
Lebanon St 26501
Ledgeview Ct 26508
Lee St 26501
Leeway St 26505
Legacy Dr 26508
Legion St 26505
Lehigh Dr 26508
Leland St 26501
Lemley St 26508
Lenora Dr 26501
Leonard St 26501
Leonidas Ln & Way 26508
Lewellyn Rd 26508
Lewis Lndg & St 26505
Lexington Ave 26501
Liberty St 26505
Lilac Ln 26501
Lillian St 26501
Lilly St 26505
W Lincoln Ave 26501
Lincova Ave 26505
Linda Ln 26508
Lindel St 26505
Linden St 26501
Linn St 26501
Linnehurst St 26505
Linwood Rd 26505
Lions Ave 26505
Listravia Ave 26505
Little Falls Rd 26508
Little Indian Creek Rd 26501
Lloyd St 26505
Loch Haven Dr 26508
Lockside Rd 26501
Lockview Ave 26501
Lockwood Dr 26508
Locust Ave 26505
Log Cabin Rd 26508
Logan Ave 26501
Lola Ln 26501
London Pl 26508
Long Aly
200-399 26501
2000-2099 26505
Long Branch Dr 26508
Longdon St 26505
Longhorn Ln 26508
Lookout Ln 26508
Lorentz St 26505
Lough St 26501
Louise Ave 26505
Lower Aarons Creek Rd 26508
Lower Booth Rd 26501
Lower Hildebrand Rd 26501
Lubbuck Ln 26508
Lucas Dr 26505
Lucille Ln 26501
Luckey Ln 26501
Lucy Ln 26501
Luke St 26508
Lydia Ln 26508
Lynch Rd 26501
Lyndhurst St 26501
Lynn Ave 26501
Lyon Tower 26506
Mackey Ln 26508
Macomb St 26501
Maczko Dr 26508
Madeline Cir 26508
Madigan Ave 26501
Madison Ave 26501
Madora Dr 26505
Magnolia Dr 26508
N Main St 26505
W Main St 26501
Majestic Dr 26508
Maleah Ct 26508
Mall Rd 26501
Mallard Run 26508
Malone Dr 26501
Manchester Dr 26505
Manor Pl 26505
Mansfield Ave 26505
Mansion St 26505
Mansman Ln 26508
Manville St 26501
Maple Ave 26501
Maple Ct 26508
Maple Dr 26505
Maple Ln 26505
Maple St 26505
Maple Grove Ave 26501
Maple Leaf Ln 26508
Mapleleaf Ln 26508
Marble Dr 26508
March Ln 26508
Marchand Dr 26501
Marco Polo Dr 26508
Marcus Ct & Dr 26501
Marcus Point Dr 26501
Maren Ln 26508
Marie Ln 26508
Mariner Vlg 26508
Mariners Plz 26508
Marion St 26505
Mark Ln 26508
Marlington Ave 26501
Marshall Ave 26501
Martin Ln 26501
Martin St 26505
Martin Hollow Rd 26501
Marvin St 26505
Marvins Gdns 26508
Mary Ln 26508
Mary Ann Ln 26501
Maryland Ave & St 26501
Mason Ave & St 26505
Mason Dixon Hwy 26501
Master Graphics Rd 26501
Mathess Ln 26508
Matthew Dr 26508
Maxey St 26505
Mayfield Ave 26505
Mayfield Rd 26508
Mccartney Ave 26505
Mccormick Hollow Rd 26508
Mccullough St 26505
Mcdonald Ln 26508
Mcgara St 26501
Mcginnis Vlg 26501
Mckinley Ave 26505
Mckinley St 26501
Mckinney Cave Rd 26508
Mclane Ave 26505
Meadow Brooke Dr 26508
Meadow Ridge Townhomes 26505
Meadow River Rd 26508
Meadow View Ln 26508
Meadowbrook Rd 26505
Meadowland Dr 26508
Meadows Dr 26505
Mechanic St 26501
Med Center Dr 26505
Medical Center Dr 26505
Medley Ridge Dr 26508
Mel Brand Rd 26501
Melrose Aly & St 26505
Melvin Fields Rd 26508
Memorial Church Dr 26501
Memory Ln 26501
Meridan St 26505
Merideth St 26508
Merrifield St 26505
Mesa St 26505
Mescal Ln E & W 26501
Meteor Dr 26508
N Metro Dr 26501
Metro Tower Ln 26505
Michelle St 26501
Michigan Ave 26501
Mid Atlantic Dr 26508
Mildred St 26501
Mileground Rd & Vlg 26505
Milford St 26505
Millan St 26501
Miller St
800-900 26505
902-998 26505
1100-1199 26508
Miller Hill Rd 26501
Milton St 26505
Mimosa Ln 26505
Mineral Ave 26505
Mingo St 26501
Miramichi Trl 26508
Mississippi St 26501
Missouri St 26501
Misty Meadow Ct 26508
Molisee Rd 26508
Molisee Vlg 26501
Mon General Dr 26505
Monarch Ct 26508
Monongahela Ave 26501
Monongahela Blvd 26505
Monongalia Ave 26505
Monroe St 26501
Mont Chateau Est & Rd 26508
Monterey Ave 26505
Montgomery Ave 26505
Montrose Ave 26505
Monument Ln 26508
Moon Valley Rd 26508
Moreland St 26505
Morgan Dr 26505
Morgan Ln 26508
Morgan St 26505
Morgan Hill Rd 26508
Morgan Pointe 26505
Morgan Run Rd 26508
Morgantown Ave 26501
Morgantown Industrial Park 26501
Morgantown Lock Rd 26501
Morningside Dr 26508
Morningside Way 26505
Morris Ave 26501
Morris St
200-300 26501
302-398 26501
1200-1299 26508
Morrison Ave 26501
Mossy Oak Dr 26508
Mountain Golf Dr 26508
Mountain Meadow Dr 26508
Mountain Ridge Rd 26508
Mountain Valley Dr 26508
Mountain View Mnr & Pl 26501
Mountain Vista Dr 26508
Mountaineer Dr 26501
Mountaineer Vlg 26508
Mountainview Rd 26508
Mulberry St 26505
Municipal Airport Rd 26505
Munsey Ave 26505
Murl Crawford Ave 26508

Street	ZIP
Murray Rd	26508
Mylan Park Ln	26501
Mystic Dr	26508
Nabors Rd	26508
Naomi St	26505
National Ln	26501
National Church Holw & Rd	26501
Nebraska Ave	26501
Negley St	26505
Nelson Dr	26508
Nestled Oak Ct	26508
New Castle Dr	26508
New Jersey St	26501
New York Ave	26501
Newberry Ln	26505
Newbrough Vlg	26508
Newlon Farm Dr & Rd	26508
Newport Ave	26501
Newton Ave	26505
Nicholson Loop	26508
Nolan St	26501
Nordic Dr	26505
Normandy St	26505
North St	
1-99	26501
601-699	26505
Northcrest Pl	26505
Northpointe Plz	26505
Northview Dr	26505
Northwest Ct & Dr	26505
Northwestern Ave	26505
E Northwoods Dr	26508
Nottingham Pl	26508
Nuce Ln	26508
Nueva Dr	26505
Number 8 Holw	26501
Oak Ct & St	26505
Oak Ridge Dr	26508
Oakland St	26505
Oakton Dr	26508
Oakview Dr	26505
Oakwood St	26505
Ocean View Dr	26505
October Way	26508
Odessa Ave	26508
Ogden St	26501
Ohio Ave	26501
Old Cheat Rd	26508
Old Fairmont Rd	26501
Old Farm Rd	26508
Old Golden Blue Ln	26505
Old House Ln	26505
Old Lock 12 Rd	26501
Old Lock 13 Rd	26501
Old River Rd	26501
Old Route 7	26508
Old Sawmill Rd	26508
Old School Rd	26508
Oliver St	26501
Olivia Way	26508
Olympia Ct	26508
Oneal Ln	26508
Ontario St	26508
Open Ridge Rd	26508
Orchard St	26501
Orchard Xing	26505
Orchard Acres Dr	26508
Oriole Way	26508
Orlando St	26505
Orthopedic Way	26505
Outlook St	26505
Overdale St	26501
Overhill St	26505
Overlake Dr	26508
Owl St	26508
Owl Creek Rd	26508
Oxford Pl	26505
Palace Dr	26508
Palisades Dr	26508
Palmetto Dr	26508
Paradise Cir	26508
Paradise Point Ct	26508
W Park Ave	26501
Park St	
100-799	26501
1100-1199	26508
Park Place Dr	26508
Park Ridge Dr	26508
Park Side Ln	26501
Parkview Dr	
100-299	26501
1100-1198	26505
1200-1399	26505
N Parkview Dr	26505
E Parkway Dr	26501
Parsons St	26505
Patriot Ln	26508
Patteson Dr	26505
Patton Dr	26505
Paul Wilson Ln	26508
Pauls Ln	26501
Paw Paw Ln	26501
Peaceful Rd	26501
Peach St	26505
Pearl Ave	26505
Pebble Rd	26508
Peninsula Blvd	26501
W Pennsylvania Ave	26501
Perdue St	26501
Perines Vlg	26508
Perry Ave	26505
Persimmon Woods Dr	26508
Petrich Rd	26508
Philip St	26501
Phillips Rd	26508
Piave Ln	26508
Pickadilly Way	26505
Pickhandle Hill Rd	26501
Pierce St	26501
S Pierpont Hts & Rd	26508
Pierpont Meadows Vlg	26508
Pierpont South Est	26508
Pietro Ct	26501
Pike Loop Rd	26508
Pin Oak Dr	26508
Pine Ln	26508
Pine St	26505
Pine Ridge Rd	26508
Pine Tree Ln	26508
Pinebrook Ln	26508
Pinecrest Dr & Plz	26505
Pinehurst Dr	26505
Pineview Dr & Pl	26505
Pinnacle Ln	26508
Pinnacle Height Dr	26505
Pinnacle Peak Ct	26508
Pioneer Villas	26508
Pittsburgh St	26501
Pixler Hill Rd	26508
S Plant St	26501
Plantation Dr	26508
Platinum Pt	26508
Pleasant St	
100-299	26505
300-399	26501
Pleasant Hill Ave	26505
Pleasant Hill Rd	26508
Pleasant Ridge Ln	26508
Pleasant View Acres	26508
Plum Cir	26505
Plymouth Ave	26505
Pocahontas Ave	26505
Point Marion Rd	
200-298	26505
300-799	26505
900-2299	26508
2900-3199	26505
3201-3567	26505
Pointe Dr	26508
Poling Ave	26501
Pond Rd	26508
Ponderosa Ponds Rd	26508
Poole Hill Rd	26508
Poplar Dr	26505
Poplar Woods Dr	26505
Porelloc Ave	26505
Postal Plz	26508
Posten Ave	26501
Pounds Holw	26508
Pounds Hollow Rd	26508
Powell Ave	26505
Powers Ct	26501
Prager Pl	26508
Prairie Ave	26501
Preston Rd	26505
Prestwick Ave	26508
Price St	
2-99	26501
501-597	26505
599-1000	26505
1000 1/2-1000 1/2	26505
Price Hill Rd	26501
Pride Ln	26505
Primrose Ln	26505
Prince Rd	26508
Princeton Ave	26505
E Prospect St	26505
Protzman St	26505
Purinton St	26505
Putnam St	26505
Pythian St	26505
Quadrilla St	26505
Quail Rd	26508
Quail Landing Way	26508
Quarry Run Rd	26508
Quarry Run Incline	26508
Quartz Dr	26508
Quay St	26505
Queen Anne Coloney	26505
Queens Ct	26508
Race St	26501
Rachel Rd	26508
Racine St	26505
Rail St	26501
Raleigh Pl & St	26501
Ralphs Rd	26508
Ramada Rd	26508
Ranch Dr	26508
Rand St	26505
Randall St	26505
Randolph Rd	26505
Raven Run	26508
Raven Rock Dr	26508
Rawley Ave & Ln	26505
Ray James Dr	26508
Raymond St	26505
Reay Aly	26501
Rebecca St	26505
Rec Center Dr	26505
Red Sky Dr	26508
Redaride	26506
Regal Dr	26501
Regan Ct	26508
Regency Ct	26505
Research Park Rd	26505
Revere St	26505
Rhinewood Ln	26508
Rhode Island Ave & Ln	26501
Rhubarb Ln	26508
Richard Pl	26505
Richard St	26501
Richland Ave	26505
Richmond Ave & St	26501
Richwood Ave	26505
Riddle Ave & Ct	26505
Ridenour Rd	26508
Ridge Pl	26505
Ridge Rd	26508
Ridge Of Summit Dr	26508
Ridge View Ave	26501
Ridgedale Rd	26508
Ridgeley Rd	26505
Ridgetop Dr	26508
Ridgeview Ests	26508
Ridgeview Ln	26508
Ridgeview St	26501
Ridgeway Ave	26505
W Ridgeway St	26501
Ridgewood Est	26508
Rifle Club Rd	26508
Riggan St	26501
Rightmire Ave	26501
Riley Ave	26505
Ringold Ln	26508
River Rd & St	26501
River Birch Dr	26508
River Ridge Ests	26501
Rivercrest Dr	26508
Rivers Bend Dr	26501
Riverside Ave & Ter	26501
Riverview Ave	26501
Riverview Ct	26501
Riverview Dr	26505
Riverview Estates Vlg	26501
Robin Ln	26508
Rock Circle Way	26508
Rock Forge Ln	26508
Rock Forge Mobile Home Park	26508
Rockland Ct	26508
Rockley Rd	26508
Rocky Top Ln	26508
Rogers St	26501
Rohrbaugh St	26501
Rolling Hls	26508
Rolling Hills Vlg	26508
Rollingwood St	26505
Roosevelt St	26505
Rose St	26501
Rosemarie Dr	26501
Ross Ln & St	26501
Rotary St	26505
Round St	26501
Round Bottom Rd	26508
Round Table Ct	26508
Rousch Dr	26501
Royal Oaks Dr	26508
Royce Ln	26508
Ruckart Dr	26508
Rucki St	26508
Rugh Ln	26508
Ruidosa Ln	26508
Rumbling Ln	26508
W Run Rd	26508
Rustic Dr	26508
Rystan Pl	26505
Sabraton Ave	26505
Saint Andrews Dr	26508
Saint Clair Hill Rd	26508
Saint Clairs Vlg	26505
E Saint Johns St	26505
Saint Joseph St	26505
Saint Mary St	26505
Saint Pauls Ln	26505
Salonika Dr	26508
Sanctuary Cv	26508
Sand Banks Rd	26508
Sand Springs Rd	26508
Sander Ln	26505
Sandstone Hl	26501
Sanford St	26501
Santa Fe Ct	26508
Santana Pl	26508
Santorini Ave	26508
Sapphire Cir	26508
Sarah St	26501
Saratoga Ave	26505
Savage Ln	26508
Savannah St	26501
Saxman Ave	26505
Saylor Rd	26501
Scenery Dr	26505
Scenic View Dr	26508
Scenic Woods Dr	26508
Schifano Dr	26501
Schley St	26501
School St	26505
Schubert Pl	26505
Scott Ave	26508
Scumaci Ln	26505
Seamans Vlg	26501
Selby Rd	26508
Sellaro Dr & Plz	26505
Seminole Way	26508
Seneca St	26501
Seneca Hills Ests	26508
Sennett St	26501
September Dr	26508
Serenity Dr	26508
Settlers Way	26508
Sewickley Dr	26501
Shadow Pines Ln	26508
Shady Grove Vlg	26505
Shadybrook Cir	26508
Shadyside Ln	26508
Shaffer Ln	26508
Shanes Villa	26501
Sharon Ave	
1-99	26501
400-499	26505
Shaw Pl	26505
Shawnee Dr	26508
Sheldon Ave	26501
Shellbark Ln	26508
Shepherds Ridge Rd	26501
Sheridan Ln	26508
Sherman Ave	26501
Sherwood Dr & St	26505
Shilling Plz	26508
Shiloh Ln	26508
Short St	
1-199	26501
500-599	26505
Shriver Mine Rd	26501
Shumiloff Ln	26501
Sibling Dr	26508
Sierra Pl	26505
Sierra Farm Rd	26501
Silver Creek Dr	26505
Silver View Ct	26505
Silverbell Dr	26508
Simpson St	26501
Sirockman Dr	26508
Skemp Ave	26505
Skyline Dr	26508
Skyview	26508
Slaton Ln	26508
Smith Ave	26505
Smith Rd	26501
Smithtown Rd	26508
Smithtown School Rd	26508
Smokey Crest Dr	26508
Smokey Drain Rd	26501
Snake Hill Rd	26508
Snider St	26505
Snowy Rd	26501
Snyder St	26501
Snyder Run Rd	26501
Sodomick Ln	26508
Solar Dr	26508
Solomon Rd	26501
Somerset St	26505
Sommavilla St	26508
Sonoma Way	26505
Southeast Ct	26505
Southern Ave	26501
Southern Galloway Ln	26508
Southpoint Cir	26501
Southridge Dr	26501
Southview St	26505
Sparrow Ln	26508
Spencer St	26501
Spring Rd	26501
Spring St	
1-99	26501
200-299	26505
Springbranch Rd	26505
Springbrook St	26505
Springdale Ave	26505
Springfield Ave	26505
Spruce St	26505
Squirrel Ln	26508
Stadium Dr	26506
Stafford St	26505
Staley Dr	26508
Stalnaker Hall	26506
Standard Ave	26501
Stanley St	26508
Starcrest Plz	26505
Starling Est	26508
State St	26505
Station St	26508
Statler St	26505
Steeplechase Dr	26508
Stephanie Dr	26501
Sterle Ave	26501
Sterling Dr	26505
Stewart Ln	26505
Stewart Pl	26505
Stewart Run	26501
Stewart St	26505
Stewartstown Rd	
1000-1098	26505
1100-1699	26505
1701-1897	26505
2000-3899	26508
Stilwell Dr	26505
Stockett Rd	26508
Stone Brook Est	26508
Stone Creek Rd	26508
Stone Gate Cir	26505
Stone Mill Ln	26508
Stone Mine Rd	26508
Stone Path Ln	26508
Stone Ridge Pl	26508
Stone Run St	26505
Stonewood Dr	26505
Stoney Meadow Ln	26508
Stony Brk	26508
Straight Ln	26508
Strawberry Ln	26501
Sturgiss Ave & St	26505
Suburban Ct	26505
Sugar Grove Rd	26501
Sugar Lane Ter	26501
Sugar Maple Hl	26508
Sumac Cir	26508
Summerfield Dr	26508
Summers Ln	26508
Summers St	26501
Summers Church Rd	26508
Summers School Rd	26508
Summit Overlook Dr	26508
Summits Rdg	26508
Sun Vly	26508
Sun Bonnett Ln	26508
Sun Valley Rd	26508
Suncrest Pl, Ter & Vlg	26505
Suncrest Town Centre Dr	26505
Sundance Dr	26508
Sundown Dr	26508
Sunridge Dr	26505
Sunrise Dr	26508
Sunset Dr	26501
Sunset Ln	26505
Sunset Beach Rd	26508
Sunset View Dr	26508
Sunshine Vlg	26508
Surrey Dr & Ln	26505
Suzanne Rd	26501
Swallowtail Dr	26508
Swan Ln	26505
Sweet Pea Rd	26501
Sweetbriar Ln	26508
Sweetwater Ln	26508
Sycamore St	26501
Sylvan Ave	26505
Sylvan Cir	26508
Sylvan Dr	26508
Sylvan Pl	26505
T And D Vlg	26508
Takoma St	26505
Tall Grass Ln	26505
Tally Ho Ln	26508
Tampa St	26501
Tappan Zee Ln	26508
Tara Pl	26505
Tarbert Ct	26508
Tartan Ln	26505
Taylor St	26505
Taylor Way	26508
Teaberry Ln	26508
Teardrop Ct	26508
Terrace View Dr	26508
Terrell Dr	26508
Theresa Dr	26501
Thistledown Ln	26508
Thorne Rd	26501
Thornhill Ave	26501
Tibbs Rd	26508
Timber Bluff Ct	26508
Timber Ridge Dr	26508
Timberline	26505
Tj Ln	26501
Toms Run Rd	26508
Top Of The Rock Dr	26508
Topeka Ave	26501
Torino Dr	26508
Tower Ln	26501
Town And Country Ct & Vlg	26501
Townhouse Way	26505
Townsend Ln	26508
Tram St	26501
Tranquility Way	26508
Tremont Ave & St	26505
Trent St	26505
Trenton Ln	26508
Trevilla Ave	26508
Treyson Ln	26505
Trierlea St	26501
Trinity Way	26505
Trinity Woods	26508
Triplett Ridge Rd	26501
Tripplets Vlg	26501
Triune Ln	26508
Trovato Dr	26505
Tuckers Path	26501
Tupelo Dr	26508
Turkey Rdg	26508
Turkey Foot Ln	26508
Turnberry Cir	26508
Turner Hollow Rd	26501
Turnstone Dr	26505
Turquoise Ln	26508
Turtle Creek Dr	26508
Twiddlebug Ln	26508
Twigg St	26501
Twilight Ln	26501
Twin Knobs	26508
Twin Maples Vlg	26508
Twin Oaks Dr	26508
Twin Pines Vlg	26508
Twin Ponds Ln	26508
Tyler St	26501
Tyrone Rd	26508
Tyrone Avery Rd	26508
Tyson St	26505
Union Ave	26505
Union Church Dr & Holw	26501
University Ave	
1000-1599	26505
1550-1600	26506
1601-3699	26505
1800-3398	26505
3400-3400	26504
3400-3698	26505
University Commons Dr	26505
University Town Centre Dr	26501
Upper Cobun Creek Rd	26508
Valencia Ct	26505
Valley Rd	26505
Valley Point Dr	26501
Valley View Ave & Dr	26505
Valley View Woods	26505
Van Gilder St	26505
Van Tassel Ct	26508
Van Voorhis Rd	
401-997	26505
999-1599	26505
1600-1704	26508
1705-1705	26505
1706-1998	26508
1707-1999	26508
Vandalia Rd	26501
Vandervort Dr	26505
Vanessa Ln	26505
Vangilder Pointe	26505
Vankirk Ln	26501
Vantage Dr	26508
Vassar St	26505
Vecchio Ln	26508
Venham St	26505
Venture Dr	26508
Vernon St	26505

Victoria Falls Dr 26508
Vienna Dr 26505
View Ct 26508
Villa Pl 26505
Villa View Dr 26505
Village Dr & Ln 26505
Village Crest Dr 26508
Village Park Dr 26508
Vincent Ave 26501
Vine St 26501
Vineyard Way 26508
Vintner Pl 26505
Virginia Ave 26505
W Virginia Ave 26501
N Vista Ct 26508
Vista Pl 26505
Vista Del Rio Dr 26508
Vitez Dr 26508
Vorbach Dr 26508
Votech Dr 26501
Wabash St 26501
Wade St 26501
Wades Rd 26501
Wades Run Rd 26501
Wagner Rd 26501
Waitman St 26501
Wake Robin Trl 26508
Wall St 26505
Walls Vlg 26508
Walnut Ln 26505
Walnut St 26505
S Walnut St 26501
Walnut Hill Rd 26501
Warm Hollow Rd 26508
Warren St 26501
Warrick St 26505
Wasco St 26508
Washington Ave & St 26501
Water St 26505
Waterfront Pl 26501
Waterside Dr 26508
Watts Aly & St 26501
Waverly St 26505
Wayland St 26505
Wayne Ave 26501
Weaver St 26505
Weaver Town Homes 26501
Webster Ave 26501
Wedgewood Dr 26505
Weirton Mine Rd 26508
Wellen St 26505
Wells St 26505
Wendys Way 26501
Werner St 26505
Wesley Dr 26508
West St 26501
Westbrook Dr & St 26508
Western Ave
1-399 26501
400-1599 26505
Westgate Dr 26508
Westlake Dr 26508
Westminister Dr 26501
Westridge Dr 26501
Westview Ave 26505
Westwood Ave 26505
Wetzel Ave 26505
Wharf St 26501
Wheelers Vlg 26505
Wheeling St 26501
Whipkey Ln 26508
Whispering Rdg 26501
Whispering Pines Dr 26508
White Ave 26501
White Day Creek Rd 26508
White Oak Dr 26505
White Tail Way 26508
White Willow Way 26505
Whites Run Ct 26508
Whitetail Ct 26508
Wichita St 26508
Wilbourn St 26505
Wild Cherry Rd 26508
Wildlife Hl 26508
Wildrose St 26508
Wildwood Lk 26508
Wildwood St 26505
Wiles St 26505
N Willey St 26505
William St 26501
Williams Ln 26508
Williams Rd 26501
Williams Way Ln 26508
Willie G Ave 26501
Willis Dr 26501
Willow Ln 26505
Willow Ridge Dr 26505
Willow Wick Dr 26505
Willowdale Rd 26505
Wilmerding St 26505
Wilson Ave 26501
Wilson Cir 26505
W Wilson St 26501
Wilson Woods Way 26508
Windin Ln 26505
Winding Hollow Dr 26508
Winding Springs Dr 26508
Windsong Ln 26508
Windsor Ave 26505
Windwood Dr & Pl 26505
Windy Rdg 26501
Wings Knob Pl 26508
Winona Ave & Ct 26505
Winsley St 26501
Wisconsin Ave 26501
Wiseman Rd 26501
Wispy Rd 26508
Wolfe Run 26508
Wood Trailer Ct 26508
Woodburn St 26505
Woodcrest Dr 26505
Woodhaven Dr 26505
Woodland Cir 26505
Woodland Dr 26505
Woodland Rd 26501
Woodland Ter 26505
Woodland Bluff Rd 26508
Woodland Cove Rd 26508
Woodlands Rdg 26508
Woodline Dr 26505
Woodridge St 26505
Woodrow St 26505
Woodruff Pl 26505
Woods Edge Ln 26508
Woofter St 26501
Wren Ln 26508
Wright Ave 26505
Wrightman St 26505
Yon Vlg 26508
Yorkshire Pl 26508
Zachary Ct 26508
Zackquill Ct 26508
Zara Dr 26508

NUMBERED STREETS

1st St 26505
W 1st St 26501
2nd St 26505
E 2nd St 26508
W 2nd St 26501
3rd Ave 26508
3rd St 26505
E 3rd St 26508
W 3rd St 26501
4th Ave 26508
4th St 26505
W 4th St 26501
5 Forks Dr 26508
5th Ave 26505
5th St 26505
400-499 26501
W 5th St 26501
6th Ave 26508
6th St 26505
7th Ave 26508
7th St 26505
8th Ave 26508
8th St 26505
9th Ave 26508
10th Ave 26508
11th Ave 26508
14th Fairway Ct 26508
17th Fairway 26508
18th Fairway 26508
20th Ave 26508
201st Memorial Hwy 26505
4h Camp Rd 26508

PARKERSBURG WV

General Delivery 26101

POST OFFICE BOXES MAIN OFFICE STATIONS AND BRANCHES

Box No.s
C - E 26102
1 - 2994 26102
3001 - 3800 26103
4001 - 4996 26104
7000 - 7025 26102

RURAL ROUTES

01, 03, 04, 05, 06, 07, 10, 11 26101
01, 02, 08, 12 26104

NAMED STREETS

Aarons Ct 26104
Abbey Village Dr 26104
Abby Vlg 26104
Acorn Ln 26101
Adams St
1-99 26104
400-599 26101
Addison Dr 26104
Agnes St 26101
W Airport Industrial Park 26104
Almeda Ct 26104
Alta Ln 26104
Altman Ave & Dr 26104
Amanda Ln 26104
Amber Ln 26101
American Dr 26101
Amicalola Way 26104
Andrew St 26101
Ann St 26101
Antler Ct 26104
Apache St 26101
Aqua Cir 26104
Aqua Isle Trailer Park 26104
Arabian Dr 26104
Arbor Ln 26101
Ardath Dr 26104
Arnold Ave 26101
Ashby Ridge Rd 26104
Ashwood Pl 26104
Aspendale Dr 26105
Audrey St 26101
Avery Ct 26101
Avery Pl 26101
Avery St
1026-A-1026-D 26101
1028-A-1028-B 26101
200-2599 26101
2600-3699 26104
Ball Rd 26104
Ball School Rd 26101
Baltimore St 26104
Barker Ln 26104
Barnhouse Ct 26101
Barnstable Dr 26101
Bartlett St 26104
Beam St 26104
Beaver St 26101
Beckner Blvd 26104
Beech St 26104
Beechwood Dr 26101
Beechwood Pl 26104
Belle St 26101
Belmont Rd 26101
Belrock Dr 26101
Benson Dr 26104
Benton Ave 26101
Berkley Dr 26104
Bernards Pl 26104
Berry St 26101
Berry Run Rd 26104
Bethel Rd 26101
Beverly St 26101
Bickel Mansion Dr 26101
Birch Dr 26105
Birch St 26101
Bird St 26101
Bird Dog Ln 26104
Birnham Wood Dr 26104
Birnham Wood Trailer Park 26104
Blackberry Ln 26104
Blenn Lake Rd 26101
Blenn Wood Ln 26101
Blennerhassett Hts 26101
Blizzard Dr 26101
Blue Front Holw 26104
Blue Heron Ln 26104
Blue Spruce Rd 26104
Bobcat Hollow Rd 26101
Boggess St 26104
Bonita Cir 26104
Bosley Ave & Pkwy 26101
Boulder Dr 26104
Boxwood Cir 26101
Boyles Ln 26104
Bradford Ave 26101
Brady Ln 26104
Branam Dr 26104
Branch Dr 26101
Braxton Dr 26101
Brayden Ln 26101
Brenda Ave 26101
Brentwood Dr & Hts 26104
Briant St 26101
Briarwood Cir & Pl 26104
Bridge St 26104
Briscoe Rd
600-799 26104
5000-5599 26105
Briscoe Run Rd 26104
Broad St
2300-3099 26101
3100-3899 26104
Broadway Ave, Cir & Ext 26101
Brook Pl 26101
Brooklyn Ave, Ct, Dr & Ter 26101
Brookside Cir 26104
Brooktree Dr 26101
Brookview St 26104
Brown Ave 26101
Buckeye St 26101
Bull Creek Rd 26104
Bungalow Dr 26104
Bunner Ln 26104
Burk St 26104
Burke St 26101
Burl Rd 26104
Burning Bush Dr 26104
Burnthouse Rd 26104
Bush St 26101
Butler St 26104
Cadillac Dr & Ext 26104
Cale St 26101
Camden Ave, Pl & St 26101
Camelot Dr 26101
Cameron Ave 26101
Campbell Dr 26104
Campus Dr 26104
Canterbury Dr 26104
Capital Cir & Dr 26101
Captain Ames Dr 26104
Captain Neals Ct 26104
Captain Parker Trl 26104
Carbine Ct 26104
Carp Rd 26104
Carpenter St 26105
Carriage Ln 26104
Catalino Dr
1-99 26101
2-98 26104
Cavalier Cir 26104
Cedar Grove Rd 26104
Cedar Rose Ln 26104
Cedar Tree Ln 26104
Celia St 26101
Center St
1-199 26104
800-999 26101
Central Ave 26104
Central Dr 26105
Central City Rd 26105
Chalfant St 26104
Charity Hill Rd 26101
Charles St 26101
Chateau Hls 26101
Cherry Ave 26101
Cherry St 26104
Chestnut St 26101
S Chichester Ln 26104
Cimaron Dr 26104
W Circle 26101
City View Dr 26101
Clay St 26101
Clegg St 26101
Clement Ave
2300-2599 26101
3200-3599 26104
Cleveland Ave 26104
Cliffside Ave 26101
Clinton Ave 26101
Clover Ln 26101
Cloverleaf Rd 26104
Clyde St 26101
Cokeley Dr 26104
College Pkwy
100-4500 26104
4501-4501 26105
4502-5098 26104
4503-5099 26104
Collegeview Acres 26105
Colonel Phelps Ct & Dr 26104
Colt Ridge Dr 26104
Columbia Ave
2-98 26105
101-199 26105
600-699 26101
Comer St 26101
Commercial Ln 26104
Congdon Dr 26104
Coolidge St 26104
Cooper St 26101
Cora Dr 26101
Coram Dr 26104
Core Rd 26104
Cornwall St 26101
Cory Dr 26104
Court Sq 26101
Covert St 26101
Cowan Ln 26104
Crabapple Ln 26104
Crawford St 26101
Crescent Ave 26104
Crescent Dr 26104
Crescent St 26101
Crescent Moon Dr 26101
Crestview Cir 26104
Crestwood Dr 26104
Cumberland Rd 26101
Curry Ct 26101
Custer St 26104
Cutlip Ln & Rd 26104
Cypress St
2300-2799 26101
3600-4599 26104
Dagg Rd 26101
Daisy Dr 26101
Daley Ln 26101
David Lee Dr 26101
Dean St 26101
Deer Ridge Rd 26104
Deerwalk Hwy 26104
Delaware St 26101
Delray Dr 26101
Dempsie Ave 26104
Dennis St 26101
Depot St 26101
Dewey St 26101
Dickel Ave 26101
Dillaway St 26101
Division St N 26101
Division Street Ext 26101
Dixie Ln 26104
Dogwood Cir 26101
Dolphin Dr 26105
Dooley Ave 26101
Doug Ln 26104
Douglas Dr 26104
Dr Judy Rd 26101
E Dry Run Rd 26104
Dudley Ave
1900-2999 26101
3000-3499 26104
Duerr Ln 26104
Duncan Ln 26104
Duncan Rd 26101
Dunsinane Dr 26104
Dupont Rd 26101
Dupont Manor Rd 26101
Dutch Ln 26104
Dutch Hills Ter 26104
Dutch Ridge Pl & Rd 26104
Eagle Ln 26101
Earl P St 26101
Earnhardt Ln 26104
East St 26101
Eastlawn Ave 26101
Eastview Dr 26104
Eastwood Dr 26104
Edendale Ln 26101
Edgelawn St 26101
Edgewood Park 26104
Edison Dr 26104
Edwin St 26101
Elder St 26101
Elk Ln 26104
Elkhorn Dr 26104
Ellis Ave 26104
Elm Cir 26101
Elm St
1000-2699 26101
2900-2998 26104
3000-3599 26104
Elm Tree Dr 26101
Elmira Ln 26104
Elmwood Ave & Dr 26101
Emerson Ave
900-5800 26104
5775-5775 26105
5801-13099 26104
5802-12998 26104
Emerson Ct 26104
Emerson Commons Blvd 26104
Emilee Trce 26101
Empire Lake Dr 26101
Erickson Blvd 26101
Erie St 26101
Euclid Dr 26104
Evandale Ter 26101
Fairfax St 26101
Fairlawn Dr 26101
Fairview Ave
800-2299 26101
2300-3299 26104
Fairview Hts 26101
Fairway Acres 26104
Faith Hill Rd 26101
Falcon Heights Rd 26104
Fallen Timber Dr 26105
Farm View Dr 26101
Federal Ct 26104
Fergueson Dr 26101
Fern St 26101
Firewood Dr 26101
Fisher Ln 26104
Florida St 26101
Foley Ave & Dr 26104
Ford St 26104
Forest Dr 26104
Forest Hills Dr 26105
Forest Hills Rd 26104
Forres Ln 26104
Fort Boreman Ave 26101
Fox Hill Dr & Ter 26104
Foxlair 26101
Frances St 26101
Franklin Ave 26104
Franklin Blvd 26101
Franklin St 26101
Franklin Court Aly 26101
Franwood Pl 26104
Freedom Dr 26101
Gale Ave 26101
Gant St
2201-2299 26101
2400-2499 26104
Garden St 26104
Gardenia Dr 26101
Garfield Ave 26101
Garrett Dr 26105
Gateman Dr 26101
George Ln & St 26101
Georgetown Rd 26104
Gihon Rd & Vlg 26101
Gihon Meadows Dr 26101
Gillespie Run Rd 26104
Gingerwood Ln 26105
Gladstone St 26101
Glendale Rd 26105
Glenn Ave 26104
Glover Rd 26101
Golden St 26104
Golden Field Dr 26105
Golf Dr 26104
Gove St 26101
Government Sq 26101
Grafton St 26101
Granada Cir, Dr & Hls 26104
Granada Hills Circle Ext 26104
Grand Ave 26101
Grand Central Ave 26105
Grand Park Dr 26105
Grandview Blvd, Mnr & St 26101
Grandview Trailer Park 26101
Grapevine Dr 26105
Green St 26101
Green Meadow Dr 26104
Green Tree Dr 26104
Greenbrier Apts 26101
Greenview Dr & Vlg 26104
Greenwood Dr 26104
Greystone Ln 26104
Hailey Hts 26104
Hall St 26101
Hamilton Ct 26104
Hamilton St 26101
Hamlet Close 26104
Hampton St 26101
Hanes St 26105
Hanover St 26104
Happy Valley Ln & Rd 26104
Harmon Ave 26104
Harper Dr 26101
Harris Hwy & St 26101
Harrison Ave
2200-2299 26101
2300-2899 26104
Harvest Dr 26105
Harvey St 26105
Hastings Ln 26104
Haught St 26104
Hawthorne St 26101
Hayes St 26104
Hays Dr 26104
Hazel St 26104
Hearthstone Dr 26101
Heath Ln 26104
Hecate Ct 26104
Helen Ave & St 26101
Helman Ln 26101

Hemlock Ave & Ct 26104
Herbershoff Ln 26101
Heritage Dr 26104
Herning Ln 26104
Hickory St
 1-199 26104
 200-500 26101
 502-598 26101
High View Ln 26104
Highland Ave
 1-899 26104
 1300-2799 26101
Highland Pl 26101
Highland Rd 26101
Highlight Trailer Park 26104
Hill Ave 26101
Hill St 26104
Hillcrest St & Ter 26101
Hillcrest Addition 26104
N Hills Dr 26104
S Hills Dr 26101
S Hills Pl 26101
Hilltop Ln 26101
Hite Dr 26104
Hoagland Rd 26104
Holden St 26104
Holiday Dr 26105
Holiday Hills Dr 26104
Holland Ave 26104
Homeland Ave 26101
Homestead Ct 26104
Homewood Rd 26101
Honeysuckle Dr 26101
Hoover Rd 26101
Hope Hill Rd 26101
Huber Dr 26104
Hudson St 26104
Hugh St 26101
Hughes Dr 26104
Hutchinson St 26101
Indiana St 26101
Industrial Blvd 26104
Inghram Dr 26105
Inverness Ln 26104
Island View Dr 26101
Ivy St 26101
Ivybrook Rd 26101
Jackson Ave 26101
James Ct
 1-99 26105
 2-98 26105
 2-98 26104
James St 26104
Jameson St 26101
Janet Dr 26104
Jean Marie Ln 26104
Jeanette Ct & St 26101
Jefferson St 26104
Jeffrey St 26101
Jester Court Ln 26105
Jesterville Rd 26105
Jewell Rd 26101
Jo Mar Dr 26104
Joan St 26101
Joann Dr 26101
John St 26101
Johnson St 26101
Johnson Creek Rd 26104
Johnson Farm Rd 26104
Johnson Run Rd 26104
Joy St 26101
Joyce Dr 26104
Joyceville Trailer Park 26101
Judgement Rd 26104
Jug Run Rd 26104
Juliana St 26101
Kanawha St 26101
Kanawha River Rd 26101
Kathys Ln 26101
Kay St 26104
Keeneland Ln 26104
Keever St 26101
Keith St 26104
Kemper St 26101
Kendall Ave 26105
Kennedy Ave 26104

Kenner St 26101
Kens Ave 26101
Kenwood St 26104
Kesterson Rd 26101
Kim St 26104
Kimberjack Trl 26105
Kings Row Ct 26104
Kingswood Dr 26104
Knopp Ln & St 26101
Knotts Ave 26101
Lair Of Ii 26101
Laird Ave 26101
Lake Dr 26104
S Lake Dr 26101
S Lake Pl 26101
Lake St 26101
Lake Hills Ct & Dr 26101
Lake Washington Rd 26101
Lakeview Ave 26101
Lakeview Ctr 26101
Lakeview Dr 26104
Landmark Dr 26104
Lantana Ln 26101
Lantern St 26101
Lantz Ter 26104
Larkmead Rd 26101
Latrobe St 26101
Lauckport Ln 26101
Laurel St 26101
Laverne St 26101
Lawrence St 26101
Layman Ln 26101
Leafy Glen Ct 26101
Leander Ln 26104
Lee St 26101
Lees Hill Rd 26104
Lemon Ln 26101
Lenore St 26101
Lewis Ave 26104
Liberty Hls 26104
Liberty St
 1-597 26101
 599-2799 26101
 3100-4099 26104
Lincoln Ave
 2100-2399 26101
 2400-2799 26104
Lincoln Dr
 1-499 26101
 900-999 26104
Lincoln St 26104
Linda Ln 26104
Linden St 26104
Linnwood Dr 26104
Little Kanawha River Rd 26101
Lizzie Ln 26104
Locust Ct 26104
Locust Hl 26105
Locust St 26101
Locust Hill Rd 26105
Lodge Ct 26101
Lodge Dr 26105
Logan Ln 26101
Lola Dr 26104
Loomis Ridge Rd 26104
Loretta Ln 26101
Lost St 26101
Lost Pavement Rd 26101
Louisiana Ave 26104
Lubeck Ave & Rd 26101
Lubeck Apartment Ln 26101
Ludwig Rd 26101
Lulu St 26101
Lynn St 26101
Madison Ave 26101
Magnolia Ave & Ln 26104
Main St 26104
Majestic Hills Dr 26101
Manor Ln 26101
Mansion Blvd 26101
Maple Cir & St 26101
Marie Hts & St 26104
Marietta Ave 26101
Marion Ave 26101

Market St
 200-1051 26101
 1050-1050 26102
 1053-1999 26101
 1100-1998 26101
Marlin St 26101
Marquis St 26101
Marrtown Rd 26101
Marshall Ct 26101
Mary St 26101
Mason St 26101
Mathoit St 26101
Maxwell Ave 26101
Mcclure Ave 26104
Mccoy Ln 26101
Mcgraw St 26104
Mckinley Ave 26104
Meadow Dr & Ln 26101
Meadow Lane Cir & Way 26101
Meadowbrook Acres 26101
Meadowcrest Dr 26104
Meadowlark Dr 26101
Meadows Mobile Home Park 26104
Meadowview Cir & Dr 26104
Meadville Rd 26104
Meldahl Rd 26101
Melinda St 26101
Merrick St 26101
Merrill Ln 26101
Miami St 26101
Michigan St 26104
Midnight Ln 26105
Midway St 26101
Mill Run Rd 26104
Mill View Dr 26104
Millbrook Dr 26104
Millbrook Ln 26101
Miller Rd 26104
Millers Lndg 26104
Millstone Ln 26104
Milton St 26101
Miner St 26101
Mineral Manor Way 26101
Minsount St 26101
Miracle Ln 26104
Mission Dr 26101
Missouri Run Rd 26101
Moats St 26105
Monogahela Ave 26104
Monongahela Ave 26104
Montana Dr 26105
Montero Dr 26104
Moore Ave 26104
Morgan Ln & Pl 26104
Morningside Ave & Cir 26101
Morrison Ln 26104
Mound St 26104
Mount Vernon Cir 26101
Mountain View Dr 26101
Mountain View Ln 26104
Moyer Ave 26101
Mulberry Ln 26104
Mullins Dr 26101
Murdoch Ave
 800-2499 26101
 2500-2598 26104
 2501-4099 26101
 2600-2998 26101
 3000-3198 26104
 3200-3798 26101
 3800-4098 26105
Murray Dr & Ln 26101
Mustang Acres 26104
Myrtle St 26101
Nash St 26101
Neal St
 400-807 26101
 806-806 26103
 808-2698 26101
 809-2699 26101
Neal Ann Dr 26104
Neal Run Blvd 26101
Neale Rd 26105
Nelson Ln 26101

New York Ave 26101
Newbank Rd 26104
Newbanks Rd 26104
Newberry Dr 26101
Niagara St 26101
Nice St 26101
Nicely Ave & Pl 26101
Nicholas Dr 26101
Nicholson Ln 26101
Nicolette Rd 26104
Nora St 26101
Northwestern Dr 26104
Northwestern Pike
 3000-3098 26101
 3500-3599 26104
E Northwestern Pike 26104
Northwood Dr 26104
Northwood Villa Ln 26104
Norwood Ave 26101
Notch Rd 26104
Nursery Rd 26105
Nuthatch Ln 26104
Oak Cir 26101
Oak Dr 26104
Oak St
 1-199 26104
 1300-2599 26101
Oak Leaf Dr 26104
Oakhurst Ave & St 26101
Oakridge Dr 26104
Oaktree Dr 26101
Oakview Dr 26101
Oakwood Est & Pl 26104
Odell Ln 26104
Ogdinville Rd 26104
Ohio Ave 26101
Ohio River Rd 26101
Old Ashby Ridge Rd 26104
Old Big Run Rd 26104
Old Cedar Grove Rd 26104
Old Dutch Ridge Rd 26104
Old Rosemar Rd
 1-99 26105
 2-98 26104
 2-98 26105
 400-998 26104
 1000-4999 26104
Old Saint Marys Pike 26104
Old Turnpike Rd 26104
Olive St
 100-199 26104
 500-1199 26101
Opal Rd 26104
Orchard Ave 26105
Orchard Dr 26104
Orchard Ln 26104
Orchard St
 1-99 26101
 3600-3699 26104
Oregon Dr 26105
Packard Ct, St & Way 26104
Paddock Ln 26105
Paddock Green Dr 26104
Paden St 26101
Pahlhurst Ct & Plz 26101
Palmer Dr 26104
Paradise Ln 26101
Park Ave, Pl & St 26101
Park Center Dr 26101
S Park Villa Trailer Ct 26101
Parker Ave & Trl 26104
Parkertowne 26104
Parkview Dr 26104
S Parkview Dr 26101
Parkview Way 26104
Parkville Dr 26101
Parkville Apts 26101
Parkwood Dr 26104
Parmaco St 26101
Parrish Ct 26104
Paul St 26101
Peach Orchard Ln 26104
Pearcy Ave 26101
Penn Ave & St 26104
Pennsylvania Ave 26101
Persimmon Ln 26104

Petal St 26101
Petina Ct 26104
Pettyville Rd & St 26101
Phillips St 26101
Phoenix St 26104
Pickering St 26101
Piersol Rd 26104
Pike St 26101
Pine St 26101
Pine Tree Ln 26101
Pinehurst Ave 26101
Pinetree Rd 26101
Pineview Cir 26104
N Pineview Cir 26104
Pineview Dr
 1-299 26101
 2-16 26104
 18-108 26101
 110-114 26104
 116-150 26101
 152-162 26104
 164-298 26101
 2200-2299 26104
N Pineview Dr 26104
Pinewood Ln 26104
Plainwood Dr 26104
Pleasant Vw 26101
Pleasant Hill Rd 26101
Pleasant Valley School Rd 26105
Pleasant Wood Dr 26104
Plum St
 1101-1197 26101
 1199-2599 26101
 3000-3699 26104
Point Dr 26101
Pointe W 26101
Pointe West Ct 26101
Pointe West Byway 26101
Polaris St 26101
Pole Rd 26104
Polk St 26101
Pope St 26101
Poplar Dr & St 26101
Porter Dr 26101
Postlewaite St 26101
Powell Dr & St 26104
Power Ave 26104
Prince Ct 26104
Princeton Cir & St 26101
Private St 26101
Produce Dr 26105
Prunty St 26101
Putnam St 26101
Quick St 26101
Quincy St 26101
Race St 26101
Rainbow Rd 26105
Raintree Rd 26104
Ramsey St 26101
Randolph Dr 26104
Rayon Dr 26101
Reamer St 26101
Rector Rd 26105
Red Hill Rd 26104
Red Hill Church Rd 26104
Red Peak Cir 26104
Reed St 26101
Regal Dr 26105
Reservoir Dr 26101
Rhodes Ln 26101
N Ridge Rd & Ter 26105
Ridgeview Cir & Ct 26104
Ridgeway Ave 26101
Ripple Rd 26101
Rita Dr 26104
Riverhill Rd 26101
Riverside Dr 26104
Riverview Dr 26104
Riverview Trailer Park 26104
Roberta Dr 26104
Rolling Hills Ct 26101
Rollins St 26104
Ronald Reagan Dr 26101
Roosevelt St 26104
Ros Mar Hts 26101

Rosebud St 26101
Roseland Ave 26104
Roselynne Ave 26101
Rosemar Cir 26104
Rosemar Ctr 26104
Rosemar Mdws 26105
Rosemar Rd
 1-699 26104
 1000-3900 26105
 3902-4798 26105
 4401-4613 26104
 4615-4799 26105
 4800-4899 26104
 4900-4999 26105
 5000-5098 26104
 5001-5899 26105
 5100-5898 26105
Rosemar Ter 26105
Rosemar Meadows Dr 26105
Roth Rd 26104
Ruble Ct 26104
Rubles Ct 26104
Rush St 26101
Russell St 26105
Ryanwood Vlg 26101
Sagamore Hl 26104
Saint Marys Ave 26101
Salvage Ln 26105
Sandstone Dr 26105
Sandy Ln 26104
Sayre Ave 26104
Scenic Dr 26101
Scenic Hls 26104
School St 26104
Schultz St 26101
Seattle St 26101
Selmar Ln 26101
Seneca Dr 26101
Seneca Ln 26104
Shadow Ln & Rd 26104
Shattuck Ave 26101
Shepard St 26105
Sherwood Dr 26104
Short St 26104
Shrewsbury Pl 26101
Sierra Pl 26104
Silver Ct 26105
Singletree Dr 26105
Skylar Dr 26101
Skyview Dr 26101
Sleepy Hollow Rd 26104
Smith St 26104
Smith Golf Dr 26101
Smithfield St 26101
Snider Hill Rd 26104
Sommerset Dr 26101
South Hts & St 26101
Southmoor Hts 26101
Soyer St 26101
Spider Ridge Rd 26104
Sports Dr 26101
Spring St 26101
Spruce Rd & St 26104
Spruce Rise Rd 26104
Stadium Dr 26101
Star Ave 26101
State St 26104
Staunton Ave
 1200-1999 26101
 2200-2299 26104
Staunton Tpke 26104
Stella Ct & St 26104
Stephens St 26101
Stephenson Ave 26101
Steven St 26101
Stewart Ave 26101
Stonebrook Dr 26104
Stout St 26101
Strawberry Ln 26104
Strimer Dr 26104
Stroehman St 26101
Studio Ln
 100-598 26105
 101-199 26104
 101-597 26105
Sugartree Rd 26104

Summers Rd & St 26101
Summit Rd 26105
Sun St 26101
Sun Valley Rd 26101
Sunrise Ave 26104
Sunset Blvd 26101
W Sunshine Ln 26104
Sure Fire Dr 26104
Sutton Pl 26104
Swann St 26101
Sycamore St 26101
Tallyho Rd 26104
Tanglewood Dr & Pl 26104
Tara Ln 26101
Tawney Ln 26104
Tefft St 26101
Television Plz 26101
Terrace Ave 26101
Terrace Hls 26104
Theodocia Dr 26101
Thomas Ln & St 26101
Thorn St 26101
Thornberry Hill Dr 26104
Thoroughbred Ln 26104
Tiffany Ln 26104
Timber Ln 26104
Timberland Dr 26104
Timberline Pkwy 26105
Tims Ln 26101
Tipper Rd 26101
Tolbert Rd 26101
Tonya Ave 26101
Tower Rd 26101
Tracewell Ave 26101
Trail Ridge Rd 26104
Triana Ln 26104
Tumbleweed Dr 26104
Tumblewood Dr 26105
Turnberry Ln 26101
Turner Farm Rd 26104
Twin Fawn Trl 26104
Twin Lakes Rd 26105
Twin Oaks Dr 26101
Tygart Ln & St 26101
Uhl St 26104
Unity Pl 26101
Upland Rd 26104
Utah Ln 26104
Vair Ave 26104
Valley Rd 26101
Valley Mills Cir, Ct, Dr & Rd 26104
Valley View Acres 26104
Vanfossen Ln 26104
Vase Rd 26101
Vaughan Ave 26101
Vaught Ter 26101
Victoria Ave 26101
Victory St 26104
Viewpoint Addition 26101
Villa Dr 26101
Vine Ave 26101
Virgil St 26101
Virginia Ave 26101
W Virginia Ave
 400-799 26101
 800-1399 26104
Viscose Rd & St 26101
Wallace Rd 26104
Walnut Dr 26101
Walnut St
 1-199 26104
 2900-3399 26101
Walton Dr 26101
Ward Pl 26101
Warren Ave & Dr 26104
Washington Ave, Hts & Rd 26101
Waterway St 26101
Watson Rd 26104
Wayside Farms Rd 26104
Webster St 26104
Wedgewood Dr & Pl 26104
Wellington Ct 26104
Wells Cir 26101
West Ln 26104

Western Hills Dr 26105
Westview Cir & Way ... 26101
Westwood Dr & Pt 26101
Westwood Landings Rd 26101
Wharton Dr 26104
Whispering Oaks Ln 26104
Whispering Pines Cir, Ct & Dr 26104
White Head Dr 26101
White Oaks Farm 26104
Whitetail Dr 26104
Whitetail Ln 26101
Whitman Rd 26101
Wigal St 26101
Wiggins Ln 26104
Wilbur St 26101
E & W Wildwood Cir & Dr 26101
Wildwood Heights Dr ... 26101
Willard Rd
1-2499 26105
2500-2599 26104
Willard St 26104
Williams Hwy 26105
Williams St 26101
Willie Ln 26101
Willoughby Dr 26101
Willow Ln 26105
Willow Ter 26104
Willow Tree Way 26104
Willowbrook Dr 26104
Wilson Aly & St 26101
Wind Dancer Ln 26101
Winding Rd 26104
Winding Heights Rd 26104
Windswept Acres Ln 26104
Windy Ln 26101
Wireless Way 26101
Wisper Pines Trailer Park 26104
Wolfe Estate Ln 26104
Wood Cir 26104
Wood St 26101
Wood County Courthouse 26101
Woodberry Cir & Ln 26104
Woodberry Commons .. 26104
Woodland Ave
11-98 26101
301-397 26104
399-599 26104
Woodland Hills Dr 26104
Woodland Park Dr 26104
Woodshire Ct & Dr 26104
Woodyard St 26101
Woodyards Cave Rd ... 26104
Workman Ln 26101
Worthington Ln 26104
Worthington St 26101
Worthington Ter 26104
Worthington Vw 26104
Worthington Creek Rd .. 26104
Worthington Trailer Park Rd 26104
Wyndemere Ct, Dr & Way 26105
Wyndham Knob 26104
Wyngate Ct & Dr 26105
Yellow Pine Dr 26105
Youngs Way 26104

NUMBERED STREETS

S 1st Ave & St 26101
S 2nd Ave & St 26101
S 3rd Ave & St 26101
S 4th Ave & St 26101
5 Mile Run 26104
S 5th 26101
6 Mile Run Rd 26104
S 6th Ave & St 26101
7 1/2 St 26101
7 Acres 26101
7 Acres Rd 26104
7th Ave 26101
7th St
200-3099 26101
3100-3198 26104
3101-3199 26101
E 7th St 26104
E 8th Ave & St 26101
9 1/2 St 26101
9th Ave & St 26101
10th Ave & St 26101
11th Ave & St 26101
12th Ave & St 26101
13th Ave & St 26101
14th Ave & St 26101
15th Ave & St 26101
16th Ave & St 26101
17th Ave & St 26101
18th Ave & St 26101
19th Ave & St 26101
20th Ave & St 26101
21st Ave 26101
22nd Ave & St 26101
23rd Ave & St 26101
24th Ave & St 26101
25th Ave 26101
25th Pl 26101
25th St
1000-2299 26101
2700-3499 26104
26th Ave 26101
26th Pl 26101
26th St
600-899 26101
900-1099 26104
1200-1999 26101
2500-2999 26104
27th Ave 26101
27th St
900-1199 26104
1600-1999 26101
2500-3299 26104
28th St
900-1299 26104
1400-1699 26101
2700-2999 26104
29th St
1-97 26101
99-799 26101
900-1199 26104
1900-2699 26101
2700-3099 26104
30th St
500-799 26101
800-1599 26104
1800-1999 26101
31st St
500-799 26101
800-1899 26104
529-1-529-5 26101
32nd St
500-799 26101
800-1899 26104
529-1-529-5 26101
33rd St
400-799 26101
800-2499 26104
34th Pl & St 26104
35th St 26104
36th St
400-599 26101
1000-2699 26104
37th St
400-599 26101
1000-2599 26104
38th St 26104
39th St 26104
40th St 26104
41st St 26104
42nd St 26104
43rd St 26104
44th Pl & St 26104
45th St 26104
46th St 26105
2000-2399 26104
60th St 26105
61st St 26105
10 1/2 St 26101
13 1/2 St 26101
17 1/2 St 26101

PRINCETON WV

General Delivery 24740

POST OFFICE BOXES MAIN OFFICE STATIONS AND BRANCHES

Box No.s
All PO Boxes 24740

RURAL ROUTES

03, 04, 06, 10 24739
02, 03, 04, 05, 10 24740

HIGHWAY CONTRACTS

68, 71 24740

NAMED STREETS

Abbony Ln 24740
Abbott Way 24739
Acorn Ln 24740
Adairs Run Rd 24739
Adonis Ln 24739
Airport Dr 24740
Alabama Ave 24739
Alfalfa Rd 24739
Alfonzo Ct 24739
Allenwood Pl 24739
Allison Ln 24739
Alloy Ct 24740
Aloe Ln 24739
Alpha Rd 24740
Alps Ave 24740
Alvis Rd 24739
Amber Hls & Ln 24740
Amble Way 24740
Ambrose Ln 24739
Amelia Pl 24740
Anderson Dr 24739
Antelope Ln 24739
Antler Ln 24739
Applegate Rd 24739
Appletree Pl 24739
Appleway Ln 24739
Aqua St 24739
Asbury Rd 24740
Asher Ln 24739
Ashley Ln 24740
Ashworth 24739
Ashworth Rd 24740
Aspen Ct 24740
Assembly Ln 24739
Aster Ln 24739
Athens Rd
100-1999 24740
2000-5799 24739
Athens Ter 24739
Atlas Pl 24739
Austin St 24740
Auto Ln 24740
Autry Pl 24739
Autumn Ln 24739
Azalea St 24739
B Ray St 24740
Babbit Ct 24740
Bacardi St 24740
Back School Rd 24739
Backwoods Ave 24739
Bailey Ln & St 24740
Bailey Hollow Rd 24740
Baker Ln 24740
Ball St 24740
Ballard St 24740
Bambi Pl 24739
Bane Ave 24740
Barberie Ln 24740
Barborosa Ln 24740
Barker St 24740
Barn Branch Ln 24740
Basin Pl 24740
Basking Pl 24740
Bayberry Ave 24739
Beagle Pl 24740
Beam St 24740
Beaman Hill Rd 24739
Bean Blossom Rd 24739
Beaver Br 24739
Beck St 24740
Beckley Rd 24740
Beckwith Ln 24739
Bee St 24740
Beechtree St 24739
Begonia Way 24740
Belcher Ln 24739
Belgian Rd 24739
Bell Ave & St 24740
Bella Dr 24739
Berg Ct 24740
Berkley St 24740
Berryhill Rd 24740
Bethel Rd 24739
Beulah Ln 24739
Big Laurel Hwy 24739
Big Oak Rd 24739
Big Spring Branch Rd .. 24739
Bighorn Ave 24740
Billy Rd 24739
Birch Ln 24739
Bish Ave 24740
Black Oak Rd 24740
Blackberry Rd 24740
Blake Ave 24740
Blake Hollow Rd 24739
Blazer Pl 24739
Blossom Rd 24740
Blue Rock Cir 24739
Bluebird Ln 24740
Bluefield Ave 24740
Bluejay Ct 24740
Blueridge Ave 24740
Blueview Farm Rd 24739
Bobolink Ct 24740
Bogey Ln 24739
Boggs St 24739
Booker Street Ext 24740
Boots Collins Ln 24739
Borage Ave 24739
Bostic St 24740
Botanical Ln 24739
Bower 24740
Bowling St 24740
Boxcar Pl 24740
Boxwood Cir 24739
Bradford Ln 24739
Bratton Ave 24740
Braxter St 24739
Bray Rd 24739
Brazil Ct 24739
Breezehill St 24739
Brick St 24740
Brickyard Rd 24739
Bridlewood Dr 24739
Brighton Cir 24739
Brim Rd 24739
Brinkley Rd 24739
Brittany Dr 24739
Broadway St 24740
Broadway Apartments .. 24739
Broadway Subdivision .. 24739
Broadway Townhouses 24739
Brock Cir 24740
Brook Ln 24739
Brooklyn Ln 24740
Brookman Ave 24740
Brookstone St 24739
Brookwood Pl 24739
Brown St 24740
Brown Cemetery Rd 24739
Brownie Pl 24740
Browning Oak Rd 24739
Browns Rd 24739
Browns Farm Rd 24739
Brush Creek Falls Rd .. 24739
Brushy Creek St 24740
Buckeye Hollow Rd 24739
Bucktail Rd 24739
Buckwheat Rd 24739
Bud Ave 24740
Burgess St 24740
Burnshire Pl 24740
Burnt Cabin Rd 24739
Butler St 24740
Butternut Dr 24740
C And W Trailer Park .. 24740
Cabell St 24740
Caboose Cir 24740
Cahill Dr 24740
Caldwell St
1-99 24740
100-999 24739
Caldwell Hollow Rd 24739
Calm Pl 24739
Camden Cir
126-127 24739
136-136 24740
Cameo Ln 24739
Campcreek Rd
1200-1299 24739
1300-1398 24740
1301-1399 24739
1500-1598 24740
1501-1599 24740
Canary Ln 24740
Candace Ct 24740
Candlelight Ln 24739
Cannon St 24740
E Canyon Ave 24740
N & S Caperton Ave ... 24740
Caraway St 24739
Cardinal Ave 24740
Career Path 24739
Carl Wade Rd 24739
Carmello Ave 24740
Carnation Ln 24740
Carnival St 24739
Carr Ln 24739
Carter Dr 24740
Casey St 24739
Cashmere Ct 24739
Cassatt Pl 24739
Catkin Ln 24740
Catskill Rd 24739
Caudill Ct 24739
Caywood Ln 24739
Cedar Ln 24740
Cedar Ridge Rd 24739
Cedarglen Ln 24739
Celtic St 24739
Center St 24740
Chadwood Ln 24739
Champ St 24740
Charlies Dr 24739
Charlotte Ave & St 24740
Charwood Ave 24739
Chase Ln 24740
Cheesy Creek Rd 24739
Chelsea Ln 24739
Chestnut Dr 24739
Chevy Rd 24739
Cheyenne Dr 24739
Chinky St 24739
Chop Ct 24740
Christian St 24740
Christian Fork Loop 24740
Christian Ridge Rd 24739
Christie Ave 24740
Christopher Ave 24740
Church Ln & St 24740
Church Hill Rd 24739
Cimarron Dr 24739
E Circle Dr 24740
City View Hts 24740
Clairmont Hills Dr 24739
Clark Est 24739
Clemons Rd 24739
Clemson Cir 24739
Cleveland Pl 24739
Clover Dew Dairy Rd ... 24739
Cloverleaf Ln 24739
Cochran Rd 24740
Cody Pl 24740
College Ave 24740
Colonial Hls 24739
Columbus Ln 24739
Combs Run Rd 24739
Comfort Ct 24739
Compact Way 24740
Conner St 24739
Cook St 24740
Copper St 24739
Cordell Rd 24740
Corine St 24739
Cornbread Ridge Rd ... 24740
Cornerstone Ln 24739
Cornfield Rd 24740
Cotton Pl 24739
Cottonwood Ct 24740
Country Field Ln 24739
Country Hill Dr 24739
Country Stroll Ln 24739
Countryside Rd 24739
Courthouse Rd 24740
Cove Br 24739
Cove St 24740
Cove Hill Ln 24739
Coxs Cutoff 24739
Coy Ave 24740
Craddock Farm Rd 24739
Craft Rd 24739
Crane Pl 24740
Crawford St 24739
Creedmore Cir 24739
Creekledge Ln 24740
Crestview Dr 24739
Crimson St 24739
Crockett Ave 24740
Crocus Way 24740
Crossing Ln 24739
Crotty St 24740
Crotty Smith Rd 24740
Growing Way 24739
Crown Pt 24740
Cumberland Rd 24739
Cup St 24740
Current Ln 24739
Curry Ln 24740
Curry Trailer Park 24740
Cyphers Rd 24740
Daisy St 24739
Dale Cir 24739
Damewood Ave 24740
Damson Ave 24739
Dandelion Dr 24739
Daniel Ave 24740
Daniely St 24739
Dans Rd 24739
Dara Heights Pl 24739
Dave Harman Rd 24739
Davis Ln 24740
Davis St 24739
Dawnridge Rd 24739
Dawnview Pl 24739
Dayton Hill Rd 24739
Daytona Dr 24739
Dead End Rd 24739
Deer Mountain Dr 24739
Deer Run Rd 24739
Deerfield Ln 24739
Deerwood Ln 24739
Delaney Ln 24739
Devin St 24739
Diane Ln 24740
Dingess St 24740
Dino Pl 24740
Dodrill Hollow Rd 24739
Doewood Dr 24740
Dogwood Ln 24740
Dogwood Flats Rd 24739
Dolittle Ln 24739
Don Morgan Dr 24739
Doral Ln 24739
Double Oaks Dr 24739
Double T Farm Rd 24740
Douglas Ave & St 24740
Dove Ln 24739
Downy Pl 24740
Doyle Cir 24740
Dreamview Pl 24739
Dryhill Pl 24739
Duncan Rd 24739
Dunn Ln 24740
Durrs Pond Rd 24739
Dusty Miller St 24740
Eads Mill Rd 24739
Eagle Ln 24739
Earlie St 24740
East Dr 24739
Easy St 24740
Echo Way 24739
Edgemont Dr 24740
Edwards Ave 24740
Ehn St 24740
Elder Ave 24739
Electric St 24740
Elgood Rd 24739
Elgood Mountain Rd 24739
Elgood Pettrey Rd 24739
Elko Way 24739
Elkview St 24739
Elm St 24740
Elmer St 24740
Elmore Rd 24739
Elmore St 24740
Elmore School Rd 24739
Emory Ave 24740
Erica Ln 24740
Esther St 24740
Estill St 24740
Et Dr 24739
Evans Pl 24739
Evergreen Ct 24739
Expert Cir 24739
Facet St 24739
Fairfield Pl 24740
Fairgrounds Rd 24739
Fairmont Dr 24739
Fairview St 24740
Faith Ln 24739
Falcon Ln 24740
Fallview Rd 24740
Family Rd 24740
Farrell Cir 24739
Fawn Ln 24739
Fayette St 24740
Faze Ct 24740
Featherbed Ln 24739
Fellers St 24740
Fennel Ln 24739
Fern St 24740
Fiddle Way 24739
Field St 24740
Fiesta Ln 24739
Finch Ave 24739
Finley Ln 24739
Fleming Ln 24739
Flint St 24740
Floral Way 24739
Foot St 24740
Foothill Ln 24739
Ford Rd 24740
Forestedge Dr 24739
Forrest St 24740
Forty Foot St 24740
Foster St 24740
Fountain Park Rd 24739
Fox Run Est 24739
Frances Ct 24739
Frazier Dr 24739
Frederick Ct 24740
Freeborn Ct 24739
Freight Station Pl 24739
Friar Ln 24740
Friendly St 24739
Frisco Ln 24739
Front St 24740
Frontage Rd 24739
Frontier Pl 24739
Frosty Ln 24740

Fuller Ln 24739
Fuschia Way 24739
Gable Ct 24739
Gadd St 24740
Galaxy Ln 24739
Gale Winds Apartments 24739
Garden Crest Rd 24740
Garden Oaks Dr 24739
Gardenia Way 24739
Gardner Rd 24740
Gardner Loop Rd 24740
Garland St 24740
Garnet St 24739
Garry Dean Ln 24740
Gavins Way 24739
Gayle St 24740
Gelding St 24740
Gentry St 24740
Georgian Manor Dr 24740
Gershman Cir 24739
Gibbs Ave 24739
Ginger Ln 24740
Glacier Ln 24740
Glade Pl 24739
Glady Fork Ln 24739
Glam Ct 24740
Glen Cv 24740
Glenair St 24739
Glendale Ave 24740
Glenfield Pl 24739
Glenridge Pl 24740
Glenwood Haven Rd 24739
Glenwood Park Rd 24739
Glory Way 24740
Glossy Ln 24739
Goldcrest Ln 24739
Golden Ln 24740
Golden Gate St 24739
Goldfinch Ct 24740
Goodwyns Chapel Rd 24739
Gorbutt Rd 24739
Gott Rd & St 24740
Grace Branch Rd 24739
Gracy St 24739
Grand Veterinary Pl 24739
Grandview Dr & Pl 24740
Grape St 24740
Grass Way 24739
Grayson Rd 24740
Graystone Ln 24740
Greasy Ridge Rd 24739
Green Acres Loop 24739
Green Springs Rd 24739
Green Tree Ln 24739
Greenback Ave 24740
Greenview Ave & Dr 24740
Greenway Rd 24739
Griffith Ln 24739
Grubb Rd 24739
Guard Dr 24740
Guilford Cir 24739
Gum St 24740
Hackberry Ln 24739
Haldy Hts 24740
Hale Ave 24740
Hale Avenue Ext 24740
Hales Gap Rd 24739
Hall Ct 24740
Halls Ridge Rd 24739
Halo Pl 24740
Hampton Ct 24740
Hardin Rd 24740
Hardwood Ln 24740
Hardy Hollow Rd 24739
Harley Dr 24739
Harley Davidson Ln 24739
Harmon Branch Rd 24739
Harmon School Rd 24739
Harmony Hill Rd 24739
Harrison St 24740
Hassam Dr 24739
Hasty St 24740
Hatcher Rd 24739
Hatcher St 24740
Hatcher Church Rd 24739
Haven Dr 24740
Haw Pond Farm Rd 24739
Hawks Nest Ave 24740
Hawthorn Ln 24739
Hayes Valley Rd 24739
Haynes Ln 24739
Hazelnut Dr 24739
Hazelwood Hill Rd 24739
Hearn Ave 24740
Heart Ln 24739
Heather Ave 24739
Hedge St 24740
Hemlock Ln 24739
Henderson St 24740
Henley Rd 24739
Henry St 24739
Heuser Ave 24740
Hickory St 24740
Hickory Gate Rd 24739
Hickory Lake Ln 24739
Hickory Ridge Rd 24740
Hidden Rd 24740
Hidden Hills Way 24739
Hidden Meadows Ln 24740
Hidden Mountain Ln 24739
Hidden Spring Ln 24740
High St 24740
High Plains Dr 24739
Highland Ave 24740
Highpoint Ln 24739
Hill St 24740
Hillcrest Dr 24740
Hillside Dr 24740
Hilltop Dr 24739
Hilltop Ln 24740
Hillview St 24740
Hines Ave 24740
Hinton St 24740
Hobbs Pl 24740
Hog Wild Pl 24739
Hoge St 24740
Holly Hill Rd 24740
Hollywood Rd 24740
Home Pl 24739
Homestead Dr 24739
Honaker Ave 24740
Honey Ln 24739
Hoot Owl Hollow Rd 24739
Hope Ln 24740
Hops St 24740
Horton Ln 24739
Howard Ln 24739
Huckleberry Ln 24739
Hudson Ln 24739
Huffman Ln 24740
Hummingbird Ave 24740
Hundley St 24740
Hunnicut Ln 24740
Hunnicutt Ln 24739
Hunt St 24740
Hunter Park 24740
Hutchins Ln 24740
Icon Ct 24739
Ideal Cir 24739
Imperial Dr 24739
Indian Rocke 24740
Industrial St 24740
Ingleside Rd
100-299 24740
300-320 24739
301-321 24740
322-13699 24739
Inglevalley Rd 24739
Inpa Ln 24739
Inspiration Ln 24740
Ira Ave 24740
Iris St 24740
Irongate Ln 24739
Ironwood Gate Dr 24740
Island St 24740
Ives Ln 24739
Ivyridge St 24740
Jade Ln 24739
Jason Ave 24740
Java Ln 24739
Jays Ln 24740
Jefferson St 24740
Jennings St 24739
Jera K St 24739
Jeremy St 24740
Jimmies Pl 24739
Jodi St 24739
N & S Johnston St 24740
Johnston School Rd 24739
Joshua St 24740
Joywood Rd 24740
Juno Pl 24739
Just Ct 24740
Justice Hollow Rd 24740
Justin Jesse St 24740
Jute Pl 24739
Kale Rd 24740
Kanawha Pl 24740
Karens Way 24739
Karnes St 24740
Katava Way 24739
Kaye Dr 24740
Kb Ln 24739
Keatley Rd 24740
Keaton Ln 24739
Kee St 24740
Kegley River Rd 24740
Kegley Trestle Rd 24740
Kelly St 24740
Kellys Tank Rd 24739
Kellysville Rd 24739
Kelp Pl 24740
Kemp Ln 24739
Kenmore Cir 24739
Kensington Ct 24740
Kent Dr 24739
Kerr Pl 24739
Keystone Ln 24739
Kiffs Rd 24739
Kim St 24740
Kimberly Ln 24739
Kingbird Way 24740
Kingsmill Way 24739
Kinsman Ct 24740
Kips Rd 24739
Kirby Ave 24740
Kirby Addition Rd 24739
Kirk St 24739
Kirkwood Ave 24740
Kittinger St 24739
Knapp Ave 24739
Knob St 24740
Kolton Rd 24740
Kramer Pl 24739
Krit Ln 24739
Kylees Pl 24739
Lacy St 24740
Ladder Ln 24740
Ladyslipper Ln 24739
Lakeview Dr 24739
Lakewood Ests & St 24740
Lakewood Subdivision 24740
Lamb Rd 24739
Lamplighter St 24739
Lance St 24740
Landonwood St 24740
Landsend Ct 24739
Lark St 24739
Larue Rd 24740
Laurel Dr 24740
Laurel Creek Rd 24739
Lavender Ln 24739
Lazenby Ave 24740
Leah Dr 24739
Lee St 24740
Lees Mobile Home Park 24740
Lenox Ln 24739
Lessie Ct 24740
Lester Ln 24740
Levi Ln 24739
Lewis St 24739
Lichen Ln 24739
Lilac Ln 24739
Lilly St 24740
Lilly Addition Rd 24740
Lilly Grove Dr 24740
Lilly Top Ln 24739
Lincoln St 24740
Linda St 24740
Lindo Gillespie Rd 24739
Linkous St 24740
Lion Rd 24740
Litchfield Ct 24739
Little Fox St 24740
Little Island Creek Rd 24739
Little Sparrow St 24740
Livisay Ct 24739
Lj St 24740
Lloyd Ln 24740
Loblolly Cir 24740
Lockridge Ln 24740
Loco Ln 24740
Locust St 24740
Lohr Ln 24740
Lomax Ln 24740
Longacre Ln 24740
Lost Farm Rd 24740
Lovell Ave 24740
Lovelock Ct 24739
Lovern Rd 24739
Low Gap Rd 24740
Low Water Rd 24740
Lowe Ln 24740
Lower Bell Ave 24740
Lower Pine St 24740
Lurray Ave 24740
Lyle Way 24740
Lyndsey Dr 24739
Lynwood Cir 24739
Lyric Ln 24739
Mabe Ln 24740
Macadamia Pl 24740
Madi Ln 24739
Magnolia St 24740
Mahood Ave 24740
Main St 24740
Mallard Way 24740
Mallow Ave 24739
Manchester Ct 24740
Mantle Ln 24739
Many Springs Rd 24739
Maple St 24740
Maple Acres Rd 24739
Mapledale Dairy Rd 24739
Maplewood Rd 24739
Marathon Ave 24740
Marie Ln 24739
Marigold Cir 24740
Marion St 24740
Maris Ct 24740
Mars Dr 24739
E Martin Ave & St 24739
Martin Luther King Jr Ave 24740
Mary I Johnson Rd 24740
Mayapple Ln 24739
Mcclure Pl 24739
Mcconnell Aly 24740
Mcdowell St 24740
Mckinley Ave 24740
Mcneil Pl 24739
N & S Mcnutt Ave 24740
Meador St 24740
Meadow St 24740
Meadowbrook St 24739
Meadowbrook Mobile Home Park 24739
Meadowfield Ln 24739
Meadowlark Ln 24740
Meadows Hill Rd 24740
Meastani Rd 24740
Melrose Ln 24739
Memory Ln 24739
Mercer St 24740
Mercer Springs Rd
201-299 24740
700-998 24740
1000-3300 24739
3302-3398 24739
Merit St 24739
Merritt Pl 24739
Mica Ln 24739
Michael Ln 24739
Middlesex Ave 24740
Midway St 24740
Mikee Rd 24740
Mill Creek Rd 24739
Mills St 24739
Mimosa St 24740
Mimosa Mobile Home Park 24740
Mingo St 24740
Mink Farm Rd 24740
Mint St 24740
Minter Pl 24739
Miracle Ln 24740
Mirkwood Ln 24739
Mirror Ln 24739
Mistletoe Ln 24739
Misty Ln 24740
Misty Hills Dr 24739
Misty Oaks Ln 24740
Mitchell Ct 24739
Mobil Ave 24739
Mockingbird Pl 24740
Modern Ln 24739
Molly Ln 24739
Monroe St 24740
Mooney Ln 24739
Moore Hollow Rd 24740
Moorehead Rd 24740
Morning Star St 24739
Morningside Dr 24740
Morris Ln 24739
Morrison Dr 24740
Mount Horeb Rd 24739
Mount Jackson Heights Rd 24739
Mountain Meadow Rd 24739
Mountain Top Dr 24740
Mountain View Dr 24739
Mulkey Ln 24740
Mum Ct 24740
Murdock St 24740
Murdock Street Ext 24740
Murphy Way 24739
Muse Ln 24740
Nance Pl 24740
Nancy Owens Rd 24739
Napolean Ln 24740
Nature Dr 24739
Needham Pl 24739
New Hope Rd
1-1099 24740
1101-1235 24740
1236-4299 24739
New Life Rd 24739
New Side Rd 24739
New Zion Rd 24739
Newhouse Rd 24739
Newkirk St 24740
Newton Rd 24739
Nice St 24740
Nickel Ln 24739
Night Rd 24739
Nimitz Pl 24739
Noble Cir 24739
Nolan Cir 24739
Norfield Rd 24739
Northfield Rd 24739
Northview Ave 24740
Norton Pl 24740
Norwood Ct 24740
Nova Ln 24740
Nowlin Way 24739
Nugget Ln 24740
Oak St 24740
Oakland Dr 24739
Oakleaf Ln 24739
Oakledge Ln 24739
Oaklimb Ln 24739
Oakvale Rd 24740
Oakwood Ave & Ln 24740
Oasis Ct 24740
Oconner Dr 24739
Old Athens Rd
1-99 24740
1000-3899 24739
3901-3999 24739
Old Bluefield Rd 24739
Old Dairy Rd 24739
Old Gardner Rd 24740
Old Logan Rd 24739
Old Oakvale Rd 24740
Old Oxley Rd 24739
Old Pepsi Plant Rd 24739
Old Pisgah Rd 24740
Old Springs Rd 24739
Olen Ave 24739
Olive St 24740
Oliver Ave 24740
Olympic Rd 24739
Omega Ln 24740
Oney Gap Rd 24739
Onyx Ct 24739
Orange Ln 24739
Orchard Ave 24740
Orchid Way 24739
Oriole Ave 24740
Osprey Pl 24740
Our Hollow Rd 24740
Ovenbird Cir 24740
Overlook Ln 24739
Overton Cir 24740
Oxley Hollow Rd 24739
Palm Pl 24739
Pansy Pl 24739
Panther Pl 24739
Paradise Ln 24739
Park Ave 24740
Parrot St 24740
Partridge Dr 24740
Paynes Fork Rd 24739
Peacock Ct 24740
Pearis St 24740
Pearl St 24740
Peck St 24740
Peggy Branch Rd 24739
Pendleton Pl 24739
Pendry Ln 24739
Pennington Ln 24739
Peppermint St 24739
Peppertree Rd 24739
Periwinkle Rd 24739
Perkins Rd 24739
Pettry Rd 24739
Petty Rd 24739
Petunia Ave 24739
Phelps St 24739
Piedra Ln 24739
Pigeon Creek Rd 24739
Pigeon Roost Trl 24740
Pike Rd 24739
Pikeview Dr 24740
Pilot St 24740
Pinch Rd 24740
Pine Plz 24740
Pine Acre Way 24739
Pine Hill Cir 24739
Pine Ridge Rd 24739
Pine Tree Ln 24739
Pinehill Cir 24739
Pineview Park 24739
Piney Branch Pl 24739
Pipeline Rd 24739
Pisgah Ln & Rd 24739
Pitzer Ln 24739
Pixy Pl 24739
Planet Dr 24739
Plato Pl 24739
Pleasant Acres 24740
Pleasant Hill Est & Rd 24739
Pleasant Valley Dr 24739
Pleasantview Rd 24740
Plover Pl 24740
Plymouth Rdg 24739
Plymouth Ridge St 24739
Poem Pl 24739
Pony Farm Ln 24739
Poole Ln 24739
Poor Farm Ln 24739
Poplar Grove Dr & Est 24739
Poppy Ct 24739
Porter Dr 24739
Possum Hollow Rd 24739
Potomac Ln 24740
Powder House Rd 24739
Powell Rd 24739
Powell Mountain Rd 24739
Powers Rd 24740
Prince St 24740
Princeton Ave & Vlg 24740
Princeton Elks St 24739
Promise Ave 24740
Providence Pl 24740
Puffin Ct 24740
Puppy Ln 24740
Puritan Pl 24740
Quail Vly 24740
Quail Valley Dr 24740
Quail Valley Medical Ctr 24740
Quailview Dr 24740
Quailwood Dr 24740
Queen Ln 24740
Rabbit Rd 24739
Rabbit Run 24740
Rabbit Hollow Rd 24739
Racetrack Rd 24740
Radio Ln 24740
Rae St 24739
Railroad Ave 24739
Rainbow Rd 24739
Raintree Ln 24739
Raleigh St 24740
Ramey Ave 24740
Ranch Ln 24740
Ranch Mobile Park 24740
Randolph Ave 24740
Red Ash Rd 24740
Red Brook Dr 24739
Red Sulpher Tpke 24739
Redfox Rd 24740
Redknot St 24740
Redmont Pl 24739
Redsky Rd 24739
Reed St 24740
Reindeer Pl 24739
Repass Rd 24740
Rest Pl 24739
E Reynolds Ave 24740
Ribern St 24740
Ridgeview Farm Rd 24739
Ridgeway Dr 24740
Ridgeway Drive Ext 24740
Riggs Dr 24739
Rimcrest Ave 24739
Ring Ln 24739
Ringo Way 24740
Ritchie St 24740
Ritter St 24740
Riverfront St 24739
Roane Ave 24740
Roark Rd 24739
Robbie Ct 24739
Robbins St 24740
Robert L White Rd 24739
Robertson Ln 24739
Robin St 24740
Rock Barn Ave 24740
Rock Garden Dr & Rd 24739
Rockledge Ave 24740
Rocky Branch Rd 24740
Rocky Hollow Rd 24739
Rogers St 24740
Roller Ln 24739
Rolling Hls 24740
Rolling Hills Dr 24740
Rome St 24740
Ronald Sizemore Rd 24739
Rooster Pl 24739
Roseland Ave 24740
Rosemary St 24739
Rosewood Dr 24740
Ross Branch Rd 24740
Roth St 24740
Round Bottom Rd 24739
Roundhouse Rd 24740
Royal St 24740
Rumble Rd 24740

Rumburg Run 24739
Rustic Way 24739
Rustic Hill Dr 24739
Ruth St 24740
Rutledge Dr 24740
Ryan Vlg 24739
Rylee Pl 24739
Sackett Rd 24739
Saddle Way 24739
Sadie Brown Rd 24739
Sagebrush Ave 24740
Sami Lea St 24739
Sammy St 24740
Sand Branch Rd 24739
Sanders Grove Rd 24739
Sandpiper Ave 24740
Sandrine Pt 24740
Sandstone Dr & Park 24740
Sanford St 24739
Santa Rita Rd 24739
Sarah Rae Ct 24740
Sargent St 24739
Sassafras Ln 24739
Saucer St 24740
S Saunders Ave 24740
Savannah Ln 24740
Saved Acres Rd 24739
Savory Ln 24739
Scarlet Oaks 24739
Scenic Valley Rd 24740
Schaub Rd 24740
Scope St 24739
Scott St 24740
Scott Knob Rd 24740
Seneca Ln 24739
Sentz Aly 24740
Shadetree Cir 24739
S Shadowood Ln 24740
Shadowwood Mobile Home Park 24740
Shaker Ln 24740
Shane Ct 24740
Sharps Turn Rd 24740
Shearwater Ct 24740
Shelby Ln 24740
Shelter Rd 24739
Shelton Ln 24740
Shenandoah Ests 24740
Sheppard Hollow Rd 24739
Shop St 24740
Shopview Ave 24740
Short St 24740
Shufflebarger St 24740
Shumate Rd 24739
Sierra Cir 24739
Silver St 24739
Silver Springs Ave 24740
Simmons Cir 24739
Singer Ln 24739
Singleton Ln 24739
Skylanding Way 24739
Skylark Ln 24740
Skyview Loop 24739
Small Trl 24739
Smoky St 24740
Soaring Eagle Ln 24740
Somerset Pl 24739
South Ave 24740
Southern Hollow Rd 24739
Southview Ct & Dr 24740
Spangler Ln 24740
Sparkles St 24740
Sparrow St 24740
Spike Ln 24739
Spray Ln 24740
Spring Grove Ave 24740
Springdale Ave 24740
Springhaven Dr 24740
Spruce Dr 24740
Stable Ln 24739
Stacey St 24740
Stafford Dr
- 500-1396 24740
- 1397-1399 24739
- 1398-1398 24740

Stafford Commons 24740
Stanley St 24740
Star Dr 24739
Starling St 24740
Starr Pt 24739
N State St 24739
Steele Sawmill Rd 24739
Steeple St 24740
Stella St 24739
Stillhouse Rd 24739
Stinson Rd 24740
Stone Cress Way 24739
Stone Mountain Dr 24739
Stone Point Ln 24739
Stone Pond Ct 24739
Stonecreek St 24739
Straley Ave 24740
Strawberry Loop 24739
Strawberry Patch Rd 24739
Strock Ln 24739
Summerfield Rd 24739
Summers St 24740
Summit St 24740
Sundown Ln 24739
Sunflower St 24739
Sunny Dr 24740
Sunnydale Loop 24740
Sunrise Ave & Ext 24740
Sunset Dr 24740
Sutton Ave 24740
Swallow Ln 24740
Swan Ln 24740
Sweet Pea Ct 24740
Sweetbriar Pl 24739
Swim Ln 24739
Swing Ridge Rd 24739
Swiss Ave 24740
Sycamore Ct 24739
Syres Ln 24740
Tame St 24739
Tanager Ln 24740
Tanglewood Dr 24740
Tango Dr 24740
Tansy Pl 24740
Target Ln 24740
Tarpon Ln 24739
Taryn Cir 24739
Tea Kettle Rd 24740
Teaberry St 24739
Teresa St 24740
Teri Cir 24740
Terry Crews Rd 24739
Tetra St 24739
Thistle St 24739
Thomas Jefferson Dr 24739
Thompson Cemetery Rd 24739
Thorn Ave & St 24740
Thornton Ave 24740
Thunder Valley Rd 24740
Thurmer St 24740
Tiger Dr 24739
Tilley Rd 24740
Timber Vw 24739
Timber Hill Dr 24739
Tip Top St 24740
Toby Ln 24739
Toler Rd 24739
Toni Ln 24740
Topaz Ave 24740
Tracy St 24740
Tranquill Ln 24739
Treeline Rd 24740
Trent St 24740
Tri City Rd 24739
Trig Ln 24740
Triple C Rd 24739
Tristan Ln 24740
Trove Pl 24740
Truelove Rd 24739
Trumpet Vine Rd 24739
Tumbleweed St 24740
Tumblewood Rd 24739
Turnbull St 24739
Turnpike Industrial Park Rd 24739
Turtle Ridge Rd 24739
Twelvemile Rd 24739
Twin Lake Ln 24739
Twin Oaks Cir 24739
Twin Pine Ln 24739
Tyler Wesley Rd 24739
Tynwald Hill Ln 24739
Undercliff Ter 24740
Union Dr 24740
Union St 24739
Unity Rd 24739
Upper Bell Ave 24740
Upper Pine St 24740
E Valley Dr & St 24740
Valley View St 24740
Valor Ct 24740
Vance Rd 24739
Vandiver Ln 24740
Vapor Way 24739
Vector Ln 24739
Vegas Ln 24739
Velum Rd 24739
Venus Dr 24739
Veterinary Pl 24739
Vicars St 24740
Vida Ln 24739
Village Glen St 24740
Village Green Cir 24739
Vine Loop 24739
Vine St 24740
Viney Cir 24739
Vintage Oak Way 24739
Vintage Oaks 24739
Violet St 24740
Virginian Industrial Park Rd 24740
Von Nida Bahn 24739
Wabash Rd 24739
Wagner Dr 24740
Wakefield Ln 24739
N & S Walker Ave & St 24740
Walkup Hill Rd 24739
Wallace St 24740
Wallingford Rd 24739
Walnut St 24740
Walnut Grove Rd 24739
Washington Ave 24740
Watts Pl 24740
Waxberry Pl 24740
Webster St 24740
Wedgewood Ave 24739
Wertville Rd 24740
West St 24740
Westfield Rd 24739
Westover Ave 24740
Westview Ave & Dr 24740
Wetzel St 24740
Wexford Cir 24739
Wheatear Way 24740
Whispering Pine Ln 24739
Whistler Pl 24739
White Horse Rd 24739
White Oak Dr & Vly 24740
White Pines Rd 24739
White School Rd 24739
Whiteoak Creek Rd 24739
Whites Xing 24739
Whitfield Ave 24740
Whitlow Rd 24739
Whitt Hill Rd 24740
Whitts Rd 24739
N & S Wickham Ave 24740
Wilburn Flats Rd 24739
Wildlife Rd 24739
Wiley St 24740
Willeva Rd 24740
Williby Farm Rd 24739
Willow Oak Dr 24739
Willow Wind Ln 24740
Willowbrook Rd 24739
Willowbrook Road Ext 24739
Willowton Rd 24739
Willowtop Dr 24739
Willowtree St 24740
Willowview Dr 24739
Wilshire Cir 24739
Wimmer Hollow Rd 24739
Windmere St 24739
Windy Acre Pl 24739
Windy Hill Dr 24739
Winfrey Ln 24739
Winfrey Mobile Home Park 24739
Winmore Rd 24739
Winslow Cir 24739
Winterhaven Ave 24739
Winterview Ln 24739
Wirt Ct 24740
Wolf Run Rd 24739
Wood Ave 24740
Woodbridge Dr 24740
Woodchuck Rd 24739
Woodcrest Dr 24740
Woodcrest Addition 24740
Woodland Ln 24740
Workshop St 24739
Worley St 24740
Worrell St 24740
Wren Pl 24740
Wyndale Dr 24739
Wynn Ct 24739
Yale Ct 24739
Yoke Ct 24740
Yorkshire Ln 24739
Young St 24740
Your Way 24740
Yukon St 24740
Zanza Ln 24740
Zena St 24739
Zinnia Ct 24740

NUMBERED STREETS

All Street Addresses 24740

Wisconsin

People QuickFacts	Wisconsin	USA
Population, 2013 estimate	5,742,713	316,128,839
Population, 2010 (April 1) estimates base	5,686,983	308,747,716
Population, percent change, April 1, 2010 to July 1, 2013	1.0%	2.4%
Population, 2010	5,686,986	308,745,538
Persons under 5 years, percent, 2013	6.0%	6.3%
Persons under 18 years, percent, 2013	22.8%	23.3%
Persons 65 years and over, percent, 2013	14.8%	14.1%
Female persons, percent, 2013	50.3%	50.8%
White alone, percent, 2013 (a)	88.1%	77.7%
Black or African American alone, percent, 2013 (a)	6.5%	13.2%
American Indian and Alaska Native alone, percent, 2013 (a)	1.1%	1.2%
Asian alone, percent, 2013 (a)	2.5%	5.3%
Native Hawaiian and Other Pacific Islander alone, percent, 2013 (a)	Z	0.2%
Two or More Races, percent, 2013	1.7%	2.4%
Hispanic or Latino, percent, 2013 (b)	6.3%	17.1%
White alone, not Hispanic or Latino, percent, 2013	82.5%	62.6%
Living in same house 1 year & over, percent, 2008-2012	85.8%	84.8%
Foreign born persons, percent, 2008-2012	4.6%	12.9%
Language other than English spoken at home, pct age 5+, 2008-2012	8.6%	20.5%
High school graduate or higher, percent of persons age 25+, 2008-2012	90.2%	85.7%
Bachelor's degree or higher, percent of persons age 25+, 2008-2012	26.4%	28.5%
Veterans, 2008-2012	423,264	21,853,912
Mean travel time to work (minutes), workers age 16+, 2008-2012	21.6	25.4
Housing units, 2013	2,633,330	132,802,859
Homeownership rate, 2008-2012	68.6%	65.5%
Housing units in multi-unit structures, percent, 2008-2012	25.3%	25.9%
Median value of owner-occupied housing units, 2008-2012	$169,000	$181,400
Households, 2008-2012	2,286,339	115,226,802
Persons per household, 2008-2012	2.42	2.61
Per capita money income in past 12 months (2012 dollars), 2008-2012	$27,426	$28,051
Median household income, 2008-2012	$52,627	$53,046
Persons below poverty level, percent, 2008-2012	12.5%	14.9%

Business QuickFacts	Wisconsin	USA
Private nonfarm establishments, 2012	138,246	7,431,808
Private nonfarm employment, 2012	2,388,855	115,938,468
Private nonfarm employment, percent change, 2011-2012	1.5%	2.2%
Nonemployer establishments, 2012	336,059	22,735,915
Total number of firms, 2007	433,797	27,092,908
Black-owned firms, percent, 2007	2.6%	7.1%
American Indian- and Alaska Native-owned firms, percent, 2007	0.6%	0.9%
Asian-owned firms, percent, 2007	1.6%	5.7%
Native Hawaiian and Other Pacific Islander-owned firms, percent, 2007	S	0.1%
Hispanic-owned firms, percent, 2007	1.3%	8.3%
Women-owned firms, percent, 2007	25.9%	28.8%
Manufacturers shipments, 2007 ($1000)	163,563,195	5,319,456,312
Merchant wholesaler sales, 2007 ($1000)	59,996,244	4,174,286,516
Retail sales, 2007 ($1000)	72,283,321	3,917,663,456
Retail sales per capita, 2007	$12,904	$12,990
Accommodation and food services sales, 2007 ($1000)	9,247,311	613,795,732
Building permits, 2012	12,041	829,658

Geography QuickFacts	Wisconsin	USA
Land area in square miles, 2010	54,157.80	3,531,905.43
Persons per square mile, 2010	105	87.4
FIPS Code	55	

(a) Includes persons reporting only one race.
(b) Hispanics may be of any race, so also are included in applicable race categories.
FN: Footnote on this item for this area in place of data
NA: Not available
D: Suppressed to avoid disclosure of confidential information
X: Not applicable
S: Suppressed; does not meet publication standards
Z: Value greater than zero but less than half unit of measure shown
F: Fewer than 100 firms
Source: US Census Bureau State & County QuickFacts

Wisconsin

3 DIGIT ZIP CODE MAP

Wisconsin

(Abbreviation: WI)

Post Office, County — ZIP Code

Places with more than one ZIP code are listed in capital letters, See pages indicated.

Abbotsford, Clark 54405
Abrams, Oconto 54101
Adams, Adams 53910
Adell, Sheboygan 53001
Afton, Rock 53501
Albany, Green 53502
Algoma, Kewaunee 54201
Allenton, Washington 53002
Allouez, Brown 54301
Alma, Buffalo 54610
Alma Center, Jackson 54611
Almena, Barron 54805
Almond, Portage 54909
Altoona, Eau Claire 54720
Alvin, Florence 54542
Amberg, Marinette 54102
Amery, Polk 54001
Amherst, Portage 54406
Amherst Junction, Portage 54407
Aniwa, Marathon 54408
Antigo, Langlade 54409
APPLETON, Outagamie
(See Page 4333)
Arbor Vitae, Oneida 54568
Arcadia, Trempealeau 54612
Arena, Iowa 53503
Argonne, Forest 54511
Argyle, Lafayette 53504
Arkansaw, Pepin 54721
Arkdale, Adams 54613
Arlington, Columbia 53911
Armstrong Creek, Forest 54103
Arpin, Wood 54410
Ashippun, Dodge 53003
Ashland, Ashland 54806
Ashwaubenon, Brown 54115
Athelstane, Marinette 54104
Athens, Marathon 54411
Auburndale, Wood 54412
Augusta, Eau Claire 54722
Avalon, Rock 53505
Avoca, Iowa 53506
Babcock, Wood 54413
Bagley, Grant 53801
Baileys Harbor, Door 54202
Baldwin, Saint Croix 54002
Balsam Lake, Polk 54810
Bancroft, Portage 54921
Bangor, La Crosse 54614
Baraboo, Sauk 53913
Barnes, Douglas 54873
Barneveld, Iowa 53507
Barron, Barron 54812
Barronett, Barron 54813
Bassett, Kenosha 53101
Bay City, Pierce 54723
Bay View, Milwaukee 53207
Bayfield, Bayfield 54814
Bayside, Milwaukee 53217
Bear Creek, Outagamie 54922
Beaver, Marinette 54114
Beaver Dam, Dodge 53916
Beetown, Grant 53802
Beldenville, Pierce 54003
Belgium, Ozaukee 53004
Belleville, Dane 53508
Bellevue, Brown 54311
Belmont, Lafayette 53510
BELOIT, Rock
(See Page 4335)
Benet Lake, Kenosha 53102
Bennett, Douglas 54873
Benoit, Bayfield 54816
Benton, Lafayette 53803
Berlin, Green Lake 54923
Big Bend, Waukesha 53103
Big Falls, Waupaca 54926
Birchwood, Washburn 54817
Birnamwood, Shawano 54414
Black Creek, Outagamie 54106
Black Earth, Dane 53515
Black River Falls, Jackson 54615
Blair, Trempealeau 54616
Blanchardville, Lafayette 53516
Blenker, Wood 54415
Bloom City, Vernon 54634
Bloomer, Chippewa 54724
Bloomington, Grant 53804
Blue Mounds, Dane 53517
Blue River, Grant 53518
Bonduel, Shawano 54107
Bonduel, Shawano 54182
Boscobel, Grant 53805
Boulder Junction, Vilas 54512
Bowler, Shawano 54416
Boyceville, Dunn 54725
Boyd, Chippewa 54726
Branch, Manitowoc 54247
Brandon, Fond Du Lac 53919
Brantwood, Price 54513
Briggsville, Marquette 53920
Brill, Barron 54818
Brillion, Calumet 54110
Bristol, Kenosha 53104
Brodhead, Green 53520
Brokaw, Marathon 54417
BROOKFIELD, Waukesha
(See Page 4336)
Brooklyn, Green 53521
Brooks, Marquette 53952
Brown Deer
(See Milwaukee)
Brownsville, Dodge 53006
Browntown, Green 53522
Bruce, Rusk 54819
Brule, Douglas 54820
Brussels, Door 54204
Bryant, Langlade 54418
Buffalo City, Buffalo 54622
Burlington, Racine 53105
Burnett, Dodge 53922
Butler, Waukesha 53007
Butte Des Morts, Winnebago 54927
Butternut, Ashland 54514
Byron, Dodge 53006
Cable, Bayfield 54821
Cadott, Chippewa 54727
Caledonia, Racine 53108
Cambria, Columbia 53923
Cambridge, Dane 53523
Cameron, Barron 54822
Camp Douglas, Juneau 54618
Camp Douglas, Juneau 54637
Camp Lake, Kenosha 53109
Campbellsport, Fond Du Lac 53010
Canton, Barron 54868
Caroline, Shawano 54928
Cascade, Sheboygan 53011
Casco, Kewaunee 54205
Cashton, Monroe 54619
Cassville, Grant 53806
Cataract, Monroe 54620
Catawba, Price 54515
Cato, Manitowoc 54230
Cavour, Forest 54511
Cazenovia, Richland 53924
Cecil, Shawano 54111
Cedar Grove, Sheboygan 53013
Cedarburg, Ozaukee 53012
Centuria, Polk 54824
Chaseburg, Vernon 54621
Chelsea, Taylor 54451
Chetek, Barron 54728
Chili, Clark 54420
Chilton, Calumet 53014
Chippewa Falls, Chippewa 54729
Clam Falls, Polk 54837
Clam Lake, Ashland 54517
Clayton, Polk 54004
Clear Lake, Polk 54005
Cleveland, Manitowoc 53015
Clinton, Rock 53525
Clintonville, Waupaca 54929
Clyman, Dodge 53016
Cobb, Iowa 53526
Cochrane, Buffalo 54622
Colby, Clark 54421
Coleman, Marinette 54112
Colfax, Dunn 54730
Colgate, Washington 53017
Collins, Manitowoc 54207
Coloma, Waushara 54930
Columbus, Columbia 53925
Combined Locks, Outagamie 54113
Comstock, Barron 54826
Conover, Vilas 54519
Conrath, Rusk 54731
Coon Valley, Vernon 54623
Cornell, Chippewa 54732
Cornucopia, Bayfield 54827
Cottage Grove, Dane 53527
Couderay, Sawyer 54828
Crandon, Forest 54520
Crivitz, Marinette 54114
Cross Plains, Dane 53528
Cuba City, Grant 53807
Cudahy, Milwaukee 53110
Cumberland, Barron 54829
Curtiss, Clark 54422
Cushing, Polk 54006
Custer, Portage 54423
Cutler, Juneau 54618
Dairyland, Burnett 54830
Dale, Outagamie 54931
Dallas, Barron 54733
Dalton, Green Lake 53926
Danbury, Burnett 54830
Dane, Dane 53529
Darien, Walworth 53114
Darlington, Lafayette 53530
De Forest, Dane 53532
De Pere, Brown 54115
De Soto, Vernon 54624
Deer Park, Saint Croix 54007
Deerbrook, Langlade 54424
Deerfield, Dane 53531
Delafield, Waukesha 53018
Delavan, Walworth 53115
Dellwood, Adams 53927
Delta, Bayfield 54856
Denmark, Brown 54208
Deronda, Polk 54001
Dickeyville, Grant 53808
Dodge, Trempealeau 54625
Dodgeville, Iowa 53533
Dorchester, Clark 54425
Dousman, Waukesha 53118
Downing, Dunn 54734
Downsville, Dunn 54735
Doylestown, Columbia 53928
Dresser, Polk 54009
Drummond, Bayfield 54832
Dunbar, Marinette 54119
Durand, Pepin 54736
Eagle, Waukesha 53119
Eagle River, Vilas 54521
East Ellsworth, Pierce 54010
East Troy, Walworth 53120
Eastman, Crawford 54626
EAU CLAIRE, Eau Claire
(See Page 4338)
Eau Galle, Dunn 54737
Eden, Fond Du Lac 53019
Edgar, Marathon 54426
Edgerton, Rock 53534
Edgewater, Sawyer 54834
Edmund, Iowa 53535
Egg Harbor, Door 54209
Eland, Marathon 54427
Elcho, Langlade 54428
Elderon, Marathon 54429
Eldorado, Fond Du Lac 54932
Eleva, Trempealeau 54738
Elk Mound, Dunn 54739
Elkhart Lake, Sheboygan 53020
Elkhorn, Walworth 53121
Ellison Bay, Door 54210
Ellsworth, Pierce 54010
Ellsworth, Pierce 54011
Elm Grove, Waukesha 53122
Elmwood, Pierce 54740
Elmwood Park, Racine 53405
Elroy, Juneau 53929
Elton, Langlade 54430
Embarrass, Waupaca 54933
Emerald, Saint Croix 54013
Endeavor, Marquette 53930
Ephraim, Door 54211
Ettrick, Trempealeau 54627
Eureka, Winnebago 54934
Eureka, Winnebago 54963
Evansville, Rock 53536
Exeland, Sawyer 54835
Fairchild, Eau Claire 54741
Fairwater, Fond Du Lac 53931
Fall Creek, Eau Claire 54742
Fall River, Columbia 53932
Fence, Florence 54120
Fennimore, Grant 53809
Fenwood, Marathon 54426
Ferryville, Crawford 54628
Fifield, Price 54524
Fish Creek, Door 54212
Fitchburg, Dane 53575
Fitchburg, Dane 53593
Florence, Florence 54121
FOND DU LAC, Fond Du Lac
(See Page 4340)
Fontana, Walworth 53125
Footville, Rock 53537
Forest Junction, Calumet 54123
Forestville, Door 54213
Fort Atkinson, Jefferson 53538
Fort Mccoy, Monroe 54656
Fountain City, Buffalo 54629
Fox Lake, Dodge 53933
Fox Point, Milwaukee 53217
Foxboro, Douglas 54836
Francis Creek, Manitowoc 54214
Franklin, Milwaukee 53132
Franksville, Racine 53126
Frederic, Polk 54837
Fredonia, Ozaukee 53021
Freedom, Outagamie 54130
Fremont, Waupaca 54940
Friendship, Adams 53934
Friesland, Columbia 53923
Friesland, Columbia 53935
Galesville, Trempealeau 54630
Galloway, Marathon 54432
Gays Mills, Crawford 54631
Genesee Depot, Waukesha 53127
Genoa, Vernon 54632
Genoa City, Walworth 53128
Germantown, Washington 53022
Gile, Iron 54525
Gillett, Oconto 54124
Gilman, Taylor 54433
Gilman, Taylor 54434
Gilmanton, Buffalo 54743
Gleason, Lincoln 54435
Glen Flora, Rusk 54526
Glen Haven, Grant 53810
Glenbeulah, Sheboygan 53023
Glendale
(See Milwaukee)
Glenwood City, Saint Croix 54013
Glidden, Ashland 54527
Goodman, Marinette 54125
Gordon, Douglas 54838
Gotham, Richland 53540
Grafton, Ozaukee 53024
Grand Chute
(See Appleton)
Grand Marsh, Adams 53936
Grand View, Bayfield 54839
Granton, Clark 54436
Grantsburg, Burnett 54840
Gratiot, Lafayette 53541
GREEN BAY, Brown
(See Page 4342)
Green Lake, Green Lake 54941
Green Valley, Shawano 54127
Greenbush, Sheboygan 53026
Greendale, Milwaukee 53129
Greenfield
(See Milwaukee)
Greenleaf, Brown 54126
Greenville, Outagamie 54942
Greenwood, Clark 54437
Gresham, Shawano 54128
Gurney, Iron 54559
Hager City, Pierce 54014
Hales Corners, Milwaukee 53130
Hamburg, Marathon 54411
Hammond, Saint Croix 54015
Hancock, Waushara 54943
Hannibal, Taylor 54439
Hanover, Rock 53542
Harshaw, Oneida 54529
Hartford, Washington 53027
Hartland, Waukesha 53029
Hatley, Marathon 54440
Haugen, Barron 54841
Haven, Sheboygan 53083
Hawkins, Rusk 54530
Hawthorne, Douglas 54842
Hayward, Sawyer 54843
Hazel Green, Grant 53811
Hazelhurst, Oneida 54531
Heafford Jct, Lincoln 54532
Heafford Junction, Lincoln 54532
Helenville, Jefferson 53137
Herbster, Bayfield 54844
Hertel, Burnett 54845
Hewitt, Wood 54441
High Bridge, Ashland 54846
Highbridge, Ashland 54846
Highland, Iowa 53543
Hilbert, Calumet 54129
Hiles, Forest 54511
Hillpoint, Sauk 53937
Hillsboro, Vernon 54634
Hillsdale, Barron 54733
Hingham, Sheboygan 53031
Hixton, Jackson 54635
Hobart, Brown 54115
Holcombe, Chippewa 54745
Hollandale, Iowa 53544
Holmen, La Crosse 54636
Honey Creek, Walworth 53138
Horicon, Dodge 53032
Hortonville, Outagamie 54944
Houlton, Saint Croix 54082
Howard
(See Green Bay)
Howards Grove, Sheboygan 53083
Hubertus, Washington 53033
Hudson, Saint Croix 54016
Humbird, Clark 54746
Hurley, Iron 54534
Hustisford, Dodge 53034
Hustler, Juneau 54637
Independence, Trempealeau 54747
Ingram, Rusk 54526
Iola, Waupaca 54945
Irma, Lincoln 54442
Iron Belt, Iron 54536
Iron Ridge, Dodge 53035
Iron River, Bayfield 54847
Ixonia, Jefferson 53036
Jackson, Washington 53037
JANESVILLE, Rock
(See Page 4342)
Jefferson, Jefferson 53549
Jim Falls, Chippewa 54748
Johnson Creek, Jefferson 53038
Johnson Creek, Jefferson 53094
Juda, Green 53550
Jump River, Taylor 54434
Junction City, Portage 54443
Juneau, Dodge 53039
Kansasville, Racine 53139
Kaukauna, Outagamie 54130
Kaukauna, Outagamie 54131
Kellnersville, Manitowoc 54215
Kempster, Langlade 54424
Kendall, Monroe 54638
Kennan, Price 54537
KENOSHA, Kenosha
(See Page 4344)
Keshena, Menominee 54135
Kewaskum, Washington 53040
Kewaunee, Kewaunee 54216
Kiel, Manitowoc 53042
Kieler, Grant 53812
Kimberly, Outagamie 54136
King, Waupaca 54946
Kingston, Green Lake 53939
Knapp, Dunn 54749
Knowles, Dodge 53048
Kohler, Sheboygan 53044
Krakow, Shawano 54137
Krakow, Oconto 54171
Kronenwetter, Marathon 54455
LA CROSSE, La Crosse
(See Page 4345)
La Farge, Vernon 54639
La Pointe, Ashland 54850
La Valle, Sauk 53941
Lac Du Flambeau, Vilas 54538
Ladysmith, Rusk 54848
Lake Delton, Sauk 53940
Lake Geneva, Walworth 53147
Lake Hallie, Chippewa 54729
Lake Mills, Jefferson 53551
Lake Nebagamon, Douglas 54849
Lake Tomahawk, Oneida 54539
Lakewood, Oconto 54138
Lancaster, Grant 53813
Land O Lakes, Vilas 54540
Lannon, Waukesha 53046
Laona, Forest 54541
Larsen, Winnebago 54947
Lebanon, Dodge 53047
Lena, Oconto 54139
Leopolis, Shawano 54948
Lewis, Polk 54837
Lily, Langlade 54491
Lime Ridge, Sauk 53942
Linden, Iowa 53553
Lisbon, Waukesha 53089
Little Chute, Outagamie 54140
Little Chute, Outagamie 54911
Little Suamico, Oconto 54141
Livingston, Grant 53554
Lodi, Columbia 53555
Loganville, Sauk 53943
Lomira, Dodge 53048
Lone Rock, Richland 53556
Long Lake, Florence 54542
Loretta, Sawyer 54896
Lowell, Dodge 53557
Loyal, Clark 54446
Lublin, Taylor 54447
Luck, Polk 54853
Luxemburg, Kewaunee 54217
Lyndon Station, Juneau 53944
Lynxville, Crawford 54626
Lynxville, Crawford 54640
Lyons, Walworth 53148
MADISON, Dane
(See Page 4346)
Maiden Rock, Pierce 54750
Malone, Fond Du Lac 53049
Manawa, Waupaca 54949
Manchester, Green Lake 53946
Manitowish Waters, Vilas 54545
MANITOWOC, Manitowoc
(See Page 4352)
Maple, Douglas 54854
Maplewood, Door 54226
Maplewood, Door 54235
Marathon, Marathon 54448
Marengo, Ashland 54846
Marengo, Ashland 54855
Maribel, Manitowoc 54227
Marinette, Marinette 54143
Marion, Waupaca 54950
Markesan, Green Lake 53946
Marquette, Green Lake 53947

Marshall, Dane 53559
Marshfield, Wood 54449
Mason, Bayfield 54816
Mason, Bayfield 54856
Mather, Juneau 54641
Mattoon, Shawano 54450
Mauston, Juneau 53948
Mayville, Dodge 53050
Mazomanie, Dane 53560
Mc Farland, Dane 53558
Mc Naughton, Oneida 54543
Medford, Taylor 54451
Medina, Outagamie 54944
Mellen, Ashland 54546
Melrose, Jackson 54642
Menasha, Winnebago 54952
MENOMONEE FALLS, Waukesha
(See Page 4352)
Menomonie, Dunn 54751
MEQUON, Ozaukee
(See Page 4353)
Mercer, Iron 54547
Merrill, Lincoln 54452
Merrillan, Jackson 54754
Merrimac, Sauk 53561
Merton, Waukesha 53056
Middle Inlet, Marinette 54114
Middleton, Dane 53562
Middleton, Dane 53597
Mikana, Barron 54857
Milan, Marathon 54411
Milladore, Wood 54454
Millston, Jackson 54643
Milltown, Polk 54858
Milton, Rock 53563
MILWAUKEE, Milwaukee
(See Page 4354)
Mindoro, La Crosse 54644
Mineral Point, Iowa 53565
Minocqua, Oneida 54548
Minong, Washburn 54859
Mishicot, Manitowoc 54228
Modena, Buffalo 54755
Mondovi, Buffalo 54755
Mondovi, Dunn 54764
Monico, Oneida 54501
Monona
(See Madison)
Monroe, Green 53566
Montello, Marquette 53949
Montfort, Grant 53569
Monticello, Green 53570
Montreal, Iron 54550
Moquah, Ashland 54806
Morrisonville, Dane 53571
Mosinee, Marathon 54455
Mount Calvary, Fond Du Lac 53057
Mount Hope, Grant 53816
Mount Horeb, Dane 53572
Mount Pleasant, Racine 53177
Mount Sterling, Crawford 54645
Mountain, Oconto 54149
Mukwonago, Waukesha 53149
Muscoda, Grant 53573
Muskego, Waukesha 53150
Nashotah, Waukesha 53058
Navarino, Shawano 54107
Necedah, Juneau 54646
NEENAH, Winnebago
(See Page 4361)
Neillsville, Clark 54456
Nekoosa, Wood 54457
Nelma, Florence 54542
Nelson, Buffalo 54756
Nelsonville, Portage 54458
Neopit, Menominee 54150
Neosho, Dodge 53059
Neshkoro, Marquette 54960
New Auburn, Chippewa 54757
NEW BERLIN, Waukesha
(See Page 4362)
New Franken, Brown 54229
New Glarus, Green 53574
New Holstein, Calumet 53061

New Lisbon, Juneau 53950
New London, Waupaca 54961
New Munster, Kenosha 53152
New Post, Sawyer 54828
New Richmond, Saint Croix 54017
Newald, Forest 54511
Newburg, Washington 53060
Newton, Manitowoc 53063
Niagara, Marinette 54151
Nichols, Outagamie 54152
North Fond Du Lac
(See Fond Du Lac)
North Freedom, Sauk 53951
North Lake, Waukesha 53064
North Prairie, Waukesha 53153
North Woods Beach, Sawyer 54843
Northfield, Jackson 54635
Norwalk, Monroe 54648
Oak Creek, Milwaukee 53154
Oakdale, Monroe 54649
Oakfield, Fond Du Lac 53065
Oconomowoc, Waukesha 53066
Oconto, Oconto 54153
Oconto Falls, Oconto 54154
Odanah, Ashland 54861
Ogdensburg, Waupaca 54962
Ogema, Price 54459
Ojibwa, Sawyer 54862
Okauchee, Waukesha 53069
Oliver, Douglas 54880
Omro, Winnebago 54963
Onalaska, La Crosse 54650
Oneida, Brown 54155
Ontario, Vernon 54651
Oostburg, Sheboygan 53070
Oregon, Dane 53575
Orfordville, Rock 53576
Osceola, Polk 54020
OSHKOSH, Winnebago
(See Page 4363)
Osseo, Trempealeau 54758
Owen, Clark 54460
Oxford, Marquette 53952
Packwaukee, Marquette 53953
Palmyra, Jefferson 53156
Pardeeville, Columbia 53954
Park Falls, Price 54552
Patch Grove, Grant 53817
Pearson, Langlade 54462
Pelican Lake, Oneida 54463
Pell Lake, Walworth 53157
Pembine, Marinette 54119
Pembine, Marinette 54156
Pence, Iron 54550
Pepin, Pepin 54759
Peshtigo, Marinette 54157
Pewaukee, Waukesha 53072
Phelps, Vilas 54554
Phillips, Price 54555
Phlox, Langlade 54464
Pickerel, Langlade 54465
Pickett, Winnebago 54964
Pigeon Falls, Trempealeau 54760
Pine River, Waushara 54965
Pittsville, Wood 54466
Plain, Sauk 53577
Plainfield, Waushara 54966
Platteville, Grant 53818
Pleasant Prairie, Kenosha 53158
Plover, Portage 54467
Plum City, Pierce 54761
Plymouth, Sheboygan 53073
Poplar, Douglas 54864
Port Edwards, Wood 54469
Port Washington, Ozaukee 53074
Port Wing, Bayfield 54865
Portage, Columbia 53901
Porterfield, Marinette 54159
Poskin, Barron 54812
Potosi, Grant 53820
Potter, Calumet 54160
Pound, Marinette 54161
Powers Lake, Kenosha 53159
Poy Sippi, Waushara 54967
Poynette, Columbia 53955

Prairie Du Chien, Crawford 53821
Prairie Du Sac, Sauk 53578
Prairie Farm, Barron 54762
Prentice, Price 54556
Prescott, Pierce 54021
Presque Isle, Vilas 54557
Princeton, Green Lake 54968
Pulaski, Brown 54162
Pulcifer, Oconto 54124
RACINE, Racine
(See Page 4365)
Radisson, Sawyer 54867
Randolph, Dodge 53956
Random Lake, Sheboygan 53075
Readfield, Waupaca 54969
Readstown, Vernon 54652
Redgranite, Waushara 54970
Reedsburg, Sauk 53958
Reedsville, Manitowoc 54230
Reeseville, Dodge 53579
Rewey, Iowa 53580
Rhinelander, Oneida 54501
Rib Lake, Taylor 54470
Rice Lake, Barron 54868
Richfield, Washington 53076
Richland Center, Richland 53581
Ridgeland, Dunn 54763
Ridgeway, Iowa 53582
Ringle, Marathon 54471
Rio, Columbia 53960
Rio Creek, Kewaunee 54201
Ripon, Fond Du Lac 54971
River Falls, Pierce 54022
River Hills
(See Milwaukee)
Roberts, Saint Croix 54023
Rochester, Racine 53167
Rock Falls, Buffalo 54755
Rock Falls, Dunn 54764
Rock Springs, Sauk 53961
Rockfield, Washington 53022
Rockland, La Crosse 54653
Rosendale, Fond Du Lac 54974
Rosholt, Portage 54473
Rothschild, Marathon 54474
Royalton, Waupaca 54961
Rubicon, Dodge 53078
Rudolph, Wood 54475
Saint Cloud, Fond Du Lac 53079
Saint Croix Falls, Polk 54024
Saint Francis, Milwaukee 53235
Saint Germain, Vilas 54558
Saint Nazianz, Manitowoc 54232
Salem, Kenosha 53168
Sanborn, Ashland 54806
Sand Creek, Dunn 54765
Sarona, Washburn 54870
Sauk City, Sauk 53583
Saukville, Ozaukee 53080
Saxeville, Waushara 54976
Saxon, Iron 54559
Sayner, Vilas 54560
Scandinavia, Waupaca 54977
Schofield, Marathon 54476
Seneca, Crawford 54654
Sextonville, Richland 53584
Seymour, Outagamie 54165
Sharon, Walworth 53585
Shawano, Shawano 54166
SHEBOYGAN, Sheboygan
(See Page 4367)
Sheboygan Falls, Sheboygan 53085
Sheldon, Rusk 54766
Shell Lake, Washburn 54871
Sherwood, Calumet 54169
Shiocton, Outagamie 54170
Shorewood, Milwaukee 53211
Shullsburg, Lafayette 53586
Silver Cliff, Marinette 54104
Silver Lake, Kenosha 53170
Sinsinawa, Grant 53824
Siren, Burnett 54872
Sister Bay, Door 54234
Slinger, Washington 53086
Sobieski, Oconto 54171

Soldiers Grove, Crawford 54655
Solon Springs, Douglas 54873
Somers, Kenosha 53171
Somerset, Saint Croix 54025
South Byron, Dodge 53006
South Milwaukee, Milwaukee 53172
South Range, Douglas 54874
South Wayne, Lafayette 53587
Sparta, Monroe 54656
Spencer, Marathon 54479
Spooner, Washburn 54801
Spring Green, Sauk 53588
Spring Valley, Pierce 54767
Springbrook, Washburn 54875
Springfield, Walworth 53176
St Francis, Milwaukee 53235
Stanley, Chippewa 54768
Star Lake, Vilas 54561
Star Prairie, Polk 54026
Stetsonville, Taylor 54480
Steuben, Crawford 54657
Stevens Point, Portage 54481
Stiles, Oconto 54139
Stitzer, Grant 53825
Stockbridge, Calumet 53088
Stockholm, Pepin 54769
Stoddard, Vernon 54658
Stone Lake, Sawyer 54876
Stoughton, Dane 53589
Stratford, Marathon 54484
Strum, Trempealeau 54770
Sturgeon Bay, Door 54235
Sturtevant, Racine 53177
Suamico, Brown 54173
Suamico, Brown 54313
Sullivan, Jefferson 53178
Summit, Waukesha 53066
Summit Lake, Langlade 54485
Sun Prairie, Dane 53590
Superior, Douglas 54880
Suring, Oconto 54174
Sussex, Waukesha 53089
Taycheedah, Fond Du Lac 54935
Taylor, Jackson 54659
Theresa, Dodge 53091
Thiensville
(See Mequon)
Thorp, Clark 54771
Three Lakes, Oneida 54562
Tigerton, Shawano 54486
Tilleda, Shawano 54978
Tipler, Florence 54542
Tisch Mills, Manitowoc 54240
Tomah, Monroe 54660
Tomahawk, Lincoln 54487
Tomahawk, Lincoln 54532
Tony, Rusk 54563
Townsend, Oconto 54175
Trego, Washburn 54888
Trempealeau, Trempealeau 54661
Trevor, Kenosha 53102
Trevor, Kenosha 53179
Tripoli, Oneida 54564
Tunnel City, Monroe 54662
Turtle Lake, Barron 54889
Twin Lakes, Kenosha 53181
Two Rivers, Manitowoc 54241
Underhill, Oconto 54124
Union Center, Juneau 53962
Union Grove, Racine 53182
Unity, Marathon 54488
Upson, Iron 54565
Valders, Manitowoc 54245
Van Dyne, Fond Du Lac 54979
Vernon
(See Waukesha)
Verona, Dane 53593
Vesper, Wood 54489
Victory, Vernon 54624
Viola, Richland 54664
Viroqua, Vernon 54665
Wabeno, Forest 54566
Waldo, Sheboygan 53093
Wales, Waukesha 53183
Walworth, Walworth 53184

Warrens, Monroe 54666
Wascott, Douglas 54838
Wascott, Douglas 54890
Washburn, Bayfield 54891
Washington Island, Door 54246
Waterford, Racine 53185
Waterloo, Jefferson 53594
WATERTOWN, Jefferson
(See Page 4368)
Waubeka, Ozaukee 53021
Waukau, Winnebago 54980
WAUKESHA, Waukesha
(See Page 4369)
Waumandee, Buffalo 54622
Waunakee, Dane 53597
Waupaca, Waupaca 54981
Waupun, Dodge 53963
WAUSAU, Marathon
(See Page 4372)
Wausaukee, Marinette 54177
Wautoma, Waushara 54982
Wauwatosa
(See Milwaukee)
Wauzeka, Crawford 53826
Webb Lake, Burnett 54830
Webster, Burnett 54893
Wentworth, Douglas 54874
West Allis
(See Milwaukee)
WEST BEND, Washington
(See Page 4374)
West Lima, Vernon 54639
West Milwaukee
(See Milwaukee)
West Salem, La Crosse 54669
Westboro, Taylor 54490
Westby, Vernon 54667
Westfield, Marquette 53964
Weston, Marathon 54476
Westport, Dane 53597
Weyauwega, Waupaca 54983
Weyerhaeuser, Rusk 54895
Wheeler, Dunn 54772
White Lake, Langlade 54491
Whitefish Bay
(See Milwaukee)
Whitehall, Trempealeau 54773
Whitelaw, Manitowoc 54247
Whitewater, Walworth 53190
Wild Rose, Waushara 54984
Willard, Clark 54493
Williams Bay, Walworth 53191
Wilmot, Kenosha 53192
Wilson, Saint Croix 54027
Wilton, Monroe 54670
Winchester, Vilas 54557
Wind Lake, Racine 53185
Wind Point, Racine 53402
Windsor, Dane 53598
Winnebago, Winnebago 54985
Winneconne, Winnebago 54986
Winter, Sawyer 54896
Wisconsin Dells, Columbia 53965
WISCONSIN RAPIDS, Wood
(See Page 4375)
Withee, Clark 54498
Wittenberg, Marathon 54432
Wittenberg, Shawano 54499
Wonewoc, Juneau 53968
Woodford, Lafayette 53599
Woodland, Dodge 53099
Woodman, Grant 53827
Woodruff, Oneida 54568
Woodville, Saint Croix 54028
Woodworth, Kenosha 53194
Wrightstown, Brown 54180
Wyeville, Monroe 54660
Wyocena, Columbia 53969
Yellow Lake, Burnett 54830
Yuba, Vernon 54634
Zachow, Shawano 54182
Zenda, Walworth 53195

APPLETON WI

General Delivery 54911

POST OFFICE BOXES MAIN OFFICE STATIONS AND BRANCHES

Box No.s
All PO Boxes 54912

NAMED STREETS

N Abendroth St 54914
W Abitz Rd 54914
S Adams St 54915
Aerotech Dr 54914
African Violet Dr 54915
Albert Way 54915
Alder Way 54915
Alex Dr 54915
N Alexander St 54911
E Alice St 54911
S Alicia Dr 54914
Allegiance Ct 54913
S Allen St 54911
Alphorn Ln 54913
N Altamont Dr 54913
N Altenhofen Dr 54913
E Alton Ct & St 54911
N Alvin St
1300-2199 54911
3700-3899 54913
Amber Dr 54913
W Amberwood Ln 54913
E Amelia St 54911
American Dr 54914
Amy Ave 54915
Andrew Dr 54915
S Angela Dr 54915
W Anita Ct & St 54913
Anita Wieckert Rd 54913
Anmarita Ct 54915
Anna Ct 54915
Anton Ct 54915
Apache Ct & Pl 54911
Apostolic Rd 54913
N Apple Rd 54913
E Apple Creek Ct & Rd 54913
E Apple Hill Blvd 54913
E Apple Tree Ln 54911
N Applebend Dr 54913
W Applegate Dr 54914
E Appleseed Dr 54913
N & S Appleton St 54911
E Appleview Dr 54913
E Aquamarine Ave 54913
Arbor Ln 54915
Ares Dr 54914
S Arlington St 54915
E Arnold St 54911
W Arrowhead Ln 54913
Arts Way 54913
Aschen Puttel Dr 54915
S Ashbrook St 54915
E Ashbury Dr 54913
N Ashford Ct 54913
Aspen Ct 54915
Associated Ct 54913
N & W Association Dr 54914
W Aster Ln 54914
E & W Atlantic St 54911
Atlantis Dr 54914
E Audrey Ln 54915
S Aurora Dr 54915
Austin Dr 54915
N Autumn Crest Dr 54913
Autumn Hills Pkwy 54913
Autumn Mist Trl 54913
N Autumn Ridge Ct 54911
S Aykens St 54915
N & S Badger Ave 54914
Bailey Dr 54915
Baldwin Ct 54915
Ballard Rd 54913
N Ballard Rd
1000-1328 54911
1330-3399 54911
3401-3499 54911
4000-6700 54913
6702-9298 54913
Balsam Ct 54913
E Banta Ct 54915
Barbara Ave 54915
Barberry Ln 54915
Barbie Ct 54915
W Barefoot Ct 54913
S Barker Ln 54915
N Barkwood Ln 54914
W Barley Way 54913
Barney Ct 54915
S Bartell Ct & Dr 54914
N Barton Ct 54913
Basswood Ln 54915
N Bateman St 54911
Baum Ln 54913
N Bay St 54911
N Bay Ridge Rd 54915
Bayberry St 54915
W Beau Ryan Ct 54913
Bedford Ln 54915
Beechwood Ct 54911
S Behm Ct 54914
Belaire Rd 54914
W Bell Ave 54914
Bellaire Ct 54911
Bellevue Pl 54913
Bellflower Ct 54915
N Bennett St 54914
S Benoit St 54914
W Bent Oak Ln 54914
E Benton Dr 54913
E Benvalley Dr 54913
N Benview Ct 54913
Berken St 54915
S Berry Dr 54915
S Berryfield Ln 54915
Better Way 54915
W Big Bend Dr 54914
N Birchbark Ct 54913
N Birchwood Ave 54914
Birds Nest Ct 54913
Bittersweet Ct 54914
Blackberry Ct 54915
S Blandist St 54915
Blazing Star Dr 54915
Block Rd 54915
Bloomingrose Ln 54915
N Blossom Dr 54914
Blue Bonnet Dr 54915
S Blue Spruce Ln 54915
W Bluebell Ln 54914
Blueberry Ln 54915
E Bluebird Ln 54915
N & S Bluemound Cir, Ct & Dr 54914
N Blueridge Dr 54914
E Bluewater Way 54913
Boardwalk Ct 54914
S Bob O Link Ln 54915
Bobby Ct 54915
Bodoh Way 54914
E Boldt Way 54911
E Bona Ave 54915
N Bountiful Ln 54913
Bouquet Dr 54915
S Bouten St 54915
W Boxwood Ln 54913
S Boyd Ct 54915
N Bracken Ct & Dr 54911
E Bradford Ave 54911
E Bradley Ln 54915
E Braeburn Dr 54913
Brandon Way 54915
W Breckenridge Ct 54914
Breezewood Dr 54915
Brenda Dr 54915
Brentwood Ct & Ln 54915
E Brewster St 54911
W Brewster St
100-699 54911
700-3499 54914
N Briarcliff Ct & Dr 54915
Briarwood Dr 54915
W Brickstone Ct 54914
Brighton Cir 54915
Brittany Dr 54915
E & W Broadway Dr 54913
Broek Dr 54915
Brokaw Pl 54911
Brookdale Ct 54911
Brookhaven Ct & Dr 54915
Brookmeadow Ct 54915
N Brookridge Ln 54913
N Brookshire Dr 54913
Brookview Dr 54913
Brookwood Ct 54914
W Browning St 54914
Brux Rd 54915
Buchanan Rd 54915
Buchanan St 54913
S Buchanan St 54915
Buckhorn Dr 54913
N Bull Rush Dr 54913
N Bunting Ct 54913
Butte Des Morts Ct 54914
Buttercup Ct 54914
E Byrd St 54911
N Calmes Dr 54913
E & W Calumet St 54915
N Cambridge Ct & Dr 54915
N Camellia Ln 54915
Camelot Ct 54915
Cameo Ct 54915
Camilia Ln 54915
Camron Dr 54915
E Canary St 54915
E Candee St 54915
Candlelite Way 54915
N Canterbury Ct & Dr 54915
E Canvasback Cir & Ln 54913
Canyon Ct & Ln 54913
Cape Cod Ave 54914
N Capitol Ct 54913
E Capitol Dr 54911
W Capitol Dr
100-699 54911
700-3635 54914
3637-3899 54914
4000-4098 54913
4100-5599 54913
5601-5699 54913
Cara Way 54915
E Cardinal Pl 54915
Caribou Ct 54911
Carleton Ave 54915
Carols Ln 54915
S Carpenter St 54915
Carriage Ln 54914
E Carrington Ln 54913
E Carroll St 54915
S Carver Ln 54915
N Casaloma Dr
100-326 54913
311-311 54912
328-3998 54913
347-3999 54913
S Casaloma Dr 54914
E Cass St 54915
E Castlebury Ln 54913
W Casual Ct 54913
N Catherine St 54911
Cathy Ct 54915
Cattail Ct 54915
W Cedar St 54914
W Cedar Crest Ct 54914
Cedar Hollow Ct 54915
E Cedar Ridge Dr 54915
E Cedarwood Dr 54915
E Celtic Xing 54913
N Center St 54911
Center Valley Rd 54913
Century Ct 54914
W Century Farm Blvd 54913
Chadbury Ln 54915
N Chadwicke Ct 54913
S Chain Dr 54915
Chalet Dr 54913
Challenger Dr 54914
Champagne Ct 54913
N Chappell Ct & Dr 54914
W Charles St 54914
N Charlotte St 54911
W Cherokee Dr 54914
Cherry Ct 54915
Cherry Meadow Dr 54915
Cherryvale Ave & Cir 54913
W Cherrywood Ct 54914
S Chestnut Ln 54915
N Chestwood Ct 54911
Cheyenne Dr 54915
S Chickadee Ln 54915
W Chicory Ct & Ln 54914
N Chippewa St 54911
S Christine St 54915
Christopher Ct & Ln 54915
E Circle St 54911
W Civic St 54914
W Clairemont Dr 54913
S Clara St 54915
N Clark St 54911
N Clayhill Dr 54913
E Clearfield Ln 54913
Clearwater Ct & Dr 54913
Cliff Dr 54915
N Cloudview Ct & Dr 54914
S Clover Ln 54915
Clover Downs Ct 54915
Clover Ridge Trl 54915
W Cloverdale Dr 54914
N Cobble Creek Dr 54913
Coburg Ct 54915
Cold Spring Rd 54914
Colin St 54915
E College Ave
1-999 54911
1300-3799 54915
W College Ave
100-699 54911
700-4399 54914
4400-4660 54913
4401-6479 54914
6162-6480 54914
Colonial Ct 54915
Colonial Dr 54914
Colony Ct 54915
N Colorado Ave 54913
Columbia Dr 54914
Commerce Ct 54911
E Commercial St 54911
W Commercial St
100-198 54911
200-619 54911
700-1899 54914
Commonwealth Ct 54914
Communication Ct & Dr 54914
N Conkey St 54911
S Connell St 54914
N Connies Ct 54914
Continental Ct 54911
Contractor Dr 54914
W Converters Dr 54913
E Coolidge Ave 54915
N Coop Rd 54915
Coral Ct 54915
N Corey Ln 54913
Cornell Ct 54915
Cornflower Dr 54915
N Corporate Ct 54913
E Corridor Dr 54913
W Corsican Pine Dr 54913
W Cortland Dr 54914
S Cotter St 54914
W Cottonwood Ct 54914
Country Ayre Ct 54915
N Country Run Dr 54914
Country View Dr 54913
County Rd N 54915
County Road A 54913
County Road Bb 54914
S County Road Cb 54914
County Road Ee 54913
County Road Jj 54913
County Road Kk 54915
County Road O 54913
County Road Pp 54913
S Covenant Ln 54915
Crab Apple Ct 54914
E Cranberry Dr 54915
N Crane Dr 54913
W Creek Valley Ln 54914
Creek Water Ct 54914
Creekside Ct 54915
Creekview Ln 54915
N Crescent Ln 54913
Crestview Ct & Dr 54915
Crestway Ct 54913
Crestwood Ct 54915
N Cripple Creek Dr 54913
S Crocus Ln 54914
Crooked Pine Ct 54915
N Crosscreek Cir 54913
Crossing Ct 54913
E & W Crossing Meadows Ln 54913
Crystal Ct & Dr 54915
Cumberland Dr 54915
N Cutter Ct 54913
S Cypress St 54915
Daffodil Dr 54915
Dahlia Dr 54915
Daisy Ct 54915
Darboy Ct & Dr 54915
W Darling St 54914
N David St 54914
Dawn Ct 54914
S Daybreak Dr 54915
W Deerview Dr 54913
W Deerwood Ct 54914
Del Rose Ln 54913
S Dellwood St 54915
E Dennison St 54915
S Derks Dr 54915
E Destination Dr 54915
Devine Dr 54913
N Devonshire Dr 54913
E Dewey St 54915
Diamond Ct 54915
Diane Ln 54915
E Dietzen Dr 54915
Discovery Dr 54914
N Division St 54911
Dogwood Ct 54914
Dons Dr 54915
N Doris Ln 54911
N & S Douglas St 54914
E Downs Rdg 54913
E Drake Ln 54913
Dream Weaver Dr 54913
N & S Drew St 54911
S Driftwood Ln 54915
S Driscoll St 54914
Duchess Ct 54914
Duck A Way Ct 54915
N Dunlap St 54911
N & S Durkee St 54911
Dusty Dr 54915
Dylan Dr 54915
N Eagle Crest Dr 54913
E Eagle Flats Pkwy 54915
W Earthrock Rd 54913
S East St 54915
Easter Lily Dr 54915
Eastfield Ct 54915
Easthaven Ct 54915
Eastowne Ct & Ln 54915
Eastwood Ct 54915
Edelweiss Ct 54913
E Edgemere Dr 54915
N Edgewood Ave 54914
E Edgewood Dr 54913
W Edgewood Dr 54913
Edgewood Trl 54913
W Edison Ave 54915
W Edmund Dr 54914
Edward St 54913
N Edward St 54914
N Edwin St 54913
Eisenhower Dr 54915
W Elberg Ave 54914
E Eldorado St 54911
N Elinor St 54914
S Elm St 54911
E Elmview Dr 54915
Elmwood Ct 54911
W Elsie St 54914
W Elsner Rd 54913
Embrey Ct 54915
Emerald Ln 54915
E Emmers Dr 54915
Emons Rd 54915
E Endeavor Dr 54915
E Enterprise Ave 54913
N Erb St 54911
S Eric Dr 54915
N Erin Dr 54914
E Esther St 54915
Estherbrook Ct 54915
Ethan Dr 54915
N Eugene St 54914
Evan St 54915
Everbreeze Cir 54913
W Everett St 54914
E & W Evergreen Ct & Dr E 54913
N Executive Dr 54911
Exploration Ave 54915
Express Ct 54915
N Fair St 54911
Fairfield Ct 54911
S Fairview St 54914
Fairway Ct 54913
Falcon Ct 54915
E Fallcreek Ln 54913
Falling Leaf Trl 54913
N Fallview Ln 54913
Farmstead Dr 54915
Feather Ridge Dr 54913
N Federated Dr 54913
Fenceline Dr 54915
N Fernmeadow Dr 54915
E Fernwood Ln 54913
S Fidelis St 54915
Fieldside Ct & Ln 54915
W Fieldwood Ln 54913
N Fiesta Ct & Dr 54911
E Flintrock Dr 54913
E Florida Ave 54911
W Florida Ave
100-399 54911
3300-3699 54914
Fontana Way 54915
E Forest St 54915
Forest Tree Ct 54914
Forest View Ct 54915
W Foster Ct & St 54915
S Fountain Ave 54915
Fox Run 54914
N Fox St 54911
Fox Pines Ct & Ln 54913
N Fox River Dr 54913
N Foxcroft Ct 54913
N Foxglove Ln 54913
E Foxmoor Ln 54911
Foxwood Dr 54914
E Frances St 54911
W Frances St 54914
E Franklin St 54911
W Franklin St
200-499 54911
410-410 54912
500-598 54911
501-699 54911
700-3099 54914
Fraser Fir Ln 54913
S Frederick St 54915
Freedom Rd 54913
E Fremont St 54915
French Rd 54913
N French Rd
1901-2297 54911
2299-2699 54911
2701-3499 54911
3800-3998 54913
4000-6199 54913
6201-8799 54913
S Friendly St 54915
W Front St 54914
Frontier Dr 54915
Fuji Ct & Dr 54913
Full Moon Ln 54913
Fullview Dr 54913
Gable Dr 54915
N Gala Ct 54913
Gales Ln 54915
Garden Ct 54915
N Gardenwood Ln 54913
Gardners Row 54915
N Garfield Pl 54911
Garnet Ct & Dr 54915
N Garys Ln 54914
N Gateway Dr 54913
E Gatewood Dr 54915
E Gazebohill Rd 54913
George St 54915
Geranium Dr 54915
Gillan Ct 54915
N Gillett St
800-3799 54914
3800-5499 54913
Gina Dr 54915
S Gladys Ave 54915
Glen Creek Pl 54914
Glenbrooke Ct 54915
E Glendale Ave 54911
W Glendale Ave
100-620 54911
622-698 54911
700-2699 54914
E Glenhurst Ln 54913
Glenn St 54913
W Glenpark Dr 54914
S Glenridge Ct 54914
W Glenwood Dr 54914
Glockenspiel Ln 54913
Gloria Ct 54915
E Glory Ln 54913
Gmeiner Rd 54915
Goldbeck Ct 54914
Golden Ct & Way 54915
Golden Eagle Ct 54915
S Goldenrod Dr 54914
Golf Terrace Ct 54914
E Goodall St 54915
E Goodland Dr 54911
Grace Ct 54915
N Graceland Ave 54911
W Grand Chute Blvd 54913
W Grand Meadows Dr 54914
N Grand View Rd 54911
W Grande Market Dr 54913
E Grant St 54911
W Grant St 54914
N Grassmere Ct 54913
N Green Bay Ct & Rd 54911
N Green Grove Rd 54911
Green Haven Ct 54911
Green Meadow Dr 54914
E Green Tree Ct 54915
E Greenbriar Dr 54911
E Greenfield St 54911
W Greenlawn Ln 54914
E Greenleaf Dr 54913
Greenspire Way 54915
S Greenview St 54915
Greenville Ctr 54914
W Greenville Dr 54913
Greenwood Rd 54913
Gregor Ct 54915
Greves Ct 54914
Greystone Ct & Ln 54915
S Grider St 54914
Grishaber Ct 54915
W Grove St 54915
N Gullwing Ct 54913
E Gunn St 54915
E Guyette Dr 54915

N Habitat Way 54913
Hacienda Ct 54911
S Hackberry Ln 54915
E Haddonstone Dr 54913
N Hall Ave 54911
E Hammond Ave 54911
Hample Rd 54913
S Hampton Ct 54915
E & W Hancock St 54911
Handel Dr 54915
Hank Dr 54915
E Hanson Dr 54915
N Hard Dr 54914
E Harding Dr 54915
S Harmon St 54915
W Harmony Ln 54913
Harold Way 54915
E Harriet St 54915
N Harriman St 54911
E Harris St 54911
W Harris St
100-198 54911
700-1599 54914
E Harrison St 54915
Harrys Gtwy 54914
Hartford Ln 54915
Hartzheim Dr 54913
Harvard Ct 54915
W Harvest Dr 54914
Harvest Trl 54913
W Haskel St 54914
N Hastings Ct 54913
W Hawes Ave 54914
N Hawthorne Dr 54915
N Haymeadow Ave 54913
Hazelnut Ln 54915
N Headwall Cir 54913
Hearthstone Dr 54915
Heartland Ct 54915
W Heather Ave 54914
Hedgerow Dr 54915
E Heideman Dr 54915
N Helen St 54911
S Hemlock Ln 54915
E Henry St 54915
S Herbert St 54914
W Heritage Ave 54914
Heritage Ct 54913
S Heritage Woods Dr 54915
W Hiawatha Dr 54914
N Hicheld Dr 54913
Hickory Ct 54914
Hickory Dr 54915
Hickory Ln 54915
N Hickory Farm Ln 54914
Hickory Meadows Ln 54914
Hickory Nut Trl 54914
Hickory Park Dr 54915
Hidden Acres Ct 54915
Hidden Trail Ln 54915
E Hietpas St 54911
W Highland Ave 54914
W Highland Park Ave 54911
E Highpond Xing 54913
Highview Dr 54913
W Highview Dr 54914
W Highway Dr 54914
W Hill Ct 54913
S Hillcrest Dr 54914
Hillock Ct 54914
N Hillsborough Dr 54911
Hillside Dr 54915
Hilltop Ct 54914
Hilltop Dr 54913
Hillview Dr 54913
Hillwood Ct 54911
N Hine St 54914
Hoelzel Way 54915
N Holiday Dr 54913
Holland Rd
N1500-N1598 54911
N1670-N2499 54913
1301-1397 54911
1399-2298 54911
Holly Ln & St 54915
Hollyhock Ct 54914
W Homestead Dr 54914
Honey Bunch Ct 54915
Honey Lou Ct 54915
W Honeysuckle Ln 54913
N Honeywood Ct 54913
E Hoover Ave 54915
Hopfensperger Rd 54915
S Horizon Dr 54915
W Hubble Ln 54913
Huckleberry Ln 54915
Hulke Dr 54915
S Hummingbird Ln 54915
Hunter St 54915
N Hunters Ln 54913
S Hycrest Ct & Dr 54914
N Ida St 54911
W Idaho Ave 54913
Imperial Ln 54915
E Incline Way 54913
W Independence Ct 54914
N Indigo Ln 54913
Inglewood Pl 54915
Innovation Ct 54914
W Integrity Way 54913
N Intertech Ct 54913
Inverness Cir 54914
Irene St 54913
S Irma St 54915
S Ivy St 54915
W Jack Pine Ct 54913
S Jackman St 54911
S Jackson St 54915
S Jade Ct & Dr 54915
E James St 54915
Jamie Ct 54913
E Janet Ln 54915
N Jarchow St 54911
E Jardin Ct & St 54911
Jared Ct 54913
S Jason Dr 54915
Jean St 54913
Jeff Ct 54915
S Jefferson St 54915
Jentz Ln 54913
Jeske Rd 54913
Jessica Ln 54915
Jochmann Dr 54915
S Johann Dr 54915
E John St
800-899 54911
901-999 54911
1300-1322 54915
1324-2800 54915
2802-2898 54915
Johnson Ct 54915
W Johnston St 54911
W Jonathon Dr 54914
Jonsch Dr 54915
Jordan St 54915
S Joseph St 54915
Joy Ln 54914
N Juanita Ln 54911
E Julie St 54915
Julius Dr 54914
Juneberry Ct 54915
E Juniper Ln 54915
Just About Ln 54915
W Justin Ct & St 54914
Kamkes Ave 54915
W Kamps Ave 54914
Karen Dr 54913
S Kasper Dr 54914
Katherine St 54915
Kathleen Ct 54915
E Kay St 54911
W Kaylee Ln 54913
Kebe Ct 54915
S Keller Park Dr 54914
N Kenilworth Ave 54911
N & S Kensington Ct &
Dr 54915
S Kernan Ave 54915
S Kerry Ln 54915
Kesting Ct 54911
E Keystone Ln 54913
E Killdeer Ln 54915
Kilsdonk Ct 54915
E Kimball St 54911
King Ct 54915
Kingfisher Ct 54915
Kirkland Ct 54911
Kisser Ct 54914
N Knollwood Ln 54913
S Kools Ct & St 54914
E Kramer Ln 54915
Krueger Rd 54913
N Kurey Rd 54913
N Kurt Ave 54913
E Ladybug Ln 54915
Lake Ct & Rd 54913
S & E Lake Park Rd &
Xing 54915
S Lakeland Dr 54915
Lamplighter Ct 54914
S Lance Ave 54915
Landon Dr 54915
E & N Lanser Ct & Ln 54913
Larkspur Dr 54915
N Latitude Ln 54913
N Laurie St 54914
Lavender Ln 54915
N Lawe St 54911
S Lawe St
100-200 54911
202-298 54911
500-2599 54915
Lawrence Ct 54911
E Lawrence St 54911
W Lawrence St
100-212 54911
214-699 54911
700-4800 54914
4802-4898 54914
E Layton Ave 54915
Leah Ln 54913
S Lee Ct & St 54915
S Lehmann Ln 54914
N Leminwah St 54911
N Leona St 54911
W Leonard St 54914
Leroy Ct 54913
Lester Ln 54913
E Lexington Dr 54915
Liberty Ln 54915
N Lightning Dr 54913
Lilac Ct 54914
N & S Lilas Dr 54914
Lillian Ct 54911
S Lily Pad Ln 54915
E Lincoln St 54915
E Lindbergh St 54911
W Lindbergh St
200-599 54911
700-1599 54914
N Linden Ln 54915
Linden Hill Dr 54915
N & S Linwood Ave 54914
N Lisa St 54914
W Little Ranch Rd 54913
N & S Locust St 54914
Logan Ln 54915
Lois Ln 54914
Lone Oak Dr 54913
S Long Ct 54914
E Longview Dr 54911
N Longwood Ln 54913
W Lorain Ct & St 54914
E Lorna Ln 54915
E Lourdes Dr 54915
W Lowelare St 54914
E Lucille St 54915
Lucy St 54915
E Lucylu Ct 54913
S Lutz Dr 54914
Lydia Ln 54915
W Lynch Ave 54915
Lynn Dr 54915
N Lynndale Dr
200-3399 54914
3401-3799 54914
3800-6299 54913
S Lynndale Dr 54914
Mackville Rd 54913
Macky Dr 54915
S Madison St 54915
N Magnolia Ct 54913
Main St 54915
N Mall Dr 54913
S Mallard Dr 54915
Manitowoc Rd 54915
Maple Dr 54913
E Maple St 54915
N Maple Edge Ct 54913
S Maple Hill Dr 54914
S Maplecrest Dr 54915
Mapleridge Ct & Dr 54915
Maplewood Ct 54915
E Marble Ln 54913
N Marcos Ln 54911
Margaret Dr 54915
N Margaret St 54913
N Mariah Ln 54911
Marie Claire Dr 54915
Marigold Ct 54914
E Marion Ave & St 54915
Mark Ct 54915
E Marnie Ln 54911
E Marquette St 54911
W Marquette St
100-198 54911
200-699 54911
700-2199 54914
N Marshall Rd 54911
N Marshall Heights
Ave 54913
Martin Ln 54915
Mary Dr 54915
N Mary St 54911
N Mary Martin Dr 54913
N & S Mason St 54914
W Mason Ridge Ct 54914
S Matthias Ct & St 54915
S Mayfair Dr 54914
E Mayfield Dr 54911
N Mayflower Dr 54913
S Mayflower Dr 54914
Mayflower Rd
N601-N2697 54913
N301-N599 54914
N2699-N3199 54913
E Mcarthur St 54911
N Mccarthy Rd 54913
S Mccarthy Rd 54914
N Mcdonald St 54911
N Mcintosh Dr 54914
Mckayla Dr 54915
E Mckinley St 54915
N Meade Pl 54911
Meade St 54913
N Meade St
100-198 54911
200-3399 54911
3401-3599 54911
3900-4398 54913
4400-5899 54913
S Meade St 54911
E Meadow Grove Blvd 54915
Meadow Row Ct 54913
Meadowbreeze Ct 54915
Meadowbrook Ct & Ln 54914
E Meadowlark Ln 54915
S Meadows Dr 54915
N Meadowsweet Ln 54911
S Meadowview Ln 54915
N Mearadwa St 54911
Medard Pl 54914
Melmar Ct 54913
E Melody Ln 54913
E Melrose Ave 54911
W Melvin St 54914
S Memorial Dr
100-999 54911
1200-2599 54915
E Memory Ln 54913
N Metro Dr 54913
W Michaels Dr 54913
Michelle Ct 54914
Michelle Way 54915
W Michigan St 54911
N Midfield Ct 54913
S Midpark Dr 54915
N Midsummer Dr 54913
E Midway Rd 54915
Mile Long Dr 54915
Milestone Ct & Dr 54913
Milky Way 54915
N Millbrook Rd 54914
N Millwood Dr 54913
E Minor St 54911
N Mistwood Ln 54914
S Misty Ln 54914
E Mitchell Ave 54915
S Mohawk Dr 54914
Monarch Dr 54915
S Monroe St 54915
W Montana Ave 54913
Montclaire Ct 54915
E Moon Beam Ct &
Trl 54915
N Moon Glow Ct 54913
Moonflower Dr 54915
E Moorpark Ave 54911
E Morning Glory Dr 54913
Morning Star Ct 54914
E Morningsun Dr 54913
N Morningview Ct 54913
N & S Morrison St 54911
Mountainash Ln 54915
Mueller Ct 54915
S Mueller St 54914
Mulberry Ct 54913
Municipal Dr 54914
E Murray Ave 54915
N Mutual Way 54913
Mutzy Way 54915
N Mya Dr 54913
Nature Trl 54914
W Natures Ln 54914
W Navitus Dr 54913
E Nawada Ct & St 54911
Nettie Dr 54915
W Neubert Rd 54913
W New Horizons Blvd 54914
E Newberry Ct & St 54915
N Newcastle Ln 54913
N Nicholas St 54914
S & W Nicolet Cir &
Rd 54914
Night Sky Ct 54913
Noe Rd 54915
W Noelle Ln 54913
Nolan Dr 54915
W Nordale Dr 54914
E Norfolk Pl 54911
Norman Ln 54913
Norrose Ln 54913
W & E North Ave &
St 54911
E North Island St 54915
Northbreeze Cir, Ct &
Dr 54911
Northbrook Ct 54915
Northern Rd 54914
E Northland Ave 54911
W Northland Ave
100-699 54911
700-2600 54914
2602-3198 54914
W Northland Ct 54914
N Northridge Ct & Ln 54914
E Northshore Blvd 54915
W Northstar Dr 54913
E Northwood Dr 54911
Nottingham Rd 54915
O Conner Way 54915
S Oak St 54911
Oak Lawn Dr 54915
Oakbrook Ct 54915
W Oakcrest Ct & Dr 54914
N Oakdale Ln 54914
Oakmeadow Ct 54915
Oakridge Ct & Dr 54915
Oakwood Ct 54911
W Oklahoma St 54914
W Old Sleigh Ln 54913
N Olde Casaloma Dr 54913
Olde Oak Tree Ct 54915
S Olde Oneida St
401-499 54911
500-1099 54915
Olde Paltzer Ct & Ln 54913
Oliver Ct 54913
S Olson Ave 54914
Omega Dr 54915
Oneida Ct 54911
Oneida St 54915
N Oneida St 54911
S Oneida St 54915
Onyx Ct 54915
Opal Ct 54915
E Opechee St 54911
Opportunity Way 54915
E Orange St 54915
S Orchard Dr 54914
Orchard Blossom Dr 54915
Oriole Ct 54915
N Orion Ln 54913
Otte Ct 54915
N & S Outagamie Ct &
St 54914
E Overland Cir, Ct &
Rd 54911
N Owaissa St 54911
E & W Pacific St 54911
W Packard St
200-298 54911
300-600 54911
602-698 54911
700-2499 54914
4700-5698 54913
5700-5799 54913
Paige Way 54915
W Palisades Dr & Ln 54915
N Palladium Ct 54913
E Paloma Ct 54913
Pamela Ct 54915
E Paris Way 54913
N Park Ave 54911
S Park Dr 54914
Park Pl 54914
N Park Drive Ln 54911
E Park Hills Dr 54915
Park Lawn Ct 54911
E & W Park Ridge
Ave 54911
Park Site Pl 54913
W Parkmoor Ct 54914
W Parkridge Ave 54914
E Parkside Blvd 54915
E Parkview Dr & Way 54913
E Parkway Blvd 54911
W Parkway Blvd
100-699 54911
700-1299 54914
4100-4699 54913
Partridge Ct 54915
Pathfinder Way 54914
Pats Dr 54915
Patti Ct 54915
E Pauline St 54911
S Peabody St 54915
Peaceful Ln 54915
N Peach Tree Ln 54911
Pearl Dr 54915
Pearl Essence St 54913
Penbrook Cir 54913
Pennsylvania Ave 54914
E Pensar Dr 54911
E Peppercorn Dr 54913
W Periwinkle Ct 54914
N & S Perkins St 54914
E Pershing St 54911
W Pershing St
200-699 54911
1300-2499 54914
E Peter St 54915
Petunia Ct 54915
Pheasant Ct 54915
N Pheasant Ln 54913
Pheasant Run Ct 54914
Philip Ln 54915
Phlox Dr 54915
Pierce Ave & Ct 54914
Pilgrim St 54914
W Pine Ct, Dr & St 54914
Pine Grove Rd 54913
Pinecrest Blvd & Ct 54915
Pinewild Ct 54913
Pinewood Ct 54915
Pintail Pl 54913
Pioneer Ct 54915
E Plank Cir & Rd 54915
N Plateau St 54911
E Plaza Dr 54915
Pleasant Rd 54913
S Pleasant St 54914
W Pleasant Way 54913
W Pleasantview Ct 54914
Plymouth St 54914
Pogrant Rd 54913
N Pointer Rd 54911
W Polaris Ct 54913
E Pollywog Way 54915
E Pondview Ct 54913
S Poplar Ln 54915
N Popp Ln 54914
W Poppy Dr 54914
N Potato Point Rd 54911
Prairie Ct 54915
N Prairie Rose Ln 54913
W Prairie Song Ln 54913
N Prairiewood Dr 54913
N Preservation Trl 54913
E Primrose Ln 54915
Priscilla Ln 54914
N Progress Dr 54911
W Prospect Ave
200-699 54911
700-5400 54914
5402-5998 54914
Prospect Ct 54914
N Providence Ave 54913
N Purdy Pkwy 54913
N Quail Ridge Dr 54913
W Quaker Ridge Ln 54914
Quarry Rd 54913
E Quietwinds Way 54913
Quintin Ct 54915
W Rachel Ln 54913
N Racine St 54911
Radio Rd 54915
E Rail Rd 54915
Railroad St 54915
Rainbow Ct 54915
N Rambling Rose Dr 54914
Ramlen Ct 54915
Ranch View Rd 54913
Randall Ave & St 54911
Randolph Dr 54913
Randys Ln 54915
N & S Rankin Ct & St 54911
E Ravenswood Ct 54913
S Ravinia Pl 54915
S Rebecca Ln 54915
W Red Barn Ct 54913
Red Clover Trl 54915
Red Leaf Dr 54913
Red Oak Ln 54915
Red Tail Ct & Ln 54915
W Red Tamarack Ct 54913
N Redcrested Ct 54913
Redhawk Dr 54914
Reef Ct 54915
W Reeve St 54914
Regal Ter 54915
Regency Ct 54915
W Reid Ct & Dr 54914
Reiland Rd 54913
Reinke Ct 54915
N Rexford St 54914
N Richmond St
100-124 54911
126-3441 54911
3443-3799 54911
3800-3998 54913
4000-6100 54913

6102-6198 54913
S Ridge Ln 54914
Ridge Haven Ln 54913
Ridge Point Rd 54913
Ridgebrook Ct 54915
Ridgefield Ct 54915
Ridgeview Cir 54911
Ridgeview Ct 54915
W Ridgeview Dr
641-699 54911
700-1299 54914
Ridgewood Ct 54915
N Rifle Range Rd 54913
Rip Van Winkle Ln 54913
Rita Ct 54915
S Ritger St 54915
W River Dr & Rd 54915
River Front Ct 54914
River Island Ct 54914
River Oaks Ct 54915
S Riverdale Dr 54914
S Riverheath Way 54915
S & W Riverview Ct, Dr & Ln 54915
W Roberts Ave 54914
E Robin Way 54915
Robincrest Ct 54915
Rock Rd 54913
E Rock A Way Rd 54915
Rocking Horse Ln 54913
Rocky Ct 54915
E Roeland Ave 54915
N Roemer Rd 54911
W Rogers Ave 54914
Rogers Ln 54915
W Rolling Meadows Ln 54913
E & W Roosevelt St 54911
Rose Ct 54913
N Rose Meadow Ln 54913
Rose Tree Dr 54913
Rosebud Ln 54915
N Rosedale Ln 54913
W Roselawn Dr 54914
Rosella Dr 54915
Roselyn Ct 54913
E & N Rosemary Dr 54913
Rosenberry Ct 54913
N Rosewood Dr 54913
Royal Ct 54915
Ruby Ct 54915
E Rubyred Dr 54913
N Russelwood Dr 54913
W Russet Ct 54914
Rustic Ct 54911
Rustic Ln 54915
E Rustic Rd 54911
Ryan St 54915
W Ryegrass Dr 54913
N Rynders St 54914
E Sableridge Dr 54913
Sage Way 54915
N Sagebrook Ln 54913
Saint Germaine Ct 54915
N Sampson St 54911
Sanctuary Ct & Dr 54914
S Sanders St 54915
E Sandpiper Ln 54913
W Sandra Dr 54913
N Sandra St 54911
Sandstone Ct 54913
Sapphire Ct 54915
Sara Ct & Ln 54915
Saratoga Dr 54915
S Scarlet Oak Ct & Ln 54915
Scarlett Way 54915
Schabo Rd 54913
S Schaefer Cir & St 54915
Schmalz Cir 54915
Schmidt Rd 54915
W Schneider Pl 54914
S School Ave 54915
Schroth Ln 54913
Schuh Rd 54913
W Scotch Pine Ct 54913
Selma Ct 54914
S Seminole Ct & Rd 54914
Seneca Ct 54911
W Seneca Dr
400-699 54911
1200-3299 54914
E Serene Way 54913
Serenity Ct 54914
E Service Rd 54911
W Settlers Ct 54914
W Seymour St 54915
E Shade Tree Ln 54915
Shady Hollow Ct 54913
Shagbark Way 54914
Shamrock Ct 54914
N Sharon St 54914
E Shasta Ln 54915
Shawnee Ave & Ln 54914
E Sheffield Ln 54913
Shepherd Ln 54915
Sherman Pl 54911
N Sherri Lin Ct 54914
Shooting Star Ln 54913
Short St 54915
W Shoshone Dr 54911
E Sienna Way 54913
E Sierra Ln 54913
N Silentwind Way 54913
Silver Ct 54915
Silver Leaf Ct 54913
Silvercrest Dr 54911
N Silverspring Dr 54913
E Silverspur Ln 54913
W Sioux Ct & Dr 54911
Skippers Ln 54915
N Skylark Dr 54914
Skyview Ct 54915
N Skyway Ct & Ln 54913
N Smoketree Pass 54913
Snapdragon Ln 54915
Snowberry Dr 54915
N Snowden Pl 54913
N Snowy Owl Ct 54913
Solar Cir 54915
Soldiers Sq 54911
S Solitude Ln 54915
Sommers Dr 54913
E Songbird Ln 54913
Sonny Ct 54915
W Sophia Ln 54913
N Sourapple Dr 54913
E South Ct & St 54911
E South Island St 54915
E South River St 54915
Southview Rd 54913
Southwood Dr 54915
Speel School Rd 54915
W Spencer Rd & St 54914
Spencer Village Ct 54914
N Spicewood Ln 54914
Spirit Ct 54913
E Spring St 54911
W Spring St
100-600 54911
602-698 54911
700-1899 54914
W Spring Hollow Dr 54914
Spring Meadow Ct 54914
Springbrook Cercle Dr 54914
Springfield Ct & Dr 54915
N & S Spruce St 54914
Squirrel Run 54914
Stames Dr 54914
Stanton Cir 54915
N Star Point Ln 54913
N Star Ridge Ln 54913
N Stargaze Dr 54913
Starlight Ct 54913
Starview Ct & Dr 54913
N & S State St 54911
State Park Ct & Rd 54915
State Road 47 54911
Steeple Dr 54913
Stillwater Trl 54915
E Stirling Pkwy 54913
N Stonebridge Ct 54913
Stonehedge Ln 54914
S Stonemeadow Way 54915
Stoney Brook Rd 54915
Stoney Creek Ct 54913
N & S Story St 54914
E Stratford Ln 54913
Strawberry Ln 54915
Strawflower Dr 54915
Streamview Ln 54913
Stroebe Rd 54914
Stroebe Island Dr & Rd 54914
N Sugar Maple Ln 54913
N Sugarberry Ln 54913
Sumac Ln 54915
E Summer St 54911
W Summer St
100-699 54911
700-1899 54914
Summerland Ct & Dr 54913
S Summerset Dr 54915
N & S Summit St 54914
Sun Valley Ct 54911
Sunbeam Ct 54915
N Suncastle Ct 54913
N Suncrest Ln 54914
E Sundance Dr 54913
S Sundown Ln 54915
Sunflower Ln 54913
W Sunflower Rd 54914
Sunlite Ct 54915
S Sunnyslope Ct 54914
Sunnyview Cir & Rd 54914
Sunray Ct 54915
N Sunridge Dr 54914
Sunrise Ct 54914
Sunrise Dr 54914
Sunrise Ln 54913
Sunrise Trl 54914
E Sunset Ave 54911
W Sunset Ave
100-699 54911
2900-3299 54914
W Sunset Ct 54914
Sunset Dr 54914
S Sunshine Dr 54915
N Superior St 54911
Sweet Clover Dr 54915
Sweet Pea Dr 54913
Sweet William Dr 54913
Sweetwood Ct 54913
S Sycamore Ln 54915
E Sylvan Ave 54915
Sylvan St 54913
N Systems Dr 54914
E Taft Ave 54915
S Tahoe Ln 54915
E Tallgrass Dr 54913
Tamarack Cir & Dr 54915
N Tanglewood Dr 54913
Tannenbaum Trl 54914
Tannery Ln 54915
W Taylor St 54914
Teakwood St 54915
Teardrop Ct 54914
Technology Cir 54914
S Telulah Ave 54915
Tempest Ct 54913
N Terraview Dr 54913
N Terri Ln 54914
Thelosen Dr 54915
E & S Theodore Ln & St 54915
Theresa Ave 54915
Therese Ct 54915
W Thistle Ln 54913
Thistle Down Ct 54915
N Thomas Ct 54913
Thornapple Ln 54913
N Thornberry Dr 54913
E Thornbrook Ln 54913
N Thornwood Dr 54913
Thyme Way 54915
N Tigerlily Dr 54913
Tilbury Ct 54913
W Tillman St 54914
Timber Row 54913
Timber Crest Ct 54914
E Timberline Ct & Dr 54913
S Timmers Ln 54914
Tom Ct 54915
N Tonka St 54911
Touchmark Ct & Dr 54914
Town Rd 54915
Towne Lakes Ave & Cir 54913
E Tracia Ln 54911
E Tracy Ct & St 54915
N Trailway Ln 54913
Trailwood Ln 54915
Tranquil Way 54915
W Trasino Way 54913
Tree Line Ct 54915
Tri Park Ct & Way 54914
Trillium Ln 54915
Trillium Trl 54913
N Trinity Ct 54913
Trumpet Ln 54915
N Turnberry Dr 54913
Turning Woods Trl 54913
E Tuscany Way 54913
Twelve Corners Rd 54913
W Twin Willow Ct 54914
W Twin Willows Dr 54914
Two Mile Rd 54914
N Ullman St 54911
N & S Union St 54911
W Utah Ave 54913
E Vail Ln 54915
Valerie Dr 54915
W Valley Ln & Rd 54915
Valley Fair Mall 54915
Valley View Ln 54913
Valleywood Ln 54913
S Van Dyke Rd 54914
Van Handel Dr 54915
Van Roy Rd 54915
Vans Rd 54915
E Venture Dr 54911
N Verbrick St 54915
S Vermillion St 54915
E Vermont Ave 54911
S Victoria St 54914
Victorian Dr 54915
N Victory Ln 54913
E & N Vine St 54911
N Viola St 54911
S Violet Ln 54914
Vista Ct 54913
S Vulcan St 54915
Wagon Wheel Dr 54913
S Walden Ave 54915
N Waldoch Dr 54913
N & S Walnut St 54911
S Walter Ave 54915
Walter Wieckert Rd 54913
E Warehouse Rd 54915
S Warner St 54915
W Warner Estates Dr 54913
E Washington St 54911
N Washington St 54915
W Washington St
101-297 54911
299-300 54911
302-398 54911
700-1799 54914
E & W Water St 54911
N & W Waterford Dr & Ln 54913
N Watershed Way 54913
Waterstone Ct 54914
W & E Wayfarer Ct & Ln 54913
N Wayman Ct 54914
N Wayne St 54911
N Wayside Ln 54913
Weatherstone Dr 54914
Wedgewood Ct 54915
N Wedgewood Dr 54913
Wege Rd 54913
W Weiland Ave
200-599 54911
701-797 54914
799-1099 54914
W Weiland Ln 54914
S Weimar Ct & St 54915
Welcome Cir 54915
N Wellington Dr 54911
W Wellspring Dr 54913
E Wentworth Ln 54913
E Werner Rd 54913
West Ave & Ct 54915
Westbrook Ct 54913
W Westchester Ct 54914
N Westfield Dr 54913
S Westhaven Pl 54914
N Westhill Blvd 54914
S Westland Dr 54914
Westowne Ct 54915
Westwood Ct 54911
S Wheatfield Ct & Dr 54915
Wheeler Rd 54914
S Whip Poor Will Ln 54915
Whispering Pine Ct 54913
S White Birch Ct & Ln 54915
White Clover Cir 54915
N White Hawk Dr 54913
N White Oak Dr 54915
Whitepine Dr 54915
Whitetail Way 54914
Whitetail Ridge Ct 54915
S Whitman Ave 54914
N Whitney Dr 54914
W Whittier Dr 54914
Wild Rose Ct & Ln 54914
S Wildberry Ln 54915
W Wildflower Ln 54914
W Wildplum Ct 54913
N William St 54914
W Willis Way 54913
S Willkie St 54915
Willow Ct 54911
Willow Brook Ct 54913
Willowcrest Ct 54915
Willowglen Way 54915
N Wilmer St 54911
E & W Wilson Ave & Ct 54915
N Windcross Dr 54913
E Windfield Pl 54911
N Windingbrook Dr 54913
N Windover Ct 54913
N Windsong Ln 54914
W Windtree Dr 54914
N Windward Ln 54911
Wine Berry Ct 54913
N Winesap Ln 54914
E Winnebago St 54911
W Winnebago St
101-197 54911
199-699 54911
700-1899 54914
Winnegamie Dr 54914
Winona Ct & Way 54911
W Winrowe Ct & Dr 54913
E Winslow Ave 54911
W Wintergreen Dr 54914
N Winterset Dr 54911
Winwood Ct 54913
Winwood Dr 54915
E Wisconsin Ave 54911
W Wisconsin Ave
100-699 54911
700-3999 54914
4100-5899 54913
Wisconsin Ct 54911
Wittmann Ct 54915
E Witzke Blvd 54911
N Wood St 54911
Woodbury Ct 54913
E Woodcrest Dr 54915
S Woodendale Way 54915
N Woodhaven Ct 54913
Woodland Ave & Ct 54911
E Woodlark Rd 54911
Woodlawn Ln 54914
W Woodman Dr 54914
Woodmere Ct 54911
N Woodridge Dr 54913
Woodrow Ct 54915
W Woods Creek Ln 54913
N Woods Edge Dr 54914
Woodsedge Ct 54915
N Woodside Ct 54913
Woodstock Ln 54915
W Woodstone Dr 54914
Woodview 54913
N Wren Dr 54913
Wundrow Ct 54915
E Wyndmere Dr 54913
Ziegler Ct 54913
Zinnia Dr 54915
N Zuehlke Dr 54911

NUMBERED STREETS

E 1st Ave 54911
100-199 54911
2500-3699 54914
W 2nd St 54914
W 3rd St
600-699 54911
700-999 54914
W 4th St
500-699 54911
700-4699 54914
W 5th St
400-699 54911
700-1199 54914
W 6th St 54911
W 7th St 54911
W 8th St
300-514 54911
516-600 54911
602-698 54911
700-2900 54914
2902-4798 54914

BELOIT WI

General Delivery 53511

POST OFFICE BOXES MAIN OFFICE STATIONS AND BRANCHES

Box No.s
All PO Boxes 53512

NAMED STREETS

Abc Dr & Pkwy 53511
E Acorn Dr 53511
Adams St 53511
Advance Dr 53511
E Adventure Ct 53511
S Afton Rd 53511
Aldrich Pl 53511
Alice Ave 53511
Allen Ct 53511
Alongi Ln 53511
W Alpine Dr 53511
W Antler Dr 53511
Apex Dr 53511
Arbor Dr 53511
Argall Ave 53511
Arlington Ave 53511
Arrowhead Dr 53511
Ashland Ave 53511
Athletic Ave 53511
Auburn Dr 53511
Austin Pl 53511
Avon Ct 53511
E Azalea Ter 53511
W B R Townline Rd 53511
S Bakke Rd 53511
Baldwin Woods Rd 53511
S Barnum Rd 53511
Barrett Pl 53511
S Bartells Dr 53511
W Bass Creek Rd 53511
Bay Dr 53511
Bayliss Ave 53511
Beach Ave 53511
S Beacon Light Rd 53511
Bee Ln 53511
W Belcrest Dr 53511
Bellevue Ave 53511
S Belmont Dr 53511
W Beloit Newark Rd 53511
E Berkshire Ct 53511
W Big Hill Ct & Rd 53511
Birch Ave 53511
Bittel St 53511
Blarney Stone Dr 53511
S Bluejay Ct 53511
Bluff St 53511
Booker St 53511
Booth Dr 53511
N Bootmaker Dr 53511
Boulder Ct & Ln 53511
Bradley St 53511
Bramble Ct 53511
W Brandherm Rd 53511
Branigan Rd 53511
Brewster Ave 53511
E Briar Ln 53511
Bridget Dr 53511
S Bristle Dr 53511
E Broad St 53511
Brooks St 53511
S Brostuen Rd 53511
Buckridge Dr 53511
S Burchfield Rd 53511
Burton St 53511
Bushnell St 53511
N Butlin Ct & Dr 53511
Butterfly Ln & Rd 53511
Caldwell Ave 53511
Calumet Ave 53511
Camelot Ct 53511
Campus Dr 53511
Candi Ln 53511
Canterbury Dr 53511
Carlyle Rd 53511
Carnegie Ave & Ct 53511
Carnforth Pl 53511
E Carolyn Dr 53511
Carpenter St 53511
W Carroll Dr & Rd 53511
Casey Ct 53511
Central Ave 53511
Centre St 53511
Chapin St 53511
Chapman Ave 53511
Chatsworth Dr 53511
Cherry St 53511
Cheshire Ln 53511
Chestnut Ave 53511
S Chippendale Dr 53511
Chippewa Trl 53511
Christilla Dr 53511
E Church St 53511
E Circlewood Dr 53511
S Claremont Dr 53511
Clary St 53511
W Cleophas Rd 53511
Cleora Dr 53511
Cleveland St 53511
Clifcorn Dr 53511
S Clinic Rd 53511
S Clover Ln 53511
Club Ln 53511
Cobblestone Ct & Ln 53511
Colby St 53511
College St 53511
E Colley Rd 53511
E Collingswood Dr 53511
Colony Ct 53511
E Columbine Dr 53511
Columbus Dr 53511
Community Dr 53511
Congress Ave 53511
Copeland Ave 53511
Cora Ct 53511
Corene Ave 53511
Cottage Ave 53511

S Country Ln 53511
E County Rd S 53511
S County Road D 53511
County Road G 53511
S & W County Road H 53511
E & S County Road J 53511
S & W County Road K 53511
E County Road X 53511
W Cove Dr 53511
Coyote Run 53511
Crane Ave 53511
Cranston Rd 53511
W Creedy Rd 53511
E & S Creek Rd 53511
W Creek View Pkwy 53511
Crescent Dr 53511
Crest Rd 53511
Crestview Dr 53511
Crist Rd 53511
Criswell Blvd 53511
Crittenden Pl 53511
Cross St 53511
Crystal Ln 53511
W Cutter 53511
E Daffodil Ln 53511
S Davis Dr 53511
Dawson Ave 53511
Daylily Ct 53511
Dearborn St 53511
Deer Path Way 53511
W Deer Run Pkwy 53511
Dell Dr 53511
Dewey Ave 53511
Division St 53511
S Doe Dr 53511
E Dogwood Dr 53511
S Duggan Rd 53511
Eagles Ridge Dr 53511
E Easy St 53511
Eaton Ave 53511
Eclipse Blvd & Ctr 53511
Edan Ct 53511
Eddy Ave 53511
S Edgewater Dr 53511
Edgewood Dr 53511
S Ehle Dr 53511
E Elaine Dr 53511
S Elk Dr 53511
Elm St 53511
Elmwood Ave 53511
S & W Emerson Rd & St 53511
E Erin Cir 53511
Euclid Ave 53511
Evergreen Ave 53511
Fairfax Ave 53511
Fairview Dr 53511
Farwell St 53511
Fawn Ct 53511
Fayette Ave 53511
Field Crest Ct & Rd 53511
Fieldstone Ln 53511
W Finley Rd 53511
Finn Rd 53511
Fir Dr 53511
S Flack Rd 53511
Florence Dr 53511
Ford St 53511
Forest Ave 53511
Franklin St 53511
Frederick St 53511
Freeman Pkwy 53511
Froebel Dr 53511
Fuller Dr 53511
E Gale Dr 53511
Garden Ln 53511
Garfield Ave 53511
Gartner Ave 53511
Gaston Dr 53511
Gateway Blvd 53511
Genevieve Ave & Ct 53511
Gerald Ave 53511
S Gesley Rd 53511
Glen Ave & Ct 53511
Glen Ellyn Ave 53511
S Glenwood Dr 53511
Golden Eagle Dr 53511
Gorton St 53511
Grace Ave 53511
E & W Grand Ave 53511
Grandview Dr 53511
Granite Ct & Ter 53511
Grant St 53511
W Gravedale Rd 53511
S Gray Bill Dr 53511
Green Dr 53511
Greenview Dr 53511
Grove St 53511
W Grove School Rd 53511
Haborn Dr 53511
Hackett St 53511
S Hamilton Dr 53511
Hancock St 53511
Harmony Ln 53511
Harrison Ave 53511
S, E & W Hart Ct & Rd 53511
Harvey St 53511
Hawthorne Dr 53511
Hayfield Ln 53511
Hazel Ave 53511
S Hazelwood Dr 53511
Heather Ter 53511
Hemlock St 53511
Henderson Ave 53511
Henry Ave 53511
Herbert Dr 53511
W Heron Dr 53511
S & W Hickory Ct, Dr & Hls 53511
S Hidden Creek Ct 53511
S High Crest Rd 53511
Highland Ave 53511
Highview Ct 53511
E Hill Rd 53511
Hillside Ave 53511
Hinsdale Ave 53511
Hobart Pl 53511
E Holiday Dr 53511
E Holly Rd 53511
Homeland Ct 53511
House St 53511
Howes Dr 53511
E Huebbe Pkwy 53511
Hull Ave 53511
Hurst St 53511
Hyacinth Ct 53511
S Idlewild Dr 53511
Indian Rd 53511
E Inman Pkwy 53511
S Iris Dr 53511
Iva Ct 53511
S Ivy Ln 53511
S Jackdaws Dr 53511
Jackson St 53511
S Jacobson Dr 53511
James Kelly Ln 53511
Janie Ln 53511
Jean Ellen Dr 53511
Jeannie Ln 53511
Jerry Thomas Pkwy 53511
Johnson Rd & St 53511
Jonquil Ct 53511
Juniper St 53511
Kadlec Dr 53511
E Kaleen Ln 53511
Keeler Ave 53511
Keep St 53511
Kelsey Rd 53511
Kennedy Dr 53511
Kensington Ln 53511
S Kenucane Rd 53511
Kenwood Ave 53511
Kettle Rd & Way 53511
Knoll View Dr 53511
S Knutson Rd 53511
S Krueger Dr 53511
Kruse Dr 53511
Kyle Ln 53511
E L T Townline Rd 53511
La Salle St 53511
W Laird Rd 53511
W Lamplighter Trl 53511
Lane Dr 53511
S Lathers Rd 53511
Laundale Dr 53511
Lawton Ave 53511
Lee Ln N 53511
Leeson Park Rd 53511
Lenox Ave & St 53511
E Leona Dr 53511
S Lexington Ct 53511
W Liberty Ave 53511
E & S Lilac Rd 53511
E Limerick Ln 53511
Lincoln Ave, Ct & Hts 53511
E Linda Ave 53511
Linway Dr 53511
Locust St 53511
N & S Lodge Dr 53511
Loma Dr 53511
Lombard Ave 53511
Lookout Dr 53511
E Lorena Dr 53511
Lori Ann Dr 53511
Lovell Ave 53511
Luety Pkwy 53511
S Luther Valley Rd 53511
S Madison Rd 53511
Manchester St 53511
Mandi Ln 53511
S Manitou Dr 53511
Manor Dr 53511
Maple Ave 53511
S Marigold Rd 53511
W Marilyn Pkwy 53511
Marinoff Dr 53511
Marion Ct 53511
Mary St 53511
Mason Rd 53511
Masters St 53511
E Mckearn Ln 53511
S Mckinley Ave & Rd 53511
Meadow Dr 53511
Meadowlark Way 53511
Meridith Dr 53511
S Merlet Rd 53511
Merrill Ave 53511
Middle St 53511
Mildred St 53511
Mill St
300-398 53511
300-300 53512
W Mill Pond Rd 53511
Millar Rd 53511
Millington Rd 53511
Milwaukee Rd 53511
E Minnie Ln 53511
Moccasin Trl 53511
S Mohican Dr 53511
S Molar Ln 53511
E Monarch Cir 53511
Monroe Ave 53511
Moore St 53511
Morgan St & Ter 53511
Morning Dove Ln 53511
E Morning Glory Ln 53511
Morse Ave 53511
Mound Ave 53511
Murphy Woods Rd 53511
E & S Nakoma Ct 53511
S & W Natures Ridge Rd 53511
E Needham Rd 53511
Nelson Ave 53511
W Newark Rd 53511
Newfield Dr 53511
North St 53511
Northfield Ln 53511
Northgate Dr 53511
S Northwest Dr 53511
W Noss Rd 53511
S Nye School Rd 53511
Oak St 53511
Oak Lane Dr 53511
Oakwood Ave 53511
Office Park Ln 53511
S Olson Rd 53511
Olympian Blvd 53511
Oxford Ln 53511
S Paddock Rd 53511
Palmer Dr 53511
W Pann Rd 53511
Park Ave 53511
E Park Avenue Plz 53511
Parker Ave & Ct 53511
Parkmeadow Dr 53511
Partridge Ave 53511
S Patrick Rd 53511
Pebble Ct & Dr 53511
Penny Ln 53511
Petunia Ln 53511
E Philhower Rd 53511
Pine St 53511
S Pinnow Grove Rd 53511
Pioneer Dr 53511
Pleasant St 53511
Plum Tree Vlg 53511
W Plymouth Church Rd 53511
Poff St 53511
Poole Ct E 53511
Poranden Ave 53511
Porter Ave 53511
Portland Ave 53511
E Post Rd 53511
S Pow Wow Trl 53511
E Powers Dr 53511
Poydras St 53511
S Prairie Ave 53511
Prince Hall Dr 53511
Prospect Ave 53511
W Provincial Ln 53511
Public Ave 53511
Rachel Ter 53511
Randall St 53511
W Ravine Dr 53511
S Read Rd 53511
Regal Oaks Ct 53511
Reynolds Dr 53511
Rice Dr 53511
E & S Ridge Rd 53511
Ridgeland Ave 53511
Ridgeway St 53511
Ritsher St 53511
S Riverside Dr 53511
Robin Rd 53511
N Robinson Dr 53511
Rockfence Ln 53511
Roger Ct 53511
Romona Ct 53511
Roosevelt Ave 53511
Rose Ct 53511
S Roy Rd 53511
Royce Ave 53511
Ryan Pkwy 53511
E Sager Ln 53511
W Saint Lawrence Ave 53511
Saint Paul Ave 53511
W Sandale Dr 53511
Sarah Ln 53511
S Satinwood Dr 53511
S Savanna Way 53511
S Schroeder Rd 53511
Schuster Dr 53511
Scotties Dr 53511
E Security Rd 53511
Shady Ln 53511
Sharon Dr 53511
Sharpes Ct 53511
Shears Ct 53511
S Shenandoah Ave 53511
Sheridan Ave 53511
Sherman Ave 53511
Sherwood Dr NE 53511
Shirland Ave 53511
Shopiere Rd 53511
Shore Dr 53511
Short St 53511
S Ski View Dr 53511
W Skinner Rd 53511
Skyline Dr 53511
W Smith Rd 53511
S Smythe School Rd 53511
E South Ave 53511
W Spring Creek Rd 53511
Springbrook Ct 53511
Spruce St 53511
Staborn Dr 53511
State St 53511
E State Line Rd 53511
S & W State Road 213 53511
E State Road 67 53511
W State Road 81 53511
E & S Stateline Rd 53511
Stewart Pl 53511
Stonehedge Ln 53511
Strasburg St 53511
E Stratford Dr 53511
Strong Ave 53511
W Stuart Rd 53511
S Suburban Dr 53511
Sumac Ct 53511
Summit Ave 53511
Sun Valley Dr 53511
Sunrise Ct 53511
Sunset Dr 53511
Sunshine Ln 53511
Sutler Ave 53511
S Swain Dr 53511
Tallgrass Ct 53511
Tara Ct 53511
Terrace Ln 53511
Terry Ct 53511
Thomas Rd 53511
Totem Rd 53511
Town Hall Rd 53511
Townline Ave 53511
Townview Ave 53511
Tremont Dr 53511
Trush Ct 53511
S & W Tucker Dr 53511
Tumbleweed Ln 53511
Turnberry Ct & Dr 53511
E Turner Dr 53511
Turtle St 53511
S Turtle Town Hall Rd 53511
Udell Dr 53511
S Us Highway 51 53511
Ute Ct 53511
Vail Ter 53511
Valley Rd 53511
W Vel Marge Pkwy 53511
Vernon Ave 53511
S Victorian Ln 53511
S Victory Dr 53511
Vine St 53511
Virginia St 53511
Vista Dr 53511
S Voyage Dr 53511
S Walker Rd 53511
Walnut St 53511
S & W Walters Rd 53511
Walton Ln 53511
Warbler Ct 53511
Washburn St 53511
S Water St 53511
S & E Waterford Ct & Dr 53511
Weirick Ave 53511
Weiser Dr 53511
Welty Ave 53511
West Dr & St 53511
E West Hart Rd 53511
Whipple St 53511
Whippoorwill Way 53511
White Ave 53511
White Oaks Ct & Dr 53511
Whitman Ct 53511
Wildflower Ct 53511
William St 53511
E Williams Dr 53511
Willowbrook Rd 53511
Wilson St 53511
Winchester Dr 53511
E Windfield Ct 53511
Windsor Ct 53511
Wisconsin Ave 53511
E & N Wood Ct, Dr & Trl 53511
E Woodland Dr 53511
Woodward Ave 53511
Wren Dr 53511
Wyetta Dr 53511
Yates Ave 53511
Yorkshire Dr 53511
E Yost St 53511
E Zick Dr 53511

NUMBERED STREETS

All Street Addresses 53511

BROOKFIELD WI

General Delivery 53045

POST OFFICE BOXES MAIN OFFICE STATIONS AND BRANCHES

Box No.s
All PO Boxes 53008

NAMED STREETS

Abbey Ct & Ln 53045
Acre View Ct & Dr 53005
Adelaide Ln 53005
Adelmann Ave & Ct 53045
Alfred St 53005
Almesbury Ave & Ct 53045
Alpine Cir 53005
Alta Louise Pkwy 53045
Alta Mesa Ct 53045
Alta Vista Cir & Dr 53045
Alverno Dr 53005
Alvin Ln 53045
Amber Ct 53045
Anders Ct & Ln 53005
Anita Ct & Dr 53045
Ann Rita Dr 53045
Anthony Ln 53045
Apache Trl 53005
Apple Tree Ln 53005
Apple Valley Ct 53005
Applegate Ct & Ln 53005
Applewood Ct 53005
Arbor Dr 53005
Arcadia Pl 53045
Arden Ave 53045
Arlyne Ct 53045
Arrowhead Pl 53005
Arroyo Rd 53045
Ashbourne Ct & Ln 53045
Ashford Ln 53045
Ashlea Dr 53045
Astolat Dr 53045
Astor Ct & Dr 53045
Atlentri Dr 53005
Auburn Ct & Dr 53045
Audrey Ln 53005
W Auer Ave 53005
Avalon Dr 53045
Avie Ct 53045
Avondale Dr 53045
Azure Ln 53045
Balmoral Ct 53005
Barberry St 53045
Bard Ln 53045
N & S Barker Rd 53045
Barrett Ct 53045
Barrington Woods Dr 53045
Bartlett Ct & Dr 53045
Bawden Cir 53045
Bay Ct 53005
Baythorn Way 53045
Beaufort Dr 53045
N & S Beaumont Ave 53005
Beaver Ln 53045
Bedford Dr 53045
Beechwood Ave 53005
Bell Tower Ct 53045
Bending Brae Ct 53005
Benington Dr 53045
Bermuda Blvd 53045
Bermuda Blvd Lower 53045
Bermuda Blvd Upper 53045
Berwick Ct 53045
Betsy Ross Ct 53045
Betty Ct 53045
Betty Ln 53005
Beverly Dr 53005
Beverly Hills Dr 53045
Bexley Dr 53045
Birch Dr 53005
Birmingham Ct 53045
Bishops Ct, Dr, Ln & Way 53005
Bishops Woods Ct 53005
Bittersweet Rd 53005
Black Forest Dr 53045
Black Walnut Ln 53045
Blue Ridge Ct 53045
W Bluemound Rd
12501-15697 53005
15699-17199 53005
17200-20399 53045
Blythe Rd 53005
N & S Bobolink Dr 53005
Bolter Ln 53045
Bonnie Ln 53045
Boxwood Ct 53045
Bradee Rd 53005
Bradford Ct & Ln 53045
Bradon Trl E & W 53045
Bramblewood Trl 53045
Brampton Ct 53045
Brandywine Ln 53045
Brehon Ct & Ln 53005
Brenner Ct & Dr 53045
Brentwood Dr 53005
Brian Ct & Dr 53045
E & W Briar Ridge Dr 53045
Briar Wood Ln 53045
Briarcliff Trl 53045
Bridgetown Ct 53045
Brighton Ct 53045
Bristol Ln 53045
Brittany Ct 53045
Brook Ln 53005
Brook Park Ct & Dr 53045
Brookdale Dr 53045
N & S Brookfield Rd 53045
Brookfield Lake Ct & Dr 53045
Brookhill Dr 53005
Brooklawn Dr 53045
Brookridge Dr 53045
Brookside Ln 53005
Brooksprings Dr 53005
Brookview Ct 53005
Buckingham Pl 53045
Buena Vista Dr 53045
Bunker Hill Dr 53005
Burlawn Ct & Pkwy 53005
Burleigh Blvd 53005
Burleigh Pl 53005
W Burleigh Rd
12400-15599 53005
17201-17797 53045
17799-18799 53045
Burnet Ct 53005
Burnet St
1000-17100 53005
17102-17198 53005
17200-17500 53045
17502-17598 53045
Burnwood Ct 53045
Butler Ct 53045
Byron Ct 53045
N & S Calhoun Rd 53005
Cambridge Cir & Ct 53045

Street	ZIP
Cambridge Circle Lower	53045
Cambridge Circle Upper	53045
Camden Ln	53045
Camelot Dr	53045
Cameron Ct	53005
Cameron Drive Lower	53005
Cameron Drive Upper	53005
Camfield Dr	53045
Cantebury Cir	53005
W Capitol Dr	
12400-17199	53005
17200-19199	53045
19201-20899	53045
Capone Ct	53045
Captains Ct	53045
Cara Marie Ct	53005
Cardinal Dr	53005
Cardinal Crest Dr	53005
Caribou Pass	53045
Carlisle Ct	53045
Carol Dr	53045
Carpenter Rd	53005
Carriage Ct	53045
Carrington Ct & Dr	53045
Carson Ct	53005
Casey Cir	53005
Castle Ct	53045
Cathedral Sq	53045
Cathy Ann Ln	53005
Cavendish Rd	53045
Cedar Dr	53045
Centennial Ct	53045
W Center St	53005
Chadburn Ct	53045
Chadwick Ct & Ln	53045
Chancery Ct	53045
Chanticleer Ct & Dr	53045
Chaparral Dr	53045
Chapel Rd	53045
Chapel Hill Ct & Dr	53045
Charleston Ct	53045
Charter Point Ct	53045
Chaucer Ct	53045
Cherokee Dr	53045
Cherry Hill Dr	53005
Cherry Stone Cir	53005
Chester St	53005
Chesterwood Ct & Dr	53005
Chestnut Grove Ct	53005
Chevy Chase St	53045
Chimney Rock Ct	53045
Chinook Ln	53045
Chipmunk Ct	53045
Choctaw Trl	53005
Churchview Dr	53005
Cindy Ct	53045
Civic Dr	
17301-17399	53045
17345-17345	53008
Clair Ct	53045
Clairmont Dr	53005
Clare Bridge Ln	53005
Clayton Ct	53045
Clearfield Ct & Rd	53045
Clearwater Dr	53005
Clifford Ct	53005
Club Cir	53005
Coach House Ct & Dr	53045
Colby Ct	53045
Colline Vue Blvd & Ct	53045
Collins Ct	53045
Colony Ct	53045
N & S Columbia Blvd	53005
Commerce Ave	53045
Commons Dr	53005
Compton Ct & Ln	53045
Concord Dr	53005
W Congress St	53005
Conservancy Dr	53005
Constitution Dr	53005
Continental Dr	53045
Coopers Ct & Ln	53045
Coral Dr	53045
Cornell Ct	53005
Corona Ct	53005
Coronado Ct	53045
N & W Corporate Dr	53045
Cotton Tail Ln	53045
Cottonwood Ct	53005
Country Ln	53045
Countryside Ct & Ln	53045
Courtland Ave	53005
Coventry Dr	53045
Crescent Ct	53005
Crest Ct	53045
Crest Hill Dr	53045
Crestview Cir	53005
Cromwell Ct E & W	53045
Crystal Dr	53005
Cullen Ct & Dr	53005
Cumberland Ct & Trl	53005
Dale Dr	53005
Danbury Ct & Dr	53045
Dane Ct E & W	53005
Dantonso Dr	53045
Dartmouth Dr	53005
Davidson Rd	53045
De Carlin Dr	53045
N & S Dechant Rd	53005
Deer Creek Pkwy	53005
Deer Park Dr	53005
Derrin Ln	53045
Devon Ct	53045
Dexter Ct	53045
Dominic Dr	53045
Donmar Ln	53005
Dorchester Ct & Dr	53045
Dorothy St	53005
Dorset Ct & Ln	53045
Douglas Dr	53005
Dover Pl	53005
Downing Ct	53005
Drake Ct	53005
Driftwood Ct	53005
Druid Ct	53005
Dublin Ct	53005
Duke Ct	53005
Dundee Rd	53005
Dustin Dr	53045
Eagle Dr	53005
Eastbrook Pl	53005
N & S Eastmoor Ave	53005
Eastview Ct	53005
Eastwood Ln	53005
Echo Ln	53045
Edge O Woods Dr	53005
Edgewater Dr	53005
Edington Ln	53005
Edmonton Ct, Dr & Ln	53045
Edwards St	53005
Egan Rd	53045
Eileen Ct	53005
El Rancho Dr	53005
Elderlawn Pkwy	53005
Eldorado Ct & Dr	53005
Elizabeth Ct	53045
Elizabeth Dr	53005
N & S Elm Grove Rd	53005
Elm Terrace Cir & Dr	53005
N & S Elmridge Ave	53005
Ely Ct	53045
Emberwood Dr	53005
Emerald Cir & Dr	53045
Emery Dr	53005
Emily Ann Ct	53005
Emling Cir	53005
Endicott Ct	53045
Engel Dr	53045
Enterprise Ave	53045
Erin Ct	53045
Esser Ct	53005
Estate Cir	53045
Eton Ct	53045
Evergreen Ct	53045
N & S Executive Dr	53005
Fairlane Ave	53005
Fairview Ct	53045
Fairview Ln	53045
Fairway Dr	53005
Falcon Dr	53005
Farm Hill Ct	53005
Fernwood Ln	53005
Fiebrantz Dr	53005
Fieldbrook Dr	53005
Fieldside Ct	53005
Fieldstone Dr	53005
Fiserv Dr	53045
Flagstaff Rd	53045
Flagstone Dr	53045
Fleetwood Ct	53045
Flora Ave	53005
Follett Dr	53045
Fordham Ct	53045
Forest Ct	53045
Forest Ln	53005
Forest Grove Cir, Ct, Ln & Rd	53005
Forest View Ct & Ln	53005
Fountain Plaza Dr	53005
Fox Hollow Run	53045
Foxglove Ct	53045
Foxkirk Ct & Dr	53045
Franklin Dr	53005
Freedom Ct	53045
Fresno Rd	53045
Galahad Ln	53045
Gareth Ln	53045
Garvens Ave	53005
Gate House Ln	53005
Gate Post Rd	53045
Gateway Ct & Rd	53045
Gaywood Ct & Dr	53045
Gebhardt Ct	53005
Gebhardt Rd	
15600-17099	53005
17101-17199	53005
17401-17497	53045
17499-20399	53045
Georges Ave	53045
Georgetown Dr	53045
Glacier Pkwy	53045
Glen Cove Ln	53005
Glen Echo Dr	53005
Glen Kerry Dr	53045
Glendale Ave	53005
Glenmaura Pl	53005
Glenoaks Dr	53045
Glenview Dr	53045
Glenwood Ln	53045
Glory Way	53005
Goetz Dr	53005
Golden Eagle Ct	53045
Golden Meadow Cir, Ct & Gln	53045
Golf Pkwy	53005
Grandview Dr	53005
Grandview Drive Lower	53005
Grandview Drive Upper	53005
Grant Ct	53005
Gray Fox Dr & Holw	53045
Green Isle Ct	53005
Green Meadow Dr	53045
Green Valley Blvd	53045
Greenbrier Dr	53045
W Greenfield Ave	
12500-17198	53005
17300-20398	53045
Greenridge Ter	53045
Greenview Dr	53045
Greenway Ter	53005
Greenwood Ct E & W	53005
Guinevere Dr	53045
Hackberry Ln	53045
Hackney Ct	53045
Hallendale Ct	53045
Hamilton Dr	53045
Hammock Hill Ln	53045
Hampstead Dr	53005
Hampton Rd	53005
Hancock Ct	53045
Harmony Cir	53045
Harrigan Ct & Dr	53005
Harvest Ln	53045
Harvey Ave	53005
Hastings Dr	53005
Havenwood Ct	53005
Hawks Ridge Rd	53045
Hawkswood Ct	53045
Hawthorne Ln	53005
Hawthorne Ridge Ct & Dr	53045
Hayden Ct	53045
Hazel Ct	53045
Heather Hill Dr	53005
Heatherview Dr	53045
Heathway Ln	53045
Helene Dr	53045
Hensley Ct	53045
Heron Pass	53045
Hi View Dr	53045
Hickory Ct	53045
Hickory Hill Ln	53045
Hidden Creek Ct & Trl	53005
Hidden Hills Dr	53005
Hidden Pond Ct	53005
High Knoll Ln	53045
High Meadow Cir & Dr	53045
Highfield Ct	53045
Highland Pass	53045
Hill Ct	53005
Hillcrest Dr	53005
N Hills Dr	53045
Hillsdale Dr	53005
Hilltop Dr	53005
Hobbs Ct	53005
Hoffman Ave	53045
Holly Ln	53045
Holly Ridge Ct	53045
Hollycrest Ct & Dr	53045
Hollyhock Ln	53005
Hollywood Ln	53045
Holsen Ct	53005
Honey Creek Dr	53045
Hope St	53005
Horseshoe Bend Ct	53045
Huff Way	53005
Hunters Ct & Run	53045
Huntington Cir	53005
Huntington Cir Lower	53005
Huntington Cir Upper	53005
Hushing Brae Ct	53045
Hyland Dr	53005
Imperial Dr	53045
Independence Ct & Dr	53045
Indian Trl	53045
Indian Creek Pkwy	53005
Indian Ridge Dr	53005
Indianwood Dr	53005
Industry Ave	53045
Intertech Dr	53045
Iris Ct	53045
Ivy Ln	53045
Jaclyn Dr	53045
James St	53005
N Janacek Ct & Rd	53045
Jean Marie Ct	53005
Jennifer Ln	53005
Jerri Ct	53005
Jewel St	53005
Jill Ct	53045
Joanne Dr	53005
Jodon Ct	53005
Jonquil Ct	53045
Judith Ln	53005
Kamala Ct & Ln	53045
Kathlynn Ct	53045
Keats Ct & Dr	53045
Keefe Ave	53005
Keller Dr	53005
Kelly Ln	53045
Kenmar Ct & Rd	53005
Kent Ave	53005
Kestrel Ct & Trl	53005
Keswick Ct	53045
Kevenauer Dr	53005
Kilkee Ct	53045
Killarney Way	53045
King Arthurs Ct	53045
Kings Ridge Ct	53005
Kingsview Ln	53005
Kinsey Park Dr	53005
Kirby St	53045
Kirkham Ct	53045
Kittridge Ct	53005
Klondike Ct	53045
Knoll Ct	53045
Kodiak Trl	53045
Kristin Ct E & W	53045
La Chandelle Ct	53045
La Fontaine Ct	53045
La Rochelle Ct	53045
La Vela Cir	53005
La Vela Circle Lower	53005
La Vela Circle Upper	53005
Lafayette Ct	53045
Lake Cir, Holw & Rd	53005
Lakeview Ct & Dr	53045
Lamplighter Ct & Ln	53045
Lancaster Ct	53045
Lancelot Dr	53045
Lansdowne Ct	53045
Larkspur Dr	53045
Laura Ln	53045
Le Chateau Dr	53045
Le Fey Ct	53045
Le Jardin Ct	53045
Leanore Ln	53005
Lees Ct	53045
Legend Ct	53045
Leland Dr	53005
Leon Ter	53005
Lewis Ave	53005
Lexington Ct	53045
Liberty Ct	53045
Lillan Rd	53005
Lilly Rd	53005
Lilly Heights Dr	53005
Limerick Ln	53045
Lincolnshire Ct	53045
Lincrest Dr	53005
Linden Ln	53005
Lindsay Dr	53005
Lindsay Ln	53045
Links Ct	53005
Linnan Ct	53005
Lionel Ct	53045
Lisa Ct & Ln	53005
W Lisbon Rd	
12401-12497	53005
12499-14499	53005
14501-17199	53005
18201-19499	53045
Locksley Ln	53045
Logan Dr	53045
Lois Ave	53045
Lola Dr	53045
Lone Elm Dr	53005
Lone Oak Cir & Ln	53045
Long Grove Rd	53045
Longview Ct	53045
Lookout Ln	53045
Lorien Ct	53045
Lothmoor Drive Lower	53045
Lothmoor Drive Upper	53045
Loughlin Ct N & S	53005
Louis Ln	53005
Lower Valley Ridge Dr	53005
Lucy Cir	53045
Luella Dr	53005
N Lynette Ln	53045
Lynnwood Ln	53005
Lyonnesse Ln	53045
Mac Henry Cir	53045
Macaulay Dr	53045
Madeline Ln	53045
Main St	53005
Mallard Ct	53045
Manchester Ct	53045
Manor Ct	53005
Maple Hill Ln	53005
Maple Ridge Ln	53045
Maple Tree Ln	53045
Maraljo Ct	53045
Marcella Ln	53005
Marie St	53005
Marie Ann Dr	53005
Mariner Ct	53045
Mark Dr	53005
Marseille Dr	53045
Martha Dr	53005
Marti Ln	53005
Martin Dr	53045
Mary Ln	53045
Mary Beth Ct	53005
Mary Cliff Ct & Ln	53005
Mary Lynn Dr	53045
Mary Rose Ct	53045
Mayer Ln	53005
Mayfair Dr	53005
Mayrose Blvd	53045
W Mc Allister Ln	53045
Mc Aurther Ln	53045
Mc Coy Ln	53045
Mcnally Ln	53045
Mcpride Ln	53045
Meadow Ct	53045
Meadow Vw E	53045
Meadow Vw W	53005
Meadow Croft Ct	53045
Meadow View Dr	53005
Meadowbrook Ln	53005
Meadowside Ct	53045
Melody Ln	53005
W Melvina St	53005
Memorial Dr	53045
Memory Ln	53045
Merlin Way	53045
Merrie Cir	53005
Mesa Ct	53005
Michael Dr	53045
Michelle Ct & Dr	53045
Midland Pl	53005
Mierow Ct & Ln	53045
Mildale St	53005
Milford Ln	53045
Milrod Ln	53005
Milton Ct	53045
Milwaukee Ave	53005
Misty Mountain Pkwy	53045
Monet Ct	53005
Monterey Blvd	53005
Montilla Ct	53005
Moor Ct	53005
N & S Moorland Rd	53005
Morningview Ct	53045
Mound Zion Woods Ct	53005
Mount Vernon Ave	53005
Mountain Dr	53005
Muirwood Dr	53045
Myrtle Ave	53005
Nancy Ln	53005
Nassau Dr	53045
Nelson Ave	53005
Neuberry Ct	53005
Newell Dr	53005
Nicholas Ct	53045
Norhardt Dr	53045
Norman Ct & Dr	53045
W North Ave	
12401-12597	53005
12599-17199	53005
17200-17522	53045
17524-21999	53045
Norwood Ln	53005
Nottingham Ct	53045
Oak Ct	53045
Oak Ln	53005
Oak Grove Rd	53005
Oak Hill Ct & Ln	53005
Oak Park Row	
16900-17199	53005
17200-17599	53045
Oak Ridge Ct	53045
Oakmont Ln	53005
Oakwood Ln	53045
Old Church Rd	53045
Old Lantern Ct & Dr	53005
Old Oak Ct	53005
Onondaga Cir	53005
Orchid Ct	53045
Oriole Ln	53005
Osage Trl	53005
Overhill Dr	53005
Overlook Cir	53045
Oxford Ct	53045
Paradise Ln	53045
Parish Dr	53045
N & S Park Blvd	53005
Parkhurst Dr	53045
Parkmoor Dr	53005
Parkside Dr	53005
Parkview Dr	53045
S Parkway Dr	53005
Partridge Ct	53045
Patricia Ln	
16200-17199	53005
17201-17205	53045
17207-17699	53045
N Patrick Blvd	53045
Patti Ln	53045
Paul Ct	53045
Penbrook Dr	53045
Penn Ct	53045
Pepper Ln	53005
Peppercorn Cir	53005
Peregrine Ln	53045
Pershing Dr	53005
Pheasant Dr	53005
Phoenix Ave	53005
Pilgrim Pkwy & Rd	53005
Pilgrim Hollow Ct	53005
Pilgrim Square Dr	53005
Pine Tree Ln	53005
Pinehurst Ct & Dr	53005
Pineview Ct	53045
Pinewood Rd	53045
Pitzka Rd	53045
Pleasant St	53045
Pleasant View Ct	53045
Plum Ct	53045
Pomona Ct & Rd	53005
Poplar Creek Dr	53045
Poplar Ridge Ct	53045
Possum Ct	53045
Post Rd	53005
Prairie Ct	53005
Prairie Falcon Ln	53045
President Ave	53045
Primrose Ln	53045
Prince George Ct	53045
Princeton Rd	53005
Prospect Dr	53005
Providence Ln	53005
Putneys Ct	53045
Quail Hollow Dr	53045
Queen Ann Dr	53005
Rackwood Ct	53045
Radiant Ct & Dr	53005
Ranch Rd	53005
Raven Ct & Dr	53005
Raven Rock Rd	53005
E & W Ravenswood Hills Cir	53045
Red Fox Dr	53045
Red Tail Ct	53045
Redvere Dr	53045
Regency Ct	53045
Regis St	53005
Revere Dr	53045
Richard Rd	53005
Richland Pkwy	53045
Ridgefield Ct	53005
Ridgeview Dr	53005
Ridgeway Rd	53045
Ridgewood Ln	53045
Ridgewood Rd	53005
Rivendell Dr	53045
N & W River Birch Dr	53045
Riverview Dr	53045
Robbie Ct	53005
Robin Ln	53005
Robinwood St	
12400-13199	53005
17200-17298	53045
17300-17400	53045
17402-17898	53045
Rockway Ln E & W	53005
Rocky Pt	53005

N & S Rolland Rd 53005
Rolling Meadow Ct & Dr 53045
N & S Rosedale Dr 53005
Rosewood Ct 53005
Roswell Dr 53005
W Roualt St 53005
Royalcrest Dr 53045
Ruby Ln 53005
Russet Dr 53045
Safer Ct 53045
Saint Andrews Ct & Ln 53045
Saint Charles Ct 53005
Saint James Rd 53045
Saint Therese Blvd 53005
San Fernando Dr 53045
San Gabriel Dr 53005
San Juan Trl 53005
San Lucas Ct & Dr 53045
San Marcos Ct & Dr 53005
San Raphael Dr 53005
Sanctuary Ct & Trl 53005
Santa Barbara Dr 53005
Santa Maria Ct & Dr 53005
Santa Rosa Dr 53005
W Sarah Ln 53045
Saratoga Ct 53045
Satinwood Ct 53005
Sauk Trl 53005
Saxon Ct 53045
Scarlet Dr 53005
Scarlet Hawthorne Ct & Rd 53045
Sceptor Ct 53045
Scheibe Dr 53005
Sean Ct 53045
Senate St 53005
Senlac Ln 53045
Serene Cir 53045
Serene Ln 53005
Shadybrook Ct & Pl 53005
Shagbark Ct & Ln 53005
Shamrock Ln 53005
Shasta Dr 53045
Shawnee Pass 53005
Sheffield Dr 53005
Shelly Ct 53045
Shepherd Ct 53045
Sheraton Ct & Rd 53005
Shetland Ln 53045
Shirley Ln 53005
Shore Line Dr 53045
Sierra Dr & Ln 53045
Siesta Ln 53005
Silver Mist Ct 53005
Simon Dr 53005
Sky Cliff Dr 53005
Sleepy Hollow Ln 53005
Smith Ct & Dr 53005
Somerset Ct & Ln 53045
Sommers Dr 53045
Spencer Ct & Ln 53045
Spring Dr 53005
Springdale Rd 53045
Springwood Ct 53005
Spruce Ln 53005
Squirrel Dr 53005
Starbridge Dr 53005
Steeple Chase 53045
Still Point Cir & Trl 53045
Stillwater Ct 53045
Stockton Ct 53005
Stonebrook Ct 53005
S Stonehedge Dr 53045
Stonewood Ct 53045
Stratford Ct 53045
Studio Ct 53045
Summerhill Ct & Ln 53045
Sundance Dr 53005
Sunny Crest Dr 53045
N & S Sunny Slope Rd 53005
Sunny View Ln 53005
Sunrise Ave 53005
Surrey Ln 53045
Talbots Ct & Ln 53045
Tall Oaks Dr 53045
Talon Ct & Trl 53045
Tamarack Dr 53045
Tanala Dr 53045
Tanglewood Ct & Dr 53045
Tara Dr 53045
Tarrytown Rd 53005
Taywood Cir 53045
Teal Ridge Ct 53045
Tennyson Dr 53045
Terrace Dr E & W 53045
Thomas Ln 53005
Thomson Dr 53045
Thornapple Ln 53005
Thornridge Ct 53045
Three Meadows Dr 53005
Tia Ct 53005
Tilton Ct & Ln 53045
Timber Pass 53045
Timberidge Trl 53005
Timberline Dr 53045
Toldt Forest Ct 53045
Toldt Woods Dr 53045
Tomahawk Trl 53005
Tower Hill Dr 53005
Town Trl 53045
Town Crier Ct 53005
W Townsend St 53005
Tralee Ct 53045
Tremont St
12400-13999 53005
17300-17498 53045
17500-17700 53045
17702-17798 53045
Trenton Ct 53045
Trilby Ct 53045
Tru Ln 53005
Tucson Dr 53005
Tulane Ct & St 53005
Turnberry Dr 53005
Turtle Creek Dr 53005
Twin Oaks Ct 53005
Tyein Pl 53045
Tyrone Ct 53045
Valiant Dr 53045
Valley Forge Ct 53045
Valley Ridge Dr 53005
Valley View Dr 53045
Vanderbilt St 53005
Ventura Cir 53045
Veranda Ct 53005
Verna Dr 53005
Vernon Dr 53005
Versailles Ave & Ct 53045
Victoria Ln 53045
Vincent Ct & Dr 53045
Virginia Ave 53005
Vista View Dr 53005
Vogel Ct 53005
Walnut Grove Ct 53005
Warwick Dr 53045
Washington Ct 53045
Washington Dr 53005
Water Tower Blvd 53045
Waynescott Rd 53005
Webster Ave 53005
Wellington Ct 53045
Wembley Cir & Rd 53045
Wembley Circle Lower 53005
Wembley Circle Upper 53005
Wessex Dr 53045
West Ln 53045
Westmoor Dr 53005
Weston Hills Ct & Dr 53045
Westview Ct 53005
Westwood Ct & Dr 53005
Wetherby Ct 53045
Wetzel Ln 53005
Wexford Ct 53005
Whipple Tree Ct & Ln 53045
Whitehall Ct & Dr 53045
Whitemont Dr 53045
Whittington Ct 53045
Wild Cherry Ct 53005
Wild Rose Ct 53045
Wilderness Ct & Way 53045
Wildwood Ct 53005
Willaura Ct 53005
Williams Ct 53045
Willow Ridge Ln 53005
Willow Spring Dr 53045
Willowick Ct 53045
Wilshire Rd 53045
Wilson Dr 53005
Windemere Rd 53045
Windwood Ct 53005
Winston Park Ct 53045
Winthrop Ct 53005
Wirth St 53005
W Wisconsin Ave
16201-17099 53005
17201-17307 53045
17309-18500 53045
18502-18798 53045
Woelfel Rd 53045
Wolf Trap Ct 53045
Wood Ln 53005
Woodberry Ct 53045
Woodbridge Ct & Rd 53005
Woodburn Ct 53005
Woodchuck Ln 53045
Woodcrest Ct 53005
Woodglen Ct 53005
Woodhill Ct 53005
Woodland Ct & Pl 53005
Woodmoor Ln 53045
Woodmount Dr 53005
Woodridge Cir & Ct 53045
Woods Edge Ct 53005
Woodside Pl 53005
Woodstock Ct 53005
W Woodview Dr 53005
Wynchester Ct 53045
Wyndham Pointe Cir 53005
Wynfield Ct & Ln 53045
Yale Ct 53005
Yorkshire Ln 53045
Yorktown Ct 53045
Yukon Rd 53045
Zacher Blvd 53005
Zinke Dr 53005

NUMBERED STREETS

N & S 124th 53005
N 126th St 53005
N 127th St 53005
N 128th St 53005
N 129th St 53005
N 130th St 53005
N 131st St 53005
N 133rd St 53005
N 134th St 53005
N 135th St 53005
N 137th St 53005
N 138th St 53005
N 142nd St 53005
N 143rd St 53005
N 144th St 53005
N 145th St 53005
N 146th St 53005
N 147th St 53005
N 148th St 53005
N 149th St 53005
N 150th St 53005
N 158th St 53005
N 159th St 53005
N 160th St 53005
N 161st St 53005
N 162nd St 53005
N 163rd St 53005
N 165th St 53005
N 166th St 53005
N & S 167th 53005
N 169th St 53005
N 178th St 53045
N 180th St 53045
N 184th St 53045
N 185th St 53045
N 186th St 53045
N 187th St 53045

EAU CLAIRE WI

General Delivery 54703

POST OFFICE BOXES MAIN OFFICE STATIONS AND BRANCHES

Box No.s
All PO Boxes 54702

NAMED STREETS

Abbe Ct 54703
Abbe Hill Dr 54703
Abbey Rd 54701
Addison Ave 54703
Agnes St 54701
Airport Rd 54703
Albright Ct 54701
Alf Ave & Ct 54701
Allemande Ct 54701
Alpine Rd 54703
Alter Rd 54703
Altoona Ave 54701
Amanda Ct 54703
American Blvd 54701
Amy Ln 54701
Anderson Dr & Rd 54703
Andover Ave 54703
Andrew Dr 54701
E & S Anita Dr 54701
Ann St 54703
Anric Dr 54701
Arbor Ct & Ln 54701
Arbor Hills Cir 54703
Arbutus Dr 54703
Archer Ln 54703
Arlen Ct 54703
Arlene Pl 54703
Armstrong Pl 54701
Arndt Rd 54701
Arnstad Pl 54703
Arrowhead Dr 54703
Arthur St 54701
Ash St 54703
Ashley Ln 54701
Aspen Ct & Ln 54703
Aspen Ridge Dr 54703
Augusta St 54701
Avenue A St 54703
Avenue B St 54703
Avenue C St 54703
Aylmer Ct 54703
Babcock St 54703
Badger Ave 54701
Balcom St 54703
Ball St 54703
Balsam Ct 54703
Balsam Rd 54701
Barland St 54701
Barron St 54703
Barry Ave 54701
N Barstow St
100-199 54703
126-126 54702
200-798 54703
201-799 54703
S Barstow St 54701
Bartlett Ct 54701
Bartusch Rd 54701
Bauer Ave 54703
Bauer St 54701
Bayview Dr 54701
Beach St 54703
Becker Rd 54703
Bell St 54703
Bellevue Ave 54703
Bellinger St 54703
Belmont Ave 54701
Bend Ct 54701
Benjamin St 54703
Bennington Ct 54703
Benrud Ln & Pkwy 54701
Benton Ave 54701
Bergen Ave 54703
Bernhardt Rd 54701
Bethel St 54703
Betz Rd 54701
Beulah Ln 54701
Beverly Hills Dr 54701
Birch Dr & St 54703
Birch Crest Ln 54701
Birch Hill Ct 54703
Birch Hills Dr & Ln 54701
Birchwood Ln 54703
Birdlawn Rd 54701
Birney St 54701
Bittersweet Rd 54701
Black Ave & Ct 54703
Blackberry Rd 54701
Blackoak Rd 54701
Blakeley Ave 54701
Blue Bird Ct 54701
Blue Valley Ct & Dr 54703
Blueberry Dr 54703
Boardwalk Cir & St 54701
Bobbie St 54703
Bogey Ave 54701
Bolles St 54703
Bonnie Ct 54701
Bonnie Vale Ct 54701
Books Dr 54703
Bordeaux Ct 54703
Boston Dr 54703
Bostrom Ct 54701
Boulevard Pl 54703
Bowe Rd 54701
Brackett Ave 54701
Bradley Ave 54701
Brandt Rd 54703
Brent Dr 54701
Brentwood Ter 54703
Brian St 54701
Briar Way 54701
Briarcrest Dr 54701
Briarwood Ct 54703
Briarwood Dr 54701
Briggs Ave 54703
Brittany Ct 54701
Broadview Blvd 54703
Broadway St 54703
Brookline Ave 54703
Brookwood Dr 54701
Buck Rub Rd 54703
N Buena Vista Rd 54703
Buffington Ct & Dr 54703
Bullis Ct 54701
Bullis Farm Rd 54701
Bunker Ln 54701
Burnell Dr 54703
Calumet Rd 54703
W Cameron St & Trl 54703
Campus Rd 54703
Canfield St 54701
Canterbury Rd 54701
Cardell Rd 54703
Cardinal Ave 54703
Carol Ct 54703
Carol Ln 54701
Carol St
700-899 54703
6600-6799 54701
Carpenter Ave 54703
Carson Park Dr 54703
Carter St 54703
Cass St 54701
Cater Rd 54701
Catherine St 54703
Catur Ln 54701
Cedar Rd 54701
Cedar St 54703
Cemetary Rd 54701
Central St 54703
Centre St 54703
Chapin St 54701
Charles St 54703
Charleston Ct & Dr 54703
Chasewood Ln 54701
Chauncey St 54701
Chayne Dr 54703
Cherry Ln 54701
Cherrywood Ln 54701
Chestnut St 54703
Chippewa St 54703
Chippewa River Dr 54703
Chokecherry Rd 54701
Christian Ave 54703
Christopher Dr 54703
Chuck Ln 54703
Chumas Dr 54701
Church St 54703
Churchill St 54703
City Line Rd 54703
City View Dr 54701
E Clairemont Ave
200-298 54701
300-2700 54701
2615-2615 54702
2702-3798 54701
3001-3799 54701
N Clairemont Ave 54703
W Clairemont Ave 54701
Clare St 54703
Clark Pl 54701
Claudette St 54701
Clay St 54701
Claymore Ln 54701
Clearwater Ridge Ct & Dr 54703
Cleveland St 54703
Cliff St 54703
Clinton Ct 54701
Close Ct 54701
Clover Dr 54701
Club House Ln 54703
Cochrane St 54703
Collins Ct 54701
Colonial Ct & Dr 54703
Coltman Ln 54701
Comet Ave & Ct 54703
Comings Rd 54701
Commerce Valley Rd 54701
Commonwealth Ave 54701
Conch Ave 54701
Concord Trl 54703
Cone Ct 54701
Congress St 54703
Conifer Ct 54703
Connell Rd 54703
Conrad St 54703
Continental Dr 54701
Coolidge Ct 54701
Cooper Ave 54703
Cornell Ct & St 54703
Corona Ave 54701
Corydon Rd 54701
Cottonwood Dr 54701
Country Club Ln 54701
County Rd E 54703
County Farm Cir & Rd 54703
County Highway X 54703
County Line Rd 54703
County Road B 54701
County Road F
W300-W399 54701
County Road H 54701
County Road Hh 54701
County Road I 54701
County Road Ii 54701
County Road T 54703
County Road Z 54701
Court Dr 54703
Coventry Ct 54701
Craig Rd 54701
Creek Ridge Dr 54703
Crescent Ave 54703
Crest Ct 54701
Crestview Ct 54701
Crestview Dr
S7600-S7799 54701
1800-2299 54703
Crestwood Rd 54703
Crocus Ln 54701
Culver St 54701
Cummings Ave & Ct 54701
Curtis Ln 54701
Curtiss St 54703
Curvue Rd 54703
Cyndi Ct 54703
Cypress St 54701
Dale Rd & St 54703
Damar Private Dr 54701
Damon Ct & St 54701
Dana St 54701
Darmel St 54703
Darryl Ln 54703
Davey Ct & St 54703
David Dr & Ln 54701
Davis Ave 54703
Davis Dr 54701
S Davis Dr 54701
E Deblene Ln 54703
Declaration Dr 54703
Dedham St 54703
Deepwood Ct 54703
Deer Park Pl 54701
Deer Park Rd 54703
Deerfield Dr 54703
Deerfield Rd 54701
Delbert Rd 54703
Dells Ct 54703
Dellview St 54703
Delrae Ct 54703
Demoe Ln 54703
N Dewey St 54703
S Dewey St 54701
Deyo Ave 54703
Diane Ln 54703
Division St 54703
Dodge St 54701
Dogwood Dr 54701
Donald Ave 54701
Donna Ct 54703
Donnellan Ln 54703
Dorbe St 54701
Dorret Rd 54703
Doty St 54701
Douglas Ln 54703
Drier Ct & Rd 54701
Driftwood Ln 54703
Drinkman Ln 54701
Drummond St 54701
Drury Ave & Ct 54703
Dulaney St 54703
Eagle Ln & Ter 54703
Eagle Ridge Ct 54703
Earl St 54701
East St 54701
Eastland Ct 54703
Eastlawn St 54703
Eastridge Ctr 54701
Eastwind Dr 54701
Eau Claire St 54701
Echo Valley Dr 54703
N Eddy Ln & St 54703
Edgewater Ct 54703
S Edgewater Dr 54701
Edgewood Ln 54703
Edwards St 54703
Eisenhower St 54701
Elayne Dr 54701
Elderberry Ln 54701
Eldorado Blvd 54701
Eliza Wilson Rd 54703
Elizabeth St 54703
Elk Creek Rd 54703
Ellis St 54701
Elm Rd 54701
Elm St 54703
Emery St 54701
Enterprise St 54701
Epiphany Ln 54703
Erica Ct 54701
Erin St 54703
Ervin Rd & St 54703
Esmond Rd 54701
Essex St 54703
Estate St 54703
Evergreen Ln 54701
Evergreen St 54703
Evergreen Ter 54701

Fairfax St 54701
Fairfax Park Dr 54701
Fairmont Ave 54703
Fairview Dr 54701
Fairway St 54701
Fall St 54703
Farr Ct 54701
N Farwell St 54703
S Farwell St 54701
Fay St 54703
Fear St 54701
Fehr Rd 54701
Fenner St 54703
Fenwick Ave 54701
Fern Ct 54703
Ferry St 54703
Fieldstone Dr 54701
E & W Fillmore Ave 54701
Fisher St 54703
Flaten Ct 54703
Fleming Ave 54701
Florence Ave & Ct 54703
Flynn Pl 54703
W Folsom St 54703
Forest St 54703
Forest Heights Dr 54701
Forest Knoll Ct & Dr 54701
Fortune Dr 54703
Fountain St 54703
Fouser Farm Rd 54701
Fox Point Trl 54701
Foxmoor Ln 54701
Francis St 54703
W Frank St 54703
Franklin St 54703
Frederic St 54701
Freedom Dr 54703
Friedeck Rd 54701
Frisbie Ln 54703
Frona Pl 54701
S Frontage Rd 54701
Frostwoods St 54703
Fuller Ave 54703
Fuller Rd 54701
Fulton St 54703
Gables Cir, Ct, Dr & Pl 54701
Gala St 54703
Galloway St 54703
Garden St 54703
Garfield Ave & Rd 54701
Garner St 54701
Gary Ln 54703
Gatehouse Dr & Ter 54701
Gateway Dr 54701
Germania St 54703
Gerrard Ave & Ct 54701
Gessner Rd 54703
Gibson St 54701
Giese Rd 54701
Gilbert Ave 54701
Gilbert St 54703
Glen Way 54701
Glen Crest Ct 54701
Glenbrooke Dr 54701
Glenhaven Pl 54703
Glenn Pl 54703
Glenwood Ave 54703
Glory Ln 54703
Goff Ave 54701
Golden Dr 54703
Goldridge Ct & Rd 54701
Golf Rd & Ter 54701
Golf View Ct & Dr 54701
N & S Gooder Ave & St 54703
Goodview Ct 54703
Graceland Ct 54701
Graff Rd 54701
Graham Ave 54701
E Grand Ave 54701
W Grand Ave 54703
Grandview Ct & Dr 54703
E & W Grant Ave 54701
Gray St 54701
Green Acres Ct 54703
Green View Dr 54703
Greendale Ct 54701
Greenfield Dr 54703
Greenway St 54701
Gregerson Dr 54703
Gregory Ln 54703
Grey Friar Ln 54701
Grissom Dr 54703
Grove St 54701
Grover Rd 54701
Guettinger Rd 54701
Gunnes Rd 54701
Guthrie Rd 54703
Haanstad Rd 54703
Hagman St 54703
Hailey Ln 54701
Hallie Ln 54701
Halsey St 54701
E & W Hamilton Ave 54701
Hampton Ct 54703
Hangar Rd 54703
Harding Ave & Ct 54701
Harlem St 54701
Harless Rd 54701
Harold St 54701
Harris St 54703
Harrison St 54703
Hart Rd 54701
Hartwood Dr 54703
Hartzell Ln 54703
Harvard Ln 54701
N Hastings Pl 54703
N Hastings Way 54703
S Hastings Way
601-697 54701
699-1200 54701
1201-3699 54701
1201-1201 54702
1202-3698 54701
Hatch St 54701
Havenwood Ln 54701
Hawkins St 54703
Hawthorne St 54703
Hazeltine Dr 54703
Hazelwood Ct 54701
Heartland Dr N & W 54701
Heather Ct & Rd 54701
Heights Dr 54701
Heimstead Rd 54703
Helen Ct 54703
Hemlock Ln 54703
Hemlock Rd 54701
Hendrickson Dr 54701
Henry Ave 54701
Heritage Dr 54703
Heron St 54703
Hester St 54701
Hewitt St 54703
Hickory Ln 54703
Hickory Rd 54701
Hidden Pl 54701
Highland Ave 54701
Highview Dr 54703
Hillsdale Rd 54703
Hillside Dr 54703
Hillside Park Rd 54701
Hilltop Cir 54701
Hillview Rd
S8102-S8198 54701
Hobart St 54703
Hogarth St 54703
Hogeboom Ave 54701
Holm Ave 54703
Holum Rd 54701
Homestead Ct & Rd 54701
Hoover Ave 54701
Hope Ave 54703
Hopkins Ave 54701
Horlacher Ln 54701
Hotchkiss Ave 54703
House Rd 54701
Howard Ave 54703
Howard Dr 54701
W Hoyem Ct & Ln 54703
N & S Hubbard Dr 54701
Hudson St 54703
Huebsch Blvd 54701
Illinois St 54703
Imperial Cir 54701
Independence Ct 54703
Indian Hills Dr 54703
Industrial Dr 54701
Ingram Dr 54701
International Dr 54701
Inwood Ct 54703
Inwood Dr 54701
Iona Beach Rd 54703
Irene Dr 54701
Ironwood Ln 54703
Isabel St 54701
Jackson St 54703
James Ln 54701
James St 54703
Jamie Ln 54701
Jannet Ave 54701
Jaybee Dr 54701
Jeanne Ln 54703
Jeffers Rd 54703
Jeffers Ridge Rd 54703
Jefferson Ct & St 54701
Jeffery Ct 54701
Jeffrey Ln 54703
Jene Rd 54701
Jennifer Ln 54701
Jensen Rd 54701
Jill Ave & Ct 54701
Jingle Ct 54703
Joan St 54703
Jodi Dr 54703
John St 54701
John Hart Pl 54703
Johnson Ln 54701
Johnson St 54703
Jones St 54701
Jopke Rd 54701
Jordan Ct 54701
Jule Ct 54703
Julius Dr 54703
Jupiter Ave 54703
Kane Ct & Rd 54703
Kappus Dr 54701
Karen Ct 54701
Kari Dr 54701
Karissa Dr 54701
Katelyn Ct 54701
Kathryn Dr 54701
Katie Ln 54703
Kay St 54701
Kaycee Dr 54703
Keith St 54701
Kelley Pl 54701
Kendall St 54703
Kenney Ave 54701
Kenora Pkwy 54703
Kensington Ct 54701
Kent Ave & Ct 54701
Kern Dr 54701
Kern St 54703
Kernan Ct 54703
Kestrel Rd 54701
Keystone Xing 54701
Kilbourne Ave 54703
Kimberly Dr 54703
King Pl 54701
Kingswood Ct 54701
Kirk Ct, Dr & St 54701
Knight St 54703
Kohlhepp Rd 54703
Kristy Rd 54701
Kucera Dr 54703
La Salle St 54703
Laddie Rd 54703
Lake Dr 54703
Lake St 54703
E Lake St 54701
Lake Shore Dr 54703
Lakeside Ave & Dr 54703
Lakeview Dr 54701
Lamans Ln 54703
Lamont Ct & St 54701
Lamplighter Ct 54703
Lana Ln 54701
Landon St 54703
Langdell Rd 54701
Lantern Ln 54703
Larchmont Rd 54701
Lark Ave 54703
Lars Rd 54703
Lassek Ct 54703
Laurel Ave 54701
Laurie Ct 54703
Lawelda Ln 54703
Lawrence St 54703
Lee St 54701
Leeds Ct 54703
Lehman St 54701
Leonard Ct & Dr 54703
Leslie Ln 54703
Lever St 54701
E Lexington Blvd 54701
Liberty Ct 54703
Lila Ln 54701
Lilac St 54703
Lincoln Ave 54701
Linda Ln 54703
Linden Pl 54703
Livingston Ln 54701
Lloyd Ave 54701
Loch Wood Ct 54703
Locust Ln & St 54703
Loken Ln 54703
London Rd 54701
Long St 54703
Lorch Ave 54703
Loriande St 54701
W Losan Ave 54703
Lotus St 54703
Louis Ave 54703
E, S & W Lowes Creek Ct & Rd 54701
Luer Rd 54701
Lyle Ln 54703
Lyndale Ave 54701
Lynnette Ct 54703
E & W Macarthur Ave 54701
E & W Madison St 54703
Madwarne St 54703
Maiden Ln 54703
Main St 54701
Malden Ave 54703
Maleda Ct & Dr 54703
Mall Dr 54701
Mandy Ln 54703
Manor Ct 54703
Maple Rd 54701
Maple St 54703
Maple Drive Rd 54701
Mappa St 54703
Marcott Ct 54703
Maren Ct 54703
Margaret Ln 54703
Margaret St 54701
Marie Ct 54703
Marilyn Dr 54701
Marion St 54701
Mark Ln 54703
Market St 54703
Marquette St 54703
Mars Ave 54703
Marshall St 54703
Marston Ave & Ct 54701
Martenson Dr 54703
Martenson St 54701
Martin St 54701
Mary Ln, Pl & St 54703
Mathews Dr 54703
Maxon St 54703
May St 54701
Mayer Rd 54701
Mayo St 54701
Maywood Dr 54703
Mcclaflin Ave 54703
Mcdonough St 54703
Mcelroy Ct & St 54701
Mcgraw St 54701
Mcgregor Dr 54703
Mcintyre Ave 54703
Mcivor St 54701
Mckai Dr 54703
Mckinley Ave 54701
Mckinley Ct 54703
Mckinley Rd 54703
Mcmillen St 54703
W Mead St 54703
Meadow Ln 54701
Meadow Lark Ln 54703
Meadowbrook Ct 54701
E Meadows Pl 54701
Meadowwood Dr 54701
Megan Ln 54703
Melanie Ln 54703
Melby St 54703
Melmar Ct 54703
Melody Ln 54703
Memory Ln 54701
Menard Dr 54703
W Menomonie St 54703
Mercantile Dr 54703
Mercury Ave 54703
Meridian Heights Dr 54703
Mesa Ridge Dr 54703
Mewhorter Ct & Rd 54701
Michael Dr 54701
Michaud St 54703
N & S Michigan St 54703
Midway St 54703
Mill Ridge Cir 54703
Mill Run Ct & Rd 54703
Miller Rd 54703
Miller St 54701
Milton Rd 54703
Milward St 54703
Minnesota St 54703
Mischler Rd 54701
E & S Mission Dr 54701
Mitchell Ave
300-1999 54701
3000-3399 54703
Mitchell Rd 54701
Mitscher Ave 54703
Mittelstadt Ln 54703
W Moholt Dr 54703
Moliter Rd 54701
Mondovi Rd 54701
Monroe St 54703
Mont Claire Rd 54703
Montaine St 54701
Monte Carlo Dr 54703
Moon Ave 54703
Moore St 54703
Morgan Ave 54701
Morningcrest Rd 54703
Morningside Dr 54703
Motycka Dr 54703
Mount Nemo Ave 54703
Mount Washington Ave 54703
Mountain View Pl 54703
Mountaray Ct & Dr 54703
Mourning Dove Ct 54701
Mulberry St 54703
Murphy Ln 54703
Necessity St 54703
Nelson Dr 54703
Neptune Ave & Ct 54703
Nestle Ave 54703
Newton St 54701
Niagara St 54703
Nicholas Dr 54703
Nimitz St 54701
Nixon Ave 54701
Noble Ct & Dr 54703
Normandale Dr 54703
Norrish Rd 54701
North Ln 54703
North Rd 54701
Northland Dr 54703
W Northstar Ct, Dr & Ln 54703
Northwinds Dr 54701
Northwoods Ct & Ln 54703
Nova Dr 54703
Oak St 54703
Oak Bluff Ct 54701
Oak Hill Pl 54703
Oak Knoll Dr 54701
Oak Park Ave 54703
Oak Ridge Dr 54701
Oak Tree Ln 54701
Oakcrest Dr 54701
Oakdale Ct 54701
Oakland St 54703
Oaklawn Dr 54703
Oakwood Pl 54701
Oakwood Hills Pkwy 54701
Oakwood Mall Dr 54701
Obrien St 54703
Ohio St 54703
Ohm Ave 54701
Old Mill Plz 54703
Old Orchard Rd 54703
Old School Ct 54701
Old Town Hall Rd 54701
Old Wells Rd 54703
Olson Dr 54703
Olson Rd 54701
Omaha St 54703
Orange St 54701
Orchard Pl 54703
Oriole Dr 54701
Orion Way 54703
Oscar 54703
Otis St 54703
Otter Rd 54701
Otter Creek Ct 54701
Otteson Ln 54701
Owen Ayres Ct 54701
N Oxford Ave 54703
Palmer Ln 54701
Palomino Rd 54701
Pamela Pl 54701
Pana Cir 54701
Paris Pl 54703
Park Ave & Pl 54701
Park Ridge Ct & Dr 54703
Parkside Cir E & W 54701
Parkwood Dr 54703
Partridge Rd 54703
Partridge Run 54701
Pascal Ct 54703
Patton St 54701
Paul St 54701
Paula Ct & Pl 54703
Paulina St 54703
Pavelski Rd 54703
Pearl Dr 54703
Peebles St 54703
Perkins Ln 54703
Pershing St 54703
Perth Dr 54703
Peters Dr 54703
Peterson Ave & St 54703
Peuse Rd 54701
Phoenix Ave 54703
Pickerign Pl 54701
Piedmont Rd 54703
Pine Ct 54703
Pine Pl 54701
Pine Lodge Rd 54701
Pine Meadow Dr 54701
Pine Park Dr 54701
Pine Ridge Rd 54703
Pinehurst Rd 54703
Pineview Rd 54703
Pinewood Rd 54701
Pinnacle Way 54701
Pioneer Ct 54701
Pitt St 54703
Plante St 54703
Platt St 54703
Pleasant St 54701
Pleasant Hill Rd 54703
Pleasant Valley Dr 54701
Pleasant View St 54701
Plum St 54703
S Pointe Ct 54701
E & W Polk Ave 54701
Pomona Dr 54701
Ponderosa Dr E & N 54701
Popular St 54703
Porter Ave 54701
Porterville Rd 54701
Potter Rd 54703
Powell St 54703
Prairie Cir N 54701
Prairie Cir S 54701
Prairie Ln 54703
E Prairie Ln 54703
Prairie Park Dr 54701
Premier Ct 54703
Prestige Ct 54703
Preston Rd 54703
Prill Rd 54701
Primrose St 54703
E & W Princeton Ave 54703
Priory Rd 54701
Promontory Ct 54701
Prospect Dr 54703
Providence Ct 54703
Putnam Dr 54701
Putnam St 54703
Putnam Glen Pl 54701
Puttor Dr 54701
Quail Ridge Rd 54701
Quail Run Rd 54701
Quarry St 54703
Quasar Dr 54703
Quetico Ct 54703
Quinnelan Dr 54703
Raber Rd 54701
Race St 54703
Raedel Rd 54703
Rainetta Dr 54701
Rambil Ct & Rd 54703
Randall St 54703
Rassbach St 54701
Ravencrest Ave 54703
Red Maple Ct & Rdg 54703
Red Pine Dr 54701
Redwood Dr 54701
Regis Ct 54701
Remington Rd 54703
Renee Ct & Dr 54703
Reno Dr 54703
Revere St 54703
Rice Ct 54701
Richard Dr 54701
W Ridge Ct 54703
W Ridge Dr 54703
Ridge Rd 54701
Ridgedale Ct & Rd 54701
Ridgeview Dr 54701
Ridgeway Dr 54701
Ridgewood Dr 54701
Riley St 54701
Rim Rock Rd 54701
Rimridge Rd 54701
Ripley Ave 54701
Rist Ave 54701
Ritsch Ct 54703
N River Dr & St 54703
River Glen Ct 54703
Rivercrest Dr 54703
Riverfront Ter 54703
Riverside Ave 54703
E Riverview Dr 54703
Robert Rd 54703
Robin Rd 54703
E Robin Meadows Ln 54701
Rock Falls Rd 54701
Roderick St 54701
Rooney Dr 54701
Roosevelt Ave 54701
Rork Ave 54703
Rose St 54701
Rosewood Ln 54703
Roshell Dr 54701
Rowe St 54703
Roy St 54701
Royal Ct & Dr 54701
Ruby Ln 54703
Rudolph Ct & Rd 54701
Running Deer Dr 54703
Runway Ave 54703
Russell Ct 54703
Rust St 54701

Ruth St 54701
Ryder Rd 54701
Rye Ct 54701
Rygg Rd 54701
Saint Andrews Cir 54701
Saint Claire St 54703
Saint Francis Dr E & W 54703
Saint Louis St 54703
Saint Thomas Dr 54703
Sandberg Rd 54701
Sandstone Rd 54701
Sandusky Dr 54703
Sanford Ln 54703
Sara St 54703
Saturn Ave 54703
Schoettl Ave 54703
Schuh Rd 54701
Schult St 54703
Scobie Ln 54703
Scotch Pine Ct 54701
Scully Dr 54701
Seaver St 54703
Seclusion Dr 54703
Selma St 54703
Service Rd 54701
Sessions Ct & St 54701
Severson St 54703
Seymour Rd 54703
Shady Grove Rd 54703
Shale Ledge Rd 54703
Shang Dr 54701
Sharon Dr 54701
Sheeder Rd 54701
Shellamie Dr 54701
Sheridan Rd 54703
Sherman St 54701
Sherman Creek Rd 54703
Sherwin Ave 54701
Sherwood Blvd & Cir 54703
Shetland Rd 54701
N Shore Dr 54703
Shoreline Ct 54703
S & W Shorewood Dr 54703
Shorewood Heights Pkwy 54703
Short Rd 54701
Short St
 100-198 54703
 700-1199 54701
Sierra Dr E & S 54701
Siewert Rd 54701
Silver Springs Ct & Dr 54701
Silvermine Dr 54703
Simon Ct 54703
Sindelar Dr 54701
Skeels Ave 54701
Sky Hawk Ct & Dr 54703
Sky Park Blvd 54701
Skyline Ct & Dr 54703
Slawson Ct 54703
Slayton Ave 54703
Sloan St 54703
S Slope Ter 54703
Snelling St 54703
Solberg Ct 54703
Solem Ln 54703
Soley Ln 54703
Somona Pkwy 54703
South Rd & St 54701
Southern Way 54701
Southgate Ct 54701
Southridge Ct & Dr 54701
Southtowne Dr & Pl 54701
Southwind Dr 54701
Southwood Ct 54701
Spehle Rd 54701
Speros Ln 54701
Sportsman Dr 54703
Spring St 54703
Springfield Dr 54701
Spruce St 54703
Star Ridge Rd 54708
Starlite Ln 54703
Starr Ave 54703
State St 54701
State Road 37 54701
State Road 85 54701
State Road 93 54701
Statz Ave 54703
Stein Blvd & Ct 54701
Steinhauer Dr 54701
Stellar Dr 54703
Stephi Rd 54703
Sterling Dr 54701
Steven Ln 54701
Stonewood Dr 54703
Stookey St 54703
Storrs Rd 54701
Suburban St 54703
Suchla Ct 54701
Sumac Ln 54701
Summer St 54701
Summerfield Dr 54701
Summit Ave 54701
Summit St 54703
Sun Vista Ct 54703
Sundance Pl 54701
Sundet Rd 54703
Sunny Ln 54703
Sunray Cir 54703
Sunridge St 54703
Sunrise Ln 54703
Sunset Dr 54703
Sunset View Dr 54701
Susan Dr 54701
Sussex Dr 54703
Taft Ave 54703
Talmadge Rd & St 54703
Tamara Dr 54701
Tamarack Ln 54701
Tartan Pl 54701
Tate Ave 54703
Taylor Creek Rd 54701
Teal Ct 54701
Terre Bone Trl 54701
Terri Ct 54703
Terry Ln 54703
Texaco Dr 54703
Thistle Ln 54703
Thomas Dr 54701
Thrush Dr 54701
Tiburon Dr 54703
Tiffany Ln 54703
Timber Ln & Rd 54701
Timber Creek Ct 54701
Timber Line Dr 54701
Timber Ridge Cir & Ln 54701
Timber Trails Ct 54701
Todd Rd 54701
Tony Ct 54701
Tower Dr 54703
Town Hall Rd 54701
N Town Hall Rd 54703
S Town Hall Rd 54703
Trenton Ct 54703
Trillium Dr 54701
Trimble St 54701
Trindal St 54703
Trinity St 54703
Truax Blvd, Ct & Ln 54703
E & W Truman Ave 54701
Tweed Dr 54703
Twilight Ln 54703
E & W Tyler Ave 54701
Uecke Ave 54703
Union St 54703
University Dr 54701
Uranus Ave 54703
Us Highway 12 54701
Us Highway 12 E 54701
Us Highway 12 W 54703
Us Highway 53 54701
Vale Ln 54703
Valley Rd N & S 54703
Valley Park Ct 54703
Valley View Dr 54701
Valley View Pl
 2200-2299 54703
 3600-3699 54701
S Valley View Pl 54701
Valmont Ave 54701
Van Buren St 54703
Van Es Pkwy 54703
Venture Dr 54703
Venus Ave 54703
Vernon St 54701
Vesta Ct 54703
Vesterheim St 54703
Vienna Ter 54703
Viking Pl 54701
Village Oaks Cir 54701
Village Terrace Ct 54701
W Vine Ct & St 54703
Vineyard St 54703
Violet Ave 54701
Virginia Ln 54703
Vista Ct 54701
Vold Ct 54701
Vollendorf Ln 54703
Wagner Ave 54703
Waller St 54703
Walnut Rd 54701
Walnut St 54703
Walnut Ridge Dr 54701
Wander Ct 54703
Ward St 54703
Warden St 54703
Washington St 54701
Water St 54701
Wayland Ct 54703
Wayne Pl 54701
Webster Ave 54701
Wedgewood Ave 54701
Wellington Dr E & W 54703
Welsh Ct & Dr 54703
Wenzel Dr 54701
Werlein Ave 54703
Western Ave 54703
Westgate Rd 54703
Westhaven Ct 54701
Westover Ln & Rd 54701
Westwood Ln 54703
Whipple St 54703
Whispering Pines Ln 54701
White Ave 54703
White Birch Ct 54701
White Oak Dr & Ln 54703
White Pine Dr 54703
White Pine Dr E 54701
White Pine Dr N 54701
White Tail Dr 54701
Wilcox St 54703
Wild Ridge Ct 54703
Wild Rose Dr 54703
Wild Rose Ln 54701
Wildon St 54703
Wildwood Ct 54701
William Ct 54701
William Dr 54701
William St 54703
Williamsburg Dr 54703
Willis Ave 54703
Willow Ln 54703
Willow Creek Rd 54701
Willow Green Cir 54701
Wilson Dr 54703
Wilson St 54701
Windsong Ct 54703
Windward Ct 54701
Winget Dr 54703
Winsor Dr 54703
Winter St 54701
Wintergreen Ct 54701
Wisconsin St 54703
Wold Ct 54701
Woodcrest Ct 54701
Woodcrest Highlands Rd 54701
Woodfield Dr & Rd 54701
Woodford Ct 54703
Woodhaven Ct & Rd 54701
Woodland Ave 54701
Woodland Ct 54703
Woodland Dr 54701
Woodridge Dr 54701
Woodstock Ct 54701
Woodtrail Ct 54703
Worbach Dr 54703
Wren Dr 54701
Xiong Blvd 54703
Yorktown Ct 54703
Zephyr Hill Ave 54703

NUMBERED STREETS

1st Ave & St 54703
1st Reserve St 54703
2nd Ave & St 54703
2nd Reserve St 54703
3rd Ave & St 54703
4th Ave & St 54703
5th Ave & St 54703
6th Ave & St 54703
7th Ave & St 54703
8th Ave & St 54703
9 Mile Creek Rd 54701
9th Ave & St 54703
10th Ave & St 54703
11th St 54703
12th Ave & St 54703
13th St 54703
14th Ave & St 54703
15th St 54703
16th St 54703
17th Ave 54703
19th Ave & St 54703
20th Ave 54703
23rd Ave S 54703
24th S 54703
25th Ave 54703
26th Ave 54703
27th Ave 54703
30th Ave 54703
33rd Ave & St 54703
34th St 54703
40th St 54703
S 41st Ave 54703
S 42nd Ave 54703
50th Ave & St 54703
N 54th Ave 54703
56th St 54703
S 57th Ave 54703
58th St 54703
N & S 60th 54703
N 62nd Ave 54703
63rd St 54703
N & S 65th 54703
N 67th Ave 54703
70th St 54703
71st St 54703
S 72nd Ave 54703
N & S 75th 54703
N 77th Ave 54703
80th St 54703
S 82nd Ave 54703
S 85th Ave 54703
86th St 54703
87th St 54703
90th Ave & St 54703
1000th St 54703
1008th St 54703
1000th St
 N1200-N1899 54701
1010th St
 N2100-N2199 54701
 N3300-N3699 54703
105th St 54703
106th St 54703
125th St 54701
140th Ave 54701
176th Ave 54701
190th Ave 54701
194th Ave 54701
331st Ave 54703
370th Ave 54703
390th Ave 54703
408th Ave 54703
410th Ave 54703
945th St 54701
950th St 54701
980th St 54701
989th St 54701
990th St 54703
996th St 54703
998th St 54703

FOND DU LAC WI

General Delivery 54935

POST OFFICE BOXES MAIN OFFICE STATIONS AND BRANCHES

Box No.s
All PO Boxes 54936

RURAL ROUTES

01, 05, 07, 11 54937

NAMED STREETS

Abel Dr 54937
Abler Rd 54937
Adams Ave 54937
Adams St 54935
Aeolus Way 54937
Alexander Ln 54937
Algoma St 54935
Allan Ct 54935
Allen St 54935
Alpine Cir 54937
Americana Dr 54935
Amory St 54935
Anchor Cir 54937
Ann St 54935
E & W Ann Randall Dr 54937
Anne St 54937
Apollo Ave 54937
Arlington Ave 54935
E & W Arndt St 54935
Artesian Rd 54937
Arvey Ln 54935
Ashberry Ave 54937
Ashbury Ct & Dr 54935
Ashland Ave 54935
Aspen Ct 54937
Atlantis Ave 54937
Auburn St 54935
Audrey Ct 54937
Aurora Ln 54935
Austin Ct & Ln 54935
Backwater Dr 54937
E & W Bank St 54935
Bark Rd 54937
Barrington Ct 54935
Baudry Ln 54937
Bayberry Ln 54935
Beachview Dr 54937
Bechaud Ave 54937
Bechaud Beach Dr 54935
N & S Bell St 54935
Belle Terre Dr 54937
Bellevue Blvd 54937
Bergens Beach Rd 54937
N & S Berger Pkwy 54935
Berkley Pl 54935
Betty Ln 54937
Beverly Pkwy 54937
Birch Rd 54937
Birchtree Ln 54935
Birchwood Ct 54935
Bischoff St 54935
Bishop Ct 54935
Bittersweet Ct & Ln 54937
Blackbird St 54937
Blodgett Ct 54937
Blue Cottage Ln 54935
Blue Heron Blvd 54937
Blue Jay Ln 54937
Bluebell Blvd 54935
Bluegill Dr 54937
Bluehill Ave 54935
N & S Boardman St 54935
Boda Ln 54937
Bowe Ln 54937
Boyd St 54935
Boyke Dr 54937
Boyle Pl 54935
Bradley Ave 54937
Bragg St 54935
Branch Ln & Rd 54937
Breister Ave 54935
Briarwood Ln 54935
Broadway St 54937
N & S Brooke St 54935
Brookfield Blvd 54935
Brookhaven Beach Rd 54937
Brookside Rd 54937
Brookview Dr 54937
Brown Rd 54937
Bruce St 54935
Brush St 54935
Bryn Mawr Cir 54935
Buena Vista Dr 54937
W Burch Ct 54937
N & S Butler St 54935
Buttermilk Creek Ct & Dr 54935
Butternut Rd 54937
Cadillac Ct 54935
Calumet St 54935
Cambridge Ct 54935
Camelot Dr 54935
Campus Dr 54935
Candlelight Ln 54937
Candy Ln 54935
Canterbury Dr & Ln 54937
Cantom Ave 54935
Capital Dr 54937
Captains Cv 54935
Cardinal Ct 54937
Carl Dr 54937
Carole Ln 54935
Caroline Ct 54935
Carpenter St 54935
Carriage Cir, Ct & Ln 54935
Carrington Dr 54937
Castle Rd 54935
Cattail Ln 54937
Cearns Ln 54937
Cedar St 54935
Center St
 1-99 54937
 200-299 54937
 300-499 54935
Central Ave 54935
Challenger Dr 54937
Champion Ave 54935
Chapleau St 54935
Chapman Ave 54937
Cherry Ln 54935
Cherrywood Dr 54937
Chester Pl 54935
Chestnut St 54935
Chickadee Ct 54937
Church Rd 54937
Churchill Ln 54935
Clark St 54935
Cleveland St 54937
Clinton St 54937
Clover Ct 54935
Clover Ln 54935
Club De Neveu Dr 54937
Cobblestone Dr 54937
Cody Rd 54937
Coffman Ave 54935
Colonial Dr 54937
Columbia Dr 54937
Commerce Ct 54937
Concord Dr 54935
Connell St 54935
Corvette Cir 54935
Cottage Ave 54935
Cottage Dr 54937
Cottage Ln 54937
E & W Cotton St 54935
Cottonwood Rd 54937
Cougar Ct 54935
N & S Country Cir, Ct & Ln 54935
Country Club Ct & Ln 54935
Country Creek Dr 54935
Country Lane Ct 54935
County Rd W 54937
County Road Ap 54937
County Road B 54937
County Road D 54937
County Road F 54937
County Road H 54937
County Road I 54937
County Road K
 N7200-N7399 54935
County Road K
 N2699-N7199 54937
 N2601-N2697 54937
 N6205A-N6207A 54937
 N6205B-N6207B 54937
 N6221C-N6223C 54937
 201-297 54937
 299-599 54937
 601-799 54937
County Road Oo 54937
County Road Ooo 54937
County Road Q 54937
County Road Qq 54937
County Road T 54937
County Road Uu 54937
County Road V
 N5512-N5699 54935
County Road Wh 54937
County Road Y 54937
Court St 54935
Coyne Rd 54937
Creek Rd 54937
Creek Vu Dr 54937
Crescent Ave 54935
Crestview Ct 54937
Crestview Ln 54935
Crestwood Dr 54937
Crowfoot Ave & Ct 54935
Cumberlynn Cir, Ct & Dr 54935
Dahl Pl 54935
Danbury Ave 54935
Danderel St 54935
Danny Ln 54937
David Dr 54937
Deadwood Point Rd 54937
Decorah Ln 54937
Deer Run 54935
Deer Path Rd 54937
Delaware Ave 54937
Deming Pl 54935
Deneveu Cir 54935
Deneveu Ln 54937
Dewberry Dr 54935
Dike Rd 54937
Discovery Dr 54937
E & W Division St 54935
Dixie St 54935
Dixon Rd 54937
Dogwood Ln
 W4400-W4599 54937
 200-299 54935
Dondor Dr 54937
Donohue Ct 54935
Doty St 54935
Douglas Ct 54935
Draeger Ln 54937
Driftwood Dr 54937
Drury Pl 54935
Duley Ct 54935
Eagle Ln 54937
Eastbrook Ln 54935
Easterlies Ct & Dr 54937
Eastgate Pl 54935
Eastman Ln 54935
Eastwind Ln 54937
Eastwood Ct 54935
Edgewater Dr 54937
Edgewood Ln 54937
Eleanore Ln 54937
Elizabeth St 54935
Ellen Ct & Ln 54935

Ellis St 54935
Elm St 54935
Elm Acres Dr 54935
Elm Beach Rd 54937
Elm Tree Ln 54935
Emerald Ct 54935
Emery Ln 54937
Emma St 54935
Empire Dr & Ln 54937
Endeavour Dr 54937
Enterprise Rd 54937
Estate Dr 54935
Esterbrook Rd 54937
Evans Dr 54935
Everett St 54935
Evergreen Ave 54935
Explorer Dr 54937
Fairfield Dr 54937
Fairlawn Ave 54937
Fairview Rd 54937
Fanna St 54935
Farwell Ave 54935
Fawn Ct 54937
Fishermans Rd 54937
Florida Ave 54937
E & W Follett St 54935
Fond Du Lac Ave 54935
Ford Dr 54937
Forest Ave
W6500-W7999 54937
1-999 54935
Forest Cir 54935
Forest Ct 54935
Forest Ln 54935
Fountain Cir 54935
Fox Ct & Dr 54937
Fox Ridge Dr 54937
Franklin Ave 54937
Franklin St 54935
Fremont St 54935
Friendship St 54937
Fulton St 54935
Galloway Ct 54935
Garden Dr 54935
Gardenia Ln 54937
Garfield St
14-48 54937
50-200 54937
202-298 54937
300-500 54935
502-598 54935
Gaslight Dr 54937
Gemini Cir & Way 54937
Gertrude Ave 54935
Giese Dr 54935
Gillett St 54935
Glacier Ct 54937
Gladstone Beach Rd 54937
Glen Echo Rd 54937
Glenwood Ct & Dr 54935
Glynn Ave 54935
Goebel Ln 54937
Golf Course Dr
W4805 1/2-W4807 1/2 54935
Golf Vu Dr 54935
N & S Gould St 54935
Grace Ave 54935
Grand Ct 54935
Grandview Rd 54937
Grandwood Dr 54937
Grant St 54935
Green St 54935
Greenbriar Ave, Cir & Ct 54935
Greenview Ct 54937
Greenwood St 54935
Griffith St 54935
Grove St 54935
W Grove St 54937
Guindon Blvd 54935
Guinette Ave 54935
Haberkorn Dr 54937
Halbach Ct 54937
Hamilton Pl 54935
Hamilton Rd 54937

Hampton Ave & Ct 54935
E & W Harbor View Dr 54935
Harrison Ct 54937
Harrison Pl 54935
Harrison St 54937
Hass Cir 54935
Hawes Ct 54937
Hawks Ct 54937
Hawkview Cir 54937
Hawthorne Ct, Dr & Pl 54935
Hazotte Ct 54935
Henning St 54935
Henry St 54935
Heritage Ct & Ln 54935
Hettwer Ln 54937
Hickory Rd
N5800-N5898 54935
N3500-N5599 54937
N5601-N5799 54937
1100-1799 54937
N Hickory St
1-469 54935
470-599 54937
S Hickory St
1-999 54935
1101-1197 54937
1199-1500 54937
1502-1598 54937
Hideaway Ct & Ln 54937
Highland Ct 54935
Highland Dr 54937
Hill St 54937
Hillcrest Ln
W3800-W3899 54937
200-399 54935
Hillcrest Rd 54937
Hillside Cir 54937
Hilltop Dr 54937
Holiday Ln 54937
Hollander Ct 54937
Holly Tree Ln 54935
Hone St 54935
Honeysuckle Ln
1-99 54937
900-1000 54935
1002-1098 54935
Honold Rd 54937
Horizon Ct 54937
Horseshoe Ln 54935
Howard Ave 54935
Hoyt St 54935
Hummingbird Ct 54937
Hunter Ave & Ln 54937
Hunters Ct 54937
Illinois Ave 54937
Immel Ln 54937
Indiana Ave 54935
Industrial Pkwy 54937
Iowa Ct 54935
Irene Dr 54937
Jefferson St 54935
Jeffrey Ct 54937
John St 54935
Johnsburg Rd 54937
Johnson Ct 54935
E Johnson St
1-1113 54935
1115-1199 54935
1755-1757 54937
W Johnson St
200-234 54935
236-899 54935
901-999 54935
1101-1299 54937
Jon Ray Dr 54935
Joseph Ct & Dr 54937
Julie Ct 54937
Jupiter Dr 54937
Kairis Ct 54935
Karen Ct 54937
Kathryn Ct 54935
Kaye St 54935
N & S Kayser St 54935
Kelly Dr 54935
Kelly Rd 54937

Kennedy Dr 54935
Keshena Ct 54935
Kiekhaefer Pkwy 54937
Kings Ct 54937
Kings Crest Ln 54935
Kingswood Ave 54935
Kinker Rd 54937
Knights Way 54935
Kohlman Rd 54937
Kramer Ct & Dr 54935
Lac Vue Ct 54937
Lake St 54937
Lakepark Ct & Dr 54935
Lakeshore Dr 54937
Lakeview Ln & Rd 54937
Lallier Ln 54935
E Lamartine Dr 54937
E & W Larsen Dr & St 54937
Laurel Ln
N7300-N7399 54937
Lavan Way 54937
Lawrence Ave 54935
Lawrence St 54937
Le Baron Ln 54935
Ledge Rd 54937
Ledgebrook Dr 54935
Ledgetop Ct & Dr 54937
Ledgeview Ave & Blvd 54935
Ledgeview Springs Dr 54937
Ledgewood Dr 54937
Lee Ct 54935
Lee Oelke Ct 54937
Lennora Cres 54935
Leonard Dr 54935
Lewis St 54935
Lexington St 54935
Liberty St 54935
Lighthouse Ln 54937
Lighthouse Village Rd 54937
N Lincoln Ave 54935
S Lincoln Ave 54935
Lincoln St 54937
Linden St 54935
Linden Beach Rd 54937
Lloyd St 54935
Loehr Rd 54937
Lost Arrow Ct & Rd 54937
Luco Rd 54935
Lynn Ave 54937
N & S Macy St 54935
Madison St 54937
Main St 54935
N Main St 54935
S Main St
N5700-N5799 54935
N5401-N5599 54937
1-1399 54935
1600-1698 54937
Maine Ave 54937
Malibu Ct 54935
Mallard Ln 54937
Manske Dr 54937
Maona Ave 54935
Maple Ave 54935
Maple Ln 54937
Maple Rd 54937
Maple Ridge Dr 54937
Maplewood Ct 54937
Maplewood Dr 54935
Maplewood Ln 54937
Marcoe St 54937
Maria Ln 54935
Mariearl Ln 54935
Mariner Cir 54937
Marquette St 54935
N & S Marr St 54935
Marshall Ave 54935
Martin Ave 54935
Martin Ln 54935
Martin Pl 54935
Martin Rd
N5400-N5598 54935
N4700-N5299 54937
Mary Hill Park Dr 54937
Mary Lee Dr 54935

Marys Ave
W4500-W4699 54937
1-159 54935
161-199 54935
Mason St 54937
Mcarthur St 54935
Mckinley St
1-327 54937
174-325 54935
327-399 54935
329-399 54937
E & W Mcwilliams St 54935
Meadow Ct 54935
Meadow Dr 54937
Meadow Ln 54935
Meadowbrook Blvd, Ct & Ln 54935
Meadowcreek Ln 54935
Meadowlark Ct 54937
Meadowview Dr 54935
Meadowview Ln 54937
Meiklejohn Dr 54937
Melody Ln 54937
Melrose Blvd 54935
Menard Dr 54937
Mengel Hill Rd 54937
Mequon Ave 54935
E Merrill Ave 54935
Merwin Way 54937
Messner Dr 54937
Meyer Ct 54937
Michael Ln 54935
Michels Dr 54937
Michigan Ave 54937
Michigan St
N7300-N7499 54935
400-499 54937
Midarenw Rd 54937
Mihill Ave 54935
N Military Rd 54935
S Military Rd
1-842 54935
844-998 54935
1100-1199 54937
Mill Rd 54937
Mill St 54935
Minawa Beach Rd 54937
Minnesota Ave & Ct 54937
Minnow Ln 54937
Miranda Way 54937
Mistral Ln 54937
Mockingbird Ln 54937
Mohawk Ave 54935
Monmouth St 54937
Montana St 54937
Moonlight Ln 54937
Morningside Dr 54935
Morris Ct & St 54935
Mosher Dr 54937
Mountain Rd 54937
Mueller Dr 54937
Muenter Ave 54935
Mulberry Ct 54935
Mullen Dr 54935
Mustang Ln 54935
Nakoma Ave 54935
N & S National Ave 54935
Neitzel Ln & Rd 54937
Nelson Rd 54937
Nelson St 54935
New Haven Ave 54935
New York Ave 54937
Newport Ave 54935
Newton Rd 54937
Niagara Ct & Ln 54937
North St 54937
Northgate St 54935
Northland Ave 54935
Northwest Way 54937
Northwestern Ave 54937
Nursery Dr 54935
Oak Rd 54937
Oak St 54935
Oak Acre Dr 54937
Oak Acres Ct 54937
Oak Hill Rd 54937

Oak Park Ave 54935
Oak Ridge Ln 54937
Oaklawn Ave 54935
Oakridge Ct 54937
Oakwood Dr 54937
Ohio Ave 54935
Olcott St 54935
Old Pioneer Rd 54935
Orchard Ct & Rd 54937
Oriole Pkwy 54937
Osage Ct 54937
Osborn Way 54937
Overland Trl 54937
Packer St 54935
Palmar Pl 54935
Panoka Pl 54935
Panorama Dr 54937
Paradise Ct & Ln 54937
N & S Park Ave, Cir & Ln 54935
Park Ridge Dr & Ln 54937
Parkview Ct 54937
Parkway Ct 54935
Pastwood Rd 54937
Patricia St 54937
Pearl Ln
405-421 54935
450-599 54937
N & S Peebles Ct & Ln 54937
Penny Ln 54937
Pennycress Ct 54935
Perch Ln 54937
Perry Ln 54937
N Peters Ave 54935
Petula Ave 54937
Pheasant Ct 54935
Pheasant Dr 54935
Pheasant Run 54937
Phoenix Dr 54937
Pier Ct 54935
Pine Lake Dr 54935
Pine Tree Dr 54935
Pioneer Ct 54935
N Pioneer Pkwy 54935
S Pioneer Pkwy 54935
E Pioneer Rd 54935
N Pioneer Rd
N7300-N7699 54937
2-148 54935
150-188 54935
165-167 54937
169-171 54935
175-185 54937
187-189 54935
195-215 54937
220-298 54935
301-349 54935
350-372 54937
369-373 54935
374-598 54937
383-385 54935
391-411 54935
413-415 54937
417-445 54935
501-699 54937
S Pioneer Rd 54935
W Pioneer Rd 54935
Pleasant St 54935
Pleasure Pl 54935
Polk St 54937
Poplar Rd 54937
Poplar St 54935
S Port Blvd 54937
Portage Pl 54937
Portage St 54935
N & S Portland St 54935
Prairie Ave 54935
Prairie Ct 54935
Prairie Pkwy 54935
Prairie Rd
W6400-W6699 54937
N6601-N7141 54935
1-148 54935
150-198 54935
N Prairie Rd 54935

Prairie Fox Ct & St 54937
Prairieview Rd 54937
Prestige Cir 54935
Primrose Ln 54935
Prospect Ave 54937
Queens Way 54935
Rademann Dr 54937
Rancho Viejo Rd 54937
Randallwood Ln 54937
Ranger Way 54937
Ray St 54935
Ray Wood Ter 54937
Red Fox Run 54937
Redwing Dr 54937
E & W Rees St 54935
Regent St 54935
Reid Ter 54935
Reilly Dr 54937
Reinhardt Rd 54937
N & S Reserve Ave 54935
Richards Rd 54937
Rickmeyer Dr 54937
Ridgeview Ct 54937
Ridgewood Ct 54937
Rienzi Rd 54935
Ritger Dr 54937
River Rd 54937
River St 54935
Riverbend Rd 54937
Riverside Ct 54935
Riverview Ct 54937
Roberta Ct 54935
Roberts Ct 54935
Robin Dr 54937
Rockrose Dr 54935
Rockwood Ct 54935
Rogersville Rd
W6400-W7299 54937
500-598 54937
600-699 54935
Rolling Hills Dr 54937
N, S & W Rolling Meadows Dr 54937
Roosevelt St 54935
Rose Ave
97-97 54935
99-351 54935
353-399 54935
1601-1699 54937
Rose St 54937
N & S Royal Ave 54935
Rubina Ln 54935
Ruggles St 54935
Russell St 54935
Safari Ln 54935
N & S Saint Joseph Ln 54935
Saint Paul Ave 54937
Salem Ave 54935
Sales Rd 54937
N & S Sallie Ave 54935
Sammy Jo Cir 54935
Sandy Beach Rd 54937
Sarah Dr 54935
Saratoga Ave 54937
Satterlee St 54935
Saturn Dr 54937
Scenic Cir 54935
Schraven Cir 54937
Schubert Ln 54935
Scott Rd 54937
E Scott St 54935
W Scott St
1-199 54935
201-263 54935
276-1399 54937
Seagull Pl 54937
Security Dr 54935
See Vue Dr 54937
Seefeld Rd 54937
Seven Hills Rd 54937
N & S Seymour St 54935
Shady Dr & Ln 54937
Shadybrook Cir 54937
Shamrock Ct 54937
Sheboygan St 54935

Sheila St 54937
Shelley Ct 54937
Sherman St 54935
Sherwood Ave 54935
N Shore Ln 54937
Shorewood 54937
Sibley St 54935
Silica Rd 54937
Silver St 54937
Sirocco St 54937
Skyline Ct 54935
Skyway Dr 54937
Somerset Ct 54937
Somerset Ln 54935
N & S Sophia St 54935
South St 54935
Southern Edge Ct & Dr 54935
Southgate Dr 54935
Southlake Cir & Ln 54935
Southview Dr 54937
Southview Rd 54935
Southwind Ln 54935
Spring St 54935
Spring Lake Dr 54935
Springs Rd 54935
Spruce Dr 54937
Stanchfield Dr 54937
Star St 54935
State St 54937
State Road 175
N4701-N4799 54937
State Road 23 54937
Stenz Rd 54937
Sterling Dr 54935
Stillwater Dr 54937
Stone Castle Dr 54935
Stoneridge Dr 54937
Stones Cir 54937
Stony Ln 54937
Stow St 54935
Streblow Dr 54937
Streeter Ct 54935
Sturgeon St 54937
Subway Rd 54937
Sullivan Dr 54937
Sumac Ct 54937
Summit Ct & Dr 54937
Sunny Ln 54937
Sunnyside Ln 54935
Sunrise Ct 54935
Sunset Cir 54935
Sunset Dr 54937
Sunset Ln 54935
Sunset Circle Dr 54937
Superior St 54935
Swan Dr 54937
Sweetflag Ave 54935
Sycamore Dr 54937
Sycamore Tree Ct & Dr 54935
Sylvan Bay Rd 54937
T Bird Dr 54935
Taft Rd 54937
Taft St 54935
Takodah Dr 54935
Tallmadge St 54935
Tap St 54935
Taycheedah Way 54935
Taylor Ct & St 54935
Temperance St 54937
Terrace Rd 54937
Thomas St 54935
Thomaswood Ct & Trl 54937
Thome Dr 54937
Thornton Ct 54935
Thorpe St 54935
Thurke Ave & Ct 54937
Timber Trl 54937
Timber Ridge Dr 54937
Tompkins St 54935
Tower Rd 54937
Towne Ln 54937
Townline Rd 54937
Trails End Ct 54937
Triangle Rd 54935

Triple T Rd 54937
Trowbridge Dr 54937
Tuxedo Ln 54935
Twilight Trl 54937
Twin Lakes Dr 54937
Twin Oaks Dr 54937
Tyler Ct 54935
Uneeda St 54935
University Dr 54935
Us Highway 151 54937
Us Highway 41 54935
Us Highway 45
  N4900-N5651 54937
Valley Ct & Dr 54937
Valley Creek Rd 54937
Van Dyne Rd 54937
Vanguard Ave 54937
Vermont St 54937
Viking Dr 54937
Vincent St 54935
Vine St 54935
Voyager Dr 54937
Wabash Ave 54935
Wakawn Ave 54935
Wakefield Ave 54935
Walker St 54935
Walnut Rd 54937
Walnut St 54935
Warber Ln 54937
Warner St 54935
Washington Ave & St 54937
Water St 54935
Waterway Dr 54937
Wedgewood Ln 54935
Weis Ave 54935
Welling Beach Rd 54937
Wells St 54937
Welsh St 54935
Wendy Ln 54937
West Ln 54937
Westbrook Ln 54937
Western Ave 54935
Westfield Cir 54935
Westfield Rd 54937
Westhaven Dr 54937
Westlake Ct 54937
Westminster Cir 54935
Westview Ct & Dr 54937
Westwind Dr 54937
Westwood Ave & Dr 54937
Wettstein Ave 54935
Whippoorwill Ln 54935
Whispering Springs Ct & Dr 54937
Whitetail Ct 54937
Wild West Ln 54937
Wildlife Dr & Ln 54937
Wildwood Ln 54935
Wilkins St 54935
William Ave 54935
Willis Ct 54937
Willow Dr 54935
Willow Rd 54937
Willow Lane Beach Rd 54937
Willow Lawn Rd 54937
Willowcreek Ct 54935
Willsher Dr 54935
Wilson Ave 54935
Winchester Ave 54935
Windsor Ave & Ct 54935
Winnebago Dr 54935
Winnebago Ln 54935
Winnebago St
  N7300-N7373 54935
  N7375-N7399 54935
  W6600-W6700 54937
  W6702-W6798 54937
  1-499 54937
Winnebago Park Rd 54937
Winnvue Ct 54937
Wisconsin Ave & Ct 54937
Wisconsin American Dr 54937
Wonser Rd 54937
Woodbine Park Rd 54935
Woodcrest Ct & Dr 54935
Woodland Ave 54935
Woods Pl 54935
Woodside Ct 54937
Woodvue Ct 54935
Woodward St 54935
Wrightway Dr 54937
Yacoub Ln 54935
Yorkshire Dr 54935
Zeller Ct 54937
Zephyrus Dr 54937

NUMBERED STREETS

E & W 1st 54935
E 2nd St 54935
W 2nd St
  1-21 54935
  23-100 54935
  99-99 54936
  102-398 54935
  121-399 54935
3rd St 54935
4th St
  2-14 54935
  16-1300 54935
  1302-1398 54935
  1400-1500 54937
  1502-1598 54937
4th Street Ct 54935
4th Street Rd
  W4800-W5199 54935
  W2100-W4660 54937
  W4662-W4698 54937
4th Street Way 54937
5th St 54935
6th St 54935
7th St 54935
8th St 54935
E & W 9th 54935
E & W 10th 54935
E & W 11th 54935
E & W 12th 54935
E & W 13th 54935
14th St 54935
15th St 54935
16th St 54935
17th St 54935
18th St 54935
19th St 54935
20th St 54935
21st St 54935

GREEN BAY WI

General Delivery 54303

POST OFFICE BOXES MAIN OFFICE STATIONS AND BRANCHES

Box No.s
A - W 54303
1 - 1972 54305
2001 - 2777 54306
3006 - 4129 54303
7000 - 7075 54307
8001 - 9998 54308
10001 - 19976 54307
22001 - 23930 54305
28000 - 28900 54324
33011 - 33304 54303

NAMED STREETS

JANESVILLE WI

General Delivery 53545

POST OFFICE BOXES MAIN OFFICE STATIONS AND BRANCHES

Box No.s
All PO Boxes 53547

NAMED STREETS

W Aberdeen Dr 53545
N Academy St 53548
S Academy St
  1-699 53548
  1001-1097 53546
  1099-1199 53546
N & S Adams St 53545
Adel St 53546
Affirmed Dr 53546
Afton Rd 53548
W Airport Rd 53546
Alden Rd 53545
Alexandria Pl 53548
Allendale Dr 53546
Alpine Dr 53546
Amber Ln 53546
Amhurst Rd 53546
Andre Ave 53545
Anthony Ave 53546
Antler Dr 53548
Apache Ct & Dr 53545
E Apollo Ln 53546
E Appleridge Dr 53545
Applewood Ln 53548
N Arabian View Dr 53545
Arbor Hill Dr 53548
Arbor Ridge Way 53548
Arbutus St 53546
N Arch St 53548
S Arch St
  2-98 53548
  100-699 53548
  1200-2399 53546
S Arizona Trl 53546
Arlington Ct 53545
E Arrowhead Ln 53546
W Arroyo Ct 53545
Ashland Ave 53548
Aspen St 53546
S Atlantis Dr 53546
N & S Atwood Ave 53545
Audubon Ave 53546
Augusta St 53545
Aurora Ln 53548
N & S Austin Rd 53548
Autumn Ln 53546
E & W Avalon Rd 53546
Avery Ln 53546
Avon St 53545
Ba Wood Ln 53545
Badger St 53545
Balmoral Dr 53548
Barberry Dr 53545
Barham Ave 53548
S Baxter Ln 53546
W Baxterwood Ln 53546
Baybrook Dr 53546
Beacon Ct 53546
Beacon Hill Dr 53546
Bedford Dr 53546
Beechwood Dr 53548
S Belding Rd 53546
Bell St 53545
Belmont Ct 53548
Beloit Ave
  800-899 53545
  1000-3000 53546
  3002-3598 53546
Bemis St 53548
Bennett St 53545
Benton Ave 53545
Berkshire Rd 53546
E Bingham Ave & Rd 53546
Birch Ct 53545
Birdsong Ln 53548
Black Bridge Rd 53545
N & S Blackhawk St 53545
Blaine Ave 53545
Blayden Dr 53546
Blue Devil Blvd 53545
Bluebird Ln 53546
Bluewing Ct & Pl 53546
Bobwhite Ln 53546
Bond Pl 53548
Bordeaux Ct & Dr 53546
Bostwick Ave 53545
Bouchard Ave 53546
Boulder Dr 53546
Boynton Ct 53545
Bradford Ave 53545
Braemore Dr 53548
Brakefield Dr 53546
Braxton Dr 53546
Briar Crest Dr 53546
Bristol Dr 53546
N Britt Rd 53548
W Brookmeadow Ln 53548
W Brookview Ct 53548
W Brown Deer Ln 53548
Browning Dr 53546
W Brownview Dr 53545
Bruin Ln 53545
Brunswick Ln 53546
Bryn Mawr Dr 53546
Buckhorn Trce 53548
Buckingham Dr 53546
N Buckskin Dr 53546
W Buggs Rd 53548
Bunting Ln 53546
E & W Burbank Ave 53546
N Burdick Rd 53548
Burnwyck Dr 53546
Burr Oak Ct 53545
W Burrwood Dr 53548
W Butler Rd 53548
Calgary Ln 53545
California Ct 53548
Cambridge Ct & Dr 53546
Camden Sq 53545
Camelot Dr 53548
Campus Ln 53545
Canary Ln 53546
Candlewood Dr 53546
Canterbury Ln 53546
Canvasback Dr 53546
Canyon Dr 53546
Capella Dr 53546
Capital Cir 53546
Cardinal Ln 53546
Cargill Ct 53545
Caroline St 53545
Carrington St 53545
Carrousel Ln 53546
Cascade Dr 53546
E Case Dr 53546
Castlemoor Dr 53546
Cedar Pointe Dr 53546
Cedar Ridge Ct & Dr 53545
S Cemetery Rd 53546
W Cemetery Rd 53548
Center Ave
  100-899 53548
  901-947 53546
  949-2599 53546
  2601-2609 53546
E Centerway 53545
W Centerway St 53548
Chadswyck Dr 53546
Champlain St 53546
Chaparral Dr 53546
Charles St 53548
Chartier St 53546
N Chatham St 53548
S Chatham St
  1-699 53548
  1200-2499 53546
N Chaucer Ct 53545
W Chelly Ln 53548
Chelsea Pl 53546
Cherokee Rd 53545
Cherry St
  100-699 53548
  1000-1299 53546
W Cherrywood Dr 53548
Chesapeake Ave 53546
Chestnut St 53548
Chickadee Ln 53546
Chickasaw Dr 53545
S Christianson Rd 53546
Church St 53548
Churchill Dr 53546
Citation Dr 53546
City Highway 11 E 53546
Claire Ct 53548
N Claremont Dr 53545
Clark St 53545
Clearview Ct 53548
Cleveland Ave 53546
Clover Ln
  100-299 53548
  1400-2599 53545
Cobblestone Ln 53546
Colby Ct & Ln 53546
College Dr 53546
S Colorado Trl 53546
Colt Dr 53548
S Columbia Dr 53546
Columbus Cir 53545
Commercial Dr
  100-198 53548
  4000-4299 53548
Commons Ave 53546
N & S Concord Dr 53545
E Conde St 53546
W Condon Rd 53548
N Connor Rd 53548
N Consolidated School Rd 53545
Conway Dr 53548
Coolidge St 53546
N Coon Island Rd 53546
N Coquette Dr 53546
Cornelia St 53545
Cornell Ave 53545
Cortland Dr 53548
Cottonwood Dr 53545
Country View Ct 53548
N County Rd E 53548
E County Road A 53546
W County Road A 53548
W County Road B 53548
S County Road D 53546
N County Road F 53545
S County Road G 53546
N County Road H 53548
S County Road J 53546
E County Road Mm 53546
E County Road O 53546
E Court St 53545
W Court St 53548
Coventry Dr 53546
Covey Dr 53546
Crabapple Ln 53548
Craig Ave 53545
Cree Ct 53545
E Creek Rd 53546
Creekside Ct, Dr & Pl 53548
E Cress Ct 53546
Creston Park Dr 53545
Crestview St 53546
Cricketeer Dr 53546
N Crosby Ave 53548
S Crosby Ave
  1-97 53548
  99-399 53548
  401-699 53548
  1300-2399 53546
Cross Prairie Dr 53546
Crown Ct 53546
N Crystal Springs Rd 53545
Cumberland Dr 53545
Curry Ln 53546
Dakota Dr 53545
Danbury Dr E & W 53546
Dani Dr 53548
Dartmouth Dr 53548
Dayton Dr 53546
Deer Crossing Dr 53546
W Deer Path Trl 53545
Deer Point Dr 53546
Deerfield Dr 53546
E & W Delavan Dr 53546
Delaware Dr 53548
Desoto Dr 53546
E Detroit Ave 53546
Devereaux Dr 53546
Devon Dr 53546
S Discovery Dr 53546
S Division St 53545
Dodge St 53548
Doe Ct & Dr 53548
Dorado Dr 53546
Dorchester Dr 53546
W Dorner Rd 53548
Doty Ct 53545
Doubletree Dr 53546
Douglas St 53545
Dover Ct 53546
Drake St 53546
Dresser Dr 53546
S Driftwood Dr 53546
S Dunbar Rd 53548
Dupont Dr 53546
Eagle Ln 53546
N Eagle Rd 53548
Eastridge Dr 53546
Eastwood Ave 53545
W Eau Claire Rd 53548
Edge Hill Dr 53548
Edgeview Ct & Dr 53545
N & W Edgewood Dr 53545
Edison Ave 53546
Edon Dr 53546
W Ehrlinger Rd 53546
Eider Ln 53546
Eisenhower Ave 53545
Elgin Ave 53546
Elida St 53545
Elizabeth St 53545
Elliott St 53546
S & W Ellis Rd 53548
E Elm Dr 53546
Elm Ln 53545
Emerald Dr 53546
N & S Emerald Grove Rd 53546
W Enterprise Dr 53546
Erie Dr 53545
Essex Dr 53546
Eventide Dr 53548
Evergreen Dr 53546
Excalibur Dr 53546
Exeter Dr 53546
Fairfax Ct 53546
Fairfield Dr 53546
Falcon Ridge Ct & Dr 53548
Fall Harvest Dr 53546
Falling Creek Cir & Dr 53548
Fawn Ln 53548
W Fenrick Rd 53548
Fieldcrest Dr 53546
W Fieldwood Dr 53545
Fillmore St 53545
Fir Ct & St 53546
N Fitzsimmons Rd 53548
Flamingo Ln 53546
N & S Footville Rd 53548
S & W Footville Hanover Rd 53548
W Forest Ln 53545
N Forest Hills Blvd 53545
Forest Park Blvd 53545
Foster Ave 53545
N Fox Rd 53548
Fox Hills Ct & Dr 53546
S Foxmoor Rd 53546
Foxwood Ct 53546
N & S Franklin St 53548
Frederick St 53548
Freedom Ln 53546
N & S Fremont St 53545
Friendship Dr 53546
Frontier Rd 53548
Fulton St 53546
Galahad Way 53548
N Galaxy Dr 53546
Galena Ln & Rd 53548
Garden Dr 53546
N & S Garfield Ave 53545
Gartland Ave 53548
General Motors Dr 53546
Gershwin Dr 53545
W Gibbs Lake Rd 53548
S Gilbert St 53548
Glen St 53545
Glenbarr Dr 53548
Glendale St 53546
N & W Glenmoor Ln 53545
Glenview Ct 53548
Goldenrod Pl 53546
W Golf Cir 53548
Golf Course Rd 53548
Grace St 53545
W Graham Dr 53548
Grand Ave 53546
N & W Grand Videre Ct & Dr 53548
N Granite Dr 53546
N Grant Ave 53548
S Grant Ave
  1-699 53548
  1100-2399 53546
Green Forest Run 53546
Green Meadow Ln 53546
Green Valley Dr 53546
Greenbriar Dr 53546
Greendale Ct & Dr 53546
W Greenfield Rd 53548
Greenview Ave 53548
Greenway Cir 53548
Greenway Point Dr 53548
Greenwich Ln 53545
Greenwood Dr 53546
Grove St 53545
Haberdale Dr 53548
N Hackbarth Rd 53548
Hamilton Ave & Ct 53548
Hampshire Rd 53546
Hancock Ln 53545
Hanover Rd & St 53548
W Happy Hollow Rd 53546
Harding St 53545
N & S Harmony Cir & Dr NE, NW, SE & SW 53545
N Harmony Town Hall Rd 53546
Harold Ave 53546
Harrison St 53545
Hartford Ln 53546
Harvard Ct & Dr 53548
N Harvest View Dr 53548
Hawaii Dr 53548
Hawkridge Ct & Dr 53546
Hawthorne Ave 53545
N & S Hawthorne Park Dr 53545
S Hayner Rd 53548
Hearthridge Dr 53546
Hearthstone Dr 53546
Heather Ct 53546
Hemmingway Ct & Dr 53545
N & S Henke Rd 53546
Heritage Ln 53546
Hermitage Ln 53546
W & N Hickory Ct & Dr 53545
N & S High St 53548
High Point Ct 53548
Highland Ave 53548
Hillcrest Dr 53545
N & W Hills Dr 53545
Hillside Ct 53545
Hilltop Dr 53548
Holiday Dr 53545
Holly Dr 53546
E Holmes St 53545
W Holmes St 53548
Home Park Ave 53545
Honeysuckle Ln 53546
Hoover St 53545
E Howorth Dr 53546
Hoya Ln 53545
Hubbard St 53546
W Hubble Rd 53548
Humes Rd
  1700-1798 53545
  1800-2699 53545
  2701-2899 53545

Street	ZIP
3200-3298	53546
4501-4599	53546
Huntinghorne Dr	53546
Huntington Ave & Ct	53546
N & S Huron Dr	53545
Hyacinth Ave	53545
Hyatt St	53545
Ice Age Way	53548
E Idaho Trl	53546
Independence Rd	53545
S Indian Lake Dr	53548
Industrial Ct & Dr	53546
Ingram Dr	53546
W Interlochen Dr	53545
W Inverness Dr	53545
W Ironwood Dr	53545
Iroquois Ct	53545
E J F Townline Rd	53545
Jackman St	53545
N Jackson St	53548
S Jackson St	
1-799	53548
801-899	53548
900-2200	53546
2202-2498	53546
Janesville St	53548
Jefferson Ave	53545
Jefferson School Dr	53545
Jerome Ave	53546
Johnson Rd & St	53548
Joliet St	53546
Jonathon Dr	53548
S Jones Rd	53546
Josephine St	53545
N Juniper Dr	53545
W Juniper Ridge Ct	53545
N Katherine Dr	53548
Kellie Ct	53548
Kellogg Ave	53546
Kells Way	53546
Kelso Dr	53546
Kennedy Rd	53545
Kensington St	53546
Kentucky Dr	53548
Kenwood Ave	53545
Kerwin Matthews Ct	53545
S Kessler Rd	53548
Kettering St	53546
N Kidder Rd	53545
Killdeer Ct & Ln	53546
King St	53546
Kingsbridge Dr	53546
Kingsford Dr	53546
Kipling Dr	53548
Klein Ave	53546
W Knilans Rd	53546
Knollview Dr	53548
N Knollwood Dr	53545
E L T Townline Rd	53546
La Mancha Dr	53546
La Salle Ct & St	53546
Labrador Dr	53546
Lafayette St	53546
Lansing Dr	53546
Lapham St	53546
Lapidary Ln	53548
S Laprairie Town Hall Rd	53546
Laramie Ln	53546
Lark Ct	53548
E Larsen Rd	53546
N Laura Dr	53548
Laurel Ave	53548
N Lazy River Rd	53545
Lee Ln	53546
N Leith Rd	53548
N & S Lexington Dr	53545
Liberty Ln	53545
Lilac Ln	53545
Lincoln St	53548
Linden Ave	53548
Linn St	53548
Little Ct & Rd	53548
Littlefield Dr	53546
N Lochwood Dr	53545
N & S Locust St	53548
Lodge Dr	53545
Logan St	53545
Lombard Ave	53545
E Lone Lane Rd	53546
N Lone Rock Rd	53548
Longwood Dr	53548
Lowell St	53545
W Lowry Rd	53548
Lucerne Dr	53545
Lucey St	53546
N Lunar Dr	53546
E & W Luther Rd	53545
Lyndhurst Dr	53545
W Lynne Dr	53548
Macarthur Dr	53548
Macfar Ln	53546
Mackinac Dr	53546
Mackintosh Dr	53548
Madison St	53548
N Main St	53545
S Main St	
1-799	53545
900-999	53546
Mallard Ln	53546
Manchester Dr	53545
E & W Manogue Rd	53545
Manor Dr	53548
Maple Ave	53548
Maple Ct	53548
E Maple Ln	53546
Margate Dr	53546
N Marion Ave	53548
S Marion Ave	53546
Markham Dr	53548
Marquette St	53546
W Marsh Creek Rd	53548
Marshall Pl	53545
N & S Martin Rd	53545
Marvog Dr	53548
Matheson St	53545
Mayapple Dr	53545
Mayfair Dr	53545
Maynard Dr	53548
Mccann Dr	53546
Mccormick Dr	53546
Mckinley St	53548
Meadow Ln	53546
Meadowlark Dr	53546
Meadowview Dr	53546
W Melrose Dr	53548
E Memorial Dr	53545
W Memorial Dr	53548
Menard St	53546
Micheart Ave	53545
Midland Ct & Rd	53546
Midvale Dr	53546
W Miles Rd	53545
N Miller Ave & Rd	53548
Milton Ave	
200-1817	53545
1818-3598	53545
1818-1818	53547
1819-3599	53545
3900-4499	53546
4501-4725	53546
N & S Milton Shopiere Rd	53546
E Milwaukee St	
1-2999	53545
3100-4599	53546
W Milwaukee St	53548
W Mineral Point Ave, Ct & Rd	53548
Mitchell St	53546
Mockingbird Ln	53546
Mohawk Rd	53545
Mohican Rd	53545
Mole Ave	53548
Monroe St	53545
S Montana Trl	53546
Monterey Ln	53546
Moreland Dr	53548
E Morgan Way	53546
Morningside Dr	53546
Morse St	53545
Mount Vernon Ave	53545
Mount Zion Ave	
1201-1297	53545
1299-2999	53545
3000-3599	53546
Muir St	53546
Mullen Dr	53546
S Murphy Rd	53548
S Murray Rd	53548
Myra Ave	53548
Nantucket Dr	53546
Navajo Ct	53545
S Nevada Trl	53546
New Haven Dr	53546
Newcastle Dr	53546
Newman St	53545
Newport Ave	53545
N Newville Rd	53545
Nicolet St	53546
Nittany Ln	53545
Northington Dr	53546
W & N Northwood Ct & Trce	53545
Norwood Rd	53545
Oak Rd	53545
Oakbrook Ct	53548
N Oakhill Ave	53548
S Oakhill Ave	53546
Oakland Ave	53545
S Oakley Rd	53546
W Oakwood Park Dr	53548
S Old 11	53548
N Old Orchard Dr	53545
Oldwyck Dr	53546
W Oleary Rd	53548
Omaha Dr	53546
W Oneil Rd	53548
Ontario Dr	53545
S Orchard St	
1-97	53548
99-699	53548
1200-2299	53546
E & N Orchard View Dr	53545
E Oregon Trl	53546
Oriole Dr	53548
Oriole Ln	53546
Orion Dr	53546
N Osborne Ave	53548
S Osborne Ave	53546
Owl Ln	53546
E Palakwia Dr	53546
N Palm St	53548
S Palm St	
1-800	53548
802-998	53546
2100-2299	53546
Palmer Dr	
1-1499	53545
2100-2198	53545
3000-3599	53546
Palomino Dr	53548
Park Ave	
300-699	53548
900-999	53548
Park Place Ln	53545
Park Ridge Rd	53546
Park View Dr	53546
N & S Parker Ct, Dr & Pl	53545
Parkside Dr	53548
Parkwood Dr	53545
Partridge Ln	53546
N & W Partridge Hollow Dr	53548
Patton Pl	53546
Peachtree St	53548
N Pearl St	53548
S Pearl St	
1-699	53548
701-799	53548
1000-2299	53546
Pease Ct	53545
N Pember Rd	53546
N & W Pennycook Rd	53545
Pershing Pl	53546
Peterson Ave	53548
Pheasant Ln & Run	53546
E Pic A Dilly Dr	53546
Pickwick Dr	53546
Pierce St	53546
N Pine St	53548
S Pine St	
1-500	53548
502-798	53548
1200-2299	53546
Pine Ridge Dr	53545
Pineview Ln	53546
Pintail Dr	53546
Pioneer Rd	53546
Plainfield Ave	53545
N Pleasant Hill Dr	53546
Pliny Ave	53546
Plum Ct	53546
Plymouth Ave	53545
N Polaris Pkwy	53546
Polk St	53546
N Polzin Rd	53548
N Pond View Ct	53548
N & S Pontiac Dr & Pl	53545
Poplar Ln	53545
Portland Dr	53546
Power Rd	53546
Prairie Ave	53545
Prairie Fox Dr	53546
Prairie Knoll Dr	53546
Primrose Ln	53545
Princeton Ct & Rd	53546
Prominence Dr	53548
Prospect Ave	53545
Purple Aster Ln	53546
Purvis Ave	53548
Putnam Ave	53546
Quail Ln	53546
Quail Ridge Dr	53546
Quebec Ln	53545
Quixote Dr	53546
Race St	53548
E Racine St	
1-2799	53545
3200-3298	53546
3300-3799	53546
W Racine St	53548
Railroad St	53545
N & S Randall Ave	53545
Randolph Rd	
1500-2999	53545
3100-4199	53546
N Ravenswood Dr	53545
Ravine St	53545
S Read Rd	53546
Red Apple Dr	53548
W Red Cedar Dr	53545
Red Hawk Dr	53546
Red Oak Dr	53546
Red Tail Ln	53546
Redstone Dr	53546
Redwood Dr	53546
N Redwood Dr	53548
Refset Dr	53545
Regent St	53546
S Reid Rd	53546
Revere Ln	53545
Richards Ct	53545
Richardson St	53545
Ridge Ct & Dr	53548
Ridge Creek Dr	53546
Ridge View Ct & Dr	53548
Ridgewood Dr	53548
Rimrock Rd	53548
N & S Ringold St	53545
NW River Dr	53548
W River Dr	53548
N River Rd	53545
S River Rd	53546
N River St	53548
S River St	53548
N River Bluff Dr	53545
N River Hills Ct	53545
W River Oaks Rd	53545
N River Valley Ct	53548
N & W Riverfield Dr	53548
N Rivers Edge Dr	53548
Riverside St	53548
Riverview Dr	53546
Robin Ln	53548
N Robinson Ln	53548
Rock St	53548
Rockingham Dr	53546
W Rockport Rd	53548
W Rockport Park Dr	53548
Rockshire Dr	53546
N Roherty Rd	53548
W Rollingwood Dr	53545
Roosevelt Ave	53546
Rosewood Dr	53546
W & E Rotamer Ct & Rd	53546
Roxbury Rd	53545
Royal Ct & Rd	53546
Royal Oaks Dr	53548
E & W Rugby Rd	53545
Ruger Ave	
1000-2999	53545
3000-4599	53546
E & W Russell Rd	53545
Rutledge Ave & Ct	53545
Ryan Rd	53545
N Saint Andrews Dr	53545
Saint George Ln	53545
Saint Lawrence Ave	53545
Saint Marys Ct	53545
Sandhill Dr	53546
Sandstone Dr	53546
Saratoga Dr	53546
Satinwood Dr	53546
E Saturn Dr	53546
Sauk Ct & Dr	53545
Savanna Ct & Dr	53546
S & W Schaffner Rd	53548
Schaller St	53546
Secretariat Dr	53546
W Seeman Rd	53546
Seminole Ct & Rd	53545
Sentinel Dr	53546
Shade Tree Ln	53545
Shadowwood Ct	53548
S Shady Ln	53546
Shady Oak Ct	53548
Shag Bark Ct	53545
Shamrock Ln	53546
Shannon Ct & Dr	53546
Sharon Rd	53546
Sharon St	53545
Sheffield Dr	53546
Sheridan St	53546
Sherman Ave	53545
Sherwood Dr	53545
Sienna Xing	53546
Sinclair St	53545
Sinnissippi Ln	53548
Sioux Ct	53545
Skylark Ln	53546
Skyline Dr	53548
Skyview Dr	53546
N Snyder Rd	53548
Solar Ave	53548
Somerset Ct & Dr	53546
Sountow Dr	53546
Sousa Ct	53545
Southridge Dr	53546
Southwyck Ct & Dr	53546
Spaulding Ave	53548
W Splendor Valley Dr	53548
N Spring Hill Dr	53545
S Spring Park Dr	53548
W Spring Valley Cors	53548
Spruce Ct & St	53546
Stafford Rd	53546
Starbrite Ln	53546
W Stark Rd	53545
Starling Ln	53546
E & W State St	53546
E State Road 11	53546
W State Road 11	
1-999	53546
W State Road 11	
400-498	53548
700-1098	53546
3001-3097	53548
3099-10099	53548
S State Road 140	53546
N State Road 26	53546
Stellar Dr	53548
Stone St	53548
Stone Ridge Dr	53548
Stonefield Ln	53546
Stonehenge Dr	53545
Stonemoor Dr	53546
Stratford Ct	53546
Stuart St	53546
Suffolk Dr	53546
N & S Sumac Ct & Dr	53545
Summerhill Dr	53546
Summit Dr	53548
W Sunny Ln	53546
Sunnyshore Ln	53545
Sunnyside St	53548
Sunrise Ln	53548
Sunset Dr	53548
Surrey Ln	53546
Sussex Dr	53546
Sutherland Ave	53545
Swallow Ln	53546
Swan Ln	53546
E Swiss Valley Dr	53545
Sycamore St	53545
Sylvester St	53546
Tamarack Ln	53545
Tanglewood Ct & Dr	53546
N & S Tarrant Rd	53546
Tay Ct	53546
Taylor Ct	53546
Teal Ln	53546
Tennyson Dr	53548
Terapin Trl	53545
Terrace Ct	53546
N Terrace St	53546
S Terrace St	53546
W Terrington Dr	53546
Texas Dr	53548
Thames Ln	53546
Thomas St	53545
W Thornapple Dr	53548
Thornecrest Ct & Dr	53546
Thornton Dr	53548
Timber Ln	53548
N Timber Rdg	53545
N Timber Trl	53548
Tisbury Dr	53546
Todd Dr	53546
E Tomahawk Ln	53546
N Touson Dr	53546
S Tower Dr	53546
W Townsend Rd	53548
S Tracey Rd	53548
N Tradition Ln	53545
Tripoli Rd	53545
W Tripp Rd	53548
Tudor Dr	53546
Turnberry Dr	53548
Tydl Dr	53546
Tyler St	53545
Union St	53548
E Us Highway 14	
200-398	53545
400-2100	53545
2102-2624	53545
3100-8599	53546
8601-9199	53546
N Us Highway 14	53546
W Us Highway 14	
1600-1698	53545
1700-2361	53545
2363-2699	53545
3000-3198	53548
3200-8199	53548
N Us Highway 51	53545
S Us Highway 51	53546
E Utah Trl	53546
Vail Ct	53545
Valencia Dr	53546
Valley Dr	53546
W Valley Springs Rd	53548
N Valleyview Dr	53546
S Van Allen Rd	53546
E Van Buren St	53545
W Van Buren St	53548
W Venture Dr	53546
E Venus Dr	53546
NW Vernesta Pl	53548
Victoria Pl	53546
Village Ct	53546
Violet St	53546
Virginia Dr	53548
Vista Ave	53545
N Vista Ln	53548
Vold Ct	53546
Walker St	53545
E Wall St	53545
W Wall St	53548
N Walnut St	53548
S Walnut St	
300-699	53548
1200-2299	53546
S Warlance Ln	53548
N Washington St	53548
S Washington St	
300-899	53548
1000-1499	53546
1501-1799	53546
S Water St	53545
Waterford Dr	53546
Waveland Rd	53548
Wedgewood Dr	53548
W Wee Croft Ct	53545
Wellington Ct & Pl	53546
Wells St	53545
W Welsh Rd	53548
Wesley Ave	53545
Westminster Rd	53546
Westridge Rd	53548
W Westward Ln	53548
Westwood Dr	53548
Wexford Rd	53546
W Wheeler Rd	53548
Wheeler St	53545
Whilden Ct	53546
White Oak Dr	53546
White Tail Ln	53545
Whitney St	53546
Widgeon Dr	53546
E Wilcox Rd	53546
Wildflower Ln	53548
W Wildlife Ln	53548
Wildrose Way	53546
S Wilke Rd	53548
N Willard Ave	53548
S Willard Ave	
1-697	53548
699-799	53548
801-899	53548
1101-1197	53546
1199-2299	53546
Williams Rd & St	53545
Williamsburg Pl	53548
S Willing Rd	53548
Willow Springs Ct	53548
N Willowdale Rd	53548
Wilshire Ln	53546
Wilson Ave	53548
Winchester Pl	53548
Windfield Way	53546
Windmill Ln	53546
Windsor Ln	53546
Windwood Dr	53546
Winesap Ct & Dr	53548
Winnebago Dr	53545
Wintergreen Way	53546
Winthrop Dr	53546
N & S Wisconsin St	53545
Wolcott St	53546
Wood St	53548
W Wood Ridge Dr	53548
N Woodbury Ln	53545
Woodcrest Dr	53546
Woodgate Dr	53546
Woodhall Dr	53546
N Woodhue Dr	53546
Woodlane Dr	53545
Woodman Rd	53545

E Woodman Rd 53546
Woodridge Ct 53546
Woodruff Blvd 53548
W Woods Edge Ln & Rd 53548
Wren Ln 53546
N & S Wright Rd 53546
N & S Wuthering Hills Dr 53546
Wynd Tree Dr 53546
S Wyoming Ct 53546
Yale Dr 53548
Yorkshire Ln 53546
Yuba St 53545
E & N Zermatt Ct & Dr 53545

KENOSHA WI

General Delivery 53140

POST OFFICE BOXES MAIN OFFICE STATIONS AND BRANCHES

Box No.s
All PO Boxes 53141

NAMED STREETS

Adams Rd 53144
Alford Park Dr 53140
Beverly Ln 53142
Birch Rd 53140
Bristol Rd 53142
Brumback Blvd 53144
Buchanan Rd 53143
Burlington Rd 53144
Chintres Ave 53140
Cooper Rd 53142
Corbett Rd 53144
Emeashil Ave 53143
Grant Rd 53142
Green Bay Rd
100-5999 53144
6000-7999 53142
8001-8199 53142
Harding Rd 53142
Harrison Rd 53142
Horton Rd 53142
Johnson Rd 53143
Lincoln Rd 53143
Madison Rd 53140
Old Green Bay Rd 53144
Peredari Ave 53142
Pershing Blvd
4500-4598 53144
4600-5999 53144
6001-6097 53142
6099-7999 53142
Petrifying Springs Rd 53144
Prairie Village Dr 53142
Roosevelt Rd
2101-2197 53143
2199-2999 53143
3000-4799 53142
Salloren Ave 53144
Sheridan Rd
700-5700 53140
5605-5605 53141
5701-5999 53140
5702-5998 53140
6001-6097 53143
6099-9099 53143
Simmons Island Dr 53140
Taft Rd 53142
University Dr 53144
Van Buren Rd 53142
Village Centre Dr 53144
Washington Rd
401-497 53140
499-2999 53140
3000-5599 53144
5601-5999 53144
Wilmot Rd 53142
Wilson Rd 53142
Wood Rd 53144

NUMBERED STREETS

1st Ave
5400-5599 53140
7100-7498 53143
1st Cir 53140
1st Pl
2300-2599 53140
4300-6099 53144
1st St 53144
2nd Ave
5400-5598 53140
6900-7500 53143
7502-7898 53143
2nd Cir 53140
2nd Pl 53140
2nd St
2200-2499 53140
5700-5999 53144
3rd Ave
5400-5498 53140
5500-5600 53140
5602-5998 53140
6000-6098 53143
6100-7899 53143
3rd St
2000-2198 53140
4800-4899 53144
4th Ave 53140
4th St 53144
5th Ave
3800-4098 53140
4100-5999 53140
6000-7899 53143
5th Ct 53143
5th Pl 53144
6th Ave
3800-5922 53140
5924-5998 53140
6600-7899 53143
6th Pl 53144
6th St
300-398 53140
4100-4599 53144
6th Avenue A 53140
7th Ave
3500-3898 53140
6001-6097 53143
7th Ct 53143
7th Pl 53140
7th St
201-297 53140
3000-4898 53144
8th Ave
3600-3798 53140
3800-5800 53140
5802-5998 53140
6000-6098 53143
6100-7899 53143
8th Pl 53140
8th St 53140
9th Ct 53143
9th Pl 53140
9th St 53140
10th Ave
3500-5999 53140
6000-6098 53143
6100-7999 53143
10th Pl
401-497 53140
499-2999 53140
6300-8799 53144
10th St
400-599 53140
6100-6299 53144
11th Ave
3500-5999 53140
6000-6098 53143
11th Pl
500-2899 53140
6300-6398 53144
11th St
500-2999 53140
8700-8798 53144
12th Ave
1500-1598 53140
1600-1899 53140
6000-7600 53143
7602-8198 53143
12th Pl
400-1999 53140
8000-9799 53144
12th St
600-2199 53140
3001-3997 53144
3999-17199 53144
13th Ave
3500-3898 53140
6001-6897 53143
13th Ct 53140
13th Ln 53144
13th Pl
500-1900 53140
3200-4499 53144
13th St
400-2199 53140
3100-5400 53144
14th Ave
2200-3098 53140
6000-8500 53143
14th Ln
2800-2999 53140
3100-3199 53144
14th Pl
500-2900 53140
3200-9899 53144
14th St
401-2297 53140
3200-9999 53144
15th Ave
1500-1899 53140
6000-9099 53143
15th Ct 53140
15th Pl 53140
15th St
1501-1697 53140
1699-1999 53140
3000-9999 53144
16th Ave
1400-1498 53140
1500-5899 53140
6000-9099 53143
16th Pl
600-2999 53140
3400-5699 53144
16th St
500-2999 53140
3200-4699 53144
4701-4899 53144
17th Ave
1500-5399 53140
6500-8799 53143
8801-9099 53143
17th Pl
600-899 53140
3700-5599 53144
17th St
600-1599 53140
3300-4999 53144
18th Ave
700-5999 53140
6000-8699 53143
18th Pl 53140
18th St
1501-1597 53140
1599-2599 53140
2601-2899 53140
3001-3397 53144
3399-9999 53144
19th Ave
1500-5999 53140
6000-8699 53143
19th Pl 53144
19th St 53140
20th Ave
700-5899 53140
5901-5999 53140
6001-6013 53143
6015-8999 53143
20th Pl
1901-2097 53140
2099-2699 53140
4300-4699 53144
21st Ave
700-5999 53140
6400-8699 53143
21st St 53140
22nd Ave
101-197 53140
199-5999 53140
6000-9099 53143
22nd Pl 53140
22nd St
1400-2999 53140
3500-5600 53144
5602-5698 53144
23rd Ave
100-5599 53140
5601-5999 53140
6000-8499 53143
23rd Pl 53144
23rd St
1700-2999 53140
3100-3498 53144
3500-3899 53144
24th Ave
200-5599 53140
6000-9226 53143
24th Pl 53144
24th St
1400-2999 53140
3000-4799 53144
25th Ave
100-5499 53140
6000-9099 53143
25th Ct 53143
25th Pl 53144
25th St
1400-1498 53140
1500-2899 53140
3000-5299 53144
26th Ave
2100-3499 53140
3501-5299 53140
6000-9299 53143
26th St
1500-2699 53140
4800-5599 53144
27th Ave
1000-2099 53140
2101-3499 53140
6300-9299 53143
27th Ct 53140
27th St
1500-2999 53140
3000-4899 53144
28th Ave
2100-5199 53140
6000-8399 53143
28th Ct 53140
28th Pl
2800-2898 53140
5300-5499 53144
28th St
1700-2699 53140
3000-5599 53144
29th Ave
1000-5199 53140
6000-9299 53143
29th Ct
1400-1499 53140
8900-8999 53143
29th Pl 53144
29th St
1700-2699 53140
3000-4599 53144
30th Ave
100-5399 53140
5401-5599 53144
6000-8000 53142
8002-9298 53142
30th Ct 53144
30th St
1700-2699 53140
3000-4599 53144
4601-4699 53144
31st Ave
3800-5999 53144
6000-8999 53142
9001-9099 53142
31st Ct 53142
31st St
1001-1597 53140
1599-2699 53140
5000-6499 53144
32nd Ave
1400-5999 53144
6000-9299 53142
32nd Ct 53144
32nd St
1700-2699 53140
5000-5499 53144
33rd Ave
100-5999 53144
6000-9199 53142
33rd Ct 53144
33rd St
1300-2699 53140
4800-5499 53144
34th Ave
1600-5999 53144
6000-8999 53142
34th Ct 53144
34th St
1800-2999 53140
5000-5599 53144
35th Ave
1300-5999 53144
6000-8899 53142
35th Ct 53142
35th Pl 53140
35th St
700-1098 53140
1100-2999 53140
5500-5699 53144
36th Ave
1600-5899 53144
6600-8799 53142
36th St 53140
37th Ave
600-5999 53144
6000-8799 53142
37th Ct 53144
37th St 53140
38th Ave
400-5999 53144
6033-6041 53142
6043-8999 53142
38th Ct 53144
38th St
800-998 53140
1000-2199 53140
6101-6397 53144
6399-17399 53144
17401-17999 53144
39th Ave
500-5999 53144
6000-9299 53142
39th St
501-597 53140
599-2099 53140
5000-5198 53144
5200-5499 53144
40th Ave
1200-5900 53144
5902-5998 53144
6000-6198 53142
40th Ct 53144
40th Pl 53140
40th St
500-698 53140
3001-3797 53144
41st Ave
1200-5999 53144
6000-6898 53142
6900-9199 53142
41st Pl 53140
41st St
1901-2099 53140
3000-5599 53144
42nd Ave
1200-5999 53144
6000-9299 53142
42nd Ct 53142
42nd St
500-2099 53140
4500-5299 53144
43rd Ave
100-5999 53144
6000-8999 53142
43rd St
400-2900 53140
2902-2998 53140
3000-6399 53144
44th Ave
2500-5999 53144
6000-8799 53142
44th Ct
2400-4999 53144
6800-6899 53142
44th Pl 53140
44th St
400-2099 53140
3300-6399 53144
45th Ave
1201-1297 53144
1299-4600 53144
4602-4898 53144
6701-6797 53142
45th St
400-498 53140
3001-3097 53144
46th Ave
1800-5999 53144
6000-8899 53142
46th Pl
500-698 53140
6200-6299 53144
46th St
500-598 53140
600-2899 53140
2901-2999 53140
3900-6999 53144
47th Ave
400-5800 53144
5802-5998 53144
6000-8899 53142
47th Ct
2300-2599 53144
7900-8300 53142
47th St
701-797 53140
4400-4498 53144
48th Ave
2300-5699 53144
6000-9299 53142
48th Ct 53144
48th St
700-798 53140
800-2999 53140
3200-3498 53144
3500-6399 53144
49th Ave
400-5799 53144
6000-8400 53142
8402-8498 53142
49th St
700-999 53140
5600-6099 53144
50th Ave
2500-5999 53144
6000-8799 53142
50th St
401-697 53140
699-2800 53140
2802-2898 53140
3500-3898 53144
3900-8799 53144
51st Ave
3800-3898 53144
3900-5799 53144
6000-7299 53142
7301-7399 53142
51st Pl 53144
51st St
700-2198 53140
2200-2899 53140
6801-6897 53144
6899-6999 53144
52nd Ave
1200-5799 53144
5801-5999 53144
6600-6698 53142
6700-7499 53142
52nd St
600-2600 53140
2602-2998 53140
3001-3197 53144
3199-8800 53144
8802-11998 53144
53rd Ave
1200-5799 53144
6300-6499 53142
53rd Ct 53144
53rd Pl 53144
53rd St
1000-2599 53140
3101-3397 53144
3399-7199 53144
54th Ave
4000-4098 53144
4100-5799 53144
6000-8299 53142
54th St
201-897 53140
899-2599 53140
5300-5398 53144
5400-7099 53144
55th Ave
2400-5799 53144
6501-6697 53142
55th Ct 53144
55th Pl 53140
55th St
200-2500 53140
3101-3697 53144
56th Ave
100-4300 53144
6001-8499 53142
56th Ct 53142
56th St
1-97 53140
3301-3697 53144
57th Ave
101-3697 53144
6000-8499 53142
57th St
300-498 53140
500-2299 53140
3500-5099 53144
58th Ave
5200-5599 53144
6100-6799 53142
58th Pl 53144
58th St
300-598 53140
600-1899 53140
3201-4297 53144
4299-5599 53144
59th Ave 53142
59th Pl 53140
59th St
401-497 53140
499-1799 53140
3400-3498 53144
3500-4099 53144
4101-4299 53144
60th Ave
100-198 53144
200-299 53144
6000-8499 53142
60th Pl
2000-2099 53143
3700-11599 53142
60th St
300-2399 53140
2401-2999 53140
3000-12699 53144
12701-12799 53144
61st Ave 53142
61st Pl 53142
61st St
300-2999 53143
3001-3697 53142

3699-11499 53142
62nd Ave 53142
62nd Pl 53142
62nd St
800-2199 53143
3700-11399 53142
63rd Ave
1000-5499 53144
6200-8228 53142
63rd St
901-1197 53143
1199-2999 53143
3201-3497 53142
3499-10699 53142
64th Ave
4401-4497 53144
4499-5500 53144
5502-5598 53144
6900-8299 53142
64th St
801-997 53143
999-2900 53143
2902-2998 53143
3000-3498 53142
3500-15099 53142
65th Ave
1100-1199 53144
8100-8299 53142
65th Pl 53142
65th St
300-2399 53143
3500-14699 53142
66th Pl
900-999 53143
5200-5899 53142
66th St
100-2500 53143
2502-2898 53143
3301-3397 53142
3399-15099 53142
67th Ave 53142
67th Pl
1300-1399 53143
4700-11099 53142
67th St
1000-2699 53143
2701-2799 53143
3200-3998 53142
4000-15599 53142
68th Ave
4501-4597 53144
4599-4900 53144
4902-5198 53144
8100-8299 53142
68th Pl
100-699 53143
4400-11099 53142
68th St
100-2299 53143
3800-3998 53142
69th Ave 53142
69th St
200-2799 53143
2801-2899 53143
3501-4697 53142
4699-15099 53142
70th Ave 53144
70th Ave 53144
7500-7700 53142
7702-7898 53142
70th Ct
5400-5599 53144
6900-7199 53142
70th St
500-2799 53143
3401-3497 53142
3499-15499 53142
71st Pl 53142
71st St
101-297 53143
299-2799 53143
3300-3498 53142
3500-11899 53142
11901-12299 53142
72nd Ave 53144
72nd St
500-2999 53143
6100-14899 53142
73rd Pl 53142
73rd St
100-298 53143
3000-15599 53142
74th Pl
1800-2099 53143
4500-9500 53142
9502-11898 53142
74th St
500-2199 53143
3001-3097 53142
3099-15599 53142
75th Pl 53142
75th St
200-298 53143
300-2999 53143
3000-12400 53142
12402-12498 53142
76th St
701-717 53143
719-2700 53143
2702-2798 53143
3100-3298 53142
3300-6399 53142
77th Ave 53142
77th St
501-597 53143
599-699 53143
3401-3697 53142
3699-12199 53142
78th Pl
1300-1498 53143
4700-6999 53142
78th St
400-498 53143
500-2200 53143
2202-2398 53143
3301-3397 53142
3399-6999 53142
79th Pl 53142
79th St
500-698 53143
700-2600 53143
2602-2898 53143
3000-3198 53142
3200-5499 53142
5501-6999 53142
80th Ave 53144
80th Pl
1901-2097 53143
2099-2599 53143
4100-4198 53142
4200-6300 53142
6302-6398 53142
80th St
1100-2899 53143
3000-5999 53142
81st Pl 53142
81st St
1400-2600 53143
3900-6499 53142
82nd Ave
1200-1299 53144
6000-6599 53142
82nd Pl 53142
82nd St
800-2599 53143
5100-6200 53142
6202-6698 53142
83rd Ave 53142
83rd Pl
2700-2799 53143
3900-5999 53142
83rd St
900-2799 53143
3900-5999 53142
84th Ave 53142
84th Pl 53143
84th St
1400-2799 53143
4700-5999 53142
85th Ave 53142
85th Pl 53142
85th St
900-1398 53143
1400-2200 53143
2202-2898 53143
3000-5099 53142
86th Ave 53142
86th Pl
1800-1999 53143
3100-3198 53142
3200-4499 53142
86th St 53142
87th Ave
1100-1199 53144
6400-6599 53142
87th Pl
1400-2199 53143
3000-4999 53142
87th St
1400-2099 53143
3400-4299 53142
88th Ave
500-798 53144
800-4999 53144
5001-5999 53144
6000-7499 53142
88th Pl
1100-1198 53143
3000-4699 53142
88th St
1700-2199 53143
3400-3699 53142
3701-4199 53142
89th Ave 53142
89th Ct 53142
89th Pl
1800-2199 53143
4200-4999 53142
5001-5099 53142
89th St
1700-2199 53143
2201-2999 53143
3000-4899 53142
90th Ct 53142
90th St
1800-2198 53143
3100-13999 53142
91st Ave 53142
91st Pl 53142
91st St
1000-2198 53143
2200-2599 53143
3900-13999 53142
92nd Ave & St 53142
93rd Ave 53144
6300-7299 53142
93rd Ct 53142
93rd St 53142
94th Ave
1400-1499 53144
6200-6599 53142
94th Ct 53142
95th Ave
1200-5799 53144
6100-7499 53142
96th Ave
3400-3799 53144
6300-7399 53142
97th Ave
1200-1499 53144
6900-7400 53142
7402-7498 53142
98th Ave
1200-1298 53144
1300-1500 53144
1502-1598 53144
6500-7499 53142
99th Ave
5300-5899 53144
6200-6899 53142
100th Ave 53144
100th Ave 53144
100th Ave 53144
6600-6799 53142
101st Ave 53144
102nd Ave 53144
6600-6999 53142
103rd Ave 53142
104th Ave 53144
6100-6798 53142
6800-6899 53142
6901-7499 53142
104th St 53142
105th Ave 53142
106th Ave 53142
107th Ave 53142
108th Ave 53142
109th Ave 53142
111th Ave & Ct 53142
112th Ave 53142
113th Ave 53142
114th Ave 53142
115th Ave 53142
116th St 53142
117th Ave 53142
118th Ave 53142
120th Ave
1100-5299 53144
6000-12799 53142
122nd Ave
1200-1298 53144
6201-7197 53142
7199-7299 53142
7301-7499 53142
125th Ave 53142
128th Ave 53144
9200-9599 53142
128th St 53142
136th Ave
2400-3799 53144
8700-12799 53142
138th Ave 53144
141st Ave 53142
142nd Ave 53142
143rd Ct 53142
144th Ave 53142
145th Ave 53142
146th Ave 53142
147th Ave 53142
148th Ave 53142
149th Ave 53142
150th Ave 53142
152nd Ave 53144
152nd Ave 53144
152nd Ave 53144
6700-12799 53142
154th Ave 53142
155th Ave & Ct 53142
168th Ave 53144
169th Ave 53144
176th Ave 53144

LA CROSSE WI

General Delivery 54601

POST OFFICE BOXES MAIN OFFICE STATIONS AND BRANCHES

Box No.s
All PO Boxes 54602

NAMED STREETS

Adams Ct & St 54601
Aiken Rd 54603
Airport Dr & Rd 54603
Alexander St 54601
Apple Orchard Ln 54601
Aspen Ct 54601
Avon St 54603
Badger St 54601
Bahr Rd 54601
Baier Ln 54601
Bainbridge Pl & St 54603
Baker Rd 54601
W Bank Dr 54601
Barlow St 54601
Barnabee Rd 54601
Battlestone Station Rd 54601
Baumgartner Dr 54603
Bayshore Dr N 54603
Bayside Ct 54601
Bayview Ct 54603
Bennett St 54601
Bennora Lee Ct 54601
Bentwood Pl 54601
Berlin Dr 54601
Birch Dr, Ln & St 54601
Birchview Cir & Rd 54601
Birchwood Ln 54601
Bissen Pl 54603
Blackhawk Pl 54601
Bliss Rd 54601
Bloomer Mill Rd 54601
Bluebird Ct & Ln 54601
Bluff Pass & St 54601
Bluffview Pl 54601
Boma Rd 54601
Bond Rd 54601
Boschert St 54601
Boulder Ct 54601
Brackenwood Ct 54601
Braleash St 54603
Brecken Rdg 54601
Breezy Point Rd 54603
Breidel Coulee Rd 54601
Briarwood Ave 54601
Brickyard Ln 54601
Broadhead Rd 54601
Broadview Pl 54601
Brook Ct 54601
Brookshire Pl 54601
Brookside Dr & Ln 54601
Brookview Rd 54601
Buchner Pl 54603
Bundy St 54601
E & W Burr Oak St 54601
Caledonia St 54603
Callaway Blvd & Ct 54603
Calvert Rd 54601
Cameron Ave 54601
E Camino Real Dr 54601
Campbell Ct 54603
Campbell Rd 54601
Campbell St 54603
Car St 54603
Cardinal Ln 54601
Carol Ct 54601
Caroline St 54603
Casa Del Sol Rd 54601
Cass St 54601
Castle Pl 54601
Causeway Blvd 54603
Cedar Rd 54601
Cedar Point Rd 54601
Center St 54601
Central Rd 54603
Charles Ct & St 54603
Chase St 54601
Cherokee Ave 54603
Cherrywood Dr 54601
Church Ct 54601
Church Dr 54603
Circle Pl 54601
City View Ln 54601
Clarence Ct 54601
Clements Rd 54601
Cliffside Dr & Pl 54601
Cliffview Ter 54601
Cliffwood Ln 54601
Clinic Ct 54601
Clinton St 54603
Commerce St 54603
Company Store Rd 54601
Concord Pl 54601
Conoco Rd 54601
Continental Ln 54601
Cook St 54601
Copeland Ave 54603
Copeland Park Dr 54603
Copus Ct 54603
Cottage Grove Ave 54601
Coulee Ave & Dr 54601
Coulee Springs Ln 54601
Country Club Ct 54601
County Road B 54601
County Road F 54601
County Road Fa 54601
County Road Fo 54601
County Road I 54601
County Road M 54601
County Road Mm 54601
County Road O 54601
County Road Oa 54601
County Road Yy 54601
Credit Union Ct 54603
Creekside Pl 54601
Crestline Pl 54601
Crestview Pl 54601
Cross St 54601
Crowley Pl 54601
Crown Blvd 54601
Crystal Dr & Ln 54601
Cunningham St 54603
Daisy Dr 54601
Dakota St 54603
Dauphin St 54603
Dawson Ave, Ct & Pl 54603
Deerfield Pl & Rd 54601
Deerview Dr 54601
Del Ray Ave 54603
Demlow Rd 54601
Denton St 54601
Diagonal Rd 54601
Division St 54601
Doll Rd 54601
Dorn Pl & St 54603
Drectrah Rd 54601
Drogseth Rd 54601
Dummer Valley Dr 54601
Eagle Ln 54601
Eagle Point Dr 54601
East Ave N & S 54601
Eastbrook Dr 54601
Easter Hts & Rd 54601
Eastwood Ln 54601
Ebner Coulee Rd 54601
Eddie Ave 54601
Edgewater Ct, Dr & Ln 54603
Edgewood Pl 54601
Elizabeth Way 54601
Elm Dr 54601
Elm St 54603
Emerald Ct 54601
Emerlert St 54601
Enterprise Ave 54603
Evergreen Ln & Pl 54601
Evergreens Trl 54601
E & W Fairchild St 54601
Fairview Dr 54603
Fairway Ct & St 54601
Fanell Dr 54601
Fanta Reed Pl & Rd 54603
Farnam Ct & St 54601
Farwell St 54601
Fen Lockney Dr 54601
Ferndale Ln 54601
Ferry St 54601
Fiesta Ct 54601
Fireclay Ct 54601
Fisherman Rd 54603
Floral Ln 54601
Forest Ridge Dr 54601
Fox Hollow Dr 54601
Fox Tail Run 54601
Franciscan Way 54601
Frank Ct 54601
Front St N & S 54601
Garbers Ct & Rd 54601
Garden St 54601
Garner Pl 54601
Geneva Ln 54601
George Pl & St 54603
Gillette Pl 54603
Gillette St
400-2199 54603
2900-3098 54601
Gladys St 54601
Glendale Ave 54601
Glenhaven Dr 54601
Glenwood Pl 54601
Goddard Pl & St 54603
Gohres St 54603
Gold St 54603
Golden Valley Trailer Ct 54601
Goodview Pl 54601
Gould St 54603
Grand St 54603
Grandad Ter 54601
Grandad Bluff Rd 54601
Grandview Pl 54601
Grandwood Pl E & W 54601
Grant Ct 54601
Green St 54601
Green Bay St 54601
Green Glen Dr 54601
Greenbriar Ct 54601
Greenhills Pl 54601
Greenspire Ln 54601
Greenwood Dr 54601
Grove St 54601
H Helke Rd 54601
Hackberry Ln 54601
Hagar St 54603
Hagen Rd 54601
Hamilton St 54603
Hanifl Rd 54601
Hanks Peak Rd 54601
Hanson Ct & Rd 54603
Harborview Plz 54601
Harvest Ln 54601
Harvey St 54603
Hass St 54601
Hauser St 54603
Hayes St 54603
Heatherwood Pl 54601
E Helke Rd 54601
Hemstock St 54603
Hengel Ct 54601
Heritage Ct 54601
Hess Rd 54601
Hewitt St 54601
Hiawatha Ave 54601
Hibbard Ct 54603
Hickory Ln & Ter 54601
Hickory Nut Ct 54601
Hidden Springs Rd 54601
Highland Dr, Pl & St 54601
Hillcrest Dr 54601
E Hills Rd 54601
Hillview Ave & Dr 54601
Hinkley Rd 54603
Hintgen Ct & Rd 54601
Hoeschler Ct & Dr 54601
Hoeth St 54601
Holly Pl 54601
Holmgren Dr 54601
Hood St 54601
Horseshoe Pl 54601
Horton St 54601
Howry St 54603
Huber Ct 54601
Hummingbird Rd 54601
Huntington Ct 54601
Hyde Ave 54601
Hypoint Dr 54601
Iga Ct 54603
Interchange Pl 54603
Irish Ct 54601
Island St 54603
Island Park Rd 54603
Jackie Ln 54603
Jackson St 54601
James St 54601
Jane St 54601
Janice Ct 54601
Jansky Pl 54601
Jason Ln 54601
Jay St 54601
Jenkins Ln 54603
Jerald St 54603
Joey Ln 54601
John Flynn Dr 54603
Johns Rd 54601
Johnson St 54601
Jordan Pl 54601

Joseph Houska Park Dr 54601
Joy Ln 54601
Juniper St 54601
Justin Rd 54601
Kammel Ct & Rd 54601
Kane St 54603
Kearns Ct 54601
Keil Coulee Rd 54601
Kelly Pl 54603
Kenton St 54601
Kertzman Pl 54601
Kime St 54603
King St 54601
Kings Ct 54601
N Kinney Coulee Rd 54601
Kleinsmith Rd 54601
Kloss Rd 54601
Knobloch Rd 54601
Kraft St 54603
Kramer St 54603
Kranc Ave 54601
Kreutz Ln 54601
Kwik Trip Way 54603
La Crescent Ct, Pl & St 54603
La Crosse St 54601
La Fond Ave 54603
Lakeshore Dr 54603
Lakeview Dr 54603
Lakota Ct & Pl 54601
Lancaster St 54603
Lang Dr 54603
Larson St 54603
Lauderdale Ct & Pl 54603
Laurel St 54601
Lauterbach Rd 54601
Lazy Acres Rd 54601
Le Jeune Rd 54601
Leonard Rd & St 54601
Leske Rd 54601
Levy Ln 54601
Lexington Heights Dr 54601
Liberty St 54603
Linbridge Ct 54601
Lincoln Ave 54601
Linden Dr 54601
Linwood Ct 54601
Livingston St 54603
Loch Nairn Ct 54601
Locust St 54603
Logan St 54603
Lombard Ct 54603
Longview Ct 54601
Loomis St 54603
Lori Pl 54603
Losey Blvd & Ct 54601
Losey Court Ln 54601
Lost Ridge Rd 54601
Luoyang Ave 54601
Mac Harley Ln 54601
Macavorson Ct 54601
Madison Pl & St 54601
Main St 54601
Malzacher Rd 54601
Maple Dr & St 54601
Marco Dr 54601
Mariah Dr N & S 54601
Marina Dr 54603
N Marion Rd 54601
S Marion Rd 54601
Marion St 54603
Mark Pl 54601
Market St 54601
Markle Rd 54601
Maryline Ct 54603
Mc Laren Rd 54601
Mccumber St 54601
Meadow Lane Pl 54601
Meadow Pond Ln 54601
Meadow Ridge Rd 54601
Meadowlark Ct & Ln 54601
Medco Ct 54601
Meir Ct 54601
Mesa Rd 54601
Mesa Grande Pl 54601

Meyer Rd 54601
Mickel Rd 54601
Mill St 54601
Millatti Ln 54601
Miller Pl 54603
Miller Rd 54601
W Miller Rd 54601
Miller St 54601
Milson Ct 54601
Milwaukee St 54603
Mississippi St 54601
Monitor St 54603
Moore St 54603
Moorings Dr 54603
Mormon Dr & Pl 54601
Mormon Coulee Ct & Rd 54601
Mount Vernon St 54601
Muenzenberger Rd 54601
Musgjerd Ln 54601
Muth Rd 54603
Myrick Park Dr 54601
Nakomis Ave 54603
Nancy Ct 54601
Nelson Pl 54601
Nolop Rd 54601
Norplex Dr 54601
Norseman Dr 54603
North St 54603
Northbrook Rd 54601
Nottingham Ave 54601
Nuttleman Rd 54601
Oak Ct 54603
Oak Dr 54601
Oak St 54603
Oakland Ln & St 54601
Ohlsun Ct 54601
Old Town Hall Rd 54601
Old Vineyard Rd 54601
Olivet Ct & St 54603
Onalaska Ave & Ct 54603
Orchard Valley Dr 54601
Oriole Ln 54601
Orion Ct 54601
Palace St 54603
Pammel Pass E & W 54601
Pammel Creek Rd 54601
Paris Angel Dr 54601
Park Ave 54601
Park Dr 54601
Park Ln 54603
Park St 54601
Park St S
1400-1498 54601
N Park St 54601
S Park St
1301-1399 54601
Park Lane Dr 54601
Park Plaza Dr 54601
Parkwood Pl 54601
Partridge Ln S 54601
Patrie Dr 54601
Paul Pl 54601
Peace St 54601
Pearl St 54601
Peters Rd 54601
S Pettibone Dr 54601
Pheasant Ln 54601
Pierce Ave 54603
Pine St 54601
Pine Bluff Rd 54601
Pinecrest Ct 54601
Pineview Dr 54601
Plainview Rd 54603
Potato Ridge Rd 54601
Powell St 54603
Prospect St 54603
Puent Rd 54601
Quail Dr 54601
Quarry Pl & Rd 54601
Queens Ave 54601
Raatz Rd 54601
Raintree Pl 54601
Ramsey Pl 54603
Ranger Dr 54603
Ray Pl 54601

Red Oaks Dr 54601
Redbird Ct 54603
Redfield St 54603
Redwing Rd 54601
Redwood Ct 54601
N & S Richard Dr 54601
Richmond St 54603
Richmond Bay Ct 54603
Ridge Dr 54601
Ridgeview Dr 54601
Ridgewood Ln 54601
Rim Of The City Rd 54601
Rio Grande Blvd 54601
Ristow Ct 54601
Rivercrest Dr N & S 54601
Riverplace Dr 54601
Riverside Dr 54601
Riverview Dr 54601
Robil Ct E 54601
Robin Hood Dr 54601
Robinsdale Ave 54601
Roesler Pl 54601
Rose Ct & St 54603
Rosehill Pl 54601
Rublee St 54603
Russian Coulee Rd 54601
Sablewood Rd 54601
Saint Andrew St 54603
Saint Cloud St 54603
Saint James St 54603
Saint Paul St 54603
N Salem Rd 54603
Sanborn St 54603
Sandpiper Ln S 54601
Scarlett Dr 54601
Scenic Dr 54601
Schams Ave 54601
Schieche Rd 54601
Schubert Pl 54601
Schultz Dr 54603
Schwartz Rd 54601
Scott Dr 54601
Seiler Ln 54601
Serenity Way 54601
Servais Rd 54601
Servais Collern Rd 54601
Seven Springs St 54601
Shady Lane Ct 54601
Shady Maple Ridge Rd 54601
Shady Pines Rd 54601
Sharon St 54603
Shelby Rd 54601
Shelly Ln 54603
Sherry Ln 54601
Sherwood Dr 54601
Shiftar Rd 54603
Shorewood Dr 54601
Sigel Ct 54601
Silha Rd 54601
Sill St 54603
Silver Morning Ln 54601
Sims Pl 54601
Sisson Dr 54601
Skemp Rd 54601
Sky Harbour Dr 54603
Skyline Blvd 54601
Smith Valley Rd 54601
Solaris Ln 54601
Sophia Ln 54601
South Ave 54601
Southdale Dr 54601
Southfield Grn 54601
Sperbeck St 54603
Spillway Dr 54603
Sprig St 54601
Springbrook Way 54601
Stanley Ct 54601
Stark Rd 54601
Starlite Dr 54601
State Rd 54601
State St
101-297 54601
299-500 54601
425-425 54602
502-2698 54601

601-2499 54601
State Road 157 54601
State Road 16 54601
State Road 33 54601
State Road 35 54601
Steele St 54601
Steven Pl 54603
Stoddard St 54603
Stone Bridge Rd 54601
Stonecrest Rd 54601
Stonehill Rd N 54601
Storandt Pl 54601
Strittmater Rd 54601
Strong Ave 54601
Sugar Pine Ln 54601
Summit Dr 54601
Sumner St 54603
Sun Valley Rd 54601
Sunny Slope Rd 54601
Sunnyside Dr 54601
Sunnyslope Dr 54601
Sunrise Dr & Pl 54601
Sunset Ct, Dr & Ln 54601
Susan Pl 54603
Swamp Rd 54601
Tamarack Rd 54601
Taylor St 54603
Tellin Ct 54603
Terrace Dr 54601
Terry Ct 54601
Thistledown Dr 54601
Thomas St 54603
Thompson St 54601
Three Town Rd 54601
Tietze Dr 54601
Timber Ln 54601
Timber Creek Trl 54601
Timber Valley Rd 54601
Tower Ct & Ln 54601
Town Hall Rd 54601
Townsend St 54601
Travis St 54601
Troy Rd 54601
Tyler Ln & St 54601
Tyson Rd 54601
Us Highway 14 61 54601
Usher St 54603
V Hawk Ct 54601
Valley Pkwy, Pl & Rd 54601
Van Loon Rd 54601
Velmar Ct 54601
Verchota St 54601
Verde Valley Rd N & S 54601
Veterans Memorial Dr 54601
Victory St 54601
Vine St 54601
Vista Ct & Dr 54601
Viterbo Ct & Dr 54601
Wall St 54603
Walnut St 54603
Ward Ave 54601
Washburn St 54603
Waterford Valley Rd 54601
Wedgewood Dr E & W 54601
Welsh Coulee Rd 54601
West Ave N & S 54601
Western Ave 54603
Weston St 54601
Westview Ct & Pl 54601
Whippoorwill Ln S 54601
Wildwood Ln 54601
William St 54603
Williams Pl 54601
Willow Dr & Way 54601
Windsor St 54603
Winnebago Ct & St 54601
Winneshiek Rd 54603
Winona St 54603
Wolf Ridge Ct 54601
Wollan Pl 54601
Wood St 54603
Woodbridge Ct 54601
Woodhaven Dr 54601
Woodland Dr & Grn 54601

Wuensch Rd 54601
Yanzer Rd 54601
Youngdale Ave 54603
Zeisler St 54601
Zephyr Cir 54601
Zion Rd 54601

NUMBERED STREETS

1st E & W 54603
2nd Ave E 54603
2nd Ave W 54603
2nd St N 54601
2nd St S 54601
3rd Ave W 54603
3rd St N 54601
3rd St S 54601
4th N & S 54601
5th N & S 54601
6th N & S 54601
7th N & S 54601
8th Pl & St 54601
9th N & S 54601
10th N & S 54601
11th Pl & St 54601
12th St N 54601
13th Ct, Pl & St N & S 54601
14th N & S 54601
15th Pl & St 54601
16th N & S 54601
17th Pl & St 54601
18th Pl S 54601
19th Pl & St 54601
20th N & S 54601
21st Pl, St & Ter N & S 54601
22nd Dr & St 54601
23rd N & S 54601
24th N & S 54601
25th St S 54601
26th Pl & St N & S 54601
27th Pl & St N & S 54601
28th Ct & St 54601
29th Ct & St 54601
30th Ct & St 54601
31st Ct, Pl & St 54601
32nd St S 54601
33rd Ct & St 54601
34th St S 54601
35th St S 54601

MADISON WI

General Delivery 53714

POST OFFICE BOXES MAIN OFFICE STATIONS AND BRANCHES

Box No.s
1 - 2999 53701
3000 - 3429 53704
5001 - 5970 53705
6001 - 6872 53716
7001 - 7999 53707
8001 - 8998 53708
10001 - 10001 53705
14011 - 14768 53708
44001 - 46654 53744
55001 - 56240 53705
70701 - 77094 53707
258001 - 259997 53725
260011 - 260368 53726

NAMED STREETS

Aaron Ct 53716
Aberg Ave 53704
Abilene Ct 53719
Acacia Ln 53716
Academy Dr 53716

Acadia Dr 53717
Acewood Blvd
100-999 53714
1000-1499 53716
Acker Rd 53704
Adams St 53711
Adams Hall 53706
Adarianc Dr 53706
Adderbury Cir & Ln 53711
Adeline Cir 53713
Adkins Ogg Hall W 53706
Admiral Dr 53716
Adobe Way 53719
Advance Rd 53718
Agate Ln 53714
Agnes Dr 53711
Agriculture Dr
2600-2900 53718
2902-2998 53718
3300-3399 53716
3600-3698 53718
Alamosa Ct 53719
Albert Ct 53714
Alden Dr 53705
Alder Rd 53716
Alena Ln 53718
Alexandria Ln 53718
Algoma St 53704
Alison Ln 53711
Allegheny Dr 53719
N & S Allen St 53726
Alliant Energy Center Way 53713
Allied Dr 53711
Allis Ave 53716
Alma Rd 53711
Almo Ave 53704
Alpine Rd 53704
Alrita Ct 53713
Altem Cir 53711
Alvarez Ave 53714
Ambassador Dr 53718
Ambleside Dr 53719
American Ln 53704
American Pkwy 53718
American Ash Dr 53704
American Family Dr 53718
Ames St 53711
Amherst Dr 53705
Ammerman Cir 53716
Amnicon Trl 53718
Amoth Ct 53704
Amsterdam Ave 53716
Anchor Dr 53714
Anchorage Ave 53705
Anderson St 53704
Andes Dr 53719
Andover Cir 53717
Andrew Way 53714
Angel Crest Way 53716
Anhalt Dr 53704
Ann St 53713
Annamark Dr 53704
Annen Ln 53711
Annestown Dr 53718
Anniversary Ct & Ln 53704
Anthony Ln 53711
Anthony Pl 53716
Antietam Ln 53705
Anvil Ln 53716
Anzinger Ct 53704
Apollo Way 53718
Apostle Is 53719
Appalachian Way 53705
Apple Hill Cir 53717
Applegate Ct & Rd 53713
Appleglen Ln 53719
Applewood Dr 53719
Appomattox Ct 53705
Arapahoe Ln 53704
Arbor Dr 53711
Arbor Vitae Pl 53705
Arbordale Ct 53713
Arboretum Dr & Ln 53713
Arctic Fox Dr 53719
Arden Ln 53711

Ardmore Dr 53713
Ardsley Cir & Ln 53713
Argosy Ct 53714
Argyle Ct 53719
Arial Cir 53719
Arial Spring Trl 53718
Arizona Cir & Pass 53704
Arkansas Ave 53704
Arlington Pl 53726
Armistice Ln 53704
Arrowhead Dr 53716
Arrowood Dr 53704
Artesian Ln 53713
Arther Ct 53713
Artisan Dr 53704
Ascot Ln 53711
Ash St 53726
Asher Cir 53716
Ashford Ln 53713
Ashland Ct 53705
Ashley Cir 53719
Ashwabay Ln 53719
Ashwood Ct 53719
Aspen Rd 53711
Aspen Way 53718
Aspen Grove Ln 53717
Aster Ln 53719
Atlas Ave & Ct 53714
Attic Angels Cir 53717
Atticus Way 53711
Atwood Ave
1900-3248 53704
3250-3398 53704
3500-3898 53714
Augusta Dr 53717
Autumn Jade Ct 53719
Autumn Leaf Ln 53704
Autumnwood Cir 53719
Avalon Ln 53719
Axel Ave 53711
Aztalan Dr 53718
Babcock Dr 53706
Backbay Cir 53717
Badeau Cir 53704
E & W Badger Ln, Pkwy & Rd 53713
Bagley Ct & Pkwy 53705
Bahr Cir 53719
Bailey Dr 53718
Bainbridge St 53716
Baird St 53713
Baker Ave 53705
Balden St 53713
N & S Baldwin St 53703
Balsam Rd 53711
Baltzell St 53711
Banding Ln 53704
Banner Cir 53718
Barby Ln 53704
Barlow St 53705
Barnard Hall 53706
Barnett St 53704
Barr Ogg Hall W 53706
Barron Ct 53705
Bartels St 53716
N & S Bartelt Ct 53704
Bartillon Dr 53704
Bartlett Ln 53711
Barton Rd 53711
Basalt Ln 53719
Bascom Mall 53706
Bascom Pl 53726
Bascom St 53726
Bascom Hall 53706
Bashford Ave 53704
Bashford Tripp Hall 53706
Basil Ct & Dr 53704
Baskerville Ave 53716
N & S Bassett St 53703
Basswood Ct 53719
Bauer Dr 53718
Bay Ave 53704
Bay Vw 53715
Bay Hill Dr 53717
Bay Ridge Rd 53716
Bayberry Trl 53717

Bayfield Ter 53705
Bayside Dr 53704
Bea Cir 53716
Beach St 53705
Beale St 53711
Beale Witte B Hall 53706
Bear Claw Way 53717
Beatty Witte B Hall 53706
Beaumont Cir 53714
Becker Dr 53704
Becker Witte B Hall 53706
N & S Bedford St 53703
Bedner Rd 53719
Beehner Cir 53714
Beihoffer Ct 53719
Beilfuss Dr 53704
Bel Aire Dr 53713
Beld St
1401-1497 53715
1499-1699 53715
1701-1797 53713
1799-1899 53713
1901-2099 53713
Belin St 53705
Bellflower Ln 53719
Bellgrove Ln 53704
Bellows Cir 53716
Belmont Cir & Rd 53714
Beloit Ct 53705
S Beltline Ct 53713
W Beltline Hwy
17-197 53713
199-2799 53713
2801-3599 53713
4201-4699 53711
Benjamin Dr 53718
Bennett Ct 53719
Bergen St 53714
Berkan St 53711
Berkley Cir & Dr 53719
Berkshire Rd 53711
Bernard Ct 53715
Bernwick Cir 53719
Berwyn Dr 53711
Bettys Ln 53711
Beverly Rd 53711
Bewick Dr 53714
Bierman Slichter Hall 53706
Big Dipper Dr 53718
Big Sky Dr 53719
N & S Biltmore Ln 53718
Birch Ave & Cir 53711
Birch Haven Cir 53716
Birch Hill Dr 53711
Birchstone Dr 53719
Birchwood Cir 53704
Birge Ter 53726
Bishops Hill Cir 53717
Bittersweet Pl 53705
Bjelde Ln 53716
Black Oak Cir & Dr 53711
Black Stone Cir 53719
Blackbird Ln 53704
N & S Blackhawk Ave & Dr 53705
Blacksmith Ln 53716
Blackwolf Dr 53717
Blaine Dr 53704
N & S Blair St 53703
Blakton Rd 53719
Blanchard St 53705
Blazing Star Dr 53718
Blettner Blvd 53714
Bleyer Bradley Hall 53706
Bliss St 53718
Blossom Ln 53716
N & S Blount St 53703
Blue Bill Park Dr 53704
Blue Maple Trl 53719
Blue Ridge Ct & Pkwy 53705
Blue Spruce Trl 53717
Bluebird Ct 53711
Bluejay Ln 53704
Bluestem Way 53704
Bluff St 53705
Bluff Point Dr 53718

Bob O Link Ln 53714
Boca Grande Way 53719
Bonner Cir & Ln 53704
Bonnie Ave 53718
Bonnie Ln 53716
Book Ct 53713
Boothbay Cir 53717
Bordner Dr 53705
Boston Ct 53711
Botkin Tripp Hall 53706
Boulder Ter 53711
Boulder Creek Cir 53717
Bowdoin Rd 53705
Bowen Ct 53715
Bowman Ave 53716
Bowman St 53704
Boyd Ave 53704
Boynton Pl 53714
Bradbury Ct & Rd 53719
Bradford Ln 53714
Bradley Pl 53711
Bradley Hall 53706
Bram St 53713
Brandenburg Way 53718
Brandie Rd 53714
Brandon Rd 53719
Brandt Pl 53716
Branford Ln E & W 53717
Braxton Pl 53715
N & S Brearly St 53703
N Breese Ter
2-398 53726
21-25 53711
S Breese Ter 53711
Breese Chadbourne 53706
Breezy Grass Way 53718
Brentwood Pkwy 53704
Bresland Ct 53715
Briar Crest St 53704
Briar Hill Rd 53711
Brickson Park Rd 53704
Bridge Rd
5700-6399 53716
6400-6598 53713
6401-6509 53713
Bridle Way 53718
Brigham Ave 53714
Brighton Pl 53713
Brindley Cir 53719
Britta Dr & Pkwy 53711
Brittany Pl 53711
S & W Brittingham Pl 53715
Broad Creek Blvd 53718
Broadmoor St 53719
E Broadway 53716
W Broadway
100-500 53716
W Broadway
502-610 53716
800-898 53713
900-2449 53713
2451-2599 53713
Brody Dr 53705
Bromley Cir 53714
Brompton Cir 53711
Brookfield Pkwy 53718
Brookins Ct 53716
N & S Brookline Dr 53719
N & S Brooks St 53715
Brookshire Ln 53714
Brookside Dr 53718
Brookwood Rd 53711
N & S Broom St 53703
Brown Ln 53704
Brown Quail Ct 53713
Browning Rd 53704
Bruce Ct 53705
Brule Cir & St 53717
Bruns Ave 53714
N & S Bryan St 53714
Bryan Sullivan Hall 53706
Bryant Rd 53713
Bryce Canyon Cir 53705
Bryn Trem Rd 53716
Brynwood Dr 53716
Buchner Ct 53718

Buck Cole Hall 53706
E Buckeye Rd 53716
Buckhorn Dr 53718
Buckingham Ln 53714
Buell St 53704
Buena Vista St 53704
Buffalo Trl 53705
Buford Dr 53718
Buhler Ct 53704
Buick St 53713
Bull Run 53718
Bullis Ogg Hall W 53706
Bultman Rd 53704
Bunge Elizabeth Waters Hall 53706
Bunker Hill Ln 53704
Bunn Ogg Hall W 53706
Bunting Ln 53704
Burbank Pl 53705
N & S Burberry Dr 53719
Burdette Ct 53713
Burke Ave 53714
Burke Rd 53718
Burnett Dr 53705
Burning Wood Ct & Way 53704
Burr Oak Ln 53713
Burrows Rd 53704
Busse St 53714
N & S Butler St 53703
Butterfield Dr 53704
Butternut Rd 53704
Buttonwood Ct & Dr 53718
Byars Cir 53719
Cable Ave 53705
Cabot Ln 53711
Cairns Ogg Hall W 53706
Caldy Pl 53711
Caliangt St 53704
Calico Dr 53718
Callahan Sellery B Hall 53706
Callisto Dr 53718
Calumet Cir 53705
Calvert Rd 53714
Calypso Rd 53704
Cambridge Ct & Rd 53704
Camden Rd 53716
Camelot Dr 53705
Cameo Ln 53714
Cameron Dr 53711
Camilla Rd 53716
Camino Way 53719
Camino Del Sol 53704
Campbell St 53711
Campbell Chadbourne 53706
E Campus Mall
2-98 53715
101-399 53715
400-498 53706
401-499 53703
Camus Ln 53705
Canter Cir & Dr 53718
Canterbury Cir & Rd 53711
Cantwell Ct 53703
Canvasback Cir 53717
Capital Ave 53705
Capitol Ct 53715
Capitol View Ter 53713
Capricorn Ln 53718
Captains Ct 53719
Carberry St 53704
Cardinal Cres 53716
Cardinal Ln 53704
Carey Ct 53704
Carillon Dr 53705
Carina Ln 53718
Carioca Ln 53704
Carling Dr 53711
Carlsbad Dr 53705
Carlton Dr 53718
Carns Dr 53719
Carns Elizabeth Waters Hall 53706
Carnwood Rd 53719
Caromar Dr 53711

Carpenter St 53704
Carrington Dr 53719
N & S Carroll St 53703
Carver St 53713
Cascade Rd 53704
Castle Pl 53703
Castle Pines Dr 53717
Castlebar Ct 53717
Catalpa Cir & Rd 53713
Cathy Ct 53711
Catlin Pl 53713
Cavendish Ct 53714
Cedar Pl 53705
Cedar St 53715
Cedar Creek Trl 53717
Celebration Pkwy 53718
Celia Ct 53711
Center Ave 53704
Center St 53713
Chadbourne Ave 53726
Chadbourne Hall 53706
Chamberlain Ave
300-2499 53726
2500-2899 53705
Chamberlin Kronshage Hall 53706
Chandler St
900-1399 53715
1400-1599 53711
Chapel Hill Rd 53711
Chapman St 53711
Charing Cross Rd 53704
Charleen Ln 53714
Charles Ln 53711
Charmany Dr 53719
N Charter St
1-299 53715
401-467 53706
469-473 53706
475-499 53706
S Charter St 53715
Chatham Ter 53711
Chautauqua Trl 53719
Chelsea Ct & St 53719
Chequamegon Bay 53719
Cherbourg Ct 53711
Cherokee Cir 53704
Cherokee Dr 53711
Cherry Ave 53714
Cherry Hill Dr 53717
Cherrywood Ct 53714
Chester Dr 53719
Chesterton Cir 53717
Chestnut St 53726
Cheyenne Cir & Trl 53705
Chicago Ave 53714
Chickadee Ct 53714
Chieftain Lookout 53711
Chinook Ln 53704
Chippewa Ct & Dr 53711
Chive Ct 53704
Christianson Ave 53714
Christine Ln 53716
Christopher Ct 53705
Churchill Dr 53713
Cimarron Trl 53719
Circle Close 53705
City View Dr 53718
Claire St 53716
Claremont Ln 53704
Clarence Ct 53715
Clarendon Ct 53704
Clark Ct 53715
Classic Cir 53719
Clear Spring Ct 53716
Clemons Ave 53704
Cleradw Dr 53705
Clerthe Rd 53711
Clifden Dr 53711
Cliff Ct 53713
Clove Dr 53704
Clover Ct 53711
Clover Ln 53714
Clyde Gallagher Ave
200-298 53704
201-399 53714

Clymer Pl 53715
Coach House Dr 53714
Cobblestone Ct 53714
Cocoa Beach Dr 53719
Cody Ln 53704
Coffey Cir 53716
Coho St 53713
Colby St 53715
E & W Coldspring Ave 53716
Cole Hall 53706
Coleman Rd 53704
Colgate Rd 53705
College Ct 53715
Collins Ct 53716
Colony Cir & Dr 53717
Colorado Ct 53704
Columbia Cir 53716
Columbia Rd 53705
Columbus Ln 53704
Comanche Gln & Way 53704
Commerce Dr 53719
Commercial Ave
1700-3099 53704
3100-4200 53714
4202-4698 53714
4901-5399 53704
Commonwealth Ave
1900-2299 53726
2300-2599 53711
Concord Ave 53714
Coney Weston Pl 53711
Congress Ave 53718
Conklin Pl 53703
Conlin St 53714
Connecticut Ct 53719
Connor Ct 53718
Conover Kronshage 53706
Conservation Pl 53713
Constitution Ln 53711
Cool Bradley Hall 53706
Coolidge St 53704
Copeland St 53711
Copernicus Way 53718
E & W Copper Cir 53717
Copper Leaf Trl 53719
Copps Ave 53716
Coral Ct 53714
Corben Ct 53704
Cordelia Cres 53704
Corinth Trl 53718
Cornell Ct 53705
Cornucopia Ct 53719
Cornwall Pl 53716
Corona Ct 53719
Coronado Ct 53705
W Corporate Dr 53714
Corry St 53704
Corscot Ct 53704
Cortina Dr 53719
Cosgrove Dr 53719
Cottage Ct 53716
Cottage Grove Rd
100-5200 53716
5202-5406 53716
5701-5997 53718
5999-6800 53718
6802-7598 53718
Cottontail Trl 53718
Cottonwood Cir 53704
Council Crst 53711
Country Ln 53719
Country Club Rd 53711
Country Glen Cir 53719
Country Grove Dr 53719
Country Rose Ct 53713
Countryside Ln 53705
Countrywood Ln 53719
County Road Cv 53704
County Road Ab 53718
County Road Bb 53718
County Road M
3500-3598 53719
County Road M
3691-3729 53719
5420-5442 53704

County Road T
3200-3298 53718
3300-3500 53718
3502-3648 53718
3700-3798 53704
6800-6898 53718
Court Of Brixham 53705
Courtland Cir 53711
Courtyard Dr 53719
Covall St 53713
Cove Cir 53716
Coventry Trl 53713
Coyier Ln 53713
Coyne Ct 53715
Coyote Ct 53717
Crabapple Ln 53711
Craig Ave 53705
Cranbrook Cir 53719
Cranchin St 53715
Crandall St 53711
Crawford Dr 53711
Crawling Stone Cir & Rd 53719
Creekside Way 53717
Crescent Rd 53711
Crescent Oaks Ct & Dr 53704
Crest Line Dr 53704
Crested Owl Ln 53718
Crestview Dr 53716
Crestwood Dr & Pl 53705
Critchell Ter 53711
Crocus Cir 53713
Cross St 53711
Cross Hill Dr 53718
Crossbridge Ct 53717
Crossroads Dr 53718
Crowley Ave 53704
Crownhardt Cir 53704
Crystal Ln 53714
Culmen St 53713
Culpepper Ln 53718
Cumberland Ln 53714
Curry Pkwy 53713
Curtis Ct 53703
Curtis Witte B Hall 53706
Cynthia Ln 53718
Cypress Way 53713
Daffodil Ln 53714
Dahle St 53704
Dahlen Dr 53705
Dairy Dr 53718
Daisy Dr 53711
Dakota Dr 53704
Dale Ave 53705
Daley Dr 53714
Dallas Dr 53719
Damon Rd 53713
Danbury St 53711
Dandaneau Trl 53719
Dane St 53713
Daniels St 53718
Danville Dr 53719
Dapin Rd 53704
Darbo Dr 53714
Darien Cir & Dr 53717
Dartmouth Rd 53705
Darwin Rd 53704
Davenport Dr 53711
David Rd 53704
Davidson St 53716
Davies St 53716
Dawe Elizabeth Waters Hall 53706
Dawes St 53714
Dawn Rd 53704
Day Tripper Dr 53718
Dayflower Dr 53719
Daystar Ct & Rd 53704
Dayton Row 53703
E Dayton St
2-598 53703
600-1400 53703
1402-1498 53703
1900-2699 53704

W Dayton St
1-297 53703
299-599 53703
601-799 53715
716-718 53706
750-1098 53715
801-899 53706
901-1099 53715
1210-1212 53706
1214-1221 53706
1223-1225 53706
1300-1399 53715
Daytona Beach Dr 53719
De Volis Pkwy 53711
E & W Dean Ave 53716
Dearholt Rd 53711
Debra Ln 53704
Debs Rd 53704
Declaration Ln 53704
Deer Hollow Ct 53717
Deer Point Trl 53719
Deer Valley Rd 53713
Deerwood Dr 53716
Dejope Hall 53706
Del Mar Dr 53704
Delaplaine Ct 53715
Delaware Blvd 53704
Dell Dr 53718
Della Ct 53714
Delladonna Way 53704
Dellwood Cir 53716
Demilo Way 53718
Deming Way 53717
Dempsey Rd
1-999 53714
3900-4100 53716
4102-4298 53716
Dennett Dr 53714
Dennis Dr 53704
Denton Cir & Pl 53711
Derby Down 53713
Derek Rd 53704
Deschamp Ct 53718
Design Pass 53719
Detling Sellery A Hall 53706
Devon Ct 53711
Dewberry Dr 53719
Dewdrop Dr 53719
Dewey Ct 53703
Dexter St 53704
Di Loreto Ave 53704
Diamond Dr 53714
N & S Dickinson St 53703
Dickson Pl 53713
Dicky Ln 53718
Dinauer Ct 53716
Discovery Ln 53719
Diving Hawk Trl 53713
Division St 53704
Dixie Ln 53716
Dixon St 53704
Dodge St 53713
Doe Crossing Trl 53704
Dogwood Pl 53705
Dolomite Ln 53719
Dolores Ct & Dr 53716
Dolphin Dr 53719
Dominion Dr 53718
Donald Dr 53704
Doncaster Dr 53711
Dondee Rd 53716
Donofrio Dr 53719
Dons Rd 53711
Door Dr 53705
Doral Cir 53719
Dorchester Cir & Way 53719
Dorfmeister Ct 53714
Dorothy Dr 53711
Dorsett Dr 53711
Dorton Cir 53704
Dottl Ct 53713
E & W Doty St 53703
Douglas Trl 53716
Dover Pl 53716
Dovetail Dr 53704
Dow Ct 53703

Downer Cir 53714
Drake St
800-898 53715
900-1399 53715
1400-1598 53711
Dream Ln 53718
Drewry Ln 53704
Drexel Ave 53716
Driftwood Ave 53705
Driscoll Dr 53718
Droster Rd 53716
Drumhill Cir 53717
Drumlin Ln 53719
Dryden Dr 53704
Duggar Ogg Hall W 53706
Duke St 53704
Dumont Cir & Rd 53711
Duncan Dr 53714
Dunn Pl 53713
Dunning St 53704
Dunraven Ct 53705
Dunwoody Dr 53713
Durose Ter 53705
Dustin Ln 53718
Dutch Mill Rd 53716
S Dutch Mill Rd 53718
Dwight Dr 53704
Dylyn Dr 53719
Eagan Rd 53704
Eagle Hts 53705
Eagle Crest Dr 53704
Eagle Summit Ct 53718
Eagles Perch Cir & Dr 53718
Easley Ln 53714
East Blf 53704
East Ln 53704
East Pass 53719
Eastbourne Cir 53717
Easterday Ln 53706
Eastgate Rd 53716
Eastland Way 53716
Eastlawn Ct 53704
Eastpark Blvd & Ct 53718
Eastridge Ct 53716
Eastwood Dr 53704
N & S Eau Claire Ave 53705
Eberhardt Ct 53715
Eddy St 53705
Edensway Rd 53719
Edgartown Ct 53719
Edgehill Dr & Pkwy 53705
Edgewood Ave & Dr 53711
Edgewood College Dr 53711
Edna Ct 53716
Edna Taylor Pkwy 53716
Edward St 53711
Ela Ter 53716
Elder Pl 53705
Elderberry Rd 53717
Eldon Ct 53716
Eldorado Ln 53716
Elgar Cir & Ln 53704
Elinor St 53716
Eliot Ln 53704
Elizabeth St 53703
Elizabeth Waters Hall 53706
Elka Ln 53704
Ellen Ave 53716
Ellenwood Dr 53714
Ellestad Dr 53716
Ellie Cir 53714
Ellis Potter Ct 53711
Elm Dr 53706
Elm St 53726
Elmside Blvd 53704
Elmwood Ct 53719
Elna Rd 53718
Elsom Bradley Hall 53706
Elver Ct 53719
Ely Pl 53726
Ely Sellery B Hall 53706
Emerald St 53715
Emerson St 53715
Emil St 53713
Emma Ct 53716
Emmet St 53704

Engel St 53713
Engelhart Dr 53713
Engineering Dr 53706
Englewood Dr 53705
Enterprise Ln 53719
Epworth Ct 53705
Erdman Pl 53717
Erie Ct 53704
Erin St 53715
Esch Ln 53704
Esker Dr 53704
Essex Ct 53713
Esther Ct 53714
Esther Beach Rd 53713
Ethan Cir 53719
Ethelwyn Rd 53713
Eton Rdg 53726
Euclid Ave 53711
Eugenia Ave 53705
Evan Acres Rd 53718
Everest Dr 53719
Everett St 53704
Everglade Cir & Dr 53717
Evergreen Ave 53704
Ewbank Sellery B Hall 53706
Excelsior Dr 53717
Expo Mall E 53713
Express Cir 53704
Eyre Ln 53711
Fahrenbrook Ct 53715
Faincou Rd 53716
N Fair Oaks Ave 53714
S Fair Oaks Ave
2-26 53714
28-99 53714
100-299 53704
N & S Fairchild St 53703
Fairfax Ct & Ln 53718
Fairfield Pl 53704
Fairgrounds Dr 53713
Fairhaven Rd 53719
Fairlane Ct 53713
Fairmont Ave 53714
Fairview Dr & St 53704
Fairway Dr 53711
Falcon Cir 53716
Falerive Dr 53717
Falles Ct 53705
Fallows Tripp Hall 53706
Fallview Ct 53704
Falmouth Ct 53719
Farley Ave 53705
Farmco Dr 53704
Farmington Ct & Way 53717
Farragut St 53704
Farrell St 53714
Farwell Ct, Dr & St 53704
Fayette Ave 53713
Fell Rd 53713
Felland Rd 53718
Felton Pl 53705
Femrite Dr
100-1100 53716
1102-1398 53716
3100-3298 53718
3300-3499 53718
3501-3599 53718
4400-4999 53716
5001-5199 53716
5200-5899 53718
5901-6699 53718
Fen Oak Ct & Dr 53718
Ferchland Pl 53714
Fern Ct 53711
Ferris Ave 53716
N & S Few St 53703
Fiedler Ln 53713
Field St 53713
Field Crest Way 53719
Field Flower Way 53718
Fieldstone Ln 53704
Fieldwood Rd 53718
Firestone Ct 53717
Fish Hatchery Rd
1000-1098 53715
1100-1399 53715

1715-1997 53713
1999-2545 53713
2547-2605 53713
Fish Ogg Hall E 53706
Fisher St 53713
Fisk Pl 53704
Fiskdale Cir 53717
Fitchrona Rd 53719
Flad Ave & Cir 53711
Flagship Dr 53719
Flagstaff Ct 53719
Flagstone Dr 53719
Flambeau Rd 53705
Flamingo Rd 53716
Fleetwood Ave 53716
Fleischman Cir 53719
Fletcher Sellery A Hall 53706
Flint Ln 53714
Flora Ln 53714
Florence Ct 53703
Flower Ln 53717
Floyd Pl 53713
Fond Du Lac Trl 53705
Ford St 53716
Fordem Ave & Ct 53704
Forest Rdg 53704
Forest St 53726
Forest Dale Ct 53704
Forest Run Ct, Rd & Way 53704
Forge Ct & Dr 53716
Forster Dr 53704
Forsythia Pl 53705
Forward Dr 53711
Fourier Dr 53717
Fox Ave 53711
Fox Point Cir 53717
Foxboro Cir 53717
Foxglove Cir 53717
Foxwood Trl 53713
N Frances St 53703
Frankenburger Tripp Hall 53706
N Franklin Ave 53705
S Franklin Ave 53705
Franklin Ct 53705
N Franklin St 53703
S Franklin St 53703
Fraust Cir 53711
Frazer Pl 53713
Frazier Ave 53713
Frederick Cir & Ln 53711
Fredericksburg Ct & Ln 53718
Freedom Ln 53718
Freedom Ring Rd 53718
Freeport Rd 53711
Freese Ct & Ln 53718
Fremont Ave & Cir 53704
Frey St 53705
Friar Ln 53711
Frigate Dr 53705
Frisby Sellery A Hall 53706
Frisch Rd 53711
Fritz Ave 53705
Frost Woods Rd 53716
Frosted Leaf Dr 53719
Frosty Ln 53705
Fulcher Witte B Hall 53706
Fuller Ct & Dr 53704
Fulton Ln 53704
Furey Ave 53714
Gale Ct 53704
Galileo Dr 53718
Galleon Run 53718
Galley Ct 53705
Gammon Ln 53719
Gammon Pl 53719
N Gammon Rd 53717
S Gammon Rd
1-47 53717
49-300 53717
302-398 53717
400-430 53719
432-3299 53719
Gannon Ave 53714

Gannon St 53711
Ganser Way 53719
Garden View Ct 53713
Garfield St 53711
Garnet Ln 53714
Garrison St 53704
Gary St 53716
Gaston Rd 53718
Gately Ter 53711
Gateway Grn 53716
Gateway Pl 53704
Gavin Slichter Hall 53706
Gay Sellery A Hall 53706
Gem Ct 53714
Gemini Dr 53718
Gene Parks Pl 53711
E & W Geneva Cir 53717
Georgetown Ct 53719
Georgiana Cir 53716
Gerald St 53704
Geronimo Cir 53713
Gerry Ct 53715
Gettle Ave 53705
Gettysburg Dr 53705
Gifford Pinchot Dr 53726
Gilbert Ct & Rd 53711
Gillin Sellery B Hall 53706
E & W Gilman St 53703
Gilman Kronshage Hall 53706
Gilmore St 53711
Gilson St 53715
Gina Ct 53704
Gisholt Dr 53713
Glacier Cir 53719
Glacier Ct 53705
Glacier Dr 53705
Glacier Hill Dr 53705
Gladstone Dr 53719
Glen Dr 53711
Glen Hwy 53705
Glen Hollow Rd 53705
Glenbrook Cir 53711
Glendale Ln 53704
Glenside Cir 53717
Glenthistle Ct & Rd 53705
Glenview Dr 53716
Glenway St
9-13 53705
15-335 53705
337-337 53705
400-598 53711
600-729 53711
731-799 53711
Glenwood St 53711
Gleriste Dr 53718
Glory Ct 53718
Goldberg Slichter Hall 53706
Golden Gate Way 53713
Golden Leaf Trl 53704
Golden Maple Rd 53718
Golden Oak Ln 53711
Goldenrod Ln 53719
Goldfinch Dr 53714
N & S Golf Gln & Pkwy 53704
Golf Course Rd 53704
Golf View Rd 53704
Goodland Dr 53704
Goodland Park Rd 53711
Gordon Ave 53716
E & W Gorham St 53703
Goucher Ln 53716
Graceland Ave 53704
Graedel Ct 53704
Grafton Cir & Rd 53716
Graham Dr 53716
Graham Pl 53718
Grainger Hall 53706
Granby Cir 53704
Grand Ave 53705
Grand Canyon Ct 53705
Grand Canyon Dr
2-98 53705
100-300 53705
302-398 53705

400-418 53719
420-600 53719
602-698 53719
Grand Teton Plz 53719
Grandview Blvd 53713
Grandwood Ct 53714
Grant St 53711
Gray Birch Trl 53717
Gray Fox Cir & Trl 53717
Grayhawk Trl 53704
Great Gray Dr 53718
Green Ave 53704
Green Lake Pass 53705
Green Ridge Ct & Dr 53704
Greenbriar Ln 53714
Greengrass Rd 53718
Greenhaven Cir 53717
Greening Ln 53705
Greenleaf Dr 53713
Greentree Rd 53711
Greenway Rd 53716
Greenway Trl 53719
Greenway Vw 53713
Greenway Cross 53713
Greenwich Dr 53711
Greenwood St 53716
Gregg Rd 53705
Gregory St 53711
Gregory Tripp Hall 53706
Grim St 53704
Groton Ln 53711
Grove Cir 53719
Groveland Ter 53716
Grover St 53704
Gull Ln 53713
Gulseth St 53704
Gunderson St 53714
Haas St 53704
Hackberry Ln 53713
Hackney Way 53714
Hagan Dr 53704
Hagen Hill Cir 53718
Haight Rd 53705
Half Moon Ct 53718
Halley Way 53718
Hallows Cir 53704
Halo Ln 53716
N & S Hamilton St 53703
Hamlet Cir & Pl 53714
Hammersley Ave 53705
Hammersley Rd 53711
Hampshire Pl 53711
Hampton Ct 53705
N & S Hancock St 53703
Hanning Eliza Waters Hall 53706
Hanover St 53704
Hanson Rd 53704
Hansons Lndg 53704
Harbor Ct 53705
Harbor House Dr 53719
Harbort Dr 53704
Harbour Town Dr 53717
Harding St 53714
Hargrove St 53714
Harley Dr 53711
Harmony Hill Dr 53714
Harper Rd 53704
Harriman Ln 53713
Harrington Ct & Dr 53718
Harrison St
1-99 53726
600-798 53711
800-1199 53711
Hartford Ct & Dr 53719
Hartleigh Ct 53705
Harvard Dr 53705
Harvest Cir 53713
Harvest Hill Rd 53717
Harvey St 53705
Harvey Ter 53703
Harwood Cir N & S 53717
Hastings Cir 53711
Hathaway Dr 53711
Hauk St 53704
Havenswood Dr 53718

Haverhill Cir 53717
Havey Rd 53704
Hawk Feather Cir 53717
Hawkweed Ln 53719
Hawser Rd 53705
Hawthorne Ct 53715
Hayes Rd 53704
Haywood Dr 53715
Hazelcrest Dr 53704
Hazeltine Sellery A Hall 53706
Hazelwood Ct 53713
Healy Ln 53716
Heartland Trl 53717
Heath Ave 53704
Heather Crst 53705
Heather Glen Dr 53719
Heatherdell Ln 53713
Heffernan Dr 53704
Hegg Ave 53716
Heim Ave 53705
Helen White Hall 53706
Helena St 53704
Helene Pkwy 53711
Helgesen Dr 53718
Hemlock Trl 53717
Hempstead Pl & Rd 53711
Henman Bradley Hall 53706
Henry Mall 53706
N Henry St 53703
S Henry St 53703
Henshue Rd 53711
Henuah Cir 53716
Hercules Trl 53718
Heritage Cir 53711
Hermina St
2700-2999 53704
3000-3199 53714
Hermsmeier Ln 53714
Herndon Dr 53718
Herrick Dr 53706
Herrick Ln 53711
Herrick Witte B Hall 53706
Herro Ln 53716
Hey Jude Ln 53718
Hiawatha Cir & Dr 53711
Hickory Dr 53705
Hickory St 53715
Hickory Hollow Dr 53705
Hickory Ridge Rd 53719
Hidden Cave Rd 53717
Hidden Hollow Trl 53717
High St 53715
High Crossing Blvd
4800-4898 53704
5100-5198 53718
5200-5499 53718
5501-5599 53718
N High Point Ct 53717
High Point Rd 53719
N High Point Rd 53717
S High Point Rd
200-299 53717
401-497 53719
499-3000 53719
3002-3198 53719
High Point Oaks Ln 53719
High Point Woods Dr 53719
High Tower Trl 53719
High Tripp Hall 53706
Highcliff Ct & Trl 53718
Highgate Cir 53717
Highland Ave 53705
N & S Highlands Ave 53705
Highridge Rd 53718
Highview Dr 53719
S Hill Dr 53705
E Hill Pkwy 53718
Hill St 53705
Hill Elizabeth Waters Hall 53706
Hillcrest Cir & Dr 53705
Hilldale Ct & Way 53705
Hillington Grn & Way 53726
N & S Hillside Ave & Ter 53705

Hilltop Dr 53711
Hillview Ter 53711
Hilton Dr 53711
Hilton Head Dr 53719
Hintze Rd 53704
Historical Society 53706
Hitching Post Ct 53714
Hoard St 53704
Hob St 53716
Hoboken Rd 53713
Hodgson Ct 53717
Hoepker Rd
3700-3798 53718
3800-3958 53718
4082-4098 53704
4100-4200 53704
4202-4402 53704
4215-4217 53718
4351-4403 53704
4901-4999 53718
Hoff Ct 53711
Hoffman St 53704
Hohlfield Ogg Hall E 53706
Holborn Cir 53718
Holiday Dr 53711
Hollister Ave 53726
Hollow Ridge Rd 53704
Holly Ave 53711
Hollybrook Ct 53716
Hollywood Dr 53713
N & S Holt Cir, Ct & Pl 53719
Holtzman Rd 53713
Holy Cross Way 53704
Homberg Ln
1500-1799 53716
4701-4899 53718
Home Ave 53714
Homer Ct 53715
Homestead Ct & Rd 53711
Homewood Cir 53704
Honeylocust Trl 53717
Honeypie Dr 53718
Honeysuckle Ln 53713
Honor Ct 53718
Hooker Ave 53704
Hoover Dr 53714
Hopewell Dr 53718
Horned Owl Ct & Dr 53718
Horseshoe Bnd 53705
Hovde Rd 53704
Hoven Ct 53715
Howard Pl 53703
Hoyt St 53726
Hudson Ave 53704
Huegel Ct 53719
Hughes Pl 53713
Hummingbird Ln 53714
Hunter Hl 53705
Huron Hl 53711
Huxley St 53704
Hynek Rd 53714
I 94 Frontage Rd 53718
Ice Age Dr 53719
Idledale Cir 53711
Ilene Ln 53704
Imagine St 53718
Independence Ln 53704
Index Rd 53713
Indian Trce 53716
Industrial Dr 53713
N & S Ingersoll St 53703
Ingraham Hall 53706
Inner Dr 53705
Interlake Dr 53716
Interlaken Pass 53719
International Ln 53704
Inverness Dr 53717
Inverrary Ct 53717
Inwood Way 53714
Iota Ct 53703
Iowa Dr 53704
Iris Ln 53711
Iris Bloom Cir & Dr 53719
Irongate Ct & Dr 53716
Ironwood Cir & Dr 53716

Iroquois Dr 53711
Irvington Way 53713
Irwin Pl 53713
Isaac Dr 53717
Island Dr 53705
Isle Royal Dr 53705
Ivy St 53714
Jaarsma Ct 53716
Jackson St 53704
Jackson Sellery B Hall 53706
Jacobs Ct & Way 53711
Jacobson Ave 53714
Jade Ln 53714
James St 53714
Jana Ln 53704
Janie Ln 53711
Jasmine Dr 53719
Jason Cir & Pl 53719
Jay Cir & Dr 53704
Jean St 53703
Jeffers Dr 53719
Jefferson St 53711
Jeffrey Cir 53716
Jeffy Trl 53719
Jenewein Rd 53711
Jenifer St
700-1599 53703
1600-2099 53704
Jenna Dr 53704
Jerome St 53716
Jetty Dr 53705
Jewel Ct 53711
John Nolen Dr
1-99 53703
600-698 53713
700-800 53713
802-1198 53713
John Q Hammons Dr 53717
Johns St 53714
E Johnson St
1-1299 53703
1301-1499 53703
1800-1998 53704
2000-2800 53704
2802-2898 53704
W Johnson St
100-599 53703
613-899 53706
700-898 53715
900-1000 53715
1002-1098 53715
1023-1119 53706
1200-1202 53706
1201-1299 53715
Jonathon Dr 53713
Jones Kronshage Hall 53706
Jonquil Ln 53713
Jonquil Rd 53711
Joshua Cir 53714
Joss Ct 53726
Joyce Rd 53716
Joylynne Dr 53716
Juaire Witte A Hall 53706
Jubilee Cir & Ln 53718
Judd St 53714
Judy Cir & Ln 53704
Julia Cir & St 53705
Junction Ct 53717
Junction Rd 53717
S Junction Rd 53719
Juneau Rd 53705
Juneberry Dr 53718
Juniper Ave 53714
Jupiter Dr 53718
Kalas St 53716
Kanazawa Cir 53718
Karen Ct 53705
Karmichael Ct 53718
E & W Karstens Dr 53704
Katherine Ct 53718
Katie Ln 53704
Kay St 53716
Keating Ter 53711
Kedzie St 53704
Keelson Dr 53705
Keighley Cir 53719

Kellogg Eliza Waters
Hall 53706
Kelly Pl 53716
Kendall Ave
1700-2499 53726
2500-2799 53705
2801-2899 53705
Kennedy Hts & Rd 53704
Kenneth St 53711
N & S Kenosha Dr 53705
Kensington Dr 53704
Kent Ln 53713
Kenward St 53713
Kenwood St 53704
Kessel Ct 53711
Keswick Ct & Dr 53719
Kevins Way 53714
Kewaunee Ct 53705
Keyes Ave 53711
Kiekhofer Cole Hall 53706
Kilgust Rd 53713
Kilpatrick Ln 53718
Kim Ln 53704
King St 53703
Kingman Ln 53719
Kings Row 53716
Kings Way 53704
Kings Mill Cir & Way 53718
Kingsbridge Rd 53714
Kingsbury Ct 53711
Kingsford Way 53704
Kingsley Way 53713
Kingston Dr 53713
Kinsman Blvd 53704
Kiowa Ct 53713
Kipling Dr 53704
Kipp St 53718
Kirkwood Ct 53718
Knickerbocker St 53711
Knightsbridge Rd 53714
Knollwood Ct & Way 53713
Knox Ln 53711
Knutson Dr 53704
Koster St 53713
Kottke Dr 53719
Kresteller Cir 53719
Kristi Cir 53716
Kristy Rd 53718
Kroncke Dr 53711
Kronshage Dr 53706
Kronshage Hall 53706
Kropf Ave 53704
Krystana Way 53711
Kurt Dr 53714
Kvamme Ln 53716
La Belle Ln 53716
La Crescenta Cir 53716
La Crosse Ln 53705
La Follette Ave 53704
La Pointe Ter 53719
La Salle St 53713
La Sierra Way 53716
Lafayette Dr 53705
Lafollette Adams 53706
Lake Ct 53715
N Lake St
300-398 53715
401-499 53715
420-698 53706
501-699 53703
Lake Edge Blvd 53716
Lake Farm Rd 53711
Lake Mendota Dr 53705
Lake Park Blvd 53713
Lake Point Dr 53713
Lake View Ave 53704
Lakeland Ave 53704
Lakelawn Pl 53703
Lakeshore Ct 53715
Lakeside St 53711
E Lakeside St 53715
W Lakeside St 53715
E & W Lakeview Ave 53716
Lakewood Blvd 53704
Lakewood Gardens Ln 53704
Lambeth Cir 53711

Lamboley Ave 53716
Lamont Ln 53716
Lamplighter Way 53714
Lancaster Ct 53719
Lancaster Dr 53718
Lancaster Ln 53719
Lance Ln
300-499 53716
3600-3698 53718
3700-3799 53718
Landfall Dr 53705
Landmark Pl 53713
Lane St 53718
Lanett Cir 53711
Langdon St
1-699 53703
700-899 53706
Langley Ln 53718
Langlois St 53705
Lansing St 53714
Laramie Ct 53719
Larch Cir 53705
Laredo Ct 53719
Larkin St 53705
Larry Ln 53704
Larsen Rd 53711
Larson Ct 53714
Latham Dr 53713
Lathrop Dr 53706
Lathrop St 53726
Laub Ln 53711
Laurel Crst 53705
Laurel Ct 53705
Laurel Ln 53704
Laurie Dr 53711
N Lawn Ave 53704
W Lawn Ave 53711
Lawrence St 53715
Leah Ct 53711
Legacy Ln 53719
Leitch Ct 53703
Leith Ogg Hall E 53706
Leland Cir & Dr 53711
Leo Cir 53704
Leo Dr 53716
Leon St 53714
Leona Ct 53716
Leonard St 53711
Leopold Sullivan Hall 53706
Lerdahl Rd 53704
Leroy Rd 53704
Leslie Ln 53718
Levine Ct 53714
Lewis Ct 53711
Lewon Dr 53711
Lexington Ave 53714
Leyton Cir & Ln 53713
Libby Rd 53711
Liberty Ln 53718
Lien Rd
3700-4999 53704
5400-5899 53718
5901-5999 53718
Lighthouse Bay Dr 53704
Lilac Ln 53711
Lily Dr 53713
Limekiln St 53719
Lincoln Dr 53706
Lincoln St 53711
N & S Lincoln Ridge
Dr 53719
Linda Vista Rd 53716
Lindbergh St 53704
Lindemann Trl 53719
Linden Ave 53704
Linden Dr 53706
Lindfield Rd 53719
Lisa Ann Dr 53718
Little Fleur Ln 53704
Littlemore Ct & Dr 53718
N & S Livingston St 53703
Loeprich Ln 53704
Loftsgordon Ave 53704
Lofty Ave 53716
Logan St 53704
Lois Ln 53714

Lois Lowry Ln 53719
Lomax Ln 53711
Londonderry Dr 53704
Lone Eagle Dr 53713
Longmeadow Cir & Rd 53717
Longnecker Dr 53711
Longview Ln 53713
Longview St 53704
Loomis Cir 53704
Loon Ln 53717
Lorch St 53706
Lordshire Rd 53719
Loreen Dr 53711
Lorena Pkwy 53713
Loretta Ct & Ln 53716
Lori Cir 53714
Lorillard Ct 53703
Lorraine Dr 53705
Loruth Ter 53711
Lotheville Rd 53704
Lotus Ln 53718
Louden Ln 53716
Lowell St 53715
Luann Ln 53713
Lucia Crst 53705
Lucy Ln 53711
Ludington Ave 53704
Luedke Slichter Hall 53706
Lukken Ct 53704
Lumbermans Trl 53716
Lumley Rd 53711
Lupine Ln 53718
Luster Ave 53704
Lynbrook Cir & Ln 53719
Lynchburg Trl 53718
Lynn Ter 53705
Lynndale Rd 53711
Lynnhaven Rd 53714
Lynville Ct 53719
Lynwood Dr 53705
Lyons Cir 53704
Macarthur Ct & Rd 53714
Mack Kronshage Hall 53706
Maclachlan Witte A
Hall 53706
Macpherson St 53704
Madeline Is 53719
Mader Dr 53719
Madison St 53711
Magdeline Dr 53704
Magnolia Cir & Ln 53713
Maher Ave 53716
E Main St
1-97 53703
99-1099 53703
1101-1499 53703
1800-2000 53704
2002-2198 53704
W Main St
1-117 53703
119-699 53703
700-799 53715
Major Ave 53716
Malabar Ln 53711
Maldwyn Ln 53716
Malibu Dr 53713
Mallard Ln 53704
Mallory Cir 53704
Maloney Dr 53713
Malvern Hill Dr 53718
Mammoth Cir & Trl 53719
Manassas Trl 53718
Manchester Ct & Rd 53719
Mandan Cir & Cres 53711
Mandrake Rd 53704
Mangrove Ln 53713
Manhasset Pl 53711
Manitou Way 53711
Manitowish Way 53704
Manitowoc Pkwy 53705
Manley St 53704
Manning Witte A Hall 53706
Manor Dr 53713
Manor Cross 53711
Manor Green Dr 53711
Manor Hill Cir 53717

Mansion Hill Ave 53719
Manufacturers Dr 53704
Maple Ave 53704
Maple Ter 53705
Maple Grove Ct & Dr 53719
Maple Park Cir 53719
Maple Point Dr 53719
Maple Run Ct & Dr 53719
Maple Valley Ct & Dr 53719
Maple View Ct & Dr 53719
Maple Wood Ln 53704
Marathon Dr 53705
Marble Cir 53719
Marconi St 53705
Marcus Ct 53713
Marcy Rd 53704
Marg St 53716
Margaret St 53714
Maria Pl 53711
Maricopa Way 53719
Marigold Dr 53713
Mariners Cove Dr 53704
Marinette Trl 53705
Marion St 53703
Mark Twain St 53705
Marlatt Chadbourne 53706
Marmot Pass 53718
N & S Marquette St 53704
Marsh Ct & Rd 53718
Marsha Dr 53705
Marshall Ct 53705
Marshall Pkwy 53713
Marston Ave 53703
Martha Cir & Ln 53714
Martin St 53713
Martin Luther King Jr
Blvd
100-211 53703
213-215 53703
215-215 53701
Martin Witte A Hall 53706
Marty Rd 53719
Marvin Ave 53711
Maryland Dr 53704
Mason St 53705
Masters Ln 53719
Masthead Dr 53705
Mathys Rd 53716
Mayer Ave 53704
Mayfair Ave 53714
Mayfield Ln 53704
Mayhew Sellery A Hall 53706
Mayhill Dr 53711
Mayo Dr 53719
Maywick Dr 53718
Maywood Rd 53716
Maywood St 53704
Mcbride Rd 53704
Mccaffrey Sullivan Hall 53706
Mccann Rd 53714
Mcclellan Dr 53718
Mccormick Ave 53704
Mcdivitt Rd 53713
Mcguffey Dr 53717
Mckee Rd 53719
Mckenna Blvd
1000-1299 53719
1301-1697 53711
1699-2799 53711
2800-2900 53719
2902-2998 53719
Mckenna Rd 53716
Mckinley St 53705
Mclean Dr 53718
N & S Meadow Ln 53705
Meadow Ridge Ln 53704
Meadow Rose Ln 53717
Meadow Sweet Dr 53719
Meadow Vale Ct 53704
Meadow Valley Dr 53704
Meadowlark Dr
1-932 53714
934-998 53714
1100-1399 53716
Meadowood Dr 53711
Meadowview Rd 53711

Medical Cir 53719
Meek Witte B Hall 53706
Meier Rd 53718
Melby Dr 53704
Melinda Dr 53716
Melody Ln 53704
Melrose St 53704
Melvin Ct 53704
Memorial Dr 53704
Memorial Library St 53706
Memphis Ave 53714
Mendota Ct 53703
Mendota St
1101-1197 53714
1199-1399 53714
1500-1699 53704
Menomonie Ct & Ln 53704
Meredithe Ave 53716
Meriter Way 53719
Merlham Dr 53705
Merrick Ct 53704
Merrill Crest Dr 53705
Merrill Springs Rd 53705
Merritt Rdg 53718
Merry St 53704
Merryturn Rd 53714
Merwood Ln 53718
Mesa Ct 53719
Mesa Rd 53716
Mesa Verde Ct 53705
Messerschmidt Rd 53704
Mesta Ln 53704
Metro Ter 53718
Metropolitan Ln 53713
Meyer Ave 53711
Miami Pass 53711
Mica Rd 53719
Michigan Ct 53704
Mickelson Pkwy 53711
Middlebury Pl 53716
Middleton St 53717
Midland Ln 53716
Midland St 53715
Midmoor Rd 53716
Midtown Rd 53719
N Midvale Blvd 53705
S Midvale Blvd
1-399 53705
400-1300 53711
1302-1398 53711
Midwood Ave 53716
E Mifflin St
2-98 53703
100-1399 53703
1900-2599 53704
W Mifflin St 53703
Mike Mckinney Ct 53711
Milford Rd 53711
Milky Way 53718
Mill Bluff Dr 53718
Mill Creek Dr 53719
Miller Ave & St 53704
Millpond Rd 53718
N Mills St
1-199 53715
223-225 53706
250-252 53706
311-399 53715
S Mills St 53715
Millstone Rd 53717
Milo Ln 53714
Milton Ct & St 53715
Milward Dr 53711
Milwaukee St
2600-2999 53704
3000-3903 53714
3902-3902 53707
3902-3902 53708
3905-5399 53714
4000-5398 53714
5701-5997 53718
5999-6899 53718
6901-6999 53718
Minakwa Dr 53711
Mineau Pkwy 53711
Mineral Point Rd
3800-6799 53705

7000-7850 53717
7852-7898 53717
8100-8200 53719
8202-8398 53719
Minocqua Cres 53705
Minton Rd 53711
Mission Cir 53713
Mitchell St 53704
Mockingbird Ln 53704
Mohawk Cir & Dr 53711
Mohican Pass 53711
Moland St 53704
Monarch Cir 53717
Mondale Ct 53705
Monica Ln 53704
Monona Dr
3701-3899 53714
3900-4698 53716
3901-5297 53716
5299-6514 53716
6516-6598 53716
Monona Pass 53716
Monona Rdg 53716
Monroe St 53711
Montana Cir 53704
Montauk Pl 53711
Montclair Ln 53711
Monterey Dr 53704
Montgomery Dr 53716
Monticello Way 53719
Monument Ln 53704
Moorland Rd
400-1300 53713
1302-1698 53713
1701-1999 53711
Moose Trl 53704
Morgan Way 53718
Morning Rd 53704
Morningdale Cir 53717
Morningside Ave 53716
Morningstar Ln 53704
Morraine View Dr 53719
Morrison Ct & St 53703
Morrow Ct 53704
Mosinee Ln 53704
Moulton Ct 53704
Mound St
1000-1399 53715
1400-1499 53711
Mount Rainier Ln 53705
Mount Vernon Ct 53719
Mountain Ash Trl 53717
Moygara Rd 53716
Muir Dr 53704
Muir Field Rd 53719
Mulberry Cir & Ln 53711
Munn Rd 53713
Murley Dr 53718
Murray Chadbourne 53706
Mustang Way 53718
Myrtle St 53704
Naheda Trl 53711
Nakoma Rd 53711
Nakoosa Trl 53714
Namekagon Ln 53704
Nana Ln 53713
Nancy Ln 53704
Nantucket Ct 53719
Nardin Sellery A Hall 53706
Natchez Trce 53705
National Ave 53716
Nautilus Dr 53705
Navajo Trl 53716
Naylor Cir 53719
Neponset Trl 53716
Neptune Ct 53714
Nesbitt Rd 53719
Nessling St 53719
Nevada Rd 53704
New Berm Ct 53719
New Castle Way 53704
New Washburn Way 53719
Newbury Cir 53711
E & W Newhaven Cir 53717
Newport Cir 53719
Nichols Rd 53716

Street	ZIP
Niemann Pl	53711
Nishishin Trl NE	53716
No Oaks Rdg	53711
Noarts St	53711
Nob Hill Rd	53713
Nobel Ln	53704
Nokomis Ct	53711
Nondahl Cir	53718
Nora Ln	53711
Norman Way	53705
Normandy Ln	53719
Norris Ct	53703
North Ave	53713
North Ct	53704
North Pass	53719
North St	53704
Northern Ct	53703
Northfield Pl	53704
Northland Dr	53704
Northport Dr	53704
Northridge Ter	53704
Northview Dr	53704
Northwestern Ave	53704
Norwalk Cir	53717
Norway Maple Cir	53704
Norwood Pl	53726
Notting Hill Way	53718
Nottingham Way	53713
Nova Way	53704
Novation Pkwy	53713
Novick Dr	53704
Noyes Adams	53706
Nygard St	53713
Oak Ct	53716
Oak St	53704
N Oak St	53704
Oak Way	53705
Oak Creek Trl	53717
Oak Crest Ave & Pl	53705
Oak Glen Ct	53717
N Oak Grove Dr	53717
Oak Valley Dr	53704
Oak View Dr	53719
S & E Oakbridge Ct & Way	53717
E & W Oakbrook Cir	53717
Oakland Ave	53711
Oakmont Dr	53717
Oakridge Ave	53704
Oakwood Cir	53719
Obrien Ct	53714
Observatory Dr	53706
Ocean Rd	53713
Ochsner Adams	53706
Oconto Ct	53705
Odana Ct	53719
Odana Ln	53711
Odana Rd	
3600-5399	53711
5501-5597	53719
5599-6999	53719
Odell St	53711
Offshore Dr	53705
Ogden St	53714
Ogg Hall	53706
Ohio Ave	53704
Ohmeda Dr	53718
Olbrich Ave	53714
Old Camden Sq	53718
Old Gate Rd	53704
Old Meier Rd	53718
Old Middleton Rd	53705
Old Sauk Ct	53717
Old Sauk Rd	
5700-5798	53705
5800-6799	53705
6800-6898	53717
6900-7799	53717
Old Shore Rd	53704
Oldfield Rd	53717
E Olin Ave	53713
W Olin Ave	53715
Olson Sullivan Hall	53706
Olympic Dr	53705
Onaway Pass	53711
Ondossagon Ct & Way	53719
Oneida Pl	53711
Oneill Ave	53704
Onsgard Rd	53704
Ontario St	53714
Onyx Ln	53714
Opal Ct	53714
Open Wood Way	53714
Orchard Dr	
300-399	53705
400-699	53711
N Orchard St	53715
S Orchard St	53715
Orin Rd	53704
Oriole Ln	53704
Orion Trl	53718
Orton Ct	53703
Osheridan St	53715
Ottawa Trl	53711
Outlook St	53716
Overlook Ter	53705
N Owen Dr	53705
S Owen Dr	
1-399	53705
400-4399	53711
Owen Rd	53716
Owl Creek Dr	53718
Oxbow Bnd & Ct	53716
Oxford Pl	53704
Oxford Rd	53705
Oxwood Cir	53717
Ozark Trl	53705
Packers Ave	53704
Page Ogg Hall E	53706
Paget Rd	53704
Pagham Ct & Dr	53719
Painted Post Dr	53716
Palace Rd	53718
Palomino Ln	53705
Pankratz St	53704
Panther Trl	53716
Park Ln	53711
Park Pl	53705
N Park St	
2-36	53715
38-98	53715
400-500	53706
502-698	53706
S Park St	
1-13	53715
15-1699	53715
1700-2499	53713
2501-2599	53713
Park Way	53705
Park Crest Ct	53711
Park Edge Dr	53719
Park Heights Ct	53711
Park Knoll Dr	53718
Park Meadow Dr	53704
Park Ridge Dr	53719
Parker Pl	53713
Parker Hill Dr	53719
Parkinson Witte B Hall	53706
Parklawn Pl	53705
Parkside Dr	53704
Parkway Dr	53716
Parkwood Ln	53714
Parman Ter	53711
Paso Roble Way	53716
N & S Paterson St	53703
Patriot Dr	53718
Patton Witte B Hall	53706
Paul Ave	53711
Pauline Ave	53705
Paunack Ave	53711
Paunack Pl	53726
Paus St	53714
Pawling St	53704
Paxson Sellery B Hall	53706
Payson Ct	53719
Peadontr Dr	53719
Pearl Ln	53714
Pearson St	53704
Pebble Beach Cir & Dr	53717
Pebblebrook Dr	53716
Pelham Ct & Rd	53713
Pelican Cir	53716
Pendleton Dr	53718
Pennsylvania Ave	53704
Penny Ln	53718
Peony Dr	53713
Pepin Pl	53705
Pepper Wood Ct	53704
Perkins Sellery A Hall	53706
Perlman Sellery B Hall	53706
Perry St	53713
Person Elizabeth Waters Hall	53706
Petra Pl	53713
Petterle Pl	53704
Pflaum Rd	
201-497	53716
499-1500	53716
1502-4498	53716
4500-4900	53718
4902-5198	53718
Pheasant Hill Rd	53716
Pheasant Ridge Trl	53713
Phillip Ln	53711
Phillips Hall	53706
Phlox Dr	53713
Phoenix Ct	53719
Piccadilly Dr	53714
Pickford St	53711
Piedmont Ct & Rd	53711
Pierstorff St	53704
Pike Dr	53713
Pilgrim Cir & Rd	53711
Pima Dr	53719
Pin Oak Trl	53717
Pinchot Ave	53716
N & S Pinckney St	53703
Pine St	53715
Pine Grove Way	53719
Pine Ridge Trl	53717
Pine View Dr	53704
Pinecrest Dr	53714
Pinehurst Cir	53717
Pinelake Dr	53719
Pinewood Ct	53714
Pintail Cir	53717
Pioneer Rd	53711
Piper Dr	53711
Piping Rock Rd	53711
Pirate Island Rd	53716
Pitman Witte A Hall	53706
Pizarro Cir	53719
Plaenert Dr	53713
W Platte Dr	53719
Plaza Dr	53719
Pleasure Dr	53704
Plover Cir	53717
Pluto St	53718
Plymouth Cir	53705
Pocahontas Dr	53716
Point Pl	53719
Polar Bear Trl	53719
Pond Rd	53718
Pond St	53704
Pontiac Trl	53711
Ponwood Cir	53717
Poplar Creek Dr	53718
Portage Rd	
2001-2997	53704
2999-5576	53704
5578-5598	53704
5601-5607	53718
5609-5899	53718
Porter Ave	53704
Portia Ct	53718
Portland Cir & Pkwy	53714
Portsmouth Way	53714
Post Rd	53713
Potawatomi Dr	53718
Potomac Ln	53719
Potter St	53715
Powers Ave	53714
Prairie Ave	53714
Prairie Rd	
1300-2700	53711
2702-2798	53711
2800-3499	53719
Prairie Dock Dr	53718
Prairie Hill Ct & Rd	53719
Prairie Rose Rd	53704
Prairie Smoke Rd	53717
Prairieview Dr	53704
Prentice Pl	53704
Prescott Cir	53719
Presidential Ln	53711
Preston Cir & Rd	53719
Price Pl	53705
Prielann Dr	53713
Prierso Rdg	53726
Primrose Ln	53713
Princeton Ave	53726
Priscilla Ln	53705
Progress Rd	53716
Progressive Ln	53716
N Prospect Ave	53726
S Prospect Ave	
2-198	53726
500-700	53711
702-798	53711
Prospect Pl	53703
Proudfit St	53715
Provo Ct	53719
Pueblo Ct	53719
Pulley Dr	53714
Putnam Rd	53711
Quail Ridge Dr	53717
Quaker Cir	53716
Quarry Park Rd	53718
Quarterdeck Dr	53705
Quartz Ln	53719
Queens Way	53716
Queensbridge Rd	53714
Quetico Dr	53705
Quiet Ln	53714
Quincy Ave	53704
Quinn Cir	53713
Racine Rd	53705
Radcliffe Dr	53719
Radford Dr	53718
Rae Ln	53711
Rahel St	53716
Railroad St	53703
Raindine Ave	53714
Ralph Cir	53714
Ramsey Ct	53704
Ramsgate Cir	53717
Ranch House Ln	53716
N Randall Ave	
1-199	53715
201-215	53706
301-315	53715
317-399	53715
400-442	53706
444-448	53706
450-498	53706
S Randall Ave	53715
Randall Ct	53715
Randolph Dr	53717
Randy Ln	53704
Rankin Rd	53718
Raskin Cir	53719
Rattman Rd	53718
Raven Ln	53704
Ravenswood Rd	53711
Rawlings Witte A Hall	53706
Ray O Vac Dr	53711
Raymond Rd	
4900-4998	53711
5000-6599	53711
6601-6699	53711
6700-8399	53719
Raywood Rd	53713
Red Birch Run	53718
Red Cedar Trl	53717
Red Cloud Ln	53704
Red Fox Trl	53717
Red Granite Rd	53719
Red Maple Trl	53717
Red Oak Trl	53717
Redland Dr	53714
Redmound Cir	53717
Redwing Ln	53704
Redwood Ln	53711
Reetz Rd	53711
Regas Rd	53714
Regent St	
700-998	53715
1000-1399	53715
1400-1499	53711
1600-2499	53726
2700-5407	53705
5409-5699	53705
Regis Cir & Rd	53711
Reid Dr	53717
Reindahl Ave	53704
Reiner Rd	53718
Reinke Dr	53704
Remington Rd	53716
Research Park Blvd	53719
Reston Heights Dr	53718
Retana Dr	53714
Rethke Ave	53714
Revival Rdg	53711
Richard St	53714
Richardson Adams	53706
Richland Ln	53705
Ridge Rd & St	53705
Ridge Oak Dr	53704
Ridgeview Ct	53704
Ridgeway Ave	53704
Ridgewood Ave	53716
Ridgewood Way	53713
Rieder Rd	53704
Rigney Ln	53704
Rimrock Rd	53713
Ring St	53714
Risser Rd	53705
Ritz Dr	53719
Riva Rd	53711
River Pl	53716
River Bend Rd	53713
Riverside Dr	53704
Roanne Ln	53718
Roberts Ct	53711
Robertson Rd	53714
Robin Cir & Pkwy	53705
Robin Hood Way	53718
N & S Roby Rd	53726
N & S Rock Rd	53705
Rockefeller Ln	53704
Rockstream Dr	53719
Rockwell Dr	53714
Rockwood Dr	53713
Rocky Ledge Ln	53705
Rodefeld Way	53718
Rodney Ct	53715
Roe Sellery B Hall	53706
Rogers St	53703
Roigan Ter	53716
Rolfsmeyer Dr	53713
Rolla Ln	53711
Romay Ct	53711
Romford Rd	53711
N Rosa Rd	53705
S Rosa Rd	
1-200	53705
202-298	53705
441-497	53719
499-599	53719
Roseberg Rd	53719
Rosedale Ave	53714
Roselawn Ave	53716
Rosemary Ave	53714
Rosenberry Rd	53711
Rosenberry Chadbourne	53706
Rosewood Cir	53711
Ross St	53705
Ross Cole Hall	53706
Roth St	53704
Rothman Pl	53716
Rough Lee Ct	53705
Round Hill Cir	53717
Rowell St	53715
Rowland Ave	53704
Rowley Ave	53726
Roxbury Rd	53704
Royal Ave	53713
Royster Ave	53714
Ruby Ct	53714
Rudi Cir	53719
Rugby Row	53726
Rushmore Ln	53711
N Rusk Ave	53713
Rusk St	53704
Ruskin St	53704
Russell St	53704
Russell Walk	53703
Russett Rd	53711
Rustic Dr	53718
Rustic Pkwy	53713
Rustic Ridge Ct	53716
Rustic Woods Ct & Dr	53716
Ruth St	53716
Rutledge Ct	53703
Rutledge St	
1030-1036	53703
1038-1599	53703
1600-2099	53704
Ryan St	53704
Rye Cir	53717
Rylant Cir	53719
Saalsaa Rd	53711
Sabertooth Ln & Trl	53719
Sachs St	53704
Sachtjen St	53704
Saddle Stone Ln	53719
Sage Cir	53704
Saint Albans Ave	53714
Saint Andrews Cir	53717
Saint Clair St	53711
Saint Croix Ln	53705
Saint Dunstan Dr	53705
Saint James Ct	53715
Saint Lawrence Cir	53717
Saint Paul Ave	
2200-2898	53704
2901-2999	53704
3100-3298	53714
Saint Teresa Ter	53716
Salem Dr	53713
Salina Ct	53719
Salisbury Pl	53711
Sams Ct	53716
Samuel Dr	53717
San Antonio Ct	53719
San Juan Trl	53705
Sanctuary Ln	53718
Sandlewood Cir	53716
Sandpiper Ln	53716
Sandsnes Ln	53719
Sandstone Dr	53719
Sandwood Way	53713
Sandy Ct	53717
Sandy Lee Ln	53718
Santa Fe Trl	53719
Sara Rd	53711
Saratoga Cir	53705
Sargent St	53714
Saturn Dr	53718
Sauk Creek Cir & Dr	53717
Sauk Ridge Trl	
700-798	53705
800-999	53717
Sauk Woods Ct	53705
Saukdale Dr, Trl & Way	53717
W Sauthoff Rd	53704
Saw Tooth Ln	53719
Sawmill Rd	53717
Sawyer Ter	53705
Saybrook Rd	53711
Sayle St	53715
Sayner Ct	53717
Scenic Ridge Dr	53719
Schenk St	53714
Schiller Ct	53704
Schley Pass	53703
Schlimgen Ave	53704
Schlough Ct	53717
Schluter Rd	53716
Schmedeman Ave	53704
Schmitt Pl	53705
Schoenemann Ct	53719
Schoenieber Chadbourne	53706
Schofield St	53716
School Rd	53704
Schroeder Ct & Rd	53711
Schultz Pl	53716
Schurz Ave	53704
Science Ct & Dr	53711
Scofield St	53704
Scorpio Ln	53718
Scott Ln	53704
Scott Chadbourne	53706
Scranton Ct	53719
Sebring Ct	53719
Secret Bluff Dr	53719
Sedona Ct	53719
N Segoe Rd	53705
S Segoe Rd	
1-327	53705
329-399	53705
400-677	53711
679-699	53711
Seiferth Rd	53716
Sellery Hall	53706
Seminary Springs Rd	53718
Seminole Hwy	53711
Seneca Pl	53711
Sequoia Trl	53713
Serenity Trl	53719
Sessler Witte B Hall	53706
Seth Cir	53716
Sethne Ct	53716
Settlement Dr	53713
Settler Hill Cir	53717
Settlers Rd	53717
Seven Nations Dr	53713
Seven Pines Ave & Ct	53718
Severn Way	53714
Severson Dr	53718
Seybold Rd	53719
Shade Tree Ct	53717
Shady Ln	53705
Shady Leaf Rd	53718
Shady Wood Way	53714
Shaffer Ave	53716
Shagbark Ct	53719
Shale Dr	53719
Sharpsburg Dr	53718
Shasta Dr	53704
Shato Ln	53716
Shaw Ct	
3000-3099	53711
5300-5399	53705
5401-5499	53705
Shawano Ter	53705
Shawnee Pass	53711
Shea Ct	53717
Shearwater St	53714
Sheboygan Ave	53705
Sheffield Rd	53711
Shefford Cir & Dr	53719
Sheldon St	53711
Shelley Ln	53704
Shenandoah Way	53705
Shepard Ter	53705
Sheridan Dr & St	53704
Sherman Ave	
1000-1299	53703
1301-1399	53703
1600-2299	53704
N Sherman Ave	53704
Sherman Ter	53704
Sherven Dr	53716
Sherwood Rd	53711
Shiloh Ct & Dr	53705
Shopko Dr	53704
S & W Shore Dr	53715
Shore Acres Rd	53716
Shoreham Dr	53711
Shorewood Blvd	53705
Short St	53715
Showerman Kronshage Hall	53706
Sidney St	53703
Siebecker Adams	53706

Sierra Ct 53713
Siggelkow Rd 53718
N Sillesto St 53703
Silver Rd 53714
Silver Dawn Dr 53718
Silverton Trl 53719
Silvertree Run 53705
Singleton Ct 53711
Sinykin Cir 53714
Sioux Trl 53716
Sirloin Strip 53713
Siskiwit Cir 53719
Ski Ct & Ln 53713
Sky Ridge Dr 53719
E & W Skyline Dr 53705
Skyview Pl 53713
Sleepy Lagoon Dr 53716
Slichter Hall 53706
Sloan Blvd 53704
Smith Hall 53715
Snow Cole Hall 53706
Snowcap Trl 53719
Snowflake Ct 53719
Snowmist Trl 53719
Snowy Pkwy 53719
Somerset Ln 53711
Sommers Ave 53704
Sonora Ct 53719
South Ct 53704
South St 53715
Southern Cir 53716
Southern Oak Pl 53719
Southern Ridge Trl 53719
Southridge Ct & Dr 53704
Southwick Cir 53717
Spaanem Ave 53716
Spaight St
800-1399 53703
1401-1599 53703
1800-1899 53704
Sparkle Ct 53703
Spear Cir 53713
Speedway Rd 53705
Spenser Ln 53704
Spicebush Ln 53714
Splint Rd 53718
Spohn Ave 53704
N Spooner St 53726
S Spooner St
1-99 53726
501-699 53711
Spooner Tripp Hall 53706
Sprague St 53711
Sprecher Rd 53718
Spring Ct 53705
Spring St 53715
Spring Trl 53711
Spring Harbor Dr 53705
Springfield Ct 53719
E Springs Dr 53704
Springview Ct 53704
Springwood Cir 53717
Spruce St 53715
E & W Spyglass Ct 53717
Squaw Cir 53716
Stacy Ln 53716
Stadium Dr 53705
Stage House Trl 53714
Stagecoach Trl 53717
Standish Ct 53705
Stang St 53704
Stanton Cir & Ln 53719
N Star Dr 53718
Star Fire Ct 53719
Star Spangled Trl 53718
Starflower Dr 53719
Starker Ave 53716
Starlight Dr 53711
Starling Ln 53704
Starr Ct 53711
Starr Grass Dr 53719
Starry Ave 53716
State St
100-699 53703
701-899 53703
728-898 53706
State Road 113 53704
Steensland Dr 53704
Stein Ave 53714
Steinhauer Trl 53716
Steinies Dr 53714
Stemp Ter 53711
Stevens St 53705
Stewart St 53713
Stockbridge Dr 53718
Stockton Ct 53711
Stone Ter 53716
Stone Corner Cir 53704
N & S Stone Creek
Cir 53719
Stone Crest Cir 53717
Stonebridge Dr 53719
Stonecreek Dr 53719
Stonefield Ter 53717
Stonehaven Dr 53716
Stonehedge Ct 53717
N Stoughton Rd
1200-1498 53714
1500-1599 53704
1601-2299 53704
S Stoughton Rd
1-299 53714
1201-1797 53716
1799-2699 53716
2701-3099 53716
Stratford Dr 53719
N & S Strathfield Cir 53717
Strathmore Ln 53711
Stratton Way 53719
Straubel Ct & St 53704
Struck St
600-699 53719
700-799 53711
733-733 53744
801-899 53711
Stuart Ct 53704
Sturbridge Cir 53717
Sudbury Way 53714
Sue Pl 53705
Suffolk Rd 53711
Sugar Maple Trl 53717
Sullivan Hall 53706
Sumac Dr 53705
Summer Ridge Dr 53704
Summertown Dr 53718
Summerview Ct 53704
Summit Ave 53726
Summit Rd 53704
Sumter Ct 53705
Sunbrook Rd 53704
Sunburst Rd 53718
Sundown Ct 53704
Sundstrom St 53713
Sunfield St 53704
Sunfish Ct 53713
Sunhill Dr 53718
Sunny Meade Ln 53713
Sunnyside Cres 53704
N & S Sunnyvale Ln 53713
Sunridge Dr 53711
E, N, S & W Sunset Ct
& Dr 53705
Superior St 53704
Surrey Cir 53704
Susan Cir & Ln 53704
Susan Davis Hall 53715
Sussex Ln 53714
Sutherland Ct 53704
Sutteridge Trl 53704
Sutton Rd 53711
Swallowtail Dr 53717
Swanton Rd 53714
Swarthmore Ct 53705
Sweetbriar Rd 53705
Swenson Kronshage
Hall 53706
Sycamore Ave
3800-4300 53714
4302-4498 53714
4600-4798 53704
5001-5099 53704
Syene Rd 53713
Sylvan Ave 53705
Sylvan Ln 53716
Taft St 53713
Tail Water Dr 53719
Talc Trl 53719
Talisman Ln 53704
Tallyho Ln 53705
Talmadge St 53704
Tamarron Ct 53719
Tanager Trl 53711
Tancho Dr 53718
Tanglewood Dr 53719
Tarragon Dr 53716
Tarrant Adams 53706
Tasman St 53714
Taunton Cir 53719
Tawhee Dr 53711
Taychopera Rd 53705
Taylor St 53713
Teal Dr 53711
Tecumseh Ave 53716
Temkin Ave 53705
Tempe Dr 53719
Temple Ct 53705
Tennessee Trl 53704
Tennyson Ln 53704
Terminal Dr 53718
Tern Cir 53716
E & W Terrace Ct &
Dr 53718
Terre Haute Ave 53705
Terry Pl 53711
Tesla Ter 53705
Texas Trl 53704
Thackeray Rd 53704
Theresa Ter 53711
Thierer Rd 53704
N Thompson Dr
1-499 53714
700-1699 53704
S Thompson Dr
1-199 53714
801-997 53716
999-2299 53716
Thorn Ln 53711
Thornebury Dr 53719
Thornhill Cir 53717
N & S Thornton Ave 53703
Thorp St 53714
Thorstrand Rd 53705
Thrush Ln 53711
Thunderbird Ln 53716
Thurber Ave 53714
Thurston Ln 53711
Tiller Trl 53719
Timber Lake Trl 53719
Timber Run Ct 53719
Timber Wolf Trl 53717
Timberwood Ct & Dr 53719
Timothy Ave 53716
Toban Dr 53704
Tocora Ln 53711
Todd Dr 53713
Toepfer Ave 53711
Togstad Glenn 53711
Tokay Blvd
4000-5199 53711
5201-5399 53711
5700-5799 53719
Tolman Ter 53711
Tomahawk Trl 53705
Tompkins Dr 53716
Tomscot Trl 53704
Tonkinese Trl 53719
Tony Dr 53704
Tonyawatha Trl 53716
Topaz Ln 53714
Topping Rd 53705
Toribrooke Ln 53719
Tormey Ln 53718
Torrey Pines Ct 53717
Tottenham Rd 53711
Town Center Dr 53718
E Towne Blvd 53704
S Towne Dr 53713
E Towne Mall 53704
W Towne Mall 53719
E Towne Way 53704
W Towne Way 53719
Traceway Dr 53713
Tradewinds Pkwy 53718
Tradition Ave 53719
Trafalger Pl 53714
Trailsway 53704
Tramore Trl 53717
Transport Ct 53704
Traveler Ln 53718
Travis Ter 53711
Tree Ln 53717
Tree Ridge Trl 53718
Treichel St 53718
Trempealeau Trl 53705
Trevor Way 53719
Trilling Eliza Waters
Hall 53706
Trillium Ct 53719
Tripp Cir 53706
Tripp Hall 53706
Troxell Eliza Waters
Hall 53706
Troy Dr 53704
Truax Ct 53704
Tucson Trl 53719
Tulane Ave 53714
Tulip Ln 53713
Tumalo Trl 53711
Turbot Dr 53713
Turnberry Rd 53719
Turner Ave 53716
Turner Kronshage Hall 53706
Turning Leaf Dr 53719
Turquoise Ln 53714
Twilight Trl 53716
Twin Oaks Dr 53714
Twin Pines Dr 53704
Twinflower Dr 53719
Twinleaf Ln 53719
Tyler Cir 53716
Underdahl Rd 53718
Union St
2600-2999 53704
3000-3099 53714
Unity Way 53718
University Ave
500-599 53703
600-739 53715
740-818 53706
741-799 53715
820-1000 53706
1001-1099 53715
1002-1430 53706
1101-1103 53706
1121-1199 53715
1217-1225 53706
1401-1499 53715
1501-1513 53706
1552-1606 53726
1608-2499 53726
2500-6099 53705
6101-6239 53705
University Row 53705
University Bay Dr 53705
University Houses 53705
Upham St 53704
Upland Dr 53705
Urich Ter 53719
Us Highway 12 And
18 53718
Us Highway 51 53704
Utah Ct 53704
Vahlen St 53704
Vale Cir 53711
E & W Valhalla Ct, Trl &
Way 53719
Valley Rd 53714
Valley St 53718
Valley Edge Dr 53704
E & W Valley Ridge
Dr 53719
Valley Stream Dr 53711
Valleyhigh Dr 53718
Valor Cir & Way 53718
Valorie Ln 53716
Van Buren St 53711
Van Deusen St 53715
Van Hise Ave
1700-2300 53726
2302-2498 53726
2500-2899 53705
Van Hise Hall 53706
Van Vleck Hall 53706
Varsity Hl 53705
Vaughn Ct 53705
Veblen Pl 53705
Veith Ave 53704
Velvet Leaf Dr 53719
Venetian Ln 53718
Venus Way 53718
Vera Ct 53704
Verde Ct 53719
Vermont Cir 53704
Vernon Ave
500-999 53714
1000-1199 53716
Vernon Blvd 53705
Vernon Rd 53704
Verona Rd 53711
Veterans Dr 53713
Viburnum Dr 53705
Vicar Ln 53714
Vicksburg Ct & Rd 53718
Victoria Ln 53704
Vidon Dr 53704
Vienna Cir & Ln 53718
View Rd 53711
S View Rd 53719
Vilas Ave
900-1399 53715
1401-2000 53711
2002-2198 53711
Vilas Rd 53718
Vilas Tripp Hall 53706
Village Ln 53704
E & W Village Crest
Dr 53719
Village Green Ln E &
W 53704
Village Park Dr 53718
Vinje Ct 53716
Violet Cir & Ln 53714
Virginia Ter 53726
Vista Rd 53726
Voges Rd 53718
Vogts Ln 53716
Vondron Rd
1400-2199 53716
2200-2418 53718
2420-2498 53718
Waban Hl 53711
Wagon Trl 53716
Waite Cir & Ln 53711
Wakefield St 53711
Wakeman St 53705
Walbridge Ave 53714
Walden Way 53719
Waldorf Blvd 53719
Wales Sellery A Hall 53706
Walker Dr 53714
Wall St 53718
Wallace Ave 53716
Wallerstein
Chadbourne 53706
Wallingford Cir 53717
Walnut St 53726
Walnut Grove Dr 53717
Walsh Rd 53714
Walter St 53714
Waltham Cir & Rd 53711
Walton Pl 53704
Walton Commons Ln 53718
Walworth Ct 53705
Wanda Pl 53711
Wanebo Ln 53719
Wanetah Trl 53711
Warbler Ln 53704
Ward Ct 53713
Warner Dr 53704
Warner Ln 53713
Warner St 53713
Warrior Ln 53704
Warwick Way 53711
Washburn Pl 53703
Washburne Witte A
Hall 53706
E Washington Ave
101-197 53703
199-1499 53703
1800-3900 53704
3902-4898 53704
W Washington Ave
100-699 53703
701-797 53715
799-800 53715
802-898 53715
Washington Pl 53703
Waterford Cir & Rd 53719
Waterman Way 53716
Watford Way 53713
Watson Ave 53713
Watts Rd 53719
Waubesa Ave 53711
Waubesa St 53704
Waucheeta Trl 53711
Waukesha St 53705
Waunona Way 53713
Waunona Woods Ct 53713
Waupaca Ct 53705
Waushara Cir 53705
Waverly Pl 53705
Waxwing Ln 53704
Wayland Dr 53713
Wayne St 53714
Wayne Ter 53718
Wayridge Dr 53704
Waywood Cir 53704
Webb Ave 53714
Weber Dr 53713
N & S Webster St 53703
Wedgewood Way 53711
Weeping Birch Cir 53704
Weir Cir 53719
Welch Ave 53704
Wellesley Rd 53705
Wells Ave 53714
Welton Dr 53719
Wembly Cir 53719
Wendy Ln 53716
Wentworth Cir & Dr 53719
West Ln 53704
Westbourne St 53719
Westbrook Cir & Ln 53711
Westbury Pl 53711
Westend Cir 53704
Westerfield Ln 53704
Western Ave 53711
Western Rd 53705
N & S Westfield Rd 53717
Westgate Mall 53711
Westgate Rd 53716
Westin Dr 53719
Westminster Ct 53714
Westmorland Blvd
200-399 53705
400-599 53711
Westover Ct 53719
Westport Rd 53704
Westridge Cir 53704
Westview Ln 53713
Westward Way 53717
Westwood Ct 53714
Westwynn Cir 53704
Whalen Ln 53713
Wheeler Ct & Rd 53704
Whenona Dr 53711
Whitacre Rd 53717
Whitbeck Sellery B
Hall 53706
Whitcomb Cir & Dr 53711
White Aspen Rd 53704
White Oaks Ln 53711
White Pine Trl 53717
Whitefish Ct 53718
Whitehall Dr 53714
Whitetail Ln 53704
Whitlock Rd 53719
N Whitney Way 53705
S Whitney Way
1-300 53705
302-398 53705
600-2299 53711
Whittier St 53715
Wichita Ct 53719
N & S Wickham Ct 53711
Wicklow Way 53711
Widgeon Way 53717
Wild Indigo Ln 53717
Wild Oak Cir 53713
Wildberry Dr 53719
Wilder Dr 53704
Wilkinson Chadbourne 53706
Willard Ave 53704
Williams Cir 53719
Williamsburg Way 53719
Williamson St 53703
Willow Dr 53706
Willow Ln 53705
Willowbrook Ct 53719
Wilshire Ln 53714
E & W Wilson St 53703
Wilton Ct 53704
Wimbledon Way 53713
Winchester St 53704
Wind Stone Dr 53718
Windflower Way 53711
Windhaven Cir 53717
Windigo Trl 53711
Windom Way 53704
Windsor Ct 53714
N Wingra Dr 53715
W Wingra Dr
401-499 53713
700-898 53715
820-820 53725
900-998 53715
Wingra St 53715
Wingra Creek Pkwy 53715
Winn Trl 53704
Winnebago St 53704
Winnemac Ave 53711
E Winnequah Dr, Rd &
Trl 53716
Winslow Ln 53711
Winslow Faville
Adams 53706
Winston Dr 53711
Winstone Dr 53711
Winter Park Pl 53719
Winterberry Trl 53717
Wintergreen Dr 53704
Winterset Cir 53717
Winterview Ct 53704
Wirth Ct 53704
Wisconsin Ave & Pl 53703
Withey Ogg Hall E 53706
Witte Hall 53706
Wittwer Rd 53714
Wolf St 53717
Wolfe Ogg Hall E 53706
Wood Cir & Ln 53705
Wood Chadbourne 53706
Wood Crest Ct 53705
Wood Reed Dr 53719
Wood Violet Way 53717
Woodburn Dr 53711
Woodcroft Cir 53719
Woodglen Ct & Trl 53716
Woodington Way 53711
Woodland Cir 53704
Woodland Way 53711
Woodlawn Dr 53716
Woodley Ln 53713
N & S Woodmont Cir 53717
Woodridge Ct 53704
Woodridge Rd 53716
Woodrow St 53711
Woods End 53711
Woodside Ter 53711
Woodstock Cir 53716
Woodstone Dr 53719
Woodvale Cir & Dr 53716

Woodview Ct 53713
Woodward Dr 53704
Woody Ln 53716
Wopat Ln 53719
World Dairy Dr 53718
Worthington Ave 53714
Wright St 53704
Wyalusing Dr 53718
Wyldewood Cir & Dr 53704
Wyldhaven Ave 53716
Wynbrook Cir 53704
Wynnwood Way 53705
Wynter Ln 53718
Wyoming Way 53704
Wyota Ave 53711
Yahara Pl 53704
Yale Rd 53705
Yarrow Cir 53719
Yellowcress Dr 53719
Yellowstone Ct 53705
N Yellowstone Dr 53705
S Yellowstone Dr
1-399 53705
401-417 53719
419-499 53719
501-599 53719
Yesterday Dr 53718
York St 53711
Yorkshire Rd 53711
Yorktown Cir 53711
Yosemite Pl & Trl 53705
Young Witte A Hall 53706
Yuma Dr 53711
Zeier Rd 53704
Zeno St 53704
Ziegler Rd 53714
Zor Shrine Pl 53719
Zuercher Ct 53711
Zwerg Dr 53705

NUMBERED STREETS

N & S 1st 53704
N & S 2nd 53704
3rd Ave 53713
3rd St 53711
N 3rd St 53704
N & S 4th 53704
N & S 5th 53704
N 6th St 53704
N 7th St 53704
N 8th St 53704

MANITOWOC WI

General Delivery 54220

POST OFFICE BOXES MAIN OFFICE STATIONS AND BRANCHES

Box No.s
All PO Boxes 54221

NAMED STREETS

All Street Addresses 54220

NUMBERED STREETS

All Street Addresses 54220

MENOMONEE FALLS WI

General Delivery 53051

POST OFFICE BOXES MAIN OFFICE STATIONS AND BRANCHES

Box No.s
All PO Boxes 53052

NAMED STREETS

Aberdeen Dr 53051
Acacia Ct 53051
Ada Ct 53051
Adamdale Dr 53051
Addison Rd 53051
Albert Pl 53051
Allen Ave 53051
Alpine Ln 53051
Amberleigh Cir 53051
Amy Ln 53051
Ann Ave & Ct 53051
Anthony Ave 53051
Antler Dr 53051
Apple Blossom Ln 53051
Apple Tree Ct 53051
Apple Valley Dr 53051
Appleton Ave 53051
Arbor Ln 53051
Arbor Vitae Ct 53051
Arrowhead Ct 53051
Arthur Ave 53051
Aryshire Ct 53051
Ash Dr 53051
Aspen Dr 53051
Auburn Ct 53051
Autumn View Ln 53051
Azalea Rd 53051
Badger Dr 53051
Balsam Ct & Dr 53051
Bancroft Dr 53051
Barberry Rd 53051
Bay Ridge Ct & Ln 53051
Beacon St 53051
Beaver Dr 53051
Beechnut Rd 53051
Beechwood Dr 53051
Belleview Blvd 53051
Bette Dr 53051
Birch Ln 53051
Bittersweet Ln 53051
Blackfoot Dr 53051
Blair Ct 53051
Blue Heron Dr 53051
Blue Spruce Ct 53051
Bluejay Ct 53051
Bobolink Ave 53051
Bonnie Ln 53051
Boundary Rd 53051
Bradley Cir 53051
Brahm Ct 53051
Brehmer Ter 53051
Brentwood Dr 53051
Brian Ct 53051
Briarwood Ter 53051
Brook Falls Dr 53051
Brookside Dr 53051
Bryn Mawr Ct 53051
Butternut Dr 53051
Caitlin Ct 53051
Camelot Ct 53051
Campbell Ct & Dr 53051
Campus Ct 53051
Canary Dr 53051
Cardinal Ct 53051
Carl Ross Dr 53051
Carmen Ave 53051
Carol Ct & Dr 53051
Caroline Dr 53051
Carters Crossing Cir 53051
Cattail Ct 53051
Cedar Ridge Ln 53051
Chapel Ct 53051
Charles Ct & Dr 53051
Chase Ave 53051
Chateau Dr 53051
Cherokee Dr 53051
Cherry Ct & Ln 53051
Cherry Hill Dr 53051
Cheryln Dr 53051
Chestnut Ct & Rd 53051
Cheyenne Dr 53051
Chippewa Dr 53051
Christman Rd 53051
Christopher Blvd & Ct 53051
Church St 53051
Cindy Cir & Ct 53051
Circle Ct 53051
Claas Rd 53051
Clare Dr 53051
Claremore Cir 53051
Cleveland Ave 53051
Clover Ln 53051
Club Circle Dr 53051
Cobblestone Ct & Dr 53051
Colony Rd 53051
Columbine Ct 53051
Commerce Dr 53051
Community Dr 53051
Continental Pkwy 53051
Cornflower Ct 53051
Corryton Ct 53051
Country Ln 53051
Country Club Ct & Dr 53051
Country Terrace Ln 53051
Countryside Dr 53051
County Line Rd 53051
Coventry Ct 53051
Crabapple Ct 53051
Creek View Ct 53051
Creekwood Xing 53051
Crestview Ter 53051
Crestwood Dr 53051
Crimson Ct 53051
Crossview Way 53051
Crossway Dr 53051
Cumberland Ct & Rd 53051
Custer Ln 53051
Danell Dr 53051
Dardis Ave & Pl 53051
Daylily Ct & Dr 53051
Deer Trl 53051
Deerfield Trl 53051
Denice Ave 53051
Destiny Dr 53051
Devon Wood Rd 53051
Dial Ct 53051
Dolores Ln 53051
Dolphin Dr 53051
Donald Ave & Ct 53051
Doris Ct 53051
Duke Ct & St 53051
Eagle Ct 53051
Eastwood Dr 53051
Edelweiss Ln 53051
Edgemont Dr 53051
Edgewood Pl 53051
Eileen Ave 53051
El Camino Dr 53051
El Portal Ct 53051
El Rio Ct & Dr 53051
Elder Ln 53051
Ellie Ct 53051
Elm Ln 53051
Elm Tree Ln 53051
Elmway Dr 53051
Elmwood Dr 53051
Elsie Ave 53051
Emerald Hills Dr 53051
Enterprise Ave 53051
Erika Rd 53051
Esquire Rd 53051
Evelyn Ter 53051
Evergreen Ln 53051
Executive Pkwy 53051
Fair Oak Ct & Pkwy 53051
Fairfield Ct 53051
Fairmount Ave 53051
Fairview Dr 53051
Fairway Ct 53051
Falls Ave & Pkwy 53051
Falls Creek Ct 53051
Fawn Ave 53051
Faye Ct 53051
Fieldcrest Ct 53051
Fillmore Dr 53051
Fleet Ave 53051
Flint Dr 53051
Flora Dr 53051
Florence Ave 53051
Fond Du Lac Ave 53051
Forest Dr 53051
Fountain Blvd 53051
Fox Ridge Ct & Dr 53051
Fox River Way 53051
Foxview Ct 53051
Franklin Dr 53051
Freedom Ct 53051
Garden Ave 53051
Garfield Dr 53051
Garwin Mace Dr 53051
Georgetown Dr 53051
Glenmeadow Ct 53051
Glenview Ct & Dr 53051
Goetz Ct 53051
Golden Fields Ct & Dr 53051
Goldenrod Dr 53051
Golfview Ct & Dr 53051
Golfway Dr 53051
Good Hope Rd 53051
Goode Ave 53051
Grand Ave 53051
Grant Ave 53051
Graysland Dr E 53051
Green Crane Dr 53051
Green Hill Ct 53051
Green Meadow Ct 53051
Greenview Ave & Ct 53051
Greenway Cir 53051
Grey Log Ln 53051
Grove St 53051
Hale Ave 53051
Hampton Ave 53051
Harding Dr 53051
Harrison Ave 53051
Hawthorne Dr 53051
Hayes Ave 53051
Haymeadow Rd 53051
Hazel K Cir 53051
Held Dr 53051
Hemlock Ct 53051
Henry Stark Rd 53051
Heritage Ct 53051
Heritage Reserve 53051
Heron Ct 53051
Hi Mount Ct 53051
Hiawatha Ave & Ct 53051
Hickory Hollow Ct 53051
Hickory Tree Ln 53051
Hidden Ln 53051
Hidden Hollow Ct 53051
Hidden Meadow Ct & Dr 53051
Hidden Way Dr 53051
High Point Ave 53051
Highland Ct & Dr 53051
Highland Heights Ct 53051
Highridge Dr 53051
Hillcrest Dr 53051
N Hills Dr 53051
Hillside Ln 53051
Hilltop Dr 53051
Hillview Dr 53051
Homestead Dr 53051
Honey Ln 53051
Honey Suckle Ln 53051
Hope Ln 53051
Horse Chestnut Ct 53051
Houston Dr 53051
How Ave 53051
Hoyt Dr 53051
Hummingbird Way 53051
Hunters Ridge Cir 53051
Imperial Ct 53051
Independence Ln 53051
Industrial Ave 53051
Invery Dr 53051
Irene Dr 53051
Jacklin Ct 53051
Jackson Dr 53051
Jacob Ln 53051
Jacobson Dr 53051
James Ave 53051
Jarod Ct 53051
Jay Dr 53051
Jefferson Ave 53051
Jerry Ln 53051
Joanne Dr 53051
Joetta Dr 53051
Joper Rd 53051
Joss Pl 53051
Judith Ln 53051
Juniper Ln 53051
Kathrn Ave 53051
Kaul Ave 53051
Keith Cir 53051
Kendel Pl 53051
Kenmore Dr 53051
Kenny Ln 53051
Kenwood Blvd 53051
King David Ct 53051
Kings Hwy 53051
Knoll Ter 53051
Kohler Ln 53051
Kolbrook Ct 53051
Kristen Ct 53051
Lake Park Dr 53051
Lakewood Ct 53051
Lambs Ln 53051
Lancaster Ave 53051
Landover Ct 53051
Lannon Rd 53051
Lari Lou Ct & Dr 53051
Larkspur Ln 53051
Laurel Ln 53051
Lavender Lilac Ln 53051
Lavergne Ave & Ct 53051
Lawrence Ave & Ct 53051
Le Mons Dr 53051
Leatherwood Ct 53051
Lee Pl 53051
Legend Ct 53051
Leon Rd 53051
Leona Ln 53051
Lexington Dr 53051
Lilac Ct & Ln 53051
Lilly Ct & Rd 53051
Lilly Creek Dr 53051
Lincoln Ln 53051
Linden Ct & Ln 53051
Lisbon Rd 53051
Lloyd Ave 53051
Logan Dr 53051
Lomas Ln 53051
Lone Oak Ln 53051
Longwood St 53051
Lost Pond Ct & Dr 53051
Lucerne Dr 53051
Lulu Ct 53051
Lund Cir & Ln 53051
Lynwood Dr 53051
Macallan Ct 53051
Macarthur Dr 53051
Maclynn Ct & Dr 53051
Madison Ave 53051
Main St 53051
Manchester Dr 53051
Manhardt Dr 53051
Manhattan Dr 53051
Manor Hills Blvd & Ct 53051
Maple Rd 53051
Maple Crest Ln 53051
Marach Rd 53051
Marcy Rd 53051
Mardene Ave 53051
Margaret Rd 53051
Marion Ct 53051
Market Dr 53051
Marshall Dr 53051
Marson Ct 53051
Martin Dr 53051
Marvel Dr 53051
Mary Ct 53051
Mary Dale Dr 53051
Maryhill Dr 53051
May Ave 53051
Mckinley Dr 53051
Mclaughlin Dr 53051
Meadow Ct 53051
Meadow Lark Ln 53051
Meadow View Rd 53051
Meadowland Dr 53051
Meastanc Dr 53051
Megal Dr 53051
Melanie Ln 53051
Melody Ln 53051
Melville Dr 53051
Memorial Ct & Dr 53051
Memory Rd 53051
Menomonee Ave 53051
Menomonee Manor Ct & Dr 53051
Menomonee River Pkwy 53051
Merrimac Dr 53051
Mesa Ct & Dr 53051
Mill Rd & St 53051
Mill Creek Ct 53051
Mill Ridge Dr 53051
Mineola Dr 53051
Monroe Ave 53051
Mulberry Ln 53051
Narrow Ln 53051
Nath Ct 53051
Nelson Ln 53051
Nicolet Ct 53051
Norman Dr 53051
Northfield Dr 53051
Northpark Dr 53051
Northpoint Ct & Dr 53051
Northway Dr 53051
Northwood Dr 53051
Norxway Ave 53051
Oak Ln 53051
Oak Ridge Trl 53051
Oakwood Dr 53051
Old Gate Rd 53051
Old Hickory Rd 53051
Old Orchard Ct & Rd 53051
One Mile Rd 53051
Orchard Ct 53051
Overlook Ct, Dr & Trl 53051
Overview Dr 53051
Oxford Ct & St 53051
Pageant Dr 53051
Papoose Dr 53051
Park Blvd 53051
Parkview Dr 53051
Parkway Dr 53051
Parkwood Ct 53051
Paseo Cir, Ct & Ln 53051
Patio Ct 53051
Patricia Pl 53051
Patrician Pkwy 53051
Patrita Dr 53051
Patton Dr 53051
Pebble Ct 53051
Pershing Ave 53051
Pheasant Ln 53051
Pilgrim Rd 53051
Pin Oak Ct 53051
Pine Tree Ct 53051
Pineview Ct 53051
Pinewood Cir & Trl 53051
Plainview Dr 53051
Plata Ct 53051
Plateau Dr 53051
Plaza Dr 53051
Pleasant St 53051
Pleasant View Dr 53051
Pocahontas Dr 53051
Pontiac Dr 53051
Poplar Ct & Dr 53051
Prairie Ln 53051
Prairie Dawn 53051
Prairie Sky Ct 53051
Premier Ln 53051
Princeway Dr 53051
Prudence Dr 53051
Pueblo St 53051
Queensway St 53051
Rainbow Dr 53051
Ranch Rd 53051
Raven Way Dr 53051
Ravenwood Dr 53051
Ravine Dr 53051
Red Cloud Ct 53051
Red Crown Trl 53051
Red Oak Ct 53051
Redbud Ln 53051
Redwood Dr 53051
Reichert Ave 53051
Remington Trl 53051
Renee Dr 53051
Revere Dr 53051
Richmond Dr 53051
Ridge Ct & Rd 53051
Ridgeline Trl 53051
Ridgeview Dr 53051
Ridgeway Ln 53051
Ridgewood Ct & Dr 53051
River Ct, Dr & Rd 53051
River Crest Dr 53051
River Heights Ct & Dr 53051
River Park Dr 53051
Riverlands Cir 53051
Riverside Bluff Rd 53051
Roanoke Ct 53051
Robert Ave 53051
Robin Cir 53051
Robinhood Dr 53051
Roger Ave 53051
Rolling Ridge Dr 53051
Roman Ct 53051
Ronald Dr 53051
Roosevelt Dr 53051
Roseway Ave 53051
Rosewood Dr 53051
Rosslyn Ave 53051
Rozanne Dr 53051
Ruby Rd 53051
Russel Ct 53051
Saint Andrews Cir, Ct & Dr 53051
Saint Francis Dr
N90W17499-N90W17699 53051
Saint George Ct 53051
Saint James Dr 53051
Saint Mark Dr 53051
Saint Regis Dr 53051
Saint Stevens Ct & Dr 53051
Saint Thomas Dr 53051
Sandhill Ct 53051
Santa Barbara Ct 53051
Saxony Dr 53051
Scenic Dr 53051
Schlafer Dr 53051
Schlei Rd 53051
Schneider Dr 53051
Scott Ln 53051
Seneca Ct & Dr 53051
Settlers Ct 53051
Shady Ln 53051
Shagbark Rd 53051
Sharonrose Ln 53051
Sharptail Ct 53051
Shawn Cir 53051
Sheffield Ct & Ln 53051
Shenandoah Dr 53051
Shepherd Dr 53051
Sheridan Dr 53051
Sherwood Dr 53051
Shore Crest Dr 53051
Silver Meadows Dr 53051
Silver Spring Dr & Rd 53051
Skyline Dr 53051
Somerset Dr 53051
Spencers Ct & Pass 53051
Spruce Ln 53051
Stanley Dr 53051
State Road 145 53051
Steven Mack Cir & Dr 53051
Stone Dr 53051
Stonefield Ct & Rd 53051
Stoneridge Ct & Dr 53051
Stonewood Cir & Dr 53051
Stony Ct 53051
Sumac Ct & St 53051
Summit Dr 53051
Sunburst Dr 53051
Sunny Cir 53051
Sunny Dale Dr 53051
Sunset Ridge Dr 53051
Sunset View Dr 53051

Susan Dr ... 53051
Sycamore Ln ... 53051
Sylvan Ln ... 53051
Tall Oak Ct ... 53051
Tall Pines Cir ... 53051
Tamarack Ct, Dr & Trl ... 53051
Tartan Cir ... 53051
Taylors Ln ... 53051
Taylors Woods Dr ... 53051
Technology Dr ... 53051
Teepee Ct ... 53051
Terrace Dr ... 53051
Terriwood Ct & Dr ... 53051
Theodore Ave ... 53051
Theresa Maria Ct ... 53051
Thomas Dr ... 53051
Thornapple Ct ... 53051
Thorndell Dr ... 53051
Thornhill Ct & Dr ... 53051
Thornwood Cir ... 53051
Thunder Rd ... 53051
Thunder Ridge Rd ... 53051
Thurston Ave ... 53051
Timber Ridge Ct ... 53051
Timms Prairie Walk Rd ... 53051
Tipp St ... 53051
Titan Ct ... 53051
Tours Dr ... 53051
Town Hall Rd ... 53051
Town Line Rd ... 53051
Trails End Ct ... 53051
Tyler Ct & Dr ... 53051
University Dr ... 53051
Upper Cir ... 53051
Valley View Dr ... 53051
Van Buren Dr ... 53051
Vera Ln ... 53051
Victory Rd ... 53051
Village Ct ... 53051
Villard Ave ... 53051
Virginia Ln ... 53051
Vista Ln ... 53051
Waldens Pass ... 53051
Walnut Ct ... 53051
Walnut Way Dr ... 53051
Wampum Dr ... 53051
Warren St ... 53051
Washington Ave ... 53051
Water St ... 53051
Water Tower Pl ... 53051
Wedge Ct ... 53051
Wellington Dr ... 53051
Westbridge Ave ... 53051
Westbrook Xing ... 53051
Westchester Dr ... 53051
Westview Ct & Dr ... 53051
Westwind Dr ... 53051
Westwood Dr ... 53051
Weyer Rd ... 53051
Wheeler Dr ... 53051
Whispering Way ... 53051
White Birch Dr ... 53051
White Oak Cir ... 53051
Whitetail Run ... 53051
Whittaker Way ... 53051
Wigwam Dr ... 53051
Wild Rose Ct ... 53051
Wildflower Dr ... 53051
Wildlife Ct & Ln ... 53051
Wildwood Dr ... 53051
Williams Pl ... 53051
Williamsburg Ct ... 53051
Willow Ct ... 53051
Wilson Dr ... 53051
Winchester Dr ... 53051
Windrift Pass ... 53051
Winter Hollow Dr ... 53051
Wood Ct ... 53051
Wood View Dr ... 53051
Woodale Dr ... 53051
Woodcrest Ct ... 53051
Woodland Dr ... 53051
Woodland Prime ... 53051
Woodlawn Dr ... 53051
Woodside Ln ... 53051
Woodward Ct ... 53051
Woody Ln ... 53051

NUMBERED STREETS

All Street Addresses ... 53051

MEQUON WI

General Delivery ... 53092

POST OFFICE BOXES MAIN OFFICE STATIONS AND BRANCHES

Box No.s
All PO Boxes ... 53092

NAMED STREETS

N Adams Ct ... 53092
W Alsace Ct ... 53092
E & W Alta Loma Cir & Dr ... 53092
N Amherst Ct ... 53097
N Andover Ct ... 53097
N Anne Ct ... 53092
N Annette Ave ... 53092
W Appletree Ct ... 53092
N Applewood Ct ... 53092
N Arbor Ln ... 53092
N & W Arrowwood Rd ... 53092
N Ash Ct ... 53092
N Ashbury Woods Dr ... 53097
Ashley Ln ... 53092
W Aspen Tree Ct ... 53092
N & W Aster Ln ... 53092
N & W Aster Woods Cir & Ct ... 53092
N & W Auburn Ct ... 53092
N Auer Ln ... 53092
N & W Augusta Ct ... 53092
N Austin Ave ... 53092
N Baehr Rd ... 53092
N Baldev Ct ... 53092
W Baldwin Ct ... 53092
N Balsam Tree Ct ... 53092
W Bancroft Ct ... 53092
E Barkwood Ct ... 53092
W Bayberry Pkwy ... 53092
E & N Beechwood Ct & Dr ... 53092
Bel Aire Ct & Dr ... 53092
W Bel Mar Dr ... 53092
N & W Bennington Ct ... 53097
Birch Ct ... 53092
Birch Creek Rd ... 53097
N Birchwood Ln ... 53097
N Bittersweet Ct ... 53092
N Bobolink Ln ... 53092
Bonness Ln ... 53097
W Bonnie Ct ... 53092
N Bonnie Lynn Dr ... 53092
N & W Bonniwell Ct & Rd ... 53097
E & W Boundary Rd & Sq ... 53092
W Bradford Dr ... 53092
N Briarhill Rd ... 53097
N Briarwood Ct ... 53092
N Bridal Path Ct ... 53097
N Bridgewater Dr ... 53092
N Brighton Pl ... 53097
W Brittany Ct ... 53092
N Brookdale Dr ... 53092
N Buntrock Ave ... 53092
W Burgundy Ct ... 53092
N & W Burning Bush Ln ... 53092
W Cairdel Ln ... 53092
N Cambridge Ct ... 53092
W Candlewick Ct ... 53092
W & N Canterbury Ct & Ln ... 53092
N & W Carriage Ct ... 53092
W Cassell Ln ... 53097
W Castlebury Ln ... 53092
E Cedar Ln ... 53092
W Cedar Ridge Ct ... 53092
N Cedarburg Rd
9600-11400 ... 53092
11402-12498 ... 53092
12800-14399 ... 53097
W Celeste Ct ... 53092
N Center Dr ... 53092
W Century Ct ... 53092
W Chantilly Ct ... 53092
W Chapel Hill Rd ... 53097
E Charter Mall ... 53092
W Chateau Ct ... 53092
W Chestnut Rd ... 53092
Cheverny Dr ... 53097
N Chicory Ln ... 53092
W Chippewa Dr ... 53092
E Chowning Sq ... 53092
E Chowning Cross St ... 53092
N Church Pl ... 53097
N, W & E Circle Dr & Rd ... 53092
W Clover Ln ... 53092
W Clubview Ct ... 53092
N Cobblestone Ct ... 53097
W Colette Ct ... 53092
N Colony Dr ... 53097
W & N Columbia Ct & Dr ... 53092
N Columbia Creek Ln ... 53092
N Commerce St ... 53092
N Concord Dr ... 53097
W Concord Dr ... 53097
Concord Pl ... 53092
N & W Concord Creek Dr ... 53092
N Corey Ln ... 53092
Coronada Ave ... 53092
Corporate Pkwy ... 53092
N Council Hills Dr ... 53097
N & W Country Ln ... 53092
N & W Country Club Dr ... 53092
N & W Country View Dr ... 53092
W County Line Rd
1400-7598 ... 53092
7600-12398 ... 53097
N Courtland Dr ... 53092
N & W Creekside Ct ... 53092
Crescent Ln ... 53092
N Crestline Rd ... 53092
N Crestwood Ct ... 53092
W Crimson Ct ... 53092
N Crossroad Dr ... 53097
N Crown Ct ... 53092
W Cumberland Ct ... 53092
N Dalewood Ln ... 53092
N & W Dandelion Ct & Ln ... 53092
W Daventry Rd ... 53097
N Davis Rd ... 53097
N & W De La Warr Cir ... 53092
N Deer Run Ln ... 53092
N Dellwood Dr ... 53097
W Dickinson Ct ... 53092
W Division St ... 53092
W Dogwood Ct ... 53092
W Donges Bay Rd
100-298 ... 53092
300-7599 ... 53092
7600-12399 ... 53097
W Dorothy Pl ... 53092
W Dunhill Dr ... 53092
W & N Eastbrook Ct & Dr ... 53092
W Eastfield Cir ... 53097
N Eastgate Dr ... 53092
Eastwood Ct ... 53092
E Eastwyn Bay Dr ... 53092
W Edward Dr ... 53092
W El Patio Ln ... 53092
W El Rancho Dr ... 53092
N Elder Tree Ct ... 53092
W & N Elderberry Ct & Ln ... 53092
W Eleanor Pl ... 53092
N & W Elizabeth Ct ... 53097
Ellenbecker Rd ... 53092
Elm St ... 53092
Elmdale Ct & Rd ... 53092
W Elmhurst Dr ... 53092
N Emily Ln ... 53092
N & W Enterprise Dr ... 53092
Essex Ct & Dr ... 53092
W Estates Dr ... 53092
N Eugene Ave ... 53092
W Evergreen Rd ... 53097
N & W Executive Ct & Dr ... 53092
N Fairfield Rd ... 53092
W Fairview Dr ... 53092
Fairway Cir & Ln ... 53092
N & W Fairway Heights Dr ... 53092
W Farkenw Rd ... 53092
N Farmdale Rd ... 53097
N Fieldwood Rd ... 53092
W Fiesta Ln ... 53092
N Flanders Ct ... 53092
Fleur De Lis Dr ... 53092
N Fontainbleau Ct ... 53092
Forest Ct & Dr ... 53092
W Forrester Ct ... 53097
W Fox Run ... 53092
N Fox Hollow Rd ... 53097
W Fox Hunt Trce ... 53092
N & W Foxkirk Cir & Dr ... 53097
Foxtail Ln ... 53097
N Franklin Ct ... 53092
E Freistadt Rd ... 53092
W Freistadt Rd
100-130 ... 53092
132-198 ... 53092
2900-3798 ... 53092
3800-7499 ... 53092
7501-7599 ... 53092
7600-12399 ... 53097
W Gateway Ct ... 53092
W & N Gazebo Hill Blvd & Pkwy E & W ... 53092
N Gettysburg Ct ... 53092
W Glen Cv ... 53092
W Glen Oaks Ln ... 53092
N & W Glenbrook Ln ... 53092
W Glenview Ct ... 53092
N Glenwood Dr ... 53097
W & N Golf Cir & Dr ... 53092
W & N Grace Ave & Ct ... 53092
Grand Ave ... 53092
N Granville Rd ... 53097
N Grasslyn Rd ... 53092
Green Bay Rd
100-700 ... 53092
702-12798 ... 53092
12800-14399 ... 53097
Greenbrier Ln ... 53092
N Greenside Ct ... 53092
Greenview Dr & Ln ... 53092
N & W Haddonstone Pl ... 53092
Haven Ave & Ct ... 53092
W & N Hawks Glen Cir & Ct ... 53097
N Hawks Landing Rd ... 53097
N & W Hawthorne Ct & Rd ... 53097
W Hawthorne Farm Ln ... 53097
N Hayden Ct ... 53097
W Heather Dr ... 53097
N Hedgewood Ln ... 53092
W Heidel Rd ... 53092
W Helen Dr ... 53092
W Hemlock Ln ... 53097
W Heritage Ct ... 53092
W Heron Pond Dr ... 53092
W Hiawatha Dr ... 53092
Hickory Ln & Rd ... 53092
Hidden Creek Ct & Dr ... 53092
W Hidden Lake Rd ... 53092
N & W Hidden Reserve Cir & Ct ... 53092
W Hidden River Dr ... 53092
N Highgate Ct ... 53097
N Highland Ave ... 53097
S Highland Ave ... 53092
N Highland Dr ... 53097
W Highland Rd
700-1398 ... 53092
1400-6900 ... 53092
6902-7298 ... 53092
7500-12399 ... 53097
12401-12699 ... 53097
W Highland Ridge Dr ... 53092
E Highview Dr ... 53092
W Hilands Ct ... 53092
W Hillcrest Dr ... 53092
N Hillside Dr ... 53097
N Hillside Ln ... 53092
N Hilltop Ln ... 53092
W Hillview Dr ... 53097
N & W Holly Rd ... 53097
N Hollyhock Ct ... 53092
N Holmes Ct ... 53092
W Homestead Trl ... 53092
W Hunt Club Cir & Dr ... 53097
W Huntington Dr ... 53097
W Hyacinth Ct ... 53092
W Indian Mound Rd ... 53092
N & W Industrial Dr ... 53092
E, N & W Ironwood Cir & Ln ... 53092
N Island Dr ... 53092
N Ivy Ct ... 53092
N Jacqueline Ct ... 53092
W Joliet Ct ... 53092
N Jonquil Ct ... 53092
E, N & W Juniper Cir, Ct, Ln & Trl ... 53092
N Justin Dr ... 53092
Kasota Ct ... 53092
W Kathleen Ln ... 53092
N & W Kenilworth Cir & Ct ... 53092
N & W Kensington Ct & Dr ... 53097
N Kent Ct ... 53097
Kenwood Dr ... 53092
W Keonah Cir ... 53092
Kieker Rd ... 53092
N Kings Cir ... 53092
Kings Crossing Way ... 53097
N Kirkland Ct ... 53092
N Klug Ln ... 53097
N & W Knightsbridge Ct & Dr ... 53097
N La Belle Ct ... 53092
N La Cresta Dr ... 53092
N & W Lafayette Pl ... 53092
W Lagoon Ct ... 53092
N Laguna Dr ... 53092
Lake Bluff Rd ... 53092
N & W Lake Forest Ct ... 53092
W Lake Isle Dr ... 53092
W Lake Park Ct ... 53092
N Lake Shore Dr
9800-9898 ... 53092
9900-12600 ... 53092
12602-12798 ... 53092
12800-14399 ... 53097
W Lake Vista Ct ... 53092
N Lakeside Rd ... 53092
Lakeview Pl & Rd ... 53092
N Lakewood Dr ... 53097
N Lamplighter Ln ... 53092
N & W Lantern Ln ... 53092
N Larkspur Ct ... 53092
Laurel Dr ... 53092
N Laurel Ln ... 53097
Laurel Lake Rd ... 53092
W Laurmark Ct ... 53092
W Laverna Ave ... 53092
N & W Le Grande Blvd ... 53092
N & W Le Mont Blvd ... 53092
N Lee Ct ... 53092
N Legacy Hills Dr ... 53097
W Liebau Rd ... 53092
Lilac Ln ... 53092
W Lilly Ln ... 53092
N Lincolnshire Dr ... 53097
N Linde Ct ... 53092
Linden Ln ... 53092
N Linnwood Ln ... 53092
W Lucerne Ct ... 53092
Luisita Rd ... 53092
N Luther Ln ... 53092
Madero Dr ... 53092
N Magnolia Dr ... 53092
N & S Main St ... 53092
N & W Manor Cir ... 53092
E Maple Ln ... 53092
N Maple Crest Ln ... 53092
W Maplewood Ct ... 53092
W Mariana Ct ... 53092
W Marigold Ct ... 53092
N & W Market St ... 53092
Marseilles Ct & Dr ... 53092
N Martin Way ... 53097
Mary Ln ... 53092
N Maryhill Ct ... 53092
W Mcintosh Ln ... 53092
N & W Meadow Cir & Ln E & W ... 53092
N Meadowbrook Dr ... 53097
W Meadowview Ct ... 53092
N Melrose Ct ... 53097
Mendota Ct ... 53092
N Mequon Pl ... 53092
E Mequon Rd ... 53092
W Mequon Rd
100-7599 ... 53092
7600-12399 ... 53097
N Mequon Trl ... 53092
W Mequon Trl ... 53092
N & W Mequon Square Dr ... 53092
W Merrimac Ct ... 53092
E, N & W Miller Ct & Dr ... 53092
W Monterey Ln ... 53092
N & W Mulberry Dr ... 53092
Nashota Ct ... 53092
W Norfolk Ct ... 53092
W Normandy Ct ... 53092
E North Point Rd ... 53092
N Northwood Ln ... 53097
N & W Norway Dr ... 53092
N O Connell Ln ... 53097
W Oak Shore Ln ... 53092
N & W Oakview Ct ... 53092
Oakwood Dr ... 53092
Obikoba Cir ... 53092
N Old Barn Rd ... 53092
N & S Orchard Ct & St ... 53092
N Oriole Ln
10800-11999 ... 53092
12800-13599 ... 53097
N Otto Rd ... 53092
W Overlook Ct ... 53092
N Oxford Ct ... 53092
W Paget Ct ... 53092
W Parc Ct ... 53092
N Park Dr ... 53092
Park Crest Dr ... 53092
Parkside Ct ... 53092
N & W Parkview Dr ... 53092
N Pebble Ln ... 53092
W Perlerle Rd ... 53097
N Pheasant Ct ... 53092
N Phillip Dr ... 53097
W Picardy Ct ... 53092
W Pierre Ct ... 53092
N Pilot Dr ... 53092
W Pine Ln ... 53092
N Pine Bluff Rd ... 53097
Pine Ridge Cir & Dr ... 53092
N Pine Tree Cir ... 53092
N Pinehurst Cir ... 53092
W Pinewood Ct ... 53092
Pioneer Rd ... 53097
Pippin Ct ... 53092
W Pleasant Dr ... 53092
W Plum Tree Ct ... 53092
W Poplar Dr ... 53097
N Port Washington Ln ... 53092
N Port Washington Rd
9900-9998 ... 53092
10000-12799 ... 53092
12800-14399 ... 53097
N Portland Ave ... 53092
W Post Ct ... 53092
N Prairie View Ln ... 53092
N Provence Ct ... 53092
W Quincy Ct ... 53092
W Rael Dr ... 53097
W Raleigh Ct ... 53092
W Ranch Rd ... 53092
W Ranchito Ln ... 53092
W & N Range Line Cir, Ct, Rd & Ter ... 53092
W Ravenna Ct ... 53092
W Ravenwood Ct ... 53097
E, N & W Ravine Ct & Dr ... 53092
W Red Cedar Ct ... 53097
N Redwood Tree Ct ... 53092
W Renee Ct ... 53092
N & W Revere Rd ... 53092
N Ridge Rd ... 53092
W Ridgeline Ct ... 53092
Ridgeview Ct & Dr ... 53092
N & W Ridgeway Ave & Ln ... 53097
W River Ct ... 53092
W River Dr ... 53097
N River Rd ... 53092
W River Bend Ct ... 53092
N & W River Birch Dr ... 53092
N & W River Forest Cir & Dr ... 53092
N River Glenn Ln ... 53092
W River Hollow Ct ... 53092
River Oaks Ln & Pl ... 53092
W & N River Ridge Ct & Dr ... 53092
W & N River Trail Ct & Rd ... 53092
N River Valley Dr ... 53092
W River Willows Ct ... 53092
Riveredge Ct ... 53092
N & W Riverlake Ct & Dr ... 53092
N Riverland Ct ... 53092
W Riverland Dr ... 53092
N Riverland Rd
11200-11800 ... 53092
11802-11898 ... 53092
13600-14399 ... 53097
N Riverside Rd ... 53092
Riverview Ct & Dr ... 53092
W Riviera Ct ... 53092
N Robin Ln ... 53092
N & W Rolling Field Dr ... 53097
Rosedale Dr ... 53092
N Rosewood Dr ... 53092
Rotary Park Ct ... 53092
N Royal Ln ... 53092
N & W Rudella Rd ... 53092
W Russet Ln ... 53092
Sabra Ct ... 53092
N & W Saddlebrook Cir & Ln ... 53097
W Saddleworth Ct ... 53092
Saint Anne Ct & Ln ... 53092
N & W Saint James Ct & Ln ... 53092
W San Jose Dr ... 53092
N San Marino Dr ... 53092
N Sandhill Cir ... 53092

Sauk Cir 53092
N Savannah Ct 53092
W Scenic Ave 53092
N Schwemer Ln 53092
W Seacroft Ct 53092
N Seminary Dr 53092
N Settlement Dr 53092
N & W Shady Ln 53097
W & N Shaker Cir & Ln 53092
N Shannon Ct 53097
W Shawnee Pass 53097
W Sherbrooke Dr 53092
N Sheridan Dr 53092
N & W Sherwood Dr 53092
W Sholes Dr 53092
N Shorecliff Ln 53092
NE Shoreland Dr 53092
NW Shoreland Dr 53097
N Shoreland Pkwy 53092
W Sierra Ln 53092
N & W Silver Ave 53097
N Silver Fox Dr 53097
W Sleepy Hollow Ln 53092
N Solar Ave 53097
Solvang Ln 53092
N & W Spring Ave & St 53092
N & W Springdale Ct 53092
E Springwood Ct 53092
N Spruce Ln 53092
W Squire Rd 53092
W & N Stanford Ct & Dr 53097
W Steffen Dr 53092
Stillwater Cir & Ct 53092
N Stone Creek Dr 53092
N & W Stonefield Ct & Rd 53092
N Stratford Pl 53092
N Sunflower Ct 53092
Sunny Ln 53092
N Sunnycrest Dr 53092
N & W Sunnydale Ln 53092
W Sunnyside Dr 53092
Sunnyvale Ct 53092
W Sunnyvale Rd 53097
N & W Sunset Ln & Rd 53092
W Sunset Woods Ln 53097
Susan Ln 53092
N Sutton Ridge Dr 53097
N Swan Rd 53097
Tamarack Ct 53092
N & W Tarrytown Ln 53092
N Thomas Dr 53097
N & W Thornapple Ln 53092
N Thorngate Rd 53097
W Thrush Ln 53092
W Tomahawk Trl 53097
N Torrey Dr 53092
N Tower Ln 53097
N & W Towne Square Rd 53092
Tremont Ct 53092
E, N & W Trillium Ct & Rd 53092
Turnberry Dr 53092
N Twin Oaks Ln 53097
N Valley Dr 53092
N Valley Hill Dr 53092
W Valleyview Ct 53092
N Vega Ave 53097
W Venture Ct 53092
Vernon Ave 53092
N Versailles Ct 53092
N & W Ville Du Parc Dr 53092
E, N & W Vintage Ct & Dr 53092
W Vista View Cir 53097
Wandawega Cir 53092
W Wartburg Cir 53092
N Wasaukee Rd 53097
Washington Ct 53092
Waterleaf Ct & Dr 53092
Waunakee Cir 53092
N Wauwatosa Rd 53097
West St 53092
N & W Westchester Ct 53092
W Westfield Rd 53092
N & W Westport Cir 53092
N Westview Ln 53092
N Westwood Cir 53097
N Whilton Rd 53097
E & W White Oak Way 53092
N Whitetail Ct 53092
N & W Wild Rose Ct 53097
N Wilderness Ct 53092
N & W Wildwood Ct & Dr 53092
Williamsburg Dr 53092
Willow Pkwy & Rd 53092
N Willow Glenn Ct 53092
W Willowbrook Ct 53092
W Willowbrook Dr 53097
N & W Winding Hollow Ln 53092
Windpointe Cir & Ct 53092
N Windsor Ct 53097
Winesap Ct 53092
W & N Winslow Ct & Dr 53092
N Winston Ct 53097
Wood Crest Ct & Dr 53092
N Woodberry Dr 53092
N & W Woodfield Ct & Dr 53092
W & N Woodland Ct & Dr 53092
W Woodlyn Dr 53092
N & W Woodside Ct & Ln 53092
W Woodview Ct 53092
N Wyngate Trce 53092
N Yvonne Dr 53092
E & W Zedler Ln 53092

MILWAUKEE WI

General Delivery 53201

POST OFFICE BOXES MAIN OFFICE STATIONS AND BRANCHES

Box No.s
26157C - 26157C 53226
1 - 3299 53201
4001 - 4958 53204
5000 - 5070 53201
5011 - 5844 53205
6001 - 6850 53206
11041 - 11982 53211
12000 - 12993 53212
13001 - 13940 53213
14001 - 14999 53214
16111 - 16974 53216
18001 - 18996 53218
20001 - 20999 53220
26001 - 26998 53226
27901 - 27915 53227
28801 - 28999 53228
44011 - 44366 53214
64001 - 64600 53204
70011 - 70980 53207
71011 - 71368 53211
72001 - 72120 53212
76001 - 76900 53216
80011 - 80790 53208
90011 - 91690 53209
100011 - 101030 53210
170001 - 171014 53217
210011 - 211086 53221
240011 - 245042 53224
250211 - 251006 53225
270001 - 270760 53227
340011 - 343940 53234
370001 - 371386 53237
510011 - 514199 53203
909951 - 909999 53209
4995 - 4997 53204
5900 - 5911 53205
70504 - 71220 53207

NAMED STREETS

A B Data Dr 53217
W Abbott Ave
600-4099 53221
4400-4498 53220
4500-5799 53220
9400-9599 53228
Aberdeen Ct 53213
W Abert Ct 53216
E Abert Pl 53212
W Abert Pl
100-699 53212
901-997 53206
999-1299 53206
E Acacia Rd 53217
W Acacia Rd
400-1099 53217
1101-1199 53217
2200-2699 53209
W Acacia St
6700-8299 53223
8700-9099 53224
N Achilles St 53212
S Acorn Ln 53221
Adams Ave & Ct 53207
Adler Ln & St 53214
Aetna Ct 53213
S Aetna Ln 53215
S Ahmedi Ave 53207
Air Cargo Way 53207
S Alabama Ave 53207
W Albany Pl 53206
Alberta Ct & Ln 53217
E Albion St 53202
W Alda Ct 53227
S Aldrich St 53207
Alice St 53213
N Allen Ln 53217
W Allerton Ave
100-599 53207
3100-3799 53221
4700-8399 53220
8400-9449 53228
9451-9535 53228
S Allis St 53207
Allyn Ct & St 53224
W Alma St 53204
N Alois St 53208
N Alpine Ave 53211
N Alpine Ln 53223
Alta Vista Ave 53213
E Alvina Ave 53207
W Alvina Ave
100-299 53207
2000-4299 53221
W Alvina Ct 53221
Amberwood Ln 53221
W American Dr 53221
N Ames Ter 53209
S Amy Pl 53204
E Anderson Ave 53204
W Andover Rd 53219
N Andrea St 53224
N & W Angela Ave 53223
N Anita Ave 53217
N Ann St 53224
W Anthony Dr 53219
N Apple Blossom Ln 53217
E Apple Tree Rd 53217
W Apple Tree Rd
100-900 53217
902-998 53217
2100-2599 53209
W Appleton Ave
5600-6499 53210
6600-6998 53216
7000-7474 53216
7476-7570 53216
7600-7799 53222
7800-8399 53218
8401-8497 53225
8499-11200 53225
11202-11298 53225
11601-11797 53224
11799-12399 53224
W Appleton Ln 53225
W Appleton Pl 53224
N & W Applewood Ln 53209
N Arbon Dr 53223
W Arbor Ave 53209
W Arch Ave
6100-6499 53223
9300-10599 53224
W Arch Ct 53224
E Archer Ave 53207
S Arctic Ave 53207
N Ardara Ave 53209
W Arden Pl
7800-7899 53218
8500-8899 53225
N Ardmore Ave
4100-4700 53211
4702-4798 53211
4800-5000 53217
5002-5198 53217
N & W Argonne Dr 53222
N Argyle Ave 53209
Arizona Ct & St 53219
N Arlington Pl 53202
W Armitage Ave 53218
E Armour Ave 53207
W Armour Ave
100-599 53207
600-3699 53221
4500-7199 53220
11000-11199 53228
W Armour Ct 53228
W Arrow St 53204
N Art Museum Dr 53202
W Arthur Ave
400-599 53207
600-3499 53215
5900-8299 53219
8301-8399 53219
8400-12099 53227
W Arthur Ct
300-399 53207
4400-4499 53219
W Arthur Pl 53227
W Ash St 53206
W Aspen St 53221
W Aspenwood Ct 53217
N Astor St 53202
S Athens St 53220
W Atkinson Ave
600-699 53212
800-1899 53206
1901-1949 53206
1950-3100 53209
3102-3198 53209
N Atwahl Dr 53209
S Au Rene Cir 53227
Auburn Ave 53213
E Auer Ave 53212
W Auer Ave
100-499 53212
2000-2098 53206
2100-2699 53206
2700-5699 53216
5701-5799 53216
7700-7998 53222
8000-10700 53222
10702-10798 53222
S Austin St 53207
W Autumn Path Ln 53217
S Avalon St 53221
Avon Ct 53213
N Avondale Blvd 53210
E Back Bay St 53202
N Baker Rd 53209
W Baldwin St 53218
W Barbee St 53205
S Barclay St 53204
W Barnard Ave
1300-4299 53221
4300-7999 53220
8001-8099 53220
9100-12399 53228
N Barnett Ln 53217
S Bartel Dr 53220
N Bartlett Ave
1900-2299 53202
2400-4799 53211
4800-4999 53217
N Bartlett Dr 53211
E & S Bay St 53207
E Bay Point Rd 53217
N Bay Ridge Ave 53217
S Bayberry Ln 53228
Bayfield Ave & Rd 53217
N Bayshore Dr 53217
N Bayside Dr 53217
Beach Ct & Dr 53217
N Beale St 53224
W Beatrice Ct
6900-8399 53223
8400-8499 53224
W Beatrice St 53224
N Beau Ave 53224
E Beaumont Ave 53217
W Beaver Creek Pkwy 53223
W Becher Pl 53219
E Becher St 53207
W Becher St
100-599 53207
600-3699 53215
6600-6698 53219
6700-8399 53219
8400-11399 53227
W Beckett Ave
7000-7499 53216
7700-8199 53218
9400-9599 53225
W Beech Ct 53223
N Beech Tree Dr 53209
W Beechwood Ave
7700-8199 53223
9600-10199 53224
W Beethoven Pl 53209
Bel Air Cir 53226
N Bel Aire Dr 53209
N Bell Rd 53217
E & W Belle Ave 53217
E Belleview Pl 53211
N Belmont Ln 53217
W Beloit Rd
4600-5799 53214
5800-8399 53219
8400-9999 53227
10000-12399 53228
W Bender Ave
7700-8300 53218
8302-8398 53218
8600-9099 53225
W Bender Ct 53218
W Bender Rd
201-397 53217
399-1199 53217
1201-1299 53217
1600-2299 53209
10500-11999 53225
E Bennett Ave 53207
W Bennett Ave 53219
Bergen Ct & Dr 53217
N Berkeley Blvd
4700-4799 53211
4800-6499 53217
W Bernard Ln 53209
W Bernhard Pl 53216
N Berwyn Ave 53209
N Bethanne Dr 53223
N Bethmaur Ln 53209
Betsy Ross Pl 53213
S Bettinger Ct 53204
W Betty Ln 53223
Beverly Pl 53226
E Beverly Rd 53211
E Birch Ave 53217
W Birch Ave
100-399 53217
1000-1299 53209
5700-6699 53218
9200-10599 53225
W Birch Ct
1300-1999 53209
6900-6999 53218
N Birch Hill Ct 53217
W Birchwood Ave 53221
N Bishop Cir 53224
N Bittersweet Ln 53217
W Black Oak Dr 53228
W Blackhawk Rd 53217
E Blackthorne Pl 53211
N Blaine Pl 53210
Blanchard St 53213
Blue Mound Ct & Rd 53208
W Bluemound Rd
5600-5798 53213
5800-8399 53213
8400-12399 53226
W Bobolink Ave
2700-3299 53209
6200-7398 53218
7400-7899 53218
7901-8399 53218
10500-10698 53225
10700-12399 53225
W Bobolink Pl 53218
W Boden Ct 53221
E Boden St 53207
S Boden St 53207
W Boden St 53207
W Boehlke Ave
4200-4299 53209
5800-6599 53223
E Bolivar Ave 53207
W Bolivar Ave
100-599 53207
1300-1398 53221
1400-2699 53221
W Bonny Pl 53216
W Boone Ave 53227
N Booth St 53212
W Bottsford Ave
100-499 53207
1600-3799 53221
4300-8299 53220
8500-9199 53228
N Bourbon St 53224
W Bow St 53204
N Boyd Way 53217
E Boylston St 53202
E Bradford Ave 53211
E Bradley Ave 53207
E Bradley Rd 53217
W Bradley Rd
100-2799 53217
2800-3099 53217
3100-3798 53209
3800-4299 53209
4300-8399 53223
8400-12199 53224
E Brady St 53202
N Braeburn Ln 53209
Brandybrook Trl 53223
W Branting Ln 53215
Brantwood Ave & Ct 53209
N Bremen St 53212
W Brentwood Ave
4700-8399 53223
8400-8899 53224
W Brentwood Ct
4600-4699 53223
9300-9399 53224
W Brentwood Ln 53217
Brewers Way 53214
E & N Briarwood Ct & Pl 53217
N Bridge Ln 53217
W Bridge St 53221
N Bridgewood Ln 53209
W Briggs Ave 53223
S Brisbane Ave 53207
W Brittany Way 53224
N Broadmoor Rd 53217
N Broadway 53202
S Brookdale Dr 53228
W Brooklyn Pl 53216
W Brookside Dr 53228
Brookside Pl 53213
E Brown St 53212
W Brown St
100-599 53212
601-699 53212
701-1097 53205
1099-2699 53205
2700-3899 53208
3901-4099 53208
W Brown Deer Pl 53224
E Brown Deer Rd 53217
W Brown Deer Rd
100-3699 53217
2700-3000 53217
3002-3098 53217
3900-4298 53209
4300-6900 53223
6821-6829 53224
6901-8399 53223
6902-8398 53223
8400-11899 53224
11901-12399 53224
E & W Bruce St 53204
E Brunks Ln 53207
S Brust Ave 53207
S Buchanan Pl 53219
E Buffalo St 53202
N Buffum St 53212
W Bungalow Pkwy 53214
N Burbank Ave 53224
E Burdick Ave 53207
W Burdick Ave
6100-8299 53219
8600-12099 53227
E Burleigh St 53212
W Burleigh St
100-699 53212
800-2699 53206
2700-7599 53210
7600-12399 53222
W Burnham St
300-2699 53204
2700-4299 53215
4301-4397 53219
4399-7199 53219
7201-8399 53219
S Burrell St 53207
W Butler Pl 53225
S Butterfield Way 53221
E Buttles Pl 53217
W Byron Pl 53222
E Bywater Ln 53217
W Caldwell Ave
7401-7497 53218
7499-7599 53218
10300-10599 53225
W Caldwell Ct 53218
S California St 53207
N Callahan Pl 53233
W Calumet Ct 53217
E Calumet Rd 53217
W Calumet Rd
100-1199 53217
1201-1399 53217
3800-4299 53209
4301-4397 53223
4399-8399 53223
8400-11500 53224
11502-11598 53224
N Cambridge Ave
1700-2299 53202
2300-2500 53211
2502-3398 53211
S Cambridge Ln 53221
W Camden Rd 53209
S Camelot Ln 53221
W Cameron Ave
2800-3400 53209
3402-3498 53209
10300-10798 53225
10800-10999 53225
W Canal St
400-699 53203
700-2599 53233
2601-2699 53233

2701-3399 53208
3500-3898 53208
N Canchenw St 53218
N Candowes St 53203
W Canterbury Rd 53221
N Cape St 53212
E Capitol Dr
100-899 53212
1101-1197 53211
1199-2799 53211
W Capitol Dr
100-699 53212
700-2699 53206
2700-7599 53216
7600-12199 53222
12201-12399 53222
S Carferry Dr 53207
W Caridar Ave 53220
E Carlisle Ave 53217
N Carlotta Ln 53223
N Carlton Pl 53210
W Carmen Ave
2700-3099 53209
5500-8399 53218
8700-8898 53225
8900-12100 53225
12102-12898 53225
E Carol St 53207
W Carolann Dr 53223
W Carpenter Ave
801-1997 53221
1999-4199 53221
6500-7199 53220
9200-12199 53228
W Carrington Ave 53221
W Carter Pl 53216
W Casper St 53223
N Cass St 53202
N Cassie Ave 53224
Cathedral Ave & Ct 53226
W Cawker Pl 53210
W Cedar Ln 53217
Cedar St 53213
N Cedar Ridge Ln 53217
N Cedarburg Rd 53209
N Celina St 53224
S Centennial Cir 53221
E Center St 53212
W Center St
100-699 53212
800-2699 53206
2700-7599 53210
7600-12399 53222
N Centerpark Way 53217
S Cesar E Chavez Dr 53204
N Chadwick Rd 53217
W Chambers Ct 53210
E Chambers St 53212
W Chambers St
100-699 53212
800-2699 53206
2700-7599 53210
7600-8098 53222
8100-12299 53222
N Chameard St 53206
W Chapman Ave
6900-7199 53220
8400-12399 53228
W Chapman Pl 53216
S Chase Ave 53207
E & W Chateau Pl 53217
E Cherokee Cir 53217
W Cherokee Cir 53217
S Cherokee Way 53221
W Cherry St
100-699 53212
700-2499 53205
2501-2699 53205
2700-5999 53208
11600-12399 53226
W Cherrywood Ln 53209
W Chester St 53214
Chestnut St 53213
W Cheyenne Ct 53224
W Cheyenne St
3700-4099 53209
8400-8999 53224

E Chicago St 53202
W Christine Dr 53226
W Christine Ln 53212
Church St 53213
E Churchill Ln 53217
W Churchill Ln 53223
W Circle Ct 53224
E Circle Dr 53217
E Citation Way 53207
W Civic Dr 53209
N Claire Ct 53217
E Clarence St 53207
W Clarendon Pl 53208
E Clarke St 53212
W Clarke St
100-699 53212
800-2499 53206
2700-5300 53210
5302-5998 53210
6000-8399 53213
8400-12099 53226
W Clayton Crest Ave
1400-2699 53221
4500-4899 53220
S Clement Ave 53207
W Cleveland Ave
600-3099 53215
4300-8299 53219
8301-8399 53219
8400-12399 53227
S Cleveland Park Dr 53219
E Clifford St 53207
W Clinton Ave
3700-4299 53209
5100-7999 53223
W Cloverleaf Ln 53223
W Clovernook Ct
6600-6699 53223
8800-8899 53224
E Clovernook Ln 53217
W Clovernook Ln 53217
W Clovernook St
6800-8299 53223
9300-9399 53224
N Club Cir 53217
W Club View Dr 53209
E Clybourn St 53202
W Clybourn St
100-199 53203
1300-2298 53233
2300-2699 53233
2700-4599 53208
Cody Cir & St 53223
W Coldspring Rd
2700-4299 53221
4300-8399 53220
8400-12399 53228
W Colfax Ct 53218
E Colfax Pl 53217
W Colfax Pl 53209
N Colgate Cir 53222
E College Ave 53207
W College Ave
100-598 53207
600-1998 53221
2000-4299 53221
W Colonial Ct 53220
N Colonial Dr 53222
W Colony Dr 53221
E Colorado St 53207
W Columbia St 53206
N Commerce St 53212
E Community Pl 53217
W Como Pl 53209
S Comstock Ave 53204
W Concord Ln 53228
E Concordia Ave 53212
W Concordia Ave
100-699 53212
800-998 53206
1000-2699 53206
2700-5300 53216
5302-5398 53216
8200-10500 53222
10502-10598 53222
S Conerent St 53214
S Conger Pl 53227

S Congo Ave 53204
E Congress St 53211
W Congress St
1400-4100 53209
4102-4298 53209
4300-8399 53218
8400-8698 53225
8700-11200 53225
9400-9498 53225
11202-11398 53225
W Connell Ave 53226
W Conrad Ln 53214
N Consaul Pl 53217
W Constance Ave 53218
E Conway St 53207
S Cooper Ct 53227
E Corcoran Ave 53202
W Cornell St 53209
W Cottage Pl 53206
Cottonwood Ct 53221
W County Line Rd
801-2997 53217
2999-3099 53217
3101-3499 53217
3901-3999 53209
4301-8399 53223
8401-12399 53224
W Court St 53212
W Courtland Ave
1600-4299 53209
5100-8399 53218
8700-11099 53225
11101-11799 53225
E Courtland Pl 53211
N Coventry Ct 53224
W Coventry Ct 53217
N Craillea St 53205
N Cramer St 53211
S Crandon Pl 53219
E Crawford Ave 53207
W Crawford Ave
100-299 53207
1500-1999 53221
4500-8399 53220
8400-9199 53228
W Crawford Ct 53228
W Creekside Dr 53223
Crescent Ct 53213
Crestview Ct 53226
Crestwood Blvd & Dr 53209
E Crocker Pl 53217
W Crossfield Ave 53225
W Crossing Blvd 53228
N Crossway Rd 53217
E Cudahy Ave 53207
W Cudahy Ave 53221
E Cumberland Blvd 53211
N Cumberland Blvd
4700-4799 53211
4800-5099 53217
5101-5199 53217
W Cumberland Ct 53217
Currie Ave & Pl 53213
E Curtis Pl 53202
S Curtis Rd 53214
W Custer Ave
1301-1397 53209
1399-3899 53209
3901-4299 53209
4301-4497 53218
4499-8299 53218
8700-10599 53225
W Cypress St 53206
E Daisy Ln 53217
W Daisy Ln 53209
E Dakota St 53207
W Dakota St
600-3799 53215
4300-4398 53219
4400-8399 53219
8600-10799 53227
W Dallas St 53224
S & W Dana Ct & St 53214
N Danbury Rd 53217
E Daphne Rd 53217
W Daphne Rd
101-897 53217

899-999 53217
2000-2599 53209
W Daphne St
5700-8299 53223
8600-11499 53224
N Darien St 53209
W Darnel Ave
6000-6599 53223
9300-10499 53224
E Day Ave 53217
W Day Ave 53217
Day Ct 53213
S Dayfield Ave 53207
N Dean Cir 53217
W Dean Ct 53217
E Dean Rd 53217
W Dean Rd
100-2599 53217
2700-2799 53217
2801-2899 53217
4300-7600 53223
7602-7798 53223
8800-10599 53224
W Dearbourn Ave 53226
W Debbie Ln 53224
N Deer Ct 53223
E Deer Pl 53207
W Deer Creek Ct 53217
W Deer Run Dr 53223
N Deerbrook Trl 53223
N Deerwood Dr
8500-8899 53209
8900-9099 53223
9101-9199 53223
S Delaware Ave 53207
N Delco Ave 53225
N Delta Pl 53223
W Denis Ave 53221
N Denmark Ct 53224
N Denmark St 53225
W Denver Ave
7600-8399 53223
8400-9099 53224
W Derby Ave 53225
W Derby Pl
4200-4299 53209
7400-8399 53218
E & W Devon St 53217
Dewey Ave 53213
E Dewey Pl 53207
W Dewey Pl 53207
N Dexter Ave 53209
W Diane Dr 53226
W Dickinson St 53214
N Diversey Blvd
4700-4799 53211
4800-5599 53217
W Dixon St 53214
W Dodge Pl 53220
W Dogwood St 53224
E Donges Ct 53217
W Donges Ct
5000-5199 53223
10500-10699 53224
E Donges Ln 53217
W Donges Ln 53223
E Donges Rd 53217
W Donna Ct 53223
W Donna Dr
4400-6399 53223
10200-10298 53224
10300-10899 53224
10901-10999 53224
W Dorothy Pl 53215
W Dosie Ave 53228
E Doty Pl 53207
W Douglas Ave
3501-3697 53209
3699-4299 53209
4301-4399 53209
5500-5598 53218
5600-7499 53218
7501-7599 53218
8500-12299 53225
N Dousman St 53212
W Dove Ct 53223
E Dover St 53207

N Downer Ave 53211
W Doyne Ave 53226
N Dr Martin Luther King Dr
1300-3699 53212
3700-3798 53206
3901-3999 53206
W Dreyer Pl
7000-8399 53219
10200-10399 53228
W Drury Ln 53215
W Duchess Ct 53217
W Duluth Ave 53220
W Dunwood Rd
100-300 53217
302-398 53217
2200-2699 53209
4400-4699 53223
S Durand Ave 53219
Eagle St 53213
W Eckel Ln 53227
W Eden Ct 53220
E Eden Pl 53207
W Eden Pl
800-1099 53221
6100-7899 53220
9000-9899 53228
N Edge O Woods Dr 53223
W Edgerton Ave
100-599 53207
1300-4299 53221
4300-7599 53220
W Edgewater Dr 53224
N Edgewater Ln 53217
E Edgewood Ave 53211
N Edgeworth Dr 53223
N Edison St 53202
W Edward Ln 53209
W Eggert Pl
1900-4199 53209
4300-4598 53218
4600-8299 53218
8701-8799 53225
W Elder Wallace Dr 53210
W Electric Ave 53219
W Elgin Ln 53204
E Elizabeth Ave 53207
W Elk Ct 53223
N Elkhart Ave
4600-4799 53211
4800-5199 53217
S Ellen St 53207
W Elliott Cir 53208
E & W Ellsworth Ln 53217
N Elm Ct 53223
W Elm St 53209
Elm Lawn St 53213
Elm Spring Ave 53226
N Elm Tree Rd
4600-4699 53209
6000-6999 53217
E Elmdale Ct 53211
W Elmhurst Pkwy 53226
N Elmhurst Rd 53216
Elmore Ave & Ct 53222
S Elmwood Ave 53219
W Ely Pl 53216
N Emery Ave 53210
N & S Emmber Ln 53233
W English Meadows Dr 53220
E Erie St 53202
W Essex Ln 53205
W Estabrook Blvd 53212
W Ester Pl 53223
E Estes St 53207
E Euclid Ave 53207
W Euclid Ave
600-4299 53215
4600-4698 53219
4700-8399 53219
8500-12399 53227
W Eula Ct 53209
N Evans St 53218
W Everett Cir 53214
W Everett St 53203
W Evergreen Ct 53217

W Evergreen Ln 53215
Fairchild Cir & Rd 53217
W Fairfield Ct
400-498 53217
500-1299 53217
1500-1799 53209
W Fairlane Ave
2000-2299 53209
6000-8399 53223
10400-10499 53224
10501-11099 53224
W Fairlane Ct 53224
E Fairmount Ave 53217
W Fairmount Ave
100-299 53217
1800-4299 53209
4301-4797 53218
4799-8399 53218
8401-8797 53225
8799-10999 53225
W Fairview Ave
5900-7999 53213
11600-12399 53226
N Fairway Cir 53217
N Fairway Dr 53217
N Fairway Pl 53223
N Fairwood Ct 53222
N Fairy Chasm Cir 53223
W Fairy Chasm Ct 53223
W Fairy Chasm Dr 53224
N Fairy Chasm Ln 53223
E Fairy Chasm Rd 53217
W Fairy Chasm Rd
100-2500 53217
2502-2698 53217
5100-6099 53223
S Falcon Glen Blvd 53228
E Falling Heath Pl 53207
W Fardale Ave 53221
N Farwell Ave
1400-2299 53202
2300-4499 53211
N Faulkner Rd 53224
Feerick Pl & St 53222
E Fernwood Ave 53207
W Fernwood Cir 53219
S Ferry St 53204
E Fiebrantz Ave 53212
W Fiebrantz Ave
500-600 53212
602-698 53212
700-1999 53209
4000-7399 53216
7600-7698 53222
7700-10999 53222
W Fiebrantz Ct 53222
N Fielding Rd 53217
W Fillmore Dr 53219
W Finger Pl 53219
W Finn Pl 53206
W Fisher Pkwy 53226
W Flagg Ave 53225
W Flanders Ave 53227
E Fleetwood Pl 53217
N Flint Rd 53209
W Floral Ln 53223
W Florence Ln 53227
E & W Florida St 53204
W Florist Ave
1700-4399 53209
5500-8200 53218
8202-8398 53218
8400-10698 53225
10700-12300 53225
12302-12398 53225
W Fond Du Lac Ave
1200-1998 53205
2000-2099 53205
2100-2198 53206
2200-2699 53206
2700-3499 53210
3500-5799 53216
5800-8399 53218
8401-8497 53225
8499-9600 53225
9602-9698 53225
9700-9798 53224

9800-10999 53224
11001-12199 53224
Forest St 53213
W Forest Garden Ct 53220
W Forest Home Ave
1300-1398 53204
1400-1999 53204
2000-4099 53215
4101-4299 53215
4300-4398 53219
4400-5299 53219
5300-7352 53220
7353-7399 53220
7353-7353 53228
7354-8398 53220
8400-9000 53228
9002-9398 53228
W Foster Ave 53221
W Fountain Ave
3800-4299 53209
4400-7899 53223
9600-10799 53224
W Fountainview Dr 53217
E Fox Ln 53217
N Fox Croft Ln 53217
W & E Fox Dale Cir, Ct & Rd 53217
S Foxwood Blvd 53228
N Franklin Pl 53202
W Fransee Ln 53217
N Fratney St 53212
W Frederica Pl 53215
N Frederick Ave 53211
E Fremont Pl 53207
W Fremont Pl 53219
W Fresh Water Way 53204
W Freshwater Way 53204
N Fresno St 53224
N Front St 53202
S Fulton St 53207
W Galena St
200-699 53212
700-2600 53205
2602-2698 53205
2700-5899 53208
5901-5999 53208
N Gallores St 53212
N Garden Grove Ln 53209
W Garden Park Dr 53209
E Garfield Ave 53212
W Garfield Ave
100-699 53212
700-998 53205
1000-2699 53205
2700-5999 53208
6000-7599 53213
10400-12399 53226
E Gauer Cir 53207
E Geneva Pl 53211
Georgia Ave & Ct 53220
Geralayne Cir & Dr 53213
W Gertrude Dr 53218
W Gilbert Ave 53226
W Girard Ave 53210
S Gladstone Pl 53207
E Glen Ave 53217
W Glen Ave 53218
W Glen Bay Ave 53217
W Glen Hills Ct 53209
N Glen Park Rd 53209
W Glen River Rd 53217
N Glen Shore Dr 53209
W Glenbrook Ct 53224
E Glenbrook Rd 53217
W Glenbrook Rd
5100-8399 53223
8400-8799 53224
Glencoe Cir 53226
Glencoe Pl 53226
E Glencoe Pl 53217
W Glencoe Pl 53217
E Glendale Ave 53211
W Glendale Ave
600-4299 53209
4400-8000 53218
8002-8198 53218
8401-8597 53225

8599-11099 53225
11101-11799 53225
W Glendale Ct 53218
Glenview Ave & Pl 53213
Glenway Ct 53222
Glenway St 53222
N Glenway St 53225
E Glover Ave 53212
W Goldcrest Ave 53221
N Goldendale Dr 53223
E & W Goldleaf Ave 53207
W Good Hope Pl 53224
E Good Hope Rd 53217
W Good Hope Rd
100-999 53217
1400-4299 53209
4301-4897 53223
4899-8399 53223
8400-8598 53224
8600-12399 53224
W Goodrich Ave 53224
E Goodrich Ct 53217
W Goodrich Ct 53224
E Goodrich Ln 53217
W Goodrich Ln 53223
Gordon Cir, Ct & Pl 53212
S Graham St 53207
W Granada St 53221
Grand Pkwy 53213
N Grandview Dr 53223
E Grange Ave 53207
W Grange Ave
100-598 53207
600-4299 53221
4300-4600 53220
4602-4898 53220
N Grant Blvd 53210
W Grant Ct 53227
W Grant St
500-599 53207
600-3899 53215
5500-5598 53219
5600-8099 53219
8101-8399 53219
8400-11099 53227
W Grantosa Ct 53218
W Grantosa Dr
6800-8399 53218
8400-8498 53225
8500-9199 53225
9401-9697 53222
9699-10799 53222
W Granville Cir 53223
N Granville Rd 53224
N Granville Woods Rd 53223
N Gray Log Ln 53217
S Greeley St 53207
W Green Ave 53221
N Green Bay Ave 53209
N Green Bay Ct 53217
N Green Bay Rd
7800-8598 53217
8001-8997 53209
8999-9500 53209
9502-9598 53209
N Green Brook Ct
8800-8899 53223
8900-9099 53217
W Green Brook Ct 53223
W Green Brook Dr
4800-5999 53223
8500-8799 53224
N Green Brook Rd 53217
W Green Brook Rd 53217
S Green Links Dr 53227
N Green Tree Ct 53217
E Green Tree Rd 53217
W Green Tree Rd
100-1299 53217
1600-4299 53209
4300-4998 53223
5000-8399 53223
9700-11799 53224
W Green View Ct 53224
S Greenbrook Ter 53220
E Greenfield Ave 53204
W Greenfield Ave
100-2699 53204
2700-4299 53215
4400-12300 53214
12302-12398 53214
S Greenleaf Ct 53228
S Greenridge Cir 53220
Greenvale Ct & Rd 53217
N Greenview Ct 53223
E Greenwich Ave 53211
W Greenwood Rd 53209
W Greenwood Ter
5200-5499 53223
8700-10699 53224
W Greves St
2600-2699 53233
2700-2798 53208
Gridley Ave 53213
S Griffen Ave 53207
S Griffin Ave 53207
W Groeling Ave 53206
N Hackett Ave 53211
E Hadley St 53212
W Hadley St
100-699 53212
800-2699 53206
2701-2917 53210
2919-7599 53210
7600-12399 53222
W Hale Ct 53227
W Hale Pl 53216
W Halsey Ave 53221
N Halyard St 53205
S Hamilton Ct 53220
E Hamilton St 53202
E Hampshire Ave 53211
W Hampton Ave
100-598 53217
800-1298 53209
1300-4299 53209
4300-8399 53218
8400-11899 53225
11901-12099 53225
E Hampton Rd 53217
N Hanchind St 53213
S Hanson Ave 53207
N Harbor Dr 53202
S Harbor Dr 53207
E Harbor Pl 53202
W Harbor House Dr 53224
N Harcourt Pl 53211
Harding Blvd 53226
N Harding Blvd 53226
W Harding Pl 53227
N Harley Davidson
Ave 53225
W Harrison Ave
200-599 53207
600-3099 53215
6101-6197 53219
6199-7199 53219
8400-11799 53227
W Harrison Pl 53227
E Hartford Ave 53211
N Hartung Ave 53210
W Harvard Ln 53226
W Harvest Ln 53225
Harvey Ave 53213
Harwood Ave 53213
W Hassel Ln 53223
N Hastings St 53224
W Hauser Ave 53209
S Hawley Ct 53214
N Hawley Rd
101-497 53213
499-999 53213
1000-1699 53208
S Hawley Rd 53214
W Hawthorne Ave 53226
N Hawthorne Rd 53217
W Hawthorne Rd 53217
W Hawthorne Trace
Rd 53209
W Hayes Ave
300-599 53207
600-3499 53215
3501-3799 53215
5201-5397 53219
5399-8199 53219
8201-8299 53219
8400-12199 53227
W Hayes Pl 53227
W Heather Ave
7600-7999 53223
8700-11399 53224
W Heather Dr
9500-9599 53228
11500-11799 53224
W Heather Ln 53217
W Helena Ave 53209
W Helena Ct 53224
W Helena St
5700-5999 53223
8401-8597 53224
8599-8999 53224
W Hemlock Rd
2100-2599 53209
5100-5499 53223
W Hemlock St
3700-3798 53209
3800-4199 53209
5600-5899 53223
8500-8699 53224
S Hencolli St 53227
Hennessey Ave 53213
E Henry Ave 53207
W Henry Ave 53221
W Henry Ct 53221
E & W Henry Clay St 53217
W Herbert Ave
6900-8399 53218
8700-8999 53225
9001-9099 53225
W Herbert Ct 53225
S Heritage Dr 53220
W Heritage Dr 53224
S Herman St 53207
E Hermitage Rd 53217
N Hi Mount Blvd 53208
W Hibbard Ave 53226
W Hickory St 53206
W Hicks St 53219
S Hidden Dr 53221
W High Life Pl 53208
E Highland Ave 53202
W Highland Ave
200-300 53203
302-598 53203
700-898 53233
900-2699 53233
W Highland Blvd 53208
N Highview Dr 53223
W Highwood Ave 53222
S Hilbert St 53207
W Hilda Pl 53215
Hill St 53226
E Hillcrest Ave 53207
Hillcrest Dr
6500-8299 53213
8400-8499 53226
W Hillcrest Dr 53221
W Hillside Ave 53222
Hillside Ct 53223
Hillside Ln 53213
W Historic Mitchell St 53204
N Holly Ct 53217
W Holly Ln 53228
N Hollywood Ave
4600-4698 53211
4700-4799 53211
4800-5599 53217
W Holmes Ave
1300-1398 53221
1400-3799 53221
4500-8399 53220
12000-12399 53228
W Holmes Ct 53221
E Holt Ave 53207
W Holt Ave
100-373 53207
700-2699 53215
2701-3899 53215
4600-8300 53219
8302-8398 53219
8400-8498 53227
8500-12399 53227
W Holt Ct 53219
N Holton St 53212
E Homer St 53207
W Homewood Ave 53226
W Honey Creek Cir 53221
S Honey Creek Ct 53219
S Honey Creek Dr
200-399 53214
3300-3399 53219
3401-3499 53219
3501-3531 53220
3533-4499 53220
5100-6099 53221
W Honey Creek Dr 53219
Honey Creek Pkwy 53213
N Honey Creek Pkwy 53213
S Honey Creek Pkwy 53214
W Honey Creek Pkwy
7600-7798 53219
8201-8399 53214
Honey Tree Ln 53221
E Hope Ave 53212
W Hope Ave
1000-2499 53209
2501-2699 53209
2901-2997 53216
2999-7499 53216
7501-7599 53216
7601-7797 53222
7799-11199 53222
N Hopkins St 53209
W Hopkins St
1300-2599 53206
2701-2897 53216
2899-3374 53216
3376-3498 53216
N Houston Ave 53218
E Howard Ave 53207
W Howard Ave
100-599 53207
701-1297 53221
1299-4299 53221
4300-8399 53220
8400-12399 53228
S Howell Ave
2200-5499 53207
5500-6298 53207
5500-5500 53237
5501-6299 53207
W Howie Pl 53216
W Hoyt Pl 53216
N Hubbard St 53212
N Humboldt Ave 53202
N Humboldt Blvd 53212
S Humboldt Park Ct 53207
W Hummingbird Ct 53223
W Hunt Club Cir 53209
W Hunter Cir 53209
W Hustis Ct
8000-8099 53223
8800-8899 53224
W Hustis St
5300-7999 53223
8700-8999 53224
N Hyacinth Ln 53217
E Hyde Way 53217
E Idaho St 53207
W Idaho St 53219
N Idlewild Ave
4600-4799 53211
4800-5299 53217
5301-5499 53217
S Illinois Ave 53207
S Imperial Cir 53220
W & N Indian Creek Ct
& Pkwy 53217
S Indiana Ave 53207
N Industrial Rd 53223
W Innovation Dr 53226
W Iona Ter 53221
S Iowa Ave 53207
E Iron St 53207
N Ironwood Ln
4600-4699 53209
6000-9299 53217
N Ironwood Rd 53217
Iroquois Ave & Rd 53217
E Irving Pl 53202
E Ivanhoe Pl 53202
N Ivy St 53223
N Jacheas Ave 53211
W Jackson Dr 53219
N Jackson St 53202
Jackson Park Blvd
7800-8399 53213
8400-9499 53226
W Jackson Park Dr 53219
N Jadam Ln 53224
S Jake Marchese Way 53204
N James Lovell St 53233
E Jarvis St 53211
S Jasper Ave 53207
N Jean Nicolet Rd 53217
N Jefferson St 53202
Jeffrey Ct & Ln 53225
W Jerelyn Pl 53219
W Jewell Ave 53221
W Joleno Ct 53223
W Joleno Ln
4800-5699 53223
9100-9299 53224
W Jonathan Ln 53217
W Jonen St 53224
E Jones St 53207
N Joseph Ave 53224
E Joseph M Hutsteiner
Dr 53207
N Joyce Ave
6100-6399 53225
8900-9399 53224
N Julia St 53212
E Juneau Ave
100-699 53202
606-606 53203
700-1298 53202
701-1199 53202
W Juneau Ave
200-298 53203
300-399 53203
401-599 53203
701-897 53233
899-2699 53233
2700-4999 53208
5001-5999 53208
W Juniper Ct
1900-3799 53209
9700-9799 53224
E Juniper Ln 53217
W Juniper Ln 53209
W Juniper St 53224
E Kane Pl 53202
S Kansas Ave 53207
W Kassner Pl 53204
S Katelyn Cir 53220
Kathryn Ave & Ct 53218
W Kaul Ave
3601-3697 53209
3699-4299 53209
6000-6198 53218
6200-6399 53218
8400-12099 53225
Kavanaugh Pl 53213
E Keefe Ave 53212
W Keefe Ave
100-699 53212
800-898 53206
900-2699 53206
3700-5899 53216
7600-10199 53222
10201-10799 53222
W Keefe Avenue
Pkwy 53216
W Kenboern Dr 53209
Kendall Ave & Ct 53209
E Kenilworth Pl 53202
E Kenmore Pl 53211
E Kensington Blvd 53211
N Kent Ave 53217
S Kentucky Ave 53221
Kenwood Ave 53213
E Kenwood Blvd 53211
Kenyon Ave 53226
W Kerney Pl 53215
E Kewaunee St 53202
W Kiehnau Ave
3301-3397 53209
3399-4299 53209
7400-8399 53223
8700-10499 53224
E Kilbourn Ave 53202
W Kilbourn Ave
100-600 53203
602-698 53203
1101-1197 53233
1199-2699 53233
2700-3799 53208
3801-3899 53208
N Kildeer Ct 53209
W Kiley Ave
3500-4199 53209
4300-4799 53223
W Kiley Ct 53223
N Killian Pl 53212
N Kimbark Pl 53217
W Kimberly Ave 53221
N King Rd 53217
S & W King Arthurs
Ct 53221
W Kingston Pl 53208
S Kinnickinnic Ave
1700-1999 53204
2000-3399 53207
3401-3499 53207
W Kinnickinnic River
Pkwy
2800-3000 53215
3002-3498 53215
4400-4498 53219
4500-7399 53219
Kinsman St 53213
W Kinzie St 53209
W Kirchhoff Ave 53209
W Kisslich Pl 53208
W Klein Ave 53221
W Klondike Pl 53207
E Knapp St 53202
W Kneeland St
600-699 53212
1300-1999 53205
Knoll Blvd & Ter 53222
W Krause Pl 53217
La Salle Ave & Ct 53209
E Lafayette Pl 53202
N Lake Dr
2000-2299 53202
2300-4799 53211
4800-9799 53217
E Lake Ter 53217
E Lake Bluff Blvd 53211
N Lake Drive Ct 53217
E Lake Forest Ave 53217
E Lake Hill Ct 53217
W Lake Park Dr 53224
N Lake Park Rd 53211
E & W Lake View Ave 53217
W Lakefield Dr
3001-3097 53215
3099-3799 53215
5801-6297 53219
6299-7299 53219
11800-12199 53227
E Lancaster Ave 53217
W Lancaster Ave
100-199 53217
2200-4299 53209
6400-8299 53218
8500-10699 53225
Land Pl 53205
E Land Pl 53202
W Land Pl 53212
N Landers St 53223
S Landl Ln 53227
W Langlade St 53225
N Lanianso Rd 53217
W Lapham Blvd 53204
W Lapham St
1600-2699 53204
2701-2897 53215
2899-3799 53215
4400-5198 53214
5200-11200 53214
11202-11298 53214
E Laramie Ln 53217
W Laramie Ln 53217
W Laramie Rd 53224
N Larkin St
4000-4799 53211
4800-5099 53217
W Larkspur Ln 53217
N Lauer St 53224
Laurel Ct 53213
W Lawn Ave
1200-2498 53209
6200-6599 53218
8700-10599 53225
E Lawnwood Pl 53211
W Lawrence Ave
1901-1999 53209
8500-9099 53225
E Layton Ave 53207
W Layton Ave
100-554 53207
555-555 53221
556-598 53207
557-599 53207
601-697 53221
699-4299 53221
4300-8399 53220
8400-12399 53228
S Layton Blvd 53215
W Leeds Pl 53215
N Lefeber Ave
2200-2699 53213
2700-2899 53210
W Legion St 53204
Lenox Pl & St 53207
W Leon Ter
4400-5599 53216
6000-6500 53218
6502-7998 53218
9900-9998 53224
10000-10699 53224
W Leroy Ave
1400-2600 53221
2602-2698 53221
5100-8299 53220
E Lexington Blvd 53217
W Lexington Blvd 53217
W Lexington Ln 53228
W Liberty Dr 53224
E Lilac Ln 53217
W Lima St 53223
Limerick Rd 53223
E Lincoln Ave 53207
W Lincoln Ave
100-599 53207
600-4299 53215
4300-8399 53219
4300-4300 53234
8400-11699 53227
11701-12399 53227
Lincoln Pl 53213
W Lincoln Creek Dr 53218
N Lincoln Memorial Dr
700-1698 53202
1700-1800 53202
1802-2298 53202
2400-3098 53211
S Lincoln Memorial Dr 53207
W & N Lincolnshire Blvd
& Cir 53223
W Linden Pl 53208
N Lindsay St 53205
S Linebarger Ter 53207
N Link Pl 53223
Links Cir & Way 53217
E Linnwood Ave 53211
E Linus St 53207
W Linwal Ln 53209
W Lisbon Ave
2400-2500 53205
2502-2698 53205
2700-2998 53208
3000-4799 53208
4800-7199 53210
7201-7599 53216

7600-9899 53222
9901-10099 53222
N Lite Ln 53208
Livingston Ave 53213
S Livingston Ter 53219
E Lloyd St 53212
W Lloyd St
100-600 53212
602-698 53212
1100-2699 53205
2901-3097 53208
3099-5699 53208
5701-5999 53208
6000-7399 53213
E Locust St
200-498 53212
500-1399 53212
1600-3099 53211
W Locust St
100-298 53212
300-600 53212
602-698 53212
800-1020 53206
1022-2600 53206
2602-2698 53206
2700-7599 53210
7600-7698 53222
7700-12299 53222
12301-12399 53222
W & N Lodgewood Ct & Rd 53217
S Logan Ave 53207
W Lolita Ave
7600-8099 53223
9500-9799 53224
9801-9899 53224
Lombard Ct 53213
Lombardy Ct & Rd 53217
N Long Island Dr 53209
N Longacre Rd 53217
Longview Ave & Dr 53209
W Loomis Rd
2900-4299 53221
4300-5099 53220
S Lorene Ave 53221
W Lorraine Pl 53222
W Louise Pl 53216
S Louisiana Ave 53221
N Lovers Lane Rd 53225
Ludington Ave & Ct 53226
W Luebbe Ln
400-599 53217
5100-5799 53223
W Luscher Ave
4200-4299 53209
4701-4797 53218
4799-7900 53218
7902-8398 53218
W Luzerne Ct 53221
N Lydell Ave
4000-4100 53212
4102-4298 53212
4800-6399 53217
Lynmar Ct & Ter 53222
W Lynndale Ave
3101-3197 53221
3199-3499 53221
4800-4999 53220
Lynx Ave & Ct 53225
E Lyon St 53202
S Mabbett Ave 53207
E Macarthur Rd 53217
N Macharic St 53223
S Madeline Ave 53221
W Madison Pl 53214
E Madison St 53204
W Madison St
200-298 53204
300-1499 53204
3100-3299 53215
5800-11800 53214
11802-12398 53214
W Magnolia St 53224
W Main St 53214
Maitland Ct & Rd 53217
N Malibu Dr 53217
E & W Mall Rd 53217
S Mallard Cir 53221
W Mallory Ave
600-2900 53221
2902-3098 53221
4300-4499 53220
E Malvern Pl 53207
W Manchester Ave 53221
E Mangold Ave 53207
W Mangold Ave
100-299 53207
1800-4200 53221
4202-4298 53221
E Manitoba St 53207
W Manitoba St
600-4099 53215
4400-8199 53219
9100-10599 53227
Manor Cir 53223
E Manor Cir 53217
W Manor Cir
200-599 53217
7800-8399 53223
N Manor Ct 53217
W Manor Ct 53224
W Manor Dr 53223
N Manor Ln 53217
W Manor Ln
1000-1699 53217
7800-8399 53223
W Manor Park Dr 53227
W Manpower Pl 53212
W Maple Ct 53214
W Maple Ln 53225
E Maple St 53204
W Maple St
100-2699 53204
3600-3700 53215
3702-3798 53215
8400-9099 53214
Maple Ter 53213
W Maple Leaf Cir 53220
W Maplewood Ct 53221
W Maplewood Dr 53220
W Marcelle Ave 53224
W Marcia Rd 53223
S & W Marcy Ln & St 53220
W Margaret Pl 53215
W Margaretta Ct 53209
N Marietta Ave 53211
S Marilyn St 53221
S Marina Dr 53207
Marine Ct & Dr 53223
N Mariners St 53224
E Marion St 53211
W Marion St
3500-7599 53216
7900-10999 53222
11001-11099 53222
N Market St 53202
N Marlborough Dr
4300-4799 53211
4800-5423 53217
5425-5599 53217
W Marne Ave
401-599 53217
1900-2399 53209
N Marshall St 53202
W Martha Dr 53226
Martha Washington Dr 53213
E Marti Ct 53217
W Martin Dr
4100-5999 53208
6000-6199 53213
W Martin Ln 53207
Mary Ellen Pl 53213
N Maryland Ave 53211
E Mason St 53202
S Massachusetts Ave 53220
N Maura Ln 53223
N Mayfair Ct 53222
N Mayfair Rd
101-197 53226
199-1600 53226
1602-2698 53226
1655-1655 53213
1655-2699 53226
2701-3097 53222
3099-3999 53222
4001-4399 53222
4400-4498 53225
4500-4600 53225
4602-4798 53225
N Mayflower Ct 53205
Maywood Ave & Ct 53226
W Mcauley Pl 53233
W Mcgeoch Ave 53219
S Mckerich St 53215
W Mckinley Ave
200-400 53212
402-698 53212
700-998 53205
1000-2499 53205
2501-2599 53205
3500-5600 53208
5602-5698 53208
6300-6399 53213
W Mckinley Blvd 53208
W Mckinley Ct 53208
W Mcmyron St 53214
Meadow Ct 53222
W Meadow Dr 53228
E Meadow Pl 53217
Meadow Creek Ct & Dr 53224
S Meadow Park Ln 53220
N Meadowlark Ln 53217
N Meadowside Ct 53223
W Medford Ave
2400-2699 53206
4400-5099 53216
6000-6098 53218
6100-8299 53218
8600-8699 53225
E Meinecke Ave 53212
W Meinecke Ave
100-699 53212
800-2699 53206
2700-3028 53210
3030-5800 53210
5802-5998 53210
6000-8399 53213
8400-11999 53226
12001-12099 53226
N Melarres St 53208
S Melinda St 53221
N Melissa Ct 53209
W Melody Ln 53228
Melrose Ave 53213
E Melvina St 53212
W Melvina St
100-699 53212
700-1298 53206
1300-2599 53206
2700-7599 53216
7600-7698 53222
7700-10499 53222
E Menlo Blvd 53211
Menomonee Dr 53213
E Menomonee St 53202
W Menomonee Park Ct 53225
Menomonee River Pkwy 53222
N Menomonee River Pkwy
1900-1998 53226
2000-2200 53226
2202-2698 53226
2700-3098 53222
3100-3129 53222
3131-3499 53222
4400-4498 53225
W Menomonee River Pkwy 53213
W Mequanigo Dr 53227
W Merco Ln 53212
E Meredith St 53207
N Merrie Ln 53217
W Merrill St 53204
W Messmer St 53209
N Met To Wee Ln 53226
W Metcalf Pl 53222
Metro Blvd 53224
W Metro Auto Mall 53224
N Michael Ct 53224
W Michael Dr 53209
N Michele St 53224
N Michelle Ct 53224
E Michigan St 53202
W Michigan St
100-699 53203
700-798 53233
800-2699 53233
2700-3899 53208
5600-5999 53213
9100-11099 53226
W Midarest Ave 53225
W Middlemass St 53215
W Midland Dr
4400-5099 53219
5100-5499 53220
W Mill Rd
1601-1797 53209
1799-4199 53209
4201-4299 53209
4500-4598 53218
4600-8399 53218
8400-12099 53225
W Mill St 53225
Miller Ct 53217
W Miller Ln 53208
Miller Park Way
1100-1198 53214
1200-1699 53214
1701-1899 53214
1900-2299 53219
Milwaukee Ave 53213
W Milwaukee Rd 53208
N Milwaukee St 53202
N Milwaukee River Pkwy 53209
S Miner St 53221
E Mineral St 53204
W Mineral St
100-2699 53204
5700-5798 53214
5800-5899 53214
E Mitchell St 53204
W Mitchell St
100-2699 53204
2700-4299 53215
4400-11599 53214
W Mobile St 53219
Mohawk Ave & Rd 53217
W Moltke Ave 53210
W Monarch Pl 53208
E Mondendo Ave 53207
W Monona Pl 53219
W Monroe St
1800-1899 53205
1901-1999 53205
2400-2599 53206
E Monrovia Ave 53217
W Monrovia Ave
100-1199 53217
8600-8999 53225
W Monrovia Way 53209
W Montana Ave
8200-8399 53219
8400-11499 53227
E Montana St 53207
W Montana St
700-3499 53215
4301-4397 53219
4399-7199 53219
E & W Montclaire Ave 53217
N Montreal St 53216
W Montrose Ave 53219
E Morgan Ave 53207
W Morgan Ave
100-399 53207
701-947 53221
949-4299 53221
4300-8399 53220
8400-12399 53228
W Morgan Oak Dr 53228
Morningside Ln 53221
N Morris Blvd 53211
N & W Mother Daniels Way 53209
N Mother Simpson Way 53206
S Mound St 53207
W Mount Royal Rd 53217
W Mount Vernon Ave
300-398 53203
901-1097 53233
1099-2299 53233
2700-3900 53208
3902-5598 53208
6300-7899 53213
7901-7999 53213
9000-11699 53226
Mountain Ave 53213
Mower Ct 53213
W Mt Zion Dr 53224
W Mulberry Ct 53217
W Muriel Pl 53218
N Murray Ave 53211
S Muskego Ave
500-2099 53204
2100-2299 53215
E Nash St 53212
W Nash St
100-198 53212
200-299 53212
800-2599 53206
2601-2699 53206
3500-3698 53216
3700-7400 53216
7402-7598 53216
8101-8197 53222
8199-10299 53222
E National Ave 53204
W National Ave
100-2699 53204
2700-4199 53215
4201-4299 53215
4400-4498 53214
4500-8200 53214
8202-8398 53214
8400-11599 53227
Navajo Ave & Rd 53217
W Nebraska Ave
5200-5399 53219
6101-6297 53220
6299-6499 53220
N & W Neil Pl 53209
S Nevada St 53207
W New Jersey Ave 53220
S New York Ave 53207
E Newberry Blvd 53211
N Newhall Ln 53211
N Newhall St
2000-2299 53202
2300-2498 53211
2500-4799 53211
4800-4999 53217
Newport Ave & Ct 53211
E Newton Ave 53211
W Newton Pl 53209
W Nicolet Ct 53217
E Nock St 53207
W Nokomis Ct 53217
W Nokomis Rd 53223
Normandy Ct & Ln 53226
E North Ave
100-1199 53212
1400-2399 53202
W North Ave
100-699 53212
800-898 53205
900-2699 53205
2700-5999 53208
6000-8399 53213
8400-12399 53226
N North Mother Daniels Way St 53209
W Northridge Ct
8301-8399 53223
8400-8499 53224
W Northridge Lakes Blvd 53223
W Northshore Dr 53217
W Norwich Ave
4400-8299 53220
9700-10599 53228
W Norwich Ct 53220
E Norwich St 53207
W Norwich St
100-599 53207
5100-5198 53220
5200-8107 53220
N Norwood Pl 53216
W Notre Dame Ct 53208
W O Connor St 53214
Oak Ct 53223
W Oak St 53206
S Oak Park Ct 53214
S Oakbrook Dr 53228
N Oakenest St 53210
Oakhill Ave 53213
N Oakland Ave
1800-2299 53202
2300-4799 53211
4800-4899 53217
4901-4999 53217
S Oakridge Ct 53228
W Oconto Pl 53219
W Odell St 53204
E Ogden Ave 53202
E Ohio Ave 53207
W Ohio Ave
600-3700 53215
3702-3898 53215
4401-4997 53219
4999-8299 53219
8301-8399 53219
8400-8598 53227
8600-12399 53227
W Ohio Ct 53219
E Oklahoma Ave 53207
W Oklahoma Ave
100-599 53207
600-4299 53215
4301-4397 53219
4399-8399 53219
8400-12399 53227
S & W Old Oaks Dr & Ln 53221
N Old World 3rd St
700-1199 53203
1200-1298 53212
N Oldennew St 53233
E Olive St 53211
W Olive St
101-197 53212
199-400 53212
402-598 53212
1200-2399 53209
4300-4699 53216
8500-8899 53222
N Olsen Ave 53211
E Ontario St 53207
W Orchard Ct 53214
W Orchard Pl 53214
E Orchard St 53204
W Orchard St
100-2699 53204
2900-4299 53215
6000-6898 53214
6900-10799 53214
E & W Oregon St 53204
W Orinda Ct 53224
W Oriole Dr 53209
S Orleans Ave 53227
E Otjen St 53207
W Oxford Pl 53226
W Pabst Ave 53215
N Palisades Rd 53217
W Pallottine Dr 53228
N Palmer St 53212
W Palmetto Ave
7600-7999 53218
8700-9199 53225
9400-9899 53222
W Palmetto Ct 53225
W & N Paradise Ct & Ln 53209
N Park Dr 53222
W Park Dr 53220
E Park Pl 53211
W Park Pl 53224
N Park Rd 53217
W Park Hill Ave
3400-3998 53208
5800-7199 53213
8800-11500 53226
11502-11598 53226
N Park Manor Dr 53224
N Park Plaza Ct 53223
W Park Ridge Ave 53222
W Parkland Ave
3900-4299 53209
4301-4397 53223
4399-8099 53223
11101-11197 53224
11199-11299 53224
W Parkland Ct
7000-8399 53223
9500-9699 53224
Parkside Ct & Dr 53225
Parkview Ct 53226
N Parkway Ave 53209
W Parkway Dr 53218
N Parlered St 53202
W Parnell Ave 53221
Pasadena Blvd 53226
S Pearl St 53204
N Pearlette Ln 53223
E Pearson St 53202
W Peck Ct 53225
W Peck Pl 53209
N Pelham Pkwy 53217
N Pelican Ln 53217
W Pelican Ln 53209
W Pemberton Ave 53210
S Pennsylvania Ave 53207
W Peregrine Way 53228
W Perkins Pl 53216
N Perry Ct 53213
W Petersik St 53224
N Pheasant Ln 53217
W Philip Pl 53216
S Phillips Ave 53221
N Pierce St 53212
W Pierce St
100-2199 53204
2201-2699 53204
2700-3799 53215
3801-3899 53215
5800-5899 53214
W Pierner Pl 53223
N Pierron Rd 53209
S Pine Ave 53207
W Pine Ridge Rd 53228
N Pine Shore Dr 53209
N Pinecrest St 53208
E Pinedale Ct 53211
N Pingree Ave 53224
E & W Pittsburgh Ave 53204
S Placid Dr 53220
E Plainfield Ave 53207
W Plainfield Ave
100-599 53207
900-3999 53221
5100-8399 53220
8800-12199 53228
W Plank Ct 53226
N Plankinton Ave 53203
W Plaza Cir 53223
Pleasant St 53213
E Pleasant St
100-199 53212
401-497 53202
499-1199 53202
W Pleasant St 53212
Pleasant View St 53226
W Poe St 53215
N Point Dr 53217
S Point Ter 53221
N Pointe St 53224
E Polk St 53202
N Poplar Dr 53217
W Port Ave
5600-7999 53223
8600-8799 53224
N Port Ct 53217
W Port Sunlight Way 53209
N Port Washington Ct 53217

N Port Washington Rd
3400-4799 53212
4800-9599 53217
W Portage Ave 53223
E Portage Rd 53217
W Portage St
3700-4299 53209
8700-9099 53224
Portland Ave 53213
W Potomac Ave
7200-7376 53216
7378-7398 53216
7700-7798 53222
7800-7900 53222
7902-7998 53222
8000-8399 53218
8500-8899 53225
E Potter Ave 53207
W Potter Rd 53226
Powell Pl 53213
S Prairie Hill Ln 53228
N Prentiss St 53218
N & W Presidio Dr & Ln 53223
Price Ave & Ct 53207
S Princeton Ave 53215
N Prospect Ave
701-997 53202
999-2299 53202
2300-4499 53211
E Providence Ave 53211
E Pryor Ave 53207
N Pulaski St 53202
W Purdue St 53209
E Quarles Pl 53217
Quincy Ave & Ct 53207
W Radcliffe Dr 53223
W Rae Ave 53225
W Rainbow Ave 53214
Raintree Ct & Dr 53223
W Raleigh Ave 53209
W Ramsey Ave 53221
E & W Randolph Ct & St 53212
W Range Ave 53223
N Range Line Rd
6400-7100 53209
7102-7798 53209
7800-8799 53217
8800-8998 53217
9000-9599 53217
Ravenswood Cir 53226
E Ravine Ln 53217
W Ravine Ln
1000-1099 53217
4500-4699 53223
E & W Ravine Baye Rd 53217
S Ravinia Dr 53221
Raymir Cir & Pl 53222
W Raymond Ln 53219
W Rebecca Ct 53228
Red Arrow Ct 53213
W Red Oaks Ct 53220
Redwood Ct & Rd 53209
Regent Ct & Rd 53217
W Reichert Pl
2700-4299 53209
9701-9799 53225
E Reindl Way 53212
N Renee St 53233
W Research Dr 53226
E Reservoir Ave 53212
W Reservoir Ave
100-699 53212
700-1098 53205
1100-1399 53205
W Rev Cecil A Fisher Ln 53212
Revere Ave 53213
W Revere Pl 53219
N Rexleigh Dr 53217
N Reynard Rd 53217
W Reynolds Pl 53204
E Rhode Island Ave 53207
W Rice St 53216
N Richards St 53212
W Richardson Pl 53208
N Richland Ct 53211
W Richmond Ave 53210
Richmond Ct 53213
W Richmond St 53210
Ridge Blvd 53226
Ridge Ct 53213
W Ridge Ct 53216
N Ridgefield Cir 53211
S Ridgewood Ln 53221
E Ring St 53212
W Ring St
100-699 53212
800-1599 53206
1601-1699 53206
W Rio St 53225
W Ripley Ave 53226
N Ripon Pl 53222
W Rita Dr 53219
W River Ct 53217
W River Ln
3701-3897 53209
3899-4200 53209
4202-4298 53209
4300-4499 53223
River Pkwy 53213
N River Rd 53217
N River Bend Ct 53217
W River Bend Dr 53219
N River Edge Dr 53209
N River Forest Dr 53209
W River Front Dr 53217
S River Glen Ln 53228
N River Park Blvd 53209
River Park Ct 53226
E River Park Ct 53211
W River Park Ln 53209
S River Ridge Blvd 53228
W River Ridge Dr 53224
N River Trail Dr 53225
N River View Ct 53224
W River Woods Pkwy 53212
N Riverboat Rd 53212
N Rivercenter Dr 53212
Rivers Bnd 53226
W Rivers Edge Cir 53209
S Rivershire Dr 53228
E Riverside Pl 53211
W Riverview Dr 53209
N Riverwalk Way
501-599 53203
1701-1797 53212
1799-1899 53212
1901-2099 53212
Riverwoods Dr 53224
E Roadsmeet St 53212
W Roberts St 53208
Robertson St 53213
S Robinson Ave 53207
W Rochelle Ave
1600-3999 53209
4400-4799 53223
9000-9799 53224
W Rock Pl 53209
N Rockledge Ave 53209
Rockway Pl 53213
W Roder Ct 53208
Rogers Ave 53213
W Rogers St
500-2699 53204
2700-3699 53215
5000-5098 53219
5100-8399 53219
8800-11599 53227
W Rohr Ave
2200-3999 53209
4400-4898 53218
4900-4999 53218
8700-10799 53225
Romona Ave 53213
W Roosevelt Dr
2000-2699 53209
2700-5999 53216
Root River Pkwy 53227
S Root River Pkwy 53228
W Rose St 53223
E Rosedale Ave 53207
W Rosedale Ave
301-499 53207
9501-9597 53227
9599-9799 53227
E Royall Pl 53202
W Ruby Ave
2200-4299 53209
6300-6598 53218
6600-8399 53218
8400-11199 53225
E Rusk Ave 53207
Ruskin Ct & St 53215
E Russell Ave 53207
W Rust Ct 53227
Ruth Pl 53209
W Ryan Ct 53224
Saint Anne Ct 53213
Saint Charles St 53213
S Saint Clair St 53207
W Saint Francis Ave
3401-3499 53221
4401-4497 53220
4499-4799 53220
4801-4899 53220
10300-11099 53228
Saint James Ct & St 53213
W Saint Johns Ct 53217
Saint Jude Ct 53213
E Saint Paul Ave 53202
W Saint Paul Ave
131-297 53203
299-400 53203
345-345 53201
401-499 53203
402-698 53203
701-897 53233
899-2500 53233
2502-2698 53233
2700-2898 53208
2900-5599 53208
5800-7199 53213
9100-9499 53226
W Saireda Ave 53221
W Salem St 53221
W Sanctuary Dr 53224
W Sandpiper Ct 53223
S Sansontr St 53219
N Santa Monica Blvd
4700-4799 53211
4800-9199 53217
W Sarah Ct 53228
W Sarasota Pl 53222
W Sarnow St 53208
E & W Saveland Ave 53207
W Scarlet Oak Ct 53228
S Schauer Ave 53219
E Schiller St 53207
W Schlinger Ave 53214
E School Rd 53217
W Schroeder Dr
4100-4199 53209
4300-4999 53223
E Scott St
100-199 53204
800-899 53207
W Scott St
101-197 53204
199-2699 53204
2700-4099 53215
4401-4497 53214
4499-5899 53214
N Scranton Ct 53224
W Scranton Pl
4600-4899 53216
4901-4999 53216
8000-8199 53218
E & W Seeboth St 53204
E Seeley St 53207
W Senator Ave 53216
Seneca Ave, Ct & Rd 53217
N Sequoia Dr 53217
N Sercombe Rd 53216
N Servite Dr 53223
N Seville Ave 53209
S Seymour Pl 53227
S Shady Lane Ct 53228
W Sharon Ln 53225
N Shasta Dr 53209
S Shea Ave 53215
N Sheffield Ave
4300-4799 53211
4800-5099 53217
W Shelby St 53223
N Shepard Ave 53211
N Sherburn Pl 53211
W Sheridan Ave
1800-4299 53209
5100-8300 53218
8302-8398 53218
9200-10600 53225
10602-10698 53225
W Sheridan Ct 53209
N Sherman Blvd
1400-2299 53208
2300-3099 53210
3100-4399 53216
4400-8099 53209
E Ship St 53212
N Sholes Ave 53210
N Shore Dr 53217
S Shore Dr 53207
N Shoreland Ave 53217
E Shorewood Blvd 53211
N Sidney Pl 53209
W Sieben Pl 53216
W Siegfried Pl 53214
N Sievers Pl 53209
S Sijan St 53207
N & W Silver Brook Ln 53223
E Silver Spring Dr 53217
W Silver Spring Dr
100-599 53217
601-699 53217
800-998 53209
1000-4299 53209
4800-5098 53218
5100-8399 53218
8400-9098 53225
9100-12399 53225
W Silver Spring Rd 53225
W Silverleaf Ln 53223
E Singer Cir 53212
Six Points Xing 53214
N Skyline Ln 53217
W Skyline Rd
1000-1199 53217
2100-2399 53209
E Skytrain Ave 53207
N Sleepy Hollow Ln 53217
W Sleske Ct 53223
E Smith St 53207
W Somers St 53205
Somerset Ln S 53221
S & W Sonata Cir & Dr 53221
W Southridge Dr 53220
W Spaulding Pl 53208
W Spencer Pl
4400-4599 53216
6000-6399 53218
10200-10599 53224
W Spokane St
6000-6799 53223
8600-11399 53224
E Spooner Rd 53217
W Spring Ln 53223
W Spring Green Rd 53228
S Springfield Ave 53207
W & N Spruce Ct & Rd 53217
W Squire Ave
4000-4299 53221
6900-7399 53220
12200-12299 53228
Stack Ct & Dr 53219
E Standish Pl 53217
N Stanley Pl 53212
N Stanton Dr 53209
W Stark St
2000-2698 53209
2700-4299 53209
4401-4597 53218
4599-7300 53218
7302-7698 53218
8601-8697 53225
8699-10999 53225
E State St 53202
W State St
200-599 53203
601-699 53203
700-2699 53233
2700-5599 53208
6000-7799 53213
N Steven Rd 53223
W Stevenson St
6000-7999 53213
9200-9299 53226
9301-9399 53226
W Stewart Ave 53222
E Stewart St 53207
Stickney Ave
7600-8399 53213
8400-9399 53226
W Stonebridge Ct 53221
S & W Stonehedge Dr 53220
N Stoneridge Ct 53223
N Story Pkwy 53208
N Story Hill Pl 53208
N Stowell Ave 53211
E Stratford Ct 53211
N Strathmore Ave 53218
S Stratton Dr 53219
S Strothmann Dr 53219
W Stuth Ave 53227
W Stuth Pl 53219
Suburban Ct & Dr 53217
W Suelane Rd 53209
W Sugar Ln 53217
W Sumac Pl 53219
N Summit Ave
1900-2299 53202
2500-3599 53211
W Sunbury Ct
2200-3599 53215
8000-8299 53219
N Sunny Point Ln 53217
N Sunny Point Rd
5600-6199 53209
6200-6599 53217
W Sunnyside Dr 53208
W Sunset Ave 53222
Sunset Ct 53226
S Sunset Dr 53220
N Sunset Ln
5600-5700 53209
5702-5798 53209
6400-6599 53217
W Sunset Ln 53228
S Sunset Sq 53220
S Superior St 53207
S Supreme Ct 53228
N Surf Ct 53223
N Sussex St 53209
Sutton Pl S 53221
S Swain Ct 53207
W & N Swallow Blvd, Ln & Rd 53223
N Swan Blvd 53226
W Swan Cir 53225
N Swan Rd
4800-4899 53225
8835-8839 53224
8841-9599 53224
N Sycamore Ct 53217
E Sylvan Ave 53217
W Sylvia St 53224
N Tacoma St 53224
Tallmadge Ct & Pl 53218
W Talon Cir 53228
W Tamarack St 53206
S Tamerlea St 53204
S Tami Ln 53221
S Tara Hill Dr 53220
Taylor Ave & Ct 53207
N Teal Ct 53223
S Tennessee Ave 53221
N Tennyson Dr 53217
W Teresa Ln 53224
Terra Ave & Ct 53224
N Terrace Ave
1900-2299 53202
2300-2398 53211
2400-2699 53211
Terrace Ct 53213
W Terry Ave 53223
W Tesch Ave
4300-8399 53220
11800-11899 53228
N Teutonia Ave
2200-2299 53205
2300-3999 53206
4000-8399 53209
E Texas Ave 53207
W Theodore Trecker Way 53214
Theresa Ct & Ln 53209
E Thomas Ave 53211
E Thorne Ln 53217
N Thrush Ln 53217
W Thurston Ave
3100-4299 53209
5400-8299 53218
8700-9700 53225
9702-9898 53225
W Thurston Cir 53218
W Thurston Ct 53218
S Todd Dr 53228
S Toldt Cir 53221
S Toldt Pkwy 53227
N Tomart Ave 53225
N & W Toronto St 53216
W Tower Ave
4400-8399 53223
8400-10599 53224
W Tower View Blvd 53222
E Townsend St 53212
W Townsend St
100-199 53212
2001-2197 53206
2199-2599 53206
2601-2699 53206
2701-3497 53216
3499-5899 53216
7600-9799 53222
9801-10799 53222
W Trenton Pl 53213
N Tridench St 53216
E Tripoli Ave 53207
W Tripoli Ave
100-299 53207
2000-2499 53221
4301-4497 53220
4499-8299 53220
8500-9899 53228
E Trowbridge St 53207
N Troy Ct 53223
Tuckaway Blvd, Cir, Ct, Dr & Ln 53221
N Tucker Pl 53222
W Tupelo Ct 53224
W Tupelo St
3800-4099 53209
8600-8699 53224
Two Tree Ln 53213
E & W Uncas Ave 53207
Underwood Ave 53213
Underwood Ct 53226
Underwood Pkwy 53226
W Underwood Pkwy 53226
S Union St 53204
W Upham Ave
1400-3100 53221
3102-4198 53221
4300-5899 53220
9500-9599 53228
W Upham Ct 53221
Upper Pkwy N & S 53213
Upper River Ct & Rd 53217
S Utah Ave 53219
W Valanna Ct 53209
N Valerlea St 53226
W Valley Forge Dr 53213
N Valley Hill Rd 53217
E Van Beck Ave 53207
W Van Beck Ave
2050-2398 53221
4400-8199 53220
8500-11799 53228
W Van Beck Way 53221
N Van Buren St 53202
S Van Dyke Pl 53219
N Van Dyke Rd 53217
E Van Norman Ave 53207
W Van Norman Ave
100-499 53207
1300-1998 53221
2000-2299 53221
6200-7199 53220
11900-11998 53228
W Van Norman Ct 53228
W Vance Pl 53216
W Vera Ave
2700-4099 53209
9400-10699 53224
S Vermont Ave 53207
W Verona Ct
2100-3599 53215
5400-7899 53219
8800-12299 53227
N Verrens St 53224
W Victory Ln 53209
W Vieau Pl 53204
E Vienna Ave 53212
W Vienna Ave
101-297 53212
299-699 53212
701-1597 53206
1599-2599 53206
2601-2699 53206
2701-2797 53216
2799-7000 53216
7002-7098 53216
7600-8398 53222
8400-10499 53222
10501-10599 53222
W Vienna Ct 53216
N View Pl 53217
W Vigo Ter 53227
W Villa Ave 53224
S Villa Cir 53227
W Villa Ln 53223
W Villard Ave
1800-4299 53209
4300-8299 53218
8301-8399 53218
8400-10899 53225
W Vilter Ln 53204
W Vincent Pl 53214
E Vine St 53212
W Vine St
100-699 53212
1100-2699 53205
2700-2798 53208
2800-5499 53208
5501-5999 53208
N Vintrado St 53222
W Virginia St 53204
Vista Ave 53213
W Vliet St
300-699 53212
700-2699 53205
2700-5999 53208
6000-6199 53213
11600-12399 53226
W Vogel Ave
200-399 53207
1400-3799 53221
6900-7199 53220
W Vogel Ct 53221
E Vollmer Ave 53207
W Vollmer Ave 53219
W Wabash Ave
4800-7299 53223
10000-10699 53224
W Wabash Ct 53223
E Wabash Pl 53217
N Wahl Ave 53211
W Wahner Ave 53223
E Wahner Pl 53217
N Wakefield Ct 53217
E Walker St 53204
W Walker St
100-1599 53204

5700-12399 53214
W Walnut Rd 53226
W Walnut St
300-699 53212
700-798 53205
800-2699 53205
2700-2898 53208
2900-5599 53208
N Walton Pl 53222
E Walworth St 53212
W Wanda Ave
1400-4299 53221
4300-4398 53220
4400-4499 53220
Warbler Ct 53223
E Ward St 53207
E Warnimont Ave 53207
W Warnimont Ave
100-599 53207
2000-2599 53221
5701-6097 53220
6099-8399 53220
8400-8999 53228
9001-9099 53228
W Warnimont Ct 53220
Warren Ave 53213
N Warren Ave 53202
N Warwick Ct 53209
N Wasaukee Rd 53224
W Washington Blvd
4700-5999 53208
6000-6599 53213
Washington Cir 53213
N Washington Ln 53217
W Washington Pl 53214
E Washington St 53204
W Washington St
100-1999 53204
5600-5698 53214
5700-12299 53214
12301-12399 53214
N Water St 53202
S Water St 53204
E Waterford Ave 53207
W Waterford Ave
100-599 53207
601-999 53221
1100-1198 53221
5500-8299 53220
8400-12399 53228
W Waterford Ct 53220
W Waterford Sq N 53228
W Waterford Sq S 53228
Watertown Plank Rd 53213
W Watertown Plank Rd 53226
S Waterview Ct 53220
Watson Ave 53213
S Waukesha Rd 53227
N Wauwatosa Ave 53213
N Waverly Dr 53217
N Waverly Pl 53202
N & W Wayside Ct & Dr 53209
Webster Ct 53222
E Webster Pl 53211
Wedgewood Ct & Dr 53220
N Weil St 53212
Wellauer Dr 53213
E Wells St 53202
W Wells St
100-399 53203
401-699 53203
700-2699 53233
2700-5599 53208
5600-7599 53213
10900-11199 53226
Wending Ct & Dr 53209
S Wentworth Ave 53207
S & W Westchester Sq & St 53214
S Westgrand Ln 53219
W Wheelhouse Rd 53208
W Whitaker Ave
1301-1497 53221
1499-3199 53221
5200-8299 53220
8301-8399 53220
8400-12399 53228
E Whitaker Ct 53207
W Whitaker Ct 53228
W White St 53204
W White Oak Dr 53228
N White Oak Ln 53217
W White Oak Ln 53217
S Whitnall Ave 53207
N Whitney Rd 53217
W Wick Pl 53219
E Wilbur Ave 53207
W Wilbur Ave
100-299 53207
1300-2199 53221
2201-3499 53221
4600-8399 53220
8400-12099 53228
W Wilbur Ct 53220
Wildcat Ct 53228
N Wildwood Ave
4300-4699 53211
4800-4999 53217
W Wildwood Ct 53227
S Wildwood Dr 53227
W Wildwood Ln 53227
W Wildwood Ter 53227
N Will Enterprise Ct 53224
S Williams St 53207
N Willis Pl 53222
W Willow Ct
400-499 53217
11600-11699 53228
E Willow Rd 53217
W Willow Rd
100-299 53217
4700-5299 53223
W Willow Ter 53217
W Willow Way 53221
N Willow Glen Ln 53209
Willowbrook Ln 53221
N Wilshire Rd 53211
Wilson Blvd 53226
N Wilson Dr 53211
E Wilson St 53207
S Winchester St 53207
N Windermere Ct 53211
W Windlake Ave
700-1099 53204
1100-1120 53215
1122-1999 53215
W Windsor Cir 53209
Windsor Ct 53226
E Windsor Pl 53202
W Winfield Ave
7700-8299 53218
8700-8900 53225
8902-8998 53225
W Wingate Ave 53209
S Wingspan Ln 53228
E Winkler Ln 53217
W Winnebago St 53205
S Winona Ln 53204
W Wirth St 53222
E Wisconsin Ave 53202
W Wisconsin Ave
100-699 53203
700-2699 53233
2700-5599 53208
5600-8399 53213
8400-11599 53226
N Witte Ln 53209
S Wollmer Rd
2900-3499 53227
3600-3699 53228
W Wood Ave 53221
E Wood Pl 53211
W Woodale Ave
4000-4299 53209
4300-4699 53223
Woodbridge Ln S 53221
N Woodburn St
4000-4098 53211
4100-4799 53211
4800-5199 53217
W Woodbury Ln 53209
W Wooded Ct 53228
W Woodland Ave
7600-8299 53213
11600-12399 53226
S Woodland Dr 53220
W Woodland Dr 53223
W Woodlawn Ct 53208
S Woodlawn Pl 53228
N Woodruff Ave
4400-4498 53211
4500-4799 53211
4800-5099 53217
5101-5199 53217
Woods Cir 53223
Woodside Ct 53226
E Woodstock Pl 53202
W Woodview Ct 53220
W Woodward Ave 53222
S Woodward St 53207
W Woolworth Ave 53218
W Wren Ave
3200-3399 53209
10700-10899 53225
10901-11299 53225
W Wren Ct 53225
E Wright St 53212
W Wright St
100-699 53212
800-2699 53206
2700-5999 53210
6000-8399 53213
8400-10299 53226
E Wye Ln 53217
E Wyoming Pl 53202
Yale Pl 53213
N Yates Rd 53217
York Ct & Pl 53222
N Yuba St 53223
W Zellman Ct 53221

NUMBERED STREETS

S 1st Pl 53207
N 1st St 53212
S 1st St
100-1999 53204
2000-6299 53207
N 2nd Ln 53212
N 2nd St
300-398 53203
400-899 53203
1500-3999 53212
S 2nd St
100-1899 53204
3400-5099 53207
N 3rd St
400-500 53203
502-598 53203
3100-3198 53212
3200-3899 53212
3901-3999 53212
S 3rd St
100-1999 53204
2300-6299 53207
N 4th St
600-1199 53203
1201-1297 53212
1299-3999 53212
S 4th St
400-1400 53204
1402-2098 53204
2100-2398 53207
2400-4399 53207
S 5th Ct 53207
S 5th Pl
1900-2099 53204
2100-4599 53207
N 5th St
400-1199 53203
1400-3999 53212
S 5th St
400-498 53204
500-1199 53204
1201-2099 53204
2100-4699 53207
N 6th Pl 53212
N 6th St
300-498 53203
1300-4199 53212
S 6th St
500-2099 53204
2100-2899 53215
3501-4597 53221
S 7th Ln 53204
N 7th St
800-998 53233
1300-2299 53205
2300-3698 53212
4000-4199 53209
S 7th St
101-199 53233
400-2099 53204
2100-3399 53215
4401-4697 53221
N 8th St
301-497 53233
499-1199 53233
1300-1999 53205
2301-3673 53206
3800-3998 53206
4000-4099 53209
S 8th St
1000-2099 53204
2300-3499 53215
3500-5499 53221
N 9th Ln 53206
S 9th Pl 53215
N 9th St
501-697 53233
1200-1799 53205
2300-2398 53206
4001-4099 53209
S 9th St
400-498 53204
2300-3499 53215
5101-5197 53221
N 10th Ln 53206
S 10th Pl 53215
N 10th St
600-900 53233
1200-2200 53205
2301-2397 53206
4100-4199 53209
S 10th St
600-1999 53204
2100-3499 53215
4100-4899 53221
N 11th Ln 53206
N 11th St
601-697 53233
1801-2097 53205
2300-3999 53206
4000-5599 53209
S 11th St
101-199 53233
400-2099 53204
2100-3499 53215
3501-3527 53221
N 12th Ln 53205
N 12th St
200-298 53233
1201-1597 53205
2300-3999 53206
4000-5599 53209
S 12th St
600-2099 53204
2200-3499 53215
3500-3599 53221
N 13th St
301-527 53233
1200-2099 53205
2401-2497 53206
4000-5599 53209
S 13th St
2001A-2099A 53204
2100-3499 53215
3500-6299 53221
N 14th Ln 53205
N 14th St
500-1199 53233
1200-1398 53205
2300-3999 53206
4000-4499 53209
S 14th St
800-2099 53204
2100-3499 53215
3500-5700 53221
S 15th Ct 53221
N 15th Ln 53206
S 15th Pl
1100-2099 53204
2100-3499 53215
3500-6199 53221
N 15th St
300-542 53233
1400-2299 53205
2300-3999 53206
4000-4399 53209
S 15th St
800-2099 53204
2100-3499 53215
3500-4999 53221
N 16th St
301-497 53233
1500-2299 53205
2300-3999 53206
4000-4399 53209
S 16th St
301-399 53233
1700-2099 53204
2100-3499 53215
3500-4400 53221
N 17th St
200-498 53233
1201-1397 53205
2300-3999 53206
4000-4399 53209
S 17th St
300-398 53233
800-2099 53204
2100-3499 53215
3500-6799 53221
N 18th Ct 53205
W 18th Ct 53205
N 18th St
500-999 53233
1200-2299 53205
2300-3999 53206
4000-4999 53209
S 18th St
800-2099 53204
2100-3499 53215
3500-6799 53221
S 19th Ct 53221
W 19th Ct 53205
N 19th Ln 53205
N 19th Pl
3700-3999 53206
4000-5199 53209
N 19th St
500-1099 53233
1200-2234 53205
2300-3999 53206
4000-5499 53209
S 19th St
300-399 53233
800-2099 53204
2100-3499 53215
3500-6899 53221
N 20th Ln
1600-1699 53205
2801-2899 53206
S 20th Pl 53221
N 20th St
500-1199 53233
1200-2299 53205
2300-3999 53206
4000-5599 53209
S 20th St
700-2099 53204
2100-3499 53215
3500-6400 53221
S 21st Ct 53221
N 21st Ln 53205
S 21st Pl 53215
N 21st St
201-697 53233
1200-2100 53205
2300-2398 53206
4000-4098 53209
S 21st St
700-1999 53204
2100-3299 53215
3600-6099 53221
S 22nd Ct 53221
S 22nd Pl
1900-1999 53204
4700-5499 53221
N 22nd St
500-1100 53233
1200-2200 53205
2400-3999 53206
4100-5199 53209
S 22nd St
700-1899 53204
2200-3499 53215
3500-6099 53221
N 23rd St
600-1099 53233
1201-1297 53205
2400-3999 53206
4000-5199 53209
S 23rd St
700-2099 53204
2100-2198 53215
3500-6299 53221
S 24th Ct 53221
N 24th Pl
1100-1199 53233
1200-2299 53205
2300-3999 53206
4000-5199 53209
N 24th St
600-798 53233
1200-2199 53205
2301-2397 53206
4000-5499 53209
S 24th St
700-2099 53204
2100-3499 53215
3500-5799 53221
S 25th Ct 53221
N 25th St
101-197 53233
1200-2299 53205
2300-3999 53206
4000-5299 53209
S 25th St
700-2099 53204
2100-3499 53215
3500-5699 53221
N 26th St
400-498 53233
1200-2299 53205
2300-3999 53206
4000-5599 53209
S 26th St
700-2099 53204
2100-3499 53215
3500-6299 53221
N 27th St
100-2199 53208
2300-2398 53210
2400-3099 53210
3100-4399 53216
4400-5799 53209
S 27th St
2300-3499 53215
3500-6299 53221
N 28th Pl 53208
N 28th St
400-2299 53208
2301-2397 53210
2399-3099 53210
3100-4399 53216
4400-5399 53209
S 28th St
600-3200 53215
3202-3298 53215
4600-5999 53221
N 29th St
3001A-3099A 53210
101-397 53208
399-2299 53208
2301-2397 53210
2399-3099 53210
3100-4399 53216
4400-5899 53209
S 29th St
600-3299 53215
5600-5699 53221
N 30th St
100-2299 53208
2300-2332 53210
2334-3099 53210
3100-4300 53216
4302-4398 53216
4400-4799 53209
S 30th St
700-3399 53215
4900-5699 53221
N 31st St
100-2299 53208
2300-2399 53210
3100-3300 53216
3302-4098 53216
4500-5599 53209
S 31st St
700-3299 53215
3501-3597 53221
3599-6299 53221
N 32nd St
100-298 53208
300-2299 53208
2300-2398 53210
2400-2899 53210
3201-3299 53216
4600-5999 53209
S 32nd St
700-3499 53215
3500-5999 53221
S 33rd Ct 53221
N 33rd St
100-2299 53208
2400-2899 53210
3100-3299 53216
4900-5899 53209
S 33rd St
900-3499 53215
3500-6199 53221
S 34th Ct 53221
N 34th St
100-2299 53208
2300-2900 53210
3100-4100 53216
4701-4797 53209
S 34th St
700-3499 53215
3500-6199 53221
N 35th St
101-197 53208
2300-2899 53210
3100-4399 53216
4501-4597 53209
S 35th St
701-897 53215
3500-6299 53221
S 36th Ct 53221
N 36th St
100-2299 53208
2300-3099 53210
3100-4399 53216
4400-6199 53209
S 36th St
700-3299 53215
3800-6199 53221
S 37th Ct 53221
N 37th Pl 53208
N 37th St
100-2299 53208
2301-2397 53210
2399-3099 53210
3100-4399 53216
4400-8299 53209
S 37th St
700-3499 53215
3800-6199 53221
N 38th Ct 53209
S 38th Ct 53221
N 38th Pl 53209
N 38th St
100-2299 53208
2300-3099 53210
3100-4399 53216
4400-8299 53209
S 38th St
700-3499 53215

3800-6299 53221
N 39th St
101-397 53208
399-2299 53208
2300-3099 53210
3100-4399 53216
4400-7599 53209
S 39th St
700-3499 53215
3800-6299 53221
N 40th Pl 53209
N 40th St
100-2299 53208
2300-3099 53210
3100-4399 53216
4400-7599 53209
S 40th St
900-3299 53215
3800-6199 53221
N 41st St
100-298 53208
300-2299 53208
2300-3099 53210
3100-4399 53216
4400-7599 53209
S 41st St
900-3299 53215
3500-6299 53221
N 42nd Pl 53216
N 42nd St
100-1198 53208
1200-2299 53208
3100-4399 53216
4400-8599 53209
S 42nd St
1400-3299 53215
4800-6199 53221
N 43rd St
100-998 53208
1000-1399 53208
5600-8799 53209
S 43rd St
2300-3499 53219
3500-5800 53220
5802-6298 53221
S 44th Ct 53220
N 44th Pl 53216
N 44th St
100-2299 53208
2300-3099 53210
3100-4399 53216
4400-5399 53218
6800-8299 53223
S 44th St
600-1398 53214
2401-2697 53219
3500-5699 53220
N 45th Pl 53216
N 45th St
100-2299 53208
2300-3099 53210
3100-4299 53216
4400-5399 53218
6800-9599 53223
S 45th St
1100-1399 53214
2700-3499 53219
3500-5699 53220
S 46th Pl 53220
N 46th St
900-2299 53208
2300-3099 53210
3100-4399 53216
4400-5399 53218
6800-8599 53223
S 46th St
200-1399 53214
2700-3400 53219
3500-5499 53220
N 47th St
1000-1198 53208
1401-2299 53208
2300-3099 53210
3100-4399 53216
4400-5399 53218
6400-9599 53223
S 47th St
1000-1399 53214

2700-3399 53219
3500-4899 53220
N 48th Ct 53223
N 48th St
100-2299 53208
2300-3099 53210
3100-4399 53216
4400-5399 53218
7100-8599 53223
S 48th St
1000-1299 53214
2700-3299 53219
3500-5499 53220
N 49th Ct 53223
N 49th St
100-2299 53208
2301-2347 53210
3100-4399 53216
4400-5399 53218
6400-9599 53223
S 49th St
1100-1399 53214
2600-2632 53219
3500-4298 53220
N 50th Pl 53208
S 50th Pl 53219
N 50th St
100-1699 53208
2300-2999 53210
3100-4399 53216
4400-5399 53218
7600-8599 53223
S 50th St
1100-1399 53214
2600-3299 53219
3801-3897 53220
N 51st Blvd
3100-4399 53216
4400-5399 53218
N 51st St
500-2299 53208
2300-2398 53210
6400-9399 53223
S 51st St
1400-1499 53214
2300-3399 53219
3500-5300 53220
S 52nd Pl 53219
N 52nd St
100-2299 53208
2300-3099 53210
3100-4399 53216
4400-4598 53218
6400-9599 53223
S 52nd St
1200-1899 53214
2300-3499 53219
3500-4599 53220
N 53rd St
100-2299 53208
2300-3099 53210
3100-4399 53216
4401-4597 53218
6400-8799 53223
S 53rd St
1200-1899 53214
1900-3399 53219
3500-3598 53220
N 54th Blvd 53216
N 54th St
100-2199 53208
2300-3099 53210
3100-4399 53216
4400-5599 53218
6400-8799 53223
S 54th St
1200-1899 53214
1900-3499 53219
3600-4399 53220
N 55th Pl 53218
N 55th St
100-998 53208
2300-3099 53210
3100-4399 53216
4400-5599 53218
6400-9099 53223
S 55th St
1400-1899 53214

1900-3431 53219
3600-5099 53220
S 56th Ct 53219
N 56th St
100-2299 53208
2300-3099 53210
3100-4200 53216
4400-5799 53218
6400-8799 53223
S 56th St
700-1899 53214
1900-3499 53219
3600-4299 53220
N 57th St
1000-2299 53208
2300-3099 53210
3300-3899 53216
4400-5799 53218
6400-8699 53223
S 57th St
700-1899 53214
1900-3499 53219
3500-4299 53220
N 58th Blvd 53216
N 58th St
800-999 53213
1000-2299 53208
2300-3099 53210
3100-3999 53216
4400-5799 53218
6400-8699 53223
S 58th St
700-798 53214
1900-3499 53219
3500-5299 53220
N 59th St
100-999 53213
1000-2299 53208
2300-3099 53210
7600-8699 53223
S 59th St
200-1899 53214
1900-2499 53219
4300-4499 53220
N 60th St
100-999 53213
1000-1298 53208
1001-1299 53213
1300-2299 53208
2300-2498 53210
3100-3398 53216
4400-6399 53218
6400-9599 53223
S 60th St
100-1899 53214
1900-3499 53219
3500-5099 53220
N 61st St
200-2699 53213
2700-3099 53210
3500-4399 53216
4400-6099 53218
6800-8399 53223
S 61st St
100-1899 53214
2000-3499 53219
3500-4699 53220
N 62nd St
100-2699 53213
2800-3099 53210
3500-4399 53216
4400-6099 53218
6401-7997 53223
S 62nd St
100-1899 53214
1900-3499 53219
4400-4617 53220
N 63rd Ct 53213
N 63rd St
100-2699 53213
2700-3099 53210
3500-4399 53216
4400-6099 53218
8400-8699 53223
S 63rd St
100-1899 53214
2100-3499 53219

3500-4499 53220
N 64th Ct 53223
N 64th St
100-2600 53213
2801-2835 53210
3500-4399 53216
4400-6399 53218
6900-8799 53223
S 64th St
100-1899 53214
2100-3499 53219
4100-4699 53220
S 65th Ct
3000-3099 53219
4900-4999 53220
N 65th St
100-2599 53213
3900-4298 53216
4400-5999 53218
8000-9599 53223
S 65th St
100-1899 53214
2000-2028 53219
4000-5099 53220
S 66th Pl 53214
N 66th St
100-2699 53213
2900-3099 53210
3801-3997 53216
4400-5999 53218
6400-8799 53223
S 66th St
100-1899 53214
2100-3499 53219
3500-5099 53220
S 67th Ct
3100-3199 53219
4900-4999 53220
S 67th Pl
1000-1399 53214
1900-2299 53219
N 67th St
100-2699 53213
2700-2999 53210
3400-4399 53216
4400-5999 53218
6400-9599 53223
S 67th St
100-699 53214
2200-3499 53219
3700-5099 53220
S 68th Pl 53214
N 68th St
100-2699 53213
2700-3099 53210
3800-4399 53216
4400-5999 53218
6400-8799 53223
S 68th St
100-198 53214
1900-3441 53219
3500-5099 53220
S 69th Pl 53214
N 69th St
100-2699 53213
2700-3099 53210
3800-4399 53216
4400-5999 53218
9000-9099 53223
S 69th St
101-197 53214
1900-3499 53219
3600-5099 53220
N 70th St
100-2699 53213
2700-3099 53210
3800-4399 53216
4400-5999 53218
6500-8798 53223
S 70th St
101-197 53214
1900-3399 53219
3900-4299 53220
N 71st St
100-2699 53213
2700-2899 53210
3900-4399 53216

4400-5999 53218
6400-6599 53223
S 71st St
100-1899 53214
1900-3499 53219
3600-4399 53220
N 72nd St
100-2699 53213
2700-3099 53210
3900-4399 53216
4400-5999 53218
8400-8799 53223
S 72nd St
100-1799 53214
1801-1899 53214
1900-3299 53219
3900-5099 53220
N 73rd St
100-2699 53213
2700-3099 53210
3700-4399 53216
4400-5999 53218
6001-6099 53218
6400-8699 53223
S 73rd St
100-1899 53214
1900-3439 53219
3800-4099 53220
N 74th St
100-2699 53213
2700-3099 53210
3100-4399 53216
4400-5999 53218
6600-6799 53223
S 74th St
100-1599 53214
1601-1699 53214
1900-3047 53219
3800-5099 53220
N 75th Ct 53218
N 75th St
9241A-9241M 53223
100-2699 53213
2700-3099 53210
3100-4399 53216
4400-5999 53218
6600-9240 53223
S 75th St
100-1899 53214
1900-3499 53219
3500-4099 53220
N 76th Pl 53223
N 76th St
100-999 53213
2700-4399 53222
4400-6399 53218
6400-9599 53223
S 76th St
100-1899 53214
1900-3499 53219
3501-3897 53220
3899-5099 53220
N 77th Ct
4700-4799 53218
6900-6999 53223
N 77th St
100-799 53213
2800-4199 53222
4400-6399 53218
6600-6899 53223
S 77th St
100-1899 53214
1900-3440 53219
3500-3900 53220
N 78th Ct
4100-4199 53222
4700-4799 53218
6900-6999 53223
N 78th St
100-2699 53213
2701-2797 53222
4500-5999 53218
6600-7999 53223
S 78th St
100-1699 53214
1900-3499 53219
3600-5099 53220

N 79th Ct 53223
N 79th St
100-799 53213
2800-4199 53222
4600-5999 53218
7400-7799 53223
S 79th St
100-1699 53214
1900-3441 53219
3443-3499 53219
3500-4999 53220
N 80th Ct 53223
N 80th St
100-2699 53213
2700-4335 53222
4400-5900 53218
6400-9499 53223
S 80th St
100-1899 53214
1900-3499 53219
3500-4100 53220
N 81st St
1800-2699 53213
2700-4399 53222
4700-5899 53218
6400-7999 53223
S 81st St
100-1799 53214
1900-3499 53219
3500-4999 53220
N 82nd Ct
5200-5799 53218
6500-6599 53223
S 82nd Ct 53219
N 82nd St
2300-2699 53213
2701-2737 53222
4400-5899 53218
6400-6498 53223
S 82nd St
300-1799 53214
1900-3499 53219
3500-4999 53220
S 83rd Pl 53219
N 83rd St
1700-1710 53213
2700-4399 53222
4400-5899 53218
6400-9299 53223
S 83rd St
300-1799 53214
1900-3499 53219
3500-4499 53220
N 84th St
1700-2699 53226
2700-4300 53222
4400-6399 53225
6400-7099 53224
9001-9099 53223
S 84th St
100-1799 53214
1900-3499 53227
3500-4999 53228
N 85th Ct 53225
N 85th St
100-2699 53226
2700-4299 53222
4400-5200 53225
5202-5898 53225
6400-9499 53224
S 85th St
400-1799 53214
2000-3499 53227
3500-4699 53228
N 86th Ct
6300-6399 53225
9100-9199 53224
N 86th Pl 53225
N 86th St
100-2699 53226
2700-4299 53222
4600-5700 53225
6400-9199 53224
S 86th St
400-1499 53214
1900-3499 53227
3500-4499 53228

N 87th Ct
4100-4199 53222
8900-8999 53224
S 87th Ct 53227
S 87th Pl 53214
N 87th St
100-1099 53226
2700-4399 53222
4500-6199 53225
6400-8699 53224
S 87th St
400-1599 53214
2000-3499 53227
3500-3899 53228
N 88th Ct 53225
N 88th St
100-2699 53226
2700-4399 53222
4400-4999 53225
S 88th St
400-1799 53214
2000-3499 53227
3500-4300 53228
4302-4898 53228
N 89th St
100-2699 53226
2700-4399 53222
4400-6399 53225
6400-7599 53224
S 89th St
400-1799 53214
1900-3399 53227
3600-4699 53228
N 90th Blvd 53224
N 90th Ct 53222
N 90th St
100-2699 53226
2700-4399 53222
4600-5799 53225
6500-7599 53224
S 90th St
400-1699 53214
1900-3399 53227
3600-4899 53228
N 91st Pl 53224
S 91st Pl
400-499 53214
4000-4299 53228
N 91st St
100-2699 53226
2700-4399 53222
4401-4697 53225
6400-8799 53224
S 91st St
400-1799 53214
1900-3499 53227
3500-4499 53228
N 92nd St
100-1099 53226
2700-4399 53222
4400-4498 53225
4500-5899 53225
S 92nd St
100-1899 53214
1900-3499 53227
3500-5099 53228
N 93rd Ct 53224
N 93rd St
100-298 53226
3100-4299 53222
5601-5697 53225
6400-8399 53224
S 93rd St
400-1699 53214
1900-3499 53227
3500-4299 53228
S 94th Pl 53214
N 94th St
500-2699 53226
2700-4399 53222
5600-5900 53225
6400-9199 53224
S 94th St
400-1699 53214
1900-3099 53227
3500-4899 53228
N 95th Ct 53225

N 95th St
300-2699 53226
2700-4399 53222
5501-5539 53225
5541-6299 53225
7300-9299 53224
S 95th St
400-1699 53214
1900-3499 53227
3500-4899 53228
N 96th Ct 53224
N 96th St
2300-2699 53226
3100-4299 53222
5600-5799 53225
5801-5899 53225
8800-9099 53224
S 96th St
700-1799 53214
1900-3499 53227
3500-4899 53228
N 97th Ct 53224
N 97th Pl 53222
N 97th St
401-2397 53226
2700-4200 53222
5600-5698 53225
7000-9099 53224
S 97th St
700-1599 53214
1900-3399 53227
3500-4299 53228
N 98th Ct 53225
S 98th Ct 53228
N 98th St
400-2699 53226
2700-4199 53222
5601-5697 53225
6800-7199 53224
S 98th St
700-1399 53214
1900-3399 53227
4100-4299 53228
S 99th Ct 53227
N 99th St
400-699 53226
3300-4299 53222
4400-5900 53225
6601-6697 53224
S 99th St
3201A-3299A 53227
3500-4799 53228
N 100th St 53226
3500-4399 53222
4400-6399 53225
6800-8499 53224
S 100th St
601-1397 53214
1399-1899 53214
2300-2498 53227
3101-3499 53227
N 101st Ct 53224
N 101st St
2300-2399 53226
3600-3899 53222
4500-6399 53225
6400-6499 53224
S 101st St
700-1599 53214
1601-1799 53214
2501-2999 53227
4000-5099 53228
N 102nd Ct 53224
N 102nd St
2200-2499 53226
3100-3946 53222
3948-3998 53222
6200-6399 53225
6800-8099 53224
S 102nd St
700-1399 53214
1900-2999 53227
3700-5099 53228
N 103rd Ct 53224
S 103rd Ct 53227
N 103rd St
400-2499 53226
3100-3199 53222
4400-6399 53225
6601-8397 53224
S 103rd St
600-1399 53214
2800-3499 53227
3500-3598 53228
N 104th Ct 53224
N 104th St
400-2299 53226
3100-4399 53222
4400-6399 53225
6400-6499 53224
S 104th St
600-1399 53214
2000-3499 53227
3500-5099 53228
N 105th St
500-2299 53226
3100-3399 53222
3401-3499 53222
4400-6399 53225
6400-8399 53224
S 105th St
500-1099 53214
1900-3299 53227
N 106th St
2201A-2299A 53226
400-2299 53226
3100-3299 53222
4400-6399 53225
6400-8699 53224
S 106th St
1100-1800 53214
1802-1898 53214
2000-3299 53227
3900-5099 53228
N 107th St
2200A-2298A 53226
400-2299 53226
3200-3500 53222
3502-3998 53222
4400-6399 53225
6400-9599 53224
S 107th St
1100-1399 53214
1900-3299 53227
5000-5098 53228
N 108th Ct 53225
N 108th Pl 53226
N 108th St
4400-5000 53225
5002-5198 53225
6700-6799 53224
S 108th St
301-497 53214
499-1899 53214
1900-3499 53227
3500-5099 53228
N 109th St
400-899 53226
4400-6099 53225
6700-7699 53224
S 109th St
700-1399 53214
2100-2799 53227
3500-4699 53228
N 110th Pl 53226
N 110th St
100-399 53226
4001-4043 53222
4400-4999 53225
6600-6700 53224
S 110th St
700-1399 53214
2100-3499 53227
4300-5099 53228
S 111th Pl 53214
N 111th St
200-2699 53226
4000-4199 53222
5800-5899 53225
8101-8197 53224
8199-8499 53224
S 111th St
700-1399 53214
2100-2899 53227
3500-4699 53228
N 112th Ct 53224
N 112th St
200-2400 53226
2800-2898 53222
6000-6199 53225
S 112th St
700-1298 53214
2700-3399 53227
3900-4799 53228
N 113th St
200-2199 53226
5800-6199 53225
6501-6699 53224
7800-7898 53224
S 113th St
700-1599 53214
3300-3499 53227
4400-4699 53228
N 114th St
200-2699 53226
2901-2997 53222
5800-6199 53225
6400-6698 53224
S 114th St
700-1399 53214
2000-3399 53227
4300-4699 53228
S 115th Ct 53214
N 115th St
200-2699 53226
6000-6198 53225
6201-6299 53225
6601-7099 53224
S 115th St 53214
N 116th Ct 53224
N 116th St
200-2699 53226
6100-6199 53225
8600-8699 53224
S 116th St
100-1899 53214
1901-1997 53227
3500-5099 53228
N 117th Pl 53222
N 117th St
500-2699 53226
2800-2900 53222
4601-5797 53225
8600-8699 53224
S 117th St
1101-1297 53214
2301-2699 53227
3900-4599 53228
N 118th Ct 53225
N 118th St
1100-2699 53226
2700-2899 53222
4501-4597 53225
4599-6399 53225
S 118th St
100-1098 53214
1100-1399 53214
2300-2699 53227
3900-4399 53228
N 119th St
500-2499 53226
4500-4798 53225
4800-6399 53225
S 119th St
700-1399 53214
3100-3499 53227
3900-4899 53228
N 120th St
100-2699 53226
2900-2999 53222
S 120th St
700-1399 53214
3500-4099 53228
S 121st Ct 53228
N 121st St
100-1999 53226
2900-3099 53222
5800-6399 53225
S 121st St
700-1399 53214
3200-3399 53227
3900-4699 53228
S 122nd Ct 53228
N 122nd St
1000-2699 53226
2700-3099 53222
6000-6199 53225
S 122nd St
700-1399 53214
3100-3499 53227
4000-4999 53228
N 123rd St
100-1699 53226
7201-7299 53224
S 123rd St
700-1399 53214
3200-3399 53227
3500-4999 53228
N 124th St
900-2698 53226
2700-4398 53222
4400-5198 53225
6800-9598 53224
S 124th St
700-1598 53214
2000-3299 53227
3500-4500 53228

NEENAH WI

General Delivery 54956

POST OFFICE BOXES MAIN OFFICE STATIONS AND BRANCHES

Box No.s
All PO Boxes 54957

NAMED STREETS

Abby Ave 54956
Acorn Rd 54956
Adams St 54956
Adelaide Rd 54956
Adella Beach Rd 54956
Agnes Ave 54956
Alcott Dr 54956
Alex Ct 54956
Alexander Dr 54956
Allison Dr 54956
Alpha Dr 54956
Alpine Ln 54956
Amber Ln 54956
Amendment Dr 54956
W American Ct & Dr 54956
Ames St 54956
Anderson Ln 54956
Andrew Ave 54956
Antelope Trail Ct 54956
Anthem Dr 54956
Antler Ct 54956
Apollo Ct 54956
Apple Blossom Dr 54956
Arena Dr 54956
Armstrong St 54956
Ashbrooke Pl 54956
Ashwood Ct 54956
Austin Ave 54956
Ava Ct 54956
Babcock St 54956
Baldwin St 54956
Balfour St 54956
Barrow Way 54956
Basil Ct 54956
Baytree Ln 54956
Bayview Rd 54956
Bear Trail Ct 54956
Beaulieu Rd 54956
Beethoven Way 54956
Behm Dr 54956
E & W Bell St 54956
Bellin St 54956
Belmont Ave & Ct 54956
Bengal Rd 54956
Benjamin Ct 54956
Bergstrom Rd 54956
Berkeley St 54956
Berry Bramble Trl 54956
Beta Dr 54956
Betty Ave 54956
Beverly Ct 54956
Birch St 54956
Birch Bark Ln 54956
Birch Haven Ct 54956
Bishops Ln 54956
Blackmoor Cir 54956
Blair Ave 54956
Blueberry Ln 54956
Bluebird Ct 54956
Bomar Ave 54956
Bond St 54956
Bondow Dr 54956
Bonheur Ct 54956
Bosworth Ct & Ln 54956
Bradford Ct 54956
Bramblewood Ct 54956
Brantwood Ct & Dr 54956
Braun Ct 54956
Breaker Trl 54956
Breezewood Ln 54956
Briar Dr & Ln 54956
Bridgeview Ct & Dr 54956
Bridgewood Dr 54956
Bridle Ln 54956
Brien St 54956
Briggs Ln 54956
Brittany Ct 54956
Brookfield Dr & Ln 54956
Brooks Ave 54956
Brookview Ct 54956
Brookwood Dr 54956
Bruce Ct & St 54956
Buck Ct 54956
Buckhorn Ln 54956
Burnette St 54956
Burr Ave 54956
Buser Dr 54956
Butte St 54956
Butte Des Morts Beach Rd 54956
Buttercup Rd 54956
Buttonbush Way 54956
Byrd Ave 54956
Cambridge Ct 54956
Cameron Cir & Way 54956
Campbell St 54956
Campers Blvd & Way 54956
Carden Dr 54956
Carey Ct 54956
Caroline St 54956
Carriage Dr 54956
Casaloma Dr 54956
Cassy Ln 54956
Castle Oak Dr 54956
Cavalry Ln 54956
Cavendish Rd 54956
E & W Cecil St 54956
Cedar St 54956
Center Rd & St 54956
Challenger Dr 54956
Chancelant Ct 54956
Chapman Ave 54956
Charles Ct 54956
Chatham Ct 54956
Cherry Ln 54956
Cherrywood Ct 54956
Cheryl Ann Dr 54956
Chestnut St 54956
Christopher Dr 54956
Church St 54956
Citation Ln 54956
Claire Ave 54956
Clairmont Ct 54956
Clark St 54956
Clayton Ave 54956
Cleveland St 54956
Clovernook Ln 54956
Clybourn St 54956
Cold Spring Rd 54956
Coleman Rdg 54956
Collins St 54956
E & W Columbian Ave 54956
Commerce Ct 54956
Commerce Plaza Dr 54956
N & S Commercial St 54956
Congress Pl & St 54956
Constitution Dr 54956
Cooke Rd 54956
Coolidge St 54956
Copperhead Dr 54956
Copperstone Pl 54956
Corona Way 54956
Cottagewood Dr 54956
Country Ln 54956
Country Woods Ct 54956
County Ln 54956
County Road A 54956
County Road Bb 54956
County Road Cb 54956
County Road G 54956
County Road Gg 54956
County Road Ii 54956
County Road Jj 54956
County Road O 54956
Courtney Ct 54956
Cowling Bay Rd 54956
Creek Side Dr 54956
Crescent Dr 54956
Crestview Ave 54956
Cricket Ct 54956
Cumings Ln 54956
Curtis Ave 54956
Dalebrook Dr 54956
Dalton Rd 54956
Daniel Ct 54956
Darrow Rd 54956
Dartmouth Dr 54956
Davis Point Ct 54956
Dawn Ct 54956
Declaration Dr 54956
Deer Crossing Ct 54956
Deer Prairie Dr 54956
Deerpath Cir 54956
Deerwood Ave & Dr 54956
Dekalb Ln 54956
Dell Ct 54956
Delta Dr 54956
Denhardt Ave 54956
Derby Ln 54956
Diane St 54956
Dickenson Ct 54956
Dieckhoff St 54956
Discovery Dr 54956
Division St 54956
Dixie Rd 54956
Dobberke Ln 54956
Doctors Dr 54956
Doe Trail Ct 54956
Dogwood Trl 54956
Dordona Dr 54956
E & W Doty Ave 54956
Douglas St 54956
Dublin Trl 54956
Eagle Dr 54956
Eagle Feather Trl 54956
Eden Dr 54956
Edgewood Dr 54956
Edna Ave 54956
Edward St 54956
Ehlers Rd 54956
Elk Trail Ct & Dr 54956
Elm St 54956
Elmwood Ct 54956
Emerald Crown Pkwy 54956
Emerson St 54956
Enterprise Dr 54956
Etten Ct 54956
Evans St 54956
Evergreen Ln 54956
Fair Oaks Dr 54956
Fairbrook Dr 54956
Fairview Ave & Rd 54956
Fairwinds Dr 54956
Fairwood Dr 54956
Fall View Ln 54956
Fallow Dr 54956
Farm Ridge Ln 54956
Fawn Dr 54956
Ferdinand St 54956
S Fieldcrest Dr 54956
Fieldstone Ct 54956
Fiesta Ct 54956
Fircrest Rd 54956
Firefly Ct & Ln 54956
Fondotto Dr 54956
E & W Forest Ave 54956
Forest Glen Rd 54956
Forest Heights Ln 54956
Forest Manor Ct 54956
Fort Dr 54956
Fox Burrow Ct 54956
Fox Point Plz & Sq 54956
E Franklin Ave 54956
W Franklin Ave
101-199 54956
130-132 54956
130-130 54957
Fredrick Dr 54956
Fury Ln 54956
Gail Ave 54956
Galaxy Dr 54956
Gateway Pl 54956
Gateway Meadows Ln 54956
Gavin Rd 54956
Gay Dr 54956
Geiger St 54956
Gershwin Ln 54956
Gilbert St 54956
Gilbertson Pl 54956
Gillingham Rd 54956
Glenayre Dr 54956
Glenview Dr 54956
Golden Field Rd 54956
Golden Harvest Dr 54956
Golden Primrose Cir 54956
Golf Bridge Dr 54956
Golf Course Dr 54956
Golf Wood Dr 54956
Grand Meadows Xing 54956
Grant Pl & St 54956
Grassy Ln 54956
Grassy Plains Dr 54956
Great Plains Dr 54956
Green St 54956
Green Acres Ln 54956
N & S Green Bay Rd 54956
Green Meadows St 54956
Green Valley Dr & Rd 54956
Greenfield St 54956
Gregory St 54956
Grove St 54956
Gruenwald Ave 54956
Guardian Ct & Ln 54956
Haase St 54956
Hansen St 54956
Harbor Light Ct 54956
Harbor Wood Ln 54956
Harrison St 54956
Harvard Dr 54956
Harvest Moon Dr 54956
Hawthorne St 54956
Haylett St 54956
Hazel St 54956
Hazelwood Ct 54956
Heather Ct & Ln 54956
Hedgerow Dr 54956
Hedgeview Dr 54956
Helen St 54956
Henry St 54956
Hewitt St 54956
Hickory Ln 54956
Hickory Hill Rd 54956
Hidden Acres Ln 54956
Hidden Creek Rd 54956
Higgins Ave 54956
High St 54956
High Meadows Ln 54956
Highland Ct & Dr 54956
Highland Park Rd 54956
Hillcrest Pl 54956

- Hillington Dr 54956
- Hillsdale Ct 54956
- Hilltop Dr 54956
- Hoffman St 54956
- Holiday Ct 54956
- Holly Ct & Rd 54956
- Honeysuckle Ln 54956
- Hoot Owl Ct 54956
- Horizon Dr 54956
- Hughes Ct 54956
- Hummingbird Ln 54956
- Hunt Ave 54956
- Hunters Point Rd 54956
- Independence Dr 54956
- Indianwood Ct 54956
- Industrial Dr 54956
- Inverness Ln 54956
- Irene St 54956
- Irish Rd 54956
- Isabella St 54956
- Island Rd 54956
- Jackson St 54956
- Jacobsen Rd 54956
- Jadetree Ter 54956
- Jameson St 54956
- Jane Ct 54956
- Janssen Dr 54956
- Jean St 54956
- Jefferson St 54956
- Jensen Rd 54956
- Jewel Dr 54956
- Jewelers Park Dr 54956
- N & S John St 54956
- Jonathon Ln 54956
- Joseph Ct & St 54956
- Joseph Peters Dr 54956
- Jule St 54956
- Julie Ct 54956
- Justine Ct 54956
- Kalfahs St 54956
- Kampo Ct & Dr 54956
- Kappell Dr 54956
- Kaufman St 54956
- Kay Kourt 54956
- Kellett Rd 54956
- Kensington Rd 54956
- Kenwood Dr 54956
- Kerwin Rd 54956
- Kessler Dr 54956
- Kiely Way 54956
- Kimberly Dr 54956
- King St 54956
- Kingswood Dr 54956
- Kittiver Ct 54956
- Kitzerow Ln 54956
- Kline St 54956
- Klompen Ct 54956
- Kluck St 54956
- Knight Ave 54956
- Knox Ln 54956
- Kraft St 54956
- Kuehn Ct 54956
- Kuettel Ct 54956
- La Quinta Ct 54956
- Lacewing Dr 54956
- Ladybird Dr 54956
- N & S Lake St 54956
- Lakecrest Dr 54956
- Lakeshore Ave 54956
- Langley Blvd 54956
- Larsen Rd 54956
- Laudan Blvd 54956
- Laurel Ct 54956
- Law St 54956
- Lee St 54956
- Lehrer Ln 54956
- Lennon Ln 54956
- Lennox St 54956
- Lexington Ct 54956
- Liberty Ct 54956
- Limekiln Dr 54956
- Lincoln St 54956
- Lind Ln 54956
- Linden Ct 54956
- Linwood Ln 54956
- Lone Oak Dr 54956
- Loper Ct 54956
- Lori Dr 54956
- Lorraine Ave 54956
- Louise Rd & St 54956
- Lowell Pl 54956
- Lynn Dr 54956
- Lynrose Ct & Ln 54956
- Lyon Dr 54956
- Madison St 54956
- Mahler Blvd 54956
- Main St 54956
- Manchester Ct & Rd 54956
- Mandella Ct 54956
- Manor Dr 54956
- Mansur Dr 54956
- Maple Ln & St 54956
- Maple Grove Dr 54956
- Marathon Ave 54956
- Margeo Dr 54956
- Mark Ct 54956
- Marten St 54956
- Martin Dr 54956
- Martingale Ln 54956
- Mary Ln 54956
- Matthews St 54956
- Mayer St 54956
- Mcgann Rd 54956
- Mckinley St 54956
- Mcmahon Rd 54956
- Meade St 54956
- Meadow Ln 54956
- Meadow Flower Ct 54956
- Meadow Green Dr 54956
- Meadow Heights Cir 54956
- Meadowbreeze Cir 54956
- Meadowbrook Dr 54956
- Meadowview St 54956
- Megan Way 54956
- Melrose Ct & St 54956
- Memorial Ct 54956
- Memory Ln 54956
- Michael Ave 54956
- Milkweed Ct 54956
- Mill Pond Ct & Ln 54956
- Millbrook Dr 54956
- Millview Dr 54956
- Mimosa Ln 54956
- Mitchell St 54956
- Monroe St 54956
- Mulberry Ln 54956
- Municipal Dr 54956
- Murray Rd 54956
- Muttart Rd 54956
- Nates Ct 54956
- Nation Ct 54956
- Nature Trail Dr 54956
- Nee Vin Rd 54956
- Neenah Ctr 54956
- Neff Ct 54956
- Nelson Ct 54956
- Nennig Rd 54956
- Nichole Hts 54956
- Nicolet Blvd 54956
- North St 54956
- E & W North Water St 54956
- Northcreek Dr 54956
- Nuthatch Ln 54956
- Oak St 54956
- Oak Hollow Ln 54956
- Oakcrest Dr 54956
- Oakridge Ln, Pl & Rd 54956
- Oakview Dr 54956
- Oakwood Ave 54956
- Old Dixie Rd 54956
- Old Glory Ln 54956
- Old Orchard Ln 54956
- Olde Buggy Dr 54956
- Olde School Rd 54956
- Oleary Rd & St 54956
- Olive St 54956
- Omaha Ave 54956
- Orchard Ct 54956
- Orchid Ln 54956
- Oriole Ct 54956
- Otto St 54956
- Oxford Ct & Dr 54956
- Oxwood Dr 54956
- Paintbrush Rd 54956
- Pansy Ct 54956
- N & S Park Ave, Ct & Dr 54956
- Park Lane Dr 54956
- Park Village Dr 54956
- Parkside Ct 54956
- Parkwood Dr 54956
- Patrick Ct 54956
- W Paynes Point Rd 54956
- E & W Peckham St 54956
- Pembrook Ct & Dr 54956
- Pemmican Ct & Trl 54956
- Pendleton Rd 54956
- Peppergrass Ln 54956
- Pilgrim Rd 54956
- Pine St 54956
- Pine Point Ct 54956
- Pinehurst Ln 54956
- Pioneer Rd 54956
- Plains Ave 54956
- Plaza Dr 54956
- Pleasant Ct 54956
- Plexus Way 54956
- Plummer Ave & Ct 54956
- Plummers Harbor Rd 54956
- Pond View Ct & Dr 54956
- Poplar Ct 54956
- E Prairie Creek Dr 54956
- Prairie Lake Cir 54956
- Prairie View Ct 54956
- Prairiewood Trl 54956
- Presidential Dr 54956
- Primrose Ct & Ln 54956
- Professional Plz 54956
- Progress Ct 54956
- Quail Pt 54956
- Quarry Ln 54956
- Radcliff Rd 54956
- Rainberry Ct 54956
- Rainbow Beach Rd 54956
- Ravenswood Ct 54956
- Reddin Ave 54956
- Redtail Dr 54956
- Redwing Dr 54956
- Reed St 54956
- Regent Pl 54956
- Remington Ct & Rd 54956
- Retlaw Dr 54956
- Rhyner Rd 54956
- Richard Ave 54956
- Rickers Bay Rd 54956
- E Ridge Pl 54956
- Ridgeside Dr 54956
- Ridgetop Dr 54956
- Ridgeway Ct & Dr 54956
- Riford Rd 54956
- Riva Ridge Ln 54956
- River Ln & St 54956
- Riverlawn St 54956
- Rock Ledge Ln 54956
- Rockwood Ln 54956
- Rogers Ct 54956
- Roosevelt St 54956
- Rose Moon Way 54956
- Royal Sierra Trl 54956
- Saddlebrook Ct 54956
- Saffron Ln 54956
- Sage Ct 54956
- Sally Ln 54956
- Sande St 54956
- Sandpoint Rdg 54956
- Saquaro Ct 54956
- Schanke St 54956
- Schramm Rd 54956
- Schultz Rd 54956
- Secretariat Ln 54956
- Seymour Ct 54956
- Shadow Bend Ct 54956
- E Shady Ln 54956
- Shady Springs Ct & Dr 54956
- Shaggy Bark Dr 54956
- Shangra La 54956
- Shannon St 54956
- Sharens Way 54956
- Shenandoah Trl 54956
- Sherri Lea 54956
- Sherry St 54956
- Shootingstar Dr 54956
- Shreve Ln 54956
- Silverwood Ln 54956
- Skyview Dr 54956
- Smith St 54956
- Smoke Tree Rd 54956
- Solar Pkwy 54956
- Specialists Ave 54956
- Spike Ct 54956
- Spring Hill Ct 54956
- Spring Meadow Ct & Dr 54956
- Spring Road Dr 54956
- Spruce St 54956
- Stanford Dr 54956
- Stanley Ct & St 54956
- State St 54956
- State Road 76 54956
- Statue Dr 54956
- Sterling Ave 54956
- Stevens St 54956
- Stillwater Ct 54956
- Stone Ave 54956
- Stone Hedge Ct 54956
- Stonecrest Ct 54956
- Stoney Bridge Rd 54956
- Stratford Ct 54956
- Strohmeyer Ct & Dr 54956
- Stuart Ct & Dr 54956
- Sturgis Ln 54956
- Sugar Tree Ln 54956
- Sunburst Ln 54956
- Sund St 54956
- Sundew Way 54956
- Sundial Ln 54956
- Sunrise Bay Rd 54956
- Sunshine Ln 54956
- Sunwood Dr 54956
- Surrey Ct & Ln 54956
- Susan Ave 54956
- Sweet Autumn Ln 54956
- Symphony Blvd 54956
- Syngentia Way 54956
- Talkeetna Rd 54956
- Tameradw St 54956
- Tanager Dr 54956
- Terra Cotta Ct & Dr 54956
- Theda Clark Medical Plz 54956
- Thomas Ct 54956
- Thrush Ln 54956
- Timber Ridge Rd 54956
- Timber Run Dr 54956
- Tonya Trl 54956
- Torrey St 54956
- Towerview Dr 54956
- Towmen Rd 54956
- Towne Ct 54956
- Trailsway Ln 54956
- Treyburn Ct 54956
- Tribute Dr 54956
- Tullar Ct & Rd 54956
- Tumblebrook Ct & Rd 54956
- Tyler St 54956
- Union St 54956
- Van St 54956
- Vassar Ln 54956
- Venture Ct 54956
- Vera Ave 54956
- Villa Dr 54956
- Vinland Center Rd 54956
- Viola St 54956
- Voyager Dr 54956
- Walnut St 54956
- Wanda Ave 54956
- Warbler Ln 54956
- Washington Ave 54956
- Wasilla Ln 54956
- Waterford Ct 54956
- Watermark Ct 54956
- Weatherwood Dr 54956
- Webster St 54956
- Wedgewood Ln 54956
- Wenban Ave 54956
- Wendy Way 54956
- Westbreeze Dr 54956
- Westcreek Ln 54956
- N & S Western Ave 54956
- Westfield Ln & Rdg 54956
- Westowne Dr 54956
- Westphal Ln 54956
- Westwind Ct & Dr 54956
- Westwood Ct & Dr 54956
- Wheeler Rd & St 54956
- Whippletree Ln 54956
- Whippoorwill Cir 54956
- Whirlaway Ct 54956
- Whispering Pines Ln 54956
- White Petal Ct 54956
- Whitenack Ct 54956
- Whitetail Dr 54956
- Whiting Ct 54956
- Whitlow St 54956
- Whittier Dr 54956
- Wick Ct 54956
- Wild Rose Ln 54956
- Wilderness Ct 54956
- Wildlife Ln 54956
- Willow Hill Dr 54956
- Wilson St 54956
- Winchester Rd 54956
- Windfield Dr 54956
- Windflower Dr 54956
- Windmar Dr 54956
- Windward Ct 54956
- Windy Way 54956
- Winncrest Rd 54956
- Winnebago Hts 54956
- E & W Winneconne Ave 54956
- Winnegamie Dr 54956
- Winter Wheat Dr 54956
- E & W Wisconsin Ave 54956
- Wismer Ln 54956
- Woodcrest Dr 54956
- Woodenshoe Ct & Rd 54956
- Woodfield Ct & Rd 54956
- Woodgate Ln 54956
- Woodhaven Ln 54956
- Woodland Ter 54956
- Woods Edge Ln 54956
- Woodside Ct & Ln 54956
- Worth Ave 54956
- Wrenwood Ln 54956
- Wright Ave 54956
- Yale Ln 54956
- Yorkshire Ct & Rd 54956
- Yosemite Ln 54956
- Yukon Ln 54956
- Zeh Ave 54956
- Zemlock Ave 54956
- Zephyr Dr 54956

NUMBERED STREETS

- All Street Addresses 54956

NEW BERLIN WI

- General Delivery 53151

POST OFFICE BOXES MAIN OFFICE STATIONS AND BRANCHES

Box No.s
- All PO Boxes 53151

NAMED STREETS

- S Abbott Ln 53151
- S Aberdeen Dr 53146
- Acredale Ct & Dr 53151
- W Addison Ave 53151
- S Adell Ave 53151
- S Albert Ave 53151
- W Allerton Ave 53151
- Allison Dr & Ln 53151
- S & W Amor Dr 53146
- S Andrae Dr 53151
- S Ann St 53146
- S & W Ann Louise Ct & Dr 53146
- W Apple Ct 53146
- W Apple Blossom Ln 53151
- S Arcadian Dr 53151
- Armour Ave & Ct 53151
- W Arrowhead Ln 53151
- Ash Ct 53151
- Aspen Ct 53151
- S Avon Dr 53151
- S Baas Dr 53146
- W Bagpipe Ct 53146
- Balboa Dr 53151
- S Balmoral Dr 53146
- S Baneberry Ct 53146
- Barbary Ct 53151
- W Barton Rd 53146
- W Bates Pl 53146
- W Beechwood Trl 53151
- W Beeheim Rd 53146
- Belgrave Rd 53151
- W Beloit Rd
  - 12400-16600 53151
  - 16602-17198 53151
  - 17200-18699 53146
- S Benfield Ct 53151
- W Beres Rd 53146
- Berkshire Ct 53151
- S Berlin Ave 53151
- S Beverly Dr 53146
- S Birchwood Ln 53146
- W Bittersweet Ln 53146
- W Blue Jay Cir 53151
- W Bobwood Rd 53151
- S Brennan Dr 53146
- S & W Brentwood Dr & Rd 53151
- W Brian Rd 53151
- W Briarwood Ln 53151
- W Broadale Dr 53146
- W Brook Dr 53151
- W Brook Hollow Ct 53151
- S Brookland Rd 53151
- Brookside Ct & Pkwy 53151
- Burdick Ave & Ct 53151
- W Butternut Trl 53151
- Caldwell Ct & Dr 53151
- S Calhoun Rd 53151
- Cambridge Dr 53151
- S Camrose Ave 53151
- S Canary Ln 53151
- S Canary Rd 53146
- S & W Cardinal Ln & Pkwy 53151
- Cari Adam Cir, Ct & Dr 53146
- Carnaby Ct & Ln 53151
- S Carriage Ln 53151
- S Casper Dr 53151
- S & W Catamount Ct & Dr 53146
- S Cavendish Rd 53151
- W Cedar Trl 53151
- Chancel Ct 53151
- W Cherrytree Ln 53151
- S Cherrywood Ct 53151
- W Chestnut Dr 53146
- W Chipmunk Ln 53151
- S Church Dr 53151
- W Churchview Dr 53151
- S Clearwater Pl 53151
- W Cleveland Ave
  - 12400-17099 53151
  - 17101-17199 53151
  - 17200-21999 53146
- S Clover Dr 53146
- S Clover Knoll Pl 53151
- S Clubhouse Dr 53151
- S & W Coachlight Dr 53151
- W Coffee Rd
  - 15100-16500 53151
  - 16502-16798 53151
  - 17200-21699 53146
- W Cold Spring Rd 53151
- W College Ave
  - 13300-14598 53151
  - 18000-19498 53146
- S Commerce Dr 53151
- S Connie Ln 53151
- S Conrad Pl 53151
- Conservancy Dr 53151
- S & W Cortez Dr 53151
- S Cottonwood Rd 53151
- S Country Ln 53146
- W Court St 53146
- Courtland Ct & Pkwy 53151
- Coventry Ct & Rd 53151
- W Crabtree Ln 53146
- S Craftsman Dr 53146
- W Crawford Dr 53151
- S & W Crescent Dr 53151
- W Crestview Dr 53151
- Crestwood Ct 53151
- Crimson Ln 53151
- S Crown Dr 53146
- W Culloden Ct 53146
- W Cynthia Dr 53151
- S Daisy Ct 53151
- Dakota Ct & St 53151
- W Dale Dr 53146
- S Danny Rd 53146
- S Deer Creek Pkwy 53151
- Deer Park Ct & Dr 53151
- S Deerwood Dr 53151
- S Delphine Dr 53151
- W Dena Dr 53146
- Desoto Ct & Ln 53151
- W Dianne Dr 53151
- S Dora Ln 53151
- W Dove Dr 53146
- W Doverhill Ln 53151
- W Downie Rd 53146
- Duncan Ln 53151
- S Dunvegan Dr 53146
- W Eagle Trce 53151
- S East Ln 53146
- Eden Ct & Trl 53151
- W Edgerton Ave 53151
- Edgewood Ave & Ct 53151
- S & W Edinbourgh Dr 53146
- S Egofske Rd 53146
- S & W El Dorado Dr 53151
- S El Sirroco Dr 53151
- W Elger Ct 53146
- Elizabeth Ct 53151
- S Elm Dr 53146
- S Elm Grove Rd 53151
- W Elmont Ln 53151
- W Elmwood Dr 53151
- W Elmwood Rd 53146
- S Emmer Dr 53151
- Euclid Ave & Ct 53151
- W Evergreen Pl 53146
- Fairfield Ct & Dr 53151
- S Fairview Dr 53146
- W Farrell Dr 53151
- Fenway Ct & Dr 53151
- W Ferguson Rd 53151
- Fieldpointe Ct & Dr 53151
- S Five Iron Ct 53151
- W Fleetwood Ln 53151
- S Fohr Dr 53151
- S & W Forest Ave & Dr 53151
- Forest Knoll Ct & Dr 53151
- S Forest Point Blvd 53151
- S Forest Ridge Dr 53151
- Fountain Ct & Dr 53151
- S Fountain Square Blvd 53151
- Fox Glen Ct 53146
- Foxglove Ct 53151
- Foxhaven Ct 53151
- Foxwood Ct & Dr 53151
- S Frances Ave 53151

Franklin Ct & Dr 53151
S Fremont Ln 53151
W Fullerton Ave 53151
Gatewood Ct & Dr 53151
W Glen Meadow Dr 53151
Glen Park Ct & Rd 53151
W Glendale Dr 53151
W Glengarry Rd 53146
Glenora Ave & Ct 53151
W Glenwood Ln 53146
Golden Rain Ct & Ln 53151
W Graham St 53151
W Grange Ave 53151
S & W Graylog Ln 53151
W Green Meadow Dr 53151
S Green Ridge Ter 53151
W Greenbriar Ln 53151
W Greenfield Ave
12401-17199 53151
17201-20397 53146
20399-21999 53146
Greenhaven Ct 53151
S Greenhill Rd 53146
Greenlawn Ct & Ter 53151
S & W Greentree Ct & Dr 53151
Guerin Ct & Pass 53151
W Handerid Dr 53151
S Hanke Dr 53146
W Hansen Dr 53151
Harcove Ct & Dr 53151
S Harland Dr 53151
Harmony Ct & Dr 53151
S & W Hawthorne Ct, Dr & Ln 53151
Hearth Ridge Ct & Dr 53151
S & W Hearthside Dr 53151
W Heatherly Dr 53151
S Heide Ln 53146
W Hemlock Dr 53151
W Heritage Ln 53151
S Hi Knoll Dr 53146
S Hi View Ct 53146
W Hickory Ct 53151
S Hickory Rd 53151
W Hickory Rd 53151
W Hickory Trl 53146
W Hickory Hills Dr 53151
W Hidden Creek Ct 53151
W Hidden Valley Dr 53146
W Highland Dr 53146
Highpointe Ct & Dr 53151
Hillcrest Ct & Dr 53146
S Hillendale Dr 53146
W Hillside Dr 53146
W Hilltop Dr 53146
Hillview Ct & Dr 53146
S Holly Ct 53151
W Homestead Dr 53151
W Honey Ln 53151
W Honey Lane Ct 53151
W Honeyager Dr 53151
S Hope St 53151
W Horizon Dr 53146
W Howard Ave 53151
S Hunter Ln 53151
W Imperial Ct 53146
W Inez Dr 53146
S Ivy Ct 53151
W Jacobs Dr 53146
W Jacobs Ridge Ct 53146
W Jacqueline Dr 53146
S James Dr 53151
Janice Ct & Pl 53151
S & W Jeffers Ct & Dr 53146
Jennifer Ct 53151
S Jessica Ct 53151
W Jills Dr 53146
S Johns Dr 53146
S Johnson Rd 53146
W Joliet Cir 53151
S Jonathan Ln 53151
S Joseph Rd 53151
W Julius Heil Dr 53146
S Karrington Ln 53151
S Katherine Dr 53151

Kelly Ct 53151
Kelton Ct 53151
W Kingsway Dr 53151
Kirkwood Dr 53151
W Kohler Ct 53146
S Koinia Cir 53146
S Kolupar Ln 53151
Kostner Ct & Ln 53151
S & W Krahn Ct & Rd 53151
S La Salle Dr 53151
W Lagoon Rd 53151
W Lakeland Dr 53151
S Langlade Dr 53151
S Laurel Dr 53151
S Laurie Ln 53146
Lawnsdale Ct & Rd 53146
Lenox Dr 53151
W Liberty Ln 53146
Library Ln 53151
S & W Lilac Ln 53151
S Lilly Ln 53146
W Lincoln Ave
14001-14397 53151
14399-17199 53151
17200-21599 53146
21601-21899 53146
W Lincoln Rd 53151
Lindenwood Dr 53151
Linfield Ct, Dr & Ln 53151
S & W Linnie Lac Ct, Dr & Pl 53146
S Lions Ct 53151
W Lochinvar Ln 53146
Lochleven Ln 53146
Loftus Ct & Ln 53151
S Lombardy Ln 53151
S Long Acre Dr 53151
W Longleaf Dr 53151
S Longview Dr 53151
W Lookout Ln 53146
S Loretta Ln 53151
S Lucylle Ln 53151
W Lynette Ln 53146
S Lynn Dr 53151
W Lynwood Ct 53151
S Maberry Ln 53146
Mac Alister Way 53151
W Mac Gregor Dr 53146
S Magdalena Dr 53151
S Magellan Dr 53151
S Majors Dr 53146
W Manitoba Ave 53151
Manor Ct & Dr 53151
Maple Ridge Ct & Rd 53151
S Maplewood Ln 53151
Maria Ct & Dr 53151
W Marietta Dr 53151
S & W Marin Way 53151
W Mark Dr 53151
S & W Marquette Ct & Dr 53151
S Mars Dr 53146
S Martha Dr 53146
S Martin Rd 53146
S Mary Ln 53151
S & W Mary Ross Dr 53151
S Maryknoll Dr 53151
Mayflower Ct & Dr 53151
S & W Maylore Ct & Dr 53151
Mcintosh Ct & Ln 53151
W Meadow Ln 53151
S Meadow Creek Ct 53146
S Meadowlark Dr 53151
S Meadowmere Pkwy 53151
Meadowshire Ct & Dr 53151
W Meantont Rd 53146
Melody Ct & Dr 53151
S Menard Dr 53151
W Michaels Rd 53146
Michelle Witmer Memorial Dr 53151
W Mill Creek Trl 53146
Mill Pond Cir 53146
S Miller Ln 53146
W Milton Ct 53151

Misty Ct 53151
W Montana Ave 53151
S & W Monterey Dr 53151
S Moorland Rd 53151
W Morningview Ct 53151
S Mulberry Cir 53146
Murray St 53151
W National Ave
12400-17199 53151
17300-17498 53146
17500-21800 53146
21802-21898 53146
W Needham Dr 53151
W Nettesheim Rd 53151
New Haven Ct 53151
S Nicole Ct 53151
S & W Nicolet Dr 53151
W Nine Iron Ct 53151
North Ct & Ln 53151
North Oak Blvd & Ct 53151
S Northfield Ave 53151
S & W Norwood Dr 53146
W Oak Dr 53146
W Oak Park Dr 53146
W Oakcrest Dr 53146
S Oakdale Dr 53151
S Oakridge Dr 53146
S Oakwood Ter 53151
W Observatory Rd
16700-17199 53151
17200-19999 53146
Ohio Ct & Dr 53151
Oklahoma Ave & Ct 53151
S & W Old Oak Ct & Ln 53151
S Old Orchard Ct 53146
W Olivia Ln 53151
W Orchard Dr 53146
Overland Dr & Trl 53151
S & W Overlook Dr 53146
S Oxford Dr 53146
Paddock Pkwy 53151
Park Ave, Ct, Dr & Ter 53151
W Park Central Blvd 53151
Parkside Ct & Dr 53151
S Parkview Ave 53151
S Parkwood Ln 53151
W Peachtree Dr 53151
S Pembrook Ct 53151
S Pfeil Ln 53146
W Pheasant Run Dr 53146
S Piccard Ct 53151
S & W Pickford Ct & Dr 53151
W Pinecrest Ln 53146
W Pinewood Dr 53146
S Pinewood Creek Ct 53151
W Plateau Ln 53146
W Pleasant Dr 53151
S Pleasant Hill Dr 53146
S & W Pleasantview Ct & Dr 53151
S Pohl Dr 53151
S Poplar Rd 53151
W Prairie Ln 53151
Preston Ln 53151
Prospect Dr & Pl 53151
Providence Ct & Dr 53146
S Quimby Ave 53151
Rachel Ct & Ln 53151
Racine Ave, Ct & Pl 53146
W Radam Dr 53151
S & W Radisson Ct & Dr 53151
S & W Rainbow Ct & Dr 53146
S Ranch Rd 53151
Rausch Ct 53151
S Raven Ln 53151
S Raymond Dr 53151
W Redwood Dr 53151
Regal Ct & Dr 53151
Regal Manor Ct & Dr 53151
S Reno Dr 53151
S Reservoir Ln 53151

W Ridge Rd 53151
S Ridge Crest Ct 53151
Ridgeway Dr & Rd 53146
W Ridgewood Ln 53146
W Rindt Ct 53146
S River Rd 53151
W Riviera Dr 53151
Robin Rd & Trl 53151
S Rock Pl 53151
Rock Ridge Rd 53151
S Rogers Ct 53146
W Rogers Dr
14200-17199 53151
17200-17999 53146
S Rolling Dr 53146
Rolling Meadow Dr 53146
S Ronke Ln 53151
W Roosevelt Ave
16700-17199 53151
17200-17999 53146
S Rose Ct 53151
Rosemary Ave 53151
S Rosetree Pass 53151
Russel Ct & Rd 53151
Rustic Ridge Ct & Dr 53146
W Ryerson Rd 53151
S Saint Andrews Dr 53146
W Saint Francis Dr 53151
S & W Saint Marys Dr 53151
W Salentine Dr 53151
San Mateo Ct & Dr 53151
S Sanctuary Dr 53151
Sandalwood Ct & Dr 53151
S Sandra Ln 53151
W Santa Rosa Blvd 53151
W Saturn Dr 53146
Scarborough Ct & Dr 53151
Scenic View Ct 53146
Schaefer Ct 53151
W Schneider Ln 53151
S Scot Dr 53151
Settlers Hollow Ln 53146
Settlers Ridge Ct 53146
W Shadow Dr 53151
S Shady Ln 53146
S Sherwood Dr 53151
W Shields Dr 53146
W Signet Ln 53151
S Skyline Dr 53151
S Small Rd 53151
W Small Rd
14800-16999 53151
17001-17199 53151
17200-17999 53146
Solitaire Ct 53151
S Sommerset Dr 53151
S South Valley Ln 53146
W Southview Ln 53146
S Sovereign Dr 53151
S Springdale Rd 53146
S Spruce Rd 53151
S & W Steven Ct & Dr 53146
S Stigler Rd 53146
S Stonegate Cir 53151
S Stonewood Rd 53151
Stratford Ct & Dr 53151
W Stratton Dr 53151
W Sumerland Ct 53151
S Summit Ln 53146
S & W Sun Valley Ct & Dr 53151
Sunburst Ct & Ln 53151
Sunbury Rd 53151
Sundown Ct & Dr 53151
S Sunny Ridge Ln 53151
S & W Sunny View Dr 53151
S & W Sunnycrest Dr 53146
S Sunnyslope Rd 53151
S Sunset Ct 53151
S Swartz Rd 53146
W Sycamore Dr 53151
S Tall Oaks Ct 53146
S Tammy Ln 53151
S Tartan Ct 53146
W Terrace Dr 53146

Terrywood Ct 53151
W Thomas Dr 53151
S & W Thornapple Ln 53146
S Tie Ave 53151
W Tiffany Pl 53151
Timber Ridge Ct & Dr 53151
S Timberlane Rd 53146
W Todd Ct 53146
W Tolbert Dr 53146
S & W Top O Hill Dr 53151
S Town Rd 53151
S Towne Dr 53151
W Treetop Ln 53146
S Triangle Ave 53151
S Trillium Dr 53146
Twilight Way 53151
S Twin Willow Dr 53146
S Two Ponds Ct 53146
W Valley Dr 53146
Valley Ridge Dr 53151
S & W Valley Spring Ct & Dr 53151
S Valley View Dr 53151
W Van Norman Ave 53151
S Ventura Dr 53151
W Venus Dr 53146
Vera Cruz Ct & Dr 53151
W Verona Dr 53151
W Victor Rd 53151
Victoria Cir & Ct 53151
S Villa Ter 53146
S & W Vista Ct & Dr 53146
S Vista Granada Dr 53151
S & W Vogel Ct & Dr 53151
W Wade Dr 53151
S Wakefield Ln 53151
Walnut Ct 53151
Waterbury Ct 53151
Waterford Ct 53151
Waterford Square Dr 53151
Waters Way 53151
Waters Edge Trl 53151
W Weather Creek Ct 53151
Weatherstone Blvd & Ct 53151
W Wedgewood Ct 53146
S Wehr Rd 53146
Wembly Ct & Dr 53151
S & W West Ln 53146
S Westbrook Pkwy 53146
W Westeria Ct 53151
Westridge Ct & Dr 53151
W Westview Ln 53146
W Westward Dr 53146
S Westwoods Rd 53146
White Ct & Dr 53151
S & W Wilbur Ct & Dr 53151
W Wildflower Ln 53151
S Wildwood Dr 53151
Williams Cir & Rd 53146
S & W Willow Rd 53146
S Willow Glen Dr 53151
Wilshire Ct & Dr 53151
W Wimbledon Dr 53151
W Windsor Dr 53146
W Winston Ct 53146
Winterberry Way 53151
S Woelfel Rd 53146
Woodfield Ln 53151
Woodhill Ct & Ln 53151
S Woodland Ct 53146
W Woodland Ct 53146
W Woodland Dr
14400-15299 53151
21300-21499 53146
21501-21599 53146
S Woodlawn Dr 53146
S Woodridge Ln 53146
Woodshire Ct & Dr 53151
S Woodside Dr 53151
S Woodsview Ct 53146
Woodview Ct & Dr 53151
Wyndridge Ct & Dr 53151
Wynfield Ct 53151
W Yuma Ct 53151

NUMBERED STREETS

S 124th St 53151
S 126th St 53151
S 127th St 53151
S 128th St 53151
S 129th St 53151
S 130th St 53151
S 131st St 53151
S 132nd St 53151
S 133rd St 53151
S 134th St 53151
145th Ct & St 53151
S 146th St 53151
S 147th St 53151
S 149th St 53151
S 152nd St 53151
S 153rd St 53151
S 157th St 53151
S 158th St 53151
S 159th St 53151
S 160th St 53151
S 162nd St 53151
S 163rd St 53151
S 164th St 53151
S 165th St 53151
S 166th St 53151
S 167th St 53151
S 168th St 53151
S 169th St 53151
S 170th St 53151
S 171st St 53151
S 179th St 53146
S 199th St 53146
S 200th St 53146

OSHKOSH WI

General Delivery 54902

POST OFFICE BOXES MAIN OFFICE STATIONS AND BRANCHES

Box No.s
All PO Boxes 54903

NAMED STREETS

Abbey Ave 54904
Abraham Ln 54904
Acorn Ct 54904
Adams Ave 54902
Addie Pkwy 54904
Alaska St 54902
Alden Ave 54901
Alexandra Ct 54902
Algoma Blvd 54901
Alida Ln 54904
Allen Ave 54901
Allerton Dr 54904
Alpine Ct 54901
Amanda Ct 54904
Amherst Ave 54901
Amy Jo Dr 54904
Anchorage Ct 54901
Anderson St 54901
Andrew St 54904
Angell Rd 54904
Angle Rd 54904
Annex Ave 54901
Apple Ct & Ln 54902
Arboretum Dr 54901
Arcadia Ave 54904
Ardmore Trl 54904
Arizona St 54902
Arlington Dr 54904
Armory Pl 54902
Arthur Ave 54902
Ashland St 54901
Atlas Ave 54904
Autumn Hills Dr 54904

Aviation Rd 54902
Babbitz Ave 54901
Bacon Ave 54901
Badger Ave 54904
Bailey Ct 54904
Baldwin Ave 54901
Balerinc St 54902
Bambi Ln 54904
Banville Rd 54904
Baron Ln 54904
Barton Rd 54904
Bauman St 54902
Bavarian Ct 54901
Bay St 54901
Bay Shore Dr 54901
Bay View Ln 54902
Bayberry Ct & Ln 54902
Beachcomber St 54902
Beech St 54901
Beechnut Dr 54904
Bell Heights Ct 54904
Bellaire Ln 54904
Bellfield Dr 54904
Bellhaven Ln 54904
Bennett Ct 54904
E & W Bent Ave 54901
Berger St 54902
Bernheim St 54904
Birch Ln 54901
Bismarck Ave 54902
Bison Point Rd 54904
Bittersweet Ln 54901
Black Oak School Rd 54902
E Black Wolf Ave 54902
Black Wolf Point Ln & Rd 54902
Blake Ct 54904
Blossom Ct 54902
Bong Ct 54901
Bonnie View Rd 54904
Bowen St 54901
Boyd St 54901
Bradley St 54902
Braeburn St 54904
W Breezewood Ln 54904
Brenland Rd 54902
Brentwood Cir & Dr 54904
British Ln 54901
Broad St 54901
Brockway Ave 54902
Bromfield Dr 54904
Brooks Ln & Rd 54904
Brookview Ct 54904
Brookwood Ct 54902
Brown St 54901
Buchanan Ave 54902
Buehring Rd 54904
Burdick St 54901
Burnwood Dr 54902
Burr Oak Rd 54904
Butler Ave 54901
Cambria Ct 54904
Cambridge Ave 54902
Camden Ln 54904
Camelot Ct 54901
N & S Campbell Rd 54902
Campus Pl 54901
Candlelight Ct 54904
Candlish Harbor Ln 54902
Canniff Ct 54901
Canterbury Dr 54902
Capital Dr 54902
Carlet Dr 54904
Carlton Rd 54904
Carr Pl 54901
Casey Trl 54904
Castle Ct 54902
Catherine Ave 54902
Ceape Ave 54901
Cedar St 54901
Cedar View Dr 54901
Central St 54901
Channel View Dr 54901
Charlie Anna Dr 54904
Chateau Ter 54901
Chatham Cir, Ct & Dr 54904

Cherokee Ln 54904
Cherry St 54901
Cherry Park Ct 54902
Chesapeake Ct 54901
Chestnut St 54901
Christensen Rd 54904
Christian Dr 54901
Church Ave 54901
Cimarron Ct 54902
Circle R Rd 54902
Ciscel Dr 54904
City Ctr 54901
Clairville Rd 54904
Clarks Ct 54901
Clay Rd 54904
Clayton Ct 54902
Clevedon Ln 54904
Cleveland Ave 54901
Cliffview Ct & Dr 54901
Clover Ln 54904
Clover St 54901
Cobblestone Ct 54901
Colleen Ct 54904
Collier Ct 54904
Columbia Ave 54901
Comanche Ln 54901
Comet St 54901
Commander Ct 54901
Commerce St 54901
Concordia Ave 54902
Conger Ct 54904
Congress Ave 54901
Conrad St 54904
Coolidge Ave 54902
Coronado Ln 54902
Cottontail Dr 54904
Cottonwood Ave 54904
Country Club Ln & Rd 54902
Country Meadow Ct 54904
Countryside Ct 54904
County Rd E 54904
County Rd N
2000-2299 54904
2900-3699 54902
3800-4899 54904
County Rd S 54904
County Road A 54901
County Road C 54904
County Road Ff 54904
County Road G 54904
County Road Gg 54904
County Road I 54902
County Road K 54904
County Road R 54902
County Road T 54904
E County Road Y 54901
W County Road Y
2-98 54901
W County Road Y
100-199 54901
201-999 54901
1400-2299 54904
County Road Z
2500-3699 54902
4100-4299 54904
E County Road Z 54902
W County Road Z 54904
Court St 54901
Courtland Ave 54901
Cove Ln 54902
Covington Dr 54904
Cozy Ln 54901
Crab Apple Ln 54904
Crane St 54901
Creek Side Dr 54904
Crest Ct 54904
Crestview Dr 54904
Crestwood Dr 54904
Crimson Ln 54902
Crown Dr 54904
Cryer Ln 54904
Crystal Springs Ave 54902
Cumberland Trl 54904
E & W Custer Ave 54901
Cutter Ct 54904
Dakota St 54902
Dale Ave 54901
Danbe Rd 54904
Daniel Ct 54904
David Dr 54904
Dawes St 54901
Decorah Ave 54902
Deerfield Dr 54904
Delaware St 54902
Dempsey Trl 54902
Devonshire Dr 54902
Dickinson Ave 54904
Division St 54901
Doctors Ct 54901
Doemel St 54901
Donegal Ct 54904
Donner Hall 54901
Doty St 54902
Dove St 54902
Doyle Ln 54902
Driftwood Ln 54901
Duchess Ln 54904
Durfee Ave 54902
N & S Eagle St 54902
Eastman St 54901
Eckardt Ct 54902
Eden Ct & Ln 54904
Eden Meadows Dr 54904
Edgewater Ln 54902
Edgewood Ln & Rd 54904
Egg Harbor Ln 54904
Eichstadt Rd 54901
Elderberry Ln 54904
Elk Ridge Dr 54904
E Elm Ln 54902
Elmhurst Ln 54904
Elmwood Ave 54901
Elo Rd 54904
Emily Anne Dr 54904
Emmers Ln 54904
Enterprise Dr & Trl 54904
Erie Ave 54902
Evans St 54901
Evans Hall 54901
Eveline St 54901
Fabry St 54902
Fahley Rd 54904
Fahrnwald Rd 54902
Fairfax St 54904
Fairlawn St 54902
Fairview St 54901
Fall Creek Ln 54904
Farmington Ave 54901
Farmstead Ln 54901
Faust Ave 54902
Faust Rd 54904
Fenzl Dr 54904
E & W Fernau Ave &
Ct 54901
Fillmore Ave 54902
Fireside Cir 54901
Fisk Ave
2600-2800 54902
2802-2898 54902
3700-6099 54904
6101-6199 54904
E Fisk Ave 54902
Fitchburg Ct 54904
Fletcher Hall 54901
Fleur De Lis Ct 54904
Florida Ave 54902
Fluor Ct 54901
Fond Du Lac Rd 54902
Forest View Rd 54904
Forte Rd 54904
Foster St 54902
Fountain Ave 54904
Fox St 54902
Fox Fire Dr 54904
Fox Tail Ln 54904
Frankfort St 54901
Franklin St 54901
Fraser Dr 54904
Frederick St 54901
Freedom Ave 54901
Fugleberg Trl 54902
Fulton Ave 54901
Galway Ct 54904
Garfield St 54901
Gaslight Ct 54904
E Gate Dr 54904
Gehres Ct 54901
Geneva St 54901
Georgia St 54902
Gibs Rd 54904
Gibson Ct 54902
Glane Ct 54902
Glen Ave 54902
Glenayre Ln 54904
Glenbrook Ln 54904
Glendale Ave 54901
Glenhurst Ln 54904
Glenkirk Ln 54904
Glenshire Ln 54904
Glenview Ln 54904
Glenwalk Dr 54904
Glenway Dr 54904
Glenwood Dr 54904
Gloria Ct 54904
Golden Ave 54904
Golden Iris Dr 54901
Goss Ct 54901
Graber St 54901
Graceland Ct & Dr 54904
Graham Ave 54902
Grand St 54901
Gray Wolf Dr 54904
Green Meadow Rd 54904
Green Valley Ct & Rd 54904
Greenbriar Ct 54901
Greenbriar Trl 54904
Greenfield Trl 54904
Greenhill Ct 54904
Greenwood Ct 54901
Greystone Ct 54902
Grimson Rd 54904
Grove St 54901
Gruenhagen Hall 54901
E & W Gruenwald Ave 54901
Grundman Ct & Ln 54901
Guenther St 54902
Gullig Ct 54904
Hallie Hollow Ct 54904
Hamilton St 54901
Hansen Rd 54904
Harbor Bay Rd 54901
Harborview Ct 54901
Harmel Ave 54902
Harney Ave 54901
Harrison St 54901
Hartland Rd 54902
Harvest Ct & Dr 54901
N Haven Ct & Ln 54904
Havenwood Dr 54904
Hawk St 54902
Hawthorne St 54902
Hayden Dr 54904
Hayward Ave 54904
Hazel St 54901
Hearthstone Dr 54901
Heidi Haven Ct & Dr 54904
Heidl Ln 54904
Hemlock Ct 54904
Hennessy St 54904
Heritage Ct & Trl 54904
Hickory Ct, Ln & St 54901
Hickory Heights Ave 54904
Hickory Ridge Rd 54904
Hidden Hollow Rd 54904
High Ave 54901
High Oak Dr 54902
Highland Shore Ln 54904
Hilltop Rd 54904
Hillwood Run 54901
Hobbs Ave 54901
Hollister Ave 54901
Holly Ct 54904
Homestead Dr 54904
Honey Creek Cir, Ct &
Rd 54904
Honeysuckle Ct 54904
Horizon Vlg 54901
Horseshoe Rd 54904
Howlett Rd 54902
Hubbard St 54902
Hudson Ave 54901
Hughes St 54902
Hunters Pl 54904
Hunters Glen Dr 54904
Huntington Pl 54902
Huron Ave & Ct 54901
I Ah May Tah Rd 54901
Ida Ave 54901
Idaho St 54902
Imperial Rd 54904
Indian Bend Rd 54904
Indian Echoes 54902
Indian Point Rd 54901
Indigo Dr 54902
Industrial Ave 54901
Iowa St 54902
Iroquois Ct 54901
E & W Irving Ave 54901
Isaac Ln 54902
Island Dr & Rd 54904
Island Estates Ct 54901
Island View Dr 54901
Ivy Ln 54904
Jackson St 54901
Jacktar Rd 54901
Jacob Ave 54902
James Ln & Rd 54904
Jefferson St 54901
Jensen Rd 54904
John Ave 54901
John Moore Dr 54904
Johnson Ave 54902
Jones Ct 54904
Josslyn St 54902
Judy Lee Ct & Dr 54904
Juniper Ln 54904
Kaitlynn Ct & Dr 54901
Kansas St 54902
Katy Ct 54904
Keenville Ln 54901
Kendall Dr 54904
Kensington Ave 54902
Kentucky St 54901
Kenwood Ct 54904
Kewaunee St 54904
Kienast Ave 54901
Killarney Ct 54904
Killdeer Ln 54901
Kincaid Ave 54904
Kings Ln 54904
Kingston Pl 54904
Kirkwood Dr 54904
Knapp St 54902
Knott Rd 54904
N & S Koeller St 54902
Koelpin Rd 54902
Kolb Rd 54904
Kope Ave 54901
Kristine St 54904
Laager Ln 54902
Lake Rd 54902
Lake St 54901
Lake Breeze Rd 54904
Lake Butte Des Morts
Dr 54904
Lake Pointe Dr 54904
Lake Rest Ave, Ct &
Ln 54902
Lakeland Dr 54904
Lakeshore Dr 54901
Lakeside Ct 54904
Lakeview Ct 54902
Lakewind Dr 54904
Lamar Ave 54901
Lampert St 54901
Lamplight Ct 54904
Lansing High Pt 54904
N & S Lark St 54902
Laurie Ave 54902
Lawndale St 54901
Leach Rd 54904
Lee Rd 54902
Lee Harbor Ln 54902
Leeward Ct W 54901
Legion Pl 54901
Leila Mae Ln 54904
Lennox St 54904
Leonard Point Ln &
Rd 54904
Libbey Ave 54901
Liberty St 54901
Lilac St 54902
Lilly Ln 54902
Lin Way 54904
E & W Lincoln Ave 54901
Lincorai Rd 54904
Linde St 54901
Linden Oaks Dr 54904
E & W Linwood Ave 54901
Little Evergreen Ave 54902
Locust St 54902
Logan Dr 54901
Lombard Ave 54902
E Lone Elm Ave 54902
Louise Ct 54901
Luebke Rd 54904
Luke Ln 54902
Lullabye Rd 54904
Macarthur Rd 54901
Madison St 54901
Magnolia Ave 54902
N Main St 54901
S Main St 54902
Maincong St 54901
Malibu Cv 54904
Mallard Ave 54901
Manor Dr 54904
Maple Ave 54902
Maricopa Dr 54904
Marine Dr 54901
Marion Rd 54901
Market St 54901
Marquette Ave 54901
Marquis Rd 54904
Marsh Creek Rd 54904
Marston Pl 54901
Marvel Dr 54902
Marway Ct 54901
Maryden Rd 54904
Mason St 54902
Maxwell Rd 54904
Maywood Ct 54901
Mccurdy St 54902
Mcintosh Ct 54904
Mckinley St 54901
N & S Meadow St 54902
Meadow View Ln 54904
Meadowbrook Ct & Rd 54904
Medalist Dr 54902
Melody Ln 54904
E & W Melvin Ave 54901
Menard Dr 54904
Menominee Dr 54901
Mereworth Ct 54904
Merrill St 54901
Merritt Ave 54901
Michigan St 54902
Milford Dr 54904
Mill St 54901
Miller Dr 54904
Miller Ln 54901
Milton Cir 54904
Minerva St 54901
Minnesota St 54902
Mission Meadows Trl 54904
Mitchell St 54901
Mockingbird Way 54904
Monroe St 54901
Montana St 54902
Montclair Pl 54904
Moon Cir 54904
Moore Is 54904
Moreland St 54902
Morgan Ave 54901
Moser St 54901
Mount Vernon St 54901
E & W Murdock Ave 54901
Murmuring Waters Ln 54901
Myrna Jane Dr 54902
National Ave 54902
Nebraska St 54902
Neighborly Rd 54904
Nekimi Ave
1-3699 54902
3700-4899 54904
Nelson Rd 54904
E & W Nevada Ave 54901
E & W New York Ave 54901
Newport Ave & Ct 54904
Nickels Dr 54904
Nicole Ct 54904
Nicolet Ave 54901
Nielsen Dr 54901
Nimrod Ct 54902
Noel Ct 54904
Norman Ct & Way 54904
Northpoint St 54901
Northwestern Ave 54901
Norton Ave 54901
Oak St 54901
Oak Crest Dr 54904
Oak Manor Dr 54904
Oak Park Dr 54904
Oakdale Ct 54904
Oakland Ln 54902
N & S Oakwood Cir, Ct,
Ln & Rd 54904
Ohio St 54902
Old Alex Ct 54904
Old Knapp Rd 54902
Old Oak Rd 54904
Old Omro Rd 54904
Old Orchard Ln 54902
Old Oregon Rd 54902
Olde Apple Ln 54904
Olive St 54901
Olson Ave 54901
Omni Dr 54904
Omro Rd
1900-1999 54902
2000-2198 54904
2200-3599 54904
Oneida Ave 54904
Ontario St 54901
Orchard Ct & Ln 54902
Oregon St 54902
Ormand Beach Ct 54904
Ormond Beach Rd 54904
Osborn Ave 54902
Osceola St 54901
Oshkosh Ave 54902
Otter Ave 54901
Overland Trl 54904
Oxford Ave 54901
E & W Packer Ave 54901
Park Ridge Ave 54901
Parkside Ct & Dr 54901
Parkview Ct 54901
E & W Parkway Ave 54901
Parkwood Dr 54904
Partridge Ct 54904
Patriot Ln 54904
Pau Ko Tuk Ln 54902
Pearl Ave 54901
E & W Pheasant Ct 54904
Pheasant Creek Dr 54904
Pickett Rd 54904
Pierce Ave 54902
Pierce Ln 54904
Pine Ridge Rd 54904
Pip Ln 54904
Planeview Dr 54904
Pleasant St 54901
Plummer St 54902
Plummers Point Rd 54904
Plymouth St 54901
Poberezny Rd 54902
N & S Point Comfort
Rd 54902
W Pointe Dr 54902
S Pond Ct 54904
Poplar Ave 54904
Porter Ave 54902
Portside Ct 54901
Powers St 54901
Prairie Ct & Ln 54901
Prairie Wood Dr 54904
Primrose Ln 54904
Progress Dr 54901
Prospect Ave 54901
Punhoqua St 54902
Purple Crest Ct & Dr 54901
Pyle Ave 54901
Quail Ct 54904
Quail Run Dr 54904
Queens Dr 54904
Raddison Ave 54904
Rahr Ave 54901
Rainbow Dr 54902
Ran Lie St 54904
Randall Pl 54901
Rasmussen Rd 54904
Rath Ln 54902
Ravine Way 54904
Rebecca Run 54904
Red Fox Rd 54904
Red Oak Ct 54902
Red Tail Way 54902
Reed Ave 54901
Reichow St 54902
Repp Ave 54902
Richards Ave 54904
Ridge Ln 54901
Ripon Ln 54902
Ripon Pl 54904
Ripple Ave 54904
E Ripple Ave 54902
W Ripple Ave 54902
River Mill Rd 54901
Riverway Dr 54901
Roberts Ave 54904
Robin Ave 54902
Rock Pl 54901
Rocky Rd 54904
Roeder Ct 54904
Rolling Green Cir 54904
Romberg Rd 54904
Roosevelt Ave 54901
Rosalia St 54901
Roselawn Ln 54904
Rosewood Ln 54904
Rugby St 54902
Ruschfield Dr 54904
Rush Ave 54902
Russett Ln 54904
Ryf Rd 54904
Saint Ives Rd 54904
Sally Lynn Ct 54904
Sand Pit Ln & Rd 54904
Sanders St 54902
Sandhill Ct 54904
Sandstone Ct 54904
N & S Sandy Beach
Ln 54902
Saratoga Ave 54901
Sawtell Ct 54902
N & S Sawyer St 54902
Sawyer Creek Dr 54904
Scarlet Oak Trl 54904
Scenic Ct & Dr 54904
Schneider Ave 54904
School Ave 54901
Scott Ave 54901
N & S Scott Hall 54901
Security Dr 54904
Sennholz Ct 54902
Sesame Street Rd 54902
Shadow Ln 54901
Shady Ln S 54902
Shambeau Dr 54901
Shammy Ln 54904
Shangri La Point Rd 54904
Sharratt Dr 54901
Shawano Ave 54901
Shawnee Ln 54901
Shea Rd 54904
Sheboygan St 54904
Sheldon Dr 54904
Shelter Ct 54901
Sheppard Dr 54904
Sheridan St 54901
Sherman Rd 54901

Sherrin St 54904
Shore Preserve 54904
Shorebird Ct 54904
Shorehaven Ct & Ln 54904
Shorelane St 54901
Shorewood Dr & Ln 54901
Short Ave 54901
Short Rd 54904
Simpson St 54902
Skeleton Bridge Rd 54904
Sky Ranch Ave 54904
Skyview Ave 54902
E & W Smith Ave 54901
E Snell Rd 54901
W Snell Rd
1-1799 54901
1801-1899 54901
1900-1969 54904
1970-1972 54901
1975-1977 54901
1979-1999 54904
Snowdon Dr 54904
Soda Creek Rd 54901
Sonshine Ln 54902
W South Park Ave 54902
Southland Ave 54902
Spencer Ct 54904
Spiegelberg Rd 54904
Spring Valley Rd 54904
Springmill Dr 54904
Spruce St 54901
Stanley Ave 54901
Star Ct 54904
Starboard Ct W 54901
State St
100-199 54901
130-130 54903
200-398 54901
201-399 54901
State Road 21 54904
State Road 26 54904
State Road 44 54904
State Road 76 54904
State Road 91 54904
Stearns Dr 54904
Sterling Ave 54901
Stevens Ct 54901
Stevens Ln 54904
Stewart Hall 54901
Stillman Dr 54901
Stillwell Ave 54901
Stonefield Ct & Dr 54902
Stonegate Ct & Dr 54904
Stonewood Ct & Dr 54902
Stoney Beach Ln, Rd & St 54902
Stoney Ridge Trl 54904
Streich Ln 54902
Sullivan St 54902
Summerset Way 54901
Summerview Dr 54901
Summit Ave 54901
Sunkist Rd 54904
E Sunny Hill Ave 54902
Sunnybrook Dr 54904
E Sunnyview Rd 54901
Sunset Point Ln 54904
Swallow Banks Ln 54904
Sweet St 54901
Swiss Rd 54902
Taft Ave 54902
Talbot Ln 54902
Tamarack Trl 54904
Tammy Rd 54904
Tank Ave 54902
Taylor Hall 54901
Templeton Pl 54904
E & W Tennessee Ave 54901
Thackery Dr 54904
Thornberry Trl 54904
Thornton Dr 54904
Timberland Dr 54902
Timberline Dr 54904
Timothy Trl 54904
Titan Ct 54901
Transport Ct 54904
Traxler Trl 54904
Trillium Trl 54904
Tumblebrook Dr 54904
Twilight Ct 54904
Tyler Ave 54902
Ulman St 54904
Union Ave 54901
Universal Ct & St 54904
Us Highway 45 54904
S Us Highway 45 54902
Valley Rd 54904
Valley Heights Rd 54904
Van Buren Ave 54902
Venture Dr 54902
Victoria Ct 54902
Viking Ct & Pl 54904
Villa Park Dr 54904
Village Ln & Rd 54904
Vine Ave 54901
Vinland St 54901
Vinland Center Rd 54904
Viola Ave 54901
Violet Ln 54904
Virginian St 54902
Wagon Trail Rd 54904
Walden Ln 54904
Waldwic Ln 54904
Walnut St 54901
Walter Ct & St 54901
N & S Washburn St 54904
Washington Ave 54901
Washington St 54904
Waugoo Ave 54901
E Waukau Ave 54902
W Waukau Ave
1-1999 54902
2300-2599 54904
Waupun Rd 54902
Weatherstone Dr 54901
Webster Hall 54901
Weisbrod St 54902
Weldon Ct 54904
Welle Dr 54902
Wellington Ct & Dr 54904
Welsh Haven Dr 54904
Westbreeze Dr 54904
Westbrook Dr 54904
Western Ct, Dr & St 54901
N & S Westfield St 54902
N & S Westhaven Cir, Ct & Dr 54904
Westmoor Ct & Rd 54904
Westowne Ave 54904
Westview Ln 54904
Westwind Rd 54904
Weyerhorst Creek Rd 54904
Wheatfield Way 54904
White Swan Dr 54901
White Tail Ln 54904
Wild Rose Ln 54904
Wilderness Pl 54904
Willow Ln 54902
Willow Way 54904
Willow Bend Ct & Ln 54904
Willow Springs Rd 54904
Wilson Ave 54901
Winchester Ave 54901
Windermere Ln 54902
Windhurst Dr 54904
Windingbrook Dr 54904
Windsong Ter 54904
Windsor St 54902
Windward Ct 54901
Winnebago Ave 54901
Wisconsin St 54901
Witzel Ave
600-1799 54902
1801-1899 54902
2000-3499 54904
3501-3599 54904
Woodduck Ct 54904
Woodland Ave 54901
Woodridge Dr 54904
Woodrose Ln 54902
Woodstock St 54904
Wright St 54901
Wylde Oak Ct & Dr 54904
Wyldeberry Ln 54904
Wyldeflower Ct 54904
Wyldewood Dr & Rd 54904
Wyoming St 54902
Yorkton Pl 54904
Zacher Dr 54901
Zarling Ave 54901
Zoar Rd 54904

NUMBERED STREETS

W 2nd Ave 54902
W 3rd Ave 54902
W 4th Ave 54902
W 5th Ave 54902
W 6th Ave 54902
E & W 7th 54902
E & W 8th 54902
W 9th Ave
1-97 54902
2000-3599 54904
9th Street Rd 54904
E & W 10th 54902
E & W 11th 54902
W 12th Ave 54902
W 14th Ave 54902
W 15th Ave 54902
W 16th Ave 54902
W 17th Ave 54902
W 18th Ave 54902
W 19th Ave 54902
W 20th Ave
200-1026 54902
1025-1025 54903
1028-1798 54902
1101-1699 54902
2000-3599 54904
W 21st Ave 54902
W 22nd Ave 54902
W 23rd Ave 54902
W 24th Ave 54902
W 25th Ave 54902
W 28th Ave 54902
W 29th Ave 54902
W 33rd Ave 54902
W 35th Ave 54902

RACINE WI

General Delivery 53401

POST OFFICE BOXES MAIN OFFICE STATIONS AND BRANCHES

Box No.s
1 - 1938 53401
2011 - 46005 53404
80731 - 85948 53408
44451 - 45042 53404
80011 - 87601 53408

RURAL ROUTES

01, 04 53402
02, 03, 05 53403

NAMED STREETS

Aberdeen Dr 53402
Acorn Trl 53402
Adams Dr 53404
Admiralty Ave 53406
Agatha Turn 53402
Airline Rd 53406
Albert St 53404
Alburg Ave 53406
Alcyn Dr 53402
Alden Ct 53405
Alexander Dr 53402
Ambassador Dr 53402
Amys Bnd 53402
Anker Rd 53405
Ann St 53403
Antoinette Trl 53402
Appaloosa Trl 53402
Apple Tree Cir & Ln 53405
Applewood Ct 53402
Arcturus Ave 53404
Arlington Ave 53403
Arrowhead St 53402
Arthur Ave 53405
Ashland Ave 53403
Aster Ct 53402
Astoria Dr 53402
Athens Ave 53406
Augusta St 53402
Austin Ave 53403
Autumn Dr & Trl 53402
Autumnwood Ct 53403
Back Nine Rd 53406
Badger St 53403
Banoch Dr 53402
Barbara Dr 53404
Barker St 53402
Bate St 53403
N Bay Dr 53402
Bay Filly Ln 53402
Bay Wood Dr 53402
Bayfield Dr 53402
Beacon Ln 53402
Beacon View Dr 53402
Beaugrand Ct 53404
Bedford Ct 53406
Beech Rd 53402
Beechnut Dr 53402
Beechwood Ct 53402
Belmar Ave 53402
Belmont Ave 53405
Ber Wil Dr 53402
Bergamot Dr 53406
Berkeley Dr 53402
Birch St 53403
Birch Creek Ln 53402
Birch View Rd 53402
Birchwood Ct 53402
Biscayne Ave 53406
Bittersweet Ct 53402
Blackhawk Dr 53402
Blaine Ave 53405
Blake Ave 53404
Blazing Star Dr 53406
Blue Jay Ct 53402
Blue River Ave 53405
Blue River Way 53402
Blue Star Cir 53406
Bluebird Ln 53406
Bluff Ave 53403
Bluffside Dr 53402
Bobolink Rd 53402
Bonita Ln 53402
Botting Rd 53402
Boyd Ave 53405
Bradford Ave 53406
Bradley Dr 53406
W Branch Trl 53402
Brandywine Ave 53404
Breeze Ter 53406
Brentwood Dr 53403
Brian Dr 53402
Briarwood Ln 53402
Broadleaf Dr 53402
Brooker St 53404
Brookhaven Dr 53406
Browns Ct 53405
Bruce Dr 53404
Buchanan St 53402
Buckley Rd 53404
Bunting Ct 53402
Burrline Rd 53402
Butternut Rd 53402
Byrd Ave
4100-4699 53405
4700-4898 53406
4900-5699 53406
5701-5799 53406
Byron Ave 53405
C A Becker Dr 53406
Caledonia St 53402
Camelot Dr 53406
E & W Campus Ct 53402
Canada Goose Xing 53403
Candle Ct 53402
Candlelight Dr 53402
Capitol Ave 53403
Cardinal Dr 53402
Carlisle Ave 53404
Carls Ave 53402
Carlton Dr 53402
Carmel Ave 53405
Caroline Ct & Dr 53405
Carpenter Ave 53403
Carrol St 53403
Carter Dr & St 53402
Case Ave 53403
Castle Ct 53406
Castleton Dr 53406
Catherine Dr 53402
Cecelia Park Dr 53404
Cedar Creek St 53402
Cedar Ridge Ln 53405
Cedarwood Ct 53402
Center St 53403
Century Way 53406
Charles St
1600-1800 53404
1802-1898 53404
1901-1997 53402
1999-6699 53402
Chatham Cir & St 53402
Cherry St 53403
Cherry Tree Ct 53402
Cherrywood Ct 53402
Chesapeake Rd 53406
Chester Ln 53402
Chestnut Dr 53402
Cheyenne Ct 53404
Chicago St 53405
Chicory Rd 53403
Chris Ct 53402
Christopher Ct 53402
Christopher Columbus 53403
Cindy Dr 53404
Circlewood Dr 53402
Citation Dr & Ln 53402
Clairmont St 53406
Clarence Ave 53405
Clark St 53403
Clayton Ave 53404
Cleveland Ave 53405
Cliff Ave 53404
Cliffside Ct & Dr 53402
Clinton Ln 53406
Clover Ln 53406
Cloverdale Dr 53403
Clubview Ln 53406
Coachlight Dr 53404
Cobblestone Dr 53405
College Ave 53403
College Point Ct 53402
Collova Dr 53406
Colorado Ct 53404
Concord Dr 53403
Conlaine Dr 53406
Connolly Ave 53405
Conrad Dr 53404
Coolidge Ave 53403
Corona Dr 53406
Coronada Dr 53402
Corporate Dr 53406
Cortland Ave 53406
Cottonwood Ct 53402
Count Dr 53402
Count Turf Ln 53402
Country Rd 53402
Country Club Dr 53406
County Line Rd
6000-6099 53402
6101-6799 53402
6700-6999 53403
6801-8099 53402
County Road C 53406
Crab Tree Cir & Ln 53406
Crabapple Dr 53405
Cramford Dr 53402
Cranberry Ln 53404
S Creek Rd 53402
Creek Ridge Dr 53402
E & W Crescent St 53403
Crestview Park Dr 53402
Cross Creek Rd 53402
Crossridge Dr 53405
Crosswinds 53403
Crown Ct 53406
Crown Chase Dr 53402
Crown Point Dr 53402
Crystal Dr & Spg 53406
Dahlia Ln 53406
Daily Double Ln 53402
Daisy Ln 53405
Dale Dr 53402
Dan Mor Ln 53404
Darby Pl 53402
David St 53404
Davis Pl 53403
De Koven Ave 53403
De Rose Ct 53404
Deane Blvd
1300-1799 53405
1800-2099 53403
Debra Ln 53403
Deepwood Dr 53402
Delamere Ave 53403
Delaware Ave 53403
Dena Cir 53402
Diane Ave 53404
Dodge St 53402
Domanik Dr 53404
Dombrowski Blvd 53405
Donegal Dr 53405
Donna Ave 53404
Dorelach St 53403
Dorset Ave 53406
Douglas Ave
1000-1399 53402
1400-1799 53404
1800-8700 53402
8702-9198 53402
Dr Martin Luther King Dr 53404
Drexel Ave 53403
Dublin Ct 53402
Duchess Dr 53406
Dundee Dr 53402
Durand Ave
1500-2548 53403
2550-3099 53403
3200-4699 53405
3901-3929 53405
5200-5598 53406
5600-5700 53406
5702-6098 53406
Dustir Dr 53402
Dutchess Dr 53405
Dwight St 53403
Eagle Point Dr 53406
East St 53402
Eastwood Rdg 53406
Eaton Ln 53404
Echo Cir & Ln 53406
Edgar Ter 53402
Edgewood Ave 53404
Ehlert St 53405
Eifler Ct 53402
Eisenhower Dr 53405
Elderberry Rd 53402
Eldorado Dr 53402
Elisa Dr 53402
Elizabeth St 53402
Ellen Dr 53405
Ellis Ave 53402
Elm Ln 53405
Elm St 53403
Elm Tree Ct 53405
E Elmwood Dr 53405
Emmertsen Rd 53406
Emstan Hills Rd 53406
English St
200-1299 53402
1800-2199 53404
Erie St 53402
Esquire Ln 53406
Evergreen Ct 53402
Fairchild Ave 53404
Fairview Ter 53403
Fairway Dr 53405
N Fairway Dr 53402
N & S Fancher Rd 53406
Fayette Dr 53402
Fenceline Rd 53406
Fergus Ave 53404
Fieldstone Ct 53402
Finch Ln 53402
Fireside Dr 53402
Fleetwood Dr 53403
Flett Ave
1400-1740 53405
1741-1899 53403
Florence Ave 53402
Flower Ln 53402
Floyd Dr 53404
Foley Rd 53402
Foothill Dr 53403
Forest St 53404
Fox Dr 53404
Foxwood Rd 53405
Frances Dr 53405
Frank Ave 53404
Franklin St 53403
Frederick St 53404
Freeland Cir 53405
Freres Ave 53405
Frontier Dr 53404
Gallant Fox Ln 53402
Garden Dr 53403
Garfield St 53404
Gas Light Cir & Dr 53403
Gates Ct 53403
Gehring Rd 53402
Gemini Ct 53406
Geneva St
900-1599 53404
1700-3300 53402
3302-3798 53402
Georgia Ave 53404
Gerry Ln 53404
Gideon Ct 53404
Gillen St 53403
Gilson St 53403
Gina Dr 53406
Gittings Rd 53406
Glen St 53405
Glendale Ave 53403
Goleys Ln 53404
Golf Ave 53404
Golf Ridge Dr 53402
Goold St
200-1499 53402
1501-1549 53402
1600-2000 53404
2002-3098 53404
Graceland Blvd
3501-4699 53405
4701-4797 53406
4799-4899 53406
Graceway Dr 53406
Graham St 53405
Grand Ave 53403
Grange Ave
1300-1398 53405
1400-1699 53405
1701-1739 53405
1741-2099 53403
Great Elms Ln 53405
Great Oak Dr 53402
Green St 53402
N Green Bay Rd 53404
S Green Bay Rd 53406
Green Meadows Ln 53405
Green Tree Ln 53402
Greenfield Rd 53402
Greenwood Ct 53402
Grove Ave 53405

Hagerer St
600-1299 53402
1700-1799 53404
Hamilton Ave 53403
Hamilton St
200-298 53402
300-621 53402
623-699 53402
700-1999 53404
Hamlin Ave 53403
Hampden Pl 53403
Hansen Ave 53405
Harborview Dr 53403
Harbridge Ave 53403
Harmony Dr 53402
Harriet St 53404
Harrington Dr 53405
Harrison St 53404
Hartman Ct 53404
Harvest Ln 53402
Harvey Dr 53405
Hastings Ct 53406
Haven Ave 53405
Hawk Hollow Ln 53403
Hawthorne Dr 53405
Hayes Ave 53405
Hazelcrest Dr 53402
Hearthside Ln 53402
Hearthward Ct 53403
Heartland Ln 53402
Heather Ln 53402
Heidi Dr 53402
Hennepin Pl 53402
Henry Cir 53404
Heritage Ct 53402
Hialeah Dr 53402
Hickory Way 53405
Hickory Grove Ave 53403
Hidden Creek Rd 53402
High St
300-398 53402
400-1100 53402
1102-1298 53402
1300-2199 53404
2201-2299 53404
W High St 53404
High Hill Cir 53402
Highcrest Dr 53404
Highland Ave 53403
Highwood Dr 53406
Hilker Pl 53403
Hill St 53404
Hillcrest Cir 53406
Hilldale Dr 53406
Holiday Dr 53402
Hollow Creek Rd 53402
Holly Grove Ct 53402
Hollyhock Ln 53406
Holmes Ave
1500-1799 53405
1800-1899 53403
Holy Cross Rd 53402
Homestead St 53404
Horlick Ave 53404
Horner Dr 53402
Horseshoe Ln 53402
Hounds Trl 53402
Howard St 53404
Howe St 53403
Howland Ave 53404
Hubbard St 53402
W Hubbard St 53404
Hummingbird Ct 53402
Hunt Club Rd 53402
Huron St 53404
Idlewood Dr 53402
N Illinois St 53405
Imperial Dr 53402
Imperial St 53405
Independence Rd 53406
Indian Trl 53402
Indiana St 53405
Indigo Dr 53406
Iris Ct 53402
Ironwood Ct 53402
Irving Pl 53403

Isabelle Ave 53402
Island Ave 53405
Ivy Ln 53402
Jacato Dr 53404
Jackson Pl 53406
Jackson St 53404
James Ave 53402
James Blvd 53403
Jay Eye See Ave 53403
Jean Ave 53404
Jefferson St 53404
Jerome Blvd 53403
Jessica Turn 53402
Jim Lin Ln 53402
Joan Ave 53402
Johnson Ave 53402
W Johnson Ave 53405
Johnston Pl 53403
Jonathon Dr 53402
Jones Ave 53402
Jones St 53404
Jonsue Ln 53402
Junction Ave 53403
Jupiter Ave 53404
Kasper St 53402
Kaywood Dr 53402
Kearney Ave
1500-1699 53405
1800-1898 53403
1900-3200 53403
3202-3398 53403
Kelsey Ct 53406
Kennedy Dr 53404
Kenrich Dr 53402
Kensington Ct 53405
Kentucky St 53405
Kentwood Dr 53402
Kenwood Dr 53403
Kewaunee St
100-198 53402
200-999 53402
1100-2099 53404
Kilbride Dr 53402
Killips Ln 53404
Kingdom Ct 53402
Kings Cir 53406
Kings Way 53403
Kings Cove Rd 53406
Kingsberry St 53406
Kingston Ave 53402
Kinzie Ave
2000-3098 53405
3100-4500 53405
4502-4698 53405
4700-7199 53406
Knoll Pl 53403
Kremer Ave 53402
Lake Ave 53403
Lake Meadow Dr 53402
Lake Pointe Cir 53402
Lake Vista Ct 53402
Lakecrest Ave 53402
Lakefield Ct 53402
Lakeshore Dr 53402
S Lakeshore Dr 53403
Lakeview Cir 53402
Lakeview Dr 53403
Lakewood Dr 53402
Lamberton Rd 53402
Lamplighter Ln 53402
Langdale Dr 53402
Langdon Ct 53406
Lansdale Ln 53402
Lanterli Dr 53406
Lasalle St
900-1499 53404
1500-4699 53402
Lathrop Ave 53405
Lawn St 53404
Lawndale Ave 53403
Layard Ave
1000-1540 53402
1542-1542 53402
1545-2400 53404
2402-2498 53404
Leawood Ln 53402

Leeward Ln 53402
Leo Ln 53406
Leslie Ann Ln 53403
Lewis St 53404
Lexington Ave 53404
Liberty St 53404
Libra Ln 53406
Lighthouse Dr 53402
Lilac Ln 53406
Lincoln St 53402
Lincoln Village Dr 53406
Lincolnwood Ct & Dr 53403
Linden Ave 53403
Linden Cir 53406
Linden Ln 53406
Lindermann Ave
3200-4699 53405
4700-5299 53406
Linwood Rd 53402
Lockwood Ave 53403
Lombard Ave 53402
Lone Elm Dr 53402
Long View Ln 53404
Longmeadow Ln 53402
Loni Ln 53406
Lora St 53402
Loraine Ave 53404
Louise Ln 53404
Luane Dr 53406
Luedtke Ave 53405
Luedtke Ct
1901-1999 53404
2000-2098 53405
Lydian Dr 53403
Lyra Ln 53406
Madison St 53403
Maiden Ln 53403
Main St
1-97 53403
99-600 53403
601-607 53401
601-1899 53403
602-1698 53403
N Main St 53402
Majestic Dr 53402
Mallard Dr 53402
Manhattan Dr 53402
Maple St 53404
Maple Grove Ave 53404
Maplewood Ct 53402
Mar Kay Dr 53402
Marboro Dr 53406
Marcia Dr 53405
Maria St 53404
Marigold Ct 53402
Mariner Dr 53406
Marion Ave 53403
Marnie Ct 53403
Marquette Dr 53402
Marquette St
700-1599 53404
1800-3799 53402
S Marquette St 53403
Mars Ave 53404
Marwood Ct & Dr 53402
Mary Drew Dr 53402
Maryland Ave
2301-2497 53403
2499-2999 53403
3500-3899 53405
4000-4399 53405
4401-4699 53405
4700-5099 53406
5101-5299 53406
Matthew Dr 53402
May St 53404
Mayfair Dr 53402
Mcarthur Pl 53405
Mckinley Ave 53404
Meachem St 53403
Mead St 53403
Meadow Dr 53402
Meadowbrook Blvd 53405
Meadowdale Ln 53402
Meadowlark Ct 53402
N Meadows Dr 53402

Medley Dr 53402
Melvin Ave
201-397 53402
399-1599 53402
1600-1898 53404
1900-2000 53404
2002-2098 53404
Memco Ln 53404
N Memorial Dr 53404
S Memorial Dr 53403
Mercury Cir & Ln 53404
Meridian Ave 53402
Merriburr Ln 53402
Merrie Ln 53405
Mertens Ave 53405
Metron Ct 53403
Michigan Blvd & Ct 53402
Michna Rd 53402
Middle Rd 53402
Mitchell St 53403
Mohr Ave 53405
Mona Park Rd 53405
Monarch Dr 53406
Monroe Ave 53405
Montclair Dr 53402
Monterey Dr 53402
Monticello Dr 53402
Monument Sq 53403
Moorland Ave 53405
Moraine Ct 53402
Morning Wood Dr 53402
Morton Ave 53403
Mound Ave 53404
Mount Pleasant St 53404
Mulberry Ln 53402
Murray Ave 53403
Myrtle Ct 53402
Nature Dr 53402
Nature Trl 53403
Navajo Trl 53404
Nelson Ct 53404
Neptune Ave & Cir 53404
Newberry Ln 53402
Newcastle Ln 53402
Newman Rd 53406
Newport Ln 53403
Nicholson Rd 53406
Nicolet Pl 53402
Nields Ct 53404
Noelle Ct 53402
North St 53402
Northbridge Dr 53404
Northdale Dr 53402
Northway Dr 53402
Northwestern Ave
2001-2097 53404
2099-2600 53404
2602-3698 53404
3700-3798 53405
3800-3899 53405
5500-5698 53406
5700-9500 53406
9502-9598 53406
Northwood Dr 53402
Norton Ave 53403
Norwood Ct & Dr 53403
Novak Rd 53402
Oak Ct & St 53404
Oak Forest Dr 53406
Oak Tree Ln 53405
Oakdale Ave 53406
Oakdale Dr 53405
Oakes Rd 53406
Oaklawn Dr 53402
Oakwood Dr 53406
N Ohio St 53405
Old Farm Rd 53402
Old Mill Dr 53405
Old Oak Ln 53402
Old Pine Cir 53402
Old Spring St 53406
Old Wood Trl 53402
Ole Davidson Rd 53405
Olive St
2101-2197 53403
2199-3099 53403

3201-3897 53405
3899-4699 53405
Ontario St 53402
Open Meadow Rd 53402
Orange St 53404
Orchard St 53405
N Oregon St 53405
Orion Cir & Ct 53406
N Osborne Blvd 53405
Ostergaard Ave 53406
Owen Ave 53403
Owen St 53404
Packard Ave 53403
Packer Dr 53404
W Palamino Dr 53402
Park Ave 53403
Park Pl 53402
Park Ridge Dr 53402
Park View Dr 53404
Parker Ave 53403
E & W Parkfield Ct 53402
Parkland Ct 53402
Parkway Dr 53402
Parkwood Ct 53402
Parry Ave 53402
Partridge Ter 53404
Patzke Ln & Rd 53405
Paul Bunyan Rd 53402
Pearl St 53403
Peck Ave 53404
Percival Ln 53406
Perry Ave
101-197 53406
199-1301 53406
1300-1300 53408
1303-1699 53406
1500-1698 53406
Pheasant Trl 53402
Phillips Ave 53403
Pierce Blvd 53405
Pilgrim Dr 53404
Pine Ridge Cir & Ln 53403
Pinehurst Ave 53403
Pinetree Cir 53402
Pinewood Ct 53402
Pleasant View Cir 53402
Poe Ave 53405
W Point Ln 53402
Point Ridge Dr 53402
E Point View Dr 53402
N Pointe Dr 53402
Pointmere Ln E & W 53402
Polaris Ave 53404
Pond View Ln 53406
Portico Dr 53406
Prairie Cir 53406
Prairie Green Dr 53406
Prince Dr 53402
Princess Pl 53406
Princeton Ln 53402
Pritchard Dr 53406
Prospect St
601-699 53402
700-2499 53404
2501-2699 53404
Quarry Springs Dr 53405
Queens Ct 53402
Quincy Ave
1300-1700 53405
1702-1798 53405
1800-2100 53403
2102-2198 53403
Rachel Gln 53402
Racine St 53403
Railroad St 53404
Randal Ln 53402
Randolph St 53404
Rapids Dr 53404
Raven Turn E 53402
Ravenswood Ln 53402
Ravine Dr 53405
Rebecca Dr 53402
Red Berry Rd 53406
Red Maple Ct 53402
Redbird Ln 53402
Redwing Ln 53402

Redwood Ct 53402
Reeds Ct 53404
Regal Ct 53406
Regency Dr 53402
Reichert Ct 53402
Reiley Ct 53403
Republic Ave 53405
Reschke Ave 53404
Revere Rd 53402
Richmond Dr 53406
Richwood Ln 53402
Rickman Ct 53404
Ridgeway Ave
4400-4699 53405
4800-5099 53406
Ridgewood Ave 53403
Rio Vista Rd 53404
Riva Rdg 53402
River Dr 53405
E River Rd 53402
River Bend Dr 53404
River Hills Rd 53402
River Meadows Turn 53402
Riverbrook Dr 53405
Riverpark Ln 53405
Riverside Dr 53404
Riverview Ter 53404
Riverwalk Ct 53405
Robin Ln 53402
Rode Ave 53404
Rodney Ln 53406
Roe Ave 53404
Romayne Ave
400-1598 53402
2100-3099 53404
Roosevelt Ave 53406
Rosalind Ave 53403
Rosemary Ln 53406
Rosewood Ln 53404
Round Table Dr 53406
Roxbury Blvd & Ct 53406
Royal Park Rd 53402
Ruby Ave 53402
Rudolph Dr 53406
Running Horse Rd 53402
Rupert Blvd 53405
Russet St 53405
Safe Harbor Ct 53403
Saint Andrews Blvd & Ct 53405
N Saint Clair St 53402
Saint Patrick St
300-1000 53402
1002-1098 53402
1100-1999 53404
Saint Rita Rd
2300-2499 53402
2500-2999 53404
San Dell Way 53402
Sandalwood Ct 53402
Sandhill Rd 53402
Sandpiper Ln 53402
Sandra Ct 53403
Sandstone Ct 53406
Sandview Ln 53406
Santa Anita Dr 53402
Santa Fe Trl 53404
Sara Ln 53402
Saratoga Ct 53405
Saturn Ave 53404
Savoy Cir 53404
Saxony Dr 53402
Schiller St 53403
Scotts Way 53402
Scout Trl 53404
Secretariat Ln 53402
September Dr 53402
Settlement Trl 53406
Settler Dr 53404
Shadow Ln 53405
Shadowood Ct 53406
Shady Ln 53402
Sheffield Dr 53402
Shelbourne Ct 53402
Shelley Dr 53405
Sheraton Dr 53402

Sheridan Rd 53403
Shirley Ave 53406
Shoop St 53404
Shore Dr 53402
Shore Acres Dr 53402
Shorecrest Dr 53402
Shoreland Dr 53402
Shorewood Ct 53402
Shorewood Dr 53404
Short Rd & St 53402
Shortridge Dr 53402
Silent Sunday Ct 53402
Sina Ln 53402
Singing Trees Dr 53406
Skyline Dr 53406
Slauson Ave 53403
South St
400-420 53402
422-1600 53402
1602-1698 53402
1701-1797 53404
1799-2300 53404
2302-2398 53404
Southwood Dr 53406
Sovereign Dr 53406
Sportsman Dr 53402
Spring Pl 53404
Spring St
1743-1799 53404
2001-2197 53405
2199-4099 53405
9601-9699 53406
Spring Lake Dr 53405
Spring Valley Dr 53405
Springfield Ln 53402
Spruce St 53403
Sprucewood Ct 53402
Standish Ln 53405
Stannard St 53403
Star Grass Ln 53406
Starlight Dr 53402
State St
200-298 53403
500-599 53402
601-699 53402
700-898 53404
900-1999 53404
State Road 31
3000-4899 53405
State Road 31
4901-4999 53405
5100-7199 53402
State Road 38 53406
Steeplechase Dr 53402
Stephan Rd 53402
Stonebridge Dr 53404
Stonewood Ct 53402
Stratford Ave 53402
Stratford Ct 53406
N Stuart Rd 53406
Sumac Dr 53402
Summerfield Way 53406
Summerset Dr 53406
Summit Ave 53404
Sun Valley Dr 53406
Sundance Ln 53402
S Sunnyslope Dr 53406
Sunrise Rd 53402
Sunshine Ln 53402
Superior St
900-1399 53404
1400-2299 53402
2301-2499 53402
Surrey Ln 53402
Sycamore Ave 53406
Sydney Dr 53402
Tabor Rd 53402
Tall Oak Ct 53406
Tammy Ln 53402
Tanglewood Ave 53402
Tara Dr 53402
Taurus Ct & Dr 53406
Taylor Ave
1500-2699 53403
2701-2799 53403
2800-3106 53405

3108-4298 53405
3131-3297 53405
3299-3600 53405
3602-4006 53405
4900-5198 53406
Tennessee Rd 53405
Tera Lee Ct 53402
Terrace Ave 53403
Terrace High 53406
Thomas St 53405
Thor Ave 53405
Thornapple Ct 53402
Thunderbird Dr 53402
Thurston Ave
1300-1699 53405
1800-2099 53403
Tiffany Dr 53402
Tower Cir 53402
Tracy Cir 53402
Trefoil Cir 53406
Trellard St 53404
Tropical Ct 53402
Tulip Ct 53402
Twin Ln 53406
Twin Elms Dr 53406
Union St 53404
Valerie Ct 53403
Valley Dr 53403
Valley Rd 53405
Valley Trl 53402
Valley Forge St 53404
Venus Cir 53404
Vermont St 53406
Victoria Dr 53403
Victorian Dr 53406
Victory Ave 53405
Viken Ln 53402
Villa St 53403
Village Dr 53406
Village Center Dr 53406
N & S Vincennes Cir 53402
Violet Ct 53402
Virginia St 53405
Vista Dr 53405
Vrana Ln 53405
Wagon Trl 53402
Walden Way 53405
Walnut St 53403
Walsh Rd 53405
Walter Raleigh Ln 53406
Walton Ave 53402
Warwick Way 53406
Washington Ave
700-2199 53403
2200-4699 53405
4700-9099 53406
9101-9799 53406
Water St 53403
Waterbury Ln 53403
Waters Edge Rd 53402
Waterview Cir 53405
Webster St 53403
Wedgewood Dr 53402
Wellacha St 53402
Wellington Dr 53403
West Blvd
301-397 53405
399-1599 53405
1601-1799 53405
1801-2999 53403
West St 53404
Western Way 53404
Westlake Dr 53402
Westlawn Ave 53405
Westminster Sq 53402
Westmore Dr 53406
Westway Ave
4400-4699 53405
4700-4999 53406
Westwood Cir & Dr 53404
Wheelock Dr 53405
Whirlaway Ln 53402
White Birch Ct 53402
White Sand Ln 53402
Whitewater St 53402
Wickford Pl 53405
Wickham Blvd 53405
Wildrose Way 53402
William St
200-1599 53402
1800-2499 53404
Williamsburg Way 53406
Willmor St 53402
Willow Spring Dr 53402
Willow Tree Cir 53405
Willowbrook Rd 53402
Willowview Rd 53402
Wilnette Spring Dr 53405
Wilshire Dr 53402
Wilson St 53404
Wind Dale Dr 53402
Wind Point Dr & Rd 53402
Windridge Dr 53402
Windsor Dr 53404
Windward Dr 53406
Winners Dr 53402
Winslow St 53404
Winstar Ln 53402
Winthrop Ave
1701-2497 53403
2499-2999 53403
4201-4299 53405
Wisconsin Ave 53403
N Wisconsin St 53402
Wolff St
200-1599 53402
2900-3099 53404
Wood Rd 53406
Wood Duck Way 53403
Woodbury Ln 53403
Woodcrest Ln 53405
Woodfield Ct 53402
Woodland Ave 53403
Woodrow Ave 53404
Woodview Ln 53404
Worsley Ln 53402
Wright Ave
2601-2697 53405
2699-4699 53405
5100-5599 53406
5601-5699 53406
Wustum Ave 53404
Wyoming Way 53404
Yorktown St 53404
Young Ct 53404
Youngblood Rd 53405
Yout St
400-598 53402
600-1400 53402
1402-1498 53402
1500-2999 53404

NUMBERED STREETS

1st Ave 53402
1st St 53403
2nd Ln, Pl & St 53403
3 Mile Rd
2-498 53402
500-1099 53402
1101-1599 53402
1900-3500 53404
3502-3598 53404
4700-5899 53406
5901-6099 53406
3rd Ave 53402
3rd St 53403
4 1/2 Mile Rd 53402
4 Mile Rd
100-2400 53402
2402-2498 53402
2600-4600 53404
4602-4698 53404
4700-6699 53402
E 4 Mile Rd 53402
4th Ave 53402
4th St 53403
5 1/2 Mile Rd 53402
5 Mile Rd 53402
5th Ave 53402
5th St 53403
6 Mile Rd 53402
6th Ave 53402
6th Pl 53403
6th St 53403
W 6th St
1301-1397 53404
1399-1899 53404
1901-1999 53404
2000-2098 53405
7 Mile Rd 53402
7th St 53403
8th Ave 53402
8th Ct 53403
8th St 53403
9th Ave 53402
9th St 53403
10th Ave 53402
10th St 53403
11th Ave & St 53403
12th St 53403
13th Ave 53403
13th St
200-498 53403
500-1800 53403
1802-1898 53403
3100-3398 53405
3400-4699 53405
5100-5199 53406
14th St 53403
15th St
200-500 53403
502-698 53403
2600-3098 53405
3100-4599 53405
4601-4699 53405
16th St
200-298 53403
300-2199 53403
2200-4699 53405
4801-4997 53406
4999-5525 53406
5527-6199 53406
17th St
200-398 53403
400-2099 53403
2300-2498 53405
2500-4699 53405
18th St 53403
19th St
2400-3099 53403
3301-3897 53405
20th St
1001-2097 53403
2099-2899 53403
2901-2999 53403
3201-3297 53405
3299-4199 53405
4201-4299 53405
21st St
600-3099 53403
3101-3197 53405
3199-4699 53405
4700-4898 53406
4900-5900 53406
5902-6098 53406
22nd Ave 53403
23rd St 53403
24th St 53403
26th Ave 53403
28th Ave 53403

SHEBOYGAN WI

General Delivery 53081

POST OFFICE BOXES MAIN OFFICE STATIONS AND BRANCHES

Box No.s
All PO Boxes 53082

NAMED STREETS

Abbey Ct 53083
Ajax St 53083
Alabama Ave 53081
Alcott Ave 53083
Alexander Ct 53081
Algonquin Trl 53081
Alyssa Ln 53083
Amanda Ln 53081
Andrae Cir 53081
Annie Ct 53083
N & W Apache Rd 53083
Appletree Rd 53083
Applewood Dr 53081
Arboleda Ln 53081
Arbor Ln 53083
Arizona Ave 53081
Armstrong Ave 53083
Arrowhead Ct 53083
Arrowhead Ln 53081
Ashby Ct 53081
Ashland Ave 53081
Ashley Ln 53083
Ashwood Dr
W1800-W1899 53083
2-98 53081
Audubon Rd 53083
Autumn Ct 53081
Autumnwood Ct 53083
Badger Rd 53083
Baronwood Way 53083
Barrett St 53081
Beach Ct 53081
Beach Park Ln 53081
Beechtree Rd 53083
Beechwood Dr 53081
Behrens Pkwy 53081
W Bell Ave 53083
Bender Ct & Rd 53083
Berrywood Ct 53081
Birch Dr 53083
Birch Hill Cir 53083
Birch Hill Ln 53081
Birch Tree Rd 53083
Birchwood Ave 53083
Birchwood Ln 53081
Birdland Rd 53083
Bismarck Cir 53083
Bittersweet Ln 53083
Black Fox Ct 53081
Black River Rd 53081
Black Walnut Trl 53081
Blackfoot Trl 53081
Blackstock Ave & Rd 53081
Blackwood Ct 53081
Bleyer Dr 53081
Blocki Ct 53081
Blue Harbor Dr 53081
Bluebell Ct 53083
Bluebird Rd 53083
Bluff Ave 53081
Bollmann Dr 53081
Bonnie Ct 53083
Briarwood Rd 53083
Broadway Ave 53081
Brookdale Rd 53083
Brookfield Ct 53081
Broughton Dr 53081
S Business Dr 53081
Butternut Highlands 53081
Calumet Dr
1600-2199 53081
2201-2229 53083
2231-2899 53083
2901-3199 53083
Cambridge Ave 53081
Camelot Blvd 53081
Campus Dr 53081
Capitol Dr 53081
W Cardinal Ct, Dr, Ln & Pkwy 53083
Carl Ave 53081
Carmen Ave 53081
Cart Path Rd 53081
Carver Ave 53083
Castle Ave 53081
Center Ave 53081
Charter Rd 53083
Cherokee Dr 53083
Cherry Ln 53081
Cherrywood Ct 53081
Chestnut Cir 53083
Cheyenne Trl 53081
Chime Ln 53081
Chippewa Trl 53081
Clara Ave 53081
Clearview Cir 53083
Clement Ave 53083
Clenerid Ave 53081
Cleveland Ave 53081
Clifton Ave 53081
Clover Ct & Ln 53083
Cloverleaf Ct 53081
Cobblestone Dr 53083
College Ave 53083
Colonial Ct 53083
Colorado Ct 53081
Columbus Ave 53083
N & S Commerce St 53081
Conrad Ct 53083
Cooper Ave 53083
Country Pl 53081
Country Meadows Dr 53083
County Road A 53081
County Road Ff 53083
County Road J 53083
County Road Ls 53083
County Road Ok W 53081
County Road V 53081
County Road Y 53083
Courtney Ln 53083
Creekside Ct 53083
Creekview Ct 53081
Crestview Ln 53083
Crestwood Cir 53081
Crocker Ave 53081
Cross Creek Dr 53083
Culla Hill Cir 53083
Curtiss Dr 53083
Custer Ave 53081
Dairyland Dr 53083
Dakota Trl 53081
David Ave 53081
Deer Path Trl 53081
Deer Trail Ln 53083
Deer Valley Dr 53083
Deerfield Dr & Ln 53083
Deerhaven Ln 53083
Dennwood Dr 53083
Depot St 53081
Dewey Ct 53081
Dillingham Ave 53081
Division Ave 53081
Douglas Fir Ln 53083
Driftwood Ct & Ln 53081
Duchess Dr 53083
Echo Ct 53083
Edgewater Rd 53081
Edgewood Rd 53083
Edison Ave 53083
Eisenhower Ct 53083
Eisner Ave & Ct 53083
Elizabeth St 53083
Elk Ln 53083
Elm Ave & Cir 53081
Elm Tree Rd 53083
Elmwood Ct & Dr 53081
Ember Ln 53081
Emerson Ave 53083
End Ct 53081
Enterprise Dr 53083
Erie Ave 53081
Erik Ln 53083
Ethan Allen Dr 53083
Euclid Ave 53083
N & S Evans St 53081
Evergreen Dr 53083
N Evergreen Dr 53083
W Evergreen Dr 53081
Evergreen Ln 53083
Evergreen Pkwy 53083
Fairfield Ln 53083
Fairway Dr 53081
Fawn Ct 53083
Ferndale Ct 53081
N Field Dr 53083
S Fields Cir 53083
Fieldstone Ln 53083
Flagstone Rd 53083
Florida Ave 53081
Folger Ct 53081
Forest Ave 53081
Forest Ct 53083
Forest Hills Dr 53083
Forsythe Ave 53081
Fox Grove Rd 53081
Fox Hill Rd 53081
Fox Ridge Ct 53081
N Franklin St 53081
N & S Frontage Rd 53081
Frost Rd 53083
Gander Rd 53083
Garden Ct 53081
Garden Grove Dr 53081
Garfield Ave 53081
Garton Ct & Rd 53083
Gateway Dr 53081
Geele Ave 53083
Georgia Ave 53081
Germaine Ave 53081
Glen Ave 53083
Glenside Cir 53081
Glenwood Ct 53081
Goldfinch Ln 53083
Golf View Dr E & W 53083
Grace Ave 53081
Grams Ct 53083
Grand Ave 53083
Granite Rd 53083
Grant Ave 53081
S Grant St 53081
Green Meadow Pl 53083
Green Valley Ln 53083
Greendale Cir & Rd 53081
Greenfield Ave 53083
Greenview Dr 53083
Greenwing Dr 53081
Greenwood Ct 53081
Gregory Dr 53083
Grey Fox Ct & Dr 53081
Grote Rd 53083
Hannah Ln 53083
Harry Ct 53083
Havenwood Ct 53081
Hawthorn Rd 53083
Hawthorne Dr 53083
Hazelnut Ct 53081
Heather Valley Rd 53083
Heatherfield Ct 53083
Heathmor Dr 53083
Hedgestone Ln 53083
Heermann Ct 53081
Heller Ave 53081
Henry St 53081
N & S Hiawatha Cir 53081
Hickory Cir & St 53081
Hickorywood Dr 53081
Hidden Creek Ct & Dr 53083
Hidden Fields Ct 53081
High Ave 53081
High Point Ct 53083
High Tech Ln 53083
Highcliff Cir & Ct 53083
Highland Ter 53083
Highview Ct & Dr 53083
Hillshire Dr 53081
Hillside Dr 53081
Hilltop Dr 53081
Homestead Ln 53083
Honeysuckle Ct 53081
Horseleap Ln 53083
Hubert Cir 53083
Humboldt Ave 53081
Hunters Glen Dr 53083
Huron Ave 53081
Idlewild Ln 53083
Illinois Ave 53081
Indian Mound Cir & Rd 53081
Indian Oaks Ln 53081
Indiana Ave 53081
Industrial Ct 53083
Iowa Ave 53081
Ironwood Dr 53081
Jackson Ave 53081
Janewood Ln 53081
Jay Rd 53083
Jefferson Ave 53081
Jefferson Cir 53083
Jens Rd 53083
John Ct 53083
Julson Ct 53081
Juniper Dr 53081
Kaat Ln 53081
Kadlec Dr 53083
Kansas Ave 53081
Karen Cir 53083
Kaufmann Ave 53081
N & W Kay Dr 53083
Kennedy Ave, Cir & Ct 53083
Kentucky Ave 53081
Kings Ct 53081
Kirkwood Ct 53081
Knoll Crest Dr 53081
Koechel Ct 53083
Koehler Dr 53083
Koehn Ave 53081
Kohler Memorial Dr 53081
Kohls Ct 53083
N & W Koning Ct & Dr 53083
Kroos Ct 53083
Kruschke Ave 53081
Lafayette Dr 53081
S Lake Ct 53081
Lake Aire Ct & Dr 53081
Lakeshore Dr 53081
Lakeshore Rd 53083
Lannon Rd 53083
Larkspur Way 53083
Lavalle Dr 53081
Lee Ave 53081
Leland Ave 53081
Lenz Ct 53081
Leon Ct 53081
Leona Ln 53081
Leys Rd 53083
Liberty Ct 53083
Lighthouse Ct 53081
Lilac Ct 53081
Lily Ct 53081
Limerick Ln 53083
Limestone Ct 53083
Lincoln Ave 53081
N Lincoln Dr 53083
S Lincoln Dr 53083
Lisa Ave 53083
Logan Ave 53083
Lone Oak Dr 53083
Lonesome Pine Rd 53081
Long Ct 53081
Long Acre Rd 53083
Longfellow Ave 53083
Los Angeles Ave 53083
Lower Falls Rd 53081
Luedke Ct 53083
Luelloff Rd 53083
S Macarthur Ave & St 53083
Madison Ave 53083
W Main Ave 53083
Mandy Cir 53081
Manor Pkwy 53083
Maple Cir & Ln 53083
Mapledale Ct & Dr 53081
Mapletree Ct & Rd 53083
Maplewood Dr 53083
Marie Ct 53081
Marion Ln 53083
E & W Mark Dr 53083
Martin Ave & Ln 53083
Marvery Rd 53081
Marvin Ct 53081
Maryland Ave 53081
Mayberry Rd 53083
Mayflower Ave & Ln 53083

Mckinley St 53081
Mead Ave 53081
Meadowbrook Ct 53081
Meadowbrook Ln 53083
Meadowland Dr 53081
Meadowlark Rd 53083
W Meadows Ct 53081
Meggers Rd 53081
Mehrtens Ave 53081
S Memorial Pl 53081
Mendocino Ln 53083
Michigan Ave 53081
Middle Rd 53081
Mill Rd & St 53083
Millersville Ave 53083
Milz Ct 53083
Moenning Rd 53081
Monarch Cir 53083
Morning Dove Cv & Dr 53083
Morning View Ct 53081
Motel Rd 53081
Mueller Rd 53083
Muth Ct 53083
Najacht Rd 53083
National Ave 53081
Navajo Trl 53081
Neumair Ct 53083
Nevada Ct 53081
New Jersey Ave 53081
New York Ave 53081
Niagara Ave 53081
Nicole Ln 53083
Norene Rd 53083
Norma Ct 53081
W North Ave & Ln 53083
Northfield Cir 53083
Northwood Ct 53081
Nutmeg Ct 53081
Oak Tree Rd 53083
Oakdale Ct 53081
Oakland Ave 53081
Oakwood Dr 53081
Ohio Ave 53081
Old Park Rd 53081
Ontario Ave 53081
Orchard Dr 53081
Orchard Rd 53083
Orchard Beach Dr 53083
Oriole Ln 53083
Ottawa Pl 53081
Page Ct 53081
Paine Ave 53081
Palmer Dr 53083
Panther Ave 53081
Park Ave 53081
Park Ct 53083
Park Pl 53083
Park Place Dr 53081
E, N & S Parke Ridge Ct & Ln 53083
Parkview Ter 53081
Parkwood Blvd 53081
Patricia Cir 53083
Pawnee Pkwy 53081
Pebble Rd 53083
Penn Cir 53081
Pennsylvania Ave 53081
S Pershing Ave & St 53083
Petra Ln 53081
Pheasant Ln 53081
S Pier Dr 53081
Pigeon St 53083
Pine Ct 53083
Pine Ln 53081
Pine Bluff Dr 53083
Pine Crest Cir 53081
Pine Grove Ave 53083
Pine Ridge Ave 53083
Pine View Dr 53083
Pineview Ct 53083
Pinewood Dr
1-99 53081
3300-3499 53083
Pioneer Rd 53081
Plainwood Cir & Dr 53081
Plath Ct 53081
Playbird Rd 53083
Plymouth Ln 53081
Point Ct & Dr 53081
Polk Ct 53081
Prairie Ridge Ct 53083
Prairie View Rd 53081
Prairie Winds Ct 53081
Primrose Ct 53081
Professional Dr 53083
Progress Dr 53081
Prospect Ave 53081
Quail Ct 53083
Racetrack Rd 53081
Rammer Ct 53081
Rangeline Rd 53083
Red Birch Ct 53081
Red Oak Ln 53081
Red Pine Ln 53081
Redwing Dr 53083
N Reineking Dr 53083
Revere Ct 53083
Ridge Rd 53083
Ridgemor Dr 53083
W Ridgeview Ave 53083
Ridgeway Cir 53081
Ridgewood Ln 53083
N River Pkwy 53083
S River St 53081
River Trl 53081
River Bluff Dr 53083
River Ridge Dr 53083
W Riverdale Ave 53081
Riverfront Dr 53081
Rivermor Dr 53083
Riverview Dr 53083
Riverview Ln 53081
Riverwoods Ct & Dr 53083
Robin Rd 53083
Rolling Meadows Dr 53083
Roosevelt Ave & Rd 53083
Rosewood Ct 53083
Rowe Rd 53083
Saemann Ave 53081
Saint Clair Ave 53081
Saint James Ct 53081
Sandstone Ln 53083
Santana Dr 53083
Sara Ct 53081
Sauk Trail Rd 53081
Savannah Cir 53083
Schetter Ave 53083
Schinker Creek Rd 53083
School Ave 53083
Schwarz Ln 53081
Scotch Pine Cir 53083
Seneca Trl 53081
Settlement Trl 53083
Shady Ln 53081
Shady Brook Ln 53083
Shamrock Dr 53083
E & W Shelly Ct 53083
Sheridan Ave 53081
Sherry Ln 53081
Sherwood Dr 53081
N Shincedg St 53083
Shircel Rd 53081
Shirley Ln 53081
Shorecrest Rd 53083
Sibley Ct 53081
Silver Fox Run 53083
Silver Leaf Ln 53083
Skylark Dr 53083
Skyline Dr 53081
Snow Goose Bay 53083
Sommer Dr 53081
Spring Ave 53081
Spring Ct 53083
Springwood Ct 53081
Spruce Ct 53081
Stahl Rd 53081
Star Ln & Rd 53083
State Highway 32 53083
State Highway 42 53083
Stone Dr 53083
Stonebridge Dr 53083
Stonefield Cir & Rd 53083
Sunflower Ave 53081
Sunnyside Ave & Ct 53081
Sunset Rd 53081
Sunset Circle Dr 53083
Superior Ave
100-198 53081
200-3999 53081
4001-4299 53081
4400-4498 53083
4500-5999 53083
6001-6399 53083
Swallow Dr 53083
Swift Ave 53081
Tacoma Trl 53081
Tanglewood Ln 53081
Tara Ct & Ln 53081
Tasswood Dr 53081
N Taylor Dr
1200-1699 53081
1701-1799 53081
2201-2297 53083
2299-2899 53083
S Taylor Dr 53081
Taylor Pkwy 53081
Technology Pkwy 53083
Telluride Dr 53083
Tennis Ln 53083
Terrace Cir 53081
Terrace View Dr 53081
Terry Ct 53081
Terry Andrae Ave & Ter 53081
Thielman Dr 53081
Timberlake Rd 53083
Timberline Ln 53081
Tivoli Ln 53081
Tomahawk Trl 53081
Tower Dr 53081
Treeline Ter 53081
Trimberger Ct 53081
Truman Cir 53083
Twin Oaks Ln 53083
Tyler Rd 53083
Union Ave 53081
W Union Ave 53081
Union Rd 53083
University Dr 53081
Van Buren Cir & Rd 53083
Vanguard Dr 53083
Venture Dr 53083
Victor Ct 53081
Vincent Dr 53081
Virginia Ave 53081
Vollrath Blvd 53081
Wahgouly Rd 53081
Warbler Rd 53083
Washington Ave 53081
Washington Ct 53081
S Washington Dr 53083
Washington Avenue S Frontage Rd 53081
N & S Water St 53081
Waveland Rd 53083
Waverly Ct 53083
Wedemeyer St 53081
Weeden Creek Rd 53081
Weiss Ct & Dr 53083
Werthmann Ln 53083
Whispering Winds Dr 53081
Whistling Ct 53083
Whitcomb Ave 53081
White Fox Dr 53081
White Oak Ln 53083
White Pine Ln 53083
Whitetail Run Ln 53081
Whittier Ave 53083
Wiemann Ave 53081
Wild Meadow Ct & Dr 53083
N & S Wildwood Ave 53081
Wilgus Ave 53081
Willow Ave 53083
Willow Cir 53083
Willow Dr 53081
W Willow Creek Ln 53083
Willowbrook Ct 53081
Willowood Dr 53081
Wilson Ave 53081
Wind Dancer Ct 53081
Windepoint Ct 53083
Windmor Dr 53083
Windsor Dr 53083
Windward Ct 53083
Winnebago Pl 53081
Winship Cir 53083
Winter Ct 53081
Wisconsin Ave 53081
N Wisconsin Dr 53083
S Wisconsin Dr 53083
Wood Ct 53081
Woodbine Dr 53081
Woodglen Dr 53083
Woodhaven Ct 53081
Woodland Rd
N6100-N6298 53083
Woodland Meadows Dr 53083
Woodside Ln 53081
Woodside Hills Dr 53083
Woodview Ave 53081
Wren Ln 53083
X-Press Ln 53081
Z Ct 53083
Zientek Ln 53081
Zimbal Ave 53081

NUMBERED STREETS

N 1st St 53081
N 2nd St 53081
N 3rd St
1300-1926 53081
1928-2198 53081
2200-2500 53083
2502-2698 53083
N 4th St
500-598 53081
600-2000 53081
2002-2098 53081
2200-2500 53083
2502-2598 53083
N 5th St
500-2099 53081
2300-2799 53083
N 6th St
500-2199 53081
2200-3699 53083
N 7th St
600-898 53081
2200-3499 53083
S 7th St 53081
N 8th St
500-2199 53081
2200-3799 53083
S 8th St 53081
N 9th St 53081
S 10th Pl 53081
N 10th St
800-998 53081
1000-2199 53081
2200-3600 53083
3602-3898 53083
S 10th St 53081
S 11th Pl 53081
N 11th St
900-1098 53081
1100-2199 53081
2200-3499 53083
S 11th St 53081
N 12th Pl 53083
S 12th Pl 53081
N 12th St
901-997 53081
999-2199 53081
2401-2497 53083
2499-3899 53083
3901-3999 53083
S 12th St 53081
N 13th St
500-2199 53081
2200-2498 53083
S 13th St 53081
N 14th St
500-1499 53081
3600-3799 53083
S 14th St 53081
N 15th St
500-2199 53081
2200-2899 53083
S 15th St 53081
N & S 16th 53081
S 17th Pl 53081
N 17th St
700-898 53081
900-1799 53081
3600-3699 53083
3701-3799 53083
S 17th St 53081
N 18th St
900-1798 53081
1800-2199 53081
2200-4798 53083
4800-4999 53083
S 18th St 53081
N 19th St
1500-2199 53081
2500-3700 53083
S 19th St 53081
N 20th Pl 53083
N 20th St
1500-2199 53081
2200-3699 53083
S 20th St 53081
N 21st St
1500-2199 53081
2700-3699 53083
S 21st St 53081
N 22nd St
1500-2199 53081
2200-2599 53083
S 22nd St 53081
N 23rd St
1001-1197 53081
2200-2599 53083
S 23rd St 53081
N 24th St
1500-2099 53081
2200-2600 53083
S 24th St 53081
N 25th St
501-597 53081
599-2100 53081
2102-2198 53081
2200-3200 53083
3202-3298 53083
S 25th St 53081
N 26th St
500-2199 53081
2200-3299 53083
S 26th St 53081
N 27th Pl
1500-2100 53081
2102-2198 53081
2200-2599 53083
N 27th St
500-2199 53081
2200-3299 53083
S 27th St 53081
N 28th St
500-2199 53081
2200-3999 53083
S 28th St 53081
N 29th St
700-798 53081
800-2099 53081
2101-2199 53081
2200-4299 53083
N 30th St
1200-1499 53081
2200-4299 53083
N 31st Pl 53083
N 31st St
1200-1499 53081
2300-4200 53083
4202-4298 53083
S 31st St 53081
S 32nd St 53081
N 33rd Pl 53081
N 33rd St 53083
N 34th St
1600-1700 53081
1702-1798 53081
2200-3699 53083
3701-3799 53083
N 35th St
1500-1799 53081
2200-3700 53083
N 36th Pl 53083
N 36th St
700-1498 53081
1500-1800 53081
1802-2198 53081
2200-2599 53083
2601-2699 53083
N 37th St
700-2199 53081
2200-2299 53083
N 38th St
600-2199 53081
2200-2599 53083
N 40th St
500-2099 53081
2101-2199 53081
2200-5299 53083
5301-5399 53083
N 43rd St 53081
N 44th St 53083
N 45th St
1300-1498 53081
3600-4099 53083
N 46th St
1400-1499 53081
3600-4199 53083
N 47th Pl 53083
N 47th St 53081
48th Pl & St 53083
N 49th Pl 53083
N 49th St
1000-1499 53081
3500-3599 53083
N 50th St 53083
N 51st St 53083
N 52nd St 53083
N 61st St 53083
N 66th St 53083
N 67th St 53083

WATERTOWN WI

General Delivery 53094

POST OFFICE BOXES MAIN OFFICE STATIONS AND BRANCHES

Box No.s
All PO Boxes 53094

RURAL ROUTES

03, 04, 06, 07, 08 53094
01, 02, 05, 07 53098

NAMED STREETS

Adam Ct 53094
Air Park Dr 53094
Airport Rd 53094
Aliceton Dr 53094
Allermann Dr 53094
Allwardt St 53098
Alvoss Rd 53094
Amber Ln 53098
American Way 53094
Ann St 53094
Anne St 53098
Apple Rd 53098
Applewood Ln 53094
W Arcade Ave 53098
Arlington Way 53094
Arthur St 53098
Ash Rd 53094
Atlantic Ave 53094
Autumn Crest Dr 53094
Aviation Way 53094
Bailey St 53094
Baneck Ln 53094
Banon Rd 53098
Barry Rd 53098
Baurichter Ln 53094
Baxter St 53094
Bayberry Dr
1000-1060 53098
1061-1079 53094
1062-1198 53098
1081-1199 53098
Beacon Dr 53098
Bee Rd 53098
Beggan Ln 53094
Belmont Dr 53094
Benton St 53094
Bernard St 53094
Berry Rd 53094
Beryl Dr 53094
Beverly Dr 53098
Birchwood Ct 53094
Bittersweet Ln 53094
Blaine Rd 53098
Blue Bird Rdg 53094
Bluebird Rd 53098
Boje Ct & Ln 53094
Bonner St 53098
Boomer St 53094
Boughton St
1000-1099 53094
1100-1198 53098
1101-1199 53094
Boulder Rd 53098
Braasch Rd 53098
Bradley St 53098
Brentwood Ln 53094
Brian Ct 53094
Briar Ct 53094
Bridge St 53094
Bridlewood Ln 53094
Brookstone Way 53094
Buchert Ln 53094
Buske Ln 53094
Buttercup Way 53094
E & W Cady St 53094
Cana Rd 53098
Canadian Ct 53094
Canary Cir 53098
Cardinal Ct 53098
Carl Schurz Dr 53094
Carlson Pl 53094
Carol St 53094
Carr St 53094
Carriage Hill Dr 53098
Casey Dr 53094
Cast Rd 53098
Cattail Dr 53094
Caughlin Rd 53098
Ceasar Rd 53094
Cemetery Rd 53098
Center St 53098
Chadwick Ct & Dr 53094
Charles St 53094
Cherokee Ct 53094
Cherrywood Ln 53094
Cheyenne Cir 53098
Christberg Rd 53098
Church Dr 53094
N Church St
100-309 53094
310-310 53098
311-311 53098
312-1199 53098
S Church St 53094
Churchill Rd 53094
Circle Dr 53094
Clark St 53094
Clay St 53094
Clement St 53094
Cleveland St 53098
Clifford Ln 53094
Clovercrest Ct 53094

Clyman St 53094
E & W Clymet Rd 53098
Cobblestone Way 53094
Coffee Rd 53094
Cole St 53094
College Ave & St 53094
Colonial Dr 53098
Comenius Ct 53098
Commerce Dr & Way 53094
N & S Concord Ave & Pl 53094
Corner St 53094
Cottonwood Ct 53098
Country Ln 53098
Country Club Ln 53098
Country Crest Ln 53098
Countryaire Ct 53094
County Rd E
N7200-N9199 53094
N1200-N1398 53098
N1400-N3399 53098
County Road A 53094
County Road B 53094
County Road Cw
W800-W3199 53094
County Road Cw
W5200-W5600 53098
W4200-W5198 53098
W5602-W5998 53098
County Road D 53094
County Road Dj 53098
County Road Em 53098
County Road G 53094
County Road J 53098
County Road Jm 53098
County Road K 53098
County Road Kw 53098
County Road L 53098
County Road M 53098
County Road Me 53098
County Road Mm 53098
County Road O 53098
County Road P 53094
County Road Q
N7900-N9699 53094
N101-N697 53098
W6900-W8599 53098
W8700-W8899 53098
W8601-W9099 53098
N699-N1299 53098
County Road Qq 53098
County Road R 53098
County Road Sc
N100-N398 53098
County Road T 53094
County Road X 53094
County Road Y 53094
Coventry Dr 53098
Creekside Ct 53094
Crest Rd 53098
Crestview Dr 53094
D Ln 53094
Dakota St 53094
Danbury Dr 53098
Davidson Rd 53098
Davies Ct 53098
Davis St 53098
Dayton St 53094
Deer Rd 53098
Deer Trl 53094
Derby Ln 53094
Dewey Ave 53098
Dewey Ln 53098
Dewey Rd
N9600-N9698 53094
N100-N399 53098
E Division St
100-998 53098
101-999 53094
W Division St
800-898 53098
801-899 53094
Doctors Ct 53094
Dodge St 53094
Donald Ln 53094
Doris St 53098

Dorothy Ln & Pl 53094
Douglas Ave 53098
Dreamfield Dr 53094
Duffy St 53094
Ebenezer Dr 53094
Edgewater Ct 53098
Eichstaedt Ln 53094
Elba St 53094
Elder Dr 53098
Elizabeth St 53098
Elk Rd 53098
Elm St 53098
Elmwood Rd 53098
Emerald Dr 53094
Emerald St 53098
Emmet St 53094
Endevour Dr 53098
Englehart Rd 53094
N Englehart Rd 53098
Evergreen Dr 53098
Fairfield Ct 53098
Fairview St 53094
Falcon Ct 53094
Faleredg Rd 53098
N & S Farmington Ln & Rd 53094
Fieldcrest Ct 53094
Fieldstone Way 53094
Five Mile Rd 53098
Fox Creek Dr 53098
Franklin St 53094
Frederick St 53094
Freitag Ln 53094
Fremont St
100-199 53094
200-499 53098
Frohling Ln 53094
Front St 53094
S Garden Rd 53098
Garfield St 53098
E Gate Dr 53094
Gateway Dr 53094
Girard St 53094
Glenwood Ct 53094
Gopher Hill Rd 53094
Grandview Ct 53098
Granite Ln 53094
E & W Green St 53098
Green Ridge Cir 53094
Green Valley Rd 53094
Greencrest Dr 53098
Grey Fox Run 53094
Groth Ln 53094
Gypsy Rd 53098
Hadley Ct 53098
Hady Ln 53094
Hall St 53094
Halter Ln 53098
Hancock Rd & St 53098
Harding St 53094
Harold St 53098
Harrison St 53098
Hart St 53094
Harvey Ave 53094
E & W Haven Dr 53094
Hazelcrest Dr 53098
Henry St 53094
Herbert Dr 53094
Heritage Ct 53098
Herman St 53098
Hiawatha St 53098
Hickory Ct 53094
Hickory Rd 53098
Hidde Dr
600-603 53094
604-800 53098
802-898 53098
Hidden Meadows Pkwy 53098
High Rd 53094
Highland Ave 53098
Highland Rd 53094
Highway Cw 53094
Hill Ct, Rd & St 53098
Hillcrest Dr 53094
W Hillcrest Rd 53098

Hillside Dr 53094
Hillside Ln 53098
Hilltop Rd 53094
Hillview Ln 53098
Hinze Ln 53098
Hoffman Dr 53094
Hoffmann Dr 53094
Holste St 53098
Homestead Ln 53098
Horn Rd 53098
E Horseshoe Rd 53094
Hospital Dr 53098
E Hubbleton Rd 53094
Huberbrooks Dr 53094
Humboldt St 53094
Hunter Oaks Blvd 53094
Hus Dr 53098
Hustisford Rd 53098
Hutson Dr 53098
Hwy 16 Frontage Rd 53094
Hyland St 53094
Indian Hill Rd 53098
Industrial Dr 53094
Irene St 53098
N & S Island View Rd 53094
James St 53098
Jamesway Dr 53098
Janet Ln 53094
Jefferson Rd & St 53094
Jenna Ct 53098
Johnson St 53098
Jones St 53094
Josephine St 53098
Juneau St 53098
Justman Rd 53098
Kaddatz Dr 53098
Kansas St 53094
Kasten Ln 53098
Kathryn Ct 53098
Kelm Rd 53094
Kensington Ct 53098
Kiewert St 53098
Kildeer Rd 53098
Kiln Dr 53098
Kohloff Ln 53094
Koschnick Rd 53098
Kossuth St 53094
Kraemer Ct 53098
Krakow Ln 53094
Kuckkan Ln 53098
Labaree St 53098
Labelle St 53098
Lafayette St 53094
Lake Dorothy Ln 53094
Lakeside Ter 53094
Lang Ln 53098
Lange Ln 53094
Lanon Rd 53098
Laurel Ct 53098
Lauren Ln 53098
Laurie Ann Cir 53098
Lawnview Ln 53098
W Leonard St 53098
Level Valley Rd 53098
Lexington Ct 53098
Liberty Ln 53098
Lincoln St 53098
Linda Ln 53094
Link St 53098
Linmar Ln 53094
Lisbon St 53098
Little Coffee Rd 53094
Livsey Pl 53098
Loam Rd 53094
Long Rd & St 53098
Louisa St 53098
Lounsbury St 53098
Lovers Lane Rd 53098
Lowell St 53098
Luttmann Dr 53098
Lyndell St 53098
Lynn St 53098
E & W Madison St 53094
Main St 53098
E Main St 53094

W Main St
100-839 53098
840-1498 53098
841-1499 53094
Majesta Ct 53094
Maple Ln 53098
N Maple St 53094
S Maple St 53094
Maple Crest Ln 53094
Margaret St 53098
Market St & Way 53094
Marsh Rd 53094
Marten Rd 53098
Martins Way 53094
Mary St 53094
Mary Knoll Ln 53098
Meadow St 53094
Meadow Lark Ln 53098
Meadowbrook Dr 53098
Memorial Dr 53098
Michael Ln 53094
Middle Rd 53098
Midway Ln 53098
Mile Rd 53098
Milford St 53094
E & W Milwaukee St 53094
N Monroe St
100-305 53094
306-499 53098
S Monroe St 53094
N Montgomery St
100-308 53094
309-699 53098
S Montgomery St 53094
Morningside Rd 53098
Mound St 53098
Mourning Dove Dr 53098
Munzel Dr 53094
Navan Rd 53094
Neenah St 53094
Nelson Ln 53098
Newcastle Ct 53098
Nimm Ln 53098
Norma Dr 53098
North Ave 53098
North Ln 53094
North Rd 53098
Northside Dr 53098
O Connell St 53094
Oak Rd & St 53098
Oak Hill Ct 53094
Oak Hill Rd
N9600-N9699 53094
W3200-W3299 53094
W4700-W4798 53098
W4901-W4999 53098
Oak Park Ave 53098
Oakland Ave 53094
Oakridge Ct 53094
Oakwood Ln 53094
Ochs Ct 53098
Oconomowoc Ave 53094
Octagon Ct 53094
Old 26 Rd 53094
Old Settlement Dr 53098
Olson Rd 53094
Omena St 53094
Oraill St 53094
Ornis Rd 53094
Otto Ln 53094
Overland Dr 53094
Pacific Ct 53094
Park St 53098
Park View Ln 53094
Pawnee St 53094
Peaceful Ln 53094
Pearl St 53094
Perry St 53098
Perry Way 53094
Petig Rd 53094
Pheasant Run 53094
Phillip Rd 53094
Pieper Rd 53098
Pine Ridge Ct 53094
Pioneer Ct & Rd 53098
Pipersville Rd 53094

Pleasant St 53098
Pleasant Valley Ln 53094
Poplar Grove Rd 53098
Praire Aire Dr 53098
Prairie Ct 53094
Pratt Rd 53098
Prospect St 53098
Provimi Rd 53098
Quarry Rd 53098
Quirk Pl 53094
Radloff Ln 53094
Ranch Rd
W2300-W4299 53098
N1417-N1499 53098
N1411-N1415 53098
Randall Rd 53098
Randolph St 53094
Reamer Rd 53094
Red Fox Ct 53094
Red Oak Cir 53094
Redwood Ln 53094
Reek Ln 53094
Reese Ln 53094
Reinhold St 53094
Remmel Dr 53094
Renner Ln 53094
Revere Way 53094
Rhine Rd 53098
Rich Rd 53098
Richards Ave 53094
Richart Rd 53098
Ridge Ln 53094
River Dr 53094
River Rd 53094
River St
N8200-N8299 53094
100-199 53098
River Bend Rd 53094
River Park Dr 53094
River Ridge Ln 53094
River View Rd 53098
Riverdale Cir & Ln 53094
Riverlawn Ave 53094
S Riverview Ln & Rd 53094
Riverwood Ct 53094
Riviera Ln 53094
Robert St 53094
Robin Rd 53098
Rock St
200-298 53098
201-399 53094
Rock River Paradise 53094
Rockview Ct 53094
Rubidell Rd 53094
Rusch Rd 53098
Rusk Rd 53098
Ruth St 53094
Sand St 53094
Sandy Ln 53098
Saucer Dr 53094
Schiller St 53098
Schmidt Rd 53094
Schmied Ln 53094
Schuman Dr 53098
Schumann Dr 53098
Schweppe Ln 53094
Scofield Rd 53094
Scot St 53094
Serenity Oaks Ter 53098
Shade Rd 53094
Shady Ln
N1700-N1998 53098
N9600-N9699 53098
Shamrock Ln 53094
Silver Dr 53094
Silver Creek Rd 53094
Smith Rd 53098
Sommers Ct 53098
South Rd & St 53094
E & W Spaulding St 53098
Spoehr Ln 53094
Spooner Rd 53094
Spring St 53094
Spruce Dr 53094
State Road 16 53094
State Road 16/60 53098

State Road 19
W4500-W4699 53094
State Road 26
N2601-N2799 53098
State Road 26
N6800-N8399 53094
Station St 53094
Staude Ln 53094
Steeplechase Dr 53094
Stimpson St 53094
Stone St 53094
Stoneridge Dr 53098
Stonewood Dr 53094
Summer Hill Ct 53098
Summit Ave 53094
Sun Val Rd 53094
Sunnyfield Ct 53098
Sunrise Dr 53098
Sunset Ave & Rd 53094
Sutton Dr 53094
Sweetbriar Ln 53098
Swift Rd 53094
Switzke Rd 53094
Terry Ln 53094
Theresa St 53094
Thomas Ave 53094
Thoren Ln 53094
Thrush Rd 53098
Timber Ridge Trl 53098
Timberline Ct 53094
Tivoli Dr 53094
Tloha Ct 53098
Tower Rd 53098
Track Rd 53098
Train Rd 53098
Trestle Rd 53098
Trieloff Dr 53094
Turf Dr 53094
Turke Ln 53094
Twain Rd 53098
Union St
300-304 53094
305-699 53098
Upham Rd 53098
Utah St 53094
Valley Dr 53098
Valview Ct 53098
Vel Rd 53098
Venus Rd 53098
Vine St 53094
Virginia Ave 53098
N Votech Dr 53094
S Votech Dr 53094
Wakoka St 53094
Waldmann Ln 53094
Waldron St 53094
Walnut Rd & St 53098
Walton Rd 53098
Warbler Way 53098
N Warren St
100-307 53094
308-599 53098
S Warren St 53094
N Washington St
100-399 53094
400-599 53098
S Washington St 53094
Water St 53098
E Water St 53094
N Water St
N500-N700 53098
N702-N898 53098
100-399 53094
400-1399 53098
S Water St 53094
Water Tower Ct 53094
Watertown Sq 53094
Wedgewood Ct & Dr 53098
Welsh Rd 53098
Werner St
600-605 53094
606-1099 53098
Wesley Rd 53094
West Rd & St 53094
Western Ave 53094
Western Meadows Dr 53098

Wilbur St 53098
Wild Rose Way 53094
Wildflower Ln 53094
Wiley Rd
N300-N599 53098
William St 53094
Willman Ct 53094
Willow Rd & St 53094
Willow Creek Pkwy 53094
Willow View Dr 53098
Willowview Dr 53094
Windsor Cir 53098
Windstone Ct 53094
Windwood Ln 53094
Winnebago Way 53094
Wisconsin St 53094
Witte Ln 53094
Wolff Rd 53094
Wood Rd 53098
Woodbridge Trl 53094
Woodchuck Ln 53094
Woodland Dr 53098
Woodland Preserve 53094
Woodside Ln 53094
Wren Rd 53098
Zillge Ln 53094

NUMBERED STREETS

N 1st St 53094
S 1st St 53094
W 1st St 53098
N 2nd St
100-599 53094
600-1699 53098
S 2nd St 53094
2nd Street Rd 53098
N & S 3rd 53094
N 4th St
100-599 53094
600-1399 53098
S 4th St 53094
N & S 5th 53094
N & S 6th 53094
N & S 7th 53094
N & S 8th 53094
N & S 9th 53094
N & S 10th 53094
S 11th St 53094
S 12th St 53094

WAUKESHA WI

General Delivery 53186

POST OFFICE BOXES MAIN OFFICE STATIONS AND BRANCHES

Box No.s
All PO Boxes 53187

NAMED STREETS

Abbey Rd 53188
Aberdeen Ct 53188
Aberdeen Way 53189
Adams St 53186
Airport Rd 53188
Albany Ct 53188
Albert St 53188
Alder Dr 53188
Alderwood Ln 53186
Aldoro Dr 53188
Algoma Ter 53188
S Allen Ln & Rd 53186
Amber Ct 53189
Amber Ln 53186
American Ave 53188
Amherst Pl 53188
Amy Ct 53189
Amy James Dr 53189

Ancestral Dr 53188
Anitol Ave 53186
Ann St 53188
Anoka Ave 53186
Antioch St 53186
Apache Pass 53188
Apple Tree Ct 53188
Applewood Dr 53189
Arbor Dr 53188
Arbor Oaks Ln 53188
Arcadian Ave 53186
Archery Dr 53188
Arlington St 53186
Arlo Dr 53189
Arrow Ridge Rd 53189
Arrowhead Trl 53188
Arthur Ct 53188
Aspen Dr 53188
Aspenwood Ln 53186
Aster Ct 53189
Atlantic Dr 53186
Auburn Ct 53189
Aurora Ave 53186
Austin Ct 53186
Autumn Haze Ct 53189
Avalon Dr 53186
Aviation Rd 53188
Avondale Ct 53186
Ayrshire Ln 53186
Badger Ct & Dr 53188
Badinger Rd 53188
Bahcall Ct 53186
Baird St 53189
Bank St 53188
Banning Way 53188
Barberry Ct 53188
Barney St 53186
N Barstow St 53186
NW Barstow St 53188
Bartel Ct & Rd 53189
Basque Ct 53188
Baxter St 53186
Bayberry Dr 53189
Bedford Ct 53186
Bedouin Ct 53188
Beechwood Ave & Ln 53186
Beeheim Rd 53189
N & W Bel Ayr Dr 53186
Belgren Rd 53186
Bell St 53186
Belmont Dr 53186
Benjamin Ct 53188
Bennet Ct & Rd 53189
Bennett Cv 53189
Benson Ave 53189
Berkshire Ct & Dr 53188
Bethesda Cir 53188
N Bethesda Cir 53188
S Bethesda Cir 53188
W Bethesda Cir 53188
Bethesda Ct
W299S2848-
W299S2898 53188
W298S2801-
W298S2899 53188
300-599 53186
Bethesda Rd 53189
Biddle St 53186
Bidwell Ave 53188
Big Bend Rd 53189
Birch Ct & Dr 53188
Birchwood Ct 53186
Birdseye Ln 53186
Black Oak Ct & Ln 53189
Blackhawk Trl 53186
Blackstone Ave 53186
Blair Ct 53188
Blodwen Dr 53188
Blue Heron Ct 53189
Bluebird Ter 53188
Bluemound Rd 53186
Bluespruce Ct 53189
Bluff Ct 53186
Bob Bell Ct 53189
Boettcher Ct 53188
Boettcher Rd
S27W29500-
S27W30099 53188
W303S2500-
W303S2699 53188
W306S2200-
W306S2499 53188
S22W30700-
S22W30999 53188
S23W30900-
S23W30999 53188
W300S3100-
W300S3299 53189
W297S3100-
W297S3399 53189
S26W29800-
S26W30099 53188
W297S2900-
W297S3099 53188
W305S2200-
W305S2699 53188
W304S2400-
W304S2699 53188
Bonnie Ln 53188
Born Pl 53186
Boulder Ct 53189
Bowling Green Dr 53186
Brad St 53188
Bramblewood Ct 53188
Brandybrook Rd 53188
Brasted Pl 53186
Brendon Way 53188
Brentwood Dr 53188
Brian Ct 53188
Briar Hedge Cir 53189
Briar Hill Dr 53188
Briarwood Ln 53186
Brighton Dr 53188
Brightside Rd 53188
Bristol Ct 53188
Broadway 53186
E Broadway
100-299 53186
E Broadway
300-1998 53186
300-300 53187
301-2199 53186
W Broadway 53186
Broken Arrow Ct 53189
Broken Bow Trl 53188
Broken Hill Ct & Rd 53188
Brook Ct 53189
Brook St 53188
Brookhill Ct 53189
Brookhill Dr 53189
Brookhill Rd
W304S3000-
W304S3099 53188
W304S3100-
W304S4699 53189
W305S3000-
W305S3099 53188
W305S3100-
W305S4699 53189
W310S4200-
W310S4299 53189
Brookridge Ct N & S 53188
Brookside Cir 53189
Brookstone Ct & Ln 53188
Brunner Ct 53186
Bryn Dr 53188
Bryn Mawr Ct 53188
Buchner Ct 53186
Buckingham Ct 53188
Buckley St 53186
Buena Vista Ave 53188
Buffalo St 53188
Burnell Dr 53189
Burningwood Ln 53186
Burr Oak Blvd & Ct 53189
Burrie Ln 53188
Burton Ct & Dr 53186
Burtsway Dr 53189
Burwood Ct 53186
Busse Rd 53188
Butler Dr 53186
Caldwell St 53188
Calico Ct 53186
Cambria Rd 53188
Cambrian Rdg 53188
Cambridge Ave 53188
Camden Ct & Way 53186
Cameron Ct & Dr 53189
Campfire Xing 53189
Candlewood Dr 53188
Candlewyck Ct 53188
Canterbury Ln 53188
Canyon View Dr 53189
Capella Ct 53186
Cardinal Ct & Dr 53186
Carlton Pl 53186
Carmarthen Ct & Dr 53188
Caroline St 53186
Carpenter Pl 53186
Carriage Dr 53188
Carroll St 53186
Cartwright Cir 53189
Cascade Dr 53188
Castle Combe Ct 53188
Cathedral Ct 53189
Catherine St 53188
Catskill Rd 53186
Cavalier Dr 53186
Cecilia Ct 53188
Cedar Ct 53189
Cedar Ln 53188
Cedar Hollow Ct 53188
Cedarwood Ct 53186
Center Rd 53189
Central Ave 53186
Century Oak Dr 53188
Chancery Ln 53188
Chapman Dr
1200-1299 53186
1400-2099 53189
Charles Dr 53189
N Charles St 53186
S Charles St 53186
Chatsworth Cir 53188
Cheaney Rd 53186
S Cherokee Dr 53186
Cherokee Trl 53188
Cherry Ln 53188
Cherrywood Ct
W221N2600-
W221N2699 53186
2400-2499 53189
Cherrywood Dr 53188
Chesterwood Ln 53188
Chestnut Ln & Trl 53189
Cheviot Chase 53186
Cheyenne Dr 53188
Chicago Ave 53188
Chicory Cir 53189
Chinook Ct 53189
Chippewa Dr 53186
Chukar Ln 53189
Churchview Dr 53188
Cider Hills Ct & Dr 53189
Claremont Ct 53186
Clarion Ln 53186
Clearview Ct & Ln 53189
Clearwater Ln 53189
Cleveland Ave 53186
Cliff Alex Ct N & S 53189
Cliffside Ct 53189
Clinton St 53186
Clover Knoll Dr 53189
Cloverview Ct 53186
Coachman Ct 53188
Cobblestone Ct 53188
Cody Ct 53188
Coldwater Creek Dr 53188
E & W College Ave 53186
Collins St 53188
Cologne Rd 53186
Colton St 53186
Columbia Ave 53186
N & S Comanche Ct &
Ln N & S 53188
Commerce Cir 53188
Commerce St 53186
Concord Ct 53189
Concordia Ave 53186
Cone View Ln 53189
Conifer Ct 53188
Cook St 53186
Coolidge Ave 53186
Copenhill Dr 53186
Coppersmith Sq 53189
Coral Dr 53186
Cornell Dr 53188
Coronado St 53189
Corporate Ct
W231N1400-
W231N1699 53186
800-899 53189
Corporate Dr 53189
Corrina Blvd 53186
Cottage Ct 53186
Cotton Ct 53186
Cottontail Trl 53189
Cottonwood Dr 53189
Country Ct 53186
Country Ln 53189
Country Club Ct 53189
Country Crest Ln 53189
Country Glen Dr 53189
County Rd E 53189
County Highway F 53186
County Road De 53189
County Road Dt 53188
County Road F 53186
Coventry Ln 53188
Coyote Xing 53189
Creek Dr 53188
Creekside Ct 53188
Creekside Dr 53189
Crest Dr 53189
Crest Ln 53188
Crestview Ct & Dr 53189
Crestwood Dr 53188
Crossbow Ct 53186
Crossroads Cir 53186
Crystal Ln 53188
N & W Cumberland Dr 53186
Cutler St 53186
Dairy Ave 53188
Daisy Ln 53189
Dale Dr 53189
Daleview Dr 53189
Dana Ct & Ln 53189
Danny St 53186
Darlene Dr 53189
Darrell Dr 53189
Dartmoor Ct 53188
David Ct 53188
Davidson Rd 53186
Davis Ln 53189
Debbie Ct & Dr 53186
Deer Ct, Path & Trl 53189
Deer Crossing Rd 53189
Deer Forest Ct 53188
Deer Path Ct 53188
Deercrest Ct 53188
Deerfield Cir 53189
Delafield St 53188
Dendon Ct 53189
Denton Dr 53188
Depot Rd 53189
Depot Hill Rd 53188
Devonshire Ct 53188
Dewitt Ct 53186
Diane Ct 53188
Diane Dr 53189
Dixie Ct & Dr 53189
Dodie Dr 53186
Dogwood Ln 53189
Dolphin Ct & Dr 53186
Dona Vista Dr 53186
Donald Dr 53189
Doneswood Dr 53186
Dopp St 53186
Doral Ln 53189
Doral Rd 53186
Douglas Ave 53186
Dover Dr 53186
Downing Dr 53186
Dresser Ave 53188
Drumlin Dr 53188
Dunbar Ave 53186
Duncan Ct 53189
Duplainville Rd 53186
Dustin Ct 53189
Eagle Ct 53189
Eales Ave 53186
N East Ave 53186
S East Ave
100-1999 53186
2000-2098 53189
2001-2199 53186
Eastmound Dr 53186
Easy St 53188
Ed Mar Cir 53188
Elder St 53188
Elder Ayre Dr 53189
Elise Ct & Dr 53189
Elizabeth St 53186
Elk Ln 53188
Elk Valley Ct & Rd 53189
Ellis St 53186
Ellsworth Pl 53186
Elm Cir 53189
Elm St 53186
Elm Tree Ln 53189
Elmhurst Dr 53188
Elmwood Dr 53189
Emberwood Ct 53186
Emerald Ct 53188
Empire Ct & Dr 53186
Emslie Ct & Dr 53188
End Ln & Rd 53188
Endfield Cir 53186
Engler Dr 53189
Enterprise St 53189
Erin Ln 53188
Ermine Ct 53189
Esser Ct & Dr 53189
Essex Xing 53189
Estberg Ave 53186
Eugene Ct 53186
Everett Dr 53188
Evergreen Dr 53188
Fairfield Way 53188
Fairlane Ct 53189
Fairlawn Way 53188
Fairmont Ave 53188
Fairview Ave 53188
Falls Ct 53186
Faringdon Ct 53189
Farm View Ct 53188
Fawn Ct 53189
Fenway Dr N & S 53188
Fern Dr 53189
Fernwood Ct
W225N2700-
W225N2799 53186
S67W23600-
S67W23799 53189
Fernwood Dr 53189
Fiddlers Creek Dr 53188
Field Dr 53188
Fieldcrest Ln 53186
Fielding Ln 53189
Fieldridge Ct & Dr 53188
Finch Ct 53189
Fisk Ave 53186
Fleetfoot Dr 53186
Forest Hill Ct 53188
Forestview Ct & Ln 53189
Foster Ct 53186
Fountain Ave 53186
Fox Ct 53189
Fox Hill Cir, Ct & Dr 53189
Fox Lake Cir 53189
Fox Point Ct & Dr 53189
Fox Ridge Dr 53189
Fox River Cir & Pkwy 53189
Fox Run Ct 53189
Fox Vale Ct 53189
Foxboro Ct 53189
Foxcroft Ln 53189
Foxhaven Run 53186
Foxview Ct 53186
Foxwood Ct 53186
Foxwood Ln 53186
Foxwood Trl 53189
Frame Ave 53186
Francis St 53188
Franklin Ave 53186
Frederick Pl 53189
Frederick St 53186
Freeman St 53189
Friedman Dr 53186
Frontier Pass 53189
Fulton St 53186
Gabriel Dr 53188
Gale St 53186
Garden Prairie Dr 53186
Garfield Ave
100-1399 53186
1400-1699 53188
E Garfield Ave 53189
Garfield Cir 53186
Garland Ave & Ct 53188
Garrett Dr 53189
Garvens Ct 53188
Gascoigne Dr 53186
Gaspar St 53186
Gate Keeper Dr 53189
Gatekeeper Ct 53188
Gateway Dr 53186
Genesee Pass 53189
Genesee Rd
W253S2201-
W253S2299 53188
S37W26999-
S37W27999 53189
S37W26501-
S37W26997 53189
S37W26901A-
S37W26999A 53189
S38W27001-
S38W27297 53189
W259S3100-
W259S3198 53189
W257S2600-
W257S2799 53188
W256S2601-
W256S2699 53188
W258S2801-
W258S3099 53188
S36W26900-
S36W26999 53189
S38W27299-
S38W27599 53189
S36W26500-
S36W26898 53189
S39W27501-
S39W27899 53189
W260S3101-
W260S3299 53189
W261S3201-
W261S3599 53189
Genesee St 53186
George Hunt Cir 53186
Georgetown Pl 53189
Gertrude St 53186
Glacier Ct 53188
Glacier Ridge Rd 53188
Glen Hollow Ln 53189
Glen Ridge Ct 53188
Glendale Rd 53189
Glendon Way 53188
Glengarry Rd 53189
N & W Glenn Dr 53188
Glenview Dr 53189
Glenwall Dr 53189
Glenwood Dr & Ln 53186
Goetz Dr 53186
Grace Ct 53189
Gramling Ln 53186
N Grand Ave 53186
S Grand Ave
100-1399 53186
1400-2199 53189
N & S Grandview Blvd &
Ct 53188
Grant St 53186
Grayfox Ct 53189
Graywood Ct 53186
Green Ln 53188
Green Rd 53186
Green Briar Rd 53189
Green Country Rd 53189
Green Mountain Dr 53189
Green Valley Dr 53189
Greenbriar Dr 53189
Greenbush St 53186
Greendale Dr 53186
N & S Greenfield Ave &
Ct 53186
S & W Greenhill Rd 53186
Greenmeadow Dr &
Ln 53188
Greenway Ter 53186
Greenwood Ave 53188
Greenwood Rd 53186
Griffith Ct 53188
Grouse Ct 53189
Grove St 53186
Gruettner Dr 53189
Grush Rd 53189
Guthrie Rd
W226S2700-
W226S2999 53186
W223S3300-
W223S4299 53189
W224S4800-
W224S6599 53189
W225S4100-
W225S4599 53189
W225S4800-
W225S6699 53189
W226S5900-
W226S5999 53189
W225S3300-
W225S4098 53189
W225S4601-
W225S4699 53189
W224S3300-
W224S4300 53189
W224S4302-
W224S4698 53189
1000-1399 53186
Habourn Ct 53189
Hamilton Ave 53186
Hamilton Dr 53189
Harding Ave 53186
Harris Dr 53186
Harris Highland Dr 53188
Harrison Ave 53186
Harrogate Dr 53188
Hartman Pl 53186
N & S Hartwell Ave 53186
Harvest Ln 53189
Harvest View Dr 53189
Harvey Ave 53186
Hasting Ct 53186
Havenridge Ct 53188
Hawks Meadow Dr 53188
Hawthorn Cir & Dr 53188
Hawthorn Hill Dr 53188
Hawthorne Hollow Dr 53189
Haymarket Rd 53189
Hazelhurst Ln 53189
Hazelwood Pl 53189
Heather Ct & Dr 53189
Heather Glen Ct 53188
Heather Ridge Dr 53189
Hemit Ave 53189
Hemlock Ln 53189
Herman St 53189
Hermie Ln 53188
Heyer Dr 53186
Hi Lo Dr 53189
Hi Ridge Ave 53186
Hi View Ct 53189
Hickory Dr 53186
Hickory Hill Dr 53188
Hickory Ridge Dr 53189
Hickorywood Ct 53186
Hidden Ct 53189
High Pointe Knoll Cir 53188
High Ridge Ct & Dr 53189
Highfield Rd 53188
Highland Ave 53186
Highland Ct 53189
Highpoint Ln 53189

Hightop Cir 53188
Highview Ln 53188
Highview Rd 53189
Hillcrest Dr 53186
Hillside Dr 53186
Hillside Rd 53189
Hilltop Dr 53188
Hillview Cir 53188
N & S Hine Ave 53188
Hinman Ave 53186
Hinsdale Rd 53186
Holiday Rd 53189
Holiday Hill Ct & Rd 53189
Holiday Oak Ct & Dr 53189
Holiday Point Dr 53189
Hollidale Dr 53186
Homewood Ct 53186
Honey Acres Ct 53189
Hoover Ave 53186
Horizon Trl 53189
Howard St 53188
Howell Ave & Ct 53186
Howlett Ln 53186
Hudson Way 53189
Hughes Ln 53188
Hunter Ct & Rd 53189
Hunters Holw 53189
Hunters Hollow Ct 53189
Hunting Ridge Rd 53188
Huntley Ct 53188
Huron Ln 53189
Hyde Park Ave 53188
Imperial Ct & Ln 53188
Indianwood Ct & Ln 53186
Industrial Ln 53189
Inverness Dr S 53186
Irene Ct 53189
Ironwood Ct 53188
Irving Pl 53189
Isabella Ct 53189
Ivy Cir 53186
Ivy Ct 53189
Jackson Ct 53186
Jacob Ct 53188
Jacquelyn Dr 53188
N & S James St 53186
Jamie Ct 53188
Jan Ave 53188
Jane Ln 53186
Jarmon Ct & Rd 53188
Jasper Ln 53188
Jays Ln 53188
Jefferson Ave 53186
Jeffery Ln 53188
Jenkins Ct 53189
Jenna Ln 53188
Jennie Ct 53188
Jennifer Ln 53186
Jenny Ct 53188
Jericho Ct & Dr 53186
Jersey Cir 53188
Jills Dr
N8W27100-
N8W27199 53188
Joanne Dr 53188
Joellen Dr 53188
John St 53188
Johns Way 53189
Johnson Dr 53186
Joris Ave 53188
Joseph Rd 53186
Josephine St 53186
Journeys Way 53189
Judith Ln 53188
Juniper Cir 53189
Juniper Ct 53189
Justin Ln 53189
Kame Ter 53188
Kame Terrace Ct N & S 53188
Kamps Ct 53189
Katherine Ct 53189
Kathryn Ct 53186
Kathy Ct 53188
Kayla Ct & Dr 53188
Kegler Rd 53186
Kensington Dr 53188
Kent Dr 53188
Keri Ct 53188
Kestrel Ct 53189
Kestrel Dr 53188
Kestrel Ln 53188
Keswick Ct 53188
Kettlefield Ct 53189
Kilps Ct & Dr 53188
Kimberly Dr 53188
King Fisher Ct 53188
King William Ct S & W 53186
Kings Ct, Dr & Way 53188
Kings Peak Ave & Ct 53189
Kioa Ct 53188
Kisdon Hill Ct & Dr 53188
Klein Ct 53186
Knollwood Ct 53188
Kossow Rd 53186
La Salle St 53186
Lacustrine Way 53188
E & W Laflin Ave 53186
Lake St 53186
Lambeth Rd 53189
Lancaster Dr 53188
Lander Ct & Ln 53189
Landmark Dr 53186
Lang Udsigt Cir 53188
Larchmont Dr 53186
Larkspur Ct 53188
Larry Ct 53186
Laura Ct & Ln 53186
Laurelwood Ct 53186
Lavine Ln 53189
Lawndale Ave 53188
Lawnsdale Ct & Rd 53189
Lawrence Ln 53186
Ledward Ct 53189
Lee Ct 53186
Legend Cir & Ct 53189
Legend Hill Ln 53189
Lemira Ave & Cir 53188
Leslie Ln 53189
Letko Ln 53188
Lexington Dr 53186
Lincoln Ave 53186
Lincolnshire Ct 53188
Linda Ct 53188
Lindbergh Ave 53186
Linden Ln & St 53188
Lindenwood Ct 53186
Lindsay Way 53186
Little John Dr 53188
Lois Ln 53189
Lombardi Way 53186
London Dr 53189
Long Beard Rd 53186
Longbow Ct 53186
Longview Ct 53189
Longview Dr
S67W25300-
S67W25399 53189
S68W25200-
S68W25399 53189
W253S6700-
W253S6799 53189
S69W24700-
S69W25299 53189
21601-21999 53189
Lookout Dr 53186
Lookout Ridge Ct 53189
Loon Holw 53189
Lorraine Dr 53189
Lowell Dr 53186
Lucille Ct 53186
Ludwig Dr 53189
Luis Ct 53188
Luke Ave
600-612 53189
601-611 53186
613-799 53186
Lyla Ct 53189
Lyles Dr 53188
Lynne Ct & Dr 53186
Lynnewood Dr 53188
Lynx Blvd 53189
Mabel Ct 53189
Mac Arthur Ct & Rd 53188
Mackenzie Ct 53189
Mackenzie Dr 53188
Madera St 53189
Madison Ct & St 53189
Magnolia Dr 53189
Main St 53186
Maitland Dr 53188
Majestic Ct 53189
Makou Ct 53189
Mallard Pointe Cir 53189
Manchester Ct & Dr 53188
Mandan Dr 53188
Manhattan Dr 53186
Manor Ct & Dr 53188
Maple Ave 53188
Maple Hill Ct & Dr 53188
Maplefields Path 53188
Mapleton Ct 53189
Maplewood Ln 53186
Maplewood Ter 53186
Marcelle Dr 53189
Margaret St 53186
Maria St 53186
Marjean Ln 53186
Mark Trl 53189
Market Pl 53189
Marlene Ln 53189
Marlin Ct 53189
Marliz Dr 53189
Marmaduke Ct 53189
Marsh Ave 53189
Marshall St 53186
Martin St 53188
Mary Ann Ct & Dr 53189
Maryanna Dr 53189
Mccall St 53186
Mcdowell Rd 53189
Mcfarlane Rd 53189
Mcgregor Ct 53189
Meadow View Ct & Dr 53189
Meadowbrook Rd 53186
Meadowdale Dr 53189
Meadowlark Ln 53186
Meadowood Ct & Ln 53186
Meadowridge Ct 53186
Meghan Ct 53189
Melissa Ct 53189
Melody Ln 53186
Merlin Ln 53189
Merrihill Pkwy 53189
Merrill Hills Ct 53189
Merrill Hills Rd
W270S3100-
W270S3699 53189
W269S3100-
W269S3698 53189
W271S2700-
W271S3099 53188
W270S1900-
W270S1998 53188
W271S2100-
W271S2698 53188
W272S2001-
W272S2599 53188
301-397 53188
399-499 53188
Merrimac Trl 53189
Merriwood Ct 53189
Mesa Ct 53188
Mesa Verde Dr 53189
Meyers Dr 53189
Michael Dr 53189
Michelle Ct 53188
Michigan Ave & Ct 53188
Midellaw Dr 53189
Midland Ave 53186
Milky Way Rd 53189
Mill Ct 53189
Mill Creek Trl 53189
Mill Reserve Dr 53188
Millers Ct 53186
Millwood Ave & Ln 53188
Milwaukee Ave 53188
Minaka Dr 53188
Minor Ln 53189
Minot Ln 53188
Misty Ln 53186
Moccasin Trl 53186
Mohawk Ln 53186
Mohawk Trl 53188
Mohican Cir & Trl 53189
Molla Dr 53189
Molly Ln N & S 53186
Moraine Ct 53189
Moraine Farm Rd 53188
E Moreland Blvd 53186
N Moreland Blvd 53188
S Moreland Blvd 53188
W Moreland Blvd 53188
Morey Ln & St 53188
Morgan Ave 53188
Morningside Cir & Dr 53186
Morris Dr 53189
Motor Ave 53188
Mount Everest Ct & Rd 53189
Mount Vernon Dr 53186
Mount Whitney Ave 53189
Mountain Ave 53188
Moyer Way 53189
Mt Rainier Dr 53189
Mucklestone Ct 53188
Mulberry Ln 53189
Murray Ave 53186
Nancys Ct 53188
Napa Trl 53188
National Ave
S14W22300-
S14W22499 53186
Navajo Ln 53186
Newcastle Ct 53188
E & W Newhall Ave 53186
Niagara Ct & St 53186
Nike Dr 53186
Noquets Dr 53189
Norms Rd 53188
North Ave 53186
E North St 53188
W North St 53188
Northview Rd 53188
Norton Ave 53188
Norwood Ct & Dr 53188
Nottingham Ct 53189
Nottingham Dr 53188
Nottingham Way 53189
Oak Cir 53189
Oak Ct 53188
Oak Grove Ln 53189
Oak Knoll Dr 53189
Oak Park Dr 53189
Oak Ridge Ct & Dr 53189
Oak Valley Ln 53189
Oak View Dr 53189
Oakcrest Dr 53188
Oakdale Ct & Dr 53189
Oakland Ave 53186
Oaklawn Ave 53186
Oakmont Dr & Trl 53188
Oakridge Dr 53189
Oakwood Dr & Ln 53186
Old Mill Rd 53186
Old Village Rd 53186
Olympia Ct N & S 53189
Orchard Ave 53188
Orchard Ln 53186
Oriole Dr 53186
Oscar St 53186
Otter Trl 53189
Overlook Ln 53189
Overton Ave 53188
Oxbow Dr 53189
Oxbridge Ct 53188
Oxford Rd 53186
Paces Dr 53189
Palmer St 53188
Pamela Cir 53188
Pamela Ct 53189
Paradise St 53188
Paramount Ct & Dr 53186
E & W Park Ave & Pl 53186
Park View Ct 53189
Parke Ln E & W 53189
Parkers Pl 53188
Parklawn Ct & Dr 53186
Parkton Dr 53186
Partridge Ct & Ln 53189
Patricia Ln
W255N100-
W255N398 53188
W227S4400-
W227S4699 53189
Patrick Ln 53188
Paul Ln 53186
Peachwood Ct 53186
Pearl St 53186
Pebble Valley Rd 53188
Pendleton Ct & Pl 53188
Penhurst Way 53186
Periwinkle Ct & Dr 53189
Perkins Ave 53186
Perkins Rd 53189
Perren Dale Rd 53189
Peterhill Ct 53186
Peters Dr 53188
Pewaukee Dr & Rd 53188
Pheasant Ct, Dr & Run 53189
Philip Dr 53186
Phoenix Dr 53186
Pilgrim Cir 53188
Pilot Ct 53186
Pin Oak Ln 53189
Pine Ct 53189
Pine St 53188
Pine Hollow Ct 53189
Pinewood Ct 53186
Pioneer Ct & Trl 53186
Plateau Ln 53186
Plaza Ct 53186
Pleasant St 53186
Pleasantview Ave 53188
Plymouth Ct 53188
Point Dr 53189
Poplar Dr 53188
Poppy Fields Rd 53189
Portage Cir 53189
N & S Porter Ave 53186
Prairie Ave 53186
Prairie Falcon Pass 53189
Prairie Song Dr 53188
Prairie Wolf Ct 53189
Prairieside Ct & Dr 53189
Preston Ct 53188
Price Ct 53188
Primrose Ln 53189
Progress Ave 53186
Prospect Ave 53186
Prospect Ct 53186
Quail Run 53189
Quail Run Dr 53189
Queens Ct 53188
Quinn Rd 53189
Racine Ave
W227S2600-
W227S2699 53186
W220S3200-
W220S3348 53189
W221S3200-
W221S3348 53189
W223S3100-
W223S3198 53189
Raintree Ct & Ln 53188
Rambling Rose Rd 53186
Ramona Rd 53186
Ramshead Ct 53188
Randall St 53188
Rapids Trl 53189
Rawlins Dr 53189
Raymond St 53186
Red Clover Dr 53189
Red Maple Way 53188
Red Oak Ct & Dr 53186
Red Wing Dr 53189
Redford Blvd 53186
Redtail Ct 53189
Redwood Ct 53186
Regency Ct 53189
Regent St 53186
Rempe Dr 53186
Rhapsody Ln 53186
Richard St 53189
Richland Pl 53188
Richmond Ct 53186
Rickert Dr 53189
Ridge Rd 53186
Ridge Creek Cir 53186
Ridge Valley Rd 53189
Ridgefield Rd 53189
Ridgeline Cir & Dr 53188
Ridgeview Ct & Pkwy 53188
Ridgeview Parkway Ct 53188
Ridgewood Ct 53186
Ridgewood Dr
W298S2700-
W298S3099 53188
W299S3000-
W299S3099 53188
800-1099 53186
Ridgewood Ln 53186
Ringneck Ct 53189
Rip Van Winkle Dr 53186
River Ct 53189
River Ln 53188
River Rd
S63W27400-
S63W27799 53189
S64W27400-
S64W27799 53189
S65W27400-
S65W27999 53189
S66W27400-
S66W29399 53189
S67W27400-
S67W29399 53189
W267S4700-
W267S5899 53189
W270S5700-
W270S5899 53189
W271S5700-
W271S5899 53189
W264S4500-
W264S5299 53189
W266S4500-
W266S5299 53189
W269S4700-
W269S5299 53189
W269S5500-
W269S5599 53189
W273S6200-
W273S6299 53189
2800-2899 53189
River Edge Ct 53189
River Hill Ct & Dr 53189
River Park Dr 53189
River Place Blvd 53189
River Point Ct 53189
River Ridge Dr 53189
River Valley Rd 53189
River View Dr 53189
Rivera Dr 53189
E Rivera Dr
100-198 53186
101-199 53189
Riverfront Plz 53186
Rivers Crossing Dr 53189
Riverton Dr 53189
Riverview Ave 53188
Riverview Dr 53189
Riverwalk Dr 53188
Riverwood Dr 53189
Roanoke Dr 53189
Robby Ln 53188
E & W Roberta Ave 53186
Roberts Ct, Rd & St N & S 53188
Robin Ct 53186
Robin Hill Cir 53189
Robinhood Ct 53188
Robyn Rd 53189
Rock St 53186
Rockridge Rd & Way 53188
Rockwood Cir 53189
Rockwood Dr 53188
Rockwood Trl 53189
Rockwood Way 53189
Rocky Creek Dr 53189
Rocky Hills Ct 53188
Rolling Green Dr 53186
Rolling Oaks Ter 53189
Rolling Ridge Ct & Dr 53188
Rolling View Dr 53188
Roosevelt Pl 53186
Rose Ct 53186
Rosemary St 53186
Rosewood Ct 53186
Roxbury Way 53186
Royal Ct 53188
Ruben Dr 53186
Ruddy Duck Run 53189
Rue Rae Ln 53188
Rushmore Dr 53188
Rustic Way 53186
Rustic Woods Ct 53188
Ruth Pl 53189
Ryan St 53186
Sadie Ln 53189
Sage Ct & Rd 53189
Saillak Dr 53188
Saint Andrews Ct 53188
Saint Davids Dr 53189
Saint James Ct & Way 53188
E Saint Paul Ave 53188
W Saint Paul Ave
100-198 53188
200-1900 53188
1902-2398 53188
2400-2498 53189
Salem Ct 53189
Salter Dr 53186
Sandpiper Br & Cir 53189
Sandra Ln 53188
Santa Barbara Dr 53189
Santa Monica Cir 53186
Saratoga Dr & Rd 53186
Saylesville Rd 53189
School Dr 53189
Scotland Dr 53189
Scott Ave 53186
Seftar Rd 53189
Seitz Dr 53186
Sentinel Dr 53189
Sentry Dr 53186
Sequoia Cir 53188
Shade Tree Ct 53188
Shadow Ridge Cir & Dr 53189
Shadywood Ct 53186
Shagbark Trl 53188
Shananagi Ln 53188
Sheffield Rd 53186
Shepherd Ct 53186
Shepherds Way 53188
Sherryl Ln 53188
Sherwood Dr 53188
Short Rd 53186
Shoshone Dr 53188
Sierra Madre Ct 53189
Silver Fox Ct 53188
Silverberry Ct 53189
Skyline Ave 53189
Skyline Ct 53189
Snow Goose Trl 53189
Snowdon Dr
W300S2700-
W300S3099 53188
Somerset Ct 53186
Sommers Hills Dr 53189
Sonya Dr 53188
South St 53186
Southampton Ct & Dr 53188
Spring St 53186
Spring City Dr & Ln 53186
Spring Crest Cir 53188
Spring Ridge Ct & Ln 53189
Springbrook N & S 53186
Springdale Rd 53186
Springview Ct 53186

Springwood Ln 53186
Square Cir 53186
Squire Ct & Rd 53189
Stardust Ct & Dr 53186
State Road 164
W233N500-
W233N599 53188
State Road 164
W238S6700-
W238S6899 53189
W239S4700-
W239S6599 53189
W240S4699-
W240S6599 53189
W241S3800-
W241S4699 53189
W239S6701-
W239S6899 53189
W240S3801-
W240S4697 53189
State Road 59
W226S2400-
W226S2499 53186
S40W28000-
S40W28199 53189
S43W28400-
S43W28799 53189
S46W29230-
S46W29899 53189
S41W28800-
S41W28898 53189
S46W30300-
S46W30398 53189
S41W28201-
S41W28299 53189
S42W28401-
S42W28499 53189
S47W29601-
S47W30199 53189
S45W29199-
S45W29299 53189
S45W29101-
S45W29197 53189
501-599 53186
1700-1740 53186
W State Road 59 53189
State Road 59 Rd 53189
State Road 83 53189
Sterling Ct 53188
Stewart Hill Dr 53188
Stigler Ln 53189
Stillwater Cir 53189
Stone Gate Ln 53189
Stone Manor Ln 53189
Stone Ridge Dr 53188
Stonebridge Rd 53188
Stonebrook Dr 53186
Stonefield Ct
1400-1499 53186
2500-2599 53188
Stonegate Ct & Rd 53189
Stonehaven Ct 53186
Stonehedge Ct & Dr 53189
Stonehenge Ct 53188
Stoneridge Ct 53189
Stonewood Ct & Ln 53186
Stony Ridge Ct & Dr 53189
N Street Ct 53188
Sugar Maple Dr 53189
Sultan Dl & St 53186
Sumac Ln 53189
Summit Ave 53188
Summit Dr 53186
Sun Valley Cir & Trl 53189
Sunkist Ave 53188
Sunny Cir 53188
Sunnycrest Dr 53186
Sunnyside Dr 53186
Sunridge Ct & Dr 53189
Sunrise Ct 53188
Sunset Cir 53186
Sunset Dr 53189
E Sunset Dr 53189
W Sunset Dr 53189
Sunset Vw 53189
Susan Cir & St 53189
Sussex Ln 53188
E Sutton Pl 53188
Swallow Ct & Rd 53189
Swartz Ct & Dr 53188
Sweetbriar Ct & Dr 53186
Swenson Dr 53186
Sycamore Dr 53189
Sylvan Ct, Ter & Trl 53188
Takoma Dr 53186
Tallgrass Cir 53188
Talon Ct & Dr 53188
Tamarack Ct & Ln 53188
Tanager Ct 53189
Tanglewood Dr 53189
Tansdale Ct & Rd 53189
Tara Hill Ct 53188
Teal Ct 53189
Tenny Ave 53186
Tensleep Ter 53188
Tesch Ct 53186
Thames Ct & Rd 53188
The Strand 53186
Thrush Ct & Ln 53189
Thunderhead Trl 53188
Tiffany St 53189
Timber Trl 53189
Timber Ridge Ct & Dr 53189
Timberwood Ct & Ln 53186
Timm Dr 53189
Tomahawk Ct & Ln 53186
Torhorst Rd 53188
Tower Pl 53188
Townline Rd 53189
Travis Ln 53189
Tree Line Ct 53188
Trefor Ct 53188
Trillium Cir 53189
Trillium Hill Ct 53189
Trinity Ln 53189
Turnberry Ct 53188
Turnberry Oak Dr 53188
Turners Pike E & W 53189
Underwood Ct 53189
Union St 53188
N & S University Ct &
Dr 53188
Valley Dr 53186
Valley Ln 53189
Valley Rd 53186
Valley Creek Dr 53189
Valley Hill Dr 53189
Valley View Dr 53189
Valley View Rd 53189
Van Winkle Ct 53186
Velma Ct & Dr 53189
Venture Dr 53189
Venture Hill Rd 53188
Verta Vista Ct & Dr 53189
Victoria Dr 53189
E View Ct 53188
S View Ct 53188
W View Ct 53188
View Dr 53189
Villa Ct & Ter 53186
Virginia Dr 53186
Vista Del Tierra 53189
E & W Wabash Ave 53186
Walden Cir 53188
Wall St 53188
Walnut Trl 53189
Walton Ave 53186
N Washington Ave 53188
Watertown Rd
N14W22000-
N14W22219 53186
Waterview Ln 53189
Waukesha Ave 53186
Waverly Pl 53186
Wayne Keith Cir 53188
Wealthy St 53188
Weber Ct & Dr 53189
Wedgewood Dr 53186
Weiland Dr 53189
Wellington Ct 53188
Welsh Ct 53188
Wensley Ct 53188
Wern Way 53189
Wern Farm Cir E & W 53189
Wesley Dr N 53189
West Ave 53186
N West Ave 53186
S West Ave
100-300 53186
301-797 53189
302-798 53186
799-1099 53189
1100-1399 53186
1400-2300 53189
2302-2398 53189
Westbrooke Pkwy 53186
Western Ave 53188
Westminster Dr 53186
Westmound Dr 53186
Westowne Ave 53188
Westwood Dr 53186
Wexford Ct & Ln 53186
Whispering Hills Ct 53189
Whitby Ct 53188
White Oak Ct & Way 53188
Whitehall St 53186
Whiterock Ave 53186
Wilbur Ave 53186
Wild Berry Ct & Ln 53188
Wild Rose Ln 53188
Wildberry Ct 53186
Wildwood Ct
N11W27500-
N11W27699 53188
W246S7100-
W246S7199 53189
W247S7100-
W247S7199 53189
Wildwood Dr 53189
Wildwood Ln 53188
Willard Ln 53188
Williams Ct 53188
Williams St 53186
Williams Way 53188
Williams Bay Ct & Dr 53188
Willow Ct 53188
Willowood Dr 53188
Willowood Ln 53186
Wills Barry Ct & Dr 53188
Wilmont Dr 53189
Wilshire Pl 53188
Wilson Ave 53186
Windcrest Dr 53189
Windemere Dr 53188
Windham Ct 53186
Windrift Ct & Ln 53188
Windsong Rdg 53189
Windsor Ct 53189
Windsor Dr 53186
Windsor Pl 53188
Winnebago Way 53188
Winston Cir 53186
Wisconsin Ave 53186
Wisteria Ln 53189
Wolf Ct & Rd 53186
Wolf Meadow Ct 53186
Wood St 53186
Wood Lilly Ln 53189
Woodburn Dr & Rd 53188
Woodbury Cir & Cmn 53189
Woodchuck Ln 53189
Woodcock Ct 53189
Woodcrest Ct & Dr 53188
Woodfield Cir 53188
Woodfield Ct 53186
Woodfield Ct E 53186
Woodfield Ct W 53186
Woodglen Ct 53188
Woodhill Way 53189
Woodland Ct 53186
Woodland Trl 53188
Woodland Hills Dr 53188
Woodlark Ct 53186
Woodmere Trce 53189
Woodridge Ct & Ln 53188
Woods Dr & Rd 53189
Woodside Ct 53189
Woodside Dr
S55W22500-
S55W22899 53189
S56W22500-
S56W22899 53189
W278N1173-
W278N1199 53188
W278N901-
W278N1171 53188
W277N800-
W277N1174 53188
W277N1176-
W277N1198 53188
Woodview Dr 53189
Woodward St 53186
Wren Ln 53189
Wright St 53186
Wyngate Way 53189
Wynnewood Ct 53188
Yorkshire Ct 53188
Yvonne St 53188

NUMBERED STREETS

All Street Addresses 53188

WAUSAU WI

General Delivery 54403

POST OFFICE BOXES MAIN OFFICE STATIONS AND BRANCHES

Box No.s
All PO Boxes 54402

NAMED STREETS

Acorn Ln 54403
Adams Ct 54403
Adams Ln 54401
Adams St 54403
Adolph St 54401
Adrian St 54401
Alexander St 54401
Anderson Rd 54403
Ankor St 54403
Antler Cir 54401
Apple Ln 54401
Arbor Ct 54401
Arctic Ln 54401
Arlington Ln 54401
Arrow Dr 54403
Arrowwood Ct & Ln 54401
Artesian Way 54401
Arthur Ave 54401
Arthur St 54403
Ashland Ave 54403
Aspen Grove Ln 54403
Aster Rd 54401
Augusta Ave 54401
Autumn Brooke Ter 54403
Azalea Ct, Ln & Rd 54401
Badger Ave 54401
Balsam Dr 54401
Baneberry Ct 54401
Barker Ave 54403
Batten Dr 54403
Battery St 54403
Bay Park Ct 54401
Bay Shore Dr 54401
Beancord Ln 54401
Becher Dr 54401
Beckman Rd 54401
Beecher Ave 54401
Beechwood Dr 54401
Begonia St 54401
Bel Aire Dr 54401
Bellflower St 54401
N & S Bellis St 54403
W Belmont Rd 54401
Bent Stick Dr 54403
Bernard St 54403
Bertha St 54403
Big Hill Ln 54401
Big Pine Ln 54401
Big Sandy Ave 54403
Birch St 54403
Birch Ridge Ct 54403
Birchwood Dr 54401
Bird St 54403
Bissell St 54401
E Bittersweet Ct & Rd 54401
Blackberry Ct & Dr 54401
Blazing Star St 54401
Bleeding Heart St 54401
Blessing Rd 54403
Blossom Rd 54403
Blue Rock Ct 54403
Bluebell Dr, Ln & Rd 54401
Blueberry Ct & Ln 54401
Bluebird Ln 54401
Bluegill Ave 54401
Bluejay Ln 54401
Bluestone Dr 54401
Bob O Link Ave 54401
Bobwhite Rd 54401
Bombardier Ct 54401
Boot Ln 54401
Bopf St 54401
E & W Bos Creek Dr 54401
Boulder Rdg 54401
Bovine Ln 54401
Brady St 54401
Brandon Cir 54401
Brentwood Rd 54401
Briarwood Ave 54403
E Bridge St 54403
W Bridge St 54401
Brisbane Ct 54401
Bristers Hill Rd 54401
Broadbill Ln 54401
Broadway Ave & Ln 54403
Broken Arrow Rd 54401
Brookdale Dr 54403
Brookfield Ln 54401
Brooks Pl 54401
Brookview Ct 54403
Brown St 54403
Bruce Dr 54403
Buck Trail Rd 54403
Buckthorn Ct 54401
Bufflehead Ave 54401
Bugbee Ave 54401
Burek Ave 54401
Burger Ln 54403
Burlington Dr 54401
Burns St 54401
Business Park Dr 54403
Butler Pl 54401
Buttercup Rd 54401
Butternut Rd
2400-2799 54403
6800-7299 54401
E Butternut Rd 54403
Calico Ln 54403
Callon St 54401
Camellia St 54401
Camp Creek Rd 54403
Camp Phillips Rd 54403
E & W Campus Dr 54401
Canary Ave 54401
Canvasback Ln 54401
Cardinal Ave 54401
Carl St 54403
Carnation Ave 54401
Carol Dr 54401
E, N & W Cassidy Cir &
Dr 54401
Castle Rock Ln 54403
Cavin Dr 54401
Cecil St 54403
Cedar St 54401
Center St 54403
Central Dr 54401
Central Bridge St 54401
E Chellis St 54401
E Cherry St 54401
Chicago Ave 54403
Chickadee Ln 54401
Christian Ave 54401
Christopher Cir 54401
Circle Dr 54401
Clarke St 54401
Clarks Is 54403
E Clayton St 54401
Cleveland Ave 54401
Cliffway Dr 54403
Clover Rd 54401
Clover Creek Rd 54403
Cloverdale Dr 54401
Cloverland Ln 54401
Coel Blvd 54403
Colonial Rd 54403
Conner Davis Dr 54401
Copper Ln 54403
Cordell St 54403
Corporate Dr 54401
Cottage St 54401
Country Ln 54401
County Rd N & W 54403
County Road A 54401
County Road G 54403
County Road J 54403
County Road K 54401
County Road O 54401
County Road Q 54403
County Road U 54401
County Road Ww 54403
N County Road X 54403
County Road Z 54403
Crabapple Rd 54401
E Crabtree Cir & Dr 54401
Crane Dr 54401
Crescent Dr 54401
Crestview Dr 54403
Crestwood Dr 54403
E Crocker St 54403
W Crocker St 54401
Crocus Rd 54401
Crystal Dr 54401
Curlers Way 54403
Daffodil Ln 54401
Dahlia Ln 54401
Daisy Rd 54401
Decator Dr 54401
Deer Rd 54403
Deer Brook Ct 54401
Deer Park Dr 54401
Deer Tail Ln 54401
Dekalb St 54403
Delta Ct 54401
Desert Dr 54401
Development Ct 54401
Devoe St 54403
Division St 54403
Dixie Ave 54401
Dogwood Rd 54401
Dove Ave 54401
Dover Ln 54401
E Dunbar St 54403
Eagle Ave 54401
Eagle Valley Ln 54403
Easthill Dr & Pl 54403
Eastview Ct & Dr 54403
Eau Claire Blvd 54403
Eden Dr 54401
Edgewood Blvd 54401
Edgewood Rd 54403
Edwards St 54401
Elderberry Rd 54401
E & W Eldred St 54401
Elk Dr 54401
Elm Ln 54403
Elm Rd 54403
Elm St 54401
Elmwood Blvd 54403
N & S Emerald Dr 54401
Emerson St 54403
Emery Dr 54401
Empire Ln 54401
Emter St 54401
Enterprise Dr 54401
Ethel St 54403
Everest Blvd 54403
Evergreen Dr 54401
Evergreen Rd 54403
Ewing St 54403
Excel Dr 54401
Fairmount St 54403
Falcon Ave, Dr & Way 54401
Falling Oaks Ln 54401
Fawn Rd 54403
Fern Ln 54401
Fernwood Dr 54401
Financial Way 54401
Firethorn Rd 54401
Flagstone Dr 54401
Flameflower Rd 54401
Flamingo Ln 54401
Flax Ln 54401
Fleet Dr 54401
Fleming St 54403
Flieth St 54401
Flint Creek Cir 54401
Flints Rd 54401
Floral Ave & Ln 54403
Forest St
101-299 54403
235-235 54402
300-398 54403
400-1199 54403
Forest Hill Rd 54403
Forest Valley Rd 54403
Fountain Hills Blvd 54403
Foxglove Rd 54401
Foxwood Ct 54401
Frank Ave 54403
Franklin Pl & St 54403
Freedom Way 54403
Frenzel St 54403
E Fulton St 54403
Fust Ln 54403
Garfield Ave 54401
Garth St 54403
Geischen Dr 54401
Geisler St 54403
Gemini Pl 54401
Genrich St 54403
Geralds Ct 54401
Gilbert St 54403
Ginger Ln 54403
Glendale Ave 54401
Glenwood Rd 54403
Goetsch Rd 54403
Golden Meadow St 54401
Goldenrod Cir, Ct &
Rd 54401
Golf Club Rd 54403
Golf View Dr 54403
Goose Ln 54401
Gowen St 54403
Graham St 54401
Grand Ave 54403
Granite Rd 54403
Granite Heights Rd 54403
Grant St 54403
Graves Ave 54403
Gray Pl 54403
Green Hill Rd 54403
Green Valley Rd 54403
Green Vistas Dr 54403
Greenfield Ave 54401
Greenhill Dr 54401
Greenhouse Rd 54401
Grouse Ln 54401
Grove Dr 54401
E Hamilton St 54403
Hampton Ave 54403
Hardwood Ln 54403
Hawthorne Ln 54403
Haymeadow Ln 54403
Helmke St 54403
Hemlock Dr 54401
Hemlock Ln 54403
Henrietta St 54403
Henry St 54403
Heron Ave 54401
Hickory Rd 54403
Hidden Creek Way 54401

Street	ZIP
Hidden Links Dr	54403
Hidden Trail Ave	54403
High Oaks Way	54401
Highland Ct	54403
Highland Dr	54401
Highland Ln	54403
Highland Rd	54403
Highland Park Blvd	54403
Highwood Ln & Rd	54403
N Hill Rd	54403
Hillcrest Ave & Dr	54401
Hillside Cir	54401
Hillside Ln	54403
Hilltop Ave	54401
Hilltop Rd	54403
Hillview Ct	54403
Hollibush Ln	54401
Hollirob Ln	54403
Hollywood Rd	54401
Holub St	54401
Homestead Rd	54403
Honeysuckle Ln	54401
Horseshoe Spring Rd	54403
Hubbill Ave	54401
Humboldt Ave	54403
Hummingbird Rd	54401
Huntington Ct	54401
Hurley Cir	54403
Imm St	54401
Independence Ln	54403
Indian Ct	54401
Indian Springs Dr	54401
Indigo Dr	54401
Industrial Dr	54401
International Dr	54401
Iris Ln	54401
Ivy Ln	54401
Jackson St	54403
Jade Ave	54401
James Ave	54403
Jay St	54403
E Jefferson St	54403
Joan Dr	54403
Jonquil Ln	54401
Joyce St	54401
Jozik St	54403
Julip Dr	54401
Junction Rd & St	54403
Juniper Ln	54401
Kaitlin Dr	54403
E Kent St	54403
Kenwood Dr	54401
Kickbusch St	54403
Kildeer Ln	54401
King St	54403
King Bird Ave	54401
Kingfisher Ln	54401
Kinglet Cir	54401
Kings Ct	54403
Kiwanis Rd	54403
E Knox St	54401
Kolter St	54403
Kreutzer Blvd	54403
La Salle St	54403
Lahr Ave	54403
Lake St	54401
Lake View Ct & Dr	54403
Lakeshore Dr	54401
Lakeview Ave	54401
Lamont St	54403
Landing Rd	54403
N Lane Dr	54401
Langsdorf St	54403
Larkspur Ln	54401
Laughlin St	54403
Laurel Rd	54401
Laurie Ann Ln	54401
Lavina Dr	54401
W Lazy Acre Rd	54401
Le Messurier St	54403
E Lemke St	54403
Lenard St	54401
Leubner St	54403
Liberty Ave	54401
Liberty Ridge Way	54401
Lilac Ave	54401
Lillie St	54403
Lily Ln	54401
Lincoln Ave	54403
Lincoln Dr	54401
Lines St	54403
Lisbeth Rd	54401
Little Brook Ct	54401
Little Cain Rd	54403
Little Rib Cir	54401
Little Trappe Rd	54403
Lockwood Ln	54403
Loganberry Ct	54401
Lomar Dr	54401
Lombardy Dr	54401
Lonely Ln	54403
Lori Jody Ln	54403
Lotus Ln	54401
Lucille St	54401
Lupine Rd	54401
Lynx Rd	54401
Macaw Ave	54401
Madison St	54401
Madonna Dr	54401
Magnolia Ave	54401
Malak Cir	54403
Mallard Ln	54401
Mandarin Ln	54401
Manson St	54403
Maple Rd	54403
Maple St	54401
Maple Hill Dr	54401
Maple Hill Rd	54403
Maple Ridge Rd	54403
Maplecrest Dr	54401
Maria Dr	54401
Marigold Rd	54401
Marmel Dr	54401
Marquardt Rd	54403
Marshall St	54403
Marshall Hill Rd	54403
Marten St	54401
Martin Ave	54401
Mary St	54403
Mary Ann Ln	54401
Mathie Rd & St	54403
Matz Ter	54403
Mccarthy Blvd	54401
Mccleary St	54401
Mcclellan St	54403
Mcdonald St	54403
Mcindoe Ct & St	54403
Mcintosh St	54403
Meadow Cir	54401
Meadow Ln	54403
Meadow Rd	54403
Meadow Ridge Rd	54401
Meadowbrook Way	54403
Meadowlark Ln	54401
Meadowview Rd	54403
Mechanics Ridge Rd	54403
Melody Ln	54403
Menard Plz	54401
Merganser Way	54401
Merrill Ave	54401
Meuret Ln	54403
Michael St	54403
Midway Blvd	54403
Mile Rd	54403
Mill Rd	54403
Miller Ave	54401
Milwaukee Ave	54403
Mint Ln	54401
Mobile Ave	54403
Mockingbird Ln	54401
Monroe St	54403
Moonlite Ave	54401
Morgan Ln	54403
Morgan Creek Dr	54401
Morning Glory Ln	54401
Mount View Blvd	54403
Mountain Ct	54401
Mountain Ln	54401
N Mountain Rd	
1800-2099	54401
2100-8998	54401
2100-2100	54402
2101-8999	54401
S Mountain Rd	54401
Mulligan Dr	54403
Myron St	54401
Nehring St	54401
Nicolet St	54401
Nightingale Ln	54401
Nina Ave	54403
Norman Ave	54403
N & S Northfork Dr	54403
Northwestern Ave	54403
Norton St	54401
Norway Dr	54401
Nowak St	54401
Nuthatch Ln	54401
Oak Ln	54403
Oak St	54401
E Oak St	54401
Oakwood Blvd & Cir	54403
Old Hwy W	54403
Old Coach Rd	54401
Orchard St	54403
Orchid Cir, Ct & Ln	54401
Oriole Ln	54401
Osprey Dr	54401
Osswald Rd	54403
Overlook Dr	
1800-2499	54401
3701-3899	54403
Owl Ln	54401
Packer Dr	54401
Pansy Ln	54401
Paradise Ln	54403
Paramount Dr	54401
Parcher St	54403
Pardee St	54401
Park Ave	54403
Park Blvd	54401
Park Rd	54403
Parrot Ln	54401
Partridge Ave & Way	54401
Pasture Ln	54403
Patriot Dr	54403
Payne St	54403
Peacock Ave	54401
Pearson St	54403
Pepperbush Ln	54401
Peppermint Ln	54401
Petunia Rd	54401
Pheasant Ave	54401
Phlox Ln	54401
Pied Piper Ln	54403
Pine Rd	54403
Pine St	54401
Pine Bluff Rd	54403
Pine Cone Ln	54403
Pine Crest Ave	54401
Pine Hills Dr	54403
Pine Ridge Blvd	54401
Pine Siskin Ln	54401
Pine Tree Rd	54403
Pine View Ln	54403
Pinewood Ln	54403
Pintail Ln	54401
Pioneer Ln	54403
Pit Rd	54403
Plarthen St	54403
Plato St	54403
Plaza Dr	54401
Pleasant St	54403
Pleasant View Ln	54403
Plover Ln	54401
Plum Dr	54401
Plumer St	54403
Polzer Dr	54401
Poplar Ln	54403
Porcupine Rd	54403
Porter St	54401
Primrose Ln	54401
Prospect Ave	54401
Quail Ave	54401
Quarry Rd	54403
Quaw St	54401
Rachel Ln	54401
Radar Rd	54403
Rainbow Ln	54401
Rainbow Ter	54403
E & W Randolph St	54401
Raspberry Ln	54401
Raven Ave	54401
Red Bud Rd	54401
Red Maple Rd	54401
Red Tail Ln	54401
Redwing Rd & Way	54401
Reservoir Ave	54401
E Rib Mountain Dr & Way	54401
Rib River Trl	54401
Richards Rd	54401
N Ridge Rd	54403
Ridge View Dr	54401
Ridgewood Dr	54401
Rimrock Rd	54401
River Dr	54403
N River Dr	54403
River St	54401
River Highlands Ct	54403
River Hills Cir & Rd	54403
Riverview Ct & Dr	54403
Roberta Ln	54401
Robin Ln	54401
Rocky Ridge Rd	54403
Roger Dr	54403
Rolling Hills Ln	54401
Rolling Meadows Ln	54401
Rookery View Dr	54401
Roosevelt St	54403
Rose Ave	54401
Rose Marie St	54401
Rosecrans St	54401
E Ross Ave	54403
Royalston Ct	54401
Ruder St	54403
Russell Dr	54403
Sage Ln	54401
Saint Austin Ave	54403
Saint Francis Way	54401
Saint Paul St	54403
Sandpiper Ave	54401
Sandy Dr	54403
Sandy Banks Dr	54403
Sandy Creek Rd	54401
Sandy Ridge Ln	54403
Sandy River Rd	54403
School Rd	54403
Schroeder Dr	54403
Schwebach St	54403
Scott St	54403
Sell St	54403
Seymour Ln	54401
Seymour St	54403
Shady Lane Rd	54403
Shenandoah Ridge Rd	54403
Sherah Dr	54401
Sheridan Rd	54401
Sherman Rd & St	54401
Sherwood Cir	54403
Short St	54403
Silver Ln	54403
Silver Spring St	54401
Single Ave	54403
Skylark Ln	54401
Skyline Dr & Ln	54403
Smoketree Ln	54401
Snowbird Ave	54401
Snowdrop Ln	54401
Snowflake Ln	54401
Snowshoe Rd	54403
Sorrel Ln	54403
Spearmint Ln	54403
Split Rock Ln	54403
Spring Cir	54401
Spring St	54403
Spring Brook Rd	54403
Springbrook Dr	54401
Springdale Ave	54401
Spruce Ln	54403
Spruce St	54401
Spur Ln	54403
Stacey Cir	54403
Star Rd	54403
Starflower Dr & Ln	54401
Stark St	54403
Starling Ln	54401
Starlite Ave	54401
N State Highway 52	54403
Statesman Dr	54403
Steel Ln	54403
Stettin Dr	54401
Stettin Ridge Ct	54401
Steuben St	54403
Stevens Dr	54401
E Stewart Ave & Pl	54401
Stone Rd	54403
Stone St	54401
Stonecrop Rd	54401
Stoneridge Dr	54403
Strawberry Ct & Ln	54401
Strawflower Cir	54401
E & W Strowbridge St	54401
Sturgeon Eddy Rd	54403
Sugar Hill Ln	54403
Summit Dr	54401
Sumner St	54403
Sunbird Ln	54401
Sunny Hill Ln	54401
Sunnyvale Ln	54401
Sunrise Ct	54401
Sunrise Dr	54401
Sunrise Ln	54401
Sunrise Rd	54403
Sunset Ave	54403
Sunset Dr	54401
Sunset Hill Ct	54403
Sunset Valley Rd	54403
Swallow Ln	54401
Swan Ave	54401
Swanee Ave	54403
Sylvan St	54403
Tall Oaks Dr	54403
Talon Ln	54403
Tanager Ridge Rd	54401
Tate Ct	54401
Teal Ave	54401
Terrace Ct	54401
E Thomas St	
100-299	54401
400-598	54403
600-909	54403
W Thomas St	54403
Thornapple Rd	54401
Thunderbird Ln	54401
Tierney Rd	54401
Timber Ln	54403
Timber River Trl	54401
Timber Trail Dr	54403
Timberline Dr	54401
Tinkers Ct	54401
Topaz Dr	54401
Torney Ave	54403
E Tower Rd	54403
Town Hall Rd	54403
Townline Rd	54403
Trappe Rd	54403
Troy St	54403
Tulip Ct & Ln	54401
Turner St	54403
Tuzigoot Ln	54403
E Union Ave	54403
W Union Ave	54401
Us Highway 51 N	54401
Valley View Rd	54403
Verbena Ave	54401
Vilas Rd	54401
Violet Ln	54401
Vista Cir	54403
Walden Blvd	54401
Walnut St	54401
Warbler Way	54401
W Washington St	54403
E Wausau Ave	54403
W Wausau Ave	54401
W Wausau Cir	54401
Wausau Ctr	54403
Waxwing Rd	54401
Wegner St	54401
Werle Ave	54401
West St	54401
Westhill Dr	54401
Weston Ave	54403
Westwood Dr	54401
Westwood Center Blvd	54401
Whippoorwill Rd	54401
Whisper Rd	54401
Whispering Pine Ave	54403
White Pine Ct	54403
Wild Rose Ln	54403
Wildwood Ln	54401
Wind Ridge Dr	54401
Windflower Ln	54401
Windtree Dr	54401
Wintergreen Rd	54401
Winton St	54403
Wisconsin St	54403
Wisconsin River Rd	54403
Wisteria Ln	54401
Wonderland Rd	54403
Wood Duck Ln	54401
Woodbine Ln	54401
Woodbury Pkwy	54403
Woodland Dr	54401
Woodland Rd	54403
Woodland Ridge Rd	54403
Woodlawn Rd	54403
Woods Pl	54403
Woodsmoke Rd	54401
Wren St	54401
Wyatt St	54401
Young St	54403
Zimmerman St	54403

NUMBERED STREETS

Street	ZIP
N 1st Ave	54401
S 1st Ave	54401
N 1st St	54403
N 2nd Ave	54401
S 2nd Ave	54401
N 2nd St	54403
N 3rd Ave	54401
S 3rd Ave	54401
N 3rd St	54403
N 4th Ave	54401
S 4th Ave	54401
N 4th St	54403
S 4th St	54403
N 5th Ave	54401
S 5th Ave	54401
N 5th St	54403
S 5th St	54403
N 6th Ave	54401
S 6th Ave	54401
N 6th St	54403
N 7th Ave	54401
S 7th Ave	54401
N 7th St	54403
S 7th St	54403
N 8th Ave	54401
S 8th Ave	54401
N 8th St	54403
N 9th Ave	54401
S 9th Ave	54401
N 9th St	54403
N 10th Ave	54401
S 10th Ave	54401
N 10th St	54403
S 10th St	54403
N 11th Ave	54401
S 11th Ave	54401
N 11th St	54403
S 11th St	54403
N 12th Ave	54401
S 12th Ave	54401
N 12th St	54403
S 12th St	54403
S 12th Avenue Ct	54401
N 13th Ave	54401
S 13th Ave	54401
13th Dr	54403
N 13th St	54403
S 13th St	54403
N 14th Ave	54401
S 14th Ave	54401
N 14th St	54403
N 15th Ave	54401
S 15th Ave	54401
N 15th St	54403
N 16th Ave	54401
S 16th Ave	54401
N 16th St	54403
N 17th Ave	54401
S 17th Ave	54401
S 17th St	54403
N 18th Ave	54401
S 18th Ave	54401
N 18th St	54403
S 19th Ave	54401
N 19th St	54403
N 20th Ave	54401
S 20th Ave	54401
S 20th St	54403
S 21st Ave	54401
S 21st Pl	54401
N 21st St	54403
S 21st St	54403
22nd Ave & Pl	54401
N 23rd Ave	54401
S 24th Ave	54401
N 24th St	54403
N & S 25th	54403
N 26th Ave	54401
N 26th St	54403
N 27th Ave	54401
N 28th Ave	54401
S 28th Ave	54401
N 28th St	54403
N 29th Ave	54401
N 29th St	54403
N 30th Ave	54401
N & S 32nd Ave & Pl	54401
N 33rd St	54403
N 34th Ave	54401
N 34th St	54403
N 35th Ave	54401
S 35th St	54403
N 36th Ave	54401
S 36th Ave	54401
S 36th St	54403
S 38th Ave	54401
N & S 39th	54401
N 40th St	54403
N 41st Ave	54401
N 41st St	54403
N 43rd Ave	54401
N 44th Ave	54401
S 44th Ave	54401
N 44th St	54403
S 45th Ave	54401
N & S 48th	54401
N 49th St	54403
S 50th Ave	54401
N 52nd Ave	54401
S 52nd Ave	54401
N 52nd St	54403
N 53rd Ave	54401
S 54th Ave	54401
N 55th Ave	54401
N 56th Ave	54401
S 56th Ave	54401
N 56th St	54403
N 57th Ave	54401
N 57th St	54403
S 57th St	54403
S 58th Ave	54401
N & S 60th	54401
S 62nd Ave	54401
N 65th St	54403
S 66th Ave	54401
S 68th Ave	54401
N 69th St	54403
N & S 72nd	54401
N 73rd Ave	54401
N 73rd St	54403
S 73rd St	54403
N 74th Ave	54401
N & S 75th	54401
N 76th Ave	54401
N & S 77th	54401
N & S 80th	54401
N 81st St	54403

N & S 84th 54401
N & S 85th 54403
S 86th Ave 54401
N 86th St 54403
S 86th St 54403
N 88th Ave 54401
N 88th St 54403
S 88th St 54403
N 89th St 54403
N & S 93rd 54403
N 96th Ave 54401
N 97th St 54403
N 98th Ave 54401
N 100th Ave 54401
S 102nd St 54403
N 104th Ave 54401
N 108th Ave 54401
N 120th Ave 54401
N 128th 54401

WEST BEND WI

General Delivery 53095

POST OFFICE BOXES MAIN OFFICE STATIONS AND BRANCHES

Box No.s
All PO Boxes 53095

RURAL ROUTES

03, 06, 07, 09, 10, 13, 18 53090
01, 02, 04, 05, 08, 11, 12, 14, 15, 16, 17 53095

NAMED STREETS

Aarons Pl 53090
Abby Rd 53095
Acadia Ave 53095
Acorn Rd 53090
Adams St 53090
Aerial Dr 53095
Alder St 53090
Alpine Ct 53090
Alpine Dr
6300-6499 53095
6500-7299 53090
Amber Pl 53095
Amys Pl 53090
Angela Ct 53090
Anna Rd 53095
Anne St 53090
Anne Marie Ct 53095
Annette Ct 53090
Annie Pl & St 53090
Apple Blossom Ln 53095
Arbor Point Ave 53095
Arbor Vitae Dr 53095
Arlene Dr 53095
Arnold Ln 53090
Arthur Pl 53095
Artist Bay Rd 53095
Aspen Pl 53095
Auburn Rd 53090
Aurora Rd
6100-6499 53095
6500-7899 53090
Autumn Dr 53090
Auxiliary Ct 53095
Babalee Ln 53090
E & W Badger Ln 53095
Balsam Pl 53095
Barber Cir 53090
Barberry Pl 53095
Barbie Dr 53090
Barney Ct 53090
Barrington Ct 53095
Barton Ave 53090
Basin Rd 53095
Bauers Dr 53095
Bavarian Ln 53090
Beaver Dam Rd 53090
Beck Ln 53090
Becky Dr 53090
Beech St 53090
Beechnut Dr 53090
Bellmann Dr 53095
Bellvue Ct 53090
Bendamar Ln 53090
Bender Rd 53090
Berkshire Ct 53095
Bernadine Cir 53090
Beverly Ln 53090
Birch Ter 53090
Birchview Rd 53095
Birchwood Ln, Rd & Trl 53095
N & S Bittersweet Cir & Dr 53095
Blue Goose Rd
3100-3699 53095
3900-4199 53090
N & S Blue Heron Dr 53095
Bluebell Dr 53090
Bobolink Ln 53095
Boettcher Dr 53095
Briar Dr 53090
Briarvale Dr 53095
Brookhaven Dr 53090
Brooks Ct 53090
Brookview Dr 53095
Buckingham Ln 53095
Buttercup Ct 53090
Butternut St 53095
Cabrini Cir 53095
Cal Dr 53095
Caleb Ct 53090
Camden Ln 53090
Canary St 53090
Canterberry Ct 53090
Canyon Ln 53090
Cardinal Dr 53090
Carla Ln 53095
Carol Ct & Ln 53095
Carriage Dr 53095
Carrie Ln 53095
Cascade Dr 53095
Cecelia Dr 53090
Cedar Ct & St 53095
Cedar Bay 53095
Cedar Creek Rd 53095
Cedar Lake Dr 53095
Cedar Park Dr 53095
Cedar Pointe Dr 53095
Cedar Ridge Dr 53095
Cedar Sauk Rd 53095
Cedar View Dr 53095
Cedardale Dr 53095
Center Ln 53095
Century Hills Ct 53095
Chapel Hill Pl 53095
Chapel Hills Dr 53090
Cheri Ln 53095
Cherokee Dr 53090
Cherry St 53090
Cherrywood Cir 53090
Cheryl Ln 53095
Chestnut St 53095
Chopper Dr 53095
Church Dr 53095
N Church Rd 53090
S Church Rd 53095
Cindy Place Rd 53090
Claire Pl 53095
Clarence Ct 53095
Clear View Dr 53090
Clover Ct 53095
Cloverview St 53095
Club Ln 53090
Cobblestone Pl 53095
Colleen Ln 53095
Colt Cir 53090
Columbia Pl 53095
Commerce St 53090
Concord Ct & Ln 53095
Congress Dr 53095
Congress St 53090
Conifer Ave 53090
Connie Dr 53090
Continental Dr 53095
Corporate Center Dr 53095
Cortland Ln 53095
Cottonwood Ct 53095
Country Creek Cir 53095
Country View Ln 53090
County Rd W 53090
County D 53090
County G 53095
County Hwy Nn 53095
County Road A 53090
County Road B 53090
County Road C 53095
County Road D 53090
County Road G 53095
County Road H 53090
County Road M
500-899 53090
County Road M
4900-6499 53095
6500-7699 53090
County Road My 53090
County Road Nn 53095
County Road P S 53095
County Road Pv 53095
County Road Ww 53090
County Road Xx 53090
County Road Y 53095
County Road Z 53095
Courtland Pl 53095
Covey Pl 53090
Creek Dr & Rd 53090
Creekside Dr & Pl 53095
Creekwood Dr & Ln 53095
Crestview Dr 53095
Crestwood Rd 53095
Crocus Ct 53095
Crystal Ln 53095
Curtis Ln 53090
Daisy Dr 53090
Daisy Lane Cir 53095
Dandelion Ln 53090
Davids Vw W 53090
Debbie Ln 53095
Decker Dr 53090
Decorah Rd 53095
Deer Creek Ln 53095
Deer Ridge Dr 53095
Deer View Ct 53095
Deerfield Dr 53090
Dennis Path 53090
Devonshire Ln 53095
Diane Dr 53090
Division Rd 53095
Division St 53090
Dollar Dr 53095
Dove Cir 53090
Dricken Ln 53090
Dubin Cir 53090
Dunst Dr 53095
Eagle Ln 53095
E & W Eagle Ridge Dr 53095
Eagles Ct 53095
Earl Stier Dr 53095
East Ave 53095
Eastern Ave 53095
Eastwood Ct & Trl 53090
Easy St 53090
Edelweiss Ln 53090
Eden Ct & Dr 53095
Eder Ln 53095
Edge O Woods Dr 53095
Edgewater Dr 53095
Edgeway Dr 53095
Edgewood Ln 53095
Edward Ct 53095
Elder Dr 53090
Elderberry St 53095
Elm Dr & St 53095
Elma Way 53095
Emerald St 53095
Enge Dr 53090
Enterprise St 53095
Erin Ct 53095
Esker Dr 53095
Esker Park Ct 53095
Evergreen Dr & St 53095
Fair St 53090
Fairfield Ct, Dr & Ln 53090
Fairview Dr 53090
Fairway Ln 53090
Fairy Chasm Rd 53095
Faith Ln 53095
Fieldstone Ct 53095
Finch Ln 53090
Firethorn Dr 53090
Fond Du Lac St 53090
Fontana Rd 53095
N & S Forest Ave 53095
Forest View Dr 53090
Forest View Rd
5500-5599 53095
7300-7899 53090
Forseth Ct 53090
Fox Hunter Ct 53090
Foxland Pl 53095
Foxtail Ct 53095
Franklin Pl 53095
Franklin St 53090
Frederick Pl 53090
Frontier Ct 53095
Fullpail Ln 53095
Gadow Ln 53090
Garden Ln 53095
Garret Dr 53090
Gateway Ct 53095
Gatewood 53095
Gehl Way 53095
George Ct 53095
German Village Rd 53095
Gilbert Cir 53095
Glacier Dr 53090
Glacier Trl 53095
Glen Ct
1300-1399 53090
6300-6499 53095
Glen Ivy Dr 53095
Glen View Cir & Pkwy 53095
Glenway Ct 53095
Glenway Dr 53095
N Glenwood Cir 53095
Goldcrest Ct 53095
Goldenrod Cir 53095
Golf Ct 53095
Golfview Dr 53095
Gonring Dr 53095
Good Luck Ln 53090
Gorman Way 53095
Grant Pl 53090
Granville Rd 53095
Grasser Dr 53095
Gravel Dr 53095
Great Forest Dr 53095
E & W Green Lake Dr 53090
Green Tree Rd 53095
Green Valley Pl 53095
Greenbriar Ct 53095
Greenway Ct & Ln 53095
Hacker Dr 53095
Hans St 53090
Harbor Ct 53090
Hargrove Pl & St 53095
Harrison Ct & St 53090
Hawkeye Dr 53095
Hawthorn Dr & Ln 53095
W Hawthorne Dr 53090
Hazelnut Ct 53095
Hazelwood Ct 53095
Heather Dr 53095
W Heights Ct 53095
Hemlock St 53090
Heron Dr 53095
Hi Mount Rd 53095
Hickory Ln 53095
Hickory Rd 53090
Hickory St 53095
Hickory Hill Dr 53090
Hickory Knoll Dr 53095
Hidden Fields Dr 53095
Hidden Forest Pl 53090
Hidden Waters Cir 53095
Hideaway Cir 53090
High St 53090
High Point Cir 53090
High Ridge Trl 53095
Highland Dr 53090
Highlandview Dr 53095
Highview Dr & Rd 53090
Highway 33 53095
Highway 45 53090
Hillcrest Dr 53095
Hillcrest Ln 53090
Hillcrest St 53095
Hillside Dr & Rd 53095
Hilltop Dr 53095
Hollow Cir 53090
Holly Ln
4400-4499 53090
6000-6099 53095
Home Dr 53095
Homestead Ct & Dr 53090
Horizon Ct 53095
Hron Rd 53095
Humar St 53095
Hummingbird Ct 53090
Hwy 33 53095
Idlewood Ave 53095
Imperial Ct 53095
S Indian Lore Ct & Rd 53090
N Indiana Ave 53090
S Indiana Ave 53095
Indiana Ct 53095
Ivy Pl 53095
Jackson Dr 53095
Jackson St 53090
Jacob Rd 53095
Jacqueline Dr 53095
James Ct 53095
Jamestown Ct, Dr & Pl 53090
Janet Pl 53095
Jansen Dr N 53090
Janz Dr 53095
Jay Rd 53090
Jay St 53095
Jeanellen Rd 53090
Jefferson St 53090
Jills Ct 53090
Jim Henry Rd 53095
John Ct 53090
Joshua Dr 53090
Joshua Ln 53095
Jubilee Ave 53095
Judith Ct 53095
Julen Cir 53095
Juniper Ct & Ln 53095
Kaelin Ln 53095
Kathryn Ln 53095
Kenny Dr 53095
Kettle Ct 53090
Kettle Moraine Dr 53090
Kettle Round St 53090
Kettle View Dr S 53090
Kevin Dr 53090
E & W Kilbourn Ave 53095
Kilkenny Ct 53095
Killarney Ct 53095
Killdeer Ct 53095
Kingfisher Dr 53095
Kings Ct 53095
Kings Ridge Ct E & W 53090
Kinross Ct 53095
Knollwood Rd 53095
Kohler Dr 53090
Koller Ln 53090
Kristine Ln 53095
Kueffner Ct 53095
N & S Kuester Ln 53090
Lagoon Ln 53095
Lake Dr 53095
Lakehaven Ct & Dr 53090
Lakeridge Ct 53090
Lakeview Rd 53090
Lang St 53090
Larkfield Dr 53095
Larkspur Ln 53090
Laurel Dr N & S 53095
Lee Ave 53090
Legion Cir 53090
Lenora Ct & Dr 53090
Lenwood Dr 53090
Lighthouse Ln 53090
Lilac Ln 53095
Lily Ave 53090
Lily Rd 53095
Lime Ridge Rd 53095
Lincoln Dr E, N, S & W 53095
Linda Dr 53090
Linden Ct 53095
E Linden Dr 53095
W Linden Dr 53095
Linden St 53090
Linwood Ter 53095
Little Cedar Ln 53095
Lockhorn Cir 53090
Locust Dr & St 53095
Lois Ln 53095
Longmeadow Dr 53095
Loretta Ln 53090
Lorrin Pl 53095
Lovers Lane Rd 53090
Lower Forest Ct 53090
Lower Woodford Cir 53090
Macintosh Ct 53095
Madison Ave 53095
Main St 53090
N Main St
100-338 53095
340-398 53095
400-2099 53090
2101-2199 53090
S Main St
100-2499 53095
2501-2999 53095
3400-3599 53095
Maple Rd & St 53095
Maple Dale Rd 53090
Maple Grove Dr 53095
Maple Ridge Ct & Dr 53095
Maplewynde Rd 53095
Marainco Dr 53090
Marcia Ave 53090
Margolis Dr 53095
Marie Ct 53095
Marshal Ct 53090
Martha Ct & Dr 53095
Mary Ln 53090
Mayer St 53090
Mayfield Rd 53095
Mayflower Rd 53090
Mckinley St 53090
Meadow Ct 53095
Meadow Rd 53090
Meadowbrook Dr 53090
Meadowlark Ct & St 53090
Mediterranean Ave 53090
Meehan Cir 53095
Meridian Ave 53095
Metalcraft Rd 53095
Michigan Ave 53095
Midland Ave 53090
Mile View Rd 53095
Mill St
501-599 53095
5700-5799 53090
Miller St 53095
Mint Dr 53090
Minz Park Cir 53095
Mitter Cir 53090
Moll Ct 53090
Monroe St 53090
Moore Ave 53090
E Moraine Hills Dr 53095
Morgan Dr 53095
Morning Glory Dr 53095
Mount Pleasant Dr 53090
Mueller Ln 53095
Mulberry Cir, Ct & Dr E & W 53090
Municipal Dr
100-198 53095
200-300 53095
302-598 53095
3500-3999 53090
6400-6498 53095
Muriel Ln 53090
Nabob Dr 53095
Nener Dr 53095
Newark Dr E 53090
Ney A Ti Ct & Hl 53095
Noah Ln 53090
Norman Dr 53090
North St
400-799 53090
3700-3799 53095
Northvue Ct 53090
Northwestern Ave 53090
Oak Ave 53095
N Oak Rd 53090
S Oak Rd 53095
Oak St 53095
W Oak St 53095
Oak Lodge Rd 53095
Oakfield St 53090
Oakwood Ct 53095
Old Apple Ln 53090
Old Farm Ln 53095
Old Hickory Pl 53095
Old Homestead Dr 53095
Orchard St 53095
Orchard Knoll Dr 53095
Orchard Valley Rd 53090
Oriole Ct 53090
E & W Overlook Cir & Ct 53095
Pamme Ct 53090
Paradise Dr 53095
Paradise Ridge Dr 53095
Park Ave 53090
Park Forest Dr 53090
Parkfield Dr 53090
Parkway Dr 53095
Partridge Ct 53095
Pathfinder Ln 53090
Patricia Dr 53090
Patrick Ct 53095
Pear Tree Ct 53090
Pebble Stone Pl 53095
Peninsula Dr 53095
Pennsylvania Ave 53095
Perresto Dr 53095
Peters Dr 53095
Pheasant Ln 53090
Pine Dr 53095
Pinecrest Ct 53095
Pintail Dr 53095
Plantation Way 53090
Pleasant Dr
600-799 53095
7100-7298 53090
Pleasant Heights Pl 53090
Pleasant Hill Dr 53095
Pleasant Valley Rd 53095
Po St 53095
Point Dr 53095
Polaris St 53095
Pond View Ln 53090
Ponderosa Rd 53095
N Poplar Rd 53090
Poplar St 53095
Prairie Ct & Dr 53095
Primrose Ln 53090
Princeton Pl 53095
E & W Progress Dr 53095
Quaas Dr 53095
Quail Cir
200-398 53095
201-239 53090
241-399 53090
Quietwood Ln 53090
Rail Pl & Way 53095
Rainbow Lake Ln 53090
Raintree Ln 53090

Raven St 53090
Ravine Forest Dr 53090
Rawhide Dr 53090
Red Cedar Ct 53095
Red Fox Ln 53095
Red Pine Ct 53090
Redwood St 53095
Reeds Dr 53095
Regent Pl 53090
Reuter Ln 53090
Rhynie Ct 53095
Richards Pl 53095
Ridge Rd
501-597 53095
599-699 53095
2900-3099 53095
Ridgewood Dr 53095
Riesch Rd 53095
River Ct 53095
River Dr N
2100-6998 53090
1753-1799 53095
W River Dr 53090
N River Rd
208-298 53095
400-7299 53090
S River Rd 53095
Rivershores Dr 53090
Riverview Dr & Pl 53095
Riverwood Ln 53095
Road 2 53095
Road 2a 53095
Robin St 53090
Rock Ridge Rd 53095
Rockingham Ct 53090
Rolfs Ave 53090
Rolling Ridge Dr 53090
Roosevelt Dr 53090
Royal Dr 53090
Rusco Dr 53095
Rustic Rd 53090
Ryan Ct 53095
Sagewood Cir 53095
Saint Augustine Rd 53095
N Salisbury Rd & St N 53090
Sand Dr 53095
Sandalwood Ave 53095
Sandra Ln 53095
Sandur Pl 53095
E Sandy Acre Ct, Dr & Rd 53090
Sandy Knoll Ct 53090
Scenic Dr 53095
Scenic Dr E
401-497 53090
499-799 53090
6300-6499 53095
Scenic Dr W 53095
Schloemer Dr 53095
Schmidt Rd 53090
Schneider Ct 53095
Schoenhaar Dr 53090
School Pl 53090
School Rd 53095
Schuster Dr 53090
Scott Ln 53095
Senior Dr 53095
Shadowood Cir 53095
Shady Lane Rd 53090
Shalom Dr 53090
Shepherds Dr 53090
Sheridan Dr 53095
Sherman Way 53090
Sherwood Pl 53090
S Shore Ave 53095
Shore Ln 53090
Silver Lake Dr 53095
N Silverbrook Dr
100-198 53095
400-798 53090
800-999 53095
1001-1199 53090
S Silverbrook Dr 53095
Silverwood Pl 53090
Singing Hill Rd 53090
Sky Ct 53095
Skyline Dr 53090
Sleeping Dragon Rd 53095
Sleepy Hollow Dr 53090
Smith Lake Rd 53090
South St 53095
Southview Cir & Ct 53090
Southwood Trl 53090
Spaeth Ct 53095
Sportsman Ln 53090
Spring Ct 53095
Spring Dr 53095
Spring Rd 53095
Spring St 53090
Spruce St 53090
Squire Ln 53090
St Anthony Rd 53090
Stand Hill Cir 53090
Stanford Ln 53090
Starlite Dr 53095
State Road 144 53095
State Road 144 N 53090
Steeple Ln 53090
Steeple View Rd 53095
Stirling Ct 53095
Stockhausen Ln 53095
Stonebridge Cir & Rd 53095
Stonefield Ct 53090
Stonewood Cir 53095
Stoney Creek Ct & Rd 53095
Stratford Rd 53090
Sumac Dr 53090
Summer St 53090
Summerhill Ave 53095
W Summit Cir 53090
Summit Ct 53095
Summit Dr 53095
Sundance Ln 53090
Sunflower Ave 53090
Sunnydale Cir 53090
Sunset Dr 53095
W Sunset Ridge Dr 53090
Sunset View Dr 53095
Susan Dr 53090
Susan Lee Ct 53090
Sycamore St 53095
Sylvan Way 53095
Tamarack Ct, Dr & Trl E & W 53095
Taylor Ln 53090
Terrace Dr 53095
Terry Dale Ct & Dr 53095
Terry Jak Dr 53090
Thekla Ln 53095
Thoma Park Dr 53095
Timber Ct 53095
Timberline Dr 53095
Timblin Dr 53090
Timmer Bay Rd 53095
Tolbert Ln 53090
Tomahawk Dr 53090
Tower Dr & Ln 53090
Town Line Rd 53090
Townline Rd 53095
Trackett Dr 53095
Trading Post Trl 53090
Tree Ln 53090
Trenton Rd
100-299 53095
6500-6799 53090
N Trenton Rd 53090
Trillium Ct 53095
Tumbleweed Ave & Cir 53095
Tuscola Ln 53095
Uncle Dicks Rd 53095
University Dr 53095
Upper Forest Ln 53090
Upper Woodford Cir 53090
Valley Ave 53095
Valley Rd 53090
Valley Trl 53095
Vern St 53090
Veterans Ave
100-198 53095
201-299 53095
501-599 53090
Victoria Dr & St 53090
Villa Park Ct & Dr 53090
Village Dr 53095
Village Green Way 53090
Vine Pl & St 53095
Vivian Ct 53090
Vogt Dr 53095
Wagner Ln 53095
N & S Wallace Lake Dr & Rd 53090
Walnut St 53095
Walsh Acres Dr 53095
Walters Dr 53090
E & W Washington Ct, Dr & St 53095
Water St 53095
Watercress Cir 53095
Wausaukee Rd 53095
Wayne Dr 53095
Wayne Rd 53090
Weatherstone Ct 53090
Webster Pl 53095
Weinert Rd 53095
Wellington Dr 53090
Werner Rd 53090
Weslyn Ct 53095
Western Ct & Pl 53095
Westminster Ct 53095
Westridge Dr 53095
Westview Rd 53090
Westwood Trl 53090
Wheat Ridge Ln 53095
Whispering Pines Dr 53095
White Sands Ct 53090
White Swan Dr 53095
Whitetail Trl 53095
Whitewater Dr 53095
Wickert Dr 53095
Wilderness Dr 53095
Wildflower Dr 53095
Wildwood Rd 53090
William Tell Dr 53095
Williams Ct 53090
Willow Ln 53095
Willow Switch Ct 53090
Willowbrook Dr 53090
Wilson Ave 53090
Windsor Pl 53090
Wingate Cir 53090
Wingate Ct 53090
Wingate Ln E 53090
Wingate Ln W 53090
Wingate St 53095
Winter Dr 53090
Wisconsin St 53095
Wolcott St 53090
Wolf Dr 53090
Wood Way 53090
Wood Duck Way 53095
Wood River Ct 53095
N & S Woodcrest Ridge Dr 53095
Woodford Dr 53090
Woodhaven Dr 53095
Woodhill Ct 53095
Woodland Dr 53095
Woodland Ln 53090
Woodland Smt 53095
Woodlawn Ave 53090
Woodridge Rd 53095
Worthington Ct 53090
Wurbro Dr 53090

NUMBERED STREETS

S 2nd Ave 53095
S 3rd Ave 53095
S 5th Ave 53095
N & S 6th 53095
N & S 7th 53095
N 8th Ave 53095
N 8th Ave
400-1299 53090
S 8th Ave 53095
N 9th Ave
100-200 53095
400-1299 53090
S 9th Ave 53095
N 10th Ave
100-300 53095
401-1097 53090
1099-1599 53090
S 10th Ave 53095
N 11th Ave 53090
S 11th Ave 53095
N 12th Ave 53090
S 12th Ave 53095
N 13th Ave 53090
N 14th Ave 53090
S 14th Ave 53095
N & S 15th 53095
N & S 16th 53095
S 17th Ave 53095
N 18th Ave 53095
500-1899 53090
S 18th Ave 53095

WISCONSIN RAPIDS WI

General Delivery 54494

POST OFFICE BOXES MAIN OFFICE STATIONS AND BRANCHES

Box No.s
All PO Boxes 54495

NAMED STREETS

Abby Ln 54494
Acorn Trl 54494
Adams Ave 54494
Ahles Ave 54494
Airport Ave 54494
Airport Hanger Dr 54494
Alder St 54494
Alkar Ave 54494
Alpine Way 54494
Altman Ct & Rd 54495
Alton St 54495
Amandale Way 54495
Amundson St 54494
Angle Dr 54494
Antler Trl 54494
Apple St 54494
Apricot St 54494
Arbor Ln 54494
Arbor Haven Ln 54494
Arbutus Dr 54494
Ash St 54494
Ashbury Dr 54494
Auburn Ave 54494
Avon St 54494
Badger Ave 54494
Badger Trl 54495
Bain Cir 54494
Bainbridge Trl 54494
Baker Dr & St 54494
Balsam Cir 54494
Baltic Dr 54494
Bambi Ln 54494
Barberry Cir & Dr 54494
Barbon Dr 54494
Bassett Pl 54494
Batavia Ave 54494
Bauer St 54494
N Beach Rd 54494
Bear St 54494
Beaver St 54494
Bell Rd 54494
Belle Isle 54494
Bellview Dr 54494
Ben Franklin Dr 54494
Big Oak Rd 54495
Big Timber Cir & Dr 54494
Birch Ave & St 54494
Biron Dr E 54494
Black Forest Dr 54494
Black Oak Cir 54495
Blue Heron Ln 54494
Blue Iris Ct 54494
Blue Ridge Ln 54494
Blue Violet Ln 54494
Blueberry Ln 54494
Bluebird Ln 54494
Bluejay Dr 54494
Bob O Link Cir & Ct 54494
Bohn Dr 54494
Boles Cir & St 54495
Bonow Ave 54495
Boone Cir 54495
Bornbach Rd 54494
Boulder Cir 54494
Bradford Ct 54494
Brahms Way 54494
Brahmstead Cir 54494
Branding Iron Ct 54494
Branwood Dr 54494
Breckenridge Ct 54494
Breezy Pine Dr 54494
Brenda Ln 54494
Brentwood Dr 54494
Brianwood Ave 54494
Brickyard Rd 54495
Bridle Path 54494
Bristol Ct 54494
Broadway St 54494
Bronson Rd 54495
Brooke Ln 54494
Brookhaven Trce 54494
Brookshire Ct 54494
Brookside Cir 54494
Brookwood Ln 54494
Brostowitz Rd 54495
Brown St 54495
Bruce Ln 54494
Buchberger Rd 54494
Buck Trl 54494
Buena Vista Rd 54494
Buffalo St 54494
Burns Dr 54494
Burt St 54494
Butler St 54495
Cama Dr 54494
Canal St 54495
Cape Vista Dr 54494
Cardinal St 54494
Carey St 54495
Carillon Dr 54494
Carousel Ct 54494
Carriage Ct 54494
Carson Cir 54495
Case Ave 54494
Cedar Ln 54494
Center St 54495
Chapel Rd 54495
Chardonay Ln 54495
Chase St 54495
Cherokee Cir, Ct & Rd 54494
Cherry St 54494
Cherrywood Ct 54494
Chestnut St 54494
Church Ave 54494
Cindy Ct 54494
N & S Circle Dr 54494
Clark St 54495
Cleveland St 54495
Cliff St 54494
Clyde Ave 54494
Coach Lantern Dr 54494
Commerce Dr 54494
Condo Dr 54495
Cook Ave 54494
Corey Ave 54494
Cottontail Trl 54494
Country Cir, Ct, Dr & Ln 54494
Country Village Dr 54494
County Rd S 54495
County Rd W 54494
County Road C 54495
County Road D 54495
County Road F
101-2697 54494
2699-3999 54494
4900-5000 54495
5001-5099 54494
5002-6898 54495
5101-6899 54495
County Road Ff 54494
County Road Hh 54495
County Road Q 54495
County Road U 54494
County Road Ww 54494
County Road Z 54494
Court St 54494
Cove Trl 54494
Cranberry Ln 54495
Cranberry Rd 54494
Crest Ridge Ct 54494
Crestwood Ct 54494
Crockett Ln 54495
Crystal Ln 54494
Crystal Brooke Ct 54494
Crystal Creek Ct 54494
Curve St 54494
D St 54494
Dakota Ct 54494
Dale St 54494
Daly Ave 54494
David Dr 54494
Davis Ave 54494
Deer Ave 54495
Deer Ln 54495
Deer Rd 54494
Deer St 54494
Deer Ridge Rd 54494
Dewberry Ln 54494
Dewey St 54494
Dove Ave 54494
Dover Ct 54494
Downing St 54494
Drake St 54494
Dry Creek Trl 54494
Duck Creek Ln 54494
Dura Beauty Ln 54495
Eagle Rd 54494
Eagle Nest Rd 54494
East Ln 54495
Eastwood Dr 54494
Edgewood Pl 54495
Elm Rd 54495
Elm St 54494
Elm Lake Ln 54495
Elmhurst Rd 54495
Enchanted Dr & Ln 54494
Engel Rd 54495
Engler Dr 54495
English Oak Dr 54495
Ervin Rd 54495
Esox Trl 54494
Essex St 54495
Estates Dr 54494
Evergreen Ave & Ln 54494
Fairview Ln 54494
Fairway Cir 54494
Falcon Ct 54494
Finup Ln 54495
Fisher Rd 54495
Forest Ln 54494
Forest Ridge Ln 54495
Forestview Dr 54494
Fountain Ave 54495
Four Mile Ln 54494
Fox Run Dr 54494
Franklin St 54495
Freedom Trl 54495
Fremont St 54495
E G St 54494
Gardner St 54495
Garfield St 54494
Gaynor Ave 54494
Genes Ct 54494
Geneva Ct 54494
George Rd 54495
Ghilloni Rd 54495
Gilbertson Ct 54494
Ginger Trl 54494
Glenwood Hts & Rd 54494
Goggins St 54495
Golden Pheasant Ct 54494
Golf Course Rd 54494
Goodnow Ave 54494
E Grand Ave
100-398 54494
320-326 54495
400-1499 54494
W Grand Ave 54495
Grand Forest Dr 54494
Grant St 54494
Grassmere Dr 54494
Greeler Ln 54494
Green Bay St 54495
Greenfield Ave 54495
Greenwood Dr 54494
Griffith Ave 54494
Grouse Trl 54494
Grove Ave 54494
Haferman Rd 54495
Hafermann Hts 54495
Hagen St 54495
Hale St 54495
Hamann Ave 54494
Hampton Ct 54494
Hanks Ln 54495
Harrison St 54495
Hasa Ln 54494
Hazelnut Trl 54494
Heiser Ln 54495
Helke Rd 54494
Hemlock Trl 54495
Henke Rd 54495
Heritage Trl 54495
Heritage Ridge Dr 54494
Hetze Rd 54495
High St 54495
High Point Ct 54494
Highland Ave 54494
Hill St 54494
Hobnail Ct 54494
Honeysuckle Ct & Ln 54494
Huffman Rd 54494
Hunters Ridge Dr 54494
Huntington Ave 54494
Hurley St 54495
Industrial Ct & St 54495
Irving St 54494
E Jackson St 54494
W Jackson St 54495
James Ct 54494
Jayne Ln 54494
Jefferson St 54495
Johnson Ave 54494
Johnson Pkwy 54494
Johnson St 54495
Juniper Ln 54494
Kahoun Rd 54494
Kauth Dr 54494
Kaye Rd 54495
Keen Ln 54495
Kellner Rd 54494
Kester Rd 54494
Kingston Rd 54494
Kirkwood Cir 54495
Klevene Cir 54494
Knuth Rd 54495
Kruger Rd 54495
Kuhn Ave 54494
Lake Ave, Dr & Rd 54494
Lakeview Dr 54494
Lakewood Ln 54494
Larry Ave 54494
Larrys Ct 54494
Larson Ave 54494
Latvia Ave 54494
Lee St 54494
Lenox Ave 54495
Leonard Rd 54495
Lexus Ln 54494
Lilac Trl 54494
Lily Ln 54494
Lincoln St 54494
Lisa Ln 54494
Locust St 54494

Log Home Ln 54494
Lone Pine Rd 54495
Lonesome Rd 54495
Love St 54494
Lovewood Dr 54494
Lundberg Rd 54495
Lynwood Ct 54495
Lyon St 54495
Madison Cir & St 54494
Magnolia Dr 54494
Mai Chee Trl 54494
Main St S 54494
Majestic Trl 54494
Manhattan Dr 54494
Manor Ln 54495
Maple St 54494
Maple Manor Dr 54494
Mapledale Ct 54494
Maria Dr 54494
Marie Cir 54494
Marigold Ave 54495
Market St 54494
Marsh Rd 54495
Martin Rd 54495
Mattheis Rd 54495
May St 54495
Maywood Ct 54495
Mckinley St 54495
Mckinney Ln 54494
Mead Cir & St 54494
Meadow Ln 54494
Meadowlark Ln 54494
Menominee St 54495
Metcalf Pl 54494
Michael Ct 54494
Midas Ct 54494
Mill Ave & Rd 54494
Miller Ave 54494
Mohawk St 54494
Moll Rd 54494
Monroe St 54494
Moon Ct 54494
Moyer St 54495
Mulberry Cir 54494
Murwin Cir 54494
Nash Rd 54495
Natures Way 54494
Needles Ln 54494
Neitzel Rd 54495
Nelson Ln 54495
Nepco Lake Rd 54494
Nordstrum Rd 54495
Norpine St 54494
North Ave & Rd 54495
Northstar Ct 54494
Norton St 54494
Norway Cir 54494
Nuber Rd 54495
Oak Ln 54495
Oak St 54494
Oak Brook Ct 54495
Oak Leaf Cir 54495
W Oak Ridge Rd 54494
Oakbrook Ct 54494
Oakbury Dr 54494
Oday Cir 54494
Old Trl 54494
Oliver St 54494
Oneida Ave 54495
Oradwarl St 54495
Oriole Ln 54494
Paradise Trl 54494
Park Ave 54495
S Park Dr 54494
N Park Rd 54494
S Park Rd 54494
Parkland Ln 54494
Parkway Ct 54494
Parkwood Dr 54494
Patrick Henry Ct 54494
Paul Revere Ct 54494
Payne St 54495
Peaceful Trl 54494
Peach St 54494
Pear St 54494
Pelot Ln 54495
Pepper Ave 54494
Peterson Ave 54494
Petes Ln 54494
Pickens Trl 54494
Piltz Ave 54494
Pine Ave 54494
Pine Ln 54495
Pine Rd 54495
Pine St 54494
Pine Haven Ct 54494
Pine Ridge Trl & Way 54494
Pineway Dr 54494
Piney Ave & Cir 54494
Pioneer Dr 54494
Pioneer Rd 54495
Pixler Ct 54494
Plantation Ct 54494
Pleasant View Dr 54494
Plover Rd & St 54494
Plum St 54494
Point Trl 54494
Point Haven Dr 54494
Pointe Pl 54494
Ponderosa Cir 54494
Poplar St 54494
Port Rd 54495
Port St 54494
Porter Ln 54495
Possum Trl 54494
Prairie Cir 54494
Prairie Ridge Dr 54494
Prairie View Dr 54494
Prospect St 54494
Pryne Rd 54495
Quarry Cir 54495
Quarry Rd 54494
Quinnell Ln 54495
Railroad St 54494
Rangeline Rd 54494
Ranger Rd 54494
Rapids St 54494
Reber Dr 54494
Red Oak Cir 54495
Reddin Rd 54495
Rhapsody Rd 54494
Richland Cv 54494
Richland Heights Ct 54494
Richland Hills Dr 54494
Ridge Rd 54495
Ridgeview Ct & Ln 54494
Ridgeway Trl 54494
Ridgewood Trl 54494
Ringer Ln 54495
River Birch Ln 54494
River Ridge Rd 54494
River Run Dr 54494
Riverview Dr 54494
E Riverview Expy 54494
W Riverview Expy 54495
Riverwood Ln 54494
Robbin Rd 54495
Robin Cir 54494
Robinson St 54495
Rockwood Ct 54495
Rose St 54495
Rosebury Dr 54494
Rosecrans St 54495
Rosemary Cir 54494
Rosewood Ave & Rdg 54494
Round Oak Ct 54495
Rounds Round 54494
Ruby Ave 54494
Rude St 54494
Russell St 54495
Ryans Way 54494
Saint Johns Rd 54495
Sampson St 54494
Sandy Rd 54495
Sarah Cir 54494
Saratoga St 54494
School Rd 54495
Schroeder Dr 54494
Schudy Rd 54495
Searles Rd 54495
Seneca Rd 54495
Sequoia Cir 54494
Seven Mile Trl 54494
Shady Ln 54494
Shady Forest Ln 54494
Shady Oak Cir 54495
Shady Pines Ave 54494
Shamrock Ln 54494
Sheila Ln 54494
Sherri Ct & Ln 54494
Sherwood Ct 54494
S Shore 54494
Shore Acres Dr 54494
Shorewood Ter 54494
Siesta Cir 54494
Silver Creek Trl 54494
Silver Fox Ct 54494
Smith Ln 54495
Smith St 54494
Snyder St 54494
Southbrook Ln 54494
Southpark Rd 54494
Sparks Ave 54494
Spencer St 54495
Spring St 54494
Springwood Ct & Dr 54494
Spruce Ave, Ln & St 54494
Squirrel Trl 54494
State Highway 13 S 54494
State Highway 13/34 54495
State Highway 173 54495
State Highway 54 E 54494
State Highway 54 W 54495
State Highway 73 54495
State Highway 73 S 54494
State Highway 80 54495
S Strawberry Ln 54494
Strodman Ave 54494
Sunrise Ln 54494
Sunset Strip 54494
Swanson Rd 54495
Sweat Ave 54494
Swedish Rd 54495
Swiggum Ln 54495
Tamarack Trl 54494
Tanglewood Trl 54494
Taylor Ave & Ln 54494
Ten Mile Ave 54494
Tenpas Rd 54495
Thalacker Ave 54494
Thousand Oaks Rd 54494
Timber Valley Dr 54494
Timber Wolfe Ct 54494
Timberland Trl 54494
Timberline Ct & Way 54494
Timm Ave 54494
Tower Rd 54494
Town Hall Rd 54495
Townline Rd 54494
Township Ave 54494
Toy Rd 54495
Travis Dr 54495
Tredalea St S 54494
Trout Trl 54494
Two Mile Ave 54494
E, S, W & N Valley Ct & Dr 54494
Van Slate St 54494
Vanburen St 54495
Vans Rd 54495
Viaduct Ave 54495
Victorian Ct & Way 54494
Wall St 54494
Warren Ct & Dr 54494
Washington St 54494
Wazeecha Ave 54494
Wazeecha Ridge Ct 54494
Webb Ave 54494
Wedgewood Cir 54494
Weeping Willow Cir, Ct & Dr 54494
Weslan Dr 54494
Westwood Dr 54494
Whip Or Will Ln 54494
Whispering Pines Ln 54494
White Pine Cir, Ct & Dr 54494
Whitrock Ave 54494
Wickham Ave 54495
Wilderness Ln 54494
Wildwood Dr 54494
Williams St 54494
Winding Trl 54494
Winnebago Ave 54495
Wintergreen Dr 54494
Wisconsin St 54494
Witter St 54494
Wolosek Ave 54494
Wood Ave 54494
Woodbine St 54495
Woodhaven Ct & Ln 54494
Woodland Dr 54494
Woodridge Trce 54495
Woodside Cir 54494
Wyatt Ave 54494
Wylie St 54494
N & S Young St 54494

NUMBERED STREETS

1st Ave N 54495
1st Ave S 54495
1st St N 54494
1st St S 54494
2nd Ave S 54495
2nd St N 54494
2nd St S 54494
3rd Ave N 54495
3rd Ave S 54495
3rd St N 54494
3rd St S 54494
4th Ave N 54495
4th St S 54494
5th Ave N 54495
5th St N 54494
5th St S 54494
6th Ave N 54495
6th Ave S 54494
6th St N 54494
6th St S 54494
7th Ave N 54495
7th Ave S 54495
7th Dr 54494
7th St N 54494
7th St S 54494
8th Ave N 54495
8th Ave S 54495
8th St N 54494
8th St S 54494
9th Ave N 54495
9th Ave S 54495
9th St N 54494
9th St S 54494
10th Ave N 54495
10th Ave S 54495
10th St N 54494
10th St S 54494
11th Ave N 54495
11th Ave S 54495
11th St N 54494
11th St S 54494
12th Ave N 54495
12th Ave S 54495
12th St N 54494
12th St S 54494
13th Ave N 54495
13th Ave S 54495
13th St N 54494
13th St S 54494
14th Ave N 54495
14th Ave S 54495
14th Pl 54494
14th St N 54494
14th St S 54494
15th Ave N 54495
15th Ave S 54495
15th Pl S 54494
15th St N 54494
15th St S 54494
16th Ave N 54495
16th Ave S 54495
16th St N 54494
16th St S 54494
17th Ave N 54495
17th Ave S 54495
17th St N 54494
17th St S 54494
18th Ave N 54495
18th Ave S 54495
18th St N 54494
18th St S 54494
19th Ave N 54495
19th Ave S 54495
19th St N 54494
19th St S 54494
20th Ave S 54495
20th Pl 54494
20th St N 54494
20th St S 54494
21st Ave N 54495
21st Ave S 54495
21st Pl S 54494
21st St N 54494
22nd Ave S 54495
22nd St N 54494
23rd Ave S 54495
23rd St N 54494
23rd St S 54494
24th Ave S 54495
24th St N 54494
24th St S 54494
25th Ave N 54495
25th Ave S 54495
25th Pl 54494
25th St N 54494
26th Ave S 54495
26th St N 54494
26th St S 54494
27th Ave S 54495
27th St N 54494
27th St S 54494
28th Ave S 54495
28th St N 54494
28th St S 54494
29th Ave N 54495
29th Ave S 54495
29th St N 54494
30th N & S 54494
31st N & S 54494
32nd N & S 54494
33rd St S 54494
35th St S 54494
36th N & S 54494
37th N & S 54494
40th N & S 54494
41st Ct S 54494
42nd N & S 54494
43rd St S 54494
44th Ct & St S 54494
45th Ct & St S 54494
46th St S 54494
47th Ct & St S 54494
48th N & S 54494
49th St S 54494
50th St S 54494
52nd N & S 54494
53rd St S 54494
54th N & S 54494
56th St S 54494
57th St S 54494
58th St S 54494
59th St S 54494
60th St S 54494
61st N & S 54494
62nd St S 54494
63rd St S 54494
64th N & S 54494
66th St S 54494
67th St S 54494
68th St S 54494
69th St S 54494
70th St S 54494
71st Ct & St S 54494
72nd N & S 54494
73rd St S 54494
74th St S 54494
75th St S 54494
76th St S 54494
77th St S 54494
78th St S 54494
80th N & S 54494
82nd Ct & St S 54494
83rd St S 54494
84th N & S 54494
85th St S 54494
86th St S 54494
87th St S 54494
88th St S 54494
90th N & S 54494
91st St S 54494
93rd St S 54494
94th St S 54494
95th N & S 54494
100th N & S 54494
110th St S 54494
130th St S 54494

Wyoming

People QuickFacts	Wyoming	USA
Population, 2013 estimate	582,658	316,128,839
Population, 2010 (April 1) estimates base	563,626	308,747,716
Population, percent change, April 1, 2010 to July 1, 2013	3.4%	2.4%
Population, 2010	563,626	308,745,538
Persons under 5 years, percent, 2013	6.6%	6.3%
Persons under 18 years, percent, 2013	23.6%	23.3%
Persons 65 years and over, percent, 2013	13.5%	14.1%
Female persons, percent, 2013	49.0%	50.8%
White alone, percent, 2013 (a)	92.7%	77.7%
Black or African American alone, percent, 2013 (a)	1.7%	13.2%
American Indian and Alaska Native alone, percent, 2013 (a)	2.6%	1.2%
Asian alone, percent, 2013 (a)	0.9%	5.3%
Native Hawaiian and Other Pacific Islander alone, percent, 2013 (a)	0.1%	0.2%
Two or More Races, percent, 2013	1.9%	2.4%
Hispanic or Latino, percent, 2013 (b)	9.7%	17.1%
White alone, not Hispanic or Latino, percent, 2013	84.1%	62.6%
Living in same house 1 year & over, percent, 2008-2012	81.8%	84.8%
Foreign born persons, percent, 2008-2012	3.2%	12.9%
Language other than English spoken at home, pct age 5+, 2008-2012	6.8%	20.5%
High school graduate or higher, percent of persons age 25+, 2008-2012	92.1%	85.7%
Bachelor's degree or higher, percent of persons age 25+, 2008-2012	24.3%	28.5%
Veterans, 2008-2012	51,203	21,853,912
Mean travel time to work (minutes), workers age 16+, 2008-2012	18.5	25.4
Housing units, 2013	265,438	132,802,859
Homeownership rate, 2008-2012	70.3%	65.5%
Housing units in multi-unit structures, percent, 2008-2012	16.1%	25.9%
Median value of owner-occupied housing units, 2008-2012	$184,400	$181,400
Households, 2008-2012	221,479	115,226,802
Persons per household, 2008-2012	2.48	2.61
Per capita money income in past 12 months (2012 dollars), 2008-2012	$28,858	$28,051
Median household income, 2008-2012	$56,573	$53,046
Persons below poverty level, percent, 2008-2012	11.0%	14.9%

Business QuickFacts	Wyoming	USA
Private nonfarm establishments, 2012	20,635	7,431,808
Private nonfarm employment, 2012	214,241	115,938,468
Private nonfarm employment, percent change, 2011-2012	2.8%	2.2%
Nonemployer establishments, 2012	46,103	22,735,915
Total number of firms, 2007	61,179	27,092,908
Black-owned firms, percent, 2007	0.2%	7.1%
American Indian- and Alaska Native-owned firms, percent, 2007	0.8%	0.9%
Asian-owned firms, percent, 2007	0.7%	5.7%
Native Hawaiian and Other Pacific Islander-owned firms, percent, 2007	0.0%	0.1%
Hispanic-owned firms, percent, 2007	2.8%	8.3%
Women-owned firms, percent, 2007	25.5%	28.8%
Manufacturers shipments, 2007 ($1000)	8,834,810	5,319,456,312
Merchant wholesaler sales, 2007 ($1000)	6,352,890	4,174,286,516
Retail sales, 2007 ($1000)	8,957,553	3,917,663,456
Retail sales per capita, 2007	$17,114	$12,990
Accommodation and food services sales, 2007 ($1000)	1,469,008	613,795,732
Building permits, 2012	2,110	829,658

Geography QuickFacts	Wyoming	USA
Land area in square miles, 2010	97,093.14	3,531,905.43
Persons per square mile, 2010	5.8	87.4
FIPS Code	56	

(a) Includes persons reporting only one race.
(b) Hispanics may be of any race, so also are included in applicable race categories.
FN: Footnote on this item for this area in place of data
NA: Not available
D: Suppressed to avoid disclosure of confidential information
X: Not applicable
S: Suppressed; does not meet publication standards
Z: Value greater than zero but less than half unit of measure shown
F: Fewer than 100 firms
Source: US Census Bureau State & County QuickFacts

Wyoming

3 DIGIT ZIP CODE MAP

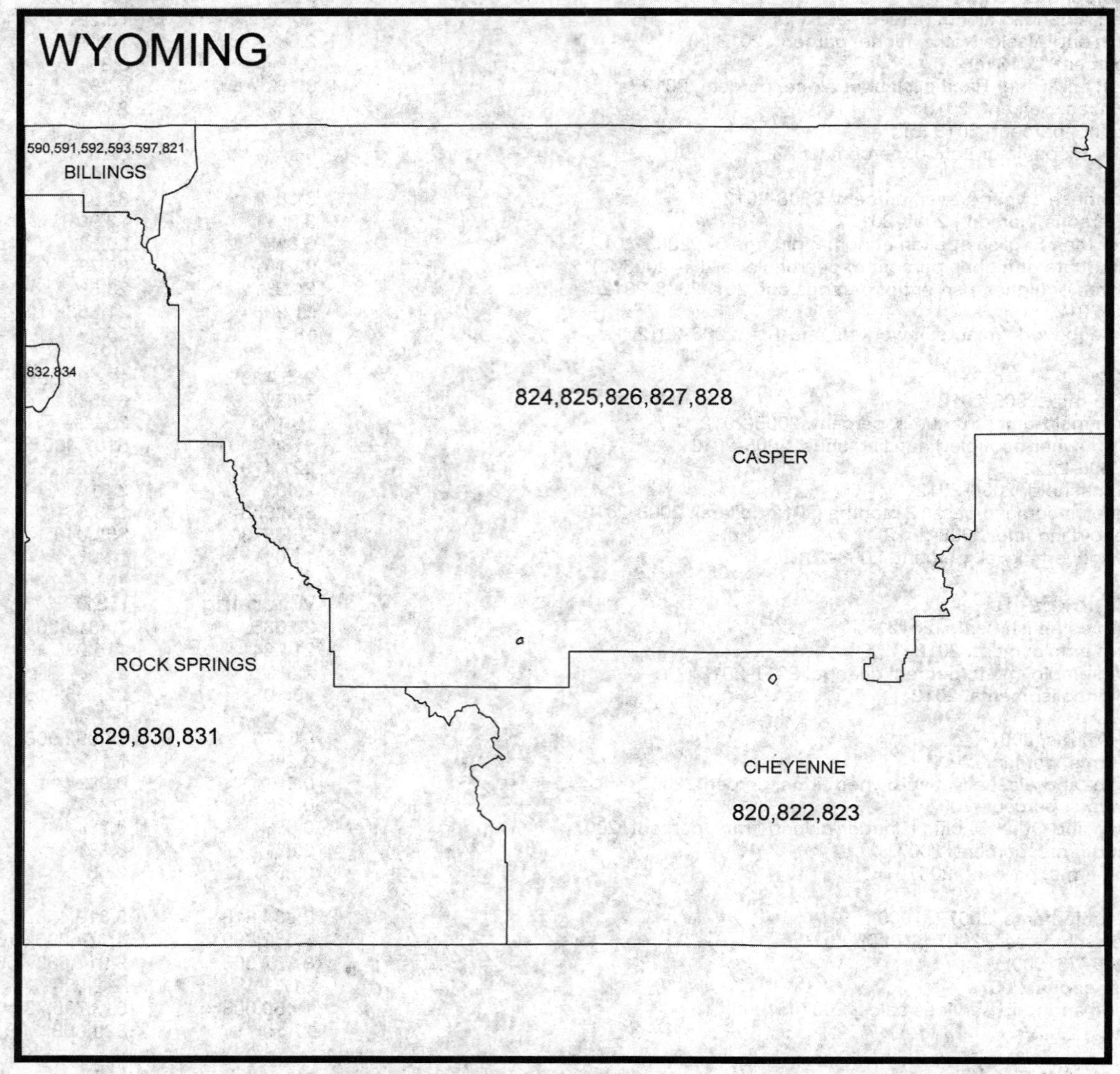

Wyoming

(Abbreviation: WY)

Places with more than one ZIP code are listed in capital letters, See pages indicated.

Post Office, County	ZIP Code
Acme, Sheridan	82839
Afton, Lincoln	83110
Aladdin, Crook	82710
Albin, Laramie	82050
Alcova, Natrona	82620
Allendale, Natrona	82609
Alpine, Lincoln	83128
Alta, Teton	83414
Alva, Crook	82711
Arapahoe, Fremont	82510
Arlington, Albany	82083
Arminto, Natrona	82630
Arvada, Sheridan	82831
Atlantic City, Fremont	82520
Auburn, Lincoln	83111
Baggs, Carbon	82321
Bairoil, Sweetwater	82322
Banner, Sheridan	82832
Bar Nunn (See Casper)	
Basin, Big Horn	82410
Bear River, Uinta	82930
Bedford, Lincoln	83112
Beulah, Crook	82712
Big Horn, Sheridan	82833
Big Piney, Sublette	83113
Bitter Creek, Sweetwater	82901
Bondurant, Sublette	82922
Bordeaux, Platte	82201
Bosler, Albany	82051
Bosler, Albany	82070
Boulder, Sublette	82923
Buffalo, Johnson	82834
Buffalo, Johnson	82840
Buford, Albany	82052
Burlington, Big Horn	82411
Burns, Laramie	82053
Burris, Fremont	82512
Byron, Big Horn	82412
Carlile, Crook	82721
Carpenter, Laramie	82054
CASPER, Natrona (See Page 4380)	
Centennial, Albany	82055
CHEYENNE, Laramie (See Page 4382)	
Chugwater, Platte	82210
Clark, Park	82435
Clearmont, Sheridan	82835
Cody, Park	82414
Cokeville, Lincoln	83114
Cora, Sublette	82925
Cowley, Big Horn	82420
Creston, Carbon	82301
Crowheart, Fremont	82512
Daniel, Sublette	83115
Dayton, Sheridan	82836
Deaver, Big Horn	82421
Devils Tower, Crook	82714
Diamond, Platte	82210
Diamondville, Lincoln	83116
Dixon, Carbon	82323
Douglas, Converse	82633
Dubois, Fremont	82513
Eden, Sweetwater	82932
Edgerton, Natrona	82635
Egbert, Laramie	82053
Elk Mountain, Carbon	82324
Elmo, Carbon	82327
Emblem, Big Horn	82422
Encampment, Carbon	82325
Ethete, Fremont	82520
Etna, Lincoln	83118
EVANSTON, Uinta (See Page 4385)	
Evansville, Natrona	82636
Fairview, Lincoln	83119
Farson, Sweetwater	82932
Fe Warren Afb, Laramie	82001
Fe Warren Afb, Laramie	82005
Fontenelle, Lincoln	83101
Fort Bridger, Uinta	82933
Fort Laramie, Goshen	82212
Fort Steele, Carbon	82301
Fort Washakie, Fremont	82514
Four Corners, Weston	82715
Foxpark (See Laramie)	
Frannie, Park	82423
Freedom, Lincoln	83120
Frontier, Lincoln	83121
Garland, Park	82435
Garrett, Albany	82058
Gas Hills, Fremont	82501
GILLETTE, Campbell (See Page 4385)	
Glendo, Platte	82213
Glenrock, Converse	82637
Granger, Sweetwater	82934
Granite Canon, Laramie	82059
Granite Canyon, Laramie	82059
Green River, Sweetwater	82935
Green River, Sweetwater	82938
Greybull, Big Horn	82426
Grover, Lincoln	83122
Guernsey, Platte	82214
Hamilton Dome, Hot Springs	82443
Hamsfork, Lincoln	83101
Hanna, Carbon	82327
Harriman, Laramie	82059
Hartville, Platte	82215
Hawk Springs, Goshen	82217
Hiland, Natrona	82638
Hillsdale, Laramie	82060
Hoback Junction, Teton	83001
Horse Creek, Laramie	82061
Hudson, Fremont	82515
Hulett, Crook	82720
Huntley, Goshen	82218
Hyattville, Big Horn	82428
Iron Mountain, Laramie	82009
JACKSON, Teton (See Page 4387)	
Jackson Hole (See Jackson)	
Jay Em, Goshen	82219
Jeffrey City, Fremont	82310
Jelm, Albany	82063
Jelm, Albany	82072
Jenny Lake, Teton	83012
Kaycee, Johnson	82639
Keeline, Niobrara	82227
Kelly, Teton	83011
Kemmerer, Lincoln	83101
Kinnear, Fremont	82516
Kirby, Hot Springs	82430
Kirtley, Niobrara	82225
Kortes Dam, Carbon	82327
La Barge, Lincoln	83123
Lagrange, Goshen	82221
Lance Creek, Niobrara	82222
Lander, Fremont	82520
LARAMIE, Albany (See Page 4388)	
Leiter, Sheridan	82837
Leo, Carbon	82327
Linch, Johnson	82640
Lingle, Goshen	82223
Little America, Sweetwater	82929
Lonetree, Uinta	82936
Lost Cabin, Fremont	82642
Lost Springs, Converse	82224
Lovell, Big Horn	82431
Lucky Maccamp, Fremont	82501
Lusk, Niobrara	82225
Lyman, Uinta	82937
Lysite, Fremont	82642
Mammoth Hot Springs, Park	82190
Manderson, Big Horn	82432
Mantua, Park	82435
Manville, Niobrara	82227
Mayoworth, Johnson	82639
Mc Kinnon, Sweetwater	82935
Mc Kinnon, Sweetwater	82938
Mcfadden, Albany	82083
Medicine Bow, Carbon	82329
Meeteetse, Park	82433
Meriden, Laramie	82081
Midval, Fremont	82501
Midwest, Natrona	82643
Mills, Natrona	82604
Mills, Natrona	82644
Moneta, Natrona	82604
Moorcroft, Crook	82721
Moose, Teton	83012
Moran, Teton	83013
Morton, Fremont	82501
Mountain Home, Albany	82072
Mountain View, Uinta	82939
Muddy Gap, Carbon	82301
Natrona, Natrona	82646
New Haven, Crook	82720
Newcastle, Weston	82701
Newcastle, Weston	82715
Node, Niobrara	82225
Opal, Lincoln	83124
Orin, Converse	82633
Osage, Weston	82723
Oshoto, Crook	82721
Otto, Big Horn	82434
Parkerton, Converse	82637
Parkman, Sheridan	82838
Pavillion, Fremont	82523
Piedmont, Uinta	82933
Pine Bluffs, Laramie	82082
Pine Haven, Crook	82721
Pinedale, Sublette	82941
Point Of Rocks, Sweetwater	82942
Powder River, Natrona	82648
Powell, Park	82435
Prairie Center, Goshen	82240
Quealy, Sweetwater	82901
Ralston, Park	82440
Ranchester, Sheridan	82839
Ranchester, Sheridan	82844
Rawlins, Carbon	82301
Rawlins, Fremont	82310
Raymond, Lincoln	83114
Recluse, Campbell	82725
Red Desert, Sweetwater	82336
Reliance, Sweetwater	82943
Riner, Carbon	82301
Riverside, Carbon	82325
Riverton, Fremont	82501
Robertson, Uinta	82944
Rock River, Albany	82058
Rock River, Albany	82083
ROCK SPRINGS, Sweetwater (See Page 4389)	
Rockeagle, Goshen	82223
Rolling Hills, Converse	82637
Rozet, Campbell	82727
Ryan Park, Carbon	82331
Saddlestring, Johnson	82840
Saint Stephens, Fremont	82524
Sand Draw, Fremont	82501
Saratoga, Carbon	82331
Savery, Carbon	82332
Shawnee, Converse	82229
Shell, Big Horn	82441
Sheridan, Sheridan	82801
Shirley Basin, Carbon	82615
Shoshoni, Fremont	82649
Sinclair, Carbon	82334
Slater, Platte	82201
Smoot, Lincoln	83126
South Pass City, Fremont	82520
Star Valley Ranch, Lincoln	83127
Story, Sheridan	82832
Story, Sheridan	82842
Sundance, Crook	82729
Sunrise, Platte	82215
Superior, Sweetwater	82945
Sussex, Johnson	82639
Sweetwater Station, Fremont	82520
Ten Sleep, Washakie	82442
Teton Village, Teton	83025
Thayne, Lincoln	83127
Thermopolis, Hot Springs	82443
Tie Siding, Albany	82084
Tipton, Sweetwater	82336
Torrington, Goshen	82240
Turnerville, Lincoln	83110
Upton, Weston	82730
Urie, Uinta	82937
Uva, Platte	82201
Van Tassell, Niobrara	82242
Veteran, Goshen	82243
Walcott, Carbon	82335
Wamsutter, Sweetwater	82336
Wapiti, Park	82450
Weston, Campbell	82731
Wheatland, Platte	82201
Willwood, Park	82435
Wilson, Teton	83014
Wolf, Sheridan	82844
Worland, Washakie	82401
Worland, Hot Springs	82430
Wright, Campbell	82732
Wyarno, Sheridan	82845
Yellowstone National Park, Park	82190
Yoder, Goshen	82244

CASPER WY

General Delivery 82609

POST OFFICE BOXES MAIN OFFICE STATIONS AND BRANCHES

Box No.s
1 - 3862 ... 82602
4001 - 4998 ... 82604
10100 - 33201 ... 82602
40001 - 40200 ... 82604
44001 - 44403 ... 82602
50001 - 56000 ... 82605

NAMED STREETS

E A St
300-1999 ... 82601
2000-2099 ... 82609
2101-2299 ... 82609
W A St ... 82601
W Abbott St ... 82604
Absaroka Trl ... 82601
Airport Pkwy ... 82604
Alcova Rte ... 82604
Ali Cir ... 82609
Allen Ave ... 82604
W Allen Rd ... 82601
Allendale Blvd ... 82601
Allyson Pl ... 82604
Alpine Dr ... 82601
Alta Vista St ... 82601
Amherst Ave ... 82601
Andrea Ln ... 82609
Andrea St ... 82601
Andy Rd ... 82601
Angus St ... 82609
Antelope Dr ... 82601
Antler Dr ... 82601
Apache Cir ... 82601
Applegate Dr ... 82604
April Ct ... 82609
Arabian Ave ... 82604
Arapahoe Rd ... 82601
Ardon Ln ... 82609
Arrowhead St ... 82604
Arroyo Dr ... 82604
Arts Way ... 82601
Aryn Ln ... 82604
N & S Ash St ... 82601
S Aspen ... 82601
W Aspen ... 82601
Aspen Dr ... 82601
Aspen Ln ... 82604
Aspen Pl ... 82604
Aster St ... 82604
Avon ... 82609
Azalea St ... 82604
E B St
100-150 ... 82601
150-150 ... 82602
600-998 ... 82601
1000-1199 ... 82601
W B St ... 82601
Badger Ave & St ... 82601
Bailey Pl ... 82604
W Balben Rd ... 82601
Barbara St ... 82601
Barnard St ... 82604
Barton Dr ... 82604
S Bates Run ... 82604
Bates Creek Ln, Rd & Rte ... 82604
W Bc St ... 82601
Beatrice St ... 82601
Beaumont Dr ... 82601
Beaver ... 82604
Beaverbrook Dr ... 82604
N & S Beech St ... 82601
Begonia St ... 82604
Bel Vista Dr ... 82601
Bell Ave ... 82604
Bell Valley Rd ... 82604
Bella Vista Dr ... 82601
Bellaire Dr ... 82604
Bello Camino ... 82604
Belmont Dr & Rd ... 82604
Bently Dr ... 82609
Bernadine St ... 82601
Bessemer Bnd & Rd S ... 82604
Bestos Rd ... 82601
N & S Beverly St ... 82609
Big Horn Rd ... 82601
Big Horn St ... 82609
Big Sky Dr ... 82604
Birch St ... 82604
Bishop Rd ... 82604
Bissacca St ... 82604
Black Widow Rd ... 82604
Blackmore Rd ... 82609
Blair Ln ... 82601
Blue Sage Ln ... 82601
Blue Springs Rd ... 82604
Blue Spruce Dr ... 82609
Bobcat ... 82604
Boles Rd ... 82604
Bolton Creek Rd ... 82604
Bon Ave ... 82609
Bonnie Brae St ... 82601
Boot Hill Rd ... 82604
Boots Dr ... 82609
S Boris Kicken Dr ... 82601
Boulder Dr ... 82601
S Boxelder St ... 82604
Boyd Ave ... 82604
Boysen St ... 82604
Brandt Rd ... 82604
Breck Ave ... 82601
Brentwood Dr ... 82604
Bretton Dr ... 82609
Brigham Young St ... 82604
Brighton St ... 82609
Bristol ... 82609
Broken Trail Dr ... 82601
N Brooks Ave ... 82604
Brookview Dr ... 82604
Bruce Ln ... 82601
Bruhn Way ... 82609
Brush Rd ... 82604
Bryan Stock Trl ... 82601
Bryan-Evansville Rd ... 82609
Buck Creek Rd ... 82604
Buckboard Rd ... 82604
Bucknum Cir & Rd ... 82604
Buffalo Run ... 82601
Buffalo St ... 82604
W Buick St ... 82604
Burd Rd ... 82601
Burke Rd ... 82601
E Burlington Ave ... 82601
N Burris Rd ... 82604
Bush Ln ... 82604
S Buthore St ... 82601
By Pass Blvd ... 82601
E C St ... 82601
Caballero Trl ... 82601
Cabin Creek Pl & Rd ... 82604
Cacti Pl ... 82604
W Cactus Ln ... 82604
Calle Bonita ... 82601
Calypso St ... 82604
Camel Back Dr ... 82604
Camellia St ... 82604
Cannon Rd ... 82601
S Cantrell Rd ... 82601
Carbide Trail Rd ... 82604
Cardiff ... 82609
Cardinal Ct ... 82604
Carefree Wind Way ... 82601
Caribou ... 82604
Carmel Dr ... 82604
Carnation St ... 82604
Carriage Ln ... 82609
Cascade Ave ... 82604
Casper St ... 82604
Casper Mountain Rd ... 82601
Castlerock St ... 82601
Cattle Trail Dr ... 82604
Cbs Ct ... 82604
S Cedar St ... 82601
Centennial Ct ... 82609
Centennial Hills Blvd ... 82609
Centennial Village Dr ... 82609
N & S Center St ... 82601
Central Dr ... 82604
W Chalk Creek Rd ... 82604
Chalmers St ... 82604
Chamberlain Rd ... 82604
Chaparral ... 82604
Chapman Pl ... 82604
Charlotte Dr ... 82604
Chase Rd ... 82604
Cheesebrough Way ... 82609
Cheney Loop ... 82609
Cherokee Ln ... 82604
S Cherry St ... 82604
Cheshire St ... 82609
S Chestnut St ... 82601
Cheyenne Trl ... 82601
Chief Washakie Rd ... 82604
Chinook Trl ... 82604
Chippewa Trl ... 82604
Chisolm Trl ... 82601
Choctaw Cir ... 82601
Chuckwagon Rd & Trl ... 82604
Cimarron Cir ... 82604
E & S Circle Dr N & S ... 82601
Circle Drive Rd ... 82604
Clark Rd ... 82604
Claude Creek Rd ... 82609
Clearfork Rd ... 82609
Cleveland St ... 82604
Clifton Ave & Ct ... 82609
Cloud St ... 82609
Clover Rd ... 82604
Clyde ... 82609
Coal Rd ... 82604
Coates Rd ... 82604
Cody Ave ... 82604
S & W Coffman Ave & Ct ... 82604
Cold Springs Rd ... 82604
Coleman Cir ... 82601
N Coleman Ln ... 82601
College Dr ... 82601
E Collins Dr ... 82601
W Collins Dr
100-899 ... 82601
901-999 ... 82601
1000-1299 ... 82601
1301-1499 ... 82604
Colorado Ave ... 82609
Columbia River Rd ... 82604
Columbine Dr ... 82604
E Columbine Dr ... 82601
Comanche Cir ... 82601
Concho Ct ... 82604
N & S Conwell St ... 82601
Coolidge Ave ... 82604
Cornwall St ... 82609
Coronado Dr ... 82609
Cotton Creek Pl ... 82604
Cottontail Ln ... 82604
S Cottonwood St ... 82604
Coulter Dr ... 82604
Country Club Rd ... 82609
Country Side Ct ... 82604
Cowpony Trl ... 82601
W Coyote Ave ... 82601
Crescent Ave & Dr ... 82604
Crest Hill Dr ... 82601
E & S Crimson Dawn Rd ... 82601
Crooked Pine Trl ... 82601
W Cross St ... 82601
Crystie Ln ... 82609
Custer Ave ... 82604
Cy Ave
300-913 ... 82601
1000-5999 ... 82604
6001-6099 ... 82604
Cyclone Blvd ... 82604
Cynthia Dr ... 82609
S Cypress St ... 82604
Daffodil St ... 82601
Dahlia St ... 82604
Daisy St
200-299 ... 82604
2001-2199 ... 82609
Dale Dr ... 82609
Dame Ave ... 82604
Dartford Ct ... 82609
N & S David St ... 82601
Davis Rd ... 82604
Davis Rd W ... 82604
Davis Way ... 82601
Dead Horse Hl ... 82604
Dee Pl ... 82609
Dee Lyle Cir ... 82604
Deer Run ... 82601
Delia Dr ... 82601
Delta Dr ... 82604
E Dencoli St ... 82609
Denis Dr ... 82604
Derby St ... 82609
N & W Derick Dr ... 82604
Derington Ave ... 82609
Desmet Dr ... 82604
Desperado Dr ... 82601
Devonshire Pl ... 82609
Dew Dr ... 82601
Dexter ... 82609
Diamond Dr ... 82601
Divine Ave ... 82601
Doane Ln ... 82601
Dodge St ... 82604
E Doe Trl ... 82601
Doggie Rd ... 82601
Donegal St ... 82609
Dorset Ct & St ... 82609
Dover Ave ... 82604
Drake Pl ... 82609
Driller Rd ... 82601
N Dry Creek Rd ... 82604
Dundee ... 82609
Dunlap Way ... 82601
Durango Ct ... 82609
N & S Durbin St ... 82601
Dusty Ln ... 82604
E & W E St ... 82601
Eagle Dr ... 82604
Eastbrook Ave ... 82601
Easthaven Ave ... 82609
Eisenhower St ... 82604
El Rio Rd ... 82604
N & S Elk St ... 82601
Elkhorn Valley Dr ... 82609
S Elm St ... 82601
N Elma St ... 82601
Elton Ct ... 82604
S Emigrant Pl ... 82604
Emigrant Trl ... 82601
E End Rd ... 82601
Energy Ln ... 82604
Engburg Rd ... 82604
English Ave & Dr ... 82601
Enterprise ... 82609
Ermine Cir ... 82604
Esmay Ave ... 82604
Essex Ave ... 82604
Events Dr ... 82601
E & W F St ... 82601
N & S Fairdale Ave & St ... 82601
Fairgrounds Rd ... 82604
Fairside Rd ... 82604
Fairview Ave
1800-2199 ... 82601
2200-2299 ... 82609
Fairway Dr ... 82604
Fairwood Commons Ave ... 82609
Falcon Crest Blvd ... 82601
Fall Creek Rd ... 82609
Farnum St
1000-1198 ... 82601
1200-2000 ... 82601
2002-2198 ... 82601
2201-2599 ... 82609
Feldspar ... 82601
N & S Fenway St ... 82601
Fetterman Ave ... 82604
W Fiddler Creek Rd ... 82604
Fitzhugh Rd ... 82604
Fleetwood Pl ... 82604
Fontenelle St ... 82604
Forbes Rd ... 82601
Ford St ... 82604
N Forest Dr
100-400 ... 82609
402-598 ... 82609
411-411 ... 82602
411-411 ... 82605
S Forest Dr ... 82609
Forget Me Not ... 82604
W Fork Rd ... 82601
Fort Caspar Rd ... 82604
Foster Rd ... 82601
Fountain Ln ... 82601
Fox ... 82604
Frances St ... 82601
Freedom Cir ... 82609
Fremont Ave ... 82604
Frontage Rd ... 82601
Frontier St ... 82601
Fuller St ... 82604
E & W G St ... 82601
Gannett St ... 82609
Garbutt Rd ... 82604
W Garden Creek Hts & Rd ... 82601
Gardenia St ... 82604
Gardner St ... 82604
S Garling Rd ... 82601
Garrett Ln ... 82604
Gary Ave ... 82609
Gila Bnd ... 82604
Glacier ... 82604
Gladstone St ... 82609
Glen Dr ... 82604
W Glen Garden Dr ... 82604
Glenaire Dr ... 82609
Glenarm St ... 82601
Glendale Ave ... 82601
Glendo St ... 82604
N Glenn Rd ... 82601
Golden Leaf Rd ... 82601
Goldenrod St ... 82604
Goodstein Dr ... 82601
Goose Creek Cir & Rd ... 82609
S & W Goose Egg Cir, Hl & Rd ... 82604
Goosewing St ... 82601
Gosfield St ... 82609
Gothberg Rd ... 82604
Granada Ave
1000-1299 ... 82601
1300-1398 ... 82604
1400-1499 ... 82604
Grandview Pl ... 82604
Granite Peak Dr ... 82609
N & S Grant Ave & St ... 82601
N Grass Creek Rd ... 82604
Green Leaf Ct ... 82601
Green Meadows Dr ... 82604
Grey Cloud Rd ... 82604
Grizzly ... 82604
Grove St ... 82609
N Gypsum Rd ... 82604
Gypsy Trl ... 82601
E & W H St ... 82601
Haigler Ave ... 82604
W Haines Rd ... 82604
Hamilton Way ... 82604
Hanly St ... 82604
Hanway Ave ... 82604
Harden Dr ... 82609
Harding Ave ... 82604
Harvard St ... 82601
Harvey Pl ... 82601
Hat Six Rd ... 82609
Hawthorne Ave ... 82604
Hazelwood Dr ... 82609
Heathrow Ave ... 82609
Heights Blvd ... 82601
Henderson Creek Pl ... 82604
Henlow Ave ... 82609
Henning Loop ... 82609
Herford Ln ... 82609
Herrington Dr ... 82604
S Hickory St ... 82604
Hidden Meadow Dr ... 82601
Hideaway Ln ... 82604
Highland Dr ... 82609
W Highway St ... 82604
Hione Rd ... 82604
Hogadon Rd & Trl ... 82601
Hogan Dr ... 82601
Holland Rd ... 82604
Holly St ... 82604
W Homa Hills Rd ... 82601
Honeysuckle St ... 82604
Hope St ... 82609
Hopi ... 82601
Horizon Dr ... 82601
Hornchurch Ave ... 82609
Horse Ranch Rd ... 82604
Horse Ranch Creek Rd ... 82601
Horseshoe Rd ... 82604
Hospitality Ln ... 82609
Howard St ... 82601
N & S Huber Dr ... 82609
Hummingbird Ln ... 82601
Hy Ave ... 82604
Hyview Dr ... 82604
S Illinois Ave ... 82609
Imperial Pl ... 82604
Inca Trl ... 82601
W Incline Rd ... 82604
Indian Paintbrush St ... 82604
Indian Scout Dr ... 82604
Indian Springs Dr ... 82604
Indian Wells Dr ... 82604
Indiana Ave ... 82609
Industrial Ave ... 82601
Industrial Way ... 82604
N & S Iowa Ave ... 82609
Iron Creek Rasmus Lee Rd ... 82604
Ivy Ln ... 82609
E & W J St ... 82601
N & S Jackson St ... 82601
Jafer Rd ... 82601
Jamaica Dr ... 82609
James ... 82601
Jane St ... 82601
Janel Dr ... 82604
Jasmine St ... 82604
Jc Rd ... 82604
N & S Jefferson St ... 82601
Jet Dr ... 82604
Jim Bridger Ave ... 82604
Johnson Lateral ... 82604
Johnstone Rd ... 82604
Jonah Dr ... 82609
Jonquil St ... 82604
Jourgensen Ave ... 82604
Jul Ln ... 82609
Junco St ... 82609
Juniper ... 82601
E & W K St ... 82601
Kalina Trl ... 82601
Kati Ln ... 82601
Kearney Ave ... 82604
Kelly Dr ... 82609
Kent ... 82609
N & S Kenwood St ... 82601
Kerry St ... 82609
Kerzell Ln ... 82601
Kestrel Ct ... 82601
Kilmer Rd ... 82601
N & S Kimball St ... 82601
King Blvd ... 82604
King Salmon Dr ... 82604
Kingsboro Rd ... 82604
Kingsbury Dr ... 82609
Kingston ... 82601
Kinzie Creek Pl ... 82604
Kirk Ave ... 82601
Kit Carson Ave ... 82604
Kitty Hawk ... 82604
Klein Dr ... 82601
Knollwood Dr ... 82604
Kodiak ... 82604
Ktwo Rd ... 82601
E & W L St ... 82601
La Hacienda ... 82601
W Lafayette St ... 82604
W Lake Rd ... 82601
N Lake Creek Rd ... 82604
N Lakeview Dr & Ln ... 82604
Lakota Trl ... 82601
Lamb Rd ... 82609
Lamplighter Ln ... 82601
N Lance Creek Rd ... 82604
Landmark Dr ... 82609
Landmark Ln ... 82604
Lanner St ... 82601
Laramie Ave ... 82604
Lark St ... 82609
S Larkspur ... 82604
Laura Dr ... 82604
S Laurel St ... 82604
Lee Ln ... 82604
Legend Ln ... 82601
Legion Ln ... 82609
Lemmers Rd ... 82601
N & S Lennox Ave & St ... 82601
Leo Ln ... 82601
N Lewis Ln ... 82601
Lexington Ave ... 82601
Liberty ... 82601
License St ... 82601
Lilac St ... 82604
Lillian Ln ... 82609
Lily St ... 82604
N & S Lincoln St ... 82601
Lind Ave ... 82601
Linda Vista Dr ... 82609
Link Dr ... 82604
Lion Ct ... 82609
Little Moon Trl ... 82604
Lobo Ln ... 82601
W Lockner Rd ... 82604
S Locust St ... 82604
E & S Lodgepole ... 82601
S Lone Tree Rd ... 82604
Long Ln ... 82609
Long Horn St ... 82609
Longhorn Dr ... 82601
N & S Loop Ave ... 82601
Lost Springs Rd ... 82604
N & S Lowell St ... 82601
Luker Dr ... 82609
Lynn Ln ... 82609
Lynwood Pl ... 82604
E M St ... 82601
M J B Rd ... 82601
E Magnolia St ... 82604
Mandan Trl ... 82601
E Manly Rd ... 82601
Manor Dr ... 82609
Maple St ... 82604
Maple Leaf ... 82604
Marigold St ... 82604
Mariposa Blvd & Ct ... 82604
W Marmon St ... 82604
Mary St ... 82609
Mary Hester Rd ... 82601
Maverick Dr ... 82601
Mcclendon Rd ... 82601
N & S Mckinley St ... 82601
Mcmurry Blvd ... 82601
Meadow Dr ... 82604
Meadowlark Dr ... 82604
Medallion Rd ... 82604
Medicine Bow St ... 82609
Meier Rd ... 82604
Melodi Ln ... 82601
N & S Melrose St ... 82601
Menard Dr ... 82609
Mercy Cir & Ln ... 82609
W Mesquite Ln ... 82604
Mica Rd ... 82601

Micro Rd 82601
Mid Way Rd 82601
Middle Springs Rd 82604
Midway Dr 82604
E & W Midwest Ave 82601
Mile Hi Dr 82604
N Mill Creek Rd 82604
Miller St 82604
Milton Ave 82601
Mink 82604
N & S Minnesota Ave 82609
Miracle Dr 82609
Missouri Ave & Cir 82609
Misty Mountain Rd 82601
S Mitchell St 82601
Mitchie Dr 82604
Moccasin Trl 82601
Mockingbird Trl 82604
Moffat 82604
Mohican 82601
S Moki 82604
Monarch Ct 82604
Moneta Service Rd 82638
N & S Montana Ave 82609
Monte Vista Dr 82601
Monument Rd 82604
Moonbeam Rd 82604
Moonstone Ln 82601
Moose 82604
Morado Dr 82609
Morgan St 82604
Morning Dove Rd 82604
Morning Glory St 82604
Mountain Way 82601
Mountain View Ave 82601
Mountain View Dr 82604
Mountain View Rd 82604
Mulberry St 82604
Mystic Moon Trl 82604
Nash St 82604
Navarre Rd 82604
N & S Nebraska Ave 82609
Neosho Rd 82601
New Market Cir 82609
Newport 82609
Nez Perce Trl 82601
Nichols Ave 82601
Nicklaus Dr 82601
N Nine Mile Rd 82604
Nob Hill Dr 82601
Northway 82609
Norwood 82609
Nottingham Dr 82609
Nuclear Dr 82604
S Oak St 82601
S Oakcrest Ave 82601
S Odell Ave 82604
W Odell Ave 82604
Odell Pl 82609
Oil Dr 82604
Oil Camp Rd 82604
Oil Field Center Rd 82604
S Okeepa 82604
Old Salt Creek Rd 82601
W Old Yellowstone Hwy 82604
Oleander St 82604
Omaha Trl 82601
Open Range Rd 82601
Opportunity Blvd 82601
Orchid St 82604
N & S Oregon Trl 82604
Oriole Ct 82604
Ormsby Rd 82601
Osage 82601
Osprey St 82601
Otter 82604
Overland Trl 82601
Overlook Dr 82601
Oxcart Ln 82604
Oxford Ln 82604
Paige St 82604
Painted Horse Trl 82604
Palmer Dr 82601
Palomino Ave 82601
Paradise Dr 82604

N & S Park St 82601
Parkview Dr 82609
Parkway Dr 82609
Partridge Ln 82604
Pathfinder Rd 82604
Pawnee Cir 82601
Payne Ave 82609
Payton Cir 82609
Pedros Pass 82604
E Pennsylvania Ave 82609
Pershing St 82601
Petunia St 82604
Pheasant Dr 82604
Phillips Ln 82604
W Pierce St 82601
Pilot Dr & St 82604
Pine Rd 82601
Pine St 82601
Pine Creek Pl 82604
Pine Ridge Rd 82604
Pineview Pl 82609
Piney Creek Rd 82604
Pioneer Ave 82604
Pittman Cir 82604
Placid Dr 82604
Plateau Pl 82604
Plateau St 82601
Platte Rd & St 82601
Player Dr 82601
Plaza Dr 82604
N Pleasant St 82601
Plumeria St 82604
Plymouth 82609
W Poison Spider Rd 82604
Pond Hill Rd 82604
Ponderosa Rd 82601
Pontiac St 82601
N & S Poplar St 82601
Poppy St 82601
S Powder Horn Grn 82604
Prairie Ln 82601
Prairie Dog Dr 82601
Prairie River Dr 82604
Pratt Blvd 82609
Preserve Cir 82609
Primrose St 82604
Pronghorn Dr & St 82601
Prospector Dr 82604
Provence Ct 82609
Puma Dr 82604
Pursel Dr 82604
Pyrite Rd 82604
Quail Ln 82604
Queen St 82604
Quivera River Rd 82604
Rabbitbrush Dr 82601
Raderville Rte 82604
Rainbow Dr 82604
Rambler St 82604
Ranch Rd
4000-4199 82604
26700-26799 82601
Ranchero Rd 82604
Ravine Ln & Rd 82604
Raymond Ln 82601
Recluse Ct 82609
Red Creek Rd 82601
N Redman Rd 82604
Redtail St 82601
W Renauna Ave 82601
Reo St 82604
Restoration Rd 82604
Revenue Blvd 82601
S Richard St 82601
Ricky Cir 82601
Ridge Ln 82601
Ridgecrest Dr 82604
S Ridgecrest Dr 82601
Rigal Rd 82601
Rimrock Dr 82601
River Cross Rd 82601
River Heights Dr 82604
River Meadows Rd 82604
River Park Dr 82604
W Riverbend Rd 82604
Rivers Gate 82604

Riverside Dr, St & Ter 82604
N & S Robertson Rd 82604
Robin St 82609
Rocking R Rd 82604
Romeo Rd 82601
Roosevelt St 82604
Rosado 82609
Rosberg Rd 82604
Rose St 82604
Ross Ridge Rd 82604
S Rotary Park Rd 82601
Round The Hill Rd 82601
Ruiz Way 82604
Runway Dr 82604
Rustic Cir, Ct, Dr & Pl 82609
S-P Rd 82604
Saber Rd 82604
Saddlestring Rd 82604
N Sage Ave & Rd 82604
Sagebrush St 82604
Sagewood Ave 82601
Saint John St 82601
Saint Mary St 82601
Saker Ct 82601
Sally Ln 82609
Salt Creek Hwy & Rte 82601
Sam Howell Rd 82604
E Sandstone Dr 82601
Saratoga Rd 82604
E & S Scenic Rte & St 82601
Schlager Rd 82604
Schulte Ave 82604
Scott Dr 82601
W Sego Lily Ct 82604
Seminoe St 82609
Sequoia Dr 82604
Seven Butte Dr 82601
Shamrock Dr 82601
Shannon Dr 82609
W Sharrock Rd 82604
Shasta Dr 82604
Shattuck Ave 82601
Sheridan Dr 82604
Sherwood Cir 82609
Shetland Rd 82604
Shinn Rd 82604
Shorinso Rd 82604
Short Horn St 82609
Shumway Ave & St 82601
Siebke Dr 82601
Silver Leaf Rd 82601
Silvertip St 82601
W Sims Creek Rd 82604
N & S Sinclair Pl 82609
Sioux Trl 82601
Siskin St 82609
Six Mile Rd 82604
Six Wn Rd 82604
Skylark Ave 82604
S Skyline Rd 82604
Skyview Dr 82601
Sleepy Ridge Rd 82609
Smoke Rise Rd 82604
N & S Socony Pl 82609
Somerset Cir 82609
Southwood St 82604
Speas Rd 82604
Spencer Rd 82604
S Springs Dr 82604
S Spruce St 82601
Squash Blossom Rd 82604
Squaw Creek Rd 82604
Stafford Ct 82609
S Stag Run 82601
Stagecoach Dr 82604
Staghorn Ridge Rd 82601
Star Ln 82604
State Highway 220 82604
State Highway 487 82604
State Highway 77 82604
Stewart St 82604
Stillwater Way 82604
Stoneridge Way 82601
Stout St 82609
Stuckenhoff St 82601

Studer Ave 82604
Summit Dr 82604
N & S Sun Dr 82609
Sundown Pl 82601
Sunflower St 82604
E & N Sunlight Dr 82601
Sunrise Dr 82604
Sunset Blvd 82601
Surrey Ct & St 82609
Sussex 82609
Swanton Ave 82609
Sweet Creek Rd 82604
Sweetbrier St 82604
Sweetwater Dr 82609
Swingle Acres Rd 82604
Sycamore St 82604
Talc Rd 82604
Talon Dr 82604
Tanager St 82609
Taxiway Dr & Pl 82604
Teapot Dr 82601
N Ten Mile Rd 82604
Terrace Dr 82604
Teton St 82609
Texas Pl 82609
Thelma Dr 82609
Thorndike Ave 82601
Three Crowns Dr 82604
Timberline Ct 82604
Tipton St 82601
E Toad Rd 82601
Tomahawk Rd 82601
Tonkawa Trl 82601
Tower Hill Rd 82601
Townsend Ln 82609
Trail Rd 82601
Trails End 82601
Trappers Trl 82604
Trevett Ln 82604
Trigood Dr 82609
Trojan Dr 82609
Trotter Rd 82604
Tubbs Rd 82604
Tuffy Rd 82604
Tulip St 82604
Tumbleweed Dr 82601
Tumbleweed Ln 82604
Turpin St 82601
W Tye Moore 82604
Umpqua River Rd 82604
University Ct 82609
Uranium Rd 82604
Us Highway 20-26 82604
S Utah Ave 82609
Ute Cir 82601
Valcaro Rd 82604
Vale Pl 82604
S Valley Dr & Rd 82604
Venture Way 82609
Verde Ct 82609
View Dr 82601
Village Dr 82604
Vista Way 82601
Vista Grande 82601
Vista Royale 82601
S Walnut St 82601
Walport St 82604
N & S Walsh Dr 82609
N Wardwell Industrial Ave 82601
N Warehouse Rd 82601
Warwick 82609
Washakie St 82609
N & S Washington St 82601
Waterford 82609
Webb Creek Rd 82604
Week Creek Rd 82609
Welsh Ave 82604
Werner 82604
Werner Ct 82601
Westash St 82601
Westcott Dr 82609
Westland Pl & Rd 82604
Weston St 82609
Westridge Cir, Ct, Dr, Pl, Ter & Way 82604

Westshore Rd 82601
Westshore Village Dr & Rd 82601
Westwood Hl 82604
Whiskey Gap Rd 82604
Whispering Springs Ct & Rd 82604
Whitcomb Rd 82601
Whitcomb Way 82609
White Deer Trl 82604
White Rock Dr 82604
Whitetail Draw Rd 82601
Whitlock Rd 82604
Wigwam Way 82601
Wilkins Cir 82601
Willer Dr 82604
S Willow St 82604
Willow Creek Rd 82604
Willy Rd 82604
Wilshire Ct 82604
N & S Wilson St 82601
Winborne St 82601
Wind River Ave 82609
Windsor Pl 82604
Winton Way 82604
S Wisconsin Ave 82609
N & S Wolcott St 82601
Wolf Creek Rd 82604
Wood Court Rd 82601
Woodglenn Pl 82609
Woolwick Ct 82609
Wyo Highway 259 82601
Wyoming Blvd SW 82604
SE Wyoming Blvd
1-499 82609
501-799 82609
3601-4097 82601
4099-4599 82601
S Yarrow 82604
N Yellow Creek Rd 82604
E Yellowstone Hwy
500-598 82601
600-1999 82601
2000-2500 82609
2502-3498 82609
W Yellowstone Hwy
200-899 82601
901-999 82601
1701-4997 82604
3600-3798 82604
3800-4899 82604
4901-4999 82604
4999-7999 82604
8001-8999 82604
Yesness Ct & Ln 82604
Yorkshire Ave 82609
Yucca Cir 82604
Zephyr Rd 82604
Zero Rd 82604
Zinnia St 82604
Zion Ln 82609
Zuni Trl 82601

NUMBERED STREETS

N 1st Ave 82604
E 1st Ln 82609
E 1st St
200-398 82601
2000-2998 82609
W 1st St
100-599 82601
1000-1698 82604
N 2nd Ave 82604
E 2nd St
100-1999 82601
2000-6651 82609
W 2nd St 82601
N 3rd Ave 82604
S 3rd Ave 82604
E 3rd St
501-697 82601
2000-3099 82609
N 4th Ave
1-799 82604

S 4th Ave
1-799 82604
E 4th St
601-697 82601
699-1900 82601
1902-1998 82601
2001-2097 82609
2099-3099 82609
N 5th Ave
1-999 82604
S 5th Ave
1-400 82604
E 5th St
100-298 82601
300-1199 82601
1201-1299 82601
2200-3199 82609
N 6 Mile Rd 82604
W 6 Wn Rd 82604
N 6th Ave 82604
S 6th Ave 82604
E 6th St
100-1299 82601
2200-2999 82609
W 6th St 82601
N 7 Mile Rd 82604
N 7th Ave 82604
E 7th St
100-298 82601
2200-2999 82609
W 7th St 82601
N & S 8 Mile 82604
N 8th Ave 82604
E 8th St
101-197 82601
199-1399 82601
2200-2398 82609
2400-4199 82609
W 8th St 82601
E 9th St
100-299 82601
2400-2699 82609
W 9th St 82601
E 10th St
100-1199 82601
1201-1299 82601
2201-2397 82609
2399-3099 82609
W 10th St 82601
E 11th St
101-197 82601
199-799 82601
801-999 82601
2600-3099 82609
W 11th St
100-999 82601
1000-1299 82604
E 12th St
101-197 82601
199-2199 82601
2200-5299 82609
W 12th St
101-197 82601
199-899 82601
901-999 82601
1000-1098 82604
1100-1499 82604
1501-1599 82604
E 13th St 82601
W 13th St
100-999 82601
1000-1098 82604
1100-1599 82604
1601-2199 82604
E 14th St
200-999 82601
2700-4099 82609
W 14th St
100-999 82601
1000-1599 82604
E 15th St
100-298 82601
300-1999 82601
2001-2099 82601
2300-5199 82609
W 15th St
100-899 82601

901-999 82601
1000-1398 82604
1400-2299 82604
E 16th St
601-697 82601
2200-5199 82609
W 16th St 82604
E 17th St
601-797 82601
799-1700 82601
1702-1798 82601
2200-5199 82609
W 17th St 82601
E 18th St
600-698 82601
700-1499 82601
2200-2998 82609
3000-5100 82609
5102-5198 82609
W 18th St 82601
E 19th St
700-798 82601
800-1399 82601
3400-3498 82609
3500-5099 82609
W 19th St
700-900 82601
902-998 82601
1000-1199 82604
E 20th St
601-697 82601
699-800 82601
802-1098 82601
3700-3898 82609
3900-5099 82609
W 20th St
700-899 82601
901-999 82601
1000-1199 82604
E 21st St
601-697 82601
699-2199 82601
3501-4397 82609
4399-5599 82609
W 21st St
600-698 82601
700-899 82601
1000-1199 82604
E 22nd St
700-2099 82601
3500-5500 82609
W 22nd St 82604
E 23rd St
600-798 82601
3500-4599 82609
W 23rd St 82604
E 24th St
1100-1198 82601
2200-4699 82609
W 24th St 82604
E 25th St
800-1799 82601
4200-4499 82609
W 25th St 82604
E 26th St 82601
E 27th St 82601
W 27th St
100-298 82601
300-400 82601
402-498 82601
1300-1699 82604
1701-1799 82604
E 29th St 82601
100-1199 82601
1300-2299 82604
30th St 82601
W 38th St 82604
W 39th St 82604
W 40th St 82604
W 41st St 82604
W 42nd St 82604
W 43rd St 82604
W 44th St 82604
W 45th St
700-899 82601
2100-3999 82604
W 46th St 82604

W 47th St 82601
W 50th St
600-799 82601
1800-1899 82604
W 51st St 82601
W 52nd St 82601
W 53rd St 82601
W 54th St 82601
W 55th St 82601
W 57th St 82601
W 58th St 82601
W 59th St 82601
W 60th St 82601
W 62nd St 82601
10 Mile Rd 82604
S 12 Mile Rd 82604
33 Mile Rd 82604

CHEYENNE WY

General Delivery 82009

POST OFFICE BOXES MAIN OFFICE STATIONS AND BRANCHES

Box No.s
All PO Boxes 82003

HIGHWAY CONTRACTS

56 82009

NAMED STREETS

A Bar A Dr 82007
Abby Rd 82007
Absaroka 82007
Acacia Dr 82001
Adams Ave 82001
Affirmed Rd 82009
Agate Rd 82009
Ahrens Ave 82007
Airport Pkwy 82001
Akes Dr 82009
Albany Ave 82001
Albin Ln 82009
Alden Dr 82005
Alder Ct 82009
Alex Ranch Rd 82007
Alexander Ave
600-798 82007
1701-2097 82001
2099-3699 82001
Alice Ct 82007
Allan Rd 82009
E & W Allison Rd 82007
Alpine Ranch Rd 82009
Alyssa Way 82009
Amber Trl 82001
Ames Ave
200-299 82007
1701-1997 82001
1999-2699 82001
Ames Ct 82001
Amherst Rd 82001
Anderson Ct 82009
Andover Dr 82001
Andra Ct 82009
Angie St 82007
Angus Ln 82009
Anna Loop Dr 82009
Annie Morgan Ct 82007
Antelope Ave 82009
Antelope Meadows Dr 82009
Anthony Rd 82009
Apache St 82009
Appaloosa Dr 82001
Apple St 82007
Appletree Ln 82009
Applewood Ct 82009
Arabian Ln 82009
Arapaho St 82009
Arbor Ln 82009
Arcadian Dr 82007
Archer Pkwy & Rd 82009
Archer Frontage Rd 82007
Archer Ranch Rd 82009
Archies Rd 82001
Arctic Willow Ct 82009
Arena Ln 82007
N & S Argonne Dr 82005
Arizona St 82009
Arkansas Ave 82005
Arkel Way 82007
Arlene Pointe 82009
Armant Ct 82009
S Arp Ave 82007
Arrow Pl 82009
Arrow Wood Ln 82009
Arrowhead Rd 82001
Artesian Rd 82007
Arthur Ave 82009
Artillery Rd 82005
Ash 82001
Ashford Ct & Dr 82007
Ashley Dr 82009
Aspen Cir & Dr 82009
Aspen Pointe Ln 82009
Astronaut Dr 82009
Atkin St 82001
Atlantic Dr 82001
Atlas Loop 82001
Aurora Pl 82001
Avenue B 82007
Avenue B2 82007
N Avenue B4 82007
Avenue B5 82007
N & S Avenue B6 82007
Avenue C 82007
Avenue C1 82007
Avenue C2 82007
Avenue C3 82007
N Avenue C4 82007
Avenue D 82007
Aviation Rd 82009
Aviator Ct 82009
Aztec Dr 82009
Bade Rd 82009
Badger Rd 82009
Bailey Ct 82001
Bailey Fae Way 82009
Baldwin Dr 82001
Ballad Ln 82007
Balmoral Ct 82009
Baltic Rd 82009
Bandemer Blvd 82009
Banjo Ct 82007
Bannock Rd 82001
Bar X Rd 82007
Barbell Ct 82001
Barberry Rdg 82009
Barrett Rd 82009
Barrington Rd 82009
Basin St 82009
Bear Ave 82007
Bear River Ave 82007
Beartooth Dr 82009
Beckle Rd 82009
Belaire Ave 82001
Bell Ln 82009
Bell Ranch Rd 82009
Belmont Ave 82009
Belvedere Ct 82009
Bennet Ct 82007
Bent Ave
200-799 82007
801-1099 82007
1501-1697 82001
1699-4000 82001
4002-4098 82001
Berkelley Rd 82009
Berwick Dr 82007
Beulah Ave 82009
Bevans St 82001
Beverly Blvd 82007
Big Horn Ave 82001
Big Prairie Blvd 82009
Big Sandy Cir 82001
Big Sky Trl 82009
Big Sur Ave 82009
Birch Pl 82001
Bishop Blvd 82009
Bison Trl 82009
Bison Run Loop 82009
Black Ct 82001
Black Bear Ct 82009
Black Jack Loop 82001
Blackhawk Dr 82007
Blackpowder Rd 82005
Blazer Rd 82009
Blazing Star Rd 82009
Blossom Ct 82007
Blue Blf 82009
Blue Bell Trl 82007
Blue Mesa Rd 82009
Blue Mountain Rd 82009
Blue Roan 82007
Blue Sky Dr 82009
Blue Willow Ln 82009
Bluegrass Cir 82009
Blues Dr 82007
Bluff Pl 82009
Bobcat Rd & Trl 82009
Bocage Dr 82009
Bomar Dr 82009
Bonanza Trl 82009
Bonita Pl 82009
Bonneville Pl 82009
Bonnie Brae Loop 82009
Booker Rd 82005
Boot Strap Ct 82001
Borough St 82007
Boston Rd 82001
Boulder Ct 82009
Boundary Rd 82009
Bourne Pl 82009
Bowie Dr 82009
Boxelder Dr 82001
Boysen Ave 82001
Bozeman Trl 82009
Bradley Ave
600-798 82007
801-899 82007
1400-1898 82001
1900-2599 82001
2601-3699 82001
Braehill Rd 82009
Brahma Rd 82009
Brandi Ln 82009
Branding Iron Dr 82009
Brave Ct 82009
Brett Pt 82009
Brianna Ct 82009
Briar Ct 82007
Briarwood Ct & Ln 82009
Bridger Dr & Trl 82009
Bridle Dr 82009
Brimmer Rd 82009
Brittany Dr 82009
Broken Arrow Rd 82007
Broken T Trl 82007
Broken Wheel Ct 82007
Brome Rd 82007
Bronco Trl 82009
Brook Ct 82009
Brookfield Ct 82009
Brooks Blvd 82009
Browning Dr 82007
Bruegman Blvd 82009
Brundage Rd 82009
Brush Creek Rd 82009
Buck Brush Rd 82009
Buckboard Rd 82009
Buckskin Trl 82009
Buffalo Ave 82009
Buick Rd 82009
Bullseye Blvd 82009
Bunn Ave 82009
Burke Dr 82009
Burns Ave 82009
Butch Cassidy Trl 82009
Buttercup Dr 82009
Caballo Trl 82007
Cable Ave 82009
Cactus Way 82009
Cactus Hill Rd 82001
Cadillac Rd 82009
Cahill Dr 82001
Calico Hills Ranch Rd 82009
Calin Ct 82009
Calumet Dr 82001
Camelot Ct 82009
Camp Carlin Dr
4400-5500 82005
5500-5999 82001
5502-6198 82005
Campbell Ave 82001
Campfire Ct & Trl 82001
Campkettle Dr 82007
Campstool Rd 82007
N & S Cannon Dr 82005
Canyon Dr & Rd 82009
Cape Ct 82001
Capitol Ave
500-598 82007
600-999 82007
1500-1598 82001
1600-2199 82001
2120-2120 82003
2201-3999 82001
2300-4098 82001
Carbine Trl 82009
Carbon Ave 82001
Carey Ave
601-697 82007
699-1099 82007
1500-4699 82001
Carina Ct 82009
Carla Dr 82009
Carlin Ave 82009
Carls Rd 82009
E & W Carlson St 82009
Carmel Dr 82009
Carmon Cir 82001
Carpenter Pl 82009
Carriage Cir & Dr 82009
Carroll Ave 82009
Carter Rd 82001
Cascade Ave 82009
Casey Ranch Rd 82009
Cattle Dr 82009
Cattlemans Dr 82009
Cedar Ave 82007
Cedar Pl 82001
Cemetery Dr 82005
Centennial Dr 82001
Central Ave
100-998 82007
1600-4099 82001
4601-5099 82009
5600-8799 82005
Century Rd 82009
Century Hills Rd 82007
Cessna Ln 82009
Chalk Bluffs Rd 82007
Chalmette Ct 82009
N & S Champagne Dr 82005
Champion Dr 82009
Channell Dr 82009
Chaparral Rd 82009
Chapel Hill Dr 82009
Charles St 82001
Charolais Ln 82009
Cherokee St 82009
Cherry Ct 82001
Cherry St 82007
Cherry Blossom Dr 82009
Cherry Wine Dr 82009
Cherry Wood Ln 82009
Cheshire Dr 82001
Chestnut Dr 82001
Chetwood Ave 82001
Chevy Rd 82009
Cheyenne Pl 82001
Cheyenne Rd 82005
Cheyenne St 82001
Chickadee Dr 82009
Chickasaw Dr 82001
Chief Twomoon Rd 82009
Chief Washakie Ave 82009
Child Rd 82009
Chinook Dr 82009
Chisolm Trl 82009
Choke Cherry Rd 82009
Chris Loop 82007
Christensen Rd
2701-2899 82007
3401-4597 82009
4599-8400 82009
8402-9398 82009
Christine Cir 82007
Chrysler Rd 82009
Chuck Wagon Rd 82009
Chugwater Dr 82009
Church Ave 82007
Cimarron Dr 82009
Cindy Ave 82009
Circle Dr 82009
Citation Rd 82009
Citrus St 82007
Cityview Ct 82009
Clark St 82009
Clear Creek Pkwy
4900-4998 82001
4900-6898 82007
4901-4999 82001
4901-6899 82007
Clear Sky Dr 82009
Clear View Cir 82009
Cleveland Ave 82001
Cleveland Pl 82007
Cliffs Rd 82007
Cloud Mesa Dr 82009
Clover Ct 82009
Clubhouse Ln 82001
Clyde Cir 82001
Cobblestone Ct 82009
Cochise Rd 82009
Cody Ln & St 82009
Cole Pl & Rd 82009
Cole Shopping Ctr 82001
E College Dr 82007
N College Dr
3200-3798 82001
3800-4100 82001
4102-4598 82001
4600-7300 82009
7302-7698 82009
S College Dr 82007
W College Dr 82007
Colonial Dr 82001
Colony Ct 82009
Colt Ct 82007
Columbia Dr 82009
Columbine Ct 82001
Columbus Dr 82007
Comanche Dr 82009
Commerce Cir 82007
Commissary Rd
1000-1999 82005
1800-5099 82001
Commons Cir & Dr 82009
Concerto Ln 82007
Concha Loop 82009
Concord Rd 82001
Conestoga Rd 82009
Connie Dr 82009
Constitution Dr 82001
Continental Pl 82001
Continental Rd 82009
Converse Ave
801-1999 82001
2001-4399 82001
4800-4800 82003
4800-4800 82009
Coolidge St 82001
Coonrod Rd 82009
Copper Mountain Ct 82009
Copperville Rd 82001
Cordova Dr 82009
Cornell Ln 82009
Corral Pl 82007
Cosgriff Ct 82001
Cottage Ln 82001
Cottonwood Dr 82001
Coulter Cir & Dr 82009
Council Blf 82009
Country Club Ave 82001
Country Dream 82009
Country West Rd 82007
Countryside Ave 82001
County Road 113 82009
Covered Wagon Dr 82007
Cowboy Rd 82009
Cowboy Walk 82001
Cowpoke Rd 82009
Cox Ct 82001
Cox Rd 82009
Craigy J Dr 82009
Crazy Horse Rd 82009
Cree Loop 82001
N & S Creek Dr 82005
Creighton St 82009
Crescent Dr 82007
Crest Park Dr 82001
Crested Butte Dr 82009
Crestline Ave 82009
Crestridge Dr 82009
Crestview Dr 82009
Crews Ct 82001
Cribbon Ave
100-198 82007
200-500 82007
502-1298 82007
2700-2798 82001
2800-3999 82001
S Cribbon Ave 82007
Crook Ave 82001
Crossbow Trl 82001
Crow Rd 82009
Crow Creek Rd 82009
Crowell Ranch Rd 82007
Crystal Ave 82001
Crystal Mountain Rd 82009
Curt Gowdy Dr 82009
Custer St 82009
Cutler Rd 82001
Cypress Ln 82009
Dakota Dr & Xing 82001
Dalcour Dr 82009
W Dale Blvd 82009
Dallas Rd 82007
Dan Ranch Rd 82009
Daniel Ct 82009
Danielle Ct 82009
Danni Grace Cir 82009
Danni Marie Cir 82009
Darby Ln 82001
Darnell Pl 82001
Dartmouth Ln 82009
Dater Rd 82009
David Ct 82007
E David St 82009
Dawson 82009
Dayshia Ln 82007
Deadwood Trl 82009
Dean Fogg Rd 82007
Dean Paul Dr 82009
Debbie Ln 82007
Deer Ave 82009
Deerbrooke Cir & Trl 82009
Degraw Dr 82009
Deike Ct 82009
Delaware St 82009
Dell Range Blvd 82009
Deming Blvd 82001
Deming Dr 82007
Denise Rd 82009
Derr Ave 82007
Desert Storm Way 82005
Desmet Dr 82007
Devils Tower Rd 82009
Dey Ave
201-221 82007
223-225 82007
227-299 82007
2001-2097 82001
2099-3900 82001
3902-3998 82001
Diamond Ave 82001
Diamond B Blvd 82009
Diamond Creek Way 82005
Dildine Rd 82001
Dillon Ave
200-1100 82007
1102-1198 82007
1601-1697 82001
1699-4099 82001
Dittman Ct 82009
Division Ave 82007
Doc Holliday Loop 82009
Dodge Ct 82001
Dodge Rd 82009
Dogwood Ave 82009
E Dona St 82009
Donald Dr 82009
Dorierie Rd 82009
Dorothy Ln 82009
Dorsey Rd 82009
Dot Ray Pl 82007
Doubletree Ln 82009
Douglas St 82009
Dover Rd 82001
Draper Rd 82007
Draw Dr 82009
Drew Ct 82007
Driftwood Dr 82009
Drummond Ave 82009
Duck Creek Ranch Rd 82007
Duesenberg Rd 82009
Duff Ave 82001
Dunn Ave 82001
Durham Rd 82001
Dusty Rd 82009
Dutch Ct 82009
Eagle Dr 82009
Eagle Crest Ct 82009
Eagle View Ln 82009
Earle Ct 82009
Eastland Ct 82001
Eastview St 82001
Easy St 82009
Echostar Dr 82007
Eda Pl 82001
Edgewater Ave 82009
Education Dr 82009
Edward Dr 82009
El Camino Dr 82001
El Camino Real 82009
Eldorado Ct 82009
Elizabeth Rd 82009
Elk Ave 82009
Elkhorn Dr 82007
Elling Rd 82009
Elm Ct 82001
Elmwood Ave & Ct 82007
Emerald Dr 82009
Emily Dr 82009
Empire Dr 82009
Eric Ln 82009
Erickson Ct 82009
Erie Ct 82001
Essex Rd 82001
Etchepare Dr 82007
Evan Pl 82009
Evans Ave
300-999 82007
1601-1697 82001
1699-3999 82001
4001-4199 82001
Evelyn St 82007
Eveningstar Ct 82009
Everglade Dr 82001
Evergreen St 82009
Evers Blvd 82009
Everton Dr 82009
F Quarter Circle Loop 82007
Factor Ln 82007
Fairfield Ave & Ct 82007
Fairview Ave 82009
Faith Dr 82009
Falcon Rdg 82009
Falling Star Loop 82009
Farthing Rd 82001
Fawn Pass 82009
Fe Warren Air Force
Ba 82005

Street	ZIP
Feather Rdg	82009
Federal Blvd	82009
Feldspar Rd	82009
Ferguson Ave	82009
Field Station Rd	82009
Fillmore Ave	82001
Fir Dr	82001
Fire Rock Dr	82009
Fire Side Dr	82001
Fire Star Dr	82009
Fire Walker Trl	82001
Firethorn Ln	82009
Fishing Brg	82009
Fishing Bridge Rd	82009
Flaming Gorge Ave	82001
Fleischli Pkwy	82001
Fogg Trl	82007
Fontenelle Cir	82001
Foothills Rd	82009
Forbes Ct	82009
Ford Rd	82009
Forest Dr	82001
S Fort Steele Way	82005
Fort Warren Ave	
1-199	82001
6800-6899	82005
Fossil Butte Rd	82009
Foster Ave	82001
E & W Four Mile Rd	82009
Fox Trl	82009
Fox Chase Rd	82009
E & W Fox Farm Rd	82007
Fox Hill Rd	82009
Fox Ridge Dr	82009
Fox Run Rd	82009
Fox Tail Rd	82007
Foxcroft Rd	82001
Foxen Ct	82001
Foxglove Dr	82009
Foxhaven Ln	82009
Foyer Ave	82001
Frank Ct	82001
Frankie Dr	82009
Frederick Dr	82009
Freedom Rd	82001
Fremont Ave	82001
Frontier Ct	82001
N Frontier Rd	82005
S Frontier Rd	82005
Frontier St	82001
Frontier Mall Dr	82009
Frontier Park Ave	82001
Fuel Rd	82005
Gabriel Ct & Dr	82009
Garden Ct	82001
Gardenia Dr	82009
Garnet Way	82009
Garrett St	82001
Garrison Loop	82005
Gateway Dr	82009
Gem Trl	82001
Geronimo Rd	82009
Gettysburg Dr	82001
Geyser Rd	82009
Giffin Gulch	82009
Gilchrist Rd	82009
Glencoe Dr	82009
Glendale Ct	82007
Glendo Ave	82001
Gold Dust Rd	82007
Golden Ct	82001
Golden Hill St	82009
Golden Meadows Ln	82009
Golden Rod Trl	82007
Golf Course Dr	82005
E & W Gopp Ct	82007
Gordon Rd	82007
Goshen Ave	82001
Gowdy Ct	82009
Grace Rd	82009
Gramercy Dr	82009
Granada Trl	82009
Grand Teton Ct	82009
Grandpre Cir	82009
Grandview Ave & Ct	82009
Granite St	82001
Granite Springs Rd	82009
Grape St	82007
Grasslands Pkwy	82001
Gray Wolf Rd	82009
N & S Greeley Hwy	82007
Green Ct	82009
Green Acres Ct	82007
Green Meadow Dr	82001
Green Mountain Rd	82009
Green Prairie Pl	82001
Green River Pl & St	82001
Green Valley Rd	82001
Greenfield Ct	82001
Greenhill Ct	82001
Greenridge Ct	82001
Greenway St	82001
Gregg Way	82009
Greybull Ave	82009
Grier Blvd	82001
Griffith Ave	82009
Grizzly Gulch	82009
Grove Dr	
3301-3497	82001
3499-3599	82001
3601-3999	82001
10900-10998	82009
Guernsey Dr	82009
Gunsmoke Rd	82001
Gysel Pl	82009
H Bar E Dr	82007
Hacienda Ct	82007
Hackamore Rd	82009
Hacker Cir & Ct	82009
Hales Ranch Rd	82007
Hamilton Ave	82009
Hanson St	82001
Happy Jack Rd	82009
Happy Trails Dr	82009
Harmon Ave	82009
Harmony Ln	82009
Hartford Ave	82007
Harvard Ln	82009
Harvest Loop	82009
Haunted Rd	82001
Hawthorne Dr	82009
Hayes Ave	82001
Hazer Ct	82009
Headquarters Dr	82005
Healy Rd	82009
Heavenly Dr	82009
Helen Ave	82007
Hellwig Rd	82007
Hemlock Ave	82009
Henderson Dr	82001
Hereford Ranch Rd	82007
Herford Ln	82009
Heritage Dr	82009
Hickory Pl	82009
Hidden Valley Dr	82009
High Plains Rd	82007
High Side Trl	82007
High Spring Rd	82001
Highland Rd	82009
Highview Ct	82009
Hilary Dr	82009
Hildreth Rd	82009
Hillcrest Rd	82001
Hillside Dr	82009
Hilltop Ave	82009
Hinesley Rd	82001
Hirst St	82009
Hitching Post Ln	82001
Hobbs Ave	82009
Hodahlee Trl	82009
Holland Ct	82009
Holly Ct	82001
Holmes St	82001
Homestead Ave	82001
Hope Ct	82001
Horizon Dr & Loop	82009
Horse Creek Ln & Rd	82009
Horse Soldier Rd	82001
Horseshoe Rd	82007
Hot Springs Ave	82001
House Ave	
300-398	82007
400-1000	82007
1002-1098	82007
1600-4000	82001
4002-4098	82001
S House Ave	82007
Hoy Rd	82009
Hr Ranch Rd	82007
Hugh Glass Trl	82009
Hugur Ave	82001
Huisman Rd	82001
Hummingbird Trl	82009
Humphrey Ln	82007
Hunters Way	82007
Huntz Dr	82009
Huron Ave	82001
Hutchins Dr	82007
Hyde Merritt Rd	82009
Hyndman Rd	82007
Hynds Ave	82007
Hynds Blvd	
3001-3999	82001
5201-9899	82009
Hynds Lodge Rd	82009
I25 Service Rd	
1-299	82007
1700-3900	82009
3902-4198	82009
I80 Service Rd	82009
E & W Idaho St	82009
Illini Ct	82009
Illinois Rd	82009
Imperial Ct	82001
Independence Dr	82001
Indiana Rd	82009
Indigo Dr	82001
S Industrial Service Rd	82007
Industry Dr	82007
E Iowa St	82009
Iriquois Dr	82009
Iron Mountain Rd & Rte	82009
Ivan St	82001
J W Ct	82001
Jack Rabbit Rd	82009
Jackpot Loop	82009
Jackson Ct & St	82009
Jackson Lake Rd	82009
Jacob Pl	82009
Jade Rd	82009
Jaker Ct	82009
James Dr	82009
James Cole Ct	82009
Jane Ln	82009
Jay Pl	82001
Jazz Dr	82007
E & W Jefferson Rd	82007
Jenkins St	82009
Jenny Lk	82009
Jessi Dr	82009
Jessica Dr	82009
Jessup Ranch Rd	82007
Jim Ct	82009
Joes Rd	82009
John Dr	82009
Johnson Ave	82001
Jonah Dr	82009
Jordann Ln	82009
Joyce St	82009
Judy Lee Rd	82007
Julia Rd	82009
Julianna Rd	82007
Juniper Dr	82009
K Mckenna Trl	82009
K2 Ranch Rd	82007
Kansas St	82009
Karen Pl	82007
Kate Cameron Dr	82009
Kay Ave	82007
Kaycee Pl	82009
Kelley Dr	82001
Kelso Rd	82007
Kemp Hill Dr	82009
Kennedy Dr	82001
Kenosha St	82001
Kentucky St	82009
Kepler Dr	82009
Kerry Ave	82009
Kersey Dr	82009
Ketcham Rd	82009
Kettle Hill Ct	82001
Kevin Ave	82009
Keystone Dr	82009
Kickapoo Loop	82001
Killarney Dr	82009
Kim Ln	82009
King Ct	82007
King Arthur Ct & Way	82009
Kingham Dr	82001
Kingswood Dr	82009
Klipstein Rd	82009
Knowlwood Rd	82009
Kooper Trl	82009
Kopsa Ct	82007
Kornegay Ct	82009
Koster Rd	82009
La Cresta Ln	82001
La Vista Ct	82001
Lacy Dr	82009
Lafayette Blvd	82009
Lajuana Ct	82001
Lake Pl	82007
Lakeshore Dr	82009
Lakota Ln	82009
Lampman Ct	82007
Land Ct	82001
Lander Ln	82009
Lapaz Dr	82009
Laramie St	82001
Laredo Ct	82009
Lariat Loop	82009
Larintr Ave	82005
Larkspur Rd	82001
Latigo Loop	82009
E & W Laughlin Rd	82009
Laura Dawn Ave	82009
Laurel Dr	82001
Lawrence Ln	82009
Lazear Ranch Rd	82007
Lazy R Ln	82009
Lazy Y Dr	82007
Leah Dr	82009
Leavey Ranch Rd	82007
Leech Blvd	82001
Leeds Pl	82001
Legacy Pkwy	82009
Legend Ln & Trl	82009
W Leisher Rd	82007
Levi Rd	82009
Lexington Ave	82007
Liberty St	82001
Lilac Ct	82001
E & W Lincolnway	82001
Linda Ct	82009
Lindbloom Ct	82007
Linden Ct	82001
Linden Way	82009
Line Ave & Ct	82007
S Lions Park Dr	82001
Little Horse Rd	82009
Little Leaf Ct	82009
Little Moon Trl	82009
Little Ridge Ct	82009
Little Shield Rd	82009
Little Star Dr	82009
Little Valley Trl	82007
Liz Ranch Rd	82009
Locust Dr	82001
Lodgepole Dr	82009
Logan Ave	82001
Logistics Dr	82009
Lone Tree Ct	82009
Lonesome Ct	82007
Long Branch Loop	82001
Long Shadow Ln	82007
Long Valley Rd	82001
E Longhorn Rd	82009
Longs Peak Dr	82009
Lookout Dr	82009
Lori Rd	82007
Lorilynn Pointe	82009
Luckie Rd	82001
Lucky Ct	82001
Lucy Ln	82007
Lummis Ct	82007
Lunsford Dr	82001
Lupe Rd	82009
Lupine Trl	82009
Lusk Pl	82009
Luther Pl	82001
Lynx Rd	82009
Macarthur Ave	82007
Macy Pl	82009
Maddies Way	82007
Madison Ave	82001
Magnolia Dr	82009
Mahogany Ct	82009
Main St	82009
Malibu Ct	82009
Mammoth Rd	82009
Mandan Ln	82009
Mandolin Way	82007
Manewal Dr	82009
Manhattan Ln	82009
Manor Ln	82009
Maple Ct	82001
Maple Way	82009
Marble Ave	82001
Maria E Ln	82009
Marian Cir	82001
Marie Ln	82009
Marjon Ct	82009
Marne Loop	82005
Maroon Dr	82001
Marsellaise Ct	82009
Marshall Rd	82009
Martin Esquibel Dr	82001
Martingale Loop	82009
Mary Way	82007
Mary Elizabeth Ln	82007
Maryland Ct	82009
Mason Rd	82009
Max Ct	82009
Maxwell Ave	
101-397	82007
399-999	82007
1501-1597	82001
1599-2800	82001
2802-3398	82001
Mcallister Ln	82009
Mccann Ave	82001
Mccomb Ave	
200-499	82007
3101-3197	82001
3199-3999	82001
Mccue Dr	82009
Mcdonald Rd	82009
Mcfarland Ave	82007
Mcgarry Dr	82009
Mcgovern Ave	82001
Mcintire Ln	82007
Mckenzie Loop	82009
Mckinley Ave	82001
Mckinney Dr	82009
Meadow Dr	82001
Meadowbrook Dr	82009
Meadowland Dr	82009
Meadowlark Ln	82009
Medicine Bow Ave	82007
Medley Loop	82007
Melody Ln	82007
Melton St	82009
Merritt Rd	82009
Mesa Ct & Trl	82009
Messerger Ct	82001
Miami Cir	82001
Michael Dr	82009
Michelle St	82009
Michelle Joy Hts	82009
Michigan St	82009
Middle Fork Trl	82007
Milatzo Ave	82007
Miles Ct	82009
Military Rd	82009
Miller Ln	82009
E, N, S & W Milliron Rd	82009
Milton Dr	82001
Minuteman Ct & Dr	82001
Miracle Pkwy	82009
Missile Dr	
1900-2698	82001
4600-7899	82005
Mission Ct	82009
Missouri Ave	82005
Mitchell Ct & Pl	82007
Moccasin Ave	82009
Monarch Dr	82009
Monroe Ave & Ct	82001
Montalto Dr	82007
Montclair Dr	82009
Monte Carlo Dr	82009
Moonlight Ct	82009
Moore Ave	82001
Moran Ave	82009
Moreland Ave	82009
Morgan Dr	82009
Morgan Ranch Rd	82007
Moriah Ln	82009
Morning Glory Trl	82007
Morningside Dr	82001
Morningstar Rd	82009
Morrie Ave	
2-498	82007
500-899	82007
1401-1697	82001
1699-2499	82001
Morrison Ct	82001
Mount Meeker Rd	82009
Mountain Ct & Trl	82009
Mountain Shadow Dr & Ln	82009
Mountain View Loop	82009
Mountainview Dr	82009
Mueller Rd	82009
Mugho Rd	82009
Mulberry Ave	82001
E & S Mule Trl	82009
Mule Deer Rd	82005
Murray Rd	82007
Murray Hill Dr	82009
Muscadine Way	82009
Musket Dr	82005
Muskogee Loop	82001
E Mustang Rd	82009
Myers Ct	82001
Mylar Park Dr	82009
Mynear St	82009
E & W Nation Rd	82007
E Nationway	82001
Natrona Ave	82001
Neal Ave	82007
Nebraska Ave	82005
Neilsen Ranch Rd	82007
New Bedford Dr	82009
New York Rd	82009
Newland Ave	82009
Newton Dr	82001
Nimmo Dr	82009
Ninemile Blvd	82009
Norma Ct	82007
Northamerican Rd	82007
Northgate Ave	82009
Northview Dr	82009
Notre Dame Ct	82009
Oak Ct	82001
Oak Valley Ln	82009
Oakhurst Dr	82009
Oasis St	82009
Obsidian Rd	82009
Ocean Ave	82001
Ocean Loop	82009
E Ogallala Pl	82009
Ogden Rd	82009
Ok Trl	82007
Old Faithful Rd	82001
Old Glory Rd	82005
Old Happy Jack Rd	
1501-2799	82001
4000-5098	82009
Old Town Ln	82009
Old Trail Rd	82001
E & W Ole Maverick Rd	82009
Olive Dr	82001
Omaha Rd	82001
Omega Rd	82009
Oneil Ave	
401-497	82007
499-1099	82007
1500-2098	82001
2100-3099	82001
3101-3199	82001
Ontario Ave	
4300-4599	82001
4600-4999	82009
Opal Dr	82009
N Orchard Dr	82009
Orchid Ct	82001
Orion Dr	82009
Osage Ave	82009
Ostdiek Ct	82001
Ottawa Dr	82001
Otto Rd	82001
Overland Trl	82009
Owl Creek Ave	82007
Oxford Dr	82001
Pacific Ave	82007
Packard Rd	82009
Paintbrush Ct	82001
Painted Horse Trl	82009
Painted Sky Rd	82009
Palen Rd	82007
Palm Springs Ave	82009
Palmer St	82001
Pamela Ln	82009
Panorama Ct & Dr	82009
Parade Rd	82005
Paradise Pointe	82009
Park Ave	82007
Park Pl	82001
Parkhill Rd	82009
Parkside Dr	82001
Parkview Dr	82001
S Parsley Blvd	82007
Parsons Pl	82001
Pasadena Dr & Rd	82009
S Pass Trl	82007
Pathfinder Ave	82001
Patio Dr	82009
Patricia Ct & Ln	82009
Patrol Rd	82005
Pattison Ave	82009
Patton Ave	82007
Pawnee Ave	82009
Peace Pointe	82009
Peacekeeper Rd	82001
Peach St	82007
Pearl Ct	82007
Pebble Bend Ct	82009
Pebrican Ave	
101-797	82007
799-999	82007
1600-2299	82001
Pegasus Pt	82009
Pennsylvania Ave	82001
Penny Ln	82009
E Pershing Blvd	
100-198	82001
200-7299	82001
7301-7999	82001
8000-9599	82009
9601-9999	82009
W Pershing Blvd	82001
Pershing Pointe Dr	82001
Persons Rd	82007
Petersen Dr	82009
Pharmond Trl	82009
Phillips Pl	82009
Phoenix Dr	82001
Piccadilly Dr	82009
Pierce Ave	82001
Pike St	82009
Pine Ave	82007
Pine Dr	82001
Pine Bluffs St	82009
Pine Tree Rd	82009
Pineridge Ave	82009
Pinion Dr	82001
Pinto Ln	82007

Pioneer Ave 82001
Piper Ln 82009
Pitchfork Rd 82007
Piute Dr
  1700-2599 82001
  1755-1799 82005
Plain View Rd 82009
W Plains Ave & Rd 82009
Plains View Dr 82009
Plainsview Ct 82009
Plateau Ct 82009
Platte Ave 82001
E & W Plaza 82005
Pleasant Valley Trl 82007
Plum Dr 82001
Plum St 82007
Point Blf 82009
Pointe Pinnacle 82009
Polar Blf 82009
Polar Star Ct 82009
Polaris Pt 82009
Pole Mountain Rd 82009
Polk Ave 82001
E & W Polo Plate 82009
Polo Ranch Rd 82009
Ponderosa Rd & Trl 82009
Pontillo Dr 82007
Pony Express Rd 82009
Pool Dr 82001
Poplar Ct 82001
Portugee Phillips Rd 82009
Post Rd 82005
Potomac St 82001
Poulos Dr 82009
Powderhouse Rd 82009
E & W Powell Rd 82009
Prairie Ave 82009
Prairie Center Cir 82009
Prairie Dog Dr 82001
Prairie Hills Cir & Dr 82009
Prairie Lark Ln 82009
Prairie Schooner Rd 82009
Prairie View Rd 82009
Prevailing Dr 82009
Primrose Trl 82007
Princeton Ln 82009
Progress Cir 82007
Pronghorn Ct 82009
Pronghorn Rd 82005
Prospect Ct 82009
E & W Prosser Rd 82007
Providence Pl 82001
Ptarmigan Ln 82009
Puma Path 82009
Quarter Circle Dr 82009
Queens Rd 82007
Quincy Rd 82009
Rachel Rd 82007
Ragtime Dr 82007
Railroad Rd 82009
Rain Dancer Trl 82001
Rainbow Rd 82001
Rainbow Rdg 82009
Ranch Ct 82007
Ranch Loop 82009
Ranch Rd 82009
Ranch House Way 82001
Ranch View Dr 82001
Randall Ave
  200-6108 82005
  300-1300 82001
  1302-1398 82001
  6109-6109 82001
  6110-7698 82005
  6111-7699 82005
Randy Rd 82001
Range Line Rd 82009
Ranger Dr 82009
Rangeview Dr 82001
Rawhide Rdg 82007
Rawlins St 82001
Rayor Ave 82001
Red Blf 82009
Red Cloud Trl 82009
Red Fox Rd 82009
Red Rocks Rd 82007
Red Sky Loop 82009
Red Tail Way 82009
Redhawk Dr 82007
Redmond Rd 82009
Redwood Ct 82009
Reed Ave
  200-1099 82007
  2300-4000 82001
  4002-4098 82001
Reese Rd 82009
Regal Ct 82001
Register Cliff Ct 82009
E & W Reiner Ct & Pl 82007
Remington Ct, Dr & Way 82007
Renee Rd 82007
Riata Rd 82007
Richardson Ct 82001
N Ridge Dr 82009
Ridge Rd
  901-997 82001
  999-4599 82001
  4701-4797 82009
  4799-9299 82009
Ridgeland St 82009
E & W Riding Club Rd 82009
Ridley Rd 82009
Rilley Rd 82009
Rim Rd 82009
Rio Verde Cir & St 82001
Rising Star 82009
Riverbend Rd 82001
Road 106 82009
Road 109 82009
Road 110 82009
Road 110a 82009
Road 118a 82009
Road 11o 82009
Road 120 82009
Road 123 82009
Road 124 82009
Road 124a 82009
Road 126 82009
Road 128 82009
Road 128a 82007
Road 132
  101-199 82007
Road 132
  3300-3599 82009
Road 134 82009
Road 135 82009
Road 136 82009
Road 137 82009
Road 138
  300-799 82007
  2500-2599 82009
Road 139 82009
Road 140 82009
Road 142 82009
Road 143 82009
Road 144 82009
Road 150 82009
Road 203 82007
Road 206 82001
Road 207 82007
Road 209 82007
Road 210 82009
Road 212 82009
Road 214 82009
Road 215 82009
Road 216 82009
Road 217 82009
Road 218 82009
Road 219 82009
Road 220 82009
Road 222 82009
Road 223 82009
Road 224 82009
Road 225 82009
Road 226 82009
Road 227 82009
Road 228 82009
Road 229 82009
Road 231 82009
Road 232 82009
Road 234 82009
Road 237 82009
Road 237a 82009
Road 238 82009
Road 240 82009
Road 242 82009
Robert Ave 82007
Robin Dr 82009
Robitaille Ct 82001
Rock Springs St 82001
Rockcrest Ct & Dr 82009
Rockwood Dr 82001
Rocky Rd 82009
Rodeo Ave & Ct 82009
Rogers Ave 82009
Rogers Dr 82005
Rogers Rd 82005
Rolling Hills Dr 82009
Rollins Ave 82001
Rooks Ave 82007
Ropers Ln 82009
Rose Ct 82009
Rosebud Rd 82001
Rosetta Ln 82007
Rough Rider Loop 82001
Roundtop Ct, Dr & Rd 82009
Roundup Rd 82009
Rozetta Cir 82009
Ruby Dr 82009
Rucker Rd 82009
Rue Royal 82009
Rue Terre 82009
Ruger Dr 82007
Russell Ave
  100-498 82007
  500-800 82007
  802-998 82007
  1500-1598 82001
  1600-2299 82001
  2301-2499 82001
Rustrali Ave 82001
Rutgers Rd 82009
Ryan Ave 82009
Saber Rd 82005
Sabrina Rd 82007
Saddle Dr 82009
Saddle Ridge Trl 82001
Saddleback Dr 82001
Sage Rd 82001
Sagebrush Ave 82009
Saint James Rd 82009
Sampson Rd 82005
Samuel Ln 82009
San Mateo Pl 82009
Sandstone Ln 82001
Santa Fe Trl 82009
Santa Marie Dr 82009
Santontr Ave 82007
Sapphire St 82001
Saratoga St 82001
Savage Dr 82007
Savannah Dr 82001
Say Kally Rd 82009
Scenic Ct 82009
Scenic Ridge Dr 82009
Schrader Ln 82009
Scofield Ct 82007
Scott Dr 82007
Scout Rd 82001
Secret Valley Trl 82007
Secretariat Rd E & W 82009
Seminoe Rd 82009
Seneca Ave 82001
Sequoia Ct 82009
Serenity Ct 82009
Seslar Ave 82009
Seymour Ave
  100-899 82007
  901-999 82007
  1600-2599 82001
Shadow Dr 82009
Shadow Mountain Cir & Trl 82009
Shadow Ridge Dr 82009
Shadow Rock Dr 82009
Shadow Valley Rd 82009
Shannon Ave 82009
Shapra Rd 82009
Shaun Ave 82009
Shaver Rd 82009
Shawnee St 82001
Shell Beach Ave 82009
Shellback Rd 82009
Shenandoah St 82001
Sheridan St 82009
Sherman Mountain Loop & Rd 82009
Sherry Rd 82009
Shooting Star Trl 82007
Shoshoni St 82009
Sierra Dr 82009
Sierra Madre St 82007
Silver Fox Ln 82009
Silver Moon Ct 82009
Silver Sage Ave 82009
Silver Spur Rd 82009
Silver Tip Dr 82009
Silvergate Ct & Dr 82001
Silverton Dr 82001
Sioux Dr 82009
Sitting Bull Rd 82009
Sky Top Rd 82009
Skyline Dr 82009
Skyview Cir 82007
Skyway Ave 82009
Smith Pl 82009
Smokebrush Ct & Dr 82009
Smoking Oak Rd 82009
Snake River Ave 82007
Snow Crest Dr 82009
Snow Mass Ct 82009
Snow Valley Ct 82009
Snowberry Dr 82009
Snowy River Rd 82001
Snyder Ave
  100-1100 82007
  1102-1198 82007
  1500-1598 82001
  1600-4099 82001
Solitude Loop 82009
Sonata Ln 82007
Southern View Dr 82007
Southfork Rd 82007
Southwest Dr 82007
Space Dr 82009
Sparks Rd 82001
Speer Rd 82007
Spencer Dr 82007
Spiker Rd 82009
Spirit Ln 82009
Split Rail Ct 82001
Split Rock Dr 82009
Spring Ct 82009
Spring Beauty Trl 82007
Spring Creek Rd 82009
Spring Valley Dr 82009
Springer Ct 82001
Springfield Dr 82007
Spruce Ct & Dr 82001
Spur Dr 82001
Squash Blossom Trl 82009
Stage Rd 82005
Stage Loop Rd 82005
Stagecoach Rd 82009
Stallion Dr 82009
Stampede Cir 82009
Stampede Ranch Rd 82007
Stanfield Ave 82007
Star Loop & Pass 82009
Star Bright Dr 82009
Star Hill Ct 82009
Star Pass Rd 82009
Star Valley Dr 82009
Star Wood Ct 82009
Stardust Trl 82009
Starfire Ct 82009
Starlight Ct 82009
State St 82009
States Rd 82009
Steamboat Ln 82009
Stephanie Ct 82007
Sterling Dr 82009
Stetson Dr 82009
Steve Ave 82007
Stevens Dr 82001
Stewart Rd 82009
Stillwater Ave 82009
Stinner Rd 82001
Stinson Ave
  200-499 82007
  1500-1598 82001
Stirrup Rd 82007
Stockman St 82009
Stone Trl 82009
Stoneridge Dr 82009
Stonewood Dr 82001
Storey Blvd 82009
Studebaker Rd 82009
Stundon Ave 82007
Sugarloaf Ln 82009
Sullivan St 82009
Summerhill Ct 82009
Summerset Dr 82001
Summit Ct & Dr 82009
Sun Ct 82009
Sun Valley Dr 82001
Sunbright Trl 82007
Sundance Ln 82007
Sundance Loop 82009
Sunflower Rd 82009
Sunlight Rd 82009
Sunny Pl 82001
Sunny Glen Ln 82009
Sunny Hill Dr 82001
Sunny Ridge Ln 82001
Sunridge Dr 82007
Sunrise Rd 82001
Sunrise Hills Dr 82009
Sunset Dr 82009
Superior Ave 82001
Surrey Rd 82009
Swan Ct & Trl 82007
Sweetwater Trl 82009
Swing 82007
Sycamore Rd 82009
Syracuse Rd 82009
N & S Table Mountain Loop 82009
Tada Ln 82009
Taft Ave 82001
Taggart Dr 82007
Talbot Ct 82001
Talon Ct 82009
Tampa Ct 82001
Targhee Ave 82007
Tate Rd 82001
Telephone Rd 82009
Telluride Dr 82009
Ten Sleep Dr 82009
Tennessee Rd 82009
Teresa Cir 82009
Territory Rd 82005
Terry Rd 82007
Terry Ranch Rd 82007
Teton St 82007
Thomas Rd 82009
Thomes Ave
  401-497 82007
  499-500 82007
  502-1098 82007
  1500-1698 82001
  1700-3199 82001
Thoroughbred Ln 82009
W Thumb Rd 82009
Thunder Rd 82009
Thunder Ridge Rd 82009
Timber Wolf Rd 82009
Timberline Ct & Rd 82009
Tom Horn Trl 82009
Tomahawk Rd 82009
Tonto Rd 82009
Topaz Dr 82009
Toria Rd 82009
Torrington Rd 82009
Tower Junction Rd 82009
Townsend Pl 82009
Trail Way Rd 82007
Trails End Dr 82009
Tranquility Rd 82009
Treadway Trl 82009
Trent Ct 82009
Trinidad Ct 82009
Trophy Dr 82009
Troyer Dr 82007
Trucker Trl 82007
Trumpeter Dr 82007
Tuckaway Ct 82007
Tumbleweed Dr 82009
Tundra Dr 82007
Tura Pkwy 82001
Turk Ave & Ct 82007
Turquoise Rd 82009
Twilight Ct 82009
Twin Mountain Rd 82009
Tyler Pl 82007
Uintah Rd 82001
Us Highway 30
  3300-6899 82001
Us Highway 30
  6901-7599 82001
  8000-11999 82009
Us Highway 85 82007
Utah St 82009
Ute Ave 82001
Valley View Ct, Dr & Pl 82009
Van Buren Ave
  3600-4399 82001
  4401-4599 82001
  4600-7699 82009
Van Lennen Ave
  100-800 82007
  802-998 82007
  1600-2799 82001
Van Velzor Ave 82009
Vandehei Ave 82009
Vaughn Ct 82007
Veda Dr 82009
Ventor Rd 82009
Ventura Dr 82009
Vera Ln 82009
Verlan Way 82009
Vermont Rd 82009
Vesle Dr 82005
Victoria Dr 82009
View Point Ct 82009
E & W Villa Cir 82009
Village Ln & Way 82009
Village View Ln 82009
Virginia Ct & Rd 82009
Vista Ln 82009
Volar Dr 82009
Vosler Pl 82009
Wadlow Ranch Rd 82009
Wagon Box Rd 82009
Wagon Trail Dr 82009
Wahoo Pl 82009
Walden Rd 82007
Walker Ln 82007
Walker Rd 82009
E & W Wallick Rd 82007
Walnut Dr 82001
Walterscheid Blvd 82007
Wapiti Dr 82005
Wapiti Trl 82007
War Admiral Rd 82009
Warren Ave
  701-1099 82007
  1600-1698 82001
  1700-3899 82001
  3901-3999 82001
Warrior Ave 82007
Wasatch St 82007
Washakie Loop 82001
Washington Ave 82001
Water Line Rd 82009
Wayne Rd 82009
Wayside Ct 82009
Weatherby Dr 82007
Weathertop Ave 82001
Weaver Rd 82009
Webster Ln 82007
Welchester Dr 82009
Wenandy Ave 82001
Wendy Ln 82009
Westedt Rd 82009
Western Way 82001
Western Hills Blvd 82009
Westland Ct & Rd 82001
Westview Dr 82007
Wheatland Dr 82009
Whirlaway Rd 82009
Whispering Hills Rd 82009
Whistler Dr 82009
White Blf 82009
White Cloud Rd 82001
White Eagle Rd 82009
White Water Ct 82009
Whitetail Rd 82009
Whitney Rd
  1900-1998 82007
  2601-3297 82001
  3299-4599 82001
  4700-6999 82009
Wild Bill Ct 82001
Wild Cat Trl 82009
Wild Rose Trl 82007
Wilderness Trl 82001
Wildflower Dr 82009
Wildhorse Trl 82009
Williams St 82007
Willow Dr 82001
Willow Way 82009
Wills Rd 82001
Willshire Blvd 82009
Willson Ct 82007
Wilson Ranch Rd 82009
Winchester Blvd 82007
Wind Dancer Rd 82009
Wind River Trl 82009
Windbreak Dr 82009
Windhaven Ln 82009
Windmill Rd
  800-898 82001
  900-1200 82001
  1202-1298 82001
  2500-2599 82009
  3600-3699 82001
  4301-4697 82009
  4699-5399 82009
Windsor Blvd 82009
Windwood Dr 82001
Woodcrest Ave 82001
Woodhaven Dr 82001
Woodhouse Rd 82001
Woods Rd 82009
Woodward Dr 82007
Worth Dr 82001
E & W Wrangler Rd 82009
Wright Ct 82001
Wyodak Loop 82001
Wyoming Ave 82005
Wyott Dr 82007
Yarina Way 82009
Yellow Bear Rd 82009
Yellowstone Rd 82009
Yellowtail Rd 82009
York Ave 82007
Yucca Rd 82001
Yuma Ct 82001
Zelma Dr 82009
Ziemann Ct 82001
Zuni St 82001

NUMBERED STREETS

E 1st Ave 82001
S 1st Ave 82007
W 1st Ave 82001
E 1st St 82007
2 Hearts Trl 82007
E 2nd Ave 82001
S 2nd Ave 82007
W 2nd Ave 82001
E 2nd St 82007
W 2nd St 82007
E 3rd Ave 82001
S 3rd Ave 82007
W 3rd Ave 82001
E 3rd St 82007
W 3rd St 82007

E 4th Ave ... 82001
S 4th Ave ... 82007
W 4th Ave ... 82001
E 4th St ... 82007
W 4th St ... 82007
E 5th Ave ... 82001
S 5th Ave ... 82007
W 5th Ave ... 82001
E 5th St ... 82007
W 5th St ... 82007
5th Cavalry Ave ... 82005
E 6th Ave ... 82001
W 6th Ave ... 82001
E 6th St
- 200-1200 ... 82007
- 1202-1298 ... 82007
- 3900-4999 ... 82001

W 6th St ... 82007
E 7th Ave ... 82001
W 7th Ave ... 82001
E 7th St
- 201-397 ... 82007
- 399-1299 ... 82007
- 2400-4999 ... 82001

W 7th St ... 82007
E 8th Ave
- 100-123 ... 82001
- 124-398 ... 82001
- 124-124 ... 82003
- 125-215 ... 82001

W 8th Ave ... 82001
E 8th St
- 200-1199 ... 82007
- 2300-3898 ... 82001
- 3900-5099 ... 82001

W 8th St ... 82007
E 9th St
- 200-1099 ... 82007
- 2100-2298 ... 82001

W 9th St ... 82007
E 10th St
- 200-599 ... 82007
- 2100-4799 ... 82001

W 10th St ... 82007
10th Cavalry Ave ... 82005
E 11th St ... 82001
W 11th St ... 82007
E 12th St ... 82001
E 13th St ... 82001
E 14th St ... 82001
E & W 15th ... 82001
15th Cavalry Ave ... 82005
E 16th St ... 82001
E & W 17th ... 82001
E & W 18th ... 82001
E & W 19th ... 82001
E & W 20th ... 82001
E & W 21st ... 82001
E & W 22nd ... 82001
E & W 23rd ... 82001
E & W 24th ... 82001
E & W 25th ... 82001
E & W 26th ... 82001
E & W 27th ... 82001
E & W 28th ... 82001
E & W 29th ... 82001
W 30th St ... 82001
W 31st St ... 82001
W 32nd St ... 82001

EVANSTON WY

General Delivery ... 82930

POST OFFICE BOXES MAIN OFFICE STATIONS AND BRANCHES

Box No.s
All PO Boxes ... 82931

NAMED STREETS

A Ave ... 82930
Agape Way ... 82930
Alecias Way ... 82930
Allegiance Cir ... 82930
Almy Road 105 ... 82930
Almy Road 107 ... 82930
Alpine Cir ... 82930
Amy Rd ... 82930
W Anderson St ... 82930
Andrea Ave ... 82930
Antelope Dr ... 82930
Apache Dr ... 82930
Appaloosa Dr ... 82930
Arapahoe Cir ... 82930
Arrowhead Cir & Dr ... 82930
Ash St ... 82930
Aspen Grove Dr E & W ... 82930
Aspen Hills Ct ... 82930
Autumn Ave ... 82930
B Ave ... 82930
Barrett Ave ... 82930
Bear Cir & Ln ... 82930
Bear River Dr ... 82930
Beckers Cir ... 82930
Benjamin Franklin St ... 82930
Bighorn Dr ... 82930
Billies Cir ... 82930
Birch St ... 82930
Bodine Ave ... 82930
Boone Ct ... 82930
Briarwood Ct ... 82930
Bridger Rd ... 82930
Broken Circle Dr ... 82930
Brookhollow Dr ... 82930
Burns Ave ... 82930
Butterfield Rd ... 82930
C Ave ... 82930
Cale Dr ... 82930
Campbell Ave ... 82930
Canyon Hollow Dr ... 82930
Carriage Dr ... 82930
Castlehale Way ... 82930
Catalina Ct ... 82930
Cedar St ... 82930
W Center St ... 82930
Champs Ave ... 82930
Chandler Ln ... 82930
Cherokee Ct ... 82930
W Cheyenne Dr ... 82930
China Mary Rd ... 82930
Citation Ln ... 82930
City View Dr ... 82930
Clark Ave ... 82930
Clarkson Ave ... 82930
Cobble Creek Dr ... 82930
Colonial Ave ... 82930
Comanche Ct ... 82930
Commerce Dr ... 82930
Constitution Ave ... 82930
Cottonwood St ... 82930
Country Way ... 82930
Country Club Dr ... 82930
County Rd ... 82930
County Road 101 ... 82930
County Road 103 ... 82930
County Road 108 ... 82930
County Road 109 ... 82930
County Road 111 ... 82930
County Road 152 ... 82930
County Road 157 ... 82930
County Road 158 ... 82930
County Road 159 ... 82930
County Road 160 ... 82930
County Road 161 ... 82930
County Road 162 ... 82930
County Road 164 ... 82930
County Road 165 ... 82930
County Road 166 ... 82930
County Road 167 ... 82930
County Road 169 ... 82930
County Road 173 ... 82930
Cox Ct ... 82930
Crane Ave ... 82930
Crestview Dr ... 82930
Crompton Rd ... 82930
Curved Way ... 82930
D Ave ... 82930
Darby Ln ... 82930
Davis Dr ... 82930
Dean Ave ... 82930
Declaration Dr ... 82930
N Deer Mountain Rd ... 82930
Del Rio Dr ... 82930
Donner Ave ... 82930
Duncomb Hollow Dr ... 82930
Dunmar Ln ... 82930
Eldorado Ct ... 82930
Elk Dr ... 82930
Elkridge Ln ... 82930
Elliot Dr ... 82930
Elm St ... 82930
Ember St ... 82930
Emerson Ave ... 82930
Erica Dr ... 82930
Evans Ln ... 82930
Expedition Dr ... 82930
Fearn Ln & Rd ... 82930
Feather Way ... 82930
Fife Ct ... 82930
Florence Ave ... 82930
Fox Point Ct ... 82930
Fox Point Loop Rd ... 82930
Freedom Dr ... 82930
Freedom Country Ln ... 82930
Front St ... 82930
Front Stretch ... 82930
Gage Ave ... 82930
Gannett Dr ... 82930
Garner Ave ... 82930
Grand View Cir ... 82930
Granite Dr ... 82930
Grass Valley Dr ... 82930
Greek St ... 82930
Green River Cir ... 82930
Gregory Ave ... 82930
Hale Cir ... 82930
Hansen Ave ... 82930
Harrison Dr
- 100-1999 ... 82930
- 100-100 ... 82931

Hathaway Ave ... 82930
Haw Patch Ln ... 82930
E Hayden Ave ... 82930
Herschler Ave ... 82930
Hickey Ave ... 82930
Hidden Hollow Ct ... 82930
Highridge Pt ... 82930
Hillcrest Park Ave ... 82930
Hillside Dr ... 82930
Holbrook Ct ... 82930
Holland Dr ... 82930
Home Stretch ... 82930
Hopi Ct ... 82930
Horn Rd ... 82930
Hoyt Cir ... 82930
Hunt Ave ... 82930
Imperial Dr ... 82930
Incline Dr ... 82930
Independence Dr ... 82930
Jamison Dr ... 82930
Jared Ln ... 82930
John Adams St ... 82930
John Hancock St ... 82930
Johnston Ln ... 82930
Jones Ave ... 82930
Juniper Ridge Ct & Dr ... 82930
Kimberly Ave ... 82930
Kindler Dr ... 82930
Kingfisher Ave ... 82930
Kings Ct ... 82930
Kirlin Dr ... 82930
Knotty Pine Dr ... 82930
Lakeview Dr ... 82930
Laramie St ... 82930
Laredo Rd ... 82930
Liberty Ave ... 82930
Lilac Way ... 82930
Lincoln Ave ... 82930
Little Falls Rd ... 82930
Lodgepole Dr ... 82930
Lombard St ... 82930
Loop Rd ... 82930
Lucas Ave ... 82930
Lucille Cir ... 82930
Lupine Dr ... 82930
W Main St ... 82930
Manderne Dr ... 82930
Maple St ... 82930
Marble Dr ... 82930
Marilyn Ave ... 82930
Marsh Ln ... 82930
Marshall Ave ... 82930
Meadow Dr ... 82930
Meadow View St ... 82930
Medicine Butte Dr ... 82930
Mesa Dr ... 82930
Michael Ave ... 82930
Mill Creek Rd ... 82930
Miller Ave ... 82930
S Mirror Lake Hwy ... 82930
Mohawk Ct ... 82930
Moon Way ... 82930
Morgan Cir & Dr ... 82930
W Morse Lee St ... 82930
Mountain Rd ... 82930
Mountain View Dr ... 82930
Mountain Village Dr ... 82930
Mustang Dr ... 82930
Nacho Rd ... 82930
Navajo Cir ... 82930
No Name St ... 82930
Oak St ... 82930
Ortega Ct ... 82930
Ottley Ln ... 82930
Overlook Ct ... 82930
Overthrust Rd ... 82930
Paddock Cir ... 82930
Palomino Dr ... 82930
Park Rd ... 82930
Pasture Dr ... 82930
Patriot Ct ... 82930
Peart Ave ... 82930
Pine St ... 82930
Piper Ct ... 82930
Pleasant View St ... 82930
Ponderosa St ... 82930
Porter Rd ... 82930
Prospector Dr ... 82930
Quarter Horse Dr ... 82930
Rail Ctr ... 82930
Randall Way ... 82930
Rapid Canyon Dr ... 82930
Rebel Dr ... 82930
Red Hawk Ave ... 82930
Red Mountain Rd & Ter ... 82930
S Red Willow Rd ... 82930
Remington Cir & Dr ... 82930
Revolution Ave ... 82930
Richard St ... 82930
Ridge Ln ... 82930
Ridgecrest Ave ... 82930
Rimrock Dr ... 82930
Riverbend Ct ... 82930
Riverside Loop ... 82930
Riverview Dr ... 82930
Roaring Fork Dr ... 82930
Roosevelt Ave ... 82930
Ross Ave ... 82930
Sac Fox Ct ... 82930
Saddle Ridge Rd ... 82930
W Sage St ... 82930
Sage Industrial Rd ... 82930
Sand Hill Cir ... 82930
Sandstone Dr ... 82930
Saunders Cir ... 82930
Sawmill Ln ... 82930
Schwitzers Ct ... 82930
Scotts Dr ... 82930
Seale Rd ... 82930
Seminole Dr ... 82930
E Service Rd ... 82930
Shady Ln ... 82930
Silver Sage Dr ... 82930
Silverwood Way ... 82930
Simpson Ave ... 82930
Sims Ln ... 82930
Sioux Dr ... 82930
Skyline Dr ... 82930
Smith Ave ... 82930
South Ave ... 82930
Southridge Rd ... 82930
Sparrow Dr ... 82930
Springbrook Dr ... 82930
Stahley Ave ... 82930
State Highway 150 S ... 82930
State Highway 89 N ... 82930
Straight And Narrow Dr ... 82930
W Summit St ... 82930
Sundance Ave ... 82930
Sunset Ave ... 82930
Superior Dr ... 82930
Thayer Cir ... 82930
Thornock Ave ... 82930
Tomahawk Dr ... 82930
Toponce Dr ... 82930
Troy Ct ... 82930
Twin Ridge Ave ... 82930
W Uinta Cir & St ... 82930
Union Cir & Dr ... 82930
Urroz Rd ... 82930
Ute Cir ... 82930
S Valley Dr ... 82930
Valley View Ave ... 82930
Village Dr ... 82930
Vista Ridge Cir ... 82930
Walker Rd ... 82930
Wall St ... 82930
Walton Ave ... 82930
Wasatch Rd ... 82930
Washakie Dr ... 82930
Washington Ave ... 82930
West St ... 82930
Westview Ct ... 82930
White Water Dr ... 82930
Wilderness Pt ... 82930
Willow Dr ... 82930
Wind River Dr ... 82930
Windy Ridge Ct ... 82930
Woodridge Ln ... 82930
Worland Cir ... 82930
Wright Way ... 82930
Yellow Creek Rd ... 82930
Yellowstone River Dr ... 82930
Zuni Ct ... 82930

NUMBERED STREETS

All Street Addresses ... 82930

GILLETTE WY

General Delivery ... 82716

POST OFFICE BOXES MAIN OFFICE STATIONS AND BRANCHES

Box No.s
All PO Boxes ... 82717

NAMED STREETS

A Ct & Ln ... 82716
Abby Ct ... 82718
Airport Rd ... 82716
Alberta Dr ... 82718
Aleute Ln ... 82716
Alex Way ... 82718
Alexis Ct ... 82718
Alison Ave ... 82718
Allen Ave ... 82718
Almon Cir & Dr ... 82718
Alpine Dr ... 82716
American Ln & Rd ... 82716
Andover St ... 82716
Andre Ct ... 82718
Angus Dr ... 82718
Antelope Rd ... 82718
Antelope Valley St ... 82718
Antler Rd ... 82718
Anvil ... 82718
Apache Cir ... 82718
Apex Ct ... 82716
Apple Blossom Way ... 82716
Apple Creek St ... 82716
Apricot St ... 82716
Arapahoe Ave ... 82718
Arcadia Ave ... 82716
Arctic Ave ... 82718
Ariel Ave ... 82718
Arizona St ... 82716
Arlington Ct ... 82718
Arrow Blvd ... 82716
Arrowhead Dr ... 82718
Ash St ... 82716
Ash Meadows Dr ... 82716
Aspen Ln ... 82716
Aster Ln ... 82716
Astoria Ave ... 82716
Augusta Cir ... 82718
Austin Dr ... 82718
S Autumn Ct ... 82718
Avalon Ct ... 82716
Axels Ave ... 82718
B Ct & Ln ... 82716
B Bar L Ln ... 82716
Badger Ave ... 82718
Bald Mountain Rd ... 82716
Bantam Ave ... 82718
Barber Creek Rd
- 1-199 ... 82718
- 800-899 ... 82716
- 1800-1899 ... 82718

Bare Buttes Rd ... 82718
Barlow Rd ... 82718
Barrel Racing Ave ... 82718
Battle Cry Ln ... 82716
Bay Ave ... 82716
Baywood St ... 82716
Beacon Ct ... 82718
W Beaver Dr ... 82718
Beech St ... 82716
Bell Rd ... 82718
Bella Colla Ln ... 82716
Belle Ct ... 82718
Belle Fourche Dr ... 82718
Bellows Rd ... 82718
Benelli Dr ... 82718
Benjamin St ... 82716
Benjamin Franklin Rd ... 82718
Bentley Ct ... 82718
Bertha Ave ... 82718
Beryl Ln ... 82716
Big Lost Ct & Dr ... 82718
Big Sky St ... 82718
Big Wood Dr ... 82718
Bighorn Cir ... 82716
Birch Ave ... 82718
Bird Dr ... 82718
Bishop Rd ... 82718
Black And Yellow Rd ... 82718
Blackbird Rd ... 82716
Blackhills St ... 82718
Blacktooth Ave ... 82718
Blaine Ct ... 82716
Blake Rd ... 82716
Blue Ave ... 82718
Blue Tick Ct & Dr ... 82718
Bluebell Ct ... 82716
Bluebird ... 82716
Bluff Blvd ... 82716
Bluffs Ridge Dr ... 82718
Bobolink Ct ... 82716
Boise Ave ... 82716
Bomber Mountain Rd ... 82716
Bonanza Cir ... 82716
Borderline Rd ... 82718
Bowers Ute Rd ... 82716
Box N Ranch Rd ... 82718
Box Wood St ... 82718
E & W Boxelder Rd ... 82718
Boysen Creek Dr ... 82716
Brahma St ... 82718
Brentwood Ct ... 82718
Bridger St ... 82716
Bridle Bit Ct ... 82718
Broadway St ... 82716
Brom St ... 82718
N & S Brooks Ave ... 82716
Brorby Blvd ... 82718
Brown Rd ... 82718
Brown Duck Dr ... 82718
Bruce Ln ... 82716
Bryan Ln ... 82716
N & S Buckboard Ct ... 82718
Buckskin Dr ... 82716
Buffalo Back Peak Rd ... 82716
Buffalo Cut Across Rd ... 82718
Bull Riding Dr ... 82718
Bullion Ct ... 82716
Bundy Ave ... 82716
Bunny Ln ... 82718
N Burma Ave ... 82716
S Burma Ave
- 100-398 ... 82716
- 501-599 ... 82716
- 800-899 ... 82718
- 901-999 ... 82718

Bush Ave ... 82718
Business Cir ... 82716
Butcher Ct ... 82716
Butler Spaeth Rd
- 400-1000 ... 82716
- 1002-1698 ... 82716
- 2001-2599 ... 82718
- 4500-4998 ... 82718

N Butler Spaeth Rd ... 82716
S Butler Spaeth Rd ... 82718
Butte Dr ... 82716
C Ct & Ln ... 82716
Cabin Ct & Dr ... 82718
Caesars Ct ... 82716
Camel Dr ... 82716
Cameo Ct ... 82718
Camillia Ct ... 82716
Canary Rd ... 82716
Canterbury Ct ... 82716
Carey Ave ... 82716
Carlisle St ... 82718
Carmel Ct ... 82716
Carrington Ave ... 82718
Carter Ave ... 82716
Casa Quinta Ave ... 82716
Cascade Ct & Dr ... 82718
Castle Pines Dr ... 82718
Catalina Ct ... 82718
Cattail Dr ... 82718
Cattle Trail Ct ... 82718
Cedar Ave ... 82718
Cedar Creek Ct & Dr ... 82718
Centennial Dr ... 82716
Chancery Ln ... 82716
Chandler Ln ... 82716
Chara Ave ... 82718
Charlie St ... 82718
Cherokee Cir ... 82718
Cherry Dr & Ln ... 82716
Cherry Creek St ... 82716
Cheryl Ave ... 82718
Chestnut Cir ... 82718
Chickadee Rd ... 82716
Chickasaw Ave ... 82718
Chicory Ct ... 82716
Chinook Ln ... 82716
Chippewa Ave ... 82718
Choctaw St ... 82718
Christenson Rd ... 82718
Christinck Ave ... 82718
Chukar Dr ... 82718
Church Ave ... 82716
Cimarron Dr ... 82716
Cindy Dr ... 82716
Circle Dr ... 82716
Clareton Hwy ... 82718
Clarion Ct & Dr ... 82718
Clarkelen Rd ... 82718
Clearview Ct ... 82716
Clemence Ave ... 82718
Cliff Davis Ave ... 82718
Cloud Peak Rd ... 82716

Clover Ave ... 82716
Coal Dust Rd ... 82718
Coal Train Rd ... 82718
Cocklebur Dr ... 82718
Cold Springs Ct ... 82718
N & S College Park Cir
& Ct ... 82718
Collins Ave ... 82718
Collins Rd ... 82716
Collins Rd E ... 82718
Colorado St ... 82716
Columbine Dr ... 82716
Comanche Ave ... 82718
Commerce Dr ... 82718
N Commercial Dr ... 82716
Concho St ... 82718
Conestoga Dr ... 82718
Constitution Dr ... 82716
Cook Rd ... 82716
Copper St ... 82716
Cotton Ave ... 82718
Cottonwood Ln ... 82718
Cottonwood St ... 82716
Coulter Ln ... 82716
Country Club Rd ... 82718
Country Side Dr ... 82716
Cowen Dr ... 82718
Coyote Ct & Trl ... 82718
Coyote Trail Rd ... 82716
Crane St ... 82718
Crazy Horse Ln ... 82716
Cressett St ... 82716
Crestfield Ave & Ct ... 82718
Crestline Cir ... 82716
Crestview Ct ... 82716
Cypress Cir ... 82718
Cysco Ct ... 82718
D Ct ... 82716
Dade Rd ... 82718
Daisy Dr & St ... 82716
Dakota Ct & St ... 82718
Dalbey Ave ... 82716
Daly Rd ... 82716
Danielle Ave ... 82718
Daredevil Ave ... 82718
Darrell St ... 82718
David Ave ... 82718
Davis St ... 82718
Dawn Dr ... 82716
Daybreak Ct & Dr ... 82718
Daylight Ct ... 82718
Decker Ct ... 82716
Declaration Ln ... 82716
Decoy Ave ... 82718
Deer Run Rd ... 82716
Del Toro Dr ... 82716
Delanie Ct ... 82716
Denver Ave ... 82716
Derringer Ct & Dr ... 82718
Desert Hills Cir ... 82716
Diamond Bar Ct ... 82718
Dietrich Ct ... 82718
Dillon Ct ... 82718
Dinwoody Dr ... 82718
Doe Ct ... 82718
Dogwood Ave ... 82718
W Donkey Creek Dr ... 82718
Dorr Way ... 82718
Doud Dr ... 82718
S Douglas Hwy
300-1299 ... 82716
1800-1898 ... 82718
1900-6199 ... 82718
6201-6599 ... 82718
Dove Rd ... 82718
Dryfork Dr ... 82718
Dubois Ln ... 82716
Duck Head Dr ... 82718
Dull Knife ... 82718
E Ct ... 82716
Eagles Nest Cir ... 82716
W Echeta Rd ... 82716
Edison Ave ... 82716
Edwards Rd & St ... 82718
El Camino Ct & Rd ... 82716
Elder St ... 82718

Elk Mountain Dr ... 82718
Elk Ridge Rd ... 82718
Elk Valley Rd ... 82718
Elm Ave & Ct ... 82716
Elon Ave ... 82716
Emerald Ave ... 82716
S Emerson Ave
200-800 ... 82716
802-898 ... 82716
1900-2799 ... 82718
Emily Ct ... 82718
Energy Ct ... 82718
Energy St ... 82716
S Enterprise Ave ... 82716
Escheta Ln ... 82716
Essex Ct ... 82718
Estes Ln ... 82716
Evening Shadow Ct ... 82718
N Exchange Ave ... 82716
Express Dr ... 82718
Ez St ... 82718
F Ct ... 82716
Fairview Rd ... 82718
Fairway Dr ... 82718
Falcon Ave ... 82718
Fawn Ct ... 82718
Federal Ave ... 82718
Fern Ave ... 82716
Fir Ave & Ct ... 82716
Fitch Dr ... 82718
Fitch Rd ... 82716
Fitzpatrick Ct & Dr ... 82718
Five Finger Peaks Rd ... 82716
Flower Cir ... 82716
E & W Flying Circle
Dr ... 82716
Flying D ... 82718
Foothills Blvd & Cir ... 82716
Force Rd
101-197 ... 82716
199-499 ... 82716
501-549 ... 82716
551-9199 ... 82718
Forge Ct ... 82718
Four-J Ct ... 82716
Fox Ln ... 82716
Fox Butte St ... 82718
Fox Park Ave ... 82718
Fox Ridge Ave ... 82718
Foxhill Ave ... 82718
Foxrun Dr ... 82718
Franklin Ave ... 82716
Freedom Rd ... 82718
Friday Ct & St ... 82718
Frisky Ct ... 82718
Frontage Rd ... 82718
Frontier Dr ... 82718
Frying Pan Lake Rd ... 82718
G Ct ... 82716
Gage Ct ... 82718
Gallery View Dr ... 82718
Game Trail Ct ... 82718
Gannett Ct ... 82718
Gap Rd ... 82718
Garden Cir ... 82716
Gargoyle Peak Ct ... 82716
Garman Ct & Rd ... 82716
Garner Lake Rd ... 82718
N Garner Lake Rd ... 82716
S Garner Lake Rd ... 82718
George Washington
Rd ... 82718
Georgia Cir ... 82718
N Gillette Ave ... 82716
S Gillette Ave
100-1099 ... 82716
1701-1897 ... 82716
1899-2299 ... 82718
Glacier St ... 82718
Glenn Ave ... 82716
Glock Ave ... 82718
Glover Ct ... 82718
Gold Rd ... 82716
Goldenrod Ave ... 82718
Gordon St ... 82718
Graham Ave ... 82716

Grand View Ct & Dr ... 82718
Grandview Cir ... 82716
Granite Ct & St ... 82718
Green Ave ... 82716
Greensburgh Ave ... 82718
Greenway Dr ... 82716
Greenwood Ave ... 82716
Grosventre Way ... 82716
Grouse Ave ... 82718
Grover Dr ... 82716
Gunpowder St ... 82718
N & S Gurley Ave ... 82716
H Ct ... 82716
Hackamore Ct ... 82718
Hackathorn Ln ... 82716
Haida Ln ... 82716
Hall Rd ... 82716
Halleluja Peak Rd ... 82716
Hamilton Rd ... 82718
Hannum Rd ... 82716
Harder Dr ... 82718
Harry St ... 82718
Hart Rd ... 82716
Harvard Dr ... 82716
Harvest Moon Dr ... 82718
Hawk Ct ... 82718
Hayfield Pl ... 82718
Hays Dr ... 82716
Hazelton Peak Rd ... 82716
Heart X Ave & Ct ... 82718
Heather Ct ... 82718
Helena Ave ... 82716
Hemlock Ave ... 82716
Hendrich Ct ... 82718
Henry Rd ... 82718
Hereford Dr ... 82718
Hessian St ... 82718
Hi Line Rd ... 82716
Hidden Valley Rd ... 82718
High Ct ... 82718
High Plains Dr ... 82716
Highcliff Ave & Ct ... 82718
Highland Ct ... 82716
Hilight Rd ... 82716
Hill Blvd ... 82718
Hill Valley Rd ... 82716
Hillcrest Dr ... 82716
Hillside Dr ... 82718
Hilltop Cir ... 82716
Hilltop Ct ... 82718
Hilltop Dr ... 82716
Hinsdale Ln ... 82718
Hitt Blvd & Dr ... 82718
Hoadley Rd ... 82716
Hoback Ave ... 82718
Hoe Creek Rd ... 82718
E & W Hogeye Dr ... 82716
Homestake Dr ... 82716
Homestead Ln ... 82716
Hope Dr ... 82716
Hopi Cir ... 82718
Horse Creek Rd ... 82716
Hudson Ave ... 82716
Hunt Ave ... 82716
Huntington Dr ... 82716
I Ct ... 82716
Iberlin Rd ... 82718
Ichabod Ave ... 82718
Idaho St ... 82718
Independence Dr ... 82716
Indian Hills Dr ... 82716
Industrial Park Dr ... 82716
Inexco Dr ... 82716
Innominate Peak Rd ... 82716
Ironwood St ... 82716
Iroquois Ln ... 82716
Irving Blvd ... 82718
Island Dr ... 82716
J Ct ... 82716
J Cross Ave ... 82718
J M Rd
1-47 ... 82716
53-151 ... 82718
Jack Ct ... 82718
Jack Plane Ln ... 82716
Jackson ... 82718

Jacobs Rd ... 82718
James Ct ... 82718
Jane Ct ... 82718
Jason Ct ... 82718
Jayhawker St ... 82718
Jicarilla Ln ... 82716
Jim Ct ... 82718
Jocelynn Ave ... 82718
Jonquil Ln ... 82718
Jordan Ct & Dr ... 82718
E & W Juniper Ln ... 82718
Jz Ct ... 82718
K Ct ... 82716
Karok Way ... 82716
Kathleen Pl ... 82716
Katrina Ave ... 82718
Keeline Rd ... 82718
Kenadie Dr ... 82718
S Kendrick Ave ... 82716
Khadfy Skoal Rd ... 82716
Kilkenny Cir ... 82716
Killdeer Rd ... 82716
Kimber Ct & Dr ... 82716
Kindt Rd ... 82718
Kingfisher Rd ... 82716
Kinner Dr ... 82718
Kiowa Ave ... 82718
Kirk Ct & St ... 82716
Kiwi Creek Ln ... 82718
Kluver Rd ... 82716
Knickerbocker St ... 82718
Knollwood Dr ... 82718
Kristan Ave ... 82718
L Ct ... 82716
L A Ln ... 82716
L J Ct ... 82718
Lafayette Dr ... 82716
Lake St ... 82716
Lakeland Hills Dr ... 82716
Lakeside Dr ... 82718
E & W Lakeway Rd ... 82716
Lamerlew Dr ... 82718
Landing Strip ... 82718
E & W Laramie St ... 82716
Larch St ... 82716
Lariat Ct ... 82716
Lariat St ... 82716
Larkspur Ln ... 82716
Latigo St ... 82716
E & W Laurel Ct & St ... 82718
Lawver Rd ... 82716
Lazy D Ave ... 82718
Le Tourneau Dr ... 82716
Ledoux Ave ... 82718
Lee Esther Ln ... 82716
Legacy Pkwy ... 82718
Lemaster Ln ... 82716
Lemon Creek Ct ... 82716
Lewis Rd ... 82716
Lexington Ave & Ct ... 82718
Liberty Ln ... 82716
Lila Rd ... 82716
Lilloct Ln ... 82716
Lime Creek Ave ... 82716
Limestone Ave ... 82716
E Lincoln St ... 82716
Linden Cir ... 82718
Links Ln ... 82718
Little Powder River Rd ... 82716
Lobo Ln ... 82718
Lodahl Ave ... 82718
Logger Rd ... 82716
Lone Cedar Ct ... 82716
Lone Ridge Rd ... 82716
Lone Tree Dr ... 82718
Longhorn Ave & Ct ... 82716
Longmont St ... 82716
Lonigan Cir ... 82716
Low Ct ... 82718
Lowery Ranch Rd ... 82716
Lunar Ave ... 82718
Lundock Ct ... 82718
Lvb Rd ... 82716
M Ct ... 82716
M M Cir ... 82716
Macallan Ln ... 82718

Madison St ... 82718
Madsen Rd ... 82716
Magnolia Ct ... 82716
Magnuson Blvd ... 82718
Mahogany Cir ... 82718
Mallard Rd ... 82716
Manchester St ... 82716
Mancor Rd ... 82716
Mandy Ln ... 82718
Manor St ... 82716
Maple Ave & Cir ... 82716
Market Street Ct ... 82718
Marlin Ct ... 82718
Mary Ct ... 82716
Mather Ave ... 82718
Matheson Rd ... 82718
Matlack Dr ... 82718
Maverik Dr ... 82718
Maycock Rd ... 82716
Mcgee Ave & Rd ... 82716
Mckenney St ... 82718
Mckenzie Rd ... 82716
Meadow Ln ... 82718
N & S Meadow Brook Ct
& Ln ... 82718
Meadow Rose Ave ... 82716
Meadowlark Ct & Rd ... 82716
Means St ... 82716
Mecent Ave ... 82718
S Medical Arts Ct ... 82716
Medicine Lodge Rd ... 82718
Meeteetse Ln ... 82716
Megans Way ... 82718
Melissa Ct & Dr ... 82716
Mercantile Dr ... 82718
Mercury Ct ... 82718
Mes Dr ... 82716
Mesa Dr ... 82716
Mesa Verde Dr ... 82716
Metz Dr ... 82718
Mica Ct & Dr ... 82716
Michelle St ... 82718
Midday Ct ... 82718
Middle Fork Dr ... 82718
Middle Prong Rd ... 82716
Midland Rd ... 82716
N & S Miller Ave ... 82716
Mills Ave & Rd ... 82718
Milne Valley Rd ... 82716
Milton St ... 82718
Mineral Ct ... 82716
Mink Ave ... 82716
Mint Ave ... 82718
Miranda Ave ... 82718
Mitchell Ave ... 82716
Mohan Rd ... 82716
Mohawk St ... 82718
Moncreiffe Ridge Rd ... 82716
Montana St ... 82716
Monte Vista Ln ... 82716
Montgomery Rd ... 82716
Moon Dancer St ... 82718
Moonlight Dr ... 82718
Moonshiner Ln ... 82718
Moore Ct & Rd ... 82718
Morning Glory Ct ... 82716
Morningside Dr ... 82716
Motor Ct ... 82718
Mountain Meadow Ln ... 82718
Mountain Shadow Dr ... 82716
Mountain View Dr ... 82716
Muscovy Dr ... 82716
Musket Ct ... 82718
Mustang Rd ... 82718
Muttin Bustin St ... 82718
N Ct ... 82716
Napier Rd ... 82718
Nathan Hale Rd ... 82718
Navajo Cir ... 82718
Nebraska St ... 82716
Needle Ct ... 82718
Nepstad Dr ... 82718
Nettle Creek Ct ... 82716
Nevada St ... 82718
Newton Rd ... 82716
Night Fall Ln ... 82718

Nine Mile Creek Rd ... 82718
Nogales Ln & Way ... 82716
Nugget Ct ... 82716
Nut Tree St ... 82716
Nutwood Ct ... 82716
O Ct ... 82716
Oak Cir ... 82718
Oakcrest Dr ... 82718
Oasis Spring Rd ... 82716
Obsidian Dr ... 82716
Oedekoven Rd ... 82716
Ogala Ln ... 82716
Ohara Dr ... 82716
Ohenry Dr ... 82716
Old Farm Rd ... 82718
Old Glory ... 82718
Olive Ave ... 82718
Olmstead Rd ... 82716
Or Dr ... 82718
Orange Creek Dr ... 82716
Orchid Ln ... 82716
Oregon Ave ... 82718
Oriva Rd ... 82716
N & S Osborne Ave ... 82716
Oshannon Dr ... 82716
Outback Ln ... 82718
Overbrook Ct & Rd ... 82718
Overdale Dr ... 82716
Overland Trl ... 82716
Owl Rd ... 82718
P Ct ... 82716
Paintbrush Dr ... 82716
Painted Pony Ln ... 82716
Palomino Rd ... 82716
Par Dr ... 82718
Park Cir & Ln ... 82718
Parkridge Ct ... 82716
Partridge Ct & Dr ... 82716
Pathfinder Cir ... 82716
Patik Rd ... 82718
Patrick Henry Rd ... 82718
Patty Ave ... 82718
Paul Revere ... 82718
Peaceful Valley Dr ... 82718
S Peak Ct, Rd & St ... 82716
Pebble Beach Dr ... 82718
Penny Ln ... 82718
Penrose Peak Rd ... 82716
Pheasant Ct & Dr ... 82718
Phillips Cir ... 82718
Phoenix Ave & Ln ... 82716
Pierce St ... 82718
Pine Dr ... 82716
Pinehurst Ct ... 82718
Pinetree Rd ... 82718
N Pineview Ct & Dr ... 82716
Pinnacle Dr ... 82718
Pintail Dr ... 82718
Pioneer Ave ... 82718
Pj Rd ... 82716
Placer Ct ... 82716
N Plains Dr ... 82716
Plum Creek Ave & Ct ... 82716
Polly Ave ... 82718
Poplar Ln ... 82716
Potter Ave ... 82718
Powder Basin Ave ... 82718
Prairie St ... 82718
Prairieview Ct & Dr ... 82718
Preamble Ln ... 82716
Primrose Dr ... 82716
Pronghorn Meadow Ln ... 82718
Prospector Pkwy ... 82716
Providence Ln ... 82716
Ptarmigan Ave ... 82718
Pumpkin Ct ... 82718
Quacker Ave ... 82718
Quail Meadows St ... 82716
Quarry Rd ... 82716
Quarter Circle Ct ... 82718
Quarter Horse Ave ... 82718
Quincy Rd ... 82718
Radio Rd ... 82718
Rafter D ... 82718
Rafter Star Rd ... 82718
E & W Railroad St ... 82716

Rain Dancer Ct ... 82718
Raintree Cir ... 82716
Rampart Dr ... 82718
Ramshorn Ave ... 82718
Ranchette Dr ... 82716
Rapid St ... 82718
Ratcliff Dr ... 82716
Rattlesnake Rd ... 82718
Raven St ... 82718
Rawhide Dr ... 82716
Raymond Dr ... 82718
Reata Dr ... 82718
Recluse Rd ... 82716
Red Fox St ... 82718
Red Hills Rd ... 82718
Red Lodge Dr ... 82718
Red Ryder Dr ... 82718
Red Stone Ct & Rd ... 82718
Red Vista Ct ... 82718
Redrock Dr ... 82716
Redtail St ... 82718
E & W Redwood St ... 82718
Reno Rd ... 82718
Republic Ln ... 82716
Richards Ave ... 82716
Ridge Way Rd ... 82716
Ridgecrest Dr ... 82718
Ridgewood Dr ... 82716
Rimrock Dr ... 82718
Roadrunner Dr ... 82718
Roanoke Ct ... 82718
Roany Rd ... 82718
Robin Dr ... 82718
Robinson St ... 82716
Rock Rd ... 82718
Rocking T Dr ... 82718
Rockpile Blvd ... 82716
Rockwood Dr ... 82716
Rocky Point Dr ... 82718
Rodeo St ... 82718
Rodgers Dr ... 82716
Rohan Ave ... 82716
Ron Don Rd ... 82716
Roper Ln ... 82718
Rose Creek Dr ... 82718
Ross Ave ... 82716
Round Up Dr ... 82718
Rourke Ave ... 82716
Ruby St ... 82716
Ruger Ct ... 82718
Rule Rd ... 82716
Running W Dr ... 82716
Runtime Hills Rd ... 82718
Russell Ct ... 82718
Saddle String Cir ... 82716
Sage Ct ... 82716
N Sage Hill Rd ... 82716
S Sage Hill Rd ... 82716
Sage Valley Dr ... 82716
Sako Dr ... 82718
Salt Box Ln ... 82716
Sammye Ave ... 82718
Samuel Adams Rd ... 82718
Sandalwood St ... 82716
Santee Dr ... 82716
Sassick St ... 82718
Saunders Blvd & Rd ... 82716
Savageton Rd ... 82718
Sawtooth Dr ... 82718
Schoonover St ... 82718
Sequoia Dr ... 82718
Shade Tree Ave ... 82716
Shale Hill Rd ... 82716
Shalom Ave ... 82718
Sherard Rd ... 82718
Ship Wheel Ln ... 82718
Shober Rd ... 82718
Shooting Park Rd ... 82718
Short Dr ... 82718
Shoshone Ave ... 82718
Sierra Cir, Dr & Way ... 82716
Silver Ave ... 82716
Silver Spur Ave ... 82718
Silverwood St ... 82716
Simpson Ln ... 82718
W Sinclair St ... 82718

Sioux Ave 82718
Sky Hi Ct 82718
Skylark Ct 82716
Skyline Dr 82718
Skyview Cir 82716
Sleepy Hollow Blvd 82718
Small Ct 82718
Smithie Rd 82718
Solar Dr 82716
Southern Dr 82718
Speigelmyer Ave 82718
Spotted Fox St 82718
Spring Hill Rd 82718
Spring Valley Ln 82716
Spur Ct 82718
Sr 4 Rd 82716
Sr 6 Rd 82716
Stacy Rd 82718
Stafford Bnd & Ct 82718
Stagecoach Dr 82716
Stampede Dr 82718
Stanley Ave 82716
Star Hope Dr 82718
State Highway 50 82718
State Highway 51 82718
State Highway 59 N 82716
State Highway 59 S 82718
Steer Roping Ave 82718
Sterling St 82718
Stetson Dr 82716
Stocktrail Ave 82716
Stone Crest Dr 82718
Stone Field Ct 82718
Stone Gate Ave 82718
Stone Lake Ave 82718
Stone Place Ave & Loop 82718
Stone Ridge Ct 82718
Stone Trail Ave & Ct 82718
Stone View Ct 82718
Streamside Ct & Dr 82718
Summerfield Ln 82718
Summit Dr 82718
Sun Dancer St 82718
Sunburst Ct 82718
Sundog Dr 82718
Sunflower Ln 82716
Sunlight Dr 82716
Sunridge Ave 82718
Sunrise Ln 82716
E & W Sunset Dr 82716
Sutherland Dr 82718
Sutherland Cove Ln 82718
Swanson Ct & Rd 82718
Swift St 82718
Sylvan Rd 82718
T-7 Ln 82718
T-7 Rd 82718
Tabiano Rd 82716
Tabor Ln 82718
Talisker Dr 82718
Tanner Dr 82718
E Tapadera St 82718
Tappan Ct 82718
Tarry St 82718
Tassel Ave 82718
Tate Ave & Ct 82718
Taylor Rd 82716
Teak St 82718
Tee Ct 82718
Teewinot Cir 82716
Tepee St 82718
Terrace Cir 82716
Teton Cir 82716
W Thomas Jefferson Rd 82718
Thomas Paine Rd 82718
E & W Timothy Ct & St 82718
Tisdale Ln 82718
Todd Rd 82718
Tong Ln 82718
Tongue River Rd 82718
E & W Tonk Ct & St 82718
Torrey Pines Ct 82718
Tory Ln 82718
Tower Ave 82718
Town Center Dr 82718
Townsend 82716
W Trail St 82718
Trails Cir 82718
Trapper Ln 82718
Tressa Rd 82718
Trinidad Ct 82716
Triple T Ct 82718
Triton Ave 82718
Turkey Track Ln 82716
Turnercrest Rd 82718
Twilight Ct 82716
Twin Butte Dr 82718
Twister Dr 82716
Tyler Ave 82716
Union Chapel Rd 82716
University Rd 82718
E Us Highway 14-16 82716
Utah St 82716
E & W Valley Dr 82716
Van Brunt Ct 82718
Van Buggenum Rd 82718
Van Ripper St 82718
Vanscoy Dr 82718
Vantage Ct 82718
Vaquero Ave 82716
Ventura Ave 82716
Villa Way 82718
Violet Ct & Ln 82716
Vista Cir 82716
Vista Hills Ct 82718
Vivian Ct & St 82718
Wagensen Rd 82718
Wagon Box 82718
Wagon Master Pl 82718
Wagon Trail St 82718
Wagon Wheel Pl 82718
Wagonhammer Ln
1200-1299 82716
1600-2299 82718
Wall Street Ct 82718
E & W Walnut St 82718
War Chant Dr 82716
E & W Warlow Dr 82716
Warren Ave 82716
Warrior Rd 82716
Washington 82718
Waterfall Rd 82718
Watsabaugh Dr 82718
Weatherby Ct & Dr 82718
Webster St 82716
Westhills Loop 82718
Westover Rd 82718
Westrali Rd 82716
Westside Dr 82718
Whitetail Ct & St 82718
Wiggins Ct 82718
Wigwam Blvd 82718
Wikaka St 82718
Wild Bronc Way 82716
Wild Cat Ct 82716
Wild Horse Creek Rd 82718
Wild Prairie Ct & Rd 82718
Wilderness Dr 82718
Willow St 82716
Willow Brook Ln 82718
Willow Lake Rd 82716
Wilson Way 82716
Wind Dancer Ct 82718
Wind River Dr 82718
Windflower 82718
S Winland Ct & Dr 82718
Wisteria Ct 82716
Wolff Rd 82718
Woodland Ave 82716
Woolsey Peak Rd 82716
Worchester Dr 82718
N Works Ave 82716
Worley Dr 82716
Wrangler Ct & Rd 82718
Wyodak Rd 82716
Wyoming Ave 82718
Zee Ct 82718

NUMBERED STREETS

E & W 1st 82716
W 2nd Ave 82716
E 2nd St
101-197 82716
199-999 82716
1001-1699 82716
2600-3699 82718
W 2nd St 82716
3 Forks Dr 82718
W & E 3rd Ave & St 82716
4 Corners Rd 82718
W & E 4th Ave & St 82716
W & E 5th Ave & St 82716
E & W 6th 82716
7 Bar 7 Dr 82718
E & W 7th 82716
E & W 8th 82716
E & W 9th 82716
E & W 10th 82716
W 11th St 82716
E & W 12th 82716
4j Ct 82716
S 4j Rd
100-298 82716
300-1099 82716
1700-2899 82718
2901-3199 82718
W 4j Rd 82718

JACKSON WY

General Delivery 83002

POST OFFICE BOXES MAIN OFFICE STATIONS AND BRANCHES

Box No.s
SKI - SKI 83001
1 - 5002 83001
6271 - 9894 83002
9993 - 9993 83001
10001 - 30000 83002

HIGHWAY CONTRACTS

64, 65, 66 83001

NAMED STREETS

Absaroka Dr 83001
S Adams Canyon Dr 83001
E Airport Rd 83001
Alpine Ln 83001
Amangani Dr 83001
W American Brant Rd 83001
W Angus Dr 83001
Apache Rd 83001
S Appaloosa Dr 83001
S Arabian Dr 83001
Arapahoe Ln 83001
Arena Rd 83001
Arnica Ct 83001
Aspen Dr 83001
Avalanche Canyon Dr 83001
Balsam Ln 83001
W Bannock Rd 83001
W Bar Bc Ranch Rd 83001
N Bar Y Rd 83001
Barberry Dr 83001
N Bear Lakes Rd 83001
S Beaverslide Dr 83001
S Bedstraw Ln 83001
Berger Ln 83001
W Big Trail Dr 83001
S Black Baldy Dr 83001
Blair Dr 83001
S Blue Crane Dr 83001
W Bohnetts Rd 83001
Boyles Hill Rd 83001
W Brahma Dr 83001
W Brangus Dr 83001
S Bridle Dr 83001
W & E Broadway Ave 83001
S Bryans Flat Rd 83001
E Buck Mountain Rd 83001
W Buck Rail Rd 83001
W Buck Rake Dr 83001
E Buckwheat Cir 83001
N Budge Dr & Ln 83001
Buffalo Way 83001
W Bugling Elk Trl 83001
W Bull Rake Dr 83001
W Bulrush Ln 83001
W Bunk House Dr 83001
Buttercup Ln 83001
N & S Cache St 83001
Cache Creek Dr 83001
W Calliope Dr 83001
Camp Creek Rd 83001
Canadian Springs Dr 83001
Carol Ln 83001
Centennial Dr 83001
Center St 83001
Central St 83001
Chickadee Cir 83001
W Cinnamon Teal Rd 83001
Clark St 83001
Clissold St 83001
E Cloudveil Rd 83001
W Clydesdale Dr 83001
Cody Dr 83001
S Cody Creek Dr 83001
Cole Canyon Rd 83001
W Collar Dr 83001
W Colt Dr 83001
Columbine Dr 83001
Coneflower Dr 83001
Corner Creek Ln 83001
Cortland Dr 83001
Cottonwood Dr 83001
Coulter Ave 83001
S Cow Camp Dr 83001
Cowboy Way 83001
Coyote Canyon Rd 83001
Crabtree Ln 83001
Creamery Ln 83001
Curlew Ln 83001
Cygnet Ln 83001
W Dairy Ln 83001
E Death Canyon Rd 83001
E & W Deer Dr 83001
Deer Creek Dr 83001
N Deland Dr 83001
E & W Deloney Ave 83001
Deyo Ln 83001
Diamond Hat Rd 83001
W Diamond Hitch Dr 83001
Dogwood Dr 83001
Dora St 83001
S Double Tree Dr 83001
Dylan Dr 83001
S Eagle View Dr 83001
W Eaglecrest 83001
N East Butte Rd 83001
W & E Elk Ave & Dr 83001
Elk Camp Rd 83001
N Elk Refuge Rd 83001
Elk Run Ln 83001
N & S Ely Springs Rd 83001
E Evans Rd 83001
S Fallen Leaf Ln 83001
E Fish Hatchery Rd 83001
Fishing Club Dr 83001
Flat Creek Dr 83001
S Fork Rd 83001
Forweal Dr 83001
N Foxtail Rd 83001
Francis Way 83001
W Fremont Rd 83001
W Fresno Dr 83001
Game Creek Rd 83001
N Gannett Rd 83001
E & W Gill Ave 83001
E Glacier Rd 83001
N & S Glenwood St 83001
Glory View Ln 83001
Glory Vista Ter 83001
Golden Currant 83001
Goldfinch Rd 83001
E Golf Creek Ln 83001
Grand Teton Cir 83001
Granite Creek Rd 83001
Gregory Ln 83001
N & S Gros Ventre Dr & St 83001
Grouse Dr 83001
N H Bar C Rd 83001
N H-C Dr 83001
E Hall Ave 83001
E & W Hansen Ave 83001
W Hansen Peak Rd 83001
N Harvest Dance Rd 83001
S Hay Loft Dr 83001
W Hay Sled Dr 83001
Henley Rd 83001
S Henrys Rd 83001
W Hereford Dr 83001
Hi Country Dr 83001
Hidden Ranch Ln & Loop 83001
Hidden Spur Ln 83001
High School Rd 83001
Hillside Dr 83001
Hoback Jct South Rd 83001
Hoback River Rd 83001
W Homestead Dr 83001
E & S Horse Creek Rd 83001
Horse Creek Mesa Rd 83001
Hoyt Ln 83001
Huckleberry Dr 83001
Huff Ln 83001
Huffsmith Hill Rd 83001
E Hwy 191 83001
S Hwy 89 83001
Ibis Ln 83001
S Indian Springs Dr 83001
W Indian Terrace Dr 83001
Iron Rock Rd 83001
J-W Dr 83001
Jackpine 83001
N & S Jackson St 83001
N & S Jean St 83001
Johnny Counts Rd 83001
N June Grass Rd 83001
S Juniper Ln 83001
E & W Karns Ave 83001
Kdc Ln 83001
E & W Kelly Ave 83001
S Kestrel Ln 83001
W Killdeer Rd 83001
N & S King St 83001
W King Eider Rd 83001
W Kingfisher Ln 83001
W Kings Hwy 83001
Knori Ln 83001
Lake Ln 83001
Lakota Ln 83001
Lariat Loop 83001
Larkspur Dr 83001
E Lebonte Rd 83001
Lilac Ln 83001
E Limber Pine Rd 83001
N Linger Longer Dr 83001
Lodgepole Ln 83001
W Longhorn Dr 83001
N Lower Cascade Dr 83001
N Lower Ridge Rd 83001
Lower Snow King Loop 83001
Lupine Dr 83001
Macleod Dr 83001
Maddox Dr 83001
Mallard Rd 83001
Maple Way
900-999 83001
1001-1299 83001
1070-1070 83002
1100-1298 83001
Marsh Hawk Ln 83001
Martin Ln 83001
S Mccoy Rd 83001
S Meadow Dr 83001
Meadowlark Ln & Rd 83001
Meander Way 83001
Melody Creek Ln 83001
Melody Ranch Dr 83001
Mercill Ave 83001
E Middle Meadow Rd 83001
Middle School Rd 83001
N & S Millward St 83001
Montana Rd 83001
Moose Dr & St 83001
Moran St 83001
W Morgan Ln 83001
Moulton Loop Rd 83001
Mtn Mahogany Ln 83001
Mule Deer Ln 83001
S Mustang Dr 83001
W Ne-Yate Rd 83001
Nelson Dr 83001
E Nez Perce Rd 83001
No Name St 83001
Old Yellowstone Rd 83001
Orourke Way 83001
W Oskie Dr 83001
Otter Ln 83001
E Owl Ln 83001
W Pack Saddle Dr 83001
Paintbrush Dr 83001
Palmer Creek Dr 83001
Palomino Dr 83001
Park Dr 83001
S Park Loop Rd 83001
S Park Ranch Rd 83001
E & W Pearl Ave & St 83001
W Pemmican Rd 83001
W Percheron Dr 83001
W Peregrine Ln 83001
Perry St 83001
E Phelps Canyon Rd 83001
Pine Dr 83001
W Pine Siskin Rd 83001
W Pintal Ln 83001
W Pinto Dr 83001
Pioneer Ln 83001
S Pitch Fork Dr 83001
W Polo Pl 83001
Polo Pony Rd 83001
Ponderosa Dr 83001
Porcupine Rd 83001
S Porcupine Creek Rd 83001
Porter Loop 83001
Powderhorn Ln 83001
Prarie Clover Ln 83001
N Pratt Rd 83001
Preston Ln 83001
Prickley Pear Ln 83001
Prince Pl 83001
W Quarterhorse Dr 83001
Queens Ln 83001
Quill Rd 83001
S Rabbit Brush Ln 83001
N Rachel Way 83001
Ranch Rd 83001
Ranch House Cir 83001
Rancher St 83001
Raptor View Ln 83001
Red House Rd 83001
N Red Tail Rd 83001
Redmond St 83001
S Redtail Hawk Ln 83001
Reed Dr 83001
Ricks Rd 83001
N Ridge View Dr 83001
E River Dr 83001
Riverbend Rd 83001
Riverfront Dr 83001
N Roberta Dr 83001
Robertson Ln 83001
Rockmore Rd 83001
Rodeo Dr & Rd 83001
Roice Ln 83001
Rosencrans 83001
Runway Rd 83001
Saddle Butte Dr & Way 83001
E & W Sagebrush Dr 83001
Sandcherry Way 83001
W Sandpiper Ln 83001
Sandy Creek Ln 83001
Scott Ln 83001
W Sena Rd 83001
Seneca Ln 83001
Shelby Ln 83001
Shidner Ln 83001
Shootin Iron Ranch Rd 83001
S Shorthorn Dr 83001
S Silver Fox Ln 83001
N Silverberry Ln 83001
Simon Ln 83001
E & W Simpson Ave 83001
S Single Tree Dr 83001
N Sleeping Indian Dr 83001
Smith Ln 83001
N Snake River Dr 83001
N Snake River Ranch Rd 83001
N Snake River Woods Dr 83001
E & W Snow King Ave, Ct, Dr & Loop 83001
W Snowshoe Ln 83001
E Solitude Dr 83001
Southpark Dr 83001
Southpark Loop Rd 83001
N & W Spirit Dance Rd 83001
N Split Creek Rd 83001
Spoiled Horse Rd 83001
Sporting Club Rd 83001
N Spring Gulch Rd 83001
S Springwater Ln 83001
Spruce Dr 83001
S Squaw Creek Rd 83001
Stacy Ln 83001
State Highway 22 83001
Stellaria Ln 83001
S Stirrup Dr 83001
S Storage Stables Ln 83001
Stormy Cir 83001
S Swan Rd 83001
Swift Creek Rd 83001
Sycamore Dr 83001
Sylvia Dr 83001
Tanager Ln 83001
W Teal Rd 83001
W Tee-Titch Rd 83001
S Ten Sleep Dr 83001
Teton Ave 83001
Trader Rd 83001
Trail Dr 83001
Trails End 83001
E Trap Club Rd 83001
S Tribal Trail Rd 83001
W Trumpeter Swan Ln 83001
W Two Rivers Rd 83001
Upper Cache Creek Dr 83001
N Upper Cascade Dr 83001
Upper Redmond Rd 83001
Upper Snow King Loop 83001
S Us Highway 191 83001
N & S Us Highway 89 83001
S V-O Ln 83001
Vantreda Dr 83001
Veronica Ln 83001
Vine St 83001
Virginian Ln 83001
N Vista Ln 83001
S Wagon Rd 83001
Walton Ranch Rd 83001
Wapiti Dr 83001
Water Cress Ln 83001
N West Ridge Rd 83001
Whitehouse Dr 83001
E Wild Rye Dr 83001
S Willow Dr & St 83001
S Wilson Rd 83001
Wind River Ln 83001
S Winding Trail Dr 83001
S Wister Ave 83001
W Wolf Dr 83001
W Woodside Dr 83001

E Zenith Dr & Rd 83001

NUMBERED STREETS

All Street Addresses 83001

LARAMIE WY

HIGHWAY CONTRACTS

69 82051

NAMED STREETS

Able Ln 82072
N & S Adams St 82070
Albin St 82072
Alsop Ln 82072
Alta Vista Dr 82072
Ames Ct 82072
Anchor Dr 82070
Antelope Ave 82072
Antelope Ridge Loop 82072
Apache Dr 82072
Arabian Dr 82070
Arapaho Dr 82072
Armory Rd 82072
Arnold St 82070
Arrowhead Dr 82070
Arrowhead Ln 82072
Artesian Ln 82072
Arthur St 82070
Asay Springs Ct 82070
Ashley St 82070
Aspen Ln 82070
Autumn Cir 82070
B And M 82070
Badger Dr & Ln 82072
E & W Baker Ln & St 82072
S Balearn St 82070
Banner Rd 82072
Banock Dr 82072
Barratt St 82070
Barricade Rd 82070
Baruch Dr 82070
Bath Ave 82072
Battle St 82072
Bear Creek Rd 82070
Beaufort St 82072
Beech St 82070
Bench Heart Dr 82070
Bennys Ln 82070
Berner Mill Rd 82070
Beryl Dr 82070
Big Hollow Rd 82070
Bill Nye Ave 82070
Binford St 82072
Black Elk Trl 82070
Blackfoot St 82070
Blake Ln 82070
Bluebird Ln 82070
Bobcat St 82072
Bobolink Ln 82070
Bonita Dr 82072
Bonneville St 82070
Boswell Dr 82070
Boswell Creek Rd 82070
Boughton Ln 82051
Boulder Dr 82070
E & W Bradley St 82072
Brandt Ln 82070
Bridger St 82070
Bridle Bit Rd 82072
Bridle Trail Rd 82070
Brittany Ln 82070
Bronco Rd 82070
Brooks Blvd & Dr 82070
Brown Bear Rd 82070
Brubaker Ln 82070
N & S Buchanan St 82070
Bucking Horse Ranch Rd 82070
Buckrail Rd 82072
Buffalo Soldier 82070
Bull Mountain Rd 82070
Burro Ln 82072
Butte Loop 82070
Cactus Flower Rd 82070
Cactus Hill Ln 82070
Calvert Rd 82070
E Canby St 82072
Canyon Ct 82070
Canyon Ranch Rd 82070
Carrington Ct 82072
Carroll Ave 82072
Carroll Lake Rd 82070
Cattle Dr 82072
Cavalryman Ranch Rd 82070
N & S Cedar St 82072
Centennial Dr 82070
Center St 82072
Chaparral Dr 82070
Cheyenne Dr 82072
S Cheyenne St 82070
Chimney Lamp Rd 82070
Chinook Dr 82070
Chokecherry Creek Rd 82070
Chugwater Dr 82070
Cinnamon Bear Rd 82070
Circle Dr 82070
E & W Clark St 82072
S Cleveland St 82070
Cliff St 82070
Clistine Rd 82051
Cloudland Rd 82070
Clydesdale 82070
Coe St 82072
Colina Dr 82072
Collins St 82072
Collins Creek Cir & Dr 82070
N & S Colorado Ave 82070
Comanche Dr 82072
Commerce Dr 82070
Connors Ave 82070
Corral Rd 82070
Corthell Rd 82070
Cottontail Dr 82070
Cottonwood Dr 82070
Coughlin St 82072
Country Ln 82070
County Shop Rd 82070
Coyote St 82072
Crane Hall 82070
Crazy Horse Way 82070
Crestridge St 82070
Crow Dr 82072
Crown 82070
E Curtis St 82072
W Curtis St 82070
E Custer St 82070
Dadisman St 82070
Dakota Dr 82072
Dale Ct 82072
Dalles Ln 82070
Deer St 82072
Desperado Dr 82070
Desperado Buttes Trce 82070
Diamond Head Ct 82072
Dillon St 82072
Dinwiddie Rd 82070
Dog Iron Ln 82070
Dog Tail Trl 82072
N Dome Rd 82070
Domino Rd 82072
Douglas Dr 82070
Douglas Creek Rd 82070
Dover Dr 82072
Downey St 82072
Downey Hall 82070
Dragonfly Trl 82070
Duna Dr 82072
Dutton Ct 82072
Dutton Creek Rd 82070
Eagle Nest Ln 82070
Eaglecrest Ct 82072
East St 82072
Easterling St 82070
Eberhart St 82070
Edward Dr 82070
Elk Willows Rd 82070
Empinado Dr 82072
W End Rd 82070
Erie St 82070
Escalera St 82072
Ethan Dr 82072
Evans St 82070
Evergreen Dr 82070
Evets Ln & Rd 82070
Fairview Dr 82070
Falcon Ct 82072
Fast Ln 82070
Fdr 561 82070
Ferrett Cir 82070
Fetterman Dr & St 82070
N & S Fillmore St 82070
Flag Rd 82070
E & W Flint St 82072
Foothills St 82070
Forbes Ln 82070
Forest St 82070
Forrest St 82070
Fort Buford Ln 82070
Fort Laramie 82070
Fort Mackenzie 82070
Fort Sanders Rd 82070
Fox Ct 82072
Fox Creek Rd 82070
Fox Hill Rd 82070
Fox Kit Ln 82072
Fox Park Cir & Ln 82070
Fox Ridge Rd 82072
Foxborough Est 82070
Franklin St 82072
E Fraternity Row 82072
E & W Fremont St 82072
French Creek Rd 82070
Frontera Dr 82072
Gabrielson Ln 82070
Gap 82070
Gardner Ln 82070
E Garfield St 82070
W Garfield St 82072
Gearhart Rd 82070
General Brees Rd 82070
N Gennerid St 82072
Gerald Pl 82070
E & W Gibbon St 82072
Gibbs Rd 82070
Gilmore Gulch 82070
Git Along Trl 82070
Glacier St 82070
Golden Prairie Ln 82070
Golden Spur Trl 82070
Grafton St 82072
Graham Dr 82070
E Grand Ave 82070
W Grand Ave 82072
Grandpas Rd 82070
Grandview Dr 82070
Granito Dr 82072
N & S Grant St 82070
Grays Gable Rd 82072
Gros Ventre St 82070
Guffy Rd 82070
Hackney Dr 82070
E Hancock St 82072
Hancori 82071
Hanson Ln 82070
Happy Jack Trl 82070
Harmony Ln 82070
Harney St 82072
Harrison St 82070
Hart Rd 82070
Harvest Dr 82070
N & S Hayes St 82070
Hayford Ave 82072
Hecht Crk 82070
Henry Dr 82072
Herrick Ln 82070
Hidalgo Dr 82072
Hidden Vly 82070
Hidden Springs Rd 82070
High Plains Rd 82072
W Hill Rd 82072
Hill Hall 82070
Hillside Dr 82070
Hilltop Dr 82072
N & S Hodgeman St 82072
Holliday Dr 82070
Horizon Ct 82072
Hornsby Rd 82070
Horseshoe Ln 82072
Howe Ln & Rd 82070
Howell Rd
1-1099 82072
1100-1799 82051
Hunt Rd 82070
Huron St 82070
Inca Dr 82072
Indian Hills Dr 82072
Industry Dr 82070
Ione Ln 82051
Irma Ct 82070
Iroquois St 82070
W Ivinson Ave 82072
E Ivinson St 82070
Jack Rabbit Rd 82070
Jackalope Ct 82070
Jackson St 82070
Jefferson St 82070
Joanna Brunner Dr 82072
N & S Johnson St 82070
Johnson 99 Ranch Rd 82070
Juniper Dr 82070
K Bar D Rd 82070
Katie Canyon Loop 82072
E Kearney St 82070
W Kearney St 82072
Kennedy St 82070
Kerr Ln 82070
Kerry Lynne Ln 82070
Kestrel Ln 82070
Kiowa Dr 82072
S Kiowa St 82070
Knadler St 82072
Knoll Ct 82070
Knoll Dr 82072
La Prele St 82070
Lake Hattie Rd 82070
Lakeview Rd 82070
Laredo Dr 82070
Lasso Ln 82070
Lawrence Rd 82070
Lazy Eight Trl 82072
Lazy G Rd 82070
Leslie Ct 82072
Lewis Rd 82070
E Lewis St 82072
W Lewis St 82072
Liberty Trl 82070
E, N & S Lincoln Hwy & St 82070
Lindsey Ct 82072
Little Worth Ln 82072
Ll Willow Trl 82072
Lodgepole Dr 82070
Lodgepole Ln 82072
E & W Lyons St 82072
Madison St 82070
Mammoth Ct 82072
Mandel Ln 82070
Mason Ln 82070
Mccollum St 82070
E Mcconnell St 82072
N Mccue St 82072
Mcgill Ln 82070
Mcintyre Hall 82070
Meadow Ln 82070
Meadow Acres Rd 82070
Meadow Plains Rd 82070
Meadow View Rd 82070
Meadowlark Ct & Ln 82070
Meadows Rd 82070
Meeboer Rd 82070
Mercil Ct 82070
Mesquite Ln 82070
Mill St 82072
Mill Iron Rd 82072
Millbrook Rd 82070
Miner Rd 82070
Misner Ln 82070
Mitchell St 82072
Mockingbird Ln 82070
Monroe St 82070
Moose Meadow Rd 82070
Mopar Dr 82070
Moraine St 82070
Morgan Dr 82070
Mortenson Rd 82070
Motley Rd 82070
Moulton Rd 82070
Mountain Air Dr 82070
Mountain Meadow Rd 82070
Mountain Mist Ct 82070
Mountain Shadow Ln 82070
Mountain Valley Dr 82070
Mule Shoe Ln 82070
Mustang 82070
Navajo Dr 82072
Nelson St 82070
Newton St 82072
Nighthawk Dr 82072
Niver 82051
Norris Rd 82070
North St 82072
Northview St 82072
Nottage Ct 82072
Old Highway 130 82070
Old Stockyard Rd 82072
Olson Ln 82070
Ord St 82070
Oriole Ln 82070
Orr Hall 82070
Osprey Rd 82070
Outlaw Rd 82070
Overland Rd 82070
Owen Ct 82072
Pahlow Ln 82070
Paint Brush Rd 82070
Palmer Dr 82070
Palomino Dr 82070
Paradise Dr 82070
Paradise Valley Rd 82070
Park Ave 82070
E Park Ave 82070
W Park Ave 82072
Park Dr 82070
Pathfinder Ln 82072
Peak Cir 82070
Pearl 82070
Peregrine Ln 82070
Person St 82070
N & S Pierce St 82070
Pierson Ct 82070
Pilot Peak Rd 82070
N & S Pine St 82072
Pioneer Rd 82070
Piper Dr & Rd 82070
Plains St 82072
Plateau St 82070
Platte River Access Rd 82070
Plaza Ct & Ln 82070
Pleasant Ct 82072
Polk St 82070
Ponderosa Ln 82070
Pope Springs Rd 82070
Porter Ranch Rd 82070
Prairie Dr 82070
Prairie Dog St 82072
Private Lake Rd 82070
Pronghorn Rd 82070
Purdy Rd 82070
W Quakey Way 82070
Quarter Horse Dr 82070
Rabbit Run Trl 82070
N Railroad St 82072
Rainbow Ave 82070
Ramble A Rd 82070
Rambler Rd 82070
Rampart Rd 82070
Rangeview Ln 82070
Raptor Ranch Rd 82072
Rawhide Rd 82070
Red Fox Rd 82070
Red Iron Rd 82072
Redtail Ct 82072
Regency Dr 82070
Remington Dr 82070
Renshaw St 82072
Reynolds St 82072
Riata Rd 82070
Ridgeview St 82072
Rifle Range 82072
River Creek Ct 82070
River Ranch Rd 82070
River Ridge Rd 82070
Riverside Dr 82070
Riverview Rd 82070
Roberts Ct 82070
Rodeo Rd 82070
Rodeo Ranch Rd 82070
Roger Canyon Rd 82072
Rosedale Rd 82070
Ruggles Way 82070
Russell St 82070
Ruthie Rd 82070
Ryff Rd 82070
Sage Dr 82070
Sage Ridge Rd 82072
Sally Port Rd 82070
Sand Creek Rd 82070
Sanders Dr & St 82070
Satanka Rd 82070
Sawmill Rd 82070
Scherer Ave 82070
Schrader St 82070
Scout Trl 82070
Seeton St 82072
Sheep Mountain Ranch Rd 82070
E Sheridan St 82070
W Sheridan St 82072
Sherman Hill Rd 82070
Shetland Dr 82070
Shield St 82072
Short Pl 82070
Silver Spur Rd 82072
Silverado Trl 82070
Simpson Springs Rd 82070
Sky View Ln 82070
Skyline Dr & Rd 82070
Snowy Range Rd
350-399 82072
401-599 82072
901-1097 82070
1099-3099 82070
Snowy View Ct & Rd 82070
Sodergreen Rd 82070
Soldier Springs Rd 82070
E Somber Hill Rd 82070
Sommers Rd 82070
E Sorority Row 82072
Soule St 82072
South St 82072
Southview Rd 82070
Sportsman Lake Rd 82070
Sprague Ln 82070
Spring Creek Dr 82070
S Spruce St 82072
Squirt Rd 82072
Stagecoach Dr 82070
Stampede Dr 82070
Star Flight Rd 82070
State St 82072
State Highway 11 82070
State Highway 130 82070
State Highway 230 82070
State Highway 34 82051
Steele St 82070
Stetson Ct 82070
Stevenson Rd 82070
Stone Rd 82070
Strom Rd 82070
Stuart St 82070
Stuart Ridge Rd 82072
Sublette St 82070
E Sully St 82072
Summit Dr 82070
Sundance Ln 82072
Sunrise Ct 82070
Sunset Dr 82070
Superior Ct 82072
Sweetwater Dr 82070
Sybille Dr 82070
Sybille Rd 82051
Symons St 82070
Tallmadge Rd 82051
Targhee 82070
N & S Taylor St 82070
Terrace 82070
Thaxton Ct 82072
Thomes St 82072
Thornburgh Dr 82070
Thunder Ridge Rd 82070
Toltec Dr 82072
Topaz Ln 82070
Trabing Ln 82072
Trotter Ln 82070
Truman St 82070
Tullis Ct 82072
E University Ave
100-198 82072
200-849 82072
1000-1099 82071
W University Ave 82072
Upper Rd 82070
Us Highway 287 82070
N Us Highway 30
600-32200 82072
N Us Highway 30
1300-2899 82051
32202-32250 82072
V Bar Ranch Rd 82070
Valley Rd 82070
Valley View Rd 82070
Van Buren St 82070
Varney Ridge Rd 82070
Vedauwoo Loop 82070
Vee Bar Ranch Rd 82070
Ventura Dr 82070
Vista Dr 82070
Vista Grande Way 82070
Walgren Rd 82070
Walsh Ct 82072
Wapiti Way 82070
Warrens Ranch Rd 82072
Washington St 82070
Wayside Rd 82051
Welsh Ln
100-198 82072
600-700 82070
601-799 82072
702-6198 82070
1001-6199 82070
West St 82072
Western Skies Rd 82070
Westview Ct & Dr 82070
Westwinds Rd 82070
Whirlwind Ln 82070
White Hall 82070
Whitman St 82070
Wicklund Ln 82070
Wild Horse Ranch Rd 82070
Wild Iris Rd 82070
Willett Dr 82072
Willow Creek Rd 82070
Wind In Wire Ranch Rd 82072
Wind River Rd 82070
Windmill Ct 82070
Windmill Ranch Rd 82070
Windy Ridge Rd 82070
Wister Dr 82070
Wyatt Ct 82070
Wyman Ct 82072
Wyocolo Rd 82070
Wyoming Ave 82070
Wyoming Ben Rd 82070
Zog Ln 82072

NUMBERED STREETS

All Street Addresses 82070

ROCK SPRINGS WY

General Delivery ... 82901

POST OFFICE BOXES MAIN OFFICE STATIONS AND BRANCHES

Box No.s
All PO Boxes ... 82902

NAMED STREETS

A St ... 82901
Adams Ave ... 82901
Adobe Cir ... 82901
Affirmed Dr ... 82901
Agate St ... 82901
Ahsay St ... 82901
Albany Cir ... 82901
Alder St ... 82901
Alpine St ... 82901
Amy Ln ... 82901
Angle St ... 82901
Ankeny Way ... 82901
Antelope Dr ... 82901
Apache Ln ... 82901
Applewood Dr ... 82901
Arabian Cir ... 82901
Arapahoe St ... 82901
Archers Trl ... 82901
Arrowhead Cir & Way ... 82901
Artesian Cir ... 82901
Arthur Ave ... 82901
Ash St ... 82901
Ashley St ... 82901
Aspen Ct, Rd & Way ... 82901
B St ... 82901
Bald Eagle Ct ... 82901
Bank Ct ... 82901
Bannock Dr ... 82901
Barlow Cir ... 82901
Bastion Dr ... 82901
Belgian Dr ... 82901
Bellview Dr ... 82901
Beverly Hills Dr ... 82901
Big Horn St ... 82901
Big Sandy Ave ... 82901
Big Sky Dr & Trl ... 82901
Billie Dr ... 82901
Birch St ... 82901
Birdie Dr ... 82901
Bitter Creek Trl ... 82901
Black Kettle Dr ... 82901
W Blair Ave ... 82901
W Blairtown Rd ... 82901
Blue Heron St ... 82901
Blue Sage Way ... 82901
Bluebonnet Cir ... 82901
Bonners Way ... 82901
Booker St ... 82901
Bordeaux Ln ... 82901
Bowker Rd ... 82901
Briarwood Ln ... 82901
Brickyard Ave ... 82901
Bridger Ave ... 82901
Brimstone St ... 82901
Bristol Ave ... 82901
Broadway St ... 82901
Burr Dr ... 82901
Bushnell Ave ... 82901
C St ... 82901
Cache Valley Dr ... 82901
Camellia Cir ... 82901
Cameron Rd ... 82901
Campbell Ln ... 82901
Carbon Cir & St ... 82901
Carlyle Ct ... 82901
Carson St ... 82901
Carter Ave ... 82901
Cascade Dr ... 82901
Cathedral Dr ... 82901
Cattle Dr ... 82901
Cedar St ... 82901
Cedar Springs St ... 82901
Cedarwood St ... 82901
Center St ... 82901
Central St ... 82901
Century Blvd ... 82901
Channel St ... 82901
Chardonnay Ln ... 82901
Cherokee Dr ... 82901
Cherry Creek Dr ... 82901
Cherrywood Ln ... 82901
Chestnut St ... 82901
Cheyenne Dr ... 82901
Chimuza ... 82901
Churchill ... 82901
Clark St ... 82901
Clearview Dr ... 82901
Cleveland Dr ... 82901
Cloud Ct ... 82901
Clubhouse Dr ... 82901
Clydesdale Dr ... 82901
Clyman Dr ... 82901
Cody St ... 82901
Coldwater Creek Dr ... 82901
Colima Dr ... 82901
College Ct, Dr & Ln ... 82901
Collins St ... 82901
Commerce St ... 82901
Commercial Way
2600-2830 ... 82901
2829-2829 ... 82902
2832-2898 ... 82901
Community Park Dr ... 82901
Conch ... 82901
Connecticut Ave ... 82901
Continental St ... 82901
Converse Ct ... 82901
Cook Dr ... 82901
Coral St ... 82901
Corso Assisi ... 82901
Cottonwood Dr & St ... 82901
Country Hills Dr ... 82901
Creek Ave ... 82901
Crestwood Ln ... 82901
Cripple Creek Dr ... 82901
Crown Point Way ... 82901
Cy St ... 82901
Cypress Cir ... 82901
D St ... 82901
Daffodil Cir ... 82901
Daisy Ave ... 82901
Dana Cir ... 82901
Darlington Ave ... 82901
Daytona Dr ... 82901
Decora Dr ... 82901
Deer Creek Dr ... 82901
Desert Blvd & Ln ... 82901
Dewar Dr ... 82901
Dickson Ave ... 82901
Dines Way ... 82901
Dinwoody Way ... 82901
Divide St ... 82901
Donalynn Dr ... 82901
Douglas Dr ... 82901
Dover Ave ... 82901
Driftwood Ln ... 82901
Duran Dr ... 82901
E St ... 82901
Eagle Way ... 82901
Edgar St ... 82901
Eisenhower Dr ... 82901
Elbow Ln ... 82901
Elias Ave ... 82901
Elk St ... 82901
Elm Dr & Way ... 82901
Emerald St ... 82901
Emigrant Dr ... 82901
N Energy Rd ... 82901
Euclid Ave ... 82901
Evans St ... 82901
Evelyn Rd ... 82901
Evergreen St & Way ... 82901
F St ... 82901
Fairview Ln ... 82901
Fairway Dr ... 82901
Fall Creek Dr ... 82901
Fancher St ... 82901
Fillmore Ave ... 82901
Fir Dr ... 82901
Firestone Rd ... 82901
Fitzpatrick Dr ... 82901
Flagstone Dr ... 82901
Folsom Dr ... 82901
Foothill Blvd ... 82901
Ford Cir ... 82901
Frainche St ... 82901
Fremont Ave & Cir ... 82901
N Front St ... 82901
Frontier Dr ... 82901
G St ... 82901
Gale St ... 82901
Gannett Dr ... 82901
Garfield Ln ... 82901
Garnet St ... 82901
Gateway Blvd ... 82901
Gobel St ... 82901
Goldenrod Dr ... 82901
Gookin White Mountain Rd ... 82901
Gopher Dr ... 82901
Goshawk Dr ... 82901
Granite Dr ... 82901
Grant St ... 82901
Greve Cir ... 82901
Gunn Cir ... 82901
H St ... 82901
Hailee Dr ... 82901
Hancock St ... 82901
Harding Ct ... 82901
Harrier Dr ... 82901
Harrison Dr ... 82901
Hassel Rd ... 82901
Hawk Dr ... 82901
Hay St ... 82901
Hemlock Dr ... 82901
Hickory St ... 82901
Highland Way ... 82901
S Highway 191 ... 82901
Hill St ... 82901
Hillcrest Dr & Ln ... 82901
Hilltop Dr ... 82901
Hillview Dr ... 82901
Homestead Ave ... 82901
Horizon Dr ... 82901
Hoskins Ln ... 82901
Hunters Cv ... 82901
I St ... 82901
I80 Service Rd ... 82901
Imperial Dr ... 82901
Independence Cir ... 82901
Industrial Dr ... 82901
Interchange Dr & Rd ... 82901
J St ... 82901
Jackman Access Rd ... 82901
Jackman Ranch Rd ... 82901
Jackson St ... 82901
Jade St ... 82901
Jaidyn Dr ... 82901
James Dr ... 82901
Jayme Ln ... 82901
Jefferson Ave ... 82901
Johnson Ave ... 82901
Jonah Dr ... 82901
Juniper Dr ... 82901
K St ... 82901
Kanda Cir ... 82901
Kappes Rd ... 82901
Kari Ln ... 82901
Kennedy Ave ... 82901
Kent Ranch Rd ... 82901
Kestrel Way ... 82901
Killpecker Dr ... 82901
Kimberly Ave & Cir ... 82901
Kitchen St ... 82901
Klondike Way ... 82901
Kolman Ranch Rd ... 82901
Koven Dr ... 82901
Kp Industrial Dr ... 82901
L St ... 82901
Lacebark Ln ... 82901
Lagoon Rd ... 82901
Lakota Dr ... 82901
Laramie St ... 82901
Layos Dr ... 82901
Lee St ... 82901
Lester Dr ... 82901
Lewis St ... 82901
Liberty Dr & St ... 82901
Lincoln Ave ... 82901
Little Moon Trl ... 82901
Little Sandy Dr ... 82901
Locust St ... 82901
Logan St ... 82901
Lombard Dr ... 82901
Long Dr ... 82901
Lowell Ave ... 82901
Lucky Springs Dr ... 82901
Ludvig St ... 82901
Lyle Ave ... 82901
M St ... 82901
Madison Dr ... 82901
Magnolia Cir & Dr ... 82901
S Main St ... 82901
Maple St & Way ... 82901
Marchant St ... 82901
Marion St ... 82901
Massachusetts Ave ... 82901
Mccabe Ave & St ... 82901
Mccarty Ave ... 82901
Mcclellan St ... 82901
Mccurtain Dr ... 82901
Mckeehan Ave ... 82901
Mckinley Ave ... 82901
Mctee St ... 82901
Meade St ... 82901
Meadow Dr ... 82901
Medina Cir ... 82901
Melody Dr ... 82901
Mesa Dr & Ln ... 82901
Midway St ... 82901
Milne St ... 82901
Mimosa Ct ... 82901
Mineral Dr ... 82901
Mini Ranch Rd ... 82901
Mitchelson St ... 82901
Moccasin Ln ... 82901
Mohawk Dr ... 82901
Monarch Cir ... 82901
Monroe Dr ... 82901
Monte Vista Rd ... 82901
Monterey Dr ... 82901
Moore Ave ... 82901
Moran St ... 82901
Morgan Ave & Cir ... 82901
Morning Glory Way ... 82901
Morningside Dr ... 82901
Moses Dr ... 82901
Mountain Dr & Rd ... 82901
Mountain Springs Rd ... 82901
Mountain View Dr ... 82901
Muir Ave ... 82901
Mustang Dr ... 82901
N St ... 82901
New Hampshire St ... 82901
Noble Dr ... 82901
Norton St ... 82901
O St ... 82901
Oak Way ... 82901
Oak Creek Dr & Ln ... 82901
Odonnell St ... 82901
Opal St ... 82901
Osprey Dr ... 82901
Overland Dr ... 82901
P St ... 82901
Pacific Dr ... 82901
Palisades Ct & Way ... 82901
Palomino St ... 82901
Par Ct ... 82901
N Park Ave & Dr ... 82901
Parkview Ave ... 82901
Patrick Draw Rd ... 82901
Paulson St ... 82901
Peachwood Dr ... 82901
Peak Rd ... 82901
Pearl St ... 82901
Pennsylvania Ave ... 82901
Peregrine St ... 82901
Perry St ... 82901
Pierce Way ... 82901
Pilot Butte Ave ... 82901
Pine St ... 82901
Pinion St ... 82901
Pinnacle Dr ... 82901
Pinto St ... 82901
Pioneer Dr ... 82901
Plainview Dr ... 82901
Plateau Rd ... 82901
Plumtree Dr ... 82901
Polk St ... 82901
Pollux Dr ... 82901
Ponderosa Way ... 82901
Poplar Ct ... 82901
Popo Agie Cir & Dr ... 82901
Port Orford Ln ... 82901
Portland Ln ... 82901
Potter St ... 82901
Powder Ridge Ln ... 82901
Powell St ... 82901
Power House Rd ... 82901
Powerline Dr ... 82901
Prairie Ave ... 82901
Prairie Dawn Cir ... 82901
Production Dr ... 82901
Pronghorn Dr ... 82901
Prospect Dr ... 82901
Province ... 82901
Pueblo Trl ... 82901
Purple Sage Rd ... 82901
Pyramid Dr ... 82901
Q St ... 82901
Quadrant Dr ... 82901
Quincy Dr ... 82901
R St ... 82901
Radar Rd ... 82901
Rahonce Dr ... 82901
Raid Cir ... 82901
Railroad Ave ... 82901
Raindance Dr ... 82901
Rampart Dr ... 82901
Ramshead Cir ... 82901
Ranchview Dr ... 82901
Randolph St ... 82901
Range Rd ... 82901
Reagan Ave ... 82901
Red Tail Dr ... 82901
Redwood Way ... 82901
Reed St ... 82901
Reliance Rd ... 82901
Rennie St ... 82901
Retford St ... 82901
Rhode Island Ave ... 82901
Ridge Ave ... 82901
Rockies Cir ... 82901
Roosevelt Way ... 82901
Rose Crown Cir ... 82901
Rosewood Dr ... 82901
Ruby St ... 82901
Rugby St ... 82901
Sage Ct & St ... 82901
Sage Brush Ln ... 82901
Sand Point Way ... 82901
Sand Pointe Cir ... 82901
Sandhill St ... 82901
Sandpiper Dr ... 82901
Sandy Rd ... 82901
Santa Ana Dr ... 82901
Santa Cruz Dr ... 82901
Sapphire St ... 82901
Scott Cir & Dr ... 82901
Seattle Slew Dr ... 82901
Secretariat Dr ... 82901
Shadow Ridge Ln ... 82901
Sheehan Rd ... 82901
Sheridan St ... 82901
Sherman St ... 82901
Sherwood Ct ... 82901
Short St ... 82901
Sidney St ... 82901
Sierra Cir & Rd ... 82901
Signal Dr ... 82901
Silver Creek Dr ... 82901
Skyline Dr ... 82901
Skyview St ... 82901
Smarty Jones Ln ... 82901
Smith St ... 82901
Sonata Ln ... 82901
Soulsby St ... 82901
Spangler Rd ... 82901
Spearhead Way ... 82901
Sphinx Way ... 82901
Spotted Tail Cir ... 82901
Springs Dr ... 82901
Sprucewood Dr ... 82901
Stable Ln ... 82901
Stagecoach Dr ... 82901
Stassinos Ranch Rd ... 82901
State Highway 371 ... 82901
State Highway 430 ... 82901
Steamboat Dr ... 82901
Stillwater Dr ... 82901
Stratton Cir ... 82901
Sublette St ... 82901
Summit Dr ... 82901
Sun Dance Ln ... 82901
Sunflower Ln ... 82901
Sunridge Dr ... 82901
Sunset Dr ... 82901
Swan St ... 82901
Swanson Dr ... 82901
Sweeney Ranch Rd ... 82901
Sweetwater Dr ... 82901
Taft Way ... 82901
Tahoe Dr ... 82901
Talladega Dr ... 82901
Tamarack Dr ... 82901
Tate Way ... 82901
Taylor St ... 82901
Temple Cir ... 82901
Temple Peak Dr ... 82901
Teton St ... 82901
Thomas St ... 82901
Thompson St ... 82901
Thorpe St ... 82901
Thunder Gulch Ln ... 82901
Tisdel St ... 82901
Topaz St ... 82901
Tri State Rd ... 82901
Truman St ... 82901
Trumpeter Dr ... 82901
Turret Dr ... 82901
Tyler St ... 82901
Uinta St ... 82901
Upland St ... 82901
Us Highway 191 ... 82901
Utah Ave ... 82901
Valley St ... 82901
Valley View Dr & Ln ... 82901
Van Buren St ... 82901
Vermont St ... 82901
Veterans Park Dr ... 82901
Via Assisi Dr ... 82901
Via Capri Dr ... 82901
Via Fabriano Dr ... 82901
Via Rucce Dr ... 82901
Via Spoleto ... 82901
Victor Dr & Rd ... 82901
View St ... 82901
Villa Ln ... 82901
Village Cir ... 82901
Virginia St ... 82901
Walnut St ... 82901
War Admiral Dr ... 82901
War Emblem Ln ... 82901
Warbonnet Rd ... 82901
Wardell Ct ... 82901
Wasatch Cir ... 82901
Washakie Dr ... 82901
Washburn Dr ... 82901
Washington Ave ... 82901
Wendt Ave ... 82901
West St ... 82901
Westgate Dr ... 82901
Westland Way ... 82901
Westridge Ct & Dr ... 82901
Westview Ave ... 82901
White Mountain Blvd, Dr & Rd ... 82901
Whitewater Dr ... 82901
Wild Buffalo Ct ... 82901
Wild Horse Rd ... 82901
Wild Rose Ln ... 82901
Wilkins Peak Dr ... 82901
Willamette Dr ... 82901
Willow St ... 82901
Wilson Way ... 82901
Windriver Dr ... 82901
Winston Dr ... 82901
Winterhawk Cir & Dr ... 82901
Winton Cir ... 82901
Wood Haven Dr ... 82901
Woodruff Ave ... 82901
Wright St ... 82901
Wyoming St ... 82901
Yalecrest Dr ... 82901
Yellowstone Rd ... 82901
Young Ave ... 82901

NUMBERED STREETS

All Street Addresses ... 82901

Numeric List of Post Offices

005

00501 Holtsville, NY
00544 Holtsville, NY

006

00601 Adjuntas, PR
00602 Aguada, PR
00603 Aguadilla, PR
00603 Ramey, PR
00604 Aguadilla, PR
00604 Ramey, PR
00605 Aguadilla, PR
00606 Maricao, PR
00610 Anasco, PR
00611 Angeles, PR
00612 Arecibo, PR
00613 Arecibo, PR
00614 Arecibo, PR
00616 Bajadero, PR
00617 Barceloneta, PR
00622 Boqueron, PR
00623 Cabo Rojo, PR
00624 Penuelas, PR
00627 Camuy, PR
00631 Adjuntas, PR
00631 Castaner, PR
00636 Rosario, PR
00637 Sabana Grande, PR
00638 Ciales, PR
00641 Utuado, PR
00646 Dorado, PR
00647 Ensenada, PR
00650 Florida, PR
00652 Garrochales, PR
00653 Guanica, PR
00656 Guayanilla, PR
00659 Hatillo, PR
00660 Hormigueros, PR
00662 Isabela, PR
00664 Jayuya, PR
00667 Lajas, PR
00669 Lares, PR
00670 Las Marias, PR
00674 Manati, PR
00676 Moca, PR
00677 Rincon, PR
00678 Quebradillas, PR
00680 Mayaguez, PR
00681 Mayaguez, PR
00682 Mayaguez, PR
00683 San German, PR
00685 San Sebastian, PR
00687 Morovis, PR
00688 Sabana Hoyos, PR
00690 San Antonio, PR
00692 Vega Alta, PR
00693 Vega Baja, PR
00694 Vega Baja, PR
00698 Yauco, PR

007

00703 Aguas Buenas, PR
00704 Aguirre, PR
00705 Aibonito, PR
00707 Maunabo, PR
00714 Arroyo, PR
00715 Mercedita, PR
00715 Ponce, PR
00716 Mercedita, PR
00716 Ponce, PR
00717 Ponce, PR
00718 Naguabo, PR
00719 Naranjito, PR
00720 Orocovis, PR
00721 Palmer, PR
00721 Rio Grande, PR
00723 Patillas, PR
00725 Caguas, PR
00726 Caguas, PR
00727 Caguas, PR
00728 Ponce, PR
00729 Canovanas, PR
00730 Ponce, PR
00731 Ponce, PR
00732 Ponce, PR
00733 Ponce, PR
00734 Ponce, PR
00735 Ceiba, PR
00735 Roosevelt Roads, PR
00736 Cayey, PR
00737 Cayey, PR
00738 Fajardo, PR
00739 Cidra, PR
00740 Puerto Real, PR
00741 Punta Santiago, PR
00742 Ceiba, PR
00742 Roosevelt Roads, PR
00744 Rio Blanco, PR
00745 Rio Grande, PR
00751 Salinas, PR
00754 San Lorenzo, PR
00757 Santa Isabel, PR
00765 Vieques, PR
00766 Villalba, PR
00767 Yabucoa, PR
00769 Coamo, PR
00771 Las Piedras, PR
00772 Loiza, PR
00773 Luquillo, PR
00775 Culebra, PR
00777 Juncos, PR
00778 Gurabo, PR
00780 Coto Laurel, PR
00780 Ponce, PR
00782 Comerio, PR
00783 Corozal, PR
00784 Guayama, PR
00785 Guayama, PR
00786 La Plata, PR
00791 Humacao, PR
00792 Humacao, PR
00794 Barranquitas, PR
00795 Juana Diaz, PR

008

00801 Charlotte Amalie, VI
00801 St Thomas, VI
00802 Charlotte Amalie, VI
00802 St Thomas, VI
00803 Charlotte Amalie, VI
00803 St Thomas, VI
00804 Charlotte Amalie, VI
00804 St Thomas, VI
00805 St Thomas, VI
00820 Christiansted, VI
00820 St Croix, VI
00821 Christiansted, VI
00822 Christiansted, VI
00823 Christiansted, VI
00823 St Croix, VI
00824 Christiansted, VI
00824 St Croix, VI
00830 Cruz Bay, VI
00830 St John, VI
00831 Cruz Bay, VI
00831 St John, VI
00840 Frederiksted, VI
00841 Frederiksted, VI
00850 Kingshill, VI
00851 Kingshill, VI

009

00901 Old San Juan, PR
00901 San Juan, PR
00901 Viejo San Juan, PR
00902 Old San Juan, PR
00902 San Juan, PR
00902 Viejo San Juan, PR
00906 Puerta De Tierra, PR
00906 San Juan, PR
00907 Condado, PR
00907 Miramar, PR
00907 San Juan, PR
00907 Santurce, PR
00908 San Juan, PR
00909 Fernandez Juncos, PR
00909 Minillas, PR
00909 San Juan, PR
00909 Santurce, PR
00910 Fernandez Juncos, PR
00910 San Juan, PR
00911 San Juan, PR
00911 Santurce, PR
00912 San Juan, PR
00912 Santurce, PR
00913 Isla Verde, PR
00913 San Juan, PR
00913 Santurce, PR
00914 San Juan, PR
00914 Santurce, PR
00915 Barrio Obrero, PR
00915 Bo Obrero, PR
00915 San Juan, PR
00915 Santurce, PR
00916 Barrio Obrero, PR
00916 San Juan, PR
00916 Santurce, PR
00917 Hato Rey, PR
00917 San Juan, PR
00918 San Juan, PR
00919 Hato Rey, PR
00919 San Juan, PR
00920 Caparra, PR
00920 Caparra Hills, PR
00920 Caparra Terrace, PR
00920 Pto Nuevo, PR
00920 Puerto Nuevo, PR
00920 San Juan, PR
00921 College Park, PR
00921 Pto Nuevo, PR
00921 Puerto Nuevo, PR
00921 Rio Piedras, PR
00921 San Juan, PR
00922 Caparra, PR
00922 Caparra Hills, PR
00922 Caparra Terrace, PR
00922 San Juan, PR
00923 San Juan, PR
00924 Rio Piedras, PR
00924 San Juan, PR
00925 Rio Piedras, PR
00925 San Juan, PR
00926 Cupey, PR
00926 Rio Piedras, PR
00926 San Juan, PR
00927 Rio Piedras, PR
00927 San Juan, PR
00928 Rio Piedras, PR
00928 San Juan, PR
00929 Rio Piedras, PR
00929 San Juan, PR
00930 Rio Piedras, PR
00930 San Jose, PR
00930 San Juan, PR
00931 Rio Piedras, PR
00931 San Juan, PR
00933 San Juan, PR
00934 Fort Buchanan, PR
00935 San Juan, PR
00936 Barrio Obrero, PR
00936 Caparra, PR
00936 Cupey, PR
00936 Minillas, PR
00936 Old San Juan, PR
00936 Rio Piedras, PR
00936 San Jose, PR
00936 San Juan, PR
00936 Santurce, PR
00937 San Juan, PR
00939 San Juan, PR
00940 Minillas, PR
00940 San Juan, PR
00940 Santurce, PR
00949 Levittown, PR
00949 Toa Baja, PR
00950 Toa Baja, PR
00951 Toa Baja, PR
00952 Sabana Seca, PR
00953 Toa Alta, PR
00954 Toa Alta, PR
00955 San Juan, PR
00956 Bayamon, PR
00957 Bayamon, PR
00958 Bayamon, PR
00959 Bayamon, PR
00960 Bayamon, PR
00961 Bayamon, PR
00962 Catano, PR
00963 Catano, PR
00965 Guaynabo, PR
00966 Guaynabo, PR
00968 Guaynabo, PR
00969 Guaynabo, PR
00970 Guaynabo, PR
00971 Guaynabo, PR
00975 San Juan, PR
00976 Trujillo Alto, PR
00977 Trujillo Alto, PR
00978 Saint Just, PR
00979 Carolina, PR
00981 Carolina, PR
00982 Carolina, PR
00983 Carolina, PR
00984 Carolina, PR
00985 Carolina, PR
00986 Carolina, PR
00987 Carolina, PR
00988 Carolina, PR

010

01001 Agawam, MA
01002 Amherst, MA
01002 Cushman, MA
01002 Pelham, MA
01003 Amherst, MA
01004 Amherst, MA
01005 Barre, MA
01007 Belchertown, MA
01008 Blandford, MA
01009 Bondsville, MA
01010 Brimfield, MA
01011 Chester, MA
01012 Chesterfield, MA
01013 Chicopee, MA
01013 Willimansett, MA
01014 Chicopee, MA
01020 Chicopee, MA
01021 Chicopee, MA
01022 Chicopee, MA
01022 Westover Afb, MA
01026 Cummington, MA
01027 E Hampton, MA
01027 Easthampton, MA
01027 Mount Tom, MA
01027 Westhampton, MA
01028 East Longmeadow, MA
01029 East Otis, MA
01030 Feeding Hills, MA
01031 Gilbertville, MA
01032 Goshen, MA
01033 Granby, MA
01034 Granville, MA
01034 Tolland, MA
01035 Hadley, MA
01036 Hampden, MA
01037 Hardwick, MA
01038 Hatfield, MA
01039 Haydenville, MA
01039 West Whately, MA
01040 Holyoke, MA
01041 Holyoke, MA
01050 Huntington, MA
01050 Montgomery, MA
01053 Leeds, MA
01054 Leverett, MA
01056 Ludlow, MA
01057 Monson, MA
01059 Amherst, MA
01059 North Amherst, MA
01060 Northampton, MA
01061 Northampton, MA
01062 Bay State Village, MA
01062 Florence, MA
01062 Northampton, MA
01063 Northampton, MA
01066 North Hatfield, MA
01068 Oakham, MA
01069 Palmer, MA
01070 Plainfield, MA
01071 Russell, MA
01072 Shutesbury, MA
01073 Southampton, MA
01074 South Barre, MA
01075 South Hadley, MA
01077 Southwick, MA
01079 Thorndike, MA
01080 Three Rivers, MA
01081 Wales, MA
01082 Hardwick, MA
01082 Ware, MA
01083 Warren, MA
01084 West Chesterfield, MA
01085 Montgomery, MA
01085 Westfield, MA
01086 Westfield, MA
01088 W Hatfield, MA
01088 West Hatfield, MA
01089 West Springfield, MA
01092 West Warren, MA
01093 Whately, MA
01094 Wheelwright, MA
01095 Wilbraham, MA
01096 Williamsburg, MA
01097 Woronoco, MA
01098 Worthington, MA

011

01101 Springfield, MA
01102 Springfield, MA
01103 Springfield, MA
01104 Springfield, MA
01105 Springfield, MA
01106 Longmeadow, MA
01106 Spfld (Long), MA
01106 Springfield, MA
01107 Springfield, MA
01108 Springfield, MA
01109 Springfield, MA
01111 Springfield, MA
01115 Springfield, MA
01116 East Longmeadow, MA
01116 Longmeadow, MA
01118 Springfield, MA
01119 Springfield, MA
01128 Springfield, MA
01129 Springfield, MA
01138 Springfield, MA
01139 Springfield, MA
01144 Springfield, MA
01151 Indian Orchard, MA
01151 Springfield, MA
01152 Springfield, MA
01199 Springfield, MA

012

01201 Pittsfield, MA
01202 Pittsfield, MA
01203 Pittsfield, MA
01220 Adams, MA
01222 Ashley Falls, MA
01223 Becket, MA
01223 Washington, MA
01224 Berkshire, MA
01224 Lanesboro, MA
01225 Cheshire, MA
01226 Dalton, MA
01227 Dalton, MA
01229 Glendale, MA
01230 Egremont, MA
01230 Great Barrington, MA
01230 New Marlboro, MA
01230 New Marlborough, MA
01230 North Egremont, MA
01230 Simons Rock, MA
01235 Hinsdale, MA
01235 Peru, MA
01236 Housatonic, MA
01237 Hancock, MA
01237 Lanesboro, MA
01237 New Ashford, MA
01238 Lee, MA
01240 Lenox, MA
01242 Lenox Dale, MA
01243 Middlefield, MA
01244 Mill River, MA
01245 Monterey, MA
01245 West Otis, MA
01247 Clarksburg, MA
01247 Florida, MA
01247 North Adams, MA
01252 North Egremont, MA
01253 Otis, MA
01254 Richmond, MA
01255 Sandisfield, MA
01256 Savoy, MA
01257 Sheffield, MA
01258 Mount Washington, MA
01258 South Egremont, MA
01259 Southfield, MA
01260 South Lee, MA
01262 Stockbridge, MA
01263 Stockbridge, MA
01264 Lee, MA
01264 Tyringham, MA
01266 Alford, MA
01266 West Stockbridge, MA
01267 Williamstown, MA
01270 Windsor, MA

013

01301 Greenfield, MA
01301 Leyden, MA
01302 Greenfield, MA
01330 Ashfield, MA
01331 Athol, MA
01331 Phillipston, MA
01337 Bernardston, MA
01337 Leyden, MA
01338 Buckland, MA
01339 Charlemont, MA
01339 Hawley, MA
01340 Colrain, MA
01340 Shattuckville, MA
01341 Conway, MA
01342 Deerfield, MA
01343 Drury, MA
01344 Erving, MA
01346 Charlemont, MA
01346 Heath, MA
01347 Lake Pleasant, MA
01349 Millers Falls, MA
01350 Monroe, MA
01350 Monroe Bridge, MA
01351 Montague, MA
01354 Gill, MA
01354 Mount Hermon, MA
01354 Northfield Mount Hermon, MA
01354 Northfield Mt Hermon, MA
01355 New Salem, MA
01360 Northfield, MA
01364 Orange, MA
01364 Warwick, MA
01366 Petersham, MA
01367 Rowe, MA
01368 Royalston, MA
01368 S Royalston, MA
01370 Shelburne Falls, MA
01373 South Deerfield, MA
01375 Sunderland, MA
01376 Turners Falls, MA
01378 Orange, MA
01378 Warwick, MA
01379 Wendell, MA
01380 Wendell Depot, MA

014

01420 Fitchburg, MA
01430 Ashburnham, MA
01431 Ashby, MA
01432 Ayer, MA
01434 Ayer, MA
01434 Devens, MA
01436 Baldwinville, MA
01438 East Templeton, MA
01440 Gardner, MA
01441 Westminster, MA
01450 Groton, MA
01451 Harvard, MA
01452 Hubbardston, MA
01453 Leominster, MA
01460 Littleton, MA
01462 Lunenburg, MA
01463 Pepperell, MA
01464 Shirley, MA
01464 Shirley Center, MA
01467 Still River, MA

01468 Templeton, MA
01469 Townsend, MA
01470 Groton, MA
01471 Groton, MA
01472 West Groton, MA
01473 Westminster, MA
01474 Townsend, MA
01474 W Townsend, MA
01474 West Townsend, MA
01475 Winchendon, MA
01477 Winchendon Springs, MA

015

01501 Auburn, MA
01503 Berlin, MA
01504 Blackstone, MA
01505 Boylston, MA
01506 Brookfield, MA
01507 Charlton, MA
01508 Charlton City, MA
01509 Charlton Depot, MA
01509 Charlton Dpt, MA
01510 Clinton, MA
01515 East Brookfield, MA
01516 Douglas, MA
01516 East Douglas, MA
01517 East Princeton, MA
01518 Fiskdale, MA
01518 Sturbridge, MA
01519 Grafton, MA
01520 Holden, MA
01521 Fiskdale, MA
01521 Holland, MA
01522 Jefferson, MA
01523 Lancaster, MA
01524 Leicester, MA
01525 Linwood, MA
01526 Manchaug, MA
01527 Millbury, MA
01529 Millville, MA
01531 New Braintree, MA
01532 Northborough, MA
01534 Northbridge, MA
01535 North Brookfield, MA
01536 North Grafton, MA
01537 North Oxford, MA
01538 North Uxbridge, MA
01540 Oxford, MA
01541 Princeton, MA
01542 Rochdale, MA
01543 Rutland, MA
01545 Shrewsbury, MA
01546 Shrewsbury, MA
01550 Southbridge, MA
01560 South Grafton, MA
01561 South Lancaster, MA
01562 Spencer, MA
01564 Sterling, MA
01566 Sturbridge, MA
01568 Upton, MA
01569 Uxbridge, MA
01570 Dudley Hill, MA
01570 Webster, MA
01571 Dudley, MA
01581 Westborough, MA
01583 West Boylston, MA
01585 West Brookfield, MA
01586 Millbury, MA
01586 West Millbury, MA
01588 Whitinsville, MA
01590 Sutton, MA
01590 Wilkinsonville, MA

016

01601 Worcester, MA
01602 Worcester, MA
01603 Worcester, MA
01604 Worcester, MA
01605 Worcester, MA
01606 Worcester, MA
01607 Worcester, MA
01608 Worcester, MA
01609 Worcester, MA
01610 Worcester, MA
01611 Cherry Valley, MA
01612 Paxton, MA
01612 Worcester, MA
01613 Worcester, MA
01614 Worcester, MA
01615 Worcester, MA
01653 Worcester, MA
01654 Worcester, MA
01655 Worcester, MA

017

01701 Framingham, MA
01702 Framingham, MA
01703 Framingham, MA
01704 Framingham, MA
01705 Framingham, MA
01718 Acton, MA
01718 Village Of Nagog Woods, MA
01719 Acton, MA
01719 Boxboro, MA
01719 Boxborough, MA
01720 Acton, MA
01721 Ashland, MA
01730 Bedford, MA
01731 Bedford, MA
01731 Hanscom Afb, MA
01740 Bolton, MA
01741 Carlisle, MA
01742 Concord, MA
01745 Fayville, MA
01745 Southborough, MA
01746 Holliston, MA
01747 Hopedale, MA
01748 Hopkinton, MA
01749 Hudson, MA
01752 Marlborough, MA
01754 Maynard, MA
01756 Mendon, MA
01757 Milford, MA
01760 Natick, MA
01770 Sherborn, MA
01772 Southborough, MA
01773 Lincoln, MA
01775 Stow, MA
01776 Sudbury, MA
01778 Wayland, MA
01784 Woodville, MA

018

01801 Woburn, MA
01803 Burlington, MA
01805 Burlington, MA
01810 Andover, MA
01812 Andover, MA
01813 Woburn, MA
01815 Woburn, MA
01821 Billerica, MA
01822 Billerica, MA
01824 Chelmsford, MA
01824 Kates Corner, MA
01824 S Chelmsford, MA
01826 Dracut, MA
01827 Dunstable, MA
01830 Haverhill, MA
01831 Haverhill, MA
01832 Haverhill, MA
01833 Georgetown, MA
01833 Haverhill, MA
01834 Groveland, MA
01835 Bradford, MA
01835 Haverhill, MA
01835 Ward Hill, MA
01840 Lawrence, MA
01841 Lawrence, MA
01842 Lawrence, MA
01843 Lawrence, MA
01844 Methuen, MA
01845 North Andover, MA
01850 Lowell, MA
01851 Lowell, MA
01852 Lowell, MA
01853 Lowell, MA
01854 Lowell, MA
01860 Merrimac, MA
01862 North Billerica, MA
01863 North Chelmsford, MA
01864 North Reading, MA
01865 Nutting Lake, MA
01866 Pinehurst, MA
01867 Reading, MA
01876 Tewksbury, MA
01879 Tyngsboro, MA
01880 Wakefield, MA
01885 West Boxford, MA
01886 Westford, MA
01887 Wilmington, MA
01888 Woburn, MA
01889 North Reading, MA
01890 Winchester, MA
01899 Andover, MA

019

01901 Lynn, MA
01902 Lynn, MA
01903 Lynn, MA
01904 East Lynn, MA
01904 Lynn, MA
01905 Lynn, MA
01905 West Lynn, MA
01906 Saugus, MA
01907 Swampscott, MA
01908 Nahant, MA
01910 Lynn, MA
01913 Amesbury, MA
01915 Beverly, MA
01921 Boxford, MA
01922 Byfield, MA
01922 Newbury, MA
01923 Danvers, MA
01929 Essex, MA
01930 Gloucester, MA
01931 Gloucester, MA
01936 Hamilton, MA
01937 Hathorne, MA
01938 Ipswich, MA
01940 Lynnfield, MA
01944 Manchester, MA
01944 Manchester By The Sea, MA
01945 Marblehead, MA
01949 Middleton, MA
01950 Newburyport, MA
01951 Newbury, MA
01951 Newburyport, MA
01952 Salisbury, MA
01952 Salisbury Beach, MA
01960 Peabody, MA
01961 Peabody, MA
01965 Prides Crossing, MA
01966 Rockport, MA
01969 Rowley, MA
01970 Salem, MA
01971 Salem, MA
01982 South Hamilton, MA
01983 Topsfield, MA
01984 Wenham, MA
01985 West Newbury, MA

020

02018 Accord, MA
02018 Hingham, MA
02019 Bellingham, MA
02020 Brant Rock, MA
02021 Canton, MA
02025 Cohasset, MA
02026 Dedham, MA
02027 Dedham, MA
02030 Dover, MA
02032 East Walpole, MA
02035 Foxboro, MA
02035 Foxborough, MA
02038 Franklin, MA
02040 Greenbush, MA
02040 Scituate, MA
02041 Green Harbor, MA
02043 Hingham, MA
02044 Hingham, MA
02045 Hull, MA
02047 Humarock, MA
02048 Mansfield, MA
02050 Marshfield, MA
02051 Marshfield Hills, MA
02052 Medfield, MA
02053 Medway, MA
02054 Millis, MA
02055 Minot, MA
02055 Scituate, MA
02056 Norfolk, MA
02059 North Marshfield, MA
02060 North Scituate, MA
02060 Scituate, MA
02061 Norwell, MA
02062 Norwood, MA
02065 Marshfield, MA
02065 Ocean Bluff, MA
02066 Scituate, MA
02067 Sharon, MA
02070 Sheldonville, MA
02071 South Walpole, MA
02072 Stoughton, MA
02081 Walpole, MA
02090 Westwood, MA
02093 Wrentham, MA

021

02108 Boston, MA
02109 Boston, MA
02110 Boston, MA
02111 Boston, MA
02112 Boston, MA
02113 Boston, MA
02114 Boston, MA
02115 Boston, MA
02116 Boston, MA
02117 Boston, MA
02118 Boston, MA
02118 Roxbury, MA
02119 Boston, MA
02119 Roxbury, MA
02120 Boston, MA
02120 Mission Hill, MA
02120 Roxbury, MA
02120 Roxbury Crossing, MA
02121 Boston, MA
02121 Dorchester, MA
02121 Grove Hall, MA
02122 Boston, MA
02122 Dorchester, MA
02123 Boston, MA
02124 Boston, MA
02124 Dorchester, MA
02124 Dorchester Center, MA
02125 Boston, MA
02125 Dorchester, MA
02125 Uphams Corner, MA
02126 Boston, MA
02126 Mattapan, MA
02127 Boston, MA
02127 South Boston, MA
02128 Boston, MA
02128 East Boston, MA
02129 Boston, MA
02129 Charlestown, MA
02130 Boston, MA
02130 Jamaica Plain, MA
02131 Boston, MA
02131 Roslindale, MA
02132 Boston, MA
02132 West Roxbury, MA
02133 Boston, MA
02134 Allston, MA
02134 Boston, MA
02135 Boston, MA
02135 Brighton, MA
02136 Boston, MA
02136 Hyde Park, MA
02136 Readville, MA
02137 Boston, MA
02137 Hyde Park, MA
02137 Readville, MA
02138 Cambridge, MA
02139 Cambridge, MA
02140 Cambridge, MA
02140 North Cambridge, MA
02141 Cambridge, MA
02141 East Cambridge, MA
02142 Cambridge, MA
02143 Somerville, MA
02144 Somerville, MA
02144 West Somerville, MA
02145 Somerville, MA
02145 Winter Hill, MA
02148 Malden, MA
02149 Everett, MA
02150 Chelsea, MA
02151 Revere, MA
02152 Winthrop, MA
02153 Medford, MA
02153 Tufts University, MA
02155 Medford, MA
02156 West Medford, MA
02163 Boston, MA
02163 Cambridge, MA
02169 Quincy, MA
02170 Quincy, MA
02170 Wollaston, MA
02171 North Quincy, MA
02171 Quincy, MA
02171 Squantum, MA
02176 Melrose, MA
02180 Stoneham, MA
02184 Braintree, MA
02185 Braintree, MA
02186 Milton, MA
02187 Milton Village, MA
02188 Weymouth, MA
02189 East Weymouth, MA
02189 Weymouth, MA
02190 South Weymouth, MA
02190 Weymouth, MA
02191 North Weymouth, MA
02191 Weymouth, MA
02196 Boston, MA
02199 Boston, MA

022

02201 Boston, MA
02203 Boston, MA
02204 Boston, MA
02205 Boston, MA
02206 Boston, MA
02210 Boston, MA
02211 Boston, MA
02212 Boston, MA
02215 Boston, MA
02217 Boston, MA
02222 Boston, MA
02228 Boston, MA
02228 East Boston, MA
02238 Cambridge, MA
02238 Harvard Square, MA
02241 Boston, MA
02266 Boston, MA
02269 Quincy, MA
02283 Boston, MA
02284 Boston, MA
02293 Boston, MA
02297 Boston, MA
02298 Boston, MA

023

02301 Brockton, MA
02302 Brockton, MA
02303 Brockton, MA
02304 Brockton, MA
02305 Brockton, MA
02322 Avon, MA
02324 Bridgewater, MA
02325 Bridgewater, MA
02327 Bryantville, MA
02330 Carver, MA
02331 Duxbury, MA
02332 Duxbury, MA
02333 E Bridgewater, MA
02333 East Bridgewater, MA
02334 Easton, MA
02337 Elmwood, MA
02338 Halifax, MA
02339 Hanover, MA
02340 Hanover, MA
02341 Hanson, MA
02343 Holbrook, MA
02344 Middleboro, MA
02344 Middleborough, MA
02345 Manomet, MA
02346 Middleboro, MA
02347 Lakeville, MA
02348 Lakeville, MA
02348 Middleboro, MA
02348 Middleborough, MA
02349 Middleboro, MA
02349 Middleborough, MA
02350 Monponsett, MA
02351 Abington, MA
02355 North Carver, MA
02356 North Easton, MA
02357 North Easton, MA
02357 Stonehill Clg, MA
02358 North Pembroke, MA
02359 Pembroke, MA
02360 Plymouth, MA
02361 Plymouth, MA
02362 Plymouth, MA
02364 Kingston, MA
02366 South Carver, MA
02367 Plympton, MA
02368 Randolph, MA
02370 Rockland, MA
02375 South Easton, MA
02379 West Bridgewater, MA
02381 White Horse Beach, MA
02382 Whitman, MA

024

02420 Lexington, MA
02421 Lexington, MA
02445 Brookline, MA
02446 Brookline, MA
02447 Brookline Village, MA
02451 North Waltham, MA
02451 Waltham, MA
02452 North Waltham, MA
02452 Waltham, MA
02453 South Waltham, MA
02453 Waltham, MA
02454 Waltham, MA
02455 North Waltham, MA
02456 New Town, MA
02457 Babson Park, MA
02458 Newton, MA
02458 Newtonville, MA
02459 Newton, MA
02459 Newton Center, MA
02459 Newton Centre, MA
02460 Newton, MA
02460 Newtonville, MA
02461 Newton, MA
02461 Newton Highlands, MA
02462 Newton, MA
02462 Newton Lower Falls, MA
02462 Newtonville, MA
02464 Newton, MA
02464 Newton Upper Falls, MA
02465 Newton, MA
02465 West Newton, MA
02466 Auburndale, MA
02467 Boston College, MA
02467 Chestnut Hill, MA
02468 Waban, MA
02471 Watertown, MA
02472 East Watertown, MA
02472 Watertown, MA
02474 Arlington, MA
02474 East Arlington, MA
02475 Arlington Heights, MA
02476 Arlington, MA
02477 Watertown, MA
02478 Belmont, MA
02479 Waverley, MA
02481 Wellesley, MA
02481 Wellesley Hills, MA
02482 Wellesley, MA
02492 Needham, MA
02493 Weston, MA
02494 Needham, MA
02494 Needham Heights, MA
02495 Newton, MA
02495 Nonantum, MA

025

02532 Bourne, MA
02532 Buzzards Bay, MA

02534 Cataumet, MA
02535 Aquinnah, MA
02535 Chilmark, MA
02535 Gay Head, MA
02536 E Falmouth, MA
02536 Ea Falmouth, MA
02536 East Falmouth, MA
02536 Hatchville, MA
02536 Teaticket, MA
02536 Waquoit, MA
02537 E Sandwich, MA
02537 East Sandwich, MA
02538 E Wareham, MA
02538 East Wareham, MA
02539 Edgartown, MA
02540 Falmouth, MA
02541 Falmouth, MA
02542 Buzzards Bay, MA
02542 Otis Angb, MA
02543 Falmouth, MA
02543 Woods Hole, MA
02552 Menemsha, MA
02553 Monument Beach, MA
02554 Nantucket, MA
02556 North Falmouth, MA
02557 Oak Bluffs, MA
02558 Onset, MA
02559 Pocasset, MA
02561 Sagamore, MA
02562 Sagamore Beach, MA
02563 Sandwich, MA
02564 Nantucket, MA
02564 Siasconset, MA
02565 North Falmouth, MA
02565 Silver Beach, MA
02568 Vineyard Haven, MA
02571 Wareham, MA
02573 Vineyard Haven, MA
02573 West Chop, MA
02574 W Falmouth, MA
02574 West Falmouth, MA
02575 West Tisbury, MA
02576 West Wareham, MA
02584 Nantucket, MA

026

02601 Hyannis, MA
02630 Barnstable, MA
02631 Brewster, MA
02632 Centerville, MA
02633 Chatham, MA
02634 Centerville, MA
02635 Cotuit, MA
02637 Cummaquid, MA
02638 Dennis, MA
02639 Dennis Port, MA
02639 Dennisport, MA
02641 East Dennis, MA
02642 Eastham, MA
02643 East Orleans, MA
02644 Forestdale, MA
02645 E Harwich, MA
02645 East Harwich, MA
02645 Harwich, MA
02646 Harwich Port, MA
02647 Hyannis Port, MA
02648 Marstons Mills, MA
02649 Mashpee, MA
02650 North Chatham, MA
02651 North Eastham, MA
02652 North Truro, MA
02653 Orleans, MA
02655 Osterville, MA
02657 Provincetown, MA
02659 South Chatham, MA
02660 South Dennis, MA
02661 South Harwich, MA
02662 South Orleans, MA
02663 South Wellfleet, MA
02664 Bass River, MA
02664 South Yarmouth, MA
02666 Truro, MA
02667 Wellfleet, MA
02668 West Barnstable, MA
02669 West Chatham, MA
02670 West Dennis, MA
02671 West Harwich, MA
02672 West Hyannisport, MA
02673 W Yarmouth, MA
02673 West Yarmouth, MA
02675 Yarmouth Port, MA

027

02702 Assonet, MA
02703 Attleboro, MA
02703 South Attleboro, MA
02712 Chartley, MA
02713 Cuttyhunk, MA
02714 Dartmouth, MA
02715 Dighton, MA
02717 East Freetown, MA
02718 East Taunton, MA
02719 Fairhaven, MA
02720 Fall River, MA
02721 Fall River, MA
02722 Fall River, MA
02723 Fall River, MA
02724 Fall River, MA
02725 Somerset, MA
02726 Somerset, MA
02738 Marion, MA
02739 Mattapoisett, MA
02740 New Bedford, MA
02741 New Bedford, MA
02742 New Bedford, MA
02743 Acushnet, MA
02743 New Bedford, MA
02744 New Bedford, MA
02745 Acushnet, MA
02745 New Bedford, MA
02746 New Bedford, MA
02747 Dartmouth, MA
02747 North Dartmouth, MA
02748 Dartmouth, MA
02748 Nonquitt, MA
02748 South Dartmouth, MA
02760 North Attleboro, MA
02762 Plainville, MA
02763 Attleboro Falls, MA
02763 North Attleboro, MA
02764 N Dighton, MA
02764 North Dighton, MA
02766 Norton, MA
02767 Raynham, MA
02768 Raynham Center, MA
02769 Rehoboth, MA
02770 Rochester, MA
02771 Seekonk, MA
02777 Swansea, MA
02779 Berkley, MA
02780 Taunton, MA
02783 Taunton, MA
02790 Westport, MA
02791 Westport Point, MA

028

02801 Adamsville, RI
02802 Albion, RI
02804 Ashaway, RI
02806 Barrington, RI
02807 Block Island, RI
02807 New Shoreham, RI
02808 Bradford, RI
02809 Bristol, RI
02812 Carolina, RI
02812 Richmond, RI
02813 Charlestown, RI
02814 Chepachet, RI
02815 Clayville, RI
02816 Coventry, RI
02817 West Greenwich, RI
02818 East Greenwich, RI
02822 Escoheag, RI
02822 Exeter, RI
02823 Fiskeville, RI
02824 Forestdale, RI
02825 Foster, RI
02826 Glendale, RI
02827 Coventry, RI
02827 Greene, RI
02828 Greenville, RI
02829 Harmony, RI
02830 Burrillville, RI
02830 Harrisville, RI
02831 Hope, RI
02832 Hope Valley, RI
02832 Richmond, RI
02833 Hopkinton, RI
02835 Jamestown, RI
02836 Kenyon, RI
02836 Richmond, RI
02837 Little Compton, RI
02838 Manville, RI
02839 Mapleville, RI
02840 Newport, RI
02841 Newport, RI
02842 Middletown, RI
02852 North Kingstown, RI
02857 North Scituate, RI
02857 Scituate, RI
02858 Oakland, RI
02859 Pascoag, RI
02860 Pawtucket, RI
02861 Pawtucket, RI
02862 Pawtucket, RI
02863 Central Falls, RI
02864 Cumberland, RI
02865 Lincoln, RI
02871 Portsmouth, RI
02872 Prudence Island, RI
02873 Rockville, RI
02874 Saunderstown, RI
02875 Richmond, RI
02875 Shannock, RI
02876 Slatersville, RI
02877 Slocum, RI
02878 Tiverton, RI
02879 Narragansett, RI
02879 Peace Dale, RI
02879 South Kingstown, RI
02879 Wakefield, RI
02880 Wakefield, RI
02881 Kingston, RI
02882 Narragansett, RI
02882 Point Judith, RI
02883 Peace Dale, RI
02883 South Kingstown, RI
02885 Warren, RI
02886 Warwick, RI
02887 Warwick, RI
02888 Warwick, RI
02889 Warwick, RI
02891 Westerly, RI
02892 Richmond, RI
02892 West Kingston, RI
02893 West Warwick, RI
02894 Wood River Junction, RI
02895 Woonsocket, RI
02896 North Smithfield, RI
02898 Richmond, RI
02898 Wyoming, RI

029

02901 Providence, RI
02902 Providence, RI
02903 Providence, RI
02904 North Providence, RI
02904 Providence, RI
02905 Cranston, RI
02905 Providence, RI
02906 Providence, RI
02907 Cranston, RI
02907 Providence, RI
02908 North Providence, RI
02908 Providence, RI
02909 Providence, RI
02910 Cranston, RI
02910 Providence, RI
02911 North Providence, RI
02911 Providence, RI
02912 Providence, RI
02914 East Providence, RI
02915 Riverside, RI
02916 Rumford, RI
02917 Smithfield, RI
02918 Providence, RI
02919 Johnston, RI
02919 Providence, RI
02920 Cranston, RI
02921 Cranston, RI
02940 Providence, RI

030

03031 Amherst, NH
03032 Auburn, NH
03033 Brookline, NH
03034 Candia, NH
03036 Chester, NH
03037 Deerfield, NH
03038 Derry, NH
03038 Londonderry, NH
03040 East Candia, NH
03041 East Derry, NH
03042 Epping, NH
03043 Francestown, NH
03044 Fremont, NH
03045 Goffstown, NH
03046 Dunbarton, NH
03047 Greenfield, NH
03048 Greenville, NH
03048 Mason, NH
03049 Hollis, NH
03051 Hudson, NH
03052 Litchfield, NH
03053 Londonderry, NH
03054 Merrimack, NH
03055 Milford, NH
03057 Mont Vernon, NH
03060 Nashua, NH
03061 Nashua, NH
03062 Nashua, NH
03063 Nashua, NH
03064 Nashua, NH
03070 New Boston, NH
03071 New Ipswich, NH
03073 North Salem, NH
03076 Pelham, NH
03077 Raymond, NH
03079 Salem, NH
03082 Lyndeborough, NH
03084 Temple, NH
03086 Wilton, NH
03087 Windham, NH

031

03101 Manchester, NH
03102 Manchester, NH
03103 Manchester, NH
03104 Manchester, NH
03105 Manchester, NH
03106 Hooksett, NH
03106 Manchester, NH
03107 Manchester, NH
03108 Manchester, NH
03109 Manchester, NH
03110 Bedford, NH
03111 Manchester, NH

032

03215 Waterville Valley, NH
03216 Andover, NH
03217 Ashland, NH
03218 Barnstead, NH
03220 Belmont, NH
03221 Bradford, NH
03222 Alexandria, NH
03222 Bristol, NH
03223 Campton, NH
03223 Ellsworth, NH
03223 Thornton, NH
03224 Canterbury, NH
03225 Center Barnstead, NH
03226 Center Harbor, NH
03227 Center Sandwich, NH
03227 Sandwich, NH
03229 Contoocook, NH
03229 Hopkinton, NH
03230 Danbury, NH
03231 East Andover, NH
03233 Elkins, NH
03234 Epsom, NH
03235 Franklin, NH
03237 Gilmanton, NH
03238 Glencliff, NH
03240 Grafton, NH
03241 East Hebron, NH
03241 Hebron, NH
03242 Henniker, NH
03243 Hill, NH
03244 Deering, NH
03244 Hillsboro, NH
03244 Hillsborough, NH
03244 Windsor, NH
03245 Holderness, NH
03246 Laconia, NH
03247 Laconia, NH
03249 Gilford, NH
03251 Lincoln, NH
03252 Lochmere, NH
03253 Meredith, NH
03254 Moultonborough, NH
03255 Mount Sunapee, NH
03255 Newbury, NH
03256 New Hampton, NH
03257 New London, NH
03258 Chichester, NH
03259 North Sandwich, NH
03260 North Sutton, NH
03261 Northwood, NH
03262 North Woodstock, NH
03263 Pittsfield, NH
03264 Plymouth, NH
03266 Dorchester, NH
03266 Rumney, NH
03268 Salisbury, NH
03269 Sanbornton, NH
03272 South Newbury, NH
03273 South Sutton, NH
03274 Stinson Lake, NH
03275 Allenstown, NH
03275 Pembroke, NH
03275 Suncook, NH
03276 Northfield, NH
03276 Tilton, NH
03278 Warner, NH
03279 Warren, NH
03280 Washington, NH
03281 Weare, NH
03282 Wentworth, NH
03284 Springfield, NH
03285 Thornton, NH
03287 Wilmot, NH
03289 Winnisquam, NH
03290 Nottingham, NH
03291 West Nottingham, NH
03293 Woodstock, NH
03298 Tilton, NH
03299 Tilton, NH

033

03301 Concord, NH
03302 Concord, NH
03303 Boscawen, NH
03303 Concord, NH
03303 Penacook, NH
03303 Webster, NH
03304 Bow, NH
03305 Concord, NH
03307 Loudon, NH

034

03431 Keene, NH
03431 North Swanzey, NH
03431 Roxbury, NH
03431 Surry, NH
03435 Keene, NH
03440 Antrim, NH
03441 Ashuelot, NH
03442 Bennington, NH
03443 Chesterfield, NH
03444 Dublin, NH
03445 Sullivan, NH
03446 Swanzey, NH
03447 Fitzwilliam, NH
03448 Gilsum, NH
03449 Hancock, NH
03450 Harrisville, NH
03451 Hinsdale, NH
03452 Jaffrey, NH
03455 Marlborough, NH
03456 Marlow, NH
03457 Munsonville, NH
03457 Nelson, NH
03458 Peterborough, NH
03458 Sharon, NH
03461 Rindge, NH
03462 Spofford, NH
03464 Stoddard, NH
03465 Troy, NH
03466 West Chesterfield, NH
03467 Westmoreland, NH
03468 West Peterborough, NH
03469 West Swanzey, NH
03470 Richmond, NH
03470 Winchester, NH

035

03561 Littleton, NH
03570 Berlin, NH
03574 Bethlehem, NH
03575 Bretton Woods, NH
03576 Colebrook, NH
03576 Dixville, NH
03576 Stewartstown, NH
03579 Errol, NH
03579 Wentworths Location, NH
03580 Franconia, NH
03581 Gorham, NH
03581 Shelburne, NH
03582 Groveton, NH
03582 Northumberland, NH
03582 Stark, NH
03582 Northumberland, NH
03583 Jefferson, NH
03584 Lancaster, NH
03585 Landaff, NH
03585 Lisbon, NH
03585 Lyman, NH
03586 Sugar Hill, NH
03588 Dummer, NH
03588 Milan, NH
03589 Mount Washington, NH
03590 North Stratford, NH
03590 Stratford, NH
03592 Clarksville, NH
03592 Pittsburg, NH
03593 Randolph, NH
03595 Twin Mountain, NH
03597 West Stewartstown, NH
03598 Carroll, NH
03598 Dalton, NH
03598 Whitefield, NH

036

03601 Acworth, NH
03602 Alstead, NH
03602 Langdon, NH
03603 Charlestown, NH
03604 Drewsville, NH
03605 East Lempster, NH
03605 Lempster, NH
03607 South Acworth, NH
03608 Walpole, NH
03609 North Walpole, NH

037

03740 Bath, NH
03741 Canaan, NH
03741 Orange, NH
03743 Claremont, NH
03745 Cornish, NH
03746 Cornish Flat, NH
03748 Enfield, NH
03749 Enfield Center, NH
03750 Etna, NH
03751 Georges Mills, NH
03752 Goshen, NH
03753 Grantham, NH
03754 Guild, NH
03755 Hanover, NH
03756 Lebanon, NH
03765 Haverhill, NH
03766 Lebanon, NH
03768 Lyme, NH
03769 Lyme Center, NH
03770 Meriden, NH
03771 Monroe, NH
03773 Croydon, NH
03773 Newport, NH

03774 North Haverhill, NH
03777 Orford, NH
03779 Piermont, NH
03780 Pike, NH
03781 Plainfield, NH
03782 Sunapee, NH
03784 West Lebanon, NH
03785 Benton, NH
03785 Woodsville, NH

038

03801 Newington, NH
03801 Portsmouth, NH
03802 Portsmouth, NH
03803 Portsmouth, NH
03804 Portsmouth, NH
03809 Alton, NH
03810 Alton Bay, NH
03811 Atkinson, NH
03812 Bartlett, NH
03812 Harts Location, NH
03813 Center Conway, NH
03813 Chatham, NH
03814 Center Ossipee, NH
03815 Center Strafford, NH
03816 Center Tuftonboro, NH
03817 Chocorua, NH
03818 Albany, NH
03818 Conway, NH
03819 Danville, NH
03820 Dover, NH
03821 Dover, NH
03822 Dover, NH
03823 Madbury, NH
03824 Durham, NH
03824 Lee, NH
03825 Barrington, NH
03826 East Hampstead, NH
03827 East Kingston, NH
03827 South Hampton, NH
03830 East Wakefield, NH
03832 Eaton Center, NH
03833 Brentwood, NH
03833 Exeter, NH
03833 Kensington, NH
03835 Farmington, NH
03836 Freedom, NH
03837 Gilmanton Iron Works, NH
03838 Glen, NH
03839 Rochester, NH
03840 Greenland, NH
03841 Hampstead, NH
03842 Hampton, NH
03843 Hampton, NH
03844 Hampton Falls, NH
03845 Intervale, NH
03846 Jackson, NH
03847 Kearsarge, NH
03848 Kingston, NH
03849 Madison, NH
03850 Melvin Village, NH
03851 Milton, NH
03852 Milton Mills, NH
03853 Mirror Lake, NH
03854 New Castle, NH
03855 New Durham, NH
03856 Newfields, NH
03857 Newmarket, NH
03858 Newton, NH
03859 Newton Junction, NH
03860 Hales Location, NH
03860 North Conway, NH
03861 Lee, NH
03862 North Hampton, NH
03864 Ossipee, NH
03865 Plaistow, NH
03866 Rochester, NH
03867 Rochester, NH
03868 Rochester, NH
03869 Rollinsford, NH
03870 Rye, NH
03871 Rye Beach, NH
03872 Brookfield, NH
03872 Sanbornville, NH
03873 Sandown, NH
03874 Seabrook, NH
03875 Silver Lake, NH
03878 Somersworth, NH
03882 Effingham, NH
03883 South Tamworth, NH
03884 Strafford, NH
03885 Stratham, NH
03886 Tamworth, NH
03887 Middleton, NH
03887 Union, NH
03890 West Ossipee, NH
03894 Wolfeboro, NH
03896 Wolfeboro Falls, NH
03897 Wonalancet, NH

039

03901 Berwick, ME
03902 Cape Neddick, ME
03903 Eliot, ME
03904 Kittery, ME
03905 Kittery Point, ME
03906 North Berwick, ME
03907 Ogunquit, ME
03908 South Berwick, ME
03909 York, ME
03910 York Beach, ME
03911 York Harbor, ME

040

04001 Acton, ME
04002 Alfred, ME
04002 Lyman, ME
04003 Bailey Island, ME
04004 Bar Mills, ME
04005 Biddeford, ME
04005 Dayton, ME
04006 Biddeford Pool, ME
04007 Biddeford, ME
04008 Bowdoinham, ME
04009 Bridgton, ME
04010 Brownfield, ME
04011 Birch Island, ME
04011 Brunswick, ME
04011 Cundys Harbor, ME
04011 Mere Point, ME
04013 Bustins Island, ME
04013 South Freeport, ME
04014 Cape Porpoise, ME
04015 Casco, ME
04016 Center Lovell, ME
04017 Chebeague Island, ME
04019 Cliff Island, ME
04020 Cornish, ME
04021 Cumberland, ME
04021 Cumberland Center, ME
04022 Denmark, ME
04024 East Baldwin, ME
04027 Lebanon, ME
04028 East Parsonsfield, ME
04029 Sebago, ME
04030 East Waterboro, ME
04032 Freeport, ME
04033 Freeport, ME
04034 Freeport, ME
04037 Fryeburg, ME
04037 North Fryeburg, ME
04037 Stow, ME
04038 Gorham, ME
04039 Gray, ME
04040 Harrison, ME
04040 Sweden, ME
04041 Hiram, ME
04042 Hollis Center, ME
04043 Kennebunk, ME
04046 Arundel, ME
04046 Kennebunkport, ME
04047 Kezar Falls, ME
04047 Parsonsfield, ME
04048 Limerick, ME
04049 Limington, ME
04050 Long Island, ME
04051 Lovell, ME
04054 Moody, ME
04055 Naples, ME
04056 Newfield, ME
04057 North Bridgton, ME
04061 North Waterboro, ME
04062 Windham, ME
04063 Ocean Park, ME
04064 Old Orchard Beach, ME
04066 Orrs Island, ME
04068 Porter, ME
04069 Pownal, ME
04070 Scarborough, ME
04071 Frye Island, ME
04071 Raymond, ME
04072 Saco, ME
04073 Sanford, ME
04074 Pine Point, ME
04074 Scarborough, ME
04076 North Shapleigh, ME
04076 Shapleigh, ME
04077 South Casco, ME
04078 South Freeport, ME
04079 Harpswell, ME
04079 South Harpswell, ME
04082 South Windham, ME
04082 Windham, ME
04083 Springvale, ME
04084 Sebago Lake, ME
04084 Standish, ME
04085 Steep Falls, ME
04086 Pejepscot, ME
04086 Topsham, ME
04087 Waterboro, ME
04088 Waterford, ME
04090 Wells, ME
04091 West Baldwin, ME
04092 Westbrook, ME
04093 Buxton, ME
04094 West Kennebunk, ME
04095 West Newfield, ME
04096 Yarmouth, ME
04097 North Yarmouth, ME
04098 Westbrook, ME

041

04101 Portland, ME
04102 Portland, ME
04103 Portland, ME
04104 Portland, ME
04105 Falmouth, ME
04105 Portland, ME
04106 Portland, ME
04106 South Portland, ME
04107 Cape Elizabeth, ME
04107 Pond Cove, ME
04107 Portland, ME
04108 Peaks Island, ME
04108 Portland, ME
04109 Cushing Island, ME
04109 Diamond Cove, ME
04109 Diamond Island, ME
04109 Great Diamond Island, ME
04109 Little Diamond Island, ME
04109 Portland, ME
04110 Cumberland Foreside, ME
04110 Portland, ME
04112 Portland, ME
04116 Portland, ME
04116 South Portland, ME
04122 Portland, ME
04123 Portland, ME
04124 Portland, ME

042

04210 Auburn, ME
04211 Auburn, ME
04212 Auburn, ME
04216 Andover, ME
04217 Albany Twp, ME
04217 Bethel, ME
04217 Gilead, ME
04217 Mason Twp, ME
04219 Bryant Pond, ME
04219 Milton Twp, ME
04220 Buckfield, ME
04220 Hartford, ME
04221 Canton, ME
04222 Durham, ME
04223 Danville, ME
04224 Carthage, ME
04224 Dixfield, ME
04225 Dryden, ME
04226 East Andover, ME
04227 East Dixfield, ME
04228 East Livermore, ME
04230 East Poland, ME
04231 E Stoneham, ME
04231 Stoneham, ME
04234 East Wilton, ME
04236 Greene, ME
04237 Hanover, ME
04238 Hebron, ME
04239 Jay, ME
04240 Lewiston, ME
04241 Lewiston, ME
04243 Lewiston, ME
04250 Lisbon, ME
04252 Lisbon, ME
04252 Lisbon Falls, ME
04253 Livermore, ME
04254 Livermore Falls, ME
04255 Greenwood, ME
04256 Mechanic Falls, ME
04257 Mexico, ME
04258 Minot, ME
04259 Monmouth, ME
04260 New Gloucester, ME
04261 Newry, ME
04261 Upton, ME
04262 North Jay, ME
04263 Leeds, ME
04265 North Monmouth, ME
04266 North Turner, ME
04267 North Waterford, ME
04268 Norway, ME
04270 Otisfield, ME
04270 Oxford, ME
04271 Paris, ME
04274 Poland, ME
04274 Poland Spring, ME
04275 Byron, ME
04275 Roxbury, ME
04276 Rumford, ME
04276 Rumford Center, ME
04276 Rumford Point, ME
04280 Sabattus, ME
04280 Wales, ME
04281 South Paris, ME
04282 Turner, ME
04284 Wayne, ME
04285 Weld, ME
04286 West Bethel, ME
04287 Bowdoin, ME
04287 W Bowdoin, ME
04288 West Minot, ME
04289 West Paris, ME
04290 Peru, ME
04291 West Poland, ME
04292 Sumner, ME
04294 Perkins Twp, ME
04294 Wilton, ME

043

04330 Augusta, ME
04330 Chelsea, ME
04330 Sidney, ME
04332 Augusta, ME
04333 Augusta, ME
04336 Augusta, ME
04338 Augusta, ME
04341 Coopers Mills, ME
04342 Dresden, ME
04343 East Winthrop, ME
04344 Farmingdale, ME
04345 Gardiner, ME
04345 Pittston, ME
04345 West Gardiner, ME
04346 Randolph, ME
04347 Hallowell, ME
04348 Jefferson, ME
04348 Somerville, ME
04349 Fayette, ME
04349 Kents Hill, ME
04350 Litchfield, ME
04351 Manchester, ME
04352 Mount Vernon, ME
04353 Whitefield, ME
04354 Palermo, ME
04355 Readfield, ME
04357 Richmond, ME
04358 China, ME
04358 South China, ME
04358 Weeks Mills, ME
04359 South Gardiner, ME
04360 Vienna, ME
04363 Windsor, ME
04364 Winthrop, ME

044

04401 Bangor, ME
04401 Glenburn, ME
04401 Hermon, ME
04401 Veazie, ME
04402 Bangor, ME
04406 Abbot, ME
04406 Blanchard Twp, ME
04408 Aurora, ME
04408 Great Pond, ME
04410 Bradford, ME
04411 Bradley, ME
04412 Brewer, ME
04413 Brookton, ME
04413 Forest City Twp, ME
04413 Forest Twp, ME
04414 Barnard Twp, ME
04414 Brownville, ME
04414 Ebeemee Twp, ME
04414 Williamsburg Twp, ME
04415 Brownville Junction, ME
04416 Bucksport, ME
04416 Verona Island, ME
04417 Burlington, ME
04418 Cardville, ME
04418 Costigan, ME
04418 Greenbush, ME
04418 Greenfield Twp, ME
04418 Olamon, ME
04419 Carmel, ME
04420 Castine, ME
04421 Castine, ME
04422 Charleston, ME
04424 Danforth, ME
04424 Weston, ME
04426 Atkinson, ME
04426 Bowerbank, ME
04426 Dover Foxcroft, ME
04426 Dvr Foxcroft, ME
04426 Sebec, ME
04427 Corinth, ME
04428 Clifton, ME
04428 Eddington, ME
04429 Dedham, ME
04429 East Holden, ME
04429 Holden, ME
04430 East Millinocket, ME
04431 East Orland, ME
04434 Etna, ME
04435 Exeter, ME
04438 Frankfort, ME
04441 Beaver Cove, ME
04441 Frenchtown Twp, ME
04441 Greenville, ME
04441 Lily Bay Twp, ME
04441 Shirley, ME
04442 Greenville Junction, ME
04443 Elliottsville Twp, ME
04443 Guilford, ME
04443 Parkman, ME
04443 Willimantic, ME
04444 Hampden, ME
04444 Newburgh, ME
04448 Edinburg, ME
04448 Howland, ME
04448 Seboeis Plt, ME
04449 Hudson, ME
04450 Kenduskeag, ME
04451 Kingman, ME
04451 Kingman Twp, ME
04451 Macwahoc Plt, ME
04453 Lagrange, ME
04453 Maxfield, ME
04454 Lambert Lake, ME
04455 Lee, ME
04456 Levant, ME
04457 Chester, ME
04457 Lincoln, ME
04457 Lincoln Center, ME
04457 Mattamiscontis Twp, ME
04457 Woodville, ME
04459 Mattawamkeag, ME
04459 Molunkus Twp, ME
04460 Grindstone Twp, ME
04460 Medway, ME
04460 Soldiertown Twp, ME
04461 Milford, ME
04462 Cedar Lake Twp, ME
04462 Indian Purchase Twp, ME
04462 Long A Twp, ME
04462 Millinocket, ME
04463 Derby, ME
04463 Lake View Plt, ME
04463 Medford, ME
04463 Milo, ME
04463 Orneville Twp, ME
04464 Monson, ME
04468 Alton, ME
04468 Argyle Twp, ME
04468 Indian Island, ME
04468 Old Town, ME
04469 Orono, ME
04471 Amity, ME
04471 Cary Plt, ME
04471 Orient, ME
04472 Orland, ME
04473 Orono, ME
04474 Orrington, ME
04475 Passadumkeag, ME
04476 Penobscot, ME
04478 Pittston Academy Grant Twp, ME
04478 Plymouth Twp, ME
04478 Rockwood, ME
04478 Seboomook Twp, ME
04478 Tomhegan Twp, ME
04479 Sangerville, ME
04481 Brownville, ME
04481 Sebec, ME
04485 Greenville, ME
04485 Shirley Mills, ME
04487 Carroll Plt, ME
04487 Lakeville, ME
04487 Prentiss Twp, ME
04487 Springfield, ME
04487 Webster Plt, ME
04488 Stetson, ME
04489 Stillwater, ME
04490 Codyville Plt, ME
04490 Topsfield, ME
04490 Waite, ME
04491 Vanceboro, ME
04492 Talmadge, ME
04492 Waite, ME
04493 Enfield, ME
04493 Lowell, ME
04493 West Enfield, ME
04495 Winn, ME
04496 Winterport, ME
04497 Bancroft, ME
04497 Drew Plt, ME
04497 Glenwood Plt, ME
04497 Haynesville, ME
04497 Reed Plt, ME
04497 Wytopitlock, ME

045

04530 Arrowsic, ME
04530 Bath, ME
04530 West Bath, ME
04535 Alna, ME
04537 Boothbay, ME
04538 Boothbay Harbor, ME
04538 Capitol Island, ME
04539 Bristol, ME
04541 Chamberlain, ME
04543 Damariscotta, ME
04544 East Boothbay, ME
04547 Friendship, ME
04548 Georgetown, ME

04548 Mac Mahan, ME
04549 Boothbay, ME
04549 Isle Of Springs, ME
04551 Bremen, ME
04551 Medomak, ME
04553 Newcastle, ME
04554 New Harbor, ME
04555 Nobleboro, ME
04556 Edgecomb, ME
04558 New Harbor, ME
04558 Pemaquid, ME
04562 Phippsburg, ME
04563 Cushing, ME
04564 Round Pond, ME
04565 Sebasco Estates, ME
04568 South Bristol, ME
04570 Boothbay Harbor, ME
04570 Squirrel Island, ME
04571 Trevett, ME
04572 Waldoboro, ME
04573 Walpole, ME
04574 Washington, ME
04575 W Boothbay Harbor, ME
04575 West Boothbay Harbor, ME
04576 Newagen, ME
04576 Southport, ME
04578 Westport Island, ME
04578 Wiscasset, ME
04579 Woolwich, ME

046

04605 Amherst, ME
04605 Ellsworth, ME
04605 Fletchers Landing Twp, ME
04605 Lamoine, ME
04605 Mariaville, ME
04605 Osborn, ME
04605 Otis, ME
04605 Trenton, ME
04605 Waltham, ME
04606 Addison, ME
04607 Gouldsboro, ME
04607 South Gouldsboro, ME
04609 Bar Harbor, ME
04611 Beals, ME
04612 Bernard, ME
04612 West Tremont, ME
04613 Birch Harbor, ME
04614 Blue Hill, ME
04616 Brooklin, ME
04617 Brooksville, ME
04619 Calais, ME
04622 Beddington, ME
04622 Cherryfield, ME
04622 Deblois, ME
04623 Centerville, ME
04623 Columbia, ME
04623 Columbia Falls, ME
04624 Corea, ME
04625 Cranberry Isles, ME
04626 Cutler, ME
04627 Deer Isle, ME
04628 Dennysville, ME
04628 Edmunds Twp, ME
04628 Marion Twp, ME
04629 East Blue Hill, ME
04629 Surry, ME
04630 East Machias, ME
04631 Eastport, ME
04634 Eastbrook, ME
04634 Franklin, ME
04635 Frenchboro, ME
04637 Grand Lake Stream, ME
04640 Hancock, ME
04642 Harborside, ME
04643 Harrington, ME
04644 Hulls Cove, ME
04645 Isle Au Haut, ME
04645 Stonington, ME
04646 Islesford, ME
04648 Jonesboro, ME
04649 Jonesport, ME
04650 Little Deer Isle, ME
04652 Lubec, ME
04652 Trescott Twp, ME
04653 Bass Harbor, ME
04654 Day Block Twp, ME
04654 Machias, ME
04654 Marshfield, ME
04654 Northfield, ME
04654 Roque Bluffs, ME
04654 Whitneyville, ME
04655 Bucks Harbor, ME
04655 Machiasport, ME
04657 Cathance Twp, ME
04657 Cooper, ME
04657 Meddybemps, ME
04658 Milbridge, ME
04660 Mount Desert, ME
04660 Otter Creek, ME
04662 Northeast Harbor, ME
04664 North Sullivan, ME
04664 Sullivan, ME
04666 Charlotte, ME
04666 Pembroke, ME
04667 Perry, ME
04667 Pleasant Point, ME
04668 Big Lake Twp, ME
04668 Grand Lake Stream, ME
04668 Greenlaw Chopping Twp, ME
04668 Indian Twp, ME
04668 Princeton, ME
04669 Prospect Harbor, ME
04671 Robbinston, ME
04672 Salsbury Cove, ME
04673 Sargentville, ME
04674 Seal Cove, ME
04675 Seal Harbor, ME
04676 Sedgwick, ME
04677 Sorrento, ME
04679 Southwest Harbor, ME
04680 Steuben, ME
04681 Stonington, ME
04683 Sunset, ME
04684 Surry, ME
04685 Minturn, ME
04685 Swans Island, ME
04686 Machias, ME
04686 Wesley, ME
04691 Whiting, ME
04693 Winter Harbor, ME
04694 Alexander, ME
04694 Baileyville, ME
04694 Baring Plt, ME
04694 Crawford, ME
04694 Woodland Washington County, ME

047

04730 Hammond, ME
04730 Hodgdon, ME
04730 Houlton, ME
04730 Linneus, ME
04730 Littleton, ME
04730 Ludlow, ME
04732 Ashland, ME
04732 Garfield Plt, ME
04732 Masardis, ME
04732 Nashville Plt, ME
04732 Sheridan, ME
04733 Benedicta, ME
04734 Blaine, ME
04735 Bridgewater, ME
04736 Caribou, ME
04736 Connor Twp, ME
04736 Woodland, ME
04737 Clayton Lake, ME
04738 Crouseville, ME
04739 Eagle Lake, ME
04739 Quimby, ME
04739 Winterville Plt, ME
04740 Easton, ME
04741 Estcourt Station, ME
04742 Fort Fairfield, ME
04743 Fort Kent, ME
04743 New Canada, ME
04743 St John Plt, ME
04744 Fort Kent Mills, ME
04745 Frenchville, ME
04745 Upper Frenchville, ME
04746 Grand Isle, ME
04746 Lille, ME
04747 Crystal, ME
04747 Dyer Brook, ME
04747 Island Falls, ME
04750 Caswell, ME
04750 Limestone, ME
04750 Loring Cm Ctr, ME
04751 Limestone, ME
04756 Madawaska, ME
04757 Castle Hill, ME
04757 Chapman, ME
04757 Mapleton, ME
04758 Mars Hill, ME
04760 Monticello, ME
04761 Houlton, ME
04761 New Limerick, ME
04762 New Sweden, ME
04763 Oakfield, ME
04764 Oxbow, ME
04765 Mount Chase, ME
04765 Patten, ME
04766 Perham, ME
04768 Portage, ME
04768 Portage Lake, ME
04769 Presque Isle, ME
04772 Saint Agatha, ME
04773 Saint David, ME
04774 Allagash, ME
04774 Saint Francis, ME
04775 Sheridan, ME
04776 Sherman, ME
04776 Sherman Mills, ME
04776 Silver Ridge Twp, ME
04777 Herseytown Twp, ME
04777 Sherman Station, ME
04777 Stacyville, ME
04779 Cross Lake Twp, ME
04779 Sinclair, ME
04780 Hersey, ME
04780 Merrill, ME
04780 Moro Plt, ME
04780 Smyrna Mills, ME
04781 Wallagrass, ME
04783 Stockholm, ME
04783 Westmanland, ME
04785 Cyr Plt, ME
04785 Hamlin, ME
04785 Van Buren, ME
04786 Wade, ME
04786 Washburn, ME
04787 Westfield, ME

048

04841 Rockland, ME
04843 Camden, ME
04847 Camden, ME
04847 Hope, ME
04848 Islesboro, ME
04849 Lincolnville, ME
04849 Northport, ME
04850 Lincolnville Center, ME
04851 Matinicus, ME
04852 Monhegan, ME
04853 North Haven, ME
04854 Owls Head, ME
04855 Port Clyde, ME
04856 Rockport, ME
04858 South Thomaston, ME
04859 Spruce Head, ME
04859 Tenants Harbor, ME
04860 Saint George, ME
04860 Tenants Harbor, ME
04861 Thomaston, ME
04862 Appleton, ME
04862 Union, ME
04863 Vinalhaven, ME
04864 Warren, ME
04865 West Rockport, ME

049

04901 Benton, ME
04901 Waterville, ME
04901 Winslow, ME
04903 Waterville, ME
04910 Albion, ME
04911 Anson, ME
04911 Starks, ME
04912 Athens, ME
04912 Brighton Plt, ME
04915 Belfast, ME
04915 Swanville, ME
04915 Waldo, ME
04917 Belgrade, ME
04918 Belgrade Lakes, ME
04920 Bingham, ME
04920 Concord Twp, ME
04920 Moscow, ME
04920 Pleasant Ridge Plt, ME
04921 Brooks, ME
04921 Jackson, ME
04922 Burnham, ME
04923 Cambridge, ME
04924 Canaan, ME
04925 Caratunk, ME
04926 China Village, ME
04926 China Vlg, ME
04927 Clinton, ME
04928 Corinna, ME
04929 Detroit, ME
04930 Dexter, ME
04930 Ripley, ME
04932 Dixmont, ME
04933 East Newport, ME
04935 East Vassalboro, ME
04936 Chain Of Ponds Twp, ME
04936 Coburn Gore, ME
04936 Eustis, ME
04936 Jim Pond Twp, ME
04937 Fairfield, ME
04938 Chesterville, ME
04938 Farmington, ME
04938 Industry, ME
04939 Garland, ME
04940 Farmington Falls, ME
04941 Freedom, ME
04941 Montville, ME
04942 Harmony, ME
04942 Kingsbury Plt, ME
04942 Mayfield Twp, ME
04942 Wellington, ME
04943 Hartland, ME
04944 Hinckley, ME
04945 Dennistown, ME
04945 Jackman, ME
04945 Johnson Mountain Twp, ME
04945 Long Pond Twp, ME
04945 Moose River, ME
04945 Parlin Pond Twp, ME
04945 Sandy Bay Twp, ME
04947 Carrabassett Valley, ME
04947 Kingfield, ME
04949 Liberty, ME
04950 Madison, ME
04951 Monroe, ME
04952 Belmont, ME
04952 Morrill, ME
04953 Newport, ME
04954 New Portland, ME
04954 North New Portland, ME
04955 New Sharon, ME
04956 New Vineyard, ME
04957 Mercer, ME
04957 Norridgewock, ME
04958 Embden, ME
04958 North Anson, ME
04961 Carrying Place Town Twp, ME
04961 Dead River Twp, ME
04961 Highland Plt, ME
04961 Lexington Twp, ME
04961 N New Portland, ME
04961 New Portland, ME
04961 North New Portland, ME
04961 Pierce Pond Twp, ME
04962 N Vassalboro, ME
04962 North Vassalboro, ME
04963 Oakland, ME
04963 Rome, ME
04964 Adamstown Twp, ME
04964 Oquossoc, ME
04965 Palmyra, ME
04966 Avon, ME
04966 Madrid Twp, ME
04966 Phillips, ME
04967 Pittsfield, ME
04969 Plymouth, ME
04970 Coplin Plt, ME
04970 Dallas Plt, ME
04970 Lang Twp, ME
04970 Rangeley, ME
04970 Sandy River Plt, ME
04971 Saint Albans, ME
04972 Sandy Point, ME
04973 Searsmont, ME
04974 Searsport, ME
04975 Shawmut, ME
04976 Cornville, ME
04976 Skowhegan, ME
04978 Smithfield, ME
04979 Solon, ME
04981 Prospect, ME
04981 Stockton Springs, ME
04982 Stratton, ME
04983 Freeman Twp, ME
04983 Salem Twp, ME
04983 Strong, ME
04984 Temple, ME
04985 East Moxie Twp, ME
04985 Indian Stream Twp, ME
04985 Moxie Gore Twp, ME
04985 The Forks Plt, ME
04985 West Forks, ME
04986 Knox, ME
04986 Thorndike, ME
04987 Troy, ME
04988 Unity, ME
04989 Vassalboro, ME
04992 West Farmington, ME

050

05001 White River Junction, VT
05030 Ascutney, VT
05031 Barnard, VT
05032 Bethel, VT
05033 Bradford, VT
05034 Bridgewater, VT
05035 Brdgewtr Cors, VT
05035 Bridgewater Corners, VT
05036 Brookfield, VT
05037 Brownsville, VT
05038 Chelsea, VT
05039 Corinth, VT
05040 East Corinth, VT
05041 East Randolph, VT
05042 East Ryegate, VT
05042 Ryegate, VT
05043 East Thetford, VT
05045 Fairlee, VT
05046 Groton, VT
05047 Hartford, VT
05048 Hartland, VT
05049 Hartland Four Corners, VT
05050 Mc Indoe Falls, VT
05051 Newbury, VT
05052 North Hartland, VT
05053 North Pomfret, VT
05054 North Thetford, VT
05055 Norwich, VT
05056 Plymouth, VT
05058 Post Mills, VT
05059 Quechee, VT
05060 Braintree, VT
05060 Randolph, VT
05060 West Brookfield, VT
05061 Randolph Center, VT
05062 Reading, VT
05065 Sharon, VT
05067 South Pomfret, VT
05068 South Royalton, VT
05069 South Ryegate, VT
05070 South Strafford, VT
05071 South Woodstock, VT
05072 Strafford, VT
05073 Taftsville, VT
05074 Thetford, VT
05075 Thetford Center, VT
05076 East Corinth, VT
05076 Topsham, VT
05077 Tunbridge, VT
05079 Vershire, VT
05081 Wells River, VT
05083 West Fairlee, VT
05084 West Hartford, VT
05085 West Newbury, VT
05086 East Orange, VT
05086 West Topsham, VT
05088 Wilder, VT
05089 West Windsor, VT
05089 Windsor, VT
05091 Woodstock, VT

051

05101 Bellows Falls, VT
05141 Cambridgeport, VT
05142 Cavendish, VT
05143 Andover, VT
05143 Athens, VT
05143 Baltimore, VT
05143 Chester, VT
05146 Grafton, VT
05148 Landgrove, VT
05148 Londonderry, VT
05149 Ludlow, VT
05150 North Springfield, VT
05151 Perkinsville, VT
05152 Peru, VT
05153 Proctorsville, VT
05153 South Reading, VT
05154 Saxtons River, VT
05155 South Londonderry, VT
05155 Stratton Mnt, VT
05155 Stratton Mountain, VT
05156 Springfield, VT
05158 Westminster, VT
05159 Westminster Station, VT
05161 Weston, VT

052

05201 Bennington, VT
05201 Woodford, VT
05250 Arlington, VT
05250 Sandgate, VT
05250 Sunderland, VT
05250 West Arlington, VT
05251 Dorset, VT
05252 East Arlington, VT
05253 East Dorset, VT
05254 Manchester, VT
05255 Manchester Center, VT
05257 North Bennington, VT
05260 North Pownal, VT
05261 Pownal, VT
05262 Shaftsbury, VT

053

05301 Brattleboro, VT
05301 Dummerston, VT
05301 Guilford, VT
05301 West Brattleboro, VT
05302 Brattleboro, VT
05303 Brattleboro, VT
05304 Brattleboro, VT
05340 Bondville, VT
05340 Winhall, VT
05341 East Dover, VT
05342 Jacksonville, VT
05343 Jamaica, VT
05344 Marlboro, VT
05345 Brookline, VT
05345 Newfane, VT
05346 East Dummerston, VT
05346 Putney, VT
05346 Westminster West, VT
05350 Readsboro, VT
05351 South Newfane, VT
05352 Readsboro, VT
05352 Stamford, VT
05353 Townshend, VT
05354 Vernon, VT
05355 Wardsboro, VT
05356 Mount Snow, VT
05356 West Dover, VT
05357 West Dummerston, VT

05358 West Halifax, VT
05359 West Townshend, VT
05359 Windham, VT
05360 Stratton, VT
05360 West Wardsboro, VT
05361 Whitingham, VT
05362 Williamsville, VT
05363 Searsburg, VT
05363 West Marlboro, VT
05363 Wilmington, VT

054

05401 Burlington, VT
05402 Burlington, VT
05403 South Burlington, VT
05404 Winooski, VT
05405 Burlington, VT
05406 Burlington, VT
05407 South Burlington, VT
05408 Burlington, VT
05439 Colchester, VT
05440 Alburg, VT
05440 Alburgh, VT
05441 Bakersfield, VT
05442 Belvidere Center, VT
05443 Bristol, VT
05443 Lincoln, VT
05444 Cambridge, VT
05445 Charlotte, VT
05446 Colchester, VT
05447 East Berkshire, VT
05448 East Fairfield, VT
05449 Colchester, VT
05450 Enosburg Falls, VT
05451 Essex, VT
05452 Essex Junction, VT
05454 Fairfax, VT
05455 Fairfield, VT
05455 Sheldon, VT
05456 Ferrisburgh, VT
05457 Franklin, VT
05458 Grand Isle, VT
05459 Highgate Center, VT
05460 Highgate Springs, VT
05461 Hinesburg, VT
05462 Huntington, VT
05463 Isle La Motte, VT
05464 Jeffersonville, VT
05465 Jericho, VT
05465 Jericho Center, VT
05466 Jonesville, VT
05468 Milton, VT
05469 Monkton, VT
05470 Montgomery, VT
05471 Montgomery Center, VT
05472 New Haven, VT
05473 North Ferrisburgh, VT
05474 North Hero, VT
05476 Richford, VT
05477 Bolton Valley, VT
05477 Richmond, VT
05478 Saint Albans, VT
05479 Saint Albans, VT
05481 Saint Albans Bay, VT
05482 Shelburne, VT
05483 Sheldon, VT
05485 Sheldon Springs, VT
05486 South Hero, VT
05487 Starksboro, VT
05488 Swanton, VT
05489 Underhill, VT
05490 Underhill Center, VT
05491 Addison, VT
05491 Panton, VT
05491 Vergennes, VT
05492 Waterville, VT
05494 Westford, VT
05495 Saint George, VT
05495 St George, VT
05495 Williston, VT

055

05501 Andover, MA
05544 Andover, MA

056

05601 Montpelier, VT
05602 Berlin, VT
05602 Middlesex, VT
05602 Middlesex Center, VT
05602 Montpelier, VT
05603 Montpelier, VT
05604 Montpelier, VT
05609 Montpelier, VT
05620 Montpelier, VT
05633 Montpelier, VT
05640 Adamant, VT
05641 Barre, VT
05641 Orange, VT
05647 Cabot, VT
05648 Calais, VT
05649 East Barre, VT
05650 East Calais, VT
05651 East Montpelier, VT
05652 Eden, VT
05653 Eden, VT
05653 Eden Mills, VT
05654 Graniteville, VT
05655 Hyde Park, VT
05656 Johnson, VT
05657 Lake Elmore, VT
05658 Marshfield, VT
05660 Moretown, VT
05660 South Duxbury, VT
05661 Elmore, VT
05661 Morristown, VT
05661 Morrisville, VT
05662 Moscow, VT
05663 Northfield, VT
05663 Riverton, VT
05663 West Berlin, VT
05664 Northfield Falls, VT
05664 Northfld Fls, VT
05665 North Hyde Park, VT
05666 North Montpelier, VT
05667 Plainfield, VT
05669 Roxbury, VT
05669 West Braintree, VT
05670 South Barre, VT
05671 Waterbury, VT
05672 Stowe, VT
05673 Waitsfield, VT
05674 Warren, VT
05675 Washington, VT
05676 Waterbury, VT
05677 Waterbury Center, VT
05678 Websterville, VT
05679 Williamstown, VT
05680 Wolcott, VT
05681 Woodbury, VT
05682 North Middlesex, VT
05682 Worcester, VT

057

05701 Mendon, VT
05701 Rutland, VT
05701 South Chittenden, VT
05702 Rutland, VT
05730 Belmont, VT
05731 Benson, VT
05732 Bomoseen, VT
05733 Brandon, VT
05733 Goshen, VT
05733 Leicester, VT
05733 Sudbury, VT
05734 Bridport, VT
05735 Castleton, VT
05736 Center Rutland, VT
05737 Chittenden, VT
05738 Cuttingsville, VT
05738 Shrewsbury, VT
05739 Danby, VT
05739 Mount Tabor, VT
05740 East Middlebury, VT
05741 East Poultney, VT
05741 Poultney, VT
05742 East Wallingford, VT
05743 Benson, VT
05743 Fair Haven, VT
05743 West Haven, VT
05744 Florence, VT
05745 Forest Dale, VT
05746 Gaysville, VT
05747 Granville, VT
05748 Hancock, VT
05750 Hydeville, VT
05751 Killington, VT
05753 Cornwall, VT
05753 Middlebury, VT
05753 Weybridge, VT
05757 Middletown Springs, VT
05758 Mount Holly, VT
05759 North Clarendon, VT
05760 Orwell, VT
05761 Pawlet, VT
05762 Pittsfield, VT
05763 North Chittenden, VT
05763 Pittsford, VT
05764 Poultney, VT
05765 Proctor, VT
05766 Ripton, VT
05767 Rochester, VT
05768 Rupert, VT
05769 Salisbury, VT
05770 Shoreham, VT
05772 Stockbridge, VT
05773 Tinmouth, VT
05773 Wallingford, VT
05774 Wells, VT
05775 West Pawlet, VT
05776 West Rupert, VT
05777 Clarendon Springs, VT
05777 West Rutland, VT
05778 West Cornwall, VT
05778 Whiting, VT

058

05819 Saint Johnsbury, VT
05819 Waterford, VT
05820 Albany, VT
05821 Barnet, VT
05822 Barton, VT
05823 Beebe Plain, VT
05824 Concord, VT
05825 Coventry, VT
05826 Craftsbury, VT
05827 Craftsbry Cmn, VT
05827 Craftsbury Common, VT
05828 Danville, VT
05829 Derby, VT
05830 Derby Line, VT
05832 East Burke, VT
05833 East Charleston, VT
05836 East Hardwick, VT
05837 East Haven, VT
05838 East Saint Johnsbury, VT
05839 Barton, VT
05839 Glover, VT
05840 Granby, VT
05841 Greensboro, VT
05842 Greensboro Bend, VT
05842 Grnsboro Bend, VT
05843 Hardwick, VT
05845 Irasburg, VT
05846 Island Pond, VT
05847 Lowell, VT
05848 Lower Waterford, VT
05849 Lyndon, VT
05850 Lyndon Center, VT
05851 Lyndonville, VT
05853 Morgan, VT
05853 Morgan Ctr, VT
05855 Newport, VT
05857 Newport Center, VT
05858 North Concord, VT
05858 Victory, VT
05859 Jay, VT
05859 Jay Peak, VT
05859 North Troy, VT
05860 Brownington, VT
05860 Orleans, VT
05861 Passumpsic, VT
05862 Peacham, VT
05863 Saint Johnsbury Center, VT
05866 Sheffield, VT
05867 Sutton, VT
05868 Troy, VT
05871 West Burke, VT
05872 West Charleston, VT
05873 West Danville, VT
05874 Westfield, VT
05875 Barton, VT
05875 West Glover, VT

059

05901 Averill, VT
05901 Canaan, VT
05902 Beecher Falls, VT
05903 Canaan, VT
05903 Lemington, VT
05904 Gilman, VT
05905 Bloomfield, VT
05905 Brunswick, VT
05905 Guildhall, VT
05905 Maidstone, VT
05906 East Concord, VT
05906 Lunenburg, VT
05907 Norton, VT

060

06001 Avon, CT
06002 Bloomfield, CT
06006 Windsor, CT
06010 Bristol, CT
06011 Bristol, CT
06013 Burlington, CT
06013 Unionville, CT
06016 Broad Brook, CT
06016 Melrose, CT
06016 Windsorville, CT
06018 Canaan, CT
06019 Canton, CT
06019 Collinsville, CT
06020 Canton Center, CT
06021 Colebrook, CT
06022 Collinsville, CT
06023 East Berlin, CT
06024 East Canaan, CT
06025 East Glastonbury, CT
06026 East Granby, CT
06027 East Hartland, CT
06028 East Windsor Hill, CT
06029 Ellington, CT
06030 Farmington, CT
06031 Falls Village, CT
06032 Farmington, CT
06033 Glastonbury, CT
06034 Farmington, CT
06035 Granby, CT
06037 Berlin, CT
06037 Kensington, CT
06039 Lakeville, CT
06040 Manchester, CT
06041 Manchester, CT
06042 Manchester, CT
06043 Bolton, CT
06045 Manchester, CT
06050 New Britain, CT
06051 New Britain, CT
06052 New Britain, CT
06053 New Britain, CT
06057 New Hartford, CT
06058 Norfolk, CT
06059 North Canton, CT
06060 North Granby, CT
06061 Pine Meadow, CT
06062 Plainville, CT
06063 Barkhamsted, CT
06063 Pleasant Valley, CT
06063 Winsted, CT
06064 Poquonock, CT
06065 Riverton, CT
06066 Vernon, CT
06066 Vernon Rockville, CT
06067 Rocky Hill, CT
06068 Salisbury, CT
06069 Sharon, CT
06070 Simsbury, CT
06071 Somers, CT
06072 Somersville, CT
06073 South Glastonbury, CT
06074 South Windsor, CT
06075 Stafford, CT
06076 Stafford Springs, CT
06076 Union, CT
06077 Staffordville, CT
06078 Suffield, CT
06079 Taconic, CT
06080 Suffield, CT
06081 Tariffville, CT
06082 Enfield, CT
06083 Enfield, CT
06084 Tolland, CT
06085 Unionville, CT
06087 Unionville, CT
06088 East Windsor, CT
06089 Weatogue, CT
06090 West Granby, CT
06091 West Hartland, CT
06092 West Simsbury, CT
06093 West Suffield, CT
06094 Winchester Center, CT
06095 Windsor, CT
06096 Windsor Locks, CT
06098 Winchester Center, CT
06098 Winsted, CT

061

06101 Hartford, CT
06102 Hartford, CT
06103 Hartford, CT
06104 Hartford, CT
06105 Hartford, CT
06106 Hartford, CT
06107 Hartford, CT
06107 West Hartford, CT
06107 West Hartfrd, CT
06108 East Hartford, CT
06108 Hartford, CT
06109 Hartford, CT
06109 Wethersfield, CT
06110 Hartford, CT
06110 West Hartford, CT
06110 West Hartfrd, CT
06111 Hartford, CT
06111 Newington, CT
06112 Hartford, CT
06114 Hartford, CT
06115 Hartford, CT
06117 Hartford, CT
06117 West Hartford, CT
06117 West Hartfrd, CT
06118 East Hartford, CT
06118 Hartford, CT
06119 Hartford, CT
06119 West Hartford, CT
06119 West Hartfrd, CT
06120 Hartford, CT
06123 Hartford, CT
06126 Hartford, CT
06127 Hartford, CT
06127 West Hartford, CT
06127 West Hartfrd, CT
06128 East Hartford, CT
06128 Hartford, CT
06129 Hartford, CT
06129 Wethersfield, CT
06131 Hartford, CT
06131 Newington, CT
06132 Hartford, CT
06133 Hartford, CT
06133 West Hartford, CT
06133 West Hartfrd, CT
06134 Hartford, CT
06137 Bishops Corner, CT
06137 Hartford, CT
06137 West Hartford, CT
06137 West Hartfrd, CT
06138 East Hartford, CT
06138 Hartford, CT
06138 Silver Lane, CT
06140 Hartford, CT
06141 Hartford, CT
06142 Hartford, CT
06143 Hartford, CT
06144 Hartford, CT
06145 Hartford, CT
06146 Hartford, CT
06147 Hartford, CT
06150 Hartford, CT
06151 Hartford, CT
06152 Hartford, CT
06153 Hartford, CT
06154 Hartford, CT
06155 Hartford, CT
06156 Hartford, CT
06160 Hartford, CT
06161 Hartford, CT
06161 Wethersfield, CT
06167 Hartford, CT
06176 Hartford, CT
06180 Hartford, CT
06183 Hartford, CT
06199 Hartford, CT

062

06226 Willimantic, CT
06230 Abington, CT
06231 Amston, CT
06232 Andover, CT
06233 Ballouville, CT
06234 Brooklyn, CT
06235 Chaplin, CT
06235 Mansfield Center, CT
06235 North Windham, CT
06237 Columbia, CT
06238 Coventry, CT
06239 Danielson, CT
06241 Dayville, CT
06242 Eastford, CT
06243 East Killingly, CT
06244 East Woodstock, CT
06245 Fabyan, CT
06246 Grosvenor Dale, CT
06247 Hampton, CT
06248 Hebron, CT
06249 Lebanon, CT
06250 Mansfield Center, CT
06251 Mansfield Depot, CT
06254 North Franklin, CT
06255 North Grosvenordale, CT
06256 North Windham, CT
06258 Pomfret, CT
06259 Pomfret Center, CT
06260 Putnam, CT
06262 Quinebaug, CT
06263 Rogers, CT
06264 Scotland, CT
06265 South Willington, CT
06266 South Windham, CT
06267 South Woodstock, CT
06268 Storrs, CT
06268 Storrs Mansfield, CT
06269 Storrs, CT
06269 Storrs Mansfield, CT
06277 Thompson, CT
06278 Ashford, CT
06278 Warrenville, CT
06279 Willington, CT
06280 Windham, CT
06281 Woodstock, CT
06282 Woodstock Valley, CT

063

06320 New London, CT
06330 Baltic, CT
06331 Canterbury, CT
06332 Central Village, CT
06333 East Lyme, CT
06334 Bozrah, CT
06335 Gales Ferry, CT
06336 Gilman, CT
06338 Ledyard, CT
06338 Mashantucket, CT
06339 Gales Ferry, CT
06339 Ledyard, CT
06340 Groton, CT
06349 Groton, CT
06350 Hanover, CT
06351 Griswold, CT
06351 Jewett City, CT
06351 Lisbon, CT
06353 Montville, CT
06354 Moosup, CT
06355 Mystic, CT
06357 Niantic, CT
06359 North Stonington, CT
06360 Norwich, CT
06365 Norwich, CT

06365 Preston, CT
06370 Oakdale, CT
06371 Lyme, CT
06371 Old Lyme, CT
06372 Old Mystic, CT
06373 Oneco, CT
06374 Plainfield, CT
06375 Quaker Hill, CT
06376 South Lyme, CT
06377 Sterling, CT
06378 Stonington, CT
06379 Pawcatuck, CT
06380 Taftville, CT
06382 Uncasville, CT
06383 Versailles, CT
06384 Glasgo, CT
06384 Voluntown, CT
06385 Waterford, CT
06387 Wauregan, CT
06388 Mystic, CT
06388 West Mystic, CT
06389 Yantic, CT
06390 Fishers Island, NY

064

06401 Ansonia, CT
06403 Beacon Falls, CT
06404 Botsford, CT
06405 Branford, CT
06408 Cheshire, CT
06409 Centerbrook, CT
06410 Cheshire, CT
06411 Cheshire, CT
06412 Chester, CT
06413 Clinton, CT
06414 Cobalt, CT
06415 Colchester, CT
06416 Cromwell, CT
06417 Deep River, CT
06418 Derby, CT
06419 Deep River, CT
06419 Killingworth, CT
06420 Colchester, CT
06420 Salem, CT
06422 Durham, CT
06423 East Haddam, CT
06424 East Hampton, CT
06424 Haddam Neck, CT
06426 Essex, CT
06437 Guilford, CT
06438 Haddam, CT
06439 Hadlyme, CT
06440 Hawleyville, CT
06441 Higganum, CT
06442 Ivoryton, CT
06443 Madison, CT
06444 Marion, CT
06447 Marlborough, CT
06450 Meriden, CT
06451 Meriden, CT
06455 Middlefield, CT
06456 Middle Haddam, CT
06457 Middletown, CT
06459 Middletown, CT
06460 Milford, CT
06461 Milford, CT
06467 Milldale, CT
06468 Monroe, CT
06469 Moodus, CT
06470 Newtown, CT
06471 North Branford, CT
06472 Northford, CT
06473 North Haven, CT
06474 North Westchester, CT
06475 Old Saybrook, CT
06477 Orange, CT
06478 Oxford, CT
06478 Seymour, CT
06479 Plantsville, CT
06480 Portland, CT
06481 Rockfall, CT
06482 Sandy Hook, CT
06483 Seymour, CT
06484 Huntington, CT
06484 Shelton, CT
06487 South Britain, CT
06488 Southbury, CT
06489 Southington, CT
06491 Stevenson, CT
06492 Wallingford, CT
06492 Yalesville, CT
06493 Wallingford, CT
06494 Wallingford, CT
06495 Wallingford, CT
06498 Westbrook, CT

065

06501 New Haven, CT
06502 New Haven, CT
06503 New Haven, CT
06504 New Haven, CT
06505 New Haven, CT
06506 New Haven, CT
06507 New Haven, CT
06508 New Haven, CT
06509 New Haven, CT
06510 New Haven, CT
06511 Hamden, CT
06511 New Haven, CT
06512 East Haven, CT
06512 New Haven, CT
06513 East Haven, CT
06513 New Haven, CT
06514 Hamden, CT
06514 New Haven, CT
06515 New Haven, CT
06516 W Haven, CT
06516 West Haven, CT
06517 Hamden, CT
06517 New Haven, CT
06517 Whitneyville, CT
06518 Hamden, CT
06518 New Haven, CT
06519 New Haven, CT
06520 New Haven, CT
06521 New Haven, CT
06524 Bethany, CT
06524 New Haven, CT
06525 New Haven, CT
06525 Woodbridge, CT
06530 New Haven, CT
06531 New Haven, CT
06532 New Haven, CT
06533 New Haven, CT
06534 New Haven, CT
06535 New Haven, CT
06536 New Haven, CT
06537 New Haven, CT
06538 New Haven, CT
06540 New Haven, CT

066

06601 Bridgeport, CT
06602 Bridgeport, CT
06604 Bridgeport, CT
06605 Bridgeport, CT
06606 Bridgeport, CT
06607 Bridgeport, CT
06608 Bridgeport, CT
06610 Bridgeport, CT
06611 Trumbull, CT
06612 Easton, CT
06614 Stratford, CT
06615 Stratford, CT
06650 Bridgeport, CT
06673 Bridgeport, CT
06699 Bridgeport, CT

067

06701 Waterbury, CT
06702 Waterbury, CT
06703 Waterbury, CT
06704 Waterbury, CT
06705 Waterbury, CT
06705 Wolcott, CT
06706 Waterbury, CT
06708 Waterbury, CT
06710 Waterbury, CT
06712 Prospect, CT
06712 Waterbury, CT
06716 Waterbury, CT
06716 Wolcott, CT
06720 Waterbury, CT
06721 Waterbury, CT
06722 Waterbury, CT
06723 Waterbury, CT
06724 Waterbury, CT
06725 Waterbury, CT
06726 Waterbury, CT
06749 Waterbury, CT
06750 Bantam, CT
06751 Bethlehem, CT
06752 Bridgewater, CT
06753 Cornwall, CT
06754 Cornwall Bridge, CT
06754 Warren, CT
06755 Gaylordsville, CT
06756 Goshen, CT
06757 Kent, CT
06758 Lakeside, CT
06759 Litchfield, CT
06762 Middlebury, CT
06763 Morris, CT
06770 Naugatuck, CT
06776 New Milford, CT
06777 New Preston Marble Dale, CT
06777 Warren, CT
06777 Washington Depot, CT
06778 Northfield, CT
06778 Thomaston, CT
06779 Oakville, CT
06779 Watertown, CT
06781 Pequabuck, CT
06782 Plymouth, CT
06783 Roxbury, CT
06784 Sherman, CT
06785 South Kent, CT
06786 Terryville, CT
06787 Thomaston, CT
06790 Torrington, CT
06791 Harwinton, CT
06791 Torrington, CT
06792 Harwinton, CT
06792 Torrington, CT
06793 Washington, CT
06793 Washington Depot, CT
06795 Watertown, CT
06796 West Cornwall, CT
06798 Woodbury, CT

068

06801 Bethel, CT
06804 Brookfield, CT
06804 Brookfld Ctr, CT
06807 Cos Cob, CT
06810 Danbury, CT
06811 Danbury, CT
06812 New Fairfield, CT
06813 Danbury, CT
06814 Danbury, CT
06816 Danbury, CT
06817 Danbury, CT
06820 Darien, CT
06824 Fairfield, CT
06825 Fairfield, CT
06828 Fairfield, CT
06829 Georgetown, CT
06830 Greenwich, CT
06831 Greenwich, CT
06836 Greenwich, CT
06838 Greens Farms, CT
06840 New Canaan, CT
06850 Norwalk, CT
06851 Norwalk, CT
06852 Norwalk, CT
06853 Norwalk, CT
06854 Norwalk, CT
06855 Norwalk, CT
06856 Norwalk, CT
06857 Norwalk, CT
06858 Norwalk, CT
06860 Norwalk, CT
06870 Old Greenwich, CT
06875 Redding Center, CT
06876 Redding Ridge, CT
06877 Ridgefield, CT
06878 Riverside, CT
06879 Ridgefield, CT
06880 Westport, CT
06881 Westport, CT
06883 Weston, CT
06888 Westport, CT
06889 Westport, CT
06890 Southport, CT
06896 Redding, CT
06896 West Redding, CT
06897 Wilton, CT

069

06901 Stamford, CT
06902 Stamford, CT
06903 Stamford, CT
06904 Stamford, CT
06905 Ridgeway, CT
06905 Stamford, CT
06906 Stamford, CT
06907 Stamford, CT
06910 Stamford, CT
06911 Stamford, CT
06912 Stamford, CT
06913 Stamford, CT
06914 Stamford, CT
06920 Stamford, CT
06921 Stamford, CT
06922 Stamford, CT
06926 Stamford, CT
06927 Stamford, CT

070

07001 Avenel, NJ
07002 Bayonne, NJ
07003 Bloomfield, NJ
07004 Fairfield, NJ
07005 Boonton, NJ
07005 Boonton Township, NJ
07006 Caldwell, NJ
07006 North Caldwell, NJ
07006 W Caldwell, NJ
07006 West Caldwell, NJ
07007 Caldwell, NJ
07007 West Caldwell, NJ
07008 Carteret, NJ
07009 Cedar Grove, NJ
07010 Cliffside Park, NJ
07011 Clifton, NJ
07012 Clifton, NJ
07013 Clifton, NJ
07014 Clifton, NJ
07015 Clifton, NJ
07016 Cranford, NJ
07017 East Orange, NJ
07018 East Orange, NJ
07019 East Orange, NJ
07020 Edgewater, NJ
07021 Essex Fells, NJ
07022 Fairview, NJ
07023 Fanwood, NJ
07024 Fort Lee, NJ
07026 Garfield, NJ
07027 Garwood, NJ
07028 Glen Ridge, NJ
07029 East Newark, NJ
07029 Harrison, NJ
07030 Hoboken, NJ
07031 North Arlington, NJ
07032 Kearny, NJ
07033 Kenilworth, NJ
07034 Lake Hiawatha, NJ
07035 Lincoln Park, NJ
07036 Linden, NJ
07036 Winfield Park, NJ
07039 Livingston, NJ
07040 Maplewood, NJ
07041 Millburn, NJ
07042 Montclair, NJ
07043 Montclair, NJ
07043 Upper Montclair, NJ
07044 Verona, NJ
07045 Montville, NJ
07046 Mountain Lakes, NJ
07047 North Bergen, NJ
07050 Orange, NJ
07051 Orange, NJ
07052 West Orange, NJ
07054 Parsippany, NJ
07055 Passaic, NJ
07057 Wallington, NJ
07058 Pine Brook, NJ
07059 Warren, NJ
07060 North Plainfield, NJ
07060 Plainfield, NJ
07061 Plainfield, NJ
07062 North Plainfield, NJ
07062 Plainfield, NJ
07063 North Plainfield, NJ
07063 Plainfield, NJ
07064 Port Reading, NJ
07065 Rahway, NJ
07066 Clark, NJ
07067 Colonia, NJ
07068 Roseland, NJ
07069 Plainfield, NJ
07069 Watchung, NJ
07070 Rutherford, NJ
07071 Lyndhurst, NJ
07072 Carlstadt, NJ
07073 East Rutherford, NJ
07074 Moonachie, NJ
07075 Wood Ridge, NJ
07076 Scotch Plains, NJ
07077 Sewaren, NJ
07078 Short Hills, NJ
07079 South Orange, NJ
07080 South Plainfield, NJ
07081 Springfield, NJ
07082 Towaco, NJ
07083 Union, NJ
07086 Weehawken, NJ
07087 Union City, NJ
07088 Vauxhall, NJ
07090 Westfield, NJ
07091 Westfield, NJ
07092 Mountainside, NJ
07093 Guttenberg, NJ
07093 West New York, NJ
07094 Secaucus, NJ
07095 Woodbridge, NJ
07096 Secaucus, NJ
07097 Jersey City, NJ
07099 Kearny, NJ

071

07101 Newark, NJ
07102 Newark, NJ
07103 Newark, NJ
07104 Newark, NJ
07105 Newark, NJ
07106 Newark, NJ
07107 Newark, NJ
07108 Newark, NJ
07109 Belleville, NJ
07110 Nutley, NJ
07111 Irvington, NJ
07112 Newark, NJ
07114 Newark, NJ
07175 Newark, NJ
07184 Newark, NJ
07188 Newark, NJ
07189 Newark, NJ
07191 Newark, NJ
07192 Newark, NJ
07193 Newark, NJ
07195 Newark, NJ
07198 Newark, NJ
07199 Newark, NJ

072

07201 Elizabeth, NJ
07202 Elizabeth, NJ
07203 Roselle, NJ
07204 Roselle Park, NJ
07205 Hillside, NJ
07205 Industrial Hillside, NJ
07206 Elizabeth, NJ
07206 Elizabethport, NJ
07207 Elizabeth, NJ
07208 Elizabeth, NJ

073

07302 Jersey City, NJ
07303 Jersey City, NJ
07304 Jersey City, NJ
07305 Jersey City, NJ
07306 Jersey City, NJ
07307 Jersey City, NJ
07308 Jersey City, NJ
07310 Jersey City, NJ
07311 Jersey City, NJ
07395 Jersey City, NJ
07399 Jersey City, NJ

074

07401 Allendale, NJ
07403 Bloomingdale, NJ
07405 Butler, NJ
07405 Kinnelon, NJ
07407 Elmwood Park, NJ
07410 Fair Lawn, NJ
07416 Franklin, NJ
07417 Franklin Lakes, NJ
07418 Glenwood, NJ
07419 Hamburg, NJ
07420 Haskell, NJ
07421 Hewitt, NJ
07422 Highland Lakes, NJ
07423 Ho Ho Kus, NJ
07424 Little Falls, NJ
07424 West Paterson, NJ
07424 Woodland Park, NJ
07428 Mc Afee, NJ
07430 Mahwah, NJ
07432 Midland Park, NJ
07435 Newfoundland, NJ
07436 Oakland, NJ
07438 Oak Ridge, NJ
07439 Ogdensburg, NJ
07440 Pequannock, NJ
07442 Pompton Lakes, NJ
07444 Pompton Plains, NJ
07446 Ramsey, NJ
07450 Ridgewood, NJ
07451 Ridgewood, NJ
07452 Glen Rock, NJ
07456 Ringwood, NJ
07457 Riverdale, NJ
07458 Saddle River, NJ
07458 Upper Saddle River, NJ
07460 Hardyston, NJ
07460 Stockholm, NJ
07461 Sussex, NJ
07461 Wantage, NJ
07462 Vernon, NJ
07463 Waldwick, NJ
07465 Wanaque, NJ
07470 Wayne, NJ
07474 Wayne, NJ
07480 West Milford, NJ
07481 Wyckoff, NJ
07495 Mahwah, NJ

075

07501 Paterson, NJ
07502 Paterson, NJ
07502 Totowa, NJ
07503 Paterson, NJ
07504 Paterson, NJ
07505 Paterson, NJ
07506 Hawthorne, NJ
07507 Hawthorne, NJ
07508 Haledon, NJ
07508 North Haledon, NJ
07508 Paterson, NJ
07508 Prospect Park, NJ
07509 Paterson, NJ
07510 Paterson, NJ
07511 Paterson, NJ
07511 Totowa, NJ
07512 Paterson, NJ
07512 Totowa, NJ
07513 Paterson, NJ
07514 Paterson, NJ
07522 Paterson, NJ
07524 Paterson, NJ
07533 Paterson, NJ
07538 Haledon, NJ
07538 Paterson, NJ
07543 Paterson, NJ
07544 Paterson, NJ

076

07601 Hackensack, NJ
07602 Hackensack, NJ
07603 Bogota, NJ
07604 Hasbrouck Heights, NJ
07605 Leonia, NJ
07606 South Hackensack, NJ
07607 Maywood, NJ
07608 Teterboro, NJ
07620 Alpine, NJ
07621 Bergenfield, NJ
07624 Closter, NJ
07626 Cresskill, NJ
07627 Demarest, NJ
07628 Dumont, NJ
07630 Emerson, NJ
07631 Englewood, NJ
07632 Englewood, NJ
07632 Englewood Cliffs, NJ
07640 Harrington Park, NJ
07641 Haworth, NJ
07642 Hillsdale, NJ
07643 Little Ferry, NJ
07644 Lodi, NJ
07645 Montvale, NJ
07646 New Milford, NJ
07647 Northvale, NJ
07647 Rockleigh, NJ
07648 Norwood, NJ
07649 Oradell, NJ
07650 Palisades Park, NJ
07652 Paramus, NJ
07653 Paramus, NJ
07656 Park Ridge, NJ
07657 Ridgefield, NJ
07660 Ridgefield Park, NJ
07661 River Edge, NJ
07662 Rochelle Park, NJ
07663 Saddle Brook, NJ
07666 Teaneck, NJ
07670 Tenafly, NJ
07675 Old Tappan, NJ
07675 River Vale, NJ
07675 Rivervale, NJ
07675 Westwood, NJ
07676 Township Of Washington, NJ
07676 Washington Twps, NJ
07677 Westwood, NJ
07677 Woodcliff Lake, NJ
07699 Teterboro, NJ

077

07701 Red Bank, NJ
07701 Tinton Falls, NJ
07702 Red Bank, NJ
07702 Shrewsbury, NJ
07703 Fort Monmouth, NJ
07703 Red Bank, NJ
07704 Fair Haven, NJ
07704 Red Bank, NJ
07709 Red Bank, NJ
07710 Adelphia, NJ
07711 Allenhurst, NJ
07711 Loch Arbour, NJ
07711 West Allenhurst, NJ
07712 Asbury Park, NJ
07712 Interlaken, NJ
07712 Ocean, NJ
07712 Tinton Falls, NJ
07715 Belmar, NJ
07716 Atlantic Highlands, NJ
07717 Avon By The Sea, NJ
07718 Belford, NJ
07719 Belmar, NJ
07719 Lake Como, NJ
07719 Wall, NJ
07719 Wall Township, NJ
07720 Bradley Beach, NJ
07721 Cliffwood, NJ
07722 Colts Neck, NJ
07723 Deal, NJ
07724 Eatontown, NJ
07724 Tinton Falls, NJ
07726 Englishtown, NJ
07726 Manalapan, NJ
07727 Farmingdale, NJ
07727 Tinton Falls, NJ
07727 Wall Township, NJ
07728 Freehold, NJ
07730 Hazlet, NJ
07731 Howell, NJ
07731 Wall Township, NJ
07732 Highlands, NJ
07732 Sandy Hook, NJ
07733 Holmdel, NJ
07734 Hazlet Township, NJ
07734 Keansburg, NJ
07735 Keyport, NJ
07735 Union Beach, NJ
07737 Leonardo, NJ
07738 Lincroft, NJ
07739 Little Silver, NJ
07740 Long Branch, NJ
07746 Marlboro, NJ
07747 Aberdeen, NJ
07747 Matawan, NJ
07748 Middletown, NJ
07748 New Monmouth, NJ
07748 North Middletown, NJ
07750 Monmouth Beach, NJ
07751 Morganville, NJ
07752 Navesink, NJ
07753 Neptune, NJ
07753 Neptune City, NJ
07753 Tinton Falls, NJ
07753 Wall Township, NJ
07754 Neptune, NJ
07755 Oakhurst, NJ
07756 Ocean Grove, NJ
07757 Oceanport, NJ
07758 Port Monmouth, NJ
07760 Locust, NJ
07760 Rumson, NJ
07760 Sea Bright, NJ
07762 Spring Lake, NJ
07763 Tennent, NJ
07764 West Long Branch, NJ
07765 Wickatunk, NJ
07799 Eatontown, NJ

078

07801 Dover, NJ
07802 Dover, NJ
07803 Dover, NJ
07803 Mine Hill, NJ
07806 Dover, NJ
07806 Picatinny Arsenal, NJ
07820 Allamuchy, NJ
07821 Andover, NJ
07821 Byram Township, NJ
07821 Green Township, NJ
07822 Augusta, NJ
07823 Belvidere, NJ
07825 Blairstown, NJ
07825 Hardwick, NJ
07825 Johnsonburg, NJ
07826 Branchville, NJ
07826 Sandyston, NJ
07827 Branchville, NJ
07827 Montague, NJ
07827 Sandyston, NJ
07828 Budd Lake, NJ
07829 Buttzville, NJ
07830 Califon, NJ
07830 Tewksbury Township, NJ
07831 Changewater, NJ
07832 Columbia, NJ
07833 Delaware, NJ
07834 Denville, NJ
07836 Flanders, NJ
07836 Roxbury Township, NJ
07837 Glasser, NJ
07838 Great Meadows, NJ
07839 Greendell, NJ
07840 Hackettstown, NJ
07842 Hibernia, NJ
07843 Hopatcong, NJ
07844 Hope, NJ
07845 Ironia, NJ
07846 Johnsonburg, NJ
07847 Kenvil, NJ
07848 Lafayette, NJ
07849 Lake Hopatcong, NJ
07850 Landing, NJ
07851 Layton, NJ
07851 Sandyston, NJ
07852 Ledgewood, NJ
07853 Long Valley, NJ
07855 Middleville, NJ
07856 Mount Arlington, NJ
07857 Netcong, NJ
07860 Fredon, NJ
07860 Fredon Township, NJ
07860 Newton, NJ
07863 Oxford, NJ
07865 Port Murray, NJ
07866 Rockaway, NJ
07869 Dover, NJ
07869 Randolph, NJ
07870 Schooleys Mountain, NJ
07871 Sparta, NJ
07874 Stanhope, NJ
07875 Stillwater, NJ
07876 Succasunna, NJ
07877 Swartswood, NJ
07878 Mount Tabor, NJ
07879 Tranquility, NJ
07880 Vienna, NJ
07881 Wallpack Center, NJ
07882 Washington, NJ
07885 Wharton, NJ
07890 Branchville, NJ

079

07901 Summit, NJ
07902 Summit, NJ
07920 Basking Ridge, NJ
07921 Bedminster, NJ
07922 Berkeley Heights, NJ
07924 Bernardsville, NJ
07926 Brookside, NJ
07927 Cedar Knolls, NJ
07928 Chatham, NJ
07928 Chatham Twp, NJ
07930 Chester, NJ
07931 Far Hills, NJ
07932 Florham Park, NJ
07933 Gillette, NJ
07934 Gladstone, NJ
07935 Green Village, NJ
07936 East Hanover, NJ
07938 Liberty Corner, NJ
07939 Basking Ridge, NJ
07939 Lyons, NJ
07940 Madison, NJ
07945 Mendham, NJ
07945 Mendham Twsp, NJ
07946 Millington, NJ
07950 Greystone Park, NJ
07950 Morris Plains, NJ
07960 Morristown, NJ
07961 Convent Station, NJ
07961 Morristown, NJ
07962 Morristown, NJ
07963 Morristown, NJ
07970 Mount Freedom, NJ
07974 New Providence, NJ
07976 New Vernon, NJ
07977 Peapack, NJ
07978 Pluckemin, NJ
07979 Pottersville, NJ
07980 Stirling, NJ
07981 Whippany, NJ
07999 Whippany, NJ

080

08001 Alloway, NJ
08002 Cherry Hill, NJ
08003 Cherry Hill, NJ
08004 Atco, NJ
08005 Barnegat, NJ
08006 Barnegat Light, NJ
08007 Barrington, NJ
08008 Beach Haven, NJ
08008 Harvey Cedars, NJ
08008 Long Beach, NJ
08008 Long Beach Township, NJ
08008 Ship Bottom, NJ
08008 Surf City, NJ
08009 Berlin, NJ
08010 Beverly, NJ
08010 Edgewater Park, NJ
08011 Birmingham, NJ
08012 Blackwood, NJ
08012 Turnersville, NJ
08014 Bridgeport, NJ
08015 Browns Mills, NJ
08016 Burlington, NJ
08016 Burlington City, NJ
08016 Burlington Township, NJ
08018 Cedar Brook, NJ
08019 Chatsworth, NJ
08020 Clarksboro, NJ
08021 Clementon, NJ
08021 Laurel Springs, NJ
08021 Lindenwold, NJ
08021 Pine Hill, NJ
08021 Pine Valley, NJ
08022 Columbus, NJ
08023 Deepwater, NJ
08025 Ewan, NJ
08026 Gibbsboro, NJ
08027 Gibbstown, NJ
08028 Glassboro, NJ
08029 Glendora, NJ
08030 Brooklawn, NJ
08030 Gloucester City, NJ
08030 Gloucstr City, NJ
08031 Bellmawr, NJ
08032 Grenloch, NJ
08033 Haddonfield, NJ
08034 Cherry Hill, NJ
08035 Haddon Heights, NJ
08035 Haddon Hts, NJ
08036 Hainesport, NJ
08036 Hainesport Township, NJ
08037 Batsto, NJ
08037 Hammonton, NJ
08038 Hancocks Bridge, NJ
08039 Harrisonville, NJ
08041 Jobstown, NJ
08042 Juliustown, NJ
08043 Kirkwd Vrhes, NJ
08043 Kirkwood, NJ
08043 Voorhees, NJ
08045 Lawnside, NJ
08046 Willingboro, NJ
08048 Lumberton, NJ
08048 Lumberton Township, NJ
08049 Magnolia, NJ
08050 Manahawkin, NJ
08050 Stafford Township, NJ
08051 Mantua, NJ
08051 West Deptford, NJ
08052 Maple Shade, NJ
08053 Evesham, NJ
08053 Marlton, NJ
08054 Mount Laurel, NJ
08055 Medford, NJ
08055 Medford Lakes, NJ
08056 Mickleton, NJ
08057 Moorestown, NJ
08059 Mount Ephraim, NJ
08059 West Collingswood Heights, NJ
08060 Eastampton, NJ
08060 Eastampton Township, NJ
08060 Mount Holly, NJ
08060 Westampton, NJ
08061 Mount Royal, NJ
08062 Mullica Hill, NJ
08062 South Harrison Township, NJ
08063 National Park, NJ
08063 West Deptford, NJ
08064 New Lisbon, NJ
08065 Palmyra, NJ
08066 Paulsboro, NJ
08066 West Deptford, NJ
08067 Pedricktown, NJ
08068 Pemberton, NJ
08069 Carneys Point, NJ
08069 Penns Grove, NJ
08070 Pennsville, NJ
08071 Pitman, NJ
08072 Quinton, NJ
08073 Rancocas, NJ
08074 Richwood, NJ
08075 Delanco, NJ
08075 Delran, NJ
08075 Riverside, NJ
08076 Riverton, NJ
08077 Cinnaminson, NJ
08077 Riverton, NJ
08078 Runnemede, NJ
08079 Mannington, NJ
08079 Salem, NJ
08080 Sewell, NJ
08081 Erial, NJ
08081 Sicklerville, NJ
08083 Hi Nella, NJ
08083 Somerdale, NJ
08084 Stratford, NJ
08085 Logan Township, NJ
08085 Swedesboro, NJ
08085 Woolwich Township, NJ
08086 Thorofare, NJ
08086 West Deptford, NJ
08087 Little Egg Harbor, NJ
08087 Little Egg Harbor Twp, NJ
08087 Mystic Islands, NJ
08087 Tuckerton, NJ
08088 Shamong, NJ
08088 Southampton, NJ
08088 Tabernacle, NJ
08088 Vincentown, NJ
08089 Chesilhurst, NJ
08089 Waterford Works, NJ
08090 Wenonah, NJ
08091 Berlin Township, NJ
08091 West Berlin, NJ
08092 West Creek, NJ
08093 West Deptford, NJ
08093 Westville, NJ
08094 Williamstown, NJ
08095 Winslow, NJ
08096 Blackwood Terrace, NJ
08096 Deptford, NJ
08096 West Deptford, NJ
08096 Woodbury, NJ
08097 Deptford, NJ
08097 Woodbury, NJ
08097 Woodbury Heights, NJ
08098 Pilesgrove, NJ
08098 Pilesgrove Township, NJ
08098 Woodstown, NJ
08099 Bellmawr, NJ

081

08101 Camden, NJ
08102 Camden, NJ
08103 Camden, NJ
08104 Camden, NJ
08104 Haddon Township, NJ
08105 Camden, NJ
08106 Audubon, NJ
08107 Collingswood, NJ
08107 Haddon Township, NJ
08107 Oaklyn, NJ
08107 West Collingswood, NJ
08107 Woodlynne, NJ
08107 Haddon Township, NJ
08108 Collingswood, NJ
08108 Haddon Township, NJ
08108 Westmont, NJ
08108 Haddon Township, NJ
08109 Merchantville, NJ
08109 Pennsauken, NJ
08110 Delair, NJ
08110 Pennsauken, NJ

082

08201 Absecon, NJ
08202 Avalon, NJ
08203 Brigantine, NJ
08204 Cape May, NJ
08204 North Cape May, NJ
08204 West Cape May, NJ
08205 Absecon, NJ
08205 Galloway, NJ
08205 Smithville, NJ
08210 Cape May Court House, NJ
08212 Cape May Point, NJ
08213 Cologne, NJ
08214 Dennisville, NJ
08215 Egg Harbor City, NJ
08215 Egg Hbr City, NJ
08217 Elwood, NJ
08218 Goshen, NJ
08219 Green Creek, NJ
08220 Leeds Point, NJ
08221 Linwood, NJ
08223 Marmora, NJ
08224 New Gretna, NJ
08225 Northfield, NJ
08226 Ocean City, NJ
08230 Ocean View, NJ
08231 Oceanville, NJ
08232 Mckee City, NJ
08232 Pleasantville, NJ
08234 Egg Harbor Township, NJ
08234 Egg Harbor Twp, NJ
08240 Pomona, NJ
08241 Port Republic, NJ
08242 Rio Grande, NJ
08243 Sea Isle City, NJ
08243 Townsends Inlet, NJ
08244 Somers Point, NJ
08245 South Dennis, NJ
08246 South Seaville, NJ
08247 Stone Harbor, NJ
08248 Strathmere, NJ
08250 Tuckahoe, NJ
08251 Del Haven, NJ
08251 Villas, NJ
08252 Whitesboro, NJ
08260 North Wildwood, NJ
08260 West Wildwood, NJ
08260 Wildwood, NJ
08260 Wildwood Crest, NJ
08270 Corbin City, NJ
08270 Woodbine, NJ

083

08302 Bridgeton, NJ
08310 Buena, NJ
08311 Cedarville, NJ
08312 Clayton, NJ
08313 Deerfield Street, NJ
08314 Delmont, NJ
08315 Dividing Creek, NJ
08316 Dorchester, NJ
08317 Dorothy, NJ
08318 Elmer, NJ
08318 Pittsgrove, NJ
08319 Estell Manor, NJ
08320 Fairton, NJ
08321 Fortescue, NJ
08322 Franklinville, NJ
08323 Greenwich, NJ
08324 Heislerville, NJ
08326 Landisville, NJ
08327 Leesburg, NJ
08328 Malaga, NJ
08329 Mauricetown, NJ
08330 Mays Landing, NJ
08332 Millville, NJ
08340 Milmay, NJ
08341 Minotola, NJ
08342 Mizpah, NJ
08343 Monroeville, NJ
08344 Newfield, NJ
08345 Newport, NJ
08346 Newtonville, NJ
08347 Norma, NJ
08348 Port Elizabeth, NJ
08349 Port Norris, NJ
08350 Richland, NJ
08352 Rosenhayn, NJ
08353 Shiloh, NJ
08360 Vineland, NJ
08361 Vineland, NJ
08362 Vineland, NJ

084

08401 Atlantic City, NJ
08402 Margate City, NJ
08403 Longport, NJ
08404 Atlantic City, NJ
08405 Atlantic City, NJ
08406 Ventnor City, NJ

085

08501 Allentown, NJ
08502 Belle Mead, NJ
08504 Blawenburg, NJ
08505 Bordentown, NJ
08505 Fieldsboro, NJ
08510 Clarksburg, NJ
08510 Millstone Township, NJ
08511 Cookstown, NJ
08512 Cranbury, NJ
08512 East Windsor, NJ
08514 Cream Ridge, NJ
08515 Chesterfield, NJ
08515 Crosswicks, NJ
08518 Florence, NJ
08520 East Windsor, NJ
08520 Hightstown, NJ
08525 Hopewell, NJ
08526 Imlaystown, NJ
08527 Jackson, NJ
08528 Kingston, NJ
08530 Lambertville, NJ
08533 New Egypt, NJ
08534 Pennington, NJ
08535 Millstone Township, NJ
08535 Perrineville, NJ
08536 Plainsboro, NJ
08540 Princeton, NJ
08541 Princeton, NJ
08542 Princeton, NJ
08543 Princeton, NJ
08544 Princeton, NJ
08550 Princeton Junction, NJ
08550 West Windsor, NJ
08551 Ringoes, NJ
08553 Rocky Hill, NJ
08554 Roebling, NJ
08555 Roosevelt, NJ
08556 Rosemont, NJ
08557 Sergeantsville, NJ
08558 Skillman, NJ
08559 Stockton, NJ
08560 Ewing, NJ
08560 Titusville, NJ
08561 Windsor, NJ
08562 Wrightstown, NJ

086

08601 Trenton, NJ
08602 Trenton, NJ
08603 Trenton, NJ
08604 Trenton, NJ
08605 Trenton, NJ
08606 Trenton, NJ
08607 Trenton, NJ
08608 Trenton, NJ
08609 Hamilton, NJ
08609 Trenton, NJ
08610 Hamilton, NJ
08610 Trenton, NJ
08611 Hamilton, NJ
08611 Trenton, NJ
08618 Ewing, NJ
08618 Trenton, NJ
08619 Hamilton, NJ
08619 Mercerville, NJ
08619 Trenton, NJ
08620 Hamilton, NJ
08620 Trenton, NJ
08625 Trenton, NJ
08628 Ewing, NJ
08628 Trenton, NJ
08628 West Trenton, NJ
08629 Hamilton, NJ
08629 Trenton, NJ
08638 Ewing, NJ
08638 Trenton, NJ
08640 Fort Dix, NJ
08641 Mc Guire Afb, NJ
08641 Trenton, NJ
08645 Trenton, NJ
08646 Trenton, NJ
08647 Trenton, NJ
08648 Lawrence, NJ
08648 Lawrence Township, NJ
08648 Lawrenceville, NJ
08648 Trenton, NJ
08650 Hamilton, NJ
08650 Trenton, NJ
08666 Trenton, NJ
08690 Hamilton, NJ
08690 Hamilton Square, NJ
08690 Trenton, NJ
08691 Hamilton, NJ
08691 Robbinsville, NJ
08691 Trenton, NJ
08695 Trenton, NJ

087

08701 Lakewood, NJ
08720 Allenwood, NJ
08721 Bayville, NJ
08722 Beachwood, NJ
08723 Brick, NJ
08723 Osbornville, NJ
08724 Brick, NJ
08724 Wall Township, NJ
08730 Brielle, NJ
08731 Forked River, NJ
08732 Island Heights, NJ
08733 Lakehurst, NJ
08733 Lakehurst Naec, NJ
08734 Lanoka Harbor, NJ
08735 Lavallette, NJ
08736 Manasquan, NJ
08738 Mantoloking, NJ
08739 Normandy Beach, NJ
08740 Ocean Gate, NJ
08741 Pine Beach, NJ
08742 Bay Head, NJ
08742 Point Pleasant Beach, NJ
08742 Point Pleasant Boro, NJ
08742 Pt Pleasant Beach, NJ
08750 Sea Girt, NJ
08751 Seaside Heights, NJ
08752 Seaside Park, NJ
08753 Toms River, NJ
08754 Toms River, NJ
08755 Toms River, NJ
08756 Toms River, NJ
08757 Toms River, NJ
08758 Waretown, NJ
08759 Lakehurst, NJ
08759 Manchester, NJ
08759 Manchester Township, NJ
08759 Whiting, NJ

088

08801 Annandale, NJ
08802 Asbury, NJ
08803 Baptistown, NJ
08804 Bloomsbury, NJ
08805 Bound Brook, NJ
08807 Bridgewater, NJ
08808 Broadway, NJ
08809 Clinton, NJ
08810 Dayton, NJ
08812 Dunellen, NJ
08812 Green Brook, NJ
08816 East Brunswick, NJ
08817 Edison, NJ
08818 Edison, NJ
08820 Edison, NJ
08821 Flagtown, NJ
08822 Flemington, NJ
08823 Franklin Park, NJ
08824 Kendall Park, NJ
08825 Frenchtown, NJ
08826 Glen Gardner, NJ
08827 Hampton, NJ
08828 Helmetta, NJ
08829 High Bridge, NJ
08830 Iselin, NJ
08831 Jamesburg, NJ
08831 Monroe, NJ
08831 Monroe Township, NJ
08832 Keasbey, NJ
08833 Lebanon, NJ
08834 Little York, NJ
08835 Manville, NJ
08836 Martinsville, NJ
08837 Edison, NJ
08840 Metuchen, NJ
08844 Hillsborough, NJ
08846 Middlesex, NJ
08848 Milford, NJ
08850 Milltown, NJ
08852 Monmouth Junction, NJ
08853 Branchburg, NJ
08853 Neshanic Station, NJ
08854 Piscataway, NJ
08855 Piscataway, NJ
08857 Old Bridge, NJ
08858 Oldwick, NJ
08859 Parlin, NJ
08861 Hopelawn, NJ
08861 Perth Amboy, NJ
08862 Perth Amboy, NJ
08863 Fords, NJ
08863 Perth Amboy, NJ
08865 Alpha, NJ
08865 Phillipsburg, NJ
08867 Pittstown, NJ
08868 Quakertown, NJ
08869 Raritan, NJ
08870 Readington, NJ
08871 Sayreville, NJ
08872 Sayreville, NJ
08873 Somerset, NJ
08875 East Millstone, NJ
08875 Somerset, NJ
08876 Branchburg, NJ
08876 North Branch, NJ
08876 Somerville, NJ
08879 Laurence Harbor, NJ
08879 South Amboy, NJ
08880 South Bound Brook, NJ
08882 South River, NJ
08884 Spotswood, NJ
08885 Stanton, NJ
08886 Stewartsville, NJ
08887 Three Bridges, NJ
08888 Whitehouse, NJ
08889 Whitehouse Station, NJ
08890 Zarephath, NJ
08899 Edison, NJ

089

08901 New Brunswick, NJ
08902 New Brunswick, NJ
08902 North Brunswick, NJ
08903 New Brunswick, NJ
08904 Highland Park, NJ
08904 New Brunswick, NJ
08906 Edison, NJ
08906 New Brunswick, NJ
08933 New Brunswick, NJ
08989 New Brunswick, NJ

100

10001 New York, NY
10002 Knickerbocker, NY
10002 New York, NY
10003 New York, NY
10004 Bowling Green, NY
10004 New York, NY
10005 New York, NY
10005 Wall Street, NY
10006 New York, NY
10006 Trinity, NY
10007 New York, NY
10008 New York, NY
10009 New York, NY
10010 New York, NY
10011 New York, NY
10012 New York, NY
10012 Prince, NY
10013 Canal Street, NY
10013 Chinatown, NY
10013 New York, NY
10014 New York, NY
10016 New York, NY
10017 New York, NY
10018 New York, NY
10019 New York, NY
10020 New York, NY
10021 New York, NY
10022 New York, NY
10023 New York, NY
10024 New York, NY
10025 New York, NY
10026 New York, NY
10027 New York, NY
10028 New York, NY
10029 New York, NY
10030 New York, NY
10031 New York, NY
10032 New York, NY
10033 New York, NY
10034 New York, NY
10035 New York, NY
10036 New York, NY
10037 New York, NY
10038 New York, NY
10038 Peck Slip, NY
10039 New York, NY
10040 New York, NY
10041 New York, NY
10043 New York, NY
10044 New York, NY
10044 Roosevelt Island, NY
10045 New York, NY
10055 New York, NY
10060 New York, NY
10065 New York, NY
10069 New York, NY
10075 New York, NY
10080 New York, NY
10081 New York, NY
10087 New York, NY
10090 New York, NY
10095 New York, NY

101

10101 New York, NY
10102 New York, NY
10103 New York, NY
10104 New York, NY
10105 New York, NY
10106 New York, NY
10107 New York, NY
10108 New York, NY
10109 New York, NY
10110 New York, NY
10111 New York, NY
10112 New York, NY
10113 New York, NY
10114 New York, NY
10115 New York, NY
10116 New York, NY
10117 New York, NY
10118 New York, NY
10119 New York, NY
10120 New York, NY
10121 New York, NY
10122 New York, NY
10123 New York, NY
10124 New York, NY
10125 New York, NY
10126 New York, NY
10128 New York, NY
10129 New York, NY
10130 New York, NY
10131 New York, NY
10132 New York, NY
10133 New York, NY
10138 New York, NY
10150 New York, NY
10151 New York, NY
10152 New York, NY
10153 New York, NY
10154 New York, NY
10155 New York, NY
10156 New York, NY
10157 New York, NY
10158 New York, NY
10159 New York, NY
10160 New York, NY
10161 New York, NY
10162 New York, NY
10163 New York, NY
10164 New York, NY
10165 New York, NY
10166 New York, NY
10167 New York, NY
10168 New York, NY
10169 New York, NY
10170 New York, NY
10171 New York, NY
10172 New York, NY
10173 New York, NY
10174 New York, NY
10175 New York, NY
10176 New York, NY
10177 New York, NY
10178 New York, NY
10179 New York, NY
10185 New York, NY
10199 New York, NY

102

10203 New York, NY
10211 New York, NY
10212 New York, NY
10213 New York, NY
10242 New York, NY
10249 New York, NY
10256 New York, NY
10257 New York, NY
10258 New York, NY
10259 New York, NY
10259 New York City, NY
10260 New York, NY
10261 New York, NY
10265 New York, NY
10268 New York, NY
10269 New York, NY
10270 New York, NY
10271 New York, NY
10272 New York, NY
10273 New York, NY
10274 New York, NY
10275 New York, NY
10276 New York, NY
10277 New York, NY
10278 New York, NY
10279 New York, NY
10280 New York, NY
10281 New York, NY
10282 New York, NY
10285 New York, NY
10286 New York, NY
10292 New York, NY

103

10301 Staten Island, NY
10302 Staten Island, NY
10303 Staten Island, NY
10304 Staten Island, NY
10305 Staten Island, NY
10306 Staten Island, NY
10307 Staten Island, NY
10308 Staten Island, NY
10309 Staten Island, NY
10310 Staten Island, NY
10311 Staten Island, NY
10312 Staten Island, NY
10313 Staten Island, NY
10314 Staten Island, NY

104

10451 Bronx, NY
10452 Bronx, NY
10453 Bronx, NY
10454 Bronx, NY
10455 Bronx, NY
10456 Bronx, NY
10457 Bronx, NY
10458 Bronx, NY
10459 Bronx, NY
10460 Bronx, NY
10461 Bronx, NY
10462 Bronx, NY
10463 Bronx, NY
10464 Bronx, NY
10465 Bronx, NY
10466 Bronx, NY
10467 Bronx, NY
10468 Bronx, NY
10469 Bronx, NY
10470 Bronx, NY
10471 Bronx, NY
10472 Bronx, NY
10473 Bronx, NY
10474 Bronx, NY
10475 Bronx, NY

105

10501 Amawalk, NY
10502 Ardsley, NY
10503 Ardsley On Hudson, NY
10504 Armonk, NY
10504 North Castle, NY
10505 Baldwin Place, NY
10506 Bedford, NY
10507 Bedford Hills, NY
10509 Brewster, NY
10510 Briarcliff Manor, NY
10510 Scarborough, NY
10511 Buchanan, NY
10512 Carmel, NY
10512 Kent Cliffs, NY
10512 Kent Lakes, NY
10514 Chappaqua, NY
10516 Cold Spring, NY
10516 Nelsonville, NY
10517 Crompond, NY
10518 Cross River, NY
10519 Croton Falls, NY
10520 Croton On Hudson, NY
10521 Crugers, NY
10522 Dobbs Ferry, NY
10523 Elmsford, NY
10524 Garrison, NY
10526 Goldens Bridge, NY
10527 Granite Springs, NY
10528 Harrison, NY
10530 Hartsdale, NY
10530 Scarsdale, NY
10532 Hawthorne, NY
10533 Irvington, NY
10535 Jefferson Valley, NY
10536 Katonah, NY
10537 Lake Peekskill, NY
10538 Larchmont, NY
10540 Lincolndale, NY
10541 Lake Lincolndale, NY
10541 Mahopac, NY
10542 Mahopac Falls, NY
10543 Mamaroneck, NY
10545 Maryknoll, NY
10546 Millwood, NY
10547 Mohegan Lake, NY
10548 Montrose, NY
10549 Bedford Corners, NY
10549 Mount Kisco, NY
10550 Mount Vernon, NY
10551 Mount Vernon, NY
10552 Fleetwood, NY
10552 Mount Vernon, NY
10553 Mount Vernon, NY
10560 North Salem, NY
10562 Ossining, NY
10566 Peekskill, NY
10567 Cortlandt Manor, NY
10570 Pleasantville, NY
10573 Port Chester, NY
10573 Rye Brook, NY
10576 Pound Ridge, NY
10577 Purchase, NY
10578 Purdys, NY
10579 Putnam Valley, NY
10580 Rye, NY
10583 Heathcote, NY
10583 Scarsdale, NY
10587 Shenorock, NY
10588 Shrub Oak, NY
10589 Somers, NY

10590 South Salem, NY
10591 North Tarrytown, NY
10591 Sleepy Hollow, NY
10591 Tarrytown, NY
10594 Thornwood, NY
10595 Valhalla, NY
10596 Verplanck, NY
10597 Waccabuc, NY
10598 Yorktown Heights, NY

106

10601 White Plains, NY
10602 White Plains, NY
10603 N White Plains, NY
10603 White Plains, NY
10604 W Harrison, NY
10604 West Harrison, NY
10604 White Plains, NY
10605 White Plains, NY
10606 White Plains, NY
10607 White Plains, NY
10610 White Plains, NY

107

10701 Yonkers, NY
10702 Yonkers, NY
10703 Yonkers, NY
10704 Yonkers, NY
10705 Yonkers, NY
10706 Hastings On Hudson, NY
10706 Yonkers, NY
10707 Eastchester, NY
10707 Tuckahoe, NY
10707 Yonkers, NY
10708 Bronxville, NY
10708 Yonkers, NY
10709 Eastchester, NY
10709 Yonkers, NY
10710 Yonkers, NY

108

10801 New Rochelle, NY
10802 New Rochelle, NY
10803 Pelham, NY
10804 New Rochelle, NY
10804 Wykagyl, NY
10805 New Rochelle, NY

109

10901 Airmont, NY
10901 Montebello, NY
10901 Suffern, NY
10910 Arden, NY
10911 Bear Mountain, NY
10912 Bellvale, NY
10913 Blauvelt, NY
10914 Blooming Grove, NY
10914 S Bloomng Grv, NY
10915 Bullville, NY
10916 Campbell Hall, NY
10917 Central Valley, NY
10918 Chester, NY
10919 Circleville, NY
10920 Congers, NY
10921 Florida, NY
10922 Fort Montgomery, NY
10923 Garnerville, NY
10924 Goshen, NY
10925 Greenwood Lake, NY
10926 Harriman, NY
10927 Haverstraw, NY
10928 Highland Falls, NY
10930 Highland Mills, NY
10931 Hillburn, NY
10932 Howells, NY
10933 Johnson, NY
10940 Middletown, NY
10940 Scotchtown, NY
10941 Middletown, NY
10941 Scotchtown, NY
10949 Monroe, NY
10950 Kiryas Joel, NY
10950 Monroe, NY
10952 Airmont, NY
10952 Kaser, NY
10952 Monsey, NY
10953 Mountainville, NY
10954 Bardonia, NY
10954 Nanuet, NY
10956 New City, NY
10958 New Hampton, NY
10959 New Milford, NY
10960 Grandview On Hudson, NY
10960 Nyack, NY
10962 Orangeburg, NY
10963 Otisville, NY
10964 Palisades, NY
10965 Pearl River, NY
10968 Piermont, NY
10969 Pine Island, NY
10970 Pomona, NY
10973 Slate Hill, NY
10974 Sloatsburg, NY
10975 Southfields, NY
10976 Sparkill, NY
10977 Chestnut Ridge, NY
10977 New Square, NY
10977 Spring Valley, NY
10979 Sterling Forest, NY
10980 Stony Point, NY
10981 Sugar Loaf, NY
10982 Tallman, NY
10983 Tappan, NY
10984 Thiells, NY
10985 Thompson Ridge, NY
10986 Tomkins Cove, NY
10987 Tuxedo Park, NY
10988 Unionville, NY
10989 Valley Cottage, NY
10990 Warwick, NY
10992 Washingtonville, NY
10993 West Haverstraw, NY
10994 West Nyack, NY
10996 West Point, NY
10997 West Point, NY
10998 Westtown, NY

110

11001 Bellerose Village, NY
11001 Floral Park, NY
11001 South Floral Park, NY
11002 Floral Park, NY
11003 Alden Manor, NY
11003 Elmont, NY
11003 Floral Park, NY
11003 Meacham, NY
11004 Floral Park, NY
11004 Glen Oaks, NY
11005 Floral Park, NY
11010 Franklin Square, NY
11020 Great Neck, NY
11020 Lake Success, NY
11021 Great Neck, NY
11021 Great Neck Plaza, NY
11022 Great Neck, NY
11023 Great Neck, NY
11024 Great Neck, NY
11024 Kings Point, NY
11026 Great Neck, NY
11027 Great Neck, NY
11030 Manhasset, NY
11030 Plandome, NY
11040 Garden City Park, NY
11040 Hillside Manor, NY
11040 Manhasset Hills, NY
11040 New Hyde Park, NY
11040 North Hills, NY
11040 North New Hyde Park, NY
11042 New Hyde Park, NY
11042 North New Hyde Park, NY
11050 Port Washington, NY
11050 Sands Point, NY
11051 Port Washington, NY
11096 Far Rockaway, NY
11096 Inwood, NY

111

11101 Astoria, NY
11101 Long Island City, NY
11102 Astoria, NY
11102 Long Island City, NY
11103 Astoria, NY
11103 Long Island City, NY
11104 Astoria, NY
11104 Long Island City, NY
11104 Sunnyside, NY
11105 Astoria, NY
11105 Long Island City, NY
11106 Astoria, NY
11106 Long Island City, NY

112

11201 Brooklyn, NY
11201 Brooklyn Heights, NY
11202 Brooklyn, NY
11203 Brooklyn, NY
11204 Brooklyn, NY
11205 Brooklyn, NY
11206 Brooklyn, NY
11207 Brooklyn, NY
11208 Brooklyn, NY
11209 Brooklyn, NY
11210 Brooklyn, NY
11211 Brooklyn, NY
11212 Brooklyn, NY
11213 Brooklyn, NY
11214 Brooklyn, NY
11215 Brooklyn, NY
11216 Brooklyn, NY
11217 Brooklyn, NY
11218 Brooklyn, NY
11219 Brooklyn, NY
11220 Brooklyn, NY
11221 Brooklyn, NY
11222 Brooklyn, NY
11223 Brooklyn, NY
11224 Brooklyn, NY
11225 Brooklyn, NY
11226 Brooklyn, NY
11228 Brooklyn, NY
11229 Brooklyn, NY
11230 Brooklyn, NY
11231 Brooklyn, NY
11232 Brooklyn, NY
11233 Brooklyn, NY
11234 Brooklyn, NY
11235 Brooklyn, NY
11236 Brooklyn, NY
11237 Brooklyn, NY
11238 Brooklyn, NY
11239 Brooklyn, NY
11241 Brooklyn, NY
11242 Brooklyn, NY
11243 Brooklyn, NY
11245 Brooklyn, NY
11247 Brooklyn, NY
11249 Brooklyn, NY
11251 Brooklyn, NY
11252 Brooklyn, NY
11252 Fort Hamilton, NY
11256 Brooklyn, NY

113

11351 Flushing, NY
11352 Flushing, NY
11354 Flushing, NY
11355 Flushing, NY
11356 College Point, NY
11356 Flushing, NY
11357 Beechhurst, NY
11357 Flushing, NY
11357 Malba, NY
11357 Whitestone, NY
11358 Auburndale, NY
11358 Flushing, NY
11359 Bayside, NY
11359 Flushing, NY
11359 Fort Totten, NY
11360 Bayside, NY
11360 Flushing, NY
11361 Bayside, NY
11361 Flushing, NY
11362 Douglaston, NY
11362 Flushing, NY
11362 Little Neck, NY
11363 Douglaston, NY
11363 Flushing, NY
11363 Little Neck, NY
11364 Bayside, NY
11364 Bayside Hills, NY
11364 Flushing, NY
11364 Hollis Hills, NY
11364 Oakland Gardens, NY
11365 Flushing, NY
11365 Fresh Meadows, NY
11366 Flushing, NY
11366 Fresh Meadows, NY
11367 Flushing, NY
11367 Kew Gardens Hills, NY
11368 Corona, NY
11368 Flushing, NY
11369 East Elmhurst, NY
11369 Flushing, NY
11370 East Elmhurst, NY
11370 Flushing, NY
11371 East Elmhurst, NY
11371 Flushing, NY
11371 La Guardia Airport, NY
11372 Flushing, NY
11372 Jackson Heights, NY
11373 Elmhurst, NY
11373 Flushing, NY
11374 Flushing, NY
11374 Rego Park, NY
11375 Flushing, NY
11375 Forest Hills, NY
11377 Flushing, NY
11377 Woodside, NY
11378 Flushing, NY
11378 Maspeth, NY
11379 Flushing, NY
11379 Middle Village, NY
11380 Elmhurst, NY
11380 Flushing, NY
11381 Flushing, NY
11385 Flushing, NY
11385 Glendale, NY
11385 Ridgewood, NY
11386 Flushing, NY
11386 Ridgewood, NY

114

11405 Jamaica, NY
11411 Cambria Heights, NY
11411 Jamaica, NY
11412 Jamaica, NY
11412 Saint Albans, NY
11413 Jamaica, NY
11413 Laurelton, NY
11413 Rosedale, NY
11413 Saint Albans, NY
11413 Springfield Gardens, NY
11414 Howard Beach, NY
11414 Jamaica, NY
11415 Jamaica, NY
11415 Kew Gardens, NY
11416 Jamaica, NY
11416 Ozone Park, NY
11417 Jamaica, NY
11417 Ozone Park, NY
11418 Jamaica, NY
11418 Richmond Hill, NY
11419 Jamaica, NY
11419 South Richmond Hill, NY
11420 Jamaica, NY
11420 South Ozone Park, NY
11421 Jamaica, NY
11421 Woodhaven, NY
11422 Jamaica, NY
11422 Rosedale, NY
11423 Hollis, NY
11423 Jamaica, NY
11424 Jamaica, NY
11424 Kew Gardens, NY
11425 Jamaica, NY
11426 Bellerose, NY
11426 Jamaica, NY
11427 Bellerose Manor, NY
11427 Jamaica, NY
11427 Queens Village, NY
11428 Bellerose Manor, NY
11428 Jamaica, NY
11428 Queens Village, NY
11429 Jamaica, NY
11429 Queens Village, NY
11430 Jamaica, NY
11430 Jf Kennedy Ap, NY
11430 John F Kennedy Airport, NY
11431 Jamaica, NY
11432 Jamaica, NY
11433 Addisleigh Park, NY
11433 Jamaica, NY
11434 Addisleigh Park, NY
11434 Jamaica, NY
11434 Rochdale Village, NY
11435 Briarwood, NY
11435 Jamaica, NY
11436 Jamaica, NY
11436 South Ozone Park, NY
11439 Jamaica, NY
11451 Jamaica, NY
11499 Jamaica, NY

115

11501 Mineola, NY
11507 Albertson, NY
11509 Atlantic Beach, NY
11510 Baldwin, NY
11510 N Baldwin, NY
11510 North Baldwin, NY
11514 Carle Place, NY
11516 Cedarhurst, NY
11518 East Rockaway, NY
11520 Freeport, NY
11530 Garden City, NY
11530 Garden City South, NY
11530 Stewart Manor, NY
11530 Village Of Garden City, NY
11531 Garden City, NY
11542 Glen Cove, NY
11545 Glen Head, NY
11547 Glenwood Landing, NY
11548 Greenvale, NY
11549 Hempstead, NY
11550 Hempstead, NY
11550 South Hempstead, NY
11551 Hempstead, NY
11552 West Hempstead, NY
11553 Uniondale, NY
11554 East Meadow, NY
11555 Uniondale, NY
11556 Uniondale, NY
11557 Hewlett, NY
11558 Island Park, NY
11559 Lawrence, NY
11560 Locust Valley, NY
11561 E Atlantic Beach, NY
11561 East Atlantic Beach, NY
11561 Lido Beach, NY
11561 Long Beach, NY
11563 Lynbrook, NY
11565 Malverne, NY
11566 Merrick, NY
11566 N Merrick, NY
11566 North Merrick, NY
11568 Old Westbury, NY
11568 Westbury, NY
11569 Point Lookout, NY
11570 Rockville Centre, NY
11572 Oceanside, NY
11572 Rockville Centre, NY
11575 Roosevelt, NY
11576 Roslyn, NY
11577 Roslyn Heights, NY
11579 Sea Cliff, NY
11580 Valley Stream, NY
11581 Valley Stream, NY
11582 Valley Stream, NY
11590 Westbury, NY
11596 East Williston, NY
11596 Williston Park, NY
11598 Woodmere, NY
11599 Garden City, NY

116

11690 Edgemere, NY
11690 Far Rockaway, NY
11690 Wave Crest, NY
11691 Far Rockaway, NY
11692 Arverne, NY
11692 Far Rockaway, NY
11693 Broad Channel, NY
11693 Far Rockaway, NY
11693 Rockaway Beach, NY
11694 Belle Harbor, NY
11694 Far Rockaway, NY
11694 Neponsit, NY
11694 Rockaway Park, NY
11695 Far Rockaway, NY
11695 Fort Tilden, NY
11697 Breezy Point, NY
11697 Far Rockaway, NY
11697 Rockaway Point, NY

117

11701 Amity Harbor, NY
11701 Amityville, NY
11702 Babylon, NY
11702 Captree Island, NY
11702 Gilgo Beach, NY
11702 Oak Beach, NY
11702 Oak Island, NY
11702 West Gilgo Beach, NY
11703 Babylon, NY
11703 North Babylon, NY
11704 Babylon, NY
11704 West Babylon, NY
11705 Bayport, NY
11706 Bay Shore, NY
11706 Fair Harbor, NY
11706 Kismet, NY
11706 Point O Woods, NY
11706 Saltaire, NY
11707 Babylon, NY
11707 West Babylon, NY
11709 Bayville, NY
11710 Bellmore, NY
11710 North Bellmore, NY
11713 Bellport, NY
11714 Bethpage, NY
11715 Blue Point, NY
11716 Bohemia, NY
11717 Brentwood, NY
11717 Edgewood, NY
11717 West Brentwood, NY
11718 Brightwaters, NY
11719 Brookhaven, NY
11720 Centereach, NY
11720 South Setauket, NY
11721 Centerport, NY
11722 Central Islip, NY
11724 Cold Spring Harbor, NY
11725 Commack, NY
11726 Copiague, NY
11727 Coram, NY
11729 Deer Park, NY
11730 East Islip, NY
11731 East Northport, NY
11731 Elwood, NY
11732 East Norwich, NY
11733 East Setauket, NY
11733 Setauket, NY
11735 Farmingdale, NY
11735 South Farmingdale, NY
11737 Farmingdale, NY
11738 Farmingville, NY
11739 Great River, NY
11740 Greenlawn, NY
11741 Holbrook, NY
11742 Holtsville, NY
11743 Halesite, NY
11743 Huntington, NY
11743 Lloyd Harbor, NY
11746 Dix Hills, NY
11746 Huntington Station, NY
11747 Melville, NY
11749 Central Islip, NY
11749 Hauppauge, NY
11749 Islandia, NY
11749 Ronkonkoma, NY
11751 Islip, NY
11752 Islip Terrace, NY
11753 Jericho, NY
11754 Kings Park, NY

1755 Lake Grove, NY
1756 Levittown, NY
1757 Lindenhurst, NY
1758 Massapequa, NY
1758 North Massapequa, NY
1760 Melville, NY
1762 Massapequa Park, NY
1763 Medford, NY
1764 Miller Place, NY
1765 Mill Neck, NY
1766 Mount Sinai, NY
1767 Nesconset, NY
1768 Fort Salonga, NY
1768 Northport, NY
1769 Oakdale, NY
1770 Ocean Beach, NY
1771 Oyster Bay, NY
1772 Davis Park, NY
1772 East Patchogue, NY
1772 Patchogue, NY
1773 Syosset, NY
1775 Melville, NY
1776 Port Jefferson Station, NY
1777 Port Jefferson, NY
1777 Port Jefferson Station, NY
1778 Rocky Point, NY
1779 Lake Ronkonkoma, NY
1779 Ronkonkoma, NY
1780 Saint James, NY
1782 Cherry Grove, NY
1782 Fire Island Pines, NY
1782 Sayville, NY
1783 Seaford, NY
1784 Selden, NY
1786 Shoreham, NY
1787 Smithtown, NY
1788 Hauppauge, NY
1788 Smithtown, NY
1789 Sound Beach, NY
1790 Stony Brook, NY
1791 Syosset, NY
1792 Wading River, NY
1793 Wantagh, NY
1794 Stony Brook, NY
1795 West Islip, NY
1796 West Sayville, NY
1797 Woodbury, NY
1798 Wheatley Heights, NY
1798 Wyandanch, NY

118

1801 Hicksville, NY
1802 Hicksville, NY
1803 Plainview, NY
1804 Old Bethpage, NY
1815 Hicksville, NY
1819 Hicksville, NY
1853 Jericho, NY
1854 Hicksville, NY

119

1901 Flanders, NY
1901 Riverhead, NY
1930 Amagansett, NY
1931 Aquebogue, NY
1932 Bridgehampton, NY
1933 Baiting Hollow, NY
1933 Calverton, NY
1934 Center Moriches, NY
1935 Cutchogue, NY
1937 East Hampton, NY
1939 East Marion, NY
1940 East Moriches, NY
1941 Eastport, NY
1942 East Quogue, NY
1944 Greenport, NY
1946 Hampton Bays, NY
1947 Jamesport, NY
1948 Laurel, NY
1949 Manorville, NY
1950 Mastic, NY
1951 Mastic Beach, NY
1952 Mattituck, NY
1953 Middle Island, NY
11954 Montauk, NY
11955 Moriches, NY
11956 New Suffolk, NY
11957 Orient, NY
11958 Peconic, NY
11959 Quogue, NY
11960 Remsenburg, NY
11961 Ridge, NY
11962 Sagaponack, NY
11963 Sag Harbor, NY
11964 Shelter Island, NY
11965 Shelter Island Heights, NY
11967 E Yaphank, NY
11967 East Yaphank, NY
11967 Shirley, NY
11967 Smith Point, NY
11968 Southampton, NY
11969 Southampton, NY
11970 South Jamesport, NY
11971 Southold, NY
11972 Speonk, NY
11973 Upton, NY
11975 Wainscott, NY
11976 Water Mill, NY
11977 Westhampton, NY
11978 Westhampton Beach, NY
11980 Yaphank, NY

120

12007 Alcove, NY
12008 Alplaus, NY
12008 Schenectady, NY
12009 Altamont, NY
12010 Amsterdam, NY
12010 West Charlton, NY
12015 Athens, NY
12016 Auriesville, NY
12016 Fultonville, NY
12017 Austerlitz, NY
12018 Averill Park, NY
12019 Ballston Lake, NY
12019 Burnt Hills, NY
12019 Charlton, NY
12020 Ballston Spa, NY
12020 Malta, NY
12022 Berlin, NY
12023 Berne, NY
12024 Brainard, NY
12025 Broadalbin, NY
12027 Burnt Hills, NY
12028 Buskirk, NY
12029 Canaan, NY
12031 Carlisle, NY
12032 Caroga Lake, NY
12033 Brookview, NY
12033 Castleton On Hudson, NY
12033 South Schodack, NY
12035 Central Bridge, NY
12036 Charlotteville, NY
12037 Chatham, NY
12040 Cherry Plain, NY
12041 Clarksville, NY
12042 Climax, NY
12043 Cobleskill, NY
12043 Lawyersville, NY
12045 Coeymans, NY
12046 Coeymans Hollow, NY
12047 Cohoes, NY
12050 Columbiaville, NY
12051 Coxsackie, NY
12052 Cropseyville, NY
12053 Delanson, NY
12054 Delmar, NY
12055 Dormansville, NY
12056 Duanesburg, NY
12057 Eagle Bridge, NY
12057 White Creek, NY
12058 Earlton, NY
12059 East Berne, NY
12060 East Chatham, NY
12061 East Greenbush, NY
12062 East Nassau, NY
12063 East Schodack, NY
12064 East Worcester, NY
12065 Clifton Park, NY
12066 Esperance, NY
12067 Feura Bush, NY
12068 Fonda, NY
12069 Fort Hunter, NY
12070 Fort Johnson, NY
12071 Fultonham, NY
12072 Fultonville, NY
12073 Gallupville, NY
12074 Galway, NY
12075 Ghent, NY
12076 Gilboa, NY
12077 Glenmont, NY
12078 Gloversville, NY
12082 Grafton, NY
12083 Greenville, NY
12083 Norton Hill, NY
12083 South Westerlo, NY
12084 Guilderland, NY
12085 Guilderland Center, NY
12086 Hagaman, NY
12087 Hannacroix, NY
12089 Hoosick, NY
12090 Hoosick Falls, NY
12092 Howes Cave, NY
12093 Jefferson, NY
12094 Johnsonville, NY
12095 Johnstown, NY

121

12106 Kinderhook, NY
12107 Knox, NY
12108 Lake Pleasant, NY
12110 Latham, NY
12110 Newtonville, NY
12115 Malden Bridge, NY
12116 Maryland, NY
12117 Mayfield, NY
12118 Mechanicville, NY
12120 Medusa, NY
12121 Melrose, NY
12122 Middleburgh, NY
12123 Nassau, NY
12124 New Baltimore, NY
12125 Lebanon Springs, NY
12125 New Lebanon, NY
12128 Latham, NY
12128 Newtonville, NY
12130 Niverville, NY
12131 North Blenheim, NY
12132 North Chatham, NY
12133 North Hoosick, NY
12134 Northville, NY
12136 Old Chatham, NY
12137 Pattersonville, NY
12138 Petersburg, NY
12138 Petersburgh, NY
12138 Taconic Lake, NY
12139 Piseco, NY
12140 Poestenkill, NY
12141 Quaker Street, NY
12143 Ravena, NY
12144 Rensselaer, NY
12147 Rensselaerville, NY
12148 Rexford, NY
12149 Richmondville, NY
12150 Rotterdam Junction, NY
12151 Round Lake, NY
12153 Sand Lake, NY
12154 Schaghticoke, NY
12155 Schenevus, NY
12156 Schodack Landing, NY
12157 Schoharie, NY
12158 Selkirk, NY
12159 Slingerlands, NY
12160 Sloansville, NY
12161 South Bethlehem, NY
12164 Speculator, NY
12165 Spencertown, NY
12166 Sprakers, NY
12167 Stamford, NY
12168 Stephentown, NY
12169 Stephentown, NY
12170 Stillwater, NY
12172 Stottville, NY
12173 Stuyvesant, NY
12174 Stuyvesant Falls, NY
12175 Summit, NY
12176 Surprise, NY
12177 Tribes Hill, NY
12180 Troy, NY
12181 Troy, NY
12182 Troy, NY
12183 Green Island, NY
12183 Troy, NY
12184 Valatie, NY
12185 Valley Falls, NY
12186 Voorheesville, NY
12187 Warnerville, NY
12188 Waterford, NY
12189 Watervliet, NY
12190 Wells, NY
12192 West Coxsackie, NY
12193 Westerlo, NY
12194 West Fulton, NY
12195 West Lebanon, NY
12196 West Sand Lake, NY
12197 Worcester, NY
12198 Wynantskill, NY

122

12201 Albany, NY
12202 Albany, NY
12203 Albany, NY
12203 Stuyvesant Plaza, NY
12204 Albany, NY
12204 Menands, NY
12205 Albany, NY
12205 Colonie, NY
12205 Roessleville, NY
12206 Albany, NY
12207 Albany, NY
12208 Albany, NY
12209 Albany, NY
12210 Albany, NY
12211 Albany, NY
12211 Loudonville, NY
12211 Siena, NY
12212 Albany, NY
12214 Albany, NY
12220 Albany, NY
12222 Albany, NY
12223 Albany, NY
12224 Albany, NY
12225 Albany, NY
12226 Albany, NY
12227 Albany, NY
12228 Albany, NY
12229 Albany, NY
12230 Albany, NY
12231 Albany, NY
12232 Albany, NY
12233 Albany, NY
12234 Albany, NY
12235 Albany, NY
12236 Albany, NY
12237 Albany, NY
12238 Albany, NY
12239 Albany, NY
12240 Albany, NY
12241 Albany, NY
12242 Albany, NY
12243 Albany, NY
12244 Albany, NY
12245 Albany, NY
12246 Albany, NY
12247 Albany, NY
12248 Albany, NY
12249 Albany, NY
12250 Albany, NY
12252 Albany, NY
12255 Albany, NY
12256 Albany, NY
12257 Albany, NY
12260 Albany, NY
12261 Albany, NY
12288 Albany, NY

123

12301 Schenectady, NY
12302 Glenville, NY
12302 Schenectady, NY
12302 Scotia, NY
12303 Schenectady, NY
12304 Schenectady, NY
12305 Schenectady, NY
12306 Rotterdam, NY
12306 Schenectady, NY
12307 Schenectady, NY
12308 Schenectady, NY
12309 Niskayuna, NY
12309 Schenectady, NY
12325 Glenville, NY
12325 Schenectady, NY
12345 Schenectady, NY

124

12401 Eddyville, NY
12401 Kingston, NY
12401 Saint Remy, NY
12402 Kingston, NY
12404 Accord, NY
12405 Acra, NY
12406 Arkville, NY
12407 Ashland, NY
12409 Bearsville, NY
12409 Shady, NY
12410 Big Indian, NY
12410 Oliverea, NY
12411 Bloomington, NY
12412 Boiceville, NY
12413 Cairo, NY
12414 Catskill, NY
12414 Cementon, NY
12416 Chichester, NY
12417 Connelly, NY
12418 Cornwallville, NY
12419 Cottekill, NY
12420 Cragsmoor, NY
12421 Denver, NY
12422 Durham, NY
12423 East Durham, NY
12424 East Jewett, NY
12424 Tannersville, NY
12427 Elka Park, NY
12428 Ellenville, NY
12429 Esopus, NY
12430 Fleischmanns, NY
12430 Halcott Center, NY
12431 Freehold, NY
12432 Glasco, NY
12433 Glenford, NY
12434 Grand Gorge, NY
12435 Greenfield Park, NY
12436 Haines Falls, NY
12438 Halcottsville, NY
12439 East Windham, NY
12439 Hensonville, NY
12440 High Falls, NY
12441 Highmount, NY
12442 Hunter, NY
12443 Hurley, NY
12444 Jewett, NY
12446 Kerhonkson, NY
12448 Lake Hill, NY
12449 Lake Katrine, NY
12450 Lanesville, NY
12451 Leeds, NY
12452 Lexington, NY
12453 Malden On Hudson, NY
12454 Maplecrest, NY
12455 Margaretville, NY
12456 Mount Marion, NY
12457 Mount Tremper, NY
12458 Napanoch, NY
12459 New Kingston, NY
12460 Oak Hill, NY
12461 Krumville, NY
12461 Olivebridge, NY
12463 Palenville, NY
12464 Phoenicia, NY
12465 Pine Hill, NY
12466 Port Ewen, NY
12468 Prattsville, NY
12469 Preston Hollow, NY
12470 Purling, NY
12471 Rifton, NY
12472 Rosendale, NY
12473 Round Top, NY
12474 Roxbury, NY
12475 Ruby, NY
12477 Saugerties, NY
12480 Shandaken, NY
12481 Shokan, NY
12482 South Cairo, NY
12483 Spring Glen, NY
12484 Stone Ridge, NY
12485 Tannersville, NY
12486 Tillson, NY
12487 Ulster Park, NY
12489 Wawarsing, NY
12490 West Camp, NY
12491 West Hurley, NY
12492 West Kill, NY
12493 West Park, NY
12494 West Shokan, NY
12495 Willow, NY
12496 Windham, NY
12498 Woodstock, NY

125

12501 Amenia, NY
12502 Ancram, NY
12503 Ancramdale, NY
12504 Annandale On Hudson, NY
12504 Red Hook, NY
12506 Bangall, NY
12507 Barrytown, NY
12507 Red Hook, NY
12508 Beacon, NY
12510 Billings, NY
12511 Castle Point, NY
12512 Chelsea, NY
12513 Claverack, NY
12514 Clinton Corners, NY
12515 Clintondale, NY
12516 Copake, NY
12517 Copake Falls, NY
12518 Cornwall, NY
12520 Cornwall On Hudson, NY
12521 Craryville, NY
12521 Taghkanic, NY
12522 Dover Plains, NY
12523 Elizaville, NY
12523 Taghkanic, NY
12524 Fishkill, NY
12525 Gardiner, NY
12526 Germantown, NY
12527 Glenham, NY
12528 Highland, NY
12529 Hillsdale, NY
12530 Hollowville, NY
12531 Holmes, NY
12533 East Fishkill, NY
12533 Hopewell, NY
12533 Hopewell Junction, NY
12533 Wiccopee, NY
12534 Hudson, NY
12537 Hughsonville, NY
12538 Hyde Park, NY
12540 Lagrangeville, NY
12541 Livingston, NY
12542 Marlboro, NY
12543 Maybrook, NY
12544 Mellenville, NY
12545 Millbrook, NY
12546 Millerton, NY
12547 Milton, NY
12548 Modena, NY
12549 Montgomery, NY
12550 Newburgh, NY
12551 Newburgh, NY
12552 Newburgh, NY
12553 New Windsor, NY
12553 Newburgh, NY
12555 Mid Hudson, NY
12555 Newburgh, NY
12561 New Paltz, NY
12563 Patterson, NY
12564 Pawling, NY
12565 Philmont, NY
12566 Pine Bush, NY
12567 Pine Plains, NY
12568 Plattekill, NY
12569 Pleasant Valley, NY

12570 Poughquag, NY
12571 Milan, NY
12571 Red Hook, NY
12572 Rhinebeck, NY
12574 Rhinecliff, NY
12575 Rock Tavern, NY
12577 Salisbury Mills, NY
12578 Salt Point, NY
12580 Staatsburg, NY
12581 Stanfordville, NY
12582 Stormville, NY
12583 Tivoli, NY
12584 Vails Gate, NY
12585 Verbank, NY
12586 Walden, NY
12588 Walker Valley, NY
12589 Wallkill, NY
12590 New Hamburg, NY
12590 Wappingers Falls, NY
12590 West Fishkill, NY
12592 Wassaic, NY
12594 Wingdale, NY

126

12601 Poughkeepsie, NY
12602 Poughkeepsie, NY
12603 Arlington, NY
12603 Poughkeepsie, NY
12604 Poughkeepsie, NY

127

12701 Monticello, NY
12719 Barryville, NY
12720 Bethel, NY
12721 Bloomingburg, NY
12722 Burlingham, NY
12723 Callicoon, NY
12724 Callicoon Center, NY
12725 Claryville, NY
12726 Cochecton, NY
12727 Cochecton Center, NY
12729 Cuddebackville, NY
12729 Godeffroy, NY
12732 Eldred, NY
12733 Fallsburg, NY
12734 Ferndale, NY
12736 Fremont Center, NY
12737 Glen Spey, NY
12738 Glen Wild, NY
12740 Grahamsville, NY
12740 Sundown, NY
12741 Hankins, NY
12742 Harris, NY
12743 Highland Lake, NY
12745 Hortonville, NY
12746 Huguenot, NY
12747 Hurleyville, NY
12748 Jeffersonville, NY
12749 Kauneonga Lake, NY
12750 Kenoza Lake, NY
12751 Kiamesha Lake, NY
12752 Lake Huntington, NY
12754 Liberty, NY
12758 Lew Beach, NY
12758 Livingston Manor, NY
12759 Loch Sheldrake, NY
12760 Long Eddy, NY
12762 Mongaup Valley, NY
12763 Mountain Dale, NY
12764 Narrowsburg, NY
12765 Neversink, NY
12766 North Branch, NY
12767 Obernburg, NY
12768 Parksville, NY
12769 Phillipsport, NY
12770 Pond Eddy, NY
12771 Port Jervis, NY
12775 Rock Hill, NY
12776 Roscoe, NY
12777 Forestburgh, NY
12777 Monticello, NY
12778 Smallwood, NY
12779 South Fallsburg, NY
12780 Sparrow Bush, NY
12780 Sparrowbush, NY
12781 Summitville, NY
12783 Swan Lake, NY
12784 Thompsonville, NY
12785 Port Jervis, NY
12785 Westbrookville, NY
12786 White Lake, NY
12787 White Sulphur Springs, NY
12788 Woodbourne, NY
12789 Woodridge, NY
12790 Wurtsboro, NY
12791 Youngsville, NY
12792 Yulan, NY

128

12801 Glens Falls, NY
12801 Queensbury, NY
12803 Glens Falls, NY
12803 South Glens Falls, NY
12804 Glens Falls, NY
12804 Queensbury, NY
12808 Adirondack, NY
12809 Argyle, NY
12810 Athol, NY
12811 Bakers Mills, NY
12812 Blue Mountain Lake, NY
12814 Bolton Landing, NY
12815 Brant Lake, NY
12816 Cambridge, NY
12817 Chestertown, NY
12819 Clemons, NY
12820 Cleverdale, NY
12821 Comstock, NY
12822 Corinth, NY
12823 Cossayuna, NY
12824 Diamond Point, NY
12827 Fort Ann, NY
12828 Fort Edward, NY
12831 Gansevoort, NY
12831 Wilton, NY
12832 Granville, NY
12833 Greenfield Center, NY
12834 Greenwich, NY
12834 Thomson, NY
12835 Hadley, NY
12836 Hague, NY
12837 Hampton, NY
12838 Hartford, NY
12839 Hudson Falls, NY
12841 Huletts Landing, NY
12842 Indian Lake, NY
12843 Johnsburg, NY
12844 Kattskill Bay, NY
12844 Pilot Knob, NY
12845 Lake George, NY
12846 Lake Luzerne, NY
12847 Long Lake, NY
12848 Middle Falls, NY
12849 Middle Granville, NY
12850 Middle Grove, NY
12851 Minerva, NY
12852 Newcomb, NY
12853 North Creek, NY
12854 North Granville, NY
12855 North Hudson, NY
12856 North River, NY
12857 Olmstedville, NY
12858 Paradox, NY
12858 Ticonderoga, NY
12859 Porter Corners, NY
12860 Pottersville, NY
12861 Putnam Station, NY
12862 Riparius, NY
12863 Rock City Falls, NY
12864 Sabael, NY
12865 East Greenwich, NY
12865 Salem, NY
12866 Saratoga Springs, NY
12870 Schroon Lake, NY
12871 Schuylerville, NY
12872 Severance, NY
12873 Shushan, NY
12874 Silver Bay, NY
12878 Stony Creek, NY
12879 Newcomb, NY
12879 Tahawus, NY
12883 Ticonderoga, NY
12884 Victory Mills, NY
12885 Thurman, NY
12885 Warrensburg, NY
12886 Wevertown, NY
12887 Whitehall, NY

129

12901 Plattsburgh, NY
12903 Plattsburgh, NY
12910 Altona, NY
12911 Au Sable Chasm, NY
12911 Keeseville, NY
12912 Au Sable Forks, NY
12913 Bloomingdale, NY
12914 Bombay, NY
12915 Brainardsville, NY
12916 Brushton, NY
12917 Burke, NY
12918 Cadyville, NY
12919 Champlain, NY
12920 Chateaugay, NY
12921 Chazy, NY
12922 Childwold, NY
12923 Churubusco, NY
12924 Clintonville, NY
12924 Keeseville, NY
12926 Constable, NY
12927 Cranberry Lake, NY
12928 Crown Point, NY
12929 Dannemora, NY
12930 Dickinson Center, NY
12932 Elizabethtown, NY
12933 Ellenburg, NY
12934 Ellenburg Center, NY
12935 Ellenburg Depot, NY
12936 Essex, NY
12936 Whallonsburg, NY
12937 Fort Covington, NY
12939 Gabriels, NY
12941 Jay, NY
12942 Keene, NY
12943 Keene Valley, NY
12943 Saint Huberts, NY
12944 Keeseville, NY
12945 Lake Clear, NY
12945 Upper Saint Regis, NY
12946 Lake Placid, NY
12949 Lawrenceville, NY
12950 Lewis, NY
12952 Lyon Mountain, NY
12953 Malone, NY
12955 Lyon Mountain, NY
12955 Merrill, NY
12956 Mineville, NY
12957 Moira, NY
12958 Mooers, NY
12959 Mooers Forks, NY
12960 Moriah, NY
12961 Moriah Center, NY
12962 Morrisonville, NY
12964 New Russia, NY
12965 Fort Jackson, NY
12965 Hopkinton, NY
12965 Nicholville, NY
12966 Bangor, NY
12966 North Bangor, NY
12966 West Bangor, NY
12967 North Lawrence, NY
12969 Owls Head, NY
12970 Paul Smiths, NY
12972 Peru, NY
12973 Piercefield, NY
12974 Port Henry, NY
12975 Port Kent, NY
12976 Rainbow Lake, NY
12977 Ray Brook, NY
12978 Redford, NY
12979 Rouses Point, NY
12980 Saint Regis Falls, NY
12981 Saranac, NY
12983 Saranac Lake, NY
12985 Schuyler Falls, NY
12986 Massawepie, NY
12986 Tupper Lake, NY
12987 Upper Jay, NY
12989 Loon Lake, NY
12989 Onchiota, NY
12989 Vermontville, NY
12992 West Chazy, NY
12993 Wadhams, NY
12993 Westport, NY
12995 Whippleville, NY
12996 Willsboro, NY
12997 Whiteface Mountain, NY
12997 Wilmington, NY
12998 Witherbee, NY

130

13020 Apulia Station, NY
13021 Auburn, NY
13021 Owasco, NY
13022 Auburn, NY
13024 Auburn, NY
13026 Aurora, NY
13027 Baldwinsville, NY
13027 Lysander, NY
13028 Bernhards Bay, NY
13029 Brewerton, NY
13030 Bridgeport, NY
13031 Camillus, NY
13032 Canastota, NY
13032 Perryville, NY
13033 Cato, NY
13034 Cayuga, NY
13035 Cazenovia, NY
13036 Central Square, NY
13037 Chittenango, NY
13039 Cicero, NY
13039 Clay, NY
13040 Cincinnatus, NY
13040 East Freetown, NY
13041 Clay, NY
13042 Cleveland, NY
13043 Clockville, NY
13044 Constantia, NY
13045 Cortland, NY
13051 Delphi Falls, NY
13052 De Ruyter, NY
13053 Dryden, NY
13054 Durhamville, NY
13056 East Homer, NY
13057 East Syracuse, NY
13060 Elbridge, NY
13061 Erieville, NY
13062 Etna, NY
13063 Fabius, NY
13064 Fair Haven, NY
13065 Fayette, NY
13066 Fayetteville, NY
13068 Freeville, NY
13069 Fulton, NY
13071 Genoa, NY
13072 Georgetown, NY
13073 Groton, NY
13074 Hannibal, NY
13076 Hastings, NY
13077 Homer, NY
13078 Jamesville, NY
13080 Jordan, NY
13081 King Ferry, NY
13082 Kirkville, NY
13083 Lacona, NY
13084 La Fayette, NY
13087 Little York, NY
13088 Liverpool, NY
13089 Liverpool, NY
13090 Bayberry, NY
13090 Liverpool, NY
13092 Locke, NY
13093 Lycoming, NY

131

13101 Mc Graw, NY
13102 Mc Lean, NY
13103 Mallory, NY
13104 Manlius, NY
13107 Maple View, NY
13108 Marcellus, NY
13110 Marietta, NY
13111 Martville, NY
13112 Memphis, NY
13113 Meridian, NY
13114 Mexico, NY
13115 Minetto, NY
13116 Minoa, NY
13117 Montezuma, NY
13118 Moravia, NY
13119 Mottville, NY
13120 Nedrow, NY
13121 New Haven, NY
13122 New Woodstock, NY
13123 North Bay, NY
13124 North Pitcher, NY
13126 Oswego, NY
13131 Parish, NY
13132 Pennellville, NY
13134 Peterboro, NY
13135 Phoenix, NY
13136 Pitcher, NY
13137 Plainville, NY
13138 Pompey, NY
13139 Poplar Ridge, NY
13140 Port Byron, NY
13141 Preble, NY
13142 Pulaski, NY
13143 Red Creek, NY
13144 Richland, NY
13145 Sandy Creek, NY
13146 Savannah, NY
13147 Scipio Center, NY
13147 Venice Center, NY
13148 Seneca Falls, NY
13152 Skaneateles, NY
13153 Skaneateles Falls, NY
13154 South Butler, NY
13155 South Otselic, NY
13156 Sterling, NY
13157 Sylvan Beach, NY
13158 Cuyler, NY
13158 East Homer, NY
13158 Truxton, NY
13159 Tully, NY
13160 Union Springs, NY
13162 Verona Beach, NY
13163 Wampsville, NY
13164 Warners, NY
13165 Waterloo, NY
13166 Weedsport, NY
13167 West Monroe, NY

132

13201 Syracuse, NY
13202 Syracuse, NY
13203 Syracuse, NY
13204 Syracuse, NY
13205 Syracuse, NY
13206 Syracuse, NY
13207 Syracuse, NY
13208 Syracuse, NY
13209 Solvay, NY
13209 Syracuse, NY
13210 Syracuse, NY
13211 Mattydale, NY
13211 Syracuse, NY
13212 North Syracuse, NY
13212 Syracuse, NY
13214 De Witt, NY
13214 Syracuse, NY
13215 Syracuse, NY
13217 Syracuse, NY
13218 Syracuse, NY
13219 Syracuse, NY
13220 Syracuse, NY
13221 Syracuse, NY
13224 Syracuse, NY
13225 Syracuse, NY
13235 Syracuse, NY
13244 Syracuse, NY
13250 Syracuse, NY
13251 Syracuse, NY
13252 Syracuse, NY
13261 Syracuse, NY
13290 Syracuse, NY

133

13301 Alder Creek, NY
13302 Altmar, NY
13303 Ava, NY
13304 Barneveld, NY
13305 Beaver Falls, NY
13305 Beaver Fls, NY
13308 Blossvale, NY
13309 Boonville, NY
13310 Bouckville, NY
13312 Brantingham, NY
13312 Glenfield, NY
13313 Bridgewater, NY
13314 Brookfield, NY
13315 Burlington Flats, NY
13316 Camden, NY
13317 Ames, NY
13317 Canajoharie, NY
13318 Cassville, NY
13319 Chadwicks, NY
13320 Cherry Valley, NY
13321 Clark Mills, NY
13322 Clayville, NY
13323 Clinton, NY
13324 Cold Brook, NY
13324 Ohio, NY
13325 Constableville, NY
13326 Cooperstown, NY
13326 Hartwick Seminary, NY
13327 Croghan, NY
13328 Deansboro, NY
13329 Dolgeville, NY
13331 Eagle Bay, NY
13332 Earlville, NY
13332 Lebanon, NY
13332 Poolville, NY
13333 East Springfield, NY
13334 Eaton, NY
13335 Edmeston, NY
13337 Fly Creek, NY
13338 Forestport, NY
13339 Fort Plain, NY
13340 Frankfort, NY
13340 Schuyler, NY
13341 Franklin Springs, NY
13342 Garrattsville, NY
13343 Glenfield, NY
13345 Greig, NY
13346 Hamilton, NY
13348 Hartwick, NY
13350 Herkimer, NY
13352 Hinckley, NY
13353 Hoffmeister, NY
13354 Holland Patent, NY
13355 Hubbardsville, NY
13357 Ilion, NY
13360 Inlet, NY
13361 Jordanville, NY
13362 Knoxboro, NY
13363 Lee Center, NY
13364 Leonardsville, NY
13365 Little Falls, NY
13367 Beaver River, NY
13367 Lowville, NY
13368 Lyons Falls, NY

134

13401 Mc Connellsville, NY
13402 Madison, NY
13403 Marcy, NY
13404 Martinsburg, NY
13406 Middleville, NY
13407 Mohawk, NY
13408 Morrisville, NY
13409 Munnsville, NY
13409 Pratts Hollow, NY
13410 Nelliston, NY
13411 New Berlin, NY
13411 South Edmeston, NY
13413 New Hartford, NY
13415 New Lisbon, NY
13416 Newport, NY
13417 New York Mills, NY
13418 North Brookfield, NY
13420 Old Forge, NY
13421 Oneida, NY
13424 Oriskany, NY
13425 Oriskany Falls, NY
13426 Orwell, NY
13428 Palatine Bridge, NY
13431 Poland, NY
13433 Port Leyden, NY
13435 Prospect, NY

3436 Raquette Lake, NY
3437 Redfield, NY
3438 Remsen, NY
3439 Richfield Springs, NY
3440 Rome, NY
3441 Rome, NY
3442 Rome, NY
3449 Rome, NY
3450 Roseboom, NY
3452 Saint Johnsville, NY
3454 Salisbury Center, NY
3455 Sangerfield, NY
3456 Paris, NY
3456 Sauquoit, NY
3457 Schuyler Lake, NY
3459 Sharon Springs, NY
3460 Sherburne, NY
3461 Sherrill, NY
3464 Smyrna, NY
3465 Solsville, NY
3468 Springfield Center, NY
3469 Stittville, NY
3470 Stratford, NY
3471 Taberg, NY
3472 Thendara, NY
3473 Turin, NY
3475 Van Hornesville, NY
3476 Vernon, NY
3477 Vernon Center, NY
3478 Verona, NY
3479 Washington Mills, NY
3480 Waterville, NY
3482 West Burlington, NY
3483 Westdale, NY
3484 West Eaton, NY
3485 West Edmeston, NY
3486 Westernville, NY
3488 Westford, NY
3489 West Leyden, NY
3490 Westmoreland, NY
3491 West Exeter, NY
3491 West Winfield, NY
3492 Whitesboro, NY
3493 Williamstown, NY
3494 Woodgate, NY
3495 Yorkville, NY

135

3501 Utica, NY
3502 Deerfield, NY
3502 Utica, NY
3503 Utica, NY
3504 Utica, NY
3505 Utica, NY
3599 Utica, NY

136

3601 Glen Park, NY
3601 Watertown, NY
3602 Fort Drum, NY
3602 Watertown, NY
3603 Fort Drum, NY
3603 Watertown, NY
3605 Adams, NY
3605 Smithville, NY
3606 Adams Center, NY
3607 Alexandria Bay, NY
3607 Point Vivian, NY
3608 Antwerp, NY
3608 Oxbow, NY
13611 Belleville, NY
13612 Black River, NY
3613 Brasher Falls, NY
3614 Brier Hill, NY
3615 Brownville, NY
13616 Calcium, NY
13617 Canton, NY
13618 Cape Vincent, NY
13619 Carthage, NY
13620 Castorland, NY
13621 Chase Mills, NY
13622 Chaumont, NY
13623 Chippewa Bay, NY
13624 Clayton, NY
13624 Frontenac, NY
13624 Grenell, NY
13624 Murray Isle, NY
13625 Colton, NY
13626 Barnes Corners, NY
13626 Copenhagen, NY
13626 South Rutland, NY
13627 Deer River, NY
13628 Deferiet, NY
13630 De Kalb Junction, NY
13631 Denmark, NY
13632 Depauville, NY
13633 De Peyster, NY
13634 Dexter, NY
13635 Edwards, NY
13636 Ellisburg, NY
13637 Evans Mills, NY
13638 Felts Mills, NY
13639 Fine, NY
13640 Fineview, NY
13640 Wellesley Island, NY
13641 Fishers Landing, NY
13642 Balmat, NY
13642 Gouverneur, NY
13643 Great Bend, NY
13645 Hailesboro, NY
13646 Hammond, NY
13647 Hannawa Falls, NY
13648 Harrisville, NY
13649 Helena, NY
13650 Henderson, NY
13650 Woodville, NY
13651 Henderson Harbor, NY
13652 Hermon, NY
13654 Heuvelton, NY
13655 Akwesasne, NY
13655 Hogansburg, NY
13656 La Fargeville, NY
13657 Limerick, NY
13658 Lisbon, NY
13659 Lorraine, NY
13660 Madrid, NY
13661 Mannsville, NY
13662 Massena, NY
13664 Morristown, NY
13665 Natural Bridge, NY
13666 Newton Falls, NY
13667 Norfolk, NY
13668 Norwood, NY
13669 Ogdensburg, NY
13670 Oswegatchie, NY
13671 Oxbow, NY
13672 Parishville, NY
13673 Philadelphia, NY
13674 Pierrepont Manor, NY
13675 Plessis, NY
13676 Potsdam, NY
13677 Pyrites, NY
13678 Raymondville, NY
13679 Redwood, NY
13680 Rensselaer Falls, NY
13681 Richville, NY
13682 Rodman, NY
13683 Rooseveltown, NY
13684 Degrasse, NY
13684 Russell, NY
13685 Sackets Harbor, NY
13687 South Colton, NY
13690 Star Lake, NY
13691 Theresa, NY
13692 Thous Is Pk, NY
13692 Thousand Island Park, NY
13693 Three Mile Bay, NY
13694 Waddington, NY
13695 Wanakena, NY
13696 West Stockholm, NY
13697 Winthrop, NY
13699 Potsdam, NY

137

13730 Afton, NY
13731 Andes, NY
13732 Apalachin, NY
13733 Bainbridge, NY
13734 Barton, NY
13736 Berkshire, NY
13737 Bible School Park, NY
13738 Blodgett Mills, NY
13739 Bloomville, NY
13740 Bovina Center, NY
13743 Candor, NY
13744 Castle Creek, NY
13745 Chenango Bridge, NY
13746 Chenango Forks, NY
13747 Colliersville, NY
13748 Conklin, NY
13749 Corbettsville, NY
13750 Davenport, NY
13751 Davenport Center, NY
13752 Delancey, NY
13753 Delhi, NY
13753 Meredith, NY
13754 Deposit, NY
13755 Downsville, NY
13755 Shinhopple, NY
13756 East Branch, NY
13757 East Meredith, NY
13758 East Pharsalia, NY
13760 Endicott, NY
13760 Endwell, NY
13761 Endicott, NY
13762 Endwell, NY
13763 Endicott, NY
13774 Fishs Eddy, NY
13775 Franklin, NY
13776 Gilbertsville, NY
13777 Glen Aubrey, NY
13778 Greene, NY
13780 Guilford, NY
13782 Hamden, NY
13783 Cadosia, NY
13783 Hancock, NY
13784 Harford, NY
13786 Harpersfield, NY
13787 Harpursville, NY
13788 Hobart, NY
13790 Johnson City, NY
13794 Killawog, NY
13795 Kirkwood, NY
13796 Laurens, NY
13797 Lisle, NY

138

13801 Mc Donough, NY
13802 Maine, NY
13803 Marathon, NY
13804 Masonville, NY
13806 Meridale, NY
13807 Milford, NY
13808 Morris, NY
13809 Mount Upton, NY
13810 Mount Vision, NY
13811 Newark Valley, NY
13812 Nichols, NY
13813 Nineveh, NY
13814 North Norwich, NY
13815 Norwich, NY
13820 Oneonta, NY
13825 Otego, NY
13826 Harpursville, NY
13826 Ouaquaga, NY
13827 Owego, NY
13830 Brisben, NY
13830 Oxford, NY
13832 Plymouth, NY
13833 Port Crane, NY
13833 Sanitaria Springs, NY
13834 Portlandville, NY
13835 Harford Mills, NY
13835 Richford, NY
13838 Sidney, NY
13839 Sidney Center, NY
13840 Smithboro, NY
13841 Smithville Flats, NY
13842 South Kortright, NY
13843 South New Berlin, NY
13844 South Plymouth, NY
13845 Tioga Center, NY
13846 Franklin, NY
13846 Treadwell, NY
13847 Trout Creek, NY
13848 Tunnel, NY
13849 Unadilla, NY
13850 Vestal, NY
13851 Vestal, NY
13856 Walton, NY
13859 Wells Bridge, NY
13860 West Davenport, NY
13861 West Oneonta, NY
13862 Whitney Point, NY
13863 Willet, NY
13864 Willseyville, NY
13865 W Windsor, NY
13865 West Windsor, NY
13865 Windsor, NY

139

13901 Binghamton, NY
13902 Binghamton, NY
13903 Binghamton, NY
13904 Binghamton, NY
13905 Binghamton, NY

140

14001 Akron, NY
14004 Alden, NY
14005 Alexander, NY
14006 Angola, NY
14008 Appleton, NY
14009 Arcade, NY
14010 Athol Springs, NY
14011 Attica, NY
14012 Barker, NY
14013 Alabama, NY
14013 Basom, NY
14020 Batavia, NY
14021 Batavia, NY
14024 Bliss, NY
14025 Boston, NY
14026 Bowmansville, NY
14027 Brant, NY
14028 Burt, NY
14029 Centerville, NY
14030 Chaffee, NY
14031 Clarence, NY
14032 Clarence Center, NY
14033 Colden, NY
14034 Collins, NY
14035 Collins Center, NY
14036 Corfu, NY
14037 Cowlesville, NY
14038 Crittenden, NY
14039 Dale, NY
14040 Darien Center, NY
14041 Dayton, NY
14042 Delevan, NY
14043 Depew, NY
14047 Derby, NY
14048 Dunkirk, NY
14048 Van Buren Bay, NY
14051 East Amherst, NY
14051 Swormville, NY
14052 East Aurora, NY
14054 East Bethany, NY
14055 Concord, NY
14055 East Concord, NY
14056 East Pembroke, NY
14057 Eden, NY
14058 Elba, NY
14059 Elma, NY
14060 Farmersville Station, NY
14061 Farnham, NY
14062 Forestville, NY
14063 Fredonia, NY
14065 Freedom, NY
14065 Sandusky, NY
14066 Gainesville, NY
14067 Gasport, NY
14068 Getzville, NY
14069 Glenwood, NY
14070 Gowanda, NY
14072 Grand Island, NY
14075 Hamburg, NY
14080 Holland, NY
14081 Irving, NY
14082 Java Center, NY
14083 Java Village, NY
14085 Lake View, NY
14086 Lancaster, NY
14091 Lawtons, NY
14092 Lewiston, NY
14092 Stella Niagara, NY
14094 Lockport, NY
14095 Lockport, NY
14098 Lyndonville, NY

141

14101 Machias, NY
14102 Marilla, NY
14103 Medina, NY
14105 Middleport, NY
14107 Model City, NY
14108 Newfane, NY
14109 Niagara University, NY
14110 North Boston, NY
14111 North Collins, NY
14112 North Evans, NY
14113 North Java, NY
14120 North Tonawanda, NY
14125 Oakfield, NY
14126 Olcott, NY
14127 Orchard Park, NY
14129 Perrysburg, NY
14130 Pike, NY
14131 Ransomville, NY
14132 Sanborn, NY
14133 Sandusky, NY
14134 Sardinia, NY
14135 Sheridan, NY
14136 Silver Creek, NY
14138 South Dayton, NY
14139 South Wales, NY
14140 Spring Brook, NY
14141 Springville, NY
14143 Stafford, NY
14144 Stella Niagara, NY
14145 Strykersville, NY
14150 Tonawanda, NY
14151 Tonawanda, NY
14166 Dunkirk, NY
14166 Van Buren Point, NY
14167 Varysburg, NY
14168 Versailles, NY
14169 Wales Center, NY
14170 West Falls, NY
14171 West Valley, NY
14172 Wilson, NY
14173 Yorkshire, NY
14174 Youngstown, NY

142

14201 Buffalo, NY
14202 Buffalo, NY
14203 Buffalo, NY
14204 Buffalo, NY
14205 Buffalo, NY
14206 Buffalo, NY
14206 Cheektowaga, NY
14206 West Seneca, NY
14207 Buffalo, NY
14208 Buffalo, NY
14209 Buffalo, NY
14210 Buffalo, NY
14210 West Seneca, NY
14211 Buffalo, NY
14212 Buffalo, NY
14212 Sloan, NY
14213 Buffalo, NY
14214 Buffalo, NY
14215 Buffalo, NY
14215 Cheektowaga, NY
14215 Snyder, NY
14216 Buffalo, NY
14217 Buffalo, NY
14217 Kenmore, NY
14217 Tonawanda, NY
14217 Town Of Tonawanda, NY
14218 Buffalo, NY
14218 Lackawanna, NY
14218 West Seneca, NY
14219 Blasdell, NY
14219 Buffalo, NY
14220 Buffalo, NY
14221 Amherst, NY
14221 Buffalo, NY
14221 Williamsville, NY
14222 Buffalo, NY
14223 Buffalo, NY
14223 Kenmore, NY
14223 Tonawanda, NY
14223 Town Of Tonawanda, NY
14224 Buffalo, NY
14224 West Seneca, NY
14225 Buffalo, NY
14225 Cheektowaga, NY
14226 Amherst, NY
14226 Buffalo, NY
14226 Eggertsville, NY
14226 Snyder, NY
14227 Buffalo, NY
14227 Cheektowaga, NY
14227 South Cheektowaga, NY
14228 Amherst, NY
14228 Buffalo, NY
14228 W Amherst, NY
14228 West Amherst, NY
14231 Buffalo, NY
14231 Williamsville, NY
14233 Buffalo, NY
14240 Buffalo, NY
14241 Buffalo, NY
14260 Amherst, NY
14260 Buffalo, NY
14261 Amherst, NY
14261 Buffalo, NY
14263 Buffalo, NY
14264 Buffalo, NY
14265 Buffalo, NY
14267 Buffalo, NY
14269 Buffalo, NY
14270 Buffalo, NY
14272 Buffalo, NY
14273 Buffalo, NY
14276 Buffalo, NY
14280 Buffalo, NY

143

14301 Niagara Falls, NY
14302 Niagara Falls, NY
14303 Niagara Falls, NY
14304 Niagara Falls, NY
14305 Niagara Falls, NY

144

14410 Adams Basin, NY
14411 Albion, NY
14411 Eagle Harbor, NY
14413 Alton, NY
14414 Avon, NY
14415 Bellona, NY
14416 Bergen, NY
14418 Branchport, NY
14420 Brockport, NY
14422 Byron, NY
14423 Caledonia, NY
14424 Canandaigua, NY
14425 Canandaigua, NY
14425 Farmington, NY
14427 Castile, NY
14428 Churchville, NY
14428 Clifton, NY
14429 Clarendon, NY
14430 Clarkson, NY
14432 Clifton Springs, NY
14433 Clyde, NY
14435 Conesus, NY
14437 Dansville, NY
14441 Dresden, NY
14443 East Bloomfield, NY
14445 East Rochester, NY
14449 East Williamson, NY
14450 Fairport, NY
14452 Fancher, NY
14453 Fishers, NY
14454 Geneseo, NY
14456 Geneva, NY
14461 Gorham, NY
14462 Groveland, NY
14463 Hall, NY
14464 Hamlin, NY
14466 Hemlock, NY

14467 Henrietta, NY
14468 Hilton, NY
14469 Bloomfield, NY
14470 Holley, NY
14470 Hulberton, NY
14471 Honeoye, NY
14472 Honeoye Falls, NY
14475 Ionia, NY
14476 Kendall, NY
14477 Kent, NY
14478 Bluff Point, NY
14478 Keuka Park, NY
14479 Knowlesville, NY
14480 Lakeville, NY
14481 Leicester, NY
14482 Le Roy, NY
14485 Lima, NY
14486 Linwood, NY
14487 Livonia, NY
14488 Livonia Center, NY
14489 Lyons, NY

145

14502 Macedon, NY
14504 Manchester, NY
14505 Marion, NY
14506 Mendon, NY
14507 Middlesex, NY
14508 Morton, NY
14510 Mount Morris, NY
14510 Tuscarora, NY
14511 Mumford, NY
14512 Naples, NY
14513 East Palmyra, NY
14513 Newark, NY
14514 North Chili, NY
14515 North Greece, NY
14516 North Rose, NY
14517 Nunda, NY
14518 Oaks Corners, NY
14519 Ontario, NY
14520 Ontario Center, NY
14521 Hayt Corners, NY
14521 Ovid, NY
14522 Palmyra, NY
14525 Pavilion, NY
14526 Penfield, NY
14527 Penn Yan, NY
14529 Perkinsville, NY
14530 Perry, NY
14532 Phelps, NY
14533 Piffard, NY
14533 Wadsworth, NY
14534 Pittsford, NY
14536 Portageville, NY
14536 Rossburg, NY
14537 Port Gibson, NY
14538 Pultneyville, NY
14539 Retsof, NY
14541 Mac Dougall, NY
14541 Romulus, NY
14542 Rose, NY
14543 Industry, NY
14543 Rush, NY
14543 West Rush, NY
14544 Rushville, NY
14545 Groveland, NY
14545 Scottsburg, NY
14546 Scottsville, NY
14547 Seneca Castle, NY
14548 Shortsville, NY
14549 Silver Lake, NY
14550 Rock Glen, NY
14550 Silver Springs, NY
14551 Sodus, NY
14551 Sodus Center, NY
14555 Sodus Point, NY
14556 Sonyea, NY
14557 South Byron, NY
14558 South Lima, NY
14559 Spencerport, NY
14560 Springwater, NY
14560 Webster Crossing, NY
14561 Stanley, NY
14563 Union Hill, NY
14564 Victor, NY
14568 Walworth, NY
14569 Warsaw, NY
14571 Waterport, NY
14572 Wayland, NY
14580 Webster, NY
14585 West Bloomfield, NY
14586 West Henrietta, NY
14588 Willard, NY
14589 Williamson, NY
14590 Wolcott, NY
14591 Wyoming, NY
14592 York, NY

146

14602 Rochester, NY
14603 Rochester, NY
14604 Rochester, NY
14605 Rochester, NY
14606 Gates, NY
14606 Rochester, NY
14607 Rochester, NY
14608 Rochester, NY
14609 Irondequoit, NY
14609 Rochester, NY
14610 Brighton, NY
14610 Rochester, NY
14611 Rochester, NY
14612 Greece, NY
14612 Rochester, NY
14613 Rochester, NY
14614 Rochester, NY
14615 Greece, NY
14615 Rochester, NY
14616 Greece, NY
14616 Rochester, NY
14617 Irondequoit, NY
14617 Rochester, NY
14618 Loehmanns Plaza, NY
14618 Rochester, NY
14619 Rochester, NY
14620 Brighton, NY
14620 Rochester, NY
14621 Rochester, NY
14622 Irondequoit, NY
14622 Rochester, NY
14623 Rochester, NY
14624 Gates, NY
14624 Rochester, NY
14624 Westgate, NY
14625 Panorama, NY
14625 Rochester, NY
14626 Greece, NY
14626 Ridgemont, NY
14626 Rochester, NY
14627 Rochester, NY
14638 Rochester, NY
14639 Rochester, NY
14642 Rochester, NY
14643 Rochester, NY
14644 Rochester, NY
14646 Rochester, NY
14647 Rochester, NY
14649 Rochester, NY
14650 Rochester, NY
14651 Rochester, NY
14652 Rochester, NY
14653 Rochester, NY
14692 Rochester, NY
14694 Rochester, NY

147

14701 Jamestown, NY
14701 West Ellicott, NY
14702 Jamestown, NY
14706 Allegany, NY
14707 Allentown, NY
14708 Alma, NY
14709 Angelica, NY
14710 Ashville, NY
14711 Belfast, NY
14712 Bemus Point, NY
14714 Black Creek, NY
14715 Bolivar, NY
14716 Brocton, NY
14717 Caneadea, NY
14718 Cassadaga, NY
14719 Cattaraugus, NY
14720 Celoron, NY
14721 Ceres, NY
14722 Chautauqua, NY
14723 Cherry Creek, NY
14724 Clymer, NY
14726 Conewango Valley, NY
14727 Cuba, NY
14728 Dewittville, NY
14729 East Otto, NY
14730 East Randolph, NY
14731 Ellicottville, NY
14732 Ellington, NY
14733 Falconer, NY
14735 Fillmore, NY
14736 Findley Lake, NY
14737 Franklinville, NY
14738 Frewsburg, NY
14739 Friendship, NY
14740 Gerry, NY
14741 Great Valley, NY
14742 Greenhurst, NY
14743 Hinsdale, NY
14743 Ischua, NY
14744 Houghton, NY
14745 Hume, NY
14747 Kennedy, NY
14748 Kill Buck, NY
14750 Lakewood, NY
14751 Leon, NY
14752 Lily Dale, NY
14753 Limestone, NY
14754 Little Genesee, NY
14755 Little Valley, NY
14756 Maple Springs, NY
14757 Mayville, NY
14758 Niobe, NY
14760 Knapp Creek, NY
14760 Olean, NY
14766 Otto, NY
14767 Panama, NY
14769 Portland, NY
14770 Portville, NY
14772 Randolph, NY
14774 Richburg, NY
14775 Ripley, NY
14777 Rushford, NY
14778 Saint Bonaventure, NY
14779 Salamanca, NY
14781 Sherman, NY
14782 Sinclairville, NY
14783 Steamburg, NY
14784 Stockton, NY
14785 Stow, NY
14786 West Clarksville, NY
14787 Westfield, NY
14788 Westons Mills, NY

148

14801 Addison, NY
14802 Alfred, NY
14803 Alfred Station, NY
14804 Almond, NY
14805 Alpine, NY
14806 Andover, NY
14807 Arkport, NY
14808 Atlanta, NY
14808 North Cohocton, NY
14809 Avoca, NY
14809 Wallace, NY
14810 Bath, NY
14810 Veterans Administration, NY
14812 Beaver Dams, NY
14813 Belmont, NY
14814 Big Flats, NY
14815 Bradford, NY
14816 Breesport, NY
14817 Brooktondale, NY
14818 Burdett, NY
14819 Cameron, NY
14820 Cameron Mills, NY
14821 Campbell, NY
14822 Canaseraga, NY
14823 Canisteo, NY
14824 Cayuta, NY
14825 Chemung, NY
14826 Cohocton, NY
14827 Coopers Plains, NY
14830 Corning, NY
14830 South Corning, NY
14831 Corning, NY
14836 Dalton, NY
14837 Dundee, NY
14838 Erin, NY
14839 Greenwood, NY
14840 Hammondsport, NY
14841 Hector, NY
14841 Valois, NY
14842 Himrod, NY
14843 Hornell, NY
14843 North Hornell, NY
14845 Horseheads, NY
14846 Hunt, NY
14847 Interlaken, NY
14850 Ithaca, NY
14851 Ithaca, NY
14852 Ithaca, NY
14853 Ithaca, NY
14854 Jacksonville, NY
14855 Jasper, NY
14856 Kanona, NY
14857 Lakemont, NY
14858 Lindley, NY
14859 Lockwood, NY
14860 Lodi, NY
14861 Lowman, NY
14863 Mecklenburg, NY
14864 Millport, NY
14865 Montour Falls, NY
14867 Newfield, NY
14869 Odessa, NY
14870 Painted Post, NY
14871 Pine City, NY
14872 Pine Valley, NY
14873 Prattsburgh, NY
14874 Pulteney, NY
14876 Reading Center, NY
14877 Rexville, NY
14878 Rock Stream, NY
14879 Savona, NY
14880 Scio, NY
14881 Slaterville Springs, NY
14882 Ithaca, NY
14882 Lansing, NY
14883 Spencer, NY
14883 West Danby, NY
14884 Swain, NY
14885 Troupsburg, NY
14886 Trumansburg, NY
14887 Tyrone, NY
14889 Van Etten, NY
14891 Watkins Glen, NY
14892 Waverly, NY
14893 Wayne, NY
14894 Wellsburg, NY
14895 Wellsville, NY
14897 Whitesville, NY
14898 Woodhull, NY

149

14901 Elmira, NY
14902 Elmira, NY
14903 Elmira, NY
14903 Elmira Heights, NY
14903 Elmira Hgts, NY
14904 Elmira, NY
14905 Elmira, NY

150

15001 Aliquippa, PA
15001 Macarthur, PA
15001 West Aliquippa, PA
15003 Ambridge, PA
15003 Fair Oaks, PA
15004 Atlasburg, PA
15005 Baden, PA
15006 Bairdford, PA
15007 Bakerstown, PA
15009 Beaver, PA
15009 Vanport, PA
15009 West Bridgewater, PA
15010 Beaver Falls, PA
15010 Patterson Heights, PA
15010 Racine, PA
15012 Belle Vernon, PA
15012 Belle Vrn Br, PA
15012 N Bell Vernon, PA
15012 N Belle Vernon, PA
15012 North Belle Vernon, PA
15014 Brackenridge, PA
15015 Bradfordwoods, PA
15017 Bridgeville, PA
15018 Buena Vista, PA
15019 Bulger, PA
15020 Bunola, PA
15021 Burgettstown, PA
15021 Eldersville, PA
15021 Paris, PA
15022 Charleroi, PA
15022 North Charleroi, PA
15024 Cheswick, PA
15025 Clairton, PA
15025 Floreffe, PA
15025 Jefferson Hills, PA
15025 Large, PA
15026 Clinton, PA
15027 Conway, PA
15028 Coulters, PA
15030 Creighton, PA
15031 Cuddy, PA
15032 Curtisville, PA
15033 Donora, PA
15034 Dravosburg, PA
15035 East Mc Keesport, PA
15037 Elizabeth, PA
15038 Elrama, PA
15042 Freedom, PA
15043 Georgetown, PA
15044 Gibsonia, PA
15045 Glassport, PA
15046 Crescent, PA
15046 Glenwillard, PA
15047 Greenock, PA
15049 Harwick, PA
15050 Hookstown, PA
15051 Indianola, PA
15052 Industry, PA
15053 Joffre, PA
15054 Langeloth, PA
15055 Lawrence, PA
15056 Leetsdale, PA
15057 Mc Donald, PA
15059 Midland, PA
15060 Midway, PA
15061 Monaca, PA
15062 Monessen, PA
15063 Monongahela, PA
15064 Morgan, PA
15065 Natrona Heights, PA
15066 New Brighton, PA
15067 New Eagle, PA
15068 Arnold, PA
15068 Barking, PA
15068 Lower Burrell, PA
15068 New Kensington, PA
15068 Parnassus, PA
15069 New Kensington, PA
15071 Noblestown, PA
15071 Oakdale, PA
15072 Pricedale, PA
15074 Rochester, PA
15075 Rural Ridge, PA
15076 Russellton, PA
15077 Shippingport, PA
15078 Slovan, PA
15081 South Heights, PA
15082 Sturgeon, PA
15083 Sutersville, PA
15084 Tarentum, PA
15085 Trafford, PA
15086 Warrendale, PA
15087 Webster, PA
15088 West Elizabeth, PA
15089 West Newton, PA
15090 Wexford, PA
15091 Wildwood, PA
15095 Warrendale, PA
15096 Warrendale, PA

151

15101 Allison Park, PA
15102 Bethel Park, PA
15104 Braddock, PA
15104 Rankin, PA
15106 Carnegie, PA
15106 Heidelberg, PA
15108 Coraopolis, PA
15108 Moon Township, PA
15108 Moon Twp, PA
15110 Duquesne, PA
15112 East Pittsburgh, PA
15116 Glenshaw, PA
15120 Homestead, PA
15120 Munhall, PA
15120 West Homestead, PA
15122 Pittsburgh, PA
15122 West Mifflin, PA
15123 West Mifflin, PA
15126 Imperial, PA
15127 Ingomar, PA
15129 Library, PA
15129 South Park, PA
15131 Mckeesport, PA
15131 White Oak, PA
15132 Mckeesport, PA
15133 Mckeesport, PA
15134 Mckeesport, PA
15135 Boston, PA
15135 Mckeesport, PA
15136 Mc Kees Rocks, PA
15137 North Versailles, PA
15139 Oakmont, PA
15140 Monroeville, PA
15140 Pitcairn, PA
15142 Presto, PA
15143 Edgeworth, PA
15143 Sewickley, PA
15144 Springdale, PA
15145 Turtle Creek, PA
15146 Monroeville, PA
15147 Verona, PA
15148 Wall, PA
15148 Wilmerding, PA

152

15201 Arsenal, PA
15201 Pittsburgh, PA
15202 Avalon, PA
15202 Bellevue, PA
15202 Bellvue, PA
15202 Ben Avon, PA
15202 Emsworth, PA
15202 Pittsburgh, PA
15203 Carson, PA
15203 Pittsburgh, PA
15204 Corliss, PA
15204 Pittsburgh, PA
15205 Crafton, PA
15205 Pittsburgh, PA
15206 East Liberty, PA
15206 Pittsburgh, PA
15207 Hazelwood, PA
15207 Pittsburgh, PA
15208 Homewood, PA
15208 Pittsburgh, PA
15209 Millvale, PA
15209 Pittsburgh, PA
15210 Mount Oliver, PA
15210 Mt Oliver, PA
15210 Pittsburgh, PA
15211 Mount Washington, PA
15211 Pittsburgh, PA
15212 Allegheny, PA
15212 Pittsburgh, PA
15213 Oakland, PA
15213 Pittsburgh, PA
15214 Observatory, PA
15214 Pittsburgh, PA
15215 Aspinwall, PA
15215 Pittsburgh, PA
15215 Sharpsburg, PA
15216 Pittsburgh, PA
15216 South Hills, PA
15217 Pittsburgh, PA
15217 Squirrel Hill, PA
15218 Pittsburgh, PA
15218 Swissvale, PA
15219 Pittsburgh, PA
15220 Pittsburgh, PA

15220 Wabash, PA
15221 Pittsburgh, PA
15221 Wilkinsburg, PA
15222 Pittsburgh, PA
15223 Etna, PA
15223 Pittsburgh, PA
15224 Bloomfield, PA
15224 Pittsburgh, PA
15225 Pittsburgh, PA
15226 Brookline, PA
15226 Pittsburgh, PA
15227 Brentwood, PA
15227 Pittsburgh, PA
15228 Mt Lebanon, PA
15228 Pittsburgh, PA
15229 Pittsburgh, PA
15229 West View, PA
15230 Pittsburgh, PA
15231 Pgh Int Arprt, PA
15231 Pittsburgh, PA
15232 Pittsburgh, PA
15232 Shadyside, PA
15233 Kilbuck, PA
15233 Pittsburgh, PA
15234 Castle Shannon, PA
15234 Pittsburgh, PA
15235 Penn Hills, PA
15235 Pittsburgh, PA
15236 Pittsburgh, PA
15236 Pleasant Hills, PA
15236 West Mifflin, PA
15237 Mc Knight, PA
15237 Mcknight, PA
15237 Pittsburgh, PA
15238 Blawnox, PA
15238 Pittsburgh, PA
15239 Pittsburgh, PA
15239 Plum, PA
15240 Pittsburgh, PA
15241 Pittsburgh, PA
15241 Upper Saint Clair, PA
15241 Upper St Clair, PA
15242 Greentree, PA
15242 Pittsburgh, PA
15243 Cedarhurst, PA
15243 Pittsburgh, PA
15244 Montour, PA
15244 Pittsburgh, PA
15250 Pittsburgh, PA
15251 Pittsburgh, PA
15252 Pittsburgh, PA
15253 Pittsburgh, PA
15254 Pittsburgh, PA
15255 Pittsburgh, PA
15257 Pittsburgh, PA
15258 Pittsburgh, PA
15259 Pittsburgh, PA
15260 Pittsburgh, PA
15261 Pittsburgh, PA
15262 Pittsburgh, PA
15264 Pittsburgh, PA
15265 Pittsburgh, PA
15267 Pittsburgh, PA
15268 Pittsburgh, PA
15270 Pittsburgh, PA
15272 Pittsburgh, PA
15274 Pittsburgh, PA
15275 Pittsburgh, PA
15276 Pittsburgh, PA
15277 Pittsburgh, PA
15278 Pittsburgh, PA
15279 Pittsburgh, PA
15281 Pittsburgh, PA
15282 Pittsburgh, PA
15283 Pittsburgh, PA
15286 Pittsburgh, PA
15289 Pittsburgh, PA
15290 Pittsburgh, PA
15295 Pittsburgh, PA

153

15301 Washington, PA
15310 Aleppo, PA
15311 Amity, PA
15312 Avella, PA
15312 Rea, PA
15313 Beallsville, PA
15314 Bentleyville, PA
15315 Bobtown, PA
15316 Brave, PA
15317 Canonsburg, PA
15317 Mc Murray, PA
15317 Mcmurray, PA
15320 Carmichaels, PA
15321 Cecil, PA
15322 Clarksville, PA
15323 Claysville, PA
15324 Cokeburg, PA
15325 Crucible, PA
15327 Dilliner, PA
15329 Prosperity, PA
15330 Eighty Four, PA
15331 Ellsworth, PA
15332 Finleyville, PA
15333 Fredericktown, PA
15334 Garards Fort, PA
15336 Gastonville, PA
15337 Graysville, PA
15338 Greensboro, PA
15339 Hendersonville, PA
15340 Hickory, PA
15341 Holbrook, PA
15342 Houston, PA
15344 Jefferson, PA
15345 Marianna, PA
15346 Mather, PA
15347 Meadow Lands, PA
15348 Millsboro, PA
15349 Davistown, PA
15349 Mount Morris, PA
15349 Mt Morris, PA
15350 Muse, PA
15351 Nemacolin, PA
15352 New Freeport, PA
15352 Pine Bank, PA
15353 Nineveh, PA
15357 Rices Landing, PA
15358 Richeyville, PA
15359 Rogersville, PA
15360 Scenery Hill, PA
15361 Southview, PA
15362 Spraggs, PA
15363 Strabane, PA
15364 Sycamore, PA
15365 Taylorstown, PA
15366 Van Voorhis, PA
15367 Venetia, PA
15368 Vestaburg, PA
15370 Waynesburg, PA
15376 West Alexander, PA
15377 West Finley, PA
15378 Westland, PA
15379 West Middletown, PA
15380 Wind Ridge, PA

154

15401 Uniontown, PA
15410 Adah, PA
15411 Addison, PA
15412 Allenport, PA
15413 Allison, PA
15415 Brier Hill, PA
15416 Brownfield, PA
15417 Brownsville, PA
15419 California, PA
15420 Cardale, PA
15421 Chalk Hill, PA
15422 Chestnut Ridge, PA
15423 Coal Center, PA
15424 Confluence, PA
15424 Listonburg, PA
15424 Ursina, PA
15425 Connellsville, PA
15425 S Connellsvl, PA
15427 Daisytown, PA
15428 Dawson, PA
15429 Denbo, PA
15430 Dickerson Run, PA
15431 Dunbar, PA
15432 Dunlevy, PA
15433 East Millsboro, PA
15434 Elco, PA
15435 Fairbank, PA
15436 Fairchance, PA
15437 Farmington, PA
15438 Fayette City, PA
15439 Gans, PA
15439 Lake Lynn, PA
15440 Gibbon Glade, PA
15442 Grindstone, PA
15443 Hibbs, PA
15444 Hiller, PA
15445 Hopwood, PA
15446 Indian Head, PA
15447 Isabella, PA
15448 Jacobs Creek, PA
15449 Keisterville, PA
15450 La Belle, PA
15451 Lake Lynn, PA
15454 Leckrone, PA
15455 Leisenring, PA
15456 Lemont Frnce, PA
15456 Lemont Furnace, PA
15458 Lamberton, PA
15458 Mc Clellandtown, PA
15459 Markleysburg, PA
15460 Martin, PA
15461 Masontown, PA
15462 Melcroft, PA
15463 Merrittstown, PA
15464 Mill Run, PA
15465 Mount Braddock, PA
15466 Newell, PA
15467 New Geneva, PA
15468 New Salem, PA
15469 Normalville, PA
15470 Ohiopyle, PA
15472 Oliver, PA
15473 Layton, PA
15473 Perryopolis, PA
15473 Whitsett, PA
15474 Point Marion, PA
15475 Republic, PA
15476 Ronco, PA
15477 Roscoe, PA
15478 Smithfield, PA
15479 Smithton, PA
15479 Van Meter, PA
15480 Smock, PA
15482 Star Junction, PA
15483 Stockdale, PA
15484 Uledi, PA
15485 Ursina, PA
15486 Vanderbilt, PA
15488 Waltersburg, PA
15489 West Leisenring, PA
15490 White, PA
15492 Wickhaven, PA

155

15501 Somerset, PA
15502 Hidden Valley, PA
15510 Somerset, PA
15520 Acosta, PA
15521 Alum Bank, PA
15522 Bedford, PA
15530 Berlin, PA
15531 Boswell, PA
15532 Boynton, PA
15533 Breezewood, PA
15534 Buffalo Mills, PA
15535 Clearville, PA
15536 Crystal Spring, PA
15537 Everett, PA
15538 Fairhope, PA
15538 Glencoe, PA
15539 Fishertown, PA
15540 Fort Hill, PA
15541 Friedens, PA
15542 Garrett, PA
15544 Gray, PA
15545 Hyndman, PA
15546 Jenners, PA
15547 Jennerstown, PA
15548 Kantner, PA
15549 Listie, PA
15550 Manns Choice, PA
15551 Markleton, PA
15552 Meyersdale, PA
15553 New Baltimore, PA
15554 New Paris, PA
15555 Quecreek, PA
15557 Rockwood, PA
15558 Salisbury, PA
15559 Schellsburg, PA
15560 Shanksville, PA
15561 Sipesville, PA
15562 Springs, PA
15563 Stoystown, PA
15564 Wellersburg, PA
15565 West Salisbury, PA

156

15601 Greensburg, PA
15605 Greensburg, PA
15606 Greensburg, PA
15610 Acme, PA
15611 Adamsburg, PA
15612 Alverton, PA
15613 Apollo, PA
15615 Ardara, PA
15616 Armbrust, PA
15617 Arona, PA
15618 Avonmore, PA
15618 Edmon, PA
15619 Bovard, PA
15620 Bradenville, PA
15621 Calumet, PA
15622 Champion, PA
15623 Claridge, PA
15624 Crabtree, PA
15625 Darragh, PA
15626 Delmont, PA
15627 Derry, PA
15628 Donegal, PA
15629 East Vandergrift, PA
15631 Everson, PA
15632 Export, PA
15632 Murrysville, PA
15633 Forbes Road, PA
15634 Grapeville, PA
15635 Hannastown, PA
15636 Harrison City, PA
15637 Herminie, PA
15638 Hostetter, PA
15639 Hunker, PA
15640 Hutchinson, PA
15641 Hyde Park, PA
15642 Irwin, PA
15642 No Huntingdon, PA
15642 North Huntingdon, PA
15642 North Irwin, PA
15644 Jeannette, PA
15646 Jones Mills, PA
15647 Larimer, PA
15650 Latrobe, PA
15655 Laughlintown, PA
15656 Leechburg, PA
15656 North Leechburg, PA
15656 West Leechburg, PA
15658 Ligonier, PA
15658 Wilpen, PA
15660 Lowber, PA
15661 Loyalhanna, PA
15662 Luxor, PA
15663 Madison, PA
15664 Mammoth, PA
15665 Manor, PA
15666 Mount Pleasant, PA
15668 Murrysville, PA
15670 New Alexandria, PA
15671 New Derry, PA
15672 New Stanton, PA
15673 North Apollo, PA
15674 Norvelt, PA
15675 Penn, PA
15676 Pleasant Unity, PA
15677 Rector, PA
15678 Rillton, PA
15679 Ruffs Dale, PA
15680 Salina, PA
15681 Saltsburg, PA
15682 Schenley, PA
15683 Scottdale, PA
15684 Slickville, PA
15685 Southwest, PA
15686 Spring Church, PA
15687 Stahlstown, PA
15688 Tarrs, PA
15689 United, PA
15690 Park, PA
15690 Vandergrift, PA
15691 Wendel, PA
15692 Westmoreland City, PA
15693 Whitney, PA
15695 Wyano, PA
15696 Youngstown, PA
15697 Youngwood, PA
15698 Yukon, PA

157

15701 Indiana, PA
15705 Indiana, PA
15710 Alverda, PA
15711 Anita, PA
15712 Arcadia, PA
15713 Aultman, PA
15714 Barnesboro, PA
15714 Northern Cambria, PA
15715 Big Run, PA
15716 Black Lick, PA
15717 Blairsville, PA
15720 Brush Valley, PA
15721 Burnside, PA
15722 Carrolltown, PA
15723 Chambersville, PA
15724 Cherry Tree, PA
15725 Clarksburg, PA
15727 Clune, PA
15728 Clymer, PA
15729 Commodore, PA
15730 Coolspring, PA
15731 Coral, PA
15732 Creekside, PA
15733 De Lancey, PA
15734 Dixonville, PA
15736 Elderton, PA
15737 Elmora, PA
15738 Emeigh, PA
15739 Ernest, PA
15741 Gipsy, PA
15742 Glen Campbell, PA
15744 Hamilton, PA
15745 Heilwood, PA
15746 Hillsdale, PA
15747 Home, PA
15748 Graceton, PA
15748 Homer City, PA
15748 Waterman, PA
15750 Josephine, PA
15752 Kent, PA
15753 La Jose, PA
15754 Lucernemines, PA
15756 Mc Intyre, PA
15757 Mahaffey, PA
15757 Mcgees Mills, PA
15758 Marchand, PA
15759 Marion Center, PA
15760 Marsteller, PA
15761 Mentcle, PA
15762 Nicktown, PA
15763 Northpoint, PA
15764 Oliveburg, PA
15765 Penn Run, PA
15767 Frostburg, PA
15767 Juneau, PA
15767 Punxsutawney, PA
15770 Ringgold, PA
15771 Rochester Mills, PA
15772 Rossiter, PA
15773 Saint Benedict, PA
15774 Shelocta, PA
15775 Spangler, PA
15776 Sprankle Mills, PA
15777 Starford, PA
15778 Timblin, PA
15779 Torrance, PA
15780 Valier, PA
15781 Walston, PA
15783 West Lebanon, PA
15784 Worthville, PA

158

15801 Du Bois, PA
15801 Dubois, PA
15821 Benezett, PA
15821 Benezette, PA
15822 Brandy Camp, PA
15823 Brockport, PA
15824 Brockway, PA
15825 Brookville, PA
15825 Hazen, PA
15827 Byrnedale, PA
15828 Clarington, PA
15829 Corsica, PA
15831 Dagus Mines, PA
15832 Driftwood, PA
15834 Emporium, PA
15840 Falls Creek, PA
15841 Force, PA
15845 Johnsonburg, PA
15846 Kersey, PA
15847 Knox Dale, PA
15848 Luthersburg, PA
15849 Penfield, PA
15851 Reynoldsville, PA
15853 Portland Mills, PA
15853 Ridgway, PA
15856 Rockton, PA
15857 Saint Marys, PA
15860 Hallton, PA
15860 Sigel, PA
15861 Sinnamahoning, PA
15863 Stump Creek, PA
15864 Summerville, PA
15865 Sykesville, PA
15866 Troutville, PA
15868 Weedville, PA
15870 Wilcox, PA

159

15901 Johnstown, PA
15902 Johnstown, PA
15904 Johnstown, PA
15905 Johnstown, PA
15906 Johnstown, PA
15907 Johnstown, PA
15909 Conemaugh, PA
15909 Johnstown, PA
15915 Johnstown, PA
15920 Armagh, PA
15921 Beaverdale, PA
15922 Belsano, PA
15923 Bolivar, PA
15924 Cairnbrook, PA
15925 Cassandra, PA
15926 Central City, PA
15927 Colver, PA
15928 Davidsville, PA
15929 Dilltown, PA
15930 Dunlo, PA
15931 Ebensburg, PA
15934 Elton, PA
15935 Hollsopple, PA
15936 Hooversville, PA
15937 Jerome, PA
15938 Lilly, PA
15940 Loretto, PA
15942 Mineral Point, PA
15943 Nanty Glo, PA
15944 New Florence, PA
15945 Johnstown, PA
15945 Parkhill, PA
15946 Portage, PA
15946 Puritan, PA
15948 Revloc, PA
15949 Robinson, PA
15951 Saint Michael, PA
15952 Salix, PA
15953 Seanor, PA
15954 Seward, PA
15955 Sidman, PA
15956 South Fork, PA
15957 Strongstown, PA
15958 Summerhill, PA
15959 Tire Hill, PA
15960 Twin Rocks, PA
15961 Vintondale, PA
15962 Wilmore, PA
15963 Windber, PA

160

16001 Butler, PA
16001 Meridian, PA

16002 Butler, PA
16003 Butler, PA
16016 Boyers, PA
16017 Boyers, PA
16018 Annandale, PA
16018 Boyers, PA
16020 Annandale, PA
16020 Boyers, PA
16021 Branchton, PA
16022 Bruin, PA
16023 Cabot, PA
16023 Marwood, PA
16024 Callery, PA
16025 Chicora, PA
16027 Connoquenessing, PA
16028 East Brady, PA
16029 East Butler, PA
16030 Eau Claire, PA
16033 Evans City, PA
16034 Fenelton, PA
16035 Forestville, PA
16036 Foxburg, PA
16037 Harmony, PA
16038 Harrisville, PA
16039 Herman, PA
16040 Hilliards, PA
16041 Karns City, PA
16045 Lyndora, PA
16046 Mars, PA
16046 Seven Fields, PA
16048 North Washington, PA
16049 Parker, PA
16050 Petrolia, PA
16051 Portersville, PA
16052 Prospect, PA
16053 Renfrew, PA
16054 Saint Petersburg, PA
16055 Sarver, PA
16056 Saxonburg, PA
16057 Slippery Rock, PA
16058 Turkey City, PA
16059 Valencia, PA
16061 West Sunbury, PA
16063 Zelienople, PA
16066 Cranberry Township, PA

161

16101 New Castle, PA
16102 New Castle, PA
16103 New Castle, PA
16105 Neshannock, PA
16105 New Castle, PA
16107 New Castle, PA
16108 New Castle, PA
16110 Adamsville, PA
16111 Atlantic, PA
16112 Bessemer, PA
16113 Clark, PA
16114 Clarks Mills, PA
16115 Darlington, PA
16116 Edinburg, PA
16117 Ellport, PA
16117 Ellwood City, PA
16120 Enon Valley, PA
16121 Farrell, PA
16123 Fombell, PA
16124 Fredonia, PA
16125 Greenville, PA
16125 Shenango, PA
16127 Grove City, PA
16130 Hadley, PA
16131 Hartstown, PA
16132 Hillsville, PA
16133 Jackson Center, PA
16134 Jamestown, PA
16134 Westford, PA
16136 Koppel, PA
16137 Mercer, PA
16140 New Bedford, PA
16141 New Galilee, PA
16142 New Wilmington, PA
16143 Pulaski, PA
16145 Sandy Lake, PA
16146 Sharon, PA
16148 Hermitage, PA
16148 Sharon, PA
16150 Sharpsville, PA
16151 Sheakleyville, PA
16153 Stoneboro, PA
16154 Transfer, PA
16155 Villa Maria, PA
16156 Volant, PA
16157 Wampum, PA
16159 West Middlesex, PA
16160 West Pittsburg, PA
16161 Wheatland, PA
16172 New Wilmington, PA

162

16201 Kittanning, PA
16210 Adrian, PA
16211 Beyer, PA
16212 Cadogan, PA
16213 Callensburg, PA
16214 Clarion, PA
16217 Cooksburg, PA
16218 Cowansville, PA
16220 Crown, PA
16221 Curllsville, PA
16222 Dayton, PA
16223 Distant, PA
16224 Fairmount City, PA
16225 Fisher, PA
16226 Ford City, PA
16228 Ford Cliff, PA
16229 Freeport, PA
16230 Hawthorn, PA
16232 Knox, PA
16233 Leeper, PA
16234 Limestone, PA
16235 Lucinda, PA
16236 Mc Grann, PA
16238 Manorville, PA
16239 Marienville, PA
16240 Mayport, PA
16242 Climax, PA
16242 New Bethlehem, PA
16244 Nu Mine, PA
16245 Oak Ridge, PA
16246 Plumville, PA
16248 Huey, PA
16248 Rimersburg, PA
16249 Rural Valley, PA
16250 Sagamore, PA
16253 Seminole, PA
16254 Shippenville, PA
16255 Sligo, PA
16256 Smicksburg, PA
16257 Snydersburg, PA
16258 Strattanville, PA
16259 Templeton, PA
16260 Vowinckel, PA
16261 Widnoon, PA
16262 Craigsville, PA
16262 Worthington, PA
16263 Yatesboro, PA

163

16301 Oil City, PA
16311 Carlton, PA
16312 Chandlers Valley, PA
16313 Clarendon, PA
16314 Cochranton, PA
16316 Conneaut Lake, PA
16317 Cooperstown, PA
16319 Cranberry, PA
16321 East Hickory, PA
16321 Endeavor, PA
16322 Endeavor, PA
16323 Franklin, PA
16326 Fryburg, PA
16327 Guys Mills, PA
16328 Hydetown, PA
16329 Irvine, PA
16331 Kossuth, PA
16332 Lickingville, PA
16333 Ludlow, PA
16334 Marble, PA
16335 Meadville, PA
16340 Pittsfield, PA
16341 Pleasantville, PA
16342 Polk, PA
16343 Reno, PA
16344 Rouseville, PA
16345 Russell, PA
16346 Seneca, PA
16347 Sheffield, PA
16350 Sugar Grove, PA
16351 Tidioute, PA
16352 Tiona, PA
16353 Tionesta, PA
16354 Titusville, PA
16360 Townville, PA
16361 Tylersburg, PA
16362 Utica, PA
16364 Venus, PA
16365 North Warren, PA
16365 Warren, PA
16366 Warren, PA
16367 Warren, PA
16368 Warren, PA
16369 Warren, PA
16370 West Hickory, PA
16371 Youngsville, PA
16372 Clintonville, PA
16373 Emlenton, PA
16374 Kennerdell, PA
16375 Lamartine, PA
16388 Meadville, PA

164

16401 Albion, PA
16401 Lundys Lane, PA
16402 Bear Lake, PA
16403 Cambridge Springs, PA
16404 Centerville, PA
16405 Columbus, PA
16406 Conneautville, PA
16407 Corry, PA
16410 Cranesville, PA
16411 East Springfield, PA
16412 Crossingville, PA
16412 Edinboro, PA
16413 Elgin, PA
16415 Fairview, PA
16416 Garland, PA
16417 Girard, PA
16420 Grand Valley, PA
16421 Harborcreek, PA
16422 Harmonsburg, PA
16423 Lake City, PA
16424 Espyville, PA
16424 Linesville, PA
16426 Mc Kean, PA
16426 Mckean, PA
16427 Mill Village, PA
16428 North East, PA
16430 North Springfield, PA
16432 Riceville, PA
16433 Saegertown, PA
16434 Spartansburg, PA
16435 Springboro, PA
16436 Spring Creek, PA
16438 Union City, PA
16440 Venango, PA
16441 Waterford, PA
16442 Wattsburg, PA
16443 West Springfield, PA
16444 Edinboro, PA
16475 Albion, PA

165

16501 Erie, PA
16502 Erie, PA
16503 Erie, PA
16504 Erie, PA
16505 Erie, PA
16506 Erie, PA
16507 Erie, PA
16508 Erie, PA
16509 Erie, PA
16510 Erie, PA
16511 Erie, PA
16512 Erie, PA
16514 Erie, PA
16515 Erie, PA
16522 Erie, PA
16530 Erie, PA
16531 Erie, PA
16534 Erie, PA
16538 Erie, PA
16541 Erie, PA
16544 Erie, PA
16546 Erie, PA
16550 Erie, PA
16553 Erie, PA
16563 Erie, PA
16565 Erie, PA

166

16601 Altoona, PA
16602 Altoona, PA
16603 Altoona, PA
16611 Alexandria, PA
16611 Barree, PA
16613 Ashville, PA
16616 Beccaria, PA
16617 Bellwood, PA
16619 Blandburg, PA
16620 Brisbin, PA
16621 Broad Top, PA
16622 Calvin, PA
16623 Cassville, PA
16624 Chest Springs, PA
16625 Claysburg, PA
16627 Coalport, PA
16629 Coupon, PA
16630 Cresson, PA
16631 Curryville, PA
16633 Defiance, PA
16634 Dudley, PA
16635 Duncansville, PA
16636 Dysart, PA
16637 East Freedom, PA
16638 Entriken, PA
16639 Fallentimber, PA
16640 Flinton, PA
16641 Gallitzin, PA
16644 Glasgow, PA
16645 Glen Hope, PA
16646 Hastings, PA
16647 Hesston, PA
16648 Hollidaysburg, PA
16650 Hopewell, PA
16651 Ginter, PA
16651 Houtzdale, PA
16652 Huntingdon, PA
16654 Huntingdon, PA
16655 Imler, PA
16656 Irvona, PA
16657 James Creek, PA
16659 Loysburg, PA
16660 Mc Connellstown, PA
16661 Madera, PA
16662 Martinsburg, PA
16663 Morann, PA
16664 New Enterprise, PA
16665 Newry, PA
16666 Osceola Mills, PA
16667 Osterburg, PA
16667 Saint Clairsville, PA
16667 St Clairsville, PA
16667 Saint Clairsville, PA
16668 Patton, PA
16669 Petersburg, PA
16670 Queen, PA
16671 Ramey, PA
16672 Riddlesburg, PA
16673 Bakers Summit, PA
16673 Roaring Spring, PA
16674 Robertsdale, PA
16675 Saint Boniface, PA
16677 Sandy Ridge, PA
16678 Saxton, PA
16679 Six Mile Run, PA
16680 Smithmill, PA
16681 Smokerun, PA
16682 Sproul, PA
16683 Spruce Creek, PA
16684 Tipton, PA
16685 Todd, PA
16686 Birmingham, PA
16686 Tyrone, PA
16689 Waterfall, PA
16691 Wells Tannery, PA
16692 Westover, PA
16693 Ganister, PA
16693 Williamsburg, PA
16694 Wood, PA
16695 Woodbury, PA
16698 Houtzdale, PA
16699 Cresson, PA

167

16701 Bradford, PA
16720 Austin, PA
16724 Crosby, PA
16725 Custer City, PA
16726 Cyclone, PA
16726 Ormsby, PA
16727 Derrick City, PA
16728 De Young, PA
16729 Duke Center, PA
16730 East Smethport, PA
16731 Eldred, PA
16732 Gifford, PA
16733 Hazel Hurst, PA
16734 James City, PA
16735 Kane, PA
16738 Lewis Run, PA
16740 Mount Jewett, PA
16740 Westline, PA
16743 Port Allegany, PA
16744 Rew, PA
16745 Rixford, PA
16746 Roulette, PA
16748 Shinglehouse, PA
16749 Smethport, PA
16750 Turtlepoint, PA

168

16801 State College, PA
16802 Penn State University, PA
16802 State College, PA
16802 University Park, PA
16803 State College, PA
16804 State College, PA
16805 State College, PA
16820 Aaronsburg, PA
16821 Allport, PA
16822 Beech Creek, PA
16823 Bellefonte, PA
16823 Hublersburg, PA
16823 Pleasant Gap, PA
16823 Wingate, PA
16825 Bigler, PA
16826 Blanchard, PA
16827 Boalsburg, PA
16828 Centre Hall, PA
16829 Clarence, PA
16830 Clearfield, PA
16832 Coburn, PA
16833 Curwensville, PA
16834 Drifting, PA
16835 Fleming, PA
16836 Frenchville, PA
16837 Glen Richey, PA
16838 Grampian, PA
16839 Grassflat, PA
16840 Hawk Run, PA
16841 Howard, PA
16843 Hyde, PA
16844 Julian, PA
16845 Karthaus, PA
16847 Kylertown, PA
16848 Lamar, PA
16849 Lanse, PA
16850 Lecontes Mills, PA
16851 Lemont, PA
16852 Madisonburg, PA
16853 Milesburg, PA
16854 Millheim, PA
16855 Mineral Springs, PA
16856 Mingoville, PA
16858 Morrisdale, PA
16859 Moshannon, PA
16860 Munson, PA
16861 New Millport, PA
16863 Olanta, PA
16864 Orviston, PA
16865 Pennsylvania Furnace, PA
16866 Philipsburg, PA
16868 Pine Grove Mills, PA
16870 Port Matilda, PA
16871 Pottersdale, PA
16872 Rebersburg, PA
16873 Shawville, PA
16874 Snow Shoe, PA
16875 Spring Mills, PA
16876 Wallaceton, PA
16877 Warriors Mark, PA
16878 West Decatur, PA
16879 Winburne, PA
16881 Woodland, PA
16882 Woodward, PA

169

16901 Wellsboro, PA
16910 Alba, PA
16910 Snydertown, PA
16911 Arnot, PA
16912 Blossburg, PA
16914 Columbia Cross Roads, PA
16915 Coudersport, PA
16915 Oswayo, PA
16917 Covington, PA
16920 Elkland, PA
16921 Gaines, PA
16922 Galeton, PA
16923 Genesee, PA
16923 North Bingham, PA
16925 Gillett, PA
16926 Granville Summit, PA
16927 Harrison Valley, PA
16927 Westfield, PA
16928 Knoxville, PA
16929 Lawrenceville, PA
16930 Liberty, PA
16932 Mainesburg, PA
16933 Mansfield, PA
16935 Middlebury Center, PA
16936 Millerton, PA
16937 Mills, PA
16938 Morris, PA
16939 Morris Run, PA
16940 Nelson, PA
16941 Genesee, PA
16941 North Bingham, PA
16942 Osceola, PA
16943 Sabinsville, PA
16945 Sylvania, PA
16946 Tioga, PA
16947 Troy, PA
16947 West Burlington Township, PA
16948 Ulysses, PA
16950 Cowanesque, PA
16950 Little Marsh, PA
16950 Westfield, PA

170

17001 Camp Hill, PA
17002 Allensville, PA
17003 Annville, PA
17004 Belleville, PA
17005 Berrysburg, PA
17006 Blain, PA
17007 Boiling Springs, PA
17009 Burnham, PA
17010 Campbelltown, PA
17011 Camp Hill, PA
17011 Shiremanstown, PA
17012 Camp Hill, PA
17013 Carlisle, PA
17013 Carlisle Barracks, PA
17014 Cocolamus, PA
17015 Carlisle, PA
17015 West Pennsboro, PA
17016 Cornwall, PA
17017 Dalmatia, PA
17018 Dauphin, PA
17019 Dillsburg, PA
17020 Duncannon, PA
17021 East Waterford, PA
17022 Elizabethtown, PA
17023 Elizabethville, PA

7024 Elliottsburg, PA
7024 Green Park, PA
7025 East Pennsboro, PA
7025 Enola, PA
7026 Fredericksburg, PA
7027 Grantham, PA
7027 Messiah College, PA
7028 Grantville, PA
7029 Granville, PA
7030 Gratz, PA
7032 Halifax, PA
7033 Hershey, PA
7034 Highspire, PA
7035 Honey Grove, PA
7036 Hummelstown, PA
7037 Ickesburg, PA
7038 Jonestown, PA
7039 Kleinfeltersville, PA
7040 Landisburg, PA
7041 Lawn, PA
7042 Cleona, PA
7042 Colebrook, PA
7042 Cornwall Borough, PA
7042 Lebanon, PA
7043 Lemoyne, PA
7043 Wormleysburg, PA
7044 Lewistown, PA
7045 Liverpool, PA
7046 Lebanon, PA
7046 Swatara Township, PA
7047 Loysville, PA
7048 Lykens, PA
7049 Mc Alisterville, PA
7050 Hampden Township, PA
7050 Mechanicsburg, PA
7050 Silver Spring Township,
A
7051 Mc Veytown, PA
7052 Mapleton Depot, PA
7053 Marysville, PA
7054 Mattawana, PA
7055 Bowmansdale, PA
7055 Mechanicsburg, PA
7056 Mexico, PA
7057 Middletown, PA
7058 Mifflin, PA
7059 Mifflintown, PA
7060 Mill Creek, PA
7061 Millersburg, PA
7062 Millerstown, PA
7063 Milroy, PA
7064 Mount Gretna, PA
7065 Mount Holly Springs, PA
7066 Mount Union, PA
7067 Myerstown, PA
7068 New Bloomfield, PA
7069 New Buffalo, PA
7070 New Cumberland, PA
7071 New Germantown, PA
7072 New Kingstown, PA
7073 Newmanstown, PA
7074 Newport, PA
7075 Newton Hamilton, PA
7076 Oakland Mills, PA
7077 Ono, PA
7078 Palmyra, PA
7080 Pillow, PA
7081 Plainfield, PA
7082 Port Royal, PA
7083 Quentin, PA
7084 Reedsville, PA
7085 Rexmont, PA
7086 Richfield, PA
7087 Richland, PA
7088 Schaefferstown, PA
7089 Camp Hill, PA
7090 Shermans Dale, PA
7093 Summerdale, PA
7094 Thompsontown, PA
7097 Wiconisco, PA
7098 Williamstown, PA
7099 Yeagertown, PA

171

7101 Harrisburg, PA
7102 Harrisburg, PA
7103 Harrisburg, PA
17103 Penbrook, PA
17104 Harrisburg, PA
17105 Harrisburg, PA
17106 Harrisburg, PA
17107 Harrisburg, PA
17108 Harrisburg, PA
17109 Harrisburg, PA
17109 Lower Paxton, PA
17109 Penbrook, PA
17110 Harrisburg, PA
17111 Harrisburg, PA
17111 Paxtang, PA
17111 Swatara, PA
17112 Harrisburg, PA
17112 Linglestown, PA
17112 Lower Paxton, PA
17112 Paxtonia, PA
17112 West Hanover, PA
17113 Bressler, PA
17113 Harrisburg, PA
17113 Oberlin, PA
17113 Steelton, PA
17120 Harrisburg, PA
17121 Harrisburg, PA
17122 Harrisburg, PA
17123 Harrisburg, PA
17124 Harrisburg, PA
17125 Harrisburg, PA
17126 Harrisburg, PA
17127 Harrisburg, PA
17128 Harrisburg, PA
17129 Harrisburg, PA
17130 Harrisburg, PA
17140 Harrisburg, PA
17177 Harrisburg, PA

172

17201 Chambersburg, PA
17202 Chambersburg, PA
17202 Guilford Township, PA
17210 Amberson, PA
17211 Artemas, PA
17212 Big Cove Tannery, PA
17213 Blairs Mills, PA
17214 Blue Ridge Summit, PA
17215 Burnt Cabins, PA
17217 Concord, PA
17219 Doylesburg, PA
17220 Dry Run, PA
17221 Fannettsburg, PA
17222 Fayetteville, PA
17223 Fort Littleton, PA
17224 Fort Loudon, PA
17225 Greencastle, PA
17228 Harrisonville, PA
17229 Hustontown, PA
17231 Lemasters, PA
17232 Lurgan, PA
17233 Mc Connellsburg, PA
17235 Marion, PA
17236 Mercersburg, PA
17237 Mont Alto, PA
17238 Needmore, PA
17239 Neelyton, PA
17240 Newburg, PA
17241 Newville, PA
17243 Orbisonia, PA
17244 Orrstown, PA
17246 Pleasant Hall, PA
17247 Quincy, PA
17249 Rockhill Furnace, PA
17250 Rouzerville, PA
17251 Roxbury, PA
17252 Saint Thomas, PA
17253 Saltillo, PA
17254 Scotland, PA
17255 Shade Gap, PA
17256 Shady Grove, PA
17257 Shippensburg, PA
17260 Mount Union, PA
17260 Shirleysburg, PA
17261 South Mountain, PA
17262 Spring Run, PA
17263 State Line, PA
17264 Three Springs, PA
17265 Upperstrasburg, PA
17266 Walnut Bottom, PA
17267 Warfordsburg, PA
17268 Waynesboro, PA
17271 Willow Hill, PA
17272 Zullinger, PA

173

17301 Abbottstown, PA
17302 Airville, PA
17303 Arendtsville, PA
17304 Aspers, PA
17306 Bendersville, PA
17307 Biglerville, PA
17309 Brogue, PA
17310 Cashtown, PA
17311 Codorus, PA
17312 Craley, PA
17313 Dallastown, PA
17313 Yoe, PA
17314 Delta, PA
17315 Dover, PA
17315 York, PA
17316 East Berlin, PA
17317 East Prospect, PA
17318 Emigsville, PA
17319 Etters, PA
17320 Fairfield, PA
17320 Greenstone, PA
17321 Fawn Grove, PA
17322 Felton, PA
17323 Franklintown, PA
17324 Gardners, PA
17325 Gettysburg, PA
17327 Glen Rock, PA
17329 Brodbecks, PA
17329 Glenville, PA
17331 Hanover, PA
17332 Hanover, PA
17333 Hanover, PA
17334 Hanover, PA
17335 Hanover, PA
17337 Idaville, PA
17339 Lewisberry, PA
17340 Littlestown, PA
17342 Loganville, PA
17343 Mc Knightstown, PA
17344 Mc Sherrystown, PA
17345 Manchester, PA
17347 Mount Wolf, PA
17349 New Freedom, PA
17350 New Oxford, PA
17352 New Park, PA
17353 Orrtanna, PA
17354 Porters Sideling, PA
17354 Spring Grove, PA
17355 Railroad, PA
17356 Red Lion, PA
17358 Rossville, PA
17360 Seven Valleys, PA
17361 Shrewsbury, PA
17362 Menges Mills, PA
17362 Spring Grove, PA
17363 Stewartstown, PA
17364 Thomasville, PA
17365 Wellsville, PA
17366 Windsor, PA
17368 Wrightsville, PA
17370 York Haven, PA
17371 York New Salem, PA
17372 York Springs, PA
17375 Peach Glen, PA

174

17401 York, PA
17402 East York, PA
17402 Springettsbury Township,
PA
17402 York, PA
17403 York, PA
17404 West York, PA
17404 York, PA
17405 York, PA
17406 Hallam, PA
17406 Hellam, PA
17406 York, PA
17406 Yorkana, PA
17407 Jacobus, PA
17407 York, PA
17408 New Salem Borough, PA
17408 West Manchester Twp,
PA
17408 York, PA

175

17501 Akron, PA
17502 Bainbridge, PA
17503 Bart, PA
17504 Bausman, PA
17505 Bird In Hand, PA
17506 Blue Ball, PA
17507 Bowmansville, PA
17508 Brownstown, PA
17509 Christiana, PA
17509 Ninepoints, PA
17512 Columbia, PA
17516 Conestoga, PA
17517 Denver, PA
17518 Drumore, PA
17519 East Earl, PA
17520 East Petersburg, PA
17521 Elm, PA
17522 Ephrata, PA
17527 Gap, PA
17528 Goodville, PA
17529 Gordonville, PA
17532 Holtwood, PA
17533 Hopeland, PA
17534 Intercourse, PA
17535 Kinzers, PA
17536 Kirkwood, PA
17537 Lampeter, PA
17538 Landisville, PA
17538 Salunga, PA
17540 Leola, PA
17543 Lititz, PA
17545 Manheim, PA
17547 Marietta, PA
17549 Martindale, PA
17550 Maytown, PA
17551 Millersville, PA
17552 Florin, PA
17552 Mount Joy, PA
17554 Mountville, PA
17555 Narvon, PA
17557 New Holland, PA
17560 New Providence, PA
17562 Paradise, PA
17563 Peach Bottom, PA
17564 Penryn, PA
17565 Pequea, PA
17566 Quarryville, PA
17567 Reamstown, PA
17568 Refton, PA
17569 Reinholds, PA
17570 Rheems, PA
17572 Ronks, PA
17572 Soudersburg, PA
17573 Lancaster, PA
17575 Silver Spring, PA
17576 Smoketown, PA
17578 Stevens, PA
17579 Strasburg, PA
17580 Talmage, PA
17581 Terre Hill, PA
17582 Washington Boro, PA
17583 West Willow, PA
17584 Willow Street, PA
17585 Witmer, PA

176

17601 Lancaster, PA
17601 Neffsville, PA
17602 Lancaster, PA
17603 Lancaster, PA
17603 Rohrerstown, PA
17604 Lancaster, PA
17605 East Lancaster, PA
17605 Lancaster, PA
17606 Lancaster, PA
17607 Lancaster, PA
17608 Lancaster, PA
17611 Lancaster, PA
17622 Lancaster, PA
17699 Lancaster, PA

177

17701 Williamsport, PA
17702 Armstrong, PA
17702 Bastress, PA
17702 Collomsville, PA
17702 Duboistown, PA
17702 Nisbet, PA
17702 S Williamspor, PA
17702 S Williamsport, PA
17702 South Williamsport, PA
17702 Sylvan Dell, PA
17702 Williamsport, PA
17703 Williamsport, PA
17705 Williamsport, PA
17720 Antes Fort, PA
17721 Avis, PA
17723 Cammal, PA
17723 Jersey Shore, PA
17724 Canton, PA
17724 Leroy, PA
17726 Castanea, PA
17727 Cedar Run, PA
17727 Jersey Shore, PA
17728 Cogan Station, PA
17729 Cross Fork, PA
17730 Dewart, PA
17731 Eagles Mere, PA
17735 Grover, PA
17737 Hughesville, PA
17739 Jersey Mills, PA
17740 Jersey Shore, PA
17740 Salladasburg, PA
17742 Lairdsville, PA
17744 Linden, PA
17745 Farrandsville, PA
17745 Flemington, PA
17745 Lock Haven, PA
17747 Loganton, PA
17747 Tylersville, PA
17748 Mc Elhattan, PA
17749 Mc Ewensville, PA
17750 Mackeyville, PA
17751 Mill Hall, PA
17752 Montgomery, PA
17754 Montoursville, PA
17756 Muncy, PA
17756 Pennsdale, PA
17758 Muncy Valley, PA
17758 Sonestown, PA
17760 North Bend, PA
17762 Picture Rocks, PA
17763 Ralston, PA
17764 Renovo, PA
17765 Roaring Branch, PA
17767 Salona, PA
17768 Shunk, PA
17769 Slate Run, PA
17771 Trout Run, PA
17772 Turbotville, PA
17774 Unityville, PA
17776 Waterville, PA
17777 Watsontown, PA
17778 Westport, PA
17779 Woolrich, PA

178

17801 Sunbury, PA
17810 Allenwood, PA
17812 Beaver Springs, PA
17812 Middle Creek, PA
17813 Beavertown, PA
17814 Benton, PA
17815 Bloomsburg, PA
17820 Catawissa, PA
17821 Danville, PA
17822 Danville, PA
17823 Dornsife, PA
17824 Elysburg, PA
17827 Freeburg, PA
17829 Hartleton, PA
17830 Herndon, PA
17831 Hummels Wharf, PA
17832 Marion Heights, PA
17833 Kreamer, PA
17834 Kulpmont, PA
17835 Laurelton, PA
17836 Leck Kill, PA
17837 Lewisburg, PA
17839 Lightstreet, PA
17840 Locust Gap, PA
17841 Mc Clure, PA
17842 Middleburg, PA
17843 Beaver Springs, PA
17843 Middle Creek, PA
17844 Mifflinburg, PA
17845 Millmont, PA
17846 Millville, PA
17847 Milton, PA
17850 Montandon, PA
17851 Mount Carmel, PA
17853 Mount Pleasant Mills,
PA
17853 Mt Pleasant Mills, PA
17855 New Berlin, PA
17856 New Columbia, PA
17857 Northumberland, PA
17858 Numidia, PA
17859 Orangeville, PA
17860 Paxinos, PA
17861 Paxtonville, PA
17862 Penns Creek, PA
17864 Port Trevorton, PA
17865 Potts Grove, PA
17866 Coal Township, PA
17866 Excelsior, PA
17866 Ranshaw, PA
17867 Rebuck, PA
17868 Riverside, PA
17870 Monroe Township, PA
17870 Selinsgrove, PA
17872 Gowen City, PA
17872 Shamokin, PA
17876 Shamokin Dam, PA
17877 Snydertown, PA
17878 Stillwater, PA
17880 Swengel, PA
17881 Trevorton, PA
17882 Troxelville, PA
17883 Vicksburg, PA
17884 Washingtonville, PA
17885 Weikert, PA
17886 Lewisburg, PA
17886 New Columbia, PA
17886 West Milton, PA
17887 White Deer, PA
17888 Wilburton, PA
17889 Winfield, PA

179

17901 Pottsville, PA
17920 Aristes, PA
17921 Ashland, PA
17921 Centralia, PA
17921 Helfenstein, PA
17922 Auburn, PA
17923 Branchdale, PA
17925 Brockton, PA
17929 Cressona, PA
17930 Cumbola, PA
17931 Frackville, PA
17932 Frackville, PA
17933 Friedensburg, PA
17934 Gilberton, PA
17935 Girardville, PA
17936 Gordon, PA
17938 Hegins, PA
17941 Klingerstown, PA
17943 Lavelle, PA
17944 Llewellyn, PA
17945 Locustdale, PA
17946 Lost Creek, PA
17948 Mahanoy City, PA
17948 Morea, PA
17948 New Boston, PA
17949 Mahanoy Plane, PA
17951 Mar Lin, PA
17952 Mary D, PA
17953 Middleport, PA
17954 Minersville, PA
17957 Muir, PA
17959 Kaska, PA
17959 New Philadelphia, PA
17960 New Ringgold, PA

17961 Orwigsburg, PA
17963 Pine Grove, PA
17964 Pitman, PA
17965 Port Carbon, PA
17966 Ravine, PA
17967 Ringtown, PA
17968 Sacramento, PA
17970 Saint Clair, PA
17972 Landingville, PA
17972 Schuylkill Haven, PA
17974 Seltzer, PA
17976 Lower Shaft, PA
17976 Shenandoah, PA
17978 Spring Glen, PA
17979 Summit Station, PA
17980 Tower City, PA
17981 Donaldson, PA
17981 Good Spring, PA
17981 Joliett, PA
17981 Tremont, PA
17981 Zerbe, PA
17982 Tuscarora, PA
17983 Valley View, PA
17985 Zion Grove, PA

180

18001 Lehigh Valley, PA
18002 Lehigh Valley, PA
18003 Lehigh Valley, PA
18010 Ackermanville, PA
18010 Bangor, PA
18011 Alburtis, PA
18012 Aquashicola, PA
18013 Bangor, PA
18013 East Bangor, PA
18013 Roseto, PA
18014 Bath, PA
18015 Bethlehem, PA
18015 Fountain Hill, PA
18016 Bethlehem, PA
18017 Bethlehem, PA
18017 Butztown, PA
18017 Freemansburg, PA
18018 Bethlehem, PA
18020 Bethlehem, PA
18025 Bethlehem, PA
18030 Bowmanstown, PA
18031 Breinigsville, PA
18032 Catasauqua, PA
18034 Center Valley, PA
18035 Cherryville, PA
18036 Coopersburg, PA
18037 Coplay, PA
18038 Danielsville, PA
18039 Durham, PA
18040 Easton, PA
18040 Forks Township, PA
18040 Stockertown Township, PA
18041 East Greenville, PA
18042 College Hill, PA
18042 Easton, PA
18042 Glendon, PA
18042 West Easton, PA
18042 Williams Township, PA
18043 Easton, PA
18043 Palmer, PA
18044 Easton, PA
18045 Easton, PA
18045 Palmer, PA
18045 Palmer Township, PA
18045 Tatamy Borough, PA
18046 East Texas, PA
18049 Emmaus, PA
18050 Bangor, PA
18050 Flicksville, PA
18051 Fogelsville, PA
18052 Hokendauqua, PA
18052 Whitehall, PA
18053 Germansville, PA
18054 Green Lane, PA
18055 Hellertown, PA
18056 Hereford, PA
18058 Kunkletown, PA
18059 Laurys Station, PA
18060 Limeport, PA
18062 Macungie, PA
18063 Martins Creek, PA
18064 Nazareth, PA
18065 Neffs, PA
18066 New Tripoli, PA
18067 Northampton, PA
18068 Old Zionsville, PA
18069 Orefield, PA
18070 Palm, PA
18071 Palmerton, PA
18072 Pen Argyl, PA
18073 Pennsburg, PA
18073 Red Hill, PA
18074 Perkiomenville, PA
18076 Red Hill, PA
18077 Riegelsville, PA
18078 Schnecksville, PA
18079 Slatedale, PA
18080 Emerald, PA
18080 Slatington, PA
18081 Springtown, PA
18083 Stockertown, PA
18084 Sumneytown, PA
18085 Tatamy, PA
18086 Treichlers, PA
18087 Trexlertown, PA
18088 Walnutport, PA
18091 Wind Gap, PA
18092 Zionsville, PA
18098 Emmaus, PA
18099 Emmaus, PA

181

18101 Allentown, PA
18102 Allentown, PA
18103 Allentown, PA
18104 Allentown, PA
18105 Allentown, PA
18106 Allentown, PA
18106 Wescosville, PA
18109 Allentown, PA
18195 Allentown, PA

182

18201 Hazle Township, PA
18201 Hazleton, PA
18202 Hazle Township, PA
18202 Hazleton, PA
18202 Pardeesville, PA
18202 W Hazleton, PA
18202 West Hazleton, PA
18210 Albrightsville, PA
18211 Andreas, PA
18212 Ashfield, PA
18214 Barnesville, PA
18216 Beaver Meadows, PA
18218 Coaldale, PA
18219 Conyngham, PA
18220 Delano, PA
18221 Drifton, PA
18222 Drums, PA
18223 Ebervale, PA
18224 Freeland, PA
18225 Harleigh, PA
18229 Jim Thorpe, PA
18230 Junedale, PA
18231 Kelayres, PA
18232 Lansford, PA
18234 Lattimer Mines, PA
18235 Lehighton, PA
18235 Lehighton Borough, PA
18235 Weissport, PA
18237 Mcadoo, PA
18239 Milnesville, PA
18240 Nesquehoning, PA
18241 Fern Glen, PA
18241 Nuremberg, PA
18242 Oneida, PA
18244 Parryville, PA
18245 Quakake, PA
18246 Rock Glen, PA
18247 Saint Johns, PA
18248 Sheppton, PA
18249 Sugarloaf, PA
18250 Summit Hill, PA
18251 Sybertsville, PA
18252 Tamaqua, PA
18254 Tresckow, PA
18255 Weatherly, PA
18256 Weston, PA

183

18301 East Stroudsburg, PA
18301 Lehman, PA
18302 East Stroudsburg, PA
18320 Analomink, PA
18321 Bartonsville, PA
18322 Brodheadsville, PA
18323 Buck Hill Falls, PA
18324 Bushkill, PA
18324 Lehman, PA
18325 Canadensis, PA
18326 Cresco, PA
18326 Paradise Valley, PA
18327 Delaware Water Gap, PA
18328 Dingmans Ferry, PA
18328 Lakeview Township, PA
18328 Lehman, PA
18330 Effort, PA
18331 Gilbert, PA
18332 Henryville, PA
18333 Kresgeville, PA
18334 Long Pond, PA
18335 Marshalls Creek, PA
18336 Matamoras, PA
18337 Milford, PA
18340 Millrift, PA
18341 Minisink Hills, PA
18342 Mountainhome, PA
18343 Mount Bethel, PA
18344 Mount Pocono, PA
18346 Pocono Summit, PA
18347 Pocono Lake, PA
18348 Pocono Lake, PA
18348 Pocono Lake Preserve, PA
18349 Pocono Manor, PA
18350 Pocono Pines, PA
18351 Portland, PA
18352 Reeders, PA
18353 Saylorsburg, PA
18354 Sciota, PA
18355 Scotrun, PA
18356 Shawnee, PA
18356 Shawnee On Delaware, PA
18357 Skytop, PA
18360 Stroudsburg, PA
18370 Swiftwater, PA
18371 Bushkill, PA
18371 Lehman, PA
18371 Tamiment, PA
18372 Tannersville, PA
18373 Bushkill, PA
18373 Unity House, PA

184

18403 Archbald, PA
18403 Eynon, PA
18405 Beach Lake, PA
18407 Carbondale, PA
18407 Childs, PA
18407 Clifford Township, PA
18407 Greenfield Township, PA
18407 Simpson, PA
18410 Chinchilla, PA
18411 Clarks Green, PA
18411 Clarks Summit, PA
18411 S Abington Twp, PA
18411 Scott Township, PA
18411 South Abington Township, PA
18413 Clifford, PA
18414 Dalton, PA
18414 North Abington Township, PA
18414 Scott Township, PA
18414 West Abington Township, PA
18415 Damascus, PA
18415 Galilee, PA
18416 Elmhurst, PA
18417 Equinunk, PA
18419 Factoryville, PA
18420 Fleetville, PA
18421 Browndale, PA
18421 Clifford Township, PA
18421 Forest City, PA
18421 Richmondale, PA
18421 Vandling, PA
18424 Clifton, PA
18424 Clifton Township, PA
18424 Covington Township, PA
18424 Gouldsboro, PA
18424 Thornhurst, PA
18425 Greeley, PA
18426 Greentown, PA
18427 Hamlin, PA
18428 Blooming Grove, PA
18428 Hawley, PA
18428 Lords Valley, PA
18430 Herrick Center, PA
18431 Bethany, PA
18431 Honesdale, PA
18433 Jermyn, PA
18433 Mayfield, PA
18433 Scott Township, PA
18434 Jessup, PA
18435 Lackawaxen, PA
18436 Cobbs Lake Preserve, PA
18436 Jefferson Township, PA
18436 Lake Ariel, PA
18436 Mount Cobb, PA
18436 Roaring Brook Twp, PA
18437 Lake Como, PA
18438 Hawley, PA
18438 Lakeville, PA
18439 Lakewood, PA
18440 La Plume, PA
18441 Clifford Township, PA
18441 Lenoxville, PA
18441 Nicholson, PA
18443 Milanville, PA
18444 Covington Township, PA
18444 Elmhurst Township, PA
18444 Madison Township, PA
18444 Moscow, PA
18444 Roaring Brook Twp, PA
18444 Spring Brook Township, PA
18445 Newfoundland, PA
18445 South Sterling, PA
18446 Clifford Township, PA
18446 Nicholson, PA
18447 Blakely, PA
18447 Dickson Cty, PA
18447 Olyphant, PA
18447 Scott Township, PA
18448 Olyphant, PA
18449 Orson, PA
18451 Paupack, PA
18452 Peckville, PA
18453 Pleasant Mount, PA
18454 Poyntelle, PA
18455 Preston Park, PA
18456 Prompton, PA
18457 Rowland, PA
18458 Shohola, PA
18459 South Canaan, PA
18460 South Sterling, PA
18461 Starlight, PA
18462 Starrucca, PA
18463 Sterling, PA
18464 Tafton, PA
18465 Thompson, PA
18466 Coolbaugh Township, PA
18466 Tobyhanna, PA
18469 Tyler Hill, PA
18470 Clifford Township, PA
18470 Union Dale, PA
18471 Waverly, PA
18472 Waymart, PA
18473 White Mills, PA

185

18501 Scranton, PA
18502 Scranton, PA
18503 Scranton, PA
18504 Scranton, PA
18505 Scranton, PA
18507 Moosic, PA
18507 Scranton, PA
18508 North Scranton, PA
18508 Scranton, PA
18509 Dunmore, PA
18509 Scranton, PA
18510 Dunmore, PA
18510 Scranton, PA
18512 Dunmore, PA
18512 Scranton, PA
18512 Throop, PA
18515 Scranton, PA
18517 Scranton, PA
18517 Taylor, PA
18518 Old Forge, PA
18518 Scranton, PA
18519 Dickson City, PA
18519 Scranton, PA
18540 Scranton, PA
18577 Scranton, PA

186

18601 Beach Haven, PA
18602 Bear Creek, PA
18603 Berwick, PA
18610 Blakeslee, PA
18611 Cambra, PA
18612 Dallas, PA
18612 Monroe Township, PA
18614 Dushore, PA
18614 Forkston Township, PA
18614 Wilmot Township, PA
18615 Falls, PA
18616 Forksville, PA
18617 Glen Lyon, PA
18618 Harveys Lake, PA
18618 Monroe Township, PA
18619 Hillsgrove, PA
18621 Hunlock Creek, PA
18621 Hunlock Township, PA
18622 Huntington Mills, PA
18623 Laceyville, PA
18624 Lake Harmony, PA
18625 Lake Winola, PA
18626 Laporte, PA
18627 Lehman, PA
18628 Lopez, PA
18629 Forkston Township, PA
18629 Mehoopany, PA
18630 Meshoppen, PA
18631 Mifflinville, PA
18632 Mildred, PA
18634 Nanticoke, PA
18635 Nescopeck, PA
18636 Forkston Township, PA
18636 Monroe Township, PA
18636 Noxen, PA
18640 Hughestown, PA
18640 Inkerman, PA
18640 Jenkins Township, PA
18640 Pittston, PA
18640 Pittston Township, PA
18640 Port Griffith, PA
18640 Yatesville, PA
18641 Avoca, PA
18641 Dupont, PA
18641 Pittston, PA
18642 Duryea, PA
18642 Pittston, PA
18643 Exeter, PA
18643 Harding, PA
18643 Pittston, PA
18643 West Pittston, PA
18644 Pittston, PA
18644 West Wyoming, PA
18644 Wyoming, PA
18651 Larksville, PA
18651 Plymouth, PA
18653 Ransom, PA
18654 Shawanese, PA
18655 Mocanaqua, PA
18655 Shickshinny, PA
18656 Sweet Valley, PA
18657 Forkston Township, PA
18657 Mehoopany Twp, PA
18657 Monroe Township, PA
18657 Tunkhannock, PA
18660 Wapwallopen, PA
18661 White Haven, PA
18690 Dallas, PA

187

18701 Wilkes Barre, PA
18702 Bear Creek Township, PA
18702 City Of Wilkes Barre, PA
18702 Hilldale, PA
18702 Hudson, PA
18702 Korn Krest, PA
18702 Plains, PA
18702 Plains Township, PA
18702 Wilkes Barre, PA
18702 Wilkes Barre Township, PA
18703 Wilkes Barre, PA
18704 Courtdale, PA
18704 Edwardsville, PA
18704 Forty Fort, PA
18704 Kingston, PA
18704 Larksville, PA
18704 Pringle, PA
18704 Swoyersville, PA
18704 Wilkes Barre, PA
18705 Hilldale, PA
18705 Hudson, PA
18705 Miners Mill, PA
18705 Parsons, PA
18705 Plains, PA
18705 Plains Township, PA
18705 Wilkes Barre, PA
18706 Ashley, PA
18706 Hanover Township, PA
18706 Laurel Run, PA
18706 Sugar Notch, PA
18706 Warrior Run, PA
18706 Wilkes Barre, PA
18706 Wilkes Barre Township, PA
18707 Mountain Top, PA
18707 Nuangola, PA
18707 Wilkes Barre, PA
18708 Jackson Township, PA
18708 Shavertown, PA
18708 Trucksville, PA
18708 Wilkes Barre, PA
18709 Luzerne, PA
18709 Wilkes Barre, PA
18710 Wilkes Barre, PA
18711 Wilkes Barre, PA
18762 Wilkes Barre, PA
18764 Wilkes Barre, PA
18765 Wilkes Barre, PA
18766 Wilkes Barre, PA
18767 Wilkes Barre, PA
18769 Wilkes Barre, PA
18773 Wilkes Barre, PA

188

18801 Montrose, PA
18810 Athens, PA
18812 Brackney, PA
18813 Brooklyn, PA
18814 Burlington, PA
18815 Camptown, PA
18816 Dimock, PA
18817 East Smithfield, PA
18818 Friendsville, PA
18820 Gibson, PA
18821 Great Bend, PA
18822 Hallstead, PA
18823 Harford, PA
18824 Hop Bottom, PA
18825 Jackson, PA
18826 Kingsley, PA
18827 Lanesboro, PA
18828 Lawton, PA
18828 Rushville, PA
18829 Le Raysville, PA
18830 Little Meadows, PA
18831 Milan, PA

18832 Monroeton, PA
18833 New Albany, PA
18834 New Milford, PA
18837 Rome, PA
18840 Sayre, PA
18840 South Waverly, PA
18842 South Gibson, PA
18843 South Montrose, PA
18844 Springville, PA
18845 Stevensville, PA
18846 Sugar Run, PA
18847 Susquehanna, PA
18848 Burlington Township, PA
18848 Towanda, PA
18850 Ulster, PA
18851 Warren Center, PA
18853 Wyalusing, PA
18854 Wysox, PA

189

18901 Doylestown, PA
18901 New Britain, PA
18902 Doylestown, PA
18910 Bedminster, PA
18911 Blooming Glen, PA
18912 Buckingham, PA
18913 Carversville, PA
18914 Chalfont, PA
18915 Colmar, PA
18916 Danboro, PA
18917 Dublin, PA
18918 Earlington, PA
18920 Erwinna, PA
18921 Ferndale, PA
18922 Forest Grove, PA
18923 Fountainville, PA
18924 Franconia, PA
18925 Furlong, PA
18927 Hilltown, PA
18928 Holicong, PA
18929 Jamison, PA
18930 Kintnersville, PA
18931 Lahaska, PA
18932 Line Lexington, PA
18933 Doylestown, PA
18933 Lumberville, PA
18934 Mechanicsville, PA
18935 Milford Square, PA
18936 Montgomeryville, PA
18938 New Hope, PA
18940 George School, PA
18940 Newtown, PA
18940 Upper Makefield, PA
18942 Ottsville, PA
18943 Penns Park, PA
18944 Perkasie, PA
18946 Pineville, PA
18947 Pipersville, PA
18949 Plumsteadville, PA
18950 Point Pleasant, PA
18951 Quakertown, PA
18953 Revere, PA
18954 Richboro, PA
18954 Southampton, PA
18955 Richlandtown, PA
18956 Rushland, PA
18957 Salford, PA
18958 Salfordville, PA
18960 Sellersville, PA
18962 Silverdale, PA
18963 Solebury, PA
18964 Souderton, PA
18964 Telford, PA
18966 Churchville, PA
18966 Holland, PA
18966 Southampton, PA
18968 Spinnerstown, PA
18969 Indian Valley, PA
18969 Telford, PA
18970 Trumbauersville, PA
18971 Tylersport, PA
18972 Upper Black Eddy, PA
18974 Hartsville, PA
18974 Ivyland, PA
18974 Warminster, PA
18974 Warwick, PA
18976 Warrington, PA
18977 Washington Crossing, PA
18977 Washington Xing, PA
18979 Woxall, PA
18980 Wycombe, PA
18981 Zionhill, PA
18991 Warminster, PA

190

19001 Abington, PA
19001 Ogontz Campus, PA
19001 Roslyn, PA
19002 Ambler, PA
19002 Lower Gwynedd, PA
19002 Maple Glen, PA
19003 Ardmore, PA
19004 Bala Cynwyd, PA
19004 Belmont Hills, PA
19006 Huntingdon Valley, PA
19007 Bristol, PA
19007 Edgely, PA
19007 Tullytown, PA
19007 West Bristol, PA
19008 Broomall, PA
19008 Radnor, PA
19009 Bryn Athyn, PA
19010 Bryn Mawr, PA
19012 Cheltenham, PA
19013 Chester, PA
19013 Chester Township, PA
19013 Eddystone, PA
19013 Upper Chichester, PA
19014 Aston, PA
19014 Chester, PA
19014 Upper Chichester, PA
19015 Brookhaven, PA
19015 Chester, PA
19015 Upland, PA
19016 Chester, PA
19017 Chester Heights, PA
19018 Aldan, PA
19018 Clifton Heights, PA
19018 Primos, PA
19018 Primos Secane, PA
19018 Secane, PA
19019 Philadelphia, PA
19020 Andalusia, PA
19020 Bensalem, PA
19020 Cornwells Heights, PA
19020 Eddington, PA
19021 Bensalem, PA
19021 Croydon, PA
19022 Chester, PA
19022 Crum Lynne, PA
19022 Eddystone, PA
19023 Collingdale, PA
19023 Darby, PA
19025 Dresher, PA
19026 Drexel Hill, PA
19026 Pilgrim Gardens, PA
19027 Elkins Park, PA
19027 Lamott, PA
19027 Melrose, PA
19027 Melrose Park, PA
19028 Edgemont, PA
19029 Essington, PA
19029 Lester, PA
19030 Fairless Hills, PA
19031 Flourtown, PA
19032 Folcroft, PA
19033 Folsom, PA
19033 Milmont Park, PA
19034 Fort Washington, PA
19035 Gladwyne, PA
19036 Glenolden, PA
19037 Glen Riddle, PA
19037 Glen Riddle Lima, PA
19037 Lima, PA
19038 Erdenheim, PA
19038 Glenside, PA
19038 Laverock, PA
19038 Wyndmoor, PA
19039 Gradyville, PA
19040 Hatboro, PA
19040 Uppr Moreland, PA
19041 Haverford, PA
19043 Holmes, PA
19044 Horsham, PA
19046 Foxcroft Square, PA
19046 Hollywood, PA
19046 Jenkintown, PA
19046 Meadowbrook, PA
19046 Rockledge, PA
19046 Rydal, PA
19047 Hulmeville, PA
19047 Langhorne, PA
19047 Penndel, PA
19047 Upper Holland, PA
19048 Fort Washington, PA
19050 East Lansdowne, PA
19050 Lansdowne, PA
19050 Yeadon, PA
19052 Lenni, PA
19053 Feasterville Trevose, PA
19053 Langhorne, PA
19053 Oakford, PA
19053 Trevose, PA
19053 Upper Holland, PA
19054 Fallsington, PA
19054 Levittown, PA
19055 Levittown, PA
19056 Levittown, PA
19056 Newportville, PA
19057 Levittown, PA
19058 Levittown, PA
19060 Boothwyn, PA
19060 Garnet Valley, PA
19060 Marcus Hook, PA
19061 Boothwyn, PA
19061 Garnet Valley, PA
19061 Linwood, PA
19061 Marcus Hook, PA
19061 Ogden, PA
19061 Trainer, PA
19061 Upper Chichester, PA
19063 Elwyn, PA
19063 Garden City, PA
19063 Glen Riddle, PA
19063 Media, PA
19063 Rose Valley, PA
19064 Springfield, PA
19065 Media, PA
19065 Moylan, PA
19066 Merion Station, PA
19067 Morrisville, PA
19067 Yardley, PA
19070 Morton, PA
19070 Ridley, PA
19070 Rutledge, PA
19072 Narberth, PA
19072 Penn Valley, PA
19073 Newtown Square, PA
19074 Norwood, PA
19075 Oreland, PA
19076 Prospect Park, PA
19078 Ridley Park, PA
19079 Sharon Hill, PA
19080 Radnor, PA
19080 Wayne, PA
19081 Swarthmore, PA
19082 Bywood, PA
19082 Highland Park, PA
19082 Kirklyn, PA
19082 Millbourne, PA
19082 Upper Darby, PA
19083 Havertown, PA
19083 Lower Merion, PA
19085 Villanova, PA
19086 Rose Valley, PA
19086 Wallingford, PA
19087 Chesterbrook, PA
19087 Radnor, PA
19087 Saint Davids, PA
19087 St Davids, PA
19087 Strafford, PA
19087 Wayne, PA
19088 Radnor, PA
19088 Wayne, PA
19089 Radnor, PA
19089 Wayne, PA
19090 Willow Grove, PA
19091 Media, PA
19092 Philadelphia, PA
19093 Philadelphia, PA
19094 Woodlyn, PA
19095 Wyncote, PA
19096 Carroll Park, PA
19096 Penn Wynne, PA
19096 Wynnewood, PA
19098 Holmes, PA
19099 Philadelphia, PA

191

19101 Phila, PA
19101 Philadelphia, PA
19102 Middle City East, PA
19102 Phila, PA
19102 Philadelphia, PA
19103 Middle City West, PA
19103 Phila, PA
19103 Philadelphia, PA
19104 Phila, PA
19104 Philadelphia, PA
19105 Phila, PA
19105 Philadelphia, PA
19106 Phila, PA
19106 Philadelphia, PA
19106 William Penn Annex East, PA
19107 Phila, PA
19107 Philadelphia, PA
19107 William Penn Annex West, PA
19108 Phila, PA
19108 Philadelphia, PA
19109 Phila, PA
19109 Philadelphia, PA
19110 Phila, PA
19110 Philadelphia, PA
19111 Phila, PA
19111 Philadelphia, PA
19112 Phila, PA
19112 Philadelphia, PA
19113 Phila, PA
19113 Philadelphia, PA
19114 Phila, PA
19114 Philadelphia, PA
19115 Phila, PA
19115 Philadelphia, PA
19116 Phila, PA
19116 Philadelphia, PA
19118 Phila, PA
19118 Philadelphia, PA
19119 Phila, PA
19119 Philadelphia, PA
19120 Phila, PA
19120 Philadelphia, PA
19121 Phila, PA
19121 Philadelphia, PA
19122 Phila, PA
19122 Philadelphia, PA
19123 Phila, PA
19123 Philadelphia, PA
19124 Phila, PA
19124 Philadelphia, PA
19125 Phila, PA
19125 Philadelphia, PA
19126 Phila, PA
19126 Philadelphia, PA
19127 Manayunk, PA
19127 Phila, PA
19127 Philadelphia, PA
19128 Phila, PA
19128 Philadelphia, PA
19129 Phila, PA
19129 Philadelphia, PA
19130 Phila, PA
19130 Philadelphia, PA
19131 Phila, PA
19131 Philadelphia, PA
19132 Phila, PA
19132 Philadelphia, PA
19133 Phila, PA
19133 Philadelphia, PA
19134 Phila, PA
19134 Philadelphia, PA
19135 Phila, PA
19135 Philadelphia, PA
19136 Phila, PA
19136 Philadelphia, PA
19137 Phila, PA
19137 Philadelphia, PA
19138 Phila, PA
19138 Philadelphia, PA
19139 Phila, PA
19139 Philadelphia, PA
19140 Phila, PA
19140 Philadelphia, PA
19141 Phila, PA
19141 Philadelphia, PA
19142 Phila, PA
19142 Philadelphia, PA
19143 Phila, PA
19143 Philadelphia, PA
19144 Phila, PA
19144 Philadelphia, PA
19145 Phila, PA
19145 Philadelphia, PA
19146 Phila, PA
19146 Philadelphia, PA
19147 Phila, PA
19147 Philadelphia, PA
19148 Phila, PA
19148 Philadelphia, PA
19149 Phila, PA
19149 Philadelphia, PA
19150 Phila, PA
19150 Philadelphia, PA
19151 Overbrook Hills, PA
19151 Phila, PA
19151 Philadelphia, PA
19152 Phila, PA
19152 Philadelphia, PA
19153 Phila, PA
19153 Philadelphia, PA
19154 Phila, PA
19154 Philadelphia, PA
19155 Phila, PA
19155 Philadelphia, PA
19160 Phila, PA
19160 Philadelphia, PA
19161 Phila, PA
19161 Philadelphia, PA
19162 Phila, PA
19162 Philadelphia, PA
19170 Phila, PA
19170 Philadelphia, PA
19171 Phila, PA
19171 Philadelphia, PA
19172 Phila, PA
19172 Philadelphia, PA
19173 Phila, PA
19173 Philadelphia, PA
19175 Phila, PA
19175 Philadelphia, PA
19176 Philadelphia, PA
19177 Phila, PA
19177 Philadelphia, PA
19178 Phila, PA
19178 Philadelphia, PA
19179 Phila, PA
19179 Philadelphia, PA
19181 Phila, PA
19181 Philadelphia, PA
19182 Phila, PA
19182 Philadelphia, PA
19183 Phila, PA
19183 Philadelphia, PA
19184 Phila, PA
19184 Philadelphia, PA
19185 Phila, PA
19185 Philadelphia, PA
19187 Phila, PA
19187 Philadelphia, PA
19188 Phila, PA
19188 Philadelphia, PA
19190 Philadelphia, PA
19191 Phila, PA
19191 Philadelphia, PA
19192 Phila, PA
19192 Philadelphia, PA
19193 Phila, PA
19193 Philadelphia, PA
19194 Philadelphia, PA
19195 Philadelphia, PA
19196 Phila, PA
19196 Philadelphia, PA
19197 Phila, PA
19197 Philadelphia, PA

192

19244 Philadelphia, PA
19255 Philadelphia, PA

193

19301 Paoli, PA
19310 Atglen, PA
19310 Steelville, PA
19311 Avondale, PA
19312 Berwyn, PA
19312 Tredyffrin, PA
19316 Brandamore, PA
19317 Chadds Ford, PA
19318 Chatham, PA
19319 Cheyney, PA
19320 Coatesville, PA
19320 East Fallowfield Township, PA
19320 Romansville, PA
19320 Valley Township, PA
19320 West Bradford, PA
19320 West Brandywine, PA
19330 Cochranville, PA
19331 Concordville, PA
19333 Devon, PA
19335 Downingtown, PA
19335 West Bradford, PA
19339 Concordville, PA
19340 Concordville, PA
19341 Exton, PA
19341 Franklin Center, PA
19342 Glen Mills, PA
19343 Glenmoore, PA
19343 West Brandywine, PA
19344 Honey Brook, PA
19344 West Brandywine, PA
19345 Immaculata, PA
19346 Kelton, PA
19347 Kemblesville, PA
19348 Kennett Square, PA
19350 Landenberg, PA
19351 Lewisville, PA
19352 Lincoln University, PA
19352 New London Township, PA
19352 Newlondon Twp, PA
19353 Exton, PA
19353 Lionville, PA
19354 Lyndell, PA
19355 Frazer, PA
19355 Malvern, PA
19357 Mendenhall, PA
19358 Modena, PA
19360 New London, PA
19362 Nottingham, PA
19363 Oxford, PA
19365 Parkesburg, PA
19366 Pocopson, PA
19367 Pomeroy, PA
19369 Sadsburyville, PA
19371 Suplee, PA
19372 Downingtown, PA
19372 Thorndale, PA
19373 Thornton, PA
19374 Toughkenamon, PA
19375 Unionville, PA
19376 Wagontown, PA
19380 West Bradford, PA
19380 West Chester, PA
19381 West Chester, PA
19382 West Chester, PA
19383 West Chester, PA
19390 Chatham, PA
19390 West Grove, PA
19395 Westtown, PA
19397 Southeastern, PA
19398 Southeastern, PA
19399 Southeastern, PA

194

19401 Black Horse, PA
19401 East Norriton, PA
19401 Norristown, PA
19403 Audubon, PA
19403 Eagleville, PA
19403 East Norriton, PA

19403 Jeffersonville, PA
19403 Norristown, PA
19403 Trooper, PA
19404 Norristown, PA
19405 Bridgeport, PA
19405 Norristown, PA
19406 King Of Prussia, PA
19406 Norristown, PA
19407 Audubon, PA
19407 Norristown, PA
19408 Eagleville, PA
19408 Norristown, PA
19409 Fairview Village, PA
19409 Norristown, PA
19415 Eagleville, PA
19421 Birchrunville, PA
19422 Blue Bell, PA
19422 Center Square, PA
19422 Penllyn, PA
19423 Cedars, PA
19424 Blue Bell, PA
19425 Chester Springs, PA
19426 Collegeville, PA
19426 Trappe, PA
19428 Conshohocken, PA
19428 Gulph Mills, PA
19428 W Cnshohocken, PA
19429 Conshohocken, PA
19430 Creamery, PA
19432 Devault, PA
19435 Frederick, PA
19436 Gwynedd, PA
19436 North Wales, PA
19436 Spring House, PA
19437 Gwynedd Valley, PA
19438 Harleysville, PA
19438 Lower Salford, PA
19440 Hatfield, PA
19440 North Penn, PA
19441 Harleysville, PA
19442 Kimberton, PA
19443 Kulpsville, PA
19444 Lafayette Hill, PA
19444 Miquon, PA
19446 Lansdale, PA
19446 Upper Gwynedd, PA
19450 Lederach, PA
19451 Harleysville, PA
19451 Mainland, PA
19453 Mont Clare, PA
19453 Phoenixville, PA
19454 Gwynedd, PA
19454 North Wales, PA
19455 North Wales, PA
19456 Oaks, PA
19457 Parker Ford, PA
19460 Phoenixville, PA
19462 Plymouth Meeting, PA
19464 Pottstown, PA
19464 Sanatoga, PA
19464 Stowe, PA
19465 Pottstown, PA
19468 Limerick, PA
19468 Linfield, PA
19468 Royersford, PA
19470 Saint Peters, PA
19472 Sassamansville, PA
19473 Collegeville, PA
19473 Delphi, PA
19473 Fruitville, PA
19473 Neiffer, PA
19473 Schwenksville, PA
19474 Skippack, PA
19475 Spring City, PA
19477 North Wales, PA
19477 Spring House, PA
19478 Spring Mount, PA
19480 Eagle, PA
19480 Uwchland, PA
19481 Valley Forge, PA
19482 Valley Forge, PA
19484 Valley Forge, PA
19486 West Point, PA
19490 Worcester, PA
19492 Zieglersville, PA
19492 Zieglerville, PA
19493 Valley Forge, PA
19494 Valley Forge, PA
19495 Valley Forge, PA
19496 Valley Forge, PA

195

19501 Adamstown, PA
19503 Bally, PA
19504 Barto, PA
19505 Bechtelsville, PA
19506 Bernville, PA
19507 Bethel, PA
19508 Birdsboro, PA
19510 Blandon, PA
19511 Bowers, PA
19512 Boyertown, PA
19516 Centerport, PA
19518 Douglassville, PA
19518 Earlville, PA
19519 Earlville, PA
19520 Elverson, PA
19522 Evansville, PA
19522 Fleetwood, PA
19522 Ruscombmanor Twp, PA
19523 Geigertown, PA
19525 Gilbertsville, PA
19526 Hamburg, PA
19529 Kempton, PA
19529 Stony Run, PA
19530 Kutztown, PA
19533 Dauberville, PA
19533 Leesport, PA
19534 Lenhartsville, PA
19535 Limekiln, PA
19536 Lyon Station, PA
19538 Maxatawny, PA
19539 Mertztown, PA
19540 Mohnton, PA
19541 Mohrsville, PA
19542 Monocacy Station, PA
19543 Morgantown, PA
19544 Mount Aetna, PA
19545 New Berlinville, PA
19547 Oley, PA
19548 Pine Forge, PA
19549 Port Clinton, PA
19550 Rehrersburg, PA
19551 Robesonia, PA
19554 Shartlesville, PA
19555 Shoemakersville, PA
19559 Strausstown, PA
19560 Temple, PA
19562 Topton, PA
19564 Virginville, PA
19565 Wernersville, PA
19567 Stouchsburg, PA
19567 Womelsdorf, PA

196

19601 Reading, PA
19602 Reading, PA
19603 Reading, PA
19604 Reading, PA
19605 Laureldale, PA
19605 Muhlenberg Township, PA
19605 Ontelaunee, PA
19605 Reading, PA
19606 Mount Penn, PA
19606 Reading, PA
19606 Reading Station, PA
19607 Reading, PA
19607 Shillington, PA
19608 Reading, PA
19608 Sinking Spring, PA
19608 South Heidelberg Twp, PA
19609 Reading, PA
19609 West Lawn, PA
19610 Reading, PA
19610 Wyomissing, PA
19611 Reading, PA
19611 West Reading, PA
19612 Reading, PA

197

19701 Bear, DE
19702 Christiana, DE
19702 Newark, DE
19703 Claymont, DE
19706 Delaware City, DE
19707 Hockessin, DE
19708 Kirkwood, DE
19709 Middletown, DE
19710 Montchanin, DE
19711 Newark, DE
19712 Newark, DE
19713 Newark, DE
19714 Newark, DE
19715 Newark, DE
19716 Newark, DE
19717 Newark, DE
19718 Newark, DE
19720 Manor, DE
19720 New Castle, DE
19721 New Castle, DE
19725 Newark, DE
19726 Newark, DE
19730 Odessa, DE
19731 Port Penn, DE
19732 Rockland, DE
19733 Saint Georges, DE
19734 Townsend, DE
19735 Winterthur, DE
19736 Yorklyn, DE

198

19801 Wilmington, DE
19802 Wilmington, DE
19803 Talleyville, DE
19803 Wilmington, DE
19804 Newport, DE
19804 Stanton, DE
19804 Wilmington, DE
19805 Elsmere, DE
19805 Wilmington, DE
19806 Wilmington, DE
19807 Greenville, DE
19807 Wilmington, DE
19808 Marshallton, DE
19808 Wilmington, DE
19809 Bellefonte, DE
19809 Edgemoor, DE
19809 Wilmington, DE
19810 Edgemoor, DE
19810 Wilmington, DE
19850 Wilmington, DE
19880 Wilmington, DE
19884 Greenville, DE
19884 Wilmington, DE
19885 Wilmington, DE
19886 Wilmington, DE
19890 Wilmington, DE
19891 Wilmington, DE
19892 Wilmington, DE
19893 Wilmington, DE
19894 Wilmington, DE
19895 Wilmington, DE
19896 Wilmington, DE
19897 Wilmington, DE
19898 Wilmington, DE
19899 Wilmington, DE

199

19901 Dover, DE
19901 Leipsic, DE
19902 Dover, DE
19902 Dover Afb, DE
19902 Dover Air Force Base, DE
19903 Dover, DE
19904 Dover, DE
19905 Dover, DE
19906 Dover, DE
19930 Bethany Beach, DE
19930 S Bethany, DE
19930 South Bethany, DE
19931 Bethel, DE
19933 Bridgeville, DE
19934 Camden, DE
19934 Camden Wyoming, DE
19934 Wyoming, DE
19936 Cheswold, DE
19938 Clayton, DE
19939 Dagsboro, DE
19940 Delmar, DE
19941 Ellendale, DE
19943 Felton, DE
19944 Fenwick Island, DE
19944 Selbyville, DE
19945 Frankford, DE
19946 Frederica, DE
19947 Georgetown, DE
19950 Farmington, DE
19950 Greenwood, DE
19951 Harbeson, DE
19952 Harrington, DE
19953 Hartly, DE
19954 Houston, DE
19955 Kenton, DE
19956 Laurel, DE
19958 Lewes, DE
19960 Lincoln, DE
19961 Little Creek, DE
19962 Magnolia, DE
19963 Milford, DE
19964 Marydel, DE
19966 Long Neck, DE
19966 Millsboro, DE
19967 Millville, DE
19967 Ocean View, DE
19968 Milton, DE
19969 Nassau, DE
19970 Clarksville, DE
19970 Millville, DE
19970 Ocean View, DE
19971 Dewey Beach, DE
19971 Rehoboth Beach, DE
19973 Blades, DE
19973 Seaford, DE
19975 Selbyville, DE
19977 Smyrna, DE
19979 Viola, DE
19980 Woodside, DE

200

20001 Washington, DC
20002 Washington, DC
20003 Washington, DC
20004 Washington, DC
20005 Washington, DC
20006 Washington, DC
20007 Washington, DC
20008 Washington, DC
20009 Washington, DC
20010 Washington, DC
20011 Washington, DC
20012 Washington, DC
20013 Washington, DC
20015 Chevy Chase, DC
20015 Washington, DC
20016 Washington, DC
20017 Washington, DC
20018 Washington, DC
20019 Washington, DC
20020 Washington, DC
20022 Washington, DC
20023 Washington, DC
20024 Fort Lesley J Mcnair, DC
20024 Fort Mcnair, DC
20024 Washington, DC
20026 Washington, DC
20027 Washington, DC
20029 Washington, DC
20030 Washington, DC
20032 Bolling Afb, DC
20032 Washington, DC
20033 Washington, DC
20035 Washington, DC
20036 Washington, DC
20037 Washington, DC
20038 Washington, DC
20039 Washington, DC
20040 Washington, DC
20041 Washington, DC
20042 Washington, DC
20043 Washington, DC
20044 Washington, DC
20045 Washington, DC
20046 Washington, DC
20047 Washington, DC
20049 Washington, DC
20050 Pentagon, DC
20050 Washington, DC
20052 Washington, DC
20053 Washington, DC
20055 Washington, DC
20056 Washington, DC
20057 Washington, DC
20058 Washington, DC
20059 Washington, DC
20060 Washington, DC
20061 Washington, DC
20062 Washington, DC
20063 Washington, DC
20064 Washington, DC
20065 Washington, DC
20066 Washington, DC
20067 Washington, DC
20068 Washington, DC
20069 Washington, DC
20070 Washington, DC
20071 Washington, DC
20073 Washington, DC
20074 Washington, DC
20075 Washington, DC
20076 Washington, DC
20077 Washington, DC
20078 Washington, DC
20080 Washington, DC
20081 Washington, DC
20082 Washington, DC
20088 Washington, DC
20090 Washington, DC
20091 Washington, DC
20097 Washington, DC
20098 Washington, DC

201

20101 Dulles, VA
20102 Dulles, VA
20103 Dulles, VA
20104 Dulles, VA
20105 Aldie, VA
20105 Stone Ridge, VA
20106 Amissville, VA
20106 Viewtown, VA
20108 Manassas, VA
20109 Manassas, VA
20109 Sudley Springs, VA
20110 Manassas, VA
20111 Manassas, VA
20111 Manassas Park, VA
20112 Manassas, VA
20113 Manassas, VA
20113 Manassas Park, VA
20115 Marshall, VA
20116 Marshall, VA
20117 Middleburg, VA
20118 Middleburg, VA
20119 Catlett, VA
20120 Centreville, VA
20120 Sully Station, VA
20121 Centreville, VA
20122 Centreville, VA
20124 Clifton, VA
20128 Orlean, VA
20129 Paeonian Springs, VA
20130 Paris, VA
20131 Philomont, VA
20132 Hillsboro, VA
20132 Purcellville, VA
20134 Hillsboro, VA
20134 Purcellville, VA
20135 Bluemont, VA
20135 Mount Weather, VA
20136 Bristow, VA
20137 Broad Run, VA
20138 Calverton, VA
20139 Casanova, VA
20140 Rectortown, VA
20141 Round Hill, VA
20142 Round Hill, VA
20143 Catharpin, VA
20144 Delaplane, VA
20146 Ashburn, VA
20147 Ashburn, VA
20148 Ashburn, VA
20148 Brambleton, VA
20148 Broadlands, VA
20149 Ashburn, VA
20151 Chantilly, VA
20151 Fairfax, VA
20152 Chantilly, VA
20152 Fairfax, VA
20152 South Riding, VA
20153 Chantilly, VA
20153 Fairfax, VA
20155 Gainesville, VA
20156 Gainesville, VA
20158 Hamilton, VA
20159 Hamilton, VA
20160 Lincoln, VA
20160 Purcellville, VA
20163 Sterling, VA
20164 Sterling, VA
20165 Potomac Falls, VA
20165 Sterling, VA
20166 Arcola, VA
20166 Dulles, VA
20166 Sterling, VA
20167 Sterling, VA
20168 Haymarket, VA
20169 Haymarket, VA
20170 Herndon, VA
20171 Herndon, VA
20171 Oak Hill, VA
20172 Herndon, VA
20175 Leesburg, VA
20176 Lansdowne, VA
20176 Leesburg, VA
20177 Leesburg, VA
20178 Leesburg, VA
20180 Lovettsville, VA
20181 Nokesville, VA
20182 Nokesville, VA
20184 Upperville, VA
20185 Upperville, VA
20186 Warrenton, VA
20187 New Baltimore, VA
20187 Vint Hill Farms, VA
20187 Warrenton, VA
20188 Vint Hill Farms, VA
20188 Warrenton, VA
20189 Dulles, VA
20190 Herndon, VA
20190 Reston, VA
20191 Herndon, VA
20191 Reston, VA
20192 Herndon, VA
20192 Reston, VA
20194 Herndon, VA
20194 Reston, VA
20195 Herndon, VA
20195 Reston, VA
20196 Herndon, VA
20196 Reston, VA
20197 Waterford, VA
20198 The Plains, VA

202

20201 Washington, DC
20202 Washington, DC
20203 Washington, DC
20204 Washington, DC
20206 Washington, DC
20207 Washington, DC
20208 Washington, DC
20210 Washington, DC
20211 Washington, DC
20212 Washington, DC
20213 Washington, DC
20214 Washington, DC
20215 Washington, DC
20216 Washington, DC
20217 Washington, DC
20218 Washington, DC
20219 Washington, DC
20220 Washington, DC
20221 Washington, DC
20222 Washington, DC
20223 Washington, DC
20224 Washington, DC
20226 Washington, DC

20227 Washington, DC
20228 Washington, DC
20229 Washington, DC
20230 Washington, DC
20232 Washington, DC
20233 Washington, DC
20235 Washington, DC
20237 Washington, DC
20238 Washington, DC
20239 Washington, DC
20240 Washington, DC
20241 Washington, DC
20242 Washington, DC
20244 Washington, DC
20245 Washington, DC
20250 Washington, DC
20251 Washington, DC
20252 Washington, DC
20254 Washington, DC
20260 Washington, DC
20261 Washington, DC
20262 Washington, DC
20265 Washington, DC
20266 Washington, DC
20268 Washington, DC
20270 Washington, DC
20277 Washington, DC
20289 Washington, DC
20299 Washington, DC

203

20301 Pentagon, DC
20301 Washington, DC
20303 Washington, DC
20306 Washington, DC
20310 Washington, DC
20314 Washington, DC
20317 Washington, DC
20318 Washington, DC
20319 Fort Mcnair, DC
20319 Washington, DC
20330 Washington, DC
20340 Washington, DC
20350 Washington, DC
20355 Washington, DC
20370 Navy Annex, DC
20370 Washington, DC
20372 Washington, DC
20373 Anacostia, DC
20373 Joint Base Anacostia Bolling, DC
20373 Naval Anacost Annex, DC
20373 Washington, DC
20374 Washington, DC
20374 Washington Navy Yard, DC
20375 Washington, DC
20376 Naval Sea Systems Command, DC
20376 Washington, DC
20376 Washington Navy Yard, DC
20380 Washington, DC
20388 Washington, DC
20388 Washington Navy Yard, DC
20389 Washington, DC
20390 Us Marine Corps Barracks, DC
20390 Washington, DC
20391 Washington, DC
20391 Washington Navy Yard, DC
20392 Washington, DC
20393 Washington, DC
20394 Washington, DC
20395 Washington, DC
20398 Washington, DC
20398 Washington Navy Yard, DC

204

20401 Washington, DC
20402 Washington, DC
20403 Washington, DC
20404 Washington, DC
20405 Washington, DC
20406 Washington, DC
20407 Washington, DC
20408 Washington, DC
20409 Washington, DC
20410 Washington, DC
20411 Washington, DC
20412 Washington, DC
20413 Washington, DC
20414 Washington, DC
20415 Washington, DC
20416 Washington, DC
20417 Washington, DC
20418 Washington, DC
20419 Washington, DC
20420 Washington, DC
20421 Washington, DC
20422 Washington, DC
20423 Washington, DC
20424 Washington, DC
20425 Washington, DC
20426 Washington, DC
20427 Washington, DC
20428 Washington, DC
20429 Washington, DC
20431 Washington, DC
20433 Washington, DC
20434 Washington, DC
20435 Washington, DC
20436 Washington, DC
20437 Washington, DC
20439 Washington, DC
20440 Washington, DC
20441 Washington, DC
20442 Washington, DC
20444 Washington, DC
20447 Washington, DC
20451 Washington, DC
20453 Washington, DC
20456 Washington, DC
20460 Washington, DC
20463 Washington, DC
20468 Washington, DC
20469 Washington, DC
20470 Washington, DC
20472 Washington, DC

205

20500 Washington, DC
20501 Washington, DC
20502 Washington, DC
20503 Washington, DC
20504 Washington, DC
20505 Washington, DC
20506 Washington, DC
20507 Washington, DC
20508 Washington, DC
20509 Washington, DC
20510 Washington, DC
20511 Washington, DC
20515 Washington, DC
20520 Washington, DC
20521 Washington, DC
20522 Washington, DC
20523 Washington, DC
20524 Washington, DC
20525 Washington, DC
20526 Washington, DC
20527 Washington, DC
20528 Washington, DC
20529 Washington, DC
20530 Washington, DC
20531 Washington, DC
20532 Washington, DC
20533 Washington, DC
20534 Washington, DC
20535 Washington, DC
20536 Washington, DC
20537 Washington, DC
20538 Washington, DC
20539 Washington, DC
20540 Washington, DC
20541 Washington, DC
20542 Washington, DC
20543 Washington, DC
20544 Washington, DC
20546 Washington, DC
20547 Washington, DC
20548 Washington, DC
20549 Washington, DC
20551 Washington, DC
20552 Washington, DC
20553 Washington, DC
20554 Washington, DC
20555 Washington, DC
20557 Washington, DC
20558 Washington, DC
20559 Washington, DC
20560 Washington, DC
20565 Washington, DC
20566 Washington, DC
20570 Washington, DC
20571 Washington, DC
20572 Washington, DC
20573 Washington, DC
20575 Washington, DC
20576 Washington, DC
20577 Washington, DC
20578 Washington, DC
20579 Washington, DC
20580 Washington, DC
20581 Washington, DC
20585 Washington, DC
20586 Washington, DC
20588 Cheltenham, MD
20588 Columbia, MD
20588 Dhs, MD
20590 Washington, DC
20591 Washington, DC
20593 Washington, DC
20594 Washington, DC
20597 Washington, DC
20598 Alexandria, VA
20598 Arlington, VA
20598 Chantilly, VA
20598 Dhs, VA
20598 Fairfax, VA
20598 Falls Church, VA
20598 Herndon, VA
20598 Lorton, VA
20598 Mc Lean, VA
20598 Mclean, VA
20598 Reston, VA
20598 Springfield, VA
20598 Sterling, VA
20599 Washington, DC

206

20601 Waldorf, MD
20602 Saint Charles, MD
20602 Waldorf, MD
20603 Saint Charles, MD
20603 Waldorf, MD
20604 Saint Charles, MD
20604 Waldorf, MD
20606 Abell, MD
20607 Accokeek, MD
20608 Aquasco, MD
20608 Eagle Harbor, MD
20609 Avenue, MD
20610 Barstow, MD
20611 Bel Alton, MD
20612 Benedict, MD
20613 Brandywine, MD
20615 Broomes Island, MD
20616 Bryans Road, MD
20617 Bryantown, MD
20618 Bushwood, MD
20619 California, MD
20620 Callaway, MD
20621 Chaptico, MD
20621 Maddox, MD
20622 Charlotte Hall, MD
20623 Cheltenham, MD
20624 Clements, MD
20625 Cobb Island, MD
20626 Coltons Point, MD
20627 Compton, MD
20628 Dameron, MD
20629 Dowell, MD
20630 Drayden, MD
20632 Faulkner, MD
20634 Great Mills, MD
20635 Helen, MD
20636 Hollywood, MD
20637 Hughesville, MD
20639 Huntingtown, MD
20640 Indian Head, MD
20640 Pisgah, MD
20643 Ironsides, MD
20645 Issue, MD
20645 Swan Point, MD
20646 Dentsville, MD
20646 La Plata, MD
20650 Leonardtown, MD
20653 Lexington Park, MD
20656 Loveville, MD
20657 Lusby, MD
20658 Marbury, MD
20658 Rison, MD
20659 Mechanicsville, MD
20660 Morganza, MD
20661 Mount Victoria, MD
20662 Nanjemoy, MD
20664 Newburg, MD
20667 Park Hall, MD
20670 Patuxent River, MD
20674 Piney Point, MD
20675 Pomfret, MD
20676 Port Republic, MD
20677 Port Tobacco, MD
20678 Dares Beach, MD
20678 Prince Frederick, MD
20680 Ridge, MD
20682 Rock Point, MD
20684 Saint Inigoes, MD
20685 Saint Leonard, MD
20686 Saint Marys, MD
20686 Saint Marys City, MD
20687 Scotland, MD
20688 Solomons, MD
20689 Sunderland, MD
20690 Tall Timbers, MD
20692 Valley Lee, MD
20693 Welcome, MD
20695 White Plains, MD
20697 Southern Md Facility, MD

207

20701 Annapolis Junction, MD
20703 Lanham, MD
20703 Lanham Seabrook, MD
20704 Beltsville, MD
20705 Beltsville, MD
20705 Calverton, MD
20706 Glenarden, MD
20706 Lanham, MD
20706 Lanham Seabrook, MD
20706 Seabrook, MD
20707 Laurel, MD
20708 Laurel, MD
20708 Montpelier, MD
20709 Laurel, MD
20709 Montpelier, MD
20710 Bladensburg, MD
20711 Lothian, MD
20712 Mount Rainier, MD
20714 Holland Point, MD
20714 North Beach, MD
20714 Rose Haven, MD
20715 Bowie, MD
20716 Bowie, MD
20716 Mitchellville, MD
20717 Bowie, MD
20717 Mitchellville, MD
20718 Bowie, MD
20719 Bowie, MD
20720 Bowie, MD
20721 Bowie, MD
20721 Mitchellville, MD
20722 Brentwood, MD
20722 Colmar Manor, MD
20722 Cottage City, MD
20722 N Brentwood, MD
20722 No Brentwood, MD
20722 North Brentwood, MD
20723 Laurel, MD
20723 Scaggsville, MD
20724 Laurel, MD
20724 Maryland City, MD
20724 Md City, MD
20724 Russett, MD
20725 Laurel, MD
20726 Laurel, MD
20731 Capitol Heights, MD
20732 Chesapeake Beach, MD
20733 Churchton, MD
20735 Clinton, MD
20736 Owings, MD
20737 Riverdale, MD
20737 Riverdale Park, MD
20738 Riverdale, MD
20740 Berwyn Heights, MD
20740 College Park, MD
20741 College Park, MD
20742 College Park, MD
20743 Capitol Heights, MD
20743 Fairmount Heights, MD
20743 Seat Pleasant, MD
20744 Fort Washington, MD
20745 Forest Heights, MD
20745 Oxon Hill, MD
20746 Camp Springs, MD
20746 Hillcrest Hgts, MD
20746 Morningside, MD
20746 Suitland, MD
20747 District Heights, MD
20747 Forestville, MD
20748 Camp Springs, MD
20748 Hillcrest Heights, MD
20748 Hillcrest Hgts, MD
20748 Marlow Heights, MD
20748 Temple Hills, MD
20749 Fort Washington, MD
20750 Oxon Hill, MD
20751 Deale, MD
20752 Suitland, MD
20753 District Heights, MD
20754 Dunkirk, MD
20755 Fort George G Meade, MD
20757 Temple Hills, MD
20758 Friendship, MD
20759 Fulton, MD
20762 Andrews Air Force Base, MD
20762 Jb Andrews, MD
20763 Savage, MD
20764 Shady Side, MD
20765 Galesville, MD
20768 Greenbelt, MD
20769 Glenn Dale, MD
20770 Greenbelt, MD
20771 Greenbelt, MD
20772 Upper Marlboro, MD
20774 Glenarden, MD
20774 Kettering, MD
20774 Largo, MD
20774 Springdale, MD
20774 Upper Marlboro, MD
20774 Upr Marlboro, MD
20775 Upper Marlboro, MD
20776 Harwood, MD
20777 Highland, MD
20778 West River, MD
20779 Tracys Landing, MD
20781 Hyattsville, MD
20782 Chillum, MD
20782 Hyattsville, MD
20782 University Park, MD
20782 West Hyattsville, MD
20783 Adelphi, MD
20783 Hyattsville, MD
20784 Cheverly, MD
20784 Hyattsville, MD
20784 Landover Hills, MD
20784 New Carrollton, MD
20785 Cheverly, MD
20785 Hyattsville, MD
20785 Landover, MD
20785 North Englewood, MD
20787 Hyattsville, MD
20787 Langley Park, MD
20788 Hyattsville, MD
20788 West Hyattsville, MD
20790 Capitol Heights, MD
20792 Largo, MD
20792 Upper Marlboro, MD
20794 Jessup, MD
20797 Southern Md Facility, MD
20799 Capitol Heights, MD

208

20810 Bethesda, MD
20811 Bethesda, MD
20812 Glen Echo, MD
20813 Bethesda, MD
20814 Bethesda, MD
20815 Bethesda, MD
20815 Chevy Chase, MD
20815 Chevy Chase Village, MD
20815 Martins Additions, MD
20815 North Chevy Chase, MD
20816 Bethesda, MD
20817 Bethesda, MD
20817 Westlake, MD
20818 Cabin John, MD
20824 Bethesda, MD
20825 Bethesda, MD
20825 Chevy Chase, MD
20827 Bethesda, MD
20827 W Bethesda, MD
20827 Westlake, MD
20830 Olney, MD
20832 Olney, MD
20833 Brookeville, MD
20837 Poolesville, MD
20838 Barnesville, MD
20839 Beallsville, MD
20841 Boyds, MD
20842 Dickerson, MD
20847 Rockville, MD
20848 Rockville, MD
20849 Rockville, MD
20850 Potomac, MD
20850 Rockville, MD
20851 Rockville, MD
20852 North Bethesda, MD
20852 Rockville, MD
20853 Rockville, MD
20854 Potomac, MD
20854 Rockville, MD
20855 Derwood, MD
20855 Rockville, MD
20857 Rockville, MD
20859 Potomac, MD
20859 Rockville, MD
20860 Sandy Spring, MD
20861 Ashton, MD
20862 Brinklow, MD
20866 Burtonsville, MD
20868 Spencerville, MD
20871 Clarksburg, MD
20871 Hyattstown, MD
20872 Damascus, MD
20874 Darnestown, MD
20874 Germantown, MD
20875 Germantown, MD
20876 Germantown, MD
20877 Gaithersburg, MD
20877 Montgomery Village, MD
20878 Darnestown, MD
20878 Gaithersburg, MD
20878 N Potomac, MD
20878 No Potomac, MD
20878 North Potomac, MD
20879 Gaithersburg, MD
20879 Montgomery Village, MD
20880 Washington Grove, MD
20882 Gaithersburg, MD
20882 Laytonsville, MD
20883 Gaithersburg, MD
20884 Gaithersburg, MD
20885 Gaithersburg, MD
20886 Gaithersburg, MD
20886 Montgomery Village, MD
20889 Bethesda, MD
20891 Kensington, MD
20892 Bethesda, MD
20894 Bethesda, MD
20895 Kensington, MD

20896 Garrett Park, MD
20897 Suburb Maryland Fac, MD
20898 Gaithersburg, MD
20899 Gaithersburg, MD

209

20901 Silver Spring, MD
20901 Takoma Park, MD
20902 Silver Spring, MD
20902 Wheaton, MD
20903 Silver Spring, MD
20904 Colesville, MD
20904 Silver Spring, MD
20905 Colesville, MD
20905 Silver Spring, MD
20906 Aspen Hill, MD
20906 Silver Spring, MD
20907 Silver Spring, MD
20908 Silver Spring, MD
20910 Silver Spring, MD
20911 Silver Spring, MD
20912 Silver Spring, MD
20912 Takoma Park, MD
20913 Silver Spring, MD
20913 Takoma Park, MD
20914 Colesville, MD
20914 Silver Spring, MD
20915 Silver Spring, MD
20915 Wheaton, MD
20916 Aspen Hill, MD
20916 Silver Spring, MD
20918 Silver Spring, MD
20993 Silver Spring, MD
20997 Silver Spring, MD

210

21001 Aberdeen, MD
21005 Aberdeen Proving Ground, MD
21009 Abingdon, MD
21010 Aberdeen Proving Ground, MD
21010 Gunpowder, MD
21012 Arnold, MD
21013 Baldwin, MD
21014 Bel Air, MD
21015 Bel Air, MD
21017 Belcamp, MD
21018 Benson, MD
21020 Boring, MD
21022 Brooklandville, MD
21023 Butler, MD
21027 Chase, MD
21028 Churchville, MD
21029 Clarksville, MD
21030 Cockeysville, MD
21030 Cockysvil, MD
21030 Hunt Valley, MD
21031 Hunt Valley, MD
21032 Crownsville, MD
21034 Darlington, MD
21035 Davidsonville, MD
21036 Dayton, MD
21037 Edgewater, MD
21040 Edgewood, MD
21041 Ellicott City, MD
21042 Ellicott City, MD
21043 Daniels, MD
21043 Ellicott City, MD
21043 Ilchester, MD
21043 Oella, MD
21044 Columbia, MD
21045 Columbia, MD
21046 Columbia, MD
21047 Fallston, MD
21048 Finksburg, MD
21048 Patapsco, MD
21050 Forest Hill, MD
21051 Fork, MD
21052 Fort Howard, MD
21053 Freeland, MD
21054 Gambrills, MD
21056 Gibson Island, MD
21057 Glen Arm, MD
21060 Glen Burnie, MD
21061 Glen Burnie, MD
21062 Glen Burnie, MD
21065 Cockys Ht Vly, MD
21065 Hunt Valley, MD
21071 Glyndon, MD
21074 Greenmount, MD
21074 Hampstead, MD
21075 Elkridge, MD
21076 Hanover, MD
21077 Harmans, MD
21078 Havre De Grace, MD
21082 Hydes, MD
21084 Jarrettsville, MD
21085 Joppa, MD
21087 Bradshaw, MD
21087 Kingsville, MD
21088 Lineboro, MD
21088 Manchester, MD
21090 Linthicum, MD
21090 Linthicum Heights, MD
21092 Long Green, MD
21093 Lutherville, MD
21093 Lutherville Timonium, MD
21093 Timonium, MD
21094 Lutherville, MD
21094 Lutherville Timonium, MD
21094 Luthvle Timon, MD
21094 Timonium, MD

211

21102 Lineboro, MD
21102 Manchester, MD
21102 Millers, MD
21104 Henryton, MD
21104 Marriottsville, MD
21104 Woodstock, MD
21105 Maryland Line, MD
21106 Mayo, MD
21108 Millersville, MD
21111 Hereford, MD
21111 Monkton, MD
21113 Odenton, MD
21114 Crofton, MD
21117 Garrison, MD
21117 Owings Mills, MD
21120 Bentley Springs, MD
21120 Parkton, MD
21122 Lake Shore, MD
21122 Pasadena, MD
21122 Riviera Beach, MD
21123 Lake Shore, MD
21123 Pasadena, MD
21123 Riviera Beach, MD
21128 Perry Hall, MD
21130 Perryman, MD
21131 Jacksonville, MD
21131 Phoenix, MD
21132 Pylesville, MD
21133 Mcdonogh Run, MD
21133 Randallstown, MD
21136 Glyndon, MD
21136 Reisterstown, MD
21139 Riderwood, MD
21140 Riva, MD
21144 Severn, MD
21146 Severna Park, MD
21150 Simpsonville, MD
21152 Glencoe, MD
21152 Sparks, MD
21152 Sparks Glencoe, MD
21153 Stevenson, MD
21154 Street, MD
21155 Fowbelsburg, MD
21155 Upperco, MD
21156 Upper Falls, MD
21157 Westminster, MD
21158 Westminster, MD
21160 Cardiff, MD
21160 Whiteford, MD
21161 White Hall, MD
21162 White Marsh, MD
21163 Granite, MD
21163 Woodstock, MD

212

21201 Baltimore, MD
21202 Baltimore, MD
21202 East Case, MD
21203 Baltimore, MD
21204 Baltimore, MD
21204 Eudowood, MD
21204 Loch Raven, MD
21204 Ruxton, MD
21204 Towson, MD
21205 Baltimore, MD
21206 Baltimore, MD
21206 Raspeburg, MD
21207 Baltimore, MD
21207 Gwynn Oak, MD
21207 Pikesville, MD
21207 Woodlawn, MD
21208 Baltimore, MD
21208 Pikesville, MD
21209 Baltimore, MD
21209 Mount Washington, MD
21210 Baltimore, MD
21210 Roland Park, MD
21211 Baltimore, MD
21212 Baltimore, MD
21212 Govans, MD
21213 Baltimore, MD
21213 Clifton, MD
21214 Baltimore, MD
21215 Arlington, MD
21215 Baltimore, MD
21216 Baltimore, MD
21217 Baltimore, MD
21217 Druid, MD
21218 Baltimore, MD
21219 Baltimore, MD
21219 Edgemere, MD
21219 Sparrows Point, MD
21220 Baltimore, MD
21220 Middle River, MD
21221 Baltimore, MD
21221 Essex, MD
21222 Baltimore, MD
21222 Dundalk, MD
21223 Baltimore, MD
21223 Franklin, MD
21224 Baltimore, MD
21224 Highlandtown, MD
21225 Baltimore, MD
21225 Brooklyn, MD
21225 Brooklyn Park, MD
21226 Baltimore, MD
21226 Carvel Beach, MD
21226 Chestnut Hill Cove, MD
21226 Clearwater Beach, MD
21226 Curtis Bay, MD
21226 Greenland Beach, MD
21226 Orchard Beach, MD
21226 Stoney Beach, MD
21227 Arbutus, MD
21227 Baltimore, MD
21227 Halethorpe, MD
21227 Lansdowne, MD
21228 Baltimore, MD
21228 Catonsville, MD
21229 Baltimore, MD
21229 Carroll, MD
21230 Baltimore, MD
21231 Baltimore, MD
21233 Baltimore, MD
21234 Baltimore, MD
21234 Parkville, MD
21235 Baltimore, MD
21236 Baltimore, MD
21236 Nottingham, MD
21237 Baltimore, MD
21237 Rosedale, MD
21239 Baltimore, MD
21239 Idlewylde, MD
21239 Loch Hill, MD
21239 Northwood, MD
21240 Baltimore, MD
21240 Millersville, MD
21241 Baltimore, MD
21244 Baltimore, MD
21244 Windsor Mill, MD
21250 Baltimore, MD
21251 Baltimore, MD
21252 Baltimore, MD
21252 Towson, MD
21263 Baltimore, MD
21264 Baltimore, MD
21270 Baltimore, MD
21273 Baltimore, MD
21275 Baltimore, MD
21278 Baltimore, MD
21279 Baltimore, MD
21280 Baltimore, MD
21281 Baltimore, MD
21282 Baltimore, MD
21282 Pikesville, MD
21284 Baltimore, MD
21284 Loch Raven, MD
21284 Towson, MD
21285 Baltimore, MD
21285 Towson, MD
21286 Baltimore, MD
21286 Loch Raven, MD
21286 Towson, MD
21287 Baltimore, MD
21288 Baltimore, MD
21289 Baltimore, MD
21290 Baltimore, MD
21297 Baltimore, MD
21298 Baltimore, MD

214

21401 Annapolis, MD
21401 Cape Saint Claire, MD
21402 Annapolis, MD
21402 Naval Academy, MD
21402 North Severn Village, MD
21403 Annapolis, MD
21403 Highland Bch, MD
21404 Annapolis, MD
21405 Annapolis, MD
21405 Sherwood Forest, MD
21409 Annapolis, MD
21411 Annapolis, MD
21412 Annapolis, MD

215

21501 Cumberland, MD
21502 Cresaptown, MD
21502 Cumberland, MD
21502 Lavale, MD
21503 Cumberland, MD
21504 Cumberland, MD
21504 Lavale, MD
21505 Cresaptown, MD
21505 Cumberland, MD
21520 Accident, MD
21521 Barton, MD
21522 Bittinger, MD
21523 Bloomington, MD
21524 Corriganville, MD
21528 Eckhart Mines, MD
21529 Ellerslie, MD
21530 Flintstone, MD
21531 Friendsville, MD
21532 Frostburg, MD
21532 Midland, MD
21536 Grantsville, MD
21536 Jennings, MD
21538 Kitzmiller, MD
21538 Shallmar, MD
21539 Lonaconing, MD
21540 Luke, MD
21540 Westernport, MD
21541 Mc Henry, MD
21541 Sang Run, MD
21542 Midland, MD
21543 Midlothian, MD
21545 Mount Savage, MD
21550 Crellin, MD
21550 Deer Park, MD
21550 Hutton, MD
21550 Loch Lynn Heights, MD
21550 Mnt Lake Park, MD
21550 Mountain Lake Park, MD
21550 Mt Lake Park, MD
21550 Oakland, MD
21555 Oldtown, MD
21556 Pinto, MD
21557 Rawlings, MD
21560 Spring Gap, MD
21561 Swanton, MD
21562 Mccoole, MD
21562 Westernport, MD

216

21601 Easton, MD
21607 Barclay, MD
21609 Bethlehem, MD
21610 Betterton, MD
21612 Bozman, MD
21613 Cambridge, MD
21617 Centreville, MD
21619 Chester, MD
21620 Chestertown, MD
21622 Church Creek, MD
21623 Church Hill, MD
21624 Claiborne, MD
21625 Cordova, MD
21626 Crapo, MD
21627 Crocheron, MD
21628 Crumpton, MD
21629 Denton, MD
21631 East New Market, MD
21632 Federalsburg, MD
21634 Fishing Creek, MD
21635 Galena, MD
21635 Golts, MD
21636 Goldsboro, MD
21638 Grasonville, MD
21639 Greensboro, MD
21640 Henderson, MD
21641 Hillsboro, MD
21643 Hurlock, MD
21644 Ingleside, MD
21645 Kennedyville, MD
21647 Mcdaniel, MD
21648 Madison, MD
21649 Marydel, MD
21650 Massey, MD
21651 Millington, MD
21652 Neavitt, MD
21653 Newcomb, MD
21654 Oxford, MD
21655 Preston, MD
21656 Church Hill, MD
21656 Price, MD
21657 Queen Anne, MD
21658 Queenstown, MD
21659 Brookview, MD
21659 Eldorado, MD
21659 Galestown, MD
21659 Rhodesdale, MD
21660 Ridgely, MD
21661 Rock Hall, MD
21662 Royal Oak, MD
21663 Saint Michaels, MD
21664 Secretary, MD
21665 Sherwood, MD
21666 Stevensville, MD
21667 Still Pond, MD
21668 Sudlersville, MD
21669 Taylors Island, MD
21670 Templeville, MD
21671 Tilghman, MD
21672 Toddville, MD
21673 Trappe, MD
21675 Wingate, MD
21676 Wittman, MD
21677 Woolford, MD
21678 Lynch, MD
21678 Worton, MD
21679 Wye Mills, MD
21690 Chestertown, MD

217

21701 Frederick, MD
21701 Lewistown, MD
21702 Fort Detrick, MD
21702 Frederick, MD
21703 Frederick, MD
21704 Frederick, MD
21704 Urbana, MD
21705 Frederick, MD
21709 Frederick, MD
21710 Adamstown, MD
21710 Doubs, MD
21711 Big Pool, MD
21713 Boonsboro, MD
21714 Braddock Heights, MD
21715 Brownsville, MD
21716 Brunswick, MD
21717 Buckeystown, MD
21718 Burkittsville, MD
21719 Cascade, MD
21719 Fort Ritchie, MD
21719 Highfield, MD
21720 Cavetown, MD
21721 Chewsville, MD
21722 Big Spring, MD
21722 Clear Spring, MD
21723 Cooksville, MD
21727 Emmitsburg, MD
21733 Fairplay, MD
21733 St James, MD
21734 Funkstown, MD
21737 Glenelg, MD
21738 Glenwood, MD
21740 Hagerstown, MD
21741 Hagerstown, MD
21742 Hagerstown, MD
21746 Hagerstown, MD
21747 Hagerstown, MD
21749 Hagerstown, MD
21750 Hancock, MD
21754 Ijamsville, MD
21755 Jefferson, MD
21756 Keedysville, MD
21757 Detour, MD
21757 Keymar, MD
21757 Middleburg, MD
21758 Brunswick, MD
21758 Knoxville, MD
21759 Ladiesburg, MD
21762 Libertytown, MD
21765 Lisbon, MD
21766 Little Orleans, MD
21767 Maugansville, MD
21769 Middletown, MD
21770 Monrovia, MD
21771 Mount Airy, MD
21773 Myersville, MD
21774 New Market, MD
21775 New Midway, MD
21776 New Windsor, MD
21777 Point Of Rocks, MD
21778 Rocky Ridge, MD
21779 Gapland, MD
21779 Rohrersville, MD
21780 Sabillasville, MD
21781 Saint James, MD
21782 Sharpsburg, MD
21783 Smithsburg, MD
21784 Eldersburg, MD
21784 Gaither, MD
21784 Sykesville, MD
21787 Taneytown, MD
21788 Graceham, MD
21788 Thurmont, MD
21790 Tuscarora, MD
21791 Linwood, MD
21791 Union Bridge, MD
21792 Unionville, MD
21793 Walkersville, MD
21794 West Friendship, MD
21795 Williamsport, MD
21797 Woodbine, MD
21798 Woodsboro, MD

218

21801 Salisbury, MD
21802 Salisbury, MD
21803 Salisbury, MD
21804 Salisbury, MD
21810 Allen, MD
21811 Berlin, MD
21811 Ocean Pines, MD
21811 Ocean Pnes, MD
21813 Bishopville, MD
21814 Bivalve, MD
21817 Crisfield, MD
21821 Chance, MD
21821 Dames Quarter, MD

21821 Deal Island, MD
21821 Wenona, MD
21822 Eden, MD
21824 Ewell, MD
21826 Fruitland, MD
21829 Girdletree, MD
21830 Hebron, MD
21835 Linkwood, MD
21836 Manokin, MD
21837 Mardela, MD
21837 Mardela Springs, MD
21838 Marion, MD
21838 Marion Station, MD
21840 Nanticoke, MD
21841 Newark, MD
21842 Ocean City, MD
21843 Ocean City, MD
21849 Parsonsburg, MD
21850 Pittsville, MD
21851 Pocomoke City, MD
21852 Powellville, MD
21853 Princess Anne, MD
21856 Quantico, MD
21857 Rehobeth, MD
21861 Sharptown, MD
21862 Showell, MD
21863 Snow Hill, MD
21864 Stockton, MD
21865 Tyaskin, MD
21866 Tylerton, MD
21867 Fairmount, MD
21867 Upper Fairmount, MD
21867 Upper Hill, MD
21869 Vienna, MD
21871 Westover, MD
21872 Whaleyville, MD
21874 Willards, MD
21875 Delmar, MD
21890 Westover, MD

219

21901 North East, MD
21902 Perry Point, MD
21903 Perryville, MD
21904 Bainbridge, MD
21904 Port Deposit, MD
21911 Rising Sun, MD
21912 Warwick, MD
21913 Cecilton, MD
21914 Charlestown, MD
21915 Chesapeake City, MD
21916 Childs, MD
21917 Colora, MD
21918 Conowingo, MD
21919 Earleville, MD
21920 Elk Mills, MD
21921 Elkton, MD
21922 Elkton, MD
21930 Georgetown, MD

220

22003 Annandale, VA
22009 Burke, VA
22009 Springfield, VA
22015 Burke, VA
22015 Springfield, VA
22025 Dumfries, VA
22025 Montclair, VA
22026 Dumfries, VA
22026 Southbridge, VA
22027 Dunn Loring, VA
22027 Vienna, VA
22030 Fairfax, VA
22031 Fairfax, VA
22032 Fairfax, VA
22033 Fairfax, VA
22034 Fairfax, VA
22035 Fairfax, VA
22036 Fairfax, VA
22037 Fairfax, VA
22038 Fairfax, VA
22039 Fairfax Station, VA
22039 Fx Station, VA
22040 Falls Church, VA
22041 Baileys Crossroads, VA
22041 Falls Church, VA
22042 Falls Church, VA
22042 Mosby, VA
22043 Falls Church, VA
22043 Pimmit, VA
22044 Falls Church, VA
22044 Seven Corners, VA
22046 Falls Church, VA
22060 Fort Belvoir, VA
22060 Ft Belvoir, VA
22066 Great Falls, VA
22067 Greenway, VA
22067 Mc Lean, VA
22079 Lorton, VA
22079 Mason Neck, VA
22081 Merrifield, VA
22082 Merrifield, VA
22095 Herndon, VA
22095 Reston, VA
22096 Herndon, VA
22096 Reston, VA

221

22101 Mc Lean, VA
22101 Mclean, VA
22102 Mc Lean, VA
22102 Mclean, VA
22102 Tysons, VA
22102 Tysons Corner, VA
22102 West Mclean, VA
22103 Mc Lean, VA
22103 Mclean, VA
22103 West Mclean, VA
22106 Mc Lean, VA
22106 Mclean, VA
22107 Mc Lean, VA
22108 Mc Lean, VA
22109 Mc Lean, VA
22116 Merrifield, VA
22118 Merrifield, VA
22119 Merrifield, VA
22121 Mount Vernon, VA
22122 Newington, VA
22124 Oakton, VA
22124 Vienna, VA
22125 Occoquan, VA
22134 Quantico, VA
22135 Quantico, VA
22150 Springfield, VA
22151 North Springfield, VA
22151 Springfield, VA
22152 Springfield, VA
22152 West Springfield, VA
22153 Springfield, VA
22156 Springfield, VA
22158 Springfield, VA
22159 Springfield, VA
22160 Springfield, VA
22161 Springfield, VA
22172 Triangle, VA
22180 Vienna, VA
22181 Vienna, VA
22182 Tysons, VA
22182 Tysons Corner, VA
22182 Vienna, VA
22183 Vienna, VA
22185 Oakton, VA
22185 Vienna, VA
22191 Woodbridge, VA
22192 Lake Ridge, VA
22192 Prince William, VA
22192 Woodbridge, VA
22193 Dale City, VA
22193 Woodbridge, VA
22194 Woodbridge, VA
22195 Woodbridge, VA
22199 Lorton, VA

222

22201 Arlington, VA
22202 Arlington, VA
22203 Arlington, VA
22204 Arlington, VA
22205 Arlington, VA
22206 Arlington, VA
22207 Arlington, VA
22209 Arlington, VA
22209 Rosslyn, VA
22210 Arlington, VA
22211 Fort Myer, VA
22211 Ft Myer, VA
22212 Arlington, VA
22213 Arlington, VA
22214 Arlington, VA
22215 Arlington, VA
22216 Arlington, VA
22217 Arlington, VA
22219 Arlington, VA
22225 Arlington, VA
22226 Arlington, VA
22227 Arlington, VA
22230 Arlington, VA
22240 Arlington, VA
22241 Arlington, VA
22242 Arlington, VA
22243 Arlington, VA
22244 Arlington, VA
22245 Arlington, VA
22246 Arlington, VA

223

22301 Alexandria, VA
22301 Potomac, VA
22302 Alexandria, VA
22303 Alexandria, VA
22303 Jefferson Manor, VA
22304 Alexandria, VA
22305 Alexandria, VA
22306 Alexandria, VA
22306 Community, VA
22307 Alexandria, VA
22307 Belleview, VA
22308 Alexandria, VA
22308 Fort Hunt, VA
22309 Alexandria, VA
22309 Engleside, VA
22310 Alexandria, VA
22310 Franconia, VA
22311 Alexandria, VA
22312 Alexandria, VA
22312 Lincolnia, VA
22313 Alexandria, VA
22314 Alexandria, VA
22315 Alexandria, VA
22315 Kingstowne, VA
22320 Alexandria, VA
22331 Alexandria, VA
22332 Alexandria, VA
22333 Alexandria, VA
22334 Alexandria, VA
22350 Alexandria, VA

224

22401 Fredericksburg, VA
22403 Falmouth, VA
22403 Fredericksburg, VA
22405 Falmouth, VA
22405 Fredericksburg, VA
22406 Falmouth, VA
22406 Fredericksburg, VA
22412 Falmouth, VA
22412 Fredericksburg, VA
22427 Bowling Green, VA
22427 Fort A P Hill, VA
22428 Bowling Green, VA
22430 Brooke, VA
22430 Stafford, VA
22432 Burgess, VA
22433 Burr Hill, VA
22435 Callao, VA
22436 Caret, VA
22436 Supply, VA
22437 Center Cross, VA
22438 Champlain, VA
22438 Chance, VA
22442 Coles Point, VA
22443 Colonial Beach, VA
22443 Oak Grove, VA
22443 Washingtons Birthplace, VA
22446 Corbin, VA
22448 Dahlgren, VA
22451 Dogue, VA
22454 Dunnsville, VA
22454 Howertons, VA
22456 Edwardsville, VA
22460 Farnham, VA
22463 Garrisonville, VA
22469 Hague, VA
22471 Hartwood, VA
22472 Haynesville, VA
22473 Heathsville, VA
22476 Hustle, VA
22480 Irvington, VA
22481 Jersey, VA
22482 Kilmarnock, VA
22485 King George, VA
22485 Shiloh, VA
22488 Kinsale, VA

225

22501 Ladysmith, VA
22503 Alfonso, VA
22503 Lancaster, VA
22503 Regina, VA
22504 Laneview, VA
22507 Lively, VA
22508 Lake Of The Woods, VA
22508 Locust Grove, VA
22508 Mine Run, VA
22509 Loretto, VA
22511 Lewisetta, VA
22511 Lottsburg, VA
22513 Merry Point, VA
22514 Milford, VA
22517 Mollusk, VA
22520 Montross, VA
22523 Morattico, VA
22524 Mount Holly, VA
22526 Ninde, VA
22528 Nuttsville, VA
22529 Oldhams, VA
22530 Ophelia, VA
22534 Partlow, VA
22535 Port Royal, VA
22538 Rappahannock Academy, VA
22539 Reedville, VA
22542 Rhoadesville, VA
22544 Rollins Fork, VA
22545 Ruby, VA
22546 Ruther Glen, VA
22547 Sealston, VA
22548 Sharps, VA
22551 Spotsylvania, VA
22552 Sparta, VA
22553 Snell, VA
22553 Spotsylvania, VA
22554 Stafford, VA
22555 Stafford, VA
22556 Stafford, VA
22558 Stratford, VA
22560 Tappahannock, VA
22565 Thornburg, VA
22567 Unionville, VA
22570 Village, VA
22572 Foneswood, VA
22572 Warsaw, VA
22576 Weems, VA
22577 Sandy Point, VA
22578 White Stone, VA
22579 Wicomico Church, VA
22580 Woodford, VA
22581 Zacata, VA

226

22601 Winchester, VA
22602 Winchester, VA
22603 Hayfield, VA
22603 Winchester, VA
22604 Winchester, VA
22610 Bentonville, VA
22610 Browntown, VA
22611 Berryville, VA
22611 Mount Weather, VA
22620 Boyce, VA
22622 Brucetown, VA
22623 Chester Gap, VA
22624 Clear Brook, VA
22625 Cross Junction, VA
22625 Whitacre, VA
22626 Fishers Hill, VA
22627 Flint Hill, VA
22627 Huntly, VA
22630 Front Royal, VA
22630 Lake Frederick, VA
22630 Riverton, VA
22637 Gore, VA
22639 Hume, VA
22640 Huntly, VA
22641 Lebanon Church, VA
22641 Strasburg, VA
22642 Linden, VA
22643 Markham, VA
22644 Maurertown, VA
22645 Middletown, VA
22646 Millwood, VA
22649 Middletown, VA
22649 Reliance, VA
22650 Rileyville, VA
22652 Fort Valley, VA
22652 Saint Davids Church, VA
22652 Seven Fountains, VA
22654 Star Tannery, VA
22655 Stephens City, VA
22656 Stephenson, VA
22657 Strasburg, VA
22660 Toms Brook, VA
22663 White Post, VA
22664 Woodstock, VA

227

22701 Culpeper, VA
22701 Raccoon Ford, VA
22701 Winston, VA
22709 Aroda, VA
22711 Banco, VA
22712 Bealeton, VA
22712 Morrisville, VA
22713 Boston, VA
22714 Brandy Station, VA
22715 Brightwood, VA
22716 Castleton, VA
22718 Elkwood, VA
22719 Etlan, VA
22719 Madison, VA
22720 Goldvein, VA
22722 Haywood, VA
22723 Hood, VA
22724 Jeffersonton, VA
22725 Leon, VA
22726 Lignum, VA
22727 Banco, VA
22727 Etlan, VA
22727 Graves Mill, VA
22727 Madison, VA
22728 Midland, VA
22729 Mitchells, VA
22730 Oakpark, VA
22731 Pratts, VA
22732 Radiant, VA
22733 Rapidan, VA
22734 Remington, VA
22735 Reva, VA
22736 Richardsville, VA
22737 Rixeyville, VA
22738 Rochelle, VA
22738 Uno, VA
22739 Somerville, VA
22740 Sperryville, VA
22741 Stevensburg, VA
22742 Sumerduck, VA
22743 Syria, VA
22746 Viewtown, VA
22747 Washington, VA
22748 Wolftown, VA
22749 Woodville, VA

228

22801 Harrisonburg, VA
22802 Harrisonburg, VA
22803 Harrisonburg, VA
22807 Harrisonburg, VA
22810 Basye, VA
22811 Bergton, VA
22812 Bridgewater, VA
22815 Broadway, VA
22820 Criders, VA
22821 Dayton, VA
22821 Montezuma, VA
22824 Edinburg, VA
22827 Elkton, VA
22830 Fulks Run, VA
22831 Hinton, VA
22832 Keezletown, VA
22833 Lacey Spring, VA
22834 Linville, VA
22835 Luray, VA
22840 Massanutten, VA
22840 Mc Gaheysville, VA
22841 Mount Crawford, VA
22842 Mount Jackson, VA
22843 Mount Solon, VA
22844 New Market, VA
22845 Orkney Springs, VA
22846 Penn Laird, VA
22847 Quicksburg, VA
22847 Shenandoah Caverns, VA
22848 Pleasant Valley, VA
22849 Shenandoah, VA
22850 Singers Glen, VA
22851 Stanley, VA
22853 Timberville, VA

229

22901 Charlottesville, VA
22902 Monticello, VA
22903 Charlottesville, VA
22903 University, VA
22904 Charlottesville, VA
22920 Afton, VA
22922 Arrington, VA
22922 Tye River, VA
22923 Barboursville, VA
22923 Burnleys, VA
22923 Eheart, VA
22924 Batesville, VA
22931 Covesville, VA
22932 Crozet, VA
22932 Yancey Mills, VA
22935 Boonesville, VA
22935 Dyke, VA
22935 Nortonsville, VA
22935 St George, VA
22936 Earlysville, VA
22937 Esmont, VA
22938 Faber, VA
22939 Fishersville, VA
22940 Free Union, VA
22940 Mission Home, VA
22942 Gordonsville, VA
22942 Zion Crossroads, VA
22943 Greenwood, VA
22945 Ivy, VA
22946 Keene, VA
22947 Boyd Tavern, VA
22947 Campbell, VA
22947 Cismont, VA
22947 Cobham, VA
22947 Keswick, VA
22947 Shadwell, VA
22948 Locust Dale, VA
22949 Lovingston, VA
22952 Lyndhurst, VA
22952 Sherando, VA
22957 Montpelier Station, VA
22958 Nellysford, VA
22959 North Garden, VA
22960 Madison Mills, VA
22960 Montford, VA
22960 Nasons, VA
22960 Orange, VA
22960 Thornhill, VA
22963 Bybee, VA
22963 Cunningham, VA
22963 Palmyra, VA
22963 Wildwood, VA
22963 Wilmington, VA
22964 Piney River, VA
22965 Quinque, VA
22967 Lowesville, VA

22967 Massies Mill, VA
22967 Roseland, VA
22967 Wintergreen Resort, VA
22968 Advance Mills, VA
22968 Ruckersville, VA
22969 Schuyler, VA
22971 Rockfish, VA
22971 Shipman, VA
22972 Somerset, VA
22973 Stanardsville, VA
22974 Troy, VA
22976 Roseland, VA
22976 Tyro, VA
22980 Waynesboro, VA
22987 White Hall, VA
22989 Woodberry Forest, VA

230

23001 Achilles, VA
23002 Amelia Court House, VA
23003 Ark, VA
23004 Arvonia, VA
23005 Ashland, VA
23009 Aylett, VA
23011 Barhamsville, VA
23014 Beaumont, VA
23015 Beaverdam, VA
23018 Bena, VA
23021 Bohannon, VA
23022 Bremo Bluff, VA
23023 Bruington, VA
23024 Bumpass, VA
23025 Cardinal, VA
23025 Miles, VA
23027 Cartersville, VA
23027 Tamworth, VA
23030 Charles City, VA
23031 Christchurch, VA
23032 Church View, VA
23035 Blakes, VA
23035 Cobbs Creek, VA
23038 Columbia, VA
23039 Crozier, VA
23040 Cumberland, VA
23043 Deltaville, VA
23045 Diggs, VA
23047 Doswell, VA
23050 Dutton, VA
23055 Fork Union, VA
23056 Foster, VA
23056 Mobjack, VA
23058 Glen Allen, VA
23059 Glen Allen, VA
23060 Glen Allen, VA
23061 Bellamy, VA
23061 Gloucester, VA
23061 Naxera, VA
23061 Pinero, VA
23061 Zanoni, VA
23062 Glou Point, VA
23062 Gloucester Point, VA
23063 Fife, VA
23063 Goochland, VA
23064 Grimstead, VA
23065 Gum Spring, VA
23066 Gwynn, VA
23067 Hadensville, VA
23068 Hallieford, VA
23069 Hanover, VA
23069 Mangohick, VA
23070 Hardyville, VA
23071 Hartfield, VA
23072 Hayes, VA
23075 Henrico, VA
23075 Highland Springs, VA
23076 Hudgins, VA
23076 Redart, VA
23079 Jamaica, VA
23081 Jamestown, VA
23081 Williamsburg, VA
23083 Jetersville, VA
23084 Kents Store, VA
23085 King And Queen Court House, VA
23086 King William, VA
23089 Lanexa, VA
23090 Lightfoot, VA
23091 Little Plymouth, VA
23092 Locust Hill, VA
23093 Louisa, VA

231

23102 Dabneys, VA
23102 Maidens, VA
23103 Manakin Sabot, VA
23105 Mannboro, VA
23106 Manquin, VA
23107 Maryus, VA
23108 Mascot, VA
23109 Beaverlett, VA
23109 Mathews, VA
23110 Mattaponi, VA
23111 Mechanicsville, VA
23112 Midlothian, VA
23113 Midlothian, VA
23114 Midlothian, VA
23115 Millers Tavern, VA
23116 Mechanicsville, VA
23117 Mineral, VA
23119 Moon, VA
23120 Moseley, VA
23123 New Canton, VA
23124 New Kent, VA
23125 New Point, VA
23126 Newtown, VA
23127 Norge, VA
23128 James Store, VA
23128 North, VA
23129 Oilville, VA
23130 Onemo, VA
23131 Ordinary, VA
23138 Bavon, VA
23138 Peary, VA
23138 Port Haywood, VA
23139 Macon, VA
23139 Powhatan, VA
23140 Providence Forge, VA
23141 Quinton, VA
23146 Rockville, VA
23147 Ruthville, VA
23148 Cauthornville, VA
23148 Indian Neck, VA
23148 Saint Stephens Church, VA
23148 St Stephens Church, VA
23149 Saluda, VA
23150 Sandston, VA
23153 Sandy Hook, VA
23154 Schley, VA
23155 Severn, VA
23156 Plain View, VA
23156 Shacklefords, VA
23160 State Farm, VA
23161 Stevensville, VA
23162 Studley, VA
23163 Shadow, VA
23163 Susan, VA
23168 Toano, VA
23169 Syringa, VA
23169 Topping, VA
23170 Trevilians, VA
23173 Richmond, VA
23175 Urbanna, VA
23175 Warner, VA
23176 Wake, VA
23177 Walkerton, VA
23178 Ware Neck, VA
23180 Water View, VA
23181 Cologne, VA
23181 West Point, VA
23183 White Marsh, VA
23184 Wicomico, VA
23185 Williamsburg, VA
23186 Williamsburg, VA
23187 Williamsburg, VA
23188 Williamsburg, VA
23190 Woods Cross Roads, VA
23192 Montpelier, VA

232

23218 Richmond, VA
23219 Richmond, VA
23220 Richmond, VA
23221 Richmond, VA
23222 Richmond, VA
23223 Richmond, VA
23224 North Chesterfield, VA
23224 Richmond, VA
23225 North Chesterfield, VA
23225 Richmond, VA
23226 Richmond, VA
23227 Richmond, VA
23228 Henrico, VA
23228 Richmond, VA
23229 Henrico, VA
23229 Regency, VA
23229 Richmond, VA
23230 Richmond, VA
23231 Henrico, VA
23231 Richmond, VA
23232 Richmond, VA
23233 Henrico, VA
23233 Richmond, VA
23233 Ridge, VA
23234 Ampthill, VA
23234 North Chesterfield, VA
23234 Richmond, VA
23235 Bon Air, VA
23235 North Chesterfield, VA
23235 Richmond, VA
23236 North Chesterfield, VA
23236 Richmond, VA
23237 North Chesterfield, VA
23237 Richmond, VA
23238 Henrico, VA
23238 Richmond, VA
23241 Richmond, VA
23242 Henrico, VA
23242 Richmond, VA
23249 Richmond, VA
23250 Henrico, VA
23250 Richmond, VA
23250 Richmond Int Airport, VA
23255 Henrico, VA
23255 Richmond, VA
23260 Richmond, VA
23261 Richmond, VA
23269 Richmond, VA
23273 Henrico, VA
23273 Richmond, VA
23274 Richmond, VA
23276 Richmond, VA
23278 Richmond, VA
23279 Richmond, VA
23282 Richmond, VA
23284 Richmond, VA
23285 Richmond, VA
23286 Richmond, VA
23288 Henrico, VA
23288 Richmond, VA
23289 Richmond, VA
23290 Richmond, VA
23291 Richmond, VA
23292 Richmond, VA
23293 Richmond, VA
23294 Henrico, VA
23294 Richmond, VA
23295 Richmond, VA
23297 Richmond, VA
23298 Richmond, VA

233

23301 Accomac, VA
23302 Assawoman, VA
23303 Atlantic, VA
23304 Battery Park, VA
23306 Belle Haven, VA
23307 Birdsnest, VA
23308 Bloxom, VA
23310 Cape Charles, VA
23313 Capeville, VA
23314 Carrollton, VA
23315 Carrsville, VA
23315 Walters, VA
23316 Cheriton, VA
23320 Chesapeake, VA
23321 Chesapeake, VA
23322 Chesapeake, VA
23323 Chesapeake, VA
23324 Chesapeake, VA
23324 South Norfolk, VA
23325 Chesapeake, VA
23326 Chesapeake, VA
23327 Chesapeake, VA
23328 Chesapeake, VA
23336 Chincoteague Island, VA
23337 Wallops Island, VA
23341 Craddockville, VA
23345 Davis Wharf, VA
23347 Eastville, VA
23350 Exmore, VA
23354 Franktown, VA
23356 Greenbackville, VA
23357 Greenbush, VA
23358 Hacks Neck, VA
23358 Hacksneck, VA
23359 Hallwood, VA
23389 Harborton, VA
23395 Horntown, VA
23396 Oak Hall, VA
23397 Isle Of Wight, VA
23398 Jamesville, VA
23399 Jenkins Bridge, VA

234

23401 Keller, VA
23404 Locustville, VA
23405 Machipongo, VA
23407 Mappsville, VA
23408 Marionville, VA
23409 Mears, VA
23410 Melfa, VA
23412 Modest Town, VA
23413 Nassawadox, VA
23413 Weirwood, VA
23414 Nelsonia, VA
23415 New Church, VA
23416 Oak Hall, VA
23417 Onancock, VA
23418 Onley, VA
23419 Oyster, VA
23420 Painter, VA
23421 Lee Mont, VA
23421 Parksley, VA
23422 Pungoteague, VA
23423 Quinby, VA
23424 Rescue, VA
23426 Sanford, VA
23427 Saxis, VA
23429 Seaview, VA
23430 Smithfield, VA
23431 Smithfield, VA
23432 Suffolk, VA
23433 Suffolk, VA
23434 Suffolk, VA
23435 Suffolk, VA
23436 Suffolk, VA
23437 Suffolk, VA
23438 Suffolk, VA
23439 Suffolk, VA
23440 Tangier, VA
23441 Tasley, VA
23442 Temperanceville, VA
23443 Townsend, VA
23450 Va Bch, VA
23450 Va Beach, VA
23450 Vab, VA
23450 Virginia Beach, VA
23451 Va Bch, VA
23451 Va Beach, VA
23451 Vab, VA
23451 Virginia Beach, VA
23452 Va Bch, VA
23452 Va Beach, VA
23452 Vab, VA
23452 Virginia Beach, VA
23456 Princess Anne, VA
23456 Va Bch, VA
23456 Va Beach, VA
23456 Virginia Beach, VA
23457 Va Bch, VA
23457 Va Beach, VA
23457 Vab, VA
23457 Virginia Beach, VA
23459 Fort Story, VA
23459 Virginia Beach, VA
23462 Va Bch, VA
23462 Va Beach, VA
23462 Vab, VA
23462 Virginia Beach, VA
23464 Va Bch, VA
23464 Va Beach, VA
23464 Vab, VA
23464 Virginia Beach, VA
23480 Wachapreague, VA
23482 Wardtown, VA
23483 Wattsville, VA
23486 Willis Wharf, VA
23487 Windsor, VA
23488 Withams, VA

235

23501 Norfolk, VA
23502 Norfolk, VA
23503 Norfolk, VA
23504 Norfolk, VA
23505 Norfolk, VA
23506 Norfolk, VA
23507 Norfolk, VA
23508 Norfolk, VA
23509 Norfolk, VA
23510 Norfolk, VA
23511 Fleet, VA
23511 Naval Base, VA
23511 Norfolk, VA
23513 Norfolk, VA
23514 Norfolk, VA
23515 Norfolk, VA
23517 Norfolk, VA
23518 Norfolk, VA
23519 Norfolk, VA
23523 Norfolk, VA
23529 Norfolk, VA
23541 Norfolk, VA
23551 Norfolk, VA

236

23601 Newport News, VA
23602 Newport News, VA
23603 Newport News, VA
23604 Fort Eustis, VA
23604 Newport News, VA
23605 Hampton, VA
23605 Newport News, VA
23606 Newport News, VA
23607 Newport News, VA
23608 Newport News, VA
23609 Newport News, VA
23612 Newport News, VA
23628 Newport News, VA
23630 Hampton, VA
23651 Fort Monroe, VA
23651 Hampton, VA
23661 Hampton, VA
23662 Hampton, VA
23662 Poquoson, VA
23663 Hampton, VA
23664 Hampton, VA
23665 Hampton, VA
23665 Langley Afb, VA
23666 Hampton, VA
23667 Hampton, VA
23668 Hampton, VA
23669 Hampton, VA
23670 Hampton, VA
23681 Hampton, VA
23690 Yorktown, VA
23691 Naval Weapons Station, VA
23691 Yorktown, VA
23692 Grafton, VA
23692 Yorktown, VA
23693 Tabb, VA
23693 Yorktown, VA
23694 Lackey, VA
23696 Seaford, VA

237

23701 Portsmouth, VA
23702 Portsmouth, VA
23703 Portsmouth, VA
23704 Portsmouth, VA
23705 Portsmouth, VA
23707 Portsmouth, VA
23708 Portsmouth, VA
23709 Portsmouth, VA

238

23801 Fort Lee, VA
23801 Petersburg, VA
23803 North Dinwiddie, VA
23803 Petersburg, VA
23803 South Chesterfield, VA
23804 Petersburg, VA
23805 North Dinwiddie, VA
23805 Petersburg, VA
23805 South Prince George, VA
23806 Petersburg, VA
23806 Virginia State University, VA
23821 Alberta, VA
23822 Ammon, VA
23824 Blackstone, VA
23827 Boykins, VA
23828 Branchville, VA
23829 Capron, VA
23830 Carson, VA
23831 Chester, VA
23832 Chesterfield, VA
23833 Church Road, VA
23834 Colonial Heights, VA
23834 South Chesterfield, VA
23836 Chester, VA
23837 Courtland, VA
23838 Chesterfield, VA
23839 Dendron, VA
23840 Dewitt, VA
23841 Dinwiddie, VA
23842 Disputanta, VA
23843 Dolphin, VA
23844 Drewryville, VA
23845 Ebony, VA
23846 Elberon, VA
23847 Emporia, VA
23850 Ford, VA
23851 Franklin, VA
23856 Freeman, VA
23857 Gasburg, VA
23860 Hopewell, VA
23860 North Prince George, VA
23866 Ivor, VA
23867 Jarratt, VA
23868 Lawrenceville, VA
23868 Triplet, VA
23870 Jarratt, VA
23872 Mc Kenney, VA
23873 Meredithville, VA
23874 Newsoms, VA
23875 Prince George, VA
23876 Rawlings, VA
23878 Sedley, VA
23879 Skippers, VA
23881 Spring Grove, VA
23882 Stony Creek, VA
23883 Surry, VA
23884 Sussex, VA
23885 Sutherland, VA
23887 Valentines, VA
23888 Wakefield, VA
23889 Warfield, VA
23890 Waverly, VA
23891 Waverly, VA
23893 White Plains, VA
23894 Wilsons, VA
23897 Yale, VA
23898 Zuni, VA
23899 Claremont, VA

239

23901 Farmville, VA
23909 Farmville, VA
23915 Baskerville, VA
23917 Boydton, VA
23919 Bracey, VA
23920 Brodnax, VA
23921 Buckingham, VA
23922 Burkeville, VA
23923 Charlotte Court House, VA

23924 Chase City, VA
23927 Clarksville, VA
23930 Crewe, VA
23934 Cullen, VA
23936 Dillwyn, VA
23936 Sprouses Corner, VA
23937 Drakes Branch, VA
23938 Dundas, VA
23939 Evergreen, VA
23941 Fort Mitchell, VA
23942 Green Bay, VA
23943 Farmville, VA
23943 Hampden Sydney, VA
23944 Kenbridge, VA
23947 Keysville, VA
23950 Blackridge, VA
23950 Forksville, VA
23950 La Crosse, VA
23952 Lunenburg, VA
23954 Meherrin, VA
23955 Nottoway, VA
23958 Darlington Heights, VA
23958 Pamplin, VA
23959 Phenix, VA
23960 Prospect, VA
23962 Randolph, VA
23963 Red House, VA
23964 Red Oak, VA
23966 Rice, VA
23967 Saxe, VA
23968 Skipwith, VA
23970 South Hill, VA
23974 Victoria, VA
23976 Wylliesburg, VA

240

24001 Roanoke, VA
24002 Roanoke, VA
24003 Roanoke, VA
24004 Roanoke, VA
24005 Roanoke, VA
24006 Roanoke, VA
24007 Roanoke, VA
24008 Roanoke, VA
24009 Roanoke, VA
24010 Roanoke, VA
24011 Roanoke, VA
24012 Roanoke, VA
24013 Roanoke, VA
24014 Roanoke, VA
24015 Roanoke, VA
24016 Roanoke, VA
24017 Roanoke, VA
24018 Cave Spring, VA
24018 Roanoke, VA
24019 Hollins, VA
24019 Hollins College, VA
24019 Roanoke, VA
24020 Hollins College, VA
24020 Roanoke, VA
24022 Roanoke, VA
24023 Roanoke, VA
24024 Roanoke, VA
24025 Roanoke, VA
24026 Roanoke, VA
24027 Roanoke, VA
24028 Roanoke, VA
24029 Roanoke, VA
24030 Roanoke, VA
24031 Roanoke, VA
24032 Roanoke, VA
24033 Roanoke, VA
24034 Roanoke, VA
24035 Roanoke, VA
24036 Roanoke, VA
24037 Roanoke, VA
24038 Roanoke, VA
24040 Roanoke, VA
24042 Roanoke, VA
24043 Roanoke, VA
24050 Roanoke, VA
24053 Ararat, VA
24054 Axton, VA
24055 Bassett, VA
24058 Belspring, VA
24059 Bent Mountain, VA
24060 Blacksburg, VA
24061 Blacksburg, VA
24062 Blacksburg, VA
24063 Blacksburg, VA
24064 Blue Ridge, VA
24065 Boones Mill, VA
24066 Buchanan, VA
24066 Lithia, VA
24067 Callaway, VA
24068 Christiansburg, VA
24069 Cascade, VA
24070 Catawba, VA
24072 Check, VA
24072 Simpsons, VA
24073 Christiansburg, VA
24076 Claudville, VA
24077 Cloverdale, VA
24078 Collinsville, VA
24079 Copper Hill, VA
24082 Critz, VA
24083 Daleville, VA
24084 Dublin, VA
24085 Eagle Rock, VA
24086 Eggleston, VA
24087 Elliston, VA
24087 Ironto, VA
24087 Lafayette, VA
24088 Charity, VA
24088 Ferrum, VA
24089 Fieldale, VA
24090 Fincastle, VA
24091 Alum Ridge, VA
24091 Floyd, VA
24092 Glade Hill, VA
24093 Glen Lyn, VA
24095 Goodview, VA

241

24101 Hardy, VA
24102 Henry, VA
24104 Huddleston, VA
24105 Indian Valley, VA
24111 Mc Coy, VA
24112 Martinsville, VA
24113 Martinsville, VA
24114 Martinsville, VA
24115 Martinsville, VA
24120 Meadows Of Dan, VA
24121 Moneta, VA
24122 Montvale, VA
24124 Narrows, VA
24126 Newbern, VA
24127 New Castle, VA
24128 Newport, VA
24129 New River, VA
24130 Oriskany, VA
24131 Paint Bank, VA
24132 Parrott, VA
24133 Patrick Springs, VA
24134 Pearisburg, VA
24136 Pembroke, VA
24137 Penhook, VA
24138 Pilot, VA
24139 Pittsville, VA
24141 Fairlawn, VA
24141 Radford, VA
24142 Radford, VA
24143 Radford, VA
24146 Redwood, VA
24147 Rich Creek, VA
24148 Ridgeway, VA
24149 Riner, VA
24150 Goldbond, VA
24150 Ripplemead, VA
24151 Rocky Mount, VA
24153 Salem, VA
24155 Roanoke, VA
24157 Roanoke, VA
24161 Sandy Level, VA
24162 Shawsville, VA
24165 Spencer, VA
24167 Staffordsville, VA
24168 Stanleytown, VA
24171 Stuart, VA
24174 Thaxton, VA
24175 Troutville, VA
24176 Union Hall, VA
24177 Vesta, VA
24178 Villamont, VA
24179 Vinton, VA
24184 Burnt Chimney, VA
24184 Wirtz, VA
24185 Woolwine, VA

242

24201 Bristol, VA
24202 Bristol, VA
24203 Bristol, VA
24205 Bristol, VA
24209 Bristol, VA
24210 Abingdon, VA
24211 Abingdon, VA
24212 Abingdon, VA
24215 Andover, VA
24216 Appalachia, VA
24216 Exeter, VA
24216 Stonega, VA
24217 Bee, VA
24218 Ben Hur, VA
24219 Big Stone Gap, VA
24220 Birchleaf, VA
24221 Blackwater, VA
24224 Castlewood, VA
24225 Cleveland, VA
24226 Clinchco, VA
24228 Clintwood, VA
24230 Coeburn, VA
24236 Damascus, VA
24237 Dante, VA
24237 Trammel, VA
24239 Davenport, VA
24243 Dryden, VA
24244 Clinchport, VA
24244 Duffield, VA
24245 Dungannon, VA
24246 East Stone Gap, VA
24248 Ewing, VA
24250 Fort Blackmore, VA
24251 Gate City, VA
24256 Haysi, VA
24258 Hiltons, VA
24260 Council, VA
24260 Elk Garden, VA
24260 Honaker, VA
24260 Venia, VA
24263 Jonesville, VA
24265 Keokee, VA
24266 Lebanon, VA
24269 Mc Clure, VA
24270 Mendota, VA
24271 Nickelsville, VA
24272 Nora, VA
24273 Norton, VA
24277 Pennington Gap, VA
24279 Pound, VA
24280 Rosedale, VA
24281 Rose Hill, VA
24282 Saint Charles, VA
24283 Saint Paul, VA
24290 Weber City, VA
24292 Whitetop, VA
24293 Wise, VA

243

24301 Pulaski, VA
24311 Atkins, VA
24312 Austinville, VA
24313 Barren Springs, VA
24314 Bastian, VA
24315 Bland, VA
24316 Broadford, VA
24317 Cana, VA
24318 Ceres, VA
24319 Chilhowie, VA
24322 Cripple Creek, VA
24323 Crockett, VA
24324 Draper, VA
24325 Dugspur, VA
24326 Elk Creek, VA
24327 Emory, VA
24328 Fancy Gap, VA
24330 Fries, VA
24333 Galax, VA
24340 Glade Spring, VA
24343 Hillsville, VA
24347 Allisonia, VA
24347 Hiwassee, VA
24348 Independence, VA
24350 Ivanhoe, VA
24351 Lambsburg, VA
24352 Laurel Fork, VA
24354 Marion, VA
24354 Seven Mile Ford, VA
24360 Fort Chiswell, VA
24360 Foster Falls, VA
24360 Max Meadows, VA
24361 Clinchburg, VA
24361 Meadowview, VA
24363 Mouth Of Wilson, VA
24363 Volney, VA
24366 Rocky Gap, VA
24368 Rural Retreat, VA
24370 Saltville, VA
24374 Speedwell, VA
24375 Sugar Grove, VA
24377 Tannersville, VA
24378 Troutdale, VA
24380 Willis, VA
24381 Woodlawn, VA
24382 Wytheville, VA

244

24401 Staunton, VA
24402 Staunton, VA
24411 Augusta Springs, VA
24412 Bacova, VA
24413 Blue Grass, VA
24415 Brownsburg, VA
24416 Buena Vista, VA
24421 Churchville, VA
24422 Clifton Forge, VA
24426 Alleghany, VA
24426 Covington, VA
24426 Jordan Mines, VA
24430 Craigsville, VA
24431 Crimora, VA
24432 Deerfield, VA
24433 Doe Hill, VA
24435 Fairfield, VA
24437 Fort Defiance, VA
24438 Glen Wilton, VA
24439 Goshen, VA
24440 Greenville, VA
24441 Grottoes, VA
24442 Head Waters, VA
24445 Hot Springs, VA
24448 Iron Gate, VA
24450 Lexington, VA
24457 Low Moor, VA
24458 Mc Dowell, VA
24459 Middlebrook, VA
24460 Millboro, VA
24463 Mint Spring, VA
24464 Montebello, VA
24465 Hightown, VA
24465 Monterey, VA
24467 Mount Sidney, VA
24468 Mustoe, VA
24469 New Hope, VA
24471 Port Republic, VA
24472 Raphine, VA
24473 Rockbridge Baths, VA
24474 Selma, VA
24476 Spottswood, VA
24476 Steeles Tavern, VA
24477 Stuarts Draft, VA
24479 Swoope, VA
24482 Verona, VA
24483 Vesuvius, VA
24484 Bolar, VA
24484 Warm Springs, VA
24485 West Augusta, VA
24486 Weyers Cave, VA
24487 Burnsville, VA
24487 Williamsville, VA

245

24501 Lynchburg, VA
24502 Lynchburg, VA
24502 Timberlake, VA
24503 Lynchburg, VA
24504 Lynchburg, VA
24505 Lynchburg, VA
24506 Lynchburg, VA
24513 Lynchburg, VA
24514 Lynchburg, VA
24515 Lynchburg, VA
24517 Altavista, VA
24520 Alton, VA
24521 Amherst, VA
24522 Appomattox, VA
24523 Bedford, VA
24526 Big Island, VA
24527 Blairs, VA
24528 Brookneal, VA
24529 Buffalo Junction, VA
24530 Callands, VA
24531 Chatham, VA
24533 Clifford, VA
24534 Clover, VA
24535 Cluster Springs, VA
24536 Coleman Falls, VA
24538 Concord, VA
24539 Crystal Hill, VA
24540 Danville, VA
24541 Danville, VA
24543 Danville, VA
24549 Dry Fork, VA
24550 Evington, VA
24551 Forest, VA
24553 Gladstone, VA
24554 Gladys, VA
24555 Glasgow, VA
24556 Goode, VA
24557 Gretna, VA
24558 Halifax, VA
24562 Howardsville, VA
24562 Scottsville, VA
24563 Hurt, VA
24565 Java, VA
24566 Keeling, VA
24569 Long Island, VA
24570 Lowry, VA
24571 Lynch Station, VA
24572 Madison Heights, VA
24574 Monroe, VA
24576 Naruna, VA
24577 Lennig, VA
24577 Nathalie, VA
24577 Republican Grove, VA
24578 Natural Bridge, VA
24579 Natural Bridge Station, VA
24580 Nelson, VA
24581 Norwood, VA
24586 Ringgold, VA
24588 Rustburg, VA
24589 Scottsburg, VA
24590 Scottsville, VA
24592 South Boston, VA
24592 Turbeville, VA
24593 Spout Spring, VA
24594 Sutherlin, VA
24595 Sweet Briar, VA
24597 Ingram, VA
24597 Vernon Hill, VA
24598 Virgilina, VA
24599 Wingina, VA

246

24601 Amonate, VA
24602 Bandy, VA
24603 Big Rock, VA
24603 Conaway, VA
24604 Bishop, VA
24605 Bluefield, VA
24605 Yards, VA
24606 Boissevain, VA
24607 Breaks, VA
24608 Burkes Garden, VA
24608 Tazewell, VA
24609 Cedar Bluff, VA
24612 Doran, VA
24613 Falls Mills, VA
24614 Grundy, VA
24619 Horsepen, VA
24620 Hurley, VA
24622 Jewell Ridge, VA
24622 Jewell Valley, VA
24624 Keen Mountain, VA
24627 Mavisdale, VA
24628 Harman, VA
24628 Maxie, VA
24630 North Tazewell, VA
24630 Tiptop, VA
24631 Oakwood, VA
24631 Patterson, VA
24634 Pilgrims Knob, VA
24635 Pocahontas, VA
24637 Pounding Mill, VA
24639 Raven, VA
24640 Red Ash, VA
24641 Richlands, VA
24646 Rowe, VA
24647 Shortt Gap, VA
24649 Swords Creek, VA
24651 Tazewell, VA
24656 Vansant, VA
24657 Whitewood, VA
24658 Wolford, VA

247

24701 Bluefield, WV
24701 Bluewell, WV
24701 Green Valley, WV
24712 Athens, WV
24714 Beeson, WV
24715 Bramwell, WV
24716 Bud, WV
24719 Covel, WV
24724 Coaldale, WV
24724 Freeman, WV
24726 Herndon, WV
24729 Hiawatha, WV
24731 Kegley, WV
24732 Kellysville, WV
24733 Lashmeet, WV
24736 Dott, WV
24736 Matoaka, WV
24737 Montcalm, WV
24738 Nemours, WV
24739 Oakvale, WV
24739 Princeton, WV
24740 Elgood, WV
24740 Oakvale, WV
24740 Princeton, WV
24747 Duhring, WV
24747 Mc Comas, WV
24747 Rock, WV
24751 Wolfe, WV

248

24801 Capels, WV
24801 Coalwood, WV
24801 Havaco, WV
24801 Hemphill, WV
24801 Skygusty, WV
24801 Superior, WV
24801 Welch, WV
24801 Wolf Pen, WV
24808 Anawalt, WV
24808 Leckie, WV
24811 Avondale, WV
24813 Bartley, WV
24815 Berwind, WV
24815 Canebrake, WV
24815 Vallscreek, WV
24816 Big Sandy, WV
24817 Bradshaw, WV
24818 Brenton, WV
24822 Clear Fork, WV
24823 Coal Mountain, WV
24826 Cucumber, WV
24827 Cyclone, WV
24828 Asco, WV
24828 Davy, WV
24828 Twin Branch, WV
24829 Eckman, WV
24830 Elbert, WV
24830 Filbert, WV
24831 Elkhorn, WV
24834 Fanrock, WV
24836 Gary, WV

24839 Hanover, WV
24843 Hensley, WV
24844 Iaeger, WV
24845 Ikes Fork, WV
24846 Isaban, WV
24847 Itmann, WV
24848 Jenkinjones, WV
24849 Jesse, WV
24850 Jolo, WV
24851 Justice, WV
24853 Kimball, WV
24853 Vivian, WV
24854 Kopperston, WV
24855 Kyle, WV
24857 Lynco, WV
24859 Marianna, WV
24859 Pineville, WV
24860 Matheny, WV
24861 Maybeury, WV
24862 Mohawk, WV
24866 Newhall, WV
24867 New Richmond, WV
24868 Algoma, WV
24868 Ashland, WV
24868 Crumpler, WV
24868 Keystone, WV
24868 Mc Dowell, WV
24868 Northfork, WV
24868 Powhatan, WV
24868 Worth, WV
24869 North Spring, WV
24870 Oceana, WV
24871 Pageton, WV
24872 Panther, WV
24873 Paynesville, WV
24874 Pineville, WV
24878 Premier, WV
24879 Raysal, WV
24880 Rock View, WV
24881 Roderfield, WV
24882 Simon, WV
24884 Squire, WV
24887 Switchback, WV
24888 Thorpe, WV
24892 Caretta, WV
24892 English, WV
24892 War, WV
24892 Yukon, WV
24894 Warriormine, WV
24895 Wilcoe, WV
24898 Wyoming, WV

249

24901 Lewisburg, WV
24902 Fairlea, WV
24910 Alderson, WV
24910 Dawson, WV
24915 Arbovale, WV
24916 Alta, WV
24916 Asbury, WV
24918 Ballard, WV
24920 Bartow, WV
24924 Buckeye, WV
24925 Caldwell, WV
24927 Cass, WV
24927 Stony Bottom, WV
24931 Clintonville, WV
24931 Crawley, WV
24931 Kieffer, WV
24931 Sam Black, WV
24934 Dunmore, WV
24935 Forest Hill, WV
24935 Indian Mills, WV
24938 Anthony, WV
24938 Frankford, WV
24938 Friars Hill, WV
24941 Gap Mills, WV
24941 Sweet Springs, WV
24943 Grassy Meadows, WV
24944 Green Bank, WV
24945 Greenville, WV
24946 Droop, WV
24946 Hillsboro, WV
24946 Mill Point, WV
24946 Seebert, WV
24951 Lindside, WV
24954 Marlinton, WV
24954 Minnehaha Springs, WV
24957 Maxwelton, WV
24962 Pence Springs, WV
24963 Bozoo, WV
24963 Peterstown, WV
24966 Auto, WV
24966 Falling Sprg, WV
24966 Renick, WV
24970 Fort Spring, WV
24970 Organ Cave, WV
24970 Ronceverte, WV
24974 Secondcreek, WV
24976 Pickaway, WV
24976 Sinks Grove, WV
24977 Meadow Bluff, WV
24977 Smoot, WV
24981 Ballengee, WV
24981 Talcott, WV
24983 Glace, WV
24983 Sarton, WV
24983 Union, WV
24983 Willow Bend, WV
24984 Waiteville, WV
24985 Wayside, WV
24986 Neola, WV
24986 White Sulphur Springs, WV
24986 Wht Sulphur S, WV
24986 Wht Sulphur Spgs, WV
24991 Trout, WV
24991 Williamsburg, WV
24993 Wolfcreek, WV

250

25002 Alloy, WV
25003 Alum Creek, WV
25005 Amma, WV
25007 Arnett, WV
25008 Artie, WV
25009 Ashford, WV
25011 Bancroft, WV
25015 Belle, WV
25015 Diamond, WV
25015 Dupont City, WV
25015 Quincy, WV
25015 Shrewsbury, WV
25015 Witcher, WV
25019 Bickmore, WV
25019 Fola, WV
25021 Bim, WV
25022 Blair, WV
25024 Bloomingrose, WV
25025 Blount, WV
25026 Blue Creek, WV
25028 Bob White, WV
25030 Bomont, WV
25031 Boomer, WV
25033 Buffalo, WV
25035 Cabin Creek, WV
25036 Cannelton, WV
25039 Cedar Grove, WV
25040 Charlton Heights, WV
25043 Clay, WV
25044 Clear Creek, WV
25045 Clendenin, WV
25045 Clio, WV
25045 Corton, WV
25045 Quick, WV
25047 Clothier, WV
25048 Colcord, WV
25049 Comfort, WV
25051 Costa, WV
25053 Danville, WV
25054 Dawes, WV
25057 Deep Water, WV
25059 Dixie, WV
25060 Ameagle, WV
25060 Dorothy, WV
25061 Drybranch, WV
25062 Dry Creek, WV
25063 Duck, WV
25063 Elmira, WV
25063 Harrison, WV
25063 Strange Creek, WV
25064 Dunbar, WV
25067 Crown Hill, WV
25067 East Bank, WV
25070 Eleanor, WV
25071 Elkview, WV
25071 Frame, WV
25075 Carbon, WV
25075 Decota, WV
25075 Eskdale, WV
25075 Kayford, WV
25075 Leewood, WV
25075 Ohley, WV
25076 Ethel, WV
25079 Falling Rock, WV
25081 Foster, WV
25082 Fraziers Bottom, WV
25082 Pliny, WV
25083 Burnwell, WV
25083 Gallagher, WV
25083 Livingston, WV
25083 Mahan, WV
25083 Standard, WV
25083 Whittaker, WV
25085 Brownsville, WV
25085 Gauley Bridge, WV
25086 Glasgow, WV
25088 Glen, WV
25090 Glen Ferris, WV
25093 Gordon, WV

251

25102 Handley, WV
25103 Hansford, WV
25106 Henderson, WV
25107 Hernshaw, WV
25108 Hewett, WV
25109 Hometown, WV
25110 Hugheston, WV
25111 Indore, WV
25112 Institute, WV
25113 Big Otter, WV
25113 Ivydale, WV
25114 Jeffrey, WV
25114 Ramage, WV
25115 Kanawha Falls, WV
25118 Kimberly, WV
25119 Kincaid, WV
25121 Lake, WV
25123 Arbuckle, WV
25123 Grimms Landing, WV
25123 Leon, WV
25123 Robertsburg, WV
25124 Liberty, WV
25125 Bentree, WV
25125 Lizemores, WV
25126 London, WV
25130 Madison, WV
25132 Mammoth, WV
25133 Maysel, WV
25134 Miami, WV
25136 Montgomery, WV
25139 Mount Carbon, WV
25140 Montcoal, WV
25140 Naoma, WV
25140 Stickney, WV
25140 Sundial, WV
25141 Nebo, WV
25142 Nellis, WV
25143 Nitro, WV
25148 Orgas, WV
25149 Ottawa, WV
25152 Page, WV
25154 Peytona, WV
25156 Pinch, WV
25159 Lanham, WV
25159 Poca, WV
25160 Pond Gap, WV
25161 Powellton, WV
25162 Pratt, WV
25164 Ovapa, WV
25164 Pigeon, WV
25164 Procious, WV
25165 Racine, WV
25168 Red House, WV
25169 Ridgeview, WV
25173 Beards Fork, WV
25173 Robson, WV
25174 Rock Creek, WV
25177 Jefferson, WV
25177 Saint Albans, WV
25180 Saxon, WV
25181 Prenter, WV
25181 Seth, WV
25183 Sharples, WV
25185 Mount Olive, WV
25186 Longacre, WV
25186 Smithers, WV
25187 Southside, WV
25193 Sylvester, WV

252

25201 Tad, WV
25202 Tornado, WV
25202 Upper Falls, WV
25203 Turtle Creek, WV
25204 Bandytown, WV
25204 Twilight, WV
25205 Uneeda, WV
25206 Van, WV
25208 Bald Knob, WV
25208 Barrett, WV
25208 Wharton, WV
25209 Garrison, WV
25209 Packsville, WV
25209 Pettus, WV
25209 Whitesville, WV
25211 Widen, WV
25213 Winfield, WV
25214 Winifrede, WV
25231 Advent, WV
25234 Arnoldsburg, WV
25234 Sand Ridge, WV
25235 Chloe, WV
25235 Floe, WV
25239 Cottageville, WV
25241 Evans, WV
25243 Gandeeville, WV
25243 Harmony, WV
25244 Gay, WV
25245 Given, WV
25245 Rock Castle, WV
25247 Hartford, WV
25247 Hartford City, WV
25248 Kenna, WV
25248 Kentuck, WV
25248 Romance, WV
25251 Left Hand, WV
25252 Duncan, WV
25252 Le Roy, WV
25252 Liverpool, WV
25253 Letart, WV
25259 Linden, WV
25259 Looneyville, WV
25259 Tariff, WV
25260 Clifton, WV
25260 Mason, WV
25261 Millstone, WV
25262 Millwood, WV
25264 Mount Alto, WV
25265 New Haven, WV
25266 Newton, WV
25266 Uler, WV
25267 Letter Gap, WV
25267 Lockney, WV
25267 Normantown, WV
25267 Stumptown, WV
25268 Minnora, WV
25268 Orma, WV
25270 Reedy, WV
25271 Ripley, WV
25271 Statts Mills, WV
25275 Sandyville, WV
25276 Spencer, WV
25285 Valley Fork, WV
25285 Wallback, WV
25286 Walton, WV
25287 Lakin, WV
25287 West Columbia, WV

253

25301 Charleston, WV
25302 Big Chimney, WV
25302 Charleston, WV
25303 Charleston, WV
25303 South Charleston, WV
25304 Charleston, WV
25305 Charleston, WV
25306 Charleston, WV
25306 Malden, WV
25309 Charleston, WV
25309 South Charleston, WV
25311 Charleston, WV
25312 Charleston, WV
25313 Charleston, WV
25313 Cross Lanes, WV
25314 Charleston, WV
25315 Charleston, WV
25315 Chesapeake, WV
25315 Marmet, WV
25317 Charleston, WV
25320 Charleston, WV
25320 Sissonville, WV
25321 Charleston, WV
25322 Charleston, WV
25323 Charleston, WV
25324 Charleston, WV
25325 Charleston, WV
25326 Charleston, WV
25327 Charleston, WV
25328 Charleston, WV
25329 Charleston, WV
25330 Charleston, WV
25331 Charleston, WV
25332 Charleston, WV
25333 Charleston, WV
25334 Charleston, WV
25335 Charleston, WV
25336 Charleston, WV
25337 Charleston, WV
25338 Charleston, WV
25339 Charleston, WV
25350 Charleston, WV
25356 Charleston, WV
25357 Charleston, WV
25358 Charleston, WV
25360 Charleston, WV
25361 Charleston, WV
25362 Charleston, WV
25364 Charleston, WV
25365 Charleston, WV
25375 Charleston, WV
25387 Charleston, WV
25389 Charleston, WV
25392 Charleston, WV
25396 Charleston, WV

254

25401 Martinsburg, WV
25402 Martinsburg, WV
25403 Martinsburg, WV
25404 Martinsburg, WV
25405 Martinsburg, WV
25410 Bakerton, WV
25411 Berkeley Springs, WV
25411 Hancock, WV
25411 Unger, WV
25413 Bunker Hill, WV
25414 Charles Town, WV
25419 Falling Waters, WV
25420 Gerrardstown, WV
25421 Glengary, WV
25422 Great Cacapon, WV
25423 Halltown, WV
25425 Bolivar, WV
25425 Harpers Ferry, WV
25427 Cherry Run, WV
25427 Hedgesville, WV
25427 Jones Springs, WV
25428 Inwood, WV
25430 Kearneysville, WV
25430 Middleway, WV
25431 Levels, WV
25432 Millville, WV
25434 Paw Paw, WV
25437 Points, WV
25438 Ranson, WV
25440 Ridgeway, WV
25441 Rippon, WV
25442 Shenandoah Junction, WV
25443 Shepherdstown, WV
25444 Slanesville, WV
25446 Summit Point, WV

255

25501 Alkol, WV
25502 Apple Grove, WV
25503 Ashton, WV
25504 Barboursville, WV
25505 Big Creek, WV
25506 Branchland, WV
25506 Palermo, WV
25506 Sias, WV
25507 Ceredo, WV
25508 Chapmanville, WV
25508 Shively, WV
25510 Culloden, WV
25511 Dunlow, WV
25512 East Lynn, WV
25514 Fort Gay, WV
25514 Glenhayes, WV
25515 Gallipolis Ferry, WV
25517 Genoa, WV
25517 Radnor, WV
25520 Glenwood, WV
25521 Griffithsville, WV
25523 Hamlin, WV
25523 Sweetland, WV
25524 Ferrellsburg, WV
25524 Harts, WV
25524 Leet, WV
25526 Hurricane, WV
25529 Julian, WV
25530 Kenova, WV
25534 Cove Gap, WV
25534 Kiahsville, WV
25535 Lavalette, WV
25537 Lesage, WV
25540 Midkiff, WV
25541 Milton, WV
25544 Myra, WV
25545 Ona, WV
25547 Pecks Mill, WV
25550 Point Pleasant, WV
25555 Prichard, WV
25557 Ranger, WV
25559 Salt Rock, WV
25560 Scott Depot, WV
25562 Shoals, WV
25564 Sod, WV
25565 Morrisvale, WV
25565 Spurlockville, WV
25567 Sumerco, WV
25569 Teays, WV
25570 Wayne, WV
25571 West Hamlin, WV
25572 Alkol, WV
25572 Woodville, WV
25573 Yawkey, WV

256

25601 Logan, WV
25601 Mitchell Hts, WV
25601 Monaville, WV
25601 Rossmore, WV
25601 West Logan, WV
25606 Accoville, WV
25607 Amherstdale, WV
25607 Robinette, WV
25608 Baisden, WV
25611 Bruno, WV
25612 Chauncey, WV
25614 Cora, WV
25617 Davin, WV
25621 Gilbert, WV
25621 Hampden, WV
25624 Henlawson, WV
25625 Holden, WV
25628 Kistler, WV
25630 Lorado, WV
25630 Lundale, WV
25632 Earling, WV
25632 Lyburn, WV
25632 Taplin, WV
25634 Mallory, WV
25635 Hunt, WV
25635 Landville, WV
25635 Man, WV
25637 Mount Gay, WV
25638 Barnabus, WV

25638 Omar, WV
25639 Peach Creek, WV
25644 Sarah Ann, WV
25646 Mc Connell, WV
25646 Stollings, WV
25647 Switzer, WV
25649 Verdunville, WV
25650 Emmett, WV
25650 Verner, WV
25651 Wharncliffe, WV
25652 Whitman, WV
25653 Wilkinson, WV
25654 Dehue, WV
25654 Yolyn, WV
25661 Nolan, WV
25661 Sprigg, WV
25661 Williamson, WV
25665 Borderland, WV
25666 Breeden, WV
25667 Chattaroy, WV
25669 Crum, WV
25670 Delbarton, WV
25670 Myrtle, WV
25670 Stirrat, WV
25671 Dingess, WV
25672 Edgarton, WV
25672 Thacker, WV
25672 Vulcan, WV
25674 Kermit, WV
25676 Lenore, WV
25678 Blackberry City, WV
25678 Lobata, WV
25678 Matewan, WV
25678 Meador, WV
25685 Naugatuck, WV
25686 Newtown, WV
25688 North Matewan, WV
25690 Ragland, WV
25691 Rawl, WV
25692 Red Jacket, WV
25696 Varney, WV
25699 Wilsondale, WV

257

25701 Huntington, WV
25702 Huntington, WV
25703 Huntington, WV
25704 Huntington, WV
25705 Huntington, WV
25706 Huntington, WV
25707 Huntington, WV
25708 Huntington, WV
25709 Huntington, WV
25710 Huntington, WV
25711 Huntington, WV
25712 Huntington, WV
25713 Huntington, WV
25714 Huntington, WV
25715 Huntington, WV
25716 Huntington, WV
25717 Huntington, WV
25718 Huntington, WV
25719 Huntington, WV
25720 Huntington, WV
25721 Huntington, WV
25722 Huntington, WV
25723 Huntington, WV
25724 Huntington, WV
25725 Huntington, WV
25726 Huntington, WV
25727 Huntington, WV
25728 Huntington, WV
25729 Huntington, WV
25755 Huntington, WV
25770 Huntington, WV
25771 Huntington, WV
25772 Huntington, WV
25773 Huntington, WV
25774 Huntington, WV
25775 Huntington, WV
25776 Huntington, WV
25777 Huntington, WV
25778 Huntington, WV
25779 Huntington, WV

258

25801 Beckley, WV
25802 Beckley, WV
25802 Sprague, WV
25810 Allen Junction, WV
25811 Amigo, WV
25812 Ansted, WV
25813 Beaver, WV
25813 Blue Jay, WV
25813 Glen Morgan, WV
25817 Bolt, WV
25818 Bradley, WV
25820 Camp Creek, WV
25823 Coal City, WV
25823 Jonben, WV
25823 Whitby, WV
25825 Cool Ridge, WV
25826 Corinne, WV
25827 Crab Orchard, WV
25831 Clifftop, WV
25831 Danese, WV
25831 Maplewood, WV
25832 Daniels, WV
25832 Glade Springs, WV
25833 Dothan, WV
25836 Eccles, WV
25837 Edmond, WV
25839 Fairdale, WV
25840 Beckwith, WV
25840 Cunard, WV
25840 Fayetteville, WV
25840 Wriston, WV
25841 Flat Top, WV
25843 Ghent, WV
25844 Glen Daniel, WV
25845 Glen Fork, WV
25846 Glen Jean, WV
25848 Glen Rogers, WV
25849 Glen White, WV
25851 Harper, WV
25853 Helen, WV
25854 Hico, WV
25855 Hilltop, WV
25857 Josephine, WV
25860 Lanark, WV
25862 Lansing, WV
25864 Lawton, WV
25864 Layland, WV
25864 Terry, WV
25865 Lester, WV
25866 Lochgelly, WV
25868 Lookout, WV
25870 Maben, WV
25871 Mabscott, WV
25873 Mac Arthur, WV
25875 Mc Graws, WV
25876 Mc Graws, WV
25876 Saulsville, WV
25878 Midway, WV
25878 Pemberton, WV
25879 Minden, WV
25880 Mount Hope, WV
25882 Mullens, WV
25888 Mount Hope, WV

259

25901 Harvey, WV
25901 Oak Hill, WV
25901 Redstar, WV
25901 Summerlee, WV
25902 Odd, WV
25904 Pax, WV
25906 Piney View, WV
25907 Prince, WV
25908 Princewick, WV
25908 Winding Gulf, WV
25909 Prosperity, WV
25911 Raleigh, WV
25913 Ravencliff, WV
25915 East Gulf, WV
25915 Mead, WV
25915 Rhodell, WV
25916 Sabine, WV
25917 Kingston, WV
25917 Scarbro, WV
25918 Abraham, WV
25918 Shady Spring, WV
25919 Skelton, WV
25920 Slab Fork, WV
25921 Mcalpin, WV
25921 Sophia, WV
25921 Tams, WV
25922 Spanishburg, WV
25927 Stanaford, WV
25928 Stephenson, WV
25932 Surveyor, WV
25936 Thurmond, WV
25938 Ramsey, WV
25938 Victor, WV
25942 Winona, WV
25943 Wyco, WV
25951 Brooks, WV
25951 Hinton, WV
25951 True, WV
25958 Bingham, WV
25958 Charmco, WV
25958 Hines, WV
25958 Orient Hill, WV
25962 Bellwood, WV
25962 Corliss, WV
25962 Hilton Village, WV
25962 Lilly Park, WV
25962 Rainelle, WV
25966 Green Sulphur Springs, WV
25966 Meadow Bridge, WV
25969 Jumping Branch, WV
25969 Streeter, WV
25971 Lerona, WV
25972 Bellburn, WV
25972 Leslie, WV
25976 Elton, WV
25976 Lockbridge, WV
25976 Meadow Bridge, WV
25977 Meadow Creek, WV
25978 Nimitz, WV
25979 Lovern, WV
25979 Pipestem, WV
25981 Crichton, WV
25981 Marfrance, WV
25981 Quinwood, WV
25984 Duo, WV
25984 Kessler, WV
25984 Rupert, WV
25985 Sandstone, WV
25986 Spring Dale, WV
25989 White Oak, WV

260

26003 Bethlehem, WV
26003 Elm Grove, WV
26003 Mozart, WV
26003 Overbrook, WV
26003 Warwood, WV
26003 Wheeling, WV
26030 Beech Bottom, WV
26031 Benwood, WV
26032 Bethany, WV
26033 Cameron, WV
26034 Chester, WV
26035 Colliers, WV
26036 Dallas, WV
26037 Follansbee, WV
26038 Glen Dale, WV
26039 Glen Easton, WV
26040 Mcmechen, WV
26041 Moundsville, WV
26047 New Cumberland, WV
26050 Newell, WV
26055 Proctor, WV
26056 New Manchester, WV
26058 Short Creek, WV
26059 Triadelphia, WV
26060 Valley Grove, WV
26062 Weirton, WV
26070 Wellsburg, WV
26074 West Liberty, WV
26075 Windsor Heights, WV

261

26101 Parkersburg, WV
26102 Parkersburg, WV
26103 Fort Neal, WV
26103 Parkersburg, WV
26104 North Hills, WV
26104 North Parkersburg, WV
26104 Parkersburg, WV
26105 Parkersburg, WV
26105 Vienna, WV
26106 Parkersburg, WV
26120 Coldwater Creek, WV
26120 Mineral Wells, WV
26121 Coldwater Creek, WV
26121 Mineral Wells, WV
26133 Belleville, WV
26134 Belmont, WV
26134 Eureka, WV
26134 Willow Island, WV
26136 Big Bend, WV
26136 Five Forks, WV
26137 Big Springs, WV
26137 Nobe, WV
26137 Tanner, WV
26138 Brohard, WV
26141 Annamoriah, WV
26141 Creston, WV
26142 Davisville, WV
26143 Elizabeth, WV
26143 Hughes River, WV
26143 Limestone Hill, WV
26143 Newark, WV
26143 Spring Valley, WV
26143 Standing Stone, WV
26146 Bens Run, WV
26146 Friendly, WV
26147 Grantsville, WV
26148 Macfarlan, WV
26149 Middlebourne, WV
26149 Wick, WV
26150 Mineral Wells, WV
26151 Mount Zion, WV
26152 Munday, WV
26155 New Martinsville, WV
26159 Paden City, WV
26160 Blue Goose, WV
26160 Lynncamp, WV
26160 Palestine, WV
26160 Sanoma, WV
26160 Sommerville Fork, WV
26160 Two Run, WV
26161 Petroleum, WV
26162 Porters Falls, WV
26164 Murraysville, WV
26164 Ravenswood, WV
26164 Sherman, WV
26167 Reader, WV
26169 Rockport, WV
26170 Saint Marys, WV
26175 Sistersville, WV
26178 Burnt House, WV
26178 Smithville, WV
26180 Freeport, WV
26180 Walker, WV
26181 New England, WV
26181 Washington, WV
26184 Waverly, WV
26187 Williamstown, WV

262

26201 Buckhannon, WV
26201 Century, WV
26201 Tennerton, WV
26202 Fenwick, WV
26203 Erbacon, WV
26205 Cottle, WV
26205 Craigsville, WV
26206 Boggs, WV
26206 Cowen, WV
26208 Camden On Gauley, WV
26208 Gauley Mills, WV
26209 Slatyfork, WV
26209 Snowshoe, WV
26210 Adrian, WV
26215 Cleveland, WV
26215 Rock Cave, WV
26217 Diana, WV
26218 Alexander, WV
26218 French Creek, WV
26219 Frenchton, WV
26222 Hacker Valley, WV
26222 Replete, WV
26224 Helvetia, WV
26228 Kanawha Head, WV
26229 Lorentz, WV
26230 Pickens, WV
26234 Rock Cave, WV
26236 Selbyville, WV
26237 Tallmansville, WV
26238 Volga, WV
26241 Elkins, WV
26250 Belington, WV
26253 Beverly, WV
26254 Bowden, WV
26254 Wymer, WV
26257 Coalton, WV
26259 Dailey, WV
26260 Canaan Valley, WV
26260 Davis, WV
26261 Richwood, WV
26263 Dryfork, WV
26264 Durbin, WV
26266 Upperglade, WV
26267 Ellamore, WV
26268 Glady, WV
26269 Hambleton, WV
26270 Harman, WV
26271 Hendricks, WV
26273 Huttonsville, WV
26275 Junior, WV
26276 Kerens, WV
26278 Mabie, WV
26280 Mill Creek, WV
26282 Monterville, WV
26283 Montrose, WV
26285 Norton, WV
26287 Parsons, WV
26287 Saint George, WV
26288 Curtin, WV
26288 Parcoal, WV
26288 Webster Springs, WV
26289 Red Creek, WV
26291 Slatyfork, WV
26292 Thomas, WV
26293 Valley Bend, WV
26294 Mingo, WV
26294 Valley Head, WV
26296 Job, WV
26296 Whitmer, WV
26298 Bergoo, WV

263

26301 Clarksburg, WV
26301 Country Club, WV
26301 Dawmont, WV
26301 Laurel Park, WV
26301 Laurel Valley, WV
26301 Nutter Fort, WV
26301 Stonewood, WV
26302 Clarksburg, WV
26306 Clarksburg, WV
26320 Alma, WV
26320 Wilbur, WV
26321 Alum Bridge, WV
26321 Vadis, WV
26323 Anmoore, WV
26325 Auburn, WV
26327 Berea, WV
26330 Bridgeport, WV
26330 Brushy Fork, WV
26330 Lake Ridge, WV
26330 Maple Lake, WV
26335 Burnsville, WV
26335 Gem, WV
26337 Cairo, WV
26338 Camden, WV
26339 Center Point, WV
26342 Coxs Mills, WV
26343 Crawford, WV
26346 Ellenboro, WV
26346 Highland, WV
26347 Astor, WV
26347 Brownton, WV
26347 Flemington, WV
26347 Wendel, WV
26348 Folsom, WV
26349 Galloway, WV
26351 Baldwin, WV
26351 Gilmer, WV
26351 Glenville, WV
26354 Belgium, WV
26354 Grafton, WV
26354 Harmony Grove, WV
26354 Haymond, WV
26354 White Day, WV
26361 Gypsy, WV
26362 Harrisville, WV
26362 Hazelgreen, WV
26362 Mahone, WV
26362 Newberne, WV
26366 Haywood, WV
26369 Hepzibah, WV
26372 Horner, WV
26374 Independence, WV
26376 Ireland, WV
26376 Wildcat, WV
26377 Alvy, WV
26377 Jacksonburg, WV
26377 Lima, WV
26378 Jane Lew, WV
26378 Kincheloe, WV
26384 Linn, WV
26385 Lost Creek, WV
26385 Mcwhorter, WV
26386 Dola, WV
26386 Lumberport, WV

264

26404 Meadowbrook, WV
26405 Kasson, WV
26405 Moatsville, WV
26408 Craigmoore, WV
26408 Mount Clare, WV
26410 Newburg, WV
26411 New Milton, WV
26412 Orlando, WV
26415 Greenwood, WV
26415 Mountain, WV
26415 Pennsboro, WV
26415 Toll Gate, WV
26416 Philippi, WV
26419 Hastings, WV
26419 Pine Grove, WV
26421 Pullman, WV
26422 Reynoldsville, WV
26424 Rosemont, WV
26425 Manheim, WV
26425 Rowlesburg, WV
26426 Bristol, WV
26426 Industrial, WV
26426 Salem, WV
26426 Wolf Summit, WV
26430 Sand Fork, WV
26430 Stouts Mills, WV
26431 Adamsville, WV
26431 Francis Mine, WV
26431 Owings, WV
26431 Peora, WV
26431 Pine Bluff, WV
26431 Saltwell, WV
26431 Shinnston, WV
26434 Shirley, WV
26435 Simpson, WV
26436 Smithburg, WV
26437 Smithfield, WV
26438 Spelter, WV
26440 Thornton, WV
26443 Troy, WV
26444 Tunnelton, WV
26447 Roanoke, WV
26447 Walkersville, WV
26448 Wallace, WV
26451 West Milford, WV
26452 Valley Chapel, WV
26452 Weston, WV
26456 Blandville, WV
26456 West Union, WV
26463 Wyatt, WV

265

26501 Morgantown, WV
26501 Westover, WV
26502 Morgantown, WV
26502 Westover, WV
26504 Morgantown, WV
26504 Star City, WV
26505 Booth, WV

26505 Everettville, WV
26505 Morgantown, WV
26505 Star City, WV
26506 Morgantown, WV
26507 Morgantown, WV
26508 Little Falls, WV
26508 Morgantown, WV
26519 Albright, WV
26520 Arthurdale, WV
26521 Blacksville, WV
26524 Bretz, WV
26525 Brandonville, WV
26525 Bruceton Mills, WV
26525 Cuzzart, WV
26525 Hazelton, WV
26527 Cassville, WV
26531 Dellslow, WV
26534 Granville, WV
26537 Kingwood, WV
26541 Core, WV
26541 Maidsville, WV
26542 Cascade, WV
26542 Masontown, WV
26543 Osage, WV
26544 Pentress, WV
26546 Pursglove, WV
26547 Reedsville, WV
26554 Fairmont, WV
26554 Jordan, WV
26554 Monongah, WV
26554 Pleasant Valley, WV
26554 White Hall, WV
26555 Fairmont, WV
26555 Monongah, WV
26555 Whitehall, WV
26559 Barrackville, WV
26560 Baxter, WV
26561 Big Run, WV
26562 Burton, WV
26562 Coburn, WV
26563 Carolina, WV
26566 Colfax, WV
26568 Enterprise, WV
26570 Fairview, WV
26571 Farmington, WV
26572 Four States, WV
26574 Grant Town, WV
26575 Hundred, WV
26576 Idamay, WV
26578 Kingmont, WV
26581 Knob Fork, WV
26581 Littleton, WV
26581 Wileyville, WV
26582 Mannington, WV
26585 Metz, WV
26586 Montana Mines, WV
26587 Rachel, WV
26588 Rivesville, WV
26590 Wadestown, WV
26590 Wana, WV
26591 Worthington, WV

266

26601 Centralia, WV
26601 Herold, WV
26601 Newville, WV
26601 Sutton, WV
26610 Birch River, WV
26611 Cedarville, WV
26611 Flower, WV
26615 Copen, WV
26617 Dille, WV
26619 Exchange, WV
26619 Riffle, WV
26621 Corley, WV
26621 Flatwoods, WV
26623 Clem, WV
26623 Frametown, WV
26623 Glendon, WV
26623 Wilsie, WV
26624 Chapel, WV
26624 Gassaway, WV
26627 Heaters, WV
26629 Little Birch, WV
26629 Tesla, WV
26631 Falls Mill, WV
26631 Napier, WV
26636 Nicut, WV
26636 Perkins, WV
26636 Rosedale, WV
26638 Shock, WV
26651 Summersville, WV
26656 Belva, WV
26660 Calvin, WV
26662 Canvas, WV
26667 Drennen, WV
26671 Gilboa, WV
26675 Keslers Cross Lanes, WV
26676 Leivasy, WV
26678 Mount Lookout, WV
26679 Mount Nebo, WV
26679 Runa, WV
26680 Nallen, WV
26680 Russelville, WV
26681 Nettie, WV
26684 Pool, WV
26690 Jodie, WV
26690 Swiss, WV
26691 Tioga, WV

267

26704 Augusta, WV
26705 Amboy, WV
26705 Aurora, WV
26707 Bayard, WV
26707 Wilson, WV
26710 Burlington, WV
26710 Medley, WV
26711 Capon Bridge, WV
26714 Delray, WV
26716 Eglon, WV
26716 Horse Shoe Run, WV
26717 Elk Garden, WV
26719 Fort Ashby, WV
26720 Gormania, WV
26722 Green Spring, WV
26726 Keyser, WV
26726 Rocket Center, WV
26726 Scherr, WV
26726 Short Gap, WV
26731 Lahmansville, WV
26739 Mount Storm, WV
26743 New Creek, WV
26750 Piedmont, WV
26753 Carpendale, WV
26753 Patterson Creek, WV
26753 Ridgeley, WV
26755 Kirby, WV
26755 Rio, WV
26757 Romney, WV
26757 Three Churches, WV
26761 Shanks, WV
26763 Springfield, WV
26764 Corinth, WV
26764 Hopemont, WV
26764 Terra Alta, WV
26767 Wiley Ford, WV

268

26801 Baker, WV
26802 Brandywine, WV
26802 Fort Seybert, WV
26804 Circleville, WV
26807 Franklin, WV
26808 High View, WV
26810 Lost City, WV
26810 Lost River, WV
26812 Mathias, WV
26814 Riverton, WV
26815 Moyers, WV
26815 Sugar Grove, WV
26817 Bloomery, WV
26818 Fisher, WV
26823 Capon Springs, WV
26833 Maysville, WV
26836 Moorefield, WV
26836 Rig, WV
26838 Milam, WV
26845 Old Fields, WV
26847 Arthur, WV
26847 Dorcas, WV
26847 Landes Station, WV
26847 Petersburg, WV
26851 Wardensville, WV
26852 Junction, WV
26852 Purgitsville, WV
26855 Cabins, WV
26865 Lehew, WV
26865 Yellow Spring, WV
26866 Upper Tract, WV
26884 Seneca Rocks, WV
26886 Onego, WV

270

27006 Advance, NC
27006 Bermuda Run, NC
27007 Ararat, NC
27009 Belews Creek, NC
27010 Bethania, NC
27011 Boonville, NC
27012 Clemmons, NC
27013 Barber, NC
27013 Cleveland, NC
27014 Cooleemee, NC
27016 Danbury, NC
27017 Dobson, NC
27018 East Bend, NC
27019 Germanton, NC
27020 Hamptonville, NC
27021 King, NC
27022 Lawsonville, NC
27023 Lewisville, NC
27024 Lowgap, NC
27025 Madison, NC
27027 Mayodan, NC
27028 Mocksville, NC
27030 Mount Airy, NC
27031 Mount Airy, NC
27031 White Plains, NC
27040 Pfafftown, NC
27041 Pilot Mountain, NC
27042 Pine Hall, NC
27043 Pinnacle, NC
27045 Rural Hall, NC
27046 Sandy Ridge, NC
27047 Siloam, NC
27048 Stoneville, NC
27049 Toast, NC
27050 Tobaccoville, NC
27051 Walkertown, NC
27052 Walnut Cove, NC
27053 Westfield, NC
27054 Woodleaf, NC
27055 Yadkinville, NC
27094 Rural Hall, NC
27098 Rural Hall, NC
27099 Rural Hall, NC

271

27101 Winston Salem, NC
27102 Winston Salem, NC
27103 Winston Salem, NC
27104 Winston Salem, NC
27105 Winston Salem, NC
27106 Winston Salem, NC
27107 Winston Salem, NC
27108 Winston Salem, NC
27109 Winston Salem, NC
27110 Winston Salem, NC
27111 Winston Salem, NC
27113 Winston Salem, NC
27114 Winston Salem, NC
27115 Winston Salem, NC
27116 Winston Salem, NC
27117 Winston Salem, NC
27120 Winston Salem, NC
27127 Winston Salem, NC
27130 Winston Salem, NC
27150 Winston Salem, NC
27152 Winston Salem, NC
27155 Winston Salem, NC
27157 Winston Salem, NC
27198 Winston Salem, NC
27199 Winston Salem, NC

272

27201 Alamance, NC
27202 Altamahaw, NC
27203 Asheboro, NC
27204 Asheboro, NC
27205 Asheboro, NC
27207 Bear Creek, NC
27208 Bennett, NC
27209 Biscoe, NC
27212 Blanch, NC
27213 Bonlee, NC
27214 Browns Summit, NC
27215 Burlington, NC
27215 Glen Raven, NC
27216 Burlington, NC
27217 Burlington, NC
27217 Green Level, NC
27228 Bynum, NC
27228 Pittsboro, NC
27229 Candor, NC
27230 Cedar Falls, NC
27231 Cedar Grove, NC
27233 Climax, NC
27235 Colfax, NC
27237 Cumnock, NC
27237 Sanford, NC
27239 Denton, NC
27242 Eagle Springs, NC
27243 Efland, NC
27244 Elon, NC
27244 Elon College, NC
27247 Ether, NC
27248 Franklinville, NC
27249 Gibsonville, NC
27252 Goldston, NC
27253 Graham, NC
27256 Gulf, NC
27258 Haw River, NC
27259 Highfalls, NC
27260 High Point, NC
27261 High Point, NC
27262 High Point, NC
27263 Archdale, NC
27263 High Point, NC
27264 High Point, NC
27265 High Point, NC
27278 Hillsborough, NC
27281 Foxfire Village, NC
27281 Jackson Springs, NC
27282 Jamestown, NC
27283 Julian, NC
27284 Kernersville, NC
27285 Kernersville, NC
27288 Eden, NC
27289 Eden, NC
27291 Leasburg, NC
27292 Lexington, NC
27293 Lexington, NC
27294 Lexington, NC
27295 Lexington, NC
27298 Liberty, NC
27299 Linwood, NC

273

27301 Mc Leansville, NC
27302 Mebane, NC
27305 Milton, NC
27306 Mount Gilead, NC
27310 Oak Ridge, NC
27311 Pelham, NC
27312 Fearrington Village, NC
27312 Pittsboro, NC
27313 Pleasant Garden, NC
27314 Prospect Hill, NC
27315 Providence, NC
27316 Coleridge, NC
27316 Ramseur, NC
27317 Randleman, NC
27320 Reidsville, NC
27323 Reidsville, NC
27325 Glendon, NC
27325 Robbins, NC
27326 Ruffin, NC
27330 Buffalo Lake, NC
27330 Colon, NC
27330 Sanford, NC
27331 Sanford, NC
27332 Sanford, NC
27340 Saxapahaw, NC
27341 Seagrove, NC
27342 Sedalia, NC
27343 Semora, NC
27344 Siler City, NC
27349 Snow Camp, NC
27350 Sophia, NC
27351 Southmont, NC
27355 Staley, NC
27356 Star, NC
27357 Stokesdale, NC
27358 Summerfield, NC
27359 Swepsonville, NC
27360 Thomasville, NC
27361 Thomasville, NC
27370 Trinity, NC
27371 Troy, NC
27373 Wallburg, NC
27374 Welcome, NC
27375 Wentworth, NC
27376 Seven Lakes, NC
27376 West End, NC
27377 Whitsett, NC
27379 Yanceyville, NC

274

27401 Greensboro, NC
27402 Greensboro, NC
27403 Greensboro, NC
27404 Greensboro, NC
27405 Greensboro, NC
27406 Greensboro, NC
27407 Greensboro, NC
27408 Greensboro, NC
27409 Greensboro, NC
27410 Greensboro, NC
27411 Greensboro, NC
27412 Greensboro, NC
27413 Greensboro, NC
27415 Greensboro, NC
27416 Greensboro, NC
27417 Greensboro, NC
27419 Greensboro, NC
27420 Greensboro, NC
27425 Amf Greensboro, NC
27425 Greensboro, NC
27427 Greensboro, NC
27429 Greensboro, NC
27435 Greensboro, NC
27438 Greensboro, NC
27455 Greensboro, NC
27495 Greensboro, NC
27497 Greensboro, NC
27498 Greensboro, NC
27499 Greensboro, NC

275

27501 Angier, NC
27502 Apex, NC
27503 Bahama, NC
27504 Benson, NC
27505 Broadway, NC
27506 Buies Creek, NC
27507 Bullock, NC
27508 Bunn, NC
27509 Butner, NC
27510 Carrboro, NC
27511 Cary, NC
27512 Cary, NC
27513 Cary, NC
27514 Chapel Hill, NC
27515 Chapel Hill, NC
27516 Chapel Hill, NC
27517 Chapel Hill, NC
27518 Cary, NC
27519 Cary, NC
27520 Clayton, NC
27521 Coats, NC
27522 Creedmoor, NC
27523 Apex, NC
27524 Four Oaks, NC
27525 Franklinton, NC
27526 Fuquay Varina, NC
27527 Clayton, NC
27528 Clayton, NC
27529 Garner, NC
27530 Goldsboro, NC
27531 Goldsboro, NC
27531 Seymour Johnson A F B, NC
27531 Seymour Johnson Afb, NC
27532 Goldsboro, NC
27533 Goldsboro, NC
27534 Goldsboro, NC
27536 Henderson, NC
27537 Henderson, NC
27539 Apex, NC
27540 Holly Springs, NC
27541 Hurdle Mills, NC
27542 Kenly, NC
27543 Kipling, NC
27544 Kittrell, NC
27545 Knightdale, NC
27546 Lillington, NC
27549 Centerville, NC
27549 Louisburg, NC
27551 Macon, NC
27552 Mamers, NC
27553 Manson, NC
27555 Micro, NC
27556 Middleburg, NC
27557 Middlesex, NC
27559 Moncure, NC
27560 Morrisville, NC
27562 New Hill, NC
27563 Norlina, NC
27565 Oxford, NC
27568 Pine Level, NC
27569 Princeton, NC
27570 Ridgeway, NC
27571 Rolesville, NC
27572 Rougemont, NC
27573 Roxboro, NC
27574 Roxboro, NC
27576 Selma, NC
27577 Smithfield, NC
27581 Stem, NC
27582 Stovall, NC
27583 Timberlake, NC
27584 Townsville, NC
27586 Vaughan, NC
27587 Wake Forest, NC
27588 Wake Forest, NC
27589 Warrenton, NC
27591 Eagle Rock, NC
27591 Wendell, NC
27592 Willow Spring, NC
27593 Wilsons Mills, NC
27594 Wise, NC
27596 Youngsville, NC
27597 Zebulon, NC
27599 Chapel Hill, NC

276

27601 Raleigh, NC
27602 Raleigh, NC
27603 Raleigh, NC
27604 Brentwood, NC
27604 Raleigh, NC
27605 Raleigh, NC
27606 Raleigh, NC
27607 Raleigh, NC
27608 Raleigh, NC
27609 Raleigh, NC
27610 Raleigh, NC
27611 Raleigh, NC
27612 Raleigh, NC
27613 Raleigh, NC
27614 Raleigh, NC
27615 Raleigh, NC
27616 Brentwood, NC
27616 Raleigh, NC
27617 Raleigh, NC
27619 Raleigh, NC
27620 Raleigh, NC
27621 Raleigh, NC
27622 Raleigh, NC
27623 Raleigh, NC
27624 Raleigh, NC
27625 Raleigh, NC
27626 Raleigh, NC
27627 Raleigh, NC
27628 Raleigh, NC
27629 Raleigh, NC

27634 Raleigh, NC
27635 Raleigh, NC
27636 Raleigh, NC
27640 Raleigh, NC
27650 Raleigh, NC
27656 Raleigh, NC
27658 Raleigh, NC
27661 Raleigh, NC
27668 Raleigh, NC
27675 Raleigh, NC
27676 Raleigh, NC
27690 Raleigh, NC
27695 Raleigh, NC
27697 Raleigh, NC
27698 Raleigh, NC
27699 Raleigh, NC

277

27701 Durham, NC
27702 Durham, NC
27703 Durham, NC
27704 Durham, NC
27705 Durham, NC
27706 Durham, NC
27707 Durham, NC
27707 Shannon Plaza, NC
27708 Durham, NC
27709 Durham, NC
27709 Research Triangle Park, NC
27710 Durham, NC
27711 Durham, NC
27711 Research Triangle Park, NC
27712 Durham, NC
27712 Eno Valley, NC
27713 Durham, NC
27715 Durham, NC
27717 Durham, NC
27722 Durham, NC

278

27801 Rocky Mount, NC
27802 Rocky Mount, NC
27803 Rocky Mount, NC
27804 Rocky Mount, NC
27804 Wesleyan College, NC
27805 Aulander, NC
27806 Aurora, NC
27807 Bailey, NC
27808 Bath, NC
27809 Battleboro, NC
27810 Belhaven, NC
27811 Bellarthur, NC
27812 Bethel, NC
27813 Black Creek, NC
27814 Blounts Creek, NC
27815 Rocky Mount, NC
27816 Castalia, NC
27817 Chocowinity, NC
27818 Como, NC
27819 Conetoe, NC
27820 Conway, NC
27820 Milwaukee, NC
27821 Edward, NC
27822 Elm City, NC
27823 Enfield, NC
27824 Engelhard, NC
27825 Everetts, NC
27826 Fairfield, NC
27827 Falkland, NC
27828 Farmville, NC
27829 Fountain, NC
27830 Eureka, NC
27830 Fremont, NC
27831 Garysburg, NC
27831 Gumberry, NC
27832 Gaston, NC
27833 Greenville, NC
27834 Greenville, NC
27835 Greenville, NC
27836 Greenville, NC
27837 Grimesland, NC
27839 Halifax, NC
27840 Hamilton, NC
27841 Hassell, NC
27842 Henrico, NC
27843 Hobgood, NC
27844 Hollister, NC
27845 Jackson, NC
27845 Lasker, NC
27846 Jamesville, NC
27847 Kelford, NC
27849 Lewiston Woodville, NC
27850 Littleton, NC
27851 Lucama, NC
27852 Macclesfield, NC
27853 Margarettsville, NC
27855 Murfreesboro, NC
27856 Momeyer, NC
27856 Nashville, NC
27857 Oak City, NC
27858 Greenville, NC
27860 Pantego, NC
27861 Parmele, NC
27862 Pendleton, NC
27863 Pikeville, NC
27864 Pinetops, NC
27865 Pinetown, NC
27866 Pleasant Hill, NC
27867 Potecasi, NC
27868 Red Oak, NC
27869 Rich Square, NC
27870 Roanoke Rapids, NC
27870 Roanoke Rapids Air Force Sta, NC
27871 Robersonville, NC
27872 Roxobel, NC
27873 Saratoga, NC
27874 Scotland Neck, NC
27875 Scranton, NC
27876 Seaboard, NC
27877 Severn, NC
27878 Sharpsburg, NC
27879 Simpson, NC
27880 Sims, NC
27881 Speed, NC
27882 Spring Hope, NC
27883 Stantonsburg, NC
27884 Stokes, NC
27885 Swanquarter, NC
27886 Leggett, NC
27886 Princeville, NC
27886 Tarboro, NC
27887 Tillery, NC
27888 Walstonburg, NC
27889 Washington, NC
27890 Weldon, NC
27891 Whitakers, NC
27892 Bear Grass, NC
27892 Beargrass, NC
27892 Williamston, NC
27893 Wilson, NC
27894 Wilson, NC
27895 Wilson, NC
27896 Wilson, NC
27897 George, NC
27897 Woodland, NC

279

27906 Elizabeth City, NC
27910 Ahoskie, NC
27915 Avon, NC
27916 Aydlett, NC
27917 Barco, NC
27919 Belvidere, NC
27920 Buxton, NC
27921 Camden, NC
27922 Cofield, NC
27923 Coinjock, NC
27924 Colerain, NC
27925 Columbia, NC
27926 Corapeake, NC
27927 Corolla, NC
27928 Creswell, NC
27929 Currituck, NC
27930 Durants Neck, NC
27930 Hertford, NC
27932 Edenton, NC
27935 Eure, NC
27936 Frisco, NC
27937 Gates, NC
27938 Gatesville, NC
27939 Grandy, NC
27941 Harbinger, NC
27942 Harrellsville, NC
27943 Hatteras, NC
27944 Durants Neck, NC
27944 Hertford, NC
27946 Hobbsville, NC
27947 Jarvisburg, NC
27948 Kill Devil Hills, NC
27949 Duck, NC
27949 Kitty Hawk, NC
27949 Southern Shores, NC
27950 Knotts Island, NC
27953 East Lake, NC
27953 Manns Harbor, NC
27954 Manteo, NC
27956 Maple, NC
27957 Merry Hill, NC
27958 Moyock, NC
27959 Nags Head, NC
27960 Ocracoke, NC
27962 Plymouth, NC
27964 Point Harbor, NC
27965 Poplar Branch, NC
27966 Powells Point, NC
27967 Powellsville, NC
27968 Rodanthe, NC
27969 Roduco, NC
27970 Roper, NC
27972 Salvo, NC
27973 Shawboro, NC
27974 Shiloh, NC
27976 South Mills, NC
27978 Stumpy Point, NC
27979 Sunbury, NC
27980 Tyner, NC
27981 Wanchese, NC
27982 Waves, NC
27983 Askewville, NC
27983 Windsor, NC
27985 Winfall, NC
27986 Winton, NC

280

28001 Albemarle, NC
28002 Albemarle, NC
28006 Alexis, NC
28007 Ansonville, NC
28009 Badin, NC
28010 Barium Springs, NC
28012 Belmont, NC
28016 Bessemer City, NC
28017 Boiling Springs, NC
28018 Bostic, NC
28018 Golden Valley, NC
28019 Caroleen, NC
28020 Casar, NC
28021 Cherryville, NC
28023 China Grove, NC
28024 Cliffside, NC
28025 Concord, NC
28026 Concord, NC
28027 Concord, NC
28031 Cornelius, NC
28032 Cramerton, NC
28033 Crouse, NC
28034 Dallas, NC
28035 Davidson, NC
28036 Davidson, NC
28037 Denver, NC
28038 Earl, NC
28039 East Spencer, NC
28040 Ellenboro, NC
28041 Faith, NC
28042 Fallston, NC
28043 Alexander Mills, NC
28043 Forest City, NC
28052 Gastonia, NC
28053 Gastonia, NC
28054 Gastonia, NC
28055 Gastonia, NC
28056 Gastonia, NC
28070 Huntersville, NC
28071 Gold Hill, NC
28072 Granite Quarry, NC
28073 Grover, NC
28074 Harris, NC
28075 Harrisburg, NC
28076 Henrietta, NC
28077 High Shoals, NC
28078 Huntersville, NC
28079 Indian Trail, NC
28079 Lake Park, NC
28080 Iron Station, NC
28081 Kannapolis, NC
28082 Kannapolis, NC
28083 Kannapolis, NC
28086 Kings Mountain, NC
28088 Landis, NC
28089 Lattimore, NC
28090 Lawndale, NC
28091 Lilesville, NC
28092 Boger City, NC
28092 Lincolnton, NC
28093 Lincolnton, NC
28097 Locust, NC
28098 Lowell, NC

281

28101 Mc Adenville, NC
28102 Mc Farlan, NC
28103 Marshville, NC
28104 Matthews, NC
28104 Stallings, NC
28104 Weddington, NC
28104 Wesley Chapel, NC
28105 Matthews, NC
28106 Matthews, NC
28107 Midland, NC
28108 Mineral Springs, NC
28109 Misenheimer, NC
28110 Monroe, NC
28110 Unionville, NC
28111 Monroe, NC
28112 Monroe, NC
28114 Mooresboro, NC
28115 Mooresville, NC
28117 Mooresville, NC
28119 Morven, NC
28120 Mount Holly, NC
28120 Mt Holly, NC
28123 Mooresville, NC
28123 Mount Mourne, NC
28124 Mount Pleasant, NC
28125 Mount Ulla, NC
28126 Newell, NC
28127 Badin Lake, NC
28127 New London, NC
28128 Norwood, NC
28129 Oakboro, NC
28129 Red Cross, NC
28130 Paw Creek, NC
28133 Peachland, NC
28134 Pineville, NC
28135 Polkton, NC
28136 Polkville, NC
28136 Shelby, NC
28137 Richfield, NC
28138 Rockwell, NC
28139 Rutherfordton, NC
28144 Salisbury, NC
28145 Salisbury, NC
28146 Granite Quarry, NC
28146 Salisbury, NC
28147 Salisbury, NC
28150 Kingstown, NC
28150 Shelby, NC
28151 Shelby, NC
28152 Shelby, NC
28159 Spencer, NC
28160 Spindale, NC
28163 Stanfield, NC
28164 Stanley, NC
28166 Troutman, NC
28167 Union Mills, NC
28168 Vale, NC
28169 Waco, NC
28170 Wadesboro, NC
28173 Marvin, NC
28173 Waxhaw, NC
28174 Wingate, NC

282

28201 Charlotte, NC
28202 Charlotte, NC
28203 Charlotte, NC
28204 Charlotte, NC
28205 Charlotte, NC
28206 Charlotte, NC
28207 Charlotte, NC
28208 Charlotte, NC
28209 Charlotte, NC
28210 Charlotte, NC
28211 Charlotte, NC
28212 Charlotte, NC
28213 Charlotte, NC
28214 Charlotte, NC
28215 Charlotte, NC
28216 Charlotte, NC
28217 Charlotte, NC
28218 Charlotte, NC
28219 Charlotte, NC
28220 Charlotte, NC
28221 Charlotte, NC
28222 Charlotte, NC
28223 Charlotte, NC
28224 Charlotte, NC
28226 Charlotte, NC
28227 Charlotte, NC
28227 Mint Hill, NC
28228 Charlotte, NC
28229 Charlotte, NC
28230 Charlotte, NC
28231 Charlotte, NC
28232 Charlotte, NC
28233 Charlotte, NC
28234 Charlotte, NC
28235 Charlotte, NC
28236 Charlotte, NC
28237 Charlotte, NC
28241 Charlotte, NC
28242 Charlotte, NC
28243 Charlotte, NC
28244 Charlotte, NC
28246 Charlotte, NC
28247 Charlotte, NC
28250 Charlotte, NC
28253 Charlotte, NC
28254 Charlotte, NC
28255 Charlotte, NC
28256 Charlotte, NC
28258 Charlotte, NC
28260 Charlotte, NC
28262 Charlotte, NC
28263 Charlotte, NC
28265 Charlotte, NC
28266 Charlotte, NC
28269 Charlotte, NC
28270 Charlotte, NC
28271 Charlotte, NC
28272 Charlotte, NC
28273 Charlotte, NC
28274 Charlotte, NC
28275 Charlotte, NC
28277 Charlotte, NC
28278 Charlotte, NC
28280 Charlotte, NC
28281 Charlotte, NC
28282 Charlotte, NC
28284 Charlotte, NC
28285 Charlotte, NC
28287 Charlotte, NC
28288 Charlotte, NC
28289 Charlotte, NC
28290 Charlotte, NC
28296 Charlotte, NC
28297 Charlotte, NC
28299 Charlotte, NC

283

28301 E Fayetteville, NC
28301 East Fayetteville, NC
28301 Fayetteville, NC
28302 Fayetteville, NC
28303 Fayetteville, NC
28304 Fayetteville, NC
28305 Fayetteville, NC
28306 Fayetteville, NC
28307 Fayetteville, NC
28307 Fort Bragg, NC
28308 Fayetteville, NC
28308 Pope Army Airfield, NC
28309 Fayetteville, NC
28310 Fort Bragg, NC
28311 Fayetteville, NC
28312 Eastover, NC
28312 Fayetteville, NC
28314 Fayetteville, NC
28315 Aberdeen, NC
28318 Autryville, NC
28319 Barnesville, NC
28320 Bladenboro, NC
28320 Butters, NC
28323 Bunnlevel, NC
28325 Calypso, NC
28326 Cameron, NC
28327 Carthage, NC
28327 Whispering Pines, NC
28328 Clinton, NC
28329 Clinton, NC
28330 Cordova, NC
28331 Cumberland, NC
28332 Dublin, NC
28333 Dudley, NC
28334 Dunn, NC
28335 Dunn, NC
28337 Elizabethtown, NC
28338 Ellerbe, NC
28339 Erwin, NC
28340 Fairmont, NC
28341 Faison, NC
28342 Falcon, NC
28343 Gibson, NC
28344 Godwin, NC
28345 Hamlet, NC
28347 Hoffman, NC
28348 Hope Mills, NC
28349 Kenansville, NC
28350 Lakeview, NC
28351 Laurel Hill, NC
28352 Laurinburg, NC
28353 Laurinburg, NC
28355 Lemon Springs, NC
28356 Linden, NC
28357 Lumber Bridge, NC
28358 Lumberton, NC
28359 Lumberton, NC
28360 Lumberton, NC
28362 Marietta, NC
28363 Marston, NC
28364 Maxton, NC
28365 Mount Olive, NC
28366 Newton Grove, NC
28367 Norman, NC
28368 Olivia, NC
28369 Orrum, NC
28370 Pinehurst, NC
28371 Parkton, NC
28372 Pembroke, NC
28373 Pinebluff, NC
28374 Pinehurst, NC
28375 Proctorville, NC
28376 Raeford, NC
28377 Red Springs, NC
28378 Rex, NC
28379 Rockingham, NC
28380 Rockingham, NC
28382 Roseboro, NC
28383 Raynham, NC
28383 Rowland, NC
28384 Saint Pauls, NC
28385 Salemburg, NC
28386 Rennert, NC
28386 Shannon, NC
28387 Southern Pines, NC
28390 Spring Lake, NC
28391 Stedman, NC
28392 Tar Heel, NC
28393 Turkey, NC
28394 Vass, NC
28395 Wade, NC
28396 Wagram, NC
28398 Bowdens, NC
28398 Warsaw, NC
28399 White Oak, NC

284

28401 Cape Fear, NC
28401 Wilmington, NC

28402 Wilmington, NC
28403 Wilmington, NC
28404 Wilmington, NC
28405 Wilmington, NC
28406 Wilmington, NC
28407 Wilmington, NC
28408 Wilmington, NC
28409 Wilmington, NC
28410 Wilmington, NC
28411 Wilmington, NC
28412 Wilmington, NC
28420 Ash, NC
28421 Atkinson, NC
28422 Bolivia, NC
28423 Bolton, NC
28424 Brunswick, NC
28425 Burgaw, NC
28425 Saint Helena, NC
28428 Carolina Beach, NC
28429 Castle Hayne, NC
28430 Cerro Gordo, NC
28431 Chadbourn, NC
28432 Clarendon, NC
28433 Clarkton, NC
28434 Council, NC
28435 Currie, NC
28436 Delco, NC
28438 Boardman, NC
28438 Evergreen, NC
28439 Fair Bluff, NC
28441 Garland, NC
28441 Ingold, NC
28442 Hallsboro, NC
28443 Hampstead, NC
28444 Harrells, NC
28445 Holly Ridge, NC
28445 Surf City, NC
28445 Topsail Beach, NC
28447 Ivanhoe, NC
28448 Kelly, NC
28449 Kure Beach, NC
28450 Lake Waccamaw, NC
28451 Belville, NC
28451 Leland, NC
28451 Navassa, NC
28451 Northwest, NC
28452 Longwood, NC
28453 Magnolia, NC
28454 Maple Hill, NC
28455 Nakina, NC
28456 East Arcadia, NC
28456 Riegelwood, NC
28456 Sandyfield, NC
28457 Rocky Point, NC
28458 Greenevers, NC
28458 Rose Hill, NC
28459 Shallotte, NC
28460 N Topsail Beach, NC
28460 Sneads Ferry, NC
28461 Bald Head Island, NC
28461 Boiling Spring Lakes, NC
28461 Saint James, NC
28461 Southport, NC
28462 Holden Beach, NC
28462 Supply, NC
28463 Tabor City, NC
28464 Teachey, NC
28465 Caswell Beach, NC
28465 Oak Island, NC
28466 Wallace, NC
28467 Calabash, NC
28467 Carolina Shores, NC
28467 Ocean Isle Beach, NC
28468 Shallotte, NC
28468 Sunset Beach, NC
28469 Ocean Isle Beach, NC
28469 Shallotte, NC
28470 Shallotte, NC
28470 South Brunswick, NC
28472 Whiteville, NC
28478 Watha, NC
28478 Willard, NC
28479 Winnabow, NC
28480 Wrightsville Beach, NC

285

28501 Kinston, NC
28502 Kinston, NC
28503 Kinston, NC
28504 Kinston, NC
28508 Albertson, NC
28509 Alliance, NC
28510 Arapahoe, NC
28510 Minnesott Beach, NC
28511 Atlantic, NC
28512 Atlantic Beach, NC
28512 Indian Beach, NC
28512 Pine Knoll Shores, NC
28513 Ayden, NC
28515 Bayboro, NC
28515 Mesic, NC
28516 Beaufort, NC
28518 Beulaville, NC
28519 Bridgeton, NC
28520 Cedar Island, NC
28521 Chinquapin, NC
28522 Comfort, NC
28523 Cove City, NC
28524 Davis, NC
28525 Deep Run, NC
28526 Dover, NC
28527 Ernul, NC
28528 Gloucester, NC
28529 Grantsboro, NC
28530 Grifton, NC
28531 Harkers Island, NC
28532 Havelock, NC
28533 Cherry Point, NC
28533 Havelock, NC
28537 Hobucken, NC
28538 Hookerton, NC
28539 Hubert, NC
28540 Jacksonville, NC
28541 Jacksonville, NC
28542 Camp Lejeune, NC
28542 Jacksonville, NC
28543 Jacksonville, NC
28543 Tarawa Terrace, NC
28544 Jacksonville, NC
28544 Midway Park, NC
28545 Jacksonville, NC
28545 Mccutcheon Field, NC
28546 Jacksonville, NC
28547 Camp Lejeune, NC
28551 La Grange, NC
28552 Lowland, NC
28553 Marshallberg, NC
28554 Maury, NC
28555 Maysville, NC
28556 Merritt, NC
28557 Morehead City, NC
28560 New Bern, NC
28561 New Bern, NC
28562 New Bern, NC
28562 Trent Woods, NC
28563 New Bern, NC
28564 New Bern, NC
28570 Bogue, NC
28570 Newport, NC
28571 Oriental, NC
28572 Pink Hill, NC
28573 Pollocksville, NC
28574 Richlands, NC
28575 Salter Path, NC
28577 Sealevel, NC
28578 Seven Springs, NC
28579 Smyrna, NC
28579 Williston, NC
28580 Snow Hill, NC
28581 Sealevel, NC
28581 Stacy, NC
28582 Stella, NC
28583 Stonewall, NC
28584 Cape Carteret, NC
28584 Cedar Point, NC
28584 Peletier, NC
28584 Swansboro, NC
28585 Trenton, NC
28586 Vanceboro, NC
28587 Vandemere, NC
28589 Williston, NC
28590 Winterville, NC
28594 Emerald Isle, NC

286

28601 Hickory, NC
28602 Hickory, NC
28603 Hickory, NC
28604 Banner Elk, NC
28604 Beech Mountain, NC
28604 Seven Devils, NC
28604 Sugar Mountain, NC
28605 Blowing Rock, NC
28606 Boomer, NC
28607 Boone, NC
28608 Boone, NC
28609 Catawba, NC
28609 Longisland, NC
28610 Claremont, NC
28611 Collettsville, NC
28612 Connelly Springs, NC
28613 Conover, NC
28615 Creston, NC
28616 Crossnore, NC
28617 Crumpler, NC
28618 Deep Gap, NC
28618 Triplett, NC
28619 Drexel, NC
28621 Elkin, NC
28622 Elk Park, NC
28623 Ennice, NC
28624 Ferguson, NC
28625 Statesville, NC
28626 Fleetwood, NC
28627 Glade Valley, NC
28628 Glen Alpine, NC
28629 Glendale Springs, NC
28630 Granite Falls, NC
28630 Sawmills, NC
28631 Grassy Creek, NC
28633 Lenoir, NC
28634 Harmony, NC
28635 Hays, NC
28636 Hiddenite, NC
28637 Hildebran, NC
28638 Hudson, NC
28640 Jefferson, NC
28641 Jonas Ridge, NC
28642 Jonesville, NC
28643 Husk, NC
28643 Lansing, NC
28644 Laurel Springs, NC
28645 Cajahs Mountain, NC
28645 Cedar Rock, NC
28645 Lenoir, NC
28646 Linville, NC
28647 Linville Falls, NC
28649 Mc Grady, NC
28650 Maiden, NC
28651 Millers Creek, NC
28651 Wilbar, NC
28652 Minneapolis, NC
28653 Montezuma, NC
28654 Moravian Falls, NC
28655 Morganton, NC
28656 North Wilkesboro, NC
28657 Frank, NC
28657 Newland, NC
28658 Newton, NC
28659 North Wilkesboro, NC
28660 Olin, NC
28661 Patterson, NC
28662 Pineola, NC
28663 Piney Creek, NC
28664 Plumtree, NC
28665 Purlear, NC
28666 Icard, NC
28667 Rhodhiss, NC
28668 Roaring Gap, NC
28669 Roaring River, NC
28670 Ronda, NC
28671 Rutherford College, NC
28671 Rutherfrd Col, NC
28672 Scottville, NC
28673 Sherrills Ford, NC
28675 Sparta, NC
28675 Whitehead, NC
28676 State Road, NC
28677 Statesville, NC
28678 Stony Point, NC
28679 Sugar Grove, NC
28680 Morganton, NC
28681 Taylorsville, NC
28682 Terrell, NC
28683 Thurmond, NC
28684 Todd, NC
28685 Traphill, NC
28687 Statesville, NC
28688 Turnersburg, NC
28689 Union Grove, NC
28690 Valdese, NC
28691 Banner Elk, NC
28691 Valle Crucis, NC
28692 Vilas, NC
28693 Warrensville, NC
28694 West Jefferson, NC
28697 Wilkesboro, NC
28698 Zionville, NC
28699 Scotts, NC

287

28701 Alexander, NC
28702 Almond, NC
28704 Arden, NC
28705 Bakersville, NC
28707 Balsam, NC
28708 Balsam Grove, NC
28709 Barnardsville, NC
28710 Bat Cave, NC
28711 Black Mountain, NC
28712 Brevard, NC
28713 Bryson City, NC
28714 Burnsville, NC
28715 Biltmore Lake, NC
28715 Candler, NC
28716 Canton, NC
28717 Cashiers, NC
28718 Cedar Mountain, NC
28719 Cherokee, NC
28720 Chimney Rock, NC
28721 Clyde, NC
28722 Columbus, NC
28723 Cullowhee, NC
28724 Dana, NC
28725 Dillsboro, NC
28726 East Flat Rock, NC
28727 Edneyville, NC
28728 Enka, NC
28729 Etowah, NC
28730 Fairview, NC
28731 Flat Rock, NC
28732 Fletcher, NC
28732 Mills River, NC
28733 Fontana Dam, NC
28734 Franklin, NC
28735 Gerton, NC
28736 Glenville, NC
28737 Glenwood, NC
28737 Marion, NC
28738 Hazelwood, NC
28739 Hendersonville, NC
28739 Laurel Park, NC
28740 Green Mountain, NC
28741 Highlands, NC
28742 Horse Shoe, NC
28743 Hot Springs, NC
28744 Franklin, NC
28745 Lake Junaluska, NC
28746 Lake Lure, NC
28747 Lake Toxaway, NC
28748 Leicester, NC
28749 Little Switzerland, NC
28750 Lynn, NC
28751 Maggie Valley, NC
28752 Marion, NC
28753 Marshall, NC
28754 Mars Hill, NC
28755 Micaville, NC
28756 Mill Spring, NC
28757 Montreat, NC
28758 Hendersonville, NC
28758 Mountain Home, NC
28759 Mills River, NC
28760 Naples, NC
28761 Nebo, NC
28762 Old Fort, NC
28763 Otto, NC
28765 Penland, NC
28766 Penrose, NC
28768 Pisgah Forest, NC
28770 Ridgecrest, NC
28771 Lake Santeetlah, NC
28771 Robbinsville, NC
28771 Tapoco, NC
28772 Rosman, NC
28773 Saluda, NC
28774 Sapphire, NC
28775 Scaly Mountain, NC
28776 Skyland, NC
28777 Spruce Pine, NC
28778 Swannanoa, NC
28779 Sylva, NC
28781 Aquone, NC
28781 Topton, NC
28782 Tryon, NC
28783 Tuckasegee, NC
28784 Tuxedo, NC
28785 Waynesville, NC
28786 Hazelwood, NC
28786 Waynesville, NC
28787 Weaverville, NC
28788 Webster, NC
28789 Whittier, NC
28790 Zirconia, NC
28791 Hendersonville, NC

288

28801 Asheville, NC
28802 Asheville, NC
28803 Asheville, NC
28803 Biltmore Forest, NC
28804 Asheville, NC
28804 Woodfin, NC
28805 Asheville, NC
28806 Asheville, NC
28810 Asheville, NC
28813 Asheville, NC
28814 Asheville, NC
28815 Asheville, NC
28816 Asheville, NC

289

28901 Andrews, NC
28902 Brasstown, NC
28903 Culberson, NC
28904 Hayesville, NC
28905 Marble, NC
28906 Murphy, NC
28909 Warne, NC

290

29001 Alcolu, SC
29002 Ballentine, SC
29003 Bamberg, SC
29006 Batesburg, SC
29006 Batesburg-Leesville, SC
29009 Bethune, SC
29010 Bishopville, SC
29010 Wisacky, SC
29014 Blackstock, SC
29015 Blair, SC
29016 Blythewood, SC
29018 Bowman, SC
29020 Camden, SC
29021 Camden, SC
29030 Cameron, SC
29030 Lone Star, SC
29031 Carlisle, SC
29032 Cassatt, SC
29033 Cayce, SC
29033 West Columbia, SC
29036 Chapin, SC
29037 Chappells, SC
29038 Cope, SC
29039 Cordova, SC
29040 Dalzell, SC
29041 Davis Station, SC
29042 Denmark, SC
29044 Eastover, SC
29045 Elgin, SC
29046 Elliott, SC
29047 Elloree, SC
29048 Eutawville, SC
29051 Gable, SC
29052 Gadsden, SC
29053 Gaston, SC
29054 Gilbert, SC
29055 Great Falls, SC
29056 Greeleyville, SC
29058 Heath Springs, SC
29059 Holly Hill, SC
29061 Hopkins, SC
29062 Horatio, SC
29063 Irmo, SC
29065 Jenkinsville, SC
29065 Monticello, SC
29067 Kershaw, SC
29069 Lamar, SC
29070 Batesburg-Leesville, SC
29070 Leesville, SC
29071 Lexington, SC
29072 Lexington, SC
29073 Lexington, SC
29074 Liberty Hill, SC
29075 Little Mountain, SC
29078 Lugoff, SC
29079 Lydia, SC
29080 Lynchburg, SC
29081 Ehrhardt, SC
29082 Lodge, SC

291

29101 Mc Bee, SC
29102 Manning, SC
29102 Paxville, SC
29104 Mayesville, SC
29104 Saint Charles, SC
29105 Monetta, SC
29107 Livingston, SC
29107 Neeses, SC
29108 Newberry, SC
29111 New Zion, SC
29112 North, SC
29113 Norway, SC
29114 Olanta, SC
29115 Orangeburg, SC
29116 Orangeburg, SC
29117 Orangeburg, SC
29118 Orangeburg, SC
29122 Peak, SC
29123 Pelion, SC
29125 Pinewood, SC
29125 Rimini, SC
29126 Pomaria, SC
29127 Prosperity, SC
29128 Borden, SC
29128 Rembert, SC
29129 Ridge Spring, SC
29130 Ridgeway, SC
29132 Rion, SC
29133 Rowesville, SC
29135 Fort Motte, SC
29135 Saint Matthews, SC
29137 Perry, SC
29137 Salley, SC
29138 Saluda, SC
29142 Santee, SC
29143 Sardinia, SC
29145 Silverstreet, SC
29146 Springfield, SC
29147 State Park, SC
29148 Summerton, SC
29150 Oswego, SC
29150 Sumter, SC
29151 Sumter, SC
29152 Shaw Afb, SC
29153 Sumter, SC
29154 Sumter, SC
29160 Swansea, SC
29161 Timmonsville, SC
29162 Turbeville, SC
29163 Vance, SC
29164 Wagener, SC
29166 Ward, SC
29168 Wedgefield, SC
29169 West Columbia, SC
29170 West Columbia, SC
29171 Cayce, SC
29171 West Columbia, SC
29172 Cayce, SC
29172 West Columbia, SC
29175 Westville, SC
29177 White Rock, SC
29178 Whitmire, SC

29180 White Oak, SC
29180 Winnsboro, SC

292

29201 Columbia, SC
29202 Columbia, SC
29203 Columbia, SC
29204 Columbia, SC
29205 Columbia, SC
29206 Columbia, SC
29207 Columbia, SC
29208 Columbia, SC
29209 Columbia, SC
29210 Columbia, SC
29211 Columbia, SC
29212 Columbia, SC
29214 Columbia, SC
29215 Columbia, SC
29216 Columbia, SC
29217 Columbia, SC
29218 Columbia, SC
29219 Columbia, SC
29220 Columbia, SC
29221 Columbia, SC
29222 Columbia, SC
29223 Columbia, SC
29224 Columbia, SC
29225 Columbia, SC
29226 Columbia, SC
29227 Columbia, SC
29228 Columbia, SC
29229 Columbia, SC
29230 Columbia, SC
29240 Columbia, SC
29250 Columbia, SC
29260 Columbia, SC
29290 Columbia, SC
29292 Columbia, SC

293

29301 Spartanburg, SC
29302 Spartanburg, SC
29303 Spartanburg, SC
29304 Spartanburg, SC
29305 Spartanburg, SC
29306 Spartanburg, SC
29307 Spartanburg, SC
29316 Boiling Springs, SC
29316 Spartanburg, SC
29319 Spartanburg, SC
29320 Arcadia, SC
29321 Buffalo, SC
29322 Campobello, SC
29323 Chesnee, SC
29324 Clifton, SC
29325 Clinton, SC
29329 Converse, SC
29330 Cowpens, SC
29331 Cross Anchor, SC
29332 Cross Hill, SC
29333 Drayton, SC
29334 Duncan, SC
29335 Enoree, SC
29336 Fairforest, SC
29338 Fingerville, SC
29340 Gaffney, SC
29341 Gaffney, SC
29342 Gaffney, SC
29346 Glendale, SC
29348 Gramling, SC
29349 Inman, SC
29351 Joanna, SC
29353 Jonesville, SC
29355 Kinards, SC
29356 Landrum, SC
29360 Laurens, SC
29364 Lockhart, SC
29365 Lyman, SC
29368 Mayo, SC
29369 Moore, SC
29370 Mountville, SC
29372 Pacolet, SC
29373 Pacolet Mills, SC
29374 Glenn Springs, SC
29374 Pauline, SC
29375 Reidville, SC
29376 Roebuck, SC
29377 Startex, SC
29378 Una, SC
29379 Union, SC
29384 Waterloo, SC
29385 Wellford, SC
29386 White Stone, SC
29388 Woodruff, SC
29395 Jonesville, SC

294

29401 Charleston, SC
29402 Charleston, SC
29403 Charleston, SC
29404 Charleston, SC
29404 Charleston Afb, SC
29404 Joint Base Charleston, SC
29405 Charleston, SC
29405 North Charleston, SC
29406 Charleston, SC
29406 North Charleston, SC
29407 Charleston, SC
29409 Charleston, SC
29410 Charleston, SC
29410 Hanahan, SC
29410 North Charleston, SC
29412 Charleston, SC
29413 Charleston, SC
29414 Charleston, SC
29415 Charleston, SC
29415 North Charleston, SC
29416 Charleston, SC
29417 Charleston, SC
29418 Charleston, SC
29418 North Charleston, SC
29419 Charleston, SC
29419 North Charleston, SC
29420 Charleston, SC
29420 North Charleston, SC
29422 Charleston, SC
29423 Charleston, SC
29423 North Charleston, SC
29424 Charleston, SC
29425 Charleston, SC
29426 Adams Run, SC
29426 Jericho, SC
29429 Awendaw, SC
29430 Bethera, SC
29430 Moncks Corner, SC
29431 Bonneau, SC
29432 Branchville, SC
29433 Canadys, SC
29434 Cordesville, SC
29435 Cottageville, SC
29436 Cross, SC
29437 Dorchester, SC
29438 Edisto, SC
29438 Edisto Island, SC
29439 Folly Beach, SC
29440 Georgetown, SC
29442 Georgetown, SC
29445 Goose Creek, SC
29446 Green Pond, SC
29446 Greenpond, SC
29447 Grover, SC
29448 Harleyville, SC
29449 Hollywood, SC
29449 Meggett, SC
29449 Yonges Island, SC
29450 Huger, SC
29451 Dewees Island, SC
29451 Isle Of Palms, SC
29452 Jacksonboro, SC
29453 Jamestown, SC
29453 Shulerville, SC
29455 Johns Island, SC
29455 Kiawah Island, SC
29455 Seabrook Island, SC
29456 Ladson, SC
29457 Johns Island, SC
29458 Mc Clellanville, SC
29461 Moncks Corner, SC
29464 Mount Pleasant, SC
29468 Pineville, SC
29469 Pinopolis, SC
29470 Ravenel, SC
29471 Reevesville, SC
29472 Ridgeville, SC
29474 Round O, SC
29475 Ruffin, SC
29476 Russellville, SC
29477 Saint George, SC
29479 Alvin, SC
29479 Saint Stephen, SC
29481 Smoaks, SC
29482 Sullivans Island, SC
29483 Carnes Crossroads, SC
29483 Knightsville, SC
29483 Summerville, SC
29484 Summerville, SC
29485 Ladson, SC
29485 Lincolnville, SC
29485 Summerville, SC
29487 Wadmalaw Island, SC
29488 Ritter, SC
29488 Walterboro, SC
29492 Cainhoy, SC
29492 Charleston, SC
29492 Daniel Island, SC
29492 Wando, SC
29493 Williams, SC

295

29501 Florence, SC
29502 Florence, SC
29503 Florence, SC
29504 Florence, SC
29505 Florence, SC
29506 Florence, SC
29506 Quinby, SC
29510 Andrews, SC
29511 Aynor, SC
29512 Bennettsville, SC
29516 Blenheim, SC
29518 Cades, SC
29519 Centenary, SC
29520 Cheraw, SC
29525 Clio, SC
29526 Conway, SC
29527 Bucksport, SC
29527 Conway, SC
29528 Conway, SC
29530 Coward, SC
29532 Darlington, SC
29536 Dillon, SC
29536 Floyd Dale, SC
29540 Darlington, SC
29541 Effingham, SC
29543 Fork, SC
29544 Aynor, SC
29544 Galivants Ferry, SC
29545 Green Sea, SC
29546 Brittons Neck, SC
29546 Gresham, SC
29547 Hamer, SC
29547 South Of The Border, SC
29550 Hartsville, SC
29551 Hartsville, SC
29554 Hemingway, SC
29555 Johnsonville, SC
29555 Poston, SC
29556 Kingstree, SC
29560 Lake City, SC
29563 Lake View, SC
29564 Lane, SC
29565 Latta, SC
29566 Little River, SC
29567 Little Rock, SC
29568 Longs, SC
29569 Loris, SC
29570 Mc Coll, SC
29571 Marion, SC
29572 Myrtle Beach, SC
29574 Mullins, SC
29575 Myrtle Beach, SC
29575 Surfside Beach, SC
29576 Murrells Inlet, SC
29577 Myrtle Beach, SC
29578 Myrtle Beach, SC
29579 Myrtle Beach, SC
29580 Nesmith, SC
29581 Nichols, SC
29582 Atlantic Beach, SC
29582 Cherry Grove Beach, SC
29582 North Myrtle Beach, SC
29582 Ocean Drive, SC
29583 Pamplico, SC
29584 Patrick, SC
29585 Litchfield, SC
29585 N Litchfield, SC
29585 Pawleys Island, SC
29587 Myrtle Beach, SC
29587 Surfside Beach, SC
29588 Myrtle Beach, SC
29589 Rains, SC
29590 Salters, SC
29590 Trio, SC
29591 Scranton, SC
29592 Sellers, SC
29593 Society Hill, SC
29594 Tatum, SC
29596 Wallace, SC
29597 North Myrtle Beach, SC

296

29601 Greenville, SC
29602 Greenville, SC
29603 Greenville, SC
29604 Greenville, SC
29605 Greenville, SC
29606 Greenville, SC
29607 Greenville, SC
29608 Greenville, SC
29609 Greenville, SC
29610 Greenville, SC
29611 Greenville, SC
29611 Powdersville, SC
29612 Greenville, SC
29613 Greenville, SC
29614 Greenville, SC
29615 Greenville, SC
29616 Greenville, SC
29617 Greenville, SC
29620 Abbeville, SC
29621 Anderson, SC
29622 Anderson, SC
29623 Anderson, SC
29624 Anderson, SC
29625 Anderson, SC
29626 Anderson, SC
29627 Belton, SC
29628 Calhoun Falls, SC
29630 Central, SC
29631 Clemson, SC
29632 Clemson, SC
29633 Clemson, SC
29634 Clemson, SC
29635 Cleveland, SC
29636 Conestee, SC
29638 Donalds, SC
29638 Shoals Junction, SC
29639 Due West, SC
29640 Easley, SC
29641 Easley, SC
29642 Easley, SC
29642 Powdersville, SC
29643 Fair Play, SC
29644 Fountain Inn, SC
29645 Gray Court, SC
29646 Greenwood, SC
29647 Greenwood, SC
29648 Greenwood, SC
29649 Greenwood, SC
29650 Greer, SC
29651 Greer, SC
29652 Greer, SC
29653 Hodges, SC
29654 Honea Path, SC
29655 Iva, SC
29656 La France, SC
29657 Liberty, SC
29658 Long Creek, SC
29659 Lowndesville, SC
29661 Marietta, SC
29662 Mauldin, SC
29664 Mountain Rest, SC
29665 Newry, SC
29666 Ninety Six, SC
29667 Cateechee, SC
29667 Norris, SC
29669 Pelzer, SC
29670 Pendleton, SC
29671 Pickens, SC
29672 Seneca, SC
29673 Piedmont, SC
29673 Powdersville, SC
29675 Richland, SC
29676 Salem, SC
29677 Sandy Springs, SC
29678 Seneca, SC
29679 Seneca, SC
29680 Simpsonville, SC
29681 Simpsonville, SC
29682 Six Mile, SC
29683 Slater, SC
29684 Starr, SC
29685 Sunset, SC
29686 Tamassee, SC
29687 Taylors, SC
29688 Tigerville, SC
29689 Townville, SC
29690 Travelers Rest, SC
29691 Walhalla, SC
29692 Ware Shoals, SC
29693 Madison, SC
29693 Westminster, SC
29695 Hodges, SC
29696 West Union, SC
29697 Williamston, SC

297

29702 Blacksburg, SC
29702 Cherokee Falls, SC
29702 Kings Creek, SC
29703 Bowling Green, SC
29704 Catawba, SC
29706 Chester, SC
29707 Fort Mill, SC
29707 Indian Land, SC
29708 Fort Mill, SC
29708 Tega Cay, SC
29709 Chesterfield, SC
29710 Clover, SC
29710 Lake Wylie, SC
29710 River Hills, SC
29712 Edgemoor, SC
29714 Fort Lawn, SC
29715 Fort Mill, SC
29716 Fort Mill, SC
29717 Hickory Grove, SC
29718 Jefferson, SC
29720 Lancaster, SC
29721 Lancaster, SC
29722 Lancaster, SC
29724 Lando, SC
29726 Mc Connells, SC
29727 Mount Croghan, SC
29728 Pageland, SC
29729 Lando, SC
29729 Richburg, SC
29730 Rock Hill, SC
29731 Rock Hill, SC
29732 Rock Hill, SC
29733 Rock Hill, SC
29734 Rock Hill, SC
29741 Ruby, SC
29742 Sharon, SC
29743 Smyrna, SC
29744 Van Wyck, SC
29745 York, SC

298

29801 Aiken, SC
29801 Vaucluse, SC
29802 Aiken, SC
29803 Aiken, SC
29804 Aiken, SC
29805 Aiken, SC
29808 Aiken, SC
29809 New Ellenton, SC
29810 Allendale, SC
29812 Barnwell, SC
29812 Kline, SC
29813 Hilda, SC
29816 Bath, SC
29817 Blackville, SC
29819 Bradley, SC
29821 Clarks Hill, SC
29822 Clearwater, SC
29824 Edgefield, SC
29826 Elko, SC
29827 Fairfax, SC
29828 Gloverville, SC
29829 Graniteville, SC
29831 Jackson, SC
29832 Johnston, SC
29834 Langley, SC
29835 Mc Cormick, SC
29836 Martin, SC
29838 Modoc, SC
29839 Montmorenci, SC
29840 Mount Carmel, SC
29841 Beech Island, SC
29841 Belvedere, SC
29841 Clearwater, SC
29841 North Augusta, SC
29842 Beech Island, SC
29842 Clearwater, SC
29843 Olar, SC
29844 Parksville, SC
29845 Parksville, SC
29845 Plum Branch, SC
29846 Sycamore, SC
29847 Trenton, SC
29848 Troy, SC
29849 Ulmer, SC
29850 Vaucluse, SC
29851 Warrenville, SC
29853 Williston, SC
29856 Windsor, SC
29860 North Augusta, SC
29861 North Augusta, SC
29899 Mc Cormick, SC

299

29901 Beaufort, SC
29902 Beaufort, SC
29903 Beaufort, SC
29904 Beaufort, SC
29905 Beaufort, SC
29905 Parris Island, SC
29906 Beaufort, SC
29907 Beaufort, SC
29907 Ladys Island, SC
29909 Bluffton, SC
29909 Okatie, SC
29910 Bluffton, SC
29911 Brunson, SC
29912 Coosawhatchie, SC
29913 Crocketville, SC
29914 Dale, SC
29915 Daufuskie Island, SC
29916 Early Branch, SC
29918 Estill, SC
29920 Fripp Island, SC
29920 Saint Helena Island, SC
29921 Furman, SC
29922 Garnett, SC
29923 Gifford, SC
29924 Hampton, SC
29925 Hilton Head, SC
29925 Hilton Head Island, SC
29926 Hilton Head Island, SC
29926 Hilton Head Island, SC
29927 Hardeeville, SC
29928 Hilton Head Island, SC
29929 Islandton, SC
29931 Lobeco, SC
29932 Luray, SC
29933 Miley, SC
29934 Pineland, SC
29935 Port Royal, SC
29936 Coosawhatchie, SC
29936 Ridgeland, SC
29938 Hilton Head, SC
29938 Hilton Head Island, SC
29939 Estill, SC
29939 Scotia, SC
29940 Seabrook, SC
29941 Sheldon, SC
29943 Tillman, SC
29944 Varnville, SC
29945 Yemassee, SC

300

30002 Avondale Estates, GA
30003 Norcross, GA
30004 Alpharetta, GA
30004 Milton, GA
30005 Alpharetta, GA
30005 Johns Creek, GA
30006 Marietta, GA
30007 Marietta, GA
30008 Marietta, GA
30009 Alpharetta, GA
30009 Milton, GA
30010 Norcross, GA
30010 Peachtree Corners, GA
30011 Auburn, GA
30012 Conyers, GA
30013 Conyers, GA
30014 Covington, GA
30014 Porterdale, GA
30015 Covington, GA
30016 Covington, GA
30016 Porterdale, GA
30017 Grayson, GA
30018 Jersey, GA
30019 Dacula, GA
30021 Clarkston, GA
30022 Alpharetta, GA
30022 Johns Creek, GA
30023 Alpharetta, GA
30024 Johns Creek, GA
30024 Suwanee, GA
30025 Social Circle, GA
30026 Duluth, GA
30026 North Metro, GA
30028 Cumming, GA
30029 Duluth, GA
30029 North Metro, GA
30030 Decatur, GA
30031 Decatur, GA
30032 Decatur, GA
30033 Decatur, GA
30034 Decatur, GA
30035 Decatur, GA
30036 Decatur, GA
30037 Decatur, GA
30038 Lithonia, GA
30039 Snellville, GA
30040 Cumming, GA
30041 Cumming, GA
30042 Lawrenceville, GA
30043 Lawrenceville, GA
30044 Lawrenceville, GA
30045 Lawrenceville, GA
30046 Lawrenceville, GA
30047 Lilburn, GA
30048 Lilburn, GA
30049 Lawrenceville, GA
30052 Loganville, GA
30052 Walnut Grove, GA
30054 Oxford, GA
30055 Mansfield, GA
30056 Newborn, GA
30058 Lithonia, GA
30060 Marietta, GA
30061 Marietta, GA
30062 Marietta, GA
30063 Marietta, GA
30064 Marietta, GA
30065 Marietta, GA
30066 Marietta, GA
30067 Marietta, GA
30068 Marietta, GA
30069 Dobbins Afb, GA
30069 Marietta, GA
30070 Porterdale, GA
30071 Berkeley Lake, GA
30071 Norcross, GA
30071 Peachtree Corners, GA
30072 Pine Lake, GA
30074 Lithonia, GA
30074 Redan, GA
30075 Roswell, GA
30076 Roswell, GA
30077 Roswell, GA
30078 Snellville, GA
30079 Scottdale, GA
30080 Smyrna, GA
30081 Smyrna, GA
30082 Smyrna, GA
30083 Stone Mountain, GA
30084 Tucker, GA
30085 Tucker, GA
30086 Stone Mountain, GA
30087 Smoke Rise, GA
30087 Stone Mountain, GA
30090 Marietta, GA
30091 Norcross, GA
30092 Berkeley Lake, GA
30092 Norcross, GA
30092 Peachtree Corners, GA
30093 Norcross, GA
30094 Conyers, GA
30095 Duluth, GA
30096 Berkeley Lake, GA
30096 Duluth, GA
30096 Peachtree Corners, GA
30097 Duluth, GA
30097 Johns Creek, GA
30097 Peachtree Corners, GA
30098 Duluth, GA
30099 Duluth, GA

301

30101 Acworth, GA
30102 Acworth, GA
30103 Adairsville, GA
30104 Aragon, GA
30105 Armuchee, GA
30106 Austell, GA
30107 Ball Ground, GA
30108 Bowdon, GA
30109 Bowdon Junction, GA
30110 Bremen, GA
30111 Clarkdale, GA
30112 Carrollton, GA
30113 Buchanan, GA
30114 Canton, GA
30114 Holly Springs, GA
30115 Canton, GA
30115 Holly Springs, GA
30116 Carrollton, GA
30117 Carrollton, GA
30118 Carrollton, GA
30119 Carrollton, GA
30120 Cartersville, GA
30120 Euharlee, GA
30121 Cartersville, GA
30122 Lithia Springs, GA
30123 Cassville, GA
30124 Cave Spring, GA
30125 Cedartown, GA
30126 Mableton, GA
30127 Powder Springs, GA
30129 Coosa, GA
30132 Dallas, GA
30133 Douglasville, GA
30134 Douglasville, GA
30135 Douglasville, GA
30137 Emerson, GA
30138 Esom Hill, GA
30139 Fairmount, GA
30140 Felton, GA
30141 Hiram, GA
30142 Holly Springs, GA
30143 Big Canoe, GA
30143 Jasper, GA
30144 Kennesaw, GA
30145 Euharlee, GA
30145 Kingston, GA
30146 Lebanon, GA
30147 Lindale, GA
30148 Marble Hill, GA
30149 Mount Berry, GA
30149 Rome, GA
30150 Mount Zion, GA
30151 Nelson, GA
30152 Kennesaw, GA
30153 Braswell, GA
30153 Rockmart, GA
30154 Douglasville, GA
30156 Kennesaw, GA
30157 Dallas, GA
30160 Kennesaw, GA
30161 Rome, GA
30162 Rome, GA
30163 Rome, GA
30164 Rome, GA
30165 Rome, GA
30168 Austell, GA
30169 Canton, GA
30170 Roopville, GA
30171 Rydal, GA
30172 Shannon, GA
30173 Silver Creek, GA
30175 Talking Rock, GA
30176 Tallapoosa, GA
30177 Tate, GA
30178 Taylorsville, GA
30179 Temple, GA
30180 Villa Rica, GA
30182 Waco, GA
30183 Waleska, GA
30184 White, GA
30185 Whitesburg, GA
30187 Winston, GA
30188 Holly Springs, GA
30188 Woodstock, GA
30189 Woodstock, GA

302

30204 Barnesville, GA
30205 Brooks, GA
30206 Concord, GA
30212 Experiment, GA
30213 Fairburn, GA
30214 Fayetteville, GA
30214 Woolsey, GA
30215 Fayetteville, GA
30216 Flovilla, GA
30217 Centralhatchee, GA
30217 Franklin, GA
30218 Gay, GA
30219 Glenn, GA
30220 Grantville, GA
30222 Greenville, GA
30222 Stovall, GA
30223 Griffin, GA
30224 Griffin, GA
30228 Hampton, GA
30229 Haralson, GA
30230 Hogansville, GA
30233 Jackson, GA
30234 Jenkinsburg, GA
30236 Jonesboro, GA
30236 Lake Spivey, GA
30237 Jonesboro, GA
30238 Jonesboro, GA
30240 Lagrange, GA
30241 Lagrange, GA
30248 Locust Grove, GA
30250 Lovejoy, GA
30251 Luthersville, GA
30252 Mcdonough, GA
30253 Mcdonough, GA
30256 Meansville, GA
30257 Milner, GA
30258 Molena, GA
30259 Moreland, GA
30260 Lake City, GA
30260 Morrow, GA
30261 Lagrange, GA
30261 Mountville, GA
30263 Newnan, GA
30263 Raymond, GA
30264 Newnan, GA
30265 Newnan, GA
30266 Orchard Hill, GA
30268 Chattahoochee Hills, GA
30268 Palmetto, GA
30269 Peachtree City, GA
30270 Fayetteville, GA
30270 Peachtree City, GA
30271 Newnan, GA
30272 Red Oak, GA
30273 Rex, GA
30274 Riverdale, GA
30275 Sargent, GA
30276 Senoia, GA
30277 Sharpsburg, GA
30281 Stockbridge, GA
30284 Sunny Side, GA
30285 The Rock, GA
30286 Thomaston, GA
30287 Morrow, GA
30288 Conley, GA
30289 Turin, GA
30290 Tyrone, GA
30291 Union City, GA
30292 Williamson, GA
30293 Woodbury, GA
30294 Ellenwood, GA
30295 Zebulon, GA
30296 Riverdale, GA
30297 Forest Park, GA
30297 Fort Gillem, GA
30297 Gillem Enclave, GA
30298 Forest Park, GA

303

30301 Atlanta, GA
30302 Atlanta, GA
30303 Atlanta, GA
30304 Atlanta, GA
30305 Atlanta, GA
30306 Atlanta, GA
30307 Atlanta, GA
30308 Atlanta, GA
30309 Atlanta, GA
30310 Atlanta, GA
30311 Atlanta, GA
30312 Atlanta, GA
30313 Atlanta, GA
30314 Atlanta, GA
30315 Atlanta, GA
30316 Atlanta, GA
30317 Atlanta, GA
30318 Atlanta, GA
30319 Atlanta, GA
30319 Sandy Springs, GA
30320 Atlanta, GA
30321 Atlanta, GA
30322 Atlanta, GA
30324 Atlanta, GA
30325 Atlanta, GA
30326 Atlanta, GA
30326 Brookhaven, GA
30327 Atlanta, GA
30327 Sandy Springs, GA
30328 Atlanta, GA
30328 Sandy Springs, GA
30329 Atlanta, GA
30331 Atlanta, GA
30332 Atlanta, GA
30333 Atlanta, GA
30334 Atlanta, GA
30336 Atlanta, GA
30337 Atlanta, GA
30337 College Park, GA
30338 Atlanta, GA
30338 Dunwoody, GA
30338 Sandy Springs, GA
30339 Atlanta, GA
30339 Sandy Springs, GA
30339 Vinings, GA
30340 Atlanta, GA
30340 Doraville, GA
30341 Atlanta, GA
30341 Chamblee, GA
30342 Atlanta, GA
30342 Sandy Springs, GA
30343 Atlanta, GA
30344 Atlanta, GA
30344 East Point, GA
30345 Atlanta, GA
30346 Atlanta, GA
30346 Dunwoody, GA
30348 Atlanta, GA
30349 Atlanta, GA
30349 College Park, GA
30350 Atlanta, GA
30350 Dunwoody, GA
30350 Sandy Springs, GA
30353 Atlanta, GA
30354 Atlanta, GA
30354 Hapeville, GA
30355 Atlanta, GA
30356 Atlanta, GA
30356 Dunwoody, GA
30357 Atlanta, GA
30358 Atlanta, GA
30358 Sandy Springs, GA
30359 Atlanta, GA
30360 Atlanta, GA
30360 Doraville, GA
30360 Dunwoody, GA
30361 Atlanta, GA
30362 Atlanta, GA
30362 Doraville, GA
30363 Atlanta, GA
30364 Atlanta, GA
30364 East Point, GA
30366 Atlanta, GA
30366 Chamblee, GA
30368 Atlanta, GA
30369 Atlanta, GA
30370 Atlanta, GA
30371 Atlanta, GA
30374 Atlanta, GA
30375 Atlanta, GA
30377 Atlanta, GA
30378 Atlanta, GA
30380 Atlanta, GA
30384 Atlanta, GA
30385 Atlanta, GA
30388 Atlanta, GA
30392 Atlanta, GA
30394 Atlanta, GA
30396 Atlanta, GA
30398 Atlanta, GA

304

30401 Covena, GA
30401 Oak Park, GA
30401 Summertown, GA
30401 Swainsboro, GA
30410 Ailey, GA
30411 Alamo, GA
30412 Alston, GA
30413 Bartow, GA
30414 Bellville, GA
30415 Brooklet, GA
30417 Claxton, GA
30420 Cobbtown, GA
30421 Collins, GA
30423 Daisy, GA
30424 Dover, GA
30425 Garfield, GA
30426 Girard, GA
30427 Glennville, GA
30428 Glenwood, GA
30429 Hagan, GA
30434 Louisville, GA
30436 Lyons, GA
30438 Manassas, GA
30439 Metter, GA
30441 Midville, GA
30442 Millen, GA
30442 Perkins, GA
30445 Mount Vernon, GA
30446 Newington, GA
30447 Norristown, GA
30448 Nunez, GA
30449 Oliver, GA
30450 Portal, GA
30451 Pulaski, GA
30452 Register, GA
30453 Reidsville, GA
30454 Rockledge, GA
30455 Rocky Ford, GA
30456 Sardis, GA
30457 Soperton, GA
30458 Statesboro, GA
30459 Statesboro, GA
30460 Statesboro, GA
30461 Statesboro, GA
30464 Stillmore, GA
30467 Hiltonia, GA
30467 Sylvania, GA
30470 Tarrytown, GA
30471 Twin City, GA
30473 Uvalda, GA
30474 Vidalia, GA
30475 Vidalia, GA
30477 Wadley, GA
30499 Reidsville, GA

305

30501 Gainesville, GA
30502 Chestnut Mountain, GA
30502 Oakwood, GA
30503 Gainesville, GA
30504 Gainesville, GA
30506 Gainesville, GA
30507 Gainesville, GA
30510 Alto, GA
30511 Baldwin, GA
30512 Blairsville, GA
30513 Blue Ridge, GA
30514 Blairsville, GA
30515 Buford, GA
30516 Bowersville, GA
30517 Braselton, GA
30518 Buford, GA
30518 Rest Haven, GA
30518 Sugar Hill, GA
30519 Buford, GA
30520 Canon, GA
30521 Carnesville, GA
30522 Cherry Log, GA
30523 Clarkesville, GA
30525 Clayton, GA
30527 Clermont, GA
30528 Cleveland, GA
30529 Commerce, GA
30530 Commerce, GA
30531 Cornelia, GA
30533 Dahlonega, GA
30534 Dawsonville, GA
30535 Demorest, GA
30536 Ellijay, GA
30537 Dillard, GA
30537 Sky Valley, GA
30538 Eastanollee, GA
30539 East Ellijay, GA
30540 East Ellijay, GA
30540 Ellijay, GA
30541 Epworth, GA
30542 Flowery Branch, GA
30543 Gillsville, GA
30545 Helen, GA
30546 Hiawassee, GA
30547 Homer, GA
30548 Hoschton, GA
30549 Arcade, GA
30549 Jefferson, GA
30552 Lakemont, GA
30553 Lavonia, GA
30554 Lula, GA
30555 Mc Caysville, GA
30557 Avalon, GA
30557 Martin, GA
30558 Maysville, GA
30559 Mineral Bluff, GA
30560 Morganton, GA
30562 Mountain City, GA
30563 Mount Airy, GA
30564 Murrayville, GA
30565 Nicholson, GA
30566 Oakwood, GA
30567 Pendergrass, GA
30568 Rabun Gap, GA
30571 Saute-Nacoche, GA
30571 Sautee, GA
30571 Sautee Nacoochee, GA
30572 Suches, GA
30573 Tallulah Falls, GA
30575 Talmo, GA
30576 Tiger, GA
30577 Toccoa, GA
30580 Turnerville, GA
30581 Wiley, GA
30582 Young Harris, GA
30597 Dahlonega, GA
30598 Toccoa Falls, GA
30599 Commerce, GA

306

30601 Athens, GA
30602 Athens, GA
30603 Athens, GA
30604 Athens, GA
30605 Athens, GA

30606 Athens, GA
30607 Athens, GA
30608 Athens, GA
30609 Athens, GA
30612 Athens, GA
30619 Arnoldsville, GA
30620 Bethlehem, GA
30621 Bishop, GA
30621 North High Shoals, GA
30622 Bogart, GA
30623 Bostwick, GA
30624 Bowman, GA
30625 Buckhead, GA
30627 Carlton, GA
30628 Colbert, GA
30629 Comer, GA
30630 Crawford, GA
30631 Crawfordville, GA
30633 Danielsville, GA
30634 Dewy Rose, GA
30635 Elberton, GA
30638 Farmington, GA
30639 Franklin Springs, GA
30641 Good Hope, GA
30642 Greensboro, GA
30643 Hartwell, GA
30645 High Shoals, GA
30646 Hull, GA
30647 Ila, GA
30648 Lexington, GA
30650 Madison, GA
30655 Between, GA
30655 Monroe, GA
30656 Between, GA
30656 Monroe, GA
30660 Philomath, GA
30660 Rayle, GA
30662 Royston, GA
30663 Rutledge, GA
30664 Sharon, GA
30665 Siloam, GA
30666 Statham, GA
30667 Maxeys, GA
30667 Stephens, GA
30668 Danburg, GA
30668 Tignall, GA
30669 Union Point, GA
30669 Woodville, GA
30671 Maxeys, GA
30673 Washington, GA
30677 Watkinsville, GA
30678 White Plains, GA
30680 Winder, GA
30683 Winterville, GA

307

30701 Calhoun, GA
30703 Calhoun, GA
30705 Chatsworth, GA
30707 Chickamauga, GA
30708 Cisco, GA
30710 Cohutta, GA
30711 Crandall, GA
30719 Dalton, GA
30720 Dalton, GA
30721 Dalton, GA
30722 Dalton, GA
30724 Eton, GA
30725 Flintstone, GA
30726 Graysville, GA
30728 La Fayette, GA
30730 Lyerly, GA
30731 Cloudland, GA
30731 Menlo, GA
30732 Oakman, GA
30733 Plainville, GA
30734 Ranger, GA
30735 Resaca, GA
30736 Ringgold, GA
30738 Rising Fawn, GA
30739 Rock Spring, GA
30740 Rocky Face, GA
30741 Rossville, GA
30742 Fort Oglethorpe, GA
30742 Rossville, GA
30746 Sugar Valley, GA
30747 Summerville, GA
30750 Lookout Mountain, GA
30751 Tennga, GA
30752 Trenton, GA
30753 Trion, GA
30755 Tunnel Hill, GA
30756 Varnell, GA
30757 Wildwood, GA

308

30802 Appling, GA
30803 Avera, GA
30805 Blythe, GA
30806 Boneville, GA
30807 Camak, GA
30808 Dearing, GA
30809 Evans, GA
30810 Edge Hill, GA
30810 Gibson, GA
30811 Gough, GA
30812 Gracewood, GA
30813 Grovetown, GA
30814 Harlem, GA
30815 Hephzibah, GA
30816 Keysville, GA
30817 Lincolnton, GA
30818 Matthews, GA
30818 Wrens, GA
30819 Mesena, GA
30820 Mitchell, GA
30821 Norwood, GA
30822 Perkins, GA
30823 Stapleton, GA
30824 Thomson, GA
30828 Warrenton, GA
30830 Waynesboro, GA
30833 Wrens, GA

309

30901 Augusta, GA
30903 Augusta, GA
30904 Augusta, GA
30905 Augusta, GA
30905 Fort Gordon, GA
30906 Augusta, GA
30907 Augusta, GA
30907 Martinez, GA
30909 Augusta, GA
30912 Augusta, GA
30914 Augusta, GA
30916 Augusta, GA
30917 Augusta, GA
30919 Augusta, GA
30999 Augusta, GA

310

31001 Abbeville, GA
31002 Adrian, GA
31003 Allentown, GA
31004 Bolingbroke, GA
31005 Bonaire, GA
31006 Butler, GA
31007 Byromville, GA
31008 Byron, GA
31008 Powersville, GA
31009 Cadwell, GA
31010 Cordele, GA
31011 Chauncey, GA
31012 Chester, GA
31013 Clinchfield, GA
31014 Cochran, GA
31014 Empire, GA
31015 Cordele, GA
31016 Culloden, GA
31017 Danville, GA
31018 Davisboro, GA
31018 Riddleville, GA
31019 Dexter, GA
31020 Dry Branch, GA
31021 Dublin, GA
31022 Dudley, GA
31023 Eastman, GA
31023 Plainfield, GA
31024 Eatonton, GA
31025 Elko, GA
31026 Eatonton, GA
31027 Dublin, GA
31027 E Dublin, GA
31027 East Dublin, GA
31028 Centerville, GA
31029 Forsyth, GA
31030 Fort Valley, GA
31031 Gordon, GA
31031 Ivey, GA
31032 Gray, GA
31033 Haddock, GA
31034 Hardwick, GA
31035 Harrison, GA
31036 Hawkinsville, GA
31037 Helena, GA
31038 Hillsboro, GA
31038 Round Oak, GA
31039 Howard, GA
31040 Dublin, GA
31041 Ideal, GA
31042 Irwinton, GA
31044 Jeffersonville, GA
31045 Jewell, GA
31046 Juliette, GA
31047 Kathleen, GA
31049 Kite, GA
31050 Knoxville, GA
31051 Lilly, GA
31052 Lizella, GA
31054 Mc Intyre, GA
31055 Mc Rae, GA
31057 Marshallville, GA
31058 Mauk, GA
31059 Milledgeville, GA
31060 Milan, GA
31061 Milledgeville, GA
31062 Milledgeville, GA
31063 Dooling, GA
31063 Montezuma, GA
31064 Monticello, GA
31065 Montrose, GA
31066 Musella, GA
31067 Oconee, GA
31068 Oglethorpe, GA
31069 Perry, GA
31070 Pinehurst, GA
31071 Pineview, GA
31072 Pitts, GA
31075 Rentz, GA
31076 Reynolds, GA
31077 Rhine, GA
31078 Roberta, GA
31079 Rochelle, GA
31081 Rupert, GA
31082 Deepstep, GA
31082 Sandersville, GA
31083 Scotland, GA
31084 Seville, GA
31085 Shady Dale, GA
31086 Smarr, GA
31087 Mayfield, GA
31087 Sparta, GA
31088 Warner Robins, GA
31089 Tennille, GA
31090 Toomsboro, GA
31091 Unadilla, GA
31092 Vienna, GA
31093 Warner Robins, GA
31094 Warthen, GA
31095 Warner Robins, GA
31096 Wrightsville, GA
31097 Yatesville, GA
31098 Robins A F B, GA
31098 Robins Afb, GA
31098 South Base, GA
31098 Warner Robins, GA
31099 Warner Robins, GA

311

31106 Atlanta, GA
31107 Atlanta, GA
31119 Atlanta, GA
31126 Atlanta, GA
31131 Atlanta, GA
31136 Atlanta, GA
31139 Atlanta, GA
31141 Atlanta, GA
31144 Kennesaw, GA
31145 Atlanta, GA
31146 Atlanta, GA
31146 Dunwoody, GA
31150 Atlanta, GA
31150 Sandy Springs, GA
31156 Atlanta, GA
31156 Sandy Springs, GA
31169 Peachtree City, GA
31192 Atlanta, GA
31193 Atlanta, GA
31195 Atlanta, GA
31196 Atlanta, GA

312

31201 Huber, GA
31201 Macon, GA
31202 Macon, GA
31203 Macon, GA
31204 Macon, GA
31204 Payne, GA
31204 Payne City, GA
31205 Macon, GA
31206 Macon, GA
31207 Macon, GA
31208 Macon, GA
31209 Macon, GA
31210 Macon, GA
31211 Macon, GA
31213 Macon, GA
31216 Macon, GA
31217 Macon, GA
31220 Macon, GA
31221 Macon, GA
31294 Macon, GA
31295 Macon, GA
31296 Macon, GA
31297 Macon, GA

313

31301 Allenhurst, GA
31302 Bloomingdale, GA
31303 Clyo, GA
31304 Crescent, GA
31305 Darien, GA
31307 Eden, GA
31308 Black Creek, GA
31308 Ellabell, GA
31309 Fleming, GA
31310 Hinesville, GA
31312 Guyton, GA
31313 Fort Stewart, GA
31313 Hinesville, GA
31314 Fort Stewart, GA
31315 Fort Stewart, GA
31315 Hinesville, GA
31316 Ludowici, GA
31318 Meldrim, GA
31319 Meridian, GA
31319 Valona, GA
31320 Midway, GA
31321 Nevils, GA
31321 Pembroke, GA
31322 Pooler, GA
31323 Riceboro, GA
31324 Richmond Hill, GA
31326 Rincon, GA
31327 Sapelo Island, GA
31328 Tybee Island, GA
31329 Springfield, GA
31329 Stillwell, GA
31331 Shellman Bluff, GA
31331 Townsend, GA
31333 Walthourville, GA

314

31401 Savannah, GA
31402 Savannah, GA
31403 Savannah, GA
31404 Savannah, GA
31404 Thunderbolt, GA
31405 Garden City, GA
31405 Garden Cty, GA
31405 Savannah, GA
31406 Savannah, GA
31406 Vernonburg, GA
31407 Port Wentworth, GA
31407 Prt Wentworth, GA
31407 Savannah, GA
31408 Garden City, GA
31408 Garden Cty, GA
31408 Savannah, GA
31409 Hunter Aaf, GA
31409 Savannah, GA
31410 Savannah, GA
31410 Thunderbolt, GA
31410 Wilmington Island, GA
31411 Savannah, GA
31412 Savannah, GA
31414 Savannah, GA
31415 Garden City, GA
31415 Garden Cty, GA
31415 Savannah, GA
31416 Savannah, GA
31418 Garden City, GA
31418 Garden Cty, GA
31418 Savannah, GA
31419 Savannah, GA
31420 Savannah, GA
31421 Savannah, GA

315

31501 Okefenokee, GA
31501 Waycross, GA
31502 Waycross, GA
31503 Waycross, GA
31510 Alma, GA
31512 Ambrose, GA
31513 Baxley, GA
31515 Baxley, GA
31516 Blackshear, GA
31518 Bristol, GA
31519 Broxton, GA
31520 Brunswick, GA
31521 Brunswick, GA
31522 Brunswick, GA
31522 Saint Simons Is, GA
31522 Saint Simons Island, GA
31522 St Simons Island, GA
31523 Brunswick, GA
31524 Brunswick, GA
31525 Brunswick, GA
31527 Brunswick, GA
31527 Jekyll Island, GA
31532 Denton, GA
31533 Douglas, GA
31534 Douglas, GA
31535 Douglas, GA
31537 Folkston, GA
31537 Homeland, GA
31539 Hazlehurst, GA
31542 Hoboken, GA
31543 Hortense, GA
31544 Jacksonville, GA
31545 Jesup, GA
31546 Jesup, GA
31547 Kings Bay, GA
31548 Kingsland, GA
31549 Lumber City, GA
31550 Manor, GA
31551 Mershon, GA
31552 Millwood, GA
31553 Nahunta, GA
31554 Nicholls, GA
31555 Odum, GA
31556 Offerman, GA
31557 Patterson, GA
31558 Saint Marys, GA
31560 Screven, GA
31561 Brunswick, GA
31561 Sea Island, GA
31562 Saint George, GA
31563 Surrency, GA
31564 Waresboro, GA
31565 Waverly, GA
31566 Waynesville, GA
31567 West Green, GA
31568 White Oak, GA
31569 Woodbine, GA
31598 Jesup, GA
31599 Jesup, GA

316

31601 Valdosta, GA
31602 Valdosta, GA
31603 Valdosta, GA
31604 Valdosta, GA
31605 Valdosta, GA
31606 Valdosta, GA
31620 Adel, GA
31622 Alapaha, GA
31623 Argyle, GA
31624 Axson, GA
31625 Barney, GA
31626 Boston, GA
31627 Cecil, GA
31629 Dixie, GA
31630 Du Pont, GA
31631 Fargo, GA
31632 Hahira, GA
31634 Cogdell, GA
31634 Homerville, GA
31635 Lakeland, GA
31636 Lake Park, GA
31637 Lenox, GA
31638 Morven, GA
31639 Nashville, GA
31641 Naylor, GA
31642 Pearson, GA
31643 Quitman, GA
31645 Ray City, GA
31647 Sparks, GA
31648 Statenville, GA
31649 Stockton, GA
31650 Willacoochee, GA
31698 Valdosta, GA
31699 Moody Afb, GA

317

31701 Albany, GA
31702 Albany, GA
31703 Albany, GA
31704 Albany, GA
31705 Albany, GA
31705 Bridgeboro, GA
31706 Albany, GA
31707 Albany, GA
31708 Albany, GA
31709 Americus, GA
31711 Andersonville, GA
31712 Arabi, GA
31714 Ashburn, GA
31716 Baconton, GA
31719 Americus, GA
31720 Barwick, GA
31721 Albany, GA
31722 Berlin, GA
31727 Brookfield, GA
31730 Camilla, GA
31733 Chula, GA
31735 Cobb, GA
31738 Coolidge, GA
31739 Cotton, GA
31743 De Soto, GA
31744 Doerun, GA
31747 Ellenton, GA
31749 Enigma, GA
31750 Fitzgerald, GA
31753 Funston, GA
31756 Hartsfield, GA
31757 Thomasville, GA
31758 Thomasville, GA
31760 Irwinville, GA
31763 Leesburg, GA
31764 Leslie, GA
31765 Meigs, GA
31768 Moultrie, GA
31768 Riverside, GA
31769 Mystic, GA
31771 Norman Park, GA
31772 Oakfield, GA
31773 Ochlocknee, GA
31774 Ocilla, GA
31775 Omega, GA
31776 Moultrie, GA
31778 Pavo, GA
31779 Pelham, GA
31780 Plains, GA
31781 Poulan, GA
31782 Putney, GA
31783 Rebecca, GA
31784 Sale City, GA

31787 Smithville, GA
31788 Moultrie, GA
31789 Sumner, GA
31790 Sycamore, GA
31791 Sylvester, GA
31792 Metcalf, GA
31792 Thomasville, GA
31793 Tifton, GA
31794 Abraham Baldwin College, GA
31794 Tifton, GA
31795 Ty Ty, GA
31796 Warwick, GA
31798 Wray, GA
31799 Thomasville, GA

318

31801 Box Springs, GA
31801 Juniper, GA
31803 Buena Vista, GA
31803 Tazewell, GA
31804 Cataula, GA
31805 Cusseta, GA
31806 Ellaville, GA
31807 Ellerslie, GA
31808 Fortson, GA
31810 Geneva, GA
31811 Hamilton, GA
31812 Junction City, GA
31814 Louvale, GA
31815 Lumpkin, GA
31816 Manchester, GA
31820 Midland, GA
31821 Omaha, GA
31822 Pine Mountain, GA
31823 Pine Mountain Valley, GA
31824 Preston, GA
31825 Richland, GA
31826 Shiloh, GA
31827 Talbotton, GA
31829 Columbus, GA
31829 Upatoi, GA
31830 Warm Springs, GA
31831 Waverly Hall, GA
31832 Weston, GA
31833 West Point, GA
31836 Woodland, GA

319

31901 Columbus, GA
31902 Columbus, GA
31903 Columbus, GA
31904 Columbus, GA
31905 Columbus, GA
31905 Fort Benning, GA
31906 Columbus, GA
31907 Columbus, GA
31908 Columbus, GA
31909 Columbus, GA
31914 Columbus, GA
31917 Columbus, GA
31993 Columbus, GA
31995 Columbus, GA
31995 Fort Benning, GA
31997 Columbus, GA
31998 Columbus, GA
31999 Columbus, GA

320

32003 Fleming Island, FL
32003 Orange Park, FL
32004 Ponte Vedra, FL
32004 Ponte Vedra Beach, FL
32006 Fleming Island, FL
32006 Orange Park, FL
32007 Bostwick, FL
32008 Branford, FL
32009 Bryceville, FL
32011 Callahan, FL
32013 Day, FL
32024 Lake City, FL
32025 Lake City, FL
32026 Raiford, FL
32030 Doctors Inlet, FL
32033 Elkton, FL
32034 Amelia Island, FL
32034 Fernandina Beach, FL
32038 Fort White, FL
32040 Glen Saint Mary, FL
32041 Yulee, FL
32042 Graham, FL
32043 Green Cove Springs, FL
32044 Hampton, FL
32046 Hilliard, FL
32050 Middleburg, FL
32052 Jasper, FL
32053 Jennings, FL
32054 Lake Butler, FL
32055 Lake City, FL
32056 Lake City, FL
32058 Lawtey, FL
32059 Lee, FL
32060 Dowling Park, FL
32060 Live Oak, FL
32061 Lulu, FL
32062 Mc Alpin, FL
32063 Macclenny, FL
32064 Boys Ranch, FL
32064 Dowling Park, FL
32064 Live Oak, FL
32065 Orange Park, FL
32066 Mayo, FL
32067 Orange Park, FL
32068 Middleburg, FL
32071 O Brien, FL
32072 Olustee, FL
32073 Orange Park, FL
32079 Penney Farms, FL
32080 Anastasia Island, FL
32080 Saint Augustine, FL
32080 Saint Augustine Beach, FL
32080 St Augustine Beach, FL
32081 Ponte Vedra, FL
32081 Ponte Vedra Beach, FL
32081 Town Of Nocatee, FL
32082 Ponte Vedra Beach, FL
32083 Raiford, FL
32084 Saint Augustine, FL
32084 Saint Augustine Beach, FL
32084 St Augustine Beach, FL
32085 Saint Augustine, FL
32086 Saint Augustine Beach, FL
32086 St Augustine Beach, FL
32087 Sanderson, FL
32091 Kingsley Lake, FL
32091 Kngsly Lk, FL
32091 Starke, FL
32092 Saint Augustine, FL
32094 Wellborn, FL
32095 Saint Augustine, FL
32096 White Springs, FL
32097 Yulee, FL
32099 Jacksonville, FL

321

32102 Astor, FL
32105 Barberville, FL
32110 Bunnell, FL
32111 Candler, FL
32112 Crescent City, FL
32113 Citra, FL
32114 Daytona Beach, FL
32115 Daytona Beach, FL
32116 Daytona Beach, FL
32116 Daytona Beach Shores, FL
32117 Daytona Beach, FL
32117 Holly Hill, FL
32118 Daytona Beach, FL
32118 Daytona Beach Shores, FL
32119 Daytona Beach, FL
32119 S Daytona, FL
32119 S Daytona Bch, FL
32119 South Daytona, FL
32120 Daytona Beach, FL
32121 Daytona Beach, FL
32121 South Daytona, FL
32122 Daytona Beach, FL
32123 Allandale, FL
32123 Daytona Beach, FL
32123 Port Orange, FL
32123 Pt Orange, FL
32124 Daytona Beach, FL
32125 Daytona Beach, FL
32125 Holly Hill, FL
32126 Daytona Beach, FL
32127 Ponce Inlet, FL
32127 Port Orange, FL
32127 Pt Orange, FL
32127 Wilbur By The Sea, FL
32128 Port Orange, FL
32128 Pt Orange, FL
32129 Port Orange, FL
32129 Pt Orange, FL
32130 De Leon Springs, FL
32131 East Palatka, FL
32132 Edgewater, FL
32133 Eastlake Weir, FL
32134 Fort Mc Coy, FL
32134 Salt Springs, FL
32135 Palm Coast, FL
32136 Beverly Beach, FL
32136 Flagler Beach, FL
32137 Palm Coast, FL
32138 Grandin, FL
32139 Georgetown, FL
32140 Florahome, FL
32141 Edgewater, FL
32142 Palm Coast, FL
32143 Palm Coast, FL
32145 Hastings, FL
32147 Hollister, FL
32148 Interlachen, FL
32149 Interlachen, FL
32157 Lake Como, FL
32158 Lady Lake, FL
32159 Lady Lake, FL
32159 The Villages, FL
32160 Lake Geneva, FL
32162 Lady Lake, FL
32162 The Villages, FL
32163 The Villages, FL
32164 Palm Coast, FL
32168 New Smyrna Beach, FL
32173 Ormond Beach, FL
32174 Ormond Beach, FL
32175 Ormond Beach, FL
32176 Ormond Beach, FL
32177 Palatka, FL
32178 Palatka, FL
32179 Ocklawaha, FL
32180 Pierson, FL
32181 Pomona Park, FL
32182 Orange Springs, FL
32183 Ocklawaha, FL
32185 Putnam Hall, FL
32187 San Mateo, FL
32189 Satsuma, FL
32190 Seville, FL
32192 Sparr, FL
32193 Welaka, FL
32195 Weirsdale, FL
32198 Daytona Beach, FL

322

32201 Jacksonville, FL
32202 Jacksonville, FL
32203 Jacksonville, FL
32204 Jacksonville, FL
32205 Jacksonville, FL
32206 Jacksonville, FL
32207 Jacksonville, FL
32208 Jacksonville, FL
32209 Jacksonville, FL
32210 Jacksonville, FL
32211 Jacksonville, FL
32212 Jacksonville, FL
32212 Jacksonville Nas, FL
32214 Jacksonville, FL
32216 Jacksonville, FL
32217 Jacksonville, FL
32218 Jacksonville, FL
32219 Dinsmore, FL
32219 Jacksonville, FL
32220 Jacksonville, FL
32221 Jacksonville, FL
32222 Jacksonville, FL
32223 Jacksonville, FL
32224 Jacksonville, FL
32225 Jacksonville, FL
32226 Jacksonville, FL
32227 Jacksonville, FL
32228 Jacksonville, FL
32228 Mayport Naval Station, FL
32229 Jacksonville, FL
32231 Jacksonville, FL
32232 Jacksonville, FL
32233 Atlantic Beach, FL
32233 Jacksonville, FL
32233 Mayport, FL
32234 Baldwin, FL
32234 Jacksonville, FL
32234 Maxville, FL
32235 Jacksonville, FL
32236 Jacksonville, FL
32237 Jacksonville, FL
32238 Jacksonville, FL
32239 Jacksonville, FL
32240 Jacksonville, FL
32240 Jacksonville Beach, FL
32241 Jacksonville, FL
32244 Jacksonville, FL
32245 Jacksonville, FL
32246 Jacksonville, FL
32247 Jacksonville, FL
32250 Jacksonville, FL
32250 Jacksonville Beach, FL
32254 Jacksonville, FL
32255 Jacksonville, FL
32256 Jacksonville, FL
32257 Jacksonville, FL
32258 Jacksonville, FL
32259 Fruit Cove, FL
32259 Jacksonville, FL
32259 Julington Creek, FL
32259 Saint Johns, FL
32259 Switzerland, FL
32260 Jacksonville, FL
32260 Saint Johns, FL
32266 Jacksonville, FL
32266 Neptune Beach, FL
32277 Jacksonville, FL

323

32301 Tallahassee, FL
32302 Tallahassee, FL
32303 Tallahassee, FL
32304 Tallahassee, FL
32305 Tallahassee, FL
32306 Tallahassee, FL
32307 Tallahassee, FL
32308 Tallahassee, FL
32309 Miccosukee, FL
32309 Tallahassee, FL
32310 Tallahassee, FL
32311 Tallahassee, FL
32312 Tallahassee, FL
32313 Tallahassee, FL
32314 Tallahassee, FL
32315 Tallahassee, FL
32316 Tallahassee, FL
32317 Tallahassee, FL
32318 Tallahassee, FL
32320 Apalachicola, FL
32321 Bristol, FL
32322 Carrabelle, FL
32323 Lanark Village, FL
32324 Chattahoochee, FL
32326 Crawfordville, FL
32327 Crawfordville, FL
32327 Wakulla Springs, FL
32328 Eastpoint, FL
32328 Saint George Island, FL
32329 Apalachicola, FL
32330 Greensboro, FL
32331 Greenville, FL
32332 Gretna, FL
32333 Havana, FL
32334 Hosford, FL
32335 Sumatra, FL
32336 Lamont, FL
32337 Lloyd, FL
32340 Madison, FL
32341 Madison, FL
32343 Midway, FL
32344 Monticello, FL
32345 Monticello, FL
32346 Alligator Point, FL
32346 Ochlockonee Bay, FL
32346 Panacea, FL
32347 Perry, FL
32348 Perry, FL
32350 Pinetta, FL
32351 Quincy, FL
32352 Mount Pleasant, FL
32352 Quincy, FL
32353 Quincy, FL
32355 Saint Marks, FL
32356 Salem, FL
32357 Shady Grove, FL
32358 Saint Teresa, FL
32358 Sopchoppy, FL
32358 St Teresa, FL
32359 Steinhatchee, FL
32360 Telogia, FL
32361 Wacissa, FL
32362 Woodville, FL
32395 Tallahassee, FL
32399 Tallahassee, FL

324

32401 Panama City, FL
32401 Panama City Beach, FL
32402 Panama City, FL
32403 Panama City, FL
32403 Tyndall Afb, FL
32404 Callaway, FL
32404 Panama City, FL
32405 Panama City, FL
32406 Panama City, FL
32407 Panama City, FL
32407 Panama City Beach, FL
32408 Panama City, FL
32408 Panama City Beach, FL
32409 Panama City, FL
32409 Southport, FL
32410 Mexico Beach, FL
32411 Panama City, FL
32412 Panama City, FL
32413 Grande Pointe, FL
32413 Inlet Beach, FL
32413 Panama City, FL
32413 Panama City Beach, FL
32413 Rosemary Beach, FL
32413 Seacrest, FL
32413 Watersound, FL
32417 Panama City, FL
32417 Panama City Beach, FL
32420 Alford, FL
32421 Altha, FL
32422 Argyle, FL
32423 Bascom, FL
32424 Blountstown, FL
32425 Bonifay, FL
32425 Caryville, FL
32425 Esto, FL
32425 Noma, FL
32426 Campbellton, FL
32427 Caryville, FL
32428 Chipley, FL
32428 Sunny Hills, FL
32430 Clarksville, FL
32431 Cottondale, FL
32431 Jacob, FL
32432 Cypress, FL
32433 Defuniak Springs, FL
32434 Mossy Head, FL
32435 Defuniak Springs, FL
32437 Ebro, FL
32438 Fountain, FL
32439 Freeport, FL
32440 Graceville, FL
32442 Grand Ridge, FL
32443 Greenwood, FL
32444 Lynn Haven, FL
32445 Malone, FL
32446 Marianna, FL
32447 Marianna, FL
32448 Marianna, FL
32449 Kinard, FL
32449 Wewahitchka, FL
32452 Noma, FL
32455 Bruce, FL
32455 Ponce De Leon, FL
32455 Red Bay, FL
32456 Cape San Blas, FL
32456 Mexico Beach, FL
32456 Overstreet, FL
32456 Port Saint Joe, FL
32459 Point Washington, FL
32459 Santa Rosa Beach, FL
32460 Sneads, FL
32461 Alys Beach, FL
32461 Panama City, FL
32461 Rosemary Beach, FL
32461 Watersound, FL
32462 Vernon, FL
32463 Wausau, FL
32464 Westville, FL
32465 Wewahitchka, FL
32466 Youngstown, FL

325

32501 Pensacola, FL
32502 Pensacola, FL
32503 Pensacola, FL
32504 Pensacola, FL
32505 Pensacola, FL
32506 Pensacola, FL
32507 Pensacola, FL
32508 Pensacola, FL
32509 Pensacola, FL
32511 Pensacola, FL
32512 Pensacola, FL
32513 Pensacola, FL
32514 Pensacola, FL
32516 Pensacola, FL
32520 Pensacola, FL
32521 Pensacola, FL
32522 Pensacola, FL
32523 Pensacola, FL
32524 Pensacola, FL
32526 Bellview, FL
32526 Pensacola, FL
32530 Bagdad, FL
32531 Baker, FL
32533 Cantonment, FL
32534 Pensacola, FL
32535 Century, FL
32536 Crestview, FL
32537 Milligan, FL
32538 Paxton, FL
32539 Crestview, FL
32540 Destin, FL
32541 Destin, FL
32542 Duke Field Afs, FL
32542 Eglin, FL
32542 Eglin Afb, FL
32544 Hurlburt Field, FL
32547 Fort Walton Beach, FL
32548 Okaloosa Island, FL
32549 Fort Walton Beach, FL
32550 Destin, FL
32550 Miramar Beach, FL
32550 Sandestin, FL
32559 Pensacola, FL
32560 Gonzalez, FL
32561 Gulf Breeze, FL
32561 Pensacola Beach, FL
32562 Gulf Breeze, FL
32563 Gulf Breeze, FL
32564 Holt, FL
32565 Jay, FL
32566 Gulf Breeze, FL
32566 Navarre, FL
32567 Laurel Hill, FL
32568 Mc David, FL
32568 Walnut Hill, FL
32569 Mary Esther, FL
32570 Milton, FL
32571 Milton, FL
32571 Pace, FL
32572 Milton, FL
32577 Molino, FL
32578 Choctaw Beach, FL

32578 Niceville, FL
32579 Shalimar, FL
32580 Valparaiso, FL
32583 Milton, FL
32588 Niceville, FL
32591 Pensacola, FL

326

32601 Gainesville, FL
32602 Gainesville, FL
32603 Gainesville, FL
32604 Gainesville, FL
32605 Gainesville, FL
32606 Gainesville, FL
32607 Gainesville, FL
32608 Gainesville, FL
32609 Gainesville, FL
32610 Gainesville, FL
32611 Gainesville, FL
32612 Gainesville, FL
32614 Gainesville, FL
32615 Alachua, FL
32615 Santa Fe, FL
32616 Alachua, FL
32617 Anthony, FL
32618 Archer, FL
32619 Bell, FL
32621 Bronson, FL
32622 Brooker, FL
32625 Cedar Key, FL
32626 Chiefland, FL
32627 Gainesville, FL
32628 Cross City, FL
32631 Earleton, FL
32633 Evinston, FL
32634 Fairfield, FL
32635 Gainesville, FL
32639 Gulf Hammock, FL
32640 Cross Creek, FL
32640 Hawthorne, FL
32641 Gainesville, FL
32643 High Springs, FL
32644 Chiefland, FL
32648 Horseshoe Beach, FL
32653 Gainesville, FL
32654 Island Grove, FL
32655 High Springs, FL
32656 Keystone Heights, FL
32658 La Crosse, FL
32662 Lochloosa, FL
32663 Lowell, FL
32664 Mc Intosh, FL
32666 Melrose, FL
32667 Micanopy, FL
32668 Morriston, FL
32669 Jonesville, FL
32669 Newberry, FL
32669 Tioga, FL
32680 Old Town, FL
32681 Orange Lake, FL
32683 Otter Creek, FL
32686 Reddick, FL
32692 Suwannee, FL
32693 Fanning Springs, FL
32693 Trenton, FL
32694 Waldo, FL
32696 Williston, FL
32697 Worthington Springs, FL

327

32701 Altamonte Springs, FL
32702 Altoona, FL
32703 Apopka, FL
32704 Apopka, FL
32706 Cassadaga, FL
32707 Casselberry, FL
32708 Casselberry, FL
32708 Winter Springs, FL
32709 Christmas, FL
32710 Clarcona, FL
32712 Apopka, FL
32713 Debary, FL
32714 Altamonte Springs, FL
32714 Forest City, FL
32715 Altamonte Springs, FL
32718 Casselberry, FL
32719 Casselberry, FL
32719 Winter Springs, FL
32720 Deland, FL
32721 Deland, FL
32722 Deland, FL
32722 Glenwood, FL
32723 Deland, FL
32724 Deland, FL
32725 Deltona, FL
32725 Enterprise, FL
32726 Eustis, FL
32727 Eustis, FL
32728 Deltona, FL
32730 Casselberry, FL
32730 Fern Park, FL
32732 Geneva, FL
32733 Goldenrod, FL
32735 Grand Island, FL
32736 Eustis, FL
32738 Deltona, FL
32739 Deltona, FL
32744 Lake Helen, FL
32745 Mid Florida, FL
32746 Heathrow, FL
32746 Lake Mary, FL
32747 Lake Monroe, FL
32750 Longwood, FL
32751 Eatonville, FL
32751 Maitland, FL
32752 Longwood, FL
32753 Debary, FL
32754 Mims, FL
32756 Mount Dora, FL
32757 Mount Dora, FL
32759 Oak Hill, FL
32762 Oviedo, FL
32763 Orange City, FL
32764 Osteen, FL
32765 Oviedo, FL
32766 Chuluota, FL
32766 Oviedo, FL
32767 Paisley, FL
32768 Plymouth, FL
32771 Sanford, FL
32772 Sanford, FL
32773 Sanford, FL
32774 Orange City, FL
32775 Scottsmoor, FL
32776 Mount Plymouth, FL
32776 Sorrento, FL
32777 Tangerine, FL
32778 Deer Island, FL
32778 Tavares, FL
32779 Longwood, FL
32779 Wekiva Springs, FL
32780 Titusville, FL
32781 Titusville, FL
32783 Titusville, FL
32784 Dona Vista, FL
32784 Umatilla, FL
32789 Winter Park, FL
32790 Winter Park, FL
32791 Longwood, FL
32791 Wekiva Springs, FL
32792 Aloma, FL
32792 Winter Park, FL
32793 Winter Park, FL
32794 Maitland, FL
32795 Lake Mary, FL
32796 Titusville, FL
32798 Zellwood, FL
32799 Mid Florida, FL

328

32801 Orlando, FL
32802 Orlando, FL
32803 Orlando, FL
32804 Orlando, FL
32805 Orlando, FL
32806 Orlando, FL
32807 Azalea Park, FL
32807 Orlando, FL
32808 Orlando, FL
32808 Pine Hills, FL
32809 Belle Isle, FL
32809 Edgewood, FL
32809 Orlando, FL
32809 Pine Castle, FL
32810 Lockhart, FL
32810 Orlando, FL
32811 Orlando, FL
32811 Orlo Vista, FL
32812 Belle Isle, FL
32812 Orlando, FL
32814 Orlando, FL
32815 Kennedy Space Center, FL
32815 Orlando, FL
32816 Alafaya, FL
32816 Orlando, FL
32817 Orlando, FL
32817 Union Park, FL
32818 Hiawassee, FL
32818 Orlando, FL
32818 Pine Hills, FL
32819 Orlando, FL
32819 Sand Lake, FL
32820 Alafaya, FL
32820 Orlando, FL
32821 Bay Lake, FL
32821 Orlando, FL
32822 Orlando, FL
32824 Orlando, FL
32825 Alafaya, FL
32825 Orlando, FL
32826 Alafaya, FL
32826 Orlando, FL
32827 Orlando, FL
32828 Alafaya, FL
32828 Orlando, FL
32829 Orlando, FL
32830 Lake Buena Vista, FL
32830 Orlando, FL
32831 Alafaya, FL
32831 Orlando, FL
32832 Orlando, FL
32833 Alafaya, FL
32833 Orlando, FL
32834 Alafaya, FL
32834 Orlando, FL
32835 Orlando, FL
32836 Golden Oak, FL
32836 Orlando, FL
32837 Orlando, FL
32839 Edgewood, FL
32839 Orlando, FL
32839 Pine Castle, FL
32853 Orlando, FL
32854 Orlando, FL
32855 Orlando, FL
32856 Orlando, FL
32857 Orlando, FL
32858 Orlando, FL
32859 Orlando, FL
32860 Orlando, FL
32861 Orlando, FL
32862 Orlando, FL
32867 Orlando, FL
32868 Orlando, FL
32869 Orlando, FL
32872 Orlando, FL
32877 Orlando, FL
32878 Alafaya, FL
32878 Orlando, FL
32885 Orlando, FL
32886 Orlando, FL
32887 Orlando, FL
32891 Orlando, FL
32896 Orlando, FL
32897 Orlando, FL
32899 Kennedy Space Center, FL
32899 Orlando, FL

329

32901 Melbourne, FL
32902 Melbourne, FL
32903 Indialantic, FL
32903 Melbourne, FL
32904 Melbourne, FL
32904 Melbourne Village, FL
32904 West Melbourne, FL
32905 Melbourne, FL
32905 Palm Bay, FL
32906 Melbourne, FL
32906 Palm Bay, FL
32907 Melbourne, FL
32907 Palm Bay, FL
32908 Melbourne, FL
32908 Palm Bay, FL
32909 Grant Valkaria, FL
32909 Melbourne, FL
32909 Palm Bay, FL
32910 Melbourne, FL
32910 Palm Bay, FL
32911 Melbourne, FL
32911 Palm Bay, FL
32912 Melbourne, FL
32912 West Melbourne, FL
32919 Melbourne, FL
32920 Cape Canaveral, FL
32920 Port Canaveral, FL
32922 Cocoa, FL
32923 Cocoa, FL
32924 Cocoa, FL
32925 Canaveral Air Station, FL
32925 Patrick Afb, FL
32925 Patrick Air Force Base, FL
32926 Cocoa, FL
32927 Cocoa, FL
32927 Port Saint John, FL
32931 Cocoa Beach, FL
32932 Cocoa Beach, FL
32934 Eau Gallie, FL
32934 Melbourne, FL
32935 Melbourne, FL
32936 Eau Gallie, FL
32936 Melbourne, FL
32937 Ind Hbr Bch, FL
32937 Indian Harbour Beach, FL
32937 Melbourne, FL
32937 Satellite Beach, FL
32940 Melbourne, FL
32940 Palm Shores, FL
32940 Viera, FL
32941 Melbourne, FL
32948 Fellsmere, FL
32949 Grant, FL
32949 Grant Valkaria, FL
32950 Malabar, FL
32951 Melbourne, FL
32951 Melbourne Beach, FL
32952 Merritt Island, FL
32955 Rockledge, FL
32955 Viera, FL
32956 Rockledge, FL
32957 Roseland, FL
32958 Sebastian, FL
32959 Sharpes, FL
32960 Vero Beach, FL
32961 Vero Beach, FL
32962 Vero Beach, FL
32963 Indian River Shores, FL
32963 Orchid, FL
32963 Vero Beach, FL
32964 Vero Beach, FL
32965 Vero Beach, FL
32966 Citrus Ridge, FL
32966 Vero Beach, FL
32967 Vero Beach, FL
32968 Citrus Ridge, FL
32968 Vero Beach, FL
32969 Citrus Ridge, FL
32969 Vero Beach, FL
32970 Wabasso, FL
32971 Winter Beach, FL
32976 Barefoot Bay, FL
32976 Micco, FL
32976 Sebastian, FL
32978 Sebastian, FL

330

33001 Long Key, FL
33002 Hialeah, FL
33004 Dania, FL
33004 Dania Beach, FL
33008 Hallandale, FL
33008 Hallandale Beach, FL
33009 Hallandale, FL
33009 Hallandale Beach, FL
33009 Halndle Bch, FL
33010 Hialeah, FL
33011 Hialeah, FL
33012 Hialeah, FL
33013 Hialeah, FL
33014 Hialeah, FL
33014 Miami Gardens, FL
33014 Miami Lakes, FL
33015 Hialeah, FL
33015 Miami Gardens, FL
33016 Hialeah, FL
33016 Hialeah Gardens, FL
33016 Miami Lakes, FL
33017 Hialeah, FL
33017 Miami Gardens, FL
33018 Hialeah, FL
33018 Hialeah Gardens, FL
33018 Miami Lakes, FL
33019 Hollywood, FL
33020 Hollywood, FL
33021 Hollywood, FL
33021 Pembroke Park, FL
33022 Hollywood, FL
33023 Hollywood, FL
33023 Miramar, FL
33023 Pembroke Park, FL
33023 Pembroke Pines, FL
33023 West Hollywood, FL
33023 West Park, FL
33024 Hollywood, FL
33024 Pembroke Pines, FL
33025 Hollywood, FL
33025 Miramar, FL
33025 Pembroke Pines, FL
33026 Hollywood, FL
33026 Pembroke Pines, FL
33027 Hollywood, FL
33027 Miramar, FL
33027 Pembroke Pines, FL
33028 Hollywood, FL
33028 Pembroke Pines, FL
33029 Hollywood, FL
33029 Miramar, FL
33029 Pembroke Pines, FL
33030 Homestead, FL
33031 Homestead, FL
33031 Redland, FL
33032 Homestead, FL
33032 Naranja, FL
33032 Princeton, FL
33032 Redland, FL
33033 Homestead, FL
33034 Flamingo Lodge, FL
33034 Florida City, FL
33034 Homestead, FL
33035 Homestead, FL
33036 Islamorada, FL
33037 Key Largo, FL
33039 Homestead, FL
33039 Homestead Afb, FL
33039 Homestead Air Force Base, FL
33040 E Rockland Key, FL
33040 East Rockland Key, FL
33040 Key West, FL
33040 Key West Naval Air Station, FL
33040 Stock Island, FL
33041 Key West, FL
33042 Big Torch Key, FL
33042 Cudjoe Key, FL
33042 Little Torch Key, FL
33042 Lower Sugarloaf Key, FL
33042 Middle Torch Key, FL
33042 Ramrod Key, FL
33042 Sugarloaf, FL
33042 Sugarloaf Key, FL
33042 Sugarloaf Shrs, FL
33042 Summerland Key, FL
33042 Upper Sugarloaf Key, FL
33043 Big Pine Key, FL
33043 Summerland Key, FL
33045 Key West, FL
33050 Conch Key, FL
33050 Duck Key, FL
33050 Grassy Key, FL
33050 Marathon, FL
33050 Marathon Shores, FL
33051 Key Colony Beach, FL
33051 Marathon, FL
33052 Marathon, FL
33052 Marathon Shores, FL
33054 Miami Gardens, FL
33054 Opa Locka, FL
33055 Carol City, FL
33055 Miami Gardens, FL
33055 Opa Locka, FL
33056 Carol City, FL
33056 Miami Gardens, FL
33056 Opa Locka, FL
33060 Pompano Beach, FL
33061 Pompano Beach, FL
33062 Hillsboro Beach, FL
33062 Pompano Beach, FL
33063 Coconut Creek, FL
33063 Margate, FL
33063 Pompano Beach, FL
33064 Lighthouse Point, FL
33064 Pompano Beach, FL
33065 Coral Springs, FL
33065 Margate, FL
33065 Pompano Beach, FL
33066 Coconut Creek, FL
33066 Pompano Beach, FL
33067 Coral Springs, FL
33067 Parkland, FL
33067 Pompano Beach, FL
33068 Margate, FL
33068 North Lauderdale, FL
33068 Pompano Beach, FL
33069 Pompano Beach, FL
33070 Tavernier, FL
33071 Coral Springs, FL
33071 Pompano Beach, FL
33072 Pompano Beach, FL
33073 Coconut Creek, FL
33073 Coral Springs, FL
33073 Margate, FL
33073 Parkland, FL
33073 Pompano Beach, FL
33074 Lighthouse Point, FL
33074 Pompano Beach, FL
33075 Coral Springs, FL
33075 Pompano Beach, FL
33076 Coral Springs, FL
33076 Parkland, FL
33076 Pompano Beach, FL
33077 Coral Springs, FL
33077 Pompano Beach, FL
33081 Hollywood, FL
33082 Pembroke Pines, FL
33082 South Florida, FL
33083 Hollywood, FL
33084 Hollywood, FL
33084 Pembroke Pines, FL
33090 Homestead, FL
33092 Homestead, FL
33092 Naranja, FL
33092 Princeton, FL
33093 Coconutcreek, FL
33093 Coconut Creek, FL
33093 Margate, FL
33093 Pompano Beach, FL
33097 Coconut Creek, FL
33097 Pompano Beach, FL

331

33101 Miami, FL
33102 Miami, FL
33106 Miami, FL
33109 Miami, FL
33109 Miami Beach, FL
33111 Miami, FL
33112 Miami, FL
33114 Coral Gables, FL
33114 Miami, FL
33116 Miami, FL
33119 Miami, FL
33119 Miami Beach, FL
33122 Doral, FL
33122 Miami, FL
33124 Coral Gables, FL

33124 Miami, FL
33125 Miami, FL
33126 Doral, FL
33126 Miami, FL
33127 Miami, FL
33128 Miami, FL
33129 Miami, FL
33130 Miami, FL
33131 Miami, FL
33132 Miami, FL
33133 Coconut Grove, FL
33133 Coral Gables, FL
33133 Miami, FL
33134 Coral Gables, FL
33134 Miami, FL
33135 Miami, FL
33136 Miami, FL
33137 Miami, FL
33138 El Portal, FL
33138 Miami, FL
33138 Miami Shores, FL
33139 Miami Beach, FL
33140 Miami, FL
33140 Miami Beach, FL
33141 Miami, FL
33141 Miami Beach, FL
33141 North Bay Village, FL
33142 Miami, FL
33143 Coral Gables, FL
33143 Miami, FL
33143 South Miami, FL
33144 Miami, FL
33144 West Miami, FL
33145 Coral Gables, FL
33145 Miami, FL
33146 Coconut Grove, FL
33146 Coral Gables, FL
33146 Miami, FL
33146 South Miami, FL
33147 Miami, FL
33149 Key Biscayne, FL
33149 Miami, FL
33150 El Portal, FL
33150 Miami, FL
33150 Miami Shores, FL
33151 Miami, FL
33152 Miami, FL
33153 Miami, FL
33153 Miami Shores, FL
33154 Bal Harbour, FL
33154 Bay Harbor Islands, FL
33154 Indian Creek Village, FL
33154 Miami, FL
33154 Miami Beach, FL
33154 Surfside, FL
33155 Miami, FL
33156 Coral Gables, FL
33156 Kendall, FL
33156 Miami, FL
33156 Pinecrest, FL
33157 Cutler Bay, FL
33157 Cutler Ridge, FL
33157 Miami, FL
33157 Perrine, FL
33157 Village Of Palmetto Bay, FL
33158 Coral Gables, FL
33158 Miami, FL
33158 Village Of Palmetto Bay, FL
33159 Miami, FL
33160 Aventura, FL
33160 Golden Beach, FL
33160 Miami, FL
33160 North Miami Beach, FL
33160 Sunny Isles Beach, FL
33161 Biscayne Park, FL
33161 Miami, FL
33161 Miami Shores, FL
33161 North Miami, FL
33162 Miami, FL
33162 North Miami Beach, FL
33162 Uleta, FL
33163 Miami, FL
33163 Ojus, FL
33164 Miami, FL
33164 North Miami Bch, FL
33164 North Miami Beach, FL
33164 Uleta, FL
33165 Miami, FL
33165 Olympia Heights, FL
33166 Doral, FL
33166 Medley, FL
33166 Miami, FL
33166 Miami Springs, FL
33166 Virginia Gardens, FL
33167 Miami, FL
33167 Miami Shores, FL
33167 North Miami, FL
33168 Miami, FL
33168 Miami Shores, FL
33168 North Miami, FL
33169 Miami, FL
33169 Miami Gardens, FL
33169 North Miami Beach, FL
33170 Goulds, FL
33170 Miami, FL
33170 Quail Heights, FL
33172 Doral, FL
33172 Miami, FL
33173 Miami, FL
33174 Miami, FL
33175 Miami, FL
33175 Olympia Heights, FL
33176 Miami, FL
33176 Village Of Palmetto Bay, FL
33177 Miami, FL
33177 Quail Heights, FL
33178 Doral, FL
33178 Medley, FL
33178 Miami, FL
33179 Miami, FL
33179 Miami Gardens, FL
33179 North Miami Beach, FL
33180 Aventura, FL
33180 Miami, FL
33181 Miami, FL
33181 North Miami, FL
33181 North Miami Beach, FL
33182 Doral, FL
33182 Miami, FL
33183 Kendall, FL
33183 Miami, FL
33184 Miami, FL
33185 Miami, FL
33185 Olympia Heights, FL
33186 Miami, FL
33187 Miami, FL
33187 Quail Heights, FL
33188 Miami, FL
33189 Cutler Bay, FL
33189 Miami, FL
33189 Quail Heights, FL
33190 Cutler Bay, FL
33190 Miami, FL
33190 Quail Heights, FL
33193 Miami, FL
33194 Miami, FL
33196 Miami, FL
33197 Miami, FL
33197 Quail Heights, FL
33199 Miami, FL

332

33206 Miami, FL
33222 Doral, FL
33222 Miami, FL
33231 Miami, FL
33233 Miami, FL
33234 Coral Gables, FL
33234 Miami, FL
33238 Miami, FL
33239 Carl Fisher, FL
33239 Miami, FL
33239 Miami Beach, FL
33242 Miami, FL
33243 Miami, FL
33243 South Miami, FL
33245 Miami, FL
33247 Miami, FL
33255 Ludlam, FL
33255 Miami, FL
33256 Kendall, FL
33256 Miami, FL
33256 Pinecrest, FL
33257 Miami, FL
33257 Perrine, FL
33261 Miami, FL
33261 North Miami, FL
33265 Miami, FL
33265 Olympia Heights, FL
33266 Miami, FL
33266 Miami Springs, FL
33269 Miami, FL
33280 Miami, FL
33283 Miami, FL
33296 Miami, FL
33299 Miami, FL

333

33301 Fort Lauderdale, FL
33304 Oakland Park, FL
33305 Fort Lauderdale, FL
33305 Lazy Lake, FL
33305 Oakland Park, FL
33305 Wilton Manors, FL
33306 Fort Lauderdale, FL
33306 Oakland Park, FL
33306 Wilton Manors, FL
33307 Fort Lauderdale, FL
33307 Oakland Park, FL
33308 Fort Lauderdale, FL
33308 Lauderdale By The Sea, FL
33308 Oakland Park, FL
33308 Sea Ranch Lakes, FL
33309 Fort Lauderdale, FL
33309 Lauderdale Lakes, FL
33309 Oakland Park, FL
33309 Tamarac, FL
33310 Fort Lauderdale, FL
33311 Lauderdale Lakes, FL
33311 Lauderhill, FL
33311 Oakland Park, FL
33311 Plantation, FL
33311 Wilton Manors, FL
33312 Davie, FL
33312 Fort Lauderdale, FL
33313 City Of Sunrise, FL
33313 Fort Lauderdale, FL
33313 Lauderdale Lakes, FL
33313 Lauderhill, FL
33313 Plantation, FL
33314 Davie, FL
33314 Fort Lauderdale, FL
33317 Davie, FL
33317 Fort Lauderdale, FL
33317 Plantation, FL
33318 Fort Lauderdale, FL
33318 Plantation, FL
33319 City Of Sunrise, FL
33319 Fort Lauderdale, FL
33319 Lauderdale Lakes, FL
33319 Lauderhill, FL
33319 Tamarac, FL
33320 Fort Lauderdale, FL
33320 Tamarac, FL
33321 Fort Lauderdale, FL
33321 Tamarac, FL
33322 City Of Sunrise, FL
33322 Fort Lauderdale, FL
33322 Plantation, FL
33323 City Of Sunrise, FL
33323 Fort Lauderdale, FL
33323 Plantation, FL
33324 Davie, FL
33324 Fort Lauderdale, FL
33324 Plantation, FL
33325 City Of Sunrise, FL
33325 Davie, FL
33325 Fort Lauderdale, FL
33325 Plantation, FL
33326 City Of Sunrise, FL
33326 Davie, FL
33326 Fort Lauderdale, FL
33326 Weston, FL
33327 Fort Lauderdale, FL
33327 Weston, FL
33328 Cooper City, FL
33328 Davie, FL
33328 Fort Lauderdale, FL
33329 Cooper City, FL
33329 Davie, FL
33329 Fort Lauderdale, FL
33330 Cooper City, FL
33330 Davie, FL
33330 Fort Lauderdale, FL
33330 Lauderdale Lakes, FL
33330 Southwest Ranches, FL
33331 Davie, FL
33331 Fort Lauderdale, FL
33331 Southwest Ranches, FL
33331 Weston, FL
33332 Davie, FL
33332 Fort Lauderdale, FL
33332 Southwest Ranches, FL
33332 Weston, FL
33334 Fort Lauderdale, FL
33334 Oakland Park, FL
33334 Wilton Manors, FL
33335 Fort Lauderdale, FL
33345 City Of Sunrise, FL
33345 Fort Lauderdale, FL
33351 City Of Sunrise, FL
33351 Fort Lauderdale, FL
33351 Lauderhill, FL
33351 Tamarac, FL
33355 Davie, FL
33355 Fort Lauderdale, FL
33359 Tamarac, FL
33388 Fort Lauderdale, FL
33388 Plantation, FL
33394 Fort Lauderdale, FL

334

33401 West Palm Beach, FL
33403 Lake Park, FL
33403 North Palm Beach, FL
33403 Palm Beach Gardens, FL
33403 Riviera Beach, FL
33403 W Plm Bch, FL
33403 West Palm Beach, FL
33404 Palm Beach Shores, FL
33404 Riviera Beach, FL
33404 Singer Island, FL
33404 West Palm Beach, FL
33406 Cloud Lake, FL
33406 Glen Ridge, FL
33406 Lake Clarke Shores, FL
33406 Palm Springs, FL
33406 West Palm Beach, FL
33407 Riviera Beach, FL
33407 West Palm Beach, FL
33408 Juno Beach, FL
33408 North Palm Beach, FL
33408 Palm Beach Gardens, FL
33408 West Palm Beach, FL
33409 Haverhill, FL
33409 West Palm Beach, FL
33410 North Palm Beach, FL
33410 Palm Beach Gardens, FL
33410 Riviera Beach, FL
33410 West Palm Beach, FL
33411 Royal Palm Beach, FL
33411 Wellington, FL
33411 West Palm Beach, FL
33412 Palm Beach Gardens, FL
33412 Royal Palm Beach, FL
33412 West Palm Beach, FL
33413 Green Acres, FL
33413 Greenacres, FL
33413 West Palm Beach, FL
33414 Royal Palm Beach, FL
33414 Village Of Wellington, FL
33414 Wellington, FL
33414 West Palm Beach, FL
33415 Green Acres, FL
33415 Greenacres, FL
33415 Haverhill, FL
33415 West Palm Beach, FL
33417 Haverhill, FL
33417 West Palm Beach, FL
33418 Palm Beach Gardens, FL
33418 Riviera Beach, FL
33418 West Palm Beach, FL
33419 Riviera Beach, FL
33419 West Palm Beach, FL
33420 Palm Beach Gardens, FL
33420 West Palm Beach, FL
33421 Royal Palm Beach, FL
33421 Wellington, FL
33421 West Palm Beach, FL
33422 Haverhill, FL
33422 West Palm Beach, FL
33424 Boynton Beach, FL
33425 Boynton Beach, FL
33426 Boynton Beach, FL
33427 Boca Raton, FL
33428 Boca Raton, FL
33429 Boca Raton, FL
33430 Belle Glade, FL
33431 Boca Raton, FL
33432 Boca Raton, FL
33433 Boca Raton, FL
33434 Boca Raton, FL
33435 Boynton Beach, FL
33435 Briny Breezes, FL
33435 Ocean Ridge, FL
33436 Boynton Beach, FL
33436 Golf, FL
33436 Village Of Golf, FL
33437 Boynton Beach, FL
33438 Bryant, FL
33438 Canal Point, FL
33440 Clewiston, FL
33441 Deerfield Beach, FL
33444 Delray Beach, FL
33445 Delray Beach, FL
33446 Delray Beach, FL
33446 West Delray Beach, FL
33448 Delray Beach, FL
33448 West Delray Beach, FL
33449 Lake Worth, FL
33449 Wellington, FL
33454 Greenacres, FL
33454 Lake Worth, FL
33455 Hobe Sound, FL
33458 Jupiter, FL
33459 Lake Harbor, FL
33460 Lake Worth, FL
33461 Lake Worth, FL
33461 Palm Springs, FL
33462 Atlantis, FL
33462 Hypoluxo, FL
33462 Lake Worth, FL
33462 Lantana, FL
33462 Manalapan, FL
33463 Greenacres, FL
33463 Lake Worth, FL
33464 Boca Raton, FL
33465 Lake Worth, FL
33465 Lantana, FL
33466 Lake Worth, FL
33467 Greenacres, FL
33467 Lake Worth, FL
33467 Wellington, FL
33468 Jupiter, FL
33469 Jupiter, FL
33469 Jupiter Inlet Colony, FL
33469 Tequesta, FL
33470 Lox, FL
33470 Loxahatchee, FL
33470 Loxahatchee Groves, FL
33470 Village Of Wellington, FL
33470 Wellington, FL
33471 Moore Haven, FL
33472 Boynton Beach, FL
33473 Boynton Beach, FL
33474 Boynton Beach, FL
33475 Hobe Sound, FL
33476 Pahokee, FL
33477 Jupiter, FL
33478 Jupiter, FL
33480 Palm Beach, FL
33480 South Palm Beach, FL
33481 Boca Raton, FL
33482 Delray Beach, FL
33483 Delray Beach, FL
33483 Gulf Stream, FL
33484 Delray Beach, FL
33484 West Delray Beach, FL
33486 Boca Raton, FL
33487 Boca Raton, FL
33487 Highland Beach, FL
33488 Boca Raton, FL
33493 South Bay, FL
33496 Boca Raton, FL
33497 Boca Raton, FL
33498 Boca Raton, FL
33499 Boca Raton, FL

335

33503 Balm, FL
33508 Brandon, FL
33509 Brandon, FL
33510 Brandon, FL
33511 Brandon, FL
33513 Bushnell, FL
33514 Center Hill, FL
33521 Coleman, FL
33523 Dade City, FL
33523 Ridge Manor, FL
33524 Crystal Springs, FL
33525 Dade City, FL
33525 Richland, FL
33526 Dade City, FL
33527 Dover, FL
33530 Durant, FL
33534 Gibsonton, FL
33537 Lacoochee, FL
33538 Lake Panasoffkee, FL
33539 Zephyrhills, FL
33540 Zephyrhills, FL
33541 Zephyrhills, FL
33542 Zephyrhills, FL
33543 Wesley Chapel, FL
33543 Zephyrhills, FL
33544 Wesley Chapel, FL
33544 Zephyrhills, FL
33545 Wesley Chapel, FL
33545 Zephyrhills, FL
33547 Lithia, FL
33548 Lutz, FL
33549 Lutz, FL
33550 Mango, FL
33556 Odessa, FL
33558 Lutz, FL
33559 Lutz, FL
33563 Plant City, FL
33564 Plant City, FL
33565 Plant City, FL
33566 Plant City, FL
33567 Plant City, FL
33568 Riverview, FL
33569 Riverview, FL
33570 Ruskin, FL
33571 Ruskin, FL
33571 Sun City Center, FL
33571 Sun City Ctr, FL
33572 Apollo Beach, FL
33572 Ruskin, FL
33573 Ruskin, FL
33573 Sun City Center, FL
33574 Saint Leo, FL
33575 Ruskin, FL
33575 Sun City Center, FL
33576 San Antonio, FL
33578 Riverview, FL
33579 Riverview, FL
33583 Seffner, FL
33584 Seffner, FL
33585 Sumterville, FL
33586 Sun City, FL
33587 Sydney, FL
33592 Thonotosassa, FL
33593 Trilby, FL
33594 Valrico, FL
33595 Valrico, FL
33596 Valrico, FL
33597 Ridge Manor Estates, FL
33597 Webster, FL
33598 Wimauma, FL

336

33601 Tampa, FL
33602 Tampa, FL

33603 Tampa, FL
33604 Tampa, FL
33605 Tampa, FL
33605 Ybor City, FL
33606 Tampa, FL
33606 University Of Tampa, FL
33607 Tampa, FL
33608 Macdill Afb, FL
33608 Tampa, FL
33609 Tampa, FL
33610 Tampa, FL
33611 Tampa, FL
33612 Tampa, FL
33613 Tampa, FL
33614 Tampa, FL
33615 Tampa, FL
33615 Town N Country, FL
33616 Tampa, FL
33617 Tampa, FL
33617 Temple Ter, FL
33617 Temple Terrace, FL
33618 Carrollwood, FL
33618 Tampa, FL
33619 Clair Mel City, FL
33619 Tampa, FL
33620 Tampa, FL
33621 Tampa, FL
33622 Tampa, FL
33623 Tampa, FL
33624 Northdale, FL
33624 Tampa, FL
33625 Carrollwood, FL
33625 Tampa, FL
33626 Northdale, FL
33626 Tampa, FL
33626 Westchase, FL
33629 Palma Ceia, FL
33629 Tampa, FL
33630 Tampa, FL
33631 Tampa, FL
33633 Tampa, FL
33634 Tampa, FL
33635 Tampa, FL
33637 Tampa, FL
33637 Temple Ter, FL
33637 Temple Terrace, FL
33646 Tampa, FL
33647 Tampa, FL
33647 Tampa Palms, FL
33650 Tampa, FL
33655 Tampa, FL
33660 Tampa, FL
33661 Tampa, FL
33662 Tampa, FL
33663 Tampa, FL
33664 Tampa, FL
33672 Tampa, FL
33673 Tampa, FL
33674 Tampa, FL
33675 Tampa, FL
33675 Ybor City, FL
33677 Tampa, FL
33679 Tampa, FL
33680 Tampa, FL
33681 Tampa, FL
33682 Tampa, FL
33684 Tampa, FL
33685 Tampa, FL
33686 Tampa, FL
33687 Tampa, FL
33687 Temple Ter, FL
33688 Carrollwood, FL
33688 Tampa, FL
33689 Tampa, FL
33694 Tampa, FL

337

33701 Saint Petersburg, FL
33706 Pass A Grille Beach, FL
33706 Saint Pete Beach, FL
33706 Saint Petersburg, FL
33706 St Petersburg Beach, FL
33706 Treasure Island, FL
33707 Gulfport, FL
33707 Saint Pete Beach, FL
33707 Saint Petersburg, FL
33707 South Pasadena, FL
33708 Madeira Beach, FL
33708 North Redington Beach, FL
33708 Redington Beach, FL
33708 Redington Shores, FL
33708 Saint Petersburg, FL
33709 Kenneth City, FL
33709 Saint Petersburg, FL
33711 Gulfport, FL
33711 Saint Petersburg, FL
33715 Tierra Verde, FL
33716 Saint Petersburg, FL
33731 St Petersburg, FL
33732 Saint Petersburg, FL
33733 St Pete, FL
33734 Saint Petersburg, FL
33734 St Petersburg, FL
33736 Saint Pete Beach, FL
33736 Saint Petersburg, FL
33738 Madeira Beach, FL
33738 Saint Petersburg, FL
33740 Treasure Island, FL
33741 Pass A Grille Beach, FL
33741 Saint Petersburg, FL
33744 Bay Pines, FL
33747 Saint Petersburg, FL
33755 Clearwater, FL
33756 Belleair, FL
33756 Clearwater, FL
33757 Clearwater, FL
33758 Clearwater, FL
33759 Clearwater, FL
33760 Clearwater, FL
33761 Clearwater, FL
33762 Clearwater, FL
33763 Clearwater, FL
33764 Clearwater, FL
33765 Clearwater, FL
33766 Clearwater, FL
33767 Clearwater Beach, FL
33769 Clearwater, FL
33770 Belleair Bluffs, FL
33770 Largo, FL
33771 Largo, FL
33772 Seminole, FL
33773 Largo, FL
33774 Largo, FL
33775 Seminole, FL
33776 Largo, FL
33776 Seminole, FL
33777 Largo, FL
33777 Seminole, FL
33778 Largo, FL
33778 Seminole, FL
33779 Largo, FL
33780 Pinellas Park, FL
33781 Pinellas Park, FL
33782 Pinellas Park, FL
33784 Saint Petersburg, FL
33785 Belleair Beach, FL
33785 Indian Rks Beach, FL
33785 Indian Rocks Beach, FL
33785 Indian Shores, FL
33786 Belleair Beach, FL
33786 Belleair Shores, FL
33786 Indian Rks Beach, FL
33786 Indian Rocks Beach, FL

338

33801 Lakeland, FL
33802 Lakeland, FL
33803 Lakeland, FL
33804 Lakeland, FL
33805 Lakeland, FL
33806 Lakeland, FL
33807 Lakeland, FL
33809 Lakeland, FL
33810 Lakeland, FL
33811 Lakeland, FL
33812 Lakeland, FL
33813 Lakeland, FL
33815 Lakeland, FL
33820 Alturas, FL
33823 Auburndale, FL
33825 Avon Park, FL
33826 Avon Park, FL
33827 Babson Park, FL
33830 Bartow, FL
33831 Bartow, FL
33834 Bowling Green, FL
33835 Bradley, FL
33836 Davenport, FL
33837 Davenport, FL
33838 Dundee, FL
33839 Eagle Lake, FL
33840 Eaton Park, FL
33841 Fort Meade, FL
33843 Frostproof, FL
33844 Haines City, FL
33845 Haines City, FL
33846 Highland City, FL
33847 Homeland, FL
33848 Intercession City, FL
33849 Kathleen, FL
33850 Lake Alfred, FL
33851 Lake Hamilton, FL
33852 Lake Placid, FL
33853 Lake Wales, FL
33854 Lake Wales, FL
33854 Lakeshore, FL
33855 Indian Lake Estates, FL
33855 Lake Wales, FL
33856 Lake Wales, FL
33856 Nalcrest, FL
33857 Lorida, FL
33858 Loughman, FL
33859 Lake Wales, FL
33860 Mulberry, FL
33862 Lake Placid, FL
33863 Nichols, FL
33865 Ona, FL
33867 Lake Wales, FL
33867 River Ranch, FL
33868 Polk City, FL
33870 Sebring, FL
33871 Sebring, FL
33872 Sebring, FL
33873 Wauchula, FL
33875 Sebring, FL
33876 Sebring, FL
33877 Waverly, FL
33880 Eloise, FL
33880 Jpv, FL
33880 Wahneta, FL
33880 Winter Haven, FL
33881 Winter Haven, FL
33882 Winter Haven, FL
33883 Winter Haven, FL
33884 Cypress Gardens, FL
33884 Winter Haven, FL
33885 Florence Villa, FL
33885 Winter Haven, FL
33888 Winter Haven, FL
33890 Zolfo Springs, FL
33896 Champions Gate, FL
33896 Davenport, FL
33897 Davenport, FL
33898 Lake Wales, FL

339

33901 Fort Myers, FL
33902 Fort Myers, FL
33903 Fort Myers, FL
33903 N Fort Myers, FL
33903 No Fort Myers, FL
33903 No Ft Myers, FL
33903 North Fort Myers, FL
33904 Cape Coral, FL
33905 Fort Myers, FL
33905 Tice, FL
33906 Fort Myers, FL
33907 Fort Myers, FL
33908 Fort Myers, FL
33909 Cape Coral, FL
33910 Cape Coral, FL
33910 Cape Coral South, FL
33911 Fort Myers, FL
33912 Fort Myers, FL
33913 Fort Myers, FL
33913 Miromar Lakes, FL
33914 Cape Coral, FL
33915 Cape Coral, FL
33916 Fort Myers, FL
33917 Fort Myers, FL
33917 N Fort Myers, FL
33917 No Fort Myers, FL
33917 No Ft Myers, FL
33917 North Fort Myers, FL
33917 North Ft Myers, FL
33918 Fort Myers, FL
33918 N Fort Myers, FL
33918 N Ft Myers, FL
33918 No Fort Myers, FL
33918 North Fort Myers, FL
33918 North Ft Myers, FL
33919 Fort Myers, FL
33920 Alva, FL
33921 Boca Grande, FL
33922 Bokeelia, FL
33924 Captiva, FL
33927 El Jobean, FL
33928 Estero, FL
33929 Estero, FL
33930 Felda, FL
33931 Fort Myers Beach, FL
33935 Fort Denaud, FL
33935 Ft Denaud, FL
33935 Labelle, FL
33936 Lehigh Acres, FL
33938 Murdock, FL
33944 Palmdale, FL
33945 Pineland, FL
33946 Cape Haze, FL
33946 Placida, FL
33947 Cape Haze, FL
33947 Placida, FL
33947 Rotonda West, FL
33948 Port Charlotte, FL
33949 Pt Charlotte, FL
33950 Punta Gorda, FL
33951 Punta Gorda, FL
33952 Port Charlotte, FL
33955 Punta Gorda, FL
33956 Saint James City, FL
33957 Sanibel, FL
33960 Venus, FL
33965 Fort Myers, FL
33966 Fort Myers, FL
33967 Fort Myers, FL
33970 Lehigh Acres, FL
33971 Lehigh Acres, FL
33972 Lehigh Acres, FL
33973 Lehigh Acres, FL
33974 Lehigh Acres, FL
33975 Labelle, FL
33976 Lehigh Acres, FL
33980 Port Charlotte, FL
33980 Punta Gorda, FL
33981 Port Charlotte, FL
33982 Punta Gorda, FL
33983 Port Charlotte, FL
33983 Punta Gorda, FL
33990 Cape Coral, FL
33991 Cape Coral, FL
33991 Matlacha Isles, FL
33993 Cape Coral, FL
33993 Fort Myers, FL
33993 Matlacha, FL
33994 Fort Myers, FL

341

34101 Naples, FL
34102 Naples, FL
34103 Naples, FL
34104 Naples, FL
34105 Naples, FL
34106 Naples, FL
34107 Naples, FL
34107 Vanderbilt, FL
34108 Coco River, FL
34108 Naples, FL
34109 Naples, FL
34110 Naples, FL
34112 Naples, FL
34113 Naples, FL
34114 Naples, FL
34116 Naples, FL
34117 Naples, FL
34119 Naples, FL
34120 Naples, FL
34133 Bonita Spgs, FL
34133 Bonita Springs, FL
34134 Barefoot Beach, FL
34134 Bonita Springs, FL
34136 Bonita Spgs, FL
34136 Bonita Springs, FL
34137 Copeland, FL
34138 Chokoloskee, FL
34139 Everglades City, FL
34140 Goodland, FL
34141 Jerome, FL
34141 Ochopee, FL
34142 Ave Maria, FL
34142 Immokalee, FL
34143 Ave Maria, FL
34143 Immokalee, FL
34145 Marco Island, FL
34146 Marco Island, FL

342

34201 Braden River, FL
34201 Bradenton, FL
34201 University Park, FL
34202 Bradenton, FL
34202 Lakewood Ranch, FL
34203 Braden River, FL
34203 Bradenton, FL
34203 Lakewood Ranch, FL
34204 Bradenton, FL
34205 Bradenton, FL
34206 Bradenton, FL
34207 Bradenton, FL
34208 Bradenton, FL
34209 Bradenton, FL
34209 Palma Sola, FL
34210 Bradenton, FL
34211 Bradenton, FL
34211 Lakewood Ranch, FL
34212 Bradenton, FL
34212 Lakewood Ranch, FL
34215 Cortez, FL
34216 Anna Maria, FL
34217 Bradenton Beach, FL
34217 Holmes Beach, FL
34218 Bradenton Beach, FL
34218 Holmes Beach, FL
34219 Duette, FL
34219 Parrish, FL
34220 Palmetto, FL
34221 Palmetto, FL
34221 Rubonia, FL
34222 Ellenton, FL
34223 Englewood, FL
34224 Englewood, FL
34224 Grove City, FL
34228 Longboat Key, FL
34229 Osprey, FL
34230 Sarasota, FL
34231 Sarasota, FL
34232 Sarasota, FL
34233 Sarasota, FL
34234 Sarasota, FL
34235 Sarasota, FL
34236 Sarasota, FL
34237 Sarasota, FL
34238 Sarasota, FL
34239 Sarasota, FL
34240 Lakewood Ranch, FL
34240 Sarasota, FL
34241 Sarasota, FL
34242 Sarasota, FL
34242 Siesta Key, FL
34243 Sarasota, FL
34250 Terra Ceia, FL
34250 Terra Ceia Island, FL
34251 Myakka City, FL
34260 Manasota, FL
34260 Sarasota, FL
34264 Oneco, FL
34265 Arcadia, FL
34266 Arcadia, FL
34266 Lake Suzy, FL
34266 Sidell, FL
34267 Fort Ogden, FL
34268 Nocatee, FL
34269 Arcadia, FL
34269 Lake Suzy, FL
34270 Tallevast, FL
34272 Laurel, FL
34274 Nokomis, FL
34275 Nokomis, FL
34275 North Venice, FL
34276 Sarasota, FL
34277 Sarasota, FL
34278 Pinecraft, FL
34278 Sarasota, FL
34280 Bradenton, FL
34280 Palma Sola, FL
34281 Bradenton, FL
34281 Trailer Estates, FL
34282 Bradenton, FL
34284 Venice, FL
34285 Venice, FL
34286 North Port, FL
34286 Venice, FL
34287 North Port, FL
34287 Venice, FL
34288 North Port, FL
34289 North Port, FL
34290 North Port, FL
34290 Venice, FL
34291 North Port, FL
34291 Venice, FL
34292 Venice, FL
34293 Venice, FL
34295 Englewood, FL

344

34420 Belleview, FL
34421 Belleview, FL
34423 Crystal River, FL
34428 Crystal River, FL
34429 Crystal River, FL
34430 Dunnellon, FL
34431 Dunnellon, FL
34432 Dunnellon, FL
34433 Citrus Springs, FL
34433 Dunnellon, FL
34434 Citrus Springs, FL
34434 Dunnellon, FL
34436 Floral City, FL
34441 Hernando, FL
34442 Citrus Hills, FL
34442 Hernando, FL
34445 Holder, FL
34446 Homosassa, FL
34446 Homosassa Springs, FL
34448 Homosassa, FL
34448 Homosassa Springs, FL
34449 Inglis, FL
34450 Inverness, FL
34451 Inverness, FL
34452 Inverness, FL
34453 Inverness, FL
34460 Lecanto, FL
34461 Lecanto, FL
34464 Beverly Hills, FL
34465 Beverly Hills, FL
34465 Pine Ridge, FL
34470 Ocala, FL
34471 Ocala, FL
34472 Ocala, FL
34473 Ocala, FL
34474 Ocala, FL
34475 Ocala, FL
34476 Ocala, FL
34477 Ocala, FL
34478 Ocala, FL
34479 Ocala, FL
34480 Ocala, FL
34481 Ocala, FL
34482 Ocala, FL
34483 Ocala, FL
34484 Oxford, FL
34487 Homosassa, FL
34488 Silver Springs, FL
34491 Summerfield, FL
34492 Summerfield, FL
34498 Yankeetown, FL

346

34601 Brooksville, FL
34602 Brooksville, FL
34603 Brooksville, FL

34604 Brooksville, FL
34604 Masaryktown, FL
34604 Spring Hill, FL
34605 Brooksville, FL
34606 Brooksville, FL
34606 Spring Hill, FL
34606 Weeki Wachee, FL
34607 Brooksville, FL
34607 Hernando Beach, FL
34607 Spring Hill, FL
34607 Weeki Wachee, FL
34608 Brooksville, FL
34608 Spring Hill, FL
34609 Brooksville, FL
34609 Spring Hill, FL
34610 Brooksville, FL
34610 Shady Hills, FL
34610 Spring Hill, FL
34611 Brooksville, FL
34611 Spring Hill, FL
34613 Brooksville, FL
34613 Spring Hill, FL
34613 Weeki Wachee, FL
34614 Brooksville, FL
34614 Weeki Wachee, FL
34636 Istachatta, FL
34637 Land O Lakes, FL
34638 Land O Lakes, FL
34639 Land O Lakes, FL
34652 New Port Richey, FL
34652 New Pt Richey, FL
34652 Nw Prt Rchy, FL
34653 New Port Richey, FL
34653 New Pt Richey, FL
34654 New Port Richey, FL
34654 New Pt Richey, FL
34655 New Port Richey, FL
34655 New Pt Richey, FL
34655 Trinity, FL
34656 New Port Richey, FL
34656 New Prt Rchy, FL
34656 New Pt Richey, FL
34660 Ozona, FL
34661 Nobleton, FL
34667 Bayonet Point, FL
34667 Hudson, FL
34667 Port Richey, FL
34668 Port Richey, FL
34669 Hudson, FL
34669 Port Richey, FL
34673 Port Richey, FL
34674 Hudson, FL
34674 Port Richey, FL
34677 Oldsmar, FL
34679 Aripeka, FL
34680 Elfers, FL
34681 Crystal Beach, FL
34682 Palm Harbor, FL
34683 Palm Harbor, FL
34684 Palm Harbor, FL
34685 Palm Harbor, FL
34688 Tarpon Spngs, FL
34688 Tarpon Springs, FL
34689 Tarpon Spngs, FL
34689 Tarpon Springs, FL
34690 Holiday, FL
34690 Tarpon Spngs, FL
34690 Tarpon Springs, FL
34691 Holiday, FL
34691 Tarpon Spngs, FL
34691 Tarpon Springs, FL
34692 Holiday, FL
34695 Safety Harbor, FL
34697 Dunedin, FL
34698 Dunedin, FL

347

34705 Astatula, FL
34711 Clermont, FL
34712 Clermont, FL
34713 Clermont, FL
34714 Clermont, FL
34715 Clermont, FL
34715 Minneola, FL
34729 Ferndale, FL
34729 Montverde, FL
34731 Fruitland Park, FL
34734 Gotha, FL
34736 Groveland, FL
34737 Groveland, FL
34737 Howey In The Hills, FL
34739 Kenansville, FL
34740 Killarney, FL
34740 Oakland, FL
34741 Kissimmee, FL
34742 Kissimmee, FL
34743 Buena Ventura Lakes, FL
34743 Kissimmee, FL
34744 Kissimmee, FL
34745 Kissimmee, FL
34746 Kissimmee, FL
34747 Celebration, FL
34747 Kissimmee, FL
34747 Reunion, FL
34748 Leesburg, FL
34749 Leesburg, FL
34753 Mascotte, FL
34755 Minneola, FL
34756 Montverde, FL
34758 Kissimmee, FL
34758 Poinciana, FL
34759 Kissimmee, FL
34759 Poinciana, FL
34760 Oakland, FL
34761 Ocoee, FL
34762 Okahumpka, FL
34769 Saint Cloud, FL
34770 Saint Cloud, FL
34771 Magnolia Square, FL
34771 Saint Cloud, FL
34772 Saint Cloud, FL
34773 Harmony, FL
34773 Saint Cloud, FL
34777 Winter Garden, FL
34778 Winter Garden, FL
34785 Wildwood, FL
34786 Windermere, FL
34787 Oakland, FL
34787 Winter Garden, FL
34788 Haines Creek, FL
34788 Leesburg, FL
34789 Leesburg, FL
34797 Howey In The Hills, FL
34797 Yalaha, FL

349

34945 Fort Pierce, FL
34946 Fort Pierce, FL
34947 Fort Pierce, FL
34948 Fort Pierce, FL
34949 Fort Pierce, FL
34949 Hutchinson Island, FL
34950 Fort Pierce, FL
34951 Fort Pierce, FL
34952 Fort Pierce, FL
34952 Port Saint Lucie, FL
34953 Fort Pierce, FL
34953 Port Saint Lucie, FL
34953 Saint Lucie West, FL
34954 Fort Pierce, FL
34956 Indiantown, FL
34957 Jensen Beach, FL
34957 Ocean Breeze Park, FL
34958 Jensen Beach, FL
34972 Basinger, FL
34972 Okeechobee, FL
34972 Yeehaw Junction, FL
34973 Okeechobee, FL
34974 Okeechobee, FL
34979 Fort Pierce, FL
34981 Fort Pierce, FL
34982 Fort Pierce, FL
34983 Fort Pierce, FL
34983 Port Saint Lucie, FL
34983 Saint Lucie West, FL
34984 Fort Pierce, FL
34984 Port Saint Lucie, FL
34985 Fort Pierce, FL
34985 Port Saint Lucie, FL
34986 Fort Pierce, FL
34986 Port Saint Lucie, FL
34986 Saint Lucie West, FL
34987 Fort Pierce, FL
34987 Port Saint Lucie, FL
34987 Saint Lucie West, FL
34988 Fort Pierce, FL
34988 Port Saint Lucie, FL
34988 Saint Lucie West, FL
34990 Palm City, FL
34991 Palm City, FL
34992 Port Salerno, FL
34994 Stuart, FL
34995 Stuart, FL
34996 Sewalls Point, FL
34996 Stuart, FL
34997 Stuart, FL

350

35004 Acmar, AL
35004 Moody, AL
35005 Adamsville, AL
35006 Adger, AL
35007 Alabaster, AL
35010 Alexander City, AL
35013 Allgood, AL
35014 Alpine, AL
35015 Alton, AL
35016 Arab, AL
35019 Baileyton, AL
35020 Bessemer, AL
35020 Brighton, AL
35021 Bessemer, AL
35022 Bessemer, AL
35022 Helena, AL
35023 Bessemer, AL
35023 Hueytown, AL
35031 Blountsville, AL
35032 Bon Air, AL
35033 Bremen, AL
35034 Brent, AL
35035 Brierfield, AL
35036 Brookside, AL
35036 Cardiff, AL
35038 Burnwell, AL
35040 Calera, AL
35042 Centreville, AL
35043 Chelsea, AL
35044 Childersburg, AL
35044 Coosa Pines, AL
35045 Clanton, AL
35046 Clanton, AL
35048 Clay, AL
35049 Cleveland, AL
35049 Nectar, AL
35051 Columbiana, AL
35052 Cook Springs, AL
35053 Crane Hill, AL
35054 Cropwell, AL
35055 Cullman, AL
35055 Dodge City, AL
35055 Good Hope, AL
35056 Cullman, AL
35057 Cullman, AL
35057 Good Hope, AL
35058 Cullman, AL
35060 Docena, AL
35061 Dolomite, AL
35062 Dora, AL
35063 Empire, AL
35064 Fairfield, AL
35068 Coalburg, AL
35068 Fultondale, AL
35070 Garden City, AL
35071 Gardendale, AL
35072 Goodwater, AL
35073 Graysville, AL
35074 Green Pond, AL
35077 Hanceville, AL
35078 Harpersville, AL
35079 Hayden, AL
35080 Helena, AL
35082 Hollins, AL
35082 Sylacauga, AL
35083 Holly Pond, AL
35085 Jemison, AL
35087 Joppa, AL
35089 Kellyton, AL
35091 Kimberly, AL
35094 Leeds, AL
35096 Lincoln, AL
35097 Locust Fork, AL
35098 Logan, AL

351

35111 Lake View, AL
35111 Mc Calla, AL
35112 Margaret, AL
35114 Maylene, AL
35115 Montevallo, AL
35116 Morris, AL
35117 Mount Olive, AL
35118 Mulga, AL
35118 Sylvan Springs, AL
35119 New Castle, AL
35120 Branchville, AL
35120 Odenville, AL
35121 Highland Lake, AL
35121 Oneonta, AL
35121 Rosa, AL
35123 Palmerdale, AL
35124 Indian Springs, AL
35124 Indian Springs Village, AL
35124 Pelham, AL
35125 Pell City, AL
35126 Dixiana, AL
35126 Pinson, AL
35127 Pleasant Grove, AL
35128 Pell City, AL
35130 Quinton, AL
35130 West Jefferson, AL
35131 Ragland, AL
35133 Remlap, AL
35135 Riverside, AL
35136 Rockford, AL
35137 Saginaw, AL
35139 Sayre, AL
35142 Shannon, AL
35143 Shelby, AL
35144 Alabaster, AL
35144 Siluria, AL
35146 Springville, AL
35147 Sterrett, AL
35147 Westover, AL
35148 Sumiton, AL
35149 Sycamore, AL
35150 Oak Grove, AL
35150 Sylacauga, AL
35150 Talladega Springs, AL
35151 Oak Grove, AL
35151 Sylacauga, AL
35160 Talladega, AL
35160 Waldo, AL
35161 Talladega, AL
35161 Waldo, AL
35171 Thorsby, AL
35172 County Line, AL
35172 Trafford, AL
35173 Trussville, AL
35175 Union Grove, AL
35176 Vandiver, AL
35178 Vincent, AL
35179 South Vinemont, AL
35179 Vinemont, AL
35179 West Point, AL
35180 Warrior, AL
35181 Watson, AL
35182 Wattsville, AL
35183 Weogufka, AL
35184 West Blocton, AL
35185 Westover, AL
35186 Wilsonville, AL
35187 Wilton, AL
35188 Woodstock, AL

352

35201 Birmingham, AL
35202 Birmingham, AL
35203 Birmingham, AL
35204 Birmingham, AL
35205 Birmingham, AL
35206 Birmingham, AL
35207 Birmingham, AL
35208 Birmingham, AL
35209 Birmingham, AL
35209 Homewood, AL
35209 Mountain Brook, AL
35210 Birmingham, AL
35210 Irondale, AL
35210 Mountain Brook, AL
35211 Birmingham, AL
35212 Birmingham, AL
35213 Birmingham, AL
35213 Crestline Heights, AL
35213 Mountain Brook, AL
35214 Birmingham, AL
35214 Forestdale, AL
35215 Birmingham, AL
35215 Center Point, AL
35216 Birmingham, AL
35216 Hoover, AL
35216 Mountain Brook, AL
35216 Vestavia, AL
35216 Vestavia Hills, AL
35217 Birmingham, AL
35218 Birmingham, AL
35218 Ensley, AL
35219 Birmingham, AL
35219 Homewood, AL
35219 Mountain Brook, AL
35220 Birmingham, AL
35220 Center Point, AL
35221 Birmingham, AL
35222 Birmingham, AL
35223 Birmingham, AL
35223 Mountain Brook, AL
35223 Vestavia, AL
35224 Birmingham, AL
35226 Birmingham, AL
35226 Bluff Park, AL
35226 Hoover, AL
35226 Vestavia, AL
35226 Vestavia Hills, AL
35228 Birmingham, AL
35228 Midfield, AL
35229 Birmingham, AL
35231 Birmingham, AL
35232 Birmingham, AL
35233 Birmingham, AL
35234 Birmingham, AL
35235 Birmingham, AL
35235 Center Point, AL
35236 Birmingham, AL
35236 Hoover, AL
35237 Birmingham, AL
35238 Birmingham, AL
35242 Birmingham, AL
35242 Meadowbrook, AL
35242 Shoal Creek, AL
35242 Vestavia, AL
35242 Vestavia Hills, AL
35243 Birmingham, AL
35243 Cahaba Heights, AL
35243 Mountain Brook, AL
35243 Vestavia, AL
35244 Birmingham, AL
35244 Bluff Park, AL
35244 Hoover, AL
35246 Birmingham, AL
35249 Birmingham, AL
35253 Birmingham, AL
35253 Mountain Brook, AL
35254 Birmingham, AL
35255 Birmingham, AL
35259 Birmingham, AL
35259 Homewood, AL
35259 Mountain Brook, AL
35260 Birmingham, AL
35261 Birmingham, AL
35266 Birmingham, AL
35266 Mountain Brook, AL
35266 Vestavia, AL
35266 Vestavia Hills, AL
35270 Birmingham, AL
35282 Birmingham, AL
35283 Birmingham, AL
35285 Birmingham, AL
35287 Birmingham, AL
35288 Birmingham, AL
35290 Birmingham, AL
35291 Birmingham, AL
35292 Birmingham, AL
35293 Birmingham, AL
35294 Birmingham, AL
35295 Birmingham, AL
35296 Birmingham, AL
35297 Birmingham, AL
35298 Birmingham, AL

354

35401 Tuscaloosa, AL
35402 Tuscaloosa, AL
35403 Tuscaloosa, AL
35404 Tuscaloosa, AL
35405 Tuscaloosa, AL
35406 Tuscaloosa, AL
35407 Tuscaloosa, AL
35440 Abernant, AL
35441 Akron, AL
35441 Stewart, AL
35442 Aliceville, AL
35442 Old Memphis, AL
35443 Boligee, AL
35444 Brookwood, AL
35446 Buhl, AL
35447 Carrollton, AL
35447 Pickensville, AL
35448 Clinton, AL
35449 Coaling, AL
35452 Coker, AL
35453 Coaling, AL
35453 Cottondale, AL
35456 Duncanville, AL
35457 Echola, AL
35458 Elrod, AL
35459 Emelle, AL
35460 Epes, AL
35461 Ethelsville, AL
35462 Eutaw, AL
35462 Union, AL
35463 Fosters, AL
35464 Gainesville, AL
35466 Gordo, AL
35468 Kellerman, AL
35469 Knoxville, AL
35470 Coatopa, AL
35470 Livingston, AL
35471 Mc Shan, AL
35473 Northport, AL
35474 Cypress, AL
35474 Havana, AL
35474 Moundville, AL
35475 Northport, AL
35476 Northport, AL
35477 Panola, AL
35478 Peterson, AL
35480 Ralph, AL
35481 Reform, AL
35482 Samantha, AL
35485 Tuscaloosa, AL
35486 Tuscaloosa, AL
35487 Tuscaloosa, AL
35490 Vance, AL
35491 West Greene, AL

355

35501 Jasper, AL
35502 Jasper, AL
35503 Jasper, AL
35504 Jasper, AL
35540 Addison, AL
35540 Arley, AL
35541 Arley, AL
35542 Bankston, AL
35543 Bear Creek, AL
35544 Beaverton, AL
35545 Belk, AL
35546 Berry, AL
35548 Brilliant, AL
35549 Carbon Hill, AL
35550 Cordova, AL
35551 Delmar, AL
35552 Detroit, AL
35553 Double Springs, AL
35554 Eldridge, AL
35555 Fayette, AL
35559 Glen Allen, AL
35560 Goodsprings, AL
35563 Gu-Win, AL

35563 Guin, AL
35564 Hackleburg, AL
35565 Haleyville, AL
35570 Hamilton, AL
35571 Hodges, AL
35572 Houston, AL
35573 Kansas, AL
35574 Kennedy, AL
35575 Lynn, AL
35576 Millport, AL
35577 Natural Bridge, AL
35578 Nauvoo, AL
35579 Oakman, AL
35580 Parrish, AL
35581 Phil Campbell, AL
35582 Red Bay, AL
35584 Sipsey, AL
35585 Spruce Pine, AL
35586 Sulligent, AL
35587 Townley, AL
35592 Vernon, AL
35593 Vina, AL
35594 Winfield, AL

356

35601 Decatur, AL
35602 Decatur, AL
35603 Decatur, AL
35609 Decatur, AL
35610 Anderson, AL
35611 Athens, AL
35612 Athens, AL
35613 Athens, AL
35614 Athens, AL
35615 Belle Mina, AL
35616 Cherokee, AL
35617 Cloverdale, AL
35618 Courtland, AL
35618 North Courtland, AL
35619 Danville, AL
35620 Elkmont, AL
35621 Eva, AL
35622 Falkville, AL
35630 Florence, AL
35630 Saint Florian, AL
35631 Florence, AL
35632 Florence, AL
35633 Florence, AL
35634 Florence, AL
35640 Hartselle, AL
35643 Hillsboro, AL
35645 Killen, AL
35646 Leighton, AL
35647 Lester, AL
35648 Lexington, AL
35649 Mooresville, AL
35650 Moulton, AL
35651 Mount Hope, AL
35652 Rogersville, AL
35653 Littleville, AL
35653 Russellville, AL
35654 Russellville, AL
35660 Sheffield, AL
35661 Muscle Shoals, AL
35662 Muscle Shoals, AL
35670 Somerville, AL
35671 Tanner, AL
35672 Town Creek, AL
35673 Trinity, AL
35674 Tuscumbia, AL
35677 Waterloo, AL
35699 Decatur, AL

357

35739 Ardmore, AL
35740 Bridgeport, AL
35741 Brownsboro, AL
35742 Capshaw, AL
35744 Dutton, AL
35745 Estillfork, AL
35746 Fackler, AL
35747 Grant, AL
35748 Gurley, AL
35749 Harvest, AL
35750 Hazel Green, AL
35751 Hollytree, AL
35752 Hollywood, AL
35754 Laceys Spring, AL
35755 Langston, AL
35756 Madison, AL
35757 Madison, AL
35758 Madison, AL
35758 Triana, AL
35759 Meridianville, AL
35760 New Hope, AL
35761 New Market, AL
35762 Normal, AL
35763 Big Cove, AL
35763 Hampton Cove, AL
35763 Owens Cross Roads, AL
35764 Paint Rock, AL
35765 Pisgah, AL
35766 Princeton, AL
35767 Ryland, AL
35768 Hytop, AL
35768 Scottsboro, AL
35769 Scottsboro, AL
35771 Section, AL
35772 Stevenson, AL
35773 Toney, AL
35774 Trenton, AL
35775 Valhermoso Sp, AL
35775 Valhermoso Spg, AL
35775 Valhermoso Springs, AL
35776 Woodville, AL

358

35801 Huntsville, AL
35802 Huntsville, AL
35803 Huntsville, AL
35804 Huntsville, AL
35805 Huntsville, AL
35806 Huntsville, AL
35807 Huntsville, AL
35808 Huntsville, AL
35809 Huntsville, AL
35810 Huntsville, AL
35811 Huntsville, AL
35812 Huntsville, AL
35813 Huntsville, AL
35814 Huntsville, AL
35815 Huntsville, AL
35816 Huntsville, AL
35824 Huntsville, AL
35893 Huntsville, AL
35894 Huntsville, AL
35895 Huntsville, AL
35896 Huntsville, AL
35897 Huntsville, AL
35898 Huntsville, AL
35898 Redstone Arsenal, AL
35899 Huntsville, AL

359

35901 Gadsden, AL
35902 Gadsden, AL
35903 East Gadsden, AL
35903 Gadsden, AL
35903 Hokes Bluff, AL
35904 Gadsden, AL
35905 Gadsden, AL
35905 Glencoe, AL
35906 Gadsden, AL
35906 Rainbow City, AL
35907 Gadsden, AL
35907 Southside, AL
35950 Albertville, AL
35951 Albertville, AL
35952 Altoona, AL
35952 Snead, AL
35952 Susan Moore, AL
35953 Ashville, AL
35954 Attalla, AL
35956 Boaz, AL
35956 Sardis City, AL
35957 Boaz, AL
35957 Sardis City, AL
35958 Bryant, AL
35959 Cedar Bluff, AL
35960 Centre, AL
35961 Collinsville, AL
35962 Crossville, AL
35963 Dawson, AL
35964 Douglas, AL
35966 Flat Rock, AL
35967 Fort Payne, AL
35968 Fort Payne, AL
35968 Pine Ridge, AL
35971 Fyffe, AL
35971 Lakeview, AL
35972 Gallant, AL
35973 Gaylesville, AL
35974 Geraldine, AL
35975 Groveoak, AL
35976 Guntersville, AL
35978 Henagar, AL
35979 Higdon, AL
35980 Horton, AL
35981 Ider, AL
35983 Leesburg, AL
35983 Sand Rock, AL
35983 Sandrock, AL
35984 Mentone, AL
35986 Powell, AL
35986 Rainsville, AL
35986 Shiloh, AL
35987 Steele, AL
35988 Sylvania, AL
35989 Hammondville, AL
35989 Valley Head, AL
35990 Walnut Grove, AL

360

36003 Autaugaville, AL
36005 Banks, AL
36006 Billingsley, AL
36008 Booth, AL
36009 Brantley, AL
36010 Brundidge, AL
36013 Cecil, AL
36015 Chapman, AL
36016 Clayton, AL
36017 Clio, AL
36020 Coosada, AL
36022 Deatsville, AL
36023 East Tallassee, AL
36023 Tallassee, AL
36024 Eclectic, AL
36025 Elmore, AL
36026 Equality, AL
36027 Bakerhill, AL
36027 Eufaula, AL
36028 Dozier, AL
36029 Fitzpatrick, AL
36030 Forest Home, AL
36031 Fort Davis, AL
36032 Fort Deposit, AL
36033 Georgiana, AL
36034 Glenwood, AL
36035 Goshen, AL
36036 Grady, AL
36037 Greenville, AL
36038 Gantt, AL
36039 Hardaway, AL
36040 Gordonville, AL
36040 Hayneville, AL
36041 Highland Home, AL
36042 Honoraville, AL
36043 Hope Hull, AL
36045 Kent, AL
36045 Tallassee, AL
36046 Lapine, AL
36047 Letohatchee, AL
36048 Louisville, AL
36049 Luverne, AL
36051 Marbury, AL
36052 Mathews, AL
36053 Midway, AL
36054 Millbrook, AL
36057 Mount Meigs, AL
36061 Banks, AL
36061 Perote, AL
36062 Petrey, AL
36064 Pike Road, AL
36065 Pine Level, AL
36066 Prattville, AL
36067 Prattville, AL
36068 Prattville, AL
36069 Ramer, AL
36071 Rutledge, AL
36072 Eufaula, AL
36075 Shorter, AL
36078 Tallassee, AL
36079 Troy, AL
36080 Titus, AL
36081 Troy, AL
36082 Troy, AL
36083 Tuskegee, AL
36087 Tuskegee Institute, AL
36089 Union Springs, AL
36091 Verbena, AL
36092 Wetumpka, AL
36093 Wetumpka, AL

361

36101 Montgomery, AL
36102 Montgomery, AL
36103 Montgomery, AL
36104 Montgomery, AL
36105 Montgomery, AL
36106 Montgomery, AL
36107 Montgomery, AL
36108 Montgomery, AL
36109 Montgomery, AL
36110 Montgomery, AL
36111 Montgomery, AL
36112 Maxwell Afb, AL
36112 Montgomery, AL
36113 Maxwell Afb, AL
36113 Montgomery, AL
36114 Maxwell Afb Gunter Annex, AL
36114 Montgomery, AL
36115 Montgomery, AL
36116 Montgomery, AL
36117 Montgomery, AL
36118 Montgomery, AL
36119 Montgomery, AL
36120 Montgomery, AL
36121 Montgomery, AL
36123 Montgomery, AL
36124 Montgomery, AL
36125 Montgomery, AL
36130 Montgomery, AL
36131 Montgomery, AL
36132 Montgomery, AL
36133 Montgomery, AL
36134 Montgomery, AL
36135 Montgomery, AL
36140 Montgomery, AL
36141 Montgomery, AL
36142 Montgomery, AL
36177 Montgomery, AL
36191 Montgomery, AL

362

36201 Anniston, AL
36202 Anniston, AL
36203 Anniston, AL
36203 Oxford, AL
36204 Anniston, AL
36204 Blue Mountain, AL
36205 Anniston, AL
36205 Fort Mc Clellan, AL
36206 Anniston, AL
36207 Anniston, AL
36250 Alexandria, AL
36251 Ashland, AL
36253 Bynum, AL
36254 Choccolocco, AL
36255 Cragford, AL
36256 Daviston, AL
36256 New Site, AL
36257 De Armanville, AL
36258 Delta, AL
36260 Eastaboga, AL
36261 Edwardsville, AL
36262 Fruithurst, AL
36263 Graham, AL
36264 Heflin, AL
36265 Jacksonville, AL
36266 Lineville, AL
36267 Millerville, AL
36268 Munford, AL
36269 Muscadine, AL
36271 Ohatchee, AL
36272 Borden Springs, AL
36272 Piedmont, AL
36273 Ranburne, AL
36274 Roanoke, AL
36275 Spring Garden, AL
36276 Wadley, AL
36277 Weaver, AL
36278 Wedowee, AL
36279 Wellington, AL
36280 Newell, AL
36280 Woodland, AL

363

36301 Dothan, AL
36301 Rehobeth, AL
36301 Taylor, AL
36302 Dothan, AL
36303 Dothan, AL
36303 Kinsey, AL
36304 Dothan, AL
36305 Dothan, AL
36305 Taylor, AL
36310 Abbeville, AL
36311 Ariton, AL
36312 Ashford, AL
36312 Avon, AL
36313 Bellwood, AL
36314 Black, AL
36316 Chancellor, AL
36317 Clopton, AL
36318 Coffee Springs, AL
36319 Columbia, AL
36320 Cottonwood, AL
36321 Cowarts, AL
36322 Daleville, AL
36322 Level Plains, AL
36323 Elba, AL
36330 Enterprise, AL
36331 Enterprise, AL
36340 Geneva, AL
36343 Gordon, AL
36344 Hartford, AL
36345 Headland, AL
36346 Jack, AL
36349 Malvern, AL
36350 Midland City, AL
36351 New Brockton, AL
36352 Newton, AL
36353 Newville, AL
36360 Ozark, AL
36361 Ozark, AL
36362 Fort Rucker, AL
36370 Pansey, AL
36371 Pinckard, AL
36373 Shorterville, AL
36374 Skipperville, AL
36375 Slocomb, AL
36376 Webb, AL

364

36401 Burnt Corn, AL
36401 Evergreen, AL
36420 Andalusia, AL
36420 Babbie, AL
36420 Carolina, AL
36420 Heath, AL
36420 Sanford, AL
36421 Andalusia, AL
36425 Beatrice, AL
36426 Brewton, AL
36426 East Brewton, AL
36427 Brewton, AL
36429 Brooklyn, AL
36432 Castleberry, AL
36435 Coy, AL
36436 Dickinson, AL
36439 Excel, AL
36441 Flomaton, AL
36442 Florala, AL
36444 Franklin, AL
36445 Frisco City, AL
36446 Fulton, AL
36449 Uriah, AL
36451 Allen, AL
36451 Grove Hill, AL
36453 Kinston, AL
36454 Lenox, AL
36455 Lockhart, AL
36456 Mc Kenzie, AL
36456 Mckenzie, AL
36457 Megargel, AL
36458 Mexia, AL
36460 Monroeville, AL
36461 Monroeville, AL
36467 Horn Hill, AL
36467 Onycha, AL
36467 Opp, AL
36470 Perdue Hill, AL
36471 Peterman, AL
36473 Range, AL
36474 Red Level, AL
36475 Repton, AL
36476 River Falls, AL
36477 Samson, AL
36480 Uriah, AL
36481 Vredenburgh, AL
36482 Whatley, AL
36483 Wing, AL

365

36502 Atmore, AL
36502 Mc Cullough, AL
36502 Mccullough, AL
36503 Atmore, AL
36504 Atmore, AL
36505 Axis, AL
36507 Bay Minette, AL
36509 Bayou La Batre, AL
36511 Bon Secour, AL
36512 Bucks, AL
36513 Calvert, AL
36515 Carlton, AL
36518 Chatom, AL
36521 Chunchula, AL
36522 Citronelle, AL
36523 Coden, AL
36524 Coffeeville, AL
36525 Creola, AL
36526 Daphne, AL
36527 Spanish Fort, AL
36528 Dauphin Island, AL
36529 Deer Park, AL
36530 Elberta, AL
36530 Perdido Beach, AL
36532 Fairhope, AL
36533 Fairhope, AL
36535 Foley, AL
36536 Foley, AL
36538 Frankville, AL
36539 Fruitdale, AL
36540 Gainestown, AL
36541 Grand Bay, AL
36542 Gulf Shores, AL
36543 Huxford, AL
36544 Irvington, AL
36545 Jackson, AL
36545 Salipta, AL
36545 Walker Springs, AL
36547 Gulf Shores, AL
36548 Leroy, AL
36549 Lillian, AL
36550 Little River, AL
36551 Loxley, AL
36553 Mc Intosh, AL
36555 Magnolia Springs, AL
36556 Malcolm, AL
36558 Bigbee, AL
36558 Millry, AL
36559 Montrose, AL
36560 Mount Vernon, AL
36561 Orange Beach, AL
36562 Perdido, AL
36564 Point Clear, AL
36567 Robertsdale, AL
36568 Saint Elmo, AL
36569 Saint Stephens, AL
36571 Saraland, AL
36572 Satsuma, AL
36574 Robertsdale, AL
36574 Seminole, AL
36575 Semmes, AL
36576 Silverhill, AL

36577 Spanish Fort, AL
36578 Stapleton, AL
36579 Stockton, AL
36580 Summerdale, AL
36581 Sunflower, AL
36582 Saltaire, AL
36582 Theodore, AL
36583 Tibbie, AL
36584 Vinegar Bend, AL
36585 Wagarville, AL
36587 Wilmer, AL
36590 Theodore, AL

366

36601 Mobile, AL
36602 Mobile, AL
36603 Mobile, AL
36604 Mobile, AL
36605 Mobile, AL
36606 Mobile, AL
36607 Mobile, AL
36608 Mobile, AL
36609 Mobile, AL
36610 Magazine, AL
36610 Mobile, AL
36610 Prichard, AL
36611 Chickasaw, AL
36611 Mobile, AL
36612 Mobile, AL
36612 Whistler, AL
36613 Eight Mile, AL
36613 Mobile, AL
36613 Prichard, AL
36615 Brookley Field, AL
36615 Mobile, AL
36616 Mobile, AL
36617 Mobile, AL
36617 Prichard, AL
36618 Mobile, AL
36619 Mobile, AL
36619 Theodore, AL
36628 Mobile, AL
36630 Mobile, AL
36633 Mobile, AL
36640 Mobile, AL
36641 Mobile, AL
36644 Mobile, AL
36652 Mobile, AL
36660 Mobile, AL
36663 Mobile, AL
36670 Mobile, AL
36671 Mobile, AL
36675 Mobile, AL
36685 Mobile, AL
36688 Mobile, AL
36689 Mobile, AL
36691 Mobile, AL
36693 Mobile, AL
36695 Mobile, AL

367

36701 Selma, AL
36701 Valley Grande, AL
36702 Selma, AL
36703 Selma, AL
36703 Valley Grande, AL
36720 Alberta, AL
36721 Annemanie, AL
36722 Arlington, AL
36723 Boykin, AL
36726 Camden, AL
36727 Campbell, AL
36728 Catherine, AL
36728 Prairie, AL
36732 Demopolis, AL
36736 Dixons Mills, AL
36738 Dayton, AL
36738 Faunsdale, AL
36740 Forkland, AL
36741 Furman, AL
36742 Gallion, AL
36742 Providence, AL
36744 Greensboro, AL
36745 Jefferson, AL
36748 Linden, AL
36749 Jones, AL
36750 Maplesville, AL
36751 Low Peach Tre, AL
36751 Lower Peach Tree, AL
36752 Burkville, AL
36752 Lowndesboro, AL
36753 Mc Williams, AL
36754 Magnolia, AL
36756 Marion, AL
36756 Sprott, AL
36758 Plantersville, AL
36759 Marion Junction, AL
36761 Minter, AL
36762 Thomasville, AL
36763 Myrtlewood, AL
36764 Nanafalia, AL
36765 Newbern, AL
36766 Oak Hill, AL
36767 Orrville, AL
36768 Pine Apple, AL
36768 Snow Hill, AL
36769 Pine Hill, AL
36769 Yellow Bluff, AL
36773 Safford, AL
36775 Sardis, AL
36776 Sawyerville, AL
36782 Sweet Water, AL
36783 Thomaston, AL
36784 Thomasville, AL
36785 Benton, AL
36785 Tyler, AL
36786 Uniontown, AL
36790 Stanton, AL
36792 Randolph, AL
36793 Lawley, AL

368

36801 Opelika, AL
36802 Opelika, AL
36803 Opelika, AL
36804 Opelika, AL
36830 Auburn, AL
36831 Auburn, AL
36832 Auburn, AL
36849 Auburn, AL
36849 Auburn University, AL
36850 Camp Hill, AL
36851 Cottonton, AL
36852 Cusseta, AL
36853 Dadeville, AL
36854 Valley, AL
36855 Five Points, AL
36856 Fort Mitchell, AL
36858 Hatchechubbee, AL
36859 Holy Trinity, AL
36860 Hurtsboro, AL
36861 Jacksons Gap, AL
36862 Lafayette, AL
36863 Lanett, AL
36865 Loachapoka, AL
36866 Notasulga, AL
36867 Phenix City, AL
36868 Phenix City, AL
36869 Phenix City, AL
36870 Phenix City, AL
36871 Pittsview, AL
36872 Valley, AL
36874 Salem, AL
36875 Seale, AL
36877 Smiths, AL
36877 Smiths Station, AL
36879 Auburn, AL
36879 Waverly, AL

369

36901 Bellamy, AL
36904 Butler, AL
36904 Lavaca, AL
36907 Cuba, AL
36908 Gilbertown, AL
36910 Jachin, AL
36912 Lisman, AL
36913 Melvin, AL
36915 Needham, AL
36916 Pennington, AL
36919 Bolinger, AL
36919 Silas, AL
36921 Toxey, AL
36922 Ward, AL
36925 York, AL

370

37010 Adams, TN
37011 Antioch, TN
37012 Alexandria, TN
37013 Antioch, TN
37013 Cane Ridge, TN
37014 Arrington, TN
37015 Ashland City, TN
37016 Auburntown, TN
37018 Beechgrove, TN
37019 Belfast, TN
37020 Bell Buckle, TN
37022 Bethpage, TN
37022 Rock Bridge, TN
37023 Big Rock, TN
37024 Brentwood, TN
37025 Bon Aqua, TN
37026 Bradyville, TN
37027 Brentwood, TN
37028 Bumpus Mills, TN
37029 Burns, TN
37030 Carthage, TN
37030 Defeated, TN
37030 So Carthage, TN
37030 South Carthage, TN
37031 Castalian Springs, TN
37032 Cedar Hill, TN
37033 Centerville, TN
37033 Pleasantville, TN
37034 Chapel Hill, TN
37035 Chapmansboro, TN
37036 Charlotte, TN
37037 Christiana, TN
37040 Clarksville, TN
37041 Clarksville, TN
37042 Clarksville, TN
37043 Clarksville, TN
37044 Clarksville, TN
37046 College Grove, TN
37047 Cornersville, TN
37048 Cottontown, TN
37048 Walnut Grove, TN
37049 Cross Plains, TN
37050 Cumberland City, TN
37051 Cumberland Furnace, TN
37052 Cunningham, TN
37055 Dickson, TN
37056 Dickson, TN
37057 Dixon Springs, TN
37058 Dover, TN
37059 Dowelltown, TN
37060 Eagleville, TN
37061 Erin, TN
37062 Fairview, TN
37063 Fosterville, TN
37064 Franklin, TN
37065 Franklin, TN
37066 Gallatin, TN
37067 Franklin, TN
37068 Franklin, TN
37069 Franklin, TN
37070 Goodlettsville, TN
37071 Gladeville, TN
37072 Goodlettsville, TN
37073 Greenbrier, TN
37074 Hartsville, TN
37075 Hendersonville, TN
37076 Hermitage, TN
37077 Hendersonville, TN
37078 Hurricane Mills, TN
37079 Indian Mound, TN
37080 Joelton, TN
37082 Kingston Springs, TN
37083 Lafayette, TN
37085 Lascassas, TN
37086 La Vergne, TN
37087 Lebanon, TN
37088 Lebanon, TN
37089 La Vergne, TN
37090 Lebanon, TN
37091 Lewisburg, TN
37095 Gassaway, TN
37095 Liberty, TN
37096 Flatwoods, TN
37096 Linden, TN
37097 Lobelville, TN
37098 Lyles, TN
37098 Wrigley, TN

371

37101 Mc Ewen, TN
37110 Centertown, TN
37110 Mc Minnville, TN
37110 Mcminnville, TN
37111 Mc Minnville, TN
37111 Mcminnville, TN
37115 Madison, TN
37116 Madison, TN
37118 Milton, TN
37119 Mitchellville, TN
37121 Mount Juliet, TN
37122 Mount Juliet, TN
37127 Murfreesboro, TN
37128 Murfreesboro, TN
37129 Murfreesboro, TN
37130 Murfreesboro, TN
37131 Murfreesboro, TN
37132 Murfreesboro, TN
37133 Murfreesboro, TN
37134 Denver, TN
37134 New Johnsonville, TN
37135 Nolensville, TN
37136 Norene, TN
37137 Nunnelly, TN
37138 Lakewood, TN
37138 Old Hickory, TN
37140 Only, TN
37141 Orlinda, TN
37142 Palmyra, TN
37143 Pegram, TN
37144 Petersburg, TN
37145 Pleasant Shade, TN
37146 Pleasant View, TN
37148 Portland, TN
37149 Readyville, TN
37150 Red Boiling Springs, TN
37151 Riddleton, TN
37152 Ridgetop, TN
37153 Rockvale, TN
37160 Royal, TN
37160 Shelbyville, TN
37161 Shelbyville, TN
37162 Shelbyville, TN
37165 Slayden, TN
37166 Smithville, TN
37167 Smyrna, TN
37171 Southside, TN
37172 Springfield, TN
37174 Spring Hill, TN
37175 Stewart, TN
37178 Tennessee Ridge, TN
37179 Thompsons Station, TN
37180 Unionville, TN
37181 Vanleer, TN
37183 Wartrace, TN
37184 Watertown, TN
37185 Waverly, TN
37186 Westmoreland, TN
37187 White Bluff, TN
37188 White House, TN
37189 Whites Creek, TN
37190 Woodbury, TN
37191 Woodlawn, TN

372

37201 Nashville, TN
37202 Nashville, TN
37203 Nashville, TN
37204 Berry Hill, TN
37204 Melrose, TN
37204 Nashville, TN
37205 Nashville, TN
37206 Nashville, TN
37207 Nashville, TN
37208 Nashville, TN
37209 Nashville, TN
37210 Nashville, TN
37211 Nashville, TN
37212 Nashville, TN
37213 Nashville, TN
37214 Nashville, TN
37215 Forest Hills, TN
37215 Nashville, TN
37216 Nashville, TN
37217 Nashville, TN
37218 Nashville, TN
37219 Nashville, TN
37220 Nashville, TN
37220 Oak Hill, TN
37221 Bellevue, TN
37221 Nashville, TN
37222 Nashville, TN
37224 Nashville, TN
37227 Nashville, TN
37228 Nashville, TN
37229 Nashville, TN
37230 Nashville, TN
37232 Nashville, TN
37234 Nashville, TN
37235 Nashville, TN
37236 Nashville, TN
37238 Nashville, TN
37240 Nashville, TN
37241 Nashville, TN
37242 Nashville, TN
37243 Nashville, TN
37244 Nashville, TN
37246 Nashville, TN
37250 Nashville, TN

373

37301 Altamont, TN
37302 Apison, TN
37303 Athens, TN
37304 Bakewell, TN
37304 Sale Creek, TN
37305 Beersheba Springs, TN
37306 Belvidere, TN
37307 Benton, TN
37308 Birchwood, TN
37309 Calhoun, TN
37310 Charleston, TN
37311 Cleveland, TN
37312 Cleveland, TN
37313 Coalmont, TN
37314 Coker Creek, TN
37315 Collegedale, TN
37316 Conasauga, TN
37317 Copperhill, TN
37317 Postelle, TN
37318 Cowan, TN
37320 Cleveland, TN
37321 Dayton, TN
37322 Decatur, TN
37323 Cleveland, TN
37324 Decherd, TN
37325 Delano, TN
37326 Ducktown, TN
37327 Dunlap, TN
37328 Elora, TN
37329 Englewood, TN
37330 Estill Springs, TN
37331 Etowah, TN
37332 Evensville, TN
37333 Farner, TN
37334 Fayetteville, TN
37335 Flintville, TN
37336 Georgetown, TN
37337 Grandview, TN
37338 Graysville, TN
37339 Gruetli Laager, TN
37340 Guild, TN
37341 Harrison, TN
37342 Hillsboro, TN
37343 Hixson, TN
37345 Huntland, TN
37347 Jasper, TN
37347 Kimball, TN
37348 Kelso, TN
37349 Manchester, TN
37350 Lookout Mountain, TN
37351 Lupton City, TN
37352 Lynchburg, TN
37353 Mc Donald, TN
37354 Madisonville, TN
37355 Manchester, TN
37356 Monteagle, TN
37357 Morrison, TN
37359 Mulberry, TN
37360 Normandy, TN
37361 Ocoee, TN
37362 Old Fort, TN
37363 College Dale, TN
37363 Ooltewah, TN
37364 Cleveland, TN
37365 Palmer, TN
37366 Pelham, TN
37367 Pikeville, TN
37369 Reliance, TN
37370 Riceville, TN
37371 Athens, TN
37373 Bakewell, TN
37373 Sale Creek, TN
37374 Sequatchie, TN
37375 Saint Andrews, TN
37375 Sewanee, TN
37376 Sherwood, TN
37377 Signal Mountain, TN
37377 Walden, TN
37378 Smartt, TN
37379 Lakesite, TN
37379 Soddy Daisy, TN
37380 New Hope, TN
37380 Orme, TN
37380 South Pittsburg, TN
37381 Spring City, TN
37381 Watts Bar Dam, TN
37382 Summitville, TN
37383 Sewanee, TN
37384 Soddy Daisy, TN
37385 Tellico Plains, TN
37387 Tracy City, TN
37388 Dickel, TN
37388 Tullahoma, TN
37389 Arnold Afb, TN
37389 Tullahoma, TN
37391 Turtletown, TN
37394 Viola, TN
37396 Whiteside, TN
37397 Powells Crossroads, TN
37397 Whitwell, TN
37398 Winchester, TN

374

37401 Chattanooga, TN
37402 Chattanooga, TN
37403 Chattanooga, TN
37404 Chattanooga, TN
37405 Chattanooga, TN
37406 Chattanooga, TN
37407 Chattanooga, TN
37408 Chattanooga, TN
37409 Chattanooga, TN
37410 Chattanooga, TN
37411 Chattanooga, TN
37411 Ridgeside, TN
37412 Chattanooga, TN
37412 East Ridge, TN
37414 Chattanooga, TN
37415 Chattanooga, TN
37415 Red Bank, TN
37416 Chattanooga, TN
37419 Chattanooga, TN
37421 Chattanooga, TN
37422 Chattanooga, TN
37424 Chattanooga, TN
37450 Chattanooga, TN

375

37501 Memphis, TN
37544 Memphis, TN

376

37601 Johnson City, TN
37602 Johnson City, TN
37604 Johnson City, TN
37605 Johnson City, TN
37614 Johnson City, TN
37615 Gray, TN
37615 Johnson City, TN
37616 Afton, TN

37617 Blountville, TN
37618 Bluff City, TN
37620 Bristol, TN
37621 Bristol, TN
37625 Bristol, TN
37640 Butler, TN
37641 Chuckey, TN
37642 Church Hill, TN
37643 Elizabethton, TN
37644 Elizabethton, TN
37645 Church Hill, TN
37645 Mount Carmel, TN
37645 Mt Carmel, TN
37650 Erwin, TN
37656 Fall Branch, TN
37657 Flag Pond, TN
37658 Hampton, TN
37659 Jonesborough, TN
37660 Kingsport, TN
37662 Kingsport, TN
37663 Colonial Heights, TN
37663 Kingsport, TN
37664 Kingsport, TN
37665 Kingsport, TN
37669 Kingsport, TN
37680 Laurel Bloomery, TN
37681 Limestone, TN
37682 Milligan College, TN
37683 Mountain City, TN
37684 Mountain Home, TN
37684 Mtn Home, TN
37686 Piney Flats, TN
37687 Roan Mountain, TN
37688 Shady Valley, TN
37690 Telford, TN
37691 Trade, TN
37692 Unicoi, TN
37694 Watauga, TN
37699 Piney Flats, TN

377

37701 Alcoa, TN
37705 Andersonville, TN
37707 Arthur, TN
37708 Bean Station, TN
37709 Blaine, TN
37710 Briceville, TN
37710 Devonia, TN
37711 Bulls Gap, TN
37713 Bybee, TN
37714 Caryville, TN
37715 Clairfield, TN
37716 Clinton, TN
37717 Clinton, TN
37719 Coalfield, TN
37721 Corryton, TN
37722 Cosby, TN
37723 Crab Orchard, TN
37724 Cumberland Gap, TN
37724 Cumberland Gp, TN
37725 Dandridge, TN
37726 Deer Lodge, TN
37727 Del Rio, TN
37729 Duff, TN
37729 La Follette, TN
37730 Eagan, TN
37731 Eidson, TN
37732 Elgin, TN
37733 Elgin, TN
37733 Rugby, TN
37737 Friendsville, TN
37738 Gatlinburg, TN
37742 Greenback, TN
37743 Greeneville, TN
37743 Tusculum Coll, TN
37744 Greeneville, TN
37745 Greeneville, TN
37745 Tusculum, TN
37748 Harriman, TN
37752 Harrogate, TN
37753 Hartford, TN
37754 Heiskell, TN
37755 Helenwood, TN
37756 Huntsville, TN
37757 Jacksboro, TN
37760 Jefferson City, TN
37762 Jellico, TN
37763 Kingston, TN
37764 Kodak, TN
37765 Kyles Ford, TN
37766 La Follette, TN
37766 Morley, TN
37769 Lake City, TN
37770 Lancing, TN
37771 Lenoir City, TN
37772 Lenoir City, TN
37773 Lone Mountain, TN
37774 Loudon, TN
37777 Louisville, TN
37778 Lowland, TN
37779 Luttrell, TN

378

37801 Maryville, TN
37802 Maryville, TN
37803 Maryville, TN
37804 Maryville, TN
37806 Mascot, TN
37807 Maynardville, TN
37809 Midway, TN
37810 Mohawk, TN
37811 Mooresburg, TN
37813 Morristown, TN
37814 Morristown, TN
37815 Morristown, TN
37816 Morristown, TN
37818 Mosheim, TN
37819 Newcomb, TN
37820 New Market, TN
37821 Newport, TN
37822 Newport, TN
37824 New Tazewell, TN
37825 New Tazewell, TN
37826 Niota, TN
37828 Norris, TN
37829 Oakdale, TN
37830 Oak Ridge, TN
37831 Oak Ridge, TN
37840 Oliver Springs, TN
37841 Oneida, TN
37843 Parrottsville, TN
37845 Petros, TN
37846 Philadelphia, TN
37847 Pioneer, TN
37848 Powder Springs, TN
37849 Powell, TN
37851 Pruden, TN
37852 Robbins, TN
37853 Rockford, TN
37854 Ozone, TN
37854 Rockwood, TN
37857 Rogersville, TN
37860 Russellville, TN
37861 Rutledge, TN
37862 Pigeon Forge, TN
37862 Sevierville, TN
37863 Pigeon Forge, TN
37863 Sevierville, TN
37864 Pigeon Forge, TN
37864 Sevierville, TN
37865 Seymour, TN
37866 Sharps Chapel, TN
37867 Shawanee, TN
37868 Pigeon Forge, TN
37868 Sevierville, TN
37869 Sneedville, TN
37870 Speedwell, TN
37871 Strawberry Plains, TN
37872 Sunbright, TN
37873 Surgoinsville, TN
37874 Sweetwater, TN
37876 Pigeon Forge, TN
37876 Pittman Center, TN
37876 Sevierville, TN
37877 Talbott, TN
37878 Tallassee, TN
37879 Tazewell, TN
37880 Ten Mile, TN
37881 Thorn Hill, TN
37881 Treadway, TN
37882 Townsend, TN
37885 Vonore, TN
37886 Walland, TN
37887 Wartburg, TN
37888 Washburn, TN
37890 Baneberry, TN
37890 White Pine, TN
37891 Whitesburg, TN
37892 Winfield, TN

379

37901 Knoxville, TN
37902 Knoxville, TN
37909 Knoxville, TN
37912 Knoxville, TN
37914 Knoxville, TN
37915 Knoxville, TN
37916 Knoxville, TN
37917 Knoxville, TN
37918 Knoxville, TN
37919 Knoxville, TN
37920 Kimberlin Heights, TN
37920 Knoxville, TN
37921 Karns, TN
37921 Knoxville, TN
37922 Concord, TN
37922 Concord Farragut, TN
37922 Knoxville, TN
37923 Knoxville, TN
37924 Knoxville, TN
37927 Knoxville, TN
37928 Knoxville, TN
37929 Knoxville, TN
37930 Knoxville, TN
37931 Knoxville, TN
37932 Knoxville, TN
37933 Farragut, TN
37933 Knoxville, TN
37934 Concord, TN
37934 Farragut, TN
37934 Knoxville, TN
37938 Knoxville, TN
37939 Knoxville, TN
37940 Knoxville, TN
37950 Knoxville, TN
37995 Knoxville, TN
37996 Knoxville, TN
37997 Knoxville, TN
37998 Knoxville, TN

380

38001 Alamo, TN
38002 Arlington, TN
38002 Lakeland, TN
38004 Atoka, TN
38006 Bells, TN
38007 Bogota, TN
38008 Bolivar, TN
38010 Braden, TN
38011 Brighton, TN
38012 Brownsville, TN
38014 Brunswick, TN
38015 Burlison, TN
38015 Gilt Edge, TN
38016 Cordova, TN
38017 Collierville, TN
38017 Fisherville, TN
38017 Piperton, TN
38018 Cordova, TN
38019 Covington, TN
38019 Garland, TN
38021 Crockett Mills, TN
38023 Drummonds, TN
38024 Dyersburg, TN
38025 Dyersburg, TN
38027 Collierville, TN
38028 Eads, TN
38029 Ellendale, TN
38030 Finley, TN
38034 Friendship, TN
38036 Gallaway, TN
38037 Gates, TN
38039 Grand Junction, TN
38040 Halls, TN
38041 Fort Pillow, TN
38041 Henning, TN
38042 Hickory Valley, TN
38044 Hornsby, TN
38045 Laconia, TN
38046 La Grange, TN
38047 Lenox, TN
38048 Macon, TN
38049 Mason, TN
38050 Maury City, TN
38052 Middleton, TN
38053 Millington, TN
38054 Millington, TN
38055 Millington, TN
38057 Moscow, TN
38058 Munford, TN
38059 Newbern, TN
38060 Oakland, TN
38060 Somerville, TN
38061 Pocahontas, TN
38063 Ripley, TN
38066 Rossville, TN
38067 Saulsbury, TN
38068 Mason, TN
38068 Somerville, TN
38069 Stanton, TN
38070 Tigrett, TN
38071 Tipton, TN
38075 Somerville, TN
38075 Whiteville, TN
38076 Moscow, TN
38076 Oakland, TN
38076 Rossville, TN
38076 Williston, TN
38077 Wynnburg, TN
38079 Tiptonville, TN
38080 Miston, TN
38080 Ridgely, TN
38083 Millington, TN
38088 Cordova, TN

381

38101 Memphis, TN
38103 Memphis, TN
38104 Memphis, TN
38105 Memphis, TN
38106 Memphis, TN
38107 Memphis, TN
38108 Memphis, TN
38109 Memphis, TN
38111 Memphis, TN
38112 Memphis, TN
38113 Memphis, TN
38114 Memphis, TN
38115 Hickory Hill, TN
38115 Memphis, TN
38116 Memphis, TN
38117 Memphis, TN
38118 Memphis, TN
38119 Memphis, TN
38120 Memphis, TN
38122 Memphis, TN
38124 Memphis, TN
38125 Hickory Hill, TN
38125 Memphis, TN
38126 Memphis, TN
38127 Memphis, TN
38128 Memphis, TN
38130 Memphis, TN
38131 Memphis, TN
38132 Memphis, TN
38133 Bartlett, TN
38133 Memphis, TN
38134 Bartlett, TN
38134 Memphis, TN
38135 Bartlett, TN
38135 Memphis, TN
38136 Memphis, TN
38137 Memphis, TN
38138 Germantown, TN
38138 Memphis, TN
38139 Germantown, TN
38139 Memphis, TN
38141 Memphis, TN
38145 Memphis, TN
38147 Memphis, TN
38148 Memphis, TN
38150 Memphis, TN
38151 Memphis, TN
38152 Memphis, TN
38157 Memphis, TN
38159 Memphis, TN
38161 Memphis, TN
38163 Memphis, TN
38166 Memphis, TN
38167 Memphis, TN
38168 Memphis, TN
38173 Memphis, TN
38174 Memphis, TN
38175 Memphis, TN
38177 Memphis, TN
38181 Memphis, TN
38182 Memphis, TN
38183 Germantown, TN
38184 Bartlett, TN
38184 Memphis, TN
38186 Memphis, TN
38187 Memphis, TN
38188 Memphis, TN
38190 Memphis, TN
38193 Memphis, TN
38194 Memphis, TN
38197 Memphis, TN

382

38201 Mc Kenzie, TN
38220 Atwood, TN
38221 Big Sandy, TN
38222 Buchanan, TN
38223 Como, TN
38224 Cottage Grove, TN
38225 Dresden, TN
38226 Dukedom, TN
38229 Gleason, TN
38230 Greenfield, TN
38231 Henry, TN
38232 Hornbeak, TN
38233 Kenton, TN
38235 Mc Lemoresville, TN
38236 Mansfield, TN
38237 Martin, TN
38238 Martin, TN
38240 Obion, TN
38241 Palmersville, TN
38242 Paris, TN
38251 Puryear, TN
38253 Rives, TN
38254 Samburg, TN
38255 Sharon, TN
38256 Springville, TN
38257 South Fulton, TN
38258 Trezevant, TN
38259 Trimble, TN
38260 Troy, TN
38261 Union City, TN
38271 Woodland Mills, TN
38281 Union City, TN

383

38301 Jackson, TN
38302 Jackson, TN
38303 Jackson, TN
38305 Jackson, TN
38308 Jackson, TN
38310 Adamsville, TN
38311 Bath Springs, TN
38313 Beech Bluff, TN
38314 Jackson, TN
38315 Bethel Springs, TN
38316 Bradford, TN
38317 Bruceton, TN
38318 Buena Vista, TN
38320 Camden, TN
38321 Cedar Grove, TN
38324 Clarksburg, TN
38326 Counce, TN
38327 Crump, TN
38328 Darden, TN
38329 Decaturville, TN
38330 Dyer, TN
38331 Eaton, TN
38332 Enville, TN
38333 Eva, TN
38334 Finger, TN
38336 Fruitvale, TN
38337 Gadsden, TN
38338 Gibson, TN
38339 Guys, TN
38340 Henderson, TN
38341 Holladay, TN
38342 Hollow Rock, TN
38343 Humboldt, TN
38343 Three Way, TN
38344 Huntingdon, TN
38345 Huron, TN
38346 Idlewild, TN
38347 Jacks Creek, TN
38348 Lavinia, TN
38351 Lexington, TN
38352 Luray, TN
38355 Medina, TN
38356 Medon, TN
38357 Michie, TN
38358 Milan, TN
38359 Milledgeville, TN
38361 Morris Chapel, TN
38362 Oakfield, TN
38363 Parsons, TN
38365 Pickwick Dam, TN
38366 Pinson, TN
38367 Eastview, TN
38367 Ramer, TN
38368 Reagan, TN
38369 Rutherford, TN
38370 Saltillo, TN
38371 Sardis, TN
38372 Savannah, TN
38374 Scotts Hill, TN
38375 Selmer, TN
38376 Shiloh, TN
38377 Silerton, TN
38378 Spring Creek, TN
38379 Stantonville, TN
38380 Sugar Tree, TN
38381 Toone, TN
38382 Trenton, TN
38387 Westport, TN
38388 Parker Crossroads, TN
38388 Wildersville, TN
38389 Yorkville, TN
38390 Yuma, TN
38391 Denmark, TN
38392 Mercer, TN
38393 Chewalla, TN

384

38401 Columbia, TN
38402 Columbia, TN
38425 Clifton, TN
38449 Ardmore, TN
38450 Collinwood, TN
38451 Culleoka, TN
38452 Cypress Inn, TN
38453 Dellrose, TN
38454 Duck River, TN
38455 Elkton, TN
38456 Ethridge, TN
38457 Five Points, TN
38459 Frankewing, TN
38460 Goodspring, TN
38461 Hampshire, TN
38462 Hohenwald, TN
38462 Kimmins, TN
38463 Iron City, TN
38464 Lawrenceburg, TN
38468 Leoma, TN
38469 Loretto, TN
38471 Lutts, TN
38472 Lynnville, TN
38473 Minor Hill, TN
38474 Mount Pleasant, TN
38475 Olivehill, TN
38476 Primm Springs, TN
38477 Prospect, TN
38478 Pulaski, TN
38481 Saint Joseph, TN
38482 Santa Fe, TN
38483 Summertown, TN
38485 Waynesboro, TN
38486 Westpoint, TN
38487 Williamsport, TN
38488 Taft, TN

385

38501 Algood, TN
38501 Cookeville, TN

38502 Cookeville, TN
38503 Cookeville, TN
38504 Allardt, TN
38505 Cookeville, TN
38506 Cookeville, TN
38541 Allons, TN
38542 Allred, TN
38543 Alpine, TN
38544 Baxter, TN
38545 Bloomington Springs, TN
38547 Brush Creek, TN
38548 Buffalo Valley, TN
38549 Byrdstown, TN
38550 Campaign, TN
38551 Celina, TN
38552 Chestnut Mound, TN
38553 Clarkrange, TN
38554 Crawford, TN
38555 Crossville, TN
38555 Fairfield Glade, TN
38556 Jamestown, TN
38557 Crossville, TN
38558 Crossville, TN
38559 Doyle, TN
38560 Elmwood, TN
38562 Gainesboro, TN
38563 Gordonsville, TN
38564 Granville, TN
38565 Grimsley, TN
38567 Hickman, TN
38568 Hilham, TN
38569 Lancaster, TN
38570 Livingston, TN
38571 Crossville, TN
38572 Crossville, TN
38573 Monroe, TN
38574 Monterey, TN
38575 Moss, TN
38577 Pall Mall, TN
38578 Pleasant Hill, TN
38579 Quebeck, TN
38580 Rickman, TN
38581 Bone Cave, TN
38581 Rock Island, TN
38582 Silver Point, TN
38583 Ravenscroft, TN
38583 Sparta, TN
38585 Spencer, TN
38587 Walling, TN
38588 Whitleyville, TN
38589 Wilder, TN

386

38601 Abbeville, MS
38602 Arkabutla, MS
38603 Ashland, MS
38603 Canaan, MS
38606 Batesville, MS
38609 Marks, MS
38610 Blue Mountain, MS
38611 Byhalia, MS
38614 Clarksdale, MS
38614 Mattson, MS
38614 Stovall, MS
38617 Coahoma, MS
38617 Rich, MS
38618 Coldwater, MS
38619 Como, MS
38620 Courtland, MS
38621 Askew, MS
38621 Crenshaw, MS
38622 Crowder, MS
38623 Darling, MS
38625 Dumas, MS
38626 Dundee, MS
38627 Etta, MS
38628 Sledge, MS
38629 Falkner, MS
38630 Farrell, MS
38631 Friars Point, MS
38632 Hernando, MS
38633 Hickory Flat, MS
38634 Holly Springs, MS
38635 Holly Springs, MS
38635 Mount Pleasant, MS
38637 Horn Lake, MS
38638 Independence, MS
38639 Jonestown, MS
38641 Lake Cormorant, MS
38642 Lamar, MS
38643 Lambert, MS
38644 Lula, MS
38645 Lyon, MS
38646 Marks, MS
38647 Michigan City, MS
38649 Holly Springs, MS
38649 Mount Pleasant, MS
38650 Myrtle, MS
38651 Nesbit, MS
38652 New Albany, MS
38654 Mineral Wells, MS
38654 Olive Branch, MS
38655 Lafayette, MS
38655 Oxford, MS
38658 Pope, MS
38659 Potts Camp, MS
38661 Red Banks, MS
38663 Ripley, MS
38664 Robinsonville, MS
38665 Sarah, MS
38665 Savage, MS
38666 Sardis, MS
38668 Senatobia, MS
38669 Clarksdale, MS
38669 Sherard, MS
38670 Sledge, MS
38671 Southaven, MS
38672 Southaven, MS
38673 Taylor, MS
38674 Tiplersville, MS
38675 Oxford, MS
38676 Tunica, MS
38677 University, MS
38679 Victoria, MS
38680 Walls, MS
38683 Walnut, MS
38685 Waterford, MS
38686 Walls, MS

387

38701 Greenville, MS
38702 Greenville, MS
38703 Greenville, MS
38703 Lamont, MS
38704 Greenville, MS
38720 Alligator, MS
38721 Anguilla, MS
38721 Nitta Yuma, MS
38722 Arcola, MS
38723 Avon, MS
38725 Benoit, MS
38726 Beulah, MS
38730 Boyle, MS
38730 Skene, MS
38731 Chatham, MS
38731 Greenville, MS
38732 Cleveland, MS
38733 Cleveland, MS
38736 Doddsville, MS
38737 Drew, MS
38738 Parchman, MS
38739 Dublin, MS
38740 Duncan, MS
38744 Glen Allan, MS
38745 Grace, MS
38746 Gunnison, MS
38748 Hollandale, MS
38749 Indianola, MS
38751 Baird, MS
38751 Indianola, MS
38753 Inverness, MS
38754 Isola, MS
38756 Elizabeth, MS
38756 Leland, MS
38759 Merigold, MS
38760 Metcalfe, MS
38761 Moorhead, MS
38762 Mound Bayou, MS
38764 Pace, MS
38765 Panther Burn, MS
38767 Rena Lara, MS
38768 Rome, MS
38769 Rosedale, MS
38771 Ruleville, MS
38772 Scott, MS
38773 Shaw, MS
38774 Shelby, MS
38776 Stoneville, MS
38778 Sunflower, MS
38780 Wayside, MS
38781 Winstonville, MS
38782 Winterville, MS

388

38801 Tupelo, MS
38802 Tupelo, MS
38803 Tupelo, MS
38804 Tupelo, MS
38820 Algoma, MS
38821 Amory, MS
38824 Baldwyn, MS
38825 Becker, MS
38826 Belden, MS
38827 Belmont, MS
38828 Blue Springs, MS
38829 Booneville, MS
38833 Burnsville, MS
38834 Corinth, MS
38834 Kossuth, MS
38835 Corinth, MS
38838 Dennis, MS
38839 Derma, MS
38841 Ecru, MS
38843 Fulton, MS
38844 Gattman, MS
38846 Glen, MS
38847 Golden, MS
38848 Greenwood Spg, MS
38848 Greenwood Springs, MS
38849 Guntown, MS
38850 Houlka, MS
38851 Houston, MS
38852 Iuka, MS
38855 Mantachie, MS
38856 Marietta, MS
38857 Mooreville, MS
38858 Nettleton, MS
38859 New Site, MS
38860 Egypt, MS
38860 Okolona, MS
38862 Plantersville, MS
38863 Pontotoc, MS
38864 Randolph, MS
38864 Sarepta, MS
38865 Rienzi, MS
38866 Saltillo, MS
38868 Shannon, MS
38869 Sherman, MS
38870 Smithville, MS
38871 Thaxton, MS
38873 Tishomingo, MS
38874 Toccopola, MS
38875 Trebloc, MS
38876 Tremont, MS
38877 Van Vleet, MS
38878 Vardaman, MS
38879 Verona, MS
38880 Wheeler, MS

389

38901 Grenada, MS
38902 Grenada, MS
38913 Banner, MS
38914 Big Creek, MS
38915 Bruce, MS
38916 Calhoun City, MS
38917 Carrollton, MS
38920 Cascilla, MS
38921 Charleston, MS
38922 Coffeeville, MS
38923 Coila, MS
38924 Cruger, MS
38925 Duck Hill, MS
38926 Elliott, MS
38927 Enid, MS
38928 Glendora, MS
38929 Gore Springs, MS
38930 Avalon, MS
38930 Greenwood, MS
38935 Greenwood, MS
38940 Holcomb, MS
38941 Itta Bena, MS
38943 Mc Carley, MS
38944 Minter City, MS
38945 Greenwood, MS
38946 Morgan City, MS
38947 North Carrollton, MS
38948 Oakland, MS
38949 Bruce, MS
38949 Paris, MS
38950 Philipp, MS
38951 Pittsboro, MS
38952 Schlater, MS
38953 Scobey, MS
38954 Sidon, MS
38955 Calhoun City, MS
38955 Slate Spring, MS
38957 Sumner, MS
38958 Charleston, MS
38958 Swan Lake, MS
38959 Swiftown, MS
38960 Tie Plant, MS
38961 Tillatoba, MS
38962 Tippo, MS
38963 Tutwiler, MS
38964 Vance, MS
38965 Water Valley, MS
38966 Webb, MS
38967 Winona, MS

390

39038 Belzoni, MS
39039 Benton, MS
39040 Bentonia, MS
39041 Bolton, MS
39042 Brandon, MS
39043 Brandon, MS
39044 Braxton, MS
39045 Camden, MS
39046 Canton, MS
39047 Brandon, MS
39051 Carthage, MS
39054 Cary, MS
39056 Clinton, MS
39057 Conehatta, MS
39058 Clinton, MS
39059 Crystal Springs, MS
39060 Clinton, MS
39061 Delta City, MS
39062 D Lo, MS
39063 Durant, MS
39066 Edwards, MS
39067 Ethel, MS
39069 Fayette, MS
39071 Flora, MS
39072 Flora, MS
39073 Florence, MS
39074 Forest, MS
39077 Gallman, MS
39078 Georgetown, MS
39079 Goodman, MS
39080 Harperville, MS
39081 Fayette, MS
39082 Harrisville, MS
39083 Hazlehurst, MS
39086 Hermanville, MS
39087 Hillsboro, MS
39088 Holly Bluff, MS
39090 Kosciusko, MS
39092 Lake, MS
39094 Lena, MS
39095 Lexington, MS
39096 Lorman, MS
39097 Louise, MS
39098 Ludlow, MS

391

39107 Mc Adams, MS
39108 Mc Cool, MS
39109 Madden, MS
39110 Madison, MS
39111 Magee, MS
39111 Sanatorium, MS
39113 Mayersville, MS
39114 Mendenhall, MS
39115 Midnight, MS
39116 Mize, MS
39117 Morton, MS
39119 Mount Olive, MS
39120 Church Hill, MS
39120 Natchez, MS
39121 Natchez, MS
39122 Natchez, MS
39130 Madison, MS
39140 Newhebron, MS
39144 Pattison, MS
39145 Pelahatchie, MS
39146 Pickens, MS
39148 Piney Woods, MS
39149 Pinola, MS
39150 Port Gibson, MS
39151 Puckett, MS
39152 Pulaski, MS
39153 Raleigh, MS
39154 Learned, MS
39154 Raymond, MS
39156 Redwood, MS
39157 Ridgeland, MS
39158 Ridgeland, MS
39159 Fitler, MS
39159 Rolling Fork, MS
39160 Sallis, MS
39161 Sandhill, MS
39162 Satartia, MS
39163 Sharon, MS
39165 Sibley, MS
39166 Silver City, MS
39167 Star, MS
39168 Taylorsville, MS
39169 Tchula, MS
39169 Thornton, MS
39170 Terry, MS
39171 Thomastown, MS
39173 Tinsley, MS
39174 Tougaloo, MS
39175 Utica, MS
39176 Vaiden, MS
39177 Valley Park, MS
39179 Pickens, MS
39179 Vaughan, MS
39180 Vicksburg, MS
39181 Vicksburg, MS
39182 Vicksburg, MS
39183 Vicksburg, MS
39189 Walnut Grove, MS
39190 Washington, MS
39191 Wesson, MS
39192 West, MS
39193 Whitfield, MS
39194 Yazoo City, MS

392

39201 Jackson, MS
39202 Jackson, MS
39203 Jackson, MS
39204 Jackson, MS
39205 Jackson, MS
39206 Jackson, MS
39207 Jackson, MS
39208 Jackson, MS
39208 Pearl, MS
39209 Jackson, MS
39210 Jackson, MS
39211 Jackson, MS
39212 Jackson, MS
39213 Jackson, MS
39215 Jackson, MS
39216 Jackson, MS
39217 Jackson, MS
39218 Jackson, MS
39218 Richland, MS
39225 Jackson, MS
39232 Flowood, MS
39232 Jackson, MS
39236 Jackson, MS
39250 Jackson, MS
39269 Jackson, MS
39271 Jackson, MS
39272 Byram, MS
39272 Jackson, MS
39282 Jackson, MS
39283 Jackson, MS
39284 Jackson, MS
39286 Jackson, MS
39288 Jackson, MS
39288 Pearl, MS
39289 Jackson, MS
39296 Jackson, MS
39298 Flowood, MS
39298 Jackson, MS

393

39301 Meridian, MS
39302 Meridian, MS
39303 Meridian, MS
39304 Meridian, MS
39305 Meridian, MS
39307 Meridian, MS
39309 Meridian, MS
39309 Naval Air Sta Meridian, MS
39320 Bailey, MS
39322 Buckatunna, MS
39323 Chunky, MS
39324 Clara, MS
39325 Collinsville, MS
39326 Daleville, MS
39327 Decatur, MS
39328 De Kalb, MS
39330 Enterprise, MS
39332 Hickory, MS
39335 Lauderdale, MS
39336 Lawrence, MS
39337 Little Rock, MS
39338 Louin, MS
39339 Louisville, MS
39341 Macon, MS
39341 Prairie Point, MS
39342 Marion, MS
39345 Newton, MS
39346 Noxapater, MS
39347 Pachuta, MS
39348 Paulding, MS
39350 Choctaw, MS
39350 Philadelphia, MS
39352 Porterville, MS
39354 Preston, MS
39355 Quitman, MS
39356 Rose Hill, MS
39358 Scooba, MS
39359 Sebastopol, MS
39360 Shubuta, MS
39361 Shuqualak, MS
39362 State Line, MS
39363 Stonewall, MS
39364 Toomsuba, MS
39365 Union, MS
39366 Vossburg, MS
39367 Waynesboro, MS

394

39401 Hattiesburg, MS
39402 Hattiesburg, MS
39403 Hattiesburg, MS
39404 Hattiesburg, MS
39406 Hattiesburg, MS
39407 Hattiesburg, MS
39421 Bassfield, MS
39422 Bay Springs, MS
39423 Beaumont, MS
39425 Brooklyn, MS
39426 Carriere, MS
39427 Carson, MS
39428 Collins, MS
39429 Columbia, MS
39436 Eastabuchie, MS
39437 Ellisville, MS
39439 Heidelberg, MS
39440 Laurel, MS
39441 Laurel, MS
39442 Laurel, MS
39443 Laurel, MS
39451 Leakesville, MS
39452 Agricola, MS
39452 Lucedale, MS
39455 Lumberton, MS
39456 Benndale, MS
39456 Leaf, MS
39456 Mc Lain, MS

39457 Mc Neill, MS
39459 Moselle, MS
39460 Moss, MS
39461 Neely, MS
39462 New Augusta, MS
39463 Nicholson, MS
39464 Ovett, MS
39465 Petal, MS
39466 Picayune, MS
39470 Poplarville, MS
39474 Prentiss, MS
39475 Purvis, MS
39476 Richton, MS
39477 Sandersville, MS
39478 Sandy Hook, MS
39479 Seminary, MS
39480 Soso, MS
39481 Stringer, MS
39482 Sumrall, MS
39483 Foxworth, MS
39483 Morgantown, MS

395

39501 Gulfport, MS
39502 Gulfport, MS
39503 Gulfport, MS
39505 Gulfport, MS
39506 Gulfport, MS
39507 Gulfport, MS
39520 Bay Saint Louis, MS
39520 Stennis Space Center, MS
39520 Waveland, MS
39521 Bay Saint Louis, MS
39522 Stennis Sp Ct, MS
39522 Stennis Space Center, MS
39525 Bay Saint Louis, MS
39525 Diamondhead, MS
39529 Bay Saint Louis, MS
39529 Stennis Sp Ct, MS
39529 Stennis Space Center, MS
39530 Biloxi, MS
39531 Biloxi, MS
39532 Biloxi, MS
39533 Biloxi, MS
39534 Biloxi, MS
39534 Keesler Afb, MS
39535 Biloxi, MS
39540 Diberville, MS
39552 Escatawpa, MS
39553 Gautier, MS
39555 Hurley, MS
39556 Kiln, MS
39558 Clermont Harbor, MS
39558 Lakeshore, MS
39560 Long Beach, MS
39561 Mc Henry, MS
39562 Moss Point, MS
39563 Kreole, MS
39563 Moss Point, MS
39563 Pascagoula, MS
39564 Ocean Springs, MS
39565 Ocean Springs, MS
39565 Vancleave, MS
39566 Ocean Springs, MS
39567 Pascagoula, MS
39568 Pascagoula, MS
39569 Pascagoula, MS
39571 Pass Christian, MS
39571 Pass Christin, MS
39572 Pearlington, MS
39573 Perkinston, MS
39574 Saucier, MS
39576 Waveland, MS
39577 Wiggins, MS
39581 Pascagoula, MS
39595 Pascagoula, MS

396

39601 Brookhaven, MS
39602 Brookhaven, MS
39603 Brookhaven, MS
39629 Bogue Chitto, MS
39630 Bude, MS
39631 Centreville, MS
39632 Chatawa, MS
39633 Crosby, MS
39635 Fernwood, MS
39638 Gloster, MS
39641 Jayess, MS
39643 Kokomo, MS
39645 Liberty, MS
39647 Mc Call Creek, MS
39648 Mccomb, MS
39649 Mccomb, MS
39652 Magnolia, MS
39653 Meadville, MS
39654 Monticello, MS
39656 Oak Vale, MS
39657 Osyka, MS
39661 Roxie, MS
39662 Ruth, MS
39663 Silver Creek, MS
39664 Smithdale, MS
39665 Sontag, MS
39666 Summit, MS
39667 Tylertown, MS
39668 Union Church, MS
39669 Woodville, MS

397

39701 Columbus, MS
39701 Columbus Afb, MS
39702 Columbus, MS
39703 Columbus, MS
39704 Columbus, MS
39705 Columbus, MS
39710 Columbus, MS
39730 Aberdeen, MS
39735 Ackerman, MS
39735 Reform, MS
39736 Artesia, MS
39737 Bellefontaine, MS
39739 Bigbee Valley, MS
39739 Brooksville, MS
39740 Caledonia, MS
39741 Cedarbluff, MS
39743 Crawford, MS
39744 Eupora, MS
39744 Tomnolen, MS
39745 French Camp, MS
39746 Hamilton, MS
39747 Kilmichael, MS
39750 Maben, MS
39751 Mantee, MS
39752 Mathiston, MS
39753 Mayhew, MS
39754 Montpelier, MS
39755 Pheba, MS
39756 Prairie, MS
39759 Starkville, MS
39760 Starkville, MS
39762 Mississippi State, MS
39766 Steens, MS
39767 Stewart, MS
39769 Sturgis, MS
39771 Walthall, MS
39772 Weir, MS
39773 West Point, MS
39776 Woodland, MS

398

39813 Arlington, GA
39815 Attapulgus, GA
39817 Bainbridge, GA
39818 Bainbridge, GA
39819 Bainbridge, GA
39823 Blakely, GA
39824 Bluffton, GA
39825 Brinson, GA
39826 Bronwood, GA
39827 Cairo, GA
39828 Cairo, GA
39829 Calvary, GA
39832 Cedar Springs, GA
39834 Climax, GA
39836 Coleman, GA
39837 Colquitt, GA
39840 Cuthbert, GA
39841 Damascus, GA
39842 Dawson, GA
39845 Donalsonville, GA
39846 Edison, GA
39851 Fort Gaines, GA
39852 Fowlstown, GA
39854 Georgetown, GA
39859 Iron City, GA
39861 Jakin, GA
39862 Leary, GA
39866 Morgan, GA
39867 Morris, GA
39870 Newton, GA
39877 Parrott, GA
39885 Sasser, GA
39886 Shellman, GA
39897 Whigham, GA

399

39901 Atlanta, GA
39901 Chamblee, GA

400

40003 Bagdad, KY
40004 Bardstown, KY
40006 Bedford, KY
40007 Bethlehem, KY
40008 Bloomfield, KY
40009 Bradfordsville, KY
40010 Buckner, KY
40011 Campbellsburg, KY
40012 Chaplin, KY
40013 Coxs Creek, KY
40013 Deatsville, KY
40013 Highgrove, KY
40013 Lenore, KY
40013 Samuels, KY
40014 Ballardsville, KY
40014 Crestwood, KY
40014 Orchard Grass Hills, KY
40018 Eastwood, KY
40019 Eminence, KY
40020 Fairfield, KY
40022 Finchville, KY
40023 Fisherville, KY
40023 Wilsonville, KY
40025 Glenview, KY
40026 Goshen, KY
40027 Harrods Creek, KY
40031 La Grange, KY
40031 Lagrange, KY
40032 La Grange, KY
40032 Lagrange, KY
40033 Calvary, KY
40033 Lebanon, KY
40036 Lockport, KY
40037 Loretto, KY
40040 Mackville, KY
40041 Masonic Home, KY
40045 Locust, KY
40045 Milton, KY
40046 Mount Eden, KY
40047 Mount Washington, KY
40048 Nazareth, KY
40049 Nerinx, KY
40050 New Castle, KY
40051 Howardstown, KY
40051 New Haven, KY
40051 Trappist, KY
40052 New Hope, KY
40055 Pendleton, KY
40055 Sulphur, KY
40056 Pewee Valley, KY
40057 Cropper, KY
40057 Defoe, KY
40057 Franklinton, KY
40057 Pleasureville, KY
40058 Port Royal, KY
40059 Prospect, KY
40059 River Bluff, KY
40060 Raywick, KY
40061 Saint Catharine, KY
40062 Saint Francis, KY
40063 Saint Mary, KY
40063 St Mary, KY
40065 Shelbyville, KY
40066 Shelbyville, KY
40067 Simpsonville, KY
40068 Smithfield, KY
40069 Maud, KY
40069 Springfield, KY
40070 Sulphur, KY
40071 Taylorsville, KY
40075 Turners Station, KY
40076 Waddy, KY
40077 Westport, KY
40078 Willisburg, KY

401

40104 Battletown, KY
40107 Boston, KY
40108 Brandenburg, KY
40109 Brooks, KY
40110 Clermont, KY
40111 Cloverport, KY
40115 Custer, KY
40115 Garfield, KY
40117 Ekron, KY
40118 Fairdale, KY
40118 Hollyvilla, KY
40119 Falls Of Rough, KY
40119 Glen Dean, KY
40119 Vanzant, KY
40121 Fort Knox, KY
40122 Fort Knox, KY
40129 Hillview, KY
40140 Constantine, KY
40140 Garfield, KY
40142 Guston, KY
40143 Hardinsburg, KY
40143 Mooleyville, KY
40143 Sample, KY
40144 Harned, KY
40144 Locust Hill, KY
40144 Se Ree, KY
40145 Hudson, KY
40146 Irvington, KY
40146 Lodiburg, KY
40150 Lebanon Junction, KY
40152 Mc Daniels, KY
40153 Mc Quady, KY
40155 Muldraugh, KY
40157 Payneville, KY
40159 Radcliff, KY
40160 Radcliff, KY
40161 Rhodelia, KY
40162 Rineyville, KY
40165 Fox Chase, KY
40165 Hebron Estates, KY
40165 Hunters Hollow, KY
40165 Pioneer Village, KY
40165 Shepherdsville, KY
40170 Stephensport, KY
40171 Union Star, KY
40175 Big Spring, KY
40175 Flaherty, KY
40175 Vine Grove, KY
40176 Raymond, KY
40176 Webster, KY
40177 West Point, KY
40178 Westview, KY

402

40201 Louisville, KY
40202 Louisville, KY
40203 Louisville, KY
40204 Louisville, KY
40205 Kingsley, KY
40205 Louisville, KY
40205 Seneca Gardens, KY
40205 Strathmoor Manor, KY
40205 Strathmoor Village, KY
40206 Louisville, KY
40207 Bellewood, KY
40207 Brownsboro Village, KY
40207 Druid Hills, KY
40207 Indian Hills, KY
40207 Louisville, KY
40207 Maryhill Estates, KY
40207 Mockingbird Valley, KY
40207 Norbourne Estates, KY
40207 Richlawn, KY
40207 Riverwood, KY
40207 Rolling Fields, KY
40207 Saint Matthews, KY
40207 Windy Hills, KY
40207 Woodlawn Park, KY
40208 Louisville, KY
40209 Louisville, KY
40210 Louisville, KY
40211 Louisville, KY
40212 Louisville, KY
40213 Audubon Park, KY
40213 Louisville, KY
40213 Lynnview, KY
40213 Poplar Hills, KY
40214 Louisville, KY
40215 Louisville, KY
40216 Louisville, KY
40216 Shively, KY
40217 Louisville, KY
40217 Parkway Village, KY
40218 Buechel, KY
40218 Louisville, KY
40218 Watterson Park, KY
40219 Heritage Creek, KY
40219 Louisville, KY
40219 Okolona, KY
40219 South Park View, KY
40220 Cambridge, KY
40220 Houston Acres, KY
40220 Hurstbourne Acres, KY
40220 Lincolnshire, KY
40220 Louisville, KY
40220 Meadowview Estates, KY
40220 Saint Regis Park, KY
40221 Louisville, KY
40222 Bancroft, KY
40222 Bellemeade, KY
40222 Crossgate, KY
40222 Glenview Hills, KY
40222 Glenview Manor, KY
40222 Graymoor Devondale, KY
40222 Hurstbourne, KY
40222 Louisville, KY
40222 Lyndon, KY
40222 Northfield, KY
40222 Norwood, KY
40222 Thornhill, KY
40223 Anchorage, KY
40223 Blue Ridge Manor, KY
40223 Louisville, KY
40223 Meadowbrook Farm, KY
40223 Moorland, KY
40223 Sycamore, KY
40223 Wildwood, KY
40224 Louisville, KY
40225 Louisville, KY
40228 Hollow Creek, KY
40228 Louisville, KY
40228 Spring Mill, KY
40229 Louisville, KY
40229 Okolona, KY
40231 Louisville, KY
40232 Louisville, KY
40233 Louisville, KY
40241 Barbourmeade, KY
40241 Broeck Pointe, KY
40241 Brownsboro Farm, KY
40241 Creekside, KY
40241 Fincastle, KY
40241 Goose Creek, KY
40241 Green Spring, KY
40241 Hickory Hill, KY
40241 Hills And Dales, KY
40241 Louisville, KY
40241 Lyndon, KY
40241 Manor Creek, KY
40241 Spring Valley, KY
40241 Ten Broeck, KY
40242 Briarwood, KY
40242 Langdon Place, KY
40242 Louisville, KY
40242 Lyndon, KY
40242 Meadow Vale, KY
40242 Murray Hill, KY
40242 Old Brownsboro Place, KY
40242 Plantation, KY
40242 Rolling Hills, KY
40243 Douglass Hills, KY
40243 Louisville, KY
40243 Middletown, KY
40243 Woodland Hills, KY
40245 Coldstream, KY
40245 Louisville, KY
40245 Worthington Hills, KY
40250 Louisville, KY
40251 Louisville, KY
40252 Louisville, KY
40252 Lyndon, KY
40253 Louisville, KY
40253 Middletown, KY
40255 Louisville, KY
40256 Louisville, KY
40256 Shively, KY
40257 Louisville, KY
40257 Saint Matthews, KY
40258 Louisville, KY
40258 Pleasure Ridge Park, KY
40259 Louisville, KY
40259 Okolona, KY
40261 Louisville, KY
40266 Louisville, KY
40268 Louisville, KY
40268 Pleasure Ridge Park, KY
40269 Jeffersontown, KY
40269 Louisville, KY
40270 Louisville, KY
40270 Valley Station, KY
40272 Louisville, KY
40272 Valley Station, KY
40280 Louisville, KY
40281 Louisville, KY
40281 Pleasure Ridge Park, KY
40282 Louisville, KY
40282 Pleasure Ridge Park, KY
40283 Louisville, KY
40283 Pleasure Ridge Park, KY
40285 Louisville, KY
40287 Louisville, KY
40289 Louisville, KY
40290 Louisville, KY
40291 Fern Creek, KY
40291 Louisville, KY
40292 Louisville, KY
40293 Louisville, KY
40294 Louisville, KY
40295 Louisville, KY
40296 Louisville, KY
40297 Louisville, KY
40298 Louisville, KY
40299 Jeffersontown, KY
40299 Louisville, KY

403

40310 Burgin, KY
40311 Carlisle, KY
40312 Clay City, KY
40312 Westbend, KY
40313 Clearfield, KY
40316 Denniston, KY
40317 Elliottville, KY
40319 Farmers, KY
40322 Frenchburg, KY
40322 Mariba, KY
40322 Scranton, KY
40324 Georgetown, KY
40328 Gravel Switch, KY
40330 Cornishville, KY
40330 Harrodsburg, KY
40334 Hope, KY
40336 Cobhill, KY
40336 Crystal, KY
40336 Irvine, KY
40336 Jinks, KY
40336 Pryse, KY
40336 West Irvine, KY
40336 Winston, KY
40337 Jeffersonville, KY
40339 Keene, KY
40340 Nicholasville, KY
40342 Lawrenceburg, KY
40346 Means, KY
40347 Midway, KY

40348 Millersburg, KY
40350 Moorefield, KY
40351 Haldeman, KY
40351 Lakeview Heights, KY
40351 Morehead, KY
40353 Camargo, KY
40353 Mount Sterling, KY
40355 New Liberty, KY
40356 Nicholasville, KY
40357 North Middletown, KY
40358 Olympia, KY
40359 Gratz, KY
40359 Owenton, KY
40359 Wheatley, KY
40360 Owingsville, KY
40361 Paris, KY
40362 Paris, KY
40363 Perry Park, KY
40366 Preston, KY
40370 Sadieville, KY
40371 Salt Lick, KY
40371 Sudith, KY
40372 Bondville, KY
40372 Salvisa, KY
40374 Bethel, KY
40374 Sharpsburg, KY
40376 Slade, KY
40379 Stamping Ground, KY
40380 Bowen, KY
40380 Patsey, KY
40380 Rosslyn, KY
40380 Stanton, KY
40383 Versailles, KY
40384 Versailles, KY
40385 Bybee, KY
40385 College Hill, KY
40385 Dreyfus, KY
40385 Waco, KY
40387 Pomeroyton, KY
40387 Wellington, KY
40390 Versailles, KY
40390 Wilmore, KY
40391 Ford, KY
40391 Winchester, KY
40392 Winchester, KY

404

40402 Annville, KY
40402 Bond, KY
40402 Dabolt, KY
40402 Moores Creek, KY
40403 Berea, KY
40404 Berea, KY
40405 Bighill, KY
40409 Brodhead, KY
40410 Bryantsville, KY
40419 Crab Orchard, KY
40422 Danville, KY
40423 Danville, KY
40434 Gray Hawk, KY
40437 Hustonville, KY
40440 Junction City, KY
40442 Kings Mountain, KY
40444 Lancaster, KY
40445 Livingston, KY
40446 Lancaster, KY
40447 Clover Bottom, KY
40447 Eberle, KY
40447 Foxtown, KY
40447 Hisle, KY
40447 Kerby Knob, KY
40447 Mc Kee, KY
40447 Morrill, KY
40447 New Zion, KY
40447 Parrot, KY
40447 Peoples, KY
40447 Wind Cave, KY
40448 Mc Kinney, KY
40452 Mitchellsburg, KY
40456 Climax, KY
40456 Conway, KY
40456 Disputanta, KY
40456 Mount Vernon, KY
40460 Johnetta, KY
40460 Orlando, KY
40461 Paint Lick, KY
40464 Parksville, KY
40468 Perryville, KY
40472 Ravenna, KY
40473 Renfro Valley, KY
40475 Richmond, KY
40476 Richmond, KY
40481 Sandgap, KY
40484 Stanford, KY
40486 Elias, KY
40486 Herd, KY
40486 Maulden, KY
40486 Tyner, KY
40488 Waneta, KY
40489 Waynesburg, KY
40492 Wildie, KY

405

40502 Lexington, KY
40503 Lexington, KY
40504 Lexington, KY
40505 Lexington, KY
40506 Lexington, KY
40507 Lexington, KY
40508 Lexington, KY
40509 Lexington, KY
40510 Lexington, KY
40511 Lexington, KY
40512 Lexington, KY
40513 Lexington, KY
40514 Lexington, KY
40515 Lexington, KY
40516 Lexington, KY
40517 Lexington, KY
40522 Lexington, KY
40523 Lexington, KY
40524 Lexington, KY
40526 Lexington, KY
40533 Lexington, KY
40536 Lexington, KY
40544 Lexington, KY
40546 Lexington, KY
40550 Lexington, KY
40555 Lexington, KY
40574 Lexington, KY
40575 Lexington, KY
40576 Lexington, KY
40577 Lexington, KY
40578 Lexington, KY
40579 Lexington, KY
40580 Lexington, KY
40581 Lexington, KY
40582 Lexington, KY
40583 Lexington, KY
40588 Lexington, KY
40591 Lexington, KY
40598 Lexington, KY

406

40601 Frankfort, KY
40601 Hatton, KY
40602 Frankfort, KY
40603 Frankfort, KY
40604 Frankfort, KY
40618 Frankfort, KY
40619 Frankfort, KY
40620 Frankfort, KY
40621 Frankfort, KY
40622 Frankfort, KY

407

40701 Corbin, KY
40701 Keavy, KY
40701 Woodbine, KY
40702 Corbin, KY
40724 Bush, KY
40729 East Bernstadt, KY
40729 Symbol, KY
40729 Victory, KY
40730 Emlyn, KY
40734 Gray, KY
40737 Keavy, KY
40740 Lily, KY
40741 London, KY
40741 Marydell, KY
40741 Sasser, KY
40741 Tuttle, KY
40742 London, KY
40743 London, KY
40744 London, KY
40745 London, KY
40750 London, KY
40755 Pittsburg, KY
40759 Meadow Creek, KY
40759 Rockholds, KY
40763 Siler, KY
40769 Cumberland College, KY
40769 Nevisdale, KY
40769 Williamsburg, KY
40771 Woodbine, KY

408

40801 Ages Brookside, KY
40803 Asher, KY
40806 Baxter, KY
40806 Keith, KY
40807 Benham, KY
40808 Big Laurel, KY
40810 Bledsoe, KY
40810 Pine Mountain, KY
40813 Calvin, KY
40815 Cawood, KY
40815 Crummies, KY
40815 Three Point, KY
40816 Chappell, KY
40818 Coalgood, KY
40819 Coldiron, KY
40819 Molus, KY
40820 Cranks, KY
40823 Chad, KY
40823 Cumberland, KY
40823 Hiram, KY
40823 Oven Fork, KY
40824 Dayhoit, KY
40826 Eolia, KY
40827 Essie, KY
40828 Bailey Creek, KY
40828 Dizney, KY
40828 Evarts, KY
40828 Louellen, KY
40828 Redbud, KY
40828 Woods, KY
40828 Yocum Creek, KY
40829 Grays Knob, KY
40830 Gulston, KY
40831 Chevrolet, KY
40831 Harlan, KY
40831 Smith, KY
40840 Harlan, KY
40840 Helton, KY
40843 Holmes Mill, KY
40844 Hoskinston, KY
40845 Hulen, KY
40847 Kenvir, KY
40849 Lejunior, KY
40854 Loyall, KY
40855 Lynch, KY
40856 Miracle, KY
40858 Mozelle, KY
40862 Partridge, KY
40863 Alva, KY
40863 Pathfork, KY
40865 Putney, KY
40868 Stinnett, KY
40870 Totz, KY
40873 Wallins Creek, KY
40874 Warbranch, KY

409

40902 Arjay, KY
40903 Artemus, KY
40906 Bailey Switch, KY
40906 Barbourville, KY
40906 Baughman, KY
40906 Crane Nest, KY
40906 Gausdale, KY
40906 Himyar, KY
40906 Jarvis, KY
40906 Kayjay, KY
40906 Swanpond, KY
40906 Tedders, KY
40906 Woollum, KY
40913 Beverly, KY
40913 Red Bird, KY
40914 Big Creek, KY
40914 Peabody, KY
40915 Bimble, KY
40921 Bryants Store, KY
40923 Cannon, KY
40927 Closplint, KY
40930 Dewitt, KY
40932 Fall Rock, KY
40935 Flat Lick, KY
40935 Mills, KY
40935 Salt Gum, KY
40939 Elys, KY
40939 Fourmile, KY
40939 Ivy Grove, KY
40940 Fonde, KY
40940 Frakes, KY
40940 Laurel Fork, KY
40941 Garrard, KY
40943 Girdler, KY
40944 Goose Rock, KY
40946 Green Road, KY
40949 Heidrick, KY
40951 Hima, KY
40953 Hinkle, KY
40955 Ingram, KY
40958 Kettle Island, KY
40962 Bluehole, KY
40962 Bright Shade, KY
40962 Chestnutburg, KY
40962 Eriline, KY
40962 Fogertown, KY
40962 Grace, KY
40962 Manchester, KY
40962 Marcum, KY
40962 Ogle, KY
40962 Plank, KY
40962 Tanksley, KY
40962 Urban, KY
40962 Wildcat, KY
40964 Mary Alice, KY
40965 Middlesboro, KY
40972 Oneida, KY
40977 Balkan, KY
40977 Callaway, KY
40977 Cary, KY
40977 Chenoa, KY
40977 Clear Creek, KY
40977 Clear Creek Springs, KY
40977 Davisburg, KY
40977 Dorton Branch, KY
40977 East Pineville, KY
40977 Field, KY
40977 Jenson, KY
40977 Log Mountain, KY
40977 Pineville, KY
40977 Tinsley, KY
40977 Wallsend, KY
40979 Roark, KY
40981 Saul, KY
40982 Scalf, KY
40983 Sextons Creek, KY
40988 Stoney Fork, KY
40995 Trosper, KY
40997 Walker, KY

410

41001 Alexandria, KY
41002 Augusta, KY
41003 Berry, KY
41004 Brooksville, KY
41005 Burlington, KY
41005 Rabbit Hash, KY
41006 Butler, KY
41007 California, KY
41007 Mentor, KY
41008 Carrollton, KY
41010 Blanchet, KY
41010 Corinth, KY
41010 Owen, KY
41011 Covington, KY
41011 Ft Mitchell, KY
41011 Ft Wright, KY
41011 Park Hills, KY
41012 Covington, KY
41014 Covington, KY
41015 Covington, KY
41015 Latonia, KY
41015 Latonia Lakes, KY
41015 Ryland Heights, KY
41015 Ryland Hght, KY
41015 Taylor Mill, KY
41016 Bromley, KY
41016 Covington, KY
41016 Ludlow, KY
41017 Bromley, KY
41017 Covington, KY
41017 Crescent Park, KY
41017 Crescent Spg, KY
41017 Crescent Springs, KY
41017 Crestview Hills, KY
41017 Edgewood, KY
41017 Erlanger, KY
41017 Fort Mitchell, KY
41017 Ft Mitchell, KY
41017 Ft Wright, KY
41017 Lakeside Park, KY
41017 South Fort Mitchell, KY
41017 Villa Hills, KY
41018 Covington, KY
41018 Edgewood, KY
41018 Elsmere, KY
41018 Erlanger, KY
41019 Covington, KY
41021 Hebron, KY
41022 Florence, KY
41025 Erlanger, KY
41030 Crittenden, KY
41031 Cynthiana, KY
41033 De Mossville, KY
41033 Demossville, KY
41034 Dover, KY
41035 Dry Ridge, KY
41037 Elizaville, KY
41039 Ewing, KY
41040 Falmouth, KY
41040 Pendleton County, KY
41041 Flemingsburg, KY
41042 Florence, KY
41043 Foster, KY
41044 Germantown, KY
41045 Ghent, KY
41046 Glencoe, KY
41048 Hebron, KY
41049 Hillsboro, KY
41051 Independence, KY
41052 Jonesville, KY
41053 Kenton, KY
41054 Mason, KY
41055 Mayslick, KY
41056 Maysville, KY
41056 Sardis, KY
41059 Melbourne, KY
41061 Milford, KY
41062 Minerva, KY
41063 Morning View, KY
41064 Mount Olivet, KY
41065 Muses Mills, KY
41071 Fort Thomas, KY
41071 Newport, KY
41071 Southgate, KY
41071 Wilder, KY
41072 Newport, KY
41073 Bellevue, KY
41073 Dayton, KY
41073 Fort Thomas, KY
41073 Newport, KY
41074 Bellevue, KY
41074 Dayton, KY
41074 Newport, KY
41075 Fort Thomas, KY
41075 Kenton Vale, KY
41075 Newport, KY
41076 Cold Sprgs-Highland Hts, KY
41076 Cold Spring, KY
41076 Highland Heights, KY
41076 Newport, KY
41076 Wilder, KY
41080 Petersburg, KY
41081 Plummers Landing, KY
41083 Sanders, KY
41085 Silver Grove, KY
41086 Sparta, KY
41091 Union, KY
41092 Verona, KY
41093 Wallingford, KY
41094 Walton, KY
41095 Napoleon, KY
41095 Warsaw, KY
41096 Washington, KY
41097 Williamstown, KY
41098 Worthville, KY
41099 Newport, KY

411

41101 Ashland, KY
41101 Summitt, KY
41101 Westwood, KY
41102 Ashland, KY
41102 Summitt, KY
41105 Ashland, KY
41105 Summitt, KY
41114 Ashland, KY
41121 Argillite, KY
41124 Blaine, KY
41128 Carter, KY
41128 Smiths Creek, KY
41129 Catlettsburg, KY
41132 Denton, KY
41135 Emerson, KY
41135 Head Of Grassy, KY
41139 Flatwoods, KY
41139 Russell, KY
41141 Garrison, KY
41142 Grahn, KY
41143 Fultz, KY
41143 Grayson, KY
41143 Johns Run, KY
41144 Greenup, KY
41144 Lloyd, KY
41144 Load, KY
41144 Oldtown, KY
41144 Wurtland, KY
41146 Hitchins, KY
41149 Isonville, KY
41159 Martha, KY
41160 Mazie, KY
41164 Lawton, KY
41164 Olive Hill, KY
41164 Stark, KY
41164 Upper Tygart, KY
41164 Wolf, KY
41166 Quincy, KY
41166 Saint Paul, KY
41168 Rush, KY
41169 Raceland, KY
41169 Russell, KY
41171 Bruin, KY
41171 Burke, KY
41171 Culver, KY
41171 Little Sandy, KY
41171 Lytten, KY
41171 Newfoundland, KY
41171 Sandy Hook, KY
41171 Stephens, KY
41173 Soldier, KY
41174 Firebrick, KY
41174 South Portsmouth, KY
41175 South Shore, KY
41179 Camp Dix, KY
41179 Concord, KY
41179 Trinity, KY
41179 Vanceburg, KY
41180 Webbville, KY
41181 Willard, KY
41183 Worthington, KY
41189 Tollesboro, KY

412

41201 Adams, KY
41201 Louisa, KY
41203 Beauty, KY
41204 Boons Camp, KY
41214 Davella, KY
41214 Debord, KY
41216 East Point, KY
41219 Elna, KY
41219 Flatgap, KY
41219 Fuget, KY
41219 Redbush, KY

41219 Volga, KY
41222 Denver, KY
41222 Hagerhill, KY
41222 Leander, KY
41224 Inez, KY
41224 Job, KY
41224 Threeforks, KY
41226 Keaton, KY
41230 Clifford, KY
41230 Fallsburg, KY
41230 Louisa, KY
41230 Richardson, KY
41231 Lovely, KY
41232 Lowmansville, KY
41234 Meally, KY
41238 Manila, KY
41238 Oil Springs, KY
41240 Nippa, KY
41240 Offutt, KY
41240 Paintsville, KY
41240 Swamp Branch, KY
41240 Thealka, KY
41240 Whitehouse, KY
41250 Laura, KY
41250 Pilgrim, KY
41254 River, KY
41255 Sitka, KY
41256 Barnetts Creek, KY
41256 Staffordsville, KY
41257 Stambaugh, KY
41260 Thelma, KY
41262 Davisport, KY
41262 Milo, KY
41262 Tomahawk, KY
41263 Tutor Key, KY
41264 Ulysses, KY
41265 Van Lear, KY
41267 Hode, KY
41267 Warfield, KY
41268 West Van Lear, KY
41271 Williamsport, KY
41274 Wittensville, KY

413

41301 Bethany, KY
41301 Burkhart, KY
41301 Campton, KY
41301 Flat, KY
41301 Gillmore, KY
41301 Lee City, KY
41301 Leeco, KY
41301 Mary, KY
41301 Maytown, KY
41301 Valeria, KY
41301 Zachariah, KY
41310 Bays, KY
41311 Beattyville, KY
41311 Fillmore, KY
41311 Old Landing, KY
41311 Primrose, KY
41311 Tallega, KY
41311 Vada, KY
41311 Widecreek, KY
41311 Yellow Rock, KY
41314 Booneville, KY
41314 Green Hall, KY
41314 Island City, KY
41314 Morris Fork, KY
41314 Pebworth, KY
41314 Sebastians Branch, KY
41314 Turkey, KY
41317 Clayhole, KY
41332 Buskirk, KY
41332 Hazel Green, KY
41332 Helechawa, KY
41332 Insko, KY
41339 Altro, KY
41339 Athol, KY
41339 Canoe, KY
41339 Decoy, KY
41339 Elkatawa, KY
41339 Frozen Creek, KY
41339 Guage, KY
41339 Guerrant, KY
41339 Haddix, KY
41339 Jackson, KY
41339 Lambric, KY
41339 Noctor, KY
41339 Quicksand, KY
41339 Saldee, KY
41339 Talbert, KY
41339 Wolf Coal, KY
41339 Wolverine, KY
41347 Lone, KY
41348 Hardshell, KY
41348 Lost Creek, KY
41348 Ned, KY
41351 Mistletoe, KY
41352 Grassy Creek, KY
41352 Mize, KY
41360 Pine Ridge, KY
41364 Ricetown, KY
41365 Rogers, KY
41366 Rousseau, KY
41367 Rowdy, KY
41368 Saint Helens, KY
41385 Vancleve, KY
41386 Vincent, KY
41390 Whick, KY
41397 Zoe, KY

414

41408 Cannel City, KY
41413 Crockett, KY
41421 Elkfork, KY
41425 Ezel, KY
41426 Falcon, KY
41451 Malone, KY
41464 Gypsy, KY
41464 Royalton, KY
41465 Bethanna, KY
41465 Burning Fork, KY
41465 Carver, KY
41465 Cisco, KY
41465 Conley, KY
41465 Cutuno, KY
41465 Cyrus, KY
41465 Duco, KY
41465 Edna, KY
41465 Elsie, KY
41465 Ever, KY
41465 Flat Fork, KY
41465 Foraker, KY
41465 Fredville, KY
41465 Fritz, KY
41465 Gapville, KY
41465 Gifford, KY
41465 Hager, KY
41465 Harper, KY
41465 Hendricks, KY
41465 Ivyton, KY
41465 Lickburg, KY
41465 Logville, KY
41465 Maggard, KY
41465 Marshallville, KY
41465 Mashfork, KY
41465 Salyersville, KY
41465 Seitz, KY
41465 Stella, KY
41465 Sublett, KY
41465 Swampton, KY
41465 Wonnie, KY
41472 Blairs Mill, KY
41472 Blaze, KY
41472 Caney, KY
41472 Cottle, KY
41472 Dingus, KY
41472 Elamton, KY
41472 Index, KY
41472 Lenox, KY
41472 Matthew, KY
41472 Mima, KY
41472 Moon, KY
41472 Ophir, KY
41472 Relief, KY
41472 Silverhill, KY
41472 Stacy Fork, KY
41472 West Liberty, KY
41472 White Oak, KY
41472 Yocum, KY
41477 Wrigley, KY

415

41501 Broad Bottom, KY
41501 Gulnare, KY
41501 Mccombs, KY
41501 Meta, KY
41501 Nelse, KY
41501 Pikeville, KY
41501 Piso, KY
41502 Pikeville, KY
41503 South Williamson, KY
41512 Ashcamp, KY
41513 Belcher, KY
41514 Aflex, KY
41514 Belfry, KY
41514 Burnwell, KY
41514 Goody, KY
41514 Hatfield, KY
41514 Toler, KY
41514 Turkey Creek, KY
41517 Burdine, KY
41519 Canada, KY
41520 Dorton, KY
41522 Draffin, KY
41522 Elkhorn City, KY
41522 Senterville, KY
41524 Biggs, KY
41524 Fedscreek, KY
41526 Fords Branch, KY
41527 Forest Hills, KY
41528 Freeburn, KY
41531 Hardy, KY
41534 Hellier, KY
41535 Huddy, KY
41537 Jenkins, KY
41537 Payne Gap, KY
41538 Jonancy, KY
41539 Kimper, KY
41540 Lick Creek, KY
41542 Lookout, KY
41543 Mc Andrews, KY
41544 Mc Carr, KY
41547 Majestic, KY
41548 Mouthcard, KY
41549 Myra, KY
41553 Jamboree, KY
41553 Paw Paw, KY
41553 Phelps, KY
41554 Phyllis, KY
41555 Mcveigh, KY
41555 Pinsonfork, KY
41557 Fishtrap, KY
41557 Jonican, KY
41557 Raccoon, KY
41558 Ransom, KY
41559 Regina, KY
41560 Robinson Creek, KY
41561 Rockhouse, KY
41562 Shelbiana, KY
41563 Shelby Gap, KY
41564 Sidney, KY
41566 Steele, KY
41567 Stone, KY
41568 Argo, KY
41568 Stopover, KY
41568 Woodman, KY
41571 Varney, KY
41572 Etty, KY
41572 Speight, KY
41572 Virgie, KY

416

41601 Allen, KY
41602 Auxier, KY
41603 Banner, KY
41603 Honaker, KY
41604 Beaver, KY
41604 Ligon, KY
41605 Betsy Layne, KY
41606 Bevinsville, KY
41606 Halo, KY
41607 Blue River, KY
41612 Bypro, KY
41615 Dana, KY
41616 David, KY
41619 Drift, KY
41621 Dwale, KY
41622 Eastern, KY
41630 Garrett, KY
41631 Grethel, KY
41632 Gunlock, KY
41632 Waldo, KY
41635 Craynor, KY
41635 Galveston, KY
41635 Harold, KY
41636 Buckingham, KY
41636 Hi Hat, KY
41636 Price, KY
41640 Elmrock, KY
41640 Hueysville, KY
41642 Ivel, KY
41643 Lackey, KY
41645 Langley, KY
41647 East Mc Dowell, KY
41647 Mc Dowell, KY
41647 Orkney, KY
41649 Hite, KY
41649 Martin, KY
41649 Risner, KY
41650 Melvin, KY
41651 Minnie, KY
41653 Emma, KY
41653 Endicott, KY
41653 Hippo, KY
41653 Prestonsburg, KY
41655 Hunter, KY
41655 Printer, KY
41659 Stanville, KY
41660 Teaberry, KY
41663 Tram, KY
41666 Estill, KY
41666 Wayland, KY
41667 Weeksbury, KY
41669 Wheelwright, KY

417

41701 Browns Fork, KY
41701 Hazard, KY
41701 Typo, KY
41701 Walkertown, KY
41702 Hazard, KY
41712 Ary, KY
41713 Avawam, KY
41714 Bear Branch, KY
41719 Blue Diamond, KY
41719 Bonnyman, KY
41719 Butterfly, KY
41721 Buckhorn, KY
41722 Bulan, KY
41722 Hardburly, KY
41722 Talcum, KY
41722 Tribbey, KY
41723 Busy, KY
41725 Carrie, KY
41727 Chavies, KY
41729 Combs, KY
41731 Cornettsville, KY
41731 Daisy, KY
41731 Leatherwood, KY
41731 Ulvah, KY
41735 Delphia, KY
41736 Dice, KY
41739 Dwarf, KY
41740 Bearville, KY
41740 Emmalena, KY
41740 Tina, KY
41743 Fisty, KY
41745 Gays Creek, KY
41746 Happy, KY
41749 Confluence, KY
41749 Dryhill, KY
41749 Hyden, KY
41749 Kaliopi, KY
41751 Jeff, KY
41754 Krypton, KY
41754 Napfor, KY
41759 Anco, KY
41759 Sassafras, KY
41760 Scuddy, KY
41762 Hyden, KY
41762 Sizerock, KY
41763 Slemp, KY
41764 Smilax, KY
41766 Thousandsticks, KY
41772 Vest, KY
41773 Allock, KY
41773 Amburgey, KY
41773 Vicco, KY
41774 Farler, KY
41774 Viper, KY
41775 Wendover, KY
41776 Cinda, KY
41776 Cutshin, KY
41776 Frew, KY
41776 Wooton, KY
41777 Big Rock, KY
41777 Yeaddiss, KY
41778 Yerkes, KY

418

41804 Blackey, KY
41804 Carcassonne, KY
41810 Cromona, KY
41812 Deane, KY
41815 Ermine, KY
41817 Garner, KY
41817 Larkslane, KY
41819 Gilly, KY
41819 Gordon, KY
41821 Hallie, KY
41821 Skyline, KY
41822 Brinkley, KY
41822 Hindman, KY
41824 Isom, KY
41825 Jackhorn, KY
41826 Jeremiah, KY
41828 Kite, KY
41831 Leburn, KY
41831 Soft Shell, KY
41832 Letcher, KY
41833 Linefork, KY
41834 Littcarr, KY
41835 Mc Roberts, KY
41836 Mallie, KY
41837 Mayking, KY
41838 Millstone, KY
41839 Mousie, KY
41840 Fleming, KY
41840 Fleming Neon, KY
41840 Hall, KY
41840 Neon, KY
41843 Pine Top, KY
41844 Hollybush, KY
41844 Pippa Passes, KY
41845 Premium, KY
41847 Redfox, KY
41848 Roxana, KY
41849 Seco, KY
41855 Thornton, KY
41858 Crown, KY
41858 Democrat, KY
41858 Dongola, KY
41858 Kona, KY
41858 Oscaloosa, KY
41858 Van, KY
41858 Whitesburg, KY
41859 Dema, KY
41861 Raven, KY
41862 Dry Creek, KY
41862 Topmost, KY

420

42001 Paducah, KY
42002 Paducah, KY
42003 Paducah, KY
42020 Almo, KY
42021 Arlington, KY
42022 Bandana, KY
42023 Bardwell, KY
42024 Barlow, KY
42025 Benton, KY
42027 Boaz, KY
42028 Burna, KY
42029 Calvert City, KY
42031 Clinton, KY
42032 Columbus, KY
42033 Crayne, KY
42035 Cunningham, KY
42036 Dexter, KY
42037 Dycusburg, KY
42038 Eddyville, KY
42039 Fancy Farm, KY
42040 Farmington, KY
42041 Crutchfield, KY
42041 Fulton, KY
42044 Gilbertsville, KY
42045 Grand Rivers, KY
42045 Iuka, KY
42047 Hampton, KY
42048 Hardin, KY
42049 Hazel, KY
42050 Hickman, KY
42051 Hickory, KY
42053 Kevil, KY
42054 Kirksey, KY
42055 Kuttawa, KY
42056 La Center, KY
42058 Ledbetter, KY
42060 Lovelaceville, KY
42061 Lowes, KY
42063 Lynnville, KY
42064 Marion, KY
42066 Mayfield, KY
42069 Melber, KY
42070 Milburn, KY
42071 Murray, KY
42076 Hamlin, KY
42076 New Concord, KY
42078 Lola, KY
42078 Salem, KY
42079 Sedalia, KY
42081 Carrsville, KY
42081 Smithland, KY
42082 Symsonia, KY
42083 Tiline, KY
42085 Water Valley, KY
42086 West Paducah, KY
42087 Blandville, KY
42087 Wickliffe, KY
42088 Wingo, KY

421

42101 Bowling Green, KY
42101 Hadley, KY
42101 Plum Springs, KY
42101 Richardsville, KY
42102 Bowling Green, KY
42103 Bowling Green, KY
42104 Bowling Green, KY
42120 Adolphus, KY
42122 Alvaton, KY
42123 Austin, KY
42124 Beaumont, KY
42127 Cave City, KY
42128 Drake, KY
42129 Edmonton, KY
42129 Subtle, KY
42129 Sulphur Well, KY
42130 Eighty Eight, KY
42131 Etoile, KY
42133 Fountain Run, KY
42134 Franklin, KY
42135 Franklin, KY
42140 Gamaliel, KY
42141 Glasgow, KY
42141 Lamb, KY
42142 Glasgow, KY
42151 Hestand, KY
42152 Hiseville, KY
42153 Holland, KY
42154 Knob Lick, KY
42156 Lucas, KY
42157 Mount Hermon, KY
42159 Oakland, KY
42160 Park City, KY
42163 Rocky Hill, KY
42164 Halfway, KY
42164 Scottsville, KY
42166 Summer Shade, KY
42166 Willow Shade, KY
42167 T Ville, KY
42167 Tompkinsville, KY
42170 Woodburn, KY
42171 Smiths Grove, KY

422

42201 Aberdeen, KY
42202 Adairville, KY
42204 Allensville, KY
42206 Auburn, KY

42206 South Union, KY
42207 Bee Spring, KY
42210 Brownsville, KY
42210 Huff, KY
42210 Lindseyville, KY
42210 Sunfish, KY
42211 Cadiz, KY
42211 Canton, KY
42211 Golden Pond, KY
42214 Center, KY
42215 Cerulean, KY
42216 Clifty, KY
42217 Crofton, KY
42219 Dunbar, KY
42220 Allegre, KY
42220 Elkton, KY
42221 Fairview, KY
42223 Fort Campbell, KY
42232 Gracey, KY
42234 Guthrie, KY
42234 Tiny Town, KY
42236 Herndon, KY
42240 Hopkinsville, KY
42241 Hopkinsville, KY
42252 Jetson, KY
42254 La Fayette, KY
42256 Lewisburg, KY
42256 Quality, KY
42259 Mammoth Cave, KY
42259 Mammoth Cave National Park, KY
42259 Ollie, KY
42261 Brooklyn, KY
42261 Huntsville, KY
42261 Logansport, KY
42261 Morgantown, KY
42261 Provo, KY
42261 Welchs Creek, KY
42262 Oak Grove, KY
42265 Olmstead, KY
42266 Pembroke, KY
42273 Rochester, KY
42274 Browning, KY
42274 Rockfield, KY
42275 Roundhill, KY
42276 Oakville, KY
42276 Russellville, KY
42280 Sharon Grove, KY
42285 Kyrock, KY
42285 Sweeden, KY
42286 Trenton, KY
42288 Woodbury, KY

423

42301 Owensboro, KY
42301 Saint Joseph, KY
42301 St Joseph, KY
42301 Stanley, KY
42302 Owensboro, KY
42303 Owensboro, KY
42304 Owensboro, KY
42320 Beaver Dam, KY
42321 Beech Creek, KY
42322 Beech Grove, KY
42323 Beechmont, KY
42324 Belton, KY
42325 Bremen, KY
42326 Browder, KY
42327 Calhoun, KY
42328 Centertown, KY
42330 Central City, KY
42330 Central Cty, KY
42332 Cleaton, KY
42333 Cromwell, KY
42334 Curdsville, KY
42337 Drakesboro, KY
42338 Dundee, KY
42339 Dunmor, KY
42339 Penrod, KY
42343 Fordsville, KY
42344 Graham, KY
42345 Greenville, KY
42347 Hartford, KY
42347 Narrows, KY
42348 Hawesville, KY
42349 Horse Branch, KY
42350 Island, KY
42351 Lewisport, KY
42352 Livermore, KY
42354 Mc Henry, KY
42355 Maceo, KY
42356 Maple Mount, KY
42361 Olaton, KY
42364 Hawesville, KY
42366 Knottsville, KY
42366 Philpot, KY
42367 Powderly, KY
42368 Reynolds Station, KY
42369 Rockport, KY
42370 Rosine, KY
42371 Rumsey, KY
42372 Sacramento, KY
42374 South Carrollton, KY
42376 Utica, KY
42377 West Louisville, KY
42378 Whitesville, KY

424

42402 Baskett, KY
42404 Blackford, KY
42404 Clay, KY
42406 Corydon, KY
42408 Dawson Springs, KY
42409 Dixon, KY
42410 Earlington, KY
42411 Fredonia, KY
42413 Hanson, KY
42419 Henderson, KY
42420 Henderson, KY
42431 Madisonville, KY
42436 Manitou, KY
42437 Henshaw, KY
42437 Morganfield, KY
42440 Mortons Gap, KY
42441 Nebo, KY
42442 Nortonville, KY
42444 Poole, KY
42445 Princeton, KY
42450 Providence, KY
42451 Reed, KY
42452 Robards, KY
42453 Saint Charles, KY
42455 Sebree, KY
42456 Slaughters, KY
42457 Smith Mills, KY
42458 Spottsville, KY
42459 Sturgis, KY
42460 Sullivan, KY
42461 Uniontown, KY
42462 Waverly, KY
42463 Wheatcroft, KY
42464 White Plains, KY

425

42501 Acorn, KY
42501 Alcalde, KY
42501 Elihu, KY
42501 Poplarville, KY
42501 Public, KY
42501 Ruth, KY
42501 Somerset, KY
42501 Stab, KY
42501 Walnut Grove, KY
42502 Somerset, KY
42503 Somerset, KY
42516 Bethelridge, KY
42518 Bronston, KY
42519 Burnside, KY
42519 Sloans Valley, KY
42528 Dunnville, KY
42533 Ferguson, KY
42539 Clementsville, KY
42539 Liberty, KY
42541 Middleburg, KY
42544 Cains Store, KY
42544 Faubush, KY
42544 Ingle, KY
42544 Jabez, KY
42544 Nancy, KY
42544 Naomi, KY
42544 Pointer, KY
42544 Trimble, KY
42553 Science Hill, KY
42558 Tateville, KY
42564 West Somerset, KY
42565 Windsor, KY
42566 Yosemite, KY
42567 Eubank, KY
42567 Pulaski, KY

426

42602 Aaron, KY
42602 Albany, KY
42602 Browns Crossroads, KY
42602 Highway, KY
42602 Seminary, KY
42602 Seventy Six, KY
42602 Snow, KY
42602 Static, KY
42603 Alpha, KY
42629 Bryan, KY
42629 Creelsboro, KY
42629 Jamestown, KY
42629 Rowena, KY
42629 Sewellton, KY
42631 Marshes Siding, KY
42633 Barrier, KY
42633 Bethesda, KY
42633 Betsey, KY
42633 Coopersville, KY
42633 Delta, KY
42633 Frazer, KY
42633 Frisby, KY
42633 Gregory, KY
42633 Mill Springs, KY
42633 Monticello, KY
42633 Mount Pisgah, KY
42633 Number One, KY
42633 Oil Valley, KY
42633 Parnell, KY
42633 Powersburg, KY
42633 Pueblo, KY
42633 Ritner, KY
42633 Rockybranch, KY
42633 Slat, KY
42633 Steubenville, KY
42633 Stop, KY
42633 Sunnybrook, KY
42633 Susie, KY
42633 Touristville, KY
42633 Windy, KY
42634 Greenwood, KY
42634 Honeybee, KY
42634 Parkers Lake, KY
42634 Sawyer, KY
42635 Pine Knot, KY
42638 Revelo, KY
42642 Russell Springs, KY
42642 Webbs Cross Roads, KY
42647 Stearns, KY
42649 Strunk, KY
42653 Whitley City, KY

427

42701 E Town, KY
42701 Elizabethtown, KY
42702 E Town, KY
42702 Elizabethtown, KY
42712 Big Clifty, KY
42713 Bonnieville, KY
42715 Breeding, KY
42716 Buffalo, KY
42717 Bakerton, KY
42717 Bow, KY
42717 Burkesville, KY
42717 Dubre, KY
42717 Kettle, KY
42717 Peytonsburg, KY
42717 Waterview, KY
42718 Campbellsville, KY
42718 Finley, KY
42719 Campbellsville, KY
42720 Cane Valley, KY
42721 Caneyville, KY
42721 Neafus, KY
42721 Spring Lick, KY
42722 Canmer, KY
42724 Cecilia, KY
42724 Stephensburg, KY
42724 Vertrees, KY
42726 Clarkson, KY
42726 Millerstown, KY
42726 Peonia, KY
42726 Rock Creek, KY
42726 Wax, KY
42728 Casey Creek, KY
42728 Columbia, KY
42728 Cundiff, KY
42728 Fairplay, KY
42728 Milltown, KY
42728 Montpelier, KY
42729 Cub Run, KY
42731 Dubre, KY
42732 Eastview, KY
42732 Meeting Creek, KY
42732 Summit, KY
42733 Elk Horn, KY
42740 Glendale, KY
42741 Glens Fork, KY
42742 Gradyville, KY
42743 Greensburg, KY
42746 Hardyville, KY
42748 Hodgenville, KY
42748 White City, KY
42749 Horse Cave, KY
42749 Park, KY
42753 Knifley, KY
42754 Leitchfield, KY
42755 Leitchfield, KY
42757 Magnolia, KY
42758 Mannsville, KY
42759 Marrowbone, KY
42762 Millwood, KY
42764 Mount Sherman, KY
42765 Munfordville, KY
42765 Rowletts, KY
42776 Sonora, KY
42782 Summersville, KY
42784 Upton, KY
42788 White Mills, KY

430

43001 Alexandria, OH
43002 Amlin, OH
43003 Ashley, OH
43004 Blacklick, OH
43005 Bladensburg, OH
43006 Brinkhaven, OH
43007 Broadway, OH
43008 Buckeye Lake, OH
43009 Cable, OH
43010 Catawba, OH
43011 Centerburg, OH
43013 Croton, OH
43014 Danville, OH
43015 Delaware, OH
43016 Dublin, OH
43017 Dublin, OH
43018 Etna, OH
43019 Fredericktown, OH
43021 Galena, OH
43022 Gambier, OH
43023 Granville, OH
43025 Hebron, OH
43026 Hilliard, OH
43027 Homer, OH
43028 Howard, OH
43029 Irwin, OH
43030 Jacksontown, OH
43031 Johnstown, OH
43032 Kilbourne, OH
43033 Kirkersville, OH
43035 Lewis Center, OH
43036 Magnetic Springs, OH
43037 Martinsburg, OH
43040 Marysville, OH
43041 Marysville, OH
43044 Mechanicsburg, OH
43045 Milford Center, OH
43046 Etna, OH
43046 Millersport, OH
43047 Mingo, OH
43048 Mount Liberty, OH
43050 Mount Vernon, OH
43054 New Albany, OH
43055 Hanover, OH
43055 Newark, OH
43056 Heath, OH
43056 Newark, OH
43058 Newark, OH
43060 North Lewisburg, OH
43061 Ostrander, OH
43062 Etna, OH
43062 Pataskala, OH
43064 Plain City, OH
43065 Powell, OH
43065 Shawnee Hills, OH
43066 Radnor, OH
43067 Raymond, OH
43068 Etna, OH
43068 Pataskala, OH
43068 Reynoldsburg, OH
43069 Reynoldsburg, OH
43070 Rosewood, OH
43071 Saint Louisville, OH
43071 St Louisville, OH
43072 Saint Paris, OH
43073 Pataskala, OH
43073 Summit Station, OH
43074 Sunbury, OH
43076 Thornville, OH
43077 Unionville Center, OH
43078 Urbana, OH
43080 Etna, OH
43080 Utica, OH
43081 Westerville, OH
43082 Westerville, OH
43083 Westville, OH
43084 Woodstock, OH
43085 Columbus, OH
43085 Worthington, OH
43086 Westerville, OH
43093 Newark, OH

431

43101 Adelphi, OH
43102 Amanda, OH
43103 Ashville, OH
43103 South Bloomfield, OH
43105 Baltimore, OH
43105 Etna, OH
43106 Bloomingburg, OH
43107 Bremen, OH
43107 Hideaway Hls, OH
43109 Brice, OH
43110 Canal Whchstr, OH
43110 Canal Winchester, OH
43111 Carbon Hill, OH
43112 Carroll, OH
43113 Circleville, OH
43115 Clarksburg, OH
43116 Commercial Point, OH
43117 Derby, OH
43119 Galloway, OH
43123 Darbydale, OH
43123 Grove City, OH
43123 Urbancrest, OH
43125 Groveport, OH
43126 Harrisburg, OH
43127 Haydenville, OH
43128 Jeffersonville, OH
43130 Lancaster, OH
43135 Laurelville, OH
43136 Lithopolis, OH
43137 Lockbourne, OH
43138 Logan, OH
43140 London, OH
43140 Summerford, OH
43142 Milledgeville, OH
43143 Mount Sterling, OH
43144 Murray City, OH
43145 New Holland, OH
43146 Darbyville, OH
43146 Orient, OH
43146 Pleasant Corners, OH
43147 Etna, OH
43147 Pickerington, OH
43148 Pleasantville, OH
43149 Rockbridge, OH
43150 Rushville, OH
43150 West Rushville, OH
43151 Sedalia, OH
43152 Laurelville, OH
43152 S Bloomingville, OH
43152 South Bloomingville, OH
43153 South Solon, OH
43154 Stoutsville, OH
43155 Sugar Grove, OH
43156 Laurelville, OH
43156 Tarlton, OH
43157 Thurston, OH
43158 Union Furnace, OH
43160 Washington Court House, OH
43162 West Jefferson, OH
43164 Williamsport, OH
43194 Lockbourne, OH
43195 Groveport, OH
43199 Groveport, OH

432

43201 Columbus, OH
43202 Columbus, OH
43203 Columbus, OH
43204 Columbus, OH
43205 Columbus, OH
43206 Columbus, OH
43207 Columbus, OH
43207 Obetz, OH
43209 Bexley, OH
43209 Columbus, OH
43210 Columbus, OH
43211 Columbus, OH
43212 Columbus, OH
43212 Grandview Heights, OH
43212 Marble Cliff, OH
43212 Upper Arlington, OH
43213 Columbus, OH
43213 Whitehall, OH
43214 Columbus, OH
43215 Columbus, OH
43216 Columbus, OH
43217 Columbus, OH
43218 Columbus, OH
43219 Columbus, OH
43220 Columbus, OH
43220 Upper Arlington, OH
43221 Columbus, OH
43221 Upper Arlington, OH
43222 Columbus, OH
43223 Columbus, OH
43224 Columbus, OH
43226 Columbus, OH
43227 Columbus, OH
43228 Columbus, OH
43228 New Rome, OH
43229 Columbus, OH
43230 Columbus, OH
43230 Gahanna, OH
43231 Columbus, OH
43232 Columbus, OH
43234 Columbus, OH
43235 Columbus, OH
43236 Columbus, OH
43240 Columbus, OH
43251 Columbus, OH
43260 Columbus, OH
43266 Columbus, OH
43268 Columbus, OH
43270 Columbus, OH
43271 Columbus, OH
43272 Columbus, OH
43279 Columbus, OH
43287 Columbus, OH
43291 Columbus, OH

433

43301 Marion, OH
43302 Marion, OH
43310 Belle Center, OH
43311 Bellefontaine, OH
43314 Caledonia, OH
43315 Cardington, OH
43316 Adrian, OH
43316 Carey, OH
43317 Chesterville, OH
43318 De Graff, OH
43319 East Liberty, OH
43320 Edison, OH

43321 Fulton, OH
43322 Green Camp, OH
43323 Harpster, OH
43324 Huntsville, OH
43325 Iberia, OH
43326 Kenton, OH
43330 Kirby, OH
43331 Lakeview, OH
43332 La Rue, OH
43333 Lewistown, OH
43334 Marengo, OH
43335 Martel, OH
43336 Middleburg, OH
43337 Morral, OH
43338 Mount Gilead, OH
43340 Mount Victory, OH
43341 New Bloomington, OH
43342 Prospect, OH
43343 Quincy, OH
43344 Richwood, OH
43345 Ridgeway, OH
43346 Roundhead, OH
43347 Rushsylvania, OH
43348 Russells Point, OH
43349 Shauck, OH
43350 Sparta, OH
43351 Upper Sandusky, OH
43356 Waldo, OH
43357 West Liberty, OH
43358 West Mansfield, OH
43359 Wharton, OH
43360 Zanesfield, OH

434

43402 Bowling Green, OH
43403 Bowling Green, OH
43406 Bradner, OH
43407 Burgoon, OH
43408 Clay Center, OH
43410 Clyde, OH
43412 Curtice, OH
43413 Cygnet, OH
43414 Dunbridge, OH
43416 Elmore, OH
43420 Fremont, OH
43430 Genoa, OH
43431 Gibsonburg, OH
43432 Elliston, OH
43432 Graytown, OH
43433 Gypsum, OH
43434 Harbor View, OH
43435 Helena, OH
43435 Millersville, OH
43436 Isle Saint George, OH
43437 Jerry City, OH
43438 Kelleys Island, OH
43439 Lacarne, OH
43440 Lakeside, OH
43440 Lakeside Marblehead, OH
43440 Marblehead, OH
43441 Lemoyne, OH
43442 Lindsey, OH
43443 Luckey, OH
43445 Bono, OH
43445 Martin, OH
43446 Middle Bass, OH
43447 Millbury, OH
43449 Oak Harbor, OH
43450 Pemberville, OH
43451 Portage, OH
43452 Port Clinton, OH
43456 Put In Bay, OH
43457 Risingsun, OH
43458 Rocky Ridge, OH
43460 Rossford, OH
43462 Rudolph, OH
43463 Stony Ridge, OH
43464 Vickery, OH
43465 Walbridge, OH
43466 Wayne, OH
43467 West Millgrove, OH
43468 Williston, OH
43469 Woodville, OH

435

43501 Alvordton, OH
43502 Archbold, OH
43504 Berkey, OH
43505 Blakeslee, OH
43506 Bryan, OH
43510 Colton, OH
43511 Custar, OH
43512 Defiance, OH
43515 Delta, OH
43516 Deshler, OH
43517 Edgerton, OH
43518 Edon, OH
43519 Evansport, OH
43519 Stryker, OH
43520 Farmer, OH
43521 Fayette, OH
43522 Grand Rapids, OH
43523 Grelton, OH
43523 Mc Clure, OH
43524 Hamler, OH
43525 Haskins, OH
43526 Hicksville, OH
43527 Holgate, OH
43528 Holland, OH
43529 Hoytville, OH
43530 Jewell, OH
43531 Kunkle, OH
43532 Liberty Center, OH
43533 Lyons, OH
43534 Grelton, OH
43534 Mc Clure, OH
43535 Malinta, OH
43536 Mark Center, OH
43537 Maumee, OH
43540 Metamora, OH
43541 Milton Center, OH
43542 Monclova, OH
43543 Holiday City, OH
43543 Montpelier, OH
43545 Florida, OH
43545 Napoleon, OH
43545 Okolona, OH
43547 Neapolis, OH
43548 New Bavaria, OH
43549 Ney, OH
43550 Napoleon, OH
43550 Okolona, OH
43551 Perrysburg, OH
43552 Perrysburg, OH
43553 Pettisville, OH
43554 Holiday City, OH
43554 Pioneer, OH
43555 Ridgeville Corners, OH
43556 Sherwood, OH
43557 Evansport, OH
43557 Stryker, OH
43558 Swanton, OH
43560 Sylvania, OH
43565 Tontogany, OH
43566 Waterville, OH
43567 Wauseon, OH
43569 Weston, OH
43570 Archbold, OH
43570 West Unity, OH
43571 Whitehouse, OH

436

43601 Toledo, OH
43603 Toledo, OH
43604 Toledo, OH
43605 Northwood, OH
43605 Oregon, OH
43605 Toledo, OH
43606 Ottawa Hills, OH
43606 Toledo, OH
43607 Toledo, OH
43608 Toledo, OH
43609 Toledo, OH
43610 Toledo, OH
43611 Toledo, OH
43612 Toledo, OH
43613 Toledo, OH
43614 Toledo, OH
43615 Ottawa Hills, OH
43615 Sylvania Township, OH
43615 Toledo, OH
43616 Oregon, OH
43617 Sylvania Township, OH
43617 Toledo, OH
43619 Northwood, OH
43620 Toledo, OH
43623 Sylvania Township, OH
43623 Toledo, OH
43635 Toledo, OH
43652 Toledo, OH
43654 Toledo, OH
43656 Toledo, OH
43657 Toledo, OH
43659 Toledo, OH
43660 Toledo, OH
43661 Toledo, OH
43666 Toledo, OH
43667 Toledo, OH
43681 Toledo, OH
43682 Toledo, OH
43697 Toledo, OH
43699 Toledo, OH

437

43701 Sonora, OH
43701 South Zanesville, OH
43701 Zanesville, OH
43702 South Zanesville, OH
43702 Zanesville, OH
43711 Ava, OH
43713 Barnesville, OH
43713 Somerton, OH
43716 Beallsville, OH
43717 Belle Valley, OH
43718 Belmont, OH
43719 Bethesda, OH
43720 Blue Rock, OH
43721 Brownsville, OH
43722 Buffalo, OH
43723 Byesville, OH
43724 Caldwell, OH
43725 Cambridge, OH
43725 Claysville, OH
43727 Chandlersville, OH
43728 Chesterhill, OH
43730 Corning, OH
43730 Hemlock, OH
43730 Rendville, OH
43731 Crooksville, OH
43732 Cumberland, OH
43733 Derwent, OH
43734 Duncan Falls, OH
43735 East Fultonham, OH
43736 Fairview, OH
43736 Quaker City, OH
43738 Fultonham, OH
43739 Glenford, OH
43740 Gratiot, OH
43746 Hopewell, OH
43747 Jerusalem, OH
43748 Junction City, OH
43749 Guernsey, OH
43749 Kimbolton, OH
43750 Cambridge, OH
43750 Kipling, OH
43752 Laings, OH
43754 Lewisville, OH
43754 Sycamore Valley, OH
43755 Lore City, OH
43756 Mcconnelsville, OH
43757 Malaga, OH
43758 Malta, OH
43759 Morristown, OH
43760 Mount Perry, OH
43761 Moxahala, OH
43762 New Concord, OH
43764 New Lexington, OH
43766 New Straitsville, OH
43767 Norwich, OH
43768 Old Washington, OH
43771 Philo, OH
43772 Pleasant City, OH
43773 Quaker City, OH
43777 Roseville, OH
43778 Salesville, OH
43779 Sarahsville, OH
43780 Senecaville, OH
43782 Shawnee, OH
43783 Somerset, OH
43786 Stafford, OH
43787 Pennsville, OH
43787 Stockport, OH
43788 Summerfield, OH
43791 White Cottage, OH
43793 Antioch, OH
43793 Woodsfield, OH

438

43802 Adamsville, OH
43803 Bakersville, OH
43804 Baltic, OH
43804 Bucks, OH
43804 Farmerstown, OH
43804 Mechanic, OH
43805 Blissfield, OH
43811 Conesville, OH
43812 Coshocton, OH
43821 Adams Mills, OH
43821 Dresden, OH
43822 Frazeysburg, OH
43824 Fresno, OH
43824 New Bedford, OH
43828 Keene, OH
43830 Nashport, OH
43832 Newcomerstown, OH
43836 Plainfield, OH
43837 Port Washington, OH
43840 Stone Creek, OH
43842 Trinway, OH
43843 Walhonding, OH
43844 Warsaw, OH
43845 West Lafayette, OH

439

43901 Adena, OH
43902 Alledonia, OH
43903 Amsterdam, OH
43905 Barton, OH
43906 Bellaire, OH
43907 Cadiz, OH
43908 Bergholz, OH
43909 Blaine, OH
43910 Bloomingdale, OH
43910 Unionport, OH
43912 Bridgeport, OH
43913 Brilliant, OH
43914 Cameron, OH
43915 Clarington, OH
43916 Colerain, OH
43917 Dillonvale, OH
43920 Calcutta, OH
43920 East Liverpool, OH
43925 East Springfield, OH
43926 Empire, OH
43927 Fairpoint, OH
43928 Glencoe, OH
43930 Hammondsville, OH
43931 Hannibal, OH
43932 Irondale, OH
43933 Armstrong Mills, OH
43933 Jacobsburg, OH
43933 Stewartsville, OH
43934 Lansing, OH
43935 Martins Ferry, OH
43937 Maynard, OH
43938 Mingo Junction, OH
43939 Mount Pleasant, OH
43940 Neffs, OH
43941 Piney Fork, OH
43942 Powhatan Point, OH
43943 Rayland, OH
43944 Richmond, OH
43945 Salineville, OH
43946 Sardis, OH
43947 Shadyside, OH
43948 Smithfield, OH
43950 Saint Clairsville, OH
43951 Lafferty, OH
43952 Steubenville, OH
43952 Wintersville, OH
43953 Steubenville, OH
43953 Wintersville, OH
43961 Stratton, OH
43962 Summitville, OH
43963 Tiltonsville, OH
43964 Toronto, OH
43967 Warnock, OH
43968 Wellsville, OH
43970 Wolf Run, OH
43971 Yorkville, OH
43972 Bannock, OH
43973 Freeport, OH
43974 Harrisville, OH
43976 Hopedale, OH
43977 Flushing, OH
43981 New Athens, OH
43983 Piedmont, OH
43984 New Rumley, OH
43985 Holloway, OH
43986 Jewett, OH
43988 Scio, OH

440

44001 Amherst, OH
44001 South Amherst, OH
44001 Vermilion, OH
44003 Andover, OH
44004 Ashtabula, OH
44005 Ashtabula, OH
44010 Austinburg, OH
44011 Avon, OH
44012 Avon Lake, OH
44017 Berea, OH
44021 Burton, OH
44022 Bentleyville, OH
44022 Chagrin Falls, OH
44022 Moreland Hills, OH
44023 Auburn Township, OH
44023 Chagrin Falls, OH
44024 Chardon, OH
44024 Concord Township, OH
44026 Chesterland, OH
44028 Columbia Station, OH
44030 Conneaut, OH
44032 Dorset, OH
44033 East Claridon, OH
44035 Elyria, OH
44035 North Ridgeville, OH
44035 Sheffield Village, OH
44036 Elyria, OH
44039 Elyria, OH
44039 North Ridgeville, OH
44040 Gates Mills, OH
44041 Geneva, OH
44044 Grafton, OH
44045 Grand River, OH
44046 Huntsburg, OH
44047 Jefferson, OH
44047 New Lyme, OH
44048 Kingsville, OH
44049 Kipton, OH
44050 Lagrange, OH
44052 Lorain, OH
44053 Lorain, OH
44054 Lorain, OH
44054 Sheffield Lake, OH
44054 Sheffield Village, OH
44055 Lorain, OH
44056 Macedonia, OH
44056 Northfield, OH
44057 Madison, OH
44060 Mentor, OH
44060 Mentor On The Lake, OH
44061 Mentor, OH
44062 Middlefield, OH
44064 Montville, OH
44065 Newbury, OH
44067 Macedonia, OH
44067 Northfield, OH
44067 Sagamore Hills, OH
44068 North Kingsville, OH
44070 North Olmsted, OH
44072 Novelty, OH
44072 Russell, OH
44073 Novelty, OH
44074 Elyria, OH
44074 Oberlin, OH
44076 East Orwell, OH
44076 Orwell, OH
44077 Concord Township, OH
44077 Fairport Harbor, OH
44077 Painesville, OH
44080 Parkman, OH
44081 Perry, OH
44082 Pierpont, OH
44084 Roaming Shores, OH
44084 Rock Creek, OH
44085 Roaming Shores, OH
44085 Rome, OH
44086 Thompson, OH
44087 Twinsburg, OH
44088 Unionville, OH
44089 Vermilion, OH
44090 Rochester, OH
44090 Wellington, OH
44092 Wickliffe, OH
44092 Willoughby Hills, OH
44093 Williamsfield, OH
44094 Kirtland, OH
44094 Waite Hill, OH
44094 Willoughby, OH
44094 Willoughby Hills, OH
44095 Eastlake, OH
44095 Lakeline, OH
44095 Timberlake, OH
44095 Willoughby, OH
44095 Willowick, OH
44096 Willoughby, OH
44097 Eastlake, OH
44097 Willoughby, OH
44099 Windsor, OH

441

44101 Cleveland, OH
44102 Cleveland, OH
44103 Cleveland, OH
44104 Cleveland, OH
44105 Cleveland, OH
44105 Garfield Heights, OH
44105 Newburgh Heights, OH
44106 Cleveland, OH
44106 Cleveland Heights, OH
44107 Cleveland, OH
44107 Edgewater, OH
44107 Lakewood, OH
44108 Bratenahl, OH
44108 Cleveland, OH
44109 Cleveland, OH
44110 Cleveland, OH
44110 East Cleveland, OH
44111 Cleveland, OH
44112 Cleveland, OH
44112 Cleveland Heights, OH
44112 East Cleveland, OH
44113 Cleveland, OH
44114 Cleveland, OH
44115 Cleveland, OH
44116 Cleveland, OH
44116 Rocky River, OH
44117 Cleveland, OH
44117 Euclid, OH
44118 Cleveland, OH
44118 Cleveland Heights, OH
44118 East Cleveland, OH
44118 Shaker Heights, OH
44118 South Euclid, OH
44118 University Heights, OH
44118 University Hts, OH
44119 Cleveland, OH
44119 Euclid, OH
44120 Cleveland, OH
44120 Shaker Heights, OH
44121 Cleveland, OH
44121 Cleveland Heights, OH
44121 South Euclid, OH
44122 Beachwood, OH
44122 Cleveland, OH
44122 Highland Hills, OH
44122 Shaker Heights, OH
44122 University Heights, OH
44122 Warrensville Heights, OH
44122 Woodmere, OH
44123 Cleveland, OH
44123 Euclid, OH
44124 Cleveland, OH
44124 Lyndhurst, OH
44124 Mayfield Heights, OH
44124 Pepper Pike, OH
44125 Cleveland, OH

44125 Garfield Heights, OH
44125 Valley View, OH
44126 Cleveland, OH
44126 Fairview Park, OH
44127 Cleveland, OH
44127 Cuyahoga Heights, OH
44127 Newburgh Heights, OH
44128 Bedford Heights, OH
44128 Cleveland, OH
44128 Garfield Heights, OH
44128 Highland Hills, OH
44128 North Randall, OH
44128 Warrensville Heights, OH
44129 Cleveland, OH
44129 Parma, OH
44130 Cleveland, OH
44130 Middleburg Heights, OH
44130 Parma, OH
44130 Parma Heights, OH
44131 Brooklyn Heights, OH
44131 Cleveland, OH
44131 Independence, OH
44131 Parma, OH
44131 Seven Hills, OH
44132 Cleveland, OH
44132 Euclid, OH
44133 Cleveland, OH
44133 North Royalton, OH
44134 Cleveland, OH
44134 Parma, OH
44135 Cleveland, OH
44136 Cleveland, OH
44136 Strongsville, OH
44137 Cleveland, OH
44137 Maple Heights, OH
44138 Cleveland, OH
44138 Olmsted Falls, OH
44138 Olmsted Twp, OH
44139 Cleveland, OH
44139 Solon, OH
44140 Bay Village, OH
44140 Cleveland, OH
44141 Brecksville, OH
44141 Cleveland, OH
44142 Brook Park, OH
44142 Brookpark, OH
44142 Cleveland, OH
44143 Cleveland, OH
44143 Euclid, OH
44143 Highland Heights, OH
44143 Highland Hts, OH
44143 Mayfield, OH
44143 Mayfield Heights, OH
44143 Mayfield Village, OH
44143 Richmond Heights, OH
44144 Brooklyn, OH
44144 Cleveland, OH
44145 Cleveland, OH
44145 Westlake, OH
44146 Bedford, OH
44146 Bedford Heights, OH
44146 Cleveland, OH
44146 Oakwood Village, OH
44146 Walton Hills, OH
44147 Broadview Heights, OH
44147 Cleveland, OH
44149 Strongsville, OH
44181 Cleveland, OH
44188 Cleveland, OH
44190 Cleveland, OH
44191 Cleveland, OH
44192 Cleveland, OH
44193 Cleveland, OH
44194 Cleveland, OH
44195 Cleveland, OH
44197 Cleveland, OH
44198 Cleveland, OH
44199 Cleveland, OH

442

44201 Atwater, OH
44202 Aurora, OH
44202 Reminderville, OH
44203 Barberton, OH
44203 New Franklin, OH
44203 Norton, OH
44210 Bath, OH
44211 Brady Lake, OH
44212 Brunswick, OH
44214 Burbank, OH
44215 Chippewa Lake, OH
44215 Medina, OH
44216 Clinton, OH
44216 New Franklin, OH
44217 Creston, OH
44221 Cuyahoga Falls, OH
44224 Hudson, OH
44224 Silver Lake, OH
44224 Stow, OH
44230 Doylestown, OH
44231 Garrettsville, OH
44232 Green, OH
44233 Hinckley, OH
44234 Hiram, OH
44235 Homerville, OH
44236 Hudson, OH
44237 Hudson, OH
44240 Kent, OH
44241 Streetsboro, OH
44242 Kent, OH
44243 Kent, OH
44250 Lakemore, OH
44251 Westfield Center, OH
44251 Westfield Ctr, OH
44253 Litchfield, OH
44254 Lodi, OH
44255 Mantua, OH
44256 Medina, OH
44258 Medina, OH
44260 Mogadore, OH
44262 Munroe Falls, OH
44264 Peninsula, OH
44265 Randolph, OH
44266 Ravenna, OH
44270 Rittman, OH
44272 Rootstown, OH
44273 Seville, OH
44274 Sharon Center, OH
44275 Spencer, OH
44276 Sterling, OH
44278 Tallmadge, OH
44280 Valley City, OH
44281 Wadsworth, OH
44282 Wadsworth, OH
44285 Wayland, OH
44286 Richfield, OH
44287 Congress, OH
44287 West Salem, OH
44288 Windham, OH

443

44301 Akron, OH
44302 Akron, OH
44303 Akron, OH
44304 Akron, OH
44305 Akron, OH
44306 Akron, OH
44307 Akron, OH
44308 Akron, OH
44309 Akron, OH
44310 Akron, OH
44311 Akron, OH
44312 Akron, OH
44313 Akron, OH
44314 Akron, OH
44315 Akron, OH
44316 Akron, OH
44317 Akron, OH
44319 Akron, OH
44319 New Franklin, OH
44320 Akron, OH
44321 Akron, OH
44321 Copley, OH
44325 Akron, OH
44326 Akron, OH
44328 Akron, OH
44333 Akron, OH
44333 Fairlawn, OH
44334 Akron, OH
44334 Fairlawn, OH
44372 Akron, OH
44396 Akron, OH
44398 Akron, OH
44398 Fairlawn, OH

444

44401 Berlin Center, OH
44402 Bristolville, OH
44403 Brookfield, OH
44404 Burghill, OH
44405 Campbell, OH
44406 Canfield, OH
44408 Columbiana, OH
44410 Cortland, OH
44411 Deerfield, OH
44412 Diamond, OH
44413 East Palestine, OH
44415 Elkton, OH
44416 Ellsworth, OH
44417 Farmdale, OH
44418 Fowler, OH
44420 Girard, OH
44422 Greenford, OH
44423 Hanoverton, OH
44424 Hartford, OH
44425 Hubbard, OH
44427 Kensington, OH
44428 Kinsman, OH
44429 Lake Milton, OH
44430 Leavittsburg, OH
44431 Leetonia, OH
44432 Lisbon, OH
44436 Lowellville, OH
44437 Mc Donald, OH
44438 Masury, OH
44439 Mesopotamia, OH
44440 Mineral Ridge, OH
44441 Negley, OH
44442 New Middletown, OH
44443 New Springfield, OH
44444 Newton Falls, OH
44445 New Waterford, OH
44446 Niles, OH
44449 North Benton, OH
44450 North Bloomfield, OH
44451 North Jackson, OH
44452 North Lima, OH
44453 Orangeville, OH
44454 Petersburg, OH
44455 Rogers, OH
44460 Salem, OH
44470 Southington, OH
44471 Struthers, OH
44473 Vienna, OH
44481 Warren, OH
44482 Warren, OH
44483 Warren, OH
44484 Warren, OH
44485 Warren, OH
44486 Warren, OH
44488 Warren, OH
44490 Washingtonville, OH
44491 West Farmington, OH
44492 West Point, OH
44493 Winona, OH

445

44501 Youngstown, OH
44502 Youngstown, OH
44503 Youngstown, OH
44504 Youngstown, OH
44505 Youngstown, OH
44506 Youngstown, OH
44507 Youngstown, OH
44509 Youngstown, OH
44510 Youngstown, OH
44511 Youngstown, OH
44512 Boardman, OH
44512 Youngstown, OH
44513 Boardman, OH
44513 Youngstown, OH
44514 Poland, OH
44514 Youngstown, OH
44515 Austintown, OH
44515 Youngstown, OH
44555 Youngstown, OH

446

44601 Alliance, OH
44606 Apple Creek, OH
44607 Augusta, OH
44608 Beach City, OH
44609 Beloit, OH
44610 Berlin, OH
44611 Big Prairie, OH
44612 Bolivar, OH
44613 Brewster, OH
44614 Canal Fulton, OH
44614 New Franklin, OH
44615 Carrollton, OH
44615 Harlem Springs, OH
44617 Charm, OH
44618 Dalton, OH
44619 Damascus, OH
44620 Dellroy, OH
44621 Dennison, OH
44622 Dover, OH
44624 Dundee, OH
44625 East Rochester, OH
44626 East Sparta, OH
44627 Fredericksburg, OH
44628 Glenmont, OH
44629 Gnadenhutten, OH
44630 Greentown, OH
44632 Hartville, OH
44633 Holmesville, OH
44634 Homeworth, OH
44636 Kidron, OH
44637 Killbuck, OH
44638 Lakeville, OH
44639 Leesville, OH
44640 Limaville, OH
44641 Louisville, OH
44643 Magnolia, OH
44644 Malvern, OH
44645 Marshallville, OH
44646 Massillon, OH
44647 Massillon, OH
44648 Massillon, OH
44650 Maximo, OH
44651 Mechanicstown, OH
44652 Middlebranch, OH
44653 Midvale, OH
44654 Millersburg, OH
44656 Mineral City, OH
44656 Zoarville, OH
44657 Minerva, OH
44659 Mount Eaton, OH
44660 Mount Hope, OH
44661 Nashville, OH
44662 Navarre, OH
44663 New Philadelphia, OH
44665 North Georgetown, OH
44666 North Lawrence, OH
44667 Orrville, OH
44669 Paris, OH
44670 Robertsville, OH
44671 Sandyville, OH
44672 Sebring, OH
44675 Sherrodsville, OH
44676 Shreve, OH
44677 Smithville, OH
44678 Somerdale, OH
44679 Stillwater, OH
44680 Strasburg, OH
44681 Sugarcreek, OH
44682 Tuscarawas, OH
44683 Uhrichsville, OH
44685 Uniontown, OH
44687 Walnut Creek, OH
44688 Waynesburg, OH
44689 Wilmot, OH
44690 Winesburg, OH
44691 Wooster, OH
44693 Deersville, OH
44695 Bowerston, OH
44697 Zoar, OH
44699 Tippecanoe, OH

447

44701 Canton, OH
44702 Canton, OH
44703 Canton, OH
44704 Canton, OH
44705 Canton, OH
44706 Canton, OH
44707 Canton, OH
44707 North Industry, OH
44708 Canton, OH
44709 Canton, OH
44709 North Canton, OH
44710 Canton, OH
44711 Canton, OH
44714 Canton, OH
44718 Canton, OH
44718 Jackson Belden, OH
44720 Canton, OH
44720 North Canton, OH
44721 Canton, OH
44721 N Canton, OH
44730 Canton, OH
44730 East Canton, OH
44735 Canton, OH
44750 Canton, OH
44767 Canton, OH
44799 Canton, OH
44799 North Canton, OH

448

44802 Alvada, OH
44804 Arcadia, OH
44805 Ashland, OH
44807 Attica, OH
44807 Carrothers, OH
44809 Bascom, OH
44811 Bellevue, OH
44813 Bellville, OH
44814 Berlin Heights, OH
44815 Bettsville, OH
44816 Birmingham, OH
44817 Bloomdale, OH
44818 Bloomville, OH
44820 Bucyrus, OH
44822 Butler, OH
44824 Castalia, OH
44825 Chatfield, OH
44826 Collins, OH
44827 Crestline, OH
44827 North Robinson, OH
44828 Flat Rock, OH
44830 Amsden, OH
44830 Fostoria, OH
44833 Galion, OH
44836 Green Springs, OH
44837 Greenwich, OH
44838 Hayesville, OH
44839 Huron, OH
44839 Shinrock, OH
44840 Jeromesville, OH
44841 Kansas, OH
44842 Loudonville, OH
44843 Lucas, OH
44844 Mc Cutchenville, OH
44845 Melmore, OH
44846 Milan, OH
44847 Monroeville, OH
44848 Nankin, OH
44849 Nevada, OH
44850 New Haven, OH
44851 New London, OH
44853 New Riegel, OH
44854 New Washington, OH
44855 North Fairfield, OH
44856 North Robinson, OH
44857 Norwalk, OH
44859 Nova, OH
44860 Oceola, OH
44861 Old Fort, OH
44862 Ontario, OH
44864 Perrysville, OH
44865 Plymouth, OH
44866 Polk, OH
44867 Republic, OH
44870 Sandusky, OH
44871 Sandusky, OH
44874 Savannah, OH
44875 Shelby, OH
44878 Shiloh, OH
44880 Sullivan, OH
44881 Sulphur Springs, OH
44882 Sycamore, OH
44883 Fort Seneca, OH
44883 Tiffin, OH
44887 Tiro, OH
44888 Willard, OH
44889 Wakeman, OH
44890 Willard, OH

449

44901 Mansfield, OH
44902 Mansfield, OH
44903 Mansfield, OH
44903 Ontario, OH
44904 Lexington, OH
44904 Mansfield, OH
44905 Mansfield, OH
44906 Mansfield, OH
44906 Ontario, OH
44907 Mansfield, OH

450

45001 Addyston, OH
45002 Cleves, OH
45003 College Corner, OH
45004 Collinsville, OH
45005 Carlisle, OH
45005 Franklin, OH
45005 Middletown, OH
45011 Fairfield, OH
45011 Hamilton, OH
45011 Liberty Township, OH
45011 Village Of Indian Springs, OH
45011 West Chester, OH
45012 Hamilton, OH
45013 Hamilton, OH
45013 Rossville, OH
45013 Village Of Indian Springs, OH
45014 Fairfield, OH
45014 Hamilton, OH
45014 Village Of Indian Springs, OH
45014 West Chester, OH
45015 Hamilton, OH
45015 Lindenwald, OH
45015 Village Of Indian Springs, OH
45018 Fairfield, OH
45018 Hamilton, OH
45030 Harrison, OH
45032 Harveysburg, OH
45033 Hooven, OH
45034 Kings Island, OH
45034 Kings Mills, OH
45036 Lebanon, OH
45039 Hamilton Township, OH
45039 Maineville, OH
45040 Mason, OH
45041 Miamitown, OH
45042 Middletown, OH
45044 Liberty Township, OH
45044 Middletown, OH
45044 Monroe, OH
45050 Liberty Tnsp, OH
45050 Liberty Township, OH
45050 Liberty Twnship, OH
45050 Monroe, OH
45051 Mount Saint Joseph, OH
45052 North Bend, OH
45053 Okeana, OH
45054 Oregonia, OH
45055 Overpeck, OH
45056 Oxford, OH
45061 Ross, OH
45062 Seven Mile, OH
45063 Shandon, OH
45064 Somerville, OH
45065 South Lebanon, OH
45066 Springboro, OH
45067 Trenton, OH
45068 Waynesville, OH
45069 Liberty Township, OH
45069 Liberty Townshp, OH
45069 West Chester, OH
45070 West Elkton, OH
45071 West Chester, OH

451

45101 Aberdeen, OH
45102 Amelia, OH

45103 Batavia, OH
45105 Bentonville, OH
45106 Bethel, OH
45107 Blanchester, OH
45111 Camp Dennison, OH
45111 Loveland, OH
45112 Chilo, OH
45113 Clarksville, OH
45114 Cuba, OH
45115 Decatur, OH
45118 Fayetteville, OH
45118 Marathon, OH
45119 Feesburg, OH
45120 Felicity, OH
45121 Brown County, OH
45121 Clermont County, OH
45121 Georgetown, OH
45122 Goshen, OH
45123 Greenfield, OH
45123 Ross County, OH
45130 Hamersville, OH
45130 Poetown, OH
45131 Higginsport, OH
45132 Highland, OH
45133 Hillsboro, OH
45135 Fayette County, OH
45135 Highland County, OH
45135 Leesburg, OH
45140 Loveland, OH
45140 Montgomery, OH
45140 Symmes Twp, OH
45142 Lynchburg, OH
45144 Adams County, OH
45144 Manchester, OH
45146 Martinsville, OH
45147 Miamiville, OH
45148 Midland, OH
45150 Day Heights, OH
45150 Milford, OH
45152 Morrow, OH
45153 Moscow, OH
45153 Point Pleasant, OH
45154 Mount Orab, OH
45155 Mowrystown, OH
45156 Neville, OH
45157 New Richmond, OH
45158 Newtonsville, OH
45159 New Vienna, OH
45160 Owensville, OH
45162 Pleasant Plain, OH
45164 Port William, OH
45166 Reesville, OH
45167 Ripley, OH
45168 Russellville, OH
45169 Clinton County, OH
45169 Lees Creek, OH
45169 Sabina, OH
45171 Buford, OH
45171 Lake Waynoka, OH
45171 Sardinia, OH
45172 Sinking Spring, OH
45174 Terrace Park, OH
45176 Williamsburg, OH
45177 Wilmington, OH

452

45201 Cincinnati, OH
45202 Cincinnati, OH
45203 Cincinnati, OH
45203 Queen City, OH
45204 Cincinnati, OH
45204 Queen City, OH
45205 Cincinnati, OH
45206 Cincinnati, OH
45206 Walnut Hills, OH
45207 Cincinnati, OH
45208 Cincinnati, OH
45209 Cincinnati, OH
45211 Cheviot, OH
45211 Cincinnati, OH
45212 Cincinnati, OH
45212 Norwood, OH
45213 Cincinnati, OH
45213 Taft, OH
45214 Cincinnati, OH
45214 Queen City, OH
45215 Arlington Heights, OH
45215 Cincinnati, OH
45215 Lockland, OH
45215 Reading, OH
45215 Wyoming, OH
45216 Cincinnati, OH
45216 Elmwood Pl, OH
45216 Elmwood Place, OH
45216 Saint Bernard, OH
45217 Cincinnati, OH
45217 Saint Bernard, OH
45218 Cincinnati, OH
45218 Parkdale, OH
45219 Cincinnati, OH
45220 Cincinnati, OH
45221 Cincinnati, OH
45222 Cincinnati, OH
45222 Roselawn, OH
45223 Cincinnati, OH
45224 Cincinnati, OH
45224 College Hl, OH
45224 North College Hill, OH
45225 Cincinnati, OH
45226 Cincinnati, OH
45227 Cincinnati, OH
45229 Avondale, OH
45229 Cincinnati, OH
45230 Anderson Township, OH
45230 Cincinnati, OH
45230 Mount Washington, OH
45231 Cincinnati, OH
45231 Mount Healthy, OH
45231 Wyoming, OH
45232 Cincinnati, OH
45232 Saint Bernard, OH
45233 Cincinnati, OH
45233 Sayler Park, OH
45234 Cincinnati, OH
45235 Cincinnati, OH
45236 Blue Ash, OH
45236 Cincinnati, OH
45236 Deer Park, OH
45236 Reading, OH
45236 Silverton, OH
45236 Taft, OH
45237 Amberley, OH
45237 Cincinnati, OH
45238 Cincinnati, OH
45239 Cincinnati, OH
45239 Colerain Township, OH
45239 Groesbeck, OH
45239 North College Hill, OH
45240 Cincinnati, OH
45240 Parkdale, OH
45241 Blue Ash, OH
45241 Cincinnati, OH
45241 Sharonville, OH
45241 West Chester, OH
45242 Blue Ash, OH
45242 Cincinnati, OH
45242 Montgomery, OH
45243 Cincinnati, OH
45243 Columbia Township, OH
45243 Madeira, OH
45244 Anderson, OH
45244 Cincinnati, OH
45244 Newtown, OH
45245 Cincinnati, OH
45246 Cincinnati, OH
45246 Glendale, OH
45246 Parkdale, OH
45246 Springdale, OH
45246 West Chester, OH
45247 Cincinnati, OH
45247 Colerain Township, OH
45247 Groesbeck, OH
45248 Cincinnati, OH
45248 Westwood, OH
45249 Cincinnati, OH
45249 Montgomery, OH
45249 Symmes, OH
45249 Symmes Twp, OH
45250 Cincinnati, OH
45251 Cincinnati, OH
45251 Colerain Township, OH
45251 Groesbeck, OH
45252 Cincinnati, OH
45252 Colerain Township, OH
45253 Cincinnati, OH
45253 Groesbeck, OH
45254 Anderson, OH
45254 Cincinnati, OH
45255 Anderson, OH
45255 Cincinnati, OH
45258 Cincinnati, OH
45262 Cincinnati, OH
45263 Cincinnati, OH
45264 Cincinnati, OH
45267 Cincinnati, OH
45268 Cincinnati, OH
45269 Cincinnati, OH
45270 Cincinnati, OH
45271 Cincinnati, OH
45273 Cincinnati, OH
45274 Cincinnati, OH
45275 Cincinnati, OH
45277 Cincinnati, OH
45280 Cincinnati, OH
45296 Cincinnati, OH
45298 Cincinnati, OH
45299 Cincinnati, OH

453

45301 Alpha, OH
45302 Anna, OH
45303 Ansonia, OH
45304 Arcanum, OH
45304 Castine, OH
45304 Gordon, OH
45304 Ithaca, OH
45305 Beavercreek, OH
45305 Beavercreek Township, OH
45305 Bellbrook, OH
45305 Sugarcreek Township, OH
45306 Botkins, OH
45307 Bowersville, OH
45308 Bradford, OH
45309 Brookville, OH
45310 Burkettsville, OH
45311 Camden, OH
45312 Casstown, OH
45314 Cedarville, OH
45315 Clayton, OH
45316 Clifton, OH
45317 Conover, OH
45318 Covington, OH
45319 Donnelsville, OH
45320 Eaton, OH
45321 Eldorado, OH
45322 Englewood, OH
45322 Union, OH
45323 Enon, OH
45324 Beavercreek, OH
45324 Beavercreek Township, OH
45324 Fairborn, OH
45325 Farmersville, OH
45325 Germantown, OH
45326 Fletcher, OH
45327 Germantown, OH
45328 Gettysburg, OH
45330 Gratis, OH
45331 Greenville, OH
45332 Hollansburg, OH
45333 Houston, OH
45334 Jackson Center, OH
45335 Jamestown, OH
45336 Kettlersville, OH
45337 Laura, OH
45337 Potsdm, OH
45338 Lewisburg, OH
45339 Ludlow Falls, OH
45340 Maplewood, OH
45341 Medway, OH
45342 Miamisburg, OH
45343 Miamisburg, OH
45344 New Carlisle, OH
45345 New Lebanon, OH
45346 New Madison, OH
45347 New Paris, OH
45348 New Weston, OH
45348 Rossburg, OH
45349 North Hampton, OH
45350 North Star, OH
45351 Osgood, OH
45352 Palestine, OH
45353 Pemberton, OH
45354 Phillipsburg, OH
45356 Piqua, OH
45358 Pitsburg, OH
45359 Pleasant Hill, OH
45360 Port Jefferson, OH
45361 Potsdam, OH
45362 Rossburg, OH
45363 Russia, OH
45365 Sidney, OH
45367 Sidney, OH
45368 South Charleston, OH
45369 South Vienna, OH
45370 Spring Valley, OH
45370 Sugarcreek Township, OH
45371 Phoneton, OH
45371 Tipp City, OH
45372 Tremont City, OH
45373 Troy, OH
45374 Troy, OH
45377 Vandalia, OH
45378 Verona, OH
45380 Versailles, OH
45381 West Alexandria, OH
45382 West Manchester, OH
45383 West Milton, OH
45384 Wilberforce, OH
45385 Beavercreek Township, OH
45385 Sugarcreek Township, OH
45385 Xenia, OH
45387 Yellow Springs, OH
45388 Yorkshire, OH
45389 Christiansburg, OH
45390 Dayton, OH
45390 Union City, OH

454

45401 Dayton, OH
45402 Dayton, OH
45403 Dayton, OH
45404 Dayton, OH
45405 Dayton, OH
45406 Dayton, OH
45406 Trotwood, OH
45409 Dayton, OH
45409 Kettering, OH
45409 Moraine, OH
45409 Oakwood, OH
45410 Dayton, OH
45412 Dayton, OH
45413 Dayton, OH
45414 Dayton, OH
45415 Dayton, OH
45416 Dayton, OH
45416 Trotwood, OH
45417 Dayton, OH
45419 Dayton, OH
45419 Kettering, OH
45419 Oakwood, OH
45420 Dayton, OH
45420 Kettering, OH
45422 Dayton, OH
45423 Dayton, OH
45424 Dayton, OH
45424 Huber Heights, OH
45426 Dayton, OH
45426 Trotwood, OH
45428 Dayton, OH
45429 Centerville, OH
45429 Dayton, OH
45429 Kettering, OH
45430 Beavercreek, OH
45430 Beavercreek Township, OH
45430 Dayton, OH
45430 Kettering, OH
45431 Beavercreek, OH
45431 Beavercreek Township, OH
45431 Dayton, OH
45431 Riverside, OH
45432 Beavercreek, OH
45432 Dayton, OH
45432 Kettering, OH
45433 Dayton, OH
45433 Wp Air Base, OH
45433 Wpafb, OH
45433 Wright Patter, OH
45433 Wright Patterson Afb, OH
45434 Beavercreek, OH
45434 Beavercreek Township, OH
45434 Dayton, OH
45435 Dayton, OH
45437 Dayton, OH
45439 Dayton, OH
45439 Kettering, OH
45439 Moraine, OH
45439 West Carrollton, OH
45439 West Carrollton City, OH
45440 Beavercreek, OH
45440 Beavercreek Township, OH
45440 Centerville, OH
45440 Dayton, OH
45440 Kettering, OH
45440 Sugarcreek Township, OH
45441 Dayton, OH
45448 Dayton, OH
45449 Dayton, OH
45449 West Carrollton, OH
45449 West Carrollton City, OH
45458 Centerville, OH
45458 Dayton, OH
45458 Sugarcreek Township, OH
45458 Washington Township, OH
45459 Centerville, OH
45459 Dayton, OH
45459 Kettering, OH
45459 Moraine, OH
45459 Sugarcreek Township, OH
45459 Washington Township, OH
45469 Dayton, OH
45470 Dayton, OH
45475 Dayton, OH
45479 Dayton, OH
45481 Dayton, OH
45482 Dayton, OH
45490 Dayton, OH

455

45501 Springfield, OH
45502 Springfield, OH
45503 Springfield, OH
45504 Springfield, OH
45505 Springfield, OH
45506 Springfield, OH

456

45601 Chillicothe, OH
45612 Bainbridge, OH
45613 Beaver, OH
45614 Bidwell, OH
45616 Blue Creek, OH
45617 Bourneville, OH
45618 Cherry Fork, OH
45619 Chesapeake, OH
45620 Cheshire, OH
45621 Coalton, OH
45622 Creola, OH
45623 Crown City, OH
45624 Cynthiana, OH
45628 Frankfort, OH
45629 Franklin Furnace, OH
45630 Friendship, OH
45631 Gallipolis, OH
45633 Hallsville, OH
45634 Hamden, OH
45636 Haverhill, OH
45638 Coal Grove, OH
45638 Hanging Rock, OH
45638 Ironton, OH
45640 Jackson, OH
45642 Jasper, OH
45643 Kerr, OH
45644 Kingston, OH
45645 Kitts Hill, OH
45646 Latham, OH
45647 Londonderry, OH
45648 Lucasville, OH
45650 Lynx, OH
45651 Allensville, OH
45651 Mc Arthur, OH
45652 Mc Dermott, OH
45653 Minford, OH
45654 New Plymouth, OH
45656 Oak Hill, OH
45657 Otway, OH
45658 Patriot, OH
45659 Pedro, OH
45660 Peebles, OH
45661 Idaho, OH
45661 Piketon, OH
45662 New Boston, OH
45662 Portsmouth, OH
45662 Sciotoville, OH
45663 Portsmouth, OH
45663 West Portsmouth, OH
45669 Athalia, OH
45669 Proctorville, OH
45671 Rarden, OH
45672 Ray, OH
45673 Richmond Dale, OH
45674 Rio Grande, OH
45675 Rock Camp, OH
45677 Scioto Furnace, OH
45678 Scottown, OH
45679 Seaman, OH
45680 South Point, OH
45681 South Salem, OH
45682 South Webster, OH
45683 Stockdale, OH
45684 Stout, OH
45685 Thurman, OH
45686 Vinton, OH
45687 Wakefield, OH
45688 Waterloo, OH
45690 Waverly, OH
45692 Wellston, OH
45693 West Union, OH
45694 Wheelersburg, OH
45695 Radcliff, OH
45695 Wilkesville, OH
45696 Willow Wood, OH
45697 Winchester, OH
45698 Zaleski, OH
45699 Lucasville, OH

457

45701 Athens, OH
45710 Albany, OH
45711 Amesville, OH
45712 Barlow, OH
45713 Bartlett, OH
45714 Belpre, OH
45715 Beverly, OH
45716 Buchtel, OH
45717 Carbondale, OH
45719 Chauncey, OH
45720 Chester, OH
45721 Coal Run, OH
45723 Coolville, OH
45724 Cutler, OH
45727 Dexter City, OH
45729 Fleming, OH
45732 Glouster, OH
45734 Graysville, OH
45734 Rinard Mills, OH
45735 Guysville, OH
45739 Hockingport, OH
45740 Jacksonville, OH
45741 Dexter, OH
45741 Langsville, OH
45742 Little Hocking, OH
45743 Long Bottom, OH
45744 Lowell, OH
45745 Lower Salem, OH
45745 Warner, OH

45746 Elba, OH
45746 Macksburg, OH
45750 Marietta, OH
45760 Middleport, OH
45761 Millfield, OH
45764 Nelsonville, OH
45766 New Marshfield, OH
45767 Fly, OH
45767 Matamoras, OH
45767 New Matamoras, OH
45767 Rinard Mills, OH
45768 Newport, OH
45769 Pomeroy, OH
45770 Portland, OH
45771 Racine, OH
45772 Reedsville, OH
45773 Reno, OH
45775 Rutland, OH
45776 Shade, OH
45777 Sharpsburg, OH
45778 Stewart, OH
45779 Syracuse, OH
45780 The Plains, OH
45782 Trimble, OH
45783 Tuppers Plains, OH
45784 Vincent, OH
45786 Waterford, OH
45787 Watertown, OH
45788 Whipple, OH
45789 Wingett Run, OH

458

45801 Lima, OH
45802 Lima, OH
45804 Lima, OH
45805 Lima, OH
45806 Cridersville, OH
45806 Fort Shawnee, OH
45806 Lima, OH
45807 Elida, OH
45807 Lima, OH
45808 Beaverdam, OH
45809 Gomer, OH
45809 Lima, OH
45810 Ada, OH
45812 Alger, OH
45813 Antwerp, OH
45814 Arlington, OH
45815 Belmore, OH
45815 Leipsic, OH
45816 Benton Ridge, OH
45817 Bluffton, OH
45819 Buckland, OH
45820 Cairo, OH
45821 Cecil, OH
45822 Carthagena, OH
45822 Celina, OH
45826 Celina, OH
45826 Chickasaw, OH
45827 Cloverdale, OH
45828 Coldwater, OH
45830 Columbus Grove, OH
45831 Continental, OH
45832 Convoy, OH
45833 Delphos, OH
45835 Dola, OH
45836 Dunkirk, OH
45837 Continental, OH
45837 Dupont, OH
45838 Elgin, OH
45839 Findlay, OH
45840 Findlay, OH
45841 Jenera, OH
45843 Forest, OH
45844 Fort Jennings, OH
45845 Fort Loramie, OH
45846 Fort Recovery, OH
45848 Glandorf, OH
45849 Grover Hill, OH
45850 Harrod, OH
45851 Haviland, OH
45853 Kalida, OH
45854 Lafayette, OH
45854 Lima, OH
45855 Latty, OH
45856 Leipsic, OH
45858 Mc Comb, OH
45859 Mc Guffey, OH
45860 Maria Stein, OH
45861 Melrose, OH
45862 Mendon, OH
45863 Middle Point, OH
45864 Miller City, OH
45865 Minster, OH
45866 Montezuma, OH
45867 Mount Blanchard, OH
45868 Mount Cory, OH
45869 New Bremen, OH
45870 New Hampshire, OH
45871 New Knoxville, OH
45872 Bairdstown, OH
45872 North Baltimore, OH
45873 Melrose, OH
45873 Oakwood, OH
45874 Ohio City, OH
45875 Gilboa, OH
45875 Ottawa, OH
45876 Ottoville, OH
45877 Pandora, OH
45879 Broughton, OH
45879 Paulding, OH
45880 Payne, OH
45881 Rawson, OH
45882 Rockford, OH
45883 Saint Henry, OH
45884 Saint Johns, OH
45885 Saint Marys, OH
45886 Scott, OH
45887 Spencerville, OH
45888 Uniopolis, OH
45889 Van Buren, OH
45890 Vanlue, OH
45891 Van Wert, OH
45893 Vaughnsville, OH
45894 Venedocia, OH
45895 Wapakoneta, OH
45896 Waynesfield, OH
45897 Williamstown, OH
45898 Willshire, OH
45899 Wren, OH

459

45999 Cincinnati, OH

460

46001 Alexandria, IN
46011 Anderson, IN
46011 Country Club Heights, IN
46011 River Forest, IN
46011 Woodlawn Heights, IN
46012 Anderson, IN
46013 Anderson, IN
46014 Anderson, IN
46015 Anderson, IN
46016 Anderson, IN
46017 Anderson, IN
46017 Chesterfield, IN
46018 Anderson, IN
46030 Arcadia, IN
46031 Atlanta, IN
46032 Carmel, IN
46033 Carmel, IN
46034 Cicero, IN
46034 Westfield, IN
46035 Colfax, IN
46036 Elwood, IN
46037 Fishers, IN
46038 Fishers, IN
46039 Forest, IN
46040 Fishers, IN
46040 Fortville, IN
46041 Frankfort, IN
46041 Hillisburg, IN
46044 Frankton, IN
46045 Goldsmith, IN
46047 Hobbs, IN
46048 Ingalls, IN
46049 Kempton, IN
46050 Kirklin, IN
46051 Lapel, IN
46052 Lebanon, IN
46052 Ulen, IN
46055 Mccordsville, IN
46056 Markleville, IN
46057 Michigantown, IN
46058 Frankfort, IN
46058 Mulberry, IN
46060 Noblesville, IN
46061 Noblesville, IN
46062 Noblesville, IN
46062 Westfield, IN
46063 Orestes, IN
46064 Pendleton, IN
46065 Rossville, IN
46067 Sedalia, IN
46068 Sharpsville, IN
46069 Sheridan, IN
46070 Summitville, IN
46071 Thorntown, IN
46072 Tipton, IN
46074 Carmel, IN
46074 Westfield, IN
46075 Whitestown, IN
46076 Windfall, IN
46077 Zionsville, IN
46082 Carmel, IN
46085 Fishers, IN

461

46102 Advance, IN
46103 Amo, IN
46104 Arlington, IN
46105 Bainbridge, IN
46106 Bargersville, IN
46107 Beech Grove, IN
46110 Boggstown, IN
46111 Brooklyn, IN
46112 Brownsburg, IN
46113 Camby, IN
46115 Carthage, IN
46117 Charlottesville, IN
46118 Clayton, IN
46120 Cloverdale, IN
46121 Coatesville, IN
46122 Danville, IN
46123 Avon, IN
46124 Atterbury, IN
46124 Camp Atterbury, IN
46124 Camp Attrbry, IN
46124 Edinburgh, IN
46125 Eminence, IN
46126 Fairland, IN
46127 Falmouth, IN
46128 Fillmore, IN
46129 Finly, IN
46130 Fountaintown, IN
46131 Franklin, IN
46133 Glenwood, IN
46135 Greencastle, IN
46140 Greenfield, IN
46140 Spring Lake, IN
46142 Greenwood, IN
46143 Greenwood, IN
46144 Gwynneville, IN
46146 Homer, IN
46147 Jamestown, IN
46148 Knightstown, IN
46149 Lizton, IN
46150 Manilla, IN
46151 Bethany, IN
46151 Centerton, IN
46151 Martinsville, IN
46154 Maxwell, IN
46155 Mays, IN
46156 Milroy, IN
46157 Monrovia, IN
46158 Mooresville, IN
46160 Morgantown, IN
46161 Morristown, IN
46162 Needham, IN
46163 New Palestine, IN
46164 Nineveh, IN
46164 Princes Lakes, IN
46165 North Salem, IN
46166 Paragon, IN
46167 Pittsboro, IN
46168 Cartersburg, IN
46168 Plainfield, IN
46170 Putnamville, IN
46171 Reelsville, IN
46172 Roachdale, IN
46173 Rushville, IN
46175 Russellville, IN
46176 Shelbyville, IN
46180 Stilesville, IN
46181 Trafalgar, IN
46182 Waldron, IN
46183 West Newton, IN
46184 New Whiteland, IN
46184 Whiteland, IN
46186 Wilkinson, IN
46186 Willow Branch, IN
46197 Plainfield, IN

462

46201 Indianapolis, IN
46202 Indianapolis, IN
46203 Indianapolis, IN
46204 Indianapolis, IN
46205 Indianapolis, IN
46206 Indianapolis, IN
46207 Indianapolis, IN
46208 Indianapolis, IN
46208 Rocky Ripple, IN
46209 Indianapolis, IN
46210 Indianapolis, IN
46211 Indianapolis, IN
46213 Indianapolis, IN
46214 Eagle Creek, IN
46214 Indianapolis, IN
46216 Indianapolis, IN
46217 Indianapolis, IN
46217 Southport, IN
46218 Indianapolis, IN
46219 Indianapolis, IN
46219 Warren Park, IN
46220 Indianapolis, IN
46221 Indianapolis, IN
46222 Indianapolis, IN
46224 Indianapolis, IN
46224 Speedway, IN
46225 Indianapolis, IN
46226 Indianapolis, IN
46226 Lawrence, IN
46227 Homecroft, IN
46227 Indianapolis, IN
46227 Southport, IN
46228 Crows Nest, IN
46228 Indianapolis, IN
46228 North Crows Nest, IN
46228 Spring Hills, IN
46228 Wynnedale, IN
46229 Cumberland, IN
46229 Indianapolis, IN
46230 Indianapolis, IN
46231 Indianapolis, IN
46234 Clermont, IN
46234 Indianapolis, IN
46235 Indianapolis, IN
46235 Oaklandon, IN
46236 Indianapolis, IN
46236 Oaklandon, IN
46237 Indianapolis, IN
46237 Southport, IN
46239 Indianapolis, IN
46239 Wanamaker, IN
46240 Indianapolis, IN
46240 Nora, IN
46240 Williams Creek, IN
46241 Indianapolis, IN
46242 Indianapolis, IN
46244 Indianapolis, IN
46247 Indianapolis, IN
46247 Southport, IN
46249 Indianapolis, IN
46250 Castleton, IN
46250 Indianapolis, IN
46251 Indianapolis, IN
46253 Eagle Creek, IN
46253 Indianapolis, IN
46254 Eagle Creek, IN
46254 Indianapolis, IN
46255 Indianapolis, IN
46256 Castleton, IN
46256 Indianapolis, IN
46259 Acton, IN
46259 Indianapolis, IN
46260 Indianapolis, IN
46260 Meridian Hills, IN
46260 Nora, IN
46262 Indianapolis, IN
46266 Indianapolis, IN
46268 Indianapolis, IN
46268 New Augusta, IN
46274 Indianapolis, IN
46275 Indianapolis, IN
46277 Indianapolis, IN
46278 Indianapolis, IN
46278 New Augusta, IN
46280 Indianapolis, IN
46280 Nora, IN
46282 Indianapolis, IN
46283 Indianapolis, IN
46285 Indianapolis, IN
46290 Indianapolis, IN
46290 Nora, IN
46291 Indianapolis, IN
46295 Indianapolis, IN
46296 Indianapolis, IN
46298 Indianapolis, IN

463

46301 Beverly Shores, IN
46301 Beverly Shrs, IN
46302 Boone Grove, IN
46303 Cedar Lake, IN
46304 Burns Harbor, IN
46304 Chesterton, IN
46304 Dune Acres, IN
46304 Porter, IN
46307 Crown Point, IN
46307 Winfield, IN
46308 Crown Point, IN
46310 Demotte, IN
46311 Dyer, IN
46312 East Chicago, IN
46319 Griffith, IN
46320 Hammond, IN
46321 Hammond, IN
46321 Munster, IN
46322 Hammond, IN
46322 Highland, IN
46323 Hammond, IN
46324 Hammond, IN
46325 Hammond, IN
46327 Hammond, IN
46340 Hanna, IN
46341 Hebron, IN
46342 Hobart, IN
46342 New Chicago, IN
46345 Kingsbury, IN
46346 Kingsford Heights, IN
46347 Kouts, IN
46348 La Crosse, IN
46349 Lake Village, IN
46350 La Porte, IN
46350 Laporte, IN
46352 La Porte, IN
46355 Leroy, IN
46356 Lowell, IN
46360 Long Beach, IN
46360 Michiana Shores, IN
46360 Michigan City, IN
46360 Pines, IN
46360 Pottawattamie Park, IN
46360 Town Of Pines, IN
46360 Trail Creek, IN
46361 Michigan City, IN
46365 Mill Creek, IN
46366 North Judson, IN
46368 Ogden Dunes, IN
46368 Portage, IN
46371 Rolling Prairie, IN
46372 Roselawn, IN
46373 Dyer, IN
46373 Saint John, IN
46374 San Pierre, IN
46375 Schererville, IN
46376 Schneider, IN
46377 Shelby, IN
46379 Sumava Resorts, IN
46380 Tefft, IN
46380 Wheatfield, IN
46381 Thayer, IN
46382 Union Mills, IN
46383 Valparaiso, IN
46384 Valparaiso, IN
46384 Valpo, IN
46385 Valparaiso, IN
46385 Valpo, IN
46390 Wanatah, IN
46391 Otis, IN
46391 Westville, IN
46392 Wheatfield, IN
46393 Wheeler, IN
46394 Whiting, IN

464

46401 Gary, IN
46402 Gary, IN
46403 Gary, IN
46404 Gary, IN
46405 Gary, IN
46405 Lake Station, IN
46406 Gary, IN
46407 Gary, IN
46408 Gary, IN
46409 Gary, IN
46410 Gary, IN
46410 Merrillville, IN
46411 Gary, IN
46411 Merrillville, IN

465

46501 Argos, IN
46502 Atwood, IN
46504 Bourbon, IN
46506 Bremen, IN
46507 Bristol, IN
46508 Burket, IN
46510 Claypool, IN
46511 Burr Oak, IN
46511 Clvr Mil Acad, IN
46511 Culver, IN
46513 Donaldson, IN
46514 Elkhart, IN
46515 Elkhart, IN
46516 Elkhart, IN
46517 Elkhart, IN
46524 Etna Green, IN
46526 Foraker, IN
46526 Goshen, IN
46527 Goshen, IN
46528 Goshen, IN
46530 Granger, IN
46531 Grovertown, IN
46532 Hamlet, IN
46534 Knox, IN
46534 Ober, IN
46536 Lakeville, IN
46537 La Paz, IN
46537 Lapaz, IN
46538 Leesburg, IN
46539 Mentone, IN
46540 Middlebury, IN
46542 Milford, IN
46543 Millersburg, IN
46544 Mishawaka, IN
46545 Mishawaka, IN
46546 Mishawaka, IN
46550 Nappanee, IN
46552 New Carlisle, IN
46553 New Paris, IN
46554 North Liberty, IN
46555 North Webster, IN
46556 Notre Dame, IN
46561 Osceola, IN
46562 Pierceton, IN
46562 Sidney, IN
46563 Inwood, IN
46563 Plymouth, IN
46565 Shipshewana, IN
46567 Syracuse, IN
46570 Tippecanoe, IN
46571 Topeka, IN
46572 Tyner, IN
46573 Wakarusa, IN
46574 Walkerton, IN
46580 Warsaw, IN
46581 Warsaw, IN

46582 Warsaw, IN
46590 Winona Lake, IN
46595 Wyatt, IN

466

46601 South Bend, IN
46613 South Bend, IN
46614 South Bend, IN
46615 South Bend, IN
46616 South Bend, IN
46617 South Bend, IN
46619 South Bend, IN
46624 South Bend, IN
46626 South Bend, IN
46628 South Bend, IN
46634 South Bend, IN
46635 South Bend, IN
46637 Roseland, IN
46637 South Bend, IN
46660 South Bend, IN
46680 South Bend, IN
46699 South Bend, IN

467

46701 Albion, IN
46702 Andrews, IN
46703 Angola, IN
46704 Arcola, IN
46705 Ashley, IN
46706 Auburn, IN
46710 Avilla, IN
46711 Berne, IN
46711 Linn Grove, IN
46713 Bippus, IN
46714 Bluffton, IN
46721 Butler, IN
46723 Churubusco, IN
46725 Columbia City, IN
46730 Corunna, IN
46731 Craigville, IN
46732 Cromwell, IN
46733 Decatur, IN
46737 Fremont, IN
46738 Garrett, IN
46740 Geneva, IN
46741 Grabill, IN
46742 Hamilton, IN
46743 Harlan, IN
46745 Hoagland, IN
46746 Howe, IN
46747 Helmer, IN
46747 Hudson, IN
46748 Huntertown, IN
46750 Huntington, IN
46755 Kendallville, IN
46759 Keystone, IN
46760 Kimmell, IN
46761 Lagrange, IN
46763 Laotto, IN
46764 Larwill, IN
46765 Leo, IN
46765 Leo Cedarville, IN
46766 Liberty Center, IN
46767 Ligonier, IN
46769 Berne, IN
46769 Linn Grove, IN
46770 Markle, IN
46771 Mongo, IN
46772 Monroe, IN
46773 Monroeville, IN
46773 Monroevl, IN
46774 New Haven, IN
46776 Orland, IN
46777 Ossian, IN
46778 Petroleum, IN
46779 Pleasant Lake, IN
46780 Pleasant Mills, IN
46781 Poneto, IN
46782 Preble, IN
46783 Roanoke, IN
46784 Rome City, IN
46785 Saint Joe, IN
46786 South Milford, IN
46787 South Whitley, IN
46788 Spencerville, IN
46789 Stroh, IN
46791 Uniondale, IN
46792 Warren, IN
46793 Waterloo, IN
46794 Brimfield, IN
46794 Wawaka, IN
46795 Wolcottville, IN
46796 Wolflake, IN
46797 Woodburn, IN
46798 Yoder, IN
46799 Zanesville, IN

468

46801 Fort Wayne, IN
46802 Fort Wayne, IN
46803 Fort Wayne, IN
46804 Fort Wayne, IN
46805 Fort Wayne, IN
46806 Fort Wayne, IN
46807 Fort Wayne, IN
46808 Fort Wayne, IN
46809 Fort Wayne, IN
46814 Fort Wayne, IN
46815 Fort Wayne, IN
46816 Fort Wayne, IN
46818 Fort Wayne, IN
46819 Fort Wayne, IN
46825 Fort Wayne, IN
46835 Fort Wayne, IN
46845 Fort Wayne, IN
46850 Fort Wayne, IN
46851 Fort Wayne, IN
46852 Fort Wayne, IN
46853 Fort Wayne, IN
46854 Fort Wayne, IN
46855 Fort Wayne, IN
46856 Fort Wayne, IN
46857 Fort Wayne, IN
46858 Fort Wayne, IN
46859 Fort Wayne, IN
46860 Fort Wayne, IN
46861 Fort Wayne, IN
46862 Fort Wayne, IN
46863 Fort Wayne, IN
46864 Fort Wayne, IN
46865 Fort Wayne, IN
46866 Fort Wayne, IN
46867 Fort Wayne, IN
46868 Fort Wayne, IN
46869 Fort Wayne, IN
46885 Fort Wayne, IN
46895 Fort Wayne, IN
46896 Fort Wayne, IN
46897 Fort Wayne, IN
46898 Fort Wayne, IN
46899 Fort Wayne, IN

469

46901 Kokomo, IN
46902 Kokomo, IN
46903 Kokomo, IN
46904 Kokomo, IN
46910 Akron, IN
46911 Amboy, IN
46912 Athens, IN
46913 Bringhurst, IN
46914 Bunker Hill, IN
46915 Burlington, IN
46916 Burrows, IN
46917 Camden, IN
46919 Converse, IN
46920 Cutler, IN
46921 Deedsville, IN
46922 Delong, IN
46923 Delphi, IN
46926 Chili, IN
46926 Denver, IN
46928 Fairmount, IN
46929 Flora, IN
46930 Fowlerton, IN
46931 Fulton, IN
46932 Galveston, IN
46933 Gas City, IN
46935 Grass Creek, IN
46935 Kewanna, IN
46936 Greentown, IN
46937 Hemlock, IN
46938 Jonesboro, IN
46939 Kewanna, IN
46940 La Fontaine, IN
46941 Lagro, IN
46942 Lake Cicott, IN
46943 Laketon, IN
46945 Leiters Ford, IN
46946 Liberty Mills, IN
46947 Logansport, IN
46950 Lucerne, IN
46951 Macy, IN
46952 Marion, IN
46953 Marion, IN
46957 Matthews, IN
46958 Mexico, IN
46959 Miami, IN
46960 Monterey, IN
46961 New Waverly, IN
46962 North Manchester, IN
46965 Oakford, IN
46967 Onward, IN
46968 Ora, IN
46970 Peru, IN
46971 Grissom Air Reserve Base, IN
46971 Grissom Arb, IN
46971 Peru, IN
46974 Roann, IN
46975 Rochester, IN
46977 Rockfield, IN
46978 Royal Center, IN
46979 Russiaville, IN
46980 Servia, IN
46982 Silver Lake, IN
46984 Somerset, IN
46985 Star City, IN
46986 Sims, IN
46986 Swayzee, IN
46987 Sweetser, IN
46988 Twelve Mile, IN
46989 Upland, IN
46990 Urbana, IN
46991 Van Buren, IN
46992 Wabash, IN
46994 Walton, IN
46995 West Middleton, IN
46996 Denham, IN
46996 Winamac, IN
46998 Young America, IN

470

47001 Aurora, IN
47003 West College Corner, IN
47006 Batesville, IN
47010 Bath, IN
47011 Bennington, IN
47012 Brookville, IN
47012 Saint Leon, IN
47016 Cedar Grove, IN
47017 Cross Plains, IN
47018 Dillsboro, IN
47019 East Enterprise, IN
47020 Florence, IN
47021 Friendship, IN
47022 Guilford, IN
47023 Holton, IN
47024 Laurel, IN
47025 Greendale, IN
47025 Lawrenceburg, IN
47030 Metamora, IN
47031 Milan, IN
47032 Moores Hill, IN
47033 Morris, IN
47034 Napoleon, IN
47035 New Trenton, IN
47036 Oldenburg, IN
47037 Osgood, IN
47038 Patriot, IN
47039 Pierceville, IN
47040 Rising Sun, IN
47041 Sunman, IN
47042 Versailles, IN
47043 Vevay, IN
47060 West Harrison, IN

471

47102 Austin, IN
47104 Bethlehem, IN
47106 Borden, IN
47106 Starlight, IN
47107 Bradford, IN
47108 Campbellsburg, IN
47108 Livonia, IN
47110 Central, IN
47110 New Amsterdam, IN
47111 Charlestown, IN
47112 Corydon, IN
47114 Crandall, IN
47115 Depauw, IN
47116 Eckerty, IN
47117 Elizabeth, IN
47117 Rosewood, IN
47118 English, IN
47118 Sulphur, IN
47119 Floyds Knobs, IN
47119 Galena, IN
47119 Navilleton, IN
47120 Fredericksburg, IN
47122 Georgetown, IN
47123 Grantsburg, IN
47124 Greenville, IN
47125 Hardinsburg, IN
47125 Rego, IN
47125 Valeene, IN
47126 Henryville, IN
47129 Clarksville, IN
47129 Jeffersonville, IN
47130 Jeff, IN
47130 Jeffersonville, IN
47130 Utica, IN
47130 Watson, IN
47131 Clarksville, IN
47131 Jeffersonville, IN
47135 Laconia, IN
47136 Lanesville, IN
47137 Alton, IN
47137 Carefree, IN
47137 Fredonia, IN
47137 Leavenworth, IN
47138 Blocher, IN
47138 Lexington, IN
47140 Hogtown, IN
47140 Marengo, IN
47141 Marysville, IN
47142 Mauckport, IN
47143 Memphis, IN
47144 Jeffersonville, IN
47145 Milltown, IN
47146 Mount Saint Francis, IN
47147 Nabb, IN
47150 New Albany, IN
47151 New Albany, IN
47160 New Middletown, IN
47161 New Salisbury, IN
47162 New Washington, IN
47163 Otisco, IN
47164 Palmyra, IN
47165 Pekin, IN
47166 Ramsey, IN
47167 Salem, IN
47170 Little York, IN
47170 Scottsburg, IN
47172 Sellersburg, IN
47172 Speed, IN
47174 Sulphur, IN
47175 Taswell, IN
47177 Underwood, IN
47190 Jeffersonville, IN

472

47201 Columbus, IN
47202 Columbus, IN
47203 Columbus, IN
47220 Brownstown, IN
47223 Butlerville, IN
47223 Muscatatuck, IN
47223 Nebraska, IN
47224 Canaan, IN
47225 Clarksburg, IN
47226 Clifford, IN
47227 Commiskey, IN
47228 Cortland, IN
47229 Crothersville, IN
47230 Deputy, IN
47231 Dupont, IN
47232 Elizabethtown, IN
47234 Flat Rock, IN
47235 Freetown, IN
47236 Elizabethtown, IN
47236 Grammer, IN
47240 Burney, IN
47240 Greensburg, IN
47243 Hanover, IN
47244 Hartsville, IN
47245 Hayden, IN
47246 Hope, IN
47247 Jonesville, IN
47249 Freetown, IN
47249 Kurtz, IN
47250 Brooksburg, IN
47250 Madison, IN
47260 Medora, IN
47261 Millhousen, IN
47263 New Point, IN
47264 Norman, IN
47265 North Vernon, IN
47270 Paris Crossing, IN
47272 Saint Paul, IN
47273 Scipio, IN
47274 Seymour, IN
47280 Taylorsville, IN
47281 Vallonia, IN
47282 Vernon, IN
47283 Westport, IN

473

47302 Muncie, IN
47303 Muncie, IN
47304 Muncie, IN
47305 Muncie, IN
47306 Muncie, IN
47307 Muncie, IN
47308 Muncie, IN
47320 Albany, IN
47322 Bentonville, IN
47324 Boston, IN
47325 Brownsville, IN
47326 Bryant, IN
47327 Cambridge City, IN
47330 Centerville, IN
47331 Connersville, IN
47334 Daleville, IN
47335 Dublin, IN
47336 Dunkirk, IN
47337 Dunreith, IN
47338 Eaton, IN
47339 Economy, IN
47340 Farmland, IN
47341 Fountain City, IN
47342 Gaston, IN
47344 Greensboro, IN
47345 Greens Fork, IN
47346 Hagerstown, IN
47348 Hartford City, IN
47351 Kennard, IN
47352 Lewisville, IN
47353 Liberty, IN
47354 Losantville, IN
47355 Lynn, IN
47356 Middletown, IN
47357 Milton, IN
47358 Modoc, IN
47359 Montpelier, IN
47360 Mooreland, IN
47361 Mount Summit, IN
47362 New Castle, IN
47366 New Lisbon, IN
47367 Oakville, IN
47368 Parker, IN
47368 Parker City, IN
47369 Pennville, IN
47370 East Germantown, IN
47370 Pershing, IN
47371 Portland, IN
47373 Redkey, IN
47374 Richmond, IN
47375 Richmond, IN
47380 Ridgeville, IN
47381 Salamonia, IN
47382 Saratoga, IN
47383 Selma, IN
47384 Shirley, IN
47385 Spiceland, IN
47386 Springport, IN
47387 Straughn, IN
47388 Sulphur Springs, IN
47390 Union City, IN
47392 Webster, IN
47393 Williamsburg, IN
47394 Winchester, IN
47396 Yorktown, IN

474

47401 Bloomington, IN
47402 Bloomington, IN
47403 Bloomington, IN
47404 Bloomington, IN
47405 Bloomington, IN
47406 Bloomington, IN
47407 Bloomington, IN
47408 Bloomington, IN
47408 Woodbridge, IN
47420 Avoca, IN
47421 Bedford, IN
47421 Fort Ritner, IN
47424 Bloomfield, IN
47426 Clear Creek, IN
47427 Coal City, IN
47429 Ellettsville, IN
47431 Freedom, IN
47432 French Lick, IN
47433 Gosport, IN
47434 Harrodsburg, IN
47435 Helmsburg, IN
47436 Heltonville, IN
47437 Huron, IN
47438 Jasonville, IN
47439 Koleen, IN
47441 Linton, IN
47443 Lyons, IN
47445 Midland, IN
47446 Mitchell, IN
47448 Nashville, IN
47449 Newberry, IN
47451 Oolitic, IN
47452 Orleans, IN
47453 Owensburg, IN
47454 Paoli, IN
47455 Patricksburg, IN
47456 Quincy, IN
47457 Scotland, IN
47458 Smithville, IN
47459 Solsberry, IN
47460 Spencer, IN
47462 Springville, IN
47463 Stanford, IN
47464 Stinesville, IN
47465 Switz City, IN
47467 Tunnelton, IN
47468 Unionville, IN
47469 West Baden Springs, IN
47470 Williams, IN
47471 Worthington, IN

475

47501 Washington, IN
47512 Bicknell, IN
47513 Birdseye, IN
47514 Branchville, IN
47515 Bristow, IN
47515 Siberia, IN
47516 Bruceville, IN
47519 Cannelburg, IN
47520 Cannelton, IN
47520 Magnet, IN
47520 Mount Pleasant, IN
47520 Tobinsport, IN
47521 Celestine, IN
47522 Crane, IN
47522 Crane Naval Depot, IN
47523 Dale, IN
47524 Decker, IN
47525 Derby, IN
47527 Dubois, IN
47528 Edwardsport, IN
47529 Elnora, IN
47531 Evanston, IN
47532 Ferdinand, IN

47535 Freelandville, IN
47536 Fulda, IN
47537 Gentryville, IN
47541 Holland, IN
47542 Huntingburg, IN
47545 Ireland, IN
47546 Jasper, IN
47547 Jasper, IN
47549 Jasper, IN
47550 Buffaloville, IN
47550 Lamar, IN
47551 Leopold, IN
47552 Lincoln City, IN
47553 Loogootee, IN
47556 Mariah Hill, IN
47557 Monroe City, IN
47558 Montgomery, IN
47561 Emison, IN
47561 Oaktown, IN
47562 Odon, IN
47564 Otwell, IN
47567 Petersburg, IN
47568 Plainville, IN
47573 Ragsdale, IN
47574 Rome, IN
47575 Kyana, IN
47575 Saint Anthony, IN
47576 Saint Croix, IN
47577 Saint Meinrad, IN
47578 Sandborn, IN
47579 Christmas Lake Village, IN
47579 Santa Claus, IN
47579 Xmas Lk Vlg, IN
47580 Schnellville, IN
47581 Shoals, IN
47584 Spurgeon, IN
47585 Stendal, IN
47586 Tell City, IN
47588 Troy, IN
47590 Velpen, IN
47591 Vincennes, IN
47596 Westphalia, IN
47597 Wheatland, IN
47598 Winslow, IN

476

47601 Boonville, IN
47610 Chandler, IN
47611 Chrisney, IN
47612 Cynthiana, IN
47613 Elberfeld, IN
47615 Grandview, IN
47616 Griffin, IN
47617 Hatfield, IN
47618 Darmstadt, IN
47618 Inglefield, IN
47619 Lynnville, IN
47620 Mount Vernon, IN
47629 Newburgh, IN
47630 Newburgh, IN
47631 New Harmony, IN
47633 Poseyville, IN
47634 Richland, IN
47635 Rockport, IN
47637 Folsomville, IN
47637 Tennyson, IN
47638 Wadesville, IN
47639 Haubstadt, IN
47640 Hazleton, IN
47647 Buckskin, IN
47648 Fort Branch, IN
47649 Francisco, IN
47654 Mackey, IN
47660 Oakland City, IN
47665 Owensville, IN
47666 Patoka, IN
47670 Princeton, IN
47683 Somerville, IN

477

47701 Evansville, IN
47702 Evansville, IN
47703 Evansville, IN
47704 Evansville, IN
47705 Evansville, IN
47706 Evansville, IN
47708 Evansville, IN
47710 Evansville, IN
47711 Evansville, IN
47712 Evansville, IN
47713 Evansville, IN
47714 Evansville, IN
47715 Evansville, IN
47716 Evansville, IN
47719 Evansville, IN
47720 Evansville, IN
47721 Evansville, IN
47722 Evansville, IN
47724 Evansville, IN
47725 Evansville, IN
47728 Evansville, IN
47730 Evansville, IN
47731 Evansville, IN
47732 Evansville, IN
47733 Evansville, IN
47734 Evansville, IN
47735 Evansville, IN
47736 Evansville, IN
47737 Evansville, IN
47740 Evansville, IN
47747 Evansville, IN
47750 Evansville, IN

478

47801 Terre Haute, IN
47802 Terre Haute, IN
47803 Terre Haute, IN
47804 Terre Haute, IN
47805 North Terre Haute, IN
47805 Terre Haute, IN
47807 Terre Haute, IN
47808 Terre Haute, IN
47809 Terre Haute, IN
47830 Bellmore, IN
47831 Blanford, IN
47832 Bloomingdale, IN
47833 Bowling Green, IN
47834 Brazil, IN
47836 Bridgeton, IN
47837 Carbon, IN
47838 Carlisle, IN
47840 Center Point, IN
47840 Centerpoint, IN
47841 Clay City, IN
47842 Clinton, IN
47845 Coalmont, IN
47846 Cory, IN
47847 Dana, IN
47848 Dugger, IN
47849 Fairbanks, IN
47850 Farmersburg, IN
47851 Fontanet, IN
47852 Graysville, IN
47853 Harmony, IN
47854 Hillsdale, IN
47855 Hymera, IN
47857 Knightsville, IN
47858 Lewis, IN
47859 Marshall, IN
47860 Mecca, IN
47861 Merom, IN
47862 Montezuma, IN
47863 New Goshen, IN
47865 Paxton, IN
47866 Pimento, IN
47868 Poland, IN
47869 Prairie Creek, IN
47870 Prairieton, IN
47871 Riley, IN
47872 Judson, IN
47872 Rockville, IN
47874 Rosedale, IN
47875 Saint Bernice, IN
47876 Saint Mary Of The Woods, IN
47878 Seelyville, IN
47879 Shelburn, IN
47880 Shepardsville, IN
47881 Staunton, IN
47882 New Lebanon, IN
47882 Sullivan, IN
47884 Universal, IN
47885 Sandford, IN
47885 West Terre Haute, IN

479

47901 La Fayette, IN
47901 Lafayette, IN
47902 La Fayette, IN
47902 Lafayette, IN
47903 La Fayette, IN
47903 Lafayette, IN
47904 La Fayette, IN
47904 Lafayette, IN
47905 Colburn, IN
47905 La Fayette, IN
47905 Lafayette, IN
47906 La Fayette, IN
47906 Lafayette, IN
47906 West Lafayette, IN
47907 La Fayette, IN
47907 Lafayette, IN
47907 West Lafayette, IN
47909 Lafayette, IN
47909 Shadeland, IN
47916 Alamo, IN
47917 Ambia, IN
47918 Attica, IN
47920 Battle Ground, IN
47921 Boswell, IN
47922 Brook, IN
47923 Brookston, IN
47924 Buck Creek, IN
47925 Buffalo, IN
47926 Burnettsville, IN
47928 Cayuga, IN
47929 Chalmers, IN
47930 Clarks Hill, IN
47932 Covington, IN
47933 Crawfordsville, IN
47940 Darlington, IN
47941 Dayton, IN
47942 Earl Park, IN
47943 Fair Oaks, IN
47944 Fowler, IN
47946 Francesville, IN
47948 Goodland, IN
47949 Hillsboro, IN
47950 Idaville, IN
47951 Kentland, IN
47952 Cates, IN
47952 Kingman, IN
47952 Tangier, IN
47954 Ladoga, IN
47955 Linden, IN
47957 Medaryville, IN
47958 Mellott, IN
47959 Monon, IN
47960 Monticello, IN
47962 Montmorenci, IN
47963 Morocco, IN
47964 Mount Ayr, IN
47965 New Market, IN
47966 Newport, IN
47967 New Richmond, IN
47968 New Ross, IN
47969 Newtown, IN
47970 Otterbein, IN
47971 Oxford, IN
47974 Perrysville, IN
47975 Pine Village, IN
47977 Remington, IN
47978 Collegeville, IN
47978 Rensselaer, IN
47980 Reynolds, IN
47981 Romney, IN
47982 State Line, IN
47983 Stockwell, IN
47984 Fowler, IN
47984 Talbot, IN
47986 Fowler, IN
47986 Templeton, IN
47987 Veedersburg, IN
47988 Wallace, IN
47989 Waveland, IN
47990 Waynetown, IN
47991 West Lebanon, IN
47992 Westpoint, IN
47993 Marshfield, IN
47993 Pence, IN
47993 Williamsport, IN
47994 Wingate, IN
47995 Wolcott, IN
47996 Lafayette, IN
47996 West Lafayette, IN
47997 Yeoman, IN

480

48001 Algonac, MI
48001 Clay, MI
48001 Pearl Beach, MI
48001 Russell Island, MI
48002 Allenton, MI
48002 Berlin, MI
48002 Berville, MI
48003 Almont, MI
48004 Anchorville, MI
48005 Armada, MI
48006 Avoca, MI
48006 Fargo, MI
48006 Greenwood, MI
48006 Kenockee, MI
48007 Troy, MI
48009 Birmingham, MI
48012 Birmingham, MI
48014 Capac, MI
48014 Mussey, MI
48015 Center Line, MI
48017 Clawson, MI
48021 East Detroit, MI
48021 Eastpointe, MI
48022 Emmett, MI
48023 Fair Haven, MI
48023 Ira, MI
48025 Beverly Hills, MI
48025 Bingham Farms, MI
48025 Franklin, MI
48026 Fraser, MI
48027 Goodells, MI
48027 Wales, MI
48028 Harsens Island, MI
48030 Hazel Park, MI
48032 Grant Township, MI
48032 Jeddo, MI
48033 Southfield, MI
48034 Southfield, MI
48035 Clinton Township, MI
48037 Southfield, MI
48038 Clinton Township, MI
48039 Cottrellville, MI
48039 Marine City, MI
48040 Marysville, MI
48041 Memphis, MI
48041 Riley, MI
48042 Macomb, MI
48043 Mount Clemens, MI
48044 Macomb, MI
48045 Harrison Township, MI
48045 Selfridge Angb, MI
48046 Mount Clemens, MI
48047 Chesterfield, MI
48047 New Baltimore, MI
48048 Lenox, MI
48048 New Haven, MI
48049 Clyde, MI
48049 North Street, MI
48049 Ruby, MI
48050 Lenox, MI
48050 New Haven, MI
48051 Chesterfield, MI
48051 New Baltimore, MI
48054 China, MI
48054 East China, MI
48059 Burtchville, MI
48059 Fort Gratiot, MI
48059 Lakeport, MI
48059 North Lakeport, MI
48060 Port Huron, MI
48061 Port Huron, MI
48062 Richmond, MI
48063 Columbus, MI
48064 Casco, MI
48065 Bruce, MI
48065 Bruce Township, MI
48065 Romeo, MI
48066 Roseville, MI
48067 Royal Oak, MI
48068 Royal Oak, MI
48069 Pleasant Ridge, MI
48070 Huntington Woods, MI
48071 Madison Heights, MI
48072 Berkley, MI
48073 Royal Oak, MI
48074 Kimball, MI
48074 Smiths Creek, MI
48075 Southfield, MI
48076 Lathrup Village, MI
48076 Southfield, MI
48079 Saint Clair, MI
48080 Saint Clair Shores, MI
48080 St Clair Shrs, MI
48081 Saint Clair Shores, MI
48081 St Clair Shrs, MI
48082 Saint Clair Shores, MI
48082 St Clair Shrs, MI
48083 Troy, MI
48084 Troy, MI
48085 Troy, MI
48086 Southfield, MI
48088 Warren, MI
48089 Warren, MI
48090 Warren, MI
48091 Warren, MI
48092 Warren, MI
48093 Warren, MI
48094 Washington, MI
48094 Washington Township, MI
48094 Washington Twp, MI
48095 Washington, MI
48095 Washington Township, MI
48095 Washington Twp, MI
48096 Ray, MI
48096 Ray Twp, MI
48097 Brockway, MI
48097 Lynn, MI
48097 Yale, MI
48098 Troy, MI
48099 Troy, MI

481

48101 Allen Park, MI
48103 Ann Arbor, MI
48104 Ann Arbor, MI
48105 Ann Arbor, MI
48106 Ann Arbor, MI
48107 Ann Arbor, MI
48108 Ann Arbor, MI
48109 Ann Arbor, MI
48110 Azalia, MI
48111 Belleville, MI
48111 Sumpter Twp, MI
48111 Van Buren Twp, MI
48112 Belleville, MI
48113 Ann Arbor, MI
48114 Brighton, MI
48115 Bridgewater, MI
48116 Brighton, MI
48117 Carleton, MI
48118 Chelsea, MI
48120 Dearborn, MI
48121 Dearborn, MI
48122 Melvindale, MI
48123 Dearborn, MI
48124 Dearborn, MI
48125 Dearborn Heights, MI
48126 Dearborn, MI
48127 Dearborn Heights, MI
48128 Dearborn, MI
48130 Dexter, MI
48131 Dundee, MI
48133 Erie, MI
48134 Brownstown, MI
48134 Brownstown Township, MI
48134 Brownstown Twp, MI
48134 Flat Rock, MI
48135 Garden City, MI
48136 Garden City, MI
48137 Gregory, MI
48138 Grosse Ile, MI
48139 Hamburg, MI
48140 Ida, MI
48141 Inkster, MI
48143 Lakeland, MI
48144 Lambertville, MI
48145 La Salle, MI
48146 Lincoln Park, MI
48150 Livonia, MI
48151 Livonia, MI
48152 Livonia, MI
48153 Livonia, MI
48154 Livonia, MI
48157 Luna Pier, MI
48158 Manchester, MI
48159 Maybee, MI
48160 Milan, MI
48161 Frenchtown, MI
48161 Monroe, MI
48161 Raisinville Twp, MI
48162 Monroe, MI
48164 Brownstown, MI
48164 Brownstown Township, MI
48164 Brownstown Twp, MI
48164 New Boston, MI
48165 New Hudson, MI
48166 Newport, MI
48167 Northville, MI
48167 Northville Township, MI
48168 Northville, MI
48169 Pinckney, MI
48170 Plymouth, MI
48173 Brownstown, MI
48173 Brownstown Township, MI
48173 Gibraltar, MI
48173 Rockwood, MI
48174 Brownstown, MI
48174 Brownstown Township, MI
48174 Brownstown Twp, MI
48174 Romulus, MI
48175 Salem, MI
48176 Saline, MI
48177 Samaria, MI
48178 South Lyon, MI
48179 South Rockwood, MI
48180 Taylor, MI
48182 Temperance, MI
48183 Brownstown, MI
48183 Brownstown Township, MI
48183 Brownstown Twp, MI
48183 Trenton, MI
48183 Woodhaven, MI
48184 Wayne, MI
48185 Westland, MI
48186 Westland, MI
48187 Canton, MI
48188 Canton, MI
48189 Hamburg Twp, MI
48189 Whitmore Lake, MI
48190 Whittaker, MI
48191 Willis, MI
48192 Riverview, MI
48192 Wyandotte, MI
48193 Brownstown, MI
48193 Brownstown Township, MI
48193 Brownstown Twp, MI
48193 Riverview, MI
48193 Wyandotte, MI
48195 Southgate, MI
48197 Ypsilanti, MI
48198 Superior Township, MI
48198 Ypsilanti, MI

482

48201 Detroit, MI
48202 Detroit, MI
48203 Detroit, MI
48203 Highland Park, MI
48204 Detroit, MI
48205 Detroit, MI
48206 Detroit, MI
48207 Detroit, MI
48208 Detroit, MI
48209 Detroit, MI

48210 Detroit, MI
48211 Detroit, MI
48211 Hamtramck, MI
48212 Detroit, MI
48212 Hamtramck, MI
48213 Detroit, MI
48214 Detroit, MI
48215 Detroit, MI
48215 Grosse Pointe Park, MI
48216 Detroit, MI
48217 Detroit, MI
48218 Detroit, MI
48218 River Rouge, MI
48219 Detroit, MI
48220 Detroit, MI
48220 Ferndale, MI
48221 Detroit, MI
48222 Detroit, MI
48223 Detroit, MI
48224 Detroit, MI
48224 Grosse Pointe Park, MI
48225 Detroit, MI
48225 Harper Woods, MI
48226 Detroit, MI
48227 Detroit, MI
48228 Detroit, MI
48229 Detroit, MI
48229 Ecorse, MI
48229 River Rouge, MI
48230 Detroit, MI
48230 Grosse Pointe, MI
48230 Grosse Pointe Farms, MI
48230 Grosse Pointe Park, MI
48230 Grosse Pointe Shores, MI
48230 Grosse Pointe Woods, MI
48231 Detroit, MI
48232 Detroit, MI
48233 Detroit, MI
48234 Detroit, MI
48235 Detroit, MI
48236 Detroit, MI
48236 Grosse Pointe, MI
48236 Grosse Pointe Farms, MI
48236 Grosse Pointe Park, MI
48236 Grosse Pointe Shores, MI
48236 Grosse Pointe Woods, MI
48237 Detroit, MI
48237 Oak Park, MI
48238 Detroit, MI
48239 Detroit, MI
48239 Redford, MI
48240 Detroit, MI
48240 Redford, MI
48242 Detroit, MI
48243 Detroit, MI
48244 Detroit, MI
48255 Detroit, MI
48260 Detroit, MI
48264 Detroit, MI
48265 Detroit, MI
48266 Detroit, MI
48267 Detroit, MI
48268 Detroit, MI
48269 Detroit, MI
48272 Detroit, MI
48275 Detroit, MI
48277 Detroit, MI
48278 Detroit, MI
48279 Detroit, MI
48288 Detroit, MI

483

48301 Bloomfield Hills, MI
48301 Bloomfield Township, MI
48301 Bloomfield Village, MI
48302 Bloomfield Hills, MI
48302 Bloomfield Township, MI
48302 Bloomfield Village, MI
48303 Bloomfield Hills, MI
48303 Bloomfield Township, MI
48303 Bloomfield Twp, MI
48303 Bloomfield Village, MI
48304 Bloomfield Hills, MI
48304 Bloomfield Township, MI
48304 Bloomfield Village, MI
48306 Goodison, MI
48306 Oakland, MI
48306 Oakland Township, MI
48306 Rochester, MI
48306 Rochester Hills, MI
48307 Rochester, MI
48307 Rochester Hills, MI
48308 Rochester, MI
48309 Rochester, MI
48309 Rochester Hills, MI
48310 Sterling Heights, MI
48315 Shelby Township, MI
48315 Utica, MI
48316 Shelby Township, MI
48316 Utica, MI
48317 Shelby Township, MI
48317 Utica, MI
48318 Shelby Township, MI
48318 Utica, MI
48320 Keego Harbor, MI
48320 Sylvan Lake, MI
48321 Auburn Hills, MI
48322 West Bloomfield, MI
48323 Orchard Lake, MI
48323 West Bloomfield, MI
48324 Orchard Lake, MI
48324 West Bloomfield, MI
48326 Auburn Hills, MI
48326 Lake Angelus, MI
48327 Waterford, MI
48328 W Bloomfld Tw, MI
48328 Waterford, MI
48329 Waterford, MI
48329 Waterford Township, MI
48330 Drayton Plains, MI
48330 Drayton Plns, MI
48330 Waterford Township, MI
48331 Farmington, MI
48331 Farmington Hills, MI
48331 Farmington Hls, MI
48332 Farmington, MI
48332 Farmington Hills, MI
48332 Farmington Hls, MI
48333 Farmington, MI
48333 Farmington Hills, MI
48333 Farmington Hls, MI
48334 Farmington, MI
48334 Farmington Hills, MI
48334 Farmington Hls, MI
48335 Farmington, MI
48335 Farmington Hills, MI
48335 Farmington Hls, MI
48336 Farmington, MI
48336 Farmington Hills, MI
48336 Farmington Hls, MI
48340 Mi Metro, MI
48340 Pontiac, MI
48341 Pontiac, MI
48342 Pontiac, MI
48343 Pontiac, MI
48346 Clarkston, MI
48346 Independence, MI
48347 Clarkston, MI
48348 Clarkston, MI
48348 Independence, MI
48350 Davisburg, MI
48350 Springfield Township, MI
48353 Hartland, MI
48356 Highland, MI
48357 Highland, MI
48359 Lake Orion, MI
48359 Orion, MI
48360 Lake Orion, MI
48360 Orion, MI
48361 Lake Orion, MI
48362 Lake Orion, MI
48362 Orion, MI
48363 Oakland, MI
48366 Lakeville, MI
48367 Addison Township, MI
48367 Leonard, MI
48370 Oxford, MI
48371 Oxford, MI
48374 Novi, MI
48375 Novi, MI
48376 Novi, MI
48377 Novi, MI
48380 Milford, MI
48381 Milford, MI
48382 Commerce Township, MI
48383 White Lake, MI
48386 White Lake, MI
48387 Union Lake, MI
48390 Commerce Township, MI
48390 Walled Lake, MI
48390 Wolverine Lake, MI
48391 Walled Lake, MI
48393 Wixom, MI
48397 Warren, MI

484

48401 Applegate, MI
48410 Argyle, MI
48411 Atlas, MI
48412 Attica, MI
48412 Lum, MI
48413 Bad Axe, MI
48414 Bancroft, MI
48415 Birch Run, MI
48416 Brown City, MI
48417 Burt, MI
48418 Byron, MI
48419 Carsonville, MI
48420 Clio, MI
48421 Columbiaville, MI
48422 Croswell, MI
48423 Davison, MI
48426 Decker, MI
48427 Deckerville, MI
48428 Dryden, MI
48429 Durand, MI
48429 Vernon City, MI
48430 Fenton, MI
48432 Filion, MI
48433 Flushing, MI
48434 Forestville, MI
48435 Fostoria, MI
48436 Gaines, MI
48437 Genesee, MI
48438 Goodrich, MI
48439 Grand Blanc, MI
48440 Hadley, MI
48441 Harbor Beach, MI
48442 Holly, MI
48444 Imlay City, MI
48445 Kinde, MI
48446 Lapeer, MI
48449 Lennon, MI
48450 Lexington, MI
48451 Linden, MI
48453 Marlette, MI
48454 Melvin, MI
48455 Metamora, MI
48456 Minden City, MI
48457 Montrose, MI
48458 Mount Morris, MI
48460 New Lothrop, MI
48461 North Branch, MI
48462 Ortonville, MI
48463 Otisville, MI
48464 Otter Lake, MI
48465 Minden City, MI
48465 Palms, MI
48466 Peck, MI
48467 Port Austin, MI
48468 Port Hope, MI
48469 Port Sanilac, MI
48470 Ruth, MI
48471 Sandusky, MI
48472 Snover, MI
48473 Swartz Creek, MI
48475 Ubly, MI
48476 Vernon, MI
48480 Grand Blanc, MI

485

48501 Flint, MI
48502 Flint, MI
48503 Flint, MI
48504 Flint, MI
48505 Flint, MI
48506 Flint, MI
48507 Flint, MI
48509 Burton, MI
48509 Flint, MI
48519 Burton, MI
48519 Flint, MI
48529 Burton, MI
48529 Flint, MI
48531 Flint, MI
48532 Flint, MI
48550 Flint, MI
48551 Flint, MI
48552 Flint, MI
48553 Flint, MI
48554 Flint, MI
48555 Flint, MI
48556 Flint, MI
48557 Flint, MI

486

48601 Saginaw, MI
48602 Saginaw, MI
48603 Saginaw, MI
48604 Saginaw, MI
48604 Zilwaukee, MI
48605 Saginaw, MI
48606 Saginaw, MI
48607 Saginaw, MI
48608 Saginaw, MI
48609 Saginaw, MI
48610 Alger, MI
48611 Auburn, MI
48612 Beaverton, MI
48613 Bentley, MI
48614 Brant, MI
48615 Breckenridge, MI
48616 Chesaning, MI
48617 Clare, MI
48618 Coleman, MI
48619 Comins, MI
48620 Edenville, MI
48621 Fairview, MI
48622 Farwell, MI
48623 Freeland, MI
48624 Gladwin, MI
48625 Harrison, MI
48626 Hemlock, MI
48627 Higgins Lake, MI
48628 Hope, MI
48629 Houghton Lake, MI
48630 Houghton Lake Heights, MI
48630 Htn Lk Hghts, MI
48631 Kawkawlin, MI
48632 Lake, MI
48632 Lake Station, MI
48633 Lake George, MI
48634 Linwood, MI
48635 Lupton, MI
48636 Luzerne, MI
48637 Merrill, MI
48638 Saginaw, MI
48640 Midland, MI
48641 Midland, MI
48642 Midland, MI
48647 Mio, MI
48649 Oakley, MI
48650 Pinconning, MI
48651 Prudenville, MI
48652 Rhodes, MI
48653 Roscommon, MI
48654 Rose City, MI
48655 Saint Charles, MI
48656 Saint Helen, MI
48657 Sanford, MI
48658 Standish, MI
48659 Sterling, MI
48661 West Branch, MI
48662 Wheeler, MI
48663 Saginaw, MI
48667 Midland, MI
48670 Midland, MI
48674 Midland, MI
48686 Midland, MI

487

48701 Akron, MI
48703 Au Gres, MI
48705 Barton City, MI
48706 Bay City, MI
48707 Bay City, MI
48708 Bay City, MI
48710 Bay City, MI
48710 University Center, MI
48720 Bay Port, MI
48721 Black River, MI
48722 Bridgeport, MI
48723 Caro, MI
48724 Carrollton, MI
48725 Caseville, MI
48725 Port Elizabeth, MI
48726 Cass City, MI
48727 Clifford, MI
48728 Curran, MI
48729 Deford, MI
48730 East Tawas, MI
48731 Elkton, MI
48732 Essexville, MI
48733 Fairgrove, MI
48734 Frankenmuth, MI
48735 Gagetown, MI
48737 Glennie, MI
48738 Greenbush, MI
48739 Hale, MI
48740 Harrisville, MI
48741 Kingston, MI
48742 Lincoln, MI
48743 Long Lake, MI
48744 Mayville, MI
48745 Mikado, MI
48746 Millington, MI
48747 Munger, MI
48748 National City, MI
48749 Omer, MI
48750 Au Sable, MI
48750 Oscoda, MI
48754 Owendale, MI
48755 Pigeon, MI
48755 Sand Point, MI
48756 Prescott, MI
48756 Roos, MI
48757 Reese, MI
48758 Richville, MI
48759 Sebewaing, MI
48760 Silverwood, MI
48761 South Branch, MI
48762 Spruce, MI
48763 Alabaster, MI
48763 Tawas City, MI
48764 Tawas City, MI
48765 Turner, MI
48766 Twining, MI
48767 Unionville, MI
48768 Tuscola, MI
48768 Vassar, MI
48770 Whittemore, MI
48787 Frankenmuth, MI

488

48801 Alma, MI
48804 Mount Pleasant, MI
48805 Okemos, MI
48806 Ashley, MI
48807 Bannister, MI
48808 Bath, MI
48809 Belding, MI
48811 Carson City, MI
48812 Cedar Lake, MI
48813 Charlotte, MI
48815 Clarksville, MI
48816 Cohoctah, MI
48817 Corunna, MI
48818 Crystal, MI
48819 Dansville, MI
48820 De Witt, MI
48820 Dewitt, MI
48821 Dimondale, MI
48822 Eagle, MI
48823 East Lansing, MI
48824 East Lansing, MI
48825 East Lansing, MI
48826 East Lansing, MI
48827 Eaton Rapids, MI
48829 Edmore, MI
48830 Elm Hall, MI
48831 Carland, MI
48831 Elsie, MI
48832 Elwell, MI
48833 Eureka, MI
48834 Fenwick, MI
48835 Fowler, MI
48836 Fowlerville, MI
48837 Grand Ledge, MI
48838 Greenville, MI
48840 Haslett, MI
48841 Henderson, MI
48841 Owosso, MI
48842 Holt, MI
48843 Howell, MI
48844 Howell, MI
48845 Hubbardston, MI
48846 Ionia, MI
48847 Ithaca, MI
48848 Laingsburg, MI
48849 Lake Odessa, MI
48850 Lakeview, MI
48851 Lyons, MI
48852 Mcbride, MI
48852 Mcbrides, MI
48853 Maple Rapids, MI
48854 Mason, MI
48855 Howell, MI
48856 Middleton, MI
48857 Morrice, MI
48858 Mount Pleasant, MI
48860 Muir, MI
48861 Mulliken, MI
48862 North Star, MI
48864 Okemos, MI
48865 Orleans, MI
48866 Ovid, MI
48867 Owosso, MI
48870 Palo, MI
48871 Perrinton, MI
48872 Perry, MI
48873 Pewamo, MI
48874 Pompeii, MI
48875 Portland, MI
48876 Potterville, MI
48877 Riverdale, MI
48878 Rosebush, MI
48879 Saint Johns, MI
48880 Saint Louis, MI
48881 Saranac, MI
48882 Shaftsburg, MI
48883 Shepherd, MI
48884 Sheridan, MI
48885 Sidney, MI
48886 Six Lakes, MI
48887 Belding, MI
48887 Smyrna, MI
48888 Stanton, MI
48889 Sumner, MI
48890 Sunfield, MI
48891 Vestaburg, MI
48892 Webberville, MI
48893 Lake Isabella, MI
48893 Weidman, MI
48894 Westphalia, MI
48895 Williamston, MI
48896 Winn, MI
48897 Woodland, MI

489

48901 Lansing, MI
48906 Lansing, MI
48908 Lansing, MI
48909 Lansing, MI
48910 Lansing, MI
48911 Lansing, MI
48912 Lansing, MI
48913 Lansing, MI
48915 Lansing, MI
48916 Lansing, MI
48917 Lansing, MI
48918 Lansing, MI
48919 Lansing, MI
48922 Lansing, MI

48924 Lansing, MI
48929 Lansing, MI
48930 Lansing, MI
48933 Lansing, MI
48937 Lansing, MI
48951 Lansing, MI
48956 Lansing, MI
48980 Lansing, MI

490

49001 Kalamazoo, MI
49002 Portage, MI
49003 Kalamazoo, MI
49004 Kalamazoo, MI
49004 Parchment, MI
49005 Kalamazoo, MI
49006 Kalamazoo, MI
49007 Kalamazoo, MI
49008 Kalamazoo, MI
49009 Kalamazoo, MI
49010 Allegan, MI
49011 Athens, MI
49012 Augusta, MI
49013 Bangor, MI
49014 Battle Creek, MI
49015 Battle Creek, MI
49015 Springfield, MI
49016 Battle Creek, MI
49017 Battle Creek, MI
49018 Battle Creek, MI
49019 Kalamazoo, MI
49020 Bedford, MI
49021 Bellevue, MI
49022 Benton Harbor, MI
49023 Benton Harbor, MI
49024 Portage, MI
49026 Bloomingdale, MI
49027 Breedsville, MI
49028 Bronson, MI
49029 Burlington, MI
49030 Burr Oak, MI
49031 Cassopolis, MI
49032 Centreville, MI
49033 Ceresco, MI
49034 Climax, MI
49035 Cloverdale, MI
49036 Coldwater, MI
49037 Battle Creek, MI
49037 Springfield, MI
49038 Coloma, MI
49039 Coloma, MI
49039 Hagar Shores, MI
49040 Colon, MI
49041 Comstock, MI
49042 Constantine, MI
49043 Covert, MI
49045 Decatur, MI
49046 Delton, MI
49047 Dowagiac, MI
49048 Kalamazoo, MI
49050 Dowling, MI
49051 East Leroy, MI
49052 Fulton, MI
49053 Galesburg, MI
49055 Gobles, MI
49056 Grand Junction, MI
49057 Hartford, MI
49058 Hastings, MI
49060 Hickory Corners, MI
49061 Jones, MI
49062 Kendall, MI
49063 Lacota, MI
49064 Lawrence, MI
49065 Lawton, MI
49066 Leonidas, MI
49067 Marcellus, MI
49068 Marshall, MI
49070 Martin, MI
49071 Mattawan, MI
49072 Mendon, MI
49073 Nashville, MI
49074 Nazareth, MI
49075 Nottawa, MI
49076 Olivet, MI
49077 Oshtemo, MI
49078 Otsego, MI
49079 Paw Paw, MI
49080 Plainwell, MI
49081 Portage, MI
49082 Quincy, MI
49083 Richland, MI
49084 Riverside, MI
49085 Saint Joseph, MI
49085 Shoreham, MI
49087 Schoolcraft, MI
49088 Scotts, MI
49089 Sherwood, MI
49090 South Haven, MI
49091 Sturgis, MI
49092 Tekonsha, MI
49093 Three Rivers, MI
49094 Union City, MI
49095 Vandalia, MI
49096 Vermontville, MI
49097 Vicksburg, MI
49098 Watervliet, MI
49099 Mottville, MI
49099 White Pigeon, MI

491

49101 Baroda, MI
49102 Berrien Center, MI
49103 Berrien Springs, MI
49106 Bridgman, MI
49107 Buchanan, MI
49107 Glendora, MI
49111 Eau Claire, MI
49112 Edwardsburg, MI
49113 Galien, MI
49115 Harbert, MI
49116 Lakeside, MI
49117 Grand Beach, MI
49117 Michiana, MI
49117 New Buffalo, MI
49119 New Troy, MI
49120 Niles, MI
49125 Sawyer, MI
49126 Sodus, MI
49127 Stevensville, MI
49128 Lakeside, MI
49128 Three Oaks, MI
49129 Union Pier, MI
49130 Edwardsburg, MI
49130 Union, MI

492

49201 Jackson, MI
49202 Jackson, MI
49203 Jackson, MI
49204 Jackson, MI
49220 Addison, MI
49221 Adrian, MI
49221 Cadmus, MI
49224 Albion, MI
49227 Allen, MI
49228 Blissfield, MI
49229 Britton, MI
49229 Ridgeway, MI
49230 Brooklyn, MI
49232 Camden, MI
49233 Cement City, MI
49234 Clarklake, MI
49235 Clayton, MI
49235 Clayton Twp, MI
49236 Clinton, MI
49237 Concord, MI
49238 Deerfield, MI
49239 Frontier, MI
49240 Grass Lake, MI
49241 Hanover, MI
49242 Hillsdale, MI
49245 Homer, MI
49246 Horton, MI
49247 Hudson, MI
49247 Rollin, MI
49248 Jasper, MI
49249 Jerome, MI
49250 Jonesville, MI
49251 Leslie, MI
49252 Litchfield, MI
49253 Manitou Beach, MI
49254 Michigan Center, MI
49255 Montgomery, MI
49256 Morenci, MI
49256 Seneca, MI
49257 Moscow, MI
49258 Mosherville, MI
49259 Munith, MI
49261 Napoleon, MI
49262 North Adams, MI
49263 Norvell, MI
49264 Onondaga, MI
49265 Onsted, MI
49266 Osseo, MI
49267 Ottawa Lake, MI
49268 Palmyra, MI
49269 Parma, MI
49270 Petersburg, MI
49271 Pittsford, MI
49271 Prattville, MI
49272 Pleasant Lake, MI
49274 Reading, MI
49276 Riga, MI
49277 Rives Junction, MI
49279 Sand Creek, MI
49281 Somerset, MI
49282 Somerset Center, MI
49283 Spring Arbor, MI
49284 Springport, MI
49285 Stockbridge, MI
49286 Tecumseh, MI
49287 Tipton, MI
49288 Waldron, MI
49289 Weston, MI

493

49301 Ada, MI
49302 Alto, MI
49303 Bailey, MI
49304 Baldwin, MI
49305 Barryton, MI
49306 Belmont, MI
49307 Big Rapids, MI
49309 Bitely, MI
49310 Blanchard, MI
49310 Millbrook, MI
49311 Bradley, MI
49312 Brohman, MI
49314 Burnips, MI
49315 Byron Center, MI
49316 Caledonia, MI
49316 Dutton, MI
49317 Cannonsburg, MI
49318 Casnovia, MI
49319 Cedar Springs, MI
49320 Chippewa Lake, MI
49321 Comstock Park, MI
49322 Coral, MI
49323 Dorr, MI
49325 Freeport, MI
49326 Gowen, MI
49327 Grant, MI
49328 Hopkins, MI
49329 Howard City, MI
49330 Kent City, MI
49331 Lowell, MI
49332 Mecosta, MI
49333 Middleville, MI
49335 Moline, MI
49336 Morley, MI
49337 Newaygo, MI
49338 Paris, MI
49339 Pierson, MI
49340 Remus, MI
49341 Rockford, MI
49342 Rodney, MI
49343 Sand Lake, MI
49344 Shelbyville, MI
49345 Sparta, MI
49346 Canadian Lakes, MI
49346 Stanwood, MI
49347 Trufant, MI
49348 Wayland, MI
49349 White Cloud, MI
49351 Rockford, MI
49355 Ada, MI
49356 Ada, MI
49357 Ada, MI

494

49401 Allendale, MI
49402 Branch, MI
49403 Conklin, MI
49404 Coopersville, MI
49405 Custer, MI
49406 Douglas, MI
49408 Fennville, MI
49409 Ferrysburg, MI
49410 Fountain, MI
49411 Free Soil, MI
49412 Fremont, MI
49413 Fremont, MI
49415 Fruitport, MI
49416 Glenn, MI
49417 Grand Haven, MI
49418 Grandville, MI
49418 Wyoming, MI
49419 Hamilton, MI
49420 Hart, MI
49421 Hesperia, MI
49422 Holland, MI
49423 Holland, MI
49424 Holland, MI
49425 Brunswick, MI
49425 Holton, MI
49426 Hudsonville, MI
49427 Jamestown, MI
49428 Georgetown Township, MI
49428 Jenison, MI
49429 Jenison, MI
49430 Lamont, MI
49431 Ludington, MI
49434 Macatawa, MI
49435 Marne, MI
49436 Mears, MI
49436 Silver Lake, MI
49437 Montague, MI
49440 Muskegon, MI
49441 Muskegon, MI
49441 Norton Shores, MI
49442 Muskegon, MI
49443 Muskegon, MI
49444 Muskegon, MI
49444 Muskegon Heights, MI
49444 Norton Shores, MI
49445 Muskegon, MI
49445 North Muskegon, MI
49446 New Era, MI
49448 Nunica, MI
49449 Pentwater, MI
49450 Pullman, MI
49451 Ravenna, MI
49452 Rothbury, MI
49453 Saugatuck, MI
49454 Scottville, MI
49455 Shelby, MI
49456 Norton Shores, MI
49456 Spring Lake, MI
49457 Twin Lake, MI
49458 Walhalla, MI
49459 Walkerville, MI
49460 West Olive, MI
49461 Whitehall, MI
49463 Sylvan Beach, MI
49463 Wabaningo, MI
49463 Whitehall, MI
49464 Zeeland, MI
49468 Grandville, MI

495

49501 Grand Rapids, MI
49502 Grand Rapids, MI
49503 Grand Rapids, MI
49503 Wyoming, MI
49504 Grand Rapids, MI
49505 Grand Rapids, MI
49506 East Grand Ra, MI
49506 East Grand Rapids, MI
49506 Grand Rapids, MI
49507 Grand Rapids, MI
49508 Grand Rapids, MI
49508 Kentwood, MI
49508 Wyoming, MI
49509 Grand Rapids, MI
49509 Wyoming, MI
49510 Grand Rapids, MI
49512 Grand Rapids, MI
49512 Kentwood, MI
49514 Grand Rapids, MI
49515 Grand Rapids, MI
49516 Grand Rapids, MI
49518 Grand Rapids, MI
49518 Kentwood, MI
49519 Grand Rapids, MI
49519 Wyoming, MI
49523 Grand Rapids, MI
49525 Grand Rapids, MI
49528 Grand Rapids, MI
49530 Grand Rapids, MI
49534 Grand Rapids, MI
49534 Walker, MI
49544 Grand Rapids, MI
49544 Walker, MI
49546 Grand Rapids, MI
49548 Grand Rapids, MI
49548 Kentwood, MI
49548 Wyoming, MI
49555 Grand Rapids, MI
49560 Grand Rapids, MI
49588 Grand Rapids, MI
49588 Kentwood, MI
49599 Grand Rapids, MI

496

49601 Cadillac, MI
49601 Hoxeyville, MI
49610 Acme, MI
49611 Alba, MI
49612 Alden, MI
49613 Arcadia, MI
49614 Bear Lake, MI
49614 Pierport, MI
49615 Bellaire, MI
49616 Benzonia, MI
49617 Beulah, MI
49618 Boon, MI
49619 Brethren, MI
49620 Buckley, MI
49621 Cedar, MI
49622 Central Lake, MI
49623 Chase, MI
49625 Copemish, MI
49626 Eastlake, MI
49627 Eastport, MI
49628 Elberta, MI
49629 Elk Rapids, MI
49630 Empire, MI
49631 Evart, MI
49632 Falmouth, MI
49633 Fife Lake, MI
49634 Filer City, MI
49635 Frankfort, MI
49636 Glen Arbor, MI
49637 Grawn, MI
49638 Harrietta, MI
49639 Hersey, MI
49640 Honor, MI
49642 Idlewild, MI
49643 Interlochen, MI
49643 Karlin, MI
49644 Irons, MI
49645 Kaleva, MI
49646 Kalkaska, MI
49648 Kewadin, MI
49649 Kingsley, MI
49650 Lake Ann, MI
49651 Lake City, MI
49651 Moorestown, MI
49653 Lake Leelanau, MI
49654 Leland, MI
49655 Leroy, MI
49656 Luther, MI
49657 Mc Bain, MI
49659 Mancelona, MI
49660 Manistee, MI
49660 Stronach, MI
49663 Manton, MI
49664 Maple City, MI
49665 Marion, MI
49666 Mayfield, MI
49667 Merritt, MI
49668 Mesick, MI
49670 Northport, MI
49673 Old Mission, MI
49674 Omena, MI
49675 Onekama, MI
49676 Rapid City, MI
49677 Reed City, MI
49679 Sears, MI
49680 South Boardman, MI
49682 Peshawbestown, MI
49682 Suttons Bay, MI
49683 Thompsonville, MI
49684 Traverse City, MI
49685 Traverse City, MI
49686 Traverse City, MI
49688 Tustin, MI
49689 Wellston, MI
49690 Williamsburg, MI
49696 Traverse City, MI

497

49701 Mackinaw City, MI
49705 Afton, MI
49706 Alanson, MI
49707 Alpena, MI
49709 Atlanta, MI
49710 Barbeau, MI
49711 Bay Shore, MI
49711 Charlevoix, MI
49712 Boyne City, MI
49713 Boyne Falls, MI
49715 Brimley, MI
49715 Raco, MI
49716 Brutus, MI
49717 Burt Lake, MI
49718 Carp Lake, MI
49719 Cedarville, MI
49720 Charlevoix, MI
49721 Cheboygan, MI
49722 Conway, MI
49723 Cross Village, MI
49724 Dafter, MI
49725 De Tour Village, MI
49726 Drummond Island, MI
49727 East Jordan, MI
49728 Eckerman, MI
49728 Strongs, MI
49729 Ellsworth, MI
49730 Elmira, MI
49733 Frederic, MI
49734 Gaylord, MI
49735 Gaylord, MI
49735 Treetops Village, MI
49736 Goetzville, MI
49736 Stalwart, MI
49737 Good Hart, MI
49737 Harbor Springs, MI
49738 Grayling, MI
49739 Grayling, MI
49740 Harbor Point, MI
49740 Harbor Springs, MI
49740 Wequetonsing, MI
49743 Hawks, MI
49744 Herron, MI
49745 Hessel, MI
49746 Hillman, MI
49747 Hubbard Lake, MI
49748 Hulbert, MI
49749 Indian River, MI
49751 Johannesburg, MI
49752 Kinross, MI
49753 Lachine, MI
49755 Levering, MI
49756 Lewiston, MI
49757 Mackinac Island, MI
49759 Millersburg, MI
49759 Ocqueoc, MI
49760 Moran, MI
49761 Mullett Lake, MI
49762 Naubinway, MI
49764 Oden, MI
49765 Onaway, MI
49766 Ossineke, MI
49768 Paradise, MI
49769 Pellston, MI
49770 Bay Harbor, MI
49770 Bay View, MI
49770 Petoskey, MI
49774 Pickford, MI
49775 Bois Blanc Island, MI
49775 Pointe Aux Pins, MI

49776 Posen, MI
49777 Presque Isle, MI
49779 Rogers City, MI
49780 Fibre, MI
49780 Rudyard, MI
49781 Saint Ignace, MI
49782 Beaver Island, MI
49783 Sault Sainte Marie, MI
49784 Kincheloe, MI
49784 Sault Sainte Marie, MI
49785 Kincheloe, MI
49785 Sault Sainte Marie, MI
49786 Kincheloe, MI
49786 Sault Sainte Marie, MI
49788 Kincheloe, MI
49788 Sault Sainte Marie, MI
49791 Topinabee, MI
49792 Tower, MI
49793 Trout Lake, MI
49795 Vanderbilt, MI
49796 Walloon Lake, MI
49797 Waters, MI
49799 Wolverine, MI

498

49801 Iron Mountain, MI
49802 Iron Mountain, MI
49802 Kingsford, MI
49805 Allouez, MI
49806 Au Train, MI
49807 Bark River, MI
49807 Hardwood, MI
49807 Schaffer, MI
49808 Big Bay, MI
49812 Carney, MI
49814 Champion, MI
49815 Channing, MI
49816 Chatham, MI
49816 Limestone, MI
49817 Cooks, MI
49818 Cornell, MI
49819 Arnold, MI
49819 Cornell, MI
49820 Curtis, MI
49821 Daggett, MI
49822 Deerton, MI
49825 Eben Junction, MI
49826 Eben Junction, MI
49826 Rumely, MI
49827 Engadine, MI
49829 Escanaba, MI
49831 Felch, MI
49831 Iron Mountain, MI
49833 Little Lake, MI
49834 Foster City, MI
49834 Hardwood, MI
49835 Garden, MI
49836 Germfask, MI
49837 Brampton, MI
49837 Gladstone, MI
49838 Gould City, MI
49839 Grand Marais, MI
49840 Gulliver, MI
49841 Gwinn, MI
49841 Princeton, MI
49845 Harris, MI
49847 Hermansville, MI
49848 Ingalls, MI
49849 Ishpeming, MI
49852 Loretto, MI
49852 Vulcan, MI
49853 Mc Millan, MI
49854 Manistique, MI
49854 Thompson, MI
49855 Harvey, MI
49855 Marquette, MI
49858 Menominee, MI
49861 Michigamme, MI
49862 Christmas, MI
49862 Munising, MI
49863 Nadeau, MI
49864 Nahma, MI
49865 Ishpeming, MI
49865 National Mine, MI
49866 Negaunee, MI
49868 Newberry, MI
49870 Norway, MI
49871 Palmer, MI
49872 Perkins, MI
49873 Perronville, MI
49874 Powers, MI
49876 Quinnesec, MI
49877 Felch, MI
49877 Ralph, MI
49878 Rapid River, MI
49879 Republic, MI
49880 Rock, MI
49881 Sagola, MI
49883 Seney, MI
49884 Shingleton, MI
49885 Skandia, MI
49886 Spalding, MI
49887 Cedar River, MI
49887 Stephenson, MI
49891 Traunik, MI
49891 Trenary, MI
49892 Vulcan, MI
49893 Wallace, MI
49894 Wells, MI
49895 Wetmore, MI
49896 Wilson, MI

499

49901 Ahmeek, MI
49902 Alpha, MI
49903 Amasa, MI
49905 Atlantic Mine, MI
49908 Baraga, MI
49908 Keweenaw Bay, MI
49910 Bergland, MI
49911 Bessemer, MI
49912 Bruce Crossing, MI
49913 Calumet, MI
49913 Laurium, MI
49915 Caspian, MI
49916 Chassell, MI
49917 Copper City, MI
49918 Calumet, MI
49918 Copper Harbor, MI
49919 Covington, MI
49920 Crystal Falls, MI
49921 Dodgeville, MI
49921 Houghton, MI
49922 Dollar Bay, MI
49925 Ewen, MI
49927 Gaastra, MI
49929 Greenland, MI
49930 Hancock, MI
49931 Houghton, MI
49934 Hubbell, MI
49935 Beechwood, MI
49935 Iron River, MI
49938 Ironwood, MI
49942 Calumet, MI
49942 Kearsarge, MI
49945 Gay, MI
49945 Lake Linden, MI
49946 Lanse, MI
49947 Marenisco, MI
49947 Merriweather, MI
49948 Mass City, MI
49950 Eagle Harbor, MI
49950 Eagle River, MI
49950 Mohawk, MI
49952 Nisula, MI
49953 Ontonagon, MI
49955 Painesdale, MI
49958 Pelkie, MI
49959 Ramsay, MI
49960 Rockland, MI
49961 Sidnaw, MI
49962 Skanee, MI
49963 South Range, MI
49964 Stambaugh, MI
49965 Toivola, MI
49967 Kenton, MI
49967 Trout Creek, MI
49968 Wakefield, MI
49969 Watersmeet, MI
49970 Watton, MI
49971 White Pine, MI

500

50001 Ackworth, IA
50002 Adair, IA
50003 Adel, IA
50005 Albion, IA
50006 Alden, IA
50006 Buckeye, IA
50007 Alleman, IA
50008 Allerton, IA
50009 Altoona, IA
50010 Ames, IA
50011 Ames, IA
50012 Ames, IA
50013 Ames, IA
50014 Ames, IA
50020 Anita, IA
50021 Ankeny, IA
50022 Atlantic, IA
50023 Ankeny, IA
50025 Audubon, IA
50026 Bagley, IA
50027 Barnes City, IA
50028 Baxter, IA
50029 Bayard, IA
50031 Beaver, IA
50032 Berwick, IA
50033 Bevington, IA
50034 Blairsburg, IA
50035 Bondurant, IA
50036 Boone, IA
50037 Boone, IA
50038 Booneville, IA
50039 Bouton, IA
50040 Boxholm, IA
50041 Bradford, IA
50042 Brayton, IA
50043 Buckeye, IA
50044 Bussey, IA
50046 Cambridge, IA
50047 Carlisle, IA
50048 Casey, IA
50049 Chariton, IA
50050 Churdan, IA
50051 Clemons, IA
50052 Clio, IA
50054 Colfax, IA
50055 Collins, IA
50056 Colo, IA
50057 Columbia, IA
50058 Coon Rapids, IA
50059 Cooper, IA
50060 Corydon, IA
50060 Sewal, IA
50061 Cumming, IA
50061 W Des Moines, IA
50061 West Des Moines, IA
50062 Dallas, IA
50062 Melcher Dallas, IA
50063 Dallas Center, IA
50064 Dana, IA
50065 Davis City, IA
50065 Pleasanton, IA
50066 Dawson, IA
50067 Decatur, IA
50068 Derby, IA
50069 De Soto, IA
50070 Dexter, IA
50071 Dows, IA
50072 Earlham, IA
50073 Elkhart, IA
50074 Beaconsfield, IA
50074 Ellston, IA
50075 Ellsworth, IA
50076 Exira, IA
50078 Ferguson, IA
50099 Boone, IA

501

50101 Galt, IA
50102 Garden City, IA
50103 Garden Grove, IA
50104 Gibson, IA
50105 Gilbert, IA
50106 Gilman, IA
50107 Grand Junction, IA
50108 Grand River, IA
50109 Granger, IA
50110 Gray, IA
50111 Grimes, IA
50112 Grinnell, IA
50112 Oakland Acres, IA
50115 Guthrie Center, IA
50116 Hamilton, IA
50117 Hamlin, IA
50118 Hartford, IA
50119 Harvey, IA
50120 Haverhill, IA
50122 Hubbard, IA
50123 Humeston, IA
50124 Huxley, IA
50125 Indianola, IA
50125 Spring Hill, IA
50126 Iowa Falls, IA
50127 Ira, IA
50128 Jamaica, IA
50129 Jefferson, IA
50130 Jewell, IA
50131 Johnston, IA
50132 Kamrar, IA
50133 Kellerton, IA
50134 Kelley, IA
50135 Kellogg, IA
50136 Keswick, IA
50137 Killduff, IA
50138 Knoxville, IA
50138 Pershing, IA
50139 Lacona, IA
50140 Lamoni, IA
50141 Laurel, IA
50142 Le Grand, IA
50143 Leighton, IA
50144 Leon, IA
50145 Liberty Center, IA
50146 Linden, IA
50147 Lineville, IA
50148 Liscomb, IA
50149 Lorimor, IA
50150 Lovilia, IA
50151 Lucas, IA
50152 Luther, IA
50153 Lynnville, IA
50154 Mc Callsburg, IA
50155 Macksburg, IA
50156 Madrid, IA
50157 Malcom, IA
50158 Marshalltown, IA
50160 Martensdale, IA
50161 Maxwell, IA
50162 Melbourne, IA
50163 Melcher, IA
50163 Melcher Dallas, IA
50164 Menlo, IA
50165 Millerton, IA
50166 Milo, IA
50167 Minburn, IA
50168 Mingo, IA
50169 Mitchellville, IA
50170 Monroe, IA
50171 Montezuma, IA
50173 Montour, IA
50174 Murray, IA

502

50201 Nevada, IA
50206 New Providence, IA
50207 New Sharon, IA
50207 Taintor, IA
50208 Newton, IA
50210 New Virginia, IA
50211 Churchville, IA
50211 Norwalk, IA
50212 Ogden, IA
50213 Osceola, IA
50214 Otley, IA
50216 Panora, IA
50217 Paton, IA
50218 Patterson, IA
50219 Pella, IA
50220 Perry, IA
50222 East Peru, IA
50222 Peru, IA
50223 Pilot Mound, IA
50225 Pleasantville, IA
50226 Polk City, IA
50227 Popejoy, IA
50228 Prairie City, IA
50229 Prole, IA
50230 Radcliffe, IA
50231 Randall, IA
50232 Reasnor, IA
50233 Redfield, IA
50234 Harvester, IA
50234 Rhodes, IA
50235 Rippey, IA
50236 Roland, IA
50237 Runnells, IA
50238 Russell, IA
50239 Saint Anthony, IA
50240 Saint Charles, IA
50241 Saint Marys, IA
50242 Searsboro, IA
50243 Sheldahl, IA
50244 Slater, IA
50246 Stanhope, IA
50247 State Center, IA
50248 Story City, IA
50249 Stratford, IA
50250 Stuart, IA
50251 Sully, IA
50252 Swan, IA
50254 Thayer, IA
50255 Thornburg, IA
50256 Tracy, IA
50257 Truro, IA
50258 Union, IA
50259 Gifford, IA
50261 Van Meter, IA
50262 Van Wert, IA
50263 Waukee, IA
50264 Weldon, IA
50265 W Des Moines, IA
50265 West Des Moines, IA
50268 What Cheer, IA
50269 Whitten, IA
50271 Williams, IA
50272 Williamson, IA
50273 Winterset, IA
50274 Wiota, IA
50275 Woodburn, IA
50276 Woodward, IA
50277 Yale, IA
50278 Zearing, IA

503

50301 Des Moines, IA
50302 Des Moines, IA
50303 Des Moines, IA
50304 Des Moines, IA
50305 Des Moines, IA
50306 Des Moines, IA
50307 Des Moines, IA
50308 Des Moines, IA
50309 Des Moines, IA
50310 Beaverdale, IA
50310 Des Moines, IA
50311 Des Moines, IA
50312 Des Moines, IA
50313 Des Moines, IA
50314 Des Moines, IA
50315 Des Moines, IA
50316 Des Moines, IA
50317 Des Moines, IA
50317 Pleasant Hill, IA
50318 Des Moines, IA
50319 Des Moines, IA
50320 Des Moines, IA
50321 Des Moines, IA
50322 Des Moines, IA
50322 Urbandale, IA
50323 Des Moines, IA
50323 Urbandale, IA
50324 Clive, IA
50324 Des Moines, IA
50324 Windsor Heights, IA
50325 Clive, IA
50325 Des Moines, IA
50327 Des Moines, IA
50327 Pleasant Hill, IA
50328 Des Moines, IA
50329 Des Moines, IA
50330 Des Moines, IA
50331 Des Moines, IA
50332 Des Moines, IA
50333 Des Moines, IA
50334 Des Moines, IA
50335 Des Moines, IA
50336 Des Moines, IA
50339 Des Moines, IA
50340 Des Moines, IA
50359 Des Moines, IA
50360 Des Moines, IA
50361 Des Moines, IA
50362 Des Moines, IA
50363 Des Moines, IA
50364 Des Moines, IA
50367 Des Moines, IA
50368 Des Moines, IA
50369 Des Moines, IA
50380 Des Moines, IA
50381 Des Moines, IA
50391 Des Moines, IA
50391 Urbandale, IA
50392 Des Moines, IA
50393 Des Moines, IA
50394 Des Moines, IA
50395 Des Moines, IA
50395 Urbandale, IA
50396 Des Moines, IA
50398 Urbandale, IA
50398 West Des Moines, IA

504

50401 Mason City, IA
50402 Mason City, IA
50420 Alexander, IA
50421 Belmond, IA
50423 Britt, IA
50424 Buffalo Center, IA
50426 Carpenter, IA
50427 Chapin, IA
50428 Clear Lake, IA
50430 Corwith, IA
50431 Coulter, IA
50432 Crystal Lake, IA
50433 Dougherty, IA
50434 Fertile, IA
50435 Floyd, IA
50436 Forest City, IA
50438 Garner, IA
50439 Goodell, IA
50440 Grafton, IA
50441 Hampton, IA
50441 Hansell, IA
50444 Hanlontown, IA
50446 Joice, IA
50447 Kanawha, IA
50448 Kensett, IA
50449 Klemme, IA
50450 Lake Mills, IA
50451 Lakota, IA
50452 Latimer, IA
50453 Leland, IA
50454 Little Cedar, IA
50455 Mc Intire, IA
50456 Manly, IA
50457 Meservey, IA
50458 Nora Springs, IA
50459 Northwood, IA
50460 Orchard, IA
50461 Mitchell, IA
50461 Osage, IA
50464 Plymouth, IA
50465 Rake, IA
50466 Riceville, IA
50467 Rock Falls, IA
50468 Rockford, IA
50469 Rockwell, IA
50470 Rowan, IA
50471 Rudd, IA
50472 Saint Ansgar, IA
50473 Scarville, IA
50475 Sheffield, IA
50476 Stacyville, IA
50477 Swaledale, IA
50478 Thompson, IA
50479 Thornton, IA
50480 Titonka, IA
50481 Toeterville, IA
50482 Ventura, IA
50483 Wesley, IA
50484 Woden, IA

505

50501 Fort Dodge, IA
50510 Albert City, IA
50511 Algona, IA
50514 Armstrong, IA
50515 Ayrshire, IA
50516 Badger, IA
50517 Bancroft, IA
50518 Barnum, IA
50519 Bode, IA
50520 Bradgate, IA
50521 Burnside, IA
50522 Burt, IA
50523 Callender, IA
50524 Clare, IA
50525 Clarion, IA
50526 Clarion, IA
50527 Curlew, IA
50528 Cylinder, IA
50529 Dakota City, IA
50530 Dayton, IA
50531 Dolliver, IA
50532 Duncombe, IA
50533 Eagle Grove, IA
50535 Early, IA
50536 Emmetsburg, IA
50538 Farnhamville, IA
50538 Rinard, IA
50539 Fenton, IA
50540 Fonda, IA
50541 Gilmore City, IA
50542 Goldfield, IA
50543 Gowrie, IA
50544 Harcourt, IA
50545 Hardy, IA
50546 Havelock, IA
50548 Humboldt, IA
50551 Jolley, IA
50552 Knierim, IA
50554 Laurens, IA
50556 Ledyard, IA
50557 Lehigh, IA
50558 Livermore, IA
50559 Lone Rock, IA
50560 Lu Verne, IA
50561 Lytton, IA
50562 Mallard, IA
50563 Manson, IA
50565 Marathon, IA
50566 Moorland, IA
50567 Nemaha, IA
50568 Newell, IA
50569 Otho, IA
50570 Ottosen, IA
50571 Palmer, IA
50573 Plover, IA
50574 Pocahontas, IA
50575 Knoke, IA
50575 Pomeroy, IA
50576 Rembrandt, IA
50577 Renwick, IA
50578 Ringsted, IA
50579 Rockwell City, IA
50581 Rolfe, IA
50582 Rutland, IA
50583 Sac City, IA
50585 Sioux Rapids, IA
50586 Somers, IA
50588 Lakeside, IA
50588 Storm Lake, IA
50590 Swea City, IA
50591 Thor, IA
50592 Truesdale, IA
50593 Varina, IA
50594 Vincent, IA
50595 Webster City, IA
50597 West Bend, IA
50598 Whittemore, IA
50599 Woolstock, IA

506

50601 Ackley, IA
50602 Allison, IA
50603 Alta Vista, IA
50604 Aplington, IA
50605 Aredale, IA
50606 Arlington, IA
50607 Aurora, IA
50608 Austinville, IA
50609 Beaman, IA
50611 Bristow, IA
50612 Buckingham, IA
50613 Cedar Falls, IA
50614 Cedar Falls, IA
50616 Charles City, IA
50619 Clarksville, IA
50620 Colwell, IA
50621 Conrad, IA
50622 Denver, IA
50623 Dewar, IA
50624 Dike, IA
50625 Dumont, IA
50626 Dunkerton, IA
50627 Eldora, IA
50628 Elma, IA
50629 Fairbank, IA
50630 Fredericksburg, IA
50631 Frederika, IA
50632 Garwin, IA
50632 Green Mountain, IA
50633 Geneva, IA
50634 Gilbertville, IA
50635 Gladbrook, IA
50636 Greene, IA
50638 Grundy Center, IA
50641 Hazleton, IA
50642 Holland, IA
50643 Hudson, IA
50643 Voorhies, IA
50644 Independence, IA
50645 Ionia, IA
50647 Janesville, IA
50648 Jesup, IA
50649 Kesley, IA
50650 Lamont, IA
50651 La Porte City, IA
50652 Lincoln, IA
50653 Marble Rock, IA
50654 Masonville, IA
50655 Maynard, IA
50657 Morrison, IA
50658 Nashua, IA
50659 New Hampton, IA
50659 North Washington, IA
50660 New Hartford, IA
50661 North Washington, IA
50662 Oelwein, IA
50664 Oran, IA
50665 Parkersburg, IA
50666 Plainfield, IA
50667 Raymond, IA
50668 Readlyn, IA
50669 Reinbeck, IA
50670 Shell Rock, IA
50671 Stanley, IA
50672 Steamboat Rock, IA
50673 Stout, IA
50674 Sumner, IA
50675 Traer, IA
50676 Tripoli, IA
50677 Bremer, IA
50677 Waverly, IA
50680 Wellsburg, IA
50681 Westgate, IA
50682 Winthrop, IA

507

50701 Waterloo, IA
50702 Washburn, IA
50702 Waterloo, IA
50703 Waterloo, IA
50704 Waterloo, IA
50707 Elk Run Heights, IA
50707 Evansdale, IA
50707 Waterloo, IA

508

50801 Creston, IA
50830 Afton, IA
50831 Arispe, IA
50833 Bedford, IA
50835 Benton, IA
50836 Blockton, IA
50836 Maloy, IA
50837 Bridgewater, IA
50839 Carbon, IA
50840 Clearfield, IA
50841 Corning, IA
50842 Cromwell, IA
50843 Cumberland, IA
50845 Diagonal, IA
50846 Fontanelle, IA
50847 Grant, IA
50848 Gravity, IA
50849 Greenfield, IA
50851 Kent, IA
50851 Lenox, IA
50853 Massena, IA
50854 Mount Ayr, IA
50857 Nodaway, IA
50858 Orient, IA
50859 Prescott, IA
50860 Delphos, IA
50860 Redding, IA
50861 Shannon City, IA
50862 Sharpsburg, IA
50863 Tingley, IA
50864 Villisca, IA

509

50936 Des Moines, IA
50940 Des Moines, IA
50947 Des Moines, IA
50950 Des Moines, IA
50980 Des Moines, IA
50981 Des Moines, IA
50982 Des Moines, IA
50983 Des Moines, IA

510

51001 Akron, IA
51002 Alta, IA
51003 Alton, IA
51004 Anthon, IA
51005 Aurelia, IA
51006 Battle Creek, IA
51007 Bronson, IA
51008 Brunsville, IA
51009 Calumet, IA
51010 Castana, IA
51011 Chatsworth, IA
51012 Cherokee, IA
51014 Cleghorn, IA
51015 Climbing Hill, IA
51016 Correctionville, IA
51018 Cushing, IA
51019 Danbury, IA
51020 Galva, IA
51022 Granville, IA
51023 Hawarden, IA
51024 Hinton, IA
51025 Holstein, IA
51026 Hornick, IA
51027 Ireton, IA
51028 Kingsley, IA
51029 Larrabee, IA
51030 Lawton, IA
51031 Le Mars, IA
51031 Struble, IA
51033 Linn Grove, IA
51034 Mapleton, IA
51035 Marcus, IA
51036 Maurice, IA
51037 Meriden, IA
51038 Merrill, IA
51039 Moville, IA
51040 Onawa, IA
51040 Turin, IA
51041 Orange City, IA
51044 Oto, IA
51045 Oyens, IA
51046 Paullina, IA
51047 Peterson, IA
51048 Pierson, IA
51049 Quimby, IA
51050 Remsen, IA
51051 Rodney, IA
51052 Salix, IA
51053 Schaller, IA
51054 Sergeant Bluff, IA
51055 Sloan, IA
51056 Smithland, IA
51058 Sutherland, IA
51060 Ute, IA
51061 Washta, IA
51062 Westfield, IA
51063 Whiting, IA

511

51101 Sioux City, IA
51102 Sioux City, IA
51103 Sioux City, IA
51104 Sioux City, IA
51105 Sioux City, IA
51106 Sioux City, IA
51108 Sioux City, IA
51109 Sioux City, IA
51111 Sioux City, IA

512

51201 Sheldon, IA
51230 Alvord, IA
51231 Archer, IA
51232 Ashton, IA
51234 Boyden, IA
51235 Doon, IA
51237 George, IA
51238 Hospers, IA
51239 Hull, IA
51240 Inwood, IA
51241 Larchwood, IA
51242 Lester, IA
51243 Little Rock, IA
51244 Matlock, IA
51245 Primghar, IA
51246 Rock Rapids, IA
51247 Rock Valley, IA
51248 Sanborn, IA
51249 Sibley, IA
51250 Sioux Center, IA

513

51301 Spencer, IA
51331 Arnolds Park, IA
51333 Dickens, IA
51334 Estherville, IA
51334 Gruver, IA
51338 Everly, IA
51340 Fostoria, IA
51341 Gillett Grove, IA
51342 Graettinger, IA
51343 Greenville, IA
51345 Harris, IA
51346 Hartley, IA
51347 Lake Park, IA
51350 Melvin, IA
51351 Milford, IA
51354 Allendorf, IA
51354 May City, IA
51354 Ocheyedan, IA
51355 Okoboji, IA
51357 Rossie, IA
51357 Royal, IA
51358 Ruthven, IA
51360 Orleans, IA
51360 Spirit Lake, IA
51363 Superior, IA
51364 Terril, IA
51365 Wallingford, IA
51366 Webb, IA

514

51401 Carroll, IA
51430 Arcadia, IA
51431 Arthur, IA
51432 Aspinwall, IA
51433 Auburn, IA
51433 Yetter, IA
51436 Breda, IA
51439 Charter Oak, IA
51440 Dedham, IA
51441 Deloit, IA
51442 Denison, IA
51443 Glidden, IA
51444 Halbur, IA
51445 Ida Grove, IA
51446 Irwin, IA
51447 Kirkman, IA
51448 Kiron, IA
51449 Lake City, IA
51450 Carnarvon, IA
51450 Lake View, IA
51451 Lanesboro, IA
51452 Lidderdale, IA
51453 Lohrville, IA
51454 Manilla, IA
51455 Manning, IA
51458 Odebolt, IA
51459 Ralston, IA
51460 Ricketts, IA
51461 Schleswig, IA
51462 Scranton, IA
51463 Templeton, IA
51465 Vail, IA
51466 Wall Lake, IA
51467 Westside, IA

515

51501 Council Bluffs, IA
51501 Manawa, IA
51502 Council Bluffs, IA
51510 Carter Lake, IA
51520 Arion, IA
51521 Avoca, IA
51523 Blencoe, IA
51525 Carson, IA
51526 Crescent, IA
51527 Defiance, IA
51528 Dow City, IA
51529 Dunlap, IA
51530 Earling, IA
51531 Elk Horn, IA
51532 Elliott, IA
51533 Emerson, IA
51534 Glenwood, IA
51535 Griswold, IA
51536 Hancock, IA
51537 Harlan, IA
51537 Tennant, IA
51540 Hastings, IA
51541 Henderson, IA
51542 Honey Creek, IA
51543 Kimballton, IA
51544 Lewis, IA
51545 Little Sioux, IA
51546 Logan, IA
51548 Mc Clelland, IA
51549 Macedonia, IA
51550 Magnolia, IA
51551 Malvern, IA
51552 Marne, IA
51553 Minden, IA
51554 Mineola, IA
51555 Missouri Valley, IA
51555 Mo Valley, IA
51556 Modale, IA
51557 Mondamin, IA
51558 Moorhead, IA
51559 Neola, IA
51560 Oakland, IA
51561 Pacific Junction, IA
51562 Panama, IA
51563 Persia, IA
51564 Pisgah, IA
51565 Portsmouth, IA
51566 Red Oak, IA
51570 Shelby, IA
51571 Silver City, IA
51572 Soldier, IA
51573 Stanton, IA
51575 Treynor, IA
51576 Underwood, IA
51577 Walnut, IA
51578 Westphalia, IA
51579 Woodbine, IA
51591 Red Oak, IA
51593 Harlan, IA

516

51601 Shenandoah, IA
51603 Shenandoah, IA
51630 Blanchard, IA
51631 Braddyville, IA
51632 Clarinda, IA
51636 Coin, IA
51637 College Springs, IA
51638 Essex, IA
51639 Farragut, IA
51640 Hamburg, IA
51645 Imogene, IA
51646 New Market, IA
51647 Northboro, IA
51648 Percival, IA
51649 Randolph, IA
51650 Riverton, IA
51651 Shambaugh, IA
51652 Sidney, IA
51653 Tabor, IA
51654 Bartlett, IA
51654 Thurman, IA
51656 Yorktown, IA

520

52001 Dubuque, IA
52002 Asbury, IA
52002 Dubuque, IA
52003 Dubuque, IA
52004 Dubuque, IA
52030 Andrew, IA
52031 Bellevue, IA
52032 Bernard, IA
52033 Cascade, IA
52035 Colesburg, IA
52036 Delaware, IA
52037 Delmar, IA
52038 Dundee, IA
52039 Durango, IA
52040 Dyersville, IA
52041 Earlville, IA
52042 Edgewood, IA
52042 Littleport, IA
52043 Elkader, IA
52044 Elkport, IA
52045 Epworth, IA
52046 Farley, IA
52047 Farmersburg, IA
52048 Garber, IA
52049 Clayton, IA
52049 Garnavillo, IA
52050 Greeley, IA
52052 Guttenberg, IA
52053 Holy Cross, IA
52054 La Motte, IA
52056 Luxemburg, IA
52057 Manchester, IA
52060 Maquoketa, IA
52064 Green Island, IA
52064 Miles, IA
52065 New Vienna, IA
52066 North Buena Vista, IA
52068 Peosta, IA
52069 Preston, IA
52070 Sabula, IA
52071 Saint Donatus, IA
52072 Saint Olaf, IA
52073 Sherrill, IA
52074 Spragueville, IA
52075 Springbrook, IA
52076 Strawberry Point, IA
52077 Volga, IA
52078 Worthington, IA
52079 Zwingle, IA
52099 Dubuque, IA

521

52101 Burr Oak, IA
52101 Decorah, IA
52132 Calmar, IA
52133 Castalia, IA
52134 Chester, IA
52135 Clermont, IA
52136 Cresco, IA
52140 Dorchester, IA
52141 Elgin, IA
52142 Fayette, IA
52144 Festina, IA
52144 Fort Atkinson, IA

52146 Harpers Ferry, IA
52147 Hawkeye, IA
52149 Highlandville, IA
52151 Lansing, IA
52154 Lawler, IA
52155 Lime Springs, IA
52155 Saratoga, IA
52156 Luana, IA
52157 Mc Gregor, IA
52158 Marquette, IA
52159 Monona, IA
52160 New Albin, IA
52161 Ossian, IA
52162 Postville, IA
52163 Protivin, IA
52164 Randalia, IA
52165 Ridgeway, IA
52166 Saint Lucas, IA
52168 Spillville, IA
52169 Wadena, IA
52170 Waterville, IA
52171 Alpha, IA
52171 Jackson Junction, IA
52171 Waucoma, IA
52172 Waukon, IA
52175 Auburn Douglas, IA
52175 Eldorado, IA
52175 West Union, IA

522

52201 Ainsworth, IA
52202 Alburnett, IA
52203 Amana, IA
52203 West Amana, IA
52204 Amana, IA
52205 Anamosa, IA
52206 Atkins, IA
52207 Baldwin, IA
52208 Belle Plaine, IA
52209 Blairstown, IA
52210 Brandon, IA
52211 Brooklyn, IA
52212 Center Junction, IA
52213 Center Point, IA
52214 Central City, IA
52215 Chelsea, IA
52216 Clarence, IA
52217 Clutier, IA
52218 Coggon, IA
52219 Prairieburg, IA
52220 Conroy, IA
52221 Guernsey, IA
52222 Deep River, IA
52223 Delhi, IA
52224 Dysart, IA
52225 Elberon, IA
52227 Ely, IA
52228 Fairfax, IA
52229 Garrison, IA
52231 Harper, IA
52232 Hartwick, IA
52233 Hiawatha, IA
52235 Hills, IA
52236 Homestead, IA
52237 Hopkinton, IA
52240 Iowa City, IA
52241 Coralville, IA
52241 Iowa City, IA
52241 Oakdale, IA
52242 Iowa City, IA
52243 Iowa City, IA
52244 Iowa City, IA
52245 Iowa City, IA
52246 Coralville, IA
52246 Iowa City, IA
52247 Kalona, IA
52248 Keota, IA
52249 Keystone, IA
52251 Ladora, IA
52252 Langworthy, IA
52253 Lisbon, IA
52254 Elwood, IA
52254 Lost Nation, IA
52255 Lowden, IA
52257 Luzerne, IA

523

52301 Marengo, IA
52302 Marion, IA
52305 Martelle, IA
52306 Mechanicsville, IA
52307 Middle, IA
52307 Middle Amana, IA
52308 Millersburg, IA
52309 Monmouth, IA
52310 Monticello, IA
52310 Scotch Grove, IA
52312 Morley, IA
52313 Mount Auburn, IA
52314 Mount Vernon, IA
52315 Newhall, IA
52316 North English, IA
52317 North Liberty, IA
52318 Norway, IA
52320 Olin, IA
52321 Onslow, IA
52322 Oxford, IA
52323 Oxford Junction, IA
52324 Palo, IA
52325 Parnell, IA
52326 Quasqueton, IA
52327 Riverside, IA
52328 Robins, IA
52329 Rowley, IA
52330 Ryan, IA
52332 Shellsburg, IA
52333 Solon, IA
52334 South Amana, IA
52335 Kinross, IA
52335 South English, IA
52336 Springville, IA
52336 Viola, IA
52336 Whittier, IA
52337 Stanwood, IA
52338 Shueyville, IA
52338 Swisher, IA
52339 Tama, IA
52340 Tiffin, IA
52341 Toddville, IA
52342 Toledo, IA
52344 Troy Mills, IA
52345 Urbana, IA
52346 Van Horne, IA
52347 Victor, IA
52348 Vining, IA
52349 Vinton, IA
52351 Walford, IA
52352 Walker, IA
52353 Washington, IA
52354 Watkins, IA
52355 Webster, IA
52356 Wellman, IA
52358 West Branch, IA
52359 West Chester, IA
52361 Williamsburg, IA
52362 Hale, IA
52362 Wyoming, IA

524

52401 Cedar Rapids, IA
52402 Cedar Rapids, IA
52403 Bertram, IA
52403 Cedar Rapids, IA
52404 Cedar Rapids, IA
52405 Cedar Rapids, IA
52406 Cedar Rapids, IA
52407 Cedar Rapids, IA
52408 Cedar Rapids, IA
52409 Cedar Rapids, IA
52410 Cedar Rapids, IA
52411 Cedar Rapids, IA
52497 Cedar Rapids, IA
52498 Cedar Rapids, IA
52499 Cedar Rapids, IA

525

52501 Ottumwa, IA
52530 Agency, IA
52531 Albia, IA
52531 Hiteman, IA
52533 Batavia, IA
52534 Beacon, IA
52535 Birmingham, IA
52536 Blakesburg, IA
52537 Bloomfield, IA
52537 West Grove, IA
52540 Brighton, IA
52542 Cantril, IA
52543 Cedar, IA
52544 Centerville, IA
52544 Numa, IA
52544 Rathbun, IA
52548 Chillicothe, IA
52549 Cincinnati, IA
52550 Delta, IA
52551 Douds, IA
52552 Drakesville, IA
52553 Eddyville, IA
52554 Eldon, IA
52555 Exline, IA
52556 Fairfield, IA
52556 Maharishi Vedic City, IA
52557 Fairfield, IA
52560 Floris, IA
52561 Fremont, IA
52562 Hayesville, IA
52563 Hedrick, IA
52565 Keosauqua, IA
52566 Kirkville, IA
52567 Libertyville, IA
52568 Martinsburg, IA
52569 Melrose, IA
52570 Milton, IA
52571 Moravia, IA
52572 Moulton, IA
52573 Mount Sterling, IA
52574 Mystic, IA
52576 Ollie, IA
52577 Keomah Village, IA
52577 Oskaloosa, IA
52580 Packwood, IA
52581 Plano, IA
52583 Promise City, IA
52584 Pulaski, IA
52585 Richland, IA
52585 Rubio, IA
52586 Rose Hill, IA
52588 Selma, IA
52590 Seymour, IA
52591 Sigourney, IA
52593 Udell, IA
52594 Unionville, IA
52595 University Park, IA

526

52601 Burlington, IA
52619 Argyle, IA
52620 Bonaparte, IA
52621 Crawfordsville, IA
52623 Danville, IA
52624 Denmark, IA
52625 Donnellson, IA
52626 Farmington, IA
52627 Fort Madison, IA
52630 Hillsboro, IA
52631 Houghton, IA
52632 Keokuk, IA
52635 Lockridge, IA
52637 Mediapolis, IA
52638 Middletown, IA
52639 Montrose, IA
52640 Morning Sun, IA
52641 Mount Pleasant, IA
52642 Rome, IA
52644 Mount Union, IA
52644 Mt Union, IA
52645 Lowell, IA
52645 New London, IA
52646 Oakville, IA
52647 Olds, IA
52648 Pilot Grove, IA
52649 Salem, IA
52650 Sperry, IA
52651 Stockport, IA
52652 Swedesburg, IA
52653 Wapello, IA
52654 Wayland, IA
52655 West Burlington, IA
52656 West Point, IA
52657 Saint Paul, IA
52657 West Point, IA
52658 Wever, IA
52659 Winfield, IA
52660 Yarmouth, IA

527

52701 Andover, IA
52720 Atalissa, IA
52721 Bennett, IA
52722 Bettendorf, IA
52722 Riverdale, IA
52726 Blue Grass, IA
52727 Bryant, IA
52728 Buffalo, IA
52729 Calamus, IA
52730 Camanche, IA
52731 Charlotte, IA
52732 Clinton, IA
52733 Clinton, IA
52734 Clinton, IA
52736 Clinton, IA
52737 Columbus City, IA
52738 Columbus Junction, IA
52739 Conesville, IA
52742 De Witt, IA
52745 Big Rock, IA
52745 Dixon, IA
52746 Donahue, IA
52747 Durant, IA
52748 Eldridge, IA
52749 Fruitland, IA
52750 Goose Lake, IA
52751 Grand Mound, IA
52752 Grandview, IA
52753 Le Claire, IA
52753 Leclaire, IA
52754 Letts, IA
52755 Lone Tree, IA
52756 Long Grove, IA
52757 Low Moor, IA
52758 Mc Causland, IA
52759 Montpelier, IA
52760 Moscow, IA
52761 Muscatine, IA
52765 New Liberty, IA
52766 Nichols, IA
52767 Pleasant Valley, IA
52768 Princeton, IA
52769 Stockton, IA
52771 Clinton, IA
52771 Teeds Grove, IA
52772 Tipton, IA
52773 Maysville, IA
52773 Walcott, IA
52774 Welton, IA
52776 West Liberty, IA
52777 Toronto, IA
52777 Wheatland, IA
52778 Wilton, IA

528

52801 Davenport, IA
52802 Davenport, IA
52803 Davenport, IA
52804 Davenport, IA
52805 Davenport, IA
52806 Davenport, IA
52807 Davenport, IA
52808 Davenport, IA
52809 Davenport, IA

530

53001 Adell, WI
53002 Allenton, WI
53003 Ashippun, WI
53004 Belgium, WI
53005 Brookfield, WI
53006 Brownsville, WI
53006 Byron, WI
53006 South Byron, WI
53007 Butler, WI
53008 Brookfield, WI
53010 Campbellsport, WI
53011 Cascade, WI
53012 Cedarburg, WI
53013 Cedar Grove, WI
53014 Chilton, WI
53015 Cleveland, WI
53016 Clyman, WI
53017 Colgate, WI
53018 Delafield, WI
53019 Eden, WI
53020 Elkhart Lake, WI
53021 Fredonia, WI
53021 Waubeka, WI
53022 Germantown, WI
53022 Rockfield, WI
53023 Glenbeulah, WI
53024 Grafton, WI
53026 Greenbush, WI
53027 Hartford, WI
53029 Hartland, WI
53031 Hingham, WI
53032 Horicon, WI
53033 Hubertus, WI
53034 Hustisford, WI
53035 Iron Ridge, WI
53036 Ixonia, WI
53037 Jackson, WI
53038 Johnson Creek, WI
53039 Juneau, WI
53040 Kewaskum, WI
53042 Kiel, WI
53044 Kohler, WI
53045 Brookfield, WI
53046 Lannon, WI
53047 Lebanon, WI
53048 Knowles, WI
53048 Lomira, WI
53049 Malone, WI
53050 Mayville, WI
53051 Menomonee Falls, WI
53056 Merton, WI
53057 Mount Calvary, WI
53058 Nashotah, WI
53059 Neosho, WI
53060 Newburg, WI
53061 New Holstein, WI
53062 New Holstein, WI
53063 Newton, WI
53064 North Lake, WI
53065 Oakfield, WI
53066 Oconomowoc, WI
53066 Summit, WI
53069 Okauchee, WI
53070 Oostburg, WI
53072 Brookfield, WI
53072 Pewaukee, WI
53073 Plymouth, WI
53074 Port Washington, WI
53075 Random Lake, WI
53076 Richfield, WI
53078 Rubicon, WI
53079 Saint Cloud, WI
53080 Saukville, WI
53081 Sheboygan, WI
53082 Sheboygan, WI
53083 Haven, WI
53083 Howards Grove, WI
53083 Sheboygan, WI
53085 Sheboygan Falls, WI
53086 Slinger, WI
53088 Stockbridge, WI
53089 Lisbon, WI
53089 Sussex, WI
53090 West Bend, WI
53091 Theresa, WI
53092 Mequon, WI
53092 Thiensville, WI
53093 Waldo, WI
53094 Johnson Creek, WI
53094 Watertown, WI
53095 West Bend, WI
53097 Mequon, WI
53097 Thiensville, WI
53098 Watertown, WI
53099 Woodland, WI

531

53101 Bassett, WI
53102 Benet Lake, WI
53102 Trevor, WI
53103 Big Bend, WI
53104 Bristol, WI
53105 Burlington, WI
53108 Caledonia, WI
53109 Camp Lake, WI
53110 Cudahy, WI
53114 Darien, WI
53115 Delavan, WI
53118 Dousman, WI
53119 Eagle, WI
53120 East Troy, WI
53121 Elkhorn, WI
53122 Elm Grove, WI
53125 Fontana, WI
53126 Franksville, WI
53127 Genesee Depot, WI
53128 Genoa City, WI
53129 Greendale, WI
53130 Hales Corners, WI
53132 Franklin, WI
53137 Helenville, WI
53138 Honey Creek, WI
53139 Kansasville, WI
53140 Kenosha, WI
53141 Kenosha, WI
53142 Kenosha, WI
53143 Kenosha, WI
53144 Kenosha, WI
53146 New Berlin, WI
53147 Lake Geneva, WI
53148 Lyons, WI
53149 Mukwonago, WI
53150 Muskego, WI
53151 New Berlin, WI
53152 New Munster, WI
53153 North Prairie, WI
53154 Oak Creek, WI
53156 Palmyra, WI
53157 Pell Lake, WI
53158 Kenosha, WI
53158 Pleasant Prairie, WI
53159 Powers Lake, WI
53167 Rochester, WI
53168 Salem, WI
53170 Silver Lake, WI
53171 Somers, WI
53172 South Milwaukee, WI
53176 Springfield, WI
53177 Mount Pleasant, WI
53177 Sturtevant, WI
53178 Sullivan, WI
53179 Trevor, WI
53181 Twin Lakes, WI
53182 Union Grove, WI
53183 Wales, WI
53184 Walworth, WI
53185 Waterford, WI
53185 Wind Lake, WI
53186 Vernon, WI
53186 Waukesha, WI
53187 Waukesha, WI
53188 Vernon, WI
53188 Waukesha, WI
53189 Waukesha, WI
53190 Whitewater, WI
53191 Williams Bay, WI
53192 Wilmot, WI
53194 Woodworth, WI
53195 Zenda, WI

532

53201 Milwaukee, WI
53202 Milwaukee, WI
53203 Milwaukee, WI
53204 Milwaukee, WI
53205 Milwaukee, WI
53206 Milwaukee, WI
53207 Bay View, WI
53207 Milwaukee, WI
53208 Milwaukee, WI
53209 Brown Deer, WI
53209 Glendale, WI
53209 Milwaukee, WI
53209 River Hills, WI
53210 Milwaukee, WI
53210 Wauwatosa, WI
53211 Glendale, WI
53211 Milwaukee, WI
53211 Shorewood, WI
53211 Whitefish Bay, WI

53212 Glendale, WI
53212 Milwaukee, WI
53213 Milwaukee, WI
53213 Wauwatosa, WI
53214 Milwaukee, WI
53214 West Allis, WI
53214 West Milwaukee, WI
53215 Milwaukee, WI
53215 West Milwaukee, WI
53216 Milwaukee, WI
53217 Bayside, WI
53217 Fox Point, WI
53217 Glendale, WI
53217 Milwaukee, WI
53217 River Hills, WI
53217 Whitefish Bay, WI
53218 Milwaukee, WI
53219 Greenfield, WI
53219 Milwaukee, WI
53219 West Allis, WI
53219 West Milwaukee, WI
53220 Greenfield, WI
53220 Milwaukee, WI
53221 Greenfield, WI
53221 Milwaukee, WI
53222 Milwaukee, WI
53222 Wauwatosa, WI
53223 Brown Deer, WI
53223 Milwaukee, WI
53224 Milwaukee, WI
53225 Milwaukee, WI
53225 Wauwatosa, WI
53226 Milwaukee, WI
53226 Wauwatosa, WI
53227 Milwaukee, WI
53227 New Berlin, WI
53227 West Allis, WI
53228 Greenfield, WI
53228 Milwaukee, WI
53228 New Berlin, WI
53233 Milwaukee, WI
53234 Milwaukee, WI
53235 Milwaukee, WI
53235 Saint Francis, WI
53235 St Francis, WI
53237 Milwaukee, WI
53259 Milwaukee, WI
53263 Milwaukee, WI
53267 Milwaukee, WI
53268 Milwaukee, WI
53274 Milwaukee, WI
53278 Milwaukee, WI
53288 Milwaukee, WI
53290 Milwaukee, WI
53293 Milwaukee, WI
53295 Milwaukee, WI

534

53401 Mount Pleasant, WI
53401 Racine, WI
53402 Racine, WI
53402 Wind Point, WI
53403 Mount Pleasant, WI
53403 Racine, WI
53404 Mount Pleasant, WI
53404 Racine, WI
53405 Elmwood Park, WI
53405 Mount Pleasant, WI
53405 Racine, WI
53406 Mount Pleasant, WI
53406 Racine, WI
53407 Racine, WI
53408 Racine, WI

535

53501 Afton, WI
53502 Albany, WI
53503 Arena, WI
53504 Argyle, WI
53505 Avalon, WI
53506 Avoca, WI
53507 Barneveld, WI
53508 Belleville, WI
53510 Belmont, WI
53511 Beloit, WI
53512 Beloit, WI
53515 Black Earth, WI
53516 Blanchardville, WI
53517 Blue Mounds, WI
53518 Blue River, WI
53520 Brodhead, WI
53521 Brooklyn, WI
53522 Browntown, WI
53523 Cambridge, WI
53525 Clinton, WI
53526 Cobb, WI
53527 Cottage Grove, WI
53528 Cross Plains, WI
53529 Dane, WI
53530 Darlington, WI
53531 Deerfield, WI
53532 De Forest, WI
53533 Dodgeville, WI
53534 Edgerton, WI
53535 Edmund, WI
53536 Evansville, WI
53537 Footville, WI
53538 Fort Atkinson, WI
53540 Gotham, WI
53541 Gratiot, WI
53542 Hanover, WI
53543 Highland, WI
53544 Hollandale, WI
53545 Janesville, WI
53546 Janesville, WI
53547 Janesville, WI
53548 Janesville, WI
53549 Jefferson, WI
53550 Juda, WI
53551 Lake Mills, WI
53553 Linden, WI
53554 Livingston, WI
53555 Lodi, WI
53556 Lone Rock, WI
53557 Lowell, WI
53558 Mc Farland, WI
53559 Marshall, WI
53560 Mazomanie, WI
53561 Merrimac, WI
53562 Middleton, WI
53563 Milton, WI
53565 Mineral Point, WI
53566 Monroe, WI
53569 Montfort, WI
53570 Monticello, WI
53571 Morrisonville, WI
53572 Mount Horeb, WI
53573 Muscoda, WI
53574 New Glarus, WI
53575 Fitchburg, WI
53575 Oregon, WI
53576 Orfordville, WI
53577 Plain, WI
53578 Prairie Du Sac, WI
53579 Reeseville, WI
53580 Rewey, WI
53581 Richland Center, WI
53582 Ridgeway, WI
53583 Sauk City, WI
53584 Sextonville, WI
53585 Sharon, WI
53586 Shullsburg, WI
53587 South Wayne, WI
53588 Spring Green, WI
53589 Stoughton, WI
53590 Sun Prairie, WI
53593 Fitchburg, WI
53593 Verona, WI
53594 Waterloo, WI
53595 Dodgeville, WI
53596 Sun Prairie, WI
53597 Middleton, WI
53597 Waunakee, WI
53597 Westport, WI
53598 Windsor, WI
53599 Woodford, WI

537

53701 Madison, WI
53702 Madison, WI
53703 Madison, WI
53704 Madison, WI
53705 Madison, WI
53706 Madison, WI
53707 Madison, WI
53708 Madison, WI
53711 Fitchburg, WI
53711 Madison, WI
53713 Fitchburg, WI
53713 Madison, WI
53713 Monona, WI
53714 Madison, WI
53714 Monona, WI
53715 Madison, WI
53716 Madison, WI
53716 Monona, WI
53717 Madison, WI
53718 Madison, WI
53719 Fitchburg, WI
53719 Madison, WI
53725 Madison, WI
53726 Madison, WI
53744 Madison, WI
53774 Madison, WI
53777 Madison, WI
53778 Madison, WI
53779 Madison, WI
53782 Madison, WI
53783 Madison, WI
53784 Madison, WI
53785 Madison, WI
53786 Madison, WI
53788 Madison, WI
53789 Madison, WI
53790 Madison, WI
53791 Madison, WI
53792 Madison, WI
53793 Madison, WI
53794 Madison, WI

538

53801 Bagley, WI
53802 Beetown, WI
53803 Benton, WI
53804 Bloomington, WI
53805 Boscobel, WI
53806 Cassville, WI
53807 Cuba City, WI
53808 Dickeyville, WI
53809 Fennimore, WI
53810 Glen Haven, WI
53811 Hazel Green, WI
53812 Kieler, WI
53813 Lancaster, WI
53816 Mount Hope, WI
53817 Patch Grove, WI
53818 Platteville, WI
53820 Potosi, WI
53821 Prairie Du Chien, WI
53824 Sinsinawa, WI
53825 Stitzer, WI
53826 Wauzeka, WI
53827 Woodman, WI

539

53901 Portage, WI
53910 Adams, WI
53911 Arlington, WI
53913 Baraboo, WI
53916 Beaver Dam, WI
53919 Brandon, WI
53920 Briggsville, WI
53922 Burnett, WI
53923 Cambria, WI
53923 Friesland, WI
53924 Cazenovia, WI
53925 Columbus, WI
53926 Dalton, WI
53927 Dellwood, WI
53928 Doylestown, WI
53929 Elroy, WI
53930 Endeavor, WI
53931 Fairwater, WI
53932 Fall River, WI
53933 Fox Lake, WI
53934 Friendship, WI
53935 Friesland, WI
53936 Grand Marsh, WI
53937 Hillpoint, WI
53939 Kingston, WI
53940 Lake Delton, WI
53941 La Valle, WI
53942 Lime Ridge, WI
53943 Loganville, WI
53944 Lyndon Station, WI
53946 Manchester, WI
53946 Markesan, WI
53947 Marquette, WI
53948 Mauston, WI
53949 Montello, WI
53950 New Lisbon, WI
53951 North Freedom, WI
53952 Brooks, WI
53952 Oxford, WI
53953 Packwaukee, WI
53954 Pardeeville, WI
53955 Poynette, WI
53956 Randolph, WI
53957 Randolph, WI
53958 Reedsburg, WI
53959 Reedsburg, WI
53960 Rio, WI
53961 Rock Springs, WI
53962 Union Center, WI
53963 Waupun, WI
53964 Westfield, WI
53965 Wisconsin Dells, WI
53968 Wonewoc, WI
53969 Wyocena, WI

540

54001 Amery, WI
54001 Deronda, WI
54002 Baldwin, WI
54003 Beldenville, WI
54004 Clayton, WI
54005 Clear Lake, WI
54006 Cushing, WI
54007 Deer Park, WI
54009 Dresser, WI
54010 East Ellsworth, WI
54010 Ellsworth, WI
54011 Ellsworth, WI
54013 Emerald, WI
54013 Glenwood City, WI
54014 Hager City, WI
54015 Hammond, WI
54016 Hudson, WI
54017 New Richmond, WI
54020 Osceola, WI
54021 Prescott, WI
54022 River Falls, WI
54023 Roberts, WI
54024 Saint Croix Falls, WI
54025 Somerset, WI
54026 Star Prairie, WI
54027 Wilson, WI
54028 Woodville, WI
54082 Houlton, WI

541

54101 Abrams, WI
54102 Amberg, WI
54103 Armstrong Creek, WI
54104 Athelstane, WI
54104 Silver Cliff, WI
54106 Black Creek, WI
54107 Bonduel, WI
54107 Navarino, WI
54110 Brillion, WI
54111 Cecil, WI
54112 Coleman, WI
54113 Combined Locks, WI
54114 Beaver, WI
54114 Crivitz, WI
54114 Middle Inlet, WI
54115 Ashwaubenon, WI
54115 De Pere, WI
54115 Hobart, WI
54119 Dunbar, WI
54119 Pembine, WI
54120 Fence, WI
54121 Florence, WI
54123 Forest Junction, WI
54124 Gillett, WI
54124 Pulcifer, WI
54124 Underhill, WI
54125 Goodman, WI
54126 Greenleaf, WI
54127 Green Valley, WI
54128 Gresham, WI
54129 Hilbert, WI
54130 Freedom, WI
54130 Kaukauna, WI
54131 Freedom, WI
54131 Kaukauna, WI
54135 Keshena, WI
54136 Kimberly, WI
54137 Krakow, WI
54138 Lakewood, WI
54139 Lena, WI
54139 Stiles, WI
54140 Little Chute, WI
54141 Little Suamico, WI
54143 Marinette, WI
54149 Mountain, WI
54150 Neopit, WI
54151 Niagara, WI
54152 Nichols, WI
54153 Oconto, WI
54154 Oconto Falls, WI
54155 Hobart, WI
54155 Oneida, WI
54156 Pembine, WI
54157 Peshtigo, WI
54159 Porterfield, WI
54160 Potter, WI
54161 Pound, WI
54162 Pulaski, WI
54165 Freedom, WI
54165 Seymour, WI
54166 Shawano, WI
54169 Sherwood, WI
54170 Shiocton, WI
54171 Krakow, WI
54171 Sobieski, WI
54173 Suamico, WI
54174 Suring, WI
54175 Townsend, WI
54177 Wausaukee, WI
54180 Wrightstown, WI
54182 Bonduel, WI
54182 Zachow, WI

542

54201 Algoma, WI
54201 Rio Creek, WI
54202 Baileys Harbor, WI
54204 Brussels, WI
54205 Casco, WI
54207 Collins, WI
54208 Denmark, WI
54209 Egg Harbor, WI
54210 Ellison Bay, WI
54211 Ephraim, WI
54212 Fish Creek, WI
54213 Forestville, WI
54214 Francis Creek, WI
54215 Kellnersville, WI
54216 Kewaunee, WI
54217 Luxemburg, WI
54220 Manitowoc, WI
54221 Manitowoc, WI
54226 Maplewood, WI
54227 Maribel, WI
54228 Mishicot, WI
54229 Green Bay, WI
54229 New Franken, WI
54230 Cato, WI
54230 Reedsville, WI
54232 Saint Nazianz, WI
54234 Sister Bay, WI
54235 Maplewood, WI
54235 Sturgeon Bay, WI
54240 Tisch Mills, WI
54241 Two Rivers, WI
54245 Valders, WI
54246 Washington Island, WI
54247 Branch, WI
54247 Whitelaw, WI

543

54301 Allouez, WI
54301 Green Bay, WI
54302 Green Bay, WI
54303 Green Bay, WI
54303 Howard, WI
54304 Ashwaubenon, WI
54304 Green Bay, WI
54305 Green Bay, WI
54306 Green Bay, WI
54307 Green Bay, WI
54308 Green Bay, WI
54311 Bellevue, WI
54311 Green Bay, WI
54313 Ashwaubenon, WI
54313 Green Bay, WI
54313 Hobart, WI
54313 Howard, WI
54313 Suamico, WI
54324 Green Bay, WI
54344 Green Bay, WI

544

54401 Wausau, WI
54402 Wausau, WI
54403 Wausau, WI
54404 Marshfield, WI
54405 Abbotsford, WI
54406 Amherst, WI
54407 Amherst Junction, WI
54408 Aniwa, WI
54409 Antigo, WI
54410 Arpin, WI
54411 Athens, WI
54411 Hamburg, WI
54411 Milan, WI
54412 Auburndale, WI
54413 Babcock, WI
54414 Birnamwood, WI
54415 Blenker, WI
54416 Bowler, WI
54417 Brokaw, WI
54418 Bryant, WI
54420 Chili, WI
54421 Colby, WI
54422 Curtiss, WI
54423 Custer, WI
54424 Deerbrook, WI
54424 Kempster, WI
54425 Dorchester, WI
54426 Edgar, WI
54426 Fenwood, WI
54427 Eland, WI
54428 Elcho, WI
54429 Elderon, WI
54430 Elton, WI
54432 Galloway, WI
54432 Wittenberg, WI
54433 Gilman, WI
54434 Gilman, WI
54434 Jump River, WI
54435 Gleason, WI
54436 Granton, WI
54437 Greenwood, WI
54439 Hannibal, WI
54440 Hatley, WI
54441 Hewitt, WI
54442 Irma, WI
54443 Junction City, WI
54446 Loyal, WI
54447 Lublin, WI
54448 Marathon, WI
54449 Marshfield, WI
54450 Mattoon, WI
54451 Chelsea, WI
54451 Medford, WI
54452 Merrill, WI
54454 Milladore, WI
54455 Kronenwetter, WI
54455 Mosinee, WI
54456 Neillsville, WI
54457 Nekoosa, WI
54458 Nelsonville, WI
54459 Ogema, WI
54460 Owen, WI
54462 Pearson, WI
54463 Pelican Lake, WI
54464 Phlox, WI
54465 Pickerel, WI
54466 Pittsville, WI

54467 Plover, WI
54469 Port Edwards, WI
54470 Rib Lake, WI
54471 Ringle, WI
54472 Marshfield, WI
54473 Rosholt, WI
54474 Rothschild, WI
54475 Rudolph, WI
54476 Schofield, WI
54476 Weston, WI
54479 Spencer, WI
54480 Stetsonville, WI
54481 Stevens Point, WI
54482 Stevens Point, WI
54484 Stratford, WI
54485 Summit Lake, WI
54486 Tigerton, WI
54487 Tomahawk, WI
54488 Unity, WI
54489 Vesper, WI
54490 Westboro, WI
54491 Lily, WI
54491 White Lake, WI
54492 Stevens Point, WI
54493 Willard, WI
54494 Wisconsin Rapids, WI
54498 Withee, WI
54499 Wittenberg, WI

545

54501 Monico, WI
54501 Rhinelander, WI
54511 Argonne, WI
54511 Cavour, WI
54511 Hiles, WI
54511 Newald, WI
54512 Boulder Junction, WI
54513 Brantwood, WI
54514 Butternut, WI
54515 Catawba, WI
54517 Clam Lake, WI
54519 Conover, WI
54520 Crandon, WI
54521 Eagle River, WI
54524 Fifield, WI
54525 Gile, WI
54526 Glen Flora, WI
54526 Ingram, WI
54527 Glidden, WI
54529 Harshaw, WI
54530 Hawkins, WI
54531 Hazelhurst, WI
54532 Heafford Jct, WI
54532 Heafford Junction, WI
54532 Tomahawk, WI
54534 Hurley, WI
54536 Iron Belt, WI
54537 Kennan, WI
54538 Lac Du Flambeau, WI
54539 Lake Tomahawk, WI
54540 Land O Lakes, WI
54541 Laona, WI
54542 Alvin, WI
54542 Long Lake, WI
54542 Nelma, WI
54542 Tipler, WI
54543 Mc Naughton, WI
54545 Manitowish Waters, WI
54546 Mellen, WI
54547 Mercer, WI
54548 Minocqua, WI
54550 Montreal, WI
54550 Pence, WI
54552 Park Falls, WI
54554 Phelps, WI
54555 Phillips, WI
54556 Prentice, WI
54557 Presque Isle, WI
54557 Winchester, WI
54558 Saint Germain, WI
54559 Gurney, WI
54559 Saxon, WI
54560 Sayner, WI
54561 Star Lake, WI
54562 Three Lakes, WI
54563 Tony, WI
54564 Tripoli, WI
54565 Upson, WI
54566 Wabeno, WI
54568 Arbor Vitae, WI
54568 Woodruff, WI

546

54601 La Crosse, WI
54602 La Crosse, WI
54603 La Crosse, WI
54610 Alma, WI
54611 Alma Center, WI
54612 Arcadia, WI
54613 Arkdale, WI
54614 Bangor, WI
54615 Black River Falls, WI
54616 Blair, WI
54618 Camp Douglas, WI
54618 Cutler, WI
54619 Cashton, WI
54620 Cataract, WI
54621 Chaseburg, WI
54622 Buffalo City, WI
54622 Cochrane, WI
54622 Waumandee, WI
54623 Coon Valley, WI
54624 De Soto, WI
54624 Victory, WI
54625 Dodge, WI
54626 Eastman, WI
54626 Lynxville, WI
54627 Ettrick, WI
54628 Ferryville, WI
54629 Fountain City, WI
54630 Galesville, WI
54631 Gays Mills, WI
54632 Genoa, WI
54634 Bloom City, WI
54634 Hillsboro, WI
54634 Yuba, WI
54635 Hixton, WI
54635 Northfield, WI
54636 Holmen, WI
54637 Camp Douglas, WI
54637 Hustler, WI
54638 Kendall, WI
54639 La Farge, WI
54639 West Lima, WI
54640 Lynxville, WI
54641 Mather, WI
54642 Melrose, WI
54643 Millston, WI
54644 Mindoro, WI
54645 Mount Sterling, WI
54646 Necedah, WI
54648 Norwalk, WI
54649 Oakdale, WI
54650 Onalaska, WI
54651 Ontario, WI
54652 Readstown, WI
54653 Rockland, WI
54654 Seneca, WI
54655 Soldiers Grove, WI
54656 Fort Mccoy, WI
54656 Sparta, WI
54657 Steuben, WI
54658 Stoddard, WI
54659 Taylor, WI
54660 Tomah, WI
54660 Wyeville, WI
54661 Trempealeau, WI
54662 Tunnel City, WI
54664 Viola, WI
54665 Viroqua, WI
54666 Warrens, WI
54667 Westby, WI
54669 West Salem, WI
54670 Wilton, WI

547

54701 Eau Claire, WI
54702 Eau Claire, WI
54703 Eau Claire, WI
54720 Altoona, WI
54721 Arkansaw, WI
54722 Augusta, WI
54723 Bay City, WI
54724 Bloomer, WI
54725 Boyceville, WI
54726 Boyd, WI
54727 Cadott, WI
54728 Chetek, WI
54729 Chippewa Falls, WI
54729 Lake Hallie, WI
54730 Colfax, WI
54731 Conrath, WI
54732 Cornell, WI
54733 Dallas, WI
54733 Hillsdale, WI
54734 Downing, WI
54735 Downsville, WI
54736 Durand, WI
54737 Eau Galle, WI
54738 Eleva, WI
54739 Elk Mound, WI
54740 Elmwood, WI
54741 Fairchild, WI
54742 Fall Creek, WI
54743 Gilmanton, WI
54745 Holcombe, WI
54746 Humbird, WI
54747 Independence, WI
54748 Jim Falls, WI
54749 Knapp, WI
54750 Maiden Rock, WI
54751 Menomonie, WI
54754 Merrillan, WI
54755 Modena, WI
54755 Mondovi, WI
54755 Rock Falls, WI
54756 Nelson, WI
54757 New Auburn, WI
54758 Osseo, WI
54759 Pepin, WI
54760 Pigeon Falls, WI
54761 Plum City, WI
54762 Prairie Farm, WI
54763 Ridgeland, WI
54764 Mondovi, WI
54764 Rock Falls, WI
54765 Sand Creek, WI
54766 Sheldon, WI
54767 Spring Valley, WI
54768 Stanley, WI
54769 Stockholm, WI
54770 Strum, WI
54771 Thorp, WI
54772 Wheeler, WI
54773 Whitehall, WI
54774 Chippewa Falls, WI

548

54801 Spooner, WI
54805 Almena, WI
54806 Ashland, WI
54806 Moquah, WI
54806 Sanborn, WI
54810 Balsam Lake, WI
54812 Barron, WI
54812 Poskin, WI
54813 Barronett, WI
54814 Bayfield, WI
54816 Benoit, WI
54816 Mason, WI
54817 Birchwood, WI
54818 Brill, WI
54819 Bruce, WI
54820 Brule, WI
54821 Cable, WI
54822 Cameron, WI
54824 Centuria, WI
54826 Comstock, WI
54827 Cornucopia, WI
54828 Couderay, WI
54828 New Post, WI
54829 Cumberland, WI
54830 Dairyland, WI
54830 Danbury, WI
54830 Webb Lake, WI
54830 Yellow Lake, WI
54832 Drummond, WI
54834 Edgewater, WI
54835 Exeland, WI
54836 Foxboro, WI
54837 Clam Falls, WI
54837 Frederic, WI
54837 Lewis, WI
54838 Gordon, WI
54838 Wascott, WI
54839 Grand View, WI
54840 Grantsburg, WI
54841 Haugen, WI
54842 Hawthorne, WI
54843 Hayward, WI
54843 North Woods Beach, WI
54844 Herbster, WI
54845 Hertel, WI
54846 High Bridge, WI
54846 Highbridge, WI
54846 Marengo, WI
54847 Iron River, WI
54848 Ladysmith, WI
54849 Lake Nebagamon, WI
54850 La Pointe, WI
54853 Luck, WI
54854 Maple, WI
54855 Marengo, WI
54856 Delta, WI
54856 Mason, WI
54857 Mikana, WI
54858 Milltown, WI
54859 Minong, WI
54861 Odanah, WI
54862 Ojibwa, WI
54864 Poplar, WI
54865 Port Wing, WI
54867 Radisson, WI
54868 Canton, WI
54868 Rice Lake, WI
54870 Sarona, WI
54871 Shell Lake, WI
54872 Siren, WI
54873 Barnes, WI
54873 Bennett, WI
54873 Solon Springs, WI
54874 South Range, WI
54874 Wentworth, WI
54875 Springbrook, WI
54876 Stone Lake, WI
54880 Oliver, WI
54880 Superior, WI
54888 Trego, WI
54889 Turtle Lake, WI
54890 Wascott, WI
54891 Washburn, WI
54893 Webster, WI
54895 Weyerhaeuser, WI
54896 Loretta, WI
54896 Winter, WI

549

54901 Oshkosh, WI
54902 Oshkosh, WI
54903 Oshkosh, WI
54904 Oshkosh, WI
54906 Oshkosh, WI
54909 Almond, WI
54911 Appleton, WI
54911 Grand Chute, WI
54911 Little Chute, WI
54912 Appleton, WI
54912 Grand Chute, WI
54913 Appleton, WI
54913 Freedom, WI
54913 Grand Chute, WI
54914 Appleton, WI
54914 Grand Chute, WI
54915 Appleton, WI
54915 Grand Chute, WI
54919 Appleton, WI
54921 Bancroft, WI
54922 Bear Creek, WI
54923 Berlin, WI
54926 Big Falls, WI
54927 Butte Des Morts, WI
54928 Caroline, WI
54929 Clintonville, WI
54930 Coloma, WI
54931 Dale, WI
54932 Eldorado, WI
54933 Embarrass, WI
54934 Eureka, WI
54935 Fond Du Lac, WI
54935 North Fond Du Lac, WI
54935 Taycheedah, WI
54936 Fond Du Lac, WI
54937 Fond Du Lac, WI
54937 North Fond Du Lac, WI
54940 Fremont, WI
54941 Green Lake, WI
54942 Greenville, WI
54943 Hancock, WI
54944 Hortonville, WI
54944 Medina, WI
54945 Iola, WI
54946 King, WI
54947 Larsen, WI
54948 Leopolis, WI
54949 Manawa, WI
54950 Marion, WI
54952 Menasha, WI
54956 Neenah, WI
54957 Neenah, WI
54960 Neshkoro, WI
54961 New London, WI
54961 Royalton, WI
54962 Ogdensburg, WI
54963 Eureka, WI
54963 Omro, WI
54964 Pickett, WI
54965 Pine River, WI
54966 Plainfield, WI
54967 Poy Sippi, WI
54968 Princeton, WI
54969 Readfield, WI
54970 Redgranite, WI
54971 Ripon, WI
54974 Rosendale, WI
54976 Saxeville, WI
54977 Scandinavia, WI
54978 Tilleda, WI
54979 Van Dyne, WI
54980 Waukau, WI
54981 Waupaca, WI
54982 Wautoma, WI
54983 Weyauwega, WI
54984 Wild Rose, WI
54985 Winnebago, WI
54986 Winneconne, WI
54990 Iola, WI

550

55001 Afton, MN
55002 Almelund, MN
55003 Bayport, MN
55005 Bethel, MN
55005 East Bethel, MN
55006 Braham, MN
55007 Brook Park, MN
55008 Cambridge, MN
55009 Cannon Falls, MN
55010 Castle Rock, MN
55011 Cedar, MN
55011 Cedar East Bethel, MN
55011 East Bethel, MN
55011 Oak Grove, MN
55012 Center City, MN
55013 Chisago City, MN
55014 Circle Pines, MN
55014 Lino Lakes, MN
55016 Cottage Grove, MN
55017 Dalbo, MN
55018 Dennison, MN
55018 Stanton, MN
55019 Dundas, MN
55020 Elko, MN
55020 Elko New Market, MN
55021 Faribault, MN
55024 Farmington, MN
55025 Columbus, MN
55025 Forest Lake, MN
55026 Frontenac, MN
55027 Bellechester, MN
55027 Goodhue, MN
55029 Grandy, MN
55030 Grasston, MN
55031 Hampton, MN
55031 New Trier, MN
55032 Harris, MN
55033 Hastings, MN
55036 Grasston, MN
55036 Henriette, MN
55037 Hinckley, MN
55038 Centerville, MN
55038 Hugo, MN
55038 Lino Lakes, MN
55040 Isanti, MN
55041 Lake City, MN
55042 Lake Elmo, MN
55043 Lake Saint Croix Beach, MN
55043 Lakeland, MN
55043 Lakeland Shores, MN
55043 Saint Marys Point, MN
55043 St Croix Beach, MN
55043 St Marys Point, MN
55044 Lakeville, MN
55045 Lindstrom, MN
55046 Lonsdale, MN
55046 Veseli, MN
55047 Marine On Saint Croix, MN
55049 Medford, MN
55051 Mora, MN
55052 Morristown, MN
55053 Nerstrand, MN
55054 Elko New Market, MN
55054 New Market, MN
55055 Newport, MN
55056 North Branch, MN
55057 Northfield, MN
55060 Owatonna, MN
55063 Beroun, MN
55063 Pine City, MN
55065 Randolph, MN
55066 Red Wing, MN
55067 Rock Creek, MN
55068 Rosemount, MN
55069 Rush City, MN
55070 Saint Francis, MN
55071 Saint Paul Park, MN
55072 Markville, MN
55072 Sandstone, MN
55073 Scandia, MN
55074 Shafer, MN
55075 South Saint Paul, MN
55076 Inver Grove Heights, MN
55076 South Saint Paul, MN
55077 Inver Grove Heights, MN
55077 South Saint Paul, MN
55077 Sunfish Lake, MN
55078 Stacy, MN
55079 Stacy, MN
55080 Stanchfield, MN
55082 Oak Park Heights, MN
55082 Oak Park Hgts, MN
55082 Stillwater, MN
55082 W Lakeland, MN
55082 West Lakeland, MN
55083 Stillwater, MN
55084 Taylors Falls, MN
55085 Vermillion, MN
55087 Warsaw, MN
55088 Webster, MN
55089 Welch, MN
55090 Willernie, MN
55092 East Bethel, MN
55092 Wyoming, MN

551

55101 Saint Paul, MN
55102 Saint Paul, MN
55103 Saint Paul, MN
55104 Saint Paul, MN
55105 Saint Paul, MN
55106 Saint Paul, MN
55107 Saint Paul, MN
55107 West Saint Paul, MN
55108 Falcon Heights, MN
55108 Lauderdale, MN
55108 Saint Paul, MN
55109 Little Canada, MN
55109 Maplewood, MN
55109 N Saint Paul, MN
55109 North Saint Paul, MN

55109 Saint Paul, MN
55110 Dellwood, MN
55110 Saint Paul, MN
55110 Vadnais Heights, MN
55110 White Bear Lake, MN
55110 White Bear Township, MN
55111 Fort Snelling, MN
55111 Saint Paul, MN
55112 Arden Hills, MN
55112 Mounds View, MN
55112 New Brighton, MN
55112 Saint Paul, MN
55113 Falcon Heights, MN
55113 Lauderdale, MN
55113 Little Canada, MN
55113 Roseville, MN
55113 Saint Paul, MN
55114 Saint Paul, MN
55115 Mahtomedi, MN
55115 Pine Springs, MN
55115 Saint Paul, MN
55115 White Bear Lake, MN
55116 Saint Paul, MN
55117 Little Canada, MN
55117 Maplewood, MN
55117 Saint Paul, MN
55118 Mendota Heights, MN
55118 Saint Paul, MN
55118 Sunfish Lake, MN
55118 W St Paul, MN
55118 West Saint Paul, MN
55118 West St Paul, MN
55119 Maplewood, MN
55119 Saint Paul, MN
55120 Eagan, MN
55120 Mendota Heights, MN
55120 Saint Paul, MN
55121 Eagan, MN
55121 Saint Paul, MN
55122 Eagan, MN
55122 Saint Paul, MN
55123 Eagan, MN
55123 Saint Paul, MN
55124 Apple Valley, MN
55124 Saint Paul, MN
55125 Saint Paul, MN
55125 Woodbury, MN
55126 Arden Hills, MN
55126 No Oaks, MN
55126 Roseville, MN
55126 Saint Paul, MN
55126 Shoreview, MN
55127 Little Canada, MN
55127 North Oaks, MN
55127 Saint Paul, MN
55127 Vadnais Heights, MN
55127 White Bear Lake, MN
55128 Landfall Village, MN
55128 Oakdale, MN
55128 Pine Springs, MN
55128 Saint Paul, MN
55129 Saint Paul, MN
55129 Woodbury, MN
55130 Saint Paul, MN
55133 Saint Paul, MN
55144 Maplewood, MN
55144 Saint Paul, MN
55145 Saint Paul, MN
55146 Saint Paul, MN
55150 Mendota, MN
55150 Saint Paul, MN
55155 Saint Paul, MN
55164 Saint Paul, MN
55165 Saint Paul, MN
55166 Saint Paul, MN
55168 Saint Paul, MN
55170 Saint Paul, MN
55171 Saint Paul, MN
55172 Saint Paul, MN
55175 Saint Paul, MN
55187 Saint Paul, MN
55188 Saint Paul, MN

553

55301 Albertville, MN
55301 Otsego, MN
55302 Annandale, MN
55303 Andover, MN
55303 Anoka, MN
55303 Nowthen, MN
55303 Oak Grove, MN
55303 Ramsey, MN
55304 Andover, MN
55304 Anoka, MN
55304 Ham Lake, MN
55305 Hopkins, MN
55305 Minnetonka, MN
55306 Burnsville, MN
55307 Arlington, MN
55308 Becker, MN
55309 Big Lake, MN
55310 Bird Island, MN
55311 Maple Grove, MN
55311 Osseo, MN
55312 Brownton, MN
55313 Buffalo, MN
55314 Buffalo Lake, MN
55315 Carver, MN
55316 Champlin, MN
55317 Chanhassen, MN
55318 Chaska, MN
55319 Clear Lake, MN
55320 Clearwater, MN
55320 Saint Augusta, MN
55321 Cokato, MN
55322 Cologne, MN
55323 Crystal Bay, MN
55324 Darwin, MN
55325 Dassel, MN
55325 Kingston, MN
55327 Dayton, MN
55328 Delano, MN
55329 Eden Valley, MN
55330 Burns Township, MN
55330 Elk River, MN
55330 Nowthen, MN
55330 Otsego, MN
55331 Excelsior, MN
55331 Greenwood, MN
55331 Minnetrista, MN
55332 Fairfax, MN
55333 Franklin, MN
55334 Gaylord, MN
55335 Gibbon, MN
55336 Biscay, MN
55336 Glencoe, MN
55337 Burnsville, MN
55338 Green Isle, MN
55339 Hamburg, MN
55340 Corcoran, MN
55340 Hamel, MN
55340 Medina, MN
55341 Hanover, MN
55342 Hector, MN
55343 Eden Prairie, MN
55343 Hopkins, MN
55343 Minnetonka Mls, MN
55343 Minnetonka, MN
55343 Minnetonka Mills, MN
55344 Eden Prairie, MN
55345 Hopkins, MN
55345 Minnetonka, MN
55346 Eden Prairie, MN
55347 Eden Prairie, MN
55348 Maple Plain, MN
55349 Howard Lake, MN
55350 Hutchinson, MN
55352 Jordan, MN
55353 Kimball, MN
55353 Saint Augusta, MN
55354 Lester Prairie, MN
55355 Litchfield, MN
55356 Long Lake, MN
55356 Orono, MN
55357 Independence, MN
55357 Loretto, MN
55358 Maple Lake, MN
55358 Silver Creek, MN
55359 Independence, MN
55359 Maple Plain, MN
55359 Minnetrista, MN
55359 Orono, MN
55360 Mayer, MN
55361 Minetonka Bch, MN
55361 Minnetonka Beach, MN
55362 Monticello, MN
55362 Otsego, MN
55363 Montrose, MN
55364 Minnetrista, MN
55364 Mound, MN
55365 Monticello, MN
55366 New Auburn, MN
55367 New Germany, MN
55368 Norwood, MN
55368 Norwood Young America, MN
55369 Maple Grove, MN
55369 Osseo, MN
55370 Plato, MN
55371 Princeton, MN
55372 Prior Lake, MN
55372 Shakopee, MN
55373 Rockford, MN
55374 Otsego, MN
55374 Rogers, MN
55375 Crown College, MN
55375 Minnetrista, MN
55375 Saint Bonifacius, MN
55376 Saint Michael, MN
55377 Santiago, MN
55378 Savage, MN
55379 Prior Lake, MN
55379 Shakopee, MN
55380 Maple Lake, MN
55380 Silver Creek, MN
55381 Silver Lake, MN
55382 Saint Augusta, MN
55382 South Haven, MN
55383 Norwood, MN
55384 Spring Park, MN
55385 Stewart, MN
55386 Victoria, MN
55387 Waconia, MN
55388 Minnetrista, MN
55388 Watertown, MN
55389 Watkins, MN
55390 Waverly, MN
55391 Wayzata, MN
55392 Navarre, MN
55393 Maple Plain, MN
55394 Young America, MN
55395 Winsted, MN
55396 Winthrop, MN
55397 Norwood Young America, MN
55397 Young America, MN
55398 Zimmerman, MN
55399 Young America, MN

554

55401 Minneapolis, MN
55402 Minneapolis, MN
55403 Minneapolis, MN
55404 Minneapolis, MN
55405 Minneapolis, MN
55406 Minneapolis, MN
55407 Minneapolis, MN
55408 Minneapolis, MN
55409 Minneapolis, MN
55410 Edina, MN
55410 Minneapolis, MN
55411 Minneapolis, MN
55412 Minneapolis, MN
55413 Minneapolis, MN
55414 Minneapolis, MN
55415 Minneapolis, MN
55416 Edina, MN
55416 Golden Valley, MN
55416 Minneapolis, MN
55416 Saint Louis Park, MN
55417 Minneapolis, MN
55418 Minneapolis, MN
55418 Saint Anthony, MN
55418 St Anthony, MN
55418 St Anthony Village, MN
55419 Minneapolis, MN
55420 Bloomington, MN
55420 Minneapolis, MN
55421 Columbia Heights, MN
55421 Fridley, MN
55421 Hilltop, MN
55421 Minneapolis, MN
55421 Saint Anthony, MN
55422 Crystal, MN
55422 Golden Valley, MN
55422 Minneapolis, MN
55422 Robbinsdale, MN
55423 Edina, MN
55423 Minneapolis, MN
55423 Richfield, MN
55424 Edina, MN
55424 Minneapolis, MN
55424 Saint Louis Park, MN
55425 Bloomington, MN
55425 Minneapolis, MN
55426 Golden Valley, MN
55426 Minneapolis, MN
55426 Saint Louis Park, MN
55427 Crystal, MN
55427 Golden Valley, MN
55427 Minneapolis, MN
55427 New Hope, MN
55428 Brooklyn Center, MN
55428 Brooklyn Park, MN
55428 Crystal, MN
55428 Minneapolis, MN
55428 New Hope, MN
55429 Brooklyn Center, MN
55429 Brooklyn Park, MN
55429 Crystal, MN
55429 Minneapolis, MN
55430 Brooklyn Center, MN
55430 Minneapolis, MN
55431 Bloomington, MN
55431 Minneapolis, MN
55432 Fridley, MN
55432 Minneapolis, MN
55432 Spring Lake Park, MN
55433 Coon Rapids, MN
55433 Minneapolis, MN
55434 Blaine, MN
55434 Minneapolis, MN
55435 Bloomington, MN
55435 Edina, MN
55435 Minneapolis, MN
55436 Edina, MN
55436 Minneapolis, MN
55436 Saint Louis Park, MN
55437 Bloomington, MN
55437 Minneapolis, MN
55438 Bloomington, MN
55438 Minneapolis, MN
55439 Edina, MN
55439 Minneapolis, MN
55440 Minneapolis, MN
55441 Medicine Lake, MN
55441 Minneapolis, MN
55441 Plymouth, MN
55442 Minneapolis, MN
55442 Plymouth, MN
55443 Brooklyn Center, MN
55443 Brooklyn Park, MN
55443 Minneapolis, MN
55444 Brooklyn Center, MN
55444 Brooklyn Park, MN
55444 Minneapolis, MN
55445 Brooklyn Park, MN
55445 Minneapolis, MN
55446 Minneapolis, MN
55446 Plymouth, MN
55447 Minneapolis, MN
55447 Plymouth, MN
55448 Coon Rapids, MN
55448 Minneapolis, MN
55449 Blaine, MN
55449 Minneapolis, MN
55450 Minneapolis, MN
55454 Minneapolis, MN
55455 Minneapolis, MN
55458 Minneapolis, MN
55459 Minneapolis, MN
55460 Minneapolis, MN
55467 Minneapolis, MN
55470 Minneapolis, MN
55472 Minneapolis, MN
55473 Minneapolis, MN
55473 Norwood Young America, MN
55474 Minneapolis, MN
55478 Minneapolis, MN
55479 Minneapolis, MN
55480 Minneapolis, MN
55483 Minneapolis, MN
55484 Minneapolis, MN
55485 Minneapolis, MN
55486 Minneapolis, MN
55487 Minneapolis, MN
55488 Minneapolis, MN

555

55550 Young America, MN
55551 Young America, MN
55552 Young America, MN
55553 Young America, MN
55554 Norwood, MN
55556 Young America, MN
55557 Young America, MN
55558 Young America, MN
55559 Young America, MN
55560 Young America, MN
55562 Young America, MN
55564 Young America, MN
55565 Monticello, MN
55566 Young America, MN
55567 Young America, MN
55568 Young America, MN
55569 Maple Grove, MN
55569 Osseo, MN
55570 Maple Plain, MN
55571 Maple Plain, MN
55572 Rockford, MN
55573 Young America, MN
55574 Maple Plain, MN
55575 Howard Lake, MN
55576 Maple Plain, MN
55577 Rockford, MN
55578 Maple Plain, MN
55579 Maple Plain, MN
55580 Monticello, MN
55581 Monticello, MN
55582 Monticello, MN
55583 Norwood, MN
55584 Monticello, MN
55585 Monticello, MN
55586 Monticello, MN
55587 Monticello, MN
55588 Monticello, MN
55589 Monticello, MN
55590 Monticello, MN
55591 Monticello, MN
55592 Maple Plain, MN
55593 Maple Plain, MN
55594 Young America, MN
55595 Loretto, MN
55596 Loretto, MN
55597 Loretto, MN
55598 Loretto, MN
55599 Loretto, MN

556

55601 Beaver Bay, MN
55602 Brimson, MN
55603 Finland, MN
55604 Grand Marais, MN
55605 Grand Portage, MN
55606 Hovland, MN
55607 Isabella, MN
55609 Knife River, MN
55612 Lutsen, MN
55613 Schroeder, MN
55614 Little Marais, MN
55614 Silver Bay, MN
55615 Tofte, MN
55616 Two Harbors, MN

557

55701 Adolph, MN
55701 Duluth, MN
55702 Alborn, MN
55703 Angora, MN
55704 Askov, MN
55705 Aurora, MN
55706 Babbitt, MN
55707 Barnum, MN
55707 Mahtowa, MN
55708 Biwabik, MN
55709 Bovey, MN
55710 Britt, MN
55711 Brookston, MN
55712 Bruno, MN
55713 Buhl, MN
55716 Calumet, MN
55717 Canyon, MN
55718 Carlton, MN
55719 Chisholm, MN
55720 Cloquet, MN
55721 Cohasset, MN
55722 Coleraine, MN
55723 Cook, MN
55723 Togo, MN
55724 Cotton, MN
55724 Kelsey, MN
55725 Crane Lake, MN
55726 Cromwell, MN
55730 Grand Rapids, MN
55731 Ely, MN
55732 Embarrass, MN
55733 Esko, MN
55734 Eveleth, MN
55735 Finlayson, MN
55736 Floodwood, MN
55736 Wawina, MN
55738 Forbes, MN
55738 Zim, MN
55741 Gilbert, MN
55741 Mckinley, MN
55742 Goodland, MN
55744 Grand Rapids, MN
55745 Grand Rapids, MN
55746 Hibbing, MN
55746 Kelly Lake, MN
55747 Hibbing, MN
55748 Hill City, MN
55749 Holyoke, MN
55749 Wrenshall, MN
55750 Hoyt Lakes, MN
55751 Iron, MN
55751 Iron Junction, MN
55752 Jacobson, MN
55753 Keewatin, MN
55756 Duquette, MN
55756 Kerrick, MN
55757 Kettle River, MN
55758 Kinney, MN
55760 Mcgregor, MN
55763 Makinen, MN
55764 Marble, MN
55765 Meadowlands, MN
55765 Toivola, MN
55766 Melrude, MN
55767 Moose Lake, MN
55768 Mountain Iron, MN
55768 Parkville, MN
55769 Nashwauk, MN
55771 Buyck, MN
55771 Gheen, MN
55771 Orr, MN
55772 Nett Lake, MN
55772 Orr, MN
55775 Pengilly, MN
55777 Virginia, MN
55779 Culver, MN
55779 Saginaw, MN
55780 Sawyer, MN
55781 Side Lake, MN
55782 Soudan, MN
55783 Sturgeon Lake, MN
55784 Swan River, MN
55785 Swatara, MN
55786 Taconite, MN
55787 Tamarack, MN
55790 Tower, MN
55791 Twig, MN
55792 Virginia, MN
55793 Warba, MN
55795 Rutledge, MN
55795 Willow River, MN
55796 Winton, MN
55797 Wrenshall, MN
55798 Wright, MN

558

55801 Duluth, MN
55802 Duluth, MN
55803 Duluth, MN
55804 Duluth, MN
55805 Duluth, MN
55806 Duluth, MN
55807 Duluth, MN
55808 Duluth, MN
55810 Duluth, MN
55810 Hermantown, MN
55810 Proctor, MN
55811 Duluth, MN
55811 Hermantown, MN
55812 Duluth, MN
55814 Duluth, MN
55814 Duluth Federal Prison, MN
55815 Duluth, MN
55816 Duluth, MN

559

55901 Rochester, MN
55902 Rochester, MN
55903 Rochester, MN
55904 Rochester, MN
55905 Rochester, MN
55906 Rochester, MN
55909 Adams, MN
55910 Altura, MN
55910 Minneiska, MN
55912 Austin, MN
55912 Mapleview, MN
55912 Nicolville, MN
55917 Blooming Prairie, MN
55918 Brownsdale, MN
55919 Brownsville, MN
55920 Byron, MN
55921 Caledonia, MN
55922 Canton, MN
55923 Chatfield, MN
55924 Claremont, MN
55925 Dakota, MN
55926 Dexter, MN
55927 Dodge Center, MN
55929 Dover, MN
55931 Eitzen, MN
55932 Elgin, MN
55933 Elkton, MN
55934 Eyota, MN
55934 Viola, MN
55935 Fountain, MN
55936 Grand Meadow, MN
55939 Granger, MN
55939 Harmony, MN
55940 Hayfield, MN
55941 Hokah, MN
55942 Homer, MN
55943 Houston, MN
55944 Kasson, MN
55945 Kellogg, MN
55945 Theilman, MN
55946 Kenyon, MN
55947 La Crescent, MN
55949 Lanesboro, MN
55949 Whalan, MN
55950 Lansing, MN
55951 Le Roy, MN
55952 Lewiston, MN
55953 Lyle, MN
55954 Mabel, MN
55955 Mantorville, MN
55956 Mazeppa, MN
55957 Millville, MN
55959 Minnesota City, MN
55960 Oronoco, MN
55961 Ostrander, MN
55962 Peterson, MN
55962 Rushford Village, MN
55963 Pine Island, MN
55964 Plainview, MN
55965 Preston, MN
55967 Racine, MN
55968 Reads Landing, MN
55969 Rollingstone, MN
55970 Rose Creek, MN
55971 Rushford, MN
55971 Rushford Village, MN
55972 Saint Charles, MN
55973 Sargeant, MN
55974 Spring Grove, MN
55975 Spring Valley, MN
55976 Stewartville, MN
55977 Taopi, MN
55979 Utica, MN
55981 Wabasha, MN
55982 Waltham, MN
55983 Wanamingo, MN
55985 West Concord, MN
55987 Goodview, MN
55987 Stockton, MN
55987 Winona, MN
55988 Stockton, MN
55990 Wykoff, MN
55991 Hammond, MN
55991 Zumbro Falls, MN
55992 Zumbrota, MN

560

56001 Mankato, MN
56001 Skyline, MN
56002 Mankato, MN
56003 Mankato, MN
56003 North Mankato, MN
56006 Mankato, MN
56007 Albert Lea, MN
56007 Manchester, MN
56007 Oakland, MN
56009 Alden, MN
56010 Amboy, MN
56011 Belle Plaine, MN
56013 Blue Earth, MN
56014 Bricelyn, MN
56016 Clarks Grove, MN
56017 Cleveland, MN
56019 Comfrey, MN
56020 Conger, MN
56021 Courtland, MN
56022 Darfur, MN
56023 Delavan, MN
56024 Eagle Lake, MN
56025 Easton, MN
56026 Ellendale, MN
56027 Elmore, MN
56028 Elysian, MN
56029 Emmons, MN
56030 Essig, MN
56031 Fairmont, MN
56032 Freeborn, MN
56033 Frost, MN
56034 Garden City, MN
56035 Geneva, MN
56036 Glenville, MN
56036 London, MN
56036 Myrtle, MN
56037 Good Thunder, MN
56039 Granada, MN
56041 Hanska, MN
56042 Hartland, MN
56043 Hayward, MN
56044 Henderson, MN
56045 Hollandale, MN
56046 Hope, MN
56047 Huntley, MN
56048 Janesville, MN
56050 Kasota, MN
56051 Kiester, MN
56052 Kilkenny, MN
56054 Lafayette, MN
56055 Lake Crystal, MN
56056 La Salle, MN
56057 Le Center, MN
56058 Le Sueur, MN
56060 Lewisville, MN
56062 Madelia, MN
56063 Madison Lake, MN
56065 Mapleton, MN
56068 Minnesota Lake, MN
56069 Montgomery, MN
56071 Heidelberg, MN
56071 New Prague, MN
56072 New Richland, MN
56073 Essig, MN
56073 Klossner, MN
56073 New Ulm, MN
56073 Searles, MN
56074 Nicollet, MN
56075 Fairmont, MN
56075 Northrop, MN
56078 Pemberton, MN
56080 Saint Clair, MN
56081 Saint James, MN
56082 Saint Peter, MN
56083 Sanborn, MN
56084 Searles, MN
56085 Cobden, MN
56085 Evan, MN
56085 Sleepy Eye, MN
56087 Springfield, MN
56088 Truman, MN
56089 Twin Lakes, MN
56090 Vernon Center, MN
56091 Waldorf, MN
56093 Meriden, MN
56093 Otisco, MN
56093 Waseca, MN
56096 Waterville, MN
56097 Walters, MN
56097 Wells, MN
56098 Winnebago, MN

561

56101 Wilder, MN
56101 Windom, MN
56110 Adrian, MN
56111 Alpha, MN
56113 Arco, MN
56114 Avoca, MN
56115 Balaton, MN
56116 Beaver Creek, MN
56117 Bigelow, MN
56118 Bingham Lake, MN
56119 Brewster, MN
56120 Butterfield, MN
56121 Ceylon, MN
56122 Chandler, MN
56123 Currie, MN
56125 Dovray, MN
56127 Dunnell, MN
56128 Edgerton, MN
56129 Ellsworth, MN
56131 Dundee, MN
56131 Fulda, MN
56131 Kinbrae, MN
56132 Garvin, MN
56134 Hardwick, MN
56136 Hendricks, MN
56137 Heron Lake, MN
56138 Hills, MN
56139 Holland, MN
56140 Ihlen, MN
56141 Iona, MN
56142 Ivanhoe, MN
56143 Jackson, MN
56144 Jasper, MN
56144 Trosky, MN
56145 Jeffers, MN
56146 Kanaranzi, MN
56147 Kenneth, MN
56149 Lake Benton, MN
56150 Lakefield, MN
56151 Hadley, MN
56151 Lake Wilson, MN
56151 Slayton, MN
56152 Lamberton, MN
56153 Leota, MN
56155 Lismore, MN
56156 Luverne, MN
56157 Lynd, MN
56158 Magnolia, MN
56159 Mountain Lake, MN
56160 Odin, MN
56161 Okabena, MN
56162 Ormsby, MN
56164 Hatfield, MN
56164 Ihlen, MN
56164 Pipestone, MN
56164 Verdi, MN
56165 Reading, MN
56166 Revere, MN
56167 Round Lake, MN
56168 Rushmore, MN
56169 Russell, MN
56170 Florence, MN
56170 Ruthton, MN
56171 Sherburn, MN
56172 Slayton, MN
56173 Steen, MN
56174 Storden, MN
56175 Amiret, MN
56175 Tracy, MN
56176 Trimont, MN
56177 Trosky, MN
56178 Tyler, MN
56180 Walnut Grove, MN
56181 Welcome, MN
56183 Dovray, MN
56183 Westbrook, MN
56185 Wilmont, MN
56186 Woodstock, MN
56187 Worthington, MN

562

56201 Willmar, MN
56207 Alberta, MN
56208 Appleton, MN
56209 Atwater, MN
56210 Barry, MN
56211 Beardsley, MN
56212 Bellingham, MN
56214 Belview, MN
56215 Benson, MN
56216 Blomkest, MN
56216 Svea, MN
56218 Boyd, MN
56219 Browns Valley, MN
56220 Canby, MN
56221 Chokio, MN
56222 Clara City, MN
56223 Clarkfield, MN
56224 Clements, MN
56225 Clinton, MN
56226 Clontarf, MN
56227 Correll, MN
56228 Cosmos, MN
56229 Cottonwood, MN
56230 Danube, MN
56231 Danvers, MN
56232 Dawson, MN
56235 Donnelly, MN
56236 Dumont, MN
56236 Johnson, MN
56237 Echo, MN
56239 Ghent, MN
56240 Graceville, MN
56241 Granite Falls, MN
56241 Hazel Run, MN
56243 Grove City, MN
56244 Hancock, MN
56245 Hanley Falls, MN
56248 Herman, MN
56249 Holloway, MN
56251 Kandiyohi, MN
56252 Kerkhoven, MN
56253 Lake Lillian, MN
56255 Lucan, MN
56256 Louisburg, MN
56256 Madison, MN
56257 Marietta, MN
56257 Nassau, MN
56258 Marshall, MN
56260 Maynard, MN
56262 Milan, MN
56263 Milroy, MN
56264 Minneota, MN
56264 Saint Leo, MN
56265 Montevideo, MN
56266 Evan, MN
56266 Morgan, MN
56267 Morris, MN
56270 Morton, MN
56271 De Graff, MN
56271 Murdock, MN
56273 Hawick, MN
56273 New London, MN
56274 Norcross, MN
56276 Odessa, MN
56277 Olivia, MN
56278 Ortonville, MN
56279 Pennock, MN
56280 Porter, MN
56281 Prinsburg, MN
56282 Raymond, MN
56283 Delhi, MN
56283 North Redwood, MN
56283 Redwood Falls, MN
56284 Renville, MN
56285 Sacred Heart, MN
56287 Seaforth, MN
56288 Spicer, MN
56289 Sunburg, MN
56291 Taunton, MN
56292 Vesta, MN
56293 Wabasso, MN
56294 Wanda, MN
56295 Watson, MN
56296 Wheaton, MN
56297 Wood Lake, MN

563

56301 Saint Augusta, MN
56301 Saint Cloud, MN
56302 Saint Cloud, MN
56303 Forada, MN
56303 Saint Cloud, MN
56303 Sartell, MN
56304 Saint Cloud, MN
56307 Albany, MN
56308 Alexandria, MN
56309 Ashby, MN
56310 Avon, MN
56311 Barrett, MN
56312 Belgrade, MN
56312 Regal, MN
56313 Bock, MN
56314 Bowlus, MN
56314 Elmdale, MN
56315 Brandon, MN
56315 Millerville, MN
56316 Brooten, MN
56317 Buckman, MN
56318 Burtrum, MN
56319 Carlos, MN
56320 Cold Spring, MN
56321 Collegeville, MN
56323 Cyrus, MN
56324 Dalton, MN
56325 Elrosa, MN
56326 Evansville, MN
56327 Farwell, MN
56328 Flensburg, MN
56329 Foley, MN
56329 Oak Park, MN
56330 Foreston, MN
56331 Freeport, MN
56331 Saint Rosa, MN
56332 Garfield, MN
56333 Gilman, MN
56334 Glenwood, MN
56334 Long Beach, MN
56334 Sedan, MN
56335 Greenwald, MN
56336 Grey Eagle, MN
56338 Hillman, MN
56339 Hoffman, MN
56340 Holdingford, MN
56341 Holmes City, MN
56342 Isle, MN
56343 Kensington, MN
56344 Lastrup, MN
56345 Little Falls, MN
56345 Sobieski, MN
56347 Little Sauk, MN
56347 Long Prairie, MN
56349 Lowry, MN
56350 Mc Grath, MN
56352 Meire Grove, MN
56352 Melrose, MN
56352 Spring Hill, MN
56353 Milaca, MN
56354 Miltona, MN
56355 Nelson, MN
56356 New Munich, MN
56357 Foley, MN
56357 Oak Park, MN
56357 Ronneby, MN
56358 Ogilvie, MN
56359 Onamia, MN
56360 Osakis, MN
56361 Parkers Prairie, MN
56362 Lake Henry, MN
56362 Paynesville, MN
56363 Pease, MN
56364 Harding, MN
56364 Pierz, MN
56367 Rice, MN
56368 Richmond, MN
56369 Rockville, MN
56371 Roscoe, MN
56372 Saint Cloud, MN
56373 Royalton, MN
56374 Saint Joseph, MN
56375 Saint Stephen, MN
56376 Saint Martin, MN
56377 Sartell, MN
56378 Sauk Centre, MN
56379 Sauk Rapids, MN
56381 Starbuck, MN
56382 Swanville, MN
56384 Upsala, MN
56385 Villard, MN
56385 Westport, MN
56386 Wahkon, MN
56387 Waite Park, MN
56388 Waite Park, MN
56389 Sauk Centre, MN
56389 West Union, MN
56393 Saint Cloud, MN
56395 Saint Cloud, MN
56396 Saint Cloud, MN
56397 Saint Cloud, MN
56398 Saint Cloud, MN
56399 Saint Cloud, MN

564

56401 Baxter, MN
56401 Brainerd, MN
56401 East Gull Lake, MN
56425 Baxter, MN
56425 Brainerd, MN
56430 Ah Gwah Ching, MN
56431 Aitkin, MN
56433 Akeley, MN
56434 Aldrich, MN
56435 Backus, MN
56436 Benedict, MN
56437 Bertha, MN
56438 Browerville, MN
56440 Clarissa, MN
56441 Crosby, MN
56442 Crosslake, MN
56442 Manhattan Beach, MN
56443 Cushing, MN
56444 Deerwood, MN
56446 Eagle Bend, MN
56447 Emily, MN
56448 Fifty Lakes, MN
56449 Fort Ripley, MN
56450 Garrison, MN
56452 Hackensack, MN
56453 Hewitt, MN
56455 Ironton, MN
56455 Riverton, MN
56456 Jenkins, MN
56458 Lake George, MN
56459 Lake Hubert, MN
56461 Laporte, MN
56464 Menahga, MN
56465 Merrifield, MN
56466 Motley, MN
56467 Nevis, MN
56468 Lake Hubert, MN
56468 Lake Shore, MN
56468 Nisswa, MN
56469 Palisade, MN
56470 Lake Itasca, MN
56470 Park Rapids, MN
56472 Breezy Point, MN
56472 Jenkins, MN
56472 Pequot Lakes, MN
56473 Pillager, MN

56474 Jenkins, MN
56474 Pine River, MN
56475 Randall, MN
56477 Sebeka, MN
56478 Nimrod, MN
56479 Staples, MN
56481 Verndale, MN
56482 Wadena, MN
56484 Walker, MN
56484 Whipholt, MN

565

56501 Detroit Lakes, MN
56502 Detroit Lakes, MN
56510 Ada, MN
56511 Audubon, MN
56514 Barnesville, MN
56514 Downer, MN
56515 Battle Lake, MN
56516 Bejou, MN
56517 Beltrami, MN
56518 Bluffton, MN
56519 Borup, MN
56520 Breckenridge, MN
56521 Callaway, MN
56522 Campbell, MN
56522 Doran, MN
56523 Climax, MN
56523 Eldred, MN
56524 Clitherall, MN
56525 Comstock, MN
56527 Deer Creek, MN
56528 Dent, MN
56529 Dilworth, MN
56531 Elbow Lake, MN
56533 Elizabeth, MN
56534 Erhard, MN
56535 Erskine, MN
56536 Felton, MN
56537 Carlisle, MN
56537 Fergus Falls, MN
56538 Fergus Falls, MN
56540 Fertile, MN
56541 Flom, MN
56542 Fosston, MN
56543 Foxhome, MN
56544 Frazee, MN
56545 Gary, MN
56546 Georgetown, MN
56547 Glyndon, MN
56548 Halstad, MN
56549 Hawley, MN
56549 Rollag, MN
56550 Hendrum, MN
56551 Henning, MN
56552 Hitterdal, MN
56553 Kent, MN
56554 Lake Park, MN
56556 Mcintosh, MN
56557 Mahnomen, MN
56560 Moorhead, MN
56561 Moorhead, MN
56562 Moorhead, MN
56563 Moorhead, MN
56565 Nashua, MN
56566 Naytahwaush, MN
56567 New York Mills, MN
56568 Nielsville, MN
56569 Ogema, MN
56570 Osage, MN
56571 Ottertail, MN
56572 Pelican Rapids, MN
56573 Perham, MN
56574 Perley, MN
56575 Ponsford, MN
56576 Richville, MN
56577 Richwood, MN
56578 Rochert, MN
56579 Rothsay, MN
56580 Baker, MN
56580 Sabin, MN
56581 Shelly, MN
56583 Tenney, MN
56583 Tintah, MN
56584 Twin Valley, MN
56585 Ulen, MN
56586 Underwood, MN
56587 Vergas, MN
56588 Vining, MN
56589 Waubun, MN
56590 Wendell, MN
56591 White Earth, MN
56592 Winger, MN
56593 Wolf Lake, MN
56594 Wolverton, MN

566

56601 Bemidji, MN
56601 Turtle River, MN
56601 Wilton, MN
56619 Bemidji, MN
56621 Bagley, MN
56623 Baudette, MN
56623 Pitt, MN
56626 Bena, MN
56627 Big Falls, MN
56628 Bigfork, MN
56629 Birchdale, MN
56630 Blackduck, MN
56631 Bowstring, MN
56633 Cass Lake, MN
56634 Clearbrook, MN
56636 Deer River, MN
56637 Talmoon, MN
56639 Effie, MN
56641 Federal Dam, MN
56644 Gonvick, MN
56646 Gully, MN
56647 Hines, MN
56649 International Falls, MN
56650 Kelliher, MN
56650 Saum, MN
56651 Lengby, MN
56652 Leonard, MN
56653 Littlefork, MN
56654 Loman, MN
56655 Longville, MN
56657 Marcell, MN
56658 Margie, MN
56659 Max, MN
56660 Mizpah, MN
56661 Northome, MN
56662 Outing, MN
56663 Blackduck, MN
56663 Pennington, MN
56666 Ponemah, MN
56667 Puposky, MN
56668 Ranier, MN
56669 Kabetogama, MN
56669 Ray, MN
56670 Redby, MN
56671 Redlake, MN
56672 Boy River, MN
56672 Remer, MN
56673 Roosevelt, MN
56676 Pinewood, MN
56676 Shevlin, MN
56678 Becida, MN
56678 Solway, MN
56679 South International Falls, MN
56680 Spring Lake, MN
56681 Squaw Lake, MN
56682 Roosevelt, MN
56682 Swift, MN
56683 Tenstrike, MN
56684 Trail, MN
56685 Waskish, MN
56686 Williams, MN
56687 Wilton, MN
56688 Wirt, MN

567

56701 Thief River Falls, MN
56710 Alvarado, MN
56711 Angle Inlet, MN
56713 Argyle, MN
56714 Badger, MN
56715 Brooks, MN
56716 Crookston, MN
56720 Donaldson, MN
56721 East Grand Forks, MN
56722 Euclid, MN
56723 Fisher, MN
56724 Gatzke, MN
56725 Goodridge, MN
56726 Greenbush, MN
56727 Grygla, MN
56728 Hallock, MN
56729 Halma, MN
56731 Humboldt, MN
56732 Karlstad, MN
56733 Kennedy, MN
56734 Lake Bronson, MN
56735 Lancaster, MN
56735 Orleans, MN
56736 Mentor, MN
56737 Middle River, MN
56738 Holt, MN
56738 Newfolden, MN
56740 Noyes, MN
56741 Oak Island, MN
56742 Oklee, MN
56744 Oslo, MN
56748 Plummer, MN
56750 Red Lake Falls, MN
56751 Pencer, MN
56751 Roseau, MN
56751 Ross, MN
56754 Saint Hilaire, MN
56755 Saint Vincent, MN
56756 Salol, MN
56757 Stephen, MN
56758 Strandquist, MN
56759 Strathcona, MN
56760 Viking, MN
56761 Wannaska, MN
56762 Angus, MN
56762 Radium, MN
56762 Warren, MN
56763 Warroad, MN

569

56901 Parcel Return Service, DC

570

57001 Alcester, SD
57002 Aurora, SD
57003 Baltic, SD
57004 Beresford, SD
57005 Brandon, SD
57005 Corson, SD
57005 Rowena, SD
57006 Brookings, SD
57007 Brookings, SD
57010 Burbank, SD
57012 Canistota, SD
57013 Canton, SD
57014 Centerville, SD
57015 Chancellor, SD
57016 Chester, SD
57017 Colman, SD
57018 Colton, SD
57020 Crooks, SD
57020 Renner, SD
57021 Davis, SD
57022 Dell Rapids, SD
57024 Egan, SD
57025 Elk Point, SD
57026 Elkton, SD
57026 Ward, SD
57027 Fairview, SD
57028 Flandreau, SD
57029 Freeman, SD
57030 Garretson, SD
57030 Sherman, SD
57031 Gayville, SD
57032 Harrisburg, SD
57033 Hartford, SD
57034 Hudson, SD
57035 Humboldt, SD
57036 Hurley, SD
57037 Irene, SD
57038 Jefferson, SD
57039 Lennox, SD
57040 Lesterville, SD
57041 Lyons, SD
57042 Madison, SD
57043 Marion, SD
57045 Menno, SD
57046 Mission Hill, SD
57047 Monroe, SD
57048 Montrose, SD
57049 Dakota Dunes, SD
57049 Mccook Lake, SD
57049 North Sioux City, SD
57050 Nunda, SD
57051 Oldham, SD
57052 Olivet, SD
57053 Parker, SD
57054 Ramona, SD
57055 Crooks, SD
57055 Renner, SD
57057 Rutland, SD
57058 Salem, SD
57059 Scotland, SD
57061 Sinai, SD
57062 Running Water, SD
57062 Springfield, SD
57063 Tabor, SD
57064 Tea, SD
57065 Trent, SD
57066 Tyndall, SD
57067 Utica, SD
57068 Valley Springs, SD
57069 Meckling, SD
57069 Vermillion, SD
57070 Viborg, SD
57071 Volga, SD
57072 Volin, SD
57073 Wakonda, SD
57075 Wentworth, SD
57076 Winfred, SD
57077 Worthing, SD
57078 Yankton, SD

571

57101 Sioux Falls, SD
57103 Sioux Falls, SD
57104 Sioux Falls, SD
57105 Sioux Falls, SD
57106 Sioux Falls, SD
57107 Buffalo Ridge, SD
57107 Sioux Falls, SD
57108 Sioux Falls, SD
57109 Sioux Falls, SD
57110 Sioux Falls, SD
57117 Sioux Falls, SD
57118 Sioux Falls, SD
57186 Sioux Falls, SD
57193 Sioux Falls, SD
57197 Sioux Falls, SD
57198 Sioux Falls, SD

572

57201 Watertown, SD
57201 Waverly, SD
57212 Arlington, SD
57212 Hetland, SD
57213 Astoria, SD
57214 Badger, SD
57216 Big Stone City, SD
57217 Bradley, SD
57217 Crocker, SD
57218 Brandt, SD
57219 Bristol, SD
57219 Butler, SD
57220 Bruce, SD
57221 Bryant, SD
57223 Castlewood, SD
57224 Claire City, SD
57225 Clark, SD
57226 Altamont, SD
57226 Clear Lake, SD
57227 Corona, SD
57231 De Smet, SD
57232 Eden, SD
57233 Erwin, SD
57234 Dempster, SD
57234 Estelline, SD
57235 Florence, SD
57236 Garden City, SD
57237 Gary, SD
57238 Bemis, SD
57238 Goodwin, SD
57239 Grenville, SD
57241 Hayti, SD
57242 Hazel, SD
57243 Henry, SD
57245 Kranzburg, SD
57246 Labolt, SD
57247 Lake City, SD
57248 Lake Norden, SD
57249 Lake Preston, SD
57251 Marvin, SD
57252 Milbank, SD
57255 New Effington, SD
57256 Ortley, SD
57257 Peever, SD
57258 Raymond, SD
57259 Albee, SD
57259 Revillo, SD
57260 Rosholt, SD
57261 Roslyn, SD
57262 Agency Village, SD
57262 Sisseton, SD
57263 South Shore, SD
57264 Stockholm, SD
57265 Strandburg, SD
57266 Summit, SD
57268 Toronto, SD
57269 Twin Brooks, SD
57270 Veblen, SD
57271 Vienna, SD
57272 Wallace, SD
57273 Waubay, SD
57274 Lily, SD
57274 Webster, SD
57276 Bushnell, SD
57276 White, SD
57278 Willow Lake, SD
57279 Wilmot, SD

573

57301 Loomis, SD
57301 Mitchell, SD
57311 Alexandria, SD
57311 Farmer, SD
57312 Alpena, SD
57313 Armour, SD
57314 Artesian, SD
57314 Forestburg, SD
57315 Avon, SD
57317 Bonesteel, SD
57319 Bridgewater, SD
57319 Dolton, SD
57321 Canova, SD
57322 Carpenter, SD
57323 Carthage, SD
57324 Cavour, SD
57325 Chamberlain, SD
57326 Chamberlain, SD
57328 Corsica, SD
57329 Dante, SD
57330 Delmont, SD
57331 Dimock, SD
57332 Emery, SD
57334 Ethan, SD
57335 Fairfax, SD
57337 Fedora, SD
57339 Fort Thompson, SD
57340 Fulton, SD
57341 Gann Valley, SD
57342 Geddes, SD
57344 Harrison, SD
57345 Highmore, SD
57346 Stephan, SD
57348 Hitchcock, SD
57349 Howard, SD
57349 Roswell, SD
57350 Huron, SD
57353 Bancroft, SD
57353 Iroquois, SD
57354 Kaylor, SD
57355 Kimball, SD
57356 Lake Andes, SD
57356 Ravinia, SD
57358 Lane, SD
57359 Letcher, SD
57361 Marty, SD
57362 Miller, SD
57363 Mount Vernon, SD
57364 New Holland, SD
57365 Oacoma, SD
57366 Parkston, SD
57367 Pickstown, SD
57368 Plankinton, SD
57369 Academy, SD
57369 Platte, SD
57370 Pukwana, SD
57371 Ree Heights, SD
57373 Saint Lawrence, SD
57374 Spencer, SD
57375 Stickney, SD
57376 Tripp, SD
57379 Virgil, SD
57380 Wagner, SD
57381 Wessington, SD
57382 Wessington Springs, SD
57383 White Lake, SD
57384 Wolsey, SD
57385 Woonsocket, SD
57386 Yale, SD
57399 Huron, SD

574

57401 Aberdeen, SD
57402 Aberdeen, SD
57420 Akaska, SD
57421 Amherst, SD
57422 Andover, SD
57424 Ashton, SD
57424 Athol, SD
57426 Barnard, SD
57427 Bath, SD
57428 Bowdle, SD
57429 Brentford, SD
57430 Britton, SD
57432 Claremont, SD
57433 Columbia, SD
57434 Conde, SD
57434 Verdon, SD
57435 Cresbard, SD
57436 Doland, SD
57437 Artas, SD
57437 Eureka, SD
57438 Faulkton, SD
57438 Miranda, SD
57438 Norbeck, SD
57438 Wecota, SD
57439 Ferney, SD
57440 Frankfort, SD
57441 Frederick, SD
57442 Gettysburg, SD
57445 Groton, SD
57446 Hecla, SD
57448 Hosmer, SD
57449 Houghton, SD
57450 Hoven, SD
57451 Ipswich, SD
57451 Mina, SD
57452 Java, SD
57454 Langford, SD
57455 Lebanon, SD
57456 Leola, SD
57457 Long Lake, SD
57460 Mansfield, SD
57461 Mellette, SD
57465 Chelsea, SD
57465 Northville, SD
57466 Onaka, SD
57467 Orient, SD
57468 Pierpont, SD
57469 Redfield, SD
57469 Zell, SD
57470 Rockham, SD
57471 Roscoe, SD
57472 Lowry, SD
57472 Selby, SD
57473 Seneca, SD
57474 Stratford, SD
57475 Tolstoy, SD
57476 Tulare, SD
57477 Turton, SD
57479 Warner, SD
57481 Westport, SD
57481 Wetonka, SD

575

57501 Pierre, SD
57520 Agar, SD
57521 Belvidere, SD
57522 Blunt, SD
57523 Burke, SD
57523 Lucas, SD
57528 Colome, SD
57529 Dallas, SD
57529 Dixon, SD
57531 Draper, SD
57532 Fort Pierre, SD
57532 Mission Ridge, SD
57533 Dixon, SD
57533 Gregory, SD
57533 Iona, SD
57534 Hamill, SD
57536 Harrold, SD
57537 Hayes, SD
57538 Herrick, SD
57540 Holabird, SD
57541 Ideal, SD
57543 Kadoka, SD
57544 Kennebec, SD
57547 Long Valley, SD
57548 Lower Brule, SD
57551 Martin, SD
57551 Vetal, SD
57552 Midland, SD
57552 Ottumwa, SD
57553 Milesville, SD
57555 Mission, SD
57559 Murdo, SD
57560 Norris, SD
57562 Okaton, SD
57563 Okreek, SD
57564 Onida, SD
57566 Parmelee, SD
57567 Philip, SD
57568 Presho, SD
57569 Reliance, SD
57570 Rosebud, SD
57571 Saint Charles, SD
57571 St Charles, SD
57572 Saint Francis, SD
57574 Tuthill, SD
57576 Vivian, SD
57577 Wanblee, SD
57579 Cedarbutte, SD
57579 White River, SD
57580 Carter, SD
57580 Clearfield, SD
57580 Keyapaha, SD
57580 Millboro, SD
57580 Wewela, SD
57580 Winner, SD
57584 Witten, SD
57585 Wood, SD

576

57601 Mobridge, SD
57620 Bison, SD
57621 Bullhead, SD
57622 Cherry Creek, SD
57623 Dupree, SD
57625 Eagle Butte, SD
57625 Parade, SD
57626 Faith, SD
57630 Glencross, SD
57631 Glenham, SD
57632 Herreid, SD
57633 Firesteel, SD
57633 Isabel, SD
57634 Keldron, SD
57636 Lantry, SD
57638 Lemmon, SD
57638 Shadehill, SD
57638 Thunder Hawk, SD
57639 Little Eagle, SD
57640 Lodgepole, SD
57641 Mc Intosh, SD
57642 Mc Laughlin, SD
57644 Glad Valley, SD
57644 Meadow, SD
57645 Morristown, SD
57646 Mound City, SD
57648 Pollock, SD
57649 Prairie City, SD
57650 Ralph, SD
57651 Reva, SD
57652 La Plant, SD
57652 Ridgeview, SD
57656 Timber Lake, SD
57657 Trail City, SD
57658 Wakpala, SD
57659 Walker, SD
57660 Watauga, SD
57661 Whitehorse, SD

577

57701 Rapid City, SD
57702 Rapid City, SD
57702 Rockerville, SD
57702 Silver City, SD
57703 Rapid City, SD
57706 Ellsworth Afb, SD
57709 Rapid City, SD
57714 Allen, SD
57716 Batesland, SD
57716 Denby, SD
57717 Belle Fourche, SD
57717 Fruitdale, SD
57718 Black Hawk, SD
57718 Summerset, SD
57719 Box Elder, SD
57720 Buffalo, SD
57722 Buffalo Gap, SD
57724 Camp Crook, SD
57724 Sky Ranch, SD
57725 Caputa, SD
57730 Crazy Horse, SD
57730 Custer, SD
57732 Deadwood, SD
57735 Ardmore, SD
57735 Burdock, SD
57735 Dewey, SD
57735 Edgemont, SD
57735 Provo, SD
57737 Enning, SD
57738 Fairburn, SD
57741 Fort Meade, SD
57744 Hermosa, SD
57745 Hill City, SD
57745 Rochford, SD
57747 Hot Springs, SD
57748 Howes, SD
57748 Plainview, SD
57750 Interior, SD
57751 Keystone, SD
57752 Kyle, SD
57754 Central City, SD
57754 Lead, SD
57755 Ludlow, SD
57756 Manderson, SD
57758 Mud Butte, SD
57758 Opal, SD
57758 Zeona, SD
57759 Nemo, SD
57760 Newell, SD
57761 New Underwood, SD
57762 Nisland, SD
57763 Oelrichs, SD
57764 Oglala, SD
57766 Oral, SD
57767 Owanka, SD
57769 Bethlehem, SD
57769 Piedmont, SD
57769 Summerset, SD
57770 Pine Ridge, SD
57772 Porcupine, SD
57773 Pringle, SD
57775 Cottonwood, SD
57775 Quinn, SD
57776 Redig, SD
57779 Saint Onge, SD
57780 Scenic, SD
57782 Smithwick, SD
57783 Spearfish, SD
57785 Hereford, SD
57785 Marcus, SD
57785 Sturgis, SD
57787 Red Owl, SD
57787 Stoneville, SD
57787 Union Center, SD
57788 Vale, SD
57790 Creighton, SD
57790 Wall, SD
57791 Elm Springs, SD
57791 Wasta, SD
57792 White Owl, SD
57793 Whitewood, SD
57794 Wounded Knee, SD
57799 Spearfish, SD

580

58001 Abercrombie, ND
58002 Absaraka, ND
58004 Amenia, ND
58005 Argusville, ND
58006 Arthur, ND
58007 Ayr, ND
58008 Barney, ND
58009 Blanchard, ND
58011 Buffalo, ND
58012 Casselton, ND
58013 Cayuga, ND
58015 Christine, ND
58016 Clifford, ND
58017 Brampton, ND
58017 Cogswell, ND
58017 Straubville, ND
58018 Colfax, ND
58021 Davenport, ND
58027 Enderlin, ND
58029 Erie, ND
58030 Fairmount, ND
58031 Alice, ND
58031 Fingal, ND
58032 Forman, ND
58033 Englevale, ND
58033 Fort Ransom, ND
58035 Galesburg, ND
58036 Gardner, ND
58036 Harwood, ND
58038 Grandin, ND
58040 Crete, ND
58040 Gwinner, ND
58041 Hankinson, ND
58042 Gardner, ND
58042 Harwood, ND
58042 Prosper, ND
58043 Havana, ND
58045 Hillsboro, ND
58045 Kelso, ND
58046 Colgate, ND
58046 Hope, ND
58047 Hickson, ND
58047 Horace, ND
58047 Oxbow, ND
58047 Wild Rice, ND
58048 Hunter, ND
58049 Hastings, ND
58049 Kathryn, ND
58051 Kindred, ND
58052 Leonard, ND
58053 Geneseo, ND
58053 Lidgerwood, ND
58054 Elliott, ND
58054 Lisbon, ND
58056 Luverne, ND
58057 Mcleod, ND
58058 Mantador, ND
58059 Durbin, ND
58059 Mapleton, ND
58060 Delamere, ND
58060 Milnor, ND
58061 Mooreton, ND
58062 Nome, ND
58063 Oriska, ND
58064 Page, ND
58065 Pillsbury, ND
58067 Rutland, ND
58068 Sheldon, ND
58069 Stirum, ND
58071 Tower City, ND
58072 Valley City, ND
58074 Wahpeton, ND
58075 Dwight, ND
58075 Galchutt, ND
58075 Great Bend, ND
58075 Wahpeton, ND
58076 Wahpeton, ND
58077 Walcott, ND
58078 Riverside, ND
58078 West Fargo, ND
58079 Chaffee, ND
58079 Embden, ND
58079 Wheatland, ND
58081 Wyndmere, ND

581

58102 Fargo, ND
58102 North River, ND
58102 Reiles Acres, ND
58103 Fargo, ND
58104 Briarwood, ND
58104 Fargo, ND
58104 Frontier, ND
58104 Prairie Rose, ND
58105 Fargo, ND
58106 Fargo, ND
58107 Fargo, ND
58108 Fargo, ND
58109 Fargo, ND
58121 Fargo, ND
58122 Fargo, ND
58124 Fargo, ND
58125 Fargo, ND
58126 Fargo, ND

582

58201 Grand Forks, ND
58202 Grand Forks, ND
58203 Grand Forks, ND
58204 Grand Forks, ND
58204 Grand Forks Afb, ND
58205 Grand Forks, ND
58205 Grand Forks Afb, ND
58206 Grand Forks, ND
58207 Grand Forks, ND
58208 Grand Forks, ND
58210 Adams, ND
58212 Aneta, ND
58214 Arvilla, ND
58216 Bathgate, ND
58218 Buxton, ND
58219 Caledonia, ND
58220 Backoo, ND
58220 Cavalier, ND
58220 Cavalier Afs, ND
58220 Concrete, ND
58222 Crystal, ND
58223 Cummings, ND
58224 Dahlen, ND
58225 Bowesmont, ND
58225 Drayton, ND
58227 Edinburg, ND
58227 Gardar, ND
58228 Emerado, ND
58229 Fairdale, ND
58230 Finley, ND
58231 Fordville, ND
58233 Forest River, ND
58233 Inkster, ND
58235 Gilby, ND
58235 Honeyford, ND
58235 Johnstown, ND
58236 Glasston, ND
58237 Grafton, ND
58237 Nash, ND
58238 Hamilton, ND
58239 Hannah, ND
58240 Hatton, ND
58241 Hensel, ND
58243 Hoople, ND
58244 Inkster, ND
58244 Orr, ND
58249 Langdon, ND
58250 Lankin, ND
58251 Larimore, ND
58251 Mccanna, ND
58254 Kloten, ND
58254 Mcville, ND
58255 Maida, ND
58256 Manvel, ND
58257 Mayville, ND
58258 Mekinock, ND
58259 Michigan, ND
58259 Whitman, ND
58260 Milton, ND
58260 Union, ND
58261 Ardoch, ND
58261 Minto, ND
58261 Voss, ND
58262 Mountain, ND
58265 Neche, ND
58266 Niagara, ND
58267 Kempton, ND
58267 Northwood, ND
58269 Osnabrock, ND
58269 Union, ND
58270 Park River, ND
58271 Joliette, ND
58271 Pembina, ND
58272 Petersburg, ND
58273 Pisek, ND
58274 Portland, ND
58275 Reynolds, ND
58276 Saint Thomas, ND
58277 Sharon, ND
58278 Thompson, ND
58281 Wales, ND
58282 Leroy, ND
58282 Walhalla, ND

583

58301 Devils Lake, ND
58310 Agate, ND
58311 Alsen, ND
58311 Loma, ND
58313 Balta, ND
58316 Belcourt, ND
58317 Bisbee, ND
58318 Bottineau, ND
58321 Brocket, ND
58323 Calvin, ND
58324 Cando, ND
58324 Maza, ND
58325 Churchs Ferry, ND
58327 Crary, ND
58327 Doyon, ND
58327 Southam, ND
58329 Dunseith, ND
58329 San Haven, ND
58330 Edmore, ND
58331 Egeland, ND
58332 Esmond, ND
58332 Fillmore, ND
58335 Fort Totten, ND
58338 Hampden, ND
58339 Hansboro, ND
58341 Hamberg, ND
58341 Harvey, ND
58341 Heimdal, ND
58341 Manfred, ND
58341 Selz, ND
58343 Knox, ND
58344 Lakota, ND
58344 Mapes, ND
58345 Lawton, ND
58346 Harlow, ND
58346 Leeds, ND
58348 Flora, ND
58348 Maddock, ND
58351 Brinsmade, ND
58351 Minnewaukan, ND
58352 Calio, ND
58352 Clyde, ND
58352 Munich, ND
58353 Mylo, ND
58355 Nekoma, ND
58356 Brantford, ND
58356 Bremen, ND
58356 New Rockford, ND
58357 Oberon, ND
58361 Pekin, ND
58362 Penn, ND
58363 Perth, ND
58365 Rocklake, ND
58366 Nanson, ND
58366 Rolette, ND
58367 Rolla, ND
58368 Orrin, ND
58368 Pleasant Lake, ND
58368 Rugby, ND
58368 Silva, ND
58369 Saint John, ND
58370 Saint Michael, ND
58372 Sarles, ND
58374 Sheyenne, ND
58377 Starkweather, ND
58379 Tokio, ND
58380 Hamar, ND
58380 Tolna, ND
58381 Warwick, ND
58382 Webster, ND
58384 Barton, ND
58384 Overly, ND
58384 Willow City, ND
58385 Wolford, ND
58386 Baker, ND
58386 York, ND

584

58401 Eldridge, ND
58401 Jamestown, ND
58401 Sydney, ND
58402 Jamestown, ND
58405 Jamestown, ND
58413 Ashley, ND
58413 Venturia, ND
58415 Berlin, ND
58415 Lamoure, ND
58416 Binford, ND
58418 Bowdon, ND
58418 Heaton, ND
58420 Buchanan, ND
58421 Bordulac, ND
58421 Carrington, ND
58421 Melville, ND
58422 Cathay, ND
58422 Emrick, ND
58423 Chaseley, ND
58424 Cleveland, ND
58424 Windsor, ND
58425 Cooperstown, ND
58426 Courtenay, ND
58428 Dawson, ND
58429 Dazey, ND
58429 Sibley, ND
58430 Denhoff, ND
58431 Dickey, ND
58433 Edgeley, ND
58433 Merricourt, ND
58436 Ellendale, ND
58436 Monango, ND
58438 Fessenden, ND
58439 Forbes, ND
58440 Fredonia, ND
58441 Fullerton, ND
58442 Gackle, ND
58443 Glenfield, ND
58443 Juanita, ND
58444 Goodrich, ND
58445 Grace City, ND
58448 Hannaford, ND
58448 Walum, ND
58451 Hurdsfield, ND
58452 Jessie, ND
58454 Alfred, ND
58454 Jud, ND
58454 Nortonville, ND
58455 Kensal, ND
58456 Kulm, ND
58458 Grand Rapids, ND
58458 Lamoure, ND
58460 Lehr, ND
58461 Litchville, ND
58463 Mcclusky, ND
58464 Mchenry, ND
58466 Marion, ND
58467 Crystal Springs, ND
58467 Medina, ND
58472 Adrian, ND
58472 Millarton, ND
58472 Montpelier, ND
58474 Guelph, ND
58474 Ludden, ND
58474 Oakes, ND
58475 Pettibone, ND

58476 Edmunds, ND
58476 Pingree, ND
58477 Regan, ND
58478 Lake Williams, ND
58478 Robinson, ND
58479 Leal, ND
58479 Rogers, ND
58480 Sanborn, ND
58481 Eckelson, ND
58481 Spiritwood, ND
58482 Steele, ND
58483 Streeter, ND
58484 Sutton, ND
58486 Sykeston, ND
58487 Tappen, ND
58488 Tuttle, ND
58490 Verona, ND
58492 Wimbledon, ND
58494 Arena, ND
58494 Wing, ND
58495 Burnstad, ND
58495 Wishek, ND
58496 Woodworth, ND
58497 Ypsilanti, ND

585

58501 Bismarck, ND
58502 Bismarck, ND
58503 Bismarck, ND
58504 Bismarck, ND
58504 Lincoln, ND
58505 Bismarck, ND
58506 Bismarck, ND
58507 Bismarck, ND
58520 Almont, ND
58521 Baldwin, ND
58523 Beulah, ND
58524 Braddock, ND
58528 Cannon Ball, ND
58529 Carson, ND
58529 Leith, ND
58530 Center, ND
58530 Fort Clark, ND
58530 Hensler, ND
58531 Coleharbor, ND
58532 Driscoll, ND
58533 Elgin, ND
58533 Heil, ND
58535 Flasher, ND
58535 Lark, ND
58538 Fort Yates, ND
58540 Emmet, ND
58540 Garrison, ND
58540 White Shield, ND
58541 Golden Valley, ND
58542 Hague, ND
58542 Westfield, ND
58544 Hazelton, ND
58545 Hazen, ND
58545 Pick City, ND
58549 Kintyre, ND
58552 Linton, ND
58552 Temvik, ND
58554 Fort Rice, ND
58554 Huff, ND
58554 Mandan, ND
58554 Saint Anthony, ND
58558 Menoken, ND
58559 Mercer, ND
58560 Moffit, ND
58561 Napoleon, ND
58562 Bentley, ND
58562 New Leipzig, ND
58563 Hannover, ND
58563 Judson, ND
58563 New Salem, ND
58564 Raleigh, ND
58565 Riverdale, ND
58566 Saint Anthony, ND
58568 Selfridge, ND
58569 Shields, ND
58570 Breien, ND
58570 Solen, ND
58571 Stanton, ND
58572 Mckenzie, ND
58572 Sterling, ND
58573 Strasburg, ND

58575 Turtle Lake, ND
58576 Underwood, ND
58577 Washburn, ND
58579 Wilton, ND
58580 Zap, ND
58581 Zeeland, ND

586

58601 Dickinson, ND
58601 New Hradec, ND
58602 Dickinson, ND
58620 Amidon, ND
58621 Beach, ND
58621 Trotters, ND
58622 Belfield, ND
58622 Fryburg, ND
58623 Bowman, ND
58623 Buffalo Springs, ND
58625 Dodge, ND
58626 Dunn Center, ND
58627 Fairfield, ND
58627 Gorham, ND
58630 Gladstone, ND
58631 Glen Ullin, ND
58632 Golva, ND
58634 Grassy Butte, ND
58636 Halliday, ND
58636 Werner, ND
58638 Hebron, ND
58639 Bucyrus, ND
58639 Haynes, ND
58639 Hettinger, ND
58640 Killdeer, ND
58641 Lefor, ND
58642 Manning, ND
58643 Marmarth, ND
58644 Marshall, ND
58645 Medora, ND
58646 Burt, ND
58646 Mott, ND
58647 New England, ND
58649 Reeder, ND
58650 Regent, ND
58651 Rhame, ND
58652 Richardton, ND
58653 Gascoyne, ND
58653 Scranton, ND
58654 Sentinel Butte, ND
58655 South Heart, ND
58656 Taylor, ND

587

58701 Minot, ND
58702 Minot, ND
58703 Minot, ND
58704 Minot, ND
58704 Minot Afb, ND
58705 Minot, ND
58705 Minot Afb, ND
58707 Minot, ND
58710 Anamoose, ND
58711 Antler, ND
58712 Balfour, ND
58713 Bantry, ND
58716 Benedict, ND
58718 Berthold, ND
58718 Blaisdell, ND
58718 Foxholm, ND
58718 Tagus, ND
58721 Bowbells, ND
58721 Coteau, ND
58722 Burlington, ND
58723 Butte, ND
58723 Kief, ND
58725 Carpio, ND
58727 Columbus, ND
58727 Larson, ND
58730 Crosby, ND
58731 Deering, ND
58733 Des Lacs, ND
58734 Coulee, ND
58734 Donnybrook, ND
58735 Douglas, ND
58736 Drake, ND
58737 Flaxton, ND
58737 Northgate, ND

58740 Glenburn, ND
58740 Wolseth, ND
58741 Granville, ND
58744 Karlsruhe, ND
58746 Kenmare, ND
58746 Norma, ND
58748 Kramer, ND
58750 Lansford, ND
58752 Lignite, ND
58755 Mcgregor, ND
58756 Makoti, ND
58757 Mandaree, ND
58758 Martin, ND
58759 Max, ND
58760 Maxbass, ND
58761 Loraine, ND
58761 Mohall, ND
58762 Newburg, ND
58763 Charlson, ND
58763 New Town, ND
58763 Sanish, ND
58765 Noonan, ND
58768 Norwich, ND
58769 Palermo, ND
58770 Parshall, ND
58771 Plaza, ND
58772 Portal, ND
58773 Battleview, ND
58773 Powers Lake, ND
58775 Roseglen, ND
58776 Ross, ND
58778 Ruso, ND
58779 Raub, ND
58779 Ryder, ND
58781 Sawyer, ND
58782 Sherwood, ND
58783 Carbury, ND
58783 Landa, ND
58783 Roth, ND
58783 Souris, ND
58784 Belden, ND
58784 Lostwood, ND
58784 Stanley, ND
58785 Surrey, ND
58787 Tolley, ND
58788 Berwick, ND
58788 Denbigh, ND
58788 Towner, ND
58789 Upham, ND
58790 Velva, ND
58792 Bergen, ND
58792 Voltaire, ND
58793 Westhope, ND
58794 White Earth, ND
58795 Hamlet, ND
58795 Wildrose, ND

588

58801 Bonetraill, ND
58801 Buford, ND
58801 Williston, ND
58802 Williston, ND
58803 Williston, ND
58830 Alamo, ND
58830 Appam, ND
58830 Corinth, ND
58831 Alexander, ND
58831 Rawson, ND
58833 Ambrose, ND
58835 Arnegard, ND
58838 Cartwright, ND
58843 Epping, ND
58843 Spring Brook, ND
58844 Colgan, ND
58844 Fortuna, ND
58845 Alkabo, ND
58845 Grenora, ND
58847 Keene, ND
58849 Ray, ND
58849 Wheelock, ND
58852 Temple, ND
58852 Tioga, ND
58853 Trenton, ND
58854 Watford City, ND
58856 Zahl, ND

590

59001 Absarokee, MT
59002 Acton, MT

59002 Molt, MT
59003 Ashland, MT
59004 Ashland, MT
59006 Ballantine, MT
59007 Bearcreek, MT
59007 Washoe, MT
59008 Belfry, MT
59010 Bighorn, MT
59011 Big Timber, MT
59012 Birney, MT
59013 Boyd, MT
59014 Bridger, MT
59015 Broadview, MT
59016 Busby, MT
59018 Clyde Park, MT
59019 Columbus, MT
59020 Cooke City, MT
59022 Crow Agency, MT
59024 Custer, MT
59025 Decker, MT
59026 Edgar, MT
59027 Emigrant, MT
59028 Fishtail, MT
59029 Fromberg, MT
59030 Gardiner, MT
59031 Garryowen, MT
59032 Grass Range, MT
59033 Greycliff, MT
59034 Hardin, MT
59035 Fort Smith, MT
59035 Yellowtail, MT
59036 Harlowton, MT
59037 Huntley, MT
59038 Hysham, MT
59038 Sanders, MT
59039 Ingomar, MT
59041 Joliet, MT
59041 Silesia, MT
59043 Lame Deer, MT
59044 Laurel, MT
59046 Lavina, MT
59047 Livingston, MT
59050 Lodge Grass, MT
59052 Mc Leod, MT
59053 Martinsdale, MT
59054 Melstone, MT
59055 Melville, MT
59057 Molt, MT
59058 Mosby, MT
59059 Musselshell, MT
59061 Nye, MT
59062 Otter, MT
59063 Park City, MT
59064 Pompeys Pillar, MT
59065 Pray, MT
59066 Pryor, MT
59067 Rapelje, MT
59068 Luther, MT
59068 Red Lodge, MT
59069 Reed Point, MT
59070 Fox, MT
59070 Roberts, MT
59071 Roscoe, MT
59072 Roundup, MT
59073 Roundup, MT
59074 Ryegate, MT
59075 Saint Xavier, MT
59076 Hysham, MT
59076 Sanders, MT
59077 Sand Springs, MT
59078 Shawmut, MT
59079 Shepherd, MT
59081 Cooke City, MT
59081 Silver Gate, MT
59082 Springdale, MT
59083 Sumatra, MT
59084 Teigen, MT
59084 Winnett, MT
59085 Two Dot, MT
59086 Wilsall, MT
59087 Cat Creek, MT
59087 Winnett, MT
59088 Worden, MT
59089 Wyola, MT

591

59101 Billings, MT
59102 Billings, MT

59103 Billings, MT
59104 Billings, MT
59105 Billings, MT
59106 Billings, MT
59107 Billings, MT
59108 Billings, MT
59111 Billings, MT
59112 Billings, MT
59114 Billings, MT
59115 Billings, MT
59116 Billings, MT
59117 Billings, MT

592

59201 Wolf Point, MT
59211 Antelope, MT
59212 Bainville, MT
59213 Brockton, MT
59214 Brockway, MT
59215 Circle, MT
59217 Crane, MT
59218 Culbertson, MT
59218 Mccabe, MT
59219 Dagmar, MT
59221 Fairview, MT
59222 Flaxville, MT
59223 Fort Peck, MT
59225 Frazer, MT
59225 Lustre, MT
59226 Froid, MT
59230 Glasgow, MT
59230 Saint Marie, MT
59231 Glasgow, MT
59231 Saint Marie, MT
59240 Glentana, MT
59241 Hinsdale, MT
59242 Homestead, MT
59243 Lambert, MT
59244 Larslan, MT
59247 Medicine Lake, MT
59248 Nashua, MT
59250 Opheim, MT
59252 Outlook, MT
59253 Peerless, MT
59254 Plentywood, MT
59255 Poplar, MT
59256 Raymond, MT
59257 Redstone, MT
59258 Reserve, MT
59259 Richey, MT
59260 Richland, MT
59261 Saco, MT
59262 Savage, MT
59263 Four Buttes, MT
59263 Scobey, MT
59270 Sidney, MT
59273 Vandalia, MT
59274 Vida, MT
59275 Westby, MT
59276 Whitetail, MT

593

59301 Miles City, MT
59311 Alzada, MT
59312 Angela, MT
59313 Baker, MT
59314 Biddle, MT
59315 Bloomfield, MT
59316 Boyes, MT
59317 Broadus, MT
59317 Sonnette, MT
59318 Brusett, MT
59319 Capitol, MT
59322 Cohagen, MT
59323 Colstrip, MT
59324 Ekalaka, MT
59324 Mill Iron, MT
59326 Fallon, MT
59327 Forsyth, MT
59330 Glendive, MT
59332 Hammond, MT
59333 Hathaway, MT
59336 Ismay, MT
59337 Jordan, MT
59338 Kinsey, MT
59339 Lindsay, MT

59341 Fallon, MT
59341 Mildred, MT
59343 Olive, MT
59344 Plevna, MT
59345 Powderville, MT
59347 Rosebud, MT
59349 Terry, MT
59351 Volborg, MT
59353 Wibaux, MT
59354 Willard, MT

594

59401 Great Falls, MT
59402 Great Falls, MT
59402 Malmstrom Afb, MT
59403 Great Falls, MT
59404 Great Falls, MT
59405 Great Falls, MT
59406 Great Falls, MT
59410 Augusta, MT
59411 Babb, MT
59412 Belt, MT
59414 Black Eagle, MT
59416 Brady, MT
59417 Browning, MT
59417 Saint Mary, MT
59418 Buffalo, MT
59419 Bynum, MT
59420 Carter, MT
59421 Cascade, MT
59422 Choteau, MT
59424 Coffee Creek, MT
59425 Conrad, MT
59427 Cut Bank, MT
59427 Santa Rita, MT
59430 Denton, MT
59432 Dupuyer, MT
59433 Dutton, MT
59434 E Glacier Par, MT
59434 E Glacier Park, MT
59434 East Glacier Park, MT
59435 Ethridge, MT
59436 Fairfield, MT
59440 Floweree, MT
59441 Forest Grove, MT
59442 Fort Benton, MT
59443 Fort Shaw, MT
59444 Galata, MT
59446 Geraldine, MT
59446 Square Butte, MT
59447 Geyser, MT
59448 Heart Butte, MT
59450 Highwood, MT
59450 Shonkin, MT
59451 Hilger, MT
59452 Hobson, MT
59453 Garneill, MT
59453 Judith Gap, MT
59454 Kevin, MT
59456 Ledger, MT
59457 Lewistown, MT
59460 Loma, MT
59461 Lothair, MT
59462 Moccasin, MT
59463 Monarch, MT
59464 Moore, MT
59465 Neihart, MT
59466 Ferdig, MT
59466 Oilmont, MT
59467 Pendroy, MT
59468 Power, MT
59469 Raynesford, MT
59471 Roy, MT
59472 Sand Coulee, MT
59472 Tracy, MT
59474 Shelby, MT
59477 Simms, MT
59479 Stanford, MT
59480 Stockett, MT
59482 Sunburst, MT
59483 Sun River, MT
59484 Sweet Grass, MT
59485 Ulm, MT
59486 Valier, MT
59487 Vaughn, MT
59489 Winifred, MT

595

9501 Havre, MT
9520 Big Sandy, MT
9521 Box Elder, MT
9522 Chester, MT
9523 Chinook, MT
9524 Dodson, MT
9525 Gildford, MT
9526 Harlem, MT
9527 Hays, MT
9528 Hingham, MT
9529 Hogeland, MT
9530 Inverness, MT
9531 Joplin, MT
9532 Kremlin, MT
9535 Lloyd, MT
9537 Loring, MT
9538 Malta, MT
9540 Rudyard, MT
9542 Turner, MT
9544 Whitewater, MT
9545 Whitlash, MT
9546 Zortman, MT
9547 Zurich, MT

596

9601 Helena, MT
9602 Helena, MT
9604 Helena, MT
9620 Helena, MT
9623 Helena, MT
9624 Helena, MT
9625 Helena, MT
9626 Helena, MT
9631 Basin, MT
9632 Boulder, MT
9633 Canyon Creek, MT
9634 Clancy, MT
9634 Montana City, MT
9635 East Helena, MT
9636 Fort Harrison, MT
9638 Jefferson City, MT
9639 Lincoln, MT
9640 Marysville, MT
9641 Radersburg, MT
9642 Ringling, MT
9643 Toston, MT
9644 Townsend, MT
9645 White Sulphur Springs, MT
9647 Winston, MT
9648 Craig, MT
9648 Wolf Creek, MT

597

9701 Butte, MT
9701 Walkerville, MT
9702 Butte, MT
9703 Butte, MT
9707 Butte, MT
9710 Alder, MT
9711 Anaconda, MT
9713 Avon, MT
9714 Belgrade, MT
9715 Bozeman, MT
9716 Big Sky, MT
9717 Bozeman, MT
9718 Bozeman, MT
9719 Bozeman, MT
9720 Cameron, MT
9721 Cardwell, MT
9722 Deer Lodge, MT
9724 Dell, MT
9725 Dillon, MT
9727 Divide, MT
9728 Elliston, MT
9729 Ennis, MT
9730 Gallatin Gateway, MT
9731 Garrison, MT
9732 Glen, MT
9733 Gold Creek, MT
9735 Harrison, MT
9736 Jackson, MT
9739 Lima, MT
9740 Mc Allister, MT
9741 Manhattan, MT
59743 Melrose, MT
59745 Norris, MT
59746 Polaris, MT
59747 Pony, MT
59748 Ramsay, MT
59749 Sheridan, MT
59750 Butte, MT
59751 Silver Star, MT
59752 Three Forks, MT
59754 Twin Bridges, MT
59755 Virginia City, MT
59756 Warm Springs, MT
59758 West Yellowstone, MT
59759 Whitehall, MT
59760 Willow Creek, MT
59761 Wisdom, MT
59762 Wise River, MT
59771 Bozeman, MT
59772 Bozeman, MT

598

59801 Missoula, MT
59802 Missoula, MT
59803 Missoula, MT
59804 Missoula, MT
59806 Missoula, MT
59807 Missoula, MT
59808 Missoula, MT
59812 Missoula, MT
59820 Alberton, MT
59821 Arlee, MT
59823 Bonner, MT
59823 Greenough, MT
59823 Potomac, MT
59824 Charlo, MT
59824 Moiese, MT
59825 Clinton, MT
59826 Condon, MT
59827 Conner, MT
59828 Corvallis, MT
59829 Darby, MT
59830 De Borgia, MT
59831 Dixon, MT
59832 Drummond, MT
59833 Florence, MT
59834 Frenchtown, MT
59835 Grantsdale, MT
59837 Hall, MT
59840 Hamilton, MT
59840 Pinesdale, MT
59841 Pinesdale, MT
59842 Haugan, MT
59843 Helmville, MT
59844 Heron, MT
59845 Hot Springs, MT
59845 Niarada, MT
59846 Huson, MT
59847 Lolo, MT
59848 Hot Springs, MT
59848 Lonepine, MT
59851 Milltown, MT
59853 Noxon, MT
59854 Ovando, MT
59855 Pablo, MT
59856 Paradise, MT
59858 Philipsburg, MT
59859 Plains, MT
59860 Polson, MT
59863 Ravalli, MT
59864 Ronan, MT
59865 Saint Ignatius, MT
59866 Saint Regis, MT
59867 Saltese, MT
59868 Seeley Lake, MT
59870 Stevensville, MT
59871 Sula, MT
59872 Superior, MT
59873 Thompson Falls, MT
59874 Trout Creek, MT
59875 Victor, MT

599

59901 Creston, MT
59901 Evergreen, MT
59901 Kalispell, MT
59903 Kalispell, MT
59904 Kalispell, MT
59910 Big Arm, MT
59911 Bigfork, MT
59911 Swan Lake, MT
59912 Columbia Falls, MT
59913 Coram, MT
59914 Dayton, MT
59915 Elmo, MT
59916 Essex, MT
59917 Eureka, MT
59918 Fortine, MT
59919 Hungry Horse, MT
59920 Kila, MT
59921 Lake Mc Donald, MT
59921 West Glacier, MT
59922 Lakeside, MT
59923 Libby, MT
59925 Marion, MT
59926 Martin City, MT
59927 Olney, MT
59928 Polebridge, MT
59929 Proctor, MT
59930 Rexford, MT
59931 Rollins, MT
59932 Somers, MT
59933 Stryker, MT
59934 Trego, MT
59935 Troy, MT
59936 West Glacier, MT
59937 Whitefish, MT

600

60001 Alden, IL
60002 Antioch, IL
60002 Old Mill Creek, IL
60004 Arlington Heights, IL
60007 Elk Grove Village, IL
60008 Rolling Meadows, IL
60009 Elk Grove Village, IL
60010 Barrington, IL
60010 Deer Park, IL
60010 Fox River Valley Gardens, IL
60010 Hoffman Estates, IL
60010 Inverness, IL
60010 Kildeer, IL
60010 Lake Barrington, IL
60010 North Barrington, IL
60010 Port Barrington, IL
60010 South Barrington, IL
60010 Tower Lakes, IL
60011 Barrington, IL
60012 Bull Valley, IL
60012 Crystal Lake, IL
60012 Prairie Grove, IL
60013 Cary, IL
60013 Oakwood Hills, IL
60013 Trout Valley, IL
60014 Crystal Lake, IL
60014 Village Of Lakewood, IL
60015 Bannockburn, IL
60015 Deerfield, IL
60015 Riverwoods, IL
60016 Des Plaines, IL
60017 Des Plaines, IL
60018 Des Plaines, IL
60018 Rosemont, IL
60019 Des Plaines, IL
60019 Rosemont, IL
60020 Fox Lake, IL
60020 Volo, IL
60021 Fox River Grove, IL
60022 Glencoe, IL
60025 Glenview, IL
60026 Glenview, IL
60029 Golf, IL
60030 Gages Lake, IL
60030 Grayslake, IL
60030 Hainesville, IL
60030 Third Lake, IL
60030 Volo, IL
60031 Gurnee, IL
60033 Harvard, IL
60034 Hebron, IL
60035 Highland Park, IL
60037 Fort Sheridan, IL
60037 Highland Park, IL
60038 Palatine, IL
60039 Crystal Lake, IL
60040 Highwood, IL
60041 Ingleside, IL
60041 Volo, IL
60042 Island Lake, IL
60043 Kenilworth, IL
60044 Lake Bluff, IL
60045 Lake Forest, IL
60045 Mettawa, IL
60046 Lake Villa, IL
60046 Lindenhurst, IL
60046 Old Mill Creek, IL
60047 Deer Park, IL
60047 Hawthorn Woods, IL
60047 Kildeer, IL
60047 Lake Zurich, IL
60047 Long Grove, IL
60048 Libertyville, IL
60048 Mettawa, IL
60050 Bull Valley, IL
60050 Holiday Hills, IL
60050 Johnsburg, IL
60050 Lakemoor, IL
60050 Mccullom Lake, IL
60050 Mchenry, IL
60051 Holiday Hills, IL
60051 Johnsburg, IL
60051 Lakemoor, IL
60051 Mchenry, IL
60051 Volo, IL
60053 Morton Grove, IL
60055 Palatine, IL
60056 Mount Prospect, IL
60060 Long Grove, IL
60060 Mundelein, IL
60061 Indian Creek, IL
60061 Vernon Hills, IL
60062 Northbrook, IL
60064 Abbott Park, IL
60064 Downey, IL
60064 North Chicago, IL
60065 Northbrook, IL
60067 Hoffman Estates, IL
60067 Inverness, IL
60067 Palatine, IL
60068 Park Ridge, IL
60069 Lincolnshire, IL
60069 Prairie View, IL
60069 Prairieview, IL
60070 Prospect Heights, IL
60071 Richmond, IL
60071 Solon Mills, IL
60072 Ringwood, IL
60073 Hainesville, IL
60073 Round Lake, IL
60073 Round Lake Beach, IL
60073 Round Lake Heights, IL
60073 Round Lake Park, IL
60073 Round Lk Park, IL
60073 Volo, IL
60074 Deer Park, IL
60074 Kildeer, IL
60074 Palatine, IL
60075 Russell, IL
60076 Skokie, IL
60077 Skokie, IL
60078 Palatine, IL
60079 Waukegan, IL
60081 Spring Grove, IL
60082 Techny, IL
60083 Beach Park, IL
60083 Old Mill Creek, IL
60083 Wadsworth, IL
60084 Lake Barrington, IL
60084 Wauconda, IL
60085 Park City, IL
60085 Waukegan, IL
60086 North Chicago, IL
60087 Beach Park, IL
60087 Waukegan, IL
60088 Great Lakes, IL
60088 North Chicago, IL
60089 Buffalo Grove, IL
60090 Wheeling, IL
60091 Wilmette, IL
60093 Northfield, IL
60093 Winnetka, IL
60094 Palatine, IL
60095 Palatine, IL
60096 Winthrop Harbor, IL
60097 Bull Valley, IL
60097 Wonder Lake, IL
60098 Bull Valley, IL
60098 Woodstock, IL
60099 Beach Park, IL
60099 Zion, IL

601

60101 Addison, IL
60102 Algonquin, IL
60102 Lake In The Hills, IL
60103 Bartlett, IL
60103 Ontarioville, IL
60104 Bellwood, IL
60105 Bensenville, IL
60106 Bensenville, IL
60107 Streamwood, IL
60108 Bloomingdale, IL
60109 Burlington, IL
60110 Carpentersville, IL
60111 Clare, IL
60112 Cortland, IL
60113 Creston, IL
60115 Dekalb, IL
60116 Carol Stream, IL
60117 Bloomingdale, IL
60118 Dundee, IL
60118 East Dundee, IL
60118 Sleepy Hollow, IL
60118 West Dundee, IL
60119 Campton Hills, IL
60119 Elburn, IL
60120 Elgin, IL
60120 Hoffman Estates, IL
60121 Elgin, IL
60122 Carol Stream, IL
60123 Elgin, IL
60124 Campton Hills, IL
60124 Elgin, IL
60124 Plato Center, IL
60126 Elmhurst, IL
60128 Carol Stream, IL
60129 Esmond, IL
60130 Forest Park, IL
60131 Franklin Park, IL
60131 Schiller Park, IL
60132 Carol Stream, IL
60133 Bartlett, IL
60133 Hanover Park, IL
60134 Geneva, IL
60135 Genoa, IL
60136 Gilberts, IL
60137 Glen Ellyn, IL
60137 Glendale Heights, IL
60138 Glen Ellyn, IL
60139 Glendale Heights, IL
60140 Campton Hills, IL
60140 Hampshire, IL
60140 Pingree Grove, IL
60141 Hines, IL
60142 Huntley, IL
60143 Itasca, IL
60144 Kaneville, IL
60145 Kingston, IL
60146 Kirkland, IL
60147 Lafox, IL
60148 Lombard, IL
60150 Malta, IL
60151 Maple Park, IL
60151 Virgil, IL
60152 Marengo, IL
60153 Broadview, IL
60153 Maywood, IL
60154 Westchester, IL
60155 Broadview, IL
60155 Maywood, IL
60156 Algonquin, IL
60156 Lake In The Hills, IL
60157 Medinah, IL
60159 Schaumburg, IL
60160 Melrose Park, IL
60161 Melrose Park, IL
60162 Hillside, IL
60163 Berkeley, IL
60163 Hillside, IL
60163 Melrose Park, IL
60164 Melrose Park, IL
60164 Northlake, IL
60165 Melrose Park, IL
60165 Stone Park, IL
60168 Schaumburg, IL
60169 Hoffman Estates, IL
60170 Plato Center, IL
60171 River Grove, IL
60172 Roselle, IL
60173 Schaumburg, IL
60174 Campton Hills, IL
60174 Saint Charles, IL
60174 St Charles, IL
60175 Campton Hills, IL
60175 Saint Charles, IL
60175 St Charles, IL
60176 Schiller Park, IL
60177 South Elgin, IL
60178 Sycamore, IL
60179 Hoffman Estates, IL
60179 Schaumburg, IL
60180 Union, IL
60181 Oakbrook Terrace, IL
60181 Villa Park, IL
60183 Wasco, IL
60184 Wayne, IL
60185 Northwoods, IL
60185 West Chicago, IL
60186 West Chicago, IL
60187 Wheaton, IL
60188 Carol Stream, IL
60189 Wheaton, IL
60190 Winfield, IL
60191 Wood Dale, IL
60192 Hoffman Estates, IL
60193 Schaumburg, IL
60194 Schaumburg, IL
60195 Hoffman Estates, IL
60195 Schaumburg, IL
60196 Hoffman Estates, IL
60196 Schaumburg, IL
60197 Carol Stream, IL
60199 Carol Stream, IL

602

60201 Evanston, IL
60202 Evanston, IL
60203 Evanston, IL
60204 Evanston, IL
60208 Evanston, IL
60209 Evanston, IL
60290 Chicago, IL

603

60301 Oak Park, IL
60302 Oak Park, IL
60303 Oak Park, IL
60304 Oak Park, IL
60305 River Forest, IL
60399 Bensenville, IL
60399 Wood Dale, IL

604

60401 Beecher, IL
60402 Berwyn, IL
60402 Forest View, IL
60402 Stickney, IL
60403 Crest Hill, IL
60403 Joliet, IL
60404 Joliet, IL
60404 Shorewood, IL
60406 Blue Island, IL
60407 Braceville, IL
60407 Godley, IL
60408 Braidwood, IL
60409 Calumet City, IL
60410 Channahon, IL
60411 Chicago Heights, IL
60411 Ford Heights, IL
60411 Lynwood, IL
60411 S Chicago Hei, IL
60411 S Chicago Heights, IL
60411 Sauk Village, IL

60411 South Chicago Heights, IL
60412 Chicago Heights, IL
60415 Chicago Ridge, IL
60416 Carbon Hill, IL
60416 Coal City, IL
60416 Diamond, IL
60417 Crete, IL
60419 Dolton, IL
60420 Dwight, IL
60421 Elwood, IL
60422 Flossmoor, IL
60422 Homewood, IL
60423 Frankfort, IL
60424 Gardner, IL
60425 Glenwood, IL
60426 Dixmoor, IL
60426 Harvey, IL
60426 Markham, IL
60426 Phoenix, IL
60428 Harvey, IL
60428 Markham, IL
60429 Hazel Crest, IL
60430 Homewood, IL
60431 Joliet, IL
60431 Shorewood, IL
60432 Joliet, IL
60433 Joliet, IL
60434 Joliet, IL
60435 Crest Hill, IL
60435 Joliet, IL
60435 Shorewood, IL
60436 Joliet, IL
60436 Rockdale, IL
60436 Shorewood, IL
60437 Kinsman, IL
60438 Lansing, IL
60439 Lemont, IL
60440 Bolingbrook, IL
60441 Homer Glen, IL
60441 Lockport, IL
60442 Manhattan, IL
60442 Wilton Center, IL
60443 Matteson, IL
60444 Mazon, IL
60445 Crestwood, IL
60445 Midlothian, IL
60446 Lockport, IL
60446 Romeoville, IL
60447 Minooka, IL
60448 Mokena, IL
60449 Monee, IL
60450 Morris, IL
60451 New Lenox, IL
60452 Oak Forest, IL
60453 Oak Lawn, IL
60454 Oak Lawn, IL
60455 Bedford Park, IL
60455 Bridgeview, IL
60455 Oak Lawn, IL
60456 Hometown, IL
60456 Oak Lawn, IL
60457 Hickory Hills, IL
60457 Oak Lawn, IL
60458 Bedford Park, IL
60458 Justice, IL
60458 Oak Lawn, IL
60459 Bedford Park, IL
60459 Burbank, IL
60459 Oak Lawn, IL
60460 Odell, IL
60461 Olympia Fields, IL
60462 Orland Park, IL
60463 Palos Heights, IL
60464 Palos Park, IL
60465 Palos Hills, IL
60466 Park Forest, IL
60466 University Park, IL
60467 Orland Park, IL
60468 Peotone, IL
60469 Posen, IL
60470 Ransom, IL
60471 Richton Park, IL
60472 Robbins, IL
60473 South Holland, IL
60474 South Wilmington, IL
60475 Chicago Heights, IL
60475 Steger, IL
60476 Thornton, IL
60477 Orland Hills, IL
60477 Tinley Park, IL
60478 Country Club Hills, IL
60478 Ctry Clb Hls, IL
60478 Tinley Park, IL
60479 Verona, IL
60480 Willow Springs, IL
60481 Custer Park, IL
60481 Wilmington, IL
60482 Worth, IL
60484 Park Forest, IL
60484 University Park, IL
60487 Orland Hills, IL
60487 Tinley Park, IL
60490 Bolingbrook, IL
60491 Homer Glen, IL
60491 Lockport, IL
60499 Bedford Park, IL
60499 South Suburban, IL

605

60501 Argo, IL
60501 Bedford Park, IL
60501 Summit, IL
60501 Summit Argo, IL
60502 Aurora, IL
60503 Aurora, IL
60504 Aurora, IL
60505 Aurora, IL
60506 Aurora, IL
60507 Aurora, IL
60510 Batavia, IL
60511 Big Rock, IL
60512 Bristol, IL
60513 Brookfield, IL
60514 Clarendon Hills, IL
60515 Downers Grove, IL
60516 Downers Grove, IL
60517 Downers Grove, IL
60517 Woodridge, IL
60518 Earlville, IL
60519 Eola, IL
60520 Hinckley, IL
60521 Hinsdale, IL
60521 Oak Brook, IL
60521 Oak Brook Mall, IL
60522 Hinsdale, IL
60522 Oak Brook, IL
60523 Hinsdale, IL
60523 Oak Brook, IL
60525 Countryside, IL
60525 Hodgkins, IL
60525 Ind Head Park, IL
60525 Ind Head Pk, IL
60525 Indian Head Park, IL
60525 Indian Head Pk, IL
60525 La Grange, IL
60525 La Grange Highlands, IL
60525 Mc Cook, IL
60526 La Grange Park, IL
60527 Burr Ridge, IL
60527 Willowbrook, IL
60530 Lee, IL
60531 Leland, IL
60532 Lisle, IL
60534 Lyons, IL
60536 Millbrook, IL
60537 Millington, IL
60538 Montgmry, IL
60538 Montgomery, IL
60539 Batavia, IL
60539 Mooseheart, IL
60540 Naperville, IL
60541 Newark, IL
60542 North Aurora, IL
60543 Oswego, IL
60544 Plainfield, IL
60545 Plano, IL
60546 North Riverside, IL
60546 Riverside, IL
60548 Sandwich, IL
60549 Serena, IL
60550 Shabbona, IL
60551 Sheridan, IL
60552 Somonauk, IL
60553 Steward, IL
60554 Sugar Grove, IL
60555 Warrenville, IL
60556 Waterman, IL
60557 Wedron, IL
60558 Western Springs, IL
60559 Westmont, IL
60560 Yorkville, IL
60561 Darien, IL
60563 Naperville, IL
60564 Naperville, IL
60565 Naperville, IL
60566 Naperville, IL
60567 Naperville, IL
60568 Aurora, IL
60572 Aurora, IL
60572 Fox Valley, IL
60585 Plainfield, IL
60586 Plainfield, IL
60598 Aurora, IL
60599 Fox Valley, IL

606

60601 Chicago, IL
60602 Chicago, IL
60603 Chicago, IL
60604 Chicago, IL
60605 Chicago, IL
60606 Chicago, IL
60607 Chicago, IL
60608 Chicago, IL
60609 Chicago, IL
60610 Chicago, IL
60611 Chicago, IL
60612 Chicago, IL
60613 Chicago, IL
60614 Chicago, IL
60615 Chicago, IL
60616 Chicago, IL
60617 Chicago, IL
60618 Chicago, IL
60619 Chicago, IL
60620 Chicago, IL
60621 Chicago, IL
60622 Chicago, IL
60623 Chicago, IL
60624 Chicago, IL
60625 Chicago, IL
60626 Chicago, IL
60628 Chicago, IL
60629 Chicago, IL
60630 Chicago, IL
60630 Jefferson Park, IL
60631 Chicago, IL
60632 Chicago, IL
60633 Burnham, IL
60633 Chicago, IL
60634 Chicago, IL
60636 Chicago, IL
60637 Chicago, IL
60638 Bedford Park, IL
60638 Chicago, IL
60639 Chicago, IL
60640 Chicago, IL
60641 Chicago, IL
60642 Chicago, IL
60643 Calumet Park, IL
60643 Chicago, IL
60644 Chicago, IL
60645 Chicago, IL
60646 Chicago, IL
60646 Lincolnwood, IL
60647 Chicago, IL
60649 Chicago, IL
60651 Chicago, IL
60652 Chicago, IL
60653 Chicago, IL
60654 Chicago, IL
60655 Chicago, IL
60655 Merrionette Park, IL
60656 Chicago, IL
60656 Harwood Heights, IL
60656 Norridge, IL
60657 Chicago, IL
60659 Chicago, IL
60660 Chicago, IL
60661 Chicago, IL
60664 Chicago, IL
60666 Chicago, IL
60668 Chicago, IL
60669 Chicago, IL
60670 Chicago, IL
60673 Chicago, IL
60674 Chicago, IL
60675 Chicago, IL
60677 Chicago, IL
60678 Chicago, IL
60680 Chicago, IL
60681 Chicago, IL
60682 Chicago, IL
60684 Chicago, IL
60685 Chicago, IL
60686 Chicago, IL
60687 Chicago, IL
60688 Chicago, IL
60689 Chicago, IL
60690 Chicago, IL
60691 Chicago, IL
60693 Chicago, IL
60694 Chicago, IL
60695 Chicago, IL
60696 Chicago, IL
60697 Chicago, IL
60699 Chicago, IL

607

60701 Chicago, IL
60706 Chicago, IL
60706 Harwood Heights, IL
60706 Norridge, IL
60707 Chicago, IL
60707 Elmwood Park, IL
60712 Lincolnwood, IL
60714 Niles, IL

608

60803 Alsip, IL
60803 Chicago, IL
60803 Merrionette Park, IL
60804 Chicago, IL
60804 Cicero, IL
60805 Chicago, IL
60805 Evergreen Park, IL
60827 Calumet Park, IL
60827 Chicago, IL
60827 Riverdale, IL

609

60901 Irwin, IL
60901 Kankakee, IL
60910 Aroma Park, IL
60911 Ashkum, IL
60912 Beaverville, IL
60913 Bonfield, IL
60914 Bourbonnais, IL
60915 Bradley, IL
60917 Buckingham, IL
60918 Buckley, IL
60919 Cabery, IL
60920 Campus, IL
60921 Chatsworth, IL
60922 Chebanse, IL
60922 Sammons Point, IL
60924 Cissna Park, IL
60926 Claytonville, IL
60927 Clifton, IL
60928 Crescent City, IL
60929 Cullom, IL
60930 Danforth, IL
60931 Donovan, IL
60932 East Lynn, IL
60933 Elliott, IL
60934 Emington, IL
60935 Essex, IL
60936 Gibson City, IL
60938 Gilman, IL
60939 Goodwine, IL
60940 Grant Park, IL
60941 Herscher, IL
60942 Hoopeston, IL
60944 Hopkins Park, IL
60945 Iroquois, IL
60946 Kempton, IL
60948 Loda, IL
60949 Ludlow, IL
60950 Manteno, IL
60951 Martinton, IL
60952 Melvin, IL
60953 Milford, IL
60954 Momence, IL
60955 Onarga, IL
60956 Papineau, IL
60957 Paxton, IL
60958 Pembroke Township, IL
60959 Piper City, IL
60960 Clarence, IL
60960 Rankin, IL
60961 Reddick, IL
60962 Roberts, IL
60963 Rossville, IL
60964 Saint Anne, IL
60964 Sun River Terrace, IL
60966 Sheldon, IL
60967 Stockland, IL
60968 Thawville, IL
60969 Union Hill, IL
60970 Watseka, IL
60973 Wellington, IL
60974 Woodland, IL

610

61001 Apple River, IL
61006 Ashton, IL
61007 Baileyville, IL
61008 Belvidere, IL
61010 Byron, IL
61011 Caledonia, IL
61012 Capron, IL
61013 Cedarville, IL
61014 Chadwick, IL
61015 Chana, IL
61016 Cherry Valley, IL
61018 Dakota, IL
61019 Davis, IL
61020 Davis Junction, IL
61021 Dixon, IL
61021 Nelson, IL
61024 Durand, IL
61025 East Dubuque, IL
61027 Eleroy, IL
61028 Elizabeth, IL
61030 Forreston, IL
61031 Franklin Grove, IL
61032 Freeport, IL
61032 Scioto Mills, IL
61036 Galena, IL
61037 Galt, IL
61038 Garden Prairie, IL
61039 German Valley, IL
61041 Hanover, IL
61042 Harmon, IL
61043 Holcomb, IL
61044 Kent, IL
61046 Lanark, IL
61047 Egan, IL
61047 Leaf River, IL
61048 Lena, IL
61049 Lindenwood, IL
61050 Mc Connell, IL
61051 Milledgeville, IL
61052 Monroe Center, IL
61053 Mount Carroll, IL
61054 Mount Morris, IL
61057 Nachusa, IL
61059 Nora, IL
61060 Orangeville, IL
61061 Oregon, IL
61062 Pearl City, IL
61063 Pecatonica, IL
61064 Polo, IL
61065 Poplar Grove, IL
61067 Ridott, IL
61068 Kings, IL
61068 Rochelle, IL
61070 Rock City, IL
61071 Rock Falls, IL
61072 Rockton, IL
61073 Roscoe, IL
61074 Savanna, IL
61075 Scales Mound, IL
61077 Seward, IL
61078 Shannon, IL
61079 Shirland, IL
61080 South Beloit, IL
61081 Coleta, IL
61081 Sterling, IL
61084 Stillman Valley, IL
61085 Stockton, IL
61087 Warren, IL
61088 Winnebago, IL
61089 Winslow, IL
61091 Woosung, IL

611

61101 Rockford, IL
61102 Rockford, IL
61103 Machesney Park, IL
61103 Rockford, IL
61104 Rockford, IL
61105 Rockford, IL
61106 Rockford, IL
61107 Rockford, IL
61108 Rockford, IL
61109 Rockford, IL
61110 Rockford, IL
61111 Loves Park, IL
61111 Machesney Park, IL
61112 Rockford, IL
61114 Rockford, IL
61115 Loves Park, IL
61115 Machesney Park, IL
61125 Rockford, IL
61126 Rockford, IL
61130 Loves Park, IL
61131 Loves Park, IL
61132 Loves Park, IL

612

61201 Rock Island, IL
61204 Rock Island, IL
61230 Albany, IL
61231 Aledo, IL
61232 Andalusia, IL
61233 Andover, IL
61234 Annawan, IL
61235 Atkinson, IL
61236 Barstow, IL
61237 Buffalo Prairie, IL
61238 Cambridge, IL
61239 Carbon Cliff, IL
61240 Coal Valley, IL
61241 Cleveland, IL
61241 Colona, IL
61241 Green Rock, IL
61242 Cordova, IL
61243 Deer Grove, IL
61244 East Moline, IL
61250 Erie, IL
61251 Fenton, IL
61252 Fulton, IL
61254 Geneseo, IL
61256 Hampton, IL
61257 Hillsdale, IL
61258 Hooppole, IL
61259 Illinois City, IL
61260 Joy, IL
61261 Lyndon, IL
61262 Lynn Center, IL
61263 Matherville, IL
61264 Milan, IL
61264 Oak Grove, IL
61265 Moline, IL
61266 Moline, IL
61270 Morrison, IL
61272 New Boston, IL
61273 Orion, IL
61274 Osco, IL
61275 Port Byron, IL
61276 Preemption, IL
61277 Prophetstown, IL
61278 Rapids City, IL
61279 Reynolds, IL
61281 Sherrard, IL
61282 Silvis, IL
61283 Tampico, IL
61284 Taylor Ridge, IL

61285 Thomson, IL
61299 Rock Island, IL

613

61301 La Salle, IL
61310 Amboy, IL
61311 Ancona, IL
61312 Arlington, IL
61313 Blackstone, IL
61314 Buda, IL
61315 Bureau, IL
61316 Cedar Point, IL
61317 Cherry, IL
61318 Compton, IL
61319 Cornell, IL
61319 Manville, IL
61320 Dalzell, IL
61321 Dana, IL
61322 Depue, IL
61323 Dover, IL
61324 Eldena, IL
61325 Grand Ridge, IL
61326 Granville, IL
61327 Hennepin, IL
61328 Kasbeer, IL
61329 Ladd, IL
61330 La Moille, IL
61331 Lee Center, IL
61332 Leonore, IL
61333 Long Point, IL
61334 Lostant, IL
61335 Mc Nabb, IL
61336 Magnolia, IL
61337 Malden, IL
61338 Manlius, IL
61340 Mark, IL
61341 Marseilles, IL
61342 Mendota, IL
61344 Mineral, IL
61345 Neponset, IL
61346 New Bedford, IL
61348 Oglesby, IL
61349 Ohio, IL
61350 Ottawa, IL
61353 Paw Paw, IL
61354 Peru, IL
61356 Hollowayville, IL
61356 Princeton, IL
61358 Rutland, IL
61359 Seatonville, IL
61360 Seneca, IL
61361 Sheffield, IL
61362 Spring Valley, IL
61363 Standard, IL
61364 Streator, IL
61367 Sublette, IL
61368 Tiskilwa, IL
61369 Toluca, IL
61370 Tonica, IL
61371 Triumph, IL
61372 Troy Grove, IL
61373 Utica, IL
61374 Van Orin, IL
61375 Varna, IL
61376 Normandy, IL
61376 Walnut, IL
61377 Wenona, IL
61378 West Brooklyn, IL
61379 Wyanet, IL

614

61401 Galesburg, IL
61402 Galesburg, IL
61410 Abingdon, IL
61411 Adair, IL
61412 Alexis, IL
61413 Alpha, IL
61414 Altona, IL
61415 Avon, IL
61416 Bardolph, IL
61417 Berwick, IL
61418 Biggsville, IL
61419 Bishop Hill, IL
61420 Blandinsville, IL
61421 Bradford, IL
61422 Bushnell, IL
61423 Cameron, IL
61424 Camp Grove, IL
61425 Carman, IL
61426 Castleton, IL
61427 Cuba, IL
61428 Dahinda, IL
61430 East Galesburg, IL
61431 Ellisville, IL
61432 Fairview, IL
61433 Fiatt, IL
61434 Galva, IL
61435 Gerlaw, IL
61436 Delong, IL
61436 Gilson, IL
61437 Gladstone, IL
61438 Good Hope, IL
61439 Henderson, IL
61440 Industry, IL
61441 Ipava, IL
61442 Keithsburg, IL
61443 Kewanee, IL
61447 Kirkwood, IL
61448 Knoxville, IL
61449 La Fayette, IL
61450 La Harpe, IL
61451 Laura, IL
61452 Littleton, IL
61453 Little York, IL
61454 Lomax, IL
61455 Macomb, IL
61458 Maquon, IL
61459 Marietta, IL
61460 Media, IL
61462 Monmouth, IL
61465 New Windsor, IL
61466 North Henderson, IL
61467 Oneida, IL
61468 Ophiem, IL
61469 Oquawka, IL
61470 Prairie City, IL
61471 Raritan, IL
61472 Rio, IL
61473 Roseville, IL
61474 Saint Augustine, IL
61475 Blandinsville, IL
61475 Sciota, IL
61476 Seaton, IL
61477 Smithfield, IL
61478 Smithshire, IL
61479 Speer, IL
61480 Stronghurst, IL
61482 Table Grove, IL
61483 Toulon, IL
61484 Vermont, IL
61485 Victoria, IL
61486 Viola, IL
61488 Wataga, IL
61489 Williamsfield, IL
61490 Woodhull, IL
61491 Wyoming, IL

615

61501 Astoria, IL
61516 Benson, IL
61517 Brimfield, IL
61519 Bryant, IL
61520 Banner, IL
61520 Canton, IL
61523 Chillicothe, IL
61524 Dunfermline, IL
61525 Dunlap, IL
61526 Edelstein, IL
61528 Edwards, IL
61529 Elmwood, IL
61530 Eureka, IL
61531 Farmington, IL
61531 Middlegrove, IL
61532 Forest City, IL
61533 Glasford, IL
61534 Green Valley, IL
61535 Groveland, IL
61536 Hanna City, IL
61537 Henry, IL
61539 Kingston Mines, IL
61540 Lacon, IL
61541 La Rose, IL
61542 Lewistown, IL
61543 Liverpool, IL
61544 London Mills, IL
61545 Cazenovia, IL
61545 Lowpoint, IL
61546 Manito, IL
61547 Mapleton, IL
61548 Germantown Hills, IL
61548 Metamora, IL
61550 Morton, IL
61552 Mossville, IL
61553 Norris, IL
61554 Marquette Heights, IL
61554 North Pekin, IL
61554 Pekin, IL
61555 Pekin, IL
61558 Pekin, IL
61559 Princeville, IL
61560 Putnam, IL
61561 Roanoke, IL
61562 Rome, IL
61563 Saint David, IL
61564 South Pekin, IL
61565 Hopewell, IL
61565 Sparland, IL
61567 Topeka, IL
61568 Tremont, IL
61569 Trivoli, IL
61570 Washburn, IL
61571 Washington, IL
61572 Yates City, IL

616

61601 Peoria, IL
61602 Peoria, IL
61603 Peoria, IL
61604 Bellevue, IL
61604 Peoria, IL
61604 West Peoria, IL
61605 Peoria, IL
61606 Peoria, IL
61607 Bartonville, IL
61607 Peoria, IL
61610 Creve Coeur, IL
61610 Peoria, IL
61611 Bayview Gardens, IL
61611 East Peoria, IL
61611 Peoria, IL
61611 Spring Bay, IL
61612 Peoria, IL
61613 Peoria, IL
61614 Peoria, IL
61615 Peoria, IL
61616 Peoria, IL
61616 Peoria Heights, IL
61625 Peoria, IL
61629 Peoria, IL
61630 East Peoria, IL
61630 Peoria, IL
61633 Peoria, IL
61634 Peoria, IL
61635 East Peoria, IL
61635 Peoria, IL
61636 Peoria, IL
61637 Peoria, IL
61638 Peoria, IL
61639 Peoria, IL
61641 Peoria, IL
61643 Peoria, IL
61650 Peoria, IL
61651 Peoria, IL
61652 Peoria, IL
61653 Peoria, IL
61654 Peoria, IL
61655 Peoria, IL
61656 Peoria, IL

617

61701 Bloomington, IL
61702 Bloomington, IL
61704 Bloomington, IL
61705 Bloomington, IL
61709 Bloomington, IL
61710 Bloomington, IL
61720 Anchor, IL
61721 Armington, IL
61722 Arrowsmith, IL
61723 Atlanta, IL
61724 Bellflower, IL
61725 Carlock, IL
61726 Chenoa, IL
61727 Clinton, IL
61728 Colfax, IL
61729 Congerville, IL
61730 Cooksville, IL
61731 Cropsey, IL
61732 Danvers, IL
61733 Deer Creek, IL
61734 Delavan, IL
61735 De Witt, IL
61735 Dewitt, IL
61736 Downs, IL
61736 Holder, IL
61737 Ellsworth, IL
61738 El Paso, IL
61738 Kappa, IL
61738 Panola, IL
61739 Fairbury, IL
61740 Flanagan, IL
61741 Forrest, IL
61742 Goodfield, IL
61743 Graymont, IL
61744 Gridley, IL
61745 Heyworth, IL
61747 Hopedale, IL
61748 Hudson, IL
61749 Kenney, IL
61750 Lane, IL
61751 Lawndale, IL
61752 Le Roy, IL
61753 Lexington, IL
61754 Mc Lean, IL
61755 Mackinaw, IL
61756 Maroa, IL
61758 Merna, IL
61759 Minier, IL
61760 Minonk, IL
61761 Merna, IL
61761 Normal, IL
61764 Pontiac, IL
61769 Saunemin, IL
61770 Saybrook, IL
61771 Secor, IL
61772 Shirley, IL
61773 Sibley, IL
61774 Stanford, IL
61775 Strawn, IL
61776 Towanda, IL
61777 Wapella, IL
61778 Waynesville, IL
61790 Normal, IL
61791 Bloomington, IL
61799 Bloomington, IL

618

61801 Urbana, IL
61802 Urbana, IL
61803 Urbana, IL
61810 Allerton, IL
61811 Alvin, IL
61812 Armstrong, IL
61813 Bement, IL
61814 Bismarck, IL
61815 Bondville, IL
61816 Broadlands, IL
61817 Catlin, IL
61818 Cerro Gordo, IL
61820 Champaign, IL
61821 Champaign, IL
61822 Champaign, IL
61824 Champaign, IL
61825 Champaign, IL
61826 Champaign, IL
61830 Cisco, IL
61831 Collison, IL
61832 Danville, IL
61832 Tilton, IL
61833 Danville, IL
61833 Tilton, IL
61834 Danville, IL
61839 De Land, IL
61840 Dewey, IL
61841 Fairmount, IL
61842 Farmer City, IL
61843 Fisher, IL
61844 Fithian, IL
61845 Foosland, IL
61846 Georgetown, IL
61847 Gifford, IL
61848 Henning, IL
61849 Homer, IL
61850 Indianola, IL
61851 Ivesdale, IL
61852 Longview, IL
61853 Mahomet, IL
61854 Mansfield, IL
61855 Milmine, IL
61856 Lodge, IL
61856 Monticello, IL
61857 Muncie, IL
61858 Oakwood, IL
61859 Ogden, IL
61862 Penfield, IL
61863 Pesotum, IL
61864 Philo, IL
61865 Potomac, IL
61866 Rantoul, IL
61870 Ridge Farm, IL
61871 Royal, IL
61872 Sadorus, IL
61873 Saint Joseph, IL
61874 Savoy, IL
61875 Seymour, IL
61876 Sidell, IL
61877 Sidney, IL
61878 Thomasboro, IL
61880 Tolono, IL
61882 Weldon, IL
61883 Westville, IL
61884 White Heath, IL

619

61910 Arcola, IL
61911 Arthur, IL
61911 Cadwell, IL
61912 Ashmore, IL
61913 Atwood, IL
61914 Bethany, IL
61917 Brocton, IL
61919 Camargo, IL
61920 Charleston, IL
61924 Chrisman, IL
61925 Dalton City, IL
61928 Gays, IL
61929 Hammond, IL
61929 Pierson Station, IL
61930 Hindsboro, IL
61931 Humboldt, IL
61932 Hume, IL
61933 Kansas, IL
61936 La Place, IL
61937 Lake City, IL
61937 Lovington, IL
61938 Mattoon, IL
61940 Metcalf, IL
61941 Murdock, IL
61942 Newman, IL
61943 Oakland, IL
61944 Paris, IL
61949 Redmon, IL
61951 Allenville, IL
61951 Kirksville, IL
61951 Sullivan, IL
61953 Tuscola, IL
61955 Vermilion, IL
61956 Villa Grove, IL
61957 Windsor, IL

620

62001 Alhambra, IL
62002 Alton, IL
62006 Batchtown, IL
62009 Benld, IL
62010 Bethalto, IL
62011 Bingham, IL
62012 Brighton, IL
62013 Brussels, IL
62013 Meppen, IL
62014 Bunker Hill, IL
62015 Butler, IL
62016 Carrollton, IL
62017 Coffeen, IL
62018 Cottage Hills, IL
62019 Donnellson, IL
62021 Dorsey, IL
62022 Dow, IL
62023 Eagarville, IL
62024 East Alton, IL
62025 Edwardsville, IL
62026 Edwardsville, IL
62027 Eldred, IL
62028 Elsah, IL
62030 Fidelity, IL
62031 Fieldon, IL
62032 Bingham, IL
62032 Fillmore, IL
62033 Dorchester, IL
62033 Gillespie, IL
62034 Glen Carbon, IL
62035 Godfrey, IL
62036 Golden Eagle, IL
62037 Grafton, IL
62040 Granite City, IL
62040 Mitchell, IL
62040 Pontoon Beach, IL
62044 Greenfield, IL
62045 Hamburg, IL
62046 Hamel, IL
62047 Hardin, IL
62048 Hartford, IL
62049 Hillsboro, IL
62050 Hillview, IL
62051 Irving, IL
62052 Jerseyville, IL
62052 Otterville, IL
62053 Kampsville, IL
62054 Kane, IL
62056 Litchfield, IL
62058 Livingston, IL
62059 Brooklyn, IL
62059 Lovejoy, IL
62060 Madison, IL
62061 Marine, IL
62062 Maryville, IL
62063 Medora, IL
62065 Michael, IL
62067 Moro, IL
62069 Mount Olive, IL
62070 Mozier, IL
62071 National Stock Yards, IL
62074 New Douglas, IL
62075 Nokomis, IL
62076 Ohlman, IL
62077 Panama, IL
62078 Patterson, IL
62079 Piasa, IL
62080 Ramsey, IL
62081 Rockbridge, IL
62082 Roodhouse, IL
62083 Rosamond, IL
62084 Roxana, IL
62085 Sawyerville, IL
62086 Sorento, IL
62087 South Roxana, IL
62088 Staunton, IL
62089 Taylor Springs, IL
62090 Venice, IL
62091 Walshville, IL
62092 White Hall, IL
62093 Wilsonville, IL
62094 Witt, IL
62095 Wood River, IL
62097 Worden, IL
62098 Wrights, IL

622

62201 East Saint Louis, IL
62201 Fairmont City, IL
62201 Sauget, IL
62202 East Saint Louis, IL
62203 Centreville, IL
62203 East Saint Louis, IL
62204 Washington Pk, IL
62205 Centreville, IL
62205 East Saint Louis, IL
62206 Cahokia, IL
62206 East Saint Louis, IL

62206 Sauget, IL
62207 Alorton, IL
62207 Centreville, IL
62207 East Saint Louis, IL
62208 Fairview Heights, IL
62214 Addieville, IL
62214 Venedy, IL
62215 Albers, IL
62215 Damiansville, IL
62216 Aviston, IL
62217 Baldwin, IL
62218 Bartelso, IL
62219 Beckemeyer, IL
62220 Belleville, IL
62220 Swansea, IL
62221 Belleville, IL
62221 Shiloh, IL
62221 Swansea, IL
62222 Belleville, IL
62223 Belleville, IL
62223 Swansea, IL
62225 Scott Air Force Base, IL
62226 Belleville, IL
62226 Swansea, IL
62230 Breese, IL
62230 Saint Rose, IL
62231 Boulder, IL
62231 Carlyle, IL
62231 Ferrin, IL
62231 Posey, IL
62231 Shattuc, IL
62232 Caseyville, IL
62233 Chester, IL
62234 Collinsville, IL
62236 Columbia, IL
62237 Coulterville, IL
62237 Swanwick, IL
62238 Cutler, IL
62239 Dupo, IL
62240 East Carondelet, IL
62241 Ellis Grove, IL
62242 Evansville, IL
62243 Freeburg, IL
62244 Fults, IL
62245 Germantown, IL
62246 Greenville, IL
62247 Hagarstown, IL
62248 Hecker, IL
62249 Highland, IL
62250 Hoffman, IL
62252 Huey, IL
62253 Keyesport, IL
62254 Lebanon, IL
62255 Lenzburg, IL
62256 Maeystown, IL
62257 Marissa, IL
62258 Fayetteville, IL
62258 Mascoutah, IL
62259 Menard, IL
62260 Millstadt, IL
62261 Modoc, IL
62261 Prairie Du Rocher, IL
62262 Mulberry Grove, IL
62263 Nashville, IL
62264 New Athens, IL
62265 New Baden, IL
62266 New Memphis, IL
62268 Oakdale, IL
62269 Belleville, IL
62269 O Fallon, IL
62269 Shiloh, IL
62271 Okawville, IL
62272 Percy, IL
62273 Pierron, IL
62274 Pinckneyville, IL
62275 Jamestown, IL
62275 Pocahontas, IL
62277 Prairie Du Rocher, IL
62278 Red Bud, IL
62278 Redbud, IL
62278 Ruma, IL
62279 Renault, IL
62280 Rockwood, IL
62281 Saint Jacob, IL
62282 Saint Libory, IL
62284 Smithboro, IL
62285 Smithton, IL
62286 Sparta, IL
62288 Steeleville, IL
62289 Summerfield, IL
62292 Tilden, IL
62293 Trenton, IL
62294 Troy, IL
62295 Valmeyer, IL
62297 Walsh, IL
62298 Waterloo, IL

623

62301 Quincy, IL
62305 Quincy, IL
62306 Quincy, IL
62311 Augusta, IL
62312 Barry, IL
62313 Basco, IL
62314 Baylis, IL
62316 Bowen, IL
62319 Camden, IL
62320 Camp Point, IL
62320 Columbus, IL
62321 Carthage, IL
62323 Chambersburg, IL
62324 Clayton, IL
62325 Coatsburg, IL
62326 Colchester, IL
62329 Colusa, IL
62330 Adrian, IL
62330 Burnside, IL
62330 Dallas City, IL
62330 Pontoosuc, IL
62334 Elvaston, IL
62336 Ferris, IL
62338 Fowler, IL
62339 Golden, IL
62340 Griggsville, IL
62341 Hamilton, IL
62343 Hull, IL
62344 Huntsville, IL
62345 Kinderhook, IL
62346 La Prairie, IL
62347 Liberty, IL
62348 Lima, IL
62349 Loraine, IL
62351 Mendon, IL
62352 Milton, IL
62353 Mount Sterling, IL
62353 Ripley, IL
62354 Nauvoo, IL
62355 Nebo, IL
62356 New Canton, IL
62357 New Salem, IL
62358 Niota, IL
62359 Paloma, IL
62360 Payson, IL
62361 Pearl, IL
62362 Perry, IL
62363 Detroit, IL
62363 Pittsfield, IL
62363 Summer Hill, IL
62365 Plainville, IL
62366 Pleasant Hill, IL
62367 Colmar, IL
62367 Plymouth, IL
62370 Rockport, IL
62373 Sutter, IL
62374 Tennessee, IL
62375 Timewell, IL
62376 Ursa, IL
62378 Versailles, IL
62379 Warsaw, IL
62380 West Point, IL

624

62401 Effingham, IL
62410 Allendale, IL
62411 Altamont, IL
62413 Annapolis, IL
62414 Beecher City, IL
62417 Bridgeport, IL
62418 Brownstown, IL
62419 Calhoun, IL
62420 Casey, IL
62421 Claremont, IL
62422 Cowden, IL
62423 Dennison, IL
62424 Dieterich, IL
62425 Dundas, IL
62426 Edgewood, IL
62426 Laclede, IL
62427 Birds, IL
62427 Flat Rock, IL
62428 Greenup, IL
62428 Hazel Dell, IL
62431 Herrick, IL
62432 Hidalgo, IL
62433 Hutsonville, IL
62434 Ingraham, IL
62435 Janesville, IL
62436 Jewett, IL
62438 Lakewood, IL
62439 Lawrenceville, IL
62440 Janesville, IL
62440 Lerna, IL
62441 Marshall, IL
62442 Martinsville, IL
62443 Mason, IL
62444 Beecher City, IL
62444 Mode, IL
62445 Montrose, IL
62446 Mount Erie, IL
62447 Neoga, IL
62448 Newton, IL
62449 Oblong, IL
62450 Olney, IL
62451 Palestine, IL
62452 Parkersburg, IL
62454 Robinson, IL
62458 Saint Elmo, IL
62459 Sainte Marie, IL
62460 Saint Francisville, IL
62461 Shumway, IL
62462 Sigel, IL
62463 Stewardson, IL
62464 Stoy, IL
62465 Strasburg, IL
62466 Sumner, IL
62467 Teutopolis, IL
62468 Toledo, IL
62469 Trilla, IL
62471 Hagarstown, IL
62471 Vandalia, IL
62473 Watson, IL
62474 Westfield, IL
62475 West Liberty, IL
62476 West Salem, IL
62477 West Union, IL
62478 West York, IL
62479 Wheeler, IL
62480 Willow Hill, IL
62481 Yale, IL

625

62501 Argenta, IL
62501 Newburg, IL
62501 Oakley, IL
62510 Assumption, IL
62512 Beason, IL
62513 Blue Mound, IL
62514 Boody, IL
62515 Buffalo, IL
62515 Buffalo Hart, IL
62515 Lanesville, IL
62517 Bulpitt, IL
62518 Chestnut, IL
62519 Cornland, IL
62520 Dawson, IL
62521 Decatur, IL
62521 Long Creek, IL
62522 Decatur, IL
62523 Decatur, IL
62524 Decatur, IL
62525 Decatur, IL
62526 Bearsdale, IL
62526 Decatur, IL
62530 Cimic, IL
62530 Divernon, IL
62531 Edenburg, IL
62531 Edinburg, IL
62532 Elwin, IL
62533 Farmersville, IL
62534 Findlay, IL
62534 Yantisville, IL
62535 Forsyth, IL
62536 Glenarm, IL
62537 Harristown, IL
62538 Harvel, IL
62539 Illiopolis, IL
62540 Kincaid, IL
62541 Lake Fork, IL
62543 Latham, IL
62544 Macon, IL
62545 Bolivia, IL
62545 Mechanicsburg, IL
62545 Roby, IL
62546 Morrisonville, IL
62547 Mount Auburn, IL
62548 Mount Pulaski, IL
62549 Hervey City, IL
62549 Mount Zion, IL
62549 Mt Zion, IL
62550 Moweaqua, IL
62550 Radford, IL
62551 Niantic, IL
62553 Oconee, IL
62554 Oreana, IL
62555 Owaneco, IL
62556 Clarksdale, IL
62556 Palmer, IL
62557 Dunkel, IL
62557 Millersville, IL
62557 Pana, IL
62558 Pawnee, IL
62558 Sicily, IL
62560 Raymond, IL
62561 Riverton, IL
62561 Spaulding, IL
62563 Berry, IL
62563 Breckenridge, IL
62563 New City, IL
62563 Rochester, IL
62565 Clarksburg, IL
62565 Duvall, IL
62565 Henton, IL
62565 Middlesworth, IL
62565 Shelbyville, IL
62565 Westervelt, IL
62567 Stonington, IL
62568 Hewittsville, IL
62568 Jeiseyville, IL
62568 Langleyville, IL
62568 Sharpsburg, IL
62568 Taylorville, IL
62568 Willeys, IL
62570 Tovey, IL
62571 Dollville, IL
62571 Hinton, IL
62571 Tower Hill, IL
62572 Atwater, IL
62572 Waggoner, IL
62573 Heman, IL
62573 Warrensburg, IL

626

62601 Alexander, IL
62610 Alsey, IL
62611 Arenzville, IL
62612 Ashland, IL
62612 Newmansville, IL
62612 Prentice, IL
62612 Yatesville, IL
62613 Athens, IL
62613 Fancy Prairie, IL
62615 Auburn, IL
62617 Bath, IL
62617 Lynchburg, IL
62617 Snicarte, IL
62618 Beardstown, IL
62621 Bluffs, IL
62621 Exeter, IL
62622 Bluff Springs, IL
62624 Bader, IL
62624 Bluff City, IL
62624 Browning, IL
62625 Cantrall, IL
62626 Carlinville, IL
62626 Comer, IL
62626 Enos, IL
62626 Womac, IL
62627 Chandlerville, IL
62627 Panther Creek, IL
62628 Chapin, IL
62629 Chatham, IL
62630 Chesterfield, IL
62630 Hagaman, IL
62631 Concord, IL
62633 Biggs, IL
62633 Easton, IL
62633 Poplar City, IL
62634 Broadwell, IL
62634 Elkhart, IL
62635 Emden, IL
62638 Clements, IL
62638 Franklin, IL
62638 Rees, IL
62639 Frederick, IL
62640 Girard, IL
62640 Mcvey, IL
62640 Standard City, IL
62642 Greenview, IL
62642 Hubly, IL
62642 Sweetwater, IL
62643 Hartsburg, IL
62644 Eckard, IL
62644 Enion, IL
62644 Havana, IL
62649 Hettick, IL
62650 Arcadia, IL
62650 Arnold, IL
62650 Jacksonville, IL
62650 Literberry, IL
62650 Lynnville, IL
62650 Merritt, IL
62650 Pisgah, IL
62650 Sinclair, IL
62650 South Jacksonville, IL
62651 Jacksonville, IL
62655 Kilbourne, IL
62656 Lincoln, IL
62659 Lincolns New Salem, IL
62660 Literberry, IL
62661 Loami, IL
62662 Lowder, IL
62663 Manchester, IL
62664 Luther, IL
62664 Mason City, IL
62664 Teheran, IL
62665 Meredosia, IL
62665 Naples, IL
62666 Middletown, IL
62667 Modesto, IL
62667 Scottville, IL
62668 Murrayville, IL
62668 Nortonville, IL
62670 Bates, IL
62670 Berlin, IL
62670 Curran, IL
62670 New Berlin, IL
62670 Old Berlin, IL
62671 New Holland, IL
62672 Nilwood, IL
62673 Oakford, IL
62674 Barr, IL
62674 Palmyra, IL
62674 Scottville, IL
62675 Atterberry, IL
62675 Petersburg, IL
62675 Tice, IL
62677 Farmingdale, IL
62677 Pleasant Plains, IL
62677 Richland, IL
62677 Salisbury, IL
62681 Pleasant View, IL
62681 Ray, IL
62681 Rushville, IL
62682 San Jose, IL
62683 Scottville, IL
62684 Barclay, IL
62684 Sherman, IL
62685 Plainview, IL
62685 Royal Lakes, IL
62685 Shipman, IL
62688 Tallula, IL
62689 Thayer, IL
62690 Virden, IL
62691 Little Indian, IL
62691 Virginia, IL
62692 Waverly, IL
62693 Williamsville, IL
62694 Riggston, IL
62694 Winchester, IL
62695 Woodson, IL

627

62701 Springfield, IL
62702 Grandview, IL
62702 Springfield, IL
62703 Southern View, IL
62703 Springfield, IL
62704 Jerome, IL
62704 Leland Grove, IL
62704 Springfield, IL
62705 Springfield, IL
62706 Springfield, IL
62707 Andrew, IL
62707 Archer, IL
62707 Bissell, IL
62707 Bradfordton, IL
62707 Clear Lake, IL
62707 Riddle Hill, IL
62707 Springfield, IL
62708 Springfield, IL
62711 Springfield, IL
62712 Springfield, IL
62715 Springfield, IL
62716 Springfield, IL
62719 Springfield, IL
62721 Springfield, IL
62722 Springfield, IL
62723 Springfield, IL
62726 Springfield, IL
62736 Springfield, IL
62739 Springfield, IL
62756 Springfield, IL
62757 Springfield, IL
62761 Springfield, IL
62762 Springfield, IL
62763 Springfield, IL
62764 Springfield, IL
62765 Springfield, IL
62766 Springfield, IL
62767 Springfield, IL
62769 Springfield, IL
62776 Springfield, IL
62777 Springfield, IL
62781 Springfield, IL
62786 Springfield, IL
62791 Springfield, IL
62794 Springfield, IL
62796 Springfield, IL

628

62801 Centralia, IL
62803 Hoyleton, IL
62806 Albion, IL
62807 Alma, IL
62808 Ashley, IL
62809 Barnhill, IL
62810 Belle Rive, IL
62811 Bellmont, IL
62812 Benton, IL
62814 Bluford, IL
62815 Bone Gap, IL
62816 Bonnie, IL
62816 Nason, IL
62817 Broughton, IL
62817 Dale, IL
62818 Browns, IL
62819 Buckner, IL
62820 Burnt Prairie, IL
62821 Carmi, IL
62822 Christopher, IL
62823 Cisne, IL
62824 Clay City, IL
62825 Coello, IL
62827 Crossville, IL
62828 Dahlgren, IL
62829 Dale, IL
62830 Dix, IL
62831 Du Bois, IL
62832 Du Quoin, IL
62833 Ellery, IL

62834 Emma, IL
62835 Enfield, IL
62836 Ewing, IL
62837 Fairfield, IL
62838 Farina, IL
62838 Iola, IL
62838 Loogootee, IL
62839 Flora, IL
62840 Frankfort Heights, IL
62841 Freeman Spur, IL
62842 Geff, IL
62843 Golden Gate, IL
62844 Grayville, IL
62846 Ina, IL
62848 Irvington, IL
62849 Iuka, IL
62850 Johnsonville, IL
62851 Keenes, IL
62852 Keensburg, IL
62853 Kell, IL
62854 Kinmundy, IL
62855 Lancaster, IL
62856 Logan, IL
62858 Bible Grove, IL
62858 Louisville, IL
62859 Dale, IL
62859 Mc Leansboro, IL
62860 Macedonia, IL
62861 Maunie, IL
62862 Mill Shoals, IL
62863 Mount Carmel, IL
62864 Mount Vernon, IL
62865 Mulkeytown, IL
62866 Nason, IL
62867 New Haven, IL
62868 Noble, IL
62869 Herald, IL
62869 Norris City, IL
62870 Odin, IL
62871 Omaha, IL
62872 Opdyke, IL
62874 Orient, IL
62875 Patoka, IL
62876 Radom, IL
62877 Richview, IL
62878 Rinard, IL
62879 Sailor Springs, IL
62880 Saint Peter, IL
62881 Salem, IL
62882 Sandoval, IL
62883 Scheller, IL
62884 Sesser, IL
62885 Shobonier, IL
62886 Sims, IL
62887 Springerton, IL
62888 Tamaroa, IL
62889 Texico, IL
62890 Akin, IL
62890 Thompsonville, IL
62891 Valier, IL
62892 Vernon, IL
62893 Walnut Hill, IL
62894 Waltonville, IL
62895 Wayne City, IL
62896 West Frankfort, IL
62897 Whittington, IL
62898 Woodlawn, IL
62899 Xenia, IL

629

62901 Carbondale, IL
62902 Carbondale, IL
62903 Carbondale, IL
62905 Alto Pass, IL
62906 Anna, IL
62907 Ava, IL
62908 Belknap, IL
62909 Boles, IL
62910 Brookport, IL
62910 Hamletsburg, IL
62910 New Liberty, IL
62912 Buncombe, IL
62914 Cache, IL
62914 Cairo, IL
62915 Cambria, IL
62916 Campbell Hill, IL
62917 Carrier Mills, IL
62918 Carterville, IL
62919 Cave In Rock, IL
62920 Cobden, IL
62921 Colp, IL
62922 Creal Springs, IL
62923 Cypress, IL
62924 De Soto, IL
62926 Dongola, IL
62927 Dowell, IL
62928 Eddyville, IL
62930 Eldorado, IL
62931 Elizabethtown, IL
62932 Elkville, IL
62933 Energy, IL
62934 Equality, IL
62935 Galatia, IL
62935 Harco, IL
62938 Brownfield, IL
62938 Golconda, IL
62938 Temple Hill, IL
62939 Goreville, IL
62940 Gorham, IL
62941 Grand Chain, IL
62942 Grand Tower, IL
62943 Grantsburg, IL
62946 Harrisburg, IL
62947 Herod, IL
62948 Herrin, IL
62949 Hurst, IL
62950 Jacob, IL
62951 Johnston City, IL
62952 Jonesboro, IL
62953 Joppa, IL
62954 Junction, IL
62955 Karbers Ridge, IL
62956 Karnak, IL
62957 Mc Clure, IL
62958 Makanda, IL
62959 Marion, IL
62960 Metropolis, IL
62961 Millcreek, IL
62962 Miller City, IL
62963 Mound City, IL
62964 Mounds, IL
62965 Muddy, IL
62966 Murphysboro, IL
62967 New Burnside, IL
62969 Olive Branch, IL
62970 Olmsted, IL
62971 Oraville, IL
62972 Ozark, IL
62972 Tunnel Hill, IL
62973 Perks, IL
62974 Pittsburg, IL
62975 Pomona, IL
62976 Pulaski, IL
62977 Raleigh, IL
62979 Ridgway, IL
62982 Rosiclare, IL
62983 Royalton, IL
62984 Shawneetown, IL
62985 Robbs, IL
62985 Simpson, IL
62987 Stonefort, IL
62988 Elco, IL
62988 Tamms, IL
62990 Gale, IL
62990 Thebes, IL
62992 Ullin, IL
62993 Tamms, IL
62993 Unity, IL
62994 Oraville, IL
62994 Vergennes, IL
62995 Vienna, IL
62996 Villa Ridge, IL
62997 Willisville, IL
62998 Wolf Lake, IL
62999 Zeigler, IL

630

63005 Chesterfield, MO
63005 Wildwood, MO
63006 Chesterfield, MO
63010 Arnold, MO
63011 Ballwin, MO
63011 Ellisville, MO
63011 Manchester, MO
63011 Wildwood, MO
63012 Barnhart, MO
63013 Beaufort, MO
63014 Berger, MO
63015 Catawissa, MO
63016 Cedar Hill, MO
63017 Chesterfield, MO
63017 Town And Country, MO
63019 Crystal City, MO
63020 De Soto, MO
63021 Ballwin, MO
63021 Ellisville, MO
63021 Manchester, MO
63021 Wildwood, MO
63022 Ballwin, MO
63023 Dittmer, MO
63024 Ballwin, MO
63025 Allenton, MO
63025 Byrnes Mill, MO
63025 Crescent, MO
63025 Eureka, MO
63025 Wildwood, MO
63026 Fenton, MO
63028 Festus, MO
63030 Fletcher, MO
63031 Florissant, MO
63032 Florissant, MO
63033 Black Jack, MO
63033 Florissant, MO
63034 Florissant, MO
63036 French Village, MO
63037 Gerald, MO
63038 Ellisville, MO
63038 Glencoe, MO
63038 Wildwood, MO
63039 Gray Summit, MO
63040 Grover, MO
63040 Wildwood, MO
63041 Grubville, MO
63042 Hazelwood, MO
63043 Hazelwood, MO
63043 Maryland Heights, MO
63044 Bridgeton, MO
63044 Hazelwood, MO
63045 Earth City, MO
63047 Hematite, MO
63048 Herculaneum, MO
63049 Byrnes Mill, MO
63049 High Ridge, MO
63050 Hillsboro, MO
63051 Byrnes Mill, MO
63051 House Springs, MO
63052 Antonia, MO
63052 Imperial, MO
63052 Otto, MO
63052 Sulphur Springs, MO
63053 Imperial, MO
63053 Kimmswick, MO
63055 Labadie, MO
63056 Leslie, MO
63057 Liguori, MO
63060 Lonedell, MO
63061 Luebbering, MO
63065 Mapaville, MO
63066 Morse Mill, MO
63068 New Haven, MO
63069 La Barque Crk, MO
63069 Pacific, MO
63069 Wildwood, MO
63070 Pevely, MO
63071 Richwoods, MO
63072 Robertsville, MO
63073 Saint Albans, MO
63074 Northwest Plaza, MO
63074 Saint Ann, MO
63077 Saint Clair, MO
63079 Stanton, MO
63080 Sullivan, MO
63084 Union, MO
63087 Valles Mines, MO
63088 Manchester, MO
63088 Twin Oaks, MO
63088 Valley Park, MO
63089 Villa Ridge, MO
63090 Washington, MO
63091 Rosebud, MO
63099 Fenton, MO

631

63101 Saint Louis, MO
63102 Saint Louis, MO
63103 Saint Louis, MO
63104 Saint Louis, MO
63105 Clayton, MO
63105 Saint Louis, MO
63106 Saint Louis, MO
63107 Saint Louis, MO
63108 Saint Louis, MO
63109 Saint Louis, MO
63110 Saint Louis, MO
63111 Saint Louis, MO
63112 Saint Louis, MO
63113 Saint Louis, MO
63114 Breckenridge Hills, MO
63114 Overland, MO
63114 Saint Louis, MO
63115 Saint Louis, MO
63116 Saint Louis, MO
63117 Clayton, MO
63117 Richmond Heights, MO
63117 Saint Louis, MO
63118 Saint Louis, MO
63119 Saint Louis, MO
63119 Webster Groves, MO
63120 Saint Louis, MO
63121 Normandy, MO
63121 Saint Louis, MO
63122 Kirkwood, MO
63122 Saint Louis, MO
63123 Affton, MO
63123 Saint Louis, MO
63124 Clayton, MO
63124 Saint Louis, MO
63125 Lemay, MO
63125 Saint Louis, MO
63126 Saint Louis, MO
63126 Sappington, MO
63127 Saint Louis, MO
63127 Sappington, MO
63128 Saint Louis, MO
63128 Sappington, MO
63129 Saint Louis, MO
63130 Saint Louis, MO
63130 University City, MO
63131 Des Peres, MO
63131 Frontenac, MO
63131 Saint Louis, MO
63132 Olivette, MO
63132 Saint Louis, MO
63133 Saint Louis, MO
63134 Berkeley, MO
63134 Saint Louis, MO
63135 Ferguson, MO
63135 Saint Louis, MO
63136 Jennings, MO
63136 Saint Louis, MO
63137 North County, MO
63137 Saint Louis, MO
63138 North County, MO
63138 Saint Louis, MO
63139 Saint Louis, MO
63140 Berkeley, MO
63140 Kinloch, MO
63140 Saint Louis, MO
63141 Creve Coeur, MO
63141 Saint Louis, MO
63143 Maplewood, MO
63143 Saint Louis, MO
63144 Brentwood, MO
63144 Saint Louis, MO
63145 Lambert Arpt, MO
63145 Saint Louis, MO
63146 Saint Louis, MO
63147 Saint Louis, MO
63150 Saint Louis, MO
63151 Saint Louis, MO
63155 Saint Louis, MO
63156 Saint Louis, MO
63157 Saint Louis, MO
63158 Saint Louis, MO
63160 Saint Louis, MO
63163 Saint Louis, MO
63164 Saint Louis, MO
63166 Saint Louis, MO
63167 Saint Louis, MO
63169 Saint Louis, MO
63171 Saint Louis, MO
63177 Saint Louis, MO
63178 Saint Louis, MO
63179 Saint Louis, MO
63180 Saint Louis, MO
63182 Saint Louis, MO
63188 Saint Louis, MO
63195 Saint Louis, MO
63197 Saint Louis, MO
63199 Saint Louis, MO

633

63301 Saint Charles, MO
63302 Saint Charles, MO
63303 Saint Charles, MO
63303 Saint Peters, MO
63303 St Peters, MO
63304 Cottleville, MO
63304 Saint Charles, MO
63304 Saint Peters, MO
63304 Weldon Spring, MO
63304 St Peters, MO
63330 Annada, MO
63332 Augusta, MO
63333 Bellflower, MO
63334 Bowling Green, MO
63336 Clarksville, MO
63336 Paynesville, MO
63338 Cottleville, MO
63339 Curryville, MO
63341 Defiance, MO
63342 Dutzow, MO
63343 Elsberry, MO
63344 Eolia, MO
63345 Farber, MO
63346 Flinthill, MO
63347 Foley, MO
63348 Foristell, MO
63349 Hawk Point, MO
63350 High Hill, MO
63351 Jonesburg, MO
63352 Laddonia, MO
63353 Louisiana, MO
63357 Lake Sherwood, MO
63357 Marthasville, MO
63359 Middletown, MO
63359 New Hartford, MO
63361 Buell, MO
63361 Danville, MO
63361 Mineola, MO
63361 Montgomery City, MO
63362 Moscow Mills, MO
63363 New Florence, MO
63365 New Melle, MO
63366 Cottleville, MO
63366 Dardenne Prairie, MO
63366 O Fallon, MO
63366 Saint Paul, MO
63366 Saint Peters, MO
63366 St Peters, MO
63367 Lake Saint Louis, MO
63367 O Fallon, MO
63368 Dardenne Prairie, MO
63368 O Fallon, MO
63369 Old Monroe, MO
63370 Olney, MO
63373 Portage Des Sioux, MO
63373 Prtg De Souix, MO
63376 Cottleville, MO
63376 O Fallon, MO
63376 Saint Peters, MO
63377 Silex, MO
63378 Treloar, MO
63379 Troy, MO
63381 Truxton, MO
63382 Vandalia, MO
63383 Truesdale, MO
63383 Warrenton, MO
63384 Wellsville, MO
63385 Wentzville, MO
63386 West Alton, MO
63387 Whiteside, MO
63388 Williamsburg, MO
63389 Winfield, MO
63390 Innsbrook, MO
63390 Wright City, MO

634

63401 Hannibal, MO
63430 Alexandria, MO
63431 Anabel, MO
63432 Arbela, MO
63433 Ashburn, MO
63434 Bethel, MO
63435 Canton, MO
63436 Center, MO
63437 Clarence, MO
63438 Durham, MO
63439 Emden, MO
63440 Ewing, MO
63441 Frankford, MO
63442 Granger, MO
63443 Hunnewell, MO
63445 Kahoka, MO
63446 Knox City, MO
63447 La Belle, MO
63447 Steffenville, MO
63448 La Grange, MO
63450 Lentner, MO
63451 Leonard, MO
63452 Lewistown, MO
63453 Luray, MO
63454 Maywood, MO
63456 Monroe City, MO
63457 Monticello, MO
63458 Newark, MO
63459 New London, MO
63460 Novelty, MO
63461 Palmyra, MO
63462 Perry, MO
63463 Philadelphia, MO
63464 Plevna, MO
63465 Revere, MO
63466 Saint Patrick, MO
63467 Saverton, MO
63468 Shelbina, MO
63469 Plevna, MO
63469 Shelbyville, MO
63471 Taylor, MO
63472 Wayland, MO
63473 Williamstown, MO
63474 Wyaconda, MO

635

63501 Kirksville, MO
63530 Atlanta, MO
63531 Baring, MO
63532 Bevier, MO
63533 Brashear, MO
63534 Callao, MO
63535 Coatsville, MO
63536 Downing, MO
63537 Edina, MO
63538 Elmer, MO
63539 Ethel, MO
63540 Gibbs, MO
63541 Glenwood, MO
63543 Gorin, MO
63544 Green Castle, MO
63545 Green City, MO
63546 Greentop, MO
63547 Hurdland, MO
63548 Lancaster, MO
63549 La Plata, MO
63551 Livonia, MO
63552 Macon, MO
63555 Memphis, MO
63556 Milan, MO
63557 New Boston, MO
63558 New Cambria, MO
63559 Novinger, MO
63560 Pollock, MO
63561 Queen City, MO
63561 Worthington, MO
63563 Rutledge, MO
63565 Unionville, MO
63566 Winigan, MO
63567 Worthington, MO

636

63601 Desloge, MO
63601 Elvins, MO
63601 Flat River, MO

63601 Frankclay, MO
63601 Leadington, MO
63601 Leadwood, MO
63601 Park Hills, MO
63601 Rivermines, MO
63620 Annapolis, MO
63620 Glover, MO
63621 Arcadia, MO
63622 Belgrade, MO
63623 Belleview, MO
63624 Bismarck, MO
63625 Black, MO
63626 Blackwell, MO
63627 Bloomsdale, MO
63628 Bonne Terre, MO
63628 Desloge, MO
63629 Bunker, MO
63630 Cadet, MO
63631 Caledonia, MO
63632 Cascade, MO
63633 Centerville, MO
63636 Des Arc, MO
63637 Doe Run, MO
63638 Ellington, MO
63640 Farmington, MO
63640 Leadington, MO
63645 Fredericktown, MO
63645 Millcreek, MO
63645 Mine La Motte, MO
63648 Irondale, MO
63650 Ironton, MO
63651 Knob Lick, MO
63653 Flat River, MO
63653 Leadwood, MO
63653 Park Hills, MO
63654 Lesterville, MO
63655 Marquand, MO
63656 Middle Brook, MO
63660 Mineral Point, MO
63662 Patton, MO
63663 Pilot Knob, MO
63664 Potosi, MO
63665 Redford, MO
63666 Reynolds, MO
63670 New Offenburg, MO
63670 Sainte Genevieve, MO
63673 Saint Mary, MO
63674 Tiff, MO
63675 Vulcan, MO

637

63701 Cape Girardeau, MO
63730 Advance, MO
63732 Altenburg, MO
63732 New Wells, MO
63735 Bell City, MO
63736 Benton, MO
63737 Brazeau, MO
63738 Brownwood, MO
63739 Burfordville, MO
63740 Chaffee, MO
63742 Commerce, MO
63743 Daisy, MO
63744 Delta, MO
63745 Dutchtown, MO
63746 Farrar, MO
63747 Friedheim, MO
63747 Perryville, MO
63748 Frohna, MO
63748 Wittenberg, MO
63750 Gipsy, MO
63751 Glenallen, MO
63751 Grassy, MO
63752 Gordonville, MO
63755 Jackson, MO
63758 Kelso, MO
63760 Leopold, MO
63763 Mc Gee, MO
63764 Lutesville, MO
63764 Marble Hill, MO
63764 Scopus, MO
63766 Millersville, MO
63767 Morley, MO
63769 Oak Ridge, MO
63770 Old Appleton, MO
63771 Oran, MO
63771 Painton, MO
63774 Perkins, MO
63775 Perryville, MO
63776 Mc Bride, MO
63776 Perryville, MO
63779 Pocahontas, MO
63780 Scott City, MO
63781 Sedgewickville, MO
63782 Sturdivant, MO
63783 Uniontown, MO
63784 Vanduser, MO
63785 Whitewater, MO
63787 Arab, MO
63787 Zalma, MO

638

63801 Miner, MO
63801 Sikeston, MO
63820 Anniston, MO
63821 Arbyrd, MO
63822 Bernie, MO
63823 Bertrand, MO
63824 Blodgett, MO
63825 Bloomfield, MO
63826 Braggadocio, MO
63827 Bragg City, MO
63828 Canalou, MO
63829 Cardwell, MO
63830 Caruthersville, MO
63833 Catron, MO
63834 Charleston, MO
63837 Clarkton, MO
63839 Cooter, MO
63840 Deering, MO
63841 Dexter, MO
63845 East Prairie, MO
63846 Essex, MO
63847 Gibson, MO
63848 Gideon, MO
63849 Gobler, MO
63850 Grayridge, MO
63851 Hayti, MO
63851 Hayti Heights, MO
63851 Pascola, MO
63852 Holcomb, MO
63853 Holland, MO
63855 Hornersville, MO
63857 Kennett, MO
63860 Kewanee, MO
63862 Lilbourn, MO
63863 Malden, MO
63866 Marston, MO
63867 Matthews, MO
63868 Morehouse, MO
63869 New Madrid, MO
63870 Parma, MO
63873 Conran, MO
63873 Portageville, MO
63874 Risco, MO
63875 Rives, MO
63876 Senath, MO
63877 Steele, MO
63878 Tallapoosa, MO
63879 Homestown, MO
63879 Wardell, MO
63880 Whiteoak, MO
63881 Wolf Island, MO
63882 Wyatt, MO

639

63901 Poplar Bluff, MO
63901 Rombauer, MO
63902 Poplar Bluff, MO
63931 Briar, MO
63932 Broseley, MO
63933 Campbell, MO
63934 Clubb, MO
63934 Silva, MO
63935 Doniphan, MO
63935 Poynor, MO
63936 Dudley, MO
63937 Ellsinore, MO
63938 Fagus, MO
63939 Fairdealing, MO
63940 Fisk, MO
63941 Fremont, MO
63942 Gatewood, MO
63943 Grandin, MO
63944 Greenville, MO
63944 Hiram, MO
63945 Harviell, MO
63950 Lodi, MO
63951 Lowndes, MO
63952 Mill Spring, MO
63953 Naylor, MO
63954 Neelyville, MO
63955 Oxly, MO
63956 Patterson, MO
63957 Piedmont, MO
63960 Puxico, MO
63961 Qulin, MO
63962 Rombauer, MO
63964 Silva, MO
63965 Van Buren, MO
63966 Wappapello, MO
63967 Williamsville, MO

640

64001 Alma, MO
64002 Lees Summit, MO
64011 Bates City, MO
64012 Belton, MO
64012 Village Of Loch Lloyd, MO
64013 Blue Springs, MO
64014 Blue Springs, MO
64015 Blue Springs, MO
64015 Lake Tapawingo, MO
64016 Buckner, MO
64017 Camden, MO
64018 Camden Point, MO
64019 Centerview, MO
64020 Concordia, MO
64021 Corder, MO
64022 Dover, MO
64024 Crystal Lakes, MO
64024 Excelsior Springs, MO
64024 Exclsor Sprgs, MO
64024 Homestead Vlg, MO
64024 Mosby, MO
64024 Wood Heights, MO
64028 Farley, MO
64029 Blue Springs, MO
64029 Grain Valley, MO
64030 Grandview, MO
64034 Greenwood, MO
64034 Lake Winnebago, MO
64035 Hardin, MO
64036 Henrietta, MO
64037 Higginsville, MO
64040 Holden, MO
64048 Holt, MO
64050 Independence, MO
64050 Sugar Creek, MO
64051 Independence, MO
64052 Independence, MO
64053 Independence, MO
64053 Sugar Creek, MO
64054 Independence, MO
64054 Sugar Creek, MO
64055 Independence, MO
64056 Independence, MO
64056 Sugar Creek, MO
64057 Independence, MO
64058 Independence, MO
64058 Sugar Creek, MO
64060 Kearney, MO
64061 Kingsville, MO
64062 Elmira, MO
64062 Excelsior Estates, MO
64062 Lawson, MO
64063 Lees Summit, MO
64064 Blue Springs, MO
64064 Lees Summit, MO
64065 Lees Summit, MO
64065 Unity Village, MO
64066 Levasy, MO
64067 Lexington, MO
64068 Liberty, MO
64068 Pleasant Valley, MO
64069 Liberty, MO
64070 Lone Jack, MO
64071 Mayview, MO
64072 Missouri City, MO
64073 Mosby, MO
64074 Napoleon, MO
64075 Oak Grove, MO
64076 Odessa, MO
64077 Orrick, MO
64078 Peculiar, MO
64079 Platte City, MO
64080 Pleasant Hill, MO
64081 Lees Summit, MO
64082 Lees Summit, MO
64083 Lees Summit, MO
64083 Raymore, MO
64084 Rayville, MO
64085 Richmond, MO
64086 Lake Lotawana, MO
64086 Lees Summit, MO
64086 Lone Jack, MO
64088 Sibley, MO
64089 Smithville, MO
64090 Strasburg, MO
64092 Waldron, MO
64093 Warrensburg, MO
64096 Waverly, MO
64097 Wellington, MO
64098 Weston, MO

641

64101 Kansas City, MO
64102 Kansas City, MO
64105 Kansas City, MO
64106 Kansas City, MO
64108 Kansas City, MO
64109 Kansas City, MO
64110 Kansas City, MO
64111 Kansas City, MO
64112 Kansas City, MO
64113 Kansas City, MO
64114 Kansas City, MO
64116 Kansas City, MO
64116 North Kansas City, MO
64117 Avondale, MO
64117 Kansas City, MO
64117 Randolph, MO
64118 Gladstone, MO
64118 Kansas City, MO
64119 Gladstone, MO
64119 Kansas City, MO
64120 Kansas City, MO
64121 Kansas City, MO
64123 Kansas City, MO
64124 Kansas City, MO
64125 Kansas City, MO
64126 Kansas City, MO
64127 Kansas City, MO
64128 Kansas City, MO
64129 Kansas City, MO
64129 Raytown, MO
64130 Kansas City, MO
64131 Kansas City, MO
64132 Kansas City, MO
64133 Kansas City, MO
64133 Raytown, MO
64134 Kansas City, MO
64136 Kansas City, MO
64137 Kansas City, MO
64138 Kansas City, MO
64138 Raytown, MO
64139 Kansas City, MO
64141 Kansas City, MO
64144 Kansas City, MO
64145 Kansas City, MO
64146 Kansas City, MO
64147 Kansas City, MO
64147 Martin City, MO
64148 Kansas City, MO
64149 Kansas City, MO
64150 Kansas City, MO
64150 Northmoor, MO
64150 Riverside, MO
64151 Houston Lake, MO
64151 Kansas City, MO
64151 Lake Waukomis, MO
64151 Northmoor, MO
64151 Platte Woods, MO
64151 Riverside, MO
64152 Kansas City, MO
64152 Parkville, MO
64152 Weatherby Lake, MO
64153 Kansas City, MO
64153 Weatherby Lake, MO
64154 Kansas City, MO
64155 Kansas City, MO
64156 Kansas City, MO
64157 Kansas City, MO
64158 Kansas City, MO
64161 Birmingham, MO
64161 Kansas City, MO
64161 Randolph, MO
64162 Kansas City, MO
64163 Ferrelview, MO
64163 Kansas City, MO
64164 Kansas City, MO
64165 Kansas City, MO
64166 Kansas City, MO
64167 Kansas City, MO
64168 Kansas City, MO
64168 Riverside, MO
64170 Kansas City, MO
64171 Kansas City, MO
64179 Kansas City, MO
64180 Kansas City, MO
64184 Kansas City, MO
64187 Kansas City, MO
64188 Kansas City, MO
64190 Kansas City, MO
64191 Kansas City, MO
64195 Kansas City, MO
64196 Kansas City, MO
64197 Kansas City, MO
64198 Kansas City, MO
64199 Kansas City, MO

644

64401 Agency, MO
64402 Albany, MO
64420 Allendale, MO
64421 Amazonia, MO
64422 Amity, MO
64423 Barnard, MO
64424 Bethany, MO
64426 Blythedale, MO
64427 Bolckow, MO
64428 Burlington Junction, MO
64429 Cameron, MO
64430 Clarksdale, MO
64431 Clearmont, MO
64432 Clyde, MO
64433 Conception, MO
64434 Conception Junction, MO
64436 Cosby, MO
64437 Bigelow, MO
64437 Corning, MO
64437 Craig, MO
64437 Fortescue, MO
64438 Darlington, MO
64439 Dearborn, MO
64440 De Kalb, MO
64441 Denver, MO
64442 Eagleville, MO
64443 Easton, MO
64444 Edgerton, MO
64445 Elmo, MO
64446 Fairfax, MO
64448 Faucett, MO
64449 Fillmore, MO
64451 Forest City, MO
64453 Gentry, MO
64454 Gower, MO
64455 Graham, MO
64456 Grant City, MO
64457 Guilford, MO
64458 Hatfield, MO
64459 Helena, MO
64461 Hopkins, MO
64463 King City, MO
64465 Lathrop, MO
64466 Maitland, MO
64467 Martinsville, MO
64468 Maryville, MO
64469 Fairport, MO
64469 Maysville, MO
64470 Mound City, MO
64471 New Hampton, MO
64473 New Point, MO
64473 Nw Point, MO
64473 Oregon, MO
64474 Osborn, MO
64475 Parnell, MO
64476 Pickering, MO
64477 Plattsburg, MO
64479 Ravenwood, MO
64480 Rea, MO
64481 Mount Moriah, MO
64481 Ridgeway, MO
64482 Rock Port, MO
64483 Rosendale, MO
64484 Rushville, MO
64485 Savannah, MO
64486 Sheridan, MO
64487 Quitman, MO
64487 Skidmore, MO
64489 Stanberry, MO
64490 Hemple, MO
64490 Stewartsville, MO
64491 Tarkio, MO
64492 Trimble, MO
64493 Turney, MO
64494 Union Star, MO
64496 Watson, MO
64497 Weatherby, MO
64498 Westboro, MO
64499 Worth, MO

645

64501 Saint Joseph, MO
64502 Saint Joseph, MO
64503 Saint Joseph, MO
64504 Saint Joseph, MO
64505 Country Club, MO
64505 Saint Joseph, MO
64506 Country Club, MO
64506 Saint Joseph, MO
64507 Saint Joseph, MO
64508 Saint Joseph, MO

646

64601 Avalon, MO
64601 Chillicothe, MO
64620 Altamont, MO
64622 Bogard, MO
64623 Bosworth, MO
64624 Braymer, MO
64625 Breckenridge, MO
64628 Brookfield, MO
64628 Saint Catharine, MO
64630 Browning, MO
64631 Bucklin, MO
64632 Cainsville, MO
64633 Carrollton, MO
64635 Chula, MO
64636 Coffey, MO
64637 Cowgill, MO
64638 Dawn, MO
64639 De Witt, MO
64640 Gallatin, MO
64641 Galt, MO
64642 Brimson, MO
64642 Gilman City, MO
64643 Hale, MO
64644 Hamilton, MO
64645 Harris, MO
64646 Humphreys, MO
64647 Jameson, MO
64648 Jamesport, MO
64649 Kidder, MO
64650 Kingston, MO
64651 Laclede, MO
64652 Laredo, MO
64653 Linneus, MO
64654 Lock Springs, MO
64655 Lucerne, MO
64656 Ludlow, MO
64657 Mc Fall, MO
64658 Marceline, MO
64659 Meadville, MO
64660 Mendon, MO
64661 Mercer, MO
64664 Mooresville, MO
64667 Newtown, MO

64668 Norborne, MO
64670 Pattonsburg, MO
64671 Polo, MO
64672 Powersville, MO
64673 Princeton, MO
64674 Purdin, MO
64676 Rothville, MO
64679 Spickard, MO
64680 Norborne, MO
64680 Stet, MO
64681 Sumner, MO
64682 Tina, MO
64683 Trenton, MO
64686 Utica, MO
64688 Wheeling, MO
64689 Winston, MO

647

64701 Harrisonville, MO
64720 Adrian, MO
64722 Amoret, MO
64723 Amsterdam, MO
64724 Appleton City, MO
64725 Archie, MO
64725 Austin, MO
64726 Blairstown, MO
64728 Bronaugh, MO
64730 Butler, MO
64730 Passaic, MO
64733 Chilhowee, MO
64734 Cleveland, MO
64734 West Line, MO
64735 Clinton, MO
64738 Collins, MO
64739 Creighton, MO
64740 Deepwater, MO
64741 Deerfield, MO
64742 Drexel, MO
64743 East Lynne, MO
64744 El Dorado Springs, MO
64745 Foster, MO
64746 Freeman, MO
64746 Lake Annette, MO
64747 Garden City, MO
64747 Latour, MO
64748 Golden City, MO
64750 Harwood, MO
64752 Hume, MO
64752 Stotesbury, MO
64755 Jasper, MO
64756 Jerico Springs, MO
64759 Iantha, MO
64759 Irwin, MO
64759 Lamar, MO
64761 Leeton, MO
64762 Liberal, MO
64763 Lowry City, MO
64765 Metz, MO
64766 Lamar, MO
64766 Milford, MO
64767 Milo, MO
64769 Mindenmines, MO
64770 Montrose, MO
64771 Moundville, MO
64772 Nevada, MO
64776 Osceola, MO
64776 Vista, MO
64778 Horton, MO
64778 Richards, MO
64779 Rich Hill, MO
64780 Rockville, MO
64781 Roscoe, MO
64783 Schell City, MO
64784 Sheldon, MO
64788 Urich, MO
64790 Walker, MO

648

64801 Joplin, MO
64802 Joplin, MO
64803 Joplin, MO
64804 Joplin, MO
64804 Loma Linda, MO
64830 Alba, MO
64831 Anderson, MO
64832 Asbury, MO
64832 Waco, MO
64833 Avilla, MO
64834 Carl Junction, MO
64835 Carterville, MO
64836 Carthage, MO
64840 Diamond, MO
64841 Duenweg, MO
64842 Fairview, MO
64843 Goodman, MO
64844 Granby, MO
64847 Lanagan, MO
64848 La Russell, MO
64849 Neck City, MO
64850 Neosho, MO
64853 Neosho, MO
64853 Newtonia, MO
64854 Noel, MO
64855 Oronogo, MO
64856 Jane, MO
64856 Pineville, MO
64857 Purcell, MO
64858 Racine, MO
64859 Reeds, MO
64861 Rocky Comfort, MO
64862 Sarcoxie, MO
64863 South West City, MO
64864 Saginaw, MO
64865 Seneca, MO
64866 Stark City, MO
64867 Stella, MO
64868 Tiff City, MO
64870 Webb City, MO
64873 Wentworth, MO
64874 Wheaton, MO

649

64999 Kansas City, MO

650

65001 Argyle, MO
65010 Ashland, MO
65011 Barnett, MO
65013 Belle, MO
65014 Bland, MO
65016 Bonnots Mill, MO
65017 Brumley, MO
65018 California, MO
65020 Camdenton, MO
65023 Centertown, MO
65024 Chamois, MO
65025 Clarksburg, MO
65026 Eldon, MO
65026 Etterville, MO
65026 Rocky Mount, MO
65032 Eugene, MO
65034 Fortuna, MO
65035 Freeburg, MO
65036 Gasconade, MO
65036 Morrison, MO
65037 Gravois Mills, MO
65038 Gravois Mills, MO
65038 Laurie, MO
65039 Hartsburg, MO
65040 Henley, MO
65041 Hermann, MO
65041 Mckittrick, MO
65042 California, MO
65042 High Point, MO
65043 Holts Summit, MO
65046 Jamestown, MO
65047 Kaiser, MO
65048 Koeltztown, MO
65049 Four Seasons, MO
65049 Lake Ozark, MO
65049 Village Of Four Seasons, MO
65050 Latham, MO
65051 Linn, MO
65052 Linn Creek, MO
65053 Lohman, MO
65054 Loose Creek, MO
65055 Mc Girk, MO
65058 Meta, MO
65059 Mokane, MO
65061 Gasconade, MO
65061 Morrison, MO
65062 Bland, MO
65062 Mount Sterling, MO
65063 New Bloomfield, MO
65064 Olean, MO
65065 Osage Beach, MO
65066 Owensville, MO
65067 Portland, MO
65068 Prairie Home, MO
65069 Rhineland, MO
65072 Eldon, MO
65072 Rocky Mount, MO
65074 Russellville, MO
65075 Saint Elizabeth, MO
65076 Saint Thomas, MO
65077 Steedman, MO
65078 Stover, MO
65079 Sunrise Beach, MO
65080 Tebbetts, MO
65081 Tipton, MO
65082 Tuscumbia, MO
65083 Ulman, MO
65084 Versailles, MO
65085 Westphalia, MO

651

65101 Cedar City, MO
65101 Jefferson City, MO
65101 Wardsville, MO
65102 Jefferson City, MO
65109 Saint Martins, MO
65110 Jefferson City, MO

652

65201 Columbia, MO
65202 Columbia, MO
65203 Columbia, MO
65205 Columbia, MO
65211 Columbia, MO
65212 Columbia, MO
65215 Columbia, MO
65216 Columbia, MO
65217 Columbia, MO
65218 Columbia, MO
65230 Armstrong, MO
65231 Auxvasse, MO
65232 Benton City, MO
65233 Boonville, MO
65236 Brunswick, MO
65237 Bunceton, MO
65239 Cairo, MO
65240 Centralia, MO
65243 Clark, MO
65244 Clifton Hill, MO
65246 Dalton, MO
65247 Excello, MO
65248 Fayette, MO
65250 Franklin, MO
65251 Fulton, MO
65254 Glasgow, MO
65255 Hallsville, MO
65256 Harrisburg, MO
65257 Higbee, MO
65258 Holliday, MO
65259 Huntsville, MO
65260 Jacksonville, MO
65261 Keytesville, MO
65262 Kingdom City, MO
65263 Madison, MO
65264 Martinsburg, MO
65265 Mexico, MO
65270 Moberly, MO
65274 New Franklin, MO
65275 Paris, MO
65276 Pilot Grove, MO
65278 Renick, MO
65279 Rocheport, MO
65280 Rush Hill, MO
65281 Salisbury, MO
65282 Santa Fe, MO
65283 Florida, MO
65283 Stoutsville, MO
65284 Sturgeon, MO
65285 Thompson, MO
65286 Triplett, MO
65287 Wooldridge, MO
65299 Columbia, MO

653

65301 Sedalia, MO
65302 Sedalia, MO
65305 Whiteman Air Force Base, MO
65320 Arrow Rock, MO
65321 Blackburn, MO
65322 Blackwater, MO
65323 Calhoun, MO
65324 Climax Springs, MO
65325 Cole Camp, MO
65326 Edwards, MO
65327 Emma, MO
65329 Florence, MO
65330 Gilliam, MO
65332 Green Ridge, MO
65333 Houstonia, MO
65334 Hughesville, MO
65335 Ionia, MO
65336 Knob Noster, MO
65337 La Monte, MO
65338 Lincoln, MO
65339 Grand Pass, MO
65339 Malta Bend, MO
65340 Marshall, MO
65340 Napton, MO
65344 Miami, MO
65345 Mora, MO
65347 Nelson, MO
65348 Otterville, MO
65349 Slater, MO
65350 Smithton, MO
65351 Sweet Springs, MO
65354 Syracuse, MO
65355 Warsaw, MO
65360 Windsor, MO

654

65401 Lecoma, MO
65401 Rolla, MO
65402 Rolla, MO
65409 Rolla, MO
65436 Beulah, MO
65438 Birch Tree, MO
65438 Teresita, MO
65439 Bixby, MO
65440 Boss, MO
65441 Bourbon, MO
65443 Brinktown, MO
65444 Bendavis, MO
65444 Bucyrus, MO
65446 Cherryville, MO
65449 Cook Sta, MO
65452 Crocker, MO
65453 Cuba, MO
65456 Davisville, MO
65457 Devils Elbow, MO
65459 Dixon, MO
65461 Duke, MO
65462 Edgar Springs, MO
65463 Eldridge, MO
65464 Elk Creek, MO
65466 Eminence, MO
65468 Eunice, MO
65470 Falcon, MO
65473 Fort Leonard Wood, MO
65479 Hartshorn, MO
65483 Houston, MO
65484 Huggins, MO
65486 Iberia, MO

655

65501 Jadwin, MO
65529 Jerome, MO
65532 Lake Spring, MO
65534 Laquey, MO
65535 Leasburg, MO
65536 Lebanon, MO
65541 Lenox, MO
65542 Licking, MO
65543 Lynchburg, MO
65546 Montier, MO
65548 Mountain View, MO
65550 Newburg, MO
65552 Plato, MO
65555 Raymondville, MO
65556 Richland, MO
65556 Swedeborg, MO
65557 Roby, MO
65559 Saint James, MO
65560 Salem, MO
65564 Solo, MO
65565 Berryman, MO
65565 Courtois, MO
65565 Steelville, MO
65566 Steelville, MO
65566 Viburnum, MO
65567 Stoutland, MO
65570 Success, MO
65571 Summersville, MO
65580 Vichy, MO
65582 Vienna, MO
65583 Waynesville, MO
65584 Saint Robert, MO
65586 Wesco, MO
65588 Winona, MO
65589 Yukon, MO
65590 Long Lane, MO
65591 Montreal, MO

656

65601 Aldrich, MO
65603 Arcola, MO
65604 Ash Grove, MO
65605 Aurora, MO
65605 Jenkins, MO
65606 Alton, MO
65607 Caplinger Mills, MO
65608 Ava, MO
65609 Bakersfield, MO
65610 Billings, MO
65611 Blue Eye, MO
65612 Bois D Arc, MO
65613 Bolivar, MO
65613 Cherokee Homestead Village, MO
65614 Bradleyville, MO
65615 Branson, MO
65616 Branson, MO
65617 Brighton, MO
65618 Brixey, MO
65619 Battlefield, MO
65619 Brookline, MO
65619 Brookline Sta, MO
65620 Bruner, MO
65622 Buffalo, MO
65623 Butterfield, MO
65623 Cassville, MO
65624 Cape Fair, MO
65624 Galena, MO
65625 Butterfield, MO
65625 Cassville, MO
65626 Caulfield, MO
65627 Cedarcreek, MO
65629 Chadwick, MO
65630 Chestnutridge, MO
65630 Saddlebrooke, MO
65631 Clever, MO
65632 Conway, MO
65633 Crane, MO
65634 Cross Timbers, MO
65635 Dadeville, MO
65636 Diggins, MO
65637 Dora, MO
65638 Drury, MO
65640 Dunnegan, MO
65641 Eagle Rock, MO
65644 Elkland, MO
65645 Morrisville, MO
65646 Everton, MO
65647 Exeter, MO
65648 Fair Grove, MO
65649 Fair Play, MO
65650 Flemington, MO
65652 Fordland, MO
65653 Forsyth, MO
65654 Freistatt, MO
65655 Gainesville, MO
65656 Galena, MO
65657 Garrison, MO
65658 Golden, MO
65660 Graff, MO
65661 Greenfield, MO
65662 Grovespring, MO
65663 Goodson, MO
65663 Half Way, MO
65664 Halltown, MO
65666 Hardenville, MO
65667 Hartville, MO
65668 Hermitage, MO
65669 Highlandville, MO
65672 Hollister, MO
65673 Hollister, MO
65674 Humansville, MO
65675 Hurley, MO
65676 Isabella, MO
65679 Kirbyville, MO
65680 Kissee Mills, MO
65681 Lampe, MO
65682 Lockwood, MO
65685 Louisburg, MO
65686 Kimberling City, MO
65688 Brandsville, MO
65689 Cabool, MO
65690 Couch, MO
65692 Koshkonong, MO

657

65702 Macomb, MO
65704 Mansfield, MO
65705 Marionville, MO
65706 Marshfield, MO
65707 Miller, MO
65708 Monett, MO
65710 Eudora, MO
65710 Morrisville, MO
65711 Mountain Grove, MO
65712 Mount Vernon, MO
65713 Niangua, MO
65714 Nixa, MO
65715 Noble, MO
65717 Norwood, MO
65720 Oldfield, MO
65721 Ozark, MO
65722 Phillipsburg, MO
65723 Pierce City, MO
65724 Pittsburg, MO
65725 Pleasant Hope, MO
65726 Point Lookout, MO
65727 Bolivar, MO
65727 Polk, MO
65728 Ponce De Leon, MO
65729 Pontiac, MO
65730 Powell, MO
65731 Powersite, MO
65732 Preston, MO
65733 Protem, MO
65734 Purdy, MO
65735 Quincy, MO
65737 Branson West, MO
65737 Reeds Spring, MO
65738 Republic, MO
65739 Ridgedale, MO
65740 Merriam Woods Village, MO
65740 Rockaway Beach, MO
65741 Rockbridge, MO
65742 Rogersville, MO
65744 Rueter, MO
65745 Seligman, MO
65746 Seymour, MO
65747 Shell Knob, MO
65752 South Greenfield, MO
65753 Sparta, MO
65754 Spokane, MO
65755 Squires, MO
65756 Stotts City, MO
65757 Strafford, MO
65759 Taneyville, MO
65760 Sycamore, MO
65760 Tecumseh, MO
65761 Dugginsville, MO
65761 Theodosia, MO
65762 Nottinghill, MO
65762 Thornfield, MO
65764 Tunas, MO
65765 Turners, MO
65766 Udall, MO
65767 Urbana, MO
65768 Vanzant, MO

65769 Verona, MO
65770 Walnut Grove, MO
65771 Walnut Shade, MO
65772 Washburn, MO
65773 Souder, MO
65773 Wasola, MO
65774 Weaubleau, MO
65775 West Plains, MO
65777 Moody, MO
65778 Myrtle, MO
65779 Wheatland, MO
65781 Willard, MO
65783 Windyville, MO
65784 Zanoni, MO
65785 Stockton, MO
65786 Macks Creek, MO
65787 Roach, MO
65788 Peace Valley, MO
65789 Pomona, MO
65790 Pottersville, MO
65791 Thayer, MO
65793 Willow Springs, MO

658

65801 Springfield, MO
65802 Springfield, MO
65803 Springfield, MO
65804 Springfield, MO
65805 Springfield, MO
65806 Springfield, MO
65807 Springfield, MO
65808 Springfield, MO
65809 Springfield, MO
65810 Springfield, MO
65814 Springfield, MO
65817 Springfield, MO
65890 Springfield, MO
65897 Springfield, MO
65898 Springfield, MO
65899 Springfield, MO

660

66002 Atchison, KS
66002 Potter, KS
66006 Baldwin City, KS
66007 Basehor, KS
66008 Bendena, KS
66010 Blue Mound, KS
66012 Bonner Springs, KS
66012 Lake Of The Forest, KS
66013 Bucyrus, KS
66014 Centerville, KS
66015 Colony, KS
66016 Cummings, KS
66017 Denton, KS
66018 De Soto, KS
66019 Clearview City, KS
66019 De Soto, KS
66020 Easton, KS
66021 Edgerton, KS
66023 Effingham, KS
66024 Elwood, KS
66025 Eudora, KS
66026 Fontana, KS
66027 Fort Leavenworth, KS
66030 Edgerton, KS
66030 Gardner, KS
66031 New Century, KS
66032 Garnett, KS
66033 Greeley, KS
66035 Highland, KS
66036 Hillsdale, KS
66039 Kincaid, KS
66040 Lacygne, KS
66040 Linn Valley, KS
66041 Huron, KS
66041 Lancaster, KS
66042 Lane, KS
66043 Lansing, KS
66043 Leavenworth, KS
66044 Lawrence, KS
66045 Lawrence, KS
66046 Lawrence, KS
66047 Lawrence, KS
66048 Leavenworth, KS
66049 Lawrence, KS
66050 Lecompton, KS
66051 Olathe, KS
66052 Linwood, KS
66053 Louisburg, KS
66054 Mc Louth, KS
66056 Mound City, KS
66058 Muscotah, KS
66060 Nortonville, KS
66061 Olathe, KS
66062 Lenexa, KS
66062 Olathe, KS
66062 Overland Park, KS
66063 Olathe, KS
66064 Osawatomie, KS
66066 Oskaloosa, KS
66067 Centropolis, KS
66067 Ottawa, KS
66070 Ozawkie, KS
66071 Paola, KS
66072 Parker, KS
66073 Perry, KS
66075 Pleasanton, KS
66076 Pomona, KS
66078 Princeton, KS
66079 Rantoul, KS
66080 Richmond, KS
66083 Spring Hill, KS
66085 Overland Park, KS
66085 Stilwell, KS
66086 Tonganoxie, KS
66087 Severance, KS
66087 Troy, KS
66088 Valley Falls, KS
66090 Wathena, KS
66091 Welda, KS
66092 Wellsville, KS
66093 Westphalia, KS
66094 White Cloud, KS
66095 Williamsburg, KS
66097 Winchester, KS

661

66101 Kansas City, KS
66102 Kansas City, KS
66103 Kansas City, KS
66103 Rosedale, KS
66104 Kansas City, KS
66105 Kansas City, KS
66106 Kansas City, KS
66109 Kansas City, KS
66110 Kansas City, KS
66111 Edwardsville, KS
66111 Kansas City, KS
66112 Kansas City, KS
66113 Edwardsville, KS
66113 Kansas City, KS
66115 Kansas City, KS
66117 Kansas City, KS
66118 Kansas City, KS
66119 Kansas City, KS
66160 Kansas City, KS

662

66201 Mission, KS
66201 Overland Park, KS
66201 Shawnee Mission, KS
66202 Countryside, KS
66202 Merriam, KS
66202 Mission, KS
66202 Overland Park, KS
66202 Prairie Village, KS
66202 Roeland Park, KS
66202 Shawnee Mission, KS
66203 Merriam, KS
66203 Overland Park, KS
66203 Shawnee, KS
66203 Shawnee Mission, KS
66204 Merriam, KS
66204 Overland Park, KS
66204 Prairie Village, KS
66204 Shawnee Mission, KS
66205 Fairway, KS
66205 Mission, KS
66205 Mission Woods, KS
66205 Roeland Park, KS
66205 Shawnee Mission, KS
66205 Westwood, KS
66205 Westwood Hills, KS
66206 Leawood, KS
66206 Overland Park, KS
66206 Prairie Village, KS
66206 Shawnee Mission, KS
66207 Overland Park, KS
66207 Prairie Village, KS
66207 Shawnee Mission, KS
66208 Mission Hills, KS
66208 Prairie Village, KS
66208 Shawnee Mission, KS
66209 Leawood, KS
66209 Overland Park, KS
66209 Shawnee Mission, KS
66210 Lenexa, KS
66210 Overland Park, KS
66210 Shawnee Mission, KS
66211 Leawood, KS
66211 Overland Park, KS
66211 Shawnee Mission, KS
66212 Overland Park, KS
66212 Shawnee Mission, KS
66213 Overland Park, KS
66213 Shawnee Mission, KS
66214 Lenexa, KS
66214 Overland Park, KS
66214 Shawnee, KS
66214 Shawnee Mission, KS
66215 Lenexa, KS
66215 Overland Park, KS
66215 Shawnee Mission, KS
66216 Lenexa, KS
66216 Shawnee, KS
66216 Shawnee Mission, KS
66217 Lake Quivira, KS
66217 Lenexa, KS
66217 Shawnee, KS
66217 Shawnee Mission, KS
66218 Shawnee, KS
66218 Shawnee Mission, KS
66219 Lenexa, KS
66219 Shawnee, KS
66219 Shawnee Mission, KS
66220 Lenexa, KS
66220 Shawnee, KS
66220 Shawnee Mission, KS
66221 Overland Park, KS
66221 Shawnee Mission, KS
66221 Stanley, KS
66222 Mission, KS
66222 Shawnee Mission, KS
66223 Overland Park, KS
66223 Shawnee Mission, KS
66223 Stanley, KS
66224 Leawood, KS
66224 Overland Park, KS
66224 Shawnee Mission, KS
66224 Stanley, KS
66225 Overland Park, KS
66225 Shawnee Mission, KS
66226 Shawnee, KS
66226 Shawnee Mission, KS
66227 Lenexa, KS
66227 Shawnee, KS
66227 Shawnee Mission, KS
66250 Lenexa, KS
66250 Shawnee Mission, KS
66251 Overland Park, KS
66251 Shawnee Mission, KS
66276 Lenexa, KS
66276 Shawnee Mission, KS
66282 Overland Park, KS
66282 Shawnee Mission, KS
66283 Overland Park, KS
66283 Shawnee Mission, KS
66285 Lenexa, KS
66285 Shawnee Mission, KS
66286 Lenexa, KS
66286 Shawnee, KS
66286 Shawnee Mission, KS

664

66401 Alma, KS
66402 Auburn, KS
66403 Axtell, KS
66404 Baileyville, KS
66406 Beattie, KS
66407 Belvue, KS
66408 Bern, KS
66409 Berryton, KS
66411 Blue Rapids, KS
66412 Bremen, KS
66413 Burlingame, KS
66414 Carbondale, KS
66415 Centralia, KS
66416 Circleville, KS
66417 Corning, KS
66418 Delia, KS
66419 Denison, KS
66420 Dover, KS
66422 Emmett, KS
66423 Eskridge, KS
66424 Everest, KS
66425 Fairview, KS
66426 Fostoria, KS
66426 Westmoreland, KS
66427 Frankfort, KS
66428 Goff, KS
66429 Grantville, KS
66431 Harveyville, KS
66432 Havensville, KS
66434 Hiawatha, KS
66434 Reserve, KS
66434 Willis, KS
66436 Holton, KS
66438 Home, KS
66439 Horton, KS
66440 Hoyt, KS
66441 Junction City, KS
66442 Fort Riley, KS
66442 Ft Riley, KS
66442 Junction City, KS
66449 Leonardville, KS
66451 Lyndon, KS

665

66501 Alma, KS
66501 Mc Farland, KS
66502 Manhattan, KS
66503 Manhattan, KS
66505 Manhattan, KS
66506 Manhattan, KS
66507 Maple Hill, KS
66508 Herkimer, KS
66508 Marysville, KS
66509 Mayetta, KS
66510 Melvern, KS
66512 Meriden, KS
66514 Milford, KS
66515 Morrill, KS
66516 Netawaka, KS
66517 Ogden, KS
66518 Oketo, KS
66520 Olsburg, KS
66521 Duluth, KS
66521 Onaga, KS
66521 Wheaton, KS
66522 Oneida, KS
66523 Osage City, KS
66524 Overbrook, KS
66526 Paxico, KS
66527 Powhattan, KS
66528 Quenemo, KS
66531 Riley, KS
66532 Leona, KS
66532 Robinson, KS
66533 Rossville, KS
66534 Sabetha, KS
66535 Saint George, KS
66536 Saint Marys, KS
66537 Scranton, KS
66538 Kelly, KS
66538 Seneca, KS
66538 St Benedict, KS
66539 Silver Lake, KS
66540 Soldier, KS
66541 Summerfield, KS
66542 Tecumseh, KS
66543 Vassar, KS
66544 Vermillion, KS
66544 Vliets, KS
66546 Wakarusa, KS
66547 Louisville, KS
66547 Wamego, KS
66548 Waterville, KS
66549 Blaine, KS
66549 Westmoreland, KS
66550 Wetmore, KS
66552 Whiting, KS
66554 Randolph, KS

666

66601 Topeka, KS
66603 Topeka, KS
66604 Topeka, KS
66605 Topeka, KS
66606 Topeka, KS
66607 Topeka, KS
66608 Topeka, KS
66609 Topeka, KS
66610 Topeka, KS
66611 Topeka, KS
66612 Topeka, KS
66614 Topeka, KS
66615 Topeka, KS
66616 Topeka, KS
66617 Topeka, KS
66618 Topeka, KS
66619 Topeka, KS
66620 Topeka, KS
66621 Topeka, KS
66622 Topeka, KS
66624 Topeka, KS
66625 Topeka, KS
66626 Topeka, KS
66629 Topeka, KS
66636 Topeka, KS
66647 Topeka, KS
66667 Topeka, KS
66675 Topeka, KS
66683 Topeka, KS
66699 Topeka, KS

667

66701 Fort Scott, KS
66701 Hiattville, KS
66710 Altoona, KS
66711 Arcadia, KS
66712 Arma, KS
66713 Baxter Springs, KS
66714 Benedict, KS
66716 Bronson, KS
66717 Buffalo, KS
66720 Chanute, KS
66720 Petrolia, KS
66724 Cherokee, KS
66725 Columbus, KS
66725 Hallowell, KS
66728 Crestline, KS
66732 Elsmore, KS
66733 Erie, KS
66734 Farlington, KS
66735 Franklin, KS
66736 Coyville, KS
66736 Fredonia, KS
66736 Lafontaine, KS
66736 New Albany, KS
66738 Fulton, KS
66739 Galena, KS
66740 Galesburg, KS
66741 Arcadia, KS
66741 Garland, KS
66742 Gas, KS
66743 Girard, KS
66746 Hepler, KS
66748 Humboldt, KS
66749 Carlyle, KS
66749 Iola, KS
66751 La Harpe, KS
66753 Mc Cune, KS
66754 Mapleton, KS
66755 Moran, KS
66756 Mulberry, KS
66757 Neodesha, KS
66758 Neosho Falls, KS
66759 New Albany, KS
66760 Opolis, KS
66761 Piqua, KS
66762 Pittsburg, KS
66762 Radley, KS
66763 Frontenac, KS
66763 Pittsburg, KS
66767 Prescott, KS
66769 Redfield, KS
66770 Riverton, KS
66771 Saint Paul, KS
66772 Savonburg, KS
66773 Carona, KS
66773 Scammon, KS
66775 Stark, KS
66776 Thayer, KS
66777 Toronto, KS
66778 Treece, KS
66779 Uniontown, KS
66780 Walnut, KS
66781 Lawton, KS
66781 Weir, KS
66782 West Mineral, KS
66783 Yates Center, KS

668

66801 Emporia, KS
66830 Admire, KS
66833 Allen, KS
66833 Bushong, KS
66834 Alta Vista, KS
66835 Americus, KS
66838 Burdick, KS
66839 Burlington, KS
66839 New Strawn, KS
66840 Burns, KS
66842 Cassoday, KS
66843 Cedar Point, KS
66843 Clements, KS
66845 Cottonwood Falls, KS
66846 Council Grove, KS
66846 Dunlap, KS
66849 Dwight, KS
66850 Elmdale, KS
66851 Florence, KS
66852 Gridley, KS
66853 Hamilton, KS
66854 Hartford, KS
66855 Lamont, KS
66855 Madison, KS
66856 Lebo, KS
66856 Olivet, KS
66857 Le Roy, KS
66858 Antelope, KS
66858 Lincolnville, KS
66859 Lost Springs, KS
66860 Madison, KS
66861 Marion, KS
66862 Matfield Green, KS
66863 Neal, KS
66864 Neosho Rapids, KS
66865 Olpe, KS
66866 Peabody, KS
66868 Reading, KS
66869 Strong City, KS
66870 Virgil, KS
66871 Waverly, KS
66872 White City, KS
66873 Council Grove, KS
66873 Wilsey, KS

669

66901 Ames, KS
66901 Concordia, KS
66901 Rice, KS
66930 Agenda, KS
66932 Athol, KS
66933 Barnes, KS
66935 Belleville, KS
66936 Burr Oak, KS
66937 Clifton, KS
66938 Clyde, KS
66939 Courtland, KS
66940 Cuba, KS
66941 Esbon, KS
66942 Formoso, KS
66943 Greenleaf, KS
66944 Haddam, KS
66945 Hanover, KS
66946 Hollenberg, KS

66948 Jamestown, KS
66949 Ionia, KS
66949 Jewell, KS
66951 Kensington, KS
66952 Bellaire, KS
66952 Lebanon, KS
66953 Linn, KS
66955 Mahaska, KS
66956 Mankato, KS
66958 Morrowville, KS
66959 Munden, KS
66960 Narka, KS
66961 Norway, KS
66962 Palmer, KS
66963 Randall, KS
66964 Republic, KS
66966 Scandia, KS
66967 Harlan, KS
66967 Smith Center, KS
66968 Washington, KS
66970 Webber, KS

670

67001 Andale, KS
67002 Andover, KS
67003 Anthony, KS
67004 Argonia, KS
67005 Arkansas City, KS
67005 Parkerfield, KS
67008 Atlanta, KS
67009 Attica, KS
67010 Augusta, KS
67012 Beaumont, KS
67013 Belle Plaine, KS
67016 Bentley, KS
67017 Benton, KS
67018 Bluff City, KS
67019 Burden, KS
67020 Burrton, KS
67021 Byers, KS
67022 Caldwell, KS
67023 Cambridge, KS
67024 Cedar Vale, KS
67025 Cheney, KS
67026 Clearwater, KS
67028 Belvidere, KS
67028 Coats, KS
67029 Coldwater, KS
67030 Colwich, KS
67031 Conway Springs, KS
67035 Cunningham, KS
67035 Penalosa, KS
67036 Danville, KS
67037 Derby, KS
67038 Dexter, KS
67039 Douglass, KS
67041 Elbing, KS
67042 El Dorado, KS
67045 Eureka, KS
67047 Fall River, KS
67049 Freeport, KS
67050 Garden Plain, KS
67051 Geuda Springs, KS
67052 Goddard, KS
67053 Goessel, KS
67054 Greensburg, KS
67055 Greenwich, KS
67056 Halstead, KS
67057 Hardtner, KS
67058 Harper, KS
67059 Haviland, KS
67060 Haysville, KS
67061 Hazelton, KS
67062 Hesston, KS
67063 Hillsboro, KS
67065 Isabel, KS
67066 Iuka, KS
67067 Kechi, KS
67068 Belmont, KS
67068 Kingman, KS
67070 Kiowa, KS
67071 Lake City, KS
67072 Latham, KS
67073 Lehigh, KS
67074 Leon, KS

671

67101 Maize, KS
67102 Maple City, KS
67103 Mayfield, KS
67104 Medicine Lodge, KS
67105 Milan, KS
67106 Milton, KS
67107 Moundridge, KS
67108 Mount Hope, KS
67109 Mullinville, KS
67110 Mulvane, KS
67111 Murdock, KS
67112 Nashville, KS
67114 Newton, KS
67117 Newton, KS
67117 North Newton, KS
67118 Norwich, KS
67119 Oxford, KS
67120 Peck, KS
67122 Piedmont, KS
67123 Potwin, KS
67124 Cullison, KS
67124 Pratt, KS
67127 Protection, KS
67131 Rock, KS
67132 Rosalia, KS
67133 Rose Hill, KS
67134 Sawyer, KS
67135 Sedgwick, KS
67137 Climax, KS
67137 Severy, KS
67138 Sharon, KS
67140 Hunnewell, KS
67140 South Haven, KS
67142 Rago, KS
67142 Spivey, KS
67143 Sun City, KS
67144 Towanda, KS
67146 Udall, KS
67147 Park City, KS
67147 Valley Center, KS
67149 Viola, KS
67150 Waldron, KS
67151 Walton, KS
67152 Wellington, KS
67154 Whitewater, KS
67155 Wilmore, KS
67156 Winfield, KS
67159 Zenda, KS

672

67201 Wichita, KS
67202 Wichita, KS
67203 Wichita, KS
67204 Park City, KS
67204 Wichita, KS
67205 Wichita, KS
67206 Eastborough, KS
67206 Wichita, KS
67207 Eastborough, KS
67207 Wichita, KS
67208 Eastborough, KS
67208 Wichita, KS
67209 Wichita, KS
67210 Wichita, KS
67211 Wichita, KS
67212 Wichita, KS
67213 Wichita, KS
67214 Wichita, KS
67215 Wichita, KS
67216 Wichita, KS
67217 Wichita, KS
67218 Wichita, KS
67219 Park City, KS
67219 Wichita, KS
67220 Bel Aire, KS
67220 Wichita, KS
67221 Mcconnell Afb, KS
67221 Wichita, KS
67223 Wichita, KS
67226 Bel Aire, KS
67226 Wichita, KS
67227 Wichita, KS
67228 Wichita, KS
67230 Wichita, KS
67232 Wichita, KS
67235 Wichita, KS
67260 Wichita, KS
67275 Wichita, KS
67276 Wichita, KS
67277 Wichita, KS
67278 Wichita, KS

673

67301 Independence, KS
67330 Altamont, KS
67332 Bartlett, KS
67333 Caney, KS
67334 Chautauqua, KS
67335 Cherryvale, KS
67336 Chetopa, KS
67337 Coffeyville, KS
67340 Dearing, KS
67341 Dennis, KS
67342 Edna, KS
67344 Elk City, KS
67345 Elk Falls, KS
67346 Grenola, KS
67347 Havana, KS
67349 Howard, KS
67351 Liberty, KS
67352 Longton, KS
67353 Moline, KS
67354 Mound Valley, KS
67355 Niotaze, KS
67356 Oswego, KS
67357 Parsons, KS
67360 Peru, KS
67361 Sedan, KS
67363 Sycamore, KS
67364 Tyro, KS

674

67401 Bavaria, KS
67401 Salina, KS
67402 Salina, KS
67410 Abilene, KS
67410 Industry, KS
67410 Manchester, KS
67416 Assaria, KS
67416 Mentor, KS
67417 Aurora, KS
67418 Barnard, KS
67420 Beloit, KS
67420 Scottsville, KS
67422 Bennington, KS
67423 Beverly, KS
67425 Brookville, KS
67427 Bushton, KS
67428 Canton, KS
67430 Cawker City, KS
67431 Chapman, KS
67432 Clay Center, KS
67432 Oakhill, KS
67436 Delphos, KS
67437 Downs, KS
67438 Durham, KS
67439 Ellsworth, KS
67441 Enterprise, KS
67442 Falun, KS
67443 Galva, KS
67444 Geneseo, KS
67445 Glasco, KS
67446 Glen Elder, KS
67447 Green, KS
67448 Carlton, KS
67448 Gypsum, KS
67449 Delavan, KS
67449 Herington, KS
67449 Latimer, KS
67450 Holyrood, KS
67451 Hope, KS
67451 Navarre, KS
67452 Hunter, KS
67454 Kanopolis, KS
67455 Lincoln, KS
67455 Westfall, KS
67456 Lindsborg, KS
67456 Smolan, KS
67457 Little River, KS
67458 Longford, KS
67459 Lorraine, KS
67460 Conway, KS
67460 Mc Pherson, KS
67460 Mcpherson, KS
67464 Marquette, KS
67466 Miltonvale, KS
67467 Ada, KS
67467 Minneapolis, KS
67467 Wells, KS
67468 Morganville, KS
67470 New Cambria, KS
67473 Osborne, KS
67474 Portis, KS
67475 Ramona, KS
67476 Roxbury, KS
67478 Simpson, KS
67480 Solomon, KS
67481 Sylvan Grove, KS
67482 Talmage, KS
67483 Tampa, KS
67484 Culver, KS
67484 Tescott, KS
67485 Tipton, KS
67487 Wakefield, KS
67490 Wilson, KS
67491 Windom, KS
67492 Woodbine, KS

675

67501 Hutchinson, KS
67501 Willowbrook, KS
67502 Hutchinson, KS
67502 Medora, KS
67504 Hutchinson, KS
67505 Hutchinson, KS
67505 South Hutchinson, KS
67510 Abbyville, KS
67511 Albert, KS
67512 Alden, KS
67513 Alexander, KS
67514 Arlington, KS
67515 Arnold, KS
67516 Bazine, KS
67518 Beeler, KS
67519 Belpre, KS
67520 Bison, KS
67521 Brownell, KS
67522 Buhler, KS
67523 Burdett, KS
67524 Chase, KS
67525 Beaver, KS
67525 Claflin, KS
67525 Odin, KS
67526 Ellinwood, KS
67529 Garfield, KS
67530 Dundee, KS
67530 Great Bend, KS
67530 Heizer, KS
67543 Haven, KS
67544 Hoisington, KS
67544 Susank, KS
67545 Hudson, KS
67546 Inman, KS
67547 Kinsley, KS
67548 La Crosse, KS
67550 Larned, KS
67550 Radium, KS
67552 Lewis, KS
67553 Liebenthal, KS
67554 Lyons, KS
67556 Mc Cracken, KS
67557 Macksville, KS
67559 Nekoma, KS
67560 Ness City, KS
67561 Nickerson, KS
67563 Offerle, KS
67564 Olmitz, KS
67565 Galatia, KS
67565 Otis, KS
67566 Partridge, KS
67567 Pawnee Rock, KS
67568 Plevna, KS
67570 Pretty Pr, KS
67570 Pretty Prairie, KS
67572 Ransom, KS
67573 Raymond, KS
67574 Rozel, KS
67575 Rush Center, KS
67575 Timken, KS
67576 Saint John, KS
67576 Seward, KS
67576 St John, KS
67578 Stafford, KS
67579 Sterling, KS
67581 Sylvia, KS
67583 Langdon, KS
67583 Preston, KS
67583 Turon, KS
67584 Utica, KS
67585 Yoder, KS

676

67601 Antonino, KS
67601 Hays, KS
67621 Agra, KS
67622 Almena, KS
67623 Alton, KS
67625 Bogue, KS
67626 Bunker Hill, KS
67627 Catharine, KS
67628 Cedar, KS
67629 Clayton, KS
67631 Collyer, KS
67632 Damar, KS
67634 Dorrance, KS
67635 Dresden, KS
67637 Ellis, KS
67638 Gaylord, KS
67639 Glade, KS
67640 Gorham, KS
67642 Hill City, KS
67643 Jennings, KS
67644 Kirwin, KS
67645 Densmore, KS
67645 Edmond, KS
67645 Lenora, KS
67645 New Almelo, KS
67646 Logan, KS
67647 Long Island, KS
67648 Lucas, KS
67649 Luray, KS
67650 Morland, KS
67651 Natoma, KS
67653 Norcatur, KS
67654 Norton, KS
67656 Ogallah, KS
67657 Palco, KS
67658 Paradise, KS
67659 Penokee, KS
67660 Pfeifer, KS
67661 Phillipsburg, KS
67661 Stuttgart, KS
67663 Codell, KS
67663 Plainville, KS
67663 Zurich, KS
67664 Prairie View, KS
67665 Russell, KS
67667 Hays, KS
67667 Schoenchen, KS
67669 Stockton, KS
67671 Victoria, KS
67672 Wa Keeney, KS
67672 Wakeeney, KS
67673 Waldo, KS
67674 Walker, KS
67675 Woodston, KS

677

67701 Colby, KS
67730 Atwood, KS
67731 Bird City, KS
67732 Brewster, KS
67733 Edson, KS
67734 Gem, KS
67735 Goodland, KS
67736 Gove, KS
67737 Grainfield, KS
67738 Grinnell, KS
67739 Herndon, KS
67740 Hoxie, KS
67740 Studley, KS
67741 Kanorado, KS
67743 Levant, KS
67744 Ludell, KS
67745 Mc Donald, KS
67747 Monument, KS
67747 Winona, KS
67748 Oakley, KS
67749 Oberlin, KS
67751 Park, KS
67752 Quinter, KS
67753 Menlo, KS
67753 Rexford, KS
67756 Saint Francis, KS
67756 Wheeler, KS
67757 Selden, KS
67758 Sharon Springs, KS
67761 Wallace, KS
67762 Weskan, KS
67764 Monument, KS
67764 Russell Springs, KS
67764 Winona, KS

678

67801 Dodge City, KS
67801 Fort Dodge, KS
67831 Ashland, KS
67834 Bucklin, KS
67835 Cimarron, KS
67835 Kalvesta, KS
67836 Coolidge, KS
67837 Copeland, KS
67838 Deerfield, KS
67839 Dighton, KS
67839 Shields, KS
67840 Englewood, KS
67841 Ensign, KS
67842 Ford, KS
67842 Kingsdown, KS
67843 Dodge City, KS
67843 Fort Dodge, KS
67844 Fowler, KS
67846 Garden City, KS
67849 Hanston, KS
67850 Healy, KS
67851 Holcomb, KS
67853 Ingalls, KS
67854 Jetmore, KS
67855 Johnson, KS
67857 Kendall, KS
67859 Kismet, KS
67860 Lakin, KS
67861 Leoti, KS
67862 Manter, KS
67863 Marienthal, KS
67863 Modoc, KS
67864 Meade, KS
67865 Bloom, KS
67865 Minneola, KS
67867 Montezuma, KS
67868 Garden City, KS
67868 Pierceville, KS
67869 Plains, KS
67870 Satanta, KS
67871 Friend, KS
67871 Scott City, KS
67876 Spearville, KS
67877 Sublette, KS
67878 Syracuse, KS
67879 Tribune, KS
67880 Ulysses, KS
67882 Wright, KS

679

67901 Liberal, KS
67905 Liberal, KS
67950 Elkhart, KS
67951 Hugoton, KS
67952 Moscow, KS
67953 Richfield, KS
67954 Rolla, KS

680

68001 Abie, NE
68002 Arlington, NE
68003 Ashland, NE
68004 Bancroft, NE
68005 Bellevue, NE
68007 Bennington, NE
68008 Blair, NE
68009 Blair, NE
68010 Boys Town, NE
68010 Boystown, NE
68014 Bruno, NE

68015 Cedar Bluffs, NE
68016 Cedar Creek, NE
68017 Ceresco, NE
68018 Colon, NE
68019 Craig, NE
68020 Decatur, NE
68022 Elkhorn, NE
68023 Fort Calhoun, NE
68025 Fremont, NE
68025 Inglewood, NE
68026 Fremont, NE
68028 Gretna, NE
68029 Herman, NE
68030 Homer, NE
68031 Hooper, NE
68033 Ithaca, NE
68034 Kennard, NE
68036 Linwood, NE
68037 Louisville, NE
68038 Lyons, NE
68039 Macy, NE
68040 Malmo, NE
68041 Mead, NE
68042 Memphis, NE
68044 Fontanelle, NE
68044 Nickerson, NE
68045 Oakland, NE
68046 Papillion, NE
68047 Pender, NE
68048 Plattsmouth, NE
68050 Prague, NE
68055 Rosalie, NE
68056 St Columbans, NE
68057 Scribner, NE
68058 South Bend, NE
68059 Richfield, NE
68059 Springfield, NE
68061 Tekamah, NE
68062 Thurston, NE
68063 Uehling, NE
68064 Leshara, NE
68064 Valley, NE
68065 Valparaiso, NE
68066 Wahoo, NE
68067 Walthill, NE
68068 Washington, NE
68069 Waterloo, NE
68070 Weston, NE
68071 Winnebago, NE
68072 Winslow, NE
68073 Yutan, NE

681

68101 Omaha, NE
68102 Omaha, NE
68103 Omaha, NE
68104 Omaha, NE
68105 Omaha, NE
68106 Omaha, NE
68107 Omaha, NE
68108 Omaha, NE
68109 Omaha, NE
68110 Omaha, NE
68111 Omaha, NE
68112 Omaha, NE
68113 Offutt Afb, NE
68113 Omaha, NE
68114 Omaha, NE
68116 Omaha, NE
68117 Omaha, NE
68118 Omaha, NE
68119 Omaha, NE
68120 Omaha, NE
68122 Omaha, NE
68123 Bellevue, NE
68124 Omaha, NE
68127 Omaha, NE
68127 Ralston, NE
68128 La Vista, NE
68128 Lavista, NE
68128 Ralston, NE
68130 Omaha, NE
68131 Omaha, NE
68132 Omaha, NE
68133 Bellevue, NE
68133 Papillion, NE
68134 Omaha, NE
68135 Omaha, NE
68136 Omaha, NE
68137 Omaha, NE
68138 La Vista, NE
68138 Omaha, NE
68139 Omaha, NE
68142 Omaha, NE
68144 Millard, NE
68144 Omaha, NE
68145 Millard, NE
68145 Omaha, NE
68147 Bellevue, NE
68147 Omaha, NE
68152 Omaha, NE
68154 Omaha, NE
68155 Omaha, NE
68157 Bellevue, NE
68157 Omaha, NE
68164 Omaha, NE
68172 Omaha, NE
68175 Omaha, NE
68176 Omaha, NE
68178 Omaha, NE
68179 Omaha, NE
68180 Omaha, NE
68182 Omaha, NE
68183 Omaha, NE
68197 Omaha, NE
68198 Omaha, NE

683

68301 Adams, NE
68303 Alexandria, NE
68304 Alvo, NE
68305 Auburn, NE
68307 Avoca, NE
68309 Barneston, NE
68310 Beatrice, NE
68310 Holmesville, NE
68313 Beaver Crossing, NE
68314 Bee, NE
68315 Belvidere, NE
68316 Benedict, NE
68317 Bennet, NE
68318 Blue Springs, NE
68319 Bradshaw, NE
68320 Brock, NE
68321 Brownville, NE
68322 Bruning, NE
68323 Burchard, NE
68324 Burr, NE
68325 Byron, NE
68326 Carleton, NE
68327 Chester, NE
68328 Clatonia, NE
68329 Cook, NE
68330 Cordova, NE
68331 Cortland, NE
68332 Crab Orchard, NE
68333 Crete, NE
68335 Davenport, NE
68336 Davey, NE
68337 Dawson, NE
68338 Daykin, NE
68339 Denton, NE
68340 Deshler, NE
68341 De Witt, NE
68342 Diller, NE
68343 Dorchester, NE
68344 Douglas, NE
68345 Du Bois, NE
68346 Dunbar, NE
68346 Lorton, NE
68347 Eagle, NE
68348 Elk Creek, NE
68349 Elmwood, NE
68350 Endicott, NE
68351 Exeter, NE
68352 Fairbury, NE
68352 Gladstone, NE
68354 Fairmont, NE
68355 Falls City, NE
68357 Filley, NE
68358 Firth, NE
68359 Friend, NE
68360 Garland, NE
68361 Geneva, NE
68362 Gilead, NE
68364 Goehner, NE
68365 Grafton, NE
68366 Greenwood, NE
68367 Gresham, NE
68368 Hallam, NE
68370 Hebron, NE
68371 Henderson, NE
68372 Hickman, NE
68372 Holland, NE
68375 Hubbell, NE
68376 Humboldt, NE
68377 Jansen, NE
68378 Johnson, NE
68379 Johnson, NE
68379 Julian, NE
68380 Lewiston, NE
68381 Liberty, NE
68382 Dunbar, NE
68382 Lorton, NE

684

68401 Mc Cool Junction, NE
68402 Malcolm, NE
68403 Manley, NE
68404 Martell, NE
68405 Milford, NE
68406 Milligan, NE
68407 Murdock, NE
68409 Murray, NE
68410 Nebraska City, NE
68413 Nehawka, NE
68414 Nemaha, NE
68415 Odell, NE
68416 Ohiowa, NE
68417 Otoe, NE
68418 Palmyra, NE
68419 Panama, NE
68420 Pawnee City, NE
68421 Peru, NE
68422 Pickrell, NE
68423 Pleasant Dale, NE
68424 Plymouth, NE
68428 Agnew, NE
68428 Raymond, NE
68429 Reynolds, NE
68430 Roca, NE
68431 Rulo, NE
68433 Salem, NE
68434 Seward, NE
68436 Shickley, NE
68437 Shubert, NE
68438 Sprague, NE
68439 Staplehurst, NE
68440 Steele City, NE
68441 Steinauer, NE
68442 Stella, NE
68443 Saint Mary, NE
68443 Sterling, NE
68444 Strang, NE
68445 Swanton, NE
68446 Syracuse, NE
68447 Table Rock, NE
68448 Talmage, NE
68450 Tecumseh, NE
68452 Ong, NE
68453 Tobias, NE
68454 Unadilla, NE
68455 Union, NE
68456 Utica, NE
68457 Verdon, NE
68458 Virginia, NE
68460 Waco, NE
68461 Walton, NE
68462 Waverly, NE
68463 Weeping Water, NE
68464 Western, NE
68465 Wilber, NE
68466 Wymore, NE
68467 York, NE

685

68501 Lincoln, NE
68502 Lincoln, NE
68503 Lincoln, NE
68504 Lincoln, NE
68505 Lincoln, NE
68506 Lincoln, NE
68507 Lincoln, NE
68508 Lincoln, NE
68509 Lincoln, NE
68510 Lincoln, NE
68512 Lincoln, NE
68514 Lincoln, NE
68516 Lincoln, NE
68517 Lincoln, NE
68520 Lincoln, NE
68521 Lincoln, NE
68522 Lincoln, NE
68523 Lincoln, NE
68524 Lincoln, NE
68526 Lincoln, NE
68527 Lincoln, NE
68528 Lincoln, NE
68529 Lincoln, NE
68531 Lincoln, NE
68532 Lincoln, NE
68542 Lincoln, NE
68544 Lincoln, NE
68583 Lincoln, NE
68588 Lincoln, NE

686

68601 Columbus, NE
68601 Richland, NE
68602 Columbus, NE
68620 Albion, NE
68620 Boone, NE
68621 Ames, NE
68622 Bartlett, NE
68623 Belgrade, NE
68624 Bellwood, NE
68626 Brainard, NE
68627 Cedar Rapids, NE
68628 Clarks, NE
68629 Clarkson, NE
68631 Creston, NE
68632 David City, NE
68632 Garrison, NE
68632 Octavia, NE
68633 Dodge, NE
68634 Duncan, NE
68635 Dwight, NE
68636 Elgin, NE
68637 Ericson, NE
68638 Fullerton, NE
68640 Genoa, NE
68641 Howells, NE
68642 Cornlea, NE
68642 Humphrey, NE
68642 Tarnov, NE
68643 Leigh, NE
68644 Lindsay, NE
68647 Monroe, NE
68648 Morse Bluff, NE
68649 North Bend, NE
68651 Osceola, NE
68652 Petersburg, NE
68653 Platte Center, NE
68654 Polk, NE
68655 Primrose, NE
68658 Rising City, NE
68659 Rogers, NE
68660 Saint Edward, NE
68661 Schuyler, NE
68662 Shelby, NE
68663 Silver Creek, NE
68664 Snyder, NE
68665 Spalding, NE
68666 Stromsburg, NE
68667 Surprise, NE
68667 Ulysses, NE
68669 Ulysses, NE

687

68701 Hadar, NE
68701 Norfolk, NE
68702 Norfolk, NE
68710 Allen, NE
68711 Amelia, NE
68713 Atkinson, NE
68714 Bassett, NE
68714 Rose, NE
68715 Battle Creek, NE
68716 Beemer, NE
68717 Belden, NE
68718 Bloomfield, NE
68719 Bristow, NE
68720 Brunswick, NE
68722 Anoka, NE
68722 Butte, NE
68723 Carroll, NE
68724 Center, NE
68725 Chambers, NE
68726 Clearwater, NE
68727 Coleridge, NE
68728 Concord, NE
68729 Bazile Mills, NE
68729 Creighton, NE
68730 Crofton, NE
68731 Dakota City, NE
68732 Dixon, NE
68733 Emerson, NE
68734 Emmet, NE
68735 Ewing, NE
68736 Fordyce, NE
68738 Hadar, NE
68739 Hartington, NE
68740 Hoskins, NE
68741 Hubbard, NE
68742 Inman, NE
68743 Jackson, NE
68745 Laurel, NE
68746 Lynch, NE
68746 Monowi, NE
68747 Mclean, NE
68748 Madison, NE
68749 Magnet, NE
68751 Maskell, NE
68752 Meadow Grove, NE
68753 Mills, NE
68755 Naper, NE
68756 Neligh, NE
68757 Newcastle, NE
68757 Obert, NE
68758 Newman Grove, NE
68759 Newport, NE
68760 Niobrara, NE
68760 Verdel, NE
68761 Oakdale, NE
68763 O' Neill, NE
68763 Oneill, NE
68764 Orchard, NE
68765 Foster, NE
68765 Osmond, NE
68766 Page, NE
68767 Pierce, NE
68768 Pilger, NE
68769 Plainview, NE
68770 Ponca, NE
68771 Randolph, NE
68771 Sholes, NE
68773 Royal, NE
68774 Saint Helena, NE
68776 South Sioux City, NE
68777 Spencer, NE
68778 Springview, NE
68779 Stanton, NE
68780 Stuart, NE
68781 Tilden, NE
68783 Verdigre, NE
68784 Wakefield, NE
68785 Waterbury, NE
68786 Wausa, NE
68787 Wayne, NE
68788 West Point, NE
68789 Winnetoon, NE
68790 Winside, NE
68791 Wisner, NE
68792 Wynot, NE

688

68801 Grand Island, NE
68802 Grand Island, NE
68803 Grand Island, NE
68810 Alda, NE
68812 Amherst, NE
68813 Anselmo, NE
68813 Milburn, NE
68814 Ansley, NE
68814 Berwyn, NE
68814 Weissert, NE
68815 Arcadia, NE
68816 Archer, NE
68817 Ashton, NE
68818 Aurora, NE
68820 Boelus, NE
68821 Brewster, NE
68822 Broken Bow, NE
68823 Burwell, NE
68824 Cairo, NE
68825 Callaway, NE
68826 Central City, NE
68827 Chapman, NE
68828 Comstock, NE
68831 Dannebrog, NE
68832 Doniphan, NE
68833 Dunning, NE
68834 Eddyville, NE
68835 Cotesfield, NE
68835 Elba, NE
68836 Elm Creek, NE
68837 Elyria, NE
68838 Farwell, NE
68840 Gibbon, NE
68841 Giltner, NE
68842 Greeley, NE
68843 Hampton, NE
68844 Hazard, NE
68845 Kearney, NE
68846 Hordville, NE
68847 Kearney, NE
68848 Kearney, NE
68849 Kearney, NE
68850 Lexington, NE
68852 Litchfield, NE
68853 Loup City, NE
68854 Marquette, NE
68855 Mason City, NE
68856 Merna, NE
68858 Miller, NE
68859 North Loup, NE
68860 Oconto, NE
68861 Odessa, NE
68862 Ord, NE
68863 Overton, NE
68864 Palmer, NE
68865 Phillips, NE
68866 Pleasanton, NE
68869 Ravenna, NE
68870 Riverdale, NE
68871 Rockville, NE
68872 Saint Libory, NE
68873 Saint Paul, NE
68874 Sargent, NE
68875 Scotia, NE
68876 Shelton, NE
68878 Sumner, NE
68879 Almeria, NE
68879 Taylor, NE
68881 Westerville, NE
68882 Wolbach, NE
68883 Prosser, NE
68883 Wood River, NE

689

68901 Hastings, NE
68902 Hastings, NE
68920 Alma, NE
68922 Arapahoe, NE
68923 Atlanta, NE
68924 Axtell, NE
68925 Ayr, NE
68926 Beaver City, NE
68927 Bertrand, NE
68928 Bladen, NE
68929 Bloomington, NE
68930 Blue Hill, NE
68930 Cowles, NE
68930 Rosemont, NE
68932 Campbell, NE
68933 Clay Center, NE
68934 Deweese, NE
68935 Edgar, NE
68936 Edison, NE
68937 Elwood, NE

68937 Johnson Lake, NE
68938 Fairfield, NE
68939 Franklin, NE
68940 Funk, NE
68941 Glenvil, NE
68942 Guide Rock, NE
68943 Hardy, NE
68944 Harvard, NE
68945 Heartwell, NE
68946 Hendley, NE
68947 Hildreth, NE
68948 Holbrook, NE
68949 Holdrege, NE
68950 Holstein, NE
68952 Inavale, NE
68954 Inland, NE
68955 Juniata, NE
68956 Kenesaw, NE
68957 Lawrence, NE
68958 Loomis, NE
68959 Minden, NE
68959 Norman, NE
68960 Naponee, NE
68961 Nelson, NE
68961 Nora, NE
68964 Oak, NE
68966 Orleans, NE
68967 Oxford, NE
68969 Holdrege, NE
68969 Ragan, NE
68970 Red Cloud, NE
68971 Huntley, NE
68971 Republican City, NE
68972 Riverton, NE
68973 Roseland, NE
68974 Ruskin, NE
68975 Saronville, NE
68976 Smithfield, NE
68977 Stamford, NE
68978 Superior, NE
68979 Sutton, NE
68980 Trumbull, NE
68981 Upland, NE
68982 Wilcox, NE

690

69001 Mc Cook, NE
69001 Mccook, NE
69020 Bartley, NE
69021 Benkelman, NE
69022 Cambridge, NE
69023 Champion, NE
69023 Lamar, NE
69024 Culbertson, NE
69025 Curtis, NE
69026 Danbury, NE
69027 Enders, NE
69028 Eustis, NE
69029 Farnam, NE
69030 Haigler, NE
69032 Hayes Center, NE
69033 Imperial, NE
69034 Indianola, NE
69036 Lebanon, NE
69037 Max, NE
69038 Maywood, NE
69039 Moorefield, NE
69040 Hamlet, NE
69040 Palisade, NE
69041 Parks, NE
69042 Stockville, NE
69043 Stratton, NE
69044 Trenton, NE
69045 Wauneta, NE
69046 Wilsonville, NE

691

69101 North Platte, NE
69103 North Platte, NE
69120 Arnold, NE
69121 Arthur, NE
69122 Big Springs, NE
69123 Brady, NE
69125 Broadwater, NE
69127 Brule, NE
69128 Bushnell, NE
69129 Chappell, NE
69130 Cozad, NE
69131 Dalton, NE
69132 Dickens, NE
69133 Dix, NE
69134 Elsie, NE
69135 Elsmere, NE
69138 Gothenburg, NE
69140 Grant, NE
69141 Gurley, NE
69142 Halsey, NE
69143 Hershey, NE
69144 Keystone, NE
69145 Kimball, NE
69146 Lemoyne, NE
69147 Lewellen, NE
69148 Lisco, NE
69149 Lodgepole, NE
69150 Madrid, NE
69151 Maxwell, NE
69152 Mullen, NE
69153 Ogallala, NE
69154 Oshkosh, NE
69155 Paxton, NE
69156 Potter, NE
69157 Purdum, NE
69160 Sidney, NE
69161 Seneca, NE
69162 Sidney, NE
69163 Stapleton, NE
69165 Sutherland, NE
69166 Brownlee, NE
69166 Thedford, NE
69167 Tryon, NE
69168 Venango, NE
69169 Wallace, NE
69170 Wellfleet, NE
69171 Willow Island, NE
69190 Oshkosh, NE

692

69201 Valentine, NE
69210 Ainsworth, NE
69211 Cody, NE
69212 Crookston, NE
69214 Johnstown, NE
69216 Kilgore, NE
69217 Long Pine, NE
69218 Merriman, NE
69219 Nenzel, NE
69220 Sparks, NE
69221 Wood Lake, NE

693

69301 Alliance, NE
69331 Angora, NE
69333 Ashby, NE
69334 Bayard, NE
69335 Bingham, NE
69336 Bridgeport, NE
69337 Chadron, NE
69339 Crawford, NE
69340 Ellsworth, NE
69341 Gering, NE
69343 Gordon, NE
69345 Harrisburg, NE
69346 Harrison, NE
69347 Hay Springs, NE
69348 Hemingford, NE
69350 Hyannis, NE
69351 Lakeside, NE
69352 Lyman, NE
69353 Mcgrew, NE
69354 Marsland, NE
69355 Melbeta, NE
69356 Minatare, NE
69357 Mitchell, NE
69358 Henry, NE
69358 Morrill, NE
69360 Rushville, NE
69361 Scottsbluff, NE
69363 Scottsbluff, NE
69365 Whiteclay, NE
69366 Whitman, NE
69367 Whitney, NE

700

70001 Metairie, LA
70002 Metairie, LA
70003 Metairie, LA
70004 Metairie, LA
70005 Metairie, LA
70006 Metairie, LA
70009 Metairie, LA
70010 Metairie, LA
70011 Metairie, LA
70030 Des Allemands, LA
70031 Ama, LA
70032 Arabi, LA
70033 Metairie, LA
70036 Barataria, LA
70037 Belle Chasse, LA
70038 Boothville, LA
70039 Boutte, LA
70040 Braithwaite, LA
70040 Carlisle, LA
70041 Buras, LA
70043 Chalmette, LA
70044 Chalmette, LA
70047 Destrehan, LA
70049 Edgard, LA
70050 Empire, LA
70051 Garyville, LA
70052 Gramercy, LA
70053 Gretna, LA
70054 Gretna, LA
70055 Metairie, LA
70056 Gretna, LA
70056 Terrytown, LA
70057 Hahnville, LA
70057 Killona, LA
70058 Harvey, LA
70059 Harvey, LA
70060 Metairie, LA
70062 Kenner, LA
70063 Kenner, LA
70064 Kenner, LA
70065 Kenner, LA
70067 Jean Lafitte, LA
70067 Lafitte, LA
70068 La Place, LA
70068 Montz, LA
70069 La Place, LA
70070 Luling, LA
70071 Lutcher, LA
70072 Marrero, LA
70073 Marrero, LA
70075 Meraux, LA
70076 Mount Airy, LA
70078 New Sarpy, LA
70079 Norco, LA
70080 Paradis, LA
70081 Pilottown, LA
70082 Davant, LA
70082 Pointe A La Hache, LA
70083 Port Sulphur, LA
70084 Reserve, LA
70085 Saint Bernard, LA
70086 Saint James, LA
70087 Saint Rose, LA
70090 Vacherie, LA
70091 Venice, LA
70092 Violet, LA
70093 Belle Chasse, LA
70094 Avondale, LA
70094 Bridge City, LA
70094 Fairfield, LA
70094 Nine Mile Point, LA
70094 Westwego, LA
70096 Westwego, LA
70097 Kenner, LA

701

70112 New Orleans, LA
70113 New Orleans, LA
70114 New Orleans, LA
70115 New Orleans, LA
70116 New Orleans, LA
70117 New Orleans, LA
70118 New Orleans, LA
70119 New Orleans, LA
70121 Jefferson, LA
70121 New Orleans, LA
70122 New Orleans, LA
70123 Elmwood, LA
70123 Harahan, LA
70123 New Orleans, LA
70123 River Ridge, LA
70124 New Orleans, LA
70125 New Orleans, LA
70126 New Orleans, LA
70127 New Orleans, LA
70128 New Orleans, LA
70129 New Orleans, LA
70130 New Orleans, LA
70131 New Orleans, LA
70139 New Orleans, LA
70141 New Orleans, LA
70142 New Orleans, LA
70143 New Orleans, LA
70145 New Orleans, LA
70146 New Orleans, LA
70148 New Orleans, LA
70150 New Orleans, LA
70151 New Orleans, LA
70152 New Orleans, LA
70153 New Orleans, LA
70154 New Orleans, LA
70156 New Orleans, LA
70157 New Orleans, LA
70158 New Orleans, LA
70159 New Orleans, LA
70160 New Orleans, LA
70161 New Orleans, LA
70162 New Orleans, LA
70163 New Orleans, LA
70164 New Orleans, LA
70165 New Orleans, LA
70166 New Orleans, LA
70167 New Orleans, LA
70170 New Orleans, LA
70172 New Orleans, LA
70174 New Orleans, LA
70175 New Orleans, LA
70176 New Orleans, LA
70177 New Orleans, LA
70178 New Orleans, LA
70179 New Orleans, LA
70181 New Orleans, LA
70182 New Orleans, LA
70183 New Orleans, LA
70184 New Orleans, LA
70185 New Orleans, LA
70186 New Orleans, LA
70187 New Orleans, LA
70189 New Orleans, LA
70190 New Orleans, LA
70195 New Orleans, LA

703

70301 Thibodaux, LA
70302 Thibodaux, LA
70310 Thibodaux, LA
70339 Pierre Part, LA
70340 Amelia, LA
70341 Belle Rose, LA
70342 Berwick, LA
70343 Bourg, LA
70344 Chauvin, LA
70345 Cut Off, LA
70346 Donaldsonville, LA
70346 Modeste, LA
70352 Donner, LA
70353 Dulac, LA
70354 Galliano, LA
70355 Gheens, LA
70356 Gibson, LA
70357 Golden Meadow, LA
70358 Grand Isle, LA
70359 Gray, LA
70360 Houma, LA
70361 Houma, LA
70363 Houma, LA
70364 Houma, LA
70371 Kraemer, LA
70372 Labadieville, LA
70373 Larose, LA
70374 Lockport, LA
70375 Mathews, LA
70377 Montegut, LA
70380 Morgan City, LA
70381 Morgan City, LA
70390 Napoleonville, LA
70391 Paincourtville, LA
70392 Patterson, LA
70393 Plattenville, LA
70394 Raceland, LA
70395 Schriever, LA
70397 Theriot, LA

704

70401 Hammond, LA
70402 Hammond, LA
70403 Hammond, LA
70404 Hammond, LA
70420 Abita Springs, LA
70421 Akers, LA
70422 Amite, LA
70422 Hillsdale, LA
70422 Montpelier, LA
70426 Angie, LA
70427 Bogalusa, LA
70429 Bogalusa, LA
70431 Bush, LA
70433 Covington, LA
70434 Covington, LA
70435 Covington, LA
70436 Fluker, LA
70437 Folsom, LA
70438 Franklinton, LA
70438 Sheridan, LA
70441 Greensburg, LA
70442 Husser, LA
70443 Independence, LA
70444 Kentwood, LA
70444 New Zion, LA
70445 Lacombe, LA
70446 Loranger, LA
70447 Madisonville, LA
70448 Mandeville, LA
70449 Maurepas, LA
70450 Mount Hermon, LA
70451 Natalbany, LA
70452 Pearl River, LA
70453 Pine Grove, LA
70454 Ponchatoula, LA
70455 Robert, LA
70456 Roseland, LA
70457 Saint Benedict, LA
70458 Slidell, LA
70459 Slidell, LA
70460 Slidell, LA
70461 Slidell, LA
70462 Springfield, LA
70463 Sun, LA
70464 Talisheek, LA
70465 Tangipahoa, LA
70466 Tickfaw, LA
70467 Angie, LA
70467 Varnado, LA
70469 Slidell, LA
70470 Mandeville, LA
70471 Mandeville, LA

705

70501 Lafayette, LA
70502 Lafayette, LA
70503 Lafayette, LA
70504 Lafayette, LA
70505 Lafayette, LA
70506 Lafayette, LA
70507 Lafayette, LA
70508 Lafayette, LA
70509 Lafayette, LA
70510 Abbeville, LA
70510 Cow Island, LA
70510 Meaux, LA
70511 Abbeville, LA
70512 Arnaudville, LA
70513 Avery Island, LA
70514 Baldwin, LA
70515 Basile, LA
70516 Branch, LA
70517 Breaux Bridge, LA
70517 Butte Larose, LA
70517 Henderson, LA
70518 Broussard, LA
70519 Cade, LA
70520 Carencro, LA
70521 Cecilia, LA
70522 Centerville, LA
70523 Charenton, LA
70524 Chataignier, LA
70525 Church Point, LA
70526 Crowley, LA
70527 Crowley, LA
70528 Delcambre, LA
70529 Duson, LA
70531 Egan, LA
70532 Elton, LA
70533 Erath, LA
70534 Estherwood, LA
70535 Eunice, LA
70537 Evangeline, LA
70538 Cypremort Point, LA
70538 Franklin, LA
70540 Garden City, LA
70541 Grand Coteau, LA
70542 Gueydan, LA
70543 Iota, LA
70544 Jeanerette, LA
70546 Jennings, LA
70548 Kaplan, LA
70549 Lake Arthur, LA
70550 Lawtell, LA
70551 Leonville, LA
70552 Loreauville, LA
70554 Mamou, LA
70555 Maurice, LA
70556 Mermentau, LA
70558 Milton, LA
70559 Midland, LA
70559 Morse, LA
70560 New Iberia, LA
70562 New Iberia, LA
70563 New Iberia, LA
70569 Lydia, LA
70570 Opelousas, LA
70571 Opelousas, LA
70575 Perry, LA
70576 Pine Prairie, LA
70577 Port Barre, LA
70578 Rayne, LA
70580 Reddell, LA
70581 Roanoke, LA
70582 Parks, LA
70582 Saint Martinville, LA
70583 Scott, LA
70584 Cankton, LA
70584 Sunset, LA
70585 Turkey Creek, LA
70586 Ville Platte, LA
70589 Washington, LA
70591 Welsh, LA
70592 Youngsville, LA
70593 Lafayette, LA
70596 Lafayette, LA
70598 Lafayette, LA

706

70601 Lake Charles, LA
70602 Lake Charles, LA
70605 Lake Charles, LA
70606 Lake Charles, LA
70607 Lake Charles, LA
70609 Lake Charles, LA
70611 Lake Charles, LA
70611 Moss Bluff, LA
70612 Lake Charles, LA
70615 Lake Charles, LA
70616 Lake Charles, LA
70629 Lake Charles, LA
70630 Bell City, LA
70631 Cameron, LA
70632 Creole, LA
70633 Dequincy, LA
70634 Deridder, LA
70637 Dry Creek, LA
70638 Elizabeth, LA
70639 Evans, LA
70640 Fenton, LA
70643 Grand Chenier, LA

70644 Grant, LA
70645 Hackberry, LA
70646 Hayes, LA
70647 Iowa, LA
70648 Kinder, LA
70650 Lacassine, LA
70651 Leblanc, LA
70652 Longville, LA
70653 Fields, LA
70653 Merryville, LA
70654 Mittie, LA
70655 Oberlin, LA
70656 Fullerton, LA
70656 Pitkin, LA
70657 Ragley, LA
70658 Reeves, LA
70659 Rosepine, LA
70660 Singer, LA
70661 Starks, LA
70662 Sugartown, LA
70663 Sulphur, LA
70664 Sulphur, LA
70665 Sulphur, LA
70668 Vinton, LA
70669 Westlake, LA

707

70704 Baker, LA
70706 Denham Springs, LA
70707 Gonzales, LA
70710 Addis, LA
70711 Albany, LA
70712 Angola, LA
70714 Baker, LA
70715 Batchelor, LA
70718 Brittany, LA
70719 Brusly, LA
70721 Carville, LA
70722 Clinton, LA
70723 Convent, LA
70725 Darrow, LA
70726 Denham Springs, LA
70726 Dennis Mills, LA
70726 Port Vincent, LA
70727 Denham Springs, LA
70728 Duplessis, LA
70729 Bueche, LA
70729 Erwinville, LA
70730 Ethel, LA
70732 Fordoche, LA
70733 French Settlement, LA
70734 Geismar, LA
70736 Glynn, LA
70737 Gonzales, LA
70738 Burnside, LA
70739 Greenwell Springs, LA
70740 Grosse Tete, LA
70743 Hester, LA
70744 Holden, LA
70747 Innis, LA
70748 Jackson, LA
70748 The Bluffs, LA
70749 Jarreau, LA
70750 Krotz Springs, LA
70752 Lakeland, LA
70753 Lettsworth, LA
70754 Livingston, LA
70755 Livonia, LA
70756 Blanks, LA
70756 Lottie, LA
70757 Maringouin, LA
70757 Ramah, LA
70759 Labarre, LA
70759 Morganza, LA
70760 New Roads, LA
70761 Norwood, LA
70762 Oscar, LA
70762 Torbert, LA
70763 Paulina, LA
70764 Plaquemine, LA
70765 Plaquemine, LA
70767 Port Allen, LA
70769 Galvez, LA
70769 Prairieville, LA
70770 Pride, LA
70772 Rosedale, LA
70773 Rougon, LA
70774 Saint Amant, LA
70775 Bains, LA
70775 Hardwood, LA
70775 Saint Francisville, LA
70775 Starhill, LA
70776 Iberville, LA
70776 Saint Gabriel, LA
70777 Slaughter, LA
70778 Sorrento, LA
70780 Sunshine, LA
70782 Tunica, LA
70783 Ventress, LA
70784 Wakefield, LA
70785 Walker, LA
70786 Watson, LA
70787 Weyanoke, LA
70788 Bayou Goula, LA
70788 White Castle, LA
70789 Wilson, LA
70791 Zachary, LA
70792 Uncle Sam, LA

708

70801 Baton Rouge, LA
70802 Baton Rouge, LA
70803 Baton Rouge, LA
70804 Baton Rouge, LA
70805 Baton Rouge, LA
70806 Baton Rouge, LA
70807 Baton Rouge, LA
70807 Scotlandville, LA
70808 Baton Rouge, LA
70809 Baton Rouge, LA
70810 Baton Rouge, LA
70811 Baton Rouge, LA
70811 Scotlandville, LA
70812 Baton Rouge, LA
70813 Baton Rouge, LA
70814 Baton Rouge, LA
70815 Baton Rouge, LA
70816 Baton Rouge, LA
70817 Baton Rouge, LA
70818 Baton Rouge, LA
70819 Baton Rouge, LA
70820 Baton Rouge, LA
70821 Baton Rouge, LA
70822 Baton Rouge, LA
70823 Baton Rouge, LA
70825 Baton Rouge, LA
70826 Baton Rouge, LA
70827 Baton Rouge, LA
70831 Baton Rouge, LA
70833 Baton Rouge, LA
70835 Baton Rouge, LA
70836 Baton Rouge, LA
70837 Baton Rouge, LA
70837 Central, LA
70873 Baton Rouge, LA
70874 Baton Rouge, LA
70879 Baton Rouge, LA
70884 Baton Rouge, LA
70891 Baton Rouge, LA
70892 Baton Rouge, LA
70893 Baton Rouge, LA
70894 Baton Rouge, LA
70895 Baton Rouge, LA
70896 Baton Rouge, LA
70898 Baton Rouge, LA

710

71001 Arcadia, LA
71002 Ashland, LA
71003 Athens, LA
71004 Belcher, LA
71006 Benton, LA
71007 Bethany, LA
71008 Bienville, LA
71008 Bryceland, LA
71009 Blanchard, LA
71016 Castor, LA
71018 Cotton Valley, LA
71019 Coushatta, LA
71021 Cullen, LA
71023 Doyline, LA
71024 Dubberly, LA
71027 Frierson, LA
71028 Gibsland, LA
71029 Gilliam, LA
71030 Gloster, LA
71031 Goldonna, LA
71032 Grand Cane, LA
71033 Greenwood, LA
71034 Hall Summit, LA
71037 Haughton, LA
71038 Haynesville, LA
71039 Heflin, LA
71040 Homer, LA
71043 Hosston, LA
71044 Ida, LA
71044 Mira, LA
71045 Jamestown, LA
71046 Keatchie, LA
71047 Keithville, LA
71048 Lisbon, LA
71049 Logansport, LA
71049 Stanley, LA
71050 Longstreet, LA
71051 Elm Grove, LA
71052 Mansfield, LA
71052 South Mansfield, LA
71055 Dixie Inn, LA
71055 Minden, LA
71058 Minden, LA
71060 Mooringsport, LA
71061 Oil City, LA
71063 Pelican, LA
71064 Plain Dealing, LA
71065 Pleasant Hill, LA
71066 Powhatan, LA
71067 Princeton, LA
71068 Ringgold, LA
71069 Rodessa, LA
71070 Chestnut, LA
71070 Creston, LA
71070 Saline, LA
71071 Sarepta, LA
71072 Shongaloo, LA
71073 Sibley, LA
71075 Springhill, LA
71078 Stonewall, LA
71079 Summerfield, LA
71080 Taylor, LA
71082 Trees, LA
71082 Vivian, LA

711

71101 Shreveport, LA
71102 Shreveport, LA
71103 Shreveport, LA
71104 Shreveport, LA
71105 Shreveport, LA
71106 Forbing, LA
71106 Shreveport, LA
71107 Dixie, LA
71107 Shreveport, LA
71108 Shreveport, LA
71109 Shreveport, LA
71110 Barksdale Afb, LA
71111 Bossier City, LA
71112 Bossier City, LA
71113 Bossier City, LA
71115 Caspiana, LA
71115 Shreveport, LA
71118 Shreveport, LA
71119 Shreveport, LA
71120 Shreveport, LA
71129 Shreveport, LA
71130 Shreveport, LA
71133 Shreveport, LA
71134 Shreveport, LA
71135 Shreveport, LA
71136 Shreveport, LA
71137 Shreveport, LA
71138 Shreveport, LA
71148 Shreveport, LA
71149 Shreveport, LA
71150 Shreveport, LA
71151 Shreveport, LA
71152 Shreveport, LA
71153 Shreveport, LA
71154 Shreveport, LA
71156 Shreveport, LA
71161 Shreveport, LA
71162 Shreveport, LA
71163 Shreveport, LA
71164 Shreveport, LA
71165 Shreveport, LA
71166 Shreveport, LA
71171 Bossier City, LA
71172 Bossier City, LA

712

71201 Monroe, LA
71202 Monroe, LA
71202 Richwood, LA
71203 Monroe, LA
71207 Monroe, LA
71209 Monroe, LA
71210 Monroe, LA
71211 Monroe, LA
71212 Monroe, LA
71213 Monroe, LA
71217 Monroe, LA
71218 Archibald, LA
71219 Baskin, LA
71220 Bastrop, LA
71221 Bastrop, LA
71222 Bernice, LA
71223 Bonita, LA
71225 Calhoun, LA
71226 Chatham, LA
71227 Choudrant, LA
71229 Collinston, LA
71230 Crowville, LA
71232 Delhi, LA
71232 Warden, LA
71232 Waverly, LA
71233 Delta, LA
71234 Downsville, LA
71235 Dubach, LA
71237 Epps, LA
71238 Eros, LA
71240 Fairbanks, LA
71241 Farmerville, LA
71242 Forest, LA
71243 Extension, LA
71243 Fort Necessity, LA
71245 Grambling, LA
71247 Hodge, LA
71249 Jigger, LA
71250 Jones, LA
71251 Jonesboro, LA
71253 Kilbourne, LA
71254 Lake Providence, LA
71256 Junction City, LA
71256 Lillie, LA
71259 Mangham, LA
71260 Linville, LA
71260 Marion, LA
71261 Mer Rouge, LA
71263 Oak Grove, LA
71263 Terry, LA
71264 Oak Ridge, LA
71266 Pioneer, LA
71268 Quitman, LA
71269 Alto, LA
71269 Girard, LA
71269 Holly Ridge, LA
71269 Rayville, LA
71270 Ruston, LA
71272 Ruston, LA
71273 Ruston, LA
71275 Simsboro, LA
71276 Sondheimer, LA
71277 Spearsville, LA
71279 Start, LA
71280 Spencer, LA
71280 Sterlington, LA
71281 Swartz, LA
71282 Mound, LA
71282 Richmond, LA
71282 Tallulah, LA
71284 Tallulah, LA
71286 Transylvania, LA
71291 West Monroe, LA
71292 West Monroe, LA
71294 West Monroe, LA
71295 Winnsboro, LA

713

71301 Alexandria, LA
71302 Alexandria, LA
71303 Alexandria, LA
71306 Alexandria, LA
71307 Alexandria, LA
71309 Alexandria, LA
71315 Alexandria, LA
71316 Acme, LA
71320 Bordelonville, LA
71322 Bunkie, LA
71322 Eola, LA
71322 Whitehall, LA
71323 Center Point, LA
71324 Chase, LA
71325 Cheneyville, LA
71326 Clayton, LA
71327 Cottonport, LA
71328 Buckeye, LA
71328 Deville, LA
71329 Dupont, LA
71330 Echo, LA
71331 Effie, LA
71331 Vick, LA
71333 Evergreen, LA
71333 Goudeau, LA
71334 Ferriday, LA
71334 Frogmore, LA
71334 Ridgecrest, LA
71336 Gilbert, LA
71339 Hamburg, LA
71340 Harrisonburg, LA
71341 Hessmer, LA
71342 Jena, LA
71343 Jonesville, LA
71343 Larto, LA
71345 Lebeau, LA
71345 Rosa, LA
71346 Lecompte, LA
71348 Libuse, LA
71350 Mansura, LA
71351 Marksville, LA
71353 Melville, LA
71354 Monterey, LA
71355 Moreauville, LA
71356 Le Moyen, LA
71356 Morrow, LA
71357 Newellton, LA
71358 Palmetto, LA
71359 Pineville, LA
71360 Camp Beauregard, LA
71360 Kolin, LA
71360 Pineville, LA
71361 Pineville, LA
71362 Plaucheville, LA
71363 Rhinehart, LA
71365 Ruby, LA
71366 Saint Joseph, LA
71367 Saint Landry, LA
71368 Sicily Island, LA
71369 Simmesport, LA
71371 Trout, LA
71373 Vidalia, LA
71375 Waterproof, LA
71377 Wildsville, LA
71378 Wisner, LA

714

71401 Aimwell, LA
71403 Anacoco, LA
71404 Atlanta, LA
71405 Ball, LA
71405 Pineville, LA
71405 Pollock, LA
71406 Belmont, LA
71407 Bentley, LA
71409 Boyce, LA
71409 Gardner, LA
71410 Calvin, LA
71411 Campti, LA
71414 Clarence, LA
71415 Clarks, LA
71416 Cloutierville, LA
71416 Derry, LA
71417 Colfax, LA
71418 Columbia, LA
71419 Converse, LA
71419 Mitchell, LA
71422 Dodson, LA
71423 Creola, LA
71423 Dry Prong, LA
71424 Elmer, LA
71425 Enterprise, LA
71426 Fisher, LA
71427 Flatwoods, LA
71428 Flora, LA
71429 Florien, LA
71430 Forest Hill, LA
71431 Gardner, LA
71432 Georgetown, LA
71433 Glenmora, LA
71433 Melder, LA
71434 Gorum, LA
71435 Grayson, LA
71438 Hineston, LA
71438 Lacamp, LA
71438 Leander, LA
71439 Hornbeck, LA
71440 Joyce, LA
71441 Kelly, LA
71443 Kurthwood, LA
71446 Hicks, LA
71446 Leesville, LA
71447 Chopin, LA
71447 Clifton, LA
71447 Lena, LA
71448 Longleaf, LA
71449 Many, LA
71450 Marthaville, LA
71452 Melrose, LA
71454 Montgomery, LA
71454 Verda, LA
71455 Mora, LA
71456 Natchez, LA
71457 Cypress, LA
71457 Natchitoches, LA
71458 Natchitoches, LA
71459 Fort Polk, LA
71459 Leesville, LA
71460 Negreet, LA
71461 New Llano, LA
71462 Noble, LA
71463 Oakdale, LA
71465 Olla, LA
71466 Otis, LA
71467 Pollock, LA
71468 Provencal, LA
71469 Robeline, LA
71471 Saint Maurice, LA
71472 Sieper, LA
71473 Sikes, LA
71474 Simpson, LA
71474 Temple, LA
71475 Slagle, LA
71477 Tioga, LA
71479 Tullos, LA
71480 Urania, LA
71483 Winnfield, LA
71485 Woodworth, LA
71486 Zwolle, LA
71496 Leesville, LA
71497 Natchitoches, LA

716

71601 Pine Bluff, AR
71602 Pine Bluff, AR
71602 White Hall, AR
71603 Pine Bluff, AR
71611 Pine Bluff, AR
71612 Pine Bluff, AR
71612 White Hall, AR
71613 Pine Bluff, AR
71630 Arkansas City, AR
71631 Banks, AR
71635 Crossett, AR
71638 Collins, AR
71638 Dermott, AR
71639 Dumas, AR
71640 Eudora, AR
71642 Fountain Hill, AR
71643 Gould, AR
71644 Grady, AR
71646 Hamburg, AR
71647 Hermitage, AR
71651 Jersey, AR
71652 Kingsland, AR
71653 Jennie, AR

71653 Lake Village, AR
71654 Mc Gehee, AR
71654 Mcgehee, AR
71655 Monticello, AR
71656 Monticello, AR
71657 Monticello, AR
71658 Montrose, AR
71659 Moscow, AR
71660 New Edinburg, AR
71661 Parkdale, AR
71662 Pickens, AR
71663 Portland, AR
71665 Rison, AR
71666 Mc Gehee, AR
71666 Mcgehee, AR
71666 Rohwer, AR
71667 Star City, AR
71670 Tillar, AR
71671 Warren, AR
71674 Watson, AR
71675 Wilmar, AR
71676 Wilmot, AR
71677 Winchester, AR
71678 Yorktown, AR

717

71701 Camden, AR
71701 East Camden, AR
71711 Camden, AR
71720 Bearden, AR
71721 Beirne, AR
71722 Bluff City, AR
71724 Calion, AR
71725 Carthage, AR
71726 Chidester, AR
71726 Reader, AR
71728 Curtis, AR
71730 El Dorado, AR
71731 El Dorado, AR
71740 Emerson, AR
71742 Fordyce, AR
71743 Gurdon, AR
71744 Hampton, AR
71745 Harrell, AR
71747 Huttig, AR
71748 Ivan, AR
71749 Junction City, AR
71750 Lawson, AR
71751 Louann, AR
71752 Mc Neil, AR
71753 Magnolia, AR
71753 Village, AR
71754 Magnolia, AR
71758 Mount Holly, AR
71759 Norphlet, AR
71762 Smackover, AR
71763 Manning, AR
71763 Sparkman, AR
71764 Stephens, AR
71765 Strong, AR
71766 Thornton, AR
71770 Waldo, AR
71772 Whelen Springs, AR

718

71801 Hope, AR
71802 Hope, AR
71820 Alleene, AR
71822 Ashdown, AR
71823 Ben Lomond, AR
71825 Blevins, AR
71826 Bradley, AR
71827 Buckner, AR
71828 Cale, AR
71831 Columbus, AR
71832 De Queen, AR
71833 Dierks, AR
71834 Doddridge, AR
71835 Emmet, AR
71836 Foreman, AR
71837 Fouke, AR
71838 Fulton, AR
71839 Garland City, AR
71840 Genoa, AR
71841 Gillham, AR
71842 Horatio, AR
71845 Lewisville, AR
71846 Lockesburg, AR
71847 Mc Caskill, AR
71851 Mineral Springs, AR
71852 Nashville, AR
71853 Ogden, AR
71854 Texarkana, AR
71855 Ozan, AR
71857 Laneburg, AR
71857 Prescott, AR
71858 Rosston, AR
71859 Saratoga, AR
71860 Stamps, AR
71861 Taylor, AR
71862 Washington, AR
71864 Willisville, AR
71865 Wilton, AR
71866 Winthrop, AR

719

71901 Fountain Lake, AR
71901 Hot Springs National Park, AR
71909 Hot Springs Village, AR
71910 Hot Springs National Park, AR
71910 Hot Springs Village, AR
71913 Hot Springs National Park, AR
71913 Lake Hamilton, AR
71914 Hot Springs National Park, AR
71920 Alpine, AR
71921 Alpine, AR
71921 Amity, AR
71922 Antoine, AR
71923 Arkadelphia, AR
71923 Caddo Valley, AR
71929 Bismarck, AR
71932 Board Camp, AR
71933 Bonnerdale, AR
71935 Caddo Gap, AR
71937 Cove, AR
71937 Hatton, AR
71940 Delight, AR
71941 Donaldson, AR
71942 Friendship, AR
71943 Glenwood, AR
71944 Grannis, AR
71945 Hatfield, AR
71949 Buckville, AR
71949 Jessieville, AR
71950 Kirby, AR
71952 Langley, AR
71953 Mena, AR
71956 Mountain Pine, AR
71957 Mount Ida, AR
71958 Murfreesboro, AR
71959 Newhope, AR
71960 Norman, AR
71961 Oden, AR
71961 Pine Ridge, AR
71962 Okolona, AR
71964 Pearcy, AR
71965 Pencil Bluff, AR
71966 Oden, AR
71966 Pine Ridge, AR
71968 Royal, AR
71969 Sims, AR
71970 Story, AR
71971 Umpire, AR
71972 Vandervoort, AR
71973 Wickes, AR
71998 Arkadelphia, AR
71999 Arkadelphia, AR

720

72001 Adona, AR
72002 Alexander, AR
72003 Almyra, AR
72004 Altheimer, AR
72005 Amagon, AR
72005 Balch, AR
72006 Augusta, AR
72007 Austin, AR
72010 Bald Knob, AR
72011 Bauxite, AR
72012 Beebe, AR
72013 Bee Branch, AR
72014 Beedeville, AR
72015 Benton, AR
72015 Bryant, AR
72015 Haskell, AR
72015 Tull, AR
72016 Bigelow, AR
72017 Biscoe, AR
72018 Benton, AR
72019 Benton, AR
72019 Bryant, AR
72020 Bradford, AR
72021 Brinkley, AR
72022 Benton, AR
72022 Bryant, AR
72023 Cabot, AR
72024 Carlisle, AR
72025 Casa, AR
72026 Casscoe, AR
72027 Center Ridge, AR
72028 Choctaw, AR
72029 Clarendon, AR
72030 Cleveland, AR
72031 Clinton, AR
72032 Conway, AR
72033 Conway, AR
72034 Conway, AR
72035 Conway, AR
72036 Cotton Plant, AR
72037 Coy, AR
72038 Crocketts Bluff, AR
72039 Damascus, AR
72039 Twin Groves, AR
72040 Des Arc, AR
72041 De Valls Bluff, AR
72041 Devalls Bluff, AR
72042 De Witt, AR
72042 Dewitt, AR
72043 Diaz, AR
72044 Edgemont, AR
72045 El Paso, AR
72046 England, AR
72047 Enola, AR
72048 Ethel, AR
72051 Fox, AR
72052 Garner, AR
72053 College Station, AR
72055 Gillett, AR
72057 Grapevine, AR
72058 Greenbrier, AR
72059 Gregory, AR
72060 Griffithville, AR
72061 Guy, AR
72063 Hattieville, AR
72064 Hazen, AR
72065 Hensley, AR
72066 Hickory Plains, AR
72067 Greers Ferry, AR
72067 Higden, AR
72068 Higginson, AR
72069 Holly Grove, AR
72070 Houston, AR
72072 Humnoke, AR
72073 Humphrey, AR
72074 Hunter, AR
72075 Jacksonport, AR
72076 Gravel Ridge, AR
72076 Jacksonville, AR
72076 Little Rock Afb, AR
72076 Lrafb, AR
72078 Jacksonville, AR
72079 Jefferson, AR
72080 Jerusalem, AR
72081 Judsonia, AR
72081 Steprock, AR
72082 Kensett, AR
72083 Keo, AR
72084 Leola, AR
72085 Letona, AR
72086 Lonoke, AR
72087 Lonsdale, AR
72088 Fairfield Bay, AR
72088 Shirley, AR
72089 Bryant, AR
72099 Jacksonville, AR
72099 Little Rock Afb, AR
72099 Little Rock Air Force Base, AR
72099 Lrafb, AR

721

72101 Fair Oaks, AR
72101 Howell, AR
72101 Mc Crory, AR
72101 Mccrory, AR
72102 Mc Rae, AR
72103 Mabelvale, AR
72103 Shannon Hills, AR
72104 Malvern, AR
72104 Rockport, AR
72105 Jones Mill, AR
72105 Malvern, AR
72106 Mayflower, AR
72107 Menifee, AR
72108 Monroe, AR
72110 Morrilton, AR
72110 Oppelo, AR
72111 Mount Vernon, AR
72112 Newport, AR
72113 Maumelle, AR
72113 North Little Rock, AR
72120 Sherwood, AR
72121 Pangburn, AR
72122 Paron, AR
72123 Patterson, AR
72124 North Little Rock, AR
72124 Sherwood, AR
72125 Perry, AR
72126 Perryville, AR
72127 Plumerville, AR
72128 Poyen, AR
72129 Prattsville, AR
72130 Prim, AR
72131 Quitman, AR
72132 Redfield, AR
72133 Reydell, AR
72134 Roe, AR
72135 Roland, AR
72136 Romance, AR
72137 Rose Bud, AR
72139 Russell, AR
72140 Saint Charles, AR
72141 Scotland, AR
72142 Scott, AR
72143 Georgetown, AR
72143 Searcy, AR
72145 Searcy, AR
72149 Searcy, AR
72150 Sheridan, AR
72152 Sherrill, AR
72153 Shirley, AR
72156 Solgohachia, AR
72157 Springfield, AR
72158 Benton, AR
72160 Stuttgart, AR
72164 Sweet Home, AR
72165 Thida, AR
72166 Tichnor, AR
72167 Traskwood, AR
72168 Tucker, AR
72169 Tupelo, AR
72170 Ulm, AR
72173 Holland, AR
72173 Vilonia, AR
72175 Wabbaseka, AR
72176 Ward, AR
72178 West Point, AR
72179 Wilburn, AR
72180 Woodson, AR
72181 Wooster, AR
72182 Wright, AR
72183 Wrightsville, AR
72190 North Little Rock, AR
72199 Camp Robinson, AR
72199 Nlr, AR
72199 No Little Rock, AR
72199 North Little Rock, AR

722

72201 Little Rock, AR
72202 Little Rock, AR
72203 Little Rock, AR
72204 Little Rock, AR
72205 Little Rock, AR
72206 Little Rock, AR
72207 Cammack Village, AR
72207 Little Rock, AR
72209 Little Rock, AR
72210 Little Rock, AR
72211 Little Rock, AR
72212 Little Rock, AR
72214 Little Rock, AR
72215 Little Rock, AR
72216 Little Rock, AR
72217 Little Rock, AR
72219 Little Rock, AR
72221 Little Rock, AR
72222 Little Rock, AR
72223 Little Rock, AR
72225 Little Rock, AR
72227 Little Rock, AR
72231 Little Rock, AR
72255 Little Rock, AR
72260 Little Rock, AR
72295 Little Rock, AR

723

72301 West Memphis, AR
72303 West Memphis, AR
72310 Armorel, AR
72311 Aubrey, AR
72312 Barton, AR
72313 Bassett, AR
72315 Blytheville, AR
72315 Gosnell, AR
72316 Blytheville, AR
72319 Blytheville, AR
72319 Gosnell, AR
72320 Brickeys, AR
72321 Burdette, AR
72322 Caldwell, AR
72324 Birdeye, AR
72324 Cherry Valley, AR
72325 Clarkedale, AR
72326 Colt, AR
72327 Crawfordsville, AR
72328 Crumrod, AR
72329 Driver, AR
72330 Dyess, AR
72331 Earle, AR
72331 Twist, AR
72332 Edmondson, AR
72333 Elaine, AR
72335 Forrest City, AR
72336 Forrest City, AR
72338 Frenchmans Bayou, AR
72339 Gilmore, AR
72340 Goodwin, AR
72341 Haynes, AR
72342 Helena, AR
72346 Heth, AR
72347 Hickory Ridge, AR
72348 Horseshoe Lake, AR
72348 Hughes, AR
72350 Joiner, AR
72351 Keiser, AR
72352 La Grange, AR
72353 Lambrook, AR
72354 Lepanto, AR
72355 Lexa, AR
72358 Luxora, AR
72359 Madison, AR
72360 Marianna, AR
72364 Marion, AR
72365 Marked Tree, AR
72366 Marvell, AR
72367 Mellwood, AR
72368 Moro, AR
72369 Oneida, AR
72370 Osceola, AR
72372 Palestine, AR
72373 Parkin, AR
72374 Poplar Grove, AR
72376 Proctor, AR
72377 Rivervale, AR
72379 Snow Lake, AR
72383 Turner, AR
72384 Turrell, AR
72386 Tyronza, AR
72387 Vanndale, AR
72389 Wabash, AR
72390 West Helena, AR
72391 West Ridge, AR
72392 Wheatley, AR
72394 Round Pond, AR
72394 Widener, AR
72395 Wilson, AR
72396 Wynne, AR

724

72401 Jonesboro, AR
72402 Jonesboro, AR
72403 Jonesboro, AR
72404 Jonesboro, AR
72410 Alicia, AR
72411 Bay, AR
72412 Beech Grove, AR
72413 Biggers, AR
72414 Black Oak, AR
72415 Black Rock, AR
72416 Bono, AR
72417 Brookland, AR
72419 Caraway, AR
72421 Cash, AR
72422 Corning, AR
72424 Datto, AR
72425 Delaplaine, AR
72426 Dell, AR
72427 Egypt, AR
72428 Etowah, AR
72429 Fisher, AR
72430 Greenway, AR
72431 Grubbs, AR
72432 Harrisburg, AR
72433 Hoxie, AR
72434 Imboden, AR
72435 Knobel, AR
72435 Peach Orchard, AR
72436 Lafe, AR
72436 Marmaduke, AR
72437 Lake City, AR
72438 Leachville, AR
72440 Lynn, AR
72441 Mc Dougal, AR
72442 Manila, AR
72443 Marmaduke, AR
72444 Maynard, AR
72445 Minturn, AR
72447 Monette, AR
72449 O Kean, AR
72450 Paragould, AR
72451 Paragould, AR
72453 Peach Orchard, AR
72454 Piggott, AR
72455 Pocahontas, AR
72456 Pollard, AR
72457 Portia, AR
72458 Powhatan, AR
72459 Ravenden, AR
72460 Ravenden Springs, AR
72461 Rector, AR
72462 Reyno, AR
72464 Saint Francis, AR
72465 Sedgwick, AR
72466 Smithville, AR
72467 State University, AR
72469 Calamine, AR
72469 Strawberry, AR
72470 Success, AR
72471 Swifton, AR
72472 Trumann, AR
72473 Tuckerman, AR
72474 Walcott, AR
72475 Waldenburg, AR
72476 Walnut Ridge, AR
72476 Williams Baptist College, AR
72478 Warm Springs, AR
72479 Weiner, AR
72482 Williford, AR

725

72501 Batesville, AR
72503 Batesville, AR

72512 Franklin, AR
72512 Horseshoe Bend, AR
72513 Ash Flat, AR
72515 Bexar, AR
72517 Brockwell, AR
72519 Calico Rock, AR
72519 Jordan, AR
72520 Camp, AR
72521 Cave City, AR
72522 Charlotte, AR
72523 Concord, AR
72524 Cord, AR
72525 Cherokee Village, AR
72526 Cushman, AR
72527 Desha, AR
72528 Dolph, AR
72529 Cherokee Village, AR
72529 Hardy, AR
72530 Drasco, AR
72531 Elizabeth, AR
72532 Evening Shade, AR
72533 Fifty Six, AR
72533 Mountain View, AR
72534 Floral, AR
72536 Franklin, AR
72537 Gamaliel, AR
72538 Gepp, AR
72539 Glencoe, AR
72540 Guion, AR
72542 Hardy, AR
72542 Highland, AR
72543 Heber Springs, AR
72544 Henderson, AR
72545 Heber Springs, AR
72546 Ida, AR
72550 Locust Grove, AR
72553 Magness, AR
72554 Mammoth Spring, AR
72555 Marcella, AR
72556 Boswell, AR
72556 Melbourne, AR
72556 Zion, AR
72560 Hanover, AR
72560 Mountain View, AR
72561 Mount Pleasant, AR
72562 Newark, AR
72564 Oil Trough, AR
72565 Oxford, AR
72566 Pineville, AR
72567 Pleasant Grove, AR
72568 Pleasant Plains, AR
72569 Poughkeepsie, AR
72571 Rosie, AR
72572 Saffell, AR
72573 Sage, AR
72575 Salado, AR
72576 Moko, AR
72576 Salem, AR
72577 Sidney, AR
72578 Sturkie, AR
72579 Sulphur Rock, AR
72581 Tumbling Shoals, AR
72583 Viola, AR
72584 Violet Hill, AR
72585 Wideman, AR
72587 Wiseman, AR

726

72601 Harrison, AR
72602 Harrison, AR
72611 Alpena, AR
72613 Beaver, AR
72615 Bergman, AR
72616 Berryville, AR
72617 Big Flat, AR
72617 Harriet, AR
72619 Bull Shoals, AR
72623 Clarkridge, AR
72624 Compton, AR
72626 Cotter, AR
72628 Deer, AR
72629 Dennard, AR
72630 Diamond City, AR
72631 Busch, AR
72631 Eureka Springs, AR
72631 Holiday Island, AR
72632 Eureka Springs, AR
72633 Everton, AR
72634 Flippin, AR
72635 Gassville, AR
72636 Gilbert, AR
72638 Green Forest, AR
72639 Cozahome, AR
72639 Harriet, AR
72640 Hasty, AR
72641 Jasper, AR
72642 Lakeview, AR
72644 Diamond City, AR
72644 Lead Hill, AR
72645 Leslie, AR
72648 Marble Falls, AR
72650 Marshall, AR
72651 Midway, AR
72653 Mountain Home, AR
72653 Salesville, AR
72654 Mountain Home, AR
72655 Bass, AR
72655 Mount Judea, AR
72657 Timbo, AR
72658 Norfork, AR
72658 Old Joe, AR
72659 Norfork, AR
72660 Oak Grove, AR
72661 Oakland, AR
72661 Price Place, AR
72662 Omaha, AR
72663 Onia, AR
72666 Parthenon, AR
72668 Peel, AR
72669 Pindall, AR
72670 Ponca, AR
72672 Pyatt, AR
72675 Saint Joe, AR
72677 Summit, AR
72679 Tilly, AR
72680 Alco, AR
72680 Timbo, AR
72682 Bruno, AR
72682 Valley Springs, AR
72683 Vendor, AR
72685 Western Grove, AR
72686 Witts Springs, AR
72687 Yellville, AR

727

72701 Fayetteville, AR
72702 Fayetteville, AR
72703 Fayetteville, AR
72704 Fayetteville, AR
72704 Wheeler, AR
72711 Avoca, AR
72712 Bentonville, AR
72714 Bella Vista, AR
72715 Bella Vista, AR
72716 Bentonville, AR
72717 Canehill, AR
72718 Cave Springs, AR
72719 Centerton, AR
72721 Combs, AR
72722 Decatur, AR
72727 Elkins, AR
72728 Elm Springs, AR
72729 Evansville, AR
72730 Farmington, AR
72730 Fayetteville, AR
72732 Garfield, AR
72733 Gateway, AR
72734 Gentry, AR
72734 Springtown, AR
72735 Goshen, AR
72736 Gravette, AR
72737 Greenland, AR
72738 Hindsville, AR
72739 Hiwasse, AR
72740 Huntsville, AR
72741 Johnson, AR
72742 Kingston, AR
72744 Lincoln, AR
72745 Lowell, AR
72747 Maysville, AR
72749 Morrow, AR
72751 Pea Ridge, AR
72752 Pettigrew, AR
72753 Prairie Grove, AR
72756 Little Flock, AR
72756 Rogers, AR
72757 Rogers, AR
72758 Rogers, AR
72760 Saint Paul, AR
72761 Siloam Springs, AR
72762 Springdale, AR
72764 Bethel Heights, AR
72764 Fayetteville, AR
72764 Springdale, AR
72765 Springdale, AR
72766 Springdale, AR
72768 Sulphur Springs, AR
72769 Summers, AR
72770 Tontitown, AR
72773 Wesley, AR
72774 West Fork, AR
72776 Witter, AR

728

72801 Russellville, AR
72802 Russellville, AR
72811 Russellville, AR
72812 Russellville, AR
72820 Alix, AR
72821 Altus, AR
72821 Wiederkehr Village, AR
72823 Appleton, AR
72823 Atkins, AR
72823 Blackwell, AR
72824 Belleville, AR
72826 Blue Mountain, AR
72827 Bluffton, AR
72828 Briggsville, AR
72829 Centerville, AR
72830 Clarksville, AR
72832 Coal Hill, AR
72833 Danville, AR
72834 Dardanelle, AR
72835 Delaware, AR
72837 Dover, AR
72838 Gravelly, AR
72839 Hagarville, AR
72840 Hartman, AR
72840 Hunt, AR
72841 Harvey, AR
72842 Havana, AR
72842 Waveland, AR
72843 Hector, AR
72845 Knoxville, AR
72846 Lamar, AR
72847 London, AR
72851 New Blaine, AR
72852 Oark, AR
72853 Ola, AR
72854 Ozone, AR
72855 Paris, AR
72856 Pelsor, AR
72857 Plainview, AR
72858 Pottsville, AR
72860 Rover, AR
72863 Scranton, AR
72865 Subiaco, AR

729

72901 Fort Smith, AR
72902 Fort Smith, AR
72903 Fort Smith, AR
72904 Fort Smith, AR
72905 Fort Chaffee, AR
72905 Fort Smith, AR
72906 Fort Smith, AR
72908 Fort Smith, AR
72913 Fort Smith, AR
72914 Fort Smith, AR
72916 Bonanza, AR
72916 Fort Smith, AR
72917 Fort Smith, AR
72918 Fort Smith, AR
72919 Fort Smith, AR
72921 Alma, AR
72923 Barling, AR
72926 Boles, AR
72927 Booneville, AR
72928 Branch, AR
72930 Cecil, AR
72932 Cedarville, AR
72933 Charleston, AR
72934 Chester, AR
72935 Dyer, AR
72936 Greenwood, AR
72937 Hackett, AR
72938 Hartford, AR
72940 Huntington, AR
72941 Central City, AR
72941 Lavaca, AR
72943 Magazine, AR
72944 Mansfield, AR
72945 Midland, AR
72946 Mountainburg, AR
72947 Mulberry, AR
72948 Natural Dam, AR
72949 Ozark, AR
72950 Parks, AR
72951 Ratcliff, AR
72952 Rudy, AR
72955 Uniontown, AR
72956 Van Buren, AR
72957 Van Buren, AR
72958 Bates, AR
72958 Waldron, AR
72959 Winslow, AR

730

73001 Albert, OK
73002 Alex, OK
73003 Edmond, OK
73004 Amber, OK
73005 Anadarko, OK
73005 Washita, OK
73006 Apache, OK
73007 Arcadia, OK
73008 Bethany, OK
73008 Woodlawn Park, OK
73009 Binger, OK
73010 Blanchard, OK
73010 Cole, OK
73011 Bradley, OK
73012 Edmond, OK
73013 Edmond, OK
73014 Calumet, OK
73015 Carnegie, OK
73016 Cashion, OK
73017 Cement, OK
73018 Chickasha, OK
73018 Norge, OK
73019 Norman, OK
73020 Choctaw, OK
73021 Colony, OK
73022 Concho, OK
73023 Chickasha, OK
73024 Corn, OK
73025 Edmond, OK
73026 Norman, OK
73027 Coyle, OK
73028 Cimarron City, OK
73028 Crescent, OK
73029 Cyril, OK
73030 Davis, OK
73031 Dibble, OK
73032 Dougherty, OK
73033 Eakly, OK
73034 Edmond, OK
73036 El Reno, OK
73038 Fort Cobb, OK
73039 Davis, OK
73040 Geary, OK
73041 Gotebo, OK
73042 Gracemont, OK
73043 Greenfield, OK
73044 Guthrie, OK
73045 Harrah, OK
73047 Bridgeport, OK
73047 Hinton, OK
73048 Hydro, OK
73049 Jones, OK
73050 Langston, OK
73051 Lexington, OK
73051 Slaughterville, OK
73052 Erin Springs, OK
73052 Lindsay, OK
73053 Lookeba, OK
73054 Luther, OK
73055 Bray, OK
73055 Central High, OK
73055 Marlow, OK
73056 Marshall, OK
73057 Maysville, OK
73058 Meridian, OK
73059 Minco, OK
73061 Morrison, OK
73062 Mountain View, OK
73063 Mulhall, OK
73064 Mustang, OK
73065 Newcastle, OK
73066 Nicoma Park, OK
73067 Ninnekah, OK
73068 Etowah, OK
73068 Noble, OK
73069 Norman, OK
73070 Norman, OK
73071 Norman, OK
73072 Norman, OK
73073 Orlando, OK
73074 Paoli, OK
73075 Pauls Valley, OK
73077 Perry, OK
73078 Piedmont, OK
73079 Pocasset, OK
73080 Purcell, OK
73082 Rush Springs, OK
73083 Edmond, OK
73084 Spencer, OK
73085 Yukon, OK
73086 Sulphur, OK
73089 Tuttle, OK
73090 Union City, OK
73092 Verden, OK
73093 Goldsby, OK
73093 Washington, OK
73095 Wayne, OK
73096 Weatherford, OK
73097 Wheatland, OK
73098 Wynnewood, OK
73099 Yukon, OK

731

73101 Oklahoma City, OK
73102 Oklahoma City, OK
73103 Oklahoma City, OK
73104 Oklahoma City, OK
73105 Oklahoma City, OK
73106 Oklahoma City, OK
73107 Oklahoma City, OK
73108 Oklahoma City, OK
73109 Oklahoma City, OK
73110 Midwest City, OK
73110 Oklahoma City, OK
73111 Oklahoma City, OK
73112 Oklahoma City, OK
73112 Warr Acres, OK
73113 Oklahoma City, OK
73114 Oklahoma City, OK
73115 Del City, OK
73115 Oklahoma City, OK
73115 Smith Village, OK
73116 Nichols Hills, OK
73116 Oklahoma City, OK
73117 Oklahoma City, OK
73118 Oklahoma City, OK
73119 Oklahoma City, OK
73120 Nichols Hills, OK
73120 Oklahoma City, OK
73120 The Village, OK
73120 Village, OK
73121 Forest Park, OK
73121 Lake Aluma, OK
73121 Oklahoma City, OK
73122 Oklahoma City, OK
73122 Warr Acres, OK
73123 Oklahoma City, OK
73123 Warr Acres, OK
73124 Oklahoma City, OK
73125 Oklahoma City, OK
73126 Oklahoma City, OK
73127 Oklahoma City, OK
73128 Oklahoma City, OK
73129 Oklahoma City, OK
73130 Midwest City, OK
73130 Oklahoma City, OK
73131 Oklahoma City, OK
73132 Oklahoma City, OK
73132 Warr Acres, OK
73134 Oklahoma City, OK
73135 Del City, OK
73135 Oklahoma City, OK
73136 Oklahoma City, OK
73137 Oklahoma City, OK
73139 Oklahoma City, OK
73140 Midwest City, OK
73140 Oklahoma City, OK
73141 Oklahoma City, OK
73142 Oklahoma City, OK
73143 Oklahoma City, OK
73144 Oklahoma City, OK
73145 Oklahoma City, OK
73145 Tinker Afb, OK
73146 Oklahoma City, OK
73147 Oklahoma City, OK
73148 Oklahoma City, OK
73149 Oklahoma City, OK
73150 Oklahoma City, OK
73151 Oklahoma City, OK
73152 Oklahoma City, OK
73153 Moore, OK
73153 Oklahoma City, OK
73154 Oklahoma City, OK
73155 Del City, OK
73155 Oklahoma City, OK
73156 Oklahoma City, OK
73157 Oklahoma City, OK
73159 Oklahoma City, OK
73160 Moore, OK
73160 Oklahoma City, OK
73162 Oklahoma City, OK
73163 Oklahoma City, OK
73164 Oklahoma City, OK
73165 Moore, OK
73165 Oklahoma City, OK
73167 Oklahoma City, OK
73169 Oklahoma City, OK
73170 Moore, OK
73170 Oklahoma City, OK
73172 Oklahoma City, OK
73173 Oklahoma City, OK
73178 Oklahoma City, OK
73179 Oklahoma City, OK
73184 Oklahoma City, OK
73185 Oklahoma City, OK
73189 Oklahoma City, OK
73190 Oklahoma City, OK
73194 Oklahoma City, OK
73195 Oklahoma City, OK
73196 Oklahoma City, OK

733

73301 Austin, TX
73344 Austin, TX

734

73401 Ardmore, OK
73401 Milo, OK
73401 Pooleville, OK
73402 Ardmore, OK
73403 Ardmore, OK
73425 Countyline, OK
73430 Burneyville, OK
73432 Coleman, OK
73433 Elmore City, OK
73433 Pernell, OK
73434 Foster, OK
73435 Fox, OK
73436 Gene Autry, OK
73437 Graham, OK
73438 Healdton, OK
73439 Kingston, OK
73440 Lebanon, OK
73441 Leon, OK
73442 Loco, OK
73443 Lone Grove, OK
73444 Hennepin, OK
73446 Madill, OK
73446 Mc Millan, OK
73446 Oakland, OK
73447 Mannsville, OK
73448 Marietta, OK

73449 Mead, OK
73450 Milburn, OK
73453 Overbrook, OK
73455 Ravia, OK
73456 Cornish, OK
73456 Ringling, OK
73458 Springer, OK
73459 Thackerville, OK
73460 Tishomingo, OK
73461 Wapanucka, OK
73463 Rubottom, OK
73463 Wilson, OK
73481 Ratliff City, OK
73487 Tatums, OK
73488 Tussy, OK
73491 Velma, OK

735

73501 Lawton, OK
73502 Lawton, OK
73503 Fort Sill, OK
73503 Lawton, OK
73505 Lawton, OK
73506 Lawton, OK
73507 Lawton, OK
73520 Addington, OK
73521 Altus, OK
73522 Altus, OK
73523 Altus, OK
73523 Altus Afb, OK
73526 Blair, OK
73527 Cache, OK
73528 Chattanooga, OK
73529 Comanche, OK
73530 Davidson, OK
73531 Devol, OK
73532 Duke, OK
73533 Duncan, OK
73533 Empire City, OK
73534 Duncan, OK
73536 Duncan, OK
73537 Eldorado, OK
73538 Elgin, OK
73539 Elmer, OK
73540 Faxon, OK
73541 Fletcher, OK
73542 Frederick, OK
73543 Geronimo, OK
73544 Gould, OK
73546 Grandfield, OK
73547 Granite, OK
73548 Hastings, OK
73549 Headrick, OK
73550 Hollis, OK
73551 Hollister, OK
73552 Indiahoma, OK
73553 Loveland, OK
73554 Mangum, OK
73554 Reed, OK
73555 Manitou, OK
73556 Martha, OK
73557 Medicine Park, OK
73558 Lawton, OK
73558 Meers, OK
73559 Mountain Park, OK
73560 Olustee, OK
73561 Oscar, OK
73561 Terral, OK
73562 Randlett, OK
73564 Cooperton, OK
73564 Roosevelt, OK
73565 Ryan, OK
73566 Snyder, OK
73567 Sterling, OK
73568 Temple, OK
73569 Grady, OK
73569 Terral, OK
73570 Tipton, OK
73571 Vinson, OK
73572 Walters, OK
73573 Sugden, OK
73573 Waurika, OK

736

73601 Clinton, OK
73620 Arapaho, OK
73622 Bessie, OK
73624 Burns Flat, OK
73625 Butler, OK
73626 Canute, OK
73627 Carter, OK
73628 Cheyenne, OK
73628 Strong City, OK
73632 Cordell, OK
73638 Crawford, OK
73639 Custer City, OK
73641 Dill City, OK
73642 Durham, OK
73644 Elk City, OK
73645 Erick, OK
73646 Fay, OK
73647 Foss, OK
73648 Elk City, OK
73650 Hammon, OK
73651 Hobart, OK
73654 Leedey, OK
73655 Lone Wolf, OK
73658 Eagle City, OK
73658 Oakwood, OK
73659 Putnam, OK
73660 Reydon, OK
73661 Rocky, OK
73662 Sayre, OK
73663 Seiling, OK
73664 Sentinel, OK
73666 Sweetwater, OK
73667 Taloga, OK
73668 Texola, OK
73669 Thomas, OK
73673 Willow, OK

737

73701 Enid, OK
73701 North Enid, OK
73702 Enid, OK
73703 Enid, OK
73705 Enid, OK
73706 Enid, OK
73716 Aline, OK
73717 Alva, OK
73717 Avard, OK
73717 Capron, OK
73718 Ames, OK
73719 Amorita, OK
73720 Bison, OK
73722 Burlington, OK
73722 Byron, OK
73724 Canton, OK
73726 Carmen, OK
73727 Carrier, OK
73728 Cherokee, OK
73728 Lambert, OK
73729 Cleo Springs, OK
73730 Covington, OK
73731 Dacoma, OK
73733 Douglas, OK
73734 Dover, OK
73735 Drummond, OK
73736 Fairmont, OK
73737 Fairview, OK
73737 Orienta, OK
73738 Garber, OK
73739 Goltry, OK
73741 Helena, OK
73742 Hennessey, OK
73743 Hillsdale, OK
73744 Hitchcock, OK
73746 Hopeton, OK
73747 Isabella, OK
73749 Jet, OK
73750 Kingfisher, OK
73753 Kremlin, OK
73754 Lahoma, OK
73755 Longdale, OK
73756 Loyal, OK
73757 Lucien, OK
73758 Manchester, OK
73759 Jefferson, OK
73759 Medford, OK
73759 Renfrow, OK
73760 Meno, OK
73761 Nash, OK
73762 Okarche, OK
73763 Okeene, OK
73764 Omega, OK
73766 Pond Creek, OK
73768 Ringwood, OK
73770 Southard, OK
73771 Wakita, OK
73772 Watonga, OK
73773 Waukomis, OK

738

73801 Woodward, OK
73802 Woodward, OK
73832 Arnett, OK
73832 Harmon, OK
73834 Buffalo, OK
73834 Selman, OK
73835 Camargo, OK
73838 Chester, OK
73840 Fargo, OK
73841 Fort Supply, OK
73842 Freedom, OK
73843 Gage, OK
73844 Gate, OK
73844 Knowles, OK
73848 Laverne, OK
73848 Logan, OK
73851 May, OK
73852 Mooreland, OK
73853 Mutual, OK
73855 Rosston, OK
73857 Sharon, OK
73858 Shattuck, OK
73859 Vici, OK
73860 Waynoka, OK

739

73901 Adams, OK
73931 Balko, OK
73932 Beaver, OK
73932 Elmwood, OK
73933 Boise City, OK
73937 Felt, OK
73938 Forgan, OK
73939 Goodwell, OK
73942 Guymon, OK
73944 Hardesty, OK
73945 Hooker, OK
73945 Optima, OK
73946 Kenton, OK
73947 Keyes, OK
73949 Texhoma, OK
73950 Baker, OK
73950 Turpin, OK
73951 Tyrone, OK
73960 Texhoma, TX

740

74001 Avant, OK
74002 Barnsdall, OK
74003 Bartlesville, OK
74004 Bartlesville, OK
74005 Bartlesville, OK
74006 Bartlesville, OK
74008 Bixby, OK
74010 Bristow, OK
74011 Broken Arrow, OK
74012 Broken Arrow, OK
74013 Broken Arrow, OK
74014 Broken Arrow, OK
74015 Catoosa, OK
74015 Fair Oaks, OK
74016 Chelsea, OK
74017 Claremore, OK
74017 Valley Park, OK
74018 Claremore, OK
74019 Claremore, OK
74020 Cleveland, OK
74020 Shady Grove, OK
74021 Collinsville, OK
74022 Copan, OK
74023 Cushing, OK
74026 Davenport, OK
74027 Delaware, OK
74028 Depew, OK
74029 Dewey, OK
74030 Drumright, OK
74031 Foyil, OK
74032 Glencoe, OK
74033 Glenpool, OK
74034 Hallett, OK
74035 Hominy, OK
74036 Inola, OK
74037 Jenks, OK
74038 Jennings, OK
74039 Kellyville, OK
74041 Kiefer, OK
74042 Lenapah, OK
74043 Leonard, OK
74044 Lawrence Creek, OK
74044 Mannford, OK
74045 Maramec, OK
74046 Milfay, OK
74047 Mounds, OK
74048 Nowata, OK
74050 Oakhurst, OK
74051 Ochelata, OK
74052 Oilton, OK
74053 Oologah, OK
74054 Osage, OK
74055 Owasso, OK
74056 Bowring, OK
74056 Pawhuska, OK
74058 Blackburn, OK
74058 Pawnee, OK
74058 Skedee, OK
74059 Perkins, OK
74060 Prue, OK
74061 Ramona, OK
74062 Ripley, OK
74063 Sand Springs, OK
74066 Sapulpa, OK
74067 Sapulpa, OK
74068 Shamrock, OK
74070 Skiatook, OK
74071 Slick, OK
74072 S Coffeyville, OK
74073 Sperry, OK
74074 Stillwater, OK
74075 Stillwater, OK
74076 Stillwater, OK
74077 Stillwater, OK
74078 Stillwater, OK
74079 Kendrick, OK
74079 Stroud, OK
74080 Talala, OK
74081 Terlton, OK
74082 Vera, OK
74083 Wann, OK
74084 Wynona, OK
74085 Yale, OK

741

74101 Tulsa, OK
74102 Tulsa, OK
74103 Tulsa, OK
74104 Tulsa, OK
74105 Tulsa, OK
74106 Tulsa, OK
74107 Tulsa, OK
74108 Tulsa, OK
74110 Tulsa, OK
74112 Tulsa, OK
74114 Tulsa, OK
74115 Tulsa, OK
74116 Tulsa, OK
74117 Tulsa, OK
74119 Tulsa, OK
74120 Tulsa, OK
74121 Tulsa, OK
74126 Tulsa, OK
74127 Tulsa, OK
74128 Tulsa, OK
74129 Tulsa, OK
74130 Tulsa, OK
74131 Tulsa, OK
74132 Tulsa, OK
74133 Tulsa, OK
74134 Tulsa, OK
74135 Tulsa, OK
74136 Tulsa, OK
74137 Tulsa, OK
74141 Tulsa, OK
74145 Tulsa, OK
74146 Tulsa, OK
74147 Tulsa, OK
74148 Tulsa, OK
74149 Tulsa, OK
74150 Tulsa, OK
74152 Tulsa, OK
74153 Tulsa, OK
74155 Tulsa, OK
74156 Tulsa, OK
74157 Tulsa, OK
74158 Tulsa, OK
74159 Tulsa, OK
74169 Tulsa, OK
74170 Tulsa, OK
74171 Tulsa, OK
74172 Tulsa, OK
74182 Tulsa, OK
74186 Tulsa, OK
74187 Tulsa, OK
74192 Tulsa, OK
74193 Tulsa, OK

743

74301 Centralia, OK
74301 Pensacola, OK
74301 Vinita, OK
74301 White Oak, OK
74330 Adair, OK
74331 Afton, OK
74331 Bernice, OK
74331 Cleora, OK
74331 Monkey Island, OK
74332 Big Cabin, OK
74333 Bluejacket, OK
74335 Cardin, OK
74337 Chouteau, OK
74337 Mazie, OK
74338 Colcord, OK
74338 West Siloam Springs, OK
74339 Commerce, OK
74340 Disney, OK
74342 Eucha, OK
74343 Fairland, OK
74344 Grove, OK
74345 Grove, OK
74346 Jay, OK
74347 Kansas, OK
74349 Grand Lake Towne, OK
74349 Ketchum, OK
74350 Langley, OK
74352 Locust Grove, OK
74354 Miami, OK
74355 Miami, OK
74358 North Miami, OK
74359 Oaks, OK
74360 Picher, OK
74361 Pryor, OK
74361 Sportsmen Acres, OK
74362 Pryor, OK
74363 Peoria, OK
74363 Quapaw, OK
74364 Rose, OK
74365 Salina, OK
74366 Spavinaw, OK
74367 Strang, OK
74368 Twin Oaks, OK
74369 Welch, OK
74370 Wyandotte, OK

744

74401 Muskogee, OK
74401 Summit, OK
74402 Muskogee, OK
74403 Muskogee, OK
74421 Beggs, OK
74421 Winchester, OK
74422 Boynton, OK
74423 Braggs, OK
74425 Canadian, OK
74426 Checotah, OK
74427 Cookson, OK
74428 Council Hill, OK
74429 Coweta, OK
74430 Crowder, OK
74431 Dewar, OK
74432 Eufaula, OK
74434 Fort Gibson, OK
74435 Gore, OK
74435 Paradise Hill, OK
74436 Haskell, OK
74437 Henryetta, OK
74437 Hoffman, OK
74438 Hitchita, OK
74439 Braggs, OK
74440 Hoyt, OK
74441 Hulbert, OK
74442 Indianola, OK
74444 Moodys, OK
74445 Morris, OK
74446 Okay, OK
74447 Okmulgee, OK
74450 Oktaha, OK
74451 Park Hill, OK
74452 Peggs, OK
74454 Porter, OK
74454 Tullahassee, OK
74455 Porum, OK
74456 Preston, OK
74457 Proctor, OK
74458 Redbird, OK
74459 Rentiesville, OK
74460 Schulter, OK
74461 Stidham, OK
74462 Stigler, OK
74463 Taft, OK
74464 Tahlequah, OK
74465 Tahlequah, OK
74467 Wagoner, OK
74468 Wainwright, OK
74469 Warner, OK
74470 Webbers Falls, OK
74471 Welling, OK
74472 Hoyt, OK
74472 Whitefield, OK
74477 Wagoner, OK

745

74501 Bache, OK
74501 Haywood, OK
74501 Mcalester, OK
74502 Mcalester, OK
74521 Albion, OK
74522 Alderson, OK
74523 Antlers, OK
74525 Atoka, OK
74525 Farris, OK
74528 Blanco, OK
74529 Blocker, OK
74530 Bromide, OK
74531 Calvin, OK
74531 Gerty, OK
74533 Caney, OK
74534 Centrahoma, OK
74535 Clarita, OK
74536 Clayton, OK
74538 Coalgate, OK
74540 Daisy, OK
74543 Finley, OK
74545 Gowen, OK
74546 Haileyville, OK
74547 Hartshorne, OK
74549 Honobia, OK
74549 Kiamichi, OK
74552 Kinta, OK
74553 Kiowa, OK
74554 Krebs, OK
74555 Lane, OK
74556 Lehigh, OK
74557 Moyers, OK
74558 Nashoba, OK
74559 Panola, OK
74560 Pittsburg, OK
74561 Quinton, OK
74562 Rattan, OK
74563 Red Oak, OK
74565 Savanna, OK
74567 Snow, OK
74569 Stringtown, OK
74570 Ashland, OK
74570 Stuart, OK
74571 Talihina, OK
74572 Tupelo, OK

74574 Tuskahoma, OK
74576 Wardville, OK
74577 Whitesboro, OK
74578 Wilburton, OK

746

74601 Ponca City, OK
74602 Ponca City, OK
74604 Ponca City, OK
74630 Billings, OK
74631 Blackwell, OK
74632 Braman, OK
74633 Burbank, OK
74636 Deer Creek, OK
74637 Fairfax, OK
74640 Hunter, OK
74641 Kaw, OK
74641 Kaw City, OK
74643 Lamont, OK
74644 Marland, OK
74646 Nardin, OK
74647 Newkirk, OK
74647 Peckham, OK
74650 Ralston, OK
74651 Red Rock, OK
74652 Foraker, OK
74652 Shidler, OK
74652 Webb City, OK
74653 Tonkawa, OK

747

74701 Durant, OK
74701 Silo, OK
74702 Durant, OK
74720 Achille, OK
74721 Albany, OK
74722 Battiest, OK
74723 Bennington, OK
74723 Wade, OK
74724 Bethel, OK
74726 Armstrong, OK
74726 Bokchito, OK
74727 Boswell, OK
74728 Broken Bow, OK
74729 Caddo, OK
74730 Calera, OK
74731 Cartwright, OK
74733 Colbert, OK
74734 Eagletown, OK
74735 Fort Towson, OK
74735 Ft Towson, OK
74736 Garvin, OK
74737 Golden, OK
74738 Grant, OK
74740 Haworth, OK
74740 Tom, OK
74741 Hendrix, OK
74741 Yarnaby, OK
74743 Hugo, OK
74745 Idabel, OK
74747 Kemp, OK
74748 Kenefic, OK
74750 Millerton, OK
74752 Pickens, OK
74753 Platter, OK
74754 Ringold, OK
74755 Rufe, OK
74756 Sawyer, OK
74759 Soper, OK
74760 Spencerville, OK
74761 Swink, OK
74764 Valliant, OK
74766 Wright City, OK

748

74801 Bethel Acres, OK
74801 Johnson, OK
74801 Shawnee, OK
74802 Shawnee, OK
74804 Shawnee, OK
74818 Seminole, OK
74820 Ada, OK
74820 Bing, OK
74820 Byng, OK
74820 Pontotoc, OK
74821 Ada, OK
74824 Agra, OK
74825 Allen, OK
74826 Asher, OK
74827 Atwood, OK
74829 Boley, OK
74830 Bowlegs, OK
74831 Byars, OK
74831 Rosedale, OK
74832 Carney, OK
74833 Castle, OK
74833 Welty, OK
74834 Chandler, OK
74836 Connerville, OK
74837 Cromwell, OK
74839 Dustin, OK
74840 Earlsboro, OK
74842 Fittstown, OK
74843 Fitzhugh, OK
74844 Francis, OK
74845 Hanna, OK
74845 Vernon, OK
74848 Holdenville, OK
74848 Horntown, OK
74848 Spaulding, OK
74848 Yeager, OK
74849 Konawa, OK
74850 Lamar, OK
74851 Dale, OK
74851 Mcloud, OK
74852 Macomb, OK
74854 Maud, OK
74855 Meeker, OK
74856 Mill Creek, OK
74857 Newalla, OK
74859 Bearden, OK
74859 Mason, OK
74859 Okemah, OK
74860 Paden, OK
74864 Prague, OK
74865 Hickory, OK
74865 Roff, OK
74866 Saint Louis, OK
74867 Sasakwa, OK
74868 Seminole, OK
74869 Sparks, OK
74871 Harden City, OK
74871 Stonewall, OK
74872 Stratford, OK
74873 Tecumseh, OK
74875 Tryon, OK
74878 Tribbey, OK
74878 Wanette, OK
74880 Clearview, OK
74880 Pharoah, OK
74880 Weleetka, OK
74881 Fallis, OK
74881 Warwick, OK
74881 Wellston, OK
74883 Wetumka, OK
74884 Lima, OK
74884 New Lima, OK
74884 Wewoka, OK

749

74901 Arkoma, OK
74902 Pocola, OK
74930 Bokoshe, OK
74931 Bunch, OK
74932 Cameron, OK
74935 Fanshawe, OK
74936 Gans, OK
74937 Heavener, OK
74939 Hodgen, OK
74940 Howe, OK
74941 Cowlington, OK
74941 Keota, OK
74942 Leflore, OK
74943 Lequire, OK
74944 Mccurtain, OK
74945 Marble City, OK
74946 Moffett, OK
74947 Monroe, OK
74948 Muldrow, OK
74949 Muse, OK
74951 Panama, OK
74953 Poteau, OK
74954 Roland, OK
74955 Sallisaw, OK
74956 Shady Point, OK
74957 Octavia, OK
74957 Smithville, OK
74959 Fort Coffee, OK
74959 Spiro, OK
74960 Stilwell, OK
74962 Vian, OK
74963 Watson, OK
74964 Watts, OK
74965 Westville, OK
74966 Wister, OK

750

75001 Addison, TX
75002 Allen, TX
75002 Lucas, TX
75002 Parker, TX
75006 Carrollton, TX
75007 Carrollton, TX
75009 Celina, TX
75010 Carrollton, TX
75011 Carrollton, TX
75013 Allen, TX
75014 Irving, TX
75015 Irving, TX
75016 Irving, TX
75017 Irving, TX
75019 Coppell, TX
75020 Denison, TX
75021 Denison, TX
75022 Flower Mound, TX
75022 Flowermound, TX
75022 Lewisville, TX
75023 Plano, TX
75024 Plano, TX
75025 Plano, TX
75026 Plano, TX
75027 Flower Mound, TX
75027 Flowermound, TX
75027 Lewisville, TX
75028 Flower Mound, TX
75028 Flowermound, TX
75028 Lewisville, TX
75029 Lewisville, TX
75030 Rowlett, TX
75032 Fate, TX
75032 Heath, TX
75032 Rockwall, TX
75033 Frisco, TX
75034 Frisco, TX
75035 Frisco, TX
75038 Irving, TX
75039 Irving, TX
75040 Garland, TX
75041 Garland, TX
75042 Garland, TX
75043 Garland, TX
75044 Garland, TX
75045 Garland, TX
75046 Garland, TX
75047 Garland, TX
75048 Garland, TX
75048 Sachse, TX
75049 Garland, TX
75050 Grand Prairie, TX
75051 Grand Prairie, TX
75052 Grand Prairie, TX
75053 Grand Prairie, TX
75054 Grand Prairie, TX
75056 Lewisville, TX
75056 The Colony, TX
75057 Lewisville, TX
75058 Gunter, TX
75060 Irving, TX
75061 Irving, TX
75062 Irving, TX
75063 Irving, TX
75065 Hickory Creek, TX
75065 Lake Dallas, TX
75067 Lewisville, TX
75068 Lakewood Village, TX
75068 Little Elm, TX
75068 Oak Point, TX
75069 Fairview, TX
75069 Mc Kinney, TX
75069 Mckinney, TX
75070 Mc Kinney, TX
75070 Mckinney, TX
75071 Mc Kinney, TX
75071 Mckinney, TX
75074 Plano, TX
75075 Plano, TX
75076 Pottsboro, TX
75077 Copper Canyon, TX
75077 Double Oak, TX
75077 Flower Mound, TX
75077 Highland Village, TX
75077 Lewisville, TX
75078 Prosper, TX
75080 Richardson, TX
75081 Richardson, TX
75082 Richardson, TX
75083 Richardson, TX
75085 Richardson, TX
75086 Plano, TX
75087 Fate, TX
75087 Rockwall, TX
75088 Rowlett, TX
75089 Rowlett, TX
75090 Sherman, TX
75090 Tom Bean, TX
75091 Sherman, TX
75092 Knollwood, TX
75092 Sherman, TX
75093 Plano, TX
75094 Murphy, TX
75094 Parker, TX
75094 Plano, TX
75097 Weston, TX
75098 Lucas, TX
75098 St Paul, TX
75098 Wylie, TX
75099 Coppell, TX

751

75101 Bardwell, TX
75102 Barry, TX
75103 Canton, TX
75104 Cedar Hill, TX
75105 Chatfield, TX
75106 Cedar Hill, TX
75109 Corsicana, TX
75110 Corsicana, TX
75114 Crandall, TX
75115 Desoto, TX
75116 Duncanville, TX
75117 Edgewood, TX
75118 Elmo, TX
75119 Ennis, TX
75120 Ennis, TX
75121 Copeville, TX
75123 Desoto, TX
75124 Eustace, TX
75125 Ferris, TX
75126 Forney, TX
75126 Heartland, TX
75126 Heath, TX
75126 Heathridge, TX
75127 Fruitvale, TX
75132 Fate, TX
75134 Lancaster, TX
75135 Caddo Mills, TX
75137 Duncanville, TX
75138 Duncanville, TX
75140 Grand Saline, TX
75141 Hutchins, TX
75142 Kaufman, TX
75143 Kemp, TX
75143 Seven Points, TX
75143 Tool, TX
75144 Kerens, TX
75146 Lancaster, TX
75147 Gun Barrel City, TX
75147 Mabank, TX
75148 Log Cabin, TX
75148 Malakoff, TX
75149 Mesquite, TX
75150 Mesquite, TX
75151 Corsicana, TX
75152 Palmer, TX
75153 Powell, TX
75154 Glenn Heights, TX
75154 Oak Leaf, TX
75154 Ovilla, TX
75154 Red Oak, TX
75155 Rice, TX
75156 Enchanted Oaks, TX
75156 Gun Barrel City, TX
75156 Mabank, TX
75157 Rosser, TX
75158 Scurry, TX
75159 Combine, TX
75159 Seagoville, TX
75160 Terrell, TX
75161 Terrell, TX
75163 Trinidad, TX
75164 Josephine, TX
75165 Waxahachie, TX
75166 Lavon, TX
75167 Waxahachie, TX
75168 Waxahachie, TX
75169 Wills Point, TX
75172 Wilmer, TX
75173 Nevada, TX
75180 Balch Springs, TX
75180 Mesquite, TX
75181 Balch Springs, TX
75181 Mesquite, TX
75182 Mesquite, TX
75182 Sunnyvale, TX
75185 Mesquite, TX
75187 Mesquite, TX
75189 Fate, TX
75189 Royse City, TX

752

75201 Dallas, TX
75202 Dallas, TX
75203 Dallas, TX
75204 Dallas, TX
75205 Dallas, TX
75206 Dallas, TX
75207 Dallas, TX
75208 Dallas, TX
75209 Dallas, TX
75210 Dallas, TX
75211 Dallas, TX
75212 Dallas, TX
75214 Dallas, TX
75215 Dallas, TX
75216 Dallas, TX
75217 Dallas, TX
75218 Dallas, TX
75219 Dallas, TX
75220 Dallas, TX
75221 Dallas, TX
75222 Dallas, TX
75223 Dallas, TX
75224 Dallas, TX
75225 Dallas, TX
75226 Dallas, TX
75227 Dallas, TX
75228 Dallas, TX
75229 Dallas, TX
75229 Farmers Branch, TX
75230 Dallas, TX
75231 Dallas, TX
75232 Dallas, TX
75233 Dallas, TX
75234 Dallas, TX
75234 Farmers Branch, TX
75235 Dallas, TX
75236 Dallas, TX
75237 Dallas, TX
75238 Dallas, TX
75240 Dallas, TX
75241 Dallas, TX
75242 Dallas, TX
75243 Dallas, TX
75244 Dallas, TX
75244 Farmers Branch, TX
75244 North Branch, TX
75246 Dallas, TX
75247 Dallas, TX
75248 Dallas, TX
75249 Dallas, TX
75250 Dallas, TX
75251 Dallas, TX
75252 Dallas, TX
75253 Dallas, TX
75254 Dallas, TX
75260 Dallas, TX
75261 Dallas, TX
75261 Dfw, TX
75261 Dfw Airport, TX
75262 Dallas, TX
75263 Dallas, TX
75264 Dallas, TX
75265 Dallas, TX
75266 Dallas, TX
75267 Dallas, TX
75270 Dallas, TX
75275 Dallas, TX
75277 Dallas, TX
75283 Dallas, TX
75284 Dallas, TX
75285 Dallas, TX
75287 Dallas, TX

753

75301 Dallas, TX
75303 Dallas, TX
75312 Dallas, TX
75313 Dallas, TX
75315 Dallas, TX
75320 Dallas, TX
75326 Dallas, TX
75336 Dallas, TX
75339 Dallas, TX
75342 Dallas, TX
75354 Dallas, TX
75355 Dallas, TX
75356 Dallas, TX
75357 Dallas, TX
75358 Dallas, TX
75359 Dallas, TX
75360 Dallas, TX
75367 Dallas, TX
75368 Dallas, TX
75370 Dallas, TX
75371 Dallas, TX
75372 Dallas, TX
75373 Dallas, TX
75374 Dallas, TX
75376 Dallas, TX
75378 Dallas, TX
75379 Dallas, TX
75380 Dallas, TX
75381 Dallas, TX
75382 Dallas, TX
75389 Dallas, TX
75390 Dallas, TX
75391 Dallas, TX
75392 Dallas, TX
75393 Dallas, TX
75394 Dallas, TX
75395 Dallas, TX
75397 Dallas, TX
75398 Dallas, TX

754

75401 Greenville, TX
75402 Greenville, TX
75403 Greenville, TX
75404 Greenville, TX
75407 Princeton, TX
75409 Anna, TX
75410 Alba, TX
75411 Arthur City, TX
75412 Bagwell, TX
75413 Bailey, TX
75414 Bells, TX
75415 Ben Franklin, TX
75416 Blossom, TX
75417 Bogata, TX
75418 Bonham, TX
75420 Brashear, TX
75421 Brookston, TX
75422 Campbell, TX
75423 Celeste, TX
75424 Blue Ridge, TX
75425 Chicota, TX
75426 Clarksville, TX
75428 Commerce, TX
75429 Commerce, TX
75431 Como, TX

75432 Cooper, TX
75433 Cumby, TX
75434 Cunningham, TX
75435 Deport, TX
75436 Detroit, TX
75437 Dike, TX
75438 Dodd City, TX
75439 Ector, TX
75440 Emory, TX
75441 Enloe, TX
75442 Farmersville, TX
75443 Gober, TX
75444 Golden, TX
75446 Honey Grove, TX
75447 Ivanhoe, TX
75448 Klondike, TX
75449 Ladonia, TX
75450 Lake Creek, TX
75451 Leesburg, TX
75452 Leonard, TX
75453 Lone Oak, TX
75454 Melissa, TX
75455 Mount Pleasant, TX
75457 Mount Vernon, TX
75457 Mt Vernon, TX
75458 Merit, TX
75459 Dorchester, TX
75459 Howe, TX
75460 Paris, TX
75461 Paris, TX
75462 Paris, TX
75462 Reno, TX
75468 Pattonville, TX
75469 Pecan Gap, TX
75470 Petty, TX
75471 Pickton, TX
75472 East Tawakoni, TX
75472 Point, TX
75473 Powderly, TX
75474 Quinlan, TX
75474 West Tawakoni, TX
75475 Randolph, TX
75476 Ravenna, TX
75477 Roxton, TX
75478 Saltillo, TX
75479 Savoy, TX
75480 Scroggins, TX
75481 Sulphur Bluff, TX
75482 Sulphur Springs, TX
75485 Westminster, TX
75486 Sumner, TX
75487 Talco, TX
75488 Telephone, TX
75489 Tom Bean, TX
75490 Trenton, TX
75491 Tom Bean, TX
75491 Whitewright, TX
75492 Windom, TX
75493 Winfield, TX
75494 Winnsboro, TX
75495 Van Alstyne, TX
75496 Wolfe City, TX
75497 Yantis, TX

755

75501 South Texarkana, TX
75501 Texarkana, TX
75501 Wake Village, TX
75503 Texarkana, TX
75504 Texarkana, TX
75505 Texarkana, TX
75507 Texarkana, TX
75550 Annona, TX
75551 Atlanta, TX
75554 Avery, TX
75555 Bivins, TX
75556 Bloomburg, TX
75558 Cookville, TX
75559 De Kalb, TX
75560 Douglassville, TX
75561 Hooks, TX
75562 Kildare, TX
75563 Linden, TX
75564 Lodi, TX
75565 Mc Leod, TX
75566 Marietta, TX
75567 Maud, TX
75568 Naples, TX
75569 Nash, TX
75570 Boston, TX
75570 New Boston, TX
75571 Omaha, TX
75572 Queen City, TX
75573 Redwater, TX
75574 Simms, TX
75599 Texarkana, TX

756

75601 Longview, TX
75602 Longview, TX
75603 Longview, TX
75604 Longview, TX
75605 Longview, TX
75606 Longview, TX
75607 Longview, TX
75608 Longview, TX
75615 Longview, TX
75630 Avinger, TX
75631 Beckville, TX
75633 Carthage, TX
75636 Cason, TX
75637 Clayton, TX
75638 Daingerfield, TX
75639 De Berry, TX
75640 Diana, TX
75640 New Diana, TX
75641 Easton, TX
75642 Elysian Fields, TX
75643 Gary, TX
75644 Gilmer, TX
75645 Gilmer, TX
75647 Gladewater, TX
75650 Hallsville, TX
75651 Harleton, TX
75652 Henderson, TX
75653 Henderson, TX
75654 Henderson, TX
75656 Hughes Springs, TX
75657 Jefferson, TX
75657 Smithland, TX
75658 Joinerville, TX
75659 Jonesville, TX
75660 Judson, TX
75661 Karnack, TX
75662 Kilgore, TX
75663 Kilgore, TX
75666 Laird Hill, TX
75667 Laneville, TX
75668 Lone Star, TX
75669 Long Branch, TX
75670 Marshall, TX
75671 Marshall, TX
75672 Marshall, TX
75680 Henderson, TX
75680 Minden, TX
75681 Mount Enterprise, TX
75682 New London, TX
75683 Ore City, TX
75684 Overton, TX
75685 Panola, TX
75686 Pittsburg, TX
75687 Price, TX
75688 Scottsville, TX
75689 Selman City, TX
75689 Turnertown, TX
75691 Tatum, TX
75692 Waskom, TX
75693 Clarksville City, TX
75693 White Oak, TX
75694 Woodlawn, TX

757

75701 Tyler, TX
75702 Tyler, TX
75703 Tyler, TX
75704 Tyler, TX
75705 Tyler, TX
75706 Lindale, TX
75706 Tyler, TX
75707 Tyler, TX
75708 Tyler, TX
75709 Tyler, TX
75710 Tyler, TX
75711 Tyler, TX
75712 Tyler, TX
75713 Tyler, TX
75750 Arp, TX
75751 Athens, TX
75752 Athens, TX
75754 Ben Wheeler, TX
75754 Edom, TX
75755 Big Sandy, TX
75755 Holly Lake Ranch, TX
75756 Brownsboro, TX
75756 Edom, TX
75757 Bullard, TX
75757 Mount Selman, TX
75758 Chandler, TX
75759 Cuney, TX
75760 Cushing, TX
75762 Flint, TX
75763 Coffee City, TX
75763 Frankston, TX
75764 Gallatin, TX
75765 Hawkins, TX
75765 Holly Lake Ranch, TX
75766 Jacksonville, TX
75770 Larue, TX
75771 Garden Valley, TX
75771 Hide A Way, TX
75771 Hideaway, TX
75771 Lindale, TX
75771 Mt Sylvan, TX
75772 Maydelle, TX
75773 Mineola, TX
75778 Murchison, TX
75779 Neches, TX
75780 New Summerfield, TX
75782 Poynor, TX
75783 Quitman, TX
75784 Reklaw, TX
75785 Dialville, TX
75785 Rusk, TX
75788 Sacul, TX
75789 Troup, TX
75790 Van, TX
75791 Whitehouse, TX
75792 Winona, TX
75797 Big Sandy, TX
75798 Tyler, TX
75799 Tyler, TX

758

75801 Palestine, TX
75802 Palestine, TX
75803 Palestine, TX
75831 Buffalo, TX
75831 Keechi, TX
75832 Cayuga, TX
75833 Centerville, TX
75834 Centralia, TX
75835 Crockett, TX
75838 Donie, TX
75839 Elkhart, TX
75839 Slocum, TX
75840 Fairfield, TX
75844 Grapeland, TX
75845 Groveton, TX
75846 Jewett, TX
75847 Kennard, TX
75848 Kirvin, TX
75849 Latexo, TX
75850 Leona, TX
75850 Midway, TX
75851 Lovelady, TX
75852 Midway, TX
75853 Montalba, TX
75855 Oakwood, TX
75856 Pennington, TX
75858 Ratcliff, TX
75859 Streetman, TX
75860 Teague, TX
75861 Tennessee Colony, TX
75862 Trinity, TX
75865 Woodlake, TX
75880 Tennessee Colony, TX
75882 Palestine, TX
75884 Tennessee Colony, TX

759

75901 Lufkin, TX
75902 Lufkin, TX
75903 Lufkin, TX
75904 Lufkin, TX
75915 Lufkin, TX
75925 Alto, TX
75925 Forest, TX
75926 Apple Springs, TX
75928 Bon Wier, TX
75929 Broaddus, TX
75930 Bronson, TX
75931 Brookeland, TX
75932 Burkeville, TX
75933 Call, TX
75934 Camden, TX
75935 Center, TX
75936 Chester, TX
75937 Chireno, TX
75938 Colmesneil, TX
75938 Rockland, TX
75939 Barnum, TX
75939 Corrigan, TX
75941 Burke, TX
75941 Diboll, TX
75942 Doucette, TX
75943 Douglass, TX
75944 Etoile, TX
75946 Garrison, TX
75948 Hemphill, TX
75949 Huntington, TX
75951 Jasper, TX
75954 Joaquin, TX
75956 Bon Ami, TX
75956 Kirbyville, TX
75956 Magnolia Springs, TX
75956 Roganville, TX
75958 Martinsville, TX
75959 Geneva, TX
75959 Milam, TX
75960 Moscow, TX
75961 Nacogdoches, TX
75962 Nacogdoches, TX
75963 Nacogdoches, TX
75964 Nacogdoches, TX
75965 Nacogdoches, TX
75966 Newton, TX
75968 Pineland, TX
75969 Pollok, TX
75972 San Augustine, TX
75973 Shelbyville, TX
75974 Tenaha, TX
75975 Timpson, TX
75976 Wells, TX
75977 Wiergate, TX
75978 Woden, TX
75979 Woodville, TX
75980 Zavalla, TX
75990 Woodville, TX

760

76001 Arlington, TX
76002 Arlington, TX
76003 Arlington, TX
76004 Arlington, TX
76005 Arlington, TX
76006 Arlington, TX
76007 Arlington, TX
76008 Aledo, TX
76008 Annetta, TX
76008 Annetta N, TX
76008 Annetta S, TX
76008 Willow Park, TX
76009 Alvarado, TX
76010 Arlington, TX
76011 Arlington, TX
76012 Arlington, TX
76013 Arlington, TX
76013 Dalworthington Gardens, TX
76013 Pantego, TX
76014 Arlington, TX
76015 Arlington, TX
76015 Pantego, TX
76016 Arlington, TX
76017 Arlington, TX
76018 Arlington, TX
76019 Arlington, TX
76020 Azle, TX
76020 Sanctuary, TX
76021 Bedford, TX
76022 Bedford, TX
76023 Boyd, TX
76028 Briaroaks, TX
76028 Burleson, TX
76028 Cross Timber, TX
76031 Cleburne, TX
76033 Cleburne, TX
76034 Colleyville, TX
76035 Cresson, TX
76036 Crowley, TX
76039 Euless, TX
76040 Euless, TX
76041 Forreston, TX
76043 Glen Rose, TX
76044 Godley, TX
76048 Brazos Bend, TX
76048 Granbury, TX
76049 Acton, TX
76049 Decordova, TX
76049 Granbury, TX
76050 Grandview, TX
76051 Grapevine, TX
76052 Haslet, TX
76053 Hurst, TX
76054 Hurst, TX
76055 Itasca, TX
76058 Joshua, TX
76059 Keene, TX
76060 Kennedale, TX
76061 Lillian, TX
76063 Mansfield, TX
76064 Maypearl, TX
76065 Midlothian, TX
76066 Cool, TX
76066 Millsap, TX
76067 Mineral Wells, TX
76068 Mineral Wells, TX
76070 Nemo, TX
76071 Newark, TX
76073 Paradise, TX
76077 Rainbow, TX
76078 Aurora, TX
76078 Rhome, TX
76082 Springtown, TX
76084 Venus, TX
76085 Weatherford, TX
76086 Weatherford, TX
76087 Brock, TX
76087 Hudson Oaks, TX
76087 Weatherford, TX
76087 Willow Park, TX
76088 Weatherford, TX
76092 Grapevine, TX
76092 South Lake, TX
76092 Southlake, TX
76093 Rio Vista, TX
76094 Arlington, TX
76095 Bedford, TX
76096 Arlington, TX
76097 Burleson, TX
76098 Azle, TX
76099 Grapevine, TX

761

76101 Fort Worth, TX
76101 Ft Worth, TX
76102 Fort Worth, TX
76102 Ft Worth, TX
76103 Fort Worth, TX
76103 Ft Worth, TX
76104 Fort Worth, TX
76104 Ft Worth, TX
76105 Fort Worth, TX
76105 Ft Worth, TX
76106 Fort Worth, TX
76106 Ft Worth, TX
76107 Fort Worth, TX
76107 Ft Worth, TX
76108 Fort Worth, TX
76108 Ft Worth, TX
76108 Lakeside, TX
76108 White Settlement, TX
76109 Benbrook, TX
76109 Fort Worth, TX
76109 Ft Worth, TX
76110 Fort Worth, TX
76110 Ft Worth, TX
76111 Fort Worth, TX
76111 Ft Worth, TX
76111 Haltom City, TX
76112 Fort Worth, TX
76112 Ft Worth, TX
76113 Fort Worth, TX
76113 Ft Worth, TX
76114 Fort Worth, TX
76114 Ft Worth, TX
76114 River Oaks, TX
76114 Westworth Village, TX
76115 Fort Worth, TX
76115 Ft Worth, TX
76116 Benbrook, TX
76116 Fort Worth, TX
76116 Ft Worth, TX
76117 Fort Worth, TX
76117 Ft Worth, TX
76117 Haltom City, TX
76117 N Richland Hills, TX
76117 North Richland Hills, TX
76118 Fort Worth, TX
76118 Ft Worth, TX
76118 N Richland Hills, TX
76118 North Richland Hills, TX
76118 Richland Hills, TX
76119 Forest Hill, TX
76119 Fort Worth, TX
76119 Ft Worth, TX
76120 Fort Worth, TX
76120 Ft Worth, TX
76121 Fort Worth, TX
76121 Ft Worth, TX
76122 Fort Worth, TX
76122 Ft Worth, TX
76123 Fort Worth, TX
76123 Ft Worth, TX
76124 Fort Worth, TX
76124 Ft Worth, TX
76126 Benbrook, TX
76126 Fort Worth, TX
76126 Ft Worth, TX
76127 Fort Worth, TX
76127 Ft Worth, TX
76127 Naval Air Station/ Jrb, TX
76129 Fort Worth, TX
76129 Ft Worth, TX
76130 Fort Worth, TX
76130 Ft Worth, TX
76131 Blue Mound, TX
76131 Fort Worth, TX
76131 Ft Worth, TX
76131 Saginaw, TX
76132 Benbrook, TX
76132 Fort Worth, TX
76132 Ft Worth, TX
76133 Fort Worth, TX
76133 Ft Worth, TX
76134 Edgecliff Village, TX
76134 Fort Worth, TX
76134 Ft Worth, TX
76135 Fort Worth, TX
76135 Ft Worth, TX
76135 Lake Worth, TX
76135 Lakeside, TX
76136 Fort Worth, TX
76136 Ft Worth, TX
76136 Lake Worth, TX
76137 Fort Worth, TX
76137 Ft Worth, TX
76137 Haltom City, TX
76137 Watauga, TX
76140 Everman, TX
76140 Forest Hill, TX
76140 Fort Worth, TX
76140 Ft Worth, TX
76147 Fort Worth, TX
76147 Ft Worth, TX
76148 Fort Worth, TX
76148 Ft Worth, TX
76148 Haltom City, TX
76148 N Richland Hills, TX
76148 North Richland Hills, TX
76148 Watauga, TX
76150 Fort Worth, TX

76150 Ft Worth, TX
76155 Fort Worth, TX
76155 Ft Worth, TX
76161 Fort Worth, TX
76161 Ft Worth, TX
76162 Fort Worth, TX
76162 Ft Worth, TX
76163 Fort Worth, TX
76163 Ft Worth, TX
76164 Fort Worth, TX
76164 Ft Worth, TX
76166 Fort Worth, TX
76166 Ft Worth, TX
76177 Fort Worth, TX
76177 Ft Worth, TX
76179 Fort Worth, TX
76179 Ft Worth, TX
76179 Saginaw, TX
76180 Fort Worth, TX
76180 Ft Worth, TX
76180 Haltom City, TX
76180 N Richland Hills, TX
76180 North Richland Hills, TX
76180 Richland Hills, TX
76181 Fort Worth, TX
76181 Ft Worth, TX
76182 Fort Worth, TX
76182 Ft Worth, TX
76182 N Richland Hills, TX
76182 North Richland Hills, TX
76185 Fort Worth, TX
76185 Ft Worth, TX
76190 Fort Worth, TX
76191 Fort Worth, TX
76191 Ft Worth, TX
76192 Fort Worth, TX
76192 Ft Worth, TX
76193 Fort Worth, TX
76193 Ft Worth, TX
76195 Fort Worth, TX
76195 Ft Worth, TX
76196 Fort Worth, TX
76196 Ft Worth, TX
76197 Fort Worth, TX
76197 Ft Worth, TX
76198 Fort Worth, TX
76198 Ft Worth, TX
76199 Fort Worth, TX
76199 Ft Worth, TX

762

76201 Denton, TX
76202 Denton, TX
76203 Denton, TX
76204 Denton, TX
76205 Denton, TX
76206 Denton, TX
76207 Denton, TX
76208 Corinth, TX
76208 Denton, TX
76208 Shady Shores, TX
76209 Denton, TX
76210 Corinth, TX
76210 Denton, TX
76225 Alvord, TX
76226 Argyle, TX
76226 Bartonville, TX
76226 Lantana, TX
76226 Northlake, TX
76227 Aubrey, TX
76227 Crossroads, TX
76227 Krugerville, TX
76227 Providence Village, TX
76227 Savannah, TX
76228 Bellevue, TX
76230 Bowie, TX
76233 Collinsville, TX
76234 Decatur, TX
76238 Era, TX
76239 Forestburg, TX
76240 Callisburg, TX
76240 Gainesville, TX
76240 Lake Kiowa, TX
76240 Oak Ridge, TX
76241 Gainesville, TX
76244 Fort Worth, TX
76244 Ft Worth, TX
76244 Keller, TX
76245 Gordonville, TX
76246 Greenwood, TX
76247 Justin, TX
76247 Northlake, TX
76248 Keller, TX
76249 Krum, TX
76250 Lindsay, TX
76251 Montague, TX
76252 Muenster, TX
76253 Myra, TX
76255 Nocona, TX
76258 Pilot Point, TX
76259 Ponder, TX
76261 Ringgold, TX
76262 Keller, TX
76262 Northlake, TX
76262 Roanoke, TX
76262 Trophy Club, TX
76262 Westlake, TX
76263 Rosston, TX
76264 Sadler, TX
76265 Saint Jo, TX
76266 Sanger, TX
76267 Slidell, TX
76268 Southmayd, TX
76270 Sunset, TX
76271 Tioga, TX
76272 Valley View, TX
76273 Whitesboro, TX

763

76301 Wichita Falls, TX
76302 Wichita Falls, TX
76305 Cashion Community, TX
76305 Dean, TX
76305 Jolly, TX
76305 Pleasant Valley, TX
76305 Wichita Falls, TX
76306 Wichita Falls, TX
76307 Wichita Falls, TX
76308 Wichita Falls, TX
76309 Wichita Falls, TX
76310 Wichita Falls, TX
76311 Sheppard Afb, TX
76351 Archer City, TX
76352 Bluegrove, TX
76354 Burkburnett, TX
76357 Byers, TX
76360 Electra, TX
76363 Goree, TX
76364 Harrold, TX
76365 Henrietta, TX
76366 Holliday, TX
76367 Iowa Park, TX
76369 Kamay, TX
76370 Megargel, TX
76371 Munday, TX
76372 Elbert, TX
76372 Newcastle, TX
76373 Oklaunion, TX
76374 Olney, TX
76377 Petrolia, TX
76379 Scotland, TX
76380 Red Springs, TX
76380 Seymour, TX
76380 Vera, TX
76384 Vernon, TX
76385 Vernon, TX
76388 Weinert, TX
76389 Windthorst, TX

764

76401 Stephenville, TX
76402 Stephenville, TX
76424 Breckenridge, TX
76426 Bridgeport, TX
76426 Runaway Bay, TX
76427 Bryson, TX
76429 Caddo, TX
76430 Albany, TX
76431 Chico, TX
76432 Blanket, TX
76433 Bluff Dale, TX
76435 Carbon, TX
76436 Carlton, TX
76437 Cisco, TX
76439 Dennis, TX
76442 Comanche, TX
76442 Hasse, TX
76443 Cross Plains, TX
76444 De Leon, TX
76445 Desdemona, TX
76446 Dublin, TX
76446 Lingleville, TX
76448 Eastland, TX
76449 Graford, TX
76450 Graham, TX
76452 Energy, TX
76453 Gordon, TX
76454 Gorman, TX
76455 Gustine, TX
76457 Hico, TX
76458 Jacksboro, TX
76459 Jermyn, TX
76460 Loving, TX
76461 Lingleville, TX
76462 Lipan, TX
76463 Mingus, TX
76464 Moran, TX
76465 Morgan Mill, TX
76466 Olden, TX
76467 Paluxy, TX
76468 Proctor, TX
76469 Putnam, TX
76470 Ranger, TX
76471 Rising Star, TX
76472 Santo, TX
76474 Sidney, TX
76475 Strawn, TX
76476 Tolar, TX
76481 Eliasville, TX
76481 South Bend, TX
76483 Throckmorton, TX
76484 Palo Pinto, TX
76485 Peaster, TX
76486 Perrin, TX
76487 Poolville, TX
76490 Whitt, TX
76491 Woodson, TX

765

76501 Temple, TX
76502 Temple, TX
76503 Temple, TX
76504 Temple, TX
76505 Temple, TX
76508 Temple, TX
76511 Bartlett, TX
76513 Belton, TX
76513 Morgans Point Resort, TX
76518 Buckholts, TX
76519 Ben Arnold, TX
76519 Burlington, TX
76520 Cameron, TX
76520 Maysfield, TX
76522 Copperas Cove, TX
76523 Davilla, TX
76524 Eddy, TX
76525 Bee House, TX
76525 Evant, TX
76526 Flat, TX
76527 Florence, TX
76528 Gatesville, TX
76528 Izoro, TX
76528 Leon Junction, TX
76528 South Mountain, TX
76530 Granger, TX
76531 Hamilton, TX
76533 Heidenheimer, TX
76534 Holland, TX
76537 Jarrell, TX
76538 Jonesboro, TX
76539 Kempner, TX
76540 Killeen, TX
76541 Killeen, TX
76542 Killeen, TX
76543 Killeen, TX
76544 Fort Hood, TX
76544 Killeen, TX
76547 Killeen, TX
76548 Harker Heights, TX
76548 Killeen, TX
76549 Killeen, TX
76550 Lampasas, TX
76554 Little River Academy, TX
76556 Milano, TX
76557 Moody, TX
76558 Mound, TX
76559 Nolanville, TX
76561 Oglesby, TX
76564 Pendleton, TX
76565 Pottsville, TX
76566 Purmela, TX
76567 Rockdale, TX
76569 Rogers, TX
76570 Rosebud, TX
76571 Salado, TX
76573 Schwertner, TX
76574 Taylor, TX
76577 Thorndale, TX
76578 Thrall, TX
76579 Troy, TX
76596 Gatesville, TX
76597 Gatesville, TX
76598 Gatesville, TX
76599 Gatesville, TX

766

76621 Abbott, TX
76622 Aquilla, TX
76623 Avalon, TX
76624 Axtell, TX
76626 Blooming Grove, TX
76627 Blum, TX
76628 Brandon, TX
76629 Bremond, TX
76630 Bruceville, TX
76631 Bynum, TX
76632 Chilton, TX
76633 China Spring, TX
76634 Clifton, TX
76634 Laguna Park, TX
76635 Coolidge, TX
76636 Covington, TX
76637 Cranfills Gap, TX
76638 Crawford, TX
76639 Dawson, TX
76640 Elm Mott, TX
76641 Frost, TX
76642 Groesbeck, TX
76642 Lake Limestone, TX
76643 Hewitt, TX
76644 Clifton, TX
76644 Laguna Park, TX
76645 Hillsboro, TX
76648 Hubbard, TX
76649 Iredell, TX
76650 Irene, TX
76651 Italy, TX
76652 Kopperl, TX
76653 Kosse, TX
76654 Leroy, TX
76655 Lorena, TX
76656 Lott, TX
76657 Mc Gregor, TX
76660 Malone, TX
76661 Marlin, TX
76664 Mart, TX
76665 Meridian, TX
76666 Mertens, TX
76667 Mexia, TX
76670 Milford, TX
76671 Morgan, TX
76673 Birome, TX
76673 Mount Calm, TX
76676 Penelope, TX
76678 Prairie Hill, TX
76679 Purdon, TX
76680 Reagan, TX
76681 Richland, TX
76682 Otto, TX
76682 Perry, TX
76682 Riesel, TX
76684 Ross, TX
76685 Satin, TX
76686 Tehuacana, TX
76687 Thornton, TX
76689 Valley Mills, TX
76690 Walnut Springs, TX
76691 West, TX
76692 Whitney, TX
76693 Wortham, TX

767

76701 Waco, TX
76702 Waco, TX
76703 Waco, TX
76704 Bellmead, TX
76704 Waco, TX
76705 Bellmead, TX
76705 Lacy Lakeview, TX
76705 Waco, TX
76706 Robinson, TX
76706 Waco, TX
76707 Waco, TX
76708 Waco, TX
76710 Waco, TX
76711 Beverly Hills, TX
76711 Waco, TX
76712 Waco, TX
76712 Woodway, TX
76714 Waco, TX
76715 Waco, TX
76716 Waco, TX
76797 Waco, TX
76798 Waco, TX
76799 Waco, TX

768

76801 Brownwood, TX
76802 Brownwood, TX
76802 Early, TX
76803 Brownwood, TX
76803 Early, TX
76804 Brownwood, TX
76820 Art, TX
76821 Ballinger, TX
76823 Bangs, TX
76824 Bend, TX
76825 Brady, TX
76825 Fife, TX
76827 Brookesmith, TX
76828 Burkett, TX
76831 Castell, TX
76832 Cherokee, TX
76834 Coleman, TX
76836 Doole, TX
76837 Eden, TX
76841 Fort Mc Kavett, TX
76842 Fredonia, TX
76844 Goldthwaite, TX
76845 Gouldbusk, TX
76848 Hext, TX
76849 Junction, TX
76852 Lohn, TX
76852 Pear Valley, TX
76853 Lometa, TX
76854 London, TX
76855 Lowake, TX
76856 Mason, TX
76857 May, TX
76858 Melvin, TX
76859 Menard, TX
76861 Miles, TX
76862 Millersview, TX
76864 Mullin, TX
76865 Norton, TX
76866 Paint Rock, TX
76869 Pontotoc, TX
76870 Priddy, TX
76871 Richland Springs, TX
76872 Rochelle, TX
76873 Rockwood, TX
76874 Roosevelt, TX
76875 Rowena, TX
76877 San Saba, TX
76878 Santa Anna, TX
76878 Whon, TX
76880 Star, TX
76882 Talpa, TX
76883 Telegraph, TX
76884 Valera, TX
76885 Valley Spring, TX
76886 Veribest, TX
76887 Voca, TX
76888 Leaday, TX
76888 Voss, TX
76890 Zephyr, TX

769

76901 Grape Creek, TX
76901 San Angelo, TX
76902 San Angelo, TX
76903 San Angelo, TX
76904 San Angelo, TX
76905 San Angelo, TX
76906 San Angelo, TX
76908 Goodfellow Afb, TX
76908 San Angelo, TX
76909 San Angelo, TX
76930 Barnhart, TX
76932 Best, TX
76932 Big Lake, TX
76932 Texon, TX
76933 Bronte, TX
76934 Carlsbad, TX
76935 Christoval, TX
76936 Eldorado, TX
76936 Eldorado Afs, TX
76937 Eola, TX
76939 Knickerbocker, TX
76940 Mereta, TX
76941 Mertzon, TX
76943 Ozona, TX
76945 Robert Lee, TX
76945 Silver, TX
76949 Silver, TX
76950 Sonora, TX
76951 Sterling City, TX
76953 Tennyson, TX
76955 Vancourt, TX
76957 Wall, TX
76958 Water Valley, TX

770

77001 Houston, TX
77002 Clutch City, TX
77002 Houston, TX
77003 Houston, TX
77004 Houston, TX
77005 Houston, TX
77005 West University Place, TX
77006 Houston, TX
77007 Houston, TX
77008 Houston, TX
77009 Houston, TX
77010 Houston, TX
77011 Houston, TX
77012 Houston, TX
77013 Houston, TX
77014 Houston, TX
77015 Houston, TX
77016 Houston, TX
77017 Houston, TX
77018 Houston, TX
77019 Houston, TX
77020 Houston, TX
77021 Houston, TX
77022 Houston, TX
77023 Houston, TX
77024 Houston, TX
77024 Piney Point Village, TX
77025 Houston, TX
77026 Houston, TX
77027 Houston, TX
77028 Houston, TX
77029 Houston, TX
77029 Jacinto City, TX
77030 Houston, TX
77030 Va Hospital, TX
77031 Houston, TX
77032 Houston, TX
77033 Houston, TX
77034 Houston, TX
77035 Houston, TX
77036 Houston, TX
77037 Houston, TX
77038 Houston, TX
77039 Houston, TX

77040 Houston, TX
77040 Jersey Village, TX
77041 Houston, TX
77041 Jersey Village, TX
77042 Houston, TX
77043 Houston, TX
77044 Houston, TX
77045 Houston, TX
77046 Houston, TX
77047 Houston, TX
77048 Houston, TX
77049 Houston, TX
77050 Houston, TX
77051 Houston, TX
77052 Houston, TX
77053 Houston, TX
77054 Gridiron, TX
77054 Houston, TX
77055 Houston, TX
77056 Houston, TX
77057 Houston, TX
77058 Houston, TX
77059 Houston, TX
77060 Houston, TX
77061 Houston, TX
77062 Houston, TX
77063 Houston, TX
77064 Houston, TX
77064 Jersey Village, TX
77065 Houston, TX
77065 Jersey Village, TX
77066 Houston, TX
77067 Houston, TX
77068 Houston, TX
77069 Houston, TX
77070 Houston, TX
77071 Houston, TX
77072 Houston, TX
77073 Houston, TX
77074 Houston, TX
77075 Houston, TX
77076 Houston, TX
77077 Houston, TX
77078 Houston, TX
77079 Houston, TX
77080 Houston, TX
77081 Houston, TX
77082 Houston, TX
77083 Houston, TX
77084 Houston, TX
77085 Houston, TX
77086 Houston, TX
77087 Houston, TX
77088 Houston, TX
77089 Houston, TX
77090 Houston, TX
77091 Houston, TX
77092 Houston, TX
77093 Houston, TX
77094 Houston, TX
77095 Houston, TX
77096 Houston, TX
77098 Houston, TX
77099 Houston, TX

772

77201 Houston, TX
77202 Houston, TX
77203 Houston, TX
77204 Houston, TX
77205 Houston, TX
77205 Humble, TX
77206 Houston, TX
77207 Houston, TX
77208 Houston, TX
77209 Houston, TX
77210 Houston, TX
77212 Houston, TX
77213 Houston, TX
77215 Houston, TX
77216 Houston, TX
77217 Houston, TX
77218 Houston, TX
77219 Houston, TX
77220 Houston, TX
77221 Houston, TX
77222 Houston, TX
77223 Houston, TX
77224 Houston, TX
77225 Houston, TX
77226 Houston, TX
77227 Houston, TX
77228 Houston, TX
77229 Houston, TX
77230 Houston, TX
77231 Houston, TX
77233 Houston, TX
77234 Houston, TX
77235 Houston, TX
77236 Houston, TX
77237 Houston, TX
77238 Houston, TX
77240 Houston, TX
77241 Houston, TX
77242 Houston, TX
77243 Houston, TX
77244 Houston, TX
77245 Houston, TX
77248 Houston, TX
77249 Houston, TX
77251 Houston, TX
77252 Houston, TX
77253 Houston, TX
77254 Houston, TX
77255 Houston, TX
77256 Houston, TX
77257 Houston, TX
77258 Houston, TX
77259 Houston, TX
77261 Houston, TX
77262 Houston, TX
77263 Houston, TX
77265 Houston, TX
77266 Houston, TX
77267 Houston, TX
77268 Houston, TX
77269 Houston, TX
77270 Houston, TX
77271 Houston, TX
77272 Houston, TX
77273 Houston, TX
77274 Houston, TX
77275 Houston, TX
77277 Houston, TX
77279 Houston, TX
77280 Houston, TX
77282 Houston, TX
77284 Houston, TX
77287 Houston, TX
77288 Houston, TX
77289 Houston, TX
77290 Houston, TX
77291 Houston, TX
77292 Houston, TX
77293 Houston, TX
77297 Houston, TX
77299 Houston, TX

773

77301 Conroe, TX
77302 Conroe, TX
77302 Grangerland, TX
77302 Woodloch, TX
77303 Conroe, TX
77303 Cut And Shoot, TX
77304 Conroe, TX
77304 Panorama Village, TX
77305 Conroe, TX
77306 Conroe, TX
77306 Cut And Shoot, TX
77315 North Houston, TX
77316 Montgomery, TX
77318 Willis, TX
77320 Huntsville, TX
77325 Humble, TX
77325 Kingwood, TX
77326 Ace, TX
77327 Cleveland, TX
77328 Cleveland, TX
77331 Coldspring, TX
77332 Dallardsville, TX
77333 Dobbin, TX
77334 Dodge, TX
77335 Goodrich, TX
77336 Huffman, TX
77337 Hufsmith, TX
77337 Tomball, TX
77338 Humble, TX
77339 Humble, TX
77339 Kingwood, TX
77340 Huntsville, TX
77341 Huntsville, TX
77342 Huntsville, TX
77343 Huntsville, TX
77344 Huntsville, TX
77345 Humble, TX
77345 Kingwood, TX
77346 Atascocita, TX
77346 Humble, TX
77346 Kingwood, TX
77347 Humble, TX
77348 Huntsville, TX
77349 Huntsville, TX
77350 Leggett, TX
77351 Livingston, TX
77351 Segno, TX
77353 Magnolia, TX
77354 Decker Prairie, TX
77354 Magnolia, TX
77354 The Woodlands, TX
77355 Decker Prairie, TX
77355 Magnolia, TX
77355 Stagecoach, TX
77356 Montgomery, TX
77357 New Caney, TX
77357 Roman Forest, TX
77358 New Waverly, TX
77359 Oakhurst, TX
77360 Onalaska, TX
77362 Pinehurst, TX
77363 Plantersville, TX
77363 Todd Mission, TX
77364 Pointblank, TX
77365 Porter, TX
77367 Riverside, TX
77368 Romayor, TX
77369 Rye, TX
77371 Shepherd, TX
77372 Patton Village, TX
77372 Splendora, TX
77373 Spring, TX
77374 Thicket, TX
77375 The Woodlands, TX
77375 Tomball, TX
77376 Votaw, TX
77377 Tomball, TX
77378 Willis, TX
77379 Klein, TX
77379 Spring, TX
77380 Shenandoah, TX
77380 Spring, TX
77380 The Woodlands, TX
77381 Shenandoah, TX
77381 Spring, TX
77381 The Woodlands, TX
77382 Spring, TX
77382 The Woodlands, TX
77383 Spring, TX
77384 Conroe, TX
77384 Shenandoah, TX
77384 The Woodlands, TX
77385 Conroe, TX
77385 Oak Ridge North, TX
77385 Shenandoah, TX
77385 The Woodlands, TX
77386 Oak Ridge North, TX
77386 Spring, TX
77386 The Woodlands, TX
77387 Spring, TX
77387 The Woodlands, TX
77388 Spring, TX
77389 Klein, TX
77389 Spring, TX
77389 The Woodlands, TX
77391 Klein, TX
77391 Spring, TX
77393 Spring, TX
77393 The Woodlands, TX
77396 Humble, TX
77399 Livingston, TX

774

77401 Bellaire, TX
77402 Bellaire, TX
77404 Bay City, TX
77404 Sargent, TX
77406 Richmond, TX
77407 Richmond, TX
77410 Cypress, TX
77411 Alief, TX
77412 Altair, TX
77413 Barker, TX
77414 Bay City, TX
77414 Clemville, TX
77414 Sargent, TX
77415 Cedar Lane, TX
77417 Beasley, TX
77418 Bellville, TX
77419 Blessing, TX
77420 Boling, TX
77422 Brazoria, TX
77423 Brookshire, TX
77423 Pattison, TX
77426 Chappell Hill, TX
77428 Collegeport, TX
77429 Cypress, TX
77430 Damon, TX
77431 Danciger, TX
77432 Danevang, TX
77433 Cypress, TX
77434 Eagle Lake, TX
77435 East Bernard, TX
77436 Egypt, TX
77437 El Campo, TX
77440 Elmaton, TX
77441 Fulshear, TX
77441 Weston Lakes, TX
77442 Garwood, TX
77443 Glen Flora, TX
77444 Guy, TX
77445 Hempstead, TX
77445 Pine Island, TX
77445 Prairie View, TX
77446 Prairie View, TX
77447 Hockley, TX
77448 Hungerford, TX
77449 Katy, TX
77449 Park Row, TX
77450 Katy, TX
77450 Park Row, TX
77451 Kendleton, TX
77452 Kenney, TX
77453 Lane City, TX
77454 Lissie, TX
77455 Louise, TX
77456 Markham, TX
77457 Matagorda, TX
77458 Midfield, TX
77459 Missouri City, TX
77459 Sienna Plantation, TX
77460 Nada, TX
77461 Needville, TX
77463 Old Ocean, TX
77464 Orchard, TX
77465 Palacios, TX
77466 Pattison, TX
77467 Pierce, TX
77468 Pledger, TX
77469 Booth, TX
77469 Clodine, TX
77469 Richmond, TX
77469 Rosenberg, TX
77470 Rock Island, TX
77471 Rosenberg, TX
77473 San Felipe, TX
77474 Sealy, TX
77475 Sheridan, TX
77476 Simonton, TX
77477 Meadows Place, TX
77477 Stafford, TX
77478 Sugar Land, TX
77479 Sugar Land, TX
77480 Sweeny, TX
77481 Thompsons, TX
77482 Van Vleck, TX
77483 Wadsworth, TX
77484 Prairie View, TX
77484 Waller, TX
77485 Wallis, TX
77486 West Columbia, TX
77487 Sugar Land, TX
77488 Wharton, TX
77489 Missouri City, TX
77491 Katy, TX
77491 Park Row, TX
77492 Katy, TX
77493 Katy, TX
77493 Park Row, TX
77494 Katy, TX
77494 Park Row, TX
77496 Sugar Land, TX
77497 Stafford, TX
77498 Sugar Land, TX

775

77501 Pasadena, TX
77502 Pasadena, TX
77503 Pasadena, TX
77504 Pasadena, TX
77505 Pasadena, TX
77506 Pasadena, TX
77507 Pasadena, TX
77508 Pasadena, TX
77510 Alta Loma, TX
77510 Santa Fe, TX
77511 Alvin, TX
77512 Alvin, TX
77514 Anahuac, TX
77514 Monroe City, TX
77515 Angleton, TX
77515 Holiday Lakes, TX
77515 Richwood, TX
77516 Angleton, TX
77517 Arcadia, TX
77517 Santa Fe, TX
77518 Bacliff, TX
77519 Batson, TX
77520 Baytown, TX
77520 Beach City, TX
77520 Cove, TX
77520 Mont Belvieu, TX
77520 Old River Winfree, TX
77521 Baytown, TX
77522 Baytown, TX
77523 Baytown, TX
77523 Beach City, TX
77523 Cove, TX
77523 Mont Belvieu, TX
77523 Old River Winfree, TX
77530 Channelview, TX
77531 Clute, TX
77531 Richwood, TX
77532 Crosby, TX
77533 Daisetta, TX
77534 Danbury, TX
77535 Dayton, TX
77535 Dayton Lakes, TX
77535 Mont Belvieu, TX
77535 Old River Winfree, TX
77536 Deer Park, TX
77538 Devers, TX
77539 Dickinson, TX
77539 San Leon, TX
77541 Freeport, TX
77541 Jones Creek, TX
77541 Oyster Creek, TX
77541 Quintana, TX
77541 Surfside Beach, TX
77542 Freeport, TX
77545 Fresno, TX
77546 Friendswood, TX
77547 Galena Park, TX
77549 Friendswood, TX
77550 Galveston, TX
77551 Galveston, TX
77552 Galveston, TX
77553 Galveston, TX
77554 Galveston, TX
77554 Jamaica Beach, TX
77554 Tiki Island, TX
77555 Galveston, TX
77560 Hankamer, TX
77561 Hardin, TX
77562 Highlands, TX
77563 Bayou Vista, TX
77563 Hitchcock, TX
77564 Hull, TX
77565 Clear Lake Shores, TX
77565 Kemah, TX
77566 Lake Jackson, TX
77566 Richwood, TX
77568 La Marque, TX
77571 La Porte, TX
77571 Shoreacres, TX
77572 La Porte, TX
77573 League City, TX
77574 League City, TX
77575 Ames, TX
77575 Liberty, TX
77577 Liverpool, TX
77578 Manvel, TX
77580 Mont Belvieu, TX
77581 Brookside Village, TX
77581 Pearland, TX
77582 Raywood, TX
77583 Arcola, TX
77583 Rosharon, TX
77584 Pearland, TX
77585 Saratoga, TX
77586 El Lago, TX
77586 Seabrook, TX
77586 Taylor Lake Village, TX
77587 South Houston, TX
77588 Pearland, TX
77590 Texas City, TX
77591 Texas City, TX
77592 Texas City, TX
77597 Wallisville, TX
77598 Webster, TX

776

77611 Bridge City, TX
77612 Buna, TX
77613 China, TX
77614 Deweyville, TX
77615 Evadale, TX
77616 Fred, TX
77617 Gilchrist, TX
77619 Groves, TX
77622 Hamshire, TX
77623 High Island, TX
77624 Hillister, TX
77625 Kountze, TX
77626 Mauriceville, TX
77627 Nederland, TX
77629 Nome, TX
77630 Orange, TX
77630 West Orange, TX
77631 Orange, TX
77632 Orange, TX
77639 Orangefield, TX
77640 Port Acres, TX
77640 Port Arthur, TX
77641 Port Arthur, TX
77642 Port Arthur, TX
77643 Port Arthur, TX
77650 Crystal Beach, TX
77650 Port Bolivar, TX
77651 Port Neches, TX
77655 Sabine Pass, TX
77656 Silsbee, TX
77657 Lumberton, TX
77657 Rose Hill Acres, TX
77659 Sour Lake, TX
77660 Spurger, TX
77661 Stowell, TX
77662 Vidor, TX
77663 Village Mills, TX
77664 Warren, TX
77665 Winnie, TX
77670 Vidor, TX

777

77701 Beaumont, TX
77702 Beaumont, TX
77703 Beaumont, TX
77704 Beaumont, TX
77705 Beaumont, TX
77705 Taylor Landing, TX
77706 Beaumont, TX
77707 Beaumont, TX

77708 Beaumont, TX
77709 Beaumont, TX
77710 Beaumont, TX
77713 Beaumont, TX
77713 Bevil Oaks, TX
77720 Beaumont, TX
77725 Beaumont, TX
77726 Beaumont, TX

778

77801 Bryan, TX
77802 Bryan, TX
77803 Bryan, TX
77805 Bryan, TX
77806 Bryan, TX
77807 Bryan, TX
77807 Mumford, TX
77808 Bryan, TX
77808 Wixon Valley, TX
77830 Anderson, TX
77831 Bedias, TX
77831 Singleton, TX
77833 Brenham, TX
77834 Brenham, TX
77835 Burton, TX
77836 Caldwell, TX
77837 Calvert, TX
77838 Chriesman, TX
77840 College Station, TX
77844 College Sta, TX
77844 College Station, TX
77845 College Station, TX
77845 College Station, TX
77850 Concord, TX
77852 Deanville, TX
77853 Dime Box, TX
77855 Flynn, TX
77856 Franklin, TX
77856 Ridge, TX
77857 Gause, TX
77859 Hearne, TX
77861 Iola, TX
77862 Kurten, TX
77863 Lyons, TX
77864 Madisonville, TX
77865 Marquez, TX
77866 Millican, TX
77867 Mumford, TX
77868 Navasota, TX
77870 New Baden, TX
77871 Hilltop Lakes, TX
77871 Normangee, TX
77872 North Zulch, TX
77873 Richards, TX
77875 Anderson, TX
77875 Roans Prairie, TX
77876 Shiro, TX
77878 Snook, TX
77879 Somerville, TX
77880 Washington, TX
77881 Wellborn, TX
77882 Wheelock, TX

779

77901 Victoria, TX
77902 Victoria, TX
77903 Victoria, TX
77904 Victoria, TX
77905 Raisin, TX
77905 Victoria, TX
77950 Austwell, TX
77951 Bloomington, TX
77954 Cuero, TX
77957 Edna, TX
77960 Fannin, TX
77961 Francitas, TX
77962 Ganado, TX
77963 Goliad, TX
77964 Hallettsville, TX
77964 Speaks, TX
77967 Hochheim, TX
77968 Inez, TX
77969 La Salle, TX
77970 La Ward, TX
77971 Lolita, TX
77973 Mcfaddin, TX
77974 Meyersville, TX
77975 Moulton, TX
77976 Nursery, TX
77977 Placedo, TX
77978 Point Comfort, TX
77979 Long Mott, TX
77979 Port Lavaca, TX
77982 Port O Connor, TX
77983 Seadrift, TX
77984 Shiner, TX
77986 Sublime, TX
77987 Sweet Home, TX
77988 Telferner, TX
77989 Thomaston, TX
77990 Tivoli, TX
77991 Vanderbilt, TX
77993 Weesatche, TX
77994 Westhoff, TX
77995 Yoakum, TX

780

78001 Artesia Wells, TX
78002 Atascosa, TX
78003 Bandera, TX
78004 Bergheim, TX
78005 Bigfoot, TX
78006 Boerne, TX
78006 Fair Oaks Ranch, TX
78007 Calliham, TX
78008 Campbellton, TX
78009 Castroville, TX
78010 Camp Verde, TX
78010 Center Point, TX
78011 Charlotte, TX
78012 Christine, TX
78013 Comfort, TX
78014 Cotulla, TX
78015 Boerne, TX
78015 Fair Oaks Ranch, TX
78016 Devine, TX
78017 Dilley, TX
78019 Encinal, TX
78021 Fowlerton, TX
78022 George West, TX
78023 Helotes, TX
78024 Hunt, TX
78025 Ingram, TX
78026 Jourdanton, TX
78027 Kendalia, TX
78028 Kerrville, TX
78029 Kerrville, TX
78039 La Coste, TX
78040 Laredo, TX
78041 Laredo, TX
78042 Laredo, TX
78043 Laredo, TX
78043 Rio Bravo, TX
78044 Laredo, TX
78045 Laredo, TX
78046 El Cenizo, TX
78046 Laredo, TX
78049 Laredo, TX
78050 Leming, TX
78052 Lytle, TX
78054 Macdona, TX
78055 Medina, TX
78056 Castroville, TX
78056 Mico, TX
78057 Moore, TX
78058 Mountain Home, TX
78059 Natalia, TX
78060 Oakville, TX
78061 Pearsall, TX
78062 Peggy, TX
78063 Lakehills, TX
78063 Pipe Creek, TX
78064 Pleasanton, TX
78065 Poteet, TX
78066 Rio Medina, TX
78067 San Ygnacio, TX
78069 Somerset, TX
78070 Spring Branch, TX
78071 Three Rivers, TX
78072 Tilden, TX
78073 Von Ormy, TX
78074 Waring, TX
78075 Whitsett, TX
78076 Zapata, TX

781

78101 Adkins, TX
78102 Beeville, TX
78104 Beeville, TX
78107 Berclair, TX
78108 Cibolo, TX
78108 Schertz, TX
78109 Converse, TX
78111 Ecleto, TX
78111 Gillett, TX
78112 Elmendorf, TX
78113 Falls City, TX
78113 Mccoy, TX
78114 Floresville, TX
78115 Geronimo, TX
78116 Gillett, TX
78117 Hobson, TX
78118 Karnes City, TX
78119 Kenedy, TX
78121 La Vernia, TX
78121 Lavernia, TX
78122 Leesville, TX
78123 Mc Queeney, TX
78123 Mcqueeney, TX
78124 Marion, TX
78124 Santa Clara, TX
78125 Kenedy, TX
78125 Mineral, TX
78130 Canyon Lake, TX
78130 New Braunfels, TX
78131 New Braunfels, TX
78132 Canyon Lake, TX
78132 New Braunfels, TX
78133 Canyon Lake, TX
78133 New Braunfels, TX
78135 New Braunfels, TX
78140 Nixon, TX
78141 Nordheim, TX
78142 Normanna, TX
78143 Pandora, TX
78144 Panna Maria, TX
78145 Pawnee, TX
78146 Pettus, TX
78147 Poth, TX
78148 Universal City, TX
78150 Jbsa Randolph, TX
78150 Randolph Air, TX
78150 Randolph Air Force Base, TX
78150 Universal City, TX
78151 Runge, TX
78152 Saint Hedwig, TX
78154 Schertz, TX
78154 Selma, TX
78155 New Berlin, TX
78155 Seguin, TX
78156 Seguin, TX
78159 Smiley, TX
78160 Stockdale, TX
78161 Sutherland Springs, TX
78162 Tuleta, TX
78163 Bulverde, TX
78164 Yorktown, TX

782

78201 Balcones Heights, TX
78201 San Antonio, TX
78202 San Antonio, TX
78203 San Antonio, TX
78204 San Antonio, TX
78205 San Antonio, TX
78206 San Antonio, TX
78207 San Antonio, TX
78208 San Antonio, TX
78209 Alamo Heights, TX
78209 San Antonio, TX
78209 Terrell Hills, TX
78210 San Antonio, TX
78211 San Antonio, TX
78212 Olmos Park, TX
78212 San Antonio, TX
78213 Castle Hills, TX
78213 San Antonio, TX
78214 San Antonio, TX
78215 San Antonio, TX
78216 San Antonio, TX
78217 San Antonio, TX
78218 San Antonio, TX
78218 Windcrest, TX
78219 Kirby, TX
78219 San Antonio, TX
78220 San Antonio, TX
78221 San Antonio, TX
78222 San Antonio, TX
78223 San Antonio, TX
78224 San Antonio, TX
78225 San Antonio, TX
78226 San Antonio, TX
78227 San Antonio, TX
78228 San Antonio, TX
78229 San Antonio, TX
78230 San Antonio, TX
78230 Shavano Park, TX
78231 San Antonio, TX
78231 Shavano Park, TX
78232 Hill Country Village, TX
78232 Hollywood Park, TX
78232 San Antonio, TX
78233 Live Oak, TX
78233 San Antonio, TX
78234 Fort Sam Houston, TX
78234 Jbsa Ft Sam Houston, TX
78234 San Antonio, TX
78235 Brooks City Base, TX
78235 San Antonio, TX
78236 Jbsa Lackland, TX
78236 Lackland Afb, TX
78236 San Antonio, TX
78236 Security Services, TX
78236 Wilford Hall Usaf Hosp, TX
78237 San Antonio, TX
78238 Leon Valley, TX
78238 San Antonio, TX
78239 San Antonio, TX
78239 Windcrest, TX
78240 San Antonio, TX
78241 San Antonio, TX
78242 San Antonio, TX
78243 San Antonio, TX
78244 San Antonio, TX
78245 San Antonio, TX
78246 San Antonio, TX
78247 San Antonio, TX
78247 Wetmore, TX
78248 San Antonio, TX
78249 San Antonio, TX
78249 Shavano Park, TX
78250 San Antonio, TX
78251 San Antonio, TX
78252 San Antonio, TX
78253 San Antonio, TX
78254 San Antonio, TX
78255 San Antonio, TX
78256 San Antonio, TX
78257 San Antonio, TX
78257 Shavano Park, TX
78258 San Antonio, TX
78259 San Antonio, TX
78260 San Antonio, TX
78261 San Antonio, TX
78263 China Grove, TX
78263 San Antonio, TX
78264 San Antonio, TX
78265 San Antonio, TX
78266 Garden Ridge, TX
78266 San Antonio, TX
78268 Leon Valley, TX
78268 San Antonio, TX
78269 San Antonio, TX
78270 San Antonio, TX
78270 Wetmore, TX
78278 San Antonio, TX
78279 San Antonio, TX
78280 San Antonio, TX
78283 San Antonio, TX
78284 San Antonio, TX
78285 San Antonio, TX
78288 San Antonio, TX
78289 San Antonio, TX
78291 San Antonio, TX
78292 San Antonio, TX
78293 San Antonio, TX
78294 San Antonio, TX
78295 San Antonio, TX
78296 San Antonio, TX
78297 San Antonio, TX
78298 San Antonio, TX
78299 San Antonio, TX

783

78330 Agua Dulce, TX
78332 Alice, TX
78333 Alice, TX
78335 Aransas Pass, TX
78336 Aransas Pass, TX
78336 City By The Sea, TX
78338 Armstrong, TX
78339 Banquete, TX
78340 Bayside, TX
78341 Benavides, TX
78342 Alice, TX
78342 Ben Bolt, TX
78343 Bishop, TX
78344 Bruni, TX
78347 Chapman Ranch, TX
78349 Concepcion, TX
78350 Dinero, TX
78351 Driscoll, TX
78352 Edroy, TX
78353 Encino, TX
78355 Falfurrias, TX
78357 Freer, TX
78358 Fulton, TX
78359 Gregory, TX
78360 Guerra, TX
78361 Hebbronville, TX
78362 Ingleside, TX
78363 Kingsville, TX
78363 Kingsville Naval Air Station, TX
78363 Kingsvl Naval, TX
78364 Kingsville, TX
78368 Lake City, TX
78368 Mathis, TX
78368 Swinney Switch, TX
78369 Mirando City, TX
78370 Odem, TX
78371 Oilton, TX
78372 Orange Grove, TX
78373 Port Aransas, TX
78374 Portland, TX
78375 Premont, TX
78376 Realitos, TX
78377 Refugio, TX
78379 Riviera, TX
78380 Robstown, TX
78381 Rockport, TX
78382 Rockport, TX
78383 Sandia, TX
78384 San Diego, TX
78385 Sarita, TX
78387 Sinton, TX
78389 Skidmore, TX
78390 Taft, TX
78391 Tynan, TX
78393 Woodsboro, TX

784

78401 Corpus Christi, TX

785

78501 Mcallen, TX
78502 Mcallen, TX
78503 Mcallen, TX
78504 Mcallen, TX
78505 Mcallen, TX
78516 Alamo, TX
78520 Brownsville, TX
78521 Brownsville, TX
78522 Brownsville, TX
78523 Brownsville, TX
78526 Brownsville, TX
78535 Combes, TX
78536 Delmita, TX
78537 Donna, TX
78538 Edcouch, TX
78538 Monte Alto, TX
78539 Edinburg, TX
78540 Edinburg, TX
78541 Edinburg, TX
78542 Edinburg, TX
78543 Elsa, TX
78545 Falcon Heights, TX
78547 Garciasville, TX
78548 Grulla, TX
78548 La Grulla, TX
78549 Hargill, TX
78550 Harlingen, TX
78551 Harlingen, TX
78552 Harlingen, TX
78552 Palm Valley, TX
78553 Harlingen, TX
78557 Hidalgo, TX
78558 La Blanca, TX
78559 La Feria, TX
78560 La Joya, TX
78561 Lasara, TX
78562 La Villa, TX
78563 Linn, TX
78564 Falcon, TX
78564 Lopeno, TX
78565 Los Ebanos, TX
78566 Bayview, TX
78566 Indian Lake, TX
78566 Los Fresnos, TX
78567 Los Indios, TX
78568 Lozano, TX
78569 Lyford, TX
78570 Mercedes, TX
78572 Mission, TX
78572 Palmhurst, TX
78572 Palmview, TX
78573 Alton, TX
78573 Mission, TX
78573 Palmhurst, TX
78574 Mission, TX
78574 Palmhurst, TX
78574 Palmview, TX
78575 Olmito, TX
78575 Rancho Viejo, TX
78576 Penitas, TX
78577 Pharr, TX
78578 Laguna Heights, TX
78578 Laguna Vista, TX
78578 Port Isabel, TX
78579 Progreso, TX
78580 Raymondville, TX
78582 Rio Grande City, TX
78583 Rio Hondo, TX
78584 Roma, TX
78585 Salineno, TX
78586 San Benito, TX
78588 San Isidro, TX
78589 San Juan, TX
78590 San Perlita, TX
78591 Santa Elena, TX
78592 Santa Maria, TX
78593 Santa Rosa, TX
78594 Sebastian, TX
78595 Sullivan City, TX
78596 Progreso Lakes, TX
78596 Weslaco, TX
78597 S Padre Isl E, TX
78597 South Padre Island, TX
78598 Port Mansfield, TX
78598 Raymondville, TX
78599 Weslaco, TX

786

78602 Bastrop, TX
78604 Belmont, TX
78605 Bertram, TX
78606 Blanco, TX
78607 Bluffton, TX
78608 Briggs, TX
78608 Oakalla, TX
78609 Buchanan Dam, TX
78610 Buda, TX
78610 Creedmoor, TX
78610 Hays, TX
78610 Mountain City, TX
78610 Mustang Ridge, TX
78611 Burnet, TX
78612 Cedar Creek, TX

78612 Lost Pines, TX
78613 Cedar Park, TX
78614 Bebe, TX
78614 Cost, TX
78615 Coupland, TX
78616 Dale, TX
78616 Mcmahan, TX
78617 Del Valle, TX
78618 Doss, TX
78619 Driftwood, TX
78620 Dripping Springs, TX
78621 Elgin, TX
78621 Webberville, TX
78622 Fentress, TX
78623 Fischer, TX
78624 Fredericksburg, TX
78626 Georgetown, TX
78627 Georgetown, TX
78628 Andice, TX
78628 Georgetown, TX
78628 Sun City, TX
78629 Gonzales, TX
78630 Cedar Park, TX
78631 Harper, TX
78632 Harwood, TX
78633 Georgetown, TX
78634 Hutto, TX
78635 Hye, TX
78636 Johnson City, TX
78638 Kingsbury, TX
78639 Kingsland, TX
78640 Kyle, TX
78640 Niederwald, TX
78640 Uhland, TX
78641 Leander, TX
78641 Volente, TX
78642 Liberty Hill, TX
78643 Llano, TX
78643 Sunrise Beach, TX
78644 Lockhart, TX
78645 Jonestown, TX
78645 Lago Vista, TX
78645 Leander, TX
78645 Point Venture, TX
78646 Leander, TX
78648 Luling, TX
78650 Mc Dade, TX
78650 Mcdade, TX
78651 Mc Neil, TX
78651 Mcneil, TX
78652 Manchaca, TX
78653 Manor, TX
78653 Webberville, TX
78654 Granite Shoals, TX
78654 Highland Haven, TX
78654 Marble Falls, TX
78654 Meadowlakes, TX
78655 Martindale, TX
78656 Maxwell, TX
78657 Cottonwood Shores, TX
78657 Horseshoe Bay, TX
78657 Marble Falls, TX
78658 Ottine, TX
78659 Paige, TX
78660 Pflugerville, TX
78661 Prairie Lea, TX
78662 Red Rock, TX
78663 Cypress Mill, TX
78663 Round Mountain, TX
78664 Round Rock, TX
78665 Round Rock, TX
78666 San Marcos, TX
78667 San Marcos, TX
78669 Briarcliff, TX
78669 Spicewood, TX
78670 Staples, TX
78671 Albert, TX
78671 Stonewall, TX
78672 Tow, TX
78673 Walburg, TX
78674 Weir, TX
78675 Willow City, TX
78676 Wimberley, TX
78676 Woodcreek, TX
78677 Wrightsboro, TX
78680 Round Rock, TX
78681 Round Rock, TX
78682 Round Rock, TX
78683 Round Rock, TX
78691 Pflugerville, TX

787

78701 Austin, TX
78702 Austin, TX
78703 Austin, TX
78704 Austin, TX
78705 Austin, TX
78708 Austin, TX
78709 Austin, TX
78710 Austin, TX
78711 Austin, TX
78712 Austin, TX
78713 Austin, TX
78714 Austin, TX
78715 Austin, TX
78716 Austin, TX
78717 Austin, TX
78718 Austin, TX
78719 Austin, TX
78720 Austin, TX
78721 Austin, TX
78722 Austin, TX
78723 Austin, TX
78724 Austin, TX
78725 Austin, TX
78726 Austin, TX
78727 Austin, TX
78728 Austin, TX
78729 Austin, TX
78730 Austin, TX
78731 Austin, TX
78732 Austin, TX
78733 Austin, TX
78733 Bee Cave, TX
78733 Bee Caves, TX
78734 Austin, TX
78734 Bee Cave, TX
78734 Bee Caves, TX
78734 Lakeway, TX
78735 Austin, TX
78735 Sunset Valley, TX
78736 Austin, TX
78736 Bee Cave, TX
78736 Bee Caves, TX
78737 Austin, TX
78738 Austin, TX
78738 Bee Cave, TX
78738 Bee Caves, TX
78738 Lakeway, TX
78738 The Hills, TX
78738 Village Of The Hills, TX
78739 Austin, TX
78741 Austin, TX
78742 Austin, TX
78744 Austin, TX
78745 Austin, TX
78745 Sunset Valley, TX
78746 Austin, TX
78746 Rollingwood, TX
78746 West Lake Hills, TX
78746 West Lake Hls, TX
78747 Austin, TX
78748 Austin, TX
78749 Austin, TX
78750 Austin, TX
78751 Austin, TX
78752 Austin, TX
78753 Austin, TX
78754 Austin, TX
78755 Austin, TX
78756 Austin, TX
78757 Austin, TX
78758 Austin, TX
78759 Austin, TX
78760 Austin, TX
78761 Austin, TX
78762 Austin, TX
78763 Austin, TX
78764 Austin, TX
78765 Austin, TX
78766 Austin, TX
78767 Austin, TX
78768 Austin, TX
78769 Austin, TX
78772 Austin, TX
78773 Austin, TX
78774 Austin, TX
78778 Austin, TX
78779 Austin, TX
78783 Austin, TX
78799 Austin, TX

788

78801 Uvalde, TX
78802 Uvalde, TX
78827 Asherton, TX
78828 Barksdale, TX
78829 Batesville, TX
78830 Big Wells, TX
78832 Brackettville, TX
78833 Camp Wood, TX
78834 Carrizo Springs, TX
78836 Catarina, TX
78837 Comstock, TX
78838 Concan, TX
78839 Crystal City, TX
78840 Del Rio, TX
78840 Laughlin Afb, TX
78841 Del Rio, TX
78842 Del Rio, TX
78843 Del Rio, TX
78843 Laughlin Afb, TX
78847 Del Rio, TX
78850 D Hanis, TX
78851 Dryden, TX
78852 Eagle Pass, TX
78853 Eagle Pass, TX
78860 El Indio, TX
78861 Dunlay, TX
78861 Hondo, TX
78870 Knippa, TX
78871 Langtry, TX
78872 La Pryor, TX
78873 Leakey, TX
78877 Quemado, TX
78879 Rio Frio, TX
78880 Rocksprings, TX
78881 Sabinal, TX
78883 Tarpley, TX
78884 Utopia, TX
78885 Vanderpool, TX
78886 Yancey, TX

789

78931 Bleiblerville, TX
78932 Carmine, TX
78933 Cat Spring, TX
78934 Columbus, TX
78935 Alleyton, TX
78938 Ellinger, TX
78940 Fayetteville, TX
78941 Flatonia, TX
78942 Giddings, TX
78943 Glidden, TX
78944 Industry, TX
78945 La Grange, TX
78946 Ledbetter, TX
78947 Lexington, TX
78948 Lincoln, TX
78949 Muldoon, TX
78950 New Ulm, TX
78951 Oakland, TX
78952 Plum, TX
78953 Rosanky, TX
78954 Round Top, TX
78956 Schulenburg, TX
78957 Smithville, TX
78959 Waelder, TX
78960 Warda, TX
78961 Round Top, TX
78961 Warrenton, TX
78962 Weimar, TX
78963 West Point, TX

790

79001 Adrian, TX
79002 Alanreed, TX
79003 Allison, TX
79005 Booker, TX
79007 Borger, TX
79007 Phillips, TX
79008 Borger, TX
79009 Bovina, TX
79010 Boys Ranch, TX
79010 Valle De Oro, TX
79011 Briscoe, TX
79012 Bushland, TX
79013 Cactus, TX
79014 Canadian, TX
79014 Glazier, TX
79015 Canyon, TX
79016 Canyon, TX
79018 Channing, TX
79019 Claude, TX
79021 Cotton Center, TX
79022 Dalhart, TX
79024 Darrouzett, TX
79025 Dawn, TX
79027 Dimmitt, TX
79029 Dumas, TX
79031 Earth, TX
79032 Edmonson, TX
79033 Farnsworth, TX
79034 Follett, TX
79035 Black, TX
79035 Friona, TX
79036 Fritch, TX
79039 Groom, TX
79040 Gruver, TX
79041 Hale Center, TX
79042 Happy, TX
79043 Hart, TX
79044 Hartley, TX
79045 Hereford, TX
79046 Higgins, TX
79051 Kerrick, TX
79052 Kress, TX
79053 Lazbuddie, TX
79054 Lefors, TX
79056 Lipscomb, TX
79057 Mclean, TX
79058 Masterson, TX
79059 Miami, TX
79061 Mobeetie, TX
79062 Morse, TX
79063 Nazareth, TX
79064 Olton, TX
79065 Pampa, TX
79066 Pampa, TX
79068 Panhandle, TX
79070 Perryton, TX
79072 Plainview, TX
79073 Plainview, TX
79077 Sam Norwood, TX
79078 Sanford, TX
79079 Shamrock, TX
79079 Twitty, TX
79080 Skellytown, TX
79081 Spearman, TX
79082 Springlake, TX
79083 Stinnett, TX
79084 Stratford, TX
79085 Summerfield, TX
79086 Sunray, TX
79087 Texline, TX
79088 Tulia, TX
79088 Vigo Park, TX
79091 Umbarger, TX
79092 Vega, TX
79093 Waka, TX
79094 Wayside, TX
79095 Wellington, TX
79096 Wheeler, TX
79097 White Deer, TX
79098 Wildorado, TX

791

79101 Amarillo, TX
79102 Amarillo, TX
79103 Amarillo, TX
79104 Amarillo, TX
79105 Amarillo, TX
79106 Amarillo, TX
79107 Amarillo, TX
79108 Amarillo, TX
79109 Amarillo, TX
79110 Amarillo, TX
79111 Amarillo, TX
79114 Amarillo, TX
79116 Amarillo, TX
79117 Amarillo, TX
79118 Amarillo, TX
79118 Palisades, TX
79118 Timbercreek Canyon, TX
79119 Amarillo, TX
79120 Amarillo, TX
79121 Amarillo, TX
79124 Amarillo, TX
79124 Bishop Hills, TX
79159 Amarillo, TX
79166 Amarillo, TX
79168 Amarillo, TX
79172 Amarillo, TX
79174 Amarillo, TX
79178 Amarillo, TX
79185 Amarillo, TX
79189 Amarillo, TX

792

79201 Childress, TX
79201 Northfield, TX
79220 Afton, TX
79221 Aiken, TX
79223 Cee Vee, TX
79225 Chillicothe, TX
79226 Clarendon, TX
79226 Howardwick, TX
79227 Crowell, TX
79227 Truscott, TX
79229 Dickens, TX
79230 Dodson, TX
79231 Dougherty, TX
79233 Estelline, TX
79234 Flomot, TX
79235 Floydada, TX
79236 Guthrie, TX
79237 Hedley, TX
79239 Lakeview, TX
79240 Lelia Lake, TX
79241 Lockney, TX
79243 Mcadoo, TX
79244 Matador, TX
79245 Memphis, TX
79247 Odell, TX
79248 Dumont, TX
79248 Paducah, TX
79250 Petersburg, TX
79251 Quail, TX
79252 Quanah, TX
79255 Quitaque, TX
79256 Roaring Springs, TX
79257 Silverton, TX
79258 South Plains, TX
79259 Tell, TX
79261 Turkey, TX

793

79311 Abernathy, TX
79312 Amherst, TX
79313 Anton, TX
79314 Bledsoe, TX
79316 Brownfield, TX
79322 Crosbyton, TX
79323 Denver City, TX
79324 Enochs, TX
79325 Farwell, TX
79326 Fieldton, TX
79329 Idalou, TX
79330 Justiceburg, TX
79331 La Mesa, TX
79331 Lamesa, TX
79336 Levelland, TX
79338 Levelland, TX
79339 Littlefield, TX
79342 Loop, TX
79343 Lorenzo, TX
79344 Maple, TX
79345 Meadow, TX
79346 Morton, TX
79347 Muleshoe, TX
79350 New Deal, TX
79351 Odonnell, TX
79353 Pep, TX
79355 Plains, TX
79356 Post, TX
79357 Cone, TX
79357 Ralls, TX
79358 Ropesville, TX
79359 Seagraves, TX
79360 Seminole, TX
79363 Shallowater, TX
79364 Ransom Canyon, TX
79364 Slaton, TX
79364 Southland, TX
79366 Ransom Canyon, TX
79367 Smyer, TX
79369 Spade, TX
79370 Spur, TX
79371 Sudan, TX
79372 Sundown, TX
79373 Tahoka, TX
79376 Tokio, TX
79377 Welch, TX
79378 Wellman, TX
79379 Whiteface, TX
79380 Whitharral, TX
79381 New Home, TX
79381 Wilson, TX
79382 Wolfforth, TX
79383 New Home, TX

794

79401 Lubbock, TX
79402 Lubbock, TX
79403 Lubbock, TX
79404 Buffalo Springs, TX
79404 Lubbock, TX
79406 Lubbock, TX
79407 Lubbock, TX
79408 Lubbock, TX
79409 Lubbock, TX
79410 Lubbock, TX
79411 Lubbock, TX
79412 Lubbock, TX
79413 Lubbock, TX
79414 Lubbock, TX
79415 Lubbock, TX
79416 Lubbock, TX
79423 Lubbock, TX
79424 Lubbock, TX
79430 Lubbock, TX
79452 Lubbock, TX
79453 Lubbock, TX
79457 Lubbock, TX
79464 Lubbock, TX
79490 Lubbock, TX
79491 Lubbock, TX
79493 Lubbock, TX
79499 Lubbock, TX

795

79501 Anson, TX
79502 Aspermont, TX
79503 Avoca, TX
79504 Baird, TX
79505 Benjamin, TX
79506 Blackwell, TX
79508 Buffalo Gap, TX
79510 Clyde, TX
79511 Coahoma, TX
79512 Colorado City, TX
79516 Dunn, TX
79517 Fluvanna, TX
79518 Girard, TX
79519 Goldsboro, TX
79520 Hamlin, TX
79521 Haskell, TX
79525 Hawley, TX
79526 Hermleigh, TX
79527 Ira, TX
79528 Jayton, TX
79529 Knox City, TX
79530 Lawn, TX
79532 Loraine, TX
79533 Lueders, TX
79534 Mc Caulley, TX
79535 Maryneal, TX

79536 Merkel, TX
79537 Nolan, TX
79538 Novice, TX
79539 O Brien, TX
79540 Old Glory, TX
79541 Ovalo, TX
79543 Roby, TX
79544 Rochester, TX
79545 Roscoe, TX
79546 Rotan, TX
79547 Rule, TX
79548 Rule, TX
79548 Sagerton, TX
79549 Dermott, TX
79549 Snyder, TX
79550 Snyder, TX
79553 Stamford, TX
79556 Sweetwater, TX
79560 Sylvester, TX
79561 Trent, TX
79562 Tuscola, TX
79563 Tye, TX
79565 Westbrook, TX
79566 Wingate, TX
79567 Winters, TX

796

79601 Abilene, TX
79602 Abilene, TX
79603 Abilene, TX
79604 Abilene, TX
79605 Abilene, TX
79606 Abilene, TX
79607 Abilene, TX
79607 Dyess Afb, TX
79608 Abilene, TX
79697 Abilene, TX
79698 Abilene, TX
79699 Abilene, TX

797

79701 Midland, TX
79702 Midland, TX
79703 Midland, TX
79704 Midland, TX
79705 Midland, TX
79706 Midland, TX
79707 Midland, TX
79708 Midland, TX
79710 Midland, TX
79711 Midland, TX
79712 Midland, TX
79713 Ackerly, TX
79714 Andrews, TX
79718 Balmorhea, TX
79719 Barstow, TX
79720 Big Spring, TX
79720 Vealmoor, TX
79721 Big Spring, TX
79730 Coyanosa, TX
79731 Crane, TX
79733 Forsan, TX
79734 Fort Davis, TX
79734 Mcdonald Observatory, TX
79735 Fort Stockton, TX
79738 Gail, TX
79739 Garden City, TX
79740 Girvin, TX
79741 Goldsmith, TX
79742 Grandfalls, TX
79743 Imperial, TX
79744 Iraan, TX
79745 Kermit, TX
79748 Knott, TX
79749 Lenorah, TX
79752 Mc Camey, TX
79752 Mccamey, TX
79754 Mentone, TX
79755 Midkiff, TX
79756 Monahans, TX
79756 Thorntonville, TX
79758 Gardendale, TX
79759 Notrees, TX
79760 Odessa, TX
79761 Odessa, TX
79762 Odessa, TX
79763 Odessa, TX
79764 Odessa, TX
79765 Odessa, TX
79766 Odessa, TX
79768 Odessa, TX
79769 Odessa, TX
79770 Orla, TX
79772 Pecos, TX
79772 Verhalen, TX
79776 Penwell, TX
79777 Pyote, TX
79778 Rankin, TX
79780 Saragosa, TX
79781 Sheffield, TX
79782 Stanton, TX
79783 Tarzan, TX
79785 Toyah, TX
79786 Toyahvale, TX
79788 Wickett, TX
79789 Wink, TX

798

79821 Anthony, TX
79821 Vinton, TX
79830 Alpine, TX
79831 Alpine, TX
79832 Alpine, TX
79834 Big Bend National Park, TX
79835 Canutillo, TX
79836 Clint, TX
79837 Dell City, TX
79838 Fabens, TX
79839 Fort Hancock, TX
79842 Marathon, TX
79843 Marfa, TX
79843 Shafter, TX
79845 Presidio, TX
79846 Presidio, TX
79846 Redford, TX
79847 Dell City, TX
79847 Salt Flat, TX
79848 Sanderson, TX
79849 San Elizario, TX
79851 Sierra Blanca, TX
79852 Lajitas, TX
79852 Terlingua, TX
79853 Tornillo, TX
79854 Valentine, TX
79855 Kent, TX
79855 Van Horn, TX

799

79901 El Paso, TX
79902 El Paso, TX
79903 El Paso, TX
79904 El Paso, TX
79905 El Paso, TX
79906 El Paso, TX
79906 Fort Bliss, TX
79907 El Paso, TX
79907 Ysleta Del Sur Pueblo, TX
79908 Biggs Field, TX
79908 El Paso, TX
79908 Fort Bliss, TX
79910 El Paso, TX
79911 El Paso, TX
79912 El Paso, TX
79913 El Paso, TX
79914 El Paso, TX
79915 El Paso, TX
79916 El Paso, TX
79916 Fort Bliss, TX
79917 El Paso, TX
79918 Biggs Field, TX
79918 El Paso, TX
79918 Fort Bliss, TX
79920 El Paso, TX
79922 El Paso, TX
79923 El Paso, TX
79924 El Paso, TX
79925 El Paso, TX
79926 El Paso, TX
79927 El Paso, TX
79927 Horizon City, TX
79927 Socorro, TX
79927 Ysleta Del Sur Pueblo, TX
79928 El Paso, TX
79928 Horizon City, TX
79928 Socorro, TX
79929 El Paso, TX
79930 El Paso, TX
79931 El Paso, TX
79932 El Paso, TX
79934 El Paso, TX
79935 El Paso, TX
79936 El Paso, TX
79937 El Paso, TX
79938 El Paso, TX
79940 El Paso, TX
79941 El Paso, TX
79942 El Paso, TX
79943 El Paso, TX
79944 El Paso, TX
79945 El Paso, TX
79946 El Paso, TX
79947 El Paso, TX
79948 El Paso, TX
79949 El Paso, TX
79950 El Paso, TX
79951 El Paso, TX
79952 El Paso, TX
79953 El Paso, TX
79954 El Paso, TX
79955 El Paso, TX
79958 El Paso, TX
79960 El Paso, TX
79961 El Paso, TX
79968 El Paso, TX
79976 El Paso, TX
79978 El Paso, TX
79980 El Paso, TX
79990 El Paso, TX
79995 El Paso, TX
79996 El Paso, TX
79997 El Paso, TX
79998 El Paso, TX
79999 El Paso, TX

800

80001 Arvada, CO
80002 Arvada, CO
80003 Arvada, CO
80003 Westminster, CO
80004 Arvada, CO
80005 Arvada, CO
80005 Westminster, CO
80006 Arvada, CO
80007 Arvada, CO
80010 Aurora, CO
80011 Aurora, CO
80011 Buckley Air Force Base, CO
80012 Aurora, CO
80012 Denver, CO
80013 Aurora, CO
80014 Aurora, CO
80014 Denver, CO
80015 Aurora, CO
80015 Centennial, CO
80016 Aurora, CO
80016 Centennial, CO
80016 Foxfield, CO
80017 Aurora, CO
80018 Aurora, CO
80019 Aurora, CO
80020 Broomfield, CO
80020 Westminster, CO
80021 Broomfield, CO
80021 Westminster, CO
80022 Commerce City, CO
80022 Denver, CO
80023 Broomfield, CO
80023 Thornton, CO
80023 Westminster, CO
80024 Dupont, CO
80025 Eldorado Springs, CO
80026 Lafayette, CO
80027 Louisville, CO
80027 Superior, CO
80030 Westminster, CO
80031 Westminster, CO
80033 Denver, CO
80033 Wheat Ridge, CO
80034 Wheat Ridge, CO
80035 Westminster, CO
80036 Westminster, CO
80037 Commerce City, CO
80038 Broomfield, CO
80040 Aurora, CO
80041 Aurora, CO
80042 Aurora, CO
80044 Aurora, CO
80045 Aurora, CO
80046 Aurora, CO
80047 Aurora, CO

801

80101 Agate, CO
80102 Bennett, CO
80103 Byers, CO
80104 Castle Rock, CO
80105 Deer Trail, CO
80106 Elbert, CO
80107 Elizabeth, CO
80108 Castle Pines, CO
80108 Castle Rock, CO
80109 Castle Rock, CO
80110 Cherry Hills, CO
80110 Cherry Hills Village, CO
80110 Englewood, CO
80110 Greenwood Village, CO
80110 Sheridan, CO
80111 Centennial, CO
80111 Cherry Hills, CO
80111 Cherry Hills Village, CO
80111 Englewood, CO
80111 Greenwood Village, CO
80112 Centennial, CO
80112 Englewood, CO
80112 Greenwood Village, CO
80113 Cherry Hills, CO
80113 Cherry Hills Village, CO
80113 Englewood, CO
80116 Franktown, CO
80117 Kiowa, CO
80118 Larkspur, CO
80120 Littleton, CO
80121 Centennial, CO
80121 Cherry Hills Village, CO
80121 Greenwood Village, CO
80121 Littleton, CO
80122 Centennial, CO
80122 Littleton, CO
80123 Bow Mar, CO
80123 Columbine Valley, CO
80123 Denver, CO
80123 Lakewood, CO
80123 Littleton, CO
80124 Littleton, CO
80124 Lone Tree, CO
80125 Littleton, CO
80125 Roxborough, CO
80126 Highlands Ranch, CO
80126 Littleton, CO
80127 Denver, CO
80127 Littleton, CO
80128 Littleton, CO
80129 Highlands Ranch, CO
80129 Littleton, CO
80130 Highlands Ranch, CO
80130 Littleton, CO
80131 Louviers, CO
80132 Monument, CO
80133 Palmer Lake, CO
80134 Parker, CO
80135 Deckers, CO
80135 Sedalia, CO
80136 Strasburg, CO
80137 Watkins, CO
80138 Parker, CO
80150 Englewood, CO
80151 Englewood, CO
80155 Englewood, CO
80155 Greenwood Village, CO
80160 Littleton, CO
80161 Centennial, CO
80161 Littleton, CO
80162 Littleton, CO
80163 Highlands Ranch, CO
80163 Littleton, CO
80165 Littleton, CO
80166 Littleton, CO

802

80201 Denver, CO
80202 Denver, CO
80203 Denver, CO
80204 Denver, CO
80205 Denver, CO
80206 Denver, CO
80207 Denver, CO
80208 Denver, CO
80209 Denver, CO
80210 Denver, CO
80211 Denver, CO
80212 Denver, CO
80212 Wheat Ridge, CO
80214 Denver, CO
80214 Edgewater, CO
80214 Lakewood, CO
80214 Wheat Ridge, CO
80215 Denver, CO
80215 Lakewood, CO
80215 Wheat Ridge, CO
80216 Denver, CO
80217 Denver, CO
80218 Denver, CO
80219 Denver, CO
80220 Denver, CO
80221 Denver, CO
80221 Federal Heights, CO
80221 Thornton, CO
80221 Westminster, CO
80222 Denver, CO
80223 Denver, CO
80224 Denver, CO
80225 Denver, CO
80225 Lakewood, CO
80226 Denver, CO
80226 Lakewood, CO
80227 Denver, CO
80227 Lakewood, CO
80228 Denver, CO
80228 Lakewood, CO
80229 Denver, CO
80229 Thornton, CO
80230 Denver, CO
80230 Lowry, CO
80230 Montclair, CO
80231 Denver, CO
80232 Denver, CO
80232 Lakewood, CO
80233 Denver, CO
80233 Northglenn, CO
80233 Thornton, CO
80234 Denver, CO
80234 North Glenn, CO
80234 Northglenn, CO
80234 Westminster, CO
80235 Denver, CO
80235 Lakewood, CO
80236 Denver, CO
80236 Lakewood, CO
80237 Denver, CO
80238 Denver, CO
80238 Montbello, CO
80239 Denver, CO
80241 Denver, CO
80241 Northglenn, CO
80241 Thornton, CO
80241 Westminster, CO
80243 Denver, CO
80244 Denver, CO
80246 Denver, CO
80246 Glendale, CO
80247 Aurora, CO
80247 Denver, CO
80248 Denver, CO
80249 Denver, CO
80250 Denver, CO
80251 Denver, CO
80252 Denver, CO
80256 Denver, CO
80257 Denver, CO
80259 Denver, CO
80260 Denver, CO
80260 Federal Heights, CO
80260 Northglenn, CO
80260 Thornton, CO
80260 Westminster, CO
80261 Denver, CO
80262 Denver, CO
80263 Denver, CO
80264 Denver, CO
80265 Denver, CO
80266 Denver, CO
80271 Denver, CO
80273 Denver, CO
80274 Denver, CO
80281 Denver, CO
80290 Denver, CO
80291 Denver, CO
80293 Denver, CO
80294 Denver, CO
80295 Denver, CO
80299 Denver, CO

803

80301 Boulder, CO
80302 Boulder, CO
80303 Boulder, CO
80304 Boulder, CO
80305 Boulder, CO
80306 Boulder, CO
80307 Boulder, CO
80308 Boulder, CO
80309 Boulder, CO
80310 Boulder, CO
80314 Boulder, CO

804

80401 Evergreen, CO
80401 Golden, CO
80401 Lakewood, CO
80402 Golden, CO
80403 Arvada, CO
80403 Golden, CO
80419 Golden, CO
80420 Alma, CO
80421 Bailey, CO
80422 Black Hawk, CO
80423 Bond, CO
80424 Blue River, CO
80424 Breckenridge, CO
80425 Buffalo Creek, CO
80426 Burns, CO
80427 Central City, CO
80428 Clark, CO
80429 Climax, CO
80429 Leadville, CO
80430 Coalmont, CO
80430 Walden, CO
80432 Como, CO
80432 Fairplay, CO
80433 Conifer, CO
80433 Foxton, CO
80434 Cowdrey, CO
80435 Dillon, CO
80435 Keystone, CO
80435 Montezuma, CO
80436 Dumont, CO
80437 Evergreen, CO
80438 Empire, CO
80439 Evergreen, CO
80439 Golden, CO
80440 Fairplay, CO
80442 Fraser, CO
80443 Frisco, CO
80444 Georgetown, CO
80446 Granby, CO
80447 Grand Lake, CO
80448 Grant, CO
80449 Hartsel, CO
80451 Hot Sulphur Springs, CO
80452 Idaho Springs, CO
80453 Idledale, CO
80454 Indian Hills, CO
80455 Jamestown, CO
80456 Fairplay, CO

80456 Jefferson, CO
80457 Kittredge, CO
80459 Kremmling, CO
80461 Leadville, CO
80463 Mc Coy, CO
80465 Morrison, CO
80466 Nederland, CO
80467 Oak Creek, CO
80468 Parshall, CO
80469 Phippsburg, CO
80470 Pine, CO
80471 Pinecliffe, CO
80473 Rand, CO
80474 Rollinsville, CO
80475 Shawnee, CO
80476 Silver Plume, CO
80477 Steamboat Spr, CO
80477 Steamboat Springs, CO
80478 Tabernash, CO
80479 Toponas, CO
80480 Walden, CO
80481 Ward, CO
80482 Winter Park, CO
80483 Yampa, CO
80487 Steamboat Springs, CO
80488 Steamboat Spr, CO
80488 Steamboat Springs, CO
80497 Silverthorne, CO
80498 Heeney, CO
80498 Silverthorne, CO

805

80501 Longmont, CO
80502 Longmont, CO
80503 Longmont, CO
80503 Niwot, CO
80504 Firestone, CO
80504 Frederick, CO
80504 Longmont, CO
80504 Niwot, CO
80510 Allenspark, CO
80511 Estes Park, CO
80512 Bellvue, CO
80513 Berthoud, CO
80514 Dacono, CO
80514 Erie, CO
80515 Drake, CO
80516 Erie, CO
80516 Frederick, CO
80517 Estes Park, CO
80520 Firestone, CO
80521 Fort Collins, CO
80522 Fort Collins, CO
80523 Fort Collins, CO
80524 Fort Collins, CO
80524 Severance, CO
80525 Fort Collins, CO
80526 Fort Collins, CO
80527 Fort Collins, CO
80528 Fort Collins, CO
80528 Windsor, CO
80530 Frederick, CO
80532 Glen Haven, CO
80533 Hygiene, CO
80534 Johnstown, CO
80534 Loveland, CO
80535 Laporte, CO
80536 Livermore, CO
80536 Virginia Dale, CO
80537 Loveland, CO
80538 Loveland, CO
80539 Loveland, CO
80540 Lyons, CO
80541 Masonville, CO
80542 Mead, CO
80543 Milliken, CO
80544 Niwot, CO
80545 Red Feather Lakes, CO
80546 Severance, CO
80547 Timnath, CO
80549 Wellington, CO
80550 Severance, CO
80550 Windsor, CO
80551 Windsor, CO
80553 Fort Collins, CO

806

80601 Brighton, CO
80602 Brighton, CO
80602 Thornton, CO
80603 Brighton, CO
80603 Lochbuie, CO
80610 Ault, CO
80610 Severance, CO
80611 Briggsdale, CO
80612 Carr, CO
80614 Eastlake, CO
80615 Eaton, CO
80615 Severance, CO
80620 Evans, CO
80621 Fort Lupton, CO
80621 Wattenburg, CO
80622 Galeton, CO
80623 Gilcrest, CO
80624 Gill, CO
80631 Garden City, CO
80631 Greeley, CO
80632 Greeley, CO
80633 Greeley, CO
80634 Evans, CO
80634 Greeley, CO
80638 Greeley, CO
80639 Greeley, CO
80640 Henderson, CO
80642 Hudson, CO
80643 Keenesburg, CO
80644 Kersey, CO
80645 Evans, CO
80645 La Salle, CO
80646 Lucerne, CO
80648 Nunn, CO
80649 Orchard, CO
80650 Pierce, CO
80651 Platteville, CO
80652 Roggen, CO
80653 Weldona, CO
80654 Hoyt, CO
80654 Wiggins, CO

807

80701 Fort Morgan, CO
80705 Fort Morgan, CO
80705 Log Lane Village, CO
80720 Akron, CO
80721 Amherst, CO
80722 Atwood, CO
80723 Brush, CO
80726 Crook, CO
80727 Eckley, CO
80728 Fleming, CO
80729 Grover, CO
80731 Haxtun, CO
80732 Hereford, CO
80733 Hillrose, CO
80734 Holyoke, CO
80735 Hale, CO
80735 Idalia, CO
80736 Iliff, CO
80737 Julesburg, CO
80740 Lindon, CO
80741 Merino, CO
80741 Willard, CO
80742 New Raymer, CO
80743 Otis, CO
80744 Ovid, CO
80745 Padroni, CO
80746 Paoli, CO
80747 Peetz, CO
80749 Sedgwick, CO
80750 Snyder, CO
80751 Sterling, CO
80754 Stoneham, CO
80755 Vernon, CO
80757 Last Chance, CO
80757 Woodrow, CO
80758 Laird, CO
80758 Wray, CO
80759 Yuma, CO

808

80801 Anton, CO
80802 Arapahoe, CO
80804 Arriba, CO
80805 Bethune, CO
80807 Burlington, CO
80808 Calhan, CO
80809 Cascade, CO
80810 Cheyenne Wells, CO
80812 Cope, CO
80813 Cripple Creek, CO
80814 Divide, CO
80815 Flagler, CO
80816 Florissant, CO
80817 Fountain, CO
80818 Genoa, CO
80819 Green Mountain Falls, CO
80820 Guffey, CO
80821 Boyero, CO
80821 Hugo, CO
80822 Joes, CO
80823 Karval, CO
80824 Kirk, CO
80825 Kit Carson, CO
80826 Limon, CO
80827 Lake George, CO
80828 Limon, CO
80829 Manitou Springs, CO
80830 Matheson, CO
80831 Falcon, CO
80831 Peyton, CO
80832 Ramah, CO
80833 Rush, CO
80834 Seibert, CO
80835 Simla, CO
80836 Stratton, CO
80840 United States Air Force Acad, CO
80840 Usaf Academy, CO
80841 Cadet Sta, CO
80841 Usaf Academy, CO
80860 Victor, CO
80861 Vona, CO
80862 Wild Horse, CO
80863 Woodland Park, CO
80864 Yoder, CO
80866 Woodland Park, CO

809

80901 Colo Spgs, CO
80901 Colorado Springs, CO
80902 Colo Spgs, CO
80902 Colorado Springs, CO
80902 Fort Carson, CO
80902 Ft Carson, CO
80903 Colo Spgs, CO
80903 Colorado Springs, CO
80904 Colo Spgs, CO
80904 Colorado Springs, CO
80905 Colo Spgs, CO
80905 Colorado Springs, CO
80906 Colo Spgs, CO
80906 Colorado Springs, CO
80907 Colo Spgs, CO
80907 Colorado Springs, CO
80908 Colo Spgs, CO
80908 Colorado Springs, CO
80909 Colo Spgs, CO
80909 Colorado Springs, CO
80910 Colo Spgs, CO
80910 Colorado Springs, CO
80911 Colo Spgs, CO
80911 Colorado Springs, CO
80912 Colo Spgs, CO
80912 Colorado Springs, CO
80912 Schriever Afb, CO
80913 Colo Spgs, CO
80913 Colorado Springs, CO
80913 Fort Carson, CO
80913 Ft Carson, CO
80914 Cheyenne Mountain Afb, CO
80914 Colo Spgs, CO
80914 Colorado Spgs, CO
80914 Colorado Springs, CO
80914 Peterson Afb, CO
80915 Colo Spgs, CO
80915 Colorado Springs, CO
80916 Colo Spgs, CO
80916 Colorado Springs, CO
80917 Colo Spgs, CO
80917 Colorado Springs, CO
80918 Colo Spgs, CO
80918 Colorado Springs, CO
80919 Colo Spgs, CO
80919 Colorado Springs, CO
80920 Co Spgs, CO
80920 Colo Spgs, CO
80920 Colorado Springs, CO
80921 Colo Spgs, CO
80921 Colorado Springs, CO
80922 Colo Spgs, CO
80922 Colorado Springs, CO
80923 Colo Spgs, CO
80923 Colorado Springs, CO
80924 Colo Spgs, CO
80924 Colorado Springs, CO
80925 Colo Spgs, CO
80925 Colorado Springs, CO
80926 Colo Spgs, CO
80926 Colorado Springs, CO
80927 Colo Spgs, CO
80927 Colorado Springs, CO
80928 Colo Spgs, CO
80928 Colorado Springs, CO
80929 Colo Spgs, CO
80929 Colorado Springs, CO
80930 Colo Spgs, CO
80930 Colorado Springs, CO
80931 Colo Spgs, CO
80931 Colorado Springs, CO
80932 Colo Spgs, CO
80932 Colorado Springs, CO
80933 Colo Spgs, CO
80933 Colorado Springs, CO
80934 Colo Spgs, CO
80934 Colorado Springs, CO
80935 Colo Spgs, CO
80935 Colorado Springs, CO
80936 Colo Spgs, CO
80936 Colorado Springs, CO
80937 Colo Spgs, CO
80937 Colorado Springs, CO
80938 Colo Spgs, CO
80938 Colorado Springs, CO
80939 Colo Spgs, CO
80939 Colorado Springs, CO
80941 Colo Spgs, CO
80941 Colorado Springs, CO
80942 Colo Spgs, CO
80942 Colorado Springs, CO
80943 Colo Spgs, CO
80943 Colorado Springs, CO
80944 Colo Spgs, CO
80944 Colorado Springs, CO
80945 Colo Spgs, CO
80945 Colorado Springs, CO
80946 Colo Spgs, CO
80946 Colorado Springs, CO
80947 Colo Spgs, CO
80947 Colorado Springs, CO
80949 Colo Spgs, CO
80949 Colorado Springs, CO
80950 Colo Spgs, CO
80950 Colorado Springs, CO
80951 Colo Spgs, CO
80951 Colorado Springs, CO
80960 Colo Spgs, CO
80960 Colorado Springs, CO
80962 Colo Spgs, CO
80962 Colorado Springs, CO
80970 Colo Spgs, CO
80970 Colorado Springs, CO
80977 Colo Spgs, CO
80977 Colorado Springs, CO
80995 Colo Spgs, CO
80995 Colorado Springs, CO
80997 Colo Spgs, CO
80997 Colorado Springs, CO

810

81001 Pueblo, CO
81001 Pueblo Depot Activity, CO
81002 Pueblo, CO
81003 Pueblo, CO
81004 Pueblo, CO
81005 Pueblo, CO
81006 Pueblo, CO
81007 Pueblo, CO
81007 Pueblo West, CO
81008 Pueblo, CO
81009 Pueblo, CO
81010 Pueblo, CO
81011 Pueblo, CO
81012 Pueblo, CO
81019 Colo City, CO
81019 Colorado City, CO
81020 Aguilar, CO
81021 Arlington, CO
81022 Avondale, CO
81022 North Avondale, CO
81023 Beulah, CO
81024 Boncarbo, CO
81025 Boone, CO
81027 Branson, CO
81029 Campo, CO
81030 Cheraw, CO
81033 Crowley, CO
81034 Ordway, CO
81036 Chivington, CO
81036 Eads, CO
81038 Fort Lyon, CO
81039 Fowler, CO
81040 Gardner, CO
81041 Granada, CO
81043 Hartman, CO
81044 Caddoa, CO
81044 Hasty, CO
81045 Haswell, CO
81046 Hoehne, CO
81047 Bristol, CO
81047 Holly, CO
81049 Kim, CO
81049 Villegreen, CO
81050 La Junta, CO
81050 Timpas, CO
81052 Lamar, CO
81054 Deora, CO
81054 Fort Lyon, CO
81054 Las Animas, CO
81054 Ninaview, CO
81055 La Veta, CO
81057 Mc Clave, CO
81058 Manzanola, CO
81059 Delhi, CO
81059 Model, CO
81059 Thatcher, CO
81059 Tyrone, CO
81062 Olney Springs, CO
81063 Ordway, CO
81064 Pritchett, CO
81064 Utleyville, CO
81067 Rocky Ford, CO
81069 Rye, CO
81071 Brandon, CO
81071 Sheridan Lake, CO
81071 Towner, CO
81073 Springfield, CO
81076 Sugar City, CO
81077 Swink, CO
81081 Trinchera, CO
81082 Cokedale, CO
81082 Jansen, CO
81082 Sopris, CO
81082 Starkville, CO
81082 Trinidad, CO
81084 Lycan, CO
81084 Two Buttes, CO
81087 Vilas, CO
81089 Farista, CO
81089 Walsenburg, CO
81090 Stonington, CO
81090 Walsh, CO
81091 Weston, CO
81092 Wiley, CO

811

81101 Alamosa, CO
81101 Great Sand Dunes National Mo, CO
81102 Alamosa, CO
81120 Antonito, CO
81121 Arboles, CO
81122 Bayfield, CO
81122 Chimney Rock, CO
81123 Blanca, CO
81124 Capulin, CO
81125 Center, CO
81126 Chama, CO
81128 Chromo, CO
81129 Conejos, CO
81130 Creede, CO
81131 Crestone, CO
81132 Del Norte, CO
81133 Fort Garland, CO
81133 Sangre De Cristo Ranches, CO
81135 Homelake, CO
81135 Monte Vista, CO
81136 Hooper, CO
81137 Ignacio, CO
81137 Southern Ute Indian Reservat, CO
81138 Jaroso, CO
81140 La Jara, CO
81141 Manassa, CO
81143 Moffat, CO
81144 Monte Vista, CO
81146 Mosca, CO
81147 Chimney Rock, CO
81147 Pagosa Springs, CO
81148 Romeo, CO
81149 Saguache, CO
81151 San Acacio, CO
81151 Sanford, CO
81152 Garcia, CO
81152 Mesita, CO
81152 San Luis, CO
81152 San Pablo, CO
81154 South Fork, CO
81155 Villa Grove, CO
81157 Pagosa Springs, CO

812

81201 Salida, CO
81210 Almont, CO
81211 Buena Vista, CO
81212 Brookside, CO
81212 Canon City, CO
81215 Canon City, CO
81220 Cimarron, CO
81221 Coal Creek, CO
81222 Coaldale, CO
81223 Cotopaxi, CO
81224 Crested Butte, CO
81225 Crested Butte, CO
81226 Florence, CO
81227 Monarch, CO
81227 Salida, CO
81228 Granite, CO
81228 Twin Lakes, CO
81230 Gunnison, CO
81231 Gunnison, CO
81232 Hillside, CO
81233 Howard, CO
81235 Lake City, CO
81236 Nathrop, CO
81237 Ohio City, CO
81239 Parlin, CO
81240 Penrose, CO
81241 Pitkin, CO
81242 Poncha Springs, CO
81243 Powderhorn, CO
81244 Rockvale, CO
81247 Gunnison, CO
81247 Sapinero, CO
81248 Sargents, CO
81251 Twin Lakes, CO
81252 Silver Cliff, CO
81252 Westcliffe, CO
81253 Wetmore, CO
81290 Florence, CO

813

81301 Durango, CO
81302 Durango, CO
81303 Durango, CO
81320 Cahone, CO
81321 Cortez, CO
81323 Dolores, CO
81324 Dove Creek, CO

81325 Egnar, CO
81325 Slick Rock, CO
81326 Hesperus, CO
81327 Lewis, CO
81328 Mancos, CO
81329 Marvel, CO
81330 Mesa Verde National Park, CO
81331 Pleasant View, CO
81332 Rico, CO
81334 Towaoc, CO
81335 Yellow Jacket, CO

814

81401 Montrose, CO
81402 Montrose, CO
81403 Montrose, CO
81410 Austin, CO
81410 Orchard City, CO
81411 Bedrock, CO
81413 Cedaredge, CO
81414 Cory, CO
81415 Crawford, CO
81415 Maher, CO
81416 Delta, CO
81418 Eckert, CO
81419 Hotchkiss, CO
81420 Lazear, CO
81422 Naturita, CO
81423 Norwood, CO
81424 Nucla, CO
81425 Olathe, CO
81426 Ophir, CO
81427 Ouray, CO
81428 Paonia, CO
81429 Paradox, CO
81430 Placerville, CO
81431 Redvale, CO
81432 Ridgway, CO
81433 Silverton, CO
81434 Somerset, CO
81435 Mountain Village, CO
81435 Telluride, CO

815

81501 Grand Junction, CO
81504 Fruitvale, CO
81504 Grand Junction, CO
81520 Clifton, CO
81521 Fruita, CO
81522 Gateway, CO
81523 Glade Park, CO
81524 Loma, CO
81525 Mack, CO
81526 Palisade, CO
81527 Whitewater, CO

816

81601 Glenwood Springs, CO
81610 Dinosaur, CO
81611 Aspen, CO
81612 Aspen, CO
81615 Snowmass Village, CO
81620 Avon, CO
81620 Beaver Creek, CO
81621 Basalt, CO
81623 Carbondale, CO
81623 El Jebel, CO
81623 Marble, CO
81623 Redstone, CO
81624 Collbran, CO
81625 Craig, CO
81626 Craig, CO
81630 De Beque, CO
81631 Eagle, CO
81632 Cordillera, CO
81632 Edwards, CO
81633 Dinosaur, CO
81633 Elk Springs, CO
81635 Battlement Mesa, CO
81635 Parachute, CO
81636 Battlement Mesa, CO
81636 Parachute, CO
81637 Gypsum, CO
81638 Hamilton, CO
81639 Hayden, CO
81640 Maybell, CO
81641 Meeker, CO
81642 Meredith, CO
81643 Mesa, CO
81645 Gilman, CO
81645 Minturn, CO
81646 Molina, CO
81647 New Castle, CO
81648 Rangely, CO
81649 Red Cliff, CO
81650 Rifle, CO
81652 Silt, CO
81653 Slater, CO
81654 Snowmass, CO
81655 Wolcott, CO
81656 Woody Creek, CO
81657 Vail, CO
81658 Vail, CO

820

82001 Cheyenne, WY
82001 Fe Warren Afb, WY
82002 Cheyenne, WY
82003 Cheyenne, WY
82005 Cheyenne, WY
82005 Fe Warren Afb, WY
82006 Cheyenne, WY
82007 Cheyenne, WY
82008 Cheyenne, WY
82009 Cheyenne, WY
82009 Iron Mountain, WY
82010 Cheyenne, WY
82050 Albin, WY
82051 Bosler, WY
82051 Laramie, WY
82052 Buford, WY
82053 Burns, WY
82053 Egbert, WY
82054 Carpenter, WY
82055 Centennial, WY
82058 Garrett, WY
82058 Rock River, WY
82059 Granite Canon, WY
82059 Granite Canyon, WY
82059 Harriman, WY
82060 Hillsdale, WY
82061 Horse Creek, WY
82063 Jelm, WY
82063 Laramie, WY
82070 Bosler, WY
82070 Foxpark, WY
82070 Laramie, WY
82071 Laramie, WY
82072 Bosler, WY
82072 Foxpark, WY
82072 Jelm, WY
82072 Laramie, WY
82072 Mountain Home, WY
82073 Laramie, WY
82081 Meriden, WY
82082 Pine Bluffs, WY
82083 Arlington, WY
82083 Mcfadden, WY
82083 Rock River, WY
82084 Tie Siding, WY

821

82190 Mammoth Hot Springs, WY
82190 Yellowstone National Park, WY

822

82201 Bordeaux, WY
82201 Slater, WY
82201 Uva, WY
82201 Wheatland, WY
82210 Chugwater, WY
82210 Diamond, WY
82212 Fort Laramie, WY
82213 Glendo, WY
82214 Guernsey, WY
82215 Hartville, WY
82215 Sunrise, WY
82217 Hawk Springs, WY
82218 Huntley, WY
82219 Jay Em, WY
82221 Lagrange, WY
82222 Lance Creek, WY
82223 Lingle, WY
82223 Rockeagle, WY
82224 Lost Springs, WY
82225 Kirtley, WY
82225 Lusk, WY
82225 Node, WY
82227 Keeline, WY
82227 Manville, WY
82229 Shawnee, WY
82240 Prairie Center, WY
82240 Torrington, WY
82242 Van Tassell, WY
82243 Veteran, WY
82244 Yoder, WY

823

82301 Creston, WY
82301 Fort Steele, WY
82301 Muddy Gap, WY
82301 Rawlins, WY
82301 Riner, WY
82310 Jeffrey City, WY
82310 Rawlins, WY
82321 Baggs, WY
82322 Bairoil, WY
82323 Dixon, WY
82324 Elk Mountain, WY
82325 Encampment, WY
82325 Riverside, WY
82327 Elmo, WY
82327 Hanna, WY
82327 Kortes Dam, WY
82327 Leo, WY
82329 Medicine Bow, WY
82331 Ryan Park, WY
82331 Saratoga, WY
82332 Savery, WY
82334 Sinclair, WY
82335 Walcott, WY
82336 Red Desert, WY
82336 Tipton, WY
82336 Wamsutter, WY

824

82401 Worland, WY
82410 Basin, WY
82411 Burlington, WY
82412 Byron, WY
82414 Cody, WY
82420 Cowley, WY
82421 Deaver, WY
82422 Emblem, WY
82423 Frannie, WY
82426 Greybull, WY
82428 Hyattville, WY
82430 Kirby, WY
82430 Worland, WY
82431 Lovell, WY
82432 Manderson, WY
82433 Meeteetse, WY
82434 Otto, WY
82435 Clark, WY
82435 Garland, WY
82435 Mantua, WY
82435 Powell, WY
82435 Willwood, WY
82440 Ralston, WY
82441 Shell, WY
82442 Ten Sleep, WY
82443 Hamilton Dome, WY
82443 Thermopolis, WY
82450 Wapiti, WY

825

82501 Gas Hills, WY
82501 Lucky Maccamp, WY
82501 Midval, WY
82501 Morton, WY
82501 Riverton, WY
82501 Sand Draw, WY
82510 Arapahoe, WY
82512 Burris, WY
82512 Crowheart, WY
82513 Dubois, WY
82514 Fort Washakie, WY
82515 Hudson, WY
82516 Kinnear, WY
82520 Atlantic City, WY
82520 Ethete, WY
82520 Lander, WY
82520 South Pass City, WY
82520 Sweetwater Station, WY
82523 Pavillion, WY
82524 Saint Stephens, WY

826

82601 Bar Nunn, WY
82601 Casper, WY
82602 Casper, WY
82604 Casper, WY
82604 Mills, WY
82604 Moneta, WY
82605 Casper, WY
82609 Allendale, WY
82609 Bar Nunn, WY
82609 Casper, WY
82615 Casper, WY
82615 Shirley Basin, WY
82620 Alcova, WY
82630 Arminto, WY
82630 Casper, WY
82633 Douglas, WY
82633 Orin, WY
82635 Edgerton, WY
82636 Evansville, WY
82637 Glenrock, WY
82637 Parkerton, WY
82637 Rolling Hills, WY
82638 Casper, WY
82638 Hiland, WY
82638 Moneta, WY
82639 Kaycee, WY
82639 Mayoworth, WY
82639 Sussex, WY
82640 Linch, WY
82642 Lost Cabin, WY
82642 Lysite, WY
82643 Midwest, WY
82644 Mills, WY
82646 Casper, WY
82646 Natrona, WY
82648 Powder River, WY
82649 Shoshoni, WY

827

82701 Newcastle, WY
82710 Aladdin, WY
82711 Alva, WY
82712 Beulah, WY
82714 Devils Tower, WY
82715 Four Corners, WY
82715 Newcastle, WY
82716 Gillette, WY
82717 Gillette, WY
82718 Gillette, WY
82720 Hulett, WY
82720 New Haven, WY
82721 Carlile, WY
82721 Moorcroft, WY
82721 Oshoto, WY
82721 Pine Haven, WY
82723 Osage, WY
82725 Recluse, WY
82727 Rozet, WY
82729 Sundance, WY
82730 Upton, WY
82731 Gillette, WY
82731 Weston, WY
82732 Gillette, WY
82732 Wright, WY

828

82801 Sheridan, WY
82831 Arvada, WY
82832 Banner, WY
82832 Story, WY
82833 Big Horn, WY
82834 Buffalo, WY
82835 Clearmont, WY
82836 Dayton, WY
82837 Leiter, WY
82838 Parkman, WY
82839 Acme, WY
82839 Ranchester, WY
82840 Buffalo, WY
82840 Saddlestring, WY
82842 Story, WY
82844 Ranchester, WY
82844 Wolf, WY
82845 Wyarno, WY

829

82901 Bitter Creek, WY
82901 Quealy, WY
82901 Rock Springs, WY
82902 Rock Springs, WY
82922 Bondurant, WY
82923 Boulder, WY
82925 Cora, WY
82929 Little America, WY
82930 Bear River, WY
82930 Evanston, WY
82931 Evanston, WY
82932 Eden, WY
82932 Farson, WY
82933 Fort Bridger, WY
82933 Piedmont, WY
82934 Granger, WY
82935 Green River, WY
82935 Mc Kinnon, WY
82936 Lonetree, WY
82937 Lyman, WY
82937 Urie, WY
82938 Green River, WY
82938 Mc Kinnon, WY
82939 Mountain View, WY
82941 Pinedale, WY
82942 Point Of Rocks, WY
82942 Rock Springs, WY
82943 Reliance, WY
82944 Robertson, WY
82945 Superior, WY

830

83001 Hoback Junction, WY
83001 Jackson, WY
83001 Jackson Hole, WY
83002 Jackson, WY
83002 Jackson Hole, WY
83011 Kelly, WY
83012 Jenny Lake, WY
83012 Moose, WY
83013 Moran, WY
83014 Wilson, WY
83025 Teton Village, WY

831

83101 Fontenelle, WY
83101 Hamsfork, WY
83101 Kemmerer, WY
83110 Afton, WY
83110 Turnerville, WY
83111 Auburn, WY
83112 Bedford, WY
83113 Big Piney, WY
83114 Cokeville, WY
83114 Raymond, WY
83115 Daniel, WY
83116 Diamondville, WY
83118 Etna, WY
83119 Fairview, WY
83120 Freedom, WY
83121 Frontier, WY
83122 Grover, WY
83123 La Barge, WY
83124 Opal, WY
83126 Smoot, WY
83127 Star Valley Ranch, WY
83127 Thayne, WY
83128 Alpine, WY

832

83201 Pocatello, ID
83202 Chubbuck, ID
83202 Pocatello, ID
83203 Fort Hall, ID
83203 Pocatello, ID
83204 Pocatello, ID
83205 Pocatello, ID
83206 Pocatello, ID
83209 Pocatello, ID
83210 Aberdeen, ID
83210 Sterling, ID
83211 Am Falls, ID
83211 American Falls, ID
83212 Arbon, ID
83213 Arco, ID
83213 Butte City, ID
83214 Arimo, ID
83215 Atomic City, ID
83217 Bancroft, ID
83218 Basalt, ID
83220 Bern, ID
83221 Blackfoot, ID
83223 Bloomington, ID
83226 Challis, ID
83227 Clayton, ID
83228 Clifton, ID
83228 Oxford, ID
83229 Challis, ID
83229 Cobalt, ID
83230 Conda, ID
83230 Soda Springs, ID
83232 Dayton, ID
83233 Dingle, ID
83234 Downey, ID
83235 Ellis, ID
83236 Firth, ID
83237 Franklin, ID
83238 Geneva, ID
83239 Georgetown, ID
83241 Grace, ID
83243 Holbrook, ID
83244 Howe, ID
83245 Inkom, ID
83246 Lava Hot Springs, ID
83250 Mccammon, ID
83251 Mackay, ID
83252 Malad City, ID
83252 Stone, ID
83253 May, ID
83253 Patterson, ID
83254 Bennington, ID
83254 Montpelier, ID
83254 Ovid, ID
83255 Darlington, ID
83255 Lost River, ID
83255 Moore, ID
83256 Moreland, ID
83261 Paris, ID
83262 Pingree, ID
83263 Preston, ID
83271 Rockland, ID
83272 Saint Charles, ID
83274 Shelley, ID
83276 Soda Springs, ID
83277 Springfield, ID
83278 Stanley, ID
83281 Swanlake, ID
83283 Grace, ID
83283 Thatcher, ID
83285 Soda Springs, ID
83285 Wayan, ID
83286 Weston, ID
83287 Fish Haven, ID

833

83301 Hollister, ID
83301 Twin Falls, ID
83302 Rogerson, ID
83302 Twin Falls, ID
83303 Twin Falls, ID
83311 Albion, ID
83312 Almo, ID
83313 Bellevue, ID
83313 East Magic, ID
83313 Gannett, ID
83314 Bliss, ID
83316 Buhl, ID
83318 Burley, ID
83320 Carey, ID

83321 Castleford, ID
83322 Corral, ID
83322 Fairfield, ID
83323 Declo, ID
83324 Dietrich, ID
83324 Shoshone, ID
83325 Eden, ID
83327 Fairfield, ID
83328 Filer, ID
83330 Gooding, ID
83332 Hagerman, ID
83333 Hailey, ID
83333 Triumph, ID
83334 Hansen, ID
83335 Hazelton, ID
83336 Heyburn, ID
83337 Hill City, ID
83338 Jerome, ID
83340 Ketchum, ID
83340 Sawtooth City, ID
83341 Kimberly, ID
83342 Elba, ID
83342 Malta, ID
83343 Minidoka, ID
83343 Rupert, ID
83344 Murtaugh, ID
83346 Oakley, ID
83347 Paul, ID
83348 Picabo, ID
83349 Richfield, ID
83350 Acequia, ID
83350 Jackson, ID
83350 Minidoka, ID
83350 Rupert, ID
83352 Lone Star, ID
83352 Shoshone, ID
83352 West Magic, ID
83353 Sun Valley, ID
83354 Elk Horn, ID
83354 Sun Valley, ID
83355 Wendell, ID

834

83401 Ammon, ID
83401 Idaho Falls, ID
83402 Idaho Falls, ID
83403 Idaho Falls, ID
83404 Idaho Falls, ID
83405 Idaho Falls, ID
83406 Ammon, ID
83406 Idaho Falls, ID
83414 Alta, WY
83415 Idaho Falls, ID
83420 Ashton, ID
83421 Chester, ID
83422 Driggs, ID
83423 Dubois, ID
83424 Felt, ID
83424 Tetonia, ID
83425 Hamer, ID
83427 Iona, ID
83428 Irwin, ID
83428 Palisades, ID
83429 Island Park, ID
83431 Lewisville, ID
83433 Island Park, ID
83433 Macks Inn, ID
83434 Menan, ID
83435 Monteview, ID
83436 Newdale, ID
83438 Parker, ID
83440 Rexburg, ID
83441 Rexburg, ID
83442 Rigby, ID
83443 Ririe, ID
83444 Roberts, ID
83445 Saint Anthony, ID
83446 Dubois, ID
83446 Spencer, ID
83448 Sugar City, ID
83449 Swan Valley, ID
83450 Terreton, ID
83451 Teton, ID
83452 Tetonia, ID
83454 Ucon, ID
83455 Victor, ID
83460 Rexburg, ID
83462 Carmen, ID
83463 Gibbonsville, ID
83464 Leadore, ID
83465 Lemhi, ID
83466 North Fork, ID
83467 Salmon, ID
83468 Tendoy, ID
83469 North Fork, ID
83469 Shoup, ID

835

83501 Lewiston, ID
83520 Ahsahka, ID
83522 Cottonwood, ID
83522 Keuterville, ID
83523 Craigmont, ID
83524 Culdesac, ID
83525 Dixie, ID
83525 Elk City, ID
83526 Ferdinand, ID
83530 Grangeville, ID
83531 Fenn, ID
83531 Grangeville, ID
83533 Cottonwood, ID
83533 Greencreek, ID
83535 Juliaetta, ID
83536 Kamiah, ID
83537 Kendrick, ID
83539 Kooskia, ID
83540 Lapwai, ID
83540 Spalding, ID
83541 Lenore, ID
83542 Lucile, ID
83543 Nezperce, ID
83544 Orofino, ID
83545 Peck, ID
83546 Headquarters, ID
83546 Pierce, ID
83547 Pollock, ID
83548 Culdesac, ID
83548 Reubens, ID
83549 Riggins, ID
83552 Clearwater, ID
83552 Harpster, ID
83552 Stites, ID
83553 Weippe, ID
83554 White Bird, ID
83555 Winchester, ID

836

83601 Atlanta, ID
83602 Banks, ID
83604 Bruneau, ID
83604 Grasmere, ID
83604 Riddle, ID
83605 Caldwell, ID
83606 Caldwell, ID
83607 Caldwell, ID
83610 Cambridge, ID
83611 Cascade, ID
83612 Council, ID
83612 Fruitvale, ID
83615 Donnelly, ID
83615 Tamarack, ID
83616 Eagle, ID
83617 Emmett, ID
83617 Montour, ID
83619 Fruitland, ID
83622 Garden Valley, ID
83623 Glenns Ferry, ID
83624 Grand View, ID
83626 Greenleaf, ID
83627 Hammett, ID
83628 Homedale, ID
83629 Horseshoe Bend, ID
83630 Huston, ID
83631 Idaho City, ID
83631 New Centerville, ID
83631 Pioneerville, ID
83631 Star Ranch, ID
83631 Steirman, ID
83632 Indian Valley, ID
83633 King Hill, ID
83634 Kuna, ID
83635 Lake Fork, ID
83635 Mccall, ID
83636 Letha, ID
83637 Lowman, ID
83638 Mccall, ID
83639 Marsing, ID
83641 Melba, ID
83642 Meridian, ID
83643 Mesa, ID
83644 Middleton, ID
83645 Midvale, ID
83646 Meridian, ID
83647 Anderson Dam, ID
83647 Featherville, ID
83647 Mountain Home, ID
83647 Mt Home, ID
83647 Mtn Home, ID
83647 Oasis, ID
83647 Paradise Hot Springs, ID
83647 Pine, ID
83647 Prairie, ID
83647 Rocky Bar, ID
83647 Tipanuk, ID
83648 Mountain Home Afb, ID
83650 Murphy, ID
83650 Oreana, ID
83651 Nampa, ID
83652 Nampa, ID
83653 Nampa, ID
83654 New Meadows, ID
83655 New Plymouth, ID
83656 Notus, ID
83657 Ola, ID
83660 Parma, ID
83661 Payette, ID
83666 Placerville, ID
83669 Star, ID
83670 Sweet, ID
83671 Warren, ID
83672 Weiser, ID
83676 Wilder, ID
83677 Yellow Pine, ID
83680 Meridian, ID
83686 Nampa, ID
83687 Nampa, ID

837

83701 Boise, ID
83702 Boise, ID
83703 Boise, ID
83703 Garden City, ID
83704 Boise, ID
83705 Boise, ID
83706 Boise, ID
83707 Boise, ID
83708 Boise, ID
83709 Boise, ID
83711 Boise, ID
83712 Boise, ID
83713 Boise, ID
83714 Boise, ID
83714 Garden City, ID
83714 Hidden Springs, ID
83715 Boise, ID
83716 Atlanta, ID
83716 Boise, ID
83717 Boise, ID
83719 Boise, ID
83720 Boise, ID
83722 Boise, ID
83724 Boise, ID
83725 Boise, ID
83726 Boise, ID
83728 Boise, ID
83729 Boise, ID
83731 Boise, ID
83732 Boise, ID
83735 Boise, ID
83756 Boise, ID
83799 Boise, ID

838

83801 Athol, ID
83802 Avery, ID
83803 Bayview, ID
83804 Blanchard, ID
83805 Bonners Ferry, ID
83806 Bovill, ID
83808 Calder, ID
83809 Careywood, ID
83810 Cataldo, ID
83811 Clark Fork, ID
83812 Clarkia, ID
83813 Cocolalla, ID
83814 Coeur D Alene, ID
83814 Fernan Lake Village, ID
83815 Coeur D Alene, ID
83815 Dalton Gardens, ID
83815 Huetter, ID
83816 Coeur D Alene, ID
83821 Coolin, ID
83822 Oldtown, ID
83823 Deary, ID
83824 Desmet, ID
83825 Dover, ID
83826 Eastport, ID
83827 Elk River, ID
83830 Fernwood, ID
83832 Genesee, ID
83833 Harrison, ID
83834 Harvard, ID
83835 Hayden, ID
83835 Hayden Lake, ID
83836 Hope, ID
83837 Kellogg, ID
83837 Wardner, ID
83839 Kingston, ID
83840 Kootenai, ID
83841 Laclede, ID
83842 Medimont, ID
83843 Moscow, ID
83844 Moscow, ID
83845 Moyie Springs, ID
83846 Mullan, ID
83847 Naples, ID
83848 Nordman, ID
83849 Osburn, ID
83850 Pinehurst, ID
83851 Plummer, ID
83852 Ponderay, ID
83853 Porthill, ID
83854 Hauser, ID
83854 Post Falls, ID
83855 Onaway, ID
83855 Potlatch, ID
83856 Priest Lake, ID
83856 Priest River, ID
83857 Princeton, ID
83858 Rathdrum, ID
83858 Twin Lakes, ID
83860 Sagle, ID
83861 Saint Maries, ID
83861 St Maries, ID
83864 Sandpoint, ID
83865 Colburn, ID
83866 Santa, ID
83867 Silverton, ID
83868 Smelterville, ID
83869 Spirit Lake, ID
83870 Tensed, ID
83871 Troy, ID
83872 Viola, ID
83873 Prichard, ID
83873 Wallace, ID
83874 Murray, ID
83874 Wallace, ID
83876 Worley, ID
83877 Post Falls, ID

840

84001 Altamont, UT
84002 Altonah, UT
84003 American Fork, UT
84003 Highland, UT
84004 Alpine, UT
84005 Eagle Mountain, UT
84005 Lehi, UT
84006 Bingham Canyon, UT
84006 Copperton, UT
84007 Bluebell, UT
84008 Bonanza, UT
84010 Bountiful, UT
84010 West Bountiful, UT
84010 Woods Cross, UT
84011 Bountiful, UT
84013 Cedar Fort, UT
84013 Cedar Valley, UT
84013 Fairfield, UT
84014 Centerville, UT
84015 Clearfield, UT
84015 Clinton, UT
84015 Sunset, UT
84015 West Point, UT
84016 Clearfield, UT
84017 Coalville, UT
84017 Wanship, UT
84018 Croydon, UT
84020 Draper, UT
84021 Bridgeland, UT
84021 Duchesne, UT
84022 Dugway, UT
84022 Terra, UT
84023 Dutch John, UT
84023 Red Canyon, UT
84024 Echo, UT
84025 Farmington, UT
84026 Fort Duchesne, UT
84026 Gusher, UT
84026 Ouray, UT
84027 Fruitland, UT
84028 Garden City, UT
84029 Grantsville, UT
84029 Lakeside, UT
84029 Skull Valley, UT
84031 Hanna, UT
84032 Daniel, UT
84032 Heber City, UT
84033 Henefer, UT
84034 Callao, UT
84034 Ibapah, UT
84035 Jensen, UT
84036 Francis, UT
84036 Hideout, UT
84036 Kamas, UT
84037 Fruit Heights, UT
84037 Kaysville, UT
84038 Laketown, UT
84039 Lapoint, UT
84040 Layton, UT
84041 Layton, UT
84042 Lindon, UT
84043 Eagle Mountain, UT
84043 Lehi, UT
84043 Saratoga Springs, UT
84044 Magna, UT
84045 Lehi, UT
84045 Saratoga Springs, UT
84046 Manila, UT
84047 Cottonwood Heights, UT
84047 Midvale, UT
84049 Midway, UT
84050 Morgan, UT
84050 Mountain Green, UT
84051 Mountain Home, UT
84052 Myton, UT
84053 Neola, UT
84054 North Salt Lake, UT
84055 Oakley, UT
84056 Hill Afb, UT
84056 Hill Air Force Base, UT
84057 Orem, UT
84057 Vineyard, UT
84058 Orem, UT
84058 Vineyard, UT
84059 Orem, UT
84060 Deer Valley, UT
84060 Park City, UT
84061 Peoa, UT
84062 Cedar Hills, UT
84062 Pleasant Grove, UT
84063 Randlett, UT
84064 Randolph, UT
84065 Bluffdale, UT
84065 Herriman, UT
84065 Riverton, UT
84066 Ballard, UT
84066 Roosevelt, UT
84067 Roy, UT
84068 Park City, UT
84069 Rush Valley, UT
84070 Sandy, UT
84071 Ophir, UT
84071 South Rim, UT
84071 Stockton, UT
84072 Tabiona, UT
84073 Talmage, UT
84074 Erda, UT
84074 Lake Point, UT
84074 Stansbury Park, UT
84074 Tooele, UT
84075 Syracuse, UT
84076 Tridell, UT
84078 Naples, UT
84078 Vernal, UT
84079 Vernal, UT
84080 Vernon, UT
84081 West Jordan, UT
84081 West Valley, UT
84081 West Valley City, UT
84082 Wallsburg, UT
84083 Greenhaven, UT
84083 Partoun, UT
84083 Trout Creek, UT
84083 Wendover, UT
84084 West Jordan, UT
84085 Whiterocks, UT
84086 Woodruff, UT
84087 West Bountiful, UT
84087 Woods Cross, UT
84088 West Jordan, UT
84089 Clearfield, UT
84090 Sandy, UT
84091 Sandy, UT
84092 Alta, UT
84092 Sandy, UT
84092 Snowbird, UT
84093 Cottonwood Heights, UT
84093 Sandy, UT
84094 Sandy, UT
84095 Riverton, UT
84095 South Jordan, UT
84096 Herriman, UT
84096 Riverton, UT
84097 Orem, UT
84098 Park City, UT
84098 Snyderville, UT

841

84101 Salt Lake City, UT
84101 Slc, UT
84102 Salt Lake City, UT
84102 Slc, UT
84103 Salt Lake City, UT
84103 Slc, UT
84104 Salt Lake City, UT
84104 Slc, UT
84105 Salt Lake City, UT
84105 Slc, UT
84106 Millcreek, UT
84106 Salt Lake City, UT
84106 Slc, UT
84106 South Salt Lake, UT
84107 Millcreek, UT
84107 Murray, UT
84107 Salt Lake City, UT
84108 Emigration Canyon, UT
84108 Salt Lake City, UT
84108 Slc, UT
84109 Millcreek, UT
84109 Salt Lake City, UT
84109 Slc, UT
84110 Salt Lake City, UT
84110 Slc, UT
84111 Salt Lake City, UT
84111 Slc, UT
84112 Salt Lake City, UT
84112 Slc, UT
84113 Salt Lake City, UT
84113 Slc, UT
84114 Salt Lake City, UT
84114 Slc, UT
84115 Salt Lake City, UT
84115 South Salt Lake, UT
84116 Salt Lake City, UT
84116 Slc, UT
84117 Holladay, UT
84117 Holladay Cottonwood, UT
84117 Millcreek, UT

84117 Murray, UT
84117 Salt Lake City, UT
84117 Slc, UT
84118 Kearns, UT
84118 Salt Lake City, UT
84118 West Valley City, UT
84119 Salt Lake City, UT
84119 South Salt Lake, UT
84119 Taylorsville, UT
84119 West Valley, UT
84119 West Valley City, UT
84120 Salt Lake City, UT
84120 West Valley, UT
84120 West Valley City, UT
84121 Brighton, UT
84121 Cottonwood, UT
84121 Cottonwood Heights, UT
84121 Cottonwood Heights City, UT
84121 Holladay, UT
84121 Holladay Cottonwood, UT
84121 Murray, UT
84121 Salt Lake City, UT
84121 Solitude, UT
84122 Salt Lake City, UT
84122 Slc, UT
84123 Murray, UT
84123 Salt Lake City, UT
84123 Slc, UT
84123 Taylorsville, UT
84124 Holladay, UT
84124 Millcreek, UT
84124 Salt Lake City, UT
84124 Slc, UT
84125 Salt Lake City, UT
84125 Slc, UT
84126 Salt Lake City, UT
84126 Slc, UT
84127 Salt Lake City, UT
84127 Slc, UT
84128 Salt Lake City, UT
84128 West Valley, UT
84128 West Valley City, UT
84129 Salt Lake City, UT
84129 Taylorsville, UT
84130 Salt Lake City, UT
84131 Slc, UT
84132 Salt Lake City, UT
84132 Slc, UT
84133 Salt Lake City, UT
84133 Slc, UT
84134 Salt Lake City, UT
84134 Slc, UT
84136 Salt Lake City, UT
84143 Slc, UT
84145 Salt Lake City, UT
84145 Slc, UT
84147 Salt Lake City, UT
84147 Slc, UT
84148 Salt Lake City, UT
84148 Slc, UT
84150 Salt Lake City, UT
84150 Slc, UT
84151 Salt Lake City, UT
84151 Slc, UT
84152 Salt Lake City, UT
84152 Salt Lake Cty, UT
84152 Slc, UT
84157 Murray, UT
84157 Salt Lake City, UT
84157 Salt Lake Cty, UT
84157 Slc, UT
84158 Salt Lake City, UT
84158 Salt Lake Cty, UT
84158 Slc, UT
84165 Salt Lake City, UT
84165 Salt Lake Cty, UT
84165 Slc, UT
84165 South Salt Lake, UT
84165 Ssl, UT
84170 Salt Lake City, UT
84170 Salt Lake Cty, UT
84170 West Valley, UT
84170 West Valley City, UT
84171 Cottonwood, UT
84171 Cottonwood Heights, UT
84171 Cottonwood Heights City, UT
84171 Salt Lake City, UT
84171 Salt Lake Cty, UT
84180 Salt Lake City, UT
84180 Slc, UT
84184 Salt Lake City, UT
84184 Slc, UT
84189 Salt Lake City, UT
84199 Slc, UT

842

84201 Ogden, UT
84244 Ogden, UT

843

84301 Bear River City, UT
84302 Brigham City, UT
84302 Perry, UT
84304 Cache Junction, UT
84305 Clarkston, UT
84306 Beaverdam, UT
84306 Collinston, UT
84307 Corinne, UT
84308 Cornish, UT
84309 Deweyville, UT
84310 Eden, UT
84310 Liberty, UT
84311 Fielding, UT
84312 Garland, UT
84313 Grouse Creek, UT
84314 Honeyville, UT
84315 Hooper, UT
84315 Kanesville, UT
84316 Howell, UT
84317 Huntsville, UT
84318 Hyde Park, UT
84319 Hyrum, UT
84320 Cove, UT
84320 Lewiston, UT
84321 Logan, UT
84321 Nibley, UT
84321 River Heights, UT
84322 Logan, UT
84323 Logan, UT
84324 Mantua, UT
84325 Mendon, UT
84326 Millville, UT
84327 Newton, UT
84328 Paradise, UT
84329 Park Valley, UT
84330 Plymouth, UT
84331 Portage, UT
84332 Providence, UT
84333 Richmond, UT
84334 Riverside, UT
84335 Amalga, UT
84335 Benson, UT
84335 Smithfield, UT
84336 Snowville, UT
84337 Elwood, UT
84337 Penrose, UT
84337 Thatcher, UT
84337 Tremonton, UT
84338 Trenton, UT
84339 Wellsville, UT
84340 Willard, UT
84341 Logan, UT
84341 North Logan, UT

844

84401 Hooper, UT
84401 Marriott Slaterville, UT
84401 Marriott-Slaterville City, UT
84401 Ms City, UT
84401 Ogden, UT
84401 Roy, UT
84401 Taylor, UT
84401 West Haven, UT
84402 Ogden, UT
84403 Ogden, UT
84403 South Ogden, UT
84403 South Weber, UT
84403 Uintah, UT
84404 Farr West, UT
84404 Harrisville, UT
84404 Marriott Slaterville, UT
84404 Marriott-Slaterville City, UT
84404 Ms City, UT
84404 North Ogden, UT
84404 Ogden, UT
84404 Plain City, UT
84404 Pleasant View, UT
84405 Ogden, UT
84405 Riverdale, UT
84405 South Ogden, UT
84405 South Weber, UT
84405 Uintah, UT
84405 Washington Terrace, UT
84407 Ogden, UT
84408 Ogden, UT
84409 Ogden, UT
84412 Ogden, UT
84414 Harrisville, UT
84414 North Ogden, UT
84414 Ogden, UT
84414 Pleasant View, UT
84415 Ogden, UT

845

84501 Price, UT
84510 Aneth, UT
84511 Blanding, UT
84511 White Mesa, UT
84512 Bluff, UT
84513 Castle Dale, UT
84515 Cisco, UT
84516 Clawson, UT
84518 Cleveland, UT
84520 East Carbon, UT
84521 Elmo, UT
84522 Emery, UT
84523 Ferron, UT
84525 Green River, UT
84526 Helper, UT
84526 Scofield, UT
84528 Huntington, UT
84529 Kenilworth, UT
84530 La Sal, UT
84531 Mexican Hat, UT
84532 Castle Valley, UT
84532 Moab, UT
84533 Bullfrog, UT
84533 Halls Crossing, UT
84533 Hite, UT
84533 Lake Powell, UT
84533 Ticaboo, UT
84534 Montezuma Creek, UT
84535 Monticello, UT
84536 Monument Valley, UT
84537 Orangeville, UT
84539 Sunnyside, UT
84540 Green River, UT
84540 Thompson, UT
84542 Wellington, UT

846

84601 Provo, UT
84602 Provo, UT
84603 Provo, UT
84604 Provo, UT
84604 Provo Canyon, UT
84604 Sundance, UT
84605 Provo, UT
84606 Provo, UT
84620 Aurora, UT
84621 Axtell, UT
84622 Centerfield, UT
84623 Chester, UT
84624 Delta, UT
84624 Deseret, UT
84624 Oasis, UT
84624 Sugarville, UT
84624 Sutherland, UT
84626 Elberta, UT
84627 Ephraim, UT
84628 Eureka, UT
84628 Mammoth, UT
84629 Fairview, UT
84629 Thistle, UT
84630 Fayette, UT
84631 Fillmore, UT
84632 Fountain Green, UT
84633 Goshen, UT
84634 Gunnison, UT
84635 Abraham, UT
84635 Hinckley, UT
84636 Holden, UT
84637 Kanosh, UT
84638 Leamington, UT
84639 Levan, UT
84640 Lynndyl, UT
84642 Manti, UT
84643 Mayfield, UT
84644 Meadow, UT
84645 Mona, UT
84645 Rocky Ridge Town, UT
84646 Moroni, UT
84647 Mount Pleasant, UT
84648 Nephi, UT
84649 Oak City, UT
84651 Elk Ridge, UT
84651 Payson, UT
84652 Redmond, UT
84653 Salem, UT
84653 Woodland Hills, UT
84654 Salina, UT
84655 Genola, UT
84655 Santaquin, UT
84656 Scipio, UT
84657 Sigurd, UT
84660 Benjamin, UT
84660 Spanish Fork, UT
84662 Spring City, UT
84663 Springville, UT
84664 Mapleton, UT
84664 Springville, UT
84665 Sterling, UT
84667 Wales, UT

847

84701 Richfield, UT
84701 Venice, UT
84710 Alton, UT
84711 Annabella, UT
84712 Antimony, UT
84713 Beaver, UT
84714 Beryl, UT
84715 Bicknell, UT
84716 Boulder, UT
84718 Cannonville, UT
84719 Brian Head, UT
84720 Cedar City, UT
84720 Enoch, UT
84720 Pintura, UT
84721 Cedar City, UT
84721 Enoch, UT
84722 Central, UT
84723 Circleville, UT
84724 Elsinore, UT
84725 Enterprise, UT
84726 Escalante, UT
84728 Garrison, UT
84729 Glendale, UT
84730 Glenwood, UT
84731 Adamsville, UT
84731 Greenville, UT
84732 Greenwich, UT
84733 Gunlock, UT
84734 Hanksville, UT
84735 Hatch, UT
84736 Henrieville, UT
84737 Apple Valley, UT
84737 Hurricane, UT
84738 Ivins, UT
84739 Joseph, UT
84740 Junction, UT
84741 Big Water, UT
84741 Canyon Point, UT
84741 Kanab, UT
84742 Kanarraville, UT
84743 Kingston, UT
84744 Burrville, UT
84744 Koosharem, UT
84745 La Verkin, UT
84746 Leeds, UT
84747 Fremont, UT
84747 Loa, UT
84749 Lyman, UT
84750 Marysvale, UT
84751 Milford, UT
84752 Minersville, UT
84753 Modena, UT
84754 Austin, UT
84754 Central Valley, UT
84754 Monroe, UT
84755 Mount Carmel, UT
84756 Newcastle, UT
84757 New Harmony, UT
84758 Orderville, UT
84759 Panguitch, UT
84760 Paragonah, UT
84761 Parowan, UT
84762 Duck Creek Village, UT
84763 Rockville, UT
84764 Bryce, UT
84764 Bryce Canyon, UT
84764 Bryce Canyon City, UT
84765 Santa Clara, UT
84766 Sevier, UT
84767 Springdale, UT
84767 Zion National Park, UT
84770 Saint George, UT
84770 St George, UT
84771 Saint George, UT
84771 St George, UT
84772 Summit, UT
84773 Teasdale, UT
84774 Toquerville, UT
84775 Torrey, UT
84776 Tropic, UT
84779 Springdale, UT
84779 Virgin, UT
84780 Washington, UT
84781 Pine Valley, UT
84782 Brookside, UT
84782 Veyo, UT
84783 Dammeron Valley, UT
84784 Hildale, UT
84790 Saint George, UT
84790 St George, UT
84791 Saint George, UT
84791 St George, UT

850

85001 Phoenix, AZ
85002 Phoenix, AZ
85003 Phoenix, AZ
85004 Phoenix, AZ
85005 Phoenix, AZ
85006 Phoenix, AZ
85007 Phoenix, AZ
85008 Phoenix, AZ
85009 Phoenix, AZ
85010 Phoenix, AZ
85011 Phoenix, AZ
85012 Phoenix, AZ
85013 Phoenix, AZ
85014 Phoenix, AZ
85015 Phoenix, AZ
85016 Phoenix, AZ
85017 Phoenix, AZ
85018 Phoenix, AZ
85019 Phoenix, AZ
85020 Phoenix, AZ
85021 Phoenix, AZ
85022 Phoenix, AZ
85023 Phoenix, AZ
85024 Phoenix, AZ
85025 Phoenix, AZ
85026 Phoenix, AZ
85027 Phoenix, AZ
85028 Phoenix, AZ
85029 Phoenix, AZ
85030 Phoenix, AZ
85031 Phoenix, AZ
85032 Phoenix, AZ
85033 Phoenix, AZ
85034 Phoenix, AZ
85035 Phoenix, AZ
85036 Phoenix, AZ
85037 Phoenix, AZ
85038 Phoenix, AZ
85039 Phoenix, AZ
85040 Phoenix, AZ
85041 Phoenix, AZ
85042 Phoenix, AZ
85043 Phoenix, AZ
85044 Phoenix, AZ
85045 Phoenix, AZ
85046 Phoenix, AZ
85048 Phoenix, AZ
85050 Phoenix, AZ
85051 Phoenix, AZ
85053 Phoenix, AZ
85054 Phoenix, AZ
85060 Phoenix, AZ
85061 Phoenix, AZ
85062 Phoenix, AZ
85063 Phoenix, AZ
85064 Phoenix, AZ
85065 Phoenix, AZ
85066 Phoenix, AZ
85067 Phoenix, AZ
85068 Phoenix, AZ
85069 Phoenix, AZ
85070 Phoenix, AZ
85071 Phoenix, AZ
85072 Phoenix, AZ
85073 Phoenix, AZ
85074 Phoenix, AZ
85075 Phoenix, AZ
85076 Phoenix, AZ
85078 Phoenix, AZ
85079 Phoenix, AZ
85080 Phoenix, AZ
85082 Phoenix, AZ
85083 Phoenix, AZ
85085 Phoenix, AZ
85086 Anthem, AZ
85086 Desert Hills, AZ
85086 Phoenix, AZ
85087 New River, AZ
85087 Phoenix, AZ
85097 Phoenix, AZ
85098 Phoenix, AZ

851

85117 Apache Jct, AZ
85117 Apache Junction, AZ
85118 Apache Junction, AZ
85118 Apache Junction, AZ
85118 Gold Canyon, AZ
85118 Queen Valley, AZ
85118 Superstition Mountain, AZ
85118 Superstition Mtn, AZ
85119 Apache Junction, AZ
85119 Tortilla Flat, AZ
85120 Apache Junction, AZ
85121 Bapchule, AZ
85122 Casa Grande, AZ
85122 Eleven Mile Corner, AZ
85123 Arizona City, AZ
85127 Chandler Heights, AZ
85128 Coolidge, AZ
85130 Casa Grande, AZ
85131 Eloy, AZ
85131 Toltec, AZ
85132 Florence, AZ
85135 Hayden, AZ
85137 Kearny, AZ
85138 Maricopa, AZ
85139 Maricopa, AZ
85139 Mobile, AZ
85140 Queen Creek, AZ
85140 San Tan Valley, AZ
85141 Picacho, AZ
85142 Chandler Heights, AZ
85142 Queen Creek, AZ
85142 San Tan Valley, AZ
85143 Queen Creek, AZ
85143 San Tan Valley, AZ
85145 Red Rock, AZ
85147 Sacaton, AZ
85172 Stanfield, AZ
85173 Superior, AZ
85178 Apache Junction, AZ
85190 Tortilla Flat, AZ
85191 Valley Farms, AZ
85192 Dudleyville, AZ

85192 Winkelman, AZ
85193 Casa Grande, AZ
85194 Casa Grande, AZ

852

85201 Mesa, AZ
85202 Mesa, AZ
85203 Mesa, AZ
85204 Mesa, AZ
85205 Mesa, AZ
85206 Mesa, AZ
85207 Mesa, AZ
85208 Mesa, AZ
85209 Mesa, AZ
85210 Mesa, AZ
85211 Mesa, AZ
85212 Mesa, AZ
85213 Mesa, AZ
85214 Mesa, AZ
85215 Mesa, AZ
85216 Mesa, AZ
85224 Chandler, AZ
85225 Chandler, AZ
85226 Chandler, AZ
85233 Gilbert, AZ
85234 Gilbert, AZ
85236 Higley, AZ
85244 Chandler, AZ
85246 Chandler, AZ
85248 Chandler, AZ
85248 Sun Lakes, AZ
85249 Chandler, AZ
85250 Scottsdale, AZ
85251 Scottsdale, AZ
85252 Scottsdale, AZ
85253 Paradise Valley, AZ
85253 Scottsdale, AZ
85254 Scottsdale, AZ
85255 Scottsdale, AZ
85256 Scottsdale, AZ
85257 Scottsdale, AZ
85258 Scottsdale, AZ
85259 Scottsdale, AZ
85260 Scottsdale, AZ
85261 Scottsdale, AZ
85262 Scottsdale, AZ
85263 Rio Verde, AZ
85263 Scottsdale, AZ
85264 Fort Mcdowell, AZ
85264 Scottsdale, AZ
85266 Scottsdale, AZ
85267 Scottsdale, AZ
85268 Fountain Hills, AZ
85268 Scottsdale, AZ
85269 Fountain Hills, AZ
85269 Scottsdale, AZ
85271 Scottsdale, AZ
85274 Mesa, AZ
85275 Mesa, AZ
85277 Mesa, AZ
85280 Tempe, AZ
85281 Tempe, AZ
85282 Tempe, AZ
85283 Guadalupe, AZ
85283 Tempe, AZ
85284 Tempe, AZ
85285 Tempe, AZ
85286 Chandler, AZ
85287 Tempe, AZ
85295 Gilbert, AZ
85296 Gilbert, AZ
85297 Gilbert, AZ
85298 Gilbert, AZ
85299 Gilbert, AZ

853

85301 Glendale, AZ
85302 Glendale, AZ
85303 Glendale, AZ
85304 Glendale, AZ
85305 Glendale, AZ
85306 Glendale, AZ
85307 Glendale, AZ
85307 Luke Air Force Base, AZ
85308 Glendale, AZ
85309 Gbafaf, AZ
85309 Glendale, AZ
85309 Luke Air Force Base, AZ
85310 Glendale, AZ
85311 Glendale, AZ
85312 Glendale, AZ
85318 Glendale, AZ
85320 Aguila, AZ
85321 Ajo, AZ
85322 Arlington, AZ
85323 Avondale, AZ
85324 Black Canyon City, AZ
85324 Rock Springs, AZ
85325 Bouse, AZ
85326 Buckeye, AZ
85327 Cave Creek, AZ
85328 Cibola, AZ
85329 Cashion, AZ
85331 Cave Creek, AZ
85332 Congress, AZ
85333 Dateland, AZ
85334 Ehrenberg, AZ
85335 El Mirage, AZ
85336 Gadsden, AZ
85337 Gila Bend, AZ
85338 Goodyear, AZ
85339 Laveen, AZ
85340 Litchfield Park, AZ
85341 Lukeville, AZ
85342 Morristown, AZ
85343 Palo Verde, AZ
85344 Parker, AZ
85345 Peoria, AZ
85346 Quartzsite, AZ
85347 Roll, AZ
85348 Salome, AZ
85349 San Luis, AZ
85350 Somerton, AZ
85351 Sun City, AZ
85352 Tacna, AZ
85353 Tolleson, AZ
85354 Tonopah, AZ
85355 Waddell, AZ
85356 Wellton, AZ
85357 Wenden, AZ
85358 Wickenburg, AZ
85359 Quartzsite, AZ
85360 Wikieup, AZ
85361 Wittmann, AZ
85362 Yarnell, AZ
85363 Youngtown, AZ
85364 Yuma, AZ
85365 Martinez Lake, AZ
85365 Yuma, AZ
85365 Yuma Proving Ground, AZ
85366 Yuma, AZ
85367 Yuma, AZ
85369 Yuma, AZ
85371 Poston, AZ
85372 Sun City, AZ
85373 Sun City, AZ
85374 Sun City, AZ
85374 Surprise, AZ
85375 Sun City, AZ
85375 Sun City West, AZ
85376 Sun City West, AZ
85377 Carefree, AZ
85378 Surprise, AZ
85379 Sun City, AZ
85379 Surprise, AZ
85380 Peoria, AZ
85381 Peoria, AZ
85382 Peoria, AZ
85383 Peoria, AZ
85385 Peoria, AZ
85387 Sun City, AZ
85387 Sun City West, AZ
85387 Surprise, AZ
85388 Surprise, AZ
85390 Wickenburg, AZ
85392 Avondale, AZ
85395 Goodyear, AZ
85396 Buckeye, AZ

855

85501 Globe, AZ
85502 Globe, AZ
85530 Bylas, AZ
85531 Central, AZ
85532 Claypool, AZ
85533 Clifton, AZ
85534 Duncan, AZ
85535 Eden, AZ
85536 Fort Thomas, AZ
85539 Miami, AZ
85540 Morenci, AZ
85541 Payson, AZ
85541 Star Valley, AZ
85542 Peridot, AZ
85543 Pima, AZ
85544 Pine, AZ
85544 Strawberry, AZ
85545 Roosevelt, AZ
85546 Safford, AZ
85547 Payson, AZ
85548 Safford, AZ
85550 San Carlos, AZ
85551 Solomon, AZ
85552 Thatcher, AZ
85553 Tonto Basin, AZ
85554 Young, AZ

856

85601 Arivaca, AZ
85602 Benson, AZ
85603 Bisbee, AZ
85605 Bowie, AZ
85606 Cochise, AZ
85607 Douglas, AZ
85608 Douglas, AZ
85609 Dragoon, AZ
85610 Elfrida, AZ
85611 Elgin, AZ
85613 Fort Huachuca, AZ
85613 Sierra Vista, AZ
85614 Green Valley, AZ
85614 Madera Canyon, AZ
85615 Hereford, AZ
85616 Huachuca City, AZ
85617 Mc Neal, AZ
85618 Mammoth, AZ
85619 Mount Lemmon, AZ
85620 Naco, AZ
85621 Nogales, AZ
85622 Green Valley, AZ
85623 Oracle, AZ
85624 Patagonia, AZ
85625 Pearce, AZ
85625 Sunsites, AZ
85626 Pirtleville, AZ
85627 Pomerene, AZ
85628 Nogales, AZ
85629 Sahuarita, AZ
85630 Saint David, AZ
85631 San Manuel, AZ
85632 Portal, AZ
85632 San Simon, AZ
85633 Sasabe, AZ
85634 Pisinemo, AZ
85634 Sells, AZ
85635 Sierra Vista, AZ
85636 Sierra Vista, AZ
85637 Sonoita, AZ
85638 Tombstone, AZ
85639 Topawa, AZ
85640 Tumacacori, AZ
85641 Corona, AZ
85641 Corona De Tucson, AZ
85641 Santa Rita Foothills, AZ
85641 Vail, AZ
85643 Ft Grant, AZ
85643 Willcox, AZ
85644 Willcox, AZ
85645 Amado, AZ
85646 Tubac, AZ
85648 Nogales, AZ
85648 Rio Rico, AZ
85650 Sierra Vista, AZ
85652 Cortaro, AZ
85653 Marana, AZ
85654 Rillito, AZ
85655 Douglas, AZ
85658 Marana, AZ
85662 Nogales, AZ
85670 Fort Huachuca, AZ
85670 Sierra Vista, AZ
85671 Sierra Vista, AZ

857

85701 Tucson, AZ
85702 Tucson, AZ
85703 Tucson, AZ
85704 Oro Valley, AZ
85704 Tucson, AZ
85705 Tucson, AZ
85706 Tucson, AZ
85707 Davis Monthan Afb, AZ
85707 Tucson, AZ
85708 Tucson, AZ
85709 Tucson, AZ
85710 Tucson, AZ
85711 Tucson, AZ
85712 Tucson, AZ
85713 Tucson, AZ
85714 Tucson, AZ
85715 Tucson, AZ
85716 Tucson, AZ
85717 Tucson, AZ
85718 Tucson, AZ
85719 Tucson, AZ
85720 Tucson, AZ
85721 Tucson, AZ
85722 Tucson, AZ
85723 Tucson, AZ
85724 Tucson, AZ
85725 Tucson, AZ
85726 Tucson, AZ
85728 Tucson, AZ
85730 Tucson, AZ
85731 Tucson, AZ
85732 Tucson, AZ
85733 Tucson, AZ
85734 Tucson, AZ
85735 Tucson, AZ
85736 Tucson, AZ
85737 Oro Valley, AZ
85737 Tucson, AZ
85738 Catalina, AZ
85738 Tucson, AZ
85739 Catalina, AZ
85739 Saddlebrooke, AZ
85739 Tucson, AZ
85740 Tucson, AZ
85741 Tucson, AZ
85742 Oro Valley, AZ
85742 Tucson, AZ
85743 Tucson, AZ
85744 Tucson, AZ
85745 Tucson, AZ
85746 Tucson, AZ
85747 Tucson, AZ
85748 Tucson, AZ
85749 Tucson, AZ
85750 Tucson, AZ
85751 Tucson, AZ
85752 Tucson, AZ
85754 Tucson, AZ
85755 Oro Valley, AZ
85755 Tucson, AZ
85756 Tucson, AZ
85757 Tucson, AZ
85775 Tucson, AZ

859

85901 Show Low, AZ
85902 Show Low, AZ
85911 Cibecue, AZ
85911 Show Low, AZ
85912 White Mountain Lake, AZ
85920 Alpine, AZ
85922 Blue, AZ
85923 Clay Springs, AZ
85924 Concho, AZ
85925 Eagar, AZ
85926 Fort Apache, AZ
85927 Greer, AZ
85928 Heber, AZ
85929 Lakeside, AZ
85930 Mcnary, AZ
85931 Forest Lakes, AZ
85931 Heber, AZ
85932 Nutrioso, AZ
85933 Overgaard, AZ
85934 Pinedale, AZ
85935 Pinetop, AZ
85936 Saint Johns, AZ
85937 Snowflake, AZ
85938 Springerville, AZ
85939 Taylor, AZ
85940 Vernon, AZ
85941 Whiteriver, AZ
85942 Snowflake, AZ
85942 Woodruff, AZ

860

86001 Flagstaff, AZ
86002 Flagstaff, AZ
86003 Flagstaff, AZ
86004 Flagstaff, AZ
86005 Flagstaff, AZ
86011 Flagstaff, AZ
86015 Bellemont, AZ
86015 Flagstaff, AZ
86016 Cameron, AZ
86016 Gray Mountain, AZ
86017 Flagstaff, AZ
86017 Munds Park, AZ
86018 Flagstaff, AZ
86018 Parks, AZ
86018 Parks Comm Po, AZ
86020 Cameron, AZ
86021 Colorado City, AZ
86022 Fredonia, AZ
86023 Grand Canyon, AZ
86024 Flagstaff, AZ
86024 Happy Jack, AZ
86025 Holbrook, AZ
86028 Holbrook, AZ
86028 Petrified Forest Natl Pk, AZ
86029 Holbrook, AZ
86029 Sun Valley, AZ
86030 Hotevilla, AZ
86031 Holbrook, AZ
86031 Indian Wells, AZ
86032 Joseph City, AZ
86033 Kayenta, AZ
86034 Keams Canyon, AZ
86035 Leupp, AZ
86036 Marble Canyon, AZ
86038 Flagstaff, AZ
86038 Mormon Lake, AZ
86039 Kykotsmovi Village, AZ
86040 Page, AZ
86042 Polacca, AZ
86043 Second Mesa, AZ
86044 Tonalea, AZ
86045 Tuba City, AZ
86046 Williams, AZ
86047 Winslow, AZ
86052 Fredonia, AZ
86052 North Rim, AZ
86053 Kaibeto, AZ
86053 Tonalea, AZ
86054 Shonto, AZ
86054 Tonalea, AZ

863

86301 Prescott, AZ
86302 Prescott, AZ
86303 Groom Creek, AZ
86303 Prescott, AZ
86304 Prescott, AZ
86305 Iron Springs, AZ
86305 Prescott, AZ
86312 Prescott Valley, AZ
86313 Prescott, AZ
86314 Prescott Valley, AZ
86320 Ash Fork, AZ
86321 Bagdad, AZ
86322 Camp Verde, AZ
86323 Chino Valley, AZ
86324 Clarkdale, AZ
86325 Cornville, AZ
86326 Cottonwood, AZ
86327 Dewey, AZ
86329 Humboldt, AZ
86331 Jerome, AZ
86332 Kirkland, AZ
86332 Peeples Valley, AZ
86333 Bensch Ranch, AZ
86333 Cordes Lakes, AZ
86333 Mayer, AZ
86333 Spring Valley, AZ
86334 Paulden, AZ
86335 Rimrock, AZ
86336 Sedona, AZ
86337 Seligman, AZ
86338 Skull Valley, AZ
86339 Sedona, AZ
86340 Sedona, AZ
86341 Sedona, AZ
86342 Lake Montezuma, AZ
86343 Crown King, AZ
86351 Sedona, AZ

864

86401 Kingman, AZ
86402 Kingman, AZ
86403 Lake Havasu City, AZ
86409 Hualapai, AZ
86409 Kingman, AZ
86411 Hackberry, AZ
86411 Kingman, AZ
86412 Hualapai, AZ
86412 Kingman, AZ
86413 Golden Valley, AZ
86413 Kingman, AZ
86426 Bullhead City, AZ
86426 Fort Mohave, AZ
86427 Bullhead City, AZ
86427 Fort Mohave, AZ
86429 Bullhead City, AZ
86430 Bullhead City, AZ
86431 Chloride, AZ
86432 Littlefield, AZ
86433 Oatman, AZ
86434 Peach Springs, AZ
86435 Supai, AZ
86436 Topock, AZ
86437 Kingman, AZ
86437 Valentine, AZ
86438 Yucca, AZ
86439 Bullhead City, AZ
86440 Mohave Valley, AZ
86441 Dolan Springs, AZ
86442 Bullhead City, AZ
86443 Temple Bar Marina, AZ
86444 Meadview, AZ
86445 Kingman, AZ
86445 White Hills, AZ
86445 Willow Beach, AZ
86446 Bullhead City, AZ
86446 Mohave Valley, AZ

865

86502 Chambers, AZ
86503 Chinle, AZ
86504 Fort Defiance, AZ
86505 Ganado, AZ
86506 Houck, AZ
86507 Chinle, AZ
86507 Lukachukai, AZ
86508 Houck, AZ
86508 Lupton, AZ
86510 Pinon, AZ
86511 Saint Michaels, AZ
86512 Sanders, AZ
86514 Teec Nos Pos, AZ
86515 Window Rock, AZ
86520 Blue Gap, AZ
86520 Pinon, AZ
86535 Dennehotso, AZ
86535 Teec Nos Pos, AZ
86538 Chinle, AZ
86538 Many Farms, AZ
86540 Ganado, AZ
86540 Nazlini, AZ
86544 Red Valley, AZ
86544 Teec Nos Pos, AZ
86545 Rock Point, AZ

86547 Chinle, AZ
86547 Round Rock, AZ
86556 Chinle, AZ
86556 Tsaile, AZ

870

87001 Algodones, NM
87001 Budaghers, NM
87001 San Felipe Pb, NM
87002 Belen, NM
87002 Rio Communities, NM
87004 Bernalillo, NM
87004 Sandia Pueblo, NM
87004 Santa Ana Pueblo, NM
87004 Tamaya, NM
87005 Bluewater, NM
87006 Bosque, NM
87007 Casa Blanca, NM
87007 Paraje, NM
87007 Seama, NM
87008 Cedar Crest, NM
87009 Cedarvale, NM
87010 Cerrillos, NM
87010 Madrid, NM
87011 Claunch, NM
87012 Coyote, NM
87013 Cuba, NM
87013 Ojo Encino, NM
87014 Cubero, NM
87014 Seboyeta, NM
87015 Edgewood, NM
87016 Estancia, NM
87016 Tajique, NM
87017 Gallina, NM
87018 Counselor, NM
87020 Grants, NM
87020 San Mateo, NM
87021 Milan, NM
87022 Isleta, NM
87023 Jarales, NM
87024 Jemez Pueblo, NM
87025 Jemez Springs, NM
87026 Canoncito, NM
87026 Laguna, NM
87026 Mesita, NM
87026 Old Laguna, NM
87026 Tohajiilee, NM
87027 La Jara, NM
87027 Llaves, NM
87028 La Joya, NM
87029 Lindrith, NM
87031 Los Lunas, NM
87032 Mcintosh, NM
87034 Acoma, NM
87034 Pueblo Of Acoma, NM
87035 Moriarty, NM
87036 Mountainair, NM
87037 Nageezi, NM
87038 Encinal, NM
87038 New Laguna, NM
87040 Paguate, NM
87041 Pena Blanca, NM
87042 Bosque Farms, NM
87042 Peralta, NM
87043 Placitas, NM
87044 Ponderosa, NM
87045 Prewitt, NM
87046 Regina, NM
87047 Golden, NM
87047 San Antonito, NM
87047 Sandia Park, NM
87048 Corrales, NM
87049 San Fidel, NM
87051 San Rafael, NM
87052 Kewa, NM
87052 Santo Domingo Pueblo, NM
87053 San Ysidro, NM
87053 Zia Pueblo, NM
87056 Stanley, NM
87059 Tijeras, NM
87060 Tome, NM
87061 Torreon, NM
87062 Veguita, NM
87063 Willard, NM
87064 Youngsville, NM
87068 Bosque Farms, NM
87068 Peralta, NM
87070 Clines Corners, NM
87072 Cochiti Pueblo, NM
87083 Cochiti Lake, NM

871

87101 Albuquerque, NM
87102 Albuquerque, NM
87103 Albuquerque, NM
87104 Albuquerque, NM
87105 Albuquerque, NM
87106 Albuquerque, NM
87106 Unm, NM
87107 Albuquerque, NM
87107 Los Ranchos De Abq, NM
87107 Los Ranchos De Albuquerque, NM
87107 Los Rnchs Abq, NM
87107 Village Of Los Ranchos, NM
87108 Albuquerque, NM
87109 Albuquerque, NM
87110 Albuquerque, NM
87111 Albuquerque, NM
87112 Albuquerque, NM
87113 Albuquerque, NM
87114 Alameda, NM
87114 Albuquerque, NM
87114 Los Ranchos De Abq, NM
87114 Los Ranchos De Albuquerque, NM
87114 Los Rnchs Abq, NM
87114 Village Of Los Ranchos, NM
87115 Albuquerque, NM
87116 Albuquerque, NM
87117 Albuquerque, NM
87117 Kirtland Afb, NM
87119 Albuquerque, NM
87120 Albuquerque, NM
87121 Albuquerque, NM
87122 Albuquerque, NM
87123 Albuquerque, NM
87124 Albuquerque, NM
87124 Rio Rancho, NM
87125 Albuquerque, NM
87131 Albuquerque, NM
87144 Rio Rancho, NM
87151 Albuquerque, NM
87153 Albuquerque, NM
87154 Albuquerque, NM
87158 Albuquerque, NM
87174 Albuquerque, NM
87174 Rio Rancho, NM
87176 Albuquerque, NM
87181 Albuquerque, NM
87184 Alameda, NM
87184 Albuquerque, NM
87185 Albuquerque, NM
87187 Albuquerque, NM
87190 Albuquerque, NM
87191 Albuquerque, NM
87192 Albuquerque, NM
87193 Albuquerque, NM
87194 Albuquerque, NM
87195 Albuquerque, NM
87196 Albuquerque, NM
87196 Univ Of New Mexico, NM
87196 Unm, NM
87197 Albuquerque, NM
87198 Albuquerque, NM
87199 Albuquerque, NM

873

87301 Gallup, NM
87301 Manuelito, NM
87302 Gallup, NM
87305 Gallup, NM
87310 Brimhall, NM
87310 Gallup, NM
87311 Church Rock, NM
87312 Continental Divide, NM
87313 Crownpoint, NM
87315 Fence Lake, NM
87316 Fort Wingate, NM
87317 Gallup, NM
87317 Gamerco, NM
87319 Gallup, NM
87319 Mentmore, NM
87320 Mexican Springs, NM
87321 Ramah, NM
87322 Rehoboth, NM
87323 Thoreau, NM
87325 Tohatchi, NM
87326 Gallup, NM
87326 Vanderwagen, NM
87327 Zuni, NM
87328 Navajo, NM
87347 Continental Divide, NM
87347 Jamestown, NM
87357 Pinehill, NM
87357 Ramah, NM
87364 Sheep Springs, NM
87365 Smith Lake, NM
87375 Gallup, NM
87375 Yatahey, NM

874

87401 Farmington, NM
87402 Farmington, NM
87410 Aztec, NM
87412 Blanco, NM
87413 Bloomfield, NM
87415 Flora Vista, NM
87416 Fruitland, NM
87417 Kirtland, NM
87418 La Plata, NM
87419 Navajo Dam, NM
87420 Shiprock, NM
87421 Waterflow, NM
87455 Newcomb, NM
87461 Sanostee, NM
87499 Farmington, NM

875

87501 Pojoaque, NM
87501 Santa Fe, NM
87502 Santa Fe, NM
87503 Santa Fe, NM
87504 Santa Fe, NM
87505 Santa Fe, NM
87506 Jaconita, NM
87506 Nambe, NM
87506 San Ildefonso Pueblo, NM
87506 Santa Fe, NM
87507 Santa Fe, NM
87508 Santa Fe, NM
87509 Santa Fe, NM
87510 Abiquiu, NM
87511 Alcalde, NM
87512 Amalia, NM
87513 Arroyo Hondo, NM
87514 Arroyo Seco, NM
87515 Canjilon, NM
87516 Canones, NM
87517 Carson, NM
87518 Cebolla, NM
87519 Cerro, NM
87520 Chama, NM
87521 Chamisal, NM
87521 Ojo Sarco, NM
87522 Chimayo, NM
87522 Cundiyo, NM
87523 Cordova, NM
87524 Costilla, NM
87525 Taos Ski Valley, NM
87527 Dixon, NM
87528 Dulce, NM
87528 Lumberton, NM
87529 El Prado, NM
87530 El Rito, NM
87531 Embudo, NM
87532 Espanola, NM
87533 Espanola, NM
87533 Fairview, NM
87535 Glorieta, NM
87537 Hernandez, NM
87538 Ilfeld, NM
87539 La Madera, NM
87540 Galisteo, NM
87540 Lamy, NM
87540 Santa Fe, NM
87543 Llano, NM
87544 Los Alamos, NM
87544 White Rock, NM
87545 Los Alamos, NM
87548 Medanales, NM
87549 Ojo Caliente, NM
87551 Los Ojos, NM
87551 Rutheron, NM
87552 Pecos, NM
87553 Penasco, NM
87554 Petaca, NM
87556 Questa, NM
87557 Ranchos De Taos, NM
87558 Red River, NM
87560 Gonzales Ranch, NM
87560 Ribera, NM
87560 Sena, NM
87562 Rowe, NM
87564 San Cristobal, NM
87565 San Jose, NM
87566 Ohkay Owingeh, NM
87566 San Juan Pueblo, NM
87567 Santa Cruz, NM
87569 Serafina, NM
87571 Taos, NM
87573 Tererro, NM
87574 Tesuque, NM
87575 Tierra Amarilla, NM
87576 Trampas, NM
87577 Tres Piedras, NM
87578 Truchas, NM
87579 Vadito, NM
87580 Valdez, NM
87581 Las Tablas, NM
87581 Vallecitos, NM
87582 Velarde, NM
87583 Villanueva, NM
87592 Santa Fe, NM
87594 Santa Fe, NM

876

87654 Spaceport City, NM

877

87701 Las Vegas, NM
87710 Angel Fire, NM
87710 Eagle Nest, NM
87711 Anton Chico, NM
87712 Buena Vista, NM
87713 Chacon, NM
87714 Cimarron, NM
87715 Cleveland, NM
87718 Eagle Nest, NM
87722 Guadalupita, NM
87723 Holman, NM
87724 La Loma, NM
87728 Maxwell, NM
87729 Miami, NM
87729 Springer, NM
87730 Mills, NM
87731 Montezuma, NM
87732 Ledoux, NM
87732 Mora, NM
87733 Albert, NM
87733 Mosquero, NM
87734 Ocate, NM
87735 Ojo Feliz, NM
87735 Wagon Mound, NM
87736 Rainsville, NM
87740 Raton, NM
87742 Rociada, NM
87743 Roy, NM
87745 Las Vegas, NM
87745 Sapello, NM
87746 Solano, NM
87747 Springer, NM
87749 Ute Park, NM
87750 Valmora, NM
87750 Watrous, NM
87752 Wagon Mound, NM
87753 Watrous, NM

878

87801 Socorro, NM
87820 Aragon, NM
87821 Datil, NM
87823 Lemitar, NM
87824 Luna, NM
87825 Alamo, NM
87825 Magdalena, NM
87827 Pie Town, NM
87828 Polvadera, NM
87829 Quemado, NM
87830 Reserve, NM
87831 San Acacia, NM
87832 Bingham, NM
87832 San Antonio, NM

879

87901 Cuchillo, NM
87901 Truth Consq, NM
87901 Truth Or Consequences, NM
87930 Arrey, NM
87931 Caballo, NM
87933 Derry, NM
87935 Elephant Butte, NM
87936 Garfield, NM
87937 Hatch, NM
87939 Monticello, NM
87940 Rincon, NM
87941 Salem, NM
87942 Williamsburg, NM
87943 Winston, NM

880

88001 Las Cruces, NM
88002 Las Cruces, NM
88002 White Sands Missile Range, NM
88003 Las Cruces, NM
88004 Las Cruces, NM
88005 Las Cruces, NM
88006 Las Cruces, NM
88007 Las Cruces, NM
88008 Santa Teresa, NM
88009 Lordsburg, NM
88009 Playas, NM
88011 Las Cruces, NM
88012 Las Cruces, NM
88013 Las Cruces, NM
88020 Animas, NM
88021 Anthony, NM
88021 Chaparral, NM
88022 Arenas Valley, NM
88022 Silver City, NM
88023 Bayard, NM
88023 Vanadium, NM
88024 Anthony, NM
88024 Berino, NM
88025 Buckhorn, NM
88026 Central, NM
88026 Santa Clara, NM
88027 Chamberino, NM
88028 Cliff, NM
88029 Columbus, NM
88030 Deming, NM
88031 Deming, NM
88032 Dona Ana, NM
88033 Fairacres, NM
88034 Faywood, NM
88036 Fort Bayard, NM
88036 Silver City, NM
88038 Gila, NM
88039 Glenwood, NM
88039 Mogollon, NM
88040 Hachita, NM
88041 Hanover, NM
88041 San Lorenzo, NM
88042 Hillsboro, NM
88043 Hurley, NM
88044 La Mesa, NM
88045 Lordsburg, NM
88045 Road Forks, NM
88045 Virden, NM
88046 Mesilla, NM
88047 Mesilla Park, NM
88048 Mesquite, NM
88049 Mimbres, NM
88051 Mule Creek, NM
88052 Organ, NM
88053 Pinos Altos, NM
88053 Silver City, NM
88054 Radium Springs, NM
88055 Lordsburg, NM
88055 Redrock, NM
88056 Rodeo, NM
88058 San Miguel, NM
88061 Silver City, NM
88062 Silver City, NM
88063 Sunland Park, NM
88065 Tyrone, NM
88072 Vado, NM
88081 Anthony, NM
88081 Chaparral, NM

881

88101 Cannon Afb, NM
88101 Clovis, NM
88102 Clovis, NM
88103 Cannon Afb, NM
88103 Clovis, NM
88112 Bellview, NM
88112 Broadview, NM
88113 Causey, NM
88114 Crossroads, NM
88115 Dora, NM
88116 Elida, NM
88118 Floyd, NM
88119 Fort Sumner, NM
88119 Lake Sumner, NM
88120 Grady, NM
88121 House, NM
88122 Kenna, NM
88123 Lingo, NM
88123 Portales, NM
88124 Melrose, NM
88125 Milnesand, NM
88126 Pep, NM
88130 Portales, NM
88132 Rogers, NM
88133 Saint Vrain, NM
88134 Taiban, NM
88135 Texico, NM
88136 Lon, NM
88136 Yeso, NM

882

88201 Border Hill, NM
88201 Pine Lodge, NM
88201 Roswell, NM
88202 Roswell, NM
88203 Roswell, NM
88210 Artesia, NM
88211 Artesia, NM
88213 Caprock, NM
88213 Tatum, NM
88220 Carlsbad, NM
88221 Carlsbad, NM
88230 Dexter, NM
88231 Eunice, NM
88232 Hagerman, NM
88240 Hobbs, NM
88240 Oil Center, NM
88241 Hobbs, NM
88242 Hobbs, NM
88244 Hobbs, NM
88250 Hope, NM
88252 Jal, NM
88253 Lake Arthur, NM
88254 Lakewood, NM
88255 Loco Hills, NM
88256 Loving, NM
88260 Lovington, NM
88262 Mcdonald, NM
88263 Malaga, NM
88264 Maljamar, NM
88265 Monument, NM
88267 Tatum, NM
88268 Whites City, NM

883

88301 Ancho, NM
88301 Carrizozo, NM

88301 Duran, NM
88301 Oscuro, NM
88301 White Oaks, NM
88310 Alamogordo, NM
88311 Alamogordo, NM
88312 Alto, NM
88314 Bent, NM
88316 Angus, NM
88316 Capitan, NM
88317 Cloudcroft, NM
88318 Corona, NM
88321 Encino, NM
88323 Fort Stanton, NM
88324 Glencoe, NM
88325 High Rolls Mountain Park, NM
88330 Holloman Air Force Base, NM
88336 Hondo, NM
88337 La Luz, NM
88338 Lincoln, NM
88339 Flying H, NM
88339 Mayhill, NM
88340 Mescalero, NM
88341 Nogal, NM
88342 Orogrande, NM
88343 Picacho, NM
88344 Pinon, NM
88345 Ruidoso, NM
88346 Ruidoso Downs, NM
88347 Sacramento, NM
88348 San Patricio, NM
88349 Sunspot, NM
88350 Cloudcroft, NM
88350 Timberon, NM
88351 Arabela, NM
88351 Tinnie, NM
88352 Tularosa, NM
88353 Vaughn, NM
88354 Weed, NM
88355 Ruidoso, NM

884

88401 Tucumcari, NM
88410 Amistad, NM
88411 Bard, NM
88411 San Jon, NM
88414 Capulin, NM
88415 Bueyeros, NM
88415 Clayton, NM
88415 Seneca, NM
88415 Stead, NM
88416 Conchas Dam, NM
88416 Tucumcari, NM
88417 Cuervo, NM
88418 Des Moines, NM
88419 Folsom, NM
88421 Garita, NM
88422 Gladstone, NM
88424 Grenville, NM
88424 Mount Dora, NM
88426 Logan, NM
88427 Mcalister, NM
88430 Nara Visa, NM
88431 Bell Ranch, NM
88431 Newkirk, NM
88433 Quay, NM
88434 Glenrio, NM
88434 San Jon, NM
88435 Pastura, NM
88435 Puerta De Luna, NM
88435 Santa Rosa, NM
88436 Sedan, NM
88439 Trementina, NM

885

88510 El Paso, TX
88511 El Paso, TX
88512 El Paso, TX
88513 El Paso, TX
88514 El Paso, TX
88515 El Paso, TX
88516 El Paso, TX
88517 El Paso, TX
88518 El Paso, TX
88519 El Paso, TX
88520 El Paso, TX
88521 El Paso, TX
88523 El Paso, TX
88524 El Paso, TX
88525 El Paso, TX
88526 El Paso, TX
88527 El Paso, TX
88528 El Paso, TX
88529 El Paso, TX
88530 El Paso, TX
88531 El Paso, TX
88532 El Paso, TX
88533 El Paso, TX
88534 El Paso, TX
88535 El Paso, TX
88536 El Paso, TX
88538 El Paso, TX
88539 El Paso, TX
88540 El Paso, TX
88541 El Paso, TX
88542 El Paso, TX
88543 El Paso, TX
88544 El Paso, TX
88545 El Paso, TX
88546 El Paso, TX
88547 El Paso, TX
88548 El Paso, TX
88549 El Paso, TX
88550 El Paso, TX
88553 El Paso, TX
88554 El Paso, TX
88555 El Paso, TX
88556 El Paso, TX
88557 El Paso, TX
88558 El Paso, TX
88559 El Paso, TX
88560 El Paso, TX
88561 El Paso, TX
88562 El Paso, TX
88563 El Paso, TX
88565 El Paso, TX
88566 El Paso, TX
88567 El Paso, TX
88568 El Paso, TX
88569 El Paso, TX
88570 El Paso, TX
88571 El Paso, TX
88572 El Paso, TX
88573 El Paso, TX
88574 El Paso, TX
88575 El Paso, TX
88576 El Paso, TX
88577 El Paso, TX
88578 El Paso, TX
88579 El Paso, TX
88580 El Paso, TX
88581 El Paso, TX
88582 El Paso, TX
88583 El Paso, TX
88584 El Paso, TX
88585 El Paso, TX
88586 El Paso, TX
88587 El Paso, TX
88588 El Paso, TX
88589 El Paso, TX
88590 El Paso, TX
88595 El Paso, TX

889

88901 The Lakes, NV
88905 The Lakes, NV

890

89001 Alamo, NV
89002 Henderson, NV
89003 Beatty, NV
89004 Blue Diamond, NV
89005 Boulder City, NV
89006 Boulder City, NV
89007 Bunkerville, NV
89008 Caliente, NV
89009 Henderson, NV
89010 Dyer, NV
89011 Henderson, NV
89012 Henderson, NV
89013 Goldfield, NV
89014 Henderson, NV
89015 Henderson, NV
89016 Henderson, NV
89017 Hiko, NV
89018 Indian Springs, NV
89019 Goodsprings, NV
89019 Jean, NV
89019 Primm, NV
89019 Sandy Valley, NV
89020 Amargosa Valley, NV
89021 Logandale, NV
89021 Moapa Valley, NV
89022 Manhattan, NV
89023 Mercury, NV
89024 Mesquite, NV
89025 Moapa, NV
89026 Jean, NV
89027 Mesquite, NV
89028 Laughlin, NV
89029 Laughlin, NV
89030 North Las Vegas, NV
89034 Mesquite, NV
89036 North Las Vegas, NV
89037 Coyote Springs, NV
89037 Moapa, NV
89039 Cal Nev Ari, NV
89039 Palm Gardens, NV
89039 Searchlight, NV
89040 Moapa Valley, NV
89040 Overton, NV
89041 Pahrump, NV
89042 Panaca, NV
89043 Pioche, NV
89044 Henderson, NV
89044 Las Vegas, NV
89045 Round Mountain, NV
89046 Cottonwood Cv, NV
89046 Searchlight, NV
89047 Silverpeak, NV
89048 Pahrump, NV
89049 Tonopah, NV
89052 Henderson, NV
89053 Henderson, NV
89054 Las Vegas, NV
89054 Sloan, NV
89060 Pahrump, NV
89061 Pahrump, NV
89067 Coyote Springs, NV
89067 Moapa, NV
89070 Indian Springs, NV
89074 Henderson, NV
89077 Henderson, NV
89081 North Las Vegas, NV

891

89101 Las Vegas, NV
89102 Las Vegas, NV
89103 Las Vegas, NV
89104 Las Vegas, NV
89105 Las Vegas, NV
89106 Las Vegas, NV
89107 Las Vegas, NV
89108 Las Vegas, NV
89109 Las Vegas, NV
89110 Las Vegas, NV
89111 Las Vegas, NV
89112 Las Vegas, NV
89113 Las Vegas, NV
89114 Las Vegas, NV
89115 Las Vegas, NV
89116 Las Vegas, NV
89117 Las Vegas, NV
89118 Las Vegas, NV
89119 Las Vegas, NV
89120 Las Vegas, NV
89121 Las Vegas, NV
89122 Las Vegas, NV
89123 Las Vegas, NV
89124 Calico Basin, NV
89124 Callville Bay, NV
89124 Cold Creek, NV
89124 Corn Creek, NV
89124 Enterprise, NV
89124 Las Vegas, NV
89124 Mount Charleston, NV
89124 Mountain Springs, NV
89124 Sloan, NV
89125 Las Vegas, NV
89126 Las Vegas, NV
89127 Las Vegas, NV
89128 Las Vegas, NV
89129 Las Vegas, NV
89130 Las Vegas, NV
89131 Las Vegas, NV
89132 Las Vegas, NV
89133 Las Vegas, NV
89134 Las Vegas, NV
89135 Las Vegas, NV
89136 Las Vegas, NV
89137 Las Vegas, NV
89138 Las Vegas, NV
89139 Las Vegas, NV
89140 Las Vegas, NV
89141 Las Vegas, NV
89142 Las Vegas, NV
89143 Las Vegas, NV
89144 Las Vegas, NV
89145 Las Vegas, NV
89146 Las Vegas, NV
89147 Las Vegas, NV
89148 Las Vegas, NV
89149 Las Vegas, NV
89150 Las Vegas, NV
89151 Las Vegas, NV
89152 Las Vegas, NV
89153 Las Vegas, NV
89154 Las Vegas, NV
89155 Las Vegas, NV
89156 Las Vegas, NV
89157 Las Vegas, NV
89158 City Center, NV
89158 Las Vegas, NV
89159 Las Vegas, NV
89160 Las Vegas, NV
89161 Las Vegas, NV
89161 Mountain Springs, NV
89162 Las Vegas, NV
89163 Las Vegas, NV
89163 The Lakes, NV
89164 Las Vegas, NV
89165 Las Vegas, NV
89166 Las Vegas, NV
89169 Las Vegas, NV
89170 Las Vegas, NV
89173 Las Vegas, NV
89177 Las Vegas, NV
89178 Las Vegas, NV
89179 Las Vegas, NV
89180 Las Vegas, NV
89183 Las Vegas, NV
89185 Las Vegas, NV
89191 Indian Springs Air Force Aux, NV
89191 Las Vegas, NV
89191 Nellis Afb, NV
89193 Las Vegas, NV
89195 Las Vegas, NV
89199 Las Vegas, NV

893

89301 Ely, NV
89310 Austin, NV
89311 Baker, NV
89314 Duckwater, NV
89315 Ely, NV
89316 Eureka, NV
89317 Lund, NV
89318 Mc Gill, NV
89319 Ruth, NV

894

89402 Crystal Bay, NV
89403 Dayton, NV
89404 Denio, NV
89405 Empire, NV
89406 Fallon, NV
89407 Fallon, NV
89408 Fernley, NV
89409 Gabbs, NV
89410 Gardnerville, NV
89411 Genoa, NV
89412 Gerlach, NV
89413 Glenbrook, NV
89414 Golconda, NV
89414 Midas, NV
89415 Hawthorne, NV
89415 Walker Lake, NV
89418 Imlay, NV
89418 Mill City, NV
89418 Unionville, NV
89419 Lovelock, NV
89420 Luning, NV
89421 Mc Dermitt, NV
89422 Mina, NV
89423 Minden, NV
89424 Nixon, NV
89425 Orovada, NV
89426 Paradise Valley, NV
89427 Schurz, NV
89428 Silver City, NV
89429 Silver Springs, NV
89429 Stagecoach, NV
89430 Smith, NV
89431 Sparks, NV
89432 Sparks, NV
89433 Sun Valley, NV
89434 Lockwood, NV
89434 Mccarran, NV
89434 Sparks, NV
89435 Sparks, NV
89436 Spanish Springs, NV
89436 Sparks, NV
89438 Valmy, NV
89439 Verdi, NV
89440 Virginia City, NV
89441 Spanish Springs, NV
89441 Sparks, NV
89442 Wadsworth, NV
89444 Wellington, NV
89445 Winnemucca, NV
89446 Winnemucca, NV
89447 Yerington, NV
89448 Zephyr Cove, NV
89449 Stateline, NV
89450 Incline Village, NV
89460 Gardnerville, NV
89496 Fallon, NV

895

89501 Reno, NV
89502 Reno, NV
89503 Reno, NV
89504 Reno, NV
89505 Reno, NV
89506 Reno, NV
89507 Reno, NV
89508 Reno, NV
89509 Reno, NV
89510 Reno, NV
89511 Reno, NV
89512 Reno, NV
89513 Reno, NV
89515 Reno, NV
89519 Reno, NV
89520 Reno, NV
89521 Reno, NV
89521 Vc Highlands, NV
89523 Reno, NV
89533 Reno, NV
89555 Reno, NV
89557 Reno, NV
89570 Reno, NV
89595 Reno, NV
89599 Reno, NV

897

89701 Carson City, NV
89702 Carson City, NV
89703 Carson City, NV
89704 Carson City, NV
89704 Washoe Valley, NV
89705 Carson City, NV
89706 Carson City, NV
89706 Mound House, NV
89711 Carson City, NV
89712 Carson City, NV
89713 Carson City, NV
89714 Carson City, NV
89721 Carson City, NV

898

89801 Elko, NV
89801 Halleck, NV
89801 Lee, NV
89802 Elko, NV
89803 Elko, NV
89815 Jiggs, NV
89815 Spring Creek, NV
89820 Battle Mountain, NV
89821 Beowawe, NV
89821 Crescent Valley, NV
89821 Emigrant Pass, NV
89822 Carlin, NV
89823 Deeth, NV
89825 Jackpot, NV
89826 Jackpot, NV
89826 Jarbidge, NV
89828 Lamoille, NV
89830 Montello, NV
89831 Mountain City, NV
89832 Owyhee, NV
89833 Ruby Valley, NV
89834 Tuscarora, NV
89835 Oasis, NV
89835 Wells, NV
89883 W Wendover, NV
89883 Wendover, NV
89883 West Wendover, NV

900

90001 Firestone Park, CA
90001 Los Angeles, CA
90002 Los Angeles, CA
90002 Watts, CA
90003 Los Angeles, CA
90004 Los Angeles, CA
90004 Oakwood, CA
90005 Los Angeles, CA
90005 Sanford, CA
90006 Los Angeles, CA
90007 Dockweiler, CA
90007 Los Angeles, CA
90008 Baldwin Hills, CA
90008 Leimert Park, CA
90008 Los Angeles, CA
90008 View Park, CA
90009 Los Angeles, CA
90009 Los Angeles Afb, CA
90010 Los Angeles, CA
90011 Los Angeles, CA
90012 Los Angeles, CA
90013 Los Angeles, CA
90014 Los Angeles, CA
90015 Los Angeles, CA
90016 Los Angeles, CA
90017 Los Angeles, CA
90018 Los Angeles, CA
90019 Los Angeles, CA
90020 Los Angeles, CA
90021 Los Angeles, CA
90022 Commerce, CA
90022 East Los Angeles, CA
90022 Los Angeles, CA
90023 Commerce, CA
90023 Los Angeles, CA
90024 Los Angeles, CA
90025 Los Angeles, CA
90025 West Los Angeles, CA
90026 Los Angeles, CA
90027 Los Angeles, CA
90028 Hollywood, CA
90028 Los Angeles, CA
90029 Los Angeles, CA
90030 Los Angeles, CA
90031 Lincoln Heights, CA
90031 Los Angeles, CA
90032 Los Angeles, CA
90033 Los Angeles, CA
90034 Los Angeles, CA
90035 Los Angeles, CA
90036 Los Angeles, CA
90037 Los Angeles, CA
90038 Los Angeles, CA
90038 West Hollywood, CA
90039 Los Angeles, CA
90040 Commerce, CA

90040 Cty Of Cmmrce, CA
90040 Los Angeles, CA
90041 Eagle Rock, CA
90041 Los Angeles, CA
90042 Highland Park, CA
90042 Los Angeles, CA
90043 Los Angeles, CA
90043 View Park, CA
90043 Windsor Hills, CA
90044 Los Angeles, CA
90045 Los Angeles, CA
90045 Westchester, CA
90046 Los Angeles, CA
90046 West Hollywood, CA
90047 Los Angeles, CA
90048 Los Angeles, CA
90048 West Hollywood, CA
90049 Los Angeles, CA
90050 Los Angeles, CA
90051 Los Angeles, CA
90052 Los Angeles, CA
90053 Los Angeles, CA
90054 Los Angeles, CA
90055 Los Angeles, CA
90056 Baldwin Hills, CA
90056 Los Angeles, CA
90056 Windsor Hills, CA
90057 Los Angeles, CA
90058 Los Angeles, CA
90058 Vernon, CA
90059 Los Angeles, CA
90060 Los Angeles, CA
90061 Los Angeles, CA
90062 Los Angeles, CA
90063 Hazard, CA
90063 Los Angeles, CA
90064 Los Angeles, CA
90064 Rancho Park, CA
90065 Glassell, CA
90065 Glassell Park, CA
90065 Los Angeles, CA
90066 Los Angeles, CA
90067 Century City, CA
90067 Los Angeles, CA
90068 Hollywood, CA
90068 Los Angeles, CA
90069 Los Angeles, CA
90069 West Hollywood, CA
90070 Los Angeles, CA
90071 Los Angeles, CA
90072 Los Angeles, CA
90073 Los Angeles, CA
90073 Veterans Admin, CA
90073 Veterans Administration, CA
90074 Los Angeles, CA
90075 Los Angeles, CA
90076 Los Angeles, CA
90077 Los Angeles, CA
90078 Hollywood, CA
90078 Los Angeles, CA
90079 Los Angeles, CA
90080 Los Angeles, CA
90081 Los Angeles, CA
90082 Los Angeles, CA
90083 Los Angeles, CA
90084 Los Angeles, CA
90086 Los Angeles, CA
90087 Los Angeles, CA
90088 Los Angeles, CA
90089 Los Angeles, CA
90090 Dodgertown, CA
90090 Los Angeles, CA
90091 Commerce, CA
90091 Cty Of Cmmrce, CA
90091 Los Angeles, CA
90093 Los Angeles, CA
90094 Los Angeles, CA
90094 Playa Vista, CA
90095 Los Angeles, CA
90096 Los Angeles, CA
90099 Los Angeles, CA

901

90189 Los Angeles, CA

902

90201 Bell, CA
90201 Bell Gardens, CA
90201 Cudahy, CA
90202 Bell, CA
90202 Bell Gardens, CA
90209 Beverly Hills, CA
90210 Beverly Hills, CA
90211 Beverly Hills, CA
90212 Beverly Hills, CA
90213 Beverly Hills, CA
90220 Compton, CA
90220 Crystal City, CA
90220 Rancho Dominguez, CA
90221 Compton, CA
90221 East Rancho Dominguez, CA
90222 Compton, CA
90222 Rosewood, CA
90223 Compton, CA
90224 Compton, CA
90224 Rancho Dominguez, CA
90230 Culver City, CA
90230 Los Angeles, CA
90231 Culver City, CA
90232 Culver City, CA
90233 Culver City, CA
90239 Downey, CA
90240 Downey, CA
90241 Downey, CA
90242 Downey, CA
90245 El Segundo, CA
90247 Gardena, CA
90248 Gardena, CA
90249 Gardena, CA
90250 Hawthorne, CA
90250 Holly Park, CA
90250 Hollyglen, CA
90251 Hawthorne, CA
90254 Hermosa Beach, CA
90255 Huntington Park, CA
90255 Walnut Park, CA
90260 Lawndale, CA
90261 Lawndale, CA
90262 Lynwood, CA
90263 Malibu, CA
90264 Malibu, CA
90265 Malibu, CA
90266 Manhattan Beach, CA
90270 Bell Gardens, CA
90270 Maywood, CA
90272 Pacific Palisades, CA
90274 Palos Verdes Estates, CA
90274 Palos Verdes Peninsula, CA
90274 Rolling Hills, CA
90274 Rolling Hills Estates, CA
90275 Palos Verdes Estates, CA
90275 Palos Verdes Peninsula, CA
90275 Rancho Palos Verdes, CA
90275 Rolling Hills Estates, CA
90277 Redondo Beach, CA
90278 Redondo Beach, CA
90280 South Gate, CA
90290 Topanga, CA
90291 Playa Del Rey, CA
90291 Venice, CA
90292 Marina Del Rey, CA
90292 Venice, CA
90293 Playa Del Rey, CA
90293 Venice, CA
90294 Venice, CA
90295 Marina Del Rey, CA
90295 Venice, CA
90296 Playa Del Rey, CA
90296 Venice, CA

903

90301 Inglewood, CA
90302 Inglewood, CA
90303 Inglewood, CA
90304 Inglewood, CA
90304 Lennox, CA
90305 Inglewood, CA
90306 Inglewood, CA
90307 Inglewood, CA
90308 Inglewood, CA
90309 Inglewood, CA
90310 Inglewood, CA
90311 Inglewood, CA
90312 Inglewood, CA

904

90401 Santa Monica, CA
90402 Santa Monica, CA
90403 Santa Monica, CA
90404 Santa Monica, CA
90405 Santa Monica, CA
90406 Santa Monica, CA
90407 Santa Monica, CA
90408 Santa Monica, CA
90409 Santa Monica, CA
90410 Santa Monica, CA
90411 Santa Monica, CA

905

90501 Torrance, CA
90502 Torrance, CA
90503 Torrance, CA
90504 Torrance, CA
90505 Torrance, CA
90506 Torrance, CA
90507 Torrance, CA
90508 Torrance, CA
90509 Torrance, CA
90510 Torrance, CA

906

90601 City Of Industry, CA
90601 Pico Rivera, CA
90601 Whittier, CA
90602 Whittier, CA
90603 Whittier, CA
90604 Whittier, CA
90605 Whittier, CA
90606 Los Nietos, CA
90606 Whittier, CA
90607 Whittier, CA
90608 Whittier, CA
90609 Whittier, CA
90610 Los Nietos, CA
90610 Whittier, CA
90620 Buena Park, CA
90621 Buena Park, CA
90622 Buena Park, CA
90623 Buena Park, CA
90623 La Palma, CA
90624 Buena Park, CA
90630 Cypress, CA
90631 La Habra, CA
90631 La Habra Heights, CA
90632 La Habra, CA
90633 La Habra, CA
90637 La Mirada, CA
90638 La Mirada, CA
90638 Lamirada, CA
90638 Mirada, CA
90639 La Mirada, CA
90640 Montebello, CA
90650 Norwalk, CA
90651 Norwalk, CA
90652 Norwalk, CA
90660 Pico Rivera, CA
90661 Pico Rivera, CA
90662 Pico Rivera, CA
90670 Santa Fe Springs, CA
90680 Stanton, CA

907

90701 Artesia, CA
90701 Cerritos, CA
90702 Artesia, CA
90703 Artesia, CA
90703 Cerritos, CA
90704 Avalon, CA
90706 Bellflower, CA
90707 Bellflower, CA
90710 Harbor City, CA
90711 Lakewood, CA
90712 Lakewood, CA
90713 Lakewood, CA
90714 Lakewood, CA
90715 Lakewood, CA
90716 Hawaiian Gardens, CA
90716 Lakewood, CA
90717 Lomita, CA
90720 Cypress, CA
90720 Los Alamitos, CA
90720 Rossmoor, CA
90721 Los Alamitos, CA
90723 Paramount, CA
90731 San Pedro, CA
90732 San Pedro, CA
90733 San Pedro, CA
90734 San Pedro, CA
90740 Seal Beach, CA
90742 Sunset Beach, CA
90743 Surfside, CA
90744 Wilmington, CA
90745 Carson, CA
90745 Long Beach, CA
90746 Carson, CA
90746 Long Beach, CA
90747 Carson, CA
90747 Long Beach, CA
90748 Wilmington, CA
90749 Carson, CA
90749 Long Beach, CA
90755 Long Beach, CA
90755 Signal Hill, CA

908

90801 Long Beach, CA
90802 Long Beach, CA
90803 Long Beach, CA
90804 Long Beach, CA
90805 Lakewood, CA
90805 Long Beach, CA
90806 Long Beach, CA
90807 Long Beach, CA
90807 Signal Hill, CA
90808 Long Beach, CA
90809 Long Beach, CA
90810 Carson, CA
90810 Long Beach, CA
90813 Long Beach, CA
90814 Long Beach, CA
90815 Long Beach, CA
90822 Long Beach, CA
90831 Long Beach, CA
90832 Long Beach, CA
90833 Long Beach, CA
90834 Long Beach, CA
90835 Long Beach, CA
90840 Long Beach, CA
90842 Long Beach, CA
90844 Long Beach, CA
90846 Long Beach, CA
90847 Long Beach, CA
90848 Long Beach, CA
90853 Long Beach, CA
90895 Carson, CA
90895 Long Beach, CA
90899 Long Beach, CA

910

91001 Altadena, CA
91003 Altadena, CA
91006 Arcadia, CA
91007 Arcadia, CA
91008 Bradbury, CA
91008 Duarte, CA
91009 Duarte, CA
91010 Bradbury, CA
91010 Duarte, CA
91010 Irwindale, CA
91011 Flintridge, CA
91011 La Canada, CA
91011 La Canada Flintridge, CA
91012 La Canada, CA
91012 La Canada Flintridge, CA
91016 Monrovia, CA
91017 Monrovia, CA
91020 Montrose, CA
91021 Montrose, CA
91023 Mount Wilson, CA
91024 Sierra Madre, CA
91025 Sierra Madre, CA
91030 South Pasadena, CA
91040 Shadow Hills, CA
91040 Sunland, CA
91041 Sunland, CA
91042 Tujunga, CA
91043 Tujunga, CA
91046 Verdugo City, CA
91066 Arcadia, CA
91077 Arcadia, CA

911

91101 Pasadena, CA
91102 Pasadena, CA
91103 Pasadena, CA
91104 Pasadena, CA
91105 Pasadena, CA
91106 Pasadena, CA
91107 Pasadena, CA
91108 Pasadena, CA
91108 San Marino, CA
91109 Pasadena, CA
91110 Pasadena, CA
91114 Pasadena, CA
91115 Pasadena, CA
91116 Pasadena, CA
91117 Pasadena, CA
91118 Pasadena, CA
91118 San Marino, CA
91121 Pasadena, CA
91123 Pasadena, CA
91124 Pasadena, CA
91125 Pasadena, CA
91126 Pasadena, CA
91129 Pasadena, CA
91182 Pasadena, CA
91184 Pasadena, CA
91185 Pasadena, CA
91188 Pasadena, CA
91189 Pasadena, CA
91199 Pasadena, CA

912

91201 Glendale, CA
91202 Glendale, CA
91203 Glendale, CA
91204 Glendale, CA
91205 Glendale, CA
91206 Glendale, CA
91207 Glendale, CA
91208 Glendale, CA
91209 Glendale, CA
91210 Glendale, CA
91214 Glendale, CA
91214 La Crescenta, CA
91221 Glendale, CA
91222 Glendale, CA
91224 Glendale, CA
91224 La Crescenta, CA
91225 Glendale, CA
91226 Glendale, CA

913

91301 Agoura, CA
91301 Agoura Hills, CA
91301 Calabasas, CA
91301 Calabasas Hills, CA
91301 Cornell, CA
91301 Oak Park, CA
91301 Saratoga Hills, CA
91302 Calabasas, CA
91302 Hidden Hills, CA
91302 Monte Nido, CA
91302 Woodland Hills, CA
91303 Canoga Park, CA
91303 Woodland Hills, CA
91304 Box Canyon, CA
91304 Canoga Park, CA
91304 West Hills, CA
91305 Canoga Park, CA
91306 Canoga Park, CA
91306 Winnetka, CA
91307 Bell Canyon, CA
91307 Canoga Park, CA
91307 West Hills, CA
91308 Canoga Park, CA
91308 West Hills, CA
91309 Canoga Park, CA
91310 Castaic, CA
91310 Santa Clarita, CA
91311 Chatsworth, CA
91313 Chatsworth, CA
91316 Encino, CA
91316 Van Nuys, CA
91319 Newbury Park, CA
91319 Thousand Oaks, CA
91320 Newbury Park, CA
91320 Thousand Oaks, CA
91321 Newhall, CA
91321 Santa Clarita, CA
91322 Newhall, CA
91322 Santa Clarita, CA
91324 Northridge, CA
91325 Northridge, CA
91325 Sherwood Forest, CA
91326 Northridge, CA
91326 Porter Ranch, CA
91327 Northridge, CA
91327 Porter Ranch, CA
91328 Northridge, CA
91329 Northridge, CA
91330 Northridge, CA
91331 Arleta, CA
91331 Hansen Hills, CA
91331 Pacoima, CA
91333 Pacoima, CA
91334 Arleta, CA
91334 Pacoima, CA
91335 Reseda, CA
91335 Tarzana, CA
91337 Reseda, CA
91340 San Fernando, CA
91341 San Fernando, CA
91342 Kagel Canyon, CA
91342 Lake View Terrace, CA
91342 Sylmar, CA
91343 North Hills, CA
91343 Northridge, CA
91343 Sepulveda, CA
91344 Granada Hills, CA
91344 San Fernando, CA
91345 Mission Hills, CA
91345 San Fernando, CA
91346 Mission Hills, CA
91346 San Fernando, CA
91350 Agua Dulce, CA
91350 Santa Clarita, CA
91350 Saugus, CA
91351 Canyon Country, CA
91351 Santa Clarita, CA
91352 Sun Valley, CA
91353 Sun Valley, CA
91354 Santa Clarita, CA
91354 Valencia, CA
91355 Santa Clarita, CA
91355 Valencia, CA
91356 Tarzana, CA
91357 Tarzana, CA
91358 Thousand Oaks, CA
91359 Thousand Oaks, CA
91359 Westlake Village, CA
91360 Thousand Oaks, CA
91361 Hidden Valley, CA
91361 Lake Sherwood, CA
91361 Thousand Oaks, CA
91361 Westlake Village, CA
91362 Thousand Oaks, CA
91362 Westlake Village, CA
91364 Woodland Hills, CA
91372 Calabasas, CA
91372 Woodland Hills, CA
91376 Agoura, CA
91376 Agoura Hills, CA
91377 Agoura Hills, CA
91377 Oak Park, CA
91380 Santa Clarita, CA
91380 Valencia, CA
91381 Newhall, CA
91381 Santa Clarita, CA
91381 Stevenson Ranch, CA
91381 Valencia, CA

91382 Santa Clarita, CA
91383 Santa Clarita, CA
91384 Castaic, CA
91384 Santa Clarita, CA
91384 Val Verde, CA
91385 Santa Clarita, CA
91385 Valencia, CA
91386 Canyon Country, CA
91386 Santa Clarita, CA
91387 Canyon Country, CA
91387 Santa Clarita, CA
91390 Agua Dulce, CA
91390 Canyon Country, CA
91390 Green Valley, CA
91390 Santa Clarita, CA
91392 Sylmar, CA
91393 North Hills, CA
91393 Sepulveda, CA
91394 Granada Hills, CA
91395 Mission Hills, CA
91396 Canoga Park, CA
91396 Winnetka, CA

914

91401 Sherman Oaks, CA
91401 Valley Glen, CA
91401 Van Nuys, CA
91402 Panorama City, CA
91402 Van Nuys, CA
91403 Sherman Oaks, CA
91403 Van Nuys, CA
91404 Van Nuys, CA
91405 Valley Glen, CA
91405 Van Nuys, CA
91406 Lake Balboa, CA
91406 Van Nuys, CA
91407 Van Nuys, CA
91408 Van Nuys, CA
91409 Van Nuys, CA
91410 Van Nuys, CA
91411 Sherman Oaks, CA
91411 Van Nuys, CA
91412 Panorama City, CA
91412 Van Nuys, CA
91413 Sherman Oaks, CA
91413 Van Nuys, CA
91416 Encino, CA
91416 Van Nuys, CA
91423 Sherman Oaks, CA
91423 Van Nuys, CA
91426 Encino, CA
91426 Van Nuys, CA
91436 Encino, CA
91436 Van Nuys, CA
91470 Van Nuys, CA
91482 Van Nuys, CA
91495 Sherman Oaks, CA
91495 Van Nuys, CA
91496 Van Nuys, CA
91499 Van Nuys, CA

915

91501 Burbank, CA
91502 Burbank, CA
91503 Burbank, CA
91504 Burbank, CA
91505 Burbank, CA
91506 Burbank, CA
91507 Burbank, CA
91508 Burbank, CA
91510 Burbank, CA
91521 Burbank, CA
91522 Burbank, CA
91523 Burbank, CA
91526 Burbank, CA

916

91601 North Hollywood, CA
91601 Toluca Terrace, CA
91601 Valley Village, CA
91602 North Hollywood, CA
91602 Studio City, CA
91602 Toluca Lake, CA
91602 West Toluca Lake, CA
91603 North Hollywood, CA
91604 Studio City, CA
91605 North Hollywood, CA
91606 Valley Glen, CA
91607 North Hollywood, CA
91607 Sherman Village, CA
91607 Studio City, CA
91607 Valley Village, CA
91608 North Hollywood, CA
91608 Universal City, CA
91609 North Hollywood, CA
91610 Toluca Lake, CA
91611 North Hollywood, CA
91614 Studio City, CA
91615 North Hollywood, CA
91617 Valley Village, CA
91618 North Hollywood, CA
91618 Universal City, CA

917

91701 Alta Loma, CA
91701 Rancho Cucamonga, CA
91702 Azusa, CA
91702 Irwindale, CA
91706 Baldwin Park, CA
91706 Irwindale, CA
91708 Chino, CA
91709 Chino Hills, CA
91710 Chino, CA
91710 Montclair, CA
91710 Ontario, CA
91711 Claremont, CA
91714 City Of Industry, CA
91722 Covina, CA
91723 Covina, CA
91724 Covina, CA
91729 Rancho Cucamonga, CA
91731 El Monte, CA
91732 City Of Industry, CA
91732 El Monte, CA
91733 El Monte, CA
91733 South El Monte, CA
91734 El Monte, CA
91735 El Monte, CA
91737 Alta Loma, CA
91737 Rancho Cucamonga, CA
91739 Etiwanda, CA
91739 Rancho Cucamonga, CA
91740 Glendora, CA
91741 Glendora, CA
91743 Guasti, CA
91744 City Of Industry, CA
91744 La Puente, CA
91745 City Of Industry, CA
91745 Hacienda Heights, CA
91745 La Puente, CA
91746 Bassett, CA
91746 City Of Industry, CA
91746 La Puente, CA
91747 La Puente, CA
91748 City Of Industry, CA
91748 La Puente, CA
91748 Rowland Heights, CA
91748 Rowland Hgts, CA
91749 La Puente, CA
91750 La Verne, CA
91752 Eastvale, CA
91752 Jurupa Valley, CA
91752 Mira Loma, CA
91754 Monterey Park, CA
91755 Monterey Park, CA
91756 Monterey Park, CA
91758 Ontario, CA
91759 Mt Baldy, CA
91761 Ontario, CA
91762 Montclair, CA
91762 Ontario, CA
91763 Montclair, CA
91764 Ontario, CA
91765 Diamond Bar, CA
91765 Pomona, CA
91766 Phillips Ranch, CA
91766 Pomona, CA
91767 Pomona, CA
91768 Pomona, CA
91769 Pomona, CA
91770 Rosemead, CA
91771 Rosemead, CA
91772 Rosemead, CA
91773 San Dimas, CA
91775 San Gabriel, CA
91776 San Gabriel, CA
91778 San Gabriel, CA
91780 Temple City, CA
91784 Upland, CA
91785 Upland, CA
91786 Upland, CA
91788 Walnut, CA
91789 City Of Industry, CA
91789 Diamond Bar, CA
91789 Walnut, CA
91790 West Covina, CA
91791 West Covina, CA
91792 West Covina, CA
91793 West Covina, CA

918

91801 Alhambra, CA
91802 Alhambra, CA
91803 Alhambra, CA
91804 Alhambra, CA
91896 Alhambra, CA
91899 Alhambra, CA

919

91901 Alpine, CA
91902 Bonita, CA
91903 Alpine, CA
91905 Boulevard, CA
91906 Campo, CA
91908 Bonita, CA
91909 Chula Vista, CA
91910 Chula Vista, CA
91911 Chula Vista, CA
91912 Chula Vista, CA
91913 Chula Vista, CA
91914 Chula Vista, CA
91915 Chula Vista, CA
91916 Descanso, CA
91917 Dulzura, CA
91921 Chula Vista, CA
91931 Guatay, CA
91932 Imperial Beach, CA
91934 Jacumba, CA
91935 Jamul, CA
91941 La Mesa, CA
91942 La Mesa, CA
91943 La Mesa, CA
91944 La Mesa, CA
91945 Lemon Grove, CA
91946 Lemon Grove, CA
91948 Mount Laguna, CA
91950 Lincoln Acres, CA
91950 National City, CA
91951 National City, CA
91962 Pine Valley, CA
91963 Potrero, CA
91976 Spring Valley, CA
91977 Spring Valley, CA
91978 Spring Valley, CA
91979 Spring Valley, CA
91980 Tecate, CA
91987 Tecate, CA

920

92003 Bonsall, CA
92004 Borrego Springs, CA
92007 Cardiff By The Sea, CA
92008 Carlsbad, CA
92009 Carlsbad, CA
92009 La Costa, CA
92010 Carlsbad, CA
92011 Carlsbad, CA
92011 La Costa, CA
92013 Carlsbad, CA
92014 Del Mar, CA
92018 Carlsbad, CA
92019 El Cajon, CA
92020 El Cajon, CA
92021 El Cajon, CA
92022 El Cajon, CA
92023 Encinitas, CA
92024 Encinitas, CA
92025 Escondido, CA
92026 Escondido, CA
92027 Escondido, CA
92028 Fallbrook, CA
92029 Elfin Forest, CA
92029 Escondido, CA
92030 Escondido, CA
92033 Escondido, CA
92036 Julian, CA
92037 La Jolla, CA
92038 La Jolla, CA
92039 La Jolla, CA
92040 Lakeside, CA
92046 Escondido, CA
92049 Oceanside, CA
92051 Oceanside, CA
92052 Oceanside, CA
92054 Camp Pendleton, CA
92054 Oceanside, CA
92055 Camp Pendleton, CA
92055 Oceanside, CA
92056 Oceanside, CA
92057 Oceanside, CA
92058 Oceanside, CA
92059 Pala, CA
92060 Palomar Mountain, CA
92061 Pala, CA
92061 Pauma Valley, CA
92064 Poway, CA
92065 Ramona, CA
92066 Ranchita, CA
92066 Warner Springs, CA
92067 Rancho Santa Fe, CA
92067 Rcho Santa Fe, CA
92068 Oceanside, CA
92068 San Luis Rey, CA
92069 San Marcos, CA
92070 Santa Ysabel, CA
92071 Santee, CA
92072 Santee, CA
92074 Poway, CA
92075 Solana Beach, CA
92078 Elfin Forest, CA
92078 San Marcos, CA
92079 San Marcos, CA
92081 Vista, CA
92082 Valley Center, CA
92083 Vista, CA
92084 Vista, CA
92085 Vista, CA
92086 Warner Springs, CA
92088 Fallbrook, CA
92091 Rancho Santa Fe, CA
92092 La Jolla, CA
92093 La Jolla, CA
92096 San Marcos, CA

921

92101 San Diego, CA
92102 San Diego, CA
92103 San Diego, CA
92104 San Diego, CA
92105 San Diego, CA
92106 San Diego, CA
92107 San Diego, CA
92108 San Diego, CA
92109 San Diego, CA
92110 San Diego, CA
92111 San Diego, CA
92112 San Diego, CA
92113 San Diego, CA
92114 San Diego, CA
92115 San Diego, CA
92116 San Diego, CA
92117 San Diego, CA
92118 Coronado, CA
92118 San Diego, CA
92119 San Diego, CA
92120 San Diego, CA
92121 San Diego, CA
92122 San Diego, CA
92123 San Diego, CA
92124 San Diego, CA
92126 San Diego, CA
92127 San Diego, CA
92128 San Diego, CA
92129 San Diego, CA
92130 San Diego, CA
92131 San Diego, CA
92132 San Diego, CA
92134 San Diego, CA
92135 Nas North Island, CA
92135 San Diego, CA
92136 San Diego, CA
92137 San Diego, CA
92138 San Diego, CA
92139 San Diego, CA
92140 San Diego, CA
92142 San Diego, CA
92143 San Diego, CA
92143 San Ysidro, CA
92145 San Diego, CA
92147 San Diego, CA
92149 San Diego, CA
92150 San Diego, CA
92152 San Diego, CA
92153 Nestor, CA
92153 San Diego, CA
92154 San Diego, CA
92155 San Diego, CA
92158 San Diego, CA
92159 San Diego, CA
92160 San Diego, CA
92161 San Diego, CA
92163 San Diego, CA
92165 San Diego, CA
92166 San Diego, CA
92167 San Diego, CA
92168 San Diego, CA
92169 San Diego, CA
92170 San Diego, CA
92171 San Diego, CA
92172 San Diego, CA
92173 San Diego, CA
92173 San Ysidro, CA
92174 San Diego, CA
92175 San Diego, CA
92176 San Diego, CA
92177 San Diego, CA
92178 Coronado, CA
92178 San Diego, CA
92179 San Diego, CA
92182 San Diego, CA
92186 San Diego, CA
92187 San Diego, CA
92190 San Diego, CA
92191 San Diego, CA
92192 San Diego, CA
92193 San Diego, CA
92195 San Diego, CA
92196 San Diego, CA
92197 San Diego, CA
92198 San Diego, CA
92199 San Diego, CA

922

92201 Chiriaco Summit, CA
92201 Indio, CA
92202 Indio, CA
92203 Bermuda Dunes, CA
92203 Indio, CA
92210 Indian Wells, CA
92210 Palm Desert, CA
92211 Palm Desert, CA
92220 Banning, CA
92222 Bard, CA
92223 Beaumont, CA
92223 Cherry Valley, CA
92225 Blythe, CA
92225 Ripley, CA
92226 Blythe, CA
92227 Brawley, CA
92230 Cabazon, CA
92231 Calexico, CA
92232 Calexico, CA
92233 Calipatria, CA
92234 Cathedral City, CA
92236 Coachella, CA
92239 Desert Center, CA
92239 Eagle Mountain, CA
92240 Desert Hot Springs, CA
92242 Big River, CA
92242 Earp, CA
92243 El Centro, CA
92244 El Centro, CA
92247 La Quinta, CA
92248 La Quinta, CA
92249 Heber, CA
92250 Holtville, CA
92251 Imperial, CA
92252 Joshua Tree, CA
92253 La Quinta, CA
92254 Mecca, CA
92255 Palm Desert, CA
92256 Morongo Valley, CA
92257 Niland, CA
92258 N Palm Springs, CA
92258 No Palm Springs, CA
92258 North Palm Springs, CA
92259 Ocotillo, CA
92260 Palm Desert, CA
92261 Palm Desert, CA
92262 Palm Springs, CA
92263 Palm Springs, CA
92264 Palm Springs, CA
92266 Palo Verde, CA
92267 Parker Dam, CA
92268 Pioneertown, CA
92270 Rancho Mirage, CA
92273 Seeley, CA
92274 Thermal, CA
92275 Salton City, CA
92275 Thermal, CA
92276 Thousand Palms, CA
92277 29 Palms, CA
92277 Twentynine Palms, CA
92278 29 Palms, CA
92278 Twentynine Palms, CA
92278 Twentynine Palms Mcb, CA
92280 Blythe, CA
92280 Vidal, CA
92281 Westmorland, CA
92282 Cabazon, CA
92282 Whitewater, CA
92283 Felicity, CA
92283 Winterhaven, CA
92284 Yucca Valley, CA
92285 Johnson Valley, CA
92285 Landers, CA
92285 Yucca Valley, CA
92286 Yucca Valley, CA

923

92301 Adelanto, CA
92301 El Mirage, CA
92304 Amboy, CA
92304 Cadiz, CA
92305 Angelus Oaks, CA
92307 Apple Valley, CA
92308 Apple Valley, CA
92308 Jess Ranch, CA
92309 Baker, CA
92309 Kelso, CA
92310 Barstow, CA
92310 Fort Irwin, CA
92311 Barstow, CA
92312 Barstow, CA
92313 Grand Terrace, CA
92314 Big Bear City, CA
92315 Big Bear Lake, CA
92316 Bloomington, CA
92317 Blue Jay, CA
92318 Bryn Mawr, CA
92320 Calimesa, CA
92321 Cedar Glen, CA
92322 Cedarpines Park, CA
92322 Cedarpines Pk, CA
92323 Cima, CA
92324 Colton, CA
92324 Grand Terrace, CA
92325 Crestline, CA
92327 Daggett, CA
92328 Death Valley, CA
92329 Phelan, CA
92331 Fontana, CA
92332 Essex, CA
92333 Fawnskin, CA
92334 Fontana, CA
92335 Fontana, CA
92336 Fontana, CA
92337 Fontana, CA
92338 Ludlow, CA

92338 Newberry Springs, CA
92339 Forest Falls, CA
92340 Hesperia, CA
92341 Green Valley Lake, CA
92341 Green Vly Lk, CA
92342 Helendale, CA
92344 Hesperia, CA
92344 Oak Hills, CA
92345 Hesperia, CA
92346 Highland, CA
92347 Hinkley, CA
92350 Loma Linda, CA
92352 Lake Arrowhead, CA
92352 Lk Arrowhead, CA
92354 Loma Linda, CA
92356 Lucerne Valley, CA
92357 Loma Linda, CA
92358 Lytle Creek, CA
92359 Mentone, CA
92363 Havasu Lake, CA
92363 Needles, CA
92364 Baker, CA
92364 Nipton, CA
92365 Newberry Springs, CA
92366 Mountain Pass, CA
92368 Oro Grande, CA
92369 Patton, CA
92371 Phelan, CA
92372 Pinon Hills, CA
92373 Redlands, CA
92374 Redlands, CA
92375 Redlands, CA
92376 Rialto, CA
92377 Rialto, CA
92378 Rimforest, CA
92382 Arrowbear Lake, CA
92382 Running Spgs, CA
92382 Running Springs, CA
92384 Shoshone, CA
92385 Skyforest, CA
92386 Big Bear City, CA
92386 Sugarloaf, CA
92389 Tecopa, CA
92391 Twin Peaks, CA
92392 Victorville, CA
92393 Victorville, CA
92394 George Afb, CA
92394 Victorville, CA
92395 Spring Valley Lake, CA
92395 Victorville, CA
92397 Wrightwood, CA
92398 Yermo, CA
92399 Oak Glen, CA
92399 Yucaipa, CA

924

92401 San Bernardino, CA
92407 Arrowhead Farms, CA
92407 Devore Heights, CA
92407 Muscoy, CA
92407 San Bernardino, CA
92407 Verdemont, CA
92408 San Bernardino, CA

925

92501 Riverside, CA
92502 Riverside, CA
92503 Riverside, CA
92504 Riverside, CA
92505 Riverside, CA
92506 Riverside, CA
92507 Riverside, CA
92508 Riverside, CA
92509 Jurupa Valley, CA
92509 Riverside, CA
92513 Riverside, CA
92514 Riverside, CA
92515 Riverside, CA
92516 Riverside, CA
92517 Riverside, CA
92518 March Air Reserve Base, CA
92518 Riverside, CA
92519 Riverside, CA
92521 Riverside, CA
92522 Riverside, CA
92530 Lake Elsinore, CA
92531 Lake Elsinore, CA
92532 Lake Elsinore, CA
92536 Aguanga, CA
92539 Anza, CA
92543 Hemet, CA
92544 Hemet, CA
92545 Hemet, CA
92546 Hemet, CA
92548 Homeland, CA
92549 Idyllwild, CA
92551 Moreno Valley, CA
92552 Moreno Valley, CA
92553 Moreno Valley, CA
92554 Moreno Valley, CA
92555 Moreno Valley, CA
92555 Rancho Belago, CA
92556 Moreno Valley, CA
92557 Moreno Valley, CA
92561 Mountain Center, CA
92562 Murrieta, CA
92563 Murrieta, CA
92564 Murrieta, CA
92567 Lakeview, CA
92567 Nuevo, CA
92570 Lake Mathews, CA
92570 Perris, CA
92571 Perris, CA
92572 Perris, CA
92581 San Jacinto, CA
92582 San Jacinto, CA
92583 Gilman Hot Springs, CA
92583 San Jacinto, CA
92584 Menifee, CA
92584 Sun City, CA
92585 Menifee, CA
92585 Romoland, CA
92585 Sun City, CA
92586 Menifee, CA
92586 Sun City, CA
92587 Canyon Lake, CA
92587 Menifee, CA
92587 Quail Valley, CA
92589 Temecula, CA
92590 Temecula, CA
92591 Temecula, CA
92592 Temecula, CA
92593 Temecula, CA
92595 Wildomar, CA
92596 Menifee, CA
92596 Winchester, CA
92599 Perris, CA

926

92602 Irvine, CA
92603 Irvine, CA
92604 Irvine, CA
92605 Huntington Beach, CA
92606 Irvine, CA
92607 Laguna Beach, CA
92607 Laguna Niguel, CA
92609 El Toro, CA
92609 Lake Forest, CA
92610 El Toro, CA
92610 Foothill Ranch, CA
92612 Irvine, CA
92614 Irvine, CA
92615 Huntington Beach, CA
92616 Irvine, CA
92617 Irvine, CA
92618 Irvine, CA
92619 Irvine, CA
92620 Irvine, CA
92623 Irvine, CA
92624 Capistrano Beach, CA
92624 Dana Point, CA
92625 Corona Del Mar, CA
92626 Costa Mesa, CA
92627 Costa Mesa, CA
92628 Costa Mesa, CA
92629 Dana Point, CA
92629 Monarch Bay, CA
92629 Monarch Beach, CA
92630 El Toro, CA
92630 Lake Forest, CA
92637 Laguna Hills, CA
92637 Laguna Woods, CA
92646 Huntington Beach, CA
92650 East Irvine, CA
92650 Irvine, CA
92651 Laguna Beach, CA
92652 Laguna Beach, CA
92653 Aliso Viejo, CA
92653 Laguna Beach, CA
92653 Laguna Hills, CA
92653 Laguna Woods, CA
92654 Laguna Beach, CA
92654 Laguna Hills, CA
92654 Laguna Woods, CA
92655 Midway City, CA
92656 Aliso Viejo, CA
92656 Laguna Beach, CA
92656 Laguna Hills, CA
92657 Newport Beach, CA
92657 Newport Coast, CA
92658 Newport Beach, CA
92659 Newport Beach, CA
92660 Newport Beach, CA
92661 Newport Beach, CA
92662 Balboa, CA
92662 Balboa Island, CA
92662 Newport Beach, CA
92663 Newport Beach, CA
92672 San Clemente, CA
92673 San Clemente, CA
92674 San Clemente, CA
92675 Mission Viejo, CA
92675 San Juan Capistrano, CA
92676 Silverado, CA
92677 Laguna Beach, CA
92677 Laguna Niguel, CA
92678 Trabuco Canyon, CA
92679 Coto De Caza, CA
92679 Dove Canyon, CA
92679 Portola Hills, CA
92679 Robinson Ranch, CA
92679 Trabuco, CA
92679 Trabuco Canyon, CA
92683 Westminster, CA
92684 Westminster, CA
92685 Westminster, CA
92688 Rancho Santa Margarita, CA
92688 Rancho Sta Marg, CA
92688 Rsm, CA
92690 Mission Viejo, CA
92690 San Juan Capistrano, CA
92691 Mission Viejo, CA
92691 San Juan Capistrano, CA
92692 Mission Viejo, CA
92692 San Juan Capistrano, CA
92694 Ladera Ranch, CA
92694 Mission Viejo, CA
92694 Rancho Mission Viejo, CA
92697 Irvine, CA
92698 Aliso Viejo, CA

927

92701 Santa Ana, CA
92702 Santa Ana, CA
92703 Santa Ana, CA
92704 Santa Ana, CA
92705 Cowan Heights, CA
92705 North Tustin, CA
92705 Santa Ana, CA
92706 Santa Ana, CA
92707 Santa Ana, CA
92708 Fountain Valley, CA
92708 Santa Ana, CA
92711 Santa Ana, CA
92712 Santa Ana, CA
92728 Fountain Valley, CA
92728 Santa Ana, CA
92735 Santa Ana, CA
92780 Tustin, CA
92781 Tustin, CA
92782 Tustin, CA
92799 Santa Ana, CA

928

92801 Anaheim, CA
92802 Anaheim, CA
92803 Anaheim, CA
92804 Anaheim, CA
92805 Anaheim, CA
92806 Anaheim, CA
92807 Anaheim, CA
92808 Anaheim, CA
92809 Anaheim, CA
92811 Atwood, CA
92812 Anaheim, CA
92814 Anaheim, CA
92815 Anaheim, CA
92816 Anaheim, CA
92817 Anaheim, CA
92821 Brea, CA
92822 Brea, CA
92823 Brea, CA
92825 Anaheim, CA
92831 Fullerton, CA
92832 Fullerton, CA
92833 Fullerton, CA
92834 Fullerton, CA
92835 Fullerton, CA
92836 Fullerton, CA
92837 Fullerton, CA
92838 Fullerton, CA
92840 Garden Grove, CA
92841 Garden Grove, CA
92842 Garden Grove, CA
92843 Garden Grove, CA
92844 Garden Grove, CA
92845 Garden Grove, CA
92846 Garden Grove, CA
92850 Anaheim, CA
92856 Orange, CA
92857 Orange, CA
92859 Orange, CA
92860 Norco, CA
92861 Orange, CA
92861 Villa Park, CA
92862 Orange, CA
92863 Orange, CA
92864 Orange, CA
92865 Orange, CA
92866 Orange, CA
92867 Orange, CA
92867 Villa Park, CA
92868 Orange, CA
92869 Orange, CA
92870 Placentia, CA
92871 Placentia, CA
92877 Corona, CA
92878 Corona, CA
92879 Corona, CA
92880 Corona, CA
92880 Eastvale, CA
92881 Corona, CA
92882 Corona, CA
92883 Corona, CA
92883 Temescal Valley, CA
92885 Yorba Linda, CA
92886 Yorba Linda, CA
92887 Yorba Linda, CA
92899 Anaheim, CA

930

93001 Ventura, CA
93002 Ventura, CA
93003 Ventura, CA
93004 Ventura, CA
93005 Ventura, CA
93006 Ventura, CA
93007 Ventura, CA
93009 Ventura, CA
93010 Camarillo, CA
93011 Camarillo, CA
93012 Camarillo, CA
93012 Santa Rosa Valley, CA
93013 Carpinteria, CA
93014 Carpinteria, CA
93015 Fillmore, CA
93016 Fillmore, CA
93020 Moorpark, CA
93021 Moorpark, CA
93022 Oak View, CA
93023 Ojai, CA
93024 Ojai, CA
93030 Oxnard, CA
93031 Oxnard, CA
93032 Oxnard, CA
93033 Oxnard, CA
93034 Oxnard, CA
93035 Oxnard, CA
93036 Oxnard, CA
93040 Piru, CA
93041 Point Mugu Nawc, CA
93041 Port Hueneme, CA
93042 Point Mugu Nawc, CA
93042 Port Hueneme, CA
93043 Port Hueneme, CA
93043 Port Hueneme Cbc Base, CA
93044 Port Hueneme, CA
93060 Santa Paula, CA
93061 Santa Paula, CA
93062 Simi Valley, CA
93063 Santa Susana, CA
93063 Simi Valley, CA
93064 Brandeis, CA
93064 Simi Valley, CA
93065 Simi Valley, CA
93066 Somis, CA
93067 Summerland, CA
93094 Simi Valley, CA
93099 Simi Valley, CA

931

93101 Santa Barbara, CA
93102 Santa Barbara, CA
93103 Santa Barbara, CA
93105 Santa Barbara, CA
93106 Santa Barbara, CA
93107 Santa Barbara, CA
93108 Montecito, CA
93108 Santa Barbara, CA
93109 Santa Barbara, CA
93110 Goleta, CA
93110 Santa Barbara, CA
93111 Goleta, CA
93111 Santa Barbara, CA
93116 Goleta, CA
93116 Santa Barbara, CA
93117 Gaviota, CA
93117 Goleta, CA
93117 Isla Vista, CA
93117 Santa Barbara, CA
93118 Goleta, CA
93118 Santa Barbara, CA
93120 Santa Barbara, CA
93121 Santa Barbara, CA
93130 Santa Barbara, CA
93140 Santa Barbara, CA
93150 Montecito, CA
93150 Santa Barbara, CA
93160 Santa Barbara, CA
93190 Santa Barbara, CA
93199 Goleta, CA
93199 Santa Barbara, CA

932

93201 Alpaugh, CA
93202 Armona, CA
93203 Arvin, CA
93203 Di Giorgio, CA
93204 Avenal, CA
93205 Bodfish, CA
93206 Buttonwillow, CA
93207 California Hot Springs, CA
93208 Camp Nelson, CA
93208 Springville, CA
93210 Coalinga, CA
93212 Corcoran, CA
93215 Delano, CA
93216 Delano, CA
93218 Ducor, CA
93219 Earlimart, CA
93220 Edison, CA
93221 Exeter, CA
93222 Frazier Park, CA
93222 Pine Mountain Club, CA
93223 Farmersville, CA
93224 Fellows, CA
93225 Frazier Park, CA
93226 Glennville, CA
93227 Goshen, CA
93230 Hanford, CA
93232 Hanford, CA
93234 Huron, CA
93235 Ivanhoe, CA
93237 Kaweah, CA
93238 Kernville, CA
93239 Kettleman City, CA
93240 Lake Isabella, CA
93240 Mountain Mesa, CA
93241 Lamont, CA
93242 Laton, CA
93243 Gorman, CA
93243 Lebec, CA
93244 Lemon Cove, CA
93245 Lemoore, CA
93246 Lemoore, CA
93246 Lemoore Naval Air Station, CA
93247 Lindsay, CA
93249 Lost Hills, CA
93250 Mc Farland, CA
93251 Mc Kittrick, CA
93252 Maricopa, CA
93254 Cuyama, CA
93254 New Cuyama, CA
93255 Onyx, CA
93256 Pixley, CA
93257 Poplar, CA
93257 Porterville, CA
93257 Woodville, CA
93258 Porterville, CA
93260 Posey, CA
93261 Richgrove, CA
93262 Sequoia National Park, CA
93263 Shafter, CA
93265 Springville, CA
93266 Stratford, CA
93267 Strathmore, CA
93268 Taft, CA
93270 Terra Bella, CA
93271 Three Rivers, CA
93272 Tipton, CA
93274 Tulare, CA
93275 Tulare, CA
93276 Tupman, CA
93277 Visalia, CA
93278 Visalia, CA
93279 Visalia, CA
93280 Wasco, CA
93282 Corcoran, CA
93282 Waukena, CA
93283 Weldon, CA
93285 Wofford Heights, CA
93286 Woodlake, CA
93287 Woody, CA
93290 Visalia, CA
93291 Visalia, CA
93292 Visalia, CA

933

93301 Bakersfield, CA
93302 Bakersfield, CA
93303 Bakersfield, CA
93304 Bakersfield, CA
93305 Bakersfield, CA
93306 Bakersfield, CA
93307 Bakersfield, CA
93308 Bakersfield, CA
93309 Bakersfield, CA
93311 Bakersfield, CA
93312 Bakersfield, CA
93313 Bakersfield, CA
93313 Pumpkin Center, CA
93314 Bakersfield, CA
93380 Bakersfield, CA
93383 Bakersfield, CA
93383 Pumpkin Center, CA
93384 Bakersfield, CA
93385 Bakersfield, CA
93386 Bakersfield, CA

93387 Bakersfield, CA
93388 Bakersfield, CA
93389 Bakersfield, CA
93390 Bakersfield, CA

934

93401 San Luis Obispo, CA
93402 Los Osos, CA
93402 San Luis Obispo, CA
93412 Los Osos, CA
93412 San Luis Obispo, CA
93420 Arroyo Grande, CA
93421 Arroyo Grande, CA
93422 Atascadero, CA
93423 Atascadero, CA
93424 Avila Beach, CA
93426 Bradley, CA
93427 Buellton, CA
93428 Cambria, CA
93429 Casmalia, CA
93430 Cayucos, CA
93432 Creston, CA
93433 Grover Beach, CA
93434 Guadalupe, CA
93435 Harmony, CA
93436 Lompoc, CA
93437 Lompoc, CA
93437 Vandenberg Afb, CA
93438 Lompoc, CA
93440 Los Alamos, CA
93441 Los Olivos, CA
93442 Morro Bay, CA
93443 Morro Bay, CA
93444 Nipomo, CA
93445 Oceano, CA
93446 Adelaide, CA
93446 Heritage Ranch, CA
93446 Paso Robles, CA
93447 Paso Robles, CA
93448 Pismo Beach, CA
93448 Shell Beach, CA
93449 Pismo Beach, CA
93449 Shell Beach, CA
93450 San Ardo, CA
93451 Parkfield, CA
93451 San Miguel, CA
93452 Ragged Point, CA
93452 San Simeon, CA
93453 Santa Margarita, CA
93454 Rancho Suey, CA
93454 Santa Maria, CA
93455 Orcutt, CA
93455 Santa Maria, CA
93456 Santa Maria, CA
93457 Orcutt, CA
93457 Santa Maria, CA
93458 Santa Maria, CA
93460 Santa Ynez, CA
93461 Shandon, CA
93463 Ballard, CA
93463 Solvang, CA
93464 Solvang, CA
93465 Templeton, CA
93475 Oceano, CA
93483 Grover Beach, CA

935

93501 Mojave, CA
93502 Mojave, CA
93504 California City, CA
93510 Acton, CA
93512 Benton, CA
93512 Bishop, CA
93513 Big Pine, CA
93514 Bishop, CA
93514 Chalfant, CA
93514 Chalfant Valley, CA
93514 Hammil Valley, CA
93514 Swall Meadows, CA
93515 Bishop, CA
93516 Boron, CA
93517 Bridgeport, CA
93518 Caliente, CA
93518 Havilah, CA
93519 Cantil, CA
93519 Mojave, CA
93522 Darwin, CA
93523 Aerial Acres, CA
93523 Edwards, CA
93523 North Edwards, CA
93524 Edwards, CA
93524 Edwards Afb, CA
93526 Independence, CA
93527 Inyokern, CA
93527 Pearsonville, CA
93528 Johannesburg, CA
93529 June Lake, CA
93530 Keeler, CA
93531 Keene, CA
93532 Elizabeth Lake, CA
93532 Lake Hughes, CA
93534 Lancaster, CA
93535 Hi Vista, CA
93535 Lake Los Angeles, CA
93535 Lancaster, CA
93536 Del Sur, CA
93536 Lancaster, CA
93536 Quartz Hill, CA
93539 Lancaster, CA
93541 Lee Vining, CA
93542 Little Lake, CA
93543 Juniper Hills, CA
93543 Littlerock, CA
93543 Sun Village, CA
93544 Crystalaire, CA
93544 Llano, CA
93545 Lone Pine, CA
93546 Crowley Lake, CA
93546 Mammoth Lakes, CA
93546 Toms Place, CA
93549 Cartago, CA
93549 Olancha, CA
93550 Lake Los Angeles, CA
93550 Palmdale, CA
93551 City Ranch, CA
93551 Leona Valley, CA
93551 Palmdale, CA
93551 Quartz Hill, CA
93552 Palmdale, CA
93553 Pearblossom, CA
93554 Johannesburg, CA
93554 Randsburg, CA
93555 Ridgecrest, CA
93556 Ridgecrest, CA
93558 Johannesburg, CA
93558 Red Mountain, CA
93560 Rosamond, CA
93560 Willow Springs, CA
93561 Bear Valley Springs, CA
93561 Golden Hills, CA
93561 Monolith, CA
93561 Stallion Springs, CA
93561 Tehachapi, CA
93562 Argus, CA
93562 Trona, CA
93563 Pearblossom, CA
93563 Valyermo, CA
93581 Tehachapi, CA
93584 Lancaster, CA
93586 Lancaster, CA
93586 Quartz Hill, CA
93590 Palmdale, CA
93591 Lake Los Angeles, CA
93591 Palmdale, CA
93592 Trona, CA
93596 Boron, CA
93599 Palmdale, CA

936

93601 Ahwahnee, CA
93602 Auberry, CA
93603 Badger, CA
93603 Miramonte, CA
93604 Bass Lake, CA
93605 Big Creek, CA
93606 Biola, CA
93607 Burrel, CA
93607 Riverdale, CA
93608 Cantua Creek, CA
93609 Caruthers, CA
93610 Chowchilla, CA
93611 Clovis, CA
93612 Clovis, CA
93613 Clovis, CA
93614 Coarsegold, CA
93615 Cutler, CA
93616 Del Rey, CA
93618 Dinuba, CA
93619 Clovis, CA
93620 Dos Palos, CA
93621 Dunlap, CA
93622 Firebaugh, CA
93623 Fish Camp, CA
93624 Five Points, CA
93625 Fowler, CA
93626 Friant, CA
93627 Helm, CA
93628 Hume, CA
93628 Miramonte, CA
93630 Kerman, CA
93631 Kingsburg, CA
93633 Kings Canyon, CA
93633 Kings Canyon National Pk, CA
93633 Kings Canyon Natl Park, CA
93633 Miramonte, CA
93634 Lakeshore, CA
93634 Shaver Lake, CA
93635 Los Banos, CA
93636 Madera, CA
93637 Berenda, CA
93637 Madera, CA
93638 Madera, CA
93639 Madera, CA
93640 Mendota, CA
93641 Miramonte, CA
93642 Mono Hot Springs, CA
93642 Shaver Lake, CA
93643 North Fork, CA
93644 Oakhurst, CA
93645 O Neals, CA
93646 Orange Cove, CA
93646 Squaw Valley, CA
93647 Orosi, CA
93648 Parlier, CA
93649 Piedra, CA
93650 Fresno, CA
93650 Pinedale, CA
93651 Prather, CA
93652 Raisin City, CA
93653 Raymond, CA
93654 Reedley, CA
93656 Riverdale, CA
93657 Sanger, CA
93660 San Joaquin, CA
93661 Santa Rita Park, CA
93662 Selma, CA
93664 Shaver Lake, CA
93665 South Dos Palos, CA
93666 Sultana, CA
93667 Tollhouse, CA
93668 Tranquillity, CA
93669 Bass Lake, CA
93669 Wishon, CA
93670 Yettem, CA
93673 Traver, CA
93675 Orange Cove, CA
93675 Squaw Valley, CA

937

93701 Fresno, CA
93702 Fresno, CA
93703 Fresno, CA
93704 Fresno, CA
93705 Fresno, CA
93706 Fresno, CA
93707 Fresno, CA
93708 Fresno, CA
93709 Fresno, CA
93710 Fresno, CA
93711 Fresno, CA
93712 Fresno, CA
93714 Fresno, CA
93715 Fresno, CA
93716 Fresno, CA
93717 Fresno, CA
93718 Fresno, CA
93720 Fresno, CA
93721 Fresno, CA
93722 Fresno, CA
93723 Fresno, CA
93724 Fresno, CA
93725 Fresno, CA
93726 Fresno, CA
93727 Fresno, CA
93728 Fresno, CA
93729 Fresno, CA
93730 Fresno, CA
93737 Fresno, CA
93740 Fresno, CA
93741 Fresno, CA
93744 Fresno, CA
93745 Fresno, CA
93747 Fresno, CA
93750 Fresno, CA
93755 Fresno, CA
93760 Fresno, CA
93761 Fresno, CA
93764 Fresno, CA
93765 Fresno, CA
93771 Fresno, CA
93772 Fresno, CA
93773 Fresno, CA
93774 Fresno, CA
93775 Fresno, CA
93776 Fresno, CA
93777 Fresno, CA
93778 Fresno, CA
93779 Fresno, CA
93786 Fresno, CA
93790 Fresno, CA
93791 Fresno, CA
93792 Fresno, CA
93793 Fresno, CA
93794 Fresno, CA

938

93844 Fresno, CA
93888 Fresno, CA

939

93901 Salinas, CA
93902 Salinas, CA
93905 Salinas, CA
93906 Salinas, CA
93907 Prunedale, CA
93907 Salinas, CA
93908 Corral De Tierra, CA
93908 Salinas, CA
93912 Salinas, CA
93915 Salinas, CA
93920 Big Sur, CA
93921 Carmel, CA
93921 Carmel By The, CA
93921 Carmel By The Sea, CA
93922 Carmel, CA
93923 Carmel, CA
93924 Carmel Valley, CA
93925 Chualar, CA
93926 Gonzales, CA
93927 Greenfield, CA
93928 Fort Hunter Liggett, CA
93928 Jolon, CA
93930 King City, CA
93932 Lockwood, CA
93933 East Garrison, CA
93933 Marina, CA
93940 Del Rey Oaks, CA
93940 Monterey, CA
93942 Monterey, CA
93943 Monterey, CA
93944 Monterey, CA
93944 Presidio Of Monterey, CA
93950 Pacific Grove, CA
93953 Pebble Beach, CA
93954 San Lucas, CA
93955 Sand City, CA
93955 Seaside, CA
93960 Soledad, CA
93962 Salinas, CA
93962 Spreckels, CA

940

94002 Belmont, CA
94005 Brisbane, CA
94010 Burlingame, CA
94010 Hillsborough, CA
94011 Burlingame, CA
94014 Colma, CA
94014 Daly City, CA
94015 Broadmoor Vlg, CA
94015 Daly City, CA
94016 Daly City, CA
94017 Daly City, CA
94018 El Granada, CA
94019 Half Moon Bay, CA
94020 La Honda, CA
94021 Loma Mar, CA
94022 Los Altos, CA
94022 Los Altos Hills, CA
94023 Los Altos, CA
94024 Los Altos, CA
94024 Los Altos Hills, CA
94025 Menlo Park, CA
94025 West Menlo Park, CA
94026 Menlo Park, CA
94027 Atherton, CA
94027 Menlo Park, CA
94028 Menlo Park, CA
94028 Portola Valley, CA
94030 Millbrae, CA
94035 Moffett Field, CA
94035 Mountain View, CA
94037 Montara, CA
94038 Moss Beach, CA
94039 Mountain View, CA
94040 Mountain View, CA
94041 Mountain View, CA
94042 Mountain View, CA
94043 Mountain View, CA
94044 Pacifica, CA
94060 Pescadero, CA
94061 Redwood City, CA
94061 Woodside, CA
94062 Emerald Hills, CA
94062 Palomar Park, CA
94062 Redwood City, CA
94062 Woodside, CA
94063 Redwood City, CA
94064 Redwood City, CA
94065 Redwood City, CA
94066 San Bruno, CA
94070 San Carlos, CA
94074 San Gregorio, CA
94080 South San Francisco, CA
94085 Sunnyvale, CA
94086 Sunnyvale, CA
94087 Sunnyvale, CA
94088 Onizuka Afb, CA
94088 Sunnyvale, CA
94089 Sunnyvale, CA

941

94102 San Francisco, CA
94103 San Francisco, CA
94104 San Francisco, CA
94105 San Francisco, CA
94107 San Francisco, CA
94108 San Francisco, CA
94109 San Francisco, CA
94110 San Francisco, CA
94111 San Francisco, CA
94112 San Francisco, CA
94114 San Francisco, CA
94115 San Francisco, CA
94116 San Francisco, CA
94117 San Francisco, CA
94118 San Francisco, CA
94119 San Francisco, CA
94120 San Francisco, CA
94121 San Francisco, CA
94122 San Francisco, CA
94123 San Francisco, CA
94124 San Francisco, CA
94125 San Francisco, CA
94126 San Francisco, CA
94127 San Francisco, CA
94128 San Francisco, CA
94129 San Francisco, CA
94130 San Francisco, CA
94131 San Francisco, CA
94132 San Francisco, CA
94133 San Francisco, CA
94134 San Francisco, CA
94137 San Francisco, CA
94139 San Francisco, CA
94140 San Francisco, CA
94141 San Francisco, CA
94142 San Francisco, CA
94143 San Francisco, CA
94144 San Francisco, CA
94145 San Francisco, CA
94146 San Francisco, CA
94147 San Francisco, CA
94151 San Francisco, CA
94158 San Francisco, CA
94159 San Francisco, CA
94160 San Francisco, CA
94161 San Francisco, CA
94163 San Francisco, CA
94164 San Francisco, CA
94172 San Francisco, CA
94177 San Francisco, CA
94188 San Francisco, CA

942

94203 Sacramento, CA
94204 Sacramento, CA
94205 Sacramento, CA
94206 Sacramento, CA
94207 Sacramento, CA
94208 Sacramento, CA
94209 Sacramento, CA
94211 Sacramento, CA
94229 Sacramento, CA
94230 Sacramento, CA
94232 Sacramento, CA
94234 Sacramento, CA
94235 Sacramento, CA
94236 Sacramento, CA
94237 Sacramento, CA
94239 Sacramento, CA
94240 Sacramento, CA
94244 Sacramento, CA
94245 Sacramento, CA
94247 Sacramento, CA
94248 Sacramento, CA
94249 Sacramento, CA
94250 Sacramento, CA
94252 Sacramento, CA
94254 Sacramento, CA
94256 Sacramento, CA
94257 Sacramento, CA
94258 Sacramento, CA
94259 Sacramento, CA
94261 Sacramento, CA
94262 Sacramento, CA
94263 Sacramento, CA
94267 Sacramento, CA
94268 Sacramento, CA
94269 Sacramento, CA
94271 Sacramento, CA
94273 Sacramento, CA
94274 Sacramento, CA
94277 Sacramento, CA
94278 Sacramento, CA
94279 Sacramento, CA
94280 Sacramento, CA
94282 Sacramento, CA
94283 Sacramento, CA
94284 Sacramento, CA
94285 Sacramento, CA
94286 Sacramento, CA
94287 Sacramento, CA
94288 Sacramento, CA
94289 Sacramento, CA
94290 Sacramento, CA
94291 Sacramento, CA
94293 Sacramento, CA
94294 Sacramento, CA
94295 Sacramento, CA
94296 Sacramento, CA
94297 Sacramento, CA
94298 Sacramento, CA
94299 Sacramento, CA

943

94301 Palo Alto, CA
94302 Palo Alto, CA

94303 East Palo Alto, CA
94303 Palo Alto, CA
94304 Palo Alto, CA
94305 Palo Alto, CA
94305 Stanford, CA
94306 Palo Alto, CA
94309 Palo Alto, CA
94309 Stanford, CA

944

94401 San Mateo, CA
94402 San Mateo, CA
94403 San Mateo, CA
94404 Foster City, CA
94404 San Mateo, CA
94497 San Mateo, CA

945

94501 Alameda, CA
94502 Alameda, CA
94503 American Canyon, CA
94503 Vallejo, CA
94505 Byron, CA
94505 Discovery Bay, CA
94506 Blackhawk, CA
94506 Danville, CA
94507 Alamo, CA
94508 Angwin, CA
94509 Antioch, CA
94510 Benicia, CA
94511 Bethel Island, CA
94512 Birds Landing, CA
94513 Brentwood, CA
94514 Byron, CA
94514 Discovery Bay, CA
94515 Calistoga, CA
94516 Canyon, CA
94517 Clayton, CA
94518 Concord, CA
94519 Concord, CA
94520 Concord, CA
94521 Concord, CA
94522 Concord, CA
94523 Concord, CA
94523 Pleasant Hill, CA
94524 Concord, CA
94525 Crockett, CA
94526 Danville, CA
94527 Concord, CA
94528 Diablo, CA
94529 Concord, CA
94530 El Cerrito, CA
94531 Antioch, CA
94533 Fairfield, CA
94534 Fairfield, CA
94534 Suisun City, CA
94535 Fairfield, CA
94535 Travis Afb, CA
94536 Fremont, CA
94537 Fremont, CA
94538 Fremont, CA
94539 Fremont, CA
94540 Hayward, CA
94541 Hayward, CA
94542 Hayward, CA
94543 Hayward, CA
94544 Hayward, CA
94545 Hayward, CA
94546 Castro Valley, CA
94546 Hayward, CA
94547 Hercules, CA
94547 Rodeo, CA
94548 Knightsen, CA
94549 Lafayette, CA
94550 Livermore, CA
94551 Livermore, CA
94552 Castro Valley, CA
94552 Hayward, CA
94553 Briones, CA
94553 Martinez, CA
94553 Pacheco, CA
94555 Fremont, CA
94556 Moraga, CA
94557 Hayward, CA
94557 Mount Eden, CA
94558 Napa, CA
94558 Spanish Flat, CA
94559 Napa, CA
94560 Newark, CA
94561 Oakley, CA
94562 Oakville, CA
94563 Orinda, CA
94564 Pinole, CA
94565 Bay Point, CA
94565 Pittsburg, CA
94566 Pleasanton, CA
94567 Pope Valley, CA
94568 Dublin, CA
94568 Pleasanton, CA
94569 Port Costa, CA
94570 Moraga, CA
94571 Rio Vista, CA
94572 Rodeo, CA
94573 Rutherford, CA
94574 Saint Helena, CA
94575 Moraga, CA
94576 Angwin, CA
94576 Deer Park, CA
94577 San Leandro, CA
94578 San Leandro, CA
94579 San Leandro, CA
94580 San Lorenzo, CA
94581 Napa, CA
94582 San Ramon, CA
94583 San Ramon, CA
94585 Birds Lndg, CA
94585 Suisun City, CA
94586 Sunol, CA
94587 Union City, CA
94588 Pleasanton, CA
94589 American Canyon, CA
94589 Vallejo, CA
94590 Vallejo, CA
94591 Vallejo, CA
94592 Vallejo, CA
94595 Walnut Creek, CA
94596 Walnut Creek, CA
94597 Walnut Creek, CA
94598 Walnut Creek, CA
94599 Yountville, CA

946

94601 Oakland, CA
94602 Oakland, CA
94602 Piedmont, CA
94603 Oakland, CA
94604 Oakland, CA
94605 Oakland, CA
94606 Oakland, CA
94607 Oakland, CA
94608 Emeryville, CA
94608 Oakland, CA
94609 Oakland, CA
94610 Oakland, CA
94610 Piedmont, CA
94611 Oakland, CA
94611 Piedmont, CA
94612 Oakland, CA
94613 Oakland, CA
94614 Oakland, CA
94615 Oakland, CA
94617 Oakland, CA
94618 Oakland, CA
94618 Piedmont, CA
94619 Oakland, CA
94620 Oakland, CA
94620 Piedmont, CA
94621 Oakland, CA
94622 Oakland, CA
94623 Oakland, CA
94624 Oakland, CA
94649 Oakland, CA
94659 Oakland, CA
94660 Oakland, CA
94661 Oakland, CA
94662 Emeryville, CA
94662 Oakland, CA
94666 Oakland, CA

947

94701 Berkeley, CA
94702 Berkeley, CA
94703 Berkeley, CA
94704 Berkeley, CA
94705 Berkeley, CA
94706 Albany, CA
94706 Berkeley, CA
94706 Kensington, CA
94707 Albany, CA
94707 Berkeley, CA
94707 Kensington, CA
94708 Berkeley, CA
94708 Kensington, CA
94709 Berkeley, CA
94710 Albany, CA
94710 Berkeley, CA
94712 Berkeley, CA
94720 Berkeley, CA

948

94801 North Richmond, CA
94801 Point Richmond, CA
94801 Richmond, CA
94802 Richmond, CA
94803 El Sobrante, CA
94803 Richmond, CA
94803 San Pablo, CA
94804 Richmond, CA
94805 Richmond, CA
94806 Hilltop Mall, CA
94806 Richmond, CA
94806 San Pablo, CA
94807 Richmond, CA
94808 Richmond, CA
94820 El Sobrante, CA
94820 Richmond, CA
94850 Richmond, CA

949

94901 San Anselmo, CA
94901 San Rafael, CA
94903 San Rafael, CA
94904 Greenbrae, CA
94904 Kentfield, CA
94912 San Rafael, CA
94913 San Rafael, CA
94914 Kentfield, CA
94915 San Rafael, CA
94920 Belvedere, CA
94920 Belvedere Tiburon, CA
94920 Tiburon, CA
94922 Bodega, CA
94923 Bodega Bay, CA
94924 Bolinas, CA
94925 Corte Madera, CA
94926 Cotati, CA
94926 Rohnert Park, CA
94927 Cotati, CA
94927 Rohnert Park, CA
94928 Cotati, CA
94928 Rohnert Park, CA
94929 Dillon Beach, CA
94930 Fairfax, CA
94931 Cotati, CA
94933 Forest Knolls, CA
94937 Inverness, CA
94938 Lagunitas, CA
94939 Larkspur, CA
94940 Marshall, CA
94941 Mill Valley, CA
94942 Mill Valley, CA
94945 Novato, CA
94946 Nicasio, CA
94947 Novato, CA
94948 Novato, CA
94949 Novato, CA
94950 Olema, CA
94951 Penngrove, CA
94952 Petaluma, CA
94953 Petaluma, CA
94954 Petaluma, CA
94955 Petaluma, CA
94956 Point Reyes Station, CA
94957 Ross, CA
94960 San Anselmo, CA
94963 San Geronimo, CA
94964 San Quentin, CA
94965 Muir Beach, CA
94965 Sausalito, CA
94966 Sausalito, CA
94970 Stinson Beach, CA
94971 Tomales, CA
94972 Valley Ford, CA
94973 Woodacre, CA
94974 San Quentin, CA
94975 Petaluma, CA
94976 Corte Madera, CA
94977 Larkspur, CA
94978 Fairfax, CA
94979 San Anselmo, CA
94998 Novato, CA
94999 Petaluma, CA

950

95001 Aptos, CA
95002 Alviso, CA
95002 San Jose, CA
95003 Aptos, CA
95004 Aromas, CA
95005 Ben Lomond, CA
95006 Boulder Creek, CA
95007 Brookdale, CA
95008 Campbell, CA
95009 Campbell, CA
95010 Capitola, CA
95011 Campbell, CA
95012 Castroville, CA
95013 Coyote, CA
95014 Cupertino, CA
95014 Monte Vista, CA
95014 Permanente, CA
95015 Cupertino, CA
95017 Davenport, CA
95018 Felton, CA
95019 Freedom, CA
95020 Gilroy, CA
95021 Gilroy, CA
95023 Hollister, CA
95024 Hollister, CA
95026 Holy City, CA
95026 Redwood Estates, CA
95030 Los Gatos, CA
95030 Monte Sereno, CA
95031 Los Gatos, CA
95032 Los Gatos, CA
95033 Los Gatos, CA
95035 Milpitas, CA
95036 Milpitas, CA
95037 Morgan Hill, CA
95038 Morgan Hill, CA
95039 Moss Landing, CA
95041 Mount Hermon, CA
95042 New Almaden, CA
95043 Paicines, CA
95044 Redwood Estates, CA
95045 San Juan Bautista, CA
95046 San Martin, CA
95050 Santa Clara, CA
95051 Santa Clara, CA
95052 Santa Clara, CA
95053 Santa Clara, CA
95054 Santa Clara, CA
95055 Santa Clara, CA
95056 Santa Clara, CA
95060 Bonny Doon, CA
95060 Santa Cruz, CA
95060 Scotts Valley, CA
95061 Santa Cruz, CA
95062 Santa Cruz, CA
95063 Santa Cruz, CA
95064 Santa Cruz, CA
95065 Santa Cruz, CA
95066 Santa Cruz, CA
95066 Scotts Valley, CA
95067 Santa Cruz, CA
95067 Scotts Valley, CA
95070 Saratoga, CA
95071 Saratoga, CA
95073 Soquel, CA
95075 Tres Pinos, CA
95076 Corralitos, CA
95076 La Selva Beach, CA
95076 Mt Madonna, CA
95076 Pajaro, CA
95076 Royal Oaks, CA
95076 Watsonville, CA
95077 Watsonville, CA

951

95101 San Jose, CA
95103 San Jose, CA
95106 San Jose, CA
95108 San Jose, CA
95109 San Jose, CA
95110 San Jose, CA
95111 San Jose, CA
95112 San Jose, CA
95113 San Jose, CA
95115 San Jose, CA
95116 San Jose, CA
95117 San Jose, CA
95118 San Jose, CA
95119 San Jose, CA
95120 San Jose, CA
95121 San Jose, CA
95122 San Jose, CA
95123 San Jose, CA
95124 San Jose, CA
95125 San Jose, CA
95126 San Jose, CA
95127 San Jose, CA
95128 San Jose, CA
95129 San Jose, CA
95130 San Jose, CA
95131 San Jose, CA
95132 San Jose, CA
95133 San Jose, CA
95134 San Jose, CA
95135 San Jose, CA
95136 San Jose, CA
95138 San Jose, CA
95139 San Jose, CA
95140 Mount Hamilton, CA
95140 San Jose, CA
95141 San Jose, CA
95148 San Jose, CA
95150 San Jose, CA
95151 San Jose, CA
95152 San Jose, CA
95153 San Jose, CA
95154 San Jose, CA
95155 San Jose, CA
95156 San Jose, CA
95157 San Jose, CA
95158 San Jose, CA
95159 San Jose, CA
95160 San Jose, CA
95161 San Jose, CA
95164 San Jose, CA
95170 San Jose, CA
95172 San Jose, CA
95173 San Jose, CA
95190 San Jose, CA
95191 San Jose, CA
95192 San Jose, CA
95193 San Jose, CA
95194 San Jose, CA
95196 San Jose, CA

952

95201 Stockton, CA
95202 Stockton, CA
95203 Stockton, CA
95204 Stockton, CA
95205 Stockton, CA
95206 Stockton, CA
95207 Stockton, CA
95208 Stockton, CA
95209 Stockton, CA
95210 Stockton, CA
95211 Stockton, CA
95212 Morada, CA
95212 Stockton, CA
95213 Stockton, CA
95215 Stockton, CA
95219 Stockton, CA
95220 Acampo, CA
95221 Altaville, CA
95221 Angels Camp, CA
95222 Angels Camp, CA
95223 Arnold, CA
95223 Bear Valley, CA
95223 Camp Connell, CA
95224 Avery, CA
95225 Burson, CA
95226 Campo Seco, CA
95226 Valley Springs, CA
95227 Clements, CA
95228 Copperopolis, CA
95229 Douglas Flat, CA
95229 Vallecito, CA
95230 Farmington, CA
95231 French Camp, CA
95232 Glencoe, CA
95233 Hathaway Pines, CA
95234 Holt, CA
95236 Linden, CA
95237 Lockeford, CA
95240 Lodi, CA
95241 Lodi, CA
95242 Lodi, CA
95245 Mokelumne Hill, CA
95246 Mountain Ranch, CA
95246 Sheep Ranch, CA
95247 Murphys, CA
95248 Rail Road Flat, CA
95249 San Andreas, CA
95251 Vallecito, CA
95252 Valley Springs, CA
95253 Victor, CA
95254 Wallace, CA
95255 West Point, CA
95257 Wilseyville, CA
95258 Woodbridge, CA
95267 Stockton, CA
95269 Stockton, CA
95296 Lyoth, CA
95296 Stockton, CA
95297 Stockton, CA

953

95301 Atwater, CA
95303 Ballico, CA
95304 Banta, CA
95304 Tracy, CA
95305 Big Oak Flat, CA
95306 Catheys Valley, CA
95307 Ceres, CA
95309 Chinese Camp, CA
95310 Columbia, CA
95311 Coulterville, CA
95312 Cressey, CA
95313 Crows Landing, CA
95315 Delhi, CA
95316 Denair, CA
95317 El Nido, CA
95318 El Portal, CA
95319 Empire, CA
95320 Escalon, CA
95321 Groveland, CA
95322 Gustine, CA
95322 Santa Nella, CA
95323 Hickman, CA
95324 Hilmar, CA
95325 Hornitos, CA
95326 Hughson, CA
95327 Jamestown, CA
95328 Keyes, CA
95329 La Grange, CA
95330 Lathrop, CA
95333 Le Grand, CA
95334 Livingston, CA
95335 Cold Springs, CA
95335 Long Barn, CA
95336 Manteca, CA
95337 Manteca, CA
95338 Mariposa, CA
95340 Merced, CA
95341 Merced, CA
95343 Merced, CA
95344 Merced, CA
95345 Midpines, CA
95346 Mi Wuk Village, CA
95347 Moccasin, CA
95348 Merced, CA
95350 Modesto, CA
95351 Modesto, CA
95352 Modesto, CA

95353 Modesto, CA
95354 Modesto, CA
95355 Modesto, CA
95356 Modesto, CA
95357 Modesto, CA
95358 Modesto, CA
95360 Newman, CA
95361 Knights Ferry, CA
95361 Oakdale, CA
95361 Valley Home, CA
95363 Diablo Grande, CA
95363 Patterson, CA
95364 Dardanelle, CA
95364 Pinecrest, CA
95365 Planada, CA
95366 Ripon, CA
95367 Riverbank, CA
95368 Salida, CA
95369 Snelling, CA
95370 Sonora, CA
95372 Soulsbyville, CA
95373 Sonora, CA
95373 Standard, CA
95374 Stevinson, CA
95375 Pinecrest, CA
95375 Strawberry, CA
95376 Tracy, CA
95377 Tracy, CA
95378 Tracy, CA
95379 Tuolumne, CA
95380 Turlock, CA
95381 Turlock, CA
95382 Turlock, CA
95383 Twain Harte, CA
95385 Vernalis, CA
95386 Waterford, CA
95387 Westley, CA
95388 Winton, CA
95389 Tuolumne Meadows, CA
95389 Wawona, CA
95389 Yosemite National Park, CA
95391 Mountain House, CA
95391 Tracy, CA
95397 Modesto, CA

954

95401 Santa Rosa, CA
95402 Santa Rosa, CA
95403 Larkfield, CA
95403 Santa Rosa, CA
95404 Santa Rosa, CA
95405 Santa Rosa, CA
95406 Santa Rosa, CA
95407 Santa Rosa, CA
95409 Kenwood, CA
95409 Santa Rosa, CA
95410 Albion, CA
95412 Annapolis, CA
95415 Boonville, CA
95416 Boyes Hot Springs, CA
95417 Branscomb, CA
95417 Laytonville, CA
95418 Calpella, CA
95418 Ukiah, CA
95419 Camp Meeker, CA
95420 Caspar, CA
95421 Cazadero, CA
95422 Clearlake, CA
95423 Clearlake Oaks, CA
95424 Clearlake Park, CA
95425 Cloverdale, CA
95426 Cobb, CA
95427 Comptche, CA
95428 Covelo, CA
95429 Dos Rios, CA
95430 Duncans Mills, CA
95431 Eldridge, CA
95432 Elk, CA
95433 El Verano, CA
95435 Finley, CA
95436 Forestville, CA
95437 Fort Bragg, CA
95439 Fulton, CA
95441 Geyserville, CA
95442 Glen Ellen, CA
95443 Glenhaven, CA
95444 Graton, CA
95445 Gualala, CA
95446 Guerneville, CA
95448 Healdsburg, CA
95449 Hopland, CA
95450 Jenner, CA
95451 Kelseyville, CA
95452 Kenwood, CA
95453 Lakeport, CA
95454 Laytonville, CA
95456 Little River, CA
95456 Littleriver, CA
95457 Lower Lake, CA
95458 Lucerne, CA
95459 Manchester, CA
95460 Mendocino, CA
95461 Loch Lomond, CA
95461 Middletown, CA
95462 Monte Rio, CA
95462 Russian River Mdws, CA
95463 Navarro, CA
95464 Nice, CA
95465 Occidental, CA
95466 Philo, CA
95467 Hidden Valley Lake, CA
95468 Point Arena, CA
95469 Potter Valley, CA
95470 Redwood Valley, CA
95471 Rio Nido, CA
95472 Freestone, CA
95472 Sebastopol, CA
95473 Sebastopol, CA
95476 Sonoma, CA
95480 Stewarts Point, CA
95481 Talmage, CA
95482 Ukiah, CA
95485 Upper Lake, CA
95486 Villa Grande, CA
95487 Vineburg, CA
95488 Westport, CA
95490 Willits, CA
95492 Windsor, CA
95493 Upper Lake, CA
95493 Witter Springs, CA
95494 Yorkville, CA
95497 The Sea Ranch, CA

955

95501 Eureka, CA
95502 Eureka, CA
95503 Eureka, CA
95511 Alderpoint, CA
95514 Blocksburg, CA
95518 Arcata, CA
95519 Mckinleyville, CA
95521 Arcata, CA
95521 Mc Kinleyville, CA
95524 Bayside, CA
95525 Blue Lake, CA
95526 Bridgeville, CA
95526 Mad River, CA
95526 Ruth, CA
95527 Burnt Ranch, CA
95528 Carlotta, CA
95531 Crescent City, CA
95532 Crescent City, CA
95534 Cutten, CA
95534 Eureka, CA
95536 Ferndale, CA
95537 Fields Landing, CA
95538 Crescent City, CA
95538 Fort Dick, CA
95540 Fortuna, CA
95542 Garberville, CA
95543 Gasquet, CA
95545 Honeydew, CA
95546 Hoopa, CA
95547 Hydesville, CA
95548 Klamath, CA
95549 Kneeland, CA
95550 Korbel, CA
95551 Loleta, CA
95552 Mad River, CA
95553 Miranda, CA
95554 Myers Flat, CA
95555 Orick, CA
95556 Orleans, CA
95558 Petrolia, CA
95559 Phillipsville, CA
95560 Redway, CA
95562 Rio Dell, CA
95563 Salyer, CA
95564 Samoa, CA
95565 Scotia, CA
95567 Smith River, CA
95568 Somes Bar, CA
95569 Redcrest, CA
95570 Trinidad, CA
95571 Weott, CA
95573 Willow Creek, CA
95585 Leggett, CA
95587 Piercy, CA
95589 Whitethorn, CA
95595 Zenia, CA

956

95601 Amador City, CA
95602 Auburn, CA
95603 Auburn, CA
95604 Auburn, CA
95604 Bowman, CA
95605 Broderick, CA
95605 Bryte, CA
95605 West Sacramento, CA
95606 Brooks, CA
95607 Capay, CA
95607 Esparto, CA
95608 Carmichael, CA
95609 Carmichael, CA
95610 Citrus Heights, CA
95612 Clarksburg, CA
95613 Coloma, CA
95614 Cool, CA
95615 Courtland, CA
95616 Davis, CA
95617 Davis, CA
95618 Davis, CA
95618 El Macero, CA
95619 Diamond Springs, CA
95620 Dixon, CA
95620 Liberty Farms, CA
95621 Citrus Heights, CA
95623 El Dorado, CA
95624 Elk Grove, CA
95625 Elmira, CA
95626 Elverta, CA
95627 Esparto, CA
95628 Fair Oaks, CA
95629 Fiddletown, CA
95630 Folsom, CA
95631 Foresthill, CA
95632 Galt, CA
95633 Garden Valley, CA
95634 Georgetown, CA
95635 Greenwood, CA
95636 Grizzly Flats, CA
95637 Guinda, CA
95638 Herald, CA
95639 Hood, CA
95640 Ione, CA
95641 Isleton, CA
95642 Jackson, CA
95644 Kit Carson, CA
95644 Pioneer, CA
95645 Knights Landing, CA
95646 Kirkwood, CA
95646 Pioneer, CA
95648 Lincoln, CA
95650 Loomis, CA
95651 Lotus, CA
95652 Mcclellan, CA
95653 Madison, CA
95654 Jackson, CA
95654 Martell, CA
95655 Mather, CA
95655 Rancho Cordova, CA
95656 Mount Aukum, CA
95658 Newcastle, CA
95659 East Nicolaus, CA
95659 Nicolaus, CA
95659 Trowbridge, CA
95660 North Highlands, CA
95661 Roseville, CA
95662 Orangevale, CA
95663 Penryn, CA
95664 Pilot Hill, CA
95665 Pine Grove, CA
95666 Pioneer, CA
95667 Kelsey, CA
95667 Placerville, CA
95668 Pleasant Grove, CA
95669 Plymouth, CA
95670 Gold River, CA
95670 Rancho Cordova, CA
95671 Represa, CA
95672 Rescue, CA
95673 Rio Linda, CA
95674 Rio Oso, CA
95675 Mount Aukum, CA
95675 River Pines, CA
95676 Robbins, CA
95677 Rocklin, CA
95678 Roseville, CA
95679 Rumsey, CA
95680 Ryde, CA
95681 Sheridan, CA
95682 Cameron Park, CA
95682 Latrobe, CA
95682 Shingle Springs, CA
95683 Rancho Murieta, CA
95683 Sloughhouse, CA
95684 Fair Play, CA
95684 Somerset, CA
95685 Sutter Creek, CA
95686 Thornton, CA
95687 Vacaville, CA
95688 Vacaville, CA
95689 Volcano, CA
95690 Walnut Grove, CA
95691 West Sacramento, CA
95692 Wheatland, CA
95693 Wilton, CA
95694 Winters, CA
95695 Woodland, CA
95696 Vacaville, CA
95697 Yolo, CA
95698 Zamora, CA
95699 Drytown, CA
95699 Sutter Creek, CA

957

95701 Alta, CA
95703 Applegate, CA
95709 Camino, CA
95712 Chicago Park, CA
95713 Colfax, CA
95713 Eden Valley, CA
95713 Iowa Hill, CA
95714 Dutch Flat, CA
95715 Alta, CA
95715 Emigrant Gap, CA
95717 Gold Run, CA
95720 Kyburz, CA
95721 Echo Lake, CA
95721 Twin Bridges, CA
95722 Meadow Vista, CA
95724 Norden, CA
95724 Soda Springs, CA
95726 Pacific House, CA
95726 Pollock Pines, CA
95728 Soda Springs, CA
95735 Twin Bridges, CA
95736 Weimar, CA
95741 Rancho Cordova, CA
95746 Granite Bay, CA
95746 Roseville, CA
95747 Roseville, CA
95757 Elk Grove, CA
95758 Elk Grove, CA
95759 Elk Grove, CA
95762 El Dorado Hills, CA
95762 Folsom, CA
95763 Folsom, CA
95765 Rocklin, CA
95776 Woodland, CA
95798 West Sacramento, CA

958

95811 Sacramento, CA
95812 Sacramento, CA
95813 Sacramento, CA
95814 Sacramento, CA
95815 Sacramento, CA
95816 Sacramento, CA
95817 Sacramento, CA
95818 Sacramento, CA
95819 Sacramento, CA
95820 Sacramento, CA
95821 Sacramento, CA
95822 Sacramento, CA
95823 Sacramento, CA
95824 Sacramento, CA
95825 Sacramento, CA
95826 Sacramento, CA
95827 Sacramento, CA
95828 Sacramento, CA
95829 Sacramento, CA
95830 Sacramento, CA
95831 Sacramento, CA
95832 Sacramento, CA
95833 Sacramento, CA
95834 Sacramento, CA
95835 Sacramento, CA
95836 Sacramento, CA
95837 Sacramento, CA
95838 Sacramento, CA
95840 Sacramento, CA
95841 Sacramento, CA
95842 Sacramento, CA
95843 Antelope, CA
95843 Sacramento, CA
95851 Sacramento, CA
95852 Sacramento, CA
95853 Sacramento, CA
95860 Sacramento, CA
95864 Sacramento, CA
95865 Sacramento, CA
95866 Sacramento, CA
95867 Sacramento, CA
95894 Sacramento, CA
95899 Sacramento, CA

959

95901 Linda, CA
95901 Loma Rica, CA
95901 Marysville, CA
95903 Beale Afb, CA
95903 Marysville, CA
95910 Alleghany, CA
95912 Arbuckle, CA
95912 College City, CA
95913 Artois, CA
95914 Bangor, CA
95915 Belden, CA
95915 Oroville, CA
95916 Berry Creek, CA
95917 Biggs, CA
95918 Browns Valley, CA
95919 Brownsville, CA
95920 Butte City, CA
95922 Camptonville, CA
95923 Canyon Dam, CA
95923 Canyondam, CA
95924 Cedar Ridge, CA
95925 Challenge, CA
95926 Chico, CA
95927 Chico, CA
95928 Chico, CA
95929 Chico, CA
95930 Clipper Mills, CA
95930 La Porte, CA
95932 Colusa, CA
95934 Crescent Mills, CA
95935 Dobbins, CA
95936 Downieville, CA
95937 Dunnigan, CA
95938 Durham, CA
95939 Elk Creek, CA
95940 Feather Falls, CA
95940 Oroville, CA
95941 Forbestown, CA
95942 Butte Meadows, CA
95942 Forest Ranch, CA
95943 Glenn, CA
95944 Goodyears Bar, CA
95945 Grass Valley, CA
95946 Penn Valley, CA
95947 Greenville, CA
95948 Gridley, CA
95949 Grass Valley, CA
95950 Grimes, CA
95951 Hamilton City, CA
95953 Live Oak, CA
95954 Magalia, CA
95955 Maxwell, CA
95956 Meadow Valley, CA
95957 Meridian, CA
95958 Durham, CA
95958 Nelson, CA
95959 Nevada City, CA
95960 North San Juan, CA
95961 Arboga, CA
95961 Olivehurst, CA
95961 Plumas Lake, CA
95961 West Linda, CA
95962 Oregon House, CA
95963 Orland, CA
95965 Butte Valley, CA
95965 Oroville, CA
95965 Pulga, CA
95965 Yankee Hill, CA
95966 Oroville, CA
95967 Paradise, CA
95968 Palermo, CA
95969 Paradise, CA
95970 Princeton, CA
95971 Quincy, CA
95971 Spring Garden, CA
95972 Rackerby, CA
95973 Chico, CA
95973 Cohasset, CA
95974 Richvale, CA
95975 Rough And Ready, CA
95976 Chico, CA
95977 Big Oak Valley, CA
95977 Smartsville, CA
95978 Stirling City, CA
95979 Stonyford, CA
95980 Belden, CA
95980 Oroville, CA
95980 Storrie, CA
95981 Strawberry Valley, CA
95982 Sutter, CA
95983 Taylorsville, CA
95984 Twain, CA
95986 Washington, CA
95987 Williams, CA
95988 Willows, CA
95991 Yuba City, CA
95992 Yuba City, CA
95993 Yuba City, CA

960

96001 Redding, CA
96002 Redding, CA
96003 Redding, CA
96006 Adin, CA
96007 Anderson, CA
96008 Bella Vista, CA
96009 Bieber, CA
96010 Big Bar, CA
96011 Big Bend, CA
96013 Burney, CA
96014 Callahan, CA
96015 Canby, CA
96016 Cassel, CA
96017 Castella, CA
96019 Central Valley, CA
96019 Shasta Lake, CA
96020 Chester, CA
96021 Corning, CA
96022 Cottonwood, CA
96023 Dorris, CA
96024 Douglas City, CA
96025 Dunsmuir, CA
96027 Etna, CA
96027 Sawyers Bar, CA
96028 Fall River Mills, CA
96029 Corning, CA
96029 Flournoy, CA
96031 Forks Of Salmon, CA
96032 Fort Jones, CA
96033 French Gulch, CA
96034 Gazelle, CA

96035 Gerber, CA
96037 Greenview, CA
96038 Grenada, CA
96039 Happy Camp, CA
96040 Hat Creek, CA
96041 Hayfork, CA
96044 Hornbrook, CA
96046 Hyampom, CA
96047 Igo, CA
96047 Ono, CA
96048 Helena, CA
96048 Junction City, CA
96049 Redding, CA
96050 Horse Creek, CA
96050 Klamath River, CA
96051 Lakehead, CA
96052 Lewiston, CA
96054 Lookout, CA
96055 Los Molinos, CA
96056 Little Valley, CA
96056 Mcarthur, CA
96057 Mccloud, CA
96058 Macdoel, CA
96059 Manton, CA
96061 Mill Creek, CA
96061 Mineral, CA
96062 Millville, CA
96063 Mineral, CA
96064 Montague, CA
96065 Montgomery Creek, CA
96067 Mount Shasta, CA
96068 Nubieber, CA
96069 Oak Run, CA
96070 Lakehead, CA
96070 Obrien, CA
96071 Old Station, CA
96073 Palo Cedro, CA
96074 Paskenta, CA
96075 Paynes Creek, CA
96076 Platina, CA
96076 Wildwood, CA
96078 Proberta, CA
96079 Central Valley, CA
96079 Project City, CA
96079 Shasta Lake, CA
96080 Red Bluff, CA
96084 Round Mountain, CA
96085 Scott Bar, CA
96086 Seiad Valley, CA
96087 Shasta, CA
96088 Shingletown, CA
96089 Shasta Lake, CA
96089 Summit City, CA
96090 Tehama, CA
96091 Trinity Center, CA
96092 Vina, CA
96093 Weaverville, CA
96094 Edgewood, CA
96094 Hammond Ranch, CA
96094 Weed, CA
96095 Whiskeytown, CA
96096 Whitmore, CA
96097 Yreka, CA
96099 Redding, CA

961

96101 Alturas, CA
96103 Blairsden, CA
96103 Blairsden-Graeagle, CA
96103 Cromberg, CA
96103 Graeagle, CA
96104 Cedarville, CA
96105 Chilcoot, CA
96106 Clio, CA
96107 Coleville, CA
96108 Davis Creek, CA
96109 Doyle, CA
96110 Eagleville, CA
96111 Floriston, CA
96112 Fort Bidwell, CA
96113 Herlong, CA
96114 Janesville, CA
96115 Lake City, CA
96116 Likely, CA
96117 Litchfield, CA
96118 Loyalton, CA
96119 Madeline, CA
96120 Hope Valley, CA
96120 Markleeville, CA
96121 Milford, CA
96122 Portola, CA
96123 Ravendale, CA
96124 Calpine, CA
96124 Sattley, CA
96125 Sierra City, CA
96126 Sierraville, CA
96127 Susanville, CA
96128 Standish, CA
96129 Beckwourth, CA
96129 Portola, CA
96130 Susanville, CA
96132 Termo, CA
96133 Topaz, CA
96134 Newell, CA
96134 Tionesta, CA
96134 Tulelake, CA
96135 Vinton, CA
96136 Wendel, CA
96137 Lake Almanor, CA
96137 Westwood, CA
96140 Carnelian Bay, CA
96141 Homewood, CA
96142 Tahoma, CA
96143 Kings Beach, CA
96145 Alpine Meadows, CA
96145 Tahoe City, CA
96146 Alpine Meadows, CA
96146 Olympic Valley, CA
96146 Tahoe City, CA
96148 Tahoe Vista, CA
96150 South Lake Tahoe, CA
96151 Fallen Leaf, CA
96151 South Lake Tahoe, CA
96160 Truckee, CA
96161 Northstar, CA
96161 Truckee, CA
96162 Truckee, CA

967

96701 Aiea, HI
96703 Anahola, HI
96704 Captain Cook, HI
96704 Ocean View, HI
96705 Eleele, HI
96706 Ewa Beach, HI
96707 Kapolei, HI
96708 Haiku, HI
96709 Kapolei, HI
96710 Hakalau, HI
96712 Haleiwa, HI
96713 Hana, HI
96714 Hanalei, HI
96715 Hanamaulu, HI
96715 Lihue, HI
96716 Hanapepe, HI
96717 Hauula, HI
96718 Hawaii National Park, HI
96719 Hawi, HI
96720 Hilo, HI
96721 Hilo, HI
96722 Princeville, HI
96725 Holualoa, HI
96726 Honaunau, HI
96727 Honokaa, HI
96727 Paauhau, HI
96728 Honomu, HI
96729 Hoolehua, HI
96730 Kaaawa, HI
96731 Kahuku, HI
96732 Kahului, HI
96733 Kahului, HI
96734 Kailua, HI
96737 Ocean View, HI
96738 Waikoloa, HI
96739 Kailua Kona, HI
96739 Keauhou, HI
96740 Kailua Kona, HI
96741 Kalaheo, HI
96742 Kalaupapa, HI
96743 Kamuela, HI
96744 Kaneohe, HI
96745 Kailua Kona, HI
96746 Kapaa, HI
96747 Kaumakani, HI
96748 Kaunakakai, HI
96749 Keaau, HI
96750 Kealakekua, HI
96751 Kealia, HI
96752 Kekaha, HI
96753 Kihei, HI
96753 Wailea, HI
96754 Kilauea, HI
96755 Kapaau, HI
96756 Koloa, HI
96757 Kualapuu, HI
96759 Kunia, HI
96760 Kurtistown, HI
96761 Lahaina, HI
96762 Laie, HI
96763 Lanai City, HI
96764 Laupahoehoe, HI
96765 Lawai, HI
96766 Lihue, HI
96767 Lahaina, HI
96768 Makawao, HI
96769 Makaweli, HI
96770 Maunaloa, HI
96771 Mountain View, HI
96772 Naalehu, HI
96773 Ninole, HI
96774 Ookala, HI
96776 Paauilo, HI
96777 Pahala, HI
96778 Pahoa, HI
96779 Paia, HI
96780 Papaaloa, HI
96781 Papaikou, HI
96782 Pearl City, HI
96783 Pepeekeo, HI
96784 Puunene, HI
96785 Volcano, HI
96786 Wahiawa, HI
96788 Pukalani, HI
96789 Mililani, HI
96790 Kula, HI
96791 Waialua, HI
96792 Waianae, HI
96793 Wailuku, HI
96795 Waimanalo, HI
96796 Waimea, HI
96797 Waipahu, HI
96799 Pago Pago, AS

968

96801 Honolulu, HI
96802 Honolulu, HI
96803 Honolulu, HI
96804 Honolulu, HI
96805 Honolulu, HI
96806 Honolulu, HI
96807 Honolulu, HI
96808 Honolulu, HI
96809 Honolulu, HI
96810 Honolulu, HI
96811 Honolulu, HI
96812 Honolulu, HI
96813 Honolulu, HI
96814 Honolulu, HI
96815 Honolulu, HI
96816 Honolulu, HI
96817 Honolulu, HI
96818 Honolulu, HI
96819 Honolulu, HI
96820 Honolulu, HI
96821 Honolulu, HI
96822 Honolulu, HI
96823 Honolulu, HI
96824 Honolulu, HI
96825 Honolulu, HI
96826 Honolulu, HI
96828 Honolulu, HI
96830 Honolulu, HI
96836 Honolulu, HI
96837 Honolulu, HI
96838 Honolulu, HI
96839 Honolulu, HI
96840 Honolulu, HI
96841 Honolulu, HI
96843 Honolulu, HI
96844 Honolulu, HI
96846 Honolulu, HI
96847 Honolulu, HI
96848 Honolulu, HI
96849 Honolulu, HI
96850 Honolulu, HI
96853 Hickam Afb, HI
96853 Jb Pearl Harbor Hickam, HI
96853 Jbphh, HI
96853 Joint Base Pearl Hbr Hickam, HI
96854 Wheeler Army Airfield, HI
96857 Schofield Barracks, HI
96858 Fort Shafter, HI
96859 Tripler Army Medical Center, HI
96860 Jb Pearl Harbor Hickam, HI
96860 Jbphh, HI
96860 Joint Base Pearl Hbr Hickam, HI
96860 Pearl Harbor, HI
96861 Camp H M Smith, HI
96863 Mcbh Kaneohe Bay, HI
96898 Wake Island, HI

969

96910 Agana Heights, GU
96910 Asan, GU
96910 Chalan Pago, GU
96910 Hagatna, GU
96910 Maite, GU
96910 Mongmong, GU
96910 Ordot, GU
96910 Sinajana, GU
96910 Toto, GU
96912 Dededo, GU
96913 Barrigada, GU
96913 Mangilao, GU
96913 Tamuning, GU
96915 Inarajan, GU
96915 Merizo, GU
96915 Piti, GU
96915 Santa Rita, GU
96915 Talofofo, GU
96915 Umatac, GU
96915 Yona, GU
96916 Merizo, GU
96917 Inarajan, GU
96919 Agana Heights, GU
96921 Barrigada, GU
96923 Mangilao, GU
96928 Agat, GU
96929 Barrigada, GU
96929 Dededo, GU
96929 Yigo, GU
96931 Tamuning, GU
96932 Hagatna, GU
96939 Palau, PW
96940 Palau, PW
96941 Pohnpei, FM
96942 Chuuk, FM
96943 Yap, FM
96944 Kosrae, FM
96950 Saipan, MP
96951 Rota, MP
96952 Tinian, MP
96960 Majuro, MH
96970 Ebeye, MH

970

97001 Antelope, OR
97002 Aurora, OR
97003 Aloha, OR
97003 Beaverton, OR
97003 Hillsboro, OR
97004 Beavercreek, OR
97005 Beaverton, OR
97006 Aloha, OR
97006 Beaverton, OR
97006 Hillsboro, OR
97007 Aloha, OR
97007 Beaverton, OR
97008 Beaverton, OR
97009 Boring, OR
97009 Damascus, OR
97010 Bridal Veil, OR
97011 Brightwood, OR
97013 Canby, OR
97014 Cascade Locks, OR
97015 Clackamas, OR
97015 Damascus, OR
97015 Happy Valley, OR
97016 Birkenfeld, OR
97016 Clatskanie, OR
97016 Westport, OR
97017 Colton, OR
97018 Columbia City, OR
97019 Corbett, OR
97020 Donald, OR
97021 Dufur, OR
97021 Friend, OR
97022 Eagle Creek, OR
97023 Estacada, OR
97024 Fairview, OR
97026 Gervais, OR
97027 Gladstone, OR
97028 Government Camp, OR
97028 Timberline Lodge, OR
97029 Grass Valley, OR
97030 Gresham, OR
97031 Hood River, OR
97032 Hubbard, OR
97033 Kent, OR
97034 Lake Oswego, OR
97034 Rivergrove, OR
97035 Lake Grove, OR
97035 Lake Oswego, OR
97036 Marylhurst, OR
97037 Maupin, OR
97038 Molalla, OR
97039 Moro, OR
97040 Mosier, OR
97041 Mount Hood Parkdale, OR
97042 Mulino, OR
97044 Odell, OR
97045 Oregon City, OR
97048 Prescott, OR
97048 Rainier, OR
97049 Rhododendron, OR
97049 Zigzag, OR
97050 Rufus, OR
97051 Saint Helens, OR
97053 Warren, OR
97054 Deer Island, OR
97055 Sandy, OR
97056 Scappoose, OR
97057 Shaniko, OR
97058 The Dalles, OR
97060 Troutdale, OR
97060 Wood Village, OR
97062 Tualatin, OR
97063 Tygh Valley, OR
97063 Wamic, OR
97064 Vernonia, OR
97065 Wasco, OR
97067 Welches, OR
97068 West Linn, OR
97070 Wilsonville, OR
97071 Woodburn, OR
97075 Beaverton, OR
97076 Beaverton, OR
97077 Beaverton, OR
97078 Aloha, OR
97078 Beaverton, OR
97080 Gresham, OR
97086 Clackamas, OR
97086 Happy Valley, OR
97086 Portland, OR
97089 Boring, OR
97089 Damascus, OR

971

97101 Amity, OR
97102 Arch Cape, OR
97103 Astoria, OR
97106 Banks, OR
97107 Bay City, OR
97108 Beaver, OR
97109 Banks, OR
97109 Buxton, OR
97110 Cannon Beach, OR
97111 Carlton, OR
97112 Beaver, OR
97112 Cloverdale, OR
97113 Cornelius, OR
97114 Dayton, OR
97115 Dundee, OR
97116 Forest Grove, OR
97116 Glenwood, OR
97117 Gales Creek, OR
97118 Garibaldi, OR
97119 Gaston, OR
97121 Hammond, OR
97122 Hebo, OR
97123 Cornelius, OR
97123 Hillsboro, OR
97124 Hillsboro, OR
97125 Banks, OR
97125 Manning, OR
97127 Lafayette, OR
97128 Mcminnville, OR
97130 Manzanita, OR
97131 Nehalem, OR
97132 Newberg, OR
97133 North Plains, OR
97134 Oceanside, OR
97135 Pacific City, OR
97136 Rockaway, OR
97136 Rockaway Beach, OR
97137 Saint Paul, OR
97138 Gearhart, OR
97138 Seaside, OR
97140 Sherwood, OR
97141 Tillamook, OR
97143 Netarts, OR
97143 Netarts Bay, OR
97144 Timber, OR
97145 Tolovana Park, OR
97146 Warrenton, OR
97147 Wheeler, OR
97148 Yamhill, OR
97149 Neskowin, OR

972

97201 Portland, OR
97202 Portland, OR
97203 Portland, OR
97204 Portland, OR
97205 Portland, OR
97206 Portland, OR
97207 Portland, OR
97208 Portland, OR
97209 Portland, OR
97210 Portland, OR
97211 Portland, OR
97212 Portland, OR
97213 Portland, OR
97214 Portland, OR
97215 Portland, OR
97216 Portland, OR
97217 Portland, OR
97218 Portland, OR
97219 Portland, OR
97220 Portland, OR
97221 Portland, OR
97222 Milwaukie, OR
97222 Oak Grove, OR
97222 Portland, OR
97223 Portland, OR
97223 Tigard, OR
97224 King City, OR
97224 Portland, OR
97224 Tigard, OR
97225 Portland, OR
97227 Portland, OR
97228 Portland, OR
97229 Portland, OR
97230 Portland, OR
97231 Portland, OR
97232 Portland, OR
97233 Portland, OR
97236 Portland, OR
97238 Portland, OR
97239 Portland, OR
97240 Portland, OR
97242 Portland, OR
97256 Portland, OR
97258 Portland, OR

97266 Portland, OR
97267 Milwaukie, OR
97267 Oak Grove, OR
97267 Portland, OR
97268 Oak Grove, OR
97268 Portland, OR
97269 Milwaukie, OR
97269 Portland, OR
97280 Portland, OR
97281 Portland, OR
97281 Tigard, OR
97282 Portland, OR
97283 Portland, OR
97286 Portland, OR
97290 Portland, OR
97291 Portland, OR
97292 Portland, OR
97293 Portland, OR
97294 Portland, OR
97296 Portland, OR
97298 Portland, OR

973

97301 Salem, OR
97302 Salem, OR
97303 Keizer, OR
97303 Salem, OR
97304 Salem, OR
97305 Brooks, OR
97305 Salem, OR
97306 Salem, OR
97307 Keizer, OR
97307 Salem, OR
97308 Salem, OR
97309 Salem, OR
97310 Salem, OR
97311 Salem, OR
97312 Salem, OR
97314 Salem, OR
97317 Salem, OR
97321 Albany, OR
97322 Albany, OR
97324 Alsea, OR
97325 Aumsville, OR
97325 West Stayton, OR
97326 Blodgett, OR
97327 Brownsville, OR
97329 Cascadia, OR
97330 Adair Village, OR
97330 Corvallis, OR
97331 Corvallis, OR
97333 Corvallis, OR
97335 Crabtree, OR
97336 Crawfordsville, OR
97338 Dallas, OR
97339 Corvallis, OR
97341 Depoe Bay, OR
97342 Detroit, OR
97343 Eddyville, OR
97344 Falls City, OR
97345 Foster, OR
97346 Gates, OR
97347 Grand Ronde, OR
97348 Halsey, OR
97350 Idanha, OR
97351 Independence, OR
97352 Jefferson, OR
97355 Lebanon, OR
97357 Logsden, OR
97358 Lyons, OR
97360 Mill City, OR
97361 Monmouth, OR
97362 Mount Angel, OR
97364 Neotsu, OR
97365 Newport, OR
97366 Newport, OR
97366 South Beach, OR
97367 Lincoln City, OR
97367 Rose Lodge, OR
97368 Otis, OR
97369 Otter Rock, OR
97370 Philomath, OR
97371 Rickreall, OR
97373 Saint Benedict, OR
97374 Scio, OR
97375 Scotts Mills, OR
97376 Seal Rock, OR
97377 Shedd, OR
97378 Sheridan, OR
97380 Siletz, OR
97381 Silverton, OR
97383 Stayton, OR
97384 Mehama, OR
97385 Sublimity, OR
97386 Sweet Home, OR
97388 Gleneden Beach, OR
97389 Tangent, OR
97390 Tidewater, OR
97391 Toledo, OR
97392 Marion, OR
97392 Turner, OR
97394 Waldport, OR
97396 Willamina, OR

974

97401 Eugene, OR
97402 Eugene, OR
97403 Eugene, OR
97404 Eugene, OR
97405 Eugene, OR
97406 Agness, OR
97407 Allegany, OR
97408 Coburg, OR
97408 Eugene, OR
97409 Alvadore, OR
97410 Azalea, OR
97411 Bandon, OR
97412 Blachly, OR
97412 Eugene, OR
97413 Blue River, OR
97413 Ckenzie Bridge, OR
97413 Mckenzie Bridge, OR
97414 Broadbent, OR
97415 Brookings, OR
97415 Harbor, OR
97416 Camas Valley, OR
97417 Canyonville, OR
97419 Cheshire, OR
97420 Charleston, OR
97420 Coos Bay, OR
97423 Coquille, OR
97424 Cottage Grove, OR
97424 Curtin, OR
97424 Saginaw, OR
97426 Creswell, OR
97429 Days Creek, OR
97430 Deadwood, OR
97430 Greenleaf, OR
97431 Dexter, OR
97432 Dillard, OR
97434 Culp Creek, OR
97434 Dorena, OR
97435 Drain, OR
97436 Elkton, OR
97437 Elmira, OR
97438 Fall Creek, OR
97438 Jasper, OR
97439 Dunes City, OR
97439 Florence, OR
97440 Eugene, OR
97441 Gardiner, OR
97442 Glendale, OR
97443 Glide, OR
97444 Gold Beach, OR
97446 Harrisburg, OR
97447 Idleyld Park, OR
97448 Junction City, OR
97449 Lakeside, OR
97450 Langlois, OR
97451 Lorane, OR
97452 Lowell, OR
97453 Mapleton, OR
97454 Marcola, OR
97455 Eugene, OR
97455 Pleasant Hill, OR
97456 Monroe, OR
97457 Myrtle Creek, OR
97458 Myrtle Point, OR
97458 Norway, OR
97458 Remote, OR
97459 North Bend, OR
97461 Noti, OR
97462 Oakland, OR
97463 Oakridge, OR
97464 Ophir, OR
97465 Port Orford, OR
97466 Powers, OR
97467 Reedsport, OR
97467 Winchester Bay, OR
97467 Winchestr Bay, OR
97469 Riddle, OR
97470 Roseburg, OR
97471 Roseburg, OR
97473 Scottsburg, OR
97475 Springfield, OR
97476 Sixes, OR
97477 Springfield, OR
97478 Springfield, OR
97479 Sutherlin, OR
97480 Swisshome, OR
97481 Tenmile, OR
97484 Tiller, OR
97486 Umpqua, OR
97487 Veneta, OR
97488 Vida, OR
97489 Leaburg, OR
97489 Walterville, OR
97490 Walton, OR
97491 Wedderburn, OR
97492 Westfir, OR
97493 Westlake, OR
97494 Wilbur, OR
97495 Winchester, OR
97496 Winston, OR
97497 Wolf Creek, OR
97498 Yachats, OR
97499 Yoncalla, OR

975

97501 Medford, OR
97502 Central Point, OR
97502 Medford, OR
97503 Medford, OR
97503 White City, OR
97504 Medford, OR
97520 Ashland, OR
97522 Butte Falls, OR
97523 Cave Junction, OR
97524 Eagle Point, OR
97525 Gold Hill, OR
97526 Grants Pass, OR
97527 Grants Pass, OR
97528 Grants Pass, OR
97530 Applegate, OR
97530 Jacksonville, OR
97531 Cave Junction, OR
97531 Kerby, OR
97532 Merlin, OR
97533 Murphy, OR
97534 O Brien, OR
97535 Phoenix, OR
97536 Prospect, OR
97537 Rogue River, OR
97538 Selma, OR
97539 Shady Cove, OR
97540 Talent, OR
97541 Trail, OR
97543 Grants Pass, OR
97543 Wilderville, OR
97544 Williams, OR

976

97601 Klamath Falls, OR
97601 Oretech, OR
97602 Klamath Falls, OR
97603 Klamath Falls, OR
97604 Crater Lake, OR
97620 Adel, OR
97621 Beatty, OR
97622 Bly, OR
97623 Bonanza, OR
97624 Chiloquin, OR
97625 Dairy, OR
97625 Klamath Falls, OR
97626 Fort Klamath, OR
97627 Keno, OR
97630 Lakeview, OR
97632 Malin, OR
97633 Merrill, OR
97634 Midland, OR
97635 New Pine Creek, OR
97636 Paisley, OR
97637 Plush, OR
97638 Silver Lake, OR
97639 Chiloquin, OR
97639 Sprague River, OR
97640 Summer Lake, OR
97641 Christmas Valley, OR

977

97701 Bend, OR
97702 Bend, OR
97707 Bend, OR
97707 Sunriver, OR
97708 Bend, OR
97709 Bend, OR
97710 Fields, OR
97711 Ashwood, OR
97712 Brothers, OR
97720 Burns, OR
97720 Lawen, OR
97721 Princeton, OR
97722 Diamond, OR
97730 Camp Sherman, OR
97731 Chemult, OR
97731 Diamond Lake, OR
97732 Crane, OR
97733 Crescent, OR
97733 Crescent Lake, OR
97734 Culver, OR
97735 Fort Rock, OR
97736 Frenchglen, OR
97737 Gilchrist, OR
97738 Hines, OR
97739 La Pine, OR
97741 Madras, OR
97741 Metolius, OR
97750 Mitchell, OR
97751 Paulina, OR
97752 Post, OR
97753 Powell Butte, OR
97754 Prineville, OR
97756 Redmond, OR
97758 Riley, OR
97759 Sisters, OR
97760 Crooked River, OR
97760 Crooked River Ranch, OR
97760 Terrebonne, OR
97761 Warm Springs, OR

978

97801 Cayuse, OR
97801 Pendleton, OR
97810 Adams, OR
97812 Arlington, OR
97813 Athena, OR
97814 Baker City, OR
97814 Medical Springs, OR
97817 Bates, OR
97818 Boardman, OR
97819 Bridgeport, OR
97820 Canyon City, OR
97823 Condon, OR
97823 Lonerock, OR
97824 Cove, OR
97825 Dayville, OR
97826 Echo, OR
97827 Elgin, OR
97828 Enterprise, OR
97830 Fossil, OR
97830 Kinzua, OR
97830 Mayville, OR
97833 Haines, OR
97834 Halfway, OR
97835 Helix, OR
97836 Heppner, OR
97837 Hereford, OR
97838 Hermiston, OR
97839 Lexington, OR
97840 Oxbow, OR
97841 Imbler, OR
97842 Imnaha, OR
97843 Ione, OR
97844 Irrigon, OR
97845 John Day, OR
97846 Joseph, OR
97848 Kimberly, OR
97850 Island City, OR
97850 La Grande, OR
97856 Fox, OR
97856 Long Creek, OR
97856 Ritter, OR
97857 Lostine, OR
97859 Meacham, OR
97861 Arlington, OR
97861 Mikkalo, OR
97862 Milton Freewater, OR
97864 Monument, OR
97865 Mount Vernon, OR
97867 North Powder, OR
97868 Pilot Rock, OR
97869 Prairie City, OR
97870 Richland, OR
97873 Seneca, OR
97874 Spray, OR
97875 Stanfield, OR
97876 Summerville, OR
97877 Granite, OR
97877 Greenhorn, OR
97877 Sumpter, OR
97880 Dale, OR
97880 Ukiah, OR
97882 Mcnary, OR
97882 Umatilla, OR
97883 Union, OR
97884 Unity, OR
97885 Wallowa, OR
97886 Weston, OR

979

97901 Adrian, OR
97902 Arock, OR
97903 Brogan, OR
97904 Drewsey, OR
97905 Durkee, OR
97906 Harper, OR
97907 Huntington, OR
97908 Ironside, OR
97909 Jamieson, OR
97910 Jordan Valley, OR
97910 South Mountain, OR
97911 Juntura, OR
97913 Nyssa, OR
97914 Ontario, OR
97917 Riverside, OR
97918 Vale, OR
97920 Westfall, OR

980

98001 Algona, WA
98001 Auburn, WA
98001 Federal Way, WA
98002 Auburn, WA
98003 Auburn, WA
98003 Federal Way, WA
98004 Beaux Arts, WA
98004 Bellevue, WA
98004 Clyde Hill, WA
98004 Hunts Point, WA
98004 Yarrow Point, WA
98005 Bellevue, WA
98006 Bellevue, WA
98007 Bellevue, WA
98008 Bellevue, WA
98009 Bellevue, WA
98010 Black Diamond, WA
98011 Bothell, WA
98012 Bothell, WA
98012 Mill Creek, WA
98013 Burton, WA
98013 Vashon, WA
98014 Carnation, WA
98015 Bellevue, WA
98019 Duvall, WA
98020 Edmonds, WA
98020 Woodway, WA
98021 Bothell, WA
98022 Enumclaw, WA
98023 Auburn, WA
98023 Federal Way, WA
98024 Fall City, WA
98025 Hobart, WA
98026 Edmonds, WA
98027 Issaquah, WA
98028 Bothell, WA
98028 Kenmore, WA
98029 Issaquah, WA
98030 Kent, WA
98031 Kent, WA
98032 Kent, WA
98033 Kirkland, WA
98033 Redmond, WA
98034 Kirkland, WA
98035 Kent, WA
98036 Brier, WA
98036 Lynnwood, WA
98037 Lynnwood, WA
98038 Maple Valley, WA
98039 Medina, WA
98040 Mercer Island, WA
98041 Bothell, WA
98042 Covington, WA
98042 Kent, WA
98043 Mountlake Terrace, WA
98045 North Bend, WA
98046 Lynnwood, WA
98047 Auburn, WA
98047 Pacific, WA
98050 Preston, WA
98051 Ravensdale, WA
98052 Redmond, WA
98053 Redmond, WA
98055 Renton, WA
98056 Newcastle, WA
98056 Renton, WA
98057 Renton, WA
98058 Renton, WA
98059 Newcastle, WA
98059 Renton, WA
98061 Rollingbay, WA
98062 Burien, WA
98062 Seahurst, WA
98063 Auburn, WA
98063 Federal Way, WA
98064 Kent, WA
98065 Snoqualmie, WA
98068 Snoqualmie Pass, WA
98070 Vashon, WA
98071 Auburn, WA
98072 Woodinville, WA
98073 Redmond, WA
98074 Redmond, WA
98074 Sammamish, WA
98075 Issaquah, WA
98075 Sammamish, WA
98077 Woodinville, WA
98082 Bothell, WA
98082 Mill Creek, WA
98083 Kirkland, WA
98087 Lynnwood, WA
98089 Kent, WA
98092 Auburn, WA
98093 Auburn, WA
98093 Federal Way, WA

981

98101 Seattle, WA
98102 Seattle, WA
98103 Seattle, WA
98104 Seattle, WA
98105 Seattle, WA
98106 Seattle, WA
98107 Seattle, WA
98108 Seattle, WA
98108 Tukwila, WA
98109 Seattle, WA
98110 Bainbridge Island, WA
98110 Seattle, WA
98111 Seattle, WA
98112 Seattle, WA
98113 Seattle, WA
98114 Seattle, WA
98115 Seattle, WA
98116 Seattle, WA
98117 Seattle, WA
98118 Seattle, WA
98119 Seattle, WA
98121 Seattle, WA

98122 Seattle, WA
98124 Seattle, WA
98125 Seattle, WA
98126 Seattle, WA
98127 Seattle, WA
98129 Seattle, WA
98131 Seattle, WA
98132 Seattle, WA
98133 Seattle, WA
98133 Shoreline, WA
98134 Seattle, WA
98136 Seattle, WA
98138 Seattle, WA
98138 Tukwila, WA
98139 Seattle, WA
98141 Seattle, WA
98144 Seattle, WA
98145 Seattle, WA
98146 Burien, WA
98146 Seattle, WA
98148 Burien, WA
98148 Des Moines, WA
98148 Normandy Park, WA
98148 Seatac, WA
98148 Seattle, WA
98154 Seattle, WA
98155 Lake Forest Park, WA
98155 Seattle, WA
98155 Shoreline, WA
98158 Seatac, WA
98158 Seattle, WA
98160 Seattle, WA
98161 Seattle, WA
98164 Seattle, WA
98165 Seattle, WA
98166 Burien, WA
98166 Normandy Park, WA
98166 Seattle, WA
98168 Burien, WA
98168 Seatac, WA
98168 Seattle, WA
98168 Tukwila, WA
98170 Seattle, WA
98174 Seattle, WA
98175 Seattle, WA
98177 Seattle, WA
98177 Shoreline, WA
98178 Seattle, WA
98178 Tukwila, WA
98181 Seattle, WA
98185 Seattle, WA
98188 Seatac, WA
98188 Seattle, WA
98188 Tukwila, WA
98189 Seattle, WA
98190 Seattle, WA
98191 Seattle, WA
98194 Seattle, WA
98195 Seattle, WA
98198 Des Moines, WA
98198 Normandy Park, WA
98198 Seatac, WA
98198 Seattle, WA
98199 Seattle, WA

982

98201 Everett, WA
98203 Everett, WA
98204 Everett, WA
98206 Everett, WA
98207 Everett, WA
98208 Everett, WA
98213 Everett, WA
98220 Acme, WA
98221 Anacortes, WA
98222 Anacortes, WA
98222 Blakely Island, WA
98223 Arlington, WA
98224 Baring, WA
98225 Bellingham, WA
98226 Bellingham, WA
98227 Bellingham, WA
98228 Bellingham, WA
98229 Bellingham, WA
98230 Blaine, WA
98231 Blaine, WA
98232 Bow, WA
98233 Burlington, WA
98235 Clearlake, WA
98236 Clinton, WA
98237 Concrete, WA
98238 Conway, WA
98239 Coupeville, WA
98240 Custer, WA
98241 Darrington, WA
98243 Deer Harbor, WA
98244 Deming, WA
98245 Eastsound, WA
98247 Everson, WA
98248 Ferndale, WA
98249 Freeland, WA
98250 Friday Harbor, WA
98250 Roche Harbor, WA
98251 Gold Bar, WA
98252 Granite Falls, WA
98253 Greenbank, WA
98255 Hamilton, WA
98256 Index, WA
98257 La Conner, WA
98258 Lake Stevens, WA
98259 North Lakewood, WA
98260 Langley, WA
98261 Lopez Island, WA
98262 Lummi Island, WA
98263 Lyman, WA
98264 Lynden, WA
98266 Maple Falls, WA
98267 Marblemount, WA
98270 Marysville, WA
98271 Marysville, WA
98271 Quil Ceda Village, WA
98271 Tulalip, WA
98272 Monroe, WA
98273 Mount Vernon, WA
98274 Mount Vernon, WA
98275 Mukilteo, WA
98276 Everson, WA
98276 Nooksack, WA
98277 Oak Harbor, WA
98278 Oak Harbor, WA
98278 Whidbey Island Naval Air, WA
98279 Olga, WA
98280 Orcas, WA
98281 Point Roberts, WA
98282 Camano Island, WA
98282 Stanwood, WA
98283 Rockport, WA
98284 Sedro Woolley, WA
98286 Shaw Island, WA
98287 Silvana, WA
98288 Skykomish, WA
98290 Snohomish, WA
98291 Snohomish, WA
98292 Stanwood, WA
98293 Startup, WA
98294 Sultan, WA
98295 Sumas, WA
98296 Snohomish, WA
98297 Waldron, WA

983

98303 Anderson Island, WA
98304 Ashford, WA
98305 Beaver, WA
98310 Bremerton, WA
98311 Bremerton, WA
98312 Bremerton, WA
98314 Bremerton, WA
98315 Silverdale, WA
98320 Brinnon, WA
98321 Buckley, WA
98322 Burley, WA
98323 Carbonado, WA
98324 Carlsborg, WA
98325 Chimacum, WA
98326 Clallam Bay, WA
98327 Dupont, WA
98328 Eatonville, WA
98329 Gig Harbor, WA
98329 Wauna, WA
98330 Elbe, WA
98331 Forks, WA
98332 Gig Harbor, WA
98333 Fox Island, WA
98335 Gig Harbor, WA
98336 Glenoma, WA
98337 Bremerton, WA
98337 Gorst, WA
98338 Graham, WA
98339 Port Hadlock, WA
98340 Hansville, WA
98342 Indianola, WA
98343 Joyce, WA
98344 Kapowsin, WA
98345 Keyport, WA
98346 Kingston, WA
98348 La Grande, WA
98349 Home, WA
98349 Lakebay, WA
98350 La Push, WA
98351 Lakebay, WA
98351 Longbranch, WA
98352 Sumner, WA
98353 Manchester, WA
98354 Milton, WA
98355 Mineral, WA
98356 Morton, WA
98357 Neah Bay, WA
98358 Nordland, WA
98359 Olalla, WA
98360 Orting, WA
98361 Packwood, WA
98362 Port Angeles, WA
98363 Port Angeles, WA
98364 Port Gamble, WA
98365 Port Hadlock, WA
98365 Port Ludlow, WA
98366 Port Orchard, WA
98366 South Park Village, WA
98367 Port Orchard, WA
98368 Port Townsend, WA
98370 Poulsbo, WA
98371 Edgewood, WA
98371 Puyallup, WA
98372 Edgewood, WA
98372 Puyallup, WA
98373 Puyallup, WA
98373 South Hill, WA
98374 Puyallup, WA
98374 South Hill, WA
98375 Puyallup, WA
98375 South Hill, WA
98376 Quilcene, WA
98377 Randle, WA
98378 Retsil, WA
98380 Seabeck, WA
98381 Sekiu, WA
98382 Sequim, WA
98383 Silverdale, WA
98384 South Colby, WA
98385 South Prairie, WA
98386 Southworth, WA
98387 Bethel, WA
98387 Spanaway, WA
98388 Steilacoom, WA
98390 Sumner, WA
98391 Bonney Lake, WA
98391 Lake Tapps, WA
98391 Sumner, WA
98392 Suquamish, WA
98393 Tracyton, WA
98394 Vaughn, WA
98395 Wauna, WA
98396 Wilkeson, WA
98397 Longmire, WA
98398 Paradise, WA
98398 Paradise Inn, WA

984

98401 Tacoma, WA
98402 Tacoma, WA
98403 Tacoma, WA
98404 Tacoma, WA
98405 Tacoma, WA
98406 Tacoma, WA
98407 Ruston, WA
98407 Tacoma, WA
98408 Tacoma, WA
98409 Lakewood, WA
98409 Tacoma, WA
98411 Tacoma, WA
98412 Tacoma, WA
98413 Tacoma, WA
98415 Tacoma, WA
98416 Tacoma, WA
98417 Tacoma, WA
98418 Tacoma, WA
98419 Tacoma, WA
98421 Tacoma, WA
98422 Tacoma, WA
98424 Fife, WA
98424 Tacoma, WA
98430 Camp Murray, WA
98430 Tacoma, WA
98431 Joint Base Lewis Mchord, WA
98431 Madigan Hospital, WA
98431 Tacoma, WA
98433 Fort Lewis, WA
98433 Ft Lewis, WA
98433 Joint Base Lewis Mchord, WA
98433 Tacoma, WA
98438 Joint Base Lewis Mchord, WA
98438 Mchord Afb, WA
98438 Tacoma, WA
98439 Joint Base Lewis Mchord, WA
98439 Lakewood, WA
98439 Mchord Afb, WA
98439 Tacoma, WA
98443 Tacoma, WA
98444 Parkland, WA
98444 Tacoma, WA
98445 Parkland, WA
98445 Tacoma, WA
98446 Parkland, WA
98446 Tacoma, WA
98447 Tacoma, WA
98448 Parkland, WA
98448 Tacoma, WA
98464 Tacoma, WA
98464 University Place, WA
98465 Tacoma, WA
98466 Fircrest, WA
98466 Tacoma, WA
98466 University Place, WA
98467 Tacoma, WA
98467 University Place, WA
98471 Tacoma, WA
98481 Tacoma, WA
98490 Tacoma, WA
98493 Tacoma, WA
98496 Lakewood, WA
98496 Tacoma, WA
98497 Lakewood, WA
98497 Oakbrook, WA
98497 Tacoma, WA
98498 Lakewood, WA
98498 Tacoma, WA
98499 Joint Base Lewis Mchord, WA
98499 Lakewood, WA
98499 Mchord Afb, WA
98499 Tacoma, WA

985

98501 Olympia, WA
98501 Tumwater, WA
98502 Olympia, WA
98503 Lacey, WA
98503 Olympia, WA
98504 Olympia, WA
98505 Olympia, WA
98506 Lacey, WA
98506 Olympia, WA
98507 Olympia, WA
98508 Olympia, WA
98509 Lacey, WA
98509 Olympia, WA
98511 Olympia, WA
98511 Tumwater, WA
98512 Olympia, WA
98512 Tumwater, WA
98513 Lacey, WA
98513 Olympia, WA
98516 Lacey, WA
98516 Olympia, WA
98520 Aberdeen, WA
98522 Adna, WA
98524 Allyn, WA
98526 Amanda Park, WA
98527 Bay Center, WA
98528 Belfair, WA
98530 Bucoda, WA
98531 Centralia, WA
98532 Chehalis, WA
98532 Napavine, WA
98533 Cinebar, WA
98535 Copalis Beach, WA
98536 Copalis Crossing, WA
98537 Cosmopolis, WA
98538 Curtis, WA
98539 Doty, WA
98540 East Olympia, WA
98541 Elma, WA
98542 Ethel, WA
98544 Galvin, WA
98546 Grapeview, WA
98547 Grayland, WA
98548 Hoodsport, WA
98550 Hoquiam, WA
98552 Humptulips, WA
98554 Lebam, WA
98555 Lilliwaup, WA
98556 Littlerock, WA
98557 Mccleary, WA
98558 Mckenna, WA
98559 Malone, WA
98560 Matlock, WA
98561 Menlo, WA
98562 Moclips, WA
98563 Montesano, WA
98564 Mossyrock, WA
98565 Napavine, WA
98566 Neilton, WA
98568 Oakville, WA
98569 Ocean City, WA
98569 Ocean Shores, WA
98570 Onalaska, WA
98571 Pacific Beach, WA
98572 Pe Ell, WA
98575 Quinault, WA
98576 Rainier, WA
98577 Raymond, WA
98579 Rochester, WA
98580 Roy, WA
98581 Ryderwood, WA
98582 Salkum, WA
98583 Satsop, WA
98584 Shelton, WA
98584 Skokomish Nation, WA
98585 Silver Creek, WA
98586 South Bend, WA
98587 Taholah, WA
98588 Tahuya, WA
98589 Tenino, WA
98590 Tokeland, WA
98591 Toledo, WA
98592 Union, WA
98593 Vader, WA
98595 Westport, WA
98596 Winlock, WA
98597 Yelm, WA
98599 Olympia, WA

986

98601 Amboy, WA
98602 Appleton, WA
98603 Ariel, WA
98604 Battle Ground, WA
98605 Bingen, WA
98605 Cook, WA
98606 Brush Prairie, WA
98607 Camas, WA
98609 Carrolls, WA
98610 Carson, WA
98611 Castle Rock, WA
98612 Cathlamet, WA
98613 Centerville, WA
98614 Chinook, WA
98616 Cougar, WA
98617 Dallesport, WA
98619 Glenwood, WA
98620 Goldendale, WA
98621 Grays River, WA
98622 Heisson, WA
98623 Husum, WA
98624 Ilwaco, WA
98625 Kalama, WA
98626 Kelso, WA
98628 Klickitat, WA
98629 La Center, WA
98631 Long Beach, WA
98632 Longview, WA
98635 Lyle, WA
98637 Nahcotta, WA
98638 Naselle, WA
98639 North Bonneville, WA
98640 Ocean Park, WA
98641 Oysterville, WA
98642 Ridgefield, WA
98643 Rosburg, WA
98644 Seaview, WA
98645 Silverlake, WA
98647 Skamokawa, WA
98648 Stevenson, WA
98649 Toutle, WA
98650 Trout Lake, WA
98651 Underwood, WA
98660 Vancouver, WA
98661 Vancouver, WA
98662 Vancouver, WA
98663 Vancouver, WA
98664 Vancouver, WA
98665 Vancouver, WA
98666 Vancouver, WA
98668 Vancouver, WA
98670 Klickitat, WA
98670 Wahkiacus, WA
98671 Washougal, WA
98672 White Salmon, WA
98673 Wishram, WA
98674 Woodland, WA
98675 Yacolt, WA
98682 Vancouver, WA
98683 Vancouver, WA
98684 Vancouver, WA
98685 Vancouver, WA
98686 Vancouver, WA
98687 Vancouver, WA

988

98801 Wenatchee, WA
98802 East Wenatchee, WA
98802 Wenatchee, WA
98807 Wenatchee, WA
98811 Ardenvoir, WA
98812 Brewster, WA
98813 Bridgeport, WA
98814 Carlton, WA
98815 Cashmere, WA
98816 Chelan, WA
98817 Chelan Falls, WA
98819 Conconully, WA
98821 Dryden, WA
98822 Entiat, WA
98823 Ephrata, WA
98824 George, WA
98826 Leavenworth, WA
98827 Loomis, WA
98828 Malaga, WA
98829 Malott, WA
98830 Mansfield, WA
98831 Manson, WA
98832 Marlin, WA
98833 Mazama, WA
98834 Methow, WA
98836 Monitor, WA
98837 Moses Lake, WA
98840 Okanogan, WA
98841 Omak, WA
98843 Orondo, WA
98844 Oroville, WA
98845 Palisades, WA
98846 Pateros, WA
98847 Peshastin, WA
98848 George, WA
98848 Quincy, WA
98849 Riverside, WA

98850 Rock Island, WA
98851 Soap Lake, WA
98852 Stehekin, WA
98853 Stratford, WA
98855 Tonasket, WA
98856 Twisp, WA
98857 Warden, WA
98858 Waterville, WA
98859 Wauconda, WA
98860 Wilson Creek, WA
98862 Winthrop, WA

989

98901 Union Gap, WA
98901 Yakima, WA
98902 Yakima, WA
98903 Union Gap, WA
98903 Yakima, WA
98904 Gleed, WA
98904 Yakima, WA
98907 Yakima, WA
98908 Yakima, WA
98909 Yakima, WA
98920 Brownstown, WA
98921 Buena, WA
98922 Cle Elum, WA
98923 Cowiche, WA
98925 Easton, WA
98926 Ellensburg, WA
98926 Kittitas, WA
98930 Grandview, WA
98932 Granger, WA
98933 Harrah, WA
98934 Kittitas, WA
98935 Mabton, WA
98936 Moxee, WA
98937 Goose Prairie, WA
98937 Naches, WA
98938 Outlook, WA
98939 Parker, WA
98940 Ronald, WA
98941 Roslyn, WA
98942 Selah, WA
98943 South Cle Elum, WA
98944 Sunnyside, WA
98946 Thorp, WA
98947 Tieton, WA
98948 Toppenish, WA
98950 Ellensburg, WA
98950 Vantage, WA
98951 Wapato, WA
98952 White Swan, WA
98953 Zillah, WA

990

99001 Airway Heights, WA
99003 Chattaroy, WA
99004 Cheney, WA
99005 Colbert, WA
99006 Deer Park, WA
99008 Edwall, WA
99009 Elk, WA
99011 Fairchild Air Force Base, WA
99012 Fairfield, WA
99013 Ford, WA
99014 Four Lakes, WA
99016 Greenacres, WA
99016 Liberty Lake, WA
99016 Spokane Valley, WA
99017 Lamont, WA
99017 Sprague, WA
99018 Latah, WA
99019 Liberty Lake, WA
99020 Marshall, WA
99021 Mead, WA
99022 Espanola, WA
99022 Medical Lake, WA
99023 Mica, WA
99023 Valleyford, WA
99025 Newman Lake, WA
99026 Nine Mile Falls, WA
99027 City Of Spokane Valley, WA
99027 Otis Orchards, WA
99027 Spokane Valley, WA
99029 Reardan, WA
99030 Rockford, WA
99031 Spangle, WA
99032 Sprague, WA
99033 Tekoa, WA
99034 Tumtum, WA
99036 Valleyford, WA
99037 City Of Spokane Valley, WA
99037 Spokane Valley, WA
99037 Veradale, WA
99039 Waverly, WA
99040 Wellpinit, WA

991

99101 Addy, WA
99102 Albion, WA
99103 Almira, WA
99104 Belmont, WA
99104 Farmington, WA
99105 Benge, WA
99107 Boyds, WA
99107 Kettle Falls, WA
99109 Chewelah, WA
99110 Clayton, WA
99111 Colfax, WA
99111 Diamond, WA
99113 Colton, WA
99114 Colville, WA
99115 Coulee City, WA
99116 Coulee Dam, WA
99117 Creston, WA
99118 Curlew, WA
99119 Cusick, WA
99121 Danville, WA
99122 Davenport, WA
99122 Deer Meadows, WA
99122 Seven Bays, WA
99123 Electric City, WA
99124 Elmer City, WA
99125 Endicott, WA
99126 Evans, WA
99126 Kettle Falls, WA
99128 Farmington, WA
99129 Fruitland, WA
99129 Hunters, WA
99130 Garfield, WA
99131 Gifford, WA
99133 Grand Coulee, WA
99134 Harrington, WA
99135 Hartline, WA
99136 Hay, WA
99137 Hunters, WA
99138 Inchelium, WA
99139 Ione, WA
99140 Keller, WA
99141 Kettle Falls, WA
99143 Lacrosse, WA
99144 Lamona, WA
99144 Odessa, WA
99146 Laurier, WA
99147 Creston, WA
99147 Lincoln, WA
99148 Loon Lake, WA
99149 Malden, WA
99150 Malo, WA
99151 Marcus, WA
99152 Metaline, WA
99153 Metaline Falls, WA
99154 Harrington, WA
99154 Mohler, WA
99155 Nespelem, WA
99156 Newport, WA
99157 Northport, WA
99158 Oakesdale, WA
99159 Odessa, WA
99160 Kettle Falls, WA
99160 Orient, WA
99161 Palouse, WA
99163 Pullman, WA
99164 Pullman, WA
99166 Republic, WA
99167 Rice, WA
99169 Ritzville, WA
99170 Plaza, WA
99170 Rosalia, WA
99171 Saint John, WA
99173 Springdale, WA
99174 Steptoe, WA
99176 Thornton, WA
99179 Uniontown, WA
99180 Usk, WA
99181 Valley, WA
99185 Wilbur, WA

992

99201 Spokane, WA
99202 Spokane, WA
99203 Spokane, WA
99204 Spokane, WA
99205 Spokane, WA
99206 Spokane, WA
99206 Spokane Valley, WA
99207 Spokane, WA
99208 Spokane, WA
99209 Spokane, WA
99210 Spokane, WA
99211 Spokane, WA
99211 Spokane Valley, WA
99212 Millwood, WA
99212 Spokane, WA
99212 Spokane Valley, WA
99213 Spokane, WA
99213 Spokane Valley, WA
99214 Spokane, WA
99214 Spokane Valley, WA
99215 Spokane, WA
99215 Spokane Valley, WA
99216 Spokane, WA
99216 Spokane Valley, WA
99217 Spokane, WA
99218 Spokane, WA
99219 Spokane, WA
99219 Sunset Hill, WA
99220 Spokane, WA
99223 Spokane, WA
99223 Spokane Valley, WA
99224 Spokane, WA
99228 Spokane, WA
99251 Spokane, WA
99252 Spokane, WA
99256 Spokane, WA
99258 Spokane, WA
99260 Spokane, WA

993

99301 Pasco, WA
99302 Pasco, WA
99302 Tri Cities, WA
99320 Benton City, WA
99321 Beverly, WA
99322 Bickleton, WA
99323 Burbank, WA
99324 College Place, WA
99326 Connell, WA
99328 Dayton, WA
99329 Dixie, WA
99330 Eltopia, WA
99333 Hooper, WA
99335 Kahlotus, WA
99336 Kennewick, WA
99337 Kennewick, WA
99338 Kennewick, WA
99341 Lind, WA
99343 Mesa, WA
99344 Hatton, WA
99344 Othello, WA
99345 Paterson, WA
99346 Plymouth, WA
99347 Pomeroy, WA
99348 Prescott, WA
99349 Desert Aire, WA
99349 Mattawa, WA
99350 Prosser, WA
99352 Richland, WA
99353 Richland, WA
99353 West Richland, WA
99354 Richland, WA
99356 Roosevelt, WA
99357 Royal City, WA
99359 Starbuck, WA
99360 Lowden, WA
99360 Touchet, WA
99361 Waitsburg, WA
99362 Walla Walla, WA
99363 Wallula, WA
99371 Washtucna, WA

994

99401 Anatone, WA
99402 Asotin, WA
99403 Clarkston, WA

995

99501 Anchorage, AK
99502 Anchorage, AK
99503 Anchorage, AK
99504 Anchorage, AK
99505 Anchorage, AK
99505 Fort Richardson, AK
99505 Jber, AK
99506 Anchorage, AK
99506 Elmendorf Afb, AK
99506 Jber, AK
99507 Anchorage, AK
99508 Anchorage, AK
99509 Anchorage, AK
99510 Anchorage, AK
99511 Anchorage, AK
99513 Anchorage, AK
99514 Anchorage, AK
99515 Anchorage, AK
99516 Anchorage, AK
99517 Anchorage, AK
99518 Anchorage, AK
99519 Anchorage, AK
99520 Anchorage, AK
99521 Anchorage, AK
99522 Anchorage, AK
99523 Anchorage, AK
99524 Anchorage, AK
99529 Anchorage, AK
99530 Anchorage, AK
99540 Anchorage, AK
99540 Bird Creek, AK
99540 Indian, AK
99545 Kongiganak, AK
99546 Adak, AK
99547 Atka, AK
99548 Chignik, AK
99548 Chignik Lake, AK
99549 King Salmon, AK
99549 Port Heiden, AK
99550 Port Lions, AK
99551 Akiachak, AK
99552 Akiak, AK
99553 Akutan, AK
99554 Alakanuk, AK
99555 Aleknagik, AK
99556 Anchor Point, AK
99556 Nikolaevsk, AK
99557 Aniak, AK
99557 Chuathbaluk, AK
99557 Stony River, AK
99558 Anvik, AK
99559 Atmautluak, AK
99559 Bethel, AK
99559 Napaskiak, AK
99559 Newtok, AK
99561 Chefornak, AK
99563 Chevak, AK
99564 Chignik, AK
99565 Chignik Lagoon, AK
99566 Chitina, AK
99567 Chugiak, AK
99568 Clam Gulch, AK
99569 Clarks Point, AK
99571 Adak, AK
99571 Cold Bay, AK
99571 Nelson Lagoon, AK
99572 Cooper Landing, AK
99573 Copper Center, AK
99574 Chenega Bay, AK
99574 Cordova, AK
99575 Crooked Creek, AK
99576 Dillingham, AK
99576 Koliganek, AK
99576 Twin Hills, AK
99577 Eagle River, AK
99578 Eek, AK
99579 Egegik, AK
99580 Ekwok, AK
99581 Emmonak, AK
99583 False Pass, AK
99585 Marshall, AK
99586 Gakona, AK
99586 Miers Lake, AK
99586 Slana, AK
99587 Girdwood, AK
99588 Glennallen, AK
99589 Goodnews Bay, AK
99590 Grayling, AK
99591 Saint George Island, AK
99591 Saint Paul Island, AK
99599 Anchorage, AK

996

99602 Holy Cross, AK
99603 English Bay, AK
99603 Fritz Creek, AK
99603 Halibut Cove, AK
99603 Homer, AK
99603 Kachemak, AK
99603 Nanwalek, AK
99603 Port Graham, AK
99604 Hooper Bay, AK
99605 Hope, AK
99606 Iliamna, AK
99606 Kokhanok, AK
99607 Kalskag, AK
99608 Karluk, AK
99609 Kasigluk, AK
99610 Kasilof, AK
99611 Kenai, AK
99611 Nikiski, AK
99612 King Cove, AK
99613 Igiugig, AK
99613 King Salmon, AK
99614 Kipnuk, AK
99615 Akhiok, AK
99615 Chiniak, AK
99615 Kodiak, AK
99619 Kodiak, AK
99620 Kotlik, AK
99621 Kwethluk, AK
99622 Kwigillingok, AK
99623 Big Lake, AK
99623 Houston, AK
99623 Meadow Lake, AK
99623 Wasilla, AK
99624 Larsen Bay, AK
99625 Levelock, AK
99626 Lower Kalskag, AK
99627 Mc Grath, AK
99628 Manokotak, AK
99629 Wasilla, AK
99630 Mekoryuk, AK
99631 Moose Pass, AK
99632 Mountain Village, AK
99633 Naknek, AK
99634 Napakiak, AK
99635 Kenai, AK
99635 Nikiski, AK
99636 New Stuyahok, AK
99637 Bethel, AK
99637 Toksook Bay, AK
99638 Nikolski, AK
99639 Ninilchik, AK
99640 Nondalton, AK
99641 Nunapitchuk, AK
99643 Old Harbor, AK
99644 Ouzinkie, AK
99645 Palmer, AK
99647 Iliamna, AK
99647 Pedro Bay, AK
99648 Perryville, AK
99649 Pilot Point, AK
99650 Pilot Station, AK
99651 Platinum, AK
99652 Big Lake, AK
99652 Wasilla, AK
99653 Port Alsworth, AK
99654 Wasilla, AK
99655 Quinhagak, AK
99656 Red Devil, AK
99657 Russian Mission, AK
99658 Saint Marys, AK
99659 Saint Michael, AK
99660 Saint Paul, AK
99660 Saint Paul Island, AK
99660 St Paul, AK
99661 Sand Point, AK
99662 Scammon Bay, AK
99663 Seldovia, AK
99664 Seward, AK
99665 Shageluk, AK
99666 Nunam Iqua, AK
99667 Skwentna, AK
99668 Sleetmute, AK
99669 Soldotna, AK
99670 South Naknek, AK
99671 Stebbins, AK
99672 Sterling, AK
99674 Chickaloon, AK
99674 Sutton, AK
99675 Mc Grath, AK
99675 Takotna, AK
99676 Talkeetna, AK
99677 Cordova, AK
99677 Tatitlek, AK
99678 Togiak, AK
99679 Bethel, AK
99679 Tuluksak, AK
99680 Bethel, AK
99680 Tuntutuliak, AK
99681 Tununak, AK
99682 Tyonek, AK
99683 Trapper Creek, AK
99683 Willow, AK
99684 Unalakleet, AK
99685 Unalaska, AK
99686 Valdez, AK
99687 Wasilla, AK
99688 Willow, AK
99689 Yakutat, AK
99690 Bethel, AK
99690 Nightmute, AK
99691 Mc Grath, AK
99691 Nikolai, AK
99692 Dutch Harbor, AK
99692 Unalaska, AK
99693 Girdwood, AK
99693 Whittier, AK
99694 Houston, AK
99695 Anchorage, AK
99697 Kodiak, AK

997

99701 Fairbanks, AK
99702 Eielson Afb, AK
99702 Fairbanks, AK
99703 Fort Wainwright, AK
99704 Clear, AK
99704 Nenana, AK
99705 Fairbanks, AK
99705 North Pole, AK
99706 Fairbanks, AK
99707 Fairbanks, AK
99708 Fairbanks, AK
99709 Fairbanks, AK
99710 Fairbanks, AK
99710 Steese, AK
99711 Badger, AK
99711 Fairbanks, AK
99712 Fairbanks, AK
99714 Fairbanks, AK
99714 Salcha, AK
99716 Fairbanks, AK
99716 Two Rivers, AK
99720 Allakaket, AK
99721 Anaktuvuk Pass, AK
99722 Arctic Village, AK
99723 Barrow, AK
99724 Beaver, AK
99725 Ester, AK
99726 Bettles Field, AK
99727 Buckland, AK
99729 Cantwell, AK
99730 Central, AK
99731 Delta Junction, AK
99731 Fort Greely, AK
99732 Chicken, AK
99733 Circle, AK

99734 Prudhoe Bay, AK
99736 Deering, AK
99737 Delta Junction, AK
99737 Dot Lake, AK
99738 Eagle, AK
99739 Elim, AK
99740 Fort Yukon, AK
99741 Galena, AK
99742 Gambell, AK
99743 Healy, AK
99744 Anderson, AK
99744 Nenana, AK
99745 Hughes, AK
99746 Huslia, AK
99747 Kaktovik, AK
99748 Kaltag, AK
99749 Kiana, AK
99750 Kivalina, AK
99751 Kobuk, AK
99752 Kotzebue, AK
99753 Koyuk, AK
99754 Koyukuk, AK
99755 Denali National Park, AK
99756 Manley Hot Springs, AK
99757 Lake Minchumina, AK
99758 Minto, AK
99759 Barrow, AK
99759 Point Lay, AK
99760 Nenana, AK
99761 Noatak, AK
99762 Diomede, AK
99762 Golovin, AK
99762 Little Diomede, AK
99762 Nome, AK
99763 Noorvik, AK
99764 Northway, AK
99765 Nulato, AK
99766 Point Hope, AK
99767 Fairbanks, AK
99767 Rampart, AK
99768 Ruby, AK
99769 Savoonga, AK
99770 Selawik, AK
99771 Shaktoolik, AK
99772 Shishmaref, AK
99773 Shungnak, AK
99774 Stevens Village, AK
99775 Fairbanks, AK
99776 Tanacross, AK
99776 Tok, AK
99777 Tanana, AK
99778 Teller, AK
99780 Mentasta Lake, AK
99780 Tok, AK
99781 Venetie, AK
99782 Wainwright, AK
99783 Wales, AK
99784 White Mountain, AK
99785 Brevig Mission, AK
99786 Ambler, AK
99788 Chalkyitsik, AK
99788 Fort Yukon, AK
99789 Barrow, AK
99789 Nuiqsut, AK
99790 Fairbanks, AK
99791 Atqasuk, AK
99791 Barrow, AK

998

99801 Juneau, AK
99802 Juneau, AK
99803 Juneau, AK
99811 Juneau, AK
99812 Juneau, AK
99820 Angoon, AK
99821 Auke Bay, AK
99821 Juneau, AK
99824 Douglas, AK
99824 Juneau, AK
99825 Elfin Cove, AK
99826 Gustavus, AK
99827 Haines, AK
99829 Hoonah, AK
99830 Kake, AK
99832 Pelican, AK
99833 Kupreanof, AK
99833 Petersburg, AK
99835 Sitka, AK
99836 Port Alexander, AK
99836 Sitka, AK
99840 Skagway, AK
99841 Tenakee Springs, AK
99850 Juneau, AK

999

99901 Edna Bay, AK
99901 Kasaan, AK
99901 Ketchikan, AK
99901 Naukati Bay, AK
99901 Saxman, AK
99903 Ketchikan, AK
99903 Meyers Chuck, AK
99918 Coffman Cove, AK
99918 Ketchikan, AK
99919 Ketchikan, AK
99919 Thorne Bay, AK
99921 Craig, AK
99922 Hydaburg, AK
99923 Hyder, AK
99925 Klawock, AK
99926 Metlakatla, AK
99927 Point Baker, AK
99928 Ward Cove, AK
99929 Wrangell, AK
99950 Edna Bay, AK
99950 Kasaan, AK
99950 Ketchikan, AK

Area Codes by State and City

Alabama

City	Area Code
Abbeville	334
Abel	256
Abernant	205
Acmar	205
Adamsville	205
Addison	256
Adger	205
Akron	205
Ala Gas Corp	205
Ala Power Co	334
Ala State Govt Mail	334
Alabama A And M	256
Alabama Port	251
Alabama Power Co	205
Alabaster	205
Alberta	334
Albertville	256
Alden	205
Alex City	256
Alexander City	256
Alexandria	256
Alfa Ins Co	334
Aliceville	205
Allen	251
Allgood	205
Alma	251
Almond	256
Alpine	256
Alton	205
Altoona	205
Andalusia	334
Anderson	256
Annemanie	334
Anniston	256
Aquilla	251
Arab	256
Ardmore	256
Ariton	334
Arkadelphia	256
Arley	256
Arlington	334
Armstrong	334
Ashford	334
Ashland	256
Ashville	205
Athens	256
Atmore	251
Attalla	256
Atwood	205
Auburn	334
Auburn Univ	334
Auburn University	334
Auburn Unvrsty	334
Autaugaville	334
Avondale	205
Axis	251
Baileyton	256
Bakerhill	334
Banks	334
Bankston	205
Barfield	256
Barlow	251
Barney	205
Bass Anglers Sports Soc	334
Bassetts Creek	251
Battens Crossroads	334
Bay Minette	251
Bayou La Batre	251
Bayou Labatre	251
Bazemore	205
Bear Creek	205
Beatrice	251
Beaverton	205
Belk	205
Bell Fountain	251
Bellamy	205
Belle Mina	256
Bellwood	334
Benton	334
Berry	205
Bertha	334
Bess	205
Bessemer	205
Bexar	205
Bham	205
Big Cove	256
Bigbee	251
Billingsley	205
Birmingham	205
Birmingham Southern College	205
Black	334
Bladon Springs	251
Blossburg	205
Blount Springs	205
Blountsville	205
Blue Cross-Shield	205
Blue Mountain	256
Blue Springs	334
Bluff	205
Bluff Park	205
Bluff Spring	256
Boaz	256
Boligee	205
Bolinger	251
Bolling	334
Bon Air	256
Bon Secour	251
Booth	334
Borden Springs	256
Boykin	334
Bradley	334
Branchville	205
Brantley	334
Brdn Sprngs	256
Bremen	256
Brent	205
Brewton	251
Bridgeport	256
Brierfield	205
Brighton	205
Brilliant	205
Bromley	251
Brookley Field	251
Brookley Fld	251
Brooklyn	251
Brookside	205
Brookwood	205
Brownsboro	256
Brundidge	334
Bryant	256
Bucks	251
Buena Vista	251
Buhl	205
Burkville	334
Burnt Corn	251
Burntout	256
Burnwell	205
Business Reply Mail	205
Butler	205
Bynum	256
Cahaba Heights	205
Cahaba Hts	205
Calera	205
Caller Boxes	205
Calvert	251
Camden	334
Camp Hill	256
Campbell	334
Campbells Crossroads	256
Canoe	251
Capshaw	256
Carbon Hill	205
Cardiff	205
Carlton	251
Carr Mill	256
Carrollton	205
Carson	251
Castleberry	251
Catherine	334
Cecil	334
Cedar Bluff	256
Center Point	205
Centerpoint	205
Central	334
Centre	256
Centreville	205
Chance	334
Chancellor	334
Chapman	334
Chastang	251
Chatom	251
Chelsea	205
Cherokee	256
Chestnut Grove	334
Chickasaw	251
Childersburg	256
Chisolm	334
Choccolocco	256
Christiana	256
Chrysler	251
Chulafinnee	256
Chunchula	251
Citronelle	251
Claiborne	251
Clanton	205
Clay	205
Clayhatchee	334
Clayton	334
Cleveland	205
Clinton	205
Clio	334
Clopton	334
Cloverdale	256
Coal City	205
Coal Fire	205
Coalburg	205
Coaling	205
Coatopa	205
Cochrane	205
Coden	251
Coffee Spgs	334
Coffee Springs	334
Coffeeville	251
Coker	205
Collinsville	256
Colonial Mortgage	334
Columbia	334
Columbiana	205
Comer	334
Compass Bank	205
Concord	205
Cook Springs	205
Coosa Pines	256
Coosada	334
Copeland	251
Cordova	205
Corinth	256
Cortelyou	251
Cottondale	205
Cottonton	334
Cottonwood	334
Courtland	256
Cowarts	334
Coy	334
Cragford	256
Crane Hill	256
Creola	251
Crestline	205
Crestline Heights	205
Crestline Hts	205
Cropwell	205
Crossville	256
Cuba	205
Cullman	256
Cusseta	334
Cypress	205
Dadeville	256
Daleville	334
Damascus	251
Dannelly	334
Danville	256
Daphne	251
Dauphin Island	251
Dauphin Islnd	251
Daviston	256
Dawson	256
Dayton	334
De Armanville	256
Deatsville	334
Decatur	256
Deer Park	251
Delmar	205
Delta	256
Demopolis	334
Dept Of Treas Bur Accts	205
Detroit	205
Dickert	256
Dickinson	251
Dixiana	205
Dixie	334
Dixons Mills	334
Dixonville	251
Docena	205
Dolomite	205
Dora	205
Dothan	334
Double Spgs	205
Double Springs	205
Douglas	205
Dozier	334
Duncanville	205
Dutton	256
E Tallassee	334
East Brewton	251
East Gadsden	256
East Tallassee	334
Eastaboga	256
Eastside	205
Echo	334
Echola	205
Eclectic	334
Eden	205
Edwardsville	256
Egreen	251
Eight Mile	251
Elba	334
Elberta	251
Eldridge	205
Elkmont	256
Elliotsville	205
Elliotsvl	205
Elliotsvle	205
Elmore	334
Elrod	205
Elsanor	251
Emelle	205
Empire	205
English Village	205
Ensley	205
Enterprise	334
Eoline	205
Epes	205
Eprise	334
Equality	334
Erin	256
Estillfork	256
Ethelsville	205
Eufaula	334
Eunola	334
Eutaw	205
Eva	256
Evergreen	251
Excel	251
Fabius	256
Fackler	256
Fair Hope	251
Fairfax	334
Fairfield	205
Fairhope	251
Falkville	256
Farmersville	251
Faunsdale	334
Fayette	205
Fellowship	251
Fernbank	205
First Alabama Bank	334
Fishhead	256
Fitzpatrick	334
Five Points	334
Flat Rock	256
Flomaton	251
Florala	334
Florence	256
Foley	251
Forest Home	334
Forestdale	205
Forester Chapel	256
Forkland	334
Fort Davis	334
Fort Deposit	334
Fort Mc Clellan	256
Fort Mitchell	334
Fort Payne	256
Fort Rucker	334
Fosters	205
Fountain	251
Franklin	251
Frankville	251
Frisco City	251
Fruitdale	251
Fruithurst	256
Ft Mc Clellan	256
Ft Mcclellan	256
Ft Payne	256
Fulton	251
Fulton Springs	205
Fultondale	205
Furman	251
Fyffe	256
Gadsden	256
Gainestown	251
Gainesville	205
Gallant	205
Gallion	334
Gantt	334
Garden City	256
Gardendale	205
Gateswood	251
Gaylesville	256
Geiger	205
Geneva	334
Georgetown	251
Georgiana	334
Geraldine	256
Gibsonville	256
Gilbertown	251
Glen Allen	205
Glen City	205
Glencoe	256
Glenwood	334
Goldville	256
Goodsprings	205
Goodwater	256
Goodway	251
Gordo	205
Gordon	334
Goshen	334
Gosport	251
Grady	334
Graham	256
Grand Bay	251
Grangeburg	334
Grant	256
Gravleeton	205
Grayson	205
Grayson Valley	205
Graysville	205
Green Pond	205
Greensboro	334
Greenville	334
Grimes	334
Grove Hill	251
Groveoak	256
Guin	205
Gulf Crest	251
Gulf Shores	251
Gunter A F B	334
Gunter A F S	334
Gunter Afb	334
Gunter Afs	334
Gunter Afs-Eci	334
Gunter Eci	334
Guntersville	256
Gurley	256
Hackleburg	205
Hacoda	334
Haleburg	334
Haleyville	205
Hamilton	205
Hammondville	256
Hampton Cove	256
Hanceville	256
Hardaway	334
Harkins Crossroads	256
Harpersville	205
Harrisburg	205
Hartford	334
Hartselle	256
Harvest	256
Hatchechubbee	334
Havana	205
Hawk	256
Hawthorn	251
Hawthorne	251
Hayden	205
Hayneville	334
Haywood	256
Hazel Green	256
Headland	334
Healing Springs	251
Heflin	256
Helena	205
Henagar	256
Heron Bay	251
Higdon	256
Highbluff	334
Highland	256
Highland Home	334
Highland Lake	205
Hightower	256
Hillsboro	256
Hodges	205
Hodgesville	334
Hokes Bluff	256
Hollins	256
Hollis Crossroads	256
Holly Pond	256
Hollytree	256
Hollywood	256
Holt	205
Holy Trinity	334
Homewd	205
Homewood	205
Honoraville	334
Hoods Crossroads	205
Hoover	205
Hope Hull	334
Hopewell	205
Horton	205
Houston	205
Hueytown	205
Huffman	205
Huggers Landing	251
Huntsville	256
Huntsville Utilities	256
Hurtsboro	334
Huxford	251
Hybart	334
Hytop	256
Idaho	256
Ider	256
Indian Spgs	205
Indian Springs	205
Indian Springs Village	205
Indn Spgs Vlg	205
Intergraph Corporation	256
Irondale	205
Irvington	251
Ivalee	256
Jachin	205
Jack	334
Jackson	251
Jacksons Gap	256
Jacksonville	256
Jasper	205
Jefferson	334
Jefferson Park	205
Jemison	205
Jones	334
Joppa	256
Josephine	251
Kansas	205
Keego	251
Kellerman	205
Kelly Springs	334
Kellyton	256
Kennedy	205
Kent	334
Killen	256
Kimberly	205
Kingville	205
Kinsey	334
Kinston	334
Knoxville	205
Koenton	251

City	Area Code
La Nett	334
Laceys Spring	256
Laf Ayette	334
Lafayette	334
Lake View	205
Lanett	334
Langdale	334
Langston	256
Lapine	334
Lavaca	205
Lawley	334
Lawrenceville	334
Leeds	205
Leesburg	256
Leighton	256
Lemoyne	251
Lenox	251
Leroy	251
Lester	256
Letohatchee	334
Levelroad	256
Lexington	256
Liberty Highlands	205
Libertyville	334
Lillian	251
Lincoln	205
Linden	334
Lineville	256
Lisman	205
Little Brooklyn	251
Little River	251
Livingston	205
Loachapoka	334
Lockhart	334
Locust Fork	205
Logan	256
Louisville	334
Low Peach Tre	334
Lower Peach Tree	334
Lowndesboro	334
Loxley	251
Luverne	334
Lwr Pch Tree	334
Lynn	205
Macedonia	256
Madison	256
Madrid	334
Mafb Gun Annx	334
Magazine	251
Magnolia	334
Magnolia Spgs	251
Magnolia Springs	251
Malcolm	251
Malone	256
Malvern	334
Maplesville	334
Marbury	334
Margaret	205
Marion	334
Marion Jct	334
Marion Junction	334
Marvel	205
Master Charge	256
Mathews	334
Maxwell Afb	334
Maxwell Afb Gunter Annex	334
Maylene	205
Maytown	205
Mc Calla	205
Mc Cullough	251
Mc Intosh	251
Mc Kenzie	334
Mc Shan	205
Mc Williams	251
Mccullough	251
Mckenzie	334
Mcmullen	205
Meadowbrook	205
Megargel	251
Mellow Valley	256
Melvin	251
Mentone	256
Meridianville	256
Mexia	251
Midfield	205
Midland City	334
Midway	334
Miflin	251
Millbrook	334
Millers Ferry	334
Millerville	256
Millport	205
Millry	251
Minter	251
Mobile	251
Mobile Gov Plz	251
Mobile P&dc	251
Mon Louis	251
Monroeville	251
Montevallo	205
Montg	334
Montgomery	334
Montgomery Business Reply Ma	334
Montrose	251
Moody	205
Mooresville	256
Morris	205
Morrisons Cafeteria	251
Morvin	334
Motley	256
Moulton	256
Moundville	205
Mount Hebron	205
Mount Hope	256
Mount Meigs	334
Mount Olive	205
Mount Vernon	251
Mountain Brk	205
Mountain Brook	205
Mountain Creek	334
Mtgy	334
Mtn Brook	205
Mulga	205
Munford	256
Munitions Missle Com Sch	256
Muscadine	256
Muscle Shoals	256
Mville	251
Myrtlewood	334
N Port	205
Nanafalia	334
Natural Brg	205
Natural Bridge	205
Nauvoo	205
Needham	205
New Brockton	334
New Castle	205
New Hope	256
New Market	256
New Site	256
Newbern	334
Newell	256
Newton	334
Newville	334
Nixburg	334
Normal	256
North Florence	256
North Johns	205
North Port	205
Northport	205
Notasulga	334
Nport	205
Oak Grove	256
Oak Hill	251
Oakhill	251
Oakman	205
Oakwood College	256
Odenville	205
Ofelia	256
Ohatchee	256
Oneonta	205
Opelika	334
Opp	334
Orange Beach	251
Orrville	334
Overton	205
Owens Cross Roads	256
Owens X Rds	256
Owens X Roads	256
Oxford	256
Oyster Bay	251
Ozark	334
Paint Rock	256
Palmerdale	205
Panola	205
Pansey	334
Parrish	205
Patsburg	334
Pelham	205
Pell City	205
Pennington	205
Perdido	251
Perdido Beach	251
Perdue Hill	251
Perote	334
Peterman	251
Peterson	205
Petrey	334
Phenix City	334
Phil Campbell	205
Pickensville	205
Piedmont	256
Pike Road	334
Pinckard	334
Pine Apple	251
Pine Hill	334
Pine Level	334
Pinegrove	251
Pinson	205
Pisgah	256
Pittsview	334
Pl Grove	205
Plantersville	334
Pleasant Grove	205
Pleasant Grv	205
Pleasant Home	334
Point Clear	251
Pollard	251
Praco	205
Prairie	334
Prattville	334
Press Register Inc	251
Prestwick	251
Prichard	251
Princeton	256
Pville	334
Pyriton	256
Quinton	205
Ragland	205
Rainbow City	256
Rainsville	256
Ralph	205
Ramer	334
Ranburne	256
Randolph	205
Range	251
Rbc	256
Red Bay	256
Red Level	334
Redstone Arsenal	256
Redstone Central	256
Redstone Fed Credit Union	256
Reece City	256
Reform	205
Regions Bank	205
Rehobeth	334
Remlap	205
Repton	251
Riderwood	205
Ridgeville	256
River Falls	334
Riverchase	205
Riverside	205
Riverview	334
Roanoke	334
Roba	334
Robertsdale	251
Rockford	256
Rockledge	256
Roebuck Plaza	205
Rogersville	256
Rome	334
Romulus	205
Rosa	205
Rose Hill	205
Rosinton	251
Ruffner	205
Russellville	256
Rutledge	334
Ryland	256
S S Payment Ctr	205
Safford	334
Saginaw	205
Saint Elmo	251
Saint Stephens	251
Salem	334
Salipta	251
Saltaire	251
Samantha	205
Samford University	205
Samson	334
Sand Rock	256
Sandrock	256
Saragossa	205
Saraland	251
Sardis	334
Sardis City	256
Satsuma	251
Sawyerville	334
Sayre	205
Scottsboro	256
Scyrene	251
Seaboard	251
Seale	334
Searles	205
Section	256
Selma	334
Seminole	251
Semmes	251
Shakespeare	334
Shannon	205
Shawmut	334
Sheffield	256
Shelby	205
Shinebone	256
Shoal Creek	205
Shorter	334
Shorterville	334
Sikesville	256
Silas	251
Siluria	205
Silver Cross	251
Silverhill	251
Sipsey	205
Skipperville	334
Skyland	205
Slocomb	334
Smiths	334
Smiths Sta	334
Smiths Station	334
Snead	205
Snow Hill	251
Snow Hl	251
Snowhill	251
Somerville	256
South Highlands	205
Southside	256
Spanish Fort	251
Spring Garden	256
Springville	205
Sprott	334
Spruce Pine	205
St Stephens	251
Stansel	205
Stanton	334
Stapleton	251
State Dept Industrial Relat	334
State Farm Ins	205
State Of Alabama Income Tax	334
State Of Alabama Revenue Dep	334
Steele	205
Sterrett	205
Stevenson	256
Stewart	205
Stockton	251
Straight Mountain	205
Straughn	334
Suggsville	251
Sulligent	205
Sumiton	205
Summerdale	251
Sumterville	205
Sunflower	251
Sunny South	334
Sweet Water	334
Sycamore	256
Sylacauga	256
Sylvan Spgs	205
Sylvan Springs	205
Sylvania	256
Talladega	256
Tallassee	334
Tanner	256
Tarrant	205
Taylor	334
Theodore	251
Thomaston	334
Thomasville	334
Thorsby	205
Three Notch	334
Tibbie	251
Timber Creek	251
Titus	334
Toney	256
Town Creek	256
Townley	205
Toxey	205
Trafford	205
Trenton	256
Triana	256
Trinity	256
Troy	334
Troy State University	334
Trussville	205
Turnerville	251
Tusc	205
Tuscaloosa	205
Tuscumbia	256
Tuskegee	334
Tuskegee Inst	334
Tuskegee Institute	334
Tuskegee University	334
Tyler	334
U S Corps Of Engineers	251
Union Grove	256
Union Springs	334
Uniontown	334
Univ Of Alabama Bir	205
Univ Of Alabama Hospital	205
Univ Of Alabama Hsv	256
Univ Of North Ala	256
University Of Alabama	205
University Of South Alabama	251
Uriah	251
Valhermoso Sp	256
Valhermoso Spg	256
Valhermoso Springs	256
Valley	334
Valley Grande	334
Valley Head	256
Vance	205
Vandiver	205
Vanity Fair Mills	251
Verbena	205
Vernant Park	251
Vernon	205
Vestavia	205
Vestavia Hills	205
Vestavia Hls	205
Veterans Admin. Fac.	334
Veterans Hospital	205
Victoria	334
Vina	256
Vincent	205
Vinegar Bend	251
Vinemont	256
Vlhrmoso Spgs	256
Vredenburgh	334
Wachovia Bank	205
Wadley	256
Wagarville	251
Walker Spgs	251
Walker Springs	251
Wallace	251
Walnut Grove	205
Ward	205
Warrior	205
Waterford	334
Waterloo	256
Watson	205
Watts Mill	256
Wattsville	205
Waverly	256, 334
Weaver	256
Webb	334
Wedowee	256
Wellington	256
Wenonah	205
Weogufka	256
West Blocton	205
West Greene	205
Westover	205
Wetumpka	334
Whatley	251
Whistler	251
Whitehead	256
Whites Chapel	205
Whitfield	205
Wilmer	251
Wilsonville	205
Wilton	205
Winfield	205
Wing	334
Woodland	256
Woodstock	205
Woodville	256
Yantley	205
Yarbo	251
Yellow Pine	251
York	205

Alaska

City	Area Code
All Points	907

American Samoa

City	Area Code
All Points	691

Arizona

City	Area Code
Agua Linda	520
Aguila	928
Ajo	520
Allentown	928
Alpine	928
Amado	520
Anthem	623
Apache Jct	480, 928
Apache Junction	480
Arivaca	520
Arizona City	520
Arizona Medical Center	520
Arizona State Lottery	480
Arizona State Univ	480
Arizona State University	480
Arlington	623
Ash Fork	928
Asu	480
Avondale	623
Avondale Goodyear	623
Avondale-Goodyear	623
Baby Rock	928
Bacobi	928
Bagdad	928
Bapchule	520
Bay Acres	520
Beaver Dam	928
Bellemont	928
Bensch Ranch	928
Benson	520
Bisbee	520
Bisbee Jct	520
Bitahochee	928
Black Canyon City	623
Black Cyn Cty	623
Black Mesa	928
Blue	928

City	Area Code
Blue Gap	928
Bonita	520
Bouse	928
Bowie	520
Buckeye	623
Bullhead City	928
Burnt Water	928
Business Reply	520
Bylas	928
Cameron	928
Camp Verde	928
Cane Beds	928
Canelo	520
Canyon De Chelly National Mo	928
Carefree	480
Carmen	520
Casa Grande	520
Cascabel	520
Cashion	623
Catalina	520
Cave Creek	480
Cedar Ridge	928
Census Bureau	602
Central	928
Chambers	928
Chandler	480
Chandler Heights	480
Chandler Hts	480
Chilchinbito	928
Chinle	928
Chino Valley	928
Chiricahua National Monument	520
Chloride	928
Cibecue	928
Cibola	928
Circle City	623
Clarkdale	928
Clay Springs	928
Claypool	928
Clifton	928
Coal Mine Mesa	928
Cochise	520
Colorado City	928
Concho	928
Concho Valley	928
Congress	928
Continental	520
Coolidge	520
Copper Queen	520
Cordes Lakes	928
Cornfields	928
Cornville	928
Corona	520
Corona De Tuc	520
Corona De Tucson	520
Coronado	928
Cortaro	520
Cottonwood	928
Cottonwood Station	928
Cowlic	520
Cross Canyon	928
Crown King	623
Ctc	602
Dateland	928
Davis Monthan Afb	520
Dennebito	928
Dennehotso	928
Desert Hills	623
Dewey	928
Dilkon	928
Dm Afb	520
Dolan Springs	928
Dos Cabezas	520
Double Adobe	520
Douglas	520
Dragoon	520
Dudleyville	520
Duncan	928
Eagar	928
Eden	928
Ehrenberg	928
El Mirage	623
Eleven Mile	520
Eleven Mile Corner	520
Elfrida	520
Elgin	520
Eloy	520
Fairbank	520
First Mesa	928
Flagstaff	928
Florence	520
Forest Lakes	928
Fort Apache	928
Fort Defiance	928
Fort Grant	520
Fort Huachuca	520
Fort Lowell	520
Fort Mcdowell	480
Fort Mohave	928
Fort Thomas	928
Fountain Hills	480
Fountain Hls	480
Fredonia	928
Fresnal Canyon	520
Fry	520
Ft Grant	520
Ft Lowell	520
Gadsden	928
Ganado	928
Gbafaf	623
Gila Bend	928
Gilbert	480
Gleeson	520
Glendale	602, 623
Glendale Luke Afb	623
Globe	928
Gold Canyon	480
Golden Shores	928
Golden Valley	928
Goodyear	623
Grand Canyon	928
Grand Canyon Caverns	928
Grand Canyon National Park	928
Grasshopper Junction	928
Gray Mountain	928
Greasewood	928
Greasewood Springs	928
Greaterville	520
Green Valley	520
Greenehaven	928
Greer	928
Groom Creek	928
Gu Achi	520
Guadalupe	480
Hackberry	928
Hano	928
Happy Jack	928
Hard Rock	928
Harshaw	520
Havasu City	928
Havasupai Indian Reservation	928
Hawley Lake	928
Hayden	520
Heber	928
Hereford	520
Higley	480
Hilltop	520
Holbrook	928
Hopi Indian Reservation	928
Hotevilla	928
Houck	928
Huachuca City	520
Huachuca Terrace	520
Hualapai	928
Hubbell Trading Post Nationa	928
Humboldt	928
Hunters Point	928
I B M Corp	520
Immanuel Mission	928
Indian Wells	928
Iron Springs	928
Jacob Lake	928
Jeddito	928
Jerome	928
Joseph City	928
Kaibab	928
Kaibab Indian Reservation	928
Kaibeto	928
Kansas Settlement	520
Kayenta	928
Keams Canyon	928
Kearny	520
Kin-Li-Chee	928
Kingman	928
Kino	520
Kinsley Ranch	520
Kirkland	928
Klagetoh	928
Klondyke	520
Kykotsmovi	928
Kykotsmovi Village	928
Lake Havasu City	928
Lake Mead Rancheros	928
Lake Montezuma	928
Lake Powell Mart	928
Lakeside	928
Laveen	602
Leupp	928
Leupp Corner	928
Litchfield	623
Litchfield Park	623
Litchfield Pk	623
Little Tucson	520
Littlefield	928
Lk Havasu Cty	928
Lk Montezuma	928
Lochiel	520
Low Mountain	928
Lowell	520
Lukachukai	928
Luke Afb	623
Lukeville	520
Lupton	928
Madera Canyon	520
Mammoth	520
Many Farms	928
Marana	520
Marble Canyon	928
Maricopa	520
Martinez Lake	928
Mayer	928
Mc Neal	520
Mcnary	928
Mcneal	520
Meadview	928
Mennonite Mission	928
Mesa	480, 928
Mescal	520
Mexican Water	928
Miami	928
Miracle Valley	520
Mishongnovi	928
Mission	520
Mobile	520
Moccasin	928
Moenave	928
Moenkopi	928
Mohave Valley	928
Morenci	928
Mormon Lake	928
Morristown	623
Mount Lemmon	520
Munds Park	928
Naco	520
Nau	928
Navajo Indian Reservation	928
Navajo Station	928
Nazlini	928
New Oraibi	928
New River	623
Nicksville	520
Nogales	520
North Rim	928
Northern Arizona University	928
Nutrioso	928
Oak Springs	928
Oatman	928
Old Oraibi	928
Oljato	928
Oracle	520
Oraibi	928
Oro Valley	520
Overgaard	928
Page	928
Palo Verde	623
Palominas	520
Paradise	520
Paradise Valley	480
Paradise Vly	480
Parker	928
Parker Lake	520
Parks	928
Parks Comm Po	928
Patagonia	520
Paul Spur	520
Paulden	928
Payson	928
Peach Springs	928
Pearce	520
Peeples Valley	928
Peeples Vly	928
Peoria	623
Peridot	928
Petrified For	928
Petrified Forest Natl Pk	928
Phoenix	480, 520, 602, 623, 928
Picacho	520
Pima	928
Pima Community College	520
Pine	928
Pine Springs	928
Pinedale	928
Pinetop	928
Pinon	928
Pipe Spring National Monumen	928
Pirtleville	520
Pisinemo	520
Pisinemo Trading Post	520
Polacca	928
Pomerene	520
Portal	520
Poston	928
Prescott	928
Prescott Valley	928
Prescott Vly	928
Quartzsite	928
Queen Creek	480, 520
Queen Valley	480
Querino	928
Rare Metals	928
Red Lake	928
Red Mesa	928
Red Rock	520
Red Valley	928
Redington	520
Richville	928
Rillito	520
Rimrock	928
Rincon	520
Rio Rico	520
Rio Verde	480
Rock Point	928
Rock Springs	623
Roll	928
Roosevelt	928
Rough Rock	928
Round Rock	928
Rucker	520
Sacaton	520
Saddlebrooke	520
Safford	928
Sahuarita	520
Saint David	520
Saint Johns	928
Saint Michaels	928
Salado	928
Salina	928
Salome	928
San Carlos	928
San Luis	928
San Manuel	520
San Simon	520
San Tan Valley	480
San Tan Vly	480
Sand Springs	928
Sanders	928
Santa Rita	520
Santa Rita Foothills	520
Sasabe	520
Scottsdale	480, 928
Second Mesa	928
Sedona	928
Seligman	928
Sells	520
Shipley	928
Shipolovi	928
Shongopovi	928
Shonto	928
Show Low	928
Shumway	928
Sichomovi	928
Sierra Bonita	520
Sierra Vista	520
Sil Nakaya	520
Skull Valley	928
Smoke Signal	928
Snowflake	928
Solomon	928
Somerton	928
Sonoita	520
South Bisbee	520
Spring Valley	928
Springerville	928
Springville	928
St Johns	928
St Michaels	928
Sta #10	928
Stanfield	520
Star Valley	928
Steamboat Canyon	928
Strawberry	928
Sun	520
Sun City	623
Sun City West	623
Sun Lakes	480
Sun Valley	928
Sunizona	520
Sunrise Springs	928
Sunset	520
Sunset Acres	928
Sunsites	520
Supai	928
Superior	520
Superstition Mtn	480
Suprston Mtn	480
Surprise	623
Surprise Dysart Retail	623
Tacna	928
Tahchee	928
Taylor	928
Teec Nos Pos	928
Tempe	480
Templ Bar Mar	928
Temple Bar Marina	928
Thatcher	928
Tintown	520
Tolacon	928
Tolani	928
Tolani Lakes	928
Tolleson	623
Toltec	520
Tombstone	520
Tonalea	928
Tonopah	623
Tonto Basin	928
Topawa	520
Topock	928
Toreva	928
Tortilla Flat	480
Toyei	928
Truxton	928
Tsail	928
Tsaile	928
Tse Bonita	928
Tsn	520
Tuba City	928
Tubac	520
Tucson	520
Tumacacori	520
Turkey Creek	520
Tusayan	928
Tuscon	520
Two Story	928
Univ Of Arizona	520
Upper Greasewood Trading Pos	928
Upper Wheatfields	928
Vail	520
Valentine	928
Valley Farms	520
Vamori	520
Vernon	928
Veterans Hospital	520
Virden	928
Waddell	623
Walpi	928
Warren	520
Wellton	928
Wenden	928
Whetstone	520
White Clay	928
White Hills	928
White Mountain Lake	928
White Mtn Lk	928
Whiteriver	928
Why	520
Wickenburg	928
Wide Ruins	928
Wikieup	928
Willcox	520
Williams	928
Willow Beach	928
Window Rock	928
Winkelman	520
Winslow	928
Winwood	520
Witch Wells	928
Wittmann	623
Woodruff	928
Woodsprings	928
Yarnell	928
Young	928
Youngtown	623
Ypg	928
Yucca	928
Yuma	928
Yuma Proving Ground	928

Arkansas

City	Area Code
Abbott	479
Aberdeen	870
Acorn	479
Adona	501
Air Base	501
Alco	870
Alexander	501
Algoa	870
Alicia	870
Alix	479
Alleene	870
Alma	479
Almyra	870
Alpena	870
Alpine	870
Alread	501
Altheimer	870
Altus	479
Amagon	870
Amity	870
Antoine	870
Aplin	501
Appleton	479
Arkadelphia	870
Arkansas City	870
Arkansas Post National Memor	870
Armorel	870
Arsenal	870
Arthur	501
Ash Flat	870
Ashdown	870
Ashton	870
Athens	870
Atkins	479
Aubrey	870
Augusta	870
Austin	501
Auvergne	870
Avery	870
Avoca	479
Back Gate	870
Balch	870
Bald Knob	501
Banks	870
Barling	479

City	Area Code
Barney	501
Barton	870
Bass	870
Bassett	870
Bates	479
Batesville	870
Baucum	501
Bauxite	501
Baxter	870
Bay	870
Bayou Meto	870
Bayou Metro	501
Bear	501
Bearden	870
Beaudry	501
Beaver	479
Bee Branch	501
Beebe	501
Beech Creek	870
Beech Grove	870
Beedeville	870
Beirne	870
Bella Vista	479
Bellaire	870
Belleville	479
Ben Lomond	870
Bengall	870
Benton	501
Bentonville	479
Berea	870
Bergman	870
Berlin	870
Berryville	870
Beryl	501
Bethel Heights	479
Bethel Hts	479
Beverage Town	501
Bexar	870
Big Flat	870
Big Fork	479
Bigelow	501
Biggers	870
Billstown	870
Bird Town	501
Birdeye	870
Biscoe	870
Bismarck	501
Black Fork	479
Black Oak	870
Black Rock	870
Blackfish	870
Blackton	870
Blackville	870
Blackwell	479
Blevins	870
Blue Hill	501
Blue Mountain	479
Blue Springs	501
Bluff City	870
Bluffton	479
Blytheville	870
Board Camp	479
Boles	479
Bonanza	479
Bonnerdale	501
Bono	870
Booker	501
Booneville	479
Boswell	870
Botkinburg	501
Boueff	870
Bovine	870
Bowen	870
Boydell	870
Bradford	501
Bradley	870
Bradley Quarters	870
Branch	479
Brewer	870
Brickeys	870
Briggsville	479
Brinkley	870
Brockwell	870
Brookland	870
Brown Springs	501
Brumley	501
Brummitt	870
Bruno	870
Brush Creek	870
Bryant	501
Buckner	870
Buckville	501
Buie	870
Bull Shoals	870
Burdette	870
Busch	479
Butlerville	501
Butterfield	501
Cabot	501
Caddo Gap	870
Caddo Valley	870
Calamine	870
Caldwell	870
Cale	870
Calico Rock	870
Calion	870
Calmer	870
Camden	870
Cammack Village	501
Cammack Vlg	501
Camp	870
Camp Robinson	501
Canaan	870
Cane Creek	870
Canehill	479
Caney Valley	870
Caraway	870
Carlisle	870
Carmel	870
Carrollton	870
Carthage	870
Casa	501
Cash	870
Casscoe	870
Catholic Point	501
Cave City	870
Cave Springs	479
Cecil	479
Cedarville	479
Center Grove	870
Center Point	870
Center Ridge	501
Centerton	479
Centerville	479
Central Baptist College	501
Central City	479, 501
Chanticleer	870
Charleston	479
Charlotte	870
Cherokee Village	870
Cherokee Vlg	870
Cherry Hill	501
Cherry Valley	870
Chester	479
Chicot	870
Chidester	870
Childress	870
Chimes	870
Choctaw	501
Clarendon	870
Clarkedale	870
Clarkridge	870
Clarksville	479
Cleveland	501
Clinton	501
Coal Hill	479
Cole Spur	870
Coleman	870
College Sta	501
College Station	501
Collins	870
Colt	870
Columbus	870
Combs	479
Cominto	870
Compton	870
Concord	870
Conway	501
Cord	870
Corinth	479
Cornerville	870
Corning	870
Cotter	870
Cotton Plant	870
Cove	870
Coy	501
Cozahome	870
Crabtree	501
Crawfordsville	870
Crawfordsvlle	870
Crigler	870
Crocketts Blf	870
Crocketts Bluff	870
Crossett	870
Crumrod	870
Crystal Hill	501
Culpeper	501
Curtis	870
Cushman	870
Cypress Valley	501
Dabney	501
Dalark	870
Dallas	479
Damascus	501
Danville	479
Dardanelle	479
Datto	870
Davenport	501
De Luce	870
De Queen	870
De Valls Blf	870
De Valls Bluff	870
De Witt	870
Deberrie	501
Decatur	479
Deer	870
Degray	870
Delaplaine	870
Delaware	479
Delight	870
Dell	870
Dennard	870
Dermott	870
Des Arc	870
Desha	870
Devalls Bluff	870
Dewey	501
Dewitt	870
Dialion	870
Diamond City	870
Diaz	870
Dierks	870
Divide	501
Doddridge	870
Dogpatch	870
Dolph	870
Donaldson	501
Dongola	870
Dover	479
Drasco	870
Driver	870
Duce	870
Dumas	870
Durian	501
Dyer	479
Dyess	870
Earle	870
East Camden	870
East Cotter	870
East End	501
Eden Isle	501
Edgemont	870
Edmondson	870
Eglantine	501
Egypt	870
El Dorado	870
El Paso	501
Elaine	870
Elizabeth	870
Elk Ranch	479
Elkins	479
Elm	870
Elm Springs	479
Emerson	870
Emmet	870
Empire	870
Enders	501
Endoka	870
England	501
Enola	501
Erbie	870
Ethel	870
Etowah	870
Euclid Heights	501
Eudora	870
Eureka	479
Eureka Spgs	479
Eureka Springs	479
Evansville	479
Evening Shade	870
Everton	870
Fair Oaks	870
Fairbanks	501
Fairfield Bay	501
Fairview	870
Fancy Hill	870
Farelly Lake	870
Farmington	479
Farmville	870
Fayetteville	479
Fendley	870
Fenter	501
Fifty Six	870
Fisher	870
Fitzgerald	870
Flag	870
Flippin	870
Floral	501
Florence	870
Fordyce	870
Foreman	870
Formosa	501
Forrest City	870
Fort Chaffee	479
Fort Hill	870
Fort Smith	479
Forty Four	870
Fouke	870
Fountain Hill	870
Fountain Lake	501
Fountain Prairie	870
Four Mile Corner	870
Fox	870
Franklin	870
Frenchman Byu	870
Frenchmans Bayou	870
Friendship	501
Fulton	870
Furlow	501
Gaines Landing	870
Galloway	501
Gamaliel	870
Garfield	479
Garland City	870
Garland Springs	501
Garner	501
Garrett Bridge	870
Gassville	870
Gateway	479
Genevia	501
Genoa	870
Gentry	479
Georgetown	501
Gepp	870
Gibbs	870
Gifford	501
Gilbert	870
Gillett	870
Gillham	870
Gilmore	870
Gleason	501
Glen Rose	501
Glencoe	870
Glendale	870
Glenwood	870
Gobblers Point	501
Gold Creek	501
Gold Lake Estates	501
Golden Ventures	479
Goodwin	870
Goshen	479
Gosnell	870
Gould	870
Gourd	870
Grady	870
Grand Lake	870
Grandview	870
Grannis	870
Grapevine	870
Gravel Hill	501
Gravel Ridge	501
Gravelly	479
Gravelridge	870
Gravesville	501
Gravette	479
Grays	870
Green Forest	870
Green Hill	870
Greenbrier	501
Greenland	479
Greenway	870
Greenwood	479
Greers Ferry	501
Gregory	870
Griffith Spring	870
Griffithtown	870
Griffithville	501
Grubbs	870
Guion	870
Gulledge	870
Gum Springs	870
Gurdon	870
Guy	501
H Spg Nat Pk	501
Hackett	479
Hagarville	479
Halley	870
Halley Junction	870
Hamburg	870
Hamilton	870
Hamiter	501
Hammonsville	501
Hampton	870
Hanover	870
Hardin	870
Harding University	501
Hardy	870
Harrell	870
Harriet	870
Harrisburg	870
Harrison	870
Hartford	479
Hartman	479
Harvey	479
Haskell	501
Hasty	870
Hatfield	870
Hattieville	501
Hatton	870
Havana	479
Hayley	870
Haynes	870
Haywood	870
Hazen	870
Hearn	870
Heber Springs	501
Hebron	870
Hector	479
Helena	870
Henderson	870
Henderson State University	870
Hensley	501
Herbine	870
Hermitage	870
Heth	870
Hickory Flat	501
Hickory Hill	501
Hickory Plains	870
Hickory Plns	870
Hickory Ridge	870
Higden	501
Higginson	501
Higgson	501
Highland	870
Hill Creek	501
Hillemann	870
Hindsville	479
Hiram	501
Hiwasse	479
Holiday Island	479
Holiday Isle	479
Holland	501
Holly Grove	870
Hollywood	870
Homewood	501
Hope	870
Hopper	870
Horatio	870
Horseshoe Bend	870
Horseshoe Bnd	870
Horseshoe Lake	870
Horseshoe Lk	870
Hot Spgs Vl	501
Hot Springs	501
Hot Springs National	501
Hot Springs National Park	501
Hot Springs Village	501
Houston	501
Howell	870
Hoxie	870
Hs	501
Huddleston	870
Hughes	870
Humnoke	501
Humphrey	870
Hunt	479
Hunter	870
Huntington	479
Huntsville	479
Huttig	870
Ida	501
Imboden	870
Indian	870
Ingleside	870
Ink	479
Ivan	870
Jacksonport	870
Jacksonville	501
Jasper	870
Jax	501
Jefferson	501
Jefferson Square	870
Jeffery	501
Jennie	870
Jericho	870
Jersey	870
Jerusalem	501
Jessieville	501
Joan	870
Johnson	479
Johnstown	870
Johnsville	870
Joiner	870
Jones Mill	501
Jonesboro	870
Jordan	870
Judsonia	501
Junction City	870
Kearney	501
Kedron	870
Keiser	870
Kelso	870
Kenseh	501
Kensen	501
Kensett	501
Keo	501
Kerr	501
Kimberley	870
Kingsland	870
Kingston	479
Kirby	870
Knobel	870
Knoxville	479
Koch Ridge	501
Kurdo	870
La Crosse	870
La Grange	870
Lacey	870
Ladelle	870
Lafe	870
Lake City	870
Lake Hamilton	501
Lake Village	870
Lakeside	501
Lakeview	870
Lamar	479

City	Area Code
ambert	501
ambrook	870
anark	870
andis	870
aneburg	870
angley	870
anty	501
avaca	479
awrenceville	870
awson	870
eachville	870
ead Hill	870
eola	870
epanto	870
eslie	870
etona	501
ewisburg	501
ewisville	870
exa	870
exington	501
ick Mountain	501
ight	870
imestone	870
incoln	479
inder	501
inwood	870
ittle Dixie	870
ittle Rck Afb	501
ittle Red	501
ittle Rock	501
ittle Rock Afb	501
ittle Rock Air Force Base	501
ockesburg	870
ocust Grove	870
odge Corner	870
odi	870
ollie	501
ondon	479
ono	870
onoke	501
onsdale	501
ookout Store	870
ost Corner	501
ouann	870
ow Gap	870
owell	479
r Afb	501
r Airforce Base	501
rafb	501
una	870
uxora	870
ynn	870
Mabelvale	501
Maberry	870
Macedonia	501
Macon	501
Macon Lake	870
Madison	870
Magazine	479
Magness	870
Magnet Cove	501
Magnolia	870
Mallet Town	501
Malvern	501
Mammoth Spg	870
Mammoth Spring	870
Manfred	870
Manila	870
Manning	870
Mansfield	479
Marble Falls	870
Marcella	870
Marche	501
Marianna	870
Marion	870
Marked Tree	870
Marmaduke	870
Marshall	870
Martinville	501
Marvell	870
Masonville	870
Maumelle	501
Mayflower	501
Maynard	870
Mays Mission	501
Maysville	479
Mazarn	501
Mc Caskill	870
Mc Crory	870
Mc Dougal	870
Mc Gehee	870
Mc Neil	870
Mc Rae	501
Mcalmont	501
Mcarthur	870
Mccrory	870
Mcgehee	870
Mcgintytown	501
Mcjester	501
Mckinney	870
Mcmilan Corner	870
Mcrae	501
Melbourne	870
Mellwood	870
Mena	479
Menifee	501
Menos	479
Meridian	870
Meroney	870
Metalton	870
Middleton	501
Midland	479
Midway	870
Milo	870
Mineral Spgs	870
Mineral Springs	870
Minturn	870
Mist	870
Mitchellville	870
Moko	870
Monette	870
Monkey Run	870
Monroe	870
Monticello	870
Montongo	870
Montrose	870
Moro	870
Morobay	870
Morrilton	501
Morrow	479
Morton	870
Moscow	870
Mossville	870
Mount Hersey	870
Mount Holly	870
Mount Ida	870
Mount Judea	870
Mount Moriah	870
Mount Olive	870
Mount Pleasant	870
Mount Sherman	870
Mount Tabor	870
Mount Vernon	501
Mountain Fork	479
Mountain Home	870
Mountain Pine	501
Mountain Valley	501
Mountain View	870
Mountainburg	479
Mozart	870
Mt Pine	501
Mt Pleasant	870
Mt Valley	501
Mtn Home	870
Mulberry	479
Murfreesboro	870
Murphys Corner	870
N L R	501
N Little Rock	501
N Lr	501
Nady	870
Nail	870
Nashville	870
Natural Dam	479
Natural Steps	501
Naylor	501
Nebo	870
New Blaine	479
New Edinburg	870
New Pr	870
Newark	870
Newhope	870
Newport	870
Nimrod	501
Nlr	501
No Little Rock	501
Norfork	870
Norman	870
Norphlet	870
North Little Rock	501
Northpoint	501
Nunley	479
O Kean	870
Oak Grove	870
Oakgrove	501
Oakland	870
Oaklawn	501
Oark	479
Oden	870
Ogden	870
Oil Trough	870
Okay	870
Okolona	870
Ola	479
Old Hickory	501
Old Joe	870
Old Milo	870
Omaha	870
One Horse Store	870
Oneida	870
Onia	870
Opal	479
Oppelo	501
Orion	501
Orlando	870
Osceola	870
Otto	501
Ouachita Baptist University	870
Owensville	501
Oxford	870
Oxley	870
Ozan	870
Ozark	479
Ozark Lithia	501
Ozone	479
Palestine	870
Palmer	870
Palmyra	870
Pangburn	501
Pansy	870
Panther Forest	870
Paragould	870
Paris	479
Parkdale	870
Parkin	870
Parks	479
Parma	870
Paron	501
Parthenon	870
Pastoria	870
Patsville	870
Patterson	870
Pea Ridge	479
Peach Orchard	870
Pearcy	501
Pearson	501
Peel	870
Pelsor	870
Pencil Bluff	870
Pendleton	870
Perla	501
Perry	501
Perrytown	870
Perryville	501
Pettigrew	479
Pettus	501
Pickens	870
Piercetown	870
Piggott	870
Pike	870
Pindall	870
Pine Bluff	870
Pine City	870
Pine Ridge	870
Pineville	870
Piney	501
Piney Grove	870
Pinnacle	501
Pisgah	870
Plainview	501
Plant	501
Pleasant Grove	870
Pleasant Grv	870
Pleasant Hill	501
Pleasant Hills	870
Pleasant Plains	501
Pleasant Plns	501
Pleasant Valley	501
Plum Bayou	501
Plumerville	501
Pocahontas	870
Point Cedar	870
Pollard	870
Ponca	870
Pontoon	501
Poplar Grove	870
Portia	870
Portland	870
Possum Fork	870
Potter	479
Potter Junction	479
Pottsville	479
Poughkeepsie	870
Powhatan	870
Poyen	870
Prague	870
Prairie Grove	479
Prattsville	870
Prescott	870
Preston	501
Preston Ferry	870
Price	501
Prim	870
Proctor	870
Providence	501
Pruitt	870
Pumpkin Bend	870
Pyatt	870
Quitman	501
Randall	870
Ratcliff	479
Ravenden	870
Ravenden Spgs	870
Ravenden Springs	870
Raymond	870
Rea Valley	870
Readland	870
Rector	870
Red Fork	870
Red Leaf	870
Red Oak	501
Redfield	501
Reedville	870
Relfs Bluff	870
Remmel	870
Republican	501
Reverie Tn	870
Rex	501
Reydell	870
Reyno	870
Richwood	870
Rison	870
Riverside	870
Rivervale	870
Riverview	501
Rixey	501
Robertsville	501
Rock Island Junction	870
Rock Springs	870
Rockport	501
Rocky	479
Roe	870
Rogers	479
Rohwer	870
Roland	501
Rolla	501
Romance	501
Rosboro	870
Rose Bud	501
Rosie	870
Rosston	870
Round Mountain	501
Round Pond	870
Rover	479
Rowell	870
Royal	501
Royal Oak	501
Rudd	870
Rudy	479
Rule	870
Rumley	870
Rupert	501
Rushing	501
Russell	501
Russellville	479
Rye	870
Saffell	870
Sage	870
Saginaw	501
Saint Charles	870
Saint Francis	870
Saint Joe	870
Saint Paul	479
Salado	870
Salem	870
Salesville	870
Saline	870
Saltillo	501
Sand Hill	870
Sandtown	501
Saratoga	870
Scholastic Parcels	501
Scotland	501
Scott	501
Scranton	479
Screeton	870
Searcy	501
Sedgwick	870
Selma	870
Shannon	870
Shannon Hills	501
Sheridan	870
Sherrill	870
Sherwood	501
Shirley	501
Shives	870
Sidney	870
Sidon	501
Siloam Spgs	479
Siloam Springs	479
Sims	870
Skunkhollow	501
Slovac	870
Smackover	870
Smearney	870
Smithville	870
Snow Lake	870
Snyder	870
Social Hill	501
Solgohachia	501
South Sheridan	870
Sparkman	870
Springdale	479
Springfield	501
Springhill	501
Springtown	479
St Joe	870
St University	870
Stamps	870
Star City	870
State Univ	870
State University	870
Staves	870
Stephens	870
Steprock	501
Stony Point	501
Story	870
Strawberry	870
Strong	870
Sturkie	870
Stuttgart	870
Subiaco	479
Success	870
Sulphur Rock	870
Sulphur Spgs	479
Sulphur Springs	479
Summers	479
Summit	870
Sumpter	870
Sweet Home	501
Swifton	870
Sylvania	501
Tafton	501
Tafton-Wrightville	501
Tamo	870
Tarry	870
Taylor	870
Tennessee	870
Texarkana	870
The Highlands	479
Thebes	870
Thida	870
Thornburg	501
Thornton	870
Tichnor	870
Tillar	870
Tilly	870
Timbo	870
Tobin	870
Toledo	870
Tollville	870
Toltec	501
Tomato	870
Tontitown	479
Traskwood	501
Trippe	870
Trumann	870
Tucker	501
Tuckerman	870
Tukertown	870
Tull	501
Tumbling Shls	501
Tumbling Shoals	501
Tupelo	870
Turner	870
Turrell	870
Twin Groves	501
Twist	870
Tyro	870
Tyronza	870
Ua Monticello	870
Uca	501
Ulm	870
Umpire	870
Uniontown	479
Univ Of Central	501
University Of Arkansas	870
University Of Central Ar	501
Urbana	870
Urbanette	870
Valley Spgs	870
Valley Springs	870
Van Buren	479
Vandervoort	870
Vanndale	870
Vendor	870
Veterans Admin Fac	501
Veterans Admin. Fac.	501
Veterans Administration Faci	501
Vick	870
Village	870
Vilonia	501
Viola	870
Violet Hill	870
Wabash	870
Wabbaseka	870
Wal-Mart Inc	479
Walcott	870
Waldenburg	870
Waldo	870
Waldron	479
Walnut Grove	501
Walnut Ridge	870
Ward	501
Warm Springs	870
Warren	870
Washington	870
Watson	870
Wattensaw	501
Waveland	479
Wayton	870
Weiner	870
Weldon	870
Wesley	479
Wesley Chapel	501
West Fork	479

City	Area Code
West Gum Springs	870
West Helena	870
West Marche	501
West Memphis	870
West Point	501
West Ridge	870
Western Grove	870
Wheatley	870
Wheeler	479
Whelen Spgs	870
Whelen Springs	870
White Hall	870
Whitetown	870
Whiteville	870
Wickes	870
Wideman	870
Widener	870
Wiederkehr Vg	479
Wiederkehr Village	479
Wilburn	501
Williams Baptist College	870
Williams Junction	501
Williford	870
Willisville	870
Willow	870
Wilmar	870
Wilmot	870
Wilson	870
Wilton	870
Winchester	870
Winslow	479
Winthrop	870
Wiseman	870
Witherspoon	870
Witter	479
Witts Springs	870
Wiville	870
Wms College	870
Wolf Bayou	870
Woodrow	870
Woodson	501
Wooster	501
Wright	501
Wrightsville	501
Wynne	870
Y City	870
Yancopin	870
Yardelle	870
Yellville	870
Yocana	479
Yorktown	870
Yukon	870
Zinc	870
Zion	870

California

City	Area Code
100 Palms	760
1000 Palms	760
29 Palms	760
A A R P	562
A A R P Pharmacy	562
A M O R C	408
Aarp	562
Aberdeen	760
Acampo	209
Acton	661
Adelaide	805
Adelanto	760
Adin	530
Aerial Acres	661
Aetna Life And Casualty	559
Afton	530
Agate Bay	530
Agoura	818
Agoura Hills	818
Agua Caliente	707
Agua Dulce	661
Aguanga	909
Ahwahnee	559
Alabama Hills	760
Alameda	510
Alameda Pt	510
Alamo	925
Albany	510
Albion	707
Alderpoint	707
Alhambra	626
Alisal	831
Aliso Viejo	949
Alleghany	530
Allendale	707
Allensworth	661
Almanor	530
Alpaugh	661
Alpine	619
Alpine Forest	661
Alpine Mdws	530
Alpine Meadows	530
Alta	530
Alta Hill	530
Alta Loma	909
Alta Sierra	530
Altadena	626
Altaville	209
Alturas	530
Alturas Rancheria	530
Alviso	408
Amador City	209
Amador Station	209
Ambassador College	626
Ambassador I C Foundation	626
Amboy	760
American Canyon	707
American Cyn	707
Anaheim	714
Anaheim Hills	714
Anchor Bay	707
Anderson	530
Anderson Springs	707
Andrus Island	916
Angels Camp	209
Angelus Oaks	909
Angwin	707
Annapolis	707
Antelope	916
Antioch	925
Anza	951
Apple Valley	760
Applegate	530
Aptos	831
Arboga	530
Arbuckle	530
Arcadia	626
Arcata	707
Arco	213
Arco-Plaza	213
Argus	760
Arleta	818
Arlington	951
Armona	559
Arnold	209
Aromas	831
Arrowbear Lake	909
Arrowbear Lk	909
Arrowhead Farms	909
Arrowhed Farm	909
Arroyo Grande	805
Artesia	562
Artois	530
Arvin	661
Asti	707
Asw Training Ctr	619
At & T	415
At&t	916
Atascadero	805
Atherton	650
Atwater	209
Atwood	714
Auberry	559
Auburn	530
Auburn Lake Trails	530
August F. Haw	323, 818
Avalon	310
Avenal	559
Avery	209
Avila Beach	805
Avon Products	626
Azusa	626
B H Springs	707
Badger	559
Baker	760
Baker Ranch	530
Bakersfield	661
Balance Rock	661
Balboa	949
Balboa Island	949
Baldwin Hills	310, 323
Baldwin Park	626
Ballarat	760
Ballard	805
Ballico	209
Bangor	530
Bank Of America	213, 415, 714
Banning	951
Banta	209
Bar Code Term Annex	818
Bard	760
Barona Rancheria	760
Barrington	310
Barstow	760
Base Line	909
Bass Lake	559
Bassett	626
Bassetts	530
Bay Point	925
Bayliss	530
Bayside	707
Baywood Park	805
Beach Center	714
Beale Afb	530
Bear River Pines	530
Bear Valley	209
Bear Valley Springs	661
Bear Vly Spgs	661
Beaumont	951
Beckwourth	530
Bel Marin Keyes	415
Bel Tiburon	415
Belden	530
Bell	310, 323
Bell Canyon	818
Bell Gardens	310
Bella Vista	530
Bellflower	562
Belmont	650
Belmont Shore	562
Belvedere	415
Belvedere Tiburon	415
Ben Lomond	831
Benicia	707
Benton	760
Berenda	559
Berkeley	510
Bermuda Dunes	760
Berry Creek	530
Bethel Island	925
Beverly Hills	310
Bicentennial	310
Bieber	530
Big Bar	530
Big Basin	831
Big Bear	909
Big Bear City	909
Big Bear Lake	909
Big Bend	530
Big Creek	559
Big Oak Flat	209
Big Oak Valley	530
Big Oak Vly	530
Big Pine	760
Big River	760
Big Sur	831
Biggs	530
Bijou	530
Biola	559
Biola University	562
Birds Landing	925
Birds Lndg	707
Bishop	760
Bixby Knolls	562
Black Meadow Landing	760
Black Point	415
Black Station	209
Blackhawk	925
Blairsden	530
Blairsden-Graeagle	530
Blocksburg	707
Bloomfield	707
Bloomington	909
Blossom Valley	650
Blrsdn-Greagl	530
Blue Canyon	530
Blue Cross	510
Blue Cross Of So Calif	818
Blue Jay	909
Blue Lake	707
Blue Shield Of Cal	530
Blythe	760
Boca	530
Bodega	707
Bodega Bay	707
Bodfish	760
Boeing	562
Bolinas	415
Bombay Beach	760
Bonds Corner	760
Bonita	619
Bonny Doon	831
Bonsall	760
Boonville	707
Boron	760
Borrego Spgs	760
Borrego Springs	760
Boston Ravine	530
Bostonia	619
Boulder Creek	831
Bouldin Island	916
Boulevard	619
Bouquet Canyon	661
Bowman	530
Box Canyon	818
Box Springs	909
Boyes Hot Spg	707
Boyes Hot Springs	707
Boyes Springs	707
Boyle Heights	323
Bradbury	626
Bradley	805
Bradley International	310
Brandeis	805
Brannan Island	916
Branscomb	707
Brawley	760
Brea	714
Brentwood	310, 925
Bridgeport	760
Bridgeville	707
Briggs	310
Briones	925
Brisbane	415
Bristol	714
Broadmoor Vlg	650
Broadway Manchester	323
Brockway	530
Broderick	916
Brookdale	831
Brookhurst Center	714
Brooks	530
Browns Valley	530
Brownsville	530
Brush Creek	530
Bryn Mawr	909
Bryte	916
Buckhorn	209
Bucks Bar	530
Bucks Lake	530
Buellton	805
Buena Park	714
Buffalo Hill	530
Bulk Mail Center	818
Burbank	818
Burbank Studios	818
Bureau Of The Census	909
Burlingame	650
Burney	530
Burnt Ranch	530
Burrel	559
Burson	209
Business Reply	818
Butte City	530
Butte Creek	530
Butte Meadows	530
Butte Valley	530
Buttonwillow	661
Byron	925
C S U Dom Hls	310
C S U Long Beach	562
Ca Brm Zip	916
Ca State Dmv	916
Ca State University Fresno	559
Cabazon	760, 909
Cabrillo	562
Cadiz	760
Cairns Corner	559
Cajon Junction	909
Cal Poly Slo	805
Cal Poly Student Dorms	805
Cal Poly University	805
Cal State Univ Dom Hills	310
Cal Tech	626
Calabasas	818
Calabasas Hills	818
Calabasas Hls	818
Calexico	760
Caliente	661
Calif City	760
Calif Hot Spg	661
Calif State Univ Long Beach	562
Calif State University Chico	530
California City	760
California Conservation Cent	530
California Correctional Inst	661
California Hot Springs	661
California Mens Colony Slo	805
California Pines	530
California State San Marcos	760
California State University	818
California Valley	805
California Water Service	408
Calimesa	909
Calipatria	760
Calistoga	707
Callahan	530
Calpella	707
Calpine	530
Calwa	559
Camanche Lake	209
Camarillo	805
Cambria	805
Cameron Park	530
Camino	530
Camp Connell	209
Camp Meeker	707
Camp Nelson	559
Camp Pendleton	760
Camp Richardson	530
Camp Roberts	805
Campbell	408
Campo	619
Campo Seco	209
Camptonville	530
Campus Crusade For Christ	909
Canby	530
Canoga Park	818
Cantil	760
Cantua Creek	559
Canyon	925
Canyon Cntry	661
Canyon Country	661
Canyon Crest	909
Canyon Dam	530
Canyon Lake	909
Canyondam	530
Capay	530
Cape Horn	530
Capistrano Beach	949
Capitola	831
Capo Beach	949
Carbondale	209
Cardiff	760
Cardiff By The Sea	760
Caribou	530
Carlotta	707
Carlsbad	760, 858
Carmel	831
Carmel By The	831
Carmel By The Sea	831
Carmel Highlands	831
Carmel Valley	831
Carmel Valley Village	831
Carmichael	916
Carnelian Bay	530
Carpinteria	805
Carson	310, 562
Cartago	760
Caruthers	559
Casa Blanca	909
Casitas Springs	805
Casmalia	805
Caspar	707
Cassel	530
Castaic	661
Castella	530
Castro Valley	510
Castroville	831
Catalina	310
Cathedral City	760
Cathedral Cty	760
Catheys Valley	209
Catheys Vly	209
Cayucos	805
Cazadero	707
Cedar Flat	530
Cedar Glen	909
Cedar Grove	530
Cedar Pines Pk	909
Cedar Ravine	530
Cedar Ridge	530
Cedarpines Park	909
Cedarpines Pk	909
Cedarville	530
Centerville	559
Central Valley	530
Central Vly	530
Century City	310
Ceres	209
Cerritos	562
Chalfant	760
Chalfant Valley	760
Chalfant Vly	760
Challenge	530
Chapmantown	530
Charter Oak	626
Chatsworth	818
Chemehuevi	760
Chemehuevi Valley	760
Cherokee	530
Cherry Valley	951
Chester	530
Chevron	925
Chevron Usa Inc	925
Chicago Park	530
Chico	530
Chilcoot	530
China Lake	760
China Lake Nwc	760
Chinese Camp	209
Chino	909
Chino Hills	909
Chiriaco Smt	760
Chiriaco Summit	760
Cholame	661
Chowchilla	559
Christian Valley	530
Chualar	831
Chula Vista	619
Cima	760
Cimarron	323
Cisco	530
Citibank	323
Citrus Heights	916
Citrus Hts	916
City Hall	909
City Industry	562, 626, 909
City National Bank	626
City Of Industry	562, 626, 909
City Of Riverside	909
City Ranch	661
Claremont	909
Clarksburg	916
Clay	209
Clayton	925
Clear Creek	530
Clearlake	707

City	Area Code
Clearlake Oaks	707
Clearlake Oks	707
Clearlake Park	707
Clearlake Pk	707
Clements	209
Cleone	707
Clinton	209
Clio	530
Clipper Gap	530
Clipper Mills	530
Cloverdale	707
Clovis	559
Clyde	925
Cmp Pendleton	760
Coachella	760
Coalinga	559
Coarsegold	559
Cobb	707
Codora	530
Cohasset	530
Cold Springs	209
Coleville	530
Colfax	530
College City	530
Colma	650
Coloma	530
Colton	909
Columbia	209
Colusa	530
Commerce	323
Comptche	707
Compton	310
Concord	925
Conejo	559
Cool	530
Copperopolis	209
Corcoran	559
Cornell	818
Corning	530
Corona	909, 951
Corona Del Mar	949
Corona Dl Mar	949
Coronado	619
Corral De Tie	831
Corral De Tierra	831
Corralitos	831
Corte Madera	415
Costa Mesa	714, 949
Cotati	707
Coto De Caza	949
Cottonwood	530
Coulterville	209
Courtland	916
Covelo	707
Covina	626
Cowan Heights	714
Coyote	408
Crenshaw	310, 323
Crescent City	707
Crescent Mills	530
Crescent Mls	530
Cressey	209
Crest	619
Crest Park	909
Crestline	909
Crestmore	909
Creston	805
Crockett	510
Cromberg	530
Crowley Lake	760
Crows Landing	209
Crystal City	310
Crystal Springs	530
Crystalaire	661
Cty Of Cmmrce	323
Cucamonga	909
Cudahy	323
Culver City	310
Culver Cty	310
Cupertino	408
Cutler	559
Cutten	707
Cuyama	661
Cypress	562, 714
Daggett	760
Dairyville	530
Daly City	415, 650
Dana Point	949
Danville	925
Dardanelle	209
Darwin	760
Davenport	831
Davis	530
Davis Creek	530
Dayton	530
Death Valley	760
Death Valley Jct	760
Death Valley Junction	760
Deer Park	707
Defense Dist Region	209
Del Kern	661
Del Mar	858
Del Monte Park	831
Del Rey	559
Del Rey Oaks	831
Del Rosa	909
Del Sur	661
Del Valle Finance	213
Delano	661
Delhi	209
Delleker	530
Deluxe Check	818
Denair	209
Department Of Gas & Water	562
Descanso	619
Desert Center	760
Desert Edge	760
Desert Hot Springs	760
Desert Lake	760
Desert Shores	760
Devore Heights	909
Devore Hghts	909
Di Giorgio	661
Diablo	925
Diamond	714
Diamond Bar	909
Diamond Spgs	530
Diamond Springs	530
Dillon Beach	707
Dinuba	559
Discovery Bay	925
Disney Productions	818
Dixon	707
Dobbins	530
Dockweiler	213, 323
Dodgertown	323
Dolomite	760
Dominguez	562
Donner	530
Donner Lake	530
Dorrington	209
Dorris	530
Dos Palos	209
Dos Rios	707
Dos Vientos Ranch	805
Douglas City	530
Douglas Flat	209
Dove Canyon	949
Downey	562
Downieville	530
Dowtown Carrier Annex	213
Doyle	530
Drytown	209
Dsrt Hot Spgs	760
Duarte	626
Dublin	925
Ducor	559
Dulzura	619
Duncans Mills	707
Dunlap	559
Dunnigan	530
Dunsmuir	530
Durham	530
Dutch Flat	530
E Palo Alto	650
E Rncho Dmngz	310
Eagle Lake Resort	530
Eagle Mountain	760
Eagle Mtn	760
Eagle Rock	323
Eagle Tree	916
Eagleville	530
Earlimart	661
Earp	760
East Gridley	530
East Irvine	949
East Long Beach	562
East Los Angeles	323
East Nicolaus	530
East Orosi	559
East Palo Alto	650
East Quincy	530
East Rancho Dominguez	310
Ebmud	510
Echo Lake	530
Echo Park	213
Eden Valley	530
Edendale	213
Edgewood	530
Edison	661
Edward	661
Edwards	661
Edwards Afb	661
Edwards Air Force Base	661
Eight Mile House	530
El Cajon	619
El Centro	760
El Cerrito	510
El Dorado	530
El Dorado Hills	916
El Dorado Hls	916
El Granada	650
El Macero	530
El Mirage	760
El Monte	626
El Nido	209
El Portal	209
El Segundo	310
El Sereno Car	626
El Sobrante	510
El Toro	949
El Verano	707
Elderwood	559
Eldridge	707
Elizabeth Lake	661
Elizabeth Lk	661
Elk	707
Elk Creek	530
Elk Grove	916
Elmira	707
Elverta	916
Emerald Hills	650
Emeryville	510
Emigrant Gap	530
Emigrant Trail	530
Empire	209
Encinitas	760
Encino	818
Escalon	209
Escondido	760
Esparto	530
Essex	760
Est Ls Angls	323
Etiwanda	909
Etna	530
Eureka	707
Exeter	559
Fair Oaks	916
Fair Oaks Ranch	661
Fair Play	530
Fairfax	415
Fairfield	707
Fairmead	559
Fairmont	661
Fall River Mills	530
Fallbrook	760
Fallen Leaf	530
Fallon	707
Fallsvale	909
Farmer Market	323
Farmers Ins	805
Farmersville	559
Farmington	209
Fawnskin	909
Feather Falls	530
Federal	213, 714, 818
Federal Home Loan Bank	909
Felicity	760
Fellows	661
Felton	831
Ferndale	707
Fetters Hot Springs	707
Fiddletown	209
Fields Landing	707
Fields Ldg	707
Fillmore	805
Finley	707
Firebaugh	559
Firemans Fund Ins	415
Firestone Park	323
Firestone Pk	323
First Interstate Bank	415
Fish Camp	209
Five Mile Terrace	530
Five Points	559
Fl River Mls	530
Flick Point	530
Flint	213
Flintridge	818
Floriston	530
Flournoy	530
Fluor Corp	949
Folsom	916
Folsom Prison	916
Fontana	909
Foothill Ranch	949
Foothill Rnch	949
Forbestown	530
Forest City	530
Forest Falls	909
Forest Knolls	415
Forest Ranch	530
Foresthill	530
Forestville	707
Forks Of Salmon	530
Fort Bidwell	530
Fort Bragg	707
Fort Dick	707
Fort Hunter Liggett	831
Fort Irwin	760
Fort Jones	530
Fort Macarthur	562
Fort Ross	707
Fortuna	707
Foster City	650
Fountain Valley	714
Fountain Vly	714
Four Corners	760
Fouts Springs	530
Fowler	559
Foy	213
Franchise Tax Board	916
Franchise Tax Brd Refunds	916
Frazier Park	661
Fredricksburg	530
Freedom	831
Freestone	707
Fremont	510
Fremont Valley	661
French Camp	209
French Corral	530
French Gulch	530
Fresh Pond	530
Fresno	559
Fresno Bee	559
Fresno City College	559
Fresno City Utilities	559
Fresno Cnty Social Svc Dept	559
Fresno State University	559
Fresno Superior Court	559
Friant	559
Friendly Valley	661
Frk Of Salmon	530
Frs	559
Fruitridge	916
Fruto	530
Ft Bidwell	530
Ft H Liggett	831
Ft Macarthur	562
Fuller Theological Seminary	626
Fullerton	714
Fulton	707
Fulton Acres	530
Galt	209
Ganser Bar	530
Garberville	707
Garden Grove	714
Garden Valley	530
Gardena	310
Garey	805
Garlock	760
Gasquet	707
Gaviota	805
Gazelle	530
Genesee	530
George Afb	760
Georgetown	530
Gerber	530
Geyserville	707
Gilman Hot Springs	951
Gilroy	408
Glassell	323
Glassell Park	323
Glen Ellen	707
Glenbrook Heights	530
Glencoe	209
Glendale	818
Glendale Galleria	818
Glendora	626
Glenhaven	707
Glenn	530
Glennville	661
Glenshire	530
Glmn Hot Spgs	951
Goffs	760
Gold Hill	530
Gold River	916
Gold Run	530
Golden Hills	661
Goleta	805
Gonzales	831
Goodyears Bar	530
Gorda	831
Gorman	661
Goshen	559
Gottschalks	559
Graeagle	530
Granada Hills	818
Grand Island	916
Grand Terrace	909
Granite Bay	916
Graniteville	530
Grant Grove	559
Grass Valley	530
Graton	707
Grayson	209
Green	323
Green Valley	661
Green Valley Lake	909
Green Vly Lk	909
Greenbrae	415
Greenfield	831
Greenmead	323
Greenview	530
Greenville	530
Greenwood	530
Grenada	530
Gridley	530
Griffith	323
Grimes	530
Grindstone Creek Rancheria	530
Grizzly Flats	530
Groveland	209
Grover Beach	805
Guadalupe	805
Gualala	707
Guasti	909
Guatay	619
Guerneville	707
Guernewood	707
Guinda	530
Gustine	209
Hacienda Heights	626
Hacienda Hts	626
Halcyon	805
Half Moon Bay	650
Hallwood	530
Hamilton City	530
Hammil Valley	760
Hammonton	530
Hams Station	209
Hancock	323
Hanford	559
Hansen Hills	818
Happy Camp	530
Harbor City	310
Harmony	805
Hat Creek	530
Hathaway Pines	209
Hathaway Pnes	209
Havasu Lake	760
Havilah	661
Hawaiian Gardens	562
Hawaiian Gdns	562
Hawthorne	310
Hayfork	530
Hayward	510
Hazard	323
Healdsburg	707
Heather Glen	530
Heber	760
Helena	530
Helendale	760
Helm	559
Hemet	909, 951
Herald	209
Hercules	510
Heritage Ranch	805
Heritage Rnch	805
Herlong	530
Hermosa Beach	310
Hesperia	760
Hi Vista	661
Hickman	209
Hidden Hills	818
Hidden Valley	805
Hidden Valley Lake	707
Hidden Vl Lk	707
Highland	909
Highland Park	323
Hills Flat	530
Hillsborough	650
Hilltop Mall	510
Hilmar	209
Hilt	530
Hinkley	760
Hobart Mills	530
Hodge	760
Holcomb Village	909
Holiday	714
Hollister	831
Holly Park	310
Hollyglen	310
Hollywood	323
Holt	209
Holtville	760
Holy City	408
Homeland	909
Homewood	530
Honcut	530
Honeydew	707
Hood	916
Hoopa	530
Hoopa Valley Indian Reservat	530
Hope Valley	530
Hopland	707
Hornbrook	530
Hornitos	209
Horse Creek	530
Household Finance	714
Howard Landing	916
Hughson	209
Hume	559
Huntingtn Bch	714
Huntington	714
Huntington Beach	714
Huntington Park	323
Huntington Pk	323
Hurleton	530
Huron	559
Hyampom	530
Hydesville	707
I B M	408
I R S	559
Idyllwild	951
Ignacio	415

Igo ... 530
Imperial ... 760
Imperial Bch ... 619
Imperial Beach ... 619
Independence ... 760
Indian Wells ... 760
Indio ... 760
Inglenook ... 707
Inglewood ... 310
Inverness ... 415
Inyokern ... 760
Ione ... 209
Iowa Hill ... 530
Iron Mountain ... 209
Irs ... 415, 559
Irs Remittance ... 415
Irvine ... 714, 949
Irwindale ... 626
Isla Vista ... 805
Isleton ... 916
Ivanhoe ... 559
J B Lansing Co ... 818
J P Morgan ... 626
Jackson ... 209
Jacumba ... 619
Jamestown ... 209
Jamul ... 619
Janesville ... 530
Jarbo ... 530
Jenner ... 707
Jess Ranch ... 760
Johannesburg ... 760
Johnson Park ... 530
Johnson Valley ... 760
Johnson Vly ... 760
Johnstonville ... 530
Johnsville ... 530
Jolon ... 831
Joshua Tree ... 760
Julian ... 760
Junction City ... 530
June Lake ... 760
June Lake Junction ... 760
Juniper Hills ... 661
Jurupa ... 951
Kagel Canyon ... 818
Kaiser Foundation Health ... 626
Kaiser Services ... 510
Kaweah ... 559
Kcnp ... 559
Keeler ... 760
Keene ... 661
Keene Summit ... 707
Kelsey ... 530
Kelseyville ... 707
Kelso ... 760
Kensington ... 510
Kent Woodlands ... 415
Kentfield ... 415
Kenwood ... 707
Kerman ... 559
Kernville ... 760
Keswick ... 530
Kettleman City ... 559
Kettleman Cty ... 559
Keyes ... 209
King ... 714
King City ... 831
Kings Beach ... 530
Kings Canyon ... 559
Kings Canyon National Pk ... 559
Kings Canyon Natl Park ... 559
Kingsburg ... 559
Kingvale ... 530
Kirkwood ... 209
Kit Carson ... 209
Klamath ... 707
Klamath Air Force Station ... 707
Klamath River ... 530
Kneeland ... 707
Knights Ferry ... 209
Knights Landing ... 530
Knights Lndg ... 530
Knightsen ... 925
Korbel ... 707
Kramer Junction ... 760

Kyburz ... 530
La ... 818
La Barr Meadows ... 530
La Canada ... 626, 818
La Canada Flintridge ... 626
La Canada Flt ... 626
La Conchita ... 805
La Crescenta ... 818
La Grange ... 209
La Habra ... 562
La Habra Heights ... 562
La Habra Hgts ... 562
La Habra Hts ... 562
La Honda ... 650
La International Service Ctr ... 562
La Jolla ... 858
La Mesa ... 619
La Mirada ... 562, 714
La Palma ... 714
La Porte ... 530
La Puente ... 626
La Quinta ... 760
La Selva Bch ... 831
La Selva Beach ... 831
La Sierra ... 951
La Tijera ... 323
La Tuna Canyon ... 818
La Verne ... 909
Ladera Ranch ... 949
Lafayette ... 925
Laguna Beach ... 949
Laguna Hills ... 949
Laguna Niguel ... 949
Laguna Woods ... 949
Lagunitas ... 415
Lake Almanor ... 530
Lake Almanor Sports & Spirit ... 530
Lake Arrowhead ... 909
Lake Balboa ... 818
Lake City ... 530
Lake Elizabeth ... 661
Lake Elsinore ... 909
Lake Forest ... 949
Lake Gregory ... 909
Lake Hughes ... 661
Lake Isabella ... 760
Lake La ... 661
Lake Los Angeles ... 661
Lake Mary ... 760
Lake Nacimiento ... 805
Lake Natoma ... 916
Lake Of The Pines ... 530
Lake San Marcos ... 760
Lake Sherwood ... 805
Lake View Ter ... 818
Lake View Terrace ... 818
Lake Wildwood ... 530
Lakehead ... 530
Lakeport ... 707
Lakeshore ... 559
Lakeshore Learning ... 310
Lakeside ... 619
Lakeview ... 909
Lakeview Terrace ... 818
Lakeville ... 707
Lakewood ... 562
Lamirada ... 714
Lamont ... 661
Lancaster ... 661
Landers ... 760
Lane ... 661
Larkfield ... 707
Larkspur ... 415
Las Plumas ... 530
Lassen Volcanic National Par ... 530
Lathrop ... 209
Laton ... 559
Latrobe ... 530
Lava Beds National Monument ... 530
Lawndale ... 310
Laws ... 760
Laytonville ... 707
Laytonville Rancheria ... 707
Lb ... 562
Le Grand ... 209
Lebec ... 661

Lee Vining ... 760
Leesville ... 530
Leggett ... 707
Leimert Park ... 323
Lemon Cove ... 559
Lemon Grove ... 619
Lemoore ... 559
Lemoore Nas ... 559
Lemoore Naval Air Station ... 559
Lennox ... 310
Leona Valley ... 661
Leucadia ... 760
Lewiston ... 530
Liberty Farms ... 707
Liberty Mutual ... 559
Likely ... 530
Lincoln ... 916
Lincoln Acres ... 619
Lincoln Heights ... 323
Lincoln Hts ... 323
Linda ... 530
Linden ... 209
Lindsay ... 559
Litchfield ... 530
Little Lake ... 209
Little River ... 707
Little Valley ... 530
Littleriver ... 707
Littlerock ... 661
Live Oak ... 530
Livermore ... 925
Livingston ... 209
Lk Arrowhead ... 909
Lk Elsinore ... 909
Llano ... 661
Loch Lomond ... 707
Locke ... 916
Lockeford ... 209
Lockhart ... 760
Lockheed Advanced Dev Co ... 661
Lockwood ... 831
Lodi ... 209
Lodoga ... 530
Loleta ... 707
Loma Linda ... 909
Loma Linda University ... 909
Loma Mar ... 650
Loma Rica ... 530
Lomita ... 310
Lompico ... 831
Lompoc ... 805
London ... 559
Lone Pine ... 760
Long Barn ... 209
Long Beach ... 310, 562
Long Beach Shared Firm ... 562
Long Island ... 916
Lookout ... 530
Loomis ... 916
Loraine ... 661
Los Alamitos ... 562
Los Alamos ... 805
Los Altos ... 650
Los Altos Hills ... 650
Los Angeles ... 213, 310, 323, 626, 818
Los Angeles Afb ... 310
Los Angeles Dodgers ... 323
Los Angeles International Ai ... 310
Los Angls Afb ... 310
Los Banos ... 209
Los Feliz ... 323
Los Gatos ... 408
Los Molinos ... 530
Los Nietos ... 562
Los Olivos ... 661
Los Osos ... 805
Lost Hills ... 661
Lotus ... 530
Lower Lake ... 707
Loyalton ... 530
Lucerne ... 707
Lucerne Valley ... 760
Lucerne Vly ... 760
Lucia ... 831
Ludlow ... 760

Lugo ... 323
Lynwood ... 562
Lyoth ... 209
Lytle Creek ... 909
Macdoel ... 530
Mad River ... 707
Madeline ... 530
Madera ... 559
Madison ... 530
Magalia ... 530
Magra ... 530
Malaga ... 559
Malibu ... 310
Mammoth Lakes ... 760
Manchester ... 707
Manchester Rancheria ... 707
Manhattan Bch ... 310
Manhattan Beach ... 310
Manila ... 707
Manteca ... 209
Manton ... 530
Manzanita ... 530
Mar Vista ... 310
March Air Reserve Base ... 951
March Arb ... 951
Mare Island ... 707
Maricopa ... 661
Marigold ... 909
Marin City ... 415
Marina ... 831
Marina Del Rey ... 310
Marina Dl Rey ... 310
Marine Corp Base ... 760
Marinwood ... 415
Mariposa ... 209
Market ... 213
Markleeville ... 530
Marshall ... 707
Martell ... 209
Martinez ... 925
Marysville ... 530
Massack ... 530
Mather ... 916
Maxwell ... 530
Maywood ... 323
Mc Farland ... 661
Mc Kinleyville ... 707
Mc Kittrick ... 661
Mcarthur ... 530
Mcclellan ... 916
Mccloud ... 530
Mckinleyville ... 707
Meadow Valley ... 530
Meadow Vista ... 530
Mecca ... 760
Medicine Lake Lodge ... 530
Meeks Bay ... 530
Meiners Oaks ... 805
Mellon Regional Lockbox Netw ... 626
Mendocino ... 707
Mendota ... 559
Menifee ... 909
Menlo Park ... 650
Menlo Pk ... 650
Mentone ... 909
Merced ... 209
Meridian ... 530
Mesa Verde ... 760
Mesa Vista ... 530
Metler Valley ... 661
Mettler ... 661
Meyers ... 530
Mi Wuk Village ... 209
Mi Wuk Vlg ... 209
Michigan Bluff ... 530
Middletown ... 707
Midpines ... 209
Midway City ... 714
Milford ... 530
Mill Creek ... 530
Mill Valley ... 415
Millbrae ... 650
Mills Orchard ... 530
Millville ... 530
Milpitas ... 408
Mineral ... 530

Minkler ... 559
Mint Canyon ... 661
Mira Loma ... 909
Miracle Mile ... 323
Mirada ... 714
Miramonte ... 559
Miranda ... 707
Mission Hills ... 818
Mission Rafael ... 415
Mission Viejo ... 949
Moccasin ... 209
Modesto ... 209
Modesto Brm Zip ... 209
Modjeska ... 949
Modjeska Canyon ... 949
Moffett Field ... 408
Moffett Field Nas ... 408
Mojave ... 661, 760
Mokelumne Hill ... 209
Mokelumne Hl ... 209
Monarch Bay ... 949
Monarch Beach ... 949
Mono City ... 760
Mono Hot Spgs ... 559
Mono Hot Springs ... 559
Mono Lake ... 760
Monolith ... 661
Monrovia ... 626, 818
Mont Park ... 323
Mont Pk ... 323
Montague ... 530
Montara ... 650
Montclair ... 909
Monte Nido ... 818
Monte Rio ... 707
Monte Sereno ... 408
Monte Vista ... 408
Montebello ... 323
Montecito ... 805
Monterey ... 831
Monterey Park ... 323, 626
Monterey Pk ... 323
Montgomery Creek ... 530
Montgomry Crk ... 530
Montrose ... 818
Moorpark ... 805
Morada ... 209
Moraga ... 925
Moreno Valley ... 909, 951
Morgan Hill ... 408
Mormon Island ... 916
Morongo Valley ... 760
Morongo Vly ... 760
Morro Bay ... 805
Moss Beach ... 650
Moss Landing ... 831
Mount Aukum ... 209
Mount Eden ... 510
Mount Hamilton ... 408
Mount Hermon ... 831
Mount Laguna ... 619
Mount Shasta ... 530
Mount Signal ... 760
Mount Wilson ... 626
Mountain Center ... 760
Mountain Ctr ... 760
Mountain Home Village ... 909
Mountain House ... 209
Mountain Mesa ... 760
Mountain Pass ... 760
Mountain Ranch ... 209
Mountain View ... 408, 650
Mt Baldy ... 760
Mt Hamilton ... 408
Mt Madonna ... 831
Mt View ... 650
Mtn House ... 209
Mtn Ranch ... 209
Muir Beach ... 415
Muir Woods ... 415
Murphys ... 209
Murrieta ... 951
Murrieta Hot Springs ... 951
Muscoy ... 909
Myers Flat ... 707
N B C ... 818

N Highlands ... 916
N Hollywood ... 818
N Palm Spgs ... 760
N Palm Springs ... 760
N Richmond ... 510
N San Juan ... 530
Nacimiento Lake ... 805
Napa ... 707
Naples ... 562
Nas Lemoore ... 559
Nas Miramar ... 858
Nashville ... 530
National City ... 619
Naval Air Warfare Ctr ... 805
Naval Amphibious Base ... 619
Naval Base Ventura County ... 805
Naval Hospital ... 619
Naval Station 32nd St ... 619
Naval Supply Ctr ... 619
Navarro ... 707
Navelencia ... 559
Needles ... 760
Neenach ... 661
Nelson ... 530
Nestor ... 619
Nevada City ... 530
New Almaden ... 408
New Cuyama ... 661
New Idria ... 831
Newark ... 510
Newberry Spgs ... 760
Newberry Springs ... 760
Newbury Park ... 805
Newcastle ... 916
Newell ... 530
Newhall ... 661, 818
Newman ... 209
Newport Beach ... 949
Newport Coast ... 949
Newtown ... 530
Newville ... 530
Nicasio ... 415
Nice ... 707
Nicolaus ... 530
Niland ... 760
Nimbus ... 916
Nimshew ... 530
Nipinnawassee ... 559
Nipomo ... 805
Nipton ... 760
No Palm Springs ... 760
Norco ... 951
Nord ... 530
Norden ... 530
North Bloomfield ... 530
North Columbia ... 530
North Edwards ... 661
North Fork ... 559
North Highlands ... 916
North Hills ... 818
North Hollywood ... 818
North Loma Linda ... 909
North Long Beach ... 562
North Palm Springs ... 760
North Richmond ... 510
North Sacramento ... 916
North San Juan ... 530
North Shore ... 760
North Tustin ... 714
Northcrest ... 707
Northridge ... 818
Northstar ... 530
Norwalk ... 562
Novato ... 415
Noyo ... 707
Nubieber ... 530
Nuevo ... 909
Nut Tree ... 707
O Neals ... 559
Oak Glen ... 909
Oak Grove ... 530
Oak Hills ... 760
Oak Park ... 818
Oak Run ... 530
Oak Shores ... 805
Oak View ... 805

Oakdale 209
Oakhurst 559
Oakland 510
Oakland Intrntl Service Ctr 510
Oakley 925
Oakville 707
Oakwood 323
Obrien 530
Occidental 707
Ocean Beach 619
Oceano 805
Oceanside 760
Ocotillo 760
Ojai 805
Olancha 760
Old Fort Jim 530
Old Station 530
Olema 415
Olinda 530
Olivehurst 530
Olivenhain 760
Olympic Valley 530
Olympic Vly 530
Omo Ranch 530
One Hundred Palms 760
Onizuka Afb 408
Ontario 909
Onyx 760
Ophir 530
Orange 714
Orange Cove 559
Orangevale 916
Orcutt 805
Ordbend 530
Oregon City 530
Oregon House 530
Orick 707
Orinda 925
Orland 530
Orleans 530
Oro Grande 760
Orosi 559
Oroville 530
Outingdale 530
Ovale 916
Oxnard 805
Pacheco 925
Pacific Area Office 415
Pacific Beach 858
Pacific Gas And Electric 559
Pacific Grove 831
Pacific House 530
Pacific Palisades 310
Pacific Plsds 310
Pacific Valley 831
Pacifica 650
Pacoima 818
Paicines 831
Paintersville 916
Pajaro 831
Pala 760, 951
Palermo 530
Palm Desert 760
Palm Springs 760
Palm Springs Municipal Airpo 760
Palmdale 661
Palms 310
Palo Alto 650
Palo Cedro 530
Palo Verde 760
Palomar Mountain 909
Palomar Mtn 909
Palomar Park 650
Palos Verdes Estates 310
Palos Verdes Peninsula 310
Panamint Springs 760
Panoche 831
Panorama City 818
Paradise 530
Paradise Park 831
Paradise Pines 530
Paramount 562
Parker Dam 760
Parkfield 805
Parlier 559
Pasadena 626
Paskenta 530
Paso Robles 805
Patterson 209
Patton 909
Patton Village 530
Pauma Valley 760
Paynes Creek 530
Peanut 530
Pearblossom 661
Peardale 530
Pearsonville 760
Pebble Beach 831
Peddler Hill 209
Pelican Bay State Prison 707
Penn Valley 530
Penngrove 707
Pennington 530
Penryn 916
Pentz 530
Permanente 408
Perris 909
Pescadero 650
Petaluma 707
Petrolia 707
Pg&e 415
Phelan 760
Philatelic Center 510
Phillips Ranch 909
Phillips Rnch 909
Phillipsville 707
Philo 707
Pico Heights 213
Pico Rivera 562
Piedmont 510
Piedmontxxx 510
Piedra 559
Pierce College 818
Piercy 707
Pike 530
Pilot Hill 530
Pine Bluff 916
Pine Grove 209
Pine Mountain Club 661
Pine Mtn Clb 661
Pine Valley 619
Pinecrest 209
Pinedale 559
Pinehurst 559
Pineridge 559
Pinnacles 831
Pinole 510
Pinon Hills 760
Pinyon Pines 760
Pioneer 209
Pioneer Point 760
Pioneertown 760
Piru 805
Pismo Beach 805
Pittsburg 925
Pittville 530
Pixley 559
Placentia 714
Placerville 530
Planada 209
Platina 530
Playa 949
Playa Del Rey 310
Playa Vista 310
Pleasant Grove 916
Pleasant Grv 916
Pleasant Hill 925
Pleasant Valley 530
Pleasanton 925
Pls Vrds Est 310
Pls Vrds Pnsl 310
Plumas Lake 530
Plymouth 209
Point Arena 707
Point Arena Air Force Statio 707
Point Mugu Nawc 805
Point Reyes Station 415
Point Richmond 510
Point Sur 831
Pollock Pines 530
Pomona 909
Pope Valley 707
Poplar 559
Port Chicago 925
Port Costa 510
Port Hueneme 805
Port Hueneme Cbc Base 805
Port Hueneme Naval Construct 805
Porter Ranch 818
Porterville 559
Portola 530
Portola Hills 949
Portola Valley 650
Portola Vally 650
Posey 661
Postal Data Center 650
Potrero 619
Potter Valley 707
Poway 858
Pozo 805
Prather 559
Prattville 530
Presidio 415
Presidio Mtry 831
Presidio Of Monterey 831
Press Telegram 562
Preuss 310
Princeton 530
Princeton By The Sea 650
Proberta 530
Project City 530
Prosser Lakeview 530
Prt Hueneme 805
Prunedale 831
Pt Mugu Nawc 805
Pt Reyes Sta 415
Pt Reyes Station 415
Pt Richmond 510
Pudding Creek 707
Pulga 530
Pumpkin Center 661
Pumpkin Ctr 661
Quail Valley 909
Quartz Hill 661
Quincy 530
Rackerby 530
Ragged Point 805
Rail Rd Flat 209
Rail Road Flat 209
Railroad Flat 209
Rainbow 760
Raisin City 559
Ralph M Parsons Co 626
Ramona 760
Ranchita 760
Rancho Belago 909
Rancho Bernardo 858
Rancho California 951
Rancho Cordova 916
Rancho Cucamonga 909
Rancho Dominguez 310
Rancho La Tuna Canyon 818
Rancho Mirage 760
Rancho Murieta 916
Rancho Palos Verdes 310
Rancho Park 310
Rancho Santa Fe 858
Rancho Santa Margarita 949
Rancho Sta Marg 949
Randall Island 916
Randsburg 760
Ravendale 530
Raymond 559
Rch Cucamonga 909
Rch Palos Vrd 310
Rcho Santa Fe 858
Rcho Sta Marg 949
Red Bluff 530
Red Mountain 760
Redcrest 707
Redding 530
Redlands 909
Redondo Beach 310
Redway 707
Redwood City 650
Redwood Est 408
Redwood Estates 408
Redwood Lodge 707
Redwood Valley 707
Redwood Vly 707
Reedley 559
Renaissance 530
Represa 916
Rescue 530
Reseda 818
Resighini Rancheria 530
Rialto 909
Richardson Springs 530
Richgrove 661
Richmond 510
Richvale 530
Ridgecrest 760
Ridgewood 530
Rimforest 909
Rimpau 323
Rimrock 760
Rio Del Mar 831
Rio Dell 707
Rio Linda 916
Rio Nido 707
Rio Oso 530
Rio Vista 707
Ripley 760
Ripon 209
River Bank 916
River Kern 760
River Pines 209
Riverbank 209
Riverdale 559
Riverside 909
Rllng Hls Est 310
Rncho Cordova 916
Rncho Domingz 310
Rncho Murieta 916
Robbins 530
Robinson Ranch 949
Robinson Rnch 949
Robinsons Corner 530
Robles Del Rio 831
Rock Creek 530
Rock Crest 530
Rocklin 916
Rockport 707
Rodale Press 323
Rodeo 510
Rogers Flat 530
Rohnert Park 707
Rolinda 559
Rolling Hills 310
Rolling Hills Estates 310
Romoland 909
Roosevelt Corner 661
Rosamond 661
Roseland 707
Rosemead 626
Roseville 916
Rosewood 310
Ross 415
Rossmoor 562
Rough And Ready 530
Rough Ready 530
Round Mountain 530
Round Mtn 530
Round Valley 760
Rovana 760
Rowland Heights 626
Rowland Hghts 626
Rowland Hgts 626
Royal Oaks 831
Rsm 949
Rubicon Bay 530
Rubidoux 951
Rumsey 530
Running Spgs 909
Running Springs 909
Russian River 707
Russian River Mdws 707
Ruth 707
Rutherford 707
Ryde 916
Ryer Island 916
S B County Offices 909
S Dos Palos 209
S El Monte 626
S Lake Tahoe 530
S Pasadena 626
S San Fran 650
S San Francisco 650
Sacramento 916
Safeway Stores 510
Saint Helena 707
Salinas 831
Salmon Creek 707
Salton City 760
Salyer 530
Samoa 707
San Andreas 209
San Anselmo 415
San Ardo 831
San Benito 831
San Bernardino 909
San Bruno 650
San Buenaventura 805
San Carlos 650
San Clemente 949
San Diego 619, 858
San Diego County Jail 619
San Diego Gas And Electric 858
San Diego State University 619
San Diego Water Utilities 858
San Dimas 909
San Fernando 818
San Francisco 415, 510, 650
San Francisco Intnl Airport 650
San Gabriel 626
San Geronimo 415
San Gregorio 650
San Jacinto 909, 951
San Joaquin 559
San Jose 408
San Jose Mercury News 408
San Jose State University 408
San Jose Water Company 408
San Juan Bautista 831
San Juan Capistrano 949
San Juan Capo 949
San Leandro 510
San Lorenzo 510
San Lucas 805
San Luis Obispo 805
San Luis Rey 760
San Marcos 760
San Marin 415
San Marino 626
San Martin 408
San Mateo 650
San Miguel 805
San Pablo 510
San Pedro 310, 562
San Quentin 415
San Rafael 415
San Ramon 925
San Simeon 805
San Ysidro 619
Sand Canyon 661
Sand City 831
Sandberg 661
Sandy Korner 760
Sanford 213
Sanger 559
Santa Ana 714
Santa Barbara 805
Santa Barbara P & D Ctr 805
Santa Catalina 310
Santa Clara 408
Santa Clara University 408
Santa Clarita 661, 818
Santa Cruz 831
Santa Fe Spgs 562
Santa Fe Springs 562
Santa Margar 805
Santa Margarita 805
Santa Maria 805
Santa Monica 310
Santa Nella 209
Santa Paula 805
Santa Rita Park 209
Santa Rita Pk 209
Santa Rosa 707
Santa Rosa Va 805
Santa Rosa Valley 805
Santa Susana 805
Santa Venetia 415
Santa Western 323
Santa Ynez 805
Santa Ysabel 760
Santee 619
Saratoga 408
Saratoga Hills 818
Saratoga Hls 818
Saticoy 805
Sattley 530
Saugus 661
Sausalito 415
Sawyers Bar 530
Schellville 707
Scotia 707
Scott Bar 530
Scotts Valley 831
Seacliff 831
Seal Beach 562
Seascape 831
Seaside 831
Sebastopol 707
Seeley 760
Seiad Valley 530
Selma 559
Seneca 530
Sepulveda 818
Seq Natl Pk 559
Sequoia National Park 559
Serene Lakes 530
Seven Oaks 909
Sf International Service Ctr 415
Shadow Hills 818
Shady Glen 530
Shafter 661
Shandon 661
Shared Firm Zip Code 323, 626
Sharon 559
Sharp Park 650
Shasta 530
Shasta Lake 530
Shaver Lake 559
Sheep Ranch 209
Sheepranch 209
Shell Beach 805
Shelter Cove 707
Sheridan 530, 707
Sherman Oaks 818
Sherman Village 818
Sherman Vlg 818
Sherwood Valley Rancheria 707
Shingle Spgs 530
Shingle Springs 530
Shingletown 530
Shoshone 760
Sierra Army Depot 530
Sierra City 530
Sierra Madre 626
Sierraville 530
Signal Hill 562
Signal Hl 562
Silver Fork 530
Silver Lake 209, 213
Silver Lakes 760
Silverado 949
Simi Valley 805
Sisquoc 805
Sites 530
Sky Valley 760
Skyforest 909
Sleepy Valley 661
Slo County Govt Ctr 805
Sloughhouse 916
Smartsville 530
Smiley Heights 909
Smith River 707
Smoke Tree 760
Sn Bernrdno 909
Sn Jun Batsta 831
Sn Luis Obisp 805
Sn Margarita 805
Snelling 209
Snowline Camp 530

So Cal Edison Co ... 626
Soda Springs ... 530
Solana Beach ... 858
Soledad ... 831
Solvang ... 805
Somerset ... 530
Somes Bar ... 530
Somesbar ... 530
Somis ... 805
Sonoma ... 707
Sonora ... 209
Soquel ... 831
Soulsbyville ... 209
South ... 323
South Dos Palos ... 209
South El Monte ... 626
South Gate ... 323
South Laguna ... 949
South Lake Tahoe ... 530
South Main ... 714
South Oroville ... 530
South Pasadena ... 626
South San Francis ... 650
South San Francisco ... 650
Southern California Gas Co ... 323
Southport ... 916
Spanish Flat ... 707
Spanish Ranch ... 530
Spaulding ... 530
Spawars System Center ... 619
Spg Valley Lk ... 760
Spreckels ... 831
Spring Garden ... 530
Spring Hill ... 530
Spring Valley ... 619
Spring Valley Lake ... 760
Springville ... 559
Squaw Valley ... 559
Ssf ... 650
Stallion Spgs ... 661
Stallion Springs ... 661
Standard ... 209
Standish ... 530
Stanford ... 650
Stanton ... 714
Starcrest Of Cal ... 909
Starlight Hills ... 818
State Farm Insurance ... 707
Stateline ... 530
Stevenson Ranch ... 661
Stevenson Rnh ... 661
Stevinson ... 209
Stewarts Point ... 707
Stewarts Point Rancheria ... 707
Stewarts Pt ... 707
Stinson Beach ... 415
Stirling City ... 530
Stkn ... 209
Stockton ... 209
Stockton Brm Zip ... 209
Stonyford ... 530
Storrie ... 530
Stove Pipe Wells ... 760
Stratford ... 559
Strathmore ... 559
Strawberry ... 209
Strawberry Point ... 415
Strawberry Valley ... 530
Strawbrry Vly ... 530
Studio City ... 818
Sugarloaf ... 909
Suisun City ... 707, 925
Sulphur Bank Rancheria ... 707
Sultana ... 559
Summerland ... 805
Summit City ... 530
Sun City ... 909
Sun Valley ... 818
Sun Village ... 661
Sunkist ... 714
Sunland ... 818
Sunnybrook ... 209
Sunnyvale ... 408
Sunol ... 925
Sunset Beach ... 562
Sunset View ... 530

Sunset Whitney Ranch ... 916
Surfside ... 714
Susanville ... 530
Sutter ... 530
Sutter Creek ... 209
Sutter Hill ... 209
Sutter Island ... 916
Swall Meadows ... 760
Swansboro Country ... 530
Swansea ... 760
Sweet Brier ... 530
Sweetland ... 530
Sycamore ... 530
Sylmar ... 818
T K Manufacturing ... 619
Taft ... 661
Tahoe City ... 530
Tahoe Donner ... 530
Tahoe Paradise ... 530
Tahoe Pines ... 530
Tahoe Valley ... 530
Tahoe Vista ... 530
Tahoma ... 530
Talmage ... 707
Tamalpais Valley ... 415
Tara Hills ... 510
Tarzana ... 818
Tassajara Hot Springs ... 831
Taylorsville ... 530
Tecate ... 619
Tecopa ... 760
Tecopa Hot Springs ... 760
Tehachapi ... 661
Tehama ... 530
Temecula ... 951
Temple City ... 626
Templeton ... 805
Terminal Island ... 562
Termo ... 530
Terra Bella ... 559
Terra Linda ... 415
Textile Boxes ... 213
Textile Finance ... 213
The Cedars ... 530
The Geysers ... 707
The Sea Ranch ... 707
Thermal ... 760
Thermalito ... 530
Thornton ... 209
Thousand Oaks ... 805
Thousand Palms ... 760
Thousand Plms ... 760
Three Points ... 661
Three Rivers ... 559
Three Rocks ... 559
Tiburon ... 415
Tierra Buena ... 530
Tionesta ... 530
Tipton ... 559
Tivy Valley ... 559
Tobin ... 530
Todd Valley ... 530
Tollhouse ... 559
Toluca Lake ... 818
Toluca Ter ... 818
Toluca Terrace ... 818
Tomales ... 707
Toms Place ... 760
Tonyville ... 559
Topanga ... 310
Topaz ... 530
Torrance ... 310
Torres Martinez Indian Reser ... 760
Tournament Of Roses Assoc ... 626
Trabuco ... 949
Trabuco Canyon ... 949
Trabuco Cyn ... 949
Tracy ... 209
Tranquillity ... 559
Travel Lodge ... 619
Traver ... 559
Travis Afb ... 707
Tres Pinos ... 831
Trinidad ... 707
Trinity Center ... 530
Trinity Ctr ... 530

Trona ... 760
Tropico Village ... 661
Trowbridge ... 530
Truckee ... 530
Tujunga ... 818
Tulare ... 559
Tulelake ... 530
Tuolumne ... 209
Tuolumne Mdws ... 209
Tuolumne Meadows ... 209
Tupman ... 661
Turlock ... 209
Tustin ... 714
Twain ... 530
Twain Harte ... 209
Twentynin Plm ... 760
Twentynine Palms ... 760
Twentynine Palms Mcb ... 760
Twin Bridges ... 530
Twin Peaks ... 909
Two Rock Coast Guard Station ... 707
Two Rock Ranch Sta ... 707
U C Berkeley ... 510
U S Purchasing Corp ... 818
U S Purchasing Exchange ... 818
Uc Berkeley ... 510
Uci ... 949
Ucla ... 310
Ucsb ... 805, 858
Ucsb Student Dorm Boxes ... 805
Ucsd ... 858
Ucsf ... 415
Ukiah ... 707
Union Bank Of California ... 415
Union City ... 510
Union Hill ... 530
United Faith Found ... 559
Univ Of Ca Riverside ... 909
Univ Of Ca Santa Barbara ... 805
Univ Of Cal Santa Barbara ... 805
Univ Of California Irvine ... 949
Univ Of The Pacific ... 209
Universal City ... 818
Universal Cty ... 818
University Of Southern Ca ... 213
Upland ... 909
Upper Lake ... 707
Us Naval Air Station ... 559
Us Purchasing Exchange ... 818
V A Hosp ... 858
Vacaville ... 707
Vafb ... 805
Val Verde ... 661
Valencia ... 661, 818
Valerie ... 760
Vallecito ... 209
Vallejo ... 707
Valley Center ... 760
Valley Ford ... 707
Valley Glen ... 818
Valley Home ... 209
Valley Of Enchantment ... 909
Valley Spgs ... 209
Valley Springs ... 209
Valley Village ... 818
Valley Vlg ... 818
Valyermo ... 661
Van Nuys ... 818
Vandenberg Afb ... 805
Vandenberg Air Force Base ... 805
Vandenberg Village ... 805
Vandenbrg Afb ... 805
Venice ... 310
Ventura ... 805
Ventura County Gov ... 805
Verdemont ... 909
Verdugo City ... 818
Vermont ... 323
Vernalis ... 209
Vernon ... 323
Verona ... 530
Verona Landing ... 530
Veterans Adm ... 310
Veterans Admin ... 310
Veterans Administration ... 310
Veterans Admn ... 310

Veterans' Hospital ... 909
Victor ... 209
Victorville ... 760
Vidal ... 760
Vidal Junction ... 760
View Park ... 323
Villa Grande ... 707
Villa Park ... 714
Villa Verona ... 530
Village ... 310
Vina ... 530
Vineburg ... 707
Vinton ... 530
Viola ... 530
Virgilia ... 530
Virner ... 530
Visalia ... 559
Vista ... 760
Vista Santa Rosa ... 760
Volcano ... 209
Volcanoville ... 530
Vorden ... 916
W Hollywood ... 310, 323
W Los Angeles ... 310
W Menlo Park ... 650
W Sacramento ... 916
W Toluca Lake ... 818
Wagner ... 323
Walker ... 530
Walker Landing ... 916
Wallace ... 209
Walnut ... 909
Walnut Creek ... 925
Walnut Grove ... 916
Walnut Park ... 323
Walsh Station ... 916
Walt Disney Co ... 818
Warner Spgs ... 760
Warner Springs ... 760
Wasco ... 661
Washington ... 530
Waterford ... 209
Watsonville ... 831
Watts ... 323
Waukena ... 559
Wawona ... 209
Weaverville ... 530
Weed ... 530
Weimar ... 530
Weitchpec ... 530
Weldon ... 760
Wells Fargo Bank ... 415, 626
Wendel ... 530
Wentworth Springs ... 530
Weott ... 707
West Adams ... 310
West Covina ... 626
West Hills ... 818
West Hollywood ... 310, 323
West Linda ... 530
West Los Angeles ... 310
West Menlo Park ... 650
West Pittsburg ... 925
West Point ... 209
West Sacramento ... 916
West Sacto ... 916
West Toluca Lake ... 818
West Truckee ... 530
Westchester ... 310
Westhaven ... 707
Westlake Village ... 805
Westlake Vlg ... 805
Westley ... 209
Westminster ... 714
Westmorland ... 760
Westport ... 707
Westvern ... 323
Westwood ... 530
Wheatland ... 530
Whiskeytown ... 530
White Rock ... 916
Whitethorn ... 707
Whitewater ... 760
Whitmore ... 530
Whittier ... 562
Wilbur Springs ... 530

Wilcox ... 323
Wildomar ... 951
Wildwood ... 530
Willaura Estates ... 530
Williams ... 530
Willits ... 707
Willow Creek ... 530
Willow Ranch ... 530
Willow Spgs ... 661
Willow Springs ... 661
Willows ... 530
Wilmington ... 310
Wilseyville ... 209
Wilshire-La Brea ... 323
Wilsona Gardens ... 661
Wilsonia ... 559
Wilton ... 916
Winchester ... 909
Windsor ... 707
Windsor Hills ... 310
Winnetka ... 818
Winterhaven ... 760
Winters ... 530
Winton ... 209
Wishon ... 559
Witter Spgs ... 707
Witter Springs ... 707
Wla ... 310
Wofford Heights ... 760
Wofford Hts ... 760
Woodacre ... 415
Woodbridge ... 209
Woodcrest ... 909
Woodfords ... 530
Woodlake ... 559
Woodland ... 530
Woodland Hills ... 818
Woodland Hls ... 818
Woodleaf ... 530
Woodside ... 650
Woodville ... 559
Woody ... 661
Wrightwood ... 760
Wyandotte ... 530
Xl Ranch Indian Reservation ... 530
Yankee Hill ... 530
Yankee Jims ... 530
Yermo ... 760
Yettem ... 559
Yolo ... 530
Yorba Linda ... 714
Yorkville ... 707
Yosemite ... 209
Yosemite National Park ... 209
Yosemite Ntpk ... 209
Yountville ... 707
Yreka ... 530
Yuba City ... 530
Yucaipa ... 909
Yucca Valley ... 760
Zamora ... 530
Zenia ... 707

Colorado

Adams City ... 303
Adams State College ... 719
Af Acctg & Finance Ctr ... 303
Af Reserve Pers Ctr ... 303
Affiliated Banks Service Co ... 303
Affliated National Bank ... 719
Agate ... 719
Aguilar ... 719
Akron ... 970
Alamosa ... 719
Allenspark ... 303
Allison ... 970
Alma ... 719
Almont ... 970
Alpine ... 719
Alpine Village ... 719
Amherst ... 970
Antlers ... 970
Anton ... 970
Antonito ... 719

Appleton ... 970
Aqua Ramon ... 719
Arapahoe ... 719
Arapahoe County Offices ... 303
Arboles ... 970
Arickaree ... 970
Ark Valley Corr Facl ... 719
Arlington ... 719
Aroya ... 719
Arriba ... 719
Arriola ... 970
Arvada ... 303
Aspen ... 970
Aspen Park ... 303
Aspen-Gerbaz ... 970
Atwood ... 970
Ault ... 970
Aurora ... 303
Austin ... 970
Avon ... 970
Avondale ... 719
Axel ... 970
Bailey ... 303
Baldwin ... 970
Bank Americard ... 303
Barton ... 719
Basalt ... 970
Battlement Mesa ... 970
Baxter ... 719
Baxterville ... 719
Bayfield ... 970
Bear Mine ... 970
Beaver Creek ... 970
Bedrock ... 970
Belle Plain ... 719
Bellvue ... 970
Bennett ... 303
Bents Fort ... 719
Bents Old Fort ... 719
Berthoud ... 970
Beshoar Jct ... 719
Bessemer ... 719
Bethune ... 719
Beulah ... 719
Big Bend ... 719
Black Forest ... 719
Black Hawk ... 303
Blackhawk ... 303
Blanca ... 719
Blende ... 719
Blue Cross Blue Shield Of Co ... 303
Blue Mountain ... 970
Bonanza City ... 719
Boncarbo ... 719
Bond ... 970
Boone ... 719
Boulder ... 303
Bountiful ... 719
Bovina ... 719
Bow Mar ... 303
Bowie ... 970
Boyero ... 719
Brandon ... 719
Branson ... 719
Breckenridge ... 970
Breen ... 970
Brewster ... 719
Briggsdale ... 970
Brighton ... 303
Bristol ... 719
Broadacre ... 719
Broomfield ... 303
Browns Park ... 970
Brush ... 970
Btlmt Mesa ... 970
Buckley Air Natl Guard Base ... 303
Buckley Ang ... 303
Buckskin Joe ... 719
Buena Vista ... 719
Buffalo Creek ... 303
Buford ... 970
Burlington ... 719
Burns ... 970
Byers ... 303
C O Interstate Gas ... 719
Caddoa ... 719

City	Area Code
Cadet Station	719
Cahone	970
Calhan	719
Campo	719
Canon City	719
Capulin	719
Carbondale	970
Cardiff	970
Carlton	719
Carmel	719
Carr	970
Cascade	719
Castle Rock	303
Cedaredge	970
Cedarwood	970
Cement Creek	970
Centennial	303
Center	719
Central City	303
Chama	719
Cheney Center	719
Cheraw	719
Cherry Hills	303
Cherry Hills Village	303
Cherry Hl Vlg	303
Chey Mtn Afb	719
Cheyenne Mountain Afb	719
Cheyenne Mt Complex	719
Cheyenne Mtn Afb	719
Cheyenne Wells	719
Cheyenne Wls	719
Chimney Rock	970
Chipita Park	719
Chivington	719
Chromo	970
Cimarron	970
Cimarron Hills	719
Clark	970
Cleora	719
Clifton	970
Climax	970
Cmafb	719
Co Spgs	719
Co Spgs Utilities	719
Coal Creek	719
Coalby	970
Coaldale	719
Coalmont	970
Cokedale	719
Collbran	970
College Heights Durango	970
Colo City	719
Colo Spgs	719
Colona	970
Colorado City	719
Colorado College	719
Colorado D M V Dept Of Rev	303
Colorado Dept Of Revenue	303
Colorado Lottery	719
Colorado National Monument	970
Colorado Spgs	719
Colorado Springs	719
Colorado State University	970
Columbine Valley	303
Columbine Vly	303
Comcast	719
Commerce City	303
Como	303
Compassion International	719
Conejos	719
Conifer	303
Consolidated Space Operation	719
Cope	970
Copper Mtn	970
Cordillera	970
Cortez	970
Cory	970
Cotopaxi	719
Cowdrey	970
Craig	970
Crawford	970
Creede	719
Crested Butte	970
Crested Butte So	970
Crestone	719
Cripple Creek	719
Crook	970
Crowley	719
Crystal	970
Crystal Hills	719
Crystola	719
Csoc	719
Cuchara	719
Current Inc	719
Dacono	303
De Beque	970
Deckers	303
Deer Trail	303
Del Norte	719
Delhi	719
Delta	970
Denver	303
Denver Federal Center	303
Deora	719
Devine	719
Dillon	970
Dinosaur	970
Divide	719
Dolores	970
Dotsero	970
Dove Creek	970
Doyleville	970
Drake	970
Dumont	303
Dunton	970
Dupont	303
Durango	970
Eads	719
Eagle	970
East Alamosa	719
East Lake	303
East Orchard Mesa	970
East Vail	970
East Weston	719
Eastlake	303
Eastman Kodak Co	970
Eaton	970
Eckert	970
Eckley	970
Edgewater	303
Edison	719
Edler	719
Edwards	970
Egnar	970
El Jebel	970
El Moro	719
El Rito	719
Elbert	719
Eldorado Sprg	303
Eldorado Springs	303
Elizabeth	303
Elk Springs	970
Elkton	719
Ellicott	719
Empire	303
Englewood	303
Ent Air Force Base	719
Erie	303
Espinoza	719
Estes Park	970
Estrella	719
Evans	970
Evergreen	303
Fair View	970
Fairmont	719
Fairplay	303, 719
Falcon	719
Falcon Afb	719
Farisita	719
Farista	719
Federal Bldg/Us Courthouse	303
Federal Correctional Complex	719
Federal Heights	303
Federal Hgts	303
Firestone	303
First View	719
Flagler	970
Fleming	970
Florence	719
Florida	970
Florissant	719
Florissant Fossil Beds Natio	719
Focus On The Family	719
Forbes Park	719
Fort Bent	719
Fort Carson	719
Fort Collins	970
Fort Garland	719
Fort Logan	303
Fort Lupton	303
Fort Lyon	719
Fort Morgan	970
Fountain	719
Fowler	719
Fox Creek	719
Foxfield	303
Foxton	303
Franktown	303
Fraser	970
Frederick	303
Freeman	719
Frisco	970
Fruita	970
Fruitvale	970
Ft Bent	719
Ft Carson	719
Ft Collins	970
Ft Garland	719
Ft Logan	303
Ft Lupton	303
Ft Lyon	719
G P O	719
Galeton	970
Garcia	719
Garden City	970
Gardner	719
Gateway	970
Gem Village	970
Genoa	719
Georgetown	303
Gilcrest	970
Gill	970
Gilman	970
Glade Park	970
Glen Haven	970
Glendale	303
Glenwood	970
Glenwood Spgs	970
Glenwood Springs	970
Golden	303
Goldfield	719
Granada	719
Granby	970
Grand Jct	970
Grand Junction	970
Grand Lake	970
Grand Mesa	970
Grand Valley	970
Granite	719
Grant	303
Grants Ranch	303
Great Sand Dunes National Mo	719
Greeley	970
Green Mountain Falls	719
Green Mtn Fls	719
Greenwood	719
Greenwood Village	303
Greenwood Vlg	303
Greystone	970
Grover	970
Guffey	719
Gunnison	970
Gypsum	970
Hale	970
Hamilton	970
Hartman	719
Hartsel	719
Hasty	719
Haswell	719
Hawley	719
Haxtun	970
Hayden	970
Heeney	970
Henderson	303
Henry	719
Hereford	970
Hermosa	970
Hesperus	970
Hghlnds Ranch	303
Highlands Ranch	303
Hillrose	970
Hillside	719
Hoehne	719
Holly	719
Holyoke	970
Homelake	719
Hooper	719
Horn Creek	719
Hot Slphr Spr	970
Hot Sulphur Springs	970
Hotchkiss	970
Hovenweep National Monument	970
Howard	719
Hoyt	970
Hudson	303
Hugo	719
Hygiene	303
I B M	303
Idaho Springs	303
Idalia	970
Idledale	303
Ignacio	970
Iliff	970
Ilse	719
Indian Agency	970
Indian Creek	719
Indian Hills	303
Iola	970
Iron City	719
Irondale	303
Jacks Cabin	970
Jamestown	303
Jansen	719
Jaroso	719
Jefferson	719
Jefferson County	303
Joes	970
John Martin Reservoir	719
Johnson Village	719
Johnstown	970
Julesburg	970
Karval	719
Keenesburg	303
Kersey	970
Keystone	970
Kim	719
Kiowa	719
Kirk	970
Kit Carson	719
Kittredge	303
Kline	970
Koen	719
Kornman	719
Kremmling	970
La Isla	719
La Jara	719
La Junta	719
La Salle	970
La Veta	719
Lafayette	303
Laird	970
Lake City	970
Lake George	719
Lakeside	303
Lakewood	303
Lamar	719
Laporte	970
Lariat	719
Larkspur	719
Las Animas	719
Las Mesitas	719
Lasauses	719
Lascar	719
Last Chance	970
Lay	970
Lazear	970
Leadville	719, 970
Lewis	970
Limon	719
Limon Correctional Fac	719
Limon Correctional Facility	719
Limon Crrctnl	719
Lindon	970
Littleton	303
Littleton City Offices	303
Livermore	970
Lobatos	719
Lochbuie	303
Log Lane Village	970
Log Lane Vlg	970
Loma	970
Lone Tree	303
Lonetree	303
Longmont	303
Los Fuertes	719
Los Pinas	719
Louisville	303
Louviers	303
Loveland	970
Lowry	303
Lubers	719
Lucerne	970
Ludlow	719
Lycan	719
Lyons	303
Mack	970
Maher	970
Manassa	719
Mancos	970
Manitou Spgs	719
Manitou Springs	719
Manzanola	719
Marble	970
Marvel	970
Masonic Park	719
Masonville	970
Massadona	970
Matheson	719
Maxey	719
Maxeyville	719
May Valley	719
Maybell	970
Maysville	719
Mc Clave	719
Mc Coy	970
Mead	970
Meeker	970
Meredith	970
Meridian Lake	970
Merino	970
Mesa	970
Mesa Verde	970
Mesa Verde National Park	970
Mesita	719
Milliken	970
Minturn	970
Mirage	719
Model	719
Moffat	719
Mogote	719
Molina	970
Monarch	719
Montbello	303
Montclair	303
Monte Vista	719
Montezuma	970
Montrose	970
Monument	719
Monument Lake Park	719
Monument Park	719
Morgan	719
Morrison	303
Mosca	719
Mount Crested Butte	970
Mount Princeton	719
Mountain Village	970
Mountain Vlg	970
Mt Crested Butte	970
Mutual	719
N Avondale	719
Nast	970
Nathrop	719
National Farmers Union	303
Naturita	970
Navajo State Park	970
Nederland	303
Neodata	303
Neodata Business Reply	303
New Castle	970
New Liberty	970
New Raymer	970
Ninaview	719
Niwot	303
No Name	970
Norrie	970
North Avondale	719
North Glenn	303
North La Junta	719
Northglenn	303
Norwood	970
Nucla	970
Numa	719
Nunn	970
Oak Creek	970
Ohio City	970
Ojo	719
Olathe	970
Old Snowmass	970
Olney Springs	719
Ophir	970
Orchard	970
Orchard City	970
Ordway	719
Ortiz	719
Otis	970
Ouray	970
Ovid	970
Oxford	970
Padroni	970
Pagoda	970
Pagosa Lakes	970
Pagosa Spgs	970
Pagosa Springs	970
Paisaje	719
Palisade	970
Palmer Lake	719
Pandora	970
Paoli	970
Paonia	970
Parachute	970
Paradox	970
Parkdale	719
Parker	303
Parlin	970
Parshall	970
Peetz	970
Penitentiary	719
Penrose	719
Peterson A F B	719
Peterson Afb	719
Peterson Air Force Base	719
Peyton	719
Phippsburg	970
Piedra	970
Piedre Park	970
Pierce	970
Pine	303
Pinecliffe	303
Pinon	719
Pinon Canyon	719
Pitkin	970
Placerville	970
Plateau City	970
Platteville	970
Plaza	719
Pleasant View	970
Poncha Spgs	719
Poncha Springs	719
Portland	719
Powderhorn	970
Pritchett	719
Prospect Heights	719
Prowers	719
Pryor	719
Pueblo	719
Pueblo Army Depot	719
Pueblo Dep Ac	719
Pueblo Depot Activity	719
Pueblo West	719
Punkin Center	719
Purgatory	970
Rainbow	970
Ramah	719
Rand	970
Rangely	970
Raymer	970

Red Cliff 970
Red Fe Lks 970
Red Feather Lakes 970
Red Mountain 970
Redmesa 970
Redstone 970
Redvale 970
Residence Halls Univ Of Co 303
Richfield 719
Rico 970
Ridgway 970
Rifle 970
Rio Blanco 970
Riverbend 970
Roberta 719
Rockrimmon 719
Rockvale 719
Rocky Ford 719
Rocky Mountain National Park 970
Rogers Mesa 970
Roggen 303
Rollinsville 303
Romeo 719
Rosita 719
Ruedi 970
Rulison 970
Rush 719
Rye 719
S Ute Indian 970
Saguache 719
Saint Elmo 719
Salida 719
San Acacio 719
San Antonio 719
San Francisco 719
San Isabel 719
San Luis 719
San Miguel 719
San Pablo 719
San Pedro 719
San Rafeal 719
Sand Dunes Mo 719
Sanford 719
Sangre De Cri 719
Sangre De Cristo Ranches 719
Sapinero 970
Sargents 970
Sargents School 719
Sawpit 970
Schriever Afb 719
Schriever Air Force Base 719
Schriever Air Station 719
Security 719
Sedalia 303
Sedgwick 970
Segundo 719
Seibert 970
Severance 970
Shady Camp 719
Shawnee 303
Sheridan 303
Sheridan Lake 719
Silt 970
Silver Cliff 719
Silver Plume 303
Silvercreek 970
Silverthorne 303
Silverton 970
Simla 719
Skyland 970
Slater 970
Slick Rock 970
Small Business Adm 303
Smeltertown 719
Snowmass 970
Snowmass Village 970
Snowmass Vlg 970
Snyder 970
So Ute Indian Res 970
Somerset 970
Sopris 719
South Fork 719
Southern Ute Indian Reservat 970
Spar City 719
Spring Creek 970
Springfield 719
Squaw Point 970
Stanley 719
Starkville 719
State Farm Ins 970
Steamboat 970
Steamboat Spr 970
Steamboat Springs 970
Sterling 970
Stoneham 970
Stoner 970
Stonewall 719
Stonington 719
Storage Technology Corp 303
Strasburg 303
Stratmoor Hills 719
Stratton 719
Sugar City 719
Summitville 719
Superior 303
Sweetwater 970
Swink 719
Swissvale 719
Tabernash 970
Tamarron 970
Tanglewood Acres 719
Tarryall 719
Taylor Park 970
Teledyne Water Pik 970
Telluride 970
Tercio 719
Texas Creek 719
Thatcher 719
Thornton 303
Tiffany 970
Timber Lake 719
Timnath 970
Timpas 719
Tincup 970
Toltec 719
Toonerville 719
Toponas 970
Torres Canon 719
Towaoc 970
Towner 719
Track City 719
Trinchera 719
Trinidad 719
Truckton 719
Turret 719
Twin Lakes 719
Twin Rock 719
Two Buttes 719
Tyrone 719
U S A F Academy 719
U S West Communications 303
United States Air Force Acad 719
Univ Of Colorado Med Ctr 303
Univ Of Northern Colorado 970
University Of Colorado 303
University Of Denver 303
Us Air Force 719
Us Bank 303
Us Bank Exchange 719
Us Court Of Appeals 10th Cir 303
Us Olympic 719
Us Olympic Committee 719
Usaf Academy 719
Ute Mountain Indian Reservat 970
Ute Pass 719
Utleyville 719
Vail 970
Vallecito 970
Vernon 970
Victor 719
Vigil 719
Vilas 719
Villa Grove 719
Villegreen 719
Vineland 719
Virginia Dale 970
Vona 719
Vroman 719
Wagon Wheel Gap 719
Wahatoya 719
Walden 970
Walsenburg 719
Walsh 719
Walter Drake 719
Ward 303
Washington 719
Watkins 303
Wattenburg 303
Waverly 719
Welby 303
Weldona 970
Wellington 970
Wells Fargo Bank 303
Wellsville 719
West Farm 719
West Glenwood 970
West Vail 970
West Village 970
Westcliffe 719
Western Area 303
Western State College 970
Westminster 303
Weston 719
Westwood Lake 719
Wetmore 719
Wheat Ridge 303
White Pine 970
Whitewater 970
Widefield 719
Wiggins 970
Wild Horse 719
Wildhorse Mesa 719
Wiley 719
Willard 970
Williamsburg 719
Windsor 970
Windy Point 970
Winter Park 970
Wolcott 970
Woodland Park 719
Woodmoor 719
Woodrow 970
Woody Creek 970
Wray 970
Yampa 970
Yellow Jacket 970
Yoder 719
Yuma 970

Connecticut

A A R P Pharmacy 860
Abington 860
Accr A Data 860
Advertising Distr Co 203
Aetna Insurance 860
Aetna Life 860
Allingtown 203
Allstate 860
Amston 860
Andover 860
Ansonia 203
Ashford 860
Avon 860
Bakersville 860
Ballouville 860
Baltic 860
Bank Of America 860
Bantam 860
Barkhamsted 860
Barry Square 860
Beacon Falls 203
Belle Haven 203
Berlin 860
Bethany 203
Bethel 203
Bethlehem 860
Bishop's Corner 860
Bishops Cor 860
Bishops Corner 860
Bissell 860
Bkln 860
Bloomfield 860
Bloomingdales By Mail Ltd 203
Blue Hills 860
Bolton 860
Borough 860
Botsford 203
Bozrah 860
Bradley International Airpor 860
Branford 203
Bridgeport 203
Bridgewater 860
Bristol 860
Broad Brook 860
Brookfield 203
Brookfield Center 203
Brookfld Ctr 203
Brooklyn 860
Burlington 860
C T Mutual Insurance Co 860
Canaan 860
Canterbury 860
Canton 860
Canton Center 860
Center Groton 860
Centerbrook 860
Centerville-Mount Carmel 203
Central 860
Central Village 860
Central Vlg 860
Champion International 203
Chaplin 860
Cherry Brook 860
Cheshire 203
Chester 860
Chesterfield 860
Chestnut Hill 860
Clairol Co 203
Clinton 860
Cobalt 860
Colbrook 860
Colchester 860
Colebrook 860
Collinsville 860
Columbia 860
Conantville 860
Conn Bank & Trust 203
Conn Bank & Trust Co 203
Conn National Bank 203
Connecticut State Prison 860
Controlled Distribution 203
Corbins Corner 860
Cornwall 860
Cornwall Brg 860
Cornwall Bridge 860
Cos Cob 203
Coventry 860
Cromwell 860
Ct Dept Of Motor Vehicles 860
Ct Gen Med Claims Office 203
Danbury 203
Danielson 860
Darien 203
Dayville 860
Deep River 860
Derby 203
Durham 860
E Glastonbury 860
E Glstnbry 860
E Hartford 860
E Haven 203
E Htfd 860
E Killingly 860
E Windsor Hl 860
E Woodstock 860
East Berlin 860
East Brooklyn 860
East Canaan 860
East End 203
East Glastonbury 860
East Granby 860
East Haddam 860
East Hampton 860
East Hartford 860
East Hartland 860
East Haven 203
East Htfd 860
East Killingly 860
East Lyme 860
East Norwalk 203
East Putnam 860
East Thompson 860
East Willington 860
East Windsor 860
East Windsor Hill 860
East Woodstock 860
Eastford 860
Easton 203
Ellington 860
Elliot 860
Elmwood 860
Enfield 860
Essex 860
Exeter 860
Fabyan 860
Fair Haven 203
Fairfield 203
Falls Village 860
Farmington 860
Fenwick 860
Fitchville 860
Forbes Village 860
Forestville 860
Fosdick Corp 203
Franklin 860
Franklin Hill 860
Ft Trumbull 860
Gales Ferry 860
Gaylordsville 860
Gecc 203
General Electric 203
Georgetown 203
Gilman 860
Glasgo 860
Glastonbury 860
Glenbrook 203
Glenville 203
Goshen 860
Granby 860
Greens Farms 203
Greenwich 203
Griswold 860
Grolier Entrprz Inc 203
Grosvenor Dale 860
Grosvenor Dl 860
Groton 860
Groton Long Point 860
Guilford 203
Gurleyville 860
Haddam 860
Haddam Neck 860
Hadlyme 860
Hamden 203
Hampton 860
Hanover 860
Hartford 860
Hartford Insurance Group 860
Hartford Natl Bank 860
Hartfrd 860
Harwinton 860
Hawleyville 203
Hazardville 860
Hebron 860
Hfd 860
Higganum 860
Hopeville 860
Hotchkiss School 860
Htd 860
Htfd 860
Huntington 203
International Masters Pub 203
Irs 860
Ivoryton 860
J C Penney Co 860
Jewett City 860
Jordan Village 860
Jupiter Point 860
Kenington 860
Kensington 860
Kent 860
Killingly 860
Killingly Center 860
Killingworth 860
Lake Garda 860
Lakeside 860
Lakeville 860
Laurel Hill 860
Lebanon 860
Ledyard 860
Lisbon 860
Litchfield 860
Lords Point 860
Lyme 860
M B I Inc 203, 860
Macys By Mail 203
Madison 203
Main Office 860
Manchester 860
Mansfield 860
Mansfield Center 860
Mansfield Ctr 860
Mansfield Depot 860
Mansfield Dpt 860
Mansfield Hollow 860
Marble Dale 860
Marion 860
Marlboro 860
Marlborough 860
Mashantucket 860
Masons Island 860
Mcdougal Correctional Fclty 860
Mechanicsville 860
Melrose 860
Meriden 203
Merrow 860
Middle Haddam 860
Middlebury 203
Middlefield 203
Middletown 860
Milford 203
Milldale 860
Millstone 860
Monroe 203
Montville 860
Moodus 860
Moosup 860
Morris 860
Mount Carmel 203
Mystic 860
N Branford 203
N Franklin 860
N Grosvenordl 860
N Haven 203
N Stonington 860
N Westchester 860
Naugatuck 203
Naval Submarine Base 860
Navsub Base 860
Nepaug 860
New Brit 860
New Britain 860
New Canaan 203
New Fairfield 203
New Hartford 860
New Haven 203
New London 860
New Milford 860
New Preston 860
New Preston Marble Dale 860
New Preston Marbledale 860
New Preston-Marble Dale 860
Newington 860
Newtown 203
Niantic 860
No Canaan 860
No Haven 203
Noank 860
Norfolk 860
Noroton 203
Noroton Heights 203
North Branford 203
North Canaan 860
North Canton 860
North Franklin 860
North Granby 860
North Grosvendale 860
North Grosvenordale 860
North Haven 203
North Lyme 860
North Sterling 860
North Stonington 860
North Thompsonville 860
North Westchester 860
North Windham 860

City	Area Code
Northeast Area	860
Northfield	860
Northford	203
Northville	860
Norwalk	203
Norwich	860
Norwichtown	860
Oakdale	860
Oakville	860
Occum	860
Old Greenwich	203
Old Lyme	860
Old Mystic	860
Old Saybrook	860
Oneco	860
Orange	203
Oxford	203
Pawcatuck	860
Pequabuck	860
Perkin Elmer Corp	203
Perkins Corner	860
Pine Meadow	860
Pitney Bowes Inc	203
Plainfield	860
Plainville	860
Plantsville	860
Plaza	203
Pleasant Valley	860
Pleasant Vly	860
Plymouth	860
Point O Woods	860
Pomfret	860
Pomfret Center	860
Pomfret Ctr	860
Pomfret Landing	860
Ponfret Center	860
Poquetanuck	860
Poquonock	860
Poquonock Bridge	860
Portland	860
Preston	860
Promotion Marketing Ser Inc	203
Promotion Systems Inc	203
Promotional Dev Inc	203
Prospect	203
Putman	860
Putnam	860
Putnam Heights	860
Putnm	860
Quaker Hill	860
Quinebaug	860
Redding	203
Redding Cen	203
Redding Center	203
Redding Ridge	203
Rhodesville	860
Ridgefield	203
Ridgeway	203
Riverside	203
Riverton	860
Rockfall	860
Rockville	860
Rocky Hill	860
Rogers	860
Rowayton	203
Roxbury	203
S Glastonbury	860
S Willington	860
S Woodstock	860
Salem	860
Salisbury	860
Sandy Hook	203
Saugatuck	203
Sawyer District	860
Scantic	860
Scitico	860
Scotland	860
Setan Industries	203
Seymour	203
Shared Zip For Brm	203
Sharon	860
Sharon Valley	860
Shawondassee	860
Shelton	203
Sherman	860
Silver Lane	860
Simbury	860
Simsbury	860
Somers	860
Somersville	860
South Britain	203
South Canaan	860
South Canterbury	860
South Chaplin	860
South Glastonbury	860
South Kent	860
South Killingly	860
South Lyme	860
South Norwalk	203
South Willington	860
South Windham	860
South Windsor	860
South Woodstock	860
Southbury	203
Southington	860
Southport	203
Sprague	860
Springdale	203
Stafford	860
Stafford Sp	860
Stafford Spgs	860
Stafford Springs	860
Staffordville	860
Stamford	203
Stepney	203
Sterling	860
Stevenson	203
Stonington	860
Storrs	860
Storrs Manfld	860
Storrs Mansfield	860
Storrs/Mansfield	860
Stratford	203
Stratmar Fulfillment Corp	203
Sub Base New London	860
Submarine Base	860
Suffield	860
Taconic	860
Taftville	860
Talcott Village	860
Talcottville	860
Tariffville	860
Terryville	860
The Exchange At Talcott Vill	860
Thomaston	860
Thompson	860
Thompsonville	860
Tokeneke	203
Tolland	860
Torrington	860
Travelers Ins	860
Trumbull	203
Turnpike	860
Twin Lakes	860
U S Coast Guard Acad	860
U S Postal Service	203
Uncasville	860
Union	860
Union Carbide Corp	203
Union City	203
Unionville	860
Uniroyal Inc	203
United States Coast Guard Ac	860
Unity Plaza	860
University Of Ct	860
University Of Ct Health Ctr	860
Upper Stepney	203
Vernon	860
Vernon Rockville	860
Vernon Rockvl	860
Vernon-Rockville	860
Versailles	860
Voluntown	860
W Hartford	860
W Haven	203
W Htfd	860
W Suffield	860
W Willington	860
Wallingford	203
Wapping	860
Warehouse Point	860
Warren	860
Warrenville	860
Washington	860
Washington Depot	860
Washington Dt	860
Washington Green	860
Waterbury	203
Waterford	860
Watertown	860
Wauregan	860
Weathersfield	860
Weatogue	860
Websters Unified	203
Wesleyan	860
West Ashford	860
West Cornwall	860
West Farms Mall	860
West Granby	860
West Hartford	860
West Hartfrd	860
West Hartland	860
West Haven	203
West Mystic	860
West Redding	203
West Simsbury	860
West Stafford	860
West Suffield	860
West Wauregan	860
West Woods	860
Westbrook	860
Weston	203
Westport	203
Westville	203
Weth	860
Wethersfield	860
Wethersfld	860
Whitneyville	203
Willimantic	860
Willington	860
Wilson	860
Wilton	203
Winchester	860
Winchester Center	860
Winchestr Ctr	860
Windham	860
Windsor	860
Windsor Locks	860
Windsorville	860
Winsted	860
Wolcott	203
Woodbridge	203
Woodbury	203
Woodstock	860
Woodstock Valley	860
Woodstock Vly	860
Wtby	203
Yalesville	203
Yantic	860

Delaware

City	Area Code
All Points	302

District Of Columbia

City	Area Code
All Points	202

Federated States Of Micronesia

City	Area Code
All Points	691

Florida

City	Area Code
Air Mail Facility	305
Alachua	352, 386
Alafaya	407
Alford	850
Allandale	386
Alligator Point	850
Alligator Pt	850
Aloma	407
Altamonte Spg	407
Altamonte Springs	407
Altha	850
Altoona	352
Alturas	863
Alva	239
Alys Beach	850
Amelia City	904
Amelia Island	904
Amelia Village	904
American Express	954
Amsouth	407
Anastasia Island	904
Anna Maria	941
Anthony	352
Apalachicola	850
Apollo Beach	813
Apopka	407
Arcadia	863, 941
Archer	352
Argyle	850
Aripeka	352
Armstrong	904
Astatula	352
Astor	352
Atlantic Bch	904
Atlantic Beach	904
Atlantis	561
Auburndale	863
Ave Maria	239
Aventura	305
Avon Park	863
Azalea Park	407
B'ton	941
Babson Park	863
Bagdad	850
Baker	850
Bal Harbour	305
Baldwin	904
Balm	813
Barberville	386
Barefoot Bay	772
Barefoot Bch	239
Barefoot Beach	239
Barry University	305
Bartow	863
Bascom	850
Basinger	863
Bay Harbor Is	305
Bay Harbor Islands	305
Bay Lake	407
Bay Pines	727
Bayonet Point	727
Bayshore Gardens	941
Bell	352
Belle Glade	561
Belle Isle	407
Belleair	727
Belleair Bch	727
Belleair Beach	727
Belleair Blf	727
Belleair Bluffs	727
Belleair Shores	727
Belleair Shrs	727
Belleview	352
Bellview	850
Beverly Hills	352
Big Pine Key	305
Big Torch Key	305
Biscayne Park	305
Blountstown	850
Boca Grande	941
Boca Raton	561
Bokeelia	239
Bonaventure	954
Bonifay	850
Bonita Beach	239
Bonita Spgs	239
Bonita Springs	239
Bostwick	386
Bowling Green	863
Boynton Beach	352, 561
Boys Ranch	386
Brad	941
Braden River	941
Bradenton	941
Bradenton Bch	941
Bradenton Beach	941
Bradington	941
Bradley	863
Brandon	813
Branford	386
Brickell	305
Briny Breezes	561
Bristol	850
Bronson	352
Brooker	352
Brooksville	352, 727
Broward Mall	954
Bruce	850
Bryant	561
Bryceville	904
Buena Ventura Lakes	407
Bunnell	386
Bushnell	352
Business Reply	813
Bvl	407
C Gables	305
Callahan	904
Callaway	850
Campbellton	850
Canal Point	561
Canaveral Air Station	321
Canaveral As	321
Candler	352
Cantonment	850
Cape Canaveral	321
Cape Coral	239
Cape Coral S	239
Cape Coral South	239
Cape Haze	941
Cape San Blas	850
Captiva	239
Carl Fisher	305
Carol City	305
Carrabelle	850
Carrollwood	813
Caryville	850
Cassadaga	386
Casselberry	407
Cecil Field	904
Cedar Hammock	941
Cedar Key	352
Celebration	407
Center Hill	352
Centerhill	352
Centerville	850
Century	850
Champions Gate	863
Champions Gt	863
Chapel Lakes	954
Chattahoochee	850
Chiefland	352
Chipley	850
Choctaw Beach	850
Chokoloskee	239
Christmas	407
Chuluota	407
Citra	352
Citrus Hills	352
Citrus Ridge	321, 772
Citrus Spgs	352
Citrus Springs	352
City Of Pensacola	850
City Of Sunrise	954
Clair Mel	813
Clair Mel City	813
Clarcona	407
Clarksville	850
Clearwater	727
Clearwater Beach	727
Clermont	352, 407
Clermont South Branch Postal	407
Clewiston	863
Cloud Lake	561
Coco River	239
Cocoa	321
Cocoa Beach	321
Coconut Creek	305, 954
Coconut Gr	305
Coconut Grove	305
Coconutcreek	954
Coleman	352
Conch Key	305
Cooper City	954
Copeland	239
Coral	305
Coral Gables	305
Coral Gbls	305
Coral Springs	954
Cortez	941
Cottondale	850
Country Lakes	305
Cpe Canaveral	321
Crawfordville	850
Crescent Beach	941
Crescent City	386
Crestview	850
Cross City	352
Cross Creek	352
Cross Key	305
Crossings	305
Crystal Beach	727
Crystal River	352
Crystal Spgs	813
Crystal Springs	813
Cudjoe Key	305
Cutler Bay	305
Cutler Ridge	305
Cypress	850
Cypress Gardens	863
Cypress Gdns	863
Dade City	352
Dania	954
Dania Beach	954
Davenport	407, 863
Davie	954
Day	386
Dayt Bch Sh	386
Daytona Beach	386
Daytona Beach Shores	386
De Leon Spgs	386
De Leon Springs	386
Debary	386, 407
Deer Island	352
Deerfield Bch	954
Deerfield Beach	954
Defuniak Spgs	850
Defuniak Springs	850
Deland	386
Delray Beach	561
Deltona	386
Destin	850
Dfafs	850
Dinsmore	904
Doctors Inlet	904
Dona Vista	352
Doral	305
Doral Branch	305
Dover	813
Dowling Park	386
Dr Martin Luther King Jr	305
Duck Key	305
Duette	941
Duke Field Afs	850
Dundee	863
Dunedin	727
Dunnellon	352
Durant	813
E Fort Myers	239
E Rockland Key	305
E Rockland Ky	305
Eagle Lake	863
Earleton	352
East Palatka	386
East Point	850
East Rockland Key	305
Eastlake Weir	352
Eastpoint	850
Eastside	850
Eaton Park	863
Eatonville	321
Eau Gallie	321
Ebro	850
Edgar	352

City	Area Code
Edgewater	386
Edgewood	321
Educ Dev Ctr Corresp	850
Eglin	850
Eglin Afb	850
El Jobean	941
El Portal	305
Elfers	727
Elgin	850
Elgin Afb	850
Elkton	904
Ellenton	941
Eloise	863
Englewood	941
Englewood Beach	941
Enterprise	386
Estero	239
Esto	850
Eustis	352
Everglades	239
Everglades Br	954
Everglades City	239
Everglades National Park	305
Evinston	352
F M	239
Fairfield	352
Fanning Spgs	352
Fanning Springs	352
Father Felix Varela	305
Fedhaven	863
Felda	863
Fellsmere	772
Fern Park	407
Fernandina	904
Fernandina Beach	904
Ferndale	352
Fiesta Key	305
Financial Plaza	954
Fisher Island	305
Five Points Hamilton	904
Fl Reg Lib Bl	386
Fl Regional Library For Blin	386
Fl State Lot	850
Fl State Univ Student	850
Flagler Beach	386
Flamingo Ldge	305
Flamingo Lodge	305
Fleming Island	904
Fleming Isle	904
Flemington	352
Flinternational Univ	305
Florahome	386
Floral City	352
Florence Vill	863
Florence Villa	863
Florida A & M	850
Florida A And M University	850
Florida City	305
Florida Dept Of Corrections	386
Florida Gulf Coast Univ	239
Florida International Univ	305
Florida Power & Light Co	305
Florida State	850
Florida State Lottery	850
Florida State Univ Admin	850
Florida State University	850
Fmy	239
Forest City	407
Fort Denaud	863
Fort Jefferson National Mon	305
Fort Lauderdale	954
Fort Mc Coy	352
Fort Meade	863
Fort Myers	239
Fort Myers Beach	239
Fort Ogden	941
Fort Pierce	772
Fort Walton Beach	850
Fort White	386
Fountain	850
Freeport	850
Frostproof	863
Fruit Cove	904
Fruitland Park	352
Fruitland Pk	352
Ft Charlotte	941
Ft Denaud	863
Ft Lauderdale	954
Ft Myers	239
Ft Myers Bch	239
Ft Myers Beach	239
Ft Ogden	941
Ft Walton Bch	850
Ft Walton Beach	850
Gables	305
Gables By The Sea	305
Gainesville	352
Ge Capital	407
Geneva	407
Georgetown	386
Gibsonia	863
Gibsonton	813
Glen Ridge	561
Glen Saint Mary	904
Glen St Mary	904
Glenwood	386
Golden Beach	305
Golden Gate	239
Golden Isles	954
Golden Isles Postal Store	954
Goldenrod	407
Gonzalez	850
Good Samaritan	407
Goodland	239
Gotha	407
Goulds	305
Graceville	850
Graham	352
Grand Island	352
Grand Ridge	850
Grande Pointe	850
Grandin	352
Grant	321, 772
Grant Valkaria	321
Grant Vlkria	321
Grassy Key	305
Green Acres	561
Green Cove Springs	904
Green Cv Spgs	904
Greenacres	561
Greensboro	850
Greenville	850
Greenwood	850
Gretna	850
Grove City	941
Groveland	352
Gulf Breeze	850
Gulf Hammock	352
Gulf Power	850
Gulf Stream	561
Gulfport	727
Haines City	863
Haines Creek	352
Hallandale	954
Hallandale Beach	954
Halndle Bch	954
Hampton	352
Harmony	407
Harris Corp	321
Harris Corporation	321
Hastings	904
Havana	850
Haverhill	561
Hawthorne	352
Hbj	321
Heathrow	407
Hernando	352
Hernando Bch	352
Hernando Beach	352
Hialeah	305
Hialeah Gardens	305
Hialeah Gdns	305
Hialeah Lakes	305
Hiawassee	407
High Springs	352, 386
Highland Bch	561
Highland Beach	561
Highland City	863
Hillcrest	954
Hilliard	904
Hillsboro Bch	954
Hillsboro Beach	954
Hobe Sound	772
Holder	352
Holiday	727
Hollister	386
Holly Hill	386
Hollywood	954
Holmes Beach	941
Holt	850
Home Shopping	727
Home Shopping Club	813
Homeland	863
Homestead	305
Homestead Afb	305
Homestead Air Force Base	305
Homosassa	352
Homosassa Spg	352
Homosassa Springs	352
Horseshoe Bch	352
Horseshoe Beach	352
Hosford	850
Houghton Mifflin Harcourt	321
Howey In Hls	352
Howey In The Hills	352
Hudson	727
Hurlburt Field	850
Hurlburt Fld	850
Hutchinson Is	772
Hutchinson Island	772
Hypoluxo	561
Immokalee	239
Ind Crk Vlg	305
Ind Hbr Bch	321
Indialantic	321
Indian Creek	305
Indian Creek Village	305
Indian Harbour Beach	321
Indian Lake Estates	863
Indian Lk Est	863
Indian River Shores	772
Indian Rk Bch	727
Indian Rks Beach	727
Indian Rocks Beach	727
Indian Shores	727
Indiantown	772
Indn Hbr Bch	321
Indn Riv Shrs	772
Inglewood	941
Inglis	352
Inlet Beach	850
Intercession City	407
Interchange Square	321
Interlachen	352
International Service Center	305
Intrcsion Cty	407
Inverness	352
Inverrary	954
Irvine	352
Islamorada	305
Island Grove	352
Istachatta	352
Jacksonville	904
Jacksonville Beach	904
Jacksonville N A S	904
Jacksonville Naval Air Stati	904
Jacksonville Naval Hospital	904
Jacob	850
Jasper	386
Jax	904
Jax Bch	904
Jax Beach	904
Jax Naval Air	904
Jax Naval Hos	904
Jay	850
Jena	352
Jennings	386
Jensen Beach	772
Jerome	239
Johns Pass	727
Jonesville	352
Jpv	863
Julington Creek	904
Julington Crk	904
Juno Beach	561
Jupiter	561
Jupiter Inlet	561
Jupiter Inlet Colony	561
Kathleen	813
Kenansville	407
Kendall	305
Kennedy Sp Ct	321
Kennedy Space Center	321
Kenneth City	727
Key Biscayne	305
Key Col Bch	305
Key Colony Beach	305
Key Largo	305
Key West	305
Key West Nas	305
Key West Naval Air Station	305
Keystone Heights	352
Keystone Hgts	352
Keystone Islands	305
Killarney	407
Kinard	850
Kingsley Lake	904
Kissimmee	407, 863
Kngsly Lk	904
Ky Wst	305
La Belle	863
La Crosse	386
Labelle	239
Lacoochee	352
Lady Lake	352, 772
Lake Alfred	863
Lake Buena Vista	407
Lake Butler	386
Lake City	386
Lake Clarke	561
Lake Clarke Shores	561
Lake Como	386
Lake Geneva	352
Lake Hamilton	863
Lake Harbor	561
Lake Helen	386
Lake Mary	407
Lake Monroe	407
Lake Panasoffkee	352
Lake Park	561
Lake Placid	863
Lake Suzy	863, 941
Lake Wales	863
Lake Worth	561
Lakeland	863
Lakeshore	863
Lakewood Ranch	941
Lakewood Rch	941
Lamont	850
Lanark Village	850
Lanark Vlg	850
Land O Lakes	727, 813
Land O' Lakes	813
Lantana	561
Largo	727
Laud By Sea	954
Laud By The Sea	954
Laud Lakes	954
Lauder Hill	954
Lauderdale By The Sea	954
Lauderdale Isles	954
Lauderdale Lakes	954
Lauderhill	954
Laurel	941
Laurel Hill	850
Lawtey	904
Layton	305
Lazy Lake	954
Ldhl	954
Lecanto	352
Lee	850
Leehigh	239, 727
Leehigh Acres	239
Leesburg	352
Lehigh	239
Lehigh Acres	239
Leisure City	305
Lghthse Point	954
Lighthouse Point	954
Lighthouse Pt	954
Lithia	813
Little Torch Key	305
Live Oak	386
Lk Buena Vis	407
Lk Panasoffke	352
Lloyd	850
Lochloosa	352
Lockhart	407
Long Boat Key	941
Long Key	305
Longboat Key	941
Longwood	407
Lorida	863
Loughman	863
Lowell	352
Lower Matecumbe Key	305
Lower Sugarloaf Key	305
Loxahatchee	561
Loxahatchee Groves	561
Ltl Torch Key	305
Ludlam	305
Lulu	386
Lutz	813
Lwr Sugarloaf	305
Lxhtchee Grvs	561
Lynn Haven	850
Macclenny	904
Macdill Afb	813
Madeira Beach	727
Madison	850
Magnolia Sq	407
Magnolia Square	407
Maitland	321
Malabar	321
Malone	850
Manalapan	561
Manasota	941
Mango	813
Mangonia Park	561
Marathon	305
Marathon Shores	305
Marathon Shrs	305
Marco Island	239
Margate	954
Marianna	850
Maricamp	352
Mary Esther	850
Masaryktown	352
Mascotte	352
Matecumbe Key	305
Matlacha	239
Matlacha Isle	239
Matlacha Isles	239
Maxville	904
Mayo	386
Mayport	904
Mayport Nav S	904
Mayport Nav Sta	904
Mayport Naval Housing	904
Mayport Naval Sta	904
Mayport Naval Station	904
Maypt Nav Hou	904
Mc Alpin	386
Mc David	850
Mc Intosh	352
Mcalpin	386
Mcintosh	352
Medley	305
Melbourne	321, 772
Melbourne Bch	321
Melbourne Beach	321
Melbourne Village	321
Melbourne Vlg	321
Melrose	352
Melrose Vista	954
Merritt Is	321
Merritt Island	321
Mexico Beach	850
Mia Shores	305
Mia Shrs	305
Miami	305
Miami Beach	305
Miami Gardens	305
Miami Lakes	305
Miami Shores	305
Miami Springs	305
Micanopy	352
Micco	772
Miccosukee	850
Mid Florida	407
Mid Torch Key	305
Middle Torch Key	305
Middleburg	904
Midway	850
Milam Dairy	305
Milligan	850
Milton	850
Mims	321
Minneola	352, 407
Miramar	954
Miramar Beach	850
Miromar Lakes	239
Modello	305
Molino	850
Monticello	850
Montverde	352
Moore Haven	863
Morales Discount Pharmacy	305
Morriston	352
Mossy Head	850
Mount Dora	352
Mount Pleasant	850
Mount Plymouth	352
Mt Pleasant	850
Mt Plymouth	352
Mulberry	863
Munson Island	305
Murdock	941
Myakka City	941
N A S A	321
N Fort Myers	239
N Ft Myers	239
N Lauderdale	954
N Miami Beach	305
N Palm Beach	561
N Port	941
N Redngtn Bch	727
Nalcrest	863
Naples	239
Naranja	305
Nas Jacksonvle	904
Nas Jax	904
Nations Bank	813
Naval Air Station Unit 2	305
Navarre	850
Neptune Beach	904
Netpmdsa Saufley Field	850
New Port Richey	727
New Prt Rchy	727
New Pt Richey	727
New Smyrna	386
New Smyrna Beach	386
Newberry	352
Niceville	850
Nichols	863
Nmb	305
No Fort Myers	239
No Ft Myers	239
No Name Key	305
No Port	941
Nobleton	352
Nocatee	941
Nokomis	941
Noma	850
Normandy	305
Normandy Isle	305
North Bay Village	305
North Bay Vlg	305
North Fort Myers	239
North Ft Myers	239
North Lauderdale	954
North Miami	305
North Miami Beach	305
North Palm Beach	561
North Port	941
North Redington Beach	727
North Venice	941
Northdale	813
Northport	941
Ntt Corry Field	850
Nw Prt Rchy	727
O Brien	386
Oak Hill	386
Oakland	407
Oakland Park	954
Ocala	352

City	Area Code
Ocean Reef Club	305
Ocean Ridge	561
Ochlockonee	850
Ochlockonee Bay	850
Ochopee	239
Ocklawaha	352, 386
Ocoee	407
Odessa	813
Ojus	305
Okahumpka	352
Okaloosa Is	850
Okaloosa Island	850
Okeechobee	863
Oklawaha	352
Old Town	352
Oldsmar	813
Olustee	904
Olympia Heights	305
Olympia Hgts	305
Ona	863
One Financial Plaza	954
Oneco	941
Opa Locka	305
Orange City	386
Orange Lake	352
Orange Park	904
Orange Pk	904
Orange Spgs	352
Orange Springs	352
Orchid	772
Orlando	321, 407
Orlo Vista	407
Ormond Beach	386
Osprey	941
Osteen	386
Otter Creek	352
Overstreet	850
Oviedo	407
Oxford	352
Ozona	727
P C Beach	850
P E Chevron Cs	954
Pace	850
Pahokee	561
Paisley	352
Palatka	386
Palm Bay	321, 772
Palm Bch Gdns	561
Palm Bch Shrs	561
Palm Beach	561
Palm Beach Gardens	561
Palm Beach Shores	561
Palm City	772
Palm Coast	386
Palm Harbor	727
Palm Shores	321
Palm Springs	561
Palm Springs North	305
Palma Ceia	813
Palma Sola	941
Palmdale	863
Palmetto	941
Palmetto Bay	305
Panacea	850
Panama City	850
Panama City Beach	850
Parkland	954
Parrish	941
Pasadena	727
Pass A Grille	727
Pass A Grille Beach	727
Patrick Afb	321
Patrick Air Force Base	321
Paxton	850
Pcola	850
Pembroke Lakes	954
Pembroke Park	954
Pembroke Pines	954
Pembroke Pnes	954
Penney Farms	904
Pensacola	850
Pensacola Bch	850
Pensacola Beach	850
Pensacola Naval Hospital	850
Perdido Key	850
Perrine	305
Perry	850
Pierson	386
Pine Castle	321, 407
Pine Hills	407
Pine Ridge	352
Pinecraft	941
Pinecrest	305
Pinecrest Postal Store	305
Pineland	941
Pinellas Park	727
Pinetta	850
Placida	941
Plant City	813
Plantation	954
Plantation Key	305
Plymouth	407
Pns	850
Pnte Vdra Bch	904
Poinciana	863
Point Washington	850
Polk City	863
Pomona Park	386
Pompano Beach	305, 954
Ponce De Leon	850
Ponce Inlet	386
Ponte Vedra	904
Ponte Vedra Beach	904
Port Canaveral	321
Port Charlotte	941
Port Everglades	954
Port Orange	386
Port Richey	727
Port Saint Joe	850
Port Saint John	321
Port Saint Lucie	772
Port Salerno	772
Port St Joe	850
Port St John	321
Port St Lucie	772
Princeton	305
Pt Canaveral	321
Pt Charlotte	941
Pt Orange	386
Pt Washington	850
Punta Gorda	941
Putnam Hall	352
Quail Heights	305
Quincy	850
Raccoon Key	305
Raiford	386
Ramrod Key	305
Rdg Mnr Est	352
Red Bay	850
Reddick	352
Redingtn Shor	727
Redington Bch	727
Redington Beach	727
Redington Shores	727
Redland	305
Reunion	407
Richland	352
Richmond Heights	305
Ridge Manor	352
Ridge Manor Estates	352
River Ranch	863
Riverview	813, 941
Riviera Beach	561
Rockledge	321
Rolling Acres	352
Roseland	772
Rosemary Bch	850
Rosemary Beach	850
Rotonda West	941
Royal Palm Beach	561
Royal Plm Bch	561
Royal Plm Beach	561
Rubonia	941
Ruskin	813
Ryl Palm Bch	561
S Daytona	386
S Daytona Bch	386
S Fort Myers	239
S Palm Bch	561
S Pasadena	727
Sabal Palm Postal Store	954
Safety Harbor	727
Saint Augustine	904
Saint Cloud	407
Saint George Island	850
Saint James City	239
Saint Johns	904
Saint Leo	352
Saint Lucie West	772
Saint Marks	850
Saint Pete Beach	727
Saint Petersburg	727
Saint Teresa	850
Salem	352
Salt Springs	352
Samoset	941
San Antonio	352
San Carlos Park	239
San Mateo	386
Sand Lake	407
Sanderson	904
Sandestin	850
Sanford	407
Sanibel	239
Santa Fe	386
Santa Rosa Beach	850
Santa Rsa Bch	850
Sarasota	941
Satellite Bch	321
Satellite Beach	321
Satsuma	386
Scottsmoor	386
Sea Ranch Lakes	954
Sea Ranch Lks	954
Seacrest	850
Sebastian	772
Sebring	863
Seffner	813
Seminole	727
Seven Springs	727
Seville	386
Sewalls Point	772
Seybold	305
Shady Grove	850
Shady Hills	352
Shalimar	850
Sharpes	321
Sidell	863
Siesta Key	941
Silver Spgs	352
Silver Springs	352
Singer Island	561
Snapper Creek	305
Sneads	850
Sopchoppy	850
Sorrento	352
South Bay	561
South Daytona	386
South Florida	954
South Miami	305
South Miami Heights	305
South Palm Beach	561
South Pasadena	727
Southport	850
Southwest Ranches	954
Sparr	352
Spring Hill	352, 727
St Augustine	904
St George Isl	850
St James City	239
St Lucie West	772
St Pete	727
St Pete Bch	727
St Pete Beach	727
St Petersburg	727
St Petersburg Beach	727
St Teresa	850
Starke	904
State Farm Ins	863
State Of Florida	850
Steinhatchee	352
Stetson University	386
Stock Island	305
Stuart	772
Sugarlf Shrs	305
Sugarloaf	305
Sugarloaf Key	305
Sugarloaf Shrs	305
Sumatra	850
Summerfield	352
Summerland Key	305
Summrlnd Key	305
Sumterville	352
Sun City	813
Sun City Center	813
Sun City Ctr	813
Sunny Hills	850
Sunny Isl Bch	305
Sunny Isles	305
Sunny Isles Beach	305
Sunrise	954
Sunset Island	305
Suntree	321
Suntrust National Bank	407
Suntrust Service Corporation	407
Surfside	305
Suwanee	352
Suwannee	352
Sw Ranches	954
Sweetwater	305
Switzerland	904
Sydney	813
Tallahassee	850
Tallevast	941
Tamarac	954
Tampa	813
Tampa Brm Unique	813
Tampa Palms	813
Tangerine	407
Tarpon Spgs	727
Tarpon Spngs	727
Tarpon Springs	727
Tavares	352
Tavernier	305
Telogia	850
Temple Ter	813
Temple Terrace	813
Tequesta	561
Terra Ceia	941
Terra Ceia Is	941
Terra Ceia Island	941
The Villages	352, 772
Thonotosassa	813
Tice	239
Tierra Verde	727
Time Cs Brm Unique	813
Time Customer Service Inc	813
Time Inc	813
Tioga	352
Titusville	321
Tn Of Nocatee	904
Town & Country Postal Store	305
Town N Country	813
Town Of Nocatee	904
Trailer Est	941
Trailer Estates	941
Treasure Is	727
Treasure Island	727
Trenton	352
Trilby	352
Trinity	727
Twn N Cntry	813
Tyndall A F B	850
Tyndall Afb	850
Ucf	407
Uleta	305
Umatilla	352
Union Park	407
Univ Of Fl Student Dorms	352
Univ Of Miami	305
Univ Of So Florida	813
Univ Of Tampa	813
University	954
University Medical Center	352
University Of	813
University Of Central Fl	407
University Of Fl	352
University Of Miami	305
University Of South Florida	813
University Of Tampa	813
University Park	941
University Pk	941
Upper Key Largo	305
Upper Matecumbe Key	305
Upper Sugarloaf Key	305
Upr Sugarloaf	305
Valkaria	321
Valparaiso	850
Valrico	813
Vanderbilt	239
Vanderbilt Beach	239
Venetian Islands	305
Venetian Shores	305
Venice	941
Venus	863
Vernon	850
Vero Beach	321
Viera	321
Village Of Golf	561
Village Of Palm Springs	561
Village Of Palmetto Bay	305
Village Of Pinecrest	305
Village Of Wellington	561
Virginia Gardens	305
Virginia Gdns	305
Vlg Of Golf	561
Vlg Wellingtn	561
W Delray Bch	561
W Hollywood	954
W Melbourne	321
W Panama City Beach	850
W Plm Bch	561
Wabasso	772
Wachovia	407
Wachovia Mortgage Corp	407
Wacissa	850
Wahneta	863
Wakulla Spgs	850
Wakulla Springs	850
Waldo	352
Walnut Hill	850
Watersound	850
Wauchula	863
Wausau	850
Waverly	863
Webster	352
Weeki Wachee	352
Weirsdale	352
Wekiva Spg	407
Wekiva Springs	407
Welaka	386
Wellborn	386
Wellington	561
Wesley Chapel	813
West Bradenton	941
West Dade	305
West Delray Beach	561
West Destin	850
West Hollywood	954
West Melbourne	321
West Miami	305
West Palm Bch	561
West Palm Beach	561
West Panama City Beach	850
West Park	954
Westchase	813
Westchester	305
Weston	954
Westside Branch	954
Westville	850
Wewahitchka	850
White Springs	386
Wilbur By Sea	386
Wilbur By The Sea	386
Wildwood	352
Williston	352
Wilton Manors	954
Wimauma	813
Windermere	407
Windley Key	305
Winter Beach	772
Winter Garden	407
Winter Haven	863
Winter Hvn	863
Winter Park	407
Winter Spgs	407
Winter Springs	407
Wintergarden	407
Woodville	850
Worthington Springs	386
Worthngtn Spg	386
Yalaha	352
Yankeetown	352
Ybor City	813
Yeehaw	863
Yeehaw Junction	863
Youngstown	850
Yulee	904
Zellwood	407
Zephyrhills	813
Zolfo Springs	863

Georgia

City	Area Code
Aaron	912
Abac	229
Abbeville	229
Abraham Baldwin College	229
Acworth	770
Adairsville	770
Adel	229
Adrian	478
Agnes	706
Ailey	912
Akin	912
Alamo	912
Alapaha	229
Albany	229
Aline	912
Allenhurst	912
Allentown	478
Alma	912
Alpharetta	770
Alston	912
Altama	912
Alto	706
Ambrose	912
Amer Fam Life Ins Brm	706
American Family Life Ins	706
Americus	229
Amity	706
Andersonville	478
Appling	706
Arabi	229
Aragon	770
Arcola	912
Argyle	912
Arlington	229
Armuchee	706
Arnoldsville	706
Ashburn	229
Ashintilly	912
At&t Universal Card Service	706
Athens	706
Atl	229, 404, 770
Atlanta	229, 404, 770
Atlanta Naval Air Station	770
Atlanta Ndc	404
Atlanta Postal Credit Union	404
Att Bellsouth	404
Attapulgus	229
Auburn	770
Augusta	706
Austell	770
Avera	706
Avon	770
Avondale Est	404
Avondale Estates	404
Axson	912
Baconton	229
Bainbridge	229
Baker-Taylor	706
Baldwin	706
Ball Ground	770
Bank Of America	404
Bankamerica Corporation	404
Barnesville	770
Barnett	706
Barney	229
Barrett Parkway	770
Bartow	478
Barwick	229
Baxley	912
Bayview	912
Bdge	229

City	Area Code
Beach	912
Beallwood	706
Bellville	912
Belvedere	404
Bemiss	229
Berkeley Lake	770
Berlin	229
Berzelia	706
Bethlehem	770
Bickley	912
Big Canoe	706
Birdsville	478
Bishop	706
Black Creek	912
Blackshear	912
Blairsville	706
Blakely	229
Bloomingdale	912
Blue Ridge	706
Bluffton	229
Blun	478
Blundale	478
Blythe	706
Bogart	770
Bolingbroke	478
Bonaire	478
Boneville	706
Boston	229
Bostwick	706
Bowdon	770
Bowdon Jct	770
Bowdon Junction	770
Bowersville	706
Bowman	706
Box Springs	706
Braselton	706
Bremen	770
Briarcliff	404
Bridgeboro	229
Brinson	229
Bristol	912
Bronwood	229
Brookfield	229
Brooklet	912
Brooks	770
Broxton	912
Brunswick	912
Bryon	478
Buchanan	770
Buckhead	706
Buena Vista	229
Buford	770
Business Reply Mail	478
Butler	478
Butts	478
Byromville	478
Byron	478
Cadley	706
Cadwell	478
Cairo	229
Calhoun	706
Calvary	229
Camak	706
Camilla	229
Camp Rogers	706
Campania	706
Canon	706
Canoochee	478
Canton	770
Cario	229
Carlton	706
Carnesville	706
Carnigan	912
Carrollton	770
Cartersville	770
Cassville	770
Cataula	706
Cave Spring	706
Cecil	229
Cedar Crossing	912
Cedar Springs	229
Cedartown	770
Center	912
Centerville	478
Centerville Branch	770
Central State Hospital	478
Chamblee	770
Charles	912
Chatsworth	706
Chatt Hills	770
Chattahoochee Hills	770
Chatterton	912
Chauncey	229
Cherry Log	706
Chester	478
Chestnut Mountain	770
Chestnut Mtn	770
Chickamauga	706
Chula	229
Cisco	706
Clarkdale	770
Clarkesville	706
Clarkston	404
Claxton	912
Clayton	706
Clermont	770
Cleveland	706
Climax	229
Clinchfield	478
Cloudland	706
Clyattville	229
Clyo	912
Cobb	229
Cobbtown	912
Cochran	478
Cogdell	912
Cohutta	706
Col	706
Colbert	706
Coleman	229
Coleman Lake	478
Colemans Lake	478
College Park	404
Collins	912
Colquitt	229
Cols	706
Columbus	706
Columbus Brm	706
Comer	706
Commerce	706
Concord	770
Conley	404
Conyers	770
Coolidge	229
Coosa	706
Cordele	229, 478
Cornelia	706
Cotton	229
Covena	478
Covington	770
Cox	912
Crandall	706
Crawford	706
Crawfordville	706
Crescent	912
Culloden	478
Cumberland	770
Cumming	770
Cusseta	706
Cuthbert	229
Dacula	770
Dahlonega	706
Daisy	912
Dallas	770
Dalton	706
Damascus	229
Danburg	706
Danielsville	706
Danville	478
Darien	912
Dasher	229
Davisboro	478
Dawson	229
Dawsonville	706
De Soto	229
Dearing	706
Decatur	404
Deepstep	478
Dellwood	478
Demorest	706
Denmark	912
Denton	912
Dewy Rose	706
Dexter	478
Dillard	706
Dixie	229
Dobbins A F B	770
Dobbins Afb	770
Dobbins Air Force Base	770
Doctortown	912
Doerun	229
Donald	912
Donalsonville	229
Doraville	404, 770
Double Branches	706
Douglas	912
Douglasville	770
Dover	912
Druid Hills	404
Dry Branch	478
Du Pont	912
Dublin	478
Dudley	478
Duluth	770
Dunaire	404
Dunwoody	404
Dville	229
E Dublin	478
East Dublin	478
East Ellijay	706
East Point	404
Eastanollee	706
Eastman	478
Eatonton	706
Eden	912
Edge Hill	706
Edison	229
El Dorado	229
Elberton	706
Elim	912
Elko	478
Ellabell	912
Ellaville	229
Ellenton	229
Ellenwood	404
Ellerslie	706
Ellijay	706
Ellwood	706
Embry Hls	404
Emerson	770
Emmalane	478
Emory University	404
Empire	478
Enigma	229
Ephesus	770
Epworth	706
Esom Hill	770
Eton	706
Euharlee	770
Eulonia	912
Evans	706
Everett	912
Excelsior	912
Experiment	770
Fairburn	770
Fairfax	912
Fairmount	706
Fargo	912
Farmington	706
Farrar	706
Fayetteville	770
Fed Law Enforcement Trng Ctr	912
Federal Correctional Inst	912
Felton	770
Fitzgerald	229
Fleming	912
Flemington	912
Flintstone	706
Flovilla	770
Flowery Br	770
Flowery Branch	770
Folkston	912
Forest	770
Forest Hills	706
Forest Park	404
Forsyth	478
Fort Benning	706
Fort Gaines	229
Fort Gillem	404
Fort Gordon	706
Fort Mcpherson	404
Fort Oglethorpe	706
Fort Screven	912
Fort Stewart	912
Fort Valley	478
Fortson	706
Fowlstown	229
Franklin	706
Franklin Spgs	706
Franklin Springs	706
Fry	706
Fs	912
Ft Gordon	706
Ft Mcpherson	404
Ft Oglethorpe	706
Ft Stewart	912
Funston	229
Ga Southern University	912
Gainesville	770
Garden City	912
Garden Cty	912
Gardi	912
Garfield	912
Gary	478
Gateway	229
Gay	706
Geico Claims	478
Geico Underwriting	478
Geneva	706
Georgetown	229
Georgia Power	770
Georgia State Penitentiary	912
Georgia State University	404
Georgia Tech	404
Gibson	706
Gillsville	706
Girard	478
Glenn	706
Glennville	912
Glenwood	912
Glynco	912
Good Hope	770
Gordon	478
Gough	706
Gracewood	706
Graham	912
Grange	478
Grantville	770
Gray	478
Grayson	770
Graysville	706
Green Way	478
Greensboro	706
Greenville	706
Greenway	478
Griffin	770
Grovania	478
Grovetown	706
Gum Branch	912
Guysie	912
Guyton	912
Haband	706
Habersham	706
Haddock	478
Hagan	912
Hahira	229
Hamilton	706
Hampton	770
Hapeville	404
Haralson	770
Hardwick	478
Harlem	706
Harrison	478
Hartsfield	229
Hartville	229
Hartwell	706
Hawkinsville	478
Hayneville	478
Hazlehurst	912
Helen	706
Helena	229
Hephzibah	706
Herndon	478
Hiawassee	706
Hickory Bluff	912
Hickox	912
Higgston	912
High Shoals	706
Hillsboro	706
Hiltonia	912
Hinesville	912
Hinsonton	229
Hiram	770
Hoboken	912
Hogansville	706
Holly Springs	770
Homeland	912
Homer	706
Homerville	912
Honora	706
Hortense	912
Hoschton	706
Howard	478
Huber	478
Hubert	912
Hull	706
Hunter Aaf	912
Hunter Army Air Field	912
Hville	478
Ideal	478
Ila	706
Indian Springs	770
Industrial	404
Iron City	229
Irs Service Center	770
Irwinton	478
Irwinville	229
Ivanhoe	912
Ivey	478
Jackson	770
Jacksonville	229
Jakin	229
Jasper	706
Jefferson	706
Jeffersonville	478
Jeffersonvlle	478
Jekyll Island	912
Jenkinsburg	770
Jersey	770
Jesup	912
Jewell	706
Johns Creek	770
Johnson Corner	912
Jones	912
Jonesboro	770
Jot Em Down Store	912
Juliette	478
Junction City	706
Juniper	706
Karo	229
Kathleen	478
Kelly	706
Kemp	478
Kennesaw	770
Keysville	706
Kibbee	912
Kings Bay	912
Kingsland	912
Kingston	770
Kite	478
Klondike	478
Knoxville	478
La Fayette	706
Lafayette	706
Lagrange	706
Lake Arrowhead	770
Lake City	770
Lake Park	229
Lake Spivey	770
Lakeland	229
Lakemont	706
Lakepark	229
Lavonia	706
Lawrenceville	404
Leah	706
Leary	229
Leathersville	706
Lebanon	770
Leesburg	229
Lenox	229
Lenox Sq Finance	404
Lenox Square Finance	404
Leslie	229
Lexington	706
Lexsy	478
Lilburn	770
Lilly	478
Lincolnton	706
Lindale	706
Lithia Spgs	770
Lithia Springs	770
Lithonia	770
Little Five Points Pstl Str	404
Lizella	478
Lockheed	770
Loco	706
Locust Grove	770
Loganville	770
Logistics & Distribution Ctr	404
Lollie	478
Lookout Mountain	706
Lookout Mtn	706
Lotts	912
Louisville	478
Louvale	229
Lovejoy	770
Ludowici	912
Lula	770
Lulaton	912
Lumber City	912
Lumpkin	229
Luthersville	770
Lyerly	706
Lyons	912
Mableton	404
Macon	478
Macon Brm	478
Madison	706
Madray Springs	912
Manassas	912
Manchester	706
Manor	912
Mansfield	770
Mar	404
Marble Hill	706
Marblehill	706
Marietta	404
Marine Corps Logistics Base	229
Marlow	912
Marshallville	478
Martin	706
Martinez	706
Matthews	706
Mauk	706
Maxeys	706
Maxim	706
Mayfield	706
Maysville	706
Mc Caysville	706
Mc Donough	770
Mc Intyre	478
Mc Rae	229
Mccaysville	706
Mcdonough	770
Mcgregor	912
Mckinnon	912
Meansville	706
Meigs	229
Meldrim	912
Mellon Bank	770
Memorial Square	770
Mendes	912
Menlo	706
Mercer University	478
Meridian	912
Mershon	912
Mesena	706
Metcalf	229
Metter	912
Midland	706
Midville	478
Midway	912
Milan	229
Milledgeville	478
Millen	478
Millwood	912

City	Area Code
Milner	770
Milton	770
Mineral Bluff	706
Mitchell	706
Modoc	478
Molena	706
Monroe	770
Montezuma	478
Monticello	706
Montrose	478
Moody A F B	229
Moody Afb	229
Moody Air Force Base	229
Moreland	770
Morgan	229
Morganton	706
Morris	229
Morrow	770
Morven	229
Moultrie	229
Moultrie Municipal Airport	229
Mount Airy	706
Mount Berry	706
Mount Vernon	912
Mount Zion	770
Mountain City	706
Mountville	706
Moxley	478
Mreta	404
Munnerlyn	706
Murrayville	770
Musella	478
Mville	478
Mystic	229
Nahunta	912
Nashville	229
Navy Supply Corps School	706
Naylor	229
Nelson	770
Nevils	912
New Branch	912
New Hope	706
Newborn	706
Newbranch	912
Newgistics	404
Newington	912
Newnan	770
Newton	229
Nicholls	912
Nicholson	706
No Macon	478
Noah	706
Norcross	770
Norman Park	229
Normantown	912
Norris	706
Norristown	478
North Atlanta	770
North Corners	770
North Decatur	404
North Georgia College	706
North Highland Finance	404
North Metro	770
North Springs	770
Northlake	404
Norwood	706
Nunez	478
Oak Grove	770
Oak Park	478
Oakfield	229
Oakman	706
Oakwood	770
Ochlocknee	229
Ocilla	229
Oconee	478
Odum	912
Offerman	912
Ogelthorpe	478
Oglethorpe	478
Ohoopee	912
Okefenokee	912
Olgethorpe	478
Oliver	912
Omaha	229
Omega	229
Orchard Hill	770

City	Area Code
Overlook Sru	770
Oxford	770
Palmetto	770
Parkway	770
Parrott	229
Patterson	912
Pavo	229
Payne City	478
Peach Orchard	706
Peachtree City	770
Peachtree City Parcel Return	770
Peachtree Corners	770
Peachtree Cty	770
Pearson	912
Pelham	229
Pembroke	912
Pendergrass	706
Penfield	706
Penfld	706
Perimeter Center Finance	404
Perkins	478
Perry	478
Petross	912
Philomath	706
Phinizy	706
Pine Grove	912
Pine Lake	404
Pine Mountain	706
Pine Mountain Valley	706
Pine Mtn Valy	706
Pinehurst	229
Pineora	912
Pineview	229
Piney Bluff	912
Pitts	229
Plainfield	478
Plains	229
Plainville	770
Pollards Corner	706
Pooler	912
Port Wentworth	912
Portal	912
Porterdale	770
Poulan	229
Powder Spgs	770
Powder Springs	770
Powersville	478
Preston	229
Pridgen	912
Primerica Financial Services	770
Prt Wentworth	912
Pulaski	912
Pumpkin Center	706
Putney	229
Quitman	229
Rabun Gap	706
Radium Springs	229
Railroad Retirement Board	706
Ranger	706
Ray City	229
Raybon	912
Rayle	706
Raymond	770
Rebecca	229
Red Oak	404
Redan	770
Reese	706
Register	912
Reidsville	912
Remerton	229
Rentz	478
Resaca	706
Retreat	912
Rex	770
Reynolds	478
Reynolds Plantation	706
Rhine	229
Riceboro	912
Richland	229
Richmond Hill	912
Ridgeville	912
Rincon	912
Ringgold	706
Rising Fawn	706
Riverdale	770
Roberta	478

City	Area Code
Robins A F B	478
Robins Afb	478
Robins Air Force Base	478
Rochelle	229
Rock Spring	706
Rockbridge	770
Rockingham	912
Rockledge	912
Rockmart	770
Rocky Face	706
Rocky Ford	912
Rome	706
Roopville	770
Roper	912
Rosier	478
Rossville	706
Roswell	770
Round Oak	706
Royston	706
Rupert	478
Rutledge	706
Rydal	706
S Macon	478
Saint George	912
Saint Marys	912
Saint Simons Is	912
Saint Simons Island	912
Sale City	229
Sandersville	478
Sandy Plains	770
Sandy Spgs	404
Sandy Springs	404
Santa Claus	912
Sapelo Island	912
Sardis	478
Sargent	770
Sasser	229
Saute Nacoche	706
Saute-Nacoche	706
Sautee Nacoochee	706
Savannah	912
Scarboro	478
Scotland	912
Scottdale	404
Screven	912
Sea Island	912
Sears	912
Senoia	770
Sessoms	912
Seville	229
Shady Dale	706
Shannon	770
Sharon	706
Sharpsburg	770
Shell Bluff	706
Shellman	229
Shellman Blf	912
Shellman Bluff	912
Shenandoah	770
Shiloh	706
Shoals	706
Siloam	706
Silver Creek	706
Sky Valley	706
Smarr	478
Smithville	229
Smoke Rise	770
Smyrna	770
Snapfinger	404
Snellville	770
Snipesville	912
So Macon	478
Social Circle	770
Soperton	912
South Base	478
South Newport	912
Southwire	770
Sparks	229
Sparta	706
Spring Bluff	912
Springfield	912
St Mountain	770
St Mtn	770
St Simons Is	912
St Simons Island	912
Stanleys Store	912

City	Area Code
Stapleton	706
State College	912
State Farm Insurance Co	770
Statenville	229
Statesboro	912
Statham	770
Stephens	706
Sterling	912
Stevens Pottery	478
Stillmore	912
Stillwell	912
Stilson	912
Stockbridge	770
Stockton	229
Stone Mountain	770
Stone Mtn	770
Stovall	706
Suches	706
Sugar Hill	770
Sugar Valley	706
Sugarhill	770
Summertown	478
Summerville	706
Sumner	229
Sunny Side	770
Suntrust	404
Surrency	912
Suwanee	770
Swainsboro	478
Sybert	706
Sycamore	229
Sylvania	912
Sylvester	229
T Mobile	404
Talbotton	706
Talking Rock	706
Tallapoosa	770
Tallulah Falls	706
Tallulah Fls	706
Talmo	706
Tarrytown	912
Tate	770
Taylorsville	770
Tazewell	229
Temple	770
Tennga	706
Tennille	478
Thalman	912
The Rock	706
Thomaston	706
Thomasville	229
Thomson	706
Thrift	478
Thunderbolt	912
Tifton	229
Tiger	706
Tignall	706
Toccoa	706
Toccoa Falls	706
Toomsboro	478
Townsend	912
Trenton	706
Trion	706
Tucker	770
Tunnel Hill	706
Turin	770
Turnerville	706
Tuxedo	404
Tville	229
Twin City	478
Ty Ty	229
Tybee Island	912
Tyrone	770
Tyty	229
U S P S Bulk Mail Ctr	404
Unadilla	478
Unidilla	478
Union City	770
Union Point	706
University Of Georgia	706
University Of West Georgia	770
Upatoi	706
Usps Official Mail	478
Uvalda	912
Valdosta	229
Valdosta State College	229

City	Area Code
Valona	912
Varnell	706
Vidalia	912
Vidette	478
Vienna	229
Villa Rica	770
Village Station	912
Vinings	770
Vinnings	770
Vista Grove	404
Wachovia	404
Waco	770
Wadley	478
Waleska	770
Walthourville	912
Waresboro	912
Warm Springs	706
Warner Robins	478
Warrenton	706
Warthen	478
Warwick	229
Washington	706
Watkinsville	706
Waverly	912
Waverly Hall	706
Waycross	912
Waynesboro	706
Waynesville	912
Wesley	478
West Bainbridge	229
West Green	912
West Point	706
Weston	229
Westside	770
Whigham	229
White	770
White Oak	912
White Plains	706
White Stone	706
Whitesburg	770
Wildwood	706
Wiley	706
Willacoochee	912
Williamson	770
Wilmington Island	912
Wilsonville	912
Winder	770
Winfield	706
Winston	770
Winters Chapel	404
Winterville	706
Woodbine	912
Woodbury	706
Woodland	706
Woodstock	770
Woodville	706
Woolsey	770
Wray	912
Wrens	706
Wrightsville	478
Yatesville	478
Young Harris	706
Zebulon	770
Zebulon Branch	478

Guam

City	Area Code
All Points	671

Hawaii

City	Area Code
All Points	808

Idaho

City	Area Code
All Points	208

Illinois

City	Area Code
3 State Farm Plaza	309
Abbott Park	847
Abingdon	309
Adair	309
Adams	217
Addieville	618
Addison	630
Aden	618
Adrian	217
Akin	618
Alba	309
Albany	309
Albers	618
Albion	618
Albright	217
Alden	815
Aledo	309
Alexander	217
Alexis	309
Algonquin	847
Alhambra	618
Allendale	618
Allentown	309
Allenville	217
Allerton	217
Allin	309
Allison	618
Alma	618
Alorton	618
Alpha	309
Alsey	217
Alsip	708
Alta	309
Altamont	618
Alto Pass	618
Alton	618
Altona	309
Alvin	217
Amboy	815
America	618
American National Bank	312
Ameritech	217
Amf Ohare	773
Anchor	309
Ancona	815
Andalusia	309
Andover	309
Andrew	217
Anna	618
Annapolis	618
Annawan	309, 815
Antioch	847
Apple River	815
Appleton	309
Arcadia	217
Archer	217
Arcola	217
Arenzville	217
Argenta	217
Argo	708
Argyle	815
Arlington	815
Arlington Heights	847
Arlington Hts	847
Armington	309
Armstrong	217
Arnold	217
Aroma Park	815
Arrington	618
Arrowsmith	309
Arthur	217
Asbury	618
Ashburn Park	773
Ashkum	815
Ashland	217
Ashley	618
Ashmore	217
Ashton	815
Assumption	217
Astoria	309
At & T	630
Athens	217
Athensville	217
Atkinson	309
Atlanta	217
Atlas	217
Atterberry	217

City	Area Code
Atterbury	217
Attila	618
Atwater	217
Atwood	217
Auburn	217
Audubon	217
Augsburg	618
Augusta	217
Aurora	630
Ava	618
Aviston	618
Avoca	815
Avon	309
Ayers	618
Babcock	309
Baden Baden	618
Bader	309
Baileyville	815
Baker	815
Bakerville	618
Balcom	618
Baldwin	618
Ballou	815
Bank Of America	312, 773
Banner	309
Bannockburn	847
Barclay	217
Bardolph	309
Bargerville	618
Barnes	309
Barnett	217
Barnett Township	217
Barnhill	618
Barr	217
Barren	618
Barrington	847
Barrington Hills	847
Barrow	217
Barry	217
Barstow	309
Bartelso	618
Bartlett	630
Bartonville	309
Basco	217
Batavia	630
Batchtown	618
Bates	217
Bath	309
Bayle	217
Baylis	217
Bayview Garde	309
Bayview Gardens	309
Beach Park	847
Bear Grove	618
Beardstown	217
Bearsdale	217
Beason	217
Beaucoup	618
Beaver Creek	618
Beaverville	815
Beckemeyer	618
Bedford Park	708
Bedford Pk	708
Beecher	708
Beecher City	217, 618
Beechville	618
Belgium	217
Belknap	618
Bell Plain	309
Belle Prairie City	618
Belle Rive	618
Belleville	618
Bellevue	309
Bellflower	309
Bellmont	618
Belltown	217
Bellview	309
Bellwood	708
Beloit	815
Belvidere	815
Bement	217
Benld	217
Bensenville	630
Benson	309
Bentley	217
Benton	618
Berkeley	708
Berlin	217
Bernadotte	309
Berry	217
Berryville	618
Berwick	309
Berwyn	708
Bethalto	618
Bethany	217
Bethel	217
Beulah Heights	618
Beverly Manor	309
Bible Grove	618
Big Mound	618
Big Rock	630
Big Spring	217
Biggs	309
Biggsville	309
Bigneck	217
Billet	618
Bingham	217
Binghampton	815
Birds	618
Birkbeck	217
Birmingham	309
Bishop	309
Bishop Hill	309
Bismarck	217
Bissell	217
Black	618
Blackstone	815
Blaine	815
Blair	618
Blairsville	618
Blandinsville	309
Blm	309
Bloomingdale	630
Bloomington	309
Bloomington Heights	309
Bloomington Normal Airport	309
Blue Island	708
Blue Mound	217
Blue Point	217
Bluff City	309
Bluff Hall	217
Bluff Springs	217
Bluffs	217
Bluford	618
Blyton	309
Boaz	618
Boden	309
Boggsville	217
Bogota	618
Boles	618
Bolingbrook	630
Bolivia	217
Bolo	618
Bond	618
Bondville	217
Bone Gap	618
Bonfield	815
Bonnie	618
Bonpas	618
Bonus	815
Boody	217
Boskydell	618
Boulder	618
Boulder Hill	630
Bourbonnais	815
Bowen	217
Bowlesville	618
Bowling Green	618
Boyd	618
Boyleston	618
Boynton	309
Braceville	815
Bradbury	217
Bradford	309
Bradford Group	630
Bradfordton	217
Bradley	815
Bradley Univ	309
Braidwood	815
Breckenridge	217
Breeds	309
Breese	618
Bremen	618
Brereton	309
Briarwood Trace	618
Brickton	815
Bridgeport	618
Bridgeview	708
Brighton	618
Brimfield	309
Bristol	630
Broadlands	217
Broadmoor	309
Broadview	708
Broadwell	217
Brocton	217
Brookfield	708
Brookhaven	815
Brooklyn	618
Brookport	618
Brookville	815
Broughton	618
Brownfield	618
Browning	309
Browns	618
Brownstown	618
Brush Hill	618
Brushy	618
Brussels	618
Bryant	309
Buckhart	217
Buckingham	815
Buckley	217
Buckner	618
Buda	309
Buffalo	217
Buffalo Hart	217
Buffalo Pr	309
Buffalo Prairie	309
Bull Valley	815
Bulpitt	217
Buncombe	618
Bungay	618
Bunker Hill	618
Burbank	708
Bureau	815
Bureau Junction	815
Burksville	618
Burlington	847
Burnham	773
Burnside	217
Burnt Prairie	618
Burr Ridge	708
Burridge	708
Burt	309
Burton	217
Bush	618
Bushnell	309
Butler	217
Byron	815
Byron Hills	309
C I P S	217
Cabery	815
Cable	309
Cache	618
Cadwell	217
Cahokia	618
Cairo	618
Caledonia	815
Calhoun	618
Calumet City	708
Calumet Park	708, 773
Calvin	618
Camargo	217
Cambria	618
Cambridge	309
Camden	217
Cameron	309
Camp Ground	618
Camp Grove	309
Camp Point	217
Campbell Hill	618
Campbells Island	309
Campton Hills	630, 847
Campus	815
Candlewick Lake	815
Canton	309
Cantrall	217
Capron	815
Carbon Cliff	309
Carbon Hill	815
Carbondale	618
Carlinville	217
Carlock	309
Carlyle	618
Carman	309
Carmi	618
Carol Stream	630, 708, 847
Carpentersville	847
Carpentersvle	847
Carrier Mills	618
Carriers Mills	618
Carrigan	618
Carrollton	217
Carterville	618
Carthage	217
Carthage Lake	309
Cartter	618
Cary	847
Casey	217
Caseyville	618
Castleton	309
Caterpillar Inc	309
Catlin	217
Cave	618
Cave In Rock	618
Cayuga	815
Cazenovia	309
Cdale	618
Cedar Point	815
Cedarville	815
Ceffco	309
Central City	618
Central Park	217
Centralia	618
Centreville	618
Cerro Gordo	217
Chadwick	815
Chaflin Bridge	618
Chambersburg	217
Chamnesstown	618
Champaign	217
Champlin	815
Chana	815
Chandlerville	217
Channahon	815
Chapin	217
Chapman	217
Charles A Hayes	773
Charleston	217
Chase Bank	312, 773, 847
Chatham	217
Chatsworth	815
Chauncey	618
Chautauqua	618
Chebanse	815
Check Row	309
Chemung	815
Chenoa	815
Cherry	815
Cherry Valley	815
Chesney Shores	847
Chester	618
Chesterfield	618
Chesterville	217
Chestline	217
Chestnut	217
Chestnut Street	312
Chgo	847
Chi	847
Chicago	312, 708, 773, 847
Chicago Heights	708
Chicago Hts	708
Chicago Lawn	773
Chicago Ridge	708
Chillicothe	309
Chrisman	217
Christopher	618
Cicero	708
Cimic	217
Cisco	217
Cisne	618
Cissna Park	815
Citicorp	630
Clare	815
Claremont	618
Clarence	217
Clarendon Hills	630
Clarendon Hls	630
Clark Center	217
Clarksburg	217
Clarksdale	217
Clarksville	217
Clay City	618
Clayton	217
Claytonville	815
Clearing	773
Cleburne	618
Clement	618
Clements	217
Cleone	217
Cleveland	309
Clifton	815
Clinton	217
Clintonia Township	217
Cloverdale	630
Cloverleaf	618
Clyde	815
Cna Center	312
Cntry Clb Hls	708
Coal City	815
Coal Hollow	815
Coal Valley	309
Coalton	217
Coatsburg	217
Cobden	618
Coe	309
Coello	618
Coffeen	217
Colchester	309
Coleta	815
Colfax	309
College Heights	618
College Hills Mall	309
Collinsville	618
Collison	217
Colmar	309
Colona	309
Colp	618
Columbia	618
Columbia Heights	309
Columbus	217
Colusa	217
Comer	217
Commonwealth Edison	312
Compton	815
Conant	618
Concord	217
Confidence	618
Congerville	309
Cooksville	309
Cooperstown	217
Coral	815
Cordova	309
Corinth	618
Cornell	815
Cornerville	618
Cornland	217
Cornwall	309
Cortland	815
Cottage Hills	618
Cottagegrove	618
Cottonwood	217
Coulterville	618
Country Club Hills	708
Countryside	708
Covell	309
Covington	618
Cowden	217, 618
Cowling	618
Crab Orchard Estates	618
Cragin	773
Crainville	618
Cramers	309
Cravat	618
Creal Springs	618
Crescent City	815
Crest Hill	708, 815
Cresthill	815
Creston	815
Crestview Terrace	618
Crestwood	708
Crete	708
Creve Coeur	309
Crisp	618
Crook	618
Cropsey	309
Crossville	618
Crouch	618
Crystal Lake	815
Ctry Clb Hls	708
Cuba	309
Cullom	815
Cumberland	217
Cumberland Heights	618
Curran	217
Custer Park	815
Cutler	618
Cypress	618
Dahinda	309
Dahlgren	618
Dakota	815
Dale	618
Dallas City	217
Dallasania	618
Dalton City	217
Dalzell	815
Damiansville	618
Dana	815
Danforth	815
Daniel J Doffyn	773
Danvers	309
Danville	217
Danway	815
Darien	630
Darmstadt	618
Davis	815
Davis Jct	815
Davis Junction	815
Dawson	217
Dawson Township	309
Dayton	815
De Land	217
De Pue	815
De Soto	618
Decatur	217
Decorra	309
Deer Creek	309
Deer Grove	815
Deer Park	847
Deer Plain	618
Deerfield	847
Deering	618
Degognia	618
Dekalb	815
Delafield	618
Delavan	309
Delhi	618
Delong	309
Denison	618
Denning	618
Dennison	217
Denver	217
Dept Of Transportation	217
Dept Public Property Cwlp	217
Depue	815
Depue Junction	815
Des Plaines	847
Despl/Rsmt Bus Rply	847
Detroit	217
Devereux Heights	217
Dewey	217
Dewitt	217
Dewmaine	618
Dhs Dept Of Mental Health	217
Diamond	815
Dieterich	217
Dillon	309
Dimmick	815
Diona	217
Div Of Postal Inspectors	312
Divernon	217
Divide	618
Dix	618
Dixmoor	708

City	Area Code
Dixon	815
Dixon Springs	618
Dodds	618
Doddsville	309
Dogtown	618
Dollville	217
Dolton	708
Dongola	618
Donnellson	217
Donovan	815
Dorchester	217
Dorsey	618
Douglas	217
Dover	815
Dow	618
Dowell	618
Downers Grove	630
Downey	847
Downs	309
Downtown Station Joliet	815
Drake	217
Drivers	618
Drivers Lic Div	217
Du Bois	618
Du Quoin	618
Dubois	618
Dudleyville	618
Duncanville	618
Dundas	618
Dundee	847
Dunfermline	309
Dunkel	217
Dunlap	309
Dunlap Lake	618
Dupo	618
Durand	815
Duvall	217
Dwight	815
Dykersburg	618
E Carondelet	618
E Galesburg	309
E Moline	309
E Saint Louis	618
E St Louis	618
Eagarville	217
Eagle Lake	708
Eagle Park	618
Eagle Point Bay	618
Earlville	815
East Alton	618
East Brooklyn	815
East Cape Girardeau	618
East Carondelet	618
East Clinton	815
East Dubuque	815
East Dundee	847
East Eldorado	618
East Fork	217
East Fulton	815
East Galesburg	309
East Gillespie	217
East Hannibal	217
East Hardin	618
East Hazel Crest	708
East Lynn	217
East Moline	309
East Peoria	309
East Saint Louis	618
East St Louis	618
East Wenona	815
Eastern	618
Eastland Commons	309
Eastland Shopping Center	309
Easton	309
Eaton	618
Echo Lake	847
Eckard	309
Eddyville	618
Edelstein	309
Eden	618
Edenburg	217
Edgewater Terrace	309
Edgewood	618
Edinburg	217
Edwards	309
Edwardsville	618
Effingham	217
Egan	815
Egyptian Hills	618
Egyptian Shores	618
Eileen	815
El Paso	309
El Vista	309
Elba	618
Elburn	630
Elco	618
Eldara	217
Eldena	815
Eldorado	618
Eldred	217
Eleanor	309
Eleroy	815
Elgin	847
Eliza	309
Elizabeth	815
Elizabethtown	618
Elk Grove Village	630, 847
Elk Grove Vlg	630
Elkhart	217
Elkton	618
Elkville	618
Ellery	618
Elliott	217
Ellis Grove	618
Ellisgrove	618
Ellison	309
Ellisville	309
Ellsworth	309
Elm River	618
Elmhurst	630
Elmira	309
Elmore	309
Elmwood	309
Elmwood Park	708
Elsah	618
Elsdon	708
Elvaston	217
Elvira	618
Elwin	217
Elwood	815
Emden	217
Emington	815
Emma	618
Energy	618
Enfield	618
Englewood	773
Enion	309
Enos	217
Enterprise	618
Eola	630
Eppards Point	815
Epworth	618
Equality	618
Erie	309
Esmond	815
Essex	815
Etherton	618
Eureka	309
Evans	815
Evanston	847
Evansville	618
Evergreen Park	773
Evergreen Pk	773
Ewing	618
Exeter	217
Eylar	815
Ezra	618
Fairbury	815
Fairdale	815
Fairfield	618
Fairman	618
Fairmont City	618
Fairmount	217
Fairview	309
Fairview Heights	618
Fairview Hieghts	618
Fairview Hts	618
Fall Creek	217
Fancher	217
Fancy Prairie	217
Fandon	309
Farina	618
Farm Ridge	815
Farmer City	309
Farmersville	217
Farmingdale	217
Farmington	309
Fayette	217
Fayetteville	618
Fayville	618
Fenton	309
Ferges	618
Fergestown	618
Ferrin	618
Ferris	217
Fiatt	309
Fidelity	618
Field Shopping Center	309
Fieldon	618
Fifth Third Bank	773
Fillmore	217
Findlay	217
Finney Heights	618
Fisher	217
Fithian	217
Flag Center	815
Flagg	815
Flanagan	815
Flat Rock	618
Fleet	312
Fletcher	309
Flora	618
Floraville	618
Florid	815
Flossmoor	708
Flowerfield	630
Foosland	217
Ford Heights	708
Forest City	309
Forest Lake	847
Forest Park	708
Forest View	708, 773
Forrest	815
Forreston	815
Forsyth	217
Fort Dearborn	312
Fort Russell	618
Fort Sheridan	847
Foster Pond	618
Fountain	618
Fountain Bluff	618
Fountain Green	217
Four Mile	618
Fowler	217
Fox Lake	847
Fox Lake Hills	847
Fox River Grove	847
Fox River Grv	847
Fox River Valley Gardens	847
Fox Rv Vly Gn	847
Fox Valley	630
Fox Valley Facility	630
Frankfort	815
Frankfort Heights	618
Frankfort Hts	618
Franklin	217
Franklin Grove	815
Franklin Grv	815
Franklin Park	847
Frederick	217
Freeburg	618
Freeman Spur	618
Freeport	815
Friendsville	618
Frisco	618
Frogtown	618
Fulton	815
Fults	618
Funkhouser	217
Funks Grove	309
Future City	618
Gages Lake	847
Galatia	618
Gale	618
Galena	815
Galena Knolls	309
Galesburg	309
Galt	815
Galva	309
Ganntown	618
Garber	217
Garden Hill	618
Garden Plain	815
Garden Pr	815
Garden Prairie	815
Gardner	815
Garfield	815
Garrett	217
Gays	217
Geff	618
Genesee	815
Geneseo	309
Geneva	630
Genoa	815
Georgetown	217
Gerlaw	309
German	618
German Valley	815
Germantown	618
Germantown Hills	309
Germantwn Hls	309
Gibson City	217
Gifford	217
Gila	217
Gilberts	847
Gilead	618
Gillespie	217
Gillum	309
Gilman	815
Gilmore	618
Gilson	309
Girard	217
Gladstone	309
Glasford	309
Glen Avon	309
Glen Carbon	618
Glen Ellyn	630
Glen Ridge	618
Glenarm	217
Glencoe	847
Glendale Heights	630
Glendale Hts	630
Glenn	618
Glenview	847
Glenwood	708
Godfrey	618
Godley	815
Golconda	618
Gold Hill	618
Golden	217
Golden Eagle	618
Golden Gate	618
Goldengate	618
Golf	847
Good Hope	309
Goode	618
Goodenow	708
Goodfield	309
Goodwine	815
Goofy Ridge	309
Gordons	618
Goreville	618
Gorham	618
Goshen	309
Gossett	618
Graceland	773
Grafton	618
Grand Chain	618
Grand Crossing	773
Grand Detour	815
Grand Oaks	309
Grand Prairie	618
Grand Ridge	815
Grand Tower	618
Grandview	217
Granite City	618
Grant Park	815
Grantfork	618
Grantsburg	618
Granville	815
Graymont	815
Grayslake	847
Grayville	618
Great Central Ins Co	309
Great Lakes	847
Great Lakes Area Office	630
Greater Peoria Airport	309
Green Creek	217
Green Oaks	847
Green Rock	309
Green Valley	309
Greenbush	309
Greenfield	217
Greenup	217
Greenview	217
Greenville	618
Greenwood	815
Gridley	309
Grigg	618
Griggsville	217
Grimsby	618
Grisham	217
Groveland	309
Grover	618
Gulfport	309
Gurnee	847
Hafer	618
Hagaman	618
Hagarstown	618
Hahnaman	815
Haines	618
Hainesville	847
Haldane	815
Half Day	847
Hallidayboro	618
Hallsville	217
Hamburg	618
Hamel	618
Hamilton	217
Hamlet	309
Hamletsburg	618
Hammond	217
Hampshire	847
Hampton	309
Hanaford	618
Hanna	309
Hanna City	309
Hanover	815
Hanover Park	630
Harco	618
Hardin	618
Harding	815
Hardinville	618
Harmon	815
Harmony	217
Harp Township	217
Harris Bank	312
Harrisburg	618
Harrisonville	618
Harristown	217
Hartford	618
Hartsburg	217
Harvard	815
Harvel	217
Harvey	708
Harwood Heights	773
Harwood Hgts	773
Harwood Hts	773
Havana	309
Hawthorn Wds	847
Hawthorn Woods	847
Hazel Crest	708
Hazel Dell	217
Healthcare And Family Serv	217
Heartville	217
Heathsville	618
Hebron	815
Hecker	618
Hegeler	217
Hegewisch	773
Helena	618
Helm	618
Helmar	815
Heman	217
Henderson	309
Henderson Grove	309
Hennepin	815
Henning	217
Henry	309
Henry Mcgee	773
Henton	217
Herald	618
Heralds Prairie	618
Herbert	815
Herborn	217
Hermon	309
Herod	618
Herrick	618
Herrin	618
Herscher	815
Hersman	217
Hervey City	217
Hettick	618
Hewittsville	217
Heyworth	309
Hickory Hills	708
Hidalgo	618
High Meadows	309
Highland	618
Highland Park	847
Highwood	847
Hillcrest	815
Hillerman	618
Hillsboro	217
Hillsdale	309
Hillside	708
Hilltop	309
Hillview	217
Hinckley	815
Hindsboro	217
Hines	708
Hinsdale	630
Hinton	217
Hittle	309
Hodgkins	708
Hoffman	618
Hoffman Est	847
Hoffman Estates	847
Holcomb	815
Holder	309
Holiday Hills	815
Holiday Shores	618
Hollis	309
Hollowayville	815
Hollywood Heights	618
Holmes Center	309
Homer	217
Homer Glen	708, 815
Hometown	708
Homewood	708
Honey Creek	815
Hookdale	618
Hoopeston	217
Hooppole	815
Hoosier	618
Hope School	217
Hopedale	309
Hopewell	309
Hopewell Estates	309
Hopkins Park	815
Hopper	309
Horace Mann Ins	217
Hord	618
Hornsby	217
Household Finance Corp	630
Household Financial Services	630
Houston	618
Howardton	618
Howe	815
Hoyleton	618
Hubbard Woods	847
Hubly	217
Hudson	309
Huegely	618
Huey	618
Hull	217
Humboldt	217
Hume	217
Hunt	618
Hunt City	618
Huntley	847
Huntsville	217
Hurst	618
Hutsonville	618
Hwy Accident Bureau	217
I L Central College	309

City	Area Code
Idlewood	618
Il Dept Reg And Educ	217
Il Mutual Life & Casualty	309
Ill Dept Human Services	217
Ill Dept Ins	217
Ill Dept Public Health	217
Ill Dept Revenue	217
Ill Office Educ	217
Ill R O Tax Div	217
Ill Secy State	217
Illinois City	309
Illinois State University	309
Illiopolis	217
Imbs	618
Ina	618
Ind Head Park	708
Ind Head Pk	708
Indian Creek	847
Indian Head Park	708
Indian Head Pk	708
Indianhead Park	708
Indianhead Pk	708
Indianola	217
Industry	309
Ingleside	847
Ingraham	618
Inktel Marketing	630
Internal Revenue Service	309
Inverness	847
Iola	618
Ipava	309
Irene	815
Irishtown	618
Iroquois	815
Irving	217
Irvington	618
Island Grove	217
Island Lake	847
Itasca	630
Iuka	618
Ivesdale	217
Jackson Park	773
Jacksonville	217
Jacob	618
Jamestown	618
Janesville	217
Jasper	618
Jefferson	773
Jefferson Park	773
Jefferson Pk	773
Jeffersonville	618
Jeiseyville	217
Jenkins	217
Jerome	217
Jersey	618
Jerseyville	618
Jewett	217
John Buchanan	773
Johnsburg	815
Johnsonville	618
Johnston City	618
Joliet	708
Jonesboro	618
Jonesville	815
Joppa	618
Joshua	309
Joy	309
Jp Morgan Chase	312, 773
Jt Weeker Isc	312, 847
Junction	618
Junction City	618
Justice	708
Kampsville	618
Kane	618
Kaneville	630
Kangley	815
Kankakee	815
Kansas	217
Kappa	309
Karbers Ridge	618
Karnak	618
Kasbeer	815
Kaufman	618
Keenes	618
Keeneyville	630
Keensburg	618
Keith	618
Keithsburg	309
Kell	618
Kellerville	217
Kemper	618
Kemper Ins Co	847
Kempton	815
Kenilworth	847
Kenney	217
Kent	815
Kernan	815
Kerrik	309
Kewanee	309
Keyesport	618
Keystone Steel And Wire	309
Kibble	618
Kickapoo	309
Kilbourne	309
Kildeer	847
Kincaid	217
Kinderhook	217
Kingman	217
Kings	815
Kingston	815
Kingston Mine	309
Kingston Mines	309
Kinkaid	618
Kinmundy	618
Kinsman	815
Kirkland	815
Kirksville	217
Kirkwood	309
Klondike	618
Knight Prairie	618
Knollwood	847
Knoxville	309
Komatsu Dresser	309
Kortcamp	217
Kumler	309
La Clede	618
La Crosse	217
La Fayette	309
La Gran Hghls	708
La Grange	708
La Grange Highlands	708
La Grange Park	708
La Grange Pk	708
La Grng Pk	708
La Harpe	217
La Moille	815
La Place	217
La Prairie	217
La Rose	309
La Salle	815
Laclede	618
Lacon	309
Ladd	815
Ladd Junction	815
Lafox	630
Lagrange Hlds	708
Lake Barrington	847
Lake Barrington Shores	847
Lake Bluff	847
Lake Camelot	309
Lake Carroll	815
Lake Centralia	217
Lake City	217
Lake Crest	618
Lake Forest	847
Lake Fork	217
Lake In The Hills	847
Lake Keho	217
Lake Lancelot	309
Lake Of The Woods	309
Lake Sara	217
Lake Tacoma	618
Lake Thunderbird	815
Lake Villa	847
Lake Wildwood	815
Lake Zurich	847
Lakemoor	815
Lakeview	773
Lakewood	217, 815
Lakewood Park	618
Lamard	618
Lamb	618
Lamotte	618
Lanark	815
Lancaster	618
Lane	217
Lanesville	217
Langleyville	217
Lansing	708
Larchland	309
Larkinsburg	618
Latham	217
Laura	309
Lawn Ridge	309
Lawndale	217
Lawrence	618
Lawrenceville	618
Le Roy	309
Leaf River	815
Lebanon	618
Lee	815
Lee Center	815
Leeds	815
Leland	815
Leland Grove	217
Lemont	630
Lena	815
Lenzburg	618
Leon Corners	815
Leonore	815
Lerna	217
Leroy	309
Levan	618
Lewistown	309
Lexington	309
Liberty	217
Libertyville	847
Lick Creek	618
Lilly	309
Lillyville	217
Lily Lake	630
Lima	217
Limerick	815
Lincoln	217
Lincoln Nw Sl	217
Lincoln Park	773
Lincolns New Salem	217
Lincolnshire	847
Lincolnshire Woods	847
Lincolnwood	773, 847
Lindenhurst	847
Lindenwood	815
Lisbon	815
Lisle	630
Litchfield	217
Literberry	217
Little America	309
Little Indian	217
Little Mackinaw	309
Little Rock	630
Little York	309
Littleton	309
Lively Grove	618
Liverpool	309
Livingston	618
Lk Barrington	847
Lk In The Hills	847
Lk In The Hls	847
Loami	217
Lockport	708, 815
Loda	217
Lodge	217
Logan	618
Lomax	217
Lombard	630
Lombardville	309
London Mills	309
Lone Tree	815
Long Grove	847
Long Lake	847
Long Point	815
Longview	217
Loogootee	618
Loraine	217
Loran	815
Lorenzo	815
Lostant	815
Lou Del	618
Louisville	618
Lovejoy	618
Loves Park	815
Lovington	217
Lowder	217
Lowell	815
Lowpoint	309
Ludlow	217
Lukin	618
Lumaghi Heights	618
Luther	217
Lynchburg	309
Lyndon	815
Lynn	309
Lynn Center	309
Lynnville	217
Lynwood	708
Lyons	708
Lyttleville	309
Macedonia	618
Machesney Park	815
Machesney Pk	815
Mackinaw	309
Macomb	309
Macon	217
Madison	618
Madonnaville	618
Maeystown	618
Magnolia	815
Mahomet	217
Makanda	618
Malden	815
Malta	815
Malvern	815
Manchester	217
Manhattan	815
Manito	309
Manlius	815
Mansfield	217
Manteno	815
Manville	815
Maple Park	815
Maple Point	217
Mapleton	309
Maquon	309
Marblehead	217
Marcelline	217
Marcoe	618
Mardell Manor	309
Marengo	815
Marietta	309
Marine	618
Marion	618
Marissa	618
Mark	815
Markham	708
Marlow	618
Maroa	217
Marquette Heights	309
Marquette Hts	309
Marrisa	618
Marseilles	815
Marshall	217
Marston	309
Martinsville	217
Martinton	815
Mary Alice Henry	773
Maryville	618
Mascoutah	618
Mason	618
Mason City	217
Matherville	309
Matteson	708
Mattoon	217
Maud	618
Maunie	618
Mayberry	618
Mayfair	309
Maytown	815
Maywood	708
Mazon	815
Mboro	618
Mc Clure	618
Mc Connell	815
Mc Cook	708
Mc Lean	309
Mc Leansboro	618
Mc Nabb	815
Mccall	217
Mcclure	618
Mcclusky	618
Mcconnell	815
Mccook	708
Mccormick	618
Mccullom Lake	815
Mcdowell	815
Mcgirr	815
Mchenry	815
Mclean	309
Mcleansboro	618
Mcnabb	815
Mcvey	217
Meadows	815
Mechanicsburg	217
Media	309
Medinah	630
Medora	618
Meersman	309
Mellon Financial Services	847
Melrose Park	708, 847
Melvin	217
Memorial Med Ctr	217
Menard	618
Mendon	217
Mendota	815
Menominee	815
Meppen	618
Mercer	309
Merchandise Mart	312
Meredosia	217
Meriden	815
Meridian Heights	618
Mermet	618
Merna	309
Merriam	618
Merrimac	618
Merrionett Pk	708, 773
Merrionette Park	708
Merritt	217
Merry Oaks	309
Mesa Lake	618
Metamora	309
Metcalf	217
Methodist Hosp	309
Metropolis	618
Mettawa	847
Michael	618
Middlegrove	309
Middlesworth	217
Middletown	217
Midland City	217
Midland Hills	618
Midlothian	708
Midway	309
Milan	309
Milford	815
Mill Shoals	618
Millbrook	630
Millcreek	618
Milledgeville	815
Miller City	618
Miller Lake	618
Millersburg	618
Millersville	217
Millington	815
Millstadt	618
Milmine	217
Milo	309
Milton	217
Mineral	309
Minier	309
Minonk	309
Minooka	815
Missal	815
Mitchell	618
Mitchellsville	618
Mobet Meadows	309
Mode	217
Modena	309
Modesto	217
Modoc	618
Mokena	708
Moline	309
Momence	815
Monee	708
Money Creek	309
Monica	309
Monmouth	309
Monroe Center	815
Monroe City	618
Monterey	309
Montgmry	630
Montgomery	630
Monticello	217
Montrose	217
Moonshine	217
Moores Prairie	618
Mooseheart	630
Morgan Park	773
Moro	618
Morris	815
Morrison	815
Morrisonville	217
Morristown	815
Morton	309
Morton Grove	847
Mossville	309
Mound City	618
Mounds	618
Mount Auburn	217
Mount Carbon	618
Mount Carmel	618
Mount Carroll	815
Mount Clare	217
Mount Erie	618
Mount Greenwood	773
Mount Morris	815
Mount Olive	217
Mount Palatine	815
Mount Prospect	847
Mount Pulaski	217
Mount Sterling	217
Mount Vernon	618
Mount Vernon Outland Airport	618
Mount Zion	217
Moweaqua	217
Mozier	618
Mt Auburn	217
Mt Carmell	618
Mt Carroll	815
Mt Greenwood	773
Mt Morris	815
Mt Olive	217
Mt Prospect	847
Mt Pulaski	217
Mt Sterling	217
Mt Zion	217
Muddy	618
Mulberry Grove	618
Mulberry Grv	618
Mulkeytown	618
Multi High Volume Firms	847
Muncie	217
Mundelein	847
Munson	309
Munster	815
Murdock	217
Murphysboro	618
Murrayville	217
N Barrington	847
N Henderson	309
N Riverside	708
Nachusa	815
Nancy B Jefferson	312
Naperville	630
Naplate	815
Naples	217
Nashville	618
Nason	618
Nat Stock Yds	618
National City Bank	312
National Stock Yards	618
Natl Stock Yd	618
Nauvoo	217
Neadmore	217
Nebo	217
Nebraska Township	815
Nekoma	309

City	Area Code
Nelson	815
Neoga	217
Neponset	309
Nettlecreek	815
Neunert	618
New Athens	618
New Baden	618
New Bedford	815
New Berlin	217
New Boston	309
New Burnside	618
New Camp	618
New Canton	217
New City	217
New Columbia	618
New Douglas	217
New Hanover	618
New Haven	618
New Hebron	618
New Holland	217
New Lenox	815
New Liberty	618
New Memphis	618
New Milford	815
New Minden	618
New Philadelphia	309
New Salem	217
New Windsor	309
Newark	815
Newburg	217
Newman	217
Newmansville	217
Newport	618
Newton	618
Niantic	217
Nicor Gas	630
Niles	847
Nilwood	217
Niota	217
Noble	618
Nokomis	217
Nora	815
Normal	309
Normandale	309
Normandy	815
Norridge	773
Norris	309
Norris City	618
North Aurora	630
North Barrington	847
North Chicago	847
North Fork	618
North Hampton	309
North Henderson	309
North Mounds	618
North Ottawa	815
North Pekin	309
North Riverside	708
North Suburban	630, 708
North Town	773
North Utica	815
Northbrook	847
Northern Il Gas	630
Northern Ill Gas Co	630
Northern Oaks	309
Northern Trust Co	312
Northfield	847
Northlake	847
Northmore Heights	217
Northtown	773
Northwestern Univ Adminstrn	847
Northwestern Univ Residental	847
Northwoods	630
Northwoods Shop Ctr	309
Nortonville	217
Norway	815
Norwood	309
Norwood Park	773
Nutwood	618
O Fallon	618
Oak Brk Mall	630
Oak Brook	630
Oak Brook Mall	630
Oak Forest	708
Oak Lawn	708
Oak Park	708
Oak Ridge	309
Oak Run	309
Oakbrook Ter	630
Oakbrook Terrace	630
Oakdale	618
Oakford	217
Oakland	217
Oakley	217
Oakwood	217
Oakwood Hills	847
Oblong	618
Oconee	217
Ocoya	815
Odell	815
Odgen	618
Odin	618
Ogden	217
Ogden Park	773
Oglesby	815
Ohio	815
Ohio Grove	309
Ohlman	217
Okawville	618
Old Berlin	217
Old Camp	618
Old Gilchrist	309
Old Kane	618
Old Mill Creek	847
Old Mill Crk	847
Old Ripley	618
Old Shawneetown	618
Old Stonington	217
Oldtown	309
Olena	309
Olive Branch	618
Oliver	217
Olmsted	618
Olney	618
Olympia Fields	708
Olympia Flds	708
Omaha	618
Omega	618
Onarga	815
Oneco	815
Oneida	309
Ontario Street	312
Ontarioville	630
Opdyke	618
Opheim	309
Ophiem	309
Oquawka	309
Orangeville	815
Oraville	618
Orchard Heights	618
Orchard Mines	309
Orchardville	618
Oreana	217
Oregon	815
Orel	618
Orient	618
Orion	309
Orland Hills	708
Orland Park	708
Ormonde	309
Osceola	309
Osco	309
Oskaloosa	618
Ospur	217
Ossami Lake	309
Oswego	630
Otego	618
Otis Grant Collins	773
Ottawa	815
Otter Creek	618
Otterville	618
Otto Mall	708
Ottoville	815
Owaneco	217
Owego	815
Ozark	618
Paderborn	618
Padua	309
Paineville	618
Palatine	847
Palestine	618
Palmer	217
Palmyra	217
Paloma	217
Palos Heights	708
Palos Hills	708
Palos Park	708
Pana	217
Panama	217
Panola	309
Panther Creek	217
Papineau	815
Paris	217
Park City	847
Park Forest	708
Park Hills	217
Park Ridge	847
Parker	217
Parkersburg	618
Parkland	309
Parrish	618
Partridge	309
Patoka	618
Patterson	217
Patton	618
Pattonsburg	815
Paw Paw	815
Pawnee	217
Paxton	217
Paynes Point	815
Payson	217
Pearl	217
Pearl City	815
Pecatonica	815
Pekin	309
Pekin Heights	309
Pekin Ins Co	309
Pekin Mall	309
Pembroke Township	815
Pembroke Twp	815
Penfield	217
Peoples Gas And Light	312
Peoria	309
Peoria Heights	309
Peoria Hts	309
Peoria Journal Star	309
Peotone	708
Percy	618
Perks	618
Perry	217
Perryton	309
Peru	815
Pesotum	217
Petersburg	217
Petrolia	618
Phillips	618
Phillipstown	618
Philo	217
Phoenix	708
Piasa	618
Pierron	618
Pierson Sta	217
Pierson Station	217
Piety Hill	815
Pilot Grove	217
Pilot Knob	618
Pilsen	773
Pinckneyville	618
Pingree Grove	847
Pinkstaff	618
Piopolis	618
Piper City	815
Pisgah	217
Pittsburg	618
Pittsfield	217
Plainfield	815
Plainview	618
Plainville	217
Plano	630
Plato Center	847
Plattville	630
Pleasant Hill	217
Pleasant Mound	618
Pleasant Plains	217
Pleasant Plns	217
Pleasant Ridge	815
Pleasant View	217
Plumfield	618
Plymouth	309
Pnc Bank	312
Pocahontas	618
Polo	815
Pomona	618
Pontiac	815
Pontoon Beach	618
Pontoosuc	217
Pope	618
Poplar City	309
Poplar Grove	815
Port Barrington	847
Port Byron	309
Portland	815
Portland Corners	815
Posen	708
Posey	618
Potomac	217
Pottstown	309
Pr Du Rocher	618
Prairie	618
Prairie Center	815
Prairie City	309
Prairie Du Rocher	618
Prairie Grove	815
Prairie View	847
Prairietown	618
Prairieview	847
Prairieville	815
Preemption	309
Prentice	217
Princeton	815
Princeville	309
Prophetstown	815
Prospect Heights	847
Prospect Hts	847
Providence	815
Pt Barrington	847
Pulaski	618
Pulleys Mill	618
Putnam	815
Quad City Airport	309
Quarry	618
Quincy	217
Raccoon	618
Raddle	618
Radford	217
Radom	618
Raleigh	618
Ramsey	217
Randolph	309
Rankin	217
Ransom	815
Rantoul	217
Rapatee	309
Rapids City	309
Rardin	217
Raritan	309
Ravenswood	773
Ray	217
Raymond	217
Reading	815
Rector	618
Red Bud	618
Red Town	618
Redbud	618
Reddick	815
Redmon	217
Rees	217
Reevesville	618
Renault	618
Renchville	309
Rend City	618
Reno	217
Rentchler	618
Replacement Lens Inc	309
Rev.Milton R.Brunson Station	773
Reynolds	309
Reynoldsburg	618
Reynoldsville	618
Richfield	217
Richland	217
Richland Grove	309
Richmond	815
Richton Park	708
Richview	618
Riddle Hill	217
Ridge Farm	217
Ridgefield	815
Ridgway	618
Ridott	815
Riffel	618
Riggston	217
Rinard	618
Ringwood	815
Rio	309
Ripley	217
Rising Sun	618
Ritchie	815
River Forest	708
River Grove	708
Riverdale	708
Riverside	708
Riverton	217
Riverwoods	847
Roaches	618
Roanoke	309
Robbins	708
Robbs	618
Robein	309
Robert Leflore Jr.	773
Roberto Clemente	773
Roberts	217
Robinson	618
Roby	217
Rochelle	815
Rochester	217
Rock City	815
Rock Creek	618
Rock Falls	815
Rock Grove	815
Rock Island	309
Rock Island Arsonal	309
Rockbridge	217
Rockdale	815
Rockford	815
Rockport	217
Rockton	815
Rockwell	815
Rockwood	618
Roger P. Mc Auliffe	773
Rogers Park	773
Rolling Mdws	847
Rolling Meadows	847
Rollo	815
Rome	309
Rome Heights	309
Romeoville	708, 815
Roodhouse	217
Rooks Creek	815
Rosamond	217
Roscoe	815
Rose Hill	618
Rosebud	618
Rosedale	618
Rosefield	309
Roseland	773
Roselle	630
Rosemont	847
Roseville	309
Rosewood	618
Rosiclare	618
Rossville	217
Round Grove	815
Round Knob	618
Round Lake	847
Round Lake Beach	847
Round Lake Heights	847
Round Lake Park	847
Round Lk Bch	847
Round Lk Hts	847
Round Lk Park	847
Rowe	815
Roxana	618
Royal	217
Royal Lake	618
Royal Lake Resort	618
Royal Lakes	618
Royalton	618
Rozetta	309
Rugby	815
Ruma	618
Rushville	217
Russell	847
Russelville	618
Rutland	815
S Barrington	847
S Chicago Hei	708
S Chicago Heights	708
S Chicago Hts	708
S Wilmington	815
Sabina	309
Sadorus	217
Sailor Spgs	618
Sailor Springs	618
Saint Anne	815
Saint Augustine	309
Saint Charles	630
Saint David	309
Saint Elmo	618
Saint Francisville	618
Saint Jacob	618
Saint Joe	618
Saint Joseph	217
Saint Libory	618
Saint Marys	217
Saint Paul	618
Saint Peter	618
Saint Rose	618
Sainte Marie	618
Salem	618
Salisbury	217
Samoth	618
San Jose	309
Sand Barrens	618
Sand Ridge	618
Sandoval	618
Sandwich	815
Santa Fe	618
Saratoga	618
Saratoga Center	309
Sauget	618
Sauk Village	708
Saunemin	815
Savanna	815
Savanna Army Depot	815
Savoy	217
Sawyerville	217
Saxton	309
Saybrook	309
Scales Mound	815
Scalesmound	815
Scarboro	815
Schaeferville	309
Schaumburg	847
Scheller	618
Schiller Park	847
Schram City	217
Schulines	618
Sciota	309
Scioto Mills	815
Scott Afb	618
Scott Air Force Base	618
Scottville	217
Scovel	815
Sears Roebuck And Company	847
Sears Tower	312
Seaton	309
Seatonville	815
Secor	309
Secy Of State Vehicle Svcs	217
Selective Service	847
Seneca	815
Serena	815
Sesser	618
Seville	309
Seward	815
Seymour	217
Shabbona	815
Shady Grove	618
Shafter	618
Shakerag	618
Shale City	309
Shanghai City	309
Shannon	815
Sharpsburg	217
Shattuc	618
Shatuc	618

City	Area Code
Shawnee	618
Shawneetown	618
Shaws	815
Sheffield	815
Shelbyville	217
Sheldon	815
Sheldons Grove	309
Sheridan	815
Sherman	217
Sherrard	309
Shields	618
Shiloh	618
Shiloh Hill	618
Shipman	618
Shirland	815
Shirley	309
Shobonier	618
Shokokon	309
Shorewood	708
Shumway	217
Sibley	217
Sicily	217
Sidell	217
Sidney	217
Sigel	217
Signal Hill	618
Silvis	309
Simpson	618
Sims	618
Sinclair	217
Six Mile	618
Skokie	847
Slap Out	618
Sleepy Hollow	847
Smithboro	618
Smithfield	309
Smithshire	309
Smithton	618
Smithville	309
Snicarte	309
Sollitt	708
Solon Mills	815
Somerset	618
Somonauk	815
Songer	618
Sorento	217
South Barrington	847
South Beloit	815
South Chicago Heights	708
South Clinton	217
South Crouch	618
South Elgin	847
South Fillmore	217
South Holland	708
South Moline	309
South Pekin	309
South Rome	309
South Roxana	618
South Streator	815
South Suburban	708
South Suburbn	708
South Twigg	618
South Wilmington	815
Southern Illinois University	618
Southern View	217
Southport	309
Sparland	309
Sparta	618
Spaulding	217
Speer	309
Spencer Heights	618
Spires	309
Spring Bay	309
Spring Garden	618
Spring Grove	815
Spring Lake	309
Spring Valley	815
Springerton	618
Springfield	217
St Anne	815
St Augustine	309
St Charles	630
St David	309
St Elmo	618
St Francis	217
St Francis Hosp	309
St Francisville	618
St Francisvle	618
St James	618
St Joe	618
St Johns Hospital	217
St Morgan	618
St Paul	618
St Peter	618
Standard	815
Standard City	217
Stanford	309
Stanton Point	847
State Farm Ins Il Region Ofc	309
State Of Il	312
State Of Illinois	217
State Park Place	618
State Rev 3386	217
State Rev 3667	217
State Rev 3707	217
State Rev Box 3547	217
Stateville	815
Staunton	618
Stavanger	815
Ste Marie	618
Steel City	618
Steeleville	618
Steger	708
Stelle	815
Sterling	815
Steward	815
Stewardson	217
Stickney	708, 773
Stillman Valley	815
Stillman Vly	815
Stillwell	217
Stiritz	618
Stites	618
Stock Yards	773
Stockland	815
Stockton	815
Stone Park	708
Stonefort	618
Stoneyville	815
Stonington	217
Stoy	618
Strasburg	217
Stratford	815
Stratton	618
Strawn	815
Streamwood	630
Streator	815
Streator East	815
Streator West	815
Stringtown	618
Stronghurst	309
Stubblefield	618
Sublette	815
Suburban Heights	618
Sugar Creek	618
Sugar Grove	630
Sullivan	217
Summer Hill	217
Summerfield	618
Summersville	618
Summerville	618
Summit	708
Summit Argo	708
Summit-Argo	708
Summum	309
Sumner	618
Sumpter	217
Sunbeam	309
Sunbury	815
Sunny Hill	309
Sunny Hill Estates	309
Sunnyside	815
Sutter	217
Swan Creek	309
Swansea	618
Swanwick	618
Swedona	309
Sweet Water	217
Swygert	815
Sycamore	815
Symerton	815
Table Grove	309
Tabor	217
Talbott	309
Tallula	217
Tamalco	618
Tamaroa	618
Tamms	618
Tampico	815
Taylor Ridge	309
Taylor Spgs	217
Taylor Springs	217
Taylorville	217
Techny	847
Teheran	217
Temple Hill	618
Tennessee	309
Teutopolis	618
Texas City	618
Texas Township	217
Texico	618
Thackeray	618
Thawville	217
Thayer	217
The Burg	815
Thebes	618
Third Lake	847
Thomas	815
Thomasboro	217
Thompson	815
Thompsonville	618
Thomson	815
Thornton	708
Tice	217
Tilden	618
Tilton	217
Timber Lake	847
Timewell	217
Timothy	217
Tinley Park	708
Tioga	217
Tipton	618
Tiskilwa	815
Todds Mill	618
Toledo	217
Tolono	217
Toluca	815
Tomahawk Bluff	815
Tompkins	309
Tonica	815
Topeka	309
Toulon	309
Tovey	217
Towanda	309
Tower Hill	217
Tower Lakes	847
Towne Oaks	309
Tremont	309
Trenton	618
Trilla	217
Trimble	618
Triple Lake Heights	618
Triumph	815
Trivoli	309
Trout Valley	847
Trowbridge	217
Troy	618
Troy Grove	815
Tunbridge	217
Tunnel Hill	618
Tunnel Hl	618
Tuscarora	309
Tuscola	217
Twenty Second Street	312
Twigg	618
Ulah	309
Ullin	618
Union	815
Union Center	217
Union Grove	815
Union Hill	815
Unionville	618
Unity	618
University Park	708
University Pk	708
Urbain	618
Urbana	217
Urbandale	618
Ursa	217
Usps District Chicago	312
Ustick	815
Utica	815
Valier	618
Valley City	217
Valley View	630, 815
Valmeyer	618
Van Burensburg	217
Van Orin	815
Vandalia	618
Varna	309
Venedy	618
Venetian Village	847
Venice	618
Vera	217
Vergennes	618
Vermilion	217
Vermilionville	815
Vermillion Estates	815
Vermont	309
Vernon	618
Vernon Hills	847
Verona	815
Versailles	217
Vets Row	309
Victoria	309
Vienna	618
Villa Grove	217
Villa Park	630
Villa Ridge	618
Village Of Lakewood	815
Viola	309
Virden	217
Virgil	815
Virginia	217
Vlg Of Lakewd	815
Volo	815, 847
Vonachen Knolls	309
W Frankfort	618
Waddams Grove	815
Wadsworth	847
Waggoner	217
Wakefield	618
Waldo	309
Walkerville	217
Walnut	815
Walnut Grove	309
Walnut Hill	618
Walpole	618
Walsh	618
Walshville	217
Walton	815
Waltonville	618
Wamac	618
Wanlock	309
Wapella	309
Ware	618
Warner	309
Warren	815
Warrensburg	217
Warrenville	630
Warsaw	217
Wartburg	618
Wartrace	618
Wasco	630
Washburn	309
Washingtn Park	618
Washington	309
Washington Pk	618
Wasson	618
Wataga	309
Waterloo	618
Waterman	815
Watertown	309
Watseka	815
Watson	217
Wauconda	847
Waukegan	847
Waverly	217
Wayne	630
Wayne City	618
Waynesville	217
Webster	217
Webster Park	815
Wedron	815
Weldon	217
Welge	618
Weller	309
Wellington	815
Wendelin	618
Wenona	815
Wenonah	217
West	309
West Brooklyn	815
West Chicago	630
West City	618
West Dundee	847
West End	618
West Frankfort	618
West Hallock	309
West Jersey	309
West Liberty	618
West Miltmore	847
West Peoria	309
West Point	217
West Salem	618
West Union	217
West York	217
Westchester	708
Western	309
Western Sprgs	708
Western Springs	708
Westervelt	217
Westfield	217
Westinghouse Air Brake	309
Westmont	630
Weston	815
Westport	618
Westville	217
Wetaug	618
Wethersfield	815
Wheaton	630
Wheeler	217
Wheeling	847
Whispering Oaks	309
White City	217
White Hall	217
White Heath	217
Whites Addition	309
Whittington	618
Wicker Park	312, 773
Wilbern	309
Wilberton	618
Wildwood	847
Willeys	217
Williamsfield	309
Williamson	618
Williamsville	217
Willisville	618
Willow Brook	708
Willow Hill	618
Willow Spgs	708
Willow Springs	708
Willowbrook	708
Wilmette	847
Wilmington	815
Wilsonville	618
Wilton Center	815
Winchester	217
Windsor	217
Wine Hill	618
Winfield	630
Wing	815
Winkle	618
Winnebago	815
Winnetka	847
Winslow	815
Winthrop Harbor	847
Winthrop Hbr	847
Wisetown	618
Witt	217
Woburn	618
Wolf Lake	618
Womac	217
Wonder Lake	815
Wood Dale	630
Wood River	618
Woodbine	815
Woodburn	618
Woodbury	217
Woodford	309
Woodhull	309
Woodland	815
Woodland Addition	815
Woodlawn	618
Woodridge	630
Woodson	217
Woodstock	815
Woodville	217
Woodyard	618
Woosung	815
Worden	618
Worth	708
Wrights	217
Wrights Corner	618
Ww Grainger Inc	847
Wyanet	815
Wynoose	618
Wyoming	309
Xenia	618
Yale	618
Yantisville	217
Yates	815
Yates City	309
Yatesville	217
Yeoward Addition	815
Yeowardville	815
Yorkville	630
Youngstown	309
Yuton	309
Zearing	815
Zeigler	618
Zenith	618
Zion	847

Indiana

City	Area Code
12 Mile	574
Abbey Dell	812
Abington	765
Acton	317
Adams	812
Adams Lake	260
Adel	812
Advance	765
Agricultural Census	812
Akron	574
Alamo	765
Albany	765
Albion	260
Alert	812
Alexandria	765
Alford	812
Alfordsville	812
Algiers	812
Allen	260
Allendale	812
Alma Lake	812
Alpine	765
Alquina	765
Alta	765
Alton	812
Altona	260
Alvarado	260
Ambia	765
Amboy	765
Amity	317
Amo	765
Anderson	765
Andersonville	765
Andrews	260
Angola	260
Annandale Est	812
Annandale Estates	812
Annapolis	765
Anthony	765
Antiville	260
Apache Acres	812
Arba	765
Arcadia	317
Arcola	260
Argos	574
Ari	260
Arlington	765
Armiesburg	765
Army Finance Center	317

City	Area Code
Army Finance Ctr	317
Arney	812
Aroma	765
Art	812
Arthur	812
Artic	260
Ashboro	812
Asherville	812
Ashley	260
Athens	574
Atherton	765
Atkinsonville	812
Atlanta	765
Atterbury	812
Attica	765
Atwood	574
Auburn	260
Auburn Junction	260
Augusta	812
Aurora	812
Austin	812
Avilla	260
Avoca	812
Avon	317
Ayrshire	812
B M G	317
Bainbridge	765
Baker	812
Bakertown	260
Balbee	260
Ball State Univ	765
Ball State University	765
Bandon	812
Bargersville	317
Barnard	765
Barnhart Town	812
Barr	812
Barrick Corner	812
Barrington Woods	260
Bartlettsville	812
Bartley	812
Bartonia	765
Bass Lake	574
Batesville	812
Bath	812
Battle Ground	765
Bean Blossom	812
Bear Lake	260
Bedford	812
Bedford Heights	812
Bedford Hts	812
Bee Ridge	812
Beech Grove	317
Belle Union	765
Bellefountain	260
Belleville	317
Bellmore	765
Belmont	812
Belshaw	219
Bengal	317
Bennington	812
Bentonville	765
Benwood	812
Berlien	260
Berne	260
Bethel	765
Bethlehem	812
Beverly Shores	219
Beverly Shrs	219
Bicknell	812
Big Lake	260
Billingsville	765
Billtown	812
Billville	812
Bippus	260
Birdseye	812
Blaine	260
Blairsville	812
Blanford	765
Blmgtn	812
Blocher	812
Bloomfield	812
Bloomingdale	765
Bloomingport	765
Bloomington	812
Blountsville	765
Blue Creek	812
Blue Lake	260
Bluff Point	260
Bluffton	260
Bo Bo	260
Bogard	812
Boggstown	317
Bogle Corner	812
Boone	812
Boone Grove	219
Boonville	812
Borden	812
Boston	765
Boston Corner	260
Boswell	765
Boundry	260
Bourbon	574
Bowerstown	260
Bowling Green	812
Bowman	812
Boyleston	765
Bracken	260
Bradford	812
Bramble	812
Branchville	812
Braxton	812
Braytown	812
Brazil	812
Breezewood Park	765
Breezewood Pk	765
Bremen	574
Bretzville	812
Brewington Wds	765
Brewington Woods	765
Brice	260
Bridgeport	317
Bridgeton	765
Brighton	260
Brimfield	260
Brimfld	260
Brinckley	765
Bringhurst	765
Bristol	574
Bristow	812
Brm South Bend	574
Bromer	812
Brook	219
Brook Knoll	812
Brooklyn	317
Brookston	765
Brookville	765
Brookville Heights	317
Brookville Hts	317
Brown Jug Corner	812
Brownsburg	317
Brownstown	812
Brownsville	765
Bruceville	812
Brunswick	219
Brushy Prairie	260
Bryant	260
Bryantsville	812
Brylane	317
Buchanan Cnr	812
Buchanan Corner	812
Buck Creek	765
Buckeye	260
Buckskin	812
Bucktown	812
Buddha	812
Buena Vista	765
Buffalo	574
Buffaloville	812
Bugtown	812
Bullocktown	812
Bunker Hill	765
Bureau Of Census Decennial	812
Bureau Of The Census	812
Burglen Hills	812
Burket	574
Burlington	765
Burnett	812
Burnettsville	574
Burney	812
Burns City	812
Burns Harbor	219
Burr Oak	260, 574
Burrows	574
Bus Rply	317
Business Reply	260, 317
Busseron	812
Butler	260
Butler Center	260
Butlerville	812
Cadiz	765
Cale	812
Calvertville	812
Cambridge City	765
Cambridge Cty	765
Camby	317
Camden	574
Cammack	765
Camp Atterbry	812
Camp Atterbury	812
Camp Attrbry	812
Campbellsburg	812
Canaan	812
Cannelburg	812
Cannelton	812
Cannelton Heights	812
Cannelton Hts	812
Capehart	812
Carbon	812
Cardonia	812
Carefree	812
Carlisle	812
Carlos City	765
Carmel	317
Carp	812
Carrollton	317
Carter	812
Cartersburg	317
Carthage	765
Castleton	317
Cataract	812
Cates	765
Catlin	765
Cato	812
Cayuga	765
Cedar Canyon	260
Cedar Creek	260
Cedar Grove	812
Cedar Lake	219
Cedar Shores	260
Cedarville	260
Celestine	812
Cemar Estates	812
Cementville	812
Centenary	765
Centerpoint	812
Centerton	765
Centerville	765
Central	812
Ceylon	260
Chalmers	219
Chambersburg	812
Champion	812
Chandler	812
Chapelhill	812
Charlestown	812
Charlottesville	765
Charlottesvle	765
Chase Bank	317
Chester	765
Chesterfield	765
Chesterton	219
Chili	765
Chrisney	812
Christmas Lake Village	812
Christmas Lk	812
Churubusco	260
Cicero	317
Cincinnati	812
Circle Park	260
City	219
Clarks Hill	765
Clarks Landing	260
Clarksburg	765
Clarksville	812
Clay City	812
Claypool	574
Clayton	317
Clear Creek	812
Clear Lake	260
Clermont	317
Clifford	812
Clinton	765
Cloud Crest Hills	812
Cloud Crst Hls	812
Cloverdale	765
Cloverland	812
Clvr Mil Acad	574
Coal Bluff	765
Coal City	812
Coalmont	812
Coatesville	765
Coe	812
Coesse	260
Coffey Subdiv	812
Coffey Subdivision	812
Colburn	765
Cold Springs	260
Colfax	765
Collamer	260
College Cnr	260
College Corner	260
Collegeville	219
Collett	260
Collins	260
Coloma	765
Columbia City	260
Columbia House P Due	812
Columbia House Prepaid	812
Columbus	812
Commiskey	812
Como	260
Concord	574
Connersville	765
Converse	765
Cook Acres	765
Coppess Corner	260
Cornettsville	812
Corning	812
Cortland	812
Corunna	260
Cory	812
Corydon	812
Cosperville	260
Cottagegrove	765
Country Terr	765
Country Terrace	765
Coveyville	812
Covington	765
Cowan	765
Coxville	765
Craigville	260
Cran Nav Dpo	812
Crandall	812
Crane	812
Crane Nav Dpt	812
Crane Nav Weap Spt	812
Crane Naval Depot	812
Crane Naval Weapons Support	812
Crawfordsville	765
Crawfordsvlle	765
Cree Lake	260
Creston	219
Crete	765
Crompton Hill	765
Cromwell	260
Crooked Lake	260
Cross Plains	812
Cross Roads	812
Crothersville	812
Crown Point	219
Crumley Crossing	765
Crumley Xing	765
Crystal	812
Culver	574
Cumberland	317
Cunot	765
Curry	812
Curtisville	765
Cutler	765
Cuzco	812
Cynthiana	812
Dabney	812
Daggett	812
Dale	812
Daleville	765
Dalton	765
Dana	765
Danville	317
Darlington	765
Darmstadt	812
Daylight	812
Dayton	765
Dayville	812
De Gonia	812
Deaconess Hospital	812
Decatur	260
Decker	812
Deedsville	765
Deer Creek	574
Deerfield	765
Delong	574
Delphi	765
Demotte	219
Denham	574
Denmark	812
Denver	765
Depauw	812
Deputy	812
Derby	812
Desoto	765
Dexter	812
Diamond	765
Diamond Lake	260
Dick Johnson	812
Dillman	260
Dillsboro	812
Diplomat	260
Diplomat Plaza	260
Dixon	260
Doans	812
Dodds Bridge	812
Domestic	260
Donaldson	574
Dover	812
Dover Hill	812
Dowden Acres	812
Dresden	812
Dresser	812
Drexel Gardens	317
Drexel Gdns	317
Dublin	765
Dubois	812
Dubois Crossroads	812
Dubois Xrds	812
Duck Creek	765
Dudley	765
Duff	812
Dugger	812
Dune Acres	219
Dunkirk	765
Dunlap	574
Dunlapsville	765
Dunreith	765
Dupont	812
Dutch Town	260
Dyer	219
E Enterprise	812
Eagle Creek	317
Earl Park	219
East Chicago	219
East Connersville	765
East Enterprise	812
East Haven	765
East Oolitic	812
East Shelburn	812
East Shoals	812
East Union	765
Eaton	765
Eckerty	812
Economy	765
Eden	317
Edgerton	260
Edinburgh	812
Edwardsport	812
Eel River	260
Ege	260
Ehrmandale	812
Ekin	765
Elberfeld	812
Eli Lilly Co	317
Elizabeth	812
Elizabethtown	812
Elkhart	574
Elkinsville	812
Ellettsville	812
Ellis	812
Elliston	812
Elmira	260
Elmore	812
Elnora	812
Elrod	812
Elwood	765
Eminence	765
Emison	812
Emporia	765
Enchanted Hills	260
Englewood	812
English	812
Enochsburg	812
Epsom	812
Etna	260
Etna Green	574
Etna-Troy	260
Eureka	812
Evanston	812
Evansville	812
Evansville Dress Regional Ai	812
Everton	765
Fair Oaks	219
Fairbanks	812
Fairfield Center	260
Fairland	317
Fairmount	765
Fairplay	812
Fairview Park	765
Falmouth	765
Farlen	812
Farmers	812
Farmers Retreat	812
Farmersburg	812
Farmland	765
Fayette	812
Fayetteville	812
Fenn Haven	812
Ferdinand	812
Ferguson Hill	812
Fiat	260
Fillmore	765
Fincastle	765
Finly	317
Fish Lake	260
Fishers	317, 765
Flat Rock	812
Flint	260
Flora	574
Florence	812
Florida	765
Floyds Knobs	812
Folsomville	812
Fontanet	765
Foraker	574
Forest	765
Forest Park Beach	260
Fort Branch	812
Fort Ritner	812
Fort Wayne	260
Fortville	317
Fountain City	765
Fountaintown	317
Fowler	765
Fowlerton	765
Fox Lake	260
Francesville	219
Francisco	812
Frankfort	765
Franklin	317
Franklin Hills	812
Franklin Hls	812
Frankton	765
Fredericksbrg	812
Fredericksburg	812
Fredonia	812
Freedom	812
Freelandville	812
Freeman	812

City	Area Code
Freeport	765
Freetown	812
Fremont	260
French Lick	812
Friendship	812
Fritchton	812
Fruitdale	812
Ft Benjamin Harrison	317
Ft Wayne	260
Fulda	812
Fulton	574
Galena	812
Galveston	574
Gambill	812
Gar Creek	260
Garrett	260
Gary	219
Gas City	765
Gaston	765
Gatchel	812
Gateway Shopping Center	765
Gateway Shopping Ctr	765
Gem	317
Geneva	260
Gentryville	812
Geo Koch Sons	812
Georgetown	812
Georgia	812
Gill	812
Gilmour	812
Glen Eden	260
Glendale	812
Glenwood	765
Glezen	812
Gnaw Bone	812
Goblesville	260
Golden Lake	260
Goldsmith	765
Goodland	219
Goose Lake	260
Goshen	574
Gosport	812
Grabill	260
Graceland Heights	765
Graceland Hts	765
Grammer	812
Grandview	812
Granger	574
Grant	812
Grant City	765
Grantsburg	812
Granville	765
Grass Creek	574
Gravel Beach	260
Graysville	812
Greater Indiana District	317
Green Center	260
Greenbrier	812
Greencastle	765
Greendale	812
Greenfield	317
Greens Fork	765
Greensboro	765
Greensburg	812
Greentown	765
Greenville	812
Greenwd	317
Greenwood	317
Greybrook Lake	812
Griffin	812
Griffith	219
Grissom A R B	765
Grissom Air Reserve Base	765
Grissom Arb	765
Grnwood	317
Grouseland	812
Grovertown	574
Guilford	812
Guion	765
Guthrie	812
Gwynneville	765
Haddon	812
Hagerstown	765
Halbert	812
Hall	812
Hamilton	260
Hamilton Park	765
Hamlet	574
Hammond	219
Hanna	219
Hanover	812
Hanover Beach	812
Harbison	812
Hardinsburg	812
Harlan	260
Harmony	812
Harrisburg	765
Harrisville	765
Harrodsburg	812
Hartford City	765
Hartleyville	812
Hartsville	812
Hashtown	812
Haskells	219
Hatfield	812
Haubstadt	812
Hayden	812
Hazelwood	260
Hazleton	812
Hebron	219
Heights Corner	812
Heilman	812
Helmer	260
Helmsburg	812
Helt	765
Heltonville	812
Hemlock	765
Hendricksville	812
Hendricksvle	812
Henry	765
Henryville	812
Hessville	219
High Lake	260
Highland	219
Hillham	812
Hillisburg	765
Hills And Dales	765
Hillsboro	765
Hillsdale	765
Hindostan Falls	812
Hindostan Fls	812
Hls & Dles	765
Hoagland	260
Hobart	219
Hobbieville	812
Hobbs	765
Hogtown	812
Holland	812
Hollandsburg	765
Holly Hills	812
Hollybrk Lk	812
Hollybrook Lake	812
Holton	812
Homer	765
Hondorus	260
Honey Creek Square	812
Hoosier Highlands	812
Hoosierville	812
Hope	812
Hopewell	317
Howard	765
Howe	260
Howesville	812
Hts Crnr	812
Hubbell	812
Hubbells Corner	812
Hudson	260
Hudson Lake	574
Hudsonville	812
Huffman	812
Huntersville	812
Huntertown	260
Huntingburg	812
Huntington	260
Huntington Bank	317
Huntsville	765
Huron	812
Hurshtown	260
Hyde Park	765
Hymera	812
I U P U I	317
Idaville	574
Indian Creek Settlement	812
Indian Crk Stlmt	812
Indian Lake	260
Indian Springs	812
Indian Village	260
Indiana Beach	574
Indiana State University	812
Indianapolis	317
Ingalls	317
Inglefield	812
Inwood	574
Ireland	812
Ironton	812
Irvington	317
Island City	812
Island Park	260
Iva	812
Jackson Hill	812
Jacksonburg	765
Jacksonville	765
Jamestown	765
Jasonville	812
Jasper	812
Jay City	260
Jeff	812
Jefferson Proving Ground	812
Jefferson Prv Grnd	812
Jeffersonville	812
Jeffersonvlle	812
Jennings	765
Jessup	765
Johnsburg	812
Jonesboro	765
Jonestown	765, 812
Jonesville	812
Jordan	812
Judah	812
Judson	765
Keller	812
Kellerville	812
Kempton	765
Kendallville	260
Kennard	765
Kennedy	812
Kentland	219
Kenwood	765
Kersey	219
Kewanna	574
Keyser	260
Keystone	260
Kimball International	812
Kimball Intl	812
Kimmell	260
Kingman	765
Kingsbury	219
Kingsford Heights	219
Kingsford Hts	219
Kingsland	260
Kingston	812
Kingswood Terra	812
Kirklin	765
Knapp Lake	260
Knight	812
Knightstown	765
Knightsville	812
Knox	574
Kokomo	765
Koleen	812
Kouts	219
Kurtz	812
Kyana	812
La Crosse	219
La Fayette	765
La Fontaine	765
La Porte	219
Laconia	812
Ladoga	765
Lafayette	765
Lagrange	260
Lagro	260
Lake Cicott	574
Lake Dalecarlia	219
Lake Edgewood	765
Lake James	260
Lake Lincoln	812
Lake Maxine	765
Lake Mccoy	812
Lake Mohee	765
Lake Noji	812
Lake Station	219
Lake Sullivan	812
Lake Village	219
Lakes Of Four Seasons	219
Lakeside	260
Laketon	260
Lakeview Estates	812
Lakeville	574
Lakewood	812
Lamar	812
Landess	765
Lanesville	812
Laotto	260
Lapaz	574
Lapel	765
Larimer Hill	812
Larwill	260
Laud	260
Laurel	765
Lawrence	317
Lawrenceburg	812
Lawrenceport	812
Lawrenceville	812
Leavenworth	812
Lebanon	765
Leesburg	574
Leesville	812
Leisure	765
Leiters Ford	574
Lena	812
Leo	260
Leopold	812
Leroy	219
Lewis	812
Lewisville	765
Lexington	812
Liber	260
Liberty	765
Liberty Center	260
Liberty Ctr	260
Liberty Mills	260
Libertyville	812
Licking	765
Liggett	812
Ligonier	260
Lilly Dale	812
Lima	260
Limedale	765
Lincoln Boyhood National Mem	812
Lincoln Boyhood Natl Mem	812
Lincoln City	812
Linden	765
Linn Grove	260
Linn Grv	260
Linton	812
Lisbon	260
Little	812
Little Point	812
Little York	812
Livonia	812
Lizton	317
Lockhart	812
Logan	812
Logansport	574
Lonetree	812
Long Beach	219
Long Lake	260
Loogootee	812
Loon Lake	260
Lorane	260
Losantville	765
Lost River	812
Lotus	765
Lowell	219
Lucerne	574
Luray	765
Luther	260
Lutheran Lake	812
Lydick	574
Lyford	765
Lynn	765
Lynnville	812
Lyons	812
Lyonsville	765
Mackey	812
Macy	574
Madison	812
Magnet	812
Mahon	260
Majenica	260
Maltersville	812
Manhattan	765
Manilla	765
Mansfield	765
Maples	260
Marco	812
Marengo	812
Mariah Hill	812
Marion	765
Marion Heights	812
Markle	260
Markleville	765
Marquette Farm	812
Mars Hill	317
Marshall	765
Marshfield	765
Martinsville	765
Martz	812
Maryland	812
Marysville	812
Marywood	812
Matthews	765
Mauckport	812
Maumee	260
Maxville	765
Maxwell	317
Mays	765
Maysville	812
Maywood	317
Mc Cordsville	317
Mccordsville	317
Mccutchanville	812
Mcnatts	765
Mead Johnson Co	812
Meadowbrook	260
Meadowood Est	765
Meadowood Estates	765
Mecca	765
Medaryville	219
Medford	765
Medora	812
Mellott	765
Memphis	812
Mentone	574
Mentor	812
Merchants Bank	317
Merom	812
Merriam	260
Merrillville	219
Messick	765
Metamora	765
Meth Mem Home	260
Methodist Mem Home	260
Methodist Memorial Home	260
Metz	260
Mexico	765
Miami	765
Mich City	219
Michiana Shores	219
Michiana Shrs	219
Michigan City	219
Michigantown	765
Middleboro	765
Middlebury	574
Middletown	765
Midland	812
Midway	812
Milan	812
Milan Center	260
Milford	574
Mill Creek	219
Mill Grove	765
Millersburg	574
Millhousen	812
Milligan	765
Milltown	812
Millville	765
Milroy	765
Milton	765
Mineral	812
Mishawaka	574
Mitchell	812
Modoc	765
Mongo	260
Monon	219
Monroe	260
Monroe City	812
Monroeville	260
Monroevl	260
Monrovia	317
Monterey	574
Montezuma	765
Montgomery	812
Monticello	574
Montmorenci	765
Montpelier	765
Moore	260
Mooreland	765
Moores Hill	812
Mooresville	317
Morgantown	812
Morocco	219
Morris	812
Morristown	765
Morton	765
Moscow	765
Mount Auburn	765
Mount Ayr	219
Mount Etna	260
Mount Meridian	765
Mount Pisgah	260
Mount Pleasant	812
Mount Saint Francis	812
Mount Summit	765
Mount Vernon	812
Mount Zion	260
Mt Meridian	765
Mt Pisgah	260
Mt Pleasant	812
Mt St Francis	812
Mulberry	765
Muncie	765
Munster	219
Muren	812
Murray	260
Muscatatuck	812
N Manchester	260
N Terre Haute	812
Nabb	812
Napoleon	812
Nappanee	574
Nashville	812
National City Bank	317
Navilleton	812
Nebraska	812
Needham	317
Needmore	812
Nevada	765
Nevada Mills	260
Nevins	765
New Albany	812
New Alsace	812
New Augusta	317
New Burlingtn	765
New Burlington	765
New Carlisle	574
New Castle	765
New Chicago	219
New Elliott	219
New Goshen	812
New Harmony	812
New Haven	260
New Haven Heights	260
New Hope	812
New Lancaster	765
New Lebanon	812
New Lisbon	765
New Marion	812
New Market	765
New Maysville	765
New Middletown	812
New Middletwn	812
New Mount Pleasant	260
New Mt Pleasant	260
New Palestine	317

City	Area Code
New Paris	574
New Pittsburg	765
New Point	812
New Richmond	765
New Ross	765
New Salisbury	812
New Trenton	812
New Washingtn	812
New Washington	812
New Waverly	574
New Whiteland	317
Newark	812
Newberry	812
Newburgh	812
Newgistics Merchandise Retrn	765
Newport	765
Newtonville	812
Newtown	765
Newville	260
Niles	765
Nineveh	317
Noble	260
Noblesville	317
Nora	317
Norland Park	260
Norman	812
North Hayden	219
North Judson	574
North Liberty	574
North Madison	812
North Manchester	260
North Oaks	260
North Park	812
North Salem	765
North Terre Haute	812
North Vernon	812
North Webster	574
Northeast	812
Northpine Estates	765
Northwest	812
Norton	812
Notre Dame	574
Nottingham	765
Nulltown	765
Numa	765
Nyesville	765
Nyona Lake	574
Oak Grove	812
Oakford	765
Oakland City	812
Oaklandon	317
Oaktown	812
Oakville	765
Oakwood	260
Oakwood Shores	260
Oatsville	812
Ober	574
Odon	812
Ogden	765
Ogden Dunes	219
Oil	812
Oldenburg	812
Onward	765
Oolitic	812
Ora	574
Orange	765
Orangeville	812
Orestes	765
Oriole	812
Orland	260
Orleans	812
Ormas	260
Osceola	574
Osgood	812
Ossian	260
Otis	219
Otisco	812
Otsego	260
Otter Lake	260
Otterbein	765
Otwell	812
Owensburg	812
Owensville	812
Oxford	765
Paint Mill Lake	812
Palmer	219
Palmyra	812
Paoli	812
Paradise	812
Paradise Lake	765
Paragon	765
Paris Crossing	812
Paris Xing	812
Park	812
Park Fletcher	317
Parker	765
Parker City	765
Parkers Settlement	812
Patoka	812
Patricksburg	812
Patriot	812
Patronville	812
Patton Hill	812
Paxton	812
Paynesville	812
Peabody	260
Peerless	812
Pekin	812
Pelzer	812
Pence	765
Pendleton	765
Penn Park	260
Penntown	812
Pennville	260
Peoga	317
Perrysville	765
Pershing	765
Perth	812
Peru	765
Petersburg	812
Peterson	260
Petroleum	260
Philomath	765
Pierceton	574
Pierceville	812
Pigeon	812
Pimento	812
Pine Ridge	812
Pine Village	765
Pinhook	812
Pipe Creek	765
Pittsboro	317
Plainfield	317
Plainville	812
Plato	260
Pleasant Lake	260
Pleasant Mills	260
Pleasant Mls	260
Pleasant Plain	260
Pleasant Run	812
Pleasantville	812
Plum Tree	260
Plummer	812
Plymouth	574
Poe	260
Point Commerce	812
Poland	812
Poling	260
Poneto	260
Pontiac	812
Popcorn	812
Portage	219
Porter	219
Portersville	812
Portland	260
Poseyville	812
Pottersville	812
Powers	260
Prairie City	812
Prairie Creek	812
Prairie Village	812
Prairieton	812
Preble	260
Pretty Lake	260
Princeton	812
Progress	765
Progress Acres	812
Prospect	812
Providence	317
Pt Commerce	812
Pumpkin Center	812
Pumpkin Ctr	812
Putnamville	765
Quailtown	812
Quaker	765
Queensville	812
Quincy	765
R R Donnelley & Sons	765
Raber	260
Raglesville	812
Ragsdale	812
Ramsey	812
Randolph	765
Ray	260
Raysville	765
Rca Mfg Co	317
Redkey	765
Reelsville	765
Reeve	812
Rego	812
Reiffsburg	260
Remington	219
Reno	765
Rensselaer	219
Reo	812
Reserve	765
Retreat	812
Reynolds	219
Riceville	812
Richland	812
Richmond	765
Richmond Sq	765
Richmond Square	765
Ridgeport	812
Ridgeville	765
Rigdon	765
Riley	812
Rising Sun	812
River Vale	812
Riverton	812
Riverview	812
Roachdale	765
Roann	765
Roanoke	260
Robertsdale	219
Rochester	574
Rockfield	574
Rockford	260
Rockport	812
Rockville	765
Rocky Fork Lake	812
Roland	812
Roll	765
Rolling Pr	219
Rolling Prairie	219
Rollins	812
Rome	812
Rome City	260
Romex	812
Romney	765
Romona	812
Rose Hill Gardens	812
Roseburg	765
Rosedale	765
Roselawn	219
Rosewood	812
Rossville	765
Round Lake	260
Royal Center	574
Royer Lake	260
Royerton	765
Rr Donnelley & Sons	765
Rural	765
Rushville	765
Russellville	765
Russels Point	260
Russiaville	765
Rutherford	812
S Bend	574
S Washington	812
Saint Anthony	812
Saint Bernice	765
Saint Croix	812
Saint Joe	260
Saint John	219
Saint Leon	765
Saint Mary Of The Woods	812
Saint Marys Medical Center	812
Saint Meinrad	812
Saint Paul	765
Salamonia	260
Salamonie	260
Salem	812
Salem Center	260
Saline City	812
Salomonia	260
Samaria	317
San Pierre	219
Sandborn	812
Sandcut	812
Sandford	812
Sandusky	812
Sandytown	765
Santa Claus	812
Saratoga	765
Sardinia	812
Scenic Heights	812
Scenic Hill	812
Scenic Hts	812
Schererville	219
Schneider	219
Schnellville	812
Scipio	812
Scotland	812
Scott	260
Scott City	812
Scottsburg	812
Sedalia	765
Sedan	260
Seelyville	812
Sellersburg	812
Selma	765
Selvin	812
Servia	260
Seymour	812
Shady Nook	260
Shamrock Lakes	765
Shamrock Lks	765
Sharpsville	765
Shawswick	812
Shawville	812
Shelburn	812
Shelby	219
Shelbyville	317
Shepardsville	765
Sheridan	317
Shideler	765
Shipshewana	260
Shirkieville	812
Shirley	765
Shoals	812
Siberia	812
Sidney	574
Silver Lake	260
Silverville	812
Simpson	260
Sims	765
Skinner Lake	260
Smithfield	765
Smithville	812
Smockville	812
Snow Hill	765
So Bend	574
Solitude	812
Solsberry	812
Somerset	765
Somerville	812
South Bend	574
South Bend Tribune	574
South Calumet Avenue	219
South Lake	812
South Milford	260
South Salem	765
South Wanatah	219
South Washington	812
South Whitley	260
Southport	317
Southtown	260
Southtown Mall	260
Southwood	812
Sparta	260
Spartanburg	765
Spdway	317
Spdwy	317
Spearsville	317
Speed	812
Speedway	317
Spelterville	812
Spencer	812
Spencerville	260
Spiceland	765
Spring Grove	765
Spring Grove Heights	765
Spring Grv Hts	765
Spring Hill Estates	812
Spring Valley Estates	812
Springersville	765
Springport	765
Springville	812
Springwood	812
Spurgeon	812
St Anthony	812
St Bernice	765
St Croix	812
St Henry	812
St Joe	260
St John	219
St Mary Of The Woods	812
St Mary Of Wd	812
St Marys	574
St Meinrad	812
St Paul	765
Stampers Creek	812
Stampers Crk	812
Stanford	812
Star City	574
Starlight	812
State Line	765
Staunton	812
Stearleyville	812
Steen	812
Stendal	812
Steuben	260
Steubenville	260
Stewartsville	812
Stilesville	765
Stinesville	812
Stockton	812
Stockwell	765
Stone	765
Stonington	812
Story	812
Straughn	765
Strawtown	317
Stroh	260
Sugar Ridge	812
Sullivan	812
Sulphur	812
Sulphur Spgs	765
Sulphur Springs	765
Sumava Resorts	219
Sumava Rsts	219
Summit Grove	765
Summitville	765
Sunman	812
Sunny Acres	260
Swan	260
Swayzee	765
Sweetser	765
Switz City	812
Sycamore Park	812
Sylvania	765
Syndicate	765
Syracuse	574
Syria	812
Tabertown	812
Talbot	765
Tampico	812
Tangier	765
Tanglewood	260
Taswell	812
Taylorsville	812
Tecumseh	812
Tefft	219
Tell City	812
Templeton	765
Tennyson	812
Tera North	812
Terre Haute	812
Thayer	219
Thomaston	219
Thorncreek	260
Thorntown	765
Thurman	260
Tillman	260
Timberhurst	260
Time Life Inc	317
Time/Life	317
Tippecanoe	574
Tipton	765
Toad Hop	812
Tobin	812
Tobinsport	812
Tocsin	260
Toledo	260
Toll Gate Heights	260
Topeka	260
Toto	574
Townley	260
Traders Point	317
Trafalgar	317
Trail Creek	219
Travisville	260
Treaty Line Museum	765
Treaty Ln Mus	765
Trevlac	812
Tri Lakes	260
Trinity Sprgs	812
Trinity Springs	812
Troy	812
Tulip	812
Tunker	260
Tunnelton	812
Turman	812
Turner	812
Twelve Mile	574
Tyner	574
Underwood	812
Union City	765
Union Mills	219
Uniondale	260
Unionport	765
Uniontown	812
Unionville	812
Universal	765
University Of Evansville	812
Upland	765
Upper Long Lake	260
Uptown	317
Urbana	260
Urmeyville	317
Usps Scanner Repair	317
Usps Symbol Repair	317
Utica	812
Valeene	812
Valentine	260
Vallonia	812
Valparaiso	219
Valpo	219
Van Buren	765
Vandalia	812
Veale	812
Veedersburg	765
Velpen	812
Vera Cruz	260
Vermillion Acres	812
Vernon	812
Versailles	812
Vevay	812
Vicksburg	812
Victoria	812
Vilas	812
Villa North	260
Vincennes	812
W Baden Spgs	812
W Baden Sprgs	812
W College Cor	765
W Harrison	812
W Lafayette	765
W Middleton	765
W Terre Haute	812
Wabash	260
Wadesville	812
Wakarusa	574
Wakefield Village	260
Waldron	765

Waldron Lake 260
Walkerton 574
Wall Lake 260
Wallace 765
Walnut Heights 812
Walnut Hts 812
Walton 574
Wanamaker 317
Wanatah 219
Wanda Lake 812
Warren 260
Warrenton 812
Warrington 765
Warsaw 574
Washington 812
Waterloo 260
Waterworks Dept 812
Watson 812
Waveland 765
Waverly 765
Wawaka 260
Wayne Center 260
Waynedale 260
Waynesburg 812
Waynetown 765
Webster 765
Weisburg 812
Wellsboro 219
West Acres 765
West Atherton 765
West Baden Springs 812
West Brook Acres 812
West College Corner 765
West Elwood 765
West Harrison 812
West Indianapolis 317
West Lafayette 765
West Lebanon 765
West Liberty 260
West Linton 812
West Middleton 765
West Muncie 765
West Newton 317
West Petersburg 812
West Terre Haute 812
West Union 765
Westchester 260
Westfield 317
Westphalia 812
Westpoint 765
Westport 812
Westport Addition 765
Westport Addn 765
Westville 219
Westwood 765
Wey Lake 812
Wheatfield 219
Wheatland 812
Wheatonville 812
Wheeler 219
Wheeling 765
Whirlpool Corp 812
Whitcomb Heights 812
Whiteland 317
Whiteoak 812
Whites Crossing 812
Whites Xing 812
Whitestown 317
Whitewater 765
Whitfield 812
Whiting 219
Widner 812
Wildwood Lake 812
Wildwood Landing 260
Wilfred 812
Wilkinson 765
Williams 812
Williamsburg 765
Williamsport 765
Williamstown 812
Willisville 812
Willow Branch 765
Willow Valley 812
Wilson Lake 260
Winamac 574
Winchester 765
Windemere Lake 812
Windfall 765
Windom 812
Windsor 765
Wingate 765
Winona Lake 574
Winslow 812
Witmer Manor 260
Wolcott 219
Wolcottville 260
Wolf Lake 260
Wolflake 260
Wonder Lake 812
Woodbridge 812
Woodburn 260
Woodbury 317
Woodgate 812
Woodgate East 812
Woodland Park 260
Woodlawn Park 765
Woodruff 260
Worthington 812
Wright 812
Wyatt 574
Xmas Lake Vlg 812
Xmas Lk Vlg 812
Yankeetown 812
Yeoman 574
Yockey 812
Yoder 260
York 260
Yorktown 765
Yost Woods 260
Young America 574
Youngs Creek 812
Youngstown 812
Youngstown Acres 812
Youngstown Meadows 812
Zanesville 260
Zionsville 317
Zoar 812
Zulu 260

Iowa

Abingdon 641
Ackley 641
Ackworth 641
Adair 641
Adaville 712
Adel 515
Adventureland Estates 515
Aegon Usa 319
Afton 641
Agency 641
Ainsworth 319
Akron 712
Albany 563
Albert City 712
Albia 641
Albion 641
Alburnett 319
Alden 515
Alexander 641
Algona 515
Alleman 515
Allendorf 712
Allerton 641
Allied Group 515
Allison 319
Alpha 563
Alta 712
Alta Vista 641
Alton 712
Altoona 515
Alvord 712
Amana 319
Amana Refrigeration Inc 319
Amber 319
Amboy 641
American College Testing 319
American Republic 515
Ames 515
Anamosa 319
Andover 563
Andrew 563
Anita 712
Ankeny 515
Anthon 712
Aplington 319
Arbor Hill 515
Arcadia 712
Archer 712
Aredale 641
Argyle 319
Arion 712
Arispe 641
Arlington 563
Armstrong 712
Arnolds Park 712
Artesian 319
Arthur 712
Asbury 563
Ashton 712
Aspinwall 712
Atalissa 563
Athlestan 641
Atkins 319
Atlantic 712
Auburn 712
Audubon 712
Aurelia 712
Aureola 641
Aurora 319
Austinville 319
Avery 641
Avoca 712
Avon 515
Avon Lake 515
Ayrshire 712
Badger 515
Bagley 641
Baldwin 563
Bancroft 515
Bankston 563
Barnes City 641
Barney 641
Barnum 515
Barrett Superette 641
Bartlett 712
Bassett 641
Batavia 641
Battle Creek 712
Baxter 641
Bayard 712
Beacon 641
Beaconsfield 641
Beaman 641
Beaver 515
Beaverdale Heights 319
Beckwith 641
Bedford 712
Beech 515
Bel Air Beach 712
Belle Plaine 319
Bellevue 563
Belmond 641
Bennett 563
Benton 641
Berea 712
Berkley 515
Bernard 563
Berne 712
Berwick 515
Bethlehem 641
Bettendorf 563
Bevington 641
Big Rock 563
Birmingham 319
Blackhawk Village 319
Bladensburg 641
Blairsburg 515
Blairstown 319
Blakesburg 641
Blanchard 712
Blencoe 712
Blockton 641
Bloomfield 641
Blue Grass 563
Bluff Park 319
Bluffton 563
Blvd Station 712
Bode 515
Bolan 641
Bonair 563
Bonaparte 319
Bondurant 515
Boone 515, 641
Booneville 515
Botna 712
Bouton 515
Boxholm 515
Boyd 641
Boyden 712
Boyer 712
Braddyville 712
Bradford 641
Bradgate 515
Brainard 563
Brandon 319
Brayton 712
Brazil 641
Breda 712
Bremer 319
Bridge Port 641
Bridgewater 641
Brighton 319
Bristow 641
Britt 641
Bronson 712
Brooklyn 641
Brooks 641
Brookside 319
Brunsville 712
Brushy 515
Bryant 563
Buchanan 563
Buck Grove 712
Buckcreek 563
Buckeye 515
Buckingham 319
Buffalo 563
Buffalo Center 641
Buffalo Ctr 641
Burchinal 641
Burlington 319
Burnside 515
Burr Oak 563
Burt 515
Bussey 641
Cairo 319
Calamus 563
Callender 515
Calmar 563
Calumet 712
Camanche 563
Cambria 641
Cambridge 515
Camp Dodge 515
Canby 641
Canton 563
Cantril 319
Capitol Heights 515
Carbon 641
Carbondale 515
Carl 641
Carlisle 515
Carmel 712
Carnarvon 712
Carnes 712
Carney 515
Carnforth 319
Carpenter 641
Carroll 712
Carson 712
Carter Lake 712
Cartersville 641
Cascade 563
Casey 641
Casino Beach 712
Castalia 563
Castana 712
Cds 515
Cds Main 515
Cedar 641
Cedar Bluff 563
Cedar City 319
Cedar Falls 319
Cedar Rapids 319
Cedar Valley 319
Cedarfalls 319
Center Grove 563
Center Jct 563
Center Junction 563
Center Point 319
Centerdale 319
Centerville 641
Central City 319
Central Heights 641
Centralia 563
Chapin 641
Chariton 641
Charles City 641
Charleston 319
Charlotte 563
Charter Oak 712
Chatsworth 712
Chelsea 641
Cherokee 712
Chester 563
Chickasaw 641
Chillicothe 641
Church 563
Churchville 515
Churdan 515
Cincinnati 641
Citigroup 515
Citigroup Brm 515
Clare 515
Clarence 563
Clarinda 712
Clarion 515
Clarksville 319
Clayton 563
Clayton Center 563
Clayworks 515
Clear Creek 641
Clear Lake 641
Clearfield 641
Cleghorn 712
Clemons 641
Clermont 563
Cleves 641
Cliffland 641
Climbing Hill 712
Clinton 563
Clio 641
Clive 515
Cloverdale 712
Clutier 319
Clyde 641
Co Bluffs 712
Coal Creek 641
Coalville 515
Coggon 319
Coin 712
Colesburg 563
Colfax 515
College Sprgs 712
College Springs 712
College Square 319
Collins 641
Colo 641
Columbia 641
Columbus City 319
Columbus Jct 319
Columbus Junction 319
Colwell 641
Communia 563
Communications Data Service 515
Communications Data Services 515
Conesville 319
Conger 641
Conover 563
Conrad 641
Conroy 319
Conway 712
Cool 515
Coon Rapids 712
Cooper 641
Coppock 319
Coralville 319
Cornelia 515
Cornell 712
Corning 641
Correctionville 712
Correctionvle 712
Corwith 515
Corydon 641
Cosgrove 319
Cotter 319
Cou Falls 319
Coulter 641
Council Blfs 712
Council Bluffs 712
Covington 319
Crandalls Lodge 712
Cranston 319
Crawfordsville 319
Crawfordsvlle 319
Crescent 712
Cresco 563
Creston 641
Crocker 515
Cromwell 641
Crossroads Center 515
Crystal Lake 641
Cumberland 712
Cumming 515
Curlew 712
Cushing 712
Cylinder 712
Dahlonega 641
Dakota City 515
Dalby 563
Dale 515
Dallas 641
Dallas Center 515
Dana 515
Danbury 712
Danville 319
Davenport 563
Davis City 641
Dawson 641
Dayton 515
Daytonville 319
De Soto 515
De Witt 563
Dean 641
Decatur 641
Decorah 563
Dedham 712
Deep River 641
Defiance 712
Delaware 563
Delhi 563
Delmar 563
Deloit 712
Delphos 641
Delta 641
Denhart 641
Denison 712
Denmark 319
Denver 319
Derby 641
Des Moines 515
Dewar 319
Dewitt 563
Dexter 515
Diagonal 641
Diamond Center 712
Dickens 712
Dike 319
Dinsdale 319
Dixon 563
Dodgeville 319
Dolliver 712
Donahue 563
Donnan 563
Donnellson 319
Doon 712
Dorchester 563
Doris 319
Douds 641
Dougherty 641
Douglas 563
Dow City 712
Downey 319
Dows 515

City	Area Code
Drakesville	641
Dubuque	563
Dudley	641
Dumont	641
Duncan	641
Duncombe	515
Dundee	563
Dunkerton	319
Dunlap	712
Durango	563
Durant	563
Durham	641
Dutchtown	563
Dyersville	563
Dysart	319
Eagle Grove	515
Eagle Point	563
Earl May Seed	712
Earlham	515
Earling	712
Earlville	563
Early	712
East Amana	319
East Des Moines	515
East Pleasant Plain	319
Eddyville	641
Edgewood	563
Edna	712
Eds	515
Eds Other	515
Eds-Proactive	515
Eds-Sc/Ye	515
Egan	563
Egralharve	712
Elberon	319
Eldon	641
Eldora	641
Eldorado	563
Eldridge	563
Elk Horn	712
Elk Run Heights	319
Elk Run Hgts	319
Elkader	563
Elkhart	515
Elkport	563
Elliott	712
Ellston	641
Ellsworth	515
Elma	641
Elon	563
Elrick	319
Elvira	563
Elwood	563
Ely	319
Emeline	563
Emerson	712
Emery	641
Emmetsburg	712
Enterprise	515
Epworth	563
Equitable Life Assurance	515
Essex	712
Estherville	712
Evans	641
Evans Junction	641
Evansdale	319
Evanston	515
Everly	712
Ewart	641
Exira	712
Exline	641
Fairbank	319
Fairfax	319
Fairfield	641
Fairview	319
Farley	563
Farmersburg	563
Farmington	319
Farnhamville	515
Farragut	712
Farrar	515
Farson	641
Faulkner	641
Fayette	563
Fenton	515
Ferguson	641
Fern	319
Fernald	515
Fertile	641
Festina	563
Fillmore	563
Finchford	319
First Interstate Bank	515
Fiscus	712
Florenceville	563
Floris	641
Floyd	641
Folletts	563
Fonda	712
Fontanelle	641
Forest City	641
Fort Atkinson	563
Fort Dodge	515
Fort Madison	319
Fostoria	712
Four Corners	319
Franklin	319
Frankville	563
Fredericksbrg	563
Fredericksburg	563
Frederika	319
Fredonia	319
Freeman	641
Freeport	563
Fremont	641
Froelich	563
Fruitland	319
Frytown	319
Fulton	563
Galbraith	515
Galesburg	641
Galland	319
Galt	641
Galva	712
Gambrill	563
Garber	563
Garden City	515
Garden Grove	641
Gardiner	515
Garfield	641
Garnavillo	563
Garner	641
Garrison	319
Garwin	641
Gaza	712
Geneva	641
Genoa Bluff	319
George	712
Georgetown	641
German Valley	515
Germantown	712
Germanville	319
Giard	563
Gibson	641
Gifford	641
Gilbert	515
Gilbertville	319
Gillett Grove	712
Gilman	641
Gilmore City	515
Gladbrook	641
Gladwin	319
Glasgow	641
Glendon	641
Glenwood	712
Glidden	712
Goddard	515
Goldfield	515
Goodell	641
Goose Lake	563
Gooselake	563
Gowrie	515
Grace Hill	319
Graettinger	712
Grafton	641
Grand Jct	515
Grand Junction	515
Grand Mound	563
Grand River	641
Grandview	319
Granger	515
Granite	712
Grant	712
Grant City	712
Granville	712
Gravity	712
Gray	712
Greeley	563
Green Castle	515
Green Island	563
Green Mountain	641
Green Mtn	641
Greene	641
Greenfield	641
Greenville	712
Grimes	515
Grinnell	641
Griswold	712
Grundy Center	319
Gruver	712
Guernsey	319
Gunder	563
Guss	712
Guthrie Center	641
Guthrie Ctr	641
Guttenberg	563
Halbur	712
Hale	563
Hamburg	712
Hamilton	641
Hamlin	712
Hampton	641
Hancock	712
Hanford	641
Hanley	641
Hanlontown	641
Hanna	515
Hanover	712
Hansell	641
Harcourt	515
Hardin	563
Hardy	515
Harlan	712
Harper	641
Harpers Ferry	563
Harris	712
Hartford	515
Hartley	712
Hartwick	319
Harvard	641
Harvester	641
Harvey	641
Haskins	319
Hastings	712
Hauntown	563
Havelock	712
Haven	641
Haverhill	641
Hawarden	712
Hawkeye	563
Hayesville	641
Hayfield	641
Hazel Green	563
Hazleton	319
Hebron	641
Hedrick	641
Henderson	712
Henry Field Seed	712
Herbert Hoover National Hist	319
Herrold	515
Hesper	563
Hiawatha	319
High	319
High Amana	319
High Point	641
Highland Park	515
Highlandville	563
Hills	319
Hillsboro	319
Hinton	712
Hiteman	641
Hobarton	515
Holbrook	319
Holiday Lake	641
Holland	319
Holmes	515
Holstein	712
Holy Cross	563
Homestead	319
Honey Creek	712
Hopeville	641
Hopkinton	563
Hornick	712
Horton	319
Hospers	712
Houghton	319
Howe	515
Hubbard	641
Hudson	319
Hull	712
Humboldt	515
Humeston	641
Huron	319
Hurstville	563
Hutchins	641
Huxley	515
Iconium	641
Ida Grove	712
Imogene	712
Independence	319
Indian Creek	319
Indianapolis	641
Indianola	515
Industry	712
Inwood	712
Ionia	641
Iowa Center	515
Iowa City	319
Iowa Falls	641
Iowa State University	515
Ira	515
Ireton	712
Ironhills	563
Irvington	515
Irwin	712
Ivy	515
Jackson Jct	563
Jackson Junction	563
Jamaica	641
James	712
Jamison	641
Janesville	319
Jefferson	515
Jerico	641
Jesup	319
Jewell	515
Joetown	319
Johnston	515
Joice	641
Jolley	712
Julien	563
Juniata	712
Kalona	319
Kamrar	515
Kanawha	641
Kellerton	641
Kelley	515
Kellogg	641
Kendallville	563
Kensett	641
Kent	641
Keokuk	319
Keomah	641
Keosauqua	319
Keota	641
Kesley	319
Keswick	319
Key West	563
Keystone	319
Kilbourn	319
Killduff	641
Kimballton	712
Kingsley	712
Kingston	319
Kinross	319
Kirkman	712
Kirkville	641
Kiron	712
Klemme	641
Klinger	319
Knierim	515
Knittel	319
Knoke	712
Knoxville	641
Kossuth	319
Koszta	319
La Motte	563
La Porte City	319
Lacey	641
Lacona	641
Ladora	319
Lake City	712
Lake Mills	641
Lake Panorama	641
Lake Park	712
Lake View	712
Lakeside	712
Lakewood	515
Lakota	515
Lambs Grove	641
Lamoni	641
Lamont	563
Lancaster	641
Lanedale	712
Lanesboro	712
Langworthy	319
Lansing	563
Lanyon	515
Laporte City	319
Larchwood	712
Larrabee	712
Last Chance	641
Latimer	641
Laurel	641
Laurens	712
Lavinia	712
Lawler	563
Lawn Hill	641
Lawton	712
Le Claire	563
Le Grand	641
Le Mars	712
Le Roy	641
Leando	641
Lebanon	712
Leclaire	563
Ledyard	515
Lehigh	515
Leighton	641
Leland	641
Lemars	712
Lenox	641
Leon	641
Lester	712
Letts	319
Lewis	712
Liberty	641
Liberty Center	641
Liberty Ctr	641
Libertyville	641
Lidderdale	712
Life Investors Inc	319
Lima	563
Limby	319
Lime City	563
Lime Springs	563
Lincoln	641
Linden	641
Lineville	641
Linn Grove	712
Lisbon	319
Liscomb	641
Little Cedar	641
Little Rock	712
Little Sioux	712
Little Turkey	563
Littleport	563
Littleton	319
Livermore	515
Livingston	641
Lockridge	319
Locust	563
Logan	712
Lohrville	712
Lone Rock	515
Lone Tree	319
Long Grove	563
Lorah	712
Lorimor	641
Lost Island Lake	712
Lost Nation	563
Lotts Creek	515
Lourdes	641
Lovilia	641
Lovington	515
Low Moor	563
Lowden	563
Lowell	319
Lu Verne	515
Luana	563
Lucas	641
Ludlow	563
Lundstrom Heights	515
Luther	515
Luton	712
Luxemburg	563
Luzerne	319
Lynnville	641
Lytton	712
Macedonia	712
Macksburg	641
Macy	641
Madrid	515
Magnolia	712
Maharishi University Of Mgmt	641
Malcom	641
Mallard	712
Maloy	641
Malvern	712
Manawa	712
Manchester	563
Manilla	712
Manly	641
Manning	712
Manson	712
Maple Heights	641
Maple Hill	712
Maple River	712
Mapleton	712
Maquoketa	563
Marathon	712
Marble Rock	641
Marcus	712
Marengo	319
Marion	319
Marne	712
Marquette	563
Marquisville	515
Marsh Inc	515
Marshalltown	641
Martelle	319
Martensdale	641
Martinsburg	641
Marysville	641
Maryville	563
Mason City	641
Masonville	319
Massena	712
Massey	563
Massillon	563
Matlock	712
Maurice	712
Maxwell	515
May City	712
Maynard	563
Maysville	563
Mc Callsburg	515
Mc Causland	563
Mc Clelland	712
Mc Gregor	563
Mc Intire	641
Mcclelland	712
Mcgraw Hill Companies	563
Mcnally	712
Mechanicsville	563
Mechanicsvile	563
Mederville	563
Mediapolis	319
Medora	515
Melbourne	641
Melcher	641
Melcher Dal	641
Melcher Dallas	641
Melrose	641
Meltonville	641

City	Area Code
Melvin	712
Menlo	641
Meriden	712
Meroa	641
Merrill	712
Meservey	641
Methodist Camp	712
Meyer	641
Midamerican Energy	515
Middle	319
Middle Amana	319
Middleburg	712
Middletown	319
Midvale	515
Midway	319
Miles	563
Milford	712
Miller	641
Millersburg	319
Millerton	641
Millnerville	712
Millville	563
Milo	641
Milton	641
Minburn	515
Minden	712
Mineola	712
Minerva	641
Mingo	641
Missouri Valley	712
Missouri Vly	712
Mitchell	641
Mitchellville	515
Mo Valley	712
Modale	712
Mondamin	712
Moneta	712
Monmouth	563
Monona	563
Monroe	641
Montezuma	641
Montgomery	712
Monticello	319
Montour	641
Montpelier	563
Montrose	319
Mooar	319
Moorhead	712
Moorland	515
Moran	515
Moravia	641
Morley	319
Morning Sun	319
Morrison	319
Morton Mills	712
Moscow	563
Moulton	641
Mount Auburn	319
Mount Ayr	641
Mount Carmel	712
Mount Pleasant	319
Mount Sterling	319
Mount Union	319
Mount Vernon	319
Moville	712
Mt Hamill	319
Mt Pleasant	319
Mt Sterling	319
Mt Union	319
Munterville	641
Murphy	319
Murray	641
Muscatine	563
Mystic	641
N Buena Vista	563
N Washington	641
Nashua	641
Nashville	563
National	563
Neils	641
Nemaha	712
Neola	712
Neptune	712
Nevada	515
New Albin	563
New Hampton	641
New Hartford	319
New Haven	641
New Liberty	563
New London	319
New Market	712
New Providence	641
New Providnce	641
New Sharon	641
New Vienna	563
New Virginia	641
New York	641
Newbern	641
Newburg	641
Newell	712
Newhall	319
Newkirk	712
Newton	641
Nichols	319
Nodaway	712
Nora Springs	641
Nordness	563
Nordstrom	319
North Branch	641
North Buena Vista	563
North Cedar	319
North English	319
North Liberty	319
North Washington	641
North Welton	563
Northboro	712
Northfield	319
Northwood	641
Norwalk	515
Norway	319
Norwood	641
Norwoodville	515
Numa	641
Oakdale	319
Oakland	712
Oakland Acres	641
Oakley	641
Oakville	319
Oakwood	641
Oasis	319
Ocheyedan	712
Odebolt	712
Oelwein	319
Ogden	515
Okoboji	712
Old Town	712
Olds	319
Olin	319
Olivet	641
Ollie	641
Onawa	712
Oneida	563
Onslow	563
Oralabor	515
Oran	319
Orange City	712
Orchard	641
Orient	641
Orillia	515
Osage	641
Osborne	563
Osceola	641
Osgood	712
Oskaloosa	641
Ossian	563
Osterdock	563
Otho	515
Otley	641
Oto	712
Otranto	641
Otter Creek	563
Otterville	319
Ottosen	515
Ottumwa	641
Ottumwa Junction	641
Owasa	641
Owego	712
Oxford	319
Oxford Jct	563
Oxford Junction	563
Oxford Mills	563
Oyens	712
Pacific Jct	712
Pacific Junction	712
Packard	319
Packwood	319
Painted Rocks	641
Palm Grove	515
Palmer	712
Palmyra	515
Palo	319
Panama	712
Panarama Park	563
Panora	641
Park Hills	641
Park View	563
Parkersburg	319
Parnell	319
Paton	515
Patterson	641
Paullina	712
Pekin	319
Pella	641
Peosta	563
Percival	712
Perkins	712
Perlee	641
Perry	515
Pershing	641
Persia	712
Peru	641
Petersburg	563
Peterson	712
Petersville	563
Pierson	712
Pilot Grove	319
Pilot Mound	515
Pioneer	515
Piper	712
Pisgah	712
Pitzer	515
Plain View	563
Plainfield	319
Plano	641
Platteville	641
Pleasant Hill	515
Pleasant Plain	319
Pleasant Valley	563
Pleasant Vly	563
Pleasanton	641
Pleasantville	515
Plover	712
Plymouth	641
Pocahontas	712
Polk City	515
Pomeroy	712
Popejoy	515
Portland	641
Portsmouth	712
Postville	563
Powersville	641
Prairie City	515
Prairie Grove	319
Prairieburg	319
Prescott	641
Preston	563
Primghar	712
Primrose	319
Princeton	563
Principal Financial	515
Prole	641
Promise City	641
Promotional Fulfillment Corp	563
Protivin	563
Pulaski	641
Quandahl	563
Quasqueton	319
Quimby	712
Radcliffe	515
Rake	641
Ralston	712
Randalia	563
Randall	515
Randolph	712
Rands	712
Rathbun	641
Raymar	319
Raymond	319
Readlyn	319
Reasnor	641
Red Line	712
Red Oak	712
Redding	641
Redfield	515
Reinbeck	319
Rembrandt	712
Remsen	712
Renwick	515
Rhodes	641
Riceville	641
Richards	712
Richland	319
Ricketts	712
Ridgeway	563
Rinard	515
Ringsted	712
Rippey	515
Risingsun	515
Ritter	712
River Junction	319
Riverdale	563
Riverside	319
Riverton	712
Robertson	641
Robins	319
Robinson	563
Rochester	563
Rock Creek	641
Rock Falls	641
Rock Rapids	712
Rock Valley	712
Rockdale	563
Rockford	641
Rockwell	641
Rockwell City	712
Rockwell Collins	319
Rodney	712
Roelyn	515
Roland	515
Rolfe	712
Rome	319
Rose Hill	641
Roselle	712
Ross	712
Rossie	712
Rossville	563
Rowan	641
Rowley	319
Royal	712
Rubio	319
Ruble	712
Rudd	641
Runnells	515
Russell	641
Ruthven	712
Rutland	515
Rutledge	641
Ryan	563
Sabula	563
Sac City	712
Sageville	563
Saint Ansgar	641
Saint Anthony	641
Saint Benedict	515
Saint Charles	641
Saint Donatus	563
Saint Joseph	515
Saint Lucas	563
Saint Marys	641
Saint Olaf	563
Saint Paul	319
Salem	319
Salina	641
Salix	712
Sanborn	712
Sand Prairie	319
Sand Spring	563
Sandusky	319
Sandyville	641
Santiago	515
Saratoga	563
Sattre	563
Saude	563
Sawyer	319
Saydel	515
Saylorville	515
Scarville	641
Schaller	712
Schleswig	712
Schley	563
Scotch Grove	319
Scotch Ridge	515
Scranton	712
Searsboro	641
Selma	641
Seneca	515
Sergeant Blf	712
Sergeant Bluff	712
Seventh Avenue	563
Sewal	641
Sexton	515
Seymour	641
Sgt Bluff	712
Shady Grove	319
Shaffton	563
Shambaugh	712
Shannon City	641
Sharon	712
Sharpsburg	641
Shawondasse	563
Sheffield	641
Shelby	712
Sheldahl	515
Sheldon	712
Shell Rock	319
Shellsburg	319
Shenandoah	712
Sheridan	641
Sherrill	563
Sherwood	712
Shipley	515
Siam	712
Sibley	712
Sidney	712
Sigourney	641
Silver City	712
Silver Lake	641
Sinclair	319
Sioux Center	712
Sioux City	712
Sioux Rapids	712
Six Mile	563
Slater	515
Slifer	515
Sloan	712
Smithland	712
Soldier	712
Solon	319
Somers	515
South Amana	319
South Des Moines	515
South English	319
South Ottumwa	641
Spencer	712
Sperry	319
Spillville	563
Spirit Lake	712
Spragueville	563
Spring Hill	515
Springbrook	563
Springdale	319
Springville	319
St Lucas	563
Stacyville	641
Stanhope	515
Stanley	319
Stanton	712
Stanwood	563
Stanzel	641
State Center	641
State Of Iowa	515
Steamboat Rk	641
Steamboat Rock	641
Stilson	641
Stockport	319
Stockton	563
Storm Lake	712
Story City	515
Stout	319
Stratford	515
Strawberry Point	563
Strawberry Pt	563
Stringtown	641
Stuart	515
Sugar Creek	563
Sully	641
Sulphur Springs	712
Summerset	515
Summitville	319
Sumner	563
Superior	712
Sutherland	712
Sutliff	319
Swaledale	641
Swan	515
Swea City	515
Swedesburg	319
Swisher	319
Tabor	712
Taintor	641
Talleyrand	641
Talmage	641
Tama	641
Tara	515
Teeds Grove	563
Templar Park	712
Templeton	712
Tennant	712
Tenville Junction	712
Terril	712
Thayer	641
The Meadows	515
Thompson	641
Thor	515
Thornburg	641
Thornton	641
Thorpe	563
Thurman	712
Ticonic	712
Tiffin	319
Tingley	641
Tipton	563
Titonka	515
Toddville	319
Toeterville	641
Toledo	641
Toolesboro	319
Toronto	563
Tracy	641
Traer	319
Treynor	712
Triboji Beach	712
Tripoli	319
Troy Mills	319
Truesdale	712
Truro	641
Turin	712
Turkey River	563
Tuskeego	641
Twin View Heights	319
Udell	641
Underwood	712
Union	641
Union Mills	641
Unionville	641
Univ Park	641
University Heights	319
University Of Northern Iowa	319
University Park	641
University Pk	641
Urbana	319
Urbandale	515
Usps Bmc	515
Ute	712
Vail	712
Valeria	515
Van Cleve	641
Van Horne	319
Van Meter	515
Van Wert	641
Varina	712
Vedic City	641
Ventura	641
Veo	319
Vernon Springs	563
Victor	319

City	Area Code
Village Creek	563
Villisca	712
Vincent	515
Vining	319
Vinton	319
Viola	319
Visa Mastercard	515
Volga	563
Volney	563
Voorhies	319
W Burlington	319
W Des Moines	515
W Okoboji	712
Wadena	563
Wahpeton	712
Walcott	563
Walford	319
Walker	319
Wall Lake	712
Wallingford	712
Walnut	712
Walnut City	641
Wapello	319
Ware	712
Washburn	319
Washington	319
Washta	712
Waterloo	319
Waterville	563
Watkins	319
Watson	563
Waubeek	319
Waucoma	563
Waukee	515
Waukon	563
Waukon Junction	563
Waverly	319
Wayland	319
Wdm	515
Webb	712
Webster	319
Webster City	515
Weldon	641
Weller	641
Wellman	319
Wells Fargo Mortgage	515
Wellsburg	641
Welton	563
Wesley	515
West Amana	319
West Bend	515
West Branch	319
West Burlington	319
West Chester	319
West Des Moines	515
West Fort Dodge	515
West Grove	641
West Liberty	319
West Okoboji	712
West Point	319
West Storm Lake	712
West Union	563
Westerville	641
Westfield	712
Westgate	563
Westphalia	712
Westside	712
Wever	319
What Cheer	641
Wheatland	563
White Elm	641
White Oak	515
White Pigeon	319
Whiting	712
Whittemore	515
Whitten	641
Whittier	319
Wick	641
Wickham Spur	712
Wieston	712
Wildwood Camp	563
Willey	712
Williams	515
Williamsburg	319
Williamson	641
Williamstown	319
Wilton	563
Windham	319
Windsor Heights	515
Windsor Hts	515
Winfield	319
Winnebago Heights	641
Winterset	515
Winthrop	319
Wiota	712
Wiscotta	515
Woden	641
Wood	563
Woodbine	712
Woodburn	641
Woodland	641
Woodward	515
Woolstock	515
Worthington	563
Wright	641
Wyman	319
Wyoming	563
Yale	641
Yarmouth	319
Yetter	712
Yorktown	712
Younkers	515
Zaneta	319
Zearing	641
Zion	641
Zook Spur	515
Zwingle	563

Kansas

City	Area Code
Abbyville	620
Abilene	785
Ada	785
Admire	620
Agenda	785
Agra	785
Albert	620
Alden	620
Alexander	785
Allen	620
Alma	785
Almena	785
Alta Vista	785
Altamont	620
Alton	785
Altoona	620
Americus	620
Ames	785
Andale	316
Andover	316
Angola	620
Antelope	620
Anthony	620
Antonino	785
Arcadia	620
Argonia	620
Arkansas City	620
Arlington	620
Arma	620
Arnold	785
Ashland	620
Ashton	620
Assaria	785
Atchison	913
Athol	785
Atlanta	620
Attica	620
Atwood	785
Auburn	785
Augusta	316
Aurora	785
Austin	620
Axtell	785
Badger	620
Baileyville	785
Baldwin	785
Baldwin City	785
Barber	620
Barnard	785
Barnes	785
Barnesville	620
Bartlett	620
Basehor	913
Bassett	620
Bavaria	785
Baxter Spgs	620
Baxter Springs	620
Bazine	785
Beattie	785
Beaumont	620
Beaver	620
Beeler	785
Bel Aire	316
Bellaire	785
Belle Plaine	620
Belleville	785
Belmont	620
Beloit	785
Belpre	620
Belvidere	620
Belvue	785
Bendena	785
Benedict	620
Bennington	785
Bentley	316
Benton	316
Bern	785
Berryton	785
Beulah	620
Beverly	785
Big Bow	620
Big Elk	620
Bird City	785
Bison	785
Blaine	785
Bloom	620
Blue Cross	785
Blue Mound	913
Blue Rapids	785
Bluff City	620
Bogue	785
Bonner Springs	913
Bonner Sprngs	913
Brazilton	620
Bremen	785
Brewster	785
Bronson	620
Brookville	785
Brownell	785
Bucklin	620
Bucyrus	913
Buffalo	620
Buffville	620
Buhler	620
Bunker Hill	785
Burden	620
Burdett	620
Burdick	785
Burlingame	785
Burlington	620
Burlington Northern Santa Fe	785
Burns	620
Burr Oak	785
Burrton	620
Bushong	620
Bushton	620
Buxton	620
Byers	620
Caldwell	620
Cambridge	620
Caney	620
Canton	620
Capaldo	620
Carbondale	785
Carlton	785
Carlyle	620
Carmean	620
Carona	620
Cassoday	620
Catharine	785
Cato	620
Cawker City	785
Cedar	785
Cedar Point	620
Cedar Vale	620
Centerville	913
Centralia	785
Centropolis	785
Chanute	620
Chapman	785
Chase	620
Chautauqua	620
Cheney	316
Cherokee	620
Cherryvale	620
Chetopa	620
Cimarron	620
Circleville	785
Claflin	620
Clay Center	785
Clayton	785
Clearview City	913
Clearview Cty	913
Clearwater	620
Clements	620
Clifton	785
Climax	620
Clyde	785
Coalvale	620
Coats	620
Cockerill	620
Codell	785
Coffeyville	620
Colby	785
Coldwater	620
Collyer	785
Colony	620
Columbus	620
Colwich	316
Comotara	316
Concordia	785
Conway	620
Conway Spgs	620
Conway Springs	620
Coolidge	620
Copeland	620
Corbin	620
Corning	785
Corwin	620
Cottonwd Fls	620
Cottonwood Falls	620
Council Grove	620, 785
Countryside	913
Courtland	785
Coyville	620
Crestline	620
Croweburg	620
Cuba	785
Cullison	620
Culver	785
Cummings	913
Cunningham	620
Curranville	620
Damar	785
Danville	620
De Soto	913
Dearing	620
Deerfield	620
Delavan	785
Delia	785
Delphos	785
Denison	785
Dennis	620
Densmore	785
Denton	785
Derby	316
Devon	620
Dexter	620
Dighton	620
Dodge City	620
Dorrance	785
Douglass	316
Dover	785
Downs	785
Dresden	785
Drywood	620
Duluth	785
Dundee	620
Dunlap	620
Duquoin	620
Durand	620
Durham	620
Dwight	785
Earlton	620
Eastborough	316
Easton	913
Edgerton	913
Edison	620
Edmond	785
Edna	620
Edson	785
Edwardsville	913
Effingham	913
El Dorado	316
Elbing	316
Elk City	620
Elk Falls	620
Elkhart	620
Ellinwood	620
Ellis	785
Ellsworth	785
Elmdale	620
Elsmore	620
Elwood	913
Emmett	785
Emporia	620
Englewood	620
Ensign	620
Enterprise	785
Erie	620
Esbon	785
Eskridge	785
Eudora	785
Eureka	620
Everest	785
Fairview	785
Fairway	913
Fall River	620
Falun	785
Farlington	620
Fellsburg	620
Florence	620
Fontana	913
Ford	620
Formoso	785
Fort Dodge	620
Fort Larned National History	620
Fort Leavenworth	913
Fort Riley	785
Fort Scott	620
Fostoria	785
Fowler	620
Frankfort	785
Franklin	620
Fredonia	620
Freeport	620
Friend	620
Frontenac	620
Ft Leavenworth	913
Ft Leavnwrth	913
Ft Riley	785
Fulton	620
Galatia	785
Galena	620
Galesburg	620
Galva	620
Garden City	620
Garden Plain	316
Gardner	913
Garfield	620
Garland	620
Garnett	785
Gas	620
Gaylord	785
Gem	785
Geneseo	620
Geuda Springs	620
Girard	620
Glade	785
Glasco	785
Glen Elder	785
Goddard	316
Goessel	620
Goff	785
Goodland	785
Gorham	785
Gove	785
Grainfield	785
Grantville	785
Great Bend	620
Greeley	785
Green	785
Green Bush	620
Greenbush	620
Greenleaf	785
Greensburg	620
Greenwich	316
Grenola	620
Gridley	620
Grinnell	785
Gross	620
Guilford	620
Gypsum	785
Haddam	785
Hallowell	620
Halstead	316
Hamilton	620
Hamlin	785
Hanover	785
Hanston	620
Harding	620
Hardtner	620
Harlan	785
Harper	620
Hartford	620
Harveyville	785
Havana	620
Haven	620
Havensville	785
Haviland	620
Hays	785
Haysville	316
Hazelton	620
Healy	620
Heizer	620
Hepler	620
Herington	785
Herkimer	785
Herndon	785
Hesston	620
Hewins	620
Hiattville	620
Hiawatha	785
Highland	785
Hilford	620
Hill City	785
Hillsboro	620
Hillsdale	913
Hoisington	620
Holcomb	620
Hollenberg	785
Holton	785
Holyrood	785
Home	785
Hope	785
Horton	785
Howard	620
Hoxie	785
Hoyt	785
Hudson	620
Hugoton	620
Humboldt	620
Hunnewell	620
Hunter	785
Huron	913
Hutchinson	620
Independence	620
Industry	785
Ingalls	620
Inman	620
Iola	620
Ionia	785
Isabel	620
Iuka	620
J C Penney Co	913
Jamestown	785
Jennings	785
Jetmore	620
Jewell	785
Johnson	620
Junction City	785
K U Med Center	913
Kalvesta	620
Kanopolis	785
Kanorado	785

Kansas City 913
Kansas Income Tax 785
Kansas University Med Center 913
Kechi 316
Kelly 785
Kendall 620
Kensington 785
Kincaid 620
Kingman 620
Kingsdown 620
Kinsley 620
Kiowa 620
Kirwin 785
Kismet 620
Ks Dept Of Revenue Taxation 785
Ks Dept Of Revenue Vehicles 785
Ks State Bd Of Health 785
La Crosse 785
La Harpe 620
Labette 620
Lacygne 913
Lafontaine 620
Lake City 620
Lake Of The Forest 913
Lake Quivira 913
Lakin 620
Lamont 620
Lancaster 913
Lane 785
Langdon 620
Lansing 913
Larned 620
Latham 620
Latimer 785
Laurence 785
Lawrence 785
Lawton 620
Le Roy 620
Leavenworth 913
Leawood 913
Lebanon 785
Lebo 620
Lecompton 785
Lehigh 620
Lenexa 913
Lenora 785
Leon 316
Leona 785
Leonardville 785
Leoti 620
Levant 785
Lewis 620
Liberal 620
Liberty 620
Liebenthal 785
Lillis 785
Lincoln 785
Lincolnville 620
Lindsborg 785
Linn 785
Linn Valley 913
Linwood 913
Little River 620
Lk Of The Fst 913
Logan 785
Long Island 785
Longford 785
Longton 620
Lorraine 785
Lost Springs 785
Louisburg 913
Louisville 785
Louisvl 785
Louisvle 785
Lowell 620
Lucas 785
Ludell 785
Luray 785
Lwrnce 785
Lyndon 785
Lyons 620
Macksville 620
Madison 620
Mahaska 785
Maize 316
Manchester 785
Manhattan 785
Mankato 785
Manter 620
Mantey 913
Maple City 620
Maple Hill 785
Mapleton 620
Marienthal 620
Marion 620
Marquette 785
Marysville 785
Material Distribution Ctr 785
Matfield Green 620
Matfield Grn 620
Mayetta 785
Mayfield 620
Mc Cracken 785
Mc Cune 620
Mc Donald 785
Mc Farland 785
Mc Louth 913
Mc Pherson 620
Mcconnell Afb 316
Mccune 620
Mcdonald 785
Mcfarland 785
Mcpherson 620
Meade 620
Medicine Ldg 620
Medicine Lodge 620
Medora 620
Melrose 620
Melvern 785
Menlo 785
Mentor 785
Meriden 785
Merriam 913
Milan 620
Milford 785
Milton 620
Miltonvale 785
Mineral 620
Minneapolis 785
Minneola 620
Mission 913
Mission Hills 913
Mission Woods 913
Modoc 620
Moline 620
Monmouth 620
Montezuma 620
Monument 785
Moran 620
Morehead 620
Morganville 785
Morland 785
Morrill 785
Morrowville 785
Moscow 620
Mound City 913
Mound Valley 620
Moundridge 620
Mount Hope 316
Mulberry 620
Mullinville 620
Mulvane 316
Munden 785
Murdock 620
Muscotah 785
Narka 785
Nashville 620
Natoma 785
Navarre 785
Neal 620
Nekoma 785
Neodesha 620
Neosho Falls 620
Neosho Rapids 620
Ness City 785
Netawaka 785
Neutral 620
New Albany 620
New Almelo 785
New Cambria 785
New Century 913
New Salem 620
New Strawn 620
Newton 316
Nickerson 620
Niotaze 620
Norcatur 785
North Newton 316
North Wichita 316
Norton 785
Nortonville 913
Norway 785
Norwich 620
Oakhill 785
Oaklawn 316
Oakley 785
Oatville 316
Oberlin 785
Odin 620
Offerle 620
Ogallah 785
Ogden 785
Oketo 785
Olathe 913
Olmitz 620
Olpe 620
Olsburg 785
Onaga 785
Oneida 785
Op 913
Opolis 620
Osage City 785
Osawatomie 913
Osborne 785
Oskaloosa 785
Oswego 620
Otis 785
Ottawa 785
Overbrook 785
Overland 913
Overland Park 913
Oxford 620
Ozawkie 785
Palco 785
Palmer 785
Paola 913
Paradise 785
Park 785
Park City 316
Parker 913
Parkerfield 620
Parsons 620
Partridge 620
Pawnee Rock 620
Paxico 785
Peabody 620
Peck 316
Penalosa 620
Penokee 785
Perry 785
Peru 620
Petrolia 620
Pfeifer 785
Phillipsburg 785
Piedmont 620
Pierceville 620
Piqua 620
Pittsburg 620
Plains 620
Plainville 785
Planeview 316
Pleasanton 913
Plevna 620
Pomona 785
Porterville 620
Portis 785
Potter 913
Potwin 620
Powhattan 785
Prairie View 785
Prairie Village 913
Prairie Vlg 913
Pratt 620
Prescott 913
Preston 620
Pretty Pr 620
Pretty Prairie 620
Princeton 785
Protection 620
Quaker 620
Quenemo 785
Quinter 785
Quivira 913
Radium 620
Radley 620
Rago 620
Ramona 620
Randall 785
Randolph 785
Ransom 785
Rantoul 785
Raymond 620
Reading 620
Redfield 620
Reece 620
Republic 785
Reserve 785
Rexford 785
Rice 785
Richfield 620
Richmond 785
Riley 785
Ringo 620
Riverdale 620
Riverton 620
Robinson 785
Rock 620
Roeland Park 913
Rolla 620
Roper 620
Rosalia 620
Rose 620
Rose Hill 316
Rosedale 913
Rosehill 316
Roseland 620
Rossville 785
Roxbury 785
Rozel 620
Rush Center 785
Russell 785
Russell Spg 785
Russell Spgs 785
Russell Springs 785
S Hutchinson 620
Sabetha 785
Saint Francis 785
Saint George 785
Saint John 620
Saint Marys 785
Saint Paul 620
Salina 785
Satanta 620
Savonburg 620
Sawyer 620
Scammon 620
Scandia 785
Schoenchen 785
Schulte 316
Scott City 620
Scottsville 785
Scranton 785
Security Benefit Life 785
Sedan 620
Sedgwick 316
Selden 785
Selkirk 620
Seneca 785
Severance 785
Severy 620
Seward 620
Sharon 620
Sharon Spgs 785
Sharon Springs 785
Shawnee 913
Shawnee Mission 913
Shawnee Msn 913
Sherwin 620
Shields 620
Sieboldt 620
Silver Lake 785
Silverdale 620
Simpson 785
Sims 620
Skidmore 620
Sm 913
Smith Center 785
Smolan 785
So Hutchinson 620
Soldier 785
Solomon 785
South Haven 620
South Hutchinson 620
Spearville 620
Spivey 620
Spring Grove 620
Spring Hill 913
Sprint Corporation 913
St Benedict 785
St Francis 785
St George 785
St John 620
St Marys 785
St Paul 620
Stafford 620
Stanley 913
Stark 620
Sterling 620
Stilwell 913
Stippville 620
Stockton 785
Strauss 620
Strong City 620
Studley 785
Stuttgart 785
Sublette 620
Summerfield 785
Sun City 620
Susank 620
Sycamore 620
Sylvan Grove 785
Sylvia 620
Syracuse 620
Talmage 785
Tampa 785
Tecumseh 785
Tescott 785
Thayer 620
Timken 785
Tipton 785
Tonganoxie 913
Topeka 785
Toronto 620
Towanda 316
Treece 620
Tribune 620
Trousdale 620
Troy 785
Turon 620
Tyro 620
Udall 620
Ulysses 620
Uniontown 620
University Of Kansas 785
Usps Offical Mail 316
Utica 785
V A Hospital 785
Valley Center 316
Valley Falls 785
Vassar 785
Vermillion 785
Vernon 620
Victoria 785
Viola 620
Virgil 620
Vliets 785
Wa Keeney 785
Wakarusa 785
Wakeeney 785
Wakefield 785
Waldo 785
Waldron 620
Walker 785
Wallace 785
Walnut 620
Walton 620
Wamego 785
Washington 785
Waterville 785
Wathena 785
Waverly 785
Webber 785
Weir 620
Welda 785
Wellington 620
Wells 785
Wellsville 785
Weskan 785
West Mineral 620
Westfall 785
Westmoreland 785
Westphalia 785
Westwood 913
Westwood Hills 913
Westwood Hls 913
Wetmore 785
Wheaton 785
Wheeler 785
White City 785
White Cloud 785
Whitewater 316
Whiting 785
Wichita 316
Wichita State University 316
Williamsburg 785
Willis 785
Wilmore 620
Wilsey 785
Wilson 785
Winchester 913
Windom 620
Winfield 620
Winona 785
Woodbine 785
Woodston 785
Wright 620
Xenia 620
Yates Center 620
Yoder 620
Zenda 620
Zimmerdale 316
Zurich 785

Kentucky

88 270
Aaron 606
Abegall 606
Aberdeen 270
Acorn 606
Adairville 270
Adams 606
Adolphus 270
Aflex 606
Ages 606
Ages Brooksde 606
Ages Brookside 606
Ajax 606
Albany 606
Alcalde 606
Alexandria 859
Allegre 270
Allen 606
Allen Springs 270
Allensville 270
Allock 606
Almo 270
Almo Heights 270
Alpha 606
Alpine 606
Altro 606
Alva 606
Alvaton 270
Amazon.Com 859
Amba 606
Amburgey 606
Anchorage 502
Anco 606
Annville 606
Argillite 606
Argo 606
Arjay 606
Arlington 270
Arrington Corner 270

City	Area Code
Artemus	606
Ary	606
Ashcamp	606
Asher	606
Ashland	606
Ashland Oil Inc	606
Athol	606
Atwood	859
Auburn	270
Augusta	606
Ault	606
Aurora	270
Austin	270
Auxier	606
Avawam	606
Avondale	270
Axtel	270
Bagdad	502
Bailey Creek	606
Bailey Switch	606
Bakerton	270
Bald Hill	606
Balkan	606
Ballardsville	502
Bandana	270
Bank One	502
Bank One Accts	502
Bank One Ky	502
Banner	606
Barbourville	606
Bardstown	502
Bardwell	270
Barkley Regional Airport	270
Barlow	270
Barnetts Creek	606
Barnetts Crk	606
Barrier	606
Baskett	270
Bath	606
Battletown	270
Baughman	606
Baxter	606
Bays	606
Bear Branch	606
Bearville	606
Beattyville	606
Beaumont	270
Beauty	606
Beaver	606
Beaver Bottom	606
Beaver Dam	270
Beaverlick	859
Bedford	502
Bee Spring	270
Beech Creek	270
Beech Grove	270
Beechburg	606
Beechmont	270
Beechville	270
Belcher	606
Belfry	606
Bell City	270
Bellefonte	606
Belleview	859
Bellevue	859
Belton	270
Benham	606
Benton	270
Berea	859
Berea College	859
Berlin	606
Berry	859
Bethanna	606
Bethany	606
Bethel	606
Bethelridge	606
Bethesda	606
Bethlehem	502
Betsey	606
Betsy Layne	606
Beulah	270
Beulah Heights	606
Beverly	606
Bevinsville	606
Big Branch	606
Big Clifty	270
Big Creek	606
Big Fork	606
Big Laurel	606
Big Ready	270
Big Rock	606
Big Spring	270
Biggs	606
Bighill	859
Bimble	606
Blackey	606
Blackford	270
Bladeston	606
Blaine	606
Blairs Mill	606
Blanchet	502
Blandville	270
Blaze	606
Bledsoe	606
Bloomfield	502
Blue Bank	606
Blue Diamond	606
Blue Level	270
Blue River	606
Blue Spring	270
Blue Water Estates	270
Bluehole	606
Board Tree	606
Boaz	270
Boles	270
Bonanza	606
Bond	606
Bondville	859
Bonnieville	270
Bonnyman	606
Booneville	606
Boons Camp	606
Boston	502
Bow	270
Bowen	606
Bowling Green	270
Bowling Grn	270
Boxville	270
Bracht	859
Bradford	606
Bradfordsville	270
Bradfordsvlle	270
Brandenburg	270
Breeding	270
Bremen	270
Bright Shade	606
Brinegar	606
Brinkley	606
Broad Bottom	606
Broadwell	859
Brodhead	606
Bromley	859
Bronston	606
Brooklyn	270
Brooks	502
Brookside	606
Brooksville	606
Browder	270
Browning	270
Brownings Corner	859
Browns Crossroads	606
Browns Fork	606
Browns Xroads	606
Brownsville	270
Bruin	606
Bryan	270
Bryants Store	606
Bryantsville	859
Buckhorn	606
Buckingham	606
Buckner	502
Buechel	502
Buena Vista	859
Buffalo	270
Bugtussle	270
Bulan	606
Bullittsville	859
Burdine	606
Burgin	859
Burke	606
Burkesville	270
Burkhart	606
Burlington	859
Burna	270
Burning Fork	606
Burnside	606
Burnwell	606
Burtonville	606
Bush	606
Buskirk	606
Busy	606
Butler	859
Butterfly	606
Bybee	859
Bypro	606
Cadiz	270
Cains Store	606
Calhoun	270
California	859
Callaway	606
Calvary	270
Calvert City	270
Calvin	606
Camelia	270
Camp Dix	606
Camp Ernest	859
Campbellsburg	502
Campbellsville	270
Campbellsvlle	270
Campsprings	859
Campton	606
Canada	606
Cane Valley	270
Caney	606
Caneyville	270
Canmer	270
Cannel City	606
Cannon	606
Canoe	606
Canton	270
Carbon Glow	606
Carbondale	270
Carcassonne	606
Carlisle	606, 859
Carntown	859
Carr Creek	606
Carrie	606
Carrollton	502
Carrs	606
Carrsville	270
Carter	606
Carthage	859
Carver	606
Cary	606
Casey Creek	270
Catlettsburg	606
Cave City	270
Cave Ridge	270
Cave Spring	270
Cavehill	270
Cawood	606
Cayce	270
Cecilia	270
Cedar Flat	270
Cedarville	606
Center	270
Centertown	270
Central City	270
Central Cty	270
Cerulean	270
Chad	606
Chaplin	502
Chappell	606
Charleston	270
Charters	606
Chavies	606
Chenoa	606
Cherokee	606
Chestnutburg	606
Chevrolet	606
Christian Appalachian	859
Cinda	606
Cisco	606
Clark Hill	606
Clarksburg	606
Clarkson	270
Claryville	859
Clay	270
Clay City	606
Clayhole	606
Clear Creek	606
Clear Creek Springs	606
Clear Crk Spg	606
Clearfield	606
Cleaton	270
Clementsville	606
Clermont	502
Cliff	606
Clifford	606
Clifty	270
Climax	606
Clinton	270
Clintonville	859
Closplint	606
Clover Bottom	606
Cloverport	270
Coalgood	606
Coalton	606
Cobhill	606
Cold Sprgs Hi	859
Cold Sprgs Highland Hts	859
Cold Sprgs-Highland Hts	859
Cold Spring	859
Cold Spring Highland Heights	859
Coldiron	606
Coldwater	270
Coleman	606
Colfax	606
College Campus	270
College Hill	859
Collista	606
Columbia	270
Columbus	270
Colville	859
Combs	606
Concord	606
Confederate	270
Confluence	606
Conley	606
Connersville	859
Constantine	270
Conway	606
Cooktown	270
Cool Springs	270
Cooperstown	270
Coopersville	606
Corbin	606
Cordell	606
Corinth	502
Cork	270
Cornettsville	606
Cornishville	859
Corydon	270
Cottle	606
Country Club Heights	606
Counts Cross Roads	606
Cov	859
Covington	859
Coxs Creek	502
Crab Orchard	606
Craintown	606
Crane Nest	606
Cranks	606
Crayne	270
Craynor	606
Creelsboro	270
Crescent Park	859
Crescent Spg	859
Crescent Spgs	859
Crescent Springs	859
Crestview	859
Crestview Hills	859
Crestview Hls	859
Crestwood	502
Crittenden	859
Crockett	606
Crofton	270
Croley	270
Cromona	606
Cromwell	270
Cropper	502
Crown	606
Crummies	606
Crutchfield	270
Crystal	606
Cub Run	270
Culver	606
Cumberland	606
Cumberland College	606
Cumberlnd Clg	606
Cumminsville	606
Cundiff	270
Cunningham	270
Curdsville	270
Custer	270
Cutshin	606
Cutuno	606
Cynthiana	859
Cyrus	606
Dabolt	606
Daisy	606
Dalesburg	606
Dana	606
Danville	859
Darfork	606
Davella	606
David	606
Davisburg	606
Davisport	606
Dawson Spgs	270
Dawson Springs	270
Day Rural	606
Dayhoit	606
Daysville	270
Dayton	859
De Mossville	859
Deane	606
Deatsville	502
Debord	606
Decoursey	859
Decoy	606
Defoe	502
Delphia	606
Delta	606
Dema	606
Democrat	606
Demossville	859
Denniston	606
Denton	606
Denver	606
Devon	859
Dewitt	606
Dexter	270
Dice	606
Dingus	606
Disputanta	606
Division Of Sales Use Tax	502
Dixie	859
Dixon	270
Dizney	606
Dock	606
Dogwood	270
Dolan	606
Donaldson	270
Dongola	606
Dorton	606
Dorton Branch	606
Douglas	606
Dover	606
Draffenville	270
Draffin	606
Drake	270
Drakesboro	270
Dreyfus	859
Drift	606
Dry Creek	606
Dry Fork	270
Dry Ridge	859
Dryfork	270
Dryhill	606
Duane	606
Dubre	270
Duco	606
Dunbar	270
Dundee	270
Dunham	606
Dunleary	606
Dunmor	270
Dunnville	606
Dwale	606
Dwarf	606
Dycusburg	270
Dyer	270
E Bernstadt	606
E Mc Dowell	606
E Pineville	606
E Town	270
E View	270
Earlington	270
East Bernstadt	606
East Jenkins	606
East Mc Dowell	606
East Pineville	606
East Point	606
Eastern	606
Eastview	270
Eastwood	502
Eberle	606
Echols	270
Eddyville	270
Edgewood	859
Edmonton	270
Edna	606
Eighty Eight	270
Ekron	270
Elamton	606
Elias	606
Elihu	606
Elizabethtown	270
Elizaville	606
Elk Horn	270
Elkatawa	606
Elkfork	606
Elkhorn City	606
Elkton	270
Elliottville	606
Elmrock	606
Elna	606
Elsie	606
Elsmere	859
Elys	606
Emerson	606
Emerson Orcutts Grocery	606
Eminence	502
Emlyn	606
Emma	606
Emmalena	606
Endicott	606
Engle	606
English	502
Enterprise	606
Eolia	606
Epworth	606
Eriline	606
Erlanger	859
Ermine	606
Essie	606
Estill	606
Etoile	270
Etty	606
Eubank	606
Evarts	606
Ever	606
Ewing	606
Ezel	606
Fairdale	502
Fairdealing	270
Fairfield	502
Fairplay	270
Fairview	270
Fairview Hill	606
Falcon	606
Fall Rock	606
Falls Of Rough	270
Falls Rough	270
Fallsburg	606
Falmouth	859
Fancy Farm	270
Farler	606
Farmers	606
Farmington	270
Faubush	606
Faxon	270
Fearisville	606
Fedscreek	606
Ferguson	606

City	Area Code
Fern Creek	502
Ferrells Creek	606
Field	606
Fillmore	606
Finchville	502
Finley	270
Firebrick	606
Fisherville	502
Fishtrap	606
Fiskburg	859
Fisty	606
Fitch	606
Flagg Spring	859
Flaherty	270
Flanary	606
Flat	606
Flat Fork	606
Flat Lick	606
Flatgap	606
Flatwoods	606
Fleet	270
Fleming	606
Fleming Neon	606
Flemingsburg	606
Flemingsburg Junction	606
Flingsville	859
Flippin	270
Florence	859
Fogertown	606
Folsomdale	270
Fonde	606
Foraker	606
Ford	859
Fords Branch	606
Fordsville	270
Forest Hills	606
Forkton	270
Fort Campbell	270
Fort Knox	502
Fort Mitchell	859
Fort Thomas	859
Fort Wright	859
Foster	606
Fountain Run	270
Four Oaks	859
Fourmile	606
Foxport	606
Foxtown	606
Frakes	606
Frances	270
Francisville	859
Frankfort	502
Franklin	270
Franklinton	502
Frazer	606
Fredonia	270
Fredville	606
Freeburn	606
Freetown	270
Fremont	270
Frenchburg	606
Frew	606
Frisby	606
Fritz	606
Frozen Creek	606
Ft Mitchell	859
Ft Thomas	859
Ft Wright	859
Fuget	606
Fulgham	270
Fulton	270
Fultz	606
Fusonia	606
Gage	270
Gainesville	270
Galveston	606
Gamaliel	270
Gapville	606
Gardnersville	859
Garfield	270
Garner	606
Garrard	606
Garrett	606
Garrison	606
Garvin Ridge	606
Gaskill	606
Gausdale	606
Gays Creek	606
General Electric Co	502
Geneva	270
Georgetown	502
Germantown	606
Gertrude	606
Ghent	502
Gifford	606
Gilbertsville	270
Gillem Branch	606
Gillmore	606
Gilly	606
Gimlet	606
Girdler	606
Glasgow	270
Glen Dean	270
Glen Springs	606
Glencoe	859
Glendale	270
Glens Fork	270
Glenview	502
Globe	606
Goddard	606
Goforth	859
Golden Pond	270
Goodluck	270
Goody	606
Goose Rock	606
Gordon	606
Gordonsville	270
Goshen	502
Grace	606
Gracey	270
Gradyville	270
Graham	270
Grahamville	270
Grahn	606
Grand Rivers	270
Grange City	606
Grants Lick	859
Grassy Creek	606
Gratz	502
Gravel Switch	859
Gray	606
Gray Hawk	606
Grays Knob	606
Grayson	606
Greasy Creek	606
Green Hall	606
Green Road	606
Greensburg	270
Greenup	606
Greenville	270
Greenwood	606
Gregory	606
Grethel	606
Grove Center	270
Guage	606
Gubser Mill	859
Guerrant	606
Gulnare	606
Gulston	606
Gum Tree	270
Gunlock	606
Guston	270
Guthrie	270
Gypsy	606
Haddix	606
Hadensville	270
Hadley	270
Hager	606
Hagerhill	606
Haldeman	606
Halfway	270
Halifax	270
Hall	606
Hallie	606
Halo	606
Hamilton	859
Hamlin	270
Hampton	270
Hanson	270
Happy	606
Hardburly	606
Hardin	270
Hardinsburg	270
Hardshell	606
Hardy	606
Hardyville	270
Harlan	606
Harned	270
Harold	606
Harper	606
Harrods Creek	502
Harrodsburg	859
Hartford	270
Hartley	606
Hatfield	606
Hatton	502
Hawesville	270
Haywood	270
Hazard	606
Hazel	270
Hazel Green	606
Head Of Grass	606
Head Of Grassy	606
Heath	270
Hebron	859
Heidelberg	606
Heidrick	606
Heiner	606
Helechawa	606
Helena	606
Hellier	606
Helton	606
Henderson	270
Hendricks	606
Hendron	270
Henshaw	270
Herd	606
Herman	270
Herndon	270
Heselton	606
Hestand	270
Hi Hat	606
Hickman	270
Hickory	270
High Point	270
Highgrove	502
Highland Heights	859
Highland Hgts	859
Highview	502
Highway	606
Hillsboro	606
Hillview	502
Hima	606
Himyar	606
Hindman	606
Hinkle	606
Hippo	606
Hiram	606
Hiseville	270
Hisle	606
Hitchins	606
Hite	606
Hode	606
Hodgenville	270
Holland	270
Hollybush	606
Holmes Mill	606
Honaker	606
Honeybee	606
Hooktown	859
Hope	606
Hopeful Heights	859
Hopkinsville	270
Horse Branch	270
Horse Cave	270
Horton	270
Hoskinston	606
Howardstown	502
Huddy	606
Hudson	270
Hueysville	606
Huff	270
Hulen	606
Hunter	606
Huntsville	270
Hustonville	606
Hyden	606
Ibex	606
Idlewild	859
Independence	859
Index	606
Inez	606
Ingle	606
Ingram	606
Insko	606
Internal Revenue	859
Ironton	270
Ironville	606
Irvine	606
Irvington	270
Island	270
Island City	606
Isom	606
Isonville	606
Iuka	270
Ivel	606
Ivy Grove	606
Ivyton	606
Jabez	606
Jackhorn	606
Jackson	606
Jamboree	606
Jamestown	270
Jarvis	606
Jeff	606
Jeffersontown	502
Jeffersonville	606
Jeffersonvlle	606
Jenkins	606
Jenson	606
Jeremiah	606
Jeriel	606
Jetson	270
Jinks	606
Job	606
Johnetta	606
Johns Creek	606
Johns Run	606
Johnson Bottom	606
Johnsville	606
Jonancy	606
Jonesville	859
Jonican	606
Joy	270
Junction City	859
Justell	606
Kaler	270
Kaliopi	606
Kayjay	606
Keaton	606
Keavy	606
Keene	859
Keith	606
Kenton	859
Kenton Hills	859
Kentontown	606
Kentonvale	859
Kentucky Lottery Corporation	502
Kentucky Oaks Mall	270
Kenvir	606
Kerby Knob	606
Kettle	270
Kettle Island	606
Kevil	270
Keysburg	270
Kilgore	606
Kimper	606
Kings Creek	606
Kings Mountain	606
Kings Mtn	606
Kinniconick	606
Kirksey	270
Kite	606
Knifley	270
Knob Lick	270
Knottsville	270
Kodak	606
Kona	606
Kosmosdale	502
Krypton	606
Kuttawa	270
Ky Dept Human Resources	502
Ky Dept Of Revenue	502
Ky Dept Of Transportation	502
Ky State Reformatory	502
Kyrock	270
La Center	270
La Fayette	270
La Grange	502
Lackey	606
Lagrange	502
Lair	859
Lake City	270
Lakeside Park	859
Lamasco	270
Lamb	270
Lambric	606
Lancaster	859
Lancer	606
Langley	606
Larkslane	606
Latonia	859
Latonia Lakes	859
Latonia Lks	859
Laura	606
Laurel Fork	606
Lawrenceburg	502
Lawton	606
Laynesville	606
Leander	606
Leatherwood	606
Lebanon	270
Lebanon Jct	502
Lebanon Jctn	502
Lebanon Junction	502
Leburn	606
Ledbetter	270
Lee City	606
Leeco	606
Lees Lick	859
Leesburg	859
Leitchfield	270
Lejunior	606
Lennut	606
Lenore	502
Lenox	606
Lenoxburg	859
Letcher	606
Levias	270
Lewisburg	270
Lewisport	270
Lexington	859
Lexmark	859
Liberty	606
Lick Creek	606
Lickburg	606
Ligon	606
Lily	606
Limaburg	859
Limestone	606
Lindseyville	270
Linefork	606
Linton	270
Lionilli	606
Littcarr	606
Little Sandy	606
Livermore	270
Livingston	606
Lloyd	606
Load	606
Lockport	502
Locust	502
Locust Grove	859
Locust Hill	270
Lodiburg	270
Log Mountain	606
Logansport	270
Logville	606
Lola	270
London	606
Lone	606
Lone Oak	270
Lookout	606
Lookout Heights	859
Loretto	270
Lost Creek	606
Louellen	606
Louisa	606
Louisville	502
Lovelaceville	270
Lovely	606
Lowes	270
Lowmansville	606
Loyall	606
Lucas	270
Ludlow	859
Lynch	606
Lyndon	502
Lynn Grove	270
Lynnville	270
Lytten	606
Maceo	270
Mackville	859
Madisonville	270
Maggard	606
Maggie	270
Magnolia	270
Majestic	606
Mallie	606
Malone	606
Mammoth Cave	270
Mammoth Cave National Park	270
Manchester	606
Manila	606
Manitou	270
Mannsville	270
Maple Grove	270
Maple Mount	270
Marcum	606
Mariba	606
Marion	270
Marrowbone	270
Marshallville	606
Marshes Sdng	606
Marshes Siding	606
Martha	606
Martha Mills	606
Martin	606
Mary	606
Mary Alice	606
Marydell	606
Mashfork	606
Mason	859
Masonic Home	502
Massac	270
Matthew	606
Mattoon	270
Maud	859
Maulden	606
Mayfield	270
Mayking	606
Mays Lick	606
Mayslick	606
Maysville	606
Maytown	606
Mazie	606
Mc Andrews	606
Mc Carr	606
Mc Daniels	270
Mc Dowell	606
Mc Henry	270
Mc Kee	606
Mc Kinney	606
Mc Quady	270
Mc Roberts	606
Mcandrews	606
Mccombs	606
Mcdaniels	270
Mchenry	270
Mckinneysburg	859
Mcquady	270
Mcveigh	606
Mcville	859
Meadow Creek	606
Meads	606
Meally	606
Means	606
Meeting Creek	270
Melber	270
Melbourne	859
Melvin	606
Mendola Village	606
Mentor	859
Meta	606
Mexico	270
Middleburg	606

City	Area Code
Middlesboro	606
Middlesborough	606
Middletown	502
Midway	859
Milburn	270
Milford	606
Mill Creek	606
Mill Springs	606
Millard	606
Millersburg	859
Millerstown	270
Mills	606
Millseat	606
Millstone	606
Milltown	270
Millwood	270
Milo	606
Milton	502
Mima	606
Minerva	606
Minnie	606
Minorsville	502
Miracle	606
Mistletoe	606
Mitchellsburg	859
Mize	606
Molus	606
Monford	270
Monterey	502
Montgomery	270
Monticello	606
Montpelier	270
Mooleyville	270
Moon	606
Moorefield	606
Moores Creek	606
Moranburg	606
Morehead	606
Morgan	859
Morganfield	270
Morganfld	270
Morgantown	270
Morning View	859
Morningglory	859
Morrill	606
Morris Fork	606
Mortons Gap	270
Moscow	270
Mount Auburn	859
Mount Carmel	606
Mount Eden	502
Mount Hermon	270
Mount Olivet	606
Mount Pisgah	606
Mount Sherman	270
Mount Sterling	859
Mount Vernon	606
Mount Washington	502
Mousie	606
Mouthcard	606
Mozelle	606
Mt Sterling	859
Mt Washington	502
Mud Lick	270
Muldraugh	502
Munfordville	270
Murphysville	606
Murray	270
Muses Mills	606
Myra	606
N Middletown	859
Nancy	606
Naomi	606
Napfor	606
Naples	606
Napoleon	859
Narrows	270
National City Bank	502
Natural Bridge	606
Nazareth	502
Neafus	270
Neave	859
Nebo	270
Ned	606
Needmore	606
Nelse	606
Neon	606
Nepton	606
Nerinx	270
Nevisdale	606
New Allen	606
New Castle	502
New Concord	270
New Cypress	270
New Haven	502
New Hope	502
New Liberty	502
New Salem	270
New Zion	606
Newfoundland	606
Newport	859
Nicholasville	859
Nicholson	859
Nineteen	270
Nippa	606
Noctor	606
North Middletown	859
Northern Kentucky University	859
Nortonville	270
Nuckols	270
Number One	606
Oak Grove	270
Oakdale	270
Oakland	270
Oakton	270
Oakville	270
Oddville	859
Offutt	606
Ogle	606
Oil Springs	606
Oil Valley	606
Okolona	502
Olaton	270
Old Allen	606
Old Landing	606
Oldtown	606
Olive Hill	606
Ollie	270
Olmstead	270
Olympia	606
Oneida	606
Ophir	606
Orangeburg	606
Orcutts Grocy	606
Orkney	606
Orlando	606
Osborn	606
Oscaloosa	606
Oven Fork	606
Overlook	270
Owen	502
Owensboro	270
Owenton	502
Owingsville	606
Paducah	270
Paducah Mall	270
Paint Lick	859
Paintsville	606
Palma	270
Paris	859
Park	270
Park City	270
Park Hills	859
Parkers Lake	606
Parksville	859
Parnell	606
Parrot	606
Partridge	606
Pathfork	606
Patsey	606
Paw Paw	606
Payne Gap	606
Payneville	270
Peabody	606
Peachgrove	859
Pebworth	606
Pecksridge	606
Pellville	270
Pembroke	270
Pendletn Cnty	859
Pendleton	502
Pendleton County	859
Penrod	270
Peonia	270
Peoples	606
Perry Park	502
Perryville	859
Petersburg	859
Petersville	606
Petra	606
Petros	270
Pewee Valley	502
Peytonsburg	270
Phelps	606
Philpot	270
Phyllis	606
Pikeville	606
Pilgrim	606
Pine Knot	606
Pine Mountain	606
Pine Ridge	606
Pine Top	606
Piner	859
Pineville	606
Pinsonfork	606
Pippa Passes	606
Piqua	606
Piso	606
Pittsburg	606
Plank	606
Pleasant Hill	859
Pleasanthill	859
Pleasure Rdge	502
Pleasure Ridge Park	502
Pleasureville	502
Plum Springs	270
Plummers Landing	606
Plummers Lndg	606
Plummers Mill	606
Plumville	606
Pnc Bank	502
Poindexter	859
Pointer	606
Pomeroyton	606
Poole	270
Poplar Flat	606
Poplar Plains	606
Poplarville	606
Port Royal	502
Portland	859
Potters Fork	606
Pottsville	270
Powderly	270
Powersburg	606
Powersville	606
Praise	606
Prater	606
Premium	606
Prentiss	270
Preston	606
Prestonsburg	606
Prestonville	502
Price	606
Pride	270
Primrose	606
Princess	606
Princeton	270
Printer	606
Prospect	502
Providence	270
Provo	270
Pryse	606
Public	606
Pueblo	606
Pulaski	606
Putney	606
Quality	270
Quebecor World	859
Quicksand	606
Quincy	606
Rabbit Hash	859
Raccoon	606
Raceland	606
Radcliff	270
Randolph	270
Ransom	606
Raven	606
Ravenna	606
Raymond	270
Raywick	270
Readers Digest	502
Rectorville	606
Red Bird	606
Redbud	606
Redbush	606
Redfox	606
Reed	270
Regina	606
Region	270
Reidland	270
Relief	606
Render	270
Renfro Valley	606
Repton	270
Revelo	606
Reynolds Sta	270
Reynolds Station	270
Rhodelia	270
Ribolt	606
Ricetown	606
Riceville	606
Richardson	606
Richardsville	270
Richelieu	270
Richmond	859
Richwood	859
Rineyville	270
Ringos Mills	606
Risner	606
Ritner	606
River	606
Road Creek Junction	606
Roaring Spring	270
Roark	606
Robards	270
Robinson Creek	606
Robinson Crk	606
Rochester	270
Rock Creek	270
Rockcastle	270
Rockdale	606
Rockfield	270
Rockholds	606
Rockhouse	606
Rockport	270
Rocky Hill	270
Rockybranch	606
Rogers	606
Rosedale	859
Rosine	270
Ross	859
Rosslyn	606
Roundhill	270
Rouse	859
Rousseau	606
Rowdy	606
Rowena	270
Rowletts	270
Roxana	606
Royalton	606
Rr Donnelly	502
Ruddels Mills	859
Rumsey	270
Rush	606
Russell	606
Russell Spgs	270
Russell Springs	270
Russellville	270
Ruth	606
Rutland	859
Ryland	859
Ryland Heights	859
Ryland Hght	859
Ryland Hgts	859
S Carrollton	270
S Ft Mitchell	859
S Newport	859
S Portsmouth	606
S Williamson	606
Sacramento	270
Sadieville	502
Saint Catharine	859
Saint Charles	270
Saint Francis	270
Saint Helens	606
Saint Johns	270
Saint Joseph	270
Saint Mary	270
Saint Matthews	502
Saint Paul	606
Saldee	606
Salem	270
Salt Gum	606
Salt Lick	606
Salvisa	859
Salyersville	606
Sample	270
Samuels	502
Sanders	502
Sandgap	606
Sandy Hook	606
Sardis	606
Sassafras	606
Sasser	606
Saul	606
Sawyer	606
Scalf	606
Schultztown	270
Science Hill	606
Scottsville	270
Scranton	606
Scuddy	606
Se Ree	270
Sebastians Br	606
Sebastians Branch	606
Sebree	270
Seco	606
Sedalia	270
Seitz	606
Seminary	606
Senterville	606
Seventy Six	606
Sewell	606
Sewellton	270
Sextons Creek	606
Shadynook	859
Shakertown	859
Shannon	606
Shared Firm Zip	502
Sharkey	606
Sharon	606
Sharon Grove	270
Sharpe	270
Sharpsburg	606
Shawhan	859
Shelbiana	606
Shelby Gap	606
Shelbyville	502
Shepherdsville	502
Shepherdsvlle	502
Sherburne	606
Sheridan	270
Sherman	859
Shiloh	270
Shively	502
Sidney	606
Siler	606
Silver Grove	859
Silverhill	606
Simpsonville	502
Sitka	606
Sizerock	606
Skyline	606
Slade	606
Slat	606
Slaughters	270
Slemp	606
Sloan	606
Sloans Valley	606
Smilax	606
Smith	606
Smith Mills	270
Smithfield	502
Smithland	270
Smiths Creek	606
Smiths Grove	270
Smoky Valley	606
Snow	606
So Baptist Theo Sem	502
So Fort Mitchell	859
So Newport	859
Soft Shell	606
Soldier	606
Somerset	606
Sonora	270
South Carrollton	270
South Fort Mitchell	859
South Newport	859
South Portsmouth	606
South Shore	606
South Union	270
South Williamson	606
Southgate	859
Sparta	859
Speight	606
Spence	859
Spottsville	270
Spring Grove	270
Spring Lick	270
Springfield	859
St Catharine	859
St Elmo	270
St Francis	270
St Joseph	270
St Mary	270
St Matthews	502
Stab	606
Stacy Fork	606
Staffordsville	606
Staffordsvlle	606
Stambaugh	606
Stamping Grd	502
Stamping Ground	502
Stanford	606
Stanley	270
Stanton	606
Stanville	606
Stark	606
Static	606
Stearns	606
Steele	606
Steff	270
Stella	606
Stephens	606
Stephensburg	270
Stephensport	270
Steubenville	606
Stinnett	606
Stone	606
Stonewall	606
Stoney Fork	606
Stop	606
Stopover	606
Straight Creek	606
Strunk	606
Sturgis	270
Sublett	606
Subtle	270
Sudith	606
Sullivan	270
Sulphur	502
Sulphur Well	270
Summer Shade	270
Summersville	270
Summit	270
Summitt	606
Sunfish	270
Sunnybrook	606
Sunrise	859
Susie	606
Sutton	606
Suwanee	270
Swamp Branch	606
Swampton	606
Swanpond	606
Sweeden	270
Symbol	606
Symsonia	270
T Ville	270
Talbert	606
Talcum	606
Tallega	606
Tanksley	606
Tateville	606
Taulbee	606
Taylor Mill	859

Taylor Mines 270
Taylorsport 859
Taylorsville 502
Teaberry 606
Tedders 606
Thealka 606
Thelma 606
Thornton 606
Thousandsticks 606
Three Point 606
Threeforks 606
Threlkel 270
Thsandsticks 606
Tiline 270
Tilton 606
Tina 606
Tinsley 606
Tiny Town 270
Toler 606
Tollesboro 606
Tolliver Town 606
Tolu 270
Tomahawk 606
Tompkinsville 270
Toonerville 606
Topmost 606
Totz 606
Toulouse 606
Touristville 606
Trace 606
Tram 606
Trammel 270
Trappist 502
Trenton 270
Tribbey 606
Tribune 270
Trigg Furnace 270
Trimble 606
Trinity 606
Trisler 270
Trosper 606
Turkey 606
Turkey Creek 606
Turners Sta 502
Turners Station 502
Tutor Key 606
Tuttle 606
Tyner 606
Typo 606
Ulvah 606
Ulysses 606
Union 859
Union Star 270
Uniontown 270
Univ Of Louisville 502
University 270
University Of Ky 859
University Of Ky Agri Dept 859
University Of Ky Med Ctr 859
University Of Ky Res Halls 859
Upper Tygart 606
Upton 270
Urban 606
Utica 270
Vada 606
Valeria 606
Valley Station 502
Valley Statn 502
Van 606
Van Cleve 270
Van Lear 606
Vanceburg 606
Vancleve 606
Vanzant 270
Varney 606
Venters 606
Verona 859
Versailles 859
Vertrees 270
Vest 606
Vicco 606
Victory 606
Villa Hills 859
Vincent 606
Vine Grove 270
Viola 270
Viper 606
Virgie 606
Visalia 859
Volga 606
W Louisville 270
Waco 859
Waddy 502
Waldo 606
Wales 606
Walker 606
Walkertown 606
Wallingford 606
Wallins 606
Wallins Creek 606
Wallsend 606
Walnut Grove 606
Walton 859
Waneta 606
Warbranch 606
Warco 606
Warfield 606
Warsaw 859
Washington 606
Water Valley 270
Watergap 606
Waterview 270
Waverly 270
Wax 270
Wayland 606
Waynesburg 606
Webbs Cross Roads 270
Webbs Crs Rds 270
Webbville 606
Webster 270
Wedonia 606
Weeksbury 606
Welchs Creek 270
Wellington 606
Wellsburg 606
Wendover 606
Wentz 606
West Buechel 502
West Fairview 606
West Irvine 606
West Liberty 606
West Louisville 270
West Paducah 270
West Point 502
West Somerset 606
West Van Lear 606
West Viola 270
Westbend 606
Westport 502
Westview 270
Westwood 606
Wheatcroft 270
Wheatley 502
Wheelwright 606
Whick 606
White City 270
White Mills 270
White Oak 606
White Plains 270
White Tower 859
Whitehouse 606
Whitesburg 606
Whitesville 270
Whitley City 606
Wickliffe 270
Widecreek 606
Wilbur 606
Wildcat 606
Wilder 859
Wildie 859
Willard 606
Williamsburg 606
Williamsport 606
Williamstown 859
Willisburg 859
Willow 606
Willow Grove 606
Willow Shade 270
Wilmore 859
Wilsonville 502
Winchester 859
Wind Cave 606
Windsor 606
Windy 606
Wingo 270
Winifred 606
Winslow Park 270
Winston 859
Wittensville 606
Wolf 606
Wolf Coal 606
Wolf Creek 270
Wolfpit 606
Wolverine 606
Wonnie 606
Woodbine 606
Woodburn 270
Woodbury 270
Woodlawn 859
Woodman 606
Woods 606
Woolcott 606
Woollum 606
Wooton 606
Worthington 606
Worthville 502
Wrigley 606
Wurtland 606
Yeaddiss 606
Yeaman 270
Yellow Rock 606
Yerkes 606
Yocum 606
Yocum Creek 606
Yosemite 606
Zachariah 606
Zoe 606

Louisiana

9 Mile Point 504
Abbeville 337
Abita Springs 985
Acme 318
Addis 225
Adner 318
Aimwell 318
Ajax 318
Akers 985
Albany 225
Alex 318
Alexandria 318
Alfalfa 318
Algiers 504
Allemand 985
Allen 318
Aloha 318
Alto 318
Ama 504
Amelia 985
Amite 985
Anacoco 318
Anandale 318
Angie 985
Angola 225
Ansley 318
Antonia 318
Arabi 504
Arcadia 318
Archibald 318
Archie 318
Arcola 985
Arizona 318
Arkansas Louisiana Gas 318
Arkla Gas 318
Armistead 318
Arnaudville 337
Ashland 318
Ashley 318
Athens 318
Atlanta 318
Avery Island 337
Avondale 504
Aycock 318
Azucena 318
Bagdad 318
Bains 225
Baker 225
Baldwin 337
Ball 318
Balmoral 318
Banks Springs 318
Barataria 504
Barksdale Afb 318
Barnet Springs 318
Barron 318
Basile 337
Baskin 318
Bastrop 318
Batchelor 225
Baton Rouge 225
Bawcomville 318
Bayou Blue 985
Bayou Current 337
Bayou Goula 225
Bayou Petite Prairie 337
Bayou Rouge 337
Bayou Vista 985
Beachview 504
Bear Creek 318
Beaver 318
Bee Bayou 318
Beekman 318
Belair 504
Belcher 318
Bell City 337
Belle Chasse 504
Belle Chasse Nas 504
Belle Point 985
Belle Rose 985
Bellevue 318
Bellview 318
Bellwood 318
Belmont 318
Bennetts Bay 318
Benson 318
Bentley 318
Benton 318
Bernice 318
Berwick 985
Bethany 318
Bethel 318
Bienville 318
Big Island 318
Big Ridge 318
Black Hawk 318
Blackburn 318
Blade 318
Blanchard 318
Blanche 318
Blanks 225
Blue Lake 318
Bodcau 318
Bodoc 318
Bogalusa 985
Bohemia 985
Boline 318
Bond 318
Bonita 318
Book 318
Boothville 985
Bordelonville 318
Borodino 318
Bosco 318
Bossier City 318
Bougere 318
Bourg 985
Boutte 985
Boyce 318
Braithwaite 504
Branch 337
Breaux Bridge 337
Breezy Hill 318
Bridge City 504
Brittany 225
Broadmoor 504
Brookwood 318
Brouillette 318
Broussard 337
Brownsville 318
Brownville 318
Bruly Saint Martin 985
Brusly 225
Bryceland 318
Buckeye 318
Bucks Landing 318
Bueche 225
Bunkie 318
Buras 985
Burns Town 318
Burnside 225
Burroughs 318
Burrwood 985
Bush 985
Bushes 318
Butte Larose 337
Bywater 504
C O Enl Pers Mgmt Cen 504
Caddo 318
Cade 337
Cadeville 318
Cal Marne Twr 337
Calcasieu 318
Calcasieu Marine Tower 337
Calhoun 318
Calloway Corners 318
Calumet 985
Calvin 318
Cameron 337
Camp Beauregard 318
Camp Claiborne 318
Camp Stafford 318
Campground 318
Campti 318
Cane River 318
Cankton 337
Carencro 337
Carlisle 504
Carlton 318
Carrollton 504
Cartwright 318
Carville 225
Caspiana 318
Castle Village 318
Castor 318
Castor Lane 318
Castor Plunge 318
Cecilia 337
Cedar Grove 318
Centenary 318
Center Point 318
Centerville 337
Central 225
Chalmette 504
Chambers 318
Chandler Park 318
Charenton 337
Charles Park 318
Chase 318
Chataignier 337
Chatham 318
Chauvin 985
Chef Menteur 504
Cheneyville 318
Cheniere 318
Cherokee Village 318
Chestnut 318
Chickama 318
Chickasaw 318
Chipola 225
Chopin 318
Choudrant 318
Choupique 318
Church Point 337
Claiborne 985
Clare 318
Clarence 318
Clarks 318
Clayton 318
Clayton Junction 318
Clearwater 318
Clifton 318
Clinton 225
Cloutierville 318
Cnb 318
Cocodrie 985
Cocoville 318
Colfax 318
Colgrade 318
Collinston 318
Colquitt 318
Columbia 318
Columbia Heights 318
Commerce Park 225
Commercial National Bank 318
Concord 318
Concordia Lake 318
Consuella 318
Convent 225
Converse 318
Coopers 337
Cooters Point 318
Copenhagen 318
Corey 318
Corinth 318
Cotile 318
Cotton Valley 318
Cottonport 318
Coushatta 318
Covington 985
Cow Island 337
Cp Beauregard 318
Crackville 318
Creole 337
Creston 318
Crew Lake 318
Crews 318
Crowley 337
Crowville 318
Cullen 318
Custom House 504
Cut Off 985
Cypremort Point 337
Cypremort Pt 337
Cypress 318
Cypress Gardens 504
Danville 318
Darrow 225
Davant 504, 985
Dean Chapel 318
Deer Park 318
Dehlco 318
Delacroix 504
Delcambre 337
Delhi 318
Delta 318
Delta Garden 318
Denham Spgs 225
Denham Springs 225
Dennis Mills 225
Dequincy 337
Deridder 337
Derry 318
Des Allemands 985
Destrehan 985
Deville 318
Dewdrop 318
Dixie 318
Dodson 318
Dogwood Terrace 337
Dona 318
Donaldsonville 225
Donaldsonvlle 225
Donner 985
Dora Bend 318
Doty Garden 318
Downsville 318
Dowus 318
Doyline 318
Drew 318, 337
Dry Creek 337
Dry Prong 318
Dubach 318
Dubberly 318
Dulac 985
Dunbarton 318
Dunn 318
Duplessis 225
Dupont 318
Duson 337
Duty Ferry 318
Dykesville 318
East Hodge 318
East Point 318
East Winnfield 318

City	Area Code
Eastside	318
Ebarb	318
Echo	318
Edgard	985
Effie	318
Egan	337
Elam	318
Elba	337
Elizabeth	318
Elm Grove	318
Elmer	318
Elmwood	504
Elton	337
Empire	985
Energy Center	337
Englewood	318
Entergy Corp	225
Enterprise	318
Eola	318
Epps	318
Erath	337
Eros	318
Erwinville	225
Esler	318
Estherwood	337
Ethel	225
Eunice	337
Eureka	318
Eva	318
Evangeline	337
Evans	337
Evergreen	318
Extension	318
Fairbanks	318
Fairgrounds	318
Fairmont	318
Fairview	318
Farmerville	318
Fellowship	318
Fenton	337
Ferriday	318
Fields	337
Fifth Ward	318
Fillmore	318
First Natl Bank Commerce	504
Fisher	318
Fishville	318
Flat Creek	318
Flatwoods	318
Fletcher	318
Flora	318
Florien	318
Flournoy	318
Flowers Landing	318
Fluker	985
Folsom	985
Fondale	318
Forbing	318
Fordoche	225
Forest	318
Forest Hill	318
Forest Park	318
Forksville	318
Fort De Russy	318
Fort Jessup	318
Fort Necessity	318
Fort Polk	337
Foules	318
Four Forks	318
Fr Settlement	225
Francis Place	504
Franklin	337
Franklinton	985
French Settlement	225
Friendship	318
Frierson	318
Frogmore	318
Frost Town	318
Ft Necessity	318
Fullerton	318
Gaars Mill	318
Gahagan	318
Galbraith	318
Galliano	985
Galvez	225
Gandy Spur	318
Gansville	318
Garden City	337
Gardner	318
Garyville	985
Gassoway	318
Gateway	225
Geismar	225
General Mail Facility	225
Gentilly	504
Georgetown	318
Gheens	985
Gibsland	318
Gibson	985
Gilark	318
Gilbert	318
Gilliam	318
Girard	318
Glenmora	318
Glenwild	985
Gloster	318
Glynn	225
Gmf	225
Golden Meadow	985
Goldman	318
Goldonna	318
Gonzales	225
Gooberville	318
Good Hope	985
Good Pine	318
Goodwill	318
Goodwood	337
Gordon	318
Gorhamtown	318
Gorum	318
Goudeau	318
Grambling	318
Gramercy	225
Grand Cane	318
Grand Chenier	337
Grand Coteau	337
Grand Isle	985
Grangeville	985
Grant	337
Gray	985
Grayson	318
Green Acres	318
Green Gables	318
Green Lawn Terrace	504
Greensburg	225
Greenwel Spgs	225
Greenwell Springs	225
Greenwood	318
Gretna	504
Grosse Tete	225
Gueydan	337
Gum Springs Road	318
Hackberry	337
Hagewood	318
Hahnville	985
Haile	318
Hall	318
Hall Summit	318
Hamburg	318
Hammet	318
Hammond	985
Hanna	318
Harahan	504
Hardwood	225
Hargis	318
Harmon	318
Harmony	318
Harrisonburg	318
Hart	318
Harvey	504
Hatcher	318
Haughton	318
Hawthorne	337
Hayes	337
Haynesville	318
Head Of Island	225
Hearn Island	318
Hebert	318
Hebron	318
Heflin	318
Helena	318
Henderson	337
Hessmer	318
Hester	225
Hi Land	504
Hibernia Natl Bk	504
Hickory	318
Hickory Grove	318
Hickory Valley	318
Hicks	337
Highland	318
Highland Park	318
Hillsdale	985
Hilly	318
Hineston	318
Hodge	318
Holden	225
Holloway	318
Holly	318
Holly Grove	318
Holly Ridge	318
Hollybrook	318
Holsey	318
Home Place	985
Homer	318
Hootenville	985
Hopedale	504
Hornbeck	318
Hosston	318
Hotwells	318
Houma	985
Houston Spur	318
Hudson	318
Husser	985
Hyde	318
Hydropolis	318
Iatt Lake	318
Iberville	225
Ida	318
Idlewild	985
Independence	985
Indian Creek	318
Indian Village	318
Industrial	318
Innis	225
Iota	337
Iowa	337
Irma	318
Ironton	985
Island Road	318
Ivan	318
Jackson	225
Jamestown	318
Jarreau	225
Jeanerette	337
Jefferson	504
Jena	318
Jennings	337
Jigger	318
Johnson Bayou	337
Johnsons Bayou	337
Jones	318
Jonesboro	318
Jonesburg	318
Jonesville	318
Jowers	318
Joyce	318
Junction City	318
Junks	318
Kadesh	318
Kaplan	337
Keatchie	318
Keithville	318
Kelly	318
Kellys	318
Kemps Landing	318
Kendricks Ferry	318
Kenilworth	504
Kenner	504
Kentwood	985
Kickapoo	318
Kilbourne	318
Killian	225
Killona	985
Kinder	337
Kingston	318
Kingsville	318
Kiroli Woods	318
Kisatchie	318
Kolin	318
Koran	318
Kraemer	985
Krotz Springs	337
Kurthwood	318
La Camp	318
La Chute	318
La College	318
La Dept Of Revenue	225
La Dept Reven	225
La Gas Serv Inc	504
La Lottery	225
La Place	985
La Power Light	504
La St Univ	225
La Tech	318
Labadieville	985
Labarre	225
Lacamp	318
Lacassine	337
Lacombe	985
Lafayette	337
Lafayette Square	504
Lafitte	504
Lake	225
Lake Arthur	337
Lake Bruin	318
Lake Charles	337
Lake Providence	318
Lake Saint John	318
Lakeland	225
Lakeshore	318
Lakeside	318
Lamkin	318
Lamourie	318
Lapine	318
Laplace	985
Larose	985
Larto	318
Latanier	318
Lawhon	318
Lawtell	337
Le Moyen	318
Leander	318
Lebeau	337
Leblanc	337
Lecompte	318
Lees Creek	985
Leesville	337
Leeville	985
Leland	318
Lemoine Town	318
Lena	318
Leonville	337
Lettsworth	318
Levee Heights	318
Levens Addition	318
Lewisburg	985
Liberty Hill	318
Libuse	318
Liddieville	318
Lillie	318
Linville	318
Lions	985
Lisbon	318
Lismore	318
Litroe	318
Little Caillou	985
Little Creek	318
Little Egypt	318
Livingston	225
Livonia	225
Lk Providence	318
Lockhart	318
Lockport	985
Locust Ridge	318
Log Cabin	318
Logansport	318
Loggy Bayou	318
Logtown	318
Lonepine	318
Longbridge	318
Longlake	318
Longleaf	318
Longstreet	318
Longville	337
Loranger	985
Loreauville	337
Lottie	225
Louisiana College	318
Louisiana Lottery	225
Louisiana Tech	318
Louisiana Tech Univ	318
Loyds Bridge	318
Lucerne	318
Lucky	318
Luling	985
Luna	318
Lutcher	225
Lydia	337
Madison Park	318
Madisonville	985
Magda	318
Magnolia	985
Mamou	337
Mandeville	985
Mangham	318
Manifest	318
Mansfield	318
Mansura	318
Mansura Junction	318
Many	318
Marco	318
Maringouin	225
Marion	318
Marksville	318
Marrero	504
Mars Hill	318
Marthaville	318
Martin Park	318
Mathews	985
Maurepas	225
Maurice	337
Mayflower	318
Mayna	318
Mccall	225
Mcdade	318
Mcintyre	318
Mcnary	318
Mcneely	318
Mcneese State University	337
Mcnutt	318
Meaux	337
Meeker	318
Melder	318
Melrose	318
Melville	337
Mer Rouge	318
Meraux	504
Mermentau	337
Merryville	337
Metairie	504
Midland	337
Midway	318
Millerton	318
Millikin	318
Milton	337
Minden	318
Minorca	318
Mira	318
Mitch	985
Mitchell	318
Mitchell City	985
Mittie	337
Modeste	225
Moncla	318
Monette Ferry	318
Monroe	318
Montcalm	318
Montecello	318
Montegut	985
Montgomery	318
Monticello	318
Montpelier	985
Montrose	318
Montz	985
Mooringsport	318
Mora	318
Moreauville	318
Moreland	318
Morgan City	985
Morganza	225
Morrow	318
Morse	337
Morville	318
Moss Bluff	337
Mound	318
Mount Airy	985
Mount Carmel	318
Mount Hermon	985
Mount Lebanon	318
Mount Olive	318
Mount Sinai	318
Mount Union	318
Mount Zion	318
Mudville	318
Myrtle Grove	985
Nantatchie	318
Napoleonville	985
Natalbany	985
Natch	318
Natchez	318
Natchitoches	318
Naval Air Sta N O	504
Naval Reserve Pers Ctr	504
Naval Supp Act East Bank	504
Naval Support Act Westbank	504
Navy Reg Data Auto Ctr	504
Nebo	318
Negreet	318
New Belledeau	318
New Era	318
New Hope	318
New Iberia	337
New Light	318
New Orleans	504
New Orleans Naval Air	504
New Orleans Pub Serv	504
New Roads	225
New Salem	318
New Sarpy	985
New Verda	318
New Verda Community	318
New Zion	985
Newellton	318
Newlight	318
Newllano	337
Noble	318
Noles Landing	318
Norco	985
North Hodge	318
North Shore	985
Northeast	318
Northeast Univ	318
Northwestern	318
Norwood	225
Notnac	318
Nsu	318
Oak Grove	318
Oak Ridge	318
Oakdale	318
Oakland	318
Oaks	318
Oberlin	337
Odenburg	318
Odra	318
Oil City	318
Okaloosa	318
Olinkraft	318
Olla	318
Omega	318
One Amer Pl	225
One American Place	225
Opelousas	337
Ormond	985
Oscar	225
Ostrica	985
Otis	318
Pace	318
Paincourtville	985
Paincourtvlle	985
Palmetto	337
Panola	318
Paradis	985
Paradise	318
Parhams	318

City	Area Code
Parks	337
Patch Leg	318
Patterson	985
Paulina	225
Pawnee	318
Pearl River	985
Peason	318
Pecan Acres	318
Peck	318
Pelican	318
Pendleton	318
Perry	337
Perryville	318
Pickering	337
Pierre Part	985
Pilottown	985
Pine Coupee	318
Pine Grove	225
Pine Prairie	337
Pineville	318
Pioneer	318
Pitkin	318
Plain Dealing	318
Plainview	985
Plaquemine	225
Plattenville	985
Plaucheville	318
Pleasant Hill	318
Pleasant Ridge	318
Point	318
Pointe A La Hache	985
Pollock	318
Ponchatoula	985
Poole	318
Port Allen	225
Port Barre	337
Port Eads	985
Port Sulphur	985
Port Vincent	225
Porterville	318
Potash	985
Powhatan	318
Poydras	504
Prairieville	225
Premier Bank	318
Pride	225
Princeton	318
Prospect	318
Provencal	318
Pt A La Hache	985
Quaid	318
Quimby	318
Quitman	318
Raceland	985
Ragley	337
Ramah	225
Rapides	318
Rattan	318
Rayne	337
Rayville	318
Red Chute	318
Red Fish	318
Red Gum	318
Reddell	337
Reeves	337
Reggio	504
Reserve	985
Rexmere	318
Rhinehart	318
Richmond	318
Richwood	318
Ridgecrest	318
Ringgold	318
Rio	985
Risinger Woods	318
River Ridge	504
Riverton	318
Riverwood	985
Roanoke	337
Robeline	318
Robert	985
Rock	318
Rock Hill	318
Rock Quarry	318
Rocky Branch	318
Rodessa	318
Rodoc	318
Rogers	318
Roosevelt	318
Rosa	337
Rosedale	225
Rosefield	318
Roseland	985
Rosepine	337
Rougon	225
Routon	318
Roxana	318
Roy	318
Ruby	318
Ruple	318
Ruston	318
Sabine	318
Sailes	318
Saint Amant	225
Saint Benedict	985
Saint Bernard	504
Saint Francisville	225
Saint Gabriel	225
Saint Gertrude	985
Saint James	225
Saint Joseph	318
Saint Landry	318
Saint Martinville	337
Saint Maurice	318
Saint Rose	985
Saline	318
Sanbeimer	318
Sandy Hill	337
Saranac	318
Sardis	318
Sarepta	318
Schriever	985
Scotlandville	225
Scott	337
Searcy	318
Selma	318
Sentell	318
Sewage Water Board	504
Shamrock	318
Sharp	318
Shaw	318
Shelburn	318
Shell Beach	504
Shell Point	318
Shelton	318
Sheridan	985
Shiloh	318
Shongaloo	318
Shreve Island	318
Shreveport	318
Shrewsbury	504
Sibley	318
Sicily Island	318
Siegle	318
Sieper	318
Sikes	318
Simmesport	318
Simms	318
Simpson	337
Simsboro	318
Singer	337
Slagle	337
Slaughter	225
Slidell	985
Sligo	318
Slu	985
Somerset	318
Sondheimer	318
Sorrento	225
South Central Bell	504
South Kenner	504
South Pass	985
Southeastern Louisiana Univ	985
Southern	225
Southern Hills	318
Southern University	225
Southfield	318
Spanish Lake	318
Spearsville	318
Spencer	318
Splane Place	318
Spokane	318
Spring Lake	318
Springcreek	985
Springfield	225
Springhill	318
Springridge	318
St Benedict	985
St Bernard	504
St Bernard Grove	504
St Charles	985
St Francisvle	225
St Genevieve	318
St Gertrude	985
St James	225
St Joseph	318
St Landry	318
St Martinvlle	337
St Maurice	318
St Rose	985
Standard	318
Starks	337
Start	318
Sterlington	318
Stonewall	318
Sugartown	337
Sulphur	337
Summer Grove	318
Summerfield	318
Summerville	318
Sun	985
Sunnyhill	985
Sunset	337
Sunset Acres	318
Sunshine	225
Swampers	318
Swartz	318
Sweet Lake	337
Swepco	318
Taconey	318
Talisheek	985
Talla Bena	318
Tallulah	318
Tangipahoa	985
Tanglewood	318
Tannehill	318
Taylor	318
Taylor Hill	318
Taylortown	318
Temple	337
Tensas Bluff	318
Terry	318
Terrytown	504
The Bluffs	225
Theriot	985
Thibodaux	985
Thomas	985
Thomastown	318
Three Bridges	318
Tickfaw	985
Timber Trails	318
Timberlake	318
Tioga	318
Toca	504
Toledo Bend	318
Torbert	225
Toro	318
Transylvania	318
Trees	318
Trinity	318
Triumph	985
Trout	318
Tullos	318
Tunica	225
Turkey Creek	337
Turtle Lake	318
Uncle Sam	225
Uneedus	985
Union Church	318
Union Grove	318
Union Hill	318
Union Springs	318
Unionville	318
University	225
University Of New Orleans	504
Upland	318
Urania	318
Utility	318
Vacherie	225
Varnado	985
Venice	985
Ventress	225
Verda	318
Vernon	318
Verret	504
Vick	318
Vidalia	318
Vienna	318
Ville Platte	337
Vines Loop	318
Vinton	337
Violet	504
Vivian	318
Vixen	318
Voorhies	318
Vowells Mill	318
Waggaman	504
Wakefield	225
Walker	225
Wall Lake	318
Wallace	985
Wallace Ridge	318
Walters	318
Ward	318
Warden	318
Wardville	318
Washington	337
Water Department	318
Waterproof	318
Watson	225
Waverly	318
Weil	318
Weldon	318
Welsh	337
West Monroe	318
West Pointe A La Hache	985
Westlake	337
Weston	318
Westwego	504
Westwood	318
Weyanoke	225
Whatley Landing	318
Wheeling	318
White Castle	225
White Sulphur Springs	318
Whitehall	318
Whiteville	318
Whitney National Bank	504
Wilda	318
Wildsville	318
Willhite	318
Williana	318
Willow Glen	318
Wilshire Park	318
Wilson	225
Wilsona	318
Winnfield	318
Winnsboro	318
Wisner	318
Womack	318
Woodardville	318
Woodside	337
Woodville	318
Woodworth	318
Workinger Bayou Road	318
Wyatt	318
Youngsville	337
Youree	318
Zachary	225
Zenoria	318
Zimmer	318
Zion	318
Zion City	225
Zwolle	318
Zylks	318

Maine

City	Area Code
All Points	207

Marshall Islands

City	Area Code
All Points	691

Maryland

City	Area Code
Abell	301
Aber Prov Grd	410
Aberdeen	410
Aberdeen Proving Ground	410
Abingdon	410
Accident	301
Accokeek	301
Adamstown	301
Adelphi	301
Allen	410
Andrews Afb	301
Andrews Air Force Base	301
Annapolis	410
Annapolis Jct	301
Annapolis Junction	301
Apg	410
Aquasco	301
Arbutus	410
Ardmore	301
Arlington	410
Arnold	410
Ashton	301
Aspen Hill	301
Avenue	301
Avondale	301
Bainbridge	410
Baldwin	410
Baltimore	410
Baltimore Sunpapers	410
Bancroft Hall	410
Bank Of America	410
Bank One	410
Barclay	410
Barnesville	301
Barstow	410
Barton	301
Beachville	301
Beallsville	301
Bel Air	410
Bel Alton	301
Belcamp	410
Beltsville	301
Benedict	410
Benson	410
Bentley Spgs	410
Bentley Springs	410
Berlin	410
Berwyn	301
Berwyn Heights	301
Berwyn Hts	301
Bethesda	301
Bethlehem	410
Betterton	410
Beverley Bch	410
Big Pool	301
Big Spring	301
Bishop	410
Bishopville	410
Bittinger	301
Bivalve	410
Bladensburg	301
Bloomington	301
Boonsboro	301
Boring	410
Bowie	301
Boyds	301
Bozman	410
Braddock Heights	301
Braddock Hts	301
Bradshaw	410
Brandywine	301
Brentwd	301
Brentwood	301
Brinklow	301
Brookeville	301
Brooklandville	410
Brooklandvl	410
Brooklyn	410
Brooklyn Park	410
Broomes Is	410
Broomes Island	410
Brownsville	301
Brunswick	301
Bryans Rd	301
Bryans Road	301
Bryantown	301
Buckeystown	301
Burkittsville	301
Burtonsville	301
Bushwood	301
Butler	410
Bwi Airport	410
Cabin John	301
California	410
Callaway	301
Calverton	301
Cambridge	410
Camp Springs	301
Cape Saint Claire	410
Capitol Heights	301
Capitol Heights Po	301
Capitol Hgts	301
Cardiff	410
Carroll	410
Carrollton	410
Cascade	301
Catonsville	410
Cavetown	301
Cecilton	410
Census Bureau	410
Centreville	410
Chance	410
Chaptico	301
Charlestown	410
Charlott Hall	301
Charlotte Hall	301
Chase	410
Cheltenham	202, 301
Chesapeak Bch	410
Chesapeake Beach	410
Chesapeake City	410
Chesapeake Cy	410
Chester	410
Chestertown	410
Cheverly	301
Chevy Chase	301
Chewsville	301
Childs	410
Chillum	301
Church Creek	410
Church Hill	410
Churchton	410
Churchville	410
Citicorp	301
Citicorp (Brm)	301
Claiborne	410
Clarksburg	301
Clarksville	410
Clear Spring	301
Clements	301
Clifton	410
Clifton East End	410
Clinton	301
Cloverly	301
Cobb Island	301
Cockeysville	410
Cockeysville Hunt Valley	410
Cockys Ht Vly	410
Cockysvil	410
Colesville	301
College Estates	301
College Park	301
Colmar Manor	301
Colora	410
Coltons Point	301
Columbia	202, 410
Compton	301
Comptroller Of The Treasury	410
Comus	301
Conowingo	410
Cooksville	410
Cordova	410
Corriganville	301
Cottage City	301

City	Code
Cpe St Claire	410
Crapo	410
Crellin	301
Cresaptown	301
Crestar Bank	410
Crisfield	410
Crocheron	410
Crofton	410
Crownsville	410
Crumpton	410
Cumberland	301
Curtis Bay	410
Damascus	301
Dameron	301
Dames Quarter	410
Daniels	410
Dares Beach	410
Darlington	410
Darnestown	301
Davidsonville	410
Dayton	301
Deal Island	410
Deale	410
Deer Park	301
Delmar	410
Denton	410
Dentsville	301
Dept Hs	202
Derwood	301
Detour	410
Dhs	202
Dickerson	301
District Heights	301
District Hts	301
Doubs	301
Dowell	410
Drayden	301
Druid	410
Dundalk	410
Dundalk Sparrows Point	410
Dunkirk	410
E New Market	410
Earleville	410
East Case	410
East End	410
East New Market	410
Eastern Correctional Inst	410
Easton	410
Easton Correctional Inst	410
Eastport	410
Eckhart Mines	301
Eden	410
Edgemere	410
Edgewater	410
Edgewater Bch	410
Edgewood	410
Edgewood Arsenal	410
Edmonston	301
Eldersburg	410
Elk Mills	410
Elkridge	410
Elkton	410
Ellerslie	301
Ellicott	410
Ellicott City	410
Elliott	410
Emmitsburg	301
Essex	410
Eudowood	410
Ewell	410
Fairhaven	410
Fairmount	410
Fairmount Heights	301
Fairmount Hgt	301
Fairplay	301
Fallston	410
Faulkner	301
Federalsburg	410
Finksburg	410
Firms-Business Reply	410
Firms-Courtesy Reply	410
Fishing Creek	410
Flintstone	301
Forest Heights	301
Forest Hill	410
Forest Hts	301
Forestville	301
Fork	410
Fort Detrick	301
Fort George G Meade	410
Fort George Meade	410
Fort Howard	410
Fort Meade	410
Fort Ritchie	301
Fort Washington	301
Fowbelsburg	410
Foxridge	410
Franklin	410
Frederick	301
Freeland	410
Friendship	410
Friendsville	301
Frostburg	301
Fruitland	410
Ft George G Meade	410
Ft Meade	410
Ft Washington	301
Fulton	301
Funkstown	301
Gaither	410
Gaithersburg	301
Galena	410
Galesville	410
Gambrills	410
Gapland	301
Garrett Park	301
Garrison	410
Geico	301
Georgetown	410
Germantown	301
Gibson Island	410
Girdletree	410
Glen Arm	410
Glen Burnie	410
Glen Echo	301
Glenarden	301
Glenburnie	410
Glencoe	410
Glenelg	410
Glenmont	301
Glenn Dale	301
Glenwood	410
Glyndon	410
Goddard Flight Center	301
Goldsboro	410
Golts	410
Govans	410
Graceham	301
Granite	410
Grantsville	301
Grasonville	410
Great Mills	301
Green Meadow	301
Greenbelt	301
Greenmount	410
Greensboro	410
Gunpowder	410
Gwynn Oak	410
Hagerstown	301
Halethorpe	410
Hamilton	410
Hampden	410
Hampstead	410
Hancock	301
Hanover	410
Harmans	410
Harwood	410
Havre De Grace	410
Hebron	410
Helen	301
Henderson	410
Henryton	410
Hereford	410
Hhs	301
Highfield	301
Highland	301
Highland Bch	410
Highlandtown	410
Hillandale	301
Hillcrest Heights	301
Hillcrest Hgts	301
Hillcrest Hts	301
Hillsboro	410
Holland Point	410
Hollywood	301
Hood College	301
Hoopersville	410
Household Bank	410
Hughesville	301
Hunt Valley	410
Huntingtown	410
Huntvalley	410
Hurlock	410
Hutton	301
Hvre De Grace	410
Hyattstown	301
Hyattsville	301
Hydes	410
Ijamsville	301
Ilchester	410
Indian Head	301
Ingleside	410
Ironsides	301
Issue	301
Jacksonville	410
Jarrettsville	410
Jefferson	301
Jennings	301
Jessup	410
Johns Hopkins	410
Johns Hopkins Hospital	410
Joppa	410
Joppatown	410
Joppatowne	410
Keedysville	301
Kennedyville	410
Kensington	301
Kettering	301
Keymar	410
Kingston	410
Kingsville	410
Kitzmiller	301
Knoxville	301
La Plata	301
Ladiesburg	410
Lake Linganore	301
Lake Shore	410
Landover	301
Landover Hills	301
Landover Hls	301
Langley Park	301
Lanham	301
Lanham Seabrook	301
Lansdowne	410
Laplata	301
Largo	301
Laurel	301
Lavale	301
Laytonsville	301
Leisure World	301
Leonardtown	301
Lewisdale	301
Lewistown	301
Lex Pk	301
Lexington Park	301
Lexington Pk	301
Libertytown	301
Lineboro	410
Linkwood	410
Linthicum	410
Linthicum Heights	410
Linthicum Hts	410
Linwood	410
Lisbon	410
Little Orleans	301
Loch Raven	410
Lonaconing	301
Long Green	410
Lothian	301
Loveville	301
Ltl Orleans	301
Luke	301
Lusby	410
Lutherville	410
Lutherville Timonium	410
Luthvle Timon	410
Lynch	410
M T Bank	410
Maddox	301
Madison	410
Magnolia	410
Manchester	410
Manokin	410
Marbury	301
Mardela	410
Mardela Spgs	410
Mardela Springs	410
Marion	410
Marion Sta	410
Marion Station	410
Marlboro	301
Marlow Heights	301
Marlow Hgts	301
Marriottsville	410
Marriottsvl	410
Marshall Hall	301
Marydel	410
Maryland City	301
Maryland Correctional System	301
Maryland Line	410
Maryland Motor Vehicle Admin	410
Massey	410
Maugansville	301
Mayo	410
Mc Henry	301
Mccoole	301
Mcdaniel	410
Mcdonogh Run	410
Mchenry	301
Md City	301
Mechanicsville	301
Mechanicsvlle	301
Middle River	410
Middleburg	410
Middletown	301
Midland	301
Midlothian	301
Millers	410
Millersville	410
Millington	410
Mitchellville	301
Mnt Lake Park	301
Monkton	410
Monrovia	301
Montgomery Village	301
Montgomry Vlg	301
Montpelier	301
Morgan State University	410
Morganza	301
Morningside	301
Mount Airy	301
Mount Rainier	301
Mount Savage	301
Mount Victoria	301
Mount Washington	410
Mountain Lake Park	301
Mt Lake Park	301
Mt Rainier	301
Mt Victoria	301
Mt Washington	410
Mtin Lk Park	301
Myersville	301
N Beach	410
N Bethesda	301
N Brentwood	301
N Englewood	301
N Potomac	301
Nanjemoy	301
Nanticoke	410
National Harbor	301
National Institute Of Health	301
National Library Of Medicine	301
National Naval Medical Ctr	301
Natl Institute Stds & Tech	301
Naval Academy	410
Neavitt	410
New Carrolltn	301
New Carrollton	301
New Market	301
New Midway	301
New Windsor	410
Newark	410
Newburg	301
Newcomb	410
No Bethesda	301
No Brentwood	301
No Potomac	301
Norbeck	301
Norrisville	410
North Beach	410
North Bethesda	301
North Brentwo	301
North Brentwood	301
North College Park	301
North East	410
North Englewood	301
North Ocean City	410
North Potomac	301
Northeast	410
Northern	301
Northwood	410
Nottingham	410
Oakland	301
Ocean City	410
Ocean Pines	410
Ocean Pnes	410
Odenton	410
Oella	410
Oldtown	301
Olney	301
Orchard Beach	410
Oriole	410
Owings	410
Owings Mills	410
Oxford	410
Oxon Hill	301
Palmer Park	301
Park Hall	301
Parkton	410
Parkville	410
Parsonsburg	410
Pasadena	410
Patapsco	410
Patterson	410
Patuxent Riv	301
Patuxent River	301
Patuxent River Naval Air Sta	301
Pdp Group Inc	410
Perry Hall	410
Perry Point	410
Perryhall	410
Perryman	410
Perryville	410
Phoenix	410
Pikesville	410
Pikesville Finance	410
Piney Point	301
Piney Pt	301
Pinto	301
Pisgah	301
Pittsville	410
Pocomoke	410
Pocomoke City	410
Point Of Rocks	301
Pomfret	301
Poolesville	301
Port Deposit	410
Port Republic	410
Port Tobacco	301
Potomac	301
Powellville	410
Pr Frederick	410
Preston	410
Price	410
Prince Frederick	410
Prince George Plaza	301
Prince Georges Metro Ctr	301
Princess Anne	410
Prnc Frederck	410
Pt Of Rocks	301
Pylesville	410
Quantico	410
Queen Anne	410
Queenstown	410
Randallstown	410
Raspeburg	410
Rawlings	301
Rehobeth	410
Reisterstown	410
Reisterstown Rd Plaza	410
Rhodes Point	410
Rhodesdale	410
Riderwood	410
Ridge	301
Ridgely	410
Rising Sun	410
Rison	301
Riva	410
Riverdale	301
Riverside	410
Riviera Beach	410
Rock Hall	410
Rock Point	301
Rock Pt	301
Rockville	301
Rocky Ridge	301
Rogers Heights	301
Rohrersville	301
Roland Park	410
Rose Haven	410
Rosedale	410
Royal Oak	410
Rumbley	410
Russett	301
Ruxton	410
S Bowie	301
Sabillasville	301
Saint Charles	301
Saint Inigoes	301
Saint James	301
Saint Leonard	410
Saint Marys	301
Saint Marys City	301
Saint Michaels	410
Salem	410
Salisbury	410
Sandy Spring	301
Sang Run	301
Savage	301
Scaggsville	301
Scotland	301
Seabrook	301
Seat Pleasant	301
Secretary	410
Severn	410
Severna Park	410
Shady Side	410
Shallmar	301
Sharpsburg	301
Sharptown	410
Sherwood	410
Sherwood Forest	410
Sherwood Frst	410
Showell	410
Silver Hill	301
Silver Spring	301
Simpsonville	410
Smithsburg	301
Snow Hill	410
Social Security Admin	410
Social Security Administrat	410
Solomons	410
Somerset	301
South Bowie	301
Southern Md Brmas	301
Southern Md Facility	301
Sparks	410
Sparks Glenco	410
Sparks Glencoe	410
Sparrows Point	410
Sparrows Pt	410
Spencerville	301
Spring Gap	301
Springdale	301
St Inigoes	301
St Leonard	410
St Marys City	301
St Michaels	410
State Farm Ins Co	301
Stevenson	410
Stevensville	410
Sthrn Md Fac	301
Still Pond	410
Stockton	410
Street	410
Subn Md Fac	301

Suburb Maryland Fac 301
Suburban Md Brmas 301
Sudlersville 410
Suitland 301
Sun Trust Bank 410
Sunderland 410
Sunshine 301
Swan Point 301
Swanton 301
Sykesville 410
T Rowe Price Associates Inc 410
Takoma Park 301
Takoma Pk 301
Tall Timbers 301
Taneytown 410
Taylors Is 410
Taylors Island 410
Temple Hills 301
Templeville 410
Thurmont 301
Tilghman 410
Timonium 410
Toddville 410
Towson 410
Towson Finance 410
Towson State University 410
Tracys Landing 410
Tracys Lndg 410
Trappe 410
Tuscarora 301
Tuxedo 301
Tyaskin 410
Tylerton 410
Union Bridge 410
Unionville 410
Unity 301
Univ Of Md Baltimore County 410
University Of Maryland 301
University Pa 301
University Park 301
Upper Fairmount 410
Upper Fairmt 410
Upper Falls 410
Upper Hill 410
Upper Marlboro 301
Upperco 410
Uppr Marlboro 301
Upr Marlboro 301
Urbana 301
Us Food And Drug Admin 301
Usa Fulfillment 410
Valley Lee 301
Verizon 410
Vienna 410
W Bethesda 301
W Bowie 301
W Friendship 410
W Hyattsville 301
Wachovia Bank 410
Walbrook 410
Waldorf 301
Walkersville 301
Warwick 410
Washingtn Grv 301
Washington Grove 301
Washington Ndc 301
Waverly 410
Welcome 301
Wenona 410
West Friendship 410
West Hyattsville 301
West Ocean City 410
West River 410
Westernport 301
Westlake 301
Westminster 410
Westover 410
Whaleyville 410
Wheaton 301
White Hall 410
White Marsh 410
White Plains 301
Whiteford 410
Whitehaven 410
Willards 410
Williamsport 301
Windsor Mill 410
Wingate 410
Wittman 410
Woodbine 410
Woodland Bch 410
Woodlawn 410
Woodsboro 301
Woodstock 410
Woolford 410
Worton 410
Wye Mills 410

Massachusetts

Abington 781
Accord 781
Acton 978
Acushnet 508
Adams 413
Aetna Life & Casualty Co 508
Agawam 413
Alford 413
Allendale 413
Allmerica 508
Allston 617
Amesbury 978
Amherst 413
Andover 978
Aquinnah 508
Arlington 617, 781
Arlington Heights 617
Arlington Hts 617
Ashburnham 978
Ashby 978
Ashfield 413
Ashland 508
Ashley Falls 413
Assinippi 781
Assoc Of Marian Helpers 413
Assonet 508
Athol 978
Attleboro 508
Attleboro Falls 508
Attleboro Fls 508
Auburn 508
Auburndale 617
Avon 781
Ayer 978
Babson Park 617
Baldwinville 978
Bank Of America 617
Baptist Corner 413
Bar Coded I R S 978
Barnstable 508
Barre 978
Bass River 508
Bay State Village 413
Bay State Vlg 413
Bay State W Tower 413
Baystate Medical 413
Beachmont 781
Becket 413
Becket Corners 413
Bedford 781
Belchertown 413
Bellingham 508
Belmont 617
Berkley 508
Berkshire 413
Berkshire Heights 413
Berlin 978
Bernardston 413
Beverly 978
Beverly Farms 978
Big Pond 413
Billerica 978
Blackstone 508
Blandford 413
Blissville 978
Bolton 978
Bondsville 413
Boston 617
Boston City Hall 617
Boston Clg 617
Boston College 617
Boston Financial Data Servic 617
Boston University 617
Bourne 508
Boxboro 978
Boxborough 978
Boxford 978
Boylston 508
Bradford 978
Braintree 781
Braintree Highlands 781
Braintree Hld 781
Braintree Phantom 781
Brant Rock 781
Brewster 508
Bridgewater 508
Bridgewater State College 508
Brighton 617
Brightwood 413
Brimfield 413
Brockton 508
Brookfield 508
Brookline 617
Brookline Village 617
Brookline Vlg 617
Bryantville 781
Buckland 413
Burlington 781
Buzzards Bay 508
Byfield 978
Cambridge 617
Cambridgeport 781
Canton 781
Carlisle 978
Carver 508
Cash Management 617
Cataumet 508
Cedarville 508
Centerville 508
Central Mass P & D Ctr 508
Chadwicks 508
Chappaquiddick Island 508
Charlemont 413
Charlestown 617
Charlton 508
Charlton City 508
Charlton Depot 508
Charlton Dept 508
Charlton Dpt 508
Chartley 508
Chatham 508
Chelmsford 978
Chelsea 617
Cherry Brook 781
Cherry Valley 508
Cheshire 413
Chester 413
Chesterfield 413
Chestnut Hill 617
Chicopee 413
Chilmark 508
Clarksburg 413
Clinton 978
Cochituate 508
Cohasset 781
Cold Spring 413
Colrain 413
Concord 978
Conway 413
Cotuit 508
Crescent Mills 413
Cummaquid 508
Cummington 413
Cushman 413
Cuttyhunk 508
Dalton 413
Danvers 978
Dartmouth 508
Dedham 781
Deerfield 413
Dennis 508
Dennis Port 508
Dennisport 508
Devens 978
Dighton 508
Dorchester 617
Dorchester Center 617
Dorchestr Ctr 617
Douglas 508
Dover 508
Dracut 978
Drury 413
Dudley 508
Dudley Hill 508
Dunstable 978
Duxbury 781
E Arlington 781
E Blackstone 508
E Boston 617
E Braintree 781
E Bridgewater 508
E Bridgewtr 508
E Brookfield 508
E Cambridge 617
E Dennis 508
E Falmouth 508
E Hampton 413
E Harwich 508
E Longmeadow 413
E Mansfield 508
E Otis 413
E Pepperell 978
E Princeton 978
E Sandwich 508
E Somerville 617
E Templeton 978
E Walpole 508
E Wareham 508
E Watertown 617
Ea Falmouth 508
Eagleville 978
East Arlington 781
East Blackstone 508
East Boston 617
East Braintree 781
East Bridgewater 508
East Brimfield 413
East Brookfield 508
East Cambridge 617
East Carver 508
East Charlemont 413
East Deerfield 413
East Dennis 508
East Douglas 508
East Falmouth 508
East Freetown 508
East Harwich 508
East Leverett 413
East Longmeadow 413
East Lynn 781
East Mansfield 508
East Millbury 508
East Milton 617
East Orleans 508
East Otis 413
East Pembroke 781
East Pepperell 978
East Princeton 978
East Sandwich 508
East Somerville 617
East Taunton 508
East Templeton 978
East Walpole 508
East Wareham 508
East Watertown 617
East Weymouth 781
East Windsor 413
Eastham 508
Easthampton 413
Easton 508
Edgartown 508
Edgemere 508
Egremont 413
Elmwood 508
Emc 508
Erving 413
Essex 978
Everett 617
Fairhaven 508
Fall River 508
Falmouth 508
Farley 413
Fayville 508
Feeding Hills 413
Fidelity Service Company 617
Field Premium Inc 617
Fiskdale 508
Fitchburg 978
Fleet Bank Boston 617
Florence 413
Florida 413
Forestdale 508
Forge Village 978
Fort Devens 978
Foxboro 508
Foxborough 508
Framingham 508
Framingham Center 508
Framingham So 508
Franklin 508
Freetown 508
Ft Devens 978
Gardner 978
Gay Head 508
General Elec Co 781
General Mail Facility-Bmc 413
Georgetown 978
Gilbertville 413
Gill 413
Glendale 413
Globe Village 508
Gloucester 978
Goshen 413
Gosnold 508
Grafton 508
Granby 413
Granville 413
Granville Center 413
Great Barrington 413
Green Harbor 781
Greenbush 781
Greendale 508
Greenfield 413
Groton 978
Grove Hall 617
Groveland 978
Gt Barrington 413
Hadley 413
Halifax 781
Halland 508
Halyoke 413
Hamilton 978
Hampden 413
Hampton 413
Hancock 413
Hanover 508
Hanscom Afb 781
Hanson 781
Hardwich 508
Hardwick 413
Hartsville 413
Harvard 978
Harvard Sq 617
Harvard Square 617
Harwich 508
Harwich Port 508
Harwichport 508
Hassanamisco Indian Reservat 508
Hastings 781
Hatchville 508
Hatfield 413
Hathorne 978
Haverhill 978
Hawley 413
Haydenville 413
Heath 413
Hingham 781
Hinsdale 413
Hntgtn 413
Holbrook 781
Holden 508
Holland 508
Holliston 508
Holyoke 413
Hoosac Tunnel 413
Hopedale 508
Hopkinton 508
Horseneck Beach 508
Houghs Neck 617
Housatonic 413
Hubbardston 978
Hudson 978
Hull 781
Humarock 781
Huntington 413
Hyannis 508
Hyannis Port 508
Hyde Park 617
Indian Orch 413
Indian Orchard 413
Inman Square 781
Interlaken 413
Internal Revenue Service 978
Ipswich 978
Irs Service Center 978
Islington 781
Jamaica Plain 617
Jefferson 508
John Hancock Mutual Ins 617
John Hancock P O Box 505 617
Kates Corner 978
Kendal Green 781
Kendall Square 617
Kenmore 617
Kingston 781
Knightville 413
Lahey Clinic Med Ctr 781
Lake Mattawa 978
Lake Pleasant 413
Lakeville 508
Lakeville Phantom 508
Lambs Grove 508
Lancaster 978
Lanesboro 413
Lanesborough 413
Lawrence 978
Lee 413
Leeds 413
Leicester 508
Lenox 413
Lenox Dale 413
Leominster 978
Leverett 413
Lexington 781
Leyden 413
Lincoln 781
Lincoln Center 781
Linwood 508
Lithia 413
Littleton 978
Longmeadow 413
Loudville 413
Lowell 978
Ludlow 413
Lunenburg 978
Lynn 781
Lynnfield 781
Magnolia 978
Malden 781
Manchaug 508
Manchester 978
Manchester By The Sea 978
Manomet 508
Mansfield 508
Marblehead 781
Marian Helpers 413
Marina Bay 617
Marion 508
Marion Fathers 413
Marlboro 508
Marlborough 508
Marshfield 781
Marshfield Hills 781
Marshfld Hls 781
Marstons Mills 508
Marstons Mls 508
Mashpee 508
Mass Mutual Life Ins Co 413
Mass Tax 617
Massachusetts District 978
Massachusetts Tax 617
Mattapan 617
Mattapoisett 508
Maynard 978
Medfield 508

Medford 617
Medway 508
Mellon Financial Services 781
Melrose 781
Mendon 508
Menemsha 508
Merrimac 978
Methuen 978
Mhead 781
Middleboro 508
Middleborough 508
Middlefield 413
Middleton 978
Milford 508
Mill River 413
Millbury 508
Millers Falls 413
Millerville 508
Millis 508
Millville 508
Milton 617
Milton Village 617
Milton Vlg 617
Minot 781
Mission Hill 617
Monponsett 781
Monroe 413
Monroe Bridge 413
Monson 413
Montague 413
Monterey 413
Montgomery 413
Monument Bch 508
Monument Beach 508
Morningdale 508
Mount Hermon 413
Mount Tom 413
Mount Washington 413
Mt Hermon 413
Mt Washington 413
N Adams 413
N Andover 978
N Attleboro 508
N Billerica 978
N Brookfield 508
N Cambridge 617
N Chatham 508
N Chelmsford 978
N Dartmouth 508
N Dighton 508
N Easton 508
N Egremont 413
N Falmouth 508
N Field 413
N Grafton 508
N Hatfield 413
N Marshfield 781
N Natick 508
N Orange 978
N Pembroke 781
N Quincy 617
N Reading 978
N Scituate 781
N Sudbury 978
N Uxbridge 508
N Weymouth 781
Nabnasset 978
Nahant 781
Nantasket Beach 781
Nantucket 508
Natick 508
National Grid 781
National Grid Co 508
Needham 781
Needham Heights 781
Needham Hgts 781
Needham Jct 781
New Ashford 413
New Bedford 508
New Braintree 413
New England Business 978
New England Business Svc Inc 978
New Marlboro 413
New Marlborou 413
New Marlborough 413
New Salem 978
New Seabury 508
New Town 617
Newbury 978
Newburyport 978
Newton 617
Newton Center 617
Newton Centre 617
Newton Cntr 617
Newton Ctr 617
Newton Highlands 617
Newton Hlds 617
Newton L F 781
Newton Lower Falls 781
Newton U F 781
Newton Upper Falls 781
Newtonville 617
No Adams 413
No Attleboro 508
No Easton 508
No Egremont 413
No Field 413
No Grafton 508
No Hatfield 413
No Natick 508
No Quincy 617
Nonantum 617
Nonquitt 508
Norfolk 508
Norfolk Downs 617
North Adams 413
North Amherst 413
North Andover 978
North Attleboro 508
North Billerica 978
North Brookfield 508
North Cambridge 617
North Carver 508
North Chatham 508
North Chelmsford 978
North Chester 413
North Dartmouth 508
North Dighton 508
North Eastham 508
North Easton 508
North Egremont 413
North Falmouth 508
North Grafton 508
North Hadley 413
North Hampton 413
North Hatfield 413
North Lancaster 978
North Leverett 413
North Marshfield 781
North Natick 508
North Orange 978
North Otis 413
North Oxford 508
North Pembroke 781
North Quincy 617
North Reading 978
North Scituate 781
North Sudbury 978
North Tisbury 508
North Truro 508
North Uxbridge 508
North Waltham 617
North Weymouth 781
Northampton 413
Northboro 508
Northborough 508
Northbridge 508
Northfield 413
Northfield Mount Hermon 413
Northfield Mt Hermon 413
Norton 508
Norwell 781
Norwood 781
Nutting Lake 978
Nuttings Lake 978
Oak Bluffs 508
Oakdale 508
Oakham 508
Ocean Bluff 781
Ocean Spray 508
Old Furnace 978
Onset 508
Orange 413, 978
Orleans 508
Osterville 508
Otis 413
Otis A F B 508
Otis Air National Guard 508
Otis Ang 508
Otis Angb 508
Otter River 978
Oxford 508
Padanaram The Packet 508
Palmer 413
Paxton 508
Peabody 978
Pelham 413
Pembroke 781
Pepperell 978
Peru 413
Petersham 978
Phillipston 978
Pigeon Cove 978
Pinehurst 978
Pingryville 978
Pittsfield 413
Plainfield 413
Plainville 508
Plum Island 978
Plymouth 508
Plympton 781
Pocasset 508
Porter Square 617
Prides Crossing 978
Prides Crssng 978
Princeton 978
Provincetown 508
Quincy 617
Quincy Center 617
Randolph 781
Raynham 508
Raynham Center 508
Raynham Ctr 508
Reading 781
Readville 617
Rehoboth 508
Revere 781
Revere Beach 781
Richardson Corners 508
Richmond 413
Risingdale 413
Riverside 617
Rochdale 508
Rochester 508
Rockdale 508
Rockland 781
Rockport 978
Rocky Nook 781
Roslindale 617
Rowe 413
Rowley 978
Roxbury 617
Roxbury Crossing 617
Roxbury Xing 617
Royalston 978
Russell 413
Rutland 508
S Attleboro 508
S Boston 617
S Chelmsford 978
S Chesterfield 413
S Dartmouth 508
S Deerfield 413
S Dennis 508
S Easton 508
S Egremont 413
S Hadley 413
S Hamilton 978
S Lancaster 978
S Lawrence 978
S Natick 508
S Royalston 978
S Walpole 508
S Wellfleet 508
S Weymouth 781
S Yarmouth 508
Sagamore 508
Sagamore Bch 508
Sagamore Beach 508
Salem 978
Salisbury 978
Salisbury Bch 978
Salisbury Beach 978
Sandersdale 508
Sandisfield 413
Sandwich 508
Saugus 781
Saundersville 508
Savoy 413
Saxonville 508
Scituate 781
Scituate Center 781
Scituate Harbor 781
Sconset 508
Seekonk 508
Shared Firm Zip Code 781
Sharon 781
Shattuckville 413
Sheffield 413
Shelburne 413
Shelburne Falls 413
Shelburne Fls 413
Sheldonville 508
Sherborn 508
Sherwood Forest 413
Shirley 978
Shirley Center 978
Shirley Ctr 978
Shrewsbury 508
Shutesbury 413
Siasconset 508
Silver Beach 508
Silver Hill 781
Silver Lake 781
Simons Rock 413
Smith College 413
So Deerfield 413
So Easton 508
So Egremont 413
So Hadley 413
So Lancaster 978
So Natick 508
So Yarmouth 508
Soldiers Field 617
Somerset 508
Somerville 617
South Amherst 413
South Ashburnham 978
South Ashfield 413
South Attleboro 508
South Barre 978
South Boston 617
South Carver 508
South Chatham 508
South Chesterfield 413
South Dartmouth 508
South Deerfield 413
South Dennis 508
South Easton 508
South Egremont 413
South Grafton 508
South Hadley 413
South Hadley Falls 413
South Hamilton 978
South Harwich 508
South Lancaster 978
South Lawrence 978
South Lee 413
South Lynnfield 781
South Mashpee 508
South Natick 508
South Orleans 508
South Quincy 617
South Sandisfield 413
South Walpole 508
South Waltham 781
South Wellfleet 508
South Weymouth 781
South Worthington 413
South Yarmouth 508
Southampton 413
Southboro 508
Southborough 508
Southbridge 508
Southfield 413
Southwick 413
Spencer 508
Spfld 413
Spfld (Long) 413
Springfield 413
Squantum 617
State Street Corporation 617
Sterling 978
Sterling Junction 978
Still River 978
Stockbridge 413
Stoneham 781
Stonehill Col 508
Stonehill Coll 508
Stonehill College 508
Stoneville 413
Stony Brook 781
Stoughton 781
Stow 978
Sturbridge 508
Sudbury 978
Sunderland 413
Sutton 508
Swampscott 781
Swansea 508
Talbots 508
Taunton 508
Teaticket 508
Templeton 978
Tewksbury 978
Thorndike 413
Three Rivers 413
Tisbury 508
Tolland 413
Topsfield 978
Townsend 978
Truro 508
Tufts Univ 617
Tufts University 617
Turners Falls 413
Tyco 978
Tyngsboro 978
Tyngsborough 978
Tyringham 413
Uphams Corner 617
Upton 508
Uxbridge 508
Van Deusenville 413
Verizon 508
Village Of Nagog Woods 978
Vineyard Haven 508
Vineyard Hvn 508
Vlg Nagog Wds 978
Vlg Of Nagog Woods 978
W Acton 978
W Barnstable 508
W Barnstble 508
W Becket 413
W Bridgewater 508
W Brookfield 413
W Chesterfld 413
W Concord 978
W Dennis 508
W Falmouth 508
W Groton 978
W Hatfield 413
W Hyannisprt 508
W Medford 617, 781
W Newton 617
W Roxbury 617
W Somerville 617
W Springfield 413
W Stockbridge 413
W Townsend 978
W Upton 508
W Wareham 508
W Warren 413
W Yarmouth 508
Waban 617
Wakefield 781
Wales 413
Walpole 508
Waltham 617
Waquoit 508
Ward Hill 978
Ware 413
Wareham 508
Warren 413
Warwick 413, 978
Washington 413
Watertown 617
Watertown Financial 617
Waverley 617
Wayland 508
Wearguard 508
Webster 508
Webster Square 508
Wellesley 617, 781
Wellesley Fms 781
Wellesley Hills 781
Wellesley Hls 781
Wellfleet 508
Wendell 413
Wendell Depot 978
Wenham 978
West Acton 978
West Barnstable 508
West Boxford 978
West Boylston 508
West Bridgewater 508
West Brookfield 413
West Chatham 508
West Chesterfield 413
West Chop 508
West Concord 978
West Cummington 413
West Deerfield 413
West Dennis 508
West Falmouth 508
West Granville 413
West Groton 978
West Hanover 781
West Harwich 508
West Hatfield 413
West Hawley 413
West Hyannisport 508
West Lynn 781
West Medford 617
West Millbury 508
West Newbury 978
West Newton 617
West Otis 413
West Peabody 978
West Quincy 617
West Roxbury 617
West Side 508
West Somerville 617
West Springfield 413
West Springfld 413
West Stockbridge 413
West Stockbridge Center 413
West Tisbury 508
West Townsend 978
West Upton 508
West Wareham 508
West Warren 413
West Whately 413
West Yarmouth 508
Westboro 508
Westborough 508
Westboylston 508
Westbrookfield 413
Westfield 413
Westford 978
Westhampton 413
Westminster 978
Weston 781
Westover Afb 413
Westport 508
Westport Point 508
Westport Pt 508
Westwood 781
Weymouth 781
Weymouth Lndg 781
Weymouth Nas 781
Whately 413
Wheelwright 413
White Horse Beach 508
Whitinsville 508
Whitman 781
Wht Horse Bch 508

City	Area Code
Wilbraham	413
Wilkinsonvile	508
Wilkinsonville	508
Williamsburg	413
Williamstn	413
Williamstown	413
Willimansett	413
Wilmington	978
Winchdon Spgs	978
Winchendon	978
Winchendon Springs	978
Winchester	781
Windsor	413
Winter Hill	617
Winthrop	617
Wmstown	413
Woburn	781
Wollaston	617
Woods Hole	508
Woodshole	508
Woodville	508
Worcester	508
Woronoco	413
Worthington	413
Wrentham	508
Yarmouth	508
Yarmouth Port	508
Yarmouthport	508
Zoar	413

Michigan

City	Area Code
Acme	231
Ada	616
Addison	517
Addison Township	248
Addison Twp	248
Adrian	517
Afton	231
Ahmeek	906
Akron	989
Alabaster	989
Alanson	231
Alba	231
Albion	517
Alden	231
Alger	989
Algonac	810
Allegan	269
Allen	517
Allen Park	313
Allendale	616
Allenton	810
Allouez	906
Alma	989
Almont	810
Almont Township	810
Alpena	989
Alpha	906
Alto	616
Amasa	906
Ameritech	989
Amway Corp	616
Anchorville	586
Andrews University	269
Ann Arbor	734
Ann Arbor Township	734
Applegate	810
Arcadia	231
Argyle	810
Armada	586
Armada Township	586
Arnold	906
Ash Twp	734
Ashley	989
At&t	989
Athens	269
Atlanta	989
Atlantic Mine	906
Atlas	810
Attica	810
Au Gres	989
Au Sable	989
Au Train	906
Auburn	989
Auburn Hills	248
Augusta	269
Augusta Twp	734
Avoca	810
Azalia	734
Bad Axe	989
Bailey	616
Baldwin	231
Bancroft	989
Bangor	269
Bank Of America	313
Bannister	989
Baraga	906
Barbeau	906
Bark River	906
Barlow Branch	231
Baroda	269
Barryton	989
Barton City	989
Barton Hills	734
Bath	517
Battle Creek	269
Bay City	989
Bay Harbor	231
Bay Port	989
Bay Shore	231
Bay View	231
Bear Lake	231
Beaver Island	231
Beaverton	989
Bedford	269
Beechwood	906
Belding	616
Bellaire	231
Belleville	734
Bellevue	269
Belmont	616
Bentley	989
Benton Harbor	269
Benzonia	231
Bergland	906
Berkley	248
Berlin	810
Berlin Township	810
Berlin Twp	810
Berrien Center	269
Berrien Ctr	269
Berrien Spgs	269
Berrien Sprgs	269
Berrien Springs	269
Berville	810
Bessemer	906
Beulah	231
Beverly Hills	248
Bham	248, 586
Big Bay	906
Big Rapids	231
Bingham Farms	248
Birch Run	989
Birmingham	248
Bitely	231
Black River	989
Blanchard	989
Blaney Park	906
Blissfield	517
Bloomfield	248
Bloomfield Hills	248
Bloomfield Township	248
Bloomfield Twp	248
Bloomfield Village	248
Bloomfld Hls	248
Bloomfld Twp	248
Bloomingdale	269
Boardwalk	989
Bois Blanc Is	231
Bois Blanc Island	231
Boon	231
Borculo	616
Boyne City	231
Boyne Falls	231
Bradley	269
Brampton	906
Branch	231
Brandon	248
Brant	989
Breckenridge	989
Breedsville	269
Brethren	231
Bridgeport	989
Bridgewater	517
Bridgman	269
Brighton	810
Brighton Twp	810
Brimley	906
Britton	517
Brockway	810
Brockway Township	810
Brohman	231
Bronson	517
Brooklyn	517
Brown City	810
Brownstown	734
Brownstown Township	734
Brownstown Twp	734
Brownstwn Twp	734
Bruce	586
Bruce Crossing	906
Bruce Township	586
Bruce Twp	586
Bruce Xing	906
Brunswick	231
Brutus	231
Buchanan	269
Buckley	231
Buick City	810
Buick Oldsmobile Cadillac	810
Burlington	517
Burnips	616
Burr Oak	269
Burt	989
Burt Lake	231
Burtchville	810
Burtchville Township	810
Burton	810
Business Reply Mail	616
Byron	810
Byron Center	616
Byron Township	616
Cadillac	231
Cadmus	517
Caledonia	616
Calumet	906
Camden	517
Camp Grayling	989
Canadian Lake	231
Canadian Lakes	231
Cannonsburg	616
Canton	734
Canton Twp	734
Capac	810
Carland	989
Carleton	734
Carney	906
Caro	989
Carp Lake	231
Carrollton	989
Carson City	989
Carsonville	810
Cascade	616
Cascade Twp	616
Casco	586
Casco Township	586
Caseville	989
Casnovia	616
Caspian	906
Cass City	989
Cassopolis	269
Cedar	231
Cedar Lake	989
Cedar River	906
Cedar Springs	616
Cedarville	906
Cement City	517
Centennial Heights	906
Centennial Hts	906
Center Line	586
Central Lake	231
Central Michigan University	989
Centreville	269
Ceresco	269
Champion	906
Channing	906
Charlevoix	231
Charlotte	517
Chase	231
Chase Bank	313
Chassell	906
Chatham	906
Cheboygan	231
Chelsea	734
Chesaning	989
Chesterfield	586
Chesterfield Township	586
Chevrolet Pontiac Canada	810
China	810
China Township	810
Chippewa Lake	231
Chippewa Reg Correction Fac	906
Chippewa Temp Correction Fac	906
Christian Reformed Church	616
Christmas	906
Chrysler Corporation	313
Clare	989
Clarklake	517
Clarkston	248
Clarksville	616
Clawson	248
Clay	810
Clay Township	810
Clay Twp	810
Clayton	517
Clayton Twp	517
Clifford	989
Climax	269
Clinton	517
Clinton Township	586
Clinton Twp	586
Clio	810
Cloverdale	269
Clyde	810
Clyde Township	810
Cohoctah	810
Coldwater	517
Coleman	989
Coloma	269
Colon	269
Columbiaville	810
Columbus	586
Columbus Township	586
Comerica	313
Comerica Incorporated	313
Comins	989
Commerce	248
Commerce Township	248
Commerce Twp	248
Comstock	269
Comstock Park	616
Concord	517
Cone	734
Conklin	616
Constantine	269
Consumers Energy	517
Conway	231
Cooks	906
Coopersville	616
Copemish	231
Copper City	906
Copper Harbor	906
Coppersville	616
Coral	231
Cornell	906
Corunna	989
Cottrellville	810
Cottrellville Township	810
Cottrellville Twp	810
Covert	269
Covington	906
Crooked Lake	810
Cross Village	231
Croswell	810
Croton	231
Crystal	989
Crystal Falls	906
Curran	989
Curtis	906
Custer	231
Cutlerville	616
Dafter	906
Daggett	906
Dansville	517
Davisburg	248
Davison	810
De Tour Village	906
De Tour Vlle	906
De Witt	517
Dearborn	313
Dearborn Heights	313
Dearborn Hts	313
Decatur	269
Decker	810
Deckerville	810
Deerfield	517
Deerton	906
Deford	989
Delhi	734
Delphi East	810
Delphi West	810
Delray	313
Delton	269
Detroit	248, 313, 517
Detroit River Station	248
Dewitt	517
Dexter	734
Dexter Twp	734
Dimondale	517
Dixboro	734
Dodgeville	906
Dollar Bay	906
Dorr	616
Douglas	269
Dover	734
Dow Chemical Mi Division	989
Dow Chemical Usa	989
Dow Corning Corporation	989
Dowagiac	269
Dowling	269
Drayton Plains	248
Drayton Plns	248
Drummond Is	906
Drummond Island	906
Dryden	810
Dte	313
Dte Energy	313
Dte Energy Brm	313
Duck Lake	517
Duncan	734
Dundee	734
Durand	989
Dutton	616
E Kingsford	906
Eagle	517
Eagle Harbor	906
Eagle River	906
East China	810
East China Township	810
East China Twp	810
East Detroit	586
East Grand Ra	616
East Grand Rapids	616
East Jordan	231
East Kingsford	906
East Lansing	517
East Leroy	269
East Tawas	989
Eastlake	231
Eastmanville	616
Eastpointe	586
Eastport	231
Eaton Rapids	517
Eau Claire	269
Eben Jct	906
Eben Junction	906
Eckerman	906
Ecorse	313
Edenville	989
Edmore	989
Edwardsburg	269
Elberta	231
Elk Rapids	231
Elkton	989
Ellsworth	231
Elm Hall	989
Elmira	231
Elsie	989
Elwell	989
Emmett	810
Emmett Township	810
Empire	231
Engadine	906
Erie	734
Escanaba	906
Essexville	989
Eureka	989
Evart	231
Ewen	906
Fair Haven	586
Fairgrove	989
Fairview	989
Falmouth	231
Fargo	810
Farmingtn Hls	248
Farmington	248
Farmington Hills	248
Farmington Hls	248
Farwell	989
Felch	906
Fennville	269
Fenton	810
Fenwick	989
Ferndale	248
Ferrysburg	616
Fibre	906
Fife Lake	231
Filer City	231
Filion	989
Flat Rock	734
Flint	810
Flushing	810
Forest Hills	616
Forest Lake	906
Forestville	989
Fort Gratiot	810
Fort Gratiot Township	810
Foster City	906
Fostoria	989
Fountain	231
Four Mile Lk	734
Fowler	989
Fowlerville	517
Frankenmuth	989
Frankenmuth Mutual Ins Co	989
Frankfort	231
Franklin	248
Fraser	586
Frederic	989
Free Soil	231
Freedom Twp	734
Freeland	989
Freeport	616
Fremont	231
Frenchtown	734
Frontier	517
Fruitport	231
Fulton	269
Gaastra	906
Gagetown	989
Gaines	989
Galesburg	269
Galien	269
Garden	906
Garden City	734
Gay	906
Gaylord	231, 989
General Motors	313
Genesee	810
Genoa Twp	810
Georgetown Township	616
Georgetown Tp	616
Georgetown Twp	616
Gerber Products Inc	231
Germfask	906
Gibraltar	734
Gilford	989
Gladstone	906
Gladwin	989
Glen Arbor	231
Glendora	269
Glenn	269
Glennie	989
Gm Service Parts Operations	810

City	Area Code
Gm Tech Center	810
Gm Truck And Bus	810
Gm Vehicle Development Ctr	810
Gobles	269
Goetzville	906
Good Hart	231
Goodells	810
Goodison	248
Goodrich	810
Gould City	906
Gowen	616
Gr	616
Gr Blanc	810
Grand Beach	269
Grand Blanc	810
Grand Haven	616
Grand Jct	269
Grand Junction	269
Grand Ledge	517
Grand Marais	906
Grand Rapids	616
Grandville	616
Grant	231
Grant Township	810
Grant Twp	810
Grass Lake	517
Grawn	231
Grayling	989
Green Oak Twp	810
Greenbush	989
Greenland	906
Greenville	616
Greenwood	810
Greenwood Township	810
Gregory	734
Grindstone City	989
Grosse Ile	734
Grosse Pointe	313
Grosse Pointe Farms	313
Grosse Pointe Park	313
Grosse Pointe Shores	313
Grosse Pointe Woods	313
Gulliver	906
Gwinn	906
Hadley	810
Hagar Shores	269
Hale	989
Hamburg	734, 810
Hamburg Twp	734
Hamilton	269
Hamtramck	313
Hancock	906
Hanover	517
Harbert	269
Harbor Beach	989
Harbor Point	231
Harbor Spgs	231
Harbor Springs	231
Hardwood	906
Harper Woods	313
Harrietta	231
Harris	906
Harrison	989
Harrison Township	586
Harrison Twp	586
Harrisville	989
Harsens Is	810
Harsens Island	810
Hart	231
Hartford	269
Hartland	810
Hartland Township	810
Harvey	906
Haslett	517
Hastings	269
Hawks	989
Hazel Park	248
Hemlock	989
Henderson	989
Hermansville	906
Herron	989
Hersey	231
Hesperia	231
Hessel	906
Hghtn Lk Hts	989
Hiawatha Temp Correction Fac	906
Hickory Corners	269
Hickory Crnrs	269
Hickory Isle	734
Higgins Lake	989
Highland	248
Highland Park	313
Highland Twp	248
Hillman	989
Hillsdale	517
Holland	616
Holly	248
Holt	517
Holton	231
Homer	517
Honor	231
Hope	989
Hopkins	269
Horton	517
Houghton	906
Houghton Lake	989
Houghton Lake Heights	989
Howard City	231
Howell	517
Hoxeyville	231
Htn Lk Hghts	989
Hubbard Lake	989
Hubbardston	989
Hubbell	906
Hudson	517
Hudson Mills	734
Hudsonville	616
Hulbert	906
Huntingtn Wds	248
Huntington Wd	248
Huntington Woods	248
Huron Twp	734
Ida	734
Idlewild	231
Imlay	810
Imlay City	810
Independence	248
Independence Township	248
Independence Twp	248
Indian River	231
Ingalls	906
Inkster	313
Interlochen	231
Ionia	616
Ira	586
Ira Township	586
Ira Twp	586
Iron Mountain	906
Iron Mtn	906
Iron River	906
Irons	231
Ironwood	906
Ishpeming	906
Ithaca	989
Jackson	517
Jackson National Life Ins Co	517
Jamestown	616
Jasper	517
Jeddo	810
Jenison	616
Jerome	517
Johannesburg	989
Jones	269
Jonesville	517
Kalamazoo	269
Kaleva	231
Kalkaska	231
Karlin	231
Kawkawlin	989
Kearsarge	906
Keego Harbor	248
Kelly Services Inc	517
Kendall	269
Kenockee	810
Kenockee Township	810
Kent City	616
Kenton	906
Kentwood	616
Kentwood Brch	616
Kewadin	231
Keweenaw Bay	906
Kimball	810
Kimball Township	810
Kincheloe	906
Kinde	989
Kingsford	906
Kingsford Retail	906
Kingsley	231
Kingston	989
Kinross	906
L Anse	906
L' Anse	906
La Salle	734
Lachine	989
Lacota	269
Laingsburg	517
Lake	989
Lake Angelus	248
Lake Ann	231
Lake City	231
Lake George	989
Lake Isabella	989
Lake Leelanau	231
Lake Linden	906
Lake Nepessing	810
Lake Odessa	616
Lake Orion	248
Lake Station	989
Lakeland	810
Lakeport	810
Lakeside	269
Lakeview	989
Lakeville	248
Lakewood Club	231
Lambertville	734
Lamont	616
Lanse	906
Lansing	517
Lansing State Journal	517
Lapeer	810
Lathrup Village	248
Lathrup Vlg	248
Laurium	906
Lawrence	269
Lawton	269
Le Roy	231
Leland	231
Lennon	810
Lenox	586
Lenox Township	586
Leonard	248
Leonidas	269
Leroy	231
Leslie	517
Levering	231
Lewiston	989
Lexington	810
Lima Center	734
Lima Twp	734
Limestone	906
Lincoln	989
Lincoln Park	313
Linden	810
Linwood	989
Litchfield	517
Little Lake	906
Livonia	248, 734
Loch Alpine	734
Lodi Township	734
London Twp	734
Long Lake	989
Loretto	906
Lowell	616
Luce Twp	734
Lucky Losers	517
Ludington	231
Lum	810
Luna Pier	734
Lupton	989
Luther	231
Luzerne	989
Lyndon Twp	734
Lynn	810
Lynn Township	810
Lyons	989
Macatawa	616
Mackinac City	231
Mackinac Is	906
Mackinac Island	906
Mackinaw City	231
Macomb	586
Macomb Township	586
Macomb Twp	586
Madison Heights	248
Madison Hts	248
Mancelona	231
Manchester	734
Manistee	231
Manistique	906
Manitou Beach	517
Manton	231
Maple City	231
Maple Rapids	989
Marcellus	269
Marenisco	906
Marine City	810
Marion	231
Marlette	989
Marne	616
Marquette	906
Marshall	269
Martin	269
Marysville	810
Mason	517
Mass City	906
Mattawan	269
Maybee	734
Mayfield	231
Mayville	989
Mc Bain	231
Mc Millan	906
Mcbrides	989
Mcmillan	906
Mears	231
Mecosta	231
Melvin	810
Melvindale	313
Memphis	810
Mendon	269
Menominee	906
Merrill	989
Merritt	231
Merriweather	906
Mesick	231
Meskegon	231
Metamora	810
Mi Department Of Revenue	517
Mi Metro	248
Michiana	269
Michigamme	906
Michigan Bankard	517
Michigan Bulb Co	616
Michigan Center	517
Michigan Ctr	517
Mid Michigan Reg Med Ctr	989
Middleton	989
Middleville	269
Middlevle	269
Midland	989
Midland Hospital Center	989
Mikado	989
Milan	734
Milan Twp	734
Milford	248
Milford Twp	248
Millbrook	989
Millersburg	989
Millington	989
Minden	989
Minden City	989
Mio	989
Mohawk	906
Moline	616
Monroe	734
Montague	231
Montgomery	517
Montrose	810
Moorestown	231
Mooreville	734
Moran	906
Morenci	517
Morley	231
Morrice	517
Moscow	517
Mosherville	517
Mott Park	810
Mottville	269
Mount Clemens	586
Mount Morris	810
Mount Pleasant	989
Mt Pleasant	989
Muir	989
Mullett Lake	231
Mulliken	517
Munger	989
Munising	906
Munith	517
Muskegon	231
Muskegon Heights	231
Muskegon Hts	231
Mussey	810
N Lakeport	810
N Muskegon	231
Nadeau	906
Nahma	906
Napoleon	517
Nashville	517
National City	989
National Mine	906
Naubinway	906
Nazareth	269
Negaunee	906
New Baltimore	586
New Boston	734
New Buffalo	269
New Era	231
New Haven	586
New Hudson	248
New Lothrop	810
New Troy	269
Newaygo	231
Newberry	906
Newport	734
Niles	269
Nisula	906
North Adams	517
North Branch	810
North Lakeport	810
North Manitou	231
North Muskegon	231
North Port	231
North Star	989
North Street	810
Northeast	810
Northfield Twp	734
Northland	906
Northport	231
Northport Point	231
Northville	248
Northville Township	248
Northville Tw	248
Northwest	810
Norton Shores	231
Norvell	517
Norway	906
Nottawa	269
Novi	248
Novi Township	248
Nunica	231
Oak Grove	517
Oak Park	248
Oakland	248
Oakland Township	248
Oakland Twp	248
Oakley	989
Oakville	734
Ocqueoc	989
Oden	231
Okemos	517
Old Mission	231
Oldsmobile	517
Olivet	269
Omena	231
Omer	989
Onaway	989
Onekama	231
Onondaga	517
Onsted	517
Ontonagon	906
Orchard Lake	248
Orion	248
Orion Township	248
Orion Twp	248
Orleans	616
Ortonville	248
Oscoda	989
Oshtemo	269
Osseo	517
Ossineke	989
Otisville	810
Otsego	269
Ottawa Lake	734
Otter Lake	989
Ovid	989
Owendale	989
Owosso	989
Oxford	248
Painesdale	906
Palmer	906
Palms	989
Palmyra	517
Palo	616
Paradise	906
Parchment	269
Paris	231
Parma	517
Paw Paw	269
Peacock	231
Pearl Beach	810
Peck	810
Pelkie	906
Pellston	231
Pentwater	231
Perkins	906
Perrinton	989
Perronville	906
Perry	517
Peshawbestown	231
Petersburg	734
Petoskey	231
Pewamo	989
Pickford	906
Pierport	231
Pierson	616
Pigeon	989
Pinckney	734
Pinconning	989
Pittsfield Twp	734
Pittsford	517
Plainwell	269
Pleasant Lake	517
Pleasant Rdg	248
Pleasant Ridge	248
Plymouth	734
Podunk	734
Point Aux Pin	231
Pointe Aux Barques	989
Pointe Aux Pins	231
Pompeii	989
Pontiac	248
Port Austin	989
Port Elizabeth	989
Port Hope	989
Port Huron	810
Port Huron Township	810
Port Sanilac	810
Port Sheldon	616
Portage	269
Portland	517
Posen	989
Potterville	517
Powers	906
Prattville	517
Prescott	989
Presque Isle	989
Princeton	906
Prudenville	989
Pt Elizabeth	989
Pullman	269
Putnam Twp	734
Quincy	517
Quinnesec	906
Raco	906
Radio Bible Class	616
Raisinville Twp	734
Raisinvl Twp	734

City	Area Code
Ralph	906
Ramsay	906
Rankin	810
Rapid City	231
Rapid River	906
Ravenna	231
Rawsonville	734
Ray	586
Ray Township	586
Ray Twp	586
Rea	734
Reading	517
Redford	313
Redford Twp	313
Reed City	231
Reese	989
Remus	989
Republic	906
Rhodes	989
Richland	269
Richmond	586
Richmond Township	586
Richville	989
Ridgeway	517
Riga	517
Riley	810
Riley Township	810
Ripley	906
River Rouge	313
Riverdale	989
Riverside	269
Riverview	734
Rives Jct	517
Rives Junction	517
Rochester	248
Rochester Hills	248
Rochester Hls	248
Rock	906
Rockford	616
Rockland	906
Rockwood	734
Rodney	231
Rogers City	989
Rollin	517
Romeo	586
Romulus	734
Roos	989
Roosevelt Pk	231
Roscommon	989
Rose City	989
Rosebush	989
Roseville	586
Rothbury	231
Roulo	734
Royal Oak	248
Royal Oak Twp	248
Ruby	810
Rudyard	906
Rumely	906
Russell Is	810
Russell Island	810
Ruth	989
S Boardman	231
S Rockwood	734
Saginaw	989
Sagola	906
Saint Charles	989
Saint Clair	810
Saint Clair Shores	586
Saint Clair Shrs	586
Saint Clair Township	810
Saint Helen	989
Saint Ignace	906
Saint James	231
Saint Joe	269
Saint Johns	989
Saint Joseph	269
Saint Louis	989
Salem	734
Saline	517
Samaria	734
Sand Creek	517
Sand Lake	616
Sand Point	989
Sandusky	810
Sanford	989
Sang	586
Saranac	616
Saugatuck	269
Sault S Marie	906
Sault Sainte Marie	906
Sawyer	269
Schaffer	906
Schoolcraft	269
Scio	734
Scio Township	734
Scotts	269
Scottville	231
Sears	231
Sebewaing	989
Secretary Of State	517
Selfridge	586
Selfridge Air Natl Guard	586
Selfridge Angb	586
Seneca	517
Seney	906
Shaftsburg	517
Sharon	734
Sharon Hollow	734
Shelby	231
Shelby Township	586
Shelby Twp	586
Shelbyville	269
Shepherd	989
Sheridan	989
Sherwood	269
Shingleton	906
Sidnaw	906
Sidney	989
Silver Lake	231
Silverwood	989
Simplicity Pattern	269
Six Lakes	989
Skandia	906
Skanee	906
Smiths Creek	810
Smyrna	616
Snover	810
Sodus	269
Somerset	517
Somerset Center	517
Somerset Ctr	517
South Boardman	231
South Branch	989
South Haven	269
South Lyon	248
South Manitou	231
South Range	906
South Rockwood	734
Southeast	810
Southfield	248
Southfield Township	248
Southgate	734
Spalding	906
Sparta	616
Spring Arbor	517
Spring Lake	616
Springfield	269
Springfield Township	248
Springfld Twp	248
Springport	517
Spruce	989
St Clair	810
St Clair Shores	586
St Clair Shrs	586
St Clair Township	810
St Clair Twp	810
St Clr Shores	586
St Clr Shrs	586
St Heights	586
St Joe	269
St Joseph	269
Stalwart	906
Stambaugh	906
Standale	616
Standish	989
Stanton	989
Stanwood	231
State Farm Ins	269
State Of Mich Dept Treasury	517
State Of Michigan	517
Stephenson	906
Sterling	989
Sterling Heights	586
Sterling Hts	586
Stevensville	269
Stockbridge	517
Stony Creek	734
Stronach	231
Strongs	906
Sturgis	269
Sumner	989
Sumpter Twp	734
Sunfield	517
Superior Township	734
Superior Twp	734
Suttons Bay	231
Swartz Creek	810
Sylvan Beach	231
Sylvan Lake	248
Sylvan Twp	734
Tawas City	989
Taylor	313
Tecumseh	517
Tekonsha	517
Temperance	734
Thompson	906
Thompsonville	231
Three Oaks	269
Three Rivers	269
Tipton	517
Toivola	906
Topinabee	231
Total Petroleum	989
Tower	989
Traunik	906
Traverse City	231
Treetops	989
Treetops Vil	989
Treetops Village	989
Trenary	906
Trenton	734
Trout Creek	906
Trout Lake	906
Troy	248
Trufant	616
Turner	989
Tuscola	989
Tustin	231
Twin Lake	231
Twining	989
U Of M	734
Ubly	989
Unadilla	734
Union	269
Union City	517
Union Lake	248
Union Pier	269
Unionville	989
Univ Ctr	989
University Center	989
University Ctr	989
Us Army Tank-Auto Command	586
Utica	586
Van Buren Twp	734
Vandalia	269
Vanderbilt	989
Vassar	989
Vehicle License Plates	517
Vermontville	517
Vernon	989
Vernon City	989
Vestaburg	989
Vicksburg	269
Vulcan	906
W Bloomfield	248
Wakefield	906
Waldron	517
Wales	810
Wales Township	810
Walhalla	231
Walker	616
Walkerville	231
Wallace	906
Walled Lake	248
Walloon Lake	231
Waltz	734
Warren	586
Washingtn Twp	586
Washington	586
Washington Township	586
Washington Twp	586
Waterford	248
Waterford Township	248
Waters	989
Watersmeet	906
Watervliet	269
Watton	906
Wayland	269
Wayne	734
Webberville	517
Webster	734
Weidman	989
Wells	906
Wellston	231
Wequetonsing	231
West Bloomfield	248
West Branch	989
West Olive	616
Westland	734
Weston	517
Westphalia	989
Westwood	269
Wetmore	906
Wheeler	989
White Cloud	231
White Lake	248
White Pigeon	269
White Pine	906
Whitehall	231
Whitmore Lake	734
Whittaker	734
Whittemore	989
Williamsburg	231
Williamston	517
Williamsville	734
Willis	734
Willow	734
Willow Run	734
Wilson	906
Winn	989
Wixom	248
Wolverine	231
Wolverine Lake	248
Wolverine Lk	248
Wolverine World Wide	616
Woodhaven	734
Woodland	269
Woodland Park	231
Worth Township	810
Wyandotte	734
Wyoming	616
Yale	810
Yankee Springs	269
York Twp	734
Ypsilanti	734
Zeeland	616
Zondervan Corp	616

Minnesota

City	Area Code
3 M	651
Abmps	612
Ada	218
Adams	507
Adolph	218
Adrian	507
Afton	651
Ah Gwah Ching	218
Aitkin	218
Akeley	218
Alango	218
Alaska	218
Albany	320
Albert Lea	507
Alberta	320
Albertville	763
Alborn	218
Alden	507
Aldrich	218
Alex	320
Alexandria	320
Alida	218
Almelund	651
Almora	218
Alpha	507
Altura	507
Alvarado	218
Alvwood	218
Amboy	507
Ameriprise Financial	612
Amiret	507
Amor	218
Andover	763
Andyville	507
Angle Inlet	218
Angora	218
Angus	218
Annandale	320
Anoka	763
Antlers Park	952
Apple Valley	952
Appleton	320
Arago	218
Arco	507
Arcturus	218
Arden Hills	651
Ardenhurst	218
Arendahl	507
Argonne	952
Argyle	218
Arlington	507
Arnesen	218
Arrowhead	218
Arrowhead Promotion Fulfillm	218
Ash Lake	218
Ashby	218
Askov	320
Aslo	320
Atwater	320
Audubon	218
Ault	218
Aurora	218
Austin	507
Averill	218
Avoca	507
Avon	320
Babbitt	218
Backus	218
Badger	218
Bagley	218
Baker	218
Balaton	507
Balkan	218
Ball Bluff	218
Balsam	218
Bar Code	651
Barclay	218
Barnesville	218
Barnum	218
Barrett	320
Barry	320
Bass Brook	218
Bassett	218
Basswood	218
Battle Lake	218
Battle River	218
Baudette	218
Baxter	218
Bayport	651
Baytown	651
Bear Creek	218
Bear Lake	218
Beardsley	320
Bearville North	218
Beaulieu	218
Beaver Bay	218
Beaver Creek	507
Becida	218
Becker	763
Bejou	218
Belgrade	320
Bellchester	651
Belle Plaine	952
Bellingham	320
Beltrami	218
Belview	507
Bemidji	218
Bena	218
Benedict	218
Bennington	507
Benson	320
Bergville	218
Berne	507
Berner	218
Beroun	320
Bertha	218
Bethany	507
Bethel	651
Beulah	218
Bible College	952
Big Falls	218
Big Lake	763
Bigelow	507
Bigfork	218
Bingham Lake	507
Birch	218
Birch Beach	218
Birchdale	218
Birchwood	651
Bird Island	320
Biwabik	218
Bixby	507
Black River	218
Blackduck	218
Blaine	763
Blind Lake	218
Blmng Prairie	507
Blomkest	320
Blooming Prairie	507
Bloomington	952
Blue Earth	507
Blueberry	218
Bluffton	218
Bock	320
Bombay	507
Boray	218
Border	218
Borup	218
Bovey	218
Bowlus	320
Bowstring	218
Boy Lake	218
Boy River	218
Boyd	320
Braham	320
Brainerd	218
Branch	651
Brandon	320
Bratsberg	507
Breckenridge	218
Breezy Point	218
Breitung	218
Bremen	320
Brevator	218
Brevik	218
Brewster	507
Bricelyn	507
Brimson	218
Britt	218
Brkston	218
Brook Park	320
Brooklyn	218
Brooklyn Center	763
Brooklyn Ctr	763
Brooklyn Park	763
Brooklyn Pk	763
Brooks	218
Brookston	218
Brooten	320
Browerville	320
Browns Valley	320
Brownsdale	507
Brownsville	507
Brownton	320
Bruno	320
Brunswick	320
Brushvale	218
Buckman	320
Buffalo	763
Buffalo Lake	320
Buhl	218
Burns Township	763
Burns Twnshp	763
Burnsville	952

City	Area Code
urtrum	320
utler	218
utterfield	507
uyck	218
yron	507
aledonia	507
allaway	218
alumet	218
ambridge	763
ampbell	218
anby	507
anisteo	507
annon Falls	507
anton	507
anyon	218
arimona	507
arlisle	218
arlos	320
arlton	218
arp	218
arver	952
ass Lake	218
astle Rock	952
edar	763
edar E Bethl	763
edar East Bethel	763
edar Mills	320
edar Valley	218
enter City	651
enterville	651
entral Lakes	218
eylon	507
hamplin	763
handler	507
hanhassen	952
harlesville	218
haska	952
hatfield	507
hengwatana	320
herry Grove	507
hickamaw Beach	218
hisago City	651
hisago Lake	651
hisholm	218
hokio	320
ircle Pines	763
lara City	320
laremont	507
larissa	218
lark	218
larkfield	320
larks Grove	507
lear Lake	320
learbrook	218
learwater	320
lements	507
lementson	218
leveland	507
limax	218
linton	320
litherall	218
lontarf	320
loquet	218
lough	320
lover	218
obden	507
ohasset	218
okato	320
old Spring	320
oleraine	218
ollegeville	320
ologne	952
Columbia Heights	763
Columbia Hts	763
Columbus	651, 763
olvin	218
omfrey	507
omstock	218
oncord	507
Concordia College	218
onger	507
ook	218
ooley	218
oon Rapids	763
Copas	651
opley	218
Corcoran	763
Cormant	218
Cormorant	218
Cornish	218
Correll	320
Cosmos	320
Cottage Grove	651
Cotton	218
Cottonwood	507
County Market	763
Courtland	507
Craigville	218
Crane Lake	218
Croftville	218
Cromwell	218
Crooked Lake	218
Crookston	218
Crosby	218
Cross Lake	218
Crosslake	218
Crown College	952
Crystal	763
Crystal Bay	763
Culver	218
Cummingsville	507
Currie	507
Cushing	218
Cusson	218
Cuyuna	218
Cyrus	320
Dakota	507
Dalbo	320
Dale	218
Dalton	218
Danforth	320
Danube	320
Danvers	320
Darfur	507
Darwin	320
Dassel	320
Dawson	320
Day	320
Dayton	763
De Graff	320
Deephaven	952
Deer Creek	218
Deer Riv	218
Deer River	218
Deerfield	507
Deerwood	218
Delano	763
Delavan	507
Delft	507
Delhi	507
Dell Grove	320
Dellwood	651
Dennison	507
Dent	218
Detroit Lakes	218
Dexter	507
Dilworth	218
Dlth Fed Pris	218
Dodge Center	507
Donaldson	218
Donnelly	320
Dora Lake	218
Doran	218
Dorset	218
Douglas	507, 651
Dover	507
Dovray	507
Downer	218
Dresbach	507
Dudley	218
Duluth	218
Duluth Federal Prison	218
Dumfries	651
Dumont	320
Dundas	507
Dundee	507
Dunnell	507
Duquette	218
Durand	218
E G Forks	218
E Grand Forks	218
E Gull Lake	218
Eagan	952
Eagle Bend	218
Eagle Lake	507
East Bethel	651, 763
East Grand Forks	218
East Gull Lake	218
East Lake	218
Easton	507
Ebro	218
Echo	507
Eckles	218
Eddy	218
Eden Prairie	952
Eden Valley	320
Edgerton	507
Edgewood	763
Edina	612, 952
Effie	218
Eitzen	507
Elba	507
Elbow Lake	218
Eldred	218
Elgin	507
Elizabeth	218
Elk River	763
Elko	952
Elkton	507
Ellendale	507
Ellsburg	218
Ellsworth	507
Elmore	507
Elrosa	320
Ely	218
Elysian	507
Embarrass	218
Emily	218
Emmons	507
Erdahl	218
Erhard	218
Erie	218
Erskine	218
Esko	218
Essig	507
Etter	651
Euclid	218
Evan	507
Evansville	218
Eveleth	218
Everdell	218
Excel Energy	612
Excelsior	952
Eyota	507
Fairbanks	218
Fairfax	507
Fairmont	507
Faith	218
Falcon Heights	651
Falcon Hgts	651
Falk	218
Fall Lake	218
Farden	218
Faribault	507
Farmington	952
Farris	218
Farwell	320
Fayal	218
Fdci	320
Federal Dam	218
Felton	218
Fergus Falls	218
Fertile	218
Fifty Lakes	218
Fillmore	507
Fine Lakes	218
Fingerhut	320
Fingerhut (Pre Paid)	320
Fingerhut Bus Reply	320
Fingerhut Sweepstakes	320
Finland	218
Finlayson	320
First Bank St Paul	651
Fisher	218
Flensburg	320
Flom	218
Floodwood	218
Florence	507
Florian	218
Foley	320
Forbes	218
Forest Grove	218
Forest Lake	651
Foreston	320
Fort Ripley	320
Fort Snelling	612
Fort Snelling Military Resv	612
Fosston	218
Fossum	218
Fountain	507
Foxhome	218
Franconia	651
Frankford	507
Franklin	507
Frazee	218
Freeborn	507
Freeburg	507
Freeport	320
Fremont	507
Fridley	763
Frontenac	651
Frost	507
Fulda	507
Funkley	218
Garden City	507
Garfield	320
Garrison	320
Garvin	507
Gary	218
Gatzke	218
Gaylord	507
Gem Lake	651
Gemmell	218
Geneva	507
Genoa	218
Genola	320
Gentilly	218
Georgetown	218
Gheen	218
Ghent	507
Gibbon	507
Giese	320
Gilbert	218
Gilman	320
Glencoe	320
Glendale	218
Glenville	507
Glenwood	320
Glyndon	218
Golden Valley	763
Gonvick	218
Good Hope	218
Good Thunder	507
Goodhue	651
Goodland	218
Goodridge	218
Goodview	507
Graceville	320
Granada	507
Grand Falls	218
Grand Lake	218
Grand Marais	218
Grand Meadow	507
Grand Portage	218
Grand Rapids	218
Grandy	763
Granger	507
Granite Falls	320
Grant	651
Grant Township	651
Grant Valley	218
Grass Lake	320
Grasston	320
Grattan	218
Great Scott	218
Green Isle	507
Greenbush	218
Greenfield	763
Greenleafton	507
Greenwald	320
Greenway	218
Greenwood	218
Grey Cloud Island	651
Grey Eagle	320
Groningen	320
Grove City	320
Grygla	218
Gully	218
Guthrie	218
Hackensack	218
Hackett	218
Hadley	507
Hagali	218
Halden	218
Hallock	218
Halma	218
Halstad	218
Ham Lake	763
Hamburg	952
Hamel	763
Hammond	507
Hampton	507
Hancock	320
Hangaard	218
Hanley Falls	507
Hanover	763
Hanska	507
Happyland	218
Hardwick	507
Harmony	507
Harnell Park	218
Harris	651
Hart	507
Hartland	507
Hassan	763
Hastings	651
Hatfield	507
Haugen	218
Havana	507
Hawick	320
Hawley	218
Hayfield	507
Haypoint	218
Hayward	507
Hazel Run	320
Hector	320
Heidelberg	952
Henderson	507
Hendricks	507
Hendrum	218
Hennepin County Govt Ctr	612
Henning	218
Henriette	320
Herman	320
Hermantown	218
Heron Lake	507
Hewitt	218
Hibbing	218
High Forest	507
Highland	507
Hill City	218
Hillman	320
Hills	507
Hilltop	763
Hinckley	320
Hines	218
Hitterdal	218
Hoffman	320
Hokah	507
Holdingford	320
Holland	507
Hollandale	507
Holloway	320
Holman	218
Holmes City	320
Holst	218
Holt	218
Holyoke	218
Homer	507
Hope	507
Hopkins	952
Hornet	218
Houston	507
Hovland	218
Howard Lake	320, 763
Hoyt Lakes	218
Hubbard	218
Hugo	651
Humboldt	218
Huntersville	218
Huntley	507
Hutchinson	320
Ihlen	507
Independence	763
Indus	218
Industrial	218
Inger	218
Inguadona	218
International Falls	218
Intl Falls	218
Inver Grove	651, 952
Inver Grove Heights	651
Iona	507
Iron	218
Ironton	218
Isabella	218
Isanti	763
Isle	320
Ivanhoe	507
Jackson	507
Jacobson	218
Janesville	507
Jasper	507
Jeffers	507
Jenkins	218
Jevne	218
Johnsburg	507
Johnson	320
Jones	218
Jordan	952
Kabetogama	218
Kanaranzi	507
Kandiyohi	320
Karlstad	218
Kasota	507
Kasson	507
Keewatin	218
Kego	218
Kelliher	218
Kellogg	507
Kelly Lake	218
Kelsey	218
Kennedy	218
Kenneth	507
Kensington	320
Kent	218
Kenyon	507
Kerkhoven	320
Kerrick	218
Kettle River	218
Kiester	507
Kilkenny	507
Kimball	320
Kinghurst	218
Kingston	320
Kinmount	218
Kinney	218
Kitzville	218
Klossner	507
Knife Falls	218
Knife Lake	320
Knife River	218
Kragnes	218
Kugler	218
La Crescent	507
La Fayette	507
La Porte	218
La Salle	507
Lafayette	507
Lake Benton	507
Lake Bronson	218
Lake City	651
Lake Crystal	507
Lake Edwards	218
Lake Elmo	651
Lake Emma	218
Lake George	218
Lake Hubert	218
Lake Itasca	218
Lake Lillian	320
Lake Nichols	218
Lake Park	218
Lake Shore	218
Lake Wilson	507
Lakefield	507
Lakeland	651

City	Area Code
Lakeville	952
Lamberton	507
Lammers	218
Lamoille	507
Lancaster	218
Landfall Village	651
Landfall Vlg	651
Lanesboro	507
Langor	218
Lansing	507
Laona	218
Laporte	218
Lastrup	320
Lauderdale	651
Lavinia	218
Lawler	218
Lawrence	218
Le Center	507
Le Roy	507
Le Sueur	507
Leech Lake	218
Leetonia	218
Leiding	218
Lengby	218
Lent	651
Leon	218
Leonard	218
Leonidas	218
Leota	507
Lester Pr	320
Lester Prairie	320
Lewiston	507
Lewisville	507
Lexington	763
Libby	218
Liberty	218
Lilydale	651
Lima	218
Lindford	218
Lindstrom	651
Lino Lakes	651, 763
Linwood	651
Lismore	507
Litchfield	320
Litomysl	507
Little Canada	651
Little Falls	320
Little Marais	218
Little Sauk	320
Little Swan	218
Littlefork	218
Lockhart	218
Logan	218
Loman	218
London	507
Lone Pine	218
Long Lake	763
Long Point	218
Long Prairie	320
Longville	218
Lonsdale	507
Loretto	763
Louisburg	320
Lowry	320
Lucan	507
Lude	218
Lutsen	218
Luverne	507
Lyle	507
Lynd	507
Lynwood	218
Mabel	507
Macville	218
Macys	612
Madelia	507
Madison	320
Madison Lake	507
Magnolia	507
Mahnomen	218
Mahtomedi	651
Mahtowa	218
Maine	218
Makinen	218
Manchester	507
Manhattan Bch	218
Manhattan Beach	218
Manitou	218
Mankato	507
Mantorville	507
Mantrap	218
Maple Grove	763, 952
Maple Hill	218
Maple Lake	320
Maple Plain	320, 763
Maple Ridge	218
Mapleton	507
Maplewood	651
Marble	218
Marcell	218
Margie	218
Marietta	320
Marine	651
Marine On Saint Croix	651
Marine On St Croix	651
Marine St Crx	651
Markham	218
Markville	320
Marshall	507
Martin Lake	651
Max	218
Mayer	952
Maynard	320
Mayo Clinic	507
Mazeppa	507
Mc Grath	320
Mcdavitt	218
Mcgregor	218
Mcintosh	218
Mckinley	218
Meadowlands	218
Medford	507
Medicine Lake	763
Medina	763
Melrose	320
Melrude	218
Menahga	218
Mendota	612
Mendota Heights	651, 952
Mendota Hts	651
Mentor	218
Meriden	507
Merrifield	218
Middle River	218
Midway	218
Miesville	507
Milaca	320
Milan	320
Millville	507
Milroy	507
Miltona	218
Minetonka Bch	952
Minetonka Mls	952
Minn	612
Minn City	507
Minn Mining Boxes	651
Minneapolis	612, 763, 952
Minneapolis Tribune	612
Minneiska	507
Minneota	507
Minnesota City	507
Minnesota Lake	507
Minnesota Lk	507
Minnetnka Bch	952
Minnetnka Mls	952
Minnetonka	952
Minnetonka Beach	952
Minnetonka Mills	952
Minnetrista	763
Minnewana	218
Minnewaska	218
Mizpah	218
Moland	507
Montevideo	320
Montgomery	507
Monticello	763
Montrose	763
Moorhead	218
Moorhead State University	218
Moose Creek	218
Moose Lake	218
Moose Park	218
Mora	320
Moran	218
Morgan	507
Morgan Park	218
Morris	320
Morrison	218
Morristown	507
Morse	218
Morton	507
Motley	218
Mound	952
Mounds View	651
Moundsview	651
Mountain Iron	218
Mountain Lake	507
Mozeppa	218
Mt Lake	507
Murdock	320
Murphy City	218
Myrtle	507
N Mankato	507
N Saint Paul	651
Nashua	218
Nashwauk	218
Nassau	320
Navarre	763
Naytahwaush	218
Nebish	218
Nelson	320
Nerstrand	507
Nett Lake	218
Nett River	218
Nevada	507
Nevis	218
New Auburn	320
New Brighton	651
New Germany	320
New Hartford	507
New Hope	763
New London	320
New Market	952
New Munich	320
New Prague	952
New Richland	507
New Scandia	651
New Trier	507
New Ulm	507
New York Mills	218
New York Mls	218
Newfolden	218
Newport	651
Newry	507
Nichols	218
Nickerson	218
Nicollet	507
Nicolville	507
Nielsville	218
Nimrod	218
Nisswa	218
No Mankato	507
No Oaks	651
Nodine	507
Nora	218
Norcross	320
Nore	218
Norman	320
North Branch	651
North Hibbing	218
North Mankato	507
North Oaks	651
North Redwood	507
North Saint Paul	651
North St Paul	651
Northcote	218
Northern	218
Northfield	507
Northland	218
Northome	218
Northrop	507
Norton	507
Norwood	952
Norwood Young America	763
Nowthen	763
Noyes	218
Nya	952
Nymore	218
O Brien	218
Oak Grove	763
Oak Island	218
Oak Park	320
Oak Park Heights	651
Oak Park Hgts	651
Oak Park Hts	651
Oakdale	651
Oakland	507
Odessa	320
Odin	507
Ogema	218
Ogilvie	320
Okabena	507
Oklee	218
Olga	218
Olivia	320
Onamia	320
Onigum	218
Orleans	218
Ormsby	507
Orono	763
Orr	218
Ortonville	320
Osage	218
Osakis	320
Oslo	218
Oslund	218
Osseo	763
Ostrander	507
Oteneagen	218
Otisco	507
Otisville	651
Otsego	763
Ottertail	218
Outing	218
Owatonna	507
Oylen	218
Palisade	218
Palmdale	651
Palo	218
Park Rapids	218
Parker	320
Parkers Pr	218
Parkers Prairie	218
Parkville	218
Partridge	320
Paynesville	320
Pease	320
Pel Rapids	218
Pelican Rapids	218
Pemberton	507
Penasse	218
Pencer	218
Pengilly	218
Pennington	218
Pennock	320
Pequot Lakes	218
Perham	218
Perley	218
Peterson	507
Pickwick	507
Pierz	320
Pike	218
Pike Bay	218
Pillager	218
Pilot Mound	507
Pine City	320
Pine Island	507
Pine Lake	218, 320
Pine River	218
Pine Springs	651
Pinecreek	218
Pineville	218
Pinewood	218
Pipestone	507
Pitt	218
Plainview	507
Plato	320
Pleasant Grove	507
Plummer	218
Plymouth	763
Ponemah	218
Ponsford	218
Ponto Lake	218
Poplar	218
Popple	218
Port Hope	218
Portage	218
Porter	507
Potsdam	507
Prairie Lake	218
Pratt	507
Predmore	507
Preston	507
Princeton	763
Prinsburg	320
Prior Lake	952
Proctor	218
Puposky	218
Quamba	320
Quiring	218
Qwest	612
Racine	507
Radium	218
Ramsey	763
Randall	320
Randolph	507
Ranier	218
Ray	218
Raymond	320
Reading	507
Reads Landing	651
Red Lake Falls	218
Red Rock	507
Red Wing	651
Redby	218
Redlake	218
Redwood Falls	507
Remer	218
Reno	507
Renville	320
Revere	507
Rheiderland	218
Rice	320
Rice River	218
Richfield	612
Richmond	320
Richville	218
Richwood	218
Rindal	218
Riverton	218
Rl Falls	218
Robbinsdale	763
Rochert	218
Rochester	507
Rock Creek	320
Rockford	763
Rockville	320
Rogers	763
Rollag	218
Rollingstone	507
Roosevelt	218
Roscoe	320
Rose Creek	507
Roseau	218
Rosemount	952
Roseville	651
Rosewood	218
Ross	218
Rothsay	218
Round Lake	507
Royalton	320
Ruby Junction	218
Runeberg	218
Rush City	320
Rushford	507
Rushford Village	507
Rushford Vlg	507
Rushmore	507
Russell	507
Ruthton	507
Rutledge	320
S Int Falls	218
S Intl Falls	218
S Saint Paul	651
Sabin	218
Sacred Heart	320
Saginaw	218
Saint Anthony	612, 763
Saint Augusta	320
Saint Bonifacius	952
Saint Charles	507
Saint Clair	507
Saint Cloud	320
Saint Francis	763
Saint Hilaire	218
Saint James	507
Saint Joseph	320
Saint Leo	507
Saint Louis Park	952
Saint Martin	320
Saint Michael	763
Saint Paul	612, 651, 952
Saint Paul Park	651
Saint Peter	507
Saint Stephen	320
Saint Vincent	218
Salo	218
Salol	218
Sanborn	507
Sand Lake	218
Sandstone	320
Sandy	218
Santiago	763
Saratoga	507
Sargeant	507
Sartell	320
Sauk Centre	320
Sauk Rapids	320
Saum	218
Savage	952
Savannah	218
Sawyer	218
Scandia	651
Scanlon	218
Schley	218
Schroeder	218
Seaforth	507
Searles	507
Sebeka	218
Sedan	320
Shafer	651
Shakopee	952
Shamrock	218
Shaw	218
Shell River	218
Shelly	218
Sherburn	507
Sheshebee	218
Shevlin	218
Shingobee	218
Shooks	218
Shoreview	651
Shorewood	952
Shotley	218
Shovel Lake	218
Side Lake	218
Silica	218
Silver Bay	218
Silver Creek	763
Silver Lake	320
Sinclair	218
Skelton	218
Skime	218
Slater	218
Slayton	507
Sleepy Eye	507
Smoky Hollow	218
Snellman	218
So Saint Paul	651
Soderville	763
Solway	218
Soudan	218
South Haven	320
South International Falls	218
South Rushford	507
South Saint Paul	651
South St Paul	651
Spalding	218
Spectacle Lake	763
Spicer	320
Spooner	218
Spring Grove	507
Spring Lake	218
Spring Lake Park	763
Spring Lk Pk	763
Spring Park	952

Spring Valley 507
Springfield 507
Squaw Lake 218
St Anthny Vlg 612
St Anthony 612, 763
St Anthony Village 612
St Bonifacius 952
St Charles 507
St Clair 507
St Croix 651
St Croix Beach 651
St Francis 763
St James 507
St Joseph 320
St Louis Park 952
St Louis Pk 952
St Martin 320
St Marys Point 651
St Paul Park 651
St Peter 507
St Stephen 320
Stacy 651
Stanchfield 320
Stanford 320
Stanton 507
Staples 218
Starbuck 320
State Offices 651
State Tax Dept 651
Steen 507
Stephen 218
Stewart 320
Stewartville 507
Stillwater 651
Stockton 507
Stokes 218
Stoney Brook 218
Storden 507
Strandquist 218
Strathcona 218
Stuntz 218
Sturgeon Lake 218
Sugar Bush 218
Summit 218, 507
Sunburg 320
Sunfish Lake 651, 952
Sunrise 651
Svea 320
Swan River 218
Swanburg 218
Swanville 320
Swatara 218
Swift 218
Sylvan 218
Syre 218
Taconite 218
Talmoon 218
Tamarack 218
Taopi 507
Target Direct 651
Taunton 507
Taylors Falls 651
Ten Lake 218
Tenney 218
Tenstrike 218
Terrace 320
Theilman 507
Thief River Falls 218
Thief Rvr Fls 218
Thomastown 218
Thunder Lake 218
Tintah 218
Todd 218
Tofte 218
Togo 218
Toimi 218
Toivola 218
Tonka Bay 952
Tower 218
Tr Falls 218
Tracy 507
Trail 218
Trelipe 218
Trimont 507
Trommald 218
Trosky 507
Troy 507
Truman 507
Turner 218
Turtle Lake 218
Turtle River 218
Twig 218
Twin Lakes 507
Twin Valley 218
Two Harbors 218
Tyler 507
Ulen 218
Underwood 218
Upsala 320
Us Bank 612, 651
Us Bank Visa 651
Usps Fac Area Office 651
Utica 507
V A 651
Vadnais Heights 651
Vadnais Hts 651
Van Buren 218
Vasa 651
Verdi 507
Verdon 218
Vergas 218
Vermilion Dam 218
Vermillion 651
Verndale 218
Vernon Center 507
Veseli 507
Vesta 507
Victoria 952
Viking 218
Villard 320
Vining 218
Viola 507
Virginia 218
W Lakeland 651
W Saint Paul 651
W St Paul 651
Waasa 218
Wabasha 651
Wabasso 507
Wabedo 218
Waconia 952
Wadena 218
Wagner 320
Wahkon 320
Waite Park 320
Walden 218
Waldorf 507
Walker 218
Walnut Grove 507
Walters 507
Waltham 507
Wanamingo 507
Wanda 507
Wannaska 218
Warba 218
Warman 320
Warren 218
Warroad 218
Warsaw 507
Waseca 507
Wasioja 507
Waskish 218
Wastedo 507
Waterford 507
Watertown 952
Waterville 507
Watkins 320
Watson 320
Waubun 218
Waukenabo 218
Waverly 320
Wawina 218
Wayzata 952
Weaver 507
Weber 651
Webster 952
Welch 651
Welcome 507
Wells 507
Wells Fargo Bank 612
Wells Fargo Home Mortgage 612
Wendell 218
West Concord 507
West Duluth 218
West Lakeland 651
West Rock 320
West Saint Paul 651
West St Paul 651
West Union 320
Westbrook 507
Whalan 507
Wheaton 320
Wheeling 507
Whipholt 218
White 218
White Bear Lake 651
White Bear Lk 651
White Bear Township 651
White Bear Tp 651
White Earth 218
White Rock 507
Whiteface 218
Wilder 507
Wildwood 218
Wilkinson 218
Willernie 651
Williams 218
Willmar 320
Willow River 320
Wilmont 507
Wilpen 218
Wilson 218, 507
Wilton 218
Windom 507
Wing River 218
Winger 218
Winnebago 507
Winona 507
Winsor 218
Winsted 320
Winthrop 507
Winton 218
Wirt 218
Wiscoy 507
Witoka 507
Wolf Lake 218
Wolverton 218
Wood Lake 507
Woodbury 651
Woodland 952
Woodrow 218
Woodstock 507
Workman 218
Worthington 507
Wrenshall 218
Wright 218
Wykoff 507
Wyoming 651
Young America 763, 952
Young America Corp 952
Zemple 218
Zerkel 218
Zim 218
Zimmerman 763
Zumbro Falls 507
Zumbrota 507

Mississippi

A H Mccoy Federal Bldg 601
Abbeville 662
Abbott 662
Aberdeen 662
Ackerman 662
Adaton 662
Agricola 601
Airey 228
Albin 662
Alcorn State University 601
Algoma 662
Alligator 662
Alma 662
Alpine 662
Altitude 662
Alva 662
Amistead 662
Amory 662
Anchor 662
Anguilla 662
Ansley 228
Antioch 601
Anvil 662
Arcola 662
Ariel 601
Arkabutla 662
Arlington 601
Arm 601
Arnold Line 601
Artesia 662
Ashland 662
Ashwood 601
Askew 662
Atlanta 662
Auburn 601
Austin 662
Avalon 662
Avent 601
Avon 662
Bacots 601
Bailey 601
Baird 662
Baldwyn 662
Ballardsville 662
Baltzer 662
Banks 662
Bankston 662
Banner 662
Barr 662
Barrontown 601
Bartahatchie 662
Barth 601
Barto 601
Basin 601
Bassfield 601
Batesville 662
Batson 601
Baugh 662
Baxterville 601
Bay Saint Louis 228
Bay Springs 601
Bay St Louis 228
Bayside Park 228
Bear Garden 662
Bear Town 601
Beasley 662
Beaumont 601
Becker 662
Beelake 662
Belden 662
Belen 662
Belle Isle 228
Bellefontaine 662
Belleville 601
Bellewood 662
Bells School 662
Belmont 662
Belzoni 662
Benndale 601
Benoit 662
Bentley 662
Benton 662
Bentonia 662
Benwood 662
Berclair 662
Bethany 662
Bethlehem 662
Beulah 662
Bewelcome 601
Bhaven 601
Big Creek 662
Big Level 601
Bigbee 662
Bigbee Valley 662
Biggersville 662
Bigpoint 228
Biloxi 228
Binford 662
Birdie 662
Bissell 662
Black Hawk 662
Blackjack 662
Blackland 662
Blackwater 662
Blair 662
Blodgett 601
Bloody Springs 662
Blue Lake 662
Blue Mount 662
Blue Mountain 662
Blue Springs 662
Bluff 662
Blx 228
Bobo 662
Boggan Bend 662
Bogue Chitto 601
Bolivar 662
Boloxi 228
Bolton 601
Bon Homme 601
Booneville 662
Bouge Chitto 601
Bourbon 662
Bovina 601
Bowdre 662
Bowman 662
Boyer 662
Boyle 662
Bradley 662
Brandon 601
Branyan 662
Braxton 601
Brazil 662
Brewer 662
Bristers 601
Bristers Store 601
Brookhaven 601
Brooklyn 601
Brooks 662
Brooksville 662
Brownfield 662
Bruce 662
Bryant 662
Buckatunna 601
Buckhorn 662
Bude 601
Buena Vista 662
Bunkley 601
Burns 601
Burnsville 662
Burrow 662
Burtons 662
Buxton 662
Byhalia 662
Byram 601
Cadamy 662
Cadaretta 662
Caesar 601
Caile 662
Caledonia 662
Calhoun 601
Calhoun City 662
Calhoun Cty 662
Calhoun Cy 662
Camden 662
Camp Shelby 601
Campbell 662
Camphill 662
Canaan 662
Cannon 662
Canton 601
Cardsville 662
Carlisle 601
Carmichael 601
Carnes 601
Carolina 662
Carpenter 601
Carriere 601
Carrollton 662
Carson 601
Carterville 601
Carthage 601
Cary 662
Cascilla 662
Cassels 601
Cayuga 601
Cedar Hill 662
Cedarbluff 662
Center 662
Centralgrove 662
Centreville 601
Chalybeate 662
Charlestn 662
Charleston 662
Chatawa 601
Chatham 662
Cheraw 601
Cherrycreek 662
Chester 662
Chesterville 662
Chiwapa 662
Choctaw 601
Chunky 601
Church Hill 601
Clack 662
Clara 601
Clarksdale 662
Clarkson 662
Clayton 662
Clayton Village 662
Cleo 601
Clermont Harbor 228
Clermont Hbr 228
Cleveland 662
Cliftonville 662
Clinton 601
Clove Hill 662
Coahoma 662
Cobbs 601
Coffeeville 662
Coila 662
Cold Water 662
Coldwater 662
Coles 601
Coles Creek 662
Collins 601
Collinsville 601
Colony Town 662
Colsub 662
Columbia 601
Columbus 662
Columbus Afb 662
Commerce 662
Como 662
Conehatta 601
Corinth 662
Cornersville 662
Corrona 662
Cotton Plant 662
Cottonville 662
Courtland 662
Cowart 662
Craig Springs 662
Crane Creek 601
Cranfield 601
Crawford 662
Crenshaw 662
Crockett 662
Crosby 601
Crossroads 601, 662
Crotts 601
Crowder 662
Cruger 662
Crystal Spgs 601
Crystal Springs 601
Cuevas 228
Cumberland 662
Cybur 601
D Lo 601
D' Lo 601
Dahomey 662
Daisy Vestry 601
Daleville 601
Dancy 662
Darbun 601
Darling 662
Darlove 662
Darracott 662
Darrington 601
Days 662
De Kalb 601
Decatur 601
Deerbrook 662
Deeson 662
Delta City 662
Delta State 662

City	Area Code
Delta State Univ	662
Dennis	662
Dennis Landing	662
Dentontown	662
Derby	601
Derma	662
Dexter	601
Diamondhead	228
Diberville	228
Dixie	601
Dixie Pine	601
Dlo	601
Doddsville	662
Doloroso	601
Donegal	601
Dorsey	662
Doskie	662
Drew	662
Dry Creek	601
Dsu	662
Dubard	662
Dubbs	662
Dublin	662
Duck Hill	662
Dumas	662
Duncan	662
Dundee	662
Dunleith	662
Durant	662
Dwiggins	662
Dwyer	662
Earlygrove	662
East Aberdeen	662
East Lincoln	601
East Moss Point	228
East Side	601
Eastabuchie	601
Eastfork	601
Eastlawn	228
Eastport	662
Eastside	228
Eatonville	601
Ecru	662
Eddiceton	601
Edinburg	601
Edwards	601
Effie	662
Eggville	662
Egypt	662
Electric Mills	662
Elizabeth	662
Ellard	662
Elliott	662
Ellistown	662
Ellisville	601
Ellisville Junction	601
Elsie	662
Eminence	601
Endville	662
Enid	662
Enon	601
Enterprise	601
Errata	601
Erwin	662
Escatawpa	228
Eskridge	662
Estill	662
Ethel	662
Etta	662
Eunice	601
Eupora	662
Europa	662
Eutaw	662
Evansville	662
Fair Oaks Springs	601
Fair River	601
Fairfield	662
Fairlane	662
Fairview	662
Falcon	662
Falkner	662
Fame	662
Farmhaven	601
Farmington	662
Farrell	662
Farwood	601
Fayette	601
Fentress	662
Fernwood	601
Fitler	662
Fitzhugh	662
Flora	601
Florence	601
Flowood	601
Fontainebleau	228
Foote	662
Fords Creek	601
Forest	601
Fort Adams	601
Foxworth	601
Francis	662
French Camp	662
Friars Point	662
Friendship	601
Ft Adams	601
Fulton	662
Furrs	662
Futheyville	662
G T Airport	662
G Wood	662
Gallman	601
Gandsi	601
Garden City	601
Gatewood	662
Gattman	662
Gautier	228
Geeslin Corner	662
Geeville	662
Georgetown	601
Gibson	662
Gillsburg	601
Glade	601
Glen	662
Glen Allan	662
Glendale	601
Glendora	662
Gloster	601
Glover	662
Gluckstadt	601
Golden	662
Golden Triangle Regional Air	662
Goldfield	662
Good Hope	601
Goodfood	662
Goodman	662
Goodyear	601
Gore Springs	662
Gpt	228
Grace	662
Grady	662
Graham	662
Grand Gulf	601
Grapeland	662
Gravel Siding	662
Gravestown	662
Greenbrier Park	601
Greenville	662
Greenwood	662
Greenwood Spg	662
Greenwood Spr	662
Greenwood Springs	662
Greenwood-Leflore Airport	662
Grenada	662
Griffith	662
Gulf Hills	228
Gulf Islands National Seasho	228
Gulf Park Estates	228
Gulfport	228
Gums	662
Gunnison	662
Guntown	662
Hamburg	601
Hamilton	662
Hampton	662
Hardy	662
Harleston	662
Harmontown	662
Harperville	601
Harriston	601
Harrisville	601
Harvey	601
Hatley	662
Hattiesbg	601
Hattiesburg	601
Hattiesburg South	601
Hazlehurst	601
Heads	662
Heathman	662
Heidelberg	601
Helena	228
Helm	662
Hendrix	662
Henleyfield	601
Hermanville	601
Hernando	662
Heucks	601
Hickory	601
Hickory Flat	662
Hickory Grove	662
Higgins	601
Highlandale	662
Highway Village	601
Hillhouse	662
Hillman	601
Hillsboro	601
Hillsdale	601
Hinchcliff	662
Hinds Junior College	601
Hinkle	662
Hintonville	601
Hohenlinden	662
Holcomb	662
Holcut	662
Hollandale	662
Hollis	662
Holly Bluff	662
Holly Grove	662
Holly Ridge	662
Holly Spgs	662
Holly Springs	662
Hollywood	662
Holmesville	601
Holts	662
Homochitto	601
Horn Lake	662
Hot Coffee	601
Houlka	662
Houston	662
Howison	228
Hoy	601
Hurley	228
Hurricane	662
Hushpuckena	662
Ida B Wells	662
Inda	601
Independence	662
Indian Springs	601
Indianola	662
Industrial	601
Ingomar	662
Inverness	662
Iowana	228
Ireland	601
Irene	601
Isola	662
Itta Bena	662
Iuka	662
Jacinto	662
Jackson	601
Jackson State University	601
Jago	662
James	662
Jamestown	601
Jax	601
Jayess	601
Jefferson	662
Jeffries	662
Jennings	601
Jericho	662
Jksn	601
Johnson	601
Johnston	601
Jonathan	601
Jonestown	662
Jug Fork	662
Jumpertown	662
Jxn	601
Keesler Afb	228
Keesler Air Force Base	228
Keesler Field	228
Kendrick	662
Keownville	662
Kerin	662
Kilmichael	662
Kiln	228
King And Anderson	662
Kinlock	662
Kirby	601
Kirkville	662
Knoxo	601
Knoxville	601
Kokomo	601
Kola	601
Kolola Springs	662
Kosciusko	662
Kossuth	662
Kreole	228
Lackey	662
Lafayette	662
Lafayette Springs	662
Lake	601
Lake Center	662
Lake Cormorant	662
Lake View	662
Lakeshore	228
Lamar	662
Lamar Park	601
Lambert	662
Lamont	662
Laneheart	601
Lantrip	662
Larue	228
Latimer	228
Latonia	601
Lauderdale	601
Laurel	601
Lawrence	601
Laws Hill	662
Leaf	601
Leakesville	601
Learned	601
Lebanon	662
Leedy	662
Leesdale	601
Leeville	601
Leland	662
Lena	601
Lessley	601
Letourneau	601
Leverett	662
Lexie	601
Lexington	662
Liberty	601
Lightsey	601
Limbert	601
Linn	662
Little Creek	601
Little Rock	601
Little Texas	662
Litton	662
Lk Cormorant	662
Lobdell	662
Locum	662
Lodi	662
Lombardy	662
Long	662
Long Beach	228
Longshot	662
Longtown	662
Longview	662
Looxahoma	662
Lorman	601
Louin	601
Louise	662
Louisville	662
Loyd	662
Lucas	601
Lucedale	601
Lucien	601
Ludlow	601
Lula	662
Lumberton	601
Lux	601
Lynn Creek	662
Lyon	662
Maben	662
Macedonia	601
Macel	662
Macon	662
Madden	601
Madison	601
Magee	601
Magenta	662
Magnolia	601
Mahned	601
Malvina	662
Mantachie	662
Mantee	662
Marie	662
Marietta	662
Marion	601
Marks	662
Mars Hill	601
Mary Holmes	662
Matherville	601
Mathiston	662
Mattson	662
Maxie	601
Maybank	601
Maybell	601
Mayersville	662
Mayhew	662
Mc Adams	662
Mc Call Creek	601
Mc Carley	662
Mc Cool	662
Mc Henry	601
Mc Lain	601
Mc Neill	601
Mccall Creek	601
Mccallum	601
Mccarley	662
Mccomb	601
Mccool	662
Mccrary	662
Mccutcheon	662
Mcelveen	601
Mcgee	601
Mchenry	601
Mclain	601
Mclaurin	601
Mcneill	601
Mcraney	601
Mcswain	601
Mdn	601
Meadville	601
Meedville	601
Meeham	601
Melba	601
Memphis	662
Mendenhall	601
Meridian	601
Merigold	662
Merrill	601
Mesa	601
Metcalfe	662
Metrocenter	601
Meyers	601
Michigan City	662
Midnight	662
Midway	662
Mile Branch	601
Mileston	662
Mill Creek	601
Millsaps College	601
Mineral Wells	662
Mingo	662
Minter City	662
Miss State	662
Mississippi State	662
Mississippi State University	662
Mississippi Test Facility	228
Mississippi Valley State Col	662
Mitchell	662
Mize	601
Mnd Bayou	662
Mocarter	662
Money	662
Monroe	601
Monte Vista	662
Monticello	601
Montpelier	662
Montrose	601
Moores Mill	662
Mooreville	662
Moorhead	662
Morgan City	662
Morgantown	601
Morriston	601
Morton	601
Moselle	601
Moss	601
Moss Point	228
Moss Pt	228
Mound Bayou	662
Mound City	662
Mount Carmel	601
Mount Olive	601
Mount Pleasant	662
Mount Vernon	662
Movella	601
Ms College	601
Ms St	662
Ms State	662
Ms State Univ	662
Msu	662
Mt Pleasant	662
Mt Plsnt	662
Muldon	662
Muldrow	662
Murdock Crossing	662
Murdock Xing	662
Murphreesboro	662
Murphy	662
Murry	662
Mvsu	662
Myrick	601
Myrtle	662
N Carrollton	662
N S T L	228
Nas Meridian	601
Nason	601
Natchez	601
National Space Technology La	228
Naval Air Sta Meridian	601
Naval Air Station	601
Naval Ocean O Graphic	228
Navocean O	228
Navy Homeport	228
Necaise	601
Neely	601
Nesbit	662
Neshoba	601
Nettleton	662
New Albany	662
New Augusta	601
New Harmony	662
New Hope	662
New Sight	601
New Site	662
New Town	662
New Wren	662
Newhebron	601
Newport	662
Newton	601
Nicholson	601
Niles	662
Nitta Yuma	662
Nixon	662
Norfield	601
North Carrollton	662
North Crossroads	662
North Haven	662
North Tunica	662
Northwest Junior College	662
Noxapater	662
Nw Jr College	662
Oak Bowery	601
Oak Grove	601
Oak Vale	601
Oakland	662
Ocean Spgs	228
Ocean Springs	228
Ofahoma	601
Okolona	662
Oktibbeha	662

Oktoc 662
Old Cairo 662
Old Hamilton 662
Old Houlka 662
Old Union 662
Oldenburg 601
Oldham 662
Olive Branch 662
Oloh 601
Oma 601
Onward 662
Ora 601
Orange Grove 228
Osborn 662
Osborne Creek 662
Osyka 601
Ouetti 601
Ovett 601
Oxberry 662
Oxford 662
Ozona 601
Pace 662
Pachuta 601
Paden 662
Padenville 662
Palmers Crossing 601
Panther Burn 662
Parchman 662
Paris 662
Pascagoula 228
Pascagoula Naval Air Station 228
Pasgoula 228
Pass Chris 228
Pass Christian 228
Pass Christin 228
Patrick 662
Pattison 601
Paul 662
Paulding 601
Paulette 662
Paynes 662
Pearl 601
Pearlhaven 601
Pearlington 228
Pecan 228
Pecan Grove 601
Pelahatchie 601
Pendorff 601
Penns 662
Penton 662
Peoples 662
Percy 662
Perkinston 601
Perrytown 601
Perthshire 662
Petal 601
Pheba 662
Philadelphia 601
Philipp 662
Phillipstown 662
Piave 601
Picayune 601
Pickens 662
Pickwick 601
Pinckneyville 601
Pine Belt Reg 601
Pine Belt Regional Airport 601
Pine Flat 662
Pine Grove 662
Pine Ridge 601
Pine Valley 662
Pinebluff 662
Pinedale 662
Pinegrove 662
Pineview 601
Piney Woods 601
Pinola 601
Pisgah 662
Pistol Ridge 601
Pittman 601
Pittsboro 662
Plantersville 662
Pleasant Grove 662
Pleasant Ridge 662
Plymouth 662
Poagville 662
Pocahontas 601
Polfry 228
Polkville 601
Pollock 662
Pontotoc 662
Pope 662
Poplar Corners 662
Poplar Creek 662
Poplar Springs 662
Poplarville 601
Port Gibson 601
Porterville 601
Possum Trot 662
Possumneck 662
Potts Camp 662
Powell 662
Powers 601
Prairie 662
Prairie Point 662
Prentiss 601
Preston 601
Pricedale 601
Prichard 662
Progress 601
Puckett 601
Pulaski 601
Pumpkin Center 662
Purvis 601
Pyland 662
Quentin 601
Quitman 601
Quito 662
Rainey 601
Raleigh 601
Randolph 662
Ratliff 662
Rawls Springs 601
Raymond 601
Red Banks 662
Redstar 601
Redwood 601
Reform 662
Refuge 662
Regions Bank 601
Reid 662
Rena Lara 662
Renova 662
Reservoir 601
Rexburg 662
Rhodes 601
Riceville 601
Rich 662
Richardson 601
Richland 601
Richmond 662
Richton 601
Ridgeland 601
Rienzi 662
Ripley 662
Rising Sun 662
Riverton 662
Robinsonville 662
Robinwood 601
Rochdale 662
Rock Hill 601
Rocky Hill 662
Roebuck 662
Rogerslacy 601
Rolling Fork 662
Rome 662
Rose Hill 601
Rosebloom 662
Rosedale 662
Rosella 601
Rosetta 601
Rough Edge 662
Roundaway 662
Roundlake 662
Roxie 601
Rudyard 662
Ruleville 662
Runnelstown 601
Russell 601
Ruth 601
Sabino 662
Sabougla 662
Sacred Heart League 662
Saint Martin 228
Saints Rest 662
Salem 601
Sallis 662
Saltillo 662
Sanatorium 601
Sand Hill 601
Sandersville 601
Sandhill 601
Sandy Hook 601
Sanford 601
Sanitorium 601
Sapa 662
Sarah 662
Sardis 662
Sarepta 662
Sartinsville 601
Satartia 662
Saucier 228
Saukum 601
Sauls 601
Savage 662
Savannah 601
Schlater 662
Scobey 662
Scooba 662
Scott 662
Sebastopol 601
Sellers 601
Seminary 601
Senatobia 662
Seneca 601
Sessums 662
Shady Grove 601
Shannon 662
Sharkey 662
Sharon 601
Shaw 662
Shelby 662
Shellmound 662
Shepherd 662
Sherard 662
Sherman 662
Sherwood 662
Shipman 601
Shivers 601
Shubuta 601
Shuqualak 662
Sibleton 662
Sibley 601
Sidon 662
Silver City 662
Silver Creek 601
Silver Run 601
Skene 662
Skuna 662
Slate Spring 662
Slayden 662
Sledge 662
Smith 601
Smithdale 601
Smithville 662
Snow Lake Shores 662
Society Hill 601
Somerville 662
Sonora 662
Sontag 601
Soso 601
South Amory 662
South Mccomb 601
Southaven 662
Sparta 662
Splunge 662
Spring Hill 662
Springdale 662
Springville 662
St Louis 228
St Martin 228
Stafford Springs 601
Star 601
Starkville 662
State College 662
State Line 601
Stateline 601
Steens 662
Steiner 662
Stennis Ctr 228
Stennis Sp Ct 228
Stennis Space Center 228
Stennis Spc Ctr 228
Stewart 662
Stoneville 662
Stonewall 601
Stovall 662
Straight Bayou 662
Strayhorn 662
Strengthford 601
Stringer 601
Strongs 662
Sturgis 662
Success 228
Summit 601
Sumner 662
Sumrall 601
Sunflower 662
Sunnycrest 662
Sunnyside 662
Sunrise 601
Swan Lake 662
Sweatman 662
Swiftown 662
Swiftwater 662
Sylvarena 601
Symonds 662
Talowah 601
Taska 662
Tatum 601
Taylor 662
Taylorsville 601
Tchula 662
Teasdale 662
Ten Mile 601
Terrell 601
Terry 601
Terza 662
Thaxton 662
Thomastown 601
Thompson 601
Thorn 662
Thornton 662
Thrashers 662
Three Rivers 228
Thyatira 662
Tibbee 662
Tibbs 662
Tie Plant 662
Tillatoba 662
Tilton 601
Tinsley 662
Tiplersville 662
Tippo 662
Tishomingo 662
Toccopola 662
Tomnolen 662
Toomsuba 601
Topeka 601
Topisaw 601
Tougaloo 601
Trebloc 662
Tremont 662
Trinity 662
Troy 662
Tuckers Crossing 601
Tula 662
Tunica 662
Tunica Resort 662
Tunica Resorts 662
Tupelo 662
Turnbull 601
Turon 662
Tutwiler 662
Tylertown 601
Tyro 662
Tyson 662
Uinversity Of Southern Ms 601
Union 601
Union Church 601
Union Hall 601
Univ Of Miss 662
University 662
University Of Mississippi 662
Us Nav Const Batt 228
Utica 601
Utica Junior College 601
Vaiden 662
Valewood 662
Valley Hill 662
Valley Park 601
Van Buren 662
Van Cleave 228
Van Vleet 662
Vance 662
Vancleave 228
Vardaman 662
Varden 662
Vaughan 662
Vburg 601
Velma 662
Vernal 601
Verona 662
Vicksburg 601
Victoria 662
Villa Ridge 601
Visa 601
Vossburg 601
Waco 662
Waddell 662
Wade 228
Wakefield 662
Wallerville 662
Wallhill 662
Walls 662
Walnut 662
Walnut Grove 601
Walters 601
Walthall 662
Wanilla 601
Wardwell 662
Washington 601
Water Valley 662
Waterford 662
Waveland 228
Waxhaw 662
Way 601
Waynesboro 601
Wayside 662
Wboro 601
Webb 662
Weir 662
Wells Town 601
Wenasoga 662
Wesson 601
West 662
West Biloxi 228
West Days 662
West Lincoln 601
West Point 662
West Poplarville 601
Wheeler 662
White Apple 601
White Cap 601
White Sand 662
Whitebluff 601
Whitehead 662
Whites 662
Whites Crossing 601
Whitfield 601
Whitney 662
Wiggins 601
Wilkinson 601
Willet 662
Williamsburg 601
Winborn 662
Windsor Park 228
Wingate 601
Winona 662
Winstonville 662
Winterville 662
Woodburn 662
Woodland 662
Woodville 601
Wortham 228
Wren 662
Wright 662
Wyatte 662
Yazoo 662
Yazoo City 662
Youngs 662
Zetus 601
Zion 662
Zumbro 662

Missouri

Acornridge 573
Adair 660
Adrian 816
Advance 573
Affton 314
Agency 816
Alba 417
Albany 660
Aldrich 417
Alexandria 660
Allbright 573
Allendale 660
Allenton 636
Allenville 573
Alley Springs 573
Alma 660
Altamont 660
Altenburg 573
Alton 417
Amazonia 816
American Nat Prop & Casualty 417
Americus 573
Amity 816
Amoret 660
Amsterdam 660
Anabel 660
Anderson 417
Annada 573
Annapolis 573
Anniston 573
Antonia 636
Apple Creek 573
Appleton City 660
Arab 573
Arbela 660
Arbor 573
Arbyrd 573
Arcadia 573
Archie 816
Arcola 417
Ardmore 660
Argyle 573
Armstrong 660
Arnold 636
Aroma 417
Arrow Rock 660
Asbury 417
Ash 660
Ash Grove 417
Ashburn 573
Asherville 573
Ashland 573
Ashton 660
Athens 660
Atlanta 660
Auburn 573
Augusta 636
Aullville 660
Aurora 417
Aurora Springs 573
Austin 816
Auxvasse 573
Ava 417
Avalon 660
Avilla 417
Avondale 816
Babbtown 573
Bachelor 573
Bagnell 573
Bahner 660
Bairdtown 660
Bakersfield 417
Ballwin 636
Bank Of America 314, 816
Baring 660
Barnard 660
Barnesville 660
Barnett 573

City	Area Code
Barnhart	636
Bass Pro Shops	417
Bates City	816
Battlefield	417
Beaman	660
Beaufort	573
Bel Nor	314
Bel Ridge	314
Belgrade	573
Bell City	573
Bella Villa	314
Belle	573
Belle Center	417
Bellefontaine Neighbors	314
Bellerive	314
Belleview	573
Bellflower	573
Belton	816
Bem	573
Bendavis	417
Bennett	573
Benton	573
Benton City	573
Berger	573
Berkeley	314
Bernie	573
Berryman	573
Bertrand	573
Berwick	417
Bethany	660
Bethel	660
Beulah	573
Beverly Hills	314
Bevier	660
Bible Grove	660
Biehle	573
Big Creek	573
Big Piney	573
Big Springs	573
Bigelow	660
Billings	417
Billingsville	660
Birch Tree	573
Birmingham	816
Bismarck	573
Bixby	573
Black	573
Black Jack	314
Black Walnut	636
Blackburn	660
Blackwater	660
Blackwell	636
Blairstown	660
Bland	573
Blodgett	573
Bloomfield	573
Bloomsdale	573
Blue Eye	417
Blue Springs	816
Bluffton	573
Blythedale	660
Boekerton	573
Bogard	660
Bois D Arc	417
Bolckow	816
Bolivar	417
Bonne Terre	573
Bonnots Mill	573
Boonesboro	660
Boonville	660
Boss	573
Bosworth	660
Boulder City	417
Bourbon	573
Bowling Green	573
Boynton	660
Bradleyville	417
Bragg City	573
Braggadocio	573
Branch	573
Brandsville	417
Branson	417
Branson West	417
Brashear	660
Braymer	660
Brazeau	573
Brazito	573
Breckenridge	660
Breckenridge Hills	314
Brecknrdg Hls	314
Brentwood	314
Brewer	573
Briar	573
Bridgeton	314, 636
Bridgeton Terrace	314
Brighton	417
Brimson	660
Brinktown	573
Briscoe	636
Brixey	417
Brington Jctn	660
Brm Springfield	417
Bronaugh	417
Brookfield	660
Brookline	417
Brookline Sta	417
Brooklyn Heights	417
Broseley	573
Browning	660
Browns Spring	417
Brownwood	573
Brumley	573
Bruner	417
Brunswick	660
Brush Creek	573
Buckhorn	573
Bucklin	660
Buckner	816
Bucyrus	417
Buell	573
Buffalo	417
Bull Creek Village	417
Bunceton	660
Bunker	573
Burfordville	573
Burke City	314
Burlingtn Jct	660
Burlington Junction	660
Butler	660
Butterfield	417
Butterfld	417
Bynumville	660
Byrnes Mill	636
Byron	573
Cabool	417
Cadet	636
Cainsville	660
Cairo	660
Caledonia	573
Calhoun	660
California	573, 660
Callao	660
Calverton Park	314
Calwood	573
Camden	816
Camden Point	816
Camdenton	573
Cameron	816
Camp Clark	417
Campbell	573
Campbellton	573, 636
Canaan	573
Canalou	573
Canton	573
Cape Fair	417
Cape Girardeau	573
Caplinger Mills	417
Caplinger Mls	417
Capps Creek	417
Cardwell	573
Carl Junction	417
Carrington	573
Carrollton	660
Carterville	417
Carthage	417
Caruth	573
Caruthersville	573
Caruthersvlle	573
Carytown	417
Cascade	573
Case	573
Cassville	417
Catawissa	636
Catron	573
Caulfield	417
Cedar City	573
Cedar Gap	417
Cedar Hill	636
Cedar Ridge	417
Cedarcreek	417
Cedron	660
Center	573
Centertown	573
Centerview	660
Centerville	573
Central City	417
Centralia	573
Chadwick	417
Chaffee	573
Chain Of Rocks	636
Chamois	573
Chariton	660
Charlack	314
Charles J Coyle	314
Charleston	573
Cherkee Hmstd	417
Cherokee Homestead Village	417
Cherry Box	660
Cherryville	573
Chesterfield	314
Chestnutridge	417
Chicopee	573
Chilhowee	660
Chillicothe	660
Chula	660
Clara	417
Clarence	660
Clark	573
Clarks Fork	660
Clarksburg	573
Clarksdale	816
Clarkson Valley	314
Clarksville	573
Clarkton	573
Clay	573
Claycomo	816
Clayton	314
Clearmont	660
Clearwater	573
Cleavesville	573
Cleveland	816
Clever	417
Clifton Hill	660
Climax Sprgs	573
Climax Springs	573
Clinton	660
Clover Bottom	636
Clubb	573
Clyde	660
Cncpton Jctn	660
Coatsville	660
Cobalt City	573
Coffey	660
Coffman	573
Coldwater	573
Cole Camp	660
College Mound	660
Collins	417
Colony	660
Columbia	573
Columbia College	573
Commerce	573
Commerce Bank	816
Conception	660
Conception Junction	660
Concordia	660
Connelsville	660
Conran	573
Conway	417
Cook Sta	573
Cooper Hill	573
Cooter	573
Cora	660
Corder	660
Corning	660
Corridon	573
Corso	573
Cosby	816
Cottleville	636
Cotton	660
Cottonwood Point	573
Couch	417
Country Club	816
Country Club Hills	314
Courtesy Reply Mail Firms	314
Courtois	573
Cowgill	660
Cpe Girardeau	573
Craig	660
Crane	417
Creighton	660
Crescent	636
Crestwood	314
Cretcher	660
Creve Coeur	314
Crocker	573
Cross Timbers	417
Crosstown	573
Crystal City	636
Crystal Lake Park	314
Crystal Lakes	816
Cuba	573
Curryville	573
Cyrene	573
Dadeville	417
Daisy	573
Dalton	660
Damascus	417
Danville	573
Dardenne	636
Dardenne Pr	636
Dardenne Prairie	636
Darksville	660
Darlington	660
Davis	636
Davisville	573
Dawn	660
De Kalb	816
De Soto	636
De Witt	660
Dearborn	816
Deepwater	660
Deer Park	573
Deer Ridge	660
Deerfield	417
Deering	573
Defiance	636
Dellwood	314
Delta	573
Denver	660
Des Arc	573
Des Peres	314
Desloge	573
Desoto	636
Detmold	573
Devils Elbow	573
Dexter	573
Diamond	417
Diehlstadt	573
Diggins	417
Dissen	573
Dittmer	636
Div Of Employment Sec	573
Div Of Family Services	573
Div Of Income Tax Due	573
Div Of Witholding Tax	573
Dixie	573
Dixon	573
Doe Run	573
Doniphan	573
Dora	417
Doss	573
Dover	660
Downing	660
Drake	573
Dresden	660
Drexel	816
Drury	417
Dudley	573
Duenweg	417
Dugginsville	417
Duke	573
Duncans Bridge	660
Dunksburg	660
Dunnegan	417
Duquesne	417
Durham	573
Dutchtown	573
Dutzow	636
Eagle Rock	417
Eagleville	660
Earth City	636
Easley	573
East Lynne	816
East Prairie	573
Easton	816
Eastwood	573
Economy	660
Edgar Springs	573
Edgerton	816
Edina	660
Edmundson	314
Edwards	573
El Dorado Spg	417
El Dorado Springs	417
Eldon	573
Eldorado Springs	417
Eldridge	417
Elk Creek	417
Elkhead	417
Elkhorn	636
Elkhurst	573
Elkland	417
Ellington	573
Ellis Prairie	417
Ellisville	636
Ellsinore	573
Elmer	660
Elmira	816
Elmo	660
Elmwood	660
Elsberry	573
Elston	573
Elvins	573
Ely	573
Emden	573
Eminence	573
Emma	660
Enon	573
Eolia	573
Equality	573
Ernestville	660
Essex	573
Estill	660
Ethel	660
Ethlyn	636
Etlah	573
Etterville	573
Eudora	417
Eugene	573
Eunice	417
Eureka	636
Evening Shade	417
Everton	417
Ewing	573
Ex Spgs	816
Ex Sprgs	816
Ex Springs	816
Excello	660
Excelsior Est	816
Excelsior Spg	816
Excelsior Springs	816
Exclsor Sprgs	816
Exeter	417
Fagus	573
Fair Grove	417
Fair Play	417
Fairdealing	573
Fairfax	660
Fairmont	660
Fairport	816
Fairview	417
Falcon	417
Farber	573
Farley	816
Farmington	573
Farrar	573
Faucett	816
Fayette	660
Federal Reserve	816
Femme Osage	636
Fenton	636
Ferguson	314
Ferrelview	816
Festus	636
Fidelity	417
Fillmore	816
Finley	417
Firstar Bank	314
Fisk	573
Flat River	573
Flemington	417
Fletcher	573
Flinthill	636
Flor	314
Flordell Hills	314
Florence	660
Florida	573
Florissant	314
Foley	636
Folk	573
Fordland	417
Forest City	660
Forest Green	660
Forest Springs	660
Foristell	636
Forsyth	417
Fort Leonard Wood	573
Fortescue	660
Fortuna	660
Foster	660
Four Seasons	573
Frankclay	573
Frankenstein	573
Frankford	573
Franklin	660
Fredericksburg	573
Fredericktown	573
Freeborn	573
Freeburg	573
Freedom	573
Freeman	816
Freistatt	417
Fremont	573
French Village	573
French Vlg	573
Friedheim	573
Fristoe	660
Frohna	573
Frontenac	314
Ft Leonard Wd	573
Ft Osage	816
Fulton	573
Gainesville	417
Galena	417
Gallatin	660
Galmey	417
Galt	660
Gamma	573
Garden City	816
Garrison	417
Garwood	573
Gasconade	573
Gatewood	573
Gentry	660
Gentryville	660
Georgetown	660
Gerald	573
Gibbs	660
Gibson	573
Gideon	573
Gilliam	660
Gilman City	660
Gilmore	636
Gipsy	573
Gladden	573
Gladstone	816
Glasgow	660
Glasgow Village	314
Glenallen	573
Glencoe	636
Glendale	314
Glensted	573
Glenwood	660
Glover	573
Gobler	573

oldberry 660
olden 417
olden City 417
oldsberry 660
ooch Mill 660
oodfellow Terrace 314
oodland 573
oodman 417
oodson 417
ordonville 573
orin 660
oss 660
ouch Mill 660
ower 816
raff 417
raham 660
rain Valley 816
ranby 417
rand Falls 417
rand Pass 660
randin 573
randview 816
ranger 660
rant City 660
ranville 660
rassy 573
ravelton 573
ravois Mills 573
ray Summit 636
rayridge 573
rays Point 417
raysville 660
reen Castle 660
reen City 660
reen Lawn 573
reen Ridge 660
reenbrier 573
reendale 314
reenfield 417
reensburg 660
reentop 660
reenview 573
reenville 573
reenwood 816
retna 417
rogan 417
rover 636
rovespring 417
rubville 636
uilford 660
umbo 636
unn City 816
uthrie 573
agars Grove 660
ale 660
alf Way 417
allsville 573
alltown 417
amilton 816
anley Hills 314
annibal 573
ardenville 417
ardin 660
arg 573
arris 660
arrisburg 573
arrisonville 816
art 417
artsburg 573
artshorn 417
artville 417
artwell 660
arvester 636
arviell 573
arwood 417
assard 573
astain 573
atfield 660
atton 573
awk Point 636
ayden 573
ayti 573
ayti Heights 573
ayward 573
aywood City 573
azelwood 314

Helena 816
Hematite 636
Hemple 816
Henley 573
Henrietta 816
Herculaneum 636
Hermann 573
Hermitage 417
Hickory Hill 573
Higbee 660
Higginsville 660
High Gate 573
High Hill 636
High Point 660
High Ridge 636
Highland 573
Highlandville 417
Hillsboro 636
Hinton 573
Hiram 573
Hoberg 417
Hoene Spring 636
Holcomb 573
Holden 816
Holland 573
Holliday 660
Hollister 417
Holt 816
Holts Summit 573
Homeland Nbc 816
Homestead Vlg 816
Homestown 573
Honey Creek 573
Hope 573
Hopewell 573
Hopkins 660
Horine 636
Hornersville 573
Hornet 417
Horton 417
House Creek 573
House Springs 636
Houston 417
Houston Lake 816
Houstonia 660
Howardville 573
Huggins 417
Hughesville 660
Hugo 573
Humansville 417
Hume 417
Humphreys 660
Hunnewell 573
Huntington 573
Huntleigh 314
Huntsdale 573
Huntsville 660
Hurdland 660
Hurley 417
Iantha 417
Iberia 573
Ibssc Acs Asc 314
Ilasco 573
Imperial 636
Income Tax Refund 573
Independence 816
Indian Creek 573
Indian Grove 660
Ink 573
Innsbrook 636
Internal Revenue Service 816
Ionia 660
Iron Gates 417
Iron Mountain 573
Irondale 573
Ironton 573
Irs Service Center 816
Irwin 417
Isabella 417
Jackson 573
Jacksonville 660
Jadwin 573
Jameson 660
Jamesport 660
Jamestown 660
Jane 417

Japan 573
Jasper 417
Jefferson City 573
Jefferson Cty 573
Jenkins 417
Jennings 314
Jerico Spgs 417
Jerico Sprgs 417
Jerico Springs 417
Jerome 573
Jonesburg 636
Joplin 417
Josephville 636
K C 816
Kahoka 660
Kaiser 573
Kampville 636
Kampville Beach 636
Kampville Court 636
Kans City 816
Kans Cty 816
Kans Cy 816
Kansas City 816
Kansas City North 816
Kansas Cty 816
Kansas Cy 816
Kaseyville 660
Kc 816
Kearney 816
Kelso 573
Kendricktown 417
Kennett 573
Kenwood 660
Keota 660
Kewanee 573
Keytesville 660
Kidder 816
Kimberling City 417
Kimberling Cy 417
Kimmswick 636
Kinder 573
King City 660
Kingdom City 573
Kingston 816
Kingsville 816
Kinloch 314
Kirbyville 417
Kirksville 660
Kirkwood 314
Kissee Mills 417
Kliever 573
Knob Lick 573
Knob Noster 660
Knox City 660
Koeltztown 573
Koenig 573
Koshkonong 417
Ks City 816
La Belle 660
La Grange 573
La Monte 660
La Plata 660
La Russell 417
Labadie 636
Labarque Crk 636
Laclede 660
Laclede Gas Co 314
Laddonia 573
Ladue 314
Lake Adelle 636
Lake Annette 816
Lake Chesterfield 636
Lake Forest 573
Lake Lafayette 816
Lake Lotawana 816
Lake Ozark 573
Lake Saint Louis 636
Lake Sherwood 636
Lake Spring 573
Lake St Louis 636
Lake Tapawingo 816
Lake Tapwingo 816
Lake Viking 660
Lake Waukomis 816
Lake Winnebago 816
Lakeland 573

Lakenan 573
Lakeside 417
Lakeview 417
Lakeview Heights 660
Lamar 417
Lambert 573
Lambert Airport 314
Lambert Arprt 314
Lamine 660
Lampe 417
Lanagan 417
Lancaster 660
Lanes Prairie 573
Lanton 417
Laquey 573
Laredo 660
Larussell 417
Latham 660
Lathrop 816
Latour 816
Laurie 573
Lawson 816
Leadington 573
Leadwood 573
Leasburg 573
Lebanon 417
Lecoma 573
Lees Summit 816
Leeton 660
Lemay 314
Lemons 660
Lenox 573
Lentner 573
Leonard 660
Leopold 573
Leslie 573
Lesterville 573
Levasy 816
Lewistown 573
Lexington 660
Liberal 417
Liberty 816
Libertyville 573
Licking 573
Liege 573
Liguori 636
Lilbourn 573
Lincoln 660
Lindbergh 573
Linden 417
Linn 573
Linn Creek 573
Linneus 660
Lithium 573
Livonia 660
Lk Lotawana 816
Lk Winnebago 816
Lock Springs 660
Lockwood 417
Locust Hill 660
Lodi 573
Lohman 573
Loma Linda 417
Lone Elm 660
Lone Jack 816
Lonedell 573
Long Lane 417
Longrun 417
Longtown 573
Longwood 660
Loose Creek 573
Louis 314
Louisburg 417
Louisiana 573
Low Ground 660
Lowndes 573
Lowry City 417
Ls 816
Lsl 636
Lucerne 660
Ludlow 660
Luebbering 573
Lupus 660
Luray 660
Lutesville 573
Luystown 573

Lynchburg 417
Lyon 573
Machens 636
Macks Creek 573
Macomb 417
Macon 660
Madison 660
Madisonville 573
Maitland 660
Malden 573
Malta Bend 660
Manchester 636
Manes 417
Mansfield 417
Mapaville 636
Maples 573
Maplewood 314
Marble Hill 573
Marceline 660
Marine Corps Finance Center 816
Marionville 417
Maritz Inc 636
Marquand 573
Marshall 660
Marshall Junction 660
Marshfield 417
Marston 573
Marthasville 636
Martin City 816
Martinsburg 573
Martinstown 660
Martinsville 660
Marvel Cav Pk 417
Marvel Cave Park 417
Marvin 573
Maryknoll 636
Maryland Heights 314
Maryland Hts 314
Marys Home 573
Maryville 660
Matson 636
Matthews 573
Maud 660
Maysville 816
Mayview 660
Maywood 573
Mc Bride 573
Mc Clurg 417
Mc Fall 660
Mc Gee 573
Mc Girk 573
Mcbaine 573
Mcfall 660
Mckittrick 573
Meadville 660
Medill 660
Mehlville 314
Memphis 660
Mendon 660
Mendota 660
Mercer 660
Mercyville 660
Merriam Vlg 417
Merriam Woods Village 417
Meta 573
Metz 417
Mexico 573
Miami 660
Mid Missouri P&df 573
Middle Brook 573
Middle Grove 660
Middletown 573
Midland 660
Midway 573
Midwest Service Center 816
Milan 660
Mildred 417
Milford 417
Mill Spring 573
Millard 660
Millcreek 573
Miller 417
Millersburg 573
Millersville 573
Millwood 573
Milo 417

Mincy 417
Mindenmines 417
Mine La Motte 573
Mineola 573
Miner 573
Mineral Point 573
Mint Hill 573
Mirabile 660
Missouri City 816
Missouri S & T 573
Missouri State University 417
Mo Dept Of Revenue 573
Moberly 660
Mokane 573
Moline Acres 314
Monett 417
Monkey Run 573
Monroe City 573
Monsanto 314
Montgomery 573
Montgomery City 573
Montgomery Cy 573
Monticello 573
Montier 573
Montreal 573
Montrose 660
Montserrat 660
Moody 417
Mooresville 660
Mora 660
Morehouse 573
Morgan Heights 417
Morley 573
Morrison 573
Morrisville 417
Morse Mill 636
Mosby 816
Moscow Mills 636
Moselle 636
Mound City 660
Moundville 417
Mount Hulda 660
Mount Moriah 660
Mount Sterling 573
Mount Vernon 417
Mountain Grove 417
Mountain Grv 417
Mountain View 417
Mt Sterling 573
Murphy 636
Murry 573
Musselfork 660
Myrtle 417
Mystic 660
N Kansas City 816
N Kc 816
Napoleon 816
Napton 660
Naylor 573
Nebo 417
Neck City 417
Neelyville 573
Nelson 660
Neosho 417
Nestle 314
Nevada 417
New Bloomfield 573
New Bloomfld 573
New Boston 660
New Cambria 660
New Florence 573
New Franklin 660
New Hamburg 573
New Hampton 660
New Hartford 573
New Haven 573
New Hope 573
New London 573
New Madrid 573
New Melle 636
New Offenburg 573
New Point 660
New Truxton 636
New Wells 573
Newark 660
Newburg 573

City	Area Code
Newtonia	417
Newtown	660
Niangua	417
Nind	660
Nixa	417
Nkc	816
No Kansas City	816
Noble	417
Noel	417
Norborne	660
Nordstrom	314
Normandy	314
North County	314
North Kansas City	816
North Kc	816
North Lilbourn	573
North Salem	660
Northmoor	816
Northwest Plaza	314
Northwoods	314
Norwood	417
Nottinghill	417
Novelty	660
Novinger	660
Number Eight	660
Nw Plaza	314
Nw Point	660
O Fallon	636
Oak Grove	816
Oak Ridge	573
Oakland	314
Oakview	816
Oakville	314
Oates	573
Ocie	417
Odessa	816
Ofallon	636
Old Alexandria	636
Old Appleton	573
Old Fredonia	660
Old Mines	636
Old Monroe	636
Old Woolam	573
Old Woollam	573
Oldfield	417
Olean	573
Olivette	314
Olney	573
Olympian Village	636
Oran	573
Orchard Farm	636
Oregon	660
Oronogo	417
Orrick	816
Osage Beach	573
Osage Bend	573
Osage Bluff	573
Osage City	573
Osborn	816
Osceola	417
Otterville	660
Otto	636
Overland	314
Overton	660
Owasco	660
Owensville	573
Owls Bend	573
Oxly	573
Ozark	417
Pacific	636
Pagedale	314
Painton	573
Palace	417
Palmyra	573
Palopinto	660
Paradise	816
Paris	660
Park Hills	573
Parker Lake	573
Parkville	816
Parma	573
Parnell	660
Pasadena Hills	314
Pasadena Park	314
Pascola	573
Passaic	660
Patterson	573
Patton	573
Pattonsburg	660
Paydown	573
Paynesville	573
Pea Ridge	573
Peace Valley	417
Peach Orchard	573
Peaksville	660
Peculiar	816
Pendleton	636
Pennville	660
Perkins	573
Perry	573
Perryville	573
Pershing	573
Petersburg	660
Pevely	636
Philadelphia	573
Philatelic Distribution Ctr	816
Phillipsburg	417
Pickering	660
Piedmont	573
Pierce City	417
Pierpont	573
Pilot Grove	660
Pilot Knob	573
Pine Lawn	314
Pineville	417
Pisgah	660
Pittsburg	417
Plainview	660
Plato	417
Platte City	816
Platte Woods	816
Plattsburg	816
Pleasant Hill	816
Pleasant Hope	417
Pleasant Valley	816
Pleasant Vly	816
Plevna	573, 660
Pocahontas	573
Point Lookout	417
Point Pleasant	573
Polk	417
Pollock	660
Polo	660
Pomona	417
Ponce De Leon	417
Pond	636
Pontiac	417
Poplar Bluff	573
Portage Des Sioux	636
Portageville	573
Portland	573
Potosi	573
Pottersville	417
Powell	417
Powersite	417
Powersville	660
Poynor	573
Prairie City	660
Prairie Hill	660
Prairie Home	660
Prairieville	573
Prathersville	573
Preston	417
Prices Branch	573
Princeton	660
Prosperity	417
Protem	417
Prtg De Sioux	636
Prtg De Souix	636
Purcell	417
Purdin	660
Purdy	417
Pure Air	660
Puxico	573
Queen City	660
Quincy	417
Quitman	660
Qulin	573
Racine	417
Racket	660
Randles	573
Randolph	816
Ravenwood	660
Raymondville	417
Raymore	816
Raytown	816
Rayville	660
Rea	816
Readsville	573
Red Bird	573
Redford	573
Redings Mill	417
Reeds	417
Reeds Spring	417
Reform	573
Reger	660
Renick	573
Rensselaer	573
Republic	417
Revere	660
Reynolds	573
Rhineland	573
Rich Fountain	573
Rich Hill	417
Richards	417
Richland	573
Richmond	816
Richmond Heights	314
Richmond Hts	314
Richwoods	573
Ridgedale	417
Ridgeway	660
Riggs	573
Risco	573
Rivermines	573
Riverside	816
Riversville	573
Riverview	314
Rives	573
Roach	573
Roanoke	660
Robertson	314
Robertsville	636
Roby	417
Rocheport	573
Rock Hill	314
Rock Port	660
Rockaway Bch	417
Rockaway Beach	417
Rockbridge	417
Rockport	660
Rockview	573
Rockville	660
Rocky Comfort	417
Rocky Mount	573
Rocky Ridge	573
Rogersville	417
Rolla	573
Rombauer	573
Rosati	573
Roscoe	417
Rosebud	573
Rosel	573
Rosendale	816
Rothville	660
Round Spring	573
Rowena	573
Rucker	573
Rueter	417
Rush Hill	573
Rushville	816
Russellville	573
Rutledge	660
S Greenfield	417
Saddlebrooke	417
Safe	573
Saginaw	417
Sagrada	573
Saint Albans	636
Saint Ann	314
Saint Anne	314
Saint Catharine	660
Saint Charles	636
Saint Clair	636
Saint Clement	573
Saint Elizabeth	573
Saint Francisville	660
Saint James	573
Saint John	314
Saint Joseph	816
Saint Louis	314, 816
Saint Martins	573
Saint Mary	573
Saint Marys	573
Saint Patrick	573
Saint Paul	636
Saint Peters	636
Saint Robert	573
Saint Roberts	573
Saint Thomas	573
Sainte Genevieve	573
Salem	573
Saline City	660
Salisbury	660
Salt Pond	660
Salt River	573
Sand Hill	660
Sandy Hook	660
Santa Fe	573
Sapp	573
Sappington	314
Sarcoxie	417
Savannah	816
Saverton	573
Schell City	417
Schluersburg	636
Scholastics Inc	573
Schubert	573
Scopus	573
Scotland	417
Scott City	573
Sedalia	660
Sedgewickville	573
Sedgewickvlle	573
Seligman	417
Senath	573
Seneca	417
Sereno	573
Seymour	417
Shannondale	573
Sharon	660
Shaw	573
Shelbina	573
Shelbyville	573
Sheldon	417
Shell Knob	417
Shelter Insurance	573
Sheridan	660
Sherman	636
Shibleys Point	660
Shook	573
Shrewsbury	314
Sibley	816
Sidney	660
Sikeston	573
Silex	573
Silva	573
Silver Dollar City	417
Silver Lake	573
Simmons	417
Skidmore	660
Slagle	417
Slater	660
Sligo	573
Smithfield	417
Smithton	660
Smithville	816
Smsu	417
Snyder	660
Solo	417
Sorrell	660
Souder	417
South Fork	417
South Gifford	660
South Greenfield	417
South River	573
South Shore	636
South Van Buren	573
South West City	417
South West Cy	417
Spalding	573
Spanish Lake	314
Sparta	417
Speed	660
Sperry	660
Spickard	660
Spokane	417
Spring Bluff	573
Spring Garden	573
Spring Lake	660
Springfield	417
Springfork	660
Springtown	573
Squires	417
St Anne	314
St Catharine	660
St Elizabeth	573
St Joseph	816
St Peters	636
St Robert	573
St Roberts	573
Stahl	660
Stanberry	660
Stanton	573
Stark City	417
Starkenburg	573
State Farm Ins	573
Ste Genevieve	573
Steedman	573
Steele	573
Steelville	573
Steffenville	660
Stella	417
Stephens	573
Stephens College	573
Stet	660
Stewartsville	816
Stockton	417
Stones Corner	417
Stoney Point	573
Stony Hill	573
Stotesbury	417
Stotts City	417
Stoutland	417
Stoutsville	573
Stover	573
Strafford	417
Strain	573
Strasburg	816
Stringtown	417
Strother	660
Sturdivant	573
Sturgeon	573
Sublette	660
Success	417
Sugar Creek	816
Sullivan	573
Sulphur Spg	636
Sulphur Springs	636
Summerfield	573
Summersville	417
Sumner	660
Sunrise Beach	573
Sunset Hills	314
Sw Mo State	417
Swedeborg	573
Sweet Springs	660
Swiss	573
Sycamore	417
Syracuse	660
Taberville	660
Tallapoosa	573
Taneyville	417
Taos	573
Tarkio	660
Tarrants	573
Taylor	573
Tebbetts	573
Tecumseh	417
Teresita	573
Thayer	417
Theodosia	417
Thomas Hill	660
Thomasville	573
Thompson	573
Thornfield	417
Tiff	573
Tiff City	417
Timber	573
Times Beach	636
Tina	66
Tipton	66
Tolona	57
Town And Country	314, 63
Tracy	81
Treloar	63
Trenton	66
Trimble	81
Triplett	66
Troy	63
Truesdail	63
Truesdale	63
Truxton	63
Tunas	41
Turners	41
Turney	81
Tuscumbia	57
Twin Oaks	63
Twn And Cntry	31
Tyrone	41
U City	31
Udall	41
Ulman	57
Umc Hospital Clinics	57
Union	63
Union City	41
Union Star	81
Uniontown	57
Unionville	66
United Missouri Bank	81
Unity School Of Christianity	81
Unity Village	81
Unity Vlg	81
Univ City	31
University City	31
University Cy	31
University Of Missouri	57
Urbana	41
Urbandale	66
Urich	66
Us Bank	31
Usps Inspection Service	31
Utica	66
Valles Mines	57
Valley City	66
Valley Park	63
Van Buren	57
Vancleve	573
Vandalia	573
Vandiver Village	573
Vanduser	573
Vanzant	417
Velda Village Hills	314
Vera	573
Verona	417
Versailles	573
Viburnum	573
Vichy	573
Vienna	573
Vigus	314
Villa Ridge	636
Village Of Four Seasons	573
Village Of Loch Lloyd	816
Village Of Oakview	816
Vineyard	417
Vinita Park	314
Viola	417
Vista	417
Vitilas Reid	314
Vlg Loch Loyd	816
Vlg Of 4 Ssns	573
Vulcan	573
W Plains	417
Waco	417
Wainwright	573
Waldron	816
Walker	417
Walnut Grove	417
Walnut Shade	417
Wappapello	573
Wardell	573
Wardsville	573
Warrensburg	660
Warrenton	636
Warsaw	660
Warson Woods	314

Washburn 417
Washington 636
Wasola 417
Watson 660
Waverly 660
Wayland 660
Waynesville 573
Weatherby 660
Weatherby Lake 816
Weaubleau 417
Webb City 417
Webster Groves 314
Webster Grvs 314
Weingarten 573
Weldon Spring 636
Weldon Spring Heights 636
Wellington 816
Wellston 314
Wellsville 573
Wentworth 417
Wentzville 636
Wesco 573
West Alton 314
West County 314
West Ely 573
West Eminence 573
West Line 816
West Plains 417
West Quincy 573
Westboro 660
Weston 816
Westphalia 573
Wheatland 417
Wheaton 417
Wheeling 660
Whitakerville 660
Whiteman Afb 660
Whiteman Air Force Base 660
Whiteoak 573
Whiteside 573
Whitewater 573
Wildwood 636
Willard 417
Williamsburg 573
Williamstown 573
Williamsville 573
Willmathsville 660
Willow Spgs 417
Willow Springs 417
Wilton 573
Winchester 636
Windsor 660
Windyville 417
Winfield 636
Winigan 660
Winona 573
Winston 660
Winthrop 816
Wisdom 660
Withers Mill 573
Wittenberg 573
Wolf Island 573
Womack 573
Wood Heights 816
Woodland 573
Woodlandville 573
Woodlawn 660
Woodlinville 573
Woodson Terrace 314
Woodville 660
Wooldridge 660
Worth 660
Worthington 660
Wright City 636
Wthrby Lake 816
Wyaconda 660
Wyatt 573
Yarrow 660
Yates 660
Youngstown 660
Yount 573
Yukon 417
Zalma 573
Zanoni 417
Zell 573

Montana

All Points 406

Nebraska

1st National Bank Of Omaha 402
Abie 402
Adams 402
Agnew 402
Ainsworth 402
Air Mail Facility 402
Air Park 402
Albany 308
Albion 402
Alda 308
Alexandria 402
Algernon 308
Allen 402
Alliance 308
Alma 308
Almeria 308
Alvo 402
Amelia 308
Ames 402
Amherst 308
Anderson 308
Angora 308
Anselmo 308
Ansley 308
Antioch 308
Arapahoe 308
Arcadia 308
Archer 308
Arlington 402
Armada 308
Arnold 308
Arthur 308
Ash Grove 308
Ashby 308
Ashland 402
Ashton 308
Assumption 402
Atkinson 402
Atlanta 308
Auburn 402
Aurora 402
Avoca 402
Axtell 308
Ayr 402
Bancroft 402
Bar Code 402
Barada 402
Barneston 402
Bartlett 308
Bartley 308
Bassett 402
Battle Creek 402
Bayard 308
Beatrice 402
Beaver City 308
Beaver Crossing 402
Beaver Xing 402
Bee 402
Beemer 402
Belden 402
Belgrade 308
Belle Prairie 402
Bellevue 402
Bellwood 402
Belvidere 402
Benedict 402
Benkelman 308
Bennet 402
Bennington 402
Benson 402
Berea 308
Bertrand 308
Berwyn 308
Bethany 402
Big Springs 308
Bignell 308
Bingham 308
Bixby 402
Bladen 402
Blair 402
Bloomfield 402
Bloomington 308
Blue Cross Blue Shield 402
Blue Hill 402
Blue River Lodge 402
Blue Springs 402
Boelus 308
Boone 402
Bostwick 402
Boys Town 402
Boystown 402
Bradshaw 402
Brady 308
Brainard 402
Brandon 308
Brayton 308
Brewster 308
Bridgeport 308
Bristol 308
Bristow 402
Broadwater 308
Brock 402
Broken Bow 308
Brownlee 308
Brownson 308
Brownville 402
Brule 308
Bruning 402
Bruno 402
Brunswick 402
Bucktail 308
Buffalo 402
Burchard 402
Burr 402
Burress 402
Burwell 308
Bushnell 308
Business Reply 402
Butte 402
Byron 402
Cabela's 308
Cabelas Inc 308
Cadams 402
Cairo 308
Callaway 308
Cambridge 308
Cameron 308
Campbell 402
Capehart 402
Carleton 402
Carroll 402
Cedar 308
Cedar Bluffs 402
Cedar Creek 402
Cedar Rapids 308
Center 402
Centerville 402
Central City 308
Ceresco 402
Chadron 308
Chambers 402
Champion 308
Chapman 308
Chappell 308
Cheney 402
Cherry Creek 308
Chester 402
Clarks 308
Clarkson 402
Clatonia 402
Clay 308
Clay Center 402
Clearwater 402
Cliff 308
Clinton 308
Cody 402
Coleridge 402
Colon 402
Colton 308
Columbus 402
Comstock 308
Concord 402
Cook 402
Cordova 402
Corner 308
Cornlea 402
Cortland 402
Cosmo 308
Cotesfield 308
Cowles 402
Cozad 308
Crab Orchard 402
Craig 402
Crawford 308
Creighton 402
Creighton Univ 402
Creston 402
Crete 402
Crofton 402
Crookston 402
Culbertson 308
Curtis 308
Cushing 308
Custer 308
Dakota City 402
Dalton 308
Danbury 308
Dannebrog 308
Dannevirke 308
Darr 308
Davenport 402
Davey 402
David City 402
Davis Creek 308
Dawson 402
Daykin 402
De Witt 402
Decatur 402
Delight 308
Denman 402
Denton 402
Denver 402
Deshler 402
Deweese 402
Dickens 308
Diller 402
Dix 308
Dixon 402
Doane 308
Dodge 402
Doniphan 402
Dorchester 402
Douglas 402
Douglas Grove 308
Du Bois 402
Dubois 402
Dunbar 402
Duncan 402
Dunlap 308
Dunning 308
Dwight 402
Eagle 402
East Custer 308
Eaton 308
Eddyville 308
Edgar 402
Edison 308
Elba 308
Elgin 402
Eli 402
Elim 308
Elk Creek 402
Elkhorn 402
Ellis 402
Ellsworth 308
Elm 308
Elm Creek 308
Elmwood 402
Elsie 308
Elsmere 308
Elwood 308
Elyria 308
Emerald 402
Emerson 402
Emmet 402
Enders 308
Endicott 402
Enterprise 308
Ericson 308
Eureka 308
Eustis 308
Ewing 402
Exeter 402
Fairbury 402
Fairfield 402
Fairmont 402
Falls City 402
Farmers 308
Farnam 308
Farwell 308
Filley 402
Firth 402
Flats 308
Florence 402
Fontanelle 402
Fordyce 402
Fort Calhoun 402
Fort Robinson 308
Foster 402
Franklin 308
Fremont 402
Friend 402
Fullerton 308
Funk 308
Gandy 308
Gardner 308
Garland 402
Garrison 402
Geneva 402
Genoa 402
Geranium 308
Gering 308
Gibbon 308
Gilead 402
Giltner 402
Gladstone 402
Glen 308
Glenover 402
Glenrock 402
Glenvil 402
Goehner 402
Good Samaritan Village 402
Gordon 308
Gothenburg 308
Graf 402
Grafton 402
Grand Island 308
Grant 308
Grattan 402
Greeley 308
Greenwood 402
Gresham 402
Gretna 402
Grover 402
Guide Rock 402
Gurley 308
Hadar 402
Haig 308
Haigler 308
Hall County Regional Airport 308
Hallam 402
Halsey 308
Hamilton 402
Hamlet 308
Hampton 402
Hanover 402
Hansen 402
Harbine 402
Hardy 402
Harrisburg 308
Harrison 308
Hartington 402
Harvard 402
Hastings 402
Hastings Imperial Mall 402
Hastings Municipal Airport 402
Havelock 402
Hay Springs 308
Hayes Center 308
Hayland 402
Hazard 308
Heartwell 308
Hebron 402
Hemingford 308
Henderson 402
Hendley 308
Henry 308
Herman 402
Hershey 308
Hickman 402
Highland 402
Hildreth 308
Hoag 402
Holbrook 308
Holdrege 308
Holdridge 308
Holland 402
Hollinger 308
Holmesville 402
Holstein 402
Homer 402
Homestead National Monument 402
Hooper 402
Horace 308
Hordville 402
Hoskins 402
Howe 402
Howells 402
Hubbard 402
Hubbell 402
Humboldt 402
Humphrey 402
Huntley 308
Hyannis 308
Imperial 308
Inavale 308
Independent 308
Indianola 308
Industry 308
Industry-Rock Falls 308
Ingleside 402
Inland 402
Inman 402
Ithaca 402
Jacinto 308
Jackson 402
Jansen 402
Johnson 402
Johnson Lake 308
Johnson Lk 308
Johnstown 402
Julian 402
Juniata 402
Kearney 308
Keene 308
Kenesaw 402
Kennard 402
Keystone 308
Kilfoil 308
Kilgore 402
Kimball 308
Kowanda 308
Kramer 402
Kronborg 402
La Platte 402
La Vista 402
Laird 308
Lake 308
Lakeside 308
Lamar 308
Lanham 402
Laurel 402
Lavista 402
Lawrence 402
Lebanon 308
Leicester 402
Leigh 402
Lemoyne 308
Leshara 402
Lewellen 308
Lewiston 402
Lexington 308
Liberty 402
Lincoln 402
Lindsay 402
Linwood 402
Lisco 308
Litchfield 308
Little Blue 402
Lodgepole 308
Long Pine 402
Loomis 308

Area Codes by State and City

City	Area Code
Lorenzo	308
Lorton	402
Louisville	402
Loup City	308
Lowell	308
Lushton	402
Lyman	308
Lynch	402
Lynn	402
Lyons	402
Macon	308
Macy	402
Madison	402
Madrid	308
Magnet	402
Malcolm	402
Malmo	402
Manley	402
Marquette	402
Marshall	402
Marsland	308
Martell	402
Martin	308
Martinsburg	402
Mascot	308
Maskell	402
Mason City	308
Max	308
Maxwell	308
Mayfield	308
Maywood	308
Mc Cook	308
Mc Cool Jct	402
Mc Cool Junction	402
Mc Grew	308
Mcclean	402
Mccook	308
Mcgrew	308
Mclean	402
Mead	402
Meadow Grove	402
Melbeta	308
Memphis	402
Merna	308
Merriman	308
Michigan	308
Midland	308
Milburn	308
Milford	402
Millard	402
Miller	308
Milligan	402
Mills	402
Milton	308
Minatare	308
Minden	308
Mirage	308
Mitchell	308
Monroe	402
Moorefield	308
Morrill	308
Morse Bluff	402
Mount Clare	402
Mullally	308
Mullen	308
Murdock	402
Murray	402
Mutual Of Omaha	402
Myrtle	308
Naper	402
Naponee	308
Nebr City	402
Nebraska City	402
Nehawka	402
Neligh	402
Nelson	402
Nemaha	402
Nenzel	402
New Helena	308
Newark	308
Newcastle	402
Newman Grove	402
Newport	402
Nickerson	402
Niobrara	402
Noble	308

City	Area Code
Nora	402
Norfolk	402
Norman	308
North Auburn	402
North Bend	402
North Franklin	402
North Loup	308
North Platte	308
Northport	308
Nysted	308
O' Neill	402
Oak	402
Oak Creek	308
Oak Grove	308
Oakdale	402
Oakland	402
Obert	402
Oconto	308
Octavia	402
Odell	402
Odessa	308
Offutt A F B	402
Offutt Afb	402
Offutt Air Force Base	402
Ogallala	308
Ohiowa	402
Omaha	402
Omaha Douglas Civic Ctr	402
Oneida	308
Oneill	402
Ong	402
Orchard	402
Ord	308
Orleans	308
Osceola	402
Oshkosh	308
Osmond	402
Otoe	402
Overton	308
Oxford	308
Page	402
Palisade	308
Palmer	308
Palmyra	402
Panama	402
Papillion	402
Parks	308
Paul	402
Pauline	402
Pawnee City	402
Paxton	308
Pender	402
Penn	308
Peru	402
Petersburg	402
Phillips	402
Pickrell	402
Pierce	402
Pilger	402
Plainview	402
Platte Center	402
Plattsmouth	402
Pleasant Dale	402
Pleasanthill	402
Pleasanton	308
Plymouth	402
Polk	402
Ponca	402
Poole	308
Potter	308
Powell	402
Prague	402
Prairie	308
Prairie Center	308
Prairie Dog	308
Prairie Home	402
Precept	308
Preston	402
Primrose	308
Princeton	402
Prosser	308
Purdum	308
Ragan	308
Ralston	402
Randolph	402
Ravenna	308

City	Area Code
Raymond	402
Red Cloud	402
Redington	308
Repub City	308
Republican City	308
Reuben	308
Reynolds	402
Richfield	402
Richland	402
Ringgold	308
Rising City	402
Riverdale	308
Riverside	402
Riverside Park	308
Riverton	402
Roca	402
Rock Falls	308
Rockford	402
Rockville	308
Rogers	402
Rohrs	402
Rokeby	402
Rosalie	402
Roscoe	308
Rose	402
Roseland	402
Rosemont	402
Royal	402
Rulo	402
Rusco	308
Rushville	308
Ruskin	402
Ryno	308
S Sioux City	402
Saint Edward	402
Saint Helena	402
Saint Libory	308
Saint Mary	402
Saint Paul	308
Salem	402
Saltillo	402
Sanborn	308
Sappa	308
Sarben	308
Sargent	308
Saronville	402
Sartoria	308
Scandinavia	308
Schaupps	308
School Creek	402
Schuyler	402
Scotia	308
Scottsbluff	308
Scribner	402
Sedan	402
Seneca	308
Seward	402
Sharon	308
Shelby	402
Shelton	308
Sheridan	308
Sherman	308
Sherman Lake	308
Shickley	402
Shields	402
Shubert	402
Sicily	402
Sidney	308
Silver Creek	308
Silver Lake	402
Smithfield	308
Snyder	402
Sodtown	308
South Bend	402
South Loup	308
South Minden	308
South Platte	402
South Sioux City	402
South Yankton	402
Spade	308
Spalding	308
Sparks	402
Spencer	402
Spencer Park	402
Sprague	402
Spring Creek	308

City	Area Code
Spring Grove	308
Spring Ranch	402
Springdale	308
Springfield	402
Springview	402
St Columbans	402
St Helena	402
St Libory	308
St Michael	308
St Paul	308
St Stephens	402
Stamford	308
Stanton	402
Staplehurst	402
Stapleton	308
State House	402
Steele City	402
Stegall	308
Steinauer	402
Stella	402
Sterling	402
Stockham	402
Stockville	308
Strang	402
Stratton	308
Stromsburg	402
Stuart	402
Sumner	308
Sunol	308
Superior	402
Surprise	402
Survey	308
Sutherland	308
Sutton	402
Swanton	402
Sweetwater	308
Syracuse	402
Table Rock	402
Talmage	402
Tamora	402
Tarnov	402
Taylor	308
Tecumseh	402
Tekamah	402
Terrytown	308
Thayer	402
Thedford	308
Thompson	402
Thornton	308
Thune	308
Thurston	402
Tilden	402
Tobias	402
Trenton	308
Triumph	308
Trumbull	308
Tryon	308
Uehling	402
Ulysses	402
Un Med Center	402
Unadilla	402
Union	402
Union Pacific Rr	402
Univ Of Ne Med Center	402
Univ Of Neb At Omaha	402
Univ Of Nebraska At Kearney	308
Univ Of Nebraska E Campus	402
University Of Nebraska	402
University Of Nebraska Medic	402
University Place	402
Upland	308
Utica	402
Valentine	402
Valley	402
Valparaiso	402
Venango	308
Verdel	402
Verdigre	402
Verdon	402
Victoria	308
Vieregg	308
Vinton	308
Virginia	402
Wabash	402
Waco	402
Wahoo	402

City	Area Code
Wakefield	402
Wallace	308
Walthill	402
Walton	402
Wanda	402
Washington	402
Waterbury	402
Waterloo	402
Wauneta	308
Wausa	402
Waverly	402
Wayne	402
Webster	308
Weeping Water	402
Weissert	308
Wellfleet	308
Wells Fargo	402
West Blue	402
West Point	402
West Union	308
Western	402
Westerville	308
Westmark	308
Weston	402
Westside	308
Whiteclay	308
Whitman	308
Whitney	308
Wilber	402
Wilcox	308
Williamsburg	308
Willow Island	308
Willowdale	402
Wilsonville	308
Winnebago	402
Winnetoon	402
Winside	402
Winslow	402
Wisner	402
Wolbach	308
Wood Lake	402
Wood River	308
Worms	308
Wymore	402
Wynot	402
Wyoming	402
Yale	308
York	402
Yutan	402
Zero	402

Nevada

City	Area Code
Alamo	775
Amargosa Valley	775
Amargosa Vly	775
Anderson Acres	775
Apache	775
Arden	702
Arthur	775
Ash Springs	775
Aurora	775
Austin	775
Babbitt	775
Baker	775
Battle Mountain	775
Battle Mtn	775
Beatty	775
Beowawe	775
Black Springs	775
Blue Diamond	702
Bordertown	775
Bottle Creek	775
Boulder City	702
Branch #1	775
Bunkerville	702
Cal Nev Ari	702
Calico Basin	702
Calico Ridge	702
Caliente	775
Callville Bay	702
Cannon International Airport	775
Carlin	775
Carp	775
Carroll Station	775

City	Area Code
Carson City	775
Carson City Mall	775
Carson Colony	775
Carson Meadows	775
Carvers	775
Caselton	775
Cave Rock	775
Centerville	775
Central Valley	775
Cherry Creek	775
Citibank	702
Citibank Nv	702
Clark Co Courthouse	702
Clear Creek	775
Coaldale	775
Cobre	775
Cold Creek	702
Cold Spring	775
Cold Springs	775
College Park	702
Contact	775
Cordero	775
Corn Creek	702
Cosgrave	775
Cottonwood Creek	775
Cottonwood Cv	702
Cover City	775
Coyote Spgs	702
Coyote Springs	702
Crescent Valley	775
Crescent Vly	775
Crystal	775
Crystal Bay	775
Crystal Springs	775
Currie	775
Dayton	775
Deeth	775
Denio	775
Dike	775
Dixie Valley	775
Dresslerville	775
Dry Valley	775
Duck Valley	775
Duckwater	775
Dunphy	775
Dyer	775
Eagle Valley	775
Echo Bay	702
Elburz	775
Elgin	775
Elk Point	775
Elko	775
Elks Point	775
Ely	775
Ely Colony	775
Embarq Telphone	702
Emigrant Pass	775
Empire	775
Enterprise	702
Eureka	775
Fallon	775
Fallon Colony	775
Fallon Naval Air Station	775
Fernley	775
Frenchman	775
Gabbs	775
Galena	775
Gardnerville	775
Genoa	775
Gerlach	775
Glenbrook	775
Golconda	775
Gold Hill	775
Gold Point	775
Golden Valley	775
Goldfield	775
Goodsprings	702
Grand Sierra Hotel	775
Grass Valley	775
Green Valley	702
Greenbrae	775
Halleck	775
Happy Valley	775
Hawthorne	775
Hawthorne Army Ammunition Pl	775
Hazen	775

łenderson ... 702, 775
lidden Valley ... 775
lighway 40 ... 775
liko ... 775
lumboldt ... 775
nlay ... 775
ncline Village ... 775
ncline Vlg ... 775
ndian Spgs ... 702
ndian Springs ... 702
ndian Springs Air Force Aux ... 702
one ... 775
safa ... 702
C Penney Co ... 775
ackass Flats ... 775
ackpot ... 775
acks Valley ... 775
ackson Mountain ... 775
arbidge ... 775
ean ... 702
iggs ... 775
ohnnie ... 775
ungo ... 775
Kelmont East ... 775
ing River ... 775
ingsbury ... 775
ingston ... 775
V Valley Water Co ... 702
ake Village ... 775
akeridge ... 775
akeview ... 775
amoille ... 775
ane ... 775
as Vegas ... 702
as Vegas Business Reply ... 702
athrop Wells ... 775
aughlin ... 702
awton ... 775
ee ... 775
ehman Caves ... 775
emmon Valley ... 775
ida ... 775
incoln Park ... 775
ockwood ... 775
ogandale ... 702
ovelock ... 775
ower Valley ... 775
und ... 775
uning ... 775
Manhattan ... 775
Marla Bay ... 775
Mason ... 775
Mc Dermitt ... 775
Mc Gill ... 775
Mccarran ... 775
Mccarran Airport ... 702
Mcdermitt ... 775
Mercury ... 775
Mesquite ... 702
Metropolis ... 775
Mgm Properties ... 702
Midas ... 775
Middlegate ... 775
Mill City ... 775
Mina ... 775
Minden ... 775
Moapa ... 702
Moapa Valley ... 702
Mogul ... 775
Montello ... 775
Mound House ... 775
Mount Charleston ... 702
Mountain City ... 775
Mountain Sprg ... 702
Mountain Springs ... 702
Mt Charleston ... 702
Mustang ... 775
N Las Vegas ... 702
Nellis Afb ... 702
Nellis Air Force Base ... 702
Nelson ... 702
Nevada Employment Security ... 775
Nevada Highway Dept ... 775
Nevada Industrial Comm ... 775
Nevada Mass ... 775
Nevada Motor Vehicle ... 775
Nevada Power ... 702
New Empire ... 775
New Washoe City ... 775
Nixon ... 775
No Las Vegas ... 702
North Fork ... 775
North Las Vegas ... 702
Oasis ... 775
Old Nevada ... 702
Olinghouse ... 775
Oreana ... 775
Orovada ... 775
Overton ... 702
Overton Beach ... 702
Owyhee ... 775
Pahrump ... 775
Palm Gardens ... 702
Palomino Valley ... 775
Panaca ... 775
Panther Valley ... 775
Paradise Hill ... 775
Paradise Valley ... 775
Paradise Vly ... 775
Parcel Return Reno ... 775
Patrick ... 775
Patsville ... 775
Pequop ... 775
Peterson ... 775
Pinewild ... 775
Pioche ... 775
Pizen Switch ... 775
Pleasant Valley ... 775
Preston ... 775
Primm ... 702
Pueblo Valley ... 775
Pyramid ... 775
Quinn River Crossing ... 775
Rabbit Hole ... 775
Rachel ... 775
Ragtown ... 775
Rancho Haven ... 775
Rebel Creek ... 775
Red House ... 775
Red Rock ... 775
Reese River ... 775
Reno ... 775
Rhyolite ... 775
Riverside ... 702
Rixie ... 775
Rose Valley ... 775
Round Hill ... 775
Round Mtn ... 775
Ruby Valley ... 775
Ruth ... 775
Rye Patch ... 775
S W Gas Co ... 702
Salt Wells ... 775
San Jacinto ... 775
Sand Pass ... 775
Sandy Valley ... 702
Schurz ... 775
Searchlight ... 702
Shafter ... 775
Shantytown ... 775
Shared Firm Zip Code ... 702
Sheelite ... 775
Sheridan ... 775
Sierra ... 775
Silver City ... 775
Silver Knolls ... 775
Silver Spgs ... 775
Silver Springs ... 775
Silverpeak ... 775
Simpson ... 775
Skyland ... 775
Sloan ... 702
Smith ... 775
Smoke Creek ... 775
So Desert Correctional Ctr ... 702
So Nev Correctional Ctr ... 702
Somersett ... 775
Spanish Spgs ... 775
Spanish Springs ... 775
Sparks ... 775
Spring Creek ... 775
Stagecoach ... 775
Stateline ... 775
Stead ... 775
Steamboat ... 775
Steptoe ... 775
Stewart ... 775
Stewarts Point ... 702
Stillwater ... 775
Sulphur ... 775
Sun Valley ... 775
Sutcliffe ... 775
Sweetwater ... 775
Tempiute ... 775
The Lakes ... 702
Thorne ... 775
Thousand Springs ... 775
Thunder Mountain ... 775
Tonopah ... 775
Topaz Lake ... 775
Topaz Lodge ... 775
Topaz Ranch Estates ... 775
Toulon ... 775
Tracy-Clark ... 775
Trinity ... 775
Tungsten ... 775
Tuscarora ... 775
Unionville ... 775
Univ Nv Las Vegas ... 702
University ... 775
Unr ... 775
Upper Valley ... 775
Ursine ... 775
V C Highlands ... 775
Valley Of Fire ... 702
Valmy ... 775
Vc Highlands ... 775
Verdi ... 775
Virginia City ... 775
Virginia Foothills ... 775
W Wendover ... 775
Wabuska ... 775
Wadsworth ... 775
Walker Lake ... 775
Warm Springs ... 775
Washoe ... 775
Washoe Valley ... 775
Weed Heights ... 775
Wellington ... 775
Wells ... 775
Wendover ... 775
Weso ... 775
West Wendover ... 775
Whiskey Flats ... 775
Wilkins ... 775
Willow Beach ... 702
Winnemucca ... 775
Winnemucca Colony ... 775
Wittell ... 775
Yerington ... 775
Zephyr Cove ... 775
Zephyr Point ... 775

New Hampshire

All Points ... 603

New Jersey

Aberdeen ... 732
Absecon ... 609
Absecon City ... 609
Absecon Heights ... 609
Absecon Highlands ... 609
Academy ... 973
Adelphia ... 732
Albion ... 856
Allamuchy ... 908
Allamuchy Twp ... 908
Allendale ... 201
Allenhurst ... 732
Allentown ... 609
Allenwood ... 732
Alloway ... 856
Allwood ... 973
Almonesson ... 856
Alpha ... 908
Alpine ... 201
Ampere ... 973
Ancora ... 609
Andover ... 973
Anglesea ... 609
Annandale ... 908
Arlington ... 201
Asbury ... 908
Asbury Park ... 732
Ashland ... 856
Atco ... 856
Atlantic City ... 609
Atlantic Highlands ... 732
Atlantic Hl ... 732
Atlantic Hlds ... 732
Auburn ... 856
Audubon ... 856
Audubon Park ... 856
Augusta ... 973
Aura ... 856
Avalon ... 609
Avenel ... 732
Avon ... 732
Avon By Sea ... 732
Avon By The Sea ... 732
Awosting ... 973
Bank Of America ... 973
Bank Of New York ... 973
Baptistown ... 908
Bargaintown ... 609
Barnegat ... 609
Barnegat Lgt ... 609
Barnegat Light ... 609
Barnegat Light Boro ... 609
Barnegat Township ... 609
Barnsboro ... 856
Barrington ... 856
Barry Lakes ... 973
Basking Ridge ... 908
Batsto ... 609
Bay Head ... 732
Bayonne ... 201
Bayville ... 732
Bayway ... 908
Beach Haven ... 609
Beach Haven West ... 609
Beachwood ... 732
Beaver Lake ... 973
Bedminster ... 908
Beemerville ... 973
Beesleys Point ... 609
Belcoville ... 609
Belford ... 732
Belle Mead ... 908
Belleplain ... 609
Belleville ... 973
Bellmawr ... 856
Belmar ... 732
Belvidere ... 908
Bergen Point ... 201
Bergenfield ... 201
Bergenline ... 201
Berkeley ... 732
Berkeley Heights ... 908
Berkeley Hts ... 908
Berkeley Township ... 732
Berkeley Twp ... 732
Berlin ... 856
Berlin Boro ... 856
Berlin Township ... 856
Berlin Twp ... 856
Bernardsville ... 908
Betsytown ... 908
Beverly ... 609
Billingsport ... 856
Birmingham ... 609
Bivalve ... 856
Blackwood ... 856
Blackwood Ter ... 856
Blackwood Terrace ... 856
Blairstown ... 908
Blawenburg ... 609
Blenheim ... 856
Bloomfield ... 973
Bloomingdale ... 973
Bloomsbury ... 908
Blue Anchor ... 609
Bogota ... 201
Boonton ... 973
Boonton Township ... 973
Bordentown ... 609
Bound Brk ... 732
Bound Brook ... 732
Braddock ... 609
Bradevelt ... 732
Bradley Beach ... 732
Branchburg ... 908
Branchville ... 973
Brant Beach ... 609
Brick ... 732
Bricktown ... 732
Bridgeboro ... 856
Bridgeport ... 856
Bridgeton ... 856
Bridgewater ... 908
Brielle ... 732
Brigantine ... 609
Brigantine City ... 609
Broadway ... 908
Brookdale ... 973
Brooklawn ... 856
Brookside ... 973
Browns Mills ... 609
Budd Lake ... 973
Buena ... 856
Buena Vista Township ... 856
Burleigh ... 609
Burlington ... 609
Burlington City ... 609
Burlington Township ... 609
Burlngtn City ... 609
Burlngtn Twp ... 609
Butler ... 973
Buttzville ... 908
Byram Township ... 973
Byram Twp ... 973
Caldwell ... 973
Califon ... 908
Camden ... 856
Cape May ... 609
Cape May Ch ... 609
Cape May Court House ... 609
Cape May Point ... 609
Cape May Pt ... 609
Carlstadt ... 201
Carmel ... 856
Carneys Point ... 856
Carneys Point Township ... 856
Carteret ... 732
Castle Point ... 201
Cecil ... 856
Cedar Beach ... 732
Cedar Bonnet Island ... 609
Cedar Brook ... 856
Cedar Grove ... 973
Cedar Knolls ... 973
Cedar Run ... 609
Cedarville ... 856
Cenlar Bank ... 973
Centerton ... 856
Changewater ... 908
Chatham ... 973
Chatham Twp ... 973
Chatsworth ... 609
Cherry Hill ... 856
Cherry Hill Township ... 856
Chesilhurst ... 856
Chester ... 908
Chesterfield ... 609
Chesterfield Township ... 609
Chestnut ... 908
Chews Landing ... 856
Cinnaminson ... 856
Cinnaminson Township ... 856
Clark ... 732
Clarksboro ... 856
Clarksburg ... 732
Clayton ... 856
Clementon ... 856
Clermont ... 609
Cliff Park ... 201
Cliffside Park ... 201
Cliffside Pk ... 201
Cliffwood ... 732
Cliffwood Bch ... 732
Cliffwood Beach ... 732
Cliffwood Lake ... 973
Clifton ... 973
Clinton ... 908
Closter ... 201
Cold Spring ... 609
Colesville ... 973
Collings Lakes ... 856
Collingswood ... 856
Cologne ... 609
Colonia ... 732
Colts Neck ... 732
Columbia ... 908
Columbus ... 609
Convent Sta ... 973
Convent Station ... 973
Cookstown ... 609
Corbin City ... 609
Cozy Lake ... 973
Cranbury ... 609
Cranford ... 908
Cream Ridge ... 609
Creamridge ... 609
Cresskill ... 201
Cross Keys ... 856
Crosswicks ... 609
Cupsaw Lake ... 973
Daretown ... 856
Darlington ... 201
Dayton ... 732
Deal ... 732
Deal Park ... 732
Deepwater ... 856
Deerfield ... 856
Deerfield St ... 856
Deerfield Street ... 856
Deerfield Twp ... 856
Del Haven ... 609
Delair ... 856
Delanco ... 856
Delanco Township ... 856
Delawanna ... 973
Delaware ... 908
Delaware Park ... 908
Delmont ... 856
Delran ... 856
Delran Township ... 856
Demarest ... 201
Dennisville ... 609
Denville ... 973
Deptford ... 856
Deptford Township ... 856
Devonshire ... 609
Dividing Creek ... 856
Dividing Crk ... 856
Division Of Revenue ... 609
Doddtown ... 973
Dominick V Daniels ... 201
Dorchester ... 856
Dorothy ... 609
Dover ... 973
Dover Annex ... 973
Dover Township ... 732
Dover Twp ... 732
Dumont ... 201
Dundee ... 973
Dunellen ... 732
E Brunswick ... 732
E Millstone ... 732
E Rutherford ... 201
E Windsor ... 609
Eaglewood Township ... 609
Earle Naval Weapons Station ... 732
East Amwell ... 908
East Amwell Township ... 908
East Amwell Twp ... 908
East Berlin ... 856
East Brunswick ... 732
East Camden ... 856
East Freehold ... 732

City	Area Code
East Haddonfield	856
East Hanover	973
East Keansburg	732
East Millstone	732
East Newark	973
East Orange	973
East Rutherford	201
East Vineland	856
East Windsor	609
Eastamptn Twp	609
Eastampton	609
Eastampton Township	609
Eatontown	732
Echelon	856
Edgewater	201
Edgewater Park	609
Edgewater Prk	609
Edison	732
Educational Testing Service	609
Egg Harbor	609
Egg Harbor City	609
Egg Harbor Cy	609
Egg Harbor Township	609
Egg Harbor Twp	609
Egg Hbr City	609
Egg Hbr Twp	609
Elberon	732
Elberon Park	732
Eldora	609
Elizabeth	908
Elizabethport	908
Ellis Island	201
Ellisburg	856
Elm	609
Elmer	856
Elmora	908
Elmwood Park	201
Elwood	609
Emerson	201
Englewd Clfs	201
Englewood	201
Englewood Cliffs	201
English Creek	609
Englishtown	732
Erial	856
Erlton	856
Erma	609
Erskine	973
Erskine Lakes	973
Essex Fells	973
Estell Manor	609
Evesboro	856
Evesham	856
Evesham Twp	856
Ewan	856
Ewing	609
Ewing Township	609
Ewing Twp	609
Fair Haven	732
Fair Lawn	201
Fairfield	973
Fairfield Twp	856
Fairlawn	201
Fairton	856
Fairview	201
Fanwood	908
Far Hills	908
Farmingdale	732
Farmington	609
Fayson Lake	973
Fayson Lakes	973
Fieldsboro	609
Finderne	908
Fishing Creek	609
Five Corners	201
Flagtown	908
Flanders	973
Flemington	908
Florence	609
Florham Park	973
Folsom	609
Fords	732
Forked River	609
Fort Dix	609
Fort Hancock	732
Fort Lee	201
Fort Monmouth	732
Fortescue	856
Franklin	973
Franklin Lakes	201
Franklin Lks	201
Franklin Park	732
Franklin Twp	732
Franklinville	856
Fredon	973
Fredon Township	973
Fredon Twp	973
Freehold	732
Frenchtown	908
Ft Dix	609
Galloway	609
Galloway Township	609
Gandys Beach	856
Garfield	973
Garwood	908
Gateway National Recreation	732
Georgia	732
Gerard	973
Germania	609
Gibbsboro	856
Gibbstown	856
Gillette	908
Gladstone	908
Glassboro	856
Glasser	973
Glen Gardner	908
Glen Ridge	973
Glen Rock	201
Glendora	856
Glenwood	973
Gloucester	856
Gloucester City	856
Gloucester Cy	856
Gloucstr City	856
Gordon Lakes	973
Goshen	609
Grassy Sound	609
Great Meadows	908
Great Notch	973
Green Bank	609
Green Brook	732
Green Creek	609
Green Pond	973
Green Township	973
Green Twp	973
Green Village	973
Greendell	973
Greenpond	973
Greenville	201
Greenwich	856
Greenwich Township	856
Greenwood Lake	973
Grenloch	856
Greystone Park	973
Greystone Pk	973
Grove	973
Groveville	609
Guttenberg	201
Hack	201
Hackensack	201
Hackettstown	908
Haddon Heights	856
Haddon Hgts	856
Haddon Hts	856
Haddon Township	856
Haddon Twp	856
Haddonfield	856
Hainesport	609
Hainesport Township	609
Hainesprt Twp	609
Haledon	973
Hamburg	973
Hamilton	609
Hamilton Sq	609
Hamilton Square	609
Hamilton Township	609
Hamilton Twp	609
Hammonton	609
Hampton	908
Hancocks Brg	856
Hancocks Bridge	856
Hardwick	908
Hardyston	973
Harmony Township	908
Harrington Park	201
Harrington Pk	201
Harrison	973
Harrison Township	856
Harrisonville	856
Harvey Cedars	609
Harvey Cedars Boro	609
Hasbrouck Heights	201
Hasbrouck Hts	201
Haskell	973
Haworth	201
Hawthorne	973
Hazlet	732
Heislerville	856
Helmetta	732
Hewitt	973
Hi Nella	856
Hibernia	973
High Bar Harbor	609
High Bridge	908
High Crest	973
High Point	973
High Point Park	973
Highland Lakes	973
Highland Lks	973
Highland Park	732
Highlands	732
Hightstown	609
Hillcrest	973
Hillsborough	908
Hillsdale	201
Hillside	973
Hilltop	856
Ho Ho Kus	201
Hoboken	201
Holmdel	732
Holmdel Village	732
Hopatcong	973
Hope	908
Hopelawn	848
Hopewell	609
Hopewell Township	609
Hopewell Twp	609
Howell	732
Hurffville	856
Ideal Beach	732
Imlaystown	609
Ind Hillside	973
Indian Mills	609
Industrial Hillside	973
Interlaken	732
Ironbound	973
Ironia	973
Irvington	973
Iselin	732
Island Heights	732
Island Hgts	732
J P Morgan Chase	973
Jackson	732
Jackson Township	732
Jackson Twp	732
Jacobstown	609
Jamesburg	732
Jefferson Township	973
Jefferson Twp	973
Jericho	856
Jersey Central Power Light	732
Jersey City	201
Jerseyville	732
Jobstown	609
Johnson & Johnson	732
Johnsonburg	908
Jp Morgan Chase	973
Juliustown	609
Keansburg	732
Kearny	201
Keasbey	848
Kendall Park	732
Kenilworth	908
Kenvil	973
Keyport	732
Kilmer Gmf	732
Kingston	609
Kinnelon	973
Kirkwd Voorhs	856
Kirkwd Vrhes	856
Kirkwood	856
Kresson	856
Lacey	609
Lacey Township	609
Lafayette	973
Lake Como	732
Lake Hiawatha	973
Lake Hopatcong	973
Lake Intervale	973
Lake Stockholm	973
Lake Swannanoa	973
Lake Tamarack	973
Lakehurst	732
Lakehurst Nae	732
Lakehurst Naec	732
Lakeland	856
Lakewood	732
Lambertville	609
Landing	973
Landisville	856
Lanoka Harbor	609
Laurel Lake	856
Laurel Spgs	856
Laurel Springs	856
Laurence Harbor	732
Laurence Hbr	732
Lavallette	732
Lawnside	856
Lawrence	609
Lawrence Township	609
Lawrence Twp	609
Lawrenceville	609
Layton	973
Lebanon	908
Ledgewood	973
Leeds Point	609
Leesburg	856
Leh	609
Lenola	856
Leonardo	732
Leonia	201
Liberty Cor	908
Liberty Corner	908
Lincoln Park	973
Lincroft	732
Linden	908
Lindenwold	856
Lindy Lake	973
Linwood	609
Lionshead Lake	973
Little Egg Harbor	609
Little Egg Harbor Twp	609
Little Falls	973
Little Ferry	201
Little Silver	732
Little Silver Point	732
Little York	908
Livingston	973
Lk Hiawatha	973
Lk Hopatcong	973
Lk Intervale	973
Loch Arbour	732
Locust	732
Lodi	201
Logan	856
Logan Township	856
Logan Twp	856
Long Bch Twp	609
Long Beach	609
Long Beach Township	609
Long Branch	732
Long Valley	908
Longport	609
Lopatcong	908
Loveladies	609
Lower Bank	609
Lower Montville	973
Ltl Egg Hbr	609
Lumberton	609
Lumberton Township	609
Lumberton Twp	609
Lyndhurst	201
Lyons	908
Lyonsville	973
Madison	973
Magnolia	856
Mahwah	201
Main Avenue Station	973
Malaga	856
Manahawkin	609
Manalapan	732
Manasquan	732
Manchester	732
Manchester Township	732
Manchester Tw	732
Manchester Twp	732
Mannington	856
Mannington Township	856
Mansfield	609
Mantoloking	732
Mantua	856
Mantua Heights	856
Manville	908
Maple Shade	856
Maplecrest	973
Maplewood	973
Margate	609
Margate City	609
Marlboro	732
Marlton	856
Marlton Lakes	856
Marmora	609
Martinsville	732
Masonville	856
Matawan	732
Mauricetown	856
Mayetta	609
Mays Landing	609
Mayville	609
Maywood	201
Mc Afee	973
Mc Guire Afb	609
Mc Guire Air Force Base	609
Mcafee	973
Mckee City	609
Meadows	201
Medford	609
Medford Lakes	609
Medford Lakes Boro	609
Medford Township	609
Mendham	973
Menlo Park	732
Mercerville	609
Merchantville	856
Meriden	973
Merrill Lynch	732
Merrill Lynch Inc	973
Metuchen	732
Miami Beach	609
Mickleton	856
Middlebush	732
Middlesex	732
Middletown	732
Middleville	973
Midland Park	201
Midland Pk	201
Midtown	973
Midvale	973
Milford	908
Millburn	973
Millhurst	732
Millington	908
Millstone	609, 732, 908
Millstone Township	609, 732
Millstone Twp	609
Milltown	732
Millville	856
Milmay	609
Mine Hill	973
Minotola	856
Mizpah	609
Monitor	201
Monmouth	732
Monmouth Bch	732
Monmouth Beach	732
Monmouth Hills	732
Monmouth Jct	732
Monmouth Junction	732
Monmouth Park	732
Monroe	732
Monroe Township	732
Monroe Twp	732
Monroeville	856
Montague	973
Montclair	973
Montgomery	609, 908
Montvale	201
Montville	973
Montville Township	973
Moonachie	201
Moorestown	856
Morgan	732
Morganville	732
Morris Plains	973
Morristown	973
Morsemere	201
Mount Arlington	973
Mount Ephraim	856
Mount Freedom	973
Mount Holly	609
Mount Holly Township	609
Mount Laurel	856
Mount Laurel Township	856
Mount Olive	973
Mount Royal	856
Mount Tabor	973
Mountain Lakes	973
Mountain Lks	973
Mountain View	973
Mountainside	908
Mt Arlington	973
Muhlenberg	908
Mullica Hill	856
Murray Hill	908
Mystic Islands	609
Mystic Islnds	609
N Arlington	973
N Brunswick	732
N Caldwell	973
N Cape May	609
N J Income Tax	609
N J Natural Gas Co	732
N J State Income Tax	609
N Middletown	732
N Milford	201
N Plainfield	732
N Wildwood	609
Nafec	609
National Park	856
Navesink	732
Neptune	732
Neptune City	732
Nesco	609
Neshanic Sta	908
Neshanic Station	908
Netcong	973
New Brunswick	732
New Egypt	609
New Gretna	609
New Jersey Bmc	201
New Lisbon	609
New Milford	201
New Monmouth	732
New Providence	908
New Providnce	908
New Vernon	908
Newark	201, 973
Newfield	856
Newfoundland	973
Newport	856
Newton	973
Newtonville	856
Nj Income Tax	609
Nj International And Bmc	201
Nnj Metro P&dc	201
Norma	856
Normandy Bch	732
Normandy Beach	732
North Arlington	973
North Beach	609
North Bergen	201
North Branch	908
North Brunswick	732
North Caldwell	973
North Cape May	609
North Center	973

City	Area Code
orth Delran	856
orth Dennis	609
orth Elizabeth	908
orth Haledon	973
orth Hanover	609
orth Marlton	856
orth Middletown	732
orth Plainfield	732, 908
orth Wildwood	609
orthfield	609
orthvale	201
orwood	201
utley	973
ak Ridge	973
ak Valley	856
akhurst	732
akland	201
aklyn	856
cean	732
cean City	609
cean Gate	732
cean Grove	732
cean View	609
ceanport	732
ceanville	609
gdensburg	973
ld Bridge	732
ld Tappan	201
ldwick	908
radell	201
range	973
rtley Beach	732
sbornville	732
utwater	973
verbrook	973
xford	908
ackanack Lake	973
ackanack Lk	973
alermo	609
alisade	201
alisades Park	201
alisades Pk	201
almyra	856
amrapo	201
aradise Lakes	856
aramus	201
ark Ridge	201
arkandbush	908
arkertown	609
arlin	732
arsippany	973
arsippany Troy Hills	973
assaic	973
assaic Park	973
aterson	973
aulsboro	856
eapack	908
edricktown	856
elican Island	732
emberton	609
ennington	609
enns Grove	856
ennsauken	856
ennsville	856
eoples Park	973
equannock	973
equannock Township	973
errineville	609
ershing	201
erth Amboy	732, 848
etersburg	609
eterstown	908
halanx	732
hillipsburg	908
icatinny Ars	973
icatinny Arsenal	973
ilesgrove	856
ilesgrove Township	856
ilesgrv Twp	856
ine Beach	732
ine Brook	973
ine Cliff Lake	973
ine Grove	856
ine Hill	856
ine Valley	856
inebrook	973
Pinehurst	609
Pines Lake	973
Piscataway	732
Pitman	856
Pittsgrov Twp	856
Pittsgrove	856
Pittsgrove Township	856
Pittstown	908
Plainfield	732, 908
Plainsboro	609
Plaza	201
Pleasantville	609
Pluckemin	908
Plumsted	609
Plumsted Township	609
Plumsted Twp	609
Point Pleasant	732
Point Pleasant Beach	732
Point Pleasant Boro	732
Pomona	609
Pompton Falls	973
Pompton Junction	973
Pompton Lakes	973
Pompton Plains	973
Pompton Plns	973
Port Elizabeth	856
Port Monmouth	732
Port Murray	908
Port Norris	856
Port Reading	732
Port Republic	609
Port-Au-Peck	732
Pottersville	908
Powerville	973
Preakness	973
Princeton	609
Princeton Jct	609
Princeton Junction	609
Princeton Township	609
Princeton Twp	609
Princeton University	609
Prospect Park	973
Prospect Pk	973
Prt Elizabeth	856
Prudential Mutual Fund Servi	732
Pt Pleas Bch	732
Pt Pleasant	732
Pt Pleasant B	732
Pt Pleasant Beach	732
Quakertown	908
Quinton	856
Radburn	201
Rahway	732
Ramsey	201
Rancocas	609
Rancocas Woods	856
Randolph	973
Raritan	908
Readington	908
Red Bank	732
Richland	609
Richwood	856
Ridgefield	201
Ridgefield Park	201
Ridgefield Pk	201
Ridgewood	201
Ringoes	908
Ringwood	973
Rio Grande	609
Ritz	973
River Edge	201
River Vale	201
Riverdale	973
Riverside	856
Riverton	856
Rivervale	201
Robbinsville	609
Rochelle Park	201
Rockaway	973
Rockaway Valley	973
Rockleigh	201
Rocky Hill	609
Roebling	609
Roosevelt	732
Rosedale	609
Roseland	973
Roselle	908
Roselle Park	908
Rosemont	609
Rosenhayn	856
Roseville	973
Roxbury Township	973
Roxbury Twp	973
Rumson	732
Runnemede	856
Rutherford	201
S Belmar	732
S Bound Brook	732
S Hackensack	201
S Harrisn Twp	856
S Harrison Twp	856
S Plainfield	732
S Seaside Pk	732
S Seaville	609
S Toms River	732
Saddle Brook	201
Saddle River	201
Salem	856
Sands Point	732
Sandy Hook	732
Sandyston	973
Sayreville	732
Schooleys Mountain	908
Schooleys Mtn	908
Scotch Plains	908
Scullville	609
Sea Bright	732
Sea Girt	732
Sea Isle City	609
Seabrook	856
Seaside Heights	732
Seaside Hgts	732
Seaside Park	732
Seaville	609
Secaucus	201
Selected Risks Insurance Co	973
Sergeantsville	908
Sergeantsvlle	908
Sewaren	732
Sewell	856
Shady Lake	973
Shamong	609
Shamong Township	609
Shark River Hills	732
Shark River Manor	732
Sharptown	856
Shaw Crest	609
Shiloh	856
Ship Bottom	609
Ship Bottom Boro	609
Short Hills	973
Shrewsbury	732
Shrewsbury Township	732
Sicklerville	856
Silver Lake	973
Singac	973
Skillman	609
Skyline Lakes	973
Smithville	609
Somerdale	856
Somers Point	609
Somerset	732
Somerville	908
South Amboy	732
South Belmar	732
South Bound Brook	732
South Branch	908
South Brunswick	732
South Camden	856
South Dennis	609
South Egg Harbor	609
South Hackensack	201
South Harrison Township	856
South Kearny	201
South Orange	973
South Paterson	973
South Plainfield	732
South River	732
South Seaside Park	732
South Seaville	609
South Toms River	732
South Vineland	856
Southampton	609
Southampton Twp	609
Sparta	973
Spotswood	732
Spring Heights	732
Spring Lake	732
Spring Lake Heights	732
Springfield	973
Stafford Township	609
Stafford Twp	609
Staffordville	609
Stanhope	973
Stanton	908
State Income Tax	609
State Of Nj Motor Vehicles	609
State Of Nj Mv	609
State Of Nj Taxation Dept	609
Steelmantown	609
Steelmanville	609
Stewartsville	908
Stillwater	973
Stirling	908
Stockholm	973
Stockton	609
Stone Harbor	609
Stow Creek Twp	856
Stratford	856
Strathmere	609
Strathmore	732
Succasunna	973
Summit	908
Summit Avenue	201
Surf City	609
Surf City Boro	609
Sussex	973
Swainton	609
Swartswood	973
Swedesboro	856
Sweetwater	609
Tabernacle	609
Tabernacle Twp	609
Tabor	973
Tansboro	856
Taurus	201
Tavistock	856
Taylortown	973
Teaneck	201
Tenafly	201
Tennent	732
Teterboro	201
Tewksbury Township	908
Tewksbury Twp	908
The Bank Of New York	973
Thompson Beach	856
Thorofare	856
Three Bridges	908
Tinton Falls	732
Titusville	609
Toms River	732
Totowa	973
Totowa Boro	973
Towaco	973
Town Bank	609
Town Center	973
Townley	908
Townsend Inlt	609
Townsends Inlet	609
Township Of Washington	201
Tranquility	973
Tremley	908
Tremley Point	908
Trenton	609
Troy Hills	973
Tuckahoe	609
Tuckerton	609
Tuckerton Boro	609
Turnersville	856
Twp Washingtn	201
Twp Washinton	201
Tyler Park	201
U Saddle Riv	201
Union	908
Union Beach	732
Union Center	908
Union City	201
Union Square	908
Upper Deerfield Twp	856
Upper Freehold	609
Upper Freehold Township	609
Upper Greenwood Lake	973
Upper Montclair	973
Upper Saddle River	201
Uppr Free Twp	609
Upr Montclair	973
Uptown	201
V A Hospital	973
Vail Homes	732
Vailsburg	973
Vanderburg	732
Vauxhall	973
Ventnor	609
Ventnor City	609
Ventnor Heights	609
Verga	856
Vernon	973
Verona	973
Victory Gardens	973
Vienna	908
Villas	609
Vincentown	609
Vineland	856
Voorhees	856
Voorhees Kirkwood	856
Voorhees Township	856
W Allenhurst	732
W Belmar	732
W Caldwell	973
W Colls	856
W Colls Hgts	856
W Keansburg	732
W Long Branch	732
W Paterson	973
W Windsor	609
W Windsor Township	609
Wachovia	732
Wachovia Bank	201
Wachovia Bnk	973
Waldwick	201
Wall	732
Wall Township	732
Wall Twp	732
Wallington	973
Wallkill Lake	973
Wallpack Center	973
Wallpack Ctr	973
Wanamassa	732
Wanaque	973
Wantage	973
Wantage Twp	973
Waretown	609
Warren	908
Warren Grove	609
Washington	908
Washington Park	973
Washington Street	201
Washington Tnshp	201
Washington Township	201
Washington Twnshp	201
Washington Twp	201
Washington Twps	201
Washington Twsp	201
Watchung	908
Waterford	856
Waterford Township	856
Waterford Wks	856
Waterford Works	856
Wayne	973
Wayside	732
Weehawken	201
Weekstown	609
Weequahic	973
Wenonah	856
West Allenhurst	732
West Amwell	609
West Arlington	201
West Atco	856
West Atlantic City	609
West Belmar	732
West Berlin	856
West Caldwell	973
West Cape May	609
West Carteret	732
West Collingswood	856
West Collingswood Heights	856
West Creek	609
West Deptford	856
West End	732
West Englewood	201
West Fort Lee	201
West Keansburg	732
West Long Branch	732
West Milford	973
West Milford Lakes	973
West New York	201
West Orange	973
West Paterson	973
West Trenton	609
West Tuckerton	609
West Wildwood	609
West Win Tow	609
West Windsor	609
Westampton	609
Westampton Township	609
Westboro	732
Westfield	908
Westmont	856
Westville	856
Westville Grove	856
Westwood	201
Weymouth	609
Wharton	973
Whippany	973
White House Station	908
White Hse Sta	908
Whitehouse	908
Whitehouse Station	908
Whitesboro	609
Whiting	732
Wickatunk	732
Wildwood	609
Wildwood City	609
Wildwood Crest	609
Wildwood Crst	609
Williamstown	856
Willingboro	609
Willow Grove	856
Windsor	609
Winfield Park	908
Winslow	609
Wood Ridge	201
Wood-Ridge	201
Woodbine	609
Woodbridge	732
Woodbury	856
Woodbury Heights	856
Woodbury Hgts	856
Woodbury Hts	856
Woodcliff	201
Woodcliff Lake	201
Woodcliff Lk	201
Woodcrest	856
Woodland Park	973
Woodlynne	856
Woodstown	856
Woolwich	856
Woolwich Township	856
Woolwich Twp	856
Wrightstown	609
Wyckoff	201
Yardville	609
Zarepath	732
Zarephath	732

New Mexico

City	Area Code
Abbott	505
Abeytas	505
Abiquiu	505
Acomita	505
Agua Fria	505
Alameda	505
Alamillo	505
Alamo	505
Alamogordo	505
Albert	505
Albuquerque	505
Alcalde	505

Algodones 505
Alire 505
Alma 505
Alto 505
Alto Crest 505
Amalia 505
Ambrosia Lake 505
Amistad 505
Anaconda 505
Ancho 505
Angel Fire 505
Angostura 505
Angus 505
Animas 505
Anthony 505
Anton Chico 505
Apache Creek 505
Apodaca 505
Arabela 505
Aragon 505
Arch 505
Arenas Valley 505
Arrey 505
Arroyo Hondo 505
Arroyo Seco 505
Artesia 505
Artesia Camp 505
Atoka 505
Aurora 505
Aztec 505
Bandelier National Monument 505
Bard 505
Barranca 505
Bayard 505
Belen 505
Bell Ranch 505
Bellview 505
Bennett 505
Bent 505
Berino 505
Bernal 505
Bernalillo 505
Bernardo 505
Beulah 505
Biklabito 505
Bingham 505
Bisti 505
Black Rock 505
Blanco 505
Bloomfield 505
Bluewater 505
Border Hill 505
Bosque 505
Bosque Farms 505
Brazos 505
Brimhall 505
Broadview 505
Broadview Acres 505
Buckeye 505
Buckhorn 505
Budaghers 505
Buena Vista 505
Bueyeros 505
Burnham 505
Caballo 505
Cameron 505
Campus 505
Canjilon 505
Cannon Afb 505
Cannon Air Force Base 505
Canoncito 505
Canones 505
Canova 505
Canyoncito 505
Capitan 505
Caprock 505
Capulin 505
Capulin Mountain National Mo 505
Carlsbad 505
Carlsbad Caverns National Pa 505
Carrizozo 505
Carson 505
Casa Blanca 505
Causey 505
Cebolla 505
Cedar Crest 505

Cedar Hill 505
Cedarvale 505
Central 505
Cerrillos 505
Cerritos 505
Cerro 505
Chaco Canyon National Monume 505
Chacon 505
Chama 505
Chamberino 505
Chamisal 505
Chamita 505
Chaparral 505
Chapelle 505
Chi Chil Tah 505
Chili 505
Chilili 505
Chimayo 505
Chloride 505
Chupadero 505
Church Rock 505
Cimarron 505
Clapham 505
Claunch 505
Clayton 505
Cleveland 505
Cliff 505
Clines Corners 505
Clines Cors 505
Cloudcroft 505
Cloverdale 505
Clovis 505
Cochiti Lake 505
Cochiti Publo 505
Cochiti Pueblo 505
Colfax 505
Columbine 505
Columbus 505
Conchas Dam 505
Cononcito 505
Continental Divide 505
Contnental Dv 505
Contreras 505
Coolidge 505
Cordova 505
Corona 505
Corrales 505
Coruco 505
Costilla 505
Cotton City 505
Counselor 505
Cowles 505
Coyote 505
Crossroads 505
Crownpoint 505
Cruzville 505
Crystal 505
Cuba 505
Cubero 505
Cuchillo 505
Cuervo 505
Cundiyo 505
Cuyamungue 505
Dahlia 505
Dalton Pass 505
Datil 505
Defiance 505
Deming 505
Denning 505
Derry 505
Des Moines 505
Des Montes 505
Dexter 505
Dilia 505
Dixon 505
Domingo 505
Dona Ana 505
Dora 505
Dulce 505
Dunken 505
Duran 505
Dusty 505
Eagle Nest 505
East Pecos 505
East Vaughn 505

Edgewood 505
El Ancon 505
El Cerrito 505
El Duende 505
El Guique 505
El Huerfano 505
El Llanito 505
El Llano 505
El Morro National Monument 505
El Portero 505
El Porvenir 505
El Prado 505
El Pueblo 505
El Rancho 505
El Rancho Loma Linda 505
El Rincon De Los Trujillos 505
El Rito 505
El Vado 505
El Valle 505
Elephant Btte 505
Elephant Butte 505
Elida 505
Elk 505
Elkins 505
Embudo 505
Encinal 505
Encino 505
Engle 505
Ensenada 505
Escobosa 505
Escondida 505
Espanola 505
Estaca 505
Estancia 505
Eunice 505
Fairacres 505
Fairview 505
Farley 505
Farmington 505
Farmington Municipal Airport 505
Faywood 505
Fence Lake 505
Fierro 505
Five Points 505
Flora Vista 505
Florida 505
Floyd 505
Flying H 505
Folsom 505
Fort Bayard 505
Fort Stanton 505
Fort Sumner 505
Fort Wingate 505
Fort Wingate Army Depot 505
Fruitland 505
Ft Bayard 505
Ft Stanton 505
Ft Sumner 505
Galisteo 505
Gallegos 505
Gallina 505
Gallinas 505
Gallup 505
Gamerco 505
Garfield 505
Garita 505
Garrison 505
Gavilan 505
Gila 505
Gila Cliff Dwellings Nationa 505
Gladstone 505
Glencoe 505
Glenrio 505
Glenwood 505
Glorieta 505
Gobernador 505
Golden 505
Golondrinas 505
Gonzales Ranch 505
Gonzales Rnch 505
Grady 505
Grants 505
Grenville 505
Guachupangue 505
Guadalupita 505
Guagolotes 505

Guique 505
Hachita 505
Hagerman 505
Hanover 505
Happy Valley 505
Hatch 505
Hayden 505
Hernandez 505
Hi Rls Mtn Pk 505
Hi Rolls Mt Park 505
High Rolls 505
High Rolls Mountain Park 505
Hillsboro 505
Hobbs 505
Holloman Afb 505
Holloman Air Force Base 505
Hollywood 505
Holman 505
Hondo 505
Hope 505
Horse Springs 505
House 505
Hurley 505
Hyde Park Estates 505
Ilfeld 505
Isleta 505
Jacona 505
Jaconita 505
Jal 505
Jamestown 505
Jarales 505
Jemez Pueblo 505
Jemez Springs 505
Jicarilla 505
Jicarilla Apache Indian Rese 505
Junta 505
Kenna 505
Kingston 505
Kirtland 505
Kirtland Afb 505
La Bolsa 505
La Cienga 505
La Cueva 505
La Jara 505
La Joya 505
La Junta 505
La Loma 505
La Luz 505
La Madera 505
La Mesa 505
La Mesilla 505
La Plata 505
La Puebla 505
La Puente 505
La Union 505
La Villita 505
Laguna 505
Lagunita 505
Lake Arthur 505
Lake Sumner 505
Lake Valley 505
Lakewood 505
Lama 505
Lamy 505
Las Cruces 505, 575
Las Nutrias 505
Las Palomas 505
Las Placitas 505
Las Tablas 505
Las Vegas 505
Lea County Correctional Fac 505
Ledoux 505
Lemitar 505
Levy 505
Leyba 505
Lincoln 505
Lindrith 505
Lingo 505
Little Walnut Village 505
Little Water 505
Llano 505
Llano Quemado 505
Llaves 505
Loco Hills 505
Logan 505
Lon 505

Lordsburg 505
Los Alamos 505
Los Chavez 505
Los Luceros 505
Los Lunas 505
Los Ojos 505
Los Pachecos 505
Los Padillas 505
Los Ranchos 505
Los Ranchos De Albuquerque 505
Los Rnchs Abq 505
Los Trujillos 505
Loving 505
Lovington 505
Lower Laposada 505
Lower Nutria 505
Lower Ranchito 505
Lower San Francisco Plaza 505
Lucy 505
Luis Lopez 505
Lumberton 505
Luna 505
Lyden 505
Madrid 505
Magdalena 505
Malaga 505
Maljamar 505
Mangas Springs 505
Manuelito 505
Manzano Base 505
Maxwell 505
Mayhill 505
Mc Alister 505
Mc Donald 505
Mcalister 505
Mccartys 505
Mcdonald 505
Mcgaffey 505
Mcintosh 505
Medalanes 505
Medanales 505
Medenales 505
Melrose 505
Mentmore 505
Mesa Poleo 505
Mescalero 505
Mescalero Apache Indian Rese 505
Mesilla 505
Mesilla Park 505
Mesita 505
Mesquite 505
Metropolitan Detention Ctr 505
Mexican Spgs 505
Mexican Springs 505
Miami 505
Midway 505
Milagro 505
Milan 505
Mills 505
Milnesand 505
Mimbres 505
Mogollon 505
Montezuma 505
Monticello 505
Monument 505
Mora 505
Moriarty 505
Mosquero 505
Mount Dora 505
Mountain Park 505
Mountainair 505
Mt Dora 505
Mule Creek 505
Nageezi 505
Nambe 505
Nara Visa 505
Naschitti 505
Navajo 505
Navajo Dam 505
Navajo Wingate Village 505
New Laguna 505
New Mexico State Capitol 505
New Mexico Tax Rev Dept 505
Newcomb 505
Newkirk 505
Nogal 505

North Carmen 50
North Hurley 50
North San Ysidro 50
Nutrias 50
Ocate 50
Ohkay Owingeh 50
Oil Center 50
Ojito 50
Ojo Caliente 50
Ojo Feliz 50
Ojo Sarco 50
Old Laguna 50
Old Picacho 50
Omega 50
Organ 50
Orogrande 50
Oscuro 50
Paguate 50
Pajarito 50
Panorama Heights 50
Paraje 50
Pastura 50
Pblo Of Acoma 50
Pecos 50
Pecos National Monument 50
Pena Blanca 50
Penasco 50
Pendaries 50
Pep 50
Peralta 50
Perea 50
Pescado 50
Petaca 50
Philmont 50
Picacho 50
Picuris 50
Pie Town 50
Pilar 50
Pine 50
Pine Lodge 50
Pine View 50
Pinedale 50
Pinehill 50
Pinon 50
Pinos Altos 50
Pintada 50
Placita 50
Placitas 50
Playas 50
Pleasant Hill 50
Pleasanton 50
Pojoaque 50
Polvadera 50
Ponderosa 50
Portales 50
Pot Creek 50
Prewitt 50
Progresso 50
Public Service Co 50
Pueblito 50
Pueblitos 50
Pueblo Of Acoma 50
Pueblo Pintado 50
Puerta D Luna 50
Puerta De Luna 50
Quarteles 50
Quay 50
Quemado 50
Querinda Park 50
Questa 50
Qway 50
Radium Spgs 50
Radium Sprgs 50
Radium Springs 50
Rainsville 50
Ramah 50
Ramah Community 50
Ramon 50
Ranch Taos 50
Ranches Of Taos 50
Ranchito 50
Ranchitos 50
Rancho Taos 50
Rancho West 50
Ranchos De Taos 50
Ranchos Taos 50

Raton 505
Red Hill 505
Red River 505
Redrock 505
Regina 505
Rehoboth 505
Rencona 505
Reserve 505
Ribera 505
Rincon 505
Rinconado 505
Rio Chiquito 505
Rio Lucio 505
Rio Rancho 505
Rito De Las Sillas 505
Riverside 505
Rnch De Taos 505
Road Forks 505
Rociada 505
Rock Canyon 505
Rodarte 505
Rodeo 505
Rodey 505
Rogers 505
Romeroville 505
Rosebud 505
Roswell 505
Roswell Industrial Air Cente 505
Rowe 505
Roy 505
Ruidoso 505
Ruidoso Downs 505
Rutheron 505
S W Indian Foun 505
Sabinal 505
Sacramento 505
Saint Vrain 505
Salem 505
San Acacia 505
San Antonio 505
San Antonito 505
San Cristobal 505
San Felipe Pb 505
San Fidel 505
San Francisco 505
San Francisco Plaza 505
San Ildefonso Pueblo 505
San Jon 505
San Jose 505
San Juan Pblo 505
San Juan Pueblo 505
San Lorenzo 505
San Mateo 505
San Miguel 505
San Patricio 505
San Pedro 505
San Rafael 505
San Ysidro 505
Sanctuario 505
Sandia Base 505
Sandia Park 505
Sandia Pueblo 505
Sanostee 505
Santa Ana Pue 505
Santa Ana Pueblo 505
Santa Clara 505
Santa Clara Pueblo 505
Santa Cruz 505
Santa Fe 505
Santa Rosa 505
Santa Teresa 505
Santo Domingo Pueblo 505
Santo Nino 505
Santo Tomas 505
Sapello 505
Scientific Lab 505
Seama 505
Seboyeta 505
Sedan 505
Sedillo 505
Sena 505
Senator Clarke Field 505
Seneca 505
Separ 505
Serafina 505
Servilleta Plaza 505
Seton Village 505
Seven Rivers 505
Sf 505
Sheep Springs 505
Sherman 505
Shiprock 505
Sierra Blanca 505
Sierra Vista 505
Sile 505
Silver City 505
Smith Lake 505
Socorro 505
Sofia 505
Soham 505
Solano 505
Sombrillo 505
South San Ysidro 505
Springer 505
Springstead 505
St Dmng Pblo 505
St Vrain 505
Standing Rock 505
Stanley 505
Stead 505
Sunland Park 505
Sunshine 505
Sunspot 505
T Or C 505
Taiban 505
Tajique 505
Talpa 505
Tamaya 505
Taos 505
Taos Pueblo 505
Taos Ski Valley 505
Taos Ski Vly 505
Tatum 505
Tererro 505
Tesuque 505
Tesuque Pueblo 505
Texico 505
Thomas 505
Thoreau 505
Three Rivers 505
Tierra Amarilla 505
Tijeras 505
Timberon 505
Tinaja 505
Tinnie 505
Tira Amarilla 505
Tocito 505
Tohajiilee 505
Tohatchi 505
Tohlakai 505
Tolar 505
Tome 505
Torreon 505
Tortugas 575
Trampas 505
Trechado 505
Trementina 505
Tres Piedras 505
Tres Ritos 505
Truchas 505
Truth Consq 505
Truth Or Consequences 505
Tucumcari 505
Tularosa 505
Turley 505
Twin Lakes 505
Two Gray Hills 505
Tyrone 505
Univ Of New Mexico 505
Univ Of Nm 505
University Park 505
Unm 505
Upper Anton Chico 505
Ute Park 505
Vadito 505
Vado 505
Valdez 505
Valle Escondido 505
Vallecitos 505
Valmora 505
Vanadium 505
Vanderwagen 505
Vaughn 505
Veguita 505
Velarde 505
Ventero 505
Villanueva 505
Virden 505
Wagon Mound 505
Waterflow 505
Watrous 505
Weed 505
West Las Vegas 505
White Oaks 505
White Rock 505
White Sands 505
White Sands Missile Range 505
White Sands National Monumen 505
Whites City 505
Whitewater 505
Willard 505
Williams Acres 505
Williamsburg 505
Winston 505
Yatahey 505
Yeso 505
Youngsville 505
Zia Pueblo 505
Zuni 505
Zuni Pueblo 505

New York

115 Crm Firms 516
115 Firms 516
Abmps 516
Accord 845
Acra 518
Adams 315
Adams Basin 585
Adams Center 315
Adams Corners 845
Adams Cove 315
Addisleigh Park 718
Addisleigh Pk 718
Addison 607
Adirondack 518
Afton 607
Afton Lake 607
Airmont 845
Akron 716
Akwesasne 518
Alabama 585
Albany 518
Albany Brm 518
Albertson 516
Albia 518
Albion 585
Alburgh 518
Alcove 518
Alden 585
Alden Manor 516
Alder Bend 518
Alder Creek 315
Alex Bay 315
Alexander 585
Alexandra Bay 315
Alexandria 315
Alexandria Bay 315
Alfred 607
Alfred Sta 607
Alfred Station 607
Allegany 716
Allens Point 315
Allentown 585
Allenwood 516
Allerton 718
Alma 585
Almond 607
Alpine 607
Alplaus 518
Alps 518
Altamont 518
Altmar 315
Alton 315
Altona 518
Amagansett 631
Amawalk 914
Amber 315
Ambierville 607
Amenia 845
Ames 518
Amf/Jfk Incoming Express Mai 718
Amherst 716
Amity Harbor 631
Amityville 631
Amsterdam 518
Ancram 518
Ancramdale 518
Andes 845
Andover 607
Angelica 585
Angola 716
Annandale 845
Annandale On Hudson 845
Annsville 315
Antwerp 315
Apalachin 607
Apex 607
Appleton 716
Apulia Sta 315
Apulia Station 315
Aquebogue 631
Arcade 716
Arden 845
Ardsley 914
Ardsley Hdsn 914
Ardsley On Hudson 914
Argo Village 516
Argyle 518
Arietta 518
Arkport 607
Arkville 845
Arlington 845
Armonk 914
Arverne 718
Asharoken 631
Ashland 518
Ashville 716
Assembly Point 518
Astoria 718
Athens 518
Athol 518
Athol Springs 716
Atlanta 585
Atlantic Bch 718
Atlantic Beach 718
Attica 585
Atwater 315
Atwell 315
Au Sable Chasm 518
Au Sable Forks 518
Au Sable Frks 518
Auburn 315
Auburn State Prison 315
Audit And Control Dept 518
Augusta 315
Aurelius 315
Auriesville 518
Aurora 315
Ausable Chasm 518
Austerlitz 518
Ava 315
Averill Park 518
Avoca 607
Avon 585
Babylon 631
Bache Halsey Stuart Shields 212
Bacon Hill 518
Bainbridge 607
Baiting Hollo 631
Baiting Hollow 631
Bakers Mills 518
Bald Mountain 518
Baldwin 516
Baldwin Harbor 516
Baldwin Place 914
Baldwinsville 315
Ballston 518
Ballston Center 518
Ballston Lake 518
Ballston Spa 518
Balmville 845
Bangall 845
Bangor 518
Bank Of America 585
Bank Of New York 212
Bank Of New York Brm 212
Banksville 914
Bar Code Church Street 212
Bar Harbor 631
Barbourville 607
Barclay Bank 212
Bardonia 845
Barker 716
Barkersville 518
Barnerville 518
Barnes Corners 315
Barnes Cors 315
Barneveld 315
Barnum Island 516
Barrytown 845
Barryville 845
Bartlett 315
Bartlett Hollow 607
Barton 607
Basom 585
Batavia 585
Bath 607
Battenville 518
Baxter Estates 516
Bay Hills 631
Bay Point 631
Bay Port 631
Bay Shore 631
Bay Terrace 718
Bayberry 315
Bayberry Point 631
Baychester 718
Baycrest 631
Bayport 631
Bayshore 631
Bayside 718
Bayside Hills 718
Bayville 516
Beach Hampton 631
Beacon 845
Bear Mountain 914
Bear Stearns 212
Bearsville 845
Beaver Dams 607
Beaver Falls 315
Beaver Fls 315
Beaver Meadow 315
Beaver River 315
Beckers Corners 518
Bedford 914
Bedford Corners 914
Bedford Cors 914
Bedford Hills 914
Bedford Village 914
Beech Croft 631
Beechhurst 718
Beekmantown 518
Belcher 518
Belden 607
Belfast 585
Belfort 315
Belgium 315
Belle Harbor 718
Belle Terre 631
Bellerose 516
Bellerose Manor 718
Bellerose Terrace 516
Bellerose Vil 516
Bellerose Village 516
Belleville 315
Bellevue 518
Bellmore 516
Bellona 585
Bellport 631
Bellrose Village 516
Bellrs Manor 718
Bellvale 845
Belmont 585
Bemis Heights 518
Bemus Point 716
Bennettsville 607
Benson Mines 315
Bergen 585
Berkshire 607
Berlin 518
Berne 518
Bernhards Bay 315
Berwyn 315
Bethel 845
Bethlehem 518
Bethlehem Center 518
Bethpage 516
Bflo 716
Bible Sch Pk 607
Bible School Park 607
Big Brook 315
Big Flats 607
Big Indian 845
Big Moose 315
Billings 845
Binghamton 607
Black Creek 585
Black River 315
Blasdell 716
Blauvelt 845
Bleecker 518
Bliss 585
Blodgett Mills 607
Blodgett Mls 607
Bloomfield 585
Blooming Grove 845
Blooming Grv 845
Bloomingburg 845
Bloomingdale 518
Bloomington 845
Bloomville 607
Blossvale 315
Blue Cross/Blue Shield 845
Blue Mountain Lake 518
Blue Mtn Lake 518
Blue Point 631
Blue Ridge 518
Bluff Point 315
Boght Corners 518
Bohemia 631
Boiceville 845
Bolivar 585
Bolton Landing 518
Bolton Lndg 518
Bombay 518
Bonney 607
Boonville 315
Borough Hall 718
Boston 716
Bouckville 315
Boulevard 718
Boultons Beach 315
Bovina Center 845
Bowens Corners 315
Bowling Green 212
Bowmansville 716
Box Hill 631
Boylston 315
Boyntonville 518
Bradford 607
Brainard 518
Brainardsville 518
Brainardsvle 518
Braman Corners 518
Bramanville 518
Branchport 315
Brandreth 518
Brandywine 518
Brant 716
Brant Lake 518
Brantingham 315
Brasher Falls 315
Brasie Corners 315
Breakabeen 518
Breesport 607
Breezy Point 718
Brentwood 631
Brewerton 315
Brewster 845
Briar Park 516
Briarcliff 914
Briarcliff Manor 914

City	Area Code
Briarcliff Mnr	914
Briarwood	718
Bridge Hampton	631
Bridgehampton	631
Bridgeport	315
Bridgewater	315
Brier Hill	315
Brighton	585
Brightside	518
Brightwaters	631
Brisben	607
Brm Customer	315
Broad Channel	718
Broadacres	607
Broadalbin	518
Brockport	585
Brocton	716
Bronx	718
Bronxville	914
Brookfield	315
Brookhaven	631
Brooklyn	718
Brooklyn Navy Yard	718
Brooktondale	607
Brookview	518
Brookville	516
Browns Hollow	518
Brownville	315
Brunswick	518
Brushton	518
Brutus	315
Buchanan	914
Bucks Bridge	315
Buel	518
Buffalo	716
Buffalo Airport Retail	716
Bullville	845
Bundyville	315
Burden Lake	518
Burdett	607
Bureau Of Census	212
Burke	518
Burlingham	845
Burlington	607
Burlington Flats	607
Burlngtn Flt	607
Burnt Hills	518
Burnwood	607
Burt	716
Burtonsville	518
Bushville	585
Business Reply	212
Buskirk	518
Butternuts	607
Byron	585
Cabinhill	607
Cadosia	607
Cadyville	518
Cairo	518
Calcium	315
Caledonia	585
Caller Firms	315
Callicoon	845
Callicoon Center	607
Callicoon Ctr	607
Calverton	631
Cambria Heights	718
Cambria Hts	718
Cambridge	518
Camden	315
Cameron	607
Cameron Mills	607
Camillus	315
Camp Bell Hall	845
Campbell	607
Campbell Hall	845
Campville	607
Camroden	315
Canaan	518
Canaan Lake	631
Canajoharie	518
Canal Street	212
Canandaigua	585
Canaseraga	607
Canastota	315
Candor	607
Caneadea	585
Canisteo	607
Canoga	315
Canton	315
Cape Vincent	315
Capitol Cities	718
Captree Is	631
Captree Island	631
Cardiff	315
Carle Place	516
Carlisle	518
Carmel	845
Caroga	518
Caroga Lake	518
Carousel Center	315
Carthage	315
Carver Park	631
Cassadaga	716
Cassville	315
Castile	585
Castle Creek	607
Castle Point	845
Castleton	518
Castleton On Hudson	518
Castorland	315
Catatonk	607
Cato	315
Catskill	518
Cattaraugus	716
Cattown	607
Cayuga	315
Cayuta	607
Caz	315
Cazenovia	315
Cedarhurst	516
Cedarville	315
Celoron	716
Cementon	518
Center Berlin	518
Center Brunswick	518
Center Cambridge	518
Center Moriches	631
Center Port	631
Centereach	631
Centerlisle	607
Centerport	631
Centerville	585
Central Brg	518
Central Bridge	518
Central Islip	631
Central Nyack	845
Central Sq	315
Central Square	315
Central Valley	845
Central Vly	845
Centre Island	516
Centre Village	607
Centuck	914
Ceres	585
Chadwick Bay	716
Chadwicks	315
Chaffee	716
Champion	315
Champion Huddle	315
Champlain	518
Chappaqua	914
Charleston Four Corners	518
Charlotteville	607
Charlottevle	607
Charlton	518
Chase Bank	516
Chase Lake	315
Chase Manhattan Bank	718
Chase Mills	315
Chaseville	607
Chateaugay	518
Chatham	518
Chatham Center	518
Chaumont	315
Chauncey	914
Chautauqua	716
Chazy	518
Chazy Landing	518
Cheektowaga	716
Chelsea	845
Chemung	607
Chenango Brg	607
Chenango Bridge	607
Chenango Fks	607
Chenango Forks	607
Chenango Lake	607
Cherry Creek	716
Cherry Grove	631
Cherry Plain	518
Cherry Valley	607
Cherryplain	518
Cherrytown	845
Chester	845
Chestertown	518
Chestnut Rdg	845
Chestnut Ridge	845
Cheviot	518
Chichester	845
Childwold	518
Chilson	518
China	607
Chinatown	212
Chippewa Bay	315
Chitt	315
Chittenango	315
Choconut Center	607
Chtg	315
Church Street	212
Church Street Boxes	212
Church Street Brm	212
Churchville	585
Churubusco	518
Cicero	315
Cincinnatus	607
Circleville	845
Citibank	212, 516
Citicorp	718
Citicorp Services Inc	212
Clare	315
Clarence	716
Clarence Center	716
Clarence Ctr	716
Clarendon	585
Clark Mills	315
Clarks Mills	518
Clarkson	585
Clarkson University	315
Clarkstown	845
Clarksville	518
Claryville	845
Claverack	518
Clay	315
Clayton	315
Clayville	315
Cleaver	607
Clemons	518
Clermont	518
Cleveland	315
Cleverdale	518
Clifton	585
Clifton Park	518
Clifton Park Center	518
Clifton Spgs	315
Clifton Springs	315
Climax	518
Clinton	315
Clinton Corners	845
Clinton Cors	845
Clinton Crn	845
Clintondale	845
Clintonville	518
Clockville	315
Clough Corners	607
Clyde	315
Clymer	716
Cobleskill	518
Cochecton	845
Cochecton Center	845
Cochecton Ctr	845
Coeymans	518
Coeymans Hollow	518
Coeymans Holw	518
Cohocton	585
Cohoes	518
Coila	518
Colchester	607
Cold Brook	315
Cold Spg Hbr	631
Cold Spring	845
Cold Spring Harbor	631
Cold Spring Hills	631
Colden	716
Colesville	607
Colgate	315
College	212
College Point	718
Colliersville	607
Collins	716
Collins Center	716
Collins Ctr	716
Collins Landing	315
Collinsville	315
Colonial Park	212
Colonie	518
Colonie Center	518
Colosse	315
Colton	315
Columbia	315
Columbia Center	315
Columbiaville	518
Columbus	607
Colvin	315
Colvin Elmwood	315
Commack	631
Comstock	518
Conesus	585
Conewango Valley	716
Conewango Vly	716
Conger Corners	315
Congers	845
Conifer	518
Conklin	607
Conklin Forks	607
Conklingville	518
Connelly	845
Conquest	315
Constable	518
Constableville	315
Constablevle	315
Constantia	315
Contest And Large Vol	718
Contest Mail	212
Cooks Corners	518
Coonrod	315
Cooper	212
Coopers Plains	607
Coopers Plns	607
Cooperstown	607
Cooperstown Junction	607
Coopersville	518
Copake	518
Copake Falls	518
Copenhagen	315
Copiague	631
Coram	631
Corbett	607
Corbettsville	607
Corfu	585
Corinth	518
Corneil Estates	631
Corning	607
Corning Inc	607
Cornwall	845
Cornwall Hdsn	845
Cornwall Hud	845
Cornwall Hudson	845
Cornwall On Hudson	845
Cornwall On The Hudson	845
Cornwallville	518
Corona	718
Cortland	607
Cortlandt Manor	914
Cortlandt Mnr	914
Cortlandville	607
Cossayuna	518
Cossayuna Lake	518
Cottekill	845
Cove Neck	516
Coventry	607
Coventryville	607
Cowlesville	585
Coxsackie	518
Crab Meadow	631
Cragsmoor	845
Cranberry Lake	315
Cranberry Lk	315
Crary Mills	315
Craryville	518
Creative Mailing Service	631
Crestview Heights	607
Crittenden	585
Crofts Corners	845
Croghan	315
Crompond	914
Cropseyville	518
Cross Lake	315
Cross River	914
Croton Falls	914
Croton Hdsn	914
Croton Hudson	914
Croton On Hudson	914
Crotona Park	718
Crotonville	914
Crown Point	518
Crugers	914
Crum Creek	518
Ctr Moriches	631
Cuba	585
Cuddebackville	845
Cuddebackvlle	845
Cullen	315
Cutchogue	631
Cuyler	607
D O T N Y	518
Dadville	315
Dale	585
Dalton	585
Dannemora	518
Dansville	585
Darien Center	585
Davenport	607
Davenport Center	607
Davenport Ctr	607
Davis Park	631
Day	518
Dayton	716
Daytonville	315
De Kalb Jct	315
De Kalb Junction	315
De Peyster	315
De Ruyter	315
De Witt	315
Deansboro	315
Decatur	607
Deer Park	631
Deer River	315
Deer Wells	631
Deerfield	315
Deerpark	631
Deferiet	315
Defreestville	518
Degrasse	315
Delancey	607
Delanson	518
Delevan	716
Delhi	607
Delmar	518
Delphi Falls	315
Demster	315
Denmark	315
Dennison Corners	315
Denver	607
Depauville	315
Depew	716
Depeyster	315
Deposit	607
Derby	716
Deruyter	315
Deutsche Bank	212
Dewitt	315
Dewittville	716
Dexter	315
Diamond	518
Diamond Point	518
Diana	315
Dickinson	607
Dickinson Center	518
Dickinson Ctr	518
Dix Hills	631
Dobbs Ferry	914
Dolgeville	315
Dominion Park	315
Don Jagoda Assc Inc	631
Doonan Corners	607
Doraville	607
Dorloo	518
Dormansville	518
Douglaston	718
Dover Plains	845
Downsville	607
Dresden	315
Dresden Station	518
Dryden	607
Duane	518
Duanesburg	518
Dundee	607
Dunham Hollow	518
Dunkirk	716
Dunsbach Ferry	518
Durham	518
Durhamville	315
E Amherst	716
E Atlantc Bch	516
E Atlantic Beach	516
E Bethany	585
E Bloomfield	585
E Concord	716
E Farmingdale	631
E Freetown	607
E Freetwn	607
E Greenbush	518
E Greenwich	518
E Hampton	631
E Hills	516
E Islip	631
E Marion	631
E Massapequa	516
E Meadow	516
E Moriches	631
E Northport	631
E Norwich	516
E Patchogue	631
E Pembroke	585
E Pharsalia	607
E Quogue	631
E Rochester	585
E Rockaway	516
E Rodman	315
E Setauket	631
E Springfield	607
E Syracuse	315
E Williamson	315
E Williston	516
E Worcester	518
E Yaphank	631
Eagle Bay	315
Eagle Bridge	518
Eagle Harbor	585
Eagle Lake	518
Eagle Mills	518
Eagleville	518
Earlton	518
Earlville	315
East Amherst	716
East Atlantic Beach	516
East Aurora	716
East Berkshire	607
East Berne	518
East Bethany	585
East Bloomfield	585
East Branch	607
East Chatham	518
East Concord	716
East Dickinson	518
East Durham	518
East Elmhurst	718
East Farmingdale	631
East Fishkill	845
East Floyd	315
East Freetown	607
East Genoa	315
East Glenville	518
East Greenbush	518
East Greenwich	518
East Hampton	631

City	Area Code
East Hebron	518
East Herkimer	315
East Hills	516
East Homer	607
East Irvington	914
East Islip	631
East Jefferson	607
East Jewett	518
East Line	518
East Maine	607
East Marion	631
East Masonville	607
East Massapequa	516
East Mcdonough	607
East Meadow	516
East Meredith	607
East Moriches	631
East Nassau	518
East Nichols	607
East Northport	631
East Norwich	516
East Oakfield	585
East Otto	716
East Palmyra	315
East Patchogue	631
East Pembroke	585
East Pharsalia	607
East Pitcairn	315
East Poestenkill	518
East Quogue	631
East Randolph	716
East Rochester	585
East Rockaway	516
East Schodack	518
East Setauket	631
East Sidney	607
East Springfield	607
East Syracuse	315
East Vestal	607
East View	914
East White Plains	914
East Williamson	315
East Williston	516
East Windham	518
East Winfield	315
East Worcester	518
East Yaphank	631
Eastchester	914
Eastman Kodak	585
Easton	518
Eastport	631
Eastwood	315
Eaton	315
Eatons Neck	631
Eben	315
Eddy	315
Eddyville	845
Eden	716
Edgemere	718
Edgemont	914
Edgewood	631
Edgewood Park	315
Edinburg	518
Edmeston	607
Edwards	315
Edwardsville	315
Eggertsville	716
Elba	585
Elbridge	315
Eldred	845
Elizabethtown	518
Elizaville	845
Elk Creek	607
Elka Park	518
Ellenburg	518
Ellenburg Center	518
Ellenburg Ctr	518
Ellenburg Dep	518
Ellenburg Depot	518
Ellenville	845
Ellicottville	716
Ellington	716
Ellisburg	315
Elm Grove	607
Elma	716
Elmdale	315
Elmhurst	718
Elmira	607
Elmira Heights	607
Elmira Hgts	607
Elmira Hts	607
Elmont	516
Elmsford	914
Elmwood	315
Elnora	518
Elsmere	518
Elwood	631
Emeryville	315
Emmons	607
Empeyville	315
Empire State	212
Empire State Plaza	518
Endicott	607
Endwell	607
Ephratah	518
Erieville	315
Erin	607
Esopus	845
Esperance	518
Esplanade	718
Essex	518
Etna	607
European American Bank	212
Evans Mills	315
Excellus Bcbs	585
Exeter	607
Fabius	315
Factory Village	518
Factoryville	518
Fair Harbor	631
Fair Haven	315
Fairdale	315
Fairfield	315
Fairport	585
Falconer	716
Fallsburg	845
Fancher	585
Far Rockaway	718
Farleys Point	315
Farmersville	585
Farmersville Station	585
Farmersvl Sta	585
Farmingdale	516, 631
Farmington	585
Farmingville	631
Farnham	716
Fayette	315
Fayetteville	315
Federal Reserve	212
Felts Mills	315
Fenner	315
Fenton	607
Fergusonville	607
Ferndale	845
Fernwood	315
Feura Bush	518
Filer Corners	607
Fillmore	585
Findley Lake	716
Fine	315
Fineview	315
Fire Is Pines	631
Fire Island	631
Fire Island Pines	631
Firm Zip Codes	716
Firms	315
Fish Creek	315
Fish House	518
Fishers	585
Fishers Island	631
Fishers Isle	631
Fishers Landing	315
Fishers Lndg	315
Fishkill	845
Fishs Eddy	607
Fivemile Point	607
Flanders	631
Flat Creek	518
Fleetwood	914
Fleischmanns	845
Fleming	315
Flemingville	607
Floral Park	516
Florence	315
Florida	845
Flowerfield	631
Floyd	315
Flushing	718
Fly Creek	607
Fonda	518
Forest Hills	718
Forest Hls	718
Forestburg	845
Forestburgh	845
Forestport	315
Forestport Station	315
Forestville	716
Forsyth	716
Fort Ann	518
Fort Covington	518
Fort Drum	315
Fort Edward	518
Fort George	212
Fort Hamilton	718
Fort Herkimer	315
Fort Hunter	518
Fort Jackson	315
Fort Johnson	518
Fort Miller	518
Fort Montgomery	845
Fort Plain	518
Fort Salonga	631
Fort Stanwix National Monume	315
Fort Tilden	718
Fort Totten	718
Fortsville	518
Foster	607
Fosterville	315
Fowler	315
Fowlersville	315
Frankfort	315
Frankfort Center	315
Franklin	607
Franklin D Roosevelt	212
Franklin Depot	607
Franklin Spgs	315
Franklin Springs	315
Franklin Sq	516
Franklin Square	516
Franklinville	716
Fraser	607
Fredonia	716
Freedom	585
Freehold	518
Freeport	516
Freetown	607
Freetown Corners	607
Freeville	607
Fremont	845
Fremont Center	845
Fremont Ctr	845
French Woods	607
Frenchville	315
Fresh Meadows	718
Fresh Pond	718
Frewsburg	716
Friendship	585
Frontenac	315
Frontier	585
Fruit Valley	315
Ft Covington	518
Ft Montgomery	845
Ft Plain	518
Fulfillment	516
Fullerville	315
Fulton	315
Fultonham	518
Fultonville	518
Furniss	315
Furniss Sta	315
G P O	212
G P O Official Mail	212
Gabriels	518
Gainesville	585
Galatia	607
Galeville	315
Gallatin	518
Gallupville	518
Galway	518
Galway Lake	518
Gansevoort	518
Garden City	516
Garden City P	516
Garden City Park	516
Garden City S	516
Garden City South	516
Gardiner	845
Garnerville	845
Garnet Lake	518
Garoga	518
Garrattsville	607
Garrison	845
Gaskill	607
Gasport	716
Gayville	315
Gdn City Park	516
Geddes	315
Gedney	914
Geers Corners	315
Genegantslet	607
General Electric	518
Geneseo	585
Geneva	315
Genoa	315
Georgetown	315
Georgetown Station	315
Geotown	315
German Flatts	315
Germantown	518
Gerry	716
Getzville	716
Ghent	518
Gilbertsville	607
Gilboa	607
Gilgo Beach	631
Gilmantown	518
Glasco	845
Glass Lake	518
Glen Aubrey	607
Glen Castle	607
Glen Cove	516
Glen Head	516
Glen Oaks	516
Glen Park	315
Glen Spey	845
Glen Wild	845
Glendale	718
Glenfield	315
Glenford	845
Glenham	845
Glenmont	518
Glens Falls	518
Glenville	518
Glenwood	716
Glenwood Landing	516
Glenwood Lndg	516
Gloversville	518
Godeffroy	845
Goldens Brg	914
Goldens Bridge	914
Goodyears Corners	315
Gordon Heights	631
Gorham	585
Goshen	845
Goulds Mill	315
Gouverneur	315
Gowanda	716
Gpo	718
Gpo Brm	212
Gracie	212
Grafton	518
Grahamsville	845
Granby	315
Granby Center	315
Grand Central	212
Grand Central Brm	212
Grand Gorge	607
Grand Island	716
Grandview	845
Grandview On Hudson	845
Grangerville	518
Granite Spgs	914
Granite Springs	914
Grant	315
Grantville	315
Granville	518
Graphite	518
Grassy Point	845
Gravesville	315
Gray	315
Great Bend	315
Great Neck	516
Great Neck Estates	516
Great Nk	516
Great River	631
Great Valley	716
Greece	585
Greeley Square	212
Green Island	518
Greenburgh	914
Greene	607
Greenfield	518
Greenfield Center	518
Greenfield Park	845
Greenfld Ctr	518
Greenfld Park	845
Greenhurst	716
Greenlawn	631
Greenport	631
Greenvale	516
Greenville	518
Greenway	315
Greenwich	518
Greenwood	607
Greenwood Lake	845
Greenwood Lk	845
Gregorytown	607
Greig	315
Grenell	315
Gridleyville	607
Grindstone	315
Groton	607
Groton City	607
Groveland	585
Grover Hills	518
Grt Neck	516
Gt Bend	315
Gt Neck	516
Guffin Bay	315
Guilderland	518
Guilderland Center	518
Guildrlnd Ctr	518
Guilford	607
Guilford Center	607
Gurn Spring	518
Hadley	518
Hagaman	518
Hagedorns Mills	518
Hague	518
Hailesboro	315
Haines Falls	518
Halcott Center	845
Halcott Ctr	845
Halcottsville	845
Hales Eddy	607
Halesite	631
Halfmoon	518
Hall	585
Hallsville	518
Hambletville	607
Hamburg	716
Hamden	607
Hamilton	315
Hamilton Grange	212
Hamlin	585
Hammond	315
Hammondsport	607
Hampton	518
Hampton Bays	631
Hancock	607
Hankins	845
Hannacroix	518
Hannawa Falls	315
Hannibal	315
Hannibal Center	315
Harbor Acres	516
Harbor Heights	631
Harbor Hills	516
Harbor Island	516
Harbor Isle	516
Harford	607
Harford Mills	607
Harkness	518
Harlequin Books	716
Harmony Corners	518
Harpersfield	607
Harpursville	607
Harrietstown	518
Harriman	845
Harris	845
Harrisburg	315
Harrison	914
Harrisville	315
Hart Lot	315
Hartford	518
Hartsdale	914
Hartwick	607
Hartwick Seminary	607
Harvard	607
Hastings	315
Hastings Hdsn	914
Hastings Hudson	914
Hastings On Hudson	914
Hatchs Corner	315
Hauppauge	631
Haverstraw	845
Hawkeye	518
Hawkinsville	315
Hawleys	607
Hawleyton	607
Hawthorne	914
Hayt Corners	607
Head Of The Harbor	631
Heathcote	914
Hebron	518
Hecla	315
Hector	607
Heer Park	631
Helena	315
Helmuth	716
Hemlock	585
Hempstead	516
Henderson	315
Henderson Harbor	315
Henderson Hbr	315
Henrietta	585
Hensonville	518
Herkimer	315
Hermon	315
Herricks	516
Herrings	315
Hessville	518
Heuvelton	315
Hewittville	315
Hewlett	516
Hewlett Bay	516
Hewlett Bay Park	516
Hewlett Harbor	516
Hewlett Neck	516
Hicksville	516
Hicksville Crm Firms	516
Hicksville Firms	516
Higgins Bay	518
Higginsville	315
High Falls	845
Highbridge	718
Highland	845
Highland Falls	845
Highland Fls	845
Highland Lake	845
Highland Mills	845
Highland Mls	845
Highmount	845
Hiler	716
Hillburn	845
Hillsboro	315
Hillsdale	518
Hillside	718
Hillside Manor	516
Hillside Mnr	516
Hilton	585
Himrod	607
Hinckley	315
Hinmans Corners	607
Hinmansville	315
Hinsdale	716

City	Area Code
Hither Plains	631
Hoag Corners	518
Hobart	607
Hoboken	607
Hoffmeister	516, 518
Hofstra Univ	516
Hogansburg	518
Holbrook	631
Holcomb	585
Holcombville	518
Holland	716
Holland Patent	315
Holland Patnt	315
Holley	585
Hollis	718
Hollis Hills	718
Hollowville	518
Holmes	845
Holmesville	607
Holtsville	631
Homer	607
Homes	845
Honeoye	585
Honeoye Falls	585
Honeywell Corners	518
Honnedaga Lake	315
Hoopers Valley	607
Hoosick	518
Hoosick Falls	518
Hoosick Junction	518
Hopewell	845
Hopewell Jct	845
Hopewell Junction	845
Hopkinton	315
Horace Harding	718
Horicon	518
Hornell	607
Horseheads	607
Hortonville	845
Hospital	607
Houghton	585
Hounsfield	315
Houseville	315
Howard Beach	718
Howardville	315
Howells	845
Howes Cave	518
Howlett Hill	315
Hrtwk Seminry	607
Hsbc	585
Hsbc Atrium	716
Hsbc Bank	212, 716
Hub	718
Hubbardsville	315
Hubbardtown	607
Hubbell Cors	607
Hudson	518
Hudson Falls	518
Hughsonville	845
Huguenot	845
Hulberton	585
Huletts Landing	518
Huletts Lndg	518
Hullsville	607
Hume	585
Humphrey	716
Hunt	585, 631
Hunter	518
Huntersland	518
Huntingtn Sta	631
Huntington	631
Huntington Bay	631
Huntington Station	631
Hunts Corners	607
Hurley	845
Hurleyville	845
Hyde Park	845
Hyndsville	518
I R S Service Center	631
Igerna	518
Ilion	315
Ind Order Of Foresters	716
Indian Lake	518
Indian River	315
Indian Village	315
Industry	585
Ingraham	518
Inlet	315
Interlaken	607
Inwood	718
Inwood Finance	718
Ionia	585
Irish Corners	518
Irona	518
Irondequoit	585
Ironville	518
Irs Service Center	631
Irving	716
Irvington	914
Irvington On Hudson	914
Ischua	716
Island Park	516
Island Trees	516
Islandia	631
Islip	631
Islip Manor	631
Islip Terrace	631
Itaska	607
Ithaca	607
Ithaca Coll	607
Ithaca College	607
Ivanhoe	607
J C Penney	212
Jackson Heights	718
Jackson Hts	718
Jacksonville	607
Jamaica	516, 718
Jamaica Est	718
Jamesport	631
Jamestown	716
Jamesville	315
Janesville	518
Jasper	607
Java Center	585
Java Village	716
Jay	518
Jefferson	607
Jefferson Park	315
Jefferson Valley	914
Jefferson Vly	914
Jeffersonville	845
Jeffersonvlle	845
Jenksville	607
Jericho	516
Jerome	718
Jewell Manor	315
Jewett	518
Jf Kennedy Ap	718
Jingo	716
John F Kennedy Airport	718
Johnsburg	518
Johnson	845
Johnson City	607
Johnsonville	518
Johnstown	518
Johnsville	518
Jonesville	518
Jordan	315
Jordanville	315
Jp Morgan Bank	212, 585
Junius	315
Kanona	607
Kasoag	315
Katonah	914
Kattelville	607
Kattskill Bay	518
Kauneonga Lake	845
Kauneonga Lk	845
Kayuta Lake	315
Keene	518
Keene Valley	518
Keeseville	518
Kelsey	607
Kendall	585
Kenilworth	516
Kenmore	716
Kennedy	716
Kenoza Lake	845
Kensington	516
Kent	585
Kent Lakes	845
Kenwood	315
Kerhonkson	845
Ketchumville	607
Keuka Park	315
Kew Garden Hl	718
Kew Gardens	718
Kew Gardens Hills	718
Kiamesha Lake	845
Kill Buck	716
Killawog	607
Killbuck	716
Kinderhook	518
King Ferry	315
Kings Ferry	315
Kings Park	631
Kings Point	516
Kings Settlement	607
Kings Station	518
Kingsbury	518
Kingston	845
Kirk	607
Kirkland	315
Kirkville	315
Kirkwood	607
Kirschnerville	315
Kismet	631
Kitchawan	914
Knapp Creek	716
Knapps Station	315
Knickerbocker	212
Knollwood Beach	631
Knowlesville	716
Knox	518
Knoxboro	315
Kodak Apparatus Division	585
Kodak Office	585
Kodak Park	585
Kortright	607
Kortright Center	607
Kringsbush	518
Krumville	845
L I Power Authority	516
La Fargeville	315
La Fayette	315
La Grange	845
La Guardia Airport	718
La Gurda Arpt	718
Lackawanna	716
Lacona	315
Lafargeville	315
Lafayette	315
Lagrangeville	845
Lairdsville	315
Lake Bonaparte	315
Lake Carmel	845
Lake Clear	518
Lake Colby	518
Lake Delaware	607
Lake Delta	315
Lake Desolation	518
Lake Gardens	516
Lake George	518
Lake Grove	631
Lake Hill	845
Lake Huntington	845
Lake Katonah	914
Lake Katrine	845
Lake Kitchawan	914
Lake Lincolnd	845
Lake Lincolndale	845
Lake Luzerne	518
Lake Mahopac	845
Lake Mohegan	914
Lake Panamoka	631
Lake Peekskill	914
Lake Placid	518
Lake Pleasant	518
Lake Ronkonkoma	631
Lake Ronkonkoma Heights	631
Lake Secor	845
Lake Success	516
Lake View	716
Lakemont	607
Lakeport	315
Lakeview	516, 716
Lakeville	585
Lakeville Estates	516
Lakewood	716
Lancaster	716
Lanesville	845
Langdon	607
Langdon Corners	315
Lansing	607
Lansingburg	518
Lapeer	607
Larchmont	914
Lassellsville	518
Latham	518
Lathams Corners	607
Lattingtown	516
Laurel	631
Laurel Hollow	516
Laurelton	718
Laurens	607
Lawrence	718
Lawrenceville	315
Lawtons	716
Lawyersville	518
Le Ray	315
Le Roy	585
Lebanon	315
Lebanon Center	315
Lebanon Spg	518
Lebanon Springs	518
Ledyard	315
Lee	315
Lee Center	315
Leeds	518
Leibhardt	845
Leicester	585
Lenox Hill	212
Leon	716
Leonardsville	315
Leonta	607
Leroy	585
Levittown	516
Lew Beach	845
Lewis	518
Lewisboro	914
Lewiston	716
Lexington	518
Leyden	315
Liberty	845
Lido Beach	516
Lily Dale	716
Lima	585
Limerick	315
Limestone	716
Lincklaen	315
Lincoln	315
Lincolndale	914
Lincolnton	212
Linden Hill	718
Lindenhurst	631
Lindley	607
Linlithgo	518
Linwood	585
Lisbon	315
Lisle	607
Little Falls	315
Little Genese	585
Little Genesee	585
Little Neck	718
Little Valley	716
Little York	607
Liverpool	315
Livingstn Mnr	845
Livingston	518
Livingston Manor	845
Livingstonville	518
Livonia	585
Livonia Center	585
Livonia Ctr	585
Lk Grove	631
Lk Huntington	845
Lk Peekskill	914
Lk Ronkonkoma	631
Lloyd Harbor	631
Lloyd Neck	631
Loch Sheldrake	845
Loch Sheldrke	845
Locke	315
Lockport	716
Lockwood	607
Locust Valley	516
Locustwood	516
Lodi	607
Loehmanns Plaza	585
Loehmanns Plz	585
Long Beach	516
Long Eddy	845
Long Is City	718
Long Island City	718
Long Lake	518
Longwood	718
Loon Lake	518
Lordville	607
Lorraine	315
Loudonville	518
Lounsberry	607
Low Hampton	518
Lower Genegantslet Corner	607
Lower Oswegatchie	315
Lower Rotterdam	518
Lowman	607
Lowville	315
Lpool	315
Luzerne	518
Lvpl	315
Lvrpool	315
Lycoming	315
Lykers	518
Lynbrook	516
Lyncourt	315
Lyndonville	716
Lyon Mountain	518
Lyons	315
Lyons Falls	315
Lyonsdale	315
Lyonsville	845
Lysander	315
M And T Bank	716
Mac Dougall	315
Macedon	315
Machias	716
Macomb	315
Macys Finance	212
Madison	315
Madison Square Brm	212
Madison Square Sta	212
Madrid	315
Madrid Springs	315
Mahopac	845
Mahopac Falls	845
Maine	607
Malba	718
Malden	845
Malden Brg	518
Malden Bridge	518
Malden Hudson	845
Malden On Hudson	845
Mallory	315
Malone	518
Malta	518
Malta Ridge	518
Maltaville	518
Malverne	516
Mamaroneck	914
Manchester	585
Mandana	315
Manhasset	516
Manhasset Hil	516
Manhasset Hills	516
Manhattan	212, 718
Manhattanville	212
Manheim	315
Manitou	845
Manlius	315
Mannsville	315
Mannville	518
Manor Park	631
Manorhaven	516
Manorville	631
Maple Grove	607
Maple Springs	716
Maple Valley	607
Maple View	315
Maplecrest	518
Mapletown	518
Maplewood	518
Marathon	607
Marcellus	315
Marcellus Falls	315
Marconiville	631
Marcy	315
Marden Kane Inc	212
Margaretville	845
Mariaville	518
Marietta	315
Marilla	716
Marine Midland	716
Marion	315
Marlboro	845
Marlborough	845
Marshville	518
Martinsburg	315
Martisco	315
Martville	315
Maryknoll	914
Maryland	607
Masonville	607
Maspeth	718
Massapequa	516
Massapequa Park	631
Massapequa Pk	631
Massawepie	518
Massena	315
Massena Center	315
Massena Springs	315
Mastic	631
Mastic Beach	631
Matinecock	516
Mattituck	631
Mattydale	315
Maybrook	845
Mayfield	518
Mayville	716
Mc Conelsvile	315
Mc Connellsville	315
Mc Donough	607
Mc Graw	607
Mc Lean	607
Mcclure	607
Mcdonough	607
Mcgraw	607
Mckeever	315
Mckownville	518
Mclean	607
Mdale	315
Mdl Granville	518
Meacham	516
Meadowmere Park	718
Mechanicville	518
Mecklenburg	607
Meco	518
Medford	631
Medina	716
Medusa	518
Mellenville	518
Melrose	518
Melville	631
Memphis	315
Menands	518
Mendon	585
Mental Hygiene Dept	518
Meredith	607
Meridale	607
Meridian	315
Merrick	516
Merrickville	607
Merrifield	315
Merrill	518
Merrill Lynch	212
Merrillsville	315
Messengerville	607
Metropolitan Museum Of Art	718
Mettacahonts	845
Mexico	315
Mid Hudson	845
Middle Falls	518
Middle Granville	518
Middle Grove	518
Middle Island	631
Middle Village	718
Middle Vlg	718

City	Area Code
Middleburg	518
Middleburgh	518
Middleport	716
Middlesex	585
Middletown	845
Middleville	315
Midtown	212
Milan	845
Milford	607
Milford Center	607
Mill Neck	516
Millbrook	845
Miller Place	631
Millers Mills	315
Millerton	518
Millport	607
Millwood	914
Milton	845
Milton Center	518
Minden	518
Mindenville	518
Mineola	516
Mineral Springs	518
Minerva	518
Minetto	315
Mineville	518
Minoa	315
Mitchell Field	516
Mldn On Hdsn	845
Model City	716
Modena	845
Mohawk	315
Mohawk Hill	315
Mohegan Lake	914
Moira	518
Mongaup Valley	845
Mongaup Vly	845
Monroe	845
Monsey	845
Montague	315
Montauk	631
Montebello	845
Montezuma	315
Montgomery	845
Monticello	845
Montour Falls	607
Montrose	914
Montville	315
Mooers	518
Mooers Forks	518
Moose River	315
Moravia	315
Morehouse	315
Morehouseville	315
Moriah	518
Moriah Center	518
Moriah Corners	518
Moriches	631
Morley	315
Morningside	212
Morris	607
Morris Park	718
Morrisania	718
Morrisonville	518
Morristown	315
Morrisville	315
Morrisville Station	315
Morton	585
Mosherville	518
Mosholu	718
Motor Vehicle Bureau	718
Mott Haven	718
Mottville	315
Mount Ivy	845
Mount Kisco	914
Mount Marion	845
Mount Merion Park	845
Mount Morris	585
Mount Ross	518
Mount Sinai	631
Mount Tremper	845
Mount Upton	607
Mount Vernon	914
Mount Vision	607
Mountain Dale	845
Mountain View	518
Mountaindale	845
Mountainville	845
Mt Sinai	631
Mt Vernon	914
Mumford	585
Munnsville	315
Munsons Corners	607
Murray Hill Brm	212
Murray Isle	315
Muscular Dystrophy	718
Muskalounge	315
Muttontown	516
N Amityville	631
N Babylon	631
N Baldwin	516
N Bay Shore	631
N Bellmore	516
N Bellport	631
N Blenheim	518
N Boston	716
N Brookfield	315
N Cohocton	585
N Collins	716
N Evans	716
N Falls	716
N Granville	518
N H P	516
N Haven	631
N Java	585
N Lawrence	315
N Lindenhurst	631
N Massapequa	516
N Merrick	516
N New Hyde Pk	516
N Patchogue	631
N Syracuse	315
N Tarrytown	914
N Tonawanda	716
N Valley Stream	516
N Wantagh	516
N White Plains	914
N White Plns	914
N Woodmere	516
N Y Agr And Mkts	518
N Y Assembly	518
N Y Civil Serv Dept	518
N Y Conservation Dept	518
N Y Dept Commerce	518
N Y Dept Of Motor Vehicles	518
N Y Educ Dept	518
N Y Empl Retirement	518
N Y Health Dept	518
N Y Hghr Educ Serv Corp	518
N Y Labor Div Empl	518
N Y Labor Unemp Ins	518
N Y Lottery	518
N Y Secretary Of State	518
N Y Soc Serv Dept	518
N Y State Campus	518
N Y State Lottery	518
N Y Tele Co	518
N Y Wrkmn Comp	518
Nanuet	845
Napanoch	845
Naples	585
Narrowsburg	845
Nassau	518
Nassau Point	631
Nat Fuel Gas Co	716
National Grid	315
Natural Brg	315
Natural Bridge	315
Natural Dam	315
Navarino	315
Nedrow	315
Nelliston	518
Nelson	315
Nelsonville	845
Neponsit	718
Nesconset	631
Neversink	845
Nevis	845
New Baltimore	518
New Berlin	607
New Berlin Junction	607
New Breman	315
New Cassel	516
New City	845
New Hamburg	845
New Hampton	845
New Hartfd	315
New Hartford	315
New Haven	315
New Hempstead	845
New Hyde Park	516
New Kingston	845
New Lebanon	518
New Lebanon Center	518
New Lisbon	607
New Milford	845
New Paltz	845
New Rochelle	914
New Russia	518
New Square	845
New Suffolk	631
New Wdstock	315
New Windsor	845
New Woodstock	315
New York	212
New York City	212
New York Mills	315
New York Mls	315
Newark	315
Newark Valley	607
Newburgh	845
Newcomb	518
Newfane	716
Newfield	607
Newport	315
Newstead	716
Newton Falls	315
Newton Hook	518
Newtonville	518
Niagara Falls	716
Niagara Univ	716
Niagara University	716
Nichols	607
Nicholville	315
Niles	315
Nimmonsburg	607
Nineveh	607
Nineveh Junction	607
Niobe	716
Niskayuna	518
Nissequogue	631
Niverville	518
No New Hyde Park	516
No Tonawanda	716
Noblesboro	315
Norfolk	315
North Afton	607
North Amityville	631
North Argyle	518
North Babylon	631
North Baldwin	516
North Bangor	518
North Bay	315
North Bay Shore	631
North Bellmore	516
North Bellport	631
North Blenheim	518
North Boston	716
North Branch	845
North Bridgewater	315
North Broadalbin	518
North Brookfield	315
North Castle	914
North Chatham	518
North Chili	585
North Chittenango	315
North Cohocton	585
North Collins	716
North Columbia	315
North Creek	518
North Evans	716
North Fenton	607
North Franklin	607
North Granville	518
North Greece	585
North Greenbush	518
North Hannibal	315
North Harpersfield	607
North Haven	631
North Hebron	518
North Highland	845
North Hills	516
North Hoosick	518
North Hudson	518
North Ilion	315
North Java	585
North Kortright	607
North Lawrence	315
North Lindenhurst	631
North Massapequa	516
North Merrick	516
North New Hyde Park	516
North Norwich	607
North Patchogue	631
North Petersburg	518
North Pharsalia	607
North Pitcher	315
North River	518
North Rose	315
North Russell	315
North Salem	914
North Sanford	607
North Stockholm	315
North Syracuse	315
North Tarrytown	914
North Tonawanda	716
North Valley Stream	516
North White Plains	914
North Wilmurt	315
North Winfield	315
North Woodmere	516
Northampton	631
Northbush	518
Northfield	607
Northport	631
Northville	518
Norton Hill	518
Norwich	607
Norwood	315
Nunda	585
Ny	212
Ny City	212
Ny Mills	315
Ny Park And Rec Dept	518
Ny Standards And Purc	518
Ny State Ins Dept	518
Nyack	845
Nyc	212
Nys Dept Of Tax & Finance	518
Nys Tax Processing Ctr	518
Oak Beach	631
Oak Hill	518
Oak Island	631
Oakdale	631
Oakfield	585
Oakland Gardens	718
Oakland Gdns	718
Oaks Corners	315
Oaksville	607
Obernburg	845
Ocean Bay Park	631
Ocean Beach	631
Oceanside	516
Odessa	607
Ogd	315
Ogdensburg	315
Ohio	315
Olcott	716
Old Bethpage	516
Old Brookville	516
Old Chatham	518
Old Chelsea Brm	212
Old Field	631
Old Forge	315
Old Mastic	631
Old Westbury	516
Old Westfield	631
Olean	716
Olive	845
Olivebridge	845
Oliverea	845
Olmstedville	518
Omar	315
Onchiota	518
Oneida	315
Oneida Castle	315
Oneonta	607
Onon Hill	315
Onondaga Nation	315
Ontario	315
Ontario Center	315
Ontario Ctr	315
Oppenheim	315
Oquaga Lake	607
Orangeburg	845
Orchard Park	716
Orient	631
Orient Point	631
Oriskany	315
Oriskany Falls	315
Oriskany Fls	315
Orwell	315
Oscawana Lake	845
Osceola	315
Ossining	914
Oswegatchie	315
Oswego	315
Oswego Center	315
Otego	607
Otisco	315
Otisco Valley	315
Otisville	845
Otsdawa	607
Otsego	607
Otselic	315
Otter Creek	315
Otter Lake	315
Otto	716
Ouaquaga	607
Ovid	607
Owasco	315
Owego	607
Owls Head	518
Oxbow	315
Oxford	607
Oyster Bay	516
Oyster Bay Cove	516
Ozone Park	718
P J S	631
Paddy Hill	315
Paines Hollow	315
Painted Post	607
Palatine Brg	518
Palatine Bridge	518
Palenville	518
Palermo	315
Palisades	845
Palmer	518
Palmyra	315
Pamelia	315
Pamelia Four Corners	315
Panama	716
Panamoka	631
Panorama	585
Paradox	518
Paradox Lake	518
Paris	315
Parish	315
Parishville	315
Parishville Center	315
Park Terrace	607
Parkside	718
Parksville	845
Patchogue	631
Patent	607
Patria	518
Patterson	845
Pattersonville	518
Pattersonvle	518
Paul Smiths	518
Pavilion	585
Pawling	845
Peakville	607
Pearl River	845
Peasleeville	518
Peck Slip	212
Peck Slip Brm	212
Peconic	631
Peekskill	914
Pelham	914
Pelham Manor	914
Pembroke	585
Pendleton	716
Penfield	585
Penn Yan	315
Pennellville	315
Perch River	315
Perkinsville	585
Perry	585
Perrys Mills	518
Perrysburg	716
Perryville	315
Perth	518
Peru	518
Peter Stuyvesant	212
Peterboro	315
Petersburg	518
Petersburgh	518
Phelps	315
Phila	315
Philadelphia	315
Philip Morris	718
Philipse Manor	914
Philipstown	845
Phillipsport	845
Philmont	518
Phoenicia	845
Phoenix	315
Piercefield	518
Pierces Corner	315
Pierceville	315
Piermont	845
Pierrepnt Mnr	315
Pierrepont	315
Pierrepont Manor	315
Piffard	585
Pike	585
Pilgrim	718
Pillar Point	315
Pilot Knob	518
Pine	518
Pine Air	631
Pine Bush	845
Pine City	607
Pine Grove	315
Pine Hill	845
Pine Island	845
Pine Lake	518
Pine Meadows	315
Pine Neck	631
Pine Plains	518
Pine Valley	607
Pine Woods	315
Pineville	607
Pioneer	518
Piseco	518
Pitcairn	315
Pitcher	315
Pittsfield	607
Pittsford	585
Pjs	631
Plainedge	516
Plainfield	315
Plainfield Center	315
Plainview	516
Plainville	315
Plandome	516
Planetarium	212
Plattekill	845
Plattsburgh	518
Pleasant Valley	845
Pleasant Vly	845
Pleasantdale	518
Pleasantville	914
Plessis	315
Plymouth	315
Pocantico Hills	914
Poestenkill	518
Point Lookout	516
Point O Woods	631
Point Rock	315
Poland	315
Pomona	845
Pomonok	718
Pompey	315

Pond Eddy 845
Poolville 315
Pope Mills 315
Poplar Ridge 315
Poquott 631
Port Byron 315
Port Chester 914
Port Crane 607
Port Dickinson 607
Port Ewen 845
Port Gibson 585
Port Henry 518
Port Jeff Sta 631
Port Jefferson 631
Port Jefferson Station 631
Port Jervis 845
Port Kent 518
Port Leyden 315
Port Ontario 315
Port Wash 516
Port Washington 516
Portageville 585
Portchester 914
Porter Corners 518
Porter Cors 518
Portland 716
Portlandville 607
Portville 585
Postal Data Center 212
Potsdam 315
Pottersville 518
Poughkeepsie 845
Poughquag 845
Pound Ridge 914
Pr Wash 516
Pr Wshngtn 516
Pratts Hollow 315
Prattsburgh 607
Prattsville 518
Preble 315
Preston 607
Preston Hlow 518
Preston Hollow 518
Preston Holw 518
Prince 212
Princetown 518
Priority Mail Ctr 718
Promised Land 631
Prospect 315
Providence 518
Prt Jeff Sta 631
Prt Jefferson 631
Prt Jefferson Station 631
Prt Washingtn 516
Pt Jefferson Station 631
Pt Jervis 845
Pt Lookout 516
Pt Wash 516
Publishers Clear House 516
Publishers Clearing House 516
Publishers Clearing Hse Brm 516
Pulaski 315
Pulteney 607
Pultneyville 315
Purchase 914
Purdy Station 914
Purdys 914
Purdys Mills 518
Purling 518
Putnam Sta 518
Putnam Station 518
Putnam Valley 845
Pyrites 315
Quaker Springs 518
Quaker Street 518
Queens Village 718
Queens Vlg 718
Queensbury 518
Quinneville 607
Quioque 631
Quogue 631
Radio City Brm 718
Radison 315
Radisson 315
Rainbow Lake 518
Randalls Island 212
Randallsville 315
Randolph 716
Ransomville 716
Raquette Lake 518
Ravena 518
Ray Brook 518
Raymertown 518
Raymondville 315
Readburn 607
Readers Digest 914
Reading Center 607
Reading Ctr 607
Reber 518
Red Creek 315
Red Falls 518
Red Hook 845
Red Mills 315
Red Rock 518
Redfield 315
Redford 518
Redwood 315
Rego Park 718
Rego Pk 718
Reidsville 518
Remsen 315
Remsenburg 631
Rensselaer 518
Rensselaer Falls 315
Rensselaerville 518
Rensselaervle 518
Rensslaer Fls 315
Retsof 585
Rexford 518
Rexville 607
Rhinebeck 845
Rhinecliff 845
Ricard 315
Riceville 518
Richburg 585
Richfield 315
Richfield Springs 315
Richfld Spgs 315
Richford 607
Richland 315
Richmond Hill 718
Richmondville 518
Richville 315
Ridge 631
Ridge Mills 315
Ridgemont 585
Ridgewood 718
Rifton 845
Riley Cove 518
Riparius 518
Ripley 716
Riverbank 518
Riverdale 718
Riverhead 631
Rivers Edge 631
Roch Gas & Elec Corp 585
Rochdale 718
Rochdale Vill 718
Rochdale Village 718
Rochester 585
Rock City Falls 518
Rock City Fls 518
Rock Glen 585
Rock Hill 845
Rock Stream 607
Rock Tavern 845
Rockaway Beac 718
Rockaway Beach 718
Rockaway Park 718
Rockaway Point 718
Rockaway Pt 718
Rockdale 607
Rockefeller Center Brm 212
Rockhurst 518
Rockville Center 516
Rockville Centre 516
Rockville Ctr 516
Rockwell Springs 315
Rockwells Mills 607
Rockwood 518
Rocky Point 631
Rodman 315
Roessleville 518
Rome 315
Romulus 315
Ronkonkoma 631
Roosevelt 516
Roosevelt Field 516
Roosevelt Isl 212
Roosevelt Island 212
Rooseveltown 315
Root 518
Roscoe 607
Rose 315
Roseboom 607
Rosedale 718
Rosendale 845
Roslyn 516
Roslyn Estates 516
Roslyn Harbor 516
Roslyn Heights 516
Roslyn Hts 516
Ross Corners 607
Rossburg 585
Rossie 315
Roswell Park Memorial Instit 716
Rotterdam 518
Rotterdam Jct 518
Rotterdam Junction 518
Rotterdam Square Branch 518
Round Lake 518
Round Top 518
Rouses Point 518
Roxbury 607
Royalton 716
Ruby 845
Ruby Corner 315
Rural Grove 518
Rural Hill 315
Rush 585
Rushford 585
Rushville 585
Russell 315
Russell Gardens 516
Russia 315
Rutland 315
Rvc 516
Rye 914
Rye Brook 914
S Bethlehem 518
S Cheek 716
S Cheektowaga 716
S Dayton 716
S Edmeston 607
S Edwards 315
S Fallsburg 845
S Farmingdale 631
S Floral Park 516
S Glens Falls 518
S Hampton 631
S Hauppauge 631
S Haven 631
S Hempstead 516
S Huntington 631
S Jamesport 631
S Kortright 607
S New Berlin 607
S Onon 315
S Ozone Park 718
S Ozone Pk 718
S Richmond Hill 718
S Richmond Hl 718
S Rutland 315
S Schodack 518
S Setauket 631
S U N Y 518
S U N Y 99 Wash 518
S Wales 716
S Westerlo 518
Sabael 518
Sabattis 518
Sabbath Day Point 518
Sackets Harbor 315
Sackets Hbr 315
Saddle Rock 516
Saddle Rock Estates 516
Sag Harbor 631
Sagaponack 631
Saint Albans 718
Saint Bonaventure 716
Saint Huberts 518
Saint James 631
Saint John University 718
Saint Johnsville 518
Saint Regis Falls 518
Saint Remy 845
Salamanca 716
Salem 518
Salina 315
Salisbury 315
Salisbury Center 315
Salisbury Ctr 315
Salisbury Mills 845
Salisbury Mls 845
Salt Point 845
Saltaire 631
Sammonsville 518
Samsonville 845
San Remo 631
Sanborn 716
Sand Hill 518
Sand Lake 518
Sandfordville 315
Sands Point 516
Sandusky 585
Sandy Creek 315
Sandy Hill 518
Sanford 607
Sangerfield 315
Sanitaria Spg 607
Sanitaria Springs 607
Santa Clara 518
Saranac 518
Saranac Lake 518
Saratoga Spgs 518
Saratoga Springs 518
Sardinia 716
Saugerties 845
Sauquoit 315
Savannah 315
Savona 607
Sayville 631
Scarborough 914
Scarsdale 914
Scarsdale Park 914
Schaghticoke 518
Schdy 518
Schenectady 518
Schenevus 607
Schodack Landing 518
Schodack Lndg 518
Schoharie 518
Schroeppel 315
Schroon Lake 518
Schuyler 315
Schuyler Falls 518
Schuyler Fls 518
Schuyler Lake 315
Schuylerville 518
Scio 585
Sciota 518
Scipio 315
Scipio Center 315
Scipioville 315
Scoreball 716
Scotchbush 518
Scotchtown 845
Scotchtown Branch 845
Scotia 518
Scott 607
Scotts Beach 631
Scotts Corners 914
Scottsburg 585
Scottsville 585
Scriba 315
Scriba Center 315
Scribner Corners 315
Sea Cliff 516
Seaford 516
Sears Corners 845
Seaview 631
Seifert Corners 315
Selden 631
Selkirk 518
Sempronius 315
Seneca Castle 585
Seneca Falls 315
Seneca Hill 315
Sennett 315
Sentinel Heights 315
Setauket 631
Severance 518
Seward 518
Shackport 607
Shady 845
Shandaken 845
Sharon Spgs 518
Sharon Springs 518
Shearson American Express 212
Sheds 315
Shekomeko 518
Shelby 716
Sheldon 585
Shelter Is 631
Shelter Is Ht 631
Shelter Island 631
Shelter Island Heights 631
Shenorock 914
Sherburne 607
Sheridan 716
Sherman 716
Sherrill 315
Sherwin Bay 315
Shinhopple 607
Shirley 631
Shokan 845
Shoreham 631
Shortsville 585
Shrub Oak 914
Shushan 518
Sidney 607
Sidney Center 607
Siena 518
Silhouette Books 716
Silver Bay 518
Silver Creek 716
Silver Lake 585
Silver Spgs 585
Silver Springs 585
Simpsonville 607
Sinclairville 716
Sissonville 315
Skan 315
Skan Fa 315
Skan Falls 315
Skaneateles 315
Skaneateles Falls 315
Slab City 315
Slate Hill 845
Slaterville Springs 607
Slatervle Spg 607
Slateville 518
Sleepy Hollow 914
Sleepy Hollow Manor 914
Slingerlands 518
Sloan 716
Sloansville 518
Sloatsburg 845
Smallwood 845
Smartville 315
Smith Point 631
Smithboro 607
Smithfield 315
Smiths Point 631
Smithtown 631
Smithville 315, 607
Smithville Center 607
Smithville Flats 607
Smithvle Flts 607
Smyrna 607
Snowden 607
Snyder 716
Snyder Square 716
Snyders Corners 518
Snyders Lake 518
So Floral Park 516
So Huntington 631
So Plymouth 607
Sodus 315
Sodus Center 315
Sodus Point 315
Solsville 315
Solvay 315
Somers 914
Somers Town 914
Somerville 315
Sonyea 585
Sound Beach 631
South Albion 315
South Apalachin 607
South Argyle 518
South Bay 315
South Bay Village 518
South Berne 518
South Bethlehem 518
South Bolivar 585
South Bombay 518
South Brookfield 315
South Butler 315
South Byron 585
South Cairo 518
South Cheektowaga 716
South Colton 315
South Columbia 315
South Danby 607
South Dayton 716
South Durham 518
South Edmeston 607
South Edwards 315
South Fallsburg 845
South Farmingdale 631
South Floral Park 516
South Glens Falls 518
South Granville 518
South Hamilton 315
South Hampton 631
South Hannibal 315
South Hauppauge 631
South Hempstead 516
South Huntington 631
South Ilion 315
South Jamesport 631
South Kortright 607
South Lebanon 315
South Lima 585
South New Berlin 607
South Nineveh 607
South Nyack 845
South Onondaga 315
South Otselic 315
South Owego 607
South Oxford 607
South Ozone Park 718
South Plattsburgh 518
South Plymouth 607
South Richmond Hill 718
South Russell 315
South Rutland 315
South Salem 914
South Schodack 518
South Setauket 631
South Trenton 315
South Vestal 607
South Wales 716
South Westerlo 518
South Worcester 607
Southampton 631
Southeast 845
Southfields 845
Southold 631
Southwest Oswego 315
Sparkill 845
Sparrow Bush 845
Sparrowbush 845
Speculator 518
Speedsville 607
Speigletown 518
Spencer 607
Spencer Settlement 315
Spencerport 585
Spencertown 518
Speonk 631
Spinnerville 315
Split Rock 315
Sprakers 518
Spring Brook 716

City	Area Code
Spring Glen	845
Spring Valley	845
Springbrook	716
Springfield Center	607
Springfield Gardens	718
Springfld Center	607
Springfld Ctr	607
Springport	315
Springvale	607
Springville	716
Springwater	585
Sprngfld Gdns	718
Sprout Brook	518
Spuyten Duyvil	718
St Bonas	716
St Bonaventure	716
St James	631
St Johnsville	518
St Lawrence Park	315
St Regis Fls	518
St Remy	845
Sta A	718
Staatsburg	845
Staatsburgh	845
Stacy Basin	315
Stadium	718
Stafford	585
Stamford	607
Standish	518
Stanfordville	845
Stanley	585
Stanwix	315
Stanwix Heights	315
Star Lake	315
Starkville	518
State Office Bldg	518
Staten Island	718
Steamburg	716
Stela Niagara	716
Stella Niagara	716
Stephentown	518
Stephentown Center	518
Sterling	315
Sterling Forest	845
Sterling Frst	845
Stetsonville	607
Steuben	315
Steuben Valley	315
Stevers Mills	518
Stewart Manor	516
Stilesville	607
Stillwater	518
Stittville	315
Stockbridge	315
Stockton	716
Stockwell	315
Stokes	315
Stone Arabia	518
Stone Mills	315
Stone Ridge	845
Stony Brook	631
Stony Creek	518
Stony Point	845
Stonybrook	631
Stoodley Corners	518
Stormville	845
Stottville	518
Stow	716
Straits Corners	607
Stratford	315
Strathmore	516
Streetroad	518
Strong Memorial Hospital	585
Strongs Neck	631
Strykersville	585
Sturges Corner	607
Stuyvesant	518
Stuyvesant Falls	518
Stuyvesant Fl	518
Stuyvesant Plaza	518
Stuyvsnt Plz	518
Suffern	845
Sugar Loaf	845
Sullivan	315
Summerhill	315
Summit	518
Summitville	845
Sundown	845
Sunken Meadow	631
Sunnyside	718
Suny Stony Brook	631
Surprise	518
Swain	585
Swan Lake	845
Swastika	518
Swormville	716
Sycaway	518
Sylvan Beach	315
Syosset	516
Syr	315
Syracuse	315
Syracuse Amf	315
Syracuse University	315
Taberg	315
Taborton	518
Taconic Lake	518
Taghkanic	845
Tahawus	518
Talcottville	315
Tallman	845
Tannersville	518
Tappan	845
Tarrytown	914
Taunton	315
Taylor	607
Terryville	631
Texas Valley	607
The Glen	518
The Terrace	516
The Vly	845
Thendara	315
Theresa	315
Thiells	845
Thomaston	516
Thompson Rdg	845
Thompson Ridge	845
Thompsons Lake	518
Thompsonville	845
Thomson	518
Thornwood	914
Thous Is Pk	315
Thousand Island Park	315
Three Mile Bay	315
Three Mle Bay	315
Throggs Neck	718
Throop	315
Thurman	518
Ticonderoga	518
Tillson	845
Times Square Brm	212
Tioga	607
Tioga Center	607
Tiona	607
Tivoli	845
Tn Of Tona	716
Tomkins Cove	845
Tompkins	607
Tompkins Corners	845
Tonawanda	716
Town Branch	845
Town Of Tonawanda	716
Townline	585
Tracy Creek	607
Trainsmeadow	718
Treadwell	607
Triangle	607
Tribes Hill	518
Triborough	212
Trinity	212
Trinity Brm	212
Troupsburg	607
Trout Creek	607
Trout Lake	518
Trout River	518
Troy	518
Trumansburg	607
Truthville	518
Truxton	607
Tuckahoe	914
Tully	315
Tunnel	607
Tupper Lake	518
Turin	315
Tuscarora	585
Tuxedo	845
Tuxedo Park	845
Twin Orchards	607
Tyner	607
Tyre	315
Tyrone	607
U S C C	845
Ulster Park	845
Unadilla	607
Unadilla Forks	315
Union Center	607
Union Hill	585
Union Mills	518
Union Springs	315
Uniondale	516, 718
Unionville	845
United States Military Acade	845
University	315
University At Buffalo	716
University Buffalo	716
University Gardens	516
University Heights	718
Upper Brookville	516
Upper Grandview	845
Upper Jay	518
Upper Lisle	607
Upper Nyack	845
Upper Saint Regis	518
Upper St Reg	518
Upper Union	518
Upperville	607
Upton	631
Us Postal Service	518
Ushers	518
Usmma	516
Utica	315
Utopia	718
Vail Mills	518
Vails Gate	845
Valatie	518
Valhalla	914
Valley Cottage	845
Valley Falls	518
Valley Mills	315
Valley Stream	516
Vallonia Springs	607
Valois	607
Van Buren	315
Van Buren Bay	716
Van Buren Point	716
Van Buren Pt	716
Van Cott	718
Van Deusenville	518
Van Etten	607
Van Hornesville	315
Van Hornesvle	315
Varysburg	585
Vassar College	845
Venice	315
Venice Center	315
Verbank	845
Verdoy	518
Verizon	212
Vermontville	518
Vernon	315
Vernon Center	315
Verona	315
Verona Beach	315
Verplanck	914
Versailles	716
Vesper	315
Vestal	607
Vestal Center	607
Vestal Gardens	607
Vet Admin Ext Care Ctr	718
Veterans Administration	607
Veterans Admn	607
Victor	585
Victory Mills	518
Vienna	315
Village	212
Virgil	607
Vischer Ferry	518
Vly Cottage	845
Volney	315
Voorheesville	518
W Amherst	716
W Babylon	631
W Bay Shore	631
W Bloomfield	585
W Brentwood	631
W Burlington	607
W Carthage	315
W Clarksville	585
W Coxsackie	518
W Davenport	607
W Falls	716
W Fulton	518
W Gilgo Beach	631
W Groton	607
W Hampton	631
W Hampton Bch	631
W Hampton Beach	631
W Harrison	914
W Haverstraw	845
W Hempstead	516
W Henrietta	585
W Hills	631
W Hurley	845
W Islip	631
W Lebanon	518
W Sand Lake	518
W Sayville	631
W Seneca	716
W Shokan	845
W Stockholm	315
W Valley	716
W Windsor	607
Waccabuc	914
Waddington	315
Wadhams	518
Wading River	631
Wadsworth	585
Wainscott	631
Waits	607
Wakefield	718
Walden	845
Wales Center	716
Walesville	315
Walker Valley	845
Wall Street	212
Wall Street Brm	212
Wallace	607
Wallkill	845
Walloomsac	518
Walton	607
Walworth	315
Wampsville	315
Wanakena	315
Wantagh	516
Wappinger	845
Wappingers Falls	845
Wappingers Fl	845
Wards Is	212
Wards Island	212
Warners	315
Warnerville	518
Warren	315
Warrensburg	518
Warsaw	585
Warwick	845
Washingtn Mls	315
Washington Bridge	212
Washington Mills	315
Washingtonville	845
Washingtonvle	845
Wassaic	845
Water Mill	631
Waterford	518
Waterloo	315
Watermill	631
Waterport	585
Watertown	315
Waterville	315
Watervliet	518
Watkins Glen	607
Watson	315
Wave Crest	718
Waverly	607
Wawarsing	845
Wayland	585
Wayne	607
Webster	585
Webster Crossing	585
Webster Crsng	585
Weedsport	315
Wegatchie	315
Welcome	607
Wellesley Is	315
Wellesley Island	315
Wells	518
Wells Bridge	607
Wellsburg	607
Wellsville	585
Weltonville	607
Wesley Hills	845
West Amherst	716
West Babylon	631
West Bainbridge	607
West Bangor	518
West Bay Shore	631
West Berne	518
West Bloomfield	585
West Branch	315
West Brentwood	631
West Burlington	607
West Bush	518
West Camp	845
West Candor	607
West Carthage	315
West Charlton	518
West Chazy	518
West Chenango	607
West Clarksville	585
West Colesville	607
West Copake	518
West Corners	607
West Coxsackie	518
West Danby	607
West Davenport	607
West Delhi	607
West Durham	518
West Eaton	315
West Edmeston	315
West Ellicott	716
West End	607
West Endicott	607
West Exeter	315
West Falls	716
West Farms	718
West Fort Ann	518
West Fulton	518
West Gilgo Beach	631
West Glens Falls	518
West Glenville	518
West Groton	607
West Group	585
West Hampton	631
West Hampton Beach	631
West Harpersfield	607
West Harrison	914
West Haverstraw	845
West Hebron	518
West Hempstead	516
West Henrietta	585
West Hills	631
West Hurley	845
West Islip	631
West Junius	315
West Kill	518
West Latham	518
West Laurens	607
West Lebanon	518
West Lee	315
West Leyden	315
West Lowville	315
West Meredith	607
West Milton	518
West Monroe	315
West Newark	607
West Nyack	845
West Oneonta	607
West Parishville	315
West Park	845
West Pierrepont	315
West Plattsburgh	518
West Point	845
West Point Military Reservat	845
West Potsdam	315
West Richmondville	518
West Rush	585
West Sand Lake	518
West Saugerties	845
West Sayville	631
West Seneca	716
West Shokan	845
West Stockholm	315
West Turin	315
West Valley	716
West Valley Falls	518
West Windsor	607
West Winfield	315
Westbrookville	845
Westbrookvle	845
Westbury	516
Westchester	718
Westchester County Airport	914
Westdale	315
Westerlo	518
Westernville	315
Westfield	716
Westford	607
Westgate	585
Westhampton	631
Westhampton Beach	631
Westhampton Dunes	631
Westmere	518
Westminster Park	315
Westmoreland	315
Weston Mills	585
Westons Mills	585
Westover	607
Westport	518
Westtown	845
Westvale	315
Westview	607
Westville	607
Westville Center	518
Wevertown	518
Whaley Lake	845
Whallonsburg	518
Wheatfield	716
Wheatland	585
Wheatley Heights	631
Wheatley Hts	631
Wheelerville	518
Whippleville	518
White Creek	518
White Lake	845
White Plains	914
White Sulphur Springs	845
Whiteface Mountain	518
Whiteface Mtn	518
Whitehall	518
Whitelaw	315
Whites Store	607
Whitesboro	315
Whitestone	718
Whitestown	315
Whitesville	607
Whitfield	845
Whitman	607
Whitney Point	607
Wht Sphr Spgs	845
Wiccopee	845
Wildwood	631
Willard	607
Willet	607
Williamsbridge	718
Williamson	315
Williamstn	315
Williamstown	315
Williamsville	716
Williston Park	516
Williston Pk	516
Willow	845
Willow Point	607
Willowvale	315
Willsboro	518
Willsboro Point	518
Willseyville	607
Willwood	631

City	Area Code
Wilmington	518
Wilna	315
Wilson	716
Wilton	518
Wincoma	631
Windham	518
Windsor	607
Winfield	315
Wingdale	845
Winthrop	315
Witherbee	518
Wolcott	315
Woodbourne	845
Woodbury	516
Woodgate	315
Woodhaven	718
Woodhull	607
Woodmere	516
Woodridge	845
Woods Corners	607
Woodsburgh	516
Woodside	718
Woodstock	845
Woodville	315
Worcester	607
Worth	315
Wtown	315
Wtr Mill	631
Wurtsboro	845
Wyandanch	631
Wykagyl	914
Wynantskill	518
Wyoming	585
Xerox	585
Yaleville	315
Yaphank	631
Yonkers	914
York	585
York College	718
Yorkshire	716
Yorktown	914
Yorktown Heights	914
Yorktown Hgts	914
Yorktown Hts	914
Yorkville	315
Youngs	607
Youngstown	716
Youngsville	845
Yulan	845

North Carolina

City	Area Code
A M F Greensboro	336
A&t State University	336
Aberdeen	910
Abshers	336
Acme	910
Adams	828
Advance	336
Aho	828
Ahoskie	252
Alamance	336
Alarka	828
Albemarle	704
Albertson	252
Alexander	828
Alexander Mills	828
Alexander Mls	828
Alexis	704
All Healing Springs	828
Allen Jay	336
Alliance	252
Allison	336
Almond	828
Altamahaw	336
Altamont	828
Amantha	828
Amf G Boro	336
Amf Greensboro	336
Amity	704
Andrews	828
Angier	919
Ansonville	704
Apex	919
Appalachian State Univ	828
Apple Grove	336
Aquadale	704
Aquone	828
Arapahoe	252
Ararat	336
Arcadia	336
Archdale	336
Archers Lodge	919
Arden	828
Ardmore	336
Arlington	336
Arnold	336
Ash	910
Ash Hill	336
Asheboro	336
Asheville	828
Ashland	336
Assembly	828
At&t	704
Atkinson	910
Atlantic	252
Atlantic Bch	252
Atlantic Beach	252
Atlanticbeach	252
Aulander	252
Aurora	252
Autryville	910
Avon	252
Ayden	252
Aydlett	252
Ayersville	336
Badin	704
Badin Air National Guard Sta	704
Badin Lake	704
Bagley	919
Bahama	919
Bailey	252
Bakersville	828
Bald Head	910
Bald Head Isl	910
Bald Head Island	910
Baldwin	336
Ball	336
Balm	828
Balsam	828
Balsam Grove	828
Bamboo	828
Bank Of America	704
Banner Elk	828
Barber	704
Barco	252
Barium Spngs	704
Barium Springs	704
Barnardsville	828
Barnesville	910
Barrett	336
Bat Cave	828
Bath	252
Baton	828
Battleboro	252
Bayboro	252
Bb&t	704
Bear Creek	919
Bear Poplar	704
Beargrass	252
Beaufort	252
Beaver Creek	336
Bedford Fair Industries	910
Beech Bottom	828
Beech Creek	828
Beech Mnt	828
Beech Mountain	828
Belew Creek	336
Belews Creek	336
Belhaven	252
Bellarthur	252
Bells Cross Roads	704
Belmont	704
Belvidere	252
Belville	910
Belwood	704
Bennett	336
Benson	919
Bermuda Run	336
Bessemer City	704
Bethania	336
Bethel	252
Bethlehem	828
Beulaville	910
Biggs Park	910
Biltmor	828
Biltmore Forest	828
Biltmore Frst	828
Biltmore Lake	828
Biscoe	910
Bixby	336
Black Creek	252
Black Mountain	828
Black Mtn	828
Blackburn	828
Bladenboro	910
Blanch	336
Blanche	336
Bling Spr Lks	910
Blounts Creek	252
Blowing Rock	828
Bluff	828
Bly	336
Boger City	704
Boiling Spg Lks	910
Boiling Spgs	704
Boiling Springs	704
Bolivia	910
Bolton	910
Bonlee	919
Boogertown	704
Boomer	336
Boone	828
Booneville	336
Boonville	336
Bostic	828
Bostic Yard	828
Boulevard	336
Bowdens	910
Bowman Gray School Of Med	336
Bradfords Cross Roads	704
Branch Bank And Trust (Bb&t)	704
Brandon	336
Branon	336
Brasstown	828
Brentwood	919
Brevard	828
Bridgeton	252
Bridgewater	828
Brightwood	336
Brindle Town	828
Broadway	919
Brook Cove	336
Brooks Cross Roads	336
Brown Mountain Beach	828
Brown Summit	336
Browns Summit	336
Brownwood	336
Broyhill Furniture	828
Brunswick	910
Bryson City	828
Buck Shoals	336
Buckhorn	919
Buffalo Lake	919
Buies Creek	910
Bullock	919
Bunn	252
Bunnlevel	910
Burgaw	910
Burkemont	828
Burl	336
Burlington	336
Burningtown	828
Burnsville	828
Busick	336
Butner	919
Butters	910
Buxton	252
Bynum	919
Calabash	910
Caldwell	704
Call	336
Calvin	828
Calypso	910
Camden	252
Cameron	919
Cameron Village	919
Camp Lejeune	910
Camp Springs	336
Canden	910
Candler	828
Candor	910
Canton	828
Cape Carteret	252
Cape Fear	910
Cape Hatteras National Seash	252
Cape Hatteras Naval Facility	252
Cape Lookout National Seasho	252
Carbonton	919
Caroleen	828
Carolina Bch	910
Carolina Beach	910
Carolina Hills	828
Carolina Power And Light Co	919
Carolina Shor	910
Carolina Shores	910
Carpenter Bottom	828
Carrboro	919
Carthage	910
Cartoogechaye	828
Cary	919
Casar	704
Cashiers	828
Castalia	252
Castle Hayne	910
Casville	336
Caswell Beach	910
Catawba	828
Catawba Heights	704
Cedar Falls	336
Cedar Grove	336
Cedar Island	252
Cedar Mountain	828
Cedar Mtn	828
Cedar Point	252
Celeste Hinkle	704
Center	336
Centerview	704
Cerro Gordo	910
Chadbourn	910
Champion	336
Chapel Hill	919
Charles	704
Charlotte	704
Charlotte Water Dept	704
Cherokee	828
Cherry Lane	336
Cherry Point	252
Cherry Point Marine Corps Ai	252
Cherrygrove	336
Cherryville	704
Chestnut Dale	828
Chestnut Hill	336
Chimney Rock	828
China Grove	704
Chinquapin	910
Chocowinity	252
Churchland	336
Cid	336
Cl Naval Hospital	910
Claremont	828
Clarendon	910
Clarkton	910
Clayton	919
Clemmons	336
Cleveland	704
Cliffside	828
Clifton	336
Climax	336
Clingman	336
Clinton	910
Clyde	828
Coats	910
Cofield	252
Coinjock	252
Colerain	252
Coleridge	336
Colfax	336
Collettsville	828
Collington	252
Colon	919
Columbia	252
Columbus	828
Comet	336
Comfort	910
Como	252
Concord	704
Conetoe	252
Connelly Spg	828
Connellys Spg	828
Connellys Springs	828
Conover	828
Conway	252
Cool Spring	704
Cooleemee	336
Copeland	336
Corapeake	252
Cordova	910
Corinth	828
Cornelius	704
Corolla	252
Correll Park	704
Cotton Grove	336
Cottonville	704
Council	910
Country Park Acres	336
Countyline	704
Courtney	336
Cove City	252
Cowee	828
Cp Lejeune Mcb	910
Cp Lejeunemcb	910
Crabtree Valley	919
Cramerton	704
Cranberry	828
Cranberry Gap	828
Creedmoor	919
Creston	336
Creswell	252
Cricket	336
Crossnore	828
Crouse	704
Crowders	704
Crumpler	336
Culberson	828
Cullasaja	828
Cullowhee	828
Cumberland	910
Cumnock	919
Currie	910
Currituck	252
Cycle	336
Dallas	704
Dalton	336
Dana	828
Danbury	336
Darby	336
Darkridge	828
Davidson	704
Davidson College	704
Davis	252
Deep Gap	336
Deep River	336
Deep Run	252
Deerfield	828
Delco	910
Delight	704
Denny	336
Denton	336
Denver	704
Devotion	336
Dillsboro	828
Dimmette	336
Dobbinsville	828
Dobson	336
Dockery	336
Dolinger	336
Doolie	704
Dortches	252
Dosier	336
Double Island	828
Double Shoals	704
Doughton	336
Dover	252
Drake	252
Draper	336
Drexel	828
Drums Crossroads	828
Duan	828
Dublin	910
Duck	252
Dudley	919
Dudley Shoals	828
Duke	919
Duke Medical Ctr	919
Duke Power	704
Duke University	919
Duncan	919
Dunn	910
Duraleigh	919
Durants Neck	252
Durham	919
E Fayettevill	910
E Fayetteville	910
E Fayettevlle	910
E Flat Rock	828
E Laurinburg	910
E P A	919
Eagle	336
Eagle Rock	919
Eagle Springs	910
Earl	704
East Bend	336
East Carolina Univ	252
East Carolina University	252
East Durham	919
East Fayetteville	910
East Flat Rock	828
East Franklin	828
East Lake	252
East Laport	828
East Laurinburg	910
East Monbo	704
East Spencer	704
Eastover	910
Eden	336
Edenton	252
Edgemont	828
Edneyville	828
Edward	252
Edwards Crossroads	336
Efland	919
Ela	828
Eliz City	252
Elizabeth City	252
Elizabeth City Coast Guard A	252
Elizabeth Cty	252
Elizabethtown	910
Elk Park	828
Elk Valley	828
Elkin	336
Ellenboro	828
Ellendale	828
Eller	336
Ellerbe	910
Ellijay	828
Ellisboro	336
Elm City	252
Elmwood	704
Elon	336
Elon College	336
Emerald Isle	252
Emerson	910
Emerywood	336
Emit	252
Enfield	252
Engelhard	252
Enka	828
Enka Village	828
Ennice	336
Eno Valley	919
Enola	828
Enterprise	336
Erastus	828
Ernul	252
Erwin	910
Erwin Heights	336
Essex	252
Estelle	336
Ether	910
Etowah	828
Eufola	704
Eure	252
Eureka	919
Eutaw	910

City	Area Code
Everetts	252
Evergreen	910
Fair Bluff	910
Fairfield	252
Fairmont	910
Fairplains	336
Fairview	828
Fairview Cross Roads	336
Faison	910
Faith	704
Falcon	910
Falkland	252
Fallston	704
Farmers Store	336
Farmington	336
Farmville	252
Fay	910
Fayetteville	910
Fayetteville Municipal Airpo	910
Fearrington	919
Fearrington Village	919
Feezor	336
Ferguson	336
Fig	336
First Citizens Bank	704
First Union Natl Bank	704
Fisher Town	704
Five Points	919
Flat Rock	828
Flat Springs	828
Flay	704
Fleetwood	336
Fletcher	828
Flint Hill	910
Flowes Store	704
Fontana Dam	828
Footsville	336
Forest City	828
Forest Oaks	336
Fork	336
Fort Barnwell	252
Fort Bragg	910
Fort Bragg Military	910
Fort Caswell	910
Fort Fisher Air Force Statio	910
Fort Macon Coast Guard Base	252
Fort Raleigh City	252
Fort Raleigh National Histor	252
Foscoe	828
Fountain	252
Fountain Hill	704
Four Oaks	919
Foxfire	910
Foxfire Village	910
Foxfire Vlg	910
Frank	828
Franklin	828
Franklinton	919
Franklinville	336
Freemans Mills	336
Fremont	919
Friendship	336
Frisco	252
Frog Pond	704
Frogsboro	336
Fulp	336
Fuquay Varina	919
Gamewell	828
Garland	910
Garner	919
Garysburg	252
Gaston	252
Gastonia	704
Gates	252
Gatesville	252
George	252
Germanton	336
Gerton	828
Gibson	910
Gibsonville	336
Gilkey	828
Glade Valley	336
Glass	704
Glen Alpine	828
Glen Raven	336
Glendale Spgs	336
Glendale Springs	336
Glendon	910
Glenola	336
Glenville	828
Glenwood	828
Gloucester	252
Gmac	704
Godwin	910
Gold Hill	704
Golden	828
Goldsboro	919
Goldston	919
Gordontown	336
Goshen	336
Grace Chapel	828
Grace Sta	828
Graham	336
Grandfather	828
Grandview Heights	828
Grandy	252
Granite Falls	828
Granite Qry	704
Granite Quarry	704
Grantsboro	252
Grassy Creek	336
Grays Chapel	336
Grayson	336
Green Level	336
Green Mountain	828
Green Mt	828
Green Mtn	828
Greenmountain	828
Greensboro	336
Greensboro Business Reply	336
Greensboro Courtesy Reply	336
Greensboro Ndc	336
Greensboro-High Point-Winsto	336
Greenville	252
Grifton	252
Grimesland	252
Grn Mountain	828
Groomtown	336
Grover	704
Groves	704
Guilford	336
Guilford College	336
Guilford Courthouse National	336
Gulf	919
Gumberry	252
Gumtree	336
Guthrie	336
H P	336
Halifax	252
Halls Mills	336
Hallsboro	910
Hamilton	252
Hamlet	910
Hampstead	910
Hamptonville	336
Hamtown	336
Handy	336
Hanes	336
Hanes Brands Inc	336
Hannersville	336
Happy Valley	828
Harbinger	252
Hare	336
Harkers Is	252
Harkers Island	252
Harmony	704
Harpers Crossroads	919
Harrells	910
Harrellsville	252
Harris	828
Harrisburg	704
Harrison Cross Roads	336
Hartman	336
Harts Store	336
Hassell	252
Hatteras	252
Havelock	252
Haw Branch	919
Haw River	336
Hayes	336
Hayesville	828
Haymount	910
Hays	336
Hazelwood	828
Healing Springs	336
Heaton	828
Hedrick Grove	336
Helton	336
Hemby	704
Hemby Bridge	704
Henderson	252
Hendersonville	828
Hendersonvlle	828
Hendrix	336
Henrico	252
Henrietta	828
Hertford	252
Hickory	828
Hickory Knoll	828
Hicks Crossroads	704
Hiddenite	704
Higdonville	828
High Pnt	336
High Point	336
High Rock	336
High Shoals	704
Highfalls	336
Highlands	828
Hildebran	828
Hillcrest	828
Hillsboro	919
Hillsborough	919
Hillsdale	336
Hilltop	336
Hobbsville	252
Hobgood	252
Hobucken	252
Hodges Gap	828
Hoffman	910
Holden Beach	910
Hollis	828
Hollister	252
Holly Grove	336
Holly Ridge	910
Holly Springs	919
Hookerton	252
Hope Mills	910
Horse Shoe	828
Hot Springs	828
Houstonville	704
Hubert	910
Hudson	828
Hughes	828
Huntersville	704
Hunting Creek	336
Hurdle Mills	336
Husk	336
Icard	828
Idlewild	336
Index	336
Indian Beach	252
Indian Trail	704
Indian Trl	704
Ingalls	828
Ingold	910
Integon Corp	336
Iotla	828
Iron Station	704
Ivanhoe	910
Jackson	252
Jackson Spgs	910
Jackson Springs	910
Jacksons Creek	336
Jacksonville	910
Jamestown	336
Jamesville	252
Jarvisburg	252
Jefferson	336
Joe	828
Jonas Ridge	828
Jonesboro Heights	919
Jonesville	336
Joy	828
Joyceton	828
Joynes	336
Jp Morgan Chase	704
Julian	336
Kannapolis	704
Kapps Mill	336
Kelford	252
Kellersville	828
Kelly	910
Kenansville	910
Kenly	919
Kennebec	919
Kennells Beach	252
Kernersville	336
Kilby	828
Kill Devil Hills	252
Kill Devil Hl	252
Kimesville	336
King	336
Kings Creek	828
Kings Mountain	704
Kings Mtn	704
Kingstown	704
Kinnakeet	252
Kinston	252
Kipling	919
Kittrell	919
Kitty Hawk	252
Knightdale	919
Knotts Island	252
Kure Beach	910
La Grange	252
Lafayette	910
Lake Junaluska	828
Lake Lure	828
Lake Park	704
Lake Santeetlah	828
Lake Toxaway	828
Lake Waccamaw	910
Lakedale	910
Lakeview	910
Landis	704
Lansing	336
Lasker	252
Lattimore	704
Laurel Hill	910
Laurel Park	828
Laurel Spgs	336
Laurel Springs	336
Laurinburg	910
Lawndale	704
Lawsonville	336
Laxon	828
Laytown	828
Leaksville	336
Leasburg	336
Leicester	828
Lejeune	910
Leland	910
Lemon Springs	910
Lenoir	828
Lenoir Rhyne	828
Level Cross	336
Lewiston	252
Lewiston Woodville	252
Lewisville	336
Lex	336
Lexington	336
Liberty	336
Liledown	828
Lilesville	704
Lillington	910
Lincolnton	704
Linden	910
Linville	828
Linville Falls	828
Linville Fls	828
Linwood	336
Little Horse Creek	336
Little River	828
Little Switzerland	828
Littleton	252
Lk Junaluska	828
Lk Santeetlah	828
Locust	704
Logan Station	828
Lomax	336
Lone Hickory	336
Long Beach	910
Long Creek	704
Long View	828
Longisland	828
Longtown	336
Longview	828
Longwood	910
Loray	704
Louisburg	919
Love Valley	704
Lovejoy	910
Lowell	704
Lower Pig Pen	828
Lowes Co Inc	336
Lowesville	704
Lowgap	336
Lowland	252
Ltl Switzrlnd	828
Lucama	252
Luck	828
Lumber Bridge	910
Lumberton	910
Lunana	252
Lynn	828
Mabel	828
Macclesfield	252
Macon	252
Madison	336
Maggie Valley	828
Magnolia	910
Maiden	828
Mamers	919
Manns Harbor	252
Manson	252
Manteo	252
Maple	252
Maple Hill	910
Maple Springs	336
Marble	828
Marcus	910
Margaretsville	252
Margarettsville	252
Margarettsvl	252
Marietta	910
Marion	828
Marler	336
Mars Hill	828
Marshall	828
Marshallberg	252
Marshville	704
Marston	910
Marvin	704
Matney	828
Matrimony	336
Matthews	704
Matthewstown	336
Maury	252
Maxton	910
Mayhew	704
Mayodan	336
Maysville	910
Mayview Park	828
Mazeppa	704
Mc Adenville	704
Mc Cutcheon Field	910
Mc Farlan	704
Mc Grady	336
Mc Leansville	336
Mcas Cherry Point	252
Mccullers	919
Mccutcheon Field	910
Mccutchn Fld	910
Mcgrady	336
Mcleansville	336
Meadow	336
Meadow Creek	336
Meadow Summit	336
Meat Camp	828
Mebane	919
Merritt	252
Merry Hill	252
Mesic	252
Micaville	828
Micro	919
Middleburg	252
Middlesex	252
Midland	704
Midway	336
Midway Park	910
Mill Spring	828
Millboro	336
Millers Creek	336
Millingport	704
Mills River	828
Milton	336
Milwaukee	252
Mineral Spgs	704
Mineral Springs	704
Minneapolis	828
Minnesott Bch	252
Minnesott Beach	252
Mint Hill	704
Misenheimer	704
Mocksville	336
Moncure	919
Monroe	704
Monroeton	336
Montezuma	828
Monticello	336
Montreat	828
Moores Creek National Battle	910
Mooresboro	828
Mooresville	704
Moratock	910
Moravian Falls	336
Moravian Fls	336
Morehead City	252
Morganton	828
Morrisville	919
Mortimer	828
Morven	704
Mount Airy	336
Mount Gilead	910
Mount Holly	704
Mount Mourne	704
Mount Olive	919
Mount Pleasant	704
Mount Tabor	336
Mount Ulla	704
Mount Vernon	704
Mount Zion	336
Mountain Home	828
Mountain Park	336
Mountain View	828
Moxley	336
Moyock	252
Mt Airy	336
Mt Holly	704
Mt Mourne	704
Mt Pleasant	704
Mt Ulla	704
Mt View	828
Muddy Creek	336
Mulberry	336
Murfreesboro	252
Murphy	828
N C Centralized Mailing	919
N C Dept Of Motor Veh	919
N C Dept Revenue	919
N C Library	919
N C Natl Bank	704
N Topsail Bch	910
N Topsail Beach	910
N Wilkesboro	336
Nags Head	252
Nakina	910
Naples	828
Nashville	252
Nathans Creek	336
National Info Syst Supt Cntr	919
National Wholesale Co Inc	336
Nationwide Ins Co	919
Naval Hos	910
Naval Hospital	910
Navassa	910
Nc Baptist Hospital	336
Nc State Univ	919
Nc State University	919
Ncsu Student Housing	919
Nebo	828
Needmore	828
Neuse	919
New Bern	252
New Hanover County Airport	910
New Hill	919

City	Area Code
New Hope Academy	336
New Leaksville	336
New London	704
New River Marine Corps Air S	910
New Salem	336
Newell	704
Newland	828
Newport	252
Newsom	336
Newton	828
Newton Grove	910
Norlina	252
Norman	910
North	336
North Albemarle	704
North Concord	704
North Durham	919
North Hills	919
North Wilkesboro	336
Northside	919
Norton	828
Norwood	704
Norwood Hollow	828
Nw London	704
Oak City	252
Oak Hill	828
Oak Island	910
Oak Park	828
Oak Ridge	336
Oakboro	704
Ocean Isl Bch	910
Ocean Isle	910
Ocean Isle Beach	910
Ocono Lufty	828
Ocracoke	252
Okeewemee	910
Old Fort	828
Old Sparta	252
Olde Farm	910
Oldtown	336
Olin	704
Olive Branch	704
Olivers Crossroads	828
Olivia	919
Ophir	910
Oregon Hill	336
Oriental	252
Orion	336
Orrum	910
Osbornville	704
Osceola	336
Osgood	919
Osmond	336
Ossipee	336
Oteen Sta	828
Otto	828
Oxford	919
Pactolus	252
Paint Rock	828
Palestine	704
Pantego	252
Parker	336
Parks Crossroads	336
Parkton	910
Parmele	252
Parsonville	336
Patetown	919
Patterson	828
Patterson Springs	704
Paw Creek	704
Paynes Store	828
Peace Haven Estates	336
Peachland	704
Peden	336
Peletier	252
Pelham	336
Pembroke	910
Pendleton	252
Penland	828
Penrose	828
Peoria	828
Perch	336
Perkinsville	828
Petersburg	828
Petersville	336
Pfafftown	336
Pikeville	919
Pilot Mnt	336
Pilot Mountain	336
Pilot Mt	336
Pilot Mtn	336
Pilot Mts	336
Pine Hall	336
Pine Knoll Shores	252
Pine Level	919
Pine View	919
Pinebluff	910
Pinehurst	910
Pineola	828
Pinetops	252
Pinetown	252
Pineville	704
Piney Creek	336
Pink Hill	252
Pinkney	704
Pinnacle	336
Pisgah Forest	828
Pittsboro	919
Pks	252
Plaza	336
Pleasant Gap	828
Pleasant Garden	336
Pleasant Gdn	336
Pleasant Gdns	336
Pleasant Grove	828
Pleasant Hill	252
Plumtree	828
Plyler	704
Plymouth	252
Point Harbor	252
Polkton	704
Polkville	704
Pollocksville	252
Ponderosa	910
Pooletown	704
Pope A F B	910
Pope Afb	910
Pope Air Force Base	910
Poplar Branch	252
Porter	704
Portsmouth	252
Potecasi	252
Powells Point	252
Powells Store	336
Powellsville	252
Prentiss	828
Price	336
Princess House	336
Princeton	919
Princeville	252
Proctorville	910
Propst Crossroads	828
Prospect Hill	336
Providence	336
Purlear	336
Pyatte	828
Quarry	336
Queen	910
Queens College	704
Quick	336
Qvc	252
Radical	336
Raeford	910
Ragan Village	704
Raleigh	919
Raleigh Business Reply	919
Ramseur	336
Randleman	336
Rankin	336
Ranlo	704
Red Oak	252
Red Springs	910
Redland	336
Reeds Cross Roads	336
Reedy Creek	336
Reese	828
Reidsville	336
Relief	828
Research Triangle Park	919
Research Triangle Pk	919
Rex	910
Rhine	336
Rhodhiss	828
Rhodhizz	828
Rich Square	252
Richfield	704
Richlands	910
Richmond Hill	336
Ridge	704
Ridgecrest	828
Ridgefield	336
Ridgeway	252
Riegelwood	910
River Haven	704
Riverside	252
Roanoke Rapid	252
Roanoke Rapids	252
Roanoke Rapids Air Force Sta	252
Roaring Creek	828
Roaring Gap	336
Roaring River	336
Robbins	910
Robbinsville	828
Robersonville	252
Rock Creek	336
Rockford	336
Rockingham	910
Rockwell	704
Rocky Mount	252
Rocky Mt	252
Rocky Point	910
Rodanthe	252
Roduco	252
Rolesville	919
Rominger	828
Ronda	336
Ronok Rpd Afs	252
Roper	252
Rose Hill	910
Roseboro	910
Rosman	828
Rougemont	336
Round Peak	336
Rowland	910
Roxboro	336
Roxobel	252
Royal	252
Royal Oaks	704
Royal Pines	828
Rtp	919
Rudd	336
Ruffin	336
Rural Hall	336
Ruth	828
Rutherford College	828
Rutherfordton	828
Rutherfrd Col	828
Rutherwood	828
S Brunswick	910
Saddle	336
Saint Pauls	910
Salemburg	910
Salisbury	704
Salter Path	252
Saluda	828
Salvo	252
Sands	828
Sandy Ridge	336
Sanford	919
Sapphire	828
Saratoga	252
Saw Mills	828
Saxapahaw	336
Scaly Mountain	828
Scaly Mtn	828
Scotland Neck	252
Scotts	704
Scottville	336
Scranton	252
Seaboard	252
Seagrove	336
Sealevel	252
Sedalia	336
Sedgefield	336
Sedges Garden	336
Selma	919
Semora	336
Senia	828
Seven Devils	828
Seven Lakes	910
Seven Springs	252
Severn	252
Seward	336
Seymour Johnson A F B	919
Seymour Johnson Afb	919
Shacktown	336
Shady Brook	704
Shallotte	910
Shallowell	919
Shannon	910
Shannon Plaza	919
Sharon	704
Sharpsburg	252
Shatley Springs	336
Shawboro	252
Shelby	704
Sherrills Ford	828
Sherrills Frd	828
Sherwood	828
Shiloh	252
Shingle Hollow	828
Shoal	336
Shulls Mills	828
Sidestown	704
Siler City	919
Silk Hope	919
Siloam	336
Silver Valley	336
Silverstone	828
Simpson	252
Sims	252
Sjafb	919
Skyland	828
Smethport	336
Smithfield	919
Smyre	704
Smyrna	252
Sneads Ferry	910
Snow Camp	336
Snow Hill	252
Soapstone Mountain	336
Sophia	336
Soul City	252
South Albemarle	704
South Brunswick	910
South Gastonia	704
South Greensboro	336
South Lexington	336
South Mills	252
South Newton	828
Southern Pines	910
Southern Pnes	910
Southern Shores	252
Southmont	336
Southport	910
Southrn Shore	252
Sparta	336
Spear	828
Speed	252
Speedwell	828
Spencer	704
Spencer Mountain	704
Spindale	828
Spray	336
Spring Creek	828
Spring Hope	252
Spring Lake	910
Spring Valley	336
Spruce Pine	828
Spurgeon	336
Stacy	252
Staley	336
Stallings	704
Stamey Branch	828
Stanfield	704
Stanley	704
Stanleyville	336
Stantonsburg	252
Star	910
Startown	828
State Rd	336
State Road	336
State University	919
Statesville	704
Statesville West	704
Stedman	910
Stella	252
Stem	919
Stokes	252
Stokesdale	336
Stoneville	336
Stonewall	252
Stonewall Jackson Training S	704
Stoney Creek	336
Stony Fork	336
Stony Knoll	336
Stony Point	704
Stonycreek	336
Stovall	919
Stratford	336
Stumpy Point	252
Sturgills	336
Sugar Grove	828
Sugar Mountain	828
Sugar Mtn	828
Summerfield	336
Summit	336
Sunbury	252
Sunny Point Military Ocean T	910
Sunnyside	828
Sunset Bch	910
Sunset Beach	910
Sunset Harbor	910
Sunshine	828
Supply	910
Surf City	910
Surf City Fin	910
Sussex	336
Swan Station	919
Swannanoa	828
Swanquarter	252
Swansboro	252
Sweetwater	828
Swepsonville	919
Sylva	828
Tabor City	910
Talleys Crossing	336
Tamarack	336
Tapoco	828
Tar Heel	910
Tarawa	910
Tarawa Ter	910
Tarawa Terrace	910
Tarawa Tr	910
Tarboro	252
Taylorsville	828
Teachey	910
Tennessee Acres	336
Terrell	828
Theta	336
Thomasville	336
Three Mile	828
Thurmond	336
Tillery	252
Timberlake	336
Toast	336
Tobaccoville	336
Todd	336
Toliver	336
Toluca	704
Topia	336
Topsail Beach	910
Topton	828
Townsville	252
Tramway	919
Traphill	336
Treetop	336
Trent Woods	252
Trenton	252
Trinity	336
Triplett	336
Troutman	704
Troy	910
Trust	828
Tryon	828
Tuckasegee	828
Tuckerdale	336
Turkey	910
Turnersburg	336
Tuxedo	828
Twin Oaks	336
Tyner	252
Tyro	336
Unc A Chapel Hill Schls Adm	919
Unc-G	336
Unc-Greensboro	336
Union	828
Union Cross	336
Union Grove	704
Union Mills	828
Univ Of Nc	919
University Of Nc	910, 919
Upper Pig Pen	828
Upton	828
Usps	704
Usps Hr Shared Svcs	336
Uwharie	910
V A	336
Valdese	828
Vale	704
Valle Crucis	828
Valley	828
Valmead	828
Vanceboro	252
Vandalia	336
Vandemere	252
Vander	910
Vashti	704
Vass	910
Vaughan	252
Victory	704
Vienna	336
View Mont	828
Viewmont	828
Vilas	828
W Asheville	828
W Field	336
W Jefferson	336
Wachovia Bank	336, 704
Wachovia Bldg Vim	336
Waco	704
Wade	910
Wadesboro	704
Wadeville	910
Wagoner	336
Wagram	910
Wake Crossroads	919
Wake Forest	919
Walkertown	336
Wallace	910
Wallburg	336
Walnut Cove	336
Walnut Creek	919
Walsh	336
Walstonburg	252
Wanchese	252
Warne	828
Warrensville	336
Warrenton	252
Warrior	828
Warsaw	910
Wash	252
Washburn Store	828
Washington	252
Watauga	828
Watha	910
Waughtown	336
Waves	252
Waxhaw	704
Waynesville	828
Weaversford	336
Weaverville	828
Webster	828
Webtown	919
Weddington	704
Welcome	336
Weldon	252
Wendell	919
Wentworth	336
Wesley Chapel	704
Wesleyan Col	252
Wesleyan College	252
West Ashville	828
West Bend	336
West End	910
West Haven	828

City	Area Code
West Hillsborough	919
West Jefferson	336
Western Hills	704
Westfield	336
Westgate	919
Westminster	828
Whaley	828
Whisper Pnes	910
Whispering Pines	910
Whitakers	252
White Hill	919
White Lake	910
White Oak	910
White Plains	336
White Rock	828
White Store	704
White Sulphur Springs	336
Whitehead	336
Whiteville	910
Whitley Heights	919
Whitsett	336
Whittier	828
Wilbar	336
Wilders Grove	919
Wilkesboro	336
Willard	910
Williamston	252
Williston	252
Willow Ridge	910
Willow Spring	919
Willow Springs	919
Wilm	910
Wilmington	910
Wilson	252
Wilsons Mill	919
Wilsons Mills	919
Wind Blow	910
Winders Cross Roads	336
Windsor	252
Windy Gap	336
Winfall	252
Wingate	704
Winnabow	910
Winston Salem	336
Winston Salem Business Reply	336
Winston Salem Courtesy Reply	336
Winston-Salem	336
Winterville	252
Winton	252
Wise	252
Woodfin	828
Woodford	336
Woodland	252
Woodleaf	336
Woodleigh	252
Woodville	252
Wright Brothers National Mem	252
Wrightsville Beach	910
Writsvlle Bch	910
Ws State Univ	336
Yadkin	336
Yadkin College	336
Yadkinville	336
Yanceyville	336
Yaupon Beach	910
Youngsville	919
Zebulon	919
Zionville	828
Zirconia	828

North Dakota

City	Area Code
All Points	701

Northern Marian Islands

City	Area Code
All Points	691

Ohio

City	Area Code
Aberdeen	937
Ada	419
Adairo	419
Adams County	937
Adams Mills	740
Adamsville	740
Addyston	513
Adelphi	740
Adena	740
Adrian	419
Ak Steel	513
Akron	330
Akron Beacon Journal	330
Akron Business Reply	330
Akron Canton Region Airport	330
Akron Public Lib	330
Albany	740
Albion	419
Alexandria	740
Alger	419
Alledonia	740
Allensburg	937
Allensville	740
Alliance	330
Allstate Ins Co	330
Alpha	937
Alvada	419
Alvordton	419
Amanda	740
Amelia	513
Ameritrust Bank	216
Amesville	740
Amf	513
Amherst	440
Amlin	614
Amos Press Inc	937
Amsden	419
Amsterdam	740
Anderson	513
Andover	440
Anna	937
Ansonia	937
Antioch	740
Antwerp	419
Apple Creek	330
Arcadia	419
Arcanum	937
Archbold	419
Arlington	419
Arlington Heights	513
Arlington Hts	513
Armstrong Mills	740
Armstrong Mls	740
Ash Ridge	937
Ashland	419
Ashley	740
Ashtabula	440
Ashville	740
Asm International	440
Athens	740
Attica	419
Attica Junction	419
Atwater	330
Auburn Township	440
Auburn Twp	440
Augusta	330
Aurora	330
Austinburg	440
Austintown	330
Ava	740
Avon	440
Avon Lake	440
Avondale	513
Bailey Lakes	419
Bainbridge	740
Bainbridge Township	440
Bairdstown	419
Bakersville	740
Baltic	330
Baltimore	740
Bank One	614
Bannock	740
Barb	330
Barberton	330
Bardwell	937
Barlow	740
Barnesville	740
Bartlett	740
Barton	740
Bascom	419
Batavia	513
Bath	330
Bay View	419
Bay Village	440
Bayard	330
Bazetta	330
Beach City	330
Beachwood	216
Beallsville	740
Beaver	740
Beaver Creek	937
Beavercreek	937
Beaverdam	419
Becks Mills	330
Bedford	440
Bedford Heights	216, 440
Bedford Hts	216
Belden Village Mall	330
Belfast	937
Bellaire	740
Bellbrook	937
Belle Center	937
Belle Valley	740
Belle Vernon	419
Bellefontaine	937
Bellefontne	937
Bellevue	419
Bellfntn	937
Bellville	419
Belmont	740
Belmore	419
Beloit	330
Belpre	740
Bentleyville	440
Benton	419
Benton Ridge	419
Bentonville	937
Berea	440
Bergholz	740
Berkey	419
Berlin	330
Berlin Center	330
Berlin Heights	419
Berlin Hts	419
Berlinville	419
Berwick	419
Bethany	513
Bethel	513
Bethesda	740
Bethlehem	419
Bettsville	419
Beulah Beach	440
Beverly	740
Bevis	513
Bexley	614
Bidwell	740
Big Prairie	330
Birmingham	440
Black Horse	330
Blacklick	614
Bladensburg	740
Blaine	740
Blainesville	740
Blake	330
Blakeslee	419
Blanchester	937
Blissfield	740
Bloomdale	419
Blooming Grove	419
Bloomingburg	740
Bloomingdale	740
Bloomingville	419
Bloomville	419
Blue Ash	513
Blue Ball	937
Blue Creek	740
Blue Cross Hosp Serv	419
Blue Rock	740
Bluffton	419
Boardman	330
Bolivar	330
Bond Hill	513
Bono	419
Botkins	937
Boughtonville	419
Bourneville	740
Bowerston	740
Bowersville	937
Bowling Green	419
Bowling Green St University	419
Bowling Green State Univ	419
Braceville	330
Bradford	937
Bradner	419
Brady Lake	330
Bradyville	937
Bratenahl	216
Brecksville	440
Bremen	740
Brewster	330
Briarwood Beach	330
Brice	614
Bridgeport	740
Bridgetown	513
Briggs	440
Brilliant	740
Brinkhaven	740
Bristolville	330
Brm Unique Firm Zip	216
Broadview Heights	440
Broadview Hts	440
Broadway	937
Bronson	419
Brook Park	216
Brookfield	330
Brooklyn	216
Brooklyn Heights	216
Brooklyn Hts	216
Brookpark	216
Brookville	937
Brookwood	513
Brown County	937
Brownhelm	440
Brownsville	740
Browntown	937
Brunswick	330
Bryan	419
Buchtel	740
Buckeye Lake	740
Buckeye Village	419
Buckland	419
Bucks	330
Bucyrus	419
Buffalo	740
Buford	937
Bunker Hill	330
Burbank	330
Burghill	330
Burgoon	419
Burkettsville	419
Burnet Woods	513
Burton	440
Burton City	330
Business Reply	330, 513
Business Reply Firm Zip	419
Butler	419
Butlerville	513
Byesville	740
Byrd	937
Cable	937
Cadiz	740
Cairo	419
Calcutta	330
Caldwell	740
Caledonia	419
California	513
Cambridge	740
Camden	937
Cameron	740
Camp Dennison	513
Camp Washington	513
Campbell	330
Campbellsport	330
Canal Fulton	330
Canal Whchstr	614
Canal Winchester	614
Canal Wnchstr	614
Canfield	330
Canton	330
Canton Business Reply	330
Carbon Hill	740
Carbondale	740
Cardington	419
Carey	419
Carlisle	937
Caroline	419
Carroll	740
Carrollton	330
Carrothers	419
Carthage	513
Carthagena	419
Casstown	937
Castalia	419
Castine	937
Catawba	937
Catawba Island	419
Cecil	419
Cedarville	937
Celeryville	419
Celina	419
Centerburg	740
Centerton	419
Centerville	937
Ceylon	419
Chagrin Falls	440
Chagrin Township	440
Chambersburg	330
Champion	330
Champion Spark Plug	419
Chandlersville	740
Chandlersvlle	740
Chapel Hill Mall	330
Chardon	440
Charlestown	330
Charm	330
Chatfield	419
Chatham	330
Chauncey	740
Chautauqua	937
Cherry Fork	937
Cherry Grove	513
Cherry Valley	440
Chesapeake	740
Cheshire	740
Chester	740
Chesterhill	740
Chesterland	440
Chesterville	419
Cheviot	513
Chickasaw	419
Chillicothe	740
Chilo	513
Chippewa Lake	330
Chippewa On The Lake	330
Christiansbg	937
Christiansbrg	937
Christiansburg	937
Chrysler Corp Toledo Assy	419
Cin Arprt Anx	513
Cincinnati	513
Cincinnati Airport Annex	513
Cincy Amf	513
Circleville	740
City View Heights	513
Clarington	740
Clarksburg	740
Clarksfield	440
Clarkson	330
Clarksville	937
Clay Center	419
Claysville	740
Clayton	937
Clear Creek	419
Clermont Cnty	937
Clermont County	937
Cleveland	216, 440
Cleveland Clinic Foundation	216
Cleveland Heights	216
Cleveland Hts	216
Cleves	513
Clifton	513, 937
Clinton	330
Clinton Cnty	937
Clinton County	937
Cloverdale	419
Clyde	419
Cnl Wnchstr	614
Coal Grove	740
Coal Run	740
Coalton	740
Coitsville	330
Coldwater	419
Colerain	513, 740
Colerain Township	513
Colerain Twp	513
Colg Hill Sta	513
College Cor	513
College Corner	513
College Hl	513
Collins	440
Collinsville	513
Cols Grove	419
Colton	419
Columbia	330
Columbia Sta	440
Columbia Station	440
Columbiana	330
Columbus	614
Columbus Grove	419
Columbus Grv	419
Commercial Accounts	513
Commercial Accts	513
Commercial Point	614
Commercial Pt	614
Concord Township	440
Concord Twp	440
Conesville	740
Congress	419
Congress Lake	330
Conneaut	440
Conneaut Harbor	440
Connorsville	740
Conotton	740
Conover	937
Consumer Direct Inc	330
Continental	419
Convoy	419
Cool Ridge Heights	419
Coolville	740
Copley	330
Cornersburg	330
Corning	740
Corryville	513
Cortland	330
Corwin	513
Coshocton	740
Country Fair	330
Courtesy Reply Firm Zip	419
Covedale	513
Covington	937
Cozaddale	513
Craig Beach	330
Craigton	330
Cream City	740
Creola	740
Crestline	419
Creston	330
Cridersville	419
Crooksville	740
Crosby	513
Crosstown	513
Croton	740
Crown City	740
Cuba	937
Cumberland	740
Cumminsville	513
Curtice	419
Custar	419
Cutler	740
Cuyahoga Falls	330
Cuyahoga Fls	330
Cuyahoga Heights	216
Cuyahoga Hts	216
Cygnet	419
Cynthiana	937
Dalton	330
Damascus	330
Danville	740
Darbydale	614
Darrtown	513
Day Heights	513

City	Area Code
Dayton	937
Dayton Business Reply Mail	937
Dayton Courtesy Reply Mail	937
De Graff	937
Decatur	937
Deer Park	513
Deerfield	330
Deersville	740
Defiance	419
Del Fair	513
Delaware	740
Delhi	513
Dellroy	330
Delphi	419
Delphos	419
Delta	419
Dennison	740
Dent	513
Dept Of Public Utilities	419
Derby	614
Derwent	740
Deshler	419
Deunquat	419
Dexter	740
Dexter City	740
Diamond	330
Dilles Bottom	740
Dillonvale	740
Dist Fulfillment Svc	614
Dola	419
Donnelsville	937
Dorset	440
Dover	330
Doylestown	330
Drakesburg	330
Dresden	740
Drexel	937
Dublin	614
Dueber	330
Dunbridge	419
Duncan Falls	740
Dundas	740
Dundee	330
Dungannon	740
Dunglen	740
Dunkirk	419
Dunlap	513
Dupont	419
E Ashtabula	440
E Cleveland	216
E Fultonham	740
E Liverpool	330
E Palestine	330
E Rochester	330
E Springfield	740
East Akron	330
East Ashtabula	440
East Canton	330
East Claridon	440
East Cleveland	216
East Conneaut	440
East Danville	937
East End	513
East Fultonham	740
East Greenville	330
East Liberty	937
East Liverpool	330
East Mansfield	419
East Monroe	937
East Orwell	440
East Palestine	330
East Rochester	330
East Sparta	330
East Springfield	740
East Townsend	440
Eastlake	440
Easton	330
Eastwood	513
Eaton	937
Eddie Bauer Co	614
Edenton	513
Edenville	740
Edgerton	419
Edgewater	216
Edgewood	440
Edinburg	330
Edison	419
Edon	419
Elba	740
Elder Beerman	937
Eldorado	937
Elgin	419
Elida	419
Elizabethtown	513
Elkton	330
Ellet	330
Elliston	419
Ellsberry	937
Ellsworth	330
Elm Grove	740
Elmore	419
Elyria	440
Empire	740
Englewood	937
Enon	937
Envir Pro Agency	513
Epworth Heights	513
Etna	740
Euclid	216, 440
Evansport	419
Evanston	513
Evendale	513
Everett	330
Ewington	740
Fairborn	937
Fairfax	513, 937
Fairfield	513
Fairhope	330
Fairlawn	330
Fairmont	513
Fairmount	513
Fairpoint	740
Fairport Harbor	440
Fairport Hbr	440
Fairview	740
Fairview Park	440
Fairview Pk	440
Farmdale	330
Farmer	419
Farmerstown	330
Farmersville	937
Farnham	440
Fayette	419
Fayette County	937
Fayetteville	513
Feed Springs	740
Feesburg	937
Felicity	513
Fidelity Investments	513
Fifth Third Bank	513
Findlay	419
Finneytown	513
Firestone Park	330
Firestone Tire	330
Firestone Tire & Rub Co	216
Fitchville	419
Five Mile	937
Flat Rock	419
Fleming	740
Fletcher	937
Florida	419
Flushing	740
Fly	740
Forest	419
Forest Park	513
Fort Jennings	419
Fort Loramie	937
Fort Recovery	419
Fort Scott Camps	513
Fort Seneca	419
Foster	513
Fostoria	419
Fowler	330
Frankfort	740
Franklin	937
Franklin Furnace	740
Franklin Frnce	740
Frazeysburg	740
Fredericksbg	330
Fredericksbrg	330
Fredericksburg	330
Fredericktown	740
Fredricktwn	740
Freedom	330
Freeport	740
Fremont	419
Fresno	740
Friendship	740
Ft Jennings	419
Ft Loramie	937
Ft Recovery	419
Fulfillment Corp Of Amer Brm	740
Fulton	419
Fultonham	740
Gahanna	614
Galena	740
Galion	419
Gallipolis	740
Galloway	614
Gambier	740
Ganges	419
Gap Inc Direct	740
Garfield	216
Garfield Heights	216
Garfield Hts	216
Garrettsville	330
Gates Mills	440
Geneva	440
Geneva On The Lake	440
Genoa	419
Georges Run	740
Georgetown	937
Germantown	937
Gettysburg	937
Gibsonburg	419
Gilboa	419
Girard	330
Gist Settlement	937
Glandorf	419
Glen Robbins	740
Glencoe	740
Glendale	513
Glenford	740
Glenmont	330
Glenwillow	440
Gloria Glens	330
Glouster	740
Gnadenhutten	740
Golf Manor	513
Gomer	419
Goodyear Tire	330
Gordon	937
Goshen	513
Grafton	440
Grand Rapids	419
Grand River	440
Grandview	614
Grandview Heights	614
Granville	740
Gratiot	740
Gratis	937
Graysville	740
Graytown	419
Green	330
Green Camp	740
Green Springs	419
Green Township	513
Greene	330
Greenfield	937
Greenford	330
Greensburg	330
Greentown	330
Greenville	937
Greenwich	419
Greer	330
Grelton	419
Groesbeck	513
Grove City	614
Groveport	614, 740
Grover Hill	419
Guernsey	740
Guilford	330
Gustavus	330
Guysville	740
Gypsum	419
Hallsville	740
Hamden	740
Hamersville	937
Hamilton	513
Hamilton Township	513
Hamilton Twp	513
Hamler	419
Hamlet	513
Hammondsville	330
Hanging Rock	740
Hannibal	740
Hanoverton	330
Harbor View	419
Harlem Spgs	330
Harlem Springs	330
Harmon	330
Harpster	740
Harrisburg	614
Harrison	513
Harrisville	740
Harrod	419
Hartford	330
Hartland	419
Hartsgrove	440
Hartville	330
Harveysburg	513
Haskins	419
Havana	419
Haverhill	740
Haviland	419
Haydenville	740
Hayesville	419
Hazelwood	513
Heath	740
Hebron	740
Helena	419
Hemlock	740
Hemlock Grove	740
Henrietta	440
Hepburn	419
Hglnd County	937
Hicksville	419
Hide Away Hills	740
Hideaway Hls	740
Higginsport	937
Highland	937
Highland County	937
Highland Heights	440
Highland Hgts	440
Highland Hills	216
Highland Hls	216
Highland Hts	440
Hilliard	614
Hillman	937
Hills And Dales	330
Hillsboro	937
Hinckley	330
Hiram	330
Hockingport	740
Holgate	419
Holiday City	419
Holland	419
Hollansburg	937
Holloway	740
Holmesville	330
Homer	740
Homerville	330
Homeworth	330
Hooven	513
Hopedale	740
Hopewell	740
Houston	937
Howard	740
Howenstein	330
Howland	330
Hoytville	419
Hubbard	330
Huber	937
Huber Heights	937
Huber Hgts	937
Huber Hts	937
Hudson	330
Hunting Valley	440
Huntington Bank	216
Huntington Nat'l Bank	513
Huntington National Bank	614
Huntsburg	440
Huntsville	937
Huron	419
Hyde Park	513
Iberia	419
Idaho	740
Independence	216
Indian Hill	513
Indian Spgs	513
Indian Springs	513
Ink	419
Internal Revenue Service	513
Irondale	740
Ironton	740
Irs Service Center	513
Irwin	937
Is St George	419
Isle Saint George	419
Isle St George	419
Ithaca	937
Ivorydale	513
Jacksn Belden	330
Jackson	740
Jackson Belden	330
Jackson Center	937
Jackson Ctr	937
Jacksontown	740
Jacksonville	740
Jacobsburg	740
Jamestown	937
Jasper	740
Jefferson	440
Jeffersonville	740
Jeffersonville	740
Jenera	419
Jeromesville	419
Jerry City	419
Jerusalem	740
Jewell	419
Jewett	740
Jnctn City	740
Johnstown	740
Junction City	740
Justus	330
Kalida	419
Kansas	419
Keene	740
Kelleys Is	419
Kelleys Island	419
Kelloggsville	440
Kenmore	330
Kennedy Heights	513
Kensington	330
Kent	330
Kent State University	330
Kenton	419
Kenwood	513
Kerr	740
Kettering	937
Kettlersville	419
Key Bank	216, 513
Key Corp	216
Kidron	330
Kilbourne	740
Kilgore	330
Killbuck	330
Kimball	419
Kimbolton	740
Kings Island	513
Kings Mills	513
Kingston	740
Kingsville	440
Kinsman	330
Kipling	740
Kipton	440
Kirby	419
Kirkersville	740
Kirtland	440
Kirtland Hills	440
Kitts Hill	740
Kunkle	419
La Fayette	419
La Rue	740
Lacarne	419
Lafayette	419
Lafferty	740
Lagrange	440
Laings	740
Lake Cable	330
Lake Fork	419
Lake Milton	330
Lake Slagle	330
Lake Waynoka	937
Lakeline	440
Lakemore	330
Lakeside	419
Lakeside Marblehead	419
Lakeside-Marblehead	419
Lakeview	937
Lakeville	330
Lakewood	216
Lancaster	740
Landon	513
Langsville	740
Lansing	740
Latham	937
Lattasburg	419
Latty	419
Laura	937
Laurel	513
Laurelville	740
Lawrence	330
Layland	330
Leavittsburg	330
Lebanon	513
Lees Creek	937
Leesburg	937
Leesville	740
Leetonia	330
Leipsic	419
Lemert	419
Lemoyne	419
Lena	937
Lenox	440
Lewis Center	740
Lewisburg	937
Lewistown	937
Lewisville	740
Lexington	419
Liberty Center	419
Liberty Ctr	419
Liberty Tnsp	513
Liberty Township	513
Liberty Townshp	513
Liberty Twnship	513
Liberty Twp	513
Lima	419
Limaville	330
Lincoln Heights	513
Lincoln Village Fin Unit	614
Lindale	513
Lindentree	330
Lindenwald	513
Lindsey	419
Linndale	216
Linwood Park	440
Linworth	614
Lisbon	330
Litchfield	330
Lithopolis	614
Little Hocking	740
Little Hockng	740
Little London	419
Little Washington	419
Little York	740
Lksid Marblhd	419
Lockbourne	614, 740
Lockhead Martin	330
Lockland	513
Lockwood	330
Lodi	330
Logan	740
London	740
Londonderry	740
Long Bottom	740
Lorain	440
Lordstown	330
Lore City	740
Losantiville	513
Loudonville	419
Louisville	330
Loveland	513
Lowell	740
Lowellville	330
Lower Salem	740

City	Area Code
Lucas	419
Lucasville	740
Luckey	419
Ludlow Falls	937
Lykens	419
Lyn May	440
Lynchburg	937
Lyndhurst	440
Lyndhurst Mayfield	440
Lyndon	740
Lynx	937
Lyons	419
Lytle	513
Macedonia	330
Mack	513
Macksburg	740
Madeira	513
Madison	440
Madison-On-The-Lake	440
Magnetic Spgs	937
Magnetic Spring	937
Magnetic Springs	937
Magnolia	330
Main Office Box Brm	614
Maineville	513
Malaga	740
Malinta	419
Malta	740
Malvern	330
Manchester	937
Mansfield	419
Mantua	330
Maple Heights	216
Maple Hts	216
Maple Valley	330
Mapleton	330
Maplewood	937
Marathon	513
Marble Cliff	614
Marblehead	419
Marengo	419
Maria Stein	419
Mariemont	513
Marietta	740
Marion	740
Mark Center	419
Marne	740
Marshallville	330
Martel	419
Martin	419
Martins Ferry	740
Martinsburg	740
Martinsville	937
Marysville	937
Mason	513
Massie	513
Massillon	330
Masury	330
Matamoras	740
Materials Park	440
Maumee	419
Maximo	330
Mayburn Corners	330
Mayfield	440
Mayfield Heights	440
Mayfield Hts	440
Mayfield Village	440
Mayfield Vlg	440
Maynard	740
Mc Arthur	740
Mc Clure	419
Mc Comb	419
Mc Cutchenville	419
Mc Cutchenvle	419
Mc Dermott	740
Mc Donald	330
Mc Guffey	419
Mcarthur	740
Mcclure	419
Mccomb	419
Mcconnelsville	740
Mcconnelsvle	740
Mccutchenville	419
Mcdermott	740
Mcdonaldsville	330
Mcguffey	419
Mckinley	330
Mczena	330
Mecca	330
Mechanic	330
Mechanicsburg	937
Mechanicstown	330
Medina	330
Medway	937
Melmore	419
Melrose	419
Mendon	419
Mentor	440
Mentor On The	440
Mentor On The Lake	440
Mesopotamia	440
Metamora	419
Metropolitan Life	937
Metropolitan Medical Claims	937
Miami	513
Miami Univ	513
Miami University	513
Miamisburg	937
Miamitown	513
Miamiville	513
Middle Bass	419
Middle Point	419
Middle Pt	419
Middlebranch	330
Middlebrg Hts	440
Middleburg	937
Middleburg Heights	440
Middleburg Hts	440
Middlefield	440
Middleport	740
Middletown	513
Midland	937
Midpark	440
Midvale	740
Milan	419
Milford	513
Milford Center	937
Milford Ctr	937
Millbury	419
Milledgeville	740
Miller City	419
Miller Cty	419
Millersburg	330
Millersport	740
Millersville	419
Millfield	740
Millville	513
Milton Center	419
Mineral City	330
Mineral Ridge	330
Minersville	740
Minerva	330
Minford	740
Mingo	937
Mingo Jct	740
Mingo Junction	740
Minster	419
Mitiwanga	419
Mogadore	330
Mohicanville	419
Mol	440
Moline	419
Monclova	419
Monroe	513
Monroe Center	440
Monroe Twp	440
Monroeville	419
Montezuma	419
Montgomery	513
Montpelier	419
Montrose	330
Montville	440
Moorefield	740
Moraine	937
Moreland Hills	440
Moreland Hls	440
Morges	330
Morning Sun	937
Morral	740
Morristown	740
Morrow	513
Moscow	513
Moultrie	330
Mount Air	614
Mount Blanchard	419
Mount Carmel	513
Mount Cory	419
Mount Eaton	330
Mount Gilead	419
Mount Healthy	513
Mount Holly	513
Mount Hope	330
Mount Liberty	740
Mount Olive	513
Mount Orab	937
Mount Perry	740
Mount Pisgah	513
Mount Pleasant	740
Mount Saint Joseph	513
Mount Sterling	740
Mount Vernon	740
Mount Victory	937
Mount Washing	513
Mount Washington	513
Mowrystown	937
Moxahala	740
Mt Auburn	513
Mt Blanchard	419
Mt Cory	419
Mt Lookout	513
Mt Pleasant	740
Mt Repose	513
Mt St Joseph	513
Mt Sterling	740
Mt Union	330
Munroe Falls	330
Munson Twp	440
Murdock	513
Murray City	740
N Baltimore	419
N Bloomfield	330
N Canton	330
N College Hl	513
N E Waterworks	330
N Fairfield	419
N Georgetown	330
N Hampton	937
N Industry	330
N Kingsville	440
N Lawrence	330
N Lewisburg	937
N Ridgeville	440
N Robinson	419
N Royalton	440
N Star	937
Nankin	419
Napoleon	419
Nashport	740
Nashville	330
National City Bank	216, 614, 937
Natl Family Opinion	419
Navarre	330
Neapolis	419
Neffs	740
Negley	330
Nelson	330
Nelsonville	740
Nevada	740
Neville	513
New Albany	614
New Alexander	330
New Alexandria	740
New Athens	740
New Baltimore	513
New Bavaria	419
New Bedford	740
New Bloomington	740
New Bloomngtn	740
New Boston	740
New Bremen	419
New Carlisle	937
New Concord	740
New Cumberland	330
New Franklin	330
New Garden	330
New Hagerstown	740
New Hampshire	937
New Harmony	513
New Harrisburg	330
New Haven	419, 513
New Holland	740
New Knoxville	419
New Lebanon	937
New Lexington	740
New London	419
New Lyme	440
New Madison	937
New Market	937
New Marshfield	740
New Marshfld	740
New Matamoras	740
New Miami	513
New Middletown	330
New Middletwn	330
New Paris	937
New Phila	330
New Philadelphia	330
New Pittsburgh	419
New Plymouth	740
New Richmond	513
New Riegel	419
New Rome	614
New Rumley	740
New Russia Township	440
New Springfield	330
New Springfld	330
New Straitsville	740
New Straitsvl	740
New Vienna	937
New Washingtn	419
New Washington	419
New Waterford	330
New Weston	937
New Winchester	419
Newark	740
Newburgh Heights	216
Newburgh Hts	216
Newbury	440
Newbury Twp	440
Newcomerstown	740
Newport	740, 937
Newton Falls	330
Newtonsville	513
Newtown	513, 740
Ney	419
Niles	330
No Baltimore	419
No Eaton	440
Noble	440
North Baltimore	419
North Bend	513
North Benton	330
North Bloomfield	330
North Canton	330
North Eaton	440
North Fairfield	419
North Georgetown	330
North Hampton	937
North Hill	330
North Industry	330
North Jackson	330
North Kingsville	440
North Lawrence	330
North Lewisburg	937
North Liberty	419
North Lima	330
North Madison	440
North Monroeville	419
North Olmsted	440
North Perry	440
North Randall	216
North Ridgeville	440
North Robinson	419
North Royalton	440
North Star	937
North Uniontown	937
North Woodbury	419
Northfield	330
Northfield Center	330
Northfield Village	330
Northridge	937
Northside	513
Northup	740
Northwood	419
Norton	330
Norwalk	419
Norwich	740
Norwood	513
Nova	419
Novelty	440
O M Scott Co	937
Oak Harbor	419
Oak Hill	740
Oakfield	330
Oakley	513
Oakwood	419, 937
Oakwood Village	440
Oakwood Vlg	440
Oberlin	440
Obetz	614
Oceola	740
Oh City	419
Ohio Casualty Ins	513
Ohio City	419
Ohio Dept Of Taxation	614
Ohio Edison Co	330
Okeana	513
Okolona	419
Old Fort	419
Old Washingtn	740
Old Washington	740
Olena	419
Olivesburg	419
Olmsted Falls	440
Olmsted Twp	440
Oneida	330
Ontario	419
Orange	440
Orange Village	216, 440
Orangeville	330
Orchard Island	937
Oregon	419
Oregonia	937
Orient	614
Orrville	330
Orwell	440
Osgood	419
Osnaburg	330
Ostrander	740
Ottawa	419
Ottawa Hills	419
Ottoville	419
Otway	740
Overpeck	513
Owens Corning	419
Owens Illinois	419
Owensville	513
Oxford	513
P Hill	937
Packard Elec Co Div Gm	330
Painesville	440
Palestine	937
Pandora	419
Paris	330
Parkdale	513
Parkman	440
Parkview	440
Parma	216
Parma Heights	440
Parral	330
Pataskala	740
Patmos	330
Patriot	740
Pattersonville	330
Paulding	419
Pavonia	419
Payne	419
Pedro	740
Peebles	937
Pekin	330
Pemberton	937
Pemberville	419
Peninsula	330
Pennsville	740
Pepper Pike	216
Perry	440
Perrysburg	419
Perrysville	419
Petersburg	330
Pettisville	419
Pg Contest Mail	513
Phillipsburg	937
Philo	740
Phoneton	937
Pickerington	614
Piedmont	740
Pierpont	440
Piketon	740
Piney Fork	740
Pioneer	419
Piqua	937
Pisgah	513
Pitsburg	937
Plain City	614
Plainfield	740
Plankton	419
Pleasant City	740
Pleasant Corners	614
Pleasant Cors	614
Pleasant Hill	937
Pleasant Home	419
Pleasant Plain	513
Pleasant Pln	513
Pleasant Ridge	513
Pleasant Run Farms	513
Pleasantville	740
Plymouth	419
Plymouth Twp	440
Pmi	937
Poetown	937
Poland	330
Polk	419
Pomeroy	740
Port Clinton	419
Port Jefferson	937
Port Washington	740
Port William	937
Portage	419
Portland	740
Portsmouth	740
Potsdam	937
Powell	740
Powhatan Point	740
Powhatan Pt	740
Price Hill	513
Princeton	513
Proctor	330
Proctorville	740
Prospect	740
Provident Bank	513
Prt Jefferson	937
Prt Washingtn	740
Pt Clinton	419
Puritas Pk	216
Put In Bay	419
Put-In- Bay	419
Quaker City	740
Queen City	513
Quincy	937
R R Donnelly	419
Racine	740
Radcliff	740
Radnor	740
Ragersville	330
Rainsboro	937
Randolph	330
Rarden	740
Ravenna	330
Rawson	419
Ray	740
Rayland	740
Raymond	937
Rdgville Cors	419
Readers Digest	740
Reading	513
Redhaw	419
Redoak	937
Reed	419
Reed Hartman	513
Reedsville	740
Reedtown	419
Reedurban	330
Reesville	937
Reily	513
Reinersville	740
Reminderville	330

City	Area Code
Reno	740
Reno Beach	419
Republic	419
Reynoldsburg	614
Riceland	330
Richfield	330
Richfield Heights	330
Richmond	740
Richmond Dale	740
Richmond Heights	440
Richmond Hts	440
Richville	330
Richwood	740
Rickenbacker Air Force Base	614
Ridgefield	419
Ridgeville	440
Ridgeville Corners	419
Ridgeway	937
Rinard Mills	740
Rio Grande	740
Ripley	937
Rising Sun	419
Risingsun	419
Rittman	330
River Corners	330
Riveredge	216
Riverlea	614
Riverside	937
Riverside Park	740
Roadway Express	330
Roaming Rock Shores	440
Roaming Shores	440
Roaming Shrs	440
Roanoke	740
Robertsville	330
Rochester	440
Rock Camp	740
Rock Creek	440
Rockbridge	740
Rockford	419
Rocky Ridge	419
Rocky River	440
Rodney	740
Rogers	330
Rome	440
Rootstown	330
Roselawn	513
Roselawn Finance	513
Roseville	740
Rosewood	937
Ross	513
Ross County	937
Rossburg	937
Rossford	419
Rossmoyne	513
Rossville	513
Roundhead	419
Rowsburg	419
Rudolph	419
Ruggles	419
Ruggles Beach	419
Rush	740
Rushsylvania	937
Rushville	740
Russell	440
Russell Township	440
Russells Point	937
Russells Pt	937
Russellville	937
Russia	937
Rutland	740
S Amherst	440
S Bloomfield	740
S Bloomingvil	740
S Bloomingville	740
S Charleston	937
S Vienna	937
S Zanesville	740
Sabina	937
Sagamore Hills	330
Sagamore Hls	330
Saint Bernard	513
Saint Clair	513
Saint Clairsville	740
Saint Henry	419
Saint Johns	419
Saint Louisville	740
Saint Louisvl	740
Saint Martin	513
Saint Marys	419
Saint Paris	937
Salem	330
Salesville	740
Salineville	330
Salt Creek	330
Samantha	937
San Margherita	614
Sandusky	419
Sandyville	330
Sarahsville	740
Sardinia	937
Sardis	740
Savannah	419
Sayler Park	513
Sayler Park Finance	513
Scio	740
Scioto Furnace	740
Scioto Furnce	740
Sciotoville	740
Scott	419
Scottown	740
Scroggsfield	330
Seaman	937
Sebring	330
Sedalia	740
Seilcrest Acres	513
Selma	937
Senecaville	740
Seven Hills	216
Seven Mile	513
Seville	330
Shade	740
Shademore	513
Shadyside	740
Shaker Heights	216
Shaker Hts	216
Shalersville	330
Shandon	513
Shanesville	330
Shared Zip Code	614
Sharon Center	330
Sharon Township	419
Sharonville	513
Sharpsburg	740
Shauck	419
Shawnee	740
Shawnee Hills	740
Sheffield	440
Sheffield Lake	440
Sheffield Lk	440
Sheffield Twp	440
Sheffield Village	440
Sheffield Vlg	440
Shelby	419
Shenadoah	419
Shenandoah	419
Sherrodsville	330
Sherwood	419
Shiloh	419
Shinrock	419
Shore	440
Short Creek	740
Shreve	330
Siam	419
Sidney	937
Silver Lake	330
Silverton	513
Sinking Spg	937
Sinking Spring	937
Smithfield	740
Smithville	330
So Amherst	440
So Bloomingville	740
So Charleston	937
So Oh Correctional Facility	740
So Vienna	937
Solon	440
Somerdale	330
Somerset	740
Somerton	740
Somerville	937
Sonora	740
South Amherst	440
South Arlington	330
South Bloomfield	740
South Bloomingville	740
South Charleston	937
South Euclid	216
South Lebanon	513
South Lorain	440
South Madison	440
South Point	740
South Russell	440
South Salem	740
South Solon	937
South Vienna	937
South Webster	740
South Zanesville	740
Southington	330
Southpoint	740
Sparta	740
Spencer	330
Spencerville	419
Spfld	937
Spg Valley	937
Spring Valley	937
Springboro	937
Springdale	513
Springfield	937
Springvale	513
St Clairsville	740
St Clairsvle	740
St Henry	419
St Johns	419
St Louisville	740
St Marys	419
St Paris	937
Stafford	740
State Departments Of Ohio	614
State Farm Insurance	740
Steam Corners	419
Steelville	513
Sterling	330
Steuben	419
Steubenville	740
Stewart	740
Stewartsville	740
Stillwater	740
Stillwell	330
Stockdale	740
Stockport	740
Stone Creek	330
Stonelick	513
Stony Ridge	419
Stout	740
Stoutsville	740
Stow	330
Strasburg	330
Stratton	740
Stream Side	740
Streetsboro	330
Stringtown	513
Strongsville	440
Struthers	330
Stryker	419
Suarez Corporation	330
Suffield	330
Sugar Grove	740
Sugar Grove Lake	419
Sugar Tree Ridge	937
Sugarcreek	330
Sullivan	419
Sulphur Spgs	419
Sulphur Springs	419
Summerfield	740
Summerford	740
Summit Sta	740
Summit Station	740
Summitville	330
Sunbury	740
Swanton	419
Sycamore	419, 513
Sycamore Twp	513
Sylvania	419
Sylvania Township	419
Sylvania Twp	419
Symmes	513
Symmes Twp	513
Syracuse	740
Taft	513
Tallmadge	330
Target	330
Tarlton	740
Taylortown	419
Terrace Park	513
Thatcher	740
The Central Trust Co	513
The First National Bank	513
The Plains	740
Thompson	440
Thornville	740
Thurman	740
Thurston	740
Tidd Dale	740
Tiffin	419
Tiltonsville	740
Timberlake	440
Tipp	937
Tipp City	937
Tippecanoe	740
Tiro	419
Toledo	419
Toledo Blade	419
Toledo Edison	419
Tontogany	419
Torch	740
Toronto	740
Trail	330
Tremont City	937
Trenton	513
Trimble	740
Trinway	740
Trotwood	937
Troy	937
Tuppers Plains	740
Tuppers Plns	740
Tuscarawas	740
Twenty Mile Stand	513
Twightwee	513
Twinsburg	330
U S P S Pm Msc Ofc	513
Uhrichsville	740
Union	937
Union City	937
Union Furnace	740
Unionport	740
Uniontown	330
Unionville	440
Unionville Center	614
Unionvlle Ctr	614
Uniopolis	419
Unique Firm Zip	216
Univ Cinc Med Sciences	513
Univ Dayton	937
Univ Of Akron	330
University Heights	216
University Hospital	513
University Ht	216
University Hts	216
University Of Cincinnati	513
University Of Dayton	937
Upper Arlington	614
Upper Arlngtn	614
Upper Sandsky	419
Upper Sandusky	419
Urbana	937
Urbancrest	614
Utica	740
Utopia	937
Valley City	330
Valley View	216
Valleydale	513
Valleyview	614
Van Buren	419
Van Wert	419
Vandalia	937
Vanlue	419
Vaughnsville	419
Venedocia	419
Vermilion	440
Vermilion On The Lake	440
Vernon	330
Verona	937
Versailles	937
Veterans Administration	937
Vickery	419
Victorias Secret	614
Vienna	330
Vincent	740
Vinton	740
W Alex	937
W Alexandria	937
W Carrollton	937
W Farmington	330
W Jefferson	614
W Lafayette	740
W Leipsic	419
W Manchester	937
W Mansfield	937
W Mansfld	937
W Middletown	513
W Millgrove	419
W Milton	937
W Portsmouth	740
Waco	330
Wadsworth	330
Waite Hill	440
Wakefield	740
Wakeman	440
Walbridge	419
Waldo	740
Walhonding	740
Walnut Creek	330
Walnut Hills	513
Walton Hills	440
Wapak	419
Wapakoneta	419
Warner	740
Warnock	740
Warren	330
Warrensville Heights	216
Warrensville Hts	216
Warrensvl Hts	216
Warsaw	740
Washingtn C H	740
Washingto Twp	937
Washington Ch	740
Washington Court House	740
Washington Township	937
Washingtonville	330
Washingtonvle	330
Waterford	740
Waterloo	740
Watertown	740
Waterville	419
Wauseon	419
Waverly	740
Wayland	330
Wayne	419, 440
Waynesburg	330
Waynesfield	419
Waynesville	513
Wellington	440
Wellston	740
Wellsville	330
West Akron	330
West Alex	937
West Alexandria	937
West American Ins	513
West Andover	440
West Carrollton	937
West Chester	513
West Clarksfield	440
West Elkton	937
West Farmington	330
West Jefferson	614
West Lafayette	740
West Leipsic	419
West Liberty	937
West Manchester	937
West Mansfield	937
West Mecca	330
West Millgrove	419
West Milton	937
West Point	330
West Portsmouth	740
West Richfield	330
West Rushville	740
West Salem	419
West Union	937
West Unity	419
Westboro	937
Westerville	614
Westfield Center	330
Westfield Ctr	330
Westlake	440
Weston	419
Westville	937
Westville Lake	330
Westwood	513
Westwood Area 2	513
Wharton	419
Wheelersburg	740
Whipple	740
White Cottage	740
White Oak	513
Whitehall	614
Whitehouse	419
Wickliffe	440
Widowville	419
Wilberforce	937
Wilkesville	740
Willard	419
Willetsville	937
Williamsburg	513
Williamsfield	440
Williamsport	740
Williamstown	419
Williston	419
Willoughby	440
Willoughby Hills	440
Willow Wood	740
Willowick	440
Willshire	419
Wilmington	937
Wilmot	330
Wiloughby Hls	440
Winchester	937
Windham	330
Windsor	440
Windsor Mills	440
Winesburg	330
Winfield	330
Wingett Run	740
Winona	330
Wintersville	740
Withamsville	513
Wolf	740
Wolf Run	740
Woodlawn	513
Woodmere	216
Woodsfield	740
Woodstock	937
Woodville	419
Wooster	330
Worthington	614
Wp Air Base	937
Wpafb	937
Wren	419
Wright Pat	937
Wright Patter	937
Wright Patterson	937
Wright Patterson Afb	937
Wrightstown	740
Wrightsville	740
Wshngtn Ct Hs	740
Wyandot	740
Wyoming	513
Xenia	937
Yale	330
Yankee Lake	330
Yankeetown	937
Yellow Spgs	937
Yellow Springs	937
Yorkshire	419
Yorkville	740
Youngstown	330
Youngstown State Univ	330
Zaleski	740
Zanesfield	937
Zanesville	740
Zoar	330
Zoarville	330

Oklahoma

City	Area Code
Achille	405, 580
Ada	580
Adair	918
Adams	580
Addington	580
Afton	918
Agra	918
Albany	580
Albert	405
Albion	918
Alderson	918
Alex	405
Aline	580
Allen	580
Altus	580
Altus Afb	580
Alva	580
Amber	405
Ames	580
Amorita	580
Anadarko	405
Antlers	580
Apache	580
Arapaho	580
Arcadia	405
Ardmore	580
Arkoma	918
Arnett	580
Asher	405
Aston	918
Atoka	580
Atwood	580
Avant	918
Avery	918
Bache	918
Bacone	918
Baker	580
Balko	580
Bank Of Oklahoma	405
Bank One	405
Barnsdall	918
Bartlesville	918
Battiest	580
Baugh	918
Bb	580
Bearden	918
Beaver	580
Beggs	918
Beland	918
Bennington	580
Bernice	918
Bessie	580
Bethany	405
Bethel	580
Big Cabin	918
Billings	580
Binger	405
Bird Island	918
Bison	405
Bixby	918
Blackwell	580
Blair	580
Blanchard	405
Blanco	918
Blocker	918
Bluejacket	918
Boise City	580
Bok Mail Service	918
Bokchito	580
Bokoshe	918
Boley	918
Bond	918
Boswell	580
Bowlegs	405
Bowring	918
Boynton	918
Bradley	405
Braggs	918
Braman	580
Bray	580
Bristow	918
Brkn Arw	918
Brkn Bow	580
Broken Arrow	918
Broken Bow	580
Bromide	580
Brtlsville	918
Buffalo	580
Bunch	918
Burbank	580
Burlington	580
Burneyville	580
Burns Flat	580
Bushyhead	918
Butler	580
Bville	918
Byars	405
Byron	580
Cache	580
Caddo	580
Calera	580
Calumet	405
Calvin	580
Camargo	580
Cameron	918
Canadian	918
Caney	580
Canton	580
Canute	580
Capron	580
Cardin	918
Carmen	580
Carnegie	580
Carney	405
Carrier	580
Carter	580
Cartwright	580
Cashion	405
Castle	918
Catoosa	918
Cement	405
Centrahoma	580
Centralia	918
Chandler	405
Chattanooga	580
Checotah	918
Chelsea	918
Cherokee	580
Chester	580
Cheyenne	580
Chickasha	405
Choctaw	405
Choska	918
Chouteau	918
Clairemore	918
Claremore	918
Clarita	580
Clayton	918
Clearview	918
Cleo Springs	580
Cleora	918
Cleveland	918
Clinton	580
Coalgate	580
Coalton	918
Colbert	580
Colcord	918
Coleman	580
Colgate	580
Collinsville	918
Colony	405
Comanche	580
Commerce	918
Concho	405
Connerville	580
Coodys Bluff	918
Cookson	918
Copan	918
Cordell	580
Corn	580
Cotoosa	918
Cottonwood	580
Council Hill	918
Countyline	580
Covington	580
Coweta	918
Cowlington	918
Coyle	405
Crawford	580
Crescent	405
Cromwell	405
Crowder	918
Cushing	918
Custer	580
Custer City	580
Cville	918
Cyril	580
Dacoma	580
Daisy	918
Dale	405
Davenport	405
Davidson	580
Davis	580
Deer Creek	580
Del City	405
Delaware	918
Depew	918
Devol	580
Dewar	918
Dewey	918
Dibble	405
Dill City	580
Disney	918
Dougherty	580
Douglas	580
Dover	405
Drummond	580
Drumright	918
Duke	580
Duncan	580
Durant	580
Durham	580
Dustin	918
Eagle City	580
Eagletown	580
Eakly	405
Earlsboro	405
Eastside	918
Edmond	405
Edna	918
El Reno	405
Eldorado	580
Elgin	580
Elk City	580
Elmer	580
Elmore City	580
Elmwood	580
Enid	580
Enterprise	918
Erick	580
Eucha	918
Eufaula	918
Eutaula	918
Fairfax	918
Fairland	918
Fairmont	580
Fairview	580
Fanshawe	918
Fargo	580
Farris	580
Faxon	580
Fay	580
Felt	580
Finley	580
First Natl Bank Mail Service	918
Fittstown	580
Fitzhugh	580
Fletcher	580
Foraker	918
Forgan	580
Fort Cobb	405
Fort Gibson	918
Fort Sill	580
Fort Supply	580
Fort Towson	580
Foss	580
Foster	580
Fox	580
Foyil	918
Francis	580
Frederick	580
Freedom	580
Ft Towson	580
Gage	580
Gans	918
Garber	580
Garvin	580
Gate	580
Geary	405
Gene Autry	580
Geronimo	580
Glencoe	580
Glenoak	918
Glenpool	918
Globe Life And Accident Co	405
Golden	580
Goldsby	405
Goltry	580
Goodwell	580
Gore	918
Gotebo	580
Gould	580
Gowen	918
Gracemont	405
Grady	580
Graham	580
Grandfield	580
Granite	580
Grant	580
Grayson	918
Greenfield	405
Grove	918
Grove City	918
Guthrie	405
Guymon	580
Hailey	918
Haileyville	918
Hallett	918
Halliburton	580
Hallis	918
Hammon	580
Hanna	918
Harden City	580
Hardesty	580
Harmon	580
Harrah	405
Hartshorne	918
Haskell	918
Hastings	580
Haworth	580
Haywood	918
Headrick	580
Healdton	580
Heavener	918
Helena	580
Hendrix	580
Hennepin	580
Hennessey	405
Henryetta	918
Herd	918
Higgins	918
Hillsdale	580
Hinton	405
Hitchcock	580
Hitchita	918
Hobart	580
Hodgen	918
Hoffman	918
Hog Shooter	918
Holdenville	405
Hollis	580
Hollister	580
Hominy	918
Honobia	918
Hooker	580
Hopeton	580
Howe	918
Hoyt	918
Hugo	580
Hulbert	918
Hunter	580
Hydro	405
Idabel	580
Inala	918
Indiahoma	580
Indianola	918
Inola	918
Isabella	580
Jay	918
Jenks	918
Jennings	918
Jet	580
Jones	405
Kansas	918
Kaw	580
Kaw City	580
Keefeton	918
Keifer	918
Kellyville	918
Kemp	580
Kendrick	918
Kenefic	580
Kenton	580
Keota	918
Ketchum	918
Keyes	580
Kiamichi	918
Kiamichi Christian Mission	918
Kiefer	918
Kildare	580
Kingfisher	405
Kingston	580
Kinta	918
Kiowa	918
Knowles	580
Konawa	580
Krebs	918
Kremlin	580
Lahoma	580
Lake Eufaula	918
Lamar	405
Lamont	580
Lane	580
Langley	918
Langston	405
Laverne	580
Lawton	580
Lebanon	580
Leedey	580
Leflore	918
Lehigh	580
Lenapah	918
Leon	580
Leonard	918
Lequire	918
Lexington	405
Lindsay	405
Loco	580
Locust Grove	918
Logan	580
Lone Grove	580
Lone Wolf	580
Longdale	580
Lookeba	405
Lotsee	918
Loveland	580
Loyal	405
Lucien	580
Luther	405
Macomb	405
Madill	580
Maimi	918
Manchester	580
Mangum	580
Manitou	580
Mannford	918
Mannsville	580
Mansford	918
Maramec	918
Marble City	918
Marietta	580
Marland	580
Marlow	580
Marshall	580
Martha	580
Martin	918
Mason	918
Maud	405
May	580
Mayfield	580
Maysville	405
Mazie	918
Mc Millan	580
Mcalester	918
Mccurtain	918
Mclain	918
Mcloud	405
Mead	580
Medford	580
Medicine Park	580
Meeker	405
Meers	580
Meno	580
Meridian	405
Miami	918
Midwest City	405
Milburn	580
Milfay	918
Mill Creek	580
Millerton	580
Milo	580
Minco	405
Moffett	918
Monkey Island	918
Monroe	918
Moodys	918
Moore	405
Mooreland	580
Morris	918
Morrison	580
Mounds	918
Mountain Park	580
Mountain View	580
Moyers	580
Muldrow	918
Mulhall	405
Muse	918
Musk	918
Muskogee	918
Mustang	405
Mutual	580
Nardin	580
Nash	580
Nashoba	918
Nelagony	918
New Lima	405
New Tulsa	918
Newalla	405
Newby	918
Newcastle	405
Newkirk	580
Nichols Hills	405
Nicoma Park	405
Ninnekah	405
Noble	405
Norfolk	918
Norman	405
North Miami	918
Nowata	918
Noxie	918
Nuyaka	918
Oakhurst	918
Oakland	580
Oaks	918
Oakwood	580
Ochelata	918
Octavia	580
Oilton	918
Ok St Unv Adm	405
Ok State Univ Admin	405
Ok State Univ Stu Housing	405
Ok Tax Comm	405
Okarche	405
Okay	918
Okc	405
Okeene	580
Okemah	918
Okesa	918
Okla Univ Health Sci Ctr	405
Oklahoma City	405
Oklahoma Natural Gas	918
Okmulgee	918
Oktaha	918
Olney	580
Olustee	580
Omega	405
Onola	918
Oologah	918
Optima	580
Oral Roberts Univ	918
Orienta	580
Orlando	580
Osage	918
Oscar	580
Overbrook	580

City	Area Code
Owasso	918
Owosso	918
Paden	405
Panama	918
Panola	918
Paoli	405
Park Hill	918
Pauls Valley	405
Pawhuska	918
Pawnee	918
Pearsonia	918
Peckham	580
Peggs	918
Pensacola	918
Peoria	918
Perkins	405
Pernell	580
Perry	580
Pershing	918
Pettit	918
Pharoah	918
Phillips	580
Phillips Petroleum	918
Picher	918
Pickens	580
Piedmont	405
Pierce	918
Pink	405
Pittsburg	918
Platter	580
Pocasset	405
Pocola	918
Ponca City	580
Pond Creek	580
Pontotoc	580
Pooleville	580
Port Of Catoo	918
Porter	918
Porum	918
Poteau	918
Pownee	918
Prague	405
Preston	918
Proctor	918
Prue	918
Pryor	918
Pryor Creek	918
Purcell	405
Putnam	580
Qualls	918
Quapaw	918
Quinton	918
Ralston	918
Ramona	918
Randlett	580
Ratliff City	580
Rattan	580
Ravia	580
Red Oak	918
Red Rock	580
Redbird	918
Reed	580
Rentiesville	918
Reydon	580
Richville	918
Ringling	580
Ringold	580
Ringwood	580
Ripley	918
Rocky	580
Roff	580
Roland	918
Roosevelt	580
Rose	918
Rosston	580
Rubottom	580
Rufe	580
Rush Springs	580
Ryan	580
S Coffeyville	918
Saint Louis	405
Salem	918
Salina	918
Sallisaw	918
Sand Springs	918
Sandsprings	918

City	Area Code
Sapulpa	918
Sasakwa	405
Savanna	918
Sawyer	580
Sayre	580
Schlegal	918
Schulter	918
Scipio	918
Seiling	580
Selman	580
Seminole	405
Sentinel	580
Sepulpa	918
Shady Point	918
Shamrock	918
Sharon	580
Shattuck	580
Shawnee	405
Shidler	918
Silver City	918
Skiatook	918
Slick	918
Smithville	580
Snow	918
Snyder	580
Soper	580
South Coffeyville	918
Southard	580
Sparks	918
Spavinaw	918
Spelter City	918
Spencer	405
Spencerville	580
Sperry	918
Spiro	918
Springer	580
Ss	918
Sterling	580
Stidham	918
Stigler	918
Stillwater	405
Stilwell	918
Stonewall	580
Strang	918
Stratford	580
Stringtown	580
Strong City	580
Stroud	918
Stuart	918
Stw	405
Sulphur	580
Summerfield	918
Summitt	918
Supulpa	918
Sweetwater	580
Swink	580
T A F B	405
Taft	918
Tahlequah	918
Talala	918
Talequah	918
Talihina	918
Tallant	918
Taloga	580
Tamaha	918
Tatums	580
Tecumseh	405
Temple	580
Terlton	918
Terral	580
Texanna	918
Texhoma	580
Texola	580
Thackerville	580
The Village	405
Thlequah	918
Thomas	580
Tiawah	918
Tinker Afb	405
Tipton	580
Tishomingo	580
Tom	580
Tonkawa	580
Tryon	405
Tullahassee	918
Tulsa	918

City	Area Code
Tulsa City Utilities	918
Tupelo	580
Turley	918
Turpin	580
Tuskahoma	918
Tuskegee	918
Tussy	580
Tuttle	405
Twin Hills	918
Twin Oaks	918
Tyrone	580
Union City	405
University Of Ok	405
Usps Oklahoma Dist	405
Valliant	580
Velma	580
Vera	918
Verden	405
Verdigris	918
Vernon	918
Vian	918
Vici	580
Village	405
Vinita	918
Vinson	580
Wade	580
Wagoner	918
Wainwright	918
Wakita	580
Walters	580
Wanette	405
Wann	918
Wapanucka	580
Wardville	918
Warner	918
Warr Acres	405
Washington	405
Washita	405
Watonga	580
Watova	918
Watson	580
Watts	918
Waukomis	580
Waurika	580
Wayne	405
Waynoka	580
Weatherford	580
Webbers Falls	918
Welch	918
Weleetka	918
Welling	918
Wellston	405
Welty	918
Westport	918
Westville	918
Wetumka	405
Wewoka	405
Wheatland	405
White Oak	918
Whitefield	918
Whitesboro	918
Wilburton	918
Williams Center	918
Willow	580
Wilson	580
Winganon	918
Wister	918
Wolco	918
Woodward	580
Wright City	580
Wyandotte	918
Wybark	918
Wynnewood	405
Wynona	918
Yale	918
Yarnaby	580
Yukon	405

Oregon

City	Area Code
Adair Village	541
Adams	541
Adel	541
Adrian	541
Agate Beach	541

City	Area Code
Agness	541
Albany	541
Allegany	541
Aloha	503
Alpine	541
Alsea	541
Alvadore	541
Amity	503
Antelope	541
Applegate	541
Arcadia	541
Arch Cape	503
Arlington	541
Arock	541
Ashland	541
Ashwood	541
Astoria	503
Athena	541
Aumsville	503
Aurora	503
Azalea	541
Baker	541
Baker City	541
Bandon	541
Banks	503
Barlow	503
Bates	541
Bay City	503
Beatty	541
Beaver	503
Beavercreek	503
Beaverton	503
Bend	541
Beulah	541
Biggs	541
Biggs Junction	541
Birkenfeld	503
Blachly	541
Black Butte Ranch	541
Blk Btte Rnch	541
Blodgett	541
Blue River	541
Bly	541
Boardman	541
Bonanza	541
Boring	503
Bridal Veil	503
Bridgeport	541
Brighton	503
Brightwood	503
Broadbent	541
Brogan	541
Brookings	541
Brooks	503
Brothers	541
Brownsville	541
Burlington	503
Burns	541
Burns Junction	541
Butte Falls	541
Butteville	503
Buxton	503
Cairo	541
Camas Valley	541
Camas Vly Cpo	541
Camp Sherman	541
Canby	503
Cannon Beach	503
Canyon City	541
Canyonville	541
Cape Meares	503
Carlton	503
Carver	503
Cascade Locks	541
Cascadia	541
Cave Junction	541
Cayuse	541
Cedar Mill	503
Celilo	541
Central Point	541
Charbonneau	503
Charleston	541
Chemult	541
Cheshire	541
Chiloquin	541
Christmas Valley	541

City	Area Code
Christmas Vly	541
Ckenzie Bridge	541
Clackamas	503
Clarno	541
Clatskanie	503
Claude	541
Cloverdale	503
Coburg	541
Colton	503
Columbia City	503
Condon	541
Coos Bay	541
Coos Head Naval Facility	541
Coquille	541
Corbett	503
Cornelius	503
Corvallis	541
Cottage Grove	541
Cove	541
Crabtree	503
Crane	541
Crater Lake	541
Crawfordsville	541
Crawfordsvlle	541
Crescent	541
Crescent Lake	541
Creswell	541
Crkd Rvr Rnch	541
Crooked River	541
Crooked River Ranch	541
Crow	541
Culp Creek	541
Culver	541
Curtin	541
Dairy	541
Dale	541
Dallas	503
Damascus	503
Danner	541
Days Creek	541
Dayton	503
Dayville	541
Deadwood	541
Deer Island	503
Depoe Bay	541
Dept Employment	503
Dept Motor Vehicle	503
Detroit	503
Dexter	541
Diamond	541
Diamond Lake	541
Dillard	541
Dodson	541
Donald	503
Dorena	541
Dover	503
Drain	541
Drewsey	541
Dufur	541
Dundee	503
Dunes City	541
Durham	503
Durkee	541
E Lake	541
Eagle Creek	503
Eagle Crest	541
Eagle Point	541
East Lake	541
Eastside	541
Echo	541
Eddyville	541
Elgin	541
Elkton	541
Elmira	541
Elsie	503
Emu U Of Or	541
Enterprise	541
Estacada	503
Eugene	541
Fairview	503
Fall Creek	541
Falls City	503
Fields	541
Finn Rock	541
Florence	541
Forest Grove	503

City	Area Code
Forest Heights	503
Fort Klamath	541
Fort Rock	541
Fossil	541
Foster	541
Fox	541
Frenchglen	541
Friend	541
Gales Creek	503
Galice	541
Gardiner	541
Garibaldi	503
Gaston	503
Gates	503
Gearhart	503
Gervais	503
Gilchrist	541
Gladstone	503
Glendale	541
Gleneden Bch	541
Gleneden Beach	541
Glenwood	503
Glide	541
Gold Beach	541
Gold Hill	541
Government Camp	503
Government Cp	503
Grand Island	503
Grand Ronde	503
Granite	541
Grants Pass	541
Grass Valley	541
Greenacres	541
Greenleaf	541
Gresham	503
Haines	541
Halfway	541
Halsey	541
Hammond	503
Happy Valley	503
Harbor	541
Harper	541
Harrisburg	541
Hebo	503
Helix	541
Helvetia	503
Heppner	541
Hereford	541
Hermiston	541
Hillsboro	503
Hines	541
Hood River	541
Hubbard	503
Hugo	541
Huntington	541
Idanha	503
Idleyld Park	541
Imbler	541
Imnaha	541
Independence	503
Interlachen	503
Ione	541
Ironside	541
Irrigon	541
Island City	541
Jacksonville	541
Jamieson	541
Jasper	541
Jefferson	541
Jennings Lodge	503
Jewell	503
John Day	541
Johnson City	503
Jonesboro	541
Jordan Valley	541
Joseph	541
Junction City	541
Juntura	541
Kah Nee Ta	541
Kahneeta	541
Keating	541
Keizer	503
Keno	541
Kent	541
Kerby	541
Kernville	541

City	Area Code
Kfalls	541
Kimberly	541
King City	503
Kingsley Field	541
Kinzua	541
Klamath Falls	541
La Grande	541
La Pine	541
Lafayette	503
Lake Grove	503
Lake Oswego	503
Lakeside	541
Lakeview	541
Langlois	541
Lawen	541
Leaburg	541
Lebanon	541
Lees Camp	503
Lexington	541
Liberal	503
Lime	541
Lincoln City	541
Logsden	541
Long Creek	541
Lorane	541
Lostine	541
Lowell	541
Lyons	503
Madras	541
Malin	541
Manhattan Beach	503
Manning	503
Manzanita	503
Mapleton	541
Marcola	541
Marion	503
Marylhurst	503
Maupin	541
Mayville	541
Maywood Park	503
Maywood Pk	503
Mc Kenzie Brg	541
Mckenzie Bridge	541
Mcminnville	503
Mcnary	541
Meacham	541
Medford	541
Medical Spgs	541
Medical Springs	541
Mehama	503
Merlin	541
Merrill	541
Metolius	541
Midland	541
Mikkalo	541
Mill City	503
Milton Freewater	541
Milton Frwtr	541
Milton-Freewater	541
Milwaukie	503
Mist	503
Mitchell	541
Mohler	503
Molalla	503
Monitor	503
Monmouth	503
Monroe	541
Monument	541
Moro	541
Mosier	541
Mount Angel	503
Mount Hood	541
Mount Hood Parkdale	541
Mount Hood-Parkdale	541
Mount Vernon	541
Mountain Park	503
Mt Hood	541
Mt Hood Prkdl	541
Mt Vernon	541
Mulino	503
Murphy	541
Murphys Camp	541
Myrtle Creek	541
Myrtle Point	541
N Powder	541
Neahkahnie	503
Nehalem	503
Neotsu	541
Neskowin	503
Netarts	503
Netarts Bay	503
New Pine Creek	541
New Pine Crk	541
Newberg	503
Newport	541
North Bend	541
North Plains	503
North Powder	541
Norway	541
Noti	541
Nyssa	541
O Brien	541
Oak Grove	503
Oak Lodge	503
Oakland	541
Oakridge	541
Oceanside	503
Odell	541
Ontario	541
Ophir	541
Oregon City	503
Oregon State Univ	541
Orenco	503
Oretech	541
Oswego	503
Otis	541
Otter Rock	541
Owyhee Corners	541
Oxbow	541
P Hill	541
Pacific City	503
Pacific Power	503
Pacificorp	503
Paisley	541
Parkdale	541
Parkrose	503
Paulina	541
Pendleton	541
Philomath	541
Phoenix	541
Pilot Rock	541
Pine Grove	541
Pistol River	541
Pleasant Hill	541
Plush	541
Port Orford	541
Portland	503
Post	541
Powell Butte	541
Powers	541
Prairie City	541
Princeton	541
Prineville	541
Progress	503
Prospect	541
Rainier	503
Redland	503
Redmond	541
Reedsport	541
Remote	541
Rhododendron	503
Richland	541
Rickreall	503
Riddle	541
Riley	541
Ritter	541
Riverside	541
Rock Creek	503
Rockaway	503
Rockaway Bch	503
Rockaway Beach	503
Rockwood	503
Rogue Elk	541
Rogue River	541
Rome	541
Rose Lodge	541
Roseburg	541
Rowena	541
Rsbg	541
Rufus	541
Rye Valley	541
Saginaw	541
Saint Benedict	503
Saint Helens	503
Saint Louis	503
Saint Paul	503
Salem	503
Sandy	503
Santa Clara	541
Scappoose	503
Scholls	503
Scio	503
Scotts Mills	503
Scottsburg	541
Seal Rock	541
Seaside	503
Selma	541
Seneca	541
Shady Cove	541
Shaniko	541
Shedd	541
Sheridan	503
Sherwood	503
Siletz	541
Silver Lake	541
Silverton	503
Sisters	541
Sixes	541
South Beach	541
Spfd	541
Spfld	541
Sprague River	541
Spray	541
Springdale	503
Springfield	541
St Benedict	503
St Helens	503
St Paul	503
Stanfield	541
State Accident Ins	503
State Government	503
Stayton	503
Sublimity	503
Summer Lake	541
Summerville	541
Sumpter	541
Sunnyvalley	541
Sunriver	541
Sutherlin	541
Sweet Home	541
Swisshome	541
Talent	541
Tangent	541
Tektronix	503
Tenmile	541
Terrebonne	541
The Dalles	541
Thurston	541
Tidewater	541
Tigard	503
Tillamook	503
Tiller	541
Timber	503
Timberline Lodge	503
Timbrline Ldg	503
Toledo	541
Tollgate	541
Tolovana Park	503
Tongue Point	503
Trail	541
Triangle Lake	541
Troutdale	503
Tualatin	503
Turner	503
Twin Rocks	503
Tygh Valley	541
Ukiah	541
Umatilla	541
Umpqua	541
Union	541
Unity	541
Vale	541
Vaughn	541
Veneta	541
Verboort	503
Vernonia	503
Vida	541
W Linn	503
Walden	541
Waldport	541
Walker	541
Wallowa	541
Walterville	541
Walton	541
Wamic	541
Wankers Corners	503
Warm Springs	541
Warren	503
Warrenton	503
Wasco	541
Weatherby	541
Wedderburn	541
Welches	503
Wemme	503
West Linn	503
West Slope	503
West Stayton	503
West Union	503
Westfall	541
Westfir	541
Westlake	541
Weston	541
Westport	503
Wheeler	503
White City	541
Wilbur	541
Wilderville	541
Willamette	503
Willamina	503
Williams	541
Willowcreek	541
Wilsonville	503
Win Bay	541
Winchester	541
Winchester Bay	541
Winchestr Bay	541
Winston	541
Wolf Creek	541
Wood Village	503
Woodburn	503
Worden	541
Yachats	541
Yamhill	503
Yoncalla	541
Zigzag	503

Palau

City	Area Code
All Points	691

Pennsylvania

City	Area Code
30th Street Train Station	215
A A R P Ins	215
Aaronsburg	814
Abbott	814
Abbottstown	717
Aberdeen	717
Abington	215
Academia	717
Accomac	717
Ackermanville	610
Acme	724
Acosta	814
Adah	724
Adamsburg	724
Adamsdale	570
Adamstown	717
Adamsville	724
Addison	814
Adrian	724
Africa	717
Airville	717
Akron	717
Alba	570
Albany	610
Albion	814
Albion Correctional Inst	814
Albrightsville	570
Albrightsvlle	570
Alburtis	610
Alcoa Center	724
Aldan	610
Aleppo	724
Alexander Spr	717
Alexander Springs	717
Alexandria	814
Alfarata	717
Alinda	717
Aline	570
Aliq	724
Aliquippa	724
Allegheny	412
Allegheny Power	724
Alleghenyville	610
Allenport	724
Allensville	717
Allentown	610
Allentown Airport Branch	610
Allenwood	570
Allison	724
Allison Park	412
Allport	814
Almedia	570
Alpine	717
Alsace Manor	610
Altamont	570
Altenwald	717
Altoona	814
Altria	570
Alum Bank	814
Alverda	724
Alverton	724
Amaranth	717
Amberson	717
Ambler	215
Ambridge	724
Amity	724
Analomink	570
Andalusia	215
Anderson	717
Andersonburg	717
Andersontown	717
Andover	717
Andreas	570
Andrews Bridge	610
Angelica	610
Anita	814
Annandale	724
Annville	717
Ansonia	570
Antes Fort	570
Anthony	570
Antis	814
Apollo	724
Aqua	717
Aquashicola	610
Arcadia	814
Arch Rock	717
Archbald	570
Arcola	610
Ardara	724
Ardmore	610
Ardsley	215
Arendtsville	717
Aristes	570
Armagh	814
Armbrust	724
Armstrong	570
Arnold	724
Arnot	570
Arnots Addition	570
Arona	724
Arsenal	412
Artemas	814
Asaph	570
Ashbury	570
Ashfield	610
Ashland	570
Ashley	570
Ashville	814
Aspers	717
Aspinwall	412
Aston	610
At & T	412
Atglen	610
Athens	570
Athens Township	570
Athol	610
Atkinsons Mills	717
Atkinsons Mls	717
Atlantic	814
Atlas	570
Atlasburg	724
Auburn	570
Audubon	610
Aughwick	814
Augustaville	570
Aultman	724
Austin	814
Austinburg	814
Austinville	570
Avalon	412
Avella	724
Avis	570
Avoca	570
Avon	717
Avon Heights	717
Avondale	610
Avonmore	724
Bachmanville	717
Baden	724
Baederwood	215
Bailey	717
Bainbridge	717
Bairdford	724
Bakers Summit	814
Bakerstown	724
Bala	610
Bala Cynwyd	610
Bald Eagle	570
Baldwin	412
Baldwin Township	412
Balls Mills	570
Bally	610
Bamford	717
Bangor	610
Bankstown	814
Bannerville	717
Barbours	570
Baresville	717
Bareville	717
Barkeyville	724
Barking	724
Barnesboro	814
Barnesville	570
Barneytown	814
Barree	814
Barrville	717
Barry	570
Bart	717
Barto	610
Bartonsville	570
Bartville	610
Basket	610
Bastress	570
Bath	610
Baumgardner	717
Baumstown	610
Bausman	717
Beach Haven	570
Beach Lake	570
Beale	717
Beallsville	724
Bear Creek	570
Bear Creek Township	570
Bear Creek Tw	570
Bear Gap	570
Bear Lake	814
Bear Valley	570
Beartown	610
Beautiful	717
Beaver	724
Beaver Falls	724
Beaver Lake	570
Beaver Mdws	570
Beaver Meadows	570
Beaver Spgs	570
Beaver Sprgs	570
Beaver Springs	570
Beaverdale	814
Beavertown	570
Beccaria	814

City	Area Code
Bechtelsville	610
Beckersville	610
Becks	570
Bedford	814
Bedminster	215
Beech Creek	570
Beech Flats	570
Beech Glen	570
Beecherstown	717
Beechview	412
Belfast	717
Bell Telephone	610
Bell Telephone Co	412
Bella Vista	570
Bellaire	717
Belle Valley	814
Belle Vernon	724
Belle Vrn Br	724
Bellefonte	814
Bellegrove	717
Bellemont	717
Belleville	717
Bellevue	412
Belltown	717
Bellvue	412
Bellwood	814
Belmont Hills	610
Belsano	814
Ben Avon	412
Ben Avon Heights	412
Bendersville	717
Bendertown	570
Benezett	814
Benezette	814
Benfer	570
Bensalem	215
Bentley Creek	570
Bentleyville	724
Benton	570
Berkley	610
Berkshire Heights	610
Berlin	814
Bermudian	717
Berne	610
Bernharts	610
Bernville	610
Berrysburg	717
Berrytown	570
Berwick	570
Berwyn	610
Bessemer	724
Bethany	570
Bethayres	215
Bethel	717
Bethel Park	412
Bethesda	717
Bethlehem	610
Beverly Hts	717
Beyer	724
Biesecker Gap	717
Big Cove Tann	717
Big Cove Tannery	717
Big Mine Run Junction	570
Big Pond	570
Big Run	814
Biggertown	570
Bigler	814
Biglerville	717
Bigmount	717
Bingham	814
Bino	717
Birchrunville	610
Bird In Hand	717
Birdsboro	610
Birdville	814
Birmingham	814
Bittersville	717
Bitumen	570
Bixler	717
Black Horse	610
Black Lick	724
Blacklog	814
Blackwell	570
Blain	717
Blainsport	717
Blair Corp	814
Blairs Mills	814
Blairsville	724
Blakely	570
Blakes	570
Blakeslee	570
Blanchard	814
Blandburg	814
Blandon	610
Blawnox	412
Bloomfield	412
Blooming Glen	215
Blooming Grove	570
Blooming Grv	570
Blooming Valley	814
Bloomsburg	570
Bloserville	717
Bloss	570
Blossburg	570
Blue Ball	717
Blue Bell	215
Blue Cross	717
Blue Hill	570
Blue Ridge Sm	717
Blue Ridge Summit	717
Blue Shield	717
Boalsburg	814
Bobtown	724
Boggstown	717
Bohrmans Mill	570
Boiling Spgs	717
Boiling Sprgs	717
Boiling Springs	717
Bolivar	724
Boltz	814
Bonneauville	717
Book Of Month	717
Booneville	570
Boothwyn	610
Bordnersville	717
Boston	412
Boston Run	570
Boswell	814
Botts	717
Bovard	724
Bowers	610
Bowman Addition	717
Bowmans	570
Bowmansdale	717
Bowmanstown	610
Bowmansville	717
Boydtown	570
Boyers	724
Boyers Junction	610
Boyertown	610
Boynton	814
Bra# 52	412
Brackenridge	724
Brackney	570
Braddock	412
Braddock Hills	412
Bradenville	724
Bradford	814
Bradfordwoods	724
Brady	570
Branch Dale	570
Branchdale	570
Branchton	724
Brandamore	610
Brandonville	570
Brandtsville	717
Brandy Camp	814
Bratton	717
Brave	724
Breezewood	814
Breezy Corner	610
Breinigsville	610
Brentwood	412
Bressler	717
Briarcliff	610
Bricker Dev	717
Brickerville	717
Bridgeport	610
Bridgeton	717
Bridgeville	412
Bridgewater Farms	610
Brier Hill	724
Brisbin	814
Bristol	215
Bro Dart	570
Broad Axe	215
Broad Top	814
Brockport	814
Brockton	570
Brockway	814
Brodbecks	717
Brodheadsville	570
Brodheadsvlle	570
Brogue	717
Brogueville	717
Brommerstown	570
Brook Park	570
Brookfield	814
Brookhaven	610
Brookland	814
Brookline	412
Brooklyn	570
Brookside	570
Brookville	814
Broomall	610
Browndale	570
Brownfield	724
Brownstone	717
Brownstown	717
Brownsville	724
Bruin	724
Brunnerville	717
Brush Valley	724
Brushtown	717
Bryan Mills	570
Bryansville	717
Bryn Athyn	215
Bryn Mawr	610
Brysonia	717
Buck	717
Buck Hill Falls	570
Buck Hill Fls	570
Buck Run	570
Buck Valley	717
Buckhorn	570
Buckingham	215
Buena Vista	412
Buffalo Mills	814
Buffalo Sprs	717
Buffalo X Rds	570
Bulger	724
Bulk Mail Ctr	724
Bulltown	610
Bungy	570
Bunker Hill	570
Bunkertown	717
Bunola	724
Bureau Of Motor Vehicles	717
Bureau Of Voc Rehab	724
Burgettstn	724
Burgettstown	724
Burlington	570
Burnham	717
Burnside	814
Burnt Cabins	814
Bushkill	570
Business Reply Mail	610
Butler	724
Buttonwood	570
Butztown	610
Buyerstown	717
Byrnedale	814
Bywood	610
Cabot	724
Cadogan	724
Cairnbrook	814
Caldwell	570
California	724
Callensburg	814
Callery	724
Calumet	724
Calvert	570
Calvin	814
Cambra	570
Cambridg Spgs	814
Cambridge Springs	814
Cammal	570
Camp Grove	570
Camp Hill	717
Campbelltown	717
Camptown	570
Canadensis	570
Canadohta Lake	814
Canoe Camp	570
Canonsburg	724
Canton	570
Capital Blue Cross	717
Carbondale	570
Cardale	724
Carlisle	717
Carlisle Barracks	717
Carlisle Brks	717
Carlton	814
Carmichaels	724
Carnegie	412
Carnegie Mellon Univ	412
Carpolis	412
Carroll Park	610
Carroll Valley	717
Carrolltown	814
Carson	412
Carsontown	570
Carsonville	717
Carter Camp	814
Carversville	215
Cascade	570
Cashtown	717
Cassandra	814
Cassville	814
Castanea	570
Castl Shannon	412
Castle	724
Castle Shann	412
Castle Shannon	412
Catasauqua	610
Catawissa	570
Cathead	814
Cecil	724
Cedar Lane	717
Cedar Ledge	570
Cedar Run	570
Cedar Springs	570
Cedarbrook	215
Cedarhurst	412
Cedars	610
Center City	570
Center Mills	717
Center Moreland	570
Center Square	215
Center Valley	610
Centerport	610
Centerville	814
Central	570
Central City	814
Central Manor	717
Centralia	570
Centre Hall	814
Chadds Ford	610
Chain	570
Chalfont	215
Chalk Hill	724
Chambersburg	717
Chambersville	724
Champion	814
Chandlers Valley	814
Chandlrs Vly	814
Chapmans	610
Charleroi	724
Charleston	570
Charlestown	717
Charmian	717
Charnita	717
Chatham	610
Cheesetown	717
Cheltenham	215
Cherokee Ranch	610
Cherry Flats	570
Cherry Grove	814
Cherry Hill	814
Cherry Run	570
Cherry Tree	814
Cherryville	610
Chest Springs	814
Chester	610, 717
Chester Heights	610
Chester Hts	610
Chester Sprgs	610
Chester Springs	610
Chester Township	610
Chester Twp	610
Chesterbrook	610
Chestnut Rdg	724
Chestnut Ridge	724
Cheswick	412
Cheyney	610
Chichester	610
Chicora	724
Childs	570
Chillisquaque	570
Chilton Co	610
Chinchilla	570
Christiana	610
Churchill	412
Churchtown	610
Churchville	215
Cigna Corporation	215
Cinram	570
Cisna Run	717
Citibank Delaware	215
Citizens Bank	814
Cito	717
Clairton	412
Clarence	814
Clarendon	814
Claridge	724
Clarington	814
Clarion	814
Clark	724
Clarks Green	570
Clarks Mills	724
Clarks Summit	570
Clarksburg	724
Clarkstown	570
Clarksville	724
Classification & Rates Admin	215
Clay	717
Clay Hill	717
Claylick	717
Claysburg	814
Claysville	724
Clayton	610
Clear Spring	717
Clearfield	814
Clearville	814
Cleona	717
Cleversburg	717
Clifford	570
Clifford Twp	570
Clifton	570
Clifton Heights	610
Clifton Hts	610
Clifton Township	570
Clifton Twp	570
Climax	814
Clinton	724
Clintondale	570
Clintonville	814
Clune	724
Cly	717
Clymer	724
Coal	570
Coal Cabin Beach	717
Coal Center	724
Coal Run	570
Coal Township	570
Coaldale	570
Coalport	814
Coatesville	610
Cobblerville	717
Cobbs Lake Preserve	570
Cobbs Lk Pres	570
Coburn	814
Cochranton	814
Cochranville	610
Cocolamus	717
Codorus	717
Coffeetown	717
Cogan House	570
Cogan Station	570
Cokeburg	724
Col X Rds	570
Colebrook	717
Colebrookdale	610
Colemanville	717
Colerain	717
Coles	570
Coles Creek	570
Colesburg	814
College Hill	610
College Misericordia	570
College Park	570
Collegeville	610
Collier Township	412
Collier Twp	412
Collingdale	610
Collinsville	717
Collomsville	570
Colmar	215
Colonial Hill	717
Colonial Penn (Brm)	215
Colonial Penn Group	215
Columbia	717
Columbia Cross Roads	570
Columbia Gas Of Pa	412
Columbia X Rd	570
Columbus	814
Columbus Boro	814
Colver	814
Colwyn	610
Comly	570
Commerce Bank	215
Commodore	724
Concord	717
Concordville	610
Conemaugh	814
Conestoga	717
Confluence	814
Congo	610
Conneaut Lake	814
Conneaut Lake Park	814
Conneaut Twp	814
Conneautville	814
Connellsville	724
Connersville	570
Connerton	570
Connoquenessing	724
Connoqunsg	724
Conoy	717
Conshohocken	610
Conway	724
Conyngham	570
Cooks Run	570
Cooksburg	814
Coolspring	814
Coon Hunter	570
Coopersburg	610
Cooperstown	814
Cooperville	610
Coplay	610
Coral	724
Coraopolis	412
Corliss	412
Cornwall	717
Cornwall Ctr	717
Cornwells Heights	215
Cornwells Hts	215
Coropolis	412
Corry	814
Corsica	814
Cosytown	717
Couchtown	717
Coudersport	814
Coulters	412
Coupon	814
Courtdale	570
Courtney	724
Cove	717
Cove Gap	717
Covington	570
Covngtn	570
Cowan	570
Cowanesque	814
Cowans Gap	717
Cowans Vlg	717
Cowansville	724
Cowley	570

City	Area Code
Coxeville	570
Crabtree	724
Crafton	412
Craigs	570
Craigsville	724
Craley	717
Cramer	814
Cranberry	814
Cranberry Township	724
Cranberry Twp	724
Cranesville	814
Crawford	570
Creamery	610
Creekside	724
Creighton	724
Crescent	724
Cresco	570
Cresmont	570
Cress	717
Cresson	814
Cressona	570
Crestmont	570
Creswell	717
Crooked Creek	570
Crosby	814
Cross Fork	814
Cross Roads	717
Crossgrove	717
Crossing Pointe	814
Crossingville	814
Crown	814
Croydon	215
Crucible	724
Crum Lynne	610
Crystal Spg	814
Crystal Spring	814
Cuba Mills	717
Cuddy	412
Cumbola	570
Cummings	570
Curllsville	814
Curryville	814
Curtisville	724
Curwensville	814
Custer City	814
Cyclone	814
Cynwyd	610
Daggett	570
Dagus Mines	814
Daisytown	724
Dale	610
Dallas	570
Dallastown	717
Dalmatia	717
Dalton	570
Damascus	570
Danboro	215
Danielsville	610
Danville	570
Danville East	570
Darby	610
Darby Township	610
Dark Water	570
Darlington	724
Darragh	724
Dauberville	610
Dauphin	717
Davidsburg	717
Davidson	570
Davidsville	814
Davistown	724
Dawson	724
Dayton	814
De Lancey	814
De Turksville	570
De Water Gap	570
De Young	814
Decatur	717
Deer Lake	570
Deerfield	814
Defense Depot	717
Defiance	814
Deiblers	570
Delano	570
Delaware Run	570
Delaware Twp	724
Delaware Water Gap	570
Dellville	717
Delmar	570
Delmont	724
Delta	717
Denbo	724
Denholm	717
Denver	717
Deodate	717
Department Of Revenue	717
Derrick City	814
Derrs	570
Derry	724
Derry Church	717
Devault	610
Devon	610
Dewart	570
Diamondtown	570
Dice	570
Dickerson Run	724
Dickey	717
Dickinson	717
Dickson City	570
Dickson Cty	570
Dieners Hill	570
Dilliner	724
Dillsburg	717
Dilltown	814
Dimock	570
Dingmans Ferry	570
Dingmans Fry	570
Direct Brands	717
Distant	814
District	610
Dixonville	724
Donaldson	570
Donegal	724
Donegal Heights	717
Donegal Springs	717
Donnally Mill	717
Donora	724
Dooleyville	570
Dormont	412
Dornsife	570
Dorset	570
Dott	717
Doubling Gap	717
Douglass	610
Douglassville	610
Doutyville	570
Dover	717
Downingtown	610
Doyles Mills	717
Doylesburg	717
Doylestown	215
Draper	570
Dravosburg	412
Drehersville	570
Dresher	610
Drexel Hill	610
Drexel Hills	717
Drexelbrook	610
Drifting	814
Drifton	570
Driftwood	814
Drocton	570
Drumore	717
Drums	570
Drury Run	570
Dry Run	717
Dry Valley	570
Dryville	610
Du Bois	814
Dublin	215
Dubois	814
Duboistown	570
Dudley	814
Duffield	717
Duguesne	412
Duke Center	814
Dun & Bradstreet	610
Dunbar	724
Duncan	570
Duncannon	717
Duncansville	814
Duncott	570
Dundore	570
Dunkelbergers	570
Dunlevy	724
Dunlo	814
Dunmore	570
Dunnstown	570
Dupont	570
Duquesne	412
Duquesne Light Co	412
Duquesne Univ	412
Durham	610
Durlach	717
Duryea	570
Dushore	570
Dysart	814
E Charleston	570
E Chillisquaq	570
E Fallowfield	610
E Freedom	814
E Greenville	215
E Lancaster	717
E Lansdowne	610
E Lawrencevle	570
E Lewisburg	570
E Mc Keesport	412
E Mckeesport	412
E Millsboro	724
E Pennsboro	717
E Petersburg	717
E Pittsburgh	412
E Smethport	814
E Smithfield	570
E Springfield	814
E Strodsburg	570
E Stroudsbg	570
E Stroudsburg	570
E Vandergrift	724
E Waterford	717
Eagles Mere	570
Eagleville	610
Earlington	215
Earlville	610
East Bangor	610
East Berlin	717
East Brady	724
East Brunswick	570
East Buffalo	570
East Butler	724
East Canton	570
East Earl	717
East Fallowfield Township	610
East Freedom	814
East Greenville	215
East Hanover	717
East Hickory	814
East Kane	814
East Keating	570
East Lancaster	717
East Lansdowne	610
East Liberty	412
East Mc Keesport	412
East Mckeesport	412
East Millsboro	724
East Mines	570
East Muncy	570
East Newport	717
East Norriton	610
East Pennsboro	717
East Petersburg	717
East Pgh	412
East Pittsburgh	412
East Prospect	717
East Renovo	570
East Salem	717
East Smethport	814
East Smithfield	570
East Springfield	814
East Stroudsburg	570
East Texas	610
East Vandergrift	724
East Waterford	717
East York	717
Eastern Area	412
Eastland Hill	717
Easton	610
Eastpoint	570
Eastville	570
Eastwick	215
Eau Claire	724
Ebenezer	717
Ebensburg	814
Ebervale	570
Echo Valley	570
Eckville	610
Eddington	215
Eddystone	610
Eden	717
Edenburg	610
Edgegrove	717
Edgely	215
Edgemont	610
Edgeworth	412
Edinboro	814
Edinboro University	814
Edinburg	724
Edisonville	717
Edmon	724
Edwardsville	570
Effort	610
Ehrenfeld	814
Eighty Four	724
Elco	724
Eldersville	724
Elderton	724
Eldora	717
Eldred	814
Eleven Mile	814
Elgin	814
Elimsport	570
Elizabeth	412
Elizabethtown	717
Elizabethville	717
Elizabethvle	717
Elizabthtwn	717
Elk	814
Elk Creek Twp	814
Elk Grove	570
Elkins Park	215
Elkland	814
Ellen Gowan	570
Ellendale	717
Elliottsburg	717
Ellisburg	814
Ellport	724
Ellsworth	724
Ellwood City	724
Elm	717
Elmer	814
Elmhurst	570
Elmora	814
Elrama	724
Elstonville	717
Elton	814
Elverson	610
Elwyn	610
Elwyn Terrace	717
Elysburg	570
Emeigh	814
Emerald	610
Emigsville	717
Emlenton	724
Emmaus	610
Emporium	814
Emsworth	412
Endeavor	814
Enders	717
Englesville	610
Englewood	570
English Ctr	570
Enola	717
Enon Valley	724
Enterline	717
Entlerville	717
Entriken	814
Ephrata	717
Equinunk	570
Erdenheim	215
Erdman	717
Erie	814
Erie Ins Exchange	814
Erly	717
Ernest	724
Erwinna	610
Eshbach	610
Eshcol	717
Espy	570
Espyville	814
Essington	610
Etna	412
Etown	717
Etters	717
Eulalia	814
Evans City	724
Evansville	610
Evendale	717
Everett	814
Everhartville	717
Everson	724
Eville	717
Ewaterfrd	717
Ewtrford	717
Excelsior	570
Exchange	570
Exeter	570
Exeter Township	570
Export	724
Exton	610
Eyers Grove	570
Eynon	570
Factoryville	570
Fagleysville	610
Fair Acres	717
Fair Oaks	724
Fairbank	724
Fairchance	724
Fairdale	724
Fairfield	717
Fairhope	814
Fairland	717
Fairlawn	570
Fairless Hills	215
Fairless Hls	215
Fairmount City	814
Fairmount Cty	814
Fairmount Spr	570
Fairplay	717
Fairview	814
Fairview Drive	717
Fairview Heights	610
Fairview Village	610
Fairview Vlg	610
Fairville	570
Fallentimber	814
Falls	215, 570
Falls Creek	814
Fallsington	215
Falmouth	717
Fannett	717
Fannettsburg	717
Farmdale	717
Farmersville	717
Farmington	724
Farragut	570
Farrandsville	570
Farrell	724
Farwell	570
Fassett	570
Fawn	717
Fawn Grove	717
Faxon	570
Fayette City	724
Fayetteville	717
Fayfield	717
Fearnot	570
Feasterville	215
Feasterville Trevose	215
Felton	717
Feltonville	610
Fenelton	724
Fermanagh	717
Fern Glen	570
Ferndale	610
Fernville	570
Fernwood	610
Fertility	717
Fetterville	610
Fields Sta	570
Finleyville	724
Firm Zip	570
Firm Zip Concept (Brm)	215, 610
Firm Zip Concept (Courtesy)	215
Fisher	814
Fisherdale	570
Fishers Ferry	570
Fishertown	814
Fisherville	717
Five Points	610
Fiveforks	717
Fivepointville	717
Fleetville	570
Fleetwood	610
Fleming	814
Flemington	570
Flicksville	610
Flinton	814
Flintville	717
Floradale	717
Floreffe	412
Florin	717
Flourtown	215
Fogelsville	610
Folcroft	610
Folsom	610
Fombell	724
Fontana	717
Forbes Rd	724
Forbes Road	724
Force	814
Ford City	724
Ford Cliff	724
Ford Motor Credit Corp	215
Forest City	570
Forest Grove	215
Forest Hills	412
Forest Knolls	717
Foresthill	570
Forestville	814
Forks Township	610
Forks Twp	610
Forksville	570
Fort Hill	814
Fort Littletn	814
Fort Littleton	814
Fort Loudon	717
Fort Robinson	717
Fort Washington	610
Fortney	717
Forty Fort	570
Fountain	570
Fountain Hill	610
Fountain Springs	570
Fountainville	215
Fox	570
Fox Chapel	412
Fox Chase Manor	215
Fox Hill	717
Foxburg	724
Foxcroft	215
Foxcroft Sq	215
Foxcroft Square	215
Frackville	570
Frailey	570
Franconia	215
Franklin	814
Franklin Center	610
Franklin Ctr	610
Franklin Furn	717
Franklin Mint	215
Franklintown	717
Frazer	610
Frederick	610
Fredericksbrg	717
Fredericksburg	717
Fredericksville	610
Fredericktown	724
Fredonia	724
Freeburg	570
Freedom	724
Freeland	570
Freemansburg	610
Freeport	724
Frenchville	814
Freysville	717
Friedens	814

City	Area Code
Friedensburg	570
Friendsville	570
Frisbie	570
Fritztown	610
Frnkln Mt Ctr	610
Frogtown	717
Frontier Communicationa	570
Frostburg	814
Fruitville	717
Fryburg	814
Frystown	717
Fstrvl Trvose	215
Ft Indiantown	717
Ft Littleton	814
Ft Loudon	717
Ft Wash	610
Ft Washington	610
Fulton	717
Furlong	215
Furniss	717
Gabelsville	610
Gaines	814
Galeton	814
Galilee	570
Gallitzin	814
Gamble	570
Ganister	814
Gans	724
Gap	717
Garards Fort	724
Garden City	610
Gardenview	717
Gardenville	215
Gardners	717
Garfield	610
Garland	814
Garnet Valley	610
Garrett	814
Gastonville	724
Gatchellville	717
Gay Street	610
Gbg	724
Geigertown	610
Geisinger Med	570
Geisinger Medical Center	570
Geisinger South	570
General Electric Co	814
Genesee	814
Geneva	814
George School	215
Georgetown	724
Germansville	610
Gettysburg	717
Gibbon Glade	724
Gibraltar	610
Gibson	570
Gibsonia	724
Gifford	814
Gilbert	610
Gilberton	570
Gilbertsville	610
Gillett	570
Ginter	814
Gipsy	814
Girard	814
Girardville	570
Gitts Run	717
Glades	717
Gladwyne	610
Glasgow	814
Glassport	412
Gleason	570
Gleasonton	570
Glen Campbell	814
Glen Carbon	570
Glen Dower	570
Glen Forney	717
Glen Hope	814
Glen Lyon	570
Glen Mawr	570
Glen Mills	610
Glen Rdl Lima	610
Glen Richey	814
Glen Riddle	610
Glen Riddle Lima	610
Glen Rock	717
Glencoe	814
Glendon	610
Gleniron	570
Glenmoore	610
Glenolden	610
Glenshaw	412
Glenside	215
Glenville	717
Glenwillard	724
Glenworth	570
Gnatstown	717
Gold	814
Goldsboro	717
Good	717
Good Spring	570
Goodhope	717
Goodville	717
Goodyear	717
Goosetown	570
Gordon	570
Gordonville	717
Gouglersville	610
Gouldsboro	570
Gowen City	570
Graceton	724
Gracey	717
Gradyville	610
Grampian	814
Grampian Hls	570
Grand Valley	814
Grangeville	717
Grantham	717
Grantville	717
Granville	717
Granville Ctr	570
Granville Smt	570
Granville Summit	570
Grapeville	724
Grassflat	814
Graterford	610
Gratz	717
Gray	814
Graysville	724
Great Bend	570
Greble	717
Greeley	570
Green Fields	717
Green Lane	215
Green Park	717
Green Point	717
Green Ridge	610
Green Springs	717
Greenbank	717
Greenbrier	570
Greenburr	570
Greenbury	570
Greencastle	717
Greene Junction	724
Greenfield Manor	610
Greenfield Township	570
Greenfild Twp	570
Greenock	412
Greenpark	717
Greensboro	724
Greensburg	724
Greenspring	717
Greenstone	717
Greentown	570
Greentree	412
Greenvillage	717
Greenville	724
Greenwich	610
Gregg	570
Greshville	610
Griesemersville	610
Grimesville	570
Grimville	610
Grindstone	724
Groffdale	717
Grovania	570
Grove City	724
Grove City Postal Retail Str	724
Grover	570
Guernsey	717
Guilford	717
Guilford Sprs	717
Gulph Mills	610
Guys Mills	814
Gwynedd	215
Gwynedd Valley	215
Gwynedd Vly	215
H I A	717
Hadley	724
Hahnstown	717
Haleeka	570
Halfville	717
Halifax	717
Hallam	717
Halls	570
Hallstead	570
Hallton	814
Hamburg	610
Hametown	717
Hamilton	814
Hamlin	570
Hammersley Fk	570
Hampden Station	717
Hampden Township	717
Hampden Twp	717
Hancock	610
Haneyville	570
Hannastown	724
Hanover	717
Hanover Direct	717
Hanover Township	570
Hanover Twp	570
Happy Valley	570
Harborcreek	814
Harding	570
Harford	570
Harleigh	570
Harlem	610
Harleysville	215
Harleysville Insurance Co	215
Harmonsburg	814
Harmony	724
Harper Tavern	717
Harriet Carter Gifts	215
Harrisburg	717
Harrison	814
Harrison City	724
Harrison Twp	814
Harrison Valley	814
Harrison Vly	814
Harrisonville	717
Harristown	717
Harrisville	724
Hartleton	570
Hartsfield	570
Hartstown	814
Hartsville	215
Harveys Lake	570
Harwick	724
Hastings	814
Hatboro	215
Hatfield	215
Haverford	610
Havertown	610
Hawk Run	814
Hawley	570
Hawstone	717
Hawthorn	814
Hays Grove	717
Hazel Hurst	814
Hazelwood	412
Hazen	814
Hazle Township	570
Hazle Townshp	570
Hazleton	570
Hbg	717
Hbg Inter Airp	717
Hebe	570
Heberlig	717
Heckschersville	570
Heckscherville	570
Hecla	724
Hector	814
Hegins	570
Heidelberg	412
Heidlersburg	717
Heilmandale	717
Heilwood	724
Helfenstein	570
Hellam	717
Hellen Mills	570
Hellertown	610
Hemlock Grove	570
Hendersonville	724
Hendersonvlle	724
Henryville	570
Hepburn	570
Hepburn Hts	570
Hepburnville	570
Hepler	570
Hereford	610
Herman	724
Herminie	724
Hermitage	724
Herndon	570
Herrick Center	570
Herrick Ctr	570
Herrville	717
Hershey	717
Hershey Heights	717
Heshbon Park	570
Hessdale	717
Hesston	814
Hibbs	724
Hickory	724
Hickox	814
Hidden Valley	814
High Mark Blue Shield	717
High Spire	717
Highland Park	610
Highmount	717
Highspire	717
Highville	717
Hill Church	610
Hilldale	570
Hiller	724
Hilliards	724
Hills Terrace	570
Hillsdale	814
Hillsgrove	570
Hillside	570
Hillsville	724
Hilltown	215
Hinkletown	717
Hobart	717
Hoernerstown	717
Hoffer	570
Hogestown	717
Hokendauqua	610
Holbrook	724
Holicong	215
Holland	215
Hollidaysburg	814
Hollsopple	814
Hollywood	215
Holmes	610
Holtwood	717
Home	724
Homer	814
Homer City	724
Homestead	412
Homesville	570
Hometown	570
Homewood	412
Honesdale	570
Honey Brook	610
Honey Grove	717
Hookstown	724
Hooversville	814
Hop Bottom	570
Hopeland	717
Hopewell	814
Hopwood	724
Horningford	717
Horsham	215
Hosiery Corp Of America	215
Host	610
Hostetter	724
Houston	724
Housum	717
Houtzdale	814
Howard	814
Howe	717
Hoytville	570
Hublersburg	814
Hubley	570
Hudson	570
Huey	814
Hughestown	570
Hughesville	570
Hulmeville	215
Hummels Store	610
Hummels Wharf	570
Hummelstown	717
Hunker	724
Hunlock Creek	570
Hunlock Township	570
Hunlock Twp	570
Hunter	570
Hunters Run	717
Hunterstown	717
Huntersville	570
Huntingdon	814
Huntingdon Valley	215
Huntingdon Vy	215
Huntington Mills	570
Huntington Ml	570
Hustontown	717, 814
Hustontwn	814
Hutchinson	724
Hyde	814
Hyde Park	724
Hydetown	814
Hyndman	814
Hyner	570
I R S Service Center	215
Ickesburg	717
Idaville	717
Imler	814
Immaculata	610
Imperial	724
Independence	570
Indian Head	724
Indiana	724
Indiana Univ Of Pa	724
Indianola	412
Industry	724
Inez	814
Inglenook	717
Inglesmith	814
Ingomar	412
Ingram	412
Inkerman	570
Intercourse	717
Iola	570
Iona	717
Ironton	610
Ironville	717
Irvine	814
Irving	570
Irvona	814
Irwin	724
Isabella	724
Island Park	570
Ithan	610
Iva	717
Ivyland	215
Jackson	570
Jackson Center	724
Jackson Ctr	724
Jackson Hall	717
Jackson Smt	570
Jackson Township	570
Jackson Twp	570
Jacksonville	610
Jacksonwald	610
Jacobs Creek	724
Jacobs Mills	717
Jacobus	717
Jalappa	610
James City	814
James Creek	814
Jamestown	724
Jamison	215
Jamison City	570
Jarrettown	610
Jay Advertising	717
Jeannette	724
Jefferson	724
Jefferson Hills	412
Jefferson Hls	412
Jefferson Township	570
Jefferson Twp	570
Jeffersonville	610
Jeffersonvlle	610
Jenkins Township	570
Jenkins Twp	570
Jenkintown	215
Jenners	814
Jennerstown	814
Jericho Mills	717
Jermyn	570
Jerome	814
Jersey Mills	570
Jersey Shore	570
Jerseytown	570
Jessup	570
Jim Thorpe	570
Joanna	610
Jobs Corners	570
Joffre	724
Johnsonburg	814
Johnstown	814
Joliett	570
Jones Mills	814
Jonestown	717
Jonestwn	717
Josephine	724
Julian	814
Juneau	814
Junedale	570
Juniata Terr	717
Kane	814
Kantner	814
Kantz	570
Kapp Heights	570
Karns City	724
Karthaus	814
Kaseville	570
Kasiesville	717
Kaska	570
Kauffman	717
Keating	570
Keating Summit	814
Keech	814
Keeneyville	570
Kehley Run Junction	570
Keisterville	724
Kelayres	570
Kelleysburg	570
Kelly	570
Kelly Point	570
Kelly X Rds	570
Kellytown	570
Kelton	610
Kemblesville	610
Kempton	610
Kendall Creek	814
Kenhorst	610
Kennedy	570
Kennerdell	814
Kennett Sq	610
Kennett Square	610
Kent	724
Kepner	570
Kerrstown	717
Kerrstown Sq	717
Kerrtown	814
Kersey	814
Kilbuck	412
Killinger	717
Kimberton	610
Kinderhook	717
Kindts Corner	610
King Of Prussia	610
Kingsdale	717
Kingsley	570
Kingston	570
Kinney	814
Kintnersville	610
Kinzers	717
Kirklyn	610
Kirkwood	717
Kissel Hill	717
Kissimmee	570
Kittanning	724

City	Area Code
Kleinfeltersv	717
Kleinfeltersville	717
Klines Corner	610
Klines Grove	570
Klingerstown	570
Klondyke	717
Knapp	570
Knauers	610
Kng Of Prussa	610
Knightsville	814
Knobsville	717
Knoebels Grv	570
Knousetown	717
Knox	814
Knox Dale	814
Knoxville	814
Kohinoor Junction	570
Koppel	724
Korn Krest	570
Kossuth	814
Kratzerville	570
Kreamer	570
Kresgeville	610
Kreutz Creek	717
Krumsville	610
Kulp	570
Kulpmont	570
Kulpsville	215
Kulptown	610
Kunkletown	610
Kutztown	610
Kylertown	814
Kyleville	717
La Belle	724
La Jose	814
La Plume	570
Laceyville	570
Lack	814
Lackawaxen	570
Ladona	814
Lafayette Hill	610
Lafayette Hl	610
Laflin	570
Lahaska	215
Lairdsville	570
Lake Ariel	570
Lake City	814
Lake Como	570
Lake Harmony	570
Lake Lynn	724
Lake Winola	570
Lakeville	570
Lakewood	570
Lamar	570
Lamartine	814
Lamberton	724
Lambs Creek	570
Lamott	215
Lampeter	717
Lancaster	717
Lancaster Junction	717
Landenberg	610
Landingville	570
Landis Store	610
Landisbg	717
Landisburg	717
Landisville	717
Lanesboro	570
Langeloth	724
Langhorne	215, 610
Lansdale	215
Lansdowne	610
Lanse	814
Lansford	570
Lapark	717
Laporte	570
Large	412
Larimer	724
Larksville	570
Larrys Creek	570
Larryville	570
Larue	717
Latrobe	724
Lattimer Mines	570
Lattimer Mnes	570
Laubachs	570
Laughlintown	724
Laurel Park	570
Laurel Run	570
Laureldale	610
Laurelton	570
Laurelville	717
Laurys Sta	610
Laurys Station	610
Lavelle	570
Laverock	215
Lawn	717
Lawncrest	215
Lawndale	215
Lawrence	724
Lawrence Park	610
Lawrenceville	570
Lawton	570
Layfield	610
Layton	724
Le Raysville	570
Leacock	717
Leaders Heights	717
Leaf Park	717
Leaman Place	717
Leb	717
Lebanon	717
Lebo	717
Leck Kill	570
Leckkill	570
Leckrone	724
Lecontes Mills	814
Lecontes Mls	814
Lederach	215
Leechburg	724
Leeper	814
Lees Cross Rd	717
Leesport	610
Leetonia	570
Leetsdale	724
Lehigh Valley	610
Lehighton	610
Lehman	570
Leibeyville	570
Leidy	570
Leisenring	724
Lemasters	717
Lemont	814
Lemont Fce	724
Lemont Frnc	724
Lemont Frnce	724
Lemont Furnace	724
Lemoyne	717
Lenhartsville	610
Lenkerville	717
Lenni	610
Lenoxville	570
Leola	717
Leolyn	570
Leraysville	570
Leroy	570
Lester	610
Letort	717
Letterkenny Army Depo	717
Level Corner	570
Levittown	215
Lewis Run	814
Lewisberry	717
Lewisburg	570
Lewistown	717
Lewistown Jun	717
Lewistwn	717
Lewisville	610
Lexington	717
Liberty	570
Liberty Square	717
Library	724
Licking Creek	717
Lickingville	814
Lightstreet	570
Ligonier	724
Lilly	814
Lima	610
Lime Ridge	570
Lime Rock	717
Lime Valley	717
Limekiln	610
Limeport	610
Limerick	610
Limestone	814
Limestonevle	570
Lincoln Colliery	570
Lincoln Heights	610
Lincoln Park	610
Lincoln Univ	610
Lincoln University	610
Linden	570
Line Lexington	215
Line Lxngtn	215
Line Mountain	570
Linesville	814
Linfield	610
Linglestown	717
Linntown	570
Linwood	610
Lionville	610
Lisburn	717
Listie	814
Listonburg	814
Lithia Sprs	570
Lititz	717
Little German	717
Little Kansas	717
Little Mahany	570
Little Marsh	814
Little Mdws	570
Little Meadows	570
Little Wash	717
Littlestown	717
Liverpool	717
Llanerch	610
Llewellyn	570
Loag	610
Lobachsville	610
Lochiel	570
Lock Haven	570
Locke Mills	717
Locust	570
Locust Gap	570
Locust Grove	717
Locust Point	717
Locust Run	717
Locustdale	570
Logan Mills	570
Loganton	570
Loganville	717
Londonderry	717
Long Pond	570
Longfellow	717
Longlevel	717
Longstown	717
Longswamp	610
Lopez	570
Lorane	610
Lorberry	570
Lords Valley	570
Lorenton	570
Loretto	814
Lost Creek	570
Lowber	724
Lower Augusta	570
Lower Burrell	724
Lower Chichester	610
Lower Gwynedd	215
Lower Longswamp	610
Lower Makefield	215
Lower Mifflin	717
Lower Paxton	717
Lower Shaft	570
Lower Swatara	717
Lowville	814
Loyalhanna	724
Loyalsock	570
Loyalsockvle	570
Loyalton	717
Loysburg	814
Loysville	717
Lucernemines	724
Lucinda	814
Lucky	717
Lucy Furnace	814
Ludlow	814
Luke Fidler	570
Lumberville	215
Lundys Lane	814
Lungerville	570
Lurgan	717
Luthersburg	814
Luxor	724
Luzerne	570
Lyc Co Airprt	570
Lycoming	570
Lykens	717
Lyndell	610
Lyndon	717
Lyndora	724
Lynn	610
Lynnewood Gardens	215
Lyon Station	610
Mable	570
Mac Arthur	724
Macarthur	724
Macedonia	717
Mackeyville	570
Macungie	610
Macys Dept Store	412
Maddensville	814
Madera	814
Madison	724
Madison Township	570
Madison Twp	570
Madisonburg	814
Mahaffey	814
Mahanoy	570
Mahanoy City	570
Mahanoy Cty	570
Mahanoy Cy	570
Mahanoy Plane	570
Mahoning	570
Mainesburg	570
Mainland	215
Mainsville	717
Mainville	570
Maitland	717
Maizeville	570
Malvern	610
Mammoth	724
Manatawny	610
Manayunk	215
Manchester	717
Mandata	570
Manhattan	814
Manheim	717
Mann	814
Manns Choice	814
Mannsville	717
Manoa	610
Manor	610, 724
Manor Ridge	717
Manorville	724
Mansfield	570
Mansville	717
Maple Glen	215
Maple Grove Park	610
Maple Hill	570
Mapleton Dep	814
Mapleton Depot	814
Mar Lin	570
Marble	814
Marchand	724
Marcus Hook	610
Marianna	724
Marienville	814
Marietta	717
Marion	717
Marion Center	724
Marion Height	570
Marion Heights	570
Markelsville	717
Markes	717
Markleton	814
Markleysburg	724
Marple Township	610
Mars	724
Marsh	610
Marsh Hill	570
Marsh Run	717
Marshalls Creek	570
Marshalls Crk	570
Marshallton	570
Marshlands	814
Marsteller	814
Marstown	570
Martic	717
Martic Forge	717
Marticville	717
Martin	724
Martindale	717
Martins Creek	610
Martinsburg	814
Marwood	724
Mary D	570
Marysville	717
Mascot	717
Mason Dixon	717
Masontown	724
Mastersonville	717
Matamoras	570
Mather	724
Mattawana	717
Mausdale	570
Maxatawny	610
Mayberry	570
Mayfield	570
Mayport	814
Maytown	717
Maze	717
Mazeppa	570
Mc Alisterville	717
Mc Alistervl	717
Mc Alistervle	717
Mc Clellandtown	724
Mc Clure	717
Mc Conelstown	814
Mc Connellsbg	717
Mc Connellsburg	717, 814
Mc Connellstown	814
Mc Donald	724
Mc Elhattan	570
Mc Ewensville	570
Mc Gees Mills	814
Mc Grann	724
Mc Intyre	724
Mc Kean	814
Mc Kees Rocks	412
Mc Knight	412
Mc Knightstown	717
Mc Murray	724
Mc Sherrystown	717
Mc Veytown	717
Mcadoo	570
Mcalistervle	717
Mcclellan	717
Mcclellandtown	724
Mcclellandtwn	724
Mcclure	717
Mcconnellsburg	717
Mccoysville	717
Mccrea	717
Mccullochs Ml	717
Mcdonald	724
Mcelhattan	570
Mcewensville	570
Mcgees Mills	814
Mcgillstown	717
Mcgrann	724
Mcintyre	724
Mckean	814
Mckeansburg	570
Mckee Half Fl	570
Mckees Rocks	412
Mckeesport	412
Mcknight	412
Mcknightstown	717
Mclane	814
Mcmurray	724
Mcnett	570
Mcsherrystown	717
Mcsparren	717
Mcveytown	717
Mcveytwn	717
Mdby Center	570
Mdt	717
Meadia Heights	717
Meadow Gap	814
Meadow Lands	724
Meadowbrook	215
Meadowview	570
Meadville	814
Mech	717
Mechancsbrg	717
Mechanics Grove	717
Mechanicsburg	717
Mechanicsville	215
Mechanicsvlle	215
Mechbg	717
Mecks Corner	717
Media	610
Mehoopany	570
Meiser	570
Meiserville	570
Melcroft	724
Mellon Bank	412
Mellon Bank 1	412
Mellon Bank East	215
Melrose	215
Melrose Park	215
Mendenhall	610
Menges Mills	717
Menno	717
Mentcle	724
Mercer	724
Mercersburg	717
Meridian	724
Merion	610
Merion Park	610
Merion Sta	610
Merion Station	610
Merrian	570
Merrittstown	724
Mertztown	610
Meshoppen	570
Messiah Coll	717
Messiah College	717
Metal	717
Mexico	717
Meyersdale	814
Mid City East	215
Mid City West	215
Middle City East	215
Middle City West	215
Middle Creek	570
Middle Paxton	717
Middle Spring	717
Middlebry Ctr	570
Middleburg	570
Middlebury	570
Middlebury Center	570
Middleport	570
Middleswarth	570
Middletown	717
Middletown Twp	215
Middletwn	717
Midland	724
Midltwn	717
Midvalley	570
Midway	724
Mifflin	717
Mifflinburg	570
Mifflintown	717
Mifflinville	570
Milan	570
Milanville	570
Mildred	570
Mile Hill	570
Mile Run	570
Milesburg	814
Milford	570
Milford Sq	215
Milford Square	215
Mill Creek	717
Mill Crk	717
Mill Grove	570
Mill Hall	570
Mill Run	724
Mill Village	814
Millardsville	717
Millbach	717
Millbach Sprs	717
Millersbg	717
Millersburg	717

City	Area Code
Millerstown	717
Millersville	717
Millerton	570
Millheim	814
Millmont	570
Millport	814
Millrift	570
Mills	814
Millsboro	724
Millvale	412
Millville	570
Millway	717
Milmont Park	610
Milnesville	570
Milnor	717
Milroy	717
Milton	570
Milton Grove	717
Mina	814
Mineral Point	814
Mineral Spgs	814
Mineral Springs	814
Miners Mill	570
Minersville	570
Mingoville	814
Minisink Hills	570
Minisink Hls	570
Miquon	610
Mlcreek	717
Mocanaqua	570
Modena	610
Mohns Hill	610
Mohnton	610
Mohrsville	610
Molino	570
Molltown	610
Monaca	724
Monessen	724
Mongul	717
Monocacy Sta	610
Monocacy Station	610
Monongahela	724
Monroe Township	570
Monroe Twp	570
Monroeton	570
Monroeville	412
Mont Alto	717
Mont Clare	610
Montandon	570
Montgomery	570
Montgomery Fy	717
Montgomery Twp	215
Montgomeryville	215
Montgomeryvle	215
Montour	412
Montoursville	570
Montrose	570
Moon Township	412
Moon Twp	412
Mooresburg	570
Moosic	570
Morann	814
Mordansville	570
Morea	570
Morea Colliery	570
Moreland	570
Morgan	412
Morgantown	610
Morris	570
Morris Run	570
Morrisdale	814
Morrisville	215
Morton	610
Morysville	610
Moscow	570
Moselem	610
Moselem Springs	610
Moshannon	814
Mosherville	570
Moulstown	717
Mount Aetna	717
Mount Allen	717
Mount Bethel	570
Mount Braddock	724
Mount Carmel	570
Mount Cobb	570
Mount Gretna	717
Mount Holly Spgs	717
Mount Holly Springs	717
Mount Hope	717
Mount Jewett	814
Mount Joy	717
Mount Lebanon	412
Mount Morris	724
Mount Nebo	717
Mount Oliver	412
Mount Patrick	717
Mount Penn	610
Mount Pleasant	724
Mount Pleasant Mills	570
Mount Pocono	570
Mount Royal	717
Mount Tabor	717
Mount Union	814
Mount Washington	412
Mount Wilson	717
Mount Wolf	717
Mount Zion	717
Mountain Home	570
Mountain Top	570
Mountainhome	570
Mountville	717
Mowersville	717
Mowry	570
Moylan	610
Mt Aetna	717
Mt Braddock	724
Mt Carmel	570
Mt Carmel Township	570
Mt Gretna	717
Mt Gretna Hts	717
Mt Holly Spgs	717
Mt Holly Springs	717
Mt Home	570
Mt Lebanon	412
Mt Morris	724
Mt Oliver	412
Mt Penn	610
Mt Pleasant	724
Mt Pleasant M	570
Mt Pleasant Mills	570
Mt Plsnt Mills	570
Mt Union	814
Mt Washington	412
Muddy Creek Forks	717
Muhlenburg Park	610
Muir	717
Muncy	570
Muncy Creek	570
Muncy Valley	570
Munhall	412
Munson	814
Murrell	717
Murrysville	724
Muse	724
Myersdale	814
Myerstown	717
Myerstwn	717
N Bell Vernon	724
N Belle Vernon	724
N Belle Vrn	724
N Bend	570
N Cambria	814
N Charleroi	724
N Cornwall	717
N Cumberld	717
N Huntingdon	724
N Leechburg	724
N Londonderry	717
N Mountain	570
N Springfield	814
N Versailles	412
N Washington	724
Naginey	717
Nanticoke	570
Nanty Glo	814
Napierville	717
Narberth	610
Narvon	610
Nashville	717
Natalie	570
National City Bank	412
National City Of Pa	814
National Fulfillment Serv	610
National Passport Agency	215
Natl Agency For Check Inqu	724
Natrona Heights	724
Natrona Hts	724
Nauvoo	570
Navy Ships	717
Navy Sup Dpt	717
Nazareth	610
Ne Madison	717
Needmore	717
Neelyton	814
Neffs	610
Neffsville	717
Nelson	814
Nemacolin	724
Nescopeck	570
Neshannock	724
Nesquehoning	570
Nether Providence	610
Network Distribution Ct	724
Neville Is	412
Neville Island	412
New Albany	570
New Alexandri	724
New Alexandria	724
New Baltimore	814
New Bedford	724
New Berlin	570
New Berlins	610
New Berlinville	610
New Berlinvle	610
New Bethlehem	814
New Bloomfield	717
New Bloomfld	717
New Boston	570
New Bridgeville	717
New Brighton	724
New Britain	215
New Buffalo	717
New Castle	724
New Cmbrlnd	717
New Columbia	570
New Cumb	717
New Cumberland	717
New Cumberland Army D	717
New Cumberlnd	717
New Danville	717
New Derry	724
New Eagle	724
New Enterprise	814
New Entrprise	814
New Florence	724
New Franklin	717
New Freedom	717
New Freeport	724
New Galilee	724
New Geneva	724
New Germanton	717
New Germantown	717
New Hanover Twp	610
New Holland	717
New Hope	215
New Jerusalem	610
New Kensingtn	724
New Kensington	724
New Kingstown	717
New Londn Twp	610
New London	610
New London Township	610
New Market	717
New Milford	570
New Millport	814
New Milltown	717
New Mines	570
New Oxford	717
New Paris	814
New Park	717
New Phila	570
New Philadelphia	570
New Process Co	814
New Providence	717
New Providnce	717
New Ringgold	570
New Salem	724
New Schaefferstown	610
New Smithville	610
New Stanton	724
New Street	570
New Texas	717
New Tripoli	610
New Wilmington	724
New Wilmngtn	724
Newberry	570
Newberrytown	717
Newburg	717
Newcmbrlnd	717
Newell	724
Newfield	814
Newfoundland	570
Newlondon Twp	610
Newmanstown	717
Newport	717
Newportville	215
Newprt	717
Newry	814
Newtn Hamltn	814
Newton Hamilton	814
Newton Hamltn	814
Newtown	215
Newtown Sq	610
Newtown Square	610
Newville	717
Niantic	610
Nicholson	570
Nickel Mines	717
Nicktown	814
Niles Valley	570
Ninepoints	610
Nineveh	724
Nisbet	570
No Huntingdon	724
Noblestown	724
Nook	717
Nordmont	570
Normalville	724
Norristown	610
North American Outdoor Group	717
North Apollo	724
North Belle Vernon	724
North Bend	570
North Bingham	814
North Charleroi	724
North East	814
North Fork	814
North Heidelberg	610
North Hills	215
North Huntingdon	724
North Irwin	724
North Lebanon	717
North Leechburg	724
North Manheim	570
North Newton	717
North Springfield	814
North Union	570
North Versailles	412
North Wales	215
North Warren	814
North Washington	724
Northampton	610
Northern Cambria	814
Northpoint	814
Northumberland	570
Northumberlnd	570
Norvelt	724
Norwood	610
Nossville	814
Nottingham	610
Noxen	570
Noyes	570
Nu Mine	724
Nuangola	570
Numidia	570
Nuremberg	570
Nw Cumb	717
Nw Cumberland	717
Nw Cumberlnd	717
Nwprt	717
Nyesville	717
Oak Grove	570
Oak Lane	215
Oak Park	570
Oak Ridge	814
Oakdale	724
Oakford	215
Oakland	412
Oakland Mills	717
Oaklyn	570
Oakmont	412
Oakryn	717
Oaks	610
Oakview	610
Oberlin	717
Observatory	412
Odin	814
Office Of Personnel Mgmt	724
Ogden	610
Ogdensburg	570
Ogontz Campus	215
Ohiopyle	724
Oil City	814
Oil Creek	814
Okome	570
Olanta	814
Old Forge	570
Old Line	717
Old Lycoming	570
Old Port	717
Old Zionsville	610
Old Zionsvlle	610
Oley	610
Oley Furnace	610
Oliphant Furnace	724
Oliveburg	814
Oliver	724
Olyphant	570
Oneida	570
Ono	717
Ontelaunee	610
Opp	570
Orange	570
Orangeville	570
Orbisonia	814
Ore Valley	717
Orefield	610
Oregon	717
Oregon Hill	570
Oreland	215
Oreville	610
Oriental	717
Oriole	570
Ormsby	814
Orrstown	717
Orrtanna	717
Orson	570
Orviston	570
Orwigsburg	570
Orwin	717
Osceola	814
Osceola Mills	814
Osterburg	814
Oswayo	814
Ottawa	570
Ottsville	215
Outwood	570
Oval	570
Overbrook Hills	215
Overbrook Hls	215
Oxford	610
Oyster Point	717
Pa Blue Shield	717
Pa Furnace	814
Pageville	814
Paintersville	717
Palm	215
Palmdale	717
Palmer	610
Palmer Township	610
Palmer Twp	610
Palmerton	610
Palmyra	717
Palo Alto	570
Paoli	610
Paradise	717
Paradise Park	717
Paradise Valley	570
Paradise Vly	570
Pardeesville	570
Paris	724
Park	724
Park Heights	717
Park Hills	717
Park Place	570
Parker	724
Parker Ford	610
Parkerford	610
Parkesburg	610
Parkhill	814
Parkland	215
Parkside	610
Parkside Manor	610
Parkville	717
Parnassus	724
Parrs Mill	570
Parryville	610
Parsons	570
Parvin	570
Passmore	610
Passyunk	215
Patterson Heights	724
Patterson Hts	724
Pattersonville	570
Patton	814
Paupack	570
Paxinos	570
Paxtang	717
Paxtonia	717
Paxtonville	570
Peach Bottom	717
Peach Glen	717
Pealertown	570
Peckville	570
Pen Argyl	610
Pen Mar	717
Penbrook	717
Penfield	814
Penllyn	215
Penn	724
Penn Avon	570
Penn Ctr	215
Penn Hill	717
Penn Hills	412
Penn Mutual Ins Co	215
Penn Run	724
Penn St Univ	814
Penn State University	814
Penn Valley	610
Penn Wynne	610
Penndel	215
Pennersville	717
Penns Creek	570
Penns Park	215
Pennsburg	215
Pennsdale	570
Pennside	610
Pennsylvania Furnace	814
Pennville	717
Penryn	717
Pequea	717
Perdix	717
Perkasie	215
Perkiomenville	610
Perkiomenvlle	610
Perry	610
Perry Square	814
Perry Village	717
Perryopolis	724
Perryville	570
Perulack	717
Peters	717
Petersburg	814
Petrolia	724
Pgh	412
Pgh Int Arprt	724
Pheaa	717
Phila	215, 610
Philadelphia	215
Philadelphia Ndc	215
Philipsburg	814
Phillipsville	814
Phoenix Park	570
Phoenixville	610
Piatt	570

City	Area Code
Picture Rocks	570
Pike	610
Pikeville	610
Pilgrim Gardens	610
Pilgrim Gdns	610
Pillow	717
Pine Bank	724
Pine Creek	570
Pine Forge	610
Pine Grove	570
Pine Grove Furnace	717
Pine Grove Mills	814
Pine Grv Mls	814
Pine Hill	570
Pine Run	570
Pine Summit	570
Pine Swamp	610
Pine Village	570
Pinedale	570
Pinetown	717
Pineville	215
Pinola	717
Pipersville	215
Pitcairn	412
Pitman	570
Pitt	412
Pitts	412
Pittsburgh	412, 724
Pittsfield	814
Pittston	570
Pittston Township	570
Pittston Twp	570
Plainfield	717
Plains	570
Plains Township	570
Plains Twp	570
Plank	570
Pleasant Gap	814
Pleasant Hall	717
Pleasant Hill	717
Pleasant Hills	412
Pleasant Hls	412
Pleasant Mount	570
Pleasant Mt	570
Pleasant Strm	570
Pleasant Unity	724
Pleasant Unty	724
Pleasant View	717
Pleasantview	717
Pleasantville	814
Pleasureville	717
Plum	412
Plumsteadville	215
Plumsteadvlle	215
Plumville	724
Plunketts Crk	570
Plymouth	570
Plymouth Meeting	610
Plymouth Mtng	610
Plymouth Valley	610
Pnc Bank	215, 814
Pnc Bank Pitts	412
Pocono Lake	570
Pocono Lake Preserve	570
Pocono Lk Prs	570
Pocono Manor	570
Pocono Pines	570
Pocono Summit	570
Pocopson	610
Pogue	814
Point Marion	724
Point Pleasant	215
Polk	724
Polktown	717
Pomeroy	610
Pond Bank	717
Pont	814
Poplar Grove	717
Port Allegany	814
Port Carbon	570
Port Clinton	610
Port Griffith	570
Port Matilda	814
Port Royal	717
Port Trevortn	570
Port Trevorton	570
Port Vue	412
Portage	814
Porter	717
Porters Sideling	717
Portersville	724
Portland	570
Portland Mills	814
Portland Mls	814
Ports Sidling	717
Potter Brook	814
Pottersdale	814
Potts Grove	570
Pottsgrove	570
Pottstown	610
Pottsville	570
Powells Vly	717
Powys	570
Poyntelle	570
Presque Isle	814
Presto	412
Preston Hill	570
Preston Park	570
Pricedale	724
Pricetown	610
Primos	610
Primos Secane	610
Primos-Secane	610
Primrose	570
Pringle	570
Proctor	570
Prompton	570
Prospect	724
Prospect Park	610
Prospectville	215
Prosperity	724
Providence	570
Providian Agon	610
Pt Allegany	814
Pt Pleasant	215
Pt Royal	717
Pulaski	724
Punxsutawney	814
Puritan	814
Quakake	570
Quakertown	215
Quarryville	717
Quecreek	814
Queen	814
Queen City	570
Quentin	717
Quiggleville	570
Quincy	717
Qvc Network Inc	610, 717
Racine	724
Radnor	610
Rahns	610
Railroad	717
Ralpho	570
Ralston	570
Ramey	814
Ramsey	570
Rankin	412
Ranshaw	570
Ransom	570
Rauchtown	570
Rauschs	570
Raven Creek	570
Raven Run	570
Ravine	570
Rawlinsville	717
Raymond	814
Rea	724
Reading	610
Reading Sta	610
Reading Station	610
Reamstown	717
Rebersburg	814
Rebuck	570
Rector	724
Red Bank	570
Red Bridge	717
Red Cross	570
Red Hill	215
Red Lion	717
Red Rock	570
Redrun	717
Reed	717
Reed Station	570
Reeders	570
Reeders Grove	570
Reeds Gap	717
Reedsville	717
Refton	717
Rehrersburg	717
Reiffton	610
Reilly	570
Reinerton	717
Reinholds	717
Reistville	717
Renfrew	724
Rennerdale	412
Reno	814
Renovo	570
Republic	724
Revere	610
Revloc	814
Rew	814
Reward	717
Rexford	814
Rexmont	717
Reynoldsville	814
Rhawnhurst	215
Rheems	717
Rices Landing	724
Riceville	814
Richards Grv	570
Richboro	215
Richeyville	724
Richfield	717
Richland	717
Richlandtown	215
Richmond Furn	717
Richmondale	570
Richvale	814
Riddlesburg	814
Ridgeville	570
Ridgewood	610
Ridgway	814
Ridley	610
Ridley Park	610
Riegelsville	610
Rife	717
Rillton	724
Rimersburg	814
Rinely	717
Ringgold	814
Ringtown	570
River View Park	610
Rixford	814
Roadside	717
Roaring Bk Tp	570
Roaring Branch	570
Roaring Brnch	570
Roaring Brook Twp	570
Roaring Creek	570
Roaring Spg	814
Roaring Spring	814
Robertsdale	814
Robeson	610
Robesonia	610
Robinson	724
Rocherty	717
Rochester	724
Rochester Mills	724
Rochester Mls	724
Rock Glen	570
Rockefeller	570
Rockhill Furn	814
Rockhill Furnace	814
Rockland	610
Rockledge	215
Rockrimmin Ridge	717
Rockton	814
Rockwood	814
Rocky Grove	814
Rodale Press	610
Roedersville	570
Rogersville	724
Roherstown	717
Rohrerstown	717
Rohrsburg	570
Romansville	610
Rome	570
Ronco	724
Ronks	717
Rook	412
Roscoe	724
Rose Tree	610
Rose Valley	610
Roseann	717
Rosecrans	570
Rosemont	610
Roseto	610
Roseville	717
Roslyn	215
Ross Siding	570
Rossiter	724
Rossville	717
Rote	570
Rothsville	717
Rough And Ready	570
Roulette	814
Rouseville	814
Rouzerville	717
Rowland	570
Roxbury	717
Royalton	717
Royersford	610
Rudytown	717
Ruffs Dale	724
Rupert	570
Rural Ridge	412
Rural Valley	724
Ruscmbmnr Twp	610
Ruscombmanor Twp	610
Rush	717
Rushland	215
Rushtown	570
Rushville	570
Russell	814
Russellton	724
Rutland	570
Rutledge	610
Rydal	215
Ryde	717
Ryeland	610
S Abingtn Twp	570
S Abington Twp	570
S Connellsvl	724
S Connelsvl	724
S Londonderry	717
S Montrose	570
S Mountain	717
S Pymatuning Twp	724
S Sterling	570
S Williamspor	570
S Williamsport	570
S Williamsprt	570
Sabinsville	814
Sacramento	570
Sadsburyville	610
Saegertown	814
Safe Harbor	717
Sagamore	724
Sagamore Hill	570
Saginaw	717
Sagon	570
Saint Benedict	814
Saint Boniface	814
Saint Clair	570
Saint Clairsv	814
Saint Clairsville	814
Saint Davids	610
Saint Johns	570
Saint Lawrence	610
Saint Marys	814
Saint Michael	814
Saint Peters	610
Saint Petersburg	724
Saint Thomas	717
Salford	215
Salfordville	215
Salina	724
Salisbury	814
Salix	814
Salladasburg	570
Salona	570
Saltillo	814
Saltsburg	724
Salunga	717
Saluvia	717
Sanatoga	610
Sandbeach	717
Sandy Lake	724
Sandy Ridge	814
Sarver	724
Sassamansville	610
Sassamansvlle	610
Saville	717
Saxonburg	724
Saxton	814
Saylorsburg	570
Sayre	570
Scandia	814
Scenery Hill	724
Schaefferstown	717
Schaefferstwn	717
Schellsburg	814
Schenley	724
Schnecksville	610
Schoeneck	717
Schoentown	570
Schofer	610
Schubert	717
Schultzville	610
Schuykl Havn	570
Schuyler	570
Schuylkill Haven	570
Schwenksville	610
Sci Cresson	814
Sci Houtzdale	814
Sci Huntingdon	814
Sci Somerset	814
Sciota	570
Scotland	717
Scotrun	570
Scott Township	570
Scott Twp	570
Scottdale	724
Scranton	570
Scyoc	717
Seagers	570
Seanor	814
Sebring	570
Secane	610
Selea	814
Selective Service System	215
Selinsgrove	570
Sellersville	215
Seltzer	570
Seminole	814
Seneca	814
Sereno	570
Seven Fields	724
Seven Pines	717
Seven Stars	717
Seven Valleys	717
Sevenpoints	570
Seward	814
Sewickley	412
Seyfert	610
Shade Gap	814
Shade Valley	814
Shady Grove	717
Shadyside	412
Shaft	570
Shamokin	570
Shamokin Dam	570
Shamrock Station	610
Shanesville	610
Shanksville	814
Shared Return Zip	610
Sharon	724
Sharon Hill	610
Sharpsburg	412
Sharpsville	724
Shartlesville	610
Shavertown	570
Shawanese	570
Shawnee	570
Shawnee On De	570
Shawnee On Delaware	570
Shawville	814
Sheakleyville	724
Sheffield	814
Shellsville	717
Shelocta	724
Shenandoah	570
Shenandoah Heights	570
Shenandoah Junction	570
Shenango	724
Shenks Ferry	717
Shepherdstown	717
Sheppton	570
Sheridan	717
Shermans Dale	717
Shermansdale	717
Shickshinny	570
Shillington	610
Shiloh	717
Shimpstown	717
Shindle	717
Shinglehouse	814
Shinglehse	814
Shintown	570
Shippen	570
Shippensburg	717
Shippenville	814
Shippingport	724
Shiremanstown	717
Shirleysburg	814
Shocks Mills	717
Shoemakers	570
Shoemakersville	610
Shoemakersvle	610
Shohola	570
Shope Gardens	717
Shorbes Hill	717
Shortsville	570
Shraders	717
Shrewsbury	717
Shumans	570
Shunk	570
Siddonsburg	717
Sidman	814
Sigel	814
Siglerville	717
Silver Creek	570
Silver Ford	814
Silver Lake	717
Silver Spring	717
Silverdale	215
Simpson	570
Singersville	717
Sinking Spg	610
Sinking Spring	610
Sinnamahoning	814
Sinsheim	717
Sipes Mill	717
Sipesville	814
Six Mile Run	814
Skippack	610
Skytop	570
Slackwater	717
Slate Hill	717
Slate Run	570
Slatedale	610
Slateville	610
Slatington	610
Slickville	724
Sligo	814
Slippery Rock	724
Slovan	724
Smethport	814
Smicksburg	814
Smithfield	724
Smithmill	814
Smithton	724
Smithville	717
Smock	724
Smokerun	814
Smoketown	717
Smyrna	610
Snedekerville	570
Snow Shoe	814
Snyder Corner	717
Snyders	570
Snydersburg	814
Snydertown	570

City	Area Code
Soc Auto Engineers	724
Social Sec Admin	570
Social Security Admin	570, 724
Solebury	215
Somers Lane	570
Somerset	814
Sonestown	570
Soradoville	717
Soudersburg	717
Souderton	215
South Abington Township	570
South Canaan	570
South Creek	570
South Enola	717
South Erie	814
South Fork	814
South Gibson	570
South Hanover	717
South Heights	724
South Hermitage	610
South Hills	412
South Hills Village	412
South Manheim	570
South Middleton	717
South Montrose	570
South Mountain	717
South Newton	717
South Park	724
South Renovo	570
South Sterling	570
South Waverly	570
South Williamsport	570
Southampton	215
Southeastern	610
Southview	724
Southwest	724
Spangler	814
Spangsville	610
Spartansburg	814
Spears Grove	717
Specktown	717
Speedwell	717
Spinnerstown	215
Sporting Hill	717
Spraggs	724
Sprankle Mills	814
Sprankle Mls	814
Spring Brook Township	570
Spring Church	724
Spring City	610
Spring Creek	814
Spring Glen	717
Spring Grove	717
Spring House	215
Spring Mills	814
Spring Mount	610
Spring Run	717
Spring Valley	610
Springboro	814
Springdale	724
Springfield	215, 610
Springhouse	215
Springmont	610
Springs	814
Springtown	610
Springvale	717
Springville	570
Sprng Brk Twp	570
Sproul	814
Spruce Creek	814
Spruce Hill	717
Spry	717
Squirrel Hill	412
St Benedict	814
St Boniface	814
St Clairsville	814
St Clrsville	814
St Davids	610
St Lawrence	610
St Marys	814
St Nicholas	570
St Peters	610
St Petersburg	724
St Thomas	717
Stack Town	717
Stahlstown	724
Stanhope	570
Star Junction	724
Starford	724
Starlight	570
Starners Station	717
Starr	814
Starrucca	570
Starview	717
State College	814
State Correctional Inst	570
State Dept Of Education	717
State Employment Security	717
State Farm Insurance	610
State General Services	717
State Line	717
State Liquor Control	717
State Of Pennsylvania	717
Steelstown	717
Steelton	717
Steelville	610
Steinsville	610
Sterling	570
Stevens	717
Stevensville	570
Stewartstown	717
Sticks	717
Stillwater	570
Stockdale	724
Stockertown	610
Stokesdale	570
Stoneboro	724
Stonersville	610
Stonetown	610
Stoneybreak	717
Stonington	570
Stony Creek Mills	610
Stony Run	610
Stonybrook	717
Stonyfork	570
Stouchsburg	610
Stoufferstown	717
Stoughstown	717
Stoverdale	717
Stoverstown	717
Stowe	610
Stoystown	814
Strabane	724
Strafford	610
Strasburg	717
Strattanville	814
Strausstown	610
Strawberry Rg	570
Strawbridge	570
Stricklerstwn	717
Strinestown	717
Strodes Mills	717
Strong	570
Strongstown	814
Stroudsburg	570
Stump Creek	814
Sturgeon	412
Sturges	570
Suedburg	570
Sugar Grove	814
Sugar Notch	570
Sugar Run	570
Sugargrove	814
Sugarloaf	570
Sullivan	570
Summerdale	717
Summerhill	814
Summerville	814
Summit	814
Summit Hill	570
Summit Sta	570
Summit Station	570
Sumneytown	215
Sunbeam	717
Sunbury	570
Sunderlinvle	814
Sunmark Industries	215
Sunnyburn	717
Sunnyside	570
Sunset Pines	570
Suplee	610
Susquehanna	570
Sutersville	724
Sw Madison	717
Swales	717
Swarthmore	610
Swartzville	717
Swatara	717
Swatara Sta	717
Sweden	814
Sweden Valley	814
Sweet Valley	570
Swengel	570
Swiftwater	570
Swineford	570
Swissdale	717
Swissvale	412
Swoyersville	570
Sybertsville	570
Sycamore	724
Sykesville	814
Sylvan	717
Sylvan Dell	570
Sylvania	570
Syner	717
T V Guide	610
Table Rock	717
Tafton	570
Talmage	717
Talmar	570
Tamaqua	570
Tamiment	570
Tannersville	570
Tarentum	724
Tarrs	724
Tatamy	610
Taylor	570
Taylorstown	724
Taylorville	570
Telford	215
Tell	814
Temple	610
Templeton	724
Terre Hill	717
Tharptown	570
The Vanguard Group	610
Thomasville	717
Thompson	570
Thompsontown	717
Thorndale	610
Thornhurst	570
Thornton	610
Three Springs	814
Throop	570
Tidioute	814
Tilden	610
Timblin	814
Times Publishing Co	814
Tinicum	610
Tinicum Township	610
Tioga	570
Tiona	814
Tionesta	814
Tipton	814
Tire Hill	814
Titusville	814
Tivoli	570
Toboyne	717
Tobyhanna	570
Todd	814
Toland	717
Tolna	717
Tomb	570
Tomstown	717
Topton	610
Torrance	724
Torresdale South	215
Toughkenamon	610
Towanda	570
Tower City	717
Towncrest Vlg	570
Townville	814
Traffic Safety	717
Trafford	412
Trainer	610
Transfer	724
Trappe	610
Tredyffrin	610
Treichlers	610
Tremont	570
Trenton	570
Tresckow	570
Trevorton	570
Trevose	215
Trexler	610
Trexlertown	610
Trindle Sprg	717
Trooper	610
Trout Run	570
Troutville	814
Troxelville	570
Troy	570
Trucksville	570
Trumbauersville	215
Trumbaursvlle	215
Trumbaversville	215
Tuckerton	610
Tullytown	215
Tulpehocken	717
Tunkhannock	570
Turbett	717
Turbotville	570
Turkey City	724
Turkey Run	570
Turkeyfoot	717
Turtle Creek	412
Turtlepoint	814
Tuscarora	570
Tuscarora Hts	717
Tusculam	717
Tv Guide Brm	610
Twin Oaks	610
Twin Rocks	814
Tyler Hill	570
Tylersburg	814
Tylersport	215
Tylersville	570
Tyrone	814
Uledi	724
Ulster	570
Ulysses	814
Union Center	570
Union City	814
Union Dale	570
Union Deposit	717
Union Fidelity Busi Reply	610
Union Fidelity Postage Pd	610
Union Mills	717
Uniontown	724
Unionville	610
Unisys	215
United	724
Unity House	570
Unityville	570
Univ Of Pittsburgh	412
Universal	412
University Park	814
University Pk	814
Upland	610
Upper Allen	717
Upper Augusta	570
Upper Bern	610
Upper Black Eddy	610
Upper Chichester	610
Upper Darby	610
Upper Dublin	610
Upper Fairfld	570
Upper Frankfd	717
Upper Gwynedd	215
Upper Holland	215
Upper Lawn	717
Upper Mahanoy	570
Upper Mahantongo	570
Upper Makefield	215
Upper Mifflin	717
Upper Mill	717
Upper Paxton	717
Upper Providence	610
Upper Saint Clair	412
Upper St Clair	412
Upper Strasbg	717
Upper Tulpehocken	610
Upperstrasbrg	717
Upperstrasburg	717
Uppr Blck Edy	610
Uppr Chichstr	610
Uppr St Clair	412
Upr Makefield	215
Ups	570
Upton	717
Urban	570
Uriah	717
Ursina	814
Usps Eastern Region Hdqtrs	215
Usps Official	717
Utica	814
Uwchland	610
Valencia	724
Valier	814
Vallamont Hls	570
Valley	570
Valley Forge	610
Valley Furnace	570
Valley Township	610
Valley Twp	610
Valley View	570
Van Meter	724
Van Voorhis	724
Van Wert	717
Vanderbilt	724
Vandergrift	724
Vandling	570
Vanport	724
Venango	814
Venetia	724
Venus	814
Verdilla	570
Vere Cruz	717
Verizon	215
Verona	412
Vestaburg	724
Veterans Administration	215
Veterans Hospital	412
Vicksburg	570
Villa Maria	724
Village Green	610
Villanova	610
Vinemont	717
Vintage	717
Vintondale	814
Vira	717
Virginville	610
Voganville	717
Volant	724
Vowinckel	814
W Alexander	724
W Aliquippa	724
W Atlee Burpee Co	215
W Brandywine	610
W Bridgewater	724
W Chester	610
W Chillisquaq	570
W Cnshohocken	610
W Elizabeth	412
W Fairview	717
W Hazleton	570
W Homestead	412
W Leechburg	724
W Leisenring	724
W Middlesex	724
W Middletown	724
W Mifflin/Pleasant Hills	412
W Milton	570
W Pennsboro	717
W Pittsburg	724
W Salisbury	814
W Springfield	814
Wabash	412
Wachovia Bank	215
Wadesville	570
Wagner	717
Wagontown	610
Walker	717
Wall	412
Wallaceton	814
Waller	570
Wallingford	610
Wallis Run	570
Walnut Bottom	717
Walnut Grove	717
Walnutport	610
Walnuttown	610
Walston	814
Waltersburg	724
Waltonville	717
Wampum	724
Wanamakers	610
Wapwallopen	570
Ward	570
Warfordsburg	717
Warminster	215
Warren	814
Warren Center	570
Warren Industries	814
Warrendale	724
Warrensville	570
Warrington	215
Warrior Run	570
Warriors Mark	814
Warwick	215
Wash	724
Wash Boro	717
Washington	724
Washington Boro	717
Washington Crossing	215
Washington Ht	717
Washington Xing	215
Washingtonville	570
Washingtonvle	570
Water Gap	717
Waterfall	814
Waterford	814
Waterloo	717
Waterman	724
Waterville	570
Watrous	814
Watsontown	570
Watsonville	570
Watts	717
Wattsburg	814
Waverly	570
Wawa	610
Waymart	570
Wayne	610
Wayne Heights	717
Waynecastle	717
Waynesboro	717
Waynesburg	724
Waynesville	717
Weatherly	570
Weaverland	717
Weavertown	610
Webster	724
Webster Mills	717
Weedville	814
Weidmanville	717
Weigh Scale	570
Weikert	570
Weishample	570
Weissport	610
Wellersburg	814
Wells	570
Wells Tannery	814
Wellsboro	570
Wellsville	717
Welsh Run	717
Weltys	717
Wendel	724
Wernersville	610
Wertzville	717
Wescosville	610
Wesleyville	814
West Acres	570
West Alexander	724
West Aliquippa	724
West Annville	717
West Bangor	717
West Beaver	717
West Bingham	814
West Bradford	610
West Branch	814
West Brandywine	610
West Bridgewater	724
West Bristol	215
West Brownsville	724
West Brunswick	570

City	Area Code
West Buffalo	570
West Cameron	570
West Chester	610
West Chester University	610
West Conshohocken	610
West Cressona	570
West Decatur	814
West Donegal	717
West Easton	610
West Elizabeth	412
West End	717
West Enola	717
West Fairview	717
West Finley	724
West Grove	610
West Hamburg	610
West Hazleton	570
West Hemlock	570
West Hickory	814
West Homestead	412
West Lancaster	717
West Lawn	610
West Lebanon	724
West Leechburg	724
West Leisenring	724
West Leroy	570
West Middlesex	724
West Middletown	724
West Mifflin	412
West Mifflin Century Mall	412
West Milton	570
West Monocacy	610
West Nanticoke	570
West Newton	724
West Penn	570
West Pennsboro	717
West Perry	717
West Pike	814
West Pittsburg	724
West Pittston	570
West Point	215
West Reading	610
West Renovo	570
West Salisbury	814
West Springfield	814
West Sunbury	724
West View	412
West Willow	717
West Wyoming	570
West Wyomissing	610
West York	717
Westbrook Park	610
Westfield	814
Westfield Ter	717
Westford	724
Westland	724
Westline	814
Westminster College	724
Westmoreland City	724
Westmrlnd Cty	724
Weston	570
Weston Place	570
Westover	814
Westport	570
Westtown	610
Wetona	570
Wexford	724
Wheatfield	717
Wheatland	724
Wheelerville	570
Whitaker	412
White	724
White Bear	610
White Deer	570
White Hall	717
White Haven	570
White Horse	717
White Mills	570
White Oak	412
White Pine	570
Whitehall	610
Whitesprings	570
Whitney	724
Whitneyville	570
Whitsett	724
Whtdeer	570
Wickhaven	724
Wiconisco	717
Widnoon	724
Wiggans	570
Wila	717
Wilburton	570
Wilcox	814
Wildwood	724
Wilkes Barre	570
Wilkes Barre General Hsptl	570
Wilkes Barre Township	570
Wilkes University	570
Wilkinsburg	412
William Penn Annex East	215
William Penn Annex West	215
Williams	717
Williams Grv	717
Williams Township	610
Williams Twp	610
Williamsburg	814
Williamson	717
Williamsport	570
Williamstown	717
Willow	717
Willow Grove	215
Willow Hill	717
Willow Street	717
Willow View Heights	717
Wilmerding	412
Wilmore	814
Wilpen	724
Winburne	814
Wind Gap	610
Wind Ridge	724
Windber	814
Windfall	570
Winding Hill	717
Windsor	717
Windsor Castle	610
Windsor Park	717
Winfield	570
Wingate	814
Witmer	717
Wlks Barr Twp	570
Wm Penn Anx E	215
Wm Penn Anx W	215
Wolfs X Rds	717
Wolverton	570
Womelsdorf	610
Wood	814
Woodbine	717
Woodbury	814
Woodchoppertown	610
Woodland	814
Woodlyn	610
Woodward	570
Woolrich	570
Worcester	610
Worleytown	717
Worman	610
Wormleysbg	717
Wormleysburg	717
Worthington	724
Worthville	814
Woxall	215
Wrightsdale	717
Wrightstown	215
Wrightsville	717
Wshngtn Xing	215
Wyalusing	570
Wyano	724
Wycombe	215
Wyncote	215
Wyndham Hills	717
Wyndmoor	215
Wynnewood	610
Wyoming	570
Wyomissing	610
Wyomissing Hills	610
Wysox	570
Yardley	215
Yatesboro	724
Yatesville	570
Yeadon	610
Yeagertown	717
Yeagertwn	717
Yellow House	610
Yocumtown	717
Yoe	717
York	717
York Haven	717
York New Salem	717
York Nw Salem	717
York Road	717
York Springs	717
Yorkana	717
Yorklyn	717
Yorkshire	717
Youngdale	570
Youngstown	724
Youngsville	814
Youngwood	724
Yukon	724
Zelienople	724
Zerbe	570
Zieglersville	610
Zieglerville	610
Zion Grove	570
Zionhill	610
Zionsville	610
Zooks Corner	717
Zooks Dam	717
Zullinger	717

Puerto Rico

City	Area Code
All Points	787

Rhode Island

City	Area Code
All Points	401

South Carolina

City	Area Code
Abbeville	864
Abney	803
Adams Run	843
Aiken	803
Alcolu	803
Alcot	803
Allendale	803
Alvin	843
And	864
Anderson	864
Andrews	843
Antioch	803
Arcadia	864
Arcadia Lakes	803
Ashland	803
Ashton	843
Atkins	803
Atlantic Bch	843
Atlantic Beach	843
Awendaw	843
Aynor	843
Ballentine	803
Bamberg	803
Baptist Medical Center	803
Barkersville	843
Barnwell	803
Barr	803
Barton	803
Batesburg	803
Batesburg-Leesville	803
Batesville	864
Bath	803
Batsbrg-Levil	803
Bayview	803
Beaufort	843
Beckhamville	803
Beech Island	803
Bell South	803
Bellinger	843
Belton	864
Belvedere	803
Bendale	803
Bennettsville	843
Berlin	803
Bethcar	803
Bethera	843
Bethune	843
Bigcreek	864
Bishopville	803
Blacksburg	864
Blackstock	803
Blackville	803
Blair	803
Blake	843
Blenheim	843
Bloomville	803
Blue Cross Blue Shield Od Sc	803
Bluff Estates	803
Bluffton	843
Blythewood	803
Bmg Columbia House Acs	864
Bmg Columbia Hse Music Club	864
Bmg Columbia Hse Video Club	864
Bob Jones University	864
Boiling Spgs	864
Boiling Springs	864
Bolen Town	803
Bon Air	803
Bonneau	843
Bordeaux	864
Borden	803
Bowling Green	803
Bowman	803
Bowyer	803
Boykin	803
Bradley	864
Branchville	803
Breeze Hill	803
Brighton	803
Brighton Beach	843
Brittons Neck	843
Britts	864
Brogdon	803
Brunson	803
Bucksport	843
Buffalo	864
Burnettown	803
Burton Branch	843
Cades	843
Cainhoy	843
Calhoun Falls	864
Callawassie Island	843
Callison	864
Camden	803
Cameron	803
Campobello	864
Canadys	843
Capitol	803
Capitol View	803
Carlisle	864
Carolina Forest	843
Cartersville	843
Cassatt	843
Catawba	803
Cateechee	864
Cayce	803
Cayce-W Cola	803
Cayce-West Columbia	803
Cedar Terrace	803
Centenary	843
Central	864
Ch Hgts	843
Chapin	803
Chappells	864
Charleston	843
Charleston Afb	843
Charleston Heights	843
Charleston Hts	843
Chas	843
Chas Afb	843
Chas Hgts	843
Cheraw	843
Cherokee Falls	864
Cherokee Fls	864
Cherry Grove	843
Cherry Grove Beach	843
Chesnee	864
Chester	803
Chesterfield	843
City Of Columbia	803
Clarks Hill	864
Clearwater	803
Clemson	864
Clemson University	864
Cleora	803
Cleveland	864
Clifton	864
Clinton	864
Clio	843
Clover	803
Clyde	843
College Park	843
Colliers	864
Columbia	803
Columbia Amf	803
Conestee	864
Congaree	803
Converse	864
Conway	843
Coosaw	843
Coosawhatchie	843
Cope	803
Cordesville	843
Cordova	803
Cornwell	803
Cottageville	843
Coward	843
Cowpens	864
Crafts Farrow	803
Crane Forest	803
Crescent Beach	843
Creston	803
Crocketville	803
Cross	843
Cross Anchor	864
Cross Hill	864
Cypress Crossroads	843
Dale	843
Dalzell	803
Daniel Island	843
Darlington	843
Dataw Island	843
Daufuskie Is	843
Daufuskie Island	843
Davis Crossroads	803
Davis Station	803
De Kalb	803
Dekalb	803
Delmar	803
Delta	803
Denmark	803
Denny Terrace	803
Dennys Corporation	864
Dewees Island	843
Dillon	843
Disney Direct Marketing	864
Dixiana	803
Donalds	864
Dorchester	843
Douglass	803
Drayton	864
Due West	864
Dunbarton	803
Duncan	864
Dunkins Mill	803
Dusty Bend	803
Dutch Fork	803
E I Dupont Co	803
Early Branch	843
Easley	864
Eastmont	803
Eastover	803
Eau Claire	803
Edgefield	803
Edgemoor	803
Edgewood	803
Edisto	843
Edisto Beach	843
Edisto Island	843
Edmund	803
Effingham	843
Ehrhardt	803
Elgin	803
Elko	803
Elliott	803
Elloree	803
Emory	864
Enoree	864
Estill	803
Eureka	803
Eutaw Springs	803
Eutawville	803
Fair Play	864
Fairfax	803
Fairfield	843
Fairfield Terrace	803
Fairforest	864
Fairview Crossroads	803
Farrow Terrace	803
Fechtig	843
Felderville	803
Fingerville	864
Five Points	803
Florence	843
Floyd Dale	843
Floyd Dl	843
Folly Beach	843
Forest Acres	803
Forest Lake	803
Foreston	803
Fork	843
Fort Jackson	803
Fort Lawn	803
Fort Mill	803
Fort Motte	803
Fountain Inn	864
Frens	803
Fripp Island	843
Frogmore	843
Fruit Hill	864
Ft Lawn	803
Ft Mill	803
Furman	803
Gable	803
Gadsden	803
Gaffney	864
Gaillard Crossroads	803
Galaxy	803
Galivants Ferry	843
Galivants Fry	843
Garden City	843
Garden City Beach	843
Gardens Corner	843
Garnett	803
Gaston	803
Georgetown	843
Gifford	803
Gilbert	803
Gillisonville	843
Glendale	864
Glenn Springs	864
Gloverville	803
Glympville	803
Goat Island Resort	803
Goose Creek	843
Gramling	864
Graniteville	803
Gray Court	864
Grays	843
Great Falls	803
Greeleyville	843
Green Pond	843
Green Sea	843
Greenbrier	803
Greenpond	843
Greenview	803
Greenville	864
Greenwood	864
Greer	864
Gresham	843
Grover	843
Gville	864
Gwd	864
H L Crossroads	803
Hagood	803
Hamer	843
Hammond Crossroads	803
Hampton	803
Hanahan	843
Harbison	803

- Harbville 843
- Hardeeville 843
- Harleyville 843
- Hartsville 843
- Haskell Heights 803
- Hazelwood Acres 803
- Heath Springs 803
- Hebron 843
- Hemingway 843
- Hibernia 803
- Hickory Grove 803
- Highway Four Forty One 803
- Hilda 803
- Hilton Head 843
- Hilton Head Island 843
- Hodges 864
- Holly Hill 803
- Hollywood 843
- Hollywood Hills 803
- Holtson Crossroads 803
- Honea Path 864
- Hopkins 803
- Horatio 803
- Horrel Hill 803
- Hosiery Corp Of America 803
- Hoyt Heights 803
- Huger 843
- Indian Land 803
- Inman 864
- Irmo 803
- Islandton 843
- Isle Of Palms 843
- Iva 864
- Jackson 803
- Jacksonboro 843
- James Island 843
- Jamestown 843
- Jamison 803
- Jefferson 843
- Jenkinsville 803
- Jericho 843
- Joanna 864
- Johns Island 843
- Johnsonville 843
- Johnston 803
- Jones Crossroads 803
- Jonesville 864
- Jordan 803
- Kathwood 803
- Kelton 864
- Kershaw 803
- Kiawah Island 843
- Killian 803
- Kinards 864
- Kings Creek 864
- Kingstree 843
- Kingville 803
- Kirkland 803
- Kirkwood 803
- Kitchings Mill 803
- Kline 803
- Kneece 803
- Knightsville 843
- La France 864
- Ladies Island 843
- Ladson 843
- Ladys Island 843
- Lake City 843
- Lake Murray 803
- Lake Murray Shores 803
- Lake View 843
- Lake Wylie 803
- Lamar 843
- Lancaster 803
- Lando 803
- Landrum 864
- Lane 843
- Langley 803
- Latta 843
- Laurel Bay 843
- Laurens 864
- Leeds 864
- Leesburg 803
- Leesville 803
- Lexington 803
- Liberty 864
- Liberty Hill 803
- Limehouse 843
- Lincolnshire 803
- Lincolnville 843
- Litchfield 843
- Little Mountain 803
- Little Mtn 803
- Little River 843
- Little Rock 843
- Livingston 803
- Lk Wylie 803
- Lobeco 843
- Lockhart 864
- Lodge 843
- Lone Star 803
- Long Creek 864
- Longs 843
- Longtown 803
- Loris 843
- Lowndesville 864
- Lucknow 803
- Lugoff 803
- Luray 803
- Lydia 843
- Lyman 864
- Lynchburg 803
- Macedon 803
- Madison 864
- Manning 803
- Manville 803
- Marietta 864
- Marion 843
- Market Center 803
- Martin 803
- Maryville 843
- Mauldin 864
- Mayesville 803
- Mayo 864
- Mc Bee 843
- Mc Clellanville 843
- Mc Coll 843
- Mc Connells 803
- Mc Cormick 864
- Mcbee 843
- Mcclellanville 843
- Mcclellanvle 843
- Mccoll 843
- Mcconnells 803
- Mccormick Correctional Inst 864
- Mccutchen Crossroads 803
- Mcentire Air National Guard 803
- Mckenzie Crossroads 843
- Mechanicsville 803
- Meeting Street 803
- Meggett 843
- Midway 803
- Miley 803
- Millford 803
- Minturn 843
- Mitchellville 843
- Mixville 803
- Modoc 864
- Moncks Corner 843
- Monetta 803
- Monticello 803
- Montmorenci 803
- Moore 864
- Moselle 843
- Motbridge 803
- Mount Carmel 864
- Mount Croghan 843
- Mount Pleasant 843
- Mountain Brook 843
- Mountain Rest 864
- Mountville 864
- Mt Pleasant 843
- Mullins 843
- Murrells Inlet 843
- Murrells Inlt 843
- Myrtle Beach 843
- N Charleston 843
- N Litchfield 843
- N Myrtle Bch 843
- N Myrtle Beach 843
- Naval Hospital 843
- Neeses 803
- Nesmith 843
- New Ellenton 803
- New Holland 803
- New Holland Crossroads 803
- New Zion 803
- Newberry 803
- Newry 864
- Nichols 843
- Ninety Six 864
- Nixville 803
- No Chas 843
- Norris 864
- North 803
- North Augusta 803
- North Charleston 843
- North Myrtle Beach 843
- North Pointe 803
- Northeast 803
- Norway 803
- Oak Dale 843
- Oakdale 843
- Oats 843
- Ocean Dr Beach 843
- Ocean Drive 843
- Ocean Drive Beach 843
- Okatie 843
- Olanta 843
- Olar 803
- Olympia 803
- Ora 864
- Orangeburg 803
- Osborn 843
- Oswego 803
- Pacolet 864
- Pacolet Mills 864
- Pageland 843
- Pamplico 843
- Panola 803
- Park Place 864
- Park Seed Co 864
- Parksville 864
- Parlers 803
- Parris Island 843
- Patrick 843
- Pauline 864
- Pawleys Is 843
- Pawleys Isl 843
- Pawleys Island 843
- Paxville 803
- Peak 803
- Pecan Way Terrace 803
- Pelion 803
- Pelzer 864
- Pendleton 864
- Peniel Crossroads 843
- Perry 803
- Pickens 864
- Piedmont 864
- Pinehaven 843
- Pineland 803
- Pineridge 803
- Pineville 843
- Pinewood 803
- Pinopolis 843
- Pisgah 803
- Pleasant Hill 803
- Pleasant Lane 803
- Plum Branch 864
- Pocataligo 843
- Pomaria 803
- Pontiac 803
- Port Royal 843
- Poston 843
- Powdersville 864
- Pritchardville 843
- Promised Land 864
- Prosperity 803
- Purysburgh 843
- Quinby 843
- Rains 843
- Rantowels 843
- Ravenel 843
- Ravenwood 803
- Red Bank 803
- Red Hill 803
- Reevesville 843
- Reidville 864
- Rembert 803
- Richburg 803
- Richland 864
- Richland Springs 864
- Ridge Spring 803
- Ridgeland 843
- Ridgeville 843
- Ridgeway 803
- Ridgewood 803
- Rimini 803
- Rion 803
- Ritter 843
- River Hills 803
- Robertville 803
- Robinson 843
- Rock Hill 803
- Rocky Springs 803
- Roebuck 864
- Round O 843
- Rowesville 803
- Ruby 843
- Ruffin 843
- Russellville 843
- S C Dept Of Motor Vehicles 803
- S C Electric And Gas 803
- S C Tax Comm 803
- S Of Border 843
- Saint Andrews 803
- Saint Charles 803
- Saint George 843
- Saint Helena Island 843
- Saint Matthews 803
- Saint Stephen 843
- Salem 864
- Salkehatchie 843
- Salley 803
- Salters 843
- Saluda 864
- Saluda Gardens 803
- Saluda Terrace 864
- Samaria 803
- Sandwood 803
- Sandy Springs 864
- Santee 803
- Sardinia 803
- Sardis 843
- Savannah River Plant 803
- Scotia 803
- Scottsville 803
- Scranton 843
- Seabrook 843
- Seabrook Isl 843
- Seabrook Island 843
- Seigling 803
- Seivern 803
- Sellers 843
- Seneca 864
- Shamokin 803
- Sharon 803
- Shaw A F B 803
- Shaw Afb 803
- Sheldon 843
- Shiloh 803
- Shirley 803
- Shoals Jct 864
- Shoals Junction 864
- Shulerville 843
- Silverstreet 864
- Simpsonville 864
- Singleton 803
- Six Mile 864
- Slater 864
- Slighs 803
- Smallwood 803
- Smoaks 843
- Smyrna 803
- Snelling 803
- Society Hill 843
- South Congaree 803
- South Lynchburg 803
- South Of The Border 843
- Spartanburg 864
- Spring Hill 803
- Spring Island 843
- Spring Mills 803
- Springdale 803
- Springfield 803
- Sptbg 864
- St Andrews 843
- St George 843
- St Helena Is 843
- St Matthews 803
- St Paul 803
- Stark Terrace 803
- Starr 864
- Startex 864
- State Hospital 803
- State Park 803
- Stateburg 803
- Steedman 803
- Stiefeltown 803
- Stockman 803
- Stokes Bridge 803
- Stoneboro 803
- Stoney Hill 803
- Stover 803
- Stuckey 843
- Sullivans Is 843
- Sullivans Island 843
- Summ 843
- Summerland 803
- Summerton 803
- Summerville 843
- Summit 803
- Sumter 803, 843
- Sun City 843
- Sunset 864
- Surfside 843
- Surfside Bch 843
- Surfside Beach 843
- Swansea 803
- Switzerland 843
- Sycamore 803
- Tamassee 864
- Tarboro 843
- Tatum 843
- Taxahaw 803
- Taylors 864
- Tega Cay 803
- The Citadel 843
- Thor 803
- Tigerville 864
- Tillman 843
- Timmonsville 843
- Townville 864
- Travelers Rest 864
- Travelers Rst 864
- Trenton 803
- Trio 843
- Troy 864
- Tuckertown 864
- Turbeville 843
- Twin Lake Hill 803
- Ulmer 803
- Una 864
- Union 864
- Union Crossroads 843
- Univ Of S C Students Mail 803
- University Of Sc 803
- Usc 803
- Van Wyck 803
- Vance 803
- Varnville 803
- Vaucluse 803
- Wachovia 803
- Wadmalaw Is 843
- Wadmalaw Island 843
- Wagener 803
- Walhalla 864
- Wallace 843
- Walterboro 843
- Wando 843
- Ward 803
- Ware Shoals 864
- Warrenville 803
- Wateree 803
- Waterloo 864
- Watsonia 803
- Wayside Nurseries 864
- Wedgefield 803
- Wellford 864
- West Columbia 803
- West Union 864
- Westminster 864
- Westover Acres 803
- Westside 864
- Westville 803
- White Bluff 803
- White Hall 843
- White Oak 803
- White Pond 803
- White Rock 803
- White Stone 864
- Whitehall 843
- Whitmire 803
- Williams 843
- Williamston 864
- Willington 864
- Williston 803
- Wilson 803
- Windsor 803
- Winnsboro 803
- Winnsboro Mills 803
- Wisacky 803
- Withrop College 803
- Woodrow 803
- Woodruff 864
- Woodward 803
- Workman 843
- Yemassee 843
- Yonges Island 843
- York 803

South Dakota

- All Points 605

Tennessee

- 1st Tennessee Bank 865
- Adams 615
- Adamsville 731
- Aetna 931
- Afton 423
- Alamo 731
- Alcoa 865
- Alexandria 615
- Algood 931
- Allardt 931
- Allisona 615
- Allons 931
- Allred 931
- Alpine 931
- Altamont 931
- Am Qui 615
- American General 615
- Andersonville 865
- Antioch 615
- Apison 423
- Ardmore 931
- Arlington 901
- Arnold A F B 931
- Arnold Air Force Base 931
- Arrington 615
- Arthur 423
- Ashland City 615
- Athens 423
- Atoka 901
- Atwood 731
- Auburntown 615
- Austin Peay St Univ 931
- Baileyton 423
- Bakewell 423
- Baneberry 865
- Baptist Hospital 615
- Barretville 901
- Bartlett 901
- Bath Springs 931
- Baxter 931
- Bean Station 865
- Beech Bluff 731
- Beechgrove 931
- Beershba Spgs 931
- Beersheba Springs 931

City	Area Code
Belfast	931
Bell Buckle	931
Bellevue	615
Bells	731
Belvidere	931
Bemis	731
Benton	423
Bethel Spgs	731
Bethel Springs	731
Bethesda	615
Bethpage	615
Big Rock	931
Big Sandy	731
Birchwood	423
Blaine	865
Blmngton Spgs	931
Bloomingdale	423
Bloomington Springs	931
Blountville	423
Bluff City	423
Bogota	731
Bolivar	731
Bon Aqua	931
Bone Cave	931
Braden	901
Bradford	731
Bradyville	931
Brentwood	615
Briceville	865
Brighton	901
Bristol	423
Brownsville	731
Bruceton	731
Brunswick	901
Brush Creek	615
Buchanan	731
Buena Vista	731
Buffalo Valley	615
Buffalo Vly	615
Bulls Gap	423
Bumpus Mills	931
Burlison	901
Burns	615
Burrville	423
Butler	423
Bybee	865
Byrdstown	931
Calhoun	423
Camden	731
Campaign	931
Cane Ridge	615
Carthage	615
Caryville	865
Castalian Spg	615
Castalian Springs	615
Castalin Spgs	615
Cedar Grove	731
Cedar Hill	615
Celina	931
Centerville	931
Chapel Hill	931
Chapmansboro	615
Charleston	423
Charlotte	615
Chatt	423
Chatta	423
Chattanooga	423
Chestnut Mnd	615
Chestnut Mound	615
Chewalla	731
Chickamauga	423
Christiana	931
Chuckey	423
Chucky	423
Church Hill	423
Clairfield	423
Clarkrange	931
Clarksburg	731
Clarksville	931
Cleveland	423
Cleveld	423
Clevelnd	423
Clifton	931
Clinton	865
Cloverdale	901
Cmbrlnd Frnce	615
Coalfield	865
Coalmont	931
Coble	931
Coker Creek	423
College Dale	423
College Grove	615
Collegedale	423
Collierville	901
Colliervl	901
Colliervle	901
Collinwood	931
Colonial Heights	423
Colonial Hgts	423
Columbia	931
Como	731
Conasauga	423
Concord	865
Concord Farr	865
Concord Farragut	865
Cookeville	931
Cookevl	931
Cookevle	931
Copperhill	423
Cordova	901
Cornersville	931
Corryton	865
Cosby	423
Cottage Grove	731
Cottontown	615
Counce	731
Covington	901
Cowan	931
Crab Orchard	931
Crawford	931
Crockett Mills	731
Crockett Mls	731
Cross Plains	615
Crosstown	901
Crossville	931
Crossvl	931
Crossvle	931
Crump	731
Cuba	901
Culleoka	931
Cumb Gap	423
Cumberland City	931
Cumberland Furnace	615
Cumberland Gap	423
Cumberland Gp	423
Cumberlnd Cty	931
Cunningham	931
Cypress Inn	931
Dandridge	865
Darden	731
Dayton	423
Decatur	423
Decaturville	731
Decherd	931
Deer Lodge	423
Defeated	615
Del Rio	423
Delano	423
Dellrose	931
Denmark	731
Denver	931
Devonia	865
Dickel	931
Dickson	615
Dixon Springs	615
Dixonville	901
Donelson	615
Dover	931
Dowelltown	615
Doyle	931
Dresden	731
Drummonds	901
Duck River	931
Ducktown	423
Duff	423
Dukedom	731
Dunlap	423
Dyer	731
Dyersburg	731
Eads	901
Eagan	423
Eagleville	615
East Acres	901
East Ridge	423
East Tn State Univ	423
Eaton	731
Eidson	423
Elgin	423
Elizabethton	423
Elkton	931
Ellendale	901
Elmwood	615
Elora	931
Emory Gap	865
Englewood	423
Enville	731
Erin	931
Erwin	423
Essary Springs	731
Estill Spgs	931
Estill Springs	931
Ethridge	931
Etowah	423
Etsu	423
Eva	931
Evensville	423
Fairfield	931
Fairfield Glade	931
Fairfld Glade	931
Fairfld Glde	931
Fairview	615
Fall Branch	423
Farner	423
Farragut	865
Fayetteville	931
Federal Express	901
Finger	731
Finley	731
First Tenn National Bank	901
Fisherville	901
Five Points	931
Flag Pond	423
Flatwoods	931
Flintville	931
Fort Donelson National Milit	931
Fort Pillow	731
Fosterville	931
Fountain City	865
Frankewing	931
Franklin	615
Fredonia	931
Friendship	731
Friendsville	865
Fruitvale	731
Gadsden	731
Gainesboro	931
Gallatin	615
Gallaway	901
Gassaway	615
Gates	731
Gatlinburg	865
Georgetown	423
Germantown	901
Gibson	731
Gilt Edge	901
Gladeville	615
Gleason	731
Glen Mary	423
Goodlettsville	615
Goodlettsvl	615
Goodlettsvle	615
Goodlettsvlle	615
Goodspring	931
Gordonsville	615
Grand Jct	731
Grand Junction	731
Grand View	423
Grandview	423
Granville	931
Gray	423
Graysville	423
Greenback	865
Greenbrier	615
Greeneville	423
Greenfield	731
Grimsley	931
Grinders	931
Gruetli	931
Gruetli Laager	931
Gruetli Laagr	931
Guild	423
Guys	731
Halls	731
Hampshire	931
Hampton	423
Happy Valley	865
Harriman	865
Harrison	423
Harrogate	423
Hartford	423
Hartsville	615
Heiskell	865
Helenwood	423
Henderson	731
Hendersonville	615
Hendersonvlle	615
Henning	731
Henry	731
Hermitage	615
Hickman	615
Hickory Hill	901
Hickory Point	931
Hickory Valley	731
Hickory Vly	731
Hilham	931
Hilldale	931
Hillsboro	931
Hixson	423
Hohenwald	931
Holladay	731
Hollow Rock	731
Home Shopping Network	423
Hornbeak	731
Hornsby	731
Humboldt	731
Huntingdon	731
Huntland	931
Huntsville	423
Huron	731
Hurricane Mills	931
Hurricne Mlls	931
I R S	901
Idlewild	731
Indian Mound	931
Ingram Entertainment Group	615
International Paper Co	901
Iron City	931
Jacks Creek	731
Jacksboro	423
Jackson	731
Jamestown	931
Jasper	423
Jc	423
Jeff City	865
Jefferson City	865
Jefferson Cty	865
Jellico	423
Jere Baxter	615
Joelton	615
Johnson City	423
Jonesboro	423
Jonesborough	423
Karns	865
Kelso	931
Kenton	731
Kerrville	901
Kimball	423
Kimberlin Heights	865
Kimberlin Hgt	865
Kimmins	931
Kingfield	615
Kingsport	423
Kingsport General	423
Kingston	865
Kingston Spgs	615
Kingston Springs	615
Knox	865
Knoxville	865
Knx	865
Kodak	865
Kville	865
Kyles Ford	423
La Fayette	615
La Follette	423
La Grange	731
La Vergne	615
Laager	931
Laconia	901
Lafayette	615
Lafollette	423
Lake City	865
Lakeland	901
Lakesite	423
Lancaster	615
Lancing	423
Lascassas	615
Laurel Blmry	423
Laurel Bloomery	423
Lavinia	731
Lawrenceburg	931
Lawton	731
Leach	731
Lebanon	615
Lenoir City	865
Lenox	731
Leoma	931
Lewisburg	931
Lexington	731
Liberty	615
Lifeway Christian Resources	615
Limestone	423
Linden	931
Livingston	931
Lobelville	931
Locke	901
Lone Mountain	423
Lookout Mountain	423
Lookout Mtn	423
Loretto	931
Loudon	865
Louisville	865
Lowland	865
Lucy	901
Lupton City	423
Luray	731
Luttrell	865
Lutts	931
Lyles	615
Lynchburg	931
Lynnville	931
Macon	901
Madison	615
Madisonville	423
Manchester	423, 931
Mansfield	731
Martin	731
Maryville	865
Mascot	865
Mason	901
Masonhall	731
Maury City	731
Maynardville	865
Mboro	615
Mc Clures Bend	615
Mc Donald	423
Mc Ewen	931
Mc Kenzie	731
Mc Lemoresville	731
Mc Lemoresvle	731
Mc Minnville	615
Mc Minnvl	615
Mc Minnvle	615
Mcewen	931
Mcghee Tyson Ang Base	865
Mclemoresville	731
Medina	731
Medon	731
Melrose	615
Mem	901
Memphis	901
Memphis Light Gas And Water	901
Memphis Networks Dist Ctr	901
Mercer	731
Michie	731
Middle Tenn State Univ	615
Middleton	731
Midtown	865
Midway	423
Milan	731
Milan Army Ammunition Plant	731
Milledgeville	731
Millersville	615
Milligan	423
Milligan Coll	423
Milligan College	423
Millingtn	901
Millington	731, 901
Milton	615
Minor Hill	931
Miston	731
Mitchellville	615
Mohawk	423
Monroe	931
Monteagle	931
Monterey	931
Mooresburg	865
Morley	423
Morris Chapel	731
Morrison	931
Morristown	423
Moscow	901
Mosheim	423
Moss	931
Mount Carmel	423
Mount Juliet	615
Mount Pleasant	931
Mountain City	423
Mountain Home	423
Mphs	901
Mt Carmel	423
Mt Juliet	615
Mt Pleasant	931
Mtn Home	423
Mulberry	931
Munford	901
Murfreesboro	615
Murfreesbr	615
Nashville	615
Nashville Elec Serv	615
Nashvl	615
Nashvle	615
National Pen Company	931
Natl Customer Support Ctr	901
Naval Hospital	901
Naval Personel Commnd	731
New Johnsonville	931
New Johsonvle	931
New Market	865
New Middleton	615
New River	423
New Tazewell	423, 865
Newbern	731
Newcomb	423
Newport	423
Niota	423
Nolensville	615
Norene	615
Norma	423
Normandy	931
Norris	865
Northeast	615
Nunnelly	931
Oak Ridge	865
Oakdale	423
Oakfield	731
Oakland	901
Obion	731
Ocoee	423
Old Fort	423
Old Hickory	615
Olivehill	931
Oliver Spgs	865
Oliver Springs	865
Oneida	423
Only	931
Ooltewah	423
Orlinda	615
Ozone	865
Pall Mall	931
Palmer	931
Palmersville	731
Palmyra	931
Paris	731
Parker Crossroads	731
Parker Xroads	731
Parrottsville	423

Parsons 731
Pegram 615
Pelham 931
Petersburg 931
Petros 423
Peytonsville 615
Philadelphia 423
Pickwick Dam 731
Pigeon Forge 865
Pikeville 423
Piney Flats 423
Pinson 731
Pioneer 423
Piperton 901
Piprtn 901
Plaza Tower 865
Pleasant Hill 931
Pleasant Shade 615
Pleasant Shde 615
Pleasant View 615
Pleasantville 931
Pocahontas 731
Portland 615
Postelle 423
Powder Spgs 865
Powder Springs 865
Powell 865
Powells Crossroads 423
Powells Crsrd 423
Primm Springs 931
Prospect 931
Pruden 423
Pulaski 931
Puryear 731
Quebeck 931
Quito 901
Ramer 731
Randolph 901
Ravenscroft 931
Readyville 615
Reagan 731
Red Bank 423
Red Blng Spgs 615
Red Boiling Springs 615
Regions Bank 615, 901
Reliance 423
Riceville 423
Rickman 931
Riddleton 615
Ridgely 731
Ridgetop 615
Ripley 731
Riverwatch 931
Rives 731
Roan Mountain 423
Robbins 423
Rock Bridge 615
Rock Island 931
Rockford 865
Rockvale 615
Rockwood 865
Rogersville 423
Rosemark 901
Rossville 901
Royal 931
Rudderville 615
Rugby 423
Russellville 423
Rutherford 731
Rutledge 865
S Pittsburg 423
Saint Andrews 931
Saint Joseph 931
Sale Creek 423
Saltillo 731
Samburg 731
Sango 931
Santa Fe 931
Sardis 731
Saulsbury 731
Savannah 731
Schering Plough Inc 901
Scotts Hill 731
Selmer 731
Sequatchie 423
Sevierville 865
Sewanee 931
Seymour 865
Shady Valley 423
Sharon 731
Sharp Electronic Manufac 901
Sharps Chapel 865
Shawanee 423
Shelbyville 615, 931
Sherwood 931
Shiloh 731
Shipps Bend 931
Signal Mountain 423
Signal Mtn 423
Silerton 731
Silver Point 931
Slayden 931
Smartt 931
Smithville 615
Smyrna 615
Sneedville 423
Soddy Daisy 423
Soddy-Daisy 423
Somerville 731, 901
South Fulton 731
South Pittsburg 423
Southside 931
Sparta 931
Speedwell 865
Spencer 931
Spring City 423
Spring Creek 731
Spring Hill 931
Springfield 615
Springville 731
St Joseph 931
Stanton 731
Stantonville 731
State Farm Ins Co 615
State Postal 615
Stewart 931
Straw Plains 865
Strawberry Plains 865
Sugar Tree 731
Summertown 931
Summitville 931
Sunbright 423
Suntrust Bank 615, 865, 901
Surgoinsville 423
Sweetwater 423
Taft 931
Talbott 865
Tallassee 865
Tate Springs 865
Tazewell 423
Telford 423
Tellico Plains 423
Tellico Plns 423
Ten Mile 865
Tenn Ridge 931
Tennessee Rdg 931
Tennessee Ridge 931
Thompsons Station 931
Thompsons Stn 931
Thorn Hill 423
Three Way 731
Tigrett 731
Tipton 901
Tiptonville 731
Tn Dept Of Revenue 615
Tn Dept Of Safety 615
Tn Ridge 931
Toone 731
Townsend 865
Tracy City 931
Trade 423
Treadway 423
Trenton 731
Trezevant 731
Trimble 731
Triune 615
Troy 731
Tullahoma 931
Turtletown 423
Tusculum Coll 423
Unicoi 423
Union City 731
Union Cty 731
Union Cy 731
Unionville 931
Univ Of Tn 901
University Of Memphis 901
University Of Tenn 865
University Of The South 931
University Of Tn 731
Us Postal Inspect Srvc 901
Vanderbilt Hospital 615
Vanderbilt University 615
Vanderbilt University Sta B 615
Vanleer 931
Viola 931
Vonore 423
Walland 865
Walling 931
Wartburg 423
Wartrace 931
Washburn 865
Watauga 423
Watertown 615
Watts Bar Dam 423
Waverly 931
Waynesboro 931
Westel 865
Westmoreland 615
Westpoint 931
Westport 731
White Bluff 615
White House 615
White Pine 865
Whites Creek 615
Whitesburg 423
Whiteside 423
Whiteville 731
Whitleyville 931
Whitwell 423
Wilder 931
Wildersville 731
Wilkinsville 901
Williamsport 931
Williston 901
Winchester 931
Winfield 423
Woodbine 615
Woodbury 931
Woodland Mills 731
Woodland Mls 731
Woodlawn 931
Woodstock 901
Wrigley 615
Wynnburg 731
Yorkville 731
Yuma 731

Texas

Abbott 254
Abernathy 806
Abilene 325
Abilene Christian Univ 325
Abram 956
Acacia Lake 956
Academy 254
Ace 936
Ackerly 432
Acton 817
Adams Gardens 956
Addicks 281
Addicks Barker 281
Addison 972
Adkins 210
Adrian 806
Afton 806
Aggieland 979
Agua Dulce 361
Agua Nueva 361
Aguilares 361
Aiken 806
Ala Coushatta Ind Res 936
Alamo 956
Alamo Heights 210
Alanreed 806
Alba 903
Albany 325
Albert 830
Aldine 281
Aledo 817
Alexanders Store 936
Alfred 361
Alfred P Hughes Unit 254
Algerita 325
Alice 361
Alief 281
Allen 972
Alleyton 979
Alliance Data Systems 210
Allison 806
Alpine 432
Alta Loma 409
Altair 979
Alto 936
Alto Springs 254
Alton 956
Alvarado 817
Alvin 281
Alvord 940
Amarillo 806
Amarillo College 806
Amarillo Globe News 806
Amarillo Hardware 806
Amer Income Life Ins 254
American Quarter Horse Assoc 806
Ames 936
Amherst 806
Ammansville 979
Anadarko 903
Anahuac 409
Anchor 979
Ander 361
Anderson 936
Andice 512
Andrews 432
Angelo State University 325
Angleton 979
Anna 972
Annona 903
Anson 325
Antelope 940
Anthony 915
Antioch 936
Anton 806
Apple Springs 936
Aquilla 254
Aransas Pass 361
Aranspass 361
Arcadia 409
Archer City 940
Arcola 281
Argenta 361
Argo 903
Argyle 940
Arlington 817, 972
Armstrong 361
Arneckeville 361
Arnett 254
Arp 903
Arroyo 956
Art 325
Artesia Wells 830
Arthur City 903
Asherton 830
Ashland 903
Ashwood 979
Asia 936
Aspermont 940
Astin 979
Astrodome 713
Astroworld 713
Atascocita 281
Atascosa 830
Ater 254
Athens 903
Atlanta 903
Aubrey 940
Augusta 936
Aurora 817
Austin 512
Austwell 361
Avalon 972
Avery 903
Avinger 903
Avoca 325
Avondale 956
Axtell 254
Azle 817
Bacliff 281
Bagwell 903
Bahia Mar 956
Bailey 903
Baileys Prairie 979
Baileyville 254
Baird 325
Balch Springs 972
Balcones 512
Balcones Heights 210
Balcones Hts 210
Baldwin 903
Ballinger 325
Balmorhea 432
Bammel 713
Bandera 830
Bangs 325
Bank Of America 214, 713, 817
Bank One 214
Bank One Mbank 512
Bank One Of Fort Worth 817
Bankersmith 830
Banquete 361
Barclay 254
Bardwell 972
Barker 281
Barkman 903
Barksdale 830
Barnes 936
Barnhart 325
Barnum 936
Barry 903
Barstow 432
Bartlett 254
Bartonville 940
Bascom 903
Bassett 903
Bastrop 512
Batesville 830
Batson 936
Baxter 903
Bay City 979
Bayou Vista 409
Bayside 361
Baytown 281
Bayview 956
Bayway 281
Beach 936
Beach City 281
Beasley 979
Beaukiss 512
Beaumont 409
Beaver Dam 903
Bebe 830
Beckville 903
Bedford 817
Bedias 936
Bee Cave 512
Bee Caves 512
Bee House 254
Beech Grove 409
Beeville 361
Belfalls 254
Bellaire 713
Bellevue 940
Bellmead 254
Bells 903
Bellview 979
Bellville 979
Bellvue 979
Belmont 830
Belott 936
Belton 254
Ben Arnold 254
Ben Bolt 361
Ben Franklin 903
Ben Hur 254
Ben Wheeler 903
Benavides 361
Benbrook 817
Benchley 979
Bend 325
Benjamin 940
Berclair 361
Berea 903
Bergheim 830
Berryville 903
Bertram 512
Best 325
Bethel 325
Beverly Hills 254
Beyersville 512
Bg Bnd Ntl Pk 432
Big Bend National Park 432
Big Lake 325
Big Sandy 903
Big Spring 432
Big Wells 830
Bigfoot 830
Biggs Field 915
Bighill 254
Billington 254
Birome 254
Bishop 361
Bivins 903
Bk Of America 214
Black 806
Blackfoot 903
Blackwell 325
Blair 325
Blanco 830
Blandlake 936
Blanket 325
Blanton 325
Bleakwood 409
Bledso 806
Bledsoe 806
Bleiblerville 979
Blessing 361
Blevins 254
Blocker 903
Blodgett 903
Bloomburg 903
Blooming Grove 903
Blooming Grv 903
Bloomington 361
Blossom 903
Blue 979
Blue Mound 817
Blue Ridge 972
Bluegrove 940
Bluetown 956
Bluff Dale 254
Bluff Springs 512
Bluffton 325
Blum 254
Blumenthal 830
Bluntzer 361
Bobville 936
Boca Chica 956
Boerne 830
Bogata 903
Boling 979
Bolivar 409
Bon Ami 409
Bon Wier 409
Bonham 903
Bonner 956
Bonney 979
Bonnie View 361
Booker 806
Booth 281
Borden 979
Bordersville 281
Borger 806
Bosqueville 254
Boston 903
Bovina 806
Bowie 940
Box Church 254
Boyd 940
Boys Ranch 806
Bracken 210
Brackettville 830
Bradford 903
Bradshaw 325

Brady	325
Brandon	254
Brashear	903
Brazoria	979
Brazos Point	254
Breckenridge	254
Bremond	254
Brenham	979
Breslau	361
Briarcliff	512
Briary	254
Bridge City	409
Bridgeport	940
Briggs	512
Brileytown	936
Briscoe	806
Broaddus	936
Brock	817
Bronson	409
Bronte	325
Brookeland	409
Brookesmith	325
Brooks Afb	210
Brooks Afb Branch	210
Brooks Cb	210
Brooks City Base	210
Brookshire	281
Brookside Village	281
Brookside Vl	281
Brookston	903
Browndell	409
Brownfield	806
Brownsboro	903
Brownsville	956
Brownwood	325
Bruceville	254
Bruceville Eddy	254
Brumley	903
Brundage	830
Bruni	361
Brushy Creek	512
Bryan	979
Bryans Mill	903
Bryson	940
Buchanan Dam	512
Buckeye	979
Buckholts	254
Buckhorn	979
Buckingham	972
Buda	512
Buffalo	903
Buffalo Gap	325
Buford	325
Bullard	903
Bulverde	830
Buna	409
Bunker Hill Village	713
Burkburnett	940
Burke	936
Burkett	325
Burkeville	409
Burleigh	979
Burleson	817
Burlington	254
Burnet	512
Burns	903
Burr	979
Burton	979
Bushland	806
Bustamante	361
Butler	903
Bville	956
Byers	940
Bynum	254
Cactus	806
Caddo	254
Caddo Mills	903
Caldwell	979
Caledonia	936
Calf Creek	325
Call	409
Calliham	361
Callisburg	940
Calvert	979
Calvin	512
Camden	936
Cameron	254
Camilla	936
Camp Mabry	512
Camp Strake	936
Camp Verde	830
Camp Wood	830
Campbell	903
Campbellton	830
Campo Alto	956
Campti	936
Canadian	806
Canton	903
Canutillo	915
Canyon	806
Canyon Lake	830
Capital Natl Tx Commrc Bank	512
Caplen	409
Caradan	325
Carbon	254
Carbondale	903
Cardinal Hall	903
Cardinal Sta	903
Carey	940
Carlisle	936
Carlos	936
Carlsbad	325
Carlton	254
Carmine	979
Carmona	936
Carolina Redemption Services	830
Carricitos	956
Carrizo Spgs	830
Carrizo Springs	830
Carrollton	972
Carterville	903
Carthage	903
Cason	903
Castell	325
Castle Hills	210
Castroville	830
Cat Spring	979
Catarina	830
Cave Springs	903
Cavitt	254
Cayuga	903
Cc	361
Cedar Creek	512
Cedar Hill	972
Cedar Lake	979
Cedar Lane	979
Cedar Park	512
Cedar Point	281
Cedar Springs	254
Cee Vee	940
Cego	254
Cele	512
Celeste	903
Celina	972
Center	936
Center Point	830
Centerview	903
Centerville	903
Central	936
Central Power & Light Co	361
Centralia	936
Cestohowa	830
Chaffee Village	254
Chalk	806
Chandler	903
Channelview	281
Channing	806
Chapel Hill	903
Chapman	903
Chapman Ranch	361
Chappell Hill	979
Charco	361
Charlotte	830
Chase Bank	713
Chase Bank Of Fort Worth	817
Chase Bank Of Texas	214
Chase Bank Of Tx	713
Chase Bank Texas	713
Chase Bank Tx	915
Chat	254
Chatfield	903
Cheapside	361
Checks In The Mail	830
Cheek	409
Cherokee	325
Cherry Spring	830
Chester	936
Chesterville	979
Chico	940
Chicota	903
Chihuahua	956
Childress	940
Chillicothe	940
Chilton	254
China	409
China Grove	210
China Spring	254
Chireno	936
Chita	936
Choice	936
Chriesman	979
Christine	830
Christoval	325
Church Hill	903
Cibolo	210
Cingular Wireless	817
Circleville	512
Cisco	254
Cistern	361
Citrus City	956
City By The Sea	361
City Of Lubbock	806
City Public Serv Board	210
City Water And Light Dept	512
Clairemont	325
Clarendon	806
Clark	281
Clarks	361
Clarksville	903
Clarksville City	903
Clarksvle Cty	903
Claude	806
Clay Hill	254
Clayton	903
Claytonville	325
Clear Creek	254
Clear Lake City	281
Clear Lake Shores	281
Clear Lk Shrs	281
Clearview	512
Cleburne	817
Clemville	979
Cleveland	281
Clifton	254
Clint	915
Clodine	281
Cloverleaf	713
Clowe And Cowan	806
Clutch City	713
Clute	979
Clyde	325
Coahoma	432
Cochran	979
Cockrell Hill	214
Coffee City	903
Colaboz	956
Coldspring	936
Coleman	325
College Hill	903
College Sta	979
College Station	979
Collegeport	361
Colleyville	817
Collinsville	903
Colmesneil	409
Cologne	361
Colonial Financial	817
Colorado City	325
Colton	512
Columbus	979
Comanche	325
Combes	956
Combine	972
Comby	956
Comfort	830
Commerce	903
Como	903
Comstock	432
Concan	830
Concepcion	361
Concord	903
Concrete	361
Cone	806
Connor	936
Conroe	281, 936
Content	325
Converse	210
Cookville	903
Coolidge	254
Cooper	903
Copano Village	361
Copeville	972
Coppell	972
Copper Canyon	972
Copperas Cove	254
Cordele	361
Corinth	940
Corley	903
Cornett	903
Corpus Christi	361
Corpus Christi Army Depot	361
Corpus Christi Naval Air Sta	361
Corral City	940
Corrigan	936
Corsicana	903
Cost	830
Cotton Center	806
Cotton Gin	254
Cottonwd Shrs	830
Cottonwood	936
Cottonwood Shores	830
Cotulla	830
County Line	903
Coupland	512
Cove	281
Cove Spring	903
Covington	254
Cox	903
Coy City	830
Coyanosa	432
Crabb	281
Crabbs Prairie	936
Craig	903
Craine Unit	254
Crandall	972
Crane	432
Cranfills Gap	254
Crawford	254
Crecy	936
Creedmoor	512
Crescent	979
Crescent Heights	903
Cresson	817
Crews	325
Crimcrest	903
Crockett	936
Crosby	281
Crosbyton	806
Cross Plains	254
Cross Roads	254
Crossroads	940
Crowell	940
Crowley	817
Crp Christi	361
Cruz Calle	361
Crystal Beach	409
Crystal City	830
Cty By The Se	361
Cuero	361
Cumby	903
Cuney	903
Cunningham	903
Currie	254
Curtis	409
Curvitas	956
Cushing	936
Cut	936
Cut And Shoot	936
Cuthbert	325
Cyclone	254
Cypress	281
Cypress Mill	830
D Hanis	830
Da Costa	361
Daffan	512
Daingerfield	903
Daisetta	936
Dalby Springs	903
Dale	512
Dalhart	806
Dallardsville	936
Dallas	214, 972
Dallas City Water Dept	214
Dalton	903
Dalworthington Gardens	817
Damon	979
Danbury	979
Danciger	979
Danevang	979
Darco	903
Darrouzett	806
Davilla	254
Davis Prairie	254
Davisville	903
Dawn	806
Dawson	254
Dayton	936
De Berry	903
De Kalb	903
De Leon	254
Deanville	979
Decatur	940
Decker Pr	281
Decker Prairie	281
Deer Park	281
Del Rio	830
Del Valle	512
Delhi	830
Dell City	432, 915
Dell Computers	512
Delmita	956
Delrose	903
Denhawken	830
Denison	903
Denning	936
Dennis	940
Denny	254
Denson Spring	936
Denton	940
Denver City	806
Deport	903
Dept Of Public Safety	512
Derby	830
Dermott	325
Desdemona	254
Desoto	972
Dessau	512
Detmold	512
Detroit	903
Devers	409
Devine	830
Deweyville	409
Dfw	972
Dfw Airport	972
Dialville	903
Diana	903
Diboll	936
Dickens	806
Dickinson	281
Dies	409
Dike	903
Dilley	830
Dilworth	830
Dime Box	979
Dimmitt	806
Dinero	361
Dinsmore	979
Dirgin	903
Divot	830
Doak Springs	979
Dobbin	936
Dodd City	903
Dodge	936
Dodson	806
Dogwood	409
Dogwood Acres	281
Dogwood City	903
Domino	903
Donie	254
Donna	956
Doole	325
Dorchester	903
Doss	830
Dot	254
Dotson	903
Double Oak	972
Doucette	409
Dougherty	806
Douglass	936
Douglassville	903
Drasco	325
Dreka	936
Dreyer	361
Driftwood	512
Dripping Spgs	512
Dripping Springs	512
Driscoll	361
Dryden	432
Dubina	979
Dublin	254
Duffau	254
Dumas	806
Dumont	806
Duncanville	972
Dundee	940
Dunlay	830
Dunn	325
Durango	254
Dyess Afb	325
E Texas Ctr	903
Eagle Lake	979
Eagle Pass	830
Early	325
Earth	806
East Bernard	979
East Columbia	979
East Hamilton	936
East Liberty	936
East Mayfield	409
East Mountain	903
East Side	903
East Tawakoni	903
Eastgate	936
Eastland	254
Easton	903
Ebenezer	903
Echo	325
Echols	254
Ecleto	830
Ector	903
Edcouch	956
Eddy	254
Eden	325
Edgar	361
Edge	979
Edgewood	903
Edgeworth	254
Edinburg	956
Edmonson	806
Edna	361
Edom	903
Edroy	361
Egypt	979
El Campo	979
El Cenizo	956
El Centro	956
El Gato	956
El Indio	830
El Jardin	956
El Lago	281
El Paso	915
El Paso Electric Co	915
El Paso Natural Gas	915
El Paso Water Utilities	915
El Sauz	956
El Toro	361
Elbert	940
Eldorado	325
Eldorado Afs	325
Electra	940
Electronic Security Services	210
Elgin	512
Eliasville	940
Elk	254
Elkhart	903
Ellinger	979

City	Area Code
Ellington Field	281
Elm Grove	979
Elm Mott	254
Elmaton	979
Elmendorf	210
Elmo	972
Elmwood	903
Eloise	254
Elroy	512
Elsa	956
Elwood	936
Elysian Fields	903
Elysian Flds	903
Emerald Bay	903
Emilee	409
Emmett	903
Emory	903
Enchanted Oak	903
Enchanted Oaks	903
Encinal	830
Encino	361
Energy	325
Engelman	956
Engle	979
Enloe	903
Ennis	972
Enoch	903
Enochs	806
Enterprise	903
Eola	325
Era	940
Erin	409
Escapees	936
Escapees Rv Club	936
Escobares	956
Escobas	361
Estelline	806
Estes	361
Etoile	936
Eula	325
Eulalie	936
Euless	817
Eulogy	254
Eustace	903
Evadale	409
Evant	254
Evergreen	281
Everitt	281
Everman	817
Ewell	903
Ezzell	361
Fabens	915
Fair Oaks	830
Fair Oaks Ranch	830
Fair Play	903
Fairchilds	979
Fairdale	409
Fairfield	903
Fairmount	409
Fairview	972
Faker	903
Falcon	956
Falcon Heights	956
Falcon Hts	956
Falcon Village	956
Falfurrias	361
Fallon	254
Falls City	830
Fannett	409
Fannin	361
Farmers Branch	972
Farmers Brnch	972
Farmersville	972
Farnsworth	806
Farrsville	409
Farwell	806
Fashing	830
Fate	972
Fayetteville	979
Faysville	956
Federal Aviation Administrat	817
Fedor	979
Fentress	512
Ferris	972
Fieldton	806
Fife	325
Figridge	409
Fincastle	903
Fink	903
Firm Cases	210
Fischer	830
Fisk	325
Fitze	936
Flat	254
Flat Fork	936
Flatonia	361
Flatwood	903
Flint	903
Flo	903
Flomot	806
Florence	254
Floresville	830
Flowella	361
Flower Mound	972
Flowermound	972
Floy	361
Floyd	903
Floydada	806
Fluvanna	806
Flynn	936
Follett	806
Fondren	281
Fords Corner	936
Fordtran	361
Forest	936
Forest Glade	254
Forest Hill	817
Forestburg	940
Forney	972
Forreston	972
Forsan	432
Fort Bliss	915
Fort Davis	432
Fort Gates	254
Fort Hancock	915
Fort Hood	254
Fort Mc Kavett	325
Fort Mckavett	325
Fort Ringgold	956
Fort Sam Houston	210
Fort Stockton	432
Fort Wolters	940
Fort Worth	817
Four Points	512
Fowlerton	830
Frame Switch	512
Francitas	361
Franklin	979
Frankston	903
Frankston Lake	903
Fred	409
Fredericksbg	830
Fredericksbrg	830
Fredericksburg	830
Fredonia	325
Freeport	979
Freer	361
Fresno	281
Freyburg	979
Friar	903
Friday	936
Friendship	512
Friendswood	281
Frio Town	830
Friona	806
Frisco	972
Fritch	806
Fronton	956
Frost	903
Fruitland	940
Fruitvale	903
Frydek	979
Ft Bliss	915
Ft Sm Houston	210
Ft Worth	817
Fulshear	281
Fulton	361
Fulton Beach	361
Furney Richardson	254
Fussel	903
Gail	806
Gainesville	940
Galena Park	713
Gallatin	903
Galloway	903
Galveston	409
Ganado	361
Gano	512
Garceno	956
Garciasville	956
Garden City	432
Garden Ridge	210
Garden Valley	903
Gardendale	432
Garfield	512
Garland	972
Garrison	936
Garth	281
Garwood	979
Gary	903
Gary City	903
Gatesville	254
Gause	512
Gay Hill	979
Geneva	409
George West	361
Georgetown	512, 979
Geronimo	830
Gholson	254
Gib Lewis Prison	409
Giddings	979
Gilchrist	409
Gill	903
Gillett	830
Gilmer	903
Girard	806
Girvin	432
Gladewater	903
Glaze City	361
Glazier	806
Glecker	979
Glen Flora	979
Glen Rose	254
Glendale	936
Glenn Heights	972
Glidden	979
Gober	903
Godley	817
Gold	830
Golden	903
Golden Acres	281
Goldsboro	325
Goldsmith	432
Goldthwaite	325
Goliad	361
Golinda	254
Gonzales	830
Goober Hill	936
Good Hope	936
Good Springs	903
Goodfellow Afb	325
Goodfellow Afb	325
Goodland	806
Goodrich	936
Goodville	254
Gordon	254
Gordonville	903
Goree	940
Gorman	254
Gouldbusk	325
Graceton	903
Graford	940
Graham	940
Granbury	817
Grand Bluff	903
Grand Prairie	214, 972
Grand Saline	903
Grandfalls	432
Grandview	817
Grange Hall	903
Granger	512
Grangerland	936
Granite Shls	830
Granite Shoals Lake Shores	325
Granjeno	956
Grape Creek	325
Grapeland	936
Grapevine	817
Gray	903
Grayburg	409
Green Lake	361
Greens Bayou	713
Greenville	903
Greenway Plaza	713
Greenwood	940
Gregg	512
Greggton	903
Gregory	361
Grey Forest	210
Grice	903
Gridiron	713
Griffin	903
Griffing	409
Griffing Park	409
Grigsby	936
Grindstone	903
Groesbeck	254
Groom	806
Grosvenor	325
Groves	409
Groveton	936
Grulla	956
Gruver	806
Gte	214
Guadalupe	361
Guajillo	361
Guerra	956
Gulf Oil	972
Gun Barrel City	903
Gun Barrel Cy	903
Gunter	903
Gustine	325
Guthrie	806
Guy	979
Guys Store	903
Haid	979
Hainesville	903
Halbert	936
Hale Center	806
Hallettsville	361
Hallsburg	254
Hallsville	903
Halsted	979
Haltom City	817
Hamby	325
Hamilton	254
Hamlin	325
Hammond	254
Hamon	830
Hamshire	409
Hankamer	409
Hanson	936
Happy	806
Happy Valley	325
Hardin	936
Hardin Simmons University	325
Hare	512
Hargill	956
Harker Heights	254
Harker Hts	254
Harkeyville	325
Harleton	903
Harlingen	956
Harmony	903
Harper	830
Harrisburg	409
Harrold	940
Hart	806
Hartley	806
Harvard	903
Harwood	830
Haskell	940
Haslam	936
Haslet	817
Hasse	325
Hatchel	325
Haukanier	409
Havana	956
Hawkins	903
Hawley	325
Headsville	254
Hearne	979
Heartland	972
Heath	972
Heathridge	972
Hebbronville	361
Hedley	806
Hedwig Village	713
Heidelberg	956
Heidenheimer	254
Heights	713
Helmic	936
Helotes	210
Hemphill	409
Hempstead	979
Henderson	903
Henkhaus	361
Henly	512
Henning	936
Henrietta	940
Henrys Chapel	903
Hereford	806
Hermleigh	325
Hewitt	254
Hext	325
Hgn	956
Hickory Creek	940
Hico	254
Hidalgo	956
Hidden Valley	936
Hide A Way	903
Hide A Way Lake	903
Hideaway	903
Higgins	806
High Hill	979
High Island	409
Highland Haven	830
Highland Havn	830
Highland Park	214
Highland Vill	972
Highland Village	972
Highlands	281
Hill	512
Hill Country Village	210
Hillcrest	979
Hillister	409
Hillje	979
Hills	512
Hillsboro	254
Hilltop Lakes	936
Hilltop Unit Tdc	254
Hilshire Village	713
Hitchcock	409
Hl Cntry Vlg	210
Hoard	903
Hobson	830
Hochheim	361
Hockley	936
Hockley Mine	936
Hodgson	903
Holland	254
Holliday	940
Holly Lake Ranch	903
Holly Lk Rnch	903
Holly Springs	409
Hollywood Park	210
Hollywood Pk	210
Holman	979
Hondo	830
Honey Grove	903
Honey Island	409
Hooks	903
Hope	361
Hopewell	936
Horizon City	915
Hornsby Bend	512
Horseshoe Bay	830
Horton	903
Houston	281, 713
Houston Heights	713
Howardwick	806
Howe	903
Howellville	281
Hoxie	512
Hoyte	254
Hubbard	254
Hubert	361
Hudson Bend	512
Hudson Oaks	817
Huffman	281
Hufsmith	281
Hughes Spgs	903
Hughes Springs	903
Hull	936
Humble	281
Hungerford	979
Hunt	830
Hunter	830
Hunters Creek Village	713
Huntington	936
Huntsville	936
Hurst	817
Hurst Springs	254
Hurstown	936
Hutchins	972
Hutto	512
Huxley	936
Hye	830
Iago	979
Iatan	325
Idalou	806
Impact	325
Imperial	432
Inadale	325
Independence	979
Indian Creek	325
Indian Gap	254
Indian Hill	409
Indian Lake	956
Indian Rock	903
Indianola	361
Industry	979
Inez	361
Ingleside	361
Ingleside On The Bay	361
Ingram	830
Inks Lake Village	512
Iola	936
Iowa Colony	281
Iowa Park	940
Ira	432
Iraan	432
Iredell	254
Ireland	254
Irene	254
Irs Service Center	512
Irving	972
Isabel	956
Island	409
Italy	972
Itasca	254
Ivanhoe	903
Iverson	972
Izoro	254
Jacksboro	940
Jacksonville	903
Jacobs	903
Jamaica Beach	409
James	936
Jamestown	409
Jarrell	512
Jarvis College	903
Jasper	409
Jayton	806
Jc Penney Company	214
Jeddo	830
Jefferson	903
Jenkins	903
Jericho	936
Jermyn	940
Jersey Village	281
Jersey Vlg	281
Jester	903
Jewett	903
Joaquin	936
Johnson City	830
Joinerville	903
Joliet	830
Jollyville	512
Jonah	512
Jones Creek	979
Jones Prairie	254
Jonesboro	254
Jonestown	512
Jonesville	903
Joppa	512

City	Area Code
ordans Store	936
osephine	972
Joshua	817
Josserand	936
Jourdanton	830
udson	903
unction	325
Justiceburg	806
Justin	817, 940
Kamay	940
Kamey	361
Kane	956
Karnack	903
Karnes City	830
Katemcy	325
Katy	281
Kaufman	972
Kayare	956
Keechi	903
Keene	817
Keller	817
Keller Corner	956
Kelly Usa	210
Kelly Usa Br	210
Kelsay	361
Kelsey	903
Kemah	281
Kemp	903
Kempner	254
Kendalia	830
Kendleton	979
Kenedy	361, 830
Kenefick	936
Kennard	936
Kennedale	817
Kennedy Shores	956
Kenneth Copeland Ministries	817
Kenney	979
Kent	432
Kerens	903
Kermit	432
Kerrick	806
Kerrville	830
Kickapoo	903
Kildare	903
Kilgore	903
Killeen	254
Kimball	254
Kimbro	512
Kingsbury	830
Kingsland	325
Kingsville	361
Kingsville Naval Air Station	361
Kingsvl Naval	361
Kingsvlle Nas	361
Kingwood	281
Kinkler	361
Kirby	210
Kirbyville	409
Kirk	254
Kirkland	940
Kirtley	512
Kirvin	903
Kittrell	936
Kleberg	214, 972
Klein	281
Klondike	903
Knickerbocker	325
Knippa	830
Knott	432
Knox City	940
Knoxville	830
Koerth	361
Kohrville	713
Kopperl	254
Kosse	254
Kountze	409
Kovar	361
Kress	806
Krugerville	940
Krum	940
Kurten	979
Kyle	512
La Blanca	956
La Casita	956
La Coste	830
La Feria	956
La Gloria	956
La Grange	979
La Joya	956
La Marque	409
La Mesa	806
La Paloma	956
La Porte	281
La Pryor	830
La Reforma	956
La Salle	361
La Tijera	956
La Vernia	830
La Villa	956
La Ward	361
Lackland	210
Lackland A F B	210
Lackland Afb	210
Lacy	936
Lacy Lakeview	254
Ladonia	903
Lafayette	903
Lafkin	956
Lago Vista	512
Laguna Heights	956
Laguna Hts	956
Laguna Park	254
Laguna Vista	956
Laird Hill	903
Lajitas	432
Lake Bridgeport	940
Lake Brownwood	325
Lake Cherokee	903
Lake City	361
Lake Creek	903
Lake Dallas	940
Lake Hills	830
Lake Jackson	979
Lake Jacksonville	903
Lake Kiowa	940
Lake Limestone	254
Lake Shore	325
Lake Victor	512
Lake Worth	817
Lakehills	830
Lakeland	936
Lakeport	903
Lakeside	817
Lakeside City	940
Lakeside Heights	325
Lakeside Village	254
Lakeview	409, 806
Lakeway	512
Lakewood	281
Lakewood Harbor	254
Lakewood Village	972
Lakewood Vlg	972
Lamar	361
Lamar University	409
Lamesa	806
Lampasas	512
Lanark	903
Lancaster	972
Landrum	956
Lane City	979
Lane Murray Prison	254
Lanely	903
Laneport	512
Laneville	903
Langtry	432
Lanham	254
Lanier	903
Lantana	940
Laredo	956
Larue	903
Las Milpas	956
Las Rusias	956
Lasara	956
Latch	903
Latex	903
Latexo	936
Laughlin A F B	830
Laughlin Afb	830
Laughlin Afb Branch	830
Laureles	956
Lavernia	830
Lavon	972
Law	979
Lawn	325
Lazbuddie	806
Leaday	325
League City	281
Leagueville	903
Leakey	830
Leander	512
Ledbetter	979
Leedale	254
Leesburg	903
Leesville	830
Lefors	806
Leggett	936
Leigh	903
Lelia Lake	806
Leming	830
Lenorah	432
Leo	979
Leon Junction	254
Leon Valley	210
Leona	903
Leonard	903
Leroy	254
Levelland	806
Leveretts Chapel	903
Levi	254
Levi Strauss	210
Levi Strauss Evacuee Ctr	210
Levita	254
Lewisville	972
Lexington	979
Liberty	936
Liberty City	903
Liberty Hill	512
Lilac	512
Lillian	817
Lily Island	936
Lincoln	979
Lindale	903
Linden	903
Lindenau	361
Lindsay	940
Lingleville	254
Linn	956
Linwood	936
Lipan	254
Lipscomb	806
Lissie	979
Littig	512
Little Elm	972
Little River Academy	254
Littlefield	806
Live Oak	210
Liverpool	979
Livingston	936
Lk Limestone	254
Llano	325
Lockhart	512
Lockney	806
Lodi	903
Loebau	979
Log Cabin	903
Lohn	325
Lolita	361
Lomax	281
Lometa	512
London	325
Lone Mountain	903
Lone Oak	903
Lone Star	903
Long Branch	903
Long Mott	361
Long Point	979
Longview	903
Longview Heights	903
Longworth	325
Loop	806
Lopeno	956
Lopezville	956
Loraine	325
Lorena	254
Lorenzo	806
Los Angeles	830
Los Coyotes	956
Los Cuates	956
Los Ebanos	956
Los Fresnos	956
Los Indios	956
Los Saenz	956
Lost Pines	512
Lott	254
Louise	979
Louisville	972
Lovelace	254
Lovelady	936
Loving	940
Lowake	325
Loyola Beach	361
Lozano	956
Lsi	214
Ltl Rvr Acad	254
Lubbock	806
Lucas	972
Luckenback	830
Lueders	325
Lufkin	936
Luling	830
Lull	956
Lumberton	409
Lund	512
Lyford	956
Lynchburg	281
Lyndon B Johnson Space Cen	281
Lyons	979
Lytle	830
Lytton Springs	512
M Bank	915
Mabank	903
Macdona	210
Mackay	979
Macune	936
Madero	956
Madisonville	936
Magnet	979
Magnolia	281, 936
Magnolia Beach	361
Magnolia Spgs	409
Magnolia Springs	409
Mahomet	512
Malakoff	903
Malone	254
Malta	903
Manchaca	512
Manda	512
Manheim	512
Manor	512
Mansfield	817
Manvel	281
Maple	806
Mapleton	936
Marathon	432
Marble Falls	830
Marfa	432
Marietta	903
Marion	830
Markham	979
Marlin	254
Marquez	903
Marshall	903
Marshall Ford	512
Mart	254
Martindale	512
Martins Mills	903
Martinsville	936
Maryneal	325
Mason	325
Massey Lake	903
Masterson	806
Matador	806
Matagorda	361
Mathis	361
Matinburg	903
Mattox	409
Maud	903
Mauriceville	409
Maurin	830
Maxdale	254
Maxwell	512
May	254
Maydelle	903
Mayflower	409
Maypearl	972
Maysfield	254
Mc Allen	956
Mc Camey	432
Mc Caulley	325
Mc Dade	512
Mc Faddin	361
Mc Gregor	254
Mc Kinney	972
Mc Leod	903
Mc Nary	915
Mc Neil	512
Mc Queeney	830
Mcadoo	806
Mcallen	956
Mcbeth	979
Mccamey	432
Mcclanahan	254
Mccoll	956
Mccoy	830
Mcdade	512
Mcdonald Obs	432
Mcdonald Observatory	432
Mcfaddin	361
Mcgregor	254
Mckinney	972
Mcknight	903
Mclean	806
Mcleod	903
Mcmahan	512
Mcmurry Univ	325
Mcnair	281
Mcnair Village	254
Mcneil	512
Mcqueeney	830
Meador Grove	254
Meadow	806
Meadowlakes	830
Meadows Place	281
Medina	830
Medina Lake	830
Meeks	254
Megargel	940
Meldrum	936
Melissa	972
Mellon	214
Melvin	325
Memorial Park	713
Memphis	806
Menard	325
Mendoza	512
Menlow	254
Mentone	432
Mercedes	956
Mereta	325
Meridian	254
Merit	903
Merkel	325
Mertens	254
Mertzon	325
Mesquite	972
Mexia	254
Meyersville	361
Miami	806
Mico	830
Middleton	903
Midfield	361
Midkiff	432
Midland	432
Midline	281
Midlothian	972
Midway	903
Milam	409
Miland	409
Milane	409
Milano	512
Mildland	409
Miles	325
Milford	972
Millersview	325
Millheim	979
Millican	979
Millsap	940
Minden	903
Mineola	903
Mineral	361
Mineral Wells	940
Minerva	512
Mings Chapel	903
Mingus	254
Mirando City	361
Mission	956
Mission Valley	361
Missouri City	281
Mixon	903
Mobeetie	806
Moffatt	254
Monadale	512
Monahans	432
Monaville	979
Monroe City	409
Mont Belvieu	281
Montague	940
Montague Village	254
Montalba	903
Monte Alto	956
Montgomery	936
Monthalia	830
Montopolis	512
Moody	254
Moore	830
Moore Station	903
Moores Crossing	512
Mooresville	254
Morales	361
Moran	325
Moravia	979
Morgan	254
Morgan Mill	254
Morgans Point	254, 281
Morgans Point Resort	254
Morris Ranch	830
Morse	806
Morton	806
Moscow	936
Mosheim	254
Moss Bluff	936
Moss Hill	936
Motor Vehicle Division	512
Moulton	361
Mound	254
Mound City	936
Mount Calm	254
Mount Enterprise	903
Mount Lucas	361
Mount Olive	361
Mount Pleasant	903
Mount Selman	903
Mount Sharp	512
Mount Union	409
Mount Vernon	903
Mountain	254
Mountain City	512
Mountain Home	830
Mozelle	325
Mt Enterprise	903
Mt Pleasant	903
Mt Sylvan	903
Mt Vernon	903
Muenster	940
Muldoon	979
Muleshoe	806
Mullin	325
Mullins Prairie	979
Mumford	979
Munday	940
Murchison	903
Murphy	972
Mustang	254
Myra	940
N Richlnd Hls	817
Nacogdoches	936
Nacogdoches S F Austin Univ	936
Nada	979
Nancy	936
Naples	903
Naruna	512
Nas/Jrb	817
Nash	903
Nassau Bay	281
Natalia	830

City	Area Code
Naval Air Station/ Jrb	817
Navarro	903
Navarro Mills	903
Navasota	936
Nazareth	806
Ncnb	713
Ncnb Nations Bank	512
Nechanitz	979
Neches	903
Nederland	409
Needville	979
Neiman Marcus	972
Nelsonville	979
Nemo	254
Nesbitt	903
Neuville	936
Nevada	972
New Baden	979
New Boston	903
New Braunfels	830
New Caney	281
New Clarkson	254
New Colony	903
New Corn Hill	512
New Deal	806
New Diana	903
New Harmony	936
New Home	806
New London	903
New Mine	903
New Mountain	903
New Salem	903
New Summerfield	903
New Summerfld	903
New Sweden	512
New Taiton	979
New Ulm	979
New Waverly	936
New York	903
Newark	817
Newby	903
Newcastle	940
Newport	940
Newton	409
Nickel	830
Niederwald	512
Nigton	936
Nile	512
Nix	512
Nixon	830
Noack	512
Nocona	940
Nogalus	936
Nolan	325
Nolanville	254
Nome	409
Noodle	325
Noonday	903
Nordheim	361
Norias	361
Normangee	936
Normanna	361
Normans Crossing	512
Norse	254
North Branch	972
North Cedar	936
North Cleveland	281
North Houston	281
North Prairie	254
North Richland Hills	817
North Texas Mpc	972
North Vidor	409
North Zulch	936
Northcrest	254
Northfield	940
Northlake	817, 940
Northrichland Hills	817
Norton	325
Norwest Bank	972
Norwood	936
Notrees	432
Novice	325
Noxville	830
Nursery	361
O Brien	940
Oak Forest	830
Oak Grove	903
Oak Hill	512
Oak Leaf	972
Oak Point	972
Oak Ridge N	281
Oak Ridge North	281
Oakalla	512
Oakhurst	936
Oakland	979
Oaks	817
Oakville	361
Oakwood	903
Oatmeal	512
Ocee	254
Odds	254
Odell	940
Odem	361
Odessa	432
Odonnell	806
Oenaville	254
Ofarrell	903
Oglesby	254
Oilton	361
Ojuelas	361
Oklaunion	940
Old Boston	903
Old Brazoria	979
Old Glory	940
Old Larissa	903
Old London	903
Old Mobeetie	806
Old Moulton	361
Old Ocean	979
Old River-Winfree	281, 936
Old Round Rock	512
Old Rvr-Wnfre	281
Old Salem	409
Old Union	254
Olden	254
Oletha	254
Olivia	361
Olmito	956
Olmos	361
Olmos Park	210
Olney	940
Olton	806
Omaha	903
Omen	903
Onalaska	936
Opelika	903
Oquinn	979
Orange	409
Orange Grove	361
Orangefield	409
Orchard	979
Ore City	903
Orla	432
Osage	979
Oscar	254
Ottine	830
Otto	254
Ovalo	325
Overton	903
Ovilla	972
Oyster Creek	979
Ozona	325
Padre Island National Seasho	361
Paducah	806
Pagoda	936
Paige	512
Paint Rock	325
Palacios	361
Palava	325
Palestine	903
Palito Blanco	361
Palm Village	956
Palmer	972
Palmhurst	956
Palmview	956
Palo Alto	361
Palo Alto Battlefield Nation	956
Palo Pinto	940
Paluxy	254
Pampa	806
Pancake	254
Pandora	830
Panhandle	806
Panna Maria	830
Panola	903
Panorama Village	936
Panorama Vlg	936
Pantego	817
Panther Creek	281
Papalote	361
Paradise	940
Paris	903
Park Row	281
Pasadena	281, 713
Patroon	936
Pattison	281
Patton	281
Pattonville	903
Pauls Store	936
Pawelekville	830
Pawnee	361
Paxton	936
Peacock	940
Pear Ridge	409
Pear Valley	325
Pearl City	361
Pearland	281
Pearsall	830
Peaster	940
Pecan Gap	903
Pecangrove	254
Pecos	432
Pedigo	409
Peggy	830
Pelham	254
Pelican Bay	817
Pendleton	254
Penelope	254
Penitas	956
Pennington	936
Penwell	432
Peoria	254
Pep	806
Percilla	936
Perezville	956
Pernitas Point	361
Perrin	940
Perry	254
Perryton	806
Perryville	903
Peters	979
Petersburg	806
Petersville	361
Petrolia	940
Petronila	361
Petteway	254
Pettibone	254
Pettit	806
Pettus	361
Petty	903
Pflugerville	512
Pharr	956
Phelps	936
Phillips	806
Pickton	903
Pidcoke	254
Pierce	979
Pierces Chapel	903
Pilot Knob	512
Pilot Point	940
Pine	903
Pine Forest	409
Pine Hill	903
Pine Valley	936
Pinehill	903
Pinehurst	281
Pineland	409
Pinewood	903
Piney Point	713
Pioneer Town	512
Pipe Creek	830
Pirtle	903
Pitner Junction	903
Pittsburg	903
Placedo	361
Plains	806
Plainview	806
Plano	972
Plantersville	936
Pleak	281
Pleasant Grove	903
Pleasant Hill	936
Pleasanton	830
Pledger	979
Pluck	936
Plum	979
Plum Grove	281
Pnc Bank	214
Po Boxes	361
Poesville	254
Point	903
Point Comfort	361
Point Enterprise	254
Point Venture	512
Pointblank	936
Pollok	936
Ponder	940
Pone	903
Pontotoc	325
Pony	325
Poolville	940
Porfirio	956
Port Acres	409
Port Alto	361
Port Aransas	361
Port Arthur	409
Port Bolivar	409
Port Isabel	956
Port Lavaca	361
Port Mansfield	956
Port Neches	409
Port O Connor	361
Port O' Connor	361
Porter	281
Porter Springs	936
Portland	361
Portway Acres	956
Post	806
Post Oak	979
Postoak	940
Poteet	830
Poth	830
Potosi	325
Pottsboro	903
Pottsville	254
Powderly	903
Powell	903
Powell Point	979
Powledge Prison	903
Poynor	903
Praesel	512
Praha	361
Prairie Dell	254
Prairie Grove	254
Prairie Hill	254
Prairie Lea	830
Prairie View	936, 979
Prayer Town	806
Premont	361
Presidio	432
Prestonwood	972
Price	903
Priddy	325
Primera	956
Primrose	903
Princeton	972
Pritchett	903
Proctor	325
Progreso	956
Progreso Lakes	956
Progreso Lks	956
Prosper	972
Providence Village	940
Provident City	979
Providnce Vil	940
Prt Mansfield	956
Pt Acres	409
Pt Isabel	956
Puerto Rico	956
Pumphrey	325
Purdon	903
Purmela	254
Pursley	903
Putnam	325
Pyote	432
Pyron	325
Quail	806
Quanah	940
Queen City	903
Quemado	830
Quinlan	903
Quintana	979
Quitaque	806
Quitman	903
Rabb	361
Rabbs	361
Rabbs Prairie	979
Raccoon Bend	979
Rachal	361
Radium	325
Rainbow	254
Raisin	361
Ralls	806
Ramah	936
Ramirez	361
Ramona	956
Ranchito	956
Rancho Viejo	956
Randolph	903
Randolph A F B	210
Randolph Afb	210
Randolph Air	210
Randolph Air Force Base	210
Ranger	254
Rangerville	956
Rankin	432
Ransom Canyon	806
Ratcliff	936
Ratibor	254
Ravenna	903
Rayburn	281
Rayford	281
Raymondville	956
Raytown	325
Raywood	936
Reagan	254
Realitos	361
Recycle	830
Red Gate	956
Red Lake	903
Red Oak	972
Red Ranger	254
Red River Army Depot	903
Red Rock	512
Red Springs	940
Redbank	903
Redford	432
Redlawn	936
Redtown	936
Redwater	903
Reedville	512
Reese	903
Refuge	936
Refugio	361
Reklaw	936
Relampago	956
Reliance	979
Reno	903
Reynard	936
Rhome	817
Rhonesboro	903
Ricardo	361
Rice	903
Rices Crossing	512
Richards	936
Richardson	972
Richland	903
Richland Hills	817
Richland Hls	817
Richland Spgs	325
Richland Springs	325
Richmond	281
Richwood	979
Ridge	979
Riesel	254
Rincon	956
Ringgold	940
Rio Bravo	956
Rio Frio	830
Rio Grande	956
Rio Grande City	956
Rio Grande Cy	956
Rio Hondo	956
Rio Medina	830
Rio Rico	956
Rio Vista	817
Rios	361
Rising Star	254
River Oaks	817
Riverside	936
Riviera	361
Riviera Beach	361
Rmx	512
Roanoke	817
Roans Prairie	936
Roaring Spngs	806
Roaring Springs	806
Robbins	903
Robert Lee	325
Robinson	254
Robstown	361
Roby	325
Rochelle	325
Rochester	940
Rock Creek	254
Rock Hill	903
Rock Island	979
Rockdale	512
Rockland	409
Rockport	361
Rocksprings	830
Rockwall	972
Rockwood	325
Rocky Branch	903
Rocky Hill	254
Roganville	409
Rogers	254
Rogers Hill	254
Rogerslacy	956
Rollingwood	512
Rolls	940
Roma	956
Roman Forest	281
Romayor	281
Roosevelt	325
Ropesville	806
Rosanky	830
Roscoe	325
Rose City	409
Rose Hill	281
Rosebud	254
Rosenberg	281
Rosenthal	254
Rosevine	409
Rosewood	903
Rosharon	281
Rosita	361
Ross	254
Rosser	972
Rosston	940
Rotan	325
Round Mountain	830
Round Mtn	830
Round Rock	512
Round Top	979
Rowena	325
Rowlett	972
Roxton	903
Royalty	432
Royse City	972
Royston	325
Rudolph	361
Rule	940
Rumley	254
Runaway Bay	940
Runge	830
Rusk	903
Rutersville	979
Rye	281
S F A	936
S F A U	936
S F Austin U	936
S F Austin Univ	936
S Padre Isl E	956
S Padre Isle	956

City	Area Code
Texarkana	903
W Bell Tele Co	210
abinal	830
abine	409
abine Pass	409
achse	972
acul	936
adler	903
agerton	940
aginaw	817
Saint Hedwig	210
Saint Jo	940
Salado	254
Salesville	940
Salineno	956
Salmon	903
Salt Flat	432
Saltillo	903
Salty	512
Sam Houston State Univ	936
Sam Norwood	806
San Angelo	325
San Antonio	210, 830
San Augustine	936
San Benito	956
San Carlos	956
San Diego	361
San Elizario	915
San Felipe	979
San Gabriel	512
San Isidro	956
San Jose	361
San Juan	956
San Juan Community	956
San Leanna	512
San Leon	281
San Marcos	512
San Patricio	361
San Pedro	361
San Perlita	956
San Saba	325
San Ygnacio	956
Sand Hill	903
Sanderson	432
Sandia	361
Sandoval	512
Sandy Corner	979
Sandy Fork	830
Sandy Point	281
Sanford	806
Sanger	940
Sansom Park	817
Santa Anna	325
Santa Catarina	956
Santa Cruz	956
Santa Elena	956
Santa Fe	409
Santa Maria	956
Santa Monica	956
Santa Rosa	956
Santo	940
Saragosa	432
Saratoga	936
Sarco	361
Sargent	979
Sarita	361
Saspamco	210
Satin	254
Satsuma	713
Sattler	830
Saturn	830
Savannah	940
Savoy	903
Sbc Att	214
Scallorn	512
Schertz	210
Schroeder	361
Schulenburg	979
Schwertner	512
Scotland	940
Scott And White Hospital	254
Scottsville	903
Scroggins	903
Scurry	972
Seabrook	281
Seadrift	361
Seagoville	972
Seagraves	806
Sealy	979
Sears	214
Seaton	254
Seawillow	512
Sebastian	956
Sebastopol	936
Security	281
Security Services	210
Security Svc	210
Segno	936
Segovia	325
Seguin	830
Sejita	361
Selective Service	214
Selma	210
Selman City	903
Seminole	432
Seven Oaks	936
Seven Pines	903
Seven Points	903
Seven Sisters	361
Sexton	936
Sexton City	903
Seymour	940
Sf Austin Univ	936
Sfa	936
Shady Grove	936
Shady Shores	940
Shafter	432
Shallowater	806
Shamrock	806
Shamrock Shores	325
Shankleville	409
Sharp	254
Sharpstown	713
Sharyland	956
Shavano Park	210
Sheffield	432
Shelby	979
Shelbyville	936
Sheldon	713
Shenandoah	281, 936
Shep	325
Shepherd	936
Sheppard Afb	940
Sheridan	979
Sherman	903
Sherwood	325
Shiloh	254
Shiner	361
Shiro	936
Shive	254
Shoreacres	281
Short	936
Sidney	254
Sienna Plant	281
Sienna Plantation	281
Sierra Blanca	915
Silas	936
Siloam	903
Silsbee	409
Silver	325
Silver City	903
Silver Valley	325
Silverton	806
Simmonsville	903
Simms	903
Simonton	281
Simsboro	254
Sinclair City	903
Singleton	936
Sinton	361
Skellytown	806
Skidmore	361
Slaton	806
Slidell	940
Slocum	903
Smiley	830
Smith Hill	903
Smithland	903
Smiths Bend	254
Smithville	512
Smyer	806
Smyrna	903
Snook	979
Snow Hill	936
Snyder	325
Socorro	915
Sodville	361
Solms	830
Somerset	830
Somerville	979
Sonora	325
Sorters	281
Soules Chapel	903
Sour Lake	409
South Bend	940
South Elm	254
South Houston	713
South Padre Island	956
South Plains	806
South Purmela	254
South San Pedro	361
South Texarkana	903
Southern Methodist Universit	214
Southern Union Gas Co	915
Southern Union Gas Company	512
Southlake	817
Southland	806
Southmayd	903
Southside Place	713
Spade	806
Spanish Camp	979
Sparks	254
Speaks	361
Spearman	806
Speegleville	254
Spicewood	512
Splendora	281
Spofford	830
Spring	281
Spring Branch	830
Spring Creek	830
Spring Valley	713
Springdale	903
Springfield	903
Springhill	254
Springlake	806
Springtown	817
Sprinkle	512
Spur	806
Spurger	409
St Louis	903
St Paul	972
Stafford	281
Stagecoach	281
Stairtown	830
Stamford	325
Stampede	254
Stamps	903
Stanton	432
Staples	830
Star	325
Starrville	903
Startzville	830
State Comptroller	512
Steeltown	409
Steep Hollow	979
Stellar	979
Stephen Creek	936
Stephen F Austin Univ	936
Stephenville	254
Sterling City	325
Stewards Mill	903
Stewart	903
Stewart Heights	281
Stinnett	806
Stith	325
Stockdale	830
Stockholm	956
Stockman	936
Stoneburg	940
Stonewall	830
Stormville	903
Stowell	409
Stratford	806
Stratigic Fulfilment	903
Stratton	361
Strawn	254
Streeter	325
Streetman	903
String Prairie	830
Structure	512
Stuart Place	956
Sublime	361
Sudan	806
Suffolk	903
Sugar Land	281
Sugar Valley	979
Sul Ross	432
Sullivan City	956
Sulphur Bluff	903
Sulphur Spgs	903
Sulphur Springs	903
Summerfield	806
Summerville	830
Sumner	903
Sun City	512
Sundown	806
Sunny Side	281
Sunnyvale	972
Sunray	806
Sunrise Beach	325
Sunset	940
Sunset Valley	512
Surfside Bch	979
Surfside Beach	979
Sutherland Springs	830
Sutherlnd Spg	830
Sw Baptist Theological Smry	817
Swan	903
Sweeny	979
Sweet Home	361
Sweetwater	325
Swinney Switch	361
Swinney Swtch	361
Swiss Alp	979
Sycamore	409
Sylvan Beach	281
Sylvester	325
Tabor	979
Taft	361
Tahoka	806
Taiton	979
Talco	903
Talpa	325
Tamega	512
Tamina	936
Tanglewood	979
Tarkington Prairie	281
Tarleton State Univ	254
Tarpley	830
Tarrant County Courthouse	817
Tarrytown	512
Tarzan	432
Tatum	903
Tavener	979
Taylor	512
Taylor Lake Village	281
Taylor Landing	409
Taylor Lk Vlg	281
Taylor Lndg	409
Teague	254
Teaselville	903
Tecula	903
Tehuacana	254
Telegraph	325
Telephone	903
Telferner	361
Tell	940
Temple	254
Tenaha	936
Tenn Colony	903
Tenn Colony Prison Beto 1	903
Tenn Colony Prison Coffield	903
Tenn Colony Prison Michael	903
Tenneryville	903
Tennessee Colony	903
Tennyson	325
Tenoka	936
Terlingua	432
Terrell	972
Terrell Hills	210
Terrys Chapel	254
Terryville	361
Texarkana	903
Texarkana Community College	903
Texas American Bank	817
Texas Christian Univ	817
Texas City	409
Texas Tech School Of Medicin	806
Texas Workforce Commission	512
Texline	806
Texon	325
Thayer	956
The Colony	972
The Hills	512
The University Of Texas	512
The Woodlands	281
Thedford	903
Thelma	254
Theon	512
Thicket	936
Thomas	903
Thomaston	361
Thompsons	281
Thompsonville	830
Thorndale	512
Thornton	254
Thrall	512
Three Point	512
Three Rivers	361
Thrifty	325
Throckmorton	940
Tidwell Prairie	254
Tiki Island	409
Tilden	361
Tilmon	512
Timber Cove	281
Timberlane Acres	281
Timpson	936
Tioga	940
Tivoli	361
Tivydale	830
Tod	281
Tokio	806
Tolar	254
Toledo	409
Tom Bean	903
Tomball	281
Tool	903
Topsey	254
Tornillo	915
Tours	254
Tow	325
Town Bluff	409
Toyah	432
Toyahvale	432
Trammells	713
Travis	254
Travis Heights	512
Trent	325
Trenton	903
Trevat	936
Tri Cities	903
Trinidad	903
Trinity	936
Trophy Club	817
Troup	903
Trout Creek	409
Troy	254
Truscott	940
Tu Electric	214
Tuleta	361
Tulia	806
Turkey	806
Turlington	903
Turnertown	903
Turney	903
Tuscola	325
Tuxedo	325
Twitty	806
Tx A & M University	979
Tx State Prison	936
Tye	325
Tyler	903
Tyler Junior College	903
Tynan	361
Type	512
U Of T Med Br At Galveston	409
U S P S Official	713
Uhland	512
Umbarger	806
Uncertain	903
Union	325
Union Chapel	903
Union Hill	903
United Marketing Of Texas	806
United Service Auto Assc	210
Univ Of Texas At Arlington	817
Univ Of Tx Elp	915
Univ Tx At Arlington	817
Universal City	210
Universal Cty	210
University Of Houston	713
University Of Texas	512
University Of Texas At Tyler	903
University Park	214
Upton	512
Usps Official Mail	972
Ut	512
Ut Sw Medical Center	214
Utopia	830
Uvalde	830
V A Hospital	713
V A Regional Office	254
Val Verde	254
Valentine	432
Valera	325
Valle De Oro	806
Valley Lodge	281
Valley Mills	254
Valley Spring	325
Valley View	940
Van	903
Van Alstyne	903
Van Horn	432
Van Vleck	979
Vance	830
Vancourt	325
Vanderbilt	361
Vanderpool	830
Vanetia	903
Vattmanville	361
Vaughan	254
Vealmoor	432
Vega	806
Venus	972
Vera	940
Verhalen	432
Veribest	325
Vernon	940
Veterans Administration	512
Viboras	361
Victoria	361
Victory City	903
Vidor	409
Vienna	361
Vigo Park	806
Vilas	254
Villa Cavazos	956
Villa Nueva	956
Village	214
Village Mills	409
Village Of The Hills	512
Villareales	956
Vinton	915
Violet	361
Virginia Point	409
Vlg O The Hls	512
Voca	325
Volente	512
Von Ormy	830
Voss	325
Votaw	936
W Univ Pl	713
Wachovia Bank And Trust	214
Waco	254
Wadsworth	979
Waelder	830
Waka	806
Wake Village	903
Wakefield	936
Walburg	512
Waldeck	979
Waldrip	325
Walhalla	979
Walkers Mill	903

Wall 325
Waller 936
Wallis 979
Wallisville 409
Walnut Grove 903
Walnut Spgs 254
Walnut Springs 254
Walton 903
Ward Prairie 903
Warda 979
Wards Creek 903
Waring 830
Warlock 903
Warren 409
Warrenton 979
Washington 936
Waskom 903
Wastella 325
Watauga 817
Water Valley 325
Waterloo 512
Waterman 936
Waters Bluff 903
Watson 512
Watt 254
Waxahachie 214, 972
Wayside 806
Wbamc 915
Weatherford 817
Webberville 512
Webster 281
Weches 936
Weedhaven 361
Weesatche 361
Weimar 979
Weinert 940
Weir 512
Welch 806
Welcome 979
Wellborn 979
Wellington 806
Wellman 806
Wells 936
Wells Fargo Bank 214
Weser 361
Weslaco 956
West 254
West Columbia 979
West End 979
West Galveston 409
West Lake Hills 512
West Lake Hls 512
West Mineola 903
West Orange 409
West Payne 979
West Point 979
West Port Arthur 409
West Tawakoni 903
West Texas A&m University 806
West Texas City 409
West University Place 713
Westbrook 325
Westhoff 830
Westlake 817
Westminster 972
Weston 214
Weston Lakes 281
Westover Hills 817
Westphalia 254
Westville 936
Westworth Village 817
Westworth Vlg 817
Wetmore 210
Whaley 903
Wharton 979
Wheeler 806
Wheelock 979
White Deer 806
White Hall 254, 936
White Oak 903
White Rock 936
White Settlement 817
Whiteface 806
Whitehouse 903
Whitesboro 903
Whitestone 512
Whitewright 903
Whitharral 806
Whitney 254
Whitsett 830
Whitson 254
Whitt 940
Whon 325
Wht Settlemt 817
Wichita Falls 940
Wickett 432
Wied 361
Wiergate 409
Wiggins 903
Wild Peach Village 979
Wilderville 254
Wildorado 806
Wildwood 409
Wilford Hall 210
Wilford Hall Usaf Hosp 210
Willamar 956
Willis 936
Willow City 830
Willow Grove 254
Willow Oak 903
Willow Park 817
Willow Springs 936
Wills Point 903
Wilmer 972
Wilmeth 325
Wilson 806
Wimberley 512
Winchester 979
Windcrest 210
Windom 903
Windsor Park Mall Evac Ctr 210
Windthorst 940
Winfield 903
Wingate 325
Wink 432
Winkler 903
Winnie 409
Winnsboro 903
Winona 903
Winslow 254
Winters 325
Witting 361
Woden 936
Wolfe City 903
Wolfforth 806
Womack 254
Wood Springs 903
Woodbranch 281
Woodbury 254
Woodcreek 512
Woodlake 936
Woodlawn 903
Woods 936
Woodsboro 361
Woodson 940
Woodville 409
Woodway 254
Woody Acres 281
Word Record Bus Reply 254
Wortham 254
Worthing 361
Wright City 903
Wrightsboro 830
Wylie 972
Xerox Corporation 956
Yancey 830
Yantis 903
Yard 903
Yarrelton 254
Yescas 956
Yoakum 361
Yorktown 361
Young 903
Youngsport 254
Zabcikville 254
Zapata 956
Zavalla 936
Zephyr 325
Zipperlenville 254

Utah

Abraham 435
Adamsville 435
Alpine 801
Alta 801
Altamont 435
Alton 435
Altonah 435
Am Fork 801
Amalga 435
American Express Co 801
American Fork 801
Anchorage 801
Aneth 435
Angle 435
Annabella 435
Antimony 435
Apple Valley 435
Arcadia 435
Arches 435
Arsenal 801
Aurora 435
Austin 435
Avon 435
Axtell 435
Ballard 435
Bauer 435
Bear River City 435
Bear River Cy 435
Beaver 435
Beaverdam 435
Beeton 435
Belmont Heights 801
Beneficial Life Insurance 801
Benjamin 801
Bennion 801
Benson 435
Beryl 435
Beryl Junction 435
Bethel 435
Bicknell 435
Big Water 435
Bingham 801
Bingham Canyon 801
Bingham Cyn 801
Birdseye 435
Black Rock 435
Blanding 435
Bloomington 435
Bloomington Hills 435
Bluebell 435
Bluff 435
Bluffdale 801
Bonanza 435
Boneta 435
Bonnie 801
Bothwell 435
Bottle Hollow 435
Boulder 435
Bountiful 801
Bowery Haven 435
Brian Head 435
Bridgeland 435
Brigham 435
Brigham City 435
Brighton 801
Brookside 435
Bryce 435
Bryce Canyon 435
Bryce Canyon City 435
Bryce Cyn Cty 435
Bullfrog 435
Bunker 801
Burbank 435
Burmester 435
Burrville 435
Bushnell 435
Byu 801
Cache Jct 435
Cache Junction 435
Caineville 435
Callao 435
Camp Williams 801
Cannonville 435
Canyon Point 435
Canyonlands 435
Capitol Reef 435
Carbonville 435
Castle Dale 435
Castle Gate 435
Castle Valley 435
Castleton 435
Cedar City 435
Cedar Fort 801
Cedar Hills 801
Cedar Pass 801
Cedar Valley 801
Center Creek 435
Centerfield 435
Centerville 801
Central 435
Central Valley 435
Central Vly 435
Charleston 435
Chester 435
Church Of Jesus Christ/Lds 801
Circleville 435
Cisco 435
Clarkston 435
Clawson 435
Clearfield 801
Cleveland 435
Clinton 801
Clover 435
Clyde 801
Coalville 435
College Ward 435
Collinston 435
Copperton 801
Corinne 435
Cornish 435
Cottonwd Hgts 801
Cottonwood 801
Cottonwood Heights 801
Cottonwood Heights City 801
Cove 435
Cove Fort 435
Cover Bridge Canyon 801
Covered Bridge 801
Crescent 801
Croydon 801
Crystal Springs 435
Cushing 801
Dammeron 435
Dammeron Valley 435
Dammeron Vly 435
Daniels 435
Deer Mountain 435
Deer Valley 435
Defas Park 435
Defense Depot Ogden 801
Delta 435
Deseret 435
Deweyville 435
Diamond Valley 435
Draper 801
Dry Fork 435
Duchesne 435
Duck Creek Village 435
Duck Crk Vlg 435
Dugway 435
Dutch John 435
Eagle Mountain 801
Eagle Mtn 801
East Carbon 435
East Layton 801
East Wellington 435
Echo 435
Eden 801
Elberta 435
Elk Ridge 801
Elmo 435
Elsinore 435
Elwood 435
Emery 435
Emigration Canyon 801
Emigratn Cyn 801
Emory 435
Enoch 435
Enterprise 435
Ephraim 435
Erda 435
Escalante 435
Eskdale 435
Etna 435
Eureka 435
Fairfield 801
Fairview 435
Farmington 801
Farr West 801
Faust 435
Fayette 435
Ferron 435
Fielding 435
Fillmore 435
First Security Bank 801
Fish Lake 435
Flowell 435
Fort Douglas 801
Fort Duchesne 435
Fountain Green 435
Fountain Grn 435
Francis 435
Fremont 435
Fruit Heights 801
Fruita 435
Fruitland 435
Fry Canyon 435
Ftn Green 435
Garden City 435
Garland 435
Garrison 435
Genola 801
Glen Canyon 435
Glendale 435
Glenwood 435
Gold Hill 435
Gooseberry 435
Goshen 801
Granger 801
Granger Hunter 801
Granite 801
Grantsville 435
Green Lake 435
Green River 435
Greendale 435
Greenhaven 435
Greenville 435
Greenwich 435
Grouse Creek 435
Grover 435
Gunlock 435
Gunnison 435
Gusher 435
Hailstone 435
Halls Crossing 435
Halls Xing 435
Hanksville 435
Hanna 435
Harrisburg Junction 435
Harrisville 801
Hatch 435
Heber 435
Heber City 435
Helper 435
Henefer 435
Henrieville 435
Herriman 801
Hideout 435
Highland 801
Hildale 435
Hill Afb 801
Hill Air Force Base 801
Hillfield 801
Hinckley 435
Hite 435
Holden 435
Holladay 801
Holladay Cottonwood 801
Holladay Ctwd 801
Honeyville 435
Hooper 801
Howell 435
Hoytsville 435
Hunter 801
Huntington 435
Huntsville 801
Hurricane 435
Hyde Park 435
Hyrum 435
Ibapah 435
Indianola 435
Ioka 435
Irish Green 435
Ivins 435
Jensen 435
Joseph 435
Junction 435
Kamas 435
Kanab 435
Kanarraville 435
Kanesville 801
Kanosh 435
Kayenta 435
Kaysville 801
Kearns 801
Keetley 435
Kenilworth 435
Key Bank 801
Kimball Junction 435
Kingston 435
Koosharem 435
La Sal 435
La Verkin 435
Lake Point 435
Lake Powell 435
Lake Shore 801
Lakeside 435
Laketown 435
Lakeview 801
Lapoint 435
Lawrence 435
Layton 801
Lds Hospital 801
Leamington 435
Leeds 435
Leeton 435
Lehi 801
Leland 801
Levan 435
Lewiston 435
Liberty 801
Lincoln 435
Lindon 801
Littleton 801
Loa 435
Logan 435
Lyman 435
Lynndyl 435
Madsen 435
Maeser 435
Magna 801
Mammoth 435
Manderfield 435
Manila 435
Manti 435
Mantua 435
Mapleton 801
Marion 435
Marriott 801
Marriott-Slaterville City 801
Martin 435
Marysvale 435
Mayfield 435
Meadow 435
Meadowville 435
Mendon 435
Mexican Hat 435
Middleton 435
Midvale 801
Midway 435
Milburn 435
Milford 435
Millville 435
Milton 801
Minersville 435
Moab 435
Modena 435
Mona 435
Monarch 435
Monroe 435
Montezuma Creek 435
Montezuma Crk 435
Monticello 435
Monument Valley 435
Monument Vly 435

Morgan 801
Moroni 435
Mount Carmel 435
Mount Pleasant 435
Mountain Green 801
Mountain Home 435
Ms City 801
Msc 801
Mt Pleasant 435
Mtn Green 801
Murray 801
Myton 435
N Logan 435
N Salt Lake 801
Naples 435
Natural Bridges 435
Neola 435
Nephi 435
New Harmony 435
Newcastle 435
Newton 435
Nibley 435
North Creek 435
North Logan 435
North Ogden 801
North Salt Lake 801
Nsl 801
Oak City 435
Oak Creek 435
Oakley 435
Oasis 435
Ogden 801
Ophir 435
Orangeville 435
Orderville 435
Orem 801
Ouray 435
Palmyra 801
Panguitch 435
Paradise 435
Paragonah 435
Park City 435
Park Valley 435
Parowan 435
Partoun 435
Payson 801
Penrose 435
Peoa 435
Perry 435
Petersboro 435
Peterson 801
Petra 435
Pickleville 435
Pine Canyon 435
Pine Cliff 435
Pine Valley 435
Pinto 435
Pintura 435
Pl Grove 801
Plain City 801
Pleasant Green 801
Pleasant Grove 801
Pleasant Grv 801
Pleasant View 801
Plymouth 435
Portage 435
Porterville 801
Price 435
Promontory 435
Providence 435
Provo 801
Questar Gas Company 801
Randlett 435
Randolph 435
Red Canyon 435
Redmond 435
Richfield 435
Richmond 435
Richville 801
River Heights 435
Riverdale 801
Riverside 435
Riverton 801
Rockport 435
Rockville 435
Rocky Rdg Twn 435
Rocky Ridge Town 435
Roosevelt 435
Rosette 435
Round Valley 435
Roy 801
Rubys Inn 435
Rush Valley 435
S Jordan 801
S Salt Lake 801
Saint George 435
Salem 801
Salina 435
Salt Lake City 801
Salt Lake County Complex 801
Salt Lake Cty 801
Sandy 801
Santa Clara 435
Santaquin 801
Saratoga 801
Saratoga Spgs 801
Saratoga Springs 801
Scipio 435
Scofield 435
Sevier 435
Sherwood Park 801
Sigurd 435
Skull Valley 435
Slaterville 801
Slc 801
Smithfield 435
Snowbird 801
Snowville 435
Snyderville 435
So Salt Lake 801
Solitude 801
South Jordan 801
South Ogden 801
South Rim 435
South Salt Lake 801
South Weber 801
Spanish Fork 801
Spring City 435
Spring Glen 435
Spring Lake 801
Springdale 435
Springville 801
Spry 435
Ssl 801
St George 435
Standardville 435
Stansbury Park 435
Stansbury Pk 435
Sterling 435
Stockton 435
Stoddard 801
Sugarville 435
Summit 435
Summit Park 435
Sundance 801
Sunnyside 435
Sunset 801
Sutherland 435
Swan Creek 435
Syracuse 801
Tabiona 435
Talmage 435
Taylor 801
Taylorsville 801
Teasdale 435
Terra 435
Thatcher 435
Thistle 435
Thompson 435
Ticaboo 435
Timpanogos 801
Tooele 435
Tooele Army Depot 435
Topaz 435
Toquerville 435
Torrey 435
Tremonton 435
Trenton 435
Tridell 435
Tropic 435
Trout Creek 435
Tuhaye 435
Uintah 801
Union 801
University Medical Ctr 801
Upalco 435
Upton 435
Us Postal Service 801
Utah State Tax Commission 801
Utah State University 435
Utida 435
Uvada 435
Val Verda 801
Venice 435
Vernal 435
Vernon 435
Veterans Administration Hosp 801
Veyo 435
Vineyard 801
Virgin 435
W Bountiful 801
W Jordan 435, 801
W Valley City 801
Wales 435
Wallsburg 435
Wanship 435
Warren 801
Washington 435
Washington Terrace 801
Washington Tr 801
Weber State University 801
Wellington 435
Wells Fargo Bank 801
Wellsville 435
Wendover 435
West Bountiful 801
West Haven 801
West Jordan 435
West Kaysville 801
West Layton 801
West Point 801
West Valley 801
West Valley City 801
West Warren 801
West Weber 801
Western I R S Center 801
Wheelon 435
White City 801
White Mesa 435
Whiterocks 435
Willard 801
Wilson 801
Winchester Hills 435
Wj 435
Wjrd 435
Woodland 435
Woodland Hills 801
Woodland Hls 801
Woodrow 435
Woodruff 435
Woods Cross 801
Young Ward 435
Zion National Park 435
Zion Ntl Park 435

Vermont

All Points 802

Virgin Islands

All Points 340

Virginia

7 Corners 703
A T & T 703
Abingdon 276
Accomac 757
Achilles 804
Advance Mills 434
Afton 540
Air Mail Facility 804
Airlie 540
Akk 804
Akunia 434
Alberta 434
Aldie 703
Alexandria 202, 703
Alfonso 804
Allegany Spring 540
Alleghany 540
Allisonia 540
Allstate Ins Co 540
Alpine 540
Altavista 434
Alton 434
Alum Ridge 540
Amelia 804
Amelia Ch 804
Amelia Court House 804
Amelia Ct Hse 804
Amherst 434
Amissville 540
Ammon 804
Amonate 276
Ampthill 804
Andersonville 804
Andover 276
Annandale 703
Anthem Bc Bs 540
Anthem/Blue Cross Blue Shiel 804
Appalachia 276
Appalachian Pwr 540
Appomattox 434
Ararat 276
Arcola 703
Ark 804
Arlington 202
Army Times 703
Aroda 540
Arrington 434
Arvonia 434
Ashaiiu 804
Ashburn 703
Ashland 804
Assawoman 757
Assistant Secretary Of Navy 703
At&t 703
Atkins 276
Atlantic 757
Augusta Spgs 540
Augusta Sprgs 540
Augusta Springs 540
Austinville 276
Axton 276
Aylett 804
Aylor 540
Bacova 540
Bacova Jnctn 540
Bacova Junction 540
Baileys Crossroads 703
Baileys Xrds 703
Banco 540
Bandy 276
Bank Of America 703, 804
Barboursville 540
Barhamsville 804
Barnett 276
Barren Spgs 276
Barren Springs 276
Baskerville 434
Bassett 276
Bassett Forks 276
Bastian 276
Basye 540
Batesville 540
Battery Park 757
Bavon 804
Bayford 757
Beach 804
Bealeton 540
Beaumont 804
Beaverdam 804
Beaverlett 804
Bedford 540
Bee 276
Belfast Mills 276
Bellamy 804
Belle Haven 757
Belleview 703
Belspring 540
Ben Hur 276
Bena 804
Bennett Springs 540
Bent Mountain 540
Bentonville 540
Bergton 540
Berryville 540
Big Island 434
Big Rock 276
Big Stone Gap 276
Birchleaf 276
Birdsnest 757
Bishop 276
Black Ridge 434
Blackridge 434
Blacksburg 540
Blackstone 434
Blackwater 276
Blairs 434
Blakes 804
Bland 276
Bland Correct 276
Bland Correctional Farm 276
Bloxom 757
Blue Grass 540
Blue Ridge 540
Bluefield 276
Bluemont 540
Bohannon 804
Boissevain 276
Bolar 540
Bolton 276
Bon Air 804
Bonsack 540
Boones Mill 540
Boonesville 434
Boston 540
Boswells Tavern 540
Bowling Green 804
Bowling Grn 804
Boy Scouts Of America 804
Boyce 540
Boyd Tavern 434
Boydton 434
Boykins 757
Bracey 434
Brambleton 703
Branchville 757
Brandy 540
Brandy Sta 540
Brandy Station 540
Breaks 276
Bremo Bluff 434
Bridgewater 540
Brightwood 540
Bristol 276
Bristol Merchandise Return 276
Bristow 703
Brm-Firm Zip 703
Broad Run 703
Broadford 276
Broadlands 703
Broadway 540
Brodnax 434
Brooke 540
Brookneal 434
Brownsburg 540
Browntown 540
Brucetown 540
Bruington 804
Buchanan 540
Buckingham 434
Buena Vista 540
Buffalo Jct 434
Buffalo Junction 434
Bumpass 540
Burgess 804
Burke 703
Burkes Garden 276
Burkeville 434
Burnleys 540
Burnsville 540
Burnt Chimney 540
Burr Hill 540
Business Reply 804
Business Reply Firms 434
Business Reply Mail 703
Butylo 804
Bybee 434
Callands 434
Callao 804
Callaway 540
Calverton 540
Cambria 540
Cameron Station 703
Camp Appalachia 540
Campbell 434
Cana 276
Cape Charles 757
Capeville 757
Capital One 804
Capitol 804
Capron 434
Cardinal 804
Caret 804
Carrollton 757
Carrsville 757
Carson 434
Cartersville 804
Carterton 276
Casanova 540
Cascade 276
Castleton 540
Castlewood 276
Catalpa 540
Catawba 540
Catharpin 703
Catlett 540
Cauthornville 804
Cave Spring 540
Cbn Brm 757
Cedar Bluff 276
Center Cross 804
Central Station 804
Centreville 703
Ceres 276
Champlain 804
Chance 804
Chantilly 703
Charity 540
Charles City 804
Charlotte C H 434
Charlotte Ch 434
Charlotte Court House 434
Charlottesville 434
Charlottesvle 434
Chase City 434
Chatham 434
Check 540
Cheriton 757
Chesapeake 757
Chester 804
Chester Gap 540
Chesterfield 804
Chesterfld 804
Chilhowie 276
Chincoteague 757
Chincoteague Island 757
Christchurch 804
Christian Brdcst Network 757
Christiansbrg 540
Christiansburg 540
Christnsbrg 540
Chuckatuck 757
Church Road 804
Church View 804
Churchville 540
Chville 434
Cinclantflt 757
Cismont 434
Claremont 757
Clarksville 434
Claudville 276
Clear Brook 540
Clearfork 276
Cleveland 276
Clifford 434
Clifford And Wills 434

City	Area Code
Clifton	703
Clifton Forge	540
Clinchburg	276
Clinchco	276
Clinchport	276
Clintwood	276
Clover	434
Cloverdale	540
Cluster Spgs	434
Cluster Springs	434
Cmp Appalchia	540
Coast Guard Finance Center	757
Coast Guard Finance Unit	804
Cobbs Creek	804
Cobham	434
Coeburn	276
Coleman Falls	434
Coles Point	804
College Of William & Mary	757
Collinsville	276
Cologne	804
Colonial Bch	804
Colonial Beach	804
Colonial Heights	804
Colonial Hgts	804
Columbia	804
Comers Rock	276
Community	703
Conaway	276
Concord	434
Copper Hill	540
Corbin	540
Council	276
County Of Henrico	804
Courtland	757
Cove Creek	276
Covesville	434
Covington	540
Craddockville	757
Craigsville	540
Crewe	434
Criders	540
Criglersville	540
Crimora	540
Cripple Creek	276
Crittenden	757
Critz	276
Crockett	276
Cross Jnct	540
Cross Junction	540
Crosskeys	540
Crozet	434
Crozier	804
Crystal City	703
Crystal Hill	434
Cullen	434
Culpeper	540
Cumberland	804
Cunningham	434
Dabneys	804
Dahlgren	540
Dale City	703
Dalecity	703
Daleville	540
Dalhart	276
Damascus	276
Dante	276
Danville	434
Darlingtn Hts	434
Darlington Heights	434
Davenport	276
Davis Wharf	757
Dayton	540
Deerfield	540
Defense General Supply Ct	804
Delaplane	540
Deltaville	804
Dendron	757
Dept Hs	202
Dept Of Commerce	703
Dept Of The Navy	703
Dept Public Utilities	804
Dewitt	804
Dhs	202
Dickensonville	276
Diggs	804
Dillwyn	804
Dinwiddie	804
Disputanta	804
Div Motor Veh	804
Doe Hill	540
Dogue	540
Dolphin	434
Dominion Virginia Power	804
Doran	276
Doswell	804
Drakes Branch	434
Draper	540
Drewryville	434
Driver	757
Dry Fork	434
Dryden	276
Dublin	540
Duffield	276
Dugspur	540
Dulles	540, 703
Dulles Air Mail Facility	540
Dulles Air Transfer Office	540
Dulles P & D Center	703
Dumfries	703
Dundas	434
Dungannon	276
Dunn Loring	703
Dunnsville	804
Dutton	804
Dye	276
Dyke	434
E Stone Gap	276
Eagle Rock	540
Earlysville	434
East Lexington	540
East Stone Gap	276
Eastville	757
Ebony	434
Edinburg	540
Edwardsville	804
Eggleston	540
Eheart	540
Elberon	757
Elevon	804
Elk Creek	276
Elk Garden	276
Elkton	540
Elkwood	540
Elliston	540
Eltham	804
Embarq	434
Emory	276
Emporia	434
Endicott	540
Engineering Support Center	703
Engleside	703
Enon	540
Esmont	434
Esserville	276
Etlan	540
Ettrick	804
Evergreen	434
Evington	434
Ewing	276
Exeter	276
Exmore	757
Faber	434
Fairfax	202
Fairfax County Government	703
Fairfax Sta	703
Fairfax Station	703
Fairfield	540
Fairlawn	540
Fairview	540
Falconerville	434
Falling Spring	540
Falling Sprng	540
Falls Church	202
Falls Mills	276
Falmouth	540
Family Fashions By Avon	757
Fancy Gap	276
Farmville	434
Farnham	804
Fbi Academy	703
Fdic	703
Fentress	757
Ferrum	540
Fieldale	276
Fife	804
Fincastle	540
Firm Zip	703
Fishers Hill	540
Fishersville	540
Fleet	757
Fleet Marine Force Atlantic	757
Flint Hill	540
Floyd	540
Foneswood	804
Ford	804
Forest	434
Forest Hill	804
Fork Union	434
Forksville	434
Fort A P Hill	804
Fort Belvoir	703
Fort Blackmore	276
Fort Chiswell	276
Fort Defiance	540
Fort Eustis	757
Fort Hill	434
Fort Lee	804
Fort Lewis	540
Fort Mitchell	434
Fort Monroe	757
Fort Myer	703
Fort Story	757
Fort Valley	540
Foster	804
Foster Falls	276
Franconia	703
Franklin	757
Franklin Heights	757
Franktown	757
Fred	540
Fredbg	540
Frederickbg	540
Frederickbur	540
Fredericksbg	540
Fredericksbrg	540
Fredericksbur	540
Fredericksburg	540
Free Union	434
Freeman	434
Fries	276
Front Royal	540
Ft Ap Hill	804
Ft Belvoir	703
Ft Blackmore	276
Ft Myer	703
Fulks Run	540
Fx Station	703
Gainesville	703
Galax	276
Gannett	703
Garden City	540
Garrisonville	540
Gasburg	434
Gate City	276
Geico Insurance	540
George Mason	703
George Washington	703
Gether	804
Glade Hill	540
Glade Spring	276
Gladstone	434
Gladys	434
Glasgow	540
Glass	804
Glen Allen	804
Glen Allenw	804
Glen Lyn	540
Glen Wilton	540
Glenallen	804
Glenns	804
Glenvar	540
Gln Alln	804
Glou Point	804
Gloucester	804
Gloucester Point	804
Gloucester Pt	804
Glouster Point	804
Goldbond	540
Goldvein	540
Goochland	804
Goode	434
Goodview	540
Gordonsville	540
Gore	540
Goshen	540
Grafton	757
Grandin Road	540
Grapefield	276
Gratton	276
Graves Mill	540
Great Falls	703
Green Bay	434
Greenbackvile	757
Greenbackville	757
Greenbay	434
Greenbush	757
Greenville	540
Greenville Correctional Ctr	434
Greenway	703
Greenwood	540
Gretna	434
Grimstead	804
Grosclose	276
Grottoes	540
Grundy	276
Gum Spring	804
Gumspring	804
Gwyme	804
Gwynn	804
Hacks Neck	757
Hacksneck	757
Hadensville	804
Hague	804
Halifax	434
Hallieford	804
Hallwood	757
Hamilton	540
Hampden Sydney	434
Hampton	757
Hampton University	757
Hanging Rock	540
Hanover	804
Hanover Direct	804
Hansonville	276
Harborton	757
Hardy	540
Hardyville	804
Harman	276
Harrisburg	540
Harrisonburg	540
Hartfield	804
Hartwood	540
Hayes	804
Hayfield	540
Haymakertown	540
Haymarket	703
Haynesville	804
Haysi	276
Haywood	540
Hburg	540
Head Waters	540
Healing Sprgs	540
Healing Springs	540
Heathsville	804
Henrico	804
Henry	540
Herndon	202
Hicksville	276
Highland Spgs	804
Highland Springs	804
Hightown	540
Hillsboro	540
Hillsville	276
Hiltons	276
Hinton	540
Hiwassee	540
Hmpden Sydney	434
Holland	757
Hollins	540
Hollins Clg	540
Hollins College	540
Home Shopping Network	540
Honaker	276
Honeycamp	276
Hood	540
Hopewell	804
Horntown	757
Horsepen	276
Hot Springs	540
Howardsville	434
Howertons	804
Huddleston	540
Hudgins	804
Hume	540
Hundon	703
Huntly	540
Hurley	276
Hurt	434
Hustle	804
Independence	276
Indian	276
Indian Neck	804
Indian Valley	540
Ingram	434
Inspection Service Forensic	703
Internal Revenue Service	804
Iron Gate	540
Ironto	540
Irvington	804
Isle Of Wight	757
Ivanhoe	276
Ivor	757
Ivy	434
J Crew	434
Jamaica	804
James Madison University	540
James Store	804
Jamestown	757
Jamesville	757
Jarratt	434
Java	434
Jefferson Manor	703
Jefferson Mnr	703
Jeffersonton	540
Jenkins Brg	757
Jenkins Bridge	757
Jersey	540
Jetersville	804
Jewell Ridge	276
Jewell Valley	276
Joint Forces Staff College	757
Jonesville	276
Jordan Mines	540
Journal Newspaper	703
Kecoughtan Veterans Hospital	757
Keeling	434
Keen Mountain	276
Keene	434
Keezletown	540
Keller	757
Kenbridge	434
Kents Store	540
Keokee	276
Kesslers Mill	540
Keswick	434
Keysville	434
Kilmarnock	804
Kimballton	540
King And Qn C H	804
King And Queen Court House	804
King George	540
King Queen Ch	804
King William	804
Kingqueen Court House	804
Kings Store	540
Kingstowne	703
Kinsale	804
Koger Executive Ctr	804
La Crosse	434
Lacey Spring	540
Lackey	757
Ladysmith	804
Lafayette	540
Lahore	540
Lake Frederick	540
Lake Montcelo	434
Lake Monticello	434
Lake Of The Woods	540
Lake Of Woods	540
Lake Ridge	703
Lambsburg	276
Lancaster	804
Laneview	804
Lanexa	757
Langley	757
Langley Afb	757
Langley Air Force Base	757
Lansdowne	703
Laurel Fork	276
Lawrenceville	434
Leakesville Junction	276
Lebanon	276
Lebanon Ch	540
Lebanon Church	540
Lee Hall	757
Lee Mont	757
Leesburg	703
Lennig	434
Leon	540
Lewisetta	804
Lexington	540
Lightfoot	757
Lignum	540
Lillian Vernon	757
Lincoln	703
Linden	540
Linville	540
Lithia	540
Little Plymouth	804
Little Plymth	804
Littlevine	276
Lively	804
Lk Frederick	540
Locust Dale	540
Locust Grove	540
Locust Hill	804
Locustville	757
Long Island	434
Loretto	804
Lorton	202
Lottsburg	804
Louisa	540
Lovettsville	540
Lovingston	434
Low Moor	540
Lowesville	434
Lowmoor	540
Lowry	540
Lucketts	703
Lunenburg	434
Luray	540
Lynch Station	434
Lynchburg	434
Lyndhurst	434
Lynn Spring	276
Machipongo	757
Maclean	703
Macon	804
Madison	540
Madison Heights	434
Madison Hts	434
Madison Mills	540
Maidens	804
Main Office	804
Main Post Office	804
Manakin	804
Manakin Sabot	804
Manassas	703
Manassas Park	703
Mangohick	804
Mannboro	804
Manquin	804
Manufactures Hanover	434
Mappsville	757
Marine Corps Institute	703
Marion	276
Marionville	757
Markham	540
Marshall	540
Martinsville	276
Maryus	804
Mascot	804
Mason Cove	540
Mason Neck	703
Massanutten	540

assies Mill 434
assies Ml 434
athews 804
atoaca 804
attaponi 804
aurertown 540
avisdale 276
ax Meadows 276
axie 276
axwell 276
c Clure 276
c Coy 540
c Dowell 540
c Gaheysville 540
c Gaheysvlle 540
c Kenney 804
c Lean 202
cb Quantico 703
cclure 276
cdowell 540
cgaheysville 540
cguire Veterans Hospital 804
ckenney 804
clean 202
leadowcreek 276
leadows Dan 276
leadows Of Dan 276
leadowview 276
lears 757
lechanicsville 804
lechanicsvlle 804
leherrin 434
lelfa 757
lelrose 540
lendota 276
leredithville 434
lerrifield 703
lerry Point 804
liddlebrook 540
liddleburg 540
liddletown 540
lidland 540
lidlothian 804
lilboro Sprgs 540
liles 804
lilford 804
lill Gap 540
lillboro 540
lillboro Springs 540
lillenbeck 804
liller Park 434
lillers 804
lillers Tavern 804
lillers Tavrn 804
lillwood 540
line Run 540
lineral 540
lint Spring 540
lission Home 434
litchells 540
lntpelier Sta 540
lobil Oil Corp 703
lobjack 804
Modest Town 757
Mollusk 804
Moneta 540
Monroe 434
Montclair 703
Montebello 540
Monterey 540
Montezuma 540
Montford 540
Monticello 434
Montpelier 804
Montpelier Station 540
Montrose 804
Montrose Heights 804
Montross 804
Montvale 540
Moon 804
Morattico 804
Morrisville 540
Mosby 703
Moseley 804
Mount Crawford 540
Mount Holly 804

Mount Jackson 540
Mount Sidney 540
Mount Solon 540
Mount Vernon 703
Mount Weather 540
Mouth Of Wilson 276
Mouth Wilson 276
Mt Crawford 540
Mustoe 540
N N 757
N Springfield 703
N Springfld 703
N Tazewell 276
Narrows 540
Naruna 434
Nasa 757
Nasons 540
Nassawadox 757
Nathalie 434
National Right To Work Comm 703
National Science Foundation 703
Nationsbank Mortgage 804
Natl Assn Letter Carriers 703
Natural Brg 540
Natural Bridge 540
Natural Bridge Station 540
Naturl Br Sta 540
Nav Wpns Sta 804
Naval Air System Command 703
Naval Amphibious Base 757
Naval Base 757
Naval Communications Area Ma 757
Naval Defense Distrib Ctr 757
Naval Supply System Command 703
Naval Surface Weapons Center 540
Naval Weapons Sta 804
Naval Weapons Station 804
Navy Federal Credit Union 703
Navy Mutual Aid Assoc 703
Navy Sea Systems Command 703
Naxera 804
Nebo 276
Nellysford 434
Nelson 434
Nelsonia 757
Neusons 757
New Baltimore 540
New Canton 804
New Castle 540
New Church 757
New Hope 540
New Kent 804
New Market 540
New Point 804
New River 540
Newbern 540
Newcomb Hall 434
Newington 703
Newport 540
Newport News 757
Newsoms 757
Newtown 804
Nickelsville 276
Ninde 540
Nokesville 703
Nomini Grove 804
Nora 276
Norfolk 757
Norfolk Naval Air Station 757
Norfolk Naval Public Works C 757
Norfolk Naval Station 757
Norfolk Southern 540
Norfolk Southern Rwy 540
Norge 757
North 804
North Garden 434
North Springfield 703
North Tazewell 276
Northern Virginia 703
Northern Virginia Facility 703
Norton 276
Nortonsville 434
Norwood 434
Nottoway 434

Nuttsville 804
Oak Grove 804
Oak Hall 757
Oak Hill 703
Oaklevel 276
Oakpark 540
Oakton 703
Oakwood 276
Occoquan 703
Office Of Naval Research 703
Oilville 804
Old Dominion University 757
Old Somerset 540
Oldhams 804
Onancock 757
Onemo 804
Onley 757
Opal 540
Ophelia 804
Orange 540
Ordinary 804
Oriskany 540
Orkney Spgs 540
Orkney Springs 540
Orkney Sprngs 540
Orlean 703
Osceola 276
Overall 540
Owens 540
Oyster 757
Paeonian Spgs 540
Paeonian Springs 540
Paint Bank 540
Paint Lick 276
Painter 757
Palmer Springs 434
Palmersprings 434
Palmyra 434
Pamplin 434
Paris 540
Park 540
Parksley 757
Parrott 540
Partlow 540
Patrick Spgs 276
Patrick Springs 276
Patterson 276
Pearisburg 540
Peary 804
Pembroke 540
Penhook 540
Penn Laird 540
Penningtn Gap 276
Pennington 276
Pennington Gap 276
Petersburg 804
Phenix 434
Philomont 540
Philpott 276
Pilgrims Knob 276
Pilot 540
Pimmit 703
Pinero 804
Piney River 434
Pittsville 434
Plain View 804
Plainview 804
Pleasant Valley 540
Pleasant Vly 540
Poages Mill 540
Pocahontas 276
Poquoson 757
Port Haywood 804
Port Republic 540
Port Royal 804
Portsmouth 757
Potomac 703
Potomac Falls 703
Pound 276
Pounding Mill 276
Powhatan 804
Powhatand 804
Powhatano 804
Pratts 540
Prices Fork 540
Prince George 804

Prince William 703
Prince Wm 703
Prospect 434
Provdence Frg 804
Providence Forge 804
Pt Republic 540
Pulaski 540
Pungoteague 757
Purcellville 540
Putnam 276
Quantico 703
Quantico Naval Hospital 703
Quicksburg 540
Quinby 757
Quinque 434
Quinton 804
Raccoon Ford 540
Radford 540
Radiant 540
Ragged Point Beach 804
Randolph 434
Raphanck Acad 804
Raphine 540
Rapidan 540
Rappahannock Academy 804
Rappnhanck 804
Raven 276
Rawley Springs 540
Rawley Sprngs 540
Rawlings 804
Rectortown 540
Red Ash 276
Red House 434
Red Oak 434
Redart 804
Redwood 540
Reedville 804
Regency 804
Regina 804
Reliance 540
Remington 540
Republican Grove 434
Republicn Grv 434
Rescue 757
Reston 202
Reva 540
Rhoadesville 540
Rice 434
Rich 804
Rich Creek 540
Rich Int Ap 804
Richardson 276
Richardsville 540
Richlands 276
Richmnd 804
Richmond 703, 804
Richmond Int Airport 804
Richmond Newspapers 804
Ridge 804
Ridgeway 276
Rileyville 540
Riner 540
Ringgold 434
Ripplemead 540
Rivermont 434
Riverton 540
Rixeyville 540
Roanoke 540
Rochelle 540
Rockbdge Bath 540
Rockbrg Baths 540
Rockbridge Baths 540
Rockfish 434
Rockville 804
Rocky Gap 276
Rocky Mount 540
Rollins Fork 540
Rose Hill 276
Rosedale 276
Roseland 434
Rosslyn 703
Round Hill 540, 703
Rowe 276
Royal City 276
Ruby 540
Ruckersville 434

Rural Retreat 276
Rustburg 434
Ruther Glen 804
Rutherglen 804
Ruthville 804
Sabot 804
Saint Charles 276
Saint Davids Church 540
Saint Paul 276
Saint Stephens Church 804
Salem 540
Saltville 276
Saluda 804
Sandston 804
Sandy Hook 804
Sandy Level 434
Sandy Point 804
Sanford 757
Sanville 276
Saunders 804
Saxe 434
Saxis 757
Schley 804
Schoolfield 434
Schuyler 434
Scottsburg 434
Scottsville 434
Scruggs 540
Seaford 757
Sealston 540
Seaview 757
Sedley 757
Selma 540
Seven Corners 703
Seven Fountains 540
Seven Fountns 540
Seven Mile Fd 276
Seven Mile Ford 276
Severn 804
Shacklefords 804
Shadow 804
Shadwell 434
Sharps 804
Shawsville 540
Shelby 540
Shenandoah 540
Shenandoah Caverns 540
Shenandoah National Park 540
Shenandoah Valley Airpot 540
Shendoah Cvrn 540
Sherando 434
Shiloh 540
Shipman 434
Shndoh Nat Pk 540
Shortt Gap 276
Simpsons 540
Singers Glen 540
Skippers 434
Skipwith 434
Smithfield 757
Snell 540
Snowden 434
Snowflake 276
Snowville 540
Somerset 540
Somerville 540
South 703
South Boston 434
South Garden 434
South Hill 434
South Jackson 540
South Norfolk 757
South Riding 703
South Roanoke 540
Southbridge 703
Southill 434
Space & Naval Warfare System 703
Sparta 804
Speedwell 276
Spencer 276
Sperryville 540
Spotsylvania 540, 804
Spottswood 540
Spout Spring 434
Spring Grove 757
Springfield 202, 703

Sprint 703
Sprouses Corn 804
Sprouses Corner 804
St Davids Ch 540
St George 434
St Stephens Church 804
St Stephns Ch 804
Stacy 276
Stafford 540
Staffordsville 540
Staffordsvlle 540
Stamp Distribution Network 703
Stanardsville 434
Stanley 540
Stanleytown 276
Staples Mill 804
Star Tannery 540
State Farm 804
State Farm Insurance 434
Staunton 540
Staunton Park 540
Steeleburg 276
Steeles Tavern 540
Steeles Tavrn 540
Stephens City 540
Stephenson 540
Sterling 202
Stevens Creek 276
Stevensburg 540
Stevensville 804
Stewart 804
Stone Ridge 703
Stonega 276
Stones Mill 276
Stony Battery 276
Stony Creek 434
Strasburg 540
Stratford 804
Stuart 276
Stuarts Draft 540
Studley 804
Sudley Spgs 703
Sudley Springs 703
Suffolk 757
Sugar Grove 276
Sully Station 703
Sumerduck 540
Sun Trust Bank 703
Suntrust Bank 804
Supply 804
Surry 757
Susan 804
Sussex 434
Sussex Correctional Facility 804
Sutherland 804
Sutherlin 434
Sweet Briar 434
Swoope 540
Swords Creek 276
Sycamore Square 804
Syria 540
Syringa 804
Tabb 757
Tamworth 804
Tangier 757
Tannersville 276
Tappahannock 804
Tasley 757
Tazewell 276
Temperanceville 757
Temperancevle 757
Thaxton 540
The Cedars 276
The Plains 540
Theological Seminary 703
Thomas Bridge 276
Thomas Road Bapt Church 434
Thornburg 540
Thornhill 540
Timberlake 434
Timberville 540
Tiptop 276
Toano 757
Toms Brook 540
Topping 804
Townsend 757

City	Area Code
Trade Center	703
Trammel	276
Trevilians	540
Triangle	703
Triplet	434
Trout Dale	276
Troutdale	276
Troutville	540
Troy	434
Tuckahoe	804
Turbeville	434
Twymans Mill	540
Tye River	434
Tyro	434
U S Air	703
U S Army Trng Support Ctr	757
U S Geological Survey	703
Un Va Med Ctr	434
Union Hall	540
Union Level	434
Unionville	540
Univ Of Rich	804
Univ Of Va Med Ctr	434
University	434
University Of Richmo	804
University Of Richmond	804
Uno	540
Upperville	540
Urbanna	804
Us Army Mat Com	703
Us Navy Accounting Office	703
Us Unmanned Aerial Vehicles	703
Usa Today	703
V A State Dept Tax	804
Vab	757
Valentines	434
Vansant	276
Varina	804
Vcu/Mcv East	804
Vcu/West	804
Venia	276
Vernon Hill	434
Verona	540
Vesta	276
Vesuvius	540
Victoria	434
Vienna	703
Viewtown	540
Village	804
Villamont	540
Vint Hill Farms	540
Vint Hill Frm	540
Vinton	540
Virgilina	434
Virginia Bch	757
Virginia Beach	757
Virginia State University	804
Virginia Tech	540
Volney	276
W Springfield	703
Wachapreague	757
Wachovia	540
Wachovia Bank	703, 804
Wake	804
Wakefield	757
Walkerton	804
Wallops Is	757
Wallops Island	757
Walmsley	804
Walnut Hill	804
Walters	757
Wardell	276
Wardtown	757
Ware Neck	804
Warfield	434
Warm Springs	540
Warner	804
Warrenton	540, 703
Warsaw	804
Wash	540
Washgtns Brhp	804
Washington	540
Washingtons Birthplace	804
Water View	804
Waterford	540
Wattsville	757
Waverly	804
Waynesboro	540
Wdberry Forst	540
Wdbg	703
Weber City	276
Weems	804
Weirwood	757
West Augusta	540
West Lexington	540
West Mclean	703
West Point	804
West Springfield	703
Westbury	804
Western State Hospital	540
Weyers Cave	540
Whaleyville	757
Whitacre	540
White Hall	434
White Marsh	804
White Plains	434
White Post	540
White Stone	804
Whitestone	804
Whitetop	276
Whitewood	276
Wicomico	804
Wicomico Chur	804
Wicomico Church	804
Wildwood	434
Williamsburg	757
Williamsville	540
Willis	540
Willis Wharf	757
Willow Tree	276
Wilmington	434
Wilsons	804
Winchester	540
Windsor	757
Wingina	434
Winston	540
Wintergreen	434
Wintergreen Resort	434
Wintergrn Rst	434
Wirtz	540
Wise	276
Withams	757
Wlmg	757
Wmsbg	757
Wolford	276
Wolftown	540
Woodberry For	540
Woodberry Forest	540
Woodbridge	703
Woodford	804
Woodlawn	276
Woods Cr Rds	804
Woods Cross Rds	804
Woods Cross Roads	804
Woods Crs Rds	804
Woodstock	540
Woodville	540
Woolwine	276
Wrights Shop	434
Wylliesburg	434
Wytheville	276
Yale	434
Yancey Mills	434
Yards	276
Yorktown	757, 804
Yorktown Naval Weapons Stati	804
Zacata	804
Zanoni	804
Zion	540
Zion Crossrds	540
Zion Crossroads	540
Zuni	757

Washington

City	Area Code
Aberdeen	360
Aberdeen Gardens	360
Acme	360
Adco	509
Addy	509
Adelaide	425
Adelma Beach	360
Adna	360
Adrian	509
Aeneas	509
Agate Beach	360
Agnew	360
Ahtanum	509
Airway Heights	509
Airway Hgts	509
Ajlune	360
Albion	509
Alder	253
Alder Grove	360
Alderton	253
Alger	360
Algona	253
Allen	360
Allyn	360
Almira	509
Aloha	360
Alpental	509
Alpha	360
Amanda Park	360
Amazon.Com	206
Amber	509
Amboy	360
American Lake	253
Ames Lake	425
Anacortes	360
Anatone	509
Anderson Is	253
Anderson Island	253
Annapolis	360
Appleton	509
Appleyard	509
Ardenvoir	509
Ariel	360
Arletta	253
Arlington	360
Artondale	253
Ashford	360
Asotin	509
Auburn	253
Ault Field	360
Avista Corp.	509
Avondale	425
Azwell	509
Bainbridge Is	206
Bainbridge Island	206
Bakerview	360
Ballard	206
Bangor	360
Bangor Submarine Base	360
Bank Of America	206
Baring	360
Basin City	509
Battle Ground	360
Battleground	360
Bay Center	360
Bay City	360
Beacon Hill	206
Beaux Arts	425
Beaux Arts Village	425
Beaver	360
Beckett Point	360
Belfair	360
Bellevue	425
Bellingham	360
Belmont	509
Bench Drive	360
Benge	509
Benton City	509
Bethel	253
Beverly	509
Bickleton	509
Bingen	509
Birch Bay	360
Bitter Lake	206
Black Diamond	360
Blaine	360
Blakely Is	360
Blakely Island	360
Blewett	509
Blyn	360
Bodie	509
Bogachiel	360
Boistfort	360
Bonney Lake	253
Bonney Lk	253
Boston Harbor	360
Bothell	425
Bow	360
Boyds	509
Brady	360
Breidablick	360
Brem	360
Bremerton	206, 360
Brewster	509
Bridgeport	509
Brier	425
Brinnon	360
Broadway	206
Browns Point	253
Brownstown	509
Brownsville	360
Brush Prairie	360
Bryant	360
Bryn Mawr	425
Buckley	360
Bucoda	360
Buena	509
Bunker	360
Burbank	509
Burien	206
Burley	360
Burlington	360
Burnett	360
Burton	206
Camano City	360
Camano Island	360
Camas	360
Camp Murray	253
Camp Murray Natl Guard	253
Camp Union	360
Cape Flattery	360
Capital One	206
Capitol Hill	206
Carbonado	360
Carlisle	360
Carlsborg	360
Carlson	360
Carlton	509
Carnation	425
Carriage Hill	360
Carrolls	360
Carson	509
Cascade	425
Cashmere	509
Castle Rock	360
Cathlamet	360
Cedar Falls	425
Cedarview	253
Cedarville	360
Cedonia	509
Center	360
Centerville	509
Central Park	360
Central Valley	360
Centralia	360
Ceres	360
Chattaroy	509
Chehalis	360
Chelan	509
Chelan Falls	509
Chelatchie	360
Cheney	509
Chenois Creek	360
Chesaw	509
Chewelah	509
Chico	360
Chimacum	360
Chinook	360
Chuckanut	360
Chumstick	509
Cinebar	360
City Of Spokane Valley	509
Clallam Bay	360
Claquato	360
Clarkston	509
Clayton	509
Cle Elum	509
Clearbrook	360
Clearlake	360
Clearview	360
Clearwater	360
Cliffdell	509
Clinton	360
Clyde Hill	425
Coal Creek	425
Cohasset Beach	360
Colbert	509
Colby	360
Colchester	360
Colfax	509
College Place	509
Colton	509
Columbia	206
Colville	509
Conconully	509
Concrete	360
Connell	509
Conway	360
Cook	509
Copalis Beach	360
Copalis Crossing	360
Copalis Xing	360
Cosmopolis	360
Cottage Lake	425
Cougar	360
Coulee City	509
Coulee Dam	509
Coupeville	360
Covington	253
Cowiche	509
Crane	360
Crescent Beach	360
Crescent Valley	253
Creston	509
Crocker	360
Cromwell	253
Crosby	360
Crown Hill	206
Crystal Mountain	360
Cty Spok Val	509
Cumberland	360
Curlew	509
Curtis	360
Cushman Dam	360
Cusick	509
Custer	360
Dabob	360
Dallesport	509
Danville	509
Darrington	360
Dash Point	253
Davenport	509
Dayton	509
Decatur Island	360
Deckerville	360
Deer Harbor	360
Deer Lake	509
Deer Meadows	509
Deer Park	509
Deming	360
Denny Creek	425
Des Moines	206
Desert Aire	509
Diablo	360
Diamond	509
Diamond Point	360
Diamond Pt	360
Dieringer	253
Disautel	509
Discovery Bay	360
Dixie	509
Dockton	206
Doebay	360
Donald	509
Doris	509
Doty	360
Douglas	509
Driftwood	253
Dryad	360
Dryden	509
Dungeness	360
Dupont	253
Duvall	425
Duwamish	425
E Wenatchee	50
Earlmount	42
East Bremerton	36
East Farms	50
East Olympia	36
East Port Orchard	36
East Quilcene	36
East Selah	50
East Union	20
East Wenatchee	50
Eastgate	42
Eastmont	42
Easton	42
Eastsound	36
Eatonville	25
Edgewood	25
Edison	36
Edmonds	206, 42
Edwall	50
Eglon	36
Elbe	36
Eldon	36
Electric City	50
Electron	36
Elger Bay	36
Elgin	25
Elk	50
Elk Plain	25
Ellensburg	509
Ellisford	50
Elma	360
Elmer City	509
Eltopia	509
Endicott	509
Enetai	360
Entiat	509
Enumclaw	360
Ephrata	509
Erlands Point	360
Espanola	509
Ethel	360
Evaline	360
Evans	509
Everett	425
Evergreen State College	360
Everson	360
Fairchild Afb	509
Fairchild Air Force Base	509
Fairfield	509
Fairhaven	360
Fairholm	360
Fairview	509
Fairwood	425
Fall City	425
Farmer	509
Farmington	509
Federal Way	253
Ferndale	360
Fernwood	360
Fife	253
Finley	509
Fircrest	253
Firdale	360
Firm Brm	360
Firwood	253
Ford	509
Fords Prairie	360
Forest	360
Forest City	360
Forest Park	206
Forks	360
Fort Flagler	360
Fort Lawton	206
Fort Lewis	253
Fort Steilacoom	253
Fort Worden	360
Four Corners	425
Four Lakes	509
Fox Is	253
Fox Island	253
Fragaria	253
Frances	360
Freeland	360
Friday Harbor	360
Fruitland	509
Fruitvale	509

City	Area Code
Flagler	360
Lewis	253
Worden	360
les Addition	360
lvin	360
rden City	360
rdiner	360
rfield	509
te	360
orge	509
bson Creek	360
ford	509
g Harbor	253
berton	360
acier	360
eed	509
en Cove	360
encove	253
enoma	360
enwood	509
old Bar	360
oldendale	509
nzaga Univ	509
oose Prairie	509
orst	360
aham	253
and Coulee	509
and Mound	360
andview	509
anger	509
anite Falls	360
ant Road Addition	509
apeview	253
ay Gables	360
ayland	360
ays Harbor City	360
ays River	360
een Bluff	509
eenacres	509
eenbank	360
eenwater	360
eenwood	206
isdale	360
otto	360
uemes	360
uemes Island	360
uerrier	360
adlock	360
amilton	360
anford Works	509
ansville	360
arbor Heights	253
armony	360
arper	360
arrah	509
arrington	509
arstine	360
artford	425
artline	509
arwood	509
atton	509
avillah	509
ay	509
azelwood	425
eather	360
eisson	360
erron Is	253
erron Island	253
ighlands	425
illgrove	360
obart	425
oko	360
olcomb	360
olden Village	509
olly	360
ome	253
oodsport	360
ooper	509
oquiam	360
orseshoe Lake	360
oughton	425
umptulips	360
unters	509
unts Point	425
usum	509
yak	509
Ilwaco	360
Inchelium	509
Index	360
Indian Is	360
Indian Island	360
Indianola	360
Inglewood	425
Inlet Island	253
Interbay	206
International	206
Ione	509
Irondale	360
Island Lake	360
Issaquah	425
Jovita	253
Joyce	360
Juanita	425
Junction City	360
Kahlotus	509
Kalalock	360
Kalama	360
Kalber	360
Kamilche	360
Kanaskat	360
Kapowsin	360
Keller	509
Kellys Korner	360
Kelso	360
Kendall	360
Kenmore	425
Kenn	509
Kennard Corner	425
Kennewick	509
Kennydale	425
Kenroy	509
Kent	253
Ketron Is	253
Ketron Island	253
Kettle Falls	509
Kewa	509
Key Center	253
Keyport	360
Kingsgate	425
Kingston	360
Kiona	509
Kirkland	425
Kitsap Lake	360
Kittitas	509
Klaber	360
Klickitat	509
Knab	360
Kosmos	360
Krain	360
Krupp	509
La Center	360
La Conner	360
La Crosse	509
La Grande	360
La Push	360
Lacamas	360
Lacey	360
Lacrosse	509
Lake Alice	425
Lake City	206
Lake Crescent	360
Lake Forest Park	206
Lake Holiday	360
Lake Joy	425
Lake Ozette	360
Lake Sawyer	253
Lake Stevens	425
Lake Tapps	253
Lakebay	253
Lakeridge	253
Lakeside	509
Lakeview Park	509
Lakewood	253
Lamona	509
Lamont	509
Langley	360
Larimers Corner	360
Latah	509
Laurier	509
Leavenworth	509
Lebam	360
Leland	360
Lemolo	360
Liberty	509
Liberty Lake	509
Liberty Park	509
Lilliwaup	360
Lincoln	509
Lind	509
Lindberg	360
Littell	360
Little Boston	360
Littlerock	360
Lk Forest Park	206
Lk Forest Pk	206
Lofall	360
Long Beach	360
Long Lake	360
Longbranch	253
Longmire	360
Longview	360
Loomis	509
Loon Lake	509
Lopez Island	360
Loveland	253
Lowden	509
Lowell	425
Lucerne	509
Lummi Island	360
Lyle	509
Lyman	360
Lynden	360
Lynnwood	425
Mabton	509
Machias	360
Macys	206
Madigan Army Medical Center	253
Madigan Hosp	253
Madigan Hospital	253
Madison Park	206
Mae	509
Magnolia	206
Makah Afb	360
Malaga	509
Malden	509
Malo	509
Malone	360
Malott	509
Maltby	360
Manchester	360
Manito	509
Manitou Beach	206
Mansfield	509
Manson	509
Maple Beach	360
Maple Falls	360
Maple Grove	360
Maple Valley	425
Maplewood	253
Marblemount	360
Marcus	509
Marietta	360
Marine Drive	360
Markham	360
Marlin	509
Marrowstone Is	360
Marrowstone Island	360
Marshall	509
Maryhill	509
Marys Corner	360
Marysville	360
Mason City	509
Matlock	360
Mats Mats	360
Mattawa	509
Maxwelton	360
Maytown	360
Mazama	509
Mc Chord Afb	253
Mc Cleary	360
Mc Kenna	253
Mcchord Afb	253
Mccleary	360
Mckenna	253
Mcmicken Heights	425
Mcneil Island	253
Mead	509
Meadowdale	360
Medical Lake	509
Medina	425
Meeker	253
Melbourne	360
Menlo	360
Mercer Island	206
Merritt	509
Mesa	509
Metaline	509
Metaline Falls	509
Metaline Fls	509
Methow	509
Miami Beach	360
Mica	509
Midway	253
Milan	509
Mill Creek	425
Millwood	509
Milton	253
Mineral	360
Mission Square	509
Moclips	360
Mohler	509
Molson	509
Monitor	509
Monroe	360
Monse	509
Montesano	360
Morganville	360
Morton	360
Moses Lake	509
Mossyrock	360
Mount Pleasant	360
Mount Vernon	360
Mount Walker	360
Mountlake Ter	425
Mountlake Terrace	425
Moxee	509
Moxee City	509
Mukilteo	425
N Bonneville	509
N Lakewood	360
Naches	509
Nahcotta	360
Napavine	360
Nas Whidbey	360
Naselle	360
National	360
Naval Station Everett	425
Navy Yard City	360
Neah Bay	360
Neilton	360
Nemah	360
Nespelem	509
New London	360
Newaukum	360
Newcastle	425
Newhalem	360
Newman Lake	509
Newport	509
Newport Hills	425
Newton	360
Nighthawk	509
Nile	509
Nine Mile Falls	509
Nine Mile Fls	509
Nisqually	360
Nisson	360
Nooksack	360
Nooksack Indian Reservation	360
Nordland	360
Normandy Park	206
North Bend	425, 509
North Bonneville	509
North City	206
North Cove	360
North Lakewood	360
North Prosser	509
Northgate	206
Northport	509
Novelty	360
Oak Bay	360
Oak Harbor	360
Oakbrook	253
Oakesdale	509
Oakville	360
Ocean City	360
Ocean Park	360
Ocean Shores	360
Oceanside	360
Ocosta	360
Odessa	509
Offutt Lake	360
Ohop	360
Okanogan	509
Olalla	253
Olalla Valley	253
Old Willapa	360
Olga	360
Oly	360
Olympia	360
Olympic View	360
Omak	509
Onalaska	360
Orcas	360
Orchard Heights	360
Orchards	360
Orient	509
Orondo	509
Oroville	509
Orting	360
Osceola	360
Oso	360
Othello	509
Otis Orchards	509
Outlook	509
Overlook	360
Oyhat	360
Oysterville	360
Ozette	360
Pacific	253
Pacific Beach	360
Pacific Lutheran University	253
Packwood	360
Palisades	509
Palmer	360
Palouse	509
Paradise Inn	253
Parker	509
Parkland	253
Parkwood	360
Pasco	509
Pateros	509
Paterson	509
Pe Ell	360
Pearcot	509
Pearson	360
Peell	360
Peshastin	509
Physt	360
Picnic Point	253
Pine Lake	425
Pinehurst	425
Pioneer Square	206
Plain	509
Plaza	509
Pleasant Valley	360
Plymouth	509
Point Fosdick	253
Point Roberts	360
Pomeroy	509
Pomona	509
Ponderosa Estates	253
Port Angeles	360
Port Gamble	360
Port Hadlock	360
Port Ludlow	360
Port Orchard	360
Port Stanley	360
Port Townsend	360
Possession	360
Poulsbo	360
Prairie Ridge	253
Preachers Slough	360
Prescott	509
Preston	425
Prosser	509
Protection Is	360
Protection Island	360
Prt Angeles	360
Pt Angeles	360
Pt Fosdick	253
Pt Orchard	360
Pt Townsend	360
Public Safety Bldg	509
Puget Island	360
Puget Sound Naval Shipyard	360
Pullman	509
Purdy	253
Puy	253
Puyallup	253
Queen Anne	206
Queensborough	425
Queensgate	425
Queets	360
Quilcene	360
Quinault	360
Quincy	509
Qwest	206
Raft Is	253
Raft Island	253
Rainier	360
Randle	360
Raugust	509
Ravensdale	360
Raymond	360
Reardan	509
Recreational Equipment Inc	253
Redmond	425
Redondo	253
Redondo Beach	206
Reg Lib Handicapped	206
Rei	253
Renton	425
Republic	509
Retsil	360
Rhododendron Park	253
Rice	509
Richland	509
Richmond Beach	206
Richmond Highlands	206
Ridgefield	360
Rimrock	509
Ritzville	509
Riverside	509
Riverton	425
Roche Harbor	360
Rochester	360
Rock Island	509
Rockford	509
Rocklyn	509
Rockport	360
Rocky Butte	509
Rocky Point	360
Rollingbay	206
Ronald	509
Roosevelt	509
Rosalia	509
Rosburg	360
Rosedale	253
Roslyn	509
Roy	253
Royal City	509
Royal Slope	509
Ruff	509
Ruston	253
Ryderwood	360
S Cle Elum	509
S Park Vil	360
S Park Vlg	360
Safeco Plaza	206
Saginaw	360
Saint John	509
Saint Urbans	360
Salkum	360
Samish Island	360
Sammamish	425
San Juan Island	360
Sandy Hook Park	360
Sappho	360
Satsop	360
Sawyer	509
Saxon	360
Scandia	360
Scenic	360
Schawana	509
Schneiders Prairie	360
Seabeck	360

Seahurst 206
Seatac 206, 425
Seatac Airport 206
Seattle 206
Seattle Naval Support Activi 206
Seaview 360
Sedro Woolley 360
Sekiu 360
Selah 509
Sequim 360
Seven Bays 509
Shadle Garland 509
Shaw Island 360
Shelton 360
Sheridan Park 206, 360
Shine 360
Shore Acres 253
Shoreline 206
Shorewood 206
Shorewood Beach 253
Silvana 360
Silver Beach 360
Silver Creek 360
Silver Lake 425
Silverdale 360
Silverlake 360
Similk Beach 360
Skamania 509
Skamokawa 360
Skok 360
Skokomish 360
Skokomish Nation 360
Skykomish 360
Skyway 425
Smokey Point 360
Snag Island 253
Snohomish 360
Snoqualmie 425, 509
Snoqualmie Pass 509
Snoqualmie Ps 509
Soap Lake 509
Sol Duc Hot Springs 360
South Aberdeen 360
South Bay 360
South Bend 360
South Broadway 509
South Cle Elum 509
South Colby 360
South Elma 360
South Hill 253
South Montesano 360
South Park Village 360
South Prairie 360
South Sound 360
Southworth 206
Spanaway 253
Spangle 509
Spo Valley 509
Spokane 509
Spokane City Trea 509
Spokane Dist Closed 509
Spokane Valley 509
Spokane Vly 509
Sprague 509
Spring Glen 425
Springdale 509
Stanwood 360
Starbuck 509
Startup 360
Stehekin 509
Steilacoom 253
Steptoe 509
Stevenson 509
Strandell 360
Stratford 509
Sultan 360
Sumach 509
Sumas 360
Summit 253
Sumner 253
Suncadia 509
Sunny Bay 253
Sunnyside 509
Sunnyslope 360
Sunrise Beach 253
Sunset Hill 509
Suquamish 360
Sylvan 253
Synarep 509
Tacoma 253
Taholah 360
Tahuya 360
Tampico 509
Tapps Island 253
Tatoosh Is 360
Tatoosh Island 360
Teanaway 509
Tekoa 509
Telma 509
Tenino 360
The Highlands 206
Thompson Place 360
Thornton 509
Thorp 509
Thrali 509
Thrashers Corner 425
Thrift 253
Tieton 509
Times Square 206
Tokeland 360
Toledo 360
Tonasket 509
Toppenish 509
Totem Lake 425
Touchet 509
Toutle 360
Townsend 360
Tracyton 360
Tri Cities 509
Trinidad 509
Trout Lake 509
Troutlake 509
Tukwila 206, 425
Tulalip 360
Tum Tum 509
Tumtum 509
Tumwater 360
Twisp 509
Tyler 509
U S Veterans Hospital 253
Underwood 509
Union 360
Union Gap 509
Union Mills 360
Uniontown 509
Univ Of Washington 206
University 206
University Of Puget Sound 253
University Pl 253
University Place 253
Upper Hoh 360
Upper Skagit Indian Reservat 360
Usk 509
Vader 360
Vail 360
Valley 509
Valleyford 509
Van Buren 360
Vancouver 360
Vantage 509
Vashon 206
Vashon Island 206
Vaughn 253
Veradale 509
Victor 253
View Park 360
Villa Beach 253
Virginia 360
Wabash 360
Wahkiacus 509
Waitsburg 509
Waldron 360
Walla Walla 509
Wallingford 206
Wallula 509
Wapato 509
Warden 509
Warren 253
Washington State Department 360
Washington State University 509
Washougal 360
Washtucna 509
Waterman 360
Waterville 509
Wauconda 509
Wauna 360
Wauna Shores 253
Waunch Prairie 360
Wautauga Beach 360
Waverly 509
Wedgwood 206
Weikel 509
Welcome 360
Wellpinit 509
Wenatchee 509
Wenatchee Heights 509
West Hills 360
West Park 360
West Richland 509
West Seattle 206
West Side 509
West Wenatchee 509
Westport 360
Westwood 206
Westwood Village 206
Wheeler 509
Whidbey Island Naval Air 360
Whidbey Nas 360
White Center 206
White Pass 509
White Salmon 509
White Swan 509
Whites 360
Whitworth University 509
Wilbur 509
Wildcat Lake 360
Wilderness Village 425
Wildwood 360
Wilkeson 360
Willapa 360
Wilson Creek 509
Winchester 509
Winlock 360
Winthrop 509
Winton 509
Wishkah 360
Wishram 509
Withrow 509
Wollochet 253
Woodinville 425
Woodland 360
Woodlawn 360
Woodmont Beach 253
Woodway 206
World Vision Brm 253
Wye Lake 360
Yacolt 360
Yakima 509
Yakima Firing Center 509
Yale 360
Yarrow Point 425
Yelm 360
Yoman Ferry 253
Zillah 509

West Virginia

All Points 304

Wisconsin

Abbotsford 715
Abrams 920
Adams 608
Adell 920
Afton 608
Alban 715
Albany 608
Albertville 715
Alden 715
Algoma 920
Allenton 262
Allouez 920
Alma 608
Alma Center 715
Almena 715
Almond 715
Altdorf 715
Altoona 715
Alvin 715
Amberg 715
American Family Ins Co 608
Amery 715
Amherst 715
Amherst Jct 715
Amherst Junction 715
Angelica 920
Aniwa 715
Antigo 715
Apostle Islands National Lak 715
Appleton 920
Arbor Vitae 715
Arcadia 608
Arena 608
Argonne 715
Argyle 608
Arkansaw 715
Arkdale 608
Arland 715
Arlington 608
Armstrong Creek 715
Armstrong Crk 715
Arnott 715
Arpin 715
Ashippun 920
Ashland 715
Ashley 715
Ashwaubenon 920
Athelstane 715
Athens 715
Atwood 715
Auburndale 715
Augusta 715
Auroraville 920
Avalon 608
Avoca 608
Babcock 715
Bad River Indian Reservation 715
Bagley 608
Baileys Harbor 920
Baileys Hbr 920
Bakerville 715
Baldwin 715
Balsam Lake 715
Bancroft 715
Bangor 608
Baraboo 608
Barnes 715
Barneveld 608
Barre Mills 608
Barron 715
Barronett 715
Bassett 262
Bateman 715
Bay City 715
Bay Mills 715
Bay View 414
Bayfield 715
Bayside 414
Bayview 414
Bear Creek 715
Beaver 715
Beaver Dam 920
Beecher 715
Beetown 608
Beldenville 715
Belgium 262
Bell Center 608
Belleville 608
Bellevue 920
Belmont 608
Beloit 608
Benet Lake 262
Bennett 715
Benoit 715
Benton 608
Berlin 920
Bethel 715
Bevent 715
Big Bend 262
Big Falls 715
Big Flats 608
Birch 715
Birchwood 715
Birnamwood 715
Biron 715
Black Brook 715
Black Creek 920
Black Earth 608
Black River Falls 715
Blackwell 715
Blair 608
Blanchardville 608
Blanchardvile 608
Blenker 715
Blk Riv Falls 715
Blk River Fls 715
Bloom City 608
Bloomer 715
Bloomingdale 608
Bloomington 608
Bloomville 715
Blue Mounds 608
Blue River 608
Boardman 715
Boaz 608
Bonduel 715, 920
Boscobel 608
Boulder Jct 715
Boulder Junction 715
Bowler 715
Boyceville 715
Boyd 715
Brackett 715
Branch 920
Brandon 920
Brantwood 715
Briggsville 608
Brill 715
Brillion 920
Bristol 262
Brodhead 608
Brokaw 715
Brookfield 262, 414
Brookfld 262
Brooklyn 608
Brooks 608
Brown Deer 414
Brownsville 920
Browntown 608
Bruce 715
Brule 715
Brussels 920
Bryant 715
Bte Des Morts 920
Buena Vista 715
Buffalo City 608
Burkhardt 715
Burlington 262
Burnett 920
Butler 262
Butte Des Morts 920
Butternut 715
Byron 920
Cable 715
Cadott 715
Cady 715
Caledonia 262
Cambria 920
Cambridge 608
Cameron 715
Camp Douglas 608
Camp Lake 262
Camp Mccoy 608
Campbell 608
Campbellsport 920
Canton 715
Carey 715
Caroline 715
Carson 715
Carter 715
Caryville 715
Cascade 920
Casco 920
Cashton 608
Cassian 715
Cassville 608
Cataract 6
Catawba 7
Cato 9
Cavour 7
Cayuga 7
Cazenovia 6
Cecil 7
Cedar 71
Cedar Falls 71
Cedar Grove 9
Cedar Rapids 71
Cedarburg 26
Center Valley 9
Centerville 6
Centuria 71
Chase Bank 41
Chaseburg 6
Chelsea 71
Chenequa 26
Chetek 71
Chili 71
Chilton 92
Chippewa Falls 71
Chippewa Fls 71
Christie 71
City Point 71
Clam Falls 71
Clam Lake 71
Clark 71
Clayton 71
Clearwater Lake 71
Clearwater Lk 71
Cleghorn 71
Cleveland 92
Clifton 71
Clinton 60
Clintonville 71
Cloverland 71
Clyman 92
Cobb 60
Cochrane 60
Coddington 71
Colby 71
Coleman 92
Colfax 71
Colgate 26
Collins 92
Coloma 71
Columbus 92
Combined Lcks 92
Combined Locks 92
Comstock 71
Connorsville 71
Conover 71
Conrath 71
Coon Valley 60
Cornell 71
Corning 71
Cornucopia 71
Cosy Valley 71
Cottage Grove 60
Couderay 71
Crandon 715
Cream 608
Crescent 715
Crivitz 715
Cross Plains 60
Cuba City 608
Cudahy 414
Cumberland 715
Curtiss 715
Cushing 715
Custer 715
Cutler 608
Cylon 715
Dairyland 715
Dale 920
Dallas 715
Dalton 920
Danbury 715
Dancy 715
Dane 608
Darien 262
Darlington 608
De Forest 608

City	Area Code
e Pere	920
e Soto	608
eer Creek	715
eer Park	715
eerbrook	715
eerfield	608
elafield	262
elavan	262
ellwood	608
elta	715
enmark	920
eronda	715
ewey	715
exterville	715
iamond Bluff	715
ickeyville	608
odge	608
odgeville	608
onald	715
orchester	715
ousman	262
owning	715
ownsville	715
oylestown	920
resser	715
rummond	715
unbar	715
urand	715
yckesville	920
Ellsworth	715
agle	262
agle Point	715
agle River	715
agleton	715
ast Ellsworth	715
ast Farmington	715
ast Troy	262
astman	608
aton	715
au Claire	715
au Galle	715
au Pleine	715
den	920
dgar	715
dgerton	608
dgewater	715
dmund	608
dson	715
gg Harbor	920
isenstein	715
l Paso	715
land	715
lcho	715
lderon	715
ldorado	920
lectronic Data Systems	608
leva	715
lk	715
lk Creek	715
lk Mound	715
lkhart Lake	920
lkhorn	262
llis	715
llison Bay	920
llsworth	715
lm Grove	262
lmwood	715
lroy	608
lton	715
mbarrass	715
merald	715
mployers Health Insure Cos	920
mployers Hlt Ins Co	920
ndeavor	608
phraim	920
rin	715
Erin Prairie	715
Esadore Lake	715
Ettrick	608
Eureka	715
Eureka Center	715
Evansville	608
Exeland	715
Fairchild	715
Fairwater	920
Fall Creek	715
Fall River	920
Fdl	920
Fence	715
Fennimore	608
Fenwood	715
Ferryville	608
Fifield	715
Figis	715
Figis Inc	715
Fish Creek	920
Fitchburg	608
Florence	715
Fond Du Lac	920
Fontana	262
Footville	608
Forest Jct	920
Forest Junction	920
Forestville	920
Fort Atkinson	920
Fort Mccoy	608
Foster	715
Fountain City	608
Fox Lake	920
Fox Point	414
Foxboro	715
Francis Creek	920
Franklin	414
Franksville	262
Franzen	715
Frederic	715
Fredonia	262
Freedom	920
Fremont	920
French Island	608
Friendship	608
Friesland	920
Galesville	608
Galloway	715
Gays Mills	608
General Casualty Co	608
Genesee Depot	262
Genoa	608
Genoa City	262
Germantown	262
Gile	715
Gillett	920
Gilman	715
Gilmanton	715
Gleason	715
Glen Flora	715
Glen Haven	608
Glenbeulah	920
Glendale	414
Glenwood City	715
Glidden	715
Goodman	715
Goodnow	715
Goodrich	715
Gordon	715
Gotham	608
Grafton	262
Grand Chute	920
Grand Marsh	608
Grand Rapids	715
Grand View	715
Granton	715
Grantsburg	715
Gratiot	608
Green Bay	920
Green Grove	715
Green Lake	920
Green Valley	920
Greenbush	920
Greendale	414
Greenfield	414
Greenleaf	920
Greenville	920
Greenwood	715
Gresham	715
Gurney	715
Hackett	715
Hager City	715
Halder	715
Hales Corners	414
Hallie	715
Hamburg	
Hammond	715
Hancock	715
Hannibal	715
Hanover	608
Hansen	715
Hansen Road	920
Harding	715
Harrison	715
Harshaw	715
Hartford	262
Hartland	262
Hatfield	715
Hatley	715
Haugen	715
Haven	920
Hawkins	715
Hawthorne	715
Hayward	715
Hazel Green	608
Hazelhurst	715
Heafford Jct	715
Heafford Junction	715
Helenville	262
Hendren	715
Herbster	715
Herrschners	715
Hersey	715
Hertel	715
Hewitt	715
High Bridge	715
Highbridge	715
Highland	608
Hilbert	920
Hiles	715
Hillpoint	608
Hillsboro	608
Hillsdale	715
Hingham	920
Hixton	715
Hoard	715
Hobart	920
Hofa Park	920
Hogarty	715
Holcombe	715
Hollandale	608
Hollister	715
Holmen	608
Honey Creek	262
Horicon	920
Hortonville	920
Houlton	715
Howard	920
Howards Grove	920
Howards Grove Br #4	920
Hubertus	262
Hudson	715
Hull	715
Humbird	715
Hunting	715
Huntington	715
Hurley	715
Hustisford	920
Hustler	608
Independence	715
Ingram	715
Institute	920
Iola	715
Irma	715
Iron Belt	715
Iron Ridge	920
Iron River	715
Isaar	920
Island Lake	715
Ixonia	262
J C Penney	262
J W Jung Seed Co	920
Jackson	262
Jacksonport	920
Janesville	608
Jc Penney	262
Jefferson	920
Jeffris	715
Jersey City	715
Jewett	715
Jim Falls	715
Joel	715
Johnson Creek	920
Jordan	715
Juda	608
Jump River	715
Junction City	715
Juneau	920
Kaiser	715
Kansasville	262
Kaukauna	920
Kellner	715
Kellnersville	920
Kelly	715
Kempster	715
Kendall	608
Kennan	715
Kenosha	262
Keshena	715
Kewaskum	262
Kewaunee	920
Kiel	920
Kieler	608
Kimball	715
Kimberly	920
King	715
Kingston	920
Kinnickinnic	715
Knapp	715
Knowles	920
Knowlton	715
Kohler	920
Krakow	920
Krause Publ Co	715
Kronenwetter	715
Kunesh	920
La Crosse	608
La Farge	608
La Pointe	715
La Valle	608
Lac Courte Oreilles Indian R	715
Lac Du Flambeau	715
Lac Du Flambeau Reservation	715
Lac Du Flambu	715
Lacrosse	608
Ladysmith	715
Lafayette	715
Lake	715
Lake Delton	608
Lake Emily	715
Lake Geneva	262
Lake George	715
Lake Hallie	715
Lake Holcombe	715
Lake Mills	920
Lake Nebagamon	715
Lake Tomahawk	715
Lake Wazeecha	715
Lake Windsor	608
Lake Wissota	715
Laketown	715
Lakewood	715
Lancaster	608
Land O Lakes	715
Lands End	608
Langes Corner	920
Lannon	262
Laona	715
Larsen	920
Lco Commercial Cent	715
Lebanon	920
Lena	920
Leopolis	715
Lewis	715
Lily	715
Lime Ridge	608
Linden	608
Lindsey	715
Linwood	715
Lisbon	262
Little Black	715
Little Chicago	715
Little Chute	920
Little Falls	715
Little Suamico	920
Livingston	608
Lk Nebagamon	715
Lodi	608
Loganville	608
Lohrville	920
Lomira	920
Lone Rock	608
Long Lake	715
Longwood	715
Loomis	715
Loretta	715
Lostcreek	715
Lowell	920
Loyal	715
Ltl Chicago	715
Ltl Suamico	920
Lublin	715
Luck	715
Luger	715
Lugerville	715
Luxemburg	920
Lymantown	715
Lyndon Sta	608
Lyndon Station	608
Lynn	715
Lynxville	608
Lyons	262
M And I Bank	414
Madison	608
Madison Business Reply Mail	608
Madison Gas And Electric	608
Maiden Rock	715
Malone	920
Manawa	920
Manchester	920
Manitowish Waters	715
Manitowoc	920
Manitowsh Wtr	715
Maple	715
Maple Bluff	608
Maplehurst	715
Maplewood	920
Marathon	715
Marathon City	715
Marengo	715
Maribel	920
Marinette	715
Marion	715
Markesan	920
Markton	715
Marquette	920
Marshall	608
Marshall And Ilsley Bank	414
Marshfield	715
Martell	715
Mason	715
Mason Shoe	715
Mather	608
Mattoon	715
Mauston	608
Mayville	920
Mazomanie	608
Mc Farland	608
Mc Naughton	715
Mcmillan	715
Mcnaughton	715
Medford	715
Medina	920
Mellen	715
Melrose	608
Menasha	920
Menekaunee	715
Menomonee Falls	262
Menomonee Fls	262
Menomonie	715
Mequon	262
Mercer	715
Merrill	715
Merrillan	715
Merrimac	608
Merton	262
Middle Inlet	715
Middle Ridge	608
Middleton	608
Mikana	715
Milan	715
Miles Kimball Co	920
Milladore	715
Millston	608
Milltown	715
Milton	608
Milwaukee	262
Mindoro	608
Mineral Point	608
Minocqua	715
Minong	715
Mishicot	920
Modena	715
Moeville	715
Mole Lake	715
Mondovi	715
Monico	715
Monona	608
Monona Grove	608
Monroe	608
Monroe Center	608
Montello	608
Montfort	608
Monticello	608
Montreal	715
Moon	715
Moquah	715
Morris	715
Morrisonville	608
Morse	715
Mosinee	715
Mount Calvary	920
Mount Hope	608
Mount Horeb	608
Mount Sterling	608
Mountain	715
Mt Sterling	608
Mukwonago	262
Muscoda	608
Muskego	262
N Fond Du Lac	920
N Woods Beach	715
Nashotah	262
Nashville	715
Navarino	715
Necedah	608
Neenah	920
Neillsville	715
Nekoosa	715
Nelma	715
Nelson	715
Nelsonville	715
Neopit	715
Neosho	920
Neshkoro	920
Neva Corners	715
New Auburn	715
New Berlin	262
New Franken	920
New Glarus	608
New Haven	715
New Holstein	920
New Johannesburg	715
New Lisbon	608
New London	920
New Munster	262
New Post	715
New Richmond	715
Newald	715
Newburg	262
Newburg Corners	608
Newton	920
Niagara	715
Nichols	920
Norrie	715
North Fond Du Lac	920
North Freedom	608
North Hudson	715
North Lake	262
North Menomonie	715
North Prairie	262
North Woods Beach	715
Northfield	715
Norwalk	608
Nye	715
Oak Creek	414
Oak Grove	715
Oakdale	608
Oakfield	920
Oconomowoc	262

City	Area Code
Oconto	920
Oconto Falls	920
Ocontofalls	920
Odanah	715
Ogdensburg	920
Ogema	715
Ojibwa	715
Okauchee	262
Oma	715
Omro	920
Onalaska	608
Oneida	920
Oneida Indian Reservation	715
Ontario	608
Oostburg	920
Oregon	608
Orfordville	608
Osceola	715
Oshkosh	920
Osseo	715
Owen	715
Oxford	608
Packwaukee	608
Paddock Lake	262
Padus	715
Palmyra	262
Pardeeville	608
Park Falls	715
Park Ridge	715
Parrish	715
Patch Grove	608
Pearson	715
Pelican	715
Pelican Lake	715
Pell Lake	262
Pembine	715
Pence	715
Pensaukee	920
Pepin	715
Peplin	715
Perkinstown	715
Peshtigo	715
Pewaukee	262
Phelps	715
Phillips	715
Phlox	715
Pickerel	715
Pickett	920
Pigeon Falls	715
Pine River	920
Pittsville	715
Plain	608
Plainfield	715
Platteville	608
Pleasant Lake	715
Pleasant Pr	262
Pleasant Prairie	262
Pleasant Valley	715
Plover	715
Plum City	715
Plum Lake	715
Plymouth	920
Polar	715
Polley	715
Polonia	715
Poniatowski	715
Poplar	715
Popple River	715
Port Edwards	715
Port Washington	262
Port Wing	715
Portage	608
Porterfield	715
Poskin	715
Post Lake	715
Potawatomi Indian Reservatio	715
Potosi	608
Potter	920
Pound	920
Powers Lake	262
Poy Sippi	920
Poynette	608
Pr Du Chien	608
Pr Du Sac	608
Prairie Du Chien	608
Prairie Du Sac	608
Prairie Farm	715
Pray	715
Preble	920
Prentice	715
Prescott	715
Presque Isle	715
Princeton	920
Prt Washingtn	262
Pulaski	920
Pulcifer	920
Racine	262
Radisson	715
Randolph	920
Random Lake	920
Range	715
Readfield	920
Readstown	608
Red Cliff	715
Red Cliff Indian Reservation	715
Redgranite	920
Redville	715
Reedsburg	608
Reedsville	920
Reeseville	920
Reeve	715
Remington	715
Rewey	608
Rhinelander	715
Rib Falls	715
Rib Lake	715
Rib Mountain	715
Rice Lake	715
Richardson	715
Richfield	262
Richford	715
Richland Center	608
Richland Ctr	608
Ridgeland	715
Ridgeway	608
Ringle	715
Rio	920
Rio Creek	920
Riplinger	715
Ripon	920
River Falls	715
River Hills	414
Roberts	715
Rochester	262
Rock Falls	715
Rock Springs	608
Rockfield	262
Rockland	608
Rome	715
Rosendale	920
Rosholt	715
Rothschild	715
Royalton	920
Rozellville	715
Rubicon	920
Rudolph	715
Rush River	715
Rusk	715
S Milwaukee	414
Saint Cloud	920
Saint Croix Falls	715
Saint Francis	414
Saint Germain	715
Saint Nazianz	920
Salem	262
Salvatorian Center	920
Salvtrian Ctr	920
Sanborn	715
Sand Creek	715
Sandlake	715
Sarona	715
Sauk City	608
Saukville	262
Saxeville	920
Saxon	715
Sayner	715
Scandinavia	715
Schley	715
Schofield	*715*
Scott	920
Seneca	608
Seneca Corners	715
Seneca Cors	715
Sevastopol	920
Sextonville	608
Seymour	920
Sharon	262
Shawano	715
Sheboygan	920
Sheboygan Falls	920
Sheboygan Fls	920
Shelby	608
Sheldon	715
Shell Lake	715
Shepley	715
Sherman	715
Sherry	715
Sherwood	920
Shiocton	920
Shorewood	414
Shorewood Hills	608
Shullsberg	608
Shullsburg	608
Silver Cliff	715
Silver Lake	262
Sinsinawa	608
Siren	715
Sister Bay	920
Skanawan	715
Slag Pile	715
Slinger	262
Sobieski	920
Society Of The Divine Savior	920
Soldier Grove	608
Soldiers Grove	608
Solon Springs	715
Somers	262
Somerset	715
Soperton	715
South Beaver Dam	920
South Byron	920
South Chase	920
South Fork	715
South Milwaukee	414
South Range	715
South Wayne	608
Sparta	608
Spencer	715
Spirit Falls	715
Split Rock	715
Spokeville	715
Spooner	715
Spring Green	608
Spring Valley	715
Springbrook	715
Springfield	262
Springstead	715
St Croix Falls	715
St Croix Fls	715
St Francis	414
St Germain	715
St Nazianz	920
Stangelville	920
Stanley	715
Stanton	715
Star Lake	715
Star Prairie	715
Starks	715
Starlake	715
State Capitol	608
Stella	715
Sterling	715
Stetsonville	715
Steuben	608
Stevens Point	715
Stiles	920
Stitzer	608
Stockbridge	920
Stockbridge Indian Reservati	715
Stockholm	715
Stockton	715
Stoddard	608
Stone Lake	715
Stoughton	608
Stratford	*715*
Strum	715
Sturgeon Bay	920
Sturtevant	262
Suamico	920
Sugar Camp	715
Sullivan	262
Summit	715
Summit Lake	715
Sun Prairie	608
Superior	715
Suring	920
Sussex	262
Swiss Colony	608
Swiss Colony Bus Reply	608
Tannery	715
Taycheedah	920
Taylor	715
The Wi Cheeseman	608
Theresa	920
Thiensville	262
Thornton	715
Thorp	715
Three Lakes	715
Thrivent Finan For Lutherans	920
Tigerton	715
Tilden	715
Tilleda	715
Tipler	715
Tisch Mills	920
Tomah	608
Tomahawk	715
Tony	715
Townsend	715
Trade Lake	715
Trego	715
Trempealeau	608
Trevor	262
Trimbelle	715
Tripoli	715
Troy	715
Tunnel City	608
Turtle Lake	715
Tustin	920
Twin Lakes	262
Two Rivers	920
U S Bank	414
Ubet	715
Underhill	920
Union Center	608
Union Grove	262
Unity	715
Univ Of Wis Hosp Hlth Sc Ctr	608
Upson	715
Valders	920
Valmy	920
Van Dyne	920
Veedum	715
Vernon	262
Verona	608
Vesper	715
Victory	608
Viola	608
Viroqua	608
W Bend	262
W Milwaukee	414
Wabeno	715
Waldo	920
Wales	262
Walworth	262
Wanderoos	715
Warren	715
Warrens	608
Wascott	715
Washburn	715
Washington	715
Washington Is	920
Washington Island	920
Waterford	262
Waterloo	920
Watertown	920
Waubeka	262
Waukau	920
Waukesha	262
Waumandee	608
Waunakee	608
Waupaca	*715*
Waupun	920
Wausau	*715*
Wausaukee	*715*
Wautoma	920
Wauwatosa	262
Wauzeka	608
Wawatosa	262
Wayside	920
We Energies	414
Webb Lake	715
Webster	715
Wentworth	715
West Allis	414
West Baraboo	608
West Bend	262
West Lima	608
West Milwaukee	414
West Salem	608
Westbend	262
Westboro	715
Westby	608
Westfield	608
Weston	715
Westport	608
Weurtsburg	715
Weyauwega	920
Weyerhaeuser	715
Wheeler	715
Whitcomb	715
White Lake	715
Whitefish Bay	414
Whitehall	715
Whitelaw	920
Whitewater	262
Whiting	715
Whittlesey	715
Wi Dept Ind Labor Human Rel	608
Wi Dept Revenue Box 268	608
Wi Dept Revenue Box 34	608
Wi Dept Revenue Box 59	608
Wild Rose	920
Wildwood	715
Willard	715
Williams Bay	262
Wilmot	262
Wilson	715
Wilton	608
Winchester	715, 920
Wind Lake	262
Windsor	608
Winnebago	920
Winneconne	920
Winter	715
Wisc Dells	608
Wisc Rapids	715
Wisconsin Child Support	414
Wisconsin Dells	608
Wisconsin Dept Transport	414
Wisconsin Lottery	608
Wisconsin Rapids	715
Withee	715
Wittenberg	715
Wolfcreek	715
Wonewoc	608
Woodboro	715
Woodford	608
Woodland	920
Woodman	608
Woodruff	715
Woodville	715
Woodworth	262
Worcester	715
Wrightstown	920
Wyalusing	608
Wyeville	608
Wyocena	608
Yellow Lake	715
York	715
Yuba	608
Zablocki Va Medical Ctr	414
Zachow	920
Zenda	262

Wyoming

City	Area Code
All Points	307

NATIONAL 5-DIGIT ZIP CODE® AND POST OFFICE DIRECTORY

Every year, the U.S. Postal Service produces the *National 5-Digit ZIP Code® and Post Office Directory* to accommodate the constantly changing geographical make-up of the United States. This 2015 edition contains all the essential information you need to get your mail where it needs to go—including updated information on new residential numbers, new street names, and new ZIP codes.

Published in two comprehensive volumes, the *National 5-Digit ZIP Code® and Post Office Directory* is designed to be easy to use, accurate, and up to date. In addition to ZIP code listings, Volume 1 contains helpful instructions on how to find ZIP codes in the *Directory* and how to properly address your mailings. Volume 2 contains useful information on symbol abbreviations, mail services, classes of mail, and much more.

Why should you order the *National 5-Digit ZIP Code® and Post Office Directory* from Bernan? Because we are the largest private distributor of U.S. government and international agency publications in the country. Because we offer several outstanding benefits, including flexible payment plans and standing orders. And, by placing the *National 5-Digit ZIP Code® and Post Office Directory* on standing order, you will automatically receive each new edition at the lowest price offered by Bernan. You may contact Bernan for additional ordering information by using the toll-free number listed below.

TO ORDER CALL 800-462-6420,
EMAIL US AT ORDER@BERNAN.COM
OR VISIT OUR WEB SITE AT WWW.ROWMAN.COM

ISBN 978-1-59888-756-3
90000
9 781598 887563